HANDBOOK OF THE BIRDS OF THE WORLD

Volume 3

Hoatzin *to* Auks

Josep del Hoyo
Andrew Elliott
Jordi Sargatal

George Archibald	*Robert Furness*	*Gordon Maclean*
David Baker-Gabb	*Jan van Gils*	*Curt Meine*
Brian Bertram	*Michael Gochfeld*	*David Nettleship*
Dana Bryan	*Luiz Gonzaga*	*Ray Pierce*
Alan Burger	*Frank Hawkins*	*Theunis Piersma*
Joanna Burger	*Philip Hockey*	*Michael Rands*
Nigel Collar	*Rob Hume*	*Peter Sherman*
Stephen Debus	*Gavin Hunt*	*Barry Taylor*
William Duckworth	*Donald Jenni*	*Betsy Thomas*
Michael Evans	*Guy Kirwan*	*Popko Wiersma*
Jon Fjeldså	*Algirdas Knystautas*	*Richard Zusi*

Colour Plates by

Norman Arlott	*Ian Lewington*
Robert Bateman	*Chris Rose*
Hilary Burn	*Lluís Sanz*
Àngels Jutglar	*Etel Vilaró*
Francesc Jutglar	*Ian Willis*

Consultant for Systematics
and Nomenclature

Walter J. Bock

Consultant for Status
and Conservation

Nigel J. Collar

Lynx Edicions

Barcelona

12599375

Editorial Council

Authors of Volume 3

Dr G. W. Archibald
Director, International Crane Foundation, Wisconsin, USA.

Dr D. J. Baker-Gabb
Director, Royal Australasian Ornithologists Union, Victoria, Australia.

R. Bateman
Artist/Naturalist, British Columbia, Canada.

Dr B. C. R. Bertram
Freelance Zoological Adviser, Fieldhead,
Amberley, England.

Dr D. C. Bryan
Chief, Division of Recreation & Parks, Bureau of Natural & Cultural Resources,
Department of Environmental Protection, Florida, USA.

Dr A. E. Burger
Associate Professor (Adjunct), Department of Biology, University of Victoria,
British Columbia, Canada.

Dr J. Burger
Graduate Program in Ecology and Evolution, Rutgers University, New Jersey, USA.

Dr N. J. Collar
Research Fellow, BirdLife International,
Cambridge, England.

S. J. S. Debus
Research Officer, Department of Zoology, University of New England, New South Wales, Australia.

Dr J. W. Duckworth
Freelance Conservation Biologist, Vientiane, Laos.

M. I. Evans
Field-survey Leader, Amman, Jordan.

Dr J. Fjeldså
Zoologisk Museum, Københavns Universitet, Denmark.

Dr R. W. Furness
Applied Ornithology Unit, Zoology Department, University of Glasgow, Scotland.

Drs J. van Gils
Netherlands Institute for Sea Research (NIOZ), Texel, The Netherlands.

Dr M. Gochfeld
UMDNJ, Robert Wood Johnson Medical School, New Jersey, USA.

L. P. Gonzaga
Assistant Professor, Departamento de Zoologia, Universidade Federal do Rio de Janeiro, Brazil.

Dr A. F. A. Hawkins
Technical Advisor to BirdLife International, Antananarivo, Madagascar.

Dr P. A. R. Hockey
Percy FitzPatrick Institute, University of Cape Town, South Africa.

R. A. Hume
Editor, Birds, Royal Society for the Protection of Birds, Sandy, England.

G. R. Hunt
Department of Ecology, Massey University,
New Zealand.

Professor D. A. Jenni
Division of Biological Sciences, University of Montana, USA.

G. M. Kirwan
Editor, Sandgrouse, *Ornithological Society of
the Middle East, England.*

Dr A. J. Knystautas
Freelance Ornithologist, Vilnius, Lithuania.

Professor G. L. Maclean
Department of Zoology & Entomology, University of Natal, South Africa.

Dr C. D. Meine
Co-ordinator, IUCN Action Plan for Cranes, International Crane Foundation, Wisconsin, USA.

Dr D. N. Nettleship
*Senior Research Scientist, Seabird Research Unit, Canadian Wildlife Service,
Environment Canada, Nova Scotia, Canada.*

Dr R. J. Pierce
Department of Conservation, Te Papa Atawhai, Northland Conservancy, New Zealand.

Dr T. Piersma
*Netherlands Institute for Sea Research (NIOZ), Texel,
and Zoological Laboratory, University of Groningen, The Netherlands.*

Dr M. R. W. Rands
Deputy Director-General, BirdLife International, Cambridge, England.

Dr P. T. Sherman
Department of Biology, University of Louisville, Kentucky, USA.

Dr P. B. Taylor
Department of Zoology & Entomology, University of Natal, South Africa.

B. T. Thomas
Independent Researcher, Venezuela; now Virginia, USA.

Drs P. Wiersma
Zoological Laboratory, University of Groningen, The Netherlands.

Dr R. L. Zusi
National Museum of Natural History, Smithsonian Institution, Washington D. C., USA.

CONTENTS

LIST OF PLATES

Having spent my whole life avidly involved with both nature and art, I have evolved a number of ideas on the relationship between these two areas of study and activity. I have been struck by the drift of so-called civilized man away from nature. This is manifested by the absence of wildlife subject matter in the mainstream of art of the Western world right into the twentieth century. All other periods of history and all other cultures have normally included wildlife as a subject matter for drawings, paintings, sculpture and decorative motifs. From the nineteenth century until the present, art involving plants and animals was seen as a handmaiden to the study of natural history. Until its partial supplanting by photography, art was used simply to describe various aspects of nature. In my own work I have used nature as an inspiration for my art rather than using my art as a way to illustrate nature. I am a painter who happens to love nature and so that is my subject matter. In the same way, Dégas painted back stage at the ballet and van Gogh painted the countryside around Arles.

I would like to explore the way in which humanity's drift away from nature has been reflected in our art. I will also comment on the way in which art, particularly in recent years, has influenced our understanding of and appreciation for nature.

From earliest times some of the greatest art produced depicted wild creatures. The most famous early works are the great cave paintings of Altamira and Lascaux, dating back to roughly 100,000-50,000 years ago. These bison and deer are depicted with sensitivity and power. Of course, the artists were very familiar with every sinew, bone and muscle of their subjects. They had no doubt quarreled over every bit of the anatomy, bargaining for the different pieces. Every part of the animal had a use and a significance. It is not surprising that most of the Paleolithic drawings have an accuracy and realism that is unsurpassed to this day.

For 90% of our history we were hunter-gatherers moving through the natural world like any other creatures. When food became scarce or difficult to obtain, we moved on and nature quickly healed over. Early humans were not necessarily backward or unsophisticated; in fact, there is evidence that in many ways our ancestors were superior to modern man. In practical knowledge and understanding of ecology, for example, an ordinary hunter or gatherer is vastly more sophisticated than a contemporary professor of ecology. Recently, an ethnobotanist visited the Penan tribe of Sarawak. He asked a tribesman to walk in the tropical rain forest and describe the attributes and uses of the plants along the way. It took a long time to cover a few metres because of the overwhelming wealth of detailed information. The average Penan can name thousands of species of plants and describe what they do. How many can an average "modern" person name?

The points I wish to make here are both general and particular. In general, since the invention of agriculture, or the Neolithic revolution, we have drifted away from knowl-

Cliff-nesting seabirds in the Pribilof Islands, Bering Sea.

Painted specially for the *Handbook of the Birds of the World* by Robert Bateman.

edge and wisdom concerning nature and have become increasingly obsessed with convenience through technology. At the end of the twentieth century we must now realize the folly and indeed tragedy of pursuing this course too far, and once again become more closely connected with nature, not only in mind and deed, but in spirit.

This leads to my particular point, that is concerning the role of nature art in our lives and perhaps in a small way in the salvation of the endangered life on this planet. If art has something to say about the human mind and spirit, then surely wildlife art should have a clear and forceful voice in contemporary culture.

In order to place the art of wild animals in historical perspective, I would like to return to the so-called Neolithic revolution. As I have mentioned above, for hundreds of thousands of years humans lived as an integrated part of the natural world. Then, about 20,000-10,000 years ago, our ancestors found ways to control nature and so make life easier for themselves. Perhaps the earliest innovation was the domestication of the goat. It has been said that this one "breakthrough" was by far the most earthshaking development in the past million years, surpassing the invention of the printing press and the splitting of the atom. Nomadic tribes in the Middle East found that they could control herds of goats, guide them to pastures and water and protect them from predators. In return, the goats gave milk, meat and skins for clothing, and fibre for weaving. Man the pastoralist became much more the enemy of nature than man the hunter. All larger predators were a threat to the flocks and had to be exterminated. This same prejudice is still with us worldwide, even for example in North America, as recently seen in the strong protests against the proposed reintroduction of wolves into Yellowstone Park, USA. In addition, grazing wild animals became competitors for pasture and water and were either killed or starved. Since most of the needs of the tribes were met by the goats, the peoples did not require detailed and complex knowledge about their neighbours of other species, either plant or animal. Over the centuries nature was seen as chaotic and irrelevant to the reorganized human condition, and the prevalence of this view increased with the domestication of certain plants and other animals. It allowed humans to live in villages which needed physical and social structure in relation to the complex and confusing web of the natural world.

Art totally changed, from the realistic renderings of the Paleolithic peoples, to highly abstracted and structural designs of village people. This work may be seen in the Geometric Period of early Greece (900-700 BC), as well as in the art of prehistoric peoples in China and Europe. There are abundant examples of Neolithic-style art being practised all over the world until the middle of the twentieth century. This would include the great tribal art of Africa, New Guinea and west coast North American natives. In each case, the art is abstract with distorted images of humans and animals and plants all done in a strong, stylized and decorative fashion. Wildlife of every kind was contorted into strong curves and dynamic lines with interlocking positive and negative shapes. Thus we see lions, ibexes, eagles, bears, fish, hornbills or crocodiles woven, carved or painted into or onto fabric, canoes, pots and almost every other man-made item. This decorative art is found even in Europe until quite recently. It may be seen in rural art, on clothing and furniture, especially in more remote and mountainous areas.

As early European tribal art evolved, it departed from nature and created mythical and magical creatures. Nature is seen as mysterious and menacing. Thus we have dragons, hobgoblins and griffons. The Church became more and more dominant over every aspect of life. Nature, even human nature was seen as the enemy. The magnificent and complex cathedrals of the Middle Ages were among the most comprehensive expressions of human endeavour. And yet true nature was either distorted out of almost all recognition, or it was left out entirely. Instead we have gargoyles, fantastic animistic demons and symbolic plant forms.

The Renaissance brought a renewal of classical interest in humanity and science, but wild animals and wilderness remained "beyond the pale". As European art developed, perspective and realism in painting animals became the norm. However, the subjects were almost entirely domestic animals, typically dogs, horses, cattle and sheep. This tendency continued through the great paintings of the seventeenth century. If wildlife was shown, it was quarry being exterminated at the end of a spear or ready for the table, being hung up by its feet with a bunch of grapes. One of the superb masterpieces of Peter Paul Rubens (*Tigers and Lions Hunt*) shows huntsmen on handsome and heroic horses spearing and trampling the magnificent carnivores. Man, the greatest predator, must exterminate all other predators, or so it would seem through most of our history. There are a few exceptions to this general pattern. Dürer produced his famous hare painting, and also an elaborate and inaccurate rhinoceros, while Rembrandt drew elephants and other zoo animals. These and the handful of other examples were created more as curiosities than anything else. For most of European history, I am not aware of any examples showing wildlife in its own domain, eye to eye, with respect.

In the eighteenth and nineteenth centuries an increasing number of artists tried their hands at accurate renderings of plants and animals. This was the great age of expeditions and a naturalist artist was an essential part of the record keeping on any such adventure. Specimens were shot, stuffed, pinned and painted. It was all part of the gathering of knowledge and accumulation of collections.

Artists such as John James Audubon struggled to show birds and mammals in scientific detail. These works were often based on freshly killed specimens arranged with appropriate plant forms. The results were sometimes artistic but to my mind they fall into the category of accomplished flower arranging. Nevertheless, the body of his work, particularly in his *Birds of America*, was a major landmark in the history of wildlife art. The great "double elephant" folio brought striking and quite accurate images of birds to a wide public.

Towards the end of the nineteenth century some powerful painters of wild animals emerged. The most famous of these, men like Richard Friese, Wilhelm Kunhert and, in the early twentieth century, Carl Rungius, catered to the big game hunter. Aristocrats had always had a taste for shooting wildlife. Now the new business elite aspired to join the "sport". These men were the patrons of a new art form, the depiction of the quarry species in its own habitat. These paintings hung on the walls along with the heads of the trophy animals. Not only the animals in the picture, but also the landscape, was intended to evoke memories of happy times in the field.

Of course, these artists were themselves big game hunters. And so, as in most great art throughout history, the artist explores what is meaningful to him in his own life. Since some of the painters were well trained and talented, they produced some excellent paintings, and indeed were on a par with the works of many of the more famous artists of that time. However, since the subject matter was outside the more conventional human-centred material, many of these pictures were not shown in major art museums. Those animal paintings which were priveleged to hang in art museums during the nineteenth century soon found their way into permanent storage as modernist curators took charge in the twentieth century.

A noteworthy exception to this practice was Bruno Llijefors (1860-1939) of Sweden. His work has always been recognized as having a position of status in Swedish art, and it continues to hang in major art museums of that country along with art of all periods, including contemporary. Llijefors enjoys a lofty reputation among wildlife artists and *aficionados* to this day. He employed great skill with brushwork and a fresh eye for his compositions. His paintings have a startling sense of verisimilitude which is almost photographic without being slavishly detailed. One definition of a masterpiece is that when you view it you feel you are seeing it for the first time, and it should seem as if it is done without effort. In my opinion, much of the work of Bruno Llijefors falls into this category. He not only produced pictures which would appeal to wealthy hunter clients, but also painted a great many pictures showing glimpses into ordinary little incidents in nature. These are treated with freshness and imagination. For this reason Bruno Llijefors has a proud place in the history of painting as an artist who looked nature eye to eye with respect.

There were others in the nineteenth century. One of the most gifted was Leopold Robert (1794-1835) of the Neuchatel area of Switzerland. He was famous as a painter of landscapes and of the human figure; a magnificent mural may be seen in the entry hall of the Neuchatel Museum. But his high position as a nature artist arises from his superb paintings of passerines and, oddly enough, of caterpillars. These are not mere scientific renderings but are small, perfect paintings showing the activities of these creatures in their habitats.

The tumultuous twentieth century has produced, not surprisingly, a multiplicity of trends in wildlife art. In the early years, artists continued to be used as illustrators of stories about animals or scientific books on natural history topics. As the century progressed, photography gradually took over this role.

There are, however, many areas of illustration in which the hand of the artist is superior to the camera. Detailed renderings of particular parts of plants or animals are shown with far greater clarity by draftsmanship, in which certain confusing relationships of the different parts of the natural world can be sorted out and simplified. Medical and botanical art are good examples of this.

A colossal breakthrough in the understanding and appreciation of natural history was developed by Roger Tory Peterson in the 1930's. His *Field Guide to the Birds* brought clear, standardized illustrations in a very accessible form to the general public. This meant that an ordinary beginner could buy the book and become a proficient birdwatcher, able to distinguish between all of the different species. The significance of the field guide has been enormous. As S. Dillon Ripley, Secretary Emeritus of the Smithsonian Institution, writes,

> "...because of the field guide, birds have become the best known animals in the world. Peterson entered a world in which identification and study of birds was the exclusive realm of the specialist with a shotgun, and he transformed us into a world of watchers. The impact Peterson has had is incalculable; in providing the means for the popularization and refinement of bird-watching, he has immeasurably furthered bird study and the conservation movement worldwide. He enables even the most untutored person to identify birds; he showcased the unparalleled beauty of birds in his painting and photography; and by getting millions of people interested he has helped to guarantee the survival of birds."

The field guide principle has now multiplied into every area of identification of plants and animals and even rocks, minerals and stars. This has the potential of bringing *Homo sapiens* full circle and gives us some hope that modern-day man may end up sharing at least some of the knowledge of our hunter-gatherer ancestors about the world of nature.

As we approach the end of this century, the most serious problem facing the planet is the disappearance of biodiversity. The extinction of species will mean an ugly and impoverished future and may even threaten the survival of our own species. How can we preserve biodiversity if we can not even identify the different living things in our own communities, let alone in the world at large?

In my view, artwork is superior to photography in all field guides. The standardization and lack of confusing poses and lighting conditions makes good illustration irreplaceable. Photography does have its place, however, in the depiction of nature. Photography at its best is truly an art form along with drawing, painting and sculpture. In the last few decades photography has made significant technological advances. In recent years, photographers as artists have been producing a plethora of beautiful books showing nature as it had never been seen before by the general public. In many cases, the artistic merit and creativity of the photography was, and still is, truly inspirational. This has played an important role in raising the consciousness of the common person, at least in the Western world, to the beauty and value of nature.

At the same time it is undeniable that films and television have had a major impact in the same direction in recent years. Nature shows are perennial favourites, perhaps reflecting a yearning among a modern populace for the purity of the Garden of Eden that we are rapidly losing. In fact, wildlife painting has experienced a historic surge in popularity since the 1970's. When I was a teenage wildlife painter in the 1940's, I knew of only three or four Canadians and a dozen or so from the USA who painted nature. Most of them were illustrators of books or magazines. A few had, as their main job, teaching or musem work. Today there are hundreds of artists supporting themselves with their nature art, and many more are serious amateurs. The limited edition production print has increasingly enjoyed enormous popularity, especially in North America. This has meant that high quality reproductions of wildlife paintings are avidly collected, bringing wildlife images into thousands of homes and offices.

Natural history art in many forms has proliferated. It may be found as decoration on coffee mugs and T-shirts. It is often enlisted in worthy causes such as to "Save the Whales" or "Stop Killing Baby Seals". It is now so much a part of our late twentieth century Western culture that an appreciation of nature seems to be akin to virtue. One scholar theorizes that, whereas in earlier centuries religious icons, for instance of the crucifix, showed that one was a good person, now wildlife images on one's clothing or wall are the new icons of virtue.

Moving to the opposite end of the creativity scale from the coffee mugs and clothing, wildlife art can be found in major paintings commanding as high prices as most other forms of contemporary art. Although only a few pieces have found their way past the "priesthood" of modern art museum curators, a few excellent museums of wildlife art have opened in recent years. In general these have much healthier attendance records than do their so-called fine art counterparts.

Wildlife art has been directly enlisted in the fight to save threatened species and habitats. Often artwork of this genre is the best fundraiser at charity art auctions. In British Columbia, where I live, a group of artists joined forces with environmental organizations to paint a particularly precious stand of old growth Sitka spruce forest on Vancouver Island. The forest was slated to be cut but, after the raising of public awareness through the production of an elegant art book and a travelling exhibition, the logging company and government were shamed into protecting the forest.

A Netherlands-based organization, the Artists for Nature Foundation, is targeting two areas of great natural significance in order to raise consciousness and save them from development, particularly industrial agriculture. One is the Biebzra wetlands of eastern Poland and the other Extremadura of western Spain. Both are ancient cultural landscapes where human activity and nature have evolved together in a gentle interface. This results in an abundance of wildlife including many species endangered or extinct in other parts of Europe. The Artists for Nature Foundation has organized groups of leading wildlife artists from various parts of the world to draw and paint these areas. As in the Vancouver Island example, beautiful books and travelling exhibitions have resulted.

On a poster for the Munich Art Museum I read "Kunst öffnet die Augen" (Art opens the eyes). If this is true, and I believe it is, then the world of nature as seen by artists has a crucial role to play not only in bringing pleasure and appreciation of that world to mankind, but also in teaching us all what to cherish, and therefore what to protect and guard.

The following quotation is attributed to Baba Dioum:

> "In the end, we will conserve only what we love, we will love only what
> we understand, we will understand only what we are taught."

Let us hope that humans will become truly civilized and drift back to a deep appreciation of nature. There are signs that wildlife art at the end of this millenium may be part of an optimistic trend.

Robert Bateman

Once again readers are referred to the detailed general introduction to the whole HBW series (see Volume 1, pages 15-33), where the aims, limits and structure of the project are set out.

It is clear that in a work covering all of the families in the class Aves, and each and every one of their constituent species, a high degree of uniformity in treatment is essential. However, it is equally clear that too rigorous a level of uniformity would present a number of drawbacks. Thus, while the structure itself remains untouchable and a large number of details must invariably be covered in similar depth in all families, it is considered that on a particular topic it may be useful to include a somewhat higher degree of detail in one family than in some others; for example, in this volume it was decided that, because of their special interest, descriptions of nests in Rallidae or downy chicks in Glareolidae deserved particular attention, though it should be remembered that these aspects are covered to some degree in all families. Another related policy is that a slightly greater degree of detail may be desirable in families for which even the basic details are not easily available to the average ornithologist.

One significant innovation in two families of the present volume is a subsection to cover voice; this is included within the Descriptive notes sections of all the species in the families Gruidae and Rallidae. The inclusion of a brief description of voice was originally intended only for the passerines, in part because there are many families, especially of non-passerines, for which a written description of voice would appear too subjective and perhaps somewhat pointless unless it could be expanded to a scale incompatible with the aims of HBW. However, it has subsequently been felt that the inclusion of this brief voice subsection might also be useful for a very limited number of non-passerine families.

The guiding taxonomic principles adopted for HBW were summarized at the outset (see Volume 1, page 16). Briefly, they can be considered fairly conservative at the macrosystematic level, becoming increasingly flexible at lower levels, to the extent that at the subspecific level HBW generally aims to follow all of the latest developments that appear to have gained reasonable acceptance.

The present volume contains what will undoubtedly prove taxonomically to be the single most significant deviation from traditional usage in the entire series. The Plains-wanderer (*Pedionomus torquatus*) has long been linked with buttonquails (Turnicidae), and has even at times been included within that family, although for some years now it has almost universally been awarded its own monotypic family, Pedionomidae, within the Gruiformes. However, quite recently a considerable body of strong evidence has been produced which suggests that the Plains-wanderer is not closely related to the buttonquails at all, but instead belongs alongside the waders or shorebirds in Charadriiformes. Unquestionably, the systematists have not had their last say on this matter (or any other!), but there is currently a reasonable degree of consensus in favour of this change. At the same time, as the species is endemic to Australia, and as recent

Australian literature appears to accept this transfer more or less unanimously, it seemed imprudent, confusing and perhaps even counterproductive for HBW to stick stubbornly to usage that has fallen into such disfavour within the species' only range country. To do so would have been clearly in contradiction to HBW's stated aim to provide the relevant information on any particular taxon in the place where the average reader expects to find it, since most workers, especially Australians, would presumably now expect to find this species in Charadriiformes.

The taxonomically controversial Hoatzin (*Opisthocomus hoazin*), sole member of the family Opisthocomidae, has traditionally been linked with the Galliformes, but more recently it has been placed with the Cuculiformes. As already explained (see Volume 2, page 18), it was decided some years back that, at any rate for the purposes of HBW, the most sensible and appropriate treatment for this taxon would be that advocated by E. Stresemann in 1934, namely its isolation in a separate monotypic order, Opisthocomiformes. The Hoatzin is the starting point of this present volume.

Another similar case, that of the sandgrouse (Pteroclidae), may also merit brief mention here. This family has usually been placed in the pigeon order Columbiformes, but in recent years there has been a call to shift it to the shorebird order Charadriiformes. Again, for HBW it has been deemed wisest to adopt the third major option, that of awarding the sandgrouse a separate order, Pterocliformes. Having accomodated these two macrosystematic modifications, the editors are now fairly confident that it is most unlikely that there will be any further alterations affecting ordinal level within the entire series. For example, the recent proposal to award the buttonquails their own independent order, Turniciformes, was considered an inappropriate change to introduce in HBW.

One matter deserving of explanation concerns scientific nomenclature, as laid out in the International Code for Zoological Nomenclature (ICZN). The policy for family names based on genera with the *-is* termination is that the termination of the family-group name can be either -idae or -ididae. For reasons of simplification, the shorter, simpler ending -idae is generally preferred. This policy is of particular relevance to the present volume, as it affects the case of the sheathbill family, which is preferably named Chionidae, rather than the form Chionididae; the latter form has been much used and is not technically incorrect, but the use of the shortened form Chionidae has been recommended, and so is adopted herein. A very similar case is that of a subfamily within the sandpiper family Scolopacidae: the name Calidrinae is now the recommended form, as opposed to longer version Calidridinae. However, there are exceptions: the name Otididae should be retained for the bustard family, as a special case, due to the possibility of nomenclatural confusion arising in the hypothetical case of the owl genus *Otus* being used as the basis of a family-group name.

With the introduction of the new IUCN criteria, as explained in Collar *et al.* (1994), pages 14-21, the Mace-Lande categories that appeared for some families in Volume 2 are no longer required; the new criteria are reaping the benefits of the experience gained with the Mace-Lande system, and provide a sounder basis for the application of categories. The categories themselves have changed slightly from the previous IUCN designations. The three threat categories in order of magnitude are Vulnerable, Endangered and Critically Endangered. Note that species classed as near-threatened belong, by definition, within the non-threatened category, although there can be no doubt that some of these species may shortly be reclassified to one of the threatened categories. One very slight discrepancy with IUCN is that, purely for the purposes of HBW, the category Extinct in the Wild is considered to belong in the threat categories, rather than in the extinct category, as herein it is understood not be extinction in the definitive, irreversible sense.

Throughout the texts the terms "shorebirds" and "waders" are used indifferently, as there appears to be no pressing need to establish a single term. At the same time, "shorebirds" in the Old World can be understood to include gulls, herons and perhaps even some crows, whereas "waders" in the New World is often understood to include herons, storks, ibises, flamingos and their various allies.

It is considered that the name Myanmar has now achieved almost universal acceptance, so this form has been adopted for Volume 3 onwards. On the other hand, the renaming of the South African provinces caught the editors unawares, too late to substitute all references to Natal with the new name KwaZulu-Natal.

Readers are asked to note that, as explained in Volume 1, the use of an exclamation mark with Other common names has a particular meaning, almost invariably that the name has been or is also applied to another species. Such, for example, is the case of the name "Purple Gallinule", which has been extensively used for both *Porphyrio porphyrio* and *Porphyrio martinica*, making it an inappropriate option in either case for HBW, due to the possible confusion that could result.

The accepted French, German and Spanish names come from the same sources as listed in the introductions to Volumes 1 and 2. Missing German names were kindly sent by Peter H. Barthel, Chairman of the Ständiges Komitee für deutsche Vogelnamen. Publication of the list of recommended Spanish names continues, the second batch appearing in *Ardeola* **41(2)**: 183-191.

Acknowledgements

As ever, museums have been very important in many aspects of the project. We are very grateful to the British Museum of Natural History at Tring (Robert Prys-Jones, Peter Colston, Michael Walters, Mark Adams). We should also like to thank the American Museum of Natural History in New York (Mary LeCroy, Paul Sweet), and the Smithsonian Institution in Washington (Gary R. Graves, Richard L. Zusi, Pamela C. Rasmussen, J. Phillip Angle, Carla Dove). Others who very kindly assisted in various ways include the National Museums of Scotland in Edinburgh (Bob McGowan), the Australian Museum in Sydney (Walter E. Boles), the Museum of Victoria in Melbourne (Rory O'Brien), the Field Museum of Natural History in Chicago (David Willard), and Liverpool Museum (Tony Parker).

Libraries too have again played a very important part in the preparation of the volume, and we are extremely grateful to the libraries of the Museu de Zoologia of Barcelona (María Angeles Iglesias), the Sociedad Española de Ornitología in Madrid (Blas Molina, Juan Carlos del Moral), the Station Biologique de la Tour du Valat in the Camargue (C. Perennou, J. P. Taris), the British Museum of Natural History at Tring (Effie Warr), the Centre de Documentació del P. N. dels Aiguamolls de l'Empordà (Rosa Llinàs), the Royal Australasian Ornithologists Union (John Peter), and the Estación Biológica de Doñana (José Cabot). Assistance in bibliographical matters was also received from several other ornithological organizations and staff involved in their publications, and we express our thanks to Penny Olsen (CSIRO), Nicholas Gould (*IZN*), Susanna Lawson (American Birding Association), Einhard Bezzel (*Journal für Ornithologie*), Harro Hieronimus (*Der Falke*), Jean Peck (*Birds of North America*), Raül Aymí (Grup Català d'Anellament), Ian Grant (Avicultural Society of Australia) and Taej Mundkur (AWB).

Visits to collections of live birds have proved very useful, both for the present volume and with an eye to the future, and we should like to extend special thanks to San Diego Zoo in USA (David Rimlinger), the Parque Ornitológico y Botánico El Retiro in Málaga, Spain (Geer Scheres, Eduardo Alba), and Hope Zoo in Kingston, Jamaica (Rhema Kerr).

Many people helped by providing information, often unpublished, and by clarifying particular issues, and we should like to extend our thanks to Sebastian (Bas) van Balen, Michel Devort, Geoffrey Field, Phil Gregory, Stuart Irwin, Paul Jepson, Jean-Paul Julliard, Carlos Keller, Bob Kennedy, Volker Konrad, Albert Martínez-Vilalta, Bob Medland, Anna Motis, Alan Peterson, Asad Rahmani, Richard Schodde, Mutsuyuki Ueta and all the others, regrettably too many to list, who have most kindly sent material of different sorts. Once again we are very grateful to Michael Patrikeev for sending us copies of the relevant pages of the manuscript for his forthcoming book *The Birds of Azerbaijan*. Sue McRae very kindly gave permission for the inclusion of material from her unpublished thesis. Once again, Alan Knox (Buckinghamshire County Museum) kindly checked details concerning several references of scientific descriptions, once again at very short notice!

The relative obscurity of several species in this volume meant that it was at times particularly difficult to locate reference material, especially for the plates, and we owe many thanks to Björn Andersson, Alexander V. Bardin, Albert Bertolero, Andrés Bosso, Marco Favero, Tim Fisher, Jon Fjeldså, Peter Harrison, Vladimir M. Loskot, Mary LeCroy, Mariano Martínez, Hernán Rodríguez Ponti, C. S. (Kees) Roselaar, Vadim G. Vysotsky and Claudia Wilds. Pica Press (Nigel Redman) kindly helped us with the publication of a photograph which we were particularly interested in including.

The materials used by artists, editors and some authors have been greatly enriched by two most useful agreements: with VIREO at the Academy of Natural Sciences of Philadelphia (Doug Wechsler), involving reference photographs; and the National Sound Archive of the British Library (Richard Ranft), involving recordings of bird vocalizations.

The 33 authors who have participated in the present volume variously express their sincere gratitude to David Allan, Gary Allport, Vania Soares Alves, Dan Anderson, Paulo de Tarso Zuquim Antas, Allan J. Baker, Mark Barter, Peter Becker, Albert J. Beintema, N. Belialov, O. Belialov, William Belton, Tom Benson, Walter J. Bock, P. D. Boersma, Marcel Boulet, Patricia Bradley, C. G. Bradshaw, Joël Bried, Don

22

Bruning, Kees Camphuijsen, John Chardine, P. A. Clancey, C. Clinning, Charlie Collins, Sheila Conant, Courtney J. Conway, John Cooper, Jack Cowrie, Robert H. Day, Scott R. Derrickson, George Divoky, David Duffy, Charles Duncan, J. Durbin, William R. Eddleman, Graeme Elliott, the Erickson family, Peter J. Ewins, Mario Fasola, P. G. H. Frost, Sean Furness, Anthony Gaston, A. Giles, B. Giles, Alex Gochfeld, David Gochfeld, Deborah Gochfeld, Petra de Goeij, Paul Goriup, P. Gowthorpe, Alfred Gross, H. Hafner, R. van Halewyn, Brian Harrington, Ross Harris, Rod Hay, Helen Hays, P. Houde, Marshall Howe, Tom Howell, Kees Hulsman, Mike Imber, Johan Ingels, Paul Isenmann, Eve Iversen, Joe Jehl, P. A. Johnsgard, Oscar W. Johnson, Ian Jones, Gary Kaiser, Brina Kessel, Mikael Kilpi, Dick Kimber, B. King, Fritz L. Knopf, B. A. Lane, Olivier Langrand, Mary LeCroy, David S. Lee, Mercedes Lee, Fred Lesser, Yves Létocart, N. M. Litvinenko, B. Loos, P. Luttikhuizen, Francisco Mallet-Rodrigues, Jeffrey S. Marks, John Maron, Rodney Martins, David S. Melville, Peter Miles, J. A. Mills, Colin Miskelly, Doug Mock, Robert Montgomerie, Ralph Morris, Guy Morrison, William Moskoff, Taej Mundkur, Luis G. Naranjo, Inês do Nascimento, M. Angela Nettleship, Ian Nisbet, Rob Norton, Storrs Olson, Lewis W. Oring, Henri Ouellet, José Fernando Pacheco, Gary W. Page, Dennis R. Paulson, Bob Paxton, Sarah Paxton, Charles Pickett, Manuel Plenge, Sarah Plimpton, John Ralph, Bill Robertson, Chris Robertson, Danny Rogers, Kees Roselaar, Rosanne Rowlett, Margaret Rubega, Marucio Rumboll, Keith Russell, C. Safina, Paul Sagar, H. Sakalauskas, Jorge Saliva, Betty Ann Schreiber, Stanley E. Senner, Dave Shealer, Roy Siegfried, Serge Sirgouant, Margaret A. Skeel, A. Sokolov, David Sonneborn, Bill Southern, Jeff Spendelow, Ann Sutton, Jean-Marc Thiollay, Pavel S. Tomkovich, Greg Transue, Dorothy Tunbridge, Tom Van der Have, R. P. Vari, Dick Veitch, Enriqueta Velarde, Christophe Verheyden, Yvonne Verkuil, J. Viksne, F. E. Warr, Michael Walters, Nils Warnock, Doug Watkins, A. Wassink, Karen Weaver, David Wells, C. P. Wilds, F. A. Wilkinson, M. Witte, Glen Wolfenden, Robin Woods, Gilson Evaritso Iack Ximenes, Pablo Yorio, Victor Zubakin and G. A. Zweers. Several authors also offer their kind thanks to others already participating as authors of this volume.

Permission was generously granted for the use of distributional data and information from species accounts of Rallidae for the forthcoming Southern African Bird Atlas. The chapter on Charadriidae is publication number 3002, and the chapter on Scolopacidae is publication number 3003 of the Netherlands Institute for Sea Research (NIOZ), Texel.

Miquel García and César Ruiz helped most efficiently in the production of the book. For help in many different ways, our grateful thanks go to Maria Josep de Andrés, Ventura Boluda, Dolors Buxó, Juan Antonio Cantí, Carles Carboneras, Fortunato Frias, Oriol Frias, Sònia Frias, Sílvia Muray, Maria Teresa Obiols, Deli Saavedra and R. D. Wooller. Last, but by no means least, our grateful thanks go to Toni Llobet for kindly providing the back cover illustration.

Order OPISTHOCOMIFORMES

Opisthocomiformes

Opisthocomidae

Hoatzin

Family OPISTHOCOMIDAE (HOATZIN)

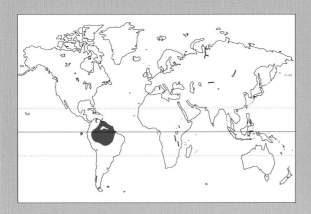

- Large, gregarious, arboreal birds, with prominent crest, long tail and large wings.
- 62-70 cm.

- N South America, E of Andes.
- Tropical forested wetlands.
- 1 genus, 1 species, 1 taxon.
- No species threatened; none extinct since 1600.

Systematics

The Hoatzin (*Opisthocomus hoazin*) is a monotypic species of uncertain affinities. Since it was first described in 1776, there has probably been more controversy regarding its systematic position than that of any other bird species. It was originally named *Phasianus hoazin* by P. L. S. Müller, implying an affinity with the Galliformes. In an 1840 publication, C. L. Nitzsch linked it with the Musophagidae, a family which is now considered to belong to the Cuculiformes. Over the years it has variously been allied to the Tinamidae, Cracidae, Rallidae, Otididae, Pteroclidae, Columbidae and Coliidae, and recently to the Cariamidae.

Most frequently, however, the Hoatzin has been considered to share some characters with the Galliformes, and it has tended to be placed near Cracidae. Nevertheless, in recent years there has been a strong move to link it with the Cuculiformes, where it is sometimes placed in close association with the anis (*Crotophaga*) and the peculiar Guira Cuckoo (*Guira guira*). The problem is that the Hoatzin is so aberrant in both morphology and behaviour that it does not fit satisfactorily alongside any other group of living birds. Apparently, it has gone through a long and independent evolution, retaining some primitive ancestral characteristics, while evolving other, more recent, specialized features.

More conservative systematists retain the Hoatzin in the order Galliformes, based on osteological and immunological data, and possibly also on account of its microscopic feather structure. In contrast, recent evidence from egg-white protein, DNA-DNA hybridization, scleral ossicles (bones of the eye-ring) and behaviour suggest its affinities are with the Cuculiformes. However, the evidence is equivocal, and the fact that the Hoatzin has the anisodactyl foot of most birds, with a single toe pointing backwards, rather than the zygodactyl foot of the cuckoos, with two toes that can be turned backwards, has been considered a major obstacle to this view. The evidence of feather lice does not appear to help, as most of the Mallophaga genera found on the Hoatzin are unique, while the one that has been found on other species occurs widely on species such as the Green Ibis (*Mesembrinibis cayennensis*), a coincidence which is assumed to be the result of these species sometimes sharing the same habitats.

Thus, the nearest living relatives of the Hoatzin, normally regarded as one of the most primitive of modern birds, remain a subject of controversy. Currently, most taxonomists award the Hoatzin at least its own suborder, Opisthocomi. However, the lack of consensus as to which are its closest relatives, combined with a fairly generalized agreement that it is quite distinct from all other birds, suggests that the most appropriate course is probably to place it in its own separate order, Opisthocomiformes, a view advocated by E. Stresemann as long ago as 1934, which has come back into favour fairly recently.

A single Tertiary fossil, *Hoazinoides magdalenae*, dating from the Miocene 18 million years ago, was discovered in Colombia and has been linked with the Cracidae. The fossil site was in the upper Magdalena Valley in the department of Huila, an inter-Andean area beyond the present day distribution of the Hoatzin, although in that period the Andes had not yet been uplifted. Interestingly, this fossil, the only avian fossil from the site, was found in close association with a fossil monkey, *Cebupitheca sarmientoi* (see Breeding). Another fossil genus, *Filholornis*, from the Upper Eocene or Lower Oligocene of France, has been linked to both the cracids and the Hoatzin.

Recently, a new fossil family of landbirds, Foratidae, from the Lower Eocene Green River Formation in Wyoming has been erected for *Foro panarium*, a new genus and new species, based on a nearly complete, associated skeleton. The skull and mandible are most similar to those of the Hoatzin, but the postcranial skeleton shows some similarities to the Musophagidae. Also of interest is a Hoatzin-like fossil fragment which has been reported from Eocene deposits in Argentina.

Since the ancient, reptilian-like, feathered dinosaur *Archaeopteryx* had three functional claws on each wing, some earlier systematists speculated that the Hoatzin was descended from it, because nestling Hoatzins have two functional claws on each wing (see Breeding). However, modern workers believe that the young Hoatzin's claws are of more recent origin, and may be a secondary adaptation resulting from its frequent need to leave the nest and climb about in dense vines and trees well before it is capable of flight.

Morphological Aspects

The generic name *Opisthocomus* comes from the Greek, meaning "wearing long hair behind" and refers to the Hoatzin's most distinctive plumage feature, its unusual crest. Much of the time the narrow, 4-8 cm long, somewhat stiffly shafted, mainly rufous crest feathers remain individually erect in a loose manner. This crest, combined with a red iris, prominent eyelashes, and a large bright blue bare orbital and facial area that extends to the bill and around and beyond the ear, gives the Hoatzin a bizarre

and somewhat startled appearance. In addition, this large, but small-headed, long-necked and long-tailed bird often crouches and peers out from between thick leaves in a suspicious manner.

The dorsal plumage is mainly bronzy olive with prominent pale buff streaks on the nape and mantle, while the brown wing-coverts are edged with three distinctive white bars. The ten rectrices of the tail are long, dark brown and very broadly tipped buffy white. The Hoatzin's primaries are chestnut, while the secondaries are brown, like the back and the tail. Below, the throat and breast are buffy white, gradually becoming rich chestnut on the thighs and the vent. The short, laterally compressed, black or dark olive-coloured bill is stout, and the strong-looking legs and large feet are also blackish. Sexes are similar, and adults weigh in the region of 700-900 g.

In general, adult Hoatzins have the appearance of a pheasant or, in the Western Hemisphere where there are no native pheasants, a cracid. Indeed, a common name for the Hoatzin in Venezuela is *Guacharaca de Agua* or "Water Chachalaca", because it seems similar to the more terrestrial and abundant Rufous-vented Chachalaca (*Ortalis ruficauda*).

Anatomically, the Hoatzin's greatest peculiarity is its unique foregut, which is far larger than its stomach, and in which it processes great quantities of vegetable matter in the manner of a ruminant (see Food and Feeding). The foregut and its contents sometimes make up 25% of the bird's total weight, while its size imposes strict constraints on much of the bird's lifestyle. In order to accommodate this large bulk, the sternum is greatly reduced, with a consequent reduction of flight muscles, which limits the Hoatzin to flying and gliding only in short, heavy bursts. While flight appears weak and awkward, a bird can cover as much as 350 metres in a single flight, though most flying involves much shorter distances. The bird's legs and feet trail below the body during these short, somewhat laboured, flights.

Birds can grasp branches, but they climb and creep about awkwardly in the often dense vegetation of their habitat, and this means of locomotion appears clumsy. Hoatzins perch in a conventional manner, but much of the time is spent in sternal perching, resting on a sternal callus, while lengthy digestion takes place. The callosity is an elliptical horny patch of skin lying over the rear tip of the sternum.

Only young Hoatzins seem able to swim well (see Breeding), and this is exclusively a predator-avoidance tactic. Adult birds found in the water have almost certainly been frightened there, and swimming by adults is generally rare. Although their legs and feet appear well developed and strong, neither adults nor young hop or walk on the ground. Their legs and feet may have evolved for clutching onto leafy branches over water, but they are not zygodactyl as in the Cuculidae (see Systematics).

The Hoatzin's anatomy and restricted locomotion can be attributed to its folivorous diet. Adults, being essentially non-swimmers, poor fliers and weak climbers, are among the most spacially restricted of all birds. Hoatzin social behaviour probably evolved as a result of their morphological limitations.

Because Hoatzins spend their lives in, and climbing through, thick arboreal vegetation, they show an unusual amount of feather wear and breakage. This is especially evident in the severe abrading of the tail, where the wide, buffy white terminal band is often extremely worn or even missing. Moult of adults takes place, as in most birds, following the breeding season, which is the early dry season. In a six month old bird, primary moult progressed outward from the first primary, but secondary moult had two centres, beginning with the tenth and first feathers. Moult on both sides of the tail began almost simultaneously with the outer and inner pairs progressing evenly towards the third pair.

Few birds have a greater reputation than the Hoatzin for an unpleasant odour; in Guyana the species is even called the "Stinking Pheasant". The smell is described as musky or like fresh cow manure, and this smell is thought to be a result of the processing of foliage in the foregut. However, several authors in Venezuela report little or no odour; this might be the result of different species of leaves being eaten there. W. Beebe cooked and ate the flesh of birds he was preparing, and he reported that although tough, the taste was "clean and appetizing as that of a curassow" (Cracidae); he doubted that the persistent odour was connected with the crop contents.

Habitat

Hoatzins are reported to be found up to an altitude of 500 m, but most birds live in the range of about 5 m above sea-level up to about 200 m. They are completely dependent on riparian vegetation in lowland habitats of the Neotropics.

The Hoatzin's range is exclusively east of the Andes, in the drainage basins of the Rivers Amazon and Orinoco, and along the Atlantic coast in Guyana, Surinam and French Guiana, where the species is associated with rivers that flow north and northeast into the ocean. The kind of water within the habitat, be it salt, brackish or fresh, appears to make little difference to the Hoatzin because it lives entirely in trees, vines and bushes, and is thus independent of the different kinds of aquatic foods that each of these water types support. In many areas the species is frequently associated with giant arums, especially those of the genus *Montrichardia*, which constitute a favourite food. In coastal zones *Avicennia* mangroves can be similarly important.

The selection of habitat depends entirely on the existence of dense fluvial-associated vegetation, beside and overhanging sluggish rivers, streams, ox-bow lakes, swamps and lagoons.

The same thick, often thorny, vegetation provides the birds with all their basic necessities for life, namely food and nesting and roosting sites. Nevertheless, Hoatzins are patchily distributed throughout their range. Often they seem plentiful in one area, but nearby there is a hiatus in seemingly acceptable habitat; perhaps this is connected with their physical limitations.

General Habits

The Hoatzin's restriction to dense trees, vines and bushes that line the waterways of Neotropical lowlands may have evolved because of the bird's evolutionary choice of a vegetarian diet, and its consequent ruminant behaviour. The anatomical modifications necessary to accommodate the bulky foregut (see Morphological Aspects), and to slow digestion, have combined to restrict the bird's capability of movement, which in turn has behavioural implications.

Hoatzins are highly social at all times of the year, and at times can be seen in groups of more than 40 birds. Two adults will sometimes perch in bodily contact with each other. During breeding, birds occupy small, densely packed, exclusive territories (see Breeding), but in the dry, non-breeding months they live in large, tight groups of as many as 100 individuals or more.

In the past, various authors reported that Hoatzins were colonial, but long-term ringing studies showed that, when breeding, they maintain exclusive, but exceedingly small, territories. Nevertheless, in Peru a non-territorial group of 28 birds was reported to nest colonially in a single tree.

Hoatzins rain-bathe while perching in trees by spreading their wings and erecting their dorsal feathers. They often climb to exposed perches to sun-bathe, turning their backs to the sun and spreading their flight-feathers. Self-preening is frequent, whereas allopreening has not been observed, either between adults, or between adults and their offspring, in spite of the large numbers of ectoparasitic eggs often clearly visible on their faces and feathers. Some of these parasites have been identified only with the Hoatzin host, but no systematic clues, that would suggest relationships to other living bird families, have been found among those parasites so far examined (see Systematics). Head scratching is direct, under the wing. Non-nesting Hoatzins spend about 75% of the day in two forms of roosting behaviour, conventional perching and sternal perching (see Morphological Aspects).

Voice

Hoatzins are noisy, and groups of birds often call in unison, when the combination of their numbers and their curious vocal repertoire can create a great commotion.

They have a large number of vocalizations including hoarse cries, grunts, croaks, growls and hissing. Many of these calls are accompanied by the spreading of the wings and tail. Contact calls, between members of a social unit, are in a series of 3-10 grunts, "oww" or "ohh". In nest defence, birds use a wheezing, raspy nasal hiss, "waaahh", which is a response to predators, humans and low-level territorial intrusions. A high-intensity raspy hiss is used in defence of young, and a gutteral 0·5 second "rrruuh" is used in the social unit, most commonly between individuals of mated pairs. Chicks out of the nest make location calls, and young will beg for food with raspy peeps.

Food and Feeding

Formerly, it was thought that Hoatzins, near-obligate folivores, ate only the leaves of arums (Araceae) and the mangrove *Avicennia*, and were thus confined to fluvial areas where these plants grew. This idea arose because early observations of Hoatzins were made in the vegetation beside saline and brackish waters of rivers in the Guianas, near the Atlantic coast.

Hoatzins are primarily social birds, living in groups all the year round. During the breeding season tight little units of 2-8 birds typically occupy and defend a territory and co-operate in the breeding effort. Outside the breeding period the groups tend to be much larger, and such large gatherings are often rather noisy. Owing to the species' limited powers of flight, and of locomotion in general, the birds are highly sedentary, and indeed are rather sluggish, being far from nimble climbers. Most feeding activity takes place in the morning and near dusk, but birds will also feed on moonlit nights when they can become extraordinarily vocal. Otherwise, apart from preening and indulging in sun- and rain-bathing occasionally, they spend a large proportion of their time simply resting in the trees.

[Opisthocomus hoazin, Photo: François Gohier/ Ardea]

The Hoatzin's fundamental habitat requirement is the existence of marshy plants, preferably giant lilies (Montrichardia) and also Avicennia mangroves, and it depends largely on such plants for its almost exclusively folivorous diet. Endowed with a peculiarly large crop, the bird, when it has eaten its fill, tends to become top-heavy and therefore unstable. At such times it typically rests on a sternal patch of horny skin which it situates on a branch, and the bird may remain in such a position for long periods at a stretch, in order to digest in comfort its bulky intake of green leaves.

[Opisthocomus hoazin, Manu National Park, Peru. Photo: Günter Ziesler]

Nowadays, they are known to eat more than 50 species of plants. In one study in the Venezuelan *llanos*, they ate 82% green leaves, 10% flowers and 8% fruits. However, their usual diet in this region consists of fewer than a dozen species of plants, while only some four or five plant species compose three quarters of this diet over the year. Hoatzins are especially partial to the leaves of tropical legume trees, many of which contain toxic compounds (see Relationship with Man). Furthermore, they are selective, choosing to eat young leaves, tender shoots and buds, which are higher in water content, as well as being both easier to digest and more nutritious.

Other leaf-eating birds, such as the Ostrich (*Struthio camelus*) and grouse (Tetraonidae), have hindgut fermentation like horses. In contrast, Hoatzins ferment their vegetable matter in the foregut like cows, sheep, deer and kangaroos. Plant-eaters obtain most of their usable sugars from the cellulose of plant cell walls, but they have to rely on microbes, such as bacteria, protozoans and fungi, which live in the gut, to break down the cellulose by means of fermentation.

The digestive tract of the Hoatzin is one of extreme adaptation. Unlike the case in other birds, the Hoatzin's crop and lower oesophagus are the main digestive organs. In this, the Hoatzin's foregut is similar to that of cows. A thick-walled, muscular crop and lower oesophagus take the place of the cow's rumen, as the site of active fermentation under constant temperature and acidity. The crop and lower oesophagus are large and voluminous, as compared with the proventriculus and gizzard, which are the main digestive organs in more typical birds. The Hoatzin's foregut contains layers of powerful muscles with folded, ridged interiors, lined with tough, horny tissue to break down the food. In addition, there are two constrictions or filters to the flow of coarse vegetable matter, which slow down the passage of food. In many bird species, the period of time for which food is retained is often measured in minutes, but the Hoatzin holds the record. In experiments, liquids were retained for about 18 hours,

and solids for 24-48 hours; these retention times are similar to those found in sheep, and are long enough to maintain stable populations of gut bacteria.

The process of the Hoatzin's foregut fermentation is complex and specialized, because it takes the place of chewing and rumination, producing usable volatile fatty acids, before the food passes through all the usual avian digestive organs. Several reasons have been suggested for this, such as the Hoatzin's high food selectivity and typical high avian energetic demands, but recent research has shown that the Hoatzin is able to digest a much higher proportion of its food than other plant-eating birds on comparable diets, and indeed that it is similar in performance to ruminants. Current speculation suggests that foregut fermentation also allows bacteria to detoxify noxious chemicals before the food can be absorbed or fed to young, while the microbial synthesis of essential amino acids and vitamins may help to give the bird a more balanced diet.

Nestling and young Hoatzins are fed from the adults' crops on this same regurgitated half-digested foliage, a sticky, greenish, pre-digested mash. It is rich in bacteria, which help to inoculate the young birds' developing crops with the necessary fermenting microbes. Because of the low nutrient value of the Hoatzin's food, the young grow very slowly.

Hoatzins rarely drink, probably because 70% of their leaf diet comprises water, but when they do drink, they tip the bill into water, then tilt the head back and upwards, like most birds. There are two reports of Hoatzins eating foods that were not vegetable, namely small fish and a crab.

The principal times of diurnal foraging are in the early morning and the early evening, and they usually last one or two hours. Birds generally forage within some 50 m of a watercourse. They spend the hot midday hours sternal perching in the shade, digesting the plant matter in their crops. On moonlit nights they typically vocalize, and travel up to 300 m from their defended

The Hoatzin's clutch usually consists of two eggs. Incubation, lasting about a month, is carried out by the monogamous pair of parent birds aided by all the group members, normally their own young of previous seasons. By day ten, the chicks have developed thick dark brown down, but their growth is very slow. Though the young birds may leave the nest at 2-3 weeks old, parents and helpers will carry on both feeding and brooding them for as much as two months. It has been calculated that breeding success can be increased substantially by the participation of helpers.

[*Opisthocomus hoazin*, Venezuela. Photo: Bruno Pambour/ Bios]

territories in order to feed. Then all the birds of a social unit, excepting those individuals that are incubating or brooding, forage close together.

Breeding

Breeding takes place during seasonal rains. Throughout much of the Hoatzin's range the climate is strongly seasonal, with six months of rain, four months of drought, and two intermediate months between the seasonal extremes; as the rains begin at quite different times of the year in the regions roughly 5° north and 5° south of the equator, the timing of breeding is better described by seasonal rainfall than by month. Furthermore, because the rainfall is bimodal in the Guianas, where early observations were made, there were conflicting reports of breeding months.

The highly gregarious Hoatzins live and breed in stable social groups of two to eight birds. Two is the most common unit and more than five is rare. The extra birds are subadult and adult helpers, and ringing has shown that nearly all helpers are the young from previous nestings of the pairs they help. A few immigrant, non-breeding helpers were found, and while they lived in the territories and were accepted by territory holders, the immigrants usually helped very little, more often in territorial defence than in rearing the young. Of all first-year birds studied, 90% stayed and helped their parents during subsequent breeding attempts. By the time helpers were four and five years old, the percentage still helping in their natal unit dropped to 20% and under 10% respectively. Most of the long-term helpers were males, because in the Hoatzin females are the dispersing sex, and most of them had left their natal units by the time they were three years old.

Hoatzin helpers take part in all breeding activities except reproductive copulation and egg-laying. In general, it was found that helpers partially emancipated female Hoatzins, and also that they significantly increased reproductive success. In territories with helpers the young were able to leave the nest, which becomes increasingly predation-prone, on average a week earlier than in territories without helpers. Helpers were particularly active in territorial defence, but they also assisted with

nest building, incubation and brooding, and fed both nestlings and fledglings. Yet, despite these apparently clear advantages, about 45% of Hoatzin territories did not have helpers.

These social units defend small, well defined, all-purpose territories throughout the breeding season. Breeding males of adjacent territories sometimes engage in aerial battles, flying at

The Hoatzin's diet is composed almost entirely of vegetable matter. When feeding the young, the parent or helper will regurgitate from its crop a semi-digested slimy mass, which the chick receives by introducing its opened bill well into the adult's gape. The chick often pecks at the adult's bill to provoke regurgitation. Although the young Hoatzin is well able to fend for itself after about three months, this begging behaviour can continue until it is 4-5 months old.

[*Opisthocomus hoazin*. Photo: F. Köster/ Survival Anglia/ Oxford Scientific Films]

each other from 3-5 m apart, and colliding in mid-air breast-to-breast, pecking and clawing at each other. Usually they fall back into the vegetation, locked together, before separating.

The prominent crest is used in social signalling. The male's crest is strongly erected when he defends his territory, at which time he also extends the neck and spreads his wings and tail. In the female, the crest is depressed and neck retracted when inviting copulation.

In the same study, the defended territories, all adjacent to watercourses, had a mean distance of 42 m along the water, and were defended up to 75 m away from the water's edge. Diurnal activities were usually confined to an area of 1000-3000 m².

Within breeding territories two kinds of copulation take place, display copulation and reproductive copulation. Display copulations constitute a defence strategy. They consist of brief mountings of females by the breeding male, that are directed towards territorial intrusions and displays by neighbouring Hoatzins. These display copulations take place throughout the year and are briefer than reproductive copulations, while the post-display vocalizations are louder and last longer than in reproductive copulations. On the other hand, reproductive copulations have been observed only between the breeding pair, not with their helpers; they occur only during the nest building period and shortly before the laying of the eggs.

The nest is a flat, unlined platform, 30-45 cm wide, made of dry twigs and sticks, sometimes so loosely constructed that the eggs can be seen from below. It is similar to the nest of the Green-backed Heron (*Butorides striatus*), which sometimes breeds nearby. The typical nest, with or without an overhead canopy, is in dense bushes or trees, 2-5 m above water. Successful nests and nest-sites are reused in subsequent years.

The usual clutch consists of 2-4 eggs, which are somewhat variable in shape from elliptical to oval, and which are said to resemble the eggs of rails (Rallidae). They are white, heavily overlaid with small dots and spots of reddish brown and lavender. The mean measurement of 111 eggs in Venezuela was 46·7 x 33·1 mm. Eggs are laid 1·5-2 days apart, and incubation begins with the laying of the second egg, lasting a total of 30-31 days; as with most other aspects of breeding, all members of the group co-operate. In the same study, renesting occurred as many as six times when a nest failed, as long as the rains continued. Successful nesting early in the season for units of 4-6 birds was followed, on rare occasions, by a second nesting.

The semi-nidicolous young hatch within a day of each other in two-egg clutches, but up to four days apart in larger clutches; the adults eat the eggshells. At hatching, the chicks weigh 17-21 g and are of a pale flesh colour, with sparse down, but by the fifth day the skin has changed to dark brown-black, and by the tenth day the nestlings are covered with a thick coat of dark brown down. Their eyes open within a day of hatching, and by the third day they move about in the nest using their wings and feet to help them; the legs and feet are very large in proportion to the size of the chicks. Growth is slow in the young birds, and their flight-feathers are only emerging from the sheaths by days 20-25.

Nestling Hoatzins are brooded continuously for up to three weeks, by both parents and their helpers. As early as their third day, young Hoatzins will jump out of their nests into the water below to avoid predators, although research has shown that these young have a lower chance of subsequent survival; if they are older, five or six days old, their chances of success are greater. Even the youngest birds, when fleeing predators, are able to swim by propelling themselves with alternate kicks of their feet. They can also dive and swim under water, using the wings synchronously. Although chicks can swim six metres or more, as soon as they reach the bushes and trees of their natal patch they climb up using the two claws on each wing, assisted sometimes by arching the neck over twigs and small branches, and by using their toes and bills. In this they are sometimes encouraged by vocalizations from the adults, but even without help, the young birds make peeping sounds that aid their parents and territorial helpers to find them. On one occasion, five birds of a territorial unit spread their wings over a young bird as it made its way into the safety of a dense cover of leaves. Early authors reported that the young find their way back to their nests. However, recent studies have found that the young do not return to the nest, but are cared for, brooded, fed and defended on various branches within the natal territory.

Undisturbed young Hoatzins leave the nest at 2-3 weeks of age, when they are sometimes coaxed away from the nest by the adults. The juvenile birds are still brooded and fed off the nest for up to two months. By days 55-65 these juveniles can fly short distances. The young shed their wing claws between days 70 and 100, but some individuals have been found to regrow them later; eight of 24 adults had non-functional, callused-over wing claws. The nestlings' claws are small, rounded hooks on digits two and three (see Volume 1, page 37); some authors,

When danger threatens, with the sudden appearance of an enemy, even a very young nestling will employ a predator-evasion mechanism by jumping out of the tree or nest into the water below. There it can swim, even under water as here, using both the wings and the feet to propel itself forwards. Eventually it manages to hoist itself onto the bank and then up into the vegetation or a tree, calling at the same time to enable a parent or helper to locate it more easily and so come to its aid.

[*Opisthocomus hoazin*, Guyana. Photo: Alan Root/ Survival Anglia/ Oxford Scientific Films]

using older systems of digit numbering, report that the claws are on digits one and two.

Successful nesting in the Venezuelan *llanos* was increased by the presence of helpers, but still only 27% of 404 nests were successful. Most failures in this study were due to predation of entire clutches of eggs or of all the chicks by the wedge-capped capuchin monkey (*Cebus olivaceus*). Other predators were the tayra (*Eira barbara*) and also ants, which sometimes attacked pipping eggs or live, newly-hatched young. The occasional disappearance of young was probably caused by avian nest predators, such as the Collared Forest-falcon (*Micrastur semitorquatus*), the Bicoloured Hawk (*Accipiter bicolor*), the Great Black Hawk (*Buteogallus urubitinga*), the Crane Hawk (*Geranospiza caerulescens*) and the Ornate Hawk-eagle (*Spizaetus ornatus*). Mammalian nest predators in a Venezuelan study area, where 58% of Hoatzin nests failed, and where neither capuchins nor tayras were present, were the common opossum (*Didelphis marsupialis*), the grison (*Galictis vittata*), the crab-eating raccoon (*Procyon cancrivorus*) and the ocelot (*Felis pardalis*). The survivorship of 60-80% that was recorded for adult Hoatzins is high.

Nestlings and fledglings are fed for several months with partially digested leaf mash, regurgitated from the crops of brooding birds; young birds will put their heads into the open bills of the adults. They beg for food by pecking at the adults' bills and making high-pitched peeps, behaviour that sometimes continues until they are four to five months old. Yet, between one and two weeks of age, nestling Hoatzins begin to sample leaves near their nests, although they do not feed independently until they are 50-70 days old.

Normally, mated pairs are monogamous, though rarely they can be polygamous, but 7% of the breeding units in one study consisted of more than a single breeding pair within a single defended territory. In these unusual circumstances, which generally occurred in units of 6-7 birds, some birds used the same nest for egg-laying and others made two separate concurrent nests in the same territory.

Rarely, Hoatzins attempt breeding as yearlings, although one such male ended up with infertile eggs. About 10% breed at two years old, whereas most start to breed when they are three years old. In the same study, the recorded nest success rate of first-time breeders was comparable or slightly lower than that of the population as a whole. One breeding male lived more than eight years, but it seems highly likely that in due course long-term studies will find much older individuals in a stable population.

Movements

In accordance with their weak flying abilities, Hoatzins are essentially sedentary. This is especially true of those with the most favourable, predator-free territories on riverine islands.

During the dry non-breeding season, the most stressful time for the birds, many Hoatzins in the Venezuelan *llanos* move short distances. In particular, those with marginal or poor quality breeding territories move to nearby sites, less than 2 km away, as the water dries off and their arboreal habitats pass through a deciduous phase.

Thus, while their preferred habitat is dense gallery forest, they can tolerate the dry season months in isolated patches of woodland, if these are beside permanent water, supporting trees and bushes that do not entirely defoliate. In the following breeding season, the territorial groups return to the same territories that they abandoned when conditions became unfavourable.

The dry season, in conjunction with the local movements it forces, is the time of greatest natural mortality amongst Hoatzins. A logical consequence of this is that drought years have a strong negative effect on their populations.

Relationship with Man

W. Beebe once described the Hoatzin as "tame to an absurd degree". Thus, the large, sedentary Hoatzin, that lives in conspicuous, highly social groups is well known to all people who share its Neotropical lowland habitat. Nevertheless, there are two quite different cultural reactions to Hoatzins which vary through the nine countries that support populations of the species.

The oldest human relationship with the Hoatzin is, of course, that of indigenous tribal people. In Brazil, these people collect the birds' eggs for consumption. They also occasionally eat the birds themselves, and will take adults for their feathers, for medicinal purposes, and again to use as fish bait. In complete contrast to this, in neighbouring Venezuela Hoatzins are generally despised because they are said to give off a repugnant odour (see Morphological Aspects). The bird's odour, or at any rate its reputation for being both smelly and inedible, has no doubt conferred a measure of protection on it in some parts of its range. Tribal people are, however, a declining element throughout South America, as they become integrated into the contemporary cultures of their sovereign states, or simply wiped out.

Very recently there has been renewed scientific interest in the Hoatzin, as microbiologists and botanists are intensively studying the bacteria and enzymes in the bird's foregut. The natural detoxifiers that it contains, if isolated and transferred to domestic grazing species, such as cows and goats, should permit these mammals safely to eat more native kinds of forage that currently remain toxic for them. This could result in important ramifications both for domestic animal husbandry and for the environment.

Status and Conservation

At present, the Hoatzin's natural habitat still covers an immense area of South America, so the total population is probably still large, and the species relatively secure, at least for the time being. However, future developments will require close monitoring.

The most serious threat to the species is the fast and permanent conversion of its habitat into agricultural concerns, most commonly for rice culture. This has already happened in Guyana, Surinam and Venezuela. Plans for the dyking and canalization of rivers on a vast scale in the Venezuelan *llanos*, if brought to fruition, would seriously affect Hoatzins in that zone. In all nine of the countries with extant Hoatzin populations, there are heavy pressures emanating from many sources that push for the "reclamation" of "useless" frontier lands, in the name of progress, and to accommodate increasing human populations.

The Hoatzin chick possesses a rather rare anatomical feature: on each wing are two claws which enable it to grip branches and clamber around in trees in a singularly awkward, almost reptilian, fashion; these features have been used for likening the species to Archaeopteryx. *The wings appear poorly developed for a chick of this size, but the feet, in contrast, look abnormally large, while there are already signs of an incipient crest.*

[*Opisthocomus hoazin*. Photo: Alan Root/ Bruce Coleman]

This adult Hoatzin, tending two chicks, reveals all its many-coloured splendour. For good reasons it is locally named "Cigana" or "Gipsy", in allusion to its extravagant apparel: the bright blue orbital and facial patch contrasts with the rufous of the crest, chestnut of the primaries, and richer chestnut of the thighs and flanks. The native populations of northern South America have, of course, long known of such a conspicuous and sedentary bird, but it is not generally accepted as a game bird on account of its frightful odour. It has, however, suffered some persecution, and in Brazil, for example, is no longer to be found in the vicinity of big cities.

[*Opisthocomus hoazin,* Tambopata Reserve, Peru. Photo: Günter Ziesler]

The preservation of small, isolated patches of intact habitat in a vast area of agriculture, although carried out with the best of intentions, is most unlikely to be of much benefit to the Hoatzin. It must be stressed that the bird's very limited capability for dispersal, in itself a probable reason for its patchy distribution in undisturbed habitat, means that it is extremely poorly designed for escape from rapid habitat changes, even though suitable unaltered habitat may be available only a few kilometres away.

The Hoatzin is a bird that thrives in its native habitat, if given sufficient protection. A good example can be seen in the Venezuelan *llanos* on the Masaguaral cattle ranch, which has been maintained as a private nature reserve for the past 30 years. It is here that much of the most recent research on the Hoatzin has taken place. In the early 1970's the Hoatzin population here was limited to about 20 individuals along the small Guárico River, on the eastern edge of the ranch. Since then, this population has expanded to over 200 birds, in part because of constant protection, and also because some Hoatzins lost their former habitat to rice fields now bordering the south-east side of the ranch. Researchers now believe that the available habitat on the east side of this ranch is saturated. In addition, an isolated area of woodland islands, 5 km to the west on the same protected ranch, and adjacent to a permanent water source maintained in the dry season by deep well pumps, has been naturally colonized from an unknown source.

Similarly, at Limoncocha, close by the River Napo in eastern Ecuador, Hoatzins were an increasing population during the 1970's around a small freshwater lake maintained and con-

trolled by a colony of missionaries. However, the missionaries have since left the station, although the consequences for the Hoatzin population remain uncertain at present. Early in the present century, in Guyana, it was noted that Hoatzins readily spread to the margins of newly constructed canals that served agriculture, if these canals were bordered with the vegetation that the Hoatzins preferred. These examples clearly suggest that existing Hoatzin populations could be maintained easily in suitable habitat in national parks, with no effort other than strict control of human activities. Unfortunately, at present there are few parks within the vast continental range of the Hoatzin that offer adequate protection.

Numerous attempts have been made to maintain Hoatzins in captivity. One zoological society sent three expeditions to Guyana in the early 1960's to collect Hoatzins, acclimatize them and bring them back live. They were unsuccessful in keeping Hoatzins alive in captivity, although a single female survived for nearly six months. In 1989, six Hoatzins were imported from Venezuela by the New York Zoological Society. One bird lived for only a year, but the others have now lived more than five years in the Bronx Zoo. These birds laid and then broke several eggs; no chicks have been hatched yet. What is perhaps more remarkable is that these birds are currently fed on readily available, standard zoological leafy greens and locally grown browse, rather than on any of the exotic, often toxic, plants of their native habitat. It took biologists and nutritionists nearly one year to adapt them gradually to their captive diets. This significant breakthrough suggests the possibility of successful captive breeding in the future.

PLATE 1

inches 7

cm 18

PLATE 1

Genus *OPISTHOCOMUS* Illiger, 1811

Hoatzin

Opisthocomus hoazin

French: Hoazin huppé   **German**: Hoatzin   **Spanish**: Hoazín

Taxonomy. *Phasianus Hoazin* P. L. S. Müller, 1776, Cayenne.
Monotypic family of uncertain affinities. Some morphological similarities with Galliformes, especially Cracidae; recent work suggests relationship with Cuculiformes, near Crotophaginae; closest relatives and position in linear hierarchy remain controversial (see page 24). Monotypic.
Distribution. E of Andes, from Colombia, Venezuela and the Guianas S to Ecuador, Peru, N & C Brazil and Bolivia.

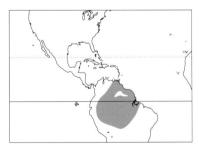

Descriptive notes. 62-70 cm; 700-900 g. Unmistakable. Above dark brown with olive reflections and large white streaks; head rufous with long, narrow, erectile crest; below pale buff to rich chestnut on thighs and vent; broad wings chestnut and brown with white bars on coverts; tail long and broad, with wide pale buffy white tip. Iris red; bare facial skin bright blue; legs, feet and smallish bill black. Female similar to male, but crest said to be slightly shorter. Immature resembles adults.
Habitat. Confined to arboreal vegetation bordering lowland waterways in Neotropics, typically alongside streams, rivers and lakes; in coastal zones, frequently associated with *Avicennia* mangroves. In dry season, some populations may be forced to occupy less favourable woodland habitats if normal preferred habitat dries out.

Food and Feeding. Near-obligate folivore; the only bird species known with foregut microbial fermentation, similar to that of ruminants; lengthy digestion of large amount of plant matter, sometimes toxic and low in nutritive value, has influenced morphology, locomotion and social behaviour (see pages 25, 26). Around 80% of intake consists of new growth of green leaves and buds, with over 50 species of plants recorded, e.g. *Montrichardia*, *Avicennia*, *Cecropia* and water hyacinth (*Eichhornia*); a few flowers and fruits taken in season. Feeds in social groups mainly in early morning and near dusk, and also on moonlit nights.
Breeding. Nests in rainy season, dates varying with locality. Monogamous pairs with up to six helpers, mostly their own young of previous season; rarely polygamous; groups defend small, all-purpose territories beside water. Nest placed in dense trees and bushes over water; unlined, open, flat platform of dry sticks. Usually 2 eggs (2-4); incubation 30-31 days, by all members of social group. Chicks have dark brown down; able to escape predators by diving into water and swimming, then clambering back up into vegetation; normally leave nest at 2-3 weeks old, but unable to fly until c. 60 days old; dependent on adults of social unit for food for 2-3 months. Sexual maturity at 2-3 years.
Movements. Highly sedentary; adults do not swim, walk or hop, and have weak flight abilities. During dry season, some social units from suboptimum habitats join others on short migrations of up to 2 km, to arboreal vegetation situated beside permanent water.
Status and Conservation. Not globally threatened. Widespread in suitable habitat, but very patchily distributed; still locally numerous, but little information available on status from most of range. In French Guiana, has declined due to persecution and is now very local; in Brazil, no longer found close to cities. Due to morphological limitations, a consequence of folivorous diet, unable to move far when habitat becomes unsuitable, notably as result of large-scale clearing, e.g. for rice cultivation or hydrological projects.

Bibliography. Amon (1978), Beddard (1889a), Beebe (1909a), Beebe *et al.* (1917), Blake (1977), Bock (1992), Brush (1979), Chubb (1916), Cracraft (1971, 1981), Domínguez-Bello, Lovera *et al.* (1993), Domínguez-Bello, Michelangeli *et al.* (1994), Domínguez-Bello, Ruiz & Michelangeli (1993), Garrod (1879), Goeldi (1896), Grajal (1991, 1995a, 1995b), Grajal & Parra (1995), Grajal & Strahl (1991), Grajal *et al.* (1989), Grimmer (1962), Haverschmidt (1968), Haverschmidt & Mees (1995), Heilmann (1926), Hellmayr & Conover (1942), Hilty & Brown (1986), Howard (1950), Lucker (1987), Meyer de Schauensee & Phelps (1978), Miller (1953), Morell (1994), Olson (1992), Ortiz & Carrión (1991), Pinto (1964), Pycraft (1895), de Queiroz & Good (1988), Quelch (1888, 1890), Ramo & Busto (1984), Ruiz *et al.* (1994), Ruschi (1979), Rutgers & Norris (1970), Rutschke (1970), Sears (1994), Sibley (1994), Sibley & Ahlquist (1972, 1973, 1990), Sibley *et al.* (1988), Sick (1985a, 1985c, 1993), Skutch (1935, 1966), Snyder (1966), Stegmann (1978), Strahl (1985, 1988), Strahl & Schmitz (1990), Stresemann & Stresemann (1966), Thiollay (1988), Thomas, B.T. (1979), Torres (1987), Tostain *et al.* (1992), Van Tyne & Berger (1959), Vanderwerf & Strahl (1990), Webb (1965), Young (1929).

Order GRUIFORMES

Gruiformes

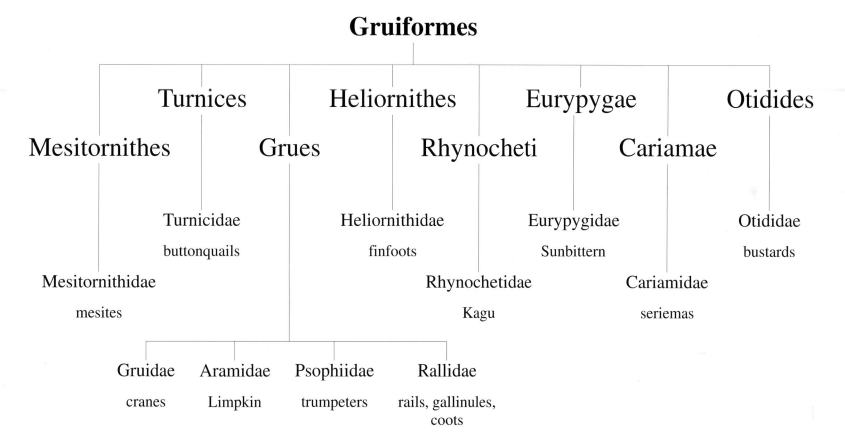

Turnices   Heliornithes   Eurypygae   Otidides

Mesitornithes   Grues   Rhynocheti   Cariamae

Turnicidae

buttonquails

Heliornithidae

finfoots

Eurypygidae

Sunbittern

Otididae

bustards

Mesitornithidae

mesites

Rhynochetidae

Kagu

Cariamidae

seriemas

Gruidae   Aramidae   Psophiidae   Rallidae

cranes   Limpkin   trumpeters   rails, gallinules, coots

Class AVES
Order GRUIFORMES
Suborder MESITORNITHES
Family MESITORNITHIDAE (MESITES)

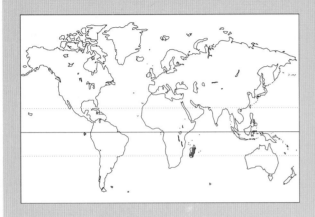

- Medium-sized terrestrial birds with long, full tail, short wings and stout legs.
- 30-32 cm.

- Madagascar.
- Forest, woodland and thicket.
- 2 genera, 3 species, 3 taxa.
- 3 species threatened; none extinct since 1600.

Systematics

The origin and nearest relatives of the mesite family remain mysterious. Since the first scientific description of the family, various authors have associated it with the Columbiformes (pigeons and doves), the Galliformes (pheasants and allies) and even the Passeriformes, in particular the family Cinclidae (dippers). On the basis of structural characters, however, current consensus places the mesites within the Gruiformes, as "primitive" relations of the rails (Rallidae). Compared with the members of that family, they lack pervious nostrils, and their ample tail is composed of 14 rectrices rather than 12, amongst a number of other differences (see Morphological Aspects). The family has always been regarded as ancient, although no fossils have ever been found, and it is frequently considered sufficiently distinct from the rest of the Gruiformes to warrant its own suborder, while some authors have gone further and awarded it a separate order of its own.

The view of the mesites as primitive is, however, open to question; many of their characters seem to be highly derived, implying that the birds have undergone considerable change since evolutionary divergence from other birds. They might better be regarded as advanced birds, early offshoots well adapted to the Madagascan environment before the arrival of humans. Unlike the vast majority of bird families, no DNA analysis has been published, although preliminary results of such research confirm that the birds do indeed belong in the gruiform assemblage.

Mesites, the name originally given by Geoffroy Saint-Hilaire to the genus now containing the White-breasted Mesite (*Mesitornis variegata*) and the Brown Mesite (*Mesitornis unicolor*), was rendered invalid upon discovery that a genus of weevils had already been given this name. The genus was re-named *Mesoenas* after Reichenbach's description of 1862, but it was eventually established that Bonaparte's name *Mesitornis* had precedence, having been published earlier, in 1855. The family name has also been changed accordingly, by tracking the generic name from Mesitidae through Mesoenatidae before reaching its current form.

The validity of the two currently recognized genera has never been challenged since their creation, which was primarily on the basis of bill form and egg structure and form. However, early authors repeatedly confused the Brown Mesite as the female of the White-breasted Mesite, and thus all records of the latter species prior to 1929 (apart from the type specimen) actually refer to the Brown Mesite. This muddle began with the original type

description of the Brown Mesite in 1845, wherein Des Murs put forward the suggestion that the two mesites might, in fact, only be two sexes of the same species. Even though Hartlaub had accepted the two species by 1877, misunderstanding was rife until the 1930's, when Lavauden finally laid to rest the belief that only a single species was involved.

No species could be described as well researched in any aspect. The White-breasted Mesite has been more extensively studied than the other two, while the Brown Mesite, in particular, remains very poorly known.

Morphological Aspects

Mesites are terrestrial birds, roughly the size of large thrushes or small doves. However, in shape they do not resemble either of these groups; they have a distinctive mien that is totally their own. The small head, the long, broad tail and the very thick and extensive undertail-coverts give an almost cylindrical look at times. The tail is usually held closed and only rarely widely fanned out. Short, rounded wings and strong legs characterize all three species and are associated with markedly terrestrial habits and infrequent flight. The bill is slightly or markedly decurved, relatively stout at the base and of short to medium length, according to the foraging specializations of each species (see Food and Feeding). The plumage is generally rather sparse. It is interesting to note that all three species lack oil glands, crops and aftershafts, while they are amongst the few Gruiformes to possess powder-downs.

All mesites are generally rufous brown, with variably paler underparts. These are blotched or spotted black or rufous brown in two of the three species. There is a pale streak above or behind the eye, with bare skin around the eye itself; the prominence of these markings varies within and between species. The legs are pale in colour and tend to be conspicuous in the gloomy conditions of the forest floor. After the post-juvenile moult there is no known variation in plumage with age or season in any species, and only the Subdesert Mesite (*Monias benschi*) is sexually dichromatic.

There is no published information on moult patterns in adult birds. The growth of the wing-feathers and their coverts in chicks seems to occur very early on, compared with the undeveloped state of the body feathers, and suggests a conspicuous relationship with other bird groups with precocial young that show delayed feather development, such as the rails.

Many physical characters seem convergent with rail-babblers (*Eupetes*) and the Sunbittern (*Eurypyga*), two other genera of terrestrial tropical forest birds, and comparisons have also been drawn with the Kagu (*Rhynochetos*) and the Neotropical earthcreepers of the genus *Upucerthia*.

Carriage is horizontal, markedly so in the two *Mesitornis* species, which hold the head and tail flat in a line with the plane of the back, accentuating their cylindrical look. The Subdesert Mesite often holds its head and tail more erect relative to its body.

Mesites generally walk slowly along the ground, never hopping, and running only when threatened, when chasing potential prey, or occasionally when crossing an open area. Each step is accompanied by a gentle head bob and tail flick in the Subdesert Mesite; the tail flick is less regular and the head bob less pronounced in *Mesitornis*. On one occasion a White-breasted Mesite was watched shivering its tail almost continuously, while walking about foraging; this movement was only visible during good close-up views using binoculars, and so may occur more commonly than is realized.

Flight has only been recorded in birds moving up to, or down from, an elevated roost-site, or as an extreme predator evasion tactic, such as when being chased by humans; the wingbeats are vigorous and noisy, like those of a gamebird, and the birds rarely fly more than 20-30 m at a stretch. One White-breasted Mesite was observed to fly for 80 m, but this is exceptional.

Habitat

Mesites occupy a variety of native forest and woodland types, from closed canopy forest through lower, stunted woodland to more open spiny subdesert thicket. No species occurs habitually in plantations, and the extent of use of open woodland varies between the species.

Traditionally, the three species were seen as allopatric, giving a pattern whereby the three major lowland forest types had their own mesite species: the Brown in the eastern humid forest; the White-breasted in the western dry forest; and the Subdesert in the south-western spiny forest. This pattern, elegant in its simplicity, was upset in 1990 by the extraordinary finding of a pair of White-breasted Mesites deep in the eastern rain forest, only 10 minutes' walk away from where sightings of the Brown Mesite had been made. The record was utterly unexpected in the light of previous knowledge, and was all the more baffling because the site, Ambatovaky, is towards the eastern edge of the widest remaining block of rain forest, and thus about as far as possible from the western forest, this species' typical habitat. Further developments are awaited with great interest.

Among all the birds of the forests of western Madagascar, the White-breasted Mesite is one of the species most limited to undisturbed forests. As a terrestrial insectivore, it is a member of a feeding guild recognized as being notably susceptible to forest change throughout the world. Too few data are available on the feeding habits of the other two mesite species to enable the drawing of similar conclusions about them.

Although local seasonal movements may occur in at least one species (see Movements), mesites do not generally move between habitats for purposes of roosting, feeding and breeding. None of the species is generally distributed throughout its main habitat type, with the possible exception of the Subdesert Mesite, but there is no indication which features of the habitat, if any, may be limiting the birds to particular geographical areas. As the Subdesert Mesite appears to be quite catholic in its choice of habitat, it is likely that its range is limited by an inability to disperse across the two large rivers which bound its range. Extensive recent work on the White-breasted Mesite has revealed differences in productivity between forest close to rivers and that at greater distance. This has important implications for conservation (see Status and Conservation).

Mesites typically feed on the ground in areas with thick leaf litter under a rather sparse herb layer. White-breasted Mesites feed preferentially in areas with larger leaves, a denser canopy and shrub layer, and a paucity of dead sticks atop the leaf litter;

The three species of mesites are endemic to Madagascar and all three are rare. Until recently they were held to be allopatric, each species occupying a different type of lowland forest habitat, but the finding of a pair of White-breasted Mesites (Mesitornis variegata) *well away from their usual western dry forest home has caused pause for thought. While further investigation into distribution is needed, it is made difficult by the elusiveness of all Mesites and the dense nature of their forest habitats. The range of the Subdesert Mesite is very restricted: it lives and breeds in the spiny forest of south-west Madagascar, an arid strip of land between the coast and the inland hills, covered in bizarre xerophytic scrub vegetation, including many endemic cactus-like plants and weird trees, such as the tall, many-branched* Didiereas *and dwarf baobabs. Like the other mesites, this species requires plenty of thick leaf litter on ground free of herbaceous growth where it is able to forage freely, probing energetically with its bill for invertebrates and vegetable material, such as seeds and small fruits. At the same time, despite its strongly terrestrial nature, it requires suitable trees or shrubs in which it can place its nest and roost at night.*

[Monias benschi, *near Ifaty, Madagascar. Photo: Peter Morris]*

The White-breasted Mesite is the best documented member of the family. Even so, data are still rather limited and the species is known from only four main sites. Monogamous, it forms a long-lasting, perhaps permanent pair-bond, and moves around the forest in small groups consisting of the parent birds and their most recent young. Pairs and groups maintain and defend territories, and territorial fights sometimes occur. White-breasted Mesites are known to rest and roost regularly in their small social units and choose sites, normally on a horizontal branch up to 4 metres off the ground, where they spend the night remaining in close bodily contact.

[Mesitornis variegata, Ankarana, Madagascar. Photo: Frank Hawkins]

such sticks would prevent the birds sifting through the litter. Nests are placed in the shrub layer, not on the ground, although birds usually walk up lianes to their nests, rather than flying up.

The White-breasted Mesite roosts 1·5-4 m up in shrubs or small trees within the forest. A roost-site of a group of Subdesert Mesites was 3·5 m above the ground, in the crown of a low, densely branched tree, on a branch 4 cm thick. Roosting sites of the Brown Mesite remain unknown as yet, but are expected to be similar to those of the other two species.

General Habits

So far as is known, mesites are exclusively diurnal. As they have distinctive and far-carrying cries, and large amounts of nocturnal survey work (for lemurs) have been carried out in some areas known to support mesites, the lack of records suggests it is unlikely that nocturnal activity is common, if it ever occurs at all. This contrasts notably with some other medium-sized terrestrial forest birds, such as woodcocks (Scolopax). White-breasted Mesites feed most intensively in the early morning and the late afternoon; the midday period, which is particularly hot in the west of the island, is spent in dense shade, the birds often mostly resting, with desultory feeding.

All three species are mainly restricted to the ground, except for roosting and nesting. The birds walk up shallowly sloping branches into trees to roost, visit their nests, or evade predators. They may rest on their tarsi when roosting, whether up a tree on a horizontal branch, on a fallen log, or sometimes on the ground itself. The Subdesert Mesite, although previously described as "apparently unable to fly", is most certainly capable in that regard. Several observers have found these birds either at dawn or dusk at their roost-sites, after hearing their loud calling. When approached, the birds may take off and fly 25-30 m away before landing. Indeed, such elevated roost-sites may be regularly used, and the Subdesert Mesite actually seems to be the species structurally best adapted for flight and arboreal locomotion. Interestingly, it retains its bobbing gait (see Morphological Aspects) while clambering around in tree crowns.

The social unit consists of the pair and their most recent young in the White-breasted Mesite, but it is larger in the Subdesert

Mesite, although precise intra-group relationships have never yet been established for this species. The pair-bond for White-breasted Mesites lasts for longer than one season and possibly for life. Adult Brown Mesites apparently live in pairs, since a high proportion of the few observations made have been of groups of two birds, even though the most widespread local name for the species (see Relationship with Man) suggests that it too occurs in family parties, perhaps containing only one young, in the post-breeding season.

Groups, at least of White-breasted Mesites, tend to move around together and approximately to co-ordinate activities such as feeding, resting or preening. Allopreening is commonly observed in the White-breasted Mesite, mostly between the members of the adult pair, but also, more rarely, between an adult and a juvenile. Feather-shaking is noticeably audible.

Within White-breasted Mesite groups, occasional disputes arise over larger food items. Pairs or groups maintain overlapping, but defended, territories. Territorial battles occur occasionally between groups of White-breasted Mesites, with individual adults fighting individual adults in the opposing group. This involves antagonists flying up in air, pecking and scratching at each other like fighting cocks. It may be that males fight males, and females females; juveniles watch but do not participate. Mesites roost and rest in close bodily contact, usually with all members of the group together.

Adult White-breasted Mesites are preyed upon by Henst's Goshawks (Accipiter henstii), but they show little reaction to passing individuals of the two sympatric species of native diurnal mongoose-like carnivores, the boky-boky (Mungotictis decemlineata) and the vontsira (Galidia elegans), suggesting that they may not be regularly attacked by these species. All species react to the presence of a major predator, such as a nearby person, by making for dense vegetation; if the stimulus is weaker, they may freeze, behaviour which makes them vulnerable to human predation.

The Brown Mesite is considered difficult to see by birdwatchers and researchers alike: O. Appert tells of how he spent six days searching a forest for the species, but managed only one brief sighting, although the "song" was easily heard (see Voice). This difficulty has traditionally been attributed to the bird's great shyness, and other surveys of suitable rain forest have had similarly poor, or even worse, sighting rates. By contrast, in one area, the Masoala Peninsula, daily sightings are possible at some seasons. The other two species are much more easily seen, probably for the simple reason that they occur at higher densities.

Appert describes a form of predator-evasion behaviour called "Camouflage-stillness", in which at the sound of human pursuit, for example, a group of Subdesert Mesites will suddenly scatter simultaneously in all directions, after which the birds stand motionless in the shadows, or fly up onto branches and then lie pressed against them, as if frozen still, for up to half an hour. This freezing behaviour is clearly similar to that shown by *Botaurus* bitterns, another genus of cryptically brown, largely terrestrial birds that inhabit densely vegetated areas. Such species tend to live in areas of low light intensity, and, provided they can remain motionless, they stand a good chance of avoiding detection by potential predators.

Voice

Vocal communication seems to be of crucial importance to mesite life, and the wide vocabularies of these birds include both resonant and harmonious sounds.

All three mesites have "songs", which in the White-breasted Mesite are known to be important in territory defence. White-breasted Mesites, and probably also Brown Mesites, have closely synchronized duets, lasting between 30 seconds and one minute, in which the male and female have different parts. The duet is started by the male, which may also sing individually, in which case the song is much shorter. Rarely, females may sing alone or may initiate duets, especially if female song is heard from a nearby group. Males frequently sing unaccompanied, particularly when the female is on the nest. Subdesert Mesites also have a song which appears to come from more than two members as a chorus. Territory holders are stimulated into vocalizing by hearing other groups calling.

White-breasted Mesites sing all year round, but more frequently in the period October to December, early in the breeding season. Duetting has interesting social implications: sometimes it certainly involves females singing to females

in other groups. It may facilitate the holding of the territory all year round by birds in which plumage is not sexually dimorphic and the adults are long-lived. Although a third member of a group, presumed to be a juvenile, sometimes joins in the duet, this individual's performance is almost always crassly timed and incomplete; usually the duet is performed solely by the male and female. These duets may parallel those performed by other visually inconspicuous birds of the tropical forest understorey, such as many Neotropical wrens, notably those of the genus *Cyphorhinus*.

The Brown Mesite's song, heard particularly between September and February, was described by Appert as a loud, far-carrying, prolonged series of calls "hütjühütjü..." (as transcribed in German), oft-repeated and somewhat reminiscent of the call of the Cuckoo-roller (*Leptosomus discolor*), and also perhaps similar to, but not really confusable with, the loud "song" of another ground-dwelling denizen of the rain forest, the Madagascar Wood-rail (*Canirallus kioloides*), which A. L. Rand well described in the 1930's as "a rather loud, sharp series of whistles, delivered with a rising inflection, that often seemed about to end several notes before it did".

Appert found that Brown Mesite singing was most intense in the early morning, in the period around half an hour on either side of sunrise, and that it was initially delivered from the roost-site, as occurs in the Subdesert Mesite. Song continued to be heard occasionally during the rest of the morning, until about 11:00 hours, but never in the afternoon or evening. This pattern of a strong peak in the early morning echoes that shown by various other highly vocal, territorial inhabitants of rain forest, most notably the gibbons (*Hylobates*) and the grand old man of the Madagascar rain forests themselves, the indri (*Indri indri*). This timing makes full use of the still, cool morning air, which allows calls to carry far and with minimal distortion; thus listening conspecifics may more easily assess the location of the territory being defended.

The Subdesert Mesite too sings mostly in the early morning: in the breeding season the song consists of strophes 33-45 seconds long, whilst outside the breeding season birds sing less frequently and employ shorter strophes. The song starts with a loud, excited series of "züzüzü zizizizi" (transcribed in German) followed by a single, precise "ürr" at a deeper pitch. This is repeated in its en-

For mesites vocal communication seems to be of paramount importance. Both males and females perform alone, in duets, and even in chorus. A certain amount of song is heard throughout the year, presumably for territory maintenance, but it is more frequent from the onset of the breeding season. The Subdesert Mesite sings quite melodiously in the early morning during the breeding season, but more sparingly at other times. The length of the phrases may vary, but a single phrase may last for up to three quarters of a minute. This species is locally known as "Naka", in imitation of its alarm calls.

[*Monias benschi*, Tuléar, Madagascar. Photo: Dominique Halleux/ Bios]

tirety, so that a rhythmic sequence develops: "züzüzü zizizizi ürr, züzüzü zizizizi zi...". The "zü... zi..." series changes somewhat during the course of a single song, such that only the sharp, high "zi" notes can be heard. The "zü..." and the "zi..." notes are probably made by the same individual, whilst the "ürr" is thought to be made by a second individual, the song thus being a duet, as in the genus *Mesitornis*.

The alarm call is rather similar in all species. It is quite loud and sharp or hissing, and is variously transcribed as "tsssk", "zik" or "tschiä", amongst others. Various other calls are much less well known; as in other aspects, the White-breasted is the best studied species.

The White-breasted Mesite shows a limited repertoire of other calls. A quiet "tschht" is given under mild alarm, accompanied by tail-wagging and head-bobbing. A very quiet "pop-pop-pop-pop-pop" while feeding is probably mostly a juvenile contact call. Birds may give a quiet "bub-bub-bub....", sounding like teeth chattering, for about five seconds, on the reunion of members of a pair or group, after they have been temporarily separated; while calling they circle around each other in a seemingly appeasing fashion, with feathers fluffed out. Another similar call, a continuous clucking noise sounding like a distant motorcycle, was heard from a lone male as he climbed up small shrubs, carrying small sticks and prospecting for nesting sites. A much louder call, associated with display, is given immediately after mating; the loud "quee-quee-quee" or "pew-pew-pew-pew" usually lasts only three or four whistles, probably to prevent predators locating the source of the sound, as, though brief, it is very penetrating. A high alarm or contact-seeking call is also given during intra-group conflict.

The Brown Mesite makes a regular, though infrequent, contact call: a distinctive sharp, but low, chicken-like "cluck" or "tschuk". As the birds forage in pairs, they may sometimes be separated, but even then they continue to give contact calls. Appert described the alarm call as a nervous "zik", repeated a few times. Subdesert Mesite chicks in the hand made sharp piping calls, like domestic hen chicks.

Despite the birds' efforts to feed quietly (see Food and Feeding), they can at least sometimes be located by the sounds of rustling leaf litter, particularly when they are probing the ground below.

Food and Feeding

All three species feed on insects, seeds and small fruit in varying proportions, with small adult and larval invertebrates predominating. Crickets, cockroaches and spiders are the dominant invertebrate groups eaten by the White-breasted Mesite, and most of those taken are less than 1 cm long. The Subdesert Mesite also feeds on cockroaches, other recorded items being grasshoppers, caterpillars, beetles, millipedes and seeds; pieces of shell and sand have also been found in the stomachs of collected specimens. Villagers also report that this species eats parts of orchids. In the White-breasted Mesite, seeds feature more in the diet during the dry season. The smallest land vertebrates in the world inhabit the forests of Madagascar, and it is not surprising that on occasion mesites may eat the tiny *Brookesia* chameleons, as some of the species are smaller than the large terrestrial invertebrates. Like them, the chameleons are common in the leaf litter.

Brown and White-breasted Mesites forage by walking slowly around suitable areas, taking a meandering path and investigating their surroundings quietly and methodically. White-breasted Mesites have been intensively studied while foraging. They use three main feeding techniques, which are, in order of importance: flicking over the uppermost dead leaves in the litter layer, and gleaning from the surface; the lifting up large leaves to look underneath for large invertebrates; and gleaning from stems and leaves in the low herb layer. Additionally, rolled-up dead leaves are picked up and thrashed against the ground or the roots or trunk of a tree to shake out any hidden prey, such as beetle larvae. In contrast, the Subdesert Mesite feeds predominantly by probing and digging below the litter layer, as might be deduced from its more robust, longer and more curved bill, but it also makes occasional pecks above ground while walking along.

The shorter and slightly curve-tipped bill of the two *Mesitornis* species is attached to the skull at an angle and position that permit the bird to lift leaves and look carefully underneath without flicking them over. Such leaves are released back to their original positions if nothing is underneath, minimizing disturbance which might flush prey, and noise which might attract predators; a sudden grab is made at any prey located beneath leaves. White-breasted and Brown Mesites may run to chase invertebrates flushed from the leaf litter. During the dry season White-breasted Mesites become more likely to dig at the ground, though they are not known to leave dimples in the soil in the way that feeding Subdesert Mesites usually do. Based on his field experience of the species in the 1970's, Appert suspected that the Brown Mesite might also be responsible for leaving such feeding dimples in the upper soil layer under the leaf litter, as well as in rotting wood, but neither he nor any subsequent observer has proved this.

White-breasted Mesites are often accompanied by Crested Drongos (*Dicrurus forficatus*) which take insects flushed by the mesites and may rob them of larger prey items. Madagascar Paradise-flycatchers (*Terpsiphone mutata*) also take insects flushed by White-breasted Mesites, and both these passerines have been observed following Subdesert Mesites. Foraging White-breasted Mesites may also attract a variety of other small birds, including Madagascar Magpie-robins (*Copsychus albospecularis*) and Long-billed Greenbuls (*Phyllastrephus madagascariensis*), and even another threatened species of similarly restricted range, Van Dam's Vanga (*Xenopirostris damii*). They are also followed by Coquerel's Couas (*Coua coquereli*) and Hoopoes (*Upupa epops*), although the reasons for this are unclear, as there is no interaction with these species; in such associations, both species may possibly enjoy better predator detection.

The diet of chicks remains entirely unknown, in part because adults become very nervous of human observers when accompanied by small chicks, making observations difficult. It is thus not clear whether the chicks are capable of feeding themselves immediately from hatching, as do many unrelated precocial birds, or whether they are absolutely dependent on parental feeding for the first few days, as is the case in other families in the order Gruiformes, such as bustards (Otididae) and rails. Such parental feeding occurs at any rate in *Monias*, with even half-grown young begging for food, but its importance remains unknown.

Mesites, at least the White-breasted, seem to drink only rarely. There is a recorded instance of a bird taking several sips from the water-filled shell of a dead African giant snail (*Achatina fulica*).

Breeding

The two *Mesitornis* species probably show a monogamous mating system, whereas there are suggestions that *Monias* is polygamous, with different females laying in the same nest. Mesites, at any rate the White-breasted, are territorial, and in this species there is some temporal and spatial overlap in territory, but when two groups meet there may be a loud singing competition or even what amounts to a pitched battle (see General Habits).

A similar phenomenon may occur in the group-living Subdesert Mesite: Appert described a kind of ritual fight display, which he saw only once, in November. There were at least three sets of two males in an unusually open, sandy, clear area, a seismic line bulldozed through the subdesert thicket. The males in each couple were opponents and jumped high in the air facing each other, rising up to 30 cm above the ground, but not touching, and staying separated by about 30 cm. In the meantime some females, and also apparently some males, ran here and there, sometimes remaining in the area of the fights, and sometimes disappearing temporarily into the thicket beside the clearing. There was a continuous chorus of loud, excited "zizi ürr zizi ürr..." calls (see Voice). The birds were spread out over 40-50 m of ground, and thus it was not always easy to distinguish the sexes. The lack of other sightings of this phenomenon he put down to the general lack of such open areas in the region where he carried out most of his observations. He heard the same long, drawn out, excited choruses on other occasions at other places in his area, but was not able to see what was going on, presumably due to the impenetrability of the thicket.

The Brown Mesite is a secretive, and thus rarely observed, bird living in remote, dimly lit parts of humid forest. Only two nests have been discovered to date, and consequently information concerning its breeding habits remains fairly scanty. The construction is of interwoven twigs and sticks, thinly lined with grass, and placed in the fork of a tree, 1-2 metres above the ground. It is situated in such a way that the bird can gain access without having to fly. Considering the size of an adult, the single egg seems disproportionately large, but as yet no explanation for this has been offered.

[*Mesitornis unicolor*, Madagascar. Photo: Dominique Halleux/ Bios]

All species breed in the rainy season, with eggs being laid between October and April; those from the latter month probably belong to replacement clutches. The main breeding season of the Subdesert Mesite is in the first half of this period, the austral summer, with a peak in November and December. However, chicks of this species have even been obtained in June, taken when they were following a female. Likewise, there is a May breeding record for the White-breasted Mesite. Copulation has been observed once in July, but this was more likely to be part of the pair-bonding process, rather than a serious attempt at fertilization; it occurred after a bout of allopreening.

The White-breasted Mesite nests so far found have all been 1-3 m above ground in rather thin clumps of vegetation. They are very difficult for human observers to locate, as the selected tangles greatly resemble numerous other clumps in the neighbouring understorey. Subdesert Mesite nests are situated in bushes or shrubby trees, 0·6-2 m above ground, and are usually reached by the birds' climbing up liane tangles. Only two Brown Mesite nests have been found to date, and both were at similar heights in forks of sloping trees well provided with low branches. In all species, the nest consists of small dry twigs, forming a rather loose, flat platform, lined with some leaves and fibres. Clutches usually number 1-3 eggs, but assessment of the number of eggs laid by individual females is complicated by the possibility of more than one female Subdesert Mesite laying in the same nest.

Eggs are in the form of a short ellipsoid, with the poles almost equally rounded. They are whitish or light yellowish brown and variably spotted reddish; the markings may appear a faded brownish or greyish when the pigmented layer is overlain by other shell layers. Surprisingly, given the similar size of adults of the three species, average egg dimensions vary between the species: the Subdesert Mesite, the largest species, lays eggs averaging 37 x 28 mm; in the White-breasted Mesite, the smallest species, the eggs measure 33 x 26 mm; Brown Mesite eggs are a surprisingly large 44 x 30 mm. It is not known why the Brown Mesite lays such anomalously large eggs, if indeed it truly does so, as only two eggs have been measured.

The division of parental care is poorly known for two of the species and utterly unknown for Brown Mesite, for which only two nests have been recorded. Both were at the incubation stage, with females sitting; so confiding were the birds that the collectors were able to remove them by hand. In the White-breasted

Mesite, females appear to do all the incubation, while males remain in the vicinity of the nest, singing occasionally. In the Subdesert Mesite, both sexes incubate and care for the young; at a nest with two eggs, one male and two females were observed. The young are nidifugous, but it is not known how they get to the ground from a nest that is usually 1-3 m up, nor when they leave the nest. In the two better known species, both adults attend the growing family and this is also extremely likely to be so for the Brown Mesite. The length of post-fledging care is unclear, but, at least in the White-breasted Mesite, it may possibly last longer than one year. Because of this extended period of chick-care, group size in the non-breeding season can be used as a measure of breeding success from the previous season. It is probable that birds do not breed every year. The age of sexual maturity is not known for any species.

There is little information on nest predators. There is a documented instance of a White-breasted Mesite nest being depredated by the large snake *Leioheterodon madagascariensis*. Otherwise, possible predators may be conjectured from the animals known to be in the area and their habits. Rodents, both of the native genera *Eliurus*, *Macrotarsomys* and *Nesomys*, and introduced rats (*Rattus*) in some areas, are likely to be the cause of some losses, although adult mesites may be capable of repelling such as these. The extent of colonization of remote forest by *Rattus* species is questionable. Although some visitors reported that these rats were swarming throughout forests several decades ago, many recent workers have found that in primary forest introduced rodents are rare or possibly even absent, and always greatly outnumbered by native species. Nonetheless, it is likely that mesites breeding at the edges of forests sustain heavy predation from rats and have low breeding success. It is likely that nests are also robbed by various birds, notably Hook-billed Vangas (*Vanga curvirostris*).

Movements

White-breasted Mesites hold stable territories of 2-15 hectares, and they tend to move roughly 0·5-1 km around their territory during the day. Roost-sites are not usually the same from one night to the next. Taken together, these findings may imply that resources are depleted by feeding, and that different parts of the territory are used from one day to the next, or they may be part of a strategy to minimize predation.

No seasonal movements are either known or likely for the white-breasted or Subdesert Mesites, but the Brown Mesite may perform altitudinal migrations. It appears to be common in forests on the Masoala Peninsula at any altitude from sea-level up to 500 m during the austral winter, but is apparently absent or much rarer in the same area during the breeding season. This may imply that the species moves uphill during the breeding season, as do many other birds on forested tropical mountains.

Relationship with Man

The three species are all well known to their human neighbours in Madagascar. The Subdesert Mesite is known as "Naka", in imitation of its calls. In the Menabe area, White-breasted Mesites are called "Agolin'ala", from "Agoly", the local name for the White-throated Rail (*Dryolimnas cuvieri*), and "ala", meaning "forest", on account of the roughly similar appearance of the two species. However, at Ampijoroa, the same mesite species is named "Tolohon'ala", from "Toloho", the name for the Madagascar Coucal (*Centropus toulou*), again combined with "ala", although in this case the reasons are less intuitively explicable. In the Ankarana region, the White-breasted Mesite is known as "Fangadiovy", meaning "excavator of yams", although this name is equally applied to many other medium-sized ground-foraging birds in Madagascar, such as ground-rollers (Brachypteraciidae). There is no evidence of any mesite species taking root crops, and indeed they would be most unlikely to do so; the name may provide extra justification for killing them, in much the same way as some lemurs, for example aye-ayes (*Daubentonia madagascariensis*), are regularly accused of stealing chickens.

The Brown Mesite is known as "Roatelo", meaning "two-three", in the northern and central rain forest areas. Although it was previously suggested that this might be a description of the repetition of elements inherent in its "song", the name in fact appears to refer to the species' occurrence in small groups. In the southern rain forests of Madagascar, this name is not recognized, and the name "Tsikozala" or "Tsikozan'ala" is used instead, based on "Tsikoza", again a local name for the White-throated Rail, and,

once again, "ala". Appert noted that the Brown Mesite shared this latter name with Madagascar Wood-rail in this area, and that local people did not distinguish these two species in the field, although they well knew the differences in the hand.

All three mesite species are hunted, especially in forest adjacent to human habitation. One of the capture methods is trapping with nooses, though these are usually intended for larger birds such as the Madagascar Crested Ibis (*Lophotibis cristata*), couas (*Coua*) or the Helmeted Guineafowl (*Numida meleagris*). Other methods include chasing on foot until the birds are exhausted, killing with a sling-shot or bow and arrow, and chasing with dogs into trees, where the birds can be knocked down with sticks or sling-shots. White-breasted Mesites become more timid, sing less and are generally unapproachable in otherwise suitable habitat near villages; densities are also very low in such habitats, implying that hunting and general disturbance have reduced populations.

In the north and central parts of the rain forest, but not in the south, the Brown Mesite is the subject of a powerful taboo, or "fady", which prevents hunting and, in some areas, even the speaking of its name. If young birds are taken, the adults are believed likely to follow the hunter back to the village; this behaviour is taken as evidence of human-like devotion to offspring, which, in turn, deserves human-like respect. In other areas this taboo engenders a terror of the birds themselves. Mesites are by no means unique in this aspect; some of the most powerful fear-inducing animals in Madagascar's forest include the tiny *Brookesia* chameleons, which may measure less than a thumbnail in length. Although this "fady" could conceivably be of occasional local importance in maintaining numbers of the species, taboos are often limited to members of individual families or groups of families, and immigrants to an area often do not respect them. Thus, they are unlikely to have a decisive effect on conservation at the species level, particularly as it is questionable whether hunting *per se* is responsible for the rarity of any of the species.

The White-breasted Mesite is not known to be associated with any taboos, although it is, of course, possible that a taboo so powerful as to preventing the speaking of the bird's name, being difficult to elucidate, could pass unnoticed. However, in areas where it occurs it is well known to local hunters as easy quarry which tastes good. Fortunately, it is not usually targeted because it is too small,

One of the few details that have been established so far as regards the breeding habits of the Brown Mesite is that incubation can be carried out by the female. The role of the male is unknown, and would be difficult to forecast based on the other species, as female White-breasted Mesites (Mesitornis variegata) *are* known to perform the entire task alone, whereas in the Subdesert Mesite (Monias benschi) *both sexes incubate.*

[*Mesitornis unicolor*, Madagascar. Photo: Dominique Halleux/ Bios]

Until recently the Brown Mesite's chick was thought to be blackish, but this photograph demonstrates that such reports were quite unfounded! In fact, an identical error was made with the chick of the White-breasted Mesite (Mesitornis variegata), illustrating just how poorly known these species were, and indeed still are. Most details of breeding have yet to be established for all three mesite species, but it seems quite likely that the chicks may be cared for by their parents for an extended period, at least in the White-breasted Mesite.

[Mesitornis unicolor, Madagascar. Photo: Dominique Halleux/ Bios]

although it is taken opportunistically. A fascinating recent "taboo" is emerging at Ampijoroa Forest Station, adjacent to Anaka-rafantsika. This site has hosted much biological research in recent decades, especially in the botanical gardens, and hunters from neighbouring villages now regard animals in this site as the property of foreigners and accordingly do not hunt them! The mesites in this area are noticeably bold with respect to people.

Status and Conservation

The mesite family is one of the most threatened of all bird families. The latest review of the conservation status of the world's birds by BirdLife International classes all mesite species as globally threatened, placing them in the category Vulnerable. Mesitornithidae is the only bird family of more than two species in which all of the species are classified as globally threatened. All three species are forecast to suffer a rapid population decline in the near future, a decline which is expected to exceed 50% over the next 20 years. This gloomy outlook is based on the high rates of destruction, degradation and fragmentation of the indigenous forest types to which the birds are restricted.

The White-breasted Mesite and the Subdesert Mesite have particularly small ranges on a global scale, rendering them especially vulnerable to habitat-related pressures, which are caused in the main by subsistence agriculture, commercial exploitation for timber and charcoal, and bush fires; hunting may have an important effect locally. In addition, the Subdesert Mesite is also considered to be at risk simply due to the very small size of its population, in conjunction with the aforementioned decline.

The precise distribution of the Brown Mesite within its range appears to be much less patchy than is that of the White-breasted Mesite, and the relative paucity of records must be at least partly due to the bird's shy and retiring nature, combined with the density of the rain forest vegetation, which easily hides the birds and greatly impedes the quiet following up of suspected mesites by observers. Also, ignorance of the bird's loud "song" has certainly inhibited progress in the process of determining the species' distribution. It will undoubtedly prove the most resilient of the three species because of its extensive geographical range, its wide altitudinal tolerance and the relatively large number of subpopulations. Nevertheless, along with all fauna strictly confined to primary rain forest, the Brown Mesite has suffered from a massive destruction and fragmentation of its habitat in the recent past, and this is set to continue at a rapid rate in the future.

As the habitat of all three species is being reduced in extent and being fragmented by humans, additional threats, such as human predation and the effects of introduced mammals, may start operating at a significant level locally, leading to the ex-

tinction of isolated populations. Recolonization of such areas would appear unlikely, even if the habitat remained suitable, since all species appear to have poor dispersal capabilities. The productivity of White-breasted Mesite populations is locally heterogeneous, with areas near water sources being the best quality habitat and holding the most successful breeding pairs, at least in the species' southern centre of distribution. These areas are thus disproportionately important in sustaining populations over a much wider area. Unfortunately, they are also a focus for subsistence agriculture and settlement by Madagascar's burgeoning human population. It is clear that the loss of these areas of forest through destruction or degradation might well cause the decline of mesite populations over much larger regions; a similar scenario may be equally applicable to the other two species.

The area of forest in Madagascar has dwindled markedly over the last thousand years, and the process is continuing at present. This suggests that the area of potential habitat for all three species has been massively reduced through human activity. The forest habitat of the two *Mesitornis* species, in particular, has declined by more than 70%. These two species both occur in several designated protected areas, but the level of real protection afforded in these areas is low. The Subdesert Mesite occurs in no protected areas. Another member of a family endemic to Madagascar, the Long-tailed Ground-roller (*Uratelornis chimaera*), also in a monotypic genus, has an almost exactly congruent range. For both of these species, identification of population centres and the development of an action plan for their conservation are high priorities.

Although it has been suggested that Brown Mesite populations may suffer through competition with Madagascar Wood-rails, no evidence has been put forward for this. Indeed, it seems from Appert's observations that the two species have different feeding methods, the rail mainly gleaning from the surface of the forest floor and leaf litter, the mesite apparently also commonly digging into the upper layer of the soil for food items (see Food and Feeding). Moreover, these species have co-existed for so many thousands of years that they are unlikely to be serious competitors anyway: population declines through interspecific competition are difficult to demonstrate, but, where they have occurred, they usually involve at least one non-native species.

No captive breeding has been attempted and, in common with the experience with several other Gruiformes, it may be barely practicable. No species is currently accorded legal protection.

General Bibliography
Appert (1985), Benson (1985), Berlioz (1948), Dee (1986), Dorst (1968), Hamsch (1987), Langrand (1990), Lavauden (1937), Lowe (1924), Mey (1993), Milon *et al.* (1973), Peters (1934), Rand (1936), Sibley & Ahlquist (1972, 1990), Sibley & Monroe (1990, 1993).

PLATE 2

inches   6

cm   15

PLATE 2

Genus *MESITORNIS*   Bonaparte, 1855

1. White-breasted Mesite
Mesitornis variegata

French: Mésite variée   **German**: Kurzfuß-Stelzenralle   **Spanish**: Mesito Pechiblanco
Other common names: (White-breasted) Roatelo

Taxonomy. *Mesites variegata* I. Geoffroy Saint-Hilaire, 1838, Madagascar.
Formerly placed in genus *Mesoenas* (see page 34). Recent anomalous record from rain forest may prove to belong to subspecifically distinct population, but no relevant specimens known to exist. Monotypic.
Distribution. Madagascar. Known only to occur in three widely separated small areas in W & N, between 12°44' S (Analamera) and 20° S (Menabe forests); however, single anomalous record from E (Ambatovaky).

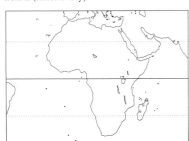

Descriptive notes. 31 cm; 103-111 g, female may be smaller and lighter, but not apparent in field. Pale creamy to white supercilium and throat; breast also pale cream, sometimes tinged rufous; black crescents on sides of breast and upper belly; back rufous brown. Development of rufous breast band linking moustachial stripes is highly variable in extent and tone in northernmost population; birds of southernmost population have thick, bright bands. Some birds have noticeably grey nape. Bare skin round eye grey to bright blue. Such variability might be related to age or sex, or both, but nothing known. Bill intermediate in length between those of *M. unicolor* and *Monias benschi*, and much less curved than that of latter; paler underparts than *M. unicolor*. No seasonal variation, nor significant changes due to feather wear. Juvenile up to 1-2 months old similar to adult, but throat and supercilium yellow-buff with smudgy blackish longitudinal marks; thenceforth probably indistinguishable from adults.
Habitat. Primarily found in dry western forests, at altitude of less than 150 m. Single recent anomalous record from lowland rain forest at 350 m.
Food and Feeding. Mainly feeds on small adult and larval invertebrates, but also takes some plant matter. Food items recorded as being taken, in order of frequency: unidentified seeds, 3-5 mm in diameter; crickets, 5-10 mm; cockroaches, 5-10 mm; spiders, 5-15 mm; beetles, adults and larvae, latter up to 20 mm long; centipedes; mantids; and moths and flies. Seeds made up 17% of items in number, rest invertebrates. Other items recorded include dwarf terrestrial chamaeleon (*Brookesia*) and crystallized exudate of homopteran bug nymphs of family Flattidae. Species inhabits seasonal environment and diet accordingly varies: small invertebrate prey commoner in dry season, larger prey more frequent in wet season. Forages on forest floor, gathering food mainly from leaf litter, but also from low vegetation. Main foraging techniques include gleaning from surface of leaf litter, low vegetation or spiders' webs, leaf-turning and leaf-lifting; also leaf-thrashing and sometimes a short chase of flushed invertebrates; occasionally probes into soil, mainly in dry season. See page 38.
Breeding. Active nests found Oct-Apr, with egg-laying peaking Nov-Jan. Apparently monogamous, with long-lasting pair-bond. Nest is loose flat platform of 20-30 sticks; placed 1-3 m up in shrub layer, in clump of dead vegetation or live bush. Clutch 1-3 eggs; incubation performed mostly or entirely by female, period unknown; chick uniform red-brown (not black as previously suggested). Post-fledging care probably long; birds live as family groups of breeding pair and most recent young.
Movements. No evidence to suggest that species is anything other than sedentary; groups maintain same territory all year round, at least in some sites.

Status and Conservation. VULNERABLE. Does not occur in at least some seemingly suitable forests between known centres; this may be due to past forest clearance and subsequent regeneration. Combined population at two main centres (Ampijoroa and Menabe) estimated at 7000-38,000 breeding adults. Group density, group size and site fidelity highest in selectively logged forest near rivers in Menabe area, and in undisturbed plateau forest at Ampijoroa. Populations at northern sites (Ankarana and Analamera) probably much smaller. Numbers at Ambatovaky and other eastern sites, if any, unknown. Major threats stem from habitat loss, caused, in order of importance, by subsistence agriculture, bush fires and intensive commercial exploitation. Birds hunted, and even taken when incubating. Selective logging may not itself threaten species, but increased hunting pressure, as result of improved access, may reduce habitat quality in logged areas. Ankarana, Analamera, Ambatovaky, Ankarafantsika, and Andranomena (part of Menabe) are all officially protected; other parts of Menabe subject to intensive commercial exploitation, as is much of Ankarafantsika. All three forests in W are subjects of current open-ended conservation management initiatives, with varying degrees of success.
Bibliography. Andriamampianina (1981), Chapman & Stewart (1986), Collar & Andrew (1988), Collar & Stuart (1985, 1988), Collar *et al.* (1994), Dee (1986), Dowsett & Forbes-Watson (1993), Forbes-Watson & Turner (1973), Hawkins, A.F.A. (1993, 1994), Hawkins, A.F.A. *et al.* (1990), King (1978/79), Langrand (1990), Lavauden (1931, 1932, 1937), Milon *et al.* (1973), Nicoll & Langrand (1989), Rand (1936), Safford & Duckworth (1990), Thompson & Evans (1991, 1992).

2. Brown Mesite
Mesitornis unicolor

French: Mésite unicolore   **German**: Einfarb-Stelzenralle   **Spanish**: Mesito Unicolor
Other common names: Brown Roatelo

Taxonomy. *Mesites unicolor* Des Murs, 1845, Madagascar.
Formerly placed in genus *Mesoenas*. Monotypic.
Distribution. E Madagascar, from near Tolagnaro (Fort Dauphin) to Marojejy; not recorded in apparently suitable Sambirano region of NW Madagascar.

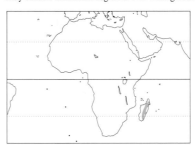

Descriptive notes. 30 cm. Sexes apparently similar in size and plumage. Whitish streak behind eye varies in intensity and extent, sometimes tapering down to form side-margin of throat; chin and throat whitish, tinged rufous, but similarly variable. Rufous brown head sometimes has pinkish grey tinge. Bill is shortest and straightest of any mesite. Eye large, giving "soft" expression. Neck can look relatively long and slender when extended. No information available on seasonal variation in plumage, on juvenile plumage, or on effects of wear.
Habitat. Humid eastern forest, especially areas with thick leaf litter and sparse covering of herbs and saplings. Most of the known sites are in remote and relatively undegraded forest. Recorded from sea-level up to c. 1100 m in Ranomafana; also found around 900 m at Perinet and 700 m in Marojejy.
Food and Feeding. Little known. Known to take invertebrates from forest floor. Forages by walking about slowly, probably for the most part using techniques similar to those recorded for *M. variegata*.
Breeding. Like other mesites, breeds in rainy season, Nov-Dec. Nest is platform of slender twigs lined with small amounts of grass, placed in fork of sloping trees 1-2 m up. Only 2 nests found to date, both initially containing 1 egg being incubated by female. Chick rich rufous buff (not blackish as previously suggested). No further information available.
Movements. Difficult to assess significance of absence of records from certain sites at given times, as species is frequently overlooked at sites where and when it is known to be present. Strong possibility

of altitudinal movement, at least on Masoala, birds being found only rarely below 700 m during breeding season, but commonly below this altitude in Apr (local winter).

Status and Conservation. VULNERABLE. Apparently present over wide area, but very patchily distributed within that habitat and possibly prefers lower-lying areas, which are the most vulnerable to human encroachment. In area of 4 km² at Ambatovaky, at least 4 pairs were found; also, 3 pairs heard calling along 2 km of path. Conservation may be complicated by possibility of species being altitudinal migrant. Threatened by forest clearance for subsistence agriculture, especially in lowlands and flat areas; also recent upsurge in commercial exploitation in what remains of lowland forest. Likely to suffer predation by rats, but there is dispute as regards degree of rat presence in forest (see page 39); certainly in relatively undisturbed areas, introduced species unlikely to be common enough to affect populations of present species. Claimed perhaps to sustain competition from Madagascar Wood-rails (*Canirallus kioloides*), but this seems unlikely (see page 41). Suffers only limited hunting pressure in some areas owing to local taboo (see page 40), but in other areas certainly hunted, with dogs used to flush birds into trees. Incubating females have been picked up live off nests. Species recently found to be present in 4 protected areas, Marojejy, Perinet, Ranomafana and Ambatovaky; the first three are currently the objects of conservation programmes.

Bibliography. Andriamampianina (1981), Bartlett (1877, 1879), Collar & Andrew (1988), Collar & Stuart (1985, 1988), Collar *et al.* (1994), Dee (1986), Delacour (1932), Dowsett & Forbes-Watson (1993), Evans *et al.* (1992), Forbes-Watson & Turner (1973), Hartlaub (1877), Humblot (1882), King (1978/79), Langrand (1990), Lavauden (1931, 1932, 1937), Milne-Edwards & Grandidier (1885), Milon *et al.* (1973), Nicoll & Langrand (1989), Rand (1936, 1951b), Safford & Duckworth (1990), Thompson & Evans (1991, 1992), Webb (1954).

Genus *MONIAS*   Oustalet & G. Grandidier, 1903

3. Subdesert Mesite

Monias benschi

French: Mésite monias   **German**: Moniasstelzenralle   **Spanish**: Mesito Monias
Other common names: Monias, Bensch's Rail

Taxonomy. *Monias Benschi* Oustalet and G. Grandidier, 1903, Vorondreo (25 km east of Toliara), Madagascar.
Monotypic.
Distribution. SW Madagascar, from R Mangoky in N to R Fiheranana in S, occupying a strip 200 km long and 70-80 km wide between coast and start of hills inland.

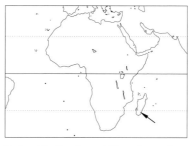

Descriptive notes. 32 cm. Bill relatively long and decurved; legs longer than in *Mesitornis*. Greyish brown above, with long white supercilium. Male has black crescents on underparts, female has extensive rufous throat and breast. No known colour variation with season, age or wear, but juveniles duller overall than adults.

Habitat. Restricted to spiny subdesert thicket, from sea-level up to 130 m. Tolerates at least some habitat disruption, perhaps because can be found even in relatively open areas provided there is access to sites rich in leaf litter. Areas where vegetation is so dense as to impede passage are eschewed, as are those entirely lacking shade.

Food and Feeding. Terrestrial invertebrates; also small amounts of vegetable material, e.g. seeds and small fruit. Digs for prey below surface of ground more than other mesites, probably leaving characteristic dimples in ground (see page 38).

Breeding. Main egg dates Dec-Jan. Species may prove to be polyandrous or polygynous, or even to have variable mating system depending on circumstances; at a nest with 2 eggs, 1 male and 2 females were observed; in another case 2 males accompanied a gravid female; species regularly occurs in groups of 2-6 birds, rarely up to 10; males and females seem equally common in an area as a whole, but proportions may vary greatly between groups. Nest is exposed, flat, open platform of few twigs with leaves and bark, 20 x 30 cm in size; situated 0·6-2 m up in bush or tree. Clutch 1-2 eggs. Sexes share incubation, feeding and care of young; chick blackish brown, sometimes described as chocolate brown, with paler markings around head and on underparts, as well as dark flecking on underparts in pattern resembling that of adult. No data available on incubation or fledging periods.

Status and Conservation. VULNERABLE. Within its limited range, species occurs patchily at high densities, but may be rare in some areas. Total area within which populations occur amounts to only 14,000 km², and parts of this are unsuitable for the species; apparently suitable habitat extends beyond its known range, but appears to be unoccupied. Forest is under pressure from subsistence exploitation for crops, grazing by goats and commercial exploitation for charcoal; rate of forest decline in the area is not known. Hunting with dogs and noose-trapping are common near villages, but, fortunately, over large areas of forest there is no surface water and little human habitation. Rats may predate nests in some areas, and hunters sometimes take adults from their nests. No protected areas within range, nor any known conservation measures in progress within species' specialized habitat. Extent of forest is undoubtedly shrinking, so overall population must be declining.

Bibliography. Appert (1968), Bangs (1918), Collar & Andrew (1988), Collar & Stuart (1985, 1988), Collar *et al.* (1994), Dee (1986), Delacour (1932), Dowsett & Forbes-Watson (1993), Forbes-Watson & Turner (1973), Griveaud (1960), Hartert (1912), King (1978/79), Langrand (1990), Lavauden (1931, 1932, 1937), Lavauden & Poisson (1929), Milon *et al.* (1973), Nicoll & Langrand (1989), Rand (1936), Rutgers & Norris (1970), Safford & Duckworth (1990), Steinbacher (1977), Turner (1981).

Class AVES
Order GRUIFORMES
Suborder TURNICES
Family TURNICIDAE (BUTTONQUAILS)

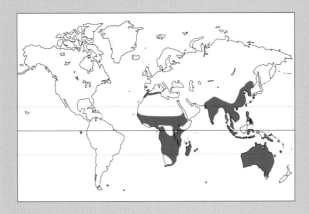

- Small, plump, quail-like terrestrial birds, with short legs, no hind toe and a rudimentary tail.
- 10-23 cm.

- Afrotropical, Oriental and Australasian Regions; peripheral in SW Palearctic.
- Grassland to forest, from sea-level up to 2500 m.
- 2 genera, 16 species, 59 taxa.
- 5 species threatened; none extinct since 1600.

Systematics

The origins and affinities of the buttonquails are obscure and disputed. There are no known pre-Pleistocene fossils to help elucidate the evolution of the family, which has variously been allied with the fowls and true quails (Galliformes), the shorebirds (Charadriiformes) and, by recent consensus, the rails and related birds (Gruiformes). Some early taxonomists saw possible connections or certain anatomical similarities with the tinamous (Tinamidae), mesites (Mesitornithidae), sandgrouse (Pteroclidae), pigeons (Columbidae) and even the passerines. Until recently, the buttonquails were almost invariably allied with the superficially similar Australian Plains-wanderer (Pedionomidae), but current opinion strongly favours the idea that the Plains-wanderer is instead related to the seedsnipes (Thinocoridae) of South America (see page 534). Recent DNA-DNA hybridization data suggest only that the buttonquails are either an ancient and distinct group without close living relatives, or a recently derived group, the rapid genetic evolution of which has obscured its connections with other families. However, an affinity with the Gruiformes should certainly not be ruled out, and it is probably most convenient to leave Turnicidae in its traditional position in that order, at any rate for the time being.

It is clear that the buttonquails only superficially resemble the true quails (*Coturnix*), and differ from them in many anatomical respects. The characters which readily distinguish the buttonquails include the lack of a crop and a hind toe, and in females an enlarged trachea and inflatable bulb in the oesophagus which combine to produce a specialized vocal organ for "booming". This is visible as an inflated, pulsating neck in calling birds. Buttonquails also have relatively larger and more "loose-fitting" wings, with greater expansion at the carpals, than the true quails, which have short wings that are often hidden by their rump feathers.

There are only two genera in the family, the large and widespread genus *Turnix* with 16 species and the monotypic, African *Ortyxelos*. The latter has traditionally been placed first in the family sequence, implying a primitive or ancestral condition, but modern taxonomists place it last, instead implying an advanced or derived condition. *Turnix* species are dumpy and generalized, with females that boom. *Ortyxelos* is tiny, gracile and longer-tailed, and its females do not boom, as they lack the necessary vocal apparatus; the species seems specialized for life in deserts.

Within the genus *Turnix*, there are recognizable groups of related species. The most widespread group is that of the Common Buttonquail (*Turnix sylvatica*) of Eurasia, which also includes the Red-backed Buttonquail (*Turnix maculosa*) of Australasia and the Black-rumped Buttonquail (*Turnix hottentotta*) of Africa. An endemic Asian group consists of the Yellow-legged (*Turnix tanki*) and Spotted Buttonquails (*Turnix ocellata*). A possible "Gondwanan remnant" group comprises the Barred Buttonquail (*Turnix suscitator*), which may have colonized Asia from the Indian plate, and the Madagascar Buttonquail (*Turnix nigricollis*). Two endemic Australasian groups seem most closely related to each other: the Black-breasted (*Turnix melanogaster*), Chestnut-backed (*Turnix castanota*), Buff-breasted (*Turnix olivii*) and Painted Buttonquails (*Turnix varia*); and Worcester's (*Turnix worcesteri*), the Sumba (*Turnix everetti*) the Red-chested (*Turnix pyrrhothorax*) and the Australian Little Buttonquails (*Turnix velox*). These Australasian species may also represent a "Gondwanan remnant", long isolated on the Australian plate, with one member, Worcester's Buttonquail, having recently colonized the Philippines via Wallacea. The Black-breasted Buttonquail may actually belong with the Madagascar and Barred Buttonquail group.

Opinion has differed on the taxonomic status of very similar, allopatric forms within *Turnix*. The Common and Red-backed Buttonquails were often considered conspecific until it was suggested that the ranges of the two forms met in the Philippines; although the existence of such sympatry is now contested, current opinion nevertheless recognizes them as separate species that probably form a superspecies. Again, the Chestnut-backed and Buff-breasted Buttonquails are often treated as conspecific, but they differ in plumage, egg colour and particularly bill size and shape. Similarly, the poorly known Worcester's and Sumba Buttonquails are suspected to be conspecific, and even possibly only subspecies of the very similar Red-chested Buttonquail; for the meantime they are probably best kept separate, pending further information. This group follows Bergmann's and Gloger's Rules: the tropical island forms, Worcester's and the Sumba Buttonquails, are smaller and more brightly pigmented than the Red-chested Buttonquail of the subtropical semi-arid zone.

In contrast, the race *nana* of the Black-rumped Buttonquail is often considered a separate species, due to constant, though minor, differences in plumage and eye colour, which may constitute a recognition signal. Also, some populations of *nana* are migratory, whereas the nominate race is sedentary, but until stronger evidence can be produced it is probably safer to treat these two forms as conspecific. Similarly, the New Caledonian race of the Painted Buttonquail is said to differ more from the nominate race than the latter does from the Buff-breasted and Chestnut-backed Buttonquails, and may therefore deserve full species status.

Taxonomic views have also differed on the validity of some subspecies described for *Turnix* species. Generally, there has been a recent trend towards a reduction in the number of recognized races, as it became apparent that some variation is individual or seasonal, or related to age and sex, rather than geographical. This is particularly the case with Australian species, and the "oversplitting syndrome" displayed by ornithologist G. M. Mathews early this century. Many of Mathews' *Turnix* "races" were based on very small series of specimens and minor variation, and are now regarded as invalid.

Morphological Aspects

Turnix buttonquails are small birds, ranging from 12 cm in length and 30 g in weight in the smallest species, to 23 cm and 130 g in the largest. The Lark Buttonquail (*Ortyxelos meiffrenii*) is even smaller at 10 cm and 20 g. In all species, the head is small, without ornamentation, and the neck rather short and slender. Buttonquails have short, laterally compressed, unspecialized bills varying from slender, in mostly insectivorous species, to stout, in mainly granivorous species. With rather short, stout legs and three forward-pointing toes, but no hind toe, they are adapted for walking and running in amongst grass and other low ground cover. The lack of a hind toe is correlated with a terrestrial way of life, and in this respect the buttonquails resemble some of the ratites and other ground-dwelling birds. A hind toe would only be a hindrance; some other terrestrial birds such as the true quails have a much-reduced hind toe raised above the level of the other toes, but the buttonquails have done away with it altogether.

The tracheal enlargement in female buttonquails is of particular note. Compared with the unspecialized trachea of the male, that of the female is slightly longer and much swollen towards its base. This greater diameter and volume of the sound-producing organ permits loud, low-frequency calls. These sounds are resonated by the enlarged oesophagus, which is inflated with air like a tiny balloon just before the female begins to boom.

The soft tail feathers of *Turnix* are so small as to be almost hidden by the overlying coverts. At rest, the wings appear short, partly because the primaries are hidden by the long tertials and inner secondaries. This is in keeping with the fact that, during the day, buttonquails only fly to escape danger. On flushing, whirring and quail-like, they reveal quite long wings and strong, rapid flight, and they often fly far. However, they are reluctant day-time fliers, and soon brake to drop and freeze, or run in cover, seldom flushing a second time in quick succession. By contrast, they readily fly under cover of darkness, and apparently make long distance seasonal movements at night (see Movements). This is probably because their white "gamebird" muscle tires quickly in bursts of escape flight, and they are vulnerable to predation during sustained flight, which is rather weaker and more fluttering. Buttonquails' day-time flight is usually low and direct, although the Painted Buttonquail often weaves between trees.

Buttonquails are shades of brown, grey and rufous, with black mottling and vermiculation and fine pale streaks, for camouflage. The dorsal surface is coloured like the bird's usual habitat. The ventral surface is paler and plainer, though often with spotting or barring on the sides. Females are larger and brighter than males, and often have stronger rufous or black markings on the foreparts. Some species, such as the Spotted and Yellow-legged Buttonquails, are strongly and attractively spotted (ocellated) on the wings. The female Black-breasted Buttonquail has black foreparts spangled white, which may not be a disadvantage on the dimly lit, litter-strewn floor of its rain forest habitat. Juveniles are small versions of adults, with duller and more mottled plumage.

The Lark Buttonquail is an exception. It is the size of the smallest *Turnix*, but is more courser-like, with a slender bill. It has somewhat longer and stiffer, white-tipped tail feathers, and longer, boldly patterned wings: white shoulder patches and trail-

ing edges contrasting with the dark flight-feathers. Its fluttering, lark-like or butterfly-like flight is wavering and erratic.

Buttonquails' normal gait is a strong walk. When feeding, they walk furtively by slinking low through cover, often slowly and jerkily, as they stop to pick at food items. When alarmed, they variously creep mouse-like into shelter, run in bursts and pauses with the head held high, or run rapidly and erratically from danger. The smaller *Turnix* species also have a peculiar gait, in which they creep slowly and stop periodically, mid-step, to rock the horizontally held body backwards and forwards on the stationary feet, much like a chameleon. Various, sometimes fanciful, explanations have been proposed for this "Rocking" gait, which appears to be an intention movement, and suggests some hesitancy or caution on the bird's part. Sometimes, this gait is used by an aggressive bird about to chase another, or by a submissive bird approaching a dominant bird. It is also used by male and female during initial stages of pairing, and if they meet during later stages of the breeding cycle. At other times it is used by a single, apparently suspicious or alert, bird creeping from one patch of cover to another.

Many, perhaps all, *Turnix* species undergo two moults per year: a complete post-breeding moult, and a partial pre-breeding moult involving the head and body only. In some species, though by no means all, the non-breeding plumage is duller, and females then tend to resemble males. Primary moult is descendant but skips from the eighth to the outermost (tenth) feather before the ninth is shed. Interrupted moult, perhaps related to seasonal conditions, is common in some species. Both sexes develop brood patches: the male two large lateral patches, and in some species an additional small central patch; the female has two lateral patches, which are smaller than the male's.

Habitat

The family Turnicidae is widely distributed in the warmer parts of Africa, Eurasia and Australasia, living in the drier parts of the tropics and subtropics, but extending to temperate regions of the Mediterranean, South Africa, East Asia and Australia. Buttonquails live almost entirely on the ground, where they obtain all their food and where they roost. They require cover in which to hide from predators and place their nests.

Buttonquails generally live in grassy or low brushy habitats, including grassland, steppe, savanna, forest clearings and secondary growth. The smallest species can live in sparse, arid grassland and deserts, remote from surface water, which they do not need. The small and medium-sized species can live in disturbed and man-modified habitats, such as agricultural landscapes, where they occur in pasture, crops and weedy fallow fields. The larger Australian

Normal notions of sexual differences are overturned where buttonquails are concerned, for it is the females which are larger and more brightly coloured than the males, their markings being much more strongly defined. This pair of Red-chested Buttonquails allows a direct comparison of the sexes as they crouch side by side. The female on the left is noticeably plumper than her partner while his plumage appears distinctly washed out beside hers.

[*Turnix pyrrhothorax*. Photo: F. Lewitzka/ Nature Focus]

Turnix *buttonquails are small, somewhat dumpy, terrestrial birds. The most apparent features of the Painted Buttonquail, one of the larger species, include the red eyes, the rather fine bill and the typically cryptic, richly patterned plumage of subtle shades. The short, sturdy legs carry three forward-pointing toes, but no hind toe, as is often the case with terrestrial birds. The wings are fairly long, endowing the bird with a surprisingly strong flight action, although buttonquails are generally rather reluctant to take to the air, and normally prefer to walk or run away from danger.*

[*Turnix varia varia*, Australia.
Photo: R. Seitre/Bios]

species live in grassy open forest or woodland with abundant litter, the two "red" species (Chestnut-backed and Buff-breasted) being found mostly on stony hills. One species, the Black-breasted Buttonquail, is exceptional in being largely restricted to the drier types of rain forest or softwood scrub, with deep leaf litter.

Buttonquails forage in accumulated mulch, and use dry soil for dust-bathing. On their daily foraging, some species follow well defined runways or trails, which are marked by their footprints in the dust. They nest amid rank or tussocky grass, sometimes near a tree, bush, log or fallen branch. The Lark Buttonquail can nest amid sparse grass and low herbaceous plants on stony or sandy soil.

During seasonal migrations or post-breeding dispersal, buttonquails sometimes appear in atypical habitats. This is probably because they migrate at night, and must descend either at dawn or wherever they become tired. At such times, individuals find themselves in hostile human environments such as urban areas, where they are easily disorientated by bright lights and sometimes collide with buildings (see Movements).

General Habits

Buttonquails are secretive and difficult to observe in the wild. They are shy and elusive, and their reaction to potential danger is to squat immobile, relying on their camouflage colours to escape detection. If approached, they creep or run away, often invisibly through cover, or, if pressed, they burst startlingly into flight. Occasionally, a bird freezing before or after an escape flight can be picked up by hand, or may be stepped upon. The presence of buttonquails is revealed by the booming calls of females, by characteristic feeding scrapes (see Food and Feeding), or by chance sightings of birds that have not been alerted to an immobile observer. The use by researchers of observation points placed above the ground, for example on raised platforms or in a low tree-fork, offers some hope of observing the normal behaviour of wild buttonquails in areas where they are common. They will respond readily to imitation of the booming call by approaching the source of the sound.

Buttonquails are active by day and night. They do most of their foraging by day, often early and late or crepuscularly, and they roost on the ground at night during sedentary phases of their life cycle. Some species of arid or semi-arid zones are suspected to be mainly nocturnal, which would assist in thermoregulation and moisture conservation. Many buttonquails also travel on migra-

tion at night, at such times frequently being attracted to bright artificial lights (see Movements). On their breeding territories, females often give their advertising calls at night, as well as during the day.

Buttonquails variously occur singly, in pairs or in small coveys. The latter are family groups consisting of a male, sometimes also with a female, and usually about four dependent young. Breeding adult *Turnix* of both sexes are solitary and aggressive towards others of their own sex, and form temporary, monogamous pair-bonds (see Breeding). However, in some species, notably the smaller ones in dry regions, post-breeding aggregations of more than one family group may occur. These amount to loose flocks numbering tens or, during irruptions of the Australian Little Buttonquail, hundreds or thousands of birds in a small area. It is unlikely that large aggregations have a coherent social structure; they may simply represent concentrations of birds in favourable habitat. Adult Lark Buttonquails occur singly or in pairs.

Buttonquails roost in circular scrapes made in the soil, often beneath a tussock or some other form of shelter, such as a clump of shrubs. Members of a family group or a mated pair roost together, often in bodily contact, by clumping side by side, and roost-sites may be used repeatedly if undisturbed. Roosts are used at night and also during the middle of the day in warm weather. In some of the smaller, more sociable species, two or more adult pairs sometimes clump together to roost.

Buttonquails sun-bathe and dust-bathe. When sun-bathing, they stretch out flat on the ground with one or both wings spread and sometimes with their plumage ruffled and their eyes closed. They may also preen beneath a spread wing. For dust-bathing, a bird first prepares a site by scratching a circular scrape with its feet and sometimes pecking at the soil. Then it squats in the scrape, wipes its head in the soil, and performs a dust-tossing movement which is different from that used by true quails. A buttonquail simultaneously loosens soil with its feet as it shuffles its body rapidly from side to side, feathers fluffed, and it thus envelops itself in a cloud of dust.

At least the smaller species of buttonquail allopreen, in the breeding season. The members of a pair preen each other's head feathers, this activity being most intense during the courtship and mating phases of the cycle. Buttonquails perform stretching exercises by simultaneously extending a wing and leg out and down on the same side, or by momentarily arching both wings above the back. They also perform jumping and fluttering exercises, one member of a pair occasionally stimulating the other to follow suit. These exercises punctuate or end periods of loafing and preening in the birds' day-time roosting scrapes.

Buttonquails drink rapidly with a continuous sucking or "bibbling" action, by immersing the bill for several seconds. In this respect they resemble the pigeons and some other birds, rather than those species that drink by repeatedly scooping and swallowing individual beakfuls. Buttonquails thus minimize the time spent in a vulnerable position and activity, at sites such as waterholes in dry country where predators may abound.

Most buttonquail aggression is related to aspects of the breeding cycle, such as defence of the territory and young (see Breeding). However, in at least the larger and more solitary species, adults are generally aggressive to members of their own sex, and females are also aggressive to males that are not their current mates. A buttonquail will chase the recipient of its aggression, and deliver pecks to the head, neck and back, sometimes grasping the nape feathers. In female Black-breasted Buttonquails, this may escalate to a short pursuit flight. In the Common Buttonquail, and perhaps others, males have a prostrate submissive posture which inhibits further aggression by a female. In small species, aggressive chases may be preceded by the aggressor approaching with "Rocking" gait and tail flicking up and down.

Voice

The characteristic buttonquail vocalization is the resonant booming, through closed bill, of female *Turnix* species which have specialized vocal organs (see Morphological Aspects). In small species the notes have a hooting or cooing quality, sometimes given in couplets by the Australian Little Buttonquail. In larger species the notes have a bovine or moaning quality, like the distant lowing of cattle. In the Black-breasted Buttonquail, each tremulous boom is really a series of drumming notes. In sympatric species, the calls of each differ in pitch or tempo, or both.

The booming calls are loud and far-carrying, an obvious advantage for such small and inconspicuous birds living at rather low densities. The calls are also ventriloquial and hence difficult to pinpoint, which would hinder attempts by a predator to locate the caller.

The booming call seems to be mainly an advertisement call to attract a male, although in the larger, more solitary species at least, it may also serve to ward off other females. A female responds aggressively to another female booming in or near her territory. In the advertisement phase, the booming notes are given deliberately from a standing position with the body upright, the bill pointing down, the abdomen drawn in and the breast and upper back inflated and pulsating in rhythm. In the Painted Buttonquail, if a male approaches a female she gives the notes explosively, in excited courtship behaviour (see Breeding). Despite the ventriloquial nature of the booming calls, prospective mates are probably able to locate each other because the male answers with soft calls; the female can turn about to project the sound towards the male when she sees or hears him, and at close range the female enhances the booms with visual signals (see Breeding). Excited individuals run and sometimes flutter about erratically, perhaps trying to locate the source of the booming.

Female *Turnix* species also give rapid purring or drumming series, with the same resonant quality as the booming calls. In the Painted Buttonquail, drumming is given softly by the female during courtship feeding (see Breeding).

Buttonquails of both sexes utter a variety of soft clucking, crooning, chattering, churring, rattling and whistling calls, through the open bill, in the normal avian manner. These are short range signals between members of a pair or family. Some small species utter a few squeaking alarm notes on being flushed. Chicks make soft peeping notes which may become more rapid and staccato if the chicks are distressed. Adult Lark Buttonquails are only known to utter soft whistling notes.

Food and Feeding

Buttonquails are rather opportunistic and generalized feeders, taking a variety of seeds, invertebrates and plant matter, which they find by walking over the ground, gleaning and scratching.

A broad and flexible diet may have enabled the buttonquails to occupy most dryland habitats within the family's range, although only in Australia is there a species living entirely within rain forest (see Habitat).

There are virtually no detailed dietary studies of any buttonquail, the limited information having come almost entirely from casual observations of a few species and the stomach contents of a few individuals of most species. Seeds eaten are small, for instance those of grasses, weeds, clover, cereal crops, legumes and *Acacia* trees, many apparently taken as fallen seed in the soil and litter. Invertebrates taken are mainly small insects, such as ants, flies, bugs, weevils, beetles, cockroaches, grasshoppers, moths and their larvae, pecked from the ground or low plants within reach or seized after a short chase of a few steps. In arid regions, termites may be important food, partly for their moisture content, as desert buttonquails may not have access to surface water. Plant material taken, also probably important for its moisture content, includes seedlings, soft green shoots, buds and small berries. Buttonquails swallow sand, grit or fine pebbles according to their body size, probably to assist in the grinding up of hard food items in the gizzard.

Some species, such as the slender-billed Common and Red-backed Buttonquails, appear to take seeds and invertebrates in similar proportions, whereas others, such as the stout-billed Australian Little and Red-chested Buttonquails, take mostly seeds including fallen grain. The large, but rather slender-billed, Black-breasted Buttonquail appears to be mainly insectivorous, living as it does on the moist rain forest floor where invertebrates abound in the deep litter. A recent study of the diet of this species, based on the microscopic analysis of faecal pellets, showed this species to take many beetles and ants, as well as spiders, whereas centipedes, millipedes and snails were also present, but were scarce in the pellets; soft-bodied prey items are most unlikely to be detected using this technique. In general, buttonquail chicks are fed mainly on small insects, although they start to cope with tiny seeds within a few days of hatching.

Buttonquails have a unique method of uncovering food on the soil surface, beneath accumulated litter. They scratch with one foot while pivoting on the other, turning a half or complete circle before changing feet and reversing direction. This method differs markedly from the alternate scratching of galliform birds. A feeding group of buttonquails presents a scene of busily "spinning" and pecking birds, which leave characteristic circular scrapes, or "platelets", as wide as the bird's body length, and numbering up to 250 platelets/5 m² in the abundant leaf litter of wooded habitats. Black-breasted Buttonquails briefly shade their scrapes with spread wings after scratching, presumably to delay the retreat of exposed prey. This spinning technique is also used to construct roost-sites, dust-bathing sites and nesting scrapes.

Buttonquails forage singly, in pairs and in family groups of an adult or two with a brood of young. Some species, such as the smaller ones, or those of dry regions, also forage in post-breed-

Highly terrestrial birds, buttonquails, such as this Barred Buttonquail, find all of their food on the ground. Whether in search of seeds or invertebrates, they forage by walking along in a rather furtive manner, scratching as they go and making curious circular scrapes in the ground by a strange spinning action in order to uncover prey.

[Turnix suscitator fasciata, Philippines. Photo: Brian J. Coates]

ing coveys or small flocks which consist of more than one family.

Buttonquails drink when water is available, but those of arid regions apparently do not need to do so, because they occur in areas lacking surface water. They probably obtain and conserve sufficient moisture from their food, but detailed physiological studies are required to prove this. They may also conserve moisture by behavioural strategies such as nocturnal activity (see General Habits).

Breeding

The mating system of the *Turnix* buttonquails has been deduced largely from captive birds, with very little information available on wild birds, although general conclusions have been confirmed in wild Painted Buttonquails from ringing studies. The usual breeding strategy is sequential polyandry with male parental care, although monogamy with limited female parental care also occurs in the Common Buttonquail and probably some other species. Perhaps food abundance determines the female's breeding condition, and hence her drive to produce multiple clutches quickly, with different mates, in a single season. Conversely, in poor seasons the chance of rearing a few young may be increased if females stay and help to rear a single brood.

The little known Lark Buttonquail is apparently monogamous, breeding solitarily in simple pairs, although male incubation would suggest the possibility of polyandry. In most *Turnix* species for which information is available, temporary monogamous pair-bonds are formed, lasting at least up to the early incubation stage and perhaps beyond, with mated females chasing away other males as well as rival females. Having presented a male with a clutch of eggs, the female then finds a new mate, if one is available, and in turn leaves him with a clutch of eggs. As already noted, in some species monogamy also occurs, at least for the duration of a breeding season. Pairs nest solitarily, with males defending their nesting territories against other males.

It follows from the mating system that the home range of a particular female, as well as covering that of her current partner, may partly overlap those of neighbouring males, although evidence is lacking. Another consequence is that males alone incubate the eggs and rear the chicks, although in some species the female may at times assist with incubation, at least in the early stages, and occasionally with the care of the young. The Black-breasted Buttonquail is puzzling, in that a wild female has been seen caring for juveniles apparently from two amalgamated broods.

In temperate regions, buttonquails usually breed in spring and summer. In the tropics and subtropics they can breed opportunistically at any time, with clutches recorded in all months, although locally breeding is episodic or seasonal in response to conditions. In areas with pronounced wet and dry seasons, they breed during or after the rains when food is most abundant. Polyandrous females lay another clutch, with a new male, in as little as two weeks after the preceding clutch. Even monogamous females can present their mate with a new clutch within two months, after the first brood has become independent. Polyandrous females can produce up to seven clutches in a season.

Female *Turnix* in breeding condition defend exclusive territories and boom frequently to attract a male. In the Painted Buttonquail, when a male appears, the female becomes excited, puffing out her breast and lowering it to the ground, cocking her tail and delivering the notes explosively as she runs around him, stopping to stamp her feet and scratch the ground. The female of the Black-breasted and Barred Buttonquails sometimes spreads her wings when drumming to a male. A courting female Common Buttonquail also makes the circular scratching motions when a male arrives, and she may be aggressive towards him at first until he stands his ground and is accepted.

In the smaller species, ensuing pairing behaviour includes the "Rocking" display by both birds, increasing synchronization of activities, male sidling up to roost or dust-bathe in bodily contact with the female, "Mutual Bowing", and allopreening. Imminent nesting is marked by the female frequently squatting in an incubating position with the tail cocked and breast puffed out. Courtship proceeds with a "Tidbitting" display, in which the female calls the male to take an item of food from her bill or the ground, and the performance of the "Scrape Ceremony" by one or both birds. The "Scrape Ceremony" consists of elements of nest-site preparation and nest construction: either bird or both, singly or together, scratches a circular scrape, squats in it with the tail cocked, and pecks the soil or pulls grass into the site, while making soft calls. At first, "reversed" false copulation may occur, the female mounting the male, but true copulation soon ensues with the male approaching and allopreening the crouching female, or the male following the female and grasping her nape feathers.

Both sexes search for a nest-site, testing several by the "Scrape Ceremony", with the female selecting the final site. The nest is a depression on the ground amongst grass, often under or

The Yellow-legged Buttonquail breeds amid grassland. The nest, a shallow depression in the ground, is lined with dry grass. Sometimes blades of grass are bent over it to form a kind of canopy and a side entrance is made. The clutch consists of four or five cryptically coloured eggs. Both incubation and rearing of the chicks is undertaken by the male, a reversal of the normal sex roles in birds, and a feature common to all species of the Turnicidae.

[*Turnix tanki blanfordii*, Russian Far East. Photo: Yuri Shibnev/ Planet Earth]

within a tussock, lined and sometimes hooded over with grass stems. Some are domed grass structures with a side entrance, and in dense cover they may have a runway leading to them. Both sexes, but mostly the female, prepare the site either by pivoting and scratching, or by using elements of the "Scrape Ceremony": pecking the soil, squatting and shuffling the body. They then pull grass stems in on themselves, moulding a compact structure by pushing, shuffling and turning, with the female again doing most of the work. The result is that the nest and incubating bird are invisible, the cryptic situation further enhanced by the adults adopting a very cautious attitude when entering and leaving. The nest of the Lark Buttonquail is a simpler structure in sparser cover; it is often rimmed by small pebbles.

Buttonquail eggs are oval to almost pyriform, and are smooth and glossy, measuring about 18 x 15 mm in the Lark Buttonquail to 29 x 24 mm in the largest *Turnix* species. They are cryptically coloured, white to buff with dark freckles, spots and blotches, particularly near the larger end. The usual clutch size is four or five, though it is only two in the Lark Buttonquail and sometimes reaches seven in some small *Turnix*. Eggs are laid at daily intervals, and incubation starts with the last egg so that hatching is synchronous. Incubation takes around 12 to 15 days, the shortest of all similarly precocial species, and little longer than in the smallest passerines. Male Common Buttonquails leave the nest about eight times per day for stints of up to 15 minutes of feeding.

Buttonquail chicks hatch downy and mobile, and desert the nest to follow the male about. They are cryptically coloured in browns and greys with dark and pale dorsal stripes. At about two grams, they are among the smallest of precocial chicks. For the first week or so they are brooded and fed by the male, which calls them, with "Tidbitting" behaviour, to take food from the tip of his bill. When threatened, they lie "frozen" with closed eyes, while the male performs an injury-feigning distraction display. If this fails and the chicks utter distress calls, the male may charge at the intruder with his wings spread, or even fly at the intruder, such as a human, with buffeting wings. The main enemies of buttonquails include raptors, mammalian carnivores and humans, and, in Australia, introduced predators such as cats and foxes.

The chicks start to feed themselves within a week, and by the second week require brooding only at night. They fend for themselves in the third week, and become fully independent in the fourth week. They perform adult behaviour such as pivoting and female booming motions, though with immature voices and anatomy, in the first week, and full maintenance behaviour and the "Rocking" gait by two weeks old.

Buttonquail chicks grow very rapidly, sprouting wing feathers on the second day, fluttering in a week and flying properly in two weeks. Body feathers quickly follow suit, with juvenile plumage attained in the third week. A post-juvenile primary moult, beginning with the innermost primary, starts at only three weeks of age, while the outermost juvenile primaries are still growing. At about this stage, when still only half-sized, chicks begin a complete moult of the juvenile plumage. Adult size is achieved in a month, adult-like plumage within two months and sexual maturity within three months of age in the smallest species.

Rapid growth and early maturity, coupled with polyandry, multiple broods per season and short breeding cycles, permit enormous potential increase in the populations of the smaller species. This is particularly the case where young hatched early in the season are themselves able to breed later in that same season when less than four months old. This capacity permits buttonquails to take full advantage of prolonged favourable conditions in climatically unpredictable semi-arid regions. However, mortality may be very high, with life expectancy in the wild perhaps only two or three years, although captive individuals have lived for up to nine years. The short generation time and rapid population turnover has apparently facilitated rapid genetic evolution in the family (see Systematics).

Movements

The movements of buttonquails are poorly understood and apparently complex, with most evidence in the form of observed fluctuations in abundance at given localities, and occasional records of buttonquails appearing in unlikely places, such as cities. In warmer temperate regions such as the Mediterranean or eastern Australia they are often considered to be resident; that is, they are always present in an area, although evidence from ringing suggests a high turnover of individuals. Conversely, some ringing data also reveal that individuals are sedentary for up to eight months at a time. In cooler temperate regions, for instance at higher latitudes and altitudes in southern Australia or east Asia, buttonquails appear to behave as spring and summer breeding migrants, wintering at lower latitudes and altitudes.

Continental populations of the smaller species make seasonal movements in those parts of the tropics and subtropics with pronounced wet and dry seasons. Generally, it appears that they are well dispersed during the wet season, when they breed, taking advantage of the abundant food supply after rains, but they then

The male Common Buttonquail incubates, admirably concealed amid tussocks of grass. Buttonquail chicks hatch after 12 to 15 days, the shortest incubation period amongst those species with precocial chicks. They develop rapidly and by the fourth week are completely independent. This short breeding cycle and the polyandrous nature of the mating system in Turnicidae can lead to multiple clutches and consequently, in good years, sizeable population increases in the smaller species.

[*Turnix sylvatica*. Photo: W. R. Tarboton]

The nest of the Painted Buttonquail is a slight cup lined with grass and forest litter, often under a tussock of grass, near a rock, or in the shelter of a small bush. The cryptic pattern and coloration of the dorsal plumage ensures that the incubating male remains virtually invisible to any inquisitive marauder.

[*Turnix varia varia*, Dryandra, West Australia. Photo: Babs & Bert Wells/ Oxford Scientific Films]

retreat to refuge areas during the dry, non-breeding season. The Australian Little Buttonquail migrates south in spring to the winter-rainfall zone of temperate regions, and north in autumn to the summer-rainfall zone of the deserts and subtropics. By doing so, this arid-adapted species follows the flush of plant growth and hence food. Buttonquails on tropical and subtropical islands, and in the more climatically stable parts of the tropics, appear to be sedentary. Even those populations in the subtropics display a tendency to extend their stay or be resident where conditions permit. On the other hand, their movements may be erratic or irruptive in response to climatic fluctuations. It is possible that some apparent "irruptions" are at least partly attributable to explosive local population growth in exceptionally favourable conditions (see Breeding).

Evidence for movement in the tropics and subtropics has come partly from a ringing station in north-eastern Australia, where there is a high turnover of individuals with none recaptured. There, and in Africa and Asia, evidence for migration has come in the form of many birds being attracted to, and sometimes colliding with, artificial lights, windows and lighthouses at night, particularly in fog after heavy rain. Nothing is known of migrating behaviour, routes or staging areas, except that many Red-backed Buttonquails "island hop" across the Torres Strait between Australia and New Guinea, with biannual movement pulses early in the wet and dry seasons. With their rather long, almost shorebird-like wings (see Morphological Aspects), it is apparent that buttonquails are capable of long-distance movements by night, and that they are stronger fliers than the gallinaceous quails.

During sedentary phases of their life cycle, buttonquails move about their home range on foot, foraging, and frequently retreat to their regular roosting scrapes to rest. Females, at least of the larger, more solitary and territorial species, also regularly patrol their territory boundaries by walking rapidly along them. The female Black-breasted Buttonquail, sometimes with her mate in tow, stops frequently to drum.

Relationship with Man

The buttonquails are secretive, cryptic and little known, and present few opportunities to observe their behaviour in the field, hence there is little raw material to form the basis of extensive folklore. They are heard, particularly with the booming call, much more often than they are seen. A mistaken belief among African tribespeople is that the booming call is made by a snake, the puff adder *Bitis arietans*. The "very human-like and heart-rending moans" of the female Yellow-legged Buttonquail must inevitably have given rise to folklore among Asian tribal peoples, but details are difficult to ascertain; rather less poetic is the comparison of the voices of both the Barred and the Yellow-legged Buttonquails to the sound of a distant two-stroke motorcycle engine!

Limited evidence suggests that buttonquails were probably significant in the ceremonial life of Aborigines in central Australia, but precise details are lacking. An Aboriginal legend from northern Australia makes possible reference to buttonquails, which a translator probably did not distinguish from the true quails. In a story explaining the long neck of the Emu (*Dromaius novaehollandiae*), Quail was one of several spirit men who changed into birds as they ate a meal obtained by trickery. Quail took the remains of the meal into long grass to eat it. An old spirit woman, who had been tricked out of her food, thought Quail's voice was coming from the sky. She threw a stick straight up, trying to hit Quail, but it fell down and lodged in her throat as she peered up. She changed into an Emu with a long neck. In this story, Quail's voice in the sky may refer to the ventriloquial booming quality of a buttonquail's call.

The buttonquails' predominant relationship with man concerns their palatability. They have long been hunted and eaten as gamebirds, although they are now not legal gamebirds in most Western countries. In developing countries, particularly in Asia, they are trapped for the pot and sold in markets. Caged or tethered females are used as decoys, and wild birds' trails, or faithful human copies, are used as sites for snares. Also in Asia, females are kept and used in "hen-fights" just as the males of galliform birds are used in cock-fights. The Australian Aborigines hunted buttonquails by means of nets set at water-holes; women and children gathered their eggs and young, and youths hunted them on drives by hurling their throwing-sticks at flushed birds.

In recent decades there has been much avicultural interest in buttonquails, with several species being bred in captivity by zoos and private individuals. This may have generated some pressure on remaining wild populations of rare species, such as the Black-breasted Buttonquail, but that particular species breeds well in aviaries. Once captive stock is established, the birds' high reproductive potential should obviate the need for further trapping of wild birds for the avicultural trade. The buttonquails have not

been truly domesticated, in the sense that no domestic strains or mutants have been developed, as has happened in the true quails.

Status and Conservation

As a family, the buttonquails seem secure, with most species adapted to, and occurring in, human pastoral and agricultural landscapes; their high reproductive output is sufficient to compensate for human predation. This is particularly the case in developing countries of the tropics and subtropics, where traditional agriculture leaves rough areas, fallow fields, forest clearings and secondary growth, and traditional pastoralism leaves sufficient grass cover. Most of the species of Africa and Asia seem to be holding their own, with the Lark Buttonquail perhaps increasing with expanding deserts. The tropical island endemics, notably the Spotted, Worcester's and Sumba Buttonquails, give cause for concern, but this may be largely because they are so poorly known. Worcester's and the Sumba Buttonquails are classified as Vulnerable, while the Spotted is considered to be near-threatened. It is difficult to foresee any real threats to these species, other than large-scale conversion to Western agricultural methods and consequent loss of habitat. The other three species currently believed to be threatened are the Black-breasted, Chestnut-backed and Buff-breasted Buttonquails, all of tropical Australia.

By contrast, the buttonquails have fared less well under highly Westernized agriculture. The Common Buttonquail has all but disappeared from Europe, under modern intensive farming methods which leave little room for wildlife, combined with at least a certain degree of hunting pressure. It is still common in sub-Saharan Africa and Asia. Similarly, several Australian species in southern, intensively farmed regions are retreating from the conversion of native grassland and grassy woodland or forest to cropland and heavily grazed pasture. These are the Painted, Red-chested and Australian Little Buttonquails. However, much habitat remains for them in northern and inland Australia where the main land use is rough grazing on native pasture. Similarly, the Red-backed Buttonquail has declined at the south-eastern periphery of its Australian range, following habitat destruction and urbanization, but it remains common in the tropics. The New Caledonian Painted Buttonquail, possibly a full species, may now even be extinct. Significantly, its habitat has been altered by Western colonists with their attendant impacts.

Two tropical Australian species, the Chestnut-backed and Buff-breasted Buttonquails, may be affected by the European grazing and fire regime in the monsoonal grassy woodlands, with some evidence that the Chestnut-backed Buttonquail's range has contracted. Frequent hot fires, late in the dry season, may be causing a decline in habitat quality and food supply. However, the biology of these species, and likewise the effects of human impact on them, are poorly known. The two species are classified, respectively, as Vulnerable and Endangered, and a strategy to redress the lack of knowledge about them has been formulated, though not yet implemented.

The most seriously threatened species is the Black-breasted Buttonquail, which is now classed as Endangered. It always had a restricted distribution, in coastal eastern Australia. Its range and numbers have seriously declined, owing to clearance of its habitat for agriculture, grazing and intensive plantation forestry. It is largely restricted to dry rain forest, although it may be adapting to native *Araucaria* plantations with an understorey of introduced *Lantana*, which forms prickly thickets. Its preferred habitat has been decimated and fragmented into small pockets, and adjoining grassy forest is frequently burnt, a process which removes the litter on which it depends. As is often the case when a rather spectacular species becomes rare, the Black-breasted Buttonquail is prone to attract the attention of illegal egg-collectors and bird-trappers; their activities have the potential to affect remnant populations seriously.

Surveys and research are being conducted in order to gather the necessary knowledge for conserving the Black-breasted Buttonquail. The emphasis of such research is mainly on the potential impact of timber harvesting in public forest, although recent surveys have located the birds also in habitat remnants within farmland. Ironically, these findings come at a time when the remnants are threatened with clearance.

The Black-breasted Buttonquail has been found recently on a large offshore island, Fraser Island, which is partly a national park. However, there is no reason to believe that this represents a recent range extension. Rather, the species was probably always present, but simply passed undetected. Extralimital reports of the species are unconfirmed, those from northern Queensland being unsupported by adequate details, and those from Victoria probably referring to the Stubble Quail (*Coturnix pectoralis*), a species that was formerly known as the "Black-breasted Quail".

On the positive side, the Black-breasted Buttonquail appears to be little affected by introduced predators, such as cats and foxes; indeed, it is not known whether the total population of any Australian buttonquail species is seriously affected by the cat or the fox, although it is suspected that they may kill many individuals. Another slightly more optimistic sign for this species lies in the fact that it has been found to respond well to the exclusion of fire from the grassy forest fringing its rain forest refuges. The main hope for its survival hangs on the preservation of all surviving remnants of its habitat, and appropriate management of wood-production forests that contain populations of the species. A fairly large captive-bred stock exists, should reintroduction become an appropriate measure.

General Bibliography
Bruning (1985), Dunning (1993), Fulgenhauer (1980), Johnsgard (1991b), Peters (1934), Ridley (1983), Sibley & Ahlquist (1990), Sibley & Monroe (1990), Sibley *et al.* (1988).

ssp *sylvatica* ♂ ♀

ssp *suluensis* ♀

ssp *whiteheadi* ♀

ssp *dussumier* ♀

1

ssp *maculosa* ♂ ♀

2

ssp *furva* ♀

ssp *mayri* ♀

ssp *nana*

ssp *horsbrughi* ♀

3

ssp *hottentotta* ♂ ♀

ssp *ocellata* ♀

ssp *tanki* ♂ ♀

ssp *benguetensis* ♂ ♀

5

4

ssp *blanfordii* ♀

ssp *suscitator* ♂

ssp *bengalensis* ♀

ssp *rufilata* ♀

6

ssp *fasciata* ♀

ssp *powelli* ♂

6

ssp *leggei* ♀

ssp *nigrescens* ♀

PLATE 3

inches 4

cm 10

Genus *TURNIX* Bonnaterre, 1791

1. **Common Buttonquail**

Turnix sylvatica

French: Turnix d'Andalousie   **German**: Laufhühnchen   **Spanish**: Torillo Andaluz
Other common names: Striped/Small/Little(!)/Kurrichane Buttonquail, Andalusian Hemipode, Bustard Quail

Taxonomy. *Tetrao sylvaticus* Desfontaines, 1787, near Algiers.
May form superspecies with *T. maculosa*, with which formerly considered conspecific, but differs in colour of plumage, bill and legs. Internal taxonomy rather complex and still somewhat provisional. Race *celestinoi* of SE Philippines sometimes referred to *T. maculosa*: Mindanao claimed to hold two sympatric forms, *celestinoi* and *masaaki*, of which former referred to *T. maculosa* and latter to present species; however, it is not at all clear that "true" *celestinoi*-type birds actually occur on Mindanao, nor that *celestinoi* and *masaaki* are indeed distinct; thus, as sympatry of two distinct forms is not demonstrated, on current evidence it appears safer to retain both forms in present species, and amalgamate *masaaki* with *celestinoi*. Several formerly recognized races now considered indistinguishable: *alleni* and *arenaria* merged into single African race *lepurana*; *mikado* merged into E Asian *davidi*. Nine subspecies normally recognized.
Subspecies and Distribution.
T. s. sylvatica (Desfontaines, 1787) - relictual in S Spain and NW African coast.
T. s. lepurana (A. Smith, 1836) - sub-Saharan Africa, except forests and deserts.
T. s. dussumier (Temminck, 1828) - W parts of SE Asia, from India to Myanmar; possibly E Iran (unconfirmed).
T. s. davidi Delacour & Jabouille, 1930 - E parts of SE Asia, from Indochina through S China to Taiwan.
T. s. whiteheadi Ogilvie-Grant, 1897 - Luzon (N Philippines).
T. s. nigrorum DuPont, 1976 - Negros (SE Philippines).
T. s. celestinoi McGregor, 1907 - Bohol and Mindanao (SE Philippines).
T. s. suluensis Mearns, 1905 - Sulu Is (SW of Mindanao).
T. s. bartelsorum Neumann, 1929 - Java and Bali.

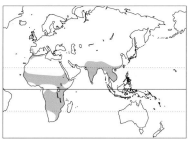

Descriptive notes. 15-16 cm; male 32-44 g, female 39-54 g; female larger. Small, largely chestnut *Turnix* with pale eyebrow, rusty breast and innerwings, scalloped upperparts, spotted flanks, pale eyes, and slender blue-grey bill. Female slightly darker and more brightly coloured than male. Non-breeding birds have duller plumage. Juvenile smaller, more heavily spotted, with dark eyes. Races differ in size and in colouring of upperparts and sides of breast; birds of SE Asia much smaller.
Habitat. Scrub, thickets, tussocky or rank grassland, crops, stubble and weedy fallow fields, sometimes near water but always on warm dry soils; in W Palearctic, found in coastal scrub of bushes and dwarf palms; occurs from sea-level up to 2400 m. Breeds among grass tussocks or low herbage.
Food and Feeding. Seeds, especially of grasses, and invertebrates including ants; usually takes more invertebrates than seeds, or takes both in about equal proportions. Chicks entirely insectivorous for first 10 days. Terrestrial; perhaps nocturnal or partly so in W Palearctic, whereas most active in early morning and late afternoon in Africa.
Breeding. Apr-Aug in W Palearctic; all months in Africa and Asia but locally only during rainy seasons. Solitary breeder; in general, females sequentially polyandrous, but locally monogamous. Nest is shallow, well concealed scrape lined with grass, under grass tussock or low vegetation; standing grass stems often pulled over to form loose canopy. Usually 4 eggs (2-5) in Palearctic, 3-4 eggs (2-7) in Africa, and 4 eggs (4-5) in Asia; incubation 12-15 days. Incubation and chick-care by male alone, except in cases of local monogamy. Chicks rufous brown with dark and pale dorsal stripes; fly at 7-11 days, independent at 18-20 days before fully-grown; first breeding within 4 months. Longevity in captivity 9 years.
Movements. Poorly understood, but seemingly rather complex. Apparently sedentary in W Palearctic. Resident and intra-tropical migrant in Africa: resident with some local movements in Nigeria, Ethiopia, E Africa, Malawi, Zambia, Zimbabwe, South Africa, and probably also in Gambia and Ghana; wet season breeding visitor to drier areas of N tropics (Chad, Sudan, Kenya) and parts of S subtropics (Namibia, Botswana); dry season non-breeding visitor to Zaire, and to Zimbabwe, Zambia and South Africa where these numbers swell resident populations. Resident and locally seasonally nomadic or semi-migratory in Asia; wet season breeding visitor to NW India. Irregular visitor or vagrant to N Yemen, SW Saudi Arabia, S Oman and Iran; formerly occurred regularly in winter in S Yemen. Migrates at night.
Status and Conservation. Not globally threatened. Nominate *sylvatica* rare and declining towards extinction in W Palearctic; now surviving locally in SW Spain and along coast of NW Africa, and perhaps also in S Portugal; extinct in Sicily not later than 1920, probably due to hunting and conversion of garigue habitat. Scarce to locally abundant in Africa: widespread W Africa, and common in Nigeria; moderately common in Sudan and Ethiopia; widespread and locally common in E Africa; common to abundant in Zambia, Zimbabwe and Malawi, and common in Kalahari zone. Uncommon to common throughout Asian range. Most widespread *Turnix* species, adapted to a variety of primary and secondary vegetation types, therefore probably secure.
Bibliography. Ali & Ripley (1980), Baker (1928b), Beaman (1994), Benson & Benson (1975), Cramp & Simmons (1980), Crouther (1994), Dickinson *et al*. (1991), Dowsett & Forbes-Watson (1993), DuPont (1971), Elgood *et al*. (1994), Étchécopar & Hüe (1964, 1978), Ginn *et al*. (1989), Gonzales & Rees (1988), Grimes (1987), Hoesch (1959, 1960), Hollom *et al*. (1988), King *et al*. (1975), Lekagul & Round (1991), MacKinnon (1988), MacKinnon & Phillipps (1993), Mackworth-Praed & Grant (1957, 1962, 1970), Maclean (1993), Newby (1980), Niethammer (1961), Pakenham (1979), Pinto (1983), Rahmani (1988), Roberts, T.J. (1991), Rutgers & Norris (1970), Smythies (1986), Sutter (1955), Trollope (1970), Urban *et al*. (1986), Urdiales (1993, 1994), Violani & Massa (1993), Wintle (1975).

2. **Red-backed Buttonquail**

Turnix maculosa

French: Turnix moucheté   **German**: Fleckenlaufhühnchen   **Spanish**: Torillo Moteado
Other common names: Black-backed/Black-spotted/Orange-breasted/Red-collared/Spotted(!) Buttonquail

Taxonomy. *Hemipodius maculosus* Temminck, 1815, Timor.
May form superspecies with *T. sylvatica*, with which formerly considered conspecific, but differs in colouring of plumage, bill and legs. Alternatively, may be closely related to *T. tanki*, although this seems less likely. Formerly recognized races *yorki* (NE Australia) and *pseutes* (NW Australia) now considered inseparable from *melanota*; *mayri* sometimes merged with similar *horsbrughi* (New Guinea). Race *T. sylvatica celestinoi* of SE Philippines often referred to present species, on grounds of sympatry of two distinct *Turnix* forms on Mindanao; however, this sympatry remains to be demonstrated, and stronger evidence required to justify range extension of present species to include Philippines. Fourteen subspecies normally recognized.
Subspecies and Distribution.
T. m. beccarii Salvadori, 1875 - Sulawesi, Muna and Tukangbesi Is.
T. m. kinneari Neumann, 1939 - Peleng (Banggai Is).
T. m. obiensis Sutter, 1955 - Obi and Kai Is (Moluccas), Babar (Lesser Sundas).
T. m. sumbana Sutter, 1955 - Sumba (Lesser Sundas).
T. m. floresiana Sutter, 1955 - Sumbawa, Komodo, Padar, Flores, Alor (Lesser Sundas).
T. m. maculosa (Temminck, 1815) - Timor, Wetar, Kisar, Moa (Lesser Sundas).
T. m. savuensis Sutter, 1955 - Sawu (Lesser Sundas).
T. m. saturata Forbes, 1882 - New Britain and Duke of York I (Bismarck Archipelago).
T. m. furva Parkes, 1949 - Huon Peninsula (NE New Guinea).
T. m. giluwensis Sims, 1954 - CE New Guinea.
T. m. horsbrughi Ingram, 1909 - S New Guinea.
T. m. mayri Sutter, 1955 - Louisiade Archipelago.
T. m. salamonis Mayr, 1938 - Guadalcanal (Solomon Is).
T. m. melanota (Gould, 1837) - N & E Australia.

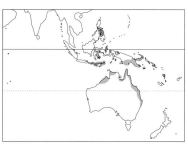

Descriptive notes. 12-16 cm; male 23-39 g, female 32-51 g; female larger. Small *Turnix* with darkish upperparts, slender yellow bill, pale eyes and yellow legs. Female brighter and more rufous than male. Non-breeding birds duller; also some individual variation in brightness. Juvenile smaller, darker, more mottled and scalloped, with dark eyes. Races vary in size and colour, some much darker overall; extent of rufous collar on hindneck varies with races, absent in some.
Habitat. Rank grassland, crops and sedgeland; also grassy ground cover in woodland, often moist or seasonally flooded; from sea-level up to 2400 m. Breeds in dense grass near water.
Food and Feeding. Seeds, e.g. of grasses, *Vicia*, *Swainsona*, *Polygonum aviculare*, *Rumex*; also green shoots and invertebrates; species more insectivorous than most *Turnix*. Swallows grit and sand, presumably to aid mechanical breakdown of seeds in gizzard, as is probably norm for family. Terrestrial, nocturnal and crepuscular; gleans and scratches in litter.
Breeding. Season Oct-Jun. Solitary breeder; females sequentially polyandrous. Nest is shallow depression on ground under grass tussock, herbage or shrub, lined with grass; surrounding grass stems bent and woven to form canopy or dome with side entrance. Usually 4 eggs (2-4); incubation 14 days. Incubation and chick-care by male alone. Chicks dusky with only traces of pale markings; self-feeding at 10 days, fully-feathered at 6 weeks, adult size at 7 weeks, adult-like plumage at 4 months.
Movements. Poorly known; apparently some populations resident, others migratory or dispersive, with some coastal concentration in dry season in Australian tropics and fluctuations in SE of Australian range. Migrates at night.
Status and Conservation. Not globally threatened. Uncommon in E Australia and has disappeared from SE extremity of Australian range, but common in N Australia. Still common in remaining habitat in Solomon Is, but most of habitat there now destroyed and race *salamonis* may now be threatened. Elsewhere, species apparently still secure, but presumably subject to habitat destruction and human predation in many areas.
Bibliography. Andrew, P. (1992), Beehler *et al*. (1986), Blaber & Milton (1991), Coates (1985), Crouther (1994), Dickinson *et al*. (1991), DuPont (1971), Gonzales & Rees (1988), Lindsey (1992), Macdonald (1988), Marchant & Higgins (1993), Mayr (1944), Olsen *et al*. (1993), Pendleton (1947), Pizzey & Doyle (1980), Rand & Gilliard (1967), Schodde & Tidemann (1986), Shephard (1989), Simpson & Day (1994), Slater *et al*. (1989), Stokes (1983), Sutter (1955), Trounson (1987), White & Bruce (1986).

3. **Black-rumped Buttonquail**

Turnix hottentotta

French: Turnix hottentot   **German**: Hottentottenlaufhühnchen   **Spanish**: Torillo Hotentote
Other common names: Dwarf/African Buttonquail; Natal Buttonquail (*nana*); Hottentott/South African Buttonquail (*hottentotta*)

Taxonomy. *Turnix hottentottus* Temminck, 1815, Cape of Good Hope.
Race *nana* often considered separate species, mainly on account of differences in eye colour and migratory habits; no intergradation reported in zone of contact, but very few recent records. Possible northern races *luciana* and *insolata* now considered inseparable from *nana*. Two subspecies normally recognized.
Subspecies and Distribution.
T. h. nana (Sundevall, 1851) - irregularly and locally in sub-Saharan Africa, mainly from Nigeria E to Uganda and Kenya, S to Angola and E South Africa; status and limits of range particularly uncertain in W Africa.
T. h. hottentotta Temminck, 1815 - mountains of S South Africa, in winter rainfall area of S Cape Province.
Descriptive notes. 14-15 cm; male 40 g, female 58-62 g; female larger. Small, rather dark *Turnix* with slender bill and orange-rufous face and breast; prominent barring on sides of breast and spotting on

On following pages: 4. Yellow-legged Buttonquail (*Turnix tanki*); 5. Spotted Buttonquail (*Turnix ocellata*); 6. Barred Buttonquail (*Turnix suscitator*).

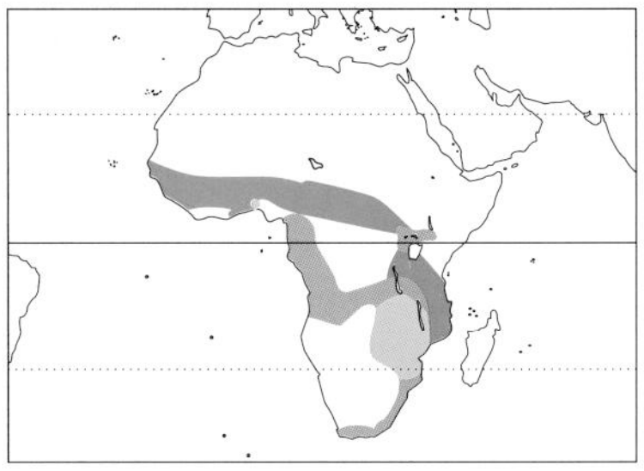

flanks; pale yellow eyes. Female has very slightly brighter red underparts. Darker, browner and generally less scalloped dorsally than partially sympatric *T. sylvatica*; calls differ. Juvenile smaller, less rufous and more heavily marked. Race *nana* has pale blue to whitish eyes, darker upperparts, richer rufous breast with less extensive black markings on sides; male much duller and more heavily marked than female.

Habitat. Short and fairly open grassland and savanna, often in moist zones; also found in fallow fields, native gardens, scrubland, areas of short herbage, and edges of thickets; occurs from sea-level up to 1800 m. Breeds in moist, open tussocky grassland; occasionally in somewhat marshy, harvested fields of sugar cane.

Food and Feeding. Little specific information available. Seeds of grasses and weeds; invertebrates including insects and their larvae. Food taken on ground.

Breeding. Laying occurs in most months, but locally during or at end of rainy seasons; nominate *hottentotta* recorded laying in Feb. Solitary breeder; females possibly polyandrous. Nest is shallow scrape, lined with grass, under grass tussock with standing stems bent to form loose canopy, or under sheaf of fallen grass without canopy. Usually 3 eggs (2-6); incubation 12-14 days. Incubation by male.

Movements. Poorly understood. Resident and local intra-African migrant; apparently itinerant over most of range, where tends to be breeding migrant during rains. Nominate race exclusively resident. Race *nana* resident in Kenya, Uganda and (formerly?) South Africa; breeding visitor to Malawi, Zimbabwe and Zambia; probably only vagrant to Nigeria, although breeding recorded; erratic appearances in Cameroon. Migrates at night.

Status and Conservation. Not globally threatened. Uncommon or locally common, but cryptic in plumage and behaviour and easily overlooked; less numerous than partially sympatric *T. sylvatica*. Nominate *hottentotta* very poorly known and restricted in range; uncommon and local, and possibly even extinct, with last breeding record in 1968. Species as a whole very rare in South Africa, where range has undergone major contraction, probably due, at least in part, to overgrazing, trampling and excessive burning of habitat; may no longer breed. Locally common in Zaire, Uganda and Kenya; widespread but local in Zambia and Malawi; uncommon and local in Mozambique and Zimbabwe, and apparently also in W Africa. Association with dry and heavily grazed grasslands, and attraction to areas disturbed by cattle, suggest that species is likely to be secure; however, overgrazing could be a threat in some areas.

Bibliography. Anon. (1995g), Benson & Benson (1975), Britton, P.L. (1980), Brooke (1984a), Brown & Britton (1980), Clancey (1967, 1970), Cyrus & Robson (1980), Dowsett & Dowsett-Lemaire (1993), Dowsett & Forbes-Watson (1993), Flieg (1973), Ginn *et al*. (1989), Kemp (1980), Lippens & Wille (1976), Mackworth-Praed & Grant (1957, 1962, 1970), Maclean (1993), Masterson (1969, 1973), Newman (1980), Pinto (1983), Short *et al*. (1990), Skead, C.J. (1967), Urban *et al*. (1986), Winterbottom (1968).

4. Yellow-legged Buttonquail

Turnix tanki

French: Turnix indien **German**: Rotnacken-Laufhühnchen **Spanish**: Torillo Tanki

Taxonomy. *Turnix tanki* Blyth, 1843, Bengal.

May be closely related to *T. maculosa*, although this proposal has not been widely accepted. Two subspecies recognized.

Subspecies and Distribution.

T. t. tanki Blyth, 1843 - Indian Subcontinent, Andaman and Nicobar Is.

T. t. blanfordii Blyth, 1863 - Myanmar through Indochina to E China, breeding N to Korea and extreme SE of Soviet Far East (S Amurland and Ussuriland).

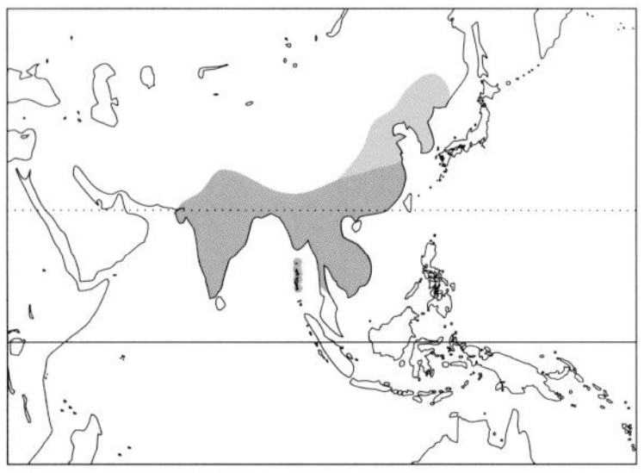

Descriptive notes. 17 cm; male 35-78 g, female 93-113 g; female larger. Fairly large, greyish *Turnix*; rather pale underparts with bold black spotting; bright yellow bill and legs. Female brighter than male, with rufous collar on hindneck. Non-breeding birds duller, female lacking rufous collar. Juvenile smaller, with more rufous mottling and more densely spotted. Race *blanfordii* slightly larger, with more distinct dorsal barring.

Habitat. Grassland, crops, secondary growth on deserted cultivation, bamboo thickets with grassy undergrowth, and scrub; occurs from sea-level up to 2200 m. Breeds in grass.

Food and Feeding. Grain, seeds, green shoots and invertebrates (ants, small beetles and grasshoppers); feeds mostly on seeds. Chicks fed mainly on minute insects, though seeds also eaten. Terrestrial forager, like congeners.

Breeding. Mar-Nov, occasionally other months; usually in rainy season Jun-Oct. Solitary breeder; females sequentially polyandrous. Nest is shallow depression on ground, lined with grass, sometimes with surrounding stems arched over to form rough dome with side entrance. Usually 4 eggs; incubation 12 days. Incubation and chick-care by male alone. Chicks can fly at 10 days, attain adult plumage at 7 weeks.

Movements. Apparently resident most areas, but nomadic or migratory in dry regions of India and Pakistan, where is breeding visitor during rainy season; summer breeding migrant in NE of range, with birds wintering in SE of range. Migrates at night.

Status and Conservation. Not globally threatened. Status and trends very poorly known. Species widespread and apparently common in much of range, e.g. in Thailand; frequent in Pakistan. Preference for disturbed and cultivated areas suggests that its future is secure.

Bibliography. Ali & Ripley (1980), Austin (1948), Baker (1928b, 1930), Beaman (1994), Deignan (1945), Étchécopar & Hüe (1978), Flint *et al*. (1984), Inskipp & Inskipp (1991), King *et al*. (1975), Knystautas (1993), Lekagul & Round (1991), Liang Qihui (1986), Meyer de Schaunsee (1984), Potapov & Flint (1987), Rahmani (1988), Ripley (1982), Roberts, T.J. (1991), Rutgers & Norris (1970), Seth-Smith (1903), Smythies (1986), Zhang Weigong & Chen Zuoping (1985).

5. Spotted Buttonquail

Turnix ocellata

French: Turnix de Luçon **German**: Riesenlaufhühnchen **Spanish**: Torillo Ocelado

Other common names: Ocellated/Philippine/Chestnut-breasted(!) Buttonquail

Taxonomy. *Oriolus ocellatus* Scopoli, 1786, Manila.

Generally regarded as polytypic, but population of Luzon may be monotypic with clinal variation in size; racial diagnosis based on few specimens. Taxonomic status of Negros population unknown. Two subspecies currently recognized.

Subspecies and Distribution.

T. o. benguetensis Parkes, 1968 - montane N Luzon; intermediate form in lowland NE Luzon (Philippines).

T. o. ocellata (Scopoli, 1786) - lowland C Luzon (Philippines).

Also occurs on Negros, but subspecies uncertain.

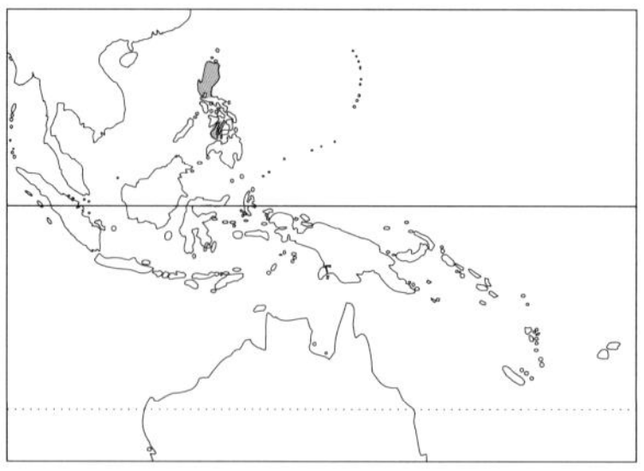

Descriptive notes. 17 cm; female larger. Fairly large, brown *Turnix* with strongly patterned head, plain rufous breast and boldly spotted wings. Female brighter, with much more boldly marked head and more prominent rufous collar. Juvenile smaller, more spotted on foreparts. Geographical or possibly altitudinal variation in size: race *benguetensis* has slightly smaller wings and bill, but intermediate specimen known; rufous of underparts also slightly brighter and often somewhat more extensive; more white markings on sides of head.

Habitat. Poorly known. Brushy grassland, ravine edges, rice fields and rarely open grassland; recorded from sea-level up to 2200 m.

Food and Feeding. No information available.

Breeding. Season Feb (chick) and May-Aug; no further information available.

Movements. No information available. Presumably sedentary, as inferred from isolation and possible subspeciation; no records outside normal range.

Status and Conservation. Not globally threatened. Currently considered near-threatened. No specific information available on status; seldom encountered by ornithologists, biology unknown. Restricted range, but apparently common as suggested by frequent capture; subject to certain amount of human predation.

Bibliography. Collar *et al*. (1994), Dickinson *et al*. (1991), DuPont (1971), Gonzales & Rees (1988), Hachisuka (1931), Hornbuckle (1994), Parkes (1968), Rabor (1955).

6. Barred Buttonquail

Turnix suscitator

French: Turnix combattant **German**: Bindenlaufhühnchen **Spanish**: Torillo Batallador

Other common names: Common(!)/Dusky/Indian/Philippine(!) Buttonquail

Taxonomy. *Tetrao Suscitator* Gmelin, 1789, Java.

Race *powelli* has on occasion been considered sufficiently distinct to merit separate species status, and is undoubtedly the most distinctive subspecies. Race *interrumpens* doubtfully distinct from *blakistoni*; validity of race *baweanus* sometimes questioned, due to similarity with Javan *suscitator*. Birds of Sumatran zone sometimes receive different subspecific designations: those of N Sumatra have been placed in race *atrogularis*; those of C Sumatra have been awarded separate race, *machetes*; and those of Belitung I sometimes awarded separate race, *kuiperi*; however, no clear patterns of geographical variation, and all three populations probably best retained in nominate *suscitator*. Eighteen subspecies recognized.

Subspecies and Distribution.

T. s. taigoor (Sykes, 1832) - India.

T. s. leggei Stuart Baker, 1920 - Sri Lanka.

T. s. plumbipes (Hodgson, 1837) - Nepal, Sikkim, Bangladesh and Assam E to NE Myanmar.

T. s. bengalensis Blyth, 1852 - lower W Bengal (India).

T. s. okinavensis Phillips, 1947 - S Kyushu and Makenoshima I (Japan) S to Ryukyu Is.

T. s. rostrata Swinhoe, 1865 - Taiwan.

T. s. blakistoni (Swinhoe, 1871) - Myanmar and N Vietnam to S China and Hainan.

T. s. pallescens Robinson & Stuart Baker, 1928 - SC Myanmar.

T. s. thai Deignan, 1946 - C Thailand.

T. s. interrumpens Robinson & Stuart Baker, 1928 - peninsular Myanmar and Thailand.

T. s. atrogularis (Eyton, 1839) - Malay Peninsula.

T. s. suscitator (Gmelin, 1789) - Sumatra, Belitung I and Bangka I to Java and Bali.

T. s. baweanus Hoogerwerf, 1962 - Bawean I (Java).

T. s. fasciata Temminck, 1815 - Luzon S to Mindoro, Sibuyan and Masbate (N Philippines).

T. s. haynaldi Blasius, 1888 - Palawan and Calamian Group (W Philippines).

T. s. nigrescens Tweeddale, 1878 - Panay and nearby islands S to Negros and Cebu (CE Philippines).

T. s. rufilata Wallace, 1865 - Sulawesi.

T. s. powelli Guillemard, 1885 - Lombok, Sumbawa, Sangeang, Flores, Lomblen and Alor (Lesser Sundas).

Contrary to some recent sources, no evidence of occurrence in Pakistan.

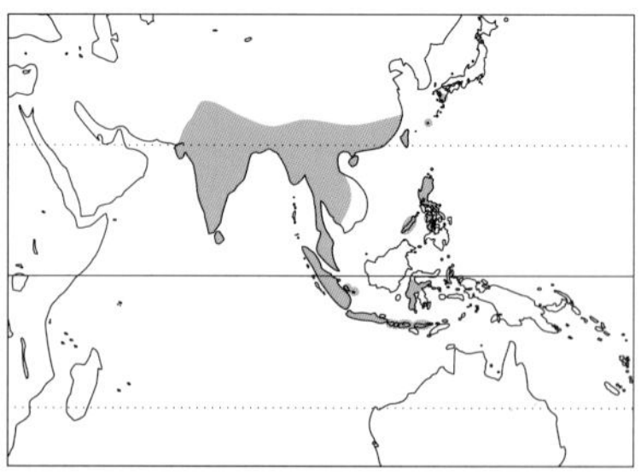

Descriptive notes. 15-17 cm; male 35-52 g, female 47-68 g; female larger. Fairly large, russet brown *Turnix* with boldly patterned head, barred underparts and greyish legs and feet. Female brighter than male, with black throat and rufous collar in some races. Non-breeding birds duller. Juvenile smaller and more buff-coloured, with underparts spotted. Races vary in size, and in patterns and coloration of plumage; sexes alike in some races; race *powelli* very different, essentially lacking rufous tones throughout plumage, and with greyish brown upperparts largely unmarked; female of race *rufilata* has throat barred black and white, rather than solid black; race *nigrescens* particularly dark rufous collar on hindneck varies considerably in extent, being totally absent in some races.

Habitat. Grassland, crops, deserted fields, secondary growth, scrub, bamboo thickets and forest edge habitats, on sandy soil, often near water; occurs from sea-level up to 2500 m. Breeds in rank ground vegetation, often near margin of more open ground.

Food and Feeding. Grass and weed seeds, invertebrates and green shoots. Terrestrial; forages among grass and leaf litter, where makes circular scrapes in mulch. Commutes to foraging sites via well defined trails, marked by footprints.

Breeding. Laying recorded in all months, but with local peaks according to seasonal conditions and possible gaps at height of rains or in driest months. Solitary breeder; females sequentially polyandrous. Nest is pad of grass in shallow depression, often in grass tuft; stems bent to form overhead dome with side entrance. Usually 4 eggs (3-6); incubation 12-14 days. Incubation and chick-care by male alone. Chicks reach adult size in 40-60 days.

Movements. Poorly known. Apparently resident in most areas, but some continental populations may be locally nomadic or migratory, according to rains.

Status and Conservation. Not globally threatened. Appears to be widespread and common in India, Sri Lanka and most parts of SE Asian range, so far as is known; very common in Thailand. Ability to live near humans and to benefit from cutting, grazing and cropping suggests that species is likely to be secure.

Bibliography. Ali & Ripley (1980), Baker (1928b), Beaman (1994), Brazil (1991), Deignan (1945), Dickinson *et al.* (1991), DuPont (1971), Étchécopar & Hüe (1978), Gonzales & Rees (1988), Henry (1971), Inskipp & Inskipp (1991), King *et al.* (1975), Kotagamana & Fernando (1994), Lekagul & Round (1991), MacKinnon (1988), MacKinnon & Phillipps (1993), Madoc (1976), Majumdar & Brahmachari (1988), van Marle & Voous (1988), Medway & Wells (1976), Phillips (1978), Prinzinger *et al.* (1993), Rabor (1977), Rutgers & Norris (1970), Smythies (1986), Starck (1991), Trollope (1970), White & Bruce (1986), Wijesinghe (1994).

PLATE 4

inches 4

cm 10

7 ♂

♀

8 ♂

♀

9 ♂

♀

10 ♂

♀

11 ♂

ssp *varia*

♂

ssp *novaecaledoniae*

♀

12 ♂

♀

13 ♀

14 ♂

♀

15 ♂

♀

16

7. Madagascar Buttonquail

Turnix nigricollis

French: Turnix de Madagascar **German**: Schwarzkehl-Laufhühnchen **Spanish**: Torillo Malgache
Other common names: Black-necked Buttonquail

Taxonomy. *Tetrao nigricollis* Gmelin, 1789, Madagascar.
Monotypic.
Distribution. Madagascar; also Mauritius, Reunion and Glorieuses Is, but possibly introduced to all of these, though may have colonized them, e.g. introduced to Reunion, but an indigenous population may have existed there already.

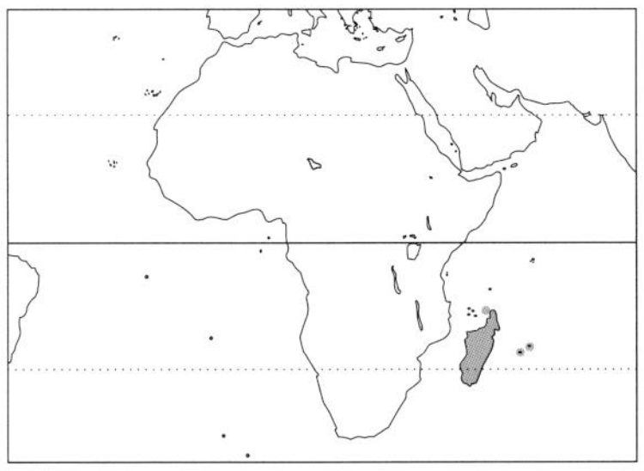

Descriptive notes. 14-16 cm; female 67-84 g; female larger. Smallish *Turnix* with blackish forehead; male has black and white barred breast; female considerably brighter, with solid black breast and deep rufous shoulder patch; no congeners within range. Juvenile smaller, with wings more rufous and more heavily spotted.
Habitat. Typically found in grassland, crops, savanna, woodland, brush and dry forest, including disturbed forest; occurs from sea-level up to 1900 m. Breeds in grassy glades in secondary growth, and among brush and tall weeds in open grassland.
Food and Feeding. Recorded as taking seeds and insects. Terrestrial and diurnal; scratches and pivots in leaf litter to form characteristic circular feeding scrapes.
Breeding. Late Aug-Feb. Solitary breeder. Nest is shallow depression or scrape, lined with grass, under grass tussock or in midst of grass beneath small tree; grasses often domed over to form canopy with side entrance, sometimes with tunnel or runway to nest. 3-5 eggs; incubation 13-16 days. Incubation by male alone. Chick brown with pale dorsal stripes; chicks self-feeding at 2 weeks, fully-feathered and flying at 3 weeks, independent in 4th week.
Movements. No specific information available, but apparently sedentary. Perhaps locally dispersive, if populations on offshore islands were self-introduced.
Status and Conservation. Not globally threatened. Common in N, W and S Madagascar, less so in E and on High Plateau. Occurs in a variety of disturbed, cultivated and secondary habitats including forest clearings, therefore probably secure. Possibly introduced population on Mauritius now extinct.
Bibliography. Appert (1972), Benson, Beamish *et al*. (1975), Benson, Colebrook-Robjent & Williams (1976-1977), Berlioz (1946), Cheke (1987), Dee (1986), Delacour (1932), Dowsett & Forbes-Watson (1993), Diamond (1987), Langrand (1990), Lever (1987), Milon (1951), Milon *et al*. (1973), Penny (1974), Rand (1936), Rutgers & Norris (1970), Salvan (1972b), Staub (1976), Watson *et al*. (1963).

8. Black-breasted Buttonquail

Turnix melanogaster

French: Turnix à poitrine noire **German**: Schwarzbrust-Laufhühnchen **Spanish**: Torillo Pechinegro

Taxonomy. *Hemipodius melanogaster* Gould, 1837, Moreton Bay, Queensland, Australia.
Variously considered to be similar to, and possibly related to, either *T. nigricollis* and *T. ocellata*, or *T. suscitator*; but affinities more likely to be with *T. varia* group, and males of *melanogaster* and *varia* resemble each other. Proposed race *goweri* (Queensland) no longer recognized because based on individual variation. Monotypic.
Distribution. Coastal E Australia, in SE Queensland and extreme NE New South Wales; recently found to occur on offshore Fraser I.

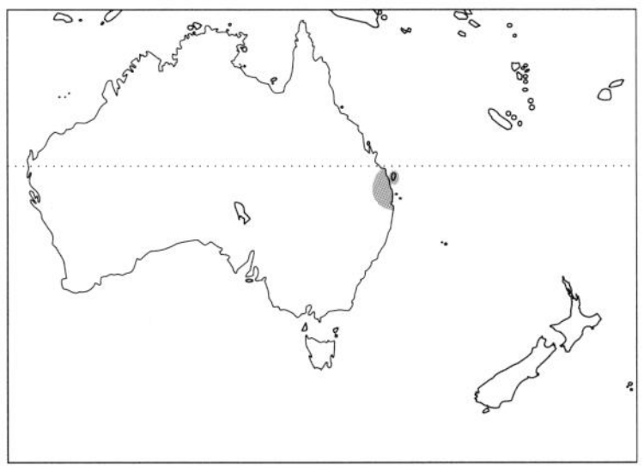

Descriptive notes. 17-19 cm; male 50-87 g, female 80-119 g; female larger. Fairly large, robust *Turnix* with relatively slender bill and pale eyes. Female, with mostly black head and breast, unmistakable. Juvenile smaller, duller, foreparts more mottled. Male and juvenile similar to those of *T. varia*, from which distinguished by details of plumage and eye colour.
Habitat. Rain forest, other moist forest, vine thicket and grassy edges, with deep leaf litter; also introduced *Lantana* thickets; sometimes found in *Araucaria* and pine plantations, rarely in grass or stubble away from forest. Occurs from sea-level up to 800 m. Breeds within rain forest or under *Lantana*.
Food and Feeding. Apparently feeds mainly on invertebrates, though seeds, including grain, also reported. In one study, commonest items were: beetles, including weevils; ants; and spiders, probably including a jumping spider (Salticidae) and a brown trapdoor (*Arbanitis variabilis*) reckoned to measure 1·5-2 cm; other items included centipedes, millipedes and land snail *Nitor pudibundus*. Terrestrial, feeding both diurnally and nocturnally. Gleans, scratches and pecks at litter; creates characteristic circular feeding scrapes by pivoting on one foot while raking with the other (see page 47), sometimes reversing direction. Sometimes shades litter with outstretched wings while scratching.
Breeding. In wild, recorded in Oct-Feb or Mar; all year but mainly Sept-Apr in captivity, if conditions sufficiently warm. Solitary breeder; females sequentially polyandrous. Nest is scrape, lined with grass and leaves, under low bush or coarse grass tussock, often with grass stems forming hood or even substantial dome with side entrance. Usually 3-4 eggs; incubation 15-16 days. Incubation and chick-care by male alone. Chicks brown with black and white dorsal stripes; start to self-feed at 8 days, but fed by male for 2 weeks; attain sexually diagnostic plumage at 8-12 weeks, breeding at 4-5 months.
Movements. Apparently mostly sedentary, with no evidence of seasonal or long distance movements, though occasional local irruptions.
Status and Conservation. ENDANGERED. CITES II. Range and numbers greatly reduced by habitat clearance for agriculture and silviculture, and remaining populations threatened by frequent fire and further habitat clearance; species now rarely seen despite searches by ornithologists. May be adapting to pine plantations and *Lantana*, but not known if these are very suitable for breeding. Extensive research required on species, especially in terms of habitat requirements, home range size, breeding biology and post-breeding dispersal, and the impact of forestry and fire; inventory and management of dry rain forest remnants also required. Some of this work has been initiated, including survey of the species and the conservation status of its habitat remnants, as well as research on impact of forestry.
Bibliography. Bennett (1985), Blakers *et al*. (1984), Brouwer & Garnett (1990), Collar & Andrew (1988), Collar *et al*. (1994), Erritzoe (1993), Garnett (1992, 1993), Hermes (1980), Holmes (1987), Hughes & Hughes (1991), Lindsey (1992), Macdonald (1988), Marchant & Higgins (1993), Olsen *et al*. (1993), Phipps (1976), Pizzey & Doyle (1980), Schodde & Tidemann (1986), Shephard (1989), Simpson & Day (1994), Slater *et al*. (1989), Trounson (1987).

9. Chestnut-backed Buttonquail

Turnix castanota

French: Turnix castanote **German**: Rotrücken-Laufhühnchen **Spanish**: Torillo Dorsicastaño

Taxonomy. *Hemipodius castanotus* Gould, 1840, Port Essington, Northern Territory.
Forms superspecies with *T. olivii* and *T. varia*; sometimes considered conspecific with former, but differs in bill size and details of plumage. Invalid races *magnifica* (NW Australia), *melvillensis* (Melville I) and *alligator* (N Australia) no longer recognized, because based on individual rather than geographical variation. Monotypic.
Distribution. NW & NC Australia and offshore islands.

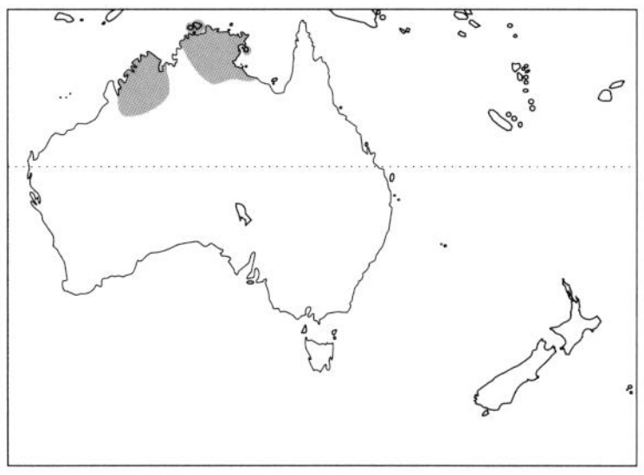

Descriptive notes. 14-20 cm; male 68-69 g, female 87-124 g; female larger. Fairly large, rufous *Turnix* with stout bill and orange-yellow eyes. Female brighter, with plainer pattern than male on upperparts. Smaller, duller and more heavily patterned than *T. olivii*. Juvenile unknown.
Habitat. Short grass in open, dry savanna woodland, often on lightly wooded, stony and litter-strewn hillsides and sandy ridges; occurs from sea-level up to at least 500 m.
Food and Feeding. Little specific information available. Takes seeds (including grass *Triodia*) and insects (beetles, ants and their eggs). Swallows grit and sand, presumably to assist mechanical breakdown in gizzard, as is probably norm for congeners. Terrestrial; nocturnal and crepuscular. Gleans and scratches in litter.
Breeding. Little known. Breeding reported to occur Dec-May, in wet season; eggs recorded Jan. Solitary breeder. Nest is depression in grass, at base of shrub or grass clump, often near water; lined with grass and leaves; sometimes domed with side entrance. Usually 4 eggs (3-4); incubation reportedly 14-15 days. Chicks rufous brown with cream dorsal stripes.
Movements. Unknown; presumably sedentary or locally nomadic, with no evidence of dispersal into other habitats nor seasonal fluctuations.
Status and Conservation. VULNERABLE. Shows cryptic behaviour and inhabits remote areas; seldom encountered by ornithologists, and biology poorly known. Has disappeared from SE extremity of range; possibly threatened by grazing and associated regular fires. Research is required on distribution, status, biology and impact of pastoralism and fire.
Bibliography. Andrew, D. (1992), Blakers *et al*. (1984), Christidis & Boles (1994), Collar *et al*. (1994), Garnett (1992, 1993), Lindsey (1992), Macdonald (1988), Marchant & Higgins (1993), Olsen *et al*. (1993), Pizzey & Doyle (1980), Rogers, D. (1995a, 1995b), Schodde & Tidemann (1986), Simpson & Day (1994), Slater *et al*. (1989), Squire (1990), Trounson (1987).

10. Buff-breasted Buttonquail

Turnix olivii

French: Turnix de Robinson **German**: Ockerbrust-Laufhühnchen **Spanish**: Torillo de Robinson
Other common names: Buff-backed/Olive's/Robinson's Buttonquail

Taxonomy. *Turnix olivii* Robinson, 1900, Cooktown, Queensland.
Forms superspecies with *T. castanota* and *T. varia*; sometimes considered conspecific with former, but differs in bill size and plainer plumage. Specific name sometimes misspelt *olivei*, but original spelling is *olivii*. Proposed race *coenensis* (from N of range) no longer recognized, because based on individual variation. Monotypic.
Distribution. Cape York Peninsula, N Queensland, Australia.

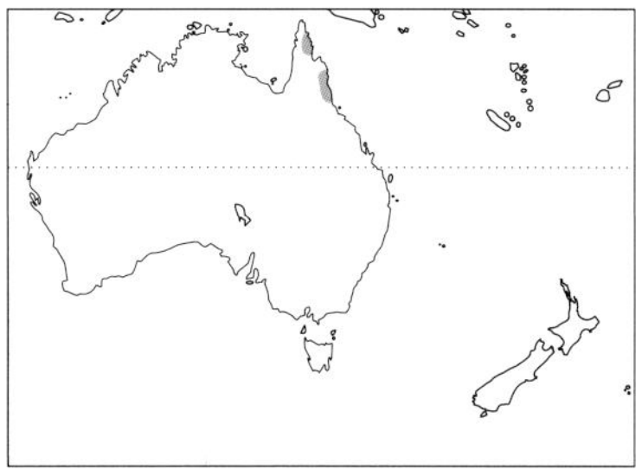

Descriptive notes. 18-22 cm; female larger. Large, rufous *Turnix* with large bill and yellow eyes. Female brighter than male, with plainer pattern. Juvenile unknown.
Habitat. Normally found in wooded grasslands and grassy fringes of forests and swamps; often on stony hillsides or ridges with sparse grass cover, within woodland or rain forest; occurs from sea-level up to 400 m. Breeds in grassy woodland.
Food and Feeding. Little known; seeds and insects recorded. Like congeners, swallows coarse sand, presumably to assist mechanical breakdown in gizzard. Terrestrial.
Breeding. Little known. Season Jan-Mar. Solitary breeder. Nest is domed structure of grass stems with side entrance, in shallow depression lined with grass and a few leaves; well hidden among grass stalks or low shrubs or under grass tussock. Usually 3-4 eggs (2-4); incubation period unknown but presumably similar to that of *T. varia*. Incubation and probably chick-care by male alone. Chicks not described.
Movements. None known; southerly expansion of range may occur during wet years.

On following pages: 11. Painted Buttonquail (*Turnix varia*); 12. Worcester's Buttonquail (*Turnix worcesteri*); 13. Sumba Buttonquail (*Turnix everetti*); 14. Red-chested Buttonquail (*Turnix pyrrhothorax*); 15. Australian Little Buttonquail (*Turnix velox*); 16. Lark Buttonquail (*Ortyxelos meiffrenii*).

Status and Conservation. ENDANGERED. Scarcely distributed in remote area, with cryptic behaviour typical of congeners; seldom encountered by ornithologists, and biology poorly known. Possibly threatened by grazing and associated frequent fires. Extensive survey and research work on ecology required.

Bibliography. Blakers *et al.* (1984), Brouwer & Garnett (1990), Christidis & Boles (1994), Collar & Andrew (1988), Collar *et al.* (1994), Garnett (1992, 1993), Lindsey (1992), Macdonald (1971, 1988), Marchant & Higgins (1993), Olsen *et al.* (1993), Pizzey & Doyle (1980), Rogers, D. (1995a, 1995b), Schodde & Tidemann (1986), Simpson & Day (1994), Slater *et al.* (1989), Squire (1990), Trounson (1987), White (1922a, 1922b).

11. Painted Buttonquail
Turnix varia

French: Turnix bariolé   **German**: Buntlaufhühnchen   **Spanish**: Torillo Pintojo
Other common names: Varied Buttonquail

Taxonomy. *Perdix varia* Latham, 1801, Sydney, New South Wales.
Forms superspecies with *T. olivii* and *T. castanota*. Proposed races *stirlingi* (SW Australia) and *subminuta* (NE Australia) no longer recognized, because based on individual rather than geographical variation. Race *novaecaledoniae* very distinct, and may be separate species. Three subspecies normally recognized.
Subspecies and Distribution.
T. v. novaecaledoniae Ogilvie-Grant, 1893 - New Caledonia.
T. v. scintillans (Gould, 1845) - Abrolhos Is (SW Australia).
T. v. varia (Latham, 1801) - SW, E & SE Australia; Tasmania.

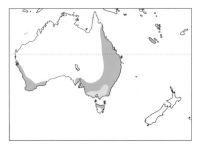

Descriptive notes. 17-23 cm; male 53-94 g, female 72-134 g; female larger. Large, rather rufous *Turnix* with fine bill and red eyes. Female brighter, more rufous than male. Juvenile smaller, more mottled and greyer, with no rufous; eyes pale. Races vary in size, and in intensity of colour and spotting: race *scintillans* smaller, browner and more boldly marked; *novaecaledoniae* small and dark with mostly black upperparts.
Habitat. Scrub, grassy forest and woodland, heath, grassy clearings within dense forest, particularly with abundant litter, and tussocky grass on stony ridges or slopes; occurs from sea-level up to at least 1500 m. Breeds in scrub, forest, woodland or rarely grassland, in sites affording extensive litter, fallen timber, saplings and clumps of grass tussocks.
Food and Feeding. Seeds (grasses, *Avena*, Fabaceae, *Trifolium*, *Erodium*, *Acacia*), fruits (*Solanum* and other wild berries), green shoots and invertebrates (fly pupae, grasshoppers, ants, beetles, weevils, bugs, moths, larvae, aquatic insects). Foraging nocturnal and crepuscular, but also diurnal; terrestrial. Like congeners, swallows grit and sand, presumably to assist mechanical breakdown in gizzard. Scratches and gleans; forms characteristic circular scrapes in litter by pivoting on one foot while raking with the other, sometimes changing feet and reversing direction.
Breeding. Aug-Mar in S, extending to May in E; all months according to local conditions in tropical N of range. Solitary breeder; females sequentially polyandrous, but monogamous bonds can be maintained for several months. Nest is cup of grass and fine litter, at least partly hooded and walled by grass stems, in scrape, sometimes with runway to entrance; normally at base of grass tussock, sapling or rock, or under small shrub. Usually 3-4 eggs (3-5); incubation 13-14 days. Incubation and chick-care by male alone. Chicks grey-brown with black and white dorsal stripes; fed by male for 7-10 days; can fly at 10 days, fully-feathered at 16 days, adult size at 23 days. For 60 eggs in 16 successful nests, 3·7 young raised per successful nest, and 2·6 young per clutch started; mean brood size 3·5 in first week, 2·3 at flying age.
Movements. Poorly understood. Mostly resident, though with high turnover of individuals and some local fluctuations in numbers. Apparently a summer breeding migrant in S of range, particularly in highlands. Migrates at night.
Status and Conservation. Not globally threatened. Generally uncommon to locally common; declining in S, particularly Tasmania where now rare. Subject to habitat clearance and degradation by urbanization, agriculture, grazing and fire. Small island population of race *scintillans* vulnerable. Poorly known on New Caledonia, where endemic race *novaecaledoniae* (possibly full species) rare, or perhaps even extinct.
Bibliography. Beruldsen (1980), Blakers *et al.* (1984), Bourne (1982), Christidis & Boles (1994), Crouther (1994), Frith (1969), Garnett (1992, 1993), Hannecart & Létocart (1980), Hobbs (1981), How & Dell (1990), Lindsey (1992), Macdonald (1971, 1988), Marchant & Higgins (1993), Mather & Rounsevell (1991), Olsen *et al.* (1993), Pedler (1982b), Pizzey & Doyle (1980), Roberts (1979), Rogers, D. (1995a, 1995b), Schodde & Tidemann (1986), Serventy & Whittell (1976), Shephard (1989), Simpson & Day (1989), Slater *et al.* (1989), Storr & Johnstone (1984), Trounson (1987), Whinray (1978).

12. Worcester's Buttonquail
Turnix worcesteri

French: Turnix de Worcester   **German**: Worcesterlaufhühnchen   **Spanish**: Torillo de Worcester

Taxonomy. *Turnix worcesteri* McGregor, 1904, probably Parañaque, Luzon.
Usually considered a separate species or conspecific with *T. everetti*, but both taxa recently proposed as races of *T. pyrrhothorax*; distinguished from latter by plumage and size. Monotypic.
Distribution. Luzon, N Philippines.

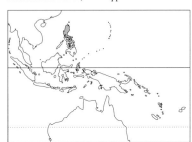

Descriptive notes. c. 14 cm; female larger. Small, stout-billed *Turnix* closely resembling allopatric *T. everetti*, which is slightly darker above; *T. pyrrhothorax* is somewhat paler dorsally, duller ventrally and normally rather larger.
Habitat. Grasslands; recorded from sea-level up to 1000 m, though perhaps mainly in the highlands.
Food and Feeding. No information available.
Breeding. No information available.
Movements. Unknown; no records outside normal range. It has been suggested that a record from a mountain pass may represent an intra-island migration point.

Status and Conservation. VULNERABLE. No specific information available; species rare and probably threatened. Restricted in range, rarely encountered by ornithologists, and biology unknown. Known from few specimens. Subject to certain degree of human predation. Populations may await discovery on other islands. Extensive research required.
Bibliography. Alonzo-Pasicolan (1992), Amadon & DuPont (1970), Christidis & Boles (1994), Collar & Andrew (1988), Collar *et al.* (1994), Dickinson *et al.* (1991), DuPont (1971), Gonzales & Rees (1988), Hornbuckle (1994), Poulsen (1995), Sutter (1955).

13. Sumba Buttonquail
Turnix everetti

French: Turnix de Sumba   **German**: Sumbalaufhühnchen   **Spanish**: Torillo de Sumba
Other common names: Everett's Buttonquail

Taxonomy. *Turnix everetti* Hartert, 1898, Waingapo, Sumba.
Usually considered a separate species or conspecific with *T. worcesteri*, but both taxa recently proposed as races of *T. pyrrhothorax*; distinguished from latter by plumage and size. In past, was considered race of *T. sylvatica*. Monotypic.
Distribution. Sumba (Lesser Sundas).

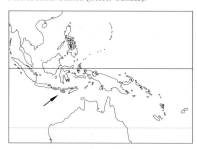

Descriptive notes. c. 14 cm; juvenile male and female 28 g; female larger. Small, stout-billed *Turnix* closely resembling allopatric *T. worcesteri*, which is slightly paler above; *T. pyrrhothorax* is paler yet dorsally, possibly slightly duller ventrally and generally somewhat larger.
Habitat. Inhabits scrubby and mostly uncultivated fields mixed with grassland; sparse grassland with scattered bushes inland from mangrove belt. Recent records were in areas of grassland with sward height of 50-70 cm, with areas of short grass interspersed. Basis of ecological separation from sympatric *T. maculosa sumbana* uncertain.
Food and Feeding. Forages on the ground, in pairs; no further information available.
Breeding. No information available.
Movements. Unknown; no records outside normal range.
Status and Conservation. VULNERABLE. Little specific information available; species apparently uncommon and considered threatened, although occurs in man-made grassland and may reach high densities (2 birds per hectare) in suitable habitat; instability of habitat combines with limited range to make species vulnerable. Repeated burning of vegetation to provide land for grazing and cultivation may have increased the area of suitable habitat. Restricted in range, rarely encountered by ornithologists, and biology unknown. Known from very few specimens. Presumably subject to some degree of human predation. Populations might await discovery on other islands. Extensive research required.
Bibliography. Andrew, P. (1992), Christidis & Boles (1994), Collar & Andrew (1988), Collar *et al.* (1994), Jones, M.J., Juhaeni *et al.* (1994), Jones, M.J., Linsley & Marsden (1995), Marsden & Peters (1992), Mayr (1944), Sutter (1955), White & Bruce (1986).

14. Red-chested Buttonquail
Turnix pyrrhothorax

French: Turnix à poitrine rousse   **German**: Rotbrust-Laufhühnchen   **Spanish**: Torillo Pechirrufo
Other common names: Chestnut-breasted/Red-breasted/Rufous-breasted/Yellow Buttonquail

Taxonomy. *Hemipodius pyrrhothorax* Gould, 1841, Aberdeen, New South Wales.
Usually regarded as monotypic, but recent proposal to treat *T. worcesteri* and *T. everetti* as races of present species. Proposed races *berneyi* (NW Australia) and *intermedia* (Queensland) no longer recognized, because based on individual rather than geographical variation. Monotypic.
Distribution. N & E Australia.

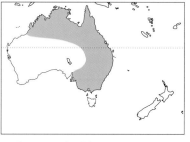

Descriptive notes. 12-16 cm; male 27-46 g, female 43-76 g; female larger. Small to medium-sized, grey and rufous *Turnix* with stout bill and pale eyes. Female brighter than male, with scalloping rarely extending onto breast. Juvenile smaller, browner and more mottled, with breast scalloped.
Habitat. Normally recorded in grassland and grassy woodland; also crops, stubble and weedy fields with dense ground cover; occurs from coastal plains around sea-level up to 1000 m. Generally found in moister, denser cover than *T. velox*, but inhabits semi-arid zones. Breeds in tussock grasslands, pastures of native grass, standing crops and stubble.
Food and Feeding. Seeds (grasses, *Triticum*, *Panicum*, Malvaceae) and insects (cockroaches, ants, flies, larvae). Terrestrial; nocturnal and crepuscular, but also diurnal. Gleans and scratches in litter; makes circular scrapes by pivoting on one foot while raking with the other.
Breeding. Little known. Eggs recorded in Feb-Jul and Sept in N, Sept-Feb in S. Solitary breeder; females sequentially polyandrous. Nest is depression lined with grass, hooded, and sheltered by grass tussock. Usually 4 eggs (2-5); incubation 13-18 days. Incubation and chick-care by male alone. Chicks grey-brown with dark and pale dorsal stripes; reach adult size in 6-8 weeks, adult-like plumage at 2-3 months.
Movements. Poorly known. Local populations variously resident, erratic or migratory. Apparently a spring-summer migrant to parts of S, and dry season (austral winter) migrant to tropical N. Migrates at night.
Status and Conservation. Not globally threatened. Generally ranges from uncommon to locally common, but cryptic behaviour makes it easily overlooked. Declining or suspected to be declining in S of range; attributed to conversion of native grasslands to agriculture.
Bibliography. Bourne (1982), Christidis & Boles (1994), Crouther (1994), Frith (1969), Fulgenhauer (1980), Lindsey (1992), Macdonald (1988), Marchant & Higgins (1993), Morris (1971), Morris & Kurtz (1977), Olsen *et al.* (1993),

Pizzey & Doyle (1980), Schodde & Tidemann (1986), Simpson & Day (1994), Slater *et al*. (1989), Sutter (1955), Trounson (1987).

15. **Australian Little Buttonquail**

Turnix velox

French: Petit Turnix   **German**: Zwerglaufhühnchen   **Spanish**: Torillo Veloz

Taxonomy. *Hemipodius velox* Gould, 1841, Yarrundi, New South Wales.
Proposed races *picturata* and *vinotincta* (NW Australia) and *leucogaster* (C Australia) no longer recognized, because based on individual variation. Monotypic.
Distribution. Continental Australia, mainly inland.

Descriptive notes. 12-16 cm; male 28-44 g, female 39-64 g; female larger. Rather small, rufous and white *Turnix* with very stout bill and pale eyes. Female brighter than male, with somewhat plainer pattern; sides of breast less scalloped. Non-breeding birds duller, and more mottled. Juvenile smaller, browner and more mottled.
Habitat. Dry grassland, grassy woodland, shrubsteppe, crops, stubble and pastures in arid and semi-arid zones; occurs from sea-level up to 1000 m. Breeds in native grasslands and crop fields.
Food and Feeding. Mostly grass seeds, including grain (*Triticum*, *Triodia*, *Danthonia*, *Chloris*, *Eragrostis*, *Panicum*, *Stipa*, Juncaceae, *Sida*, *Rumex*, *Portulaca*); some green shoots (*Citrullus* and *Cucumis* seedlings) and insects (crickets, grasshoppers, bugs, beetles, ants, moth larvae). Like congeners, swallows grit, presumably to assist mechanical breakdown in gizzard. Mainly nocturnal; also diurnal and crepuscular. Terrestrial; gleans and scratches in litter.
Breeding. Poorly known. Sept-Mar in S, Mar-Dec (usually Aug-Nov) in N; recorded in almost all months but varies locally according to rains. Solitary breeder; females sequentially polyandrous. Nest is scrape lined and sometimes hooded over with grass, or domed grass structure with runway to side entrance, under grass tussock, small shrub or fallen branch, or in dense grass or crops. 3-4 eggs; incubation 15 days. Incubation and chick-care by male alone. Chicks brown with dark and pale dorsal stripes; start to self-feed at 3 days; sexually mature at 3 months.
Movements. Poorly known. Resident, migratory and dispersive populations apparently exist; erratic or irruptive in some regions according to local rains and plant growth. General southward and coastward shift in spring-summer to regions of winter rainfall, and northward and inland in winter to regions of summer rainfall. Migrates at night.
Status and Conservation. Not globally threatened. Generally uncommon to common, but may be locally abundant during irruptions. Has declined in some intensively cultivated areas in S, but has also colonized areas where forest and scrub have been converted to pasture. Farm machinery causes much mortality during harvesting, with birds crushed or sucked in; others may catch in barbed wire, when trying to escape. Some predation by cats recorded.
Bibliography. Bourne (1982), Crouther (1994), Eckert (1972), Frith (1969), Lendon (1938), Lindsey (1992), Macdonald (1988), Marchant & Higgins (1993), Morris & Kurtz (1977), Olsen *et al*. (1993), Pizzey & Doyle (1980), Roberts (1979), Schodde & Tidemann (1986), Shephard (1989), Simpson & Day (1994), Slater *et al*. (1989), Trounson (1987).

Genus *ORTYXELOS*   Vieillot, 1825

16. **Lark Buttonquail**

Ortyxelos meiffrenii

French: Turnix à ailes blanches   **German**: Lerchenlaufhühnchen   **Spanish**: Torillo Alaudino
Other common names: Lark-quail, Quail-plover

Taxonomy. *Turnix Meiffrenii* Vieillot, 1819, Senegal.
Differs from *Turnix* in morphology, ecology and behaviour (see page 44); shape and structure, especially of wings and tail, and colour pattern of upperwing quite different. Monotypic.
Distribution. Tropical Africa, from Senegal E to Sudan and Kenya; breeds in S Ghana and possibly elsewhere in W Africa.

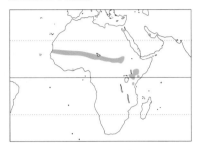

Descriptive notes. 10-13 cm; male 16-20 g; female larger. Distinctive tiny, courser-like buttonquail, with longer wings and tail than *Turnix*; shows conspicuous white wing flashes and also narrow pale tail tip. Female has slightly more rufous brown breast, and more whitish in tail. Juvenile duller and paler; more mottled and scalloped.
Habitat. Arid to semi-arid and coastal grassland; also savanna and sparse scrub to dense shrubland; occurs from sea-level up to 2000 m. In Sudan, closely associated with grass *Cenchrus catharticus*; in Chad, with grass *Aristida papposa*. Breeds on ground among sparse vegetation. Does not require access to water.
Food and Feeding. Little specific information available. Recorded taking grass seeds and insects, including termites. Terrestrial.
Breeding. Little known. Egg-laying Sept-Mar, in cool dry season. Solitary breeder; possibly monogamous. Nest is scrape in bare ground, lined with leaves and stalks, near base of plant, and often rimmed with small pebbles. 2 eggs; incubation by male alone. No further information available.
Movements. Poorly understood. Resident in some areas, elsewhere intra-African migrant, with some birds apparently breeding on coast in cool dry season; variously present only in wet season or only in dry season in some parts of range. Resident in E (Sudan, Ethiopia, Kenya) and possibly parts of W Africa; breeding visitor to S Ghana.
Status and Conservation. Not globally threatened. Uncommon to locally common; expanding range in some parts, and possibly favoured by expanding deserts. Uncommon and local in Mauritania, Niger, Ghana, Nigeria, Cameroon, Ethiopia, Uganda and Kenya; in Senegal, may have become less common since 1930's; locally common in Mali, Chad and Sudan; spreading southwards in Kenya. No threats currently known.
Bibliography. Britton, P.L. (1980), Brown & Britton (1980), Dowsett & Forbes-Watson (1993), Elgood *et al*. (1994), Glen (1994), Gore (1990), Grimes (1987), Lack (1975), Lamarche (1988), Lamm & Horwood (1958), Lynes (1925), Mackworth-Praed & Grant (1957, 1970), Newby (1980), Nikolaus (1987), Pearson (1986), Short *et al*. (1990), Snow (1978), Urban *et al*. (1986).

Class AVES
Order GRUIFORMES
Suborder GRUES
Family GRUIDAE (CRANES)

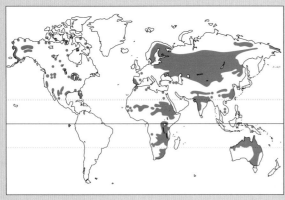

- Large, graceful wading and terrestrial birds, with long neck and legs, and mainly grey or white plumage.
- 90-176 cm.

- All regions except Antarctic, but only marginal in Neotropical; greatest diversity of genera in Africa, of species in Asia.
- Wide expanses of shallow wetlands and grasslands from the Arctic to the tropics.
- 4 genera, 15 species, 24 taxa.
- 7 species threatened; none extinct since 1600.

Systematics

The crane family is divided into two subfamilies, the crowned cranes (Balearicinae) and the "typical" cranes (Gruinae). Crowned cranes date back in the fossil record to the Eocene, 54-37 million years before the present, and as many as eleven species of crowned cranes are known to have existed in Europe and North America over the last 50 million years. The two species that survive are found exclusively in Africa. Modern crowned cranes can not withstand extreme cold, and it is conjectured that as the earth cooled these cranes died out on the northern continents and held on only in Africa, where tropical conditions were maintained throughout the ice ages. The typical cranes, by contrast, are more cold hardy. They first appear in the fossil record in the Miocene, 24-5 million years ago, the age of grasslands, and it was during this period that the thirteen surviving species of Gruinae evolved. At least seven other species of Gruinae cranes are known to have become extinct during this period.

Although there is no convincing evidence, it is generally agreed that the order Gruiformes is probably most closely related to Charadriiformes and Galliformes. This degree of uncertainty is not too surprising as Gruiformes itself is a rather heterogeneous assemblage of families, most of which do not appear to be very closely related to one another, an impression commonly reflected by the division of the order into anything from six to ten suborders. However, a number of common morphological features, mainly of the skeleton, the musculature, the digestive tract and the circulatory system, can be considered to link these different families, and the evidence of DNA supports the grouping together of virtually all of the families traditionally placed in Gruiformes.

Within the Gruiformes, cranes appear to be closely related to the Limpkin (Aramidae), which has similar flight patterns and loud calls; the trumpeters (Psophiidae), which resemble crowned cranes in their dances and plumage; and the bustards (Otididae), which are also large, long-legged, long-necked birds of open lands. Recent studies of morphology, ethology and DNA have confirmed these relationships. Also traditionally linked with the Gruidae are the Rallidae, and these two families have frequently been considered the main "core" families of the order.

Crowned cranes are distinguished from the typical cranes by their lack of a coiled trachea, their loose body plumage and their inability to withstand severe cold. They retain the ability to roost in trees, and indeed are the only cranes able to do so. Their calls

are also simpler than those of the typical cranes. There are two species, the Grey Crowned Crane (*Balearica regulorum*) of savannas from Uganda and Kenya to South Africa, and the Black Crowned Crane (*Balearica pavonina*) of the Sahel zone from Senegal to Ethiopia and Kenya. Until recently, the two were considered conspecific, but recent research suggests that it is probably better to consider them as two closely related species.

The typical cranes are divided into three genera, *Anthropoides*, *Bugeranus*, and *Grus*. The Demoiselle Crane (*Anthropoides virgo*) and the Blue Crane (*Anthropoides paradisea*) have bustard-like short toes and bills, and like the bustards live in grasslands. Although the morphological features of the *Anthropoides* species and the larger Wattled Crane (*Bugeranus carunculatus*) are dramatically different, studies of their behaviour and DNA indicate a close relationship between them. The Wattled Crane is a much more aquatic species, and

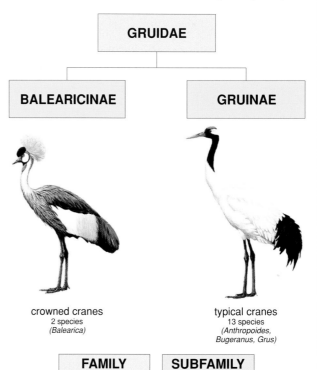

Subdivision of the Gruidae.

[Figure: Hilary Burn]

Cranes usually take off into the wind, from a running start, both of which are means of helping them lift their considerable bulk off the ground. This elegant Florida Sandhill Crane demonstrates the essential features of the crane family: the slender, elongated neck, body and legs, the fairly long bill and toes, the rather plain pale plumage, and the contrasting colour pattern on the head.

[*Grus canadensis pratensis*, Florida, USA. Photo: Tom Vezo]

undoubtedly its large size is an evolutionarily convergent feature that it shares with many of the *Grus* species that also are primarily aquatic.

The ten species of the genus *Grus* can be placed in four natural groups: the Siberian Crane (*Grus leucogeranus*) stands alone; likewise the Sandhill Crane (*Grus canadensis*); the "Group of Three" includes the Sarus Crane (*Grus antigone*), the Brolga (*Grus rubicunda*) and the White-naped Crane (*Grus vipio*); and the "Group of Five" is comprised of the Eurasian Crane (*Grus grus*), the Hooded Crane (*Grus monacha*), the Whooping Crane (*Grus americana*), the Black-necked Crane (*Grus nigricollis*) and the Red-crowned Crane (*Grus japonensis*).

The differences between the Siberian Crane and the other *Grus* species are greater than those that separate the remaining nine species. In fact, there are some morphological and ethological similarities between the Siberian Crane and the Wattled Crane, but DNA evidence suggests that these are due to convergent evolution, and several authors hold that the Siberian Crane should be placed within its own distinct genus, *Sarcogeranus*. The Sandhill Crane has features in common with both the Group of Three and the Group of Five, which suggests that it might be, or might resemble, the common ancestor of the two groups. Although the Sarus Crane and the Brolga are similar morphologically, DNA analysis suggests that the Brolga and White-naped Crane are actually more closely related. Despite the accepted sequence of species, the Eurasian Crane is probably closest to the Whooping Crane, and the Hooded Crane closest to the Black-necked Crane. Within the Group of Five, the Red-crowned Crane is the species most distantly related to the others.

At the infraspecific level, cranes show relatively little diversification, and only four species are normally considered polytypic (only three, if one considers the two crowned cranes conspecific). Again, the subspecies that are recognized do not tend to be particularly well marked, and, while four distinct forms of crowned crane are relatively apparent, with two races accepted for each species, the six generally recognized races of Sandhill Crane differ little in size and colour. Likewise, of the three extant races normally considered valid in the Sarus Crane, two differ primarily in size, while there is insufficient information to determine whether the probably extinct Philippine form was really a distinct race. The Eurasian Crane and the Brolga have at

times been divided into two subspecies, but these divisions are not now usually deemed valid.

Morphological Aspects

Cranes are large to very large birds with long necks and legs, streamlined bodies and long, rounded wings. They are readily recognized by their imposing size and graceful proportions. Cranes are among the world's tallest birds, ranging in length from 90 to more than 150 cm. The shortest is the Demoiselle Crane, while the tallest is the Sarus Crane. The Indian race of the Sarus, which can stand as high as 176 cm, is the world's tallest flying bird. The Red-crowned Crane is the heaviest crane, weighing up to 12 kg when fat deposits peak in the autumn. Male and female cranes of all species are identical in their external features, although males are usually somewhat larger than females. Compared to the other tall wading birds, cranes generally have longer legs and hold their necks straighter than the day-herons; have proportionally larger bodies than the egrets; and have longer legs, lighter bodies and smaller bills than the storks.

Distinctive features within the family reflect the varied evolutionary history and ecological niches of the cranes. Crowned cranes have a long, prehensile hallux, or hind toe, that allows them to roost in trees. Demoiselle and Blue Cranes have short, bustard-like toes that are adapted for rapid running in their grassland habitats. The relatively short bills of these cranes allow them to forage more efficiently for seeds, insects and other food items in upland habitats. All the other cranes display adaptations to more aquatic conditions: elongated necks and bills, long bare legs and broader feet. The Siberian Crane, the most aquatic of all cranes, has the longest bill and toes, adaptations for probing and walking in mud. The Brolga, which uses salt-marshes and other saline wetlands more extensively than the other species, has specialized salt glands near the eyes, through which it is able to secrete concentrated salts.

The length and positioning of the trachea are critical features of crane anatomy, and shape the distinctive voices of the various species. The two Balearicinae cranes have shorter tracheas that are, at most, impressed only slightly against the sternum, whereas in Gruinae cranes the trachea penetrates the

The Sandhill Crane is the most abundant of the 15 crane species. Its population of over 500,000 individuals is equivalent to those of all the other crane species put together. It also has the most races, six, the northern ones migrating considerable distances through North America. The dark pigment in the primary feathers serves to strengthen them structurally, so aiding long distance flight in migration. Cranes use thermal soaring when they can, but most flight is muscle-powered, with the birds often travelling in V-formation.

[*Grus canadensis*, Bosque del Apache, New Mexico, USA. Photo: Günter Ziesler]

sternum to varying degrees. On the sternum of the Siberian and Wattled Cranes the trachea makes a slight indentation that is twice as deep as that found in the *Anthropoides* cranes. With the exception of the Siberian Crane, the trachea of all *Grus* species actually coils on the vertical plane within the sternum. In the Brolga and the Sandhill and Sarus Cranes, the coiled trachea fills most of the anterior half of the sternum, while in the White-naped, Eurasian, Hooded, Whooping, Black-necked and Red-crowned Cranes the trachea penetrates the entire sternum. The bony rings of the trachea fuse with the sternum to create thin plates, and when the cranes vocalize, the plates vibrate. This produces the cranes' amplified calls, which can carry several kilometres (see Voice).

The varied features on the heads of the fifteen species are distinctive and diagnostic. Crowned cranes have elaborate tawny crests, bare cheeks and a gular wattle; unlike any of the typical cranes, mated crowned cranes preen one another's head plumage. Demoiselle and Blue Cranes have completely feathered heads, and during display they elongate the plumes on the sides of the head. This show is especially pronounced in the Blue Crane, and gives this species its unusual "cobra-like" appearance. The Wattled Crane is similarly able to raise the feathers on the sides of its head. The Wattled and Siberian Cranes have bare red skin on the front of the face that extends down the upper mandible to the nares, and in the Wattled Crane continues further down the front of the two fleshy dewlaps that hang from its cheeks. The Siberian Crane can expand the dorsal portion of its mask backward when displaying, whereas the Wattled Crane can elongate its wattles downwards. The White-naped Crane has a red comb, which in this species covers the face to a point behind the ear. In the Brolga the red skin surrounds the back of the head, while in the Sarus Crane it covers the sides and back of the head and continues several centimetres down the neck. In sharp contrast, the red comb in the remaining species is on the top of the head and expands down the back of the head only during display.

The cranes that dwell in vast open wetlands, where they are generally able to avoid undue pressure from terrestrial predators, are either entirely white, as in the Siberian, Whooping and Red-crowned, or partially white, as in the White-naped and Wattled, and they are generally larger birds. Their size and bright white plumage makes them conspicuous to conspecifics, and presumably facilitates defence of the breeding territory. The cranes that nest in smaller or forested wetlands are generally smaller

and coloured various shades of grey. Their size and colour may help them to keep a low profile on their nests. At the onset of the breeding season, Sandhill and Eurasian Cranes "paint" their feathers with mud, staining them russet brown, which makes them much more difficult to see on their nests than unpainted cranes. At the onset of its breeding period, the Siberian Crane paints dark mud on the base of its neck, but this behaviour is part of the species' sexual display rather than a camouflaging exercise.

Juvenile Demoiselle, Blue, and Wattled Cranes and Brolgas are, for reasons unknown, predominantly grey at the time of fledging. Juveniles of all the other species are russet brown, providing them with cryptic coloration as a defence against predation. This is of particular importance to young Siberian, Whooping and Red-crowned Cranes, which are destined to be primarily white as adults. During the second year of growth, adult plumage gradually replaces the juvenile plumage, and by the end of their second year many juvenile cranes are difficult to distinguish from adults.

Cranes have ten functional primary feathers, and in most species a vestigial eleventh, and 18-25 secondaries. With the exception of the Red-crowned Crane, which has white primary flight-feathers, all species have black or dark grey primaries, including the mostly white Siberian and Whooping Cranes. The dark pigment apparently strengthens the feathers structurally, thereby improving their effectiveness on long migrations. Red-crowned Cranes may once have been predominantly non-migratory, as they are today in northern Japan, and they could thus "afford" to sacrifice durability for display. The inner secondaries of many species are elongated, and when the wings are folded produce the impression of a prominent "tail" or "bustle". This "tail" is most pronounced in the Blue, Demoiselle, Wattled and White-naped Cranes, while the "bustle" is most conspicuous in the Eurasian, Hooded and Black-necked. In most species, adults moult annually during the post-breeding period. The main flight-feathers are lost at this time, rendering the birds flightless. Moulting patterns, however, vary among and within species. The wing moult in Brolgas, Demoiselle and crowned cranes occurs gradually, so that these species do not actually experience an extended flightless period.

Cranes take flight with a running start, usually into the wind, quickly gaining speed before lifting into the air with a push of the wings. When flap-flying, cranes flick their wings with a distinctive rhythm, pushing deliberately on the downstroke and rising rapidly on the upstroke. This rhythm is especially apparent when cranes are disturbed or otherwise eager to gain height quickly. Cranes, like storks, flamingos, geese and swans, and unlike the larger herons, fly with their necks stretched straight forward. With their long legs trailing directly behind them along the same axis as their bills, necks and bodies, cranes in flight present an elegant silhouette, resembling perhaps most closely that of the flamingos. When flying in cold weather, birds sometimes pull their legs in against their bodies. When landing, they approach the ground with the head semi-erect, the wings extended and the legs dangling. They descend with the wings and tail spread out and down, and, with a final flapping of the wings, alight in a normal standing stance.

Habitat

Cranes are cosmopolitan in their distribution, occurring from the North American and Asian tundra to Southern North America and the Asian, Australian and African tropics. East Asia, with eight species, has the highest level of species diversity. Five species occur at some point in the year in the Indian Subcontinent. Africa supports four species all year round; resident and wintering populations of a fifth, the Demoiselle; and wintering populations of a sixth, the Eurasian. Why cranes never colonized South America remains a mystery.

Most of the cranes prefer relatively open spaces and require territories with a wide range of visibility. Space and solitude are especially important requirements during the breeding season. Most of the species nest in shallow wetlands, where they meet both their feeding and nest building needs. The crowned cranes roost in trees, nest in wetlands and forage predominantly in grasslands. At sundown, adult crowned cranes may hide their chicks in the wetlands, and then go to roost safely in nearby trees. The *Anthropoides* species usually nest, and almost invariably feed, in expanses of open grassland, but they tend to roost in wetlands. In Central Asia, the Demoiselle Crane will nest in arid grasslands, and even in true deserts, as long as water is available.

The degree to which cranes use and require wetlands varies widely among, and within, species. The Cuban race *nesiotes* of the Sandhill Crane lives in pine and palm savanna, and nests and rears its young on dry ground. Other Sandhill Cranes and the Sarus, Brolga, White-naped, Eurasian and Black-necked Cranes nest in wetlands; however, soon after the chicks hatch they are led to neighbouring uplands to forage, returning to the wetlands to spend the night. Wattled Cranes, in the enormous floodplains of Central Africa, nest when water levels peak during the annual floods, but they remain in the wetlands throughout much of the year. In the montane wetlands of South Africa, Zimbabwe and Ethiopia the same species nests at the end of the dry season on small wetlands bordered by grassland. The large white cranes, the Siberian, Whooping and Red-crowned, remain in wetlands throughout the nesting and rearing periods, as may the Hooded Crane, which nests in isolated larch (*Larix*) swamps.

In the migratory species, family groups join together into flocks at pre-migration staging areas, soon after the chicks fledge. A staging area usually contains safe roosting sites as well as a dependable source of food. The number of cranes using a staging area continues to increase over the days until inclement weather forces the birds to move south and join even larger pre-staging congregations. Then the major portion of the migration flight is initiated, along which there are no traditional staging areas. Most species of migratory cranes remain in large flocks throughout the winter non-breeding period, roosting at night in shallow wetlands and foraging during the day in wetlands and upland areas, including agricultural fields.

Non-migratory cranes also gather in groups during the non-breeding season. They are somewhat opportunistic and nomadic in choosing habitats, moving from area to area in search of food and security. Although the availability of food is always of paramount importance during these times, social needs, such as pairing and the introduction of juveniles to flocks, also contribute to habitat choice and flocking behaviour in the non-migratory cranes.

The Red-crowned Crane, also known as the Japanese or Manchurian Crane, is the heaviest species, with birds weighing up to 12 kg in the autumn when their subcutaneous fat deposits are at their maximum. The larger cranes are wetland specialists: they require shallow wetland areas for both feeding and nesting. These more aquatic species have longer toes and bills, adapting them well for walking in soft, muddy substrates and for probing under water for food.

[Grus japonensis. Photo: Orion Service and Trading Co. Inc./ Bruce Coleman]

The smaller crane species
tend to be more terrestrial
than most of the larger
ones. They have shorter
toes and are better
runners. They have
shorter bills too, another
adaptation associated with
obtaining food in
grasslands rather than in
wetlands. They tend also
to be rather more
attractively coloured,
with more ornate feathers.
The exquisite Blue Crane,
South Africa's national
bird, has longish plumes
on the sides of the head,
which can be enlarged
to surprising effect
during display.

[Anthropoides paradisea,
Stanford-Napier,
South-western Cape,
South Africa.
Photo: Albert Masó/
VISION]

Cranes generally try to maintain a distance of at least several kilometres between themselves and areas of human activity. If, however, they are not harmed or disturbed, they can quickly become accustomed to the presence of people. Thus, Sarus Cranes in India have adapted to the high human population density in the country, and commonly nest and roost in small village ponds and *jheels*. The recovering populations of Eurasian Cranes in Europe and Sandhill Cranes in North America have in recent decades taken to using smaller, less isolated, and lower quality wetlands that are closer to human settlements. In parts of Kazakhstan and the Ukraine, the Demoiselle Crane has been able to continue breeding in steppes that have been converted to agriculture, as long as farming operations are timed so as to minimize disturbance.

The advent of agriculture has had varying consequences on cranes and their habitats. Drainage of wetlands for agriculture has negatively affected the habitat of most cranes to one degree or another, with the greatest impact on the more wetland dependent species, the Wattled, Siberian, Whooping and Red-crowned Cranes. Other species have adapted to, and even benefited from, agriculture. For some cranes, wetlands bordered by agricultural fields often provide better breeding habitat than pristine regions where wetlands are surrounded by forests. In general, cranes that subsist on gleanings of waste grain in agricultural fields during migration and in their wintering grounds are currently faring better than those species that depend exclusively upon wetlands throughout the year (see Status and Conservation).

General Habits

In general, cranes are isolated on their territories during the breeding season and gregarious during the non-breeding period. Among the migratory species during winter, those that feed primarily on abundant sedge tubers and other aquatic vegetation, such as the Sandhill, White-naped and Siberian Cranes, tend to forage in flocks, while those that feed mainly on animals, for example the Whooping and the Red-crowned, are territorial and forage in family groups.

All cranes are basically diurnal in their habits. During the day they forage, rest and preen, attend to their young during the breeding season, and socialize within flocks in the non-breeding season. At night during the breeding season, most cranes stay on or near their nests, brooding their chicks and standing guard against predators and other sources of disturbance. In the non-breeding season, they roost at night in more or less large flocks at traditional roosting sites.

The non-breeding season pattern of feeding by day and roosting by night is universal. Roosting provides security for the flock and offers juvenile and "single" birds opportunities for pair formation. Crowned cranes roost in trees (see Morphological Aspects), whereas the other species usually roost in shallow water, but occasionally use dry ground, mudflats or sandbars. Within roosting flocks, each crane stands about a "peck distance" apart from its neighbours. At night, cranes rest with the head and neck tucked on or under a shoulder. They stand on one leg, though during the course of a night they may switch from one leg to the other several times. They defecate at regular intervals. One unfamiliar sound or alarm call from a flock member is all that is required for the birds to become alert and ready to fly.

At dawn the cranes awaken, stretch, preen and drink, before beginning the day's activity. They fly off in small groups to an open upland area near the evening's roost, the post-roosting staging area, where they land and continue to preen. Cranes from several roosting sites may join together at the same staging area. From there, initially in small groups but then in larger congregations, they will move on to the day's feeding areas. Perhaps those cranes that located a good feeding spot the previous day will be the first to depart, and will thus lead the others to that area.

Depending on the availability of food, cranes feed for extended periods in the early morning, and then move to loafing areas. In these areas they drink, preen and engage in social displays to facilitate the pairing of unmated birds and to establish a pecking order among families. If temperatures are unusually hot, the birds may escape the heat by spiralling skyward on rising thermals, eventually disappearing from view. Later in the day they return to feeding or watering areas, where they again forage, before moving to pre-roosting staging areas. Here they may again engage in social displays before flying to the evening's roost, where they remain silent and still unless disturbed.

The behaviour of individual cranes can be divided into those activities that are self-directed and those that are undertaken in response to other cranes and other external stimuli. In addition to such fundamental activities as eating, drinking, sleeping, walking and flying, self-directed activities include preening, bathing, shaking, stretching, ruffling, scratching and feather painting. Behavioural studies of cranes have revealed some 90 more specific behavioural patterns within these categories.

The social behaviour of cranes includes a wide array of visual displays. These ritualized displays serve many intra- and interspecific functions, and are often accompanied by vocal displays (see Voice). Among the thirteen species that have bare red skin in the region of the head, this skin too plays an important role in communication. Cranes can vary the extent of skin displayed by contracting or relaxing the subcutaneous muscles, and can change the intensity of the colour of the skin by engorging it. The colour and exposure of the skin change in response to various stimuli, often in association with other behavioural displays.

When cranes are aggressive, they assume an upright posture with their body feathers sleeked, thighs protruding and head features expanded. They walk in a stilted manner that has been likened to the goose-step of parading soldiers. They will follow this threatening posture with a variety of flaps, ruffles, bows, bouts of false preening, stomps, nasal snorts and growls. If a crane takes to the air in this excited state, it will fly with rigid flaps in narrow arcs, with its feet and neck arched upward.

Cranes also engage in a variety of more circumscribed threat gestures. In the "Crouch Threat", the crane bends its legs, lowers itself to the ground, folds its wings loosely against its body and the ground, and places its head forward with the red patch prominent. In the "Ruffle Threat", the bird raises the feathers of its neck, wings and back, partially opens and lowers its wings, ruffles them alternately, and then lowers its bill to its lower breast or leg in a preening movement, often concluding this sequence with a low growl. In a "Charge", the bird points its neck and head straight down and lifts the feathers along its neck and back, holding this stance for several seconds. In all such threat displays, the patch of red skin appears bright and conspicuous.

A crane that is frightened, for example when confronting a predator, spreads its wings, arches forward as if ready to strike, and approaches the feared animal. A submissive crane, by contrast, lowers its neck, elevates its body feathers, and diminishes the threatening display of its head features by lowering the feathers and decreasing the comb size. In this state of deference, the crane walks loosely and warily.

Of all forms of behaviour exhibited by cranes, none is as spectacular or as well known as their elaborate and enthusiastic dancing. Cranes are not the only birds known to dance; trumpeters and egrets, for example, engage in somewhat similar displays, although not so habitually. All species of crane dance. It is apparently an ancient and complex form of behaviour within the family, and serves a variety of functions. Dancing is undertaken by even very young birds, as a part of their behavioural and physical development. Unpaired subadult birds probably dance more than any other age group, and for these birds, dancing facilitates the processes of socialization and pair formation. In adults, dancing can be a form of displacement activity when they are nervous. Within pairs, it may serve to maintain pair-bonds and synchronize sexual response prior to breeding: new pairs dance during courtship; well established pairs, on the other hand, have less need to synchronize their behaviour or to ward off rivals, and hence dance less often. Cranes do not always dance in response to readily apparent stimuli. Within flocks, it is often a contagious activity that spreads easily among the excited birds.

The pattern and intensity of dancing vary somewhat among the crane species, but the dances of all cranes consist of long, intricate sequences of co-ordinated bows, leaps, runs and short flights. In the course of dancing, cranes pick up in their bills whatever small objects, sticks, moss, grass or feathers, happen to be in the area, randomly tossing them into the air. Dancing tends to be most energetic in the smaller species, such as the Demoiselle and the two crowned cranes. Crowned cranes perhaps dance most distinctively, bobbing their heads up and down prior to bowing, spreading their wings, leaping and flapping their wings, then often landing and circling one another. The sequence

Outside the breeding season, most cranes are gregarious. After roosting in quite large flocks, they spread out a little to feed, and may then gather in loafing areas where they preen, drink, bathe, rest and interact with other conspecifics, as can be seen in this group of Eurasian Cranes. Really large concentrations may be encountered, for example, at pre-migratory staging areas, but also in winter, when hierarchies among families become established, and unmated birds go about the business of attempting to pair up.

[Grus grus, Lake Hornborga, Västergötland, Sweden. Photo: Francisco Márquez]

Measuring up to 176 cm, the Sarus Crane is the world's tallest flying bird. It demonstrates its size during some of its displays. The huge spread wings, sometimes spanning almost three metres, combine effectively with the forward arching posture and the pointing bill, and may serve to deter some predators, as well as indicating a degree of ambivalence in the bird itself. The degree of vividness of the red skin on the head of most crane species varies with the bird's motivation, and helps to communicate its intentions to others of its species.

[*Grus antigone antigone*, Keoladeo National Park, Bharatpur, India. Photo: Günter Ziesler]

of courtship dancing in Blue Cranes has been observed to last for as long as four hours. The dance of the Demoiselle Crane has been described as "more ballet-like" than those of the *Grus* species, with fewer, less theatrical, jumps. In the *Grus* cranes, dancing is slightly more deliberate, and is punctuated frequently with high, flapping leaps.

Voice

Cranes have evolved elaborate vocal displays to help them communicate with one another. From barely audible contact calls to trumpet-like notes that can carry out across their extensive territories, cranes employ a variety of calls with different meanings. The typical volume and tone likewise varies widely from species to species: the crowned cranes have soft honks; the voices of *Anthropoides* are low and raspy; and those of *Grus* are high-pitched and extremely loud. The Sandhill Crane has a distinctive low-pitched rattle, while the Siberian Crane's voice is noted for its clear, flute-like quality.

The "languages" of the various cranes develop differently, depending on the nature of the adult voice, but in all cases the "vocabulary" begins to emerge early in life. Hatching chicks emit high-pitched peeps that will subsequently persist through the first year of life. Newly-hatched chicks quickly acquire a low, purring contact call to maintain regular contact with their parents and a louder, more insistent stress call to draw their more immediate attention. Within a day or so of hatching, chicks develop a food-begging call, a soft peeping that signals the parents to provide food, and within their first year of life, the young birds also learn the "Flight-intention" and alarm calls.

By the end of a bird's first year, the voice deepens and gains strength and volume. The contact, "Flight-intention", and alarm calls are retained, while additional new ones develop: the "Guard Call" is generally given as an intraspecific threat; the "Location Call" allows a newly mobile bird to gain its bearings, if visual contact is and the "Pre-copulatory Call" begins to be heard at about the age of 24 months. Fully adult cranes augment these calls with an assortment of other specialized vocalizations.

The most penetrating of all the calls in the vocal repertoire of cranes, and among the most spectacular of all avian sounds, are the special duets of mated pairs. The duets, known as "Unison Calls", can last from a few seconds to as long as one minute, and may be repeated regularly through the course of a day; they are most commonly heard prior to the breeding season. Unison calling begins to develop in the second or third year of a bird's life. It serves a variety of important functions in the individual and social lives of cranes. First and foremost, it plays a critical role in the initiation, development and maintenance of pair-bonds.

Bathing helps to keep the plumage in good condition, but in order for it to be effective, the bird must ruffle up its feathers and shake itself vigorously in the water. Mutual preening is also indulged in by crowned cranes, reaching those parts that are inaccessible to a bird's own bill. Grey Crowned Cranes forage in grassland and agriculture, nest at wetland edges, and, unlike other cranes, roost in trees. This species is the national bird of Uganda.

[*Balearica regulorum*. Photo: Norman O. Tomalin/ Bruce Coleman]

The unison calls of recently formed pairs are typically loosely co-ordinated, in comparison with the highly synchronous calls of well established pairs. Unison calling perhaps helps partners to come into breeding condition at the same time. The call is also used more generally to demarcate territories, to ward off potential intruders and to respond to other threats.

Unison calls vary among the species. During sexual displays, crowned cranes lower their heads to shoulder level, inflate their gular sacs, and emit a long sequence of low booming calls. The unison calls of Gruinae species can be used by researchers to determine the sex of individual cranes: the female usually has the higher-pitched voice. In the case of the Siberian Crane, the pitch of the call is the only outward diagnostic feature that allows one to distinguish males from females. In *Anthropoides* and the Wattled Crane, the male and female assume distinct postures during the unison call: the female Demoiselle Crane calls with her bill pointing upward, while the male calls with the bill held horizontal; male Blue and Wattled Cranes elevate their wings at the conclusion of the unison call. All *Grus* species, except the Siberian Crane, have sexually distinct voices during the unison call, with the female emitting two or three calls for every call produced by the male. Male Sarus, Brolga and White-naped Cranes always raise their wings over their backs and droop their primaries during the unison call. In the Eurasian, Hooded, Whooping, Black-necked and Red-crowned Cranes, the amount of wing-posturing depends on the intensity of the aggression associated with the display.

Food and Feeding

Although some species are more specialized than others, most cranes are generalists and opportunists, feeding on a remarkably wide variety of plant and animal foods. Among cranes that use upland areas, the diet includes seeds, leaves, acorns, nuts, berries, fruits, waste grains, worms, snails, grasshoppers, beetles and other insects, snakes, lizards, rodents and other small mammals, and even small birds. Wetland food items include the roots, bulbs, rhizomes, tubers, sprouts, stems and seeds of submergent and emergent plants, as well as molluscs, aquatic insects, crustaceans, small fish and frogs. Cranes readily shift their feeding

strategies on a daily or seasonal basis to take advantage of available food items. For example, Eurasian Cranes wintering in the Iberian Peninsula subsist primarily on cereal grains in the early part of the winter, switch to acorns of the holm oak in mid-winter, and may turn again to germinating cereals and legumes in the late winter.

Cranes are catholic, flexible and busy feeders. A wide diversity of animal and plant food is consumed as available. Animal food includes amphibians, fish, molluscs, crustaceans and other aquatic invertebrates when foraging in wetlands, and rodents, reptiles, worms, snails and insects from grasslands. Plant matter include roots and tubers, leaves and stems, and a range of seeds, berries, nuts and fruits. The long, powerful bill of the Brolga is particularly suited to digging for submerged foods in wetland mud. Crops grown by humans comprise a food resource sometimes abundantly available and sometimes, therefore, heavily used. Cranes may spend half to three quarters of their daylight hours feeding.

[*Grus rubicunda*, Australia. Photo: Harald Lange/ Bruce Coleman]

The anatomy of cranes reveals much about their feeding preferences. Those species with shorter bills usually feed in the dry uplands, while those with longer bills usually feed in wetlands. Crowned cranes stamp the ground to scare up insects, which they then grasp in their short bills. These cranes, together with the two *Anthropoides* species, and the Sandhill, Eurasian, Hooded and Black-necked Cranes, also use their shorter bills for grazing in a goose-like manner. The taller cranes with the largest and longest bills, the Wattled, Siberian, Sarus, Brolga and White-naped, are diggers, and use their powerful mandibles to excavate tubers and roots from the muddy soils of wetlands. The long-billed Whooping and Red-crowned Cranes use their bills to probe gently in the bottom of shallow wetlands for mudfish and crustaceans.

The foraging behaviour of cranes reflects their varied strategies, niches and food items. The diggers usually stay in the same area for extended periods of time, excavating holes that are continually enlarged to expose the tubers that proliferate in certain types of wetland soil. Unlike herons, which stand motionless and wait for the moment to strike at prey, hunting cranes walk slowly through the water searching and probing for prey to grab. The upland feeders usually walk with their heads lowered, hunting and pecking at the ground for insects, seeds and other morsels. The generalist feeders will use different strategies in different circumstances. Sarus Cranes, for example, often dig for tubers and other sub-surface plant materials, but they are effective upland foragers and hunters, and have also been observed stripping grains of rice from their stalks.

Where several crane species occur together, the varied feeding strategies and adaptations tend to minimize the degree of niche overlap. This occurs most noticeably in wintering areas in China, where four species may co-exist in the same area. Thus, at Poyang Lake in Jiangxi Province, Siberian Cranes will feed in the shallow water and on mudflats, White-naped Cranes along the wetland borders, Hooded Cranes in adjacent dry sedge meadows, and White-naped, Hooded and Eurasian Cranes in agricultural fields. When Sarus and Siberian Cranes have occurred together at Keoladeo National Park (Bharatpur) in India, the Siberians have foraged for sedge tubers in deeper waters while the Sarus fed on a broader variety of plants and animals in shallower waters. A somewhat analogous situation has been observed in parts of Australia where Brolgas and Sarus Cranes are sympatric, the former tending to restrict themselves to lowland sedge marshes and the latter tending to use drier habitats.

Many species of cranes benefit from the food provided by agricultural fields during either the breeding or the non-breeding phases of their annual cycle, or in some cases both. At one time or another, most cranes forage in cropland and pastures that border wetlands where they nest or roost. At migration stopovers and on wintering grounds, those species that feed on gleanings from agricultural fields usually find an abundance of food, and interfere minimally with farming operations. For example, the great spring congregations of migrating Sandhill Cranes along the Platte River, in the central USA, subsist largely on waste corn gleaned from nearby fields. In some parts of the world, however, crop damage can be a serious problem. This usually occurs during autumn migration or early in winter, when crops are being harvested, or in early spring, when new crops are germinating. During these times, not only are the crops available as food, but the cranes are usually present in large flocks.

For several species, artificial feeding has come to play an important role not only in their annual cycle, but in the very survival and recovery of the species. Some 80% of the world's Hooded Cranes, and about 40% of all White-naped Cranes, are sustained by artificial feeding at Izumi on the Japanese island of Kyushu, a programme that was initiated in 1952. The Hokkaido population of Red-crowned Cranes, about one third of the total world population, has also used feeding stations since 1952. In both cases, artificial feeding has contributed to rapid growth of the small remnant populations. Again, in both cases, the challenge is now to avoid problems associated with overconcentration of the populations, by dispersing the birds and diversifying their feeding opportunities.

Breeding

Cranes are monogamous. Mated birds stay together throughout the year, and generally remain paired until one bird dies. The age of sexual maturity has been studied in Sandhill and Whooping Cranes. In these species, birds begin to establish pairs in their second or third years, with successful breeding usually occurring in the fourth or fifth year. Pair-bonds may be formed at any time, but many, if not most, pairs fail to breed successfully in their initial attempts. In the Sandhill Crane, the species most extensively studied, it has been shown that pairs that are unsuccessful in their first attempts to breed often dissolve, while successful pairs remain together. A strong pair-bond is maintained as long as the pair successfully reproduces. However, if breeding efforts continually fail, the pair-bond weakens and new mates are eventually taken. Most studies of this species indicate that individuals do not successfully reproduce until they are between four and eight years old. Other species may share this general pattern.

Securing a breeding territory is a prerequisite of reproduction, and in areas where all the available territories are occupied, the young birds may need to wait in order to breed. Cranes of the northern temperate and Arctic zones begin to establish breeding territories soon after their arrival from the wintering grounds, usually between mid-April and mid-June. The breeding seasons of cranes in the tropical and subtropical zones are much more variable, but generally coincide with the local rainy seasons. In the Brolga and the Sarus Crane breeding is closely associated with the distinct monsoons of south-east Asia and Australia. By contrast, Sarus Cranes in India and Wattled Cranes and Grey Crowned Cranes in southern Africa may breed throughout the year, although breeding usually peaks in response to localized conditions. Such variability is evident even within species: Sandhill Cranes breeding in Alaska produce almost all of their eggs in June; the breeding season for Florida Sandhill Cranes extends from December to June, with most eggs produced from February to April.

Breeding density and territory size are highly variable depending on food availability and topography. In India, for example, nesting territories as small as one hectare are sufficient for Sarus Cranes, if the quality of the water and vegetation is adequate and human disturbance is minimized. In Cambodia, on the other hand, Sarus Cranes have larger nesting territories in remote, isolated wetlands. A pair of Red-crowned Cranes may successfully breed on relatively small, isolated wetlands of perhaps 500 hectares, but on a larger wetland with excellent visibility they might defend several thousand hectares. Similarly, Eurasian and Sandhill Cranes have both adapted to human presence by establishing breeding territories in smaller, less natural wetlands. Once territories are established, pairs defend them through unison calls (see Voice), threat postures and attacks. The male is primarily responsible for defence, while the female is more involved in looking after the nest.

New pairs engage in long bouts of dancing before attempting copulation, whereas established pairs copulate with facility and without tension. The copulatory sequence can be initiated by either sex. One member of the pair will elevate its bill, arch slightly forward and emit a low purr-like call. If its mate reciprocates with similar behaviour, one bird, usually the male, will circle the other with exaggerated steps. The female then spreads her wings and the male approaches. With wings flapping, he jumps on her back and crouches down. The female elevates her tail as the male lowers his, and their cloacae meet. The male then jumps forward over his mate's head, and performs threat displays for a few seconds. Both members of the pair then engage in a long sequence of preening. Cranes copulate repeatedly for

A great many social interactions take place within wintering crane groups, as birds strive to impress and select potential mates, support existing mates, and establish or reinforce positions in fluid hierarchies. In migratory species, such as the Eurasian Crane, flock size diminishes once the birds have returned north in the spring to breed, but aggressive encounters are frequent as birds stake out their claims. The prominent "bustles" of this species are typically raised in threat displays, as the challenging bird cranes its neck forward at its opponent; the "bustles" are simply elongated inner secondary feathers.

[Grus grus,
Lake Hornborga,
Västergötland, Sweden.
Photo: Sture Traneving]

A male Wattled Crane displays to his mate, with his facial wattles elongated and the bare red skin on his face flushed. During courtship in this species, spreading the huge wings is often the prelude to a short run followed by a jump into the air. As usual in cranes, the male is a little larger than the female. From the colour rings, it is known that the birds were ringed as chicks in 1987. They were not seen again until in 1994 they turned up as a breeding pair, 12 and 217 miles from where they had been raised, the female having dispersed farther and, interestingly, from a population previously thought to be genetically isolated.

[*Bugeranus carunculatus.* Photo: W. R. Tarboton]

several weeks in advance of laying. Copulation usually occurs before sunrise, although it can take place at any time during the daylight hours.

Both sexes participate in nest building. They select a secluded spot within their territory and unison call from that spot. Walking away from the selected spot, they take nesting materials, mainly the stems and leaves of sedges, cat-tails and other wetland plants, and toss them over their shoulders. They return to the nest-site and pull in the material within their reach, before walking slowly away from the nest and throwing more material behind them. As they repeat this sequence many times, large quantities of nesting material accumulate at the low, platform nest, while a "moat" of water forms around the platform.

This nest building behaviour holds for those species that nest within wetlands, but two species, the Blue and Demoiselle Cranes, nest on dry ground. In both species, the eggs are usually laid directly on the ground; the birds may gather together some small stones or vegetation to provide protection and camouflage, but otherwise the nests show little preparation, if any. In some parts of its range, the Sandhill Crane also nests on dry sites. On rare occasions, Grey Crowned Cranes will nest in trees, and they have even been observed using the abandoned nests of other large tree-nesting species.

Cranes almost invariably lay two eggs. The exceptions are the crowned cranes, which regularly lay three and sometimes four eggs, and the Wattled Crane, which usually lays only one. Eggs are ovule-pointed and in most species are heavily pigmented. The species that inhabit tropical and subtropical areas lay either pale bluish eggs, as in the case of the crowned cranes, or white eggs, as in the case of the Sarus and the Brolga. In contrast, those inhabiting the coldest regions, the Siberian, Black-necked and Lesser Sandhill (*G. c. canadensis*) Cranes, produce darker eggs. This tendency for eggs to be pale in warmer climates and dark in colder climates is undoubtedly an adaptation to environmental conditions, allowing the eggs to reflect heat in the former case and absorb heat in the latter. Red-crowned Cranes lay both white and pigmented eggs, an indication that the species may have evolved under warmer climatic conditions.

The extent to which multiple clutching can or does occur in cranes is little known. Repeat clutches have, however, been reported for Grey Crowned, Blue, Wattled, Sandhill, Eurasian, White-naped and Red-crowned Cranes, while Florida Sandhill Cranes (*G. c. pratensis*) have been known to lay third, and in one case even fourth, clutches. Cranes of the northern latitudes, including the Whooping and Siberian Cranes, experience such short growing seasons that even if they did produce second clutches, it would be very difficult for them to fledge the young in time to undertake migration. In captivity, however, females of these and other species have been induced to lay repeatedly through the removal of the eggs, either one at a time or as whole clutches. In this manner, females have regularly produced up to ten or more eggs in a single breeding season.

In the crowned cranes, incubation begins after the clutch is complete, but in the remaining species, incubation begins after the first egg is laid, lasting an average of 28-32 days in most species. The Wattled Crane, at 33-36 days, has the longest incubation period, whereas species breeding in higher latitudes and altitudes tend to have the shortest periods, of under 30 days. The female usually incubates at night, but during the day the sexes exchange incubation duties several times. Once relieved, the off-duty member of the pair normally flies to a favourite feeding area far from the nest.

In accordance with the respective patterns of incubation, crowned crane chicks hatch synchronously, whereas those of Gruinae do so asynchronously. Wattled and Siberian Cranes have been observed to leave the nest after only the first egg has hatched, and typically only a single chick is raised in these species. In other species, the parents frequently rear two chicks, but one of these soon becomes dominant, and, if food is scarce, the weaker chick often dies.

The chicks of most crane species are predominantly brown. The exceptions are the Demoiselle and Blue Cranes and the Brolga, which all have silvery grey chicks. The egg tooth drops off within a few days, and the initial coat of down is replaced by a second down, which, in turn, is replaced by feathers. The rate of chick growth is astonishing, especially in chicks of the northernmost species. The legs grow rapidly during the first six weeks, followed by more rapid development of the wings.

Crane parents begin to feed their chicks almost immediately after hatching occurs, and both parents contribute to the feeding of young. The adults carry small food items to the chicks and either present the food directly to them by holding it at the tip of

Cranes are famous for their dancing, which is performed by all species. Some other bird groups dance too, but none do so as extensively, nor, simply because of their smaller size, as beautifully to human eyes. Dancing in cranes has a number of separate components in different combinations. There are elements of jerky bouncing, of graceful leaping up in the air, and of wild running with wings outstretched. Bowing, with bent legs and raised wings, is frequent, and is often followed by a jump. Stick-tossing is often incorporated, the bird seizing a piece of stick or vegetation and tossing it up in the air as the bill is flung upwards and opened. Dancing is most frequent in unpaired, young adult birds, but is by no means confined to them. Indeed, even chicks less than two days old have been seen to dance. Dancing may strengthen the pair-bond or helps to synchronize or stimulate reproductive condition, and it may, of course, have different functions at different ages. Thus it may be largely exercise and play for chicks but communicatory in adults, perhaps particulary in stifling aggression. Established breeding pairs do not dance much: their aggression towards one another is probably slight, and their breeding synchronization already good. Dancing can also be a displacement activity in situations of anxiety. Whatever its motivation, it is a delight to observe.

[Above: *Grus japonensis*, Hokkaido, Japan. Photo: Steven C. Kaufman/ Bruce Coleman.

Below: *Grus grus*, Lake Hornborga, Västergötland, Sweden. Photo: Sture Traneving]

Gregarious out of the breeding season, pairs of cranes separate from others to reproduce. Grey Crowned Cranes will sometimes display within the flock, when the activity of one pair can act as a stimulus to other pairs to follow suit, and up to 60 have been observed displaying simultaneously. All crane species are monogamous. They apparently remain paired for life as long as they breed successfully, but failure may precipitate a change of mate.

[Balearica regulorum. Photo: Günter Ziesler]

the bill or by dropping it before them. The chicks eventually begin to follow their parents to nearby food sources, although in some cases adults will continue to bring food until the chicks are several months old. Demoiselle Crane are especially noted for the high degree of mobility that young birds quickly exhibit.

Adults care for their chicks continuously through the pre-fledging period. The length of the fledging period varies widely. It is shortest in those species that inhabit upland areas, such as the Grey Crowned, Black Crowned, Demoiselle and Blue, and those that nest in the high Arctic, namely the Siberian and the Lesser Sandhill. In general, chicks of these species fledge at 50-90 days, and the Demoiselle Crane has the shortest average fledging period, usually 55-60 days. The species that inhabit permanent wetlands in warmer climates, the Wattled and Sarus Cranes and the Brolga, have the longest fledging periods, usually lasting 85-100 days, or more; the Wattled Crane has the longest fledging period at about 90-130 days.

The productivity of a given crane population can be measured in several ways, but is most easily determined by counting the number of juveniles in the flocks during the non-breeding period. In general, about 10-15% of a healthy population will consist of non-breeding juveniles.

The juvenile cranes remain with their parents throughout the non-breeding period, but at its conclusion they either leave their parents voluntarily or are driven off by the adults, after the family has returned to the breeding territory. Unpaired juvenile birds gather in non-breeding flocks and are often nomadic throughout the breeding period. By the end of their second year, juvenile birds have usually initiated their own attempts to form pair-bonds.

Movements

In terms of their movements, cranes can be divided into two groups: migratory and non-migratory. Non-migratory cranes move relatively short distances between their breeding and non-breeding areas, and also gather in large flocks prior to the onset of the breeding period. Local and seasonal movements of varying lengths are typical of the lower latitude species, the crowned cranes, the Blue, Wattled and Sarus Cranes, and the Brolga of

Australia and New Guinea. In most cases, their breeding seasons, and hence their movements, are tied to, and vary with, the duration and intensity of the local rainy seasons. Local and seasonal movements are also characteristic of southern, non-migratory populations of some of the northern migratory species. This may be seen among populations of the Demoiselle Crane in north-

Copulation starts a few weeks before the first egg is laid. It requires good co-ordination between the two birds, the female adopting a solicitation posture with open wings, and the male maintaining his balance by flapping his wings. After a copulation lasting 4-5 seconds, the male dismounts forwards, and both birds ruffle their feathers. Displays often precede and follow copulation. Eurasian Cranes reach sexual maturity at about five years old.

[Grus grus, Lake Hornborga, Västergötland, Sweden. Photo: Francisco Márquez]

Both sexes build the nest, pulling at the vegetation nearby, tossing it towards the nest-site, and subsequently collecting it in to form a thick mat. In typical cranes, such as the White-naped Crane, two eggs make up a normal clutch. In captivity this species will readily lay again about ten days later if the clutch is removed, and will do so several times over, thus producing a fair number of eggs over a single season. Crane eggs weigh 130-240 g, and, although the larger species produce eggs that are larger in absolute terms they are relatively smaller in comparison with the weight of the adult bird. The two eggs are laid two or three days apart, incubation beginning with the laying of the first. Both sexes play a part in incubation, changing over several times a day, with the off-duty bird usually away feeding. The bird on the nest rises to adjust the nest or roll the eggs at intervals averaging 30 to 80 minutes. Incubation lasts 30-33 days in White-naped Cranes, and 27-36 days in the Gruidae as a whole. The birds at this nest are in the process of delivering a unison call.

[*Grus vipio*, Zhalong Crane Sanctuary, Heilongkiang, China. Photo: Sture Traneving]

ern Africa and also in Sandhill Cranes in Cuba, Florida and Mississippi.

Such limited and seasonal movements are modest in comparison with the epic migrations of the northern cranes. Some of the migration routes stretch thousands of kilometres, during which the cranes must confront broad deserts, high mountain ranges and other formidable obstacles. This achievement is even more remarkable for the northernmost species, the Siberian and Sandhill Cranes breeding in the Arctic latitudes of Eurasia and North America. In these populations, the young of the year must in one short growing season gain the size, strength and endurance to join their adult companions on the long journey south.

Migratory cranes spend several days or weeks at premigration staging areas, building up their fat reserves and integrating into the life of the flock. Then they begin their migration. After feeding for several hours in the early morning, on a clear day with breezes gusting, they start to climb. Flap-flying in wide circles and lifted by thermals, they rise into the sky. After climbing as high as 2000 metres, they stop flapping, extend their wings, assume a V-formation and glide southwards, propelled by gravity and the wind. After losing a certain amount of altitude, they repeat the cycle, again spiralling skyward and gliding south. While flying over land, they follow this pattern throughout the day. However, when forced to fly over water, where they can not rely on thermals to gain height, they flap-fly in V-formation. Young birds fly close to their parents, and during their first migration south learn the migration route. While migrating, cranes call constantly; their voices can often be heard even before the birds are spotted as tiny specks against the blue sky.

Migratory movements have been studied closely in several species. Whooping Cranes, for example, have been shown to migrate as far as 800 km in a single day, although 300 km is more typical. In one study, Sandhill Cranes flew 575 km without stopping, over a period of nine and a half hours. Flight speeds in most estimates average 60-80 km/h.

Several crane migrations stand out as especially impressive. Eurasian Cranes from central Eurasia fly over the Himalayas at altitudes approaching 10,000 metres, while Demoiselle Cranes also negotiate the passes between these highest of all mountains. Other Demoiselles migrate across the wide deserts of the Middle East and northern Africa to wintering grounds in the upper reaches of the Nile Basin. Lesser Sandhill Cranes from eastern Siberia undertake the longest of all crane migrations, moving east across the Bering Sea into North America and continuing south to as far as northern Mexico.

An understanding of crane migratory patterns and behaviour is critically important in assessing the conservation status and needs of the different species. The problems cranes face during migration often constitute the weak links in the chain of conservation actions. Even if the cranes are secure in their breeding and wintering areas, they may be vulnerable to habitat changes at traditional staging and resting areas, and often face other dangers associated with human activity along the migration routes. Historically, for example, collisions with utility lines and accidental shooting have been important mortality factors along the Whooping Crane's narrow migration corridor. For this reason, biologists have in recent years devoted much time and effort to the study of crane migration through ringing, radio telemetry and satellite tracking programmes. Such studies have been especially important in developing recovery and reintroduction plans for the Siberian and Whooping Cranes. Because the knowledge of migration routes is passed along to new generations of cranes by experienced older birds, conservation programmes for these most threatened species must emphasize the maintenance of existing routes and the development of new techniques for teaching migration. Perhaps most significant, the conservation needs of cranes during migration have necessitated extensive co-operation across national boundaries, sometimes among countries otherwise in conflict with one another.

Relationship with Man

Since time immemorial, cranes have evoked strong emotional responses in people. Their size, behaviour, social relations, unique calls, graceful movements and stately appearance have inspired expression through human art, artifacts, mythology and legend in cultures around the world. This appreciation of cranes was first conveyed in prehistoric cave paintings in Africa, Australia and Europe.

In the western tradition, evidence of cranes dates to the ancient Egyptians, whose tombs were adorned with Demoiselle Cranes. The ancient Greeks are known to have domesticated cranes, and according to myth the flight of cranes inspired the god Hermes to invent the Greek alphabet. Throughout the classical period, cranes provided symbolic meaning in allegories and stories. They frequently appear in the literature of the ancient Greeks and Romans, for instance in the works of Homer, Aristotle, Cicero, Pliny and Plutarch. The Latin word for crane, *grues*, is thought to have been an imitation of their call. In later Christian expressions, cranes came to signify watchfulness, steadiness and mutual aid.

In the east, cranes have for millennia occupied a prominent place in religious traditions and mythology. In China, cranes have long symbolized longevity, and often appear in artwork carrying the souls of the departed to heaven after death. Similar spiritual and symbolic associations appear in various forms in many parts of Asia. In China, Korea and Japan, the Red-crowned Crane symbolizes happiness, good luck, long life and marital bliss, and appears regularly in paintings, ceramics and other decorative arts. The Emperor's throne in Beijing's Forbidden City is flanked by statues of cranes. Cranes are featured on bridal kimonos in Japan, and one of Japan's most popular folk tales concerns a crane that transforms itself into a lady.

In the New World, cranes begin to appear in pictographs, petroglyphs and ceramics from what is now the North American South-west after the year AD 900. Modified crane bones also first

Sarus Cranes, like Brolgas (Grus rubicunda), lay white eggs, and it has sometimes been remarked that the tropical members of the family show a tendency to lay paler eggs than their higher latitude counterparts. After a period of 31-34 days of incubation, the two Sarus chicks hatch asynchronously, two or three days apart. The chicks are very weak when they hatch, and they remain in the nest for a couple of days; by that stage they can walk quite well and swim very well, and they leave the nest accompanied by the adults. Unlike the sibling young of some bird families, notably birds of prey, the two chicks are not aggressive towards one another. However, the second hatched tends to be subordinate, and may well die if food is not abundant.

[Grus antigone antigone, Keoladeo National Park, Bharatpur, India. Photo: Belinda Wright/ Oxford Scientific Films]

Chicks of the Sandhill Crane have been rather thoroughly studied. The adult feeds small pieces of the eggshell to the newly hatched chicks, and subsequently offers them food, either held in the bill or dropped in front of them. Right from the start the chicks grow fast. They may leave the nest when only six hours old, perhaps even swimming at that very early age. Rapid growth and elongation of the legs and bill take place in the first six weeks, and the young are fully feathered by about three months old.

[*Grus canadensis pratensis*, Alachua County, Florida, USA. Photo: Stephen A. Nesbitt]

appear from middens of this era in other parts of North America. Crane clans developed among the Hopis and Zunis in the Southwest, while cranes served as totems for the Ojibwa and other tribal groups. Warriors of the Crow and Cheyenne made small whistles from the wing bones of Sandhill Cranes, and blew upon them in preparing for battle.

Crane-associated dances have been recorded in many parts of the world, including the Mediterranean, China, Siberia and Australia. A "dance of the white cranes" is known from 500 BC in China. Aboriginal Australians named the Brolga after a young woman whose exquisite dancing drew attention from numerous suitors, all of whose proposals of marriage she refused. Among these was an evil magician who, in his rage, transformed her into a crane.

Cranes continue to be used in new symbolic ways around the world. Crowned cranes are the national birds of Nigeria and Uganda, as are Blue Cranes of South Africa. The coins and stamps of many countries have borne cranes. In part, perhaps, because of their beauty in flight, cranes have also been selected as the corporate logos for several commercial airlines. The emergence of the conservation movement, and in particular the near demise of the Whooping Crane, invested cranes with added symbolic value as emblems of civilization's changing relationship with nature. Perhaps the best known, and most poignant, example of the enduring symbolic significance of cranes emerged from the ashes of the Second World War. A young Japanese girl who had lived through the bombing of Hiroshima, but who was fatally stricken during its impact, resolved to fold a thousand paper cranes during her effort to recover. Although she was not able to complete the task, other children soon took up the challenge. Since then, children have annually prepared paper cranes to symbolize the hope for peace.

The human relationship with cranes extends beyond the symbolic. Cranes have occasionally been used as a source of food, although this has rarely been a widespread custom. Historically, crane hunting was a leading factor behind the Eurasian Crane's extirpation from much of Europe, but hunting of cranes is now illegal in most countries where they occur. In areas, however, where hunger is a persistent problem, cranes and other large birds are seen as an excellent source of food, and are still occasionally taken.

Cranes have long been popular birds in private collections and, more recently, in zoos. Records of cranes being kept in captivity by the Chinese nobility date back more than two thousand years. Marco Polo described Kublai Khan's efforts at crane "management" in the thirteenth century. Several of the species had already bred in captivity by the late nineteenth century; all fifteen have now been bred under artificial conditions. In general, most species breed readily in captivity if they are provided with space, privacy and a balanced diet. This facility for captive propagation is now an important conservation tool for the threatened cranes, and many techniques first developed for cranes have subsequently been employed for other threatened species.

The relationship between cranes and people is by no means idyllic. Throughout the world, crane populations have been profoundly affected by development and degradation of their wetland and grassland habitats, and by other, more direct threats (see Status and Conservation).

Status and Conservation

The cranes are among the most severely threatened of all bird families. Seven of the fifteen species are now considered to be threatened; four more may shortly be added in accordance with new classification criteria of the World Conservation Union (IUCN). In addition, several subspecies are also threatened.

The loss and degradation of wetlands and grasslands have been the leading factors behind the decline of cranes around the world. In particular, the drainage and conversion of wetlands to agriculture and other human uses has deprived the birds of extensive portions of their ancestral habitat. Direct exploitation in the form of hunting and trapping, and other anthropogenic threats, including poisoning and disturbance, have also taken their toll. Populations of crowned, Sarus and Demoiselle Cranes have been affected, in some cases seriously, by the trade in live birds. Those species that face growing pressures on their natural habitats have in some cases turned to using cultivated lands. In most circumstances there is little conflict with farmers' interests, but in some situations, especially when cranes gather in large flocks during migration and in winter, they can inflict serious damage on crops.

The Demoiselle Crane is the smallest species of crane. Most Demoiselle populations are migratory, moving from breeding grounds right across eastern Euorpe and Asia to wintering grounds in North Africa and India. In travelling between these zones they pass over high mountain ranges, at altitudes up to 8000 m, and they also cross arid desert regions. The numbers that assemble for such journeys can be rather impressive, for example, many thousands of birds together.

[*Anthropoides virgo*, Blue Nile, El Kamlin, near Khartoum, Sudan. Photo: Sture Traneving]

In response, cranes have sometimes been intentionally poisoned or shot.

Even as the world's cranes have declined in response to these multiple threats, their cultural value, conspicuousness extraordinary beauty, dramatic migrations and striking behaviour have inspired widespread conservation efforts. The special characteristics of cranes have provided conservationists with unique opportunities for action. Because cranes require large territories and are among the most prominent inhabitants of wetlands, they have served as important symbols for wetland protection, and conservation activities undertaken on their behalf have benefited a wide range of other plant and animal species. Because most crane species have extensive ranges, they have been responsible for stimulating many innovative conservation measures at the international level. These same qualities also make them effective vehicles for conveying lessons in conservation education and environmental awareness. In addition, captive propagation and reintroduction programmes have been undertaken for several species, providing important experience in the combining of *in situ* and *ex situ* conservation methods for other threatened species.

Of the many conservation sagas associated with cranes, none is more dramatic than that of the Whooping Crane. The story of the species' decline, near extinction, and slow recovery is among the best known and most closely followed chapters in the annals of wildlife conservation. The Whooping Crane once frequented the vast prairie wetlands of the north central USA and south central Canada, from present day Chicago to Alberta, a region that has now been largely converted to intensive agricultural production. Beginning in the mid-1800's, European settlers drained the wetlands to build farms and cities and hunted the great white birds for their meat. As Whooping Cranes became scarce, oologists contributed to their decline by collecting eggs from the known nesting areas. Were it not for a tiny remnant flock nesting in the impenetrable muskeg in the remote Northwest Territories of Canada, the species would undoubtedly have become extinct early in the 1900's.

The Whooping Crane and its habitats continued to disappear through the early decades of the twentieth century. The population of migratory Whooping Cranes reached its historical low in 1941, when only 15 birds were counted at the wintering grounds along the Gulf Coast of Texas in the southern USA. A separate, non-migratory flock existed in Louisiana until 1950, when the last lone individual was taken into captivity. The precarious state of the species stimulated intensive efforts, beginning in the late 1930's, to protect the species' wintering grounds and to locate its breeding grounds. Since then, the establishment of refuges, the development of careful monitoring and protection programmes, and education of hunters along the narrow migration route have permitted the number of Whooping Cranes in the traditional flock to increase slowly to its current size of approximately 150 birds. This population, however, remains highly vulnerable to pollution, storms and other potentially catastrophic events in its winter range, and to genetic and demographic problems associated with the small population size.

More intensive steps have also been taken in efforts to speed the recovery of the species. Whooping Cranes lay two eggs but seldom rear two chicks. By removing second eggs and hatching them elsewhere, crane conservationists have been able to establish a captive population of more than 100 birds. If eggs are collected from the captive birds, one pair may produce several clutches in a single breeding season. Using the available "surplus" eggs from the wild and captive flocks, conservationists have attempted to establish new wild populations of Whooping Cranes. Between 1976 and 1989, in the north-western state of Idaho, USA, 289 Whooping Crane eggs were substituted into the nests of wild Greater Sandhill Cranes (*G. c. tabida*). From these eggs, 84 juveniles were fledged, and these birds accompanied their foster-parents along a 1300 km migration route to New Mexico. The Whooping Cranes learned to feed in the niche of the Sandhill, and they learned a new migration route. Unfortunately, however, they also learned to be sexually attracted to Sandhill Cranes through the process of sexual imprinting. As a result, conspecific pairs did not form and the experiment was discontinued in the late 1980's.

Since 1992, an experiment has been under way in central Florida to establish a non-migratory flock of Whooping Cranes using captive-reared birds. Through a technique known as "isolation rearing", chicks are reared in enclosures by people in crane costumes, using hand puppets that resemble the heads and necks of adult cranes. In an adjacent area, adult Whooping Cranes provide "imprint models" for the chicks; the chicks are exposed to

What with their northern breeding grounds, their intermediate staging posts, and their southern wintering areas, Eurasian Cranes are in effect distributed over the whole of Europe and Asia. Spain lies towards the northern limits of the species' wintering zone, and even here, where they escape the worst of a European winter, winter temperatures can drop quite low. One of the major sites for both passage migrants and winterers of this species in Spain is the lake at Gallocanta, where up to 54,000 birds have been seen together.

[*Grus grus*, Laguna de Gallocanta, Aragón, Spain. Photo: Francisco Márquez]

uncostumed people only to condition them to be afraid of humans. Chicks fledged using these methods have then been released on the Kissimmee Prairie in Florida, where scattered wetlands amidst grazed fields provide prime habitat for Florida Sandhill Cranes. As of 1994, this new experimental flock of Whooping Cranes contained approximately 25 birds.

The Florida project was undertaken in part because no artificial technique has yet been developed for teaching cranes to migrate. In the future, Whooping Crane recovery projects will have to overcome this barrier if new migratory populations are to be established. Research to develop such techniques is now under way. One promising method, already used successfully to teach migration to young Canada Geese, is to teach chicks to follow an ultralight aeroplane, which can then be used to guide the fledged young along a new migration route. However, the development of such techniques is highly intensive in terms of time, labour and money, and the focus in recovery programmes for this and other crane species has been on maintaining the existing migratory populations, with their ancestral knowledge of migration routes.

The Red-crowned Crane, with between 1600 and 1900 birds in the wild, is the second rarest crane. It is divided into two allopatric populations: 1100-1400 in a migratory flock on mainland Asia; and 600 in a non-migratory flock in Japan. It is estimated that as much as 90% of the species' wetland breeding habitat in northern China has been destroyed through drainage for agriculture since the 1950's. China views the vast wetlands of former Manchuria as its "great northern food basket", and development of these areas has proceeded on a massive scale. Although several nature reserves have been established to protect the nesting habitat of the Red-crowned Cranes in China, the reserves are seriously affected by changes in hydrology due to development of neighbouring areas. Reintroduction of captive-reared Red-crowned Cranes has taken place on a limited basis at three natural breeding sites: at Kushiro Natural Crane Park in Hokkaido; at the Zhalong Nature Reserve in northern China; and at the Khinganski Reserve in south-eastern Russia. For the species as a whole, however, the critical need is to protect the existing habitats against looming threats.

A large portion of the Red-crowned Crane's mainland population winters along the delta of the River Yangtze, where sev-

eral hundred metres of "new" land are created each year by the deposit of sediments. However, the world's largest power dam is being planned for construction across the Yangtze at the Three Gorges. If, as a result of the dam, the deposit of sediments downstream is insufficient to overcome erosion losses on the delta, there could be a net annual loss in wetland area, and thus rapid loss of prime winter habitat for as many as 800 Red-crowned Cranes.

Another portion of the mainland population of Red-crowned Cranes breeds in south-eastern Russia and neighbouring areas of China, and winters in the Cholewon Basin of the Korean Demilitarized Zone. If North and South Korea are united, plans to build factories in the Demilitarized Zone, using capital from the South and labour from the North, will likely move forward at a rapid pace, thus destroying the winter habitat of about 300 Red-crowned Cranes. The impact would be all the greater as the Demilitarized Zone also provides important migratory and wintering habitat for the threatened White-naped Crane.

The Red-crowned Cranes in northern Japan are much more secure that those on the mainland. Considered extirpated from Japan for half a century, a tiny population of about 30 birds was discovered in 1924 in south-eastern Hokkaido. They fed along streams and near hot springs throughout the winter, and their failure to migrate turned out to be their salvation. In 1952, however, severe cold covered their feeding areas in ice. Seeing that the cranes might starve, school children in the area scattered corn on the ice. The cranes readily accepted the food and the tradition of feeding cranes thus had its beginning in Japan. Today, three major crane feeding stations and several smaller stations are sponsored by the Japanese government. The number of cranes has increased to approximately 600 and thousands of tourists visit the feeding stations each winter to observe and photograph the Red-crowned Cranes. This concentration of the population, however, brings with it an increased risk of disastrous mortality, should a disease break out during the winter.

Although not the rarest of the cranes, the Siberian Crane is perhaps the most seriously threatened. Unlike Whooping and Red-crowned Cranes, which during the non-breeding period can feed in upland habitats alongside their more abundant cousins, such as Sandhill and Eurasian Cranes, Siberian Cranes are restricted to wetlands, where they dig in the mud for roots and tubers. Thus, the challenge for Siberian Crane conservationists in southern Asia, a region heavily populated and intensively used by people, is to protect, manage and restore vital wetland habitats. Siberian Cranes are also highly vulnerable to hunting along their migration routes.

There are three major wintering areas for Siberian Cranes: the Caspian lowlands of Iran; the Gangetic Plains of northern India; and the Yangtze lowlands of China. The wintering flock in Iran has been reduced to 9-12 birds, the Indian flock is nearly extinct, and the China flock amounts to perhaps 3000 birds; the breeding grounds of the Iranian flock remains a mystery. The Indian flock has probably been decimated by sport hunters in Afghanistan and Pakistan. The fragile wetlands used by wintering Siberian Cranes, as well as White-naped and other cranes, in China may be seriously affected by the proposed dam across the Yangtze.

Since 1977, when the collecting of "second" eggs from wild Siberian Cranes in eastern Siberia began, captive flocks have been established in Germany, Russia and the USA. These flocks now form a "species bank" to provide insurance, should the wild cranes be lost, and to supplement the dwindling wild populations. Experiments are now under way to use captive-raised birds to bolster the Iranian flock and to revive the Indian population.

The intensive conservation work undertaken for the Whooping, Red-crowned and Siberian Cranes reflects the vulnerability of their small populations and their restricted habitats. Three other threatened species, the Wattled, White-naped and Black-necked Cranes, still exist in the low thousands, while a fourth, the Blue Crane, may still be slightly more numerous, but appears to be declining rapidly. Unless these birds and their habitats are protected, they could easily follow the path of the Whooping Crane and the western flocks of Siberian Cranes.

The Wattled Crane, with a total estimated population of 13,000-15,000 birds, is the rarest of the six crane species occurring in Africa. The population of the species has been declining throughout its range over the last several decades. The Wattled Crane is the most wetland dependent of the African cranes, preferring in particular the expansive riparian marshes of the Zambezi, Okavango and other large river systems in southern Africa. The species has thus suffered disproportionately from the loss of wetlands to development and the disruption of floodplain hydrological cycles due to dam construction and other water development projects. In areas where Wattled Cranes use smaller wetlands, as in the highlands of Ethiopia and South Africa, human disturbance also constitutes an important threat. Since the early 1980's, conservation measures involving Wattled Cranes have expanded throughout the species' range, most extensively in South Africa. These measures include regular counts and surveys in many portions of the range, marking and relocation of utility lines, adoption of habitat conservation practices by private landowners, initiation of a limited release programme, and development of special education schemes. Reserves have also been established to protect several key wetland complexes used by the species in Zambia, Namibia and Botswana.

The population of the White-naped Crane reached its historic low in the years immediately following the Second World War, and has since recovered to a current estimated total of about 5000 birds. However, the species may be declining again in parts of its Russian and Chinese breeding grounds, due largely to agricultural expansion in the Amur Basin and elsewhere in northern China. The preferred habitat of the White-naped Crane, wetland margins and adjacent grassland, are especially attractive for conversion to agriculture. Other threats include the potential development of non-breeding habitat in the Korean Demilitarized Zone, proposed dams along the Amur and Yangtze Rivers, and an elevated risk of disease due to the concentration of wintering cranes at Izumi, in southern Japan. Along with the other east Asian cranes, the White-naped has benefited in recent years from expanded international co-operation, involving legal protection, research, surveys, and establishment of

Young cranes grow remarkably quickly, on the varied food that their parents help them to acquire. Those 57-97% of young that survive are able to fly by the age of about three months. The young birds learn the traditional migration routes from their parents, whom they accompany for almost a year. After their first return journey back to the breeding grounds, they leave their parents' territory, or are expelled from it. Thereafter, in often nomadic non-breeding groups, they will initiate the process of forming their own pair-bonds.

[*Grus canadensis pratensis*, Florida, USA.
Photo: Bates Littlehales/ Animals Animals]

Perhaps the least studied crane, the Black-necked is, nonetheless, known to be in difficulty. In general, the species has been protected in its breeding grounds, both by legislation recently and by Buddhist respect for wildlife for centuries beforehand. In its wintering grounds in areas where fire-arms are more numerous, hunting has become a significant problem. In addition, the wetlands themselves are under threat through drainage, conversion and pollution. The lake of Cao Hai (meaning "Sea of Grass") in China was unsuccessfully drained for agriculture in 1971, but reflooded and made into a Nature Reserve in 1985.

[Grus nigricollis, Cao Hai Nature Reserve, China. Photo Sue Earle/ Planet Earth]

Since 1971, the Hooded Crane has been considered a National Monument in South Korea. Its fortunes have fluctuated over the past 70 years. Three quarters of the world population of around 10,000 birds are sustained by artificial winter feeding at Izumi in Japan; with such numbers close together there is clearly a risk of disease. There is an international studbook and captive breeding programme in the world zoo community, containing about 100 birds.

[Grus monacha, Fuji, Japan. Photo: T. Shimba/VIREO]

protected areas. In particular, the combined efforts of Chinese, Mongolian and Russian conservationists have provided greater protection for the species on its breeding grounds. Captive-raised White-naped Cranes have been released on a limited basis at the Zhalong Nature Reserve in China and the Khinganski Reserve in Russia.

The Black-necked Crane population, estimated at 5600-6000 birds, seems to have stabilized since the 1970's, after many decades of decline. Local Buddhist traditions of respect for wildlife have played an important role in safeguarding the species across much of its breeding range in the Tibet-Qinghai Plateau in China and adjacent parts of Bhutan and India. The major threats to the species occur at the lower altitudes where the birds winter. In these areas, wetlands have been extensively lost or degraded due to drainage, dam construction, river canalization and other environmental modifications. The species' main winter food, surplus barley and wheat, is increasingly scarce due to widespread changes in traditional agricultural practices. At the same time, hunting of Black-necked Cranes has increased, as formerly remote areas have become accessible, and firearms more available. Since the late 1970's, the species has drawn closer attention from conservationists. Key wintering habitats have been protected in reserves in China and Bhutan. Regular surveys have been carried out, especially in the wintering areas, allowing for much more accurate estimates of the population. Field research on the species in general has expanded dramatically in these years. Although these measures have done much to safeguard the species, it remains highly vulnerable to poaching, changing land uses, and habitat deterioration, especially in its wintering grounds.

South Africa's endemic Blue Crane, with a population estimated at 21,000 birds, is still relatively abundant in some portions of its range. However, since 1980 its numbers have declined significantly in many portions of its range due to intentional and unintentional poisoning, as well as the extensive loss of its grassland habitat to afforestation. As a result of these alarming trends, and in the absence of accurate total population estimates, the Blue Crane has been added to the list of globally threatened species. Since the mid-1980's, conservation efforts for this species have increased, and it is to be hoped that the decline can be halted before numbers slump much further.

The Hooded Crane's total population, estimated at about 9400-9600 birds, is probably as high as it has been at any point since the 1920's. The species is somewhat more secure than the other rare endemic cranes of eastern Asia, due mainly to the relative inaccessibility and low development potential of its boggy breeding grounds in south-eastern Russia and northern China. However, even these areas are subject to increased economic pressures. At the same time, wintering habitats in Korea and China are subject to intensified agricultural and commercial development. Some 80% of the total Hooded Crane population winters at Izumi, on the Japanese island of Kyushu. Sustained by artificial feeding, these birds, along with White-naped Cranes, are densely concentrated, and thus highly sus-

Siberian Cranes provide a fine illustration of varied conservation problems. Their long migrations across international borders, the existence of tiny populations, together with our lack of knowledge about them and the difficulties in enforcing protection measures all combine to produce an uncertain future for the species in the wild. The three wild populations are faring very differently. The western population, which winters in the Caspian lowlands of Iran, is apparently down to only about 10 individuals; where they breed in northern Russia is unknown, but this might soon be revealed by satellite radio tracking. The central population breeds in an apparently secure remote region of northern Russia, and winters at Bharatpur and other Indian wetlands where it is protected. But in between, its staging posts are being disturbed, and the birds are often shot at in Afghanistan and Pakistan. This minute population was believed extinct when none showed up in 1994 or 1995, but four birds reappeared at Bharatpur in 1996. The eastern population was discovered only in the 1980's, wintering at Lake Poyang in China. It numbers about 3000 birds, which breed in Yakutia and Siberian Arctic regions. The huge Three Gorges dam being constructed on the River Yangtze may well damage the wintering wetlands on which the birds depend.

[*Grus leucogeranus*, Keoladeo National Park, Bharatpur, India. Photo: Jean-Paul Ferrero/ Auscape

Grus leucogeranus, Lake Poyang, Jiangxi Province, China. Photo: Sture Traneving]

The Whooping Crane has come pretty well as close to extinction as any species can: no more than 16 individuals remained in the early 1940's. Careful protection and management of both wild and captive populations brought world numbers up to 330 birds by August 1995, including some 150 wild birds, a success story that can be put down, in large part, to the management practice of removing second eggs for incubation and rearing elsewhere. Reintroduction attempts are under way and have met with some success, but one particularly exasperating problem is how to teach the migration routes to the inexperienced birds.

[Grus americana, Aransas National Wildlife Refuge, Texas, USA. Photo: Jeff Foott/ Bruce Coleman]

ceptible to outbreaks of disease. Like the White-naped Crane, the Hooded has benefited from international agreements and co-operative conservation actions. At present, however, the long-term security of the species is compromised by the lack of alternative feeding and roosting sites for wintering populations in southern Japan and Korea.

Other crane taxa are of concern from a conservation standpoint. Since the 1970's, the population of Black Crowned Cranes has declined precipitously in much of its range in sub-Saharan West Africa, mainly as a result of heavy human population and development pressures, compounded by long-term drought in the region. The species has been, or is on the verge of being, extirpated from several countries, including Nigeria, where it is the national bird. The population of Grey Crowned Cranes has also declined during this period. These declines may warrant the listing of both species as threatened.

The Indian race of the Sarus Crane, though still common in the north, is declining in numbers, and has been extirpated from much of its historical range. The south-east Asian race of the Sarus has been reduced to perhaps several thousand birds, mainly in Cambodia and Laos. In the meantime, the Philippine population of the Sarus has probably become extinct, without its taxonomic status ever having been clarified (see Systematics). Although the Sandhill Crane is the most abundant of the world's cranes, two of its six recognized races are severely threatened. The population of the Mississippi race *pulla*, augmented by the release of captive-produced birds, numbers approximately 100 birds, while the Cuban race *nesiotes* may amount to some 300 birds at nine widely scattered locations. Several other species have some small isolated populations with conservation needs that are poorly known. These include, for example, populations of Demoiselle Cranes in Morocco and Turkey, Eurasian Cranes in Turkey and Tibet Wattled Cranes in Ethiopia, Blue Cranes in Namibia and Brolgas in New Guinea.

It is not only the currently threatened cranes that are of interest from a conservation perspective. The most abundant and extensively distributed crane species, the Sandhill, Demoiselle and Eurasian, offer other lessons and challenges. All three of these species have experienced declines, sometimes severe, in portions of their historical ranges, while some of their populations have also recovered dramatically. For example, the numbers of Greater Sandhill Cranes in the Great Lakes region of North America and of Eurasian Cranes in parts of Europe have increased steadily in recent decades. At the same time, these species are being forced to adapt to dynamic forces affecting their habitats, distribution and population structure. All three species have been affected to one degree or another by fragmentation of formerly contiguous populations. This has probably occurred, for example, in the south-eastern USA, where resident Sandhill Cranes were more abundant in the past. Similarly, the Demoiselle and Eurasian Crane populations across Eurasia are becoming increasingly concentrated in discrete populations.

In addition to these internal changes in populations, external changes in their habitats make the future of these abundant species unpredictable. Changes in land use in Western Europe will play a key role in determining the future of the Eurasian Crane in that sector of its range. Similarly, the rapid conversion of the Eurasian steppes to cropland is forcing the Demoiselle Crane to adapt to artificial conditions during its breeding period. Changes in hydrology and vegetation along the Platte River in the central USA have affected habitat conditions in an area used by roughly 80% of the total population of Sandhill Cranes during spring migration. Furthermore, these abundant species occasionally cause crop damage, presenting conservationists with different challenges for harmonizing the interests of cranes and people. Large-scale and long-term factors such as these are of vital importance to these species, if they are to avoid the declines that have affected the more threatened members of their family.

General Bibliography

Archibald (1976), Archibald & Mirande (1985), Archibald & Pasquier (1987a), Bankovics (1987b), Beilfuss *et al.* (1996), Cheng Tsohsin (1986), Collar (1985c), Cooley (1993), Cracraft (1973), Halvorson *et al.* (1995), Haney & Eiswerth (1992), Harris (1991b, 1992b), Hendrickson (1969), Higuchi & Minton (1994), Ingold *et al.* (1989), Johnsgard (1983, 1991a), Krajewski (1989), Krajewski & Fetzner (1994), Lewis (1976a, 1979a, 1982, 1987), Lewis & Masatomi (1981), Litvinenko & Neufeldt (1982, 1988), Ma Yiqing (1986), Meine (1993), Meine & Archibald (1996), Neufeldt (1982), Neufeldt & Kespaik (1987), Peters (1934), Porter *et al.* (1992), Prange *et al.* (1995), Sibley & Ahlquist (1990), Sibley & Monroe (1990), Soothill & Soothill (1982), Stahlecker (1992), Walkinshaw (1973), Wood (1979).

1

ssp *gibbericeps*

ssp *regulorum*

2

ssp *ceciliae*

ssp *pavonina*

PLATE 5

inches   16

cm   40

3

4

6

ssp *tabida*

7

5

ssp *canadensis*

Subfamily BALEARICINAE

Genus *BALEARICA* Brisson, 1760

1. Grey Crowned Crane

Balearica regulorum

French: Grue royale   **Spanish**: Grulla Coronada Cuelligrís
          German: Südafrikanischer Kronenkranich
Other common names: Blue-necked/Royal Crane; East African Crowned Crane (*gibbericeps*); South African Crowned Crane (*regulorum*)

Taxonomy. *Anthropoïdes Regulorum* Bennett, 1834, South Africa.
Formerly considered conspecific with *B. pavonina*, with species labelled as *B. pavonina* or sometimes, incorrectly, as *B. regulorum*; but differences revealed by electrophoresis, together with those in vocalizations, bare parts and plumage, advocate recognition of two species constituting a superspecies. Two subspecies recognized.
Subspecies and Distribution.
B. r. gibbericeps Reichenow, 1892 - Uganda and Kenya S to N Zimbabwe and N Mozambique.
B. r. regulorum (Bennett, 1834) - S Angola and N Namibia E through Botswana to Zimbabwe, then S to SE South Africa.

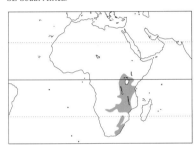

Descriptive notes. 100-110 cm; 3000-4000 g; wingspan 180-200 cm. Iris pale grey to pale blue. Shares distinctive crown of yellow feathers with *B. pavonina*; differs in pale grey neck and larger red throat wattles; white cheek patch has red only at top. Juvenile generally grey, with brown crown and nape, grey to brown body, and brown iris. Race *gibbericeps* has more red in cheek patch than nominate *regulorum*. VOICE: Calls are mellow honks, generally low-pitched.
Habitat. Mixture of wetlands and open grassland or savanna. In E Africa, now found mostly in human-modified habitats, including pastures, cropland, fallow fields, irrigated areas, and ranches. In S Africa, marshes and *vleis* in grassland and savanna, and also agricultural land. Will roost in water, in trees, or on utility line posts; present species and *B. pavonina* are only cranes able to perch in trees.
Food and Feeding. Generalist. Feeds on seed heads (e.g. of *Cyperus* sedges) and fresh tips of grasses; insects, including grasshoppers, crickets, locusts, cutworms and army worms; and other small animals, e.g. frogs, lizards and *Potamon* crabs. Forages in grassland and agricultural land. Takes food with rapid pecks; plants may be uprooted; sometimes stamps feet to disturb insects; associates with grazing herbivores, perhaps benefiting from increased abundance of prey, and also from prey items disturbed.
Breeding. Season variable in response to rains: all year round in E Africa, with peaks during drier periods; in drier portions of S Africa, breeds mainly during rainy periods, c. Oct-Apr, peaking Dec-Feb. Nests in or along margins of wetlands, very rarely in trees; nest consists of uprooted grasses and sedges piled and flattened into circular platform, concealed by surrounding aquatic vegetation. Eggs 1-4; average clutch size 2·5+, largest of any crane; clutch size can vary with altitude. Incubation 28-31 days; chicks umber to brown with buff head; fledging period variable, perhaps 56-100 days. Sexually mature at three (rarely two) years.
Movements. Non-migratory. Variable local and seasonal movements depending on abundance and distribution of food, nest-sites and rainfall. More sedentary in E Africa. Local and seasonal movements both more extensive in drier portions of range, e.g. Namibia and parts of South Africa; in these drier areas, flocking most marked during dry seasons.
Status and Conservation. Not globally threatened. CITES II. Most abundant African crane, with total population estimated at 85,000-95,000 birds; race *gibbericeps* comprises more than 90% of total. Since mid-1980's, population has declined by estimated 10%, as indicated by surveys in Kenya, Uganda and South Africa, with contractions in range reported from South Africa, Namibia and Zambia. This decline reflects widespread threats to habitats resulting from rapid human population growth, drought-related changes in land use, and other factors; loss and deterioration of wetland breeding areas, mainly due to drainage or overgrazing, has been most significant; other habitat problems include heavy pesticide use, declines in the practice of fallowing, high rates of sedimentation, and altered hydrological patterns due to dam construction and groundwater extraction. Live-trapping, trade, egg-collecting and hunting are also of concern. In many areas, local cultural traditions of reverence have provided protection. Research on species remains relatively limited, although field studies have expanded in 1980's and 1990's. Counts and surveys have been conducted intermittently in several range countries. Community-based wetland conservation projects involving the species have been undertaken in Kenya. Non-governmental organizations have been active in conservation projects in several countries, especially Kenya, Uganda and South Africa. Twelve range countries prepared preliminary crane and wetland action plans at 1993 African Crane and Wetland Training Workshop in Botswana. Species breeds readily in captivity. Release and reintroduction programmes have not been necessary.
Bibliography. Allan (1994a), Archibald (1992a), Benson & Benson (1975), Benson *et al*. (1971), Berry (1995), Blossom (1992), Britton, P. L. (1980), Brown, C. J. (1992), Colahan (1990), Dowsett & Dowsett-Lemaire (1993), Dowsett & Forbes-Watson (1993), Filmer & Holtshausen (1992), Frame (1982, 1985), Gichuki (1993), Gichuki & Gichuki (1991), Ginn *et al*. (1989), Johnson (1992), Johnson & Barnes (1986), Kanyawimba (1996), Katenekwa (1996), Katondo (1996), Konrad (1987), Mackworth-Praed & Grant (1957, 1962, 1970), Maclean (1993), Mafabi (1991), Mmari (1996), Morris (1987), Mundy (1994), Pinto (1983), Pomeroy (1980a, 1980b, 1987), Rutgers & Norris (1970), Siegfried (1985), Steyn & Ellman-Brown (1974), Steyn & Tredgold (1977), Tarboton (1992a, 1992b), Tarboton, Kemp & Kemp (1987), Tarsnane (1981), Taylor (1992), Urban (1985, 1996), Urban *et al*. (1986), Vernon *et al*. (1992), Walkinshaw (1964).

2. Black Crowned Crane

Balearica pavonina

French: Grue couronnée   **German**: Kronenkranich   **Spanish**: Grulla Coronada Cuellinegra
Other common names: Dark Crowned Crane; West African Crowned Crane (*pavonina*); Sudan Crowned Crane (*ceciliae*)

Taxonomy. *Ardea pavonina* Linnaeus, 1758, Cape Verde, Senegal.
Formerly considered conspecific with *B. regulorum*, with species labelled as *B. pavonina* or sometimes, incorrectly, as *B. regulorum*; but differences revealed by electrophoresis, together with those in vocalizations, bare parts and plumage, advocate recognition of two species constituting a superspecies. Two subspecies recognized.
Subspecies and Distribution.
B. p. pavonina (Linnaeus, 1758) - scattered populations in sub-Saharan W Africa from Senegambia to L Chad.
B. p. ceciliae Mitchell, 1904 - sub-Saharan Africa from Chad to Sudan, Ethiopia and Kenya, especially in basin of upper R Nile.

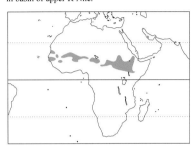

Descriptive notes. 100-105 cm; 3000-4000 g; wingspan 180-200 cm. Iris pale grey to pale blue. Distinguished from *B. regulorum* by darker neck, small wattles, and red in lower part of cheek patch. Juvenile generally grey, with brown crown and nape, grey to brown body, and brown iris. Race *ceciliae* has red extending somewhat more than half way up cheek patch (only up to about half way in nominate *pavonina*). VOICE: Calls are mellow honks, generally low-pitched, with some differences from those of *B. regulorum*..
Habitat. Mixture of shallow wetlands and grassland. In W Africa, affects flooded lowlands, riverbanks, rice fields and wet cropland, and upland fields. In E Africa, found in extensive marshes, wet meadows, and in margins of ponds, lakes and rivers. Will nest and forage in uplands, but always close to wetlands.
Food and Feeding. Generalist. Feeds on insects, including grasshoppers and flies; other invertebrates, including molluscs, millipedes and crustaceans; fish, amphibians and reptiles; and seed heads and tips of grasses, and also crops, e.g. millet, corn, rice. Normally pecks food off surface, rarely digs; sometimes stamps feet, probably trying to disturb invertebrate prey; in dry season, frequently forages near herds of domestic livestock, where invertebrates occur in greater abundance.
Breeding. Jul-Oct, but variable in response to rains. Nest is circular platform of grasses and sedges built within or along edge of densely vegetated wetlands. Eggs 2-3; average clutch size c. 2·5, similar to that of *B. regulorum*. Incubation 28-31 days; plumage of chicks undescribed; soon after hatching, chicks forage with parents in nearby uplands; fledging period perhaps 60-100 days. Age of sexual maturity undetermined.
Movements. Non-migratory. Daily and seasonal movements, up to perhaps several dozen kilometres, between feeding and roosting areas. Often flocks in large numbers during dry season, dispersing from large permanent wetlands to breed in smaller temporary wetlands during rainy season.
Status and Conservation. Not globally threatened. CITES II. In past, species was probably more numerous and more evenly distributed. Population of race *ceciliae* estimated at 55,000-60,000 birds and considered relatively stable. Population of race *pavonina*, estimated at 11,500-17,500 birds, has fallen dramatically since 1970's due to drought, human population pressures, and habitat loss; contraction of range of this race has led to near or total extirpation in several countries, including Nigeria (where it is the national bird); not recorded in Sierra Leone since 1930's, when was not uncommon in small groups; has become much less common in Ghana, and is now rare. Habitat loss and degradation continue to be the most serious threats; drought-related declines in wetlands have been compounded by intensive agricultural development and expansion and by large-scale dam, drainage and irrigation projects; although most pressing in W Africa, these factors also affect the species in E of range. Hunting and trade are of concern in some areas. Species protected by law in most range countries. Several surveys undertaken at local level. In 1992, *International Conference on the Black Crowned Crane and Its Wetlands Habitat in West and Central Africa* was held in Nigeria, and a Black Crowned Crane Co-ordinating Centre was established. Several range countries prepared crane and wetland action plans at 1993 African Crane and Wetland Training Workshop. Reintroductions of subspecies *pavonina* currently under consideration; several releases have taken place on an experimental basis.
Bibliography. Akinyemi & Iyoha (1983), Archibald & Pasquier (1987b), Daddy & Ayeni (1996), Dowsett & Dowsett-Lemaire (1993), Dowsett & Forbes-Watson (1993), Fry (1981, 1987), Garba (1996), Goodman *et al*. (1989), Gore (1990), Grimes (1987), Mackworth-Praed & Grant (1957, 1970), Meduna *et al*. (1988), Mustafa & Durbunde (1992), Newby (1979), Newton (1996a), Parker (1971), Rutgers & Norris (1970), Tréca & Ndiaye (1996), Urban (1981, 1987, 1996), Urban & Gichuki (1991), Urban *et al*. (1986), Walkinshaw (1964, 1966, 1981b).

Subfamily GRUINAE

Genus *ANTHROPOIDES* Vieillot, 1816

3. Demoiselle Crane

Anthropoides virgo

French: Grue demoiselle   **German**: Jungfernkranich   **Spanish**: Grulla Damisela

Taxonomy. *Ardea Virgo* Linnaeus, 1758, India.
Genus sometimes merged with *Grus*, but usually considered sufficiently distinct. Monotypic.
Distribution. C Eurasia, from Black Sea E to Mongolia and NE China. Winters in Indian Subcontinent and in sub-Saharan Africa from L Chad to Ethiopia. Small, disjunct breeding populations in Turkey and in Atlas Mts, NW Africa.
Descriptive notes. c. 90 cm; 2000-3000 g; wingspan c. 150-170 cm. Smallest crane; male slightly larger than female. Present species and *A. paradisea* are the only cranes with entirely feathered head, and lacking red skin on head. Uniform grey, except for black head and neck, black-tipped secondaries, and distinctive white ear tufts extending from behind eye to upper nape; elongated black plumage of foreneck hangs down below breast. Iris reddish orange. Juvenile generally duller grey with paler head and neck; ear tufts less distinct. VOICE: Calls are low-pitched and raspy.
Habitat. Primarily savanna, steppe and other grassland types, often in close proximity to streams, shallow lakes and other wetlands. Inhabits semi-desert and true deserts where water is available. Occurs up to 3000 m in C Asia. Is adapting to agricultural fields in Kazakhstan and Ukraine. Also uses agricultural

On following pages: 4. Blue Crane (*Anthropoides paradisea*); 5. Wattled Crane (*Bugeranus carunculatus*); 6. Siberian Crane (*Grus leucogeranus*); 7. Sandhill Crane (*Grus canadensis*).

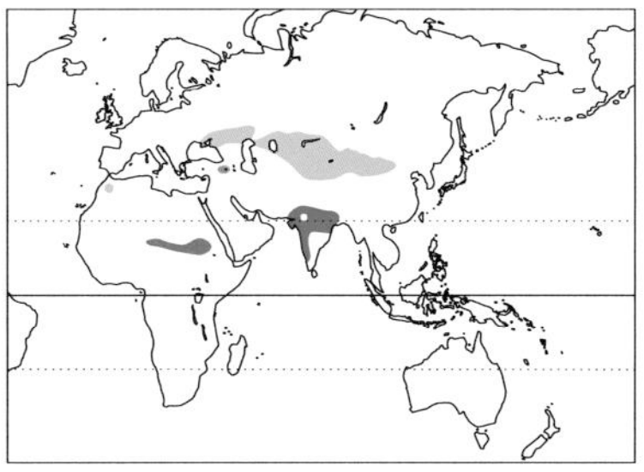

fields in wintering areas in India, roosting in nearby shallow waters and wetlands; affects *Acacia* savanna, grassland and riparian wetlands in African wintering grounds.

Food and Feeding. Mainly seeds (especially of grasses) and other plant materials; also insects, especially beetles (Coleoptera) in summer; worms, lizards and other small vertebrates. Walks slowly while foraging. Large flocks at migration staging areas and in Indian wintering grounds forage in cultivated fields, sometimes causing damage to cereal and legume crops.

Breeding. Spring breeder, mainly Apr-May, but as late as Jun in north. Nest is minimally prepared in open patches of grass, in cultivated areas, or on gravel; pebbles and some plant material may be gathered, but eggs are often laid directly on ground. Usually 2 eggs; incubation 27-29 days; chicks pale brown above, greyish white below; fledging 55-65 days, the shortest period in any crane. May reach sexual maturity by second year.

Movements. Migratory, with possible exception of small population in Turkey; in past, species wintered in Mugan Steppe, SE Azerbaijan. Birds from W Eurasia winter in E sub-Saharan Africa. Birds from C Asia, Mongolia and China winter in Indian Subcontinent. Small population of Atlas Plateau may move to L Chad in winter.

Status and Conservation. Not globally threatened. CITES II. Current population estimated at 200,000-240,000 birds. Generally abundant throughout most of historical range, but during last 100 years species has been extirpated from Iberian Peninsula, Balkan Peninsula, and parts of N Africa and W Eurasia. Steppes of E Eurasia are stronghold of species, although even the large eastern populations have become vulnerable to habitat loss. Declines have been noted in C Asia and Kazakhstan in recent decades due mainly to agricultural development of the steppes. Little known about populations of Turkey and Atlas Plateau; latter may now number only 10-12 individuals. Habitat loss and degradation are principal threats across range, especially in steppe regions, but also along migration routes and in wintering areas. Other threats include human disturbance, especially in India and Sudan; and intensive use of pesticides, e.g. in India, Sudan and Morocco. About 5000 cranes (*G. grus* and *G. leucogeranus* are also affected) are taken by sport hunters annually along migration route in Afghanistan and Pakistan. Shooting and intentional poisoning are problems in some areas where crop damage occurs. Extensive research and conservation efforts undertaken in many portions of range over last 20 years. Information exchanged at several international crane conferences, and at a species-specific meeting in Kazakhstan in 1988. Monitoring and survey programmes established in India, Ukraine and Saudi Arabia. Habitat-related research most advanced in Ukraine and Kazakhstan. Efforts to regulate hunting and provide education in Pakistan started in mid-1980's. Breeds well in captivity; no active reintroduction programmes at present, but releases being considered for areas where species is extinct or exists in critically low numbers.

Bibliography. Abuladze (1995), Ali & Ripley (1980), Andryushchenko (1995), Bankovics (1987a), Beaman (1994), Berlijn (1991), Brazil (1991), Chekmenev (1960), Cramp & Simmons (1980), Dementiev & Gladkov (1951a), Ding Hanlin *et al.* (1987), Dowsett & Dowsett-Lemaire (1993), Dowsett & Forbes-Watson (1993), Fan Zhongmin *et al.* (1994), Flint (1984b), Fujita *et al.* (1994), Gao Zhongxin & Pan Weili (1986), Gavrilov (1977), Glutz von Blotzheim *et al.* (1973), Gole (1993a), Goodman *et al.* (1989), Harris (1991a), Irisov & Irisova (1995), Kasparek (1988), Knystautas (1993), Kovshar (1987), Kovshar & Neufeldt (1991), Kovshar *et al.* (1995), Kydyraliyev (1995), Landfried *et al.* (1995), Ma Ming *et al.* (1993), Mackworth-Praed & Grant (1957, 1970), Newby (1979), Newton (1996a, 1996b), Newton & Symons (1993), Patrikeev (1995), Paz (1987), Perennou *et al.* (1994), Ponomarena (1985), Potapov & Flint (1987), Prokofiev (1995), Roberts, T. J. (1991), Roberts, T. J. & Landfried (1987), Rogacheva (1992), Rutgers & Norris (1970), Shirihai (1996), Simeonov *et al.* (1990), Smythies (1986), Soni (1995), Tong Junchang (1986), Ullman (1991), Urban (1996), Urban *et al.* (1986), Vasilchenko (1995), Winter (1991), Winter *et al.* (1995), Yang Xueming & Tong Junchang (1991).

4. Blue Crane

Anthropoides paradisea

French: Grue de paradis **German**: Paradieskranich **Spanish**: Grulla del Paraíso
Other common names: Stanley/Paradise Crane

Taxonomy. *Ardea paradisea* Lichtenstein, 1793, inner South Africa.
Genus sometimes merged with *Grus*, but usually considered sufficiently distinct. "Emendation" of species name to *paradiseus* is not justified. Monotypic.

Distribution. E & S South Africa; small disjunct population in Etosha Pan region of Namibia.

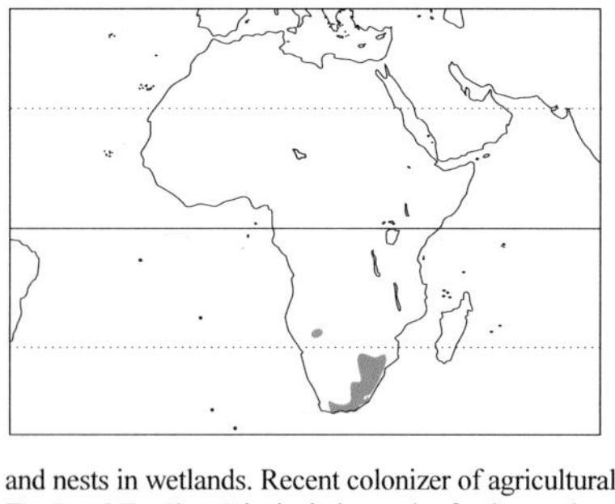

Descriptive notes. 110-120 cm; 4900-5300 g; wingspan 180-200 cm; male larger than female. Present species and *A. virgo* are the only cranes with entirely feathered head, and lacking red skin on head. Uniform bluish grey on head, neck and body. Loose feathers of cheek and upper nape give head distinctive "cobra" shape. Elongated secondaries, black-tipped and almost reaching ground. Iris dark brown. Juvenile paler grey; lacks extended secondaries. VOICE: Calls are low-pitched, raspy and broken, similar to those of *A. virgo*.

Habitat. Primarily dry upland natural grassland dominated by grasses and sedges. Also roosts and nests in wetlands. Recent colonizer of agricultural areas, using pastures, cropland and fallow fields.

Food and Feeding. Diet includes seeds of sedges and grasses, roots and tubers; also insects, especially locusts and grasshoppers, and worms, crabs, fish, frogs, reptiles and small mammals; in agricultural areas, feeds on waste cereal grain, e.g. maize and wheat. Some use of artificial foods recorded in livestock feedlots. Forages by searching on ground surface and vegetation; sometimes digs for food.

Breeding. Mainly Oct-Dec, but on occasion as late as Mar. Nests primarily in grasslands near water, but also in pastures, crop fields, and marshes; nest platform of small stones and wetland vegetation, but often only minimally prepared; eggs laid in grass or on bare ground. Usually 2 eggs; incubation 30-33 days; chicks generally grey with yellowish head and neck, and white breast and lower throat; fledging period variable, with earliest at c. 85 days. Sexually mature at 3-5 years.

Movements. Non-migratory. Local seasonal movements within South Africa. Vagrant in other parts of S Africa, e.g. Botswana, Lesotho, Swaziland, Zimbabwe.

Status and Conservation. VULNERABLE. CITES II. Population recently estimated at 21,000 birds, but reliable range-wide data lacking. Population in SW Cape Province expanding into agricultural areas, while Namibian population appears steady at c. 80 individuals. Overall population, however, has fallen since 1980, with dramatic declines in many areas; population declines of as much as 90% confirmed in Transvaal, Natal and E Cape Province during 1980's, with similar losses likely in Orange Free State. Main factors in decline have been intentional and unintentional poisoning in farming regions and commercial afforestation of South Africa's grasslands. Other threats include intensive livestock grazing, disturbance, urban and agricultural expansion, and collisions with utility lines and fences. Some young birds illegally taken into captivity. Expanded conservation efforts since mid-1980's, including adoption of stricter legal protection, local and national surveys in South Africa, increasing research on species' biology and ecology, habitat protection and management programmes (especially on private land), establishment of local conservation organizations, and development of educational facilities, programmes and publications.

Bibliography. Allan (1992, 1993, 1994a), Anon. (1995b), Archibald (1992a), Archibald & Pasquier (1987b), Aucamp (1994, 1996), Brown, C. J. (1992), Colahan (1990), Collar *et al.* (1994), D'Eath (1972), Dowsett & Dowsett-Lemaire (1993), Dowsett & Forbes-Watson (1993), Filmer & Holtshausen (1992), Geldenhuys (1984), Ginn *et al.* (1989), Holtshausen & Ledger (1985), Johnson (1992), Johnson & Barnes (1986), Keep (1985), Lotter (1975), Mackworth-Praed & Grant (1962), Maclean (1993), Oatley (1969), Rutgers & Norris (1970), Scott, A. (1993), Siegfried (1985), Stretton (1992), Tarboton (1992b), Tarboton, Kemp & Kemp (1987), Urban (1985, 1996), Urban *et al.* (1986), Van Ee (1966, 1981), Vernon *et al.* (1992), Walkinshaw (1963).

Genus *BUGERANUS* Gloger, 1842

5. Wattled Crane

Bugeranus carunculatus

French: Grue caronculée **German**: Klunkerkranich **Spanish**: Grulla Carunculada
Other common names: Great African Wattled Crane

Taxonomy. *Ardea carunculata* Gmelin, 1789, Cape of Good Hope.
Previously placed in *Grus* by some researchers, although recent ethological and DNA analysis suggests a closer relationship with *Anthropoides* species; both genera sometimes merged with *Grus*, but usually considered sufficiently distinct. Species has been considered congeneric with *Grus leucogeranus* alone, on basis of some morphological and behavioural similarities. Three main populations, but not considered subspecifically distinct. Monotypic.

Distribution. Ethiopia; Zaire, Zambia and Tanzania to Botswana and Mozambique, with outlying populations in Angola, Namibia and South Africa.

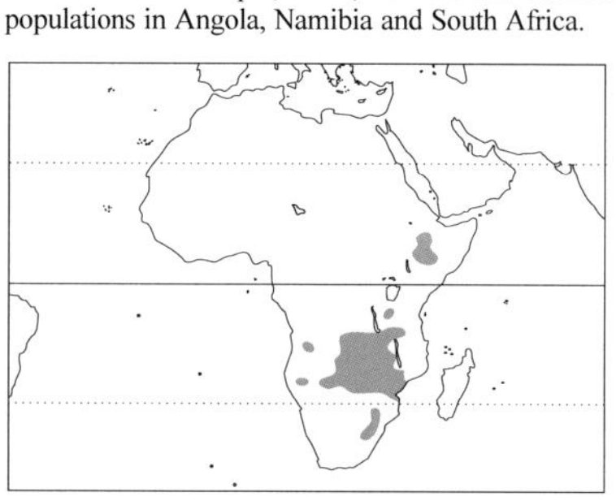

Descriptive notes. c. 175 cm; male 8300-8500 g, female 7100-7900 g; wingspan 230-260 cm. Only African crane with white neck; prominent wattles, mostly white with some red skin. As in *A. paradisea*, elongated inner secondaries extend beyond tail almost to ground. Iris orange to red. Juvenile similar to adult, but with shorter tertials and white crown; lacks red patch of facial skin, and wattles not fully developed.. VOICE: High-pitched piercing calls.

Habitat. Most dependent on wetlands of all African cranes. Large wetlands in riparian floodplains, primarily in Zambezi and Okavango Basins. Smaller permanent and seasonal wetlands in highlands of Ethiopia and South Africa. Specialized breeder in shallow sedge-dominated wetlands. Tends to breed above 2000 m, but normally occurs below 1000 m outside breeding season.

Food and Feeding. Primarily tubers and rhizomes of aquatic vegetation, e.g. *Cyperus*, *Eleocharis dulcis* and water-lilies (*Nymphaea*); also insects (Orthoptera, Coleoptera), snails, frogs and other small vertebrates. Typically uses large bill for digging in wetland and soft upland soils. Will forage in agricultural fields when convenient.

Breeding. Season highly variable, depending on water levels: mainly Jul-Aug in Ethiopia; mainly Apr-Oct in S population. Nests typically in wet grasslands and sedge marshes when water levels provide new vegetation growth and open water around nests; nest usually consists of wetland vegetation piled into a mound and surrounded by "moat" of open water 4 m wide; nest is 120-180 cm in diameter, and situated in water up to c. 60 cm deep. Usually 1 egg, sometimes 2; average clutch size 1·4, smallest of any crane. Incubation 33-36 days, longest of any crane; chicks pale to dark brown, with slightly developed wattles; fledging period 90-130 days. Sexually mature at 3-4 years.

Movements. Non-migratory, but irregularly nomadic in response to water availability. Movements poorly studied. Birds in permanent wetlands generally less mobile than those inhabiting seasonal riparian and upland wetlands.

Status and Conservation. VULNERABLE. CITES II. Total estimated population of 13,000-15,000 birds remained constant between mid-1980's and mid-1990's, but this was mainly due to more thorough surveying: during this period, core population in Zambia fell from estimated 11,000 to 7000-8000 birds; discovery of 2500 birds in Mozambique in early 1990's partially compensated for this loss. N population of Ethiopia, estimated in 100's, apparently remained constant during that same period. The most important threats to species are loss and degradation of wetlands due to intensified agriculture, indiscriminate use of wetland resources, and dam construction and subsequent changes in flooding regimes. Other threats include human disturbance, poisoning, and collisions with utility lines. Conservation measures have been undertaken most extensively in South Africa, but are expanding in other range countries. Species strictly protected in most countries. Protected areas have been established in several of the key wetlands, especially in Zambia, Namibia and Botswana. Field surveys and studies of the species have increased greatly since early 1980's. In South Africa, efforts have been made to encourage private landowners to protect and manage habitat, to mark and relocate utility lines, and to develop education and awareness programmes. Species is somewhat more difficult to breed in captivity than other cranes. Habitat conservation needs have taken priority over release or reintroduction programmes.

Bibliography. Allan (1994a), Banda (1996), Beall (1996), Beilfuss (1995), Benson & Benson (1975), Bousfield (1986), Brooke (1984a), Brooke & Vernon (1988), Colahan (1990), Collar & Andrew (1988), Collar & Stuart (1985), Collar *et al.* (1994), Conway & Hamer (1977), Cooper (1969), Dodman (1996), Douthwaite (1974), Dowsett & Dowsett-Lemaire (1993), Dowsett & Forbes-Watson (1993), Dyer (1992), Field (1978), Filmer & Holtshausen (1992), Ginn *et al.* (1989), Goodman (1992), Herholdt & Bernitz (1995), Hines (1996), Johnson & Barnes (1985, 1986, 1991), Johnson & Sinclair (1983), Kamweneshe (1996), Konrad (1981), Macartney (1968), Mackworth-Praed & Grant (1957, 1962, 1970), Maclean (1993), Malambo & Chabwela (1992), Mangubuli (1996), Masterson (1986), Nhlane (1993), Pinto (1983), Rutgers & Norris (1970), Tarboton (1984, 1995), Tarboton & Johnson (1992), Tarboton, Barnes & Johnson (1987), Tarboton, Kemp & Kemp (1987), Urban (1996), Urban & Walkinshaw (1967), Urban *et al.* (1986), Vernon & Boshoff (1986), Walkinshaw (1965), Wennrich (1985), West (1963, 1976, 1982), Williams, J. (1987), Woolcock (1983a, 1983b, 1984a, 1984b).

Genus *GRUS* Pallas, 1766

6. Siberian Crane

Grus leucogeranus

French: Grue de Sibérie **German**: Schneekranich **Spanish**: Grulla Siberiana
Other common names: Great/Siberian/Asiatic White Crane

Taxonomy. *Grus Leucogeranus* Pallas, 1773, central Siberia along Ischim, Irtysh and Ob' Rivers.
Formerly considered congeneric with *Bugeranus carunculatus*, based on morphological and behavioural similarities. Alternatively proposed to merit separate monospecific genus, *Sarcogeranus*. Three wintering subpopulations, but no evidence as yet of geographical variation. Monotypic.
Distribution. Arctic W & EC Siberia; possibly also extreme NW Russia. Three wintering areas: middle R Yangtze in China; Keoladeo (Bharatpur) and other wetlands in India; and S Caspian Sea in Iran.

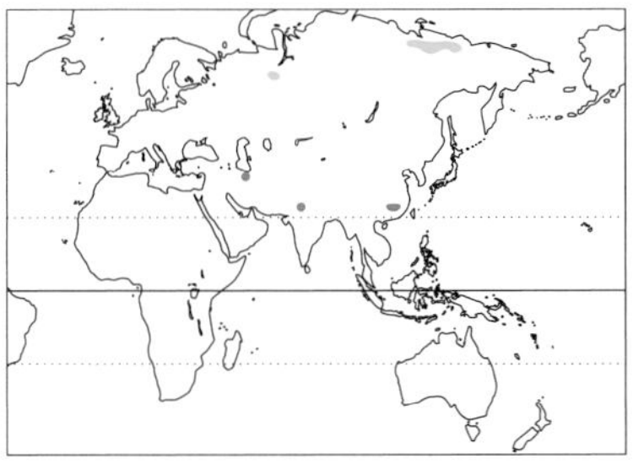

Descriptive notes. 140 cm; 4900-8620 g; wingspan 210-230 cm; male slightly larger than female. Distinguished from other white cranes, *G. americana* and *G. japonensis*, by entirely white cap with dark red mask extending from bill to behind eye. Iris yellow. Juvenile has mask feathered; neck and body plumage buff or cinnamon. VOICE: Calls flute-like and musical, quite different from those of other cranes.
Habitat. Most aquatic member of family, using exclusively wetlands for nesting, feeding and roosting. Breeding habitat in lowland tundra and taiga-tundra transition zone includes tidal flats, bogs, marshes and other wetland depressions with unrestricted visibility. Migration resting areas and stopovers in large, isolated wetlands. In China, winters in shallows and mudflats of seasonal lakes of Yangtze Basin; winter habitats in India and Iran consist of artificial water impoundments and flooded rice fields.
Food and Feeding. Omnivorous. Summer diet is broader, consisting primarily of roots, rhizomes, seeds, sprouts of sedges, and other plant materials, but also insects, fish, rodents and other small animals. On migration and in wintering areas, eats mainly roots, bulbs, tubers (especially of sedges), rhizomes, sprouts, and stems of aquatic plants; aquatic animals consumed if readily available. Generally forages by wading and digging in shallow water, up to 30 cm deep.
Breeding. Spring breeder, with start of laying varying with weather conditions: eggs generally laid from late May to mid-Jun, peaking in first week of Jun. Nest is flat mound of grass and sedge 50-80 cm in diameter, elevated 12-15 cm above water level; surrounding water may be 25-60 cm deep. Usually 2 eggs; incubation 29 days; chicks yellowish to chestnut brown; fledging 70-75 days. High rate of post-hatching mortality, due in part to aggressiveness between chicks, usually resulting in only one fledging successfully. Age of sexual maturity uncertain, but probably 3 years.
Movements. Three wintering populations. Birds from main, "eastern" population migrate between breeding grounds in Yakutia and wintering grounds along middle R Yangtze in SC China; traditional stopovers in E Russia and E China, including wetlands now protected in Xianghai, Momoge and Zhalong Nature Reserves in China. A second "central" population of 4 known birds (Feb 1996) migrates between breeding grounds in W Siberia, probably in lower basin of R Kunovat, and wintering grounds in Rajasthan, NW India; presumed migration route passes through Kazakhstan, Uzbekistan, Turkmenistan, Afghanistan and Pakistan, with traditional stopovers at L Akusat and Nar Zum wetlands in Russia, and Ab-i-Estada in Afghanistan. A third "western" population of c. 10 birds migrates between undetermined breeding grounds in W Siberia, or NW European Russia, and wintering grounds at a single marsh at Fereindoonkenar on S coast of Caspian Sea in N Iran; current information suggests a migration route that follows W coast of Caspian Sea with a traditional stopover point at the Astrakhan Nature Reserve at mouth of R Volga; in past, unrecorded numbers wintered in Mugan Steppe, SE Azerbaijan, but declined for unknown reasons, and was already only very rare migrant by 1940's.
Status and Conservation. ENDANGERED. CITES I. Although probably never common in historical times, species has suffered dramatic contraction of range and decline in numbers since 1800's. Total population was estimated in 100's until 1980's, when Chinese ornithologists discovered wintering flock at L Poyang, near R Yangtze. Most reliable surveys suggest total current population of 2900-3000 birds, most of which belong to E population. Because of peculiar distribution and specialized habitat requirements, species has been and remains more vulnerable to habitat loss and exploitation than most other cranes. In general, the three populations are secure on their remote breeding grounds, but face wide array of threats outside breeding range, including: heavy human demands upon migratory and wintering habitats, even those within protected areas, in China and India; potential hydrological changes in primary wintering area in China as result of planned dam on R Yangtze, at Three Gorges; human disturbance at many stopover points and in wintering areas; ineffective management of existing protected areas; sport hunting of cranes along C population's migration route in Afghanistan and Pakistan; and, for C and W populations, genetic and demographic problems related to their critically small population sizes. Intensive conservation efforts began in early 1970's. Protected areas have been established at several key migration stopover points and wintering areas. Winter censuses are conducted annually in all known wintering areas. Field research on species has expanded significantly, and information exchanged at regular international meetings. *Memorandum of Understanding Concerning Conservation Measures for the Siberian Crane* recently prepared and signed by most range countries. In 1992, a population and habitat viability assessment was prepared for species. A captive propagation and reintroduction programme initiated in mid-1970's, and captive-raised birds now being released in effort to bolster C and W populations.
Bibliography. Ali & Ripley (1980), Anon. (1995a), Archibald (1992b, 1994, 1995), Archibald & Landfried (1993), Ashtiani (1987), Azarov (1977), Brazil (1991), Collar & Andrew (1988), Collar *et al*. (1994), Cramp & Simmons (1980), Degtyaryev & Labutin (1991), Dementiev & Gladkov (1951a), Dey (1993), Ding Wenning (1986), Ding Wenning & Zhou Fuzhang (1991), Fan Zhongmin *et al*. (1994), Flint (1984a), Flint & Kistchinski (1981), Flint & Sorokin (1981), Gole (1993a), Gui Xiaojie (1991), Harris (1986, 1992b), Hunt, M.C. (1994), King (1978/79), Knystautas (1993), Lall & Raman (1994), Landfried *et al*. (1995), Li Fangman & Li Peixun (1991), Li Jinlu & Feng Kemin (1985, 1990), Liu Zhiyong & Chen Bin (1991), Liu Zhiyong *et al*. (1987a), Luthin *et al*. (1986), Mahan & Simmers (1992), Müller (1995), Neufeldt (1974, 1982), Nordin (1995), Patrikeev (1995), Perennou *et al*. (1994), Perfiliev (1963, 1965), Potapov, E. (1992), Potapov, R.L. & Flint (1987), Putnam & Archibald (1987), Roberts, T. J. (1991), Roberts, T. J. & Landfried (1987), Rogacheva (1992), Rutgers & Norris (1970), Sauey (1976, 1979, 1985, 1987), Sauey *et al*. (1987), Sharma & Sharma (1991), Singh *et al*. (1987), Sludski (1959), Sorokin & Kotyukov (1987), Spitzer (1979, 1981), Stewart (1987), Swengel (1992), Tang Xiyang (1984), Vuosalo-Tavakoli (1991, 1995), Williams *et al*. (1991), Wu Zhigang, Han Xiaodong & Wang Li (1991), Xu Jie *et al*. (1986), Zhou Fuzhang & Ding Wenning (1982, 1987), Zhou Fuzhang *et al*. (1981), Zhou Haizhong *et al*. (1986).

7. Sandhill Crane

Grus canadensis

French: Grue du Canada **German**: Kanadakranich **Spanish**: Grulla Canadiense
Other common names: Little Brown/Canadian Crane; Lesser Sandhill Crane (*canadensis*); Canadian Sandhill Crane (*rowani*); Greater Sandhill Crane (*tabida*); Mississippi Sandhill Crane (*pulla*); Florida Sandhill Crane (*pratensis*); Cuban Sandhill Crane (*nesiotes*)

Taxonomy. *Ardea canadensis* Linnaeus, 1758, Hudson Bay, Canada.
Races *canadensis*, *rowani* and *tabida* probably form cline, with gradual changes in morphology, and random pairing among them; these three intergrade along limits of their ranges. Race *tabida* subdivided into five populations; morphological differences among these populations have been noted, but not analysed in terms of taxonomic importance. Subspecies status of *pulla* has not been definitively established; first described in 1972, based mainly on colour differences with *pratensis*; remnant population in Mississippi was probably more widespread in past, and likely to have intergraded with *pratensis*. Six subspecies normally recognized.
Subspecies and Distribution.
G. c. canadensis (Linnaeus, 1758) - Arctic and subarctic North America and E Siberia; winters in SW USA and NC Mexico.
G. c. rowani Walkinshaw, 1965 - subarctic Canada, from British Columbia to N Ontario; winters on Texas coast of Gulf of Mexico, and in SW USA and NC Mexico.
G. c. tabida (J. L. Peters, 1925) - five breeding populations in mid-continental North America from Vancouver I to Great Lakes region; winters in NC Mexico and S USA, from California to Georgia and Florida.
G. c. pulla Aldrich, 1972 - Mississippi, USA.
G. c. pratensis (F. A. A. Meyer, 1794) - Georgia and Florida, USA.
G. c. nesiotes Bangs & Zappey, 1905 - Cuba and I of Pines.

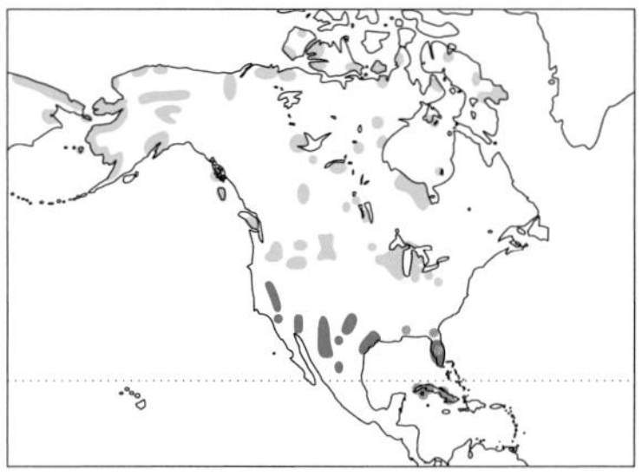

Descriptive notes. Up to 120 cm; average weight ranges from male 3750 g and female 3350 g in *canadensis*, to male 5390 g and female 4300 g in *tabida*; wingspan 160-210 cm. Grey body; only member of *Grus* with fully-feathered grey neck and head, apart from bare red forecrown; iris orange. Juvenile similar to adult, but wing-coverts, nape and back reddish brown toward edges. Races generally very similar, differing more in size than in coloration; plumage of migratory races often stained brown with mud in summer. VOICE: Calls are loud, low-pitched and rattling.
Habitat. Mainly in open wetlands, shallow marshes and wet meadows. During breeding season, the three migratory races occur in wide variety of northern wetland communities, including muskeg, sphagnum bogs, fens, sedge meadows, cat-tail marshes, stream banks and lake shores. Habitats along migration routes tend to be large, open marshes near agricultural areas. Especially important are submerged sandbars and shallows of wide rivers, especially Platte R (C USA). Wintering habitats include coastal and riparian wetlands, wet meadows, playa lakes, oak savannas, and agricultural fields and pastures. Florida and Mississippi races occur in matrix of shallow wetlands, wet prairie, pastures, and savanna. Cuban race uses relatively dry grassland in uplands, also patches of woodland adjacent to marshes (hammocks), and pine and palmetto savannas.
Food and Feeding. Omnivorous. Diet highly varied depending on season and location; common items include tubers, corms, berries, acorns, waste corn and other grains, insects, earthworms, snails and rodents; waste grain in agricultural fields is significant when available. Feeds by probing and gleaning on land and in shallow wetlands.
Breeding. Generally in spring, but more variable in S races: Apr-Jun in N populations; Mar-Apr in Mississippi; mainly Jan-Mar in Florida and Cuba. Nest is usually slight mound of dried and green wetland plants, varying in size depending on available materials; in tundra zone and in Florida and Cuba, nests on drier sites. Usually 2 eggs; incubation 29-32 days; chicks brown above, pale tawny below, with white throat; fledging period varies with race, 50-90 days. Sexually mature at 2-3 years.
Movements. S races essentially sedentary. N races migrate along several major migration routes: W populations follow routes along Pacific coast, E of Cascade Range, through Intermountain West, and through C Rocky Mts to wintering areas in California, Arizona, New Mexico and N Mexico; C populations follow routes across Great Plains to wintering areas in New Mexico and Texas; E populations follow routes from Great Lakes region to C Florida.
Status and Conservation. Not globally threatened. CITES II. Total population estimated at 500,000 birds; the most abundant of all cranes. Races *pulla* and *nesiotes* endangered, numbering 120 and 300 respectively. Hunting, agricultural expansion, drainage of wetlands and other habitat changes in 18th and 19th centuries resulted in extirpation from many parts of breeding range, as well as declines in non-migratory populations. Since 1930's, populations in Great Lakes and Rocky Mts regions have recovered dramatically. Loss and degradation of wetland habitats pose most significant threat to species as a whole. Critical spring staging areas along Platte R in C USA have diminished as result of changes in river's flow, and further threatened by water withdrawals and dam construction projects. W populations subject to regulated hunting. Key habitats are protected in reserves in many areas, including Cuba, Florida, Georgia, Mississippi and New Mexico. Restoration of wetlands has been important factor in recovery of Great Lakes population. Surveys are conducted regularly in most portions of range, and field studies of species have been most extensive for any crane. Recovery plan for race *pulla* has been in effect since 1976; under this plan, since 1981 captive-raised birds have been released to supplement wild population; in 1992, a population and habitat viability assessment (PHVA) was prepared for race *pulla*. In 1994, first comprehensive survey of habitats in Cuba to determine status and needs of population.
Bibliography. Aldrich (1972), Anon. (1991a, 1992a), Armstrong (1983), Baldwin (1977), Bennett (1989), Bishop, M.A. (1988a), Boise (1976), Brazil (1991), Carlisle & Tacha (1983), Cramp & Simmons (1980), Davis & Vohs (1993), Drewien (1973), Drewien & Bizeau (1974, 1978), Drewien & Lewis (1987), Drewien, Brown & Kendall (1995), Drewien, Littlefield *et al*. (1975), Ehrlich *et al*. (1992), Ellis, Olsen *et al*. (1992), Faanes (1990b), Flather *et al*. (1994), Folk & Tacha (1990), Frith, C. R. (1976), Galvez & Perera (1995), Gee *et al*. (1995), González *et al*. (1995), Grooms (1992), Guthery & Lewis (1979), Herter (1982), Horwich (1986), Howell & Webb (1995a), Hunt, M.C. (1994), Iverson *et al*. (1985, 1987), Johnsgard (1991a), Johnson & Stewart (1973), Kessel (1984), King (1978/79), Krapu *et al*. (1984), Krechmar *et al*. (1978), Labutin & Dregayev (1988), Lewis (1974, 1976b, 1979b), Littlefield (1981, 1995), Littlefield & Thompson (1979), Liu Peiqi (1988), Lovvorn & Kirkpatrick (1981, 1982), Luthin *et al*. (1986), Mahan & Simmers (1992), McIvor & Conover (1994), McMillen (1988), Melvin & Temple (1982), Nesbitt (1975, 1987, 1988, 1989, 1992), Nesbitt & Carpenter (1993), Nesbitt & Williams (1990), Piao Renzhu (1989), Potapov & Flint (1987), Quale (1976), Reinecke & Krapu (1986), Rutgers & Norris (1970), Smith & Valentine (1987), Sparling & Krapu (1994), Sykes *et al*. (1995), Tacha (1984, 1987), Tacha & Nesbitt (1994), Tacha, Nesbitt & Vohs (1992), Tacha, Vohs & Warde (1985), Valentine (1981, 1982), Valentine & Noble (1970), Walkinshaw (1949, 1981a, 1982a), Williams (1978), Wenner & Nesbitt (1987), Williams & Phillips (1972), Windingstad (1988), Wingate (1993), Yosef (1994).

PLATE 6

inches 16

cm 40

ssp *sharpii*

ssp *antigone*

8

9

10

11

12

13

14

15

8. **Sarus Crane**

Grus antigone

French: Grue antigone **German**: Saruskranich **Spanish**: Grulla Sarus
Other common names: Sharpe's Crane (*sharpii*)

Taxonomy. *Ardea Antigone* Linnaeus, 1758, India.
Recently described race *gilliae* sometimes still included within *sharpii*. Possible race *luzonica*, endemic to Philippines, now presumed extinct; possibly synonymous with *gilliae* or *sharpii*, or both. Three extant subspecies normally recognized.
Subspecies and Distribution.
G. a. antigone (Linnaeus, 1758) - N India, Nepal and (formerly?) Bangladesh.
G. a. sharpii Blanford, 1895 - Cambodia and S Laos; winters in Vietnam; status in E India and Myanmar uncertain.
G. a. gilliae Schodde, 1988 - N Australia, mainly in Queensland only scattered populations elsewhere.

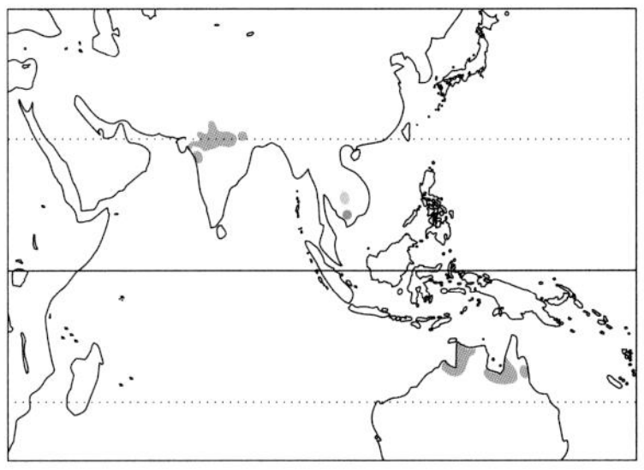

Descriptive notes. Up to 176 cm; 6800-12,240 g (*antigone*), 5400-8400 g (*sharpii*), 5200-8400 g (*gilliae*); wingspan 220-280 cm; male larger than female. Tallest of all flying birds; red skin covers head, throat and upper neck, with sparse black feathers on neck; body generally grey; iris orange. Juvenile tinged brown, head and neck feathered. Races differ notably in size, less markedly in plumage: *sharpii* smaller than nominate, *gilliae* smaller still; both lack white collar and tertials of nominate race. VOICE: High-pitched penetrating calls, loudest of any crane.
Habitat. Adapted to human presence in India, using canals, irrigation ditches, village ponds, shallow marshes, *jheels* and cultivated and fallow fields. Breeding habitat in interior wetlands of SE Asia poorly known; in dry season, shallow wetlands, dry sedge meadows, rice fields and wet grasslands of Mekong Delta. In Australia, sympatric with *G. rubicunda*, but shows greater use of upland agricultural fields and grassland during dry season.
Food and Feeding. Generalist: diet widely varied, including sedge tubers, other wetland plants, upland grasses and groundnuts, waste rice and other grains; also snails, crustaceans, grasshoppers and other insects, fish, frogs, snakes and other small vertebrates. Walks along slowly with head down, searching for food; does not dig. Forages in both wetlands and uplands.
Breeding. Nesting associated with wet season throughout range: in India, breeds throughout year (except May and Jun) with Jul-Sept peak; in SE Asia, during monsoon season, Jun-Oct; in N Australia, during wet season, generally Jan-Mar. Nest consists of wetland vegetation and other available materials; in India, breeds in large wetlands and also scattered sites amid human settlements, e.g. irrigation ditches, village ponds,*jheels*; in SE Asia, isolated wetlands; in N Australia, uses similar nest-sites to those of *G. rubicunda*, but often more shaded. Usually 2 eggs, occasionally 3; incubation 31-34 days; chicks yellowish brown, with two darker brown lines down back, and white on breast, belly and base of wings; fledging 85-100 days. Sexually mature at 2-3 years.
Movements. Non-migratory in India and Australia, but some seasonal movement, especially during periods of drought. SE Asian populations undertake limited migration from isolated breeding areas of upper basin of Mekong to delta in Vietnam.
Status and Conservation. Not globally threatened. CITES II. Currently considered near-threatened. Estimated total population 13,500-15,500 birds. Nominate *antigone* common, perhaps numbering 10,000 birds, but declining; extirpated from much of former range within and beyond India; extinct in Pakistan, probably due to human persecution, as still numerous just across border in parts of India; may still survive in Bangladesh, but only one recent record. Race *sharpii* has been devastated throughout SE Asia, and since 1960 has disappeared from S China, Thailand and other portions of its historical range; estimated population 500-1500 birds. Race *gilliae* has population of perhaps 5000 birds; considered secure. Probably extirpated from Philippines (possible race *luzonica*), where early in present century moulting birds were reported to be hunted and lassoed from horseback; no recent records, despite surveys in 1970's and 1980's. Most significant threats are loss and degradation of wetlands due to agricultural expansion, drainage, industrial development, pollution, warfare and heavy pesticide use. In India and Vietnam, human population pressures compound these threats and increase the level of human disturbance of cranes; eggs are occasionally stolen and chicks captured and raised for food; some trading reported in India, Cambodia and Thailand. Species protected by local traditions and religious beliefs in many parts of range, especially N India, W *terai* of Nepal, and Vietnam. Conservation efforts have been most intensive in SE Asia, where international agreements and collaborative conservation projects have expanded significantly since mid-1980's. In 1990, *International Sarus Crane and Wetland Conservation Workshop* was conducted in Vietnam. Comprehensive field studies of the species have been conducted in India and Nepal. There have been several surveys of wintering grounds in Vietnam, and of potential breeding grounds in Cambodia. Tram Chim National Reserve in Vietnam provides partial protection for winter habitat of race *sharpii*; ecological restoration and management of Tram Chim wetlands have been undertaken. A national wetland management plan is being developed in Cambodia, in part to protect breeding habitat. The species has also been centrepiece of environmental education programmes in Vietnam, Nepal and India. No captive-raised birds being released at present, but reintroduction plans have been advanced in Thailand and other portions of historical range.
Bibliography. Ali (1958), Ali & Ripley (1980), Anon. (1994g), Archibald (1992c), Archibald & Swengel (1987), Barzen (1991, 1994), Brownsmith (1978), Christidis & Boles (1994), Deignan (1945), Delacour & Mayr (1946), Desai (1980), Dickinson *et al.* (1991), Duc (1990, 1991), Gill (1969), Gole (1987, 1989a, 1989b, 1991, 1992, 1993a), Harris (1987, 1992a), Hesch (1987), Iqubal (1992), Kemf (1988), Lavery & Blackman (1969), Luthin *et al.* (1986), Madsen (1981), Marchant & Higgins (1993), Medway & Wells (1976), Mundkur *et al.* (1995), Perennou *et al.* (1994), Roberts, T. J. (1991), Rothschild (1930), Rutgers & Norris (1970), Smythies (1986), Suwal (1994), Swengel (1992), Tanner & Jaensch (1988), Yang Lan (1987, 1991).

9. **Brolga**

Grus rubicunda

French: Grue brolga **German**: Brolgakranich **Spanish**: Grulla Brolga
Other common names: Australian Crane

Taxonomy. *Ardea rubicunda* Perry, 1810, Botany Bay, New South Wales.
N and S populations formerly placed in separate races, with *argentea* for N birds; subspecific division no longer widely accepted, although the two populations are probably independent. Monotypic.
Distribution. N & E Australia; small populations in New Guinea, in basin of R Sepik and in Trans-Fly.
Descriptive notes. c. 160 cm; male 4761-8729 g, female 3628-7255 g; wingspan 200-230 cm; male slightly larger than female. Iris orange. Distinguished from similar *G. antigone* by slightly smaller size, small dewlap, uniform grey body and darker legs; bare skin patch in *G. rubicunda* limited to head. Juvenile has head entirely feathered, iris dark brown. VOICE: Calls lower, more guttural than in other *Grus* species, except *G. canadensis*.

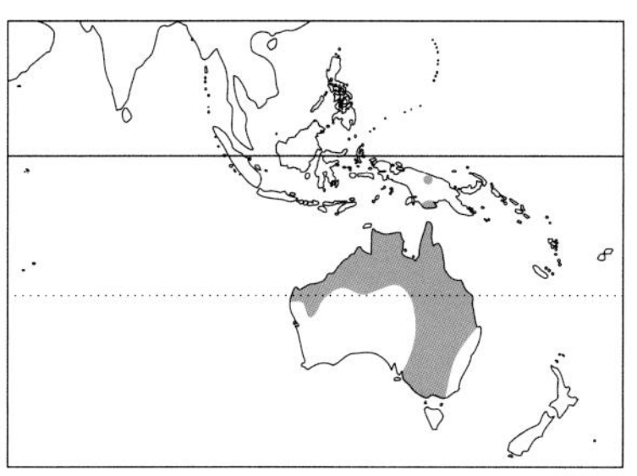

Habitat. Varies by season, and between N and S Australia. S birds prefer shallow freshwater marshes, with water less than 50 cm deep; also use deeper marshes, wet meadows and brackish wetlands; move to traditional flocking areas, including permanent wetlands, upland pastures and other drier foraging areas in summer, Dec-May. N birds more tolerant of saline conditions; use coastal freshwater sedge marshes; partial dispersal to suitable nesting areas in ephemeral inland marshes with onset of wet season in Dec. Habitat in New Guinea unstudied.
Food and Feeding. Widely varied diet. Major food item is sedge tubers, which are excavated from mud of drying marshes. Bulkuru sedge (*Eleocharis dulcis*) is especially important in N. Also takes insects, crustaceans, molluscs, frogs, small mammals and birds; cereal grains and nut crops in cultivated areas. Feeds by digging with large bill, especially in drier areas; also forages in shallow waters and wetlands, including freshwater and saltwater marshes.
Breeding. In Australia, breeding coincides with wet season in N, peaking in Feb-Mar; season less distinct in S, Jul-Nov. Nest is large mound, up to 1·5 m in diameter, of grass and sedge stems, built in densely vegetated wetlands as water levels rise. Usually 2 eggs; incubation 28-31 days; chicks grey with buff head and neck; fledging c. 100 days. Sexually mature at 3-5 years.
Movements. Non-migratory. Local movements in response to seasonal conditions. In Queensland and Northern Territory, substantial dispersal during wet season to upstream sections of coastal floodplains and to inland nesting sites; birds return gradually to coasts and form flocks as dry season advances. Inland dispersal has probably increased with proliferation of stock ponds and other small water developments. In S Australia, disperses to isolated wetlands during breeding season, returning to traditional flocking sites as dry season advances. Movements of New Guinea population unknown.
Status and Conservation. Not globally threatened. CITES II. No range-wide surveys, but current population estimated at 20,000-100,000 birds, generally stable with local declines. Still occupies most of historical range; is apparently expanding into W Australia, with retraction of range in Victoria and other portions of SE. No information available on status of New Guinea populations, but species is locally common in Trans-Fly, occurring in flocks of up to 600 birds; no recent records from Sepik region. In Australia, most significant threats are loss and degradation of wetlands due to soil erosion and sedimentation, vegetation change, and, especially in S, land reclamation for agriculture. S Australian birds also affected by land subdivision, utility lines and predation by introduced red fox (*Vulpes vulpes*). Degree of legal protection varies in Australian states. Limited field studies, concentrated in SE & E Australia. Since mid-1980's, private wetland management and restoration efforts have expanded, especially in Victoria. Surveys and education programmes conducted by "Friends of the Brolga", established in 1991.
Bibliography. Archibald (1974), Archibald & Swengel (1987), Arnol *et al.* (1984), Beehler *et al.* (1986), Blackman (1971, 1977), Blakers *et al.* (1984), Bransbury (1991), Brownsmith (1978),Christidis & Boles (1994), Coates (1985), Goldstraw & DuGuesclin (1991), Hesch (1987), Jaensch & Vervest (1990), LaRue (1979), Lavery (1965), Lavery & Blackman (1969), Marchant & Higgins (1993), Morton *et al.* (1993), Rand & Gilliard (1967), Rutgers & Norris (1970), Serventy & Whittell (1976), Storr (1977, 1980), White (1987).

10. **White-naped Crane**

Grus vipio

French: Grue à cou blanc **German**: Weißnackenkranich **Spanish**: Grulla Cuelliblanca
Other common names: Japanese White-necked Crane

Taxonomy. *Grus vipio* Pallas, 1811, Transbaikalia. Monotypic.
Distribution. NE Mongolia, NE China and extreme SE Russia. Winters in Korea, S Japan and CE China, along middle and lower R Yangtze.

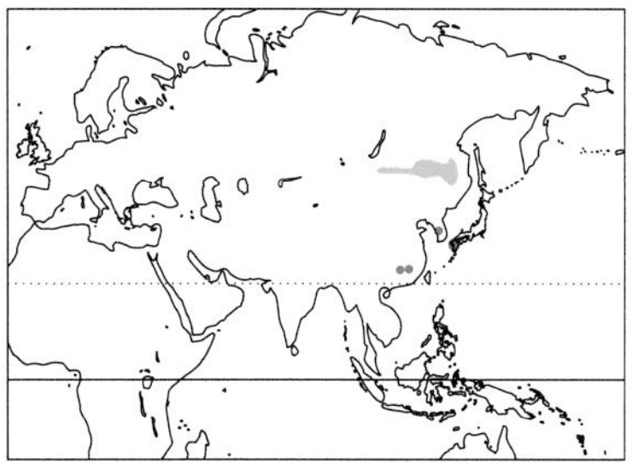

Descriptive notes. 125+ cm; 4750-6500 g; wingspan 200-210 cm. Slate grey body with white throat and distinctive vertical white stripe from crown down back of neck; iris orange. Juvenile has head entirely brown, with pale throat. VOICE: High-pitched penetrating calls.
Habitat. Breeds in shallow open wetlands and wet meadows in broad river valleys and along lake edges. Also frequents grassland and cropland adjacent to breeding areas. During migration and on wintering grounds, will use both fallow fields and wetlands, e.g. riparian and brackish marshes, rice paddies and estuarine mudflats. On Chinese wintering grounds, niche intermediate between sympatric congeners: less so than *G. leucogeranus*, but more aquatic than *G. grus* and *G. monacha*.
Food and Feeding. Feeds on roots and tubers of sedges and other wetland plants; also insects, small vertebrates, seeds and rice gleanings. During non-breeding season, consumes relatively more waste grain, seeds and tubers; rice and other cereal grains provided at winter feeding stations in Japan. Digs for roots and tubers, but forages at large for animal prey and grain; more territorial when digging.
Breeding. Spring breeder, with eggs laid from Apr to late May. Nest is mound of dried sedges and grasses in open wetlands. Usually 2 eggs; incubation 28-32 days; chicks brownish yellow with darker spots; fledging 70-75 days. Sexually mature at 2-3 years.
Movements. Birds from E portion of breeding range migrate through Korean Peninsula: several hundred birds overwinter in the Demilitarized Zone between North and South Korea; as many as 2100 birds continue S to Kyushu, S Japan, where they join the main wintering population of *G. monacha*. About 3000 birds from W portion of breeding range migrate across C & E China to wintering grounds in Hunan, Jiangxi, Anhui and Jiangsu Provinces.
Status and Conservation. VULNERABLE. CITES I. Formerly more abundant and more extensively distributed than at present, but declined steadily through first half of 1900's due to habitat loss, hunting and effects of warfare. Population began to recover in 1950's and is currently estimated at 5000 birds. Most significant threat is extensive loss and alteration of habitat in the Amur Basin, the Sanjiang Plain in NE China, and other portions of breeding range, primarily as result of agricultural conversion. Migration and wintering habitats in China and Korea, especially Korean Demilitarized Zone, are also under heavy development pressure. In S Japan, concentration of c. 40% of total population winters at Izumi, SW Kyushu, where artificial feeding began in 1952; susceptible to outbreak of disease and other catastrophic events. Species is legally protected in all range countries; has benefited from a series of bilateral migratory bird

On following pages: 11. Eurasian Crane (*Grus grus*); 12. Hooded Crane (*Grus monacha*); 13. Whooping Crane (*Grus americana*); 14. Black-necked Crane (*Grus nigricollis*); 15. Red-crowned Crane (*Grus japonensis*).

agreements in E Asia, and international agreements to protect key habitats at L Khanka on China-Russia border, and in China-Russia-Mongolia border region; these efforts were advanced at *International Workshop on Cranes and Storks of the Amur Basin* in 1992 and *International Symposium on the Future of Cranes and Wetlands* in Japan in 1993. Winter counts have been carried out regularly in Japan since early 1950's, in Korea since 1970's and in China since early 1980's. Field studies of species have expanded greatly in all portions of range since mid-1970's. Several non-governmental organizations, including Wild Bird Society of Japan, Socio-Ecological Union of Russia, National Audubon Society, and International Crane Foundation, have been active in conservation efforts for the species. Breeds readily in captivity and release of semi-wild birds has taken place on a limited basis at Zhalong Nature Reserve in China and Khinganski Nature Reserve in Russia.

Bibliography. Andreev (1974), Andronov (1988), Archibald (1981, 1992d), Brazil (1991, 1994), Chen Bin *et al.* (1987), Chong (1987), Chong *et al.* (1992), Christidis & Boles (1994), Collar & Andrew (1988), Collar *et al.* (1994), Dementiev & Gladkov (1951a), Duan Wenrui *et al.* (1991), Fan Zhongmin *et al.* (1994), Flint (1978), Formozov & Smirin (1987), French & Young (1992), Fujita *et al.* (1994), Halvorson & Kaliher (1995), Harris, J. (1991a, 1992b, 1994), Higuchi (1991a, 1993), Higuchi, Ozaki, Golovushkin *et al.* (1994), Higuchi, Ozaki, Soma *et al.* (1992), Hunt, M.C. (1994), Kaliher (1993), King (1978/79), Knystautas (1993), Li Fangman *et al.* (1991), Li Peixun, Li Fangman & Yu Xuefeng (1991), Li Peixun, Yuan Tao *et al.* (1987), Mahan & Simmers (1992), Nagano *et al.* (1992), Neufeldt (1982), Ohsako (1987), Ozaki (1991), Ozaki & Baba (1994), Pae & Pyong-Oh Won (1994), Perennou *et al.* (1994), Potapov & Flint (1987), Rutgers & Norris (1970), Shibaev & Surmach (1994), Smirenski (1980), Sonobe & Izawa (1987), Su Liying (1993), Su Liying *et al.* (1991), Swengel (1992), Tian Xiuhua *et al.* (1992), Williams, Bakewell *et al.* (1991), Williams, Carey *et al.* (1992), Won (1981, 1988), Won & Koo (1986), Xu Xinjie *et al.* (1991), Yang Ruoli *et al.* (1991), Yang Xueming *et al.* (1986), Yuan Tao & Li Peixun (1991), Zhou Chenyao (1986).

11. Eurasian Crane

Grus grus

French: Grue cendrée **German**: Kranich **Spanish**: Grulla Común
Other common names: Common Crane

Taxonomy. *Ardea Grus* Linnaeus, 1758, Sweden.
Sometimes divided into W and E races, with *lilfordi* for E birds; division based on plumage colour variations, due in part to differences in feather-painting behaviour, and no longer widely accepted. Monotypic.
Distribution. Scandinavia and NE Europe to NC China and Russian Far East; also Turkey and Caucasus, in Armenia and possibly Azerbaijan. Winters in France, Iberian Peninsula, NW & NE Africa, Middle East, Pakistan, India and S & E China.

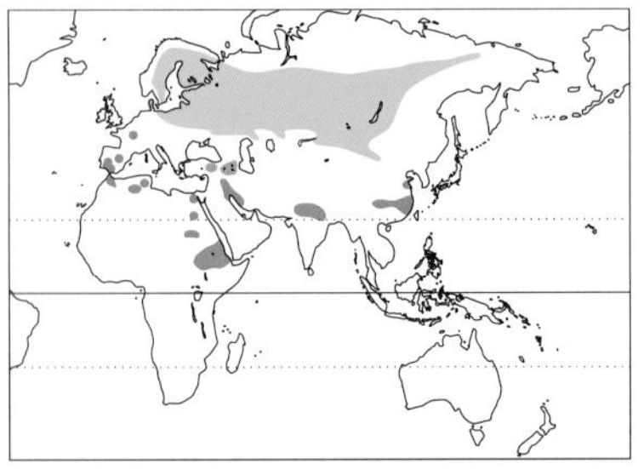

Descriptive notes. c. 115 cm; male 5100-6100 g, female 4500-5900 g; wingspan 180-200 cm. Slate grey body, with black primaries; dark head has white stripe starting behind eye and extending down nape; red skin patch on crown; iris yellow to orange. Similar to *G. nigricollis*, but has extensive white on head. Juvenile has crown feathered; body plumage tipped with yellowish brown. VOICE: Calls high-pitched and penetrating.
Habitat. Breeds in wide variety of shallow wetlands, including forested swamps (especially of birch and alder), sedge meadows and bogs. In Europe, has adapted to use of smaller natural, artificial and restored wetlands. Throughout winter range, forages in agricultural fields and pastures, and roosts in nearby wetlands or other shallow waters.
Food and Feeding. Omnivorous. Plant items generally more important, especially outside breeding season: roots, rhizomes, tubers, stems, shoots, leaves, berries, seeds of emergent wetland plants, grasses, forbs and crop plants; also takes acorns, nuts, legumes and waste grain. Animal items more frequent in summer diet: mainly invertebrates, including worms, snails, insects and other arthropods; also frogs, snakes, lizards, fish and rodents. Forages on land and in water by probing and picking.
Breeding. Spring breeder; most eggs laid in May. Nest is mound, c. 80 cm wide, of wetland vegetation; situated in shallow marsh or bog, often near trees. Usually 2 eggs; incubation 28-31 days; chicks dark brown above, pale brown below; fledging c. 65-70 days. Sexually mature at 4-6 years.
Movements. Major migration routes: from Scandinavia and N continental Europe through W Europe to wintering areas in France, Spain, Portugal and Morocco; from NE Europe through C Europe and Italy to wintering areas in Tunisia, Libya and Algeria; from E Europe and W Russia, through Balkans and across and around Black Sea to wintering areas in E Africa, Middle East and Asia Minor; from C Russia around Caspian Sea to SE Iraq and SW Iran; from W Siberia through Afghanistan and Pakistan to wintering areas in W & C India; from N China and C Siberia across China to wintering areas along middle R Yangtze; and from Xinjiang and Qinghai Provinces on Tibetan Plateau to wintering areas in S China. Small breeding population in Turkey; may breed in Azerbaijan, where until fairly recently species regularly overwintered at several sites.
Status and Conservation. Not globally threatened. CITES II. Total estimated population 220,000-250,000 birds, but only European and European Russian populations reliably surveyed on regular basis. Extirpated as breeding species in much of historical range in S, W & E Europe: last breeding known in England c. 1600, Italy c. 1880, Austria c. 1885, Hungary 1952, Greece 1965. Species as a whole stable, but W populations recovering, while some E populations may be declining. Threats include loss and degradation of wetlands throughout breeding range, human pressures on wetlands in wintering grounds, changes in beneficial agricultural land uses, and persecution due to crop damage. Hunting is of concern in some areas, particularly in Afghanistan and Pakistan. Conservation efforts mainly focused on W portion of range, co-ordinated through regular international meetings of European Crane Working Group. Key migration and wintering habitats protected in reserves and in agreements with landowners, especially in Germany, France and Spain. Populations monitored closely in Europe, and species often included in waterbird surveys in other portions of range. Ringing and telemetry studies of migration routes in Europe, W Siberia and E Asia. Extensive field studies in Europe, Russia, Ukraine, Pakistan, India, Nepal and China. Focus of education projects in W Europe, Pakistan, Russia and elsewhere.

Bibliography. Alerstam (1975), Ali & Ripley (1980), Alonso, J.A. & Alonso (1990), Alonso, J.A., Alonso, Martínez-Vicente & Bautista (1991), Alonso, J.A., Alonso, Muñoz-Pulido (1990), Alonso, J.C. & Alonso (1991, 1992a, 1993), Alonso, J.C., Alonso & Bautista (1994), Alonso, J.C., Alonso, Cantos & Bautista (1990), Alonso, J.C., Veiga & Alonso (1984, 1987), Andreev (1974), Bankovics (1987b), Bautista *et al.* (1992), Brazil (1991), Bylin (1987), Cheng Tsohsin (1981), Cramp & Simmons (1980), Dementiev & Gladkov (1951a), Deppe (1991), Dombrowolski & Halba (1987), Dowsett & Forbes-Watson (1993), Fan Zhongmin *et al.* (1994), Farhadpour (1987), Fernández-Cruz (1981), Fernández-Cruz & Araújo (1987), Génard & Lanusse (1992), Génard *et al.* (1991), George (1993), Glutz von Blotzheim *et al.* (1973), Gole (1993a), Goodman *et al.* (1989), Gorman (1995), Harris (1992b), Higuchi, Nagendren *et al.* (1994), Khachar *et al.* (1991), Knystautas (1993), Kovács (1987), Levy & Yom-Tov (1991), Liu Zhiyong *et al.* (1987b), Liu Zuomo (1988), Ma Ming *et al.* (1993), Ma Yiqing (1991), Mackworth-Praed & Grant (1957), Makatsch (1987), Melnikov, I. I. (1994), Muñoz-Pulido (1989), Muñoz-Pulido *et al.* (1988), Neufeldt (1982), Neufeldt & Kespaik (1987, 1989), Neumann (1987), Newton (1996a), Nowald (1994), Patrikeev (1995), Paz (1987), Perennou *et al.* (1994), Potapov & Flint (1987), Prange (1989, 1991, 1994), Prange & Mewes (1989, 1991a, 1991b), Prange & Petersen (1995), Prange *et al.* (1995), Priklonski & Markin (1982), Roberts, T. J. (1991), Robertson, I.S. (1992), Rogacheva (1992), Sai Daojian *et al.* (1991), Sánchez *et al.* (1993), Shirihai (1995), Smythies (1986), Svanberg (1994), Swanberg (1987), Swengel (1992), Traneving (1993), von Treuenfels (1989), Urban *et al.* (1986), van der Ven (1981), Wang Youhui (1991), Wu Zhigang & Wang Youhui (1986), Yang Dehua (1982), Zhang Yuewen *et al.* (1993).

12. Hooded Crane

Grus monacha

French: Grue moine **German**: Mönchskranich **Spanish**: Grulla Monje

Taxonomy. *Grus monacha* Temminck, 1835, Hokkaido and Korea.
Monotypic.
Distribution. SE Russia and N China. Winters mainly in S Japan; also South Korea and C & E China.

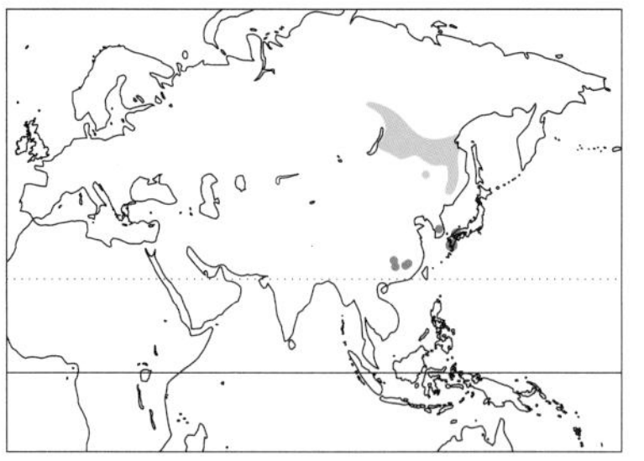

Descriptive notes. c. 100 cm; male 3280-4870 g, female 3400-3740 g; wingspan 160-180 cm. Grey body; head white except for "hood" of bare red skin above eye on forecrown; iris orange to red. Similar to *G. vipio*, but smaller, with fully white neck. Juvenile plumage tinged brown; crown black and white. VOICE: Loud, high-pitched calls.
Habitat. In breeding range, occupies isolated bogs and higher altitude forested wetlands, e.g. of larch (*Larix*). Non-breeders use open wetlands, grassland and agricultural fields. Winter habitat more diverse: shores of rivers and shallow lakes, grassy marshes, rice paddies and agricultural fields. Found at feeding stations and in agricultural fields in Korea and Japan.
Food and Feeding. In breeding areas, feeds on aquatic plants, berries, insects, frogs and salamanders. In winter, rhizomes, seeds and grains; artificial foods, rice and other waste cereal grains in Korea and Japan. In both breeding and natural wintering grounds, forages by digging and by picking food off surface.
Breeding. Spring breeder; eggs laid in late Apr or early May. Nest constructed of damp moss, peat, sedge stalks and leaves, and branches of larch and birch; situated in sphagnum bog with widely scattered larch trees. Usually 2 eggs; incubation 27-30 days; chicks dark brown above, paler below; fledging c. 75 days. Sexually mature at 3-4 years.
Movements. Migrates through NE China. Most of population (c. 8000 birds) crosses Korean Peninsula between breeding range and wintering grounds on Kyushu, S Japan. Smaller populations winter along R Naktong near Taegu, South Korea, and in S Honshu, S Japan. Several hundred birds migrate down coastal China to wintering grounds on R Yangtze in Hubei, Anhui, Hunan and Jiangxi Provinces. Non-breeders occasionally occur W to NE Mongolia.
Status and Conservation. Not globally threatened. CITES I. Conservation Dependent. Total population estimated at 9000-11,000 birds. Numbers known to have risen and fallen dramatically since 1920's. After artificial feeding began in 1952 at Izumi, SW Kyushu, population began to increase steadily. Although species might still be threatened, it is somewhat more secure than the other declining cranes of E Asia, due to absence of intensive human economic activity in its remote breeding grounds. Held in high regard in Japan, species nonetheless remains vulnerable to pressures associated with high human population density, including conflicts with farmers. Faces other critical threats, including drainage of wetlands and intensified logging pressure in taiga forests, alteration of wetlands in wintering areas of China, rapid development of key wintering areas in Korean Peninsula, and high risk of disease outbreak in the concentrated flocks at winter feeding stations in Japan. Legally protected throughout range, and has benefited from international agreements, conferences and co-operative measures to protect cranes and wetlands in E Asia. Population surveyed annually in wintering areas. Field studies were extremely limited until late 1970's; research has since expanded, especially studies of breeding habitats, winter ecology and migration routes. Key winter habitats have been secured in several protected areas. Species is well represented in captive propagation programmes, but does not breed consistently; reintroduction programmes have not been necessary to date.

Bibliography. Abe (1989), Ali & Ripley (1980), Andreev (1974), Bohmke (1992), Brazil (1991), Chen Bin & Wang Zuoyi (1991), Cheng Tsohsin (1981), Cho & Won (1990), Chong *et al.* (1992), Collar & Andrew (1988), Collar *et al.* (1994), Dementiev & Gladkov (1951a), Eguchi *et al.* (1991), Fan Zhongmin *et al.* (1994), Flint (1978), Formozov & Smirin (1987), Halvorson & Kaliher (1995), Harris (1992b), Higuchi (1991a, 1991b, 1993), Higuchi, Ozaki, Golovushkin *et al.* (1994), Higuchi, Ozaki, Soma *et al.* (1992), Jo & Won (1989), Kawamura (1981, 1991), King (1978/79), Knystautas (1993), Li Lin (1993), Liu Bowen & Sun Zhaofeng (1992), Liu Zhiyong *et al.* (1987b), Nagano *et al.* (1992), Neufeldt (1977, 1981, 1982), Ohsako (1987, 1989), Ozaki (1991), Ozaki & Baba (1994), Perennou *et al.* (1994), Potapov & Flint (1987), Pukinski (1977), Pukinski & Ilyinski (1977), Rogacheva (1992), Roslyakov (1995), Sonobe & Izawa (1987), Swengel (1992), Vorbiev (1963), Wang Liantie & Du Wei (1989), Wang Qishan (1988, 1991), Wang Qishan & Hu Xiaolong (1987), Williams, Bakewell *et al.* (1991), Williams, Carey *et al.* (1992), Zhao Haizhong (1991).

13. Whooping Crane

Grus americana

French: Grue blanche **German**: Schreikranich **Spanish**: Grulla Trompetera
Other common names: Whooper (!), Big White Crane

Taxonomy. *Ardea americana* Linnaeus, 1758, Hudson Bay, Canada. Monotypic.
Distribution. WC Canada (Wood Buffalo National Park). Winters on Texas coast of Gulf of Mexico (Aransas National Wildlife Refuge). Small experimental flock introduced in Rocky Mts, W USA; experimental non-migratory flock currently being established in Florida, SE USA.

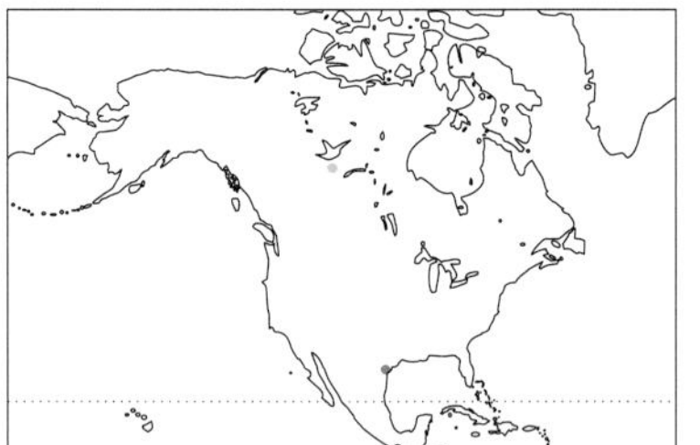

Descriptive notes. 130-160 cm; 4500-8500 g; wingspan 200-230 cm; male slightly larger than female. Tallest North American bird; pure white apart from dark red crown, dark red or black elongated malar stripe, and black primaries and alulae; iris yellow. Of the other two primarily white cranes: *G. leucogeranus* has white head, mask of bare red skin, and black primaries; *G. japonensis* has blackish neck and black secondaries. Juvenile has fully-feathered pale brown head; mottled white and cinnamon body. VOICE: Calls loud and trumpet-like.
Habitat. Historical breeding habitat was mainly potholes and other wetlands of northern plains and prairies of North America. Birds of remaining wild population nest in poorly drained area of intermixed ponds, marshes, muskeg and boreal forest; emergent vegetation of nesting grounds consists primarily of bulrush, with cat-tail and sedge common. During migration, uses wide variety of feeding and roosting habitats, including riparian marshes, other wetlands, reservoir margins, submerged sandbars and cropland. Winter habitat comprises mainly brackish bays, saltflats and coastal marshes. Experimental flock in Rocky Mts uses intermountain lacustrine and riparian wetlands; experimental flock in Florida established in savannas, wet meadows and shallow marshes and lake margins of Kissimmee Prairie region.
Food and Feeding. Omnivorous. Summer diet includes insects, small fish, frogs, small birds and rodents, and berries. During migration will also consume tubers and waste grain. Winter diet consists primarily of animal food, especially blue crabs and clams, with occasional foraging in uplands for acorns and invertebrates. Feeds by probing soil with bill and also by taking items from surface.

Breeding. Spring breeder; eggs laid from late April to mid-May. Nesting territory averages 7·2 km², but wide range of 1·3-47 km². Nest built of wetland plants; 60-150 cm in diameter, and up to 45 cm above surrounding water. Usually 2 eggs; incubation 28-31 days; chicks cinnamon brown above, pale grey or brownish white below; fledging 80-90 days. Individuals recorded forming pairs at 2 years old, and nesting at 3 years; but, on average, eggs first produced at slightly over 4 years. Maximum longevity in wild believed to be 22-24 years; captive individuals have lived up to 40 years old.
Movements. Birds of remaining wild flock migratory, as are those of experimental Rocky Mts flock. Main migration route follows a corridor, 100-300 km wide, across 9 provinces and states of Canada and USA, with important resting and staging areas at several large marshes and riparian wetlands along the way, especially along Platte R. Birds of experimental Rocky Mts population migrate between E Idaho and C New Mexico. Birds released into experimental flock in C Florida, though non-migratory, have dispersed up to 120 km from release site.
Status and Conservation. ENDANGERED. CITES I. Intensively protected, studied and monitored since reaching brink of extinction in 1930's and 1940's. Probably never very abundant in historical times; decimated by hunting, collecting and habitat loss during European settlement of North America. Main historical breeding range was in N prairies and plains of North America, from Alberta to L Michigan; wintered in highlands of N Mexico, USA Gulf Coast in Texas and Louisiana, and S Atlantic coast of USA; a non-migratory flock occurred in Louisiana. Species declined rapidly in late 1800's and early 1900's due to hunting and conversion of habitat to agriculture in main breeding range. By late 1930's, only two populations remained: the non-migratory population in Louisiana, which disappeared in late 1940's; and the remaining migratory population, which reached a low of 15 or 16 birds in 1941. This population hovered between 20 and 40 birds until 1960's, when it began slow, but steady, increase to its current level of c. 150 birds. Partial recovery of wild population has been accomplished through strict legal protection, extensive public awareness campaigns, co-operative international research and management, careful monitoring and surveying programmes, development of co-ordinated Whooping Crane Recovery Plans, and protection of the species' breeding, migration and wintering habitat. Threats include continuing loss and degradation of migration and winter habitats; pollution; vulnerability to catastrophic accidents and storms; human disturbance; collision with utility lines; illegal and accidental shooting; and loss of genetic diversity within the species. In 1975, efforts were undertaken to establish a second migratory flock by placing eggs from the wild flock into nests of *G. canadensis*, in W USA; this cross-fostering experiment proved unsuccessful, however, when the resulting birds failed to form pair-bonds with conspecifics, and hence failed to reproduce; the experiment was curtailed in 1989. An active programme of captive propagation has been under way since mid-1960's, using eggs removed from nests of wild birds; first eggs were produced in captivity in 1975. Birds are now maintained at three captive propagation centres: at Patuxent, Maryland, USA; at the International Crane Foundation in Baraboo, Wisconsin, USA; and at Calgary Zoo in Calgary, Alberta, Canada. In 1994, there were c. 120 birds in captivity at these and several other locations. Birds raised in captivity have been used to establish the non-migratory population in Florida; the first birds were released there in 1993. Further efforts to establish a self-sustaining migratory population in the wild are planned for late 1990's.
Bibliography. Allen (1952, 1956), Anon. (1994a, 1995i, 1995j), Archibald (1988), Archibald & Mirande (1985), Armbruster (1990), Bent (1926), Binkley & Miller (1983), Bishop, M.A. (1988b), Blankinship (1976, 1987), Boyce & Miller (1985), Carlson & Trost (1992), Collar & Andrew (1988), Collar, Crosby & Stattersfield (1994), Collar, Gonzaga *et al.* (1992), Cooch *et al.* (1988), Derrickson & Carpenter (1982), Didiuk (1976), Doughty (1989), Drewien & Bizeau (1978, 1981), Drewien & Kuyt (1979), Drewien *et al.* (1995), Edwards *et al.* (1994), Ehrlich *et al.* (1992), Ellis, Lewis *et al.* (1992), Erickson (1976), Erickson & Derrickson (1981), Faanes *et al.* (1992), Flather *et al.* (1994), Garton *et al.* (1989), Gollop (1978), Gómez (1992), Howe (1987, 1989), Howell & Webb (1995a), Johns (1986, 1987), Johnsgard (1991a), Kepler (1976, 1978), King (1978/79), Kuyt (1976, 1981, 1987, 1992, 1993), Labuda & Butts (1979), Lewis, J.C. (1986, 1991, 1992, 1995), Lewis & Cooch (1992), Lingle (1987), Lingle *et al.* (1991), Luthin *et al.* (1986), May (1992), May & Henry (1995), McNulty (1966), Miller *et al.* (1974), Mirande *et al.* (1993), Nedelman *et al.* (1987), Nelson *et al.* (1995), Nesbitt (1982, 1994), Novakowski (1966), Olsen *et al.* (1980), Piao Renzhu (1989), Shenk & Ringelman (1992), Sherrod & Medina (1992), Smith *et al.* (1986), Stehn (1992a, 1992b), Stehn & Johnson (1987), Stephen (1979), Stevenson & Griffith (1946), Zimmerman (1975).

14. Black-necked Crane

Grus nigricollis

French: Grue à cou noir **German**: Schwarzhalskranich **Spanish**: Grulla Cuellinegra

Taxonomy. *Grus nigricollis* Przevalski, 1876, Tsinghai Province, China. Monotypic.
Distribution. E Ladakh (NW India) through Tibet to Xinjiang, Qinghai, Gansu and Sichuan (W & C China). Winters from S Tibet-Qinghai Plateau, Bhutan and NW Arunachal Pradesh (NE India) E to Yunnan-Guizhou Plateau (SC China).

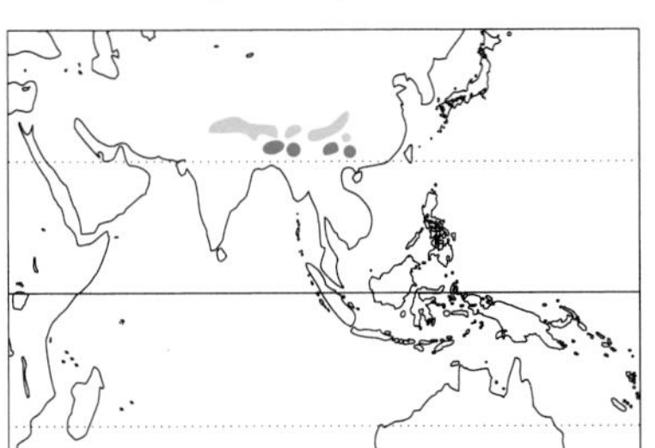

Descriptive notes. c. 115 cm; 5000-7000 g; wingspan 180-200 cm. The only grey crane with black primaries and secondaries; black neck and tail distinctive; iris yellow. Juvenile plumage greyish yellow; neck mixed black and white. VOICE: Calls high-pitched and penetrating.
Habitat. Summer habitat at high altitudes of 2950-4900 m: grassy wetlands, boggy meadows, marshes along shores of lakes and small streams, and pastures; often near human settlements. In winter occurs at much lower altitudes, down to 1375 m, typically in open country on agricultural land, e.g. deserted paddyfields.
Food and Feeding. Feeds on plant roots and tubers, snails, fish, shrimps, frogs, lizards and voles. In wintering areas, consumes waste barley, spring wheat and other cultivated crops, as well as tubers, seeds, earthworms, insects and, snails. In breeding zone, forages in wetlands, streams and pastures; in winter, mainly in agricultural fields and pastures.
Breeding. Spring breeder; eggs laid from early May to mid-Jun; in C & W Tibet, most laying in late May. Nest built in shallow peat wetlands on small, grassy islands or in water; constructed of sedges, grass, other aquatic vegetation and mud. Usually 2 eggs; incubation 31-33 days; chicks brown; fledging c. 90 days.
Movements. Limited migration between high altitude breeding areas and lower altitude agricultural valleys in SC & E Tibet, C & NE Bhutan, NW Arunachal Pradesh, NW & NE Yunnan and W Guizhou; formerly also in N Myanmar and N Vietnam, though no recent records; occasionally wanders to Nepal. Birds arrive on wintering grounds from mid-Oct to early Dec, remaining until Mar or mid-Apr.
Status and Conservation. VULNERABLE. CITES I. Total population currently estimated at 5600-6000 birds. Species has evidently declined in many portions of range since 1950's. Although numbers for species as a whole may be stabilizing, declines in wintering sub-populations have been documented since 1970's in Tibet, Bhutan and Yunnan. Loss and degradation of habitat constitute principal threats to the species; drainage and conversion of wetlands, canalization of rivers, hydroelectric projects, overgrazing, peat mining, siltation and industrial pollution have affected habitat throughout winter range and in some breeding areas. Recent studies in Tibet indicate that changing agricultural practices, especially autumn ploughing and adoption of winter wheat varieties, have reduced availability of winter food. Species has long been protected by religious traditions in many areas, and enjoys complete legal protection throughout range. Nevertheless, increasing availability of firearms has made hunting a more significant threat, especially in Arunachal Pradesh and Yunnan. Regular surveys of population have been conducted in India since mid-1970's, in Bhutan since 1978, and in China since 1988; during this period, field studies of species have expanded dramatically throughout range, and protected areas have been established at several important wintering areas in Tibet, Bhutan, Yunnan and Guizhou. Concerted programme of habitat protection and management, community development, and watershed planning has been undertaken at one especially important wintering site, Cao Hai Nature Reserve in Guizhou Province, SC China. A variety of national and international conservation organizations have worked with government authorities to support and co-ordinate surveys, research, habitat management, training and education programmes.
Bibliography. Ali & Ripley (1980), Anon. (1994d), Archibald & Mirande (1985), Archibald & Oesting (1981), Bishop (1989, 1991, 1993), Chacko (1992, 1994), Cheng Tsohsin (1981), Clements & Bradbear (1986), Collar & Andrew (1988), Collar *et al.* (1994), Delacour (1925), Dolan (1939), Dorji (1987), Dwyer *et al.* (1992), Gole (1981a, 1981b, 1993a, 1993b, 1995), Guo Juting (1981), Huang Guozhu (1990), Hussain (1985), Jin Ni Wang (1988), Khacher (1981), King (1978/79), Li Dehao (1987), Liao Yanfa (1986, 1987), Liao Yanfa *et al.* (1991), Lu Zhongbao (1983, 1986), Lu Zhongbao *et al.* (1980), Ludlow (1928), Narayan *et al.* (1986), Perennou *et al.* (1994), Qiu Guoxin (1990), Rank (1990), Rutgers & Norris (1970), Schäfer (1938), Scott, D.A. (1993), Walton (1946), Wang Youhui *et al.* (1991), Wu Zhigang & Li Ruoxian (1985), Wu Zhigang, Li Zhumei, Wang Youhui, Jang YaMeng *et al.* (1993), Wu Zhigang, Li Zhumei, Wang Youhui & Li Ruoxian (1991), Wu Zhigang, Wang Youhui *et al.* (1991), Yao Jianchu (1982, 1986), Yao Jianchu & Liao Yanfa (1984), Yu Yuqun *et al.* (1993), Zhou Fuzhang *et al.* (1987).

15. Red-crowned Crane

Grus japonensis

French: Grue du Japon **German**: Mandschurenkranich **Spanish**: Grulla Manchú
Other common names: Japanese/Manchurian Crane

Taxonomy. *Ardea (Grus) Japonensis* P. L. S. Müller, 1776, Japan.
Subspecies status formerly suggested for mainland and Japanese breeding populations, based on differences in vocalization patterns; some variation between these populations exists in morphology, coloration and egg size, but preliminary DNA analysis has shown no significant genetic distinction. Monotypic.
Distribution. Resident on Hokkaido, N Japan. Also breeds in NE China and adjacent extreme SE Russia. Winters in Korea and in and around Jiangsu, CE China.

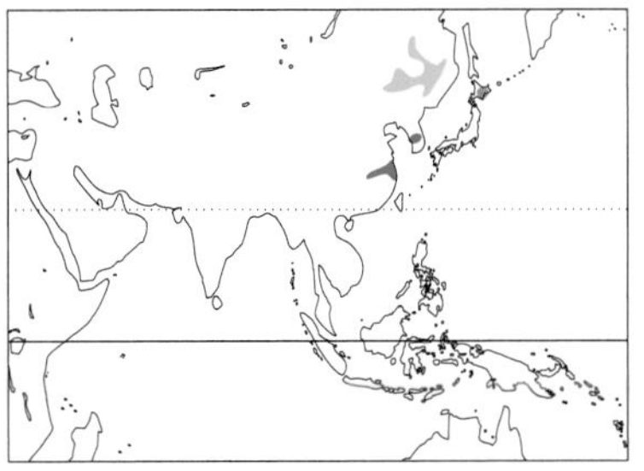

Descriptive notes. c. 150 cm; 7000-10,000 g (up to 12,000 g in winter); wingspan 220-250 cm. White primaries unique in cranes; iris dark brown or dark green. Differs from other mainly white cranes, *G. leucogeranus* and *G. americana*, by black secondaries and blackish neck with white nape; *G. nigricollis* has black neck, but is smaller, with grey body. Juvenile also white, but primaries tipped black, neck and secondaries dull brown or grey. VOICE: Calls high-pitched and penetrating.
Habitat. More aquatic than other sympatric cranes. In summer, frequents deeper portions of reed, sedge and cat-tail marshes, and extensive bogs and wet meadows. On Hokkaido, birds found in open low meadows and sparsely wooded boggy areas. Sometimes forages in crop fields, typically along dykes. In winter, occurs at rivers, freshwater wetlands, coastal salt-marshes and mudflats, and paddyfields.
Food and Feeding. Generalist. Feeds on insects, aquatic invertebrates, fish, amphibians and rodents; also reeds, grasses and other plants. Waste rice and other grains taken during winter in Japan and Korea; Hokkaido birds use feeding stations in winter. Uses "walk-and-peck" more than probing or digging.
Breeding. Spring breeder; eggs laid mainly in Apr, but also in May. Breeding territories vary widely in size, from c. 1-7 km² in Japan, to 2-3·2 km² in China, to 4-12 km² in Russia. Nest of reeds and grass built in relatively deep water, up to 50 cm deep; will only nest in areas with dead standing reeds 30-200 cm tall. Usually 2 eggs; incubation 29-34 days; chicks brown with white spot at base of wing; fledging c. 95 days. Age of sexual maturity 3-4 years.
Movements. Mainland populations migrate across NE China, dividing into 3-4 wintering sub-populations: birds from E portion of breeding range move across North Korea to wintering areas in and near Korean Demilitarized Zone; birds from W migrate along N China Sea to coastal wintering areas in and around Jiangsu. Hokkaido population essentially sedentary: some family groups remain in breeding area; others move up to 150 km to wintering areas in Kushiro District of Hokkaido. Vagrant to Mongolia.
Status and Conservation. VULNERABLE. CITES I. Second rarest crane with current population estimated at 1700-2000 birds. Population has fluctuated over last 100 years, reaching lowest point in years following Second World War. Hokkaido population has risen from 33 birds in 1952, when feeding stations were established, to over 600 in 1990's. Loss and degradation of wetlands due to agricultural and industrial development constitute main threat to the species' breeding areas in Hokkaido, the Sanjiang Plain in NE China, and Amur Basin in extreme SE Russia; proposed dams on R Amur may affect breeding populations. Wintering area in Korean Peninsula threatened by potential for conflict or development in Demilitarized Zone. Chinese wintering areas threatened by potential loss of coastal marshes due to upstream dam on R Yangtze. Other anthropogenic threats include overharvesting of wetland resources, human disturbance, intentional setting of fires in breeding areas, and poisoning. Species has benefited from intensive conservation efforts since early 1950's. Hunting prohibited in all range nations. Several international agreements have been developed to benefit this and other E Asian cranes. Wintering populations counted annually. Nature reserves provide protection for key breeding, migration and winter habitats. Marking of utility lines in Hokkaido in 1971 resulted in 70% decline in death rate from collisions. Co-operative international telemetry studies have provided information on migration routes and timing. Several international symposia and meetings have been held to exchange information on this and other E Asian crane species, most recently in 1993, in Japan. Population and habitat viability analysis conducted in 1992. Extensive education projects undertaken in Russia, China and Japan. Species breeds readily in captivity; captive-raised birds have been released into the wild at three natural breeding sites.
Bibliography. Andronov (1988), Andronov *et al.* (1988), Anon. (1976, 1981b), Archibald, G.W. (1981), Archibald, G.W. & Mirande (1985), Archibald, K. (1987), Belterman & King (1993), Bold *et al.* (1995), Borodin *et al.* (1984), Brazil (1991), Chong (1988), Collar & Andrew (1988), Collar *et al.* (1994), Fan Zhongmin *et al.* (1994), Feng Kemin & Li Jinlu (1985, 1986), Flint & Smirenski (1977), Harris, J. (1992b, 1994), Higuchi (1990, 1991a, 1991b), Higuchi *et al.* (1992), Hunt, M.C. (1994), Ilyashenko (1988), Inouye (1981), Jiang Fuling (1984), Kaliher (1993), Kamata & Tomioka (1991), King (1978/79), Knystautas (1993), Li Jinlu & Feng Kemin (1985), Ma Guoen (1982), Ma Yiqing & Jin Longrong (1987), Ma Yiqing & Li Xiaomin (1991, 1995), Mahan & Simmers (1992), Masatomi (1981, 1985a, 1985b, 1988, 1991, 1993), Masatomi & Kitagawa (1974, 1975), Masatomi *et al.* (1985), Momose & Nakamura (1983), Neufeldt (1982), Pae & Pyong-Oh Won (1994), Perennou *et al.* (1994), Potapov & Flint (1987), Rutgers & Norris (1970), Shibaev (1985), Shibaev & Andronov (1995), Shibaev & Surmach (1994), Smirenski (1980, 1992a, 1992b), Smirenski *et al.* (1988), Sonobe & Izawa (1987), Su Liying (1992, 1993), Su Liying *et al.* (1987), Swengel (1987, 1992), Tan Yaokuang (1983), Waki & Tomioka (1992), Winter (1981), Won (1981, 1988), Xue Jie *et al.* (1991), Zhou Shie (1988), Zhou Zonghan & Huan Baoqing (1984).

Class AVES
Order GRUIFORMES
Suborder GRUES
Family ARAMIDAE (LIMPKIN)

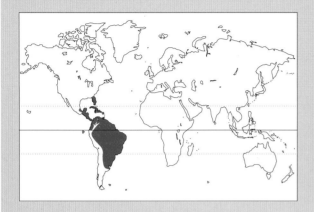

- Large brown, rail-like or ibis-like wading birds, with long bill, neck and legs.
- 56-71 cm.

- Tropical and subtropical parts of the Americas.
- Mainly in and around freshwater wetlands; also mangroves, and occasionally much drier zones.
- 1 genus, 1 species, 4 taxa.
- No species threatened; none extinct since 1600.

Systematics

The Limpkin (*Aramus guarauna*) is traditionally placed in a monospecific family within the Gruiformes, which also includes cranes (Gruidae), rails (Rallidae), bustards (Otididae), and an assemblage of other specialized birds. The cranes, Limpkin, trumpeters (Psophiidae) and rails are generally thought to constitute the core group, with the other eight as satellite families.

The Limpkin has been characterized as having had a somewhat stormy nomenclatural career. It has been variously thought to be related to the shorebirds or waders, the gallinaceous birds, and the herons, but most consistently has been positioned as a connecting link between the cranes and rails. In certain aspects it is more crane-like, notably in general anatomy; osteology and skeletal structure, especially the skull morphology; musculature; and feather patterns. However, the morphology of the bill and feet, certain external characteristics, wing size and shape, digestive system, behaviour, nesting, feather lice and egg-white protein patterns are all more rail-like. Yet another author claimed that its feather lice pointed to a relationship with the ibises and spoonbills (Threskiornithidae). Recent DNA-DNA hybridization evidence surprisingly suggests the Limpkin to be most closely related to the Sungrebe (*Heliornis fulica*), and on this basis it has been speculatively placed in Heliornithidae, alongside the three traditional members of the finfoot family; the Heliornithidae are sometimes considered to be more closely related to the cranes than to the rails.

The extant limpkin species ranges from Florida, USA, south through Central and much of South America to Buenos Aires, Argentina. However, the earliest fossil aramids were recorded from Wyoming, USA, in 54 million year old sediments of the early Eocene, and they are known to have occurred as far south as Patagonia, Argentina, in the Middle Miocene. The genus first appears in the Lower Pliocene in Nebraska, while the modern day species is known from the Pleistocene.

During the period 1856-1934, the Limpkin was regularly considered to constitute two separate species, northern birds being treated as distinct from the nominate South American form, but subsequently it has received almost universal treatment as a single species, with four races. The South American race, *guarauna*, has on occasion been split into two races, the division coming somewhere around southern central Brazil, but this proposal has now generally been rejected. Slight size differences, the darkness of the plumage, and the extent of white markings distinguish the four currently accepted races. Curiously, John James Audubon's painting of the Florida Limpkin in his 1840 *Birds of America* shows white markings only on the head, neck and mantle, suggesting that his model specimen might have been of the South American form.

Morphological Aspects

The Limpkin is a large brown rail-like or ibis-like wading bird, with long bill, neck and legs. It measures about 56-71 cm in overall length, with a 10-12 cm bill, and tarsi 11-13 cm long. In the northern race *pictus*, breeding males weigh 1130-1370 g, while there is a slight overlap in the range of the sexes, with breeding females weighing 1050-1170 g.

The deep brown colour of the plumage, shading from umber to olive brown, has a bronzy iridescence. Feathers on the head, neck, breast, upper back, scapulars and upperwing-coverts have white streaks along their shafts, while each of these, in turn, narrows to a point at the end of its feather. On the neck and head, the feathers are very small and predominantly white, giving a whitish cast. On the back, scapulars and wing-coverts, the larger overlapping feathers create broad bright white triangles, producing a striking speckled appearance; however, this feature is variable between subspecies, and is greatly reduced or even absent in nominate *guarauna*. The sexes are similar, although the white wing markings of males usually appear distinctly larger than in females, at least in the race *pictus*. Juveniles are similar, but are paler brown with thinner white markings, which appear as streaks from a distance. Chick down is lost by the fifth week. In Florida a complete pre-breeding moult occurs from February to April, and a complete post-breeding moult from August to November.

The wings are broad, fairly long, and rounded, with 26 remiges, and, when stretched out, are 100 cm or more across. The outermost primary is short, sickle-shaped, and clubbed at the end, and is used to produce a buzzing winnow during territorial and night flights. The tail is short and broad, with twelve rounded feathers. When the bird has its wings folded, the tail extends roughly to their tips and is covered by them.

The Limpkin's bill is dark greenish yellow and dusky towards the tip of both mandibles, while the eyes are hazel-coloured. The long, slightly decurved bill is notable because of a bend it takes to the right in the last centimetre or so, probably because of frequent blows and insertions into its most common

food, the right-handed apple snail (*Pomacea*). Also, the very tip of the (lower) mandible is twisted almost horizontally and sharpened against the tip of the maxilla (or upper mandible). This knife-edge is used to wedge under the snail's operculum and cut the attaching muscle, a technique that recalls that used by the two openbills (*Anastomus*), which have even stranger bills (see Volume 1, page 443). The tongue extends almost to the end of the bill and ends in split horny filaments, suggesting some specialized use during snail extraction.

The blackish olive legs are long, with the tibiae partially bare. The toes are long and slender and the claws are long and sharp, allowing the bird both to walk on mats of floating vegetation and move about easily in trees; similar developments can be seen to varying degrees in other birds that regularly move about on floating vegetation, such as the jacanas (Jacanidae) and the Shoebill (*Balaeniceps rex*).

Although appearing somewhat awkward, Limpkins are strong fliers, fast runners and good swimmers. The choice of retreat by flying as opposed to running is apparently dependent only on the situation. In order to take flight, a bird rises with a quick spring, and for short distances dangles its long legs, but on longer flights stretches them out behind. Flight has usually been described as crane-like, with the wing strokes fairly deep and steady, about two per second, and at the top of the high upstroke a noticeable upward flick of the wings. The neck is stretched forward and down at an angle, making the back appear somewhat humped in distant silhouette. Most flights are for relatively short distances within the territory, but in open marshes a bird may fly for a kilometre or more, if cover is not available. Long flights are usually carried out at higher altitudes, perhaps about 15 metres above ground, when birds occasionally sail on set wings. At the end of a flight, the Limpkin pitches abruptly downward with the wings held high, and, if alarmed, scampers quickly into cover.

When at ease, a Limpkin walks slowly with the body axis parallel to the ground and the upper neck almost vertical. Its head and neck often bob with each step, in a manner recalling rails. When foraging in shallow water, it will step high so that its long toes clear the vegetation. When surprised on the ground it typically tends to run from danger; early American artist J. J. Audubon reported that few birds excelled it in speed and it could not be caught even by the best dogs. Limpkins, including even newly-hatched chicks, are capable of swimming well, although they do so relatively infrequently; birds swim high on the water and elevate the wing tips and tail.

Habitat

Limpkins are typically found where habitat is suitable for their favoured prey, *Pomacea* apple snails, as well as for other aquatic snails and mussels. The apple snails themselves need sufficient year round water depths, sufficient submerged aquatic plants on which to forage, sufficient water hardness to manufacture shells, emergent vegetation on which to lay eggs, and fairly stable water levels in their breeding season to prevent egg inundation. Limpkins, furthermore, need water depths that are shallow enough for wading, and thus are most often found on or near the marshy or wooded shorelines of lakes and slow-moving rivers. They can also occur throughout very shallow marshes, notably in the Everglades of Florida, and well out into deeper rivers and lakes, wherever dense floating vegetation can support their weight. These aquatic habitats are used throughout the species' range, even where it occurs at higher elevations, for example up to 1500 m in Costa Rica.

However, in some parts of its range, the Limpkin uses a greater diversity of habitats. For example, in Jamaica and Haiti historically it has ranged into mid-level humid forests, wooded mountain gullies (especially in summer months), and mountain rivers. In Puerto Rico, it also occurred in dense wet forest usually on steep slopes, reportedly eating land snails and lizards; however, it is now very rare or even extirpated in this area, since much forest has been cleared. In Mexico, the species can also occupy arid brush, savanna, pastureland, hillsides and humid forests far from water, and it can be found near mountain streams at altitudes again up to 1500 m. In Panama and Brazil, birds are reported to occur in flooded farmland. Because nesting locations range from a few centimetres above water level in marshes to high tree limbs in wooded swamps, nesting requirements do not normally seem to limit acceptable habitat.

General Habits

The Limpkin is one of the many remarkable birds of the Americas, with its unique appearance, unusual diet and extraordinary calls. The use of an unusual variety of nesting sites, ritualistic courtship feeding, and a mix of monogamy and polyandry are less known characteristics. It is generally a very unaggressive bird, seemingly indifferent to other species and only infrequently fighting with its own kind over disputed territory boundaries. Indeed, in the hand, it is very calm and is not prone to peck its handler. Aggression between juveniles, including downy young, is virtually never seen, even to the extent that while one juvenile is fed repeatedly by a parent, all other siblings may stand nearby in total calm.

To date, detailed behavioural studies have only been carried out in Florida, but general notes from throughout the species' range suggest similar behaviour. Breeding territories in north and central Florida are defended by males, and most are held all year round. Territorial males will fly at intruders, calling loudly in flight, chasing them closely behind or displacing them by landing virtually onto them. Territories are also ritualistically defended with counter-calling, counter-positioning in tall trees, charging displays and occasional foot-fighting at territory boundaries. Despite strong territoriality in some areas even in the non-breeding season, elsewhere in the species' range birds readily aggregate and flock in large groups to exploit local abundances of food. There have been two reports of a crippled wing display, but the commonest distraction display is limited to the male clucking loudly and walking about prominently while the female leads the brood into hiding.

Limpkins frequently stand on one leg, like other wading birds, and perform unilateral wing-leg stretches and, less commonly, double wing stretches over the back. They do not jump-dance like cranes, although they do occasionally jump. The resting posture, day and night, is usually hunched, on one or both legs, with the neck drawn in and the eyes closed. Adults sometimes droop the wings while resting in the sun. Sitting is brief and rarely observed, although it is common in chicks and juveniles.

Limpkins usually roost in trees or shrubs at night, although when the female incubates overnight on a nest close to the water level, the male usually stands nearby. Occasionally at night adults will tuck the head under the scapulars. Nocturnal foraging is common year round, and nocturnal calling and territorial flights are common during the nesting season.

Voice

Several male Limpkins calling at once has been referred to as "one of the weirdest cacophonies of nature". A quite extraordinary variety of descriptions can be found: "a hoarse rattling cry like the gasp of person being strangled"; "little boys lost in the swamps forever"; "an unearthly shriek"; "a quality of unutterable sadness"; and "some lost spirit on the swamps, or Nickar the soulless himself, shrieking and crying"! The adult male trachea is twisted in loops and convolutions resulting in an amplified voice distinctly audible two miles away; this modified trachea is said to be similar to that of cranes (see page 61).

Males use two loud call types, which are almost always emitted in series of several to many calls. Both calls may be started or ended, or both, with a throaty rattling sound which seems to emphasize agitation. "Kreow" calls are given apparently spontaneously from perches, and are used in counter-calling with adjacent males, and also during territorial flights. Calling can be contagious and up to seven or eight males may end up calling simultaneously. "Kow" calls are loud and persistent, and are given at a quicker rate, about one per second. They are used especially in the mating season, day and night, by unpaired territorial males in order to attract mates. Up to 80 consecutive calls have been counted without pause, and such calling can continue for hours on end.

Females are characteristically silent, but they have a single common call type, "gon". When heard alone, it is usually as a single or double call when other females or juveniles enter the breeding territory, or during an incubation switch. However, female calls are most noticeable when given in a short antiphonal duet with the mate during his "kreow" or "kow" calls. Juveniles make "wheeteee" calls when adults approach with food, songbird-like chirps, and other sounds. Both males and females also give an impressive diversity of rattles and loud clucks, either spontaneously or when predators are nearby, and soft call notes to the mate and the young. Subspecific variation in calls has not been reported.

Food and Feeding

Throughout most of its range, the Limpkin eats almost exclusively apple snails (*Pomacea*), and, to a lesser extent, freshwater mussels (Unionidae) and other smaller snail species. When foraging, a bird will apparently pick up and open any species or size individual that it encounters. In the West Indies, in areas away from water, Limpkins eat terrestrial snails and lizards. Elsewhere in their range during drought or flooding they are observed readily to switch from their normal diet to other prey, including earthworms, woodworms, slugs, insects, crayfish, small crabs, frogs and geckos. In Florida and Jamaica, the eating of small amounts of rotten wood, usually before or after foraging on normal prey, is occasionally noted.

In riparian habitats, Limpkins forage by wading on the bottom or by walking on dense mats of floating vegetation. In terrestrial habitats or during drought, they grab at moving prey, or chase it, or probe into cracks in the mud for aestivating snails. Foraging in water is performed by means of visual searching or by touch alone. The latter method involves either jabbing through the surface vegetation and catching a snail before it drops off and sinks, or probing the bottom sediments with the head alternatively above or under the water. After capturing a snail or mussel, the bird moves to a solid base to extract the meat, where it sometimes creates characteristic shell piles. In rare cases, a bird will extract a snail from its shell under water. Where snails are abundant, Limpkins can capture and eat a mollusc every two to three minutes.

In order to open a snail, a Limpkin places it on a relatively solid surface with its aperture up and its spire towards the bird's feet. If the operculum is shut tight, it drives a blow or two at its inner edge; inserts the lower bill between the operculum and the columella, while bracing the upper bill against the outside of the shell; inserts the curved tip of the lower bill around the bend inside the aperture; uses the bill as forceps to cut the muscle; removes the snail's body; and detaches the operculum with scissor-like motions of the bill. The orange-coloured yolk gland of *Pomacea* females is routinely shaken loose and rejected. The entire procedure of opening a snail can take as little as 10-20 seconds, but, despite such speed, the thin shell is rarely broken.

To open a bivalve, a Limpkin places it hinge downward and directs several hard blows to the ventral posterior end where the valves meet, as this is the thinnest area of the shell; when the hole is sufficient, the lower bill is inserted and the adductor muscles are cut.

Breeding

Territories are chiefly defended by males, although females contribute, especially by displacing other females. Where water levels are steady and food is abundant, territories are held all year round, whereas poorer quality territories are defended only seasonally. On one Florida river, a colour-ringed and frequently censused male was never seen outside his territory in his 12 years of life. Territories are relatively large, averaging 2-4 ha on Florida rivers and marshes, but they can also vary considerably in size, depending on prey abundance and foraging space. Territories are usually aggregated, occurring edge to edge in suitable river and lake habitat, and also are clumped in vast and apparently uniform marshes.

In Florida, nesting typically occurs from February through to June, a few weeks later in the north than in the south; however, markedly early and late nests are fairly common. In Jamaica nesting occurs from April to November; in Cuba nests were reportedly found in every month; while in Costa Rica nesting occurs from the middle of the wet season to early in the dry season, from July to December. In South America, the nesting season varies but can generally be situated between August and January.

During the courtship period, mated pairs forage and rest side by side. Courtship feeding occurs during final nest building, and involves the male capturing and extracting snails for the waiting female. She approaches and crouches below the male or stands beside him, and will take the snail from his bill as does a juvenile being fed by an adult.

In Florida, nest-sites include an impressively wide variety of situations, including nests on piles of slowly sinking aquatic veg-

Various facets of the Limpkin's lifestyle are remarkable, none more so than the wide diversity of sites used for nesting. Nests may be built in marshland grass, shrubs or trees, or on water. Aided by its partner, this bird has piled up aquatic vegetation to form a floating raft where the eggs have been laid in a slight, unlined depression. Incubation of the largish, variably coloured eggs lasts an average of 27 days and is undertaken by both parents.

[*Aramus guarauna pictus*, Florida.
Photo: Stan Osolinski/
Oxford Scientific Films]

etation, among tall marsh grasses, in tangles of vine-covered shrubs, between bald cypress (*Taxodium distichum*) knees, on live oak (*Quercus virginiana*) tree limbs, in parasitic vegetation on trees, in cabbage palm (*Sabal palmetto*) tree tops, on cypress branches up to 14 m up, and even in more unusual sites, such as an abandoned Osprey (*Pandion haliaetus*) nest, or a large tree cavity. Nests seem to be situated to give the occupant a clear view of the immediate surroundings; reuse of the approximate or exact same nest-site is fairly common. Similar nesting habitat is described elsewhere in the Limpkin's range, and, additionally, ground-nesting is reported from Colombia and Jamaica.

The nests themselves are also quite varied. When on the water, they are constructed of floating aquatic vegetation that is merely piled up, or of dead pieces of reeds and grasses which are piled or crudely woven among growing reeds. When elevated, they are constructed of vines, sticks, palm fronds or any other materials that are within reach, and can be pulled to the nest-site; the carrying of materials to the nest site is very unusual. Nests of sticks and vines are usually lined with finer materials, while those of aquatic plants are usually unlined. Nests are roughly circular, about 40-60 cm in diameter and 20 cm deep, with a shallow egg cup depression. Nest building is generally started by the male, and he may build a few partial nests before pair-bonding takes place. The female contributes relatively equally to final nest building, and to all other aspects of nesting and the care of the young.

Eggs are laid daily. Most Florida clutches are of 4-7 eggs, averaging 5·5 eggs, and second-year and older females usually lay 6-7 eggs, while first-year females usually lay 4-5 eggs. The eggs are large for the size of the bird; in Florida, on average they measured 60·08 x 43·98 mm and weighed 57·4 g; dimensions of Argentine eggs are similar. The colour of eggs within and between sets is quite variable, but they are generally a buff or greyish white ground colour, blotched with light, purplish or chocolate brown, especially at the larger end.

Incubation is sometimes delayed until the last egg is laid, but not always. It averages 27 days and is shared, although only the female incubates at night. All eggs hatch during a period of 18-24 hours, and the adults immediately lead the downy young as a group to a newly constructed brooding platform, situated at ground or water level, near a productive foraging area. The brooding platform is about the size of a nest, but consists merely of piled or trampled aquatic vegetation. It is used only for about a week before the family relocates, either for better foraging opportunities or because of some form of disturbance. One initial platform was noted to be as much as 85 m away from the nest,

but this presents no problem, as the downy chicks swim, walk and run very ably soon after hatching.

Newly-hatched chicks are described as black by some workers and brown by others; in any case, they almost immediately lighten to cinnamon brown. Young juveniles appear to have disproportionately large legs, and the wings are late to develop. By the end of the sixth week, juveniles are almost as large as an adult but with a slightly shorter bill. Six week old juveniles can fly short distances and can find and open snails, albeit slowly.

Both parents feed the young, but by the end of the seventh week they begin to withhold food. After parental feeding stops at 8-9 weeks, the previously close sibling group dissolves. As early as 11 weeks after hatching, juvenile males begin establishing sub-territories within the parents' territory. Juveniles can start dispersing as early as at 12-14 weeks, but more usually they do so at 15-17 weeks. Second clutches are common and are usually laid when care for the first brood ends. In cases where adults have disappeared, both male and female juveniles have been observed to inherit their parents' territories. When parents remain, they eventually chase the juveniles from the territory, presumably to search for suitable unoccupied habitat elsewhere.

Adult females stay entirely within the territories of their mates during courtship, incubation and the five week downy young stage. At 1-5 weeks after the downy stage, however, females often leave the family and begin to forage and rest in distant parts of the territory, and such abandonment is especially common when high mortality of juveniles has occurred. The wandering female will forage in the neighbouring territory, when no female is present. Most of these females return to their previous mates for a second clutch, but some will pair and mate with an unpaired territorial neighbour that is still advertising with the repetitive "kow" call, thereby engaging in serial polyandry. On one occasion, a subsequent return of the female to the original mate was recorded.

Juvenile survivorship information is sparse, but one observer recorded that in 51 hatchings where the final outcome was known, 25 (49%) produced flying birds. However, the present author once followed 26 hatchings, of which none survived. The maximum known longevity is twelve years, recorded in a colour-ringed male.

Movements

In many parts of its range the Limpkin readily deserts its typical habitats as flooding or drought affect food availability. It subsequently aggregates in unusual numbers or in unusual places, where

food can still be found. Post-breeding dispersal has also been documented by a wing-tagging study, which recovered a bird from central Florida some 325 km away. Such dispersal probably accounts for the rare vagrant records in eight other south-eastern states of the USA, all occurring between April and November. One intriguing report documents a January 1901 observation of a group of nine Limpkins flying by a Bahama lighthouse well out at sea; some authors speculate on a migration between Cuba and Florida, noting about 20 records from the Florida Keys and the isolated Dry Tortugas, but others suggest this is simple vagrancy.

The Limpkin is usually described as being non-migratory and a year round resident. In parts of Brazil, however, Limpkins emigrate from their breeding marshes in the dry season, after breeding, and return with start of the rains. In addition, a partial migration has been documented on Florida rivers even though water levels remain stable. At two different sites, most post-breeding females, some of them colour-ringed, and a few males, disappeared after spring breeding, and remained absent until mid-winter, when they gradually reappeared at their previous season's breeding territories. Some females paired and successfully mated with the previous year's mates, which had been in continuous residence.

In autumn and winter, in south Florida, many Limpkins gather in the wet prairies and savannas, some in remarkably large groups. A distinct flock of 101 individuals was counted by the author, and the combination of their silence and their small white wing markings support his speculation that the group might be female migrants. It seems reasonable to suppose that migrations may occur elsewhere in the Limpkin's range, but that they have simply gone unnoticed, because some individuals remain in residence year round, as observed in Florida.

Relationship with Man

The Limpkin's common name is said to have come from a characteristic limping gait, but this feature is by no means apparent to all observers, although nervous birds do make some characteristic movements, including wing-flicking, tail-bobbing and neck-jerking. Many vernacular names mimic its calls: "Guareáo" in Cuba; "Carão" and "Guarauna" in Brazil; "Correa" in Costa Rica; "Carrao" in Venezuela and Puerto Rico; "Carau" in Argentina; and "Carrara" in the Dominican Republic. Some descriptive common names are colourful: "Mad, Crazy or Mourning Widow"; "Lamenting Bird"; "Crying Bird"; "Screamer"; "Clucking Hen"; and "Crippled Bird". Only one example of the bird's participation in folklore is reported: in Amazonia, when the Limpkin begins to call, local inhabitants believe that water levels of rivers will not rise any further.

The tame and unsuspicious nature of the species is remarkable. In the early days of European settlement in Florida, Limpkins were reportedly shot standing still, having no fear of man or gun, and they could frequently be caught by hand on their nests. In an open marsh in the 1950's, many Limpkins were observed to remain on their nests even while a deafening airboat approached to within 3-4 m. This tameness is still apparent today in areas where no hunting occurs; Limpkins often let canoes approach closely, even pecking at a paddle while they incubate on the nest. Beyond this simple tolerance, Limpkins also readily utilize man-made habitats when molluscs are not available, foraging for insects on residential lawns and in gardens, and in one case even feeding on mash put out for domestic ducks.

Status and Conservation

Throughout the Limpkin's range, the species is typically described as being locally common in appropriate freshwater marshes and swamp forest habitats. However, this was not always the case. Its tame nature, large size and excellent flavour all caused it to be heavily hunted in Florida around the turn of the century, and most populations within easy access were eliminated. Likewise, in Cuba in 1923, Limpkins were said to be rare due to hunting in their upland habitat. In Puerto Rico, hunting, forest clearing and the introduced mongoose *Herpestes auropunctatus* were blamed for the decline of a formerly abundant population, and, although rumored still to be present, Limpkins have not been recorded there since 1959. The populations of Haiti and Jamaica were also decimated, as the Limpkin was considered the best-tasting of the game birds. In all those areas where hunting pressure was great, populations were described as having been reduced to those individuals living in relatively inaccessible swamps and marshes.

Further problems occurred in Florida, as wetlands were drained for agriculture, permanently reducing the historical distribution of the species, especially in the upper Everglades, the upper St Johns River Valley, and the Kissimmee River Valley. For example, the St Johns Marsh, on the east coast of central Florida, was documented to have lost thousands of breeding Limpkins due to agricultural drainage in the 1950's. Fortunately, in recent years greater environmental regulation and major hydrological restoration projects have begun to restore more natural hydro-periods, for example, in the Everglades and the Kissimmee River Valley. Despite this, a recent analysis of Limpkin population trends in Florida, using Breeding Bird Survey data, indicates a further decline from 1966 through to 1993, although the more recent years of that period are almost stable. The Limpkin is listed as a "species of special concern" by the Florida Game and Fresh Water Fish Commission.

Except for apparently long-term declines within upland habitats of the West Indies, and a possible extirpation on the Pacific Slope in El Salvador, Limpkins apparently remain locally common throughout their range in their typical marsh habitats. However, where drainage and land conversion, hunting and severe disturbance continue to occur, local populations will be affected. Yet, because the Limpkin lives in some very inaccessible wetland habitats, populations will probably remain locally robust wherever apple snails and mussels are abundant. Fortunately, the wide distribution throughout Central and South America may allow eventual recolonization, if local populations do become extirpated.

The current proliferation of invasive exotic aquatic plants in many freshwater habitats is a modern potential threat. The native plants eaten by the apple snail are easily shaded or crowded out by floating and rooted exotics, which themselves may not fulfil the molluscs' ecological needs. As if to exacerbate the situation, repeated herbicide treatments of the exotics to keep boat channels open also threaten the health of the aquatic ecosystem. While such herbicide treatments are not suspected to be directly dangerous to Limpkins, they may harm the molluscs and certainly introduce abnormally large amounts of dead plant material, as muck, onto the river or lake bottom. If apple snail populations are adversely affected, Limpkins are bound to suffer related effects.

All the eggs hatch within 24 hours. Almost immediately the nidifugous chicks are led away in a troop by their parents to a special brooding platform, usually formed of aquatic plant material placed at ground or water level and strategically near a good foraging area. The young are fed by both parents for six to seven weeks, after which time they are almost adult size and are beginning to master the difficult art of dealing with apple snails.

[*Aramus guarauna pictus*, Alexander Srings, Florida. Photo: Dana C. Bryan]

PLATE 7

inches 7

cm 18

ssp *guarauna*

ssp *pictus*

Family ARAMIDAE (LIMPKIN)
SPECIES ACCOUNTS

PLATE 5

Genus *ARAMUS* Vieillot, 1816

Limpkin
Aramus guarauna

French: Courlan brun   **German**: Rallenkranich   **Spanish**: Carrao

Taxonomy. *Scopolax* [sic] *Guarauna* Linnaeus, 1766, Cayenne.
Shows morphological affinities with Gruidae and Rallidae; recent work with DNA suggests possible grouping with finfoots in family Heliornithidae. In past, N birds were considered to constitute a separate species, *A. pictus*. Present species formerly known as *A. scolopaceus*, but species name pre-dated by *guarauna*; in past, on occasion, South American birds were split into two races, *scolopaceus* (Colombia to C Brazil) and *carau* (S Brazil to Paraguay, Uruguay and N Argentina). Monotypic.
Subspecies and Distribution.
A. g. pictus (F. A. A. Meyer, 1794) - Florida, Cuba and Jamaica.
A. g. elucus J. L. Peters, 1925 - Hispaniola and Puerto Rico.
A. g. dolosus J. L. Peters, 1925 - SE Mexico to Panama.
A. g. guarauna (Linnaeus, 1766) - South America, except arid W coast, Andes and extreme S.
Descriptive notes. 56-71 cm; in race *pictus*, male 1130-1370 g, female 1050-1170 g; wingspan 100+ cm. All darkish oily brown, with white marks on feathers, giving speckled appearance; distinctively shaped long bill. Resembles some immature ibises (Threskiornithidae), but has much straighter, somewhat thicker bill. Female very similar to male, but usually slightly smaller. Juvenile similar to adults, but appears streaked, not speckled, with white. Races differ in extent of white markings, size and deepness of brown coloration; nominate can have virtually no white markings on body plumage.
Habitat. Freshwater river and lake margins, open freshwater marshes, margins of mangroves, and in some areas arid brush, savanna and humid forests; recorded up to 1500 m in some areas, e.g. in Costa Rica.
Food and Feeding. Feeds primarily on apple snails (*Pomacea*), but also takes other aquatic snails, and mussels; in terrestrial habitats, diet includes land snails, lizards and variety of other small prey. Wades in shallow water locating molluscs by sight and by touch; modified bill facilitates extraction of snails and bivalves from shells (see page 91). Nocturnal foraging not uncommon.
Breeding. Nesting season varies with region: Feb-Jun in Florida, all months in Cuba, Apr-Nov in Jamaica, Jul-Dec in Costa Rica, generally Aug-Jan in South America. Some pairs monogamous but some females switch mates for second clutch. Inviolate territories defended by males year round, or at least seasonally, by distinctive loud calls, chasing and ritualistic charging displays at territory boundaries; unpaired males call monotonously day and night to attract mates; courtship feeding accompanies nest building. Nest-sites diverse, from piles of aquatic vegetation to stick nests on high tree branches,

and even ground-nests. Clutch usually 5-7 eggs, averaging 5·5; incubation 26-28 days; chicks have black or dark brown down, quickly lightening to cinnamon brown; nidifugous, moving to a brooding platform of aquatic vegetation; almost fully grown at c. 7 weeks; disperse at c. 15-17 weeks. All parental duties shared. Young reach sexual maturity during following breeding season; record longevity 12 years.
Movements. Sedentary in many areas, although in Florida partial migration occurs in some breeding habitats, mostly involving females; migration also noted in Brazil, but details not well known; most numerous in *llanos* of Venezuela during period Jun-Oct; distinct local movements also noted in Costa Rica, in relation to varying water levels. Elsewhere pronounced movements occur during periods of flooding or drought.
Status and Conservation. Not globally threatened. Locally common with extensive distribution. In Florida and West Indies, many populations decimated by hunting in late 19th century and early 20th century, as species highly favoured as game bird. Wetland drainage and conversion to agriculture have also had impact on species in Florida, but loss has been slowed through regulation. Populations of Puerto Rico and Pacific slope of El Salvador have been greatly reduced or extirpated, with hunting, habitat destruction and introduced predators amongst the causes; otherwise apparently stable throughout range. Rare to uncommon and local in Panama, apparently due to scarcity of suitable habitat; very local in French Guiana; locally abundant in parts of lowland E Bolivia. Spread of invasive exotic plants in freshwater habitats is additional threat to native ecosystems, although widespread adverse effects on mollusc populations not yet noted. Drainage for development and hunting likely to continue as problems, at least locally. Nevertheless, relative inaccessibility of many wetland habitats may allow species to remain locally common wherever apple snails and mussels are naturally abundant.

Bibliography. Allen, G.M. (1925), Allen, R.P. (1961), Anon. (1983a), Bailey (1934), Barbour (1943), Beddard (1902), Belton (1984), Bent (1926), Biaggi (1983), Blake (1977), Bonhote (1903), Bourne, G.R. (1993), Brodkorb (1967), Bryan (1981, 1992, 1996), Burleigh (1958), Canevari *et al.* (1991), Collett (1977), Cottam (1936), Cox *et al.* (1994), Cracraft (1973), Garrod (1876), Gibson (1920), Hall (1950), Harper (1936, 1941), Haverschmidt (1968), Haverschmidt & Mees (1995), Hebard (1945), Hellmayr & Conover (1942), Hendrickson (1969), Hilty & Brown (1986), Howell, A.H. (1932), Howell, S.N.G. & Webb (1995a), Hudson (1920), Ingalls (1972), Jackson (1887), Klimaitis & Moschione (1987), Krajewski & Fetzner (1994), Land (1970), Lowery & Dalquest (1951), Meyer de Schauensee & Phelps (1978), Miller, B.W. & Tilson (1985), Miller, W.D. & Griscom (1921), Mitchell (1915), Monroe (1968), Nesbitt (1978), Nesbitt *et al.* (1976), Nicholson (1928), Palmer (1985), de la Peña (1992), Peters (1925), Pinto (1964), Ridgely & Gwynne (1989), Ridgway & Friedmann (1941), Rutgers & Norris (1970), Shufeldt (1916), Sibley & Ahlquist (1972, 1990), Sick (1985c, 1993), Slud (1964), Snyder, D.E. (1966), Snyder, N.F.R. & Snyder (1969), Solem (1986), Sprunt (1948b, 1954), Stevenson & Anderson (1994), Stiles & Skutch (1989), Terres (1982), Thomas, B.T. (1979), Tostain *et al.* (1992), Truslow (1958), Walkinshaw (1982b), Wetmore (1916, 1965), Wetmore & Swales (1931).

Class AVES
Order GRUIFORMES
Suborder GRUES
Family PSOPHIIDAE (TRUMPETERS)

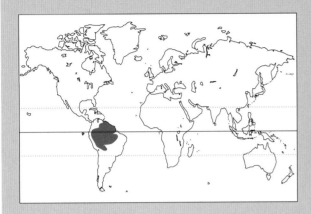

- Medium-sized terrestrial birds, with fairly long neck and legs, short, stout bill and hump-backed appearance.
- 45-52 cm.

- N South America.
- Dense tropical forest.
- 1 genus, 3 species, 7 taxa.
- No species threatened; none extinct since 1600.

Systematics

Although systematists agree that the trumpeters (Psophiidae) belong in a family of their own in the order Gruiformes, there is rather less of a consensus regarding which of the other gruiform families is most closely related to them. This problem essentially arises from the combination of a lack of psophiid fossils and differences in opinion as to which characteristics of living psophiids best indicate their evolutionary relationships with other families.

In the late nineteenth century, several of the earliest taxonomists to examine psophiids in detail decided that they were most closely related to the seriemas (Cariamidae) and the Kagu (Rhynochetidae). This view was held by most systematists until 1930, when A. Wetmore proposed that cranes (Gruidae) and limpkins (Aramidae) were trumpeters' closest relatives. This second construct has been supported for the most part by subsequent systematists, including J. J. Morony, W. J. Bock and J. Farrand, who in their 1975 publication grouped trumpeters, cranes, the Limpkin (*Aramus guarana*) and rails together in the suborder Grues.

However, more recent work by J. Cracraft, comparing derived characters of the skeletal anatomy of fossil and living gruiform families, suggests that trumpeters may be most closely related to the seriemas and an extinct family of birds, the Phororhacidae, and second most closely related to the Kagu (*Rhynochetos jubatus*) and the Sunbittern (*Eurypyga helias*, Eurypygidae). In light of these findings, Cracraft proposed expanding the suborder Grues to include these four families, in addition to the trumpeters, cranes and Limpkin, and placing the rails by themselves in their own suborder. Alternatively, C. G. Sibley and J. E. Ahlquist's comparisons of the DNA of living species suggests that trumpeters are most closely related to cranes, the Limpkin and finfoots (Heliornithidae), and second most closely related to the seriemas and the Kagu. They place these six families, along with the Sunbittern and the bustards (Otididae) in the same suborder.

Both the paleontological evidence and DNA comparisons suggest that the psophiids probably originated some time in the late Cretaceous or early Tertiary approximately 70-60 million years ago. The trumpeter family currently consists of a single genus and three species which occupy non-overlapping ranges in the northern half of South America. The three species are almost entirely separated by major rivers: the Grey-winged Trumpeter (*Psophia crepitans*) occurs north of the Amazon; the Pale-winged Trumpeter (*Psophia leucoptera*) is found mostly south of the Amazon and west of the Madeira; and the Dark-winged Trumpeter (*Psophia viridis*) occurs south of the Amazon and east of the Madeira. The three species are very similar in appearance, and differ primarily in the coloration of their wings and lower throat (see Morphological Aspects). J. T. Zimmer proposed combining the Grey-winged and the Pale-winged into a single species, but H. W. and M. Koepcke report that local hunters around Iquitos, Peru, claim that these two species co-exist there and do not interbreed, which if verified, would mean that they merit treatment as two legitimate species.

The three trumpeter species are further divided into subspecies based on subtler differences in their coloration and differences in their distribution, which again appears to have been determined in part by the course of the River Amazon and some of its larger tributaries. Within the Grey-winged Trumpeter, nominate *crepitans* occurs mainly to the east of the Rio Negro, a northern tributary of the Amazon, while the race *napensis* occurs mainly to the west of this river. In the Pale-winged Trumpeter, nominate *leucoptera* occurs south of the Amazon, while *ochroptera* is found north of it. Based on aspects of its appearance, such as its ochraceous wing patch (see Morphological Aspects), *ochroptera* has traditionally been considered to be a subspecies of the Pale-winged Trumpeter; some systematists, however, feel that the geographical location of *ochroptera*, on the opposite side of a wide stretch of the Amazon from nominate *leucoptera*, and its distribution, nestled between the ranges of the two accepted races of the Grey-winged, make it more likely to be a race of that species. Nevertheless, the western portion of the *ochroptera* population is thought to be in contact with race *napensis* of the Grey-winged, and there is no strong evidence that these two forms have interbred, which supports the idea that *ochroptera* is a race of the Pale-winged rather than of the Grey-winged.

Three subspecies of Dark-winged Trumpeter are found south of the Amazon, and appear to have been separated into distinct populations by some of its large southern tributaries. Nominate *viridis* is separated from *P. l. leucoptera* to its west by the Madeira, and from *P. v. dextralis* to its east by the Tapajós. The *dextralis* population extends to the east, where it is separated from *P. v. obscura* by the Tocantins River. A fourth subspecies, *P. v. interjecta*, was described by L. Griscom and J. C. Greenway based on a single specimen. They suggested that this race formed a population on the western bank of the Tocantins, but subsequent descriptions of this form suggest that it is probably only an intermediate population which represents an intergradation between the *dextralis* and *obscura* populations.

It has been proposed that the three trumpeter species arose during the Pleistocene period, at which time the rain forests of South America underwent a series of contractions and expansions, which paralleled the growth and decline of the major glaciers in the temperate zone. During glacial episodes, the broad expanse of Amazonian rain forest is thought to have shrunk into a number of smaller isolated patches, or refugia, which were separated from each other by more arid savanna zones. It is thought that what was once a single pan-Amazonian species of trumpeter prior to the Pleistocene, began to differentiate into separate species when different parts of the population became restricted to several isolated Pleistocene rain forest refugia. As the rain forest re-expanded following these periods of contraction, the Amazon River and its major tributaries helped to act as barriers to keep these ecologically similar species separated. It is also thought that these rivers separated populations of the same species as they re-expanded into their prior range, leading to the creation of the various trumpeter subspecies that are recognized.

Morphological Aspects

Trumpeters are about the size of a domestic chicken, measuring in the region of 49 cm and weighing up to 1·5 kg. They have a somewhat hump-backed appearance, and superficially resemble some of the larger gallinaceous birds more than they resemble other Gruiformes. Trumpeters appear to have stout bodies, but this is largely a result of the wings being held in a slightly arched and fanned-out manner, so that they completely cover the sides and back of the body and the very short tail. When the wings are lifted, the true slightness of the body is revealed.

The head and neck are covered with short, dense, velvety-looking feathers, which contribute to making the head appear somewhat small in relation to the rest of the body and to making the neck look thin. The eyes are large and dark, and the neck is long and is typically held in an S-shaped posture, which gives the bird a rhea-like profile and accentuates the hump-backed appearance. The bill bears some resemblance to those of gallinaceous birds, being short, relatively stout, slightly curved, and with a sharp tip. It is used for feeding on a range of different-sized objects, from tiny insect larvae to fruits up to 25 mm in diameter which are swallowed whole, and it is also used for removing fruit pulp surrounding the seeds of larger fruits, and occasionally for killing small vertebrates such as snakes (see Food and Feeding).

As is true for many avian species with terrestrial habits, a trumpeter's legs are strong and quite long. The front toes are sturdy, and the hind toe is elevated, as it is in a number of the other Gruiformes, including the cranes and the rails. Trumpeters spend most of their day walking around their territory, foraging for fruit and invertebrates on the forest floor. Pale-winged Trumpeters normally travel at a pace about equivalent to that of a person on a leisurely walk, but they are also able to run very fast. Among undisturbed trumpeters, running is most commonly observed among individuals that are playing or are chasing intruders off their territory (see General Habits). Trumpeters also run or fly off to safety when they encounter terrestrial predators, such as jaguars, ocelots or humans.

The wings are short and rounded, and, although the birds have relatively large pectoral muscles, their powers of flight are weak, allowing them to fly for short distances only. Trumpeters are more inclined to walk around a small obstacle, such as standing water, than to fly over it. Flight is usually limited to getting to and from trees where they roost and nest, escaping from terrestrial predators, and the occasional crossing of narrow streams or channels. Although trumpeters have been reported by some authors to be able to swim, they appear only to do so when they exhaust their powers of

The trumpeters, three allopatric species of somewhat chicken-like birds, are found only in the humid equatorial forests of the Amazon Basin. In overall appearance the three are very similar, but they are differentiated most notably by the coloration of the wings and, to a lesser extent, of the lower foreneck. The Pale-winged Trumpeter, for example, has a striking white to ochre hind-wing patch with iridescent wing-coverts. The seeming corpulence of the body is deceptive: the wings are held somewhat arched and distended, thus concealing the rather slight body structure, and contributing to give the bird a hunch-backed look; this is accentuated by the small head and slender neck, the latter habitually held in an S-bend position.

[*Psophia leucoptera leucoptera*, Tambopata Reserve, Peru. Photo: Günter Ziesler]

The trumpeter's short, dense neck and head feathers contrast strongly with the much laxer soft plumage of the wings and mantle. This Dark-winged Trumpeter is easily identified by the dull greenish colouring on the upperparts; it also shows off the iridescent purple on the lower part of the foreneck. Note the large, dark eye and the stout, downcurved bill with its sharp tip, handy for removing pulp from large fruits and similarly for dealing a deathblow to a small snake.

[Psophia viridis viridis, Amazonas, Brazil. Photo: Luiz Claudio Marigo]

flight, as they attempt to fly across water, for instance to escape from gunfire. Under normal conditions, they do not swim and do not attempt to cross rivers or other wide bodies of water.

Male and female trumpeters are identical in appearance, although adult male Pale-winged Trumpeters weigh on average about 10% more than adult females; data on adult weights are scant for the other two species. Trumpeters have a predominantly black plumage with the exception of their secondaries and inner wing-coverts, which are grey in the Grey-winged, ochre to white in the Pale-winged, and dark green in the Dark-winged. When the wings are held in their resting position, the contrastingly coloured secondaries and wing-coverts form a large distinctive oval patch that covers much of the back, the sides and the rump. This "hind-wing patch" is given a soft and uniform appearance by the similarly coloured, overlying, long hair-like filaments present on the lower portions of the inner wing-coverts.

The contrastingly coloured hind-wing patch appears to facilitate maintenance of visual contact among individuals in groups that are travelling or foraging. It also appears to play a role in accentuating some of the inter-individual social displays that are performed with the wings (see General Habits). Additionally, the patch appears to convey some information about the age of the individual bird. In Pale-winged Trumpeters, the parts of the secondaries that form the hind-wing patch are darker brown in young individuals than in birds that are a year old or more, with the result that young birds have a hind-wing patch that is darker than older birds; it is not known whether this phenomenon also occurs in the other species.

Once a young Pale-winged Trumpeter's first full set of feathers has grown in, it initiates a pattern of gradual year round moult, replacing one to several primaries or secondaries at a time. The moult patterns of the other two species are not known, but are presumed to be similar.

Habitat

Trumpeters live in dense tropical forests in the Amazon and Orinoco Basins of South America, where they are year round residents. They are found in the cloud forest that covers the eastern foothills of the Andes at elevations as high as 750 m, and their range extends far into the eastern lowland rain forests of Amazonia. Trumpeters tend to be heavily hunted near human settlements (see Status and Conservation), and for this reason are most abundant in the interior of large areas of forest in which there has been no long-term detrimental impact by humans.

Although little is known about Dark-winged Trumpeters, Pale-winged Trumpeters defend, and Grey-winged Trumpeters appear to defend, permanent year round territories, on which they feed, roost and breed. In a five-year study of wild Pale-winged Trumpeters, the present author found that territories were very large, ranging from 58 ha to 88 ha, with an average of 72 ha, and that all forested habitat was occupied by territorial groups. A series of experimental manipulations of the density of fallen ripe fruit on Pale-winged Trumpeters' territories at different times of year produced results which suggest that the territories need to be large to provide the resident group with sufficient quantities of fruit during periods of low food abundance, such as occur during the dry season.

Trumpeters' territories can contain a variety of different forest types, including mature forest, late and early successional forest, and small areas of seasonally flooded swamps. Pale-winged Trumpeters feed throughout the area encompassed by their territories, but most heavily utilize areas of forest that are in late successional or mature stages, where there is a high diversity of plant species, a high density of trees, and a relatively open understorey, allowing for ease of travel and facilitating detection of predators. Trumpeters also forage in early successional forest that is growing back, in regions where rivers have shifted course and laid down new muddy beaches, or where vegetation is growing back over sediment-filled lakebeds. As forests begin to recolonize such regions, they pass through a series of successional stages, some of which contain relatively high densities of fruiting trees, such as *Cecropia tesmanii* or *Ficus*, which produce fruit that is eaten by trumpeters. The areas of early successional forest that are used by Pale-winged Trumpeters have an understorey that ranges from moderately dense to fairly open, and a moderate density of trees that provide a covering canopy. All three species appear to be wary of entering regions of the forest that have a low density of trees or other covering vegetation.

Trumpeters obtain their drinking water throughout the year from streams or channels in the forest, or from pools that form on the forest floor as a result of rainfall. Much of the lowland rain forest that they inhabit becomes partially flooded during the rainier portion of the year, at which time the birds walk around or fly across the areas of standing water that form on their territories. J. Price noted that on average about 15% of a Pale-winged Trumpeter group's territory might be covered with water at the peak of the rainy season, but the present author found that the substantial increase in the abundance of fallen fruit at this time of year more than offsets the loss of feeding area due to flooding.

As a general rule, trumpeters roost in the branches of trees in different parts of their territory from one night to the next, and lay their clutches in elevated, hollowed out, hole-like cavities in tree trunks. Pale-winged Trumpeters show a special preference for cavities that have been excavated in the elevated bulge that is characteristic of *Iriartia* palm trees. These palms grow in mature forest, and are harvested in settled areas both for their bark, which is used to make strong, termite-proof wood planks, and for the delectable "heart of palm" that grows in the centre of the tree crown.

General Habits

Trumpeters live all year round in groups of 3-13 individuals. Although very few data are available on wild Grey- or Dark-winged Trumpeters, Pale-winged Trumpeter groups contain an average of seven birds, which usually include three unrelated adult males, two unrelated adult females, and sexually immature offspring.

Trumpeter groups are quite cohesive and social, and members travel, forage, defend their territory, preen, play, bathe and roost together. On a typical day, a Pale-winged Trumpeter group flies down from the night-time roost to the forest floor at first light. There usually follows a short period of social interaction, during which young birds and subordinate adults approach more dominant birds and "Wing-spread", crouching before the dominant bird, spreading the primaries and secondaries horizontally, and giving a high-pitched twittering call that mimics the twittering call of young chicks (see Voice). This display of subordinance is given by individuals of all ages, from newly hatched chicks to adults, and is always directed towards individuals that are higher in dominance rank than the displaying bird.

Within Pale-winged Trumpeter groups, adult individuals have a within-sex dominance hierarchy, and usually limit social display to other individuals of the same sex. Chicks that are three months of age or younger perform the Wing-spread display frequently to all birds in their group, and older birds perform the display regularly during social interactions that occur throughout the day. The Wing-spread display puts the displaying individual in a vulnerable position, and also prominently exhibits the secondaries, which are darker in juvenile birds than in adults (see Morphological Aspects). By displaying their juvenile plumage, or mimicking juvenile birds, subordinate individuals appear to be acknowledging their subordinate status to more dominant individuals. Dominant individuals frequently respond to subordinates that perform the Wing-spread display with a "Wing-flick" display, during which the dominant bird rapidly flicks its folded wings forward to a vertical position and then drops them back down to cover the back, several times in succession. The Wing-flick display appears to be a means by which a dominant trumpeter may non-aggressively affirm its dominance over a subordinate individual.

After several minutes of social interaction, the group sets off walking, and usually travels directly to a large fruiting tree, where the birds feed on ripe fruits that have fallen to the ground. The group typically spends the day traversing its territory, feeding at different fruiting trees and hunting for arthropods in the

Trumpeters live in well organized social groups, and bathing is one of the many activities that are performed in small parties, as is also the case, for example, of foraging, preening and roosting. Bathing is important for cleaning the plumage and helping to remove any unwanted parasites. This Grey-winged Trumpeter enjoys a dip in a shallow forest pool, immersing itself partly and moving the wings vigorously about. It has been reported that trumpeters are capable of swimming, although when they encounter major water barriers, they normally prefer to walk round or fly over.

[Psophia crepitans, Brazil.
Photo: R. Seitre/Bios]

leaf litter. During the course of its daily travels, a group may detect another group intruding on its territory. Trumpeters have excellent hearing and can detect the presence of groups that are several hundred metres distant, and inaudible to the human ear. When they detect an intruding group, Pale-winged Trumpeters respond immediately, running silently at full speed towards them. If the intruders hear the residents coming and retreat rapidly, they may be able to escape, leaving the territory before the resident group catches up with them, but usually the residents catch the intruders while they are still trespassing and a fight ensues.

During territorial fights between two groups, the residents chase the intruders towards the residents' territorial boundary. Resident birds chase after individuals of the same sex in the opposing group with their heads lowered, and their wings "back-arched", or held slightly arched above their backs, with their flight-feathers fanned down so that they almost touch the ground. If a resident catches up with an intruder, it may peck it and then jump into the air, flapping its wings and kicking forward like a fighting cock. If it succeeds in knocking the other bird over, it may continue to alternate between pecking and kicking forward until the fallen bird is able to get up and either flee or fight back.

During territorial fights, in addition to chasing and attacking intruders, the resident birds give the loud territorial call for which the trumpeters have received their vernacular name (see Voice). It is usually the females and juveniles that stand and call, while the males continue to chase after individuals in the other group. After a resident Pale-winged Trumpeter group has fought an intruding group and chased it to a territorial boundary, males in the two groups sometimes interact in a less aggressive manner, approaching each other to perform subordinate Wing-spread and dominant Wing-flick displays, and occasionally offering food to each other, in a manner described in more detail below.

Subordinate adult male Pale-winged Trumpeters sometimes transfer between groups during territorial fights. The lower the rank of the male, the more likely he is to transfer. These transfers appear to allow males to assess whether reproductive opportunities may be better in other groups (see Breeding), as a male always returns to his original group within a few weeks, unless he attains a position of higher dominance status in the new group.

The amount of time that Pale-winged Trumpeter groups spend in loafing activities is related to the amount of ripe fallen fruit that is available on their territories. When little fallen fruit is available, groups spend most of the day actively searching for food. When there is an abundance of fallen fruit, they tend to follow a more relaxed schedule, travelling slowly and occasionally flipping over leaves to look for arthropods (see Food and Feeding), and taking longer breaks to preen or, on hot days, to bathe and to sun.

Preening is frequently a social activity among Pale-winged Trumpeters. Adults of the same sex will approach each other and solicit preening by bowing down their heads before one another, and juveniles will approach other juveniles or adults and do the same. A trumpeter will preen mites and small bits of dried skin from another bird's head and upper neck, rapidly opening and closing its bill in these regions. The sensation caused by such preening appears to be pleasurable to the recipient, which usually closes its eyes, further lowers its head, and, at times, relaxes to the point where it may briefly lose its balance. The individual that has been preened usually reciprocates by preening the preener. Dominant individuals preen subordinates and vice versa, and observations show that either of the birds is equally likely to be the first to solicit and receive preening from the other.

When food is relatively abundant, feeding is also sometimes a social activity. A Pale-winged Trumpeter will pick up a fruit or an arthropod in its bill, hold its head high with its wings slightly arched over its back, and parade around giving a repeated, medium-pitched single note call. Birds of the same sex or juveniles will then run over and beg for the food, crouching down, giving a food-begging call (see Voice) and twittering

submissively. The individual carrying the food usually keeps it for several seconds, or sometimes several minutes, before offering to feed it to one of the begging birds. The food is usually eaten immediately by the begging bird, but sometimes it can be passed back and forth several times between the donor and the recipient before one of them finally swallows it. Dominant individuals will beg for food from subordinate birds, but the dominant bird may stop behaving submissively and grab the food away, if the subordinate does not relinquish it after several seconds.

Play is a loafing activity that can involve a single bird, several birds or the whole group. During play, Pale-winged Trumpeters engage in many forms of behaviour that are similar to those observed during territorial fights. Individuals flap their wings, jump into the air and run in short bursts, with the head lowered and the wings back-arched. Birds also attack objects such as leaves or fallen twigs, alternating between pecking and kicking forward at them. When more than one bird plays, the individuals involved usually alternate between attacking objects by themselves and chasing after one another. In the middle of a chase, two birds will sometimes face off, raise their necks, and peck at each other without making contact for a short period of time, and then split up and chase after other individuals. Bouts of play by one or more individuals usually do not last more than a few minutes.

The trumpeters' day comes to an end after the sun has set and the forest has begun to darken, when they fly 8-15 m up to roost in the branches of trees. Individuals within a group usually spread out onto different branches in the same tree or in several different trees. Groups do not have specific roosting sites that they use on a regular basis.

Voice

In general, trumpeters are quite vocal birds, and produce a variety of different calls which serve a wide range of functions. The call for which trumpeters are named does not sound very trumpet-like, but is quite loud and consists of a quick descending series of 3-5 staccato notes followed by a long, low-pitched, descending resonant vibrato "Oh-oh-oh-oh-oooooooooh". All birds except chicks can produce this call, and it is most frequently used by resident groups to proclaim their territorial occupancy. During territorial fights the resident group calls and chases the intruding group, while the intruders usually remain silent until they have retreated back onto their own territory, at which point they return the territorial call. At night, all groups produce this territorial call from their roosts more or less simultaneously. Starting about two hours after sunset, members of one group will call and then other groups will respond, each group calling for a total of about one to two minutes. These calling bouts appear to be used to announce territorial occupancy, and continue throughout the night at intervals of about two and a half hours. When two territorial groups roost in close proximity to each other near a shared territorial boundary, the following morning, after flying down from their night-time roost, they will usually run towards the shared boundary, where each group will then stand on its respective side and exchange territorial calls.

Various other types of call are produced by Pale-winged Trumpeters during social interactions. An aggressive threat call is quite similar to the staccato notes that make up the first part of the trumpeters' territorial call, except that it has a harsher, more cackling sound and often consists of ascending notes. The high-pitched twittering that is one of the first calls produced by newly hatched chicks is retained into adulthood, and is given frequently by subordinate individuals during social interactions with more dominant birds. The chicks' food-begging call, consisting of two short pure tones, the second higher in pitch than the first, is also used by adults when they beg for food from another individual (see General Habits). An individual carrying food which it intends to feed to another bird gives a somewhat nasal "enhh-enhh-enhh-enhh..." call that consists of a soft, medium-pitched short note that is repeated at medium speed.

Trumpeters are highly frugivorous. It is estimated that 90% of their diet consists of fruit pulp, the remaining 10% being made up of arthropods and small vertebrates. The Pale-winged Trumpeter forages on the forest floor, for the most part relying on the large primates to knock down ripe fruits from the branches above. There is no need to follow the monkeys as they search for fruiting trees, as the competitors for fallen fruit are few.

[*Psophia leucoptera leucoptera*, Manu National Park, Peru. Photo: Peter T. Sherman]

This same call may be given by adult males or females during the short period of solicitation that may precede copulations (see Breeding).

Pale-winged Trumpeters also produce distinct calls to alert other group members to potential predators. Individuals react to terrestrial predators, such as felids or humans, or to other types of terrestrial disturbance, by producing loud, sharp squawks. Individuals react to potential aerial predators, such as raptors perched in trees or flying overhead, by producing a low-pitched, low-volume call that is a mixture of a hum and a growl. Pale-winged Trumpeters also produce a distinctive "hm-hm-hm-hm-hm..." call on encountering a snake. This call consists of a short, rapidly repeated medium-pitched note that is given by the individual that discovers the snake, and by other individuals which join it, while they investigate the snake from a distance of some 50-100 cm away. Small non-poisonous snakes under 25 cm long are usually investigated briefly, and then killed and eaten, while larger snakes are investigated for several minutes or longer, throughout which time all of the birds investigating the snake produce this unmistakable call.

Food and Feeding

Trumpeters are primarily frugivorous. C. Érard, M. Théry and D. Sabatier found that fruit pulp accounted for 90% of the dry weight stomach contents of Grey-winged Trumpeters that were collected at different times of year in French Guiana. Similarly, the pulp of ripe fruit accounted for 90% of the dry weight, and 88% of the total calories, ingested by adult Pale-winged Trumpeters throughout the year. Trumpeters are unable to remove husks from most fruit, and thus feed mainly on soft fruits that lack thick protective coverings. Small fruits of under 20 mm are usually swallowed whole, while pulp may be pecked away from larger fruits. All seeds that are swallowed are defecated intact and unscarred.

Although trumpeters remove fruit from some small plant species that grow close to the forest floor, the majority of the fruit that they ingest comes from tree species of medium to large height and crown diameter, that produce substantial quantities of fruit. When ripening fruit is present, these tree species attract a variety of arboreal frugivores, which, in the process of feeding, knock some of this ripe fruit to the ground. Fruit-eating birds such as guans (Cracidae), toucans and aracaris (Ramphastidae) knock down small amounts of ripe fruit, but trumpeters are primarily dependent on primates, such as spider monkeys (*Ateles*), capuchins (*Cebus*) and squirrel monkeys (*Saimiri*), which knock much greater quantities of ripe fruit to the ground when they feed. Although Pale-winged Trumpeters commonly forage below trees in which primates are feeding, they rarely follow primate troops from one fruiting tree to another to eat ripe fruit as it is being knocked down. Most species of ripe fruit on which trumpeters feed persist for several days to a week on the ground before they begin to rot or mould, and there are very few animals which compete with trumpeters to feed on fallen fruit.

Invertebrates and small vertebrates make up the remaining 10% of the trumpeters' diet. Wild Pale-winged Trumpeters consume a wide variety of arthropods, including beetles and beetle larvae, caterpillars, cicadas, grasshoppers, katydids, spiders, millipedes, centipedes, scorpions, and ants and termites and their larvae. Stinging or biting arthropods are usually disabled by repeated pecking before being swallowed. The larger species of millipedes eaten by trumpeters exude hydrogen cyanide droplets when disturbed, and Pale-winged Trumpeters wipe these species against the contour feathers below their wings before eating them, the preliminary rubbing often lasting several minutes. It is quite common for a pair of Pale-winged Trumpeters to take turns, one bird wiping a millipede against its own contour feathers for a short while before dropping it, after which the other picks it up and takes over for another brief turn. After several minutes of this behaviour, the two birds usually share in eating the millipede. In addition to removing some of the noxious exudate from the millipede before it is eaten, rubbing millipedes against the feathers and skin probably also serves to repel some of the trumpeter's ectoparasites in the same way that "anting" behaviour is thought to serve a similar function in other birds. Grey-winged Trumpeters have also been observed to rub their feathers with millipedes, as have two other avian species, the Jungle Myna (*Acridotheres fuscus*) and the European Robin (*Erithacus rubecula*).

Trumpeters locate arthropods in several ways. One common method is to use the bill to flip over dead leaves and other vegetation during periods of slow travel or rest. All three species also feed commonly on arthropods that are flushed from the leaf litter on the forest floor by swarms of foraging army ants. When a trumpeter group locates a foraging army ant swarm, the birds stand close to the areas in which the ants are hunting prey, and dash in to grab arthropods that are attempting to escape from the ants. Trumpeters also occasionally feed on arthropods that drop or fly to the ground when large groups of primates, such as squirrel monkeys, engage in bouts of arboreal insect-foraging. At such times, trumpeters follow along beneath the primate troop, catching mainly grasshoppers and katydids. They also feed on alate termites which periodically emerge and fly away from their colonies in large numbers, and termite and ant larvae, if these are being transported across the surface of the forest floor.

Small vertebrates are only occasionally eaten. Pale-winged Trumpeters periodically kill and eat small snakes, usually under 25 cm long, and on very rare occasions they scavenge, eating dead frogs or lizards, and on one occasion a dead mouse.

Although adults are highly frugivorous, newly hatched chicks are fed large numbers of arthropods. For the first several weeks after they hatch, Pale-winged Trumpeter chicks consume about twice as many arthropods as fruits, but the proportion of fruit in their diet then increases gradually.

Breeding

Both wild Pale-winged Trumpeters and captive Grey-winged Trumpeters form co-operatively breeding groups: although only a few individuals in the group breed, all group members help raise the chicks. In Pale-winged Trumpeter groups, only the dominant female contributes eggs to the clutch; adult males in the group are usually unrelated; and the three highest ranking males copulate with the dominant female. This mating system in which several males copulate with a single breeding female and then help to raise a single brood is a special type of co-operative breeding known as co-operative polyandry. The strategy of co-operative polyandry is extremely rare, and has been reported for only eight other avian species, including the Tasmanian Native-hen (*Gallinula mortierii*), the Galapagos Hawk (*Buteo galapagoensis*), the Dunnock (*Prunella modularis*) and the Stripe-backed Wren (*Campylorhynchus nuchalis*).

Trumpeters' breeding appears to be timed so that chicks hatch around the beginning of the rainy season, at which time the abundance of fruit and arthropods begins to increase steadily in South American rain forests. Pale-winged Trumpeters start showing the first signs of breeding activity when the dominant male and the dominant female in each group begin to investigate nesting cavities, about two and a half months before the breeding female begins to lay the clutch. The majority of the cavities investigated are holes in tree trunks that have been excavated by other animals, such as parrots, and are protected from the rain. Occasionally, Pale-winged Trumpeters lay clutches in roofless, naturally occurring cavity-like spaces, formed where a tree trunk splits into two halves. During the investigation of nesting cavities, one member of the dominant pair, or occasionally both, flies up and enters the cavity, remaining inside for anything from ten seconds to several minutes. The individual sometimes kicks or tosses out leaves and other debris from the cavity floor, and may occasionally sit down as if to incubate.

Investigation of nesting cavities increases in frequency up to the time when the breeding female begins laying her clutch. Pale-winged Trumpeters investigate 10-12 different nesting cavities on their territories, but begin to focus their attention on a single cavity about a week before laying. Preparation of the chosen cavity is undertaken either by the dominant male or by the dominant female, and consists simply of clearing out any loose debris, leaving a thin layer of well packed decayed wood on the cavity floor, on top of which the eggs are laid. Nesting cavities used by Pale-winged Trumpeters are located an average of 11 m above the ground, and have a shallow lip between the cavity floor and entrance, presumably to make it easier for chicks to climb out of the cavity the day after they hatch.

About a month after the dominant pair begin investigating cavities, and a month and a half before the breeding female begins to lay the clutch, adult male Pale-winged Trumpeters begin to feed the breeding female fruit and arthropods. Although males offer and feed food to each other throughout the year (see General Habits), they only provide food to the breeding female during the breeding season. The dominant male feeds the breeding female most of the food that she receives from other birds; he locates most of this food himself, but receives some, and grabs some away, from other adult males in the group.

Trumpeters rarely copulate outside the breeding season. In Pale-winged Trumpeter groups, males begin to copulate with the breeding female about six weeks before she begins to lay. P. Eason and P. Sherman estimated that during the first four weeks of this period, it is still too early for the breeding female's eggs to be fertilized, and at this time males in a group disrupt each other's copulations about half of the time. Eggs can potentially be fertilized during the final two weeks before laying begins up until 24 hours before the final egg is laid, and during this time the three most highly ranked males in a group all try to guard the breeding female closely, and attempt to interrupt all of each other's copulation attempts. The dominant male wins the battle, obtaining about two thirds of the copulations with the breeding female during her fertile period. He is unable to prevent subordinate males from sneakily obtaining the remainder of the suc-

All three species live in highly organized hierarchical groups and practise co-operative polyandry, a rare breeding system in which several males copulate with one breeding female and, together with the rest of their group, help to raise a single brood. The nest-hole is normally sited well up a tree trunk. The hole, often previously excavated by another species, is cleared of loose debris after which the clutch, normally of three eggs, is laid. Pale-winged Trumpeters have been extensively observed in the wild and it is known that incubation is carried out by the dominant female, with the aid of the first three dominant males. When an incubating bird is due to be relieved at the nest, the whole group assembles below the nest-site, waiting for the change-over to take place, a real co-operative effort.

[*Psophia leucoptera leucoptera*, Manu National Park, Peru. Photo: Peter T. Sherman]

The three chicks of a normal clutch hatch synchronously after some four weeks' incubation. Highly precocial at one day old, the chicks quite literally launch themselves into society as they "freefall" from the rim of the nest cavity, accompanied by the encouraging calls of the attendant group 10-11 metres below. Covered with stripy russet down, they blend in well with the leaf-covered forest floor, but are mainly reliant on older group members for protection against predators. This month-old Pale-winged Trumpeter chick is still being fed by an adult; by three months old it will have become almost fully independent, although it may continue to beg some food.

[Psophia leucoptera leucoptera, Manu National Park, Peru. Photo: Peter T. Sherman]

cessful matings, of which the second highest ranked adult male (the Beta male) obtains about three quarters, and the third highest ranked adult male (the Gamma male) obtains about a quarter.

Mating in Pale-winged Trumpeters is often preceded by a short period of solicitation, during which the female crouches and presents her rump to the male, and the male stands close behind, stretches his neck and walks in partial circles, while the female pivots to keep her rump facing the male as he circles. These solicitations usually last about 5-10 seconds, after which the male mounts the female and they copulate. Although several general accounts report that trumpeters engage in noisy and acrobatic courtship dances, the authors of these accounts give perfect descriptions of the actions and behaviour exhibited during play within groups and in territorial fights between groups (see General Habits), and thus appear to have mistaken these activities for courtship display.

Trumpeters lay white eggs that have a somewhat rough shell and measure about 60 x 48 mm. Wild Pale-winged and captive Grey-winged Trumpeters lay clutches ranging from two to four eggs, and averaging about three. Eggs are laid at two day intervals, and incubation does not begin until the final egg is laid, after which the clutch is incubated continuously.

In a captive Grey-winged Trumpeter group of three individuals, C. Horning, M. Hutchins and W. English found that the male and two females all shared incubation. In wild Pale-winged Trumpeter groups, the dominant female incubates from dusk through to late morning, and one of the adult males incubates during the rest of the day. In this species, the dominant male takes about 75% of the late morning to dusk incubation shifts, while the remaining 25% of these shifts are split about equally by the group's Beta and Gamma males. When it is time for a male to replace the dominant female, or vice versa, the entire group travels to the nesting cavity and waits while the change occurs. Subsequently, the group and the replaced individual leave the vicinity of the nesting cavity, to travel and forage elsewhere on the group's territory.

For all three species, incubation lasts about four weeks. The chicks hatch simultaneously, and leave the nesting cavity the following day. While the group members call from the ground, each Pale-winged Trumpeter chick climbs onto the entrance lip of the nesting cavity and then jumps. After hitting the ground following the free-fall descent of up to 11 m, the chicks initially appear stunned, but within seconds they are on their feet and begging for food.

When chicks hatch, they are covered with down that is primarily russet-coloured. A stripe runs across the top of the head and several run down the back, creating a pattern that is highly effective in helping them to blend in with the dead and decaying vegetation on the forest floor. By ten days of age, the black contour feathers and flight-feathers have grown out enough to become just visible. By six weeks of age, the chicks are beginning to look like small versions of adults, and are able to fly for short distances.

Trumpeter chicks are precocial and are able to walk, run and climb the day after they hatch. Although newly hatched chicks peck at the ground, they do not pick up anything edible and are completely dependent upon older birds to provide them with food for about three weeks. By four weeks of age, wild Pale-winged Trumpeter chicks provide themselves with about 25% of their daily food intake, and by three months old, they are feeding almost completely independently, although they continue to beg food from older individuals in their group.

Newly hatched chicks are also dependent upon older individuals in their group to help protect them from predators. In a captive Grey-winged Trumpeter trio and wild Pale-winged Trumpeter groups, all individuals helped with the chick-care, albeit to varying degrees. During four years of observation on wild Pale-winged Trumpeter groups, the dominant male and female and the group's previous offspring all fed young chicks roughly equal amounts of food. The subordinate adult female, however, always fed the chicks significantly less than the dominant female, and the Beta male always fed the chicks significantly more than the dominant male. The Gamma male fed chicks more food than the dominant male during two years, and roughly equivalent amounts during the other two years.

Potential predators of both chicks and adults include raptors, felids and snakes. In Pale-winged Trumpeter groups, the dominant male was most frequently involved in protecting chicks from predators, and the subordinate adult female was least frequently involved, while the remainder of the group contributed about equally at an intermediate level. Beta and Gamma males' participation in incubation, feeding and protecting chicks may be due in part to their having some probability of fathering one or more of the chicks through their copulations with the breeding female during her fertile period. Similarly, the subordinate adult female's lack of participation in these same activities may be due partially to her lack of relatedness to the chicks or other group members.

In Pale-winged Trumpeter groups, if one or more of the chicks from the first clutch survive, no subsequent clutch is laid until the next breeding season. If a clutch is lost before or after the chicks hatch, the breeding female will lay a subsequent clutch, as long as the breeding season has not yet ended. About half of the clutches incubated by Pale-winged Trumpeters failed to produce young, and appeared to have been lost to arboreal egg predators such as primates or snakes. Additionally, about half of the Pale-winged Trumpeter chicks that hatched disappeared during their first month of life. This seems to be due in part to roosting chicks' vulnerability to predators such as ocelots and other felids, or snakes. Until they are able to fly, Pale-winged Trumpeter chicks roost alone, climbing up lianas or sloping trunks of small trees. For their first three weeks chicks roost about 1-2 m above the ground, but for the next three weeks roost height increases to 3-5 m. Adult Pale-winged Trumpeters roost at heights of 8-15 m in the trees above the chicks, and, lacking the ability to see in the dark, are unable to protect the chicks from predators. All Pale-winged Trumpeter chicks that survived their first month of life lived to adulthood, at which time they left their natal groups.

The offspring of wild Pale-winged Trumpeters usually help to raise one clutch of siblings before dispersing from their natal group. Males, and presumably females, reach sexual maturity at two years of age, and it is around this time that individuals of both sexes independently disperse from their natal groups and join other groups. In wild Pale-winged Trumpeter groups, offspring rarely obtain a breeding position in their natal group due to a combination of the longevity of established breeding individuals and incest avoidance. Additionally, all forested habitat is occupied by other territorial trumpeter groups (see Habitat), making it extremely difficult for offspring to establish a new territory of their own. Sexually mature Pale-winged Trumpeter offspring are thus left with the option of staying "at home" and not breeding, or dispersing and attempting to obtain a breeding position in another group.

Dispersing is an easier task for males than for females: whereas adult males are readily accepted by the dominant individuals in new groups, adult females that attempt to transfer into new groups are treated aggressively and are frequently chased off. The acceptance of unrelated adult male Pale-winged Trumpeters into a territorial group may be related to the group's need to contain several adult males in order to defend successfully a territory that is large enough to provide sufficient quantities of food throughout the year (see Habitat).

This need may have helped to set the stage for the evolution of co-operative polyandry in Pale-winged Trumpeters. When adult males in a group are unrelated to the breeding female, there is the possibility for these males to copulate with her. Although a group's dominant male attempts to maintain exclusive paternity of the clutch by aggressively guarding the breeding female during her fertile period, the female co-operates with subordinate adult males in her group during all of their copulation attempts. As explained above, subordinate adult males provide a significant amount of help with raising the group's chicks. It has been shown for several other co-operatively breeding avian species, such as the Dunnock and the Acorn Woodpecker (*Melanerpes formicivorus*), that the amount of help that males contribute to rearing chicks appears to be related to their probability of paternity. Thus a breeding female Pale-winged Trumpeter may be able to increase her fitness, as measured by the likelihood of her offspring surviving and successfully reproducing, by copulating with all males in her group as equally as possible. Whether subordinate male Pale-winged Trumpeters would contribute equivalent amounts of help to raising chicks if they did not obtain any copulations with the breeding female is not known.

Movements

Trumpeters are non-migratory. Although little is known about the Dark-winged, the Pale-winged defends, and the Grey-winged appears to defend large, year round territories with stable boundaries (see Habitat). Although Pale-winged groups occasionally trespass in the areas that lie just outside their territorial boundaries, they spend the majority of their time on their own territories.

Typically, a Pale-winged Trumpeter group spends the morning visiting a succession of different fruiting trees on the territory, and feeding at them. The afternoon is more likely to be spent walking around different parts of the territory and foraging for arthropods, with occasional visits to fruiting trees. If there is a lot of fallen fruit available below one tree and little fruit available elsewhere on the territory, the group may remain near that tree for much of the morning, alternating between feeding at the tree and preening or foraging for leaf litter arthropods a short distance away. Usually there is a limited amount of edible fruit available below any given tree, and after feeding for 2-6 minutes, the group travels, often in a straight and direct path, to another fruiting tree. In the course of a day, Pale-winged Trumpeter groups traverse much of their territory, travelling an average of 3·7 km on a typical day.

Relationship with Man

There are several legends concerning trumpeters. Some Brazilian tribes consider them to be amongst their ancestors. At the turn of the century, natives of Guyana told naturalists that trumpeters learned how to make their loud trumpeting call from the rooster, and that tame trumpeters were used in Brazil to herd cattle, and were especially skilled at making strays rejoin the herd.

Trumpeters' local names vary from region to region. In Surinam, the common name for the trumpeter is "Kamee-kamee", or "camel-back", derived from the Dutch word *kameel* for camel. In Brazil and elsewhere, the trumpeter is commonly known as the "Jacamim", which in the language of the Tupi Indians means "bird with a small head". In the Pará region of Brazil, and in French Guiana, the common name for the trumpeter is "Agami", a name which the French have adopted as their standard vernacular name for these birds. The English name "Trumpeter" and the German "Trompetervogel" derive from *oiseau trompette*, the eighteenth century French scientist-explorer C. M. de La Condamine's translation of *trompetero*, the name given to the birds by Spanish colonists of Maynas on the upper Amazon, to describe the trumpeters' loud territorial call, which was considered to have a trumpet-like quality.

Linnaeus named the genus *Psophia* based on the Greek word *psophos*, meaning an "inarticulate sound", and referring to the belief that trumpeters produced their loud call with their anus, while breaking wind. Although this notion was contested by Pallas in 1766 and Vosmaer in 1768, the belief persisted into the twentieth century. In 1908, F. and A. Penard reported: "Long before science discovered it, natives knew the booming call (of trumpeters) was made by the anus and not the beak". These authors further report that the Guyanan Indians believe that trumpeters stole this trick from the rooster, who cries over its loss every morning.

Trumpeters are commonly kept as pets by the local people living in or near South American rain forests. Pet trumpeters are generally acquired by capturing young birds from the wild or by removing eggs from nesting cavities and then adding them to clutches being incubated by hens. Trumpeter chicks that are raised in captivity become tame and very affectionate towards their human masters. Chicks raised from a young age often imprint on people and come to recognize the individuals associated with their household as members of their "group". A tame trumpeter, when approached by a familiar person after some period of absence, will frequently behave subordinately, running over to him to Wing-spread at his feet. Tame trumpeters will

Trumpeters do not appear to be in any imminent danger of extinction, but it is known that their populations are dwindling. The main threat comes from deforestation, for trumpeters need extensive undisturbed areas in which to live and breed. While they make delightful, very tame pets, unfortunately they are not easily bred in captivity. To date, very few chicks have been reared successfully in zoos, almost all of them Grey-winged Trumpeters.

[Psophia crepitans, San Diego Zoo, California. Photo: Kenneth W. Fink]

also solicit preening and beg for food from familiar people in the same manner that wild trumpeters carry out these social activities with each other (see General Habits).

Pet trumpeters are also valued by their owners for their utility as "watch dogs". Tame trumpeters respond to unfamiliar people, potential predators and disturbances with the loud, squawking alarm call used in the wild to draw other group members' attention to terrestrial predators (see Voice). Although trumpeters have a reputation for being excellent snake hunters, in normal circumstances they will only attack and kill small snakes (see Food and Feeding). They do have a keen eye for spotting snakes, and will draw attention to larger snakes by standing close to them and producing a distinct call for several minutes or sometimes longer (see Voice). Pet trumpeters are often kept with poultry and they are commonly considered to help protect them from potential harm.

Status and Conservation

Although trumpeters are not currently considered to be in immediate danger of extinction, their populations are in a state of decline and their future remains uncertain. The main threat is deforestation. As trumpeters occur only in dense tropical forest, partial or total clearing of rain forests, as is occurring in South America at an ever-increasing pace, makes areas uninhabitable for trumpeters. The fact that they need to defend very large areas to provide themselves with a year round supply of food (see Habitat) further contributes to the problem. Animals like trumpeters that require large areas of undisturbed habitat for survival are more severely affected by deforestation than those that are able to survive within smaller or more disturbed habitat patches. As large tracts of relatively undisturbed rain forest become increasingly scarce, habitat suitable for sustaining trumpeter populations is declining correspondingly. At present, stable populations of trumpeters are found only in large protected reserves and in remote areas which have remained largely unexploited by humans due to their inaccessibility.

The hunting of all three species throughout their range has also significantly contributed to the decline of populations. They are attractive game species: their meat is considered to taste good, and their social habits usually allow for the simultaneous harvest of several individuals. Hunters can locate groups by imitating the territorial call, which frequently elicits an approach or a response in kind from the group. This allows hunters to attract groups during the day or locate them on their roost at night. During the day, capture of several birds is facilitated by trumpeters' tendency to remain near wounded group members allowing several birds to be shot. At night, hunters spotlight groups from below and the birds' disorientation, combined with their poor night vision, also allows the harvest of several birds. The ease with which trumpeters can be hunted leads to their rapid extirpation in the vicinity of settled areas.

A secondary effect on trumpeters of both deforestation and hunting is their negative impact on the primate populations, upon which trumpeters depend to knock down the ripe fleshy fruits that make up the majority of their diet. Primates are sloppy feeders, and most of the ripe fruit with soft unprotected pulp that falls to the ground in Neotropical rain forests falls as a result of being dropped or knocked free by primates. As the population density of forest-living non-human primates declines, the amount of edible fruit available to trumpeters decreases, leading to a further reduction in the size of the trumpeter population that can be sustained within a given area of rain forest.

Attempts to breed trumpeters in captivity have for the most part been unsuccessful. Although they have been kept by zoos and private aviculturists since the late 1800's, only a small number of females have been reported to lay eggs, and an even smaller number of chicks have hatched. People who live in or near South American rain forests and keep trumpeters as pets also claim that they never breed in captivity. To date, one Dark-winged and eight Grey-winged Trumpeters are reported to have been hatched and reared successfully in captivity. There is no record of captive Pale-winged Trumpeters ever having bred successfully.

General Bibliography
Cracraft (1973, 1982), Dunning, J.B. (1993), Dunning, J.S. (1982), Haffer (1974), Haverschmidt (1985), Hellmayr & Conover (1942), Hendrickson (1969), Meyer de Schauensee (1982), Peters (1934), Rutgers & Norris (1970), Sibley & Ahlquist (1990), Sibley & Monroe (1990), Sick (1968, 1993), Willis (1983).

1

2

ssp *napensis*   ssp *crepitans*

ssp *ochroptera*

ssp *leucoptera*

PLATE 8

inches   9

cm   23

3

3

ssp *viridis*   ssp *dextralis*

ssp *obscura*

PLATE 8

Family PSOPHIIDAE (TRUMPETERS)
SPECIES ACCOUNTS

Genus *PSOPHIA*   Linnaeus, 1758

1. Grey-winged Trumpeter
Psophia crepitans

French: Agami trompette   **German**: Grauflügel-Trompetervogel   **Spanish**: Trompetero Aligrís
Other common names: Common Trumpeter

Taxonomy. *Psophia crepitans* Linnaeus, 1758, Cayenne.
Forms superspecies with *P. leucoptera* and *P. viridis*. Present species sometimes treated as conspecific with *P. leucoptera*; alternatively, considered to include race *P. l. ochroptera*, because distribution of *ochroptera* appears more compatible with that of present species, and plumage pattern intermediate; however, apparent lack of interbreeding in areas of overlap between *P. l. ochroptera* and *P. c. napensis* indicates that these two races probably belong to separate species (see page 96). Two subspecies normally recognized.
Subspecies and Distribution.
P. c. napensis P. L. Sclater & Salvin, 1873 - SE Colombia through E Ecuador to NE Peru, and extreme NW Brazil (N of R Amazon/Solimões and mostly W of R Negro).
P. c. crepitans Linnaeus, 1758 - SE Colombia through E & S Venezuela to the Guianas and S to N Brazil (N of R Amazon and E of R Negro).

Descriptive notes. 45-52 cm; 1000-1500 g. Uniform black, with reddish brown band above ash grey hind-wing patch; lower throat has purple and green iridescence; legs pale greenish grey. Juvenile similar to adult. Races differ only in coloration, race *napensis* having iridescence almost entirely purple, and paler grey hind-wing patch.
Habitat. Mature dense tropical moist forest, from lowlands up to 750 m, in areas distant from human settlement.
Food and Feeding. Mainly pulp of ripe fruit, constituting 90% dry weight of food ingested; fruit eaten includes Moraceae, Lauraceae, Euphorbiaceae, Arecaceae, Myrtaceae, Cucurbitaceae. Also takes arthropods and other invertebrates, occasionally small vertebrates. Fruit primarily picked up from forest floor, occasionally removed from small plants. All seeds ingested with fruit are defecated intact.
Breeding. Season Dec-Jun in Guianas; in Venezuela, collected birds had enlarged reproductive organs in Feb, others observed breeding in Mar; presumably during main rainy season in other locations. Appears to live in co-operatively breeding groups. Nest-site is in elevated cavity; no nest constructed. Clutch 3 eggs (2-4); eggs white, 56-61 x 46-50 mm; incubation 28 days. Chick has russet face and wings, dark grey crown and back, cream-coloured underparts and black bib covering throat and upper breast; russet stripe bisects crown, extending from rear of upper mandible to base of neck; similar stripes run lengthwise down back.

Movements. Appears to be sedentary and territorial.

Status and Conservation. Not globally threatened. Apparently widespread in undisturbed rain forest, in large protected reserves and remote areas which remain essentially unexploited by humans. Uncommon in suitable habitat in Colombia, usually far from presence of humans. In French Guiana, still locally common in remote undisturbed forest, but overall population has declined greatly, and species has virtually been exterminated from coastal plain; main problem is hunting, especially near areas of human habitation; opening up of new roads facilitates access deeper into forest for hunters. Rare or absent in many parts of former range where previously common; population decline principally due to deforestation and hunting, but data on rate and severity of decline not available.

Bibliography. Beebe, M.B. & Beebe (1910), Beebe, W. *et al.* (1917), Blake (1977), Chubb (1916), Dathe (1970), Érard & Sabatier (1988), Érard & Théry (1994), Érard *et al.* (1991), Gregory (1907), Haverschmidt (1952, 1963a, 1968), Haverschmidt & Mees (1995), Hilty & Brown (1986), Horning *et al.* (1988), Kowalczyk & McNeal (1984), Lloyd (1897), Male (1989), Meyer de Schauensee & Phelps (1978), Ortiz & Carrión (1991), Penard & Penard (1908-1910), Röhl (1959), Ruschi (1979), Schomburgk (1848), Sick (1985c, 1993), Snyder (1966), Stokes (1926), Thiollay (1988), Tostain *et al.* (1992), Willis (1983).

2. Pale-winged Trumpeter

Psophia leucoptera

French: Agami à ailes blanches   **Spanish**: Trompetero Aliblanco
German: Weißflügel-Trompetervogel
Other common names: White-winged Trumpeter

Taxonomy. *Psophia leucoptera* Spix, 1825, Rio Negro; error = left bank of Rio Madeira, Brazil.
Forms superspecies with *P. crepitans* and *P. viridis*. Present species sometimes treated as conspecific with *P. crepitans*; alternatively, race *ochroptera* transferred to that species, because distribution appears more compatible with that of *P. crepitans*, and plumage pattern intermediate; however, apparent lack of interbreeding in areas of overlap between *P. l. ochroptera* and *P. c. napensis* indicates that these two races probably belong to separate species (see page 96). Two subspecies normally recognized.

Subspecies and Distribution.
P. l. ochroptera Pelzeln, 1857 - NW Brazil (N of R Amazon/Solimões and W of R Negro).
P. l. leucoptera Spix, 1825 - E Peru, CW Brazil (generally S of R Amazon/Solimões and W of R Madeira) and NE Bolivia.

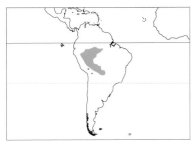

Descriptive notes. 45-52 cm; male 1280-1440 g, female 1180-1320. Uniform black, with similar appearance to *P. crepitans*, but hind-wing patch white to ochre, lower throat lacks green iridescence, and outer wing-coverts tipped in iridescent purple, green and bronze. Juvenile similar to adult, except for dark brown edging at tips of contour feathers of body. Races differ mainly in coloration, race *ochroptera* having an ochraceous hind-wing patch, as opposed to white of nominate race.

Habitat. Mature dense tropical moist forest, from lowlands up to 750 m, in areas distant from human settlement.

Food and Feeding. Mainly pulp of ripe fruit constituting 90% dry weight, 88% calories of food ingested; fruit eaten includes Moraceae, Lauraceae, Euphorbiaceae, Icacinaceae, Annonaceae, Verbenaceae. Also feeds on arthropods, occasionally annelids, and small vertebrates. Fruit primarily picked up from forest floor, occasionally removed from small plants. All seeds ingested with fruit are defecated intact. In wild, individuals ingest average of 260 kJ of food per day during periods of low fruit abundance, and 470 kJ food/day during periods of high fruit abundance.

Breeding. Season Sept-Apr. Forms co-operatively polyandrous groups. Nest-site is in elevated hollowed-out hole in tree trunk, at average of 11 m above ground; no nest constructed. Clutch 3 eggs (2-4); eggs white, 60-69 x 47-50 mm; incubation 23-29 days. Chick predominantly russet with

cream-coloured underparts and black bib covering throat and upper breast; one black bordered white stripe runs from rear of upper mandible to base of neck; four similar stripes run lengthwise down back. Chicks jump from nesting cavity on morning after hatching; completely dependent on adults for food for first 3 weeks, and partially dependent on adults for food until 3 months old. Sexual maturity at 2 years. Longevity in wild probably 10-15 years.

Movements. Groups defend year round territories with stable boundaries.

Status and Conservation. Not globally threatened. Apparently widespread in undisturbed rain forest, in large protected reserves and remote areas which remain essentially unexploited by humans. Population density under ideal conditions in remote undisturbed rain forest in Manu National Park, Peru, is c. 8 birds/km². Species rare or absent in many parts of former range where previously common; population decline principally due to habitat destruction and hunting pressure; latter has grown over past century with the increased availability of firearms; data on rate and severity of population decline not available.

Bibliography. Blake (1977), Eason & Sherman (1995), Forrester (1993), Koepcke & Koepcke (1971), Parker *et al.* (1982), Pinto (1964), Price (1985), Remsen & Traylor (1989), Ruschi (1979), Sherman (1991, 1995a, 1995b), Sick (1985c, 1993).

3. Dark-winged Trumpeter

Psophia viridis

French: Agami vert   **German**: Grünflügel-Trompetervogel   **Spanish**: Trompetero Aliverde
Other common names: Green-winged Trumpeter

Taxonomy. *Psophia viridis* Spix, 1825, Parintins, Lower Amazon.
Forms superspecies with *P. crepitans* and *P. leucoptera*. Proposed race *interjecta* differs only slightly from races *dextralis* and *obscura* and adjoins their ranges; generally thought to represent an intergradation between populations of these two races. Three subspecies usually recognized.

Subspecies and Distribution.
P. v. viridis Spix, 1825 - C Brazil (S of R Amazon, between R Madeira and R Tapajós).
P. v. dextralis Conover, 1934 - EC Brazil (S of R Amazon, between R Tapajós and R Tocantins).
P. v. obscura Pelzeln, 1857 - NE Brazil (S of R Amazon, in NE Pará E of R Tocantins).

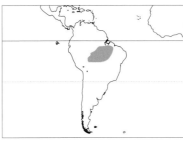

Descriptive notes. 45-52 cm. Uniform black, with similar appearance to *P. crepitans*, but hind-wing patch dark green to olive brown and typically more extensive; lower throat has purple iridescence, and outer wing-coverts tipped in iridescent purple; bill and feet green to olive. Juvenile similar to adult. Races differ only in coloration, with hind-wing patch dark green in nominate race, but olive brown in race *dextralis*, darker olive brown in race *obscura*; latter two races have dusky brown bill and feet.

Habitat. Mature dense lowland tropical moist forest in areas distant from human settlement.

Food and Feeding. Little information available. Known to feed on fruit, arthropods, small vertebrates and carrion.

Breeding. Few data available. Female shot near Pará in Jan had large eggs in ovary. In captivity, 5 eggs incubated in one clutch, of which 1 egg hatched after 27 days. Published black and white photo of chick is similar in appearance to chick of *P. leucoptera*.

Movements. Probably sedentary and territorial.

Status and Conservation. Not globally threatened. Appears to be widespread in undisturbed rain forest, in large protected reserves and remote areas which remain unexploited by humans. Rare or absent in many parts of former range where previously common; population decline principally due to deforestation and hunting pressure; no data available on rate and severity of decline. Very poorly known.

Bibliography. Anon. (1981a), Ayres *et al.* (1991), Blake (1977), Dathe (1974), Forrester (1993), Pinto (1964), Ruschi (1979), Sclater (1898), Sick (1985c, 1993), Willis (1983).

Class AVES
Order GRUIFORMES
Suborder GRUES
Family RALLIDAE
(RAILS, GALLINULES AND COOTS)

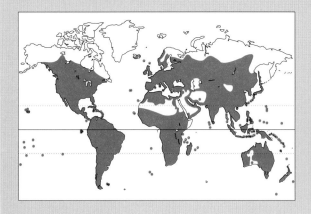

- Small to medium-sized terrestrial, marsh and aquatic birds, with short and deep to long and slender bill, moderately long neck, broad wings, short, soft tail and strong legs.
- 12-63 cm.

- Worldwide, except for polar regions and waterless deserts; widely distributed on oceanic islands.
- Many types of wetland; also grassland, forest and dense scrub.
- 33 genera, 133 species, 309 taxa.
- 33 species threatened; probably 2 of these, as well as 14 other species and 4 subspecies, extinct since 1600.

Systematics

The Rallidae form by far the largest family in the Gruiformes, comprising 147 species, 133 extant and 14 recently extinct. The family is cosmopolitan, having one of the widest distributions of any family of terrestrial vertebrates.

The order consists essentially of ground-living birds and its only other widespread family is Gruidae (cranes). The relationships of the Gruiformes to other orders are unclear but they are probably closest to the Charadriiformes and the Galliformes. In a few classifications the rails have been assigned to an order Ralliformes, while some classifications have allied the Rallidae to the Charadriiformes, and it has also been suggested that the charadriiform family Jacanidae may be derived from *Gallinula*-like stock, and could be placed within the Rallidae.

The fossil record tells very little about the origins and relationships of the Rallidae. The earliest fossils which can be assigned to the family are from the Lower Eocene, about 50 million years ago, and they reveal little about how these birds may have resembled modern rails. It is possible that the family existed earlier than the Eocene, but there is no solid evidence for this, although recent DNA-DNA hybridization studies have indicated that the rails may have diverged from the other gruiform groups as much as 86 million years ago, in the Upper Middle Cretaceous. Only in the Upper Oligocene and Lower Miocene, 20-30 million years ago, are three genera of fossil rails to be found which are based on adequate and diagnostic material, and by this period these birds had achieved a morphology not greatly different from that of modern rallids. Fossil rails occur fairly regularly in various younger Tertiary deposits from Europe, Asia and North America, and most continental fossil rails from Pliocene and Pleistocene deposits have been assigned to modern genera. As well as the Tertiary evidence in continental deposits, the more recent late Quaternary deposits of oceanic islands have produced numerous well preserved specimens of extinct rails, most of which can be assigned to modern genera; indeed, the discovery of many more fossil species on oceanic islands may be predicted. Only five extinct genera of island rails are known, and of these *Hovacrex* may be synonymous with *Gallinula*, while *Capellirallus* and *Diaphorapteryx* of New Zealand, *Aphanapteryx* of the Mascarenes, and the enigmatic *Nesotrochis* from the Greater Antilles, are valid, being morphologically quite distinct from modern genera.

The relationships of the Rallidae to the other gruiform families have not been clearly resolved. The family is commonly placed in its own superfamily (Ralloidea) within the suborder Grues, together with Aramidae (Limpkin), Psophiidae (trumpeters) and Gruidae. Skeletal morphology suggests a close alliance of Rallidae, Psophiidae and Heliornithidae (finfoots). The Aramidae, Eurypygidae (Sunbittern) and Cariamidae (seriemas) of South America, The Rhynochetidae (Kagu) of New Caledonia and the extinct Aptornithidae of New Zealand are also closely related, and it has been proposed that some of these families could be included as subfamilies within the Rallidae. However, DNA-DNA hybridization evidence suggests that the Rallidae form a distinct cluster, which is separate from cranes and their allies, and has had a distinct lineage for a long time; in line with this, it has been proposed that the rallids should be elevated to their own suborder, Ralli, alongside Grues.

Arrangements within the Rallidae have varied, and several classifications have been proposed. The first really modern one, published by R. B. Sharpe in 1894, listed 50 genera and 165 species of recent rails, while in 1934 J. L. Peters listed 52 genera and 138 species. The family was traditionally divided into three subfamilies, Rallinae, Gallinulinae and Fulicinae, although there had been little justification for this treatment, and in 1957 R. Verheyen proposed a subdivision into five subfamilies, but with no solid supporting arguments. In 1973, S. L. Olson produced a new classification for the family, reducing the number of genera to 35 and the number of subfamilies to two, Himantornithinae and Rallinae, the former being intermediate between the Rallinae and Psophiidae and containing only the Nkulengu Rail (*Himantornis haematopus*), of West and west-central Africa. Olson provided no sequence of species but discussed about 135. The more recent 1975 classification of J. J. Morony, W. J. Bock and J. Farrand listed 152 species of rails.

Olson considered *Himantornis* to be the most primitive and distinctive rallid. Its downy young are uniquely patterned in the Rallidae, and its skull is unlike that of any other rail but is very similar to that of the Psophiidae, while several elements of its postcranial skeleton are also distinct from those of other rails and closer to *Psophia*. He found that all other rails were so alike morphologically that further subfamilial separation was unwarranted. As he pointed out, one of the difficulties of rallid taxonomy arises from the relative homogeneity of the family, rails for the most part being rather generalized birds, with few groups clearly defined by morphological modifications. As a result, some particularly well marked genera had previously been elevated to subfamilial rank on the basis of characters which, in more diverse families, would not be considered significant.

Although S. D. Ripley subsequently reduced the number of rallid genera to 18, Olson's classification has found general acceptance. The most significant subsequent reappraisal of relationships within the Rallidae has been made by C. G. Sibley and J. E. Ahlquist on the basis of DNA-DNA hybridization. These workers found that the flufftails (*Sarothrura*) of Africa and Madagascar diverged from the rest of the group about 60 million years ago, in the Paleocene, and they therefore proposed that the flufftails be placed in a separate family, the Sarothruridae, within its own superfamily, Sarothruroidea; they subsequently suggested that confirmation of this arrangement should wait until further genetic material becomes available. The flufftails are a distinctive genus within the rallids: they are strongly sexually dimorphic in plumage and they lay white, unmarked eggs, both of which characters are rare in the family; they also have distinctive hooting or moaning voices. Olson had proposed that *Sarothrura* was closely allied to the *Rallicula* (herein included in *Rallina*) forest-rails of New Guinea, mainly on the basis of plumage characters and the fact that *Rallina* species also lay white eggs. He had also suggested a possible link with the genera *Coturnicops* and *Micropygia*, small species which have a similar build and ecological preferences to those of flufftails; furthermore, the three *Coturnicops* species have white secondaries, a character which they share with the White-winged Flufftail (*Sarothrura ayresi*), and which is found in no other rallid. Lack of genetic material from *Rallina*, *Coturnicops* and *Micropygia* prevented Sibley and Ahlquist from commenting on these possible relationships, and the problem of the affinities of the flufftails remains unresolved.

This work follows the taxonomic treatment of Olson, modified in some cases by more recent morphological studies. It follows Sibley and Monroe in emphasizing the distinctiveness of the genus *Sarothrura* by placing it at the beginning of the family but not assigning it to a separate subfamily. However, this has the disadvantage that the primitive and distinctive genus *Himantornis* can not be given the subfamilial rank which it probably deserves.

Most works on the family recognize, for convenience, two broad "natural groups" within it: the crakes, rails and wood-rails, most of which are terrestrial; and the gallinules (including moorhens) and coots, which tend to be more aquatic. The term "rail" is applied generally to the whole family and also to longer-billed species in many genera, while "crake" is applied mostly to the smaller, short-billed species, particularly in the genera *Laterallus* and *Porzana*. Neither term has a precise taxonomic meaning, and different species in different genera are sometimes called by either name, while crake-like birds seem to have evolved independently several times. The term "gallinule" can cover all the birds in the second group except the coots, though it is sometimes restricted to certain species of *Gallinula* and *Porphyrio*.

The greatest number of rallid species and of peculiar genera, and the most primitive species, are found in the Old World tropics. The New World has relatively fewer groups, most of which are apparently derived from Old World stem groups, and a few genera appear to have specialized and radiated in the New World, some of them subsequently re-invading the Old World. Olson suggested that the most primitive rallids are found in forest, and that an adaptation to aquatic habitats and grassland (see Habitat) may be a more recent development, but he admitted that such adaptation could have evolved several times in different groups.

In attempting to determine relationships within the Rallidae, *Himantornis* provides some clues as to which species may be the most primitive, useful indications being *Psophia*-like skeletal characters, long, slender tarsi, patterned natal down and forest habitat. Flightlessness has evolved many times in rallids (see Morphological Aspects), and therefore has no major phylogenetic significance; the incidence of flightlessness and its associated morphology can be used as a taxonomic character in the family only at the specific or subspecific levels.

The primitive nature of the forest-dwelling genus *Canirallus*, of Africa and Madagascar, is indicated by its sharing two primitive skeletal characters with *Himantornis* and by the possession of patterned natal down in the Madagascar Wood-rail (*Canirallus kioloides*). There are significant similarities in the plumage, structure and natal down of *Canirallus* and the four forest-rails (sometimes called "chestnut rails") endemic to New Guinea which were formerly placed in the genus *Rallicula*, and Olson suggested maintaining *Rallicula* as a subgenus of *Canirallus*. However, on

The nominate race of the White-throated Rail is endemic to Madagascar, where it frequently occurs along forest and woodland streams and feeds readily in shallow water, immersing the head and digging and raking vigorously with the strong bill. The bill is also a useful weapon; indeed, the Aldabra race, aldabrensis, *successfully defends itself against introduced rats by pecking forcefully at them. The white areas of plumage are prominent in signalling: in greeting and threat displays, and when singing, the bird stretches its neck vertically to display the white throat patch, while the undertail-coverts are spread during song, in the threat display, and by the female when soliciting copulation.*

[*Dryolimnas cuvieri cuvieri*, Madagascar. Photo: Patryck Vaucoulon/ Bios]

The Spot-flanked Gallinule is a rather atypical small Gallinula *species which was originally placed in a monospecific genus,* Porphyriops. *In shape it resembles a large* Porzana *crake rather than a* Gallinula, *but its behaviour is typical of gallinules: it feeds while swimming, seldom walking on vegetation or on the ground; it is not shy and is easily observed; it occurs in family parties and occasionally in flocks; and it tends to be quarrelsome, birds often chasing each other and pattering across the water. Its frontal shield is small and it is the only member of its genus to have profusely spotted flanks and lobed toes, the lobes being small and difficult to see.*

[*Gallinula melanops.* Photo: Hector Rivarola/ Bruce Coleman]

the basis of plumage similarities, Ripley included them in the genus *Rallina*, along with four species of forest and marshland from Asia and Australia, even though the latter species differ in not being sexually dichromatic. Olson regarded *Rallina* as a separate group, apparently in transition from the woodland habitat of the more primitive rails to the wetland habitat more typical of the family. Opinions still differ as to whether the forest-rails should be placed in *Rallicula* or *Rallina*.

The sequence of the first six genera in the currently adopted classification is unsatisfactory in several ways. Interposing the genera *Coturnicops* and *Micropygia* between the genera of the *Canirallus-Rallina* group is somewhat arbitrary, and reflects the assumed affinity of these small grassland and marsh crakes with the flufftails, as described above, while also acknowledging the aforementioned possible affinities between the flufftails and the *Rallina* group and attempting to reflect the primitive status of *Himantornis* and *Canirallus*.

Two New World genera of small crakes, *Anurolimnas* and *Laterallus*, appear to be derived from Old World *Rallina* stock, some *Laterallus* species showing striking plumage similarities to *Rallina*; indeed, the forest- and thicket-dwelling Chestnut-headed Crake (*Anurolimnas castaneiceps*) was formerly placed in *Rallina*. The other two *Anurolimnas* species were formerly included in *Laterallus* but are more properly included with the Chestnut-headed Crake in a distinct genus. The nine species remaining in *Laterallus* form a group of small crakes, predominantly of marsh and wet grassland, the South American representatives of which are relatively poorly known. A recently discovered and very distinctive form (*tuerosi*) of the Black Rail (*Laterallus jamaicensis*) is confined to marshes fringing Lake Junín, central Peru, and is reckoned to be endangered. It is sometimes treated as a separate species, and this may be justified because it differs from the other forms of the Black Rail as much as does the Galapagos Rail (*Laterallus spilonotus*); awarding it specific status emphasizes the conservation priorities which should be accorded to it.

The relationships of the group of barred-winged rails currently placed in the genus *Gallirallus* have been greatly obscured by the combination of some species with the more specialized species of *Rallus*, and by the creation of several unnecessary genera for flightless forms of the group. The Weka (*Gallirallus australis*), a large, flightless species endemic to New Zealand, at first sight appears to be a strange and distinctive rail, and it was originally the only species placed in the genus. Early classifiers were deceived by the neotenic characters associated with flightlessness and considered it a peculiar, primitive form without close relatives. However, it shows marked similarities, in both plumage and skeletal characters, to the volant Buff-banded Rail (*Gallirallus philippensis*), and the differences in the wings, the pectoral girdle, and some plumage features of the adults, are simply recently derived neotenic characters. It occurs alongside the Buff-banded Rail, this situation reflecting the multiple invasion of New Zealand by *G. philippensis*-like stock. The presence of two fossil relatives, one on North Island and one on an offshore island, indicates that the Weka has a long history of isolation on the New Zealand islands.

Other possible insular derivatives of *G. philippensis* stock are the recently extinct Tahiti Rail (*Gallirallus pacificus*) and the Lord Howe Rail (*Gallirallus sylvestris*), both flightless species. The flightless New Caledonian Rail (*Gallirallus lafresnayanus*) is now also regarded as a possible *G. philippensis* derivative, although Olson could see no indication of a relationship between it and the Lord Howe Rail, and regarded it as having diverged so far that any external resemblance to a possible common ancestor has been obscured. He accordingly placed it in *Tricholimnas*, moving the only other species in that genus, the Lord Howe Rail, to *Gallirallus*. Other flightless or weak-flying *Gallirallus* species endemic to oceanic islands and possibly derived from *G. philippensis* stock are the Guam Rail (*Gallirallus owstoni*) and the recently described Roviana Rail (*Gallirallus rovianae*), as well as the recently extinct Chatham Rail (*Gallirallus modestus*), Wake Rail (*Gallirallus wakensis*) and

Dieffenbach's Rail (*Gallirallus dieffenbachii*), the last of these sometimes being considered conspecific with *G. philippensis*.

An interesting, though confusing, situation has arisen concerning an extinct form of rail, apparently from the Kiribati (Gilbert) Islands in the Pacific, and known only from a specimen preserved in alcohol in the Harvard Museum of Comparative Zoology. This form, designated the Gilbert Rail (*Tricholimnas conditicius*), was subsequently dismissed by J. C. Greenway as an immature specimen of the Lord Howe Rail, the locality from which the bird was collected being in doubt. Subsequently, however, on reviewing the historical and morphological evidence, M. Walters concluded that the original designation was probably correct, but since then Olson, also reviewing morphological and historical evidence, has concluded that the bird is indeed an immature Lord Howe Rail and that the confusion is probably traceable to a misassociated specimen label.

Another subgroup within *Gallirallus* is formed by the Barred Rail (*Gallirallus torquatus*) of South-east Asia and the New Britain Rail (*Gallirallus insignis*), to which can be added the recently described flightless Okinawa Rail (*Gallirallus okinawae*). The recently extinct volant Sharpe's Rail (*Gallirallus sharpei*), known from a long-overlooked single specimen of unknown origin, is most similar to the Buff-banded Rail but differs from it strikingly in coloration and plumage pattern. The remaining species in the genus, the Slaty-breasted Rail (*Gallirallus striatus*), is the only member of the group found in continental Asia and is considered by Olson to be an advanced form of the genus that has paralleled the evolution of the *Rallus* group towards a slender marsh-dwelling build.

The species of *Rallus* are much more specialized than those of *Gallirallus* and are highly adapted to a semi-aquatic existence in reedy marshes. The genus appears to have radiated in the New World, with only three allopatric species found in the Old World. The Water Rail (*Rallus aquaticus*) of Eurasia is one of the few Palearctic rallids which does not migrate to sub-Saharan Africa, where it is replaced by the African Rail (*Rallus caerulescens*). The third species, the Madagascar Rail (*Rallus madagascariensis*) is endemic to Madagascar. All three probably had their origins in a single invasion of *Rallus* from the New World.

The recognition of the King Rail (*Rallus elegans*) as a distinct species, rather than a form of the Clapper Rail (*Rallus longirostris*), has long provoked argument, and even recent mitochondrial DNA studies have yielded inconclusive results. Although the separation is currently accepted by many authorities, the problem is likely to fuel discussion for some time to come.

The genus *Lewinia* comprises three species which are often treated as one. Olson regarded the Brown-banded Rail (*Lewinia mirificus*) of Luzon in the Philippines as a well marked form of Lewin's Rail (*Lewinia pectoralis*), while the Auckland Rail (*Lewinia muelleri*) is also regarded by some authorities as being conspecific with the latter. Furthermore, Lewin's Rail is sometimes placed in the genus *Rallus*, although its skeleton differs in several respects from the true *Rallus* type. However, its skeleton is almost identical to that of the much larger White-throated Rail (*Dryolimnas cuvieri*) of Madagascar and the Aldabra atoll, and Olson placed it too in *Dryolimnas*, regarding the genus as rather primitive and forming part of a pro-*Rallus* group.

The central South Atlantic islands served as habitat for a complex of *Rallus*-related species which presumably arose from accidental dispersal. Of these, the genus *Atlantisia* was represented by three flightless species, two of which were exterminated by introduced mammals, while the third, the Inaccessible Rail (*Atlantisia rogersi*), survives on one island of the Tristan da Cunha group. Olson considers that these species represent neotenic relict forms of ancestors of the pro-*Rallus* group *Dryolimnas-Atlantisia*.

One of the most difficult problems in rallid taxonomy concerns the proper allocation of the species included in the genera *Porzana* and *Amaurornis*. *Porzana* is a possibly polyphyletic genus and is very difficult to categorize because of differing taxonomic treatments: for example, Ripley lists 27 species but Olson only 13. The five *Amaurornis* species *akool, isabellinus, olivaceus, moluccanus* and *phoenicurus* form a rather basic stock from which both the *Porzana* assemblage and the gallinules could have arisen, and some *Amaurornis* species have previously been included in *Porzana* and *vice versa*. A natural group within *Porzana* is formed by five living species, *parva, pusilla, porzana, fluminea* and *carolina*, and the recently extinct Laysan Crake (*Porzana palmeri*). The probably extinct Kosrae Crake (*Porzana monasa*) and the Henderson Crake (*Porzana atra*) are very close

The occupation of forest habitat, and the possession of patterned natal down, are regarded as primitive characters in the Rallidae. Canirallus is a primitive genus comprising two species of forest-dwelling rails, the Grey-throated Rail (Canirallus oculeus) of West Africa and the Madagascar Wood-rail. In the latter the black natal down is patterned with rufous brown, a character which it shares with the forest-dwelling Rallina rails endemic to New Guinea. The plumage characters relevant to racial separation in the Madagascar Wood-rail are imperfectly described, while the population of the Bemaraha Reserve, in north-west Madagascar, probably belongs to an undescribed race.

[*Canirallus kioloides kioloides*, Madagascar.
Photo: Dominique Halleux/ Bios]

The genus Laterallus comprises nine species of small crakes from the Americas, with one confined to the Galapagos Islands. Typically birds of marsh and wet grassland, they have trilling, churring or rattling calls, they eat invertebrates and seeds, and most species are poorly known.
The Red-and-white Crake is possibly the most strikingly marked member of the genus, which is perhaps one reason why it is kept in captivity more frequently than are many other small rails.
It is unique in the genus, and unusual among rallids, in laying pure white eggs.

[*Laterallus leucopyrrhus*, San Diego Zoo, USA. Photo: Kenneth W. Fink]

to the Spotless Crake (*Porzana tabuensis*) and could have been derived from it.

Amaurornis-like stock could also have given rise to the assemblage of New World rails in the genera *Cyanolimnas*, *Neocrex* and *Pardirallus*. All the species in these genera share a similar drab plumage, with the exception of the Spotted Rail (*Pardirallus maculatus*), which, however, has a similar dark morph of its juvenile plumage. The long-billed *Pardirallus* rails are often mistakenly placed in *Rallus*, from which they differ markedly in skeletal characters. Another line probably derived from *Amaurornis* comprises the Australasian genera *Eulabeornis*, *Habroptila* and *Megacrex*.

The purple gallinules, formerly separated into the three genera *Porphyrula*, *Porphyrio* and *Notornis*, are considered by Olson to form an obviously monophyletic group, as was originally suggested by E. Mayr in 1949. *Porphyrula* differs from *Porphyrio* only in its smaller size, less massive bill and more oval nostril, while the two genera share a number of specialized characters. The three species sometimes placed in *Porphyrula* are closer to each other than to *Porphyrio*, so a case could be made for maintaining them as a subgenus, but they would not seem to merit a separate genus. The Takahe (*Porphyrio mantelli*), although formerly awarded the monotypic genus *Notornis*, is now generally regarded as simply a large, flightless derivative of *Porphyrio*.

Despite the distinctive appearance of the extinct Samoan Moorhen (*Gallinula pacifica*) and both the San Cristobal Moorhen (*Gallinula silvestris*) and the Tristan Moorhen (*Gallinula nesiotis*), which previously resulted in their separation in different genera, it is now generally accepted that they are most suitably placed in *Gallinula*. Similarly, it is no longer regarded as appropriate to place the Spot-flanked Gallinule (*Gallinula melanops*) in the monotypic genus *Porphyriops*, or the Black-tailed Native-hen (*Gallinula ventralis*) and the Tasmanian Native-hen (*Gallinula mortierii*) in the genus *Tribonyx*: the skeletons of all three species show no differences which can be considered of generic significance when compared to *Gallinula*.

The coots (*Fulica*) are very similar to *Gallinula* both skeletally and in their adult and juvenile plumages, and are derived from a *Gallinula*-like stock which has become adapted for diving. Their centre of species diversity is South America and it seems likely that they originated there and later spread to the

Old World. The genus is well defined and has diverged relatively little from its ancestral stock. The Hawaiian Coot (*Fulica alai*) has only recently been treated as a species distinct from the American Coot (*Fulica americana*), while the Caribbean Coot (*Fulica caribaea*) is sometimes regarded as merely a morph of the American Coot, although West Indian populations mate assortatively without evidence of crossing.

A new phylogenetic study of the Rallidae, using morphological characters, is currently being undertaken by B. Livezey, and this may well shed new light on some of the unresolved problems discussed above.

Two new living rallid species, both from islands and both flightless, have been described in the last 20 years. The Okinawa Rail was first seen on the island of Okinawa, in the Ryukyu Islands, in 1978 and was described in 1981. It is considered to belong to the superspecies containing the volant Barred Rail and the flightless New Britain Rail, and to have evolved from a progenitor of the Barred Rail. An unnamed fossil rallid from Okinawa may also be ancestral to the Okinawa Rail. The fact that the Okinawa Rail should have remained undescribed for so long may seem surprising, especially as the bird occurs on a densely populated island which is ornithologically well known, but it is found only in the largely uninhabited forests of the north, whereas most of the island's human population lives in the south.

The Roviana Rail from the Solomon Islands is known from the holotype, collected in 1977; it was first seen in the wild by an ornithologist as recently as 1994, and is known to local people on several islands in the group. It belongs to the widespread group of Pacific *Gallirallus* species that includes the volant Buff-banded Rail; it is most similar to that species and to the flightless Guam Rail and the extinct flightless Wake Rail, and is probably derived from an ancestor similar to the Buff-banded Rail.

In view of these recent discoveries, it seems highly likely that there are other forms of rallid still probably awaiting discovery by the ornithological world. For example, a hitherto undescribed chestnut rail from the uninhabited Foja Mountains in north-west New Guinea was frequently seen in October 1979 and may be either an undescribed form of Forbes's Forest-rail (*Rallina forbesi*) or a new species.

Morphological Aspects

The Rallidae are a large but rather homogeneous family of small to medium-sized terrestrial, marsh and aquatic birds. Their bodies are short, and are often laterally compressed for ease of movement through dense, low vegetation, whence the expression "thin as a rail". In the Virginia Rail (*Rallus limicola*) the very flexible vertebral column is thought to facilitate movement through dense marsh vegetation, but possibly to reduce the bird's effectiveness in flight. The neck is short to moderately long, with 14-15 cervical vertebrae.

Rails range in length from 12 cm to 63 cm and in mass from 20 g to over 3000 g. The smallest species is the Black Rail of the Americas, while the Inaccessible Rail, with a length of as little as 13 cm and a mean mass of 40 g, has the distinction of being the smallest flightless bird known to exist. The largest species is the flightless Takahe of New Zealand, males of which weigh 2250-3250 g, while the Giant Coot (*Fulica gigantea*) can reach 2500 g. In most species the sexes are very similar in size, although the male is often slightly larger than the female. Marked sexual dimorphism in size occurs in only a few rallids, and in all cases the male is the larger sex; the greatest size differences occur in the Watercock (*Gallicrex cinerea*), in which the male averages 50% heavier than the female, and the Weka, in which the male averages 42% heavier. The Dusky Moorhen (*Gallinula tenebrosa*) shows remarkable racial variation in size, nominate Australian birds averaging as much as 58% heavier than *neumanni* of New Guinea.

The wings are short, broad and rounded. There are normally ten primaries, fewer in some flightless forms, and a minute eleventh primary is present in some of the larger species. There are 10-20 secondaries, and the wing is usually diastataxic, with the fifth secondary absent. In some species the alula has a sharp, curved claw which may be used by the young, and possibly also by the adults, to assist in climbing. In volant species, flight over short distances usually appears low, weak, and generally not sustained, and the birds usually fly with dangling legs. Small crakes will often pitch or flop abruptly into cover after a short flight, almost as though they had suddenly lost the use of their wings. Notwithstanding this apparent inability to fly strongly, some species migrate or disperse over long distances and the family is renowned for its ability to colonize remote oceanic islands. In fact, in terms of their morphology and their ability to accumulate food reserves, rails are perfectly capable of sustained and very long flights, but their flight performance is relatively poor and they tend to migrate at low altitudes. The high degree of vagrancy in the Rallidae is indicative of the readiness with which the birds are apparently blown off course by unfavourable winds (see Movements).

One of the best known features of the family is the incidence of flightlessness in island taxa. Flightlessness is widespread among various avian orders, and numerous flightless forms exist, but the Rallidae show a particular proclivity to flightlessness. There are 53 rallid species living, or extinct since 1600, which are known only from islands (including New Guinea and Madagascar) and of these, 32 species (59%) are flightless or nearly so. Flightlessness has evolved many times within the Rallidae, often and repeatedly on islands without predators and probably independently each time. Selection reduces the flight muscles and pectoral girdle, probably through neoteny, and there is usually a corresponding increase in the development of the leg muscles. These modifications may involve only a few genetic changes, for example in genes controlling the relative growth rate of different body parts. The selective force involved is presumably the high energetic cost of flight and the weight burden of flight muscle: where such costs are not balanced by the benefits of dispersal and escape from predators, it is obviously to the bird's advantage to become flightless.

The frequency with which flightlessness is developed by rails suggests that they are predisposed to it, and they are certainly pre-adapted to coping with some of the restrictions which it imposes. For example, many volant species are behaviourally flightless, preferring to avoid predators by running; in common with several other groups containing flightless forms, many volant

Like most of its congeners the Grey-necked Wood-rail frequents swampy forests and coastal mangroves, but it is also found in many other habitats, including deciduous woodland, marshes and marshy thicket, rice fields, and even grassland with bushes and pools. It is normally associated with dense cover and is sometimes described as shy, skulking and difficult to see, especially when calling. However, it will forage in the open and is generally regarded as less of a skulker than most other rails. It walks with an upright carriage, flicking its short black tail, and, when disturbed, especially by dogs, may fly up to perch on a branch or tree stump. This bird has found a handy temporary perch on top of a strategically situated hornero (*Furnarius*) nest.

[*Aramides cajanea cajanea*, Argentina. Photo: Wayne Lynch/DRK]

The Tasmanian Native-hen is a large, flightless gallinule endemic to Tasmania. It inhabits open pasture, grassland, newly sown crops and cleared land around permanent or seasonal freshwater wetlands with abundant cover. Its grassland habitat may be tussocky, infested with weeds, or lightly wooded, and it breeds near water in dense vegetation such as reeds, rushes and bracken. It requires short-grazed pasture year round for foraging, and is a secondary grazer, depending on primary grazers to provide its foraging habitat. In the past suitable swards were maintained by grazing marsupials and by fire, but the job is now done by introduced rabbits, sheep and cattle.

[Gallinula mortierii, Tasmania. Photo: John Cancalosi/ Bruce Coleman]

rails are temporarily flightless during wing moult, when they become particularly secretive and elusive; and the post-natal development of flight in most species is slow.

Flightlessness may evolve in a very short period of time. For example, the White-throated Rail has a volant race on Madagascar and a flightless race on Aldabra; these differ markedly in size but very little in plumage pattern and colour, and have obviously diverged very recently.

The tail contains 6-16 rectrices, normally 12. It is short, square to rounded, arched and soft, and is sometimes decomposed, especially in flightless species and flufftails. It is often raised or flicked to show the signalling colours of the undertail-coverts, which in many species are contrastingly coloured or patterned.

The structure of the bill is variable. It is sometimes quite slender, straight or slightly downcurved, and slightly longer than the head, for instance in *Rallus* and *Aramidopsis*; it is often quite short and somewhat laterally compressed, as in crakes, and most gallinules and coots; or it may be massive and deep or laterally compressed, as in some *Porphyrio* species. Long-billed rails probe in soft ground and litter, and species with small, fine bills often take primarily insects and small seeds, while species with large, stout bills may graze, dig out roots and tubers, or tear off vegetation. Many species tend to be omnivorous and therefore have unspecialized bills.

The bill is often brightly coloured, contrasting with the plumage of the head, and in some species it has a patch of a different colour at its base. Gallinules and coots have a smooth, plate-like, horny frontal shield, continuous with the outer covering of the bill, which may be coloured similarly or contrastingly to the bill. In some species, the colours of the bill and shield become duller in the non-breeding season, when the shield may also shrink. The male Watercock has the frontal shield continued into a long red horn which almost disappears outside the breeding season, while the Horned Coot (*Fulica cornuta*) has a long, extensible and erectile black proboscis with two tufts at its base; the functions of this strange appendage are unknown. The Invisible Rail (*Habroptila wallacii*) and the New Guinea Flightless Rail (*Megacrex inepta*) also have small frontal shields.

Except in *Porphyrio*, the nostrils are usually in a large depression, and they are pervious in most species, perforate in some. The olfactory process is well developed in most species, and the

ample supply of nasal glands and ducts, with the relative size of the olfactory bulb of the brain, indicate that rails can easily discriminate odours, presumably a help in food-gathering. Rails of littoral habitats have adapted readily to salt water and are able to secrete salt by means of adapted nasal glands; they thus share with ducks and seabirds the ability to adapt to the absorption of sea water for drinking. The White-throated Rail, for example, drinks sea water on Aldabra.

As an adaptation to their primarily terrestrial existence, rails have well developed legs which may be rather long to quite short, are often slender but usually strong, and may be laterally compressed. The toes are often long and slender, but in fully terrestrial species of predominantly dry habitats they may be rather short and heavy. The hind toe is slightly raised, and is used as a plantar toe, helping in the balance of the foot structure. In most gallinules, and also in some crakes, notably the Yellow-breasted Crake (*Porzana flaviventer*) and the White-browed Crake (*Porzana cinerea*) the toes are particularly elongated and the legs modified for walking, jacana-like, on mud and floating or emergent vegetation. Many species can climb well: gallinules, for example, are often seen clambering around high in reeds, and the American Purple Gallinule (*Porphyrio martinica*) climbs easily in bushes and trees up to 20 m above the ground. In some species the legs and feet are brightly coloured and, as with bill colour, leg colour may be brighter during the breeding season. Leg colour may also change as birds mature, and can be helpful in determining a bird's age; for example, in the breeding season, American Coots may be aged on tarsal colour, which progresses through green at one year old; yellow-green at two; and yellow at three; to orange-red at four years or more.

Rails often walk with strong, precise strides. Being accustomed to cover, they often move continuously without long pauses for visual orientation, pausing mainly to feed. When moving through low vegetation, they slip beneath low horizontal stems or arched projecting roots, or raise the feet high to step over such obstacles, and one often gains the impression that the birds are avoiding making substantial vertical changes in the position of the body relative to the substrate. In dense cover rails are adept at walking, and even running, without causing any noise or movement of the vegetation. When reacting to alarm, they melt quietly and rapidly into cover, often lowering the head and stretching

The genus Fulica originated in South America, where the largest coots occur on ponds and lakes in the high, arid puna zone of the central Andes. The Giant Coot is adapted to waters which normally lack reeds and rushes; large populations occur on lakes with extensive shallows supporting dense growths of water weeds such as Myriophyllum, Potamogeton, Zanichellia and Ruppia, on which the birds feed and from which they build their enormous nests. Lauca National Park in northern Chile holds about 12,000 Giant Coots, the largest known population of this generally scarce species. Adult Giant Coots are probably flightless, and are normally attached to both territory and nest for life, but immatures are smaller and disperse by flying between lakes at night, sometimes visiting reedy lakes at lower altitudes.

[Fulica gigantea, Lake Chungara, Lauca National Park, Chile. Photo: Luiz Claudio Marigo]

The forest habitats occupied by rails are usually stable and permanently suitable for them, and forest-rails tend to be sedentary. However, species that are dependent on moist substrates and forest streams may make seasonal movements in response to dry conditions. The Red-necked Crake is one such species. An inhabitant of rain forest, swamp forest, monsoon forest and secondary growth, it forages for invertebrates in shallow streams and in leaf litter. In north Queensland it is regarded as a wet season visitor from New Guinea, leaving when the forest floor dries out in winter.

[Rallina tricolor, north Queensland, Australia. Photo: Hans & Judy Beste/Ardea]

out the neck, and they compress the body to allow easy passage between stems. They often walk with bobbing head and flicking tail, the head movement possibly being connected with acuity of vision, as in other birds such as pigeons and chickens: the head moves forwards relative to the surroundings and, at the end of the forward thrust, is temporarily stationary while the rest of the body catches up, this brief stationary phase being an adaptation to allow a motionless view (with the central fovea) of the bird's surroundings. The tail jerk possibly functions in visual orientation and signalling between individuals, especially when the tail is jerked and spread in alarm before the bird runs into cover; if accompanied by a short pause in forward gait, the jerk allows the bird an instantaneous clear view from a stationary position. It has also been suggested that such tail-jerking movements may act as a signal of fitness designed to deter predators (see page 460).

All rails can swim; they also dive easily and can sink, using the wings under water if necessary. Some species, such as the Striped Crake (*Aenigmatolimnas marginalis*) and the Clapper Rail, will dive and cling to submerged vegetation to escape pursuit or when wounded. In coots, which are fully aquatic, the pelvis and legs are modified for diving, and all but one species, the Red-fronted Coot (*Fulica rufifrons*), have toes with enlarged lateral lobes to aid swimming. The Spot-flanked Gallinule also has narrowly lobed toes, while those of the Common Moorhen (*Gallinula chloropus*) are somewhat emarginated.

The plumage of rails is often dull and cryptic, common colours being sombre browns, chestnut, black, blue-grey and grey; in the genus *Porphyrio*, however, the plumage is predominantly iridescent purple, blue or green. The upperparts are frequently spotted, barred or streaked, but are uniform in some species. The flanks are often strongly barred, for example in most *Rallus*, *Gallirallus* and *Porzana* species, and the vent and undertail-coverts may contrast strongly with the rest of the plumage. The Weka and the Chestnut Rail (*Eulabeornis castaneoventris*) both have different plumage morphs. In most species the sexes are alike or very nearly so: marked sexual dimorphism in plumage occurs only in the flufftails, the *Rallina* forest-rails endemic to New Guinea, the Striped Crake, the Little Crake (*Porzana parva*) and the Watercock, while several other species show much slighter differences.

With the exception of the Watercock, no species in the family shows any significant seasonal change in plumage colour or pattern. Most minor differences which exist between breeding and non-breeding plumages are difficult to see in the field, and are often caused by abrasion.

The downy plumage of rallid chicks is typically black (sometimes iridescent, or grizzled with brown or chestnut) or dark brown, and exceptions to this plumage pattern are few. In the Andaman Crake (*Rallina canningi*) the chick is rich chestnut, while in the Madagascar Wood-rail and Forbes's Forest-rail the grizzled chick has rufous colouring on the head and neck and, in the former species, a rufous stripe along the side of the body. The chick of the Chestnut Forest-rail (*Rallina rubra*) is black, grizzled with russet or chestnut, and the black chicks of the Buff-banded Rail and the Lord Howe Rail may have grey on the eyestripe or the cheek. In the Nkulengu Rail, however, the chick is distinctively patterned with brown, black and white; this presumably cryptic pattern more closely resembles that of the precocial chicks of other orders, whereas the black down of most other rails is a wide departure from that of typical precocial chicks. The natal down of the Nkulengu Rail probably represents a relatively primitive state, while the black down of typical rails appears to be a specialized, derived condition and may be an adaptation for hiding in dense vegetation.

The downy young of some rallids have distinctively coloured filoplumes or bristles, these being developed most markedly in the Common Coot (*Fulica atra*), which has red papillae on the face as well as black bristles on the crown, and yellow-tipped down on the neck and body. Downy young of the coots native to the Americas have yellow or orange bristles on the neck or throat. The Sora (*Porzana carolina*) also has orange throat bristles, while the American Purple Gallinule has grey bristles on the head, two other *Porphyrio* species have pale filoplumes on the head and body, and two *Gallinula* species have pale down-tips or plumes on the neck. *Fulica*, *Porphyrio* and *Gallinula* chicks also have brightly coloured bare skin on the head. It is thought that the bright colours of the bill and throat act as signals for feeding, and in the Common Coot this probable signal effect remains conspicuous as long as the young are totally dependent on parental care. J. Fjeldså has suggested that, in the Common Coot, the colours of the bare skin on the head have an appeasement func-

Coots are the most aquatic members of the Rallidae, occurring on fresh to brackish waters and also quiet inshore sea waters. Most species are gregarious, and both the American Coot and the Common Coot (Fulica atra) form large monospecific flocks outside the breeding season, while during the breeding season non-breeding birds also flock near occupied territories. Both species also congregate in large flocks to undergo their post-breeding moult, when the remiges are moulted simultaneously and the birds may be flightless for up to four weeks.

[Fulica americana americana, Merritt Island, Florida, USA. Photo: Arthur Morris]

tion, which may well be necessary in such pugnacious birds. The downy chicks of many rallid species, especially those which nest in dense vegetation, have brightly coloured or patterned bills and it has been widely suggested that this prominent feature serves to assist the parents in directing food to the chick's bill in the dim light conditions prevailing in dense vegetation.

Juvenile (post-natal) and immature (post-juvenile) plumages are undescribed for many rail species. Even when details are available, it is sometimes not possible to determine whether the described plumage is juvenile or immature, or whether there is, in fact, any difference between the two. In some species the juvenile plumage is similar to the adult plumage, but in others it may be paler or duller than in the adult, and less contrastingly barred or patterned; sometimes, for example in most flufftails, it is plain. The White-spotted Flufftail (*Sarothrura pulchra*) is apparently unique among rallids in having its juvenile plumage patterned like that of the strongly sexually dimorphic adult of the corresponding sex, and this makes it possible to sex the young as soon as post-natal moult starts. As far as can be determined, the immature plumage of rallids is usually almost identical to that of the adult.

Post-juvenile moult is partial, resulting in an immature non-breeding plumage. The following first pre-breeding moult is partial in some species and complete in others, and it may often follow the post-juvenile moult almost immediately, thus suppressing a distinct immature non-breeding plumage. In some cases the post-juvenile moult leads directly to the first breeding plumage. There are variations to these basic patterns: for example, in the Galapagos Rail the change from juvenile to adult-type plumage is gradual, no distinctive immature plumage being attained.

In adults, post-breeding moult is complete though its timing is variable, and there is usually a partial pre-breeding moult. In the Western Palearctic, migratory rallids moult the flight-feathers after breeding and before migrating, while sedentary species in Africa may undergo remex moult during the breeding season. In South Africa, the Red-knobbed Coot (*Fulica cristata*) has been found to replace the body and tail plumage continuously, while Striped Crakes in captivity had two complete moults per year, a pattern not known in any other rallid.

In some rallids, notably of the genera *Laterallus*, *Gallirallus*, *Rallus*, *Porzana*, *Pardirallus*, *Porphyrio*, *Gallinula* and *Fulica*, remex moult is simultaneous, resulting in a flightless period. In others, notably of the genera *Sarothrura*, *Himantornis*, *Canirallus*, *Rallina* and *Anurolimnas*, it is sequential.

Habitat

The wide distribution of the family is a reflection of the ability of rails to adapt to a very diverse range of habitat types, both natural and artificial. Rails are cosmopolitan and occur almost everywhere except in polar regions, completely waterless deserts and mountainous regions above the permanent snow-line. The greatest variety of species is found in wetlands, where rails occupy virtually all types of terrestrial, estuarine and littoral wetland habitats. Some species are found at coastal wetlands such as lagoons, bays, salt-marshes, tidal creeks and mudflats, and mangrove swamps. For example, the mangrove habitats of South America are home to four of the *Aramides* wood-rails, the other three species being found predominantly in forest. In Australia the Buff-banded Rail, which occurs in a wide range of habitat types including freshwater wetlands, forest, woodland, heathland, grassland and crops, sometimes also inhabits salt-marshes, tidal mudflats and mangroves, and it even occurs on coral cays and other offshore islands.

Rails occupy many types of freshwater wetland including swamps, peat bogs, marshes, dambos (seasonally wet drainage lines in African woodland), floodplains, permanent and seasonal pans and ponds, ditches, paddyfields and wet sugar cane fields, and the marginal and emergent vegetation of streams, rivers, canals, dams and lakes. Some species, such as the Grey-breasted Crake (*Laterallus exilis*), the Sakalava Rail (*Amaurornis olivieri*), the Yellow-breasted and White-browed Crakes, and the *Porphyrio* gallinules, have a preference for floating vegetation, and one factor responsible for the threatened status of the Sakalava Rail of Madagascar is probably the continued loss of this habitat type.

The most aquatic rallids, the coots, occupy water bodies ranging from freshwater lakes and ponds to brackish water, and bays and arms of the sea. They frequently occur alongside waterfowl (Anatidae) but, unlike some ducks, have not become adapted to a purely saltwater environment. The two largest species, the Giant Coot and the Horned Coot, frequent barren highland lakes of the Andean *puna* zone, occurring to altitudes of over 5000 m, while the Andean Coot (*Fulica ardesiaca*) and the White-winged Coot (*Fulica leucoptera*) occur to almost as high an elevation in similar habitats. The Red-fronted Coot, which occurs at lower altitudes in South America, appears to prefer semi-open waters with much floating and emergent vegetation, and is the only member of the genus in which the lobes on the toes are not greatly enlarged as an aid to frequent and prolonged swimming.

Other rails inhabit warm forests from lowland to highland areas, including the interior and edge of primary and secondary growth, monsoon forest, swamp forest, sago swamps, gallery forest, dense riverine forest, forested ravines, partially cleared forest and dense scrub, overgrown and abandoned cultivation at forest margins, banana groves, cassava and arrowroot plantations, and dense evergreen or deciduous thickets. Forest habitats may have clear substrates with leaf litter, moist ground or mud, or may have ground vegetation. Some species, for example the Nkulengu Rail, the Grey-throated Rail (*Canirallus oculeus*) and Woodford's Rail (*Nesoclopeus woodfordi*), are typically associated with wet habitats such as forest streams, swampy areas and muddy patches, and are never far from water, whereas the four wood-rails endemic to New Guinea appear not to be associated with wet areas. Others, such as the Rufous-necked (*Aramides axillaris*) and Grey-necked Wood-rails (*Aramides cajanea*) extend their ranges from forest into deciduous woodland. The Buff-spotted Flufftail (*Sarothrura elegans*) occupies a wide range of habitat types, from stable forest habitats to deciduous thickets which may be occupied only seasonally depending on the cover and the substrate moisture, and consequently also the availability of food.

Other species are associated with predominantly grassland habitats, ranging from mosaics of hygrophilous grassland and sedge meadow, and the marginal zones of grassland savanna with pockets of marsh, to predominantly dry grassland including savanna, *pampas*, hayfields, meadows, rough pasture, alfalfa and crop fields, occasionally crop stubble, and also golf courses and airstrips; the grass may be tall or relatively short, but it is usually dense. In New Zealand, both the Weka and the Takahe occur in subalpine tussock grassland, the latter exclusively, except when forced to move down to subalpine scrub and beech forest when snow covers the grassland in winter. In Africa, the Striped Flufftail (*Sarothrura affinis*) occurs in both upland grassland and, in the south-western Cape, in mesic mountain fynbos, a macchia-type vegetation dominated by heaths (Ericaceae), proteas (Proteaceae) and the grass- and sedge-like restios (Restioanceae) on dry to seasonally waterlogged ground; it is the only rallid to occur in this habitat type. Grassland habitats may be permanently or seasonally occupied: for example, those occupied by the African Crake (*Crex egregia*) and the Streaky-breasted Flufftail (*Sarothrura boehmi*) in central and southern Africa are typically seasonally moist to wet and are frequently burned during the dry season, forcing the birds to emigrate after breeding.

The non-breeding habitats of most rails are similar to their breeding habitats, but some wetland and grassland species, especially those which migrate, may occupy different habitats in different seasons, and many species occupy a wider range of habitats outside the breeding season. During the rainy season in central and southern Africa, sedentary species such as the Red-chested Flufftail (*Sarothrura rufa*) and the African Rail move out from permanently wet reedbeds and sedgebeds to occupy peripheral seasonally wet grassland which provides good nesting habitat but may be burned in the dry season. In North America the winter habitat of the Black Rail includes smaller, more linear and more fragmented wetland patches than does the preferred summer habitat, while in some areas the Yellow Rail (*Coturnicops noveboracensis*) appears to prefer the drier portions of coastal marshes in winter, and the Virginia Rail occupies salt-marshes more widely in winter than in the breeding season. The Little, Baillon's (*Porzana pusilla*) and the Spotted Crakes (*Porzana porzana*) and also the Sora all occupy a wider range of palustrine wetland habitats outside the breeding season, while Spotted Crakes wintering in central Africa occupy very temporary habitats not used by breeding Afrotropical species. In winter, the Water Rail, when displaced by frost, may use drainpipes, rubbish dumps,

open ditches and other artefacts as refuges, and it can occur in gardens. There is even a record of the threatened Austral Rail (*Rallus antarcticus*) wintering in a garden and subsequently moving back into its normal reedbed habitat. A narrower habitat tolerance in the breeding season may result from restrictions imposed by breeding-habitat requirements, and also from seasonal differences in food requirements (see Food and Feeding).

Any rallid is likely to make use of atypical habitats, often artificial and sometimes of very limited extent or with relatively poor cover, when on migration or undergoing dispersal or irruptive movements. Thus wetland species may occur at sewage ponds, flooded patches of grass or forbs, flooded thickets, and predominantly dry grassy areas such as lawns, pastures and hayfields, while species normally inhabiting freshwater sites may temporarily use brackish or saline wetlands. Grassland species may make use of airstrips, golf courses and crop fields. The highly eruptive Black-tailed Native-hen of Australia takes advantage of many wetland, grassland and scrub habitats, especially during influxes, and is also known to occur in urban areas and in arid country, sandhills, and coastal flats and scrub.

The ability to capitalize on this great diversity of habitats throughout the world indicates that the family shows great adaptive plasticity. Rails are also predominantly of generalist habits, for example many are omnivorous. These two characteristics allow many species to exploit highly ephemeral or atypical habitats. The great adaptive plasticity of rails also allows them to be successful colonists of oceanic islands. Their ability to make use of open land allows them to colonize islands where, in the absence of competitors, they can radiate to occupy almost any available terrestrial niche. They are capable of adapting to remote oceanic islands of volcanic origin, where conditions are harsh and vegetation is sparse or even almost non-existent. For example, the recently extinct *Atlantisia elpenor* lived on Ascension Island, where the terrestrial environment is hostile in the extreme, consisting mainly of bare, waterless tracts of lava and ash. This medium-sized rail, about the size of the Virginia Rail, apparently obtained its food and water from the eggs and regurgitated prey of the seabirds which formerly nested on the island in great numbers. Another *Atlantisia* species, the Inaccessible Rail, apparently occupies the niche of a mouse on its namesake island. It makes tunnels through the vegetation and forages on boulder beaches, making use of natural connecting cavities under boulders when moving around. The Spotless Crake is a good example of a species with a wide habitat tolerance which has successfully colonized islands. It normally occurs in a great variety of wetland habitats and also in ferns, heath and scrub, but on some islands it occupies dry, sterile, rocky or stony habitats with no standing water. Similarly, the nominate, Madagascar race of the White-throated Rail occurs in forest, wetlands and mangroves, but the Aldabra race, *aldabranus*, is adapted to coral scrub habitat.

The habitat requirements of few rail species have been studied in great detail, but it has been demonstrated that, for some wetland and forest species which feed chiefly on invertebrates, the structure of the vegetation and the nature of the substrate may be the most important factors influencing habitat suitability. For example, the Virginia Rail is known to avoid marshes with high stem densities or large amounts of residual vegetation, features which are common in older marshes and which impede the birds' movement, whereas vegetation height is not important as long as there is adequate overhead cover. These birds need shallow water and a substrate with a high invertebrate abundance, and are most common in areas with 40-70% upright emergent vegetation interspersed with patches of open water, mudflats or matted vegetation. When breeding, they may select those areas of the marsh with a greater abundance of emergent vegetation.

Red-chested Flufftails occur in a very wide variety of wetland vegetation types and, like Virginia Rails, avoid areas where the vegetation is very dense and moribund, such vegetation being difficult to move through and providing few good nest-sites and relatively little invertebrate food. In southern Africa they are adapted to fire-modified wetland habitats, and periodic burning results in improvement in habitat quality expressed in terms of the increased availability of vegetation suitable for occupation

During the breeding season coots are highly territorial and are notoriously aggressive, especially towards conspecifics but also to other waterbird species. The aggressive displays and fighting behaviour of most coots have been described in some detail; warning, patrolling, Charging-attack and Splattering-attack behaviour appear to be very similar in all taxa. The Splattering-attack, a high intensity threat, is shown in the upper photograph of Giant Coots. The attacking bird splatters noisily towards the intruder, running over the surface of the water aided by the flapping wings, extending the neck forwards and holding the tail down. The attacked bird flees in a similar manner, but with its head more erect (Splattering-retreat). To avoid violent confrontation, when close to the victim the attacker usually brakes sharply by closing its wings, raising its body and "churning" or treading water vigorously. In the Common Coot, as seen in the lower photograph, fighting generally follows Charging-attacks, when the antagonists swim towards each other at high speed and neither gives way. It involves violent, often prolonged, striking with the feet, clawing at the opponent's breast and stabbing with the bill; both birds usually spread and hold back the wings as they try to unbalance each other. The weaker bird is often forced onto its back or is held under water, and may escape by swimming under water or by fleeing in the Splattering-retreat. Fights may result in injury, and death has even been known to occur.

[Above:
Fulica gigantea,
Lauca National Park, Chile.
Photo: Günter Ziesler.

Below:
Fulica atra atra,
Arundel, England.
Photo: Roger Wilmshurst/
FLPA]

and an increase in the density of permanently resident pairs. The timing of their return to burned territories is mainly influenced by the development of adequate canopy cover (at least 55% and usually over 65% cover is required) and to the substrate water content, for they do not reoccupy seasonally wet areas until the substrate is moist or flooded; the effect of vegetation height is less important but is complementary to that of cover in that birds will return to very tall vegetation, such as *Typha*, while cover values are still relatively low.

The Buff-spotted Flufftail also occupies a wide variety of habitat types encompassing both natural forest and thickets, and also areas dominated by alien vegetation: in southern Africa it has extended its range locally by occupying exotic vegetation around human habitations. Its primary food consists of macroinvertebrates, for which it forages in leaf litter and damp earth; such prey is as abundant on substrates below exotic vegetation as on those below indigenous plants.

Although most rails inhabit wetland habitats, it does not necessarily follow that the family has an aquatic or paludicoline origin. Olson has pointed out that the most primitive living rail, the Nkulengu Rail, is a forest bird, as are the members of other primitive or unspecialized relict genera such as *Aramides*, *Canirallus* and *Gymnocrex*, while the most specialized and derived genera such as *Rallus*, *Porphyrio* and *Fulica* contain aquatic or marsh-dwelling species. Thus it would appear that the progression from generalization to specialization in the family is from forest forms to aquatic forms.

General Habits

Because of the difficulties involved in observing rails in dense cover, and the often secretive nature of the birds, the social behaviour of most species is very poorly known, and most detailed studies have been made on the larger, more obvious species such as gallinules, moorhens and coots. In general, rails are solitary or occur only in pairs, family parties or other small groups. The most gregarious species are the coots, with the exception of the Giant Coot: species such as the Common, American, Red-knobbed, White-winged and Andean Coots frequently associate in large monospecific flocks outside the breeding season, while non-breeding birds of the first two species also flock near breeding territories during the breeding season. Some flocks may be very large, numbering over 10,000 birds in the Common Coot, in which some of these agglomerations may be moulting groups. Coots tend to feed in loose flocks, often alongside ducks. In the breeding season coots are territorial and often very pugnacious, but the Horned Coot occasionally nests in loose colonies.

Some gallinules also associate in loose flocks when not breeding, examples being the Purple Swamphen (*Porhyrio porphyrio*), and the Common and Dusky Moorhens. In flocks of Common Moorhens, and in all social groups of Purple Swamphens, a social hierarchy may be seen, males being dominant to females and adults dominant to immatures. The Black-tailed Native-hen is usually gregarious and may occur in enormous flocks during its periodic irruptions, when flocks of up to 20,000 birds are recorded. It may also feed gregariously, but it breeds in isolated pairs or in small colonies of up to five nests. Populations of the Takahe are often concentrated into loose colonies, but within these, solitary pairs defend secluded territories.

Most other species are normally solitary, although population densities can be very high in some wetlands. Black Crakes (*Amaurornis flavirostris*), Lesser Moorhens (*Gallinula angulata*) and Allen's Gallinules (*Porphyrio alleni*) are known to occur and breed at high densities in the emergent vegetation of irregularly flooded river systems in the Afrotropics.

After breeding, many rails relinquish their territories and remain solitary until the next breeding season. Winter feeding territories are known to be maintained by the Water Rail, by the migrant Spotted Crake, and possibly also by the Corncrake (*Crex crex*), in their African wintering quarters, and by the African Crake, and this phenomenon is probably more widespread than is known. Some sedentary species which defend permanent territories and remain in pairs throughout the year, such as the Red-chested and White-spotted Flufftails, may allow immatures to remain in the territory throughout the non-breeding period, during which time the young birds assist with territory defence; the adults will then eject the offspring at the start of the next breeding season. Even species such as the Black Crake, which are territorial only during the breeding season, may retain a loose association between family members during the non-breeding period.

The distinctive song of the Corncrake, from which the bird's scientific and common names are derived, is a monotonous rasping call given only by the male. It may be imitated by mechanical means such as rubbing a piece of bone or wood against another with notches cut in it, or even against a comb. The call serves to proclaim ownership of a territory, to challenge conspecific intruders, and probably also to attract females. It is given most frequently early in the breeding season, when birds often call for hours on end, both day and night. The male calls from the ground, or sometimes from an elevated perch such as a wall; this bird is calling from a low bush at night.

[*Crex crex*, Ireland. Photo: Frances Furlong/ Survival Anglia/ Oxford Scientific Films]

Many rails, whether or not they are defending breeding territories, appear to be aggressive towards conspecifics, and also towards other rail and other bird species. There are few published observations of rails feeding in close proximity to other bird species, but Spotted and Baillon's Crakes, in non-breeding habitat in central and East Africa, will forage on muddy substrates alongside small sandpipers (*Tringa*, *Calidris*) and Greater Painted-snipes (*Rostratula benghalensis*), and they will also feed close to each other.

The daily activity patterns of rails have been poorly studied, but it is known that many species are active during the day and roost at night. Many species are predominantly crepuscular and most show peak activity, including intensive feeding, soon after they emerge from the roost, and again in the late afternoon and early evening. The middle of the day is often spent sheltering and resting. Some species are thought to be mainly nocturnal, but it is difficult to find solid evidence for regular nocturnal activity in more than a few species, and what is loosely described as nocturnal activity may often refer only to crepuscular activity. Some species, such as the flufftails, give advertising calls throughout the night during the breeding season but are not active in any other way at night: they remain in one spot and will not move around in response to taped playback, and they do not forage at night.

Similarly, the King Rail calls much at night during the courtship period, and to a lesser extent at other times of the year, but captive birds move little at night; nothing is known of their roosting habits in the wild. The Plumbeous Rail (*Pardirallus sanguinolentus*) gives advertising calls at night, and is also active during the night in marshes or adjacent cultivated fields. Other terrestrial and marsh species which are known to forage at night as well as by day are the Weka, the Grey-necked Woodrail, and the Chestnut, Inaccessible, Guam and Buff-banded Rails; however the last two are most active at dawn and dusk. The Weka is semi-nocturnal, becoming active in the late afternoon and being active in open habitat on clear moonlit nights. Common Coots and Common Moorhens are sometimes active on moonlit nights and on floodlit waters, and it is possible that nocturnal foraging in rallids is largely confined to species which occupy open habitats where the visibility at night is relatively good, for example coots and those species which inhabit open mudflats. Rails which forage in tidal areas must presumably be active nocturnally when low tides occur at night.

Rails usually roost solitarily, or seasonally in pairs or family groups, except in flocking species. They generally roost on the ground in dense cover, but sometimes above the ground in dense vegetation such as bushes and trees. Some forest-rails, including some flightless species, roost in trees to avoid ground predators, and the Red-necked Crake (*Rallina tricolor*) may use communal roosting platforms. The Plain Bush-hen (*Amaurornis olivaceus*) is also known to build roosting platforms, and other species roost in groups on patches of flattened vegetation. When breeding, many species roost in nests with their offspring, and some may roost in nests at other times of the year: in the New Guinea forests, Forbes's Forest-rail constructs a domed roosting nest in which up to seven adults may sleep, and the White-striped Forest-rail (*Rallina leucospila*) roosts in pairs in a roofed shelter of dried leaves and moss which, according to local people, has nothing to do with nesting and is merely a shelter from the rain, although admittedly this bird's nest remains undescribed but is possibly domed. In harsh environments shelter at night may be important, as is suggested by the case of a captive Inaccessible Rail which was inadvertently left outside in one of the island's frequent gales; although it dug a hole almost 30 cm deep near the roots of a tussock plant, it died.

When resting, rails stand, sometimes on one leg and mostly in a hunched posture with the head sunk on the shoulders, or they lie down on the belly. They often sleep with the head on the back and the bill tucked into the feathers. They bathe freely, mainly by standing in shallow water, alternately ducking the head into the water and flipping water over the back, as well as beating the half-open wings in the water; they may also move the body up and down in the water, or dip the tail. Coots sometimes bathe while swimming. After bathing, the birds leave water to oil and preen. In captive Yellow Rails, bathing activity peaked in the evening at around 19:00 hours and was less frequent in the morning. Captive Red-chested Flufftails bathed daily, always after midday and with peaks in the hottest part of the day and in the early evening, while wild Buff-spotted Flufftails bathed throughout the day, the frequency of this activity increasing during the day to a peak in the two hours before the birds went to roost; chicks also bathed regularly from the age of 10-11 days.

The Water Rail, like most rallids, is omnivorous. It eats predominantly animal matter, especially in spring and summer, consuming more plant material in autumn and winter. Its animal foods include many invertebrates, and it also eats small vertebrates such as fish, amphibians, birds and mammals, which it either kills or scavenges. It occupies many types of dense vegetation over water. On migration and in winter, especially in severe weather, it exploits a much wider range of habitats, and it may venture some distance into the open away from cover to feed, even tolerating human presence.

[*Rallus aquaticus aquaticus*. Photo: Hellio-Van Ingen/ Auscape]

After bathing, the birds preen vigorously. When conditions permit, they will often sun themselves after bathing and preening. Many species are known to stand in a characteristic sunning posture, with partly open wings spread backwards over the sides of the tail. A similar posture, with shuffling movements, is also used to dry the wings, and is the source of reports of so-called rain-bathing. Purple Swamphens will also sometimes sun by crouching with the legs extended forwards, toes splayed and pointed forwards, and wings closed. In Red-chested Flufftails, bathing is solitary but sunbathing may be a social activity, involving a pair or a family group; the birds either crouch or lie flat on the ground with the tail spread and the wings open, drooped, raised, partially or fully extended, or with the wingtips crossed across the back; they frequently preen vigorously while sunning. In captivity, these flufftails were found to sunbathe for the longest periods, lasting 4-10 minutes, in the cool of early morning, as soon as warm sunlit patches became available on the ground or on top of dense vegetation; thereafter, they sunbathed for shorter periods throughout the day. Social sunbathing and preening are also recorded in captive Red-and-white Crakes (*Laterallus leucopyrrhus*).

Allopreening is common, between pair members (often reciprocally), adults and offspring, and siblings; it probably involves functional feather-care to some extent, as well as being of social significance. Head-scratching is direct.

Thermoregulatory behaviour has been little studied in rails. Tasmanian Native-hens often face the breeze on hot days and pant to keep cool, and when shade temperatures exceed 27°C they stop feeding in the open and seek shade or move beneath dense masses of vegetation. On small islands, the Buff-banded Rail is known to shelter in shearwater and petrel burrows and under coralline rocks during the heat of the day.

Voice

Most rails are very vocal, as is to be expected in birds which inhabit dense cover where visual contact is often very limited and communication by sound is important. Red-chested and White-spotted Flufftails, for example, are strongly territorial species which inhabit very dense vegetation, and which may in-dulge in prolonged bouts of territorial calling with neighbours at a common boundary without apparently being in visual contact, even though the birds may be within 1 m of each other on the ground.

The calls of rails vary from sweet to harsh, and include screams, squeals, trills, whistles, booms, rattles, trumpets, grunts and barks. The advertising and territorial calls of many species are given in rather repetitive series and are often loud. Calling may occur at any time of the day or night, but many species call most commonly in the early morning and the evening. Most species are mainly silent when not breeding, and therefore not territorial, but those that are permanently territorial call throughout the year, as do social species, many of which have loud rallying cries. Non-vocal sound signals include wing-clapping, used by Purple Swamphens to distract predators from the young and to attract relief when incubating, beating the water with the wings, used by coots and moorhens in aggressive displays and by many rails during distraction displays in defence of chicks, and slapping noises made with the feet, these characteristically being made by moorhens and coots in defence displays.

Authors describe many rail calls as harsh or monotonous, such as "tack", "kak" or "crek", and many species include a call of this type in their vocal repertoire, sometimes given in a series as an advertising call and sometimes given singly as an aggressive, alarm or warning call. The calls of some small species such as the Yellow Rail may be likened to the noise made by knocking two large pebbles together, and the birds may be induced to respond to sounds produced in this way. Other small crakes produce a sequence of notes rather like a trill, such as is made by small grebes. Some gallinules have booming calls, holding the head and neck in such a way as to produce a resonant note, smaller in volume but similar to that produced by rheas (Rheidae) and cassowaries (Casuariidae). Some of the larger rail species can scream loudly when caught.

Characteristic call types are sometimes shared by most or all members of a genus, and some examples will serve to illustrate the range of calls used. Crakes of the genera *Anurolimnas* and *Laterallus* have trilling, churring or rattling calls, flufftails have hooting advertising calls, *Rallina* crakes often have croaking or nasal calls, and *Gallirallus* species typically give screeches, whistles, squeals or grunts. The *Aramides* wood-rails, which in-

Coots are largely herbivorous, most species feeding predominantly in open water and some also on land. They employ a variety of foraging techniques, two of which are illustrated in these photographs of Common Coots. In shallow water, the Common Coot will immerse the head and neck to scrape algae from stones, stems and tree stumps under water, and to glean food items from the bottom. It may upend in water as much as 40 cm deep, occasionally immersing the whole body. It also dives, usually to 1-2 m but as far down as 6·5 m. A bird presses the air out of the feathers, leaping upwards and then tilting forwards and diving almost vertically with the neck extended. Dives are usually short, lasting up to 20 seconds, and are made to secure water weed, invertebrates and occasionally fish. Coots are less adept at diving than are other bottom-feeding birds: in a given depth of water the duration of their dives is much less, and food is brought to the surface rather than eaten at the bottom.

[Above:
Fulica atra.
Photo: Kim Taylor/
Bruce Coleman.

Below:
Fulica atra.
Photo: Chris Knights/
Survival Anglia/
Oxford Scientific Films]

Clapper Rails inhabit mainly saltwater and brackish marshes. They eat invertebrates, including molluscs, crustaceans and insects, and also take small vertebrates such as fish and frogs, and sometimes, as in this photo, mice. Vegetable matter is also eaten. The race obsoletus of central California is one of three races of this species currently considered to be endangered in the USA. It suffered first from excessive hunting and then from extensive loss of habitat, and its numbers have declined rapidly from an estimated 4200-6000 birds in the early 1970's to only about 400 in 1991. Most of its remaining population is found in San Francisco Bay, where much of its habitat has been destroyed by development.

[*Rallus longirostris obsoletus,* San Francisco Bay, California, USA. Photo: Jeff Foott/Auscape]

habit mangroves, swamps and lowland forest in Central and South America, have a wide range of remarkably loud and far-carrying yelps, shrieks, cackles, barks, grunts and pops, which are characteristic sounds of the areas in which they occur, and which have given rise to onomatopoeic local names for the birds. The voices of the Grey-necked and the Giant Wood-rails (*Aramides ypecaha*) are particularly arresting: both species call in chorus, the former having a varied series of crazed-sounding rollicking, popping and clicking notes, and the latter congregating in groups in the evening to set up a deafening chorus of screams, shrieks and wheezes. The vocabulary of most *Porzana* crakes includes trills, rattles, purrs, chattering, knocking, grating or ticking notes; some also have whistling calls. Most *Gallinula* species emit crowing or clucking calls, and most *Fulica* species have short, explosive, aggressive calls variously rendered "pit", "hic" or "pssi".

Calling in some species is recorded as being ventriloquial, so that the position of the caller is difficult to pinpoint, and one way in which this effect is produced has been observed in the Buff-spotted Flufftail. The male gives loud, hollow, hooting "ooooooo......" notes, each lasting 3-4 seconds, usually from a completely concealed low perch in dense woody vegetation. The call is often given throughout the night and is one of the most characteristic and evocative sounds of the African forest, and has given rise to legends and superstitions (see Relationship with Man). While uttering the note the male continually turns his head slowly from side to side, possibly to broadcast the sound effectively in all directions, and this creates the impression that the call varies greatly in volume and makes the source very difficult to locate.

Duetting is reported in several genera. As normally applied to rails, the term may cover three different forms of vocalizations: true antiphonal duetting, in which a mated pair will make precisely timed alternate calls; calling in precise unison by two birds; and two or more birds calling simultaneously or in chorus, but not in unison or antiphonally. A few species are described as making calls of the second type, notably the Virginia, White-throated and Chestnut Rails and the Tasmanian Native-hen, all of which are also said to duet antiphonally. The White-throated Rail's calls are not made precisely in unison, nor is there apparently any published sonagraphic evidence that those of the other species are. Likewise, most descriptions of antiphonal singing in rails are not backed by sonagraphic evidence to show the precise synchrony of the calls and, in many instances where reasonable evidence is available, it seems that true synchrony is not achieved but that individuals may sing according to their own internally derived rhythm. Species claimed to sing antiphonally include some flufftails, the Nkulengu, New Britain, Okinawa and Water Rails, the Rufous-necked and Grey-necked Wood-rails, the Black Crake, the Rufous-tailed Bush-hen (*Amaurornis moluccanus*), the Spotted and Henderson Crakes and the Chestnut Rail; some of these species also call in chorus. The other species recorded as duetting, such as the Red-necked Crake, the Weka, the Lord Howe and African Rails and the Giant Wood-rail, call either in asynchronous duet or in chorus.

Duetting, including simultaneous song and chorus singing, in rails appears to be principally related to co-operative territorial defence and advertisement, but in some species duetting and simultaneous calling probably help to maintain and reinforce the pair-bond and may also be part of pre-copulatory behaviour. At least in the Black Crake, chorus singing may also assist in the maintenance of the extended family group during the breeding season. Much remains to be discovered about duetting in rails, especially because the calls of so many species, particularly from the tropics, remain undescribed.

Many rails have an extensive vocal repertoire, using calls to communicate in a wide variety of situations. Distinctive advertising calls are frequently uttered, both in territorial advertisement and maintenance and to attract mates. Courtship calls, pre-copulatory and mating calls, contact calls, rallying calls, aggressive calls, warning, alarm and distress calls, and food-soliciting and food-offering calls are among the many vocalizations described for the better known species. Advertis-

Display behaviour, including heterosexual behaviour, is very similar in the Common Moorhen to that found in the Common Coot (Fulica atra). The female solicits copulation by performing the standing Arch-bow display, in which the body is held upright but the head bent down so that the bill points towards the toes. This leads to the Squat-bow, when the female crouches on bent legs in a similar posture and the male steps on to her back to copulate. The male sometimes adopts the standing Arch-bow as a post-copulatory display, and this may lead to reversed mounting, when the female mounts the male, at times a not uncommon occurrence.

[Gallinula chloropus cachinnans, Florida Everglades, USA. Photo: George McCarthy/ Bruce Coleman]

ing calls are frequently far-carrying; for example, the whistle call of the Spotted Crake is audible for at least 2 km in calm weather, while the hoot of the Buff-spotted Flufftail is well audible for up to 1 km through forest and woodland and up to 2·8 km over open ground.

In seasonally territorial species, the frequency and variety of calling often peak during the establishment of the breeding territory, courtship and the early part of the breeding season, falling off after egg-laying and remaining at a relatively low level while the young are reared. In some species there may be a resurgence of territorial calling at the end of the breeding season and this has been shown, in the African Rail and probably in the Clapper Rail, to reflect inclusion of juvenile calls at this time of the year. In those species which do not hold permanent territories, advertising calling usually decreases markedly, or ceases completely, at the end of the breeding season, but species which hold permanent territories continue to make territorial advertising calls throughout the year, although usually at a reduced level outside the breeding season. The Lord Howe Rail is less vocal during its post-breeding moult, as probably are other permanently territorial species. Some species are known to call in flight when migrating, but many migrant species are described as being silent on their non-breeding grounds.

Food and Feeding

Although some species are predominantly vegetarian and some almost entirely dependent on invertebrate food, rails as a group are characteristically omnivorous and non-specialized feeders, often opportunistic, and well able to adapt to new habitats and food sources. Many species appear to feed largely on the most abundant plant or animal foods available at any time, and thus the proportions of different invertebrates in the diet, or of different seeds and vegetative parts of plants, often reflect the relative availability of these foods in the environment. While there

is much information on the diet of a few well studied species, mainly from Europe, North America and Australasia and particularly the large, easily studied species such as gallinules and coots, little or nothing is known about the food and feeding habits of many others. Even for most well studied species, good quantitative analyses of diet are lacking.

Plant foods include a wide range of vascular plant material, including seeds and drupes, shoots, stems and leaves, tubers, bulbs, rhizomes and roots, as well as marine and filamentous algae, fungi and lichens. Some species take cultivated plant matter and fruit, such as young vegetables and cereal crops, fodder crops, grain (including rice and maize), tomatoes, melons, apples, drying apricots, bananas and taro. Invertebrates are an important part of the diet of many species, and include worms (Annelida and particularly Oligochaeta), nematodes, flatworms, leeches, molluscs, woodlice (Isopoda), millipedes (Diplopoda), centipedes (Chilopoda), amphipods, copepods, crabs and crayfish, springtails (Collembola), Arachnida (mainly spiders), and a wide variety of insects and their larvae. Some species take small fish and fish spawn, amphibians and their tadpoles, reptiles (lizards and their eggs, small snakes, and turtle eggs and hatchlings), the eggs and young of other birds, the droppings of gulls and ducks, rodents (mice and rats), young rabbits, carrion (ranging from small birds and rodents to the carcass of a cow), and various household items including bread, porridge, stew, dog food, chicken food, biscuits, butter and chocolate, while the Lord Howe Rail has even been known to eat rat poison, and presumably to survive!

In general, the most aquatic species, such as the gallinules and coots, are largely herbivorous, while those that inhabit terrestrial and palustrine habitats are either omnivorous or predominantly carnivorous, at least seasonally. Forest-dwelling species are relatively poorly known but they probably eat fewer plant foods than do rails in other habitats. Forest species such as the Andaman Crake and the Grey-throated, New Caledonian, Okinawa, Woodford's and Bare-eyed Rails (*Gymnocrex*

plumbeiventris) are recorded as taking very little plant material, if any.

Species with long, thin bills probe for invertebrate food in shallow water, soft ground and litter, while species with small, fine bills tend to take many small invertebrates and seeds from the substrate, shallow water and low vegetation. Those with relatively unspecialized, straight bills of moderate length and depth take a wide variety of small to large food items, chiefly by probing, gleaning, digging, sifting litter, stabbing at large prey and raking in soft earth and mud. Thick-billed species tear and slice vegetation, and dig or pull up the underground parts of plants. Some gallinules graze, for example the Purple Swamphen and the Tasmanian Native-hen, as also do the coots. Only coots regularly dive for food; Common Moorhens do so rarely, and Rouget's Rail (*Rougetius rougetii*) of wetlands in the Ethiopian highlands has been seen to dive into a stream like a dipper (*Cinclus*) when foraging, while the Little and Baillon's Crakes are also said to dive. Coots and *Gallinula* species regularly upend when feeding, and other species such as the King Rail may upend occasionally when foraging in deep water.

Terrestrial species which forage in leaf litter and soil use the bill to move or toss aside leaves and debris, and to turn over small stones, while searching for invertebrates; some species also use the feet to move debris aside and scratch in the ground. The Weka and the Lord Howe Rail will pull apart bark and rotten wood to extract food, while the latter chisels harder wood and will also pull aside palm fronds to search for food beneath them. Some species, such as the Rufous-tailed Bush-hen, the Sora and the Spotted Crake, run grass heads through the bill to strip seeds from them. The White-browed Crake often feeds while swimming, floating with the neck extended parallel with the surface and suddenly reaching out with the fine-pointed bill to capture water insects.

Large, live food items are usually killed and dismembered before being swallowed. The Water Rail first paralyses frogs and fish by making vertical blows with its bill behind the prey's head and then kills the prey by repeatedly striking it with the bill, while the King Rail hacks large prey items, such as crayfish, to pieces before eating them, and the Rufous-tailed Bush-

hen crushes frogs in the bill before swallowing them. Large insects, such as grasshoppers, are shaken and battered before being swallowed. The Buff-banded Rail captures live prey by stabbing with the slightly open bill, pecks large snail shells to break them, crushes fish in the bill, and holds crabs by the legs in its bill while flicking its head from side to side until the legs break off. Other species knock large prey animals on the ground to immobilize or kill them before swallowing them. Several species spear eggs with the bill and either eat the contents *in situ* or carry the egg away to deal with. Large prey may be carried into cover or, if caught while the bird is in water, brought ashore to be dealt with. Rallids often wash food in water, this behaviour being recorded in aquatic, palustrine and terrestrial genera alike.

Using the foot to grasp and manipulate food is recorded in some *Porphyrio* species, such as the Purple Swamphen, Allen's Gallinule, the Takahe, and the extinct White Gallinule (*Porphyrio albus*). The Purple Swamphen uses its powerful bill to pull out grass tillers or to nip them off at the base, and to pull out emergent plants such as *Typha* and *Eleocharis*; it then grasps them in the foot while it chews or slices off the soft fleshy bases. It also holds down *Typha* stems with the foot while stripping off leaves with the bill to eat the leaf bases. Items such as stems, water-lily buds and figs are held in the foot and lifted towards the bill, which tears off small pieces or crushes the item before swallowing; plant material is held for eating by the opposition of the hind toe to the three closed fore toes. The fore toes are also used to comb through weed dangling from the bill, to strip casing from plants, or to harvest aquatic plants for nest material, and the feet are also used to hold down large food items, such as fish and carrion, while the bird pecks at them. This same species also climbs well in reedbeds and even into low trees to take eggs and nestlings, when the feet grip whole bunches of leaves and stems to give the bird sufficient support. It also grazes clover and pasture, digs for rhizomes and roots, and moves gravel and stones with the bill to find invertebrates. It is primarily vegetarian, plant material being recorded as making up 75-90% of its diet.

The Takahe holds food items in the feet in a similar way, and also strips seeds from grasses with the bill while holding the stalks in the foot. Allen's Gallinule turns over water-lily leaves with its bill and holds them down with the feet while gleaning food items from their undersurfaces. It is also partial to developing water-lily seedheads, which it breaks off with the bill and transfers to one foot before tearing off pieces with the bill, and it sometimes carries other food items in the foot to the bill. The Weka and the Dusky Moorhen also hold down food items with the foot while pecking or hammering at them, but they do not grasp or manipulate them in the foot as do the gallinules.

All rails ingest grit or small stones to help break up food in the gizzard and in some herbivorous species, such as the Takahe, this material may be ingested in considerable quantities. The Buff-spotted Flufftail, which forages in the leaf litter of forest and thickets, frequently ingests large quantities of the small, hard seeds of common trees such as bugweed (*Solanum mauritianum*) and pigeonwood (*Trema orientalis*), probably in lieu of grit, sufficient quantities of which may be hard to find.

Coots are almost entirely herbivorous but they do take some aquatic insects, molluscs and crustaceans, and will sometimes eat eggs, fish, carrion, duck-food pellets and even food scraps from camp-sites. The Common Coot feeds both in water and on land, employing a variety of foraging techniques. It scrapes algae off stems, stones and tree stumps under water, picks food from the water surface while swimming, breaks off young emergent shoots, feeds among vegetation stirred up by other waterfowl, leaps upwards to bring down leaves, seedheads and insects, upends in water up to 40 cm deep, occasionally immersing the whole body, and dives to bring up plant material and occasionally also invertebrates and fish, subsequently eating its spoils on the surface. Dives are usually short, no more than 20 seconds long, and normally to only 1-2 m, although a depth of 6·5 m is recorded. These birds also fish for shrimps in flocks of up to 100 birds, sometimes with ducks. They graze on land in flocks, or sometimes solitarily, particularly when winds cause high waves on the water.

The Spotless Crake builds a cupped nest of woven dry grass, sedges or rushes, usually very well concealed in dense vegetation such as a sedge clump or a grass tussock, and often situated over water.
The eggs are dull creamy brown with numerous small chestnut brown flecks and weigh about 9-9·5 g, roughly 23% of the female's mean weight. The clutch size is 2-6, typically 3-4, though clutches laid later in the season are apparently larger on average than the earlier ones, while island populations may lay smaller clutches than mainland birds. Both sexes incubate, and hatching may be either synchronous or, in larger clutches, asynchronous.

[Porzana tabuensis tabuensis.
Photo: Don Hadden/
Ardea]

Rails which forage in mangrove habitats appear to feed largely on crabs, these crustaceans being the main food items recorded for species such as the Chestnut Rail and the Rufous-necked and Grey-necked Wood-rails. The Chestnut Rail probes crab burrows and catches small fiddler crabs from among mangrove prop-roots, tapping them against a root before eating them. Black Crakes are apparently unique among rails in gleaning ectoparasites from the backs of large mammals, while the Nkulengu Rail and the Grey-necked Wood-rail are the only species known to follow army ant columns, presumably to feed on invertebrates that the ants disturb; other forest-rails probably do so too.

Seasonal variations in the proportions of animal and plant food taken are reported for a number of species, and reflect seasonal changes in the availability of food, the use of different habitats when birds are on migration or in wintering areas, and the possible need for a greater consumption of protein in the breeding season to satisfy the requirements for egg-laying. Many species increase their intake of animal food in the spring and summer, and of plant food in the autumn and winter. A quantitative study on the King Rail found that, during the year at one site, animal material constituted 95% by volume of foods in spring, 90% in summer, 74% in autumn and 58% in winter. In the Virginia Rail, animal foods predominate in summer, comprising 85-97% by volume of the diet, insects accounting for nearly 62% of the diet, whereas in autumn and winter 32% and 21% respectively of the diet consists of the seeds of marsh plants.

Very little information is available on the diet of the chicks of most rail species, but it would seem that the young of most species, even of herbivorous species, are fed primarily on insects and other animal food. Thus, aquatic insects comprise 45-85% of the diet of young chicks of the American Coot. Again, invertebrates form a large proportion of the diet of Takahe chicks for 4-6 weeks, the chicks becoming predominantly vegetarian when 6-8 weeks of age. Sora chicks are fed largely on invertebrates, although plant material constitutes a large proportion of the summer diet of the adults. The young of the Dusky Moorhen are fed on annelids, molluscs and insects for the first few weeks, after which plants are taken increasingly. There are conflicting accounts of the proportion of invertebrates fed to young Common Coots, but at least some are fed chiefly on invertebrates for the first 10 days, while the vegetarian Giant Coot feeds small young on both weed and invertebrates, and the American Coot feeds large quantities of aquatic insects to its chicks during the first week after hatching.

Kleptoparasitism is recorded in coots and gallinules. The Common Coot will snatch food from conspecifics and also from swans and both surface-feeding and diving ducks. The American Coot robs Canvasbacks (*Aythya valisineria*), Redheads (*Aythya americana*) and Ring-necked Ducks (*Aythya collaris*). Conversely, it has also been seen to be kleptoparasitized by American Wigeons (*Anas americana*) and Gadwalls (*Anas strepera*) and to relinquish food passively to them, apparently to gain time to dive a second time and eat food unmolested. Allen's Gallinules will chase and rob conspecifics of water-lily seedheads, and will also snatch them from African Pygmy-geese (*Nettapus auritus*).

Few studies have been made of foraging behaviour in rails. Wekas are known to search large areas of leaf litter, loosening it to a depth of 5-8 cm with the bill and covering up to 50 m² of dry litter per day. The Lord Howe Rail forages intensively in small areas, covering about 0·5 m² in 20-30 minutes. The Water Rail, in both breeding and winter territories, uses definite paths for foraging, the course of which is fixed by the position of favourable food sources, and it repeatedly visits successful hunting spots. The Madagascar Wood-rail is said to cover ground swiftly when probing leaf litter, and sometimes to return several times to areas which have just been searched. In Kakamega Forest, Kenya, pairs of White-spotted Flufftails holding permanent territories along small forest streams foraged over part of the terri-

Some African rallids undergo regular seasonal migrations, moving both north and south away from the equator to breed during the rains. One such species is Allen's Gallinule, which often breeds at seasonally inundated grasslands and floodplains. It may be locally very numerous in such breeding habitat during seasons of good rainfall. Juveniles only 2-3 months old are known to migrate with adults, while on the Nyl floodplain, South Africa, a newly arrived population included birds in all plumages from full juvenile to adult, suggesting that breeding may take place throughout the year. This species is well known for its vagrancy, and is unique in being the only Afrotropical bird species which straggles to Europe.

[*Porphyrio alleni.* Photo: Clem Haagner/ Ardea]

tory each day, one pair with two chicks using about 20% of the territory area each day and changing this foraging area every 2-4 days, the timing apparently depending on the availability of food and the amount of shallow streamside habitat available for foraging. Also in Kenya, Baillon's Crakes, feeding on plentiful invertebrates at drying shallow pools on mud in tall reedbeds, intensively searched small pools, up to about 4 m² in area, for up to 30 minutes and sometimes returned to the same sites several times per hour.

Breeding

Detailed studies have been made of the social organization, mating systems and breeding of only a few rallid species in the wild, notably some of those in the genera *Sarothrura*, *Gallirallus*, *Rallus*, *Crex*, *Porzana*, *Porphyrio*, *Gallinula* and *Fulica*, and in captivity of some of these species plus others such as the Yellow Rail and the Striped Crake. Unfortunately, little is known about the breeding of many other rails and the list of those species for which the nest, eggs and young are not even described is depressingly long.

Available evidence suggests that rails are seasonally or permanently territorial, living either in pairs or family groups, and that the majority form monogamous pair-bonds of at least seasonal duration. Monogamy is to be expected as the predominant mating system in the group because, although rail chicks are precocial or semi-precocial, they need intensive parental care at an early age, when they do not feed themselves but follow the parents and are fed, guarded and brooded by them. Some form of non-monogamous mating system is known to occur in the wild in only five rail species, the Corncrake, the Purple Swamphen, the Common and Dusky Moorhens and the Tasmanian Native-hen; in captivity it occurs in the Yellow Rail and the Striped Crake, and in the latter probably also in the wild. Although only a few species are involved, the strategies used are fascinating in their variety and complexity, and are worth examining in detail.

The Corncrake was formerly assumed to be monogamous, with the pair-bond lasting throughout the breeding season, but early observations indicated that it sometimes formed polygynous associations: males did not regard additional females as territorial intruders, closely neighbouring broods and clutches were sometimes associated with several birds, only one of which was a male, and chicks were often brooded and fed by the female alone. All these are indicative of polygyny, and recent work has shown that, although monogamy does occur, serial polygyny is regular in this species: males occupy shifting and overlapping home ranges and mate with two or more females; each female incubates the clutch and rears the young. In the congeneric African Crake, an association of one male and two females has also been observed in the breeding season. Serial polygyny has been recorded too in captive Yellow Rails, in which one male became dominant over others, claimed the entire enclosure as his territory and then paired with a female, seeking to mate with a second female when the first began to incubate; the male took no part in incubation or in caring for the young.

The reverse situation has been seen in captive Striped Crakes, which show serial polyandry. The sexes are rather different in plumage, and it is the female that makes advertising calls and establishes a breeding territory, mating with two or more males in succession and taking no part in incubation or in the rearing of the chicks. Evidence from limited observations of wild birds suggests that males normally incubate, indicating that polyandry may occur, although monogamy is also possible. One case of possible polyandry has also been reported for the Henderson Crake, in which a female made four nesting attempts with one male and one interim attempt with a male from an adjacent territory.

Monogamy is usual when both parents are needed to rear the young successfully. In situations where less parental care is needed, for example when the young are precocial and nidifugous, and especially if they can find their own food, it may not be necessary for more than one parent to tend the young. Breeding habitats such as wetlands and lush grasslands are structurally simple and may be highly productive, with food concentrated in a narrow spatial range. In such conditions it may be possible for males to control territories in which two or more females can breed, relegating less successful males to sub-optimal territories, or to none at all. This situation may apply to the Yellow Rail, and possibly also to the Corncrake. Polyandry in the Striped Crake, an Afrotropical migrant which often breeds in unpredict-

The Madagascar Flufftail is unusual among wetland and grassland Sarothrura species in building a domed, rather than a cup-shaped, nest. Like other flufftails, it lays white eggs. Although only the female is known to incubate, this photo shows the male leaving the nest. This species is very similar in plumage to the Striped Flufftail (Sarothrura affinis) of Africa, and likewise it occurs in grassland, but it also uses habitats, such as forest edge, bush, cultivation and marshes, which in Africa are occupied by other Sarothrura species. Unlike African flufftails it lacks a hooting song, but its advertising call resembles the Striped Flufftail's territorial call.

[Sarothrura insularis, Madagascar. Photo: Dominique Halleux/ Bios/Foto Natura]

The nests of coots are normally built either within emergent vegetation, in some species with little attempt at concealment, or in open water. The Red-knobbed Coot's nest is a typical bulky platform of leaves and stems of water plants, lined with finer material and usually with a ramp at one side. When situated within emergent vegetation, such as the Schoenoplectus sedges in the photograph, the nest is often constructed on a foundation of bent and trampled stems. It is built by both sexes, sometimes with the help of immatures; it is rearranged and added to during incubation; and it is built higher if the water level rises. Red-knobbed Coots occur on many types of open fresh water ranging from large natural lakes to small artificial farm dams, and can breed on waters 1 ha or less in extent; in some areas they have benefited considerably from the proliferation of artificial water bodies.

[Fulica cristata, Lake Naivasha, Kenya. Photo: Alan Root/ Survival Anglia/ Oxford Scientific Films]

ably ephemeral wetland habitat, may have evolved in response to the great variability in breeding conditions and the availability of abundant food in the breeding habitat. The situation may be comparable with that seen in some waders which breed in the far north or in montane areas and have "rapid, multi-clutch" mating systems which enable them to increase their reproductive output when conditions suitable for breeding are short-lived. In these species, such as Temminck's Stint (*Calidris temminckii*) and the Eurasian Dotterel (*Charadrius morinellus*) the female either lays two or more clutches in quick succession for different males or lays two clutches, one of which is incubated by the male and the other by herself.

The social structure and mating systems of the promiscuous *Porphyrio* and *Gallinula* species are more complex. The Common Moorhen normally forms monogamous pair-bonds, usually for the breeding season only but sometimes for up to several years; it tends to be solitary and territorial when breeding. Immatures from earlier broods, and sometimes one or more additional mature birds, often help to tend and feed chicks. Polyandrous trios, where a female forms pair-bonds with two males, also occur at a low frequency. Co-operative nesting also occurs, in which two females, sometimes more, are paired to the same male and lay in the same nest, subsequently sharing parental care. In a recent study by S. McRae, most co-operative breeding groups

consisted of a core pair and their previous offspring; in many cases a daughter laid in a communal nest with her mother and, if there was only one male in the group, he gained full paternity of his daughter's offspring, which had a low survival rate. Furthermore, brood parasitism regularly occurred: females laid eggs in neighbours' nests, often in addition to laying their own clutches. It was considered that co-operative breeding might be the only breeding option for first-year females that hatch late and overwinter on their natal territories, and that brood parasitism was a highly opportunistic reproductive strategy used by females that could produce more eggs than they could rear, or by those whose nests had been destroyed, or by "professional parasites" which achieved little reproductive success.

The flightless Tasmanian Native-hen defends a permanent territory and is either monogamous or polygamous, in the latter case usually polyandrous. The breeding unit consists of an adult pair or a trio of two males, often brothers, and a female; however, there may be up to five members, rarely including two females, always sisters. Adults normally associate for life. All males copulate with all females in the group, and the females all lay in one nest. Nest building, incubation and parental care are shared by all adults, sometimes assisted by young of an earlier brood or by young of the previous year which have not yet left the group. This strategy is believed to have arisen as a result of an unequal

Black-tailed Native-hens usually build a well concealed nest in low, dense vegetation, but they sometimes nest on the ground. Clutch size is usually 5-7 and hatching is normally asynchronous. The newly hatched chick has a white egg tooth and a black bill with a pink base to the upper mandible and a small greyish saddle, all of which features are visible here. Occurring over much of Australia, the species is dispersive and highly irruptive, and breeds opportunistically, sometimes arriving in an area in large numbers shortly after heavy rain and breeding in colonies, when laying is probably synchronous throughout the colony. It may nest in any month.

[Gallinula ventralis, Byro, West Australia. Photo: Babs & Bert Wells/ Oxford Scientific Films]

sex ratio in the species, as there is an excess of males among immatures, and it is cited as an example of kin selection.

The Dusky Moorhen is either sedentary or dispersive and is territorial only during the breeding season, when birds form breeding groups of 2-7 apparently unrelated birds in which the sex ratio usually favours males. Individuals sometimes switch groups between seasons. Simultaneous promiscuity occurs, all males copulating with all females, which all lay in one nest, and all members of the group defend the territory and share all breeding tasks; older siblings also sometimes help to care for the young. No explanation has been forthcoming for the evolution of this strategy in this species.

In Western Palearctic populations, the Purple Swamphen maintains a monogamous pair-bond, but in New Zealand the species has a complex social structure and mating system. Most birds occur in communal groups of up to 12 birds; stable groups, in which the birds remain together all year, usually consist of kin, while unstable groups are non-kin. Stable, communally breeding, groups which maintain permanent territories are polygamous and usually consist of 2-7 breeding males, 1-2 breeding females, and up to seven non-breeding helpers, which are offspring from previous matings. Unstable groups may be considered promiscuous, are characterized by much aggression and many male members, and are usually unsuccessful. Within the stable group mate-sharing is total, incestuous matings are common and homosexual matings also occur. Some males are dominant, but multiple paternity is prevalent. Only the most dominant females breed, laying in a common nest or a twin-bowl nest, and all birds in the group, including young from previous broods, care for the young. Most offspring remain as non-breeders before eventually becoming breeders. In this environment, habitat saturation and a shortage of prime breeding territories appear to be responsible for the communal breeding strategy.

A further ten species are known to live in extended family groups, at least during the breeding season, and to receive assistance, from other adults or young in the group, in feeding and rearing the chicks. This situation is normal in the Black Crake, which is territorial only in the breeding season, though it may associate in loose family groups at other times, and is multi-brooded, young of early broods helping to rear chicks of later broods; in some cases, young from one season remain with the family in the following season, when they also assist in rearing chicks. Cases of young birds helping to rear chicks of later broods are also reported in the Red-chested Flufftail, the Lord Howe Rail, the American Purple Gallinule, the Tristan Moorhen, the Common Coot and, in captivity, the Rufous-sided Crake (*Laterallus melanophaius*), while in the Weka, both large young and an extra adult have been seen to help. Some Henderson Rail territories were found to contain one or two extra birds of either sex which assisted with the defence of the chicks; it is not known whether these additional birds were fully adult, or whether they were related to the breeding pair. The Takahe is monogamous, maintains a permanent pair-bond, holds a territory during the breeding season, and breeds in family groups: older young, and sometimes offspring up to two years old, help to rear the chicks. In some of these cases, habitat saturation and a potential shortage of prime breeding territories may be reasons why mature offspring remain in the natal territory as opposed to establishing their own breeding units.

Little or no information on breeding seasonality and timing is available for many species, but most rails appear to breed seasonally, during the spring and summer in temperate regions and in or near the wet seasons in the tropics. There are exceptions to this generalization, however, most of them involving species of tropical or subtropical regions which may have extended or ill-defined breeding periods. Thus, some flufftails breed seasonally in central and southern Africa but have an indeterminate breeding season near the equator, while the African Rail breeds in both the wet and dry seasons in the tropics but is mainly restricted to summer breeding in southern Africa. Many forest species are reported to breed during, or at the start or end of, wet periods, but the Roviana Rail is reported to breed in the dry season, when excess water is not a problem on the forest floor in its habitat.

Some species may breed throughout the year if conditions remain suitable, examples from Africa being the Black Crake; the Common Moorhen in western Cape Province, South Africa, and in Zimbabwe; and the Red-knobbed Coot in Transvaal, South Africa. Elsewhere, breeding throughout the year is reported in the Guam Rail, the Lord Howe Rail, and the Giant Coot of high altitude lakes in the Andes. Over some of its range, the Buff-banded Rail is also known to breed throughout the

year, while the Weka of New Zealand has a variable breeding season, the start and duration of which are influenced by climate, food supplies and population size, and which may continue throughout the year in periods when its populations are expanding.

A study of the breeding seasons of waterbirds in southwestern Australia showed that for the rails the laying period was best correlated with increasing day length, increasing temperature and, in most cases, peak rainfall. The timing of vegetation development is often important to the initiation of nesting in rails of marshy habitats, and migratory or seasonally displaced species may not be able to colonize wetlands, or to begin nesting, until the vegetation has developed to a suitable height and density. In the USA, peak nest initiation of the Common Moorhen occurs when the height of *Typha* is 45-100 cm and its growth rate is greatest, and the nesting of American Purple Gallinules is delayed in some habitats until the plant density is adequate. The breeding season of the Tasmanian Native-hen is determined by rainfall, as it depends on fresh young plant growth. Flooding conditions may also influence the start of breeding: for example, the breeding of the Spotless Crake in Australia may be delayed by flooding by up to six weeks, while the period of laying is correlated with water depth. Breeding timing may also vary with altitude, as a result of the later development of suitable conditions at higher altitudes: in Natal, South Africa, the start of breeding in the Buff-spotted Flufftail may be 1-2 months earlier in coastal regions than at altitudes above 1200 m.

The establishment of the breeding territory and the initiation of breeding activity are usually marked by greatly increased calling. Communication by sound is important and many species have loud and distinctive advertising and territorial calls, which are often uttered most frequently and continuously at the start of the breeding season (see Voice). Pair-forming and courtship behaviour are poorly known and little studied except in the larger, more conspicuous and less secretive species such as gallinules, moorhens and coots, but it is clear that sexual display has a limited repertoire in the family. Courtship feeding and allopreening are common, and aggressive-looking courtship chases often lead to copulation. Courtship displays are usually simple and in some species, such as the Buff-banded Rail and Baillon's Crake, copu-

lation occurs with no preceding display at all. In some other species, the male's courtship display involves bowing, with head down and tail up, and either raising the wings, as in the Water Rail, or spreading them and holding them down, as in the Corncrake. The males of the King and African Rails walk around the female with the tail raised and the white undertail-coverts fanned, while the male Virginia Rail runs around the female with raised wings, stretched neck and a high-stepping gait. Male flufftails invariably vibrate their tails rapidly from side to side during courtship displays, which may involve a bowing or an upright stance, and the head and neck feathers are always raised. Courtship displays often involve the display of bold flank patterns or contrastingly coloured undertail-coverts, or both. Calling often accompanies courtship displays.

The male Purple Swamphen has upright, horizontal and hunched display postures, and also presents waterweed in his bill to the female, bowing repeatedly, while the American Purple Gallinule has billing, bowing, swaying and "Squat-arch" displays in pairing and courtship. Coots and moorhens share similar components in their courtship displays, including a "Bowing-and-nibbling" ceremony, in which one bird is submissive while the other preens it, and also an upright stance with neck arched and head down, the "Arch-bow". In coots, the threat display is very similar to pairing behaviour, showing a parallel repertoire between display elicited by the excitement of sexual stimulation and the desire to ward off strangers from the territory. Although coots and moorhens may display in water, even coots usually copulate out of water, on land or on specially built platforms.

Most species nest solitarily and are generally well separated, but in some wetland habitats, especially where nesting habitat is scarce or territories are small, nests may be very close together. For example, nests of the Little Crake may be as little as 10-15 m apart and those of the Common Moorhen as close as 8 m, while in Nigeria four nests of the Lesser Moorhen were recorded within a radius of 20 m. In restricted habitats some species such as the Purple Swamphen, may nest in loose colonies, while the nests of the Australian Crake (*Porzana fluminea*) are sometimes clumped, with up to 30 nests reported in a group. Populations of the Takahe are normally concentrated into loose colonies but with spaced-out territories within these, while the Black-tailed Native-hen breeds in isolated pairs or in colonies of 5-500 nests or more, with nests 7-10 m apart.

In many species the nest-site is selected by the male, but sometimes it may be chosen either by the female or by both members of the pair together. Nests are usually concealed in thick vegetation, often near water or in it, but some species nest on the ground far from water or in forest, or up to 10 m high in trees when they may use old nests of other birds. Nest materials are usually gleaned from any available vegetation, and nests are often built by both sexes, though sometimes by the male or the female alone. The nest is usually cup-shaped and well lined, and often fairly deep. It is domed in some species, notably the White-spotted and Buff-spotted Flufftails, the Chestnut Forest-rail, the Russet-crowned Crake (*Anurolimnas viridis*), the Inaccessible Rail, and *Coturnicops* and *Laterallus* species. Some nests of the Henderson Crake are also domed, but others are open cups. Domed nests of forest species are often made of leaves but that of the Russet-crowned Crake is a ball of dead grass with a side entrance, sometimes with a ladder-like entrance ramp, hidden about 1 m up in branches of shrubs, or in coarse herbage, in dense vegetation. *Laterallus* nests are also woven balls placed in grass, reeds or bushes, but the Black Rail has a bowl-shaped nest with a woven canopy.

Nests in grass, and in emergent vegetation such as reeds, often have the surrounding and overhanging vegetation pulled down or woven into a canopy for concealment from above, while nests in wetlands often have pathways or ramps up to the bowl. Some species build nests that float or are attached to aquatic vegetation, and nests on water may be substantial structures to cope with flooding, or may be built up rapidly as the water level rises. Non-functional nests are often found in gallinules and moorhens, and in some other species; these and many other species build nursery nests in which the family members roost.

The Giant Coot builds an enormous permanent nest of aquatic vegetation which forms a raft up to 3 m long projecting 50 cm above the water. The nest is in water about 1 m deep, and large nests usually rest on the bottom; the original structure compacts into peat in the centre. The Horned Coot also builds an enormous nest of water weed, but this is usually placed on a conical mound of stones, up to 4 m in diameter at its base and about 60 cm high, ending just below the water surface in a platform about 1 m across. The weight of the stone structure has

been estimated as about 1·5 t! Each stone weighs up to 450 g and both adults collect stones from the lake bed in shallow water and carry them to the nest-site in the bill. Sometimes the nest is built on a large stone just above the water level, while, in very shallow water, nests may be built on natural hillocks on the muddy bottom, but in lakes with very dense vegetation the birds build a floating platform of water weeds. After the coot's breeding season, the nest-site may be used by other birds such as ducks, grebes and gulls. Even the Horned Coot lines its nest well with water weed and tends to have a waterway slide of dried and decaying weeds on the entrance side of the nest.

Rail eggs are blunt oval, smooth, and usually fairly glossy. The ground colour is off-white to dark tan, usually more or less blotched or spotted with red-brown, grey, mauve, black and so on. *Rallina* and *Sarothrura* species lay unmarked white eggs, as also do the Russet-crowned and Red-and-white Crakes. Clutch size varies from 1-19 eggs, but most frequently numbers 5-10; dumping or laying by more than one female in the same nest may complicate the estimation of the clutch size laid by an individual. It has been said that, of semi-precocial birds, only the family Rallidae has clutch sizes which approach those of fully precocial birds such as galliformes and anatids, which do not feed their young, and that particularly large clutch sizes in species such as the King Rail may reflect the unpredictability of their freshwater habitats.

The laying interval between successive eggs is usually of 24-48 hours, but of 48-72 hours in the Takahe. Incubation is usually performed by both sexes but in some species only the female incubates, whereas in the polyandrous Striped Crake only the male does so. In many species the male incubates by day and the female by night. The incubation period is 13-31 days per egg, usually 15-19, and the start of incubation varies from the time of laying of the first egg to that of the last egg, so that hatching may be synchronous or asynchronous according to the species. The Sora has a large clutch size and asynchronous hatching, which may be advantageous by distributing the high energetic cost of feeding the young over a longer period. Eggshells are often removed but they may be left in the nest.

The Chestnut Forest-rail is unusual in that it lays only one large egg, which is equivalent to about 27% of the mean adult weight; incubation is at least 34 days, and possibly over 37 days,

As well as brightly coloured bills and contrastingly coloured bare skin on the head, the chicks of the Common (Gallinula chloropus) *and Dusky Moorhens also have bright bare skin on the wings; all these areas are prominent in the chicks' begging display. Dusky Moorhen chicks are fed intensively until they are four weeks old, and then with decreasing frequency for a further five weeks. The chick approaches an adult, extends its neck, waves its wings, which have conspicuous orange-yellow patches on the leading edge, and emits a high, piping call. It then further stimulates the adult to present food by pecking at the yellow tip of the adult's bill.*

[Gallinula tenebrosa tenebrosa, Sydney, Australia. Photo: Jean-Paul Ferreo/ Auscape]

the longest of any rallid. Incubation is by both sexes and the incubated egg is often left to become cold.

Rail chicks hatch covered in down, and are precocial or semi-precocial. The young stay in or near the nest until all have hatched, and they usually leave the nest within 1-3 days of hatching. They may return to the "egg nest" to be brooded at night by the parents, but in many species they roost in nursery nests. Chicks are brooded at night and in poor weather while small: they rapidly become chilled if not brooded at night, and suffer from exposure if left out in rain. Newly hatched young may swim and dive in case of need but all, even those of coots, are prone to wetting and rapidly become chilled in water. They are therefore reluctant to stay long in water during their first days of life, except in emergency situations.

Chicks are at first fed bill to bill and they become self-feeding only after a period varying from a few days to over eight weeks. The young are normally tended by both parents, sometimes by one parent only and, in a few species, also by adult helpers or the offspring of previous broods, or both. The parents may split broods for foraging and brooding. Some species, such as the Virginia Rail, may carry young in the bill; both this species and the Buff-banded Rail will also carry eggs in the bill, moving the clutch to an alternative nest if the original site is disturbed. The American Purple Gallinule has been seen to carry young in its bill when in flight, and the Red-chested Flufftail will brood a small chick under one closed wing, lifting the chick off the ground in doing so, and even sometimes carrying it like this for short distances.

In general, the fledging period of rails is 4-8 weeks, although in the Giant Coot it is about four months. The chicks' legs and feet grow rapidly, reaching full size before the rest of the body; in contrast, the growth of the wings is generally much retarded. The first body feathers begin to appear after 6-15 days, usually about 7; the tail develops quite late in the sequence, and the down on the head and neck is often the last to be replaced. A recent study of the Buff-spotted Flufftail showed that full juvenile plumage was attained in 27-32 days, mean adult mass was reached at about 45 days, the bill attained full length after 16-17 days, the tarsus after about 26 days, the tail after about 40 days and the wings not until about 90 days; the young made their first short flights at 19 days of age, an early age for small rallids, when the

wings were 79% grown and the mass 74% of the mean adult mass. Soras and Virginia Rails show a comparable rate of development, the tarsus being fully grown, and full juvenile plumage attained, at 28 days. Spotless Crake chicks were found to reach asymptotic weight at one month, with fully grown tarsi at 27-28 days.

The young usually become independent as soon as they are fully fledged, occasionally before and sometimes after fledging. The time of independence varies from 3-4 weeks, for example 20-21 days in the Buff-spotted Flufftail, to 15 weeks in the Weka and the Henderson Rail. The chicks may be ejected from the territory as soon as they are independent, after which the parents may nest again immediately. In other cases the young may stay in the natal territory for the rest of the breeding season, often helping to rear chicks of subsequent broods, before leaving at the end of the season or later. In the Sora, a migratory species, the family group disperses from the home range when the young are 16-22 days old.

Usually one or two broods are reared, and replacement laying may occur up to three times after egg loss. In species with extended breeding seasons several broods may be reared, and many species have the capability to extend the breeding season, or to raise more broods per breeding period, when food is plentiful or conditions remain favourable for longer than normal. The adaptive plasticity of rails allows some species to exploit breeding habitats as and when they appear, and to cope with sudden changes in habitat conditions. For example, American Coots in Colorado adapted well to artificial alteration of water level in a marsh, rapidly deserting areas when habitats deteriorated and recolonizing them when habitats improved. The birds were not tied to a strict seasonal breeding cycle, so could colonize ephemeral nesting sites, and when conditions changed could quickly relocate and produce a replacement brood. The Black-tailed Native-hen of Australia is widely dispersive and irruptive, and often appears in great numbers after local rain to begin breeding immediately; birds will breed continuously throughout the winter and summer if conditions remain favourable.

The age of first breeding is usually one year, but sometimes less. The Lord Howe Rail, and the White-throated Rail of Aldabra, attain sexual maturity at nine months, whereas the Guam Rail can breed at only 16 weeks old, a feature which has consider-

Clapper Rail chicks leave the nest immediately after hatching, and follow their parents in search of food. They can swim at one day old, and are adept at hiding in dense marsh vegetation. They are fed and cared for by both parents for 5-6 weeks, after which they become independent. As in other rails, the legs and feet grow fast, reaching full size long before the chick is fully grown, while the remiges develop late: the young are not able to fly until they are 10 weeks old, by which time they are fully grown and have moulted from the plain, greyish juvenile plumage into immature plumage, which is almost identical to that of the adult.

[Rallus longirostris saturatus, Anahuac National Wildlife Refuge, Texas, USA. Photo: Mike Wilkes/Aquila]

ably helped the captive breeding programme of this threatened species.

Movements

Rails have a wide variety of movement and dispersal patterns. Some species are long distance migrants, many are dispersive, some are strongly irruptive, some nomadic, and others show limited local movements in response to changing environmental conditions. The movement patterns of many species are unknown, or at best poorly known, due to a combination of factors such as the birds' tendency to move at night and the difficulty involved in locating birds when they are not breeding, when their silence and secretive behaviour render them easily overlooked; in this way, reported absences are sometimes more supposed than real.

Migrating rails fly at night and at low altitudes, usually singly or in small groups, with the exception of highly sociable species such as the coots. Virginia Rails often follow the courses of rivers in low, level ground, and may fly less than 1 m above the ground. Both they and Soras gather in numbers in marshes before moving, but there is no evidence that they migrate in groups. Migrating rails are frequently attracted to lights of many kinds, from lighthouses and floodlights to lighted house windows, and they often strike towers, buildings, overhead power lines, telephone wires, fences and other obstacles.

Most Holarctic species undertake substantial migrations and winter further south in Africa, southern Asia and South America. In the Western Palearctic, seven of nine breeding species are wholly or largely migratory, five crossing the Sahara to winter to the south and one, the Water Rail, wintering far into the Sahara; only the Purple Swamphen and the Red-knobbed Coot are mainly resident. The Water Rail migrates on broad fronts and crosses mountains such as the Alps. The Corncrake's main routes into Africa are in the west, between Morocco and Algeria, and in the east via Egypt; few cross the Mediterranean between these two flyways. It overflies North Africa and the Mediterranean region on its return passage, which is more rapid than the southward passage, unlike the migratory *Porzana* species which overfly these regions in the autumn and not the spring. The Common and American Coots are the only rallids known to have a specific moult migration, and particularly large flocks of flightless Common Coots are recorded from the Black Sea in August.

All rails breeding in North America are to some extent migratory, with at least some populations wintering to the south of the breeding range, although the Clapper Rail is largely resident. The Yellow Rail and the American Coot do not winter as far south as Central or South America. Some species, such as the Black and Yellow Rails, are known to move over a broad front, while the Sora apparently migrates along the coast and is prone to drift in strong winds, sometimes being recorded far out to sea. Migrant Clapper Rails fly overland and also along the coast.

Relatively little is known about the migrations of those species which breed from India east across Asia to China and Japan and occur south through the Oriental Region. Many are known or suspected to be at least partially migratory, evidence suggesting that they are either predominantly winter visitors to the southern parts of their range, as in the case of the Watercock, or that resident populations in the south are augmented by visitors from the north in the winter. A typical example is the Red-legged Crake (*Rallina fasciata*), which is both resident and migratory over its normal range but is largely a winter visitor to the southern regions, and is probably also dispersive. The Slaty-legged Crake (*Rallina eurizonoides*) is both a resident and migrant species in India, and moves at the beginning and end of the south-west monsoon. The Slaty-breasted Rail has local movements in India during drought or flood, and may make migratory movements elsewhere in its range. The Band-bellied Crake (*Porzana paykullii*) is a recognized migrant, but even it has an imperfectly known winter distribution.

Less is known about the movements of South American rails than about those of any other continent or subcontinent, but the great majority of the species known or suspected to be migratory or dispersive are inhabitants of palustrine wetlands or wet grass-land, habitats which have apparently received relatively little attention from ornithologists. For a few of the more obvious species, such as the coots, there is sufficient evidence to show that movements do occur: thus immature Giant Coots are known to disperse widely at night, while the Horned Coot has altitudinal movements or displacements in harsh weather. At least local movements are recorded for the Spotted Rail. Species such as the Ocellated (*Micropygia schomburgkii*), Colombian (*Neocrex colombianus*) and Grey-breasted Crakes are suspected to have migratory or dispersal movements only because individuals have flown into lighted windows at night. The Ash-throated Crake (*Porzana albicollis*) is suspected of having seasonal movements in Colombia because appearances in different parts of the country occur at different periods.

Much more is known about the movements of African rallids, but even this knowledge is very incomplete. Some species, such as the Striped and African Crakes, the Streaky-breasted Flufftail and Allen's Gallinule, move away from the equator to breed during the rains. However, such species are not necessarily always migratory: where conditions remain suitable, the African Crake may remain after breeding, while the Streaky-breasted Flufftail is sedentary in Gabon. Other species, such as the Black Crake and the African Rail, are normally regarded as sedentary but may be locally migratory in some parts of their range, appearing with the rains and disappearing in the dry season, and they may occupy temporary wetlands anywhere within their range. The Buff-spotted Flufftail has complex and poorly understood movements which are related to its wide habitat tolerance: it is largely sedentary in stable forest habitat but of seasonal occurrence in habitats, such as deciduous thickets, which are only suitable in the rains. The Striped Flufftail has seasonal altitudinal movements in Natal, South Africa, moving to lower altitudes after breeding; in some cases the distance moved may be as little as 30-40 km.

A typical dispersive and adaptable species is the Buff-banded Rail of South-east Asia and Australasia. It has a very wide habitat tolerance and is able to colonize small islands, it eats a wide range of food, and it can breed throughout the year. It may move in response to availability of water, switching from dry to wet areas depending on rainfall. The Spotless Crake is known to be a highly dispersive species which has spread widely across the Pacific. The Rufous-tailed Bush-hen is possibly nomadic in Australia, where it moves into some regions with the onset of rain and may retire to areas with permanent water in the dry season. Similar behaviour is recorded for the Dusky Moorhen, which is dispersive or nomadic in Australia but does not undergo large-scale irruptive movements. The Black-tailed Native-hen, however, is a classic dispersive and regularly irruptive species which breeds opportunistically whenever and wherever it can. Its irruptions are probably associated with a period of favourable breeding conditions which allows a population build-up and which is followed by harsh conditions that force the birds to move.

Irruptions and movements also occur in flightless species. In New Zealand, the Weka can move for significant distances: immatures may move more than 9 km from the natal area; subadults can walk more than 4 km in a day; while the greatest recorded natural movement is of 35 km, by an adult male. Rivers and lakes are apparently no barrier to the bird's movements. Mass migrations, associated with the disappearance of many populations on North Island, have occurred for unknown reasons, while rapid increases in populations are also recorded, apparently due to short-term changes in food supply. The Weka's homing ability is also remarkable, the longest return being recorded as 130 km. Also in New Zealand, the Takahe undergoes altitudinal movements of 5-10 km, possibly up to 30 km, when winter snow covers its grassland feeding territories, while chicks are recorded moving 400-800 m within a few days of hatching. Immature Tasmanian Native-hens disperse widely and are recorded as moving up to 40 km. Both adult and juvenile Lord Howe Rails make altitudinal movements over short distances.

A lack of knowledge of the distribution and status of many species sometimes makes it difficult to judge whether isolated occurrences are indicative of long distance movements, or whether movements are primarily eruptive or migratory. For example, recent distributional data suggest that the Speckled Rail

The Weka normally lays 2-4 eggs, and the young are cared for by both parents. Some young are able to feed independently at 21-40 days, and all parental care ceases after 40-108 days; most young have dispersed from their parental territories by 4-6 months after independence. Although flightless, normally sedentary and often permanently territorial, Wekas can move over significant distances: they walk up to 1 km from the territory to feed; young birds may disperse 9 km or more from the natal territory; and mass migrations and rapid local population increases are recorded, possibly due to changes in food supply. Some individuals show a remarkable homing ability, and one bird returned "home" after relocation some 130 km away!

[*Gallirallus australis australis*, Golden Bay, South Island, New Zealand. Photo: Tui de Roy/ Oxford Scientific Films]

Small crakes of dense vegetation in grassland and terrestrial wetland habitats are particularly vulnerable to the effects of fire, which may cause direct mortality, may expose them to predation, and may result in increased mortality as a result of habitat destruction and consequent forced emigration. The Ocellated Crake, a near-threatened species of dense grasslands in South America, is caught in numbers for food by local people who set fire to grassland and catch birds which are overcome by the smoke. At the same time, the vulnerable birds are often preyed upon by Aplomado Falcons (Falco femoralis).

[Micropygia schomburgkii chapmani, Das Emas National Park, Goiás, Brazil. Photo: Luiz Claudio Marigo]

(*Coturnicops notatus*) is unlikely to have regular migrations in South America, while a lack of knowledge of its distribution means that the possibility of its undergoing random long distance eruptions can not be confirmed; the best that can be said is that it must undergo post-breeding dispersal. The enigmatic White-winged Flufftail is known only from wetlands in Ethiopia and South Africa, and the morphological similarity between these two populations suggests that migration may occur between the centres of distribution. However the paucity of records from intervening regions, with a very few acceptable records from only Zimbabwe and Zambia, and an overlap in occurrence dates make this unlikely, and it is thought that in both regions it may undergo periodic long distance dispersal when numbers are high, allowing gene exchange between the two populations.

Although most forest habitats are stable and permanent, some species dependent on moist conditions may have to move at least locally if conditions become dry. In New Guinea, both the Red-necked Crake and the Bare-eyed Rail move out of some forests when the ground dries out seasonally, the former possibly migrating to north-east Australia, where it is a wet season visitor to the Cape York Peninsula, leaving again when the forest floor dries out. In Africa, the White-spotted Flufftail may move locally in response to drought conditions and habitat disturbance.

The widespread occurrence of rails on oceanic islands provides ample evidence of these birds' powers of dispersal and their tendency towards vagrancy. The available evidence shows that the phenomenon of dispersal to islands, or to continental habitats far from their home range, is widespread in rallids, and a large number of living, recently extinct and fossil taxa have been found on islands. All types of rail are involved in long distance vagrancy, and the high degree of vagrancy in the family is indicative not only of the birds' dispersive ability but also of the readiness with which they are apparently blown off course by unfavourable winds, as a result of their relatively poor flight performance. Long distance vagrancy, especially involving ocean crossings, is often associated with bad weather and prevailing winds. An example is the occurrence of American Purple Gallinules in South Africa, whereas there are no instances of African migrant rallids occurring in the Americas because the prevailing winds are against the crossing. Another factor relevant to rallids landing on oceanic islands and surviving is that they

are virtually forced to do so: to leave would mean their having to reorientate themselves from a completely unfamiliar location, and to accumulate sufficient food reserves to sustain them in a long return crossing, probably against prevailing winds. In such a situation they are well served by their ability to adapt to marginal habitats and to colonize open areas, and their tendency to omnivory. They may not be the only types of bird to reach remote islands by accident, but they are certainly amongst the best survivors in such hazardous situations. They also have the potential for rapid breeding to establish a viable population.

One of the most notable vagrants in the family is the American Purple Gallinule, which occurs from the USA south to Argentina, its northernmost and southernmost populations being migratory. This species is regularly reported from the island of Tristan da Cunha, some 3800 km from the South American mainland, has also occurred on St Helena, about 6400 km from South America, and is of almost annual occurrence in south-west Cape Province, South Africa. Of 21 vagrants to the south-western Cape, almost all have occurred from late April to early July and most were juveniles. It appears that birds starting north from Buenos Aires Province, Argentina, or from Uruguay, are caught in strong westerly winds and carried across the Atlantic, to appear in South Africa exhausted and emaciated. The majority of vagrant individuals are immatures, suggesting that adults are not inclined to stray so far off course. Another inveterate wanderer, Allen's Gallinule of sub-Saharan Africa and Madagascar, has occurred in North Africa, in Europe north to Denmark, and on offshore islands in the Atlantic Ocean as far away as the Azores, Ascension Island and St Helena, 1900 km from the African continent, and also in the Indian Ocean in the Comoros and on Rodrigues, 1500 km east of Madagascar. The Corncrake, which breeds in Eurasia and winters mainly in sub-Saharan Africa, has a remarkable range as a vagrant, having been recorded as far afield as North America, the Bahamas, India, Sri Lanka, the Seychelles and Australia.

The process of dispersal is continuous and an example of the recent colonization of islands by a rail species is that of the nominate race of the Paint-billed Crake (*Neocrex erythrops*) in the Galapagos. This race, which was formerly known only from coastal Peru, was first recorded from the Galapagos in only 1953, but it is now an abundant breeding bird on Santa Cruz, and is also recorded from Santa Maria. It had not been found by expeditions which had

By 1987 the Guam Rail had become extinct in the wild. Its decline is one of the most spectacular examples of the damage caused by an introduced species, in this case the brown tree snake (Boiga irregularis), which has caused dramatic declines and extinctions in Guam's native forest birds. A programme of captive breeding, set up in 1983, has been very successful: the original birds showed good genetic diversity, and captive numbers have grown rapidly because the birds breed throughout the year and are sexually mature at only four months. The species has been introduced to the nearby snake-free island of Rota, where it recently bred for the first time.

[Gallirallus owstoni, San Diego Zoo, USA. Photo: Kenneth W. Fink]

made extensive collections of the Galapagos avifauna in the previous hundred years, and is thus likely to be a very recent colonist, although it has been suggested that the species was possibly overlooked for some time before its discovery. The Paint-billed Crake is not known to have regular migrations, but the nominate race has also been recorded as a vagrant in Texas, USA; there are many instances of the race *olivascens* occurring outside its normal range in South America and even occasionally in Central America, and once (probably *olivascens*) in Virginia, USA. Too little is known about this bird's status and distribution to ascertain to what extent it is migratory or has vagrant habits.

Relationship with Man

Unlike many other groups of wetland birds, including members of the Pelicaniformes, Ciconiiformes and Anseriformes, the Rallidae have had no significant association or relationship with man and have no special place in art or in popular legend and myth. Virtually the only superstitions or legends which exist about rails are local ones, such as those held by certain groups of people in Africa to explain the source and meaning of the birds' strange calls heard, often at night, from forest or marsh. The remarkable song of the Buff-spotted Flufftail, one of the most evocative sounds of the African rain forest, has been the object of much superstition and speculation. It is believed to be the wail of a banshee, has been attributed to snakes, lizards, snails and mammals, and is also said to be the noise made by a chameleon in the agonies of giving birth and the sound of a chameleon mourning for his mother, whom he killed in an argument over some mushrooms. The probably extinct Kosrae Crake of the Caroline Islands remains a legend among the islanders to this day, since it had been regarded as a sacred bird before the onslaught of Christian missionaries upon the indigenous religion. The species rapidly became extinct after the islands were overrun by rats from the whaling ships which began to visit the islands from the 1830's.

A very few cases are recorded in which rails are used by man. In the Cocos (Keeling) Islands, the Buff-banded Rail is said to be used when on the nest to hatch out chicken eggs in place of domestic hens. In Bangladesh, the Watercock is used as a fighting bird on which wagers are placed, as in cockfighting. It is said that people

collect the eggs from nests and hatch them using the heat of their own bodies, the eggs being placed in a half coconut shell tied against the belly with a cloth and carried like this until they hatch after 24 days. In South America, the Giant Wood-rail is often kept in captivity, and individuals are sold commonly in village shops. If allowed to run about with chickens, however, they soon dominate the flock and become a nuisance by stealing eggs.

Although they are not now regarded as being of economic importance, rails have long been hunted for food in many parts of the world and, in some regions such as the USA and Europe, for sport, although it is difficult to see what sport or skill there can be in shooting flying rails other than coots, except perhaps the skill involved in actually inducing the more secretive species to fly. The Common Coot, much hunted in the past, is still heavily shot in Mediterranean countries today, for both sport and food, while in Pakistan, Afghanistan and neighbouring countries these coots are still eaten by fishermen on the larger lakes or *jheels*. In Europe, the Corncrake was commonly hunted for food in the past, and its flight-feathers used to be regarded as excellent for the manufacture of flies for the angler. It is still caught in Egypt during the ancient practice of quail-netting. The Water Rail and the smaller crakes were also formerly hunted with dogs in Europe. In the USA, the non-threatened larger rails may still be hunted legally, but interest by hunters is often low. In J. J. Audubon's time, Soras and Clapper Rails were popular with hunters: Soras were killed at night by being knocked on the head when they approached a light suspended from a pole on a boat, while Clapper Rails were shot indiscriminately and in large numbers.

Rail eggs are regarded as highly palatable, as indeed are the rails themselves, and Common Moorhens were formerly extensively exploited for their eggs in Asia, over 100,000 eggs being collected per year. The Giant Coot is also exploited for its eggs, many of which are taken at some sites. Forest-rails are often trapped or netted by people in Africa, southern Asia and Latin America, or hunted with dogs as in New Guinea, the Solomon Islands and New Caledonia, while marsh rails are widely hunted in southern Asia.

The larger rails may occasionally damage crops or pasture. The Common Moorhen is thought to cause damage to growing crops in the Low Countries of Europe. The Tasmanian Native-hen has been accused of damaging livestock pasture and young oat crops by grazing, although this is not the case, but the species was

Although widespread in highland areas of Ethiopia and Eritrea, and formerly regarded as common to locally abundant, Rouget's Rail is now considered near-threatened because recent visits to areas where it was formerly not uncommon have yielded very few sightings.
This rail inhabits marshy situations in montane grassland and moorland, and sometimes forages in open meadows.
The reasons for its apparent decline are thought to be habitat destruction as a result of increased grazing pressure in marshes and along streams, coupled with the ploughing up of grasslands for cereal growing. Recent droughts have probably also caused reductions in numbers.

[Rougetius rougetii, Bale Mountain National Park, Ethiopia. Photo: Michel Gunther/ Bios]

at one stage declared vermin. The Purple Swamphen is said to do considerable damage to growing rice crops in India and Bangladesh, but such damage is likely to be highly localized. In New Zealand this species is known to dig up potatoes, pull out young maize plants and eat maize cobs. It eats eggs and ducklings and on some islands it is considered a pest in taro and yam crops, and in banana groves. The American Purple Gallinule is regarded as a pest in some parts of the Neotropics where it occurs in rice plots.

The flightless Weka of New Zealand has a remarkable ability to exist alongside man in rural and urban areas. Wekas are inquisitive and curious, and their propensity for snapping up bright and shiny objects sometimes apparently leads them to be regarded as a nuisance. They are sometimes considered a pest because they pull up seedling crops, kill chickens and young ducks, and spear hen and duck eggs with the bill, but they also eat pest insects. They were formerly hunted extensively for food, but are currently protected in most places.

Status and Conservation

Current evidence indicates that 33 (25%) of the 133 listed rallid species are globally threatened, while the subspecies *tuerosi* of the Black Rail, sometimes considered a distinct species, is equally in serious danger. A further seven species are classed as near-threatened, and four more as Data Deficient. Thus the survival of 44 species (33%) of possibly extant rallids gives cause for concern. Indeed, two of the 33 can almost certainly be added to the list of extinct species: the Bar-winged Rail (*Nesoclopeus poecilopterus*), not definitely recorded since 1890; and the Kosrae Crake, with no records since its discovery in 1827/28.

Flightless species are particularly vulnerable, and 13 of the 18 surviving flightless or virtually flightless species are threatened: the Guam Rail is Extinct in the Wild; the New Caledonian Rail and the Zapata Rail (*Cyanolimnas cerverai*) are Critical; five species are Endangered and another five Vulnerable. A further three species are near-threatened or Data Deficient and, amongst the flightless species, only the New Britain Rail and the Tasmanian Native-hen are currently not globally threatened. However, even the New Britain Rail should not be regarded as completely safe: it has a restricted distribution confined to New Britain, there is no

current estimate of its status, and it is known to be trapped and eaten by local people. The Tasmanian Native-hen is apparently still very numerous, despite some drastic local declines in recent years, thought to be a result of disease. It has a history of persecution which continues today: it is traditionally regarded as an agricultural pest, though most claims are unsubstantiated; nevertheless, thousands were killed in the 1950's, when the species was declared a pest. It is not protected, is still controlled by shooting and round-ups, and is attacked by feral cats and dogs.

Of the 20 rallid taxa which have probably become extinct since 1600 (see Table), 18 (90%) were flightless. The extinction of these flightless island rails provides a classic example of the particular vulnerability of island endemics, which arises as a result of their long isolation from predators and competitors, and is one of the major factors involved in island extinctions. The worst period for recorded extinctions since 1600 was the late nineteenth and early twentieth centuries, when many oceanic islands were rapidly developed and altered. The factors which led to these extinctions are worth examining, as some of them are still applicable to threatened rails today.

The principal causes of extinctions among island rails were introduced mammalian predators such as cats, dogs, rats, mongooses and pigs, indiscriminate hunting by the first people to visit the islands and, to a lesser extent, habitat destruction by introduced goats, rabbits and fire. Hunting wiped out the larger flightless species very quickly, the White Gallinule, the Mauritian Red Rail (*Aphanapteryx bonasia*), Leguat's Rail (*Aphanapteryx leguati*) and the nominate race of the Tristan Moorhen (*Gallinula nesiotis*) all being destroyed in this way. Introduced predators have probably been responsible for more extinctions than any other single cause, although some species have been wiped out by a combination of this factor and the destruction of habitat. The Laysan Crake (*Porzana palmeri*) is an example of this, and also of a lost opportunity. It was common and fearless at the time of the arrival of the first Europeans in 1828, and was not molested by the guano diggers, but in 1903 rabbits were introduced and by 1923 had destroyed the grass and thickets in which the crakes lived and nested. They survived on two tiny islets on the Midway Atoll, to which they had been introduced. They were known to hop on to the laps of sailors stationed on Midway during the Second World War and to forage for crumbs around the tables in the mess; they were treated,

The largest living rallid, the flightless Takahe of New Zealand is also one of the most threatened members of the family. Formerly widespread on both North and South Islands, its grassland habitat was reduced by the spread of forests in the late Pleistocene-Holocene, although in the past it probably also inhabited forest ecosystems. In addition, its numbers were reduced by hunting and, more recently, by competition from, and predation by, introduced mammals. It was thought extinct by the 1930's but was rediscovered in Fiordland, South Island, in 1948. Since then its population has experienced a steady decline and now stands at about 190 birds: 150 in Fiordland, occupying apparently suboptimal habitat of alpine tussock grassland; and 40 on four islands to which it has been introduced. Extensive conservation efforts are being made on its behalf, and the Takahe Recovery Plan aims to increase the Fiordland population to 500 birds and to establish populations on at least three predator-free islands.

[Porphyrio mantelli hochstetteri, South Island, New Zealand. Photo: Paul H. Reinsch/ Aquila]

affectionately, as pets. But in 1943 rats invaded the islands from a naval craft, and by 1944 they had exterminated the rails. Unfortunately, no-one had thought to reintroduce them to Laysan, where the rabbits had been eliminated by 1924.

The Guam Rail was brought to extinction in the wild by another type of predator. Although the rail was taken by local people with dogs and snares, and despite the presence of introduced predators such as cats and pigs, it held its own on Guam until the spread of the accidentally introduced brown tree snake (*Boiga irregularis*), which has caused a precipitous decline and extinction among Guam's native forest birds. The snake is nocturnal and arboreal, and probably did not prey significantly on adults but took mainly eggs and chicks. This is the first time that a snake has been implicated as an agent of extinction.

Hunting is still a threat to some endangered species with very small populations. The San Cristobal Moorhen, Critically Endangered and possibly already extinct, has suffered from hunting by local people with dogs, and has also probably been affected by introduced predators such as cats. A similar situation affects the Invisible Rail, but it is also threatened by habitat destruction.

Several island species which are currently holding their own, having stable populations in secure habitats, are still at risk from the possible accidental introduction of mammalian predators to their islands. The Gough Island race *comeri* of the Tristan Moorhen is one such case, although precautions have been taken to minimize the chances of accidental introductions occurring. The Inaccessible Rail is another, and it is also vulnerable to fire and agricultural development, as long as Inaccessible Island continues to lack protected status. Similarly, the survival of the Auckland Rail (*Lewinia muelleri*) depends on the continued exclusion of mammalian predators. The Henderson Crake is another in this situation, and it was recently threatened by human impact when a millionaire sought to make the island his home. The Okinawa Rail, which is threatened by deforestation, is also vulnerable to the effects of the brown tree snake, which has been seen on Okinawa.

Habitat destruction, in many forms, is certainly a major threat to many continental rail species, although its impact on threatened island rails is less clear at present. The Zapata Rail is restricted to the Zapata Swamp in Cuba, where its habitat is under serious threat from dry season burning, although introduced rats and mongooses are also a serious problem for this almost flightless species. The Plain-flanked Rail (*Rallus wetmorei*) has a very restricted distribution in coastal Venezuela, where its mangrove and lagoon habitats are being destroyed by housing development, oil exploration and dyking, and the one wildlife refuge in which it occurs is also under threat. The White-winged Flufftail is under severe threat from wetland habitat destruction and modi-

fication in both of its centres of occurrence, the principal problems being damming, draining, overgrazing and afforestation, although disturbance by birdwatchers is a problem in South Africa, where only four sites regularly hold these birds and they are vulnerable to disturbance and trampling.

Great efforts have been made to save some threatened species, involving captive breeding and reintroduction of birds into the wild, habitat management and predator control. After it had been written off as extinct, but was subsequently rediscovered, the Takahe has undergone a steady decline in numbers, and its population currently stands at about 150 individuals. It has been the subject of extensive conservation efforts, including: brood manipulation, involving the transfer of eggs to other nests so that all nesting pairs have one viable egg; artificial rearing, originally to establish a captive population, and recently also to provide yearlings for release into the wild; and establishment of birds on four offshore islands, which now hold 19% of the total population. The offshore island populations are breeding successfully, and the survival rate of yearlings is good. The Takahe Recovery Plan aims to establish a self-sustaining population of over 500 birds on the mainland, to establish populations on three or more predator-free islands, and to promote public awareness.

A captive breeding programme was set up for the Guam Rail in 1983, four years before the species became extinct in the wild. The captive population has grown rapidly, because the birds attain sexual maturity at only four months of age and breed throughout the year. By 1991 there were over 180 rails in captivity on Guam and in 14 zoos in the USA, and efforts are being made to establish a self-sustaining population on the snake-free island of Rota, the intention being to eliminate the brown tree snake from Guam before reintroducing the rail to its former range. The first release on Rota was unsuccessful, birds being killed by cats and by vehicles on roads, but successful breeding was reported in 1996 and further releases are planned at sites with less traffic, while efforts are being made to control feral cats.

Many rails seem to be undergoing a continuous population decline, largely through loss of forest, marsh and grassland habitats. The continued wholesale and enormous destruction of indigenous forests is a severe threat to some species, especially in South-east Asia and South America. The Bald-faced Rail (*Gymnocrex rosenbergii*) and the Snoring Rail (*Aramidopsis plateni*) are both threatened by forest destruction. However, the forest-rails of New Guinea, including six endemic species, seem relatively secure because no major threats to their habitats are apparent at present.

Palustrine wetlands are under threat everywhere in the world and are disappearing at an alarming rate. It is only in recent years

RAIL TAXA EXTINCT SINCE 1600

Species

Mauritian Red Rail	*Aphanapteryx bonasia*	1675-1700	Mauritius
Leguat's Rail	*Aphanapteryx leguati*	c. 1730	Rodrigues I (Mascarenes)
Wake Rail	*Gallirallus wakensis*	1945	Wake I (N Pacific)
Tahiti Rail	*Gallirallus pacificus*	post-1844 (?)	Tahiti
Dieffenbach's Rail	*Gallirallus dieffenbachii*	c. 1842	Chatham Is
Chatham Rail	*Gallirallus modestus*	c. 1900	Chatham Is
Sharpe's Rail	*Gallirallus sharpei*	date unknown	perhaps Indonesia (?)
Ascension Rail	*Atlantisia elpenor*	1656	Ascension I
Tahiti Crake	*Porzana nigra*	post-1784 (?)	Tahiti
Laysan Crake	*Porzana palmeri*	1944	Laysan I (Hawaiian Is)
Hawaiian Crake	*Porzana sandwichensis*	1884	Hawaii
White Gallinule	*Porphyrio albus*	c. 1834	Lord Howe I
Samoan Moorhen	*Gallinula pacifica*	1874	Savai'i (Western Samoa)
Mascarene Coot	*Fulica newtoni*	c. 1863	Mauritius and possibly Reunion

Almost certainly extinct

38. Bar-winged Rail	*Nesoclopeus poecilopterus*	c. 1973 (?)	Fiji
95. Kosrae Crake	*Porzana monasa*	1828 (?)	Caroline Is

Subspecies

[45. Buff-banded Rail]	*Gallirallus philippensis macquariensis*	1880	Macquarie I
[74. Uniform Crake]	*Amaurolimnas concolor concolor*	c. 1890	Jamaica
[61. White-throated Rail]	*Dryolimnas cuvieri abbotti*	pre-1937	Assumption I (Mascarenes)
[116. Tristan Moorhen]	*Gallinula nesiotis nesiotis*	1861	Tristan da Cunha

Probably extinct

[59. Lewin's Rail]	*Lewinia pectoralis clelandi*	c. 1932	SW Australia

Rallidae has probably lost more species in historical times than any other bird family. This is clearly due in part to the high incidence of flightlessness among rails: all of the species now reckoned extinct were island endemics, and probably succumbed to predators introduced by man. If one looks further back in time the list grows steadily. An interesting case is that of the Takahe (Porphyrio mantelli), which was known as a subfossil species before it was ever found to survive as an extant species; indeed, the nominate race is still known only from subfossils, whence its absence from the table.

[Table: Barry Taylor]

To the surprise of the ornithological world, a new rail species was discovered on Okinawa in 1978, in the largely uninhabited northern forests of this otherwise densely populated island. The Okinawa Rail is considered Endangered: its population is estimated at about 1800 birds and it is threatened by continuing deforestation within its very small range. It is almost flightless, but has strong legs and runs swiftly to escape from predators. It is normally difficult to observe, and is most visibly active in the morning and late afternoon, when it visits pools to bathe. At night it roosts in large trees, standing on sloping trunks and branches.

[*Gallirallus okinawae*, Knigami, Okinawa, Ryukyu Islands. Photo: Kouzô Maki/ Photo Library Myojo]

that the threats to these habitats have been fully appreciated and the great importance of these wetlands realized, and, even now, there is only limited appreciation of the significance to rallids and other birds of small palustrine wetland patches. Many rails which inhabit these wetlands are threatened by habitat loss and modification. In Asia, Swinhoe's Rail (*Coturnicops exquisitus*), a migratory species which is considered Vulnerable because of its apparent rarity, is threatened by the destruction and modification of wetlands in both its breeding and wintering areas. In South America the Rufous-faced Crake (*Laterallus xenopterus*) is also considered Vulnerable, although it may be more widespread than is currently known; wholesale destruction of wetland habitats in Brazil by drainage and adjacent afforestation with *Eucalyptus* plantations may have serious effects on hitherto undiscovered populations of this poorly known species. All the savanna and *páramo* marsh habitats of the Bogota Rail (*Rallus semiplumbeus*) in Colombia are seriously threatened in many ways, for example by drainage, encroachment, pollution, tourism, hunting, burning, trampling, and fluctuating water levels. In Madagascar, the Endangered Slender-billed Flufftail (*Sarothrura watersi*) requires small wetland patches adjacent to rain forest; although its habitat may be widely distributed, the totally inadequate protection of wetlands in Madagascar gives no cause for optimism regarding this bird's long-term chances of survival.

Small crake species, such as the Black Rail, which inhabit the edge regions of marshes are generally more threatened by habitat destruction, and, for example, by disturbance from grazing or agriculture, than are other marsh rallids which live in the interiors of palustrine wetlands or alongside open water.

Prime grassland habitats are also disappearing and their rail populations are under threat. A typical example of the threats facing rails in these habitats is that of the Striped Flufftail of eastern and southern Africa. In South Africa its distribution is fragmented and its grassland habitats are disappearing rapidly as a result of agriculture and, increasingly more importantly, widespread commercial afforestation.

Another grassland species, the Corncrake, is the only globally threatened rail for the conservation of which any kind of international effort is being made. The species breeds in 31 countries and is threatened mainly on its breeding grounds, where mechanized hay mowing causes heavy losses of breeding birds, eggs and young. All large populations of Corncrakes with over 10,000 males now

occur in countries where hand mowing of hay remains a common practice. A Birdlife International European Workshop on the Corncrake was held in Poland in October 1994, to discuss the extent of its decline and possible measures to prevent further population decreases. In Britain, a major research project of the Nature Conservancy Council and the Royal Society for the Protection of Birds in the mid-1980's, and subsequent studies, identified the main reasons for the decline, and a draft action plan to halt the decline was produced in 1989. An important conservation effort was then initiated, involving government, conservation and farming bodies in the UK, Ireland and France. As a result of the implementation of conservation management measures, Corncrake numbers in Britain have recently shown a modest increase.

So little is known about many rails that their status and even their distribution can not be established with any degree of confidence. In order to address this problem, a considerable amount of work needs to be done urgently in many parts of the world. Particularly poorly known genera include the South American *Anurolimnas* and *Laterallus*, and other typical examples are to be found among the *Aramides* species. The Little Wood-rail (*Aramides mangle*) is a poorly known species of potentially restricted distribution, with habitat preferences that have not yet been properly established. The Slaty-breasted (*Aramides saracura*) and Red-winged Wood-rails (*Aramides calopterus*), although not regarded as globally threatened, are potentially at risk because of the destruction of forest habitats, and their status is in urgent need of investigation. These few examples indicate that, unless appropriate steps are taken, the lengthy list of threatened rallids is highly likely to continue to grow; serious efforts are already required to prevent the lengthy list of extinct rallids from following such a pattern.

General Bibliography

Bang (1968), Brown & Dinsmore (1986), Carpenter & Stafford (1970), Cracraft (1973), Craig & Jamieson (1990), Diamond (1991), Dunning (1993), Fjeldså (1990), Fullagar *et al.* (1982), Fuller (1987), Griese *et al.* (1980), Haig *et al.* (1990), Hendrickson (1969), Johnson & Stattersfield (1990), Keith *et al.* (1970), Kuroda *et al.* (1984), Olson (1973a, 1973b, 1974a, 1975b, 1986, 1989, 1991), Peters (1934), Remsen & Parker (1990), Ripley (1977), Ripley & Beehler (1985), Rundle & Frederickson (1981), Sibley & Ahlquist (1990), Sibley & Monroe (1990), Sibley *et al.* (1993), Tacha & Brown (1994), Williams *et al.* (1995).

ssp *pulchra*

♂

1

♀

ssp *zenkeri*

♂

♀

♂

2

♀

♂

3

♀

♀

♂

4

♀

5

♂

♀

6

ssp *affinis*

♂

ssp *antonii*

♂

♀

♂

7

♂

8

♀

♂

9

♀

PLATE 9

inches   4

cm   10

Genus *SAROTHRURA* Heine, 1890

1. White-spotted Flufftail
Sarothrura pulchra

French: Râle perlé **German**: Perlenralle **Spanish**: Polluela Pulcra

Taxonomy. *Crex Pulchra* J. E. Gray, 1829, Sierra Leone.
Genus sometimes merged into *Coturnicops*, which is more likely to be a derivative of *Sarothrura* stock. Birds of W Cameroon highlands formerly awarded race *tibatiensis*, but now reckoned to be synonymous with nominate; *batesi* has sometimes been considered synonymous with either *zenkeri* or *centralis*. Four subspecies normally recognized.
Subspecies and Distribution.
S. p. pulchra (J. E. Gray, 1829) - Gambia and S Senegal E to SW Niger, Nigeria (except extreme SE) and N & C Cameroon; possibly extreme SW Mali.
S. p. zenkeri Neumann, 1908 - extreme SE Nigeria, coastal Cameroon and Gabon.
S. p. batesi Bannerman, 1922 - interior S Cameroon.
S. p. centralis Neumann, 1908 - Congo and N Angola E through Zaire to extreme S Sudan, W Kenya extreme NW Tanzania and extreme NW Zambia.

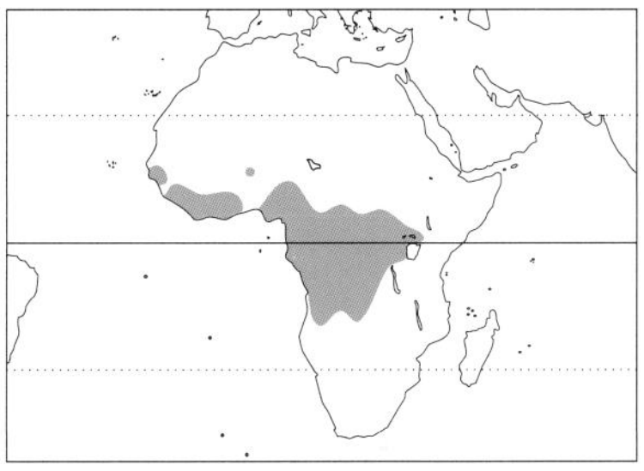

Descriptive notes. 16-17 cm; 39-53 (46) g. Tail short, not noticeably fluffy. In male, white-spotted black upperparts and red tail diagnostic. Female unlike that of any other flufftail: foreparts as male; body blackish, barred reddish buff; tail chestnut, barred black. Immature almost identical to adult but duller. Juvenile unique in genus in showing adult pattern; areas chestnut and red in adults are dark brown, as are underparts; upperparts blackish brown with pale brown to buff markings, with some whitish spots on wings of male. Races separated on: relative width of black and reddish buff bars in female; richness of plumage colours, *zenkeri* brightest; and size, *zenkeri* and *batesi* smaller. VOICE. Vocal repertoire extensive. Characteristic call of male, given all year, a series of 3-14 short, hollow "goong" notes, reminiscent of call of Golden-rumped Tinkerbird (*Pogoniulus bilineatus*); double notes "gui", rising in pitch, often included; call series often repeated for several minutes; weaker version given by female. Also gives series of 4-8 shorter, faster notes. Other calls include rapidly repeated "ker", high-pitched "ki" and ringing "klee" notes, and growls, grunts, gulps and hisses. Does not call at night.
Habitat. Mainly lowland rain forest, usually in association with water, e.g. forest swamps, streams and pools, and riverbanks. Also occurs on forest floor away from water: population in disturbed forest at Malava, W Kenya, 2 km from nearest stream. Not usually deep inside primary forest away from water. Also occupies dense shrubbery and cassava plantations in almost completely cleared areas. Follows rivers and streams out into gallery forest, dense thickets, shrubby growth, neglected cultivation and other rank herbage. Exceptionally in papyrus and other vegetation by lakes. Occurs up to 1600 m in some areas but does not frequent montane forest. Requires dense cover over foraging areas of leaf litter, mud, sand, gravel or shallow water.
Food and Feeding. Diet consists chiefly of invertebrates: earthworms, nematodes, small leeches, small gastropods, myriapods, spiders and many insects, including ants, beetles, bugs (Hemiptera), flies and small moths; takes terrestrial and aquatic insect larvae, including those of chironomids, mayflies, beetles and Lepidoptera; also small frogs. Occasionally consumes a little vegetable matter, including small seeds. Takes much food from surface of humus, mud and water; also probes with bill and turns over leaf litter. Feeds in water up to 2 cm deep; rarely immerses head; stirs up muddy stream bed with one foot to disturb prey. Searches low-growing plants for insects, chases flying insects, and digs blow-fly larvae out of cowpats. In Kenya feeds largely on the most abundant suitable invertebrate prey available at any time. Forages throughout day, with peaks in early morning and late afternoon; changes foraging area within territory every 2-4 days; one pair with 2 chicks foraged over c. 20% of territory each day.
Breeding. Seasons poorly known: in most areas breeds during rains, probably more seasonally in S areas with a marked rainy season, but in W Kenya lays Jan-Mar, in months of low rainfall; lays in Liberia, Sept; in Nigeria, Sept, breeding condition Jun, Aug, Dec; in Cameroon, Sept-Oct, breeding condition Apr, Jun; in Gabon, Mar; in Zaire, Apr-May, Nov; in Uganda Mar-Apr; nest building in Gambia, Aug. Monogamous and permanently territorial, forming strong permanent pair-bond. Nest in forest, in leaf litter on damp ground, or by pool, or on rotten tree root in shallow water in swamp; oval mound of dry or wet dead leaves, 10 cm high x 23 cm long, sometimes concealed by covering of dead leaves; lined with dry leaves, grass, etc.; entrance is slit at side. Eggs 2; incubation 14 days, by both sexes; black downy chick has black bare parts; chicks precocial and nidifugous; fed by both parents but tend to follow parent of same sex; capable of feeding themselves from early age, but remain in close association with parents until fully grown and feathered at 6-7 weeks, when post-juvenile partial moult begins; this is complete at 14-16 weeks. In W Kenya some young disperse at c. 3 months old; others may remain in parental territory for up to 9 months, disappearing by start of next breeding season. Juvenile mortality probably low; age of first breeding 1 year; adult mortality low. In W Kenya, only 1 brood per season.
Movements. Normally entirely sedentary and permanently territorial, but there is some evidence for local movements occurring in Sierra Leone, and also in W Kenya in disturbed and unusually dry habitats.
Status and Conservation. Not globally threatened. Common to locally abundant over most of range. In W Kenya distribution along streams essentially linear, one pair per 100-130 m of stream, mean territory size 0·85 ha. Catholic in choice of habitat and well adapted to forest disturbance, as long as suitable cover remains or develops: successfully colonizes cleared areas in forest, and remains along streams after forest clearance. However numbers must be decreasing with continuing large-scale destruction of forest habitat.
Bibliography. Benson *et al*. (1971), Brosset & Érard (1986), Chapin (1939), Dowsett & Forbes-Watson (1993), Elgood *et al*. (1994), Field (1995), Gore (1990), Grimes (1987), Jackson & Sclater (1938), Keith *et al*. (1970), Lippens & Wille (1976), Mackworth-Praed & Grant (1957, 1962, 1970), Pinto (1983), Pye-Smith (1950), Serle (1957), Short *et al*. (1990), Snow (1978), Taylor (1994), Taylor & Taylor (1986), Urban *et al*. (1986), Wacher (1993).

2. Buff-spotted Flufftail
Sarothrura elegans

French: Râle ponctué **German**: Tropfenralle **Spanish**: Polluela Elegante

Taxonomy. *Gallinula elegans* A. Smith, 1839, near Durban, Natal, South Africa.
Genus sometimes merged into *Coturnicops*. Possible races *buryi*, *loringi* and *languens* known from single localities in Somalia, Kenya and Tanzania respectively, and not nowadays accepted. Two subspecies recognized.
Subspecies and Distribution.
S. e. reichenovi (Sharpe, 1894) - Sierra Leone E to Zaire and Uganda, and S to N Angola.
S. e. elegans (A. Smith, 1839) - S Ethiopia; extreme S Sudan and W Kenya S through Zambia and Tanzania to E & S South Africa.

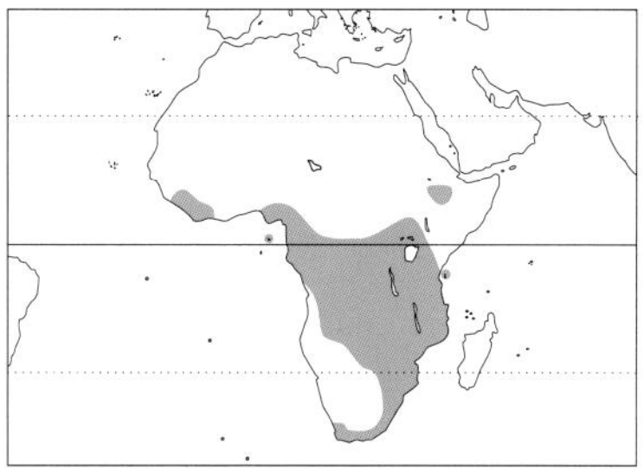

Descriptive notes. 15-17 cm; 40-61 (47·3) g; wingspan 25-28 cm. Tail short, not fluffy. Distinguished by spotted plumage and wooded habitat from all other *Sarothrura* except *S. pulchra*, from which male is separable by buff spots on upperparts, black-banded tail and lack of chestnut on mantle; female almost golden brown with small black-edged buff spots on upperparts, spotted and barred underparts, and barred tail. Immature very similar to adult but duller; female darker brown. Juvenile almost plain sepia brown, paler on face and belly, with relatively dull buff bars and spots on growing remiges. Male of race *reichenovi* darker above, with larger, coarser spots. VOICE. Vocal repertoire very extensive. Remarkable and unique song of male a series of hollow, hooting "ooooooo..." notes, like tuning fork, each of 3-4 seconds and given 5-8 times per minute. Usually calls at night, in morning and evening, and in overcast or rainy weather; may call continuously for 12 hours or more; call audible for 1 km through dense forest. Mating calls of male include low-pitched hoot followed by high-pitched whine: "mooooo-eeeee". Both sexes have a quiet, low-pitched "ooo" contact call, a rapidly-repeated, loud, nasal "né" of aggression, and various other hoots, gulps, grunts, growls, squeaks and moaning and whining notes.
Habitat. Occupies wide range of habitats associated with forest or thick bush, from sea-level to 3200 m. Occurs in interior and at edges of many forest types; particularly favours clearings, secondary growth and scrub. Occurs widely outside forest in dense evergreen and deciduous thickets; also frequents banana groves, arrowroot plantations, neglected cultivation and, in South Africa, dense exotic cover in suburban and farm gardens. Not typically associated with water, but in Gabon frequents floors of muddy valleys, in Sudan swampy patches in forest areas, and outside range of *S. pulchra* sometimes associated with forest streams. In winter in Natal, South Africa, sometimes feeds in marshes adjacent to normal forest habitat. Requires dense, low overhead cover (e.g. secondary growth or thickets), usually some dense ground cover, and clear ground or leaf litter for foraging. On migration occurs in atypical habitats.
Food and Feeding. Studies in Natal show that species takes wide variety of invertebrate prey, principally earthworms, Amphipoda, Isopoda, Diplopoda, small ants, termites, beetles, bugs and flies, but also small gastropods, Chilopoda, Nematoda, Collembola, spiders, ticks, cockroaches, Lepidoptera, grasshoppers and crickets. Larval insects taken frequently. Grass seeds eaten occasionally and hard, rough seeds of trees such as bugweed (*Solanum mauritianum*) and pigeonwood (*Trema orientalis*) frequently taken, probably to assist in grinding food in gizzard. Food items 1-32 mm long (earthworms up to 100 mm); given good selection of prey sizes, birds appear to select larger available items. Daily energy intake of adults c. 170 kJ. Forages throughout day, mostly during morning and late afternoon. Forages most frequently in leaf litter; also on open ground and mossy rocks, in short grass, dense ground cover in forest, and garden flower beds. Turns over dead leaves, digs and probes with bill, scratches with feet, and readily takes prey from shallow water.
Breeding. In S Africa breeds during rains (Sept-May), but few data from other regions: Cameroon, May, Sept, Oct; Zaire, Sept; Kenya, breeding condition Feb, Apr, May. Monogamous and territorial; pair-bond maintained at least throughout breeding season. Nest placed on ground, often in small excavated depression, usually well hidden in dense ground vegetation, tangled cover or under leaves of large plant. Most nests domed, with entrance hole at one end; made of dead leaves or grass, often with moss, twigs, roots and bark, and lined with fine grass, rootlets, moss or leaf fragments; external length 16-19 cm, width 13-20 cm, height 8·5-10 cm; nest chamber length 8-10·5 cm, width 8 cm, height 6-7·5 cm; some nests are open shallow cups with roofing cover of low vegetation; built by male. Eggs 3-5, laid at daily intervals; incubation 15-16 days, male by day, female at night; chicks precocial and nidifugous, leave nest after 1-2 days, fed by both parents; black downy chicks have black bare parts; body feathers and remiges begin to appear at 6-7 days; body almost fully feathered at independence; independent at 19-21 days, when driven off by parents; young can fly at 19 days; fully grown at 6 weeks. Adults often renest immediately after independence of young. Post-juvenile moult begins at 3-4 weeks, complete by 10 weeks. Age of first breeding 1 year; adult mortality probably high. Clutch losses low; juvenile mortality high. Up to 4 broods per season, Natal; interval between clutches 30-40 days (mean 36 days).
Movements. Poorly understood: seasonality of occurrence and extent of movements highly complex and imperfectly known (not shown on map). Normally regarded everywhere as sedentary but throughout range there are isolated records indicative of both vagrancy and migration; probable vagrants recorded in N Somalia (Wagar Mts), N Kenya (L Turkana), N Botswana (Maun) and Namibia (Omateva and Oranjemund). In some habitats, such as deciduous or exotic thickets, occurrence may be confined to the rains, when sufficient food and cover exist. In Natal some birds remain throughout year wherever suitable conditions persist, but strong evidence for regular movements, both altitudinal and coastal, possibly over long distances and involving more first-year birds than adults. In Natal, immatures disperse from vicinity of parental territory when c. 7 weeks old.
Status and Conservation. Not globally threatened. Widespread; locally common, especially in South Africa. Although forest destruction must have adversely affected its numbers in some areas, species probably holding its own by virtue of its ability successfully to colonize degraded forest habitats, overgrown cultivation and exotic vegetation in suburban gardens. In Natal, has extended its range locally in

On following pages: 3. Red-chested Flufftail (*Sarothrura rufa*); 4. Long-toed Flufftail (*Sarothrura lugens*); 5. Streaky-breasted Flufftail (*Sarothrura boehmi*); 6. Striped Flufftail (*Sarothrura affinis*); 7. Madagascar Flufftail (*Sarothrura insularis*); 8. White-winged Flufftail (*Sarothrura ayresi*); 9. Slender-billed Flufftail (*Sarothrura watersi*).

recent past, following the creation of habitats associated with human habitation. However, in residential areas it suffers heavy predation from domestic cats, which may have serious local effects on its numbers.

Bibliography. Ash (1978b), Astley-Maberly (1935a, 1935b), Basilio (1963), Bates (1927), Benson & Benson (1975), Brosset & Érard (1986), Chapin (1939, 1948), Cottrell (1949), Dowsett & Dowsett-Lemaire (1991), Dowsett & Forbes-Watson (1993), Ginn et al. (1989), Keith (1973), Keith et al. (1970), Lewis & Pomeroy (1989), Lippens & Wille (1976), Mackworth-Praed & Grant (1957, 1962, 1970), Maclean (1993), Manson (1986), Pakenham (1943, 1979), Pinto (1983), Rand (1951a), Serle (1954), Short et al. (1990), Taylor (1994), Taylor & Taylor (1986), Urban et al. (1986).

3. Red-chested Flufftail
Sarothrura rufa

French: Râle à camail   **German**: Rotbrustralle   **Spanish**: Polluela Rufa

Taxonomy. *Rallus rufus* Vieillot, 1819, Cape Province.
Genus sometimes merged into *Coturnicops*. Race *ansorgei* proposed for birds of Angola. Three subspecies recognized.
Subspecies and Distribution.
S. r. bonapartii (Bonaparte, 1856) - scattered records from Sierra Leone E to Nigeria; more continuously in Cameroon, Gabon and Congo.
S. r. elizabethae van Someren, 1919 - Ethiopia; Central African Republic and NE Zaire E to Uganda and W Kenya.
S. r. rufa (Vieillot, 1819) - C Kenya through Tanzania, S Zaire and Angola to South Africa.

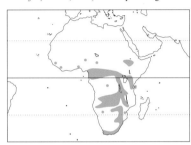

Descriptive notes. 15-17 cm; 29-47 (37·4) g; wingspan c. 25 cm. Tail noticeably long, often fluffed out. In male, chestnut extends to mantle and lower breast; tail black, spotted white. Female paler, more golden brown, than females of other wetland or grassland flufftails; spots and bars predominantly buff. Immature resembles adult but in male chestnut is duller and white markings fewer, mostly spots, female very dark brown with paler, less numerous spots on upperparts and more extensive markings on underparts. Juvenile has upperparts dull black, underparts dull grey-black except for whitish chin, throat and centre of belly. Males of races *elizabethae* and *bonapartii* have longer white streaks on upperparts and white streaks, not spots, on tail; upperparts of female *elizabethae* mainly barred, of female *bonapartii* mainly crescent-shaped; *bonapartii* smaller. Voice. Vocal repertoire very extensive. Song of male a series of high-pitched short hoots "woooo", 0·5-0·8 seconds long, repeated every 0·5-1 seconds and often continuing for several minutes; hoot sometimes rises in pitch "wooaa"; given during breeding season, both day and night. Common territorial call of male a series of loud notes, each rising in pitch at end, "dueh"; notes become more strident and lower-pitched as aggression increases; female has similar call. Gulps or grunts may accompany these and other calls. Has loud territorial "kevic" call and sharp "ki" and "ker" calls of alarm; also wide variety of other hooting, squeaking, rattling, moaning, hissing, humming, buzzing, bubbling and ticking notes.
Habitat. Wide range of wetland vegetation types, from seasonally wet hygrophilous grassland and sedge meadow as short as 55 cm to permanently flooded reedbeds up to 3 m tall, including papyrus swamp; normally avoids deeply flooded vegetation. In forested areas of W Africa also occurs in dry grass, sometimes near human habitation. Requires dense cover and foraging areas of mud, firm ground or short vegetation. In South Africa widespread from sea-level to 2100 m, above which altitude suitable cover does not grow; occurs up to 2700 m in Kenya.
Food and Feeding. Takes wide variety of invertebrate prey, including earthworms, small gastropods, spiders, and adults and larvae of many insects, including termites and small ants. Seeds, mainly of grasses, eaten frequently, but not fed to chicks, and may form large part of diet in non-breeding season. Daily energy intake of adults 140-150 kJ. Forages throughout day, with peaks in early morning and late afternoon. Searches low-growing plants for insect prey; forages on dry to wet substrates, digging with bill among roots, moss and in soft ground; takes active prey on and below surface of shallow water.
Breeding. Season indeterminate in equatorial regions; Sierra Leone, May, Jul; Nigeria, Dec; Cameroon, Mar-Jul; Gabon, Nov-Dec, Mar; Zaire, Jan-Feb, May, Jul-Aug; Angola, breeding condition May; Uganda, Oct; Kenya, May; Pemba Jan-Apr; Tanzania, Feb, Mar, breeding condition Apr, Jul; normally breeds during rains (Nov-May) in S Africa but Aug-Dec nesting recorded in SW Cape, under winter rainfall regime (Apr-Sept). Monogamous and permanently territorial, forming strong permanent pair-bond. Nest is a cup of grass or dead plants, sometimes with slight dome; well hidden in or under clump of grass or herbs 8-30 cm above ground or water surface; often nests in damp to shallowly flooded grass at edge of marshy areas; external diameter 13 cm, internal diameter 8-9·5 cm, depth of cup 3-4 cm. Usually 2-3 eggs (2-5), laid at daily intervals; incubation usually 16-18 days (14-18), male by day, female at night; chicks precocial and nidifugous, leave nest after 2-3 days, fed by both parents; black downy chicks have pronounced fluffy tail and black bare parts, bill with white tip and pink base; body fully feathered at 23 days; normally independent after 3-4 weeks, but may solicit food until 8-9 weeks old; remiges and rectrices fully grown at 6 weeks, when young fly; post-juvenile partial moult then begins, complete at 10-11 weeks. Age of first breeding 1 year; adult mortality low. Clutch losses, from predation or flooding, sometimes high; juvenile mortality possibly low. Usually 1-3 (1-4) broods per season; interval between clutches 4½-9 weeks; in captivity, in Zimbabwe up to 6 clutches laid Aug-May. Young may help feed chicks of subsequent broods; young of last brood often remain in parental territory during non-breeding season, being ejected by start of next breeding season.
Movements. No evidence for regular movements; pairs entirely sedentary and permanently territorial when conditions permit. Very local movements occur in non-breeding season when habitat is drastically reduced, e.g. by burning or drying out. Immatures disperse widely outside breeding season.
Status and Conservation. Not globally threatened. Widespread, sometimes locally common; occurs at densities of 2-6 pairs/ha in Natal, South Africa; a successful colonist of artificially created, sometimes very small, habitat patches. However, overall numbers must be decreasing with the continual destruction of wetland habitats throughout its range.

Bibliography. Ash (1978b), Benson (1956), Benson & Benson (1975), Benson et al. (1971), Broekhuysen et al. (1964), Brosset & Érard (1986), Dowsett & Forbes-Watson (1993), Ginn et al. (1989), Hopkinson & Masterson (1984), Irwin (1981), Keith et al. (1970), Lippens & Wille (1976), Liversidge (1968), Mackworth-Praed & Grant (1957, 1962, 1970), Maclean (1993), Pakenham (1943, 1979), Pinto (1983), Short et al. (1990), Steyn & Myburgh (1986), Taylor (1994), Taylor & Hustler (1993), Urban et al. (1986), Wintle (1988).

4. Long-toed Flufftail
Sarothrura lugens

French: Râle à tête rousse   **German**: Ugallaralle   **Spanish**: Polluela Cabecirroja
Other common names: Chestnut-headed Flufftail

Taxonomy. *Crex lugeus* [sic] Böhm, 1884, Ugalla District, Tanzania.
Genus sometimes merged into *Coturnicops*. Two subspecies recognized.
Subspecies and Distribution.
S. l. lugens (Böhm, 1884) - Cameroon to Zaire, Rwanda and W Tanzania.
S. l. lynesi (Grant & Mackworth-Praed, 1934) - C Angola and Zambia.
Specimen from Nyanga, Zimbabwe, is immature female *S. rufa*; recent sight and sound records from Zimbabwe and Malawi probably also referable to *S. rufa*.

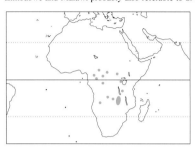

Descriptive notes. c. 15 cm. Tail even longer than in *S. rufa*, often fluffed out. Male has rich chestnut on head down to hindneck and malar region; chin and throat off-white; tail black, spotted white; upperparts finely streaked white; underparts with broad white streaks. Female distinctive, streaked chestnut and black where male is chestnut; body is dark brown-black with broader white streaks than in male; wings predominantly spotted or barred. Immature resembles adult but duller, with fewer streaks on upperparts; female streaked buff, not chestnut, on head and more heavily streaked on underparts. Juvenile blackish with dingy white chin. Race *lynesi* smaller. Voice. Poorly known. Song of male a series of moaning, rather guttural hoots "whooo", repeated with hardly a pause for up to 1 minute; speed and pitch variable. Call a series of loud, rapid, far-carrying, pumping "koh" notes, given for up to 45 seconds and often in crescendo, dying away to a grunt; sometimes calls in asynchronous duet.
Habitat. Patches of savanna in lowland forest; grass-grown marshes in savanna; lakeside marshes; rank grass and sedges in dambos (wet drainage lines in woodland). In forest of NE Gabon, also inhabits moist post-cultivation growth dominated by *Aframomum* and arrowroot plants. Prefers dense, lush vegetation 0·7-1·5 m high. Often occurs alongside *S. rufa*.
Food and Feeding. Little known. Stomach of adults contained insects and seeds; of a chick, small black ants.
Breeding. Laying months, derived from young birds and collected females containing eggs: Cameroon, Apr, Jul, Sept; Zaire Mar, Apr; Zambia, Mar, Dec. Nest and eggs undescribed; black downy chick has black bill with white base and tip.
Movements. Unknown; probably entirely sedentary, with perhaps very local displacement outside breeding season following habitat reduction by burning, etc.
Status and Conservation. Not globally threatened. Generally uncommon, but locally common in NE Zambia. Has been described as a relict species in unsuccessful competition with *S. rufa*. In view of its fragmented distribution, the fact that it appears to be generally uncommon, and the continual destruction of wetland habitats, species should perhaps be considered Vulnerable.

Bibliography. Benson & Benson (1975), Benson et al. (1971), Brosset & Érard (1986), Chapin (1939), Dowsett & Forbes-Watson (1993), Gibbon (1989), Keith et al. (1970), Lippens & Wille (1976), Louette (1981), Mackworth-Praed & Grant (1957, 1962, 1970), Pinto (1983), Roux & Benson (1969), Short et al. (1990), Snow (1978), Taylor (1994), Taylor & Hustler (1993), Urban et al. (1986).

5. Streaky-breasted Flufftail
Sarothrura boehmi

French: Râle de Böhm   **German**: Boehmralle   **Spanish**: Polluela de Boehm
Other common names: Boehm's Flufftail

Taxonomy. *Sarothrura böhmi* Reichenow, 1900, Likulwe, Haut Luapula, SE Zaire.
Genus sometimes merged into *Coturnicops*. Proposed race *danei* known only from type specimen taken at sea. Monotypic.
Distribution. Imperfectly known. Scattered localities from Nigeria and Cameroon E to Kenya, and S through NE Zaire to E Angola and N South Africa.

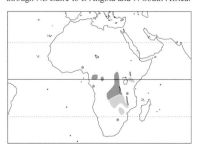

Descriptive notes. 15-17 cm; 31-42 (35·8) g, 1 female (juvenile?) 21 g, 1 juvenile 27 g. Tail short, not fluffy; outer web of outermost primary white. Male has chestnut paler than in *S. rufa* and extending only to hindneck and upper breast; tail black, streaked white; white streaks on upperparts longer than in *S. rufa*. Female dark, with mainly scallopy off-white markings on upperparts. Immature resembles adult but duller, with fewer, less pronounced upperparts markings. Juvenile is dull sooty black, with white chin, throat and centre of belly; male has faint white markings on upperwing-coverts. Voice. Song of male a deep, hollow, hooting "hooo", repeated every 2 seconds. Also a short, higher-pitched pumping toot "oo" or "oe", repeated every 0·5-0·7 seconds, each note preceded by a low grunt; series sometimes trails off into softer agitated "wu" notes. Annoyance call a repeated low "cuk".
Habitat. Breeding habitat in E & S Africa is short grass, temporarily inundated during rains, such as that at edges of rivers, drainage lines and marshes; also grass flats and pans. In Zambia occurs in grass 30-70 cm tall, on ground flooded to maximum depth of 10 cm. Often occurs alongside *Aenigmatolimnas marginalis*; prefers shorter, less dense and often drier vegetation than *S. rufa*; however, in W Africa occurs alongside *S. rufa* in dry grassland, in NE Gabon frequenting areas with large tussocks of tall grass scattered in continuous cover of shorter grass.
Food and Feeding. Poorly known. Stomach contents were small seeds, especially grass seeds, and small insects; in captivity eats much less seed than *S. rufa*. Chicks fed on insects.
Breeding. Breeds during rains: in S Africa Nov-Mar, possibly May-Jul in Kenya. Monogamous; apparently territorial; captive males have primitive communal display. Nest often in relatively short or sparse grass; a pad or shallow bowl of grass, c. 2·5 cm thick, placed in grass tuft, with growing blades pulled over it in dome; usually 2·5-7·5 cm above wet to dry (not flooded) ground. Usually 3-5 eggs (2-

5); incubation 16-18 days, male by day, female at night; chicks leave nest after 1-3 days, fed by both parents; black downy chicks have black bare parts; feathers begin to grow at 7 days; young fully grown and able to fly at 5 weeks, when post-juvenile partial moult begins. Clutch losses from predation often high. Some breeding records must be treated with caution because of confusion with *S. rufa*.

Movements. Imperfectly known. Apparently sedentary in NE Gabon, though breeding not yet recorded; in E & S Africa migrates, breeding mainly in S tropics and retreating towards equatorial regions in dry season when much of habitat dries out and is grazed and burnt. Recorded in Kenya May-Sept, and from Zambia and Angola southwards only in Nov-Apr. At Mufindi, S Tanzania, migrants attracted to lights at night in May-Jun: all were exhausted and were probably moving N after breeding. A presumed off-course migrant was taken at sea in Jun, 150 km off coast of Guinea. May migrate when only 5-6 weeks old: one in juvenile plumage flew into a building at night in Kenya, Jul.

Status and Conservation. Not globally threatened. Status difficult to assess because, like other flufftails, species is frequently overlooked. Often uncommon but may be locally numerous in good rainfall years: 100+ calling males were heard on a grass plain in Zambia in Jan 1978. Locally common in NE Gabon (Makokou), where it occurs in similar numbers to *S. rufa*. Numbers in E & S Africa must have been adversely affected by habitat loss resulting from overgrazing and the damming and draining of wetlands.

Bibliography. Baker *et al.* (1984), Benson & Benson (1975), Benson *et al.* (1971), Brosset & Érard (1986), Brown & Britton (1980), Chapin (1939), Dowsett & Forbes-Watson (1993), Farmer (1979), Ginn *et al.* (1989), Hopkinson & Masterson (1984), Irwin (1981), Keith *et al.* (1970), Lippens & Wille (1976), Mackworth-Praed & Grant (1957, 1962, 1970), Maclean (1993), Neuby Varty (1953), Pinto (1983), Short *et al.* (1990), Snow (1978), Taylor (1987, 1994), Urban *et al.* (1986), Wintle (1988).

6. Striped Flufftail

Sarothrura affinis

French: Râle affin **German**: Streifenralle **Spanish**: Polluela Estriada
Other common names: Red-tailed/Chestnut-tailed Flufftail

Taxonomy. *Crex affinis* A. Smith, 1828, Cape Province, South Africa.
Genus sometimes merged into *Coturnicops*. Forms superspecies with *S. insularis*. Two subspecies recognized.

Subspecies and Distribution.
S. a. antonii Madaràsz & Neumann, 1911 - extreme S Sudan S to E Zimbabwe.
S. a. affinis (A. Smith, 1828) - South Africa.

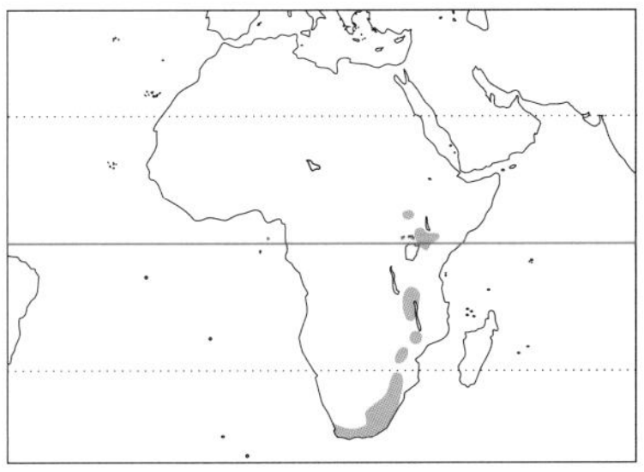

Descriptive notes. 14-15 cm; male 25-30 (28·5) g; wingspan 23-24 cm. Tail short and fluffy; upperparts heavily streaked whitish with yellowish wash. Normally the only flufftail in its habitat; male distinguished from sympatric wetland species by chestnut tail; female by chestnut and black barring on tail and orange-brown wash on face. Immature resembles adult; in race *antonii*, male has white streaks on mantle and almost no chestnut on upper breast, while female has deeper chestnut wash to upperparts streaks, fewer spots on belly, and streaks, rather than spots, on breast. Juvenile dull blackish, paler on underparts. Race *antonii* larger; chestnut on head of male extends to upper breast. VOICE. Vocal repertoire extensive. Song of male a hoot, lower-pitched than that of *S. rufa*, lasting c. 1 second and given at intervals of 1·5-2 seconds for up to 10 minutes, often continuing intermittently throughout night; also calls during day. Territorial call of male a series of loud, rapidly repeated, sharp, tinny "ki" notes, usually followed immediately by similarly loud and rapid series of lower-pitched strident "ker" notes; either series may be repeated or given without the other; female has a quiet, faster version of this call. Also various gulps, rattles, barks, low-pitched short hoots, and ticking, buzzing and bubbling notes.

Habitat. Under existing climatic conditions, distribution essentially discontinuous and relict. Over most of range typically inhabits dry upland grassland, sometimes with bracken, brambles or *Protea*, or near forest edges; also occurs in crops, e.g. lucerne, millet. In South Africa, where descends to sea-level, found in *Psoralea-Osmitopsis* fynbos in extreme SW Cape. Although frequently associated with small streams and marshy patches in grassland, no convincing evidence that species occupies larger wetland areas alongside *S. rufa* except under severe drought conditions. Requires dense cover with clear ground for foraging; in Natal, South Africa, occurs in grass 35-100 cm tall and avoids rocky areas and steep or convex slopes. Ascends to 3700 m in Kenya, 2300 m in C Africa, and 2100 m in South Africa.

Food and Feeding. Takes insects, including beetles, bugs, adult and larval Lepidoptera, ants, termites, grasshoppers, crickets and flies; also earthworms, small spiders, grass and sedge seeds and some vegetable matter. Forages throughout the day; searches clear ground, very short vegetation, low-growing plants and bases of grass tussocks; moves aside dead plant material; catches small ants around nests; probably also forages on wet substrates and in shallow water.

Breeding. Normally breeds during the rains. Sudan, breeding condition May; Kenya, May; Tanzania, Jan; Zambia, breeding condition Jan; Malawi, Apr; Zimbabwe, Jan; South Africa Dec-Mar, but SW Cape Sept (end of winter rains). Four clutches reported from South Africa are referable to other species. Monogamous; apparently permanently territorial, with permanent pair-bond when sedentary. Nest a bowl of dry grass or rootlets built into grass tuft. Usually 4 eggs, sometimes 5; incubation probably 15 days, by both sexes; black downy chicks have black bare parts; chicks precocial and nidifugous; may leave nest within a day of hatching; cared for by both parents.

Movements. Normally regarded as sedentary, with local movements when grassland habitat becomes too dry or is burnt. In Natal, sedentary at lower altitudes, where cover and food remain at suitable levels all year, but in upland areas (over 1400 m) departs Apr-Jun and returns Oct-Jan, exodus associated with drop in invertebrate numbers and arrival with increasing invertebrate numbers and development of cover after burning; movements probably altitudinal, possibly over as little as 35-40 km, to altitudes below 1000 m.

Status and Conservation. Not globally threatened. Uncommon in some parts of range, and classed as Rare in South African Red Data Book. Race *antonii* has not been recorded in Sudan for over 50 years; now rarely recorded in Kenya, although 70 years ago was considered locally common; in Zambia, may be locally common; in Zimbabwe, may be more widespread than is known. In South Africa grassland habitats of nominate race have disappeared at alarming rate and are now severely restricted in extent; very few birds are found in farming areas, where grazing renders vegetation too short and sparse for occupation, and disturbance is too intense; however, species still locally common at some protected or well managed grassland and fynbos sites. In view of continuing habitat loss, future of species is not secure.

Bibliography. Anon. (1995g), Benson & Benson (1975), Benson & Holliday (1964), Brooke (1984a), Dowsett & Forbes-Watson (1993), Ginn *et al.* (1989), Hockey, Underhill & Neatherway (1989), Irwin (1981), Kakebeeke (1993), Keith *et al.* (1970), Lewis & Pomeroy (1989), Mackworth-Praed & Grant (1957, 1962), Maclean (1993), Masterson & Child (1959), Short *et al.* (1990), Snow (1978), Tarboton, Kemp & Kemp (1987), Taylor (1994), Urban *et al.* (1986).

7. Madagascar Flufftail

Sarothrura insularis

French: Râle insulaire **German**: Hovaralle **Spanish**: Polluela Malgache

Taxonomy. *Corethrura insularis* Sharpe, 1870, Nossi Vola, Madagascar.
Genus sometimes merged into *Coturnicops*. Forms superspecies with *S. affinis*. Monotypic.

Distribution. Madagascar, mainly in E.

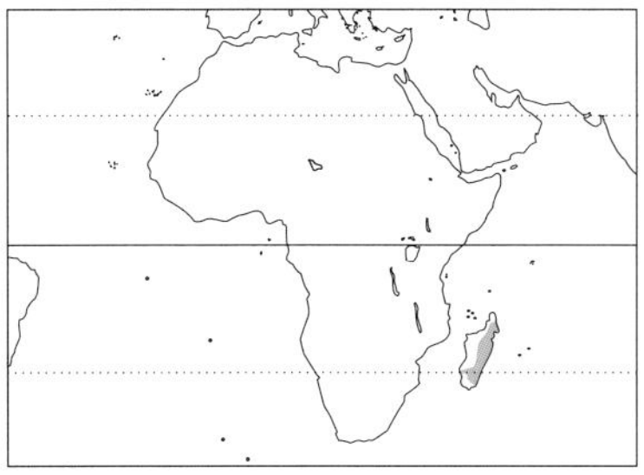

Descriptive notes. 14 cm. Tail short and fluffy. Male distinctive, with rich chestnut head, neck, breast and tail; black body with yellowish streaks on upperparts and white streaks on underparts. Female also distinctive, with dark upperparts streaked and barred buff to chestnut; ochraceous underparts with black spots on breast and bars on rest of underside; deep chestnut tail with black bars. Immature male probably resembles adult; immature female similat to adult but duller, with spotting of underparts extending to belly. Juvenile male probably almost entirely dark sooty brown. VOICE. Common call, probably given by both sexes, a characteristic, loud, high-pitched, ringing series of rapidly repeated single "kee" and double "keekee" notes, given in various combinations but often with several monosyllabic notes at beginning and end of series; volume diminishes towards end of call, which may be preceded by short trills "drr" and terminated by repeated "kik" or rapidly repeated "ki" notes, or both. Other calls include short versions of, or excerpts from, the full call.

Habitat. Tolerant of wide variety of habitats: grassland of edges and clearings of undisturbed and degraded forest; secondary bush, including that comprising large ferns, thick grass, and *Philippia* (Ericaceae); dense cultivation, although not recorded from cassava fields; also seen on forest floor, and occurs in marshes with long grass, reeds and sedges, and sometimes rice paddies. Recorded from sea-level to 2300 m.

Food and Feeding. Only insects and seeds recorded.

Breeding. Poorly known. Lays Oct, probably also Sept. Probably monogamous; apparently territorial at least while breeding and possibly also in non-breeding season. Nest a ball of broad grass blades, thickly lined with finer plant material; external length 17 cm, width 12 cm; internal length and width 8 cm; built on ground in dense grass. Eggs 3-4; incubation by female only; chicks have sooty down; young may remain with parents after start of post-juvenile moult.

Movements. Unknown: probably none.

Status and Conservation. Not globally threatened. Widespread, apparently common over most of its range, especially in E region; seems to adapt readily to degraded environments.

Bibliography. Albignac (1970), Benson *et al.* (1976-1977), Dee (1986), Delacour (1932), Dowsett & Forbes-Watson (1993), Keith (1973), Keith *et al.* (1970), Langrand (1990), Milon *et al.* (1973), Rand (1936), Snow (1978), Wilmé & Langrand (1990).

8. White-winged Flufftail

Sarothrura ayresi

French: Râle à miroir **German**: Spiegelralle **Spanish**: Polluela Especulada

Taxonomy. *Coturnicops ayresi* Gurney, 1877, Potchefstroom, south-west Transvaal, South Africa.
Sometimes placed in genus *Coturnicops*, normally with, but on occasion without, other flufftail species. Ethiopian birds first described as *Ortygops macmillani*. Forms species pair with *S. watersi*. Monotypic.

Distribution. Ethiopia, Zimbabwe and South Africa; to date only one reliable record from Zambia (Chingola); sound records from Rwanda questionable, apparently referable to Grey Crowned Crane (*Balearica regulorum*).

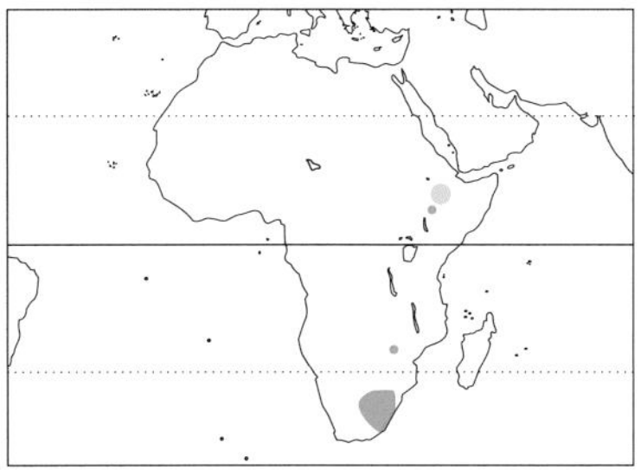

Descriptive notes. 14-16 cm. Small flufftail; unlike other species, often easy to flush and has strong, direct flight on more pointed wings. Both sexes easily identified by white secondaries, which form conspicuous white wing-patch in flight, and distinguished from all other marsh and grassland *Sarothrura* species except female *S. affinis* by chestnut and black bars on tail; outermost long primary has prominent white outer web. Sexual dimorphism less marked than in other *Sarothrura* species. Immature resembles adult, but male has upperwing-coverts spotted white (streaked in adults), mantle feathers with broader dark tips, almost no chestnut on face, less extensive white on underparts and less chestnut on sides of breast; female has browner upperparts with duller, less distinct pale markings and fewer spots on upperwing-coverts, is duller on head, neck and breast and whiter on chin and throat. Juvenile male predominantly dull grey-brown, paler on underparts, with small white spots on upperparts and white throat and centre of belly; female blackish brown with small tawny and white spots on upperparts, whitish flecks on breast, and white throat and centre of belly; juvenile tail as adult. VOICE. Common call a low-pitched, short "oop" note, repeated every second and continued for up to 3 minutes; often given in asynchronous duet, the second bird having a higher-pitched note. In South Africa, calling usually occurs only briefly, at dawn and dusk. Very similar to a roosting call of *Balearica regulorum* which, however, is louder, usually a double note or a more complex series of calls, and often given by several birds together. Other calls, rarely heard, include deep mooing notes and high-pitched short and long hoots.

Habitat. Ethiopian breeding habitat is shallowly, sometimes seasonally, flooded short, dense grassland or marsh. In Zambia, one bird found in a pan-like marsh with emergent grass. In Zimbabwe habitat varies: grass 50-100 cm tall on dry to moist ground; also muddy to shallowly flooded marshy ground with grass and sedge cover. Non-breeding birds in South Africa occur for short periods alongside breeding *S. rufa* in dense grass, sedges and rushes averaging 1 m tall, on moist to shallowly flooded substrates, and for up to 4½ months in dense sedges, reeds (*Phragmites*) and reedmace (*Typha*), 1-2 m tall, on moist to deeply flooded ground not commonly inhabited by *S. rufa*.

Food and Feeding. Stomach contents included water insects, grain seeds and vegetable mush. No information on foraging habits.

Breeding. In Ethiopia breeds during rains, Jul-Aug; despite claims to contrary, no acceptable evidence that species breeds in South Africa. Nest and eggs undescribed, but 2 clutches of 3 eggs found on seasonally flooded ground at Mazowe, Zimbabwe, in 1950's (probably Feb) may be of this species; nests were shallow cups of grass built in reedy vegetation 10-12 cm above water 30 cm deep, with growing vegetation pulled over them in a dome.

Movements. Lack of subspeciation suggests that migration may occur between centres of distribution in Ethiopia and South Africa but paucity of records from intervening regions, and overlap in occurrence dates, makes this unlikely. C Ethiopian highland breeding habitat, where birds recorded Jun-Sept, is unsuitable in non-breeding season, when birds may migrate SW to lower altitude permanent marshes, and recorded at Kaffa in May. In South Africa, where species may be purely nomadic, recorded Aug-Mar and May; in both regions may undergo periodic long distance dispersal when numbers are high, allowing gene exchange between N and S populations; records from Zambia and Zimbabwe may reflect such dispersal.

Status and Conservation. ENDANGERED. One of rarest and least known of African endemics. Total population probably very small, habitats under severe threat from damming, draining and overgrazing, and its future is precarious. In Ethiopia seen only once since 1957, with 1 bird at Sululta swamps in 1984, until small numbers found again at Sululta in Aug-Sept 1995. In Zimbabwe recently recorded only in 1977 and 1979. Since early 1980's, 4 sites in South Africa have held small numbers, 3 of them annually in 1990-1992, when regular observations were made; reliable counts of 1-17 birds. In South Africa, the lack of recent records from coastal localities suggests that species is now confined to higher altitude wetlands.

Bibliography. Ash (1978b), Atkinson *et al.* (1996), Bannerman (1911), Benson & Irwin (1971), Brooke (1984a), Collar & Andrew (1988), Collar & Stuart (1985), Collar *et al.* (1994), Dowsett & Forbes-Watson (1993), Érard (1974), Ginn *et al.* (1989), Guichard (1948), Hopkinson & Masterson (1977, 1984), Keith *et al.* (1970), Mackworth-Praed & Grant (1957, 1962), Maclean (1993), Massoli-Novelli (1988c), Mendelsohn *et al.* (1983), Taylor (1994), Urban *et al.* (1986), Wolff & Milstein (1976).

9. Slender-billed Flufftail

Sarothrura watersi

French: Râle de Waters   **German**: Lemurenralle   **Spanish**: Polluela de Waters
Other common names: Waters's Flufftail

Taxonomy. *Zapornia watersi*, Bartlett, 1880, south-east Betsileo Country, Madagascar.
Genus sometimes merged into *Coturnicops*. Forms species pair with *S. ayresi*. Monotypic.
Distribution. Madagascar.

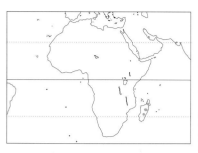

Descriptive notes. 14-17 cm; 1 male 26·5 g. Tail short, slightly fluffy; bill long and slender. Male has distinctive, relatively plain plumage with dull chestnut head, neck, breast and mantle, whitish chin and throat; dull dark brown upperparts with rather indistinct darker streaks; ashy brown unmarked underparts; tail chestnut with black feather tips. Female also plain, with chocolate brown upperparts; pale supercilium; pale brown face; whitish chin, throat and centre of breast; rest of underparts plain dark brown; tail black with narrow white and broader chestnut bars. Immature male undescribed; female duller than adult, with small white spots scattered over upperparts, wings and sides of breast. Juvenile undescribed. VOICE. Muffled, solemn call, uttered during the day and over long periods without break; described as consisting of 2 or 3 notes repeated every 0·3-0·4 seconds, the 2-note version with first syllable accentuated "goo goo"; calls vary in pitch.

Habitat. Small elevated wetlands with *Cyperus* sedges, and adjacent dense, grassy terrain or even rice paddies, near rain forest. Altitudinal range 950-1800 m. It has been suggested that this species may replace the common *S. insularis* at higher altitudes, and that temperature may control its montane distribution; however, its distribution is more probably determined by that of the rain forest.

Food and Feeding. No information available.

Breeding. Unknown; possibly breeds during rains. Male and female in breeding condition Andapa, Sept; male called Ranomafana, Oct and Nov. Adult and juvenile reported near Antananarivo, May, but occurrence there disputed.

Movements. No evidence for any movements.

Status and Conservation. ENDANGERED. Known only from five localities in E Madagascar: "SE Betsileo", "near Andapa", Antananarivo, Périnet Analamazaotra and Ranomafana. Was considered rare, possibly a relict species on its way to early extinction, until its uncorroborated discovery in the 1200 km² area around Antananarivo in 1970/71, where it was reported from three sites and was suspected to occur in all suitable marshes at density of 1 pair per 2 ha; doubt has been cast on these observations and species not reliably recorded elsewhere between 1930 and 1986. Considering only the reliable records, its distribution appears coincident with that of the much-pressurized eastern rain forest; its particular microhabitat is widely but patchily distributed in small blocks over a broad forest zone and is presumably becoming increasingly rare, but suitable habitat also possibly occurs at 9 other localities. The Madagascar system of protected areas, which includes wetlands only occasionally, incorportates only one known site of occurrence; in view of the need to expand rice cultivation, it is unlikely that wetlands will be included in new protected areas. There is an urgent need for distributional and population surveys at all sites of occurrence, and for an evaluation of sites suitable for protection.

Bibliography. Andriamampianina (1981), Benson *et al.* (1976-1977), Collar & Andrew (1988), Collar & Stuart (1985), Collar *et al.* (1994), Dee (1986), Delacour (1932), Dowsett & Forbes-Watson (1993), Keith *et al.* (1970), Langrand (1990), Milon *et al.* (1973), Rand (1936), Salvan (1972b), Snow (1978), Wilmé & Langrand (1990).

PLATE 10 ➤

PLATE 10

inches 6
cm 15

birds showing
range of variation

10

11

ssp *berliozi*

12

ssp *kioloides*

13

♀
14

15

16

♂

♀
17

♀
18

♀
19

♀
20

♂
♂
♂

Genus *HIMANTORNIS* Hartlaub, 1855

10. **Nkulengu Rail**

Himantornis haematopus

French: Râle à pieds rouges **German**: Rotfußralle **Spanish**: Rascón Nkulenga

Taxonomy. *Himantornis haematopus* Hartlaub, 1855, Dabocrom, Ghana.
Has been placed in its own subfamily (Himantornithinae) on basis of primitive skeletal characters, which suggest link with trumpeters of family Psophiidae (see page 108). Sometimes divided into three races, with recognition of *petiti* of Gabon to C Zaire, and *whitesidei* of SC & E Zaire, but in view of great individual variation in plumage within ranges of all three proposed races, and overlap of characters between "races", species probably best treated as monotypic until more extensive studies made. Monotypic.
Distribution. Sierra Leone E to W Uganda and S to coastal and C Zaire.

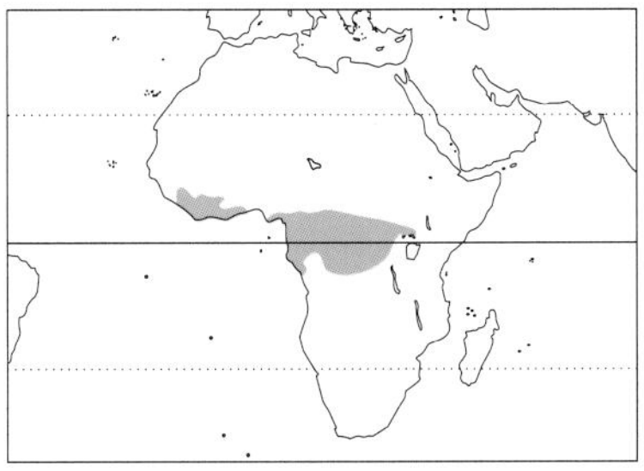

Descriptive notes. 43 cm; 1 female 390 g. Variably scaly or mottled plumage pattern more reminiscent of francolin than rail, but overall shape, leg length and behaviour are obviously rallid. Easily separated from other forest rails by large size, heavy bill and red legs. Plumage very variable, particularly in extent of grey scaling on underparts. Sexes alike. Immature similar to adult but upperpart feathers have dark centres and tawny margins; underparts pale grey-brown, with whitish chin, throat and belly; eye, legs and feet duller than in adult. VOICE. Call a rhythmical, antiphonal duet; described as series of phrases of 6 notes "ko-káw-zi-káw-hu-hóooo", each lasting c. 1·5 seconds and repeated in quick succession for several minutes. Notes are loud, raucous and far-carrying; reminiscent of monkey calls or even of "men cutting trees". Calls throughout year, mainly at night, especially at full moon, and most often just before dawn.
Habitat. Lowland rain forest, usually dense primary or old secondary growth, where inhabits rank vegetation along streams and rivers, on islands and sometimes in swampy or marshy areas; occasionally in mangroves. Also found in forest away from water, and in areas disturbed by logging.
Food and Feeding. Snails, millipedes, insects including ants and beetles, small amphibians and hard seeds. Probably takes larger prey, and forages on drier substrates, than does sympatric *Canirallus oculeus*. Forages on ground, usually in groups of 2-3 (once 8), searching for prey among dead leaves and sticks. In Gabon, seen with large parties of insectivorous birds in dry season, and also in bird parties following driver ant columns. Most active in morning and evening but also feeds during day.
Breeding. Almost unknown. Breeding recorded Cameroon, Sept; Gabon, fresh nest Feb; Zaire, Feb, probably also Mar and Sept. Probably monogamous and territorial; characteristic antiphonal duet given for long periods at dusk and during night from high in tree, and by day from ground. Only 2 nests described: 1 in Gabon was substantial structure of coarse tangled twigs and leaves, 35 cm wide and deep, placed 1·2 m above ground on heap of brushwood in undergrowth of plateau forest far from water; another nest was said to be placed in a tree. 1 clutch of 3 eggs found. Unlike most rails, downy young distinctively patterned: broad blackish brown stripe from forehead over head and back to tail; lores to ear-patch black; stripe over eye, side of head, chin, throat and underparts creamy white; brown band across breast; rest of body dull light brown; eye dull brown; legs and feet dull pink; upper mandible blackish; lower mandible grey.
Movements. Apparently sedentary.
Status and Conservation. Not globally threatened. Frequent to common throughout most of its range; in Gabon, spacing of singing birds suggested density of 3 pairs per 200 ha. No recent records in Nigeria; in 1990, was thought to be widespread in Bwamba Forest, W Uganda, whence there was only 1 previous record. Widespread destruction of its forest habitat must have reduced its numbers in many areas and species sometimes trapped for food by local people.
Bibliography. Brosset & Érard (1986), Chapin (1939), Chappuis (1975), Dowsett & Dowsett-Lemaire (1991), Dowsett & Forbes-Watson (1993), Dowsett-Lemaire *et al.* (1993), Elgood *et al.* (1994), Field (1995), Gatter (1988), Grimes (1987), Lippens & Wille (1976), Mackworth-Praed & Grant (1970), Olson (1973b), Pinto (1983), Sharpe (1907), Snow (1978), Thiollay (1985), Urban *et al.* (1986).

Genus *CANIRALLUS* Bonaparte, 1856

11. **Grey-throated Rail**

Canirallus oculeus

French: Râle à gorge grise **German**: Augenralle **Spanish**: Rascón Carigrís

Taxonomy. *Gallinula oculea* Hartlaub, 1855, Rio Butri, Ghana.
Birds from Cameroon eastward sometimes treated as separate race, *batesi*, but differ too little from other populations to merit subspecific status. Monotypic.
Distribution. Sierra Leone E across N Zaire to W Uganda and SW to coastal Congo. Occurrence in N Central African Republic (Manovo-Gounda-Saint Floris National Park) doubtful.

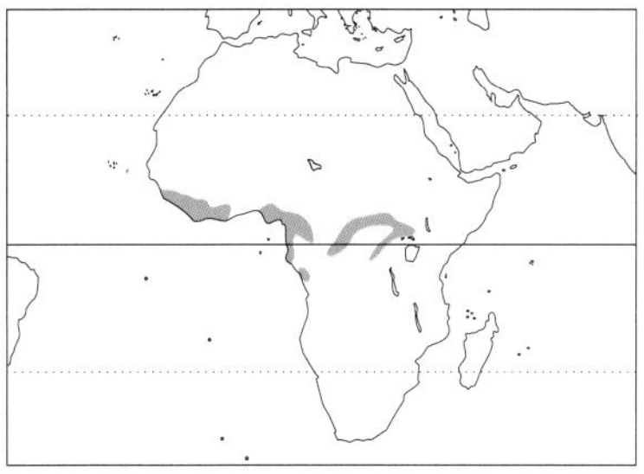

Descriptive notes. 30 cm. Plumage unlike that of any other rail in its habitat. White spots on remiges, and pale spots or bars on wing-coverts, would be obvious in flight but species is unlikely to flush; underwing also boldly spotted white. Sexes alike. Immature has forehead, face and throat brown instead of grey, upperparts with russet wash and underparts dark reddish brown. VOICE. Song lasts 2-3 minutes; starts with hollow notes like double drumbeats; after 20 seconds intersperses soft "dou" or "douah" notes, which increase towards end of call as drumbeats fade; far-carrying and ventriloquial; given both day and night, with peak at dawn. Also loud, explosive booming of 3-6 notes on descending scale of half-tones "oue-oue-oue...", lasting 0·5-1 seconds. Probable alarm calls rendered "ptik-ptik-ptik..." , "douk-douk-douk..." and muffled "thouk-thouk...".
Habitat. Primary and secondary lowland rain forest, occurring in ravines and along creeks and forest streams overhung by trees and bordered by rank undergrowth; also flooded or swampy forest, including areas with mud, tall arrowroot plants and tree ferns, and marshes within forest regions (Ghana). Records from "floodplain" in savanna-park zone of N Central African Republic very doubtful.
Food and Feeding. Skinks, snails, slugs, small crabs, millipedes and insects including ants, caterpillars and other larvae, and beetles. Seen foraging on half-dry bed of small forest stream by removing dead leaves with jerking movements of the bill.
Breeding. Breeds during rains: Cameroon, Feb, Apr, Jul; Zaire, breeding condition Sept, Nov, Dec. 2 nests described: one, of broad grass leaves, on a stump in swampy bottom of ravine among *Raphia* palms and *Canna*-like plants; the other among roots of uprooted tree over stream bank. Eggs 2; downy chicks blackish brown.
Movements. None recorded.
Status and Conservation. Not globally threatened. Regarded as locally numerous only in Congo, elsewhere apparently uncommon or rare; however, its extreme secretiveness, and lack of familiarity of most observers with its calls, render it very easy to overlook and make its abundance difficult to assess. Forest destruction must have affected its numbers over much of range; species probably extinct in Nigeria and has not been recorded in W Uganda in recent years.
Bibliography. Bates (1927), Brosset & Érard (1986), Chapin (1939), Demey & Fishpool (1994), Dowsett & Dowsett-Lemaire (1991), Dowsett & Forbes-Watson (1993), Gatter (1988), Grimes (1987), Lippens & Wille (1976), Mackworth-Praed & Grant (1957, 1970), Olson (1973b), Serle *et al.* (1977), Snow (1978), Thiollay (1985), Urban *et al.* (1986).

12. **Madagascar Wood-rail**

Canirallus kioloides

French: Râle à gorge blanche **German**: Graukehlralle **Spanish**: Rascón Kioloide
Other common names: Kioloides Rail, Grey-throated Wood-rail

Taxonomy. *Gallinula kioloides* Pucheran, 1845, Madagascar.
Formerly placed in monospecific genus *Mentocrex* on basis of imperforate nostrils (those of *C. oculeus* are perforate), but this character is not now considered generically important. Birds from Bemaraha apparently differ sufficiently in plumage coloration to be regarded as a further, as yet undescribed, race. Two subspecies currently recognized.
Subspecies and Distribution.
C. k. kioloides (Pucheran, 1845) - E half of Madagascar.
C. k. berliozi (Salomonsen, 1934) - Sambirano, NW Madagascar.

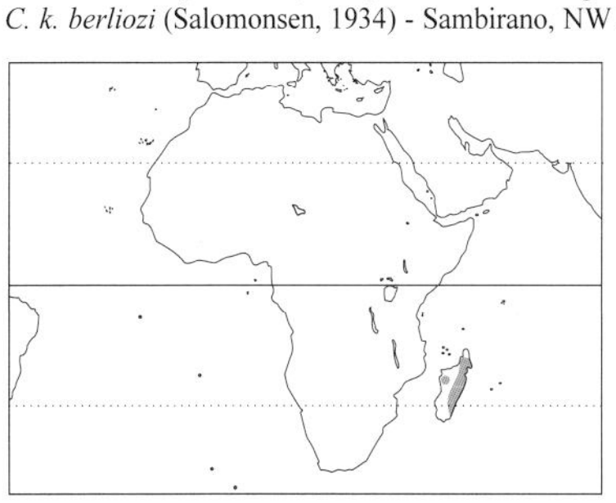

Descriptive notes. 28 cm; 258-280 (269) g. Sexes alike. Distinguished from sympatric and vaguely similar *Dryolimnas cuvieri* by smaller size, colour of head and upperparts, dark undertail-coverts, and short bill. Immature duller than adult; less extensively grey on head; yellow spots on undertail-coverts. Race *berliozi* slightly larger and paler; grey on forehead and white on throat more extensive; mantle pale greenish olive. VOICE. Rather vocal and easily located by its common call, a series of loud, piercing whistles with rising inflexion. Feeding birds constantly emit muffled, throaty chortles reminiscent of contact call of Brown Lemur (*Lemur fulvus*), very brief, sharp metallic notes and staccato "nak" notes sometimes speeded up into rattle. Also utters muffled "bub" notes and harsh clucks.
Habitat. Undisturbed rain forest; slightly degraded contiguous secondary growth with fairly sparse herbaceous ground cover; woodland water courses; edges of ponds and marshes with reeds and papyrus; also seen in dry deciduous forest. Occurs from sea-level to 1550 m.
Food and Feeding. Only insects, amphibians and seeds recorded. Normally forages in pairs. Secretive; covers ground swiftly in underbrush, stops suddenly to probe litter and then moves on, sometimes returning several times to area just searched.
Breeding. Lays May, Jun, Nov; breeding condition Oct. Nest a bowl of grass and leaves, placed 2-3 m above ground in bush or tangle of creepers. Eggs 2. Downy chick has black head and upperparts, except for light rufous brown stripe along side of back and rump, and rufous brown forehead, supercilium, ear-coverts, throat and sides of neck; wings black, flecked tawny; upper breast rufous brown; lower breast black, flecked rufous brown; belly rufous brown; all brown down on head, neck and underparts is tipped black, giving mottled appearance to these regions; iris, legs and feet black; bill grey-black, tipped whitish.
Movements. None.
Status and Conservation. Not globally threatened. Race *kioloides* confined to E and High Plateau; regarded as common in 1929-1931 but by 1970's much of habitat on coastal plain had been destroyed; at present, common at middle altitudes but affected by the general and serious continued destruction of forest habitat, chiefly by slash-and-burn itinerant cultivation and exploitation for firewood. Race *berliozi* apparently still fairly common in Sambirano Domain but forest habitats in this relatively small area are severely threatened, principally by clearing for rain-fed rice growing and coffee, and have been much degraded outside reserves. It occurs in Special Reserve of Manongarivo, the forest of which is still largely intact. It is not known which subspecies occurs on nearby Tsaratanana massif, which includes large forest blocks and a Strict Nature Reserve; *berliozi* should be regarded as near-threatened due to habitat destruction, unless its occurrence there is confirmed. Birds from Bemaraha, perhaps bellonging to an undescribed subspecies, restricted to humid forest in the Tsingy foothills; this population may be small but is relatively safe because the whole of Tsingy is legally protected.

On following pages: 13. Swinhoe's Rail (*Coturnicops exquisitus*); 14. Yellow Rail (*Coturnicops noveboracensis*); 15. Speckled Rail (*Coturnicops notatus*); 16. Ocellated Crake (*Micropygia schomburgkii*); 17. Chestnut Forest-rail (*Rallina rubra*); 18. White-striped Forest-rail (*Rallina leucospila*); 19. Forbes's Forest-rail (*Rallina forbesi*); 20. Mayr's Forest-rail (*Rallina mayri*).

Bibliography. Benson *et al.* (1976-1977), Dee (1986), Delacour (1932), Dowsett & Forbes-Watson (1993), Keith (1978), Langrand (1990), Milon *et al.* (1973), Olson (1973b), Rand (1936), Ripley (1977), Snow (1978).

Genus *COTURNICOPS* G. R. Gray, 1855

13. Swinhoe's Rail

Coturnicops exquisitus

French: Râle de Swinhoe **German**: Mandschurensumpfhuhn **Spanish**: Polluela Exquisita
Other common names: Swinhoe's Yellow/Siberian Rail

Taxonomy. *Porzana exquisita* Swinhoe, 1873, Yantai (Chefoo), Shandong, China.
Sometimes considered conspecific with *C. noveboracensis*, with which forms Holarctic superspecies. Monotypic.
Distribution. SE Transbaikalia and S Ussuriland and E Heilongjiang (Manchuria). Winters from Japan and Korea through Ryukyu Is to S China.

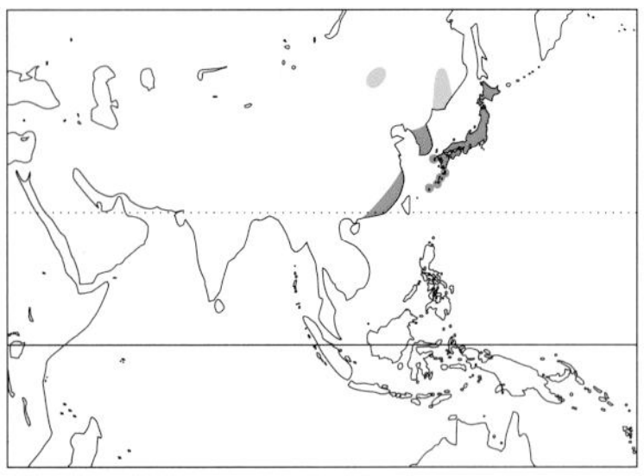

Descriptive notes. 13 cm. Sexes alike. Differs from markedly larger *C. noveboracensis* by greyer face, with close dark speckling and less distinct stripe through eye; feather edges of upperparts darker, more rufous-tinged; foreneck and sides of breast reddish brown with dusky bars; more extensive white on lower breast and belly; flanks barred deep reddish brown; legs brownish flesh. A very small rail, easily separable from all sympatric rallids by white secondaries. Immature and juvenile not described. VOICE. Not recorded; presumably similar to that of *C. noveboracensis*.
Habitat. Breeds in wet meadows and short grass marshes; habitat probably similar to that of *C. noveboracensis*. On migration and on wintering grounds frequents marshes, wet meadows and rice fields.
Food and Feeding. Nothing recorded: presumably similar to *C. noveboracensis*.
Breeding. No information available. Breeding habits probably similar to those of closely related, possibly conspecific *C. noveboracensis*.
Movements. Migratory, wintering S to SE China (Fujian and Guangdong); rare winter visitor to Japan, occurring on Hokkaido, Honshu, Shikoku and Kyushu; regarded as transient or wintering in N & S Korea and Ryukyu Is (Miyako-jima, and Amami-oshima or Okinawa). Recorded in Japan between early Aug and mid-May; most records Oct-Apr.
Status and Conservation. VULNERABLE. Regarded as very rare in SE Siberia and rare in Japan. Known from only a few breeding localities; recently recorded at Zhalong Nature Reserve, Heilongjiang, and Khanka L, N of Vladivostok. Seldom recorded on passage or in winter, recent records being of small numbers on autumn passage at Beidaihe (E China), and 1 at Poyang L (S China) in 1989. Species presumably threatened by destruction and modification of wetlands, which are occurring in both its breeding and wintering ranges.
Bibliography. Austin (1948), Austin & Kuroda (1953), Brazil (1991), Cheng Tsohsin (1987), Collar & Andrew (1988), Collar *et al.* (1994), Étchécopar & Hüe (1978), Flint *et al.* (1984), Knystautas (1993), Meyer de Schauensee (1984), Potapov & Flint (1987), Scott (1989), Sonobe (1982), Williams, M.D. (1986), Williams, M.D. *et al.* (1992).

14. Yellow Rail

Coturnicops noveboracensis

French: Râle jaune **German**: Gelbralle **Spanish**: Polluela Amarillenta
Other common names: American Yellow Rail

Taxonomy. *Fulica noveboracensis* Gmelin, 1789, New York.
Forms superspecies with *C. exquisitus*, with which sometimes regarded as conspecific. Two subspecies recognized.
Subspecies and Distribution.
C. n. noveboracensis (Gmelin, 1789) - SC & SE Canada to NC & NE USA, with isolated population in NW USA; winters in S & SE USA.
C. n. goldmani (Nelson, 1904) - marshes of R Lerma, C Mexico.

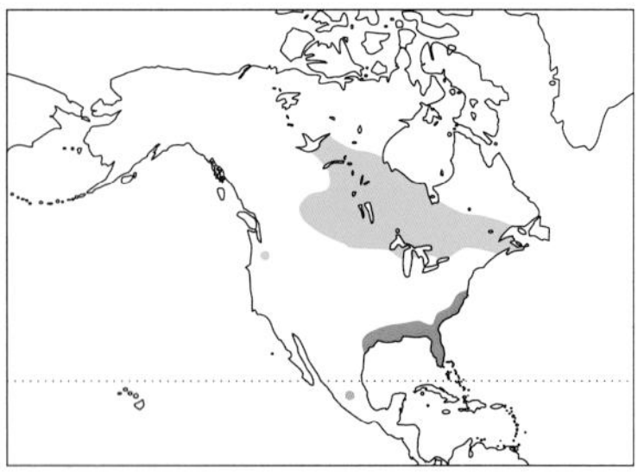

Descriptive notes. 16-19 cm; male 52-68 (59) g, female 41-61 (52) g. Easily distinguishable from all other North American rallids on size and plumage; similar to *Porzana flaviventer*, which is smaller, lacks white on secondaries and has white-streaked upperparts. Sexes alike, but male slightly larger than female; bill of breeding male corn yellow, of female and non-breeding male dark olivaceous to black. Two conflicting descriptions of immature plumage: either much darker than adult, with buffy white supercilium, entire upperparts black margined tawny and barred or spotted with narrow white lines, lower neck, breast and sides darker buff; or lighter and more buff overall than adult, with crown to upper back more brownish and buff, appearing striped, back to rump as adult but with less white barring and wider buff feather edges, upperwing-coverts browner than adult, throat buff-white, breast unmarked light buff, flanks barred brown, and belly white. Juvenile plumage not properly described. Race *goldmani* larger, with blackish crown and black stripes on nape. VOICE. Breeding-season song of male 4-5 metallic clicks, like 2 stones tapped together. Calls mostly at night, sometimes by day. Also gives cackles, clunks and croaks when breeding, and squeaks and wheezes in hostile encounters. Young peep and bark.
Habitat. Breeding habitat comprises the higher, drier margins of fresh- and brackish-water marshes dominated by sedges and grasses; also swampy meadows, sedge meadows dominated by *Carex lasiocarpa*, and occasionally wet, cut-over hay fields; rarely found in *Typha* stands. In autumn also found in hay and grain fields, and wet meadows; winters in coastal marshes, favouring drier parts of cordgrass (*Spartina patens*) marshes. Encroachment of woody vegetation in the absence of fire decreases quality of breeding habitat. Race *goldmani* recorded up to 2500 m in Mexico.
Food and Feeding. Earthworms, small freshwater snails, crustaceans (including Isopoda), spiders, beetles, cockroaches, bugs, grasshoppers, crickets, ants and fly larvae; also seeds of sedges, rushes (*Scleria*), grass (*Setaria*) and *Polygonum* in autumn and winter. Probably only diurnally active, foraging in areas with shallow water concealed by dense vegetation. Takes food from ground, from vegetation and from water, sometimes from 3-4 cm below water surface. Sometimes feeds while swimming.
Breeding. In USA, lays May-Jul; Mexico, flightless juvenile Sept. All further information for nominate race. Presumed territorial and monogamous but activity areas of breeding males overlap, suggesting gregariousness, while serial polygyny observed in captive birds, and nests of 2 females once located in territory of one male. Allopreening and courtship feeding observed in captive pairs. Nest a cup of fine sedges and grasses; external diameter 7-12 cm, depth 3-9 cm, thickness 2·5-4 cm; cup diameter 7 cm; covered with canopy of dead vegetation; built in sedges, rushes or grass on damp ground; placed on ground, or up to 15 cm above it, beneath dead, procumbent vegetation. Both sexes hollow out crude scrapes in vegetation but female builds nest; 1 or more extra nests sometimes used as brood nests. Mean 8 eggs (5-10), laid at daily intervals; incubation 17-18 days, by female; chicks leave nest after 1-2 days; downy chicks all black except for bright pink bill, which becomes black as juvenile plumage grows, legs and feet grey-brown; young largely feathered at 18 days of age; fed and brooded by female for 3 weeks; can fly at 35 days; age of independence not known. Normally one brood per season; may renest after failure.
Movements. Occupies breeding areas from late Apr or May to Sept-Oct. Thought to migrate over broad front; at least some move in groups; sometimes strikes towers, suggesting nocturnal migration. In Michigan, young depart from natal site late Sept to early Oct. Also recorded in summer from SE Alaska, S British Columbia and Colorado; on migration recorded Arizona and New Mexico, and irregularly in most of USA E of Rocky Mts; vagrant to Grand Bahama (1 record).
Status and Conservation. Not globally threatened. Nominate race is local breeder over wide area of Canada and N USA. Breeding range has decreased: formerly bred in N California, and possibly also in NE USA, S to c. 40° N; in 19th century described as resident in Florida and S Louisiana. Local breeding population in S Oregon, thought extirpated, was rediscovered in 1982. Drainage of wetlands probably responsible for loss of southernmost breeding areas during present century; in Canada many suitable wetlands lost since 1950 to drainage and possibly also after building dykes and barriers. Ditching and draining have destroyed several summering sites in Oregon since 1985. Grazing pressure probably adversely affects marsh-edge habitat, but mowing may help perpetuate breeding habitat. Race *goldmani* known only from Mexico, where formerly a local resident in upper R Lerma Valley; has not been seen since 1964 but may still survive, despite the fact that much of the area has been drained.
Bibliography. Anderson (1977), Bart *et al.* (1984), Bent (1926), Bookhout (1995), Bookhout & Stenzel (1987), Burt (1994), Dickerman (1971), Easterla (1962), Eddleman *et al.* (1988), Elliot & Morrison (1979), Gibbs *et al.* (1991), Godfrey (1986), Griese *et al.* (1980), Harrison, C. (1978), Harrison, H.H. (1975), Howell & Webb (1995a), King (1978/79), Martin, A.C. *et al.* (1951), Martin, E.M. & Perry (1981), Peabody (1922), Pulich (1962), Reid (1989), Reynard (1974), Robert & Laporte (1993, 1994), Small (1994), Stalheim (1974), Stenzel (1982), Stern *et al.* (1993), Terrill (1943), Walkinshaw (1939, 1991).

15. Speckled Rail

Coturnicops notatus

French: Râle étoilé **German**: Darwinralle **Spanish**: Polluela de Darwin
Other common names: Darwin's Rail

Taxonomy. *Zapornia notata* Gould, 1841, Rio de la Plata, Uruguay.
Monotypic.
Distribution. S Brazil to N Argentina; also Colombia, Venezuela and Guyana; status uncertain in much of apparent range, e.g. probably breeds in province of Córdoba, Argentina.

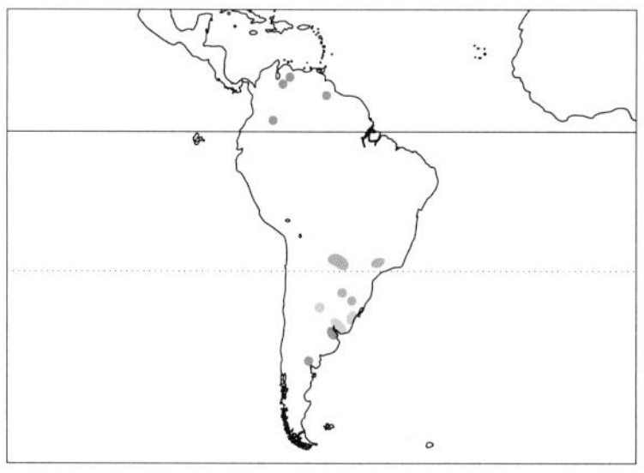

Descriptive notes. 13-14 cm; unsexed 30 g. Sexes alike. White on secondaries distinguishes from all sympatric rallids. *Laterallus jamaicensis* is similar in size and overall colour but lacks white markings on head, neck and breast, has prominent white bars only from flanks and lower belly to undertail-coverts, and has olive brown to blackish brown legs and feet. *Porzana spiloptera* is another very dark small wetland crake but has white spots and bars of upperparts confined to upperwing-coverts and remiges, white barring on underparts only from belly and flanks to undertail-coverts, and brown legs and feet. Easily distinguished from all other sympatric small rallids by very dark plumage with white spots and bars. Probable immatures have fewer spots on upperparts, some tending to be barred rather than spotted; white streaks and mottling, rather than roundish white spots, on lower throat and breast; undertail-coverts mostly sandy cinnamon rather than olive brown barred with white. Juvenile undescribed. VOICE. Vocalizations unobtrusive; easily masked by other marsh sounds. Has "kooweee-cack" call, first syllable high and brief, second louder and drier; also whistling "keeee" of alarm and high "kyu". Although diurnal, a captive bird called frequently at night.
Habitat. Grassy savanna, dense marshy vegetation, swamps, rice and alfalfa fields; also crop stubble and humid woodland edges. Inhabits lowlands up to 1500 m.
Food and Feeding. One stomach contained 80% small grass seeds, 15% arthropod remains and 5% fine gravel.
Breeding. Uruguay, brood of 3 young in Dec, in wheat stubble; Venezuela, breeding condition Aug; Brazil, breeding condition Dec.
Movements. Speculated to undertake migrations between N & S South America, but unlikely in view of occurrence in Apr-Aug in E Brazil (Taubaté) and Apr-Jun in Paraguay and Uruguay, and enlarged gonads of an Aug Venezuela specimen. One from Colombia (Mar 1959), and 2 from ships at sea have led to suggestion that birds occasionally erupt large distances randomly from centres of distribution in tropical savannas of N & E South America, but no proper evidence that centres of distribution are in tropical savannas and range may be wider and more continuous than currently known. Twice taken on ships at sea, the holotype being collected on the Beagle in 1831 at mouth of R de la Plata, while one flew aboard ship off Cabo Santa María, Uruguay, in Nov or Dec 1875; such records probably indicative at least of post-breeding dispersal. Also possible record from Falkland Is, Apr 1921, probably a straggler.

Status and Conservation. Not globally threatened. Data Deficient. Occurs over very large area but records very sparse, with few in any country, and species normally described as very rare. However, apparent occurrence throughout the year at Taubaté, Brazil, where it is not common but not rare, was taken to indicate that species is difficult to find rather than scarce; this may well be so, but, until further evidence is forthcoming, best considered genuinely rare.

Bibliography. Arballo (1990), Blake (1977), Canevari et al. (1991), Chebez (1994), Collar, Crosby & Stattersfield (1994), Collar, Gonzaga et al. (1992), Hayes (1995), Hellmayr & Conover (1942), Hilty & Brown (1986), Meyer de Schauensee (1962), Meyer de Schauensee & Phelps (1978), Nores & Yzurieta (1980), Olivares (1959), de la Peña (1992), Rutgers & Norris (1970), Sick (1985c, 1993), Snyder (1966), Teixeira & Puga (1984), Wege & Long (1995).

Genus *MICROPYGIA* Bonaparte, 1856

16. Ocellated Crake
Micropygia schomburgkii

French: Râle ocellé   **German**: Schomburgkralle   **Spanish**: Polluela Ocelada
Other common names: Ocellated Rail, Dotted Crake

Taxonomy. *Crex Schomburgkii* Schomburgk, 1848, interior of Guyana.
Sometimes placed in *Coturnicops* but differs in vocalizations, nest construction and some anatomical details. Two subspecies recognized.

Subspecies and Distribution.
M. s. schomburgkii (Schomburgk, 1848) - Costa Rica, Colombia, Venezuela and the Guianas; also SE Peru and Bolivia (racial affinities not clear).
M. s. chapmani (Naumburg, 1930) - C to SE Brazil.

Descriptive notes. 14-15 cm; male 40 g, female 24 g, unsexed 32 g. Distinctive small crake; tail quite well developed, despite genus name. Sexes similar but female usually has head more spotted; rich colour of forehead and crown less extensive. Overall colour and pattern easily distinguish species from all other small wetland rallids of region except perhaps *Porzana flaviventer*, which has distinctive face pattern and heavily barred flanks. Immature has grey-brown upperparts with spots only on wing-coverts, scapulars, side of neck, and sometimes on crown; underparts more extensively white or cream than adult, with pale, diffuse ochraceous breast band and flanks; sides and flanks barred grey. Juvenile not described. Race *chapmani* larger and has paler, more orange-brown, upperparts with reduced spotting; rump and uppertail-coverts often unmarked. VOICE. Song a sequence of clear, strong "pr-pr-pr" notes, lasting 20-30 seconds. Calls most frequently at dawn and dusk. Alarm call a harsh whirring, likened to sound of oil sizzling in frying pan.

Habitat. Variety of dense grassland habitats, both well drained and seasonally flooded, from almost pure open grasslands to those with abundance of shrubs and small trees; sometimes occurs near marshes or forest borders. Ground may be muddy or shallowly flooded. Grass height ranges from c. 1 m to very tall grass along drainage channels. Uses tunnels of rodents, e.g. *Cavia*, in dense vegetation. Occurs in lowlands up to 1400 m.

Food and Feeding. Beetles (Carabidae, Scarabaeidae), stoneflies, grasshoppers (Acridioidea), cockroaches and many ants. One caught in trap baited with oatmeal. Forages on ground, usually in grass or low scrub but occasionally in the open.

Breeding. Brazil, Oct-Mar; Costa Rica, probably during rainy season; Colombia breeding condition Mar. Monogamous; territorial, possibly throughout year. One nest was ball of dry grass with large side entrance, 50 cm above ground, completely concealed in dense wet grassland near palm (*Mauritia flexuosa*) grove. Nest was angled upwards at 45°; external length 20 cm, width 14 cm, height 17 cm; nest cavity length 11 cm, width 7 cm, height 9 cm. Eggs 2; incubation by female.

Movements. None recorded, but occasionally flies into lighted open windows at night. Doubtful record of vagrant in Galapagos.

Status and Conservation. Not globally threatened. Currently considered near-threatened. Regarded as scarce and locally distributed in many areas, probably existing in small populations, but this assessment of status may reflect the difficulty experienced in locating and observing the birds rather than actual scarcity. Apparently widespread and numerous in grasslands of N & C Bolivia, and locally common in C Brazil. Local people catch many for food by setting fire to grasslands and catching birds overcome by smoke; at such times Aplomado Falcons (*Falco femoralis*) often take the crakes.

Bibliography. Blake (1977), Dickerman (1968b), Graham et al. (1980), Hellmayr & Conover (1942), Hilty & Brown (1986), Meyer de Schauensee & Phelps (1978), Negret & Teixeira (1984a, 1984b), Parker et al. (1991), Ripley (1977), Sick (1985c, 1993), Snyder (1966), Stiles & Skutch (1989), Tostain et al. (1992).

Genus *RALLINA* G. R. Gray, 1846

17. Chestnut Forest-rail
Rallina rubra

French: Râle marron   **German**: Kastanienralle   **Spanish**: Polluela Castaña
Other common names: New Guinea Chestnut Rail

Taxonomy. *Rallicula rubra* Schlegel, 1871, northern peninsula of New Guinea.
The four *Rallina* species of New Guinea show marked sexual dimorphism and therefore sometimes retained in *Rallicula*. Possible race *subrubra* merged with *klossi* because of overlapping measurements and lack of significant colour differences. Three subspecies recognized.

Subspecies and Distribution.
R. r. rubra (Schlegel, 1871) - W New Guinea, in Arfak Mts.
R. r. klossi (Ogilvie-Grant, 1913) - WC New Guinea, from Weyland Mts to Oranje Mts.
R. r. telefolminensis (Gilliard, 1961) - C New Guinea, in Victor Emmanuel and Hindenburg Mts and Tari Gap.

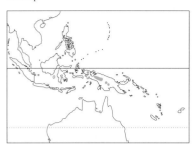

Descriptive notes. 18-23 cm; 3 male *klossi* 84-91 (87·7) g, 2 male *telefolminensis* 71 and 76 g. Smallest *Rallina*. Reddish chestnut plumage of male makes confusion possible only with very similar but allopatric male *R. mayri*, which is darker, with indistinct narrow black bars on tail. Female has back and upperwings black with small buff spots; resembles females of *R. forbesi* and *R. mayri* but has spotted upper mantle and lacks blackish barring on underparts; very similar to female *R. leucospila* but lacks narrow black tail bars of this and the other two species. Subadult male has grey base to black bill, and dark wine-brown legs and feet; juvenile not described. Races separated on: colour of nape, tinged black in *rubra*; overall colour, *klossi* palest chestnut; and biometrics, *telefolminensis* smallest. VOICE. Shrill, sharp "krill" or "keow", often repeated many times; sometimes more squeaky. Duetting recorded, when calls may become more rapid and sharper, "kee" or "kek".

Habitat. Inhabits floor of montane forest interior, at 1500-3050 m. At Tari Gap found in mossy mixed lower montane beech forest. In areas of sympatry with *R. forbesi*, present species occurs at higher altitudes.

Food and Feeding. No information available.

Breeding. Lays Oct-Nov, and either Aug or Sept, i.e. at end of period of highest rainfall. Apparently monogamous. Two adult males responded to one female's alarm call at nest, suggesting possibility of co-operative breeding. Nest a large domed structure of moss, grass, leaf skeletons, fibres and fern fronds; lined with fine fibres, rootlets and fragments of fern fronds; base extended at one side into ramp leading up to side entrance. Nest typically placed c. 2 m up between frond bases in *Pandanus* palm crown. Mean overall length 38·5 cm (ramp 15 cm) and height 25·5 cm; mean nest chamber length 21·5 cm and height 13 cm. Lays 1 egg only, large (27% of adult weight); incubation at least 34 days, possibly over 37 days, the longest of any rallid, performed by both sexes, egg often left to become cold; 2 newly hatched chicks weighed 13·4 and 14·4 g and had black down grizzled with russet or chestnut, dark brown iris, blackish legs and feet and blackish bill with white tip and egg tooth. One young chick possibly killed by torrential rain at night.

Movements. None recorded.

Status and Conservation. Not globally threatened. Widespread in Irian Jaya, where races *rubra* and *klossi* apparently abundant; race *telefolminensis* apparently uncommon in the vicinity of Telefomin in the Victor Emmanuel and Hindenburg ranges, but the population common in Tari Gap forests is presumably also of this race.

Bibliography. Andrew, P. (1992), Beehler et al. (1986), Coates (1985), Frith & Frith (1988, 1990), Gilliard & LeCroy (1961), Rand & Gilliard (1967), Ripley (1964, 1977).

18. White-striped Forest-rail
Rallina leucospila

French: Râle vergeté   **German**: Strichelralle   **Spanish**: Polluela Listada
Other common names: White-striped Chestnut Rail

Taxonomy. *Corethrura? leucospila*, Salvadori, 1875, Arfak Mountains, New Guinea.
Sometimes placed in *Rallicula*. Forms superspecies with *R. forbesi* and *R. mayri*. Monotypic.
Distribution. Tamrau, Arfak and Wandammen Mts of Vogelkop, NW New Guinea.

Descriptive notes. 20-23 cm; 2 males 114, 125 g. Fine white streaks on black upperparts easily separate male from the other *Rallina* species of New Guinea. Female spotted rather than streaked, and closely resembles female of smaller *R. rubra* but has narrow black tail bars and less extensive chestnut on upper mantle; females of *R. forbesi* and *R. mayri* have extensive unspotted chestnut on upper mantle and latter species is generally darker, duller and more uniform. Immature and juvenile not described. VOICE. Gives chuckling notes "ko..ko..ko"; contact call a low mewing note.

Habitat. Floor of montane forest interior at 1350-1850 m.

Food and Feeding. No information available.

Breeding. Nothing known. Pairs roost in roofed shelters of dried leaves and moss, so breeding nest may also be domed structure, as in *R. rubra*.

Movements. None recorded.

Status and Conservation. Not globally threatened. Data Deficient. Shy, secretive and apparently uncommon. No recent information available on status, but there is no reason to expect species to be threatened, as its montane forest habitat is likely to be secure, although local hunting with dogs occurs throughout the Vogelkop.

Bibliography. Andrew, P. (1992), Beehler et al. (1986), Collar et al. (1994), Frith & Frith (1990), Rand & Gilliard (1967), Ripley (1977).

19. Forbes's Forest-rail
Rallina forbesi

French: Râle de Forbes   **German**: Nymphenralle   **Spanish**: Polluela de Forbes
Other common names: Red-backed Forest-rail

Taxonomy. *Rallicula forbesi* Sharpe, 1887, Owen Stanley Range, New Guinea.
Sometimes placed in *Rallicula*. Forms superspecies with *R. leucospila* and *R. mayri*. Population occurring in Foja Mts, NC New Guinea, may be referable to present species or to new, as yet undescribed, form. Four subspecies recognized.

Subspecies and Distribution.
R. f. steini (Rothschild, 1934) - C New Guinea, from Weyland Mts E to Bismarck Mts.
R. f. parva Pratt, 1982 - NE New Guinea, on Mt Mengam (Adelbert Range).
R. f. dryas (Mayr, 1931) - NE New Guinea, on Huon Peninsula.
R. f. forbesi (Sharpe, 1887) - SE New Guinea, from Herzog Mts to Owen Stanley Mts.

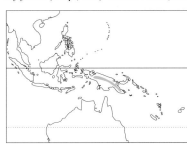

Descriptive notes. 20-25 cm; male 78-106 (88) g, female 65-96 g, 1 subadult female 81 g. Male distinguished from other mountain forest *Rallina* species by unpatterned black or dark brown lower mantle, back and upperwings; *R. tricolor*, of moist forest at low altitudes, is larger with a more extensive and more solid area of dark brown covering most of upperparts and tail, more extensive underpart barring, green or yellow bill and dark olive legs. Female has black-margined buff spots on upperparts; distinguished from female *R. rubra* and *R. leucospila* by extensive chestnut upper mantle; similar to, but considerably brighter than, female of *R. mayri*, which does not occur within range of present species. Subadult blackish to dark olive brown on back and wings; dull reddish or greyish brown below, barred with black; bill black with grey tip; some immatures have dark olive brown back and wings; juvenile not described. Races separated on biometrics, especially tail length; *parva* smallest, and also has dark olive brown back, finely and obscurely barred in both sexes, with small spots in female. Voice. Utters a low, frog-like "quaaak", slowly repeated; also a rapid "ko..ko..ko", as well as other chuckling notes.
Habitat. Floor of primary mid-montane and montane forest at 1100-3000 m. In areas of sympatry with *R. rubra*, mostly occurs at lower altitudes.
Food and Feeding. Takes mostly insects; also some seeds. Usually seen in small parties; forages deliberately in dry leaves, calling quietly.
Breeding. Social and sexual behaviour unknown; roosting nests may contain pairs or 3-7 adults of both sexes. One roosting nest a domed structure of leaf skeletons and moss, placed 2·75 m up in *Pandanus* palm crown. Breeding nests thought to be similar, and located on ground or in tree ferns, *Microsorium* cane or epiphytic ferns, but the only one described was a thick platform of dry vegetable fibre and leaf skeletons, external measurements 18 x 25 cm, placed 5-6 m up on horizontal fork of small tree in primary forest. Thought to lay 4-5 eggs; chicks have black down with rusty tips and rusty crown, face and throat.
Movements. None recorded.
Status and Conservation. Not globally threatened. Not uncommon locally in E New Guinea but apparently scarce or rare in W half of range, where overlaps with *R. rubra*. Recently-described race *parva* known only from single locality. Species regularly trapped for food. A hitherto unnamed chestnut rail from uninhabited Foja Mts, NC New Guinea, frequently seen in Oct 1979, may be either this or a new species.

Bibliography. Andrew, P. (1992), Beehler (1978), Beehler *et al.* (1986), Coates (1985), Diamond (1972b, 1985), Gilliard & LeCroy (1961), Majnep & Bulmer (1977), Mayr & Gilliard (1954), Pratt (1982), Rand & Gilliard (1967), Ripley (1977), Ripley & Beehler (1985), Schmid (1993).

20. Mayr's Forest-rail
Rallina mayri

French: Râle de Mayr **German**: Zyklopenralle **Spanish**: Polluela de Mayr
Other common names: Black-tailed Forest-rail

Taxonomy. *Rallicula rubra mayri* Hartert, 1930, Cyclops Mountains, New Guinea.
Sometimes retained in *Rallicula*. Forms superspecies with *R. leucospila* and *R. forbesi*. Two subspecies recognized.
Subspecies and Distribution.
R. m. mayri (Hartert, 1930) - Cyclops Mts, NE Irian Jaya.
R. m. carmichaeli (Diamond, 1969) - Torricelli and Bewani Mts, NW Papua New Guinea.

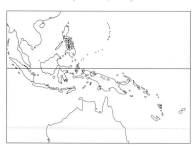

Descriptive notes. 20-23 cm; male 123-136 (128) g, 3 females 112-123 (118) g. The only *Rallina* species of montane forest within its range. Predominantly reddish chestnut plumage of male similar to that of brighter male *R. rubra*, which lacks bars on tail. Female has dark chestnut brown back and upperwing with large black-margined buff spots; similar to female *R. forbesi* and *R. leucospila*, both also having indistinct blackish bars on belly and thighs, but present species considerably duller; female *R. rubra* lacks bars on underparts and tail, and has spotted upper mantle. Immature and juvenile undescribed. Races separated on overall colour, *carmichaeli* darker brown. Voice. Unknown.
Habitat. Floor of montane forest, at 1100-2200 m.
Food and Feeding. No information available.
Breeding. Nothing known.
Movements. None recorded.
Status and Conservation. Not globally threatened. Data Deficient. Although range restricted to three isolated coastal mountain ranges, species was apparently common in secure habitat in late 1980's; however, not found more recently on visit to Cyclops Mts. In view of its localized and highly specific habitat, total numbers are probably small.
Bibliography. Andrew, P. (1992), Beehler *et al.* (1986), Coates (1985), Collar *et al.* (1994), Diamond (1969), Rand & Gilliard (1967), Ripley (1977).

PLATE 11 ➤

PLATE 11

inches 5
cm 13

21

23

22

ssp *amauroptera*

ssp *formosana*

ssp *eurizonoides*

24

ssp *minahasa*

ssp *coccineipes*

25

ssp *castaneiceps*

ssp *brunnescens*

26

27

ssp *oenops*

29

28

ssp *viridis*

ssp *cerdaleus*

ssp *cinereiceps*

31

ssp *melanophaius*

30

ssp *albigularis*

32

ssp *tuerosi*

33

34

35

36

ssp *jamaicensis*

ssp *salinasi*

21. Red-necked Crake
Rallina tricolor

French: Râle tricolore   **German**: Dreifarbenralle   **Spanish**: Polluela Tricolor
Other common names: Red-necked Rail

Taxonomy. *Rallina tricolor* G. R. Gray, 1858, Aru Islands.
Up to six races have been recognized on basis of size and plumage differences, with *tricolor* of E Indonesia, Australia, New Guinea and outlying islands (including *maxima* of New Guinea, and *robinsoni* of Queensland), *victa* of Tanimbar Is, sometimes including *laeta* of St Matthias I, and *convicta* of New Ireland and New Hanover Is; however, individual variation considerable and geographical variation in size not well understood. Monotypic.
Distribution. New Guinea and offshore islands, Bismarck Archipelago, and N & E Queensland (Australia); also spottily in S Moluccas and E Lesser Sundas, where status unclear.

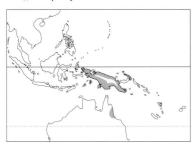

Descriptive notes. 23-30 cm; male 143-231 (164) g, 2 females 194, 200 g, 2 probable migrants 109, 115 g; wingspan 37-45 cm. Distinguished from sympatric forest rails by combination of large size, unmarked dark brown upperparts and tail, green or yellow bill and olive legs; paler fine barring on dark brown underparts varies from indistinct to virtually absent; white bars on remiges usually hidden, except when bird runs to cover with partly spread wings. Sexes alike. Immature not described. Juvenile uniform dark olive brown above and dark brown below. VOICE. Territorial call, given by pairs mostly in evening and during night, a harsh, penetrating note quickly repeated in descending scale with emphasis on first note "nárk-nak-nak..." or "káre-kar-kar..."; also monotonous repeated "tock" note uttered by pairs, sometimes continuously for hours well into night; contact calls low grunts and a repeated soft "plop" note.
Habitat. In Papua New Guinea mostly rain forest and swamp forest; also monsoon forest during rains, sago swamps, gallery forest, secondary growth and once in mangroves; occurs mostly in lowlands, but locally up to 1370 m; normally requires moist habitat, preferably with pools or creeks. In Queensland tropical rain forest, usually with dense understorey; also vine-thicket and monsoon scrub; always near permanent streams or swamps; mostly below 700 m but up to 1250 m; also sometimes in suburban gardens with dense vegetation, and occasionally in *Lantana camara* thickets.
Food and Feeding. Mainly invertebrates, including annelids, oligochaetes, molluscs, crustaceans, terrestrial amphipods, spiders, and adult and larval insects; also frogs and tadpoles; seeds, including beans, also recorded. Mainly crepuscular and nocturnal, but sometimes seen during day. Forages methodically, along shallow stream beds and stream margins, in leaf litter and occasionally along edge of salt water at low tide; rakes through leaf litter with feet and bill; turns over small stones with bill; probes pools, moss and debris.
Breeding. In Queensland lays throughout wet season, Nov-Mar, with Dec-Feb peak; in Papua New Guinea lays early in rains, Nov. Monogamous, with strong pair-bond; some pairs maintain permanent territories; one record of 3 birds attending 2 nests. Nest a shallow cup of dead leaves, twigs and tendrils, diameter 15-20 cm, in dense vegetation or bush or on tree stump 0·6-2 m above ground; or a depression in ground lined with few dead leaves. Usually 5 eggs (3-7), laid at daily intervals; incubation 18-22 days, by both sexes; black downy chicks have black bill and grey to brown (later black) legs and feet; chicks fed by both parents; leave nest soon after hatching but may return to roost for several days; still fed by adults at 5 weeks; leave parents before they can fly; fully-feathered at 4-6 weeks. May form pairs when 4-5 months old.
Movements. Regarded as sedentary over much of range, but partly migratory in NE Australia, where regarded as wet season migrant to Cape York Peninsula from New Guinea, leaving when forest floor dries out in winter. Sedentary further S in Queensland, where rain falls throughout year. Recorded from several islands of Torres Strait, where often heard overhead at night and recorded striking lighthouse. Only record from Ambon (Moluccas) is of 1 coming to a light at night in mid-Jun, possibly migrant from New Guinea. In Port Moresby area, Papua New Guinea, moves away from forest where ground becomes hard and surface water disappears in prolonged dry periods, but remains near permanent water.
Status and Conservation. Not globally threatened. Little information available on status because birds are typically shy and seldom seen. In Papua New Guinea apparently locally common. Australian population declining due to massive and continuing loss of lowland rain forest habitat for agriculture and residential development. Able to occupy dense vegetation in some suburban gardens. Little information on status elsewhere.
Bibliography. Barnard (1911), Beehler *et al.* (1986), Blakers *et al.* (1984), Campbell & Barnard (1917), Coates (1985), Draffan *et al.* (1983), Gill, H. B. (1970), Gill, R. G. (1965), Gregory (1995b), MacGillivray (1914), Magarry (1991), Marchant & Higgins (1993), Mason *et al.* (1981), Mayr (1949), Mees (1965), Ripley (1977), Ripley & Beehler (1985), Serventy (1985), White & Bruce (1986).

22. Andaman Crake
Rallina canningi

French: Râle des Andaman   **German**: Andamanenralle   **Spanish**: Polluela de Andamán
Other common names: Andaman Banded Crake

Taxonomy. *Euryzona canningi* Blyth, 1863, Port Canning, Andaman Islands.
Monotypic.
Distribution. Andaman Is.
Descriptive notes. 34 cm. Largest *Rallina*; easily distinguished by glossy chestnut plumage, extensive bold barring on underparts, unbarred undertail-coverts and relatively bright apple green bill with narrow whitish tip; barring on wings confined to primaries, outer secondaries and some median and greater coverts; tail noticeably long and fluffy. Sexes alike. Immature duller chestnut; areas barred in

adult are dark grey with chestnut tinge, narrowly banded and streaked with dirty white. Juvenile undescribed. VOICE. A deep croak "kroop"; alarm note a sharp "chick".
Habitat. Marshland in forest; large, open areas of marshland and also recorded in a small marsh on edge of secondary forest.
Food and Feeding. Largely worms, molluscs and insects (including beetles, grasshoppers and caterpillars); possibly also small fish. Large grasshoppers are shaken and battered before being swallowed.
Breeding. Breeds Jun-Aug, during summer. Nest a collection of grass and leaves, placed at foot of large forest tree or under tangled forest undergrowth, not always close to water. Clutch size unknown; incubation by both sexes. Downy chick rich chestnut, slightly greyish under wings, with dusky olive bill.
Movements. Apparently sedentary.
Status and Conservation. VULNERABLE. Precise range not clear: recorded from at least North Andaman and South Andaman Is, and possibly occurs on Great Coco or Little Coco Is (Myanmar). Formerly regarded as common but there appear to be only 2 recent records of single birds. Forest cover remains extensive in Andamans but is suffering slow though continuous loss; introduced predators may also be a threat.
Bibliography. Ali & Ripley (1980), Collar *et al.* (1994), Frith & Frith (1990), Olson (1973b), Pande *et al.* (1991), Ripley (1977, 1982).

23. Red-legged Crake
Rallina fasciata

French: Râle barré   **German**: Malaienralle   **Spanish**: Polluela Patirroja
Other common names: Malaysian (Banded) Crake

Taxonomy. *Rallus fasciatus* Raffles, 1822, Bengkulu, west Sumatra.
Monotypic.
Distribution. Lowlands from NE India (Cachar) and S Myanmar E to Philippines and S to Sumatra and Flores; spottily elsewhere through Greater and Lesser Sundas and Moluccas.

Descriptive notes. 23-25 cm. Sexes similar; female somewhat more cinnamon on head and neck, with narrower black bars on belly and flanks. Easily distinguished from *R. eurizonoides* and *R. tricolor* by boldly barred wings and red legs, and from latter also by white barring on underparts; superficially similar *Porzana paykullii* has white bars on wings confined to some upperwing-coverts (sometimes missing), dark olive brown crown, nape and upperparts, and orange-pink legs; *P. fusca* has unbarred wings, is olive brown from rear crown to tail and has less extensive underpart barring. Immature has poorly defined bars on upperwing-coverts; head, neck and breast brown, and rest of underparts whitish, obscurely barred brown-black; legs and feet brownish. VOICE. Advertising call described as loud "gogogogok" given at night, and during day in rainy weather; also a "girrrr" call. Territorial call is loud series of nasal "pek" noises given at dawn and dusk in breeding season; also slow descending trill.
Habitat. Reedy swamps and marshes, rice paddies and taro fields, rivers, water courses, riparian thickets and wet areas in forest and secondary growth. In Philippines, also occurs on open hillsides and in cogon grasslands. Confined to low altitudes up to c. 800 m, except when on migration, when recorded at c. 1400 m.
Food and Feeding. No information.
Breeding. Myanmar, Aug-Sept; Thailand, Aug; Borneo, Apr; Java, Mar; Sumatra, Jan; no date given for Flores. Nest undescribed. Eggs 3-6; both sexes incubate; downy young dark smoky brown. No further information available.
Movements. Movements not properly understood, but species is both resident and migratory in normal range; also probably dispersive; considered predominantly winter visitor in S part of range. Resident Thailand; resident and migrant Malaysia; in Borneo, most of population resident but may be augmented by visitors in winter; probably resident in Philippines. Local resident throughout Greater Sundas, numbers augmented by winter visitors from mainland Asia; normally considered migrant to Wallacea but recorded Apr-Dec, and apparently resident on Flores. Vagrants: Lanyu I (off Taiwan) in Jun; Palau (Micronesia) no date; and Western Australia in Jul.
Status and Conservation. Not globally threatened. Status uncertain, as birds difficult to observe or flush; widely distributed but apparently not particularly common anywhere. Apparently rare in S Vietnam.
Bibliography. Ali & Ripley (1980), Boyd & Alley (1948), Dickinson *et al.* (1991), Harrison & Parker (1967), Hellebrekers & Hoogerwerf (1967), Lekagul & Round (1991), MacKinnon & Phillipps (1993), Marchant & Higgins (1993), van Marle & Voous (1988), Medway & Wells (1976), Ripley (1977, 1982), Schmutz (1977, 1978), Serventy, D.L. (1958), Serventy, V.N. (1985), Smythies (1981, 1986), White & Bruce (1986), Wildash (1968).

24. Slaty-legged Crake
Rallina eurizonoides

French: Râle de forêt   **German**: Hinduralle   **Spanish**: Polluela de Jungla
Other common names: (Slaty-legged) Banded/Ryukyu/Philippine Crake

Taxonomy. *Gallinula eurizonoïdes* Lafresnaye, 1845, no locality (probably Philippines)
Seven subspecies recognized.

Subspecies and Distribution.
R. e. amauroptera (Jerdon, 1864) - Pakistan and India E to E Assam; winters in Sri Lanka and possibly Sumatra.
R. e. telmatophila Hume, 1878 - Myanmar and Thailand E to C Vietnam and SE China (Yunnan and Guangxi); winters in S Thailand and Sumatra, reaching W Java.
R. e. sepiaria (Stejneger, 1887) - Ryukyu Is.
R. e. formosana Seebohm, 1894 - Taiwan and Lanyu I.
R. e. eurizonoides (Lafresnaye, 1845) - Philippines and Palau Is.
R. e. alvarezi Kennedy & Ross, 1987 - Batan Is (N Philippines).
R. e. minahasa Wallace, 1863 - Sulawesi and Sula Is.
Also occurs on Hainan, race undetermined.

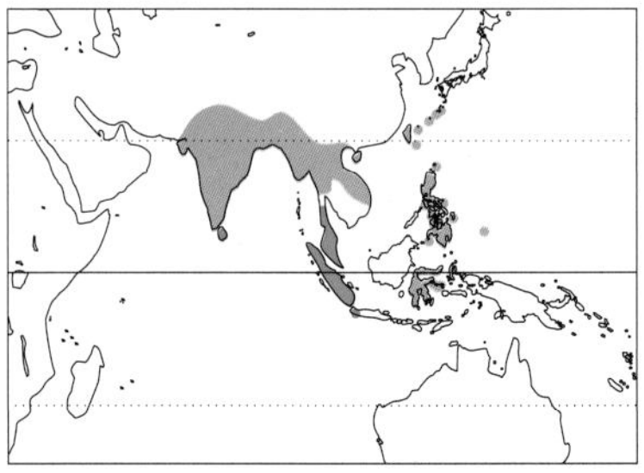

Descriptive notes. 21-25 cm; 2 males 118, 128 g, 3 females 99, 105, 180 (with oviduct egg) g, 2 adults 110, 112 g; wingspan 47·5 cm. Sexes alike. Distinguished from *R. fasciata* by darker, browner upperparts, white bars on wings confined to inner webs of remiges (not usually visible) and a few coverts, and greenish grey to black legs and feet. *R. tricolor* lacks white barring on underparts and wing-coverts, and has green or yellow bill. *Porzana fusca* and *P. paykullii* are brown from rear crown to tail and lack white bars on remiges; *P. fusca* has less extensive barring on underparts, and red legs; *P. paykullii* has white bars (sometimes missing) on some upperwing-coverts, and orange-pink legs. Immature has chestnut replaced by dark olive brown, more ashy on side of head and neck; scapulars and wing-coverts have sparse white and black bars; iris brown, legs grey. Juvenile has blackish grey upperparts, and sooty grey underparts with some white flecks on breast and belly; iris dark olive brown; bill and legs black. Races separated on: biometrics, *sepiaria* largest; colour of throat, pale rufous in *minahasa* and *eurizonoides*, purer white in *formosana*; shade of upperparts, *alvarezi* darkest; and width of white bars on underparts, narrower in *amauroptera*, *alvarezi* and *minahasa*. Voice. Repeated "kek-kek" or nasal "ow-ow", often given persistently during night, even in nocturnal flight; also nasal "kok" to other individuals, a long drumming croak and a hissing, spitting call to intruders at nest.

Habitat. Inhabits forests, well wooded areas and dense scrub, including forest edges, forest floor inside dense patches of remnant original forest vegetation, banks of forest streams, and long grass with dense bushes; also recorded from paddy and taro fields, and from mangroves. Principally lowlands, in well watered habitats up to 1600 m.

Food and Feeding. Takes worms, molluscs, insects, and shoots and seeds of marsh plants. Said to be partly nocturnal.

Breeding. India, Jun-Sept (during SW monsoon); Ryukyu Is, Apr-Jul; Sulawesi, Apr; no date in Palau; juvenile Luzon, Nov. Nests in densest forest as well as more open scrub. Nest an untidy pad of dead leaves, grass and thin twigs, with slight central depression; built on ground in clumps of bamboo or masses of tangled creepers, or on top of tree stumps up to 1 m above ground; not necessarily near water. Eggs 4-8; both sexes incubate eggs and tend young; chick has black down. No further details available.

Movements. Resident and migrant in India, moving at beginning and end of SW monsoon; birds arrive on W coast of Sri Lanka from India in Oct-Nov, spend a few days in lowlands and then move up to winter in hills, leaving Mar-Apr. Migrant Malaysia; winter visitor Sumatra (Nov and Mar-May) and occasionally W Java; resident Ryukyu Is, SE China, Taiwan and Lanyu I; some Palau birds possibly migrant visitors. Moves almost entirely at night, often flying into houses when attracted by lights. Race *telmatophila* straggles to E Himalayas (Nepal, West Bengal, Bhutan) and *eurizonoides* to W Micronesia.

Status and Conservation. Not globally threatened. Apparently races *amauroptera*, *alvarezi* and *telmatophila* are not uncommon over much of their ranges, but the last is uncommon in Sumatra and perhaps only a vagrant to W Java where no recent records. In Ryukyu Is, *sepiaria* decreased in numbers and range on some islands in 1980's, coincident with a rapid increase in numbers of *Amaurornis phoenicurus*, with which it may be in unsuccessful competition for food or nesting sites or both. Status of other races generally unknown, but *eurizonoides* is uncommon in Palau Is.

Bibliography. Ali & Ripley (1980), Brazil (1991), Deignan (1945), Dickinson *et al.* (1991), Étchécopar & Hüe (1978), Kennedy & Ross (1987), King *et al.* (1975), Lekagul & Round (1991), MacKinnon & Phillipps (1993), van Marle & Voous (1988), Medway & Wells (1976), Perennou *et al.* (1994), Phillips (1978), Pratt, Bruner & Berrett (1987), Pratt, Enbring *et al.* (1980), Ripley (1982), Roberts, T.J. (1991), Smythies (1986), White & Bruce (1986).

Genus *ANUROLIMNAS* Sharpe, 1893

25. Chestnut-headed Crake

Anurolimnas castaneiceps

French: Râle à masque rouge **German**: Rotmaskenralle **Spanish**: Polluela Pituro
Other common names: Chestnut-headed Rail

Taxonomy. *Porzana castaneiceps* P. L. Sclater and Salvin, 1868, Río Napo, eastern Ecuador.
Sometimes placed in *Rallina*, but lacks wing barring and has very short tail. Two subspecies recognized.

Subspecies and Distribution.
A. c. coccineipes Olson 1973 - S Colombia and NE Ecuador.
A. c. castaneiceps (P. L. Sclater & Salvin, 1868) - E Ecuador and N Peru; presumably this race in extreme NW Bolivia (Pando).

Descriptive notes. 19-22 cm; 1 female 126 g. Tail very short. Sexes alike. Distinguished from *A. viridis* by dark brown underparts and entirely rufous face; from *A. fasciatus* by unbarred underparts; from both by unpatterned underwing-coverts and greenish tinge to bill. Very similar *Amaurolimnas concolor* has brown-tinged face, more extensively rufous underparts, and different voice. Immature like adult but duller, with rufous areas largely brown or brownish olive; entire breast and belly dull brown; scattered adult-type chestnut feathers on cheeks, sides of neck and breast; throat light greyish buff. Juvenile not described. Race *coccineipes* has browns of upperparts and underparts tinged more greenish, and has bright red legs and feet. Voice. Song is a synchronized duet, one bird making loud,

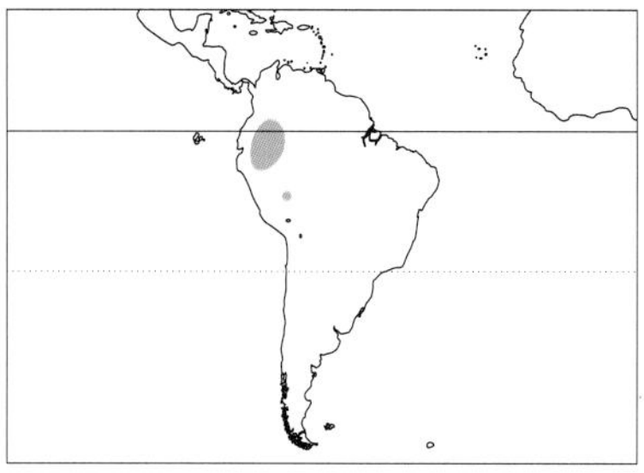

high-pitched "ti-too" call and the other answering with "ti-turro" sometimes trilled at end; this antiphonal duet may continue for 3-4 minutes. When disturbed, utters growls and soft "tuk" or "tik" notes.

Habitat. Normally said to inhabit humid *terra firme* forest and banks of forest streams, but in NW Bolivia frequents tall secondary growth and overgrown gardens surrounded by forest; in old gardens found in dark, damp thickets with almost impenetrable cover of broad-leaved *Heliconia*-like plants and decaying trunks and branches of trees in areas shaded by stands of trees 4-10 m tall and tall banana plants; similar habitat occupied elsewhere in Amazonia. Occurs E of Andes, from 200 up to 1500 m.

Food and Feeding. Food not recorded, but species presumably feeds on insects and other small invertebrates. Forages on ground inside dense thickets, flicking fallen leaves and probing debris and rotting wood.

Breeding. Bolivia, nearly grown young Jun (egg laid May?); Colombia, breeding condition Jun. Nest, eggs and young undescribed.

Movements. None recorded.

Status and Conservation. Not globally threatened. Regarded as uncommon to rare throughout its range, and possibly of rather local distribution. Status difficult to assess, as birds very wary and difficult to observe.

Bibliography. Blake (1977), Butler (1979), Donahue (1994), Hellmayr & Conover (1942), Hilty & Brown (1986), Meyer de Schauensee (1982), Olson (1973b), Parker & Remsen (1987), Parker *et al.* (1982), Remsen & Traylor (1989), Ripley (1977).

26. Russet-crowned Crake

Anurolimnas viridis

French: Râle kiolo **German**: Indioralle **Spanish**: Polluela Coronirrufa
Other common names: Cayenne Crake

Taxonomy. *Rallus viridis* P. L. S. Müller, 1776, Cayenne, French Guiana.
Sometimes placed in *Laterallus*, which it resembles in voice. Two subspecies recognized.

Subspecies and Distribution.
A. v. brunnescens (Todd, 1932) - E Colombia (middle Magdalena Valley).
A. v. viridis (P. L. S. Müller, 1776) - S Venezuela, through the Guianas and Brazil, SW to E Ecuador, E Peru and extreme N Bolivia (Beni).

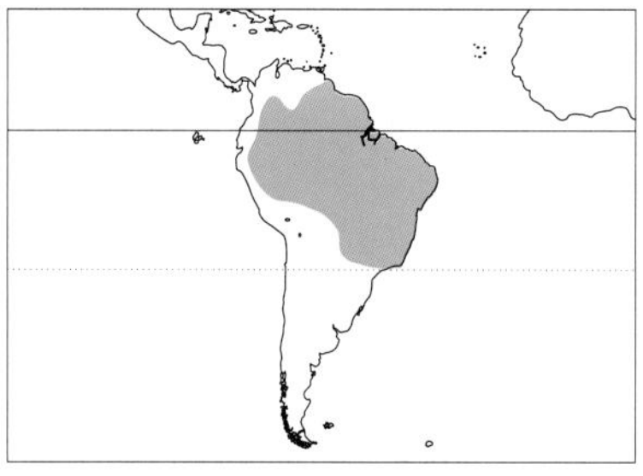

Descriptive notes. 16-18 cm; male 55-63 g, female 69-73 g. Smallest *Anurolimnas*, with relatively long tail. Sexes alike. Distinguished from *A. castaneiceps* and *A. fasciatus* by grey face and entirely rufous underparts; also from *A. castaneiceps* by mottled ashy brown and rufous underwing-coverts, and black bill. Very similar *Amaurolimnas concolor* has brown-tinged face, is more uniform rufous brown above and below, and has yellowish green bill. Immature and juvenile undescribed. Race *brunnescens* browner on upperparts, paler on head and underparts, and slightly larger. Voice. Loose, churring rattle, similar to calls of *Laterallus melanophaius* and *L. albigularis* but slower and louder; also resembles call of *A. fasciatus*. Most vocal in evening and early morning.

Habitat. Dense thickets of secondary growth saplings at forest edge, thickly overgrown wasteland, damp grassy or bushy pastures, overgrown roadsides, and gardens at edges of towns and villages. Not normally a marsh bird, but in Venezuela recorded from swamps. Mainly terrestrial, but climbs freely in branches of bushes. Occurs up to 1200 m.

Food and Feeding. Very little information available. Insects, including ants, and grass seeds. Forages within cover.

Breeding. Breeds Jan-Jun. Nest a ball of dead grass with a side entrance, sometimes with a ladder-like entrance ramp, hidden c. 1 m up in branches of shrubs, or in coarse herbage, in dense vegetation. Eggs 1-3. No other information.

Movements. None recorded.

Status and Conservation. Not globally threatened. Seldom seen because of skulking habits, but calls frequently; race *viridis* is thought to be common over much of its extensive range; status of *brunnescens* not known but is likely to be similar.

Bibliography. Blake (1977), Haverschmidt (1968), Haverschmidt & Mees (1995), Hellmayr & Conover (1942), Hilty & Brown (1986), Meyer de Schauensee & Phelps (1978), Olson (1973b), Parker *et al.* (1991), Ripley (1977), Sclater & Salvin (1879), Sick (1985c, 1993), Snyder (1966), Tostain *et al.* (1992).

27. Black-banded Crake

Anurolimnas fasciatus

French: Râle fascié **German**: Streifenbauchralle **Spanish**: Polluela Barreada

Taxonomy. *Porzana fasciata* P. L. Sclater & Salvin, 1867, near Caracas, Venezuela.
Sometimes placed in *Laterallus*, which it resembles in voice, but pattern of primary moult differs from that of *Laterallus* and is similar to that of *A. castaneiceps*. Species formerly known as *L. hauxwelli*, as name *fasciatus* erroneously thought to be incompatible with the older species name of *Rallina fasciata*. Monotypic.

Distribution. S & SE Colombia S to E Ecuador and E Peru, and E across W Amazonian Brazil to R Purús.

Descriptive notes. 18-20 cm. Tail short. Sexes alike. Distinguished from *A. castaneiceps* and *A. viridis* by rufous underparts with black bars, and uniform rufous head and neck; also from *A. castaneiceps* by mottled cinnamon and dusky underwing-coverts, and black bill. Immature and juvenile undescribed. Voice. Song a low churring rattle, similar to that of *A. viridis*, *L. albigularis* and *L. melanophaius*; often given simultaneously by both members of a pair, possibly antiphonal. Often vocal, especially in early morning and late evening.

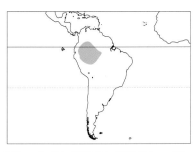

Habitat. Tall wet grass and marsh vegetation, including that fringing streams and pools. Occurs in lowlands E of Andes, up to 500 m.

Food and Feeding. Nothing recorded.

Breeding. Colombia, Jun. One nest was domed and bulky, of grass with a side entrance, 1·7 m up on a vine-covered fallen limb in a clearing. No other details recorded.

Movements. None recorded.

Status and Conservation. Not globally threatened. Status difficult to assess because of skulking habits in tall wet grass, but species is probably more widespread than the few existing records indicate.

Bibliography. Blake (1977), Butler (1979), Hellmayr & Conover (1942), Hilty & Brown (1986), Meyer de Schauensee (1982), Olson (1973b), Parker *et al.* (1982), Pinto (1964), Ripley (1977), Sick (1985c, 1993), Traylor (1958).

Genus *LATERALLUS* G. R. Gray, 1855

28. Rufous-sided Crake
Laterallus melanophaius

French: Râle brunoir   **German**: Rothalsralle   **Spanish**: Polluela Burrito
Other common names: Rufous-sided Rail

Taxonomy. *Rallus melanophaius* Vieillot, 1819, Paraguay.
Sometimes considered to include *L. albigularis*. Two subspecies recognized.

Subspecies and Distribution.
L. m. oenops (P. L. Sclater & Salvin, 1880) - SE Colombia, E Ecuador, E Peru and W Brazil.
L. m. melanophaius (Vieillot, 1819) - coastal Venezuela E to Surinam and S through C & E Brazil to E Bolivia, Paraguay, Uruguay and N Argentina.

Descriptive notes. 14-18 cm; 1 male 60 g, female 53-54 g; unsexed 46-57 (51) g. Bill relatively long and medium-slender; occasionally shows some narrow white barring on upperwing-coverts and scapulars, and some birds show buffy ochraceous colour from foreneck to breast. Sexes alike. Differs from *L. albigularis* in more extensive white from throat to belly, and plain rufous undertail-coverts. Easily confused with *L. leucopyrrhus* which, however, has rufous tinge to upperparts, sharp demarcation between rufous and white on sides of neck and breast, white lateral undertail-coverts, yellow bill base, and coral red legs and feet. Immature apparently similar to adult but not described; juvenile undescribed. Race *oenops* has lighter, more olivaceous upperparts and paler rufous tinge to forehead and face. VOICE. Abrupt, loose churring, very similar to call of *L. albigularis*. Calls frequently.

Habitat. Marshes, especially in dense vegetation along edges; also wet meadows and grassland; often some way from water. In Venezuela also recorded from forest, mudflats, lagoons and dry grassland. In Bolivia, when occurring alongside *L. exilis* in wet pasture, present species apparently more restricted to marsh grasses around patches of open water. Lowlands up to 1000 m.

Food and Feeding. Insects, especially beetles (Curculionidae), spiders, and bugs (Homoptera); captive birds ate mealworms (*Tenebrio* larvae) and blowfly larvae, and occasionally seeds. Forages on the ground and in shallow water.

Breeding. SE Brazil, 2 young Nov. Captive pair built 3 nests, 2 in bushes 0·6 m and over 1 m above ground, and 1 in nestbox on ground. Eggs 2-3; young of first brood fed chicks of second brood; downy chicks black; adult plumage attained at c. 4 months of age.

Movements. None recorded.

Status and Conservation. Not globally threatened. Apparently uncommon in Argentina and in Rio Grande do Sul, SE Brazil; status not recorded elsewhere as birds difficult to observe.

Bibliography. Belton (1984), Blake (1977), Canevari *et al.* (1991), Contreras *et al.* (1990), Gronow (1969), Haverschmidt (1968), Haverschmidt & Mees (1995), Hayes (1995), Hellmayr & Conover (1942), Hilty & Brown (1986), Meyer de Schauensee & Phelps (1978), de la Peña (1992), Ripley (1977), Sick (1985c, 1993), Snyder (1966), Storer (1981).

29. Rusty-flanked Crake
Laterallus levraudi

French: Râle de Levraud   **German**: Venezuelaralle   **Spanish**: Polluela Venezolana

Taxonomy. *Porzana levraudi* P. L. Sclater & Salvin, 1868, Caracas, Venezuela.
Monotypic.

Distribution. Venezuela N of R Orinoco. Specimen from NE Brazil (Paraiba) is a subadult *L. exilis*.

Descriptive notes. 14-16·5 cm. Upperwing-coverts variably spotted with rufous in some birds. Sexes alike. Closely resembles the three allopatric *Anurolimnas* crakes, two of which (*A. castaneiceps* and *A. viridis*) normally inhabit forest and thicket; *A. castaneiceps* differs in dark brown belly, and *A. viridis* has grey face and very short rufous tail; marsh-dwelling *A. fasciatus* has distinctive blackish barring from lower breast to undertail-coverts. Sympatric *L. melanophaius* has barred underparts, while similar but larger *Amaurolimnas concolor* of dense thickets has rufous-tinged upperwing-coverts, brown belly to undertail-coverts, and yellowish green bill. Immature apparently similar to adult but not described; juvenile undescribed. VOICE. Not described.

Habitat. Inhabits swamps, marshes, lakesides, lagoons and flooded pastures in lowlands from 20 up to 600 m.

Food and Feeding. No information available.

Breeding. No information available.

Movements. None recorded.

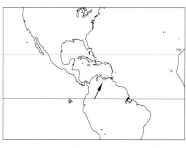

Status and Conservation. VULNERABLE. Confined to Caribbean slope of NW Venezuela, where it has been recorded infrequently from few localities. Recent records are from only 3 areas, at 2 of them in man-made habitats, a pool and a reservoir: in Yacambú National Park (Lara), Morrocoy National Park (Falcón) and Embalse de Taguaiguai (Aragua). In 1940's, species was at least locally common but present status unclear; although considered still locally common in 1980's, population at Yacambú National Park was then small and only 6-12 birds were seen in c. 3-4 ha of habitat at Embalse de Taguaiguai. Numbers are probably declining as a result of the general degradation of wetlands caused by industrial waste, pesticides and the lowering of water levels. Assessment of species' ecological requirements urgently needed, so that conservation strategy may be developed; surveys required in order to determine overall status of species and to assess threats to its survival.

Bibliography. Blake (1977), Collar & Andrew (1988), Collar, Crosby & Stattersfield (1994), Collar, Gonzaga *et al.* (1992), Hellmayr & Conover (1942), Meyer de Schauensee (1982), Meyer de Schauensee & Phelps (1978), Ripley (1977), Storer (1981), Teixeira *et al.* (1989), Wege & Long (1995).

30. Ruddy Crake
Laterallus ruber

French: Râle roux   **German**: Rubinralle   **Spanish**: Polluela Rojiza
Other common names: Red Crake

Taxonomy. *Corethrura rubra* P. L. Sclater and Salvin, 1860, Vera Paz, Guatemala.
In past, up to three races proposed, *ruber*, *ruberrimus* and *tamaulipensis*. Monotypic.

Distribution. S & E Mexico (Guerrero and Tamaulipas) S to Honduras, N Nicaragua and NW Costa Rica (N Guanacaste).

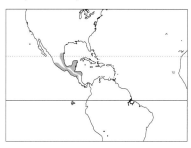

Descriptive notes. 14-16·5 cm; 42-49 (45) g. Sexes alike, but female richer, more chestnut, from lower back to uppertail-coverts; averages slightly smaller, especially in culmen length. Very similar to allopatric *L. levraudi*, but has uniform underparts; within its own range a distinctive small crake. Distinguished from congeners by dark slate top and sides of head, which contrast with chestnut mantle and sides of neck; also unbarred cinnamon to chestnut underparts with paler chin; olive green legs and feet. Immature like adult but paler on belly and with rump to uppertail-coverts like adult male. Juvenile sooty grey; almost black on crown, rump and tail; interscapular region has brownish cast; throat whitish; breast and flanks dark grey; belly pale grey to cream; iris grey-white; bill pinkish to dark horn; legs and feet greenish grey. VOICE. Explosive descending trill similar to that of *L. albigularis*, typically preceded by quiet piping notes; calls frequently during breeding season, even until midday. Also a dry, insect-like chatter or churr (a scolding note), sometimes followed by quiet rasps. Calls throughout year.

Habitat. Marshes, including brushy edges; also flooded fields, wet meadows and roadside ditches; pastures with tall grass or weeds; inhabits lowlands up to 1500 m along both slopes of Middle America.

Food and Feeding. No information available.

Breeding. Honduras, Jul-Sept; Nicaragua, Jul. Nest a rather tightly woven ball of dry grass stems, reeds and leaves, lined with finer grass, with a side entrance; one nest with external depth 20 cm and diameter 13 cm, was placed in centre of small tuft of reeds 20 cm above water. Eggs 3-6; black downy chick has pink bill, and grey legs and feet. No other details of breeding recorded.

Movements. Considered resident throughout most of normal range but possibly only a visitor to NW Costa Rica.

Status and Conservation. Not globally threatened. Difficult to observe; current status unclear, but in 1970's species was regarded as fairly common in some areas, possibly the most abundant crake over much of its range in Mexico, where its calls were heard throughout Atlantic coastal marshes in spring. Apparently rare and local at its two known Costa Rican sites, Miravalles and Orosi. No recent information on status in rest of range.

Bibliography. Blake (1977), Dickerman (1968a), Dickey & van Rossem (1938), Edwards (1989), González-García (1993), Hellmayr & Conover (1942), Howell & Webb (1995a), Land (1970), Monroe (1968), Peterson & Chalif (1973), Saab & Petit (1992), Slud (1964), Stiles & Skutch (1989).

31. White-throated Crake
Laterallus albigularis

French: Râle à menton blanc   **German**: Weißkehlralle   **Spanish**: Polluela Carrasqueadora

Taxonomy. *Corethrura albigularis* Lawrence, 1861, Atlantic side of Isthmus of Panama.
Sometimes considered conspecific with *L. melanophaius*, which replaces present species E of Andes; however, may be closer to *L. exilis*. Three subspecies recognized.

Subspecies and Distribution.
L. a. cinereiceps (Lawrence, 1875) - SE Honduras and Caribbean slope of Nicaragua through Costa Rica to NW Panama (W Veragua).
L. a. albigularis (Lawrence, 1861) - Pacific lowlands of SW Costa Rica (Gulf of Nicoya) through Panama and N & W Colombia to W Ecuador.
L. a. cerdaleus Wetmore, 1958 - E Colombia (Córdoba to Santa Marta region).

Descriptive notes. 14-16 cm; male mean 50 g, female mean 45 g. Occasionally has remiges faintly mottled or barred with white. Sexes alike. Only sympatric *Laterallus* is *L. ruber*, which lacks barring on underparts. Differs from *L. melanophaius* in less extensive white on throat and only onto upper breast; undertail-coverts clearly barred. Immature similar to adult but duller; pale tips to head feathers; sides of head to sides of breast grey, flecked with cinnamon; belly dark brown, very narrowly barred whitish. Juvenile not described. Races separated on plumage: *cinereiceps* has grey face, *cerdaleus* has fairly uniform reddish brown head and throat. VOICE. Abrupt, explosive descending trill or churr, similar to that of *L. ruber*; alarm note a sharp "chip".

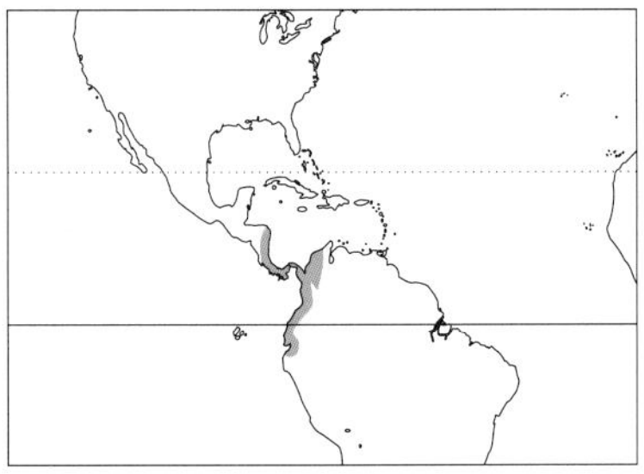

Habitat. Marshes, wet fields and damp grassy pastures, overgrown banks of ditches, canals, ponds and streams, and drying stream beds; also thickets and forest clearings. Does not require standing water; more associated with grass than with marshes in Colombia. Inhabits lowlands up to 1600 m.

Food and Feeding. Takes insects, spiders, seeds of grasses and sedges, and algae. Although normally confined to dense vegetation, ventures into more open spots to feed at dawn and dusk or in dull, rainy weather.

Breeding. Breeds Costa Rica in wet season; Colombia, breeding condition Dec-Aug. Nest a ball, with a side entrance, of woven grass stems and leaves, placed up to 60 cm above ground or water in grass tussock or bush. Eggs 2-5; black downy chick has pale brownish white bill with black band anterior to nostril.

Movements. Resident throughout range, but in wet season may wander to higher ground with low cover.

Status and Conservation. Not globally threatened. Very difficult to see and status unclear; considered common over much of its range in 1970's and 1980's, but in 1960's race *albigularis* was relatively uncommon except in some lowland regions.

Bibliography. Blake (1977), Davis (1972), Hellmayr & Conover (1942), Hilty & Brown (1986), Monroe (1968), Ridgely (1981), Ridgely & Gwynne (1989), Ripley (1977), Sclater & Salvin (1879), Slud (1964), Stiles & Levey (1988), Stiles & Skutch (1989), Storer (1981), Wetmore (1965).

32. **Grey-breasted Crake**

Laterallus exilis

French: Râle grêle **German**: Amazonasralle **Spanish**: Polluela Pechigrís

Taxonomy. *Rallus exilis* Temminck, 1831, Cayenne, French Guiana.
Monotypic.

Distribution. Guatemala and Belize S through Panama to Colombia and N Ecuador; Venezuela and the Guianas S through Amazonian Brazil and W to E Peru and N Bolivia; extreme SE Brazil; also S Paraguay (Villa Hayes), where status uncertain.

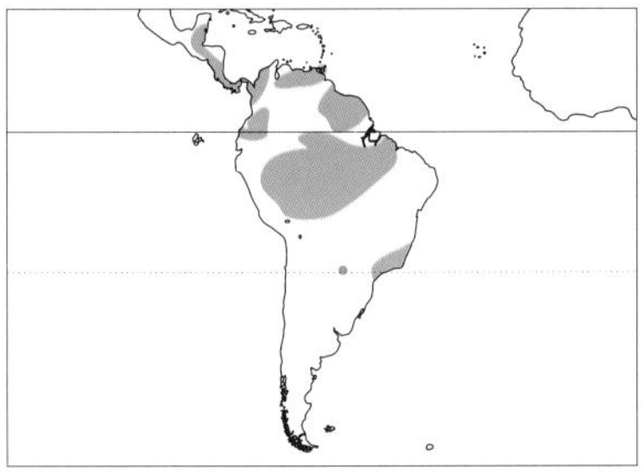

Descriptive notes. 14-15·5 cm; male 26·5-39 (32) g, female 29-43 (36) g. Variable amount of narrow white barring on upperwing-coverts, sometimes absent. Sexes alike. Easily distinguished from congeners with barred flanks by pale grey head to breast, chestnut nape and upper mantle, and olive brown upperparts. Three other superficially similar grey-breasted crakes with barred flanks are sympatric, but all are larger and lack chestnut on nape and mantle: *Neocrex erythrops* has red base to bill and red legs; *Porzana albicollis* and *P. carolina* have patterned upperparts and different head pattern, former has purplish brown legs, latter has white undertail-coverts. Immature has fuscous brown upperparts and medium grey underparts, lacks chestnut on nape and upper mantle, has duller, more restricted barring on underparts, brown iris and largely horn brown bill. Juvenile sooty black with whitish throat and centre of breast; iris and bill as immature. Voice. Call a series of 2-10 "tink" or "keek" notes; also descending musical rattle and quiet, sharp "check".

Habitat. Marshes, riverbanks, lake edges and wet grassy habitats with dense, short to fairly tall vegetation of 50-100 cm; also flooded rice fields and floating mats of *Paspalum* grass on river. Usually in areas with shallow standing water, 5-15 cm deep; sometimes in dry habitat such as pasture, fields of tall grass in a new housing area, and airfields. Occurs alongside *L. melanophaius* in marshes, and also in habitat similar to that occupied by *L. ruber*. Uses "runways" under grass; Peruvian specimen trapped on runway used by swamp rats (*Holochilus brasiliensis*). Lowlands up to c. 1700 m.

Food and Feeding. Earthworms, spiders, insects (Orthoptera, Homoptera, Coleoptera, Hemiptera, Heteroptera and larval Lepidoptera), and seeds.

Breeding. Surinam, Dec, Feb; Colombia, breeding condition Feb; Panama, possibly Jul; record from Trinidad, Jul, possibly not of this species. Nest spherical with a side entrance, typical of genus; made of woven grass and weed stems. Eggs 3; chick covered with black down.

Movements. Regarded as sedentary, but in Surinam 2 birds were caught at night at lighted houses in Jul and Feb. Not known whether S Paraguay bird, taken in early Aug 1979, was migrant, stray or part of a resident population.

Status and Conservation. Not globally threatened. Fragmented distribution suggests that species may be more widespread than is known, but birds are secretive and very difficult to see. Common in Bolivia and Amazonian Brazil; not uncommon in Surinam and Costa Rica; at Paramaribo, Surinam, many birds recorded in grass fields at new housing project, Dec 1972. Apparently local and uncommon to rare elsewhere, especially in Central America where may be generally less numerous than in South America, a distribution pattern which might be expected in a species retreating from a formerly greater range.

Bibliography. Blake (1977), Contreras & Contreras (1994), Haverschmidt (1968, 1974a), Haverschmidt & Mees (1995), Hayes (1995), Hellmayr & Conover (1942), Hilty & Brown (1986), Howell & Webb (1995a), Howell *et al*. (1992), Meyer de Schauensee (1962), Meyer de Schauensee & Phelps (1978), Monroe (1968), Olson (1974a), Parker *et al*. (1991), Pearson (1975), Ridgely (1981), Ridgely & Gwynne (1989), Sick (1985c, 1993), Snyder (1966), Stiles (1988), Stiles & Levey (1988), Stiles & Skutch (1989), Storer (1981), Texieira, Nacinovic & Luigi (1989), Texieira, Nacinovic & Tavares (1986), Tostain *et al*. (1992), Wetmore (1965).

33. **Black Rail**

Laterallus jamaicensis

French: Râle noir **German**: Schieferralle **Spanish**: Polluela Negruzca

Taxonomy. *Rallus jamaicensis* Gmelin, 1789, Jamaica.
Distinctive race *tuerosi* sometimes treated as separate species. Five subspecies normally recognized.

Subspecies and Distribution.
L. j. coturniculus (Ridgway, 1874) - California and Baja California.
L. j. jamaicensis (Gmelin, 1789) - E USA and E Central America; winters from S USA to Guatemala and Greater Antilles.
L. j. murivagans (Riley, 1916) - coastal Peru.
L. j. tuerosi Fjeldså, 1983 - L Junín, Peru.
L. j. salinasi (Philippi, 1857) - C Chile and extreme W Argentina.
Also 2 presumed Colombian specimens, labelled "Bogotá" and "Nouvelle Grenade".

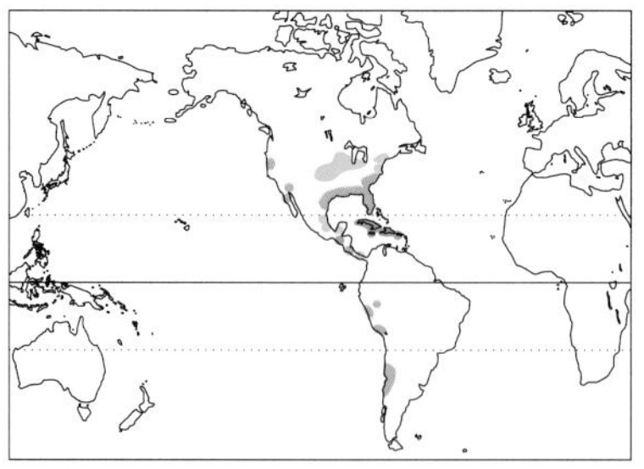

Descriptive notes. 12-15 cm; *jamaicensis* male 29-43 (35) g, female 29-44 (36) g; *coturniculus* male 21-34 (28) g, female 23-46 (30) g; wingspan 22-28 cm. Sexes similar; female has paler underparts. Very small rail, easily distinguished from congeners and most sympatric rallids by very dark plumage with white spotting and barring (although young of most rallids are black). *Porzana spiloptera* has blackish streaks on dark olive brown upperparts, white spots and bars of upperparts confined to upperwing-coverts and remiges, white barring on belly, flanks and undertail-coverts, and brown legs and feet. Possibly sympatric *Coturnicops notatus* similar in size and colour but has white spotting on head and neck, white chin, white markings on neck and breast, rest of underparts barred, and black legs and feet. Immature similar to adult; iris and legs gradually attain adult colours. Juvenile has dark brown upperparts, more rufous from nape to upper back, with variable small white spots on middle back and wings; face and underparts grey, with white chin, throat and centre of belly; flanks and undertail-coverts browner, barred white; iris brown; legs and feet darker than adult. Races separated on: colour of undertail-coverts, cinnamon or buff in *murivagans* and *tuerosi*; colour of mantle and back, chestnut-brown in *jamaicensis*, more rufous in others, more extensive in *salinasi*; nature of pattern of back to tail and upperwing, boldly barred white in *tuerosi*, variably spotted in others; white barring on flanks, broader in *salinasi*; and size, *coturniculus* smallest. Voice. Male gives "kic-kic-kerr" call ending in a downward slur; female gives low "croo-croo-croo". Also growls and barking notes.

Habitat. Marshes, both fresh and saline, and wet meadows and savanna. In North America occupies sites with shallower water (under 3 cm in Arizona) than other rallids; most breeding areas have fine-stemmed emergent plants, and substrate of ideal habitat usually moist soil with scattered small pools. In dense vegetation probably uses runways of mice. Birds in salt-marsh habitats require surrounding higher vegetation for escape during extreme high tides. Structure apparently more important than plant species composition in determining suitability of habitat. Race *tuerosi* inhabits wide rushy (*Juncus*) zones with open spaces of partly flooded moss or short matted grass in marshes fringing L Junín at 4080 m in C Peruvian Andes. Race *salinasi* occurs in salt-marsh and inundated fields. Sometimes in hay fields during migration.

Food and Feeding. Takes mainly small (under 1 cm) aquatic and terrestrial invertebrates, including snails, Amphipoda, Isopoda, spiders, ants, aphids, grasshoppers, beetles, bugs, earwigs and flies; also seeds of *Typha* and *Scirpus*; eats more seeds in winter. Foraging poorly known; active throughout day and probably forages on or near substrate at edges of stands of emergent vegetation.

Breeding. USA, May-Aug; Panama, Jul; Peru, end of dry season through rainy season; Chile, Nov-Dec. Monogamous; territorial when breeding. Nest a bowl of dominant local grasses, rushes etc., with woven canopy of dead or living vegetation and ramp of dead vegetation from substrate to entrance; external diameter 11-15 cm, height 8-10 cm; internal diameter 7-8 cm; depth of cup 3-7 cm; built in thick marsh vegetation having both dead and living plant components; usually placed low down in centre of vegetation clump over moist substrate or very shallow water; sometimes in depression in ground; may build nest up in response to high tides. Eggs 4-13 (7·6) in *jamaicensis*, 3-8 (6) in *coturniculus*, 3-7 (4·9) in *salinasi*, 2 in *tuerosi*; incubation 17-20 days, by both sexes; black downy chick has sepia bill; chicks semi-precocial, brooded for first few days; both parents, sometimes only female, care for chicks; juvenile plumage attained by 6 weeks; immature plumage acquired in autumn or early winter. Age of first breeding probably 1 year. May lay replacement and second clutches. Nest success high in Arizona; adult survival apparently high in stable habitats, despite predation by herons and other birds during extreme high tides, a major source of mortality for populations in tidal marshes.

Movements. E USA populations winter in coastal E USA (S through Florida and rarely N to New Jersey) and also S to Cuba, Jamaica and Guatemala. Recorded only in breeding season in S Mexico, Belize and Panama; only in winter in Guatemala and Jamaica; most Cuban records are of winter residents; transient in Bahamas; may winter more widely than is known in West Indies and in Central American breeding range; may breed very locally in Greater Antilles; present all year in Costa Rica. USA spring migration mid-Mar to early May; autumn migration early Sept to early Nov, mostly mid-Sept to mid-Oct; migrates at night along broad front; sometimes strikes towers and buildings. Accidental Canada (Ontario, Quebec), Maine, Rhode I, and Bermuda. Adults of Californian race (*coturniculus*) sedentary but juveniles may disperse erratically. South American races apparently sedentary.

Status and Conservation. Not globally threatened. Race *tuerosi*, sometimes treated as full species, considered Endangered; known only from L Junín, where recorded from 2 sites on SW shore (near Ondores and Pari) but likely to occur through large portions of the 15,000 ha of marshland surrounding the lake; nearby lakes do not have suitable habitat. This form at risk from pollution and water level changes which have affected the lake since at least 1955; in particular, strong desiccation of reedmarshes caused by drought and unsustainable water management by Electro Peru, and also occasional flooding with very acid water from Cerro de Pasco mines; however, *tuerosi* still survived in Jan 1995. All other races are locally distributed, often rare or infrequently recorded. Both races occurring in USA regarded as threatened in most states; in USA, breeding range has contracted seriously this century, both of *jamaicensis* at inland sites, where no confirmed nesting recorded since 1932, and of both races at coastal sites, where populations must have declined drastically before 1970's when laws protecting coastal wetlands were enacted. More susceptible than other marsh rallids to disturbance from grazing and agriculture because habitat is at edge of marshes. Race *coturniculus* threatened by marsh subsidence caused by groundwater removal, dyking of salt-marshes, water level fluctuation, and wildfires. Continued massive degradation and loss of shallow wetland habitats gives cause for greater concern in future. In South America *salinasi* is rare, and was not recorded from Chile for 25 years until a dead bird was found in Oct 1994. Race *jamaicensis* no longer occurs on Puerto Rico.

Bibliography. Bent (1926), Biaggi (1983), Blake (1977), Burt (1994), Canevari *et al*. (1991), Collar & Andrew (1988), Collar, Crosby & Stattersfield (1994), Collar, Gonzaga *et al*. (1992), Dod (1992), Eddleman, Flores & Legare (1994), Eddleman, Knopf *et al*. (1988), Ehrlich *et al*. (1992), Evens & Page (1986), Evens, Page, Laymon & Stallcup (1991), Evens, Page, Stenzel & Warnock (1986), Fjeldså (1983b), Fjeldså & Krabbe (1990), Flores (1991), Flores & Eddleman (1992, 1993, 1995), Griese *et al*. (1980), Harty (1964), Howell & Webb (1995a, 1995b), Howell *et al*. (1992), Johnson (1965b), Kerlinger & Wiedner (1990), Moreno (1953), Orians & Paulson (1969), de la Peña (1992), Repking (1975), Repking & Ohmart (1977), Reynard (1974), Ridgely & Gwynne (1989), Root (1988), Stiles & Skutch (1989), Todd (1977), Wege & Long (1995), Weske (1969), Wetmore (1965), Williams (1995a).

34. **Galapagos Rail**

Laterallus spilonotus

French: Râle des Galapagos **German**: Galapagosralle **Spanish**: Polluela de Galápagos

Taxonomy. *Zapornia spilonota* Gould, 1841, Santiago (James) Island, Galapagos.
Sometimes considered a race of *L. jamaicensis*, of which it is an insular derivative. Monotypic.
Distribution. Galapagos Is, occurring on Pinta, Fernandina, Isabela, Santiago, Santa Cruz, Floreana and San Cristóbal.

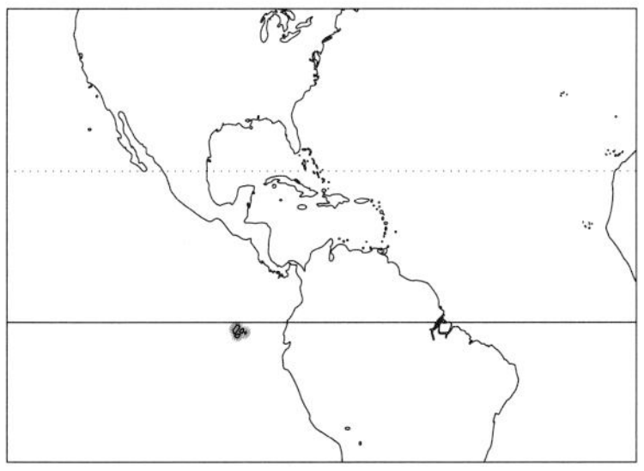

Descriptive notes. 15·5 cm; 35-45 g (no precise data). Sexes similar but female sometimes has paler throat. Very similar in plumage to *L. jamaicensis*, with blackish face, dark chocolate brown upperparts with small white spots on wings and from mantle to uppertail-coverts, dark slate grey neck and breast, chocolate brown flanks and belly with small white spots, and blackish undertail-coverts with white bars; lacks bold barring on flanks of *L. jamaicensis*, and white markings on upperparts far less distinct. Non-breeding adult has white spots on upperparts reduced or absent. Juvenile has blackish grey upperparts, greyer on face and throat; sooty brown underparts with no white spots. Change from juvenile to adult-type plumage gradual, with no distinctive immature plumage; involves mantle and back becoming increasingly brown, white spotting increasing, iris colour changing from black through brown and orange to crimson, and bill gradually darkening to black. Voice. Vocal repertoire extensive, including cackles, clucks, warbles, trills and hisses. Territorial advertising call of adults, frequently heard, is a rapid "chi-chi-chi-chirroo", the "rroo" being a falling slur; similar in form to advertising call of *L. jamaicensis*.
Habitat. Historically recorded from 2 habitat types: coastal mangroves, from which no longer known, and in grass and forest of highland moist regions, where occurs in deep thickets and in dense ground cover. Recorded from *Psychotria* thickets on Santiago; from *Scalesia* forest, shrubby *Miconia robinsoniana* belt, patches of bracken (*Pteridium aquilinum*), open sedge-fern meadows and moist farming regions on Santa Cruz; and from highland fern belt on Pinta. Generally tolerant of man-modified habitats, e.g. agricultural land, but does not venture into overgrazed short-grass pasture. Precise altitudinal limits not known: occurs on all islands higher than 500 m; may ascend to 1700 m on Isabela.
Food and Feeding. Primarily invertebrates: snails, Isopoda, Amphipoda, spiders, dragonflies, moths, Hemiptera, ants and caterpillars; also some seeds. Feeds throughout day; normally forages on ground, walking with depressed tail, darting head from side to side, jabbing bill rapidly into litter, picking up and tossing or moving aside leaves and twigs. Also takes prey from stems and overhanging leaves; frequently probes into moss and other epiphytes on *Miconia* trunks; sometimes climbs 0·5 m up into vegetation to forage. Also forages at pools, streams and *Sphagnum* bog patches; wades breast-deep and takes small prey from water surface.
Breeding. Breeds Sept-Apr, from middle of cool season to end of hot season. Monogamous and territorial. Nest a deep, semi-domed cup with side entrance; made of herbaceous stems; built on ground and covered by dense, low vegetation. Eggs 3-6; incubation 23-25 days, by both parents, with change-overs every c. 50 minutes; newly hatched downy chicks black, with black iris and white bill with black tip, weigh 8-9 g; chicks leave nest soon after hatching, and cared for and fed by both parents; juveniles feed themselves but stay with parents until almost fully grown; adult-type plumage fully attained by 80-85 days. May raise two broods per season. Age of first breeding 1 year.
Movements. None.
Status and Conservation. Not globally threatened. Currently considered near-threatened. Now known only from islands high enough to have an extensive moist region. In late 1970's species was considered still common in highland habitats, especially on Santiago and Santa Cruz, and population on Santa Cruz appeared stable, but no recent assessment of status has been made. Birds fly weakly and possibly vulnerable to introduced predators, e.g. dogs, cats and pigs; black rats (*Rattus rattus*) appear not to be significant nest predators, probably as a result of incubating adult's aggressive behaviour towards intruders. Short-eared Owl (*Asio flammeus*) may be natural predator. Introduced animals are threat to habitat: on Pinta no rails found after goats destroyed dense ground vegetation in 1968-1970 but, after introduction of hunting in 1971 to reduce goat population, vegetation regenerated and rails were again common in 1973. Most of archipelago is under national park protection and programme to eradicate introduced predators exists. Reasons for abandonment of mangrove habitat not known: unlikely to be simply a result of introduced predators or competitors because rails have also disappeared from mangroves on Fernandina, where no introductions have occurred. Much of habitat protected within Galapagos National Park but all islands where species occurs, except Fernandina, have introduced mammals; rail populations should be surveyed regularly to monitor status.
Bibliography. Collar *et al*. (1994), Franklin *et al*. (1979), Gifford (1913), Harris (1973, 1982), Ortiz & Carrión (1991), Ripley (1977), Ripley & Beehler (1985), Rosenberg (1990), Salvin (1876), Storer (1981).

35. **Red-and-white Crake**

Laterallus leucopyrrhus

French: Râle blanc et roux **German**: Weißbrustralle **Spanish**: Polluela Rojiblanca

Taxonomy. *Rallus leucopyrrhus* Vieillot, 1819, Paraguay.
Monotypic.
Distribution. SE Brazil, Paraguay and Uruguay to NE Argentina (S to Buenos Aires).
Descriptive notes. 14-16 cm; 1 female 46·5 g, 10 unsexed 34-52 (45) g. Distinctively patterned crake: pure white throat and centre of breast sharply demarcated from adjacent bright rufous areas; flanks boldly barred black and white; undertail-covert pattern unique in genus, black in centre and white laterally; bill has broad yellow base and lower mandible, rest blackish; legs and feet bright coral red.

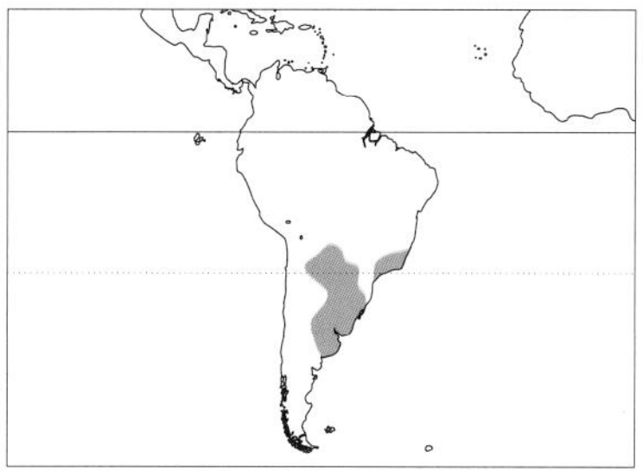

Some birds have diffuse rufous barring on upperwing-coverts, while a few have more prominent white barring, sometimes bordered with black. Sexes alike. *L. melanophaius* lacks sharp demarcation between rufous and white at sides of neck and breast, and has rufous undertail-coverts, all-dark bill and olive brown legs; *L. xenopterus* has buffy ochraceous breast, strong black and white barring on wings, black tail and undertail-coverts, rather heavy blue-grey bill and blue-grey legs. Immature similar to adult; juvenile has dark brown upperparts, grey underparts, blackish bill and black legs. Voice. Utters a prolonged throaty chatter; contact call is a low squeak or whistle.
Habitat. Open marshy areas in lowlands. Inhabits dense tussocky or matted grasses (sometimes heavily grazed) 30-50 cm tall, on moist ground or in water 2-4 cm deep; also coarse grass, 1·5-2+ m tall, with scattered tree-ferns on moist or flooded ground. Uses runways on ground beneath dense matted vegetation; in captivity, also climbs freely in bushes.
Food and Feeding. Forages by searching ground and occasionally prodding dead leaves or twigs. Captive birds ate earthworms, insects and millet seed.
Breeding. Argentina, Oct. Monogamous. Nest spherical with side entrance, made of grasses; one aviary nest was large pile of wet leaves, 18 cm deep and 23 cm across, placed 2 m up in dense honeysuckle (*Lonicera*). All following information from captive birds: eggs 2-3; incubation 23-24 days, by both sexes; black downy chicks have black bare parts, and one weighed 7·8 g; chicks leave nest soon after hatching and can feed themselves immediately, but adults normally feed and care for them; young of first brood, aged c. 8 weeks, also fed young of second brood; independent at c. 4 weeks; fully grown and feathered at 6 weeks, when eye and legs show red tinge; rufous feathers appear from 5-7 weeks of age.
Movements. None recorded.
Status and Conservation. Not globally threatened. No recent information. Formerly regarded as locally common in Argentina and Paraguay but rare in Rio Grande do Sul, Brazil. Kept in captivity relatively frequently and, at least in 1970's, was more available through the bird trade than many other small rails, suggesting that it may have been fairly common.
Bibliography. Belton (1984), Blake (1977), Canevari *et al*. (1991), Contreras *et al*. (1990), Essenberg (1984), Everitt (1962), Forrester (1993), Gibson, L. (1979), Hayes (1995), Hellmayr & Conover (1942), Kleefisch (1984), Klimaitis & Moschione (1987), Levi (1966), Meise (1934), Meyer de Schauensee (1982), Narosky & Yzurieta (1987), Olrog (1984), de la Peña (1992), Pereyra (1931), van Praet (1980), Rutgers & Norris (1970), Sick (1985c, 1993), Storer (1981).

36. **Rufous-faced Crake**

Laterallus xenopterus

French: Râle de Conover **German**: Rotgesichtralle **Spanish**: Polluela Guaraní
Other common names: Horqueta Crake

Taxonomy. *Laterallus xenopterus* Conover, 1934, Horqueta, Paraguay.
Monotypic.
Distribution. SC Brazil (Federal District) and C Paraguay.

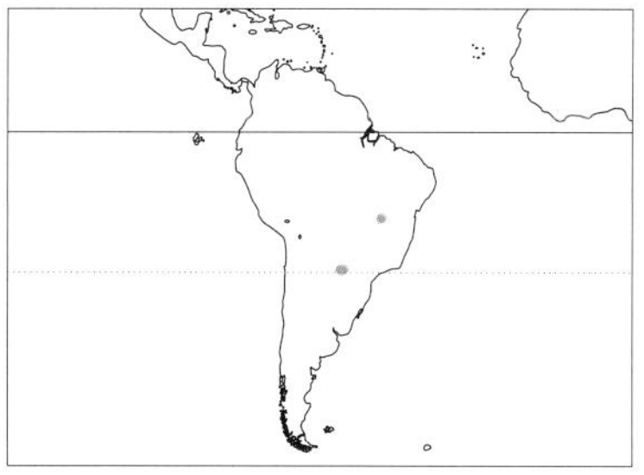

Descriptive notes. 14 cm; 3 unsexed 51-53 g. Tail relatively long, bill stout and tarsus short. Sexes alike. Distinguished from other *Laterallus* by buffy ochraceous foreneck to breast, normally rather duller than in *L. melanophaius*; from sympatric *L. melanophaius* and *L. leucopyrrhus* by boldly barred inner secondaries, upperwing-coverts and scapulars, black tail and undertail-coverts, heavy blue-grey bill and blue-grey legs and feet; some individuals of both of the above species have diffuse or narrow rufous or white barring on upperwing-coverts and scapulars, but never as extensive or as prominent. Voice. Not described.
Habitat. Inhabits coarse, tussocky or matted grass on moist to shallowly flooded substrates in marshes. Reported from tussocky grass 30-50 cm tall growing on moist ground or in 3-4 cm of water; also in coarse grass 1·5-2 m tall in 2-3 cm of water; such marshes (wet *campos*) commonly form in low areas of E Paraguay and adjacent parts of Brazil. Occurs alongside *L. leucopyrrhus* in these habitats.
Food and Feeding. Nothing recorded. Specimens captured in traps baited with peanut butter, rolled oats, cracked maize and banana.
Breeding. No information available.
Movements. None recorded.
Status and Conservation. VULNERABLE. Reliably known from only 3 areas. In C Paraguay the type was collected at Horqueta in 1933 and 4 birds were collected in Curuguaty area in 1976-1979. Over 1200 km to NE there were several sight records, and one specimen, from Brasília area during period 1978-1989. Species presumably occurs in wetlands between these two centres. Population not known but doubtless more widespread and numerous than existing records suggest, because areas of occurrence poorly studied and birds difficult to locate; judged relatively frequent around Brasília. No known threats in Paraguay. In Brazil, wholesale loss of wet *campo* habitats from drainage and adjacent *Eucalyptus* plantations may have serious effects on hitherto undiscovered populations; fire is also a potential threat. Work is needed to rediscover populations in Paraguay; voice should be recorded, enabling use of taped playback to ascertain range and status of species.
Bibliography. Blake (1977), Collar & Andrew (1988), Collar, Crosby & Stattersfield (1994), Collar, Gonzaga *et al*. (1992), Conover (1934), Hayes (1995), Hellmayr & Conover (1942), Meyer de Schauensee (1982), Myers & Hansen (1980), Negret & Teixeira (1984a), Pinto (1964), Sick (1979, 1985c, 1993), Storer (1981), Wege & Long (1995).

ssp *immaculatus*

ssp *tertius*

37

37

38

ssp *woodfordi*

dark bird

ssp *australis*

pale bird

ssp *greyi*

39

ssp *hectori*

PLATE 12

inches 8

cm 20

40

41

42

ssp *sulcirostris*

43

ssp *wilkinsoni*

ssp *celebensis*

44

45

ssp *torquatus*

ssp *philippensis*

ssp *meyeri*

47

48

46

ssp *striatus*

ssp *gularis*

Genus *NESOCLOPEUS* J. L. Peters, 1932

37. Woodford's Rail
Nesoclopeus woodfordi

French: Râle de Woodford   **German**: Salomonenralle   **Spanish**: Rascón de las Salomón
Other common names: Solomons Rail

Taxonomy. *Rallina Woodfordi* Ogilvie-Grant, 1889, Aola, Guadalcanal, Solomon Islands.
Sometimes placed in *Rallina* or even *Rallus*, but *Nesoclopeus* differs in structural characters, and may provide link between *Rallina* and *Gallirallus*. Forms superspecies with *N. poecilopterus*, with which may be conspecific. Three subspecies recognized.
Subspecies and Distribution.
N. w. tertius Mayr, 1949 - Bougainville I.
N. w. immaculatus Mayr, 1949 - Santa Isabel I.
N. w. woodfordi (Ogilvie-Grant, 1889) - Guadalcanal I.
Also reported from Malaita and Choiseul (Solomon Is); sightings from New Georgia and Kolombangara may be referable to *Gallirallus rovianae*.

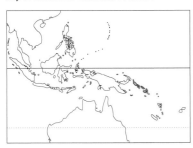

Descriptive notes. 30 cm. Fairly large, very dark rail with long, powerful bill; probably flightless. Sexes alike. Much darker than *N. poecilopterus* with less marked facial pattern; lacks tawny bars on remiges. Immature similar to adult but has white on chin, and browner underparts with pale edges to breast feathers. Juvenile undescribed. Race *tertius* smallest, *immaculatus* largest; *woodfordi* has white spots on primaries, and obscure ventral barring; *immaculatus* blacker overall, and lacks white on remiges and wing-coverts; *tertius* has belly and flanks faintly mottled buff, undertail-coverts vaguely barred white, and white barring on primaries; nominate has black bill, grey legs and red eye, *immaculatus* has greyish bill, dark greenish yellow legs and orange-red eye, and *tertius* has pale yellowish horn bill and grey legs.
Voice. Unmusical series of metallic shrieks of unvarying pitch, generally delivered in threes.
Habitat. Lowland forest, secondary growth and swamp forest, occasionally up to 1000 m; on Santa Isabel apparently prefers riparian habitats, including abandoned gardens, up to 300 m.
Food and Feeding. Worms, snails, insects, frogs, lizards and small snakes; also young shoots of taro plants. Occasionally digs in gardens.
Breeding. Bougainville, Aug. Eggs 2-4. A nest, purported to be of this species, from Santa Isabel in Jul 1988 was situated under small bush in lowland forest near stream; made of rootlets, leaves and other plant matter, measured c. 25 cm across and had shallow depression c. 15 cm across in which were 6 eggs almost identical to known eggs of this species. No further information available.
Movements. None.
Status and Conservation. ENDANGERED. May be close to extinction. Nominate race from Guadalcanal is known only from the type specimen and may be extinct, having fallen victim to introduced predators: cats have wiped out most terrestrial mammals on Guadalcanal. There were three observation of *immaculatus* from Santa Isabel in 1987 and 1988, where this bird occasionally forms part of the local human diet when caught by dogs or in traps set for the Pacific Black Duck (*Anas superciliosa*). No records of *tertius* from Bougainville between 1936 and 1985, when one bird was seen in forest which has since been logged.
Bibliography. Blaber (1990), Coates (1985), Collar & Andrew (1988), Collar *et al.* (1994), Diamond (1987, 1991), Finch (1985), Hadden (1981), Harrison & Parker (1967), Kaestner (1987), Olson (1973b), Ripley (1977), Sibley (1951), Webb (1992).

38. Bar-winged Rail
Nesoclopeus poecilopterus

French: Râle des Fidji   **German**: Fidschiralle   **Spanish**: Rascón de las Fiji
Other common names: Fiji Rail

Taxonomy. *Rallina pœciloptera* Hartlaub, 1866, Viti Levu, Fiji Islands.
Sometimes placed in *Rallina* or even *Rallus*. Forms superspecies with *N. woodfordi*, with which may be conspecific. Monotypic.
Distribution. Viti Levu and Ovalau, S Fiji. Almost certainly extinct on Taveuni, N Fiji.

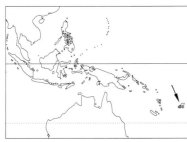

Descriptive notes. 33 cm. Probably flightless. Sexes alike; female possibly slightly larger. Very similar to *N. woodfordi*, but differs in having brown upperparts, medium dark slate grey underparts with faint pale barring from flanks to undertail-coverts, somewhat more marked facial pattern, tawny bars on remiges, white bars on all underwing-coverts, brown eye, yellow or orange-yellow bill and yellow legs. Immature and juvenile undescribed. **Voice**. Not described.
Habitat. Remote forested areas, secondary forest, old taro fields and possibly swamps.
Food and Feeding. No information available.
Breeding. Recorded nesting Oct-Dec and possibly Mar. One nest, "of sedges", contained 6 eggs; on another occasion a male and 4 eggs were obtained by local people. No other information.
Movements. None.

Status and Conservation. Almost certainly EXTINCT. An unconfirmed record from N of Waisa, near Vunidawa, Viti Levu, in 1973, the first record since 1890; however, species is thought unlikely to have survived there because a number of other ground-dwelling species, including two non-endemic volant rails (*Gallirallus phillipensis* and *Porphyrio porphyrio*), have disappeared as a result of predation by introduced mongooses and feral cats. Almost certainly extinct on Taveuni, where it was probably rare even before the introduction of mongooses and was regularly hunted by dogs. Known from 12 specimens collected on Viti Levu and Ovalau in 19th century; no estimate ever made of its abundance because it was shy and seldom seen.
Bibliography. Collar & Andrew (1988), Collar *et al.* (1994), Diamond (1991), Fullagar *et al.* (1982), Greenway (1967), Hay (1986), Holyoak (1979), King (1978/79), Layard (1875, 1876), Mayr (1945), Olson (1973b), Pratt *et al.* (1987), Ripley (1977), Watling (1982).

Genus *GALLIRALLUS* Lafresnaye, 1841

39. Weka
Gallirallus australis

French: Râle wéka   **German**: Wekaralle   **Spanish**: Rascón Weka

Taxonomy. *Rallus australis* Sparrman, 1786, Dusky Sound, South Island, New Zealand.
Includes *G. troglodytes*, now regarded as a black morph of present species. Considerable geographical variation, with up to eight races accepted in past; situation complicated by extensive individual variation. Four subspecies currently recognized.
Subspecies and Distribution.
G. a. greyi (Buller, 1888) - North I.
G. a. australis (Sparrman, 1786) - N & W South I.
G. a. hectori (Hutton, 1874) - formerly E coast and interior of South I but now confined to Chatham Is, where introduced.
G. a. scotti (Ogilvie-Grant, 1905) - Stewart I.
Introduced to many islands: *greyi* to Kapiti, Rakitu, Mokoia and Kawau, and to Bay of Islands; nominate to Kapiti, Chatham and Macquarie (now extinct on last); *hectori* to Chatham; and *scotti* to Solander and other outlying islands off Stewart I, and also to Kapiti and Macquarie (now extinct on latter).

Descriptive notes. Male 50-60 cm, 532-1605 (1049) g, wingspan 50-60 cm; female 46-50 cm, 350-1035 (737) g. Unmistakable: large, hefty, thickset, flightless species with stout bill, legs and feet; tail remarkably long for a flightless rail. Sexes similar but female smaller and may have narrower dark pink base and creamier tip to bill. Nominate and race *scotti* very variable, and commonly grouped into chestnut, grey and black morphs, although degree of individual variation has led some authors to group chestnut and grey birds together into single morph: typical chestnut morph bird has mottled red-brown underparts; grey morph has predominantly greyish underparts below brown breast band; and black morph extensively black with dark red-brown streaking on upperparts. Immature similar to adult. Juvenile similar to adult of same morph, but generally darker, though paler in *hectori*; upperparts appear less streaked because dark feather centres less distinct, almost lacking in some *greyi*; underparts may be more uniform and breast band indistinct; flanks often blotched, not barred; dark forms often have brown spots in plumage; bill grey-black; iris brown; legs grey-brown. Race *greyi* very dark, with extensive dark grey belly, reduced breast band, little barring on flanks, and dark legs; *hectori* more yellowish buff-brown; *scotti* smaller than nominate.
Voice. Adult "spacing call" a repeated shrill whistle "coo-eet", rising in pitch; most often heard at dawn and dusk and in early evening; often given by pair in duet; heard throughout year. Resonating boom call "doon-doon-doon" given during territorial or aggressive encounters.
Habitat. Frequently inhabits forest, sometimes edges only; also woodland, scrub and grassland, including subalpine tussock grassland. Occurs on beaches, particularly those with rotting seaweed, and at tidal creeks and bays; found at margins of estuarine and freshwater wetlands. Also occupies modified habitats such as lawns, rough pasture, cultivated land and plantations. Inhabits hills, mountains, cliffs, moraine, sandy and rocky shores, sand dunes and urban environments. Prefers low vegetation which gives cover but does not hinder movement; avoids forest with no suitable dense understorey. Occurs from sea-level up to c. 1500 m; may prefer low altitudes in some areas.
Food and Feeding. Omnivorous and opportunistic, taking mainly native fruit and invertebrates, sometimes vertebrates; eats more vegetable matter in winter. Takes foliage, roots, fruit and seeds of many vascular plants; also fungi and seaweed. Invertebrate prey includes earthworms, molluscs, wide variety of crustaceans, myriapods, arachnids and insects; marine animals. Vertebrate prey includes frogs, lizards, and eggs and young of other birds; may kill chickens and young ducks; also eats rats, mice and young rabbits, and scavenges carcasses. Diurnal and nocturnal; avoids forest; feeds mainly on ground. Scratches in litter with bill to depth of 8 cm, covering up to 50 m²/day; lifts dead *Rhopalostylis* palm leaves to search below them; searches seaweed and debris on beaches; searches in tree hollows; takes petrels from burrows; follows wild pigs, searching where they have rooted; climbs in trees; scavenges at camp-sites. Spears eggs with bill and runs off with them. Hammers large objects with bill to kill or break up; holds down objects in feet.
Breeding. Season highly variable, depending on climate, food and size of population; start recorded Aug-Nov, end recorded Nov-Mar, but when population expanding may breed throughout year. Monogamous; often permanently territorial; pair-bonds often permanent; non-monogamous associations (two females with one male) recorded twice. Nest on dry ground; situated in or under tussocks, in burrows, under logs, stumps or rocks, in tree-hollows, also concealed in outbuildings; up to 7 sites per territory, used for many years; nest of sedges, grasses, lilies, twigs and moss, lined with finer grasses and sometimes feathers, wool, hair or leaves; built by both sexes (captivity) or by male only. Usually

On following pages: 40. New Caledonian Rail (*Gallirallus lafresnayanus*); 41. Lord Howe Rail (*Gallirallus sylvestris*); 42. Okinawa Rail (*Gallirallus okinawae*); 43. Barred Rail (*Gallirallus torquatus*); 44. New Britain Rail (*Gallirallus insignis*); 45. Buff-banded Rail (*Gallirallus philippensis*); 46. Guam Rail (*Gallirallus owstoni*); 47. Roviana Rail (*Gallirallus rovianae*); 48. Slaty-breasted Rail (*Gallirallus striatus*).

2-4 eggs (1-6), laid 2+ days apart; incubation 26-28 days, usually by female during day, male at night; hatching asynchronous; downy chicks brown-black with black bill, brown iris and dark purple to pink-grey legs; chicks leave the nest after 2-3 days; feathered at 4 weeks; fed and cared for by parents for 40-108 days. Co-operative breeding occasional, chicks being fed either by extra adult or (captivity) by young of previous broods. Age of first breeding 1 year but can breed in first year. May rear up to 4 broods per year.

Movements. Although sedentary and flightless, can move for significant distances. Normally confined to territory all year; may walk up to 1 km away to good feeding areas. Most subadults disperse up to 6 months after independence, set up their own core areas and either stay at one site, or move between core areas, until they establish territory or die; dispersal distance may exceed 9 km; subadults can walk 4+ km/day and on islands may swim or wade at low tide. Greatest natural movements 9 km (subadult) and 35 km (adult male), both involving crossing major rivers or lakes. Mass migrations, associated with disappearance of many populations in North I, reported from 1890 to 1930's; reasons for these movements unknown. Rapid increases in populations recorded, one in South I due to movement associated with plagues of mice; others also possibly due to short-term changes in food supply. Seasonal altitudinal movement, and movement from forest to open ground in summer, also recorded. Sudden disappearances may be due to disease. Homing ability well documented; longest returns include 130 km, and 72 km in 6 weeks.

Status and Conservation. Not globally threatened. Currently considered near-threatened. Race *hectori* CITES II. Formerly occurred throughout North I and much of South I, D'Urville I and Stewart I, and some inshore islands. Current range greatly reduced and fragmented, but in some areas species is recolonizing previous range. Introduced to many offshore and outlying islands, sometimes unsuccessfully. Locally rare to common; population sizes can also fluctuate markedly, possibly due to variations in climate and food availability. Local irruptions occur and birds readily recolonize areas, but some attempts to re-establish species have been unsuccessful. Sometimes adversely affects native fauna (e.g. lizards and petrels) and flora on offshore islands to which it has been introduced, e.g. since 1960's has affected native vegetation and fauna, especially Fiordland Penguins (*Eudyptes pachyrhynchus*), on Taumaka I, where introduced early this century. In some places eradication has been undertaken, though need for this on some islands is disputed. Formerly hunted extensively for food but currently protected in most places; sometimes considered a pest because birds pull up seedling crops, kill poultry and eat eggs, but they also eat pest insects. Poisoned bait for mammals has reduced populations locally, while recolonization may be hindered by predators. Many killed on roads when populations are high.

Bibliography. Beauchamp (1986, 1987a, 1987b, 1988), Beauchamp *et al.* (1993), Blackburn (1968), Brothers & Skira (1984), Bull *et al.* (1985), Carroll (1963a, 1963b, 1963c), Chambers (1989), Coleman *et al.* (1983), Cooper & Morrison (1984), Cooper *et al.* (1986), Fullagar *et al.* (1982), Guthrie-Smith (1910, 1914), Lever (1987), Lindsay *et al.* (1959), Macmillan (1990), Marchant & Higgins (1993), Miskelly (1981, 1987), Moncrieff (1928), Pracy (1969), Robertson (1976), St. Clair & St. Clair (1992), Turbott (1967), Wilkinson (1927), Williams (1979).

40. New Caledonian Rail
Gallirallus lafresnayanus

French: Râle de Lafresnaye   **German**: Pelzralle   **Spanish**: Rascón de Nueva Caledonia
Other common names: New Caledonian Wood-rail

Taxonomy. *Gallirallus Lafresnayanus* J. Verreaux and Des Murs, 1860, New Caledonia.
Sometimes placed in genus *Tricholimnas*, or in *Rallus*. Monotypic.
Distribution. New Caledonia.

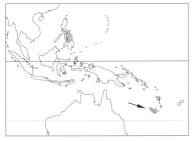

Descriptive notes. 45-48 cm. Although flightless, has fairly longish tail. Sexes alike but female somewhat smaller. Lacks rufous and dark barring on remiges which is noticeable character of the possibly closely allied *G. sylvestris*, and also of *G. australis*. Immature largely black, washed chocolate brown on upperparts apart from head, and slightly richer chocolate at sides of neck and breast. Juvenile undescribed. References to fluffy and decomposed plumage may refer to first-year birds which have retained some juvenile feathers. VOICE. Unknown.
Habitat. Dense humid forest, now probably only in relatively inaccessible areas, but formerly also in forested river valleys near coast.

Food and Feeding. Captive birds ate raw meat and vegetable matter, and caught rats. Diet thought to be similar to that of *G. sylvestris*, i.e. almost any invertebrate, and suggested to include worms and snails. Foraging methods possibly also similar to those of *G. sylvestris*. Said to be nocturnal (captivity) but possibly largely diurnal and crepuscular.
Breeding. No information available.
Movements. None.
Status and Conservation. CRITICALLY ENDANGERED. Until recently, thought to be extinct because had not been recorded by ornithologists during present century, last having been collected in 1890. However, occasional local reports this century suggest that species may still survive in relatively inaccessible areas of forest, albeit in very small numbers. Not found during a search of 3 areas of the island in 1976, but there was an unsubstantiated sighting from N New Caledonia in 1984. Species likely to be threatened by introduced species such as dogs, cats, rats, deer and especially pigs. Its habit of crouching when chased makes it vulnerable to dogs.
Bibliography. Collar & Andrew (1988), Collar *et al.* (1994), Delacour (1966), Fullagar *et al.* (1982), Greenway (1967), Hannecart (1988), Hannecart & Létocart (1983), Layard & Layard (1882), Olson (1973b), Ripley (1977), Stokes (1979), Vuilleumier & Gochfeld (1976), Warner (1947).

41. Lord Howe Rail
Gallirallus sylvestris

French: Râle sylvestre   **German**: Waldralle   **Spanish**: Rascón de la Lord Howe
Other common names: Woodhen

Taxonomy. *Ocydromus sylvestris* P. L. Sclater, 1869, Lord Howe Island.
Sometimes placed in *Tricholimnas* or *Rallus*. Includes *G. (Tricholimnas) conditicius*, known from one specimen and sometimes thought to be specifically distinct, but now generally regarded as an immature of present species (see page 111). Monotypic.
Distribution. Lord Howe I.

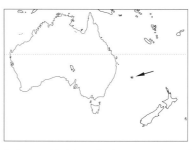

Descriptive notes. Male 34-42 cm, 410-780 (536) g, wingspan 49-52 cm; female 32-37 cm, 330-615 (456) g, wingspan 47-49 cm. Flightless, with short tail and rather long, downcurved bill. Sexes alike, female smaller. Predominantly plain olive brown bird, oldest individuals developing white cheeks and occasionally white nape; rufous and dark brown barring on remiges, a character shared by *G. australis* and *G. philippensis*, but lacking in *G. lafresnayanus*. Immature like adult, but pointed juvenile remiges retained; iris orange. Juvenile very similar to adult but upperparts slightly more reddish brown and underparts browner; bill initially shorter, grey-black becoming browner; remiges pointed; iris dark grey; legs and feet duller. VOICE. Advertising call a loud, repeated piercing whistle "coo-eet", often given in duet by pair, and often answered by neighbours; calls during day and occasionally at night. Alarm call a loud explosive "brr-deep". Contact call of adults and young deep drumming "booomp" notes, audible at close range.
Habitat. Subtropical forest. Before human settlement, probably occurred over most of island at low to high altitudes, but subsequently restricted to highest parts of mountains, up to 825 m, in gnarled moss-forest (not a preferred habitat) dominated by *Bubbia*, *Dracophyllum*, *Negria*, *Leptospermum* and palms, with understorey of tree-ferns (*Cyathea*) and litter-covered floor. Now re-established in some lowland forest areas, where inhabits closed megaphyllous broad sclerophyll forests, particularly stands of palm *Howea forsteriana* on igneous soils, and also *Ficus*, *Drypetes* and *Cryptocarya*. Occurs in forest bordering pasture and gardens, and such open areas may be included in territories. Rarely occurs in rain forest, the most widespread vegetation on the island, possibly because less food available near soil surface. Occurs on boulder-covered slopes, steep scree, in valleys, on plateaux, often near cliffs and sometimes near coast.
Food and Feeding. Mainly worms, crustaceans and insect larvae; also molluscs, myriapods, spiders and Hemiptera. Takes eggs and chicks of shearwaters, petrels and domestic fowl. Also eats lichens, fungi, pteridophytes, and flowers and fruits of vascular plants. Will eat meat, stew, butter, porridge, biscuits, bread, chocolate and rat poison. Forages on forest floor among leaf litter, palm leaves, rotten logs, moss and lichens, raking litter aside with bill but not using feet. Chisels wood; enlarges holes in soil with bill and probes to 10 cm deep; pulls aside large fallen palm leaves to glean underneath; probes rotten logs and moss. Also frequents areas inhabited or regularly visited by people. Obtains water from streams, pools and droplets on moss.
Breeding. Normally lays Aug-Jan; one lowland pair laid 11 times in 18 months, Jan 1982 to Jun 1983. Monogamous and permanently territorial; pair-bond normally permanent. Nest a shallow depression in ground, lined with dry grass, ferns, moss, palm fronds and leaves; 10-25 cm across and 7·5 cm deep; cavity depth 2·5 cm; nest well hidden in thick vegetation, under tree roots or log, or in petrel burrow; built by both sexes. Eggs 1-4 in captivity, laid at intervals of 24-36 hours; incubation 20-23 days, by both sexes; downy chick sooty black, with dark legs and iris; chicks fed and cared for by both parents; move from nest to nursery (brood nest) within 2 days of hatching; fully feathered at 28 days; almost fully grown at 65 days, when in heavy post-juvenile moult. Young of previous brood often feed and defend young of next brood and assist in territorial defence. Can pair and breed when 9 months old. Breeding success greater in lowlands than on Mt Gower, and greatest in Settlement area, where birds receive food and water from islanders.
Movements. Largely sedentary, but birds move from mountains to lower areas, such movements taking place at night, when most roadkills occur. Juveniles disperse from natal territories in Jun-Jul, when 3-5 months old, and then inhabit occupied or marginal territories, usually disappearing before next breeding season.
Status and Conservation. ENDANGERED. CITES I. When island first discovered in 1788, species was apparently widespread and common, particularly in lowlands, but in 1853, only 19 years after settlement, was restricted to mountainous regions and by 1930 occurred only in the summit regions of Mt Lidgbird and Mt Gower, where c. 30 birds (at most 10 breeding pairs) survived in 1980. Reason for virtual extinction was combination of habitat degradation by introduced pigs and goats, and predation by introduced cats, dogs, pigs and possibly people. Land clearance occurred over only small part of island, so unlikely to have had major effect. In 1980, 3 pairs were removed for captive breeding and over the next 4 years 85 captive-bred birds were released into the wild, where they have become re-established in some lowland areas; effective predator control measures were also introduced. Recent estimates suggest population of 170-200 birds, with 40-50 breeding pairs. Major current threat to population is predation by Masked Owl (*Tyto novaehollandiae castanops*), introduced in 1920's to control rats; efforts are being made to eliminate owls from the island. Rats not considered a problem, and rails sometimes kill them. Rail population small, vulnerable, largely derived from limited genetic pool, and may be limited by suitable habitat, so constant monitoring recommended. It is intended to set up a captive breeding colony to provide reservoir of birds to augment wild population if necessary.
Bibliography. Brouwer & Garnett (1990), Collar & Andrew (1988), Collar *et al.* (1994), Disney (1974a, 1974b, 1976), Disney & Fullagar (1984), Disney & Smithers (1972), Fullagar (1985), Fullagar & Disney (1975, 1981), Fullagar *et al.* (1982), Garnett (1993), Greenway (1952), Harden & Robertshaw (1987, 1988), Hindwood, K.A. (1940), King (1978/79), Lourie-Fraser (1982), Marchant & Higgins (1993), Mathews (1928), McKean & Hindwood (1965), Miller & Kingston (1980), Miller & Mullette (1985), Olson (1991), Peters & Griscom (1928), Recher & Clark (1974), Walters (1987).

42. Okinawa Rail
Gallirallus okinawae

French: Râle d'Okinawa   **German**: Okinawaralle   **Spanish**: Rascón de Okinawa

Taxonomy. *Rallus okinawae* Yamashina and Mano, 1981, near Mt Fuenchiji, Kunigami-Gun, north Okinawa.
Forms superspecies with *G. torquatus* and *G. insignis*. Monotypic.
Distribution. N Okinawa, Ryukyu Is.
Descriptive notes. 30 cm; 1 adult 433 g, 1 fully grown 435 g; wingspan 50 cm. Almost flightless; tail very short and decomposed; legs long and strong. Scarcely visible chestnut feathers are present on side of breast; some white barring on primaries. Most similar to races *sulcirostris* and *limarius* of larger, volant *G. torquatus*, but differs in having reduced white facial stripe, and reddish bill and legs. Flightless *G. insignis* larger, has different head pattern, black undertail-coverts, black bill and pink legs and feet. Immature like adult but has darker bill tip and culmen. Juvenile has paler, olive-tinged upperparts and head, mottled rather than barred underparts, brownish bill, brown iris and fleshy yellow-ochre legs and feet. VOICE. Highly vocal. Calls include "kwi kwi kwi ki-kwee ki-kwee", "ki-ki-ki", "kyip kyip kyip kyip", a rolling "kikirr krarr" followed by "kweee" notes on rising scale and

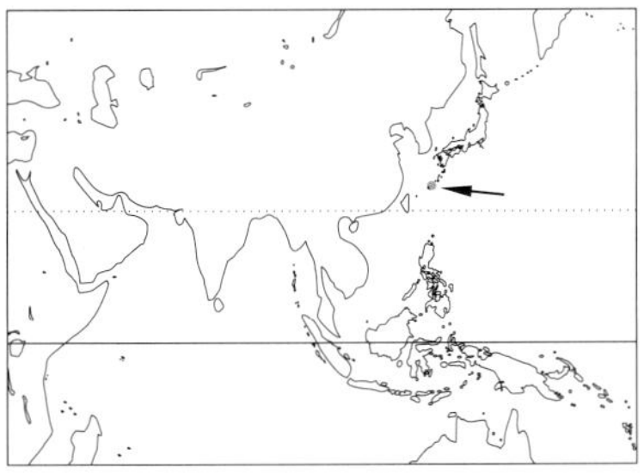

becoming almost pig-like squeals, a call rather reminiscent of neighing of horse, and deep bubbling. Normally calls only in early morning, late afternoon and evening, when voice carries further in calm conditions.

Habitat. Subtropical broadleaf evergreen forest with dense undergrowth and some water; occurs in primary and secondary forest, along forest edges and in small forest patches; also in scrub and around cultivated areas close to forest, where ground is damp or streams, pools or reservoirs occur. Found from sea-level up to highest hilltops at 498 m in mountainous areas. Requires standing water for bathing; roosts in trees.

Food and Feeding. Insects, particularly locusts, and lizards, taken on forest floor; possibly also takes some food from shallow water when visiting pools to bathe and drink.

Breeding. Lays May-Jul. Monogamous and territorial; pair-bond apparently permanent. Nest placed on ground. Eggs 2-3; incubation period unknown; downy chick black, bill white with blackish base and tip, iris black, legs and feet yellowish.

Movements. Sedentary, but in winter some may wander to reach areas just S of main distribution; ages of birds involved in these movements unknown.

Status and Conservation. ENDANGERED. Confined to largely uninhabited forests of N quarter (Yambaru) of Okinawa I, N from the Shioya to Higashi-son line; S Okinawa is highly developed and overcrowded. Species apparently reasonably common in its very small range, population estimated at c. 1800 birds; widespread wherever suitable habitat remains. Threatened by continuing deforestation: in recent years pace of development has increased in N, with building of golf courses, dams and public roads in hitherto continuous pristine forests, and its S distributional boundary is gradually moving N into the Itaji forest. Predators probably include domestic cats, dogs and indigenous snakes; cats are often observed along forest roads. Potential introduced predators include weasel (*Mustela itatsi*) and mongoose (*Herpestes edwardsi*), which are spreading into the rail's original habitat. Roosting in trees is probably adaptive in avoiding snake predation, but arboreal, nocturnal brown tree snake (*Boiga irregularis*), which has extirpated tree-roosting *G. owstoni* from Guam, has been observed on Okinawa and may have potential to establish itself.

Bibliography. Brazil (1984, 1985, 1991), Collar & Andrew (1988), Collar *et al.* (1994), Harato & Ozaki (1993), Ikenaga (1983), Ikenaga & Gima (1993), Kuroda (1993), Kuroda *et al.* (1984), Miyagi (1989), Ripley & Beehler (1985), Sonobe (1982), Thiede (1982), Vuilleumier *et al.* (1992), Yamashina & Mano (1981), Yanagisawa *et al.* (1994).

43. **Barred Rail**

Gallirallus torquatus

French: Râle à collier **German**: Zebraralle **Spanish**: Rascón Acollarado

Taxonomy. *Rallus torquatus* Linnaeus, 1766, Philippines.

Sometimes placed in *Rallus* or *Hypotaenidia*. Forms superspecies with *G. okinawae* and *G. insignis*. Five subspecies recognized.

Subspecies and Distribution.

G. t. torquatus (Linnaeus, 1766) - Philippines.

G. t. celebensis (Quoy & Gaimard, 1830) - Sulawesi and adjacent islands.

G. t. sulcirostris (Wallace, 1863) - Peleng (Banggai) and Sula Is, off EC Sulawesi.

G. t. kuehni (Rothschild, 1902) - Tukangbesi Is, SE of Sulawesi.

G. t. limarius (J. L. Peters, 1934) - Salawati I and N Irian Jaya.

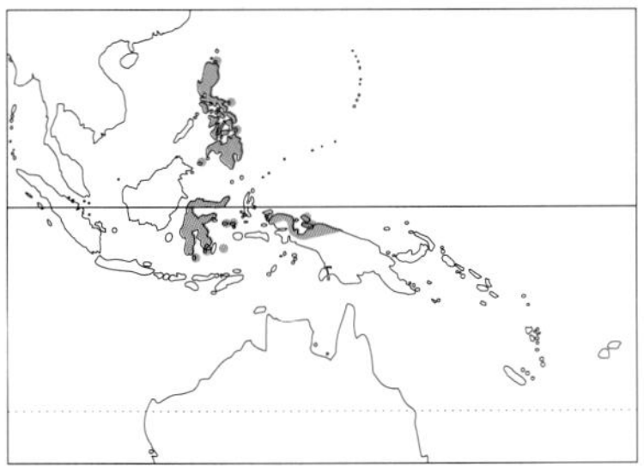

Descriptive notes. 33-35 cm; 1 female 241 g. Sexes alike; some white barring on inner webs of outer primaries. Easily separable from sympatric rallids on plumage. *G. insignis* and *G. okinawae* are almost flightless and differ in head pattern; *G. okinawae* has reddish bill and legs, and *G. insignis* black undertail-coverts and pink legs. Immature duller than adult; often washed buffy on underparts; throat whitish; in nominate race, breast band olive-brown and undertail-coverts reddish brown bordered with white. Juvenile not described. Races separated on plumage and size: *celebensis* lacks rufous breast band, and has variable proportions of black and barring on throat and upper breast; *sulcirostris* has deep rufous brown upperparts and an intensely black throat; *kuehni* largest, with dark upperparts; *limarius* has long bill. VOICE. Loud, very discordant, harsh croaking, often lasting several seconds.

Habitat. Occurs in open grassland, rice and maize fields, dry second growth and coastal swamps, and at edges of marshes. Often prefers areas where grassland, marshy spots and small groves of trees intermingle. Found in elephant grass; avoids closed forest and extensive crop fields; not restricted to sites with water but favours moist or wet areas. Occurs from sea-level up to 1000 m.

Food and Feeding. Food not recorded. Sometimes forages along roadsides.

Breeding. Luzon, Apr, Nov; Sulawesi, Dec. Nest not described; built on ground. Usually 3 eggs, sometimes 4; female known to incubate. No other information.

Movements. None recorded.

Status and Conservation. Not globally threatened. Very shy and retiring; no information on current status. Nominate race formerly common on Philippines; *celebensis* reported as common in N Sulawesi in 1980's; *limarius* formerly regarded as quite rare.

Bibliography. Andrew, P. (1992), Baltzer (1990), Beehler *et al.* (1986), Diamond (1991), Dickinson *et al.* (1991), DuPont (1971), Eck (1976a), Olson (1973b), Parkes (1971), Perennou *et al.* (1994), Rand & Gilliard (1967), Rand & Rabor (1960), Ripley & Beehler (1985), Rozendaal & Dekker (1989), Stresemann (1941), Watling (1983), White & Bruce (1986).

44. **New Britain Rail**

Gallirallus insignis

French: Râle de Nouvelle-Bretagne **German**: Bartralle **Spanish**: Rascón de Nueva Bretaña
Other common names: Bismarck/Pink-legged/Sclater's Rail

Taxonomy. *Rallus insignis* P. L. Sclater, 1880, Kahabadai, New Britain.

Sometimes placed in *Rallus*, or in monospecific *Habropteryx*, although affinities are clearly with *G. torquatus*. Forms superspecies with *G. okinawae* and *G. torquatus*. Monotypic.

Distribution. New Britain.

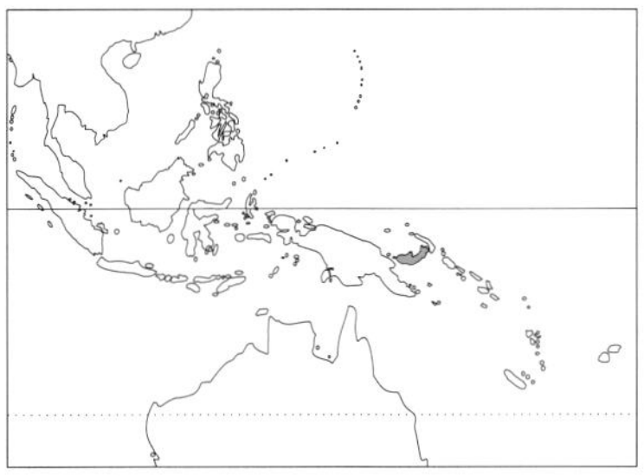

Descriptive notes. 33 cm. Probably almost flightless, although some reports that it may fly well; tail very short and decomposed; some white barring on inner webs of primaries. Sexes alike. *G. torquatus* and *G. okinawae* differ in having distinctive head pattern and barred undertail-coverts; *G. torquatus* is volant and has longer tail and brown legs; *G. okinawae* has reddish bill and legs. Immature and juvenile not described. VOICE. Loud, short calls, suggestive of dog or pig, uttered by day and night. Duetting birds call alternately to each other for several minutes. Groups reported to follow a leader, which regularly utters loud screams, often from elevated calling site, when followers utter low, nasal gulping notes.

Habitat. Heavy damp forests and mountain valleys; also swampy cane grass; wanders into gardens when foraging. Occurs from sea-level to at least 1130 m.

Food and Feeding. Snails, insects (including beetles) and vegetable matter.

Breeding. Social organization not known; commonly occurs in parties. Nests on the ground. No further information available.

Movements. None recorded.

Status and Conservation. Not globally threatened. No recent assessment of status but regarded as locally common in 1980's. Snared and eaten by local people. Extensive research required on ecology, biology and status.

Bibliography. Bishop (1983), Coates (1985), Diamond (1972a), Gilliard & LeCroy (1967), Mayr (1949), Meyer (1936), Schönwetter (1935).

45. **Buff-banded Rail**

Gallirallus philippensis

French: Râle tiklin **German**: Bindenralle **Spanish**: Rascón Filipino
Other common names: Banded/Land Rail, Banded Land-rail

Taxonomy. *Rallus philippensis* Linnaeus, 1766, Philippines.

Sometimes placed in *Rallus*. Forms superspecies with *G. owstoni*, and perhaps with *G. rovianae*; probably also with extinct *G. wakensis*, *G. pacificus*, *G. dieffenbachii* and *G. modestus*. Great geographical variation, with up to 26 subspecies recognized; validity of some racial distinctions, e.g. *tounelierie*, questionable in view of individual plumage variation, minor sexual size differences, and changes due to age and wear; possible race *wahgiensis* included in *reductus*; *randi*, *norfolkensis*, *australis* and some *yorki* in *mellori*; other *yorki* in *tounelierie*. Extinct form *dieffenbachii* sometimes included as race, but now generally considered specifically distinct. Race *macquariensis* of Macquarie I recently extinct. Twenty extant races currently recognized.

Subspecies and Distribution.

G. p. andrewsi (Mathews, 1911) - Cocos (Keeling) Is.

G. p. philippensis (Linnaeus, 1766) - Philippines; Sulawesi E to Buru; Sumba (race?), Alor, Sawu, Roti and Timor.

G. p. pelewensis (Mayr, 1933) - Palau Is.

G. p. xerophilus (van Bemmel & Hoogerwerf, 1941) - Gunungapi (Lesser Sundas).

G. p. wilkinsoni (Mathews, 1911) - Flores.

G. p. lacustris (Mayr, 1938) - N New Guinea.

G. p. reductus (Mayr, 1938) - C highlands and NE coastal New Guinea, including Long I.

G. p. anachoretae (Mayr, 1949) - Kaniet (Anchorite) Is, NW of Ninigo Is.

G. p. admiralitatis (Stresemann, 1929) - Admiralty Is.

G. p. praedo (Mayr, 1949) - Skoki (Admiralty Is).

G. p. lesouefi (Mathews, 1911) - New Hanover, Tabar and Tanga Is, and possibly New Ireland (Bismarck Archipelago).

G. p. meyeri (Hartert, 1930) - New Britain and Witu Is (Bismarck Archipelago).

G. p. christophori (Mayr, 1938) - Solomon Is.

G. p. mellori (Mathews, 1912) - S & SW New Guinea, Australia and Norfolk I.

G. p. assimilis (G. R. Gray, 1843) - New Zealand.

G. p. tounelierie Schodde & de Naurois, 1982 - Coral Sea islets, from SE New Guinea archipelagos and Great Barrier Reef E to Surprise group (off N New Caledonia).

G. p. swindellsi (Mathews, 1911) - New Caledonia and Loyalty Is.

G. p. sethsmithi (Mathews, 1911) - Vanuatu and Fiji.

G. p. ecaudatus (J. F. Miller, 1783) - Tonga.

G. p. goodsoni (Mathews, 1911) - Samoa and Niue I.

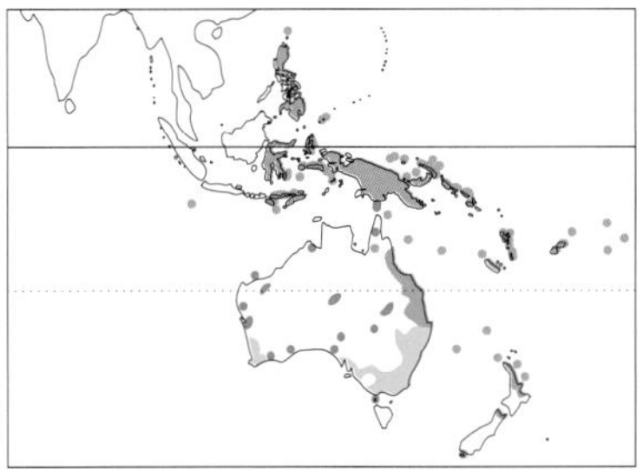

Descriptive notes. 25-33 cm; male 126-234 (185) g, female 115-265 (172) g, unsexed 130-303 (189) g; wingspan 40-52 cm. Tail relatively long; distinguished from congeners by combination of head pattern, variably spotted and barred upperparts and upperwing-coverts, rufous and blackish bars on all remiges except outer 2 which are barred black and white; white chin, grey throat, buff breast band (most races); barred underparts, including undertail-coverts; pink bill and pinkish grey legs. Sexes similar; female may be slightly smaller. Immature like adult but retains worn juvenile remiges; also has narrow or obscured nuchal collar but some adults may perhaps show this feature; iris probably yellow-brown. Juvenile duller than adult; head pattern less distinct and with little chestnut; throat mottled; smaller spots, usually olive-buff, on upperparts; breast band, if present, less distinct; underparts barred grey, not grey-black; bill grey-black; iris brown. Races separated on plumage pattern, including: extent of breast band, variable even within races; darkness of upperparts; extent of spotting on upperparts; pattern of uppertail-coverts, spotted, barred or plain; and pattern and extent of barring on underparts; also differ in lengths of wing, culmen and tarsus. VOICE. Repeated, squeaky, harsh "kreek" note, mostly heard in morning and evening, especially in breeding season; probably territorial. Also low-pitched growl, quiet repeated grunts (probably contact notes), and explosive hisses with deep growls when chicks threatened.

Habitat. Many types of wetland, including marshes, swamps, lakes, pans, rivers, streams, temporary inundations, estuaries, coastal lagoons, mangrove swamps, salt-marsh and tidal mudflats; also sewage ponds, farm dams and drainage channels. Occurs on beaches, reef flats, sandbanks and coral cays. Also found in wet to dry grass, bushed grassland, heathland, scrub, woodland, forest, and rocky and grassy uplands; in crops, pasture, gardens and parks, and on golf courses and airstrips. Favours dense, rank vegetation such as tall grass, rushes, reeds, etc.; also inhabits islands with little cover and no surface water, and may be flushed from petrel burrows. From sea-level up to 3600 m.
Food and Feeding. Worms, molluscs, crustaceans (including crabs), insects, spiders, small fish, frogs and tadpoles, eggs of birds and turtles, young of Sooty Tern (*Sterna fuscata*), fruits, seeds, young plants and other vegetable matter; also carrion from roadkills, chicken feed, bread and grain. Feeds at all times of day and night, but mostly crepuscular. Forages on ground; feeds at edges of reedbeds and other dense cover, among bushes and mangroves, and in pastures; scavenges along strandline; forages at rubbish dumps. Probes and pecks in mud and shallow water; captures prey by stabbing with slightly open bill; pecks at animals encrusting mangrove trunks; takes seeds from plants or ground. Pecks large snail shells until broken; spears eggs with bill. Once recorded hoarding food.
Breeding. Cocos (Keeling), Jan, May, Jun; Philippines, May, Nov; Lesser Sundas, Apr, Aug, but all year on Flores; Moluccas, Jul/Aug; New Guinea, mainly in rains but also in dry season; Australia, mainly Aug-Mar, but eggs and chicks recorded all months in tropics (N Queensland); Norfolk I, Dec; New Zealand, Sept-Dec, Mar; Vanuatu, mainly Oct-Mar; Samoa, chicks Jan, Mar-Apr, Jul-Sept, but breeds all year on Apia; Niue I, Jul; Tonga, Feb, Jul. Monogamous and territorial. Nest a cup of dry grass and stems, sometimes with interwoven dead rooted stems; or roughly woven platform of grass and rushes with depression on top; sometimes with flimsy canopy of growing vegetation; external diameter 10-23 cm; platform height 17 cm; internal cavity depth 2·5-6·5 cm. Placed on or above ground (sometimes above water) in long grass, marsh vegetation or crops (oats, lucerne); also in sheltered position under bush, tree, banana leaf, or in hollow; sometimes in tree or shrub, or on sand. Usually 4-8 eggs (2-8), with larger clutches (up to 12) probably from 2 females laying in same nest; eggs laid at daily intervals; incubation 18-19 days, by both parents; if nest disturbed, adult may carry eggs in bill to hastily constructed nest nearby; chicks leave nest soon after hatching; fed and cared for by both parents, possibly largely by female; black downy chicks have grey eyestripe or cheek patch, black legs and bill, and brown iris; feathers begin to appear at 5 days; attain adult weight at 3 weeks; evicted by parents when 5-9 weeks old; fly at 2 months, when post-juvenile moult begins. Age of first breeding probably 1 year. In Western Samoa, chick mortality high from feral cat predation. May breed up to 3 times (Australia) or 5 times (Western Samoa) per year.
Movements. Regarded as sedentary throughout much of range but is widely dispersive and possibly also migratory. No autumn or winter records in much of S Australia, but present all year in N with reduced reporting rate in winter. Some evidence for migration or dispersal on Cape York and across Torres Strait; movements also suggested between islands in Coral Sea. Recorded New Zealand all months except Jul, mostly in summer. May move in response to availability of water, e.g. from dry areas to areas of high rainfall. Flies at night; sometimes hits telegraph wires, street lights and lighthouses. Vagrant to Tasmania; ephemeral populations on Lord Howe I probably derived from vagrants; vagrant to Mauritius (no details).
Status and Conservation. Not globally threatened. Race *andrewsi* of Cocos (Keeling) Is regarded as Endangered, and now confined to North Keeling and West Is, with total population of c. 100 birds; extirpated elsewhere by cats, rats, habitat destruction and hunting. Locally common in Philippines and (less so than previously) Palau Is; locally common to abundant in New Guinea. Race *anachoretae* considered very scarce in 1970's, due to trapping by foreign labourers; current status unknown. Common to uncommon in Australia and New Zealand, but has declined markedly in New Zealand this century as a result of habitat destruction and predation; habitat loss caused by wetland drainage, and stock grazing and trampling, but may be offset locally to some extent by the birds' use of artificial wetlands and other man-created habitats. On some islands, populations reduced or eliminated (e.g. Macquarie and probably Solander) by introduced cats, rats and *G. australis*; these may prevent colonization on others. In Fiji, race *sethsmithi* probably extirpated from Vanua Levu and Viti Levu by introduced mongooses, but thriving on Taveuni I. Locally common in Western Samoa; very common on Niue I and in some Tonga islands.
Bibliography. Beehler *et al*. (1986), Blaber (1990), Blakers *et al*. (1984), Bravery (1970), Bregulla (1992), Bull *et al*. (1985), Chambers (1989), Coates (1985), Cooper *et al*. (1986), Crawford (1972), Diamond (1991), Dickinson *et al*. (1991), Draffan *et al*. (1983), Dunlop (1970), Elliott (1983, 1987, 1989), Garnett (1993), Gibbs (1996), Gill (1970), Guthrie-Smith (1925), Hindwood, K.A. (1940), MacGillivray (1917, 1928), Marchant & Higgins (1993), Mayr & Gilliard (1954), McKean *et al*. (1976), Parkes (1971), Reithmüller (1931), Rinke (1987), Robinson (1995), Rutgers & Norris (1970), Schodde & de Naurois (1982), Serventy (1959, 1985), Sharland (1981), Stokes (1983), Stokes *et al*. (1984), Stresemann (1941), Vestjens (1963, 1977), White & Bruce (1986).

46. Guam Rail
Gallirallus owstoni

French: Râle de Guam **German**: Guamralle **Spanish**: Rascón de Guam

Taxonomy. *Hypotaenidia owstoni* Rothschild, 1895, Guam.
Sometimes placed in *Hypotaenidia* or *Rallus*. Forms superspecies with *G. philippensis*, and perhaps with *G. rovianae*; probably also with extinct *G. wakensis*, *G. pacificus*, *G. dieffenbachii* and *G. modestus*. Monotypic.
Distribution. Guam (extinct in wild).
Recently introduced to nearby Rota I.

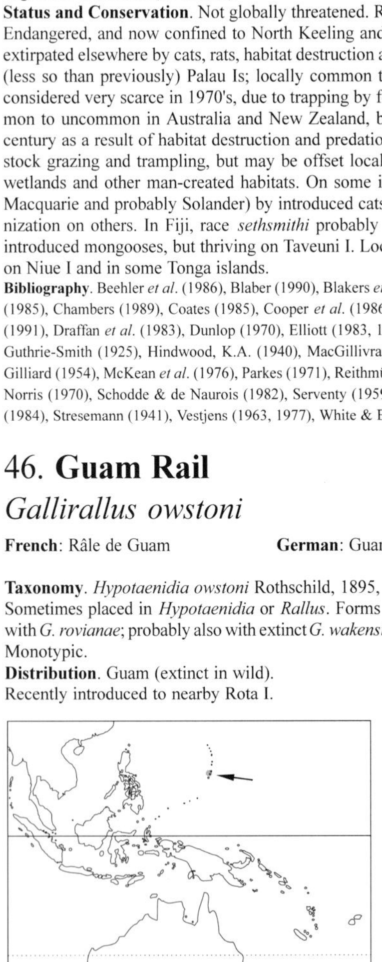

Descriptive notes. 28 cm; male 174-303 (241) g, female 170-274 (220) g. Virtually flightless; can fly for only 1-3 m; tail very short and decomposed; toes very short. In fresh plumage, has indistinct, dull olive-buff breast band which becomes abraded to leave breast clear grey; some individuals have pronounced reddish tinge on nape. Sexes alike but female smaller. Darker than *G. philippensis* and lacks chestnut on face, breast and usually nape; black and white barring on more remiges, decreasing from extensive, bold barring on outer primaries to narrow barring on secondaries as brown of feather centres becomes broader; uniform brown upperparts with no spots or bars; black bill with grey base. Duller underparts than *G. rovianae* and has different facial pattern and more extensive white wing markings. Juvenile similar to adult but with less extensive areas of grey on neck, breast and supercilium. Voice. During breeding season makes loud penetrating screeches "keee-yu"; also a series of short "kip" notes.
Habitat. Formerly occurred in most habitats on Guam, including forest, secondary grassland, mown grass, e.g. along roads and under telephone lines; scrub, mixed woodland and scrub, and fern thickets. Absent from interior of mature forest and wetland habitats.
Food and Feeding. Snails, slugs, insects (Orthoptera, Dermaptera and Lepidoptera), geckos and some vegetable matter; also fish, tomatoes, melon, palm leaves, and carrion, e.g. amphibians crushed by cars. Introduced giant African snail (*Achatina fulica*) became an important food when it expanded its range into most of the island's habitats. Takes food items from ground surface; chases low-flying insects, especially butterflies; takes seeds and flowers from low grasses and shrubs, stretching up to reach items 40 cm above ground. Often forages along field edges and roadsides, but seldom far from cover. Most active at dawn and dusk; also forages at night.
Breeding. Breeds throughout year, but possibly with peak period during rains, Jul-Nov. Monogamous and territorial. Nest located on dry ground in dense grass; a shallow cup of interwoven loose and rooted grass; built by both sexes. Eggs 3-4; incubation 19 days, by both sexes; hatching asynchronous; black downy chick has black bare parts; chicks leave nest within 24 hours of hatching; fed and cared for by both parents; chick begins to attain juvenile feathers during 4th week; reaches adult weight at 7 weeks; post-juvenile moult apparently complete at 16 weeks, when birds become sexually mature. Number of broods per year unknown.
Movements. None recorded.
Status and Conservation. EXTINCT IN THE WILD. In past, widely distributed and abundant, although taken by local people with dogs and snares, and despite presence of introduced predators such as feral pigs and cats. Before 1960's population was estimated as 10,000's; declined rapidly during 1970's, along with most other indigenous birds, as a result of the spread throughout the island of the introduced brown tree snake (*Boiga irregularis*); by 1981 population reduced to c. 2000 birds, by 1983 to less than 100, and species became extinct in the wild by 1987. In 1983 a captive breeding programme was set up, and c. 180 breeding birds are now located on Guam and in 16 zoos in USA. Captive breeding has been very successful, the founding birds showed surprisingly good genetic diversity, and efforts are being made to establish a self-sustaining experimental population on the snake-free island of Rota in S Northern Mariana Is; action also being taken to extirpate brown tree snake from Guam, so as to permit reintroduction there; birds released on Rota recently bred for first time (reported 1996), and further introductions planned in order to bolster population on Rota.
Bibliography. Aguon (1983), Baker (1951), Beck (1988), Beck & Savidge (1990), Carpenter & Stafford (1970), Collar & Andrew (1988), Collar *et al*. (1994), Derrickson (1996), Diamond (1991), Engrbring & Pratt (1985), Haig *et al*. (1990, 1993), Hay (1986), Jenkins (1979, 1983), King (1978/79), Lint (1968), Pérez (1968), Pratt *et al*. (1979, 1987), Savidge (1987), Strophlet (1946), Witteman & Beck (1991), Witteman *et al*. (1991).

47. Roviana Rail
Gallirallus rovianae

French: Râle roviana **German**: Rovianaralle **Spanish**: Rascón de Roviana

Taxonomy. *Gallirallus rovianae* Diamond, 1991, near Munda, New Georgia, Solomon Islands. May form part of *G. philippensis* superspecies. Birds from Kolombangara recently suggested to be subspecifically distinct. Monotypic.
Distribution. C Solomon Is, on New Georgia, Kolombangara, Wana Wana, Kohinggo and Rendova.

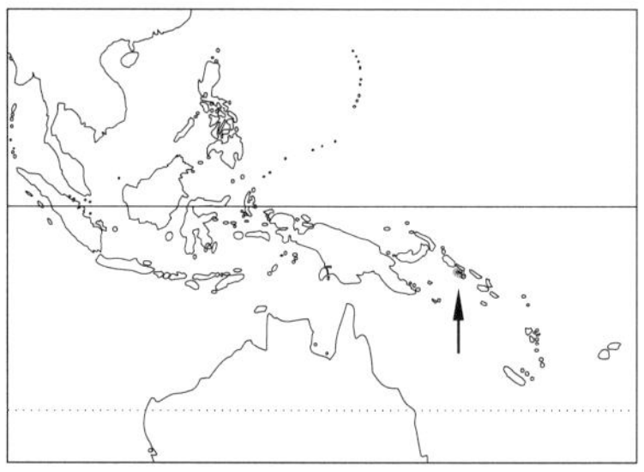

Descriptive notes. 30 cm. Known only from the holotype, sex and age unknown, but apparently fully grown. Medium-sized rail, flightless or nearly so, but with long tail; unmarked upperparts almost uniform dark chestnut brown, showing slightly richer colour on nape which continues into richer, more reddish chestnut mask through eye; wing barring restricted to small white spots on primary coverts; colours of bare parts in life not known (for purposes of plate, predicted from closest relatives). Closest in plumage to *G. philippensis* and *G. owstoni*, but appears less boldly patterned than former and has longer tarsus; underpart barring brown, not black; also has reduced barring on wings. Birds recently observed on Kolombangara reported to be generally darker and to lack breast band. Voice. Call said to be rapidly repeated high-pitched note, which has given rise to its Roviana name "Kitikete".
Habitat. Described as occurring in forest, especially second growth, where young trees grow on abandoned garden sites; also recorded in open ground on grassy airstrip.
Food and Feeding. Said to be omnivorous, taking worms, small crabs, seeds, coconut shoots, and potatoes and taro from gardens.
Breeding. Reported to breed in dry season, Jun, when rainwater is not a problem on forest floor. Nest said to be depression in the ground, lined with debris. Reported 2-3 eggs. No further information available.
Movements. None.
Status and Conservation. Not globally threatened. Currently considered near-threatened. Listed distribution mainly based on reports by local people on the islands concerned; in 1994 sighted on Kolombangara, where reported to be common. May also occur on nearby islands of Vangunu and Tetipari, where it has not yet been sought. Apparently does not occur on the other major islands near New Georgia (Vella Lavella, Ranongga, Simbo, Gizo and Nggatokai), as local inhabitants do not know it. Seems to be widespread on New Georgia; current status elsewhere not known, but its extremely restricted distribution gives cause for concern.
Bibliography. Collar *et al*. (1994), Diamond (1991), Gibbs (1996).

48. Slaty-breasted Rail
Gallirallus striatus

French: Râle strié **German**: Graubrustralle **Spanish**: Rascón Rufigrís
Other common names: Blue-breasted Banded Rail

Taxonomy. *Rallus striatus* Linnaeus, 1766, Manila, Philippines.
Sometimes placed in *Rallus* or *Hypotaenidia*. Seven subspecies recognized.
Subspecies and Distribution.
G. s. albiventer (Swainson, 1838) - India and Sri Lanka to SC China (SE Yunnan) and Thailand; some may winter in S Thailand and Malaysia.
G. s. obscurior (Hume, 1874) - Andaman and Nicobar Is.
G. s. jouyi (Stejneger, 1886) - SE China and Hainan.

G. s. taiwanus (Yamashina, 1932) - Taiwan.

G. s. gularis (Horsfield, 1821) - Vietnam and Cambodia through Malaysia to Sumatra, Java and S Borneo.

G. s. striatus (Linnaeus, 1766) - Philippines, Sulu Is, N Borneo and also Sulawesi, where may not be resident.

G. s. paratermus (Oberholser, 1924) - Samar I, EC Philippines.

Descriptive notes. 25-30 cm; adult 100-142 g. Flight often described as weak. Distinctive medium-sized rail, easily distinguished from sympatric rallids by combination of chestnut crown and nape, blue-grey breast, narrow white bars and spots on upperparts and wings, white-barred underparts, and fairly long, reddish bill. Female duller on upperparts, and more whitish on belly. Immature like adult but white barring less distinct; upperparts, including crown and hindneck, indistinctly streaked darker; breast more brownish; underparts paler. Juvenile imperfectly described: probably less patterned than immature, with white bars on upperparts largely absent. Races separated on: size, *jouyi* largest; and overall colour, with nominate *obscurior* and *paratermus* darkest, *gularis* and *taiwanus* palest. VOICE. Said to call infrequently. Has sharp whistle, repeated sharp "kerrek", and noisy "ka-ka-ka". Race *obscurior* utters deep croak, apparently reminiscent of sympatric *Rallina canningi*.

Habitat. Wetlands of many types, including marshy meadows, reedmarsh, paddy fields, and mangroves. Also occurs in *Imperator* grassland and dry rice fields, in gardens and damp areas near villages, drainage ditches; dry scrub and bush near country roads (Sumatra), and forest (Andamans). Recorded most commonly up to 1000 m, but also up to 1500 m and rarely (Sri Lanka) to 1850 m.

Food and Feeding. Worms, molluscs, crustaceans, insects (including ants) and their larvae, spiders, and the seeds and shoots of marsh plants. Takes much food from surface of ground, but also takes seeds and insects from vegetation by jumping up, or by perching on plants. Probes soft soil with bill for earthworms and insect larvae; picks up and sweeps aside fallen leaves and grasses; does not scratch with feet. Observed feeding along edges of tidal water and paddy fields, in the latter instance apparently taking aquatic insects. Swims and dives well.

Breeding. India and Sri Lanka, Jun-Oct; Sumatra, Jun, Dec; Java, Jan-Jul and Sept-Nov, but most in Mar-May; Philippines, Aug-Sept. Monogamous. Nest well concealed in thick vegetation at marsh edge, or in forest (Andamans); a pad of matted weeds, reed stems and grass, c. 25 cm in diameter, built on the ground or on dead reed debris; both sexes build, predominantly the male. Eggs 5-9, in captivity laid at daily or more frequent intervals; incubation 19-22 days, by both sexes, predominantly by female; black downy chicks have blackish bill, grey iris and dark brown legs and feet; leave nest soon after hatching; fed and cared for by both parents.

Movements. Normally regarded as resident and no regular movements recorded, but it is speculated that some winter birds in S Thailand and Peninsular Malaysia may be migrant *albiventer*; species may be merely migrant to Sulawesi. In India moves locally under stress of drought or flood; in Philippines considerable post-breeding dispersal occurs. Records from Bali, Sawu and Timor may refer to vagrants.

Status and Conservation. Not globally threatened. Little recent information available: *striatus* apparently uncommon, but very secretive, in Philippines. Formerly, *albiventer* widespread and quite common in India and Sri Lanka; *obscurior* probably common in Andamans and Nicobars; *gularis* uncommon in South Vietnam, but common in Peninsular Malaysia, Sumatra, Java and Borneo; *taiwanus* apparently fairly common; *paratermus* known only from type locality on Samar; no information available for race *jouyi*.

Bibliography. Ali & Ripley (1980), Butler (1899), Deignan (1945), Delacour (1947), Dickinson *et al.* (1991), Étchécopar & Hüe (1978), Hellebrekkers & Hoogerwerf (1967), Hoogerwerf (1949), King *et al.* (1975), Lekagul & Round (1991), MacKinnon & Phillipps (1993), Madoc (1976), McClure (1974), van Marle & Voous (1988), Medway & Wells (1976), Neelakantan (1991), Perennou *et al.* (1994), Phillips (1978), Rabor (1977), Rensch (1931), Smythies (1981, 1986), Stresemann (1941), Timmis (1974), White & Bruce (1986), Wildash (1968).

PLATE 13

inches   8
cm   20

ssp *saturatus*

olive morph

ssp *obsoletus*

brown morph

ssp *longirostris*

49

49

ssp *levipes*

ssp *scotti*

dark morph

ssp *elegans*

50

ssp *tenuirostris*

51

pale morph

52

53

54

ssp *semiplumbeus*

ssp *peruvianus*

55

57

ssp *indicus*

56

ssp *aquaticus*

ssp *insulsus*

59

58

60

ssp *exsul*

ssp *pectoralis*

Genus *RALLUS* Linnaeus, 1758

49. **Clapper Rail**

Rallus longirostris

French: Râle gris **German**: Klapperralle **Spanish**: Rascón Piquilargo

Taxonomy. *Rallus longirostris* Boddaert, 1783, Cayenne, French Guiana.
This largely saltwater and brackish water species is often considered conspecific with the largely freshwater-marsh *R. elegans*; provisionally treated as forming superspecies. Californian races *levipes*, *obsoletus* and *yumanensis* sometimes placed in *R. elegans*; race *tenuirostris* of *R. elegans* sometimes transferred to present species. Hybridization with *R. elegans* occurs occasionally in areas of sympatry, and mitochondrial DNA studies of the two species have yielded inconclusive results. Twenty-one subspecies currently recognized.
Subspecies and Distribution.
R. l. obsoletus Ridgway, 1874 - C California, mainly in San Francisco Bay.
R. l. levipes Bangs, 1899 - coastal C California to N Baja California.
R. l. yumanensis Dickey, 1923 - SE California, S Arizona and NW Mexico.
R. l. beldingi Ridgway, 1882 - S Baja California.
R. l. crepitans Gmelin, 1789 - coastal Connecticut S to NE North Carolina.
R. l. waynei Brewster, 1899 - coastal SE North Carolina to E Florida.
R. l. saturatus Ridgway, 1880 - Gulf coast from SW Alabama to extreme NE Mexico (Tamaulipas).
R. l. pallidus Nelson, 1905 - coastal Yucatán (SE Mexico).
R. l. grossi Paynter, 1950 - Quintana Roo (SE Mexico).
R. l. belizensis Oberholser, 1937 - Ycacos Lagoon, Belize.
R. l. scotti Sennett, 1888 - coastal Florida.
R. l. insularum W. S. Brooks, 1920 - Florida Keys.
R. l. coryi Maynard, 1887 - Bahamas.
R. l. leucophaeus Todd, 1913 - I of Pines (Cuba).
R. l. caribaeus Ridgway, 1880 - Cuba to Puerto Rico and Lesser Antilles E to Antigua, also Guadeloupe.
R. l. cypereti Taczanowski, 1877 - coasts from extreme SW Colombia (Nariño) through Ecuador to extreme NW Peru (Tumbes).
R. l. phelpsi Wetmore, 1941 - extreme NE Colombia and extreme NW Venezuela.
R. l. margaritae Zimmer & Phelps, 1944 - Margarita I (Venezuela).
R. l. pelodramus Oberholser, 1937 - Trinidad.
R. l. longirostris Boddaert, 1783 - coasts of Guyana, Surinam and French Guiana.
R. l. crassirostris Lawrence, 1871 - coastal Brazil from Amazon estuary to Santa Catarina.

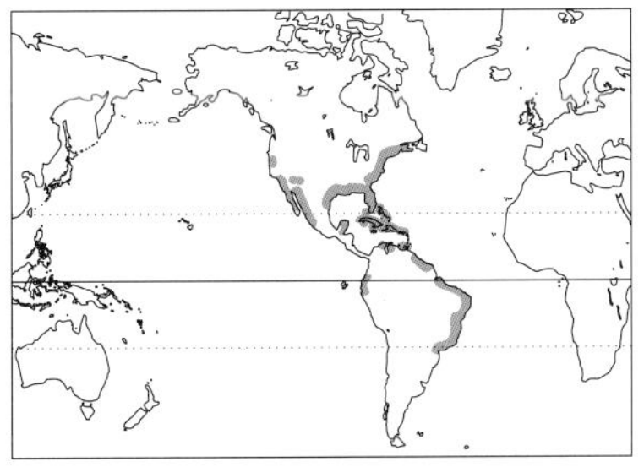

Descriptive notes. 31-40 cm; male 300-350 (322) g, female 248-301 (268) g. Large rail with long, slender, slightly decurved bill. Normally divided into two groups: *longirostris* group, comprising 4 races of W North and Central America, which resemble *R. elegans* in large size and brightness of feather fringes on upperparts; and *obsoletus* group containing all other races. Races *obsoletus*, *levipes* and *scotti* have two colour morphs: brown, in which upperpart feathers have dark brown to brown-black centres and buff-brown fringes; and olive, in which upperpart feathers have darker, blacker centres and duller, more olive, fringes. Race *ramsdeni* has at least two colour morphs, in which upperpart feathers margined with variety of olive-greys and browns. It is not clear to what extent these colour variations may be explained by age-related plumage differences. Sexes alike, but female smaller. Races sympatric with *R. elegans* differ from that species in having more grey on face, variably duller fringes to upperpart feathers, and duller neck, breast, upperwing-coverts and flank barring. Possibility of hybrids is potential complication. Markedly larger than sympatric *R. limicola*, which is darker overall with brighter rufous upperwing-coverts. Immature similar to adult but with duller bare parts. Juvenile darker (blackish in some races) on upperparts, with brownish feather edges; underparts duller cinnamon, mottled grey, belly more white and flank bars absent or indistinct; eye brown. Races separated on size, and on plumage, e.g. extent of grey on face, and general tone of upperpart and underpart colours. Voice. Very similar to that of *R. elegans*. Advertising call of both sexes ("clapper" call) a series of loud, rapid "kak" notes. Courtship call of male a series of harsh "kek" notes. Also has grunting call and very low "hoo" note; during breeding season female gives series of 1-5 "kek" notes followed by "burr".
Habitat. Salt and brackish marshes, particularly those with tidal sloughs; in California favours marshes with tall, dense cordgrass (*Spartina foliosa*) and *Salicornia*; mangrove swamps; also locally, mostly in lower Colorado River Valley (race *yumanensis*) in tropical and subtropical freshwater marshes with *Typha* and *Scirpus*.
Food and Feeding. Molluscs, leeches, crustaceans (including crayfish and many crabs), aquatic insects (especially dytiscid beetles), grasshoppers, spiders, small fish, frogs and tadpoles, and mice; also seeds (including rice), berries, green plant material and tubers of woody plants; water snake and adult Savanna Sparrow (*Passerculus sandwichensis*) recorded once. Feeds opportunistically on most readily available foods; eats more vegetable matter in winter. Apparently hunts by sight; probes exposed and shallowly flooded mud and sand; takes crabs from burrows by probing, sometimes inserting head and neck into burrow; gleans items from substrate; throws aside surface litter with bill and seizes small invertebrates hiding under it; catches fish while wading, swimming and sometimes diving; scavenges dead fish and forages at grassy edges of mangroves. Mostly forages on substrates adjacent to cover; most active at low tide, and during morning and early evening.
Breeding. USA, Mar-Jul, mostly Apr-Jun; Mexico, Mar; Trinidad, Apr-Dec, mostly May-Jun; Venezuela, Apr. Monogamous; pair-bond maintained only during breeding season, when birds territorial. Nest a platform or cup of rushes, sedges and marsh grass; or of sticks and dead leaves; built on ground in clump of vegetation, often in *Spartina* or *Juncus*, 60-120 cm tall; race *yumanensis* nests in *Typha* and *Scirpus*; situated on dry hummock, under low shrubs, or among mangrove roots; sometimes with base in water; often with canopy of dead or growing material; rim up to 45 cm above substrate; many have ramp from ground to rim. External diameter 18-35 cm; cavity diameter 12-15 cm, depth 1-6 cm; thickness 7-15 cm; height of nest mass up to 30 cm. Male most active in nest-building. Up to six brood nests (with no canopy) constructed near breeding nest; built of dead vegetation, these may float with rising tide. Eggs 3-14, laid daily; second broods smaller; replacement clutches may be only 4-6 eggs; incubation 18-29 days, by both sexes; hatching asynchronous; chicks semi-precocial; downy chicks jet black with greenish gloss on upperparts, dark brown eyes, grey legs, and white or pink bill with black base; leave nest as soon as hatched but use brood nests for first few days; feathers growing at 4 weeks; fed and cared for by both parents for 5-6 weeks; independent thereafter; fully feathered at 7-8 weeks; fly at 10 weeks, when wings fully grown; at 10+ weeks resemble adults except for dull bare parts. Nesting success 40-90% (usually high); egg success also high; initial losses usually followed by persistent renesting attempts; most failures due to flooding by extreme high tides, but on high ground predation is problem; Californian birds suffer heavy predation by rats (*Rattus norvegicus*). Normally 1 brood, but 2 recorded in most USA races.
Movements. In North America primarily resident, but northernmost populations partially migratory and some evidence from ringing and observation that birds in SE make movements, sometimes over long distances, which probably involve migration as well as dispersal and wandering. Movements appear to be overland as well as coastal. In North Carolina, in autumn large numbers have been forced down by heavy fog, and have been found dead under telephone wires. In winter, race *crepitans* ranges S to Florida, where occurs alongside at least 3 other races. W coast race *yumanensis* formerly thought to be migratory but radio telemetry studies indicate most birds resident, although some possibly winter on W coast of Mexico from Sonora to Nayarit. Casual wandering by birds of *obsoletus* group recorded on Pacific coast to Farallon Is, N to N California and S to S Baja California; by *longirostris* group on Atlantic coast N to New Brunswick, Prince Edward Island, Nova Scotia and Newfoundland, and inland to C Nebraska, C New York, Vermont, W Pennsylvania, West Virginia and C Virginia. South American populations sedentary.
Status and Conservation. Not globally threatened. In USA, 3 races considered Endangered. Race *levipes* has declined mainly because of habitat loss; less than 25% of its original habitats remain in USA, where population estimated at 190 pairs in 1990, with c. 240 pairs left in Mexico; severe threats posed by habitat destruction and modification, and by predators. About 85% of habitat of *obsoletus* has been dyked or destroyed; urban development poses continuing threat, together with pollution and introduced predators. Most of remaining population (c. 400 birds in 1991) occurs in San Francisco Bay, where development pressure greatest. Race *yumanensis* has experienced recent contractions and expansions of its freshwater and brackish water marsh habitats, and in 1992 population S to Colorado Delta estimated at c. 2000 birds; it is threatened by wetland loss and high water flows, being susceptible to effects of development projects along Colorado R. Recovery plans for these races include acquisition of habitat, habitat improvements, restoration of normal tidal flows, eliminating pollution, establishment of refuges, and captive breeding. All North American races vulnerable to habitat destruction and the effects of pesticides and contaminants, although species shows high tolerance to DDT and DDD. Species also hunted extensively in E and Gulf coastal states, where effects largely unknown; hunting pressure low in W coast areas where threatened races occur. Probably more widespread in Colombia than the few known localities suggest. Race *coryi* regarded as locally common in Bahamas (Cat I), as is nominate in French Guiana; current status of other races not known, but some were formerly considered locally common.
Bibliography. Abbott (1940), Adams & Quay (1958), Anderson & Ohmart (1985), Anon. (1983b, 1984, 1985a), Avise & Zink (1988), Bang (1968), Banks & Tomlinson (1974), Benito-Espinal & Hautcastel (1988), Bennett & Ohmart (1978), Bent (1926), Biaggi (1983), Blake (1977), Bledsoe (1988), Buden (1987), Conway *et al.* (1993), Crawford *et al.* (1983), Dickerman (1971), Eddleman & Conway (1994), Eddlemann *et al.* (1988), Ehrlich *et al.* (1992), ffrench (1973), Godfrey (1986), Harvey (1988), Harrison, C. (1978), Harrison, H.H. (1975), Harvey (1988), Haverschmidt (1968), Haverschmidt & Mees (1995), Hellmayr & Conover (1942), Hilty & Brown (1986), Hon *et al.* (1977), Howell & Webb (1995a), Johnson (1973), Jorgensen (1975), King (1978/79), Kozicky & Schmidt (1949), Lewis & Garrison (1983), Massey & Zembal (1987), Massey *et al.* (1984), Meanley (1965b), Meanley & Wetherbee (1962), Meyer de Schauensee & Phelps (1978), Ohmart & Tomlinson (1977), Paynter (1955), Remsen & Parker (1990), Root (1988), Roth *et al.* (1972), Sick (1985c, 1993), Smith, P.M. (1975), Snyder (1966), Speight (1981), Stewart (1954), Todd (1986), Tomlinson & Todd (1973), Tostain *et al.* (1992), van Velzen & Kreitzer (1975), Wilbur (1974b), Wilbur & Tomlinson (1976), Wilbur *et al.* (1979), Williams, S.O. (1989), Zembal & Fancher (1988), Zembal & Massey (1985, 1987), Zimmer & Phelps (1944).

50. **King Rail**

Rallus elegans

French: Râle élégant **German**: Königsralle **Spanish**: Rascón Elegante

Taxonomy. *Rallus elegans* Audubon, 1834, Charleston, South Carolina.
This largely freshwater-marsh bird is often considered conspecific with the largely saltwater-inhabiting *R. longirostris*; provisionally treated as forming superspecies. Race *tenuirostris* of C Mexico sometimes considered specifically distinct, or transferred to *R. longirostris*; Californian races of *R. longirostris* (*levipes*, *obsoletus*, *yumanensis*) sometimes placed in present species. Hybridization with *R. longirostris* occurs occasionally in areas of sympatry, and mitochondrial DNA studies of the two species have yielded inconclusive results. Three subspecies currently recognized.
Subspecies and Distribution.
R. e. elegans Audubon, 1834 - E Canada and NE USA; winters S to E Mexico.
R. e. tenuirostris Ridgway, 1874 - C Mexico.
R. e. ramsdeni Riley, 1913 - Cuba and I of Pines.
Descriptive notes. Race *elegans* 38-48 cm, male 340-490 (416) g, female 253-325 (306) g; *tenuirostris* 33-42 cm, male 271-331 g, female 220-268 g. Large rail with long, slender bill, slightly decurved near tip and usually orangish at base. Sexes alike, but female smaller. Polymorphic in nominate race: pale morph has upperpart feathers edged buff; dark morph with tawny olive feather edges. Much larger than *R. limicola*, which is blue-grey on side of head and duller overall, with brighter rufous upperwing-coverts. Differs from sympatric races of *R. longirostris* in having brighter fringes to upperpart feathers (not so evident in comparison with W & S USA populations of *R. longirostris*); little or no grey on face; richer and more chestnut upperwing-coverts; brighter cinnamon neck and breast; and bolder flank barring. Possibility of hybrids is potential complication. Immature similar to adult but duller, with light brown to yellowish bill. Juvenile duller and darker, largely fuscous-black on upperparts, with brown feather edges; pale cinnamon to buff or white on underparts with indistinct barring on sides and flanks; has yellow tongue and mouth lining (orange-red in adult). Races separated on size, nominate largest; also on plumage, *ramsdeni* resembling pale morph nominate, and *tenuirostris* less boldly

On following pages: 51. Plain-flanked Rail (*Rallus wetmorei*); 52. Virginia Rail (*Rallus limicola*); 53. Bogota Rail (*Rallus semiplumbeus*); 54. Austral Rail (*Rallus antarcticus*); 55. Water Rail (*Rallus aquaticus*); 56. African Rail (*Rallus caerulescens*); 57. Madagascar Rail (*Rallus madagascariensis*); 58. Brown-banded Rail (*Lewinia mirificus*); 59. Lewin's Rail (*Lewinia pectoralis*); 60. Auckland Rail (*Lewinia muelleri*).

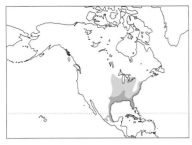

marked on upperparts and paler on underparts. VOICE. Very similar to that of *R. longirostris*. Breeding-season advertising call of both sexes a series of "cheup" or "chac" notes, slower and more regular than advertising call of *R. longirostris*. Courtship call, heard both day and night, is loud, harsh series of "kik" or "kuk" notes. Also has a soft, rapid "tuk" call, a deep boom (male only), a purring call (female) and a "rak-k-k" or "chur-ur-ur" distress call.

Habitat. Freshwater and locally brackish marshes; successional stages of marsh-shrub swamp, rice fields, flooded farmland, river margins, and upland fields near marshes. Occasionally in salt-marsh during migration. Preferred vegetation types include grasses (Poaceae), sedges (Cyperaceae), rushes (Juncaceae) and *Typha*; in coastal plain marshes, where present species most abundant, *Scirpus*, *Spartina*, *Zizaniopsis*, *Panicum*, *Cladium*, *Echinochloa* and *Polygonum* predominate. Occurs up to 2500 m in Mexico, where uses seasonal, as well as permanent, freshwater wetlands.

Food and Feeding. Principally crustaceans, especially crayfish and crabs; also molluscs, aquatic and terrestrial insects, spiders, fish, frogs, and seeds of aquatic plants. Mainly diurnal; forages within or close to cover; usually in aquatic habitats with shallow water, immersing part or all of bill; also, especially on autumn migration, forages in deep water, immersing head, neck and sometimes body; probes in mud; also feeds on dry land, picking food items from substrate.

Breeding. Lays Florida early Feb to mid-Jul; elsewhere in North America Mar/Apr to Jun/Aug; Mexico, May-Aug, possibly Apr-Sept. Monogamous and territorial. Nest-site usually over shallow water in marsh; also in roadside ditches, rice fields, swamps and upland fields. Nest a platform or cup of dead, dry grasses, sedges or rushes; at wet sites on base of wet decaying vegetation or flattened stems; usually with canopy of grass and entrance ramp. Outside diameter 20-28 cm, inside depth of cup 1·5 cm. Nest placed in grass clump or between tussocks, on ground or up to 45 cm (usually up to 30 cm) above highest water mark; may be raised as water rises after heavy rain. Male may be most active in building. Several brood nests constructed near breeding nest. Usually 10-12 eggs (3-15), laid at daily intervals; late clutches contain fewer eggs; incubation 21-24 days, by both sexes; chicks precocial; black down of chicks has faint greenish sheen, bill grey-black on basal half, white around nostrils and flesh-coloured on distal half; leave nest soon after hatching; fed and cared for by both parents; juvenile plumage evident at 4 weeks; young fly at 9-10 weeks, when post-juvenile moult is under way; independent at 6-10 weeks; post-juvenile moult apparently complete by Nov. Nest success usually high. Age of first breeding 1 year. May rear 2 broods per season in S USA.

Movements. Winters primarily from S Georgia, Florida and S Texas to Mexico and Cuba; occurs casually in winter throughout most of breeding range; temperature important in determining winter distribution, and species avoids areas where marshes freeze. Spring arrivals noted Apr-May. Migrates alone and at night; strikes buildings, telephone lines, etc., and appears in cities during migration. In Mexico, occupation of seasonal wetlands indicative of local movements and dispersal. Casual or accidental Newfoundland, Prince Edward Island, Maine, E Colorado and Dry Tortugas Is (Florida).

Status and Conservation. Not globally threatened. Listed as vulnerable in Canada (1985); in USA listed as endangered in 6 states, and threatened or of special concern in 6 others. Severe declines evident in N part of range since 1940's, mainly as result of loss, modification and degradation of wetland habitats, and pesticide use. Populations in S USA appear more stable. Birds often killed in muskrat (*Ondatra zibethicus*) traps, and are frequent road casualties when forced to move during floods in breeding season. Best chance for long-term survival in North America is considered to be offered by wildlife refuges, where a complex of habitats should be encouraged, including tussocky, shallowly flooded, densely vegetated sites for cover and nesting, and drying patches for brood foraging. Race *tenuirostris* has limited range, confined to freshwater marshes of C Mexico; its habitats are under threat from increasing agricultural, industrial and urban development. Current status of race *ramsdeni* not clear.

Bibliography. Andrews (1973), Avise & Zink (1988), Baird (1974), Bang (1968), Bent (1926), Bledsoe (1988), Dempsey (1991), Dickerman (1971), Eddleman *et al.* (1988), Ehrlich *et al.* (1992), Godfrey (1986), Harrison, C. (1978), Harrison, H.H. (1975), Howell & Webb (1995a), Meanley (1953, 1956, 1957, 1965b, 1969, 1992), Meanley & Meanley (1958), Meanley & Wetherbee (1962), Regan (1994), Reid (1989), Reid *et al.* (1994), Risen (1992), Root (1988), Speight (1981), Warner & Dickerman (1959).

51. Plain-flanked Rail
Rallus wetmorei

French: Râle de Wetmore   **German**: Wetmoreralle   **Spanish**: Rascón de Wetmore
Other common names: Wetmore's Rail

Taxonomy. *Rallus wetmorei* Zimmer and Phelps, 1944, La Ciénaga, Aragua, Venezuela.
Suggested to be conspecific with *R. longirostris*, but ranges overlap. Monotypic.
Distribution. Coastal N Venezuela.

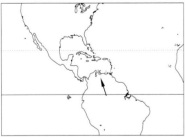

Descriptive notes. 24-27 cm. Possibly flies poorly: remiges and rectrices appear soft. Sexes alike. Similar to sympatric *R. longirostris phelpsi*, but smaller; lacks grey on side of head and has plain brown underparts, lacking all barring; bill brown, iris reddish brown. These features also serve to distinguish it from allopatric *R. limicola*, which also differs in being smaller and having rufous upperwing-coverts, dusky and red bill, and red iris. Immature and juvenile undescribed. VOICE. Undescribed.

Habitat. Coastal mangroves, "mangrove swamp", and shallow saltwater or brackish lagoons and marshes with emergent vegetation.

Food and Feeding. Nothing recorded; presumably similar to *R. longirostris*.
Breeding. Breeding condition: female, Apr; male, May. A Sept specimen is apparently a juvenile. Nothing else known.
Movements. Apparently sedentary.
Status and Conservation. ENDANGERED. Extremely rare and very poorly known. Restricted to coast of N Venezuela, where known from at most 8 localities in 3 states: near Chichiriviche (unconfirmed sighting), Cuare Wildlife Refuge and Tucacas in E Falcón; Puerto Cabello, Borburata and Patanemo in N Carabobo; and La Ciénaga and Playa de Cata in Aragua. Not recorded in Carabobo State since 1945, and only recent records are from Playa de Cata in Apr 1991, and from Chichiriviche

and Cuare Wildlife Refuge (both possibly referring to same bird) in 1980's. Probably at least locally common when discovered, 11 specimens being collected at Tucacas in May 1951, and 9 at Puerto Cabello in Sept 1945. Since these localities are easily accessible, it is likely that the paucity of subsequent records indicates a considerable population decline. Its mangrove habitats are being destroyed by housing development and by expanding oil exploration. Cuare Wildlife Refuge threatened by squatters, hotels, tourist pressure, illegal hunting, pollution and restriction of water flow from the sea; Playa de Cata lagoon has been closed off from the sea by a dyke.

Bibliography. Blake (1977), Collar & Andrew (1988), Collar, Crosby & Stattersfield (1994), Collar, Gonzaga *et al.* (1992), Hellmayr & Conover (1942), Meyer de Schauensee (1982), Meyer de Schauensee & Phelps (1978), Mountfort (1988), Ripley (1977), Scott & Carbonell (1986), Wege & Long (1995), Zimmer & Phelps (1944).

52. Virginia Rail
Rallus limicola

French: Râle de Virginie   **German**: Virginiaralle   **Spanish**: Rascón de Virginia

Taxonomy. *Rallus limicola* Vieillot, 1819, Pennsylvania.
Forms superspecies with *R. semiplumbeus* and *R. antarcticus*; latter sometimes considered a race of present species. Three subspecies recognized.
Subspecies and Distribution.
R. l. limicola Vieillot, 1819 - S Canada and W, C & NE USA; winters from SW Canada and E Great Lakes through S USA and Mexico to Guatemala.
R. l. friedmanni Dickermann, 1966 - volcanic belt of CS Mexico to extreme S Mexico to Guatemala.
R. l. aequatorialis Sharpe, 1894 - extreme SW Colombia, and Andes of Ecuador.
Birds from coastal Peru (Trujillo S to Pisco) are of an unnamed race.

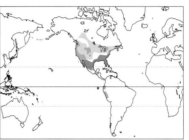

Descriptive notes. 20-25 cm; male 64-124 (94) g, female 67-80 (74) g. Sexes alike, female smaller. Much smaller than *R. longirostris* and *R. elegans*, with slightly decurved bill, extensive blue-grey on side of head, and duller upperparts with brighter rufous upperwing-coverts. Immature very similar to adult, but darker. Juvenile has sooty black upperparts with olive-brown feather edges; dull sepia-tinged upperwing-coverts; grey face, pale chin and throat, blackish underparts with white mottling, poorly defined flank barring and whitish centre to breast and belly; cinnamon-tipped undertail-coverts; grey-brown iris, blackish upper and brownish lower mandibles; dusky brown legs and feet; juvenile *aequatorialis* has much less white mottling on underparts. Races separated on: overall appearance and size, *aequatorialis* duller and smaller; colour of upperparts, darkest in *limicola*; and underparts, palest in *friedmanni*. Peruvian birds smaller and more brightly coloured. VOICE. Territorial advertising call of male a series of loud, rapid "kid kid kidic kidic" sequences. Other calls include loud series of "kik" notes followed by "queeah", and a descending series of pig-like grunts.

Habitat. Freshwater marshes with stands of robust emergent vegetation, e.g. rushes, sedges, *Typha* and tall grasses; wet meadows and irrigated hay fields; also brackish marshes and occasionally coastal salt-marshes; *páramo* bog in Andes. Prefers moist to shallowly flooded (under 15 cm) habitats with muddy, unstable foraging substrates. On migration uses areas of flooded annual grasses or forbs. In winter also found in moist coastal grasslands and brackish or saltwater marshes. Occurs in subtropical and temperate zones, from sea-level to 3660 m. In winter normally frequents regions warm enough to prevent marshes from freezing; presence in colder areas of USA in winter possibly results from use of wetlands artificially warmed by hot-water discharge from electricity-generating plants. Often occurs alongside *Porzana carolina* but prefers less deeply flooded to saturated sites.

Food and Feeding. Earthworms, molluscs, crayfish, amphipods, many insects (including Hymenoptera) and their larvae, small fish, frogs and small snakes; also variety of aquatic plants, including seeds of many marsh plants; more plant material eaten in autumn and winter. Feeds mainly by probing in mud and shallow water; also probes under matted or floating vegetation; will climb in pursuit of food. Forages primarily at dawn and dusk; usually remains in or next to cover but may feed in open at dusk.

Breeding. North America, Apr-Jul; Ecuador, chick/juvenile Aug. Monogamous; pair-bond maintained only during breeding season, when territorial. Female probably selects nest-site. Nest almost always in freshwater marsh or in rank vegetation near fresh water; platform or cup of coarse grass, reeds and *Typha*, well concealed in sedge tussocks, at base of *Typha* clumps or on piles of broken reeds or driftwood; sometimes over water; loose canopy of growing vegetation often constructed. Placed up to 60 cm above substrate, sometimes with entrance runway, or built up from substrate to height of 20 cm; external diameter 14-20 cm, height 7-8 cm; internal diameter 10-13 cm; depth of cup 1-6 cm. Both sexes build. Male builds 1-5 brood nests near breeding nest. Eggs 4-13 (mean 8·5), laid daily; incubation 18-20 days, by both sexes; all eggs hatch within 48 hours; chicks precocial; leave nest within 3-4 days of hatching; black downy chick has greenish gloss on back, black iris, brownish black legs and feet, and pink or buff bill with black band across middle; cared for by both parents; fed until 2-3 weeks old; feathers grow from 2nd week; independent at 3-4 weeks, flying at 4 weeks; full juvenile plumage attained at 6 weeks; post-juvenile moult begins at 12-14 weeks. Overall nesting success (North America) 53%; chick mortality probably high; predators of eggs and young include fish, frogs, snakes, birds and mammals; many nests lost to flooding in some areas. Both sexes can breed in first year. In USA may produce 2 broods per season, especially in S.

Movements. Most North American populations migratory. Migrants arrive on breeding grounds in USA Mar-May, most in Apr; arrivals possibly influenced by weather and vegetation development; males arrive first on breeding grounds. Departs Aug-Nov, timing possibly influenced by weather conditions; birds congregate at larger marshes prior to autumn migration. Wintering birds present in Mexico late Aug to Apr. Migrates at night, at low altitudes; sometimes strikes towers, telephone lines or wire fences. Casual or accidental to Bermuda, Cuba and Greenland; one sight record Puerto Rico.

Status and Conservation. Not globally threatened. In USA still locally common but has suffered considerable habitat reduction as wetlands have been lost to agriculture and to urban, industrial and reservoir development; palustrine and riverine wetlands are currently among the most threatened habitats in USA. In North America, populations declined 2·2% annually from 1982 to 1991, during a period when natural droughts also reduced availability of wetlands; total population now considered relatively stable. Winter habitat inland is possibly increased by hot-water discharge from power plants, and occurrence of species in other inland areas may be influenced by presence of wildlife refuges, some of which hold the densest winter populations. Legally hunted in 37 states and in Ontario, Canada, with liberal bag limits which may not be tenable, as causes of population declines not understood; current annual harvest probably within sustainable levels but harvest surveys needed. Preservation, restoration and proper management of inland freshwater wetlands are major priorities to safeguard habitats. Fairly common to uncommon but local in Mexico. Status in Colombia unclear. In Ecuador rare, local and probably declining; agriculture and siltation may have resulted in little habitat remaining in Andes. One of rarest sedentary waterbirds in Peru, where occurs in only a few of the remaining coastal marshes; these are under serious threat from drainage for agriculture and urban development, and from pollution and reed-cutting.

Bibliography. Andrews (1973), Baird (1974), Bang (1968), Bent (1926), Berger (1951), Billard (1948), Binford (1973), Blake (1977), Conway (1990, 1995), Conway & Eddleman (1994), Conway *et al*. (1994), Dickerman (1971), Eddleman *et al*. (1988), Fjeldså (1990), Fjeldså & Krabbe (1990), Glahn (1974), Godfrey (1986), Griese *et al*. (1980), Harrison (1978), Hellmayr & Conover (1942), Hilty & Brown (1986), Horak (1970), Howell & Webb (1995a), Irish (1974), Johnson & Dinsmore (1985, 1986a, 1986b), Kaufmann (1971, 1977, 1983, 1987b, 1988c, 1989), Loery (1993), Mousley (1937, 1940), Pospichal & Marshall (1954), Reynard (1974), Root (1988), Rundle & Fredrickson (1981), Sayre & Rundle (1984), Tanner & Hendrickson (1954), Walkinshaw (1937), Wiens (1966), Zimmerman (1984).

53. Bogota Rail
Rallus semiplumbeus

French: Râle de Bogota   **German**: Bogotáralle   **Spanish**: Rascón de Bogotá
Other common names: Peruvian Rail (*peruvianus*)

Taxonomy. *Rallus semiplumbeus* P. L. Sclater, 1856, Bogotá, Colombia.
Forms superspecies with *R. limicola* and *R. antarcticus*; sometimes considered conspecific with latter. Race *peruvianus*, known only from type specimen, might merit specific status. Two subspecies normally recognized.

Subspecies and Distribution.
R. s. semiplumbeus P. L. Sclater, 1856 - E Andes of Colombia.
R. s. peruvianus Taczanowski, 1886 - locality unknown: Peru?
Unconfirmed record from Ecuador (Laguna Kingora, Sigsig).

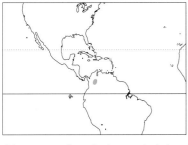

Descriptive notes. 25-30 cm. Sexes alike. Plumbeous grey head, breast and upper belly separate from structurally similar *R. limicola*; irregular white barring on flanks tinged brownish towards rear flanks; dull red bill and legs. Differs from much smaller *R. antarcticus* in olive brown feather edges to dorsal plumage and less regularly spaced and narrower white barring on flanks. Immature not described. Juvenile like adult but with slightly sooty feather tips on breast, and whitish throat. Race *peruvianus* probably less uniform; darker chestnut on upperwing-coverts; more extensive pale throat. VOICE. Variety of squeaks, grunts, and whistling and piping notes, usually starting low, growing in intensity, then wavering and trailing off rather abruptly. Also brief, rapid "tititititirr" when disturbed. Does not call at night.

Habitat. Restricted to the savanna and *páramo* marshes of temperate zone of E Andes of Colombia, characteristically occurring in dense, tall fringing reeds and rushes (e.g. *Scirpus, Typha, Juncus*, some *Cortadera*) and vegetation-rich shallows with *Elodea, Myriophyllum* and *Potamogeton*. Found in rushy fields, reedbeds, often with open, regenerating burned areas; reed-filled ditches and fens fringed with dwarf bamboo (*Swallenochloa*). May also tolerate modified habitats where floating mats of *Azolla, Ludwigia* and *Limnobium* replace emergent vegetation; avoids *Eichhornia crassies*. Once seen at a small roadside pool. Altitudinal range 2100-4000 m.

Food and Feeding. Primarily aquatic invertebrates and insect larvae, but also worms, molluscs, dead fish, frogs, tadpoles and plant material. Active from dawn to dusk; forages in areas with thin carpet of floating plants, at edges of reedbeds, on marshy shoreline, in flooded grass and marsh, and on patches of dead waterlogged vegetation.

Breeding. Dependent juveniles Jul-Aug; these and other observations suggest breeding Jul-Sept; also empty nest Oct. Apparently monogamous and territorial. No details of nest or eggs available; black downy chick has white upper mandible with central black bar, and black lower mandible; young cared for by both parents.

Movements. None recorded.

Status and Conservation. ENDANGERED. Uncommon to locally fairly common; restricted to departments of Cundinamarca and Boyaca in E Andes of Colombia, where healthy populations remain in a few areas, notably Laguna de Tota with c. 400 birds, Laguna de la Herrera with c. 50 territories, and Parque La Florida with 54 pairs. All major savanna wetland localities are seriously threatened, mainly from drainage but also from encroachment, agrochemicals and other pollution, tourism, hunting, burning, cattle trampling, cultivation, fluctuating water levels and water loss to irrigation. Throughout its range species has suffered enormous habitat loss caused by drainage, and few suitable characteristically vegetated marshes (with high plant productivity) remain because of pollution and siltation. Apparently able to survive in small patches of remaining habitat; breeding territories are 0·2-0·45 ha in area.

Bibliography. Blake (1959, 1977), Collar & Andrew (1988), Collar, Crosby & Stattersfield (1994), Collar, Gonzaga *et al*. (1992), Fjeldså (1990), Fjeldså & Krabbe (1990), Hellmayr & Conover (1942), Hilty (1985), Hilty & Brown (1986), King (1978/79), Lozano (1993), Meyer de Schauensee (1982), Ripley (1977), Varty *et al*. (1986), Wege & Long (1995).

54. Austral Rail
Rallus antarcticus

French: Râle austral   **German**: Magellanralle   **Spanish**: Rascón Pidén

Taxonomy. *Rallus Antarcticus* King, 1828, Straits of Magellan.
Sometimes regarded as conspecific with *R. limicola* or *R. semiplumbeus*, with both of which forms superspecies. Monotypic.

Distribution. C Chile and N Argentina patchily S to Tierra del Fuego.

Descriptive notes. 20 cm. In fresh plumage, breast and sides washed olive brown. Sexes alike. Similar to *R. semiplumbeus* but smaller, with sandy buff (not brown) edges to dorsal plumage, and broad, regularly spaced, black and white bars on flanks. Immature undescribed; juvenile like adult but with white throat and sooty grey feather tips on breast. VOICE. Undescribed.

Habitat. Wet fields, rushy parts of meadows, rushy lake shores and reedbeds, mostly adjacent to coast. In Chile, some birds spent winter months in garden of house, where they appeared very tame, before returning to adjacent dense reedbeds.

Food and Feeding. One stomach contained caddisflies (*Limnophilus meridionalis*, Trichoptera). Birds wintering in a garden fed on grubs found underneath decomposing leaves, and even ate left-over dog food. Diet probably similar to that of *R. limicola*.

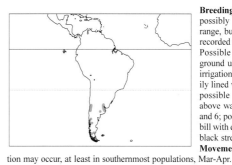

Breeding. Chile, Oct, possibly Nov; Argentina, possibly Nov; probably breeds throughout its range, but data lacking. Only definite nest was recorded from "C Chile", but locality not given. Possible nest of this species was placed on ground under thick bramble (*Rubus*) bordering irrigation canal; eggs were in depression scantily lined with grass stems and rushes; two other possible nests were in grass tussocks 20 cm above water in lagoon. Eggs 8, possibly also 4 and 6; possible chick of this species had whitish bill with distal half of upper mandible black, and black streak on lower mandible.

Movements. Northward post-breeding migration may occur, at least in southernmost populations, Mar-Apr.

Status and Conservation. CRITICALLY ENDANGERED. Known from up to 19 localities, with additional records from unspecified sites, but seems to have disappeared in course of last 100 years: only two specimens have been collected since 1901, and there have been no certain records since 1959 (when the last was collected) despite species occurring in a region where ornithological activity has not been insignificant. Possibly already rare at start of this century. Reasons for decline unclear, although overgrazing and disappearance of practically all the tall grass habitat in Patagonia has been suggested. Reported to be seen occasionally near El Bolsón, Río Negro (SC Argentina); when its calls become known, species may possibly be found with more certainty and regularity; immediate priority is to locate remaining populations.

Bibliography. Blake (1977), Canevari *et al*. (1991), Chebez (1994), Collar & Andrew (1988), Collar, Crosby & Stattersfield (1994), Collar, Gonzaga *et al*. (1992), Fjeldså (1990), Fjeldså & Krabbe (1990), Hartert & Venturi (1909), Hellmayr & Conover (1942), Humphrey *et al*. (1970), Johnson (1965b), Meyer de Schauensee (1982), Narosky & Yzurieta (1987), Navas (1962), Oates (1901), Olrog (1984), de la Peña (1992), Wege & Long (1995).

55. Water Rail
Rallus aquaticus

French: Râle d'eau   **German**: Wasserralle   **Spanish**: Rascón Europeo

Taxonomy. *Rallus aquaticus* Linnaeus, 1758, Great Britain.
Forms superspecies with *R. caerulescens* and *R. madagascariensis*. Four subspecies recognized.

Subspecies and Distribution.
R. a. hibernans Salomonsen, 1931 - Iceland.
R. a. aquaticus Linnaeus, 1758 - Europe, N Africa and W Asia to upper basin of R Ob'; winters S to N Africa and Turkmenistan.
R. a. korejewi Zarudny, 1905 - Aral Sea and L Balkhash S to Iran, Kashmir and WC China; winters patchily from Iraq to coastal E China.
R. a. indicus Blyth, 1849 - N Mongolia and E Siberia (upper R Yenisey and middle R Lena) to Manchuria, Korea, Sakhalin and N Japan; winters from E Bengal and Assam, Myanmar, N Thailand and N Laos E to SE China and Hainan, Taiwan and S Japan.

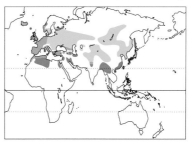

Descriptive notes. 25-28 cm; male 88-190 (128) g, female 74-138 (102) g; wingspan 38-45 cm. Female smaller, with shorter bill. In c. 60% of nominate birds, variable number of greater and median upperwing-coverts have white bars, black-bordered or on black feathers; white markings may also occur on alula, primary coverts and even remiges, while some have white speckles on mantle, back or rump; undertail-coverts usually appear white but may have variable amounts of buff, and sometimes show black barring; pattern has been used for individual recognition. Differs from all American congeners, except *R. wetmorei*, in lacking contrasting rufous or chestnut on upperwing-coverts. *R. caerulescens* of sub-Saharan Africa is larger, with unstreaked, deep vinous brown upperparts and brighter red legs and feet. Immature very like adult but duller, with whiter chin, small pale supraloral streak, olive brown patch on ear-coverts, olive brown tinge on breast, and duller legs and feet. Juvenile may have duller upperparts; grey of head and underparts replaced by buff or white with brown to black bars and feather tips; flanks buff with dark brown to black bars; undertail-coverts often appear entirely buff; bare parts dull. Races separated on plumage: *hibernans* and *korejewi* paler on underparts, and *korejewi* also on upperparts; *indicus* has brown streak through eye, whiter chin, brown tinge to breast and sides and more extensive wing barring. VOICE. Announcement call ("sharming") comprises grunting notes rising in middle of call to high-pitched, trilling whistles, likened to piglets squealing; pair members often call antiphonally in duet, male giving lower notes. Courtship-song rendered "tyick-tyick-tyick", often ending with trill "tyüirr"; also gives series of ticks followed by wheezy scream, and various groans, grunts, purrs and whistles. Calls usually given from cover; vocal by day throughout year; may call all night early in breeding season.

Habitat. Occupies almost any type of dense riparian and aquatic vegetation at still or slow-moving water; usually requires muddy ground for foraging; suitable habitat may form small pockets or narrow strips in other habitat types. Breeding habitat includes reedbeds and other emergent vegetation of swamps, marshes and fens, and at fringes of open water; also occurs on floating islands, rice paddies and lotus ponds; on Japanese offshore islands found amongst grasses and dwarf bamboo stands. Occurs at both fresh and saline lakes and marshes. On migration and in winter exploits wider range of habitats, such as farm sewage outfalls, island bracken, flooded thickets of blackberry (*Rubus*), gravel pits and other very small wetland patches; even, when displaced by frost, drainpipes, rubbish dumps, open ditches and gardens. In Iceland in winter largely dependent on marshy areas with warm water from volcanic springs. Vulnerable to extreme conditions, e.g. ice or severe floods. Mainly lowland, but resident up to 2000 m.

Food and Feeding. Worms, leeches, molluscs, shrimps, crayfish, spiders, many terrestrial and aquatic insects and their larvae (including Dermaptera, Odonata, Trichoptera, Hemiptera, Coleoptera, Diptera, Lepidoptera, Orthoptera), and small vertebrates (killed or as carrion) including amphibians, fish, birds and mammals. Plant foods include shoots, roots, seeds, berries and fruits; eats more plant material in autumn and winter. Forages on dry ground or mud near water; also wades in shallow water, taking items on and below surface, and from emergent vegetation; sometimes feeds while swimming, rarely by diving. Leaps up to take insects from vegetation; climbs in vegetation to take berries; flies into apple trees to remove fruit.

Breeding. W & C Europe, late Mar to Aug; Morocco and Algeria, May-Jun; Tunisia, Jun; Egypt, Apr-Jun; former USSR, May; Kashmir, Jun-Aug. Monogamous; highly territorial when breeding. Nest a substantial cup of dead leaves and plant stems; usually in thick vegetation of reeds or rushes on ground near or in water, rarely on tree stump or in open; surrounding vegetation often pulled down into loose canopy. External diameter 13-16 cm; height c. 7 cm; may be built up if water level rises. Both sexes build. Usually 6-11 eggs (5-16), laid at daily intervals; incubation 19-22 days, by both sexes; chicks precocial; black downy chick has visible patch of red skin on hind crown, white bill with black base and tip, grey to brown-black iris and grey-brown to blackish legs and feet; fed and cared for by both parents, apparently only until 20-30 days old; initially brooded and fed mainly in nest; begin to feed themselves at c. 5 days; fully independent and capable of flight at 7-8 weeks; post-juvenile moult starts soon after fledging (c. 10 weeks) and is usually finished by Jul-Oct. Age of first breeding 1 year. 2 broods normal; replacements laid after egg loss.
Movements. Nominate race both sedentary and migratory, birds from N of range moving S & SW to winter in Mediterranean basin, N Africa (extending far into Sahara, in Algeria and Libya) and E to S Caspian area. In Europe and Russia autumn migration begins Aug, peaks Sept-Oct, ends Dec; spring migration begins Feb, peaks Mar to mid-Apr and ends by May. Passes through Morocco Sept, Algeria Sept-Oct, Egypt Sept-Nov; occurs coastal Libya Oct-Apr and at Saharan sites Dec-Apr. Passage recorded Azerbaijan Sept-Nov and Mar-May. Scarce passage migrant in Oman, occasionally overwintering; occurs Aug-May. Has bred in Cyprus and wanders to Spitsbergen, Madeira, Canary Is and Azores. Race *hibernans* probably migrates to Faeroes in winter, occurs on passage at Scottish islands and in winter in Ireland, and wanders to Greenland and Jan Mayen. Race *korejewi* partly migratory and wanders to Sind and NW India, and to E Arabia. Race *indicus* largely migratory, occurring in winter S to Borneo (3 records, Brunei and Sarawak); occurs N Japan May-Oct and winters S Japan to Yaeyama Is Oct-Mar/Apr. Migrates at night, on broad fronts, and even crosses mountain systems such as Alps.
Status and Conservation. Not globally threatened. No evidence of significant changes in status of nominate race, which is regarded as locally common over much of range, including N Africa and Azerbaijan, although wetland habitat loss must have affected its numbers. Has benefited locally in UK from increased habitat provided by gravel pits and disused canals. Race *hibernans* is most numerous in S of Iceland; current status not clear but probably scarce in some areas. Current status of races *korejewi* and *indicus* unclear in many areas but formerly regarded as at least locally common; however *indicus* is uncommon throughout Japan. Range in Asia probably more extensive than is known.
Bibliography. Ali & Ripley (1980), Becker, P. (1995), Bengtson (1967), Boyd & Alley (1948), Brazil (1991), Cramp & Simmons (1980), Deignan (1945), Dementiev & Gladkov (1951b), Étchécopar & Hüe (1964, 1978), Evans (1994), Feindt (1968), Fjeldså (1977), Glutz von Blotzheim *et al.* (1973), Goodman *et al.* (1989), Heinroth & Heinroth (1928), Hüe & Étchécopar (1970), Jenkins & Meiklejohn (1960), King, B. (1980), King, B.F. *et al.* (1975), Knystautas (1993), Koenig (1943), Ledant *et al.* (1981), MacKinnon & Phillipps (1993), Mayaud (1982), Patrikeev (1995), Paz (1987), Perennou *et al.* (1994), Potapov & Flint (1987), Roberts, T.J. (1991), Rogacheva (1992), Rutgers & Norris (1970), Shirihai (1996), Sigmund (1959), Simeonov *et al.* (1990), Smythies (1986), Stiefel & Berg (1975), Urban *et al.* (1986), Witherby *et al.* (1941).

56. African Rail
Rallus caerulescens

French: Râle bleuâtre **German**: Kapralle **Spanish**: Rascón Cafre
Other common names: African Water/Cape/Kaffir Rail

Taxonomy. *Rallus cærulescens* Gmelin, 1789, Cape of Good Hope.
Forms superspecies with *R. aquaticus* and *R. madagascariensis*. Monotypic.
Distribution. Sub-Saharan Africa, principally from Ethiopia to E Zaire and Kenya and S to Cape of Good Hope. Status uncertain in W Africa; occurrence in NE Central African Republic and coastal Kenya requires confirmation.

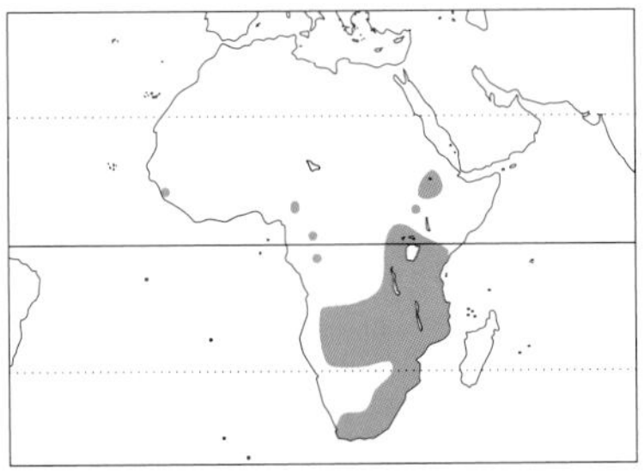

Descriptive notes. 27-28 cm; male 146-205 (180) g, female 120-170 (146) g. Unpatterned, deep vinous brown upperparts are unique character within genus. Sexes similar but female smaller; face to breast may be greyer, less slaty blue, with some pale markings; may have a little brown on sides of neck and breast and less regular barring on flanks. Larger than *R. aquaticus*, which has streaked upperparts; similar-sized *Rougetius rougetii* of Ethiopia has cinnamon-rufous underparts. Immature similar to adult but duller; chin and throat white; sides of neck and breast brown; flanks brownish black barred rufous buff to white; outer undertail-coverts tipped rufous buff; eye, bill, legs and feet brown, becoming redder with age. Juvenile has darker upperparts; face, sides of neck and breast dark brown; breast brown, mottled pale; flanks to undertail-coverts blackish brown, barred rufous; centre of breast and belly buff; eye brown; bill, legs and feet dark brown. Voice. Common territorial call, given by both sexes, often in duet or chorus, is loud high trill winding down into spaced single notes and falling in pitch and volume. Also wheezy "kreee" during territorial and aggressive encounters, shrill "ri-ri-ri" when fighting, loud rattle, deep "krock", and various growls, squeaks, short trills and clunking notes.
Habitat. Reedbeds and dense rank growth in permanent and temporary swamps and marshes, and beside lakes, pools, rivers and streams; sometimes on mature pans; tolerates brackish conditions; in breeding season moves out into seasonally inundated dense hygrophilous grassland and sedge meadow adjoining permanent cover, and occupies seasonally wet sugar cane adjacent to marshes. In W Africa also in paddy fields; in Sudan in thick secondary growth along rivers. Prefers shallowly flooded areas with mud and/or floating vegetation for foraging. Recorded from sea-level to 3000 m, but occurrence at low altitude and in coastal areas mainly confined to regions S of 20° S.
Food and Feeding. Worms, crabs, spiders, aquatic and terrestrial insects and their larvae, small fish and small frogs; also some vegetable matter, including seeds; occasionally carrion (crayfish, crabs, small mammals). Forages mainly on moist to shallowly flooded ground, sometimes on dry ground; probes mud, clumps of wet grass and mats of floating vegetation; while wading takes food from water surface and also by immersing head and neck; takes prey from low vegetation. Climbs readily in tall reedbed vegetation, sometimes probably to forage. Feeds both within and outside cover; most active in early morning and late afternoon.
Breeding. Ethiopia, Aug; SW Zaire, "dry season"; Kenya, May-Jun; Malawi, Feb-Mar; Zambia, Jan, breeding condition May; Zimbabwe, Jan-May; Mozambique, Jan; South Africa, Jul-Mar, in suitable habitat winter breeding possibly occurring more frequently than is known. Monogamous; strongly territorial when breeding. Nest is a shallow cup of aquatic plants (reeds, sedges, rushes); well concealed in aquatic vegetation, usually over water; external diameter 15-20 cm; depth 5-10 cm; depth of cup 2-5 cm; nest rim 10-40 cm above water. Both sexes build, and also construct brood platforms 20-50 cm above water. Eggs 2-6; incubation c. 20 days, by both sexes; chicks leave nest soon after hatching; black downy chicks have greyish eyes, slate legs and feet, and pink bill with black distal half; fed and cared for by both parents until 6-8 weeks old; body feathers appear at 2-3 weeks, remiges at 4-5 weeks; well feathered by 6-7 weeks; remiges fully grown at 8-9 weeks. Post-juvenile moult begins at 6-7 months; complete at 8-9 months. Age of first breeding 1 year. Not known to be multiple-brooded; will relay if clutch fails.
Movements. No evidence for regular migrations. Most seasonal variations in numbers explained by dispersal of immatures or by local movements to and from habitat rendered temporarily unsuitable by burning, drying out or reduction of cover. Possibly some seasonal movements in N Namibia and N Botswana. Known occurrence in W Africa is erratic: W Sierra Leone, May-Oct; Cameroon, Jan, Feb, Oct; NE Gabon, Oct-Nov; Congo, Feb. One came to lights at night, Tsavo West, SE Kenya, Dec 1985. Vagrant to São Tomé I (undated skin).
Status and Conservation. Not globally threatened. Regarded as widespread and locally common over much of main range, though undoubtedly under-recorded in many areas. Rare and erratic in W Africa; uncommon to rare in Ethiopian highlands and in S Sudan, where known only from Imatong Mts. Although its wetland habitats are continually being reduced, in South Africa species is under no immediate threat and is able to colonize relatively small, artificially created, wetland patches.
Bibliography. Benson & Benson (1975), Benson *et al.* (1971), Bocage (1877), Britton, P.L. (1980), Brosset & Érard (1986), Carroll, R.W. (1988), Chapin (1939), Clancey (1964b, 1971a), Dowsett & Dowsett-Lemaire (1989), Dowsett & Forbes-Watson (1993), Field (1995), Fotso (1990), Ginn *et al.* (1989), Hopkinson & Masterson (1984), Irwin (1981), Jackson & Sclater (1938), Lewis & Pomeroy (1989), Louette (1981), Mackworth-Praed & Grant (1957, 1962, 1970), Maclean (1993), Nikolaus (1987), Parrott (1979), Pinto (1983), Schmitt (1976), Sclater (1906), Shore-Baily (1929), Short *et al.* (1990), Skead, D.M. (1967), Snow (1978, 1979), Tarboton, Kemp & Kemp (1987), Taylor (1994), Urban *et al.* (1986).

57. Madagascar Rail
Rallus madagascariensis

French: Râle de Madagascar **German**: Madagaskarralle **Spanish**: Rascón Malgache

Taxonomy. *Rallus Madagascariensis* J. Verreaux, 1833, Madagascar.
Forms superspecies with *R. aquaticus* and *R. caerulescens*. Monotypic.
Distribution. E Madagascar.

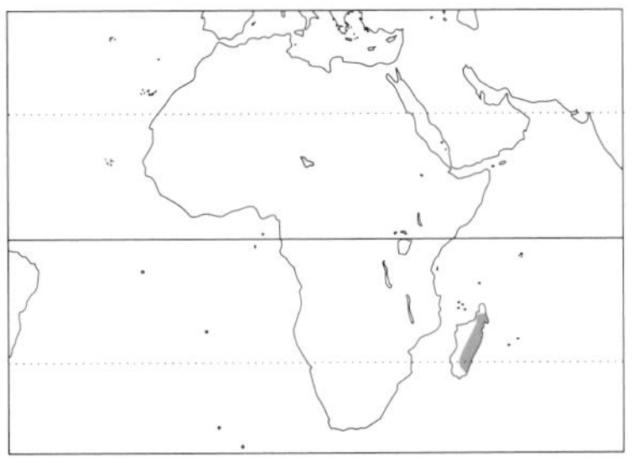

Descriptive notes. 25 cm; 1 male 148 g. Sexes alike. Distinguished from other medium-sized Madagascar rails by long, slender, decurved bill, lack of white on throat, unbarred flanks, and olive brown upperparts flecked with black; from *Canirallus kioloides* also by white undertail-coverts. Immature duller than adult, with brownish bill and brown eyes. Voice. Sharp "tsi-ka" when flushed; also "kik-kik". Calls frequently during day, from dense cover.
Habitat. Small to large marshes with dense long grass, reeds and sedges; river margins; grassland at forest edges; dense herbaceous vegetation of wet woodland and forest. Occurs from sea-level to 1800 m, more frequently at high altitudes.
Food and Feeding. Only invertebrates recorded. Moves about slowly in dense aquatic vegetation, searching for food and probing mud with long bill.
Breeding. Very poorly known. Lays Aug-Oct. Nest not described; built on ground in aquatic vegetation. No data on clutch size or downy young.
Movements. Suggested to be possibly migratory, but no evidence found.
Status and Conservation. Not globally threatened. Becoming rare throughout range as result of pressure on natural habitats in E half of Madagascar, to which species is confined and where it was formerly (1929-1931) common, especially at high altitudes. Direct destruction of wetland habitats continues, especially to create rice paddies for feeding Madagascar's rapidly growing population, and no Madagascan wetland has full legal protection; in view of the need to expand rice cultivation, it is unlikely that wetlands will be included in new protected areas. Another threat is habitat alteration through effects of deforestation, such as variations in quantity, quality and frequency of water available from wetland catchments, and siltation as result of extensive soil erosion; fertilizers and pesticides from rice paddies are also affecting wetlands and their invertebrate communities. Has been listed in 2 Special Reserves and may occur in others, but is easily overlooked because of its shyness. Still relatively common in some pristine wetlands, e.g. Torotofotsy marsh, near Périnet; but only small populations exist in the few areas which are protected. Long-term survival depends on implementation of a wetland protection programme and creation of additional protected areas.
Bibliography. Benson *et al.* (1976-1977), Dee (1986), Delacour (1932), Dowsett & Forbes-Watson (1993), Langrand (1990), Milon *et al.* (1973), Olson (1973b), Rand (1936), Ripley (1977), Salvan (1972a), Snow (1978).

Genus *LEWINIA* G. R. Gray, 1855

58. Brown-banded Rail
Lewinia mirificus

French: Râle de Luçon **German**: Luzonralle **Spanish**: Rascón de Luzón
Other common names: Luzon Rail

Taxonomy. *Rallus mirificus* Parkes and Amadon, 1959, Aritao, Luzon, Philippines.
Sometimes placed in genus *Dryolimnas*. Forms superspecies with *L. pectoralis* and *L. muelleri*; on occasion regarded as distinctive race of *L. pectoralis*. Monotypic.
Distribution. Luzon, N Philippines.
Descriptive notes. 20 cm. Sexes alike. Differs from *L. pectoralis* in absence of black streaks on less brightly coloured head and hindneck, whiter throat and lack of prominent barring on upperwings. Distinguished from sympatric *Gallirallus* species by smaller size, and by relative extent of pale markings on upperparts and barring on underparts; from sympatric *Porzana* species by longer bill, rufous crown and nape, and pattern of upperparts. Immature duller than adult: dark greyish brown on crown

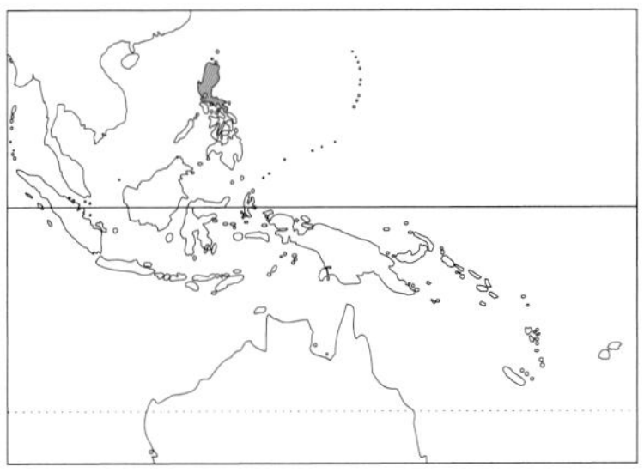

and hindneck, and greyer on cheeks and upper breast; bill darker than that of adult. Juvenile undescribed. VOICE. Not described.

Habitat. Precise habitat unknown, but species recorded from wet grassy areas; unlike congeners, may have strict ecological requirements. All records to date are from mountain foothills, migrating birds being recorded at altitude of c. 1000 m.

Food and Feeding. Unknown; food and feeding habits presumably similar to those of *L. pectoralis*.

Breeding. Unknown; probably breeds during rainy season.

Movements. In 1965-1970, total of 191 birds trapped at Dalton Pass in May-Jun and Oct-Dec, apparently while undertaking post-breeding dispersal or intra-island migration, the latter possibly between Cagayan Valley and Central Plain or between Sierra Madre and Cordillera Central. Also recorded elsewhere in mountain foothills in Dec-Jan.

Status and Conservation. ENDANGERED. Uncommon and secretive; recorded only from Luzon, where known from records of migrating birds at Dalton Pass in Sierra Madre Mts, and from six other localities in Nueva Écija, Nueva Vizcaya, Camarines Norte, Benguet and Mountain Provinces. Paucity of known localities, and lack of records since 1979, suggest that species is probably becoming increasingly rare.

Bibliography. Amadon & DuPont (1970), Collar & Andrew (1988), Collar *et al.* (1994), Danielsen *et al.* (1994), Dickinson *et al.* (1991), DuPont (1971), Hornbuckle (1994), McClure & Leelavit (1972), Parkes & Amadon (1959), Paynter (1963), Poulsen (1995), Ripley (1977).

59. **Lewin's Rail**

Lewinia pectoralis

French: Râle à poitrine grise **German**: Krickralle **Spanish**: Rascón Pectoral
Other common names: Slate-breasted Rail, Lewin's Water Rail

Taxonomy. *Rallus pectoralis* Temminck, 1831, New South Wales.
Sometimes placed in *Dryolimnas* or *Rallus*. Forms superspecies with *L. mirificus* and *L. muelleri*, both of which are on occasion considered races of present species. Eight subspecies recognized.

Subspecies and Distribution.
L. p. exsul (Hartert, 1898) - Flores (Lesser Sundas).
L. p. mayri (Hartert, 1930) - Arfak Mts, W New Guinea.
L. p. captus (Mayr & Gilliard, 1951) - C New Guinea.
L. p. insulsus (Greenway, 1935) - Herzog Mts, E New Guinea.
L. p. alberti (Rothschild & Hartert, 1907) - mountains of SE New Guinea.
L. p. clelandi (Mathews, 1911) - SW Australia (probably extinct).
L. p. pectoralis (Temminck, 1831) - E & SE Australia.
L. p. brachipus (Swainson, 1838) - Tasmania.

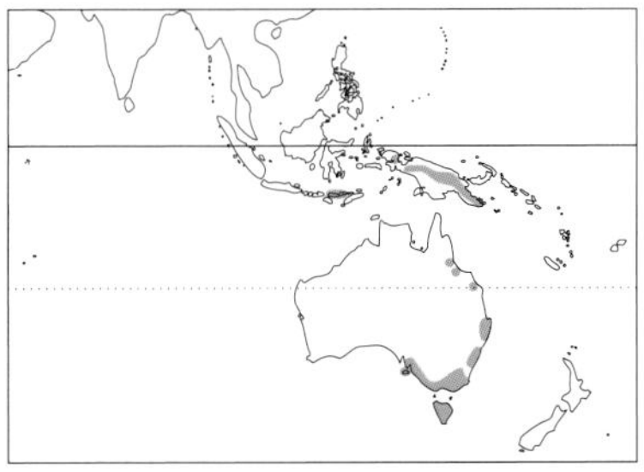

Descriptive notes. 18-27 cm; male 65-112 (88) g, female 63-111 (82) g, juvenile 42-78 (66) g; wingspan 31-35 cm. Female slightly smaller and has duller rufous head and hindneck with heavier black streaking. Differs in plumage from *L. mirificus* and *L. muelleri* in having noticeable streaks on head and hindneck, prominently dark-streaked upperparts and prominently barred upperwings. Distinguished from sympatric *Gallirallus* species by smaller size, and by pattern of upperparts, upperwings and underparts; from sympatric *Porzana* species by longer bill, rufous crown and nape, and pattern of upperparts and upperwings. Immature as adult. Juvenile has similar pattern to adult but much darker overall; lacks rufous on head and hindneck; barring on underparts less distinct and extends to upper breast; bill grey-black. Races separated on prominence of crown streaks, colour of crown, upperparts and breast, extent of white on throat, and on biometrics. VOICE. Commonest calls an accelerating series of loud notes likened to two coins being tapped together, and loud "crek"; also pig-like grunts.

Habitat. In Australia most often occurs at freshwater to saline wetlands, either permanent or ephemeral and usually with standing water: swamps, marshes, inundations, creeks, lakes, pools, farm dams, marshy streams, salt-marshes and estuaries. Requires dense fringing or emergent cover of long or tussocky grass, reeds, rushes, sedges or bracken; occasionally in thickets of wetland shrubs; sometimes uses wetlands in rain forest, woodland, riverine forest or wet heathland. Occasionally occurs away from water in parks, gardens, pasture, hay fields, lucerne, tangles of bramble or *Lantana*, and even in dry grass and ferns under canopy of scrub. In New Guinea occurs in medium-height, dense, dry upland grassland at 1040-2600 m, as well as in thick cover near water.

Food and Feeding. Largely earthworms, molluscs and arthropods, especially insects and crustaceans; occasionally frogs and eggs of birds; takes some vegetable matter; captive birds also ate meat. Crepuscular and diurnal; forages on dry ground, dry peat, soft soil and mud, and often in shallow water (less than 5 cm deep) at wetland edges, small pools and channels; usually forages within, or close to, dense vegetation, emerging from cover only briefly. Occasionally feeds on garden lawns and in short pasture. Pecks and probes; often immerses head in water; probe rate 1 per second; drills vigorously with long bill; foraging bouts interrupted by sudden dashes into cover, especially with large prey items.

Breeding. Season in Australia usually Aug-Jan; in New Guinea breeds Sept-Mar, and possibly also Jun-Aug, during both rainy and dry seasons. All following information from Australian populations. Probably monogamous and territorial. Nest a shallow cup or saucer-shaped structure, well hidden in clumps of grass or sedge at edge of marsh or other flooded area; usually above water but also on dry ground near water; sometimes solid platform in denser cover; often has approach runway or ladder. Nests often at high density along drainage areas and river flats. Average height above ground 64 cm; external diameter 18 cm and depth 8 cm; cavity diameter 12-13 cm and depth 4 cm. Woven from rushes or dead grass stems; lined with fine green stems; often with canopy woven from overhanging vegetation; construction takes 4 days to over 1 week. Eggs 3-8; colour differences and largest clutch size suggest occasional laying by 2 females; eggs laid at daily intervals; incubation 19-20 days, probably by female only; black downy chicks have black bill and iris, and grey legs; chicks remain in nest for up to 24 hours; young fed by both parents. May raise two broods per season; last brood may remain with parents during following autumn. Hatching success of 18 eggs 72%; eggs taken by water rat (*Hydromys chrysogaster*); young and adults taken by cats, dogs, Variable Goshawks (*Accipiter novaehollandiae*) and Kelp Gulls (*Larus dominicanus*).

Movements. Virtually unknown, as sightings rare and observation difficult; seldom seen to fly. In Australia present at some sites all year but in S the lack of records and lower reporting rates in winter may reflect some seasonal absence; may move to coastal and sub-coastal New South Wales to breed; no records S South Australia Jun-Aug. In Tasmania birds may move locally in response to changing conditions. Movements appear to be nocturnal and one bird struck window at night; birds probably fly c. 12 km to and fro between Maatsuyker I and mainland Tasmania. No movements recorded in New Guinea or Flores.

Status and Conservation. Not globally threatened. Race *exsul* known only from a few specimens from S & W Flores and last recorded in 1959. Race *clelandi* of SW Australia known from four specimens collected at 2-3 localities; has not been seen since 1932, despite being regarded as reasonably common at that time; it is probably extinct as result of draining, burning, grazing and trampling of its wetland habitats. Races *pectoralis* and *brachipus* widespread and uncommon to common throughout their ranges, with no recent declines noted; birds are able to occupy disturbed and artificially created habitats, and to occur close to human habitation and even in industrial areas. In New Guinea, race *captus* may be fairly common but other races may be uncommon to rare.

Bibliography. Beehler *et al.* (1986), Blakers *et al.* (1984), Coates (1985), Czechura (1983), Fletcher (1913), Garnett (1993), Gilbert (1936), Gilliard & LeCroy (1961), Harrison, C.J.O. (1975), Jaensch *et al.* (1988), Leicester (1960), Marchant & Higgins (1993), Milledge (1972), Olson (1973b), Rand & Gilliard (1967), Serventy (1985), Skemp (1955), Watson (1955), White & Bruce (1986).

60. **Auckland Rail**

Lewinia muelleri

French: Râle d'Auckland **German**: Aucklandralle **Spanish**: Rascón de las Auckland

Taxonomy. *Rallus muelleri* Rothschild, 1893, Auckland Island.
Sometimes placed in genus *Dryolimnas*. Forms superspecies with *L. mirificus* and *L. pectoralis*; on occasion regarded as race of *L. pectoralis*. Monotypic.

Distribution. Aucklands Is of Adams and Disappointment.

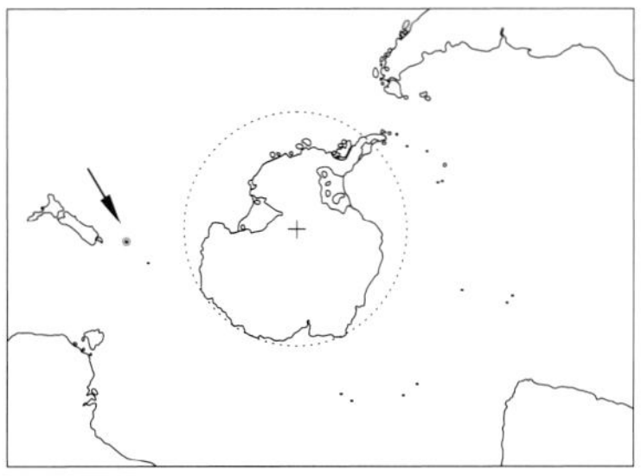

Descriptive notes. 17-18 cm; 1 female 63 g, 4 adults 89-100 (93) g, 1 juvenile 63 g. Sexes similar, but may differ in extent of rufous on head and neck, with female possibly duller, as in *L. pectoralis*. Differs from *L. pectoralis* in much smaller size, slightly straighter bill, and somewhat softer, denser plumage with little streaking on head and none on hindneck, olive brown upperparts with sparse, narrow dark streaks, restricted sparse barring on upperwing-coverts and reduced spots on primaries. Immature undescribed; juvenile apparently similar to that of *L. pectoralis* but with darker lores and ear-coverts, and with pale streaking occupying 30% of crown and 60% of upperparts. VOICE. Commonest calls a loud descending "crek" repeated at 1 per second, and a loud, sharp, whistle-like call at 4 per second; also makes grunts and clicks.

Habitat. Frequents herbaceous vegetation on damp to wet, flat to steeply sloping ground with clear areas at ground level and dense canopy c. 1 m above. Occurs in herb fields with megaherbs and sedges, and grasslands with sedges, ferns, low woody shrubs and tussocks; also ventures into scrubby forest with 2·5 m high canopy and 1 m sub-canopy over dense patches of grass and sedge. Occurs from sea-level to 500 m.

Food and Feeding. Little information, but food and foraging methods probably very similar to those of *L. pectoralis*. Once seen foraging at a rubbish dump. Active from just before sunrise to just after sunset; possibly also for some time after darkness falls.

Breeding. Season probably Oct-Dec. Probably monogamous and territorial. Two nests described: both in wetlands, in tussocks of *Carex appressa* and *Chionochloa antarctica*, sheltered by overhanging or interlaced vegetation and with well defined entrance runway. Nest a shallow cup of grasses and/or sedges; external diameter 14-23 cm and depth 7-16 cm; internal diameter 7 cm and depth 2-7 cm; cup 13-15 cm above ground. One clutch of 2 eggs recorded; incubation period probably similar to that of *L. pectoralis*; downy young not described.

Movements. Probably none, but observations difficult. Can fly but apparently does so only infrequently.

Status and Conservation. VULNERABLE. Probably eliminated on Auckland I by feral cats and/or pigs in 1860's, and thought to be extinct on other islands until a population of several hundred was discovered on Adams I (10,000 ha) in 1989, and one of c. 500 on Disappointment I (400 ha) in 1993. These islands are part of the Auckland Islands Nature Reserve and access is strictly controlled; survival of species depends on the continued exclusion of mammalian predators, especially rats, cats and pigs. Adams I has no introduced mammals but has New Zealand Falcons (*Falco novaeseelandiae*) and Brown Skuas (*Catharacta antarctica*), possible predators of present species.

Bibliography. Collar *et al.* (1994), Elliott *et al.* (1991), Falla (1967), Falla *et al.* (1981), Greenway (1967), Johnstone (1985), King (1978/79), Marchant & Higgins (1993), Robertson (1985), Soper (1976).

ssp *cuvieri*

61

62

♀

63

♂

64

♂

65

♀

66

67

ssp *cajanea*

68

ssp *albiventris*

69

ssp *plumbeicollis*

70

71

72

73

ssp *guatemalensis*

74

ssp *castaneus*

75

76

PLATE 14

inches 7

cm 18

Genus *DRYOLIMNAS* Sharpe, 1893

61. White-throated Rail

Dryolimnas cuvieri

French: Râle de Cuvier **German**: Cuvierralle **Spanish**: Rascón de Cuvier
Other common names: Cuvier's Rail

Taxonomy. *Rallus Cuvieri* Pucheran, 1845, Mauritius.
Sometimes included in the genus *Canirallus*, but skeletally very close to *Lewinia pectoralis* with which sometimes considered congeneric. Race *abbotti*, of Assumption I, recently extinct. Two extant subspecies recognized.
Subspecies and Distribution.
D. c. cuvieri (Pucheran, 1845) - Madagascar; formerly also Mauritius.
D. c. aldabranus (Günther, 1879) - Aldabra Is, Indian Ocean.

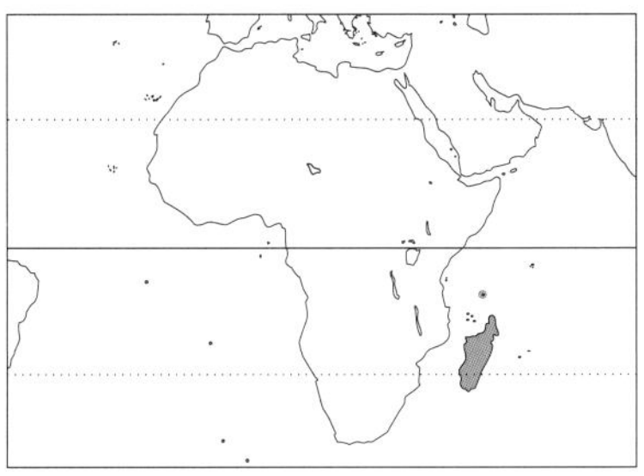

Descriptive notes. 30-33 cm; volant race *cuvieri*, male 276 g, female 258 g; flightless race *aldabranus*, male 145-218 (189) g, female 138-223 (176) g. Fairly large rail with striking, well defined plumage pattern. Distinguished from other rails on Madagascar by larger size, dusky abdomen and thighs with narrow white barring; white on throat and undertail-coverts; and straight, bill of medium length with reddish at base sometimes extending well towards tip and covering much of bill. Sexes alike, but female *aldabranus* has bright pink base to upper mandible, male dull or dark red base. Immature duller than adult, with brownish bill and brown eyes; juvenile *aldabranus* duller than adult. Race *aldabranus* smaller and paler, with dusky streaks on upperparts faint or absent, but very variable and can be much more similar to nominate; extinct *abbotti* also smaller and paler, with more extensive white on throat. Voice. Rather vocal. Contact call a muffled staccato grunt "mp", often followed by "yeah"; when agitated, utters grunt followed by click; also gives loud click of warning, sometimes followed by whistle, and a squeal of distress. Song, usually uttered towards evening, sometimes during night, begins with "mp yeah" notes and develops into a series of loud, piercing whistles, rising in pitch and intensity and developing frequency changes; often duets.
Habitat. Inhabits a wide variety of diverse habitats on Madagascar: forest with luxuriant herbaceous ground cover; woodland water courses; stream edges with tall, dense herbaceous growth; wetlands, including marshes with long grass, reeds and sedges, and rice paddies; mangroves and coral islet beaches; ranges from sea-level to 1800 m, but less numerous above 1100 m. On Aldabra, occurs mainly on extremely rough, heavily dissected coral limestone covered with very dense scrub dominated by *Pemphis acidula*; also in less dense vegetation and mangroves; presence of feral cats appears to eliminate species from otherwise suitable habitat.
Food and Feeding. Diet consists chiefly of invertebrates, including small molluscs, ghost crabs and many types of insect, including flies, beetles, termites and the eggs and larvae of ants; birds sometimes scavenge dead crabs. Takes tortoise droppings, possibly to extract insects; gleans parasites from carapaces of tortoises; takes insects and their eggs from decaying tortoise carcasses; eats eggs and hatchlings of green turtle (*Chelonia mydas*) at nests on beach, extracting buried hatchlings with bill after probing. Forages in leaf litter, including *Casuarina* needles on Aldabra, where also feeds at litter disturbed by passing tortoises, in mud among mangroves, and on rocky or sandy shores. When feeding in water, submerges head and rakes vigorously into mud with bill. In coastal areas species is known to drink salt water.
Breeding. In Madagascar, possibly breeds mostly during rains, laying Oct, Feb, Mar, and breeding condition Nov, Jan; on Aldabra lays Dec. Monogamous and permanently territorial, forming permanent pair-bond; unmated females also hold territories. Female normally selects nest-site, to which male is led. Nest flimsy, few twigs and leaves placed in depression among rocks, or more substantial deep bowl of interwoven leaves and grass placed on ground in dense vegetation. Usually 3-4 eggs (3-6); downy chick black with olive tinge, bare parts black, iris olive green; both parents tend young, which are fed until they become independent at 12-15 weeks, after which parents become aggressive to them, but immatures may stay near parents until onset of next breeding season. In *aldabranus* typically only 1 young per brood survives, probably due to predation. Age of first breeding 9 months or more; longevity at least 5-6 years.
Movements. On Aldabra populations may be transient to some degree, and large numbers of birds may be attracted to long-term campsites, dispersing when people leave; not attracted to temporary camps. No evidence of any significant movements occurring in Madagascar.
Status and Conservation. Not globally threatened. Race *aldabranus* has been considered Rare. Abundant over much of range in Madagascar but generally appears to be rarer on central plateaux, probably as result of hunting; obviously very adaptable, occupying wide range of habitat types. On Aldabra, race *aldabranus* occurs on 2 major and several smaller islands, having apparently been wiped out on other islands shortly after introduction of cats in c. 1890; current population c. 8000 individuals but distribution continues to contract; territory size 1-2 ha; no known significant predators of adults, although birds are occasionally eaten by humans; population probably stable; threat posed by feral cats currently not serious but colonization by cats may constitute major long-term threat, so establishment of captive breeding populations has been recommended; can apparently tolerate large populations of rats (*Rattus rattus*) but these may take eggs and chicks as do land crabs (*Cardisoma carnifex*). Race *abbotti* exterminated on Assumption I before 1937, probably after introduction of cats.
Bibliography. Albignac (1970), Benson (1967), Benson *et al.* (1976-1977), Collar (1994), Dee (1986), Dowsett & Forbes-Watson (1993), Frith (1977), Hambler *et al.* (1993), Huxley & Wilkinson (1977, 1979), King (1978/79), Langrand (1990), Milon *et al.* (1973), Penny (1974), Penny & Diamond (1971), Rand (1936), Salvan (1972b), van Someren (1947), Stoddart (1971), Wilkinson & Huxley (1978).

Genus *CREX* Bechstein, 1803

62. African Crake

Crex egregia

French: Râle des prés **German**: Steppensumpfhuhn **Spanish**: Guión Africano

Taxonomy. *Ortygometra (Crex) egregia* W. K. H. Peters, 1854, Tete, Zambezi.
Sometimes placed in genus *Porzana* on the basis of a superficial resemblance to *P. albicollis*, but plumage and skeletal differences make the relationship untenable. Sometimes placed in monospecific genus *Crecopsis* but probably more appropriately included in *Crex* on basis of similarities to *C. crex*. Monotypic.
Distribution. Sub-Saharan Africa from Senegal E to Kenya and S to Cape Province, South Africa, except arid areas of SW & S Africa, where W limits correlate with 300-mm summer rainfall isohyet.

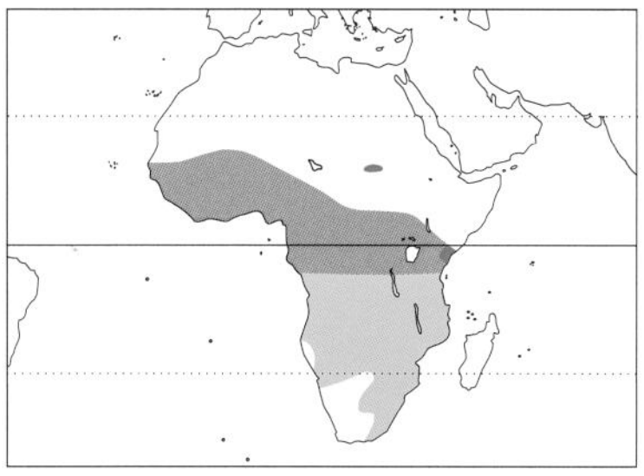

Descriptive notes. 20-23 cm; 3 males 121-141 (133) g, 16 unsexed 92-137 (117·5) g; wingspan 40-42 cm. Sexes similar but female normally looks slightly smaller, with less contrasting head pattern, duller grey face to breast, less regular underpart barring with narrower black bars, and almost unbarred centre belly. Easily separable from *C. crex* by smaller size, darker upperparts, lack of rufous on wing-coverts, entirely grey face, foreneck and breast, and black and white bars from flanks to undertail-coverts. Other sympatric crakes (*Porzana*, *Aenigmatolimnas*) smaller, with white markings on upperparts, different underpart pattern and short bill; *Rallus caerulescens* has dark, unpatterned upperparts, long red bill and red legs and feet. Immature similar to adult but duller; grey breast has brownish wash; underpart barring brown-black and off-white; iris hazel; orbital ring yellow-brown; bill, legs and feet grey. Juvenile has duller, darker upperparts; dark grey-brown face, foreneck and entire underparts, with no barring; whitish belly; blackish to dark brown bill; grey iris, legs and feet. Voice. Advertising call of male a series of rapid, grating "krrr" notes. Both sexes give sharp, loud "kip" call, often repeated and sometimes modified to descending double note "kiu", with aggressive, territorial and alarm functions, and also given in flight by nocturnal migrants. Also a wheezy "kraaa" when mating.
Habitat. Predominantly occurs in grasslands, from those (often seasonally moist or inundated) at edges of freshwater swamps, marshes and open waters to dry grassland in lightly wooded country; also in rice, maize and cotton fields, neglected cultivation, rank herbage, moist sugar cane adjacent to marshy areas, and on airfields; may occur close to human habitation. At Ndola, Zambia, occupied tussocky damp grassland 0·3-1 m tall. Grassland territories often include thickets, or large termite mounds with dense vegetation, apparently used as refuges. Recorded from sea-level up to at least 2000 m, but rare in high altitude grasslands. Grassland habitat frequently burnt in dry season, forcing emigration of birds.
Food and Feeding. Feeds on earthworms, molluscs, insects and their larvae (especially termites, ants, beetles and grasshoppers), and small frogs; also consumes seeds (especially grass seeds) and vegetable matter (grass blades, green shoots and leaves). Forages within cover, and in open on roads and tracks; picks up insects and seeds from ground; turns over dead grass and litter; probes bases of grass tussocks; digs in moist or dry ground with bill; makes rapid runs to catch fast-moving prey; stretches up to take prey from low-growing plants. Generally most active early and late in day, after rain and during light rain.
Breeding. Breeds during rains; Senegal Jul; Sierra Leone, Jun-Aug; Ivory Coast, chicks Apr, May, Oct; Ghana, Apr; Nigeria, Jul-Sept in N, Jun-Sept in C, Apr-Nov in S; Zaire, Jan; C & W Kenya, May-Jun, breeding condition Jul; N Tanzania, Jun; S Tanzania Jan-Mar; Angola, Apr; Malawi, Jan-Mar; Zambia and Zimbabwe, Dec-Mar; Botswana, Jan; South Africa, Oct-Mar. Possibly largely monogamous, but association of 1 male and 2 females recorded; pair formation may occur before leaving wintering area; territorial on both breeding and wintering grounds. Nest a shallow cup of grass blades, placed in scrape or depression on dry to moist ground, hidden under grass tussock or small bush; sometimes 2-15 cm above dry ground or standing water in dense grass or other plants; occasionally floating; loose canopy of grass blades often present; external diameter 21-23 cm, depth 4-9 cm; cup diameter 11-12 cm, depth 2-5 cm; building continues during egg-laying. Eggs 3-9, laid daily; incubation variously estimated 14-24 days, by both sexes; hatching asynchronous; black downy chicks have blackish brown bare parts; chicks leave nest soon after hatching; fed and cared for by one or both parents; fledging 4-5 weeks; young can fly when two-thirds grown.
Movements. Seasonality of occurrence too complex and poorly documented to be mapped accurately (map largely hypothetical). Moves away from equator, both N & S, to breed during rains, being primarily wet-season breeding visitor S of c. 5° S. Main periods of occurrence: S Tanzania, Dec-Apr; Zambia, Zimbabwe and Botswana, Nov-May; Malawi, Dec-Apr; Mozambique, Oct-Mar; Namibia and South Africa, Nov-May; scattered dry-season records from SE Tanzania, Zambia, Zimbabwe, Namibia and South Africa show that some birds remain after breeding when suitable habitat persists. Stragglers to Namib Desert and Namibian W coast attributed to effect of prolonged E winds. In E Africa, occurs in W & C Kenya mostly Apr-Dec; occurs W Sudan only in rains (probably breeds). Apparently resident throughout year in some W African countries, but shows marked N-S seasonal movements in Nigeria, where many move N in rains to breed, and most records from S are in dry season; similar movements noted Senegal, Gambia, Ivory Coast and Cameroon; May-Jul passage noted in SW Central African Republic; local movements noted Sierra Leone. Seasonally occurring non-breeding populations located coastal Kenya, May-Dec, and NE Gabon, Oct-Mar (not mapped). Migrates at night, when hits lighted windows and is found in city centres; caught at lights in mist, S Tanzania and SE Kenya, May and Nov. Vagrant to São Tomé and Bioko I.
Status and Conservation. Not globally threatened. Widespread and locally common throughout most of range except in rain forest and arid regions; distribution and status relatively well documented, as species is less secretive than other crakes. Overgrazing, cultivation and wetland destruction must have

On following pages: 63. Corncrake (*Crex crex*); 64. Rouget's Rail (*Rougetius rougetii*); 65. Snoring Rail (*Aramidopsis plateni*); 66. Inaccessible Rail (*Atlantisia rogersi*); 67. Little Wood-rail (*Aramides mangle*); 68. Rufous-necked Wood-rail (*Aramides axillaris*); 69. Grey-necked Wood-rail (*Aramides cajanea*); 70. Brown Wood-rail (*Aramides wolfi*); 71. Giant Wood-rail (*Aramides ypecaha*); 72. Slaty-breasted Wood-rail (*Aramides saracura*); 73. Red-winged Wood-rail (*Aramides calopterus*); 74. Uniform Crake (*Amaurolimnas concolor*); 75. Bald-faced Rail (*Gymnocrex rosenbergii*); 76. Bare-eyed Rail (*Gymnocrex plumbeiventris*).

reduced habitats in many areas: e.g. early this century, not uncommon around Durban (Natal) in marshes which have since been drained. Despite this, and despite the fact that numbers are killed for food in some regions, species appears to be under no immediate threat. As for *C. crex*, some of grassland habitats may have increased locally in recent years.

Bibliography. Avery *et al.* (1988), Benson (1964b), Benson & Benson (1975), Benson & Winterbottom (1968), Benson *et al.* (1971), Britton, P.L. (1980), Brosset & Érard (1986), Chapin (1939), Cheke & Walsh (1980), Clancey (1964b, 1971a), Demey & Fishpool (1991), Dowsett & Forbes-Watson (1993), Elgood, Fry & Dowsett (1973), Elgood, Heigham *et al.* (1994), Field (1995), Ginn *et al.* (1989), Gore (1990), Green, A.A. (1984), Green, A.A. & Carroll (1991), Grimes (1987), Haagner & Reynolds (1988), Halleux (1994), Hines (1993), Hopkinson & Masterson (1984), Irwin (1981), Lamarche (1980), Lewis & Pomeroy (1989), Mackworth-Praed & Grant (1957, 1962, 1970), Maclean (1993), Masterson (1991), Nikolaus (1987), Penry (1994), Pinto (1983), Serle (1939b), Short *et al.* (1990), Shuel (1938), Snow (1978), Tarboton, Kemp & Kemp (1987), Taylor, P.B. (1984a, 1985a), Thiollay (1985), Urban *et al.* (1986).

63. **Corncrake**

Crex crex

French: Râle des genêts **German**: Wachtelkönig **Spanish**: Guión de Codornices

Taxonomy. *Rallus Crex* Linnaeus, 1758, Sweden.
Great variation in colour within all populations renders impractical recognition of race *similis* of Kazakhstan. Monotypic.
Distribution. W & NW Europe (from British Is) E to NW China and C Siberia. Winters mainly from E Zaire and S Tanzania S to E South Africa.

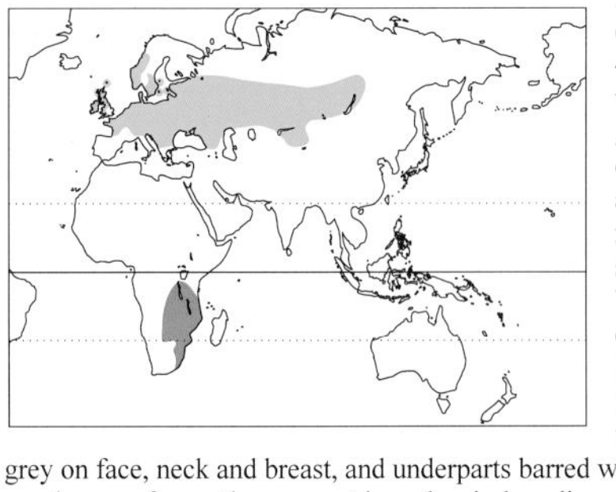

Descriptive notes. 27-30 cm; male 129-210 (165·5) g, female 138-158 (145) g; wingspan 42-53 cm. Sexes similar, but female has slightly warmer buff upperparts, narrower and duller grey streak over eye, and sometimes less grey on cheeks, neck and breast. Non-breeding plumage similar to breeding, but upperparts more rufous brown, less grey; male has less grey on side of head, and little or none on neck and breast; female has faint grey tinge in streak over eye, and often none on cheeks, neck and breast. Separable from *C. egregia*, which is sympatric in wintering areas, by larger size, paler upperparts, chestnut upperwing-coverts, less grey on face, neck and breast, and underparts barred with red-brown and white; easily distinguishable on plumage from other sympatric crakes in breeding and wintering ranges. Immature very like adult but probably with limited barring on upperwing-coverts. Juvenile like adult but has narrower, more buff-yellow-tinged, brown feather fringes on upperparts; less barring on upperwing-coverts; grey of sides of head, foreneck and breast replaced with buff-brown, sometimes with white dots on breast; less contrastingly barred flanks; duller iris; dark grey legs and feet. Voice. Advertising call of male a monotonous, rasping double call "krek-krek"; calls from ground or low perch; early in breeding season may call for hours, both day and night. Male also has "growling-mew" call, like grunting squeal of small pigs, used when aggressive and in sexual display. Also various grunts, whistles, cheeps, clicks and quacking notes.
Habitat. Breeding habitat essentially dry to moist meadows and other grasslands, including alpine meadows, marsh fringes and cleared forest areas; prefers dense herbage from head height to c. 50 cm tall. Avoids very marshy areas, standing water, and open ground with rocks, gravel or sand. Locally inhabits fields of cereals, potatoes or fodder plants, especially after breeding, when adults may also move into tall vegetation along ditches, roads and dams. Occupies similar habitats on wintering grounds: predominantly in dry grassland and savanna, often in areas burnt during dry season; in Zambia occurs in dry to moist grass 0·3-2 m high; also frequents rank grass (especially near rivers, sewage ponds and pools), pastures, hay and lucerne fields, fallow fields, neglected cultivation, airfields, and even suburban gardens; in South Africa also in moist to shallowly flooded sedges and reedbeds. On migration, also found in wheatfields and at golf courses. From sea-level up to c. 3000 m.
Food and Feeding. Earthworms, molluscs, Isopoda, Diplopoda, Arachnida and insects (including Coleoptera, Diptera, Dermaptera, Orthoptera, Odonata, Dictyoptera and Hymenoptera); also small frogs, small mammals and birds (in captivity), green parts of plants, and seeds (especially grasses and grain). Diet similar in wintering areas; in South Africa takes many ants, termites and dung beetles (Scarabaeinae). In wintering areas normally forages within cover, occasionally on open grassy tracks or dirt roads; takes food from ground, low-growing plants and interior of grass tussocks; shifts and probes litter with bill; runs to catch active prey. Most active at dawn and dusk, after rain and during drizzle.
Breeding. Season Apr-Aug. Monogamous pair-bond of seasonal duration formerly assumed, but serial polygyny regularly occurs, males occupying shifting and overlapping home ranges, and mating with 2 or more females, remaining with a female only until second half of laying period. Nest-site in grassland; sometimes in safer sites along hedgerows, near isolated trees, or in bushy or weedgrown areas. Nest built on ground, in dense continuous vegetation or in tussock; sometimes only a scrape but usually shallow cup of grass, weeds and brambles, lined with dead leaves; often with surrounding stems pulled over top in loose canopy; average external diameter 12-15 cm; depth 3-4 cm; probably built by female only. Usually 8-12 eggs (6-14), laid at daily intervals; clutches of up to 19 by 2 females; incubation 16-19 days, by female only; hatching synchronous; chick has sooty brown-black down, tinged rufous brown on upperparts, grey-brown iris, pale pink bill (soon becoming black-brown), and black legs and feet; chicks precocial, leave nest soon after hatching; cared for by female alone, sometimes by 2 adults (not clear if 2nd is male or female); self-feeding after 3-4 days; independent at fledging or earlier; fledging 34-38 days, when capable of flight; post-juvenile moult then begins and is completed after c. 1 month. Age of first breeding 1 year. 1-2 broods, in W Europe 2 broods normal, first hatching mid-Jun, second in late Jul; replacements laid after egg loss.
Movements. Almost wholly long distance migrant, although numerous Dec-Feb records from W Europe, especially in 19th century when breeding population much larger. Main flyways into Africa: W route via Morocco and Algeria; and more important E route via Egypt; few cross Mediterranean between these flyways. Some, probably from E Palearctic, enter Egypt and Sudan via Arabia and Red Sea. Autumn movements Aug-Nov (peak Sept) in Europe; passes through Morocco and Egypt Aug-Oct (mainly Sept); arrives Sudan Sept-Oct and most pass through Kenya Oct-Dec; few recorded S of equator before mid-Nov. Most reach C & S Africa late Nov-Dec, and leave late Feb-Apr; return passage more rapid, birds crossing Mediterranean late Mar to mid-May; W Palearctic breeding grounds occupied from mid-Apr. Passage recorded Azerbaijan Sept-Nov and Apr-May. Occasionally winters Mediterranean basin and N Africa. Migrates at night, at low altitude; often strikes lighthouses. Vagrant W to Canary Islands, Azores, Madeira, Iceland, Greenland (c. 20 records), North America (c. 17 records) from Baffin I along Atlantic coast and S to Bermuda; S & SE to India/Pakistan (2), Sri Lanka (3), Seychelles, and Australia (New South Wales and off W Australia); New Zealand record not accepted; in Africa very rare or vagrant to Libya (2), W Mauritania (2), Mali, SW Niger, Chad (2), Nigeria (4), W Somalia (4), Ivory Coast, Ghana, Cameroon, Gabon (3), Congo (3), Angola (2), W Namibia (1) and W Cape (1). High degree of vagrancy indicative of dispersive ability and of readiness with which birds are blown off course by opposing winds.
Status and Conservation. VULNERABLE. Although apparently still common and widespread in parts of range, there is clear evidence of very steep long-term population decline, c. 50% over 20 years, detected in Europe, Russia and Africa; this decline continues and status critical in some W European countries. In breeding areas, drainage of sites, agricultural intensification and changes in grassland management are main causes of habitat loss and of heavy losses of breeding birds, eggs and young. Does not appear to be threatened on African wintering grounds, where grassland habitats may be increasing as woods are felled and some agricultural areas no longer farmed, although grassland habitats suffering locally as result of overgrazing and cultivation. Conservation action includes: establishing reserves in key breeding areas; management to protect nests, adults and young from destruction when cutting meadows for hay or silage; supporting traditional land management practices which benefit species; encouraging continued production of hay; investigating mortality on migration, and seeking ways to reduce such mortality. Integrated national and international conservation approach required. In Britain, numbers have recently shown modest increases in areas where conservation management measures have been implemented successfully.

Bibliography. Ali & Ripley (1980), Anon. (1995o, 1996), Archer & Godman (1937-1961), Baha el Din (1993), Benson *et al.* (1971), van den Bergh (1991), Bezzel & Schöpf (1991), Braaksma (1962), Britton, P.L. (1980), Brown (1938), Broyer (1987, 1991, 1994), Broyer & Rocamora (1994), Cave & Macdonald (1955), Cempulik (1991), Chacón (1993), Clancey (1964b, 1971a), Collar & Andrew (1988), Collar *et al.* (1994), Cramp & Simmons (1980), Deceuninck (1995), Dementiev & Gladkov (1951b), Dowsett & Forbes-Watson (1993), Étchécopar & Hüe (1964, 1978), Evans (1994), Flade (1991), Gilmour (1972), Ginn *et al.* (1989), Glutz von Blotzheim *et al.* (1973), Goodman *et al.* (1989), Grimmett & Jones (1989), Hashmi (1991), Hudson *et al.* (1990), Hüe & Étchécopar (1970), Ingold (1930), Irwin (1981), Jackson & Sclater (1938), Knystautas (1993), Lewis & Pomeroy (1989), Mackworth-Praed & Grant (1957, 1962, 1970), Maclean (1993), Mason (1940, 1941, 1944, 1945, 1947, 1950, 1951), Mayes (1993), Mayes & Stowe (1989), Moody (1932), Nikolaus (1987), Norris (1947), Patrikeev (1995), Paz (1987), Pinto (1983), Potapov & Flint (1987), Rogacheva (1992), Salamolard (1995), Salathé (1991), Sauvage (1993), Schäffer (1995), Schneider-Jacoby (1991), Sclater (1906), Shirihai (1996), Simeonov *et al.* (1990), Stiefel (1991), Stowe & Becker (1992), Stowe & Hudson (1991a, 1991b), Stowe *et al.* (1993), Szep (1991), Taylor, P.B. (1984a, 1985a), Tomialojc (1994a), Urban *et al.* (1986), Vaurie (1965), Voous (1960), Weid (1991), Williams *et al.* (1995), Witherby *et al.* (1941).

Genus *ROUGETIUS* Bonaparte, 1856

64. **Rouget's Rail**

Rougetius rougetii

French: Râle de Rouget **German**: Rougetralle **Spanish**: Rascón Etíope
Other common names: Abyssinian Rail

Taxonomy. *Rallus Rougetii* Guérin-Méneville, 1843, Ethiopia.
Affinities uncertain. Monotypic.
Distribution. Ethiopia and Eritrea.

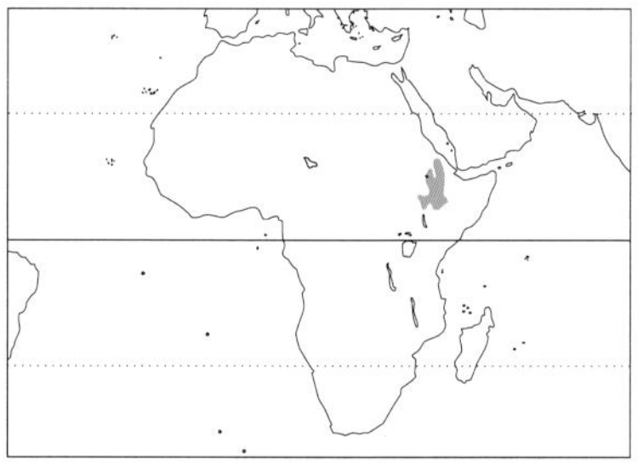

Descriptive notes. 30 cm. Combination of unstreaked olive brown upperparts, cinnamon-rufous underparts and white undertail-coverts unique among African rallids. Sexes alike. Immature paler than adult, with brown eye and bill; juvenile undescribed. Voice. Advertising call a loud, ringing, repeated "wreeeee-creeeeuw", given during day and on moonlit nights but mainly in morning and evening; several birds may call together. Alarm call a shrill, piercing "dideet" or "di-dii".
Habitat. Ethiopian and Eritrean highlands at 2000-4100 m, where frequents marshy situations in montane grassland and moorland. Found in lush grass, reeds and bushes at margins of pools and streams, in marshy meadows, in patches of tussocky marsh grass and lobelias in wet hollows, and in *Alchemilla* bogs; also among *Alchemilla* or heaths on dry ground.
Food and Feeding. Diet includes seeds, aquatic insects (especially water beetles), crustaceans and small snails. Recorded foraging in open meadows and on bare mud; also in shallow water, hopping from stone to stone; seen to dive into water at waterfall like dipper (*Cinclus*), subsequently reappearing in calmer water.
Breeding. Lays Mar-Oct. Monogamous; solitary nester. Nest is a pad of dead rushes on wet ground among high rushes or in rushes over water. Eggs 4-5, laid at daily intervals; incubation performed by female, probably also by male; both parents tend chicks, which apparently remain with adults until fully grown; one chick was accompanied by 10 adults, suggesting some degree of co-operative breeding.
Movements. None recorded.
Status and Conservation. Not globally threatened. Currently considered near-threatened. Widespread in highland areas from Eritrea to Kaffa (Maji Plateau) and regarded as common to locally abundant, but visits in 1989 to areas where species had been not uncommon in 1975 yielded extremely few sightings; the observers concluded that the greatly increased grazing pressure in marshlands and along streams had depleted vegetation cover to the extent that much habitat had become unsuitable. Grassland habitats are also being ploughed up for cereal growing. Such habitat changes have presumably affected populations in some areas, while recent droughts have probably also caused reductions in numbers.

Bibliography. Ash & Gullick (1989), Cheesman & Sclater (1935), Collar *et al.* (1994), Dowsett & Forbes-Watson (1993), von Erlanger (1905), Harrison & Parker (1967), Mackworth-Praed & Grant (1957), van Perlo (1995), Snow (1978), Urban (1980), Urban *et al.* (1986).

Genus *ARAMIDOPSIS* Sharpe, 1893

65. **Snoring Rail**

Aramidopsis plateni

French: Râle de Platen **German**: Schnarchralle **Spanish**: Rascón de Platen
Other common names: Platen's/Celebes Rail

Taxonomy. *Rallus plateni* A. W. H. Blasius, 1886, Rurukan, Sulawesi.
Sometimes retained in *Rallus*, but bill shape and plumage are somewhat similar to a pro-*Rallus* group (*Dryolimnas-Atlantisia*), near to which present species is provisionally placed. Monotypic.
Distribution. N, NC & SE Sulawesi.

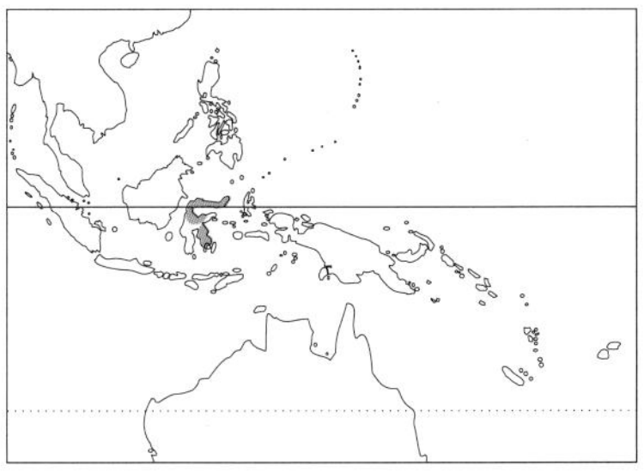

Descriptive notes. 30 cm. Flightless; heavy legs and feet; appears tailless in the field, with slightly downcurved bill. Sexes similar but female has brighter rufous hindneck and often less white on chin; base of bill and iris reddish (yellowish in male). Occurs alongside similar-sized but quite different *Gymnocrex rosenbergii*; only other sympatric rallids with which may be confused are similar-sized *Gallirallus philippensis*, which can occur near forest and has patterned head, upperparts and breast, and smaller, marsh-dwelling *G. striatus*, which has similarly coloured underparts and chestnut nape, but has distinctively barred upperparts. Immature and juvenile undescribed. Voice. Distinctive rather quiet call, lasting 1-2 seconds, rendered "ee-orrrr": very brief wheeze followed by longer snoring noise. May be uttered frequently. Possibly similar to call of *Gymnocrex rosenbergii*. Also brief, quiet, deep sigh "hmmmm".
Habitat. Dense liana and bamboo secondary growth on borders of lowland or highland forest; occasionally enters adjacent primary forest. On Minahasa Peninsula recorded from secondary growth on mountainsides skirted at base by plains of elephant grass and small bushes. In Lore Lindu National Park commonest in wet, impenetrable secondary vegetation, and in 1987 observations were made in old secondary growth (little different in structure from primary forest), with dense understorey dominated by rattans, on very wet and peaty ground bordering a fast stream. Reference to species entering rice fields could result from confusion with *Gallirallus philippensis*.
Food and Feeding. Possibly largely crabs; lizards also recorded. Captive bird survived on crabs for some time. Forages for crabs in mountain streams; also seen foraging in a shallow muddy gulley.
Breeding. Only record is of an adult foraging with 2 chicks on 18th Aug 1983.
Movements. None.
Status and Conservation. VULNERABLE. Locally distributed, rare and elusive; known from 11 specimens, all but one collected before 1940, and from 4 sightings between 1983 and 1992. Vulnerable to deforestation, which is already rather widespread in parts of Sulawesi, and also to introduced or feral predators. On Minahasa Peninsula was apparently quite common locally in past but, even as long ago as 1941, was described as threatened by increasing deforestation along R Menado, and was said to have been almost extirpated in some areas by large-scale snaring.
Bibliography. Andrew, P. (1992), Andrew, P. & Holmes (1990), Collar & Andrew (1988), Collar *et al.* (1994). Coomans de Ruiter (1947a), Lambert (1989), Ripley (1977), Stresemann (1941), Watling (1983), White & Bruce (1986).

Genus *ATLANTISIA* Lowe, 1923

66. **Inaccessible Rail**

Atlantisia rogersi

French: Râle atlantis **German**: Atlantisralle **Spanish**: Rasconcillo de Tristan da Cunha

Taxonomy. *Atlantisia rogersi* Lowe, 1923, Inaccessible Island, Tristan da Cunha.
Monotypic.
Distribution. Inaccessible I, Tristan da Cunha group.

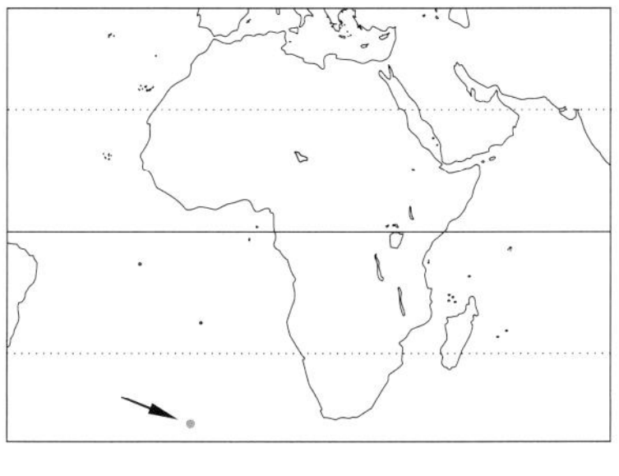

Descriptive notes. 13-15·5 cm; male 35-49 (40·5) g, female 34-42 (37) g. Smallest flightless bird in the world. Plumage decomposed and hair-like; adults easily distinguishable by chestnut-brown back and obvious white barring on flanks and belly. Sexes similar; female smaller and paler grey, most noticeably on head, throat and breast, with faint brown wash on underparts. Immature male blackish grey with no brown on underparts, no white barring, and orange-red iris; immature female medium to pale slate grey with brown wash, buffy or faint white barring, and brown or orange-red iris. Juvenile black, with no white barring; iris brown. Voice. Highly vocal. Pair members give loud trill when meeting and in threat display to other adults. Aggressive calls include loud squealing followed by prolonged twitter, a hard "tchick", and a "weechup". Contact calls include variants of quiet, repeated "tchik" and "chip" notes; alarm call a hard "chip".
Habitat. Occurs in all native vegetation types at all altitudes. Population density highest in coastal tussock-grass (*Spartina arundinacea*), sometimes mixed with ferns (*Blechnum penna-marina*), and in patches of sedges (*Carex thouarsii*, *Scirpus sulcatus*) on the peaty plateau; also occurs in fern-bush and island-tree thickets (with *Phylica* and *B. palmiforme*) on the plateau, and in *Empetrum* and *Scirpus* heath at highest altitudes. Apparently absent from short dry tussocks on cinder cones. Also forages on boulder beaches. Frequently makes use of natural connecting cavities under boulder beaches, and small tunnels (formed by regular use) through *Blechnum* and sedge mats, for access and concealment.

Food and Feeding. Earthworms, amphipods, isopods, mites, centipedes, insects (weevils, beetles, flies, moths, caterpillars); also berries of *Empetrum* and *Nertera*, and seeds of dock (*Rumex*). Does not eat fish or bird carrion. Forages in every available habitat, including very short vegetation, boulder beaches and marshy seepage zones. Foraging actions slow and deliberate, rather mouse-like, and species appears to occupy the ecological niche of a mouse; when foraging out of cover, is extremely wary. Active mainly during day but also forages at night.
Breeding. Lays Oct-Jan. Monogamous; pair-bond permanent; apparently has loose, flexible territorial system. Nest built on ground, at base of tussock grass clump or in ferns under dense cover of fallen tussock grass; oval or pear-shaped, with entrance at narrower end and access track or tunnel extending up to 0·5 m through vegetation; nest thinly domed or sturdily roofed; constructed of vegetation in which sited (either dead tussock leaves or dead sedges); one nest had external length 17 cm, external width and height 13 cm, cavity diameter 9 cm and entrance diameter 4 cm. Eggs 2, large (c. 25% of female's mass); both sexes incubate (period unknown); eggs hatch 12·5-32 hours apart; black downy chicks have dark brown iris, and black bill, legs and feet; chicks leave nest within 1 day of hatching; fed and cared for by both parents; fledging period unknown; at least some young still with parents when subadult. Immature plumage may be retained for 1-2 years, suggesting delayed maturity. In 1982, of 8 eggs found, 5 (63%) hatched, indicating low fertility and low breeding success; chick mortality high, chiefly from predation by Tristan Thrushes (*Nesocichla eremita*); wet weather also believed to cause losses.
Movements. None.
Status and Conservation. VULNERABLE. Abundant within its very restricted range and in no immediate danger. Total population estimated at c. 8400 birds, living at high density; population probably at carrying capacity, with regulatory mechanisms such as low fertility and delayed maturity operating to limit productivity. Most important potential threat is risk of mammalian predators (especially cats and rats) becoming established on the island as result of the infrequent visits by Tristan islanders. Two other *Atlantisia* rails, *A. elpenor* of Ascension I and *A. podarces* of St Helena, have become extinct since advent of man to the islands. Last century, goats and pigs were present on Inaccessible and did much damage to vegetation, but eradicated by 1950. Only significant natural predator of adults is Brown Skua (*Catharacta antarctica*), which apparently does not pose a threat. In 1872 and 1909 the island's tussock grass was burnt; these events would probably have killed many rails. Alien plants and invertebrates occur but apparently have no adverse effect, while introduced centipedes may be important food item of the rails. Proposed conservation measures include introduction of the rails to Gough I or Nightingale I, as safety measure, but this might adversely affect these islands' endemic invertebrates. Captive breeding has also been recommended to build up reserve stocks. Inaccessible has no protected area status, and agricultural development is still advocated; granting of full protection to the island, and prohibition of agriculture, strongly recommended to help ensure survival of the island's birds.
Bibliography. Anon. (1995p), Barrow (1910), Broekhuysen & Macnae (1949), Collar & Andrew (1988), Collar & Stuart (1985), Collar *et al.* (1994), Elliott (1953, 1957), Flint (1967), Fraser (1989), Fraser *et al.* (1992), Hagen (1952), Holdgate & Wace (1961), Lowe (1928), Olson (1973a), Richardson (1984), Rothschild (1928), Ryan *et al.* (1989), Voous (1962), Wace & Holdgate (1976).

Genus *ARAMIDES* Pucheran, 1845

67. **Little Wood-rail**

Aramides mangle

French: Râle des palétuviers **German**: Küstenralle **Spanish**: Cotara de Manglar

Taxonomy. *Gallinula mangle* Spix, 1825, coast of Bahia, Brazil.
Genus sometimes merged into *Eulabeornis*. Monotypic.
Distribution. E Brazil.

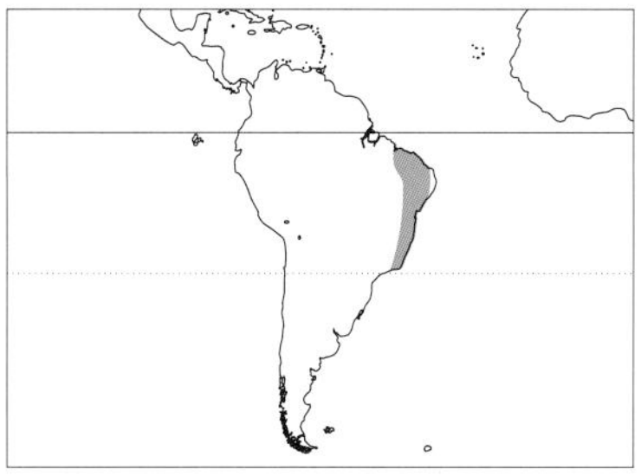

Descriptive notes. 27-29 cm; 1 female 164 g. Sexes alike. Smallest member of genus; differs from all congeners in having greenish bill with red base, and from all except *A. calopterus* and *A. axillaris* in underwing-coverts black narrowly barred white or cinnamon, instead of rufous with black bars; lacks grey underparts of *A. saracura* and *A. calopterus*, and extensive grey on head and foreneck of *A. cajanea* and *A. ypecaha*; *A. axillaris* rufous on head, neck and underparts; *A. wolfi* darker, especially on underparts, and has yellow patch on forehead. Immature and juvenile not described. Voice. Not described.
Habitat. Mainly coastal swamps and lagoons, including mangrove swamps; details of inland habitats not recorded. Larger sympatric *A. cajanea* occurs locally in mangroves, but apparently occurs more widely in swampy forests, woodland, on riverbanks, at pools and on dry ground with grass and bushes; also sympatric *A. saracura* inhabits forest.
Food and Feeding. Nothing known. At low tide, in estuary of R Traripe, Bahia, birds seen emerging from mangroves to feed on banks of river.
Breeding. Unknown.
Movements. None recorded.
Status and Conservation. Not globally threatened. Status unclear; known from NE Pará, Maranhão, Ceará, Bahia, Pernambuco and Alagoas S to São Paulo; between these limits probably less widespread than indicated on map, as species apparently confined largely to coastal localities in NE & E Brazil, with only a few inland localities known. In view of its potentially restricted distribution, the almost total lack of knowledge about its natural history, and the possibility of threats to its wetland habitats (similar to those facing *A. wolfi*), species should at least be considered Data Deficient and worthy of urgent investigation.
Bibliography. Blake (1977), Forrester (1993), Hellmayr & Conover (1942), Meyer de Schauensee (1982), Pinto (1964), Ripley (1977), Ruschi (1979), Sick (1985c, 1993).

68. **Rufous-necked Wood-rail**

Aramides axillaris

French: Râle à cou roux **German**: Braunkappenralle **Spanish**: Cotara Cuellirrufa

Other common names: Rufous-crowned Wood-rail

Taxonomy. *Aramides axillaris* Lawrence, 1863, Barranquilla, Colombia.
Genus sometimes merged into *Eulabeornis*. Monotypic.
Distribution. Coastal Mexico and Belize; Honduras to Panama; NW Colombia locally S to W Ecuador and NW Peru (unconfirmed), and E to Guyana (including Trinidad).

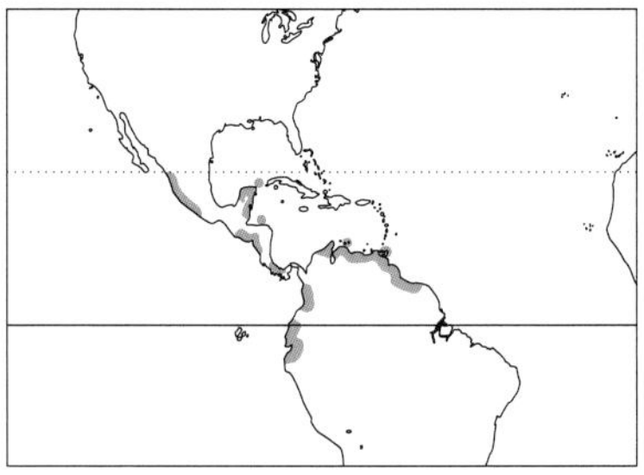

Descriptive notes. 28-30 cm; male 262-327 g, unsexed mean 275 g. Sexes alike. Only slightly larger than *A. mangle*, like which has underwing-coverts black, barred white or rufous. Differs from all congeners in lacking grey on head, neck, breast, sides and upper belly, these regions being rufous to chestnut; also has orange-brown, rather than red, eye. Immature and juvenile duller than adult; crown dull grey-brown; side of head pale grey; mantle darker grey; throat greyish buff; neck and underparts ashy grey-brown; eye brownish. Voice. Incisive, loud "pik-pik-pik" or "pyok-pyok-pyok", also described as a yelp, repeated c. 8 times, often antiphonally; also gruff "kik" of alarm. Often calls at night.
Habitat. Mangrove swamps, coastal marshes, lagoons and mudflats, and swamp forest; in South America, also dense forest undergrowth, forest edge and deciduous woodland. Mainly occurs in coastal and low altitude areas in Central America, but in South America ascends to 1800 m in open cloud forest.
Food and Feeding. Eats mainly crabs. Most active at dawn and dusk; seldom leaves dense cover but immatures venture onto open mudflats to catch crabs.
Breeding. Trinidad, Jul, Oct; Peru, Feb (unconfirmed). Nest a bowl or platform of small twigs, lined weed stems and dead and green leaves; placed 1·8-3 m up in small tree or vine tangle, or on dead stump; sometimes over water. Eggs 5. No further information available.
Movements. None recorded.
Status and Conservation. Not globally threatened. Although common in a few isolated localities, generally seems to be uncommon to rare throughout range.
Bibliography. Best *et al*. (1993), Blake (1977), ffrench (1973), Haverschmidt (1968), Haverschmidt & Mees (1995), Hellmayr & Conover (1942), Hilty & Brown (1986), Howell & Webb (1995a), Meyer de Schauensee & Phelps (1978), Monroe (1968), Parker *et al*. (1995), Peterson & Chalif (1973), Ridgely (1981), Ridgely & Gwynne (1989), Schaldach (1963), Slud (1964), Snyder (1966), Stiles & Skutch (1989), Tostain *et al*. (1992), Wetmore (1965).

69. Grey-necked Wood-rail
Aramides cajanea

French: Râle de Cayenne **German**: Cayenneralle **Spanish**: Cotara Chiricote
Other common names: Cayenne Wood-rail

Taxonomy. *Fulica Cajanea* P. L. S. Müller, 1776, Cayenne, French Guiana.
Genus sometimes merged into *Eulabeornis*. The form labelled as "*A. gutturalis*", known only from a single specimen from Lima, Peru, is a poorly prepared specimen of present species. Eight subspecies recognized.
Subspecies and Distribution.
A. c. mexicanus Bangs, 1907 - S Mexico.
A. c. albiventris Lawrence, 1867 - Yucatán to Belize and N Guatemala.
A. c. vanrossemi Dickey, 1929 - S Mexico (Oaxaca) to S Guatemala and El Salvador.
A. c. pacificus A. H. Miller & Griscom, 1921 - Caribbean slope of Honduras, and Nicaragua.
A. c. plumbeicollis Zeledon, 1888 - NE Costa Rica.
A. c. latens Bangs & Penard, 1918 - San Miguel and Viveros (Pearl Is, Panama).
A. c. morrisoni Wetmore, 1946 - San José and Pedro González (Pearl Is, Panama).
A. c. cajanea (P. L. S. Müller, 1776) - Costa Rica to Colombia, E through Venezuela and Trinidad to Brazil, and S to N Argentina and Uruguay.

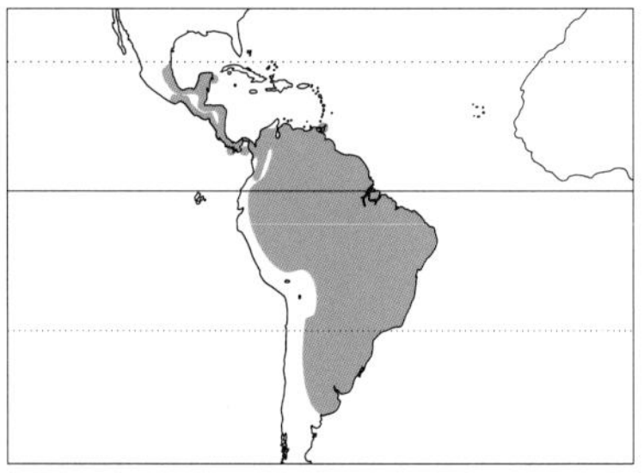

Descriptive notes. 33-40 cm; 350-466 g. Sexes alike. Large wood-rail and only member of genus with entirely grey head and neck (with rufous or dark patch on occiput and grey extending to upper mantle) and, in two races, white on belly; underwing-coverts cinnamon with black bars. Immature similar to adult. Juvenile duller than adult: belly sooty black, flecked with buff; bill and legs dusky; eyes brownish. Races separated on colour of occiput, brown or black in *cajanea*, *latens* and *morrisoni*, rufescent in the rest; presence of white patch between black belly and orange breast in *albiventris* and *mexicanus*; intensity of rufous on mantle, brightest in *plumbeicollis*; overall colour, *latens* palest; and size, *latens* and *morrisoni* smallest, *vanrossemi*, *cajanea* and *mexicanus* largest. Voice. Very vocal, calling most often at dawn, dusk, and at night; often in chorus or duet. Commonest call a prolonged and varied series of loud, crazed-sounding, rollicking, popping and clucking notes, variable in form and rendered "chirin co chirin co-co-co", "kook-kooky, kook-kooky, ko-ko-ko", etc. Alarm call a loud, harsh cackle or clucking shriek.
Habitat. Swampy forest, forest streams and rivers, secondary growth and deciduous woodland; coastal swamps and mangroves; marshes and marshy thickets, particularly in forested areas; rice fields, and even cane fields and scrubby pastures as long as they include wet areas; also seasonal pools near woodland; in Colombia sometimes occurs some distance from water. Normally in dense cover. Lowlands up to 2000 m, rarely 2300 m.
Food and Feeding. In mangroves preys heavily on crabs; elsewhere takes molluscs, arthropods (including Diplopoda, cockroaches and locusts), frogs, seeds, berries and palm fruits; once a water snake 30 cm long. Also takes maize, rice (dry or cooked) and bananas. Hammers large snails with bill to extract them from shell; jumps high to break off clusters of berries. Normally wary and secretive but sometimes forages openly in short grass close to thickets, wades in streams or forages on muddy tracks. Probes and moves aside leaf litter and other debris with partly open bill. Sometimes accompanies other birds following army ants. Apparently often feeds at night.
Breeding. Mexico, breeding condition Jan, May; Costa Rica, Apr-Sept; Panama, Apr; Colombia, breeding condition Mar-Jun; Venezuela, Jul-Sept; Trinidad, May-Aug; Surinam, Mar-Jun. Monogamous; pair-bond apparently permanent. Nest a deep bowl of twigs, dried weed stems and similar materials, or a compact, bulky mass of dead leaves and twigs with a shallow central depression; usually placed 1-7 m up in a bush, vine, low tree or on tree stump, often over or near water, sometimes on ground; external diameter 30-36 cm. Eggs 3-7; incubation 20+ days, by both parents (in captivity, male incubated by day and female by night); black downy chicks have brownish head, dull reddish bare skin around dark eyes, and black bill with flesh-coloured base; chicks leave nest after 1-2 days; young up to 40 days old sometimes use a brood nest; chicks fed and cared for by both parents; in captivity, young independent at 29 days, when 75% grown; at 25 days, one downy young appeared greyish, it was almost fully grown at 7 weeks and disappeared c. 1 week later.
Movements. None recorded, but records at 2300 m in Colombia probably of wanderers from lower elevations.
Status and Conservation. Not globally threatened. Apparently still fairly common to common over much of its extensive range, although must be adversely affected by habitat destruction; locally distributed in Guyana. In 1970's race *latens* known only from four specimens; present status unknown. Able to adapt to habitat modification: in Costa Rica persists in remnant streamside woods amid pasture or agricultural lands.
Bibliography. Belton (1984), Blake (1977), Canevari *et al*. (1991), Contreras *et al*. (1990), Dickey & van Rossem (1938), ffrench (1973), Friedmann & Smith (1950), Haverschmidt (1968), Haverschmidt & Mees (1995), Hellmayr & Conover (1942), Hilty & Brown (1986), Howell & Webb (1995a), Kilham, L.A. (1979), Lowery & Dalquest (1951), Meyer de Schauensee & Phelps (1978), Monroe (1968), Olson (1974a), de la Peña (1992), Ridgely (1981), Ridgely & Gaulin (1980), Ridgely & Gwynne (1989), Rutgers & Norris (1970), Sick (1985c, 1993), Skutch (1994), Slud (1964), Snyder (1966), Stiles & Skutch (1989), Tostain *et al*. (1992), Wetmore (1965).

70. Brown Wood-rail
Aramides wolfi

French: Râle de Wolf **German**: Esmeraldasralle **Spanish**: Cotara Morena
Other common names: Brown-backed Wood-rail

Taxonomy. *Aramides wolfi* Berlepsch and Taczanowski, 1884, Chimbo, Ecuador.
Genus sometimes merged into *Eulabeornis*. Monotypic.
Distribution. W Colombia to SW Ecuador and extreme NW Peru.

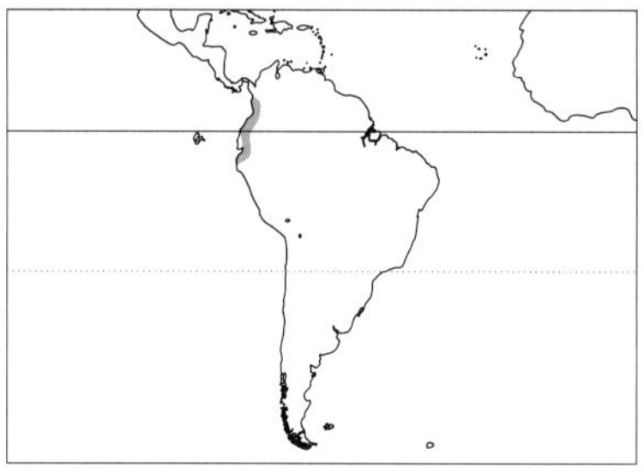

Descriptive notes. 33-36 cm. Sexes alike. Relatively large wood-rail, mainly brightish to darkish brown above and below, with ashy grey head and nape, and bare yellow patch on forehead; underwing-coverts chestnut with black bars. Differs from *A. cajanea*, *A. ypecaha*, *A. saracura* and *A. calopterus* in having no grey on foreneck or underparts; from *A. axillaris* in size and also in lack of rufous or chestnut on head; and from *A. mangle* in size, overall darker colouring, blackish lower flanks and belly, and bill colour. Immature and juvenile undescribed. Voice. Frequently repeated "kui-co-mui", apparently much like call of *A. cajanea*.
Habitat. Forest, secondary growth, forested rivers and mangroves; also riverine marsh and swampy woodland. Recorded up to 900 m.
Food and Feeding. No information available.
Breeding. Not described. Black downy chick has grey-black legs and feet, and reddish brown bill with yellow tip.
Movements. None recorded.
Status and Conservation. VULNERABLE. A very poorly known species which has a restricted range and appears to have become extremely rare, at least in Ecuador, owing to extensive destruction of its mangrove habitats. Its inability to survive in isolated patches of humid forest is predicted from observations of one such habitat island in Ecuador. It has been unreported for years from Colombia, and is recorded only once from Peru (Puerto Pizarro, Department of Tumbes, Sept 1977), so that a recent record from Ecuador (Feb 1994) is welcome evidence of its survival. There is an urgent need for further investigation of its status and natural history.
Bibliography. Blake (1977), Boyd & Alley (1948), Butler (1979), Clay *et al*. (1994), Collar *et al*. (1994), Graves (1982), Hellmayr & Conover (1942), Hilty & Brown (1986), Leck (1979), Meyer de Schauensee (1982), Olivares (1957), Ripley (1977), Ripley & Beehler (1985).

71. Giant Wood-rail
Aramides ypecaha

French: Râle ypécaha **German**: Ypecaharalle **Spanish**: Cotara Ipacaá

Taxonomy. *Rallus ypecaha* Vieillot, 1819, Paraguay.
Genus sometimes merged into *Eulabeornis*. Monotypic.
Distribution. E & SE Brazil, Paraguay, Uruguay and NE Argentina.

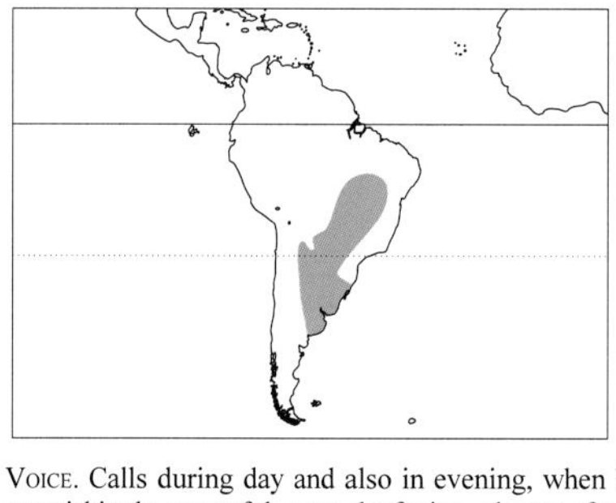

Descriptive notes. 41-45 (possibly up to 53) cm; 1 female 765 g. Sexes alike; female slightly smaller. Largest *Aramides*; handsome bird, with pale bluish grey face and foreneck, olive upperparts, and delicate brownish pink flanks and upper belly; underwing-coverts chestnut with black bars; stance upright, gait elegant. *A. cajanea* has rufous or brown-black patch on nape, but grey hindneck; *A. saracura* and *A. calopterus* darker and extensively grey below, and latter has striking reddish chestnut on side of neck and upperwing-coverts. Immature slightly duller than adult; legs brownish red; bill has brownish tinge. Juvenile not described. Voice. Calls during day and also in evening, when birds congregate in selected spots and set up an astonishingly powerful, even deafening, chorus of screams, shrieks and wheezes, rushing frenziedly about with wings spread and bill raised vertically. Calls described as: reminiscent of a hysterical human saying "all..wacky....all..wacky"; also a piercing, high, single "eeeeeeok", a bark, a low "keaaw" and an explosive "puk".

Habitat. Open marshes, lightly wooded swampy areas, fields and pastures near water and cover, and gallery forests; more likely than other *Aramides* species to appear in the open. Restricted to lowland areas.

Food and Feeding. Not recorded in the wild. In captivity, eats insect larvae, eggs, minced meat, apple and meal.

Breeding. Nest of grasses and weed stems, c. 30 cm in diameter, built 1+ m above water, in shrub or broken-down vegetation. Eggs 4-5; chicks dark mahogany brown. Other information from captive breeding: eggs laid at daily intervals; incubation 24 days; by both sexes; chicks left nest after 3-4 days; fed and cared for by both parents for 8-9 weeks; last brood stayed with parents for over 3 months; chicks half-grown at 5 weeks; renesting occurred when young of first brood 6 weeks old; 3 clutches laid in season.

Movements. None recorded.

Status and Conservation. Not globally threatened. Formerly common to abundant in much of its range; in 1980's was common in Rio Grande do Sul, Brazil, where it is a frequent victim of steel traps set in marshes for fur-bearing animals. Often kept in captivity in South America. No recent information on status, but species must have decreased in numbers as a result of extensive habitat destruction.

Bibliography. Belton (1984), Blake (1977), Brown (1974), Canevari *et al.* (1991), Contreras *et al.* (1990), Friedmann (1927), Hellmayr & Conover (1942), Hudson (1920), Klimaitis & Moschione (1987), Meyer de Schauensee (1982), Narosky & Yzurieta (1987), Olrog (1984), de la Peña (1992), Pinto (1964), Ripley (1977), Rutgers & Norris (1970), Shore-Baily (1926), Sick (1985c, 1993).

72. Slaty-breasted Wood-rail
Aramides saracura

French: Râle saracura   **German**: Saracuraralle   **Spanish**: Cotara Saracura
Other common names: Saracura Wood-rail

Taxonomy. *Gallinula saracura* Spix, 1825, Brazil.
Genus sometimes merged into *Eulabeornis*. Monotypic.
Distribution. SE Brazil, from S Minas Gerais E to Espírito Santo and S to Rio Grande do Sul, whence W to NE Argentina (Misiones) and Paraguay.

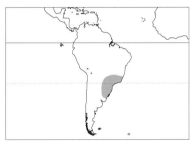

Descriptive notes. 34-37 cm; 1 male 540 g. Sexes alike. Only *Aramides* with grey of head and neck extending as far as belly apart from *A. calopterus*, which has maroon-chestnut ear-coverts and sides of neck, and median and greater upperwing-coverts. Differs from all congeners in having green bill with bluish base, and duller reddish or yellowish brown legs and feet; underwing-coverts chestnut with black bars. Immature and juvenile undescribed. VOICE. Variety of loud, resounding, noisy cries, including "po-quit kwaa kwaa kwaa", "po-peek" and "po-pereek". Often calls continuously for several minutes; usually in duet but not in unison. Also an irritated, rapidly repeated series of "quir" notes. Calls most frequently during day.

Habitat. Forests and woodland patches; prefers swampy or boggy areas or stream edges, but is not dependent on such sites. Occasionally enters house gardens. Not usually seen in open marshes.

Food and Feeding. Not recorded.

Breeding. One nest recorded: found at Novo Hamburgo (Rio Grande do Sul), spring 1961; situated 2 m above ground in thick bush; eggs 4 or 5.

Movements. None recorded.

Status and Conservation. Not globally threatened. Shy and infrequently observed; status unknown over most of range, but common in N & E Rio Grande do Sul in 1980's. Status elsewhere in need of investigation, especially in view of the potential adverse effects of continued destruction of its forest habitat. Because of this, and because nothing is known of its natural history, species should probably be classified as a Data Deficient species.

Bibliography. Belton (1984), Blake (1977), Canevari *et al.* (1991), Hayes (1995), Hellmayr & Conover (1942), Lowen *et al.* (1995), Meyer de Schauensee (1982), Narosky & Yzurieta (1987), Olrog (1984), de la Peña (1992), Pinto (1964), Ripley (1977), Sick (1985c, 1993).

73. Red-winged Wood-rail
Aramides calopterus

French: Râle à ailes rouges   **German**: Rotflügelralle   **Spanish**: Cotara Alirrufa

Taxonomy. *Aramides calopterus* P. L. Sclater & Salvin, 1878, Sarayacu, Ecuador.
Genus sometimes merged into *Eulabeornis*. Monotypic.
Distribution. E Ecuador, NE Peru (Loreto) and Brazil in SW Amazonas (upper R Jurua and R Urucu).

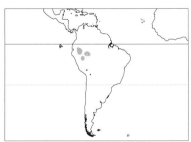

Descriptive notes. 31-33 cm. Sexes alike. Rather dark; separated from all congeners except *A. saracura* in grey of head and neck extending to belly; maroon-chestnut ear-coverts, sides of neck, and median and greater upperwing-coverts; underwing-coverts black with white bars, a character shared only with *A. mangle* and *A. axillaris*. Immature similar to adult but with blackish bill, legs and feet. Juvenile undescribed. VOICE. Not described.

Habitat. Seasonally flooded *igapó* forest, forest in the vicinity of streams and creeks.

Food and Feeding. No information available.

Breeding. Unknown.

Movements. None recorded.

Status and Conservation. Not globally threatened. Very rarely observed; status unknown over most of range, but described as rare in Amazonas earlier this century and uncommon on upper R Urucu, Amazonas, in late 1980's; status elsewhere in urgent need of investigation. In view of its scarcity in some areas, its restricted distribution in threatened habitats and the lack of knowledge of its natural history, species should be classified as a Data Deficient species.

Bibliography. Blake (1977), Butler (1979), Gyldenstolpe (1945), Hellmayr & Conover (1942), Meyer de Schauensee (1982), Parker *et al.* (1982), Peres & Whittaker (1991), Ripley (1977).

Genus *AMAUROLIMNAS* Sharpe, 1893

74. Uniform Crake
Amaurolimnas concolor

French: Râle concolore   **German**: Einfarbralle   **Spanish**: Cotara Café

Taxonomy. *Rallus concolor* Gosse, 1847, Jamaica.
Sometimes included, with *Aramides*, in *Eulabeornis*. Possibly derived from *Aramides* stock, and has identical bill structure to the smaller *Aramides* species. Nominate *concolor* of Jamaica recently extinct. Two extant subspecies recognized.
Subspecies and Distribution.
A. c. guatemalensis (Lawrence, 1863) - S Mexico S to Ecuador.
A. c. castaneus (Pucheran, 1851) - Venezuela, the Guianas, Brazil, E Peru and E Bolivia.

Descriptive notes. 20-23 cm; 1 male 133 g, unsexed mean 95 g. Sexes alike. An entirely brown to rufous brown bird; superficially resembles a diminutive *Aramides* species in build, posture and bare parts colours, but has no grey in plumage and lacks the barred underwing-coverts, and the black hindbody and tail, characteristic of *Aramides*. Differs from rather similar *Anurolimnas castaneiceps* and *A. viridis* in brown-tinged face, more extensively rufous underparts, yellowish green bill, and different voice. Immature similar to adult but more dusky on both upperparts and underparts, with white shaft streaks to feathers of throat and breast, and yellow eyes. Juvenile has brownish eyes and dull legs. Races separated on size, with *guatemalensis* smallest of the three; colour of upperparts, rufous in *concolor*, olivaceous in other races; and colour of underparts, most rufous in *castaneus*. VOICE. Loud, arresting whistled calls, reminiscent of *Aramides*. Song is series of 6-20 upslurred "tooee" whistles, loudest during middle of sequence; pair members give clear, but not loud, whistled "tooo" notes to each other; alarm call a sharp, nasal "kek".

Habitat. Forested swamps, moist and flooded forests, damp ravines, and heavy vine-tangled thickets along edges of streams; locally at edges of mangroves; often found away from water in dense second growth adjoining forest, especially favouring areas with hanging dead and decaying leaves in *Heliconia* thickets, and also in dense thickets bordering cultivation. Essentially confined to lowlands, occurring from sea-level up to c. 1000 m.

Food and Feeding. Earthworms, insects, spiders, small frogs and lizards; also seeds and berries. Normally remains in cover; forages deliberately, walking slowly and pecking into leaf litter, detritus and dead leaves hanging from plants; also probes in wet earth to depth of bill and digs with bill in soft mud.

Breeding. Costa Rica, breeding condition Jul, most song Aug-Dec, one probable nest Nov; Pearl Is (Panama), eggs found (possibly of this species) in Sept. Probably monogamous and territorial. Costa Rica nest was a loose cup of leaves filling hollow in top of vine-covered stump in treefall clearing in swamp forest, c. 5 m from stream and 1 m from dense thicket; contained 4 eggs, which agreed in size and colour with the only egg of this species definitely known.

Movements. None recorded.

Status and Conservation. Not globally threatened. Formerly considered to be locally distributed; by 1970's *guatemalensis* was regarded as very rare except in NE Costa Rica, where it was locally fairly common, while *castaneus*, known from only a few specimens, was also regarded as rare. In 1980's, *guatemalensis* described as rare in Panama and Colombia, while *castaneus* described as apparently rather common in coastal Alagoas, Brazil. Because of its secretive habits species is undoubtedly overlooked, and is possibly more widely distributed than currently known, but certainly adversely affected by destruction of its forest habitats. Given present state of knowledge, it should be considered Data Deficient and worthy of investigation, and possibly rare and threatened in some parts of its range. Nominate race was last reported from Jamaica in 1881, its extirpation presumably being due to the introduction of a mongoose species. The only record of race *castaneus* from French Guiana is a specimen from Cayenne, collected in 1833.

Bibliography. Blake (1977), Dickerman (1971), Gosse (1847), Hellmayr & Conover (1942), Hilty & Brown (1986), Howell & Webb (1995a), Howell *et al.* (1992), Kiff (1975), Meyer de Schauensee & Phelps (1978), Monroe (1968), Orians & Paulson (1969), Ridgely (1981), Ridgely & Gwynne (1989), Sick (1985c, 1993), Slud (1964), Snyder (1966), Stiles (1981), Stiles & Skutch (1989), Teixeira *et al.* (1986), Tostain *et al.* (1992), Wetmore (1965).

Genus *GYMNOCREX* Salvadori, 1875

75. Bald-faced Rail
Gymnocrex rosenbergii

French: Râle de Rosenberg   **German**: Rosenbergralle   **Spanish**: Cotara Cariazul
Other common names: Rosenberg's (Bare-eyed) Rail

Taxonomy. *Rallina rosenbergii* Schlegel, 1866, Kema, Sulawesi.
Sometimes merged, with *Aramides*, in *Eulabeornis*; genus shows some similarities to *Aramides*, possibly being derived from same stock. Monotypic.
Distribution. N & NC Sulawesi and Peleng (Banggai Is).

Descriptive notes. 30 cm. Can fly for short distances. Highly distinctive appearance, with conspicuous patch of pale cobalt blue bare skin behind eye, and black underparts. Sexes similar. Immature and juvenile undescribed. VOICE. A snoring sound, which could possibly be confused with call of *Aramidopsis plateni*; also a quiet clucking call when disturbed.

Habitat. Primary and old secondary forest; also bushy, abandoned rice fields. In Lore Lindu National Park recorded with *Aramidopsis plateni* in old secondary forest, but differing in its preference for drier areas with a thick understorey of small saplings, some bamboo clumps, and less dense rattan; when

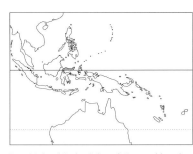

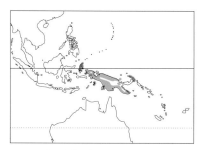

disturbed, one bird ran into the wetter, more impenetrable habitat occupied by the other rail species. Recorded from lowlands and hills.

Food and Feeding. Very little information available. Apparently feeds principally on insects and snails.

Breeding. No information available.

Movements. None.

Status and Conservation. VULNERABLE. Difficult to observe and apparently rare, but almost certainly greatly under-recorded. Known from one Sulawesi specimen and three from Peleng, other specimens having been lost; also recent records from Lore Lindu and Dumoga-Bone National Parks, Sulawesi. Presumably vulnerable to forest destruction and degradation, which are already quite widespread in parts of Sulawesi. May be trapped for food in some areas.

Bibliography. Andrew, P. (1992), Collar & Andrew (1988), Collar *et al*. (1994). Coomans de Ruiter (1947a, 1947b), Eck (1976a), Lambert (1989), Rozendaal & Dekker (1989), Stresemann (1941), Watling (1983), White & Bruce (1986).

76. Bare-eyed Rail
Gymnocrex plumbeiventris

French: Râle à ventre gris   **German**: Rostschwingenralle   **Spanish**: Cotara Moluqueña

Taxonomy. *Rallus plumbeiventris* G. R. Gray, 1862, Misool Island, off north-west New Guinea.
Sometimes placed in *Eulabeornis*, but has more in common with *Aramides*. Validity of subspecies questionable. Two subspecies recognized.

Subspecies and Distribution.

G. p. plumbeiventris (G. R. Gray, 1862) - N Moluccas, Misool, Aru Is, New Guinea (except S), Karkar and New Ireland.

G. p. hoeveni (von Rosenberg, 1866) - Aru Is and S New Guinea (Setekwa R to Fly R).

Descriptive notes. 30-33 cm; estimated 300 g. Bare orbital skin pink; eyering is salmon or reddish; long bill; axillaries and underwing-coverts barred greyish black and white; much individual variation in plumage. Sexes alike. A distinctively plumaged rail, similar in overall colouring and pattern to *Aramides* rails; also somewhat similar to much larger *Eulabeornis castaneoventris*, which, however, has grey head, entirely pinkish brown underparts, greenish bill and yellow or green legs. All similar-sized sympatric rails of wet habitats have barring on underparts, except *Amaurornis olivaceus* which is olive brown above and grey below, with buffy-rufous belly and undertail-coverts, greenish yellow legs and a short bill. Immature and juvenile undescribed. Race *hoeveni* duller and has underparts washed rufous brown. VOICE. Loud gulping "wow-wow-wow-wow", only heard at start of wet season and probably a territorial call. When foraging, a repeated pig-like grunt.

Habitat. Floor of primary forest; also marshy forests, swamps and wet grassy areas near rivers and lakes. Occurs in lowlands, up to 1200 m; in E New Guinea also recorded from Mt Hagen area at 1600 m.

Food and Feeding. Eats insects; probably also a variety of other small animals. Seen to attack a Common Paradise-kingfisher (*Tanysiptera galatea*) which was digging for food.

Breeding. Misool, Nov; Karkar, Feb; breeds in wet season. Territorial, at least when breeding; occurs in pairs or family parties. In Sepik region, New Guinea, nest said to be of grass, built on the ground when water level low, and eggs said to be white; however, this does not agree with nest at Karkar, which was situated between roots of large tree and contained patterned eggs. Possible nest near Port Moresby in Feb was a few fragments of dead leaves on bare ground, and contained 1 egg. Nothing further recorded.

Movements. Sedentary; locally nomadic in New Guinea. In Port Moresby area mostly seen Dec-May, but records also for Aug-Sept; birds vacate lowland rain forest near Brown R during long periods of dry weather, when ground becomes very hard. One bird found perched in tree in urban Port Moresby, Jan, indicative of movements.

Status and Conservation. Not globally threatened. Very little information available, but species is apparently not uncommon throughout its sizeable range, though very shy and difficult to observe.

Bibliography. Andrew, P. (1992), Beehler *et al*. (1986), Coates (1985), Gilliard & LeCroy (1966), Gregory (1995b), Rand & Gilliard (1967), Ripley (1964, 1977), Rothschild & Hartert (1915), White & Bruce (1986).

PLATE 15 ➤

ssp *akool*

77

ssp *coccineipes*

78

79

ssp *ruficrissus*

80

ssp *ultimus*

ssp *insularis*

ssp *moluccanus*

81

ssp *leucomelanus*

82

83

ssp *phoenicurus*

ssp *palustris*

ssp *intermedia*

84

ssp *pusilla*

85 ♂

85 ♀

86

PLATE 15

inches 6

cm 15

87

88 ♂

88 ♀

89 ♂

89 ♀

90

91

92

93

ssp *fusca*

ssp *erythrothorax*

Genus *AMAURORNIS* Reichenbach, 1853

77. Brown Crake

Amaurornis akool

French: Râle akool   **German**: Braunbauch-Kielralle   **Spanish**: Gallineta Akool

Taxonomy. *Rallus Akool* Sykes, 1832, Deccan.
Two subspecies recognized.
Subspecies and Distribution.
A. a. akool (Sykes, 1832) - India, Bangladesh and W Myanmar.
A. a. coccineipes (Slater, 1891) - SE China to NE Vietnam.

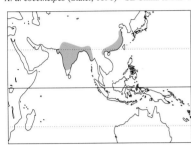

Descriptive notes. 26-28 cm; male 114-170 g, female 110-140 g. Very plain with olive brown upperparts, white throat, dark slate grey underparts shading to olive brown from belly to undertail-coverts, and indistinct pale supercilium. Sexes alike; female averages smaller. Smaller sympatric *A. bicolor* has rufous brown upperparts contrasting with grey head, neck and underparts; tail black; also differs in bare part colours. Immature similar to adult but with brown iris. Juvenile not described. Race *coccineipes* larger, with brighter, redder legs. VOICE. Short plaintive note, heard at daybreak and just before sunset; shrill rattle (attributed to this species but not proved); and long vibrating whistle, gradually falling in pitch.
Habitat. Dense swamps, *Pandanus* palm groves, sugar cane fields, riparian reedbeds and other dense herbage, and irrigation channels. Occurs from lowlands up to 800 m, possibly higher.
Food and Feeding. Worms, molluscs, adult and larval insects, and seeds of marsh plants. Largely crepuscular, emerging cautiously at edges of reedbeds and bushes to feed in early morning and evening.
Breeding. Mar-Oct, chiefly May-Aug; varies with locality. Monogamous. Nest a pad of grasses, rush blades and sticks, with slight central depression, well concealed in grass tussocks in or near edge of swamp; 1 nest was 1·5 m above ground, in flood-deposited debris on small *Acacia* tree on riverbank. Eggs 5-6; incubation by both sexes; chick has black down.
Movements. Resident, but possibly also migrant over relatively short distances, N populations wintering in S of range; extent of seasonal occurrence not clear.
Status and Conservation. Not globally threatened. Infrequently seen because of its shy and secretive nature, but formerly regarded as fairly common throughout range; no information available on current status.
Bibliography. Ali & Ripley (1980), Étchécopar & Hüe (1978), Harvey (1990), Inskipp & Inskipp (1991), King *et al.* (1975), Meyer de Schauensee (1984), Perennou *et al.* (1994), Ripley (1977, 1982), Ripley & Beehler (1985), Roberts, T.J. (1991), Smythies (1986).

78. Isabelline Bush-hen

Amaurornis isabellinus

French: Râle isabelle   **German**: Isabellkielralle   **Spanish**: Gallineta Isabelina
Other common names: Sulawesi/Isabelline Waterhen

Taxonomy. *Rallina isabellina* Schlegel, 1865, Gorontalo, Sulawesi.
Monotypic.
Distribution. Sulawesi.

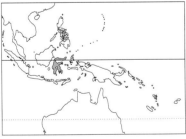

Descriptive notes. 35-40 cm. Sexes alike. Largest *Amaurornis*; paler plumage than congeners, and easily distinguishable by grey-tinged, olive-brown upperparts and entirely vinous chestnut to rufous underparts, including underwing-coverts and axillaries; bill pale green, legs and feet brownish green. Immature and juvenile undescribed. VOICE. Very striking, loud, discordant call, apparently resembling that of *Gallirallus torquatus* but usually ending with loud, clear "tak-tak-tak-tak", from which local name "Taktak" is presumably derived. Several birds usually call together.
Habitat. Grass with low bushes near streams and rivers with forested edges; also in *alang-alang* (*Imperata cylindrica*) grasslands and at edges of rice and maize fields; may occur far from water. Relatively common in dry, rank vegetation, especially old, fallow gardens in first stages of reversion to forest. Occurs from sea-level up to 800 m.
Food and Feeding. Noted foraging along a vehicle track in secondary woodland and *alang-alang*.
Breeding. Young found in May, including record of 2 adults with 5 chicks in late May 1986. No further information available.
Movements. None recorded.
Status and Conservation. Not globally threatened. Definitely known only from N Sulawesi S to Tawaya, and from the SE; occurrence elsewhere in Sulawesi requires investigation. Current status unknown, but species was regarded as relatively common at least locally in 1980's. In view of its restricted range, and lack of information on its ecology, species should probably be regarded as Data Deficient, in urgent need of investigation.
Bibliography. Andrew, P. (1992), Andrew, P. & Holmes (1990), Ripley (1977), Rozendaal & Dekker (1989), Stresemann (1941), Watling (1983), White & Bruce (1986).

79. Plain Bush-hen

Amaurornis olivaceus

French: Râle des Philippines   **German**: Philippinenkielralle   **Spanish**: Gallineta Filipina
Other common names: Bush-hen

Taxonomy. *Gallinula olivacea* Meyen, 1834, Manila, Philippines.
Formerly considered conspecific with *A. moluccanus*, but sufficiently distinctive in plumage to merit separation; probably best considered as forming superspecies. Monotypic.
Distribution. Philippines, except Palawan.

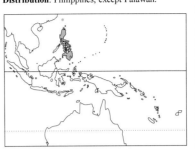

Descriptive notes. 24-31 cm. Sexes alike. Very similar to *A. moluccanus*, but somewhat larger and darker, with more olive-tinged upperparts, dark slaty grey underparts, including thighs, and dark rufous brown undertail-coverts; bill pale green; iris blood red; legs and feet yellowish brown. Immature and juvenile undescribed. VOICE. No description available, but presumably similar to that of *A. moluccanus*.
Habitat. Waterside grass clumps, flooded scrub and swampy grassland; nests in swampy conditions but also ranges through neighbouring grassland and forest edge.
Food and Feeding. Not recorded: likely to be similar to *A. moluccanus*. Shy and secretive.
Breeding. Feb, May and Sept. Nests in swampy conditions. No further details available; presumably similar to *A. moluccanus*.
Movements. None recorded.
Status and Conservation. Not globally threatened. Formerly considered common, but regarded as rare in 1991. In view of this suggested change in status, and general lack of information about biology and ecology, species should probably be regarded as Data Deficient; current status should be investigated in detail.
Bibliography. Dickinson, Kennedy & Parkes (1991), Dickinson, Kennedy, Read & Rozendaal (1989), DuPont (1971), Parkes (1971), Rand & Rabor (1960), Ripley (1977).

80. Rufous-tailed Bush-hen

Amaurornis moluccanus

French: Râle des Moluques   **German**: Rotsteiß-Kielralle   **Spanish**: Gallineta Moluqueña
Other common names: Eastern/Rufous-vented Bush-hen

Taxonomy. *Porzana moluccana* Wallace, 1865, Ambon and Ternate, Moluccas.
Formerly considered conspecific with *A. olivaceus*, but sufficiently distinctive in plumage to merit separation; probably best considered as forming superspecies. Four subspecies recognized.
Subspecies and Distribution.
A. m. moluccanus (Wallace, 1865) - Sangihe Is, Moluccas, Misool I and W & N New Guinea.
A. m. nigrifrons (Hartert, 1926) - Bismarck Archipelago and Solomon Is.
A. m. ultimus Mayr, 1949 - E Solomon Is.
A. m. ruficrissus (Gould, 1869) - S & E New Guinea, and NE & E Australia.

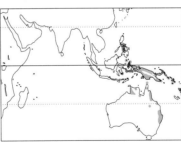

Descriptive notes. 23-30 cm; male *ruficrissus* 129-208 (177) g, *ultimus* 189-248 g; female *ultimus* 135-192 g, other races 161-205 (183) g; wingspan 45-49 cm. Sexes alike; female slightly smaller. Very similar to *A. olivaceus* but smaller and paler, with browner (less olive) upperparts, paler grey underparts, thighs vinaceous to rufous as undertail-coverts; olive yellow legs and feet. Immature very similar to adult, but throat whitish. Juvenile *ruficrissus* also similar to adult but has white throat; in worn plumage has slightly browner upperparts than adult and olive brown or light brown breast and belly; iris dark brown; bill blackish brown; legs and feet olive grey. Races separated on: bill colour, *ruficrissus* has reddish, swollen base to culmen; colour of undertail-coverts, more rufous in *ruficrissus*, pinkish red in nominate, tawny or vinaceous in other races; shade of underparts; and shade of upperparts, more olive-tinged in *nigrifrons*; in non-breeding *ruficrissus* green of bill fades, and red patch on culmen shrinks in size and fades to grey-brown. VOICE. Common call a loud shriek or wail, repeated 8-10 times; often given by pair in antiphonal duet. Also persistent and monotonous piping while feeding; clicking call given near nest; and soft but far-carrying clucking, often given by several birds in unison. Calls day and night.
Habitat. Dense stands of grass and reeds, sometimes bamboo, with pockets of dense bushes, near still or running fresh water; flooded scrub and swampy grasslands; floor of dry to swampy rain forest, often near marshes and lagoons, or in remnant patches or secondary growth; also sometimes in farmland adjacent to forest, *Lantana camara* thickets, sugar cane, and pasture and cleared land far from water; also recorded near human habitation, even in suburban gardens. On islands in Torres Strait occurs in areas bordering mangroves. Usually inhabits tallest, densest available vegetation, up to 2-4 m tall. Primarily in lowlands, but occurs up to 1500 m in New Guinea.
Food and Feeding. Earthworms, Orthoptera, Coleoptera, Lepidoptera (adults and larvae), frogs; also vegetable matter, including seeds of grass (Poaceae) and green shoots. Forages within or at edges of wetland vegetation, in cane fields and pasture, on ground in forest, at roadsides, and in shallow water; occasionally swims. Reaches or leaps up to take seeds or insects on vegetation or in air; runs grass heads through bill to remove seeds; probes into leaf litter. Shy and secretive; diurnal and crepuscular.
Breeding. Bacan (Moluccas), Sept; New Guinea, Sept-Apr; Australia, Oct-Apr. Normally seen in pairs or family groups; probably monogamous; territorial at least during breeding season. Nest usually

---

On following pages: 81. White-breasted Waterhen (*Amaurornis phoenicurus*); 82. Black Crake (*Amaurornis flavirostris*); 83. Sakalava Rail (*Amaurornis olivieri*); 84. Black-tailed Crake (*Amaurornis bicolor*); 85. Little Crake (*Porzana parva*); 86. Baillon's Crake (*Porzana pusilla*); 87. Spotted Crake (*Porzana porzana*); 88. Australian Crake (*Porzana fluminea*); 89. Sora (*Porzana carolina*); 90. Dot-winged Crake (*Porzana spiloptera*); 91. Ash-throated Crake (*Porzana albicollis*); 92. Ruddy-breasted Crake (*Porzana fusca*); 93. Band-bellied Crake (*Porzana paykullii*).

near or over water; often in bushy vegetation; also near forest edge or in secondary growth; often adjacent to tree, stump or fence post. Nest bowl-shaped, of grass, sometimes with dry leaves; built in tall, dense grass, sometimes in reeds or weeds, or on branches of *Lantana*; grass stems are bent down to form base and sides and loosely interwoven into rough canopy; ramp of trampled vegetation often present. External diameter 20-30 cm, depth 10-13 cm; cavity diameter 10-15 cm, depth 4-6·5 cm; built 10-200 cm above ground or water. Eggs 4-7; 1 clutch of 13 probably from 2 females; incubation up to 25 days, by both sexes, possibly mostly by female; hatching asynchronous; chicks semi-precocial; downy chick black, possibly fading later to black-brown on body and wings, iris dark brown, bill, legs and feet blackish; fed and cared for by both parents; usually fed in cover; no information on chick growth and development; post-juvenile moult recorded Australia, Mar-Apr. Hatching success (Australia) 32%; causes of loss include predation, flooding and desertion. May nest twice per season (Australia): first clutch usually 6-7 eggs, second usually 4-5; re-lays 14-21 days after clutch loss; one pair made 4 nesting attempts in 10 weeks.

Movements. Considered resident over most of range, and recorded throughout range in all seasons. Possibly nomadic in Australia, moving into some regions with onset of rains; may retire to areas with permanent water in dry season and move out to seasonally wet habitats in rains; thought to cross Torres Strait between Australia and New Guinea regularly; arrivals reported Cape York late Jan, and birds noted flying at night S from Cape York region at onset of wet season. Vagrant to Palau (W Micronesia), a bird found dead in sea, May 1979.

Status and Conservation. Not globally threatened. Formerly regarded as common and widespread in New Guinea, and common in Solomon Is (Santa Isabel). No current accurate estimates of abundance in Australia, where species may be widespread along coast of Northern Territory and Queensland, local and uncommon to reasonably common. In Australia, obviously well able to exploit man-modified habitats, especially on farmland, at artificial wetlands, and in gardens.

Bibliography. Beehler *et al*. (1986), Beruldsen (1975, 1976), Blakers *et al*. (1984), Clarke (1975), Coates (1985), Czechura (1983), Diamond (1972b), Diamond & Terborgh (1968), Draffan *et al*. (1983), Fraser & Mendel (1976), Gill (1970), Gilliard & LeCroy (1966, 1967), Hadden (1981), MacGillivray (1914), Marchant & Higgins (1993), Mayr (1949), McAllan & Bruce (1988), Mckean & Read (1979), Morgan & Morgan (1968), Serventy (1985), Sibley (1951), Storr (1973), Webb (1992), White (1922b, 1946), White & Bruce (1986), Wolters (1982).

81. White-breasted Waterhen

Amaurornis phoenicurus

French: Râle à poitrine blanche **German**: Weißbrust-Kielralle **Spanish**: Gallineta Pechiblanca

Taxonomy. *Gallinula phoenicurus* Pennant, 1769, Sri Lanka.
Possible races *chinensis* and *javanicus* included within nominate due to overlapping measurements, but may well be valid. Four subspecies recognized.

Subspecies and Distribution.
A. p. phoenicurus (Pennant, 1769) - Pakistan, India, Maldives and Sri Lanka to E China, Taiwan and Ryukyu Is, and S through SE Asia and Philippines to Greater Sundas; N populations winter to S, ranging W to Arabia. Currently expanding N into Japan.
A. p. insularis Sharpe, 1894 - Andaman and Nicobar Is.
A. p. midnicobaricus Abdulali, 1978 - C Nicobar Is.
A. p. leucomelanus (S. Müller, 1842) - Sulawesi, W Moluccas and Lesser Sundas.

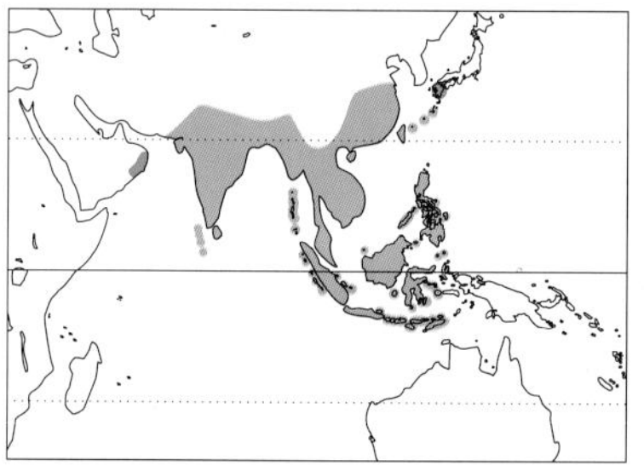

Descriptive notes. 28-33 cm; male 203-328 (228·5) g, female 166-225 (196·5) g. Relatively large, distinctive species; unmistakable, with combination of dark slate grey upperparts and flanks, prominent white face and underparts, and rufous rear flanks, vent and undertail-coverts. Female smaller, sometimes with duller bill. Some birds have grey sides of breast strongly barred with olive; partial albinism seems to occur in some areas, e.g. Andamans, Nicobars and Wallacea. In non-breeding season, male's bill becomes olive, washed brown on upper mandible. Immature duller than adult: upperparts more olive-brown, white of face obscured by brown feather tips; underparts tinged brownish; rufous areas duller; bill darker and duller. Juvenile similar but white of underparts, especially chin, throat and sides of breast, more heavily tinged dull brown; bill dark; legs and feet brownish yellow. Races separated on: extent of grey on head, in *leucomelanus* usually extending at least to forehead, and in birds from Lesser Sundas to ear-coverts and lores, not extending below eyes in nominate, and reaching only half way over top of head in *midnicobaricus* and *insularis*; extent and shade of grey on flanks, most extensive in *leucomelanus*, blackish in *insularis*; and colour of underparts, more olive in *midnicobaricus*. Head pattern very variable, and unstable mixed populations exist in Sulawesi and Lesser Sundas. Considerable individual variation and overlap with nominate race apparently prevents recognition of the races *chinensis* and *javanica*. Voice. Characteristic very loud call comprises variety of roars, grunts, croaks and chuckles, followed by a monotonous "kru-ak, kru-ak, kru-ak-a-wak-wak"; calling may continue for 15 minutes or more; calls most in early morning and in evening, also through night; often calls from perch in top of shrub or bamboo. Very vocal during breeding season; silent thereafter.

Habitat. Reedy or grassy swamps, marshes, tall grass with reeds and shrubs, bamboo stands, wet scrub, rice fields and sugar cane, sewage ponds, and shores of rivers, ponds, ditches and lakes; also thick forest (Andaman and Nicobar Is), forest edges and clearings, mangrove swamps, and scrub and bushes far from water. Often occurs close to human habitation, e.g. at village ponds, and enters compounds and public parks; runs about under roadside hedges. Occurs from lowlands up to 1500 m, to 2000 m in Nilgiri Hills, SW India.

Food and Feeding. Worms, molluscs, insects (beetles, grasshoppers, etc.) and their larvae, spiders and small fish; also grass seeds, and shoots and roots of marsh plants. Usually not particularly shy, and often seen out of cover. Gleans from ground; pecks seeds from standing grass. Forages in the open along water margins; feeds on beaches at low tide (Maldives). Climbs in bushes and trees, swims, and occasionally dives.

Breeding. India and Pakistan, Jun-Oct (SW monsoon); Andaman and Nicobar Is, Jun-Jul; Ryukyu, Apr-Oct; Sumatra, Jan, May, Jul, Sept, Nov; Java, all months except Apr, Oct and Nov; Lesser Sundas, downy chicks Apr-May; in Borneo, and probably on other tropical islands, may breed in almost any month. Normally seen singly or in pairs, sometimes in groups of up to 5; presumed monogamous, with pair-bond at least for duration of breeding season when apparently territorial. Nest a shallow cup-shaped pad of twigs, creeper stems and *Typha* leaves, placed on ground in grass or tangled undergrowth at margin of pond, ditch or flooded rice field, or concealed in shrub, bamboo clump or *Pandanus* palm thicket up to 2 m above ground, sometimes far from water. Eggs 4-9; incubation 20 days, by both sexes; downy chick black, with blackish bill and legs; chicks leave nest soon after hatching; fed and cared for by both parents. Probably multi-brooded in Ryukyu Is, which has aided rapid expansion there in recent years.

Movements. Resident throughout most of range, but N populations winter S to Lesser Sundas, occurring W to Arabia, where 13 recorded in Oman (Oct-Jan), 1 United Arab Emirates (Nov) and 1 Yemen (Mar). Wintering birds occur in Sumatra Nov-Apr. Extent of migration from northernmost breeding areas and seasonality of occurrence not clear; current expansion northwards into Japan indicative of mobility of species; recorded E to Bonin Is.

Status and Conservation. Not globally threatened. Formerly regarded as common throughout range. Currently common in Borneo, Sumatra, Java and Bali, and fairly common though local in Philippines. Accidental in Japan before 1970, after which has undergone major range extension, becoming common breeding resident in Ryukyu Is (Okinawa and in Yaeyama Is); now so common on Iriomote-jima that is thought to be ousting *Rallina eurizonoides*; expansion northwards is continuing, and now also occurs fairly regularly on main Japanese islands, having bred on Kyushu.

Bibliography. Abdulali (1978), Ali (1977), Ali & Ripley (1980), Bang (1968), Brazil (1991), Deignan (1945), Dickinson *et al*. (1991), Étchécopar & Hüe (1978), Evans (1994), Gallagher & Rogers (1980), Hellebrekers & Hoogerwerf (1967), Holmes & Nash (1991), King *et al*. (1975), Kirwan (1994), Lekagul & Round (1991), MacKinnon & Phillipps (1993), Madoc (1976), van Marle & Voous (1988), Medway & Wells (1976), Perennou *et al*. (1994), Phillips (1978), Rabor (1977), Rensch (1931), Ripley (1982), Roberts, T.J. (1991), Schmutz (1977), Smythies (1981, 1986), Stresemann (1941), Watling (1983), White & Bruce (1986), Wildash (1968), Yan Anhou & Pang Bingzhang (1986).

82. Black Crake

Amaurornis flavirostris

French: Râle à bec jaune **German**: Mohrensumpfhuhn **Spanish**: Polluela Negra Africana

Taxonomy. *Gallinula flavirostra* Swainson, 1837, Senegal.
Sometimes included in *Porzana*, or placed in monospecific *Limnocorax*, but inseparable from *Amaurornis* on skeletal characters. Forms superspecies with *A. olivieri*. Monotypic.

Distribution. Sub-Saharan Africa, from N edge of Sahel zone S to Cape, except in desert regions of NE & SW.

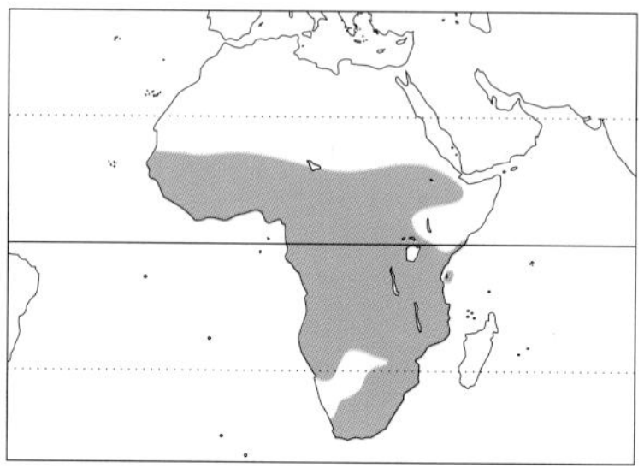

Descriptive notes. 19-23 cm; male 78-118 (96·5) g, female 70-110 (81) g; 159 both sexes 69-118 (89·5) g; weight varies greatly during year. Sexes alike. Non-breeding birds have duller red legs and feet. Very similar to *A. olivieri*, but upperparts washed olive-chestnut (in the field appearing slaty black, like rest of plumage) as opposed to rich dark brown; bright red orbital ring, legs and feet. Immature paler than adult; upperparts olivaceous brown; throat whitish; head, neck and underparts grey; bare parts duller than in adult. Juvenile entirely brown; bill blackish, changing to darkish green; iris grey to brown, changing to dark red; legs and feet blackish, changing to dull red. Voice. Very characteristic advertising call is a duet: one bird gives harsh repeated chatter "krrrok-krraaa", the other joins in with soft, purring notes. Either sex may give either call; duet not always antiphonal; sometimes other family members join in; all calling birds may crouch in circle, heads facing inwards. Alarm a sharp "chip"; contact calls soft, "pu" or "bup". Much less vocal outside breeding season.

Habitat. Occupies many types of freshwater wetland, normal requirements including moderate vegetation cover and some permanent flooding. Inhabits rank grass, sedges, reedbeds, papyrus, swampy thickets, bushes and other vegetation beside flowing and still waters; occurs in dense undergrowth of boggy clearings in forest; in open areas may occupy grassy marshes. Often found on ponds covered with *Nymphaea* and other floating vegetation; likes tangled vegetation, in which climbs, roosts and sometimes nests. Very adaptable, and in dry regions will occupy tiny streams with thin cover. Occurs close to human habitation and is quite bold and tolerant of disturbance, emerging to feed some distance from cover. Occurs from sea-level to 3000 m; in Natal, South Africa, most widespread and numerous below 1200 m, rarely recorded above 1800 m.

Food and Feeding. Worms, molluscs, crustaceans, adult and larval insects, small fish, frog tadpoles and small frogs; also seeds and other parts of water plants. Takes eggs and nestlings, including those of herons; kills small birds caught in mist-nets. Scavenges carcasses of crabs, crayfish and small birds. Often feeds in the open along shorelines, on floating vegetation, in short grass or cultivation, and on dry or burned ground; may venture some distance from cover. Takes food from surface of ground, water and vegetation, and from shallow water; probes into mud and dead vegetation; shifts fallen vegetation to search beneath. Readily perches and feeds on backs of hippopotami (*Hippopotamus amphibius*); perches on warthogs (*Phacochoerus aethiopicus*), apparently gleaning ectoparasites. Diurnal; markedly active after rain.

Breeding. In suitable conditions breeding may occur throughout year, with seasonal peaks in most regions, during or following rains: Senegal and Gambia, Dec-Mar, May-Jun, Aug-Sept; Sierra Leone, Jan, Mar, Oct, Dec; Liberia, Nov; Ghana, Jun, chicks Mar; Nigeria, Jan, Jun, Aug-Nov; Gabon, Mar, Jul; Zaire, almost all months; Sudan (Darfur) Oct; Ethiopia, Apr-Oct; Burundi, Mar; Uganda and W Kenya, all months (peaks Apr, Nov); rest of Kenya and NE Tanzania, all months (peaks Apr-Jun, Oct); rest of Tanzania, Apr, Oct-Nov; Zambia, Nov-Aug (peak Dec-Mar); Malawi, Mar-May, Jul-Sept, Dec; Mozambique, May-Jun; Zimbabwe, all months except May and Jul (peak Jan-Feb); Botswana, Aug-Oct; South Africa, Aug-May (peaks Nov, Jan-Mar). Monogamous; territorial when breeding. Nest a deep, bulky bowl of reeds, rushes, sedges, creepers, grasses or other water plants; placed in vegetation over water with rim 20-50 cm above water, but sometimes floating; also on ground or in grass tussock near water; sometimes up to 3 m high in bushes, possibly as protection against sudden flooding. External diameter 10-30 cm, depth 8-18 cm; cup depth 5-9 cm. Both sexes build, sometimes helped by young of previous broods; male may build extra nests or platforms for roosting. Usually 3 eggs (2-6), laid at daily intervals; 2 females once laid 6 and 4 eggs in same nest; incubation 13-19 days, by both parents, sometimes assisted by immatures; hatching asynchronous; black downy chicks have grey iris, pink bill with black band around centre, and slate legs and feet; chicks leave nest 1-3 days after hatching; fed and cared for by parents, helped by young of previous broods, for at least 3-6 weeks; juvenile plumage attained by 4-6 weeks; young fly at 5-6 weeks; may still beg for food when 2-3 months old; post-juvenile moult occurs between 2 and 4 months of age. Able to breed within 1 year of hatching. Up to 4 broods recorded per season; clutches may be laid when young of previous brood are as little as 3 weeks old. Co-operative breeding normal, young remaining within family group until end of breeding season, sometimes (Natal) until 16 months old.

Movements. Largely sedentary but also locally migratory. In drier N parts of range, in N Ghana, N Nigeria and Sahel zone of Sudan, appears with rains and disappears in dry season; moves in Zimbabwe when habitats dry out; occupies temporary waters in E Africa and NE Namibia; presumed migrant captured at night, Tsavo West (SE Kenya), in Dec. Seasonal variations in calling frequency, and in relative visibility of birds, may explain fluctuating reporting rates in other areas. Vagrant to Madeira, Jan 1895.

Status and Conservation. Not globally threatened. Commonest and most widespread crake in Africa; less secretive than other terrestrial wetland rallids of region, and has well known advertising call, so occurrences are relatively well documented. Common to abundant over most of range, but very localized and rare in drier W & C regions of S Africa. In favourable conditions, population density may be very high in some areas. Must have been affected by loss of wetland habitats, but is under no immediate threat anywhere. Readily occupies artificially created wetlands and temporary habitats.

Bibliography. Ash & Miskell (1983), Bannerman & Bannerman (1965), Benson & Benson (1975), Benson & Wagstaffe (1972), Benson et al. (1971), Britton, P.L. (1980), Brooke (1975), Brosset & Érard (1986), Brown & Britton (1980), Cave & Macdonald (1955), Chapin (1939), Cheesman & Sclater (1935), Clancey (1964b, 1971a), Dowsett & Dowsett-Lemaire (1980), Dowsett & Forbes-Watson (1993), Earlé & Grobler (1987), Elgood et al. (1994), Ginn et al. (1989), Gore (1990), Grimes (1987), Hopkinson & Masterson (1984), Irwin (1981), Jackson & Sclater (1938), Lewis & Pomeroy (1989), Mackworth-Praed & Grant (1957, 1962, 1970), Maclean (1993), Nikolaus (1987), Pakenham (1979), Penry (1994), Pinto (1983), Pitman (1929), Rutgers & Norris (1970), Schmitt (1975), Short et al. (1990), Sick (1930), Snow (1978), Tarboton, Kemp & Kemp (1987), Urban et al. (1986), Verheyen (1953), Watson (1969).

83. Sakalava Rail

Amaurornis olivieri

French: Râle d'Olivier   **German**: Malegassensumpfhuhn   **Spanish**: Polluela Negra Malgache
Other common names: Olivier's Crake

Taxonomy. *Porzana Olivieri* Grandidier and Berlioz, 1929, Antsalova, Province of Maintirano, west Madagascar.
Although sometimes placed in *Porzana*, has close affinities with *A. flavirostris*, with which forms superspecies. Monotypic.
Distribution. WC Madagascar.

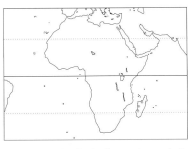

Descriptive notes. 19 cm. Distinctive: dark slate grey plumage with rich dark brown from mantle to rump and on upperwing-coverts; greenish yellow bill, pinkish red legs and eyelids, and red eye. Sexes alike. Immature and juvenile not properly described, but probably browner overall than adult. VOICE. Unknown.
Habitat. Streams and marshes offering stretches of open water, patches of floating vegetation especially water-lily (*Nymphaea*) leaves for foraging, and adjacent dense cover of reedbeds (*Phragmites*) for shelter; also among grass and bushes emerging from water in a clearing of a flooded palm-covered valley.

Food and Feeding. Food unknown. Apparently forages on floating vegetation near cover, as does *A. flavirostris*, but is less active and bold.
Breeding. Lays Mar; well grown young also seen late Mar. One nest was placed 50 cm above ground level in bulrushes (*Typha*) near water, in marshy area dominated by *Nymphaea* and *Phragmites* and with stretches of open water. This nest held 2 eggs, probably a complete clutch; downy chicks black.
Movements. None described.
Status and Conservation. CRITICALLY ENDANGERED. Known from three widely separated localities in the Sakalava country of lowland W Madagascar: Antsalova and the region of L Masama and L Bemamba; Ambararatabe near Soalala; and Nosy-Ambositra on R Mangoky. Rare and localized, with very few records. Like Madagascar Grebe (*Tachybaptus pelzelnii*), has possibly suffered from loss of lilypad habitat owing to rice cultivation and the impact of introduced fish. May suffer from systematic exploitation for food: the eggs from the only recorded nest were eaten by local people. Not seen since 1962, despite searches since mid-1980's in suitable habitat. Not very shy, so thought unlikely to have been overlooked in accessible habitat, but some potential wetland habitats are not severely threatened, and populations may survive between Antsalova and Mahajanga.
Bibliography. Benson & Wagstaffe (1972), Collar & Andrew (1988), Collar & Stuart (1985), Collar et al. (1994), Dee (1986), Delacour (1932), Dowsett & Forbes-Watson (1993), Grandidier & Berlioz (1929), Langrand (1990), Milon et al. (1973), Rand (1936), Snow (1978).

84. Black-tailed Crake

Amaurornis bicolor

French: Râle bicolore   **German**: Zweifarben-Kielralle   **Spanish**: Polluela Bicolor
Other common names: Elwes's Crake

Taxonomy. *Porzana bicolor* Walden, 1872, Rungbee, Darjeeling.
Sometimes retained in *Porzana*. Monotypic.
Distribution. NE India and Myanmar E to SC China (S Sichuan, Guizhou, Yunnan), and S to N Thailand, NW Vietnam and N Laos; recent possible record from EC Nepal.

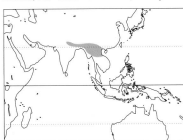

Descriptive notes. 20-22 cm. Rufous brown upperparts contrast with ashy grey head, neck and underparts; tail black; bill pale bluish green with pale tip and red patch near base; iris blood red; orbital skin pink; legs and feet dull to bright red. Sexes alike. Sympatric *A. akool* larger and duller, with uniformly olive brown upperparts, including head and neck, and olive brown from belly to undertail-coverts. Paler and larger than rather similar *A. olivieri* of Madagascar. Immature similar to adult but with brown iris. Juvenile not described. VOICE. Song has initial rasping "waak-waak" call, followed by long descending trill, with interval of 5-15 minutes before repetition; given mainly at dusk, but also heard in early morning.

Habitat. Forest patches in and around rice cultivation; swampy patches and streams in forest; grass-bordered streams and pools, often shaded by trees; small marshes in grass and cultivation; sometimes wet grassland; often in very dense cover, but will feed in open. Recorded from lowlands, but primarily a highland species, occurring at 1000-3600 m.

Food and Feeding. Worms, molluscs, insects, and seeds of marsh plants. Recorded feeding with rapid pecking motion, wings drooped, tail cocked and frequently jerked. A great skulker; emerges at edge of cover to feed in early morning and evening, but if alarmed, rapidly retreats to cover, if necessary flying or swimming; recently recorded feeding at open site near people in mid-afternoon.
Breeding. Mid-May to Aug in Khasi Hills, SC Meghalaya (NE India); 2 adults with 3 young in early Aug at Doi Inthanon (NW Thailand). Monogamous. Nest a rough pad of loosely assembled twigs and grass, with a slight central depression; built on wet ground in forest undergrowth; sometimes placed 1-2 m (once c. 7 m) above ground in bushes or trees; both sexes build. Eggs 5-8; incubation by both sexes; green-glossed black downy chick has hazel eye, pale bill and dusky legs.
Movements. Resident, but to date recorded as occurring in N Vietnam and Laos only in winter; extent of seasonal occurrence not clear.
Status and Conservation. Not globally threatened. Infrequently recorded because of its skulking habits, but formerly regarded as locally common. Several recent records (from mid-1980's) from Doi Inthanon National Park, NW Thailand, where species has been recorded year round, and breeding confirmed. No further information on current status, but habitat destruction has probably affected its numbers adversely.
Bibliography. Ali (1977), Ali & Ripley (1980), Étchécopar & Hüe (1978), Inskipp & Round (1989), King et al. (1975), Lekagul & Round (1991), Meyer de Schauensee (1984), Ripley (1977, 1982), Ripley & Beehler (1985), Sériot et al. (1986), Smythies (1986).

Genus *PORZANA*   Vieillot, 1816

85. Little Crake

Porzana parva

French: Marouette poussin   **German**: Kleines Sumpfhuhn   **Spanish**: Polluela Bastarda

Taxonomy. *Rallus parvus* Scopoli, 1769, probably from Carniola.
Monotypic.
Distribution. Locally in Europe E across Transcaucasus, SE Transcaspia, W Tadjikistan, Kazakhstan and W Xinjiang (Tien Shan and Tarim Basin E to Lop Nur), NW China. Winters from Mediterranean S to W Africa (Senegal, Niger, Nigeria) and E Africa (Uganda, Kenya), and E through Arabia to W Pakistan and NW India.

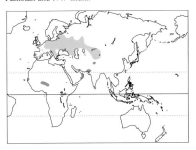

Descriptive notes. 18-20 cm; male 30-72 (50) g, female 36-65 (49·5) g; wingspan 34-39 cm. Marked sexual dimorphism in plumage: male has blue-grey face and underparts, with narrow white bars on rear flanks and black and white barring on undertail-coverts; in female blue-grey replaced by buff except for pale ash grey supercilium, lores and cheeks, and whitish chin and throat, while barring from flanks to undertail-coverts paler and less distinct. Slim shape, produced by relatively long neck, wings, tail and legs, is useful distinction from sympatric *Porzana* species. Unlike *P. porzana* and *Aenigmatolimnas marginalis*, has barred undertail-coverts. Confusion most likely with *P. pusilla* but has paler, duller brown, more uniform upperparts and upperwing-coverts, lacking contrasting white markings except on centre of mantle, but with obvious pale olive brown stripe along scapulars (these characters noticeable at rest and in flight); broad pale inner edge to tertials, red spot at base of green bill; green legs and feet; much greater primary projection in folded wing; longer tail (often not obvious in the field); and stronger, less fluttering flight; male also separable by fainter underpart barring starting only on lower flanks and belly. All ages separable from juvenile *P. pusilla* on structure, and on upperpart pattern, including pale lines on scapulars and tertials; adult female also differs from juvenile *P. pusilla* in having pale brown-buff underparts; juvenile less strongly barred than *P. pusilla* on underparts and has fewer white markings on upperparts and wings. From post-juvenile moult through first breeding season male and female retain some juvenile whitish markings on scapulars and upperwing-coverts (absent in full adult); male has olive wash on belly and pale edges to some blue-grey underparts feathers; female has paler buff underparts. Birds in first winter have red-brown iris. Juvenile resembles female but has more white spots on upperwing-coverts and scapulars, almost white supercilium, darker brown cheeks and ear-coverts, buff and cream mottling on sides of breast, and dark brown and whitish barring from breast to rear flanks and undertail-coverts; iris becomes olive green and then brown; bill becomes olive green and then horn with greener lower mandible; legs and feet olive brown, becoming olive green. VOICE. Advertising call of male a loud, barking "quack" or "quek" repeated every 1-2 seconds for up to several minutes before accelerating and descending in pitch, ending on softer, more guttural notes; sings mainly at night, sometimes during day. Female's advertising call a fast, hard trill, often preceded by 1-2 sharp "quek" notes; also a sharp "kik" often given in duet with mate. Alarm a sharp "tyiuck"; contact calls include subdued trills, "quek" and "gug" notes.
Habitat. In breeding season occurs typically in temperate and steppe zones, usually in lowlands but occasionally to c. 2000 m. Frequents dense emergent vegetation of freshwater wetlands, including margins of lakes and rivers, and flooded woodland; in breeding season differs from sympatric congeners in favouring monospecific or mixed stands of tall plants such as *Scirpus*, *Typha*, *Carex*, *Sparganium*, and also *Phragmites* which has both dead and living stems; such stands may be in fairly deep water and include horizontal stems which form bridges. Outside breeding season may share similar habitat with *P. porzana* and *P. pusilla*, and also occurs in seasonally inundated grassland. Frequents rice fields in both breeding and wintering areas. Prefers more deeply flooded habitats than *P. porzana*. Moves freely over floating vegetation and climbs easily up stems. On migration occurs in atypical habitats.
Food and Feeding. Mostly insects, especially water beetles (Hydrophilidae) and also Hemiptera, Neuroptera, and adult and larval Diptera, and also seeds of aquatic plants (*Carex*, *Sparganium*, *Polygonum* and *Nymphaea*); worms, gastropods, spiders and water mites (Arachnida), and aquatic vegetation such as young shoots. Forages while swimming, wading or walking over stems and leaves; takes food from mud, water surface or vegetation but does not probe; also dives.
Breeding. C Europe, May-Aug; bred once in Egypt, Apr. Monogamous and territorial, pair-bond maintained only during breeding season. Nest a shallow cup of plant stems and leaves; placed in thick vegetation near or over water, often raised on tussock or platform of dead material; external diameter 11-20 cm, internal diameter 10-16 cm, height 2-9 cm. In favourable habitat, nests frequently only 30-

35 m apart. Both sexes probably build; male also builds brood platforms around breeding nest. Usually 7-9 eggs (4-11), laid at daily intervals; replacements laid after egg loss; incubation 21-23 days (15-17 days per egg), by both sexes; hatching asynchronous; black downy chick has green gloss on upperparts, head and throat, with iris grey-brown to brown-black, bill white with yellow or pink tinge and grey base, legs and feet grey-brown to blackish; chicks precocial and nidifugous; fed and cared for by both parents while small; become self-feeding after a few days; probably brooded in nest for much of breeding period; young can fly at 45-50 days, when fully fledged, but are independent and probably deserted by parents before this. 2 broods quite frequent. Post-juvenile moult Sept-Nov or Nov-Mar. Age of first breeding 1 year.

Movements. Distribution imperfectly known due to secretive behaviour, and few wintering sites known (map tentative). W Palearctic breeders probably winter in Mediterranean basin, Africa (including Egypt), Arabia (Oman and possibly elsewhere), Iraq and Iran; winters occasionally in C Europe, and W to Britain. S movements late Aug-Nov, probably peaking Sept-Oct; occurs as migrant on all larger Mediterranean islands; passes through N Africa (Morocco to Egypt) late Aug-Oct, Sudan Sept-Nov and Somalia Sept-Oct; present Oman Aug-Apr. Presumed wintering birds recorded Senegal Sept-Nov, N Nigeria Dec and Feb-Mar, S Niger Sept, Oct and Jan, W Uganda Dec (1901) and C Kenya Jan (1983); probably winters regularly S to equator in Kenya and Uganda. Like *P. porzana*, probably itinerant in African wintering areas in response to habitat changes. Return passage noted N Africa Mar-May (sometimes Jun) and Mediterranean late Feb-May; also 1 presumed migrant Ethiopia Apr; most arrive on breeding grounds late Mar-Apr. Most N African records are in spring, suggesting that autumn migrants may overfly region. Vagrant or uncommon (overlooked?) winter visitor to Liberia (no dates), Zambia (Mar 1980) and possibly Ivory Coast (1 questionable Jun record); accidental Ireland, Denmark, Norway, Finland, Lebanon, Syria, Azores, Canary Is and Madeira. Little information on movement of E populations: in Azerbaijan passage noted Nov and Mar-Apr; formerly remained during warm winters but no recent information. Normally migrates singly; concentrations rarely recorded, possibly because species secretive.

Status and Conservation. Not globally threatened. Current status poorly known; formerly thought to be less severely affected than congeners by wetland drainage and reclamation, and in some areas possibly favoured by habitat changes. Formerly regarded as uncommon to scarce breeder in Europe, but increases reported in Netherlands after 1942, and in Hungary with introduction of rice cultivation and expansion of fish ponds. In former USSR, in past regarded as rare in N but common to fairly abundant in S, with total numbers fairly large; in Azerbaijan currently regarded as uncommon in summer, probably breeding. Transient in much of W Xinjiang, but may breed in Tarim Basin; uncommon in winter, W Pakistan (Baluchistan, Sind) and NW India (Gilgit, 1 record Bombay). Rarely recorded Oman, on passage and in winter. Apart from considerable numbers recorded on passage through N Africa, including many recent records from Algeria and Libya, records from Africa are very few: total of 15 birds recorded Senegal, 12 N Nigeria, 4+ S Niger, 7 W Uganda, 3 C Kenya, 1 Zambia; uncommon Sudan (recorded only in autumn); rare Ethiopia and Eritrea; 2 old records NW Somalia. However, apparently large numbers breeding in W of former USSR, considerable passage through N Africa, and occurrence in deserts of Algeria and Libya suggest broader sub-Saharan distribution and greater numbers than currently known. Bred Algeria mid-19th century, and recent breeding suspected; bred once Egypt.

Bibliography. Ali & Ripley (1980), Archer & Godman (1937-1961), Ash (1990), Bauer (1960a, 1960b), Becker, P. (1995), Bradshaw (1993b), Clarke (1985), Cramp & Simmons (1980), Dementiev & Gladkov (1951b), Dowsett & Forbes-Watson (1993), Elgood *et al*. (1994), Étchécopar & Hüe (1964, 1978), Evans (1994), Gatter (1988), Giraudoux *et al*. (1988), Glayre & Magnenat (1977), Glutz von Blotzheim *et al*. (1973), Goodman *et al*. (1989), Hogg *et al*. (1984), Hüe & Étchécopar (1970), Jackson & Sclater (1938), Knystautas (1993), Koenig (1943), Mackworth-Praed & Grant (1957, 1970), Morel & Roux (1966), Nikolaus (1987), Patrikeev (1995), Paz (1987), Potapov & Flint (1987), Roberts, T.J. (1991), Shirihai (1996), Simeonov *et al*. (1990), Taylor, P.B. (1980c), Thiollay (1985), Urban *et al*. (1986), Vaurie (1965), Wilkinson *et al*. (1982).

86. Baillon's Crake

Porzana pusilla

French: Marouette de Baillon **German**: Zwergsumpfhuhn **Spanish**: Polluela Chica
Other common names: Marsh/Tiny Crake

Taxonomy. *Rallus pusillus* Pallas, 1776, Dauria.
Forms superspecies with recently extinct *P. palmeri* of Laysan I (Hawaii). Race *mayri* possibly synonymous with *palustris*. Possible race *obscura*, of sub-Saharan Africa and Madagascar, doubtfully valid. Six subspecies normally recognized.

Subspecies and Distribution.
P. p. intermedia (Hermann, 1804) - Europe E to Asia Minor, and S locally in Morocco, Tunisia and Ethiopia, then from E Zaire to C Kenya and S to Angola, Namibia and South Africa, and also Madagascar; European birds winter in Africa.
P. p. pusilla (Pallas, 1776) - R Dnestr E through C & E Asia to Amurland, N China, N Korea and Japan, S to Iran and N India and irregularly in Sumatra and Sulawesi; winters in India, Sri Lanka and Myanmar, and from S China to Indonesia and Philippines.
P. p. mira Riley, 1938 - Borneo.
P. p. mayri Junge, 1952 - New Guinea.
P. p. palustris Gould, 1843 - E New Guinea, Australia and Tasmania.
P. p. affinis (J. E. Gray, 1846) - New Zealand and Chatham Is.

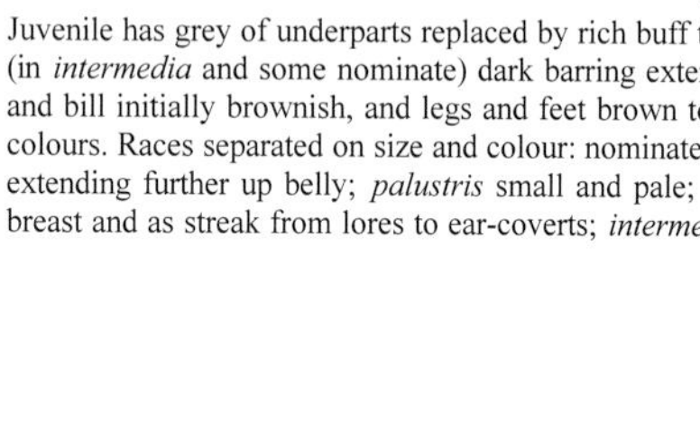

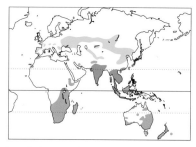

Descriptive notes. 17-19 cm; male 23-45 (35·5) g, female 17-55 (34) g, unsexed 20-52 (33) g; wingspan of *intermedia* 33-37 cm, of *palustris* 23-25 cm. Sexes similar but female often has rufous-brown streak, varyingly from over ear to complete eyestripe; sometimes paler grey on underparts than male (nominate race); pale patch on chin larger in female and in both sexes in non-breeding season, but may not be a consistent character. Separable on plumage, size and structure from sympatric congeners; legs and feet often said to be flesh-coloured, but usually greenish grey, olive or yellowish and thus may resemble those of *P. parva*. Immature like adult. Juvenile has grey of underparts replaced by rich buff to white, often mottled from face to breast, and (in *intermedia* and some nominate) dark barring extending forwards to upper flanks and breast; iris and bill initially brownish, and legs and feet brown to grey-flesh, but bare parts rapidly attain adult colours. Races separated on size and colour: nominate and *intermedia* largest, with underpart barring extending further up belly; *palustris* small and pale; nominate has some rufous brown on sides of breast and as streak from lores to ear-coverts; *intermedia* richly coloured and boldly patterned; *mira* has white throat and breast; races from Australasia and New Guinea paler grey on underparts. Voice. Advertising call of male a hard, dry rattle (in African birds identical to rattle call of *Rallus caerulescens*) lasting 1-3 seconds and repeated every 1-2 seconds; calls mainly at night. Probable alarm call a series of loud, rapidly repeated grating notes, often in a phrase such as "kraa-kraa-kraa-chachachachacha". Alarm call of both sexes a sharp "tac" or "tyiuk".

Habitat. Freshwater to saline, permanent to ephemeral palustrine wetlands with dense vegetation and often floating plants, including marshes, swamps, flooded meadows, margins of open water, peat bogs, interdune pans, irrigated crops, temporarily inundated depressions and marshy artificial wetlands; occasionally salt-marsh. Breeding habitat usually characterized by relatively fine, low, dense, tussocky or continuous vegetation such as flooded sedges and grasses (*Eleocharis*, *Carex*, *Cyperus*, *Juncus*, *Scirpus*, *Phalaris*, *Leersia*, etc.). Outside breeding season occurs in wider variety of habitats, including: tussocky cover interspersed with mud patches around ponds and lakes; interior and edges of tall reedbeds (*Phragmites*, *Typha*, sometimes with *Sesbania* bushes) with extensive mud and shallow puddles, in Kenya; flooded *Polygonum* beds; damp grassland; sewage ponds; and dense grassy vegetation of parks, golf courses, airfields, etc. in Australia. Occurs up to 1500 m, but to 2450 m in New Guinea.

Food and Feeding. Mostly adult and larval aquatic insects, including Coleoptera, Hemiptera, Odonata, Plecoptera, Phryganeidae (caddisflies) and Culicidae; also Annelida, molluscs, small crustaceans, small fish, green plant material, and seeds (including *Carex*); in captivity also small lizards and geckos. Forages on mud, probing and taking prey from surface, and in shallow water, occasionally to belly depth, immersing bill to seize prey; probes into bases of decaying plants and among or under detritus, dead stems and roots; often forages while walking on floating vegetation and broken reeds, and while swimming; reported to dive for food. Non-breeding birds in C Kenya fed largely on the most abundant small aquatic invertebrates available, including Ostracoda and Copepoda longer than 1·5 mm, showing preference for feeding in very shallow drying puddles, where prey most concentrated. Normally forages close to, or within, dense cover; most active in early morning and from late afternoon to evening.

Breeding. Europe, May-Jul; Morocco, May, breeding condition Apr; Egypt (formerly), Apr; Ethiopia, Jul; Tanzania, breeding condition Apr; Malawi, Jun, breeding condition Mar; Zimbabwe, Jan-Mar; Botswana, breeding condition Jan; South Africa, Sept, Nov-Mar; in former USSR from May; Kashmir, May-Aug; Sumatra, Feb; Japan, May-Aug; Australia, Sept-Jan, exceptionally also Feb-Mar; New Zealand, Oct-Nov; nests during or just after wet season. Monogamous and territorial; pair-bond maintained only while breeding. Nest a shallow cup or platform of material available nearby, e.g. dead leaves, dry rush stems, grass or water weed; often with vegetation pulled over to form canopy; on ground in thick vegetation close to water, in soft grass or on tussock in water; built 4-60 cm above water level; sometimes anchored in water amongst growing rice crops or on floating vegetation; occasionally in or under low bush. Rather flimsy; material added during incubation, especially if water rises. External diameter 9-15 cm, height 8-15 cm, internal diameter 7-10 cm, cup depth 1-3 cm. Both sexes probably build. Some nests have adjoining platform where young sit after hatching. Eggs 4-11 (mean 7·4) in Europe, 4-7 (5·9) Australia, 2-7 (4) Africa; laid at daily intervals; incubation 16-20 days, by both sexes; hatching asynchronous (W Palearctic) or within 24 hours (Australia); black downy chick has bottle-green gloss, iris bluish brown to black, bill bone white to straw yellow, legs and feet grey-brown to black; young precocial and nidifugous; fed and cared for by both parents, and brooded when small; become self-feeding after a few days; independent before fledging; fledging c. 35-45 days. Age of first breeding 1 year. 2 broods recorded in former USSR.

Movements. Extent of migrations unclear (map highly conjectural). In Europe, most *intermedia* move S late Aug to Oct, migrants occurring all round Mediterranean and probably overflying N Africa to winter in sub-Saharan Africa, where distribution poorly known because of close resemblance to resident birds; presumed Palearctic birds obtained in Somalia in Sept, N Sudan in Apr and Sept-Oct, and Senegal in Nov and Jan, but Kenya occurrences referable to African breeding population; return passage Mar-May, most returning migrants in N Africa being recorded Mar-Apr; returns to C Europe May. Migrants recorded Asia Minor, and birds of unknown origin winter in Iraq and Israel; occurs Oman Aug-Dec. African populations usually considered resident but at least local movements recorded in E, C and S Africa in response to seasonal habitat changes. Nominate birds winter to S of breeding range; migrants recorded in Azerbaijan, Apr; recorded once from Egypt; in Japan most occur May-Sept; regarded as winter visitor to Philippines and Sumatra, but recorded Philippines Aug, Oct, Jan and Mar-Jun, and probably breeds irregularly in Sumatra; local seasonal movements recorded in S Vietnam. Race *palustris* possibly migratory in Australia, where many disappear from S part of range Apr-Sept, probably migratory immatures recorded Northern Territory Jul, and some birds probably cross Torres Strait; erratic movements also recorded in response to vegetation changes, drought and flooding; sometimes hits lighthouses, bridges and buildings; vagrant to Macquarie I. Migratory status of races *mira*, *mayri* and *affinis* unknown.

Status and Conservation. Not globally threatened. Some races rare or poorly known. In W Palearctic, *intermedia* now regarded as rare and very local, having declined considerably since 19th century; formerly bred N Algeria (L Zana) and Egypt (Nile Delta) and may still do so; breeds Morocco and possibly Tunisia; uncommon to rare Ethiopia; widely distributed and still locally common in sub-Saharan Africa, but status unclear in some areas; local in Madagascar. Status of nominate race largely unclear but in past bred abundantly in Kashmir; no recent records from Azerbaijan, apparently uncommon in Indonesia and Philippines, and uncommon to rare in Japan. Race *mira* known from type specimen collected from R Mahakam in E Borneo in 1912 but may be relatively widespread in that area and perhaps elsewhere in Borneo; also suggested to occur in Malay Peninsula, N Sumatra and Java. Race *mayri*, endemic to New Guinea, probably very rare and local, known only from Wissel Lakes region and Weyland Mts, Irian Jaya. In Australia, *palustris* widespread and apparently locally common in E, SE & SW, but reclamation of wetlands has reduced available habitat; apparently rare and local in Tasmania and New Guinea. Race *affinis* probably widespread throughout New Zealand. Like most other wetland rallids, present species locally threatened throughout range by habitat destruction and modification, and overall numbers are declining. Frequently uses ephemeral or seasonal wetlands, and such habitats are frequently drained, overgrazed or cultivated; however, species does also occupy artificially created wetlands.

Bibliography. Ali & Ripley (1980), Archer & Godman (1937-1961), Barlow & Sutton (1975), Becker, P. (1995), Beehler *et al*. (1986), Benson (1964a), Benson & Benson (1975), Benson & Pitman (1966), Blakers *et al*. (1984), Bradshaw (1993b), Brazil (1991), Brooke (1984a), Bryant (1942), Bryant & Amos (1949), Chambers (1989), Clancey (1964b, 1971a), Coates (1985), Cramp & Simmons (1980), Dementiev & Gladkov (1951b), Dickinson *et al*. (1991), Dowsett & Forbes-Watson (1993), Draffan *et al*. (1983), Elliott (1989), Étchécopar & Hüe (1964, 1978), Evans (1994), Ginn *et al*. (1989), Glayre & Magnenat (1977), Glutz von Blotzheim *et al*. (1973), Goodman *et al*. (1989), Hobbs (1967), Hüe & Étchécopar (1970), Irwin (1981), Kaufmann (1987a), Kaufmann & Lavers (1987), Knystautas (1993), Koshelev (1994), Kraus & Lischka (1956), Langrand (1990), Lekagul & Round (1991), MacKinnon & Phillipps (1993), Mackworth-Praed & Grant (1957, 1962, 1970), Maclean (1993), Marchant & Higgins (1993), van Marle & Voous (1988), Mason & Wolfe (1975), Moore (1983), Nikolaus (1981), Patrikeev (1995), Paz (1987), Perennou *et al*. (1994), Pinto (1983), Potapov & Flint (1987), Ripley (1982), Roberts, T.J. (1991), Rogacheva (1992), Rutgers & Norris (1970), Sclater (1906), Serventy (1985), Shirihai (1996), Short *et al*. (1990), Simeonov *et al*. (1990), Smythies (1981, 1986), Snow (1978), Stokes (1983), Szabó (1970), Taylor (1987), Urban *et al*. (1986), Wheeler (1948), White & Bruce (1986).

87. Spotted Crake

Porzana porzana

French: Marouette ponctuée **German**: Tüpfelsumpfhuhn **Spanish**: Polluela Pintoja
Other common names: Eurasian Spotted Crake

Taxonomy. *Rallus Porzana* Linnaeus, 1766, France.
Monotypic.
Distribution. British Is and Spain E across S Scandinavia, N Mediterranean and Balkans to W & C Russia, Caucasus and Iran, continuing to Kazakhstan, SW Siberia (Suva) and NW China (W Xinjiang). Winters from Mediterranean and Middle East S to W Africa, and from Ethiopia S to South Africa and W to Angola and Namibia; Pakistan, India and W Myanmar; irregularly on SW Caspian Sea.

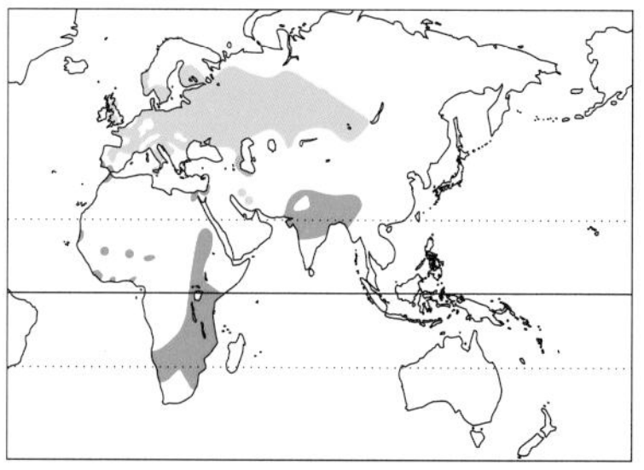

Descriptive notes. 22-24 cm; unsexed 57-147 (87·5) g; wingspan 37-42 cm. Rather plump crake, readily distinguished from sympatric rallids on size, structure and plumage: spotted appearance, lack of extensive grey on underparts (can be somewhat greyer than illustrated), buff undertail-coverts; yellow bill with greenish tip and orange-red spot at base of upper mandible; white leading edge to wing well visible in flight. Sexes similar; male in non-breeding plumage has less grey and more spotting on face and underparts; female has less grey and more spots than male on these areas in both plumages. Rare variations in colour of undertail-coverts from dark feather tips to black and white barring. *P. carolina* differs most obviously in colour and pattern of head, neck and breast, and lack of red on bill. Immature similar to non-breeding adult but has more white spots on side of head, and narrower black margins to white markings on breast; bill changes from yellow-brown with yellow base to olive green with orange base. Juvenile similar to immature but has streak over eye brown or cream with tiny white spots, neck mottled grey-brown and off-white, breast olive brown to bright brown with white or buff markings, and flanks less contrastingly barred; eye greenish; bill olive brown to greenish horn, darker at tip and more orange at base; legs dull green. Voice. Advertising call of male a short, sharp ascending whistle "whitt", suggesting whiplash, repeated about once per second for up to several minutes; given mainly from dusk through night; female has softer version, sometimes given in duet. Also quiet "hui" notes, a loud repetitive ticking call, a hard "eh" of alarm and a warning "tshick".
Habitat. Freshwater wetlands with dense cover of sedges and rushes (*Carex*, *Eleocharis*, *Cyperus*, *Juncus*, etc.), grass (e.g. *Panicum*, *Poa*, *Deschampsia*), *Polygonum*, *Iris*, *Equisetum* and other emergents; sometimes with trees such as *Acacia*, *Sesbania*, *Betula*, *Salix* and *Alnus*; frequents areas where substrate moist, muddy or flooded to c. 15 cm. Optimum conditions found in wetlands with range of water depths or where suitable foraging areas produced by variations in water level. Occurs in marshes (permanent or seasonal) and fens, at sewage ponds, pools in flooded grassland, and at margins of dams, lakes and sluggish rivers. On migration may occur in atypical habitats. In African winter quarters often occupies ephemeral habitats, with rapidly changing water levels, not normally inhabited by breeding Afrotropical rallids. Recorded up to 2420 m.
Food and Feeding. Omnivorous; mainly small aquatic invertebrates and parts of aquatic plants. Takes earthworms, molluscs, Arachnida, insects and their larvae (Trichoptera, Odonata, Diptera, Coleoptera, Hemiptera, Lepidoptera and ants), and small fish stranded in drying pools. Plant material includes algae, shoots, leaves and roots, and seeds (*Panicum*, *Oryza*, *Carex* and *Schoenoplectus*). Forages in water up to 7 cm deep, and on wet to dry mud, usually keeping close to cover; picks food from surface of substrate and immerses head in water; sometimes feeds 10-15 m from cover with groups of shorebirds such as Wood Sandpipers (*Tringa glareola*); stretches up to strip seeds from grass inflorescences; also walks on floating vegetation and gleans from underside of water-lily (*Nymphaea*) leaves; swims occasionally. Most active early and late in the day.
Breeding. Europe, Apr-Jul; former USSR, May-Jul. Monogamous; pair-bond maintained only during breeding season. Territorial when breeding and also in winter quarters. Nest a thick-walled cup of dead leaves and stems of available vegetation; placed in thick vegetation close to or over standing water, in tussock or built up well above water level; concealing vegetation often pulled over to form canopy; external diameter 12-14 cm, height 8-10 cm. Both sexes build. Usually 8-12 eggs (6-14), laid at rate of 1 per 1·5 days; replacements laid after clutch loss; incubation 18-19 days per egg, up to 24 days for clutch, by both sexes; hatching asynchronous, taking 3 days; black downy chick has green gloss on head, throat and upperparts, iris grey to brown-black, upper mandible red at base, yellow in middle and white at tip, lower mandible black with red-brown base, white band and black band in middle, and white tip, legs and feet grey-brown to black; chicks precocial and nidifugous; fed and cared for by both parents; remain in nest until all clutch hatched, then leave in 8-10 hours; become self-feeding after several days; fledging up to 45 days; post-juvenile moult late Jul to Oct. Hatching success 83%. Age of first breeding 1 year. Usually double-brooded.
Movements. European birds move S to SW in autumn; some winter S Europe and N Africa (Egypt and Morocco), others in W, E & SE Africa; relative paucity of wintering records from Africa attributed to secretiveness and inaccessibility of habitat. Autumn dispersal begins Jul; some birds halt in Aug to moult, and are flightless for 2-3 weeks; marked S movement Aug-Sept; most reach or pass Mediterranean by mid-Nov; passage recorded Egypt and Sudan Sept-Oct, Kenya Nov-Jan. Recorded Sudan and Ethiopia Sept-May; E Africa Nov to early May; C to S Africa Nov-Apr, with peak numbers Jan-Mar. In W Africa occurs Senegal Sept-Feb; isolated Sept-Mar records Mauritania, Mali, Chad, Niger, Liberia, Ivory Coast, and Nigeria (several); probably commoner and more widespread than records indicate. Itinerant in African wintering areas; in Zambia arrives at flooded sites soon after local rain and departs when conditions become too dry, maximum period of residence being 23 days. Passage through N Africa and Mediterranean more marked in spring, suggesting that more birds overfly these regions in autumn; return movements recorded Morocco to Libya and Sudan Mar-May, Kenya Apr-May, and Europe Mar-Apr; European breeding grounds reoccupied Apr. Birds of unknown origin pass through Iraq and Near East; passage Saudi Arabia and Aden Apr and Nov, Oman Sept-Dec; may overwinter regularly. Movements noted former USSR Aug-Oct and Mar-May, in Azerbaijan Oct-Dec and Mar-Apr; sometimes winters in Azerbaijan. Arrives N India Sept-Oct; return movements noted NW Pakistan Mar-Apr. Vagrant to Iceland, Greenland (9 records), Lesser Antilles and Seychelles; regarded as vagrant to Djibouti, Somalia, Socotra, Yemen and C Thailand. One individual found at same wintering site, Transvaal, in 2 successive years.
Status and Conservation. Not globally threatened. Numbers fluctuate widely in most areas, due to nature of preferred habitat, but decreases evident over most of European range during present century due to wetland drainage; now local and uncommon to rare in most regions. In Africa regarded as locally common in winter in Egypt, Senegal and Burundi but scarce elsewhere except in major known wintering region comprising Zambia, Malawi, Zimbabwe and probably Mozambique, within which region possibly not uncommon but overall numbers difficult to assess because of erratic occurrence and annual fluctuations. Generally uncommon in S Africa but locally common at temporary pans in extreme NE Namibia; 1 unconfirmed oversummering record Lesotho. Wintering habitat in Africa probably decreasing as result of wetland destruction. Formerly numerous in S & C USSR, and locally abundant further N and in Transcaucasia; still common in Azerbaijan and elsewhere, but decreasing in some areas. Status in other regions difficult to assess: in past, said to be commoner than supposed in India and Pakistan. In long term, vulnerable to changes in water levels, whether caused by wetland modification and drainage or by climatic changes, but can occupy artificially created habitats, especially in winter quarters.
Bibliography. Ali & Ripley (1980), Becker, P. (1995), Bengtson (1962), Benson & Benson (1975), Brooke (1974), Cramp & Simmons (1980), Dementiev & Gladkov (1951b), Dowsett & Forbes-Watson (1993), Étchécopar & Hüe (1964, 1978), Evans (1994), Glutz von Blotzheim *et al.* (1973), Goodman *et al.* (1989), Heim de Balsac & Mayaud (1962), Hines (1993), Hopkinson & Masterson (1984), Hüe & Étchécopar (1970), Knystautas (1993), Koenig (1943), Mackworth-Praed & Grant (1957, 1962, 1970), Mauro (1994), Nikolaus (1987), Parnell (1967), Patrikeev (1995), Pauler (1968), Paz (1987), Phillips (1984), Potapov & Flint (1987), Ripley (1982), Roberts, T.J. (1991), Rogacheva (1992), Roux & Morel (1964), Rutgers & Norris (1970), Salvan (1968), Sauvage (1993), Sharrock (1980), Shirihai (1996), Short *et al.* (1990), Simeonov *et al.* (1990), Smythies (1986), Szabó (1970), Tarboton, Kemp & Kemp (1987), Taylor (1987), Thonnerieux *et al.* (1989), Urban *et al.* (1986).

88. Australian Crake

Porzana fluminea

French: Marouette d'Australie **German**: Flußsumpfhuhn **Spanish**: Polluela Australiana
Other common names: Australian Spotted/Water Crake

Taxonomy. *Porzana fluminea* Gould, 1843, New South Wales.
Monotypic.
Distribution. Australia and Tasmania.

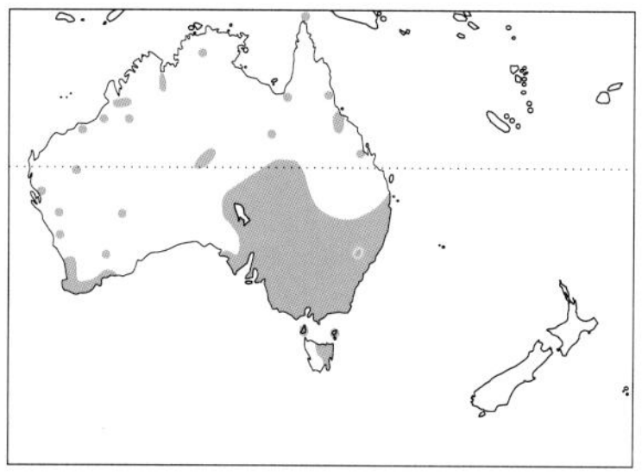

Descriptive notes. 19-23 cm; male 50-75 (65·5) g, female 50-61 (57) g, unsexed 57-81 (68) g; wingspan 27-33 cm. Female somewhat smaller than male; also differs in having duller olive upperparts, brown stripe across upper lores, grey of face to breast paler and more uniform, more extensive white spotting on breast and throat, and duller, less swollen, spot at base of culmen. Male may show slight seasonal variation in appearance of spot at base of culmen: swelling may disappear and colour may fade to brownish yellow. Sympatric *P. pusilla* smaller and paler, with richer cinnamon brown upperparts, paler grey underbody, no spots on sides of neck and breast, barred undertail-coverts, and no red or orange spot at base of bill. Immature very similar to adult, but has narrow white fringes to grey breast feathers in fresh plumage; upperwing-coverts patterned like juvenile. Juvenile similar to adult on upperparts but white spots lack black borders and are thus less striking; rump and uppertail-coverts lack white marks; secondary coverts all have white tips; grey areas of face and underparts have white spotting and whitish feather tips; sides of breast olive brown, spotted white; belly off-white; underpart barring dark brown and white; bill grey-olive with darker culmen and tip; iris dark brown. Juvenile female has less cinnamon, more olive, ground colour to upperparts and breast. Voice. Poorly known. Common call a sharp, metallic double note. Also a chattering call similar to "ratchet call" (rattle) of *P. pusilla*; a prolonged wheezing note; and a sharp or querulous single-note call.
Habitat. Well vegetated margins of permanent or ephemeral freshwater, brackish or saline wetlands. Occurs at estuaries, tidal creeks, mangroves, salt-marshes, swamps, marshes, lakes, ponds, lagoons, clay-pans and floodplains; also among water-lilies (*Nymphaea*). Prefers edges of drying wetlands rather than more deeply flooded areas. Sometimes in scrubby cover round salt-marshes and salt-works; may occur some distance from water. Often at artificial wetlands, such as salt-works, sewage ponds, gravel pits, and drains; occasionally in grassy areas, e.g. lawns, pastures, golf courses; also recorded at rubbish dump.
Food and Feeding. Molluscs, crustaceans, adult and larval insects (Dermaptera, Orthoptera, Hemiptera, Coleoptera, Diptera, Lepidoptera, Hymenoptera including ants), spiders, and frog tadpoles; also algae, plant material and seeds. Forages mainly at wetland margins on mud or peat, or in shallow water; near or among grass, marsh vegetation or shrubs; also among floating plants. Wades and swims, probing and lunging under water and at emergent vegetation. Unobtrusive, but generally bolder than other crakes; diurnal; particularly active early and late in day.
Breeding. Aug-Apr, most Aug-Jan. Monogamous; pair-bond may be maintained outside breeding season; probably territorial when breeding. Nest varies from flat, flimsy structure to cup of fine woven material; of wet or dry rushes, or dry grass; sometimes has dome or canopy of interlaced rushes; external diameter 7-9 cm, depth 5 cm; some have ramp from substrate to rim. Usually built 2-50 cm above water, in rushes, sedges, grass, low bushes, among overhanging tree branches, or in water-lilies; often in centre of clump or tussock; one built on ground. Eggs 3-7, probably laid at daily intervals; incubation by both sexes, period unknown; hatching asynchronous; black downy chicks have greenish sheen on upperparts (later, body colour fades to dark brown), iris black, bill black with red base, legs and feet dark olive-green or blue-black; chicks precocial; tended by both parents, possibly until after fledging; no information on growth or development; post-juvenile moult recorded Jan-Apr. May sometimes rear 2 broods per year.
Movements. Possibly dispersive. No seasonal movements suggested; in some areas present all year, but in others apparently occurs only in autumn and winter; higher reporting rates in summer possibly related to increased calling. May move across Torres Strait, where recorded on Booby I in Jan and May, and across Bass Strait, where recorded on King I and Flinders I. Numbers fluctuate with changing habitat conditions: becomes abundant after floods and heavy rain, and known to congregate at edges of drying wetlands. May be irruptive, as exceptional numbers sometimes appear and depart suddenly.
Status and Conservation. Not globally threatened. Endemic to Australia, occurring mainly in SE & SW, and sparsely elsewhere. Locally rare to common. Habitat loss has occurred through wetland drainage and modification, but species readily occupies artificial wetlands; construction of these provides some compensation for wetland losses, and has also allowed expansion of range into previously uninhabitable areas.
Bibliography. Badman (1979), Blakers *et al.* (1984), Bright & Taysom (1932), Bryant & Amos (1949), Campbell (1906), Cox & Pedler (1977), Draffan *et al.* (1983), Ford (1962), Jaensch (1989), Jaensch *et al.* (1988), Marchant & Higgins (1993), Roberts, G.J. (1980), Serventy (1985), Stokes (1983), Storr (1973), Watson (1955).

89. Sora

Porzana carolina

French: Marouette de Caroline **German**: Carolinasumpfhuhn **Spanish**: Polluela Sora
Other common names: Sora/Carolina Rail/Crake

Taxonomy. *Rallus carolinus* Linnaeus, 1758, Hudson Bay.
Monotypic.
Distribution. SE Alaska, Canada and USA. Winters from S USA, Mexico and West Indies S to C Peru and E to the Guianas.

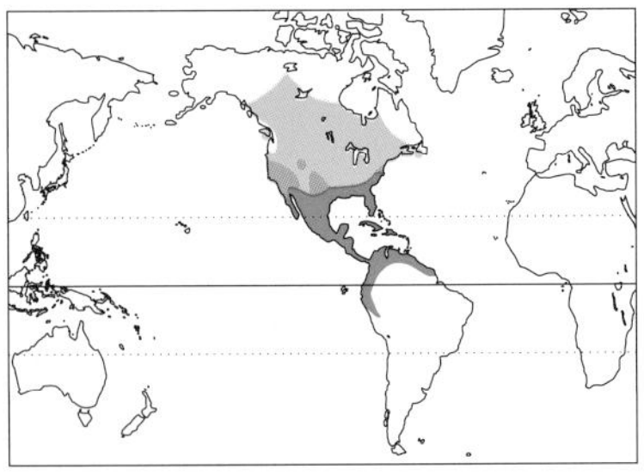

Descriptive notes. 19-25 cm; unsexed 51-126 (85) g; wingspan 35-40 cm. Black mask and small white patch behind eye. Sexes similar but female slightly smaller, with darker bill and less prominent head pattern; more white dots on upperparts and upperwing-coverts. Non-breeding adult in fresh plumage has grey tips to black throat feathers and white tips to grey breast feathers. Similar to *P. porzana* in size and bulk, but longer-necked and with striking head pattern, and yellow bill with greenish tip; grey foreneck and breast with no spots. Head pattern and extensive barring on flanks separate from smaller *P. fluminea*. Immature like adult but black patch on chin and throat less extensive and mottled grey; cheeks and sides of neck paler grey, and grey breast often tinged olive. Juvenile has upperparts and wings like adult but with more white streaks; predominantly olive brown to buff on head, neck and breast in areas where adult is grey; has black only on lores and at eye; white chin and throat, duller flank barring than adult, brown iris, and green-yellow bill. Juvenile differs from juvenile *P. porzana* in having crown and side of head brown with no spots and streaks, central crown streak and lores black, breast uniform buff, and bill green-yellow. VOICE. Characteristic breeding-season territorial and contact call, given by both sexes, a high-pitched descending whinny; occasionally heard in non-breeding season. Also plaintive, ascending, whistled "kerwee" given in spring, various peeping calls and a short, sharp "keek" when alarmed.
Habitat. Preferred habitats throughout year are freshwater emergent wetlands but often occurs in marshes of brackish and salt water during migration, and occasionally when breeding. Optimal habitat in North America is marshes with shallow and intermediate water depths, and high interspersion of fine-leaved and robust emergents, flooded annuals, and patches of open water; attracted to areas with abundant floating and submerged vegetation, probably because of good substrates for invertebrate prey near water surface. Dominant plants at freshwater nest-sites include *Typha*, *Carex* and sometimes *Scirpus*; in marshes of brackish or salt water, nests occasionally in *Spartina* or *Phragmites*. Also feeds in upland fields and row crops in late summer, and visits grass fields, rank weed growth and brushy hillsides; migrants feed in cultivated rice fields; wintering birds also occur in mangroves, and at mudflats, drainage ditches and edges of ponds. Breeds up to altitude of 3500 m in USA; recorded to 4080 m in C Peru (L Junín).
Food and Feeding. Omnivorous; common plant foods include duckweed (*Lemna*), and seeds of wild or cultivated rice (*Zizania*), *Polygonum*, sedges and grasses; invertebrate foods include molluscs, crustaceans, and insects (Diptera, Odonata, Coleoptera, Orthoptera and Lepidoptera). Plant material forms large part of diet in summer and autumn; autumn migrants in salt-marshes feed more on invertebrates; spring migrants in Missouri take largely invertebrates and seeds of *Carex*. Forages on mud and in shallow water, and on floating vegetation by raking mats of duckweed with feet and pulling aside other vegetation with bill; strips seeds from grass panicles and picks seeds from substrate; swims and dives readily. Diurnal; emerges from cover to feed in early morning and evening.
Breeding. USA Apr-Jul. Monogamous and territorial; pair-bond maintained during breeding season. Nest a loosely woven basket of available vegetation, either supported by surrounding stems or built within vegetation clump; usually built over standing water near borders of vegetation types or patches of open water. External diameter c. 15 cm, height c. 13 cm but may be built up to 48 cm high to overcome flood conditions; internal diameter 7-8 cm and depth 5 cm; ramp of vegetation often constructed to lip of nest. Several brood nests or resting platforms often constructed nearby. Usually 10-12 eggs (5-18), laid at daily intervals; incubation 16-19 days, by both sexes, starting when clutch incomplete; hatching asynchronous, over 2-17 days; one adult tends first-hatched chicks while other continues incubation; chick has glossy black down with orange throat bristles, black iris, bill whitish with red cere (later darkening to greenish), legs and feet pink (changing to grey and then yellow-green); chicks precocial; leave nest soon after all are hatched; cared for by both parents; become self-feeding after a few days but are also fed for 3 weeks and brooded for up to 1 month; feathers begin to emerge at 2-3 weeks; dispersal of family group from home range occurs when young 16-32 days old; able to fly at 4-5 weeks; full juvenile plumage attained in 6th week; post-juvenile moult begins at 12-14 weeks.
Movements. Migratory. Movement begins late summer and early autumn, when birds gather in numbers around lakes and freshwater and brackish marshes; birds are cold-sensitive and depart with advent of frosts ~~in~~ Sept-Oct. Migrates on broad front, over land and sea; prone to drifting in strong winds and occasionally taken far out to sea. Present Mexico mid-Aug to May, Panama Sept-Apr, Costa Rica Oct-Apr, West Indies and Venezuela Sept-May, and Colombia Oct-May (oversummering recorded). Return noted to S USA from Mar; spreads N in Apr, reaching Canada early May. Main passages Atlantic coast (Maryland) mid-Apr to mid-May, and mid-Aug to late Oct. Accidental EC Alaska, Queen Charlotte Is, S Labrador, Bermuda, Greenland and W Europe.
Status and Conservation. Not globally threatened. Most abundant and widely distributed North American rail. Current population trends uncertain, but habitat continues to decline throughout much of range, at least in North America, where habitat loss and degradation probably limit population size. Presence of power plants discharging hot water into rivers may allow birds to extend wintering range into colder regions. Traditionally a game species, hunted in 31 USA states and 2 Canadian provinces, with bag limits of 10-25 birds per day; as interest and participation in hunting are currently low, annual kill is probably within sustainable levels; surveys to monitor harvest and population trends have been lacking but improved estimates of harvest are now possible. Some are killed in traps for fur-bearers, while pesticides and ingested lead shot may also pose threat. Preservation and proper management of emergent wetlands are major priorities to safeguard and improve habitats; standardized taped-playback surveys could be used to monitor population trends. Elsewhere, species common to frequent throughout Mexico, where possibly breeds locally in N Baja California; local in Costa Rica; locally common in Venezuela and at 2000-3000 m in Andes of Colombia and Ecuador.
Bibliography. Andrews (1973), Armstrong (1983), Artmann & Martin (1975), Baird (1974), Becker, P. (1995), Bent (1926), Berger (1951), Biaggi (1983), Billard (1948), Blake (1977), Brown & Dinsmore (1986), Contreras (1992), Conway (1990), Conway *et al.* (1994), Cramp & Simmons (1980), Eddleman *et al.* (1988), Fannucchi *et al.* (1986), Fjeldså & Krabbe (1990), Gochfeld (1972), Godfrey (1986), Greenlaw & Miller (1982), Griese *et al.* (1980), Harrison, C. (1978), Harrison, H.H. (1975), Hilty & Brown (1986), Horak (1970), Howell & Webb (1995a), Johnson & Dinsmore (1985, 1986a), Kaufmann (1971, 1977, 1983, 1987b, 1988c, 1989), Lowther (1977), Meanley (1960, 1965a), Melvin & Gibbs (1994), Meyer de Schauensee & Phelps (1978), Mousley (1937), Pospichal & Marshall (1954), Ridgely (1981), Ridgely & Gwynne (1989), Root (1988), Rundle & Frederickson (1981), Rundle & Sayre (1983), Sayre & Rundle (1984), Slud (1964), Snyder (1966), Sorenson (1995), Stewart & Robbins (1958), Stiles & Skutch (1989), Tanner & Hendrickson (1956), Walkinshaw (1940), Webster (1964), Wetmore (1965), Zimmerman (1984).

90. Dot-winged Crake

Porzana spiloptera

French: Marouette maillée **German**: Fleckensumpfhuhn **Spanish**: Polluela Overa
Other common names: Dot-winged Rail

Taxonomy. *Porzana spiloptera* Durnford, 1877, Belgrano, Buenos Aires, Argentina.
Sometimes placed in genus *Laterallus*. Monotypic.
Distribution. S Uruguay and N Argentina.

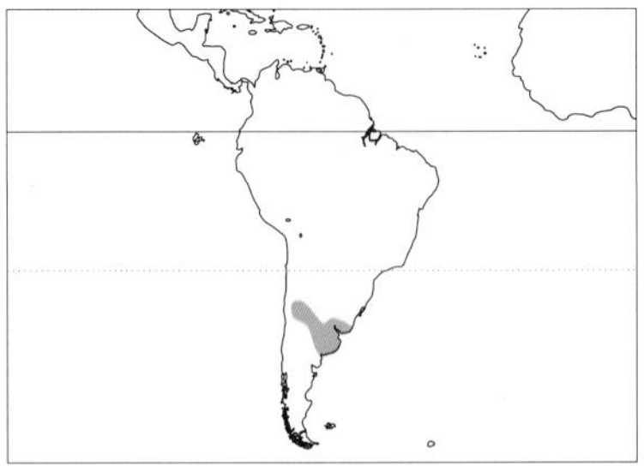

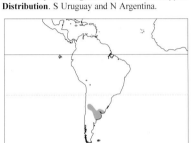

Descriptive notes. 14-15 cm. Small dark crake, with blackish streaks (feather centres) on dark olive brown upperparts; white markings on upperparts confined to upperwing-coverts and remiges; black and white bars on undertail-coverts. Sexes alike. Superficially very similar to *Laterallus jamaicensis* in size and overall colour, but latter has nape and upper back chestnut to russet, rest of upperparts dark brown to black, and white markings from lower back to tail; *L. j. murivagans* and *L. j. tuerosi* have cinnamon undertail-coverts. *Coturnicops notatus* also similar in size and colour but has white chin, white markings on head, neck and breast, white barring on rest of underparts, and black legs and feet. Larger *Neocrex erythrops* has unmarked olive brown upperparts, paler grey underparts, olive green bill with red base, and coral red legs and feet. Presumed immature described as blackish brown above, with feathers tipped vinaceous buff to vinaceous cinnamon; many upperwing-coverts with subterminal white bar; face, chin and throat whitish, washed grey-buff; breast and belly dull grey; flanks vinaceous grey with buff to cinnamon bars; undertail-coverts blackish with vinaceous tips and dull white to buff markings. VOICE. Unknown.
Habitat. Freshwater and brackish wetlands, including tidal and temporary marshes, swamps, wet marshy meadows, and wet to dry grassland; also cord grass and riparian scrub. Holotype taken in a garden almost in city of Buenos Aires. In R Luján marshes, habitat is dominated by *Spartina densiflora* and some *Eryngium*, and birds have occurred in dense *Spartina* up to 70 cm tall, with permanent brackish surface water; elsewhere, found in *Paspalum* grass.
Food and Feeding. Recorded as feeding on insects, seeds and marsh weeds. No information on feeding habits.
Breeding. Only recorded nest was found near Buenos Aires, but no further details were given. In addition, a juvenile was seen with an adult at Punta Norte, Cape San Antonio (NE Argentina), some time in 1987/88.
Movements. None recorded.
Status and Conservation. VULNERABLE. In Argentina, recorded from only 6 provinces, 3 of them doubtfully: the single records from La Rioja and San Juan possibly refer to *L. jamaicensis*; occurrence in San Luis unconfirmed. In Córdoba, up to 10 birds observed at one locality in 1973/74; in Santa Fé one collected in 1906. In Buenos Aires Province, species known from 15 localities, records from up to 7 of them falling within the last 10 years; records are all of 1-2 birds. In Uruguay, recorded only from Arroyo Pando (Canelones Department) before 1926, and Arroyo Solís Grande in 1973. Status of this poorly known and secretive crake is unclear. Formerly regarded as locally frequent to abundant in Buenos Aires Province, where currently considered locally rare (or very difficult to locate) to fairly common; lack of sightings may be attributable to paucity of observers. Formerly considered rare in La Rioja but common at the one known site in Córdoba; status in other provinces unclear. Regarded as rare and local in Uruguay. Reclamation and burning of marsh areas, flooding, intrusion by cattle, overgrazing, burning, disturbance by visitors, and projected development are cited as current risks to survival. Numbers apparently declining both at R Luján and Punta Rasa, areas considered to hold healthy populations. Reserves exist at 3 sites known to hold the species. Distributional surveys urgently needed within species' limited range; voice should be recorded; and possibly beneficial effect of better management of cattle should be studied.
Bibliography. Blake (1977), Canevari *et al.* (1991), Chebez (1994), Collar & Andrew (1988), Collar, Crosby & Stattersfield (1994), Collar, Gonzaga *et al.* (1992), Durnford (1877), Gibson (1920), Gore & Gepp (1978), Hartert & Venturi (1909), Hellmayr & Conover (1942), Meyer de Schauensee (1982), Narosky (1985), Narosky & Yzurieta (1987), Nores & Yzurieta (1980), Olrog (1984), de la Peña (1992), Wege & Long (1995).

91. Ash-throated Crake

Porzana albicollis

French: Marouette plombée **German**: Wieselsumpfhuhn **Spanish**: Polluela Turura
Other common names: White-necked/White-throated Crake

Taxonomy. *Rallus albicollis* Vieillot, 1819, Paraguay.
Race *olivacea* includes proposed race *typhoeca*. Two specimens from extreme SE Peru are as large as *albicollis* but show plumage characters of *olivacea*. Two subspecies recognized.
Subspecies and Distribution.
P. a. olivacea (Vieillot, 1819) - Colombia, Venezuela and Trinidad to the Guianas and extreme N Brazil.
P. a. albicollis (Vieillot, 1819) - E & S Brazil, N & E Bolivia, Paraguay and extreme N Argentina; probably this race in SE Peru.
Descriptive notes. 21-24 cm; male 90-114 g; 1 female 105 g. Sexes alike. Slightly smaller *P. carolina* has white streaks on upperparts, distinctive face pattern, more extensive white flank bars, white and buff undertail-coverts, bright yellow bill, and greenish legs and feet. *Neocrex erythrops*, the only other sympatric, short-billed crake of similar size with grey breast and barred flanks, has unmarked olive-brown upperparts, olive green bill with red base, and coral red legs and feet. Larger *Cyanolimnas cerverai* has unpatterned brownish olive upperparts, dark slate flanks with faint white bars, white undertail-coverts, yellowish green bill with red base, and red legs and feet. Immature similar to adult but duller, with brownish wash on grey underparts. One presumed juvenile has off-white chin, predominantly olive brown face, throat, foreneck and underparts, and no barring from flanks to undertail-

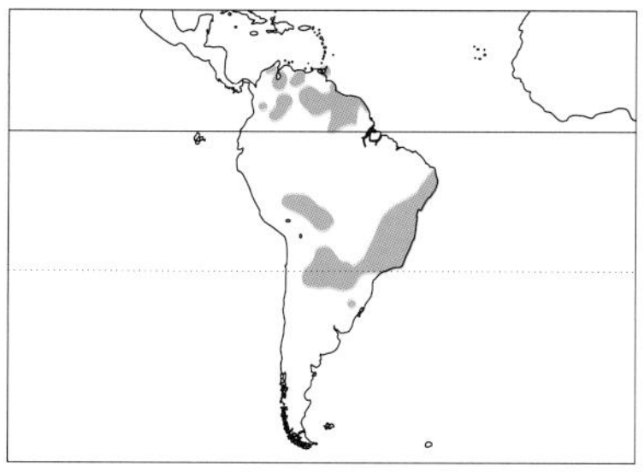

coverts but deeper brown wash in these regions. Races separated on overall colour and size, *albicollis* being larger and darker. VOICE. Song a repeated, loud, fast series of vibrating notes, sounding like machine-gun "d'd'd'd'd'-ou". Call a sharp "tuk". Calls most in early morning and evening.

Habitat. Freshwater marshes, marshy lakes, Moriche swamps, rice fields, drainage ditches, savanna, dry to damp taller grass of grazing lands, tall reeds along roadsides, and secondary growth. In marshy habitats appears to prefer drier areas, and in Surinam regarded as less of a marsh bird than other small rails. Inhabits lowlands up to 1200 m.

Food and Feeding. Insects and their larvae (Lepidoptera, Formicidae, Coleoptera), and grass seeds. Occasionally emerges partially into the open near cover, presumably feeding.

Breeding. Trinidad and Tobago, probably Jul-Oct; Guyana, Feb-Jul with peak in May, but possibly nesting throughout year. Nest a large open bowl of roughly woven coarse dry grass and sometimes a few leaves; placed on or just above ground between clumps of savanna grass or in reeds; often near base of tree stump, sheltered by roots. External diameter c. 20 cm, depth c. 10 cm; cup diameter c. 10 cm, depth c. 5 cm. Eggs usually 2-3, possibly up to 6. No other information.

Movements. Nothing definitely recorded, but some seasonal movements possible in Colombia, records from NE Meta being Dec-Mar and from W Meta Mar-Sept, while birds reported to move into *Typha* marsh during dry season at Ciénaga Grande. In French Guiana an exhausted bird was found on a bridge in Jul.

Status and Conservation. Not globally threatened. Race *olivacea* formerly regarded as quite common to abundant in Guyana, local in Colombia and rare in Trinidad; no information about past status of race *albicollis*. Apparently not uncommon in extreme SE Peru (Pampas de Heath) in 1977. Little information available on current status of species: common along littoral zone in French Guiana and probably of local occurrence in many other regions. Distribution is probably more continuous than currently thought. Species is solitary, shy and difficult to observe.

Bibliography. Belton (1984), Benson & Winterbottom (1968), Blake (1977), Canevari *et al.* (1991), Contreras *et al.* (1990), Darlington (1931), ffrench (1973), Graham *et al.* (1980), Haverschmidt (1968), Haverschmidt & Mees (1995), Hellmayr & Conover (1942), Hilty & Brown (1986), Meyer de Schauensee (1962), Meyer de Schauensee & Phelps (1978), de la Peña (1992), Sick (1985c, 1993), Snyder (1966), Tostain *et al.* (1992).

92. Ruddy-breasted Crake

Porzana fusca

French: Marouette brune **German**: Zimtsumpfhuhn **Spanish**: Polluela Pechirrufa
Other common names: Ruddy Crake(!)

Taxonomy. *Rallus fuscus* Linnaeus, 1766, Philippines.
Sometimes placed in *Amaurornis*. Possible race *bakeri* included in nominate. Four subspecies recognized.

Subspecies and Distribution.
P. f. fusca (Linnaeus, 1766) - Pakistan and N India to SC China (Yunnan) and Vietnam, Malay Peninsula, Philippines and W Indonesia.
P. f. zeylonica (Stuart Baker, 1927) - W India and Sri Lanka.
P. f. erythrothorax (Temminck & Schlegel, 1849) - Japan, E & S China and Indochina; N populations winter to S.
P. f. phaeopyga Stejneger, 1887 - Ryukyu Is.

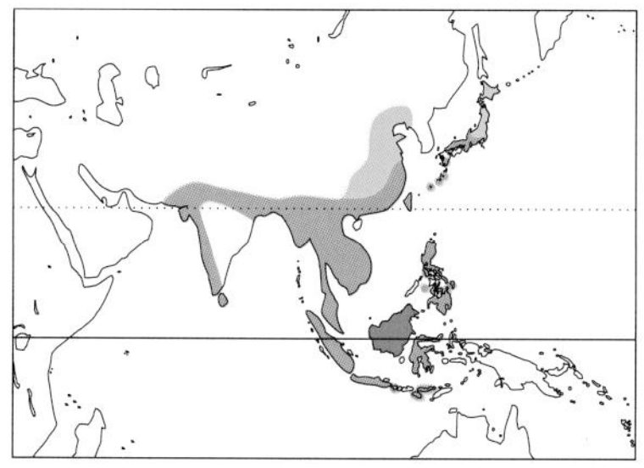

Descriptive notes. 21-23 cm; unsexed mean 60 g. Sexes alike but female generally paler, with whiter throat. *P. paykulli* similar in size but has white bars (sometimes missing) on some upperwing-coverts, bold black and white barring on lower underparts, and orange-pink legs and feet. *Rallina fasciata* larger and brighter, with bold black and white barring on remiges, upperwing-coverts and underparts, darker bill, and more prominent red orbital ring. *R. eurizonoides* has white bars on inner webs of remiges, bold underpart barring and grey legs. Immature similar to adult but darker; duller on underparts; chin, throat and centre of belly white; iris red-brown. Juvenile has darker upperparts than adult; supercilium and sides of head and neck dull white; underparts mostly dull white, barred dusky brown; flanks and thighs dull olive brown; undertail-coverts as adult; iris brown. Races separated on size and on shade of underparts, dark in nominate and *zeylonica*, which are also smallest. VOICE. Usually silent, but in early morning and evening during breeding season utters hard "tewk" or "kyot" notes (likened to knocking on a door) every 2-3 seconds, often speeding up and usually followed by bubbling call similar to that of Australasian Grebe (*Tachybaptus novaehollandiae*); utters short "chuck" when foraging.

Habitat. Reedy swamps, marshes and stream banks, reedbeds, wet grassland at edges of lakes, ditches and canals, edges of rice paddies; also bushland and forest paths, possibly during post-breeding dispersal; sometimes on dry cultivated vegetable fields, in Japan. Normally occurs in lowlands, but breeds up to c. 2000 m in Himalayas.

Food and Feeding. Eats molluscs, aquatic insects and their larvae, seeds, and shoots of marsh plants. Probably feeds mainly in cover; occasionally ventures out to edges of reedbeds; may be mainly crepuscular.

Breeding. Kashmir and NW Pakistan, Jun-Aug; Bengal and NE Pakistan, Jun-Sept; Japan, Mar-Sept; Philippines Aug-Sept; Sumatra, Dec, Mar; Singapore, Nov. Probably monogamous. Nest a pad of dry grass, rush, rice straw, roots and leaves of aquatic plants; placed on swampy ground among grass, reeds or rice; sometimes among low bushes; growing plants sometimes bent over to form canopy. Both sexes build. Eggs 3-9; incubation 20 days; glossy black downy chick has bronze-green sheen on upperparts, underparts browner, bill black with pink base and tip, legs and feet reddish black; both parents feed and care for young.

Movements. Largely resident, but migratory in some regions. Status of some populations unclear, especially on Asian mainland (demarcation on map between resident and seasonal occurrences is largely hypothetical). N populations of *erythrothorax* move S to winter in S China (S of Yangtze R) and Indochina; this race is summer breeding visitor to Japan (May-Oct), small numbers also wintering in S; in Sri Lanka numbers of *zeylonica* augmented by migrants which arrive Oct-Nov and leave Mar-Apr. Probably resident throughout Wallacean range; scarce winter visitor to Borneo. Race *phaeopyga* resident in Ryukyu Is. Vagrant to Christmas I (Indian Ocean), with 2 specimens, Aug and Sept.

Status and Conservation. Not globally threatened. Extremely shy and difficult to flush, thus poorly known, but formerly considered common to abundant over much of its range. Currently regarded as locally common to abundant in Sumatra, Java and Bali, and uncommon Philippines; race *erythrothorax* is the commonest rallid in Japan.

Bibliography. Ali & Ripley (1980), Brazil (1991), Deignan (1945), Delacour & Mayr (1946), Dickinson *et al.* (1991), Étchécopar & Hüe (1978), Hellebrekers & Hoogerwerf (1967), Hoogerwerf (1949), Knystautas (1993), Lekagul & Round (1991), MacKinnon & Phillipps (1993), Marchant & Higgins (1993), van Marle & Voous (1988), Medway & Wells (1976), Perennou *et al.* (1994), Phillips (1978), Potapov & Flint (1987), Ripley (1982), Roberts, T.J. (1991), Smythies (1986), White & Bruce (1986).

93. Band-bellied Crake

Porzana paykullii

French: Marouette mandarin **German**: Mandarinsumpfhuhn **Spanish**: Polluela Mandarín
Other common names: Siberian Ruddy/Chinese Banded Crake

Taxonomy. *Rallus Paykullii* Ljungh, 1813, Banjarmasin, Borneo, and Jakarta, Java.
Sometimes placed in genus *Rallina*; further study of relationships required. Monotypic.

Distribution. Russian Far East (SW Amurland and S Ussuriland), NE China (Heilongjiang, Hebei and N Henan) and Korea. Winters in SE Asia, Sumatra, Java and Borneo. One specimen from Basilan, Philippines, is a *Rallina fasciata*.

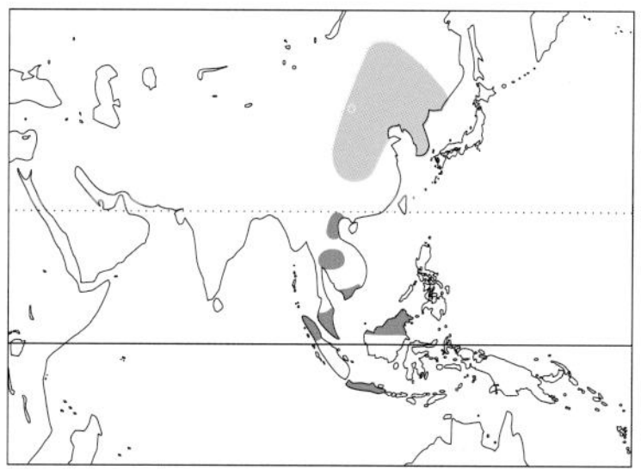

Descriptive notes. 20-22 cm. Sexes similar; in female, dark bars of underparts brown rather than black, and white markings on coverts may be less conspicuous. Outermost primary mottled white on outer web; white tips to greater and median upperwing-coverts sometimes inconspicuous or absent. Similar to *Rallina fasciata* and *R. eurizonoides*, which are larger, with chestnut crown and nape, and more extensive underpart barring; *R. fasciata* also has richer brown upperparts, boldly barred primaries and outer secondaries, more extensively barred upperwing-coverts, more extensive underpart barring with broader white bars, and red legs and feet; *R. eurizonoides* has no bars on upperwing-coverts, barring on inner webs of remiges, and greenish grey to black legs and feet. Sympatric *P. fusca* has unbarred wings, and only narrow and inconspicuous white barring on flanks, belly and undertail-coverts, and red legs and feet. Immature similar to adult but chestnut of face, neck and breast duller; legs purplish brown. Juvenile darker on upperparts, with more extensive white tips to upperwing-coverts; face, neck and breast buffy brown with obscure dark brown bars; barring on flanks, belly and undertail-coverts less regular than in adult, and white bars tinged buff; chin, throat and belly off-white. VOICE. Call distinctive: likened to intermittent drumbeats and also to sound of a wooden rattle; uttered most frequently at dusk and dawn, and at night.

Habitat. Breeds in lowland marshes and meadows with tussocks, thickets or small trees; also in marshy or damp situations in mountains, woodland and forests. Avoids open water; prefers damp to dry situations with thick grass; often found near villages and along field edges and fences. Wintering habitat described as wet grass and paddyfields (Greater Sundas), and grassy hummocks with bushes or small trees in meadows and swamps (Vietnam). Apparently mainly a lowland species.

Food and Feeding. Mostly crustaceans and insects (including Coleoptera); also seeds. Forages in damp situations, sometimes in drier areas near gardens and dwellings. May be partly nocturnal.

Breeding. In Russian Far East, breeds from late May. Usually solitary; presumed monogamous; sometimes occurs in densely populated colonies. Nests in hummocky, not too damp meadows, and swamps with thickets. Nest usually built in depression in ground in grass or shrubs; lined with fine twigs and grass stalks. Eggs 5-9. No further information.

Movements. Winters in C Thailand, Vietnam (Tonkin and Cochinchina), Peninsular Malaysia, N Sumatra, Java and N Borneo. Also one record from S Sulawesi, Apr 1979. Winter distribution imperfectly known. Transient in Inner Mongolia and Shandong, southwards through S China.

Status and Conservation. Not globally threatened. Currently considered near-threatened. Very little information available on status and distribution. In past, locally common in USSR, occasional in Borneo. Currently regarded as scarce in Greater Sundas, where recorded in N Sumatra, N Borneo and Java; only two records from Sumatra, both specimens, the second in Jan 1918. Status and distribution urgently require investigation, especially in wintering range.

Bibliography. Austin (1948), Dementiev & Gladkov (1951b), Dickinson (1984), Escott & Holmes (1980), Étchécopar & Hüe (1978), Flint *et al.* (1984), King *et al.* (1975), Knystautas (1993), Lekagul & Round (1991), MacKinnon & Phillipps (1993), van Marle & Voous (1988), Medway & Wells (1976), Potapov & Flint (1987), Ripley (1977), Smythies (1981), White & Bruce (1986), Wildash (1968).

94

95

96

97

ssp *colombianus*

98

99 ♂ ♀

100

101

ssp *ripleyi*

102

ssp *maculatus*

103

ssp *insolitus*

ssp *nigricans*

104

ssp *caucae*

ssp *sanguinolentus*

105

ssp *luridus*

olive morph

106

ssp *sharpei*

chestnut morph

ssp *castaneoventris*

107

ssp *inepta*

108

ssp *pallida*

109 ♂ ♀

PLATE 16

inches 7

cm 18

94. Spotless Crake
Porzana tabuensis

French: Marouette fuligineuse   **German**: Südsee-Sumpfhuhn   **Spanish**: Polluela de Tongatapu
Other common names: Sooty Crake

Taxonomy. *Rallus tabuensis* Gmelin, 1789, Tongatapu Group, Tonga.
Forms superspecies with *P. atra* and *P. monasa*. Geographical variation slight, and validity of subspecies requires confirmation. Possible race *plumbea* of S Australia and New Zealand included in nominate *tabuensis*. Three subspecies currently recognized.
Subspecies and Distribution.
P. t. tabuensis (Gmelin, 1789) - Philippines (Luzon) through Australia, Tasmania, New Zealand and Chatham Is to New Caledonia and SW Pacific islands and E through Micronesia and Polynesia.
P. t. edwardi Gyldenstolpe, 1955 - W & C New Guinea.
P. t. richardsoni Rand, 1940 - Oranje Mts in C Irian Jaya (W New Guinea).

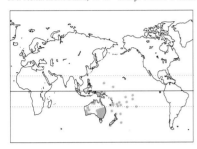

Descriptive notes. 15-18 cm; male 34-56 (45·5) g, female 21-58 (40) g; wingspan 26-29 cm. Sexes alike. Easily distinguished from all sympatric small crakes: reddish chocolate brown upperparts, dark slate grey head, neck and underparts, white outermost primary and leading edge of wing, black and white bars on undertail-coverts, red iris and orbital ring, black bill, and salmon pink legs and feet. Immature like adult. Juvenile similar to adult but dark brown from forehead to hindneck and on lores; brownish wash on face and sides of throat; white chin and throat; upperparts less red-brown than in adult, and underparts dark grey-brown; some have narrow white supercilium extending to above eye; bill black with pink base; iris brownish orange; legs and feet grey-brown to brownish flesh. Races separated on: size, *tabuensis* smallest; and colour of upperparts, olive brown in *richardsoni*, deep chocolate in *edwardi*. VOICE. Calls distinctive. Commonest calls, given during breeding season: loud trilling purr, resembling motor or sewing machine and preceded by soft quarrelling sequence; and single or repeated loud, sharp, high-pitched "pit", often interspersed with harsh nasal "harr" and trilling whistle. Also has soft bubbling and murmuring contact calls.
Habitat. Usually dense vegetation in, or at margins of, freshwater or saline wetlands, either permanent or ephemeral. Occurs in marshes, swamps, salt-marsh and peat bogs; also at margins of rivers, streams, tidal creeks, ponds and lakes. May prefer wetlands with shallow, slow-flowing water; overstorey of willows (*Salix*), or tall reedbed vegetation such as *Typha orientalis*, may be important requirement of breeding habitat in New Zealand. Frequently inhabits artificial wetlands such as salt-works, sewage farms, rice paddies, taro ponds, irrigation channels, farmland, golf courses, lawns and gardens. Also occurs on fern-covered hillsides, and in heathy flats and coastal scrub; on some islands occupies low forest and also rocky or stony habitats without standing water. Ranges from sea-level up to c. 3300 m in New Guinea, where most widespread in highlands.
Food and Feeding. Molluscs, crustaceans (ostracods and amphipods), Collembola, adult and larval insects (Ephemeroptera, Coleoptera, Diptera and Orthoptera), spiders; eggs of shearwaters, petrels and terns; seeds, fruit and shoots of grasses and aquatic plants. Also recorded feeding on carcass of cow. Crepuscular and diurnal; usually feeds on ground, but also in trees (Kermadec Is), foraging among foliage and nests of noddies (*Anous*); swims readily. Forages on mud and in shallow water, in or near marsh vegetation, along tidelines adjacent to dense vegetation, at margins of still and flowing water, and in short grass; also in and around petrel burrows; searches leaf litter in forests, scratching with feet and moving or turning over litter with bill; sometimes feeds in thickets.
Breeding. Australia, Sept-Jan; New Zealand, Aug-Jan; New Caledonia, Oct; Vanuatu, probably Sept-Feb; Society Is, Jul. Monogamous; possibly pairs for life. Record of 3 adults accompanying young. Territorial, possibly throughout year. Nest shallowly to deeply cupped, of woven dry grass and rushes; placed in clump of sedges or rushes, centre of grass tussock, or small bush in reedbed; often placed over water, sometimes on ground; also against stump of tree-fern, under tangled ferns, brambles or dense bushes. External diameter 10-23 cm, depth 5-20 cm; cup diameter c. 8 cm, depth c. 4 cm; height above water 3-150 cm. Role of male in building uncertain; female bends reeds to form canopy over nest; one or more ramps of nesting material constructed from water to rim; pair often build several roosting nests for use by family. Usually 3-4 eggs (2-6), laid at daily intervals; later clutches larger than earlier ones; island populations may lay smaller clutches than mainland birds; incubation 19-22 days, by both sexes; hatching synchronous, or asynchronous in large clutches; black down of chick has greenish sheen, bill black with pink saddle at base of upper mandible (later pink base to both mandibles), iris black or blue-grey, legs and feet dark brown-grey, pink at rear of tarsus; chicks leave nest after 1-2 days; fed and cared for by both parents, probably being attended until 4-5 months old; first feathers appear at c. 15 days; captive birds were almost fully feathered at 40 days, but remiges were not fully grown at 66 days; post-juvenile moult recorded Sept-May. May have 2 broods in Australia and New Zealand; if nesting delayed, may raise 1 large brood rather than 2 smaller broods; relays after clutch loss.
Movements. Generally regarded as resident over much of range. In Australia relatively few records in S during winter may suggest movement, while possibly regularly migratory in Queensland (recorded in N only Oct-May) and on islands in Torres Strait, where casualties recorded Dec-Feb and May; sudden or seasonal changes in numbers may occur in response to rainfall or receding water, and irruptions, probably induced by good rainfall, are recorded; birds also sometimes occur well outside normal range. On Poor Knights Is (N New Zealand) young disperse to drier habitats. One from Tiur (SE Moluccas) in Jan 1899 was presumably vagrant; species known to be highly dispersive, having spread widely E across Pacific through Polynesia, and vagrancy is to be expected.
Status and Conservation. Not globally threatened. In Australia suitable habitat lost through drainage of wetlands, but species probably still plentiful in many areas, though overlooked: birds readily occupy artificial wetlands, farmland and sometimes garden habitats, and in some areas rise in water table due to irrigation has possibly enhanced habitat. Widespread and sparse to common in New Zealand, where wetland habitats have been reduced; on Aorangi, Poor Knights Is, increased from 1930's with development of low mixed forest after human occupation ceased and pigs were re-moved (pigs adversely affected habitat by restricting regeneration of low forest, destroying nesting cover and disturbing leaf litter); declined from 1950's as low mixed forest was replaced by tall forest. Has become rare on Norfolk I, where population reduced by rats, and extinct on Raoul I (Kermadecs). Elsewhere formerly regarded as either genuinely uncommon or overlooked, except that *edwardi* was thought fairly common within its restricted range. Currently regarded as rare in Philippines, but possibly more widespread than is known. Distribution and status in New Guinea imperfectly known; apparently locally rare to common. Appears to have suffered population reductions and local extinction throughout Pacific islands, often where it has encountered man and his introduced commensals. Local and uncommon in Vanuatu, where could face extinction as result of swamp pollution or destruction. In E Polynesia disappeared from Gambier Is in 1920's but still occurs in Marquesas and Tuamotus, and on Oeno (Pitcairn group), where population very small. In 1985 rediscovered on Ta'u I, American Samoa, where population small and probably decreasing as habitat diminishes with reduction in subsistence agriculture.

Bibliography. Amadon & DuPont (1970), Banks (1984), Beehler *et al.* (1986), Blakers *et al.* (1984), Bregulla (1992), Bryant & Amos (1949), Buddle (1941a, 1941b), Chambers (1989), Coates (1985), Crouther (1994), Dickinson *et al.* (1991), Draffan *et al.* (1983), Engbring & Engilis (1988), Fletcher (1913, 1914, 1916a, 1916b), Fraser (1972), Hadden (1970, 1972, 1993), Halse & Jaensch (1989), Hannecart & Létocart (1983), Hobbs (1967), Holyoak & Thibault (1984), Kaufmann (1987a, 1988b), Kaufmann & Lavers (1987), Marchant & Higgins (1993), Morton (1953), O'Donnell (1994), Onley (1982a, 1982b), Serventy (1985), Serventy & Whittell (1976), Skinner (1979), Soper (1969b), Stokes (1983), Storr (1973), Temme (1974), White & Bruce (1986), Whitlock (1914), van't Woudt & Dobbs (1988).

95. Kosrae Crake
Porzana monasa

French: Marouette de Kusaie   **German**: Kosraesumpfhuhn   **Spanish**: Polluela de las Carolinas
Other common names: Kusaie/Ponape/Kittlitz's Crake

Taxonomy. *Rallus monasa* Kittlitz, 1858, Kosrae Island, Caroline Islands.
Formerly sometimes placed in monotypic genus *Aphanolimnas*. Forms superspecies with *P. atra* and *P. tabuensis*. Monotypic.
Distribution. Kosrae (Kusaie) I in E Caroline Is.

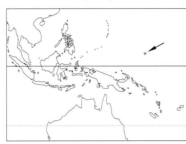

Descriptive notes. 18 cm. Flightless crake; plumage largely black, with bluish grey reflections; chin and throat paler; remiges and rectrices somewhat browner; inner upperwing-coverts brownish with white spots; undertail-coverts spotted white; iris, legs and feet red; bill black. Immature and juvenile not described. VOICE. No precise descriptions available, but species was said to have an alluring and resounding voice.
Habitat. Occupied a variety of habitats, including swamps and marshes near sea-level as well as taro patches and wet, shady places in forest.
Food and Feeding. Nothing recorded.
Breeding. No information available.
Movements. None.
Status and Conservation. Almost certainly EXTINCT. Following its discovery, and the collection of 2 specimens, in 1827/28, this crake has not been recorded, despite searches. Formerly considered sacred by the islanders, and thus remained unmolested; within 50 years of the arrival of Christian missionaries, and of rats from whaling ships, the species had most likely become extinct.

Bibliography. Engbring & Pratt (1985), Fuller (1987), Greenway (1967), Neufeldt (1978), Olson (1973b), Pratt *et al.* (1987), Ripley (1977).

96. Henderson Crake
Porzana atra

French: Marouette de Henderson   **German**: Tuamotusumpfhuhn   **Spanish**: Polluela de la Henderson
Other common names: North's Crake

Taxonomy. *Porzana atra* North, 1908, Henderson Island.
In past sometimes assigned to monotypic genus *Nesophylax*. Forms superspecies with *P. tabuensis* and *P. monasa*. Monotypic.
Distribution. Henderson I, in C Pitcairn Group.

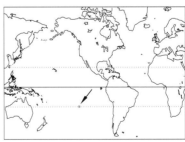

Descriptive notes. 18 cm; male 69-87 (80) g, females 66-88 (74·5) g. Flightless; legs well developed for running. Entire plumage deep black with slight greyish gloss; iris, eyering, legs and feet red; bill blackish, yellowish green at base and along culmen. Sexes alike, but female has less yellowish green on bill (if present, this colour is confined to culmen ridge), and legs plain red to orange (red mottled with black in male); male's red eyering often blotched with black. Immature similar to adult but orbital ring dark, and legs and feet dusky. Juvenile greyer than adult on throat and underparts; iris brown; legs and feet black. VOICE. Contact call a nasal "kak", repeated in rapid series as an alarm call. Also has loud, continuous churring call uttered simultaneously as duet by pair members, sometimes joined by other family members. Most vocal at dawn and dusk.
Habitat. Thick *Pisonia* forest to open *Pisonia/Xylosma* forest, and *Timonius* thickets, of the island plateau, and *Pandanus-Thespesia-Argusia* embayment forest on some beaches; also in coconut groves. Absent only from low vegetation and pinnacled limestone at exposed S end of island.
Food and Feeding. Diet includes large nematodes, terrestrial molluscs, insects (Coleoptera, and adult and larval Lepidoptera), spiders, and eggs of the skink *Emoia cyanura*. Opportunistic feeder, taking

On following pages: 97. Yellow-breasted Crake (*Porzana flaviventer*); 98. White-browed Crake (*Porzana cinerea*); 99. Striped Crake (*Aenigmatolimnas marginalis*); 100. Zapata Rail (*Cyanolimnas cerverai*); 101. Colombian Crake (*Neocrex colombianus*); 102. Paint-billed Crake (*Neocrex erythrops*); 103. Spotted Rail (*Pardirallus maculatus*); 104. Blackish Rail (*Pardirallus nigricans*); 105. Plumbeous Rail (*Pardirallus sanguinolentus*); 106. Chestnut Rail (*Eulabeornis castaneoventris*); 107. Invisible Rail (*Habroptila wallacii*); 108. New Guinea Flightless Rail (*Megacrex inepta*); 109. Watercock (*Gallicrex cinerea*).

advantage of seasonal increases in prey species. Forages by turning over leaf litter with bill, head-tossing litter aside, and scratching with feet; gleans prey items (including skink eggs) from undersides of leaves. Bold and curious. Active throughout the day.

Breeding. Jul-Feb. Monogamous, with permanent pair-bond; presumably permanently territorial. Possible polyandry once recorded, female making 4 nesting attempts with one male and 1 with a male from an adjacent territory. Some nests spherical, c. 20 cm in diameter with opening c. 10 cm wide, of shredded *Pandanus* palm leaves, placed up to 30 cm above ground in *Pandanus* leaf clump or at base of *Pandanus* trunk; others open-topped, built in low vegetation or up to 60 cm above ground in *Asplenium nidus* ferns. Male does most nest-building. Also builds roosting nests for use after hatching. Eggs 2-3; incubation 21 days, by both sexes; hatching synchronous; chicks have deep velvety black down, and black bill, legs and feet; leave nest soon after hatching; fed and cared for by both parents, helped by young of the previous brood and by other adults in family group; helpers also assist in protecting eggs and chicks from crabs and rats; young fully feathered and capable of independent foraging at c. 1 month, but remain associated with parents for much longer, sometimes being fed occasionally even when 15 weeks old. Many juveniles disperse from natal territories in Mar-Apr, but some remain with parents even when adult. Some pairs lay second clutch when young of first clutch are c. 1 month old; will also lay replacement clutches after loss of eggs or chicks. Annual adult survival at least 43%; reproductive success high, 2·45 chicks surviving for at least 6 months per pair per year. Recruitment rate not known, but probably compensates easily for annual losses, so that population is stable.

Movements. None.

Status and Conservation. VULNERABLE. Endemic to Henderson I, a 37-km² uninhabited raised-reef island with no permanent fresh water. Population estimated at c. 6200 birds in 1992, probably the carrying capacity of the island, as most territories (average size c. 1 ha) held more than 2 adults. Main predator is Polynesian rat (*Rattus exulans*), introduced by man centuries ago; rats take eggs and chicks but apparently do not pose threat to survival of species, and the crakes are very aggressive towards them. However, any inadvertent introduction of a more aggressive predator (e.g. another *Rattus* species) to the island could well result in the crake's rapid decline and extinction, as has happened with many other island rails. Species still vulnerable to possible human impacts: in 1982-83 a millionaire sought to make the island his home.

Bibliography. Bourne & David (1983), Collar & Andrew (1988), Collar *et al*. (1994), Forsberg *et al*. (1983), Graves (1992), Hay (1986), Jones, P. *et al*. (1995), Murphy (1924), Olson (1973b), Pratt *et al*. (1987), Ripley (1977).

97. Yellow-breasted Crake

Porzana flaviventer

French: Marouette à sourcils blancs **German**: Gelbbrust-Sumpfhuhn **Spanish**: Polluela Pálida

Taxonomy. *Rallus flaviventer* Boddaert, 1783, Cayenne, French Guiana.

Does not closely resemble any other *Porzana* crake; because of similarities in face pattern and bill structure sometimes placed, with *P. cinerea*, in genus *Poliolimnas*, a separation which may be appropriate. Five subspecies recognized.

Subspecies and Distribution.

P. f. gossii (Bonaparte, 1856) - Cuba and Jamaica.
P. f. hendersoni Bartsch, 1917 - Hispaniola and Puerto Rico.
P. f. woodi van Rossem, 1934 - S Mexico to NW Costa Rica.
P. f. bangsi Darlington, 1931 - N Colombia.
P. f. flaviventer (Boddaert, 1783) - Panama and Colombia to Venezuela, Trinidad and the Guianas, and S to N, EC & S Brazil, E Bolivia, Paraguay and N Argentina.

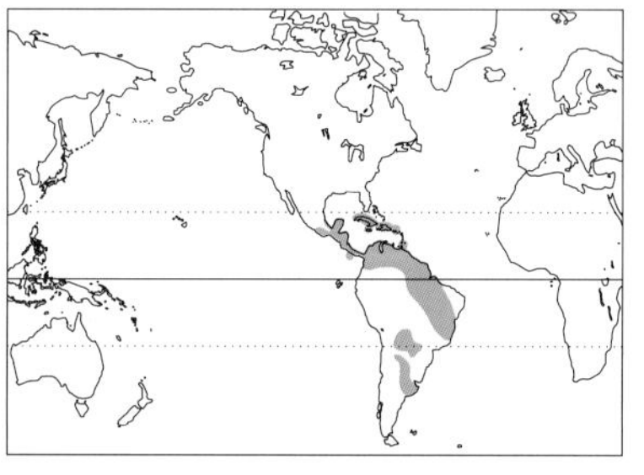

Descriptive notes. 12·5-14 cm; male 22-29 (26) g; female 20-28 (24) g. Sexes alike. Very small crake, with long toes which enable it to walk on floating vegetation; facial pattern of dark line through eye and pale buff-white supercilium diagnostic, and unique among New World rallids. Only other sympatric crake of similar size and overall colour is *Micropygia schomburgkii*, which has more extensive white markings (and no dark streaking) on upperparts, unbarred flanks and undertail-coverts, and red or orange-red legs and feet. Slightly larger *Coturnicops noveboracensis* has white secondaries, lacks white streaks on upperparts, and breeding male has yellow bill. Immature similar to adult but flank barring continues to side of breast. Juvenile has indistinct dusky barring on neck and breast. Races separated on: size, *gossii* and *flaviventer* largest; and on colour shades, *bangsi* has darkest upperparts, *flaviventer* darkest neck and breast, and *hendersoni* palest upperparts. Voice. Low, harsh, rolled or churring "k'kuk kurr-kurr"; plaintive, squealing, single or repeated "kreer" or "krreh" reminiscent of *P. carolina*; and high-pitched, whistled "peep".

Habitat. Freshwater marshes, grassy edges of lakes and ponds, flooded fields, rice fields, and floating aquatic vegetation such as water hyacinth (*Eichhornia*); rarely in saltwater habitats. Occurs from sea-level up to 2500 m.

Food and Feeding. Small gastropods, insects and seeds, taken from water, mud and vegetation. Forages among emergent plants; emerges from cover in early morning and evening to feed at marsh edge; runs across floating plants and climbs easily in tangled reedy growth.

Breeding. El Salvador, male in breeding condition Aug; Costa Rica, Jul; Trinidad, male in breeding condition Feb; Colombia, "immature" Feb. Nest loosely built among water plants or marsh grass. Eggs 3-5. No other information.

Movements. Normally regarded as sedentary, and no definite movements recorded, but seen only Mar-Jul at Hacienda Corocora, W Meta, Colombia. In Costa Rica probably makes local movements associated with changing water levels. One found at night under village street light, Veracruz (Mexico) in May.

Status and Conservation. Not globally threatened. Formerly regarded as locally abundant in Cuba, locally common in Mexico, and locally common in Trinidad, El Salvador and Panama. Currently regarded as a frequent to uncommon but local resident in Mexico, locally common in Colombia and Costa Rica, and local on the littoral plain in French Guiana; undoubtedly more widespread than is known.

Bibliography. Belton (1984), Biaggi (1983), Blake (1977), Barbour (1923), Canevari *et al*. (1991), Contreras *et al*. (1990), Dickerman (1971), Dickerman & Warner (1961), Dickey & van Rossem (1938), Gochfeld (1972, 1973a), Haverschmidt (1968), Haverschmidt & Mees (1995), Hayes (1995), Hellmayr & Conover (1942), Hilty & Brown (1986), Howell & Webb (1995a), Meyer de Schauensee & Phelps (1978), Olson (1970), Orians & Paulson (1969), de la Peña (1992), Peterson & Chalif (1973), Ridgely (1981), Ridgely & Gwynne (1989), Sick (1985c, 1993), Snyder (1966), Stiles & Skutch (1989), Tostain *et al*. (1992), Wetmore (1965), Wetmore & Swales (1931).

98. White-browed Crake

Porzana cinerea

French: Marouette grise **German**: Weißbrauen-Sumpfhuhn **Spanish**: Polluela Cejiblanca
Other common names: Ashy/Grey-bellied Crake

Taxonomy. *Porphyrio cinereus* Vieillot, 1819, Java.

On basis of bill structure and face pattern, which render it distinct from *Porzana* crakes, sometimes placed in genus *Poliolimnas* with *Porzana flaviventer*, which shows similar characters; this separation may well be valid. Until recently several races commonly recognized, notably *brevipes*, *ocularis*, *micronesiae*, *leucophrys*, *meeki* and *tannensis*; but differences between them are slight, not well defined, and subject to overlap. Monotypic.

Distribution. Malaysia and Greater Sundas through Philippines, Sulawesi, Moluccas and Lesser Sundas to New Guinea and N Australia, and E through Micronesia and Melanesia (S to Vanuatu and New Caledonia) to WC Polynesia (Fiji and Samoa); formerly also Volcano Is.

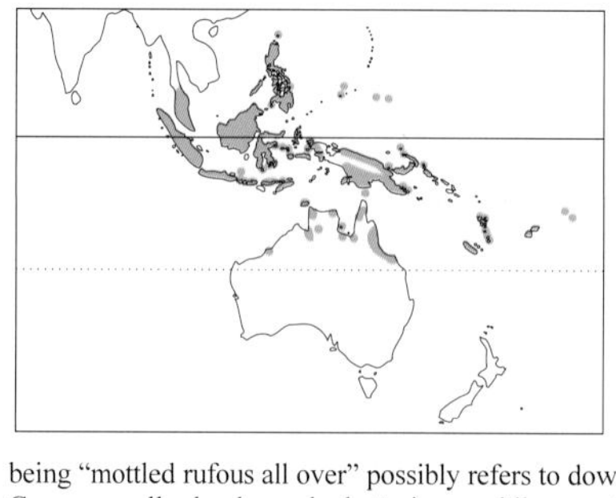

Descriptive notes. 15-20 cm; unsexed 40-62·5 (52) g; wingspan 27 cm. Small, slim-bodied crake with relatively long legs and toes. Easily distinguished from sympatric crakes by striking diagnostic face pattern. In fresh plumage forehead and crown grey, becoming black with wear. Sexes alike. Immature apparently like adult. Juvenile shows adult plumage pattern but grey and black on head replaced by brown, and white facial stripes tinged yellow-brown, making facial pattern less distinct; grey of neck, breast and flanks replaced by buff to pale brown; bill has thin orange band at base; legs and feet olive, blue-green or light blue-grey. A reference to young being "mottled rufous all over" possibly refers to down mixed with emerging juvenile plumage. Voice. Common call a loud, nasal, chattering, rapidly repeated "chika", made by both members of pair, and sometimes by several pairs in response to disturbance. Also sharp, loud "kek-kro" while feeding; quiet, repeated "charr-r" of alarm; and various plaintive, squeaky cries.

Habitat. Well vegetated coastal and terrestrial wetlands, both freshwater and saline, especially those with abundant floating vegetation; habitat may be seasonal or ephemeral. Inhabits swamps, marshes, creeks, rivers, pools, inundations, lakes, dams and sewage ponds. Uses flooded areas, and observed among flood debris. Also occurs in grassland and agricultural areas, including grazed land, rice fields and taro patches; thickets, mature or degraded forest, palm groves and mangroves. Occurs in lowlands; rarely up to 1830 m in New Guinea.

Food and Feeding. Earthworms, slugs, leeches, insects, water spiders, frog spawn, and small fish; also seeds and leaves of aquatic plants. Forages at mud patches and along margins of water courses, both in and out of cover; frequently forages on floating vegetation, dashing around in stop-start manner; also catches flying insects. Often swims, gleaning from water surface; also floats quietly with neck extended, picking up insects with short, sudden thrusts of bill. Occasionally runs up marsh vegetation or along branches. Active throughout day, particularly in early morning and evening.

Breeding. Borneo, Apr-Jun; Philippines, Jul-Aug, and downy young Oct; New Guinea, Dec-Mar, May, chicks Jun and Oct-Nov; Solomon Is, Jan, Jun-Jul, Sept; Vanuatu, possibly Sept-Mar; Australia, Jan-May, also small young in Sept-Nov, N Queensland. Monogamous; may remain paired outside breeding season; possibly permanently territorial. Nest a saucer-shaped platform of rushes, coarse grass or herbage, lined grass and other fine material; built on ground, on trampled blades of tussock, or in grassy marsh vegetation over water, sometimes more than 1 m deep; once in fork of mangrove tree; growing vegetation often woven into thin canopy. External diameter c. 15 cm, depth c. 3.5 cm; built up to 1 m above ground; runway of reed stems often leads from ground to nest rim. Usually 4 eggs (3-7), laid at daily intervals; incubation c. 18 days, by both sexes; downy chick coal black; a large chick, with emergent body feathers and remiges, had black bill with broad pink-white saddle between nostrils, dark brown iris, black eyering, and grey legs and feet; young fed and cared for by both parents for c. 4 weeks; post-juvenile moult probably begins shortly after fledging. In Australia has 1, sometimes 2, broods per year.

Movements. Imperfectly known; considered resident over much of range but probably partially migratory in some regions. Regarded as wet-season migrant in N Australia: although recorded throughout year, more records in summer months and apparently absent from some areas in winter; regular migration along wetlands of Cape York suggested; occurs on islands in Torres Strait, where 112 birds struck Booby I lighthouse between Dec 1975 and Jun 1976. Vagrant to Bikini, Marshall Is.

Status and Conservation. Not globally threatened. Less shy and elusive than most rails and formerly regarded as locally fairly common to fairly abundant throughout most of range, except in Palau, Mariana and Caroline Is, New Caledonia, Vanuatu, Fiji and Samoa. Putative form *brevipes*, confined to Volcano Is (S of Japan), generally regarded as having been extinct since 1911, although said to have been observed in 1924/25; extinction probably caused by introduced rats and cats. Species apparently disappeared from Guam in 1970's concurrent with the draining and development of many of the island's freshwater wetland habitats. Currently widespread and locally common in Greater Sundas and Philippines; local and uncommon in Vanuatu; status uncertain in Australia, but local and apparently not generally common; status elsewhere possibly largely unchanged.

Bibliography. Aumann (1991), Barnard (1914), Beehler *et al*. (1986), Blakers *et al*. (1984), Boekel (1980), Bravery (1970), Brazil (1991), Bregulla (1992), Cairns (1953), Coates (1985), Crawford (1972), Dickinson *et al*. (1991), Draffan *et al*. (1983), Givens (1948), Hadden (1981), Hellebrekers & Hoogerwerf (1967), Hoogerwerf (1949, 1964), Jenkins (1983), Le Souëf (1903), Lekagul & Round (1991), MacGillivray (1914), MacKinnon & Phillipps (1993), Marchant & Higgins (1993), Marin & Sheldon (1987), van Marle & Voous (1988), Mason & Wolfe (1975), Medway & Wells (1976), Mees (1982), Momiyama (1930), Olson (1970), Potapov & Flint (1987), Pratt *et al*. (1980), Rabor (1977), Reed (1980), Serventy (1985), Smythies (1981), Stokes (1983), Stresemann (1941), White & Bruce (1986).

Genus *AENIGMATOLIMNAS* J. L. Peters, 1932

99. Striped Crake

Aenigmatolimnas marginalis

French: Marouette rayée **German**: Graukehl-Sumpfhuhn **Spanish**: Polluela Culirroja

Taxonomy. *Porzana marginalis* Hartlaub, 1857, Gabon.
Often retained in *Porzana* on basis of plumage characters, but differs in skull structure and in having longer legs and toes. Monotypic.
Distribution. N Ivory Coast patchily E to Cameroon and S to coastal Congo; more continuously from E Zaire to Kenya, S and W to Zimbabwe and extreme SE Angola; scattered localities in South Africa, where may breed in wet years.

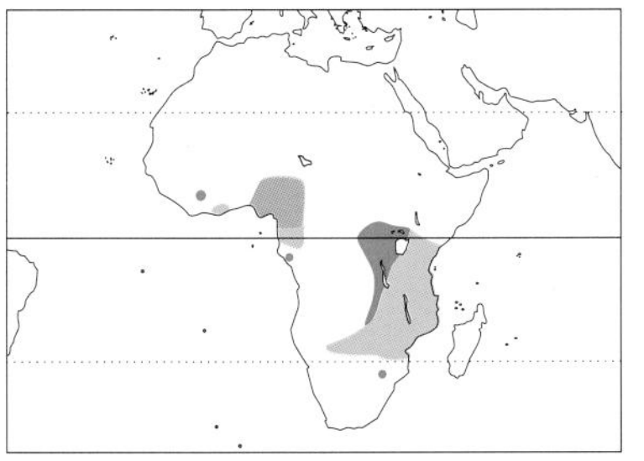

Descriptive notes. 18-21 cm; 2 females, 41·5 and 61 g. Both sexes have diagnostic reddish cinnamon lower flanks and undertail-coverts, visible in flight; other distinctive features include white-striped upperparts, short, deep, apple green bill, and very long toes. Sexually dimorphic: male buff-brown to cinnamon-brown on head, neck, and breast; female grey in these regions, with eye-ring often pale green. Non-breeding birds have eye-ring orange and less prominent; legs and feet duller. Immature resembles adult, with less prominent upperpart streaking and dull bare parts; male paler and more rufous on head, neck, breast and flanks; female has only vague pale markings on neck and breast, and has brownish tinge to grey of head, neck and sides of breast. Juvenile plumage duller and less patterned, males being darker brown, females duller grey; bare parts duller. VOICE. Advertising call of female a series of rapidly repeated ticking notes, lasting up to 1 minute. Answering call, presumably of male, a short series of rapidly-repeated, high-pitched, grating "graa" notes. Contact call "chup"; also has grunts and growls of alarm.
Habitat. Typical breeding habitat is seasonally inundated grasslands which dry out and are often burned in dry season. Occurs in temporary pans, short-grass dambos, old rice fields and edges of marshes, ponds and ditches. Avoids dense, tall vegetation in permanent marshes, and areas with water more than 20-30 cm deep; prefers areas with shallow pools, muddy patches and fine grasses up to 1 m tall. Habitat outside breeding season less well known but apparently similar.
Food and Feeding. Earthworms, small snails, spiders, beetles, grasshoppers, flies, moths, insect larvae, small fish, and tadpoles. Forages on grass and mud, at pool edges and in shallow water; walks deliberately, searching ground and short vegetation; probes into mud; immerses head in water; chases flying insects. Feeds very actively from late afternoon to dusk. Chicks are fed on insects and other small invertebrates.
Breeding. Breeds during rains: Ghana, Jun; Nigeria, Aug, breeding condition Jun; Cameroon, breeding condition Jun; Gabon, breeding condition Nov; Kenya, Jun, breeding condition May, nest building Nov; Tanzania, breeding condition Jan; Malawi, Jan-Feb; Zambia, Jan-Feb, breeding condition Dec; Zimbabwe, Dec-Mar; Namibia Feb-Mar. Captive birds show sequential polyandry, female mating with 2 or more males in succession; polyandry probably also prevalent in the wild, where 6 of 9 records of incubating birds refer to males and 2 to probable males; occasional monogamy also possible. Nest a strongly built shallow bowl or platform of grass, sometimes rushes or sedges, c. 8 cm in diameter; typically well concealed in tuft of grass, sometimes green but often old and dry; usually 10-25 cm above water but occasionally floating or above damp ground, rarely on ground; surrounding vegetation pulled down to form roof over nest. Sometimes builds dummy nests which are abandoned before completion. Usually 4-5 eggs (in captivity 2-6), laid at 1-2 day intervals; incubation 17-18 days, usually by male only; parental care in captivity exclusively by male; black downy chick has cream bill with dark band, but bill becomes predominantly greenish after 10 days; chicks leave nest after 4-5 days; in captivity feathers begin to grow at 8 days, young fully grown and able to fly at 6-7 weeks, post-juvenile moult begins at 13-15 weeks and is complete at 21 weeks; age of first breeding 1 year. Clutch losses from predation often high. In captivity normally 1-2, sometimes 3, broods per season; up to 4 clutches if repeat nesting occurs after failures; female can lay more than 6 clutches for 2 males per season.
Movements. Imperfectly known. In W Africa recorded Ghana only in rains but status uncertain; resident Nigeria but breeds in N only in rains, and latitudinal movements probably occur, night migrants being recorded Dec; in N Gabon occurs irregularly Nov-Mar and night migrants recorded; status elsewhere uncertain. Present Kenya May-Sept and Nov; breeds during rains; night migrants recorded May and coastal movements May-Jul. From Tanzania southwards recorded in breeding areas Dec-Mar; much breeding habitat ephemeral so occurrences irregular and periods of residence may be short; odd birds may remain during dry season if suitable habitat persists. Night migrants recorded S Tanzania, May and Dec, and N Zambia, Mar. Sept record from S Namibia, and 7 scattered records from South Africa (Mar-Jun), are attributed to vagrancy, possible coastal and inland migration, and birds displaced from normal wintering areas by drought conditions; rains records from Nyl floodplain, Transvaal, suggest that breeding range may extend to South Africa in years of good rainfall. In S Africa assumed to be a wet-season breeding visitor which retreats towards equatorial regions after breeding. Vagrant to Algeria in Jan, Libya in Feb, and Aldabra in Dec.
Status and Conservation. Not globally threatened. A highly secretive and poorly known species, undoubtedly overlooked but generally uncommon throughout its range, which may be more extensive and continuous than is known. Like *Sarothrura boehmi*, sometimes locally common in large areas of breeding habitat in good rainfall years but, like that species, its numbers must have been adversely affected by habitat loss resulting from overgrazing and the damming and draining of wetlands.
Bibliography. Andersson & Gurney (1872), Benson (1964b), Benson & Benson (1975), Benson *et al.* (1971), Brosset & Érard (1986), Cramp & Simmons (1980), Dowsett & Forbes-Watson (1993), Elgood *et al.* (1994), Étchécopar & Hüe (1964), Ginn *et al.* (1989), Grimes (1987), Hopkinson & Masterson (1975, 1984), Irwin (1981), Mackworth-Praed & Grant (1957, 1962, 1970), Maclean (1993), Pitman (1965a), Serle (1939b), Short *et al.* (1990), Snow (1978), Taylor (1987), Taylor *et al.* (1994), Urban *et al.* (1986), White (1945), Wintle & Taylor (1993).

Genus *CYANOLIMNAS* Barbour & J. L. Peters, 1927

100. Zapata Rail
Cyanolimnas cerverai

French: Râle de Zapata **German**: Kubaralle **Spanish**: Gallineta de Zapata

Taxonomy. *Cyanolimnas cerverai* Barbour and J. L. Peters, 1927, Santo Tomás, Peninsula de Zapata, Cuba.
Monotypic.
Distribution. Zapata Swamp, WC Cuba.

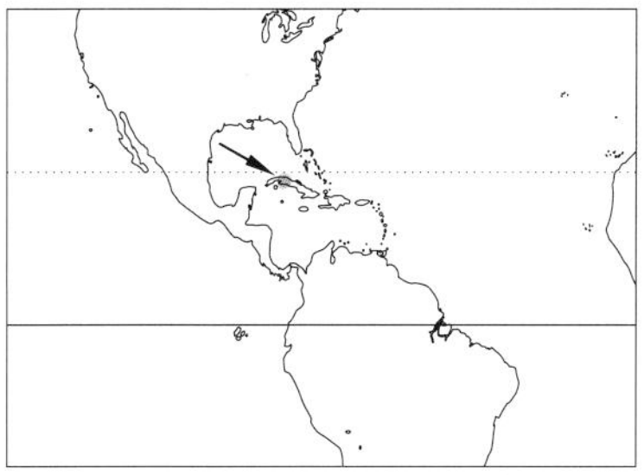

Descriptive notes. 29 cm. Apparently almost flightless; wings very short; tail short and decomposed. Dark rail without streaks or spots, faintly barred on lower belly and thighs and with white undertail-coverts. Sexes alike. Easily separable on plumage from sympatric rallids but resembles smaller *Neocrex colombianus* and *N. erythrops*; former differs in unbarred cinnamon-buff flanks and undertail-coverts; latter has much heavier barring from flanks to undertail-coverts. Considered intermediate in plumage characters between *N. colombianus* and larger *Pardirallus sanguinolentus*, which has unbarred dusky brown to blackish rear flanks and undertail-coverts, and a much longer, slightly decurved, greenish yellow bill with blue and red at base. Immature and juvenile undescribed. VOICE. Alarm call a loud "kwowk", much like that of Limpkin (*Aramus guarauna*).
Habitat. Dense bush-covered swamp with low trees, where *Myrica cerifera* and sawgrass (*Cladium jamaicense*) are common, near higher ground.
Food and Feeding. No information available.
Breeding. Sept; males in breeding condition, Jan. One nest found, situated c. 60 cm above water level in a hummock of sawgrass; contained 3 eggs.
Movements. None.
Status and Conservation. CRITICALLY ENDANGERED. Known from only two sites, c. 65 km apart, in Zapata Swamp. Four were collected near Santo Tomás in 1927 and species was easily found in 1931; subsequently no records, despite occasional searches, until 1970's, when voice was recorded and birds were found at a second locality, Laguna del Tesoro. Despite likely occurrence in other areas of the swamp, the very small number of records in recent decades suggests that population is very small. Serious threats include dry-season burning of habitat, potentially devastating for the species and still occurring, and also the existence of introduced predators, namely a mongoose (*Herpestes*) and rats (*Rattus*). The swamp has so far escaped serious drainage. Species has been afforded protection with an area of 10,000 ha in the Corral de Santo Tomás Faunal Refuge, while Laguna del Tesoro is within a Nature Tourism Area; the benefits of this protection are unknown. Survey of the bird's distribution urgently needed, and dry-season burning of its habitats must be controlled. Former distribution was wider, and fossil bones attributable to this species have been found in cave deposits in Pinar del Rio and on I of Pines.
Bibliography. Abreus & Criado (1994), Anon. (1993f), Barbour & Peters (1927), Bond, J. (1971, 1973, 1984, 1985), Clements (1979), Collar & Andrew (1988), Collar, Crosby & Stattersfield (1994), Collar, Gonzaga *et al.* (1992), Criado *et al.* (1995), Garrido (1985), King (1978/79), Morton (1979), Olson (1973b, 1974b), Regalado (1981), Ripley (1977), Sulley & Sulley (1992).

Genus *NEOCREX* P. L. Sclater & Salvin, 1868

101. Colombian Crake
Neocrex colombianus

French: Râle de Colombie **German**: Kolumbiensumpfhuhn **Spanish**: Polluela Colombiana

Taxonomy. *Neocrex colombianus* Bangs, 1898, Palomino, Santa Marta, Colombia.
Sometimes placed in *Porzana*. Forms superspecies with *N. erythrops*, and sometimes considered conspecific, but differs in plumage and in bill structure. Two subspecies recognized.
Subspecies and Distribution.
N. c. ripleyi Wetmore, 1967 - C Panama and NW Colombia.
N. c. colombianus Bangs, 1898 - N & W Colombia and W Ecuador.

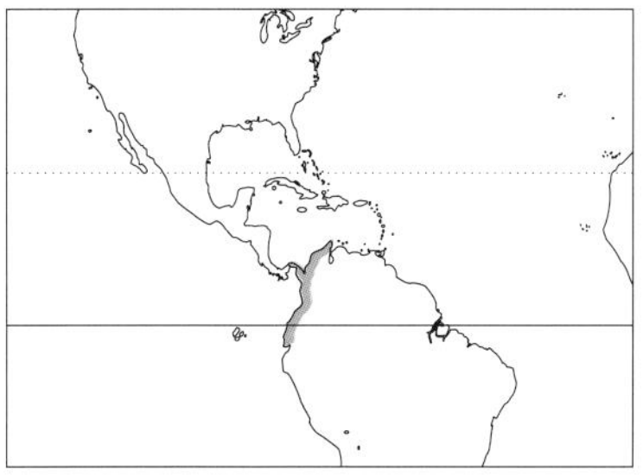

Descriptive notes. 18-20 cm. Sexes alike; underwing-coverts are white. Allopatric *N. erythrops* differs in having flanks to undertail-coverts barred blackish and white, underwing-coverts often barred with black and bill greener with bright red base. Larger *Cyanolimnas cerverai* similar in both plumage and bare parts colours, but has dark slate flanks with faint white bars, and white undertail-coverts. Immature and juvenile undescribed. Races separated on overall colour, *ripleyi* markedly darker. VOICE. Not recorded.
Habitat. Marshes, swamps, wet savannas, wet grass, pastures, and overgrown forest edges; not restricted to areas with water. Occurs up to 2100 m.
Food and Feeding. No information; presumably similar to *N. erythrops*.
Breeding. Colombia, male in breeding condition Jan, 3 birds near breeding condition Dec-Jan; in Panama, an apparently non-flying juvenile recorded in Feb 1982.
Movements. Regarded as sedentary. Three birds, all near breeding condition, flew into lighted windows in Colombian W Andes, Dec and Jan.
Status and Conservation. Not globally threatened. Currently considered near-threatened. Very little information available on status and distribution. Nominate race regarded as rare throughout range, with scattered records across most of N Colombia and S on both slopes of W Andes through W Ecuador. Race *ripleyi* rare in C Panama, where was apparently known from only one specimen (holotype of race), collected in 1965 at Achiote Road on NW boundary of Canal Zone in W Colón, before several were seen at Tocumen marshes in Feb 1982; also apparently rare in NW Colombia, where known from one specimen, collected at Acandi, Gulf of Urabá, near Panama border. Investigation of current status and distribution, and study of natural history, are urgently required. Possibly occurs in E Costa Rica, where a sighting near Hitoy Cerere in Mar 1985 was claimed to be either this species or *N. erythrops*.
Bibliography. Anon. (1983a), Behrstock (1983), Blake (1977), Butler (1979), Collar *et al.* (1994), Fjeldså & Krabbe (1990), Hellmayr & Conover (1942), Hilty & Brown (1986), Miller (1963), Olson (1973b), Ridgely (1981), Ridgely & Gwynne (1989), Ripley (1977), Ripley & Beehler (1985).

102. **Paint-billed Crake**

Neocrex erythrops

French: Râle à bec peint **German**: Goldschnabel-Sumpfhuhn **Spanish**: Polluela Picopinta

Taxonomy. *Porzana erythrops* P. L. Sclater, 1867, Lima, Peru.
Sometimes placed in *Porzana*. Forms superspecies with *N. colombianus*, and sometimes considered conspecific, but differs in plumage and in bill structure. Two subspecies recognized.
Subspecies and Distribution.
N. e. olivascens Chubb, 1917 - E Colombia, Venezuela and the Guianas through C & E Brazil to N & E Bolivia, NW Argentina and Paraguay; also Costa Rica and Panama, where status unclear.
N. e. erythrops (P. L. Sclater, 1867) - coastal Peru, and Galapagos Is (Santa Cruz and Santa María).

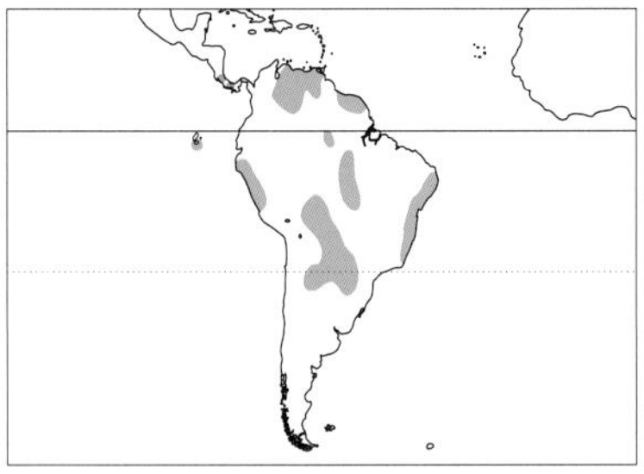

Descriptive notes. 18-20 cm; 2 males 51 and 67 g, 2 females 43 and 61 g, 3 unsexed 55-70 (62) g. Sexes alike; underwing-coverts white, often barred with black. Very similar to allopatric *N. colombianus*, which differs in having unbarred cinnamon-buff flanks and undertail-coverts, unbarred underwing-coverts, and yellower bill with orange base. Larger *Cyanolimnas cerverai* similar in plumage but has dark slate flanks with faint white bars, and white undertail-coverts. Sympatric *Laterallus exilis* smaller, with chestnut nape and upper mantle, variable amount of narrow white barring on upperwing-coverts, dusky green bill, and dusky yellow or brownish legs and feet. Immature not properly described but one had duller bill, grey iris, and pale brown legs and feet. Juvenile has pale grey, faintly barred belly, and darker, greener bill with no red at base. Race *olivascens* darker, with less white on throat. Voice. Song a long, gradually accelerating and descending series of up to 36 staccato notes followed by 3-4 short churring notes which fall in pitch, the last being a 3-second flat trill. Also loud, frog-like, guttural, buzzy, single notes rendered "qurrrk" and "auuk". Alarm a sharp "twack".
Habitat. Reedbeds, lagoons, grassy marshes, rank grass, wet to dry pastures, rice fields, corn fields, gardens, drainage ditches, overgrown bushy areas, and humid woodlands. In Panama found in same habitat as *Laterallus albigularis*. In South America described as possibly preferring dense swamp vegetation and damp secondary woodland in flooded savanna, and as mainly a crake of grass and thickets. Occurs from tropical to temperate zones; recorded up to 3375 m.
Food and Feeding. Very little information available. Known to feed on Diplopoda, insects (including Coleoptera) and seeds (including grass seeds). Takes invertebrates from soil and leaf litter; forages at puddles, sometimes along dirt roads, and in open patches adjacent to dense vegetation, at dawn and dusk.
Breeding. Venezuela, breeding condition Jul; Galapagos, Nov-Feb. Frequently seen in pairs. Nest a bowl of green grass, placed on or near ground, in grassy vegetation; recorded sites include "agricultural fields" and in Venezuela corn fields. Eggs 3-7; incubation at least 23-25 days.
Movements. No evidence for regular movements, but many records outside normal range indicative of either migration or vagrant habits. One record (presumably *olivascens*) from NC Costa Rica at Río Frío, Sarapiqui lowlands, Aug 1987, and may also occur in E Costa Rica, where sighting near Hitoy Cerere in Mar 1985 was claimed to be either this species or *N. colombianus*; also 2 *olivascens* collected at Changuinola, Bocas del Toro (W Panama), Nov 1981 but not noted in Apr or Jul and believed to be of seasonal occurrence. Several records at c. 2600 m on savannas of Bogotá and Ubaté, Colombia, mostly in MarApr, including one from streets of Bogotá; one at 3375 m in suburban garden of La Paz, Bolivia. In N Venezuela, has been attracted to lighted windows in May-Jun at Rancho Grande (Henri Pittier National Park), and was reported by hunters to be of seasonal occurrence at Caicara, appearing in numbers during Aug. Accidental in USA: *erythrops* from Texas, Feb 1972; probable *olivascens* from Virginia, Dec 1978; has also occurred in Nov (no details available).
Status and Conservation. Not globally threatened. Status in some areas difficult to assess: species very furtive and difficult to observe, but often flies when disturbed. Status unclear in Central America, could be accidental, migrant or rare resident, perhaps overlooked. Race *olivascens* formerly regarded as locally common in Colombia, Venezuela and Argentina (Tucumán), and probably less rare in French Guiana than the one existing record (Aug 1981) suggests; only one verifiable record from Guyana (Aug 1977) and recorded from scattered localities in Amazonian and C & E Brazil. Race *erythrops* possibly rare in Peru but abundant on Santa Cruz, Galapagos; known from Galapagos since 1953, but possibly overlooked for some time before that, and could occur on San Cristóbal and Isabela. Current status and distribution need investigation, as do movements and breeding.
Bibliography. Arnold (1978), Behrstock (1983), Blake (1977), Blem (1980), Bowman (1960), Brosset (1963), Canevari *et al.* (1991), Contreras *et al.* (1990), Fjeldså & Krabbe (1990), Friedmann & Smith (1950, 1955), Harris (1973, 1982), Haverschmidt (1968), Haverschmidt & Mees (1995), Hayes (1995), Hellmayr & Conover (1942), Hilty & Brown (1986), Meyer de Schauensee (1962), Meyer de Schauensee & Phelps (1978), Olivares (1969, 1974), Osborne & Beissinger (1979b), de la Peña (1992), Remsen & Traylor (1983), Ridgely & Gwynne (1989), Sick (1985c, 1993), Stiles & Skutch (1989), Teixeira *et al.* (1986), Tostain *et al.* (1992).

Genus *PARDIRALLUS* Bonaparte, 1856

103. **Spotted Rail**

Pardirallus maculatus

French: Râle tacheté **German**: Fleckenralle **Spanish**: Rascón Overo

Taxonomy. *Rallus maculatus* Boddaert, 1783, Cayenne, French Guiana.
Sometimes placed in *Rallus*. Possible race *inoptatus* of W Cuba included in nominate. Two subspecies recognized.
Subspecies and Distribution.
P. m. insolitus (Bangs & Peck, 1908) - Mexico to Costa Rica.
P. m. maculatus (Boddaert, 1783) - W Cuba, Hispaniola, Jamaica, Trinidad and Tobago; Colombia E to the Guianas and E Brazil, and S to Peru and Argentina.
Also occurs in Panama, subspecies unknown.

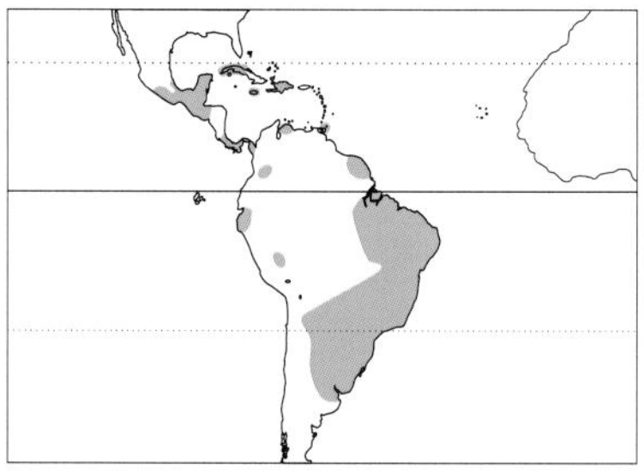

Descriptive notes. 25-28 cm; male 148-219 (189) g, female 130-190 (156) g, unsexed 140-198 (171) g. Sexes alike; female probably slightly smaller. Differs from all other rallids in strikingly variegated plumage and long greenish yellow bill with red spot at base. Immature not properly described. Juvenile has brownish iris, and duller bill and legs; plumage variable, of 3 colour morphs: dark morph, with almost plain, dark brown upperparts, and sooty, dark-tipped ventral feathers with no white bars; pale morph, with throat and breast pale greyish brown, and breast weakly barred white; barred morph, with throat grey, spotted white, and breast and belly sharply barred white. Dark morph juvenile (*maculatus*) has almost plain plumage and is similar to *P. sanguinolentus* and *P. nigricans*, both of which, however, have paler upperparts and bright red legs and feet; *P. sanguinolentus* is larger, with grey chin and throat, and grey-brown vent contrasting with slaty grey underparts; *P. nigricans* has black vent and tail. Races separated on upperpart pattern, *maculatus* streaked, *insolitus* spotted; and colour of juvenile undertail-coverts, grey or white tipped buff in *maculatus*, and white tipped grey in *insolitus*. Voice. Loud, repeated, rasping, groaning screech, usually preceded by grunt or pop, "g'reech" or "pum-kreep", probably territorial or aggressive. Also an accelerating series of deep, gruff, pumping notes, like distant motor starting up; and sharp, repeated "gek" when disturbed. Sometimes calls at night.
Habitat. Inhabits marshes, including those predominantly of *Typha* or *Polygonum*, swamps, rice paddies and other irrigated fields, grassy ditches, and wet grasslands; one occupied site in Costa Rica had *Panicum purpurescens* 45 cm to 1 m tall; also recorded from tall grass on abandoned airfield. Requires dense cover of emergent plants, grass or tangled second growth. Occurs from lowlands up to 2000 m.
Food and Feeding. Earthworms, adult and larval insects (Coleoptera, Hemiptera, Diptera and Odonata), and other invertebrates; small fish; also pondweed *Potamogeton epihydrus*. Normally keeps within cover but may feed in fairly open situations at any time of day, especially in early morning and late evening. Forages at water's edge or while wading; probes in mud.
Breeding. Cuba, late summer to early autumn, at least to Sept; Hispaniola, breeding condition Jun; Trinidad, Jun-Aug; Costa Rica, breeding condition Jul; Colombia, 2 young Dec. Monogamous; apparently territorial, at least during breeding season. Nest a cupped platform of grass or a bowl of dead rushes, built low down in wet grass or other marsh vegetation, often just above shallow water. Eggs 2-7.
Movements. None recorded, but may show widespread dispersal or vagrancy. In Surinam, one entered house at night in Paramaribo, far from suitable habitat, in Jan. Moves locally in response to adverse conditions such as drought (Surinam) or changing water levels (Costa Rica). Accidental in North America, with records from Pennsylvania and Texas, both possibly man-assisted; also Juan Fernández Is (off Chile).
Status and Conservation. Not globally threatened. Locally distributed; in past often regarded as uncommon to rare, but locally common in Zapata Swamp (Cuba), Costa Rica, Colombia and Surinam. Current status unclear in many areas, but locally frequent to uncommon in Mexico, where is more widespread than was formerly known and may be increasing (or previously overlooked); local in French Guiana; few records in Panama. Undoubtedly overlooked, especially when breeding, and probably more widespread within range than existing records suggest. Thought to have been extirpated from Jamaica, but at least one recent sight record. Predation by the introduced mongoose *Herpestes auropunctatus* was thought to have drastically reduced the population in drained agricultural lands of Cuba by 1960's, while disappearance of species from Jamaica was also attributed to mongoose predation.
Bibliography. Belton (1984), Blake (1977), Birkenholz & Jenni (1964), Bond (1980), Canevari *et al.* (1991), Clements (1979), Contreras *et al.* (1990), Dickerman (1971), Dickerman & Haverschmidt (1971), Dickerman & Parkes (1969), Dickerman & Warner (1961), Dod (1980, 1992), Emanuel (1980), ffrench (1973), Friedmann (1949), Haverschmidt (1968), Haverschmidt & Mees (1995), Hayes (1995), Hellmayr & Conover (1942), Hilty & Brown (1986), Howell & Webb (1995a), Meyer de Schauensee & Phelps (1978), Orians & Paulson (1969), Parkes *et al.* (1978), de la Peña (1992), Ridgely (1981), Ridgely & Gwynne (1989), Sick (1985c, 1993), Slud (1964), Stiles & Skutch (1989), Tostain *et al.* (1992), Watson (1962), Wetmore (1965).

104. **Blackish Rail**

Pardirallus nigricans

French: Râle noirâtre **German**: Trauerralle **Spanish**: Rascón Negruzco

Taxonomy. *Rallus nigricans* Vieillot, 1819, Paraguay.
Sometimes placed in *Rallus*, or referred to genus *Ortygonax*. In past sometimes regarded as conspecific with *P. sanguinolentus*. Two subspecies recognized.
Subspecies and Distribution.
P. n. caucae (Conover, 1949) - SW Colombia (Cauca Valley S to Nariño).
P. n. nigricans (Vieillot, 1819) - E Ecuador, E Peru, N Bolivia, W, SC & E Brazil, Paraguay and extreme NE Argentina.

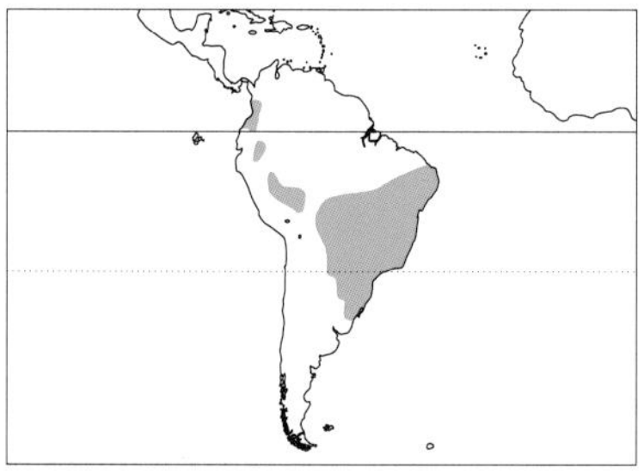

Descriptive notes. 27-29 cm; 1 male 217 g. Sexes alike. Closely resembles partially sympatric *R. sanguinolentus*, which differs in being larger and having grey chin and throat, broad dusky centres to feathers of mantle to rump and inner secondaries, olive brown uppertail-coverts and tail, grey-brown vent, and more decurved, greenish yellow bill with red and blue at base. Immature similar to adult but browner, especially on lower upperparts. Juvenile not described. Race *caucae* larger, with paler underparts, especially noticeable on vent, and usually larger, whiter throat patch. Voice. Descriptions include: very fast, metallic "tii'd'dit"; complaining "keeeeaaa" resembling call of small hawk; rapid, repeated "chchchee"; sharp double squeak; and very sharp, loud, penetrating, repeated "whuueeee" or "wheee", a form of song probably given by male. Often calls in late afternoon.
Habitat. Marshes, vegetation-choked waterways, flooded rice fields, tall damp grass, and swampy, lightly wooded areas. Predominantly lowlands, but occurs at 800-2200 m in Andes, exceptionally 4080 m.

Food and Feeding. No information on food; presumably feeds on insects and other invertebrates. Occasionally forages in the open: on muddy shores with other waterbirds or in small clear areas in marsh vegetation. Recorded venturing 5 m into restaurant garden for food scraps.
Breeding. Brazil, male with somewhat enlarged testes, Jul. Nest of aquatic grasses, placed on or near the ground in tall damp grass. Possible nest of this species (or of *P. sanguinolentus*), from Rio Grande do Sul, Brazil, in Jan, was cup-shaped and placed on low stump among heavy second-growth shoots in swampy scrub. Eggs 3 (2 in captivity); incubation (captivity) 18-21 days; both parents feed and care for young, which leave nest soon after hatching; downy chicks black, with black bare parts.
Movements. None recorded, but a stray record from Junín, NC Peru, at 4080 m.
Status and Conservation. Not globally threatened. Past and present status difficult to assess, as species usually secretive and difficult to observe, but both races generally regarded as uncommon and patchily distributed. Only two records from Bolivia (Pando and N La Paz). Locally fairly common in Rio Grande do Sul, SE Brazil.
Bibliography. Belton (1984), Blake (1977), Canevari *et al.* (1991), Fjeldså & Krabbe (1990), Hellmayr & Conover (1942), Hilty & Brown (1986), Mitchell (1957), Naranjo (1991a), Pacheco & Whitney (1995), Parker & Remsen (1987), Parker *et al.* (1991), de la Peña (1992), Pryor (1969), Ripley (1977), Sclater & Salvin (1879), Sick (1985c, 1993).

105. **Plumbeous Rail**

Pardirallus sanguinolentus

French: Râle à bec ensanglanté **German**: Grauralle **Spanish**: Rascón Gallineta

Taxonomy. *Rallus sanguinolentus* Swainson, 1838, Brazil and Chile.
Sometimes placed in *Rallus*, or referred to genus *Ortygonax*. In past, sometimes regarded as conspecific with *P. nigricans*. Formerly listed as *P. rytirhynchos*, but this name is unidentifiable. Six subspecies recognized.
Subspecies and Distribution.
P. s. simonsi Chubb, 1917 - Pacific slope of Peru S to N Chile.
P. s. tschudii Chubb, 1919 - temperate zone of Peru (S from upper Marañón) to C & SE Bolivia.
P. s. zelebori (Pelzeln, 1865) - SE Brazil.
P. s. sanguinolentus (Swainson, 1838) - Paraguay, extreme SE Brazil, Uruguay, and Argentina S to Río Negro.
P. s. landbecki (Hellmayr, 1932) - C Chile (Atacama S to Llanquihue), and SW Argentina.
P. s. luridus (Peale, 1848) - S Chile and S Argentina to Tierra del Fuego (including Isla Grande); doubtful record from Falkland Is.

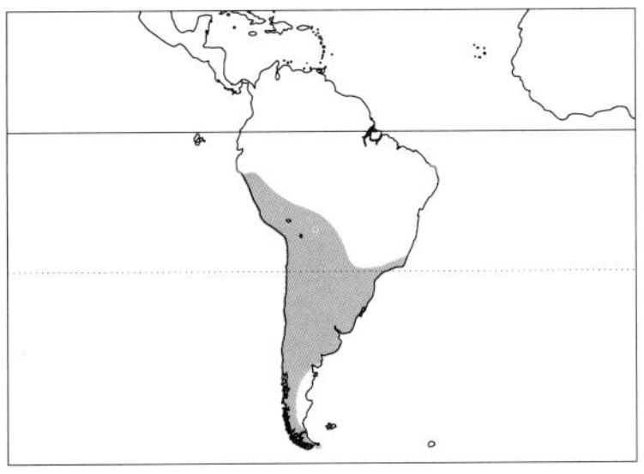

Descriptive notes. 30-38 cm; 3 males 170-213 (197) g, 1 female 233 g. Sexes alike. Very similar to sympatric *P. nigricans*, which differs in being smaller and having whitish chin and throat, lighter and more olivaceous upperparts with no dark feather centres, dark inner remiges (sometimes with narrow olive brown edges), black vent and tail, and straighter, greenish bill with a yellowish base. Immature somewhat duller than adult above, with slightly darker tail; brown-grey below; bill greenish, sometimes with darker base; iris brown; legs red-brown. Juvenile similar on upperparts; underparts all brown, with buffy white throat and belly; bill, legs and feet black. Races separated on: size, *zelebori* smallest, *luridus* largest; upperpart pattern and colour, *luridus* and *landbecki* have no mottling, *landbecki* and *simonsi* more olive-brown; and shade of underparts, paler in *luridus*, *simonsi* and *tschudii*. VOICE. Song a series of high, penetrating, rolling squeals "rrueet'e", "pu-rueet" or "huyr", etc., often with simultaneous low, deep "hoo" notes (duet). Calls are repeated "giyp" or "wit" notes. Sings both day and night, one song often giving rise to chorus.
Habitat. Reed-marsh, sometimes of small area, especially around muddy creeks and ponds with much floating vegetation (*Ranunculus*, *Hydrocotyle*). Locally also in waterside thickets, irrigated areas such as alfalfa crops, ditches through rushy pasture in cultivated parts of semi-arid valleys, and oases in arid regions. May be found wherever there is water and sufficient vegetation cover. Occurs in lowlands, also locally up to 2500 m, and patchily up to c. 4000 m.
Food and Feeding. Grubs, worms and insects. Mainly crepuscular, but also active during night, in marsh or adjacent cultivated fields; can also be seen foraging by day. Sometimes swims.
Breeding. Peru, Oct, chicks Jan; Chile, Oct-Jan; SE Brazil, breeding condition Nov; Argentina, Oct-Dec. Recorded as occurring in pairs. Nest poorly constructed, of dry grasses; built on ground among bushes, reeds and long grass bordering water. Eggs 4-6; downy chicks dark brown, darker on upperparts and wings, bill black, legs and feet pale brown.
Movements. No definite information, but thought to be migratory over part of range; birds of inland marshes on SW *pampas* thought to move N in winter, while those of Atlantic seaboard marshes, where shelter and temperature remain suitable in winter, are sedentary.
Status and Conservation. Not globally threatened. Nominate race, *simonsi* and *landbecki* formerly regarded as locally common; past status of others unknown. Current status difficult to assess in many areas, but abundant on N Altiplano around Junín, Peru (*tschudii*); common on Isla Grande, Tierra del Fuego (*luridus*). Probably more widespread than is currently known.
Bibliography. Belton (1984), Blake (1977), Canevari *et al.* (1991), Contreras, J.R. (1980), Contreras, J.R. *et al.* (1990), Fjeldså & Krabbe (1990), Harris (1981), Hayes (1995), Hellmayr & Conover (1942), Hudson (1920), Humphrey *et al.* (1970), Johnson (1965b), de la Peña (1992), Rasmussen *et al.* (1996), Remsen *et al.* (1985), Roe & Rees (1979), Sick (1985c, 1993), Weller (1967), Wetmore (1926), Zimmer (1930).

Genus *EULABEORNIS* Gould, 1844

106. **Chestnut Rail**

Eulabeornis castaneoventris

French: Râle à ventre roux **German**: Mangroveralle **Spanish**: Cotara Australiana
Other common names: Chestnut-bellied Rail

Taxonomy. *Eulabeornis castaneoventris* Gould, 1844, Flinders River, Gulf of Carpentaria.
Genus sometimes enlarged to include *Aramides*, *Amaurolimnas* and *Gymnocrex*. Two subspecies recognized.
Subspecies and Distribution.
E. c. sharpei Rothschild, 1906 - Aru Is.
E. c. castaneoventris Gould, 1844 - N coasts of Australia from N Western Australia through Northern Territory to NW Queensland.

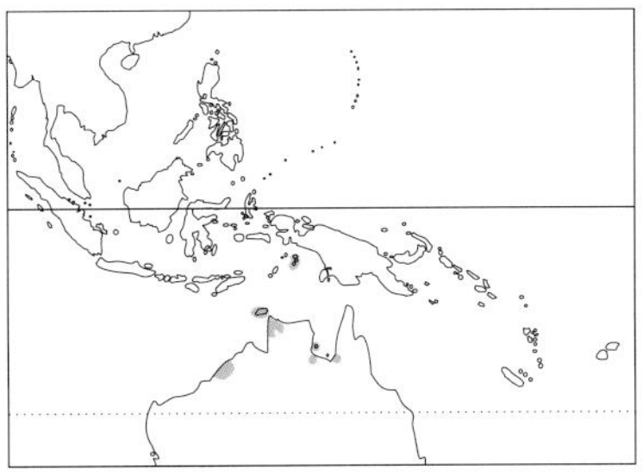

Descriptive notes. Male 52 cm, 626-910 (752) g; female 44-52 cm, 550-710 (628) g. Largest rallid in its habitat; thickset species with longish tail, long, heavy, greenish bill and pale yellow or green legs; head and upper portion of neck grey; chin white; underparts pinkish brown, varying considerably in brightness. Polymorphic, varying mainly in colour of upperparts: dark chestnut brown in chestnut morph, Northern Territory; olive in olive morph, Western Australia; olive brown in olive brown morph, Northern Territory and Queensland. Sexes similar, but female smaller. Immature undescribed; one possible juvenile identical to adult chestnut morph. Race *sharpei* like chestnut morph; has deeper, heavier bill, green with yellow tip and red around nostrils. VOICE. Poorly known. Normal call a harsh screech, preceded by grunt and usually repeated c. 12 times; sequence also described as beginning with deep drumming (grunting?) followed by loud pig-like squealing, or as barking, trumpeting or donkey-like notes; usually uttered by single bird; heard throughout year at all times of day. Contact call a loud, repeated "chuck", with occasional grunts; gives quiet grunts when disturbed.
Habitat. Tropical estuaries, preferring mangrove forests, tidal channels and flats, especially seaward mudflats; uncommon along creeks with only narrow fringe of mangroves. Occasionally in adjacent grassy flats, reedy swamps and open woodland, sometimes because normal mangrove habitat flooded.
Food and Feeding. Takes mainly crabs and other crustaceans; also small molluscs, insects and centipedes. Both diurnally and nocturnally active. Forages in soft mud or shallow water within mangrove zone, along tidal channels and on tidal flats as tide falls. Moves slowly, often flicking tail; makes short runs to chase prey; most food taken from ground or water; often immerses bill and forehead into mud or water; also gleans and pecks at bases and roots of mangroves, and probes e.g. into crab burrows. Pair members feed close together.
Breeding. Very poorly known. Breeds Sept-Feb. Monogamous; territorial when breeding. Nest a large, loose platform of dead sticks, grass, leaves, bark and seaweed, rather like flat-topped pyramid, built 0·6-3 m above ground in mangrove tree; birds often choose slanting tree for ease of access; platform 35-50 cm across, 20 cm deep; cavity 20 cm across, 6 cm deep. 2 nests 1·5 m up had gangways of sticks running up over prop-roots, from ground to nest. Nest may be refurbished and used for several years. Eggs 4-5, laid at daily intervals; downy chick dark sooty brown; chicks leave nest soon after hatching.
Movements. Probably sedentary; no long distance movements recorded. When feeding, moves to higher ground as tide rises and back to creeks as water recedes.
Status and Conservation. Not globally threatened. Patchily recorded, with several apparent gaps in distribution which may be due to incomplete coverage by observers; status uncertain because birds very shy and difficult to see in dense habitat; more often located by characteristic loud, raucous call. Probably moderately common in good habitat, and density at one site was c. 8 birds/km²; breeding territory size estimated at 10 ha. No known threats to species or its habitat, but lack of recent records from S coast of Gulf of Carpentaria is puzzling. May become accustomed to disturbance from power boats.
Bibliography. Andrew, P. (1992), Beehler *et al.* (1986), Blakers *et al.* (1984), Flegg & Madge (1995), Lindsey (1992), Macdonald (1988), Marchant & Higgins (1993), Olson (1973b), Pizzey & Doyle (1980), Ragless (1977), Rand & Gilliard (1967), Ripley (1977), Ripley & Beehler (1985), Schodde & Tidemann (1986), Serventy (1985), Simpson & Day (1994), Trounson (1987).

Genus *HABROPTILA* G. R. Gray, 1860

107. **Invisible Rail**

Habroptila wallacii

French: Râle de Wallace **German**: Trommelralle **Spanish**: Rascón de Wallace
Other common names: Wallace's/Halmahera/Drummer Rail

Taxonomy. *Habroptila wallacii* G. R. Gray, 1860, Halmahera.
Sometimes placed in *Rallus* for no good reason, but probably derived from *Amaurornis*; very close to *Megacrex*, which is its ecological counterpart in New Guinea. Monotypic.
Distribution. Halmahera (N Moluccas).

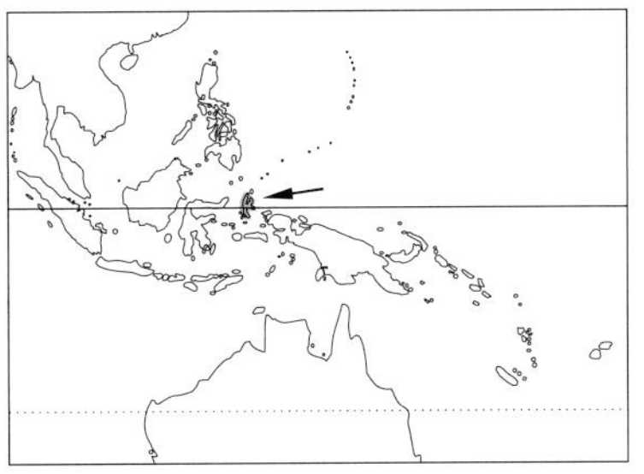

Descriptive notes. 35 cm. Sexes alike. Rather distinctive large, flightless rail of striking appearance, with very dark slate and dark brown plumage, and bright red bare parts including eye-ring and frontal shield; bill long and heavy. Immature and juvenile undescribed. VOICE. Described as a low drumbeat interspersed with a loud scream.
Habitat. Dense, impenetrable, swampy thickets, particularly areas of heavy sago swamp; also the edges of marshes, preferring peninsulas of land jutting out into marshy expanses. A report that it occurs in *alang-alang* (*Imperata cylindrica*) grass is thought to have resulted from confusion with *Amaurornis moluccanus*.
Food and Feeding. Diet and feeding habits virtually unknown. Mainly young plant shoots and beetles recorded.

Breeding. The only information is that an adult was reported with 4-5 striped chicks; if correct, this would be an atypical downy plumage for the family.

Movements. None recorded.

Status and Conservation. VULNERABLE. Probably scarce; a report that it was locally common in grassland is believed to have resulted from confusion with the common *Amaurornis moluccanus*. Only recent records are of specimens collected in early 1980's and early 1990's, and a sighting in a sago swamp in 1995. Threatened by habitat destruction, and sago swamps have been extensively destroyed on Halmahera. Snared for food by local people and caught with dogs; species is also likely to be vulnerable to other introduced predators.

Bibliography. Andrew, P. (1992), Anon. (1995q), Collar & Andrew (1988), Collar *et al.* (1994), de Haan (1950), Heinrich (1932, 1956), Olson (1973b), Ripley (1977), Ripley & Beehler (1985), Stresemann (1931), White & Bruce (1986).

Genus *MEGACREX*

D'Albertis & Salvadori, 1879

108. **New Guinea Flightless Rail**

Megacrex inepta

French: Râle géant **German**: Baumralle **Spanish**: Rascón Inepto
Other common names: Papuan Flightless/Grey-faced Rail

Taxonomy. *Megacrex inepta* D'Albertis and Salvadori, 1879, Fly River, New Guinea.
Very close to *Habroptila wallacii*; sometimes placed in *Habroptila*, or in *Amaurornis*; probably derived from latter. Two subspecies recognized.

Subspecies and Distribution.
M. i. pallida Rand, 1938 - NC New Guinea, from R Taritatu (Idenburg) to R Sepik.
M. i. inepta D'Albertis & Salvadori, 1879 - SC New Guinea, from R Setekwa and R Noord (Lorentz) to R Digul and R Fly.

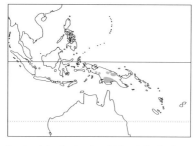

Descriptive notes. 36-38 cm. Sexes alike. Large, powerful flightless rail, with long heavy legs and very short, decomposed tail; easily distinguished from sympatric rallids on structure, size and plumage. Runs strongly, and flicks wings upwards while moving around. Young bird has brownish black hairy plumes on crown and in lines on side of head and on throat; mantle browner than in adult. Race *pallida* has paler, more buffy sides of lower neck and body. VOICE. Harsh but shrill call "aaah-aaah", reminiscent of the squeal of a baby pig; also a short complaining whistle.
Habitat. Mangrove forests, wet thickets, swamp forest and riverine bamboo thickets in lowlands.

Food and Feeding. Nothing recorded.

Breeding. Undescribed; two downy young obtained at L Daviumbu, near R Fly in Sept (latter part of dry season). Downy chick is black on head, and brownish black on body, with upperparts darker than underparts.

Movements. None recorded.

Status and Conservation. Not globally threatened. Data Deficient. Very rarely seen, but regarded by local people as not uncommon near Kiunga (on upper R Fly). No obvious threats except perhaps from feral pigs, and possibly from casual hunting by local people while collecting sago; powerful enough to frighten dogs by kicking and stabbing before escaping into dense cover or up into trees. Initial populations probably small because of specialized habitat requirements.

Bibliography. Andrew, P. (1992), Beehler *et al.* (1986), Coates (1985), Collar *et al.* (1994), Diamond (1975), Olson (1973b), Rand & Gilliard (1967), Ripley (1964, 1977).

Genus *GALLICREX* Blyth, 1852

109. **Watercock**

Gallicrex cinerea

French: Râle à crête **German**: Wasserhahn **Spanish**: Gallineta Crestada

Taxonomy. *Fulica cinerea* Gmelin, 1789, China.
Monotypic.

Distribution. Pakistan, India, Maldives and Sri Lanka E to C & E China, Korea and Ryukyu Is, and S through Andamans, Nicobars and SE Asia to Sumatra and Philippines. Winters S to Greater and Lesser Sundas and Sulawesi; now annual visitor to S Japan, mostly during winter.

Descriptive notes. Male 42-43 cm, 300-650 g; female 36 cm, 200-434 g; wingspan 68-86 cm. Large moorhen-like rail with slimmer, long-necked appearance. Male black with upperpart feathers fringed grey and usually brown, giving scaled appearance; undertail-coverts barred black and buff; bill yellow, and iris, base of upper mandible, frontal shield, horn, legs and feet bright red. Female markedly smaller; darkish brown above with buff-brown scalloping, rufous buff below with fine wavy dark barring. Non-breeding male as female. Immature and juvenile like adult female, but juvenile more tawny overall and less barred below. VOICE. Noisy in breeding season, with 3 types of call, all produced fairly continuously and rhythmically with short silence between each series: 10-12 "kok" notes with head raised; then 10-12 deeper, faster, hollow metallic "utumb" notes with head lowered; and finally 5-6 "kluck" notes with head raised. Generally silent in winter.

Habitat. Reedy or grassy swamps, flooded pasture, rice fields, irrigated sugar cane, and rush-bordered channels, rivers, ponds and ditches; sometimes brackish swamps.

Food and Feeding. Feeds largely on seeds and shoots of "green crops", and wild and cultivated rice, but also takes worms, molluscs, aquatic insects and their larvae, and grasshoppers. Swims well and will cross open water. Skulking and largely crepuscular; also emerges to feed in overcast and rainy weather.

Breeding. India and Pakistan, mostly Jun-Sept (monsoon months); Sri Lanka, May, also Jan-Feb and possibly Jul-Aug; Maldives, Jun-Jul; Ryukyu Is, Aug; Philippines, May-Jul and Sept; Sumatra, Dec (female and eggs collected). Probably monogamous, and territorial when breeding. Nest a large concave or deep cup-shaped pad of sedges, rushes, rice blades or grass, built low down in reeds or rice, or on clump of coarse grass; stems and seedheads turned down to form platform on which more material added; sometimes domed over to form bower; occasionally builds on heap of vegetable rubbish. Usually 3-6 eggs (3-10); incubation period unknown, but c. 24 days with artificial incubation. Normally rears 2 broods.

Movements. Most birds from N China and Korea apparently migrate or disperse S for winter, but extent of movements unclear, and evidence somewhat conflicting, with species also reported to be resident even in NE China (Liaoning); absent from Hong Kong, and apparently from Korea, in winter. Regarded as largely a visitor to S part of range, with winter occurrences from Borneo, Java, Sumatra, Flores and Sulawesi; also May-Jul in Sumatra and breeding recorded; migrants present in Japan mainly Sept to mid-Jan (most Oct-Nov) with occasional spring records. In India and Pakistan, resident in well watered areas but disperses widely during monsoon with creation of marshy conditions in otherwise dry lowlying areas. Vagrant to Kamchatka, Christmas I (Indian Ocean) Dec-Jan, and possibly to Palau Is.

Status and Conservation. Not globally threatened. Formerly reckoned to be common over much of range. Currently regarded as common winter visitor Sumatra (perhaps breeding only exceptionally) but uncommon in rest of Greater Sundas; fairly common resident in Philippines. In Wallacea, where assumed to be winter visitor, only 4 records: Sulawesi in Dec-Feb, and Flores May. Uncommon resident in Yaeama Is (S Ryukyu Is); rare but annual visitor to main islands of Japan.

Bibliography. Ali & Ripley (1980), Brazil (1991), Deignan (1945), Dickinson *et al.* (1991), Étchécopar & Hüe (1978), Knystautas (1993), Lekagul & Round (1991), MacKinnon & Phillipps (1993), Madoc (1976), Marchant & Higgins (1993), van Marle & Voous (1988), Medway & Wells (1976), Paynter (1963), Perennou *et al.* (1994), Phillips (1978), Rabor (1977), Ripley (1982), Roberts, T.J. (1991), Smythies (1981, 1986), White & Bruce (1986).

PLATE 17 ➤

ssp *porphyrio*

ssp *poliocephalus*

ssp *pulverulentus*

ssp *viridis*

ssp *indicus*

110

ssp *melanotus*

110

ssp *madagascariensis*

ssp *bellus*

111

113

112

116

114

115

ssp *chloropus*

ssp *pyrrhorrhoa*

ssp *orientalis*

ssp *sandvicensis*

117

ssp *cachinnans*

ssp *garmani*

PLATE 17

inches   8

cm   20

Genus *PORPHYRIO* Brisson, 1760

110. **Purple Swamphen**

Porphyrio porphyrio

French: Talève sultane **German**: Purpurhuhn **Spanish**: Calamón Común
Other common names: Purple Gallinule(!)

Taxonomy. *Fulica Porphyrio* Linnaeus, 1758, Asia, America (= lands bordering the western Mediterranean Sea).
Races *madagascariensis*, *pulverulentus* and *poliocephalus* (incorporating all remaining races except nominate) have at times been considered separate species; *melanotus* and *bellus* too might be separate species. Numerous other races described. Thirteen subspecies recognized.
Subspecies and Distribution.
P. p. porphyrio (Linnaeus, 1758) - E & S Spain, S France and Sardinia to Morocco, Algeria and Tunisia.
P. p. madagascariensis (Latham, 1801) - Egypt, sub-Saharan Africa and Madagascar.
P. p. caspius Hartert, 1917 - Caspian Sea, NW Iran and Turkey.
P. p. seistanicus Zarudny & Härms, 1911 - Iraq and S Iran to Afghanistan, Pakistan and NW India.
P. p. poliocephalus (Latham, 1801) - India and Sri Lanka through Bangladesh, Andamans, Nicobars and N Myanmar to SC China (Yunnan) and N Thailand.
P. p. viridis Begbie, 1834 - S Myanmar, S Thailand and Peninsular Malaysia through Indochina to S China.
P. p. indicus Horsfield, 1821 - Greater Sundas to Bali and Sulawesi.
P. p. pulverulentus Temminck, 1826 - Philippines.
P. p. pelewensis Hartlaub & Finsch, 1872 - Palau Is.
P. p. melanopterus Bonaparte, 1856 - Moluccas and Lesser Sundas to New Guinea.
P. p. bellus Gould, 1841 - SW Australia.
P. p. melanotus Temminck, 1820 - N & E Australia and Tasmania to New Zealand, Kermadec Is and Chatham Is; migrates to New Guinea.
P. p. samoensis Peale, 1848 - Admiralty Is S to New Caledonia and E to Samoa.

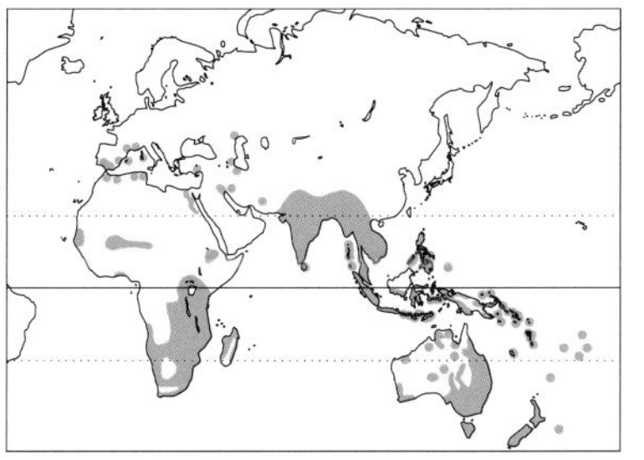

Descriptive notes. 38-50 cm; *madagascariensis* male 528-687 (636) g, female 480-737 (556) g; nominate male 720-1000 (869) g, female 520-870 (724) g; *melanotus* male 785-1310 (1089) g, female 679-1252 (881) g; wingspan 90-100 cm (nominate), 70-86 cm (*melanotus*, *bellus*). Very large, ponderous rail, much larger than all other congeners except flightless *P. mantelli*, with massive triangular red bill, red shield, red legs and long, slender toes; most races predominantly blue to violet on head and body, with contrastingly blackish or greenish back and upperwing-coverts. Female smaller, with smaller frontal shield. Immature similar to adult but duller; some juvenile body feathers often retained. Juvenile duller than adult; face, foreneck and breast washed grey and throat almost white (nominate, *madagascariensis*); wings as adult; bare parts duller than adult. Races separated on plumage and size, with six subspecies groups: (1) nominate *porphyrio* has purple back and wings; (2) *madagascariensis* has bronze-green or blue-green back and scapulars; (3) *poliocephalus* group has cerulean blue scapulars, upperwing-coverts, face, throat and breast, and dark blue back; size declines eastwards, with *caspius* largest, *seistanicus* smaller and *poliocephalus* smallest; (4) *indicus* group often has large shield, upperparts and upperwing-coverts black with green tinge (less green in *indicus*), and throat and breast turquoise green to cerulean blue; side of head blackish in *indicus*, cerulean blue in *viridis*; (5) *pulverulentus* has olive-chestnut mantle and scapulars, and whole body strongly tinged ashy grey; (6) *melanotus* group can have relatively small shield, and has short toes, black upperparts, and variably cobalt to violet throat and breast; *melanotus* has purple throat and breast, *bellus* cerulean blue in these regions, *samoensis* similar to *bellus* but smaller and often has greenish brown tinge to back; *melanopterus* very variable and differs from *melanotus* and *bellus* in having blue lesser upperwing-coverts and being smaller; *pelewensis* similar to *melanopterus* but has greener gloss on upperparts and more purple tinge to lesser upperwing-coverts and breast.
Voice. Very vocal; repertoire rich and variable. Male has low, sonorous calls, sometimes ending with hoarse trumpet notes; female has shriller, softer calls. Notes include "chuck" or "n'yip" contact and rallying calls, nasal rallying calls, explosive trumpeting alarm call, crowing territorial calls, and harsh, grating threat calls. Song a powerful series of plaintive nasal rattles, with crescendo. Flight call a loud shrieking series of cackling notes. Also has various grunts, whistles and bell-like notes.
Habitat. Fresh or brackish, sheltered open waters, still or slow-flowing, fringed or overgrown by *Phragmites*, *Typha*, *Carex*, *Cyperus*, etc. Sometimes at saline, eutrophic or turbid wetlands. Inhabited wetlands often extensive but birds also found on small waters. Habitat normally permanent but in Africa also occupies, and breeds in, seasonal and temporary wetlands. Inhabits ponds, lakes, dams, marshes, swamps, rivers, floodplains, artesian and seismic bores, and sewage farms; also lakes in towns, and islands on R Nile. Extends into open habitats adjacent to wetlands, such as grassland, agricultural land, parks, gardens, roadside verges, hedgerows, forest margins and even chicken runs. Occurs from sea-level to c. 2300 m (New Zealand) and 2500 m (Africa).
Food and Feeding. Omnivorous, but primarily vegetarian, taking shoots, leaves, roots, stems, flowers and seeds of aquatic and semi-aquatic plants. Principal food items include *Typha* (especially leaf bases and pith), *Scirpus* (pith from stems), young rice plants, seeds of grasses, sedges, *Rumex*, *Polygonum*, etc., and vegetative parts (especially tubers) of water-lilies. Animal foods normally small proportion of diet, including molluscs, leeches, small crabs, insects and their larvae, spiders, fish and their eggs, frogs and their eggs, lizards, snakes, birds, their eggs and nestlings, small rodents, and carrion. Forages in cover, at edge of cover on muddy, sandy or hard shoreline, in shallow water and on floating vegetation. Swims relatively little, but will dabble near shallow margins like Mallard (*Anas platyrhynchos*); picks insects from water surface. Climbs freely to strip flowers and seeds from reeds, etc., and to take bird eggs and nestlings. Uses bill to cut, dig up or pull out plants, to move stones and gravel, to turn over matted vegetation, and to dismember food items, and foot to grasp and manipulate food (see page 126). Adaptable: will forage in pasture, scrub and mown fields; grazes clover and grass; also feeds in rice fields. Builds platforms for feeding and roosting. Feeds mainly in early morning and late evening; sometimes at night.
Breeding. Mediterranean, mainly Mar-Jun; India and Pakistan, mainly Jun-Sept (SW monsoon); sub-Saharan Africa, in rainy season (possibly two breeding seasons in areas with bimodal rainfall regime); Madagascar, Jan; Australia, all months, main breeding correlated with peak rainfall, temperature and increase in photoperiod; New Zealand, Aug-Feb (mainly Sept-Dec); Vanuatu, mainly Aug-Jan. Social structure and mating system complex (see page 130). Mainly permanently territorial. Monogamy apparently prevails in W Palearctic races and in *madagascariensis*, but elsewhere at least races *poliocephalus* and *melanotus* live in communal groups (the former in captivity). In *melanotus*, groups contain breeding males and females, and non-breeding helpers (offspring from previous matings); mate-sharing occurs and females lay in communal nest; all group members care for young. Nest in shallow water (occasionally up to 180 m from water), concealed in thick emergent vegetation; large, substantial structure of dead stems and leaves of water plants, with shallow cup, usually built on platform of beaten-down vegetation; normally just above water but sometimes floating; surrounding stems often pulled over to form canopy; 1-2 access ramps provided. Outside diameter of nest c. 30 cm, depth 10-20 cm; cavity diameter 19-30 cm, depth 3-10 cm; material often added during incubation. Both sexes build, sometimes with assistance from helpers. Eggs 3-5 (W Palearctic, *caspius*), 3-7 (*poliocephalus*), 2-6 (*madagascariensis*, *melanotus*); laid at daily intervals; in communal breeders all breeding females in group lay eggs in same nest, sometimes in double bowl; lays up to 3 replacement clutches after losses; incubation 23-27 days, by both sexes and helpers; hatching synchronous or asynchronous; chicks precocial and nidifugous; can leave nest soon after hatching but often remain on nest for first few days; fed and cared for by parents and helpers; black downy chick has white filoplumes on head, neck, mantle and wing; skin of forehead red and eyelids purple; iris slate; bill white with purple-red at nostril and base; legs and feet rosy-flesh; young begin feeding themselves at 10-14 days, but fed for 25-40 days; fledged at 60 days or more; independent at 6-8 weeks. Age of first breeding 1-2 years. May raise two broods per season in some regions.
Movements. No regular long distance migrations. Local seasonal movements, in response to changing habitat conditions, in many regions, including SW Europe, Sardinia, N and sub-Saharan Africa, Volga Delta (most move S in winter), Caspian (numbers increase in S in winter), Azerbaijan, India and Pakistan, and Australasia (may migrate regularly across Torres Strait); possibly prone to irruptive movements in some parts of Australia and New Zealand, but fluctuations in numbers may be partly associated with modifications to habitat. In Gambia, is only non-breeding dry season visitor. Local movements in Andalusian marshes (Spain) believed to be largely made on foot and at night. Some wandering reported, in Europe confused by escapes, but genuine vagrant to Germany, former Czechoslovakia, Austria, Hungary, former Yugoslavia, Lebanon, Israel, Kuwait and Cyprus; in Africa wandering also reported to Pemba I and to scattered desert localities. In Syria, recorded at Bahrat Homs, where unlikely to breed, but may breed in Euphrates Valley.
Status and Conservation. Not globally threatened. In 20th century, nominate race has suffered marked decrease in already restricted range, often because of wetland drainage and also through hunting and effects of pesticides; requires strict protection and habitat management. Races *caspius, seistanicus* and *poliocephalus* locally common in past; current status unclear but Azerbaijan breeding population of *caspius* at least 10,000-15,000 pairs. Status in Syria uncertain: recorded at Bahrat Homs, but unlikely to breed. Race *madagascariensis* locally common to uncommon in E, C & S Africa, and in Madagascar, where heavily hunted locally; has declined recently in Nigeria. Race *melanotus* widespread and locally common in Australia and New Zealand, where range has expanded due to construction of artificial lakes. Race *pulverulentus* uncommon and local; *pelewensis* rare and probably endangered. Vulnerable to wetland drainage and to frequent disturbance; numbers reduced locally throughout range by removal of marginal wetland vegetation and by drainage. Some artificially created habitat has been provided by forest clearance, swamp drainage and creation of impoundments; on Norfolk I and Lord Howe I (off E Australia), has become established only since vegetation clearance has produced suitable habitats. Sometimes considered a pest because may damage fruit, vegetables, grain crops and pastures, and sometimes raids chicken-houses for eggs. Several successful reintroductions in W Mediterranean in recent years.
Bibliography. Ali & Ripley (1980), Beehler *et al.* (1986), Benson & Benson (1975), Blakers *et al.* (1984), Bravery (1970), Bregulla (1992), Brown & Brown (1977), Bull *et al.* 1985), Carroll (1966, 1969), Chambers (1989), Clapperton (1983), Clapperton & Jenkins (1984, 1987), Coates (1985), Craig (1976, 1977, 1979, 1980a, 1980b, 1982), Craig & Jamieson (1990), Craig *et al.* (1980), Cramp & Simmons (1980), Czechura (1983), Dementiev & Gladkov (1951b), Dickinson *et al.* (1991), Dowsett & Forbes-Watson (1993), Elgood *et al.* (1994), Engbring & Pratt (1985), Étchécopar & Hüe (1964, 1978), Evans (1994), Fagan *et al.* (1976), Fjeldså (1977), Flint *et al.* (1984), Fordham (1983), Ginn *et al.* (1989), Glutz *et al.* (1973), Goodman *et al.* (1989), Halse & Jaensch (1989), Hamling (1949), Heim de Balsac & Mayaud (1962), Hindwood, K.A. (1940), Holyoak (1970), Hopkinson & Masterson (1984), Hüe & Étchécopar (1970), Irwin (1981), Jamieson & Craig (1987a, 1987b), Knystautas (1993), Langrand (1990), Lekagul & Round (1991), MacKinnon & Phillipps (1993), Mackworth-Praed & Grant (1957, 1962, 1970), Maclean (1993), Máñez (1994), Marchant & Higgins (1993), van Marle & Voous (1988), Medway & Wells (1976), Moon (1960), Norman & Mumford (1985), Patrikeev (1995), Perennou *et al.* (1994), Phillips (1978), Pinto (1983), Potapov & Flint (1987), Ripley (1982), Roberts, T.J. (1991), Rodríguez & Hiraldo (1975), Rutgers & Norris (1970), Sánchez-Lafuente *et al.* (1992), Shirihai (1996), Short *et al.* (1990), Smythies (1981, 1986), Stokes (1983), Tunnicliffe (1985), Urban *et al.* (1986), Vieillard (1974), White & Bruce (1986).

111. **Takahe**

Porphyrio mantelli

French: Talève takahé **German**: Takahe **Spanish**: Calamón Takahe

Taxonomy. *Notornis Mantelli* Owen, 1848, Waingongoro, North Island, New Zealand.
Occasionally still placed in genus *Notornis* (see page 112). Nominate race of North I, New Zealand, recently extinct. One extant subspecies recognized.
Subspecies and Distribution.
P. m. hochstetteri (A. B. Meyer, 1883) - SW South I, New Zealand.
Race *hochstetteri* introduced to Tiritiri Matangi, Kapiti, Mana and Maud Is.
Descriptive notes. 63 cm; stands c. 50 cm tall; male 2250-3250 (2673) g, female 1850-2600 (2268) g. Largest living rallid; thickset, flightless species with reduced wings, massive bill and powerful legs and feet; plumage loose and has silken sheen. Female slightly smaller. Unmistakable: much larger and more robust than *Porphyrio porphyrio*. Immature like adult but slightly duller; bill pinkish with bluish cast; legs and feet dull red or pale brownish orange; iris attains adult colour by 5-6 months. Juvenile predominantly brownish grey on head, neck and upperparts; face and throat mottled white; upperparts

On following pages: 112. Allen's Gallinule (*Porphyrio alleni*); 113. American Purple Gallinule (*Porphyrio martinica*); 114. Azure Gallinule (*Porphyrio flavirostris*); 115. San Cristobal Moorhen (*Gallinula silvestris*); 116. Tristan Moorhen (*Gallinula nesiotis*); 117. Common Moorhen (*Gallinula chloropus*).

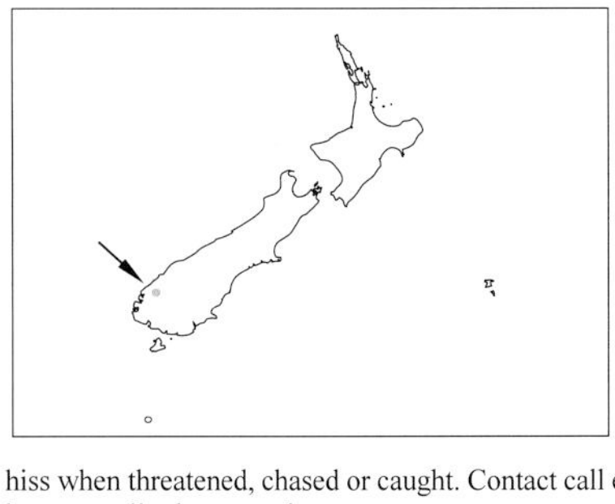

attain brownish tinge with wear; breast and upper flanks dull purplish blue; rear flanks to vent cream-buff; undertail-coverts white; wing feathers grow last and resemble those of adult; iris dark brown to grey; bill and developing frontal shield almost black, later fading to light brown or pinkish; legs and feet horn to dark purplish brown. Races differ in skeletal measurements, *hochstetteri* having shorter leg bones (nominate race known only from subfossils). VOICE. Contact call a single rising squawk "klowp". Alarm call a low, resonant "boomp" or percussive "oomp", repeated slowly. Also various clucking calls when feeding, and a loud screech or hiss when threatened, chased or caught. Contact call easily confused with that of *Gallirallus australis*, but generally deeper and more resonant.

Habitat. Alpine tussock grassland; also subalpine scrub and beech forest in winter, when snow covers grassland; before population decline may also have inhabited coastal sand ridges and open shrubland. Alpine grassland dominated by snow tussock grass (*Chionochloa*) c. 1 m high, with sedges (*Carex*, *Schoenus*), short grass (*Festuca*, *Poa*), herbs and shrubs. Forest dominated by beech *Nothofagus*, with understorey of shrubs, ferns and grass. In Fiordland National Park occurs in area of heavy snows and very high rainfall (2500-4800 mm per annum), commonly above tree-line at 1050-1520 m. Where introduced on islands, occurs in pastures of exotic grasses (*Bromus*, *Holcus*, *Dactylis*) and clovers (*Trifolium*). Frequents mountain lakes, rivers, streams and bogs; often by fast-flowing streams; some areas prone to flooding.

Food and Feeding. Eats predominantly leaf bases of *Chionochloa* tussocks and other alpine grass species; leaf bases of Cyperaceae, grass seeds and fern (*Hypolepis*) rhizomes taken seasonally, mainly in winter; rarely takes invertebrates and small reptiles. On islands eats leaf blades, leaf bases and seeds of many introduced grasses, also leaves and bases of clovers, all parts of chickweed (*Stellaria media*), and occasionally dead sticks, grass and flax stalks. Pulls tussock tillers out with bill, transferring them to foot to hold them parrot-fashion; strips seeds from seedheads by running partly open bill along stalk, sometimes first biting off stem and holding it in foot; digs up fern rhizomes with bill. Feeds selectively, taking plant bases richest in nitrogen, phosphorus, calcium, sodium, potassium and soluble sugars. Active throughout day; in winter to 22:00 hours. Energy requirement c. 2·0-2·2 kcal/g/day.

Breeding. Mainly Oct-Dec; eggs occasionally to mid-Feb and small young late Mar (probably from re-nesting after failure). Monogamous; pair-bond permanent, at least for 12 years and probably for life. Territorial within loose colonies; territory maintained while breeding, thereafter pairs remain in semi-communal and overlapping home ranges; holds same territory each year; territory size 2-60 ha. Breeds in family groups; juveniles sometimes ejected but first-year birds may assist with incubation and care of young; multiple male helpers reported in captivity. Nest built on well drained ground among tussocks; typically has 2 entrances connecting with runways; has latrine nearby. Nest a deep bowl of fine grass and tussock leaves, placed in saucer-like scrape in ground; both sexes build. Trial and/or brood nests often also built. Usually 2 eggs (1-3), with laying interval 48-72 hours; incubation 29-31 days, by both parents; hatching asynchronous; chicks precocial and nidifugous; usually leave nest soon after hatching; black downy chick has black-brown iris, bill white with black base and frontal shield, legs and feet pale pink, becoming purple-brown; down fades to black-brown (pale brown to whitish from face to breast) and replaced by grey second down at 4-5 weeks; body feathers develop at 5-8 weeks, tail at 14-18 weeks, wings at 9-20 weeks; young fed and brooded by both parents; dependent on adults for food for c. 4 months; post-juvenile moult occurs at c. 4 months; develop adult calls at c. 4·5 months; usually remain with parents for winter and disperse in following spring, some remaining for up to 2 years. Fostering recorded in captivity. Age of first breeding 2 years; sometimes 1 year. Egg fertility 70-80%; hatching success 67-76%; survival to 1 year 27-71%, dependent on weather and locality; usually only 1 young raised to independence; adult survival 73-88% per year. Second brood recorded only once.

Movements. Sedentary and flightless. Holds grassland territories until snow prevents feeding, when descends into forest or scrub, some birds wandering 5-10 km, possibly up to 30 km, from territories. Moves within territory when breeding, ascending in mid-Dec to higher altitude zones where preferred foods grow. Temporary immigration of adults recorded in 2 areas, 1972/73; known to move across and between valleys; young may move greater distances than adults, in search of territory or mate.

Status and Conservation. ENDANGERED. Formerly widespread on both North I and South I. Race *hochstetteri* thought extinct by 1930's but rediscovered W of Lake Te Anau in Murchison Mts in 1948, when population c. 260 pairs and range 750-800 km²; range then contracted, by 1966 total of 180-200 pairs occupying c. 600 km². In 1980 wild population c. 120 birds; in 1990, total of 60 pairs known; in 1992 only 41 pairs remained after hard weather and stoat predation; in 1994, c. 150 birds survived in c. 650 km² of Murchison and Stuart Mts in Fiordland. Introduced to 4 mainly predator-free nearshore islands, 1968-1992; has bred successfully on all 4, and island population now c. 40 birds. Main causes of recent decline: severe competition for food from introduced red deer (*Cervus elaphus*), which have modified habitat by overgrazing, eliminating most nutritious plants and preventing some grasses from seeding; and predation by introduced stoats (*Mustela erminea*), which take eggs and all ages of birds. Habitat also reduced by spread of forest in post-glacial Pleistocene-Holocene, leaving birds more vulnerable to hunting by Polynesian colonists, who arrived c. 1000 years ago. Probably once widespread in both forest and grassland down to sea-level; modern distribution probably in suboptimal habitat because of low hunting pressure. Removal of deer and fertilizing tussock lands allow vegetation to recover, while stoat numbers have been reduced by trapping. Captive breeding, begun in 1950's, initially had little success; since 1987, methods have improved, with 90% of viable eggs hatching and 74% of chicks surviving to maturity. Overall population continues to decline, and trends still uncertain, but recovery plans aim: to establish self-sustaining population of over 500 birds in Fiordland; to boost island populations; to introduce birds to other island or mainland sites; and to promote public awareness. Nominate race known only from subfossils.

Bibliography. Chambers (1989), Clout & Craig (1995), Collar & Andrew (1988), Collar *et al*. (1994), Crouchley (1994), Eason & Rasch (1993), Falla (1949, 1951), Fleming (1951), King (1978/79), Lavers & Mills (1984), Marchant & Higgins (1993), Mills (1973a, 1975, 1976), Mills & Lavers (1974), Mills & Mark (1977), Mills, Lavers & Lee (1984), Mills, Lee *et al*. (1980), Morris (1977), Reid (1967, 1971, 1974a, 1974b, 1977), Sibson (1982), Suttie & Fennessy (1992), Williams (1952, 1957, 1960), Williams & Given (1981), Williams & Miers (1958).

112. **Allen's Gallinule**

Porphyrio alleni

French: Talève d'Allen **German**: Bronzesultanshuhn **Spanish**: Calamoncillo Africano

Taxonomy. *Porphyrio Alleni* Thomson, 1842, Idda, Niger River.
Sometimes placed in *Gallinula* or *Porphyrula*. Forms superspecies with *P. martinica*. Monotypic.

Distribution. Senegal and Gambia E to Ethiopia and Somalia and S to South Africa, excluding arid SW; also Madagascar, Comoro Is, and (probably introduced) Mauritius.

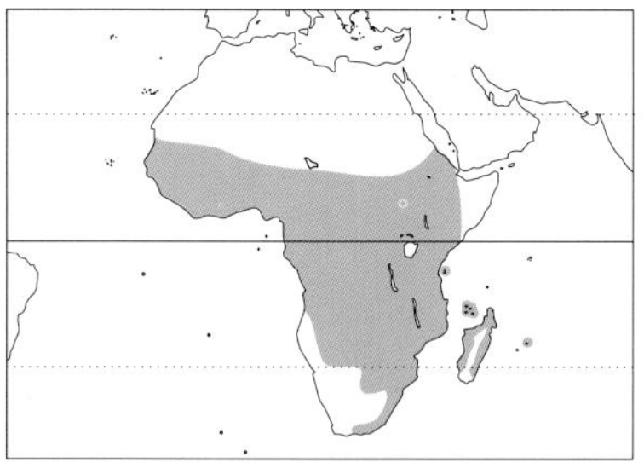

Descriptive notes. 22-26 cm; male 132-172 (154) g, female 112-145 (125) g; wingspan 48-52 cm. Superficially resembles *P. porphyrio* but much smaller, with less robust bill, blue-green frontal shield and no pale blue on face or throat. Similar to *P. martinica* but noticeably smaller and has black head, dark blue-violet neck, breast and flanks, red legs and feet, all red bill, slightly darker frontal shield, and dark central undertail-coverts, giving white undertail patch an inverted heart-shape. Sexes alike but female smaller; early in breeding season shield of male bright turquoise blue and that of female apple green, but after chicks hatch both adults have blue shield which becomes purplish to red-brown in non-breeding season; iris of breeding birds coral red, of non-breeding birds brown; leg colour duller red in non-breeding birds. Immature duller than non-breeding adult in plumage and bare parts colours. Juvenile has dark brown crown to hindneck, paler on sides of head and buff on neck and cheeks, cream chin and throat, dark brown upperparts with pale feather edges, buff underparts and undertail-coverts, and white belly; remiges as adult and outer upperwing-coverts have blue-green centres; legs and feet brown, iris grey-brown to orange, bill red-brown and shield grey to grey-brown; juvenile *P. martinica* lacks pale feather edges on upperparts. VOICE. Variety of harsh, often nasal, calls, including dry "keck" and drawn-out "kerk" (sometimes repeated); series of sharp "kik" notes ending in churring "kurr" notes; harsh quacking; high-pitched repeated "kli" call in flight; and sharp "click" of alarm.

Habitat. Freshwater marshes, reedbeds, inundated grassland and floodplains, especially with flooded *Oryza longistaminata* and *Cyperus fastigiatus*; papyrus swamps, rice fields, and thick vegetation such as sedges, reeds and rank grass beside lakes, rivers, ponds and temporary pools. Normally prefers wetlands with *Nymphaea*, *Nymphoides*, *Ottelia* and other floating-leaved vegetation. Occurs up to 1900 m in E Africa.

Food and Feeding. Flowers and seeds of reeds and sedges; seeds, stems and leaves of grasses and other marsh plants; unripe seedheads of water-lilies; fruits of thorn bush *Drepanocarpus lunatus*; also earthworms, molluscs, crustaceans, insects, spiders, fish eggs and small fish. Aggressive towards conspecifics when feeding, and sometimes kleptoparasitizes other species, e.g. robs African Pygmy-geese (*Nettapus auritus*) of water-lily seedheads. Feeds most actively in early morning and late afternoon but also in middle of day and on moonlit nights. Swims well: forages while swimming, taking insects and plant material from water; also forages while walking on floating vegetation, and occasionally in short grass bordering water. Turns over floating lily leaves with bill and gleans food from underside while holding leaf down with feet. Breaks off water-lily seedheads with bill and holds in foot while pulling apart with bill; also carries food in toes to bill. Climbs bushes to feed on fruits; climbs up to 2 m on reed stems, both to feed and to preen; said to construct platforms for feeding on flowers and seeds of reeds high above water.

Breeding. Sierra Leone, Sept, Nov; Nigeria, May-Oct; Ghana, Jun; Cameroon, Aug; Gabon, May; Ethiopia, Apr, Jun, Sept-Oct; Kenya and NE Tanzania, Apr-Oct; Zanzibar & Pemba Is, May-Aug; in E Africa prefers dry months following long rains; SE Zaire, probably begins Jan-Feb (second half of rains); Zambia, Dec-Apr; Malawi, Feb-Apr, Jun, Sept-Dec; Zimbabwe, mainly Dec-Apr, also May, Sept; Namibia, Apr; Botswana, Nov-Dec; South Africa (N Transvaal), Dec-Apr; Madagascar, Jan. Monogamous; occurs in pairs throughout year; territorial when breeding. Nest typically in reeds, grasses or tangled vegetation at edge of water; also in open marshes and rice fields; quite flimsy; loosely constructed of reed stems and blades, dry sedges and other plants, with deep or shallow cup; placed just above water; sometimes woven into surrounding vegetation, which may be bent down to form foundation and pulled over in dome. Eggs 3-8 (mean 4·4); incubation by both sexes c. 15 days, starting with 1st egg; hatching asynchronous; chicks precocial; chick has black down, browner on underparts, with silvery tips around face and chin; fed and cared for by both parents. No further details available.

Movements. Some birds resident year round in permanent wetlands, but with onset of rains in N tropics most migrate N (Nigeria, Cameroon and Chad), while most in S tropics move S to breed in rains. Mainly resident in Zaire but possible migrant birds reported Jun. Resident in some parts of E Africa, but seasonal occurrences also reported, e.g. in Kenya non-breeding birds present at Mombasa, Sept-Mar, and breeding birds present L Baringo, May-Jun and SW Tanzania only during Dec-Jan floods; wanders to desert areas, e.g. to L Turkana, N Kenya (Jun). Little evidence of movements in Malawi; some resident Zambia and Zimbabwe but many appear and breed during rains (Dec-Apr). Rains breeding visitor to NE Botswana (present Feb-May only), and to N Transvaal, South Africa, but also resident on permanent waters of N Botswana and NE Namibia. Vagrancy widely reported, with extralimital records from N Africa, 8 W European countries (peak occurrences Dec), Azores and possibly Madeira; from Ascension I and St Helena, 1600 km and 1900 km from African continent; Comoro Is; Rodrigues I, 1500 km E of Madagascar; also Gulf of Guinea islands. Stragglers also recorded from SW African region (SW Cape Province and SW Namibia).

Status and Conservation. Not globally threatened. Erratic nature of occurrence in very seasonal habitats makes populations difficult to assess, but may be locally very numerous in suitable breeding habitat during seasons of good rainfall, e.g. at least 10,000 pairs were thought to be present on the Nyl floodplain, N Transvaal, in early 1996, during an exceptionally wet season. However, the destruction and modification of wetlands, by drainage, damming and grazing, throughout the bird's range, and especially the loss of suitable seasonally flooded habitats, must have affected its numbers adversely.

Bibliography. Anon. (1995f), Benson (1960), Benson & Benson (1975), Benson *et al*. (1971), Britton, P.L. (1980), Brooke (1968), Brosset & Érard (1986), Cramp & Simmons (1980), Dowsett & Forbes-Watson (1993), Elgood, Fry & Dowsett (1973), Elgood, Heigham *et al*. (1994), Étchécopar & Hüe (1964), Fry (1966), Ginn *et al*. (1989), Gore (1990), Grimes (1987), Hudson (1974), Irwin (1981), Langrand (1990), Lewis & Pomeroy (1989), Lippens & Wille (1976), Mackworth-Praed & Grant (1957, 1962, 1970), Maclean (1993), Milon *et al*. (1973), Pakenham (1979), Penry (1994), Pinto (1983), Serle (1939b), Short *et al*. (1990), Snow (1978), Tarboton, Kemp & Kemp (1987), Taylor, P.B. (1985b), Urban *et al*. (1986), Wood (1977).

113. **American Purple Gallinule**

Porphyrio martinica

French: Talève violacée **German**: Zwergsultanshuhn **Spanish**: Calamoncillo Americano
Other common names: Purple Gallinule(!)

Taxonomy. *Fulica martinica* Linnaeus, 1766, Martinique, West Indies.
Sometimes placed in *Gallinula* or *Porphyrula*. Forms superspecies with *P. alleni*. Monotypic.

Distribution. Interior E USA; Pacific coast from Nayarit and Atlantic coast from Maryland and Delaware, S through SE USA, Central America, West Indies and N & C South America S to S Peru and N Argentina. N populations winter S from Texas and Florida.

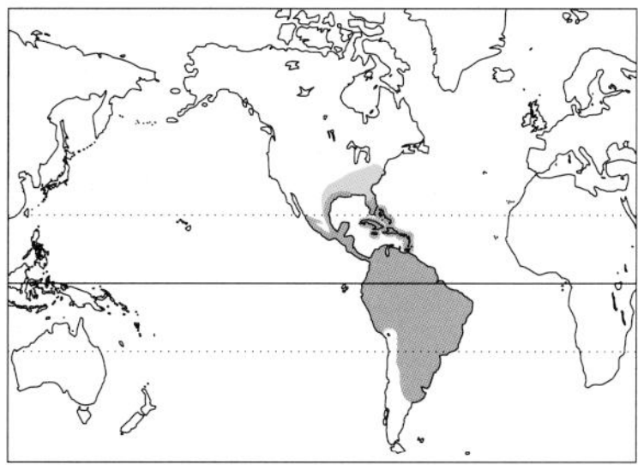

Descriptive notes. 27-36 cm; male 203-305 g, female 142-291 g; wingspan 50-55 cm. Similar to *P. alleni*, but noticeably larger with purple head, paler neck, breast and flanks, yellow legs, feet, and bill tip, slightly paler frontal shield, and entirely white undertail-coverts. Sexes alike, but female smaller. Bare parts duller outside breeding season. Immature similar to adult. Juvenile warm brown from crown to hindneck, pale buff-brown neck and sides of head, cream chin and throat; brown upperparts with bronze-green tinge on back, scapulars and upperwing-coverts; buff-brown underparts, palest on belly and vent; white undertail-coverts; outer upperwing-coverts similar to adult but less blue; legs and feet pale yellow or brownish, iris brown to pale orange, bill yellow-green with pale tip and brown-pink base, and shield brown or grey. Juvenile *P. alleni* has pale edges to upperpart feathers. Voice. Typical calls a sharp, high-pitched "kyik", sometimes with booming undertone; and loud "kur", often preceded by series of "cook" notes when commonly modified to "cu-kúr-cu". Also has wailing scream; rapid "ka-ka-ka"; gruff, repeated "kruk"; cackling "kek kek kek" in flight; low ticking; and low, reedy buzz.

Habitat. Occurs mainly in subtropical and tropical lowlands and coastal fringes, in lush wetlands, notably grassy marshes and overgrown swamps, and on pools, ponds, and channels of slow-moving water down to size of roadside ditches. Breeding habitat primarily fresh to intermediately saline wetlands, including deepwater marshes with water 25-100 cm deep, lakes, and impoundments (primarily coastal but also inland), with stable water levels and good interspersion of dense stands of floating, emergent and submerged vegetation; seldom uses areas of open water free of vegetation. Dependent on floating vegetation, and also submergents, for brood rearing, such vegetation providing food, cover and protection from aquatic predators. Rice fields also important nesting habitat. During movements, frequents wetlands at higher altitudes in E Andes of Colombia up to at least 3020 m, and recorded at 4080 m in Peru.

Food and Feeding. Predominantly plant material, including pondweed, sedges, willows, water-lilies, fruits, seeds of annual grasses and sedges and of floating and submerged vegetation, flowers of *Eichhornia crassipes*, and cultivated rice grains. Also eats insects, including Odonata adults and nymphs, Noctuidae (moth) larvae and pupae, Coleoptera, Hemiptera, Hymenoptera, Orthoptera (grasshoppers), and fly larvae and pupae (Corydalidae, Cyclorrhapha); worms, molluscs, spiders, frogs, and eggs and young of herons and jacanas; may occasionally scavenge. Walks on floating vegetation to feed; turns over lily pads to glean food from undersides, holding leaf down with foot; swims and dives easily. Climbs easily to feed in bushes and trees for up to 20 m from ground. Visits rice fields and fields of ripe grain in autumn, climbing stalks to feed on seedheads. Opportunistic, taking advantage of locally abundant foods. Usually remains close to cover, but feeds in open by day; when encouraged becomes tame, visits gardens and will pick up food dropped by humans.

Breeding. USA, May-Aug, in some habitats, e.g. rice fields, nesting delayed until plant density adequate; El Salvador, Jul-Aug; Panama, Mar-Nov; Colombia, May-Oct; Surinam, Jan, Mar-Jul; Argentina, Dec. Monogamous and territorial during breeding season; migrants arrive paired on breeding grounds or pair immediately on arrival. In Costa Rica, non-migratory birds live in extended family groups in which immatures and juveniles help with feeding and defending chicks, and with territory defence. Nest built on floating mats of vegetation, e.g. *Eichhornia* and *Alternanthera*, or in emergent vegetation, e.g. *Typha*, *Thalia* and *Zizaniopsis*; those in emergent vegetation normally near edge, where interface occurs with open water areas containing submergents such as *Ceratophyllum* and *Potamogeton*, or floating vegetation. Nest bulky, made from readily available plant materials, e.g. leaves of *Typha* or rice plants, usually obtained very close to nest-site. External diameter 16-28 cm, depth 6-20 cm; cup depth 2-9 cm; placed 20-60 cm above water. Partial canopy of growing vegetation often made; extensive ramp up to nest usually constructed; both sexes build. Eggs 6-10 (Florida), 3-12 (West Indies), 4-8 (Mexico), 3-7 (Costa Rica), 4-5 (Panama); laid at daily intervals; incubation 18-20 days, by both sexes; chicks precocial; black downy chicks have silver tips to down of head, neck and back, bill red with black tip, shield flesh; fed in nest for 2-4 days after hatching; fed and cared for by both parents; return to nest for brooding; separate brood nest sometimes constructed; chicks begin to feed themselves at 7-10 days; become self-feeding at c. 21 days; juvenile plumage attained, and young capable of flight, at 5-7 weeks. North American birds sometimes renest if first attempt fails; in Costa Rica pairs produce clutch every 2-4 months throughout year. Age of first breeding probably 1 year.

Movements. North American birds migrate S over Gulf of Mexico, Oct-Nov, a few remaining to Dec. Returning birds arrive in breeding areas in Georgia, Texas and Louisiana in mid-Apr. South American populations not migratory, except at S end of range, where birds move N into tropics for austral winter. Influx noted to coast of Brazil (Maranhão), Feb-Oct; present Rio Grande do Sul (SE Brazil) May-Sept. Well known for numerous instances of long distance vagrancy, both N and S of equator; migrants meeting cyclonic storms especially prone to being blown well beyond normal range. Recorded throughout much of USA, W to California, and into Canada, N to Labrador. Low pressure systems moving up coastal USA carry birds almost annually to Bermuda and New England, and sometimes beyond. Vagrant to S Greenland, Azores, Flores, Europe (Britain, Norway, Switzerland), and to islands in Atlantic and Pacific oceans: South Georgia, Tristan da Cunha (frequent), Galapagos, Falkland Is, Ascension I and St Helena. Quite regular in South Africa (W Cape), Apr-Aug, when birds are migrating N from Argentina, Uruguay and S Brazil, whence African vagrants may originate; also recorded off Liberian coast. S vagrants nearly all immatures.

Status and Conservation. Not globally threatened. Little information on current populations and population trends but, as wetland habitat quality and quantity are keys to population stability, populations are probably decreasing throughout range as result of freshwater wetland loss in USA and throughout South and Central America. In USA it is a game species but harvest is likely to be small because of low hunter interest and the fact that the birds migrate S prior to the late autumn hunting season in many states. In USA, conservation and management of freshwater wetlands along lower Atlantic and Gulf Coast states are critical for the species; there is also an urgent need to monitor population status, trends and harvest, and to provide information on annual productivity, recruitment and survival rates.

Bibliography. Belton (1984), Bent (1926), Biaggi (1983), Blake (1977), Canevari *et al.* (1991), Contreras *et al.* (1990), Cramp & Simmons (1980), Dickey & van Rossem (1938), Eddleman *et al.* (1988), Elliott (1957), Fjeldså & Krabbe (1990), Godfrey (1986), Haverschmidt (1968), Haverschmidt & Mees (1995), Hayes (1995), Helm (1982, 1994), Helm *et al.* (1987), Hellmayr & Conover (1942), Hilty & Brown (1986), Howell & Webb (1995b), Hunter (1987a, 1987b), Johnson (1965b), Matthews (1983), Monroe (1968), Mulholland (1983), Mulholland & Percival (1982), Olson (1973a, 1974c), de la Peña (1992), Reagan (1977), Remsen & Parker (1990), Ridgely (1981), Ridgely & Gwynne (1989), Root (1988), Sick (1985c, 1993), Siegfried & Frost (1973), Silbernagl (1982), Slud (1964), Snyder (1966), Stiles & Skutch (1989), Tostain *et al.* (1992), Urban *et al.* (1986), Wetmore (1965).

114. **Azure Gallinule**

Porphyrio flavirostris

French: Talève favorite **German**: Azursultanshuhn **Spanish**: Calamoncillo Celeste
Other common names: Little Gallinule

Taxonomy. *Fulica flavirostris* Gmelin, 1789, Cayenne.
Formerly listed as *P. parvus*, but this name preoccupied. Sometimes placed in *Gallinula* or *Porphyrula*. Monotypic.

Distribution. E Colombia through CS Venezuela to the Guianas and S to E Ecuador and N Peru E across NC Brazil; SE Peru, N Bolivia, W & C Brazil and C Paraguay to extreme N Argentina; also extreme SE Brazil.

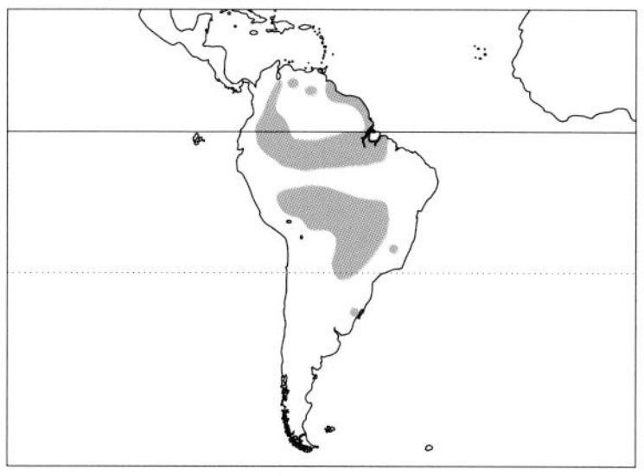

Descriptive notes. 23-26 cm; male 92-111 g, female 92-107 g. Smallest *Porphyrio*, delicately proportioned and markedly different in appearance to congeners; plumage looks washed-out: crown and hindneck to back pale brownish olive with indistinct dusky streaks, lower back to tail dark brown, upperwing-coverts azure or greenish blue, remiges grey-blue, sides of head, neck and breast blue-grey, throat and underparts pure white; bill and frontal shield pale greenish yellow; legs and feet dull to bright yellow; iris reddish brown. Immature browner above, with contrasting dark rump and tail in flight, buffy sides of head, neck and breast; bill as adult but frontal shield and culmen green; legs and feet yellowish orange; iris amber-yellow. Voice. Usually rather quiet; sometimes utters a short trill.

Habitat. Freshwater marshes, especially those with fairly deep water and thick cover of marsh grass (e.g. *Paspalum* up to 1 m tall) or other emergent or floating vegetation; also rice paddies, wet savannas, swampy stream and river margins and marshy shores of lakes (including oxbow lakes), lagoons and permanent or seasonal ponds. Occurs alongside *P. martinica* but prefers shorter, smaller-leaved vegetation and avoids areas with bushes and *Heliconia*; often flushed from emergent grass 15-30 cm tall. Normally occurs in lowlands, up to 500 m, but recorded casually on savanna of Bogotá in E Andes at 2600 m.

Food and Feeding. Grass seeds, insects (including Hemiptera and Coleoptera) and spiders recorded. Forages in cover and on floating vegetation. Climbs on grass stalks to bend them to the water and eat seeds. Seldom swims.

Breeding. Surinam, May-Aug; E Amazonian Brazil, probably May-Jun; Ecuador, oviduct egg Jun; season may extend Mar-Aug, possibly Oct, and non-breeding season may be Sept-Dec. Monogamous; probably territorial when breeding. Nest an open cup of dead leaves or rushes, concealed in marsh vegetation. Eggs 4-5; both sexes incubate. No other information available.

Movements. Highly seasonal in occurrence in parts of range. Present throughout year in much of Amazonia, but seasonal in the Guianas, almost all records Apr-Aug; also in SW Amazonia and Paraguay, mostly Oct-Jan. Near equator seasonality not so pronounced but still evident from specimen records: most specimens from E Amazonian Brazil are Feb-Aug, while specimens from W Amazonia peak in Jan and observations along upper Amazon (Iquitos and Leticia) indicate birds present only Jan-Jul. Occurrence may be timed to coincide with wet or high-water seasons; apparently present seasonally in areas at periphery of range. Arrival noted Tambopata Reserve, Madre de Dios (SE Peru), early Nov; possibly absent elsewhere in region Jun-Dec. Recorded from *llanos* of Venezuela only Aug-Dec. Apparently resident in Ecuador and S Colombia, but in C Colombia (W Meta) occurs only Mar-Jul, and migrants present Mar-May in savanna of Bogotá. Vagrancy or occurrence in atypical habitats also recorded: occurred at Escorial in Venezuelan Andes at 3000 m (Oct); twice in Bogotá city at 2600 m (Dec); on escarpment above forest in S Venezuela (Jan); and in Rio Grande do Sul, Brazil (Nov); also recorded Trinidad, where most occurrences since 1978; a specimen from New York, USA, (Dec) could be wild bird. After breeding in May-Jul, most of population in N South America may disperse S c. 1800 km to S periphery of Amazonia, returning N in Feb-Mar.

Status and Conservation. Not globally threatened. Formerly regarded as fairly common in some parts of its range, which has been conflictingly regarded as either fragmented or continuous. Apparently fairly common in the Guianas but uncommon in Colombia, E Peru and N Bolivia; probably more widespread in Amazonia than the relatively limited records indicate. Currently regarded as probably occurring regularly in summer in marshes of W São Paulo, SE Brazil, but likely to disappear as rivers become reservoirs.

Bibliography. Blake (1977), Boyle *et al.* (1987), Canevari *et al.* (1991), ffrench (1985), Fjeldså & Krabbe (1990), Haverschmidt (1968), Haverschmidt & Mees (1995), Hayes (1995), Hellmayr & Conover (1942), Hilty & Brown (1986), Meyer de Schauensee & Phelps (1978), Nicéforo & Olivares (1965), Norton (1965), Parker (1982), de la Peña (1992), Remsen & Parker (1990), Sick (1985c, 1993), Snyder (1966), Tallman *et al.* (1977), Tostain *et al.* (1992), Willis & Oniki (1993).

Genus *GALLINULA* Brisson, 1760

115. **San Cristobal Moorhen**

Gallinula silvestris

French: Gallinule d'Édith **German**: Blaustirn-Pfuhlhuhn **Spanish**: Gallineta de San Cristóbal
Other common names: Mountain Rail

Taxonomy. *Edithornis silvestris* Mayr, 1933, San Cristobal Island.
Sometimes placed in genus *Pareudiastes*, with extinct Samoan Moorhen (*G. pacifica*), on basis of construction of bill, skull and tarsus, and plumage pattern. Monotypic.

Distribution. San Cristobal, Solomon Is.

Descriptive notes. 26·5 cm (1 male); 450 g. Male entirely plain: head, neck and breast dark bluish slate, almost blackish on chin and face; scapulars, wing-coverts and secondaries brown-black, tinged olive; rest of body dull brownish black; iris chocolate; legs, feet and bill bright scarlet; shield dark grey-blue; tail very short, with hair-like rectrices; secondaries soft and decomposed; bill strong and laterally compressed; legs and feet slender; flies very little, if at all. Voice. Unknown.

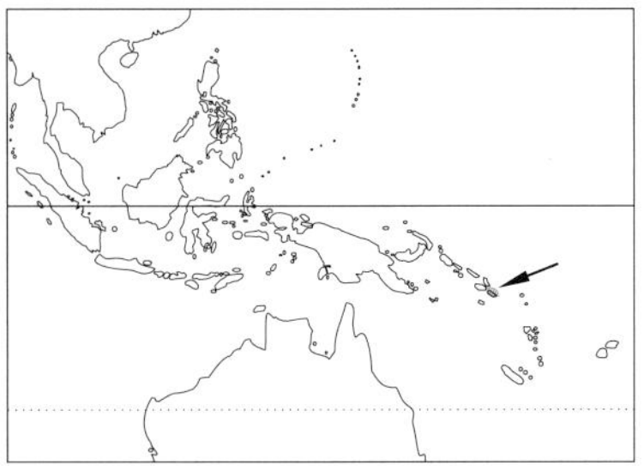

Habitat. Dense undergrowth of primeval mountain forest on steep slopes; type specimen obtained at altitude of 580 m, but mountains in the vicinity ascend to 1200 m; the area has many streams and creeks cutting deep into mountain slopes, but no standing water. Also reported as occurring in rocky valleys below 425 m.
Food and Feeding. No information: diet of extinct *G. pacificus*, of similar habitat, was apparently almost entirely animal matter.
Breeding. Unknown.
Movements. No information available.
Status and Conservation. CRITICALLY ENDANGERED. Known only from the holotype, collected in Dec 1929 in the central mountains of San Cristobal. Even then apparently rare, and hunted by local people with dogs. The only subsequent observations are of one seen by an expedition member in 1953, when it was reported apparently to be not uncommon in rocky valleys below Wuranakumau, on Naghasi ridge, and a report by local people of its presence in 1974; however, the forests where it was originally found have not been visited by ornithologists since 1950's. It is likely to have been affected by introduced mammalian predators, such as cats, which have wiped out most native terrestrial mammals on nearby Guadalcanal.
Bibliography. Cain & Galbraith (1956), Collar & Andrew (1988), Collar *et al.* (1994), Hay (1986), King (1978/79), Lees (1991), Mayr (1933), Olson (1973b, 1975b), Ripley (1977), Ripley & Beehler (1985).

116. **Tristan Moorhen**

Gallinula nesiotis

French: Gallinule de Tristan **German**: Tristanteichhuhn **Spanish**: Gallineta de Gough
Other common names: Gough Moorhen (*comeri*)

Taxonomy. *Gallinula nesiotis* P. L. Sclater, 1861, Tristan da Cunha.
In past, sometimes placed in genus *Porphyriornis*. Nominate race of Tristan da Cunha recently extinct. One extant subspecies recognized.
Subspecies and Distribution.
G. n. comeri (Allen, 1892) - Gough I, S Atlantic.
Race *comeri* introduced to Tristan da Cunha.

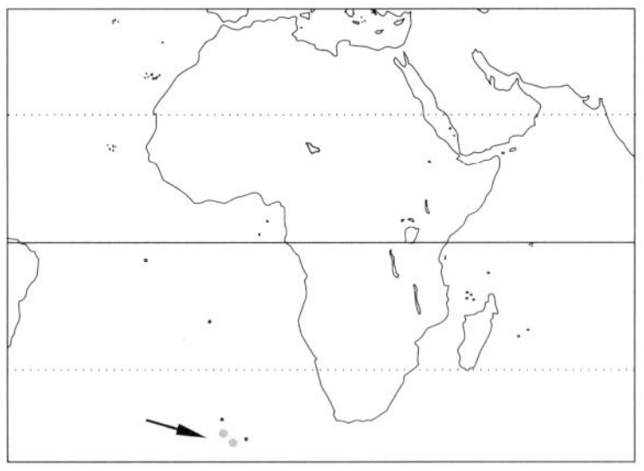

Descriptive notes. 25 cm; 3 adult *comeri* 505-530 (513) g. Sexes alike. Superficially resembles *G. chloropus* but smaller, much more strongly built, short-winged, and almost completely flightless but able to climb well and partially fly over obstacles; also differs in plumage, having black, not grey, neck and underparts, no white on flanks, and red legs heavily blotched with greenish yellow. Immature largely greyish brown, with dark sooty grey head, chestnut brown upperparts and sooty grey belly with cream feather tips; shield shiny red; bill dull, dark red with yellow-green tip. Juvenile predominantly brown, belly paler with cream feather tips; two dirty cream undertail bars; shield and bill dull green, bill with whitish tip; tibiae yellow; tarsi and feet green. Races differ only in skeletal measurements, *nesiotis* being slightly smaller and lighter. Voice. Voice metallic and loud. Common call a harsh, staccato, high-pitched, far-carrying "koo-ik", often repeated, and taken up by surrounding birds; also loud, screaming series of "koo-ik" notes; and low-pitched, monotonous, whispered, repeated "ik" or "ook" given by pair members and audible at close range. Female gives harsh repeated call near nest.
Habitat. Race *comeri* occurs throughout Gough I in very dense vegetation of tussock grass and bushes in the shrub and tree-fern zones, generally below 500 m and mainly close to coast in boggy areas and along streams. On Tristan da Cunha, where introduced, inhabits rugged, luxuriant, inaccessible fern-bush (*Blechnum*), with dense *Phylica arborea* trees, at 300-900 m.
Food and Feeding. Gough I birds appear to feed as much on vegetable matter, seeds and carrion as on invertebrates. Generally remains in cover but feeds in open if undisturbed. Eats grass, and takes grass-heads with scythe-like motion of bill. Scavenges from carcasses of Soft-plumaged Petrels (*Pterodroma mollis*) and Broad-billed Prions (*Pachyptila vittata*) partly eaten by Brown Skuas (*Catharacta antarctica*); also feeds on garbage at meteorological station. Enters petrel burrows, apparently in search of food, and seen foraging in abandoned albatross nests, presumably for invertebrates; also scavenges around active albatross nests.
Breeding. On Gough lays Sept-Mar; on Tristan probably breeds Dec-Mar. Monogamous and territorial; pair-bond apparently permanent. Nest circular and cup-shaped; made of sticks; bowl diameter 14-20 cm; rim 10-15 cm above ground (in captivity 75 cm above ground); placed in grass (*Poa flabellata*) tussock, with access tunnel from edge of tussock to nest; both sexes build. Eggs 2-5 (up to 6 in captivity); incubation 21 days, by both sexes; downy chick black, with fringe of long silky hairs on throat, bill crimson at base, blue-grey towards tip, with white spot on top of upper mandible, legs and feet black; young fed by both parents; seen to be given fresh flesh from bird carcasses. Immature plumage retained into second year. 2 broods per season recorded, with c. 14 weeks between clutches; young of first brood help to feed second brood.
Movements. None. One at Cape Town in 1893 apparently an escape.
Status and Conservation. VULNERABLE. Numbers difficult to assess because of secretive nature. Race *comeri* common on Gough I, where total population probably 2000-3000 pairs; territory size c. 0·5 ha; no avian competitors, but egg predation by skuas recorded. Introduced to Tristan da Cunha in 1956, whence nominate race was extirpated by around 1900; current population c. 250 pairs. Both populations appear stable, and habitats unlikely to change significantly, but there is permanent risk of mammalian predators becoming established on the islands; however, chances of this happening have been minimized. Re-establishment on Tristan da Cunha successful despite large population of black rats (*Rattus rattus*); earlier extinction there was attributed to rat predation but possibly more due to combination of habitat destruction, predation by cats and pigs, and hunting with dogs. Captive stock exists in a few European zoos, and species breeds successfully in captivity, but hybridization with *G. chloropus* occurs and must be avoided.
Bibliography. Beintema (1972), Broekhuysen & Macnae (1949), Clancey (1981a), Collar & Andrew (1988), Collar & Stuart (1985), Collar *et al.* (1994), Cooper & Ryan (1994), Eber (1961), Elliott (1953, 1957), Holdgate (1957), Olson (1973a), Richardson (1984), Ripley (1977), Voisin (1979), Voous (1961b, 1962), Wace & Holdgate (1976), Watkins & Furness (1986), Wilson & Swales (1958).

117. **Common Moorhen**

Gallinula chloropus

French: Gallinule poule-d'eau **German**: Teichhuhn **Spanish**: Gallineta Común
Other common names: Common Gallinule

Taxonomy. *Fulica Chloropus* Linnaeus, 1758, England.
Sometimes considered conspecific with *G. tenebrosa*, or to form superspecies, but the two are sympatric in Wallacea. Many other races described; possible races *correiana* and *indica* included in nominate. Twelve subspecies recognized.
Subspecies and Distribution.
G. c. chloropus (Linnaeus, 1758) - Europe, North Africa, Azores, Canaries and Cape Verde Is E through W, C & S Asia to Japan, S to Sri Lanka and C Malaysia; N populations winter S to Mediterranean region, sub-Saharan Africa and S Asia.
G. c. meridionalis (C. L. Brehm, 1831) - sub-Saharan Africa and St Helena.
G. c. pyrrhorrhoa A. Newton, 1861 - Madagascar, Reunion, Mauritius and Comoros Is.
G. c. orientalis Horsfield, 1821 - Seychelles, Andamans, S Malaysia and Greater & W Lesser Sundas to Philippines and Palau Is.
G. c. guami Hartert, 1917 - Northern Mariana Is.
G. c. sandvicensis Streets, 1877 - Hawaiian Is.
G. c. cachinnans Bangs, 1915 - SE Canada and USA through Central America to W Panama, also Bermuda and Galapagos; N populations winter S to Panama and possibly beyond.
G. c. cerceris Bangs, 1910 - Greater & Lesser Antilles.
G. c. barbadensis Bond, 1954 - Barbados.
G. c. pauxilla Bangs, 1915 - E Panama, N & W Colombia, W Ecuador and coastal NW Peru.
G. c. garmani Allen, 1876 - Andes of Peru, Chile, Bolivia and NW Argentina.
G. c. galeata (Lichtenstein, 1818) - Trinidad and the Guianas S through Brazil to N Argentina and Uruguay.

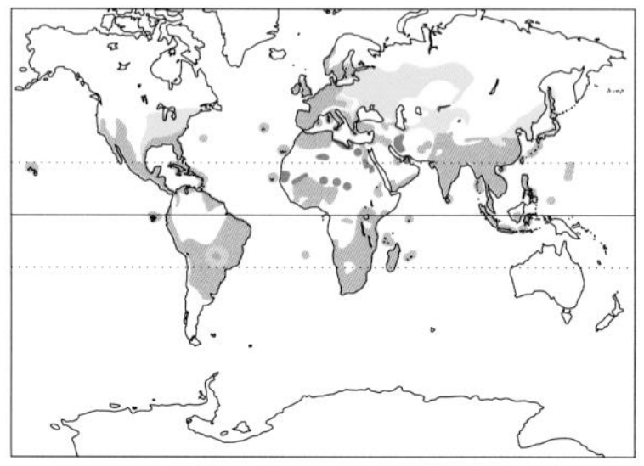

Descriptive notes. 30-38 cm; male 249-493 (339) g, female 192-343 (271) g (*chloropus*), unsexed 173-335 (245) g (*meridionalis*); wingspan 50-55 cm. Medium-sized gallinule, plumage appearing essentially black at any distance, with prominent yellow-tipped red bill and red frontal shield, prominent white line along top of flanks, and white lateral undertail-coverts rendered obvious by constantly flicking of tail; legs and feet bright yellow-green to yellow, upper half of tibia orange. Sexes similar, but female smaller. Immature similar to juvenile, gradually attaining adult bare parts colours. Juvenile has crown, hindneck and upperparts brown to grey (depending on race), duller than in adult; underparts paler, becoming whitish on throat and belly; wings, white flank line, tail and undertail-coverts like adult; iris brownish, bill and shield greenish brown, olive-grey or pinkish; legs and feet olive-grey. Racial variation mostly clinal, mainly involving size, colour of upperparts and upperwing-coverts, and size and shape of shield: Old World birds have elliptical shield, widest in middle and with rounded top, New World birds mostly have truncated shield, top almost square and widest near top; races *meridionalis* and *orientalis* smaller with slaty blue-grey upperwing-coverts but without the olive wash; *orientalis* also has relatively large shield; *pyrrhorrhoa* has buff undertail-coverts; *guami* darker than nominate; *cachinnans* like nominate but has different shield shape and relatively long bill, tarsus and toes; *cerceris* has less brown on upperparts than *cachinnans*; *sandvicensis* has large frontal shield and red on front of tarsus; *pauxilla* smaller than *cachinnans*, with greyer brown upperparts; *garmani* larger, darker and more uniformly plumbeous; *galatea* also deep plumbeous above but smaller than *garmani*; *barbadensis* like *cerceris* but body plumage much brighter and head and neck paler. Voice. Wide variety of clucking and chattering calls, sometimes repeated for long periods in American races, but not in Old World races. Most familiar calls are advertising call (crowing), a loud, explosive, single "krrrruk", and a similar "kurr-ik" and "kark". Anger or alarm indicated by loud "kik-kik" or "cuk", sometimes rapidly repeated; fighting birds emit short clicking chatter. Also has soft, musical, repeated "kook" call (murmur-call) used in various displays; loud "keh-keh"; "chuck" of distress; and familiar "kittick" of mild alarm.
Habitat. Exploits wide range of natural and man-made freshwater wetlands with fringing emergent vegetation; occurs on both still and moving water; tolerant of wide range of climatic conditions but vulnerable to freezing. Occurs on rivers, streams, canals, ditches, lakes, dams, pools, ponds, disused gravel pits, rice fields, swamps and marshes, and at seasonally flooded sites; avoids oligotrophic or saline situations, but inhabits brackish waters on Namibian coast and in Galapagos. Requires ready access to some open fresh water with adequate plant cover; occupies sites with small open water surfaces, such as ponds and pools only a few metres across; prefers waters sheltered by woodland or tall emergent plants; avoids very open sites, especially those exposed to wind and wave action. Occurs alongside *Fulica atra* at wetland margins but less prone to venture far out into open water. Normally occurs most commonly in lowlands, but reaches 1700 m in C Europe, 2400 m in Kashmir, 3000 m in Kenya and 4200 m in Argentina.
Food and Feeding. Omnivorous; proportions of plant and animal food vary. Plants include filamentous algae, moss, vegetative parts of *Lemna*, *Wolffia*, *Potamogeton*, *Juncus*, *Phragmites*, *Veronica*, *Hydrilla*, *Ceratophyllum* and grasses, seeds of *Typha*, *Sparganum*, *Potamogeton*, *Carex*, *Scirpus*, *Rumex*, *Polygonum*, *Nymphaea*, *Nuphar*, *Ranunculus*, *Ulmus*, *Zizaniopsis* and cereals, flowers of *Eichhornia*, berries of *Taxus*, *Rubus*, *Sorbus*, *Rosa*, *Crataegus*, *Rhamnus*, *Hedera*, *Sambucus* and *Hippophae*, and various orchard fruits. Animal foods include earthworms, molluscs, crustaceans, adult and larval insects (especially Ephemeroptera, Hemiptera, Trichoptera, Coleoptera, Lepidoptera and Diptera), spiders, small fish, tadpoles and occasionally eggs of birds; also takes carrion, rubbish (vegetable scraps), duck food and fish food. Feeds while swimming and while walking on floating vegetation, either in cover or in open; also feeds on land, grazing and gleaning over open grass or in arable farmland, usually near cover. In water, obtains food by dipping head, surface sifting, upending and rarely by diving. Gleans insects, seeds and fruits from ground and plants; often clambers over leaves and stems; climbs and perches well. May be opportunistic, feeding on most abundant food types. Kleptoparasitizes other birds, e.g. Great Crested Grebe (*Podiceps cristatus*). Normally diurnal but sometimes active on moonlit nights.
Breeding. Europe, Mar-Aug; N Africa, Apr-Aug; W Africa, Jun-Aug but all year S Ghana, except at peak of wet season; E Africa, all year, peaking in wet months; C Africa, Feb-Sept, Nov-Dec; S Africa all months, peaking Jan-Apr and Jun-Aug in Zimbabwe and Sept-Oct in W Cape; Madagascar, Oct-Mar; Indian Subcontinent, Mar-Sept; Philippines, Jul-Sept; Borneo, Apr; Lesser Sundas, May; Guam, Mar, Jun, Dec; North America, Apr-Jun (season 5-6 weeks longer in S than in N); Panama, mostly Dec-Jan; in Andes, Jul-Sept and in rainy season. Monogamous and territorial; territory may be perma-

nent; pair-bond sometimes maintained for several years. Polyandrous trios of 1 female and 2 males also occur; co-operative nesting of 2 or more females mated to 1 male also recorded; brood parasitism regularly occurs (see page 129). Nest saucer-shaped or more substantial, of twigs, reeds, rushes and sedges, with shallow to deep cup; on, or up to 1 m above, water; often built in emergent vegetation or on solid platform of branches or matted vegetation, in water; sometimes floating, less often in ground vegetation or low bush on bank, usually within few metres of water; occasionally in bushes and trees up to 8 m above ground. Floating nests often have entrance ramp. External diameter 24-30 cm, depth 10-20 cm; cup diameter 12-17 cm, depth 3-7 cm. Both sexes build, helped by other group members; material often added during incubation; also builds brood nests or platforms. Eggs 2-17, mostly 5-9 (W Palearctic), 3-9 (Africa), 7-9 (North America); laid at daily intervals; clutches larger than 13-14 probably from 2 females; up to 5 replacement clutches laid after egg loss; incubation 17-22 days, by both sexes; hatching usually synchronous for first clutches and asynchronous for replacements and later clutches, but asynchronous for all clutches in USA; black downy chick has bare skin of crown rose-red and blue, skin of throat yellow and of wing pink, iris grey-brown, bill orange with yellow tip, legs and feet black; chicks precocial and nidifugous; remain in nest for 1-2 days; swim well by 3rd day and dive at 8 days; fed and cared for by both parents, by immatures of previous broods and by other adults in group; brood division may occur; chicks use spur on alula to climb and grasp vegetation, and to enter brood nests; brooded frequently until c. 14 days old; become self-feeding at 21-25 days, but fed for up to 45 days; fledging 45-50 days, rarely 70 days; independent at 52-99 days (mean 72 days). May rear up to 3 (occasionally 4) broods per season; interval between broods 20-30 days; in South Africa, nested continuously in suitable conditions, although supplementary food was available. Age of first breeding 1 year.

Movements. In W Palearctic, resident or dispersive in S and extreme W, partially migratory to migratory elsewhere, extent of movement increasing further to N & E. Almost wholly summer visitor to former USSR and Finland, while relatively few remain in N Scandinavia, N Germany and Poland in winter. N European birds winter S to Iberia, Italy, Balkans and N Africa. Autumn movements mainly SW from N Europe and S-SE from C Europe; main S movements Sept-Dec, juveniles dispersing from Jul; return passage Mar-May. British and French populations resident but both receive winter migrants from NW Europe. Palearctic birds of unknown origins winter (Nov-Mar) in sub-Saharan Africa, in Senegal, Gambia, Mali, N Nigeria, C Chad and N Sudan. Winter range of emigrant Russian birds, and extent of dispersal by Near East birds, unknown. Passage noted Azerbaijan Mar-Apr and Oct-Nov. Numbers in India and Pakistan greatly augmented by winter visitors; passage noted Oct and Mar-May; occurs Japan Mar-Oct. Race *meridionalis* resident, with some local movements in response to changing conditions; wanders to temporary pools. In North America most of E population migratory, wintering along coast and S to Panama, West Indies and possibly South America; breeding migrants arrive Apr-Jun; some seasonal altitudinal movements occur in W populations (Arizona and Mew Mexico), and also some migration, extent of which unknown. Some seasonal movements noted in South America; winter migrants possibly occur Costa Rica, and Colombia Oct-Feb; presumed winter influx from S noted in Rio Grande do Sul, Brazil. Success in colonizing high proportion of suitable, often scattered, habitats, indicates effective prospecting on wing, largely at night and in lower airspace. Accidental to Iceland, Spitsbergen and São Tomé; *meridionalis* vagrant to NE Chad.

Status and Conservation. Not globally threatened. Most races at least locally common. Nominate generally common throughout range; has expanded range in N Europe since mid-19th century; common in NW Europe, where populations fluctuate markedly due to hard winters; overall increase in Fenno-Scandia and Britain; widespread in N Africa. Race *meridionalis* patchily distributed and uncommon to locally abundant in sub-Saharan Africa; increasing locally as result of man-made dams and ponds. Race *cachinnans* widespread and rare to locally abundant in North America. Race *sandvicensis* of Hawaii now restricted to a few hundred birds on 3 islands and is endangered; Mariana race *guami* also endangered, with only c. 300 birds remaining in greatly reduced wetland habitats. Locally uncommon to abundant throughout range in Central and South America. Readily exploits newly created habitats and is tenacious of occupied areas, not being displaced easily by changes or human disturbance; adapts well to situations at urban sites, where total acceptance of human presence is necessary in order to occupy suitable habitat of tree-lined ornamental waters and lawns. In North American rice fields, rice harvesting is harmful to nests and young broods. Estimated USA harvest averages 44,500 birds per year.

Bibliography. Ali & Ripley (1980), Anderson (1975), Belton (1984), Beltzer *et al.* (1991), Benson (1960), Benson & Benson (1975), Bent (1926), Blake (1977), Brackney & Bookhout (1982), Brazil (1991), Byrd & Zeillemaker (1981), Cramp & Simmons (1980), Dickinson *et al.* (1991), Dowsett & Forbes-Watson (1993), Drost (1968), Eber (1961), Eddleman *et al.* (1988), Eden (1987), Engbring & Pratt (1985), Étchécopar & Hüe (1964, 1978), Evans (1994), Fagan *et al.* (1976), Fjeldså (1977), Fjeldså & Krabbe (1990), Fredrickson (1971), Gibbons (1986, 1987, 1989), Ginn *et al.* (1989), Glutz *et al.* (1973), Godfrey (1986), Goodman *et al.* (1989), Greij (1994), Helm *et al.* (1987), Hilty & Brown (1986), Howell & Webb (1995a), Hüe & Étchécopar (1970), Huxley & Wood (1976), Johnson (1965b), Karhu (1973), King (1978/79), Knystautas (1993), Langrand (1990), Leonard *et al.* (1989), Mackworth-Praed & Grant (1957, 1962, 1970), Maclean (1993), Marchant *et al.* (1990), van Marle & Voous (1988), Medway & Wells (1976), de Naurois (1994), Patrikeev (1995), Paz (1987), Perennou *et al.* (1994), Petrie (1983, 1984), Phillips (1978), Pinto (1983), Potapov & Flint (1987), Rabor (1977), Ripley (1982), Ritter & Sweet (1993), Roberts, T.J. (1991), Root (1988), Rost (1995), Rutgers & Norris (1970), Shirihai (1996), Short *et al.* (1990), Sick (1985c, 1993), Siegfried & Frost (1975), Sigmund (1959), Simeonov *et al.* (1990), Slud (1964), Smythies (1981, 1986), Snow (1978), Stiles & Skutch (1989), Stinson *et al.* (1991), Urban *et al.* (1986), Wetmore (1965), White & Bruce (1986), Wood (1974).

ssp *tenebrosa*

118

ssp *neumanni*

119

♂ ♀

ssp *crassirostris* 120

ssp *melanops*

121

122

ssp *novaeguinea*

with red frontal shield

125

123

124

ssp *atra*

ssp *americana*

ssp *columbiana*

with yellow
frontal shield

126

127

128

129

pale-fronted morph

red-fronted
morph

130

131

132

133

PLATE 18

inches 8

cm 20

118. **Dusky Moorhen**

Gallinula tenebrosa

French: Gallinule sombre **German**: Papuateichhuhn **Spanish**: Gallineta Enlutada

Taxonomy. *Gallinula tenebrosa* Gould, 1846, South Australia.
Sometimes considered conspecific with *G. chloropus*, or to form superspecies, but the two are sympatric in Wallacea. Three subspecies recognized.
Subspecies and Distribution.
G. t. frontata Wallace, 1863 - SE Borneo and Sulawesi through S Moluccas and Lesser Sundas to W & SE New Guinea.
G. t. neumanni Hartert, 1930 - N New Guinea.
G. t. tenebrosa Gould, 1846 - Australia.

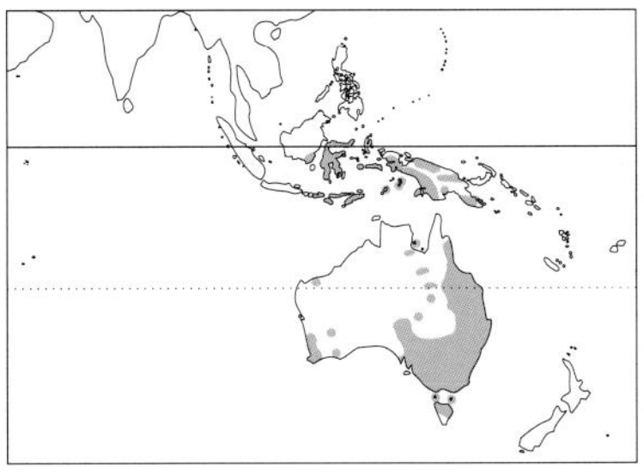

Descriptive notes. 35-40 cm (New Guinea birds 25-32 cm); nominate 336-720 (525) g, *neumanni* 290-370 (333) g; wingspan 55-65 cm. Darker and more uniform in plumage than Eurasian *G. c. chloropus*, but differs from marginally sympatric *G. c. orientalis* only in absence of prominent white line along top of flanks, only infrequently showing narrow or broken line; orange to red legs and feet with dark soles and joints. Separated from other sympatric congeners by dark plumage, white outer rectrices and lateral undertail-coverts, and bare part colours. Sexes similar. Non-breeding adult has bill dull red (most often in males) to olive-black, shrunken shield olive green or darker, red on tarsus and toes fades to olive green or yellow. Immature similar to adult but iris dark brown, bill, shield and tibia olive black or olive brown, and tarsus olive green. Juvenile duller than adult, browner on upperparts, paler on throat and underparts, with feathers of lower breast and belly extensively fringed white; bill and shrunken shield pale red, becoming dark olive brown; iris dark brown; legs and feet dark olive green or olive brown. Races separated on size and colour: *neumanni* smaller and darker; *frontata* slightly smaller than nominate, darker below, with front of tarsus and top of toes bright red (differences in leg and foot colour need further investigation). Voice. Territorial advertising call a raucous, crowing "kurk"; calls sometimes repeated or run together. Also various short, sharp alarm calls (including harsh squawks and shrieks) and a series of widely spaced staccato calls made by swimming or preening birds.

Habitat. Inhabits permanent or ephemeral wetlands, usually freshwater but sometimes brackish or saline: swamps, creeks, rivers, lagoons and estuaries. Also occupies artificial wetlands such as reservoirs, farm dams, and ornamental ponds and lakes in parks and gardens. Requires open water, which usually has fringing cover such as reeds, rushes and grass, and often has floating, emergent or aquatic vegetation; however, waters choked with water hyacinth (*Eichhornia*) are avoided. Occasionally frequents rubbish dumps and polluted water. Seldom found far from wetland edge, except when foraging in surrounding short vegetation. Uncommon on saline and ephemeral waters; rarely in mangroves.

Food and Feeding. Vegetable matter, including algae, and vegetative parts, seeds and fruits of plants of: Azollaceae, Hydrocharitaceae, Potomogetonaceae, Lemnaceae, Poaceae, Typhaceae, Polygonaceae, Portulacaceae, Solanaceae and Nymphaeaceae. Also worms, molluscs, arachnids, insects and their larvae (Odonata, Orthoptera, Hemiptera, Coleoptera, Lepidoptera and Hymenoptera), amphibians, fish, carrion, bread, and droppings of gulls and ducks. Diurnal; forages in open water and among floating vegetation, usually within 100 m of cover; also on adjacent land; often on grass and herbfields near water; rarely among tall terrestrial vegetation. Gleans and pecks on ground or low vegetation; while swimming gleans from surface and upends for 2-7 seconds, with tail and legs above water, taking food up to 30 cm below surface; does not dive. Sometimes chases insects; rarely stretches up on toes to take food; sometimes pins food item to ground with foot.

Breeding. Sulawesi, possibly Apr, downy young Mar; Seram, juvenile, May; New Guinea, small young May-Jun; Australia, Aug-Mar. Territorial when breeding. Simultaneously promiscuous, forming breeding groups of 2-7 apparently unrelated birds; individuals sometimes switch groups between seasons. Within group, all males copulate with all females. All group members defend territory, build nests, incubate, and care for young; older siblings sometimes help to care for young. Nest usually built up to 180 cm above water (occasionally on ground) in grass tussocks, reeds (especially *Typha*, *Phragmites*), rushes, bushes or trees; also on water-lilies, floating in clear water, and in stumps or hollow logs; recorded building inside metal drum and wire netting. In addition to egg-nest, may build 1-2 false nests, abandoned before completion; 1-2 brooding nests built after eggs hatch. Nest a bulky platform or shallow cup of reeds, rushes, twigs, bark, leaves and waterweed; external diameter 25-30 cm; bowl 15-20 cm wide, 6-8 cm deep. Eggs 5-18 (mean 8); large clutches probably from 2 or more females; laying irregular for first few days, then daily; in Australian study, one egg was laid per day by each female in group until clutch of 5-8 per female complete; incubation 19-24 days; hatching asynchronous, within 1-5 days; chick has black down, tipped silver on throat and neck, bill red with yellow base, skin of crown orange-brown or red, skin round eye bright blue, skin on leading edge of wing orange-yellow; chicks semi-precocial and nidifugous; leave nest after 3-4 days; fed intensively and brooded until c. 4 weeks old, then fed less frequently until c. 9 weeks old; begin to feed independently after 3-4 weeks; fully feathered at 1 month, brown with light grey streaks on cheeks; fly at 8 weeks; post-juvenile moult possibly occurs during autumn of first year, Australia. Most birds enter breeding groups when more than 20 months old. In Australian study, early nesting groups lost 13·4% eggs per group and fledged 1·97 young per female, while late nesting groups lost 38·5% eggs per group and fledged 0·5 young per female; Australian nest record cards show overall hatching success of 55·5%. Normally single-brooded; may lay twice per season in Australia.

Movements. In Australia sedentary, nomadic or dispersive, possibly partly migratory. Apparently occurs seasonally in some areas, and also shows seasonal fluctuations in numbers, but atlas reporting rates do not suggest large-scale seasonal pattern of movement. Appears at intermittent inland waters and isolated wetlands, and immatures disperse either in autumn or after wintering in flocks. Possibly moves to areas of high rainfall or surface water, to floodwaters or abundant food sources, and away from flooded areas where vegetation destroyed and from wetlands covered with *Eichhornia*. Unlike *G. ventralis*, does not undertake large-scale irruptive movements. Moves at night. Regarded as locally nomadic in New Guinea. Vagrant to New Zealand and Lord Howe I.

Status and Conservation. Not globally threatened. In Australia, nominate race widespread and common in E and inland range is expanding: small population recently established in N Western Australia and first breeding recorded recently in some parts of W Queensland and E South Australia. First bred on Flinders I 1935 and King I 1960's; has colonized N Tasmania since 1976. Favoured by construction of artificial wetlands, but habitat losses occur through wetland drainage. Race *frontata* formerly regarded as common over most of range; present overall status uncertain, but both this race and *neumanni* are currently widespread and locally common in lowlands of New Guinea. On the five islands where sympatry with *G. chloropus* is recorded, *G. chloropus* is apparently replacing present species on Sulawesi and Sumba, while present species has not been recorded from Borneo, Flores and Sumbawa since 19th century.

Bibliography. Beehler *et al*. (1986), Black (1919), Blakers *et al*. (1984), Bryant (1940b), Coates (1985), Czechura (1983), Eskell & Garnett (1979), Fleming (1976), Garnett (1978, 1980), Gilliard & LeCroy (1966), Green (1989), Gyldenstolpe (1955), Halse & Jaensch (1989), Hindwood (1953), Lord (1936, 1956), MacKinnon & Phillipps (1993), Marchant & Higgins (1993), Martin *et al*. (1979), Perennou *et al*. (1994), Serventy, D.L. & Whittell (1976), Serventy, V. (1985), Smythies (1981), Stresemann (1941), Vestjens (1977), Watling (1983), Watson (1955), White, C.M.N. (1976), White, C.M.N. & Bruce (1986), White, S.A. (1918).

119. **Lesser Moorhen**

Gallinula angulata

French: Gallinule africaine **German**: Zwergteichhuhn **Spanish**: Gallineta Chica

Taxonomy. *Gallinula angulata* Sundevall, 1851, Lower Caffraria, (= Natal), South Africa.
Monotypic.
Distribution. Senegal and Gambia E to Ethiopia, and S to N & E Namibia, Botswana and E South Africa.

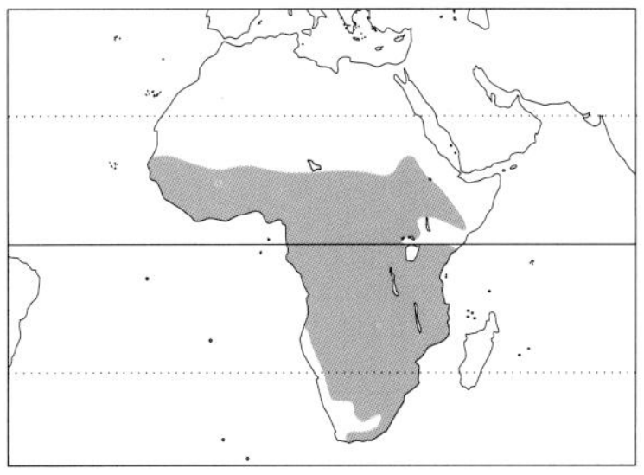

Descriptive notes. 22-23 cm; male 145-164 (155) g, female 92-137 (109) g, 1 unsexed 149 g. Like small version of *G. chloropus*, but paler overall, appearing mainly grey in flight with darker wings; bright yellow bill, scarlet culmen, scarlet pointed frontal shield (rounded in *G. chloropus*); legs and feet yellow-green, sometimes green, orange, flesh or pinkish red, with no red "garter". Female has paler, browner upperparts, light grey face with black only round base of bill, silvery grey throat, and paler grey underparts, especially on belly; frontal shield smaller, duller and orange next to feathers. Immature has crown, upperwing-coverts and upperparts olive brown, greyer on mantle; scapulars and tertials edged pale buff; sides of head and neck buffy brown; chin to lower breast and belly creamy white, shading to light grey on flanks; undertail-coverts white at sides, black in centre; bill brownish yellow with dusky base to culmen; legs and feet greyish green to dull yellow-green; may breed in this plumage. Voice. Calls resemble those of *G. chloropus* and include: rapid series of clucking notes; series of subdued chuckling or pumping notes; and sharp clicking and squeaky calls. Alarm a sharp "tik" or "tek".

Habitat. Permanent and temporary freshwater wetlands, such as papyrus swamps, reedbeds, marshes with rushes and open water, ponds with water-lilies, floodplains and pans with emergent grass or sedge cover and often floating plants; rank fringing vegetation on ponds, dams, rivers and forest streams; rice fields, flooded farmland, sewage ponds and seasonally inundated grassland. Occurs at "coastal lagoons" in Ghana. Normally occupies different habitat to that utilized by *G. chloropus*, preferring temporary waters with abundant cover of emergent vegetation as opposed to permanent waters with fringing vegetation, but both species sometimes occur together. In E Africa occurs up to 2000 m.

Food and Feeding. Molluscs, insects (especially beetles), vegetable matter including seeds and flowers of reeds; also (in captivity) termites. Forages while swimming or while walking at edge of water, on floating vegetation such as lily pads, or on open mud. Usually shy, remaining in cover while foraging. Not aggressive when feeding.

Breeding. Senegal and Gambia, breeding condition Aug; Sierra Leone, Nov; Nigeria, Jul-Sept; Ghana, Jun; Gabon, Feb; Chad, Aug; Sudan, Aug; Somalia, May; Zaire, high plateau of SE, Jan-Mar, at lower altitudes possibly Apr-May; Angola, Jan, Mar; Kenya and NE Tanzania, Mar, May-Jun; Tanzania Dec-Mar; Zambia and Malawi, Jan-Mar; Zimbabwe, Dec-Apr; Namibia, Feb-Mar, probably Sept; Botswana, Feb; South Africa, Dec-Apr. Monogamous; territorial when breeding. Nest smaller and more compact than that of *G. chloropus*; pad of grass or sedges with shallow cup; placed on or up to 5 cm above water (recorded water depth 20-100 cm) in emergent grasses or sedges up to 1·5 m tall, with surrounding stems often bent down over nest and bound together to form canopy; entrance ramp of grass and sedge stems sometimes built from water to lip of cup. External diameter 15-20 cm; thickness 6-10 cm; depth of cup 2·5-5 cm. Nests usually well separated but in Nigeria 4 pairs nested in radius of 20 m. Eggs 3-9 (mean 5); incubation 19-20 days, probably by both sexes, starting before clutch complete; black downy chick has black bill with white tip and pink base, frontal shield and base of culmen pale red-brown, pale purple next to forehead, eye dark brown, legs and feet bluish grey; fledging 35-38 days. No information on parental care.

Movements. Some birds resident year round in permanently suitable habitats, but many are rains migrants. In W Africa some resident in wet S areas but in dry N areas numbers increase during rains, when birds breed, and decrease as seasonal habitats dry out. Occurs Senegal and Gambia mainly in wet season; seasonal movements in Ivory Coast; almost all records in Nigeria Mar-Sept; occurs Ghana mainly Jun-Sept; resident in Chad except in Sahel zone, where purely a rains migrant. Probable migrants found Cameroon, Nov, and Zaire (Kivu) May-Jun; migrants arrive Gabon, Nov-Dec. Present all year near Entebbe, Uganda. Occurs Kenya and NE Tanzania most months but commonest Apr-Jul; night migrants attracted to lights, E Kenya, Dec-Jan. Largely rainy season visitor in S Africa: 88% of specimens from SE Zaire to South Africa taken Dec-Apr (38% in Jan). In Zambia, largely absent Jun-Nov; night migrant found Apr. In Zimbabwe and Botswana breeds in semi-arid areas at pans and other temporary waters which disappear in dry season; occurs Botswana Oct-Jun, mainly Dec-Apr. In South Africa, occurs Transvaal Dec-May; probable migrant found Natal Feb.

On following pages: 120. Spot-flanked Gallinule (*Gallinula melanops*); 121. Black-tailed Native-hen (*Gallinula ventralis*); 122. Tasmanian Native-hen (*Gallinula mortierii*); 123. Red-knobbed Coot (*Fulica cristata*); 124. Common Coot (*Fulica atra*); 125. Hawaiian Coot (*Fulica alai*); 126. American Coot (*Fulica americana*); 127. Caribbean Coot (*Fulica caribaea*); 128. White-winged Coot (*Fulica leucoptera*); 129. Andean Coot (*Fulica ardesiaca*); 130. Red-gartered Coot (*Fulica armillata*); 131. Red-fronted Coot (*Fulica rufifrons*); 132. Giant Coot (*Fulica gigantea*); 133. Horned Coot (*Fulica cornuta*).

Status and Conservation. Not globally threatened. Widespread and locally common over much of range but, as with *Porphyrio alleni*, erratic nature of its occurrence in seasonal habitats makes numbers difficult to assess. Sometimes locally very numerous in suitable breeding habitat during seasons of good rainfall, e.g. at least 50,000 pairs thought to be present on the Nyl floodplain, N Transvaal, in early 1996, during an exceptionally wet season; concentrations of over 1000 seen on Kafue Flats, Zambia, at end of rainy season. In Ivory Coast, outnumbers *G. chloropus* in Korhogo marshes; numerous in S Cameroon; frequent in Nigeria, except SE; locally abundant during rains in Kenya, Zambia and Zimbabwe. Much habitat loss must have occurred in recent years as a result of the draining, damming and grazing of its wetland habitats, but overall effect of this is unclear.

Bibliography. Benson & Benson (1975), Benson & Irwin (1965), Benson *et al.* (1971), Britton, P.L. (1980), Brosset & Érard (1986), Dowsett & Forbes-Watson (1993), Elgood *et al.* (1994), Ginn *et al.* (1989), Gore (1990), Grimes (1987), Hopkinson & Masterson (1984), Irwin (1981), Jackson & Sclater (1938), Lewis & Pomeroy (1989), Lippens & Wille (1976), Mackworth-Praed & Grant (1957, 1962, 1970), Maclean (1993), Penry (1994), Pinto (1983), Sclater (1906), Serle (1939b), Short *et al.* (1990), Snow (1978), Tarboton, Kemp & Kemp (1987), Urban *et al.* (1986), Verheyen (1953), White (1945).

120. Spot-flanked Gallinule

Gallinula melanops

French: Gallinule à face noire **German**: Maskenpfuhlhuhn **Spanish**: Gallineta Pintada
Other common names: Little Waterhen

Taxonomy. *Rallus melanops* Vieillot, 1819, Paraguay.
Sometimes placed in *Porphyriops*. Three subspecies recognized.
Subspecies and Distribution.
G. m. bogotensis (Chapman, 1914) - E Andes of Colombia.
G. m. melanops (Vieillot, 1819) - E Bolivia and Paraguay, E & S Brazil to extreme NE Argentina and Uruguay.
G. m. crassirostris (J. E. Gray, 1829) - Chile and Argentina, except extreme S.

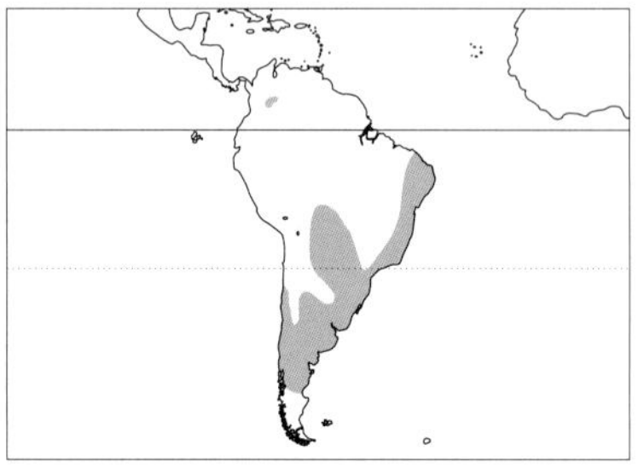

Descriptive notes. 22-30 cm; 1 unsexed 154 g. Distinctive gallinule, in shape resembling more a large *Porzana* crake than *Gallinula*; black face, grey and olive body, flanks heavily spotted white, prominent white undertail-coverts; iris red, bill stout and lime green, frontal shield green to pale bluish green, legs and feet greenish. Unique in genus in having lobed toes. On water appears flat-backed with scarcely raised rear end. Sexes alike. Shield may become duller in non-breeding season. Immature not described. Juvenile uniform olive brown, paler below and with rather faint flank spots. Races separated on colour of axillaries, white in *bogotensis*, barred in others; and size, *crassirostris* smaller than nominate, with thicker bill (variable). Voice. Common call is hollow cackling, resembling sudden burst of hysterical laughter, the notes beginning loud and long and becoming brief and hurried as they die away. Calls mainly in evening.
Habitat. Ponds, ditches, marshes, lagoons, and lake margins with often extensive floating-leaved vegetation; also wet savannas, and said to frequent dense reeds and rushes along rivers. Occurs in temperate zones; inhabits lowlands of Argentina up to 750 m; in E Andes of Colombia, occurs at 2000-3000 m.
Food and Feeding. Food not described. Feeds mostly by swimming, picking food from floating vegetation or sometimes from water; seldom walks on marsh vegetation or on land. Normally conspicuous and easily seen.
Breeding. Colombia, Feb and Jun, but also breeds in other seasons; Chile, Oct-Nov (spring); SE Brazil, season prolonged, feathered young seen with adults from mid-Oct to Mar; Argentina, Oct-Jan. Nest built among reeds or on damp ground, slightly above water rather than floating; built of dry rushes, which are also used to form half-dome. Eggs 4-8; downy young described as blackish brown. No other information.
Movements. None recorded, but at Cape San Antonio, E Argentina, birds were first seen in Sept and were gone by late May. Regarded as resident in SE Brazil.
Status and Conservation. Not globally threatened. Locally common in SE Brazil, widespread in SW Brazil, Paraguay, E Bolivia and lowlands of N & C Argentina, and thought to be spreading southwards. Race *bogotensis* has small range in Colombia, but is apparently locally common, e.g. at Parque La Florida, near Bogotá.

Bibliography. Belton (1984), Blake (1977), Canevari *et al.* (1991), Contreras *et al.* (1990), Fjeldså & Krabbe (1990), Forrester (1993), Hayes (1995), Hellmayr & Conover (1942), Hilty & Brown (1986), Johnson (1965b), Klimaitis & Moschione (1987), Meyer de Schauensee (1982), Narosky & Yzurieta (1987), Olrog (1984), de la Peña (1992), Pinto (1964), Remsen & Traylor (1989), Sick (1985c, 1993), Varty *et al.* (1986), Weller (1967).

121. Black-tailed Native-hen

Gallinula ventralis

French: Gallinule aborigène **German**: Rotfuß-Pfuhlhuhn **Spanish**: Gallineta Patirroja

Taxonomy. *Gallinula ventralis* Gould, 1837, Swan River, West Australia.
In past sometimes placed in genus *Tribonyx*; although most appropriately retained in *Gallinula*, may merit separate subgenus along with *G. mortierii* on basis of morphological features. Monotypic.
Distribution. Australia.
Descriptive notes. 30-38 cm; male 250-530 (412) g, female 322-405 (364) g; wingspan 55-66 cm. Large, thickset rail with vertically fanned black tail, black undertail-coverts, long wings, orange-yellow iris, nimble gait and somewhat bantam-like shape; gregarious; swims readily, with buoyant carriage and erect tail; these characters, and preference for foraging in groups in drier habitats, distinguish from all sympatric rallids. *G. mortierii* is much larger, flightless and appears much shorter-winged; has red iris, olive-yellow bill and grey or grey-olive legs and feet. Sexes similar, but female slightly smaller, and slightly duller and paler overall; dark band round base of bill reduced or absent and white spots on sides of belly smaller. Immature very similar to adult, but some retain smaller juvenile white flank spots; bare part colours identical to adult. Juvenile resembles adult female but has smaller white flank spots; in worn plumage is paler, with off-white lores, face, chin and throat, and paler underparts contrasting more with blackish vent and undertail-coverts; bill greenish yellow with dusky tip; iris blackish; legs and feet brownish pink. Voice. Virtually unknown. Usually silent, but both sexes have sharp "kak" of alarm and rapid, harsh, metallic cackle.

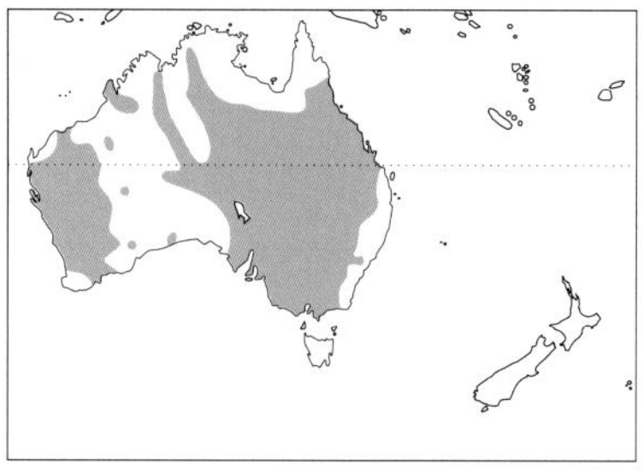

Habitat. Opportunistic, especially during influxes. Normally occurs in low rainfall areas at permanent or ephemeral terrestrial wetlands, including shallow lakes, swamps, pools, floodplains and flats of rivers and creeks, and inundated depressions; favours fresh or brackish waters but often on shallow and more saline drying ephemeral wetlands; rarely in dry *Banksia* woodland, and at mangroves and tidal pools. Habitat often characterized by dense clumps of lignum, canegrass, or scrub; sometimes sparsely wooded. Also occurs at artificial wetlands, e.g. dams, margins of reservoirs, sewage ponds; in pasture, crops or fallow lands. May occur in urban areas, e.g. streets, gardens, parks, golf courses and racecourses; and in unusual situations such as arid country, sandhills, undulating hills and valleys, coastal flats, and among samphire and coastal shrubs. May occur far from water.
Food and Feeding. Takes seeds, plant material and invertebrates (especially insects). Plant food includes grain, seeds of *Polygonum*, *Triticum* and *Hordeum*, young vegetables and cereal crops, fodder crops, fresh green growth of annuals, aquatic plants, and drying apricots; invertebrate food includes molluscs, and adult and larval insects (Orthoptera, Coleoptera, Lepidoptera, and Hymenoptera in form of ants). Diurnal; forages gregariously or in pairs; feeds at grassy or muddy wetland margins, on open ground near wetlands, in pastures and crops, and in scrub and sand dunes; sometimes feeds with domestic fowl and at piggeries. Gleans from ground, alternately running and stopping in order to disturb insects. Also feeds from surface of water and submerges head and shoulders.
Breeding. E & S Australia, usually Aug-Dec, but timing influenced by rainfall, especially after drought, when may breed any month; in SW, Jun-Nov; in SE breeds after large influxes, continuously through winter and summer; breeds opportunistically, often soon after arrival following heavy rain, or as water dries up after flooding; laying time correlated with peak rainfall + 2-3 months. Social organization unclear; on existing evidence, appears monogamous, and territorial when breeding; often nests in colonies. Nest usually well concealed low in dense vegetation, such as clumps of grass, reeds, bushes, and herbage; also on tree stump, in tree fork or branches, on debris on log in water, in shallow depression in ground, in wooden box in tree, and under wire fence enclosure. Nest cup-shaped, of any available vegetation, including lignum, reeds, twigs, leaves, grass and bark; often with partial roof of woven stems; sometimes with approach ramp of broken reeds; external diameter 26 cm, depth 10 cm; height above ground 0-80 cm. Usually 5-7 eggs (4-12); larger clutches possibly from 2 females; laying probably synchronous in large colonies where arrival virtually simultaneous; incubation probably begins before clutch complete, period unknown; hatching asynchronous but probably within 24-48 hours; chicks precocial and nidifugous; black downy chick has greenish sheen, colour fading to black-brown on body, bill black with large white egg-tooth, pink basal third of upper mandible and narrow white or grey central saddle, iris blackish, legs and feet grey-black; chicks remain in nest for unknown time after hatching; timing of chick development not recorded, and no information on parental care; date of post-juvenile moult presumably depends on hatching date, recorded Jan-Apr, but birds with fresh plumage and no moult collected May and Jul.
Movements. May make regular seasonal movements: reported as regular visitor in extreme SW, and reporting rates in N increase in summer; however in some areas present at most times of year. Dispersive and highly irruptive; since 1833 irruptions have occurred on average once every 2·7 years. Irruptions probably associated with favourable breeding conditions in N allowing build-up of numbers, followed by harsh conditions such as drought and decreasing food supplies which force birds to leave interior. Irruptions sometimes characterized by sudden appearance and disappearance of large numbers of birds over period of as little as 12 hours. Movements often linked with rain: often appears after rain and after cyclonic disturbances; also claimed to appear before rain actually falls; possibly moves in response to cloud banks. May move into flooded areas and areas with lush green growth, and away from areas subjected to drying-out, drought or hot weather. During irruptions possibly disperses in all directions, but in Queensland may move towards coast. Possibly moves back to normal range after rainfall. May move at night, and can fly long distances. Vagrant to Tasmania (3 records) and New Zealand (4 records); these and mainland vagrant occurrences often coincide with irruptions.
Status and Conservation. Not globally threatened. Generally widespread inland S of 20° S and W of Great Dividing Range, with scattered records from coastal and sub-coastal regions. Australian Atlas records no breeding N of 22° S. Locally common; wide fluctuations in numbers recorded, large concentrations of 10,000-20,000 birds recorded during irruptions. Annual indices of relative abundance, obtained in 1983-1989 and covering wetlands in c. 12% of land area in E Australia, were between 2222 and 25,424 (61-100% of total numbers were counted). Irruptions more frequent 50-100 years ago; lower frequency in recent years possibly because of reduced extent of breeding grounds following drainage of swamps and control of flooding on inland rivers. During irruptions, causes damage to crops and vegetable gardens by trampling and eating plants, and may pollute water supplies. Artificial habitats are often used, especially during irruptions.

Bibliography. Alexander (1923), Badman (1979), Berney (1907), Blakers *et al.* (1984), Carter (1904), Chaffer (1940), Christian (1909), Cox & Pedler (1977), Ford (1906), Green (1963), Halse & Jaensch (1989), Hobbs (1973b), MacGillivray (1914), Marchant & Higgins (1993), Masters & Milhinch (1974), Matheson (1978), McGilp (1923), Nicholls (1905), Patterson (1989b), Rich (1973), Roberts (1975), Schrader (1974), Serventy, D.L. (1953), Serventy, D.L. & Whittell (1976), Serventy, V. (1985), Stone (1912), Storr (1973), Wheeler (1973).

122. Tasmanian Native-hen

Gallinula mortierii

French: Gallinule de Tasmanie **German**: Grünfuß-Pfuhlhuhn **Spanish**: Gallineta Tasmania

Taxonomy. *Tribonyx mortierii* Du Bus de Gisignies, 1840, Tasmania.
Although most appropriately retained in *Gallinula*, may merit separate subgenus along with *G. ventralis* on basis of morphological features. Monotypic.
Distribution. Tasmania.
Introduced to Maria I (off E Tasmania).
Descriptive notes. 42-51 cm; male (mean) 1334 g, female (mean) 1251 g. Large, thickset, flightless rail, rather bantam-like, with long, narrow tail, and stout bill and legs; conspicuous, active, noisy, demonstrative and aggressive; walks with short wings partly drooped and tail constantly jerked up and down or carried erect; runs very swiftly with tail erect, opening wings to balance. *G. ventralis* much smaller and longer-winged, with dark area round base of bill, white spots on sides of belly sometimes covering rear flanks, no pale tips to upperwing-coverts, orange-yellow iris, pale green bill with red base to lower mandible, and pinkish red legs and feet. Sexes alike. Immature like adult except for narrower juvenile remiges. Juvenile duller and paler overall; as plumage becomes worn, white patch

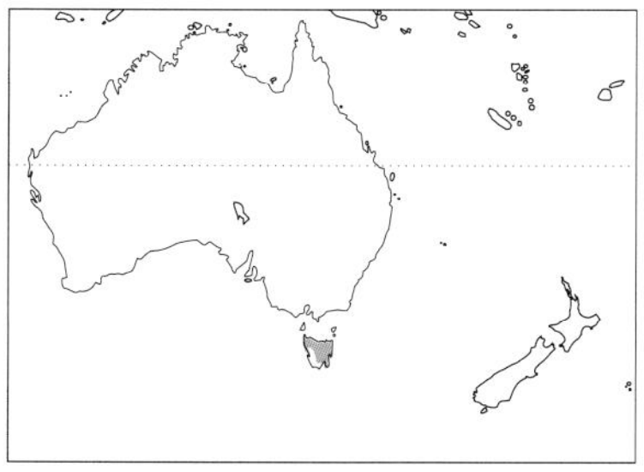

develops on lores and buff tips show from back to uppertail-coverts; feathers of breast and belly have whitish tips; bare parts as in adult, but bill initially dusky. VOICE. Characteristic aggressive call of pairs is loud, rasping, antiphonal "see-saw". Also various grunts, a repeated click call, sharp and harsh alarm calls, and screaming calls when chased or attacked. Noisy early in morning and in evening; also calls at night.

Habitat. Open pasture, grassland, crops (newly sown cereals or legumes) and other cleared land round permanent or seasonal freshwater wetlands which include marshes, lakes, dams, creeks, rivers and streams; rarely round saline wetlands. Grassland may be lightly timbered or infested with alien weeds; usually frequents wetland areas with abundant cover of rushes, reeds, sedges, tussocks, bracken or willows for shelter and nesting. Occasionally enters adjacent woodland, or penetrates forest along tracks and in clearings. Occurs throughout agricultural areas, especially where farming less intense; absent from heath dominated by button-grass in SW. Requires short-grazed pasture all year for foraging; currently dependent on swards maintained by introduced species (rabbits, sheep and cattle); swards formerly maintained by grazing marsupials and by fire. Always breeds near water.

Food and Feeding. Mostly seeds and leaves of: Poaceae, Cyperaceae, Restionaceae, Juncaceae, Polygonaceae, Portulaceae, Caryophyllaceae, Brassicaceae, Rosaceae, Fabaceae, Geraniaceae, Thymelaceae, Apiaceae, Epacridaceae, Primulaceae, Convolvulaceae, Boraginaceae, Scrophulariaceae, Plantaginaceae, Rubiaceae, Asteraceae and Hydrocharitaceae; also cereal crops; diet varies with availability of plant species. Also takes a few insects (Orthoptera, Coleoptera, Diptera and Lepidoptera); in captivity eats meat and fish. Herbage eaten most in winter and spring, seeds and insects in summer. Young chicks given worms, insects and tadpoles as well as plant material; by 14 days of age, diet as adult. Diurnal; forages on ground in pastures and paddocks; also on exposed mud. Gleans and pecks at ground and seedheads; grasps herbage and pulls seeds off with tip of bill; in orchards takes fruit from ground or low branches, sometimes hopping onto branches; chases flying moths. A secondary grazer, requiring primary grazers to maintain suitable habitat.

Breeding. Jul-Jan, usually Aug-Nov; determined by rainfall, as dependent on fresh young plant growth. Monogamous or polygamous, usually polyandrous; permanently territorial in groups of 2-17 birds consisting of 2-5 breeding adults, plus young usually up to 2 years old. Breeding unit usually adult pair, or trio of 2 males (often brothers) and 1 female; rarely has 2 females (sisters). Adults normally associate for life. All males perform copulations. Sex-ratio biased towards males. Adults share all territorial and breeding duties; young of previous year sometimes help with breeding duties; first-brood young sometimes feed and brood second-brood chicks. Nest a bulky woven cup of grass, reeds or herbage, well concealed in tall, thick vegetation such as rushes, reeds, sedges, tussocks, ferns, prickly bushes, occasionally thistles. Built 10-120 cm above ground or over water, almost always on edge of stream, dam, lagoon or pond; sometimes under overhang or in hole in creek bank; concealed overhead with woven stems; entrance leads towards water. Also constructs 1-7 brood nests after eggs hatch; usually in exposed location and often untidier and bulkier than egg-nests. Usually 5-8 eggs (3-9), laid at daily intervals; incubation 19-25 days (usually 22); eggs normally hatch within 48 hours; downy chick black (fading to dark brown), bill black with large white egg-tooth, pink base to upper mandible, and narrow lavender saddle, iris black, legs and feet grey-black; chicks semi-precocial and nidifugous; leave nest 1-2 days after hatching; become self-feeding after 1-2 weeks but fed for 8 weeks; tended closely for 3-4 weeks and then less frequently until 6 weeks old; usually remain with parents until 9-15 months; post-juvenile moult occurs before first winter. Able to breed in first year. Hatching success 89%; survival of young to 4 months 46% in adult pairs and 61% in trios; survival higher in adult groups than first-year groups. Often rears 2 broods per season, sometimes 3.

Movements. Sedentary, but some groups recorded as disappearing in summer. Many young disperse from natal area at end of first year, but on Maria I 20-30% of young were still in natal territories at end of 2nd year. Movements of up to 15 km recorded; once 40 km.

Status and Conservation. Not globally threatened. Distribution has not changed substantially in recent past, although has expanded into newly opened land. Introduced to Maria I in 1969. Has benefited from introduction of rabbits as well as clearance of wooded land for grazing and crops, and construction of artificial wetlands. Road construction may provide corridors for range expansion. Very numerous, despite some local declines. Drastic decline near Geeveston, S Tasmania, in 1989, thought to be result of disease. Decline reported in Midlands after introduction of myxomatosis and consequent reduction of rabbits; recent spread of rabbit calicivirus on Australian mainland, if extending to Tasmania, could have similar effect. Not protected: traditionally regarded as agricultural pest: claimed to trample, graze and foul pasture and crops; most claims unsubstantiated, but species may reduce sprouting oats by up to 8%. Declared vermin in 1950, and thousands were killed in 1955-1958; still controlled by shooting and round-ups. Attacked by feral cats and dogs. Killed by road traffic; appears particularly susceptible on elevated sections of roads. Formerly occurred on mainland Australia (SE Queensland to Victoria and SE South Australia); thought to have become extinct 20,000-12,000 years ago during a period of severe aridity; however recent finding of remains only 4700 years old suggests that final disappearance coincided roughly with arrival of dingo (*Canis familiaris dingo*). In Tasmania survives predation by cats as well as native species such as Tasmanian devil (*Sarcophilus harrisi*).

Bibliography. Baird (1984, 1986, 1991), Blakers *et al*. (1984), Fletcher (1909, 1912), Goldizen *et al*. (1993), Green (1965), Kraus *et al*. (1975), Littler (1910), Marchant & Higgins (1993), Maynard Smith & Ridpath (1972), Napier (1969), Olson (1975a), Ridpath (1964, 1972a, 1972b, 1972c), Ridpath & Meldrum (1968a, 1968b), Serventy (1985), Sharland (1925), Stresemann & Stresemann (1966), Taylor & Mooney (1991), Thomas, D.G. (1979).

Genus *FULICA* Linnaeus, 1758

123. **Red-knobbed Coot**

Fulica cristata

French: Foulque à crête **German**: Kammbläßhuhn **Spanish**: Focha Moruna
Other common names: Crested Coot

Taxonomy. *Fulica cristata* Gmelin, 1789, Madagascar.
Forms superspecies with *F. atra*, *F. alai*, *F. americana*, *F. caribaea*, *F. leucoptera* and *F. ardesiaca*. Monotypic.

Distribution. S Spain and N Morocco; Ethiopia, Eritrea, Kenya and Uganda S through Rwanda, Burundi, E Zaire and Tanzania, W to Angola and S to South Africa; also Madagascar.

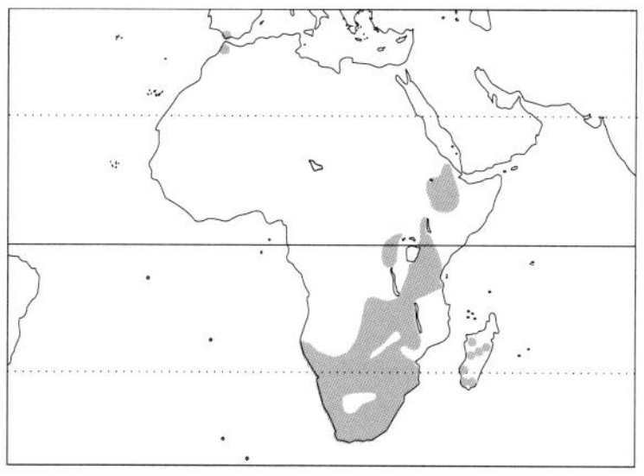

Descriptive notes. 35-42 cm; male 770-910 g, female 455-790 g, unsexed 363-1236 (737) g; wingspan 75-85 cm. Differs from *F. atra* in overall slightly darker appearance, no white tips to secondaries, rounded projection of loral feathering between bill and shield, red knobs at top of frontal shield. Sexes alike, but female smaller. Non-breeding adult has small knobs (often very hard to see), red-brown iris, duskier tinge at sides of bill, and dull slate legs and feet. Immature like adult but feathers of chin, throat, breast and underparts fringed white; upperparts often have dusky olive tinge. Juvenile has crown and upperparts dark brown with olive tinge, sides of head, neck and flanks dark olive brown mottled off-white, lores, chin and throat white, and underparts pale ash grey; iris grey-brown to dark brown; bill dull grey; legs and feet dark grey. VOICE. Vocabulary wide. Commonest calls: sharp, shrill "kik" or "krik"; low, reedy "kek"; shrill, trilled "krrt"; double clucking note; and deep, "koop" or "kup". Also has hollow "hoo"; deep, nasal, frog-like croak; drawn-out "ker"; "coo-dooc"; metallic ringing "croo-oo-k" or snorting "tcholf" of alarm; and high-pitched, nasal, repeated "hue" group alarm call.

Habitat. Chiefly frequents open fresh water of lakes, lagoons, ponds, permanent and temporary dams and vleis, and floodplains. Also occurs in swamps with reeds and papyrus, and at sewage ponds; sometimes found on rivers and tidal lagoons but generally prefers still water. When breeding, frequents waters with fringing or emergent vegetation, but at other times may occur on completely open waters; requires submerged aquatic vegetation for food. Habitat very similar to that of *F. atra*, which it replaces over most of range. Occurs up to 3000 m in E Africa.

Food and Feeding. Omnivorous; takes mainly aquatic vegetation, especially non-rooting submerged or floating plants and including filamentous algae (Chlorophyceae), water plants such as *Marsilia*, *Aeschynomene fluitans* (stems, flowers, fruits and aerial roots), *Polygonum limbatum* (stems, leaves and fruits), *Najas pectinata* (stems and leaves), *Potamogeton pectinatus*, *Ruppia maritima* and *Eichhornia crassipes*, grass (e.g. leaves of *Panicum repens*) and seeds. Also eats molluscs (Gastropoda), crustaceans and arthropods (including insects), and occasionally carrion (e.g. ducks washed up on shore). Feeding techniques similar to those of *F. atra*, with emphasis on aquatic modes such as diving down and pulling up underwater vegetation; diving ability better developed than in *F. atra*; S of Sahara feeds mostly in water. Also feeds from surface, either while swimming or when standing in shallow water. Feeds much less often on land than does *F. atra*, but grazes short grass near water, especially when food scarce (bill has shearing edge adapted to grazing). On Kafue Flats, Zambia, grazes where vegetation trampled by lechwe (*Kobus leche*); in Natal, overgrazes green crops planted near dams.

Breeding. Spain and N Africa, May; Morocco, Feb-Sept; Ethiopia, Apr-Jul, Sept-Dec; Kenya and NE Tanzania, all months; W Kenya and Uganda, all months except Feb; Zambia, Apr-Jul; Malawi, Jun-Jul; Zimbabwe, Jan-Sept; South Africa, all months; Madagascar, Dec-May. Gregarious outside breeding season but monogamous and territorial when breeding; some birds apparently also paired in winter flocks. Nest a bulky platform of leaves and stems of water plants; usually with ramp at one side; in shallow water, or floating and anchored to vegetation, built either in open water or within emergent vegetation, with no attempt at concealment. Both sexes build, occasionally with help of immatures; building renewed if platform settles or water rises; material also added during incubation. Builds many "false nests", used as resting platforms. Normally 5-7 eggs (3-11), laid at daily intervals; 2 females known to have laid in 1 nest; incubation 18-25 days, by both sexes; hatching asynchronous; downy chick ashy or grey-black, paler below, with golden yellow down on neck, bare skin of crown pink and blue, down of mantle and back with white tips, iris brown, bill red with narrow white subterminal band, legs and feet pale grey-green with pink tinge; chicks precocial; leave nest after 1 day; able to dive soon after hatching, suggesting capability for independent feeding at early age; fed and cared for by both parents, sometimes with help of immatures from earlier brood, particularly when food and nesting habitat abnormally abundant; broods often divided between parents; fledging 55-60 days. In South Africa, 42% of nests produced fledged young. Often only 1 brood, unless conditions very favourable; possibly double-brooded in Morocco.

Movements. Mainly sedentary; also nomadic and opportunistic. Local movements evident from degree of winter flocking, e.g. in Morocco, and from fluctuations in numbers on permanent waters throughout range. Erratic winter wandering beyond normal range reported in past from Morocco and Spain; in 19th century, when range extended to Algeria and Tunisia, wandered in winter to Portugal, S France, Sardinia, Sicily, Italy, and Malta. Flocks in Africa often sedentary on suitable waters but birds may move considerable distances outside breeding season, e.g. up to 1070 km in South Africa. At Barberspan, South Africa, factors influencing fluctuations include rainfall, water level and availability of favourite food; ringing recoveries show mean distance travelled from Barberspan 270 km, 70% recovered within 300 km; longest distances travelled Jan-Apr, when population drops during rainy season. Birds ringed Rondevlei, South Africa, disperse up to 400 km; birds ringed in Ngorongoro Crater, Tanzania, recovered at Eldoret and Naivasha, Kenya. On Kafue Flats, Zambia, present Feb-Oct, most Mar-Jun. Wanders to S Somalia.

Status and Conservation. Not globally threatened. Range has decreased in both Europe and N Africa; now close to extinction in Europe; reasons for decline not clear. Locally common to abundant in sub-Saharan Africa, including Ethiopia, E Africa (L Victoria, L Naivasha and many highland dams and lakes), Zimbabwe, Namibia and Botswana; sometimes up to 27,000 birds at Barberspan and over 30,000 at de Hoop Vlei, South Africa; formerly common on Kafue Flats, Zambia. Uncommon in Angola, occurring mainly on coastal plain, and in Mozambique. In some areas, especially in South Africa and Zimbabwe, has benefited from the proliferation of farm dams and other artificial water bodies, especially as can breed on very small waters.

Bibliography. Benson & Benson (1975), Cramp & Simmons (1980), Dean (1980), Dean & Skead (1979b), Douthwaite (1978), Dowsett & Forbes-Watson (1993), Étchécopar & Hüe (1964), Fernández-Palacios (1994), Fernández-Palacios & Raya (1991), Forsman (1991), Ginn *et al*. (1989), Hockey, Underhill & Neatherway (1989), Jackson & Sclater (1938), Keijl *et al*. (1993), Langrand (1990), Mackworth-Praed & Grant (1957, 1962, 1970), Maclean (1993), Milon *et al*. (1973), Pinto (1983), Sánchez (1992), Short *et al*. (1990), Skead (1980), Snow (1978), Stewart & Bally (1985), Tarboton, Kemp & Kemp (1987), Urban *et al*. (1986), Watson *et al*. (1970), Winterbottom (1966), Wood (1975).

124. **Common Coot**

Fulica atra

French: Foulque macroule **German**: Bläßhuhn **Spanish**: Focha Común
Other common names: (Eurasian/Black) Coot

Taxonomy. *Fulica atra* Linnaeus, 1758, Sweden.
Forms superspecies with *F. cristata*, *F. alai*, *F. americana*, *F. caribaea*, *F. leucoptera* and *F. ardesiaca*. Four subspecies recognized.
Subspecies and Distribution.
F. a. atra Linnaeus, 1758 - Europe, N Africa, Azores and Canaries E through C Asia to Japan and S to Indian Subcontinent and Sri Lanka; winters S to W & NE Africa, SE Asia and Philippines.
F. a. lugubris S. Müller, 1847 - E Java (formerly?) and NW New Guinea.
F. a. novaeguineа Rand, 1940 - C New Guinea.
F. a. australis Gould, 1845 - Australia, Tasmania and New Zealand.

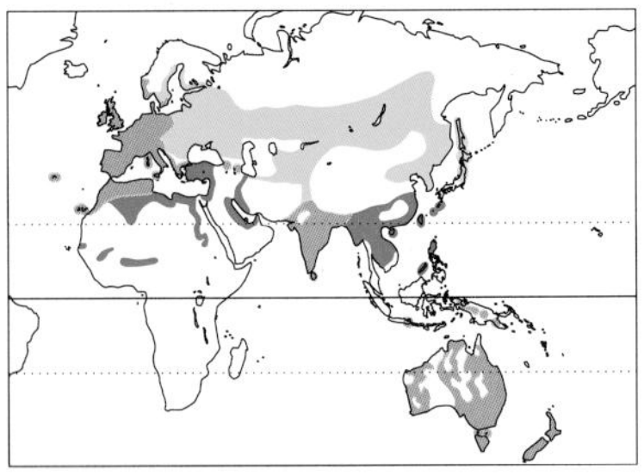

Descriptive notes. 36-39 cm; nominate male 610-1200 (902) g, female 610-1150 (770) g; race *australis* male 481-660 (568) g, female 476-609 (552) g, unsexed 305-725 (511) g; wingspan 70-80 cm in nominate, 56-64 cm in *australis*. Distinguished from *F. cristata* by greater contrast between black head and neck and somewhat paler body, white tips to secondaries (nominate and *lugubris*), lack of red knobs at top of frontal shield, and pointed projection of loral feathering between bill and shield. Differs from *F. americana* in colours of bill, shield, legs and feet, dark undertail-coverts, and less contrast between dark head and paler body. Sexes alike, female averages smaller. Immature like adult but upperparts more washed with olive brown and feathers of throat, cheeks and underparts with broader white tips, giving variably mottled appearance; attains adult bare part colours between autumn and spring. Juvenile has crown, hindneck and upperparts dark brown to dark olive brown, rest of head and neck mixed dark grey and white (whitest on throat), flanks olive brown, breast whitish and belly to vent white with grey suffusion; iris dark grey to pale brown; bill dusky grey, pink towards tip in *australis*; legs and feet grey. Races separated on: amount of white on tips of secondaries, much reduced or absent in *novaeguinea* and *australis*; size, nominate larger than *lugubris*; and underpart colour, darker in *novaeguinea* than *australis*; *novaeguinea* has deeper black head and neck. Voice. Combat call of male a sharp, explosive "pssi", of female a short, croaking "ai"; alarm call of male a sharp variant of combat call, of female a rapid sequence of "ai-oeu" sounds. Typical contact call a single, short "kow", "kowk", "kup", or sharper "kick"; sometimes 2 notes combined, e.g. "kick-kowp"; male also has mechanical "p" or "ta" calls and female a high, short, falsetto "oeu". Calls often metallic, resonant, querulous or explosive, particularly sharp and high when birds agitated. Often noisy.
Habitat. Mainly large, still or slow-moving waters. Inhabits lakes, pools, ponds, reservoirs, barrages, gravel pits, canals, drainage channels, dykes, rivers, creeks, oxbow lakes, open marshes, floodlands and lagoons; also lakes and pools in towns, and salt-pans and clay-pans. Exploits temporary pools and seasonal marshes for breeding. Prefers fairly shallow waters with room to dive and with muddy bottom well furnished with marginal, emergent, floating or submerged vegetation; requires some open water but when breeding not normally far from banks or from emergent or floating vegetation. In winter will resort to quiet estuarine or inshore sea waters, and often occurs on open water of lakes and reservoirs. Avoids small pools and streams; sometimes occurs on fast rivers where suitable vegetation flourishes. Makes little use of cover, either in water or on land. Normally occurs in lowlands, but up to 1000 m in Europe, 2000 m in Tadjikistan and Iran, 2500 m in Kashmir; occurs up to 3500 m in New Guinea, where resident at montane lakes.
Food and Feeding. Omnivorous, but primarily vegetarian. Eats mainly vegetative parts and seeds of aquatic and sometimes terrestrial plants, including algae (*Chara*, *Vaucheria*, *Cladophora*, *Spirogyra*, *Ectocarpus* and *Nostoc*), vegetative parts of *Potamogeton*, *Ruppia*, *Zannichellia*, *Elodea*, *Zostera*, *Vallisnaria*, *Lemna*, *Ceratophyllum*, *Ranunculus*, *Polygonum*, *Myriophyllum*, *Najas*, *Scirpus*, *Typha*, *Phragmites*, *Phalaris*, *Sparganium* and grasses; also seeds of *Ruppia*, *Sparganium*, *Potamogeton*, *Carex*, *Nymphaea*, grasses and cereals. Takes plant debris drifting on water surface. Animal food eaten includes worms, leeches, molluscs, shrimps, adult and larval insects (especially Diptera, Trichoptera, Odonata, Lepidoptera, Coleoptera and Hemiptera), spiders, fish, fish eggs, frogs, birds and their eggs, and small mammals. Takes fish food and duck food. Employs diverse foraging methods (see page 126), including scraping algae from hard substrates, gleaning, dabbling, upending, diving and grazing. Feeds in flocks on land, grazing near water, especially when wind causes high waves. Kleptoparasitizes conspecifics as well as swans and ducks. Large food items are shaken to break them up, or may be chopped up by bill on ground. Diurnal, but often active at night on moonlit nights or on floodlit waters.
Breeding. Europe, Feb-Sept, mostly Mar-Jul; Azerbaijan, Apr-Jun; N Africa, Mar-Jun; Kashmir and N India, May-Sept; S India, Nov-Dec; Australia, mainly Aug-Feb, also other months; New Zealand, Sept-Feb. Gregarious, but monogamous, territorial and pugnacious when breeding. Some birds territorial all year where climate and food availability permit; pair-bonds may sometimes be retained in flocking and migratory populations. Nest almost always in shallow water, normally in emergent vegetation but sometimes in open; normally resting on bottom or trampled foundation of vegetation, occasionally floating; artificial platforms, rafts, tree stumps, tree forks, or islands sometimes used. Receding water level can leave nest some way from water. Nest bulky, of dead and live stems and leaves, sometimes also twigs, bark and roots; external diameter 25-55 cm, height 8-35 cm; cup diameter 16-30 cm, depth 6-13 cm; nest may be built up if water level rises. Both sexes build; brood platforms for family also built by male. Usually 6-10 eggs (1-14), larger clutches may be laid by 2 females; eggs laid daily, sometimes at intervals of 1-2 days; up to 3 replacements laid after egg loss; incubation 21-26 days; by both parents; hatching asynchronous; black downy chick has orange to yellow tips to down of neck and side of head, wings and mantle, and red tips on lores and around shield, iris hazel to grey-brown, bare skin of crown red and blue, bill and shield red, bill white distally and black at tip, legs and feet slate grey; chicks precocial and nidifugous; brooded on nest for 3-4 days; fed and cared for by both parents, which may divide brood temporarily or permanently; older young help feed chicks of later broods; young begin to dive at 3-5 weeks; become self-feeding at 30 days; fledging 55-60 days; fed by parents for up to 2 months; independent at 6-8 weeks; fly at 8-11 weeks; remain in parental territory for up to 14 weeks, possibly helping in territory defence. Age of first breeding 1 year (usually older). May have 2 broods per season.
Movements. Present all year in warm and temperate regions, although not necessarily resident, but mainly migratory in N Eurasia under influence of continental climate. In W Palearctic, N populations winter from North Sea, Baltic, EC Europe, Black and Caspian Seas, Iraq and Arabia S to Senegal, Mali, N Nigeria, S Niger, WC Chad, desert oases in Morocco and S Algeria, and N Sudan (along R Nile). Movement through continental Europe on broad front, W to S, and coastal movement via Baltic brings birds from as far E as Moscow into North Sea area; S movements occur Sept-Nov and return passage Mar-May. Crosses Sahara on broad front, reaching W African wintering areas Nov and departing Mar-Apr. Birds wintering Black and Caspian Seas S to Iraq are presumably from former USSR; movements noted Azerbaijan Sept-Dec and Feb-Apr. Moult migrations occur; little studied but some involve non-breeding adults, while moulting concentrations occur Jun-Sept in Denmark, Bavaria, Bodensee, Black Sea, and probably much more widely. Further E in Asia, N populations winter on Indian Subcontinent, with N passage observed in Afghanistan and Pakistan, Feb-May; also in SE Asia S to Thailand, Cambodia, Vietnam and Philippines (recorded Nov-Mar); and E to S Japan and Ryukyu Is, stragglers reaching Northern Mariana Is. Dispersive in Australia, where large changes in abundance occur, possibly in response to weather conditions and changes in water levels, as birds move to flooded areas, breed and then depart; such patterns may not be seasonal, but seasonal changes occur in some areas; in New Zealand, numbers may fluctuate seasonally. Probably often crosses Bass Strait and Tasman Sea; also crosses other oceans, and recorded occasionally on Norfolk I, Lord Howe I and Macquarie I. Birds seen irregularly in New Guinea lowlands may be vagrants from Australia. Accidental in Alaska, Labrador, Newfoundland, Greenland, Iceland, Spitsbergen and Faeroes.
Status and Conservation. Not globally threatened. Nominate race has expanded range in Europe since late 19th century; marked population fluctuations in many areas due to hard winters, but has probably increased generally, aided by eutrophication, new man-made habitats, and adaptation to urban environments. In 1970's, populations of 40,000-100,000 pairs estimated for several European countries, while Jan counts for NW Europe totalled 438,000-646,000 birds, and European sector of former USSR held over 580,000 pairs in summer and 804,000 birds in winter; area of Mediterranean and Black Seas held 1,035,000-1,296,000 birds in 1969-1971 winters. Has bred in Iceland, but only very sporadically. Declining in Azerbaijan due to hunting and oil pollution. Locally common breeder in N Africa. Formerly abundant in winter, India and Pakistan; present status not clear. Uncommon and local New Guinea; increasing Japan; occurs only rarely in Borneo, Bali and Java; formerly bred in Java but no recent records. Widespread in Australia and New Zealand; locally common in Australia, counts in Victoria in 1991/92 totalling 110,000 and 131,000 birds, with populations stable. Displaced by wetland drainage but rapidly colonizes suitable artificial habitats such as dams, while in arid areas artificial wetlands act as refuges.
Bibliography. Ali & Ripley (1980), Alley & Boyd (1950), Allouche (1988), Anderson (1975), Askaner (1959), Badman (1979), Bakker & Fordham (1993), Beehler *et al.* (1986), Blakers *et al.* (1984), Bopp (1959), Brazil (1991), Brooker *et al.* (1979), Brown & Brown (1980), Chambers (1989), Coates (1985), Collinge (1936), Cramp & Simmons (1980), Czechura (1983), Dementiev & Gladkov (1951b), Dowsett & Forbes-Watson (1993), Étchécopar & Hüe (1964, 1978), Evans (1994), Fjeldså (1973, 1977), Flint *et al.* (1984), Glutz *et al.* (1973), Goodman *et al.* (1989), Halse & Jaensch (1989), Horsfall (1984a, 1984b, 1984c), Hüe & Étchécopar (1970), Hurter (1972), Huxley & Wood (1976), van Impe & Lieckens (1993), Jackson & Lyall (1964), Kochan (1992), Knystautas (1993), Kornowski (1957), Lelek (1958), MacDonald (1966, 1968), MacKinnon & Phillipps (1993), Mackworth-Praed & Grant (1957, 1970), Marchant, J.H. *et al.* (1990), Marchant, S. & Higgins (1993), Martin *et al.* (1979), Patrikeev (1995), Paz (1987), Perennou *et al.* (1994), Phillips (1978), Potapov & Flint (1987), Ripley (1982), Roberts, T.J. (1991), Rogacheva (1992), Rost (1995), Rutgers & Norris (1970), Shirihai (1996), Sigmund (1959), Simeonov *et al.* (1990), Smythies (1986), Snow (1978), Urban *et al.* (1986), Visser (1974), Watson (1955), White & Bruce (1986).

125. Hawaiian Coot
Fulica alai

French: Foulque des Hawaï **German**: Hawaiibläßhuhn **Spanish**: Focha Hawaiana

Taxonomy. *Fulica alai* Peale, 1848, Hawaiian Islands.
Sometimes regarded as a race of *F. americana*. Forms superspecies with *F. cristata*, *F. atra*, *F. americana*, *F. caribaea*, *F. leucoptera* and *F. ardesiaca*. Monotypic.
Distribution. Hawaiian Is.

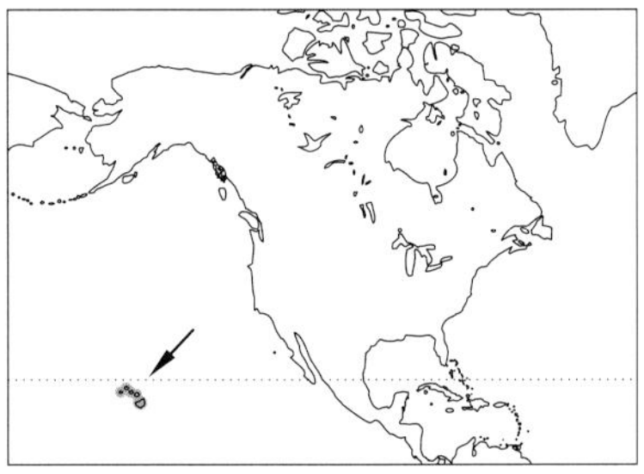

Descriptive notes. 39 cm. Differs from *F. americana* in shorter wing, pale grey or bluish legs and feet, and more swollen frontal shield which extends back to crown; bill and shield white in most birds, but colour varies from bluish white to yellow to dark blood red; in c. 15% of birds shield is red and bill has broken, reddish brown to black, subterminal ring (as in *F. americana*); white undertail-coverts often not visible in swimming birds; leading edge of wing white at bend, but outermost primary has no white. Sexes alike. Immature has white throat and breast, dark bill and small frontal shield. Voice. Chicken-like "keck-keck" calls and other clucks and creaks.
Habitat. All types of wetland, including fresh and saltwater ponds, estuaries and marshes, irrigation ditches and flooded agricultural lands.
Food and Feeding. Limited information available. Mainly vegetarian; food apparently similar to that of *F. americana*.
Breeding. Breeds throughout year, mostly Apr-Aug. Monogamous; territorial when breeding. Nest floating, usually built among robust emergent aquatic vegetation near open water and anchored to surrounding vegetation; sometimes in open water, anchored to dense algal mats, or on mats of *Bacopa* or *Paspalum*; twice recorded nesting on islands, near water. Nest platform substantial, made from buoyant stems of nearby emergent plants, particularly *Scirpus*; broader base of nests built in open water probably serves to improve stability and reduce effects of wave action. Average nesting density 1·6-12·5 nests/ha. Eggs 1-10 (mean 4·9), laid at daily intervals; replacements laid after clutch loss; incubation 23-27 days, by both parents; hatching asynchronous; black downy chick has reddish orange bristles on head; chicks precocial; details of care and development presumably similar to those for *F. americana*. Nesting success high (over 90%); hatching success averages 80%; chick mortality high. 2 broods per year occasional.
Movements. No information; apparently wanders between islands.
Status and Conservation. VULNERABLE. Resident on all main Hawaiian Is from Niihau eastward, except Lanai, with stragglers reaching as far W as Kure Atoll in NW Hawaiian Is. Suitable water bodies are scattered and very limited in area, and species has suffered from wetland destruction as result of drainage for cultivation and other development. Also, herbicides used to clear canals and drainage ditches serving sugar cane plantations may have poisoned coots directly or indirectly. When nesting, species also vulnerable to introduced predators such as dogs, cats and mongooses. Population probably fluctuates between 2000 and 4000 birds, 80% of which probably occur on Kauai, Oahu and Maui. Hunting prohibited in 1939 and species is fully protected. Management recommendations include: habitat management to promote optimum conditions, i.e. 50:50 ratio of open water and sparse emergent cover, and water depth of c. 30 cm; a better study of seasonality of breeding; more detailed studies of food requirements and breeding success; and a study of local movements.
Bibliography. Berger (1972), Byrd *et al.* (1985), Collar *et al.* (1994), Engilis & Pratt (1993), King (1978/79), Munro (1960), Pratt (1987, 1993), Pratt *et al.* (1987), Schwartz & Schwartz (1952), Stephens (1974), Udvardy (1960).

126. American Coot

Fulica americana

French: Foulque d'Amérique   **German**: Amerikanisches Bläßhuhn   **Spanish**: Focha Americana

Taxonomy. *Fulica americana* Gmelin, 1789, North America.
Sometimes considered to include *F. alai*, *F. caribaea* and *F. ardesiaca* as races; forms superspecies with these, and with *F. cristata*, *F. atra* and *F. leucoptera*. Proposed race *grenadensis* included in nominate. Two subspecies recognized.
Subspecies and Distribution.
F. a. americana Gmelin, 1789 - SE Alaska E to Nova Scotia, and S to West Indies, Nicaragua and Costa Rica; winters to W to Hawaii and S to Panama.
F. a. columbiana Chapman, 1914 - Colombia and N Ecuador.

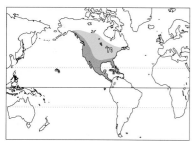

Descriptive notes. 34-43 cm; male 576-848 (742) g, female 427-628 (560) g; wingspan 60-70 cm. Differs from American congeners in having white bill with broken subterminal chestnut or maroon ring, rather small white frontal shield with dark chestnut or red-brown horny callus at top (in breeding birds sometimes covering entire shield), yellow to orange legs and feet, red tibiae and pale blue-grey toe lobes. Differs from *F. atra* in white undertail-coverts, and greater contrast between blackish head and breast and paler mantle and flanks; secondaries have small white tips. Sexes alike, but female smaller. Immature similar to adult; legs and feet become green, and tibiae red, by spring; tarsal colour then progresses through yellow-green and yellow to become orange-red after 4 years. Juvenile dark olive-brown on crown and upperparts, pale ash grey on sides of head and body, flanks and underparts; bill and shield uniform ivory-grey with small, pale red callus, most birds attaining adult colours at c. 4 months; legs and feet blue-grey or grey-green. Race *columbiana* has longer tarsus and toes, heavier and longer bill with yellow base, larger, higher, more rounded frontal shield, darker plumage (especially on underparts) and less white on underwing-coverts and tips of secondaries. Voice. Loquacious; has variety of cackling and clucking notes, often repeated. Alarm call of male "puhlk" and of female "poonk"; under stress male also gives plaintive, crowing "puhk-cowah" or "pow-ur" and female a simpler "cooah"; aggressive male gives explosive "hic".
Habitat. Reed-fringed lakes and ponds, open marshes and sluggish rivers; also estuaries and bays. Nominate race has maximum nesting densities on well flooded, semi-permanent and persistent wetlands with good interspersion of emergent vegetation and open water; nests usually found where foundations (e.g. mats of algae) are available; uses seasonal wetlands when water levels high. Race *columbianus* has peak abundance in areas with mosaics of low *Bidens* and *Limnobium*, and open water with much submerged vegetation outside fringing reeds. Prefers fresh water but sometimes forced in winter to shift temporarily to salt water and salt-marshes on sheltered coasts or estuaries; in winter uses man-made wetlands including brackish impoundments, crayfish and catfish ponds, and coal mine sediment ponds; *Hydrilla* cover may be an important component of wintering habitat in S USA. Occupies similar niche in Nearctic to that of *F. atra* in W Palearctic. In Colombia occurs up to 1000 m and in E Andes at 2100-3250 m.
Food and Feeding. Principally aquatic vegetation, mostly submerged plants, especially *Chara* and other algae, *Potamogeton*, *Lemna*, *Myriophyllum* and *Scirpus*, but also grass, sprouting grain and waste grain. Also takes aquatic insects and molluscs (especially Trichoptera and Diptera larvae, Coleoptera and Gastropoda), more frequently during breeding season; aquatic invertebrates may constitute large proportion of diet of young chicks. Feeds from surface, immerses head and neck, dives in shallow water; sometimes upends; also grazes on land or floating matted vegetation; sometimes scavenges. Sometimes feeds in association with Canvasbacks (*Aythya valisineria*), taking rootstocks of *Potamogeton* disturbed by the diving ducks; associations with other waterfowl species also recorded. Kleptoparasitism by some duck species on coots also recorded (see page 127).
Breeding. North America, Apr-Jul (peak Apr-May), winter breeding reported in Florida; Colombia, laying peaks Jun-Jul but also lays Sept, building reported Mar; usually begins nesting within 10-14 days of arrival on breeding grounds. Gregarious, but monogamous, territorial and pugnacious when breeding; both sexes assist in territory defence. Nest a large floating pile of aquatic vegetation, usually in, and anchored to, residual emergent vegetation, preferably of *Typha* or *Scirpus* although *Carex*, *Scholochloa* or *Salix* sometimes used; nests late in season sometimes in new-growth emergents; nest usually built within 1-5 m of open water, sometimes in open, and resting on mass of old matted reeds. Both sexes build. Eggs 6-15 (3-5 in *columbiana*), laid at daily intervals; some females are intraspecific brood parasites, laying eggs in other nests before producing their own clutches; incubation by both sexes, 22-27 days, starting with 3rd-6th egg; hatching asynchronous; black downy chick greyer on underside, with blue and orange to red skin on top of head, dense yellow to red bristles round neck and red bill shading to pink distally and with black to whitish tip; chicks precocial, leave nest soon after hatching; return to nest or brood platforms for frequent brooding; cared for by both parents; fed for first 2 weeks; gradually become independent over next 3-10 weeks; juvenile plumage acquired from c. 3 weeks of age; fledging 60-70 days. Nest parasitism by Ruddy Duck (*Oxyura jamaicensis*) occurs rarely. Age of first breeding 1 year; breeding performance increases with age, especially between 1 and 2 years of age. Nest success usually over 80%; hatching success 80-100%; renesting may occur up to 4 times after clutch or brood loss. Two sequential broods occasionally raised in S parts of breeding range; elsewhere, 2nd clutch may be laid while 1st still being incubated.
Movements. Mainly migratory, especially in North America E of Rocky Mts. Many apparently migrate to larger N wetlands for post-breeding moult. Winters in Pacific and Atlantic coastal states N to British Columbia and Maryland; most winter in S USA and Mexico. Birds ringed in Alberta winter mainly in California and W Mexico; those from Saskatchewan and Manitoba mainly E Mexico to Louisiana, some reaching Caribbean islands. All populations mix in Gulf states in winter. Birds nesting more to S move furthest S in winter, e.g. 32% of recoveries of those ringed in Iowa found in Cuba. Winters throughout Central America S to Panama and possibly Colombia; small numbers reach larger Hawaiian islands in winter. Migrates at night, singly or in loose flocks, probably on broad front; birds often hit powerlines. Males and non-breeders congregate in late summer and move S ahead of females and juveniles. Autumn passage late Aug to Dec; peaks in Mississippi flyway late Oct; wintering birds present Louisiana and Mexico Oct-Mar, Costa Rica Oct-Apr, and Panama Oct to late Apr. Spring migration occurs late Feb through to mid-May; males and older birds migrate first; birds arrive on N breeding grounds from late Mar. Many cases of birds wandering N of breeding range in summer and autumn, as far as Newfoundland, Labrador, Franklin and S Greenland; vagrant to Iceland. Numbers increase in Colombia Oct-Apr, but origins of birds involved not clear.

Status and Conservation. Not globally threatened. In North America considered abundant and is a game species; annual harvest over last 3-4 decades averaged c. 8000 birds in Canada and 880,000 in USA, and has declined in recent years in both countries. North American populations have increased since breeding-ground surveys began in 1950's, although reliability of estimates unknown. Major population management requirements include: evaluation of breeding-ground and wintering-ground surveys; establishment of surveys in Mexico; updated estimates of survival and recovery rates; and assessment of possible bias in harvest surveys. Traditionally, wetland habitats have not been managed for coots but the birds appear to benefit from many waterfowl management activities; however, wetland loss has reduced potential breeding population in areas such as Iowa and Minnesota. Species's ability to pioneer new habitats enables it to take advantage of wetland restoration efforts. Sometimes regarded as an urban and agricultural pest in winter, e.g. on golf courses and in rice fields. Locally common in Panama in winter. Race *columbiana* is locally common in Colombia.
Bibliography. Alisauskas (1987), Alisauskas & Arnold (1994), Anderson, M.G. (1974), Arnold (1989, 1990, 1992, 1993), Bent (1926), Bergan & Smith (1986), Bergman (1973), Biaggi (1983), Blake (1977), Briggs (1989), Burger (1973a), Burton (1959), Cosens (1981), Cramp & Simmons (1980), Crawford, R.D. (1978, 1980), Desroschers & Ankney (1986), Driver (1988), Eddleman (1983), Eddleman & Knopf (1985), Eddleman, Knopf, Meanley *et al.* (1988), Eddleman, Knopf & Patterson (1985), Fjeldså (1983c), Fjeldså & Krabbe (1990), Fredrickson (1970, 1977), Godfrey (1986), Gorenzel *et al.* (1981a, 1981b, 1982), Gullion (1952, 1953a, 1953b, 1954), Harrison (1978), Hellmayr & Conover (1942), Hill, W.L. (1986, 1988), Hilty & Brown (1986), Howell & Webb (1995a), Jones (1940), Kiel (1955), Lang (1991), Lyon (1991), Monroe (1968), Nudds (1981), Paton *et al.* (1985), Paullin (1987), Pratt (1987), Ridgely (1981), Ridgely & Gwynne (1989), Roberson & Baptista (1988), Root (1988), Ryan (1981), Ryan & Dinsmore (1979, 1980), Ryder (1963), Slud (1964), Stiles & Skutch (1989), Sugden (1979), Sutherland (1991), Sutherland & Maher (1987), Varty *et al.* (1986), Weller & Fredrickson (1974), Wetmore (1965), White & James (1978), Woolfenden (1979).

127. Caribbean Coot

Fulica caribaea

French: Foulque à cachet blanc   **German**: Karibenbläßhuhn   **Spanish**: Focha Caribeña

Taxonomy. *Fulica caribæa* Ridgway, 1884, St John, Virgin Islands.
Sometimes regarded as conspecific with *F. americana*. Forms superspecies with *F. cristata*, *F. atra*, *F. alai*, *F. americana*, *F. leucoptera* and *F. ardesiaca*. Monotypic.
Distribution. S Bahamas (N Caicos) through Greater Antilles (except I of Pines) and Lesser Antilles (S to Grenada and Barbados) to Trinidad, Curaçao and NW Venezuela. Records of birds from North American localities all refer to *F. americana*.

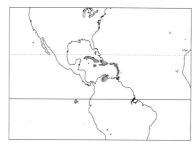

Descriptive notes. 33-38 cm. Differs from *F. americana* in having frontal shield entirely white, sometimes tinged yellow, broader, oval or elliptical; bill entirely white or with reddish brown spot near tip of both mandibles; extent of white on outer web of outermost primary and tips of secondaries very variable in both species and apparently not a distinguishing character. Undertail-coverts white; legs and feet dull olive to yellowish. Sexes alike, but female averages smaller. Immature and juvenile presumably similar to those of *F. americana*. Voice. Similar to that of *F. americana*: a variety of cackling and clucking notes.
Habitat. Freshwater lakes, ponds and marshes; also less frequently in coastal brackish lagoons. Lowlands, up to 500 m in Venezuela.
Food and Feeding. No information: presumably similar to *F. americana*.
Breeding. Poorly known; details presumably similar to *F. americana*. Virgin Is, May-Jun and Sept-Oct; season elsewhere not recorded. Eggs 4-7.
Movements. None recorded.
Status and Conservation. Not globally threatened. Formerly regarded as locally uncommon to rare throughout range; current status not clear. Much research required.
Bibliography. Anon. (1983a), Benito-Espinal & Hautcastel (1988), Biaggi (1983), Blake (1977), Bond (1985), Clark (1985), Herklots (1961), Kautesk (1985), Meyer de Schauensee (1982), Meyer de Schauensee & Phelps (1978), Raffaele (1989), Ripley (1977), Ripley & Beehler (1985), Roberson & Baptista (1988), Stockton (1978), Sykes (1975).

128. White-winged Coot

Fulica leucoptera

French: Foulque leucoptère   **German**: Weißflügel-Bläßhuhn   **Spanish**: Focha Aliblanca

Taxonomy. *Fulica leucoptera* Vieillot, 1817, Paraguay.
Forms superspecies with *F. cristata*, *F. atra*, *F. alai*, *F. americana*, *F. caribaea* and *F. ardesiaca*. Monotypic.
Distribution. Chile, E & SE Bolivia, Paraguay and extreme SE Brazil S through Argentina to Tierra del Fuego.

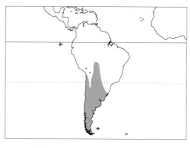

Descriptive notes. 35-43 cm; 5 females 400-500 and 607 g. Darker than *F. americana* on body; distinguished from congeners by yellow to greenish yellow bill, occasionally with a dark spot near tip, and small pale yellow to orange-yellow shield, rounded at top giving round-headed appearance; legs and feet pale sea green to yellow-green, with grey to blackish toes and joints. Some birds have predominantly bluish pink or pinkish grey bill, others have pink to light reddish shield; colour variations in Brazilian birds could be age-related. White undertail-coverts very conspicuous as bird swims away with raised tail; white line formed by broad white tips to secondaries conspicuous in flight. Sexes alike. Immature has grey-brown upperparts and paler underparts, whitish from chin to breast; brown iris, dusky olivaceous bill, greenish grey legs and feet. Juvenile dark drab grey, with white head and neck mottled dusky. Voice. Vocal, with variety of loud, hollow cackling calls and clucking notes; some calls resemble peals of laughter. Aggressive male has explosive "huc" note.

Habitat. Freshwater lagoons, river backwaters, ponds and marshes; prefers grassy or vegetation-free shores, waters with many submerged plants, or *Lemna* duckweed-covered waters. Upland breeding sites usually barren, with no fringing reeds but with much floating *Myriophyllum*. Occasionally occurs on sea, close to shore. Sometimes occurs alongside *F. armillata*.
Food and Feeding. Eats mostly aquatic weeds. Chiefly a surface feeder, but dives occasionally; pecks at surface and upends frequently. Also grazes on land some distance from marsh edges. Sometimes pulls seeds from bent-over grass-heads. Gregarious; normally seen in large flocks.
Breeding. Lowlands of C Argentina, mainly Apr-Nov; uplands, Nov-Jan; season very prolonged in Rio Grande do Sul, Brazil, where species nests throughout spring and summer. Monogamous; territorial when breeding. Nest a floating platform of rushes, green grass or other aquatic plants, often among emergent vegetation but also floating offshore on beds of aquatic plants; slight canopy sometimes built over nest. May nest alongside *F. armillata*. Eggs 10-12 (3 also recorded); black downy chick has partly naked pink and blue crown, orange tips to down of head and dense yellow bristles around neck, blood red bill with black tip, and greenish brown legs and feet; both parents feed young. No other information available.
Movements. Present all year in Rio Grande do Sul but makes considerable local movements, with most or all birds absent from some breeding areas in autumn or winter.
Status and Conservation. Not globally threatened. Formerly regarded as widespread, and common to locally abundant; recorded in flocks of thousands on large marshy lagoons of Argentine *pampas*. At present reckoned to be generally common.
Bibliography. Belton (1984), Blake (1977), Canevari *et al.* (1991), Clark (1986), Contreras *et al.* (1990), Fjeldså (1983a), Fjeldså & Krabbe (1990), Friedmann (1927), Hayes (1995), Heimsath *et al.* (1993), Hellmayr & Conover (1942), Johnson (1965b), Klimaitis & Moschione (1987), Meyer de Schauensee (1982), Mosso & Beltzer (1993), Narosky & Yzurieta (1987), Olrog (1984), de la Peña (1992), Pinto (1964), Remsen & Traylor (1989), Remsen *et al.* (1985), Sick (1985c, 1993), Weller (1967), Woods (1988).

129. Andean Coot
Fulica ardesiaca

French: Foulque ardoisée **German**: Andenbläßhuhn **Spanish**: Focha Andina
Other common names: Slate-coloured Coot

Taxonomy. *Fulica ardesiaca* Tschudi, 1843, Lake Junín, Peru.
Chestnut- and white-fronted birds formerly treated as separate species, *F. americana peruviana* and *F. ardesiaca*, and later lumped as *F. americana ardesiaca*. Forms superspecies with *F. cristata*, *F. atra*, *F. alai*, *F. americana*, *F. caribaea* and *F. leucoptera*. Two subspecies recognized.
Subspecies and Distribution.
F. a. atrura Fjeldså, 1983 - S Colombia, Ecuador and coastal Peru.
F. a. ardesiaca Tschudi, 1843 - interior Peru, C & W Bolivia, N Chile and NW Argentina.

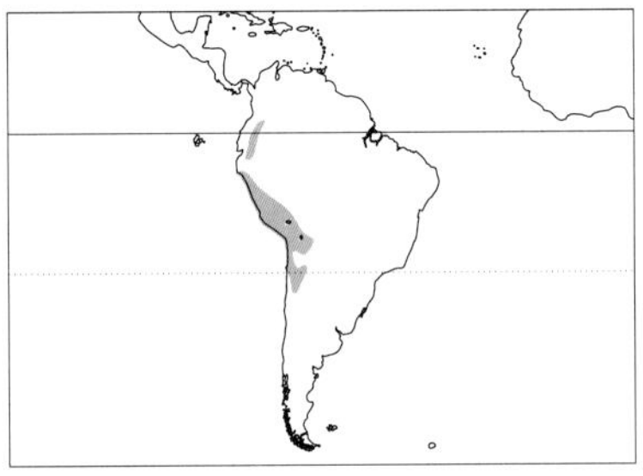

Descriptive notes. 40-43 cm. Stocky coot with large, rounded frontal shield giving round head shape; secondaries usually have white tips; undertail-coverts white to almost black; iris red to reddish yellow. Two colour morphs: red-fronted, with more solid, deep chestnut frontal shield, chrome yellow bill becoming pale yellow to green (sometimes white) near tip, and green legs and feet; and pale-fronted, with white bill, white or orange-yellow frontal shield, and slaty legs and feet. Other variants also exist: bill may be flesh-coloured, shield variably pale to primrose yellow, and legs and feet sometimes grey or lavender. Smaller than *F. armillata*; larger than *F. americana* with sometimes paler slate-coloured body plumage contrasting more with blackish head and neck. Sexes alike. Immature not described. Juvenile dark drab grey with paler underparts and mainly white face; iris dark brown; bill dark greyish horn with paler tip; legs and feet greyish horn with darker joints. Races separated on colour of undertail-coverts: all white in nominate, and with black inner webs to almost completely black in *atrura*. Voice. Usual call a low "churr" or harder "hrrp", often repeated. Females give low chitter.
Habitat. Ponds, lakes, rivers and marshes. Mostly in fairly large lakes with extensive shallows having dense submerged vegetation, fringed by reeds, but also breeds in barren lakes lacking reeds. Except furthest S, there is a tendency for red-fronted birds to dominate in well vegetated lakes and white-fronted birds to dominate in barren high altitude lakes with *Chara* as principal submerged plant. Nominate race occurs from 2100 to 4700 m; *atrura* occurring in coastal Peru and tablelands of Ecuador and Colombia, found at 2200-3600 m in Colombia.
Food and Feeding. Mainly aquatic vegetation, especially *Chara*, but also *Myriophyllum* and *Elodea*. Feeds in areas of shallow water with dense submerged or floating vegetation; generally gregarious and sometimes in mixed flocks. Dives for food at depths of 2-5 m; also feeds by walking on floating vegetation and on beaches.
Breeding. Poorly known; breeding behaviour apparently close to that of *F. americana*. Colombia, Feb; N Chile, Nov-Jan; Peru, Apr and Jun-Nov; Bolivia, adults feeding small chicks, Aug; laying peaks in dry season (Jul-Aug) but may nest in any season. Generally gregarious; monogamous, territorial and pugnacious when breeding. Mixed pairs of red-fronted and white-fronted birds often occur but there may be a tendency for assortative mating. Nest placed among reeds, or open to view in floating water weeds. Clutch size most frequently 4-5; black downy chick has red and blue skin on crown, short orange bristles on throat, and red bill with dark subterminal bar and orange tip. Second clutches likely to occur, as juveniles seen feeding downy chicks.
Movements. Seasonal population movements occur, not properly described.
Status and Conservation. Not globally threatened. No precise data available, but species is locally common to abundant, sometimes assembling in thousands.
Bibliography. Blake (1977), Canevari *et al.* (1991), Fjeldså (1982, 1983a, 1983c), Fjeldså & Krabbe (1990), Gill (1964), Harris (1981), Hellmayr & Conover (1942), Hilty & Brown (1986), Hughes (1980), Johnson (1965b, 1972), Koepcke (1970), Meyer de Schauensee (1982), Morrison (1939a, 1939b), Olrog (1984), Parker *et al.* (1982), de la Peña (1992), Remsen & Traylor (1989), Rocha & Peñaranda (1995).

130. Red-gartered Coot
Fulica armillata

French: Foulque à jarretières **German**: Gelbschnabel-Bläßhuhn **Spanish**: Focha de Ligas

Taxonomy. *Fulica armillata* Vieillot, 1817, Paraguay.
Monotypic.
Distribution. C & S Chile, and SE Brazil and Uruguay S through Argentina to Tierra del Fuego; possibly also Paraguay and Falkland Is.

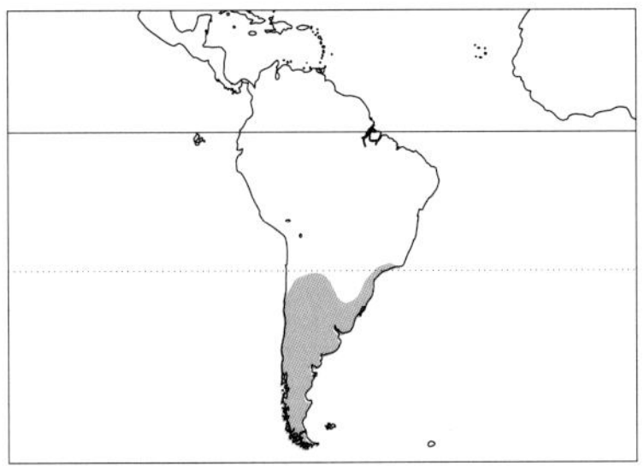

Descriptive notes. 43-51 cm. Large coot, with white undertail-coverts and no white on secondaries; pointed frontal shield, giving somewhat angular profile, and distinct red mark along base of culmen, separating yellow of bill and shield. Colours of bill and shield may vary: shield may be paler yellow than bill; bill sometimes reddish. Legs and feet orange-yellow to yellow, with pale red "garter" above ankle joint; iris usually reddish but can be yellow. Sexes alike. Immature has horn-coloured bill but soon acquires yellow shield; legs and feet olive; in second or third year birds have duller, more olive, legs and feet than adult. Juvenile dull drab grey-brown with white head and neck, mottled dusky from crown to hindneck. Voice. Alarm call of male a short, whistled "huit"; also an explosive "pit" and repeated "wuw" of aggression; repeated soft "cuit" when near female. Female has "yec" of alarm and loud, repeated "terr".
Habitat. Lakes, large ponds, rivers, marshes and deep, clear roadside ditches; rarely seen on small pools but occasionally feeds in protected waters associated with lakes. Sometimes occurs alongside *F. leucoptera* and *F. rufifrons*. On Patagonian uplands breeds mainly on exposed shallow lakes with extensive carpets of floating *Myriophyllum*. Occurs mainly in lowlands, but ascends to 1200 m on barren plateaux of inland Patagonia, up to 1000 m on lakes of S Andes, and breeds at 2100 m in L Volcán, Jujuy (NW Argentina). In winter, can form large agglomerations on sheltered marine bays.
Food and Feeding. Eats primarily aquatic plants. A skilled diver, obtaining most of food in open, fairly deep water; also upends. Occasionally raids water weeds pulled about by Rosy-billed Pochards (*Netta peposaca*) and Black-headed Ducks (*Heteronetta atricapilla*).
Breeding. Chile, Oct-Nov with replacement clutches until Jan; Brazil, Nov, large young Feb; Argentina, two peaks, mid-Sept and mid-Oct (latter possibly due to renesting). Normally gregarious, but monogamous, strongly territorial and pugnacious when breeding. Nest a loosely built platform of dried rushes with rim built up; usually in tules of moderate density near open water; sometimes floating; nest area usually free of floating vegetation. May nest alongside *F. leucoptera*. Eggs 2-8 (mean 5·3); after chicks hatch, nest built up to serve as brood site, or brood nests or platforms often constructed; black downy chick has partly naked pink and blue crown, small orange bristles on throat, black bill with orange band and red shield; young fed by both parents; able do dive quite early in life. Replacement clutches laid after egg loss. Nest parasitism by *Heteronetta atricapilla* recorded once.
Movements. Apparently normally sedentary; in Rio Grande do Sul present all year but given to considerable movement and local concentration; has strayed to Tristan da Cunha.
Status and Conservation. Not globally threatened. Formerly regarded as abundant, and still regarded as common, but very few data available. Concentration of c. 10,400 birds counted in coastal inlet at Puerto Natales, Aug 1992, in company of small numbers of *F. leucoptera*. No recent record from Paraguay.
Bibliography. Belton (1984), Blake (1977), Canevari *et al.* (1991), Clark (1986), Contreras *et al.* (1990), Fjeldså & Krabbe (1990), Forrester (1993), Heimsath *et al.* (1993), Hellmayr & Conover (1942), Johnson (1965b), Klimaitis & Moschione (1987), Meyer de Schauensee (1982), Narosky & Yzurieta (1987), Navas (1956, 1960, 1970), Olrog (1984), de la Peña (1992), Pinto (1964), Sick (1985c, 1993), Weller (1967), Woods (1988).

131. Red-fronted Coot
Fulica rufifrons

French: Foulque à front rouge **German**: Rotstirn-Bläßhuhn **Spanish**: Focha Frentirroja

Taxonomy. *Tulica* [sic] *rufifrons* Philippi and Landbeck, 1861, Chile.
Monotypic.
Distribution. Coastal S Peru; extreme SE Brazil; coastal C Chile E to S Paraguay, NE Argentina and Uruguay, and S to N Tierra del Fuego; also Falkland Is (formerly?). Erroneous records from N Argentina based on confusion with *F. armillata*.

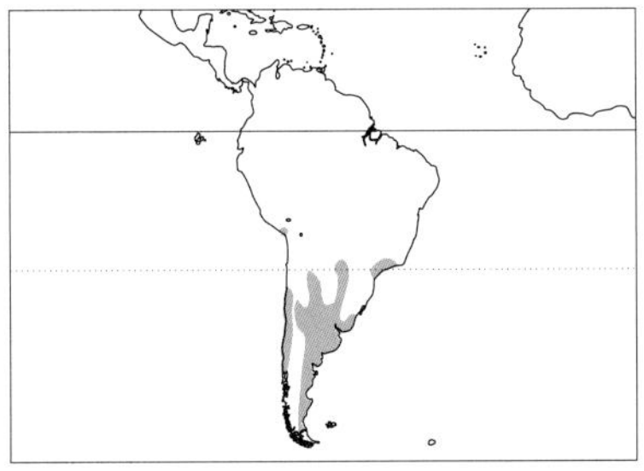

Descriptive notes. 38-43 cm; 1 male 685 g, 1 female 550 g. Unlike other coots, lacks greatly enlarged lobes on feet. Dark slate grey, blacker on head and neck; prominent white undertail-coverts form inverted heart shape; characteristic profile with almost straight line from bill tip to knob-like top of elongated frontal shield; bill yellow, ridge and frontal shield dark chestnut-red; legs and feet olive. Sexes alike. Juvenile rather uniform grey-brown, with diagnostic pointed shield and white undertail-coverts (inverted heart-shaped); some white spots on throat; bill blackish. Voice. A long, chattering series of calls, described as "togo togo togo..., cu cu cu..., puhúh puhúh puhúh...", etc. Alarm note "tuc".
Habitat. Semi-open marshes and reedy lakes, especially with much floating duckweed and water-ferns and often with very shallow water; usually found among vegetation, rarely venturing far from cover. Inhabits lowlands up to 800 m; casual up to 2100 m in NW Argentina.
Food and Feeding. Primarily a surface feeder, pecking at *Azolla* and duckweed mats, but also dives skilfully and grazes in upland areas adjacent to water when marshes dry up seasonally. Generally in loose flocks, sometimes with *F. armillata*.
Breeding. In Chile lays Sept-Oct; Argentina, May-Nov; Peru, Sept-Jan. Monogamous. Nest of plant material; rather small for the genus; generally well hidden and low in water; species very adaptable in nest-site selection. Eggs 2-9 (mean 5·6); late clutches smaller than early ones; downy chick black, crown partly naked pink and blue, throat with some broad, flat, orange bristles, bill red with 2-3 black bands; after chicks hatch, nest often relined with more delicate material, and serves as brood platform for at least 4 days. Nest success high (83%) at Cape San Antonio, E Argentina, and second broods common, but deserted readily, mostly as result of human intrusion, even when clutch well incubated. Present species is apparently main host of parasitic Black-headed Duck (*Heteronetta atricapilla*); few desertions associated with parasitism.
Movements. No regular movements recorded, but records of casual birds and occasional influxes indicate some wandering or dispersal. Apparently a migrant at São Paulo, Brazil; at Cape San Antonio,

Argentina, most birds left during winter when marshes dried up, the birds remaining being mostly immatures.

Status and Conservation. Not globally threatened. Not uncommon over most of range, and abundant in *pampas* marshes, but scarce in Rio Grande do Sul. Population apparently stable. Not recorded in Falkland Is since 1924, where may perhaps never have been more than vagrant.

Bibliography. Belton (1984), Blake (1977), Canevari *et al.* (1991), Clark (1986), Contreras *et al.* (1990), Fjeldså & Krabbe (1990), Friedmann (1927), Hayes (1995), Hellmayr & Conover (1942), Johnson (1965b), Klimaitis & Moschione (1987), Meyer de Schauensee (1982), Narosky & Yzurieta (1987), Navas (1956), Olrog (1984), Parker *et al.* (1982), de la Peña (1992), Pinto (1964), Pulido (1991), Tallman *et al.* (1978), Sick (1985c, 1993), Weller (1967), Woods (1988).

132. **Giant Coot**
Fulica gigantea

French: Foulque géante   **German**: Riesenbläßhuhn   **Spanish**: Focha Gigante

Taxonomy. *Fulcia* [sic] *gigantea* Eydoux and Souleyet, 1841, Peru.
Monotypic.
Distribution. S Peru through W Bolivia to N Chile and NW Argentina.

Descriptive notes. 48-59 cm; c. 2000-2500 g. Adult deep slaty, inclining to black on head and neck; variable white streaking on lateral undertail-coverts; very heavy-bodied with relatively small head, concave forehead and high knobs formed by enlarged orbital rims; also distinguished from all other coots by deep red legs and feet; bill deep red, ridge white, sides and shield yellow. Sexes alike. Adult normally too heavy to fly but immature smaller, not much larger than *F. ardesiaca*, and can fly readily. Immature has dark grey breast and belly, duller bill and pale greyish red legs and feet. Juvenile dull dark grey, foreneck and side of head below eye white, bare parts dusky. VOICE. Male gives alternating gobbling or laughing "houehouhouhouhoou" and low, growling "hrr" or "horr" sounds; sometimes utters only growls. Female has low, crackling "chee-jrrrh", low squeaking or cracking sounds sometimes becoming a soft chittering, and soft "hi-hirr hirrr hirrr..." when with male.

Habitat. Ponds and lakes in barren highlands of Andean *puna* zone; most numerous on lakes with extensive weedy shallows. Occurs on lakes with emergent vegetation but always stays outside cover. Probably requires wide shallows with abundant weeds for nesting, thus restricting the number of good breeding sites. Occurs chiefly at 3600-5000 m, but up to 6540 m.

Food and Feeding. Vegetarian: takes much aquatic vegetation, especially *Myriophyllum*, *Potamogeton*, *Zanichellia*, *Ruppia*; also some filamentous algae; feeds on grass on shore; unlike sympatric *F. ardesiaca* does not eat *Chara*. Feeds from surface of water with sideways throwing movement; occasionally upends like dabbling duck; also dives occasionally.

Breeding. Breeds at any season but laying peaks in local winter, Jun-Jul, often with second clutch Nov-Feb. Monogamous and permanently territorial. Nest enormous, of aquatic vegetation, forming raft up to 3 m long and projecting 50 cm above water. Nest has high rim and deep cup; maintained and enlarged over several years, the original structure having compacted into peat in centre; pairs probably hold same platform for life. Nests in water c. 1 m deep with dense water weeds rising to surface, sometimes on miry clay; small new nests usually float but large old ones rest on bottom. Both adults build; fresh weed constantly added to rim while young on raft. Eggs 3-7 (mean 4·4); both parents incubate; downy chick c. 40 g at hatching, sooty black, browner on underparts with few orange bristles on throat, pink skin of crown hardly visible, bill pink with yellow tip and magenta base separated by black bands; young fed until 2 months old; in captive juvenile, plumage complete after 67 days, fully fledged at 4 months, post-juvenile moult occurred some time later. Because of frequent strong, cold winds, chicks spend much time in nest, feeding on fresh nest material from rim. Adults often feed chicks in nest, offering weed fragments and invertebrates such as amphipods; captive young ate plants (*Elodea*, *Oxalis*), small fish, tadpoles and a small frog; immatures from previous broods often feed young. Many eggs taken by people at some sites, but survival of young high: pre-fledging mortality estimated at 36%.

Movements. Immatures disperse widely by flying at night but adults normally attached to territory and nest for life; when small breeding ponds freeze, may walk to larger ice-free lakes. Although normally confined to high altitudes, straggles to lower elevations, occasionally to Pacific coast.

Status and Conservation. Not globally threatened. Scarce through most of range, but large populations exist in some areas, including c. 12,000 in Lauca National Park, N Chile. Populations seem to have exploded in Chile and Peru, as consequence of control on use of fire-arms.

Bibliography. Blake (1977), Canevari *et al.* (1991), Chebez (1994), Fjeldså (1981), Fjeldså & Krabbe (1990), Harris (1981), Hellmayr & Conover (1942), Hughes (1980), Johnson (1964c, 1965b), Koepcke (1970), McFarlane (1975), Meyer de Schauensee (1982), Narosky & Yzurieta (1987), Olrog (1984), Parker *et al.* (1982), de la Peña (1992), Pulido (1991), Remsen & Traylor (1989), Roe & Rees (1979).

133. **Horned Coot**
Fulica cornuta

French: Foulque cornue   **German**: Rüsselbläßhuhn   **Spanish**: Focha Cornuda

Taxonomy. *Fulica cornuta* Bonaparte, 1853, Potosí, Bolivia.
Monotypic.
Distribution. N Chile, SW Bolivia and NW Argentina.

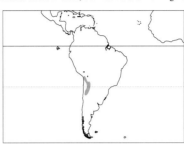

Descriptive notes. 46-53 cm; 1 male 2100 g, 2 females 1600 and 1900 g, 2 juveniles 1360 and 1500 g. Adult slate grey, darkest on head and neck; undertail-coverts black with two white stripes; bill greenish yellow with dull orange base and black ridge; long, extensible and erectile black proboscis which normally rests on ridge of bill, and has two black tufts at base; legs and feet olive with dark joints. Shape and size like *F. gigantea*, but differs strikingly in bare part colours and forecrown structure. Sexes alike. Juvenile greyer, with extensively white chin and throat; bill black, tinged greenish; proboscis reduced or absent. VOICE. Apparently similar to that of *F. gigantea*, although only a low grunting series of 3-5 syllables, and loud sharp grunts, are described.

Habitat. Barren Andean high altitude lakes, both freshwater and brackish, with dense submerged aquatic plants. Occurs chiefly at 3000-5200 m in desert *puna*.

Food and Feeding. Poorly known. Eats mainly aquatic plants, especially *Myriophyllum*, *Potamogeton* and *Ruppia*; also grass and some seeds.

Breeding. Breeds mainly Oct-Feb, although nest building recorded as early as Sept. Monogamous; may breed in colonies of up to 80 pairs. Nest enormous, resembling that of *F. gigantea* but usually built on conical mound of up to 1·5 t of stones, up to 4 m in basal diameter and built up from lake bed to height of c. 60 cm, ending just below water surface in platform c. 1 m² on which nest of water weed is placed. Both adults build; fresh material (usually *Ruppia* or *Myriophyllum*) constantly added to rim while nest in use; nest often used over many years, and also serves as nest-site for other waterbirds after coots have bred. Eggs 3-5; downy chick black with feathered crown, bill light grey with yellow base and tip, legs black; young fed by both parents; when adults bring fresh material to nest, seed pods are torn off and given to young. Chick mortality estimated at 25%.

Movements. May fly from one feeding ground to another. Local populations fluctuate greatly between periods of drought and inundation; altitudinal movements or displacements, some over long distances, may occur in harsh weather, especially in winter when food becomes locally unavailable as some lakes freeze, and at such times birds recorded as low as 2000 m. Moves at night.

Status and Conservation. VULNERABLE. Probably in decline. Normally occurs at low densities: 1-10 nesting pairs at some sites with up to 70-80 at a few; concentrations of over 100 birds (up to 780) reported occasionally; 2800 birds reported on Laguna Pelada, Bolivia, in Nov 1989. Total numbers not known; Chilean population estimated at 620 birds; 180-200 birds and 70-80 nests counted at Laguna Meñique in Nov 1993, with 30-40 birds at adjacent Laguna Miscanti; little known about population trends and no definite evidence of recent decline. Lakes at which species occurs, although remote, remain vulnerable to contamination and effects of trampling by cattle, while from some, water is pumped to coastal cities and towns and to mines. Also suffers from hunting and egg-harvesting. Predation by Andean Gull (*Larus serranus*) reported as an occasional threat. Some lakes at which species occurs have been protected, including the important Laguna Pelada. Officially considered "vulnerable" in Chile, where census work, surveillance and other studies are being carried out.

Bibliography. Behn & Millie (1959), Blake (1977), Canevari *et al.* (1991), Chebez (1994), Collar & Andrew (1988), Collar, Crosby & Stattersfield (1994), Collar, Gonzaga *et al.* (1992), Fjeldså & Krabbe (1990), Hellmayr & Conover (1942), Howell & Webb (1995b), Johnson (1965a, 1965b), King (1978/79), Meyer de Schauensee (1982), Narosky & Yzurieta (1987), Olrog (1984), de la Peña (1992), Remsen & Traylor (1989), Ripley (1957a, 1957b), Santoro *et al.* (1988), Vides-Almonacid (1988), Wege & Long (1995).

Class AVES
Order GRUIFORMES
Suborder HELIORNITHES
Family HELIORNITHIDAE (FINFOOTS)

- Medium-sized largely aquatic birds, with brightly coloured lobed toes.
- 26-59 cm.

- Pantropical.
- Thickly vegetated margins of rivers, lakes and swamps.
- 3 genera, 3 species, 6 taxa.
- 1 species threatened; none extinct since 1600.

Systematics

Rather few bird families are as poorly known and infrequently observed as the Heliornithidae, or finfoots. These birds have long been included within the Gruiformes on the classical taxonomic basis of the skeletal and musculature arrangements, but where they should be placed within this diverse order of birds is open to question. There is no fossil evidence of any of the Heliornithidae to provide any guidance, although the wide geographical distribution of this small family across three continents suggests an ancient lineage. On the grounds of superficial similarities to some rails, as well as similar Mallophaga, or feather lice, the family has usually been considered as close to the Rallidae, but, as with the even greater resemblance to the grebes (Podicipedidae), such similarities may well be misleading.

The limited DNA-DNA hybridization work carried out so far indicates that, of those species examined, the closest relative of the Sungrebe (*Heliornis fulica*) might be the Limpkin (*Aramus guarauna*); however, in that particular study no material was available for either of the other members of Heliornithidae, the African Finfoot (*Podica senegalensis*) and the Masked Finfoot (*Heliopais personata*), and such comparisons would clearly be highly desirable. A close relationship with the Limpkin has apparently never been suggested on the basis of an examination of morphological characters.

The three species are placed in three separate genera, but these are not considered equidistant from one another. The Masked Finfoot and most African Finfoots are much larger than the Sungrebe, and both of these Old World genera have stiffened rectrices, quite markedly so in the case of the African Finfoot. The differences between the hatchlings are considerably greater still: those of the African Finfoot and Masked Finfoot are down-covered and nidifugous, while the newly-hatched chicks of the Sungrebe are thoroughly altricial, in being blind, naked and helpless. On the basis of this considerable degree of difference among them, the recognition of two distinct subfamilies was proposed: Podicinae, containing the African and Masked Finfoots; and Heliornithinae, containing the Sungrebe alone.

Morphological Aspects

The three finfoot genera share a number of features that are clearly related to their way of life. They range in body length from the 26 cm of a female Sungrebe to the 59 cm of a large male African Finfoot. All birds have a long neck, slender body, pale underside, sharp pointed bill, brightly coloured lobed feet, sharp claws and a long broad tail.

The lobed feet, like those of coots (*Fulica*) and grebes, are clearly adapted to a largely aquatic way of life. They enable a powerful degree of propulsion through the water, yet do not encumber the bird on land, where the long body is carried relatively erect. Reports of finfoots' movements when on solid ground emphasize their nimbleness and the fact that they can, and do, run fast. They can also clamber into trees and move around in them in a moderately agile manner that a fully webbed foot would make impossible.

The legs and feet are brightly coloured, with striking differences between the species. The African Finfoot has bright orange or salmon red legs and feet, with bright yellow claws; the Masked Finfoot has bright pea green ones; and the Sungrebe has yellow and black banded and striped feet and legs respectively. There are no obvious behavioural reasons for this conspicuousness: for example, no courtship or other behaviour has been reported which particularly displays the feet. The latter trail behind the bird when it flies, but are obscured by the tail, and, in any case, the birds do not usually fly in company. Yellow and black striping is a classic warning colour combination in nature, for instance in wasps, snakes and caterpillars, and such colours might deter some underwater predators, such as large South American fish, although this explanation seems less applicable to the bright foot colours of the Old World finfoots.

The African Finfoot has markedly stiffened retrices with conspicuous pale shafts, and the bird often swims with the tail spread flat on the surface of the water. The function of the stiffening is not clear: presumably it does not influence the bird's flight, but it may well enable it to manoeuvre better in or on the water. It appears to be helpful to birds when they are clambering out of the water, on land or among tree branches. It is not clear why, if this stiffening is beneficial to the African Finfoot for this or any other purpose, the Masked Finfoot manages with less stiffening, and the Sungrebe with none at all. It may be that these other two species clamber and climb less, but the observations to support or refute such a suggestion are lacking.

A second possible adaptation for climbing is also found in the African Finfoot, which has a well developed claw on its wing, on the end of an independently mobile first digit that is 12-18 mm in length. This claw might be helpful when the bird is clambering among vegetation, apparently with half-open wings, rather as the young Hoatzin (*Opisthocomus hoazin*) does with its two claws. The claw on the wing of the African Finfoot is present in adults as well as in young. Both the claw and the digit are easily overlooked in a fresh specimen, and, because they shrivel when the bird is dead and dry, they are almost undetectable in dried museum skins. With far fewer specimens collected, it is not clear whether there is ever any trace of this claw and digit in the Masked Finfoot or in the Sungrebe.

The similarity between the African Finfoot, in particular, and the male Torrent Duck (*Merganetta armata*) of South America is striking, and has been commented on. It obviously has no genetic basis, but may well reflect adaptation to similar aspects of the birds' ways of life. Both birds have bright red bills and legs, elongated bodies, stiffened tail feathers, white and dark lines from either side of the eye going down the side of the neck, and a carpal spur or claw which is used in scrambling on rocks or in trees. All three finfoots have the white longitudinal neck stripes, which presumably help with the birds' concealment by breaking up the outline of head and eye.

Finfoots are to a fair extent at home in four domains, in and on the water, in the air, on the ground, and in trees and bushes. Like darters (Anhingidae), they swim with exaggerated backward and forward movements of the head and neck, presumably in time with each propulsive foot stroke. They will sometimes swim low in the water, and when alarmed may have only the head and neck above the surface. They rarely dive, for food or when disturbed, but they may lower themselves further in the water, and generally swim away to cover at the water's edge. If pressed, a bird often patters over the surface, beating its wings. Finfoots do not take to the air very readily, although they clearly are capable of long aerial journeys (see Movements). They generally fly low, with steady, fast wingbeats and with the long tail spread. They do not usually fly to a perch, but land on water and climb up to the resting place.

The African Finfoot shows a great deal of variation in size, and birds from South Africa may weigh twice as much as those from West Africa. The reasons for this cline in size are totally unknown, and the other two genera do not show any consistent variation in size over similarly large geographical ranges. The African Finfoot also exhibits considerable variation in its plumage, independent of the variation in size. One race, *camerunensis*, is much darker than the nominate race, to the extent that in some individuals the whole body, both above and below, may be largely black. The races mostly intergrade, and birds with intermediate characteristics are found. Within all four races, some birds are more blotched or barred below than others, particularly towards the rear, while some have more, and others less, white spotting on the back, which in turn may be browner or greyer. The causes and possible significance of this variation are quite unknown, and, again, the other two species do not exhibit variability of this sort: a Sungrebe looks much the same, wherever it comes from.

The greater amount of geographical variation in size in the African Finfoot than in the other two species is also reflected in the much greater degree of sexual dimorphism in the African species, where males are considerably larger than females, sometimes as much as 25%. This sexual size difference caused confusion in the past, in attempts to delineate the geographical races of this species on the basis of very small numbers of birds collected. Not enough is known of the mating systems of the three species to say whether these differences in the extent of sexual dimorphism are related to greater male competition for mates or for territory in the African Finfoot.

Habitat

Over their enormous range, finfoots are found in a wide variety of habitats where the two essential components, water and cover, are present together. Such habitats range from coastal creeks up to some wetlands about 2000 m above sea-level. In many places,

Though seemingly rare, the African Finfoot is widely distributed over the whole continent from sub-Saharan regions southwards, and it occurs wherever undisturbed perennial streams and other bodies of water offer well vegetated banks. In coloration strikingly similar to the Torrent Duck (Merganetta armata) of South America, its behaviour is really more similar to that of darters (Anhingidae). The body lies flat in the water, the head is relatively small, the neck slender and the broad tail with its stiffened rectrices is often spread as the bird swims with strong to-and-fro movements of neck and head. The adult breeding male is colourful with bright red bill and reddish orange feet, while the female is similar but with more muted plumage. This juvenile bird recalls an adult female, but can be separated by the buff on the neck and breast, but most readily by the dark bill.

[Podica senegalensis petersii, Kwazulu, Natal, South Africa. Photo: Nigel J. Dennis/ NHPA]

In common with the other finfoots, the New World Sungrebe frequents mainly slow-moving waters, usually in forested country. Apart from water it has two other essential requirements: dense riparian vegetation and freedom from disturbance. Finfoots are shy birds that often pass undetected, and the paucity of information about them is typified by the fact that it is not yet known whether they spend more time on water or on land. Clearly, the lobed feet equip them well for movement on both elements. When disturbed on water, they invariably clamber ashore to hide among vegetation. In addition, although most of their food is taken from the surface of the water, they are also known to forage on land.

[*Heliornis fulica*, La Encrucijada, Mexico. Photo: A. de Sostoa & X. Ferrer]

finfoots inhabit mangrove swamps by the shore, while at the other extreme they are found from mountain streams downwards. They may frequent quite fast-flowing streams, but in general they are most often in still or relatively slow-moving water, in streams, rivers, ponds, lakes and estuaries. On large water bodies, they are always to be found relatively close to the shore, in places where there is thick vegetation along the water's edge, particularly overhanging and emergent vegetation.

The finfoots also inhabit areas of humid and flooded rain forest, papyrus swamps, and reedbeds with shrubs, trees and creepers. Many of the tropical wetlands they inhabit experience unpredictable or seasonal changes in rainfall, and in water flow and water levels, and the birds are clearly able to cope with such variations.

It is not clear what factors determine which habitats are acceptable to the birds. Food supply and avoidance of disturbance are likely to be significant. Clearly, vegetation cover appears to be important, for reasons that are not understood: why should finfoots be so particularly keen on cover? Absolutely nothing is known of their natural predators, except for one report of a chick disappearing under the water with a sudden splash! Not being particularly proficient divers, finfoots out in open water are likely to be vulnerable to birds of prey, while both birds roosting and nests along the water's edge may be at risk from terrestrial predators. The activities of human beings nowadays are likely to be reducing the amount of suitable habitat available to the birds (see Status and Conservation).

General Habits

Finfoots are relatively unsocial birds. They are usually encountered singly, but sometimes in pairs, with or without accompanying young. As far as is known, they do not gather into any larger aggregations for any purpose. The indications are that they are territorial, individuals driving away others that may come into their own stretch of water. A male Sungrebe holds a year round territory of about 200 m of stream banks, driving out and fighting with intruding birds.

Finfoots are almost invariably described as being elusive, shy, wary and skulking. It is not at all clear why this family, in particular, should be so determined to avoid human beings and presumably many other animals too. The birds certainly never make themselves at all conspicuous, and this, of course, is why they are so often overlooked. Many experienced ornithologists in Africa count on the fingers of one hand the number of their sightings of African Finfoots in decades of birdwatching. It is only when the birds are on or beside the water on streams, rivers or lakes that the vegetation may be open enough for them to be observed at all. Their habit of seeking cover on land when in any way disturbed means that the great majority of observations are of birds on the water. It is not known where, in fact, they spend most of their time. They obviously swim very well, but there are no data on what proportion of their day they spend in the water; what is known is that, when on the water, they stay close to the banks and the concealment that the edge vegetation provides. They also use the alternative strategy of freezing motionless and semi-submerged if surprised when away from cover.

Like many other birds, finfoots are reported to be most active early in the morning and late in the afternoon, and to be relatively inactive in the middle of the day. Sungrebes watched in Mexico spent from about 09:00 hours until about 16:00 hours either floating on the water or, more often, perched on a low branch above the water, essentially resting; while on the perch, they preened sometimes, or occasionally dropped into the water below to catch an insect that was drifting by.

At dusk, the finfoot clambers up, rather than flying up, into a higher concealed roosting place in thick vegetation, from which, if disturbed, it can drop down into the safety of the water. Otherwise, the bird will remain inactive roosting there for the night.

Voice

Parallel to the finfoots' apparent determination to remain inconspicuous, they are not noted as being highly vocal. The sounds they make have been rather poorly described, although they do seem to be remarkably diverse.

The African Finfoot is reported to produce occasionally, and particularly during the breeding season, a repeated low booming sound, either loud or soft. It is likely that the bird's indigenous local name of "Mumbooma" in the Upper Zambezi region is onomatopoeic. This species apparently also utters a number of explosive or staccato croaks, barks or chatters.

The Masked Finfoot utters a bubbling call, fairly high-pitched, apparently like the sound of air being blown through a tube into water. It may be that this sound has given rise to the local Burmese name of "Ye-balon".

Sungrebes produce a characteristic territorial call, which M. Álvarez del Toro described phonetically as "eeyooo, eeyoo, eeyoo-eeyaaa, eeyaa, rather similar to the calls of some grebes". The sound is made more when a bird is advertising territorial ownership, and particularly before and after territorial disputes. Male and female utter soft clucking sounds during their mutual courtship displays, and when relieving one another at the nest.

Apart from these few, mostly rather anecdotal, descriptions, there are reports of squawking or growling noises being made by captured birds held in the hand or in traps, but in such circumstances the noises made are unlikely to be of any great significance.

Food and Feeding

The members of Heliornithidae are catholic feeders, consuming many of the range of small animals that can be found and caught along riverbanks or the margins of other water bodies. There are no quantitative data on their diets, and it is regrettable that the collectors of most museum specimens did not manage to supply information on the gut contents of their quarry. With so few data available, no meaningful dietary differences between the species have been noted.

Insects are the most frequent component of their diets, particularly the adults and aquatic larval stages of midges, mayflies and dragonflies; in addition, of other insect foods, there are records of their eating grasshoppers, flies, beetles, a butterfly and a mantis egg case. Mollusc food is common, in the form of many small snails, of which the opercula are easily recognizable in the stomach. There are records of worms, spiders and millipedes, and of crustaceans such as shrimps, prawns and crabs. Some vertebrate prey is taken, particularly tadpoles and frogs, with one record of a snake, and indications of small fish having been consumed. Vegetable matter is also eaten, including seeds as well as leaves, but in apparently small amounts. Nothing is known of the birds' preferences, and it seems quite likely that they eat virtually whatever animal matter they encounter and can catch.

The food is obtained in a number of different ways. Significant amounts are simply found drifting on the water surface, and can be picked off by the swimming bird. Such food may also be detected by a bird perched nearby, which then drops down onto the water to secure it.

Swimming finfoots are sometimes seen picking insects off rocks or off the leaves or stems of riverside vegetation, sometimes jumping clear of the water in order to do so. One was observed taking fairly large pieces of leaf in the same way, and another was seen jumping up off the water surface to catch a flying insect. Unlike coots and grebes, finfoots do not feed by diving and bringing up material from below.

Finfoots also feed on land, but the extent to which they do so is unknown, because they are so rarely observed there. The ground does not generally constitute such a convenient collecting system for insect casualties as does a moving water surface; on the other hand, there are many underwater competitors, such as fish, that are quick to seize any insects that end up in the water.

Breeding

Although data are scanty, and there is clearly some variation, it appears that all three species generally breed at times of, or soon after, high water levels, which often means during the summer rainy season. Thus, the African Finfoot in southern Africa usually nests between September and December, whereas in East Africa it is more likely to nest in the period March to June. There are no reliable data on the nesting season of the Masked Finfoot, although it is reported to take place during the rains. The Sungrebe

Thinly distributed over a vast area extending from Bangladesh eastwards through to Cambodia and Vietnam, the Masked Finfoot frequents varied habitats including swamps and mangroves. Like the other Heliornithidae, it is essentially a secretive species which keeps well hidden in thick riparian vegetation, although this individual has allowed itself to be caught by the camera as it forages on a more open stretch of mangrove shoreline. Data on its food requirements are scanty, but items are known to include aquatic insects, molluscs, fish, frogs and some vegetable matter.

[Heliopais personata, Krabi, Thailand. Photo: Jerry Warne]

nests in spring to early summer in Mexico in the north of its range.

The birds are apparently territorial when nesting, and probably for much of the year. They remain in a stretch of water several hundred metres long, which they defend.

There are changes in appearance related to the breeding season in one sex or the other in all three species. Thus, a breeding male Masked Finfoot develops a small fleshy knob above the base of his bill; this is present only in the breeding season, and is almost undetectable at other times. The male African Finfoot when ready to breed acquires a greyness over his white chin, throat and foreneck. On the other hand, in the Sungrebe it is the female that changes in the breeding season: her bill becomes scarlet, her eyelids turn from brown to red, and her cheeks and the sides of her neck acquire a rusty cinnamon patch.

The nest is a fairly untidy construction of sticks, twigs and reeds, in the form of a shallow bowl, lined with dead leaves. It is usually situated over water, often among thick overhanging vegetation. Favoured nesting sites, for all three species, are the masses of tangled dead vegetation remaining caught in low riverside branches or fallen trees after flood waters have subsided and left their flotsam behind them; on top of these, the finfoot constructs its nest using additional material that it has collected.

The nesting behaviour of the Masked Finfoot has not been observed, so almost nothing is known of the breeding of this species. Courtship has been observed in the African Finfoot; it takes place on the water, with one bird, probably the male, swimming repeatedly out from cover, raising and opening its wings on each side alternately; meanwhile its mate, from a position in cover, makes a snapping sound, probably with its bill, and makes forays out to escort the first bird back into cover. In Sungrebe courtship, as in their aggressive displays, the two birds swim in counter circles, with their necks stretched out low over the water and their wings half raised; copulation takes place when the two birds meet as their circles decrease in size.

Usually two, but sometimes three, eggs constitute the clutch in the African Finfoot and the Sungrebe. By contrast, the Masked Finfoot is reputed to lay 5-7 eggs.

In the Sungrebe, both male and female take part in nest building, and both sexes also share incubation duties, with the male taking the middle of the day shift from about 09:00-10:00 hours until 16:00-18:00 hours, and the female sitting on the nest for the remainder of the daylight hours and overnight. Observations of African Finfoots at the nest indicate that only the female incubates, although the male is fairly often nearby; it is not known whether earlier on he plays a part in nest construction. In the face of disturbance, the female will sit tightly, before eventually slipping off the nest and dropping quietly into the water. When returning, she swims back nearby, then clambers quietly up the branches to her nest.

The incubation period of the African Finfoot is unknown, except that it lasts at least 12 days. The downy young are able to leave the nest and swim strongly only a couple of days after hatching, although whether they usually leave the nest quite as early as that is not known. It is likely that both parents help to care for them.

The Sungrebe is reported to have an astonishingly short incubation period of only 10-11 days, which rivals even the short incubation periods of the small passerines. Whereas the young African Finfoot is precocial, the newly-hatched Sungrebe is highly altricial and completely helpless. It is blind, with the eyelids tightly joined. It is almost naked, with pale pink skin but with a little short sparse down only along the future feather tracts. Its bill and feet are short and poorly formed.

More astonishing still, the male is able to transport these helpless offspring, even in flight. M. Álvarez del Toro, who observed a nesting pair in Mexico, discovered that the male has a shallow pocket under each wing into which the two young can fit. The pocket is formed by a pleat of skin, and made more secure by the feathers on the side of the body just below. The heads of the chicks could be seen from below as the bird flew. Álvarez del Toro collected the bird in order to examine it and confirm the unlikely discovery. Subsequently, he found it confirmed also by a report published by Prince Maximilian of Wied

138 years earlier but apparently ignored, forgotten or not believed.

This adaptation is unique among birds: in no other species is there any mechanism whereby altricial young can be transported. Of course, the precocial young of some swans and grebes may hitch rides on their swimming parents' backs, and a male jacana can transport his chicks about holding them between his wings and body (see page 286), but neither of these cases applies when the adults are in flight. There are also occasional reports of young galliforms dropping from a flying adult, but it is likely that these are chicks which were not disentangled from a parent's legs or feathers in time before the parent took off, and no systematic transport system or adaptation has been suggested.

The transport system of the Sungrebe raises numerous further questions. How do the chicks get into the pocket? Are they put in by the male? Does he feed them in there? Do they stay inside, or get in and out? Why does the female not have similar pockets? And indeed, why do other species not have similar adaptations? The African and Masked Finfoots both have downy precocial young. If the Masked Finfoot's clutch actually does regularly consist of 5-7 eggs, transporting a whole clutch in this way might be impracticable. No such pockets have been reported in the African or Masked Finfoot, but again these features are not detectable in dried skins. Even if they are present in fresh material, unless they were particularly searched for they would probably be overlooked, as the African Finfoot's first digit and claw so often has been.

Movements

All the signs are that all three species of finfoots are largely static and resident. There is no evidence of any regular migration. However, a fair amount of travelling obviously does take place, with all species widely distributed and occurring on a variety of changing water bodies. Colonization of new areas of aquatic habitat, such as newly created lakes, takes place reasonably soon, which implies that there are birds which are moving around in search of habitat in which to settle. Without gene interchange as a result of such travel, each species would very likely have given rise to many more localized variations than is the case. It is only the African Finfoot which exhibits any noticeable regional variation.

Occasionally, individual birds crop up outside the species' normal ranges. For example, Sungrebes turn up from time to time in Trinidad, and Masked Finfoots have occurred in west Java, where they are not known to breed. It is extraordinary that a bird which is not normally prepared to venture more than a few metres away from the protection of the vegetated water's edge will sometimes undertake flights out to sea.

Relationship with Man

Finfoots must be amongst those bird families that have had least impact on the lves of men over the centuries. Their wetland haunts are on the whole not very densely populated by human beings, and the birds' avoidance of people is so strong that they very rarely come into any sort of contact. Finfoot population densities are apparently so low that they are nowhere a significant item in the hunting bags or diet of humans, although the flesh of the Masked Finfoot was described as "delicious" by W. Davison, and both the birds themselves and their eggs are said to be relished in places by the local people. Again, their diet, consisting mainly of small aquatic invertebrates, does not bring them in any way into conflict or competition for food resources that people value. The birds apparently do not feature significantly in local legends.

As far as is known, there is no finfoot in captivity anywhere in the world. Certainly, no zoo that contributes to the International Species Inventory System (ISIS) records their presence in their collections, and zoo literature does not report the keeping of them. It is likely that the birds' reclusiveness deters zoos and bird collections from trying to get hold of birds that would probably do their best not to be seen by the public, quite apart from the difficulties of finding and capturing birds, and then of inducing them to change their diet to one that could be suitably provided for in captivity.

The name *Heliornis* is derived from the Greek *helios* meaning "sun" and *ornis* meaning "bird", reflecting the original vernacular name "Sunbird". It is not at all clear why this name should have been applied to a bird which so particularly haunts shaded thick cover and water, both of which are antitheses of the sun. Other names are related to the sun theme, notably *Heliopais* meaning "sun-child", or are descriptive. Thus, *Podica* means "belonging to the foot" and draws attention to the lobed feet, as, of course, does the common name "finfoot". The species name *personata* means "wearing a mask", in reference to the black front of the face of the Masked Finfoot. The Sungrebe's species name, *fulica*, is Latin for "coot", as coots too have lobed feet. The French term *Grébifoulques* for the Heliornithidae means "Grebe-coots".

Status and Conservation

The three members of the Heliornithidae are the kind of species that are likely in the long term to be casualties of the further spread of human activities over the coming decades. Although the available evidence suggests that they are nowhere deliberately persecuted or even systematically hunted, they are nonetheless vulnerable for several reasons.

First, and primarily, the birds' wetland habitats are themselves almost everywhere under threat, from a wide range of hostile factors. Tropical wetland areas, with abundant water and sun, are highly productive, and so are often converted by mankind for his own agricultural needs, such as rice production. Many mangrove swamps are cleared for timber. Many wetlands are completely lost through drainage for urban development or mining. Others may be destroyed by water abstraction and its diversion elsewhere, so that their water supply is lost.

Second, the water supply may be modified, as a result of silt run-off in the catchment areas, or through seepage of fertilizers or other chemicals into the water system. In either case, the riverine micro-habitat is likely to be changed, and the invertebrate fauna on which the finfoots depend may well become insufficient to maintain them.

Third, finfoots do not need just water, but also cover and freedom from disturbance as well. An increase in human activity along a waterway, or the clearing of some of the waterside vegetation, can render the habitat undesirable or apparently uninhabitable to finfoots.

Due to their secretive habits, finfoots are observed too infrequently for their status to be evaluated satisfactorily. However, they are increasingly threatened as their wetland habitats suffer relentless exploitation by man. Nowhere is this threat more patent than in South-east Asia, the home of the Masked Finfoot, where native forests, including mangroves, are disappearing fast. This species is currently classed as Vulnerable, and undoubtedly requires a concerted research effort.

[Heliopais personata, Krabi, Thailand. Photo: Jerry Warne]

Fourth, despite their wide distribution, because they are at or near the top of their food chain finfoots occur only at low population densities almost throughout their range. Therefore, even if highly effective conservation measures are in place for protecting a particular area and its ecological integrity, that area will still hold only relatively few individuals of species such as finfoots. Destructive activities outside protected areas result in fragmentation of the population. Small populations are always at greater risk than larger ones, for stochastic reasons as well as inbreeding.

And fifth, the terrain in between areas of adequate safe habitat are becoming less habitable to any finfoots that may be travelling in search of mates or of new areas to colonize.

The Masked Finfoot is the finfoot most at risk. It is the only member of the family currently classed as a globally threatened species, and has been classified by BirdLife International (ICBP) as Vulnerable. Its total population is estimated to number fewer than 10,000 birds, and is considered likely to decline by more than 20% over the next 10 years; it is suffering from severe fragmentation of its wetland habitat. The Masked Finfoot has a smaller geographical range than the other two species, and South-east Asia is one of the most densely populated regions of the whole world. That high and growing human population is exploiting lowland forest and mangrove swamps at a disturbing and often unsustainable rate, is spreading its successful aquacultural practices in the region, and is producing increased traffic and development along the waterways of the region. There are threats to 94% of the wetlands of international importance in South-east Asia.

Although the African Finfoot was included in the South African Red Data Book, with indeterminate category, the species, and indeed even the race *petersii* of South Africa, occurs predominantly further north and west. Nothing is known of its population size or of trends in the rest of Africa, but the habitat the birds need is definitely being reduced and will continue to shrink. Also, there are many dam projects which alter local wetland ecology, and the amount of disturbance and waterside clearance will continue to increase, so the long-term outlook for the species is not encouraging. Nonetheless, human population pressures on the African Finfoot are not as great as those confronting the Masked.

The Sungrebe's large range is generally less densely populated by humans than are the ranges of the other two finfoots. Nevertheless, the same pressures apply, with large-scale drainage of wetlands to claim them for human agriculture, industry or settlement. Water supplies are being lost through deforestation of catchment areas, being diverted for irrigation, or being disrupted by dams for hydro-electric power. Domestic and industrial pollution from urban centres, and pesticide and fertilizer pollution from agricultural areas, are both damaging wetlands. And, as elsewhere, human beings are increasingly penetrating the wetland habitats where Sungrebes try to live undisturbed.

It may be that their protective shyness could in the end be the downfall of the finfoots. At present, their timidity means that they can not inhabit areas with more than minimal human activity and disturbance. That may not necessarily always be the case, however, as several species regularly characterized as being shy have ultimately been found able to adapt to an environment dominated by people. It would be interesting to discover whether finfoots could ever adapt themselves to living alongside humans. Properly organized attempts at captive breeding, by means of artificial incubation and rearing, might prove valuable, if this meant that the wild populations could be provided with the safety net of viable captive populations, which might be available in appropriate cases for restocking or reintroductions. Field studies too, although undoubtedly offering a major challenge, would surely prove worthwhile, as such a great deal remains to be learnt about the finfoot family.

General Bibliography

Benson (1968a), Brooke (1984b), Dugan (1993), Dunning (1993), Elliott (1985), Finlayson & Moser (1991), Glenny (1967), Hendrickson (1969), Houde & Braun (1988), Peters (1934), Sibley & Ahlquist (1990), Sibley & Monroe (1990).

ssp *senegalensis*

1

ssp *petersii*

ssp *camerunensis*

1

2

3

PLATE 19

inches 7
cm 18

Family HELIORNITHIDAE (FINFOOTS)

PLATE 19

SPECIES ACCOUNTS

Genus *PODICA*   Lesson, 1831

1. African Finfoot
Podica senegalensis

French: Grébifoulque d'Afrique   **German**: Binsenralle   **Spanish**: Avesol Africano
Other common names: Peters's Finfoot (*petersii*)

Taxonomy. *Heliornis senegalensis* Vieillot, 1817, Senegal.
Suggested subdivision of family into two subfamilies places present species in Podicinae alongside *Heliopais personata*. A cline in size, increasing towards south and east of range. Race *camerunensis* may apparently intermix with *senegalensis* in S Cameroon. Birds from Loango coast (extreme NW Angola) formerly awarded separate race *albipectus*, being intermediate in size and range, but not reliably separable. Four subspecies currently recognized.
Subspecies and Distribution.
P. s. senegalensis (Vieillot, 1817) - Senegal E mainly through forested belt of W Africa to E Zaire, Uganda, NW Tanzania and Ethiopia.
P. s. somereni Chapin, 1954 - Kenya and NE Tanzania.
P. s. camerunensis Sjöstedt, 1893 - S Cameroon, Gabon, Congo and N Zaire.
P. s. petersii Hartlaub, 1852 - Angola E to SE Zaire, Zambia and Mozambique, and S to E South Africa.
Descriptive notes. 35-59 cm; 340-880 g. Retrices stiffened markedly; small bony knob on carpal joint; first digit carries sharp claw; legs and feet bright salmon red to orange. Extensive grey colouring on male's chin, throat and foreneck gives way to white outside breeding season. Female resembles non-breeding male, but smaller and browner, with more extensive white on head and neck. Immature similar to female, but generally warmer brown above, unmarked with white; buff breast and flanks, latter with faint spotting. Generally an extraordinarily variable species, with considerable difference between individuals even within races, especially in amount of white spotting on back, blotching and barring below, and overall tone of plumage coloration; race *camerunensis* small like nominate race,

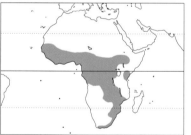

but variably darker, without spots or neck stripes; *petersii* resembles nominate race, but larger; *somereni* resembles *camerunensis*, but larger and not quite so dark.
Habitat. Permanent streams, rivers, pools and lakes, with well vegetated banks, particularly with reeds and overhanging tree branches; also occurs among mangroves and flooded rain forest. Typically found in forest zone, but also in wooded savannas. Occasionally observed further out in the open. Occurs from sea-level up to c. 1800 m.
Food and Feeding. A variety of invertebrates, particularly larvae and adults of mayflies, dragonflies, beetles, grasshoppers; spiders, millipedes; crustaceans, small snails, frogs, small fish; occasionally vegetation. Feeds both on water and on land; swimming bird often picks insects off surface; will take prey off rocks and vegetation up to 50 cm above water surface.
Breeding. Season varies with location, corresponding with high water levels; Sept in Sierra Leone; chicks in Nov-Dec in Liberia, in Oct in Nigeria; birds in breeding condition Apr-Jul in Zaire; laying Apr-May in Kenya, Oct and Jan-Feb in Zambia, and Sept-Dec and Apr in Zimbabwe. Pairs territorial. Nest is an untidy flat structure of reeds and twigs, lined with a few leaves; often placed over water, 1-3 m up, on mass of flood debris on overhanging or fallen branch. Usually 2 eggs, sometimes 3; incubated by female only, although male often nearby; incubation period reputedly short; downy chicks white below grading to dark above, with red legs; chicks leave nest within very few days.
Movements. Resident, but colonizes new locations regularly; in South Africa, and probably elsewhere, some wandering takes place, perhaps involving immatures looking for a suitable territory in which to install themselves. No evidence of migration.
Status and Conservation. Not globally threatened. Widespread, but never at high population densities; usually considered to be scarce because is so elusive and so rarely observed. Not uncommon in suitable habitat in Ghana and Nigeria, and probably also in Gambia and Sierra Leone; relatively abundant in Gabon; generally uncommon in E Africa; considered to be threatened in South Africa, and is absent from a number of areas with apparently suitable habitat. Undisturbed patches of forested

rivers are declining throughout the species' range; as species is so difficult to observe, any population declines might easily pass unnoticed.

Bibliography. Beddard (1890), Benson & Benson (1975), Benson & Schuz (1967), Brooke (1984a), Carver & Carver (1979), Chapin (1954b), Chubb (1908), Dennis & Tarboton (1993), Dowsett & Forbes-Watson (1993), Elgood *et al.* (1994), Érard & Benson (1975), Gerhart (1980), Ginn (1977a, 1977b), Ginn *et al.* (1989), Gore (1990), Grimes (1987), Hosken (1966), Johnson (1964b), Jubb (1982), Krienke (1943), Lawson (1966), Mackworth-Praed & Grant (1957, 1962, 1970), Maclean (1993), Mitchell (1977), Percy (1963), Pinto (1983), Pitman (1962), Rutgers & Norris (1970), Sassoon (1974), Schepers & Marteijn (1993), Short *et al.* (1990), Skead (1962), Snow (1978), Urban *et al.* (1986), Vernon (1983b), Whateley (1982), White (1965).

Genus *HELIOPAIS*   Sharpe, 1893

2. Masked Finfoot

Heliopais personata

French: Grébifoulque d'Asie   **German**: Maskenbinsenralle   **Spanish**: Avesol Asiático
Other common names: Asian Finfoot

Taxonomy. *Podica personata* G. R. Gray, 1849, Malacca.
Suggested subdivision of family into two subfamilies places present species in Podicinae alongside *Podica senegalensis*. Monotypic.
Distribution. Bangladesh and NE India (Assam) through Myanmar and Thailand to Cambodia and Vietnam; status uncertain in Malaysia and Sumatra, but recently recorded all year round in NW Sumatra.

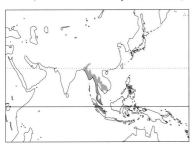

Descriptive notes. 43-55 cm. Retrices somewhat stiffened, but not as much as in *Podica senegalensis*, and tail appears broad and rounded in flight; slight barring on pale underside; legs and feet green. Small fleshy knob above base of bill present only in male, and only in breeding season. Female somewhat smaller than male; has white patch on chin, throat and forehead. Juvenile resembles female, but lacks black on crown.
Habitat. Fairly varied: well vegetated wetlands, including swamps and overgrown ponds, lake edges, streams, slow-moving forest waterways; flooded forest, including swamp forest; tidal creeks; often among mangroves. Especially found among overhanging vegetation at water's edge. Recent sightings on former tin mining pools and ornamental lakes might suggest some possible degree of adaptability to man-modified sites, or simply reflect rapid disappearance of suitable habitat.
Food and Feeding. Very few data available. Reported to feed on aquatic insects, molluscs, frogs, crustaceans, small fish and some vegetable matter. Food is gathered on water and on land. One bird reported to forage by stirring shallow lake bottom detritus with its feet.
Breeding. Very poorly known. Breeding season reputed to be during rains. Nest is a thick pad of small sticks, hidden amongst vegetation up to 2-3 m above water. Clutch reported to comprise 5-7 eggs; downy chicks dark above, pale below; chicks apparently nidifugous; roles of sexes and further breeding details unknown.
Movements. Little known. Thought to be essentially sedentary throughout most, if not all, of range, but scarcity of records impedes clear view of movement patterns, e.g. in Thailand usually considered resident, but may merely be uncommon passage migrant and winter visitor. Status uncertain in Peninsular Malaysia and Sumatra, where breeding not recorded, and species traditionally classed as possible winter visitor; recently, evidence suggests possible breeding in Malaysia; in NW Sumatra, species recently found to occur all year round in area of swamp forest, so breeding may also be likely. Occasional vagrant to Java.
Status and Conservation. VULNERABLE. World population estimated at fewer than 10,000 birds. Considered to be threatened because of small and declining population, which is severely fragmented. Extensive distribution probably masks low population densities almost everywhere in its range, and species may have restricted breeding range. Main threats include disturbance and development along

rivers, as well as rapid loss of lowland forest and mangrove swamps throughout most of range. Protected species in Malaysia.

Bibliography. Ali & Ripley (1980), Chong (1994), Collar & Andrew (1988), Collar *et al.* (1994), Deignan (1945), Harvey (1990), Hawkins & Silvius (1986), Hopwood (1921), King *et al.* (1975), Komolphalin (1993), Lekagul & Round (1991), MacKinnon & Phillipps (1993), van Marle & Voous (1988), Medway & Wells (1976), Milton (1985), Mundkur *et al.* (1995), Perennou *et al.* (1994), Robson (1992), Round (1988), Scott (1989), Smythies (1986), Ticehurst (1929), Wells (1990).

Genus *HELIORNIS*   Bonnaterre, 1791

3. Sungrebe

Heliornis fulica

French: Grébifoulque d'Amérique   **German**: Zwergbinsenralle   **Spanish**: Avesol Americano
Other common names: American Finfoot

Taxonomy. *Colymbus fulica* Boddaert, 1783, Cayenne.
Suggested subdivision of family into two subfamilies places present species alone in Heliornithinae. DNA analysis suggests possible link between present species and Aramidae. Monotypic.
Distribution. SE Mexico S through Central America and throughout most of N South America mainly E of the Andes, as far S as Bolivia and NE Argentina.

Descriptive notes. 26-33 cm; 120-150 g. Unmistakable. Smallest member of Heliornithidae; lacks the stiffened retrices of *Podica* and *Heliopais*; white tip to tail conspicuous in flight; feet conspicuously banded, legs striped, yellow and black. Male has bill dark above, pale horn below. Female slightly smaller than male, with cinnamon patch on cheeks and side of neck, scarlet eyelids and red upper mandible. Outside breeding season, most of these features lacking and female resembles male; bill retains same colour pattern, but duller. Juvenile similar to non-breeding adult, but generally duller.
Habitat. Forest streams and rivers, especially quiet backwaters; also freshwater lakes and ponds. Typically found along margins of water with thick and overhanging vegetation.
Food and Feeding. Little known. Mostly takes aquatic insects (adults and larvae), including dragonflies; ants, beetles and spiders that have fallen into the water; also crustaceans, amphibians and small fish; some seeds. Normally feeds from water surface, but also known to forage on land.
Breeding. Males reported to be more territorial during spring breeding season in N of range; elsewhere probably related to rains; laying Jun-Jul in Panama, female in breeding condition in Jan in Colombia. Nest is platform of twigs in tangle of vegetation 1-2 m above water. Usually 2 eggs, sometimes 3; incubation by both sexes, for period reported as only lasting 10-11 days; chicks altricial, carried by male in special skin pockets beneath wings (see page 214).
Movements. Local resident. No indication of migration, but birds may turn up as accidentals outside normal range.
Status and Conservation. Not globally threatened. Like other members of family, rarely observed so numbers unknown. Wide distribution, with apparently low population density. Suitable undisturbed habitat is disappearing in much of range in the face of human activity and development. Uncommon to fairly common in Mexico; uncommon and local in Panama, Colombia and French Guiana. In Brazil, species can survive in dammed water-holes beside highways; at night, birds sometimes caught in nets by fishermen.

Bibliography. Álvarez del Toro (1970, 1971), Anon. (1983a), Blake (1977), Canevari *et al.* (1991), Carbonell (1987), Contreras *et al.* (1990), González-García (1993), Haverschmidt (1968), Haverschmidt & Mees (1995), Hayes (1995), Hellmayr & Conover (1942), Hilty & Brown (1986), Howell & Webb (1995a), Land (1970), Lowery & Dalquest (1951), Meyer de Schauensee & Phelps (1978), Monroe (1968), Ortiz & Carrión (1991), Parera (1987), de la Peña (1992), Ridgely & Gwynne (1989), Rumiz (1983), Scott & Carbonell (1986), Sick (1985c, 1993), Slud (1964), Snyder (1966), Stiles & Skutch (1989), Tostain *et al.* (1992), Wetmore (1965), Wied-Neuwied (1833b).

Class AVES
Order GRUIFORMES
Suborder RHYNOCHETI
Family RHYNOCHETIDAE (KAGU)

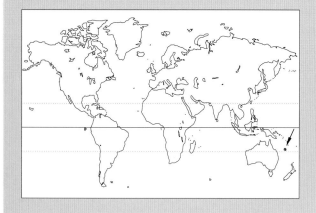

- Medium-sized flightless birds, with long crest feathers, and distinctively banded wings.
- 55 cm.

- New Caledonia.
- Forests and certain types of shrubland.
- 1 genus, 1 species, 1 taxon.
- 1 species threatened; none extinct since 1600.

Systematics

The Kagu (*Rhynochetos jubatus*) is the only extant species in a monotypic family, Rhynochetidae, within the order Gruiformes. Another, larger species, *Rhynochetos orarius*, has been described from sub-fossils found in Holocene deposits on the coast of New Caledonia, which date back some 2000-4000 years. The distinction between the two forms is based almost entirely on a slight size difference, and this raises doubts as to whether or not it really is a separate species.

The Kagu was first placed with the Ardeidae because of similarities in plumage coloration with herons and egrets; the Kagu's powder-downs are also characteristic of members of the Ardeidae. Since 1862, it has been placed with the Gruiformes because of greater similarities in internal anatomy, agility of movement on land, the coloration of the chicks and eggs, and the change in coloration between the chick and the adult (see Morphological Aspects). Amongst the Gruiformes, the Eurypygidae of South America and the Mesitornithidae of Madagascar have been cited as probable near relatives of the Kagu, and these associations have been considered to suggest a close link between the Kagu and the original fauna of Gondwanaland. Another gruiform family recently suggested to be related to Rhynochetidae is the extinct Messelornithidae of Europe and Northern America.

Over the years, systematists have found that the determination of the Kagu's closest affinities within the Gruiformes is problematic, and to date this still remains a matter for speculation. The species has features that are not shared with other Gruiformes, and, in some cases, with other birds: the unique rolled corns that cover the nasal openings, and were used to give the species its genus name, *Rhynochetos*, from the Greek *rhis* meaning "nose", and *chetos* meaning "corn"; a unique blood composition, with one third of the red blood cells and three times the haemoglobin content of those found in all other birds so far analysed; and large eyes. DNA hybridization evidence has so far been unable to establish clear relationships. Karyotype comparisons suggest that the Kagu is close to the Gruidae, which are hypothesized to be representative of the ancestral Gruiformes, which, if correct, would imply that, as a family, Rhynochetidae does not appear to have evolved recently. In the long term, further genetic comparisons should help to provide a clearer picture of the Kagu's relationships to the other families within the order Gruiformes.

Morphological Aspects

Kagus are flightless, with an appearance of something between a small heron and a rail. An obvious feature is their ash grey and white plumage, somewhat unusual for ground-living forest birds, which tend to be cryptically coloured. The long crest feathers, which extend to the lower back, are a distinguishing characteristic, but are often difficult to detect unless displayed. Adults vary considerably in weight between about 700 and 1100 g, depending on seasonal and individual size variation, as no sexual size dimorphism is known.

A striking feature of the Kagu, and usually concealed, is the patterning on the upper side of the primary wing feathers. A dominant background of alternating lateral black and white bands radiates out from the feather bases. Appearing to overlie the bands is a finer pattern of brown, black and grey coloured "stripes" extending across the primaries, mainly between black bands two and three (counting from the feather tips). An initial investigation of wild birds showed that the striped pattern tended to be much more extensive on females, so this could provide a simple method to sex quite a high percentage of birds. No other sexual dimorphism is evident.

Although the wings do not appear reduced in size, and total wingspan amounts to roughly 77·5 cm, the musculature necessary for sustained flight is lacking. Birds use the wings to assist their movement, when they are forced to flee from danger, over steep descents, or when they are climbing in difficult terrain. At these times, the birds often flap their wings, but they can also glide during airborne descents. The wings are also important for behavioural displays, in which the strikingly patterned primaries are particularly evident (see General Habits).

The large, dark red eyes and longish orange-red legs and bill are prominent features associated with the Kagu's lifestyle. The eyes are positioned in such a way as to give the Kagu excellent binocular vision, which should aid in the capture of small soil and litter fauna, particularly in the reduced light of the forest understorey. The longish bill measures about 60 mm; it is narrow, pointed and strong, and is often used for shallow digging in soil and humus to capture prey (see Food and Feeding). The rolled corns, or flaps, covering the nasal openings would seem to be designed to keep particles from entering them during probing activities.

Considerable agility in movement, aided by the longish, strong legs and relatively compact build, enables birds to travel

The Kagu is a highly improbable-looking bird to find inhabiting a subtropical forest floor. Its shape is vaguely pigeon-like and reminiscent of an upright clockwork toy, the greyish and white plumage and brightly coloured bill and legs looking bizarrely out of place against the forest background. It has two features not found elsewhere in Gruiformes: the large eyes and the rolled corns or flaps that cover the nasal openings. The narrow, pointed bill is well adapted for digging to find prey and the longish, sturdy legs equip the bird for walking long distances without undue effort. Although flightless, it uses its wings extensively in displays and to help it glide or flap over sometimes difficult terrain. The spectacular crest and splendid patterning of the primary feathers are unsuspected when the bird is at rest.

[*Rhynochetos jubatus*, New Caledonia. Photo: Michel Gunther/ Bios]

long distances relatively quickly, over a wide range of types of terrain (see Movements), and run surprisingly fast, for example to escape danger. When foraging, their movements are usually slow and measured, with their heads tilted forward to detect prey, except when they are making a dash to capture food (see Food and Feeding). When they are not foraging, their movements can involve running, for example in disputes and interactions with other Kagus. When standing still, investigating a human intruder, birds commonly move their heads, and to a lesser extent their bodies, in sudden discontinuous movements. Birds can hold their tail feathers in a raised position somewhat in the manner of rails, but this behaviour does not appear common. As with their over-all appearance, their movements too are a mixture of those of a small heron and a rail.

Powder-downs may also be beneficial for the Kagu in the New Caledonian environment. These relatively abundant feathers are distributed in tracts over much of the body, and may provide a degree of waterproofing and insulation from extremes of tropical weather. The presence of powder-downs provides another similarity with the herons.

The start of moult appears to be closely linked with the first substantial summer rains, which tend to come around January.

The timing coincides with increased food supplies associated with the hot, wet weather. Completion of primary feather moult can take about two to five months, probably depending on food levels over the rainy season. Overlap of moult and breeding activity can occur in late nesting pairs (see Breeding).

The plumage of chicks consists of a combination of light and dark browns, with fawny streaks on upperparts, making chicks nearly invisible amongst the leaf litter on the forest floor. Juvenile plumage first appears when chicks are about 20 days old, and is complete by the time they are three to four months of age. Initially, the plumage is finely banded grey and brown, making it duller than that of adults, except on the head, crest and primary wing feathers, which are adult-like in colour. The change to adult plumage is mostly complete after about two to three years. However, some remnants of juvenile plumage patterning, such as faded banding on wing-coverts, secondaries and tail feathers, appear to be present on some birds for longer than this, so the complete change could be a gradual process. By the time full adult plumage has been attained, the bird is whitish on the underparts, with paler ash greys on the breast, head and crest feathers, and darker shades on the back, tail, wing-coverts and secondary wing feathers.

Habitat

Special morphological features allow the Kagu to move freely over most terrain and catch a wide range of prey in a variety of vegetation types, rather than limiting its choice of habitat (see Morphological Aspects). Thus, the bird is considered a generalist in selection of foraging areas, as long as sufficient soil and litter prey is available for it to eat. The species was widespread in mainland forests in the past and its now restricted distribution is due to human-associated factors (see Status and Conservation).

Kagus still occur from near sea-level up to mountain summits over 1400 m in altitude, principally in habitat ranging from rain forest to the drier forest at lower altitudes. They are occasionally found in certain shrublands associated with the island's ultrabasic rocks where prey is sufficiently numerous, for example along water systems or at higher altitudes, but they do not occur in the sclerophyll forest remnants along the west coast. Birds are not known to forage in thick undergrowth, such as ferns and grasses, where movement is restricted, or in the open and short shrubland associations on the ultrabasic rocks, where suitable ground prey is in very limited availability. However, they do negotiate through these vegetation types between foraging areas, often using tracks made by feral pigs or humans.

Birds usually roost within their foraging areas, but occasionally choose sites outside them, for example in neighbouring open shrubland. Steeper terrain tends to be selected, especially for ground roosts which are commonly in sheltered positions created by rocks (see General Habits). Nesting sites are sited within a pair's territory, commonly close to good food supplies.

General Habits

A Kagu pair occupies a permanent territory of about 20 hectares, defending it year round against other Kagus. Territorial disputes between birds can involve close contact fights, when the wings and bill are used against the other bird. Such disputes are not known to result in serious injury in the wild, but they can do so in captivity.

Defence and threat display behaviour mainly involves the use of the wings and the crest. When adults are threatened, they fully open their wings to show the patterned primary feathers, but the wings are not usually flapped. A parent defending a chick, though, can flap its fully opened wings on the ground in a typical distraction display, feigning injury. In these defensive displays the crest feathers are partially raised in "Roman helmet" fashion, but they are not usually fanned. When captured, birds right up from the age of young chicks instinctively spread their wings forward in a "shield" showing the banded primary feathers. In the case of an adult bird, the "shield" often covers the bird's head. Wing patterning may have acted to confuse or intimidate past predators, such as large reptiles. In disputes with other Kagus, and in courtship, the wings are used in a "Strutting" display: birds adopt an upright posture and hold their wings down and forward in the form of a cape, while circling each other. In this display, the wing patterning is concealed, and the crest is fully raised and fanned.

Kagus are diurnal, foraging most of the day while there is sufficient light, especially outside the summer rainy season, when food supplies are less plentiful. During the rainy season birds can rest between foraging bouts, when they often preen themselves. Preening activity is mostly carried out at night at the roost-site, either in the early evening before birds sleep, or the early morning before they leave their roost. Within pairs, birds tend to be solitary outside the breeding season, coming together occasionally to sing or roost, or while foraging. During this time partners can have different, but overlapping, foraging areas.

Kagus are rarely known to drink in the wild and appear to obtain most of their water needs from their food (see Food and Feeding). Water is scarce during the annual dry periods, which last for up to several months, and at these times water is commonly unavailable at high altitudes. Because of their relatively sedentary lifestyle, birds would benefit from a physiology which reduced the need for drinking water.

Temperature influences roosting behaviour at higher altitudes. Here, Kagus mostly roost sheltered on the ground in cooler months. When average minimum temperatures in the forest are above about 12°C, birds roost more often above ground level, mostly on low branches. The closely inverse relationship between increases in the minimum temperature and ground roosting frequency suggests that Kagus are sensitive to temperature change, and alter their roosting behaviour accordingly. Thus, it appears that birds seek shelter on cold nights to try to keep warm, perhaps to limit loss of body weight (see Food and Feeding). In the Rivière Bleue Park, in low altitude habitat, birds rarely roost on the ground, doing so mainly in strong wind or heavy rain during summer cyclones. Although average minimum temperatures are several degrees warmer at lower altitudes, winter night temperatures in the park can fall well below 12°C, when, interestingly, Kagus there still roost mainly above ground level. Factors such as habit or type of terrain may also influence whether birds roost on or above the ground.

Ground roost-sites in sheltered positions are mainly those naturally created by rocks, but they can be sited under tree roots or in cavities in dirt banks. Birds at higher altitudes also very occasionally roost on the ground on warm nights, but in unsheltered positions. Excrement at ground roosts sheltered from the rain is often preserved, the build-up of deposits at some sites suggesting their regular use over many years. Because Kagus have particular preferred roosting areas, sheltered ground roost-sites can be close together. This has probably led to the mistaken reports of multiple "nests" at the same site (see Breeding).

Kagus perch above the ground mainly on live and dead branches or tree trunks, but they sometimes use vines, raised roots or isolated rocks. Perches average about 30 cm in diameter; they are usually in climbable positions about 1·5 m above the ground, but they may be up to about 4 m high.

Roost-sites can be located throughout a bird's home range, but they tend to be grouped in favourite areas. While some sites are used regularly, others are used infrequently, or even only once. At high altitude, some ground roosts and above ground roosts are used seasonally, in association with cold and warm temperatures, respectively. A roost-site can be used by both partners, either when birds are separate or when they are together, but ground sites are rarely shared on the same night. During breeding activity, partners often share the same perch or are only several metres apart.

Voice

The sound created by Kagus singing has been likened to something between a rooster crowing and the bark of a young dog, and is distinctly different between the sexes. The female's song is shorter and more rapid than the male's. The initial "gou gou gou...", call which both sexes can make before singing, is also used by partners to locate each other. It is quite loud before duet song, but softer when used alone as a locating call.

Pairs sing a duet in the early morning, usually beginning at first light, but rarely at other times. The singing constitutes territorial behaviour, the birds often turning to broadcast their song in different directions. However, birds of either sex can sing alone, and this may be more related to the business of searching for a mate or partner than to territorial behaviour. Kagu song can be heard up to about 2 kilometres away in the wild, depending on the terrain and weather conditions. Juveniles make their first singing attempts from about six months old, or possibly earlier, joining in with their parents when they duet in the mornings.

Pairs in the same vicinity tend to sing one after the other. Generally, the higher the bird density, the longer the morning singing period. Singing can last up to about one hour when many birds are present, during which period two or more pairs often duet at the same time, and individual pairs often sing more than once. Duets, usually initiated by males, can last up to about 15 minutes. Birds sing in all months, but more frequently over the breeding season.

Kagus have a range of different soft calls, for example a warning hiss, another for communicating with a chick, and a

soft clucking which is made during disputes with other conspecifics.

Food and Feeding

Kagus find most of their prey in the litter or soil, and less commonly just above the ground on rocks and vegetation, and on and in old logs. Birds also apparently foraged on beaches in the past, and they are reported to try to catch small animals in fresh water, from the edge of shallow pools. The species is only known to eat animal prey, taking a wide range of available fauna including larvae, spiders, centipedes, bugs, cockroaches, millipedes, beetles, snails, worms and lizards. The last five of these prey types are considered to be the most important. Amphipoda and Orthoptera species are relatively common in the forest litter at high altitudes, where the birds feed on them too, despite the rapid springing movements used by such animals when disturbed.

Kagus spend a considerable amount of foraging time standing motionless, often on one foot, listening and watching for prey. They sometimes stand on wood or rocks in an apparent attempt to get a better view of the forest floor around them. While standing on one leg, some birds try to flush out prey by gently brushing the litter with the open or half closed foot of the free leg. Once prey is detected, the bird will either move closer and stand still again with its head down and bill pointed directly at the probable prey area, or make a rapid "Run-strike" attack to catch the prey. Prey is often not caught on the first prey attack, and the bird must then use its bill to move litter and sticks or dig in the soil, pulling out soil in its bill, before finally catching its quarry. The feet are not used to move litter or soil, or scratch away debris. The relative importance of both hearing and sight in foraging is not known, but the number of prey items detected by sound may be considerable. Kagu digging marks in soil are obvious signs of their presence, and a hole about 7 cm deep by 5 cm wide remains, with soil spread out on one side of it. A consequence of searching for prey in soil is the large amount of this material that is present in the Kagu's excrement.

The Kagu is adept at pulling worms from soil. It usually pulls the worm out complete, but, if it breaks, the bird can drop the broken section then pull the remainder out, eating the dropped section last. The species also eats large millipedes, which are common in forest at low altitude. Most other birds avoid these animals as potential prey because of the noxious substance they secrete, but the Kagu simply breaks them into pieces before eating them; no ill effects have been recorded. The bird also regurgitates pellets, mainly in summer months, and these generally consist of entire snail shells or the parts of large nocturnal beetles.

New Caledonia's subtropical climate can be extremely variable, largely due to the cyclical El Niño effect (see Volume 1, page 341), which brings drier conditions to the island. However, a general seasonal weather pattern exists, which is responsible for changing the prey availability for Kagus, and also the prey type taken. Warm temperatures between September and March see prey such as beetles, millipedes, centipedes and lizards much more common. Worms and snails are far less numerous for the first two to four months of this period, the main dry season, but they become plentiful over the summer rainy season, from January to March. Prey is most abundant during the passage of summer cyclones in the rainy season, as these bring hot, wet weather. Dry conditions can also occur between periods of rain in summer, because of high temperatures, and resulting in lower food supplies for the birds. In the cool season, from April to August, soil conditions are generally damp, but a short dry period in the first two months is common. Kagu prey, such as lizards and beetles, are less active or in larval stages, respectively, over the cool season, when night temperatures can drop to below 5°C in July and August. Cockroaches are common year round in the forest litter, but their importance to Kagu diet is unknown.

The precise period when the Kagu's prey is least abundant is not known, but it definitely occurs some time in the main dry season. Changes in the body weights of non-breeding birds gives an indication of low prey levels, although cold temperatures may also cause a certain deterioration in body condition (see General Habits). At high altitude, body weight is generally lowest around late October, just before there is a significant change to wetter and warmer weather in the dry season. Body weight data for birds at low altitude are limited, but weights may be lowest around October as well, if not later, because of the hotter and drier conditions compared to high altitudes. Kagu body weights are highest at the end of the rainy season about March and April, when maximum weights for individuals can be as much as 20% or more above their lowest levels.

Breeding

Kagus have a low rate of reproduction, almost always raising at most one chick per year. This is not unusual for an island bird which evolved with little or no predation, and which displays notable longevity, commonly living over 20 years in captivity, as this facet potentially enables an individual to raise many offspring during its lifetime. Species showing these characteristics are extremely vulnerable to disturbance, such as increased predation (see Status and Conservation).

Kagus are monogamous, and pair establishment is generally long term, perhaps normally for life, although separation and remating have been recorded. Pairs breed on their territories (see General Habits). In the Rivière Bleue Park the main nesting period is from June to August, and most eggs are laid in July, but late breeding pairs nest up until December. Thus, breeding usually begins in mid-winter, before the start of the main dry season in September. This means that worms, for example, are quite

Display as a defence mechanism is common among Kagus even from an early age. The chick cornered by the photographer tries to escape detection by crouching down instinctively and extending its wings forwards and around it in a wide fan. The banded primary feathers are already developing, the mainly fawn and dark brown coloration helping the chick to melt into the leaf litter around it.

[*Rhynochetos jubatus*, New Caledonia. Photo: R. Seitre/Bios]

plentiful for feeding to young chicks. The two known nesting dates at high altitude were in early December, suggesting a much later breeding season there than in the Rivière Bleue Park, probably associated with the colder climate at higher altitude.

The factors influencing the timing of breeding are poorly known, but both availability of sufficient food supplies (see Food and Feeding) and tropical weather patterns are probably important determinants. Birds can lose some 200 g during incubation, so they probably need to start off with substantial body weight, or at least with access to adequate food supplies. Incubation generally seems to end before the summer rainy season begins, even though it is associated with plentiful food supplies; this wet season may not be ideal for nesting, and it is used by the birds for moulting.

Pairs generally breed each year in the Rivière Bleue Park. In the park, the loss of an egg or chick usually results in a second, often successful, nesting attempt two to four months later, starting well into the dry season, but before January. Birds may need the relatively long inter-nesting period to regain body condition after the first attempt. Nesting frequency at high altitude is little known, but two pairs on the same peak apparently failed to breed in 1993, a dry El Niño year.

The members of a pair remain in close proximity for about three weeks before the egg is laid. Little is known about Kagu courtship in the wild because it is difficult to observe, but captive pairs perform the "Strutting" courtship display (see General Habits), which often ends in copulation; the display may only be used in the early stages of breeding activity. After the "Strutting" display, one captive male performed what appeared to be ritualized nesting behaviour while holding a leaf in his bill.

Nests can be little more than the leaves, or the ground, that the egg is laid on, but most are simple constructions of layered leaves, 10-35 cm in diameter, gathered from around the nest-site. In the Rivière Bleue Park, nest-sites are not well concealed, if at all, but are often placed up against low vegetation, tree trunks or old logs. The only nest-site described at high altitude, at 1100 m, was well sheltered amongst rocks. Kagus lay a clutch of a single egg, which measures 43-47 x 59-65 mm and weighs 60-75 g. The egg carries smallish dots and blotches, umber and darkish grey in colour, that are intermingled with, and often overlie,

similar light grey markings, scattered over a light creamy brown background.

Breeding duties are shared equally by the pair. The birds take 24 hour shifts when incubating, changing over around noon, which allows both of them to forage for a considerable period each day. Some ritual "Leaf-tossing" is carried out by the bird moving off the nest. At dawn, the incubating bird will sometimes leave the nest or young chick for over 30 minutes, in order to sing with its partner, perhaps also taking the opportunity to forage. Incubation lasts 33-37 days, which is rather long for an egg of this size.

Chicks are semi-precocial. Most chicks hatch with their eyes closed, and they do not usually move from the nest until they are about three days old. Parents will incite a chick less than 24 hours old to leave the nest, if they feel that it is threatened. While in the nest, the chick is fed and brooded by its parents, which take more or less alternate shifts of about one hour each. Chicks gradually move away from their nests after about three days, walking awkwardly at first between rests. Some travel up to 150 m from the nest in the first week. Chicks are fed on most of the typical items that adults eat, especially worms if available. Parents are exceedingly patient when feeding young chicks: an adult holds prey in its bill, close to the chick's head, and softly calls until it opens its bill, a procedure which can take quite some time; the parent then places the food in the chick's mouth. After about two weeks, chicks actively demand food, taking it from the parent's bill.

Chicks are cryptically coloured amongst the forest floor litter. When the parents signal danger, the chick remains motionless, or quickly hides amongst cover, until it is called again. The parents, sometimes helped by older offspring, will defend a chick, by trying to distract or intimidate the source of the threat. As an indication of the parents' determination to defend their chicks, captive birds will even attack a human intruder by biting at the intruder's legs.

Until the chick is around six weeks old it is brooded by one parent at night. The parent arranges a rough bed of leaves on the ground, usually up against cover, for the chick to sleep on. After six weeks, no bed of leaves is made, but the chick continues to sleep on the ground in the company of one of its parents. At 8-10 weeks of age, the chick begins to perch at night, at first on wide objects, such as fallen tree trunks.

The parents continue to feed the chick until it is about 14 weeks old, around which time it becomes independent. After this, they gradually spend more and more time away from it. A juvenile can remain on its parents' home range for up to six years or perhaps more, often leaving it for short periods. Consequently, a pair with high breeding success can have several offspring of varying ages in the vicinity, and as many as five have been recorded at the same site. Males can start breeding at two years of age; the age of first breeding for females remains unknown at present.

Movements

Movements vary considerably for individual birds, depending on their social status. Established pairs mostly stay within their territories, especially when neighbouring territories surround them. Territory boundaries do not appear well defined, and some overlap of foraging areas between neighbouring birds occurs; this is probably more likely outside the breeding season or when prey is not plentiful. Birds can travel widely within their home range during the day, for example foraging on one side of their range in the afternoon and roosting 500 m away on the other side that same night. They move regularly around their current foraging ranges, possibly on a more or less rotational basis.

In the Rivière Bleue Park, pairs with territories encompassing both damper, low-lying ground and adjacent sloping terrain "migrate" within their territories. When weather conditions are dry they forage almost exclusively on the flat, damper areas, but when soils are wet they also forage on the slopes.

At Pic Ningua, the deaths of many Kagus due to dog predation (see Status and Conservation) resulted in the remaining birds leaving, or changing their existing territories. The survivors increased their home ranges into areas where birds had been killed, and three widowed females quit their territories and wandered widely over the mountain. Two of these females made short visits to surrounding valleys at around 500 m in altitude, where other Kagus lived, away from their usual foraging areas at about 1250 m in altitude. One ascended 750 m in altitude over two days. The third female was found at an altitude of 300 m, perching with another bird; it may have repaired there and established a new territory.

Again in the Rivière Bleue Park, juveniles from about 11 months old make excursions from their natal area before pairing and establishing a territory. At first, they usually make short visits of only one to several days into neighbouring territories. Older juveniles can travel several kilometres away before returning, and in one case a bird stayed away for over a year. Two females aged 30 and 38 months left their natal areas and established territories about 2 km and 8 km away respectively. The age at which males may leave their natal areas on a permanent basis is unknown.

Relationship with Man

The Kagu's place in indigenous Kanak culture varies between tribal regions. Around Hienghène, it is not prominent in legends, but plays an important role in tribal traditions. People are given the bird's name ("Kavu" in the local language), Kagu feathers were used in the chiefs' war head-dresses, and their song is sung in war dances. Also, the various calls of the Kagu are seen as different "messages": those hearing these messages would go to the chief for an explanation, for example a call to war. In the Houaïlou area, Kanaks call the Kagu ("Kagou" in their language) the "Ghost of the Forest", possibly due to its ghost-like coloration and its often elusive behaviour.

Before the arrival of Europeans, Kanaks snared and ate Kagus, thus viewing them as a food source on an island where terrestrial game was limited. A drawing in 1774 by a crew member of Captain Cook's Endeavour showed a Kagu next to a tribal house, and this has drawn some speculation that Kanaks had domesticated the birds. The introduction of dogs by Captain Cook facilitated the hunting of the species (see Status and Conservation). In the past, European colonizers and mine labourers also ate the birds, which were thought a delicacy.

The Kagu created much scientific interest among early taxonomists after its description in 1860, because it did not fit easily into any of the known bird families. This resulted in live birds and specimens being sent abroad for study.

Soon after the European colonization of New Caledonia began around 1853, it became fashionable to keep Kagus as pets, and in the past their plumes adorned women's hats. A demand for captive birds created commerce in the species, giving income to some Kanak people. However, the period 1977-1982 saw the ringing of all Kagus known to be held in private hands, a total of 94 individuals, during a campaign to stop the capture of the species. Many of these 94 birds are still living because of the Kagu's long life span. Domestication of birds is unknown, although they can become surprisingly tame in captivity.

In New Caledonia today the Kagu has a high profile because it is rare and the emblem of this French Territory. The species is an attraction for tourists and local inhabitants alike. Because of this, its image and name are used extensively on commercial and administrative logos, and Kagu-related souvenirs are common in tourist shops. Thus, the Kagu's continued survival is important for New Caledonia's image and economy.

Status and Conservation

The Kagu is Endangered and is listed on Appendix I of CITES, with full legal protection in New Caledonia. On a survey in 1991 covering much of the unprotected Kagu habitat, 491 birds were found, including 208 pairs. Most birds were in the Southern Province, with 177 pairs, whereas only a few were located in the Northern Province, with 31 pairs. Thus, birds in most areas appeared to be at low densities, those at higher densities occurring in the remoter areas of intact forest. With the 163 birds, including 63 pairs, known in the protected Rivière Bleue Park, the minimum total population in the wild in 1991 amounted to 654 individuals. The actual population was not estimated to be substantially greater.

Kagus were reportedly still in most of the island's forests earlier this century. Thus, their numbers and distribution have declined severely in recent times, and birds are now unnaturally restricted within their habitat.

The introduction of dogs to the island by Captain Cook in 1774 appears to have been the main reason, direct and indirect,

This adult male Kagu has been bamboozled into a "Strutting" defence display by a dummy bird placed on its territory in the wild. This display involves the adoption of an upright posture, the erection and fanning of the crest feathers and a subsequent spreading of the wings, which are held down and forwards like a cape, while normally the two birds would circle each other. Territorial rights are fiercely defended and infringements can lead to hotly disputed fights, but serious injuries are not usually suffered by birds in the wild.

[Rhynochetos jubatus, Pic Ningua, New Caledonia. Photo: Gavin Hunt]

for the subsequent decline of the Kagu in its habitat. First, dogs facilitated Kagu hunting for the Kanaks, and were probably used for this purpose from soon after 1774, as the pair introduced by Cook is thought to have survived and bred successfully. This may have contributed to the apparent disappearance of the birds from the Panié Range in the north-east of the island, which is close to where the first dogs were introduced. There is no indication of the numbers of birds eaten, and no records to suggest that the practice has continued in any significant way during the last 50 years.

Second, dogs allowed the easy capture of live birds for sale as pets to Europeans. This resulted in localized reductions in the numbers of Kagus, particularly along the east coast. However, this activity cannot account for the species' widespread decline. The practice of keeping birds was significantly reduced from 1977, when existing Kagu protection laws were enforced.

Last, dog predation of Kagus appears to offer an explanation for the continued and widespread decline in their numbers within their habitat. Dogs are numerous on the island, especially in and around the dispersed tribal villages where they are often uncared for. Stray dogs are also common in municipal zones, where they are rarely controlled. However, much of the evidence linking dog predation to the Kagu's decline is circumstantial. For example, Kagus are not found in large numbers near settlements, but only in remoter habitat. This distribution pattern appears to rule out significant long-term impacts of two other introduced predators, pigs and rats, because they co-exist with high densities of Kagus in remoter areas.

In the past, actual evidence of dog predation on Kagus consisted mainly of reports by hunters whose dogs accidentally killed birds. In 1993, a doctoral research project on the Kagu, funded by BirdLife International and the Royal Society for the Protection of Birds (RSPB), documented the dog-related deaths of at least 21 birds at the study site on Pic Ningua. Dogs which strayed from a nearby tribal village killed or injured birds in a series of attack episodes over a period of 14 weeks. The behaviour of the dogs showed how dangerous they are to Kagus, as they returned repeatedly and attacked birds until only a few remained, and they also left birds injured or uneaten, thus killing many more than they needed for eating. They also climbed over 1000 m in altitude to reach the peak, demonstrating that Kagus on mountain tops are not necessarily naturally safe from such attacks. The attacks were detected because the birds there were under study, and many wore radio transmitters; similar attacks on Kagus have probably occurred regularly since dogs were introduced, but have gone unnoticed. The attacks provided graphic evidence that dog predation is presently the number one threat to Kagus in their habitat.

Introduced cats and pigs, and probably rats, also directly threaten Kagus at some stages in their life cycle, but there is little real evidence that their impact on the species is important. Feral cats are not known to kill chicks or adult birds, but one did kill a year old captive-bred juvenile newly released in the wild. Pigs destroyed two of the 26 nests observed in the Rivière Bleue Park during the period 1986-1991, and can thus be seen to have some direct affect on reproductive success. Rats are not known to prey on Kagu eggs in the park, but ship rats are suspected of preying on chicks up to about the age of ten days old. Survival rates of chicks increased when rat poison was distributed in a 100 m radius around nest-sites when incubation began, and again one week before hatching occurred. Further work is needed, though, to verify that the increased chick survival was really due to rat control.

Exploitation activities, such as agriculture, mining and forestry, are also, indirectly, responsible for the Kagu's decline, because their access roads greatly facilitate the entry of stray dogs, and hunters with their dogs, to Kagu habitat. For example, only low numbers of Kagus were recorded in unprotected logged forest in 1991. Logging of Kagu habitat is continuing, and is planned north-east of Mount Do, where the largest concentration of unprotected Kagus, 135 birds, was recorded during the 1991 census. In addition, only a small amount of Kagu habitat is fully protected from mining activities, the main industry on the island.

Pigs, widespread on the island, may have an indirect impact on Kagus, by limiting their numbers through competition in two ways. First, the pigs' habit of uprooting the forest floor causes enormous damage to the forest, and this probably reduces the amount of food available for Kagus. Second, they also eat some of the same prey items as the birds, notably insects and worms, and in relatively large numbers.

The diminishing area of suitable habitat also threatens Kagus in the long term, as only about 20% of the once extensive mainland forests remain. Annual dry season fires, often associated with agriculture, mining and forestry, are the main cause of forest loss, and these have been gradually reducing and fragmenting the Kagu's habitat since human arrival on the island. Habitat directly lost through exploitation activities is also a problem, especially as lowland forests are the most severely affected, further isolating Kagus from each other by restricting them to higher altitudes.

A saving grace for the Kagu is its receptivity to captive management. The first captive-bred bird was raised in Australia around 1920. Since 1977, four permanent breeding pairs have been kept in separate enclosures, totalling one hectare in area, in sclerophyll forest at the Nouméa Zoo, in New Caledonia. From 1977 to late 1994, 61 Kagus were raised with a 44% egg to adult success rate. Pairs at the zoo commonly raise two offspring during the course of a year. Since 1989, the Nogeyama Zoo, Yokohama (Japan), has also been developing a captive breeding programme for Kagus.

In a continuing successful local introduction programme, 32 Kagus bred at the Nouméa Zoo were released in the Rivière Bleue Park between 1983 and 1992, after about 12 weeks of adjustment to natural conditions in a one hectare enclosure situated within the park. Four released males are known to have paired and bred successfully with wild females, but the overall figure is likely to be much higher, as the fate of most of the released birds is unknown.

The successful turn around in Kagu numbers in the Rivière Bleue Park, from an estimated 60 in 1980 to 163 in 1991, has come about through introductions of birds, predation control, and the halt to hunting. Along with the 32 captive-bred birds, ten wild ones had also been introduced by 1992. Dogs, cats and pigs are subjected to continuing control measures, but the latter two species are not well controlled in the park. The management of humans, introduced predators and Kagus has been carried out simultaneously, but dog control is believed to be the principal management technique responsible for the large increase in the bird's numbers.

The future for Kagus in unprotected habitat is extremely precarious because of the dog menace, and the number of pairs protected in the Rivière Bleue Park is insufficient for the long-term persistence of the species. The recent establishment of the Upper Pourina River Valley Reserve bordering the park will protect additional birds and their habitat. However, the number of birds there is small, with only 21 recorded in 1991, and no predator control measures are planned for the area. Undoubtedly, additional managed reserves are still needed to protect significant numbers of breeding pairs. Also needed are efforts to try to reduce the risk of dogs preying on unprotected birds, for example by enforcement of appropriate dog control laws, and promoting increased responsibility about dog ownership by the public.

The Kagu conservation programme in the Rivière Bleue Park, managed by the Southern Province, should continue into the foreseeable future. The current work on Kagus there is focusing on the dispersal, pairing and territorial establishment behaviour of juveniles. The recently completed (1992-1995) fieldwork for the BirdLife International/RSPB research project concentrated on the frequency, timing and success of the Kagu's breeding attempts, and also on possible competition for prey from wild pigs, in high altitude habitat. Future projects centred on the conservation of the Kagu, for example the Biodiversity Project initiated by the Ligue pour la Protection des Oiseaux and funded by the European Union and the RSPB, will likely concentrate on awareness campaigns, to promote the establishment of additional managed Kagu reserves.

PLATE 20

inches   7
cm   18

Family RHYNOCHETIDAE (KAGU)
SPECIES ACCOUNTS

PLATE 20

Genus *RHYNOCHETOS*

J. Verreaux & Des Murs, 1860

Kagu

Rhynochetos jubatus

French: Kagou huppé   **German**: Kagu   **Spanish**: Kagú
Other common names: Cagou

Taxonomy. *Rhynochetos jubatus* J. Verreaux & Des Murs, 1860, New Caledonia.
Relationships unclear (see page 218). Monotypic.
Distribution. New Caledonia.

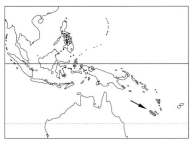

Descriptive notes. 55 cm; c. 900 g. Flightless, but wings appear full-sized. Distinctive ash grey and white plumage, with contrasting longish orange-red bill and legs; underparts whitish, head, breast and crest paler ash grey; back, wings and tail darker. Long crest; large binocularly positioned eyes, iris dark red; rolled nasal corns; and abundant powder-downs. Black and white laterally banded primaries, with smaller area of brown, black and grey stripes (see page 218); striped area tends to be more extensive on females, with no other sexual dimorphism evident. Juvenile similar to adult, but browner and finely banded; bill and legs brown to orange; adult

plumage attained at c. 2-3 years of age.
Habitat. Native forests, and occasionally damper and taller shrubland, from sea-level up to mountain summits over 1400 m. Species is generalist in choice of habitat, if sufficient prey available. Usually nests near good foraging areas.
Food and Feeding. Eats wide range of soil and litter prey, especially millipedes, snails, beetles, lizards and worms. Seasonality in prey abundance and in species taken; prey least abundant in the dry season, and most abundant during summer rains. Stands motionless until prey detected by sight or sound; can flush prey by gently brushing litter with foot. Uses bill, but not feet, to move material or dig in soil. Adept at pulling worms from soil. Apparently foraged on beaches in the past.

Breeding. Pairs monogamous, breeding on permanent territories of c. 20 ha. Main nesting period at low altitude Jun-Aug, with most eggs laid in Jul; possibly later at high altitude, due to colder climate, but before Jan; timing probably linked to food supplies and tropical weather patterns. Simple nest of layered leaves on ground, little hidden; sometimes no nest. Clutch 1 egg; incubation 33-37 days; parents share incubation and chick care; chick pale and dark brown with fawny marks; chick semi-precocial, fed by parents until independent at c. 14 weeks old. Successful renesting 2-4 months after loss of first egg or chick common at low altitude; no data at high altitude. Parents, and sometimes older offspring, protect chick. Juveniles can stay on parents' home range for 6 years, maybe more, thus several offspring can be present at same time (up to 5 recorded). Sexual maturity for males c. 2 years; unknown for females. In captivity, oldest bird lived at least 31 years; oldest breeding female aged at least 29 years.
Movements. Established pairs generally sedentary; some overlap of foraging areas between pairs. Moves widely within foraging areas, perhaps rotationally; can "migrate" within territory following food supplies. Females that lose partners can quit their territories and wander widely. Juveniles make short excursions from natal area before leaving permanently; 2 females were aged 30 and 38 months when they left and established territories with partners. Birds agile and capable of moving long distances relatively quickly over most terrain, e.g. ascent of 750 m over 2 days recorded.
Status and Conservation. ENDANGERED. CITES I. Drastic decline since European arrival on island. Within suitable habitat, species now unnaturally restricted mostly to remoter intact areas at higher altitudes. Minimum total population in 1991 was 654 birds (271 pairs); only 163 of these birds (63 pairs) were in protected and managed habitat, the Rivière Bleue Park. Predation by stray and hunting dogs is thought to be main current threat to species. Cats and pigs, and probably rats, also prey on species, but long-term impact may not be important. Pigs may limit densities of species through competition. Exploitation activities have important indirect impacts by facilitating access of dogs to habitat, and causing habitat loss by fires; continuing loss and fragmentation of habitat by fire, especially in lowland areas, further isolates birds from each other by restricting them to higher altitudes. Breeds readily in captivity; a 44% egg to adult success rate achieved. In Rivière Bleue Park, numbers of present species increased substantially, from c. 60 to 163 birds, after bolstering of population by introductions of birds, predator control, and termination of hunting activity; captive-bred birds introduced in park have bred with wild ones. Unprotected birds likely to disappear over time, because of dog predation. Insufficient pairs protected, thus new managed reserves required, and also efforts to reduce risk of dogs entering areas of unprotected habitat.

Bibliography. Balouet & Olson (1989), Barrau (1963), Bartlett (1862), Beddard (1891), Beland (1975), Belterman & De Boer (1984), Bennett (1863), Bregulla (1987), Campbell (1905a, 1905b), Collar & Andrew (1988), Collar *et al.* (1994), Delacour (1966), Duplaix-Hall (1974), Finckh (1915), Fisher *et al.* (1969), Grant-Mackie (1980), Greenway (1967), Hannecart (1988), Hannecart & Létocart (1980), Hara (1990), Hara & Hori (1992), Hay (1986), Hesse (1988), Hunt, G.R. (1992, 1993, 1994, 1995, 1996), Hunt, G. R. *et al.* (1996), Jeggo (1978), King (1978/79), Létocart (1984, 1989, 1991, 1992),Mitchell (1915), Neyrolles (1978), Neyrolles & de Naurois (1985), North (1901-1903), Pandolfi (1986), Petter *et al.* (1988), Pouget (1875), Rutgers & Norris (1970), Sarasin (1913), Sibley & Ahlquist (1972, 1990), Steinbacher (1968), Thiollay (1989), Vassart (1988), Vuilleumier & Gochfeld (1976), Wada *et al.* (1993), Warner (1947, 1948).

Class AVES
Order GRUIFORMES
Suborder EURYPYGAE
Family EURYPYGIDAE (SUNBITTERN)

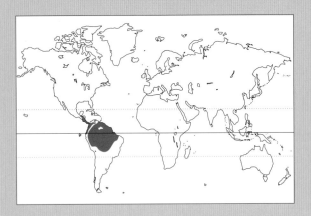

- Medium-sized heron-like birds, with long bill and neck and beautifully patterned plumage.
- 43-48 cm.

- Central and South America.
- Humid tropical and lower subtropical forest, near water.
- 1 genus, 1 species, 3 taxa.
- No species threatened; none extinct since 1600.

Systematics

The Sunbittern (*Eurypyga helias*) is a monotypic species sufficiently different from other living birds that it is placed in its own family, Eurypygidae. At one time it was thought to comprise two species, *E. helias* and *E. major*, but now there is general consensus that it is a single species with three quite distinctive races differentiated by plumage characters, size and apparently non-overlapping ranges, or allopatry. There may also be differences in micro-habitat and food preferences, and probably in behaviour too, but no one has studied all three subspecies in the wild.

The nominate race, *helias*, occurs east of the Andes in lowland tropical South America. It covers a vast range from the Orinoco basin south through the Amazonian area, east and northeast to the Atlantic Ocean, from near sea-level up to 400 m. The other two subspecies are generally found at higher altitudes: *major* from southern Mexico to Ecuador, from tropical up to lower subtropical altitudes; and *meridionalis* only in the lower subtropical zone of southern central Peru at 800-1830 m. Within this huge range encompassing as many as 16 countries, representatives of both the higher and low altitude subspecies occur in only four, Venezuela, Colombia, Ecuador and Peru. This suggests that the Sunbittern was long ago separated by vicariant events, notably the uplifting of the Andes. In Central America, which has had a different geological history, the subspecies *major* is found at altitudes from near sea-level up to 1000 m, and often on both sides of the continental divide.

No fossil Sunbitterns are known, but, in the absence of their possible evidence, relationships with two other living bird families have been suggested. Well over 100 years ago it was found that the Sunbittern shares some morphological and behavioural characteristics with the poorly-known Kagu (*Rhynochetos jubatus*), a bird of the Australasian avifauna that is restricted to New Caledonia (see page 218). More recently, egg-white protein evidence has also implied this affinity. The other relationship may be with the painted-snipes (Rostratulidae), two species, one southern Neotropical and the other Old World, which share with Sunbitterns some behavioural characteristics (see General Habits). However, egg-white protein evidence supports the traditional view that the painted-snipes are Charadriiformes, and the resemblances may be a case of convergence.

In a study of the skeletal anatomy of gruiform birds, J. Cracraft postulated strong links between the Kagu and the Sunbittern. He suggested that their phylogenetic relationship and their distribution both indicate that they originate from the Mesozoic biota of Gondwanaland, the supercontinent that was broken up and separated by continental drift in the late Cretaceous and early Cenozoic. If this is indeed the case, a relationship between these two widely separated species is not so surprising. Although the gross anatomy of the Sunbittern and Kagu are dissimilar, they share the same kind of soft, lax feathers. The primaries of the otherwise nearly uniform pale grey Kagu are coloured, striped and vermiculated much like those of the Sunbittern.

Morphological Aspects

Male and female adult Sunbitterns are very similar in appearance, but small differences in the feather patterns of the head and throat make it possible to distinguish the sexes between individuals attending a nest. Occasionally, the female is reported to be paler. The weight of one adult in the wild was 188·5 g, and those of twelve unsexed captive birds were within the range 180-220 g.

The Sunbittern looks somewhat like a horizontal heron, as both the scientific and English vernacular names testify (see Relationship with Man). It has a fairly long, straight, pointed bill, a long, slender neck, a long protruding tail, and legs shorter than in most herons, more reminiscent of those of some Charadriiformes. The legs and feet are orange-yellow in the lowland birds east of the Andes, but in the Central American race they are sometimes much redder. The hallux is short, as in shorebirds and rails. Observations of foraging birds suggest that the species may have binocular vision.

Plumage and overall coloration are particularly striking in this species. The head is black with two prominent white stripes, above and below the eye, and the iris is bright red, while the bill is dark above, and bright orange-yellow on the lower mandible. The throat is white, the neck and breast brown finely striped black, and in some birds there is a long, dark, irregular stripe down the centre of the neck onto the breast. The buff-coloured belly is offset by the white undertail-coverts.

Most attractive of all is the handsome and beautifully variegated dorsal pattern, which is highly cryptic. The nape is brown with fine black stripes, while the back is barred with blackish stripes and vermiculated stripes of olive, grey and white in the subspecies *major* and *meridionalis*, as opposed to nominate *helias*, in which the dark stripes are broader and the vermiculated

Observers of Sunbittern behaviour initially interpreted the wing flash display as having sexual significance, but it is now known to be defensive in purpose. An adult on a nest indulges in a threat display to startle an intruder and thus shows off to perfection the dazzling plumage of its upperwings and uppertail in a sudden explosion of colour and pattern. The impression of terrific size and the eye-like appearance of the roundish chestnut patches are well calculated to strike terror into the eye of any would-be predator.

[*Eurypyga helias major*, Costa Rica. Photo: Michael & Patricia Fogden]

stripes are mixed with buff; the dorsal aspect of the three races is noticeably different. In a generally cryptic bird like the Sunbittern, such variation probably reflects the different amounts of strong sunlight in the lowland and higher altitude habitats. The tail, with rectrices of generally the same length, is irregularly mottled grey and white with two broad blackish bands edged towards the body with chestnut. When folded, the wings continue the cryptic stripes of the back, but display a line of large white dots along the upperwing-coverts.

When open in display and rotated toward the observer, the Sunbittern's wings appear enormous, greatly expanding the apparent size of the bird. On the dorsal surface each wing displays two conspicuous, large, bright, semi-circular chestnut patches, edged with black and white, and set against a vermiculated field of buffy-yellow and grey. These spots might be mistaken by a startled predator for large, intimidating eyes. When fully displayed the long tail is fanned and tipped forward, revealing two broad black bands edged with chestnut, that effectively join the wings in display. The effect of the whole has been frequently been likened to a sudden appearance of the sun (see Relationship with Man).

The bird's feathers are generally lax and soft, like those of owls (Strigiformes) and the Kagu, and this accounts for the silence of the species' flight. Like the herons and the Kagu, the Sunbittern possesses powder-downs, which are absent in all other Gruiformes except the mesites of Madagascar.

As in most bird species, moult takes place after breeding. The ten primaries, with a vestigial eleventh, moult in descendent order. The secondaries are diastataxic, as in many Gruiformes, and moult commences from three centres each proceeding inward in ascending manner, starting with the first, the fifth and the tenth secondaries, but there are some irregularities. The twelve rectrices moult normally, from the centre outwards. Young birds are hatched with abundant down, but have no juvenile plumage, gaining adult-like feathers even before they leave the nest (see Breeding).

The Sunbittern flies with quick flicks and long glides of its broad wings, and, when over water, its flight is low, roughly 1·5 m above the water surface. There are no reports of it swimming. Although the species has sometimes been characterized as a poor flier, one adult, accidentally caught in a mist-net set over mudflats for shorebirds, easily flew more than 150 m across a lagoon, after being released. When Sunbitterns are nesting, their flights from the ground up to nest branches as much as seven metres off the ground is noticeably light, buoyant and precise. These examples, coupled with their display flights above the 10-15 m high canopy at the beginning of the breeding season, suggest that they can fly better than is usually thought.

Habitat

The typical habitat of the Sunbittern is in humid Neotropical forests, generally with an open understorey, and near rivers and streams. Those birds that live at higher altitudes are found in the vicinity of rushing mountain torrents, while those of low altitudes live near slower-flowing rivers and streams, or likewise the pools that are often left standing as the result of flooding during the rainy season.

The association of the species with freshwater sites is no doubt rooted in the fact that much of its food is to be found there (see Food and Feeding). Nests are saddled on tree branches, but always under a closed canopy (see Breeding). The importance of an open understorey is conjectural: did the birds evolve their elaborate displays and vocalizations as a result of the open understorey which enhances both sight and sound, or did they choose this habitat because it makes their displays and vocalizations more effective?

General Habits

Sunbitterns tend to be wary but not shy. They appear elegant because of their slow, deliberate, stately manner, and these cryptic birds are masters of the slow, "melting" move. Rarely, when encountered, do they flee in abrupt haste, as so often is the case with other largish birds, but instead they frequently turn directly toward an intruder and abruptly flash open the large wings, displaying the spectacular ocelli, which look like huge eyes.

In aspect, rather like a heron but with the body held horizontally, the Sunbittern's feeding behaviour is similar to a heron's too. This species is very much at home on swift-flowing forested torrents where it will dart with agile movements from rock to rock or wade in shallow water to stalk its prey, the head drawn back and the formidable bill ready to make a sudden stab forwards as prey comes within striking distance; its accuracy is remarkable. Both vertebrates and invertebrates are included in the diet, and, curiously, food items are often washed, especially when destined for the chicks.

[Eurypyga helias major, Costa Rica.
Photo: Roger Tidman/ NHPA]

Although early observers suggested that the Sunbittern wing flash, or "Frontal Display", was used in sexual display, numerous accounts show conclusively that the wing flash, and also its variation of a single wing display toward an intruder, is defensive (see Breeding). The "Frontal Display" sometimes lasts for over one minute, and the broad wings are not only fully opened, but are rotated forward, toward the observer, while the tail is raised almost vertically and fanned, as the bird bends its legs, so that the breast is lowered, while the bird itself looks directly toward the viewer.

While standing on the ground, and on and beside nests, Sunbitterns often gently swivel their bodies slowly from side to side in an arc, which, within the context of the use of this common behaviour, might indicate a measure of stress, or a mild threat. A variation of the "Frontal Display" is the "Broken-wing Display", which is used for distraction: the dorsal plumage is ruffled and one open wing is dragged lightly on the ground, while the bird gives rattles, hissing or trilled sounds. Other displays given by adults from the nest are a bittern-like facing, expanding the plumage, serpentine body-swaying, forward bill-darting and treading. The Greater Painted-snipe (*Rostratula benghalensis*) is reported to use many of the same threat displays in Australia, with the same startling effect, using the pattern on its open wings, lowered breast and fanned tail; it also hisses and makes "kak-kak-kak-kak" calls like the Sunbittern, and even its two week old chicks make threat displays (see page 220). The Kagu too uses its patterned wings in similar displays that are associated with threats (see page 298).

Rarely are two Sunbitterns found together, except quite briefly at the nest. In the forest understorey when two birds are seen together it is sometimes an adult still guarding and feeding a juvenile that looks very similar to, and nearly the same size as, its parent.

Voice

In the open understorey of the humid forests inhabited by Sunbitterns, vocalizations are far-carrying. The birds communicate with each other using a number of different kinds of trill,

ascending or descending, long or short, harsh or soft. Trill communication has been suggested as being of great importance to the species, because even chicks as young as six days old, while they are still nest-bound, exchange trills with attending adults. Trills are also sometimes combined with bill-clatters, bill-snaps and vocal rattles.

A long, plaintive, somewhat ventriloquial whistle that is sometimes heard may be territorial, and the loud "kak-kak-kak-kak", often made by zoo birds, as well as those in the wild, is thought to serve for advertisement. This loud call also accompanies the aerial flight display (see Breeding). The only duetting reported is the vocal rattle recorded during the display of a pair (see Breeding). Defensive hissing with neck swaying, in the manner of a snake, is a frequent form of nest defence behaviour by both adults and nestlings, when confronted by an intruding animal, such as a human.

Food and Feeding

A large number of different kinds of prey have been identified as being eaten by adult Sunbitterns, and also fed to nestlings. The most numerous invertebrate prey are flies, spiders, dragonfly and dobsonfly larvae, cockroaches, katydids, water beetles, snails and crustaceans, such as crabs and shrimps; earthworms and moths, both larvae and adults, are occasionally taken. Vertebrate prey is frequent, including small fish, tadpoles and frogs. In the *llanos* of Venezuela, small freshwater eels (*Symbranchus marmoratus*) are eaten, as are toads (*Eleutherodactylus*) and lizards (*Norops lionotus, Ameva festiva*) in the mountains of Costa Rica. Sunbitterns often wash their food, particularly prey items intended for nestlings.

The Sunbittern stalks its prey with the neck retracted, by walking very slowly along the forest floor or in shallow water; it appears to have binocular vision. Often its stealthy movement is frozen, one leg in the air, just before it makes a lightning-fast head-dart toward prey, and this seldom misses. It will also pick and glean in the forest litter, and in thick moss. In Costa Rica, birds walk slowly upstream in shallow rushing torrents to hunt for dobsonfly (*Corydalis*) larvae. When prey is sighted the birds poise with the head motionless for up to two minutes before stabbing at the intended victim.

There appear to be few published accounts of feeding in this species. In Venezuela, a Sunbittern foraged along the edge of a muddy pond sometimes wading in to a depth of about 4 cm, and making 15 strikes in ten minutes. The bird appeared to be feeding on small water-skippers (Hydrobatidae) only about 1 cm in size. After stalking for about two metres in one direction in the dappled shade of trees at the pond edge, the bird frequently reversed direction and reworked the same area again. Foraging beside it were Wattled Jacanas (*Jacana jacana*), a Grey-necked Wood-rail (*Aramides cajanea*) and a migrant Solitary Sandpiper (*Tringa solitaria*).

Breeding

Sunbitterns start nesting in the early wet season, which corresponds to late March in Costa Rica, or early May in Venezuela. In the dry season, at a study site in Venezuela, before breeding started, birds frequently made flight displays 10-15 m high, just above the tops of the gallery forest trees. They called the sharp "kak-kak-kak-kak" call, finishing with a trill, while gliding downward with wings outstretched but hanging down from the body, so that the colourful pattern was thus highly visible from a side view. This behaviour is believed to be related to courtship or pair formation.

Once, at this same study site, a case of what appeared to be pair-bonding occurred. At a nest with a single nine day old chick, one of the birds, believed to be the female, began to perform exaggerated begging behaviour, when its mate came to feed the chick, but the presumed female was never fed. The following day, the adults of this nest met on the ground below it after the presumed male made several loud "kak-kak-kak-kak" calls. This bird slightly opened its wings at the wrist and gave an accelerating vocal rattle, finishing with its bill raised vertically and its head tilted over its back. The female orientated herself parallel to him, facing the same direction, and the pair repeatedly gave the head-tilting display in synchrony, usually duetting the vocal rattle. Then the birds began to dip their heads rapidly with their necks stretched forward and their bills held horizontally. Following several head-dips, their heads were thrown back and they duetted with vertically pointing bills. The pair then parted and walked in opposite directions around a pool five metres wide beneath the nest, giving vocal rattles and trills that were not

duetted. On meeting, the birds again began the synchronous head-dipping and duetted rattles. This display lasted for nearly five minutes. A few Horned Screamers (*Anhima cornuta*) share the same area as these Sunbitterns, and a form of behaviour described as pair-bonding for screamers (Anhimidae) may be similar (see Volume 1, page 532).

The presumed female of the Venezuelan Sunbittern pair was not seen again, but the male continued to care for the nestling until it fledged. At another Venezuelan nest, a single adult was present during the final nestling days. In Costa Rica one adult, on the nest, also began giving the begging display to its mate and one parent was later seen nearby, but no longer attended the lone nestling on the last five days before fledging. These fragmentary observations suggest that Sunbitterns maintain permanent pair-bonds, and that, when a nestling required only the care of a single adult, the other bird departed, either so that the nest would become less conspicuous, or in order to begin a second nesting attempt. To date, there are no studies of ringed birds that can confirm the permanence of the pair-bond or that second nesting attempts occur in the wild.

A single copulation was observed in the wild, lasting eight seconds. It took place after the close association of a pair that stood together engaging in extensive self-preening, which was also repeated afterwards. Later, the male made a single-wing display, while standing close to the female, and following a series of low trills; this might be interpreted as mate-guarding.

Although Sunbitterns probably maintain permanent breeding territories, this too has not yet been proved with field studies. In Venezuela, at all times of the year, Sunbitterns are found in open understorey gallery forest near permanent water, such as rivers, streams, ponds and lagoons. Nests are always sited under a closed canopy, but often in open, leafless sites, on bare branches over trails or woodland pools of water. The nest, constructed by both sexes, is saddled on a smooth, fairly horizontal tree branch, approximately 1-7 m high. Frequently the nest is set at the site of a small side branch or with some other lateral support, but sometimes without any extra support. The mean outside diameter of the slightly oval cup is about 21·5 x 16·5 cm, but the inside is nearly always about 13 x 13 cm, with depths of 5·4-7 cm on the exterior and 3 cm inside the cup. These fairly bulky nests are usually on small branches of 5-8 cm diameter, but a larger branch of 13·5 cm was used in two successive years. The nest foundations are made of long grass fibres, wrapped into an oval shape and attached to the branch with mud. On this base the birds build up the sides, using leaves, rootlets, moss and mud; the cup walls

An adult Sunbittern removes fragments of eggshell from the nest which now houses the newly hatched chick and a second egg. The normal clutch of one or two pale irregularly spotted eggs requires a full month of incubation, a task shared between the parents. The chicks hatch covered in abundant down varying from pale brown to cream, according to race, though all show black stripy markings on the head, neck and back. They are nidicolous and fairly helpless until about the tenth day when they start to develop more quickly.

[Eurypyga helias major, Costa Rica. Photo: Michael & Patricia Fogden]

When the Sunbittern
chicks hatch, duties are
shared by the parent
birds, one searching for
food and bringing it to the
nest and the other
brooding the young. These
two captivating scenes
feature the same two
chicks being fed at the
same nest. In the first
instance, an adult
presents a titbit of
manageable proportions to
the young, while the
brooding parent stands
aside, seemingly to
supervise the feeding
operation. In the second, a
gargantuan meal of a
whole lizard is on offer to
the first greedy taker! The
seemingly precarious
nature of the nest
emplacement is worthy of
note. The leaves and
vegetation used in the
construction are bound
together by mud, a
requisite which means that
Sunbitterns are unable to
undertake breeding before
the beginning of the rainy
season. Often leaves from
the support tree are built
into the structure, and tiny
seeds may begin to sprout
on the outside of the nest,
all of which helps in
camouflage so that
eventually, at a casual
glance, the nest
appears to be a sort of
natural excrescence
of the tree itself.

[Eurypyga helias major,
Costa Rica.
Photo: Michael &
Patricia Fogden]

are deeper on the low side of a sloping branch, so that the cup itself is horizontal. Leaves incorporated into nests are most often from the nest-support tree, or from nearby vegetation. In some nests the bottom of the cup consists of layered leaves and mud, but in others so little material is used that the branch support may be visible. Occasionally seeds sprout in the mud, and increase the cryptic nature of the nest. Nests of this style could not be built without mud; in the Sunbittern's highly seasonal habitats, mud is not readily available until the beginning of the rainy season.

The clutch consists of one or two eggs. The eggs form a short ellipsoid, and are very smooth and moderately glossy; they are pinkish buff, with irregular purplish spots concentrated at the large end. Six Venezuelan eggs averaged 42·7 x 33·7 mm. Incu-

Having swallowed the body, but not yet the tail, of the crushed lizard, this chick has become so bloated that its smothered sibling is scarcely visible alongside it. The parent responsible for feeding the chicks has departed once again in search of further victuals, while its partner has resumed the business of brooding the chicks. Small chicks are brooded continuously for their first six days, and they continue to receive parental care throughout most of their first month of life, until they fledge.

[*Eurypyga helias major*, Costa Rica. Photo: Michael & Patricia Fogden]

bation is carried out by both the male and female and lasts for 29-30 days. In Costa Rica, incubation was continuous and shared equally, with sessions as long as two days early during the incubation period, and one-day sessions during the last twelve days. Costa Rican chicks of the race *major* hatched with pale brown down marbled with black.

Venezuelan chicks of the race *helias* hatch with abundant cream-coloured down, which is marked with black lines on the top of the head, the sides of the neck and the back. One chick at hatching weighed 17·8 g, gave a high-pitched peeping and gaped, but it was unable to grasp with its feet, or hold up its head for more than five seconds. By the third day, chicks still could not stand up or hold the head up for more than 15 seconds, but they shuffled to the edge of the nest on their tarsi, in order to defecate over the edge. Between the seventh and tenth days, nestlings begin to develop more rapidly. Thus, the young chicks, although appearing similar to plovers or snipes at hatching, are nidicolous, and are cared for by the parents until fledging at 22-30 days old. They are brooded continuously by both parents, with shared diurnal sessions of 2-4 hours, until they are six days old.

The off-duty parent brings food for the nestlings and feeds them, while the brooding parent leans aside or stands beside the nest during feeding sessions. Nestling Sunbitterns have a bright pinkish orange gape. They pick single items of food from the tip of the adult's bill, although a two day old chick was sometimes fed by regurgitation, putting its bill inside the adult's mouth. If the chick does not take the food, this is offered repeatedly until accepted. When food is dropped from the nest, the adult will fly down, retrieve it and present it again to the nestling. Most of the regular prey items of the species (see Food and Feeding) have been observed being fed to nestlings, except for moths and shrimps.

On about the nestling's ninth day, the sheaths of the primaries begin to show through the down, and by day 19 the emerging contour feathers are similar to the adults'. There is no apparent juvenile plumage. Around the time that nestlings are no longer continuously brooded, they begin to make a number of adult-like defensive displays in the nest. They practise the wing-spread "Frontal Display" with hissing, the body-sway, head-darting with serpentine neck weaving, and the bittern-stare. Such early development of these forms of behaviour by nestlings suggests that

visual defence by Sunbitterns is very important. Two fledglings, perhaps premature, weighed 83 g and 115 g, well below an adult weight of 188·5 g. A 60 day old juvenile followed, and was fed by, an adult on the forest floor; it was nearly adult size, but had yellowish irides and mottled browner plumage.

In Venezuela, two Sunbittern eggs were seen to be taken by wedge-capped capuchin monkeys (*Cebus olivaceus*), but numerous other mammalian and avian predators of eggs and nestlings may account for nest losses. The tayra (*Eira barbara*), the grison (*Galictis vittata*), the ocelot (*Felis pardalis*), the Collared Forest-falcon (*Micrastur semitorquatus*) and the Ornate Hawk-eagle (*Spizaetus ornatus*) are some of the most likely other predators in this study area.

On three occasions, Hook-billed Kites (*Chondrohierax uncinatus*) harassed adult Sunbitterns brooding very young nestlings, but were rebuffed by the Sunbitterns using visual displays, mainly the "Frontal Display", while standing on or beside their nest. Once a pair of Green Ibises (*Mesembrinibis cayennensis*) spent 3 hours attacking a brooding Sunbittern. Singly and together the adults of this nest defended it by using visual displays, most often the "Frontal Display", which intimidated the far larger ibises. This was a dispute over the nest-branch itself and not an attempt to take the chick. Following the successful Sunbittern fledging, that branch was taken over by Green Ibises, which made a nest two metres from the deserted Sunbittern nest-site.

Captive Sunbitterns often lay replacement clutches after a failure. In Venezuela, several times a second nest was found close to the site of an early failed nest, and it was believed the nests were made by the same pair, although none of the adults had been ringed. More than once captive Sunbitterns have raised a second chick after the first fledged in the same season. Therefore, it is quite possible that wild Sunbitterns might, if the rainy season continued, make a second nest after a first successful one, which could explain the early release of one bird, particularly the female, from parental duties at the first nest. Because several nests have been found in subsequent years on exactly the same branches, it has been suggested that Sunbitterns mate permanently. In captivity, both sexes can breed at the age of two.

Sunbittern chicks are unusual in that they develop no apparent juvenile plumage, but shed their downy coats to assume adult feathering directly. This young bird still on the nest shows adult coloration and patterning, but traces of down feathers are still plainly visible. Even at a tender age, the bird is already rehearsing the "Frontal Display", a clear indication of the great significance of this defence mechanism in Sunbitterns.

[*Eurypyga helias major*, Costa Rica. Photo: Michael & Patricia Fogden]

Movements

Sunbitterns do not migrate, and some birds may maintain territories all year round. In a highly seasonal habitat such as the *llanos* of Venezuela, and perhaps throughout much of the range of the race *helias*, where there is a long dry season, birds may be forced to move short distances temporarily to occupy forest areas bordering permanent water, because they feed on so many water-dependent organisms. Subsequently, they reoccupy traditional territories in the following breeding season. However, members of the subspecies *major* that occupy less seasonal sites at higher altitudes might not need to leave their territories.

Relationship with Man

Native people in both Brazil and Venezuela, and perhaps in other Neotropical countries, occasionally keep tamed Sunbitterns around their houses. The birds, taken from the wild when young, are semi-domesticated, free-roaming, and are not pinioned. William Beebe reported such a Sunbittern riding around on the shoulder of its Indian owner. These pet birds are prized for their fly- and spider-catching abilities. F. B. and A. P. Penard said that once brought inside a house, a Sunbittern would take all the insects within a few days. Since tame birds are so tranquil, it is not surprising that the species readily adapts to life in zoos.

The Sunbittern's spectacular displays have repeatedly been the object of awe. Eighteenth century Europeans, on seeing the flashy patches on the wings as resembling a sunburst, called the bird "Sonnenvogel" (Sunbird), "Sonnenreyger" (Sunheron) and "Oiseau du Soleil" (Bird of the Sun), and much earlier than this Spanish speakers had already named it "Ave Sol". In fact, the scientific name originally given to the bird by Pallas in 1781 was *Ardea helias* (Heron of the Sun). Both the heron and sun motifs are perpetuated in the vernacular English name. When Illiger named the genus in 1811, he called attention to another semi-circular feature: when fully displayed the long tail is fanned in conjunction with the wings; the name *Eurypyga* refers to the wide circle created by the tail.

Status and Conservation

Those authors who attempt to assess the relative abundance of the Sunbittern in Central America, where it is represented by the race *major*, describe it as very rare, local or uncommon, whereas nominate *helias* is described as fairly common in the Orinoco basin. Whether there is a genuine difference in the abundance of these two subspecies is uncertain, but precise comparisons between them have not been made.

The earliest behavioural observations of the nesting of Sunbitterns were made in 1865 in the London Zoological Garden, where a pair successfully raised two successive nestlings. There are abundant records of Sunbitterns living in captivity for 25-30 years, but there are no longevity records for wild birds. Zoological birds, both wild-caught and captive-raised, seldom lay more than a single egg in a clutch. An analysis of the Sunbittern Studbook in the USA for 1990 shows that, although 42% of the nestlings died before fledging, 57% lived a year or more. It would appear that enough Sunbitterns are raised in captivity to supply the zoological market, so that the bird, although not at present a listed CITES species, should no longer be taken from the wild for the trade.

Evidence of at least a certain degree of hunting pressure appeared during the 1960's, when P. Slud reported that local country people in Costa Rica said that Sunbitterns were good to eat. A. Wetmore said that they were once spread widely in Panama, "but hunting and casual killing have destroyed it over extensive areas". There are no first hand observations of human hunting of Sunbitterns for food, perhaps because the birds can not be found so easily, as the far more common, typical game species.

In so far as is known, all three races of the Sunbittern would appear to be secure, but extensive loss of their forested habitat to timber extraction or agricultural development is always a threat. Those populations that occupy higher altitude habitats might be the first to come under threat, as these cooler regions are more attractive for settlement to the ever-expanding human populations in the Neotropics. In particular, the subspecies *meridonalis*, which is reported to occur only in the departments of Junín and Cuzco in Peru, would be liable to become threatened much more quickly than the other two races, simply because of its highly restricted range. The other two subspecies have far more expansive distributions, not merely in terms of geographical surface area, but also with their occupation of a wider range of altitudes. Any form of extensive damming or channelling of rivers is likely to be highly detrimental to the survival of local Sunbittern populations.

The single most important effort man can make for the well being of the species is to preserve, and protect adequately, large areas of suitable habitat where Sunbitterns are presently known to occur. Such reserves would, of course, also protect the bird's prey species, as well as a wide diversity of other birds and other organisms.

PLATE 21

inches 7

cm 18

ssp *helias*

ssp *major*

ssp *meridionalis*

Family EURYPYGIDAE (SUNBITTERN)
SPECIES ACCOUNTS

PLATE 21

Genus *EURYPYGA* Illiger, 1811

Sunbittern
Eurypyga helias

French: Caurale soleil   **German**: Sonnenralle   **Spanish**: Tigana

Taxonomy. *Ardea helias* Pallas, 1781, north-eastern Amazonian Brazil.
Some morphological and behavioural affinities with Rhynochetidae and Rostratulidae respectively. Three subspecies recognized.
Subspecies and Distribution.
E. h. major Hartlaub, 1844 - Guatemala to W Ecuador; possibly also S Mexico.
E. h. meridionalis Berlepsch & Stolzmann, 1902 - SC Peru (Junín and Cuzco).
E. h. helias (Pallas, 1781) - Colombia, Venezuela and the Guianas S through Amazonia to E Bolivia and C Brazil.
Descriptive notes. 43-48 cm; one bird 188·5 g. Unmistakable. Cryptically coloured, with straight bill, slender neck and long tail; two white lines cross blackish head; upperparts vermiculated brown, black and grey; throat and vent white, belly pale buff; iris red, lower mandible and legs orange-yellow. Juvenile similar to adult, but iris yellowish, not red. Races separated mainly on pattern of upperparts and size: *major* larger, greyer above with thinner, dark bars, and sometimes with bill and legs much redder; *meridionalis* slightly smaller than nominate, and generally greyer above with very dark bars.
Habitat. Humid forests with open understorey, near water, in form of stream, river, pond or lagoon; from near sea-level up to 1830 m. Race *meridionalis* occurs only in lower subtropical zone, nominate *helias* only in tropical zone, race *major* straddles both zones.
Food and Feeding. Many aquatic organisms, both invertebrate and vertebrate, including flies, spiders, dragonflies, beetles, cockroaches, katydids, larvae, crabs, shrimps, snails and earthworms, as well as fish, tadpoles, frogs, eels, lizards and toads. Stalks prey by stealthy approach, with neck and head

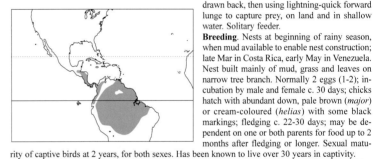

drawn back, then using lightning-quick forward lunge to capture prey, on land and in shallow water. Solitary feeder.
Breeding. Nests at beginning of rainy season, when mud available to enable nest construction; late Mar in Costa Rica, early May in Venezuela. Nest built mainly of mud, grass and leaves on narrow tree branch. Normally 2 eggs (1-2); incubation by male and female c. 30 days; chicks hatch with abundant down, pale brown (*major*) or cream-coloured (*helias*) with some black markings; fledging c. 22-30 days; may be dependent on one or both parents for food up to 2 months after fledging or longer. Sexual maturity of captive birds at 2 years, for both sexes. Has been known to live over 30 years in captivity.
Movements. Sedentary. Short displacements may occur in highly seasonal habitats where water dries up, birds moving to nearby permanent water-bordered sites.
Status and Conservation. Not globally threatened. Status poorly known, due to inconspicuous nature; no figures available for overall numbers or densities. Species widespread, but relative abundance varies from fairly common in some areas to very rare in others: rare to uncommon in N Guatemala, Honduras and Panama; declining in Costa Rica; widespread but naturally uncommon in French Guiana; traditionally said to occur in Chiapas, S Mexico, but no museum skins known, and no recent records from the area. Total dependence on forest with water makes species sensitive to habitat changes on both large and small scales. Easily tamed, and readily lives and breeds in captivity.
Bibliography. Bartlett (1866), Beebe (1909b), Blake (1977), Chubb (1916), Coimbra-Filho (1965), Cracraft (1982), Deignan (1936), Delacour (1923), Frith (1978), Haffer (1968), Haverschmidt (1968), Haverschmidt & Mees (1995), Haye (1989), Hellmayr & Conover (1942), Hendrickson (1969), Hilty & Brown (1986), Howell & Webb (1995a), Levi (1968), Lyon & Fogden (1989), Meyer de Schauensee & Phelps (1978), Monroe (1968), Ortiz & Carrión (1991), Penard & Penard (1908-1910), Pinto (1964), Ridgely & Gwynne (1989), Riggs (1948), Ruschi (1979), Rutgers & Norris (1970), Sibley & Ahlquist (1972, 1990), Sick (1985c, 1993), Skutch (1947, 1985), Slud (1964), Snyder (1966), Stiles & Skutch (1989), Thomas, B. T. (1979), Thomas, B. T. & Ingels (1995), Thomas, B. T. & Strahl (1990), Tostain *et al.* (1992), Wennrich (1981), Wetmore (1965).

Class AVES
Order GRUIFORMES
Suborder CARIAMAE
Family CARIAMIDAE (SERIEMAS)

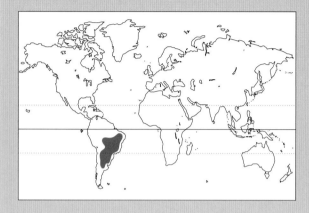

- Large, long-legged terrestrial birds, with hawk-like head and long neck and tail.
- 70-90 cm.

- C & E South America.
- Grassland, savanna, dry woodland and open forests.
- 2 genera, 2 species, 2 taxa.
- No species threatened; none extinct since 1600.

Systematics

The seriema family comprises two very closely related and perhaps even congeneric species, which have been placed in the monotypic genera *Cariama* and *Chunga*. The oldest fossil pertaining to the suborder Cariamae comes from the Paleocene of Itaboraí in Brazil, and several other records of related fossil families are known from the Oligocene-Pleistocene of South and North America. More distantly related fossil birds, pertaining to the family Phororhacidae, have been found in deposits of the Oligocene in France and the Eocene of Germany. Some of these extinct, flightless, sometimes giant, gruiform birds of the Tertiary, collectively known as phorusrhacoids, are thought to be the ancestors of present day seriemas.

The systematic relationships of the seriemas within the Gruiformes are uncertain, and even their placement within this order has been disputed at times. However, the prevalent view has been that they are more closely related to the cranes (Gruidae) and their allies than to any other birds, although their peculiarities have been considered sufficient to keep them in a separate suborder, in which they form the only extant family. They superficially resemble certain diurnal birds of prey, especially the Secretarybird (*Sagittarius serpentarius*) of African savannas, which is itself a bird of uncertain affinities, and which was even grouped with the seriemas in some older classifications.

A number of morphological characters shared by the seriemas and the trumpeters (Psophiidae) could point to a close relationship between these two groups, but the seriemas have normally been placed instead nearer the bustards (Otididae), which have quite similar cestode parasites. Adding to these uncertainties, recent work on DNA suggests that seriemas might perhaps be grouped with the Kagu (*Rhynochetos jubatus*), a species which, on a morphological basis, had never been suggested to be among their closest allies. Indeed, seriemas and Kagus do share some plumage and behavioural similarities, such as a nuchal crest and contrastingly barred flight-feathers that are displayed in similar manners during courtship and aggressive encounters, as well as similar loud barking cries. Nevertheless, the DNA evidence available for the Kagu was apparently rather limited, so this possible link should be regarded as highly tentative. Amidst all this uncertainty, for the time being at least it seems that the allocation of the seriemas to the Gruiformes is warranted, an idea reinforced by the evidence of DNA.

Morphological Aspects

The seriemas are among the largest ground-dwelling birds endemic to the Neotropics, and, in fact, are surpassed in size only by the rheas (Rheidae), with which they share a great deal of the same habitat and range, as well as a few convergent morphological and behavioural features.

The Red-legged Seriema (*Cariama cristata*) can measure up to 90 cm and weigh 1·5 kg, and is thus only slightly larger than the Black-legged Seriema (*Chunga burmeisteri*), which measures 70-85 cm and weighs around 1·2 kg. Standing up in a normal posture, they can reach 60-70 cm, which is approximately only half the height of the Greater Rhea (*Rhea americana*).

Seriemas have soft, somewhat loose-webbed plumage, especially on the neck and the underparts, and both species have elongated feathers on the hindneck that form an inconspicuous nuchal crest, rather reminiscent of that of the Kagu. A noticeable frontal crest, unique among South American birds, is found only in the Red-legged Seriema, and is certainly its most outstanding morphological feature. This crest is formed by a tuft of slender, slightly stiffened feathers that are inserted in the forehead around the base of bill. These feathers are kept permanently raised, partially directed forwards, and can be 7-10 cm long, thus exceeding the entire length of the culmen.

The greyish plumage of the seriemas is generally tinged with shades of brown, being lighter on the underparts and showing fine vermiculations on the upperparts. The belly is whitish, and the long tail is patterned black and white, as are the flight-feathers. These wing and tail patterns, however, are seldom appreciable, as seriemas possess short, rounded wings and rarely take flight. The sexes are alike or nearly so in plumage coloration. Immature plumage is similar to that of adults, but with the head, neck and back more strongly marked. The general coloration of seriemas frequently has a cryptic effect in their seasonal, often semi-arid habitats. The aberrant melanistic coloration recorded in a captive Red-legged Seriema, supposedly from Paraguay, may have been induced by some extrinsic factor such as high humidity, and has been interpreted as possibly corresponding to an hypothetical pattern of coloration of the ancestors of *Cariama*.

The vivid colours of the bill and legs of the adult Red-legged Seriema contrast with its dull body coloration, as with its pale yellow eyes, that stand out from bluish periophthalmic areas of bare skin. Young birds, however, have these parts dark grey or blackish, as does the adult Black-legged Seriema. The moder-

ately long, stout bill of seriemas has a strongly decurved culmen and ends in a small hook, thus resembling that of raptors.

Seriemas have very long, rather slender legs with extensively bare tibiae, and proportionally long necks. They stalk slowly about while not disturbed, but, like rheas, are swift runners, and, when chased, a Red-legged Seriema may attain speeds of 25-40 or even 70 km/hour. The running of the Black-legged Seriema has been described as "a graceful glide, at once both swift and deceiving". Birds only take flight occasionally, and this is usually not sustained for long, consisting of a burst of rapid flapping followed by a glide. Birds typically take flight only in order to escape an obstinate, hard-pressing pursuer, or in order to reach an elevated roost, although lower perches tend to be reached by jumping.

In accordance with the birds' cursorial adaptations, their feet have three short front toes and an elevated smaller hind toe. This conformation means that seriemas, like New World vultures (Cathartidae), are unable to catch prey with their feet, which are used instead, for instance, to step on food items while these are torn into smaller pieces with the bill (see Food and Feeding). Nevertheless, aided by very sharp claws, especially the large claws of the innermost toes, they may cling to the bark and thus climb the trunks of small trees, or similarly jump through the branches of vegetation with the aid of occasional flaps of the wings.

Habitat

Seriemas range over a variety of semi-open and relatively dry areas in the South American tableland east of the Andes and south of the Amazon. Included are some of the drier landscapes of the continent, such as the thorny scrub and other semi-arid woodland areas in the region of the *caatinga* in north-eastern Brazil and the Chaco in parts of Bolivia, Paraguay and Argentina.

The stronghold of the Red-legged Seriema is in the grassy, savanna-like *cerrados* of upland central Brazil. These usually occur on deep soils in a markedly seasonal sub-humid, tropical climate, with rainfall concentrated in the six summer months. Termite mounds, scattered over grassland areas, are one of the most characteristic features of this landscape. They may be locally extremely common and provide favourite look-out and singing posts for seriemas. Further south, the species is also found in

the grasslands and *monte* woodland in subtropical parts of its range in south Brazil, Uruguay and Argentina.

The Black-legged Seriema seems to favour xeric wooded habitats in more lowland situations, being restricted basically to the Chaco and *monte* woodlands, while the Red-legged has expanded its range by colonizing man-created "grassland" and other semi-open habitats in parts of Brazil which of old were covered by tropical forest (see Status and Conservation). The two species are partially sympatric from southern Bolivia through the Paraguayan Chaco to Argentina. Locally, in northern Argentina and Brazil, the Red-legged Seriema occurs further upland and may reach elevations of 2000 m, for instance above the tree-line in the Itatiaia massif in south-eastern Brazil. At a study site in the Paraguayan Chaco, the two species were sympatric but appeared to be segregated by means of seasonal asynchrony controlled by the temperature, as the Red-legged became less abundant during the warm season, whereas the Black-legged was less frequent during the cool season. However, home ranges were apparently exclusive within, but not between, species, implying that other ecological differences are likely to exist.

Red-legged Seriemas, like other large predators in central Brazil, are not scared away by fires, which rule the region of *cerrados* during the annual dry season and are also still regularly used as common agricultural practice in many other parts of South America. On the contrary, they may often be seen in recently burned or grazed areas, where injured or disabled large arthropods and small vertebrates are more readily available as prey.

Although seriemas may forage in extensive *campos* or cultivation in which trees are non-existent, they tend to avoid these areas unless woods are present nearby, as their nests are invariably placed in trees, either in a more or less isolated situation or at the forest edge.

General Habits

Most frequently, seriemas are seen singly or in pairs, but they also occur at times in small groups of three or more birds; each group is almost certainly composed of a pair and their offspring. The members of a pair or of a larger group forage together and keep close to each other; they are very wary and always alert to the least disturbance, and when one of them is startled and runs, it is quickly followed by the other or others. In certain circumstances, a bird may prefer not to run to try to escape a pursuer, but instead it hides by lying down quietly, for instance behind a fallen log, waiting until the danger has passed. When a bird is under imminent threat of being captured, it may try to overawe the enemy by spreading its wings and tail to display the contrasting pattern (see Morphological Aspects), while the plumage of the neck and the head is ruffled. Ruffling of the whole body plumage occurs when birds defecate.

Seriemas are diurnal birds, although in the breeding season their songs can also be heard before dawn. At night, they roost high in trees, and members of a family group may sleep perched side by side on the same branch. A roosting bird will squat on the branch and, rather than hiding its head in the plumage of the back, it keeps it forward, with the neck shrunk in. During the day, birds rest by sitting on the legs and belly on the ground, and they sometimes sun-bathe, rolling the body over onto one side and spreading the free wing to expose the flank. Dust baths are also taken by both species.

Voice

One of the most outstanding features of the seriemas is, without doubt, their queer voice, which is at the same time the most characteristic and best known of bird sounds in their range. It has attracted the attention of virtually everyone who has travelled through the open landscapes of the South American wilderness, and references to it can be found in the accounts of some of the first European naturalists to visit the continent, such as Marcgraf in the seventeenth century and Wied early in the nineteenth century.

The full song of seriemas is a long, dramatic sequence of very loud yelping cries that form phrases, with a staggered variation in pitch. The quality of these cries has been described as being turkey-like, or recalling the yaps of young dogs, or as somewhat similar to the cries of an *Aramides* wood-rail (Rallidae). This noise can be heard for several kilometres, and may sound rather melodious at a distance. Singing activity is concentrated

in the morning, but songs may be heard any time from before daybreak until late in the evening.

Singing certainly has an important role in the defence of the presumably large territory that is required to support a pair of seriemas and their young. One member of a pair usually responds to the song of the other by joining it in a duet, and sometimes a rather discordant chorus may be formed by more than two members of a family group singing together. An apparently continuous song may result from the partial overlap and frequent repetition of individual songs. Often, several such concerts can be heard at once, coming from different individual birds or different groups that are far apart and are responding to each other. In order that their vocal performances may carry farther, birds normally sing from a perch, which may be a termite mound, a fence post or a tree. A singing bird opens its mouth wide, and bends its neck, throwing its head back until it nearly touches its back during the loudest portions of the song. Members of a pair may leave their positions and continue singing while moving forward to inhibit the progress of a conspecific intruder of their territory. Young seriemas start singing the adult song by the age of 2-3 weeks, soon after leaving the nest, and thus may help their parents to defend a territory.

A low-intensity begging call of a single note has been reported in a two week old Black-legged Seriema. Other sounds recorded include a "growl" given by an irritated adult Red-legged Seriema; this species also may utter a "squeak" when courting and sometimes when resting.

Food and Feeding

The diet of seriemas consists largely of animal food, notably including a large variety of arthropods, especially: large grasshoppers, such as *Tropidacris* and *Schistocerca*; beetles, for instance Buprestidae, Scarabeidae, Cicindelidae, Curculionidae, Carabidae and Cerambycidae; and other insects. Birds often forage in areas with cattle and horses, and thus probably benefit by catching insects disturbed by these animals or those that may proliferate around their dung. Other favourite prey items include small vertebrates, such as frogs, lizards, snakes (see Relationship with Man), bird chicks and rodents. Green leaves, wild fruits and seeds are also taken, as well as corn (*Zea*) grains, beans and other cultivated crops, but these items certainly constitute only an occasional and secondary proportion of the diet. Odd as it may seem, the Red-legged Seriema has even been recorded consuming tree gum. Adults of this species brought snakes and worm-lizards to a nest that contained two young.

When foraging, birds walk deliberately, scrutinizing the ground and the lower parts of the vegetation, in search of prey, which is caught with the bill after a careful approach. Seriemas, like raptors, swallow smaller prey items whole, head first, but can use the bill and feet to tear to pieces larger animals, such as a snake or a rat (see Morphological Aspects). In order to kill a vertebrate, such as a frog or a chick, a seriema will hold it in its bill, and either beat it, or, rearing up to its full height, throw it against the ground or some other hard surface; this action may be repeated several times, until the prey is dead. A similar technique may be used to break open an egg, of which the contents alone are eaten, or a snail shell.

Breeding

At present, little has been documented of the breeding behaviour of the seriemas in the wild, and even the information obtained from captive birds is relatively scant. Particularly poorly known in this regard is the Black-legged Seriema; most of the following account thus refers to what is known about the Red-legged Seriema, although a fairly large amount of extrapolation would probably be not unreasonable.

The start and duration of the breeding season possibly vary locally throughout the birds' range, which encompasses areas under the influence of very different climates. Most of the breeding activity seems to occur in the period from September to May,

Seriemas are much more frequently heard than seen. The lengthy song, well known to local people and travellers alike, is remarkable for its loudness and has been likened to the yelping of young dogs or the gobbling of turkeys; indeed, so far does the sound carry that it can be heard at several kilometres' distance. Standing on a termite mound, the bird holds forth with its mouth wide open, a posture beautifully illustrated by this captive Black-legged Seriema. Such vocal performances can be heard throughout the day, but they tend to be most concentrated in the morning.

[Chunga burmeisteri, San Diego Zoo, California. Photo: Kenneth W. Fink]

Perhaps slightly surprisingly for such terrestrial birds, seriemas invariably build their nests in trees. The nest-site can be in an isolated tree or on the fringe of woodland. The Red-legged Seriema's nest is placed 1-5 metres up the tree, occasionally higher, and the bird typically gains access to it in stages, by jumping up from branch to branch. It is a fair-sized construction of small sticks, twigs and branches, lined with leaves and mud or cattle dung. Both parents help in the building process which may last as much as 30 days.

[Cariama cristata, Mato Grosso, Brazil. Photo: François Gohier/ Ardea]

which in central Brazil corresponds to the rainy season (see Habitat), and to be concentrated in the spring and early summer, at least from this region southwards, while it may extend to the autumn and early winter further north in the semi-arid region of north-east Brazil.

Seriemas are solitary in their breeding habits and usually silent in the immediate vicinity of the nest. Pairs keep at a considerable distance from each other, and nests may be scattered over a large area. Fights involving birds kicking one another have been observed during the breeding season, or at the start of it; these were not apparently linked to a particular nest-site, but rather to the establishment or maintenance of a larger territory. In one of these fights involving two birds on one side and one on the other, the entire fight, a long, tenacious conflict, was accompanied by intense vocalization, which continued after the single bird had been forced away.

Courtship displays of the Red-legged Seriema include an exhibition to the female of the male's contrastingly barred flight-feathers, which are exposed by lateral stretching, accompanied by a twist of the wings. There is also a ceremonial strutting walk, during which the male slightly raises its nuchal crest to one side, while the bill is held pointing vertically downward.

The nest is always placed in a tree, usually one to five metres above ground level, but on occasions as high as nine metres up. It is situated so that the adults can approach it on foot, generally reaching it by means of a series of jumps with the odd flutter. In order to facilitate such access, the nest may be sited on a sloping tree, or where a series of nearby branches may act as stepping stones. The nest itself is a large, rough platform of sticks and twigs, lined with leaves and clay or cattle dung. It is constructed by both members of the pair in roughly 30 days.

Seriemas usually lay two eggs, sometimes three. These measure 57-72 x 46-50 mm in the Red-legged and 56-61 x 42-46 mm in the Black-legged, and are white with a few brownish and pale purple spots, though they may become stained brown by the nest lining and the adults' feet. Incubation is carried out chiefly by the female and lasts 24-30 days.

The chicks are nidicolous and are covered with thin pale brown down, mottled darker brown on the back; the down is remarkably long and hair-like on the head. The young birds are fed by both parents, leaving the nest by the age of about 14 days,

when they jump down to the ground and immediately follow their parents on foot. It appears that sometimes only one chick is reared, but it is not clear how often this happens or why. In captivity, young of the Red-legged Seriema fledged at about one month old. A newly-hatched chick of this species may weigh a mere 40 g; adult-like plumage, and adult weight of about 1·5 kg, may not be attained until the birds are 4-5 months old. The age at which they reach sexual maturity is not known.

Movements

Seriemas are generally sedentary and territorial. However, in the Paraguayan Chaco some local movements related to temperature were inferred from changes in the relative abundance of the two species in an area of sympatry (see Habitat).

Some sort of long distance dispersal must be involved in the colonization by Red-legged Seriemas from central Brazil of man-modified habitats in the Amazon zone and the south-east of the country, following deforestation in these areas (see Status and Conservation). This species has also reached the isolated, rocky grasslands on the high plateau of the Itatiaia Mountains in south-eastern Brazil. However, an alternative explanation of its presence there is that this may be a relict population from the Pleistocene, when the savannas of central South America were at times more widely distributed than at present.

Relationship with Man

The generic name *Cariama* is a straightforward derivation from the Tupi native Indian word "Çariama", meaning "the one that bears an erect crest" or, more simply, "crested". The popular Brazilian names "Sariema" and "Seriema" originated from the Tupi by influence of the name "Ema", which is used in Brazil to designate the Greater Rhea. Seriemas are, in fact, the only other large terrestrial birds of South American tableland, and, owing to their peculiar appearance, their loud voice and their habits, people have long been interested in them.

In Brazil, as well as in Argentina, seriemas are reputed among countrymen to eat large numbers of venomous snakes and other

The female Red-legged Seriema undertakes most of the month-long incubation of her two brown-spotted whitish eggs. Upon hatching, the nidicolous chicks are covered in long pale brown down which stands up hair-like on the head. They are fed by both parents and, about a fortnight after hatching, they jump down from the nest, and then proceed to follow in the wake of their parents. The young birds develop rather slowly, and may take up to 5 months to attain adult plumage. For reasons as yet undetermined, often only one of the chicks survives.

[Cariama cristata, Goiás, Brazil. Photo: Richard Matthews/ Planet Earth]

unwanted animals, and are therefore considered to deserve particular protection. In certain parts of Brazil, it is even said that "where there are seriemas there are no snakes". Although seriemas are known to include snakes in their diet, this popular belief is obviously an exaggeration, as is the one that they are immune to snake poison, which was demonstrated experimentally not to be true.

Seriemas have been kept and bred in aviaries around the world since at least the nineteenth century. Captive birds are easily fed and may survive long: in Uruguay, one bird in captivity in 1972 was known to have been caught more than 30 years before. In their native countries, tame birds kept as pets among fowls around houses may act as sentinels, giving warning of an approaching person or animal.

Owing to their wary nature and their capacity for running, adult seriemas are difficult to catch, but young birds adapt easily to captivity and become tame when taken from the nest only half-grown. Capturing an adult Red-legged Seriema alive may require a skilful horseman, a fast horse, and a long, stressful chase, as some authors reported having witnessed in Brazil. In one of these instances, the horseman died a few days later of heart failure, apparently as a consequence of the effort.

Egg-collecting and the hunting of seriemas for human consumption are not apparently widespread practices, but they certainly occur occasionally around settlements, mainly in the semi-arid areas within their ranges, and the birds may represent an additional source of food for the poor people of these regions. At the beginning of this century, the boiled meat of seriemas served with vegetables constituted a valued dish in the north of Argentina.

Status and Conservation

Neither of the seriema species is globally threatened. Possible threats are large-scale agricultural development of their native habitats and hunting, but these factors are not known to have affected either of the two species, except perhaps locally (see Relationship with Man).

Loss of habitat in the Brazilian tableland is a real threat to a number of grassland and savanna birds that are unable to adapt to man-modified and other semi-open habitats, but this does not seem to be the case of the Red-legged Seriema, which has colonized deforested areas in Amazonian Brazil, for example along the Belém-Brasília highway; and in parts of the states of Minas Gerais and Rio de Janeiro, such as the valley of the River Paraíba

do Sul. This species was even found once in southern Brazil inside a large plantation of exotic *Acacia* trees that were otherwise nearly devoid of birdlife, which may also serve to demonstrate, to some extent, its exploratory nature and corresponding colonizing potential. Thus, at least in theory, birds might be able to recolonize areas from which they have been extirpated by hunting, provided this has ceased. Nevertheless, the Red-legged Seriema seems to be much scarcer in any of these secondary areas than in the core of its range. The Black-legged Seriema historically occurs in a much smaller area, and it is not known to be expanding this. Black-legged Seriemas were reportedly hunted by native Indians in the Paraguayan Chaco around the beginning of this century, and this was interpreted at that time as a potential source of local extinctions.

Although precise censuses have not been carried out, both species almost certainly occur at low densities throughout their respective ranges; at one study site in the Paraguayan Chaco Black-legged Seriemas were present at a density of 0·38 individuals per square kilometre. Their far-carrying, easily detectable loud songs probably evolved in association with this, and may be a source of overestimation of their real numbers in any given area by a stationary observer. However, even rough estimates of the present limits of distribution and regional abundance of seriemas are scanty and fragmentary.

While, for instance, the Red-legged Seriema has been considered one of the most frequently seen, and even more frequently heard, large birds in parts of central Brazil, it was rated uncommon in the extreme south of this country, and a scarce and probably vanishing bird in Uruguay. In Argentina, its apparent abundance varies from locally common to scarce, and an isolated population, recently rediscovered in the extreme north-east, is considered to be under pressure from habitat destruction and hunting, as may be populations in the semi-arid region of northeast Brazil. In north-eastern and south-eastern Brazil, Red-legged Seriemas are occasionally offered for sale by local illegal traders of live birds. The Black-legged Seriema seems to be at least a fairly common bird in Argentina, while the situation of both species in the Paraguayan Chaco and in Bolivia remains very poorly documented.

General Bibliography

Alvarenga (1985), Cicchino (1982), Cracraft (1968), Cuello (1994), Dunning (1993), Meyer de Schauensee (1966, 1982), Mourer-Chauviré (1981), Peters (1934), Rutgers & Norris (1970), Schönwetter (1967), Sibley & Ahlquist (1990), Sibley & Monroe (1990), Sick (1985b, 1993), Tonni & Tambussi (1988).

PLATE 22

inches 15
cm 38

1

2

Family CARIAMIDAE (SERIEMAS)
SPECIES ACCOUNTS

PLATE 22

Genus *CARIAMA*   Brisson, 1760

1. **Red-legged Seriema**
Cariama cristata

French: Cariama huppé   **German**: Rotfußseriema   **Spanish**: Chuña Patirroja
Other common names: Crested Seriema

Taxonomy. *Palamedea cristata* Linnaeus, 1766, north-eastern Brazil.
Monotypic genus, but could perhaps be merged with *Chunga*. Proposed races *leucofimbria* (S Mato Grosso), *bicincta* (Goiás and Mato Grosso), *schistofimbria* (N Mato Grosso) and *azarae* (Paraguay and S Brazil to Argentina) invalid, as based upon individual variants rather than geographical variation. Monotypic.
Distribution. C & E Brazil through E Bolivia and Paraguay to Uruguay and C Argentina.

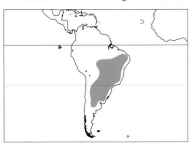

Descriptive notes. 75-90 cm; 1·5 kg. Unmistakable, due to prominent loose crest on forehead, red bill and salmon-coloured legs; elongated feathers on hindneck; large, pale yellow eyes, contrasting with bluish periophthalmic areas of bare skin; black eyelashes on upper eyelids; flight-feathers banded black and white. Immature has dark brown bars on crown, neck and mantle; legs and bill grey, recalling pattern of partially sympatric *Chunga burmeisteri*, which lacks conspicuous crest.
Habitat. Open woodland, thorny scrub, savanna and ranchland; also hilly grassland with nearby woods in S Brazil and Uruguay. Typical habitats include *caatinga*, *cerrado* and Chaco. Occurs from near sea-level locally up to c. 2000 m in Argentina and SE Brazil.

Food and Feeding. Mainly arthropods (including grasshoppers, beetles, ants and spiders), insect larvae, lizards, snakes, rodents and other small vertebrates; corn (*Zea*) grains and other crops, wild fruits and tree gum have been recorded occasionally. In captivity, also seen to eat eggs and chicks of other birds. Usually feeds alone or in pairs, seasonally in small family parties; forages by walking slowly, searching for prey on ground or in low vegetation, when foraging bird often remains concealed due to cryptic colours of plumage; some vertebrate prey grabbed in bill, beaten to death against ground and torn into pieces with bill and claws, before being swallowed.
Breeding. Timing apparently varies throughout range: Feb-Jul in NE Brazil; Sept-Jan in C Brazil; Nov-Dec in Argentina. Solitary. Nest is rough, round structure of sticks and twigs, lined with leaves and clay or cattle dung; built on branches of small trees, normally 1-5 m above ground. Usually 2 eggs, sometimes 3; incubation 24-30 days, mainly by female; chicks have pale brown down mottled with darker brown on back, remarkably long and hair-like on head; leave nest at c. 14 days; fledging (in captivity) c. 1 month; adult-like plumage acquired in 4-5 months.
Movements. Sedentary. Some local movements inferred in Chaco zone (see page 237).
Status and Conservation. Not globally threatened. Widespread, but probably at low densities; at most, is commonly recorded at some sites, but certainly nowhere abundant, although frequently heard far-carrying call may give a false idea of abundance in many areas. Hunted for meat in places, but believed to be an important consumer of snakes and rodents, so in other areas is protected by farmers. Under pressure from habitat disturbance and conversion in southern parts of range, but deforestation in SE and Amazonian Brazil has allowed species to expand to new areas of favourable open habitat. Adapts well to captivity, and is easily bred.

Bibliography. Almeida (1988), Barlow & Cuello (1964), Belton (1984), Benirschke (1977), Blake (1977), Burmeister (1937), Canevari *et al.* (1991), Chebez & Maletti (1990), Contreras *et al.* (1990), Frieling (1936), Heinroth (1924), Hellmayr & Conover (1942), Miranda-Ribeiro (1937), Mitchell (1957), Moojen *et al.* (1941), Narosky & Yzurieta (1987), Newton (1889), Nogueira-Neto (1973), Ollson (1979), Olrog (1984), Olson (1973c), de la Peña (1992), Pinto (1964), Redford & Peters (1986), Redford & Shaw (1989), Rodrigues (1962), Schneider (1957), Schubart *et al.* (1965), Seth-Smith (1912), Short (1975), Sick (1985c, 1993), Sick & Teixeira (1979), Vigil (1973), Wied-Neuwied (1820-1821, 1833a).

Genus *CHUNGA*   Hartlaub, 1860

2. **Black-legged Seriema**
Chunga burmeisteri

French: Cariama de Burmeister   **German**: Schwarzfußseriema   **Spanish**: Chuña Patinegra
Other common names: Burmeister's/Lesser Seriema

Taxonomy. *Dicholophus burmeisteri* Hartlaub, 1860, Tucumán and Catamarca, Argentina.
Monotypic genus, but could perhaps be merged with *Cariama*. Monotypic.
Distribution. S & SE Bolivia through W Paraguay to C Argentina.

Descriptive notes. 70-85 cm; 1·2 kg. Similar to partially sympatric *Cariama cristata*, but averages smaller, with an inconspicuous frontal crest, black bill and legs, and dark eyes. Immature has back and upperwing-coverts spotted white; head, neck and breast distinctly barred.
Habitat. Dry woodland, savanna and open forests, typically in Chaco and *monte* woodlands. Apparently restricted to lower altitudes than *Cariama cristata*, and may favour warmer temperatures.
Food and Feeding. Stomachs of a few specimens from Tucumán, NW Argentina, contained beetles, grasshoppers, an entire rodent, green leaves, grass and a few hard seeds. Has been observed near cattle and horses, and may benefit by increased availability of insects disturbed by them. Tame birds ate mainly arthropods, including grasshoppers, cockroaches, beetle larvae, spiders and myriapods, as well as water snails, small frogs, lizards, bats, mice and dead rats and birds; also fruits and green leaves; the corpse of a large bird was beaten against ground before being swallowed.
Breeding. In Paraguayan Chaco, breeds in local summer, season starting Nov-Dec; in Argentina, young caught in Dec. Nests in trees. 2 eggs. No further information available.
Movements. Sedentary. Some local movements inferred in Chaco zone (see page 237).
Status and Conservation. Not globally threatened. Little information available, but species has been considered common in Argentina. As with *Cariama cristata*, however, true numbers may be difficult to estimate due to often heard far-carrying voice; densities are probably low in general, e.g. 0·38 birds/km² recorded in Paraguayan Chaco. At least at beginning of present century, eggs were collected and adult birds hunted for food by natives of N Argentina and W Paraguay.

Bibliography. Beddard (1889b), Bertoni (1929), Blake (1977), Boyle (1917), Brooks (1995), Canevari *et al.* (1991), Contreras *et al.* (1990), Eisentraut (1935), Farnell (1983), Hellmayr & Conover (1942), Insfram (1929), Müller (1973), Narosky & Yzurieta (1987), Nores *et al.* (1983), Olrog (1984), de la Peña (1992), Schmitt & Cole (1981), Schmitt *et al.* (1986), Sclater (1870), Short (1975), Takagi & Sasaki (1980), Vigil (1973).

Class AVES
Order GRUIFORMES
Suborder   OTIDIDES
Family OTIDIDAE (BUSTARDS)

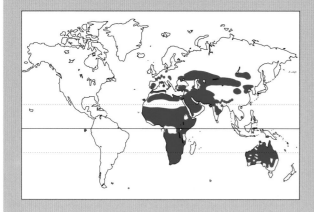

- Large to medium-sized stocky terrestrial birds, with long neck and legs.
- 40-120 cm.

- Old World, with greatest diversity in Africa.
- Flat grassy plains, sometimes with scrub or light woodland, in tropical and warm temperate zones.
- 11 genera, 25 species, 44 taxa.
- 4 species threatened; none extinct since 1600.

Systematics

The bustards constitute a distinctive, homogeneous Old World family which most systematists, in this century and the last, have judged to have its ancient origins with the cranes and crane-like birds (Gruiformes), although at one time or another they have been placed with the ratites and the Galliformes. Recent DNA studies confirm the gruiform identity, but place all other members of the order in the infraorder Gruides, while the bustards remain apart in their own infraorder, established over 70 million years ago. This distinctiveness was also suggested by now abandoned work using egg-white proteins.

While certain behavioural traits appear to stress a link with the cranes, wide differences in display structures within the family itself indicate considerable evolutionary isolation. Anatomical features that render bustards distinct from other gruiform birds are the absence of a hind toe and preen gland, dense powderdown tinged pink with light-sensitive porphyrins, and hexagonal rather than transverse tarsal scutellation.

The generic limits recognized within the family continue to fluctuate, as various attempts to simplify the situation come up against genuine and interesting levels of difference. For years it was common for the heaviest and lightest of species, the Great Bustard (*Otis tarda*) and the Little Bustard (*Tetrax tetrax*), to be regarded as congeneric, and for members of both *Neotis* and *Ardeotis* to be placed alongside both, in the genus *Otis*. In more recent times there have been moves to reduce the genera of the smaller species by placing all within *Eupodotis*, although this plays down the very considerable differences not only in morphology but also in behaviour that these species exhibit. If generic separation is a guide to biological diversity within a family, then *Afrotis*, *Lissotis*, *Lophotis*, *Houbaropsis* and *Sypheotides* should all continue to be recognized as reasonable distinctions reflecting long isolated lineages, while *Eupodotis* serves to identify the five ecologically, behaviourally and morphologically most similar species.

The connections between genera, used to determine the lineages and sequence of species, are more vexatious still. *Chlamydotis*, for all its apparent uniqueness, may actually belong close to *Neotis*, given the similarity of its display pattern to that of *N. denhami*, and its seeming replacement of *N. nuba* on the northern fringes of the Sahara. *Ardeotis* and *Neotis* are uncontroversially close, but their relation to *Otis*, with which they share characteristics of size and display type, is confused by considerable morphological differences and by the traditionally assumed proximity of *Otis* to *Tetrax*, based on their sympatry and similarity of bill shape. *Tetrax* seems otherwise to show features, such as size, display type and wing feather modification, closest to *Sypheotides*, which in turn would seem inevitably close, in terms of colour pattern and biogeography, to *Houbaropsis*. These two Indian floricans have reversed sexual size dimorphism, the only bustards to do so, and this sets them at some distance from the black-bellied species in Africa, to which they are at least superficially similar, and with which they have commonly been lumped.

Whether the small African bustards are all more closely related to each other than they are to other genera is a further uncertainty. The "black-bellied" forms seem likely to represent offshoots from a single ancestral unit. *Lophotis*, with its retractile pink nuchal crest, is perhaps the most distinctive genus; but both the stocky *Afrotis* and tall, slender *Lissotis* also appear to be at considerable evolutionary distances from other genera. If, however, only females are compared, it is possible to suggest close links between the black-bellied *Afrotis* and *Lophotis*, and between the white-bellied *Lissotis* and *Eupodotis*. The situation is ripe for revision.

The white-bellied genus *Eupodotis* holds the most species, five, of which the White-bellied Bustard (*Eupodotis senegalensis*) itself, being the most widespread, is presumably the oldest. In southern Africa the Blue (*Eupodotis caerulescens*), the Karoo (*Eupodotis vigorsii*) and Rüppell's Bustards (*Eupodotis rueppellii*) are judged to have evolved from a common ancestor and to have radiated into grassland, karoo and desert steppe respectively. All three are superficially similar in habits and calls. The Little Brown Bustard (*Eupodotis humilis*) of Somalia and Ethiopia would appear to be very closely related to these three species, reflecting that important link between the grassland avifaunas of South Africa and the Horn of Africa, which is otherwise so strongly expressed in the larks (Alaudidae).

While most commentaries refer non-committally to up to 26 species in the family, recent treatments have been conservative in restricting the number to 22. Evidence accepted here suggests this total might better be 25, with the splitting of *Lophotis* (*Eupodotis*) *ruficrista* into three and of *Afrotis* (*Eupodotis*) *afra* into two. If number of species is a reliable guide to origin, then Africa is the first home of the bustards, with 21 present on the continent. Of these, 16 are purely Afrotropical African, and two more, both essentially Sahelian endemics, are almost so: the Ara-

bian Bustard (*Ardeotis arabs*), which penetrates into the Afrotropical part of the Arabian Peninsula, has colonized the Palearctic in north-west Africa, and the Nubian Bustard (*Neotis nuba*) has been recorded just inside the debatable limits of the Palearctic in Mauritania. Three species are Palearctic, although they all occur in North Africa, another three are purely Oriental, confined to the Indian Subcontinent (with one remarkable outlying population in Indochina), and one is Australasian, occurring in Australia and southern New Guinea.

Within Africa the two centres of speciation are East Africa in a triangle formed by the Horn and the Nile above Lake Victoria, and southern Africa south of the Zambezi. Two species of *Eupodotis*, one *Lissotis* and one *Neotis* are endemic to the former region, and four *Eupodotis*, both *Afrotis* and one *Neotis* only occur in the latter. The Kori Bustard (*Ardeotis kori*) is endemic to both, and all the other exclusively Afrotropical species have major populations in them, while extending elsewhere within the continent. Superspecies are formed by the Kori with the Arabian; also by the congeneric Great Indian (*Ardeotis nigriceps*) with Australian (*Ardeotis australis*); by Denham's (*Neotis denhami*) with Heuglin's (*Neotis heuglinii*), unless the latter is closer to the Nubian; by the Black-bellied (*Lissotis melanogaster*) with Hartlaub's (*Lissotis hartlaubii*); and by Savile's (*Lophotis savilei*) with the Buff-crested (*Lophotis gindiana*) and Red-crested (*Lophotis ruficrista*). The southern African Black (*Afrotis afra*) and White-quilled Bustards (*Afrotis afraoides*), and Rüppell's and Karoo Bustards, are parapatric species pairs.

No hybridization has been recorded, except at one point in the contact zone between the Black and White-quilled Bustards. In general, the similarity of female bustards might suggest that the family is more homogeneous than the variety represented by the sexually selected males might imply, but the absence of hybrids may possibly owe itself in part to the nature of the copulation ceremony, greatly protracted in those bustard species in which it has been witnessed. This may be a key mechanism for the prevention of wasted parental investment.

Morphological Aspects

All bustards are highly terrestrial, never using trees, lacking as they do a hind toe with which to grip a perch, although an Arabian Bustard was once found roosting on a bush, apparently seeking to avoid predation at night by jackals. Bustards fly relatively little, and it seems probable that individuals of all species pass entire days, at some seasons possibly weeks, without taking wing. The word bustard comes from the Latin *avis* and a lost Spanish word *tarda*, which does not mean "slow" but is related to the English word "tread", and signifies walking: bustards are birds that walk, generally speaking at a deliberate, measured pace, although they commonly stand motionless for periods at a time. The smallness of their feet suggests that they run very little, especially the heavier species. When they do take wing, however, they prove to be capable of strong sustained flight, the larger species using slow deliberate strokes, sometimes slightly "flicked" at the end of the downbeat, while the smallest species have a much quicker, more duck-like tempo.

All bustards combine somewhat stout if tapering bodies with long legs and necks topped with rather flattened heads and short, straight bills. The proportions are roughly equal from the largest to the smallest species. Tails are all broad, with 18-20 feathers, but are medium-short, the longest being that of the Houbara (*Chlamydotis undulata*). The wings have 10 primaries and 16-24 secondaries, and in flight appear broad and rounded. The legs are quite stout, but the three toes are short, with thick soles and broad claws.

The largest and heaviest bustards are the mature males of the genera *Otis* and *Ardeotis*, which reach over a metre in height, and routinely weigh up to 10 kg, with a staggering 19 kg recorded for the Kori Bustard. The Great Bustard has been known to reach 18 kg, and hunters have claimed 24 kg for the species, which would place it on a level with the Mute Swan (*Cygnus olor*) as the heaviest flying bird in the world. In these genera, females reach roughly two thirds the height and one third the weight of the males, and are very roughly matched in size, but often surpassed in weight, by males of the genera *Neotis* and *Chlamydotis*. Females of these latter are again proportionately smaller and lighter than the males, and they are matched in turn by males of the genus *Lissotis*, but beyond this point mensural dimorphism becomes much less pronounced. The smallest bustards are the three *Lophotis* species, especially Savile's Bustard, the Lesser Florican (*Sypheotides indica*) and the Little Bustard. At a mere 450 g the Lesser Florican is only half the weight of many Little Bustards, although the latter's shorter neck and legs make it a much lower-standing bird.

Bustard plumages are all predominantly cryptic. The mantle, wings and tail are coloured in sand, tawny and buff tones barred, vermiculated or arrowed with sepia or black. White underparts supply counter-shading in open country species, although those that live in high vegetation have black on their bellies and

Strongly terrestrial like all members of the family, Great Bustards are most likely to be seen walking sedately across open grasslands in search of food. They fly little but when they do take to the air, their flight is powerful and majestic, the wingbeats slow and regular. The head and neck are stretched out in front while the legs are held straight beneath the tail, scarcely protruding; no other bustard species displays so much white in the wings or has such a pale head. When flying, these huge birds become highly conspicuous, yet on the ground it is amazing how easily they blend into the landscape.

[*Otis tarda*, Villafáfila, Zamora, Spain. Photo: Jorge Sierra]

sometimes on their necks, presumably enhancing their appearance during the flight displays their habitat requires them to make. The necks of many species are at least partly grey or bluish grey, and there is often rufous on the hindneck and sides of the breast. Black or white commonly features on the head, and most species have an individual crown pattern, often with a slight crest. The bill is usually dull horn and the legs dull yellow, but in a few species these parts are brighter, notably in the two *Afrotis*. The wings in flight often reveal large areas of white on both surfaces, notably in males that in breeding plumage have black on the neck or belly.

The most sexually dimorphic bustards, in terms of plumage, are those in which only the males possess black feathers on the neck (Little Bustard) or on the undersides in general (both floricans, both *Afrotis*, and both *Lissotis*), although non-breeding Little Bustards and Lesser Floricans revert to female-type dress. Otherwise the plumage differences between the sexes are ones of degree, with males chiefly having much brighter colours, at least when courting, than females. In the breeding season males of many species, *Otis*, *Ardeotis*, *Neotis*, *Chlamydotis*, *Lissotis* and *Houbaropsis*, develop elongated filamentous breast plumes that are puffed up in display. The most exaggerated are those of the Houbara, sometimes referred to as the Ruffed Bustard on account of such feathers running either side of the neck as well as down the breast itself. Male Great Bustards grow bushy grey "moustaches" from the base of their lower mandibles, and male Lesser Floricans have a few delightful spatulate feathers on long, bare, upcurved shafts growing from the cheeks.

The mechanisms whereby the filamentous breast plumes are displaced for display are not well understood, although the Great Bustard develops a gular pouch into which exhaled air is diverted through an aperture under the tongue, so that the entire neck becomes grossly inflated. In the Australian Bustard, a similar distortion is achieved by means of a modified oesophagus, and it seems likely that this feature is present in many other species. The Houbara also has elongated crest-plumes that are generally kept concealed. The three *Lophotis* bustards have a curious pinkish nuchal crest which likewise is only revealed in display, and which in shape is akin to the bouffant crest of the crowned cranes (*Balearica*). The male Little Bustard develops a fleshy hindcollar that allows its "hackles" to rise when calling.

The precocial chicks have a plush down subtly camouflaged with dark lines and mottling on paler ground colours varying from buff to tan. However, many chicks, including those of such widespread species as the Arabian Bustard and the three *Lophotis* species, remain to be described. In the Great Bustard, the first contour feathers and bloodquills begin to show after one week, and this first juvenile plumage is replaced by a second within three months, with an immature pre-breeding partial moult at the end of the first year. The adult pre-breeding moult is also partial, affecting the head, neck and breast only. The post-breeding moult is complete, occupying around three months, with flight-feather replacement serially descendant, starting in the primaries with the innermost, although wings may have several active moult centres.

The feathers of bustards are relatively loose, not densely packed, reflecting the high temperatures of their environments for the most part. The birds' down and plumulaceous parts of contour feathers, particularly on the wings and undersides, are tinged basally rose pink with light-sensitive porphyrins. Bustards compensate for their missing preen gland by producing powder-down instead, and they maintain and waterproof their feathers by grooming them with the bill, transferring the powder to all surfaces. They also frequently dust-bathe.

The bill itself is a stout dagger-shaped all-purpose tool, slightly decurved at the culmen. The shorter, broader and more curved bills of the two most northerly species possibly reflects their proportionately greater dependence on vegetable food at least seasonally, the shape converging on that typical of herbivores like grouse. However, the caeca in all bustards are well developed, indicating the dependence of the family as a whole on fibrous parts of plants, while the absence of a crop suggests strategic adaptation to steady rates of ingestion.

Habitat

Bustards are classic denizens of temperate and tropical grassy plains, mostly open in character, largely at elevations well below 2000 m, and always in areas that are at least seasonally dry. They have colonized all major tracts of such habitat in the Old World, also pushing into near-desert and salt steppe on the one

A Kori Bustard makes a most imposing sight as it moves at a stately pace across the open plains, sometimes in the company of big game herds. The African continent boasts 21 out of the world total of 25 bustard species and most of them are endemic, the Kori Bustard being the largest one found south of the Sahara. A male can measure as much as 120 cm tall and weigh up to 19 kg! Although the sexes are similar in plumage, the female is considerably smaller. Two distinct populations exist, one in east Africa and the other in the southern part of the continent, but the differences between them are minor ones of size and plumage detail. Fairly plainly-clad, the Kori Bustard shows certain noteworthy features, especially when seen at close quarters; the bill is dagger-like, the crest backward lying and dishevelled, the throat and neck ashy white with fine darker vermiculations, the tarsi are covered in hexagonal scales, and the feet, small for the size of the bird, have three short, rather broad toes, but no hallux.

[*Ardeotis kori kori*, Kruger National Park, South Africa. Photo: Nigel J. Dennis/ NHPA]

Most bustards are found
on open plains, where
they can scan far into the
distance and have early
warning of any danger.
Seven of the smaller
African species, among
them the White-quilled
Bustard, opt for less open
bush country, clearings in
thorn scrub and savanna
with tall grass cover,
where danger is less
readily detected, but
concealment easier. This
male White-quilled
Bustard slinks away into
cover with neck and head
held in a characteristic
alarm posture.

[Afrotis afraoides
damarensis,
Kalahari Gemsbok
National Park,
South Africa.
Photo: Richard Packwood/
Oxford Scientific Films]

hand, and dense bushland and thorny country on the other. This radiation has led to some interesting behavioural and morphological adaptations.

Altogether 18 species, representing the full complement of the genera *Ardeotis*, *Eupodotis*, *Houbaropsis*, *Neotis*, *Otis*, *Sypheotides* and *Tetrax*, are chiefly or exclusively to be found in flat or rolling, broad, open landscapes with vegetation low enough to allow long distance vision. They feed, sleep, display and nest in these habitats, and among these species are those that are most geared to follow rainfall, and indeed to move into burnt areas. The selection of terrain with wide horizons must certainly in part serve as an anti-predator strategy, since the birds are clearly major potential targets for the larger aerial and middle-sized terrestrial carnivores; the strategy trades off the risk of being seen against the advantage of early warning. Planting of hedges and shelterbelts is a common cause of site desertion by Palearctic bustards.

Many of the species above, however, show varying degrees of tolerance to partially closed terrain. The Great Bustard, in the western Iberian Peninsula at least, has a moderate tolerance of oak parkland. The Arabian Bustard also penetrates open woodland in places, and indeed there are some accounts by early observers that suggest an unusual degree of acceptance of such habitat. The only good field observations of the Moroccan race *lynesi* were in a now cleared tract of land actually called the Forest of Marmora, the observer noting that the bird could be found in all but the thickest parts. Kori and Denham's Bustards occupy savanna in parts of their ranges, and the Kori at least is known to retreat into the shade of woodland during the hot dry season in Kenya, and has been reliably reported as sometimes using dense closed-canopy miombo woodland in Zimbabwe. The two Indian floricans occupy grassland tall enough to reach beyond eye level for much of the year.

Seven species, all those in the black-bellied genera *Afrotis*, *Lissotis* and *Lophotis*, generally prefer "bush" in its various forms: light woodland, thorn country, high scrub and tall grass cover in dense savanna or on the fringes of water bodies; there is some evidence that they actively shun, rather than seek, burnt areas. These species have reversed the strategy of the others, having presumably gained in a trade-off between enhanced levels of concealment and the increased risk of ambush; but they are all smaller bustards, and are therefore more capable of rapid take-off in the event of a close-range attack. The flight displays of the males, which also distinguish this group from the others, with the exception of the floricans, are quite possibly used by females to gauge the quality of individual flying, and hence fleeing, capacity.

Male bustards commonly select small prominences from which to display, so such features, although very common, may play some part in the general location of exploded leks within a uniform landscape. Decaying termitaria are much used for calling and display-flight launch "stalls" by the savanna-dwelling Black-bellied and *Afrotis* bustards. The repeated presence of a male in a chosen display stall renders the site identifiable, with the herb layer trampled or the ground flattened. Little Bustard males enhance their bare stalls by defecating on them (see Breeding).

Female nest-site selection is poorly understood, as so few nests have been found for so many species. In general, there seems to be little evidence of differential habitat use between displaying males and breeding females, but Bengal Florican (*Houbaropsis bengalensis*) hens breed in taller, denser grassland than their "mates" use for display, and, similarly, many female Great Bustards choose to nest in the shelter of high cereal crops or dense patches of oak or olive where canopy cover may be as much as 50%; Kori Bustards in Zimbabwe also use semi-open groves of trees. Many one-off accounts refer to nests being placed near small landscape features such as grass clumps, fallen branches, and the like, and it is at least possible that some such bias in site selection exists in this regard, but for what reason remains obscure.

Measures of climate and altitude can sometimes be used to indicate habitat partitioning in species. In East Africa, the 500 mm isohyet generally marks the boundary between the more temperate-dwelling Denham's Bustard and its close relative, the arid-country Heuglin's; the sub-humid Black-bellied occurs mostly above the 1500 m contour, while the semi-arid Hartlaub's remains almost entirely below that level. In south-central Africa, the Red-crested Bustard is apparently replaced by the White-quilled in more open areas; the White-quilled, in turn, is replaced to the north of its range by the White-bellied. This last replacement involves the most open country species of the seven closed country types and perhaps the most closed country species of the 18 open country types; indeed in Kenya, White-bellied Bustards retreat from grassland into woodland shade in the middle hours of the day.

Many species of bustard are tolerant of farmland, so long as it is worked in a traditional, labour-intensive way. In Europe the Great and Little Bustard live exclusively on land cleared and worked by human hand. In many parts of its range the Houbara will forage in crop fields. In South Africa, Denham's, Ludwig's (*Neotis ludwigii*) and Blue Bustards live for large parts of the year on cultivated areas. Disturbed substrates often result in the strongest flushes of vegetation or the most intense outbreaks of

A female White-quilled Bustard peers over the tall savanna grass to see if danger is lurking. This species tends to prefer aeas of grassland where the grass is about 50-100 cm tall. While the male is noisy and conspicuous, the female is secretive and is seldom observed. In general, bustard plumages are all cryptic, but the male boasts brighter colours than the female, as befits their roles: the male's mission is to attract a mate, whereas the female, left alone to nest and rear the young, needs to escape detection at all costs.

[Afrotis afraoides, southern Africa. Photo: Peter Pickford/ NHPA]

insects, and so locally benefit some species. Nevertheless, for the most part bustards prefer relatively pristine conditions, and their future will largely depend on such conditions prevailing in the face of increasing human pressures.

General Habits

All larger bustards are known or thought to be at least mildly gregarious. The most markedly sociable of them is the Great Bustard, which is commonly to be found in flocks, usually fairly small and often loose aggregations, although sometimes ranging into groups of 50 or more. The least sociable are perhaps the most desert-adapted forms, the Houbara and Nubian Bustards. Some of the other species flock loosely on migration or when feeding, but most of them are often solitary. Flocks tend to be larger in the non-breeding period, especially in winter, and small or virtually non-existent over the breeding season.

In the larger species the sexes remain segregated by flock and mingle only rarely, as when, for example, two flocks converge temporarily at a particular food source. Males tend to be more consistently sociable; in Ludwig's Bustard any groups appear to be male, while females remain alone. Males also tend to be more philopatric: display grounds are traditional, and in the Great Indian Bustard an individual male will occupy the same territory in repeated seasons. Pair-bonds are not certainly known to form in any of these species, and the frequent reports of "pairs" in many cases seem likely to reflect mistaken, self-perpetuating assumptions about pair-bonding in birds or else refer to female parent and male offspring.

The small African bustards break down into two types: those with black underparts are solitary, occupy less open habitat, and perform spectacular aerial displays; while those with light underparts are gregarious and group-territorial, occupy open terrain, and use their voices for display with no accompanying flight. In three of the latter type, the closely related Blue, Karoo and Rüppell's Bustards, the birds are commonly encountered in small groups composed of parents and the previous year's offspring. Group size is apparently a function of habitat quality, and increases in response to increased intruder pressure, thereby keeping defence costs to a minimum.

In the Karoo Bustard, there is a highly significant negative correlation between group size and rainfall, with the largest group sizes occurring in low rainfall areas. As rainfall decreases, groups tend to be larger and more widely dispersed. In the Blue Bustard, which forms the largest family groups, group size varies season-

ally from a mean of 2·8 birds in summer (September-February) to 3·5 in winter, but it is not known whether this fluctuation, presumably produced by breeding recruitment, is accompanied by an expansion of territory size.

By far the most gregarious of all bustards is the smallest species, the Little Bustard. In Iberia and at least formerly in Russia, flocks of many thousands form from autumn through to early spring. There appears to be no clear sexual segregation in these flocks, which evidently reflect a response to predation, the species being much targeted by eagles and large falcons.

Many species, particularly the larger ones and usually when already in small flocks, have been noted to form loose, short-lived associations with herbivorous mammals. This is likely to assist with predation avoidance, although the birds may conceivably be seeking to forage for dung-living insects. On the other hand, the association between the Kori Bustard and Carmine Bee-eaters (*Merops nubicus*) appears to benefit only the bee-eaters, which use the bustard as a "beater", perching on its back and flying up to catch insects flushed from the grass as it passes, although the bustard's apparent indifference suggests that it possibly gains from the bee-eaters' additional vigilance for predators. The Great Indian Bustard is rather less tolerant, however, when used as beater and perch for Black Drongos (*Dicrurus adsimilis*), and as beater for White-eyed Buzzards (*Butastur teesa*) and Red-necked Falcons (*Falco chicquera*), all of which can provoke aggressive responses from the bustard.

The idea that bustards themselves associate with large animals in order to forage on insects that the latter flush has not received confirmation in field observations. However, Ludwig's Bustards assembling at locust outbreaks have been seen to string out in lines to "drive" the insects and thus profit from each other's presence. Very rarely, two species of bustard may group temporarily together: this has been observed in Zimbabwe with Kori and Denham's Bustards, which tolerated each other in spite of their presumed ecological competitiveness.

Known enemies of bustards in Africa include Martial Eagles (*Polemaetus bellicosus*), Tawny Eagles (*Aquila rapax*), Verreaux's Eagles (*Aquila verreauxii*) and Verreaux's Eagle-owls (*Bubo lacteus*). The result is that the open country species, in particular, are highly vigilant, pausing frequently and scanning, necks raised like periscopes. Rüppell's Bustard, a common target of Martial Eagles, makes sudden, very rapid and twisting manoeuvres when in normal flight, particularly when taking off or landing, and these are speculated to be innate "exercising" reflexes that betray a permanent condition of exposure to the risk of avian predation.

In India, nesting female Great Indian Bustards exhibit strong avoidance behaviour towards Egyptian Vultures (*Neophron percnopterus*), whereas other vulture species elicit little or no response. This difference is believed to be due to the Egyptian's singular ability to break open large eggs of ground-nesting birds, so presumably similar responses will be found in African bustards. Other known or suspected nest predators include baboons, warthogs, mongooses and monitor lizards.

The seasonal abundance of food in grasslands, and the fact that these birds are long-lived, slow breeding species with reduced clutch size and precocial young, have led males, apart from those of the genus *Eupodotis*, to abandon pair-bonding and care of their offspring, since this can be undertaken by the female alone. Predator avoidance during nesting is of cardinal importance, and the breakdown of pair formation may even also have resulted in part from the additional conspicuousness of two parents rather than one in open terrain. At any rate, females of all species become supreme mistresses of secrecy and evasion in this season, combining their cryptic coloration with an astonishing physical ability to vanish, by pressing very close to the ground in almost snake-like fashion, even in thin, boot-high grass. They also disperse rather widely to nest, often selecting very secluded and sometimes partially wooded habitat for the purpose; because they are so efficient at hiding, it is very uncertain how far they actually spread for this purpose! The young imprint themselves on their mother over a period of several days after hatching and respond acutely to her different vocalizations, including those that prompt silent, still, hiding behaviour. There are few bird families which invest so extensively in stealth and crypsis to avoid breeding failure.

Faced with ground predators threatening themselves or their eggs or young, bustards have a shock-display in which the bird will face the source of alarm, tilt the body forwards, raise the tail in a broad fan and partially open the wings, the carpals pointing downwards. The effect of this is greatly and suddenly to increase the apparent size of the bird, and must serve to discourage closer approach; the same display is sometimes used towards conspecifics. Females in greater adversity sometimes resort to injury-feigning distraction displays.

The four common activities of bustards over the course of the day are feeding, walking, resting and feather maintenance.

Like the majority of diurnal birds in tropical and subtropical regions, bustards are most active in the early mornings and late afternoons, and this is when most feeding takes place. Even so, feeding is, like walking and feather maintenance, conducted with a cautious, steady rhythm, and is rarely hurried. Feather maintenance involves much dust-bathing, birds shuffling on their tarsi, writhing their necks in powdery earth and flipping it back into their ruffled feathers, then grooming the plumage attentively with the bill. Resting, often by simply standing still, but frequently also by dropping onto the tarsi with the belly against the earth and head drawn down, is most characteristic of the period from midday till four or five in the afternoon.

In Houbaras, research using movement-activated transmitters has shown that on moonlit nights males, at least, can be very active indeed, females much less so, but the nature of the activity remains unknown. The Great Bustard has been recorded displaying during moonlit nights. Otherwise, birds at night are assumed to roost with minimal activity, moving slowly in the last light to a place of some seclusion or vantage, but not a traditional site; Great Indian Bustards have been recorded seeking open, bare areas, apparently in response to the presence of wolves (*Canis lupus*) in the region.

Voice

All bustards have some vocalizations, but many of these are confined to situations in which they would not be heard by a field observer, for example contact notes between the female parent and her offspring. Some of these informal sounds are attractive and endearing, but for the most part the self-advertising repertoire of the bustards is composed of relatively primitive booming, grunting and grating noises of little beauty or charm.

The larger bustards are all very silent birds. The females are silent throughout the year, in keeping with their typically unobtrusive demeanour. Male Great and Houbara Bustards behave likewise, relying entirely on visual signals to advertise their presence during the breeding season, although excitable young male Great Bustards can sometimes be heard making a gruff nasal cough (basically an alarm note) as they move around in a group. All male *Ardeotis* produce a guttural far-carrying sound when

On the whole bustards are rather silent birds; most of the vocalizations they make are usually connected with displays during the breeding season. The three members of the genus Lophotis are unique amongst bustards in producing clear whistles. The Red-crested starts off its advertisement call with an accelerating series of loud tongue clicks. These are followed by long, increasingly loud "kyip" notes, with a ventriloquial quality. Finally, the performance draws to a close with a series of piping "ki-kiwii ki-kiwii ki-kiwii" cries. Bustards often utter their calls from slight elevations such as termite mounds.

[*Lophotis ruficrista*, Kruger National Park, South Africa. Photo: Janos Jurka/ Bruce Coleman]

displaying, characterized as a roar in the Australian Bustard, a deep boom in the Great Indian, a series of drumming notes in the Kori, and a liquid double-note in the Arabian, sounds that all carry a kilometre or more in still air. Of the four *Neotis*, only Ludwig's Bustard is known to produce a display call, a loud boom. Denham's may do so, but reported observations of displaying birds have been too distant or in too windy conditions to be sure; however, it is authoritatively described as largely silent.

This is certainly true of Bengal Floricans. When startled, or threatening intruders and chasing them away, they emit a "chik" call, given roughly every ten seconds. This rare call is also a component of the display-flight, being given every second for around five seconds in the middle of the flight; but the wing-clapping in its display-flight is a more powerful signal. Lesser Floricans likewise use their wings to produce a noise during their display-leaps, a wing-rattle at the peak of the leap so guttural as to be described as a "harsh frog-like croak" and widely assumed to be vocal in origin. Very few true calls from this species have been reported.

Perhaps the best known sound produced mechanically by a bustard is the whistling of the Little Bustard, from which the Spanish name "Sisón" is derived. The seventh primary is emarginated, and the resulting sound is heard throughout the breeding period, when the male characteristically flies with very shallow, rapid wingbeats. The sound figures in ground displays and display-leaps at dawn and dusk, both briefly preceded by specially amplified, but not far-carrying, foot-stamping accelerandos. The male Little Bustard also has a brief sneezing snort-call, "prrret", which features at the climax of the above displays, but which he also gives repeatedly throughout the spring day.

The small African bustards are much the noisiest of the family. The Black-bellied has a "song" which involves three different notes, a moaning "oooo" followed by a snoring "waaak" or "chikk", then "pop!" Hartlaub's, its close relative, goes "click" very quietly, followed by "tok" and then "boooom". The two *Afrotis* species have almost identical display calls, a clattering, raucous "kerrak-kerrak-kerrak" that continues for several minutes at a time. These species also have similar ground calls, but the White-quilled appears to have two calls not given by the Black Bustard. The songs of the three *Lophotis* species differ

somewhat from each other, Savile's being the most distinct, but the species are united in being the only bustards to produce clear whistles. The Red-crested's starts with an accelerating series of clicks followed by long, increasingly loud "kyip" notes, to end in a minutes-long series of piping "ki-kiwii ki-kiwii ki-kiwii" calls.

The group-forming, white-bellied species have fairly similar advertising calls. The widest-spread species, the White-bellied Bustard, has a loud, far-carrying, crowing croak, "kak-warat", close to the Blue Bustard's normally disyllabic "kok-aw". Advertising calls in both Karoo and Rüppell's Bustards are in the form of duets in which the male leads, with his "squark" or "kwaaka": "squark-kok, squark-kok, squark-kok..." in the Karoo Bustard; and "kwaaka-kokka, kwaaka-kokka, kwaaka-kokka..." in Rüppell's. Young males in the family group also participate in this antiphonal calling, falteringly at first but rapidly becoming synchronized with the parent male's voice. The calls of all these *Eupodotis* species carry considerable distances, and commonly trigger response-calling by neighbouring pairs and groups.

Voices of birds are very variously transcribed, and they are very variously interpreted. In due course tape-recordings may reveal that there is a relatively small number of types of vocalization that are common across the family. The alarm call mentioned above for Great Bustard, a gruff cough, "ogh!", is certainly one that many other species appear to possess and use in similar contexts of excitement and stress. The vocabulary of pleasant, quiet calls between mother and young may also prove to be shared by many family members.

Food and Feeding

Bustards are omnivorous and highly opportunistic in their food habits, taking advantage of any local abundance whether of animal or plant, and seemingly capable of maintaining themselves on that single source for at least short periods. Nevertheless, although such biases are frequent in records of bustard food, there is generally a balance that all members of the family strike between animal and vegetable components of their diet. The bustard bill, shortish, straight and stout, is a simple, powerful, all-purpose instrument for snipping off, snapping up, probing, grasping

Bustards are well adapted to life in semi-arid conditions where water is scarce, and in the wild they are not often seen to drink, whereas in captivity where water is freely available they drink readily. It is supposed that wild bustards obtain most of the moisture they need from their food, which includes a large quantity of vegetable matter, but pools, puddles and other sources of water, when encountered, are certainly not disdained. Note the manner in which these Great Indian Bustards set about drinking by resting on their tarsi to reach the water more easily. The bird on the left, its mouth already full, will tilt the head right back before swallowing.

[*Ardeotis nigriceps*, Rajasthan, India. Photo: Joanna Van Gruisen/ Ardea]

Equipped with an all-purpose bill, bustards are omnivorous and opportunistic feeders. They are well known for taking advantage of swarming locusts and grasshoppers, and certain species gather at bush fires to feed on the victims, dead and dying insects and also vertebrates. Almost all bustard species take vertebrate prey at times, mainly small snakes and lizards, like this Kori Bustard. At the same time, research has shown that vegetable matter makes up a surprisingly large proportion of the bustard diet.

[Ardeotis kori kori, Kalahari, Africa. Photo: Régis Cavignaux/ Bios]

and crushing, and as such it serves its owner in a wide variety of foraging contexts.

It is commonly assumed that bustards are primarily insectivorous and take vegetable matter as a supplement. However, detailed studies of the gut contents of certain species have shown that vegetation constitutes a very significant proportion of the diet. In the case of the Karoo Bustard, the stomachs of 15 birds all contained animal material, but this made up only 6% of the aggregate volume and 12% of the aggregate mass, and it seems likely that this proportion will be found to exist for most bustard species in normal conditions (that is, when no local infestation of insects is taking place), as post-mortem assessments of diet may often underestimate or ignore the bulk of unrecognizable plant matter found in the stomachs of birds that do not possess a crop.

Bustards take all kinds of vegetable matter. They are keen consumers of green shoots, flowerheads and fresh leaves of plants in the herb layer, with Compositae much favoured in the European steppes. In a recent study of Karoo Bustard stomach contents, leaves were found to have contributed some 40% of the samples, indicating their considerable importance, perhaps chiefly as a source of water, though possibly also as a source of salt, for the more desert-adapted bustards. Soft roots, bulbs and corms are dug up and consumed, and seeds, fruits and berries are taken in season.

Palearctic and Indian bustards commonly forage in cultivated areas. They have a particular taste for legumes such as clover (Trifolium) and lucerne (Medicago sativa), and for crucifers such as black mustard (Brassica nigra) and turnip (Brassica napus), and in the past, at least, could become pest species at certain times of year. Any strong-tasting food, which bustards appear to prefer, supposedly taints their flesh, and it used to be claimed that birds that have fed on garlic are inedible.

In the Sahel and other parts of Africa, Acacia gum is much utilized, although perhaps this is as much for its water content as for its nutritional value. Perhaps best known for this habit is the Arabian Bustard, which in some gum-growing regions of Chad is regarded as a pest. The species is also, however, well known for its depredations on locusts and swarming grasshoppers. Stomachs of shot specimens have been found packed with Orthoptera, and the economic, and indeed direct human, benefit of such con-

sumption may be far greater than credited. A rough calculation suggests that a single White-quilled Bustard might consume around 200,000 termites a year, and that this and other species may well play a significant role in reducing the impact of agricultural pests. There has even been a case of a Denham's Bustard defending a termitarium during an emergence from the attentions of other avian species, but this is clearly unusual. Such opportunism in exploiting local abundances of insects is mirrored in the way certain species gather at bush fires to seize fleeing, dying or dead insects and small vertebrates. Indeed, the carrion habit appears to extend to roadkills, as both Kori and Black-bellied Bustard have been found at the roadside carrying or eating the corpses of birds.

Beetles and grasshoppers are the chief animal food of bustards, although any ground- or grass-dwelling invertebrates, crickets, termites, mantises, caterpillars, ants and bugs among the insects, spiders, scorpions, centipedes and snails among the rest, are readily taken. It may be that grassland bustards take more Orthoptera, bushland bustards more Coleoptera, and there may be some interesting niche adaptations, yet to be elucidated, reflected in the bill morphology of the various genera.

Almost every species of bustard has been reported taking vertebrate prey at least occasionally. Mostly the victims are small snakes and lizards, but the eggs and nestlings of ground-nesting birds must be very common seasonal prey items. Small mammals are also taken occasionally, or even relatively frequently by Great Bustards, in the more northerly parts of their range. Amphibians are also sometimes reported, and some curious observations exist that appear to refer to this source of food: in one case a Denham's Bustard seen wading thigh-deep in a pool was assumed to be foraging for frogs on emergent vegetation; in another case, in New Guinea, Australian Bustards gathered to feed in shallow water, although the presumed or known food was not specified.

In captivity, it has been noted that bustards have a liking for bright objects, a trait they share with the Ostrich (Struthio camelus), while in Chad it has been found that all species there commonly take coloured beads, notably yellow and white ones. Over half of all stomachs examined contained them, and one held no fewer than 41. Presumably such objects are taken in the belief that they are or were animate, the only other such shiny

Male bustard behaviour in the breeding season varies widely according to the species and displays can be of several types. The Houbara Bustard is in a category all of its own, since no other species has the so-called "Trotting" or "Running" display. Male Houbaras defend quite extensive territories and during the breeding season are scattered out over the plains with at least 500 m between individual birds. Their displays take place at certain slightly elevated spots within the territory. The bird will begin by depressing his tail, then fanning out the normally hidden white crown feathers. As the head is retracted onto the back, he begins to trot or strut in a bizarrely erratic fashion. After a minute or so the neck plumes cover the head completely; at this stage, seemingly headless, his vision is totally obscured and birds have been seen to crash into obstacles!

[*Chlamydotis undulata macqueenii*, Saudi Arabia. Photo: Xavier Eichaker/ Bios/Foto Natura]

objects presumably being certain beetles. However, bustards frequently and regularly ingest gastroliths, which are important in abetting the digestion of plant matter. Indeed, all species investigated have well developed caeca, often associated with a heavily vegetarian diet, although this feature may also be of importance to those species of more arid environments, implying possible physiological and thermoregulatory functions as well as a digestive adaptation.

Whether seeking animal or vegetable food, a bustard always commences a feeding bout walking slowly in a posture with the body oriented slightly downwards, the neck somewhat bent back on itself, and the bill pointing down. When a vegetable item is encountered, the bird pauses, maintaining its hunched posture,

and gives repeated, short, precise pecks at the object. If the item or items are on the ground, whether plant or small animals such as ants, the body is tilted forward and the precise short pecks are given, although for items in, rather than on, the substrate the bill is used to probe and work the ground. Animals larger than grasshoppers are generally held in and processed by the bill for a short time, the body angled forward so that the head is low, ready to release and avoid, or release and recapture, the animal with maximum ease. Birds will sometimes run briefly, head forward, to capture a moving prey item, and even jump to attempt to catch passing insects or to take berries from bushes.

The timing of breeding in bustards appears to reflect the need to hatch young at the start of the period of maximum insect availability in the annual cycle, since, as in many granivorous species, young birds need easily digested protein-rich food sources for rapid growth. Nonetheless, even very small chicks soon peck at green stems and leaves, and so begin ingesting vegetable matter at a very early age.

Bustards are adapted to arid environments, and seem to be able to survive well for extended periods without access to water, presumably, as suggested above, obtaining their needs from vegetable material. Nevertheless, opportunities to drink in the wild, at rain puddles, along small watercourses, are not missed, and in captivity most species appear to drink very freely on a daily basis. Large bustards often sit on their tarsi to drink: water can either be drawn in directly by a pumping action of the throat or else drawn into the mouth and then emptied down the neck, the head being lifted and tilted back.

Breeding

Palearctic bustards breed in the spring, although the season may be very protracted in the case of the Houbara, where local rainfall may produce suitable conditions at different times in different areas within the same year. At the foot of the Himalayas, the Bengal Florican also breeds within the period of the northern spring, as do the species in the Horn of Africa and Ethiopia. Species in the Sahel and West African savannas generally breed with the rains from July onwards, as does the Lesser Florican in western India. In East Africa there may be several breeding seasons, directly related to the rainfall regime, but all species have been recorded breeding within the period from December to May. In Central and southern Africa the season lies generally between October and March. The Great Indian Bustard has a protracted season, being distributed within three rainfall regimes; and the Australian Bustard is aseasonal in northern Australia, simply responding to unpredictable rains, but breeds from April to November in the south.

It is in the mating system and associated displays of bustards that their most obvious biological interest and aesthetic appeal lie. Twenty years ago only a very small proportion of the family had been the subject of even qualitative, anecdotal studies, yet although in the intervening period there has been some important work on the behavioural ecology of several species, the ob-

stacles to quantitative investigations have barely begun to be overcome. Chief among these obstacles are the difficulty in capturing and marking birds, the difficulty of making sustained observations owing to their often cryptic dress and wary behaviour, and the sheer remoteness and inhospitability of the habitats they occupy. Moreover, as K-selected species, long-lived and low in reproductive output, bustards take many years to furnish data that can be tested for significance. None of this is conducive to academic programmes of study, nor even to sustained observational work by committed field ornithologists working independently of tight academic reporting schedules.

The upshot is that even now there are three species, the Nubian, Heuglin's and the Little Brown Bustards, of which mating systems and displays are entirely unknown and can only be inferred from their generic position. It was only in the past few years that casual observations (by two observers once) have shown that Hartlaub's Bustard has a display-flight. Even more surprisingly, the Arabian, Denham's and the Black-bellied Bustards, supposedly familiar birds given their size and their ranges, have only been subject to brief, non-quantitative studies of their display behaviour in the wild. The display behaviour of the Australian and Kori Bustards, despite the latter's presence in many of the more accessible East and southern African reserves, has been described in detail only in captive studies.

Inevitably, therefore, the function and nature of bustard displays in relation to mate attraction, rival deterrence and territorialism remain largely unclear. What is emerging with increasing certainty, however, is that the majority of bustard species establish no true pair-bond, depending instead on "dispersed lek" behaviour in which males advertise themselves on traditional areas, often at traditional individual sites, at least sometimes in moderately clumped groupings although still preserving distances of one or several hundred metres between each other. The females are left entirely alone to undertake nesting, incubation and rearing of the young.

Observations of the seven Palearctic, Indian and Australian species indicate that this is unequivocally the case in all these birds, and the evidence from Africa matches the pattern, except in the case of the sexually rather similar white-bellied *Eupodotis* bustards. In these open country species there is evidently a strong need to defend a resource base for survival and reproduction, and all the indications are that this is achieved by an apparently year round monogamous pair-bond and territorial defence, often with the additional help of an extra bird, which, in those species studied, is a male offspring of the pair. Group-territorial behaviour is best documented in Rüppell's, the Karoo and the Blue Bustards, seems likely to occur in the closely related Little Brown Bustard of the Horn of Africa, and appears to exist in the White-bellied, although this last has such an extensive range that different ecological conditions may result in different strategies. Nevertheless, all five certainly appear to be recorded as monogamous breeding birds.

The fact that a pair of *Eupodotis* bustards will often allow a male offspring to remain on their territory to help with its defence may be attributable to the fact that young males even in these pair-forming species defer their maturity by a year or so and hence present no threat to the parent male. What happens in the other small African bustards, and indeed in the small Indian ones, is unknown, but males of the larger species certainly exhibit delayed maturity of up to six years, whereas females may take as little as two before starting to breed.

Deferred maturity in these cases is the result of sexual selection acting on males by female choice: if the females are to be left to undertake all parental responsibilities with no assistance whatsoever, and their only social contact with adult males is at the moment of copulation, then they clearly must choose males with characteristics most desirable to pass on to their offspring, including, of course, the capacity to mate with as many females as possible. Hence, males in these species grow to be larger and many times heavier than females, which inevitably takes time, and meanwhile the older, more mature males tend to be left to compete among themselves while suppressing the attempts and opportunities of younger birds to become established as rivals for female attention.

Hartlaub's Bustard is generally rather scarce and it has a much more restricted range than the very similar Black-bellied Bustard (Lissotis melanogaster). *Little seems to be known about either its feeding or its breeding behaviour, and only recently has it been observed to perform aerial displays. Here a male presents a splendid sight as, standing on a slight eminence, he inflates his throat and neck in the so-called "Balloon-display" in which he takes on a shape distinctly recalling an hourglass.*

[Lissotis hartlaubii, Kenya.
Photo: N. Gore/FLPA]

At the beginning of the breeding season, the male Great Bustard chooses a conspicuous elevated site on which to make his spectacular display and thus to attract a mate. First, the gular sac is inflated, and the tail is raised and laid flat on the back, exposing the white undertail-coverts. In addition, the inner secondaries are twisted over and fanned out. At the peak of his performance he seems to have turned himself inside out to become, in a matter of seconds, a brilliant white ball visible at a distance of several kilometres. Highly convoluted and utterly transformed, he may remain stationary like this for some time in the expectation that some female will succumb to his many gorgeous attractions.

[Otis tarda tarda, La Moraña, Avila, Spain. Photo: Carlos Sánchez Alonso]

In the case of the Great Bustard this situation results in a high proportion of under-age males in any healthy population. Outside the breeding season it is difficult, if not impossible, to distinguish these birds, as the winter plumage of all males is largely uniform by the second autumn. However, at the onset of spring the fully mature birds begin to break away from the winter flocks for increasing periods of time to display separately on the dispersed lek, leaving the younger males to roam together in and around this area. Year by year these younger birds develop more fully the appearance of the mature birds, but are presumably lighter and less experienced. They behave as an unruly gang, becoming highly excited by events amongst and around them, adopting incomplete display postures, which are chiefly aggressive in signal, and sometimes singling out members of the group for sudden concerted aggression.

The general impression from these groups is that these young males are developing and testing their strength and display repertoire prior to the time when they will contest a place on the dispersed lek itself. Fighting in male Great Bustards is not frequent, doubtless because the genuinely mature males maintain respectful distances from each other, while newcomers will only put themselves forward for combat when their condition really matches that of their opponents. Most confrontations involve a long preliminary face-to-face, but when and if a struggle ensues it is a violent and bitter event; it may well be that to lose in such an encounter involves such physical stress that no further attempts at self-establishment would be made within the season.

In the course of the spring, and almost certainly from year to year, a hierarchical order builds up among male Great Bustards. The most powerful males dominate the lek area, but there is no territorialism, although very occasionally an unmovable male may, at least in appearance, hold a given piece of land over one or more seasons. The dominant males move slowly about on the lek, displaying at different places for extended periods. Females concentrate on the fringes of the area and move slowly through

it, feeding and watching the performances. A female approaches a displaying male very cautiously, and is often quite slowly drawn into the protracted copulation sequence. However, because the males, although dispersed, have no territorial boundaries inhibiting one another, copulation sequences are often interrupted by other males attracted to the spot, particularly if the courting male is a relatively young bird that has managed to infiltrate the area.

It is usual to describe this mating system as promiscuous, inasmuch as successful males mate with several females and no bond is apparent. However, it is by no means certain that females choose at random among males, and it is at least possible that research with marked birds might reveal repeated selection of a given male by a female over successive years, indicating some vestigial type of bond. Such selection may also occur in other species, and this may be the explanation for the apparently anomalous "courtship feeding" and nest-site attendance witnessed in Kori and Denham's Bustards respectively.

The Great Bustard is perhaps unique in possessing a non-territorial dispersed lek system, and it is the only species of bustard that remains silent throughout its display. In the other very large bustards of the genus *Ardeotis*, males appear to establish territories from which other males are excluded. In the case of the Great Indian Bustard these territories are of considerable size, with evidence that display by a potential rival up to a kilometre distant may not be tolerated, although this is probably extreme. In the closely related Australian Bustard, male territories are sometimes solitary but are generally clustered so as to render the birds within sight or sound of each other, and they may be as close as 50 m apart. The territories are located near abundant food, mainly at the interface of treeless plains and shrublands, the birds using a slight eminence or low rise on which to perform. The occasional acceptance of clearly subordinate males in the territories of both species suggests that it is less the resource base of the area that is being defended than the incumbents' access to any female within it. The other two *Ardeotis* show similar behaviour,

A male Little Bustard
performs its "Jumping-
display" from a raised site
of bare earth. The
sequence begins with a
bout of foot-stamping; then
the bird leaps more than a
metre into the air, at the
same time giving its nasal
"prrt" call, while the wings
produce the characteristic
"sisisisi" sound which has
given rise to its Spanish
name of "Sisón". The
whole performance, aimed
supposedly at attracting a
female, takes about a
second and is given both
at dusk and dawn.

[Tetrax tetrax,
Pinto, Madrid, Spain.
Photo: L. M. Ruiz Gordon]

with males spaced a hundred metres or so apart, using small rises on which to display.

In a South African population of Denham's Bustard, the only *Neotis* species in which breeding behaviour has been described, males established territories in a dispersed lek in which each bird was at least 700 m from the next and occupied an area of approximately 60 ha. In Kenya, males of this species have actually been seen in boundary displays, walking parallel to each other at the evident borders of their territories. There have been observations on the Nyika Plateau in Malawi of extended associations between male and female Denham's Bustards, even to the point of their appearing to share incubation duties, but this circumstance appears anomalous, and may have involved a mother and her yearling male offspring, a combination recorded in the Great Indian Bustard; the sexual size dimorphism of the species, and other evidence available, suggests the absence of bonding behaviour between the sexes.

Ludwig's Bustard also possesses traditional display territories and has a similar display to Denham's, except that the brown foreneck produces a dark rectangle on the front of the otherwise white balloon, and, apparently unlike Denham's, a loud booming call is produced. It seems likely that Heuglin's and Nubian Bustards would show broadly similar display behaviour to their two congeners. However, to some extent the Nubian is the ecological equivalent on the Sahara's southern fringes of the Houbara: if environmental factors determine breeding systems and behaviour, it may turn out that the Nubian is the least typical *Neotis* in this regard.

The Houbara itself, which arguably shows affinities, albeit distant, to *Neotis* through its display pattern, also maintains display areas or territories that are roughly a kilometre apart, although sometimes half that distance. Territories are used in successive years, and females also tend to nest close to earlier successful nests, but again there seems to be no contact between the sexes except for copulation. This is true also of both Bengal and Lesser Floricans and the Little Bustard. The first, much the largest of the three and approximately the size of the Houbara, maintains territories which allow the nearest neighbouring males no closer than 350 m, although not necessarily within visual or acoustic range. Territory size in this species is certainly around 1 km² and probably much larger, although mostly only 20-30 ha are used for foraging and 3-10 ha for display purposes. In the Lesser Florican as many as three territories have been found in a 9 ha area of grassland, but the average territory density is 4·7 per km². This is a similar value to those for the only slightly smaller Little Bustard over much of its range, although in particularly favourable areas it reaches territorial densities of nearly 14 per km².

The various species of black-bellied bustard in Africa, namely the Black, White-quilled, Black-bellied, Hartlaub's, Savile's, Buff-crested and Red-crested, are too little studied to permit complete confidence, but all of them appear to conform to the family norm: none appears to establish a pair-bond. All these birds tend to inhabit well developed bushland habitat, and all, except apparently Savile's Bustard, advertise themselves with aerial flights over their territories.

The best studied of the five presumed monogamous members of the family is the Karoo Bustard. Pairs of this species defend territories year round, but these are "plastic", in that their boundaries shift concentrically to the pair during the course of the year in situations where resource availability is not constant. The area defended covers between 0·5 and 3 km². Young male offspring often help defend the territory, and the size of the resulting groups, though mostly three, can reach as many as five. Chief means of territorial advertising is the song, initiated by the male, given in the half-light at daybreak and dusk, or else in response to intrusion by conspecifics or to an outbreak of duetting by a neighbouring pair. Males play a greater role in territorial defence than do females, initiating the duet in response to territorial intrusion, and taking longer to return to foraging after a dispute, which can take the form of direct fighting. Inasmuch as the territory moves with the pair, it would seem that its function has also to do with mate-guarding, in other words the prevention of courtship of the mated female by other males, and as a spacing mechanism to help avoid conflict, as well as with physical resource protection.

Even where three individuals have been witnessed at the nest, there is no evidence that the extra birds involved in groups contribute directly to breeding success by helping with the care of, or food provision to, newlyhatched birds, but simply make those things more feasible by reducing the parental burden in territorial defence. Whether any males of these species actively help at the nest with incubation, brooding or food provision appears still to be unresolved.

Display in the *Eupodotis* bustards (as here constituted) is basically confined to their vocal signals. The male Karoo Bustard

Two phases of a typical male Kori Bustard display have been caught by different cameras. This display, one of the "Balloon" type, is very similar to that performed by the other members of the genus Ardeotis. The male struts to and fro, often on a low rise, then standing upright he inflates the neck until it turns into a giant white puffball. With the neck thus inflated, the tail cocked and flattened down the back to reveal white undertail-coverts, and the wings drooping so as almost to touch the ground, he may stand still or strut around, at times emitting a drum-like booming.

[Above: *Ardeotis kori kori*, Kruger National Park, South Africa. Photo: Nigel. J. Dennis/ NHPA

Below: *Ardeotis kori struthiunculus*, Masai Mara, Kenya. Photo: Hubert Klein/Bios]

Unique among bustards with its attractive blue-grey coloration, the Blue Bustard, like most other members of the family, nests in a small scrape on bare ground, in the midst of tufts of grass which provide camouflage. The eggs greenish with darker streaks can number one to three, but most commonly there are two. The female is responsible for the entire process of incubating the eggs and rearing of the young, while the male's contribution, as in most bustard species, would appear to be minimal.

[*Eupodotis caerulescens*. Photo: W. R. Tarboton]

puffs the black feathers of his throat in agonistic situations, and male White-bellied and Blue Bustards erect the feathers of the crown and neck in a ruff during courtship of females, with much rapid bobbing of the head in the latter species. However, this is the only group that does not undertake the wonderful and often astonishingly convoluted displays that the remaining 20 members perform.

In terms of display, these other species break down into two main types: those that give exclusively terrestrial displays; and those with self-advertisement that is primarily aerial. Terrestrial displaying bustards are the ten species that make up the genera *Otis*, *Ardeotis*, *Neotis* and *Chlamydotis*, while aerial displays are performed by the eight species of *Lissotis*, *Lophotis* (except, apparently, *savilei*), *Afrotis*, *Sypheotides* and *Houbaropsis*. The last two make more of a display leap, although both travel several metres into the air. Fitting neither or both of these types is the sole member of *Tetrax*, with rarely observed twilight displays that are clearly aerial in spirit but inescapably terrestrial in nature.

The display of the Great Bustard is the most remarkable, transforming a largely cryptic animal into an involuted mass of billowing white feathers, a shining ball discernible over many kilometres. The sequence begins with the inflation of a huge gular sac which extends right down the neck. This is done as the bird exhales, the air being diverted into the sac through an aperture under the tongue. Two bare dark strips of skin either side of the grey-white neck are exposed as the "balloon" swells massively. As this happens, several other contortions take place roughly simultaneously. The front of the body tilts forward, and the head itself sinks back and down as the inflated neck pushes up the long white feathers of the "beard", so that they point upwards, partly screening the eyes. The tail cocks flat along the back, so that the tips are under the head, and this exposes the pure white vent and undertail-coverts. The wings, with flight-feathers still tightly folded, are lowered so that the forewing from the shoulder to the carpal joint stretches down and slightly backwards, and the secondary coverts and tertials are lifted, exposing their pure white in a great cascading rosette. The position is held often for many minutes, the bird every so often shifting its orientation with a shuffle of feet and a shaking of body, redoubling the intensity of the posture. No sound is emitted: the signal is entirely visual.

Both *Ardeotis* and *Neotis* bustards also have neck-inflation or "Balloon-displays", but the Great Bustard's is very different and the taxonomic proximity of *Otis* to these two genera based on this character and on similarities in size remains largely assumed. However, the displays of the four *Ardeotis* bustards certainly reveal that they cannot be regarded, as they have in the past, as one species. The genus has a clear two-way split, with the Kori and Arabian on one side, and the Australian and Great Indian on the other. Each pair is, however, very closely related, as their displays clearly demonstrate.

In the Australian Bustard, the male performs at a repeatedly used spot within his territory. He tilts his body and head slightly upwards, and begins to inflate the oesophagal sac, which drops from the breast until it brushes the ground. The body of the bird tilts more upright, the neck extends vertically, the head points upwards and the tail cocks flat on the back; the neck appears inflated in two places, in the cheeks and down the throat, and in the broad dangling bag hanging from the breast. The bird then rotates on the spot, causing the sac to swing about, and opens and closes its bill in a stereotyped sequence, repeated ten times or more before commencing the calling sequence in which second-long guttural roars are produced every twelve seconds or so, the bird swinging its sac as it turns in various directions to deliver its call. The Great Indian Bustard appears to have an identical display, although it is possible that the oesophagal sac does not distend so far as to sweep the ground, and the calls may or may not be different in timbre and timing.

The other two *Ardeotis* species are far less well known, but the displays of the Arabian Bustard have recently been shown to be similar to those of the Kori. The male adopts a still, upright posture, and his neck balloons out. He then walks to a set position on a slight prominence (in Yemen, the only sites used were the tops of irrigation banks) where there he intensifies the neck inflation to become a huge whitish oblong, while his wings droop and his tail is raised into a laterally visible fan. In this position, at roughly half-minute intervals he appears to gulp in air as his head retracts into the balloon, and he then emits a liquid "puk-puk", which carries over a wide area; this is the sound described at the turn of the century as exactly like water running from a bottle. From time to time, the bird rotates on the spot through 90° or 180°. During the bout, the fan of the tail gradually folds and falls.

This description closely matches those for Kori Bustards in Namibia and Tanzania, and in captivity. The bird struts about on a low rise with tail cocked, occasionally stopping and fully inflating his neck, raising his crest and letting his wings droop so that the primaries trail along the ground. He then delivers a six note drum-like booming, which is evidently different from the two note call of the Arabian Bustard. However, more work is needed to show how different or similar the routines of the two species really are.

In Denham's Bustard, the male lets his head sink backwards close to his back, droops his wings slightly and erects, presumably through the inflation of a gular sac, the feathers of his white foreneck, breast and belly so that they billow out in a conspicuous ball in front of him, visible over several kilometres. In this posture he walks at varying speeds, sometimes rapidly, and occasionally breaking into fifteen minute periods of "Display-strutting", in which he balloons his neck more fully and then struts straight forward for up to 30 m, and for up to around one minute, then stops to raise his body in "Vertical-display", but with the head still mostly obscured by the balloon and by the raised and flared orange hindneck, which appears to be aimed at the object of display. After eight seconds the body shudders and the bird appears to call, although observations have been at too great a distance to be sure. He maintains his position for around 20 seconds, sometimes rotating slowly to display in other directions, before resuming his Display-strut. In one incomplete courtship sequence, the struts became shorter and the Vertical-display longer, the nape being turned each time towards the female.

Previously, the performances of *Otis*, *Ardeotis* and *Neotis* have been grouped together as Balloon-displays, with *Chlamydotis* classed on its own for performing a "Trotting-display". However, it is clear from what we now know of Denham's Bustard that the Houbara's display is by no means anomalous, and it may well be that when the repertoires of the other members of *Neotis* are known, the taxonomic position of the seemingly aberrant *Chlamydotis* will be resolved.

Houbara males defend fairly large territories, but they appear to have core areas within them in which they perform their displays. These are likely to be vantage points within the territory, with as few obstacles as possible, and range from 0·5 to 2·5 ha in extent, although even within these areas there may be stalls a few metres across where repeated circling displays flatten the ground. The male begins by an untidy-looking ruffling of the crown, neck and breast plumes: the black feathers of the neck sweep back, as the white ones of the breast fan out in front, first downwards, then upwards; presumably there is some inflatable pouch that causes this. As the bird begins a forward, high-stepping trot, the head drops backwards onto the back, causing the white breast plumes to rise up and over the front of the body in a loose white ball. In zig-zags, circles and long lines and curves, the seemingly headless bird runs for a minute or two, then abruptly halts, his head lifting slightly in watchfulness, before he resumes the performance.

Both Denham's and the Houbara have, very rarely, been seen to give some brief, sharply upward flight as if in display, but these seem unlikely to have any clear significance in their behavioural repertoire. Males of both species are perhaps too heavy to expend energy on display leaps and flights, which are characteristic of the lighter bustards. The intermediary between the two display types is perhaps *Houbaropsis*, the Bengal Florican, which, like other large ground-displaying bustards, has a display involving the erection of the neck plumes, the "Neck-fluff Display", although this lasts only half a minute or so. In over half the cases observed, this display then results in a flight display, in which the bird rises with loudly clapping wings 3-4 m into the air, descends with 4-6 "chik" calls to within a metre of the ground, then rises sharply with wings stiffly quivering, stalls, half folds his wings, and drops steeply back to earth.

The energetic costs of such a display in a bird weighing around 1·5 kg may be the reason why this performance is relatively little given, often only a few times an hour in the early morning and late afternoon. Curiously, these flight displays are often triggered by the calls of unrelated species, notably the Indian Peafowl (*Pavo cristatus*), and their number and distribution within and between dawn and dusk periods varies inexplicably from day to day.

In the similar-sized but somewhat heavier Black-bellied Bustard, two distinct display types are judged to have two distinct functions. An irregular and relatively uncommon flight display advertises the bird's presence over a wide area, well beyond the limits of his territory: this involves him rising to 7-15 m above the ground and flying with deep wingstrokes for 50-200 m, then gliding a further 50-150 m with wings held up in a V, head and neck angled upwards. In some reports, the breast feathers are greatly fluffed out during and at the end of these flights, and there is one account in which an extended version of the display-

Of sober, cryptic but finely vermiculated brown-grey plumage, the Karoo Bustard inhabits dry, open treeless regions. Only few data have been collected so far concerning its breeding system, though groups are known to be strongly territorial and to defend small areas. The nest is a scarcely perceptible depression on bare, often stony, ground and the clutch normally consists of a single egg, buff-olive in colour streaked with brown. It is remarkable how well both egg and bird merge into the stark surroundings.

[Eupodotis vigorsii. Photo: Peter Steyn/Ardea]

In all bustard species it is the female that selects the nest-site, incubates the eggs and rears the young. The male Denham's Bustard, one of the larger members of the family, has been observed apparently attending a nest, but to date there is not even circumstantial evidence that male bustards actively participate in incubation or caring for the chicks. The clutch of 1-2 eggs is laid in a bare scrape in tussocky grass and the female relies heavily on her beautifully patterned cryptic plumage to escape unwanted attention from predators.

[Neotis denhami. Photo: Roger Tidman/ FLPA]

flight took the performer so high in the sky as to be unidentifiable without binoculars, before dropping with wings horizontal and white primaries fluttering loudly to about 300 m, then briefly folding wings, cocking tail and retracting neck in typical (*Lophotis*) "rocketing" position, before rising again to repeat the performance.

Much more persistently given is a ground display thought to be intended for females already inside a male's territory. This is delivered from one of several traditionally used stalls within the territory, typically a patch of open, bare, raised ground, often a decomposed termite-mound; it involves standing upright, letting the neck angle forward then sharply upright, head and bill skyward, emitting a groaning "oooo" that shows off the bird's black chin patch. Then the head is drawn down onto the back for a few seconds before the bird makes a rumbling snore followed by a "pop", like a cork coming out of a bottle, and a slight shaking of the wings which shows off the white panel in sharp contrast to the black flanks.

Only very recently has it been established that the other *Lissotis*, Hartlaub's Bustard, also gives a display-flight in which the male rises steeply to 15-20 m, then descends in a glide, wings in a shallow V and legs trailing. Its ground display is similar to the Black-bellied's, although the sequence is approximately reversed and the volume much lower.

The parapatric Black Bustard and White-quilled Bustard have apparently identical display-flights, in which the male flies up and cruises round in circles, often for some time, while giving his incessant, raucous self-advertising call, then slowly parachuting or exaggeratedly "windmilling" down with wings held in a V and bright yellow legs dangling. Like the Black-bellied, these birds have one or more vantage points, usually termite mounds, on which to stand and call. In prime habitat, territories may be spaced only 300-500 m apart, and flying males commonly pursue each other.

The aerial displays of the Red-crested and Buff-crested Bustards of southern and East Africa are, by contrast, more vertical than horizontal, quickly over and, usually, given without warning, which makes them all the more dramatic. The bird flies up vertically for about 20-30 m, well above the canopy, then semi-somersaults backwards, feet up, head back, nuchal crest and breast puffed out, then rocks back forward and drops in a

fluffed-up ball to the ground, pulling out in a glide just before impact. In East Africa, less dramatic, parabolic flights have also been observed. Puzzlingly, the West African counterpart, Savile's Bustard, has never been recorded making an aerial display, although, given the way so many displays of African bustards have been overlooked for years or remain unrecorded, it may yet turn out to do so. All three species use traditional calling stalls, but unlike other bustards these are not exposed or raised sites and appear to be deliberately selected for their inconspicuousness.

The two last species to consider, the Lesser Florican and the Little Bustard, both live in grasslands and both make their presence known through sustained bouts of short leaps just above the level of the grass. At the peak of the season the florican may perform well over 500 leaps per day, mostly, but not always, from a chosen stall within his territory. He stands erect, shuffles or stamps his feet, then abruptly retracts his head, crouches and springs flapping into the air to a height of 1·5-2 m, using his half-opened wings as a parachute in the short descent. The whole event lasts about a second. A loud rattling as the bird flutters up is produced by modified primary feathers.

In very similar fashion, the Little Bustard performs a "Jumping-display" from a chosen stall that commences with a short burst of foot-stamping; he then leaps 1·5 m into the air, giving his snort-call as he does so, while the wings, again owing to a modified primary, produce their characteristic "sisisisi". The event also lasts only about one second. The leap is given at dawn and dusk, but at slightly higher light intensities than a similar display in which a much stronger foot-stamping precedes a flashing of the wings without the bird becoming airborne. It is thought that this latter display is more agonistic in intent, exaggerating the sound of a forward attack; the bird's stall is a small patch of clear ground on which it tramples its faeces, so as to enhance the sound of its foot-stamping. The display-leap is thought to be more targeted at females. Throughout the full daylight hours, however, only the snort-call is given.

Copulation in bustards often involves protracted sequences of behaviour, at least in the larger species. They are rarely witnessed, partly because the absence of a pair-bond means that the event need only occur once between any two birds. Where they have been observed, there are some clear similarities in the ritualized procedure.

The most widely known is the Great Bustard. An apparently passing female shows her interest simply by wandering close to the male. Occasionally, a female may show sufficient interest to peck lightly at the cloacal area of the displaying male before becoming embroiled in the protracted mating sequence. Mostly, however, it is the male which, despite his posture, approaches the female and initiates the sequence, walking round her and weakly banging one of his carpal joints on her back until she eventually squats, always assuming that the event is not interrupted by other males, as it usually is! Then the male stands over her, pecking at her crown, often for many minutes, and as she eventually rises, tail lifted forward, insemination very rapidly occurs.

In captive Australian Bustards, the male leaves his display stall to follow a passing female, turns side on to her and calls, then continues following. The sequence can last up to 25 minutes, with the male calling every 7-8 seconds. The female, if receptive, will duly sit, and the male then circles her repeatedly, but gradually reducing his calling frequency the more he stays behind the female, trampling on the spot, and pecking gently at her head. This may last as long as 33 minutes before the male lowers himself on his tarsi, both birds outstretch their wings for balance, and insemination rapidly occurs. As in the Great Bustard, the female then immediately moves from under the male, flapping and ruffling feathers, to begin grooming at a short distance, and soon walking away.

In close courtship the Houbara repeatedly throws its head back on its mantle, and turns it from side to side. The Black-bellied Bustard makes a ruff of his neck, then stretches it forward, up and back in a sinuous, snake-like sequence. The Bengal Florican approaches a female with head retracted, breast feathers billowing, then stops, raises his head and jerks his neck from side to side, swinging his breast plumes. The Lesser Florican runs after the female with neck outstretched, auricular plumes over his head, stops in front of her, lowers his posterior to the ground, snaps back his head and simultaneously flashes open his wings. Little Bustard males chase females for long periods, the head retracted into the neck, stopping repeatedly to call and throw the head and body from side to side. Copulation in all species involves the male pecking repeatedly at some part of the female's head.

The female is entirely responsible for nest-site selection, incubation of the eggs and, with the possible exception of the *Eupodotis* bustards, rearing of the young to fledging. Male Kori Bustards both in the wild and captivity have been seen to offer food items to females, and male Denham's Bustards have been watched apparently attending nests, yet no clear evidence has ever been furnished that in these, or any other species, the male truly contributes to parental duties. In many cases, it appears that the female removes herself entirely from the general area in which males are clustered in their dispersed leks. Consequently, the nests and patterns of nesting dispersion of many species remain virtually unknown.

The nest is always on bare ground, sometimes having been scraped clear of vegetation and perhaps slightly moulded, and occasionally bits of grass may be pulled down to form a weak rim. Statements about the nest being near to bushes, clumps or other minor landscape features are sufficiently frequent to suggest that there is often a deliberate choice by the female not to sit in the complete open, but the extent to which one or two observations have become generalized is not clear. Certainly many nests of some species have been found far from any distinguishing landscape feature.

The eggs of bustards are similar to those of cranes in shape and pattern, generally being matt olive green or buffish grey with rough blotches and dapplings of dark or reddish brown and grey around the big end. However, the eggs of species adapted to particular substrates or habitats show variations from this, and those of *Lophotis* are glossy. Clutch size is generally two to three in the three Palearctic species, although the largest has been known to lay four, the middle five and the smallest six; singletons are rare. Only the Lesser Florican, as small as the Little Bustard, lays a comparable clutch of three to five eggs; this relatively large investment in offspring probably reflects the relatively un-

stable conditions under which the species has to pursue patchy rainfall in both breeding and non-breeding periods. Otherwise, only the Australian Bustard and three of the five *Eupodotis* species have been recorded laying as many as three eggs; the remaining *Eupodotis* and *Ardeotis*, plus *Neotis*, *Lissotis*, *Afrotis* and *Lophotis*, lay one or two only.

The incubation period is 20-22 days in the Little Bustard, 24-25 days in the Australian and Great Bustards, and almost certainly between these extremes for the remaining species, although very minor variations owing to climate and season may occur. Hatching is asynchronous, suggesting that incubation starts with the first egg.

The young are precocial, but not immediately nidifugous, requiring several hours, in some cases a day or more, to develop the capacity to walk. When all young are able, the female leads them from the nest and broods them for the night at any secure site reached during the subsequent days. She draws attention to food items by pecking gently at them or dropping them in front of the young: the young themselves quickly learn to peck at grass stems, pebbles and small invertebrates. Parent and offspring maintain contact through very quiet purrs and trills.

Fledging occurs at four to five weeks, although the young are still only half-grown at that stage. These first weeks of life are lived in such secrecy that in all probability the young only disclose that they have fledged during comfort behaviour, when stretching and flapping wings. Unless hard pressed to escape from a predator, many young bustards may not truly take wing until weeks after "fledging" occurs.

Independence certainly occurs only when the young are full-sized, which may be several months after fledging. In Palearctic species the parental bond therefore lasts into the autumn, and there is circumstantial evidence that it can last through the winter. Female Great Indian Bustards have been watched incubating in the presence of highly attentive offspring, suggesting a year long association; circumstantial evidence indicates the young may be of either sex. In *Eupodotis* bustards, as noted above, single young males may stay with their parents into the following year, helping with territorial defence; young of both sexes may do so in the Blue Bustard, in which group size sometimes reaches five. Some, probably all, small female bustards are capable of breeding after one year, but females of the largest species usually only commence breeding when three years old. Maturity in males, meanwhile, is to some extent an artefact of the breeding system, so that breeding condition may be behaviourally suppressed. There are no studies on wild populations of large bustards that

A female Rüppell's Bustard with chick in tow walks with deliberate tread across a stony arid plain, the typical habitat of this species. Young bustards tend to become independent only when they are fully grown, several months after fledging. The breeding biology and ecology of Rüppell's Bustard are very poorly known.

[Eupodotis rueppellii, Namibia. Photo: J. J. Brooks/Aquila]

disclose age of first breeding, but in the Great Bustard, for example, the received wisdom is that six years is probably the age at which first copulations are likely.

Breeding success is virtually unknown and unquantified in any species, although it is inevitably low in intensively farmed areas (see Status and Conservation).

Movements

It is not certain that any species of bustard is completely migratory, in the sense that none of its populations is completely sedentary. At the other end of the scale, only a handful of species are believed to be sedentary, and even in those cases there must be considerable doubt whether all populations are entirely so. Most species appear to be at least dispersive, some outrightly nomadic. The largest species tend to move in small flocks, and the Little Bustard can do so in large assemblages. Migration appears to take place chiefly, though not exclusively, at night. The height at which birds move may vary between species, but the largest species remain fairly low.

Areas of low resource availability, such as the seasonally influenced grassland and savanna in which bustards dwell, are characterized by high temporal and spatial concentrations of resources, mostly in the form of annual plants, but also outbreaks of orthopterans and mass emergence of curculionid beetles, and concentrations of both types are usually triggered by rainfall. These variations appear to dictate breeding schedules, and they must lie behind most, if not ultimately all, local and long distance movements that bustards make.

The two main regions in which bustards are strongly migratory are, first, Eurasia through Central Asia to eastern Russia and China, and, second, the Sahelian and savanna zones of the southern borderlands of the Sahara. All three bustards occurring in the first area, Great, Little and Houbara, are compelled by long, cold winters to move southwards from the steppes into warmer areas within the region. The first two, for the most part, remain to the north of the great mountain barriers to the Indian Subcontinent and the Middle East, but the Houbara moves from its cold Kazakh deserts into both regions in large numbers, crossing to the Arabian Peninsula. Patterns of movement in the easternmost populations of Great and Houbara, in Mongolia and China, are poorly understood, but the Great Bustard is a regular, if scarce, migrant at the major Chinese watchpoint of Beidaihe, east of Beijing.

The movements of the Houbara coming down into, and beyond, the deserts of Iran and Baluchistan are basically unknown. Weather conditions may compel nomadism over the winter quarters, just as they do in the remainder of the species's range in Arabia and North Africa, or perhaps there is pressure from already resident or later arriving populations. Very recently, it has been possible to capture and fit birds with radio transmitters, and track them from satellites. It will take many years to build up a picture from which robust generalizations can be made, but already this study is providing some valuable insights, such as suggesting that males returning to the breeding grounds may pause at several localities, possibly displaying in each of them in an attempt to obtain a mating.

In the remainder of their range, the three Palearctic bustards are largely sedentary or dispersive rather than migratory, although the Little Bustard still makes clear north-south movements in France and the Great Bustard clears off the Anatolian Plateau in winter, moving into the warmer, lower plains on the Turkish border with Syria. In Iberia, both species wander in winter, and indeed the disappearance of birds after the spring display period is an uncanny phenomenon: the females are clearly on nests and keeping a low profile, but the males also melt away so that by late June it is difficult to find any, and all the evidence points to a general diaspora from the lekking centres deep into distant cropland.

Rainfall in the savanna and Sahelian zone in the period June to September causes a greening of the region and hence an influx of bustards from further south. Most prominent among these are the larger species, the Arabian and Denham's Bustards, but with the exception of the Nubian Bustard the smaller species in

the region, the Black-bellied, White-bellied and Savile's, also then show some displacement northwards. All of them appear to breed at this time, although this is presumably dependent on sufficient rainfall. Some, at least, may also or alternatively breed in the southern parts of their West African ranges, if conditions are then more favourable. Black-bellied Bustards, in particular, seem to wander in response to rain patterns, and may well breed opportunistically as local conditions allow.

In north-east, East and Central Africa, very poorly defined local movements occur in the bustards of less arid habitats. Denham's, Hartlaub's, Black-bellied and Buff-crested have all been reported as appearing or increasing seasonally in certain areas. Even the Kori Bustard moves into woodland areas in the dry season, apparently on foot, although in this species, as in others, the displacements may concern only a certain class of the population, for instance non-breeding birds.

It is in southern Africa that the majority of the sedentary bustards occur, all of them small. The two *Afrotis*, the endemic *Lophotis* and all three endemic *Eupodotis* species are, so far as is known, essentially resident, moving over very short distances from one season to the next. The non-endemic *Eupodotis*, the White-bellied Bustard, is also sedentary, as it apparently is in East Africa. Given that all *Eupodotis* are known or believed to be group-territorial throughout the year, it seems only likely that these birds should be sedentary. Denham's and Black-bellied Bustards both tend to wander in response to local conditions, although there appears to be, or to have been, a small summer breeding population of Denham's on the tropical coastal Zululand plain.

Recently, an analysis of records, coupled with aerial surveys and questionnaires to farmers, has established at least partial migratory behaviour in Ludwig's Bustard. Individuals of this large species follow seasonal rainfall patterns, moving from the more inland summer rainfall regions south and west into the coastal winter rainfall regions. Another finding of this study, that despite the evidence for such a migration there was nothing to indicate a seasonal decrease in density in the summer rainfall regions, is explained first by the species being a partial migrant, and second by the fact that birds resident in the summer rainfall areas are much easier to see in winter. Counts of other, entirely resident bustard species in the summer rainfall area actually increased in winter, indicating the extent to which lush vegetation can hide bustards and obscure their true status in an area.

This indeed may be what happens to the Bengal Florican, which, like the Great and Little Bustards in Iberia, virtually disappears after breeding, probably dispersing over short distances, although perhaps simply remaining in the deep obscurity of long grass in quiet parts of the reserves to which, as a breeding bird, it is now almost totally confined. Easily the greatest mystery in this species surrounds the provenance of birds supposedly of a different race that have been recorded in tiny numbers in winter in Cambodia and Vietnam, with one bird even found in a Bangkok bird market. Recent records all refer to southern Vietnam and all appear to be from February and March. The area is so distant from the Indian Subcontinent that there is no real expectation that these birds are migrants from known breeding areas; yet it seems only marginally more plausible that they are members of an undetected population from some remnant natural grassland area in south-east Asia.

The Lesser Florican is more certainly known to travel considerable distances with the seasons. It migrates into north-west India with the rains in August, seeking out the most appropriate habitat, with the result that its density at given sites varies greatly from year to year. Afterwards it disperses south and east, although being so small, unobtrusive and unpredictable it is nowadays very rarely recorded anywhere in the non-breeding period.

The closely related Great Indian and Australian Bustards have closely related migratory habits, both being dispersive and nomadic, with some evidence of seasonality, always with rainfall, or its absence, being the key determinant of any movement. One challenge to field biologists is to confirm or deny the report that the population of Australian Bustards in southern New Guinea migrates across the Torres Strait to Australia: this may be the only regular movement the species undertakes.

Relationship with Man

Bustards and human beings are largely incompatible, and have little to do with each other. However, cave drawings and rock engravings depicting Great and Kori Bustards indicate that prehistoric man valued these species, perhaps chiefly as game but possibly for less material reasons: the Kori certainly features in dances and songs performed by Botswana's Bushmen. Moreover, the Great and Little Bustard benefited from prehistoric human actions in clearing large areas of Europe of its original forest cover. It is difficult to judge what their ranges looked like in the immediate post-glacial period, but their survival now in part depends on the management of certain key areas in Iberia and Central Europe in which they cannot have been present a few thousand years ago.

Both species have at times been considered minor pests. In Germany in the eighteenth century Great Bustards were so common that royal edicts were issued to address the damage to crops they caused, with children being given time off school to go to the fields to drive them away. In Spain in this century a NATO airbase had to import Peregrine Falcons (*Falco peregrinus*) to reduce and disperse the flocks of Little Bustards feeding by the runways. Even today, flocks of either species can still be large enough to damage growing crops in Iberia and Russia. Houbaras on the Canary Islands used to harm chick-pea crops, and doubtlessly they do small-scale damage elsewhere. The only other significant impact is that of the Arabian Bustard on *Acacia* gum production in parts of the Sahel.

In general, however, bustards must be judged highly beneficial. Most importantly, they help control insect plagues, at times consuming huge quantities of grasshoppers and locusts, as well as termites, beetles, mice and other economically injurious creatures. These advantages have been noted from Germany south to Cape Province. There may also be an important role in seed dispersal. Karoo Bustards have been found to consume high numbers of seeds of early successional "nurse plants", and may therefore play a role in the spread of karoo pioneer vegetation and the reclamation of degraded areas.

More obviously, bustards and their eggs have, at least in the past, been much used by man for food, especially in Europe and Asia and on both fringes of the Sahara. Great Bustards were served in the courts of European nobility. Little Bustards were once a common delicacy in Tunis hotels. British imperial servants ate their way through the Indian florican populations; indeed, the Bengal Florican was even once known as *Otis deliciosa*! Local people in Chad hunt the Arabian Bustard for food, and frequently rob its nests, although eggs may be left at least until their presence has helped capture the incubating bird: in much the most remarkable bustard-hunting technique on record, a child is buried right next to a nest, with only a hand free under the eggs in the sand, so that when the female returns and sits, the child tries to grab its feet, and hangs on until help arrives.

Much the most important relation with man lies in the high significance attached to the Houbara as the chief quarry in the Arabian practice of falconry. Oil-rich royal dignitaries seeking to retain cultural links with their ancestors see the wintering hunting party as a vital expression of their roots, even though the nature of the hunt has been transformed out of recognition by the full engagement of modern technology. Camels, hardship and chance have been supplanted by desert-adapted, radio-equipped luxury vehicles that trawl in fleets across the terrain, supported by fleets of petrol tankers, mobile kitchens and other logistical palliatives. Dozens of falcons are used, and gyroscopically mounted rifles often assist in the pursuit.

The result is that thousands of Houbaras have been caught and killed annually since the mid-1970's throughout the species's massive range within Islamic countries, causing serious conservation alarm. However, the situation remains very unclear, with local declines and disappearances claimed, but with no certainty in many cases that these are real, or else that hunting has been their cause. Indeed, the resilience of the persistently hunted populations that winter in Pakistan has prompted the quantification of various data, revealing that the total number of birds breeding in Kazakhstan alone is in the order of 50,000, a far better situation than was once believed. Nevertheless, the immoderate hunting of the Houbara, often resulting in great piles of discarded corpses or feathers after the "sport" is over, remains a cause for concern, chiefly because it is by no means clear that populations south and west of Pakistan have similar levels of resilience, but also because of the risks to desert ecosystems, indirectly through the "vacuuming out" of a possibly keystone species, and directly through the impact of the vehicles on desert substrates and floras.

Arabian dignitaries have, however, discovered that other species of bustard can be hunted with the same relentlessness in the Sahel, and this has placed a serious burden notably on the Arabian and Nubian Bustards. Moreover, an interest in keeping and breeding bustards, and in purchasing various species in volume for target practice by falcons, has caused the market in traded birds to burgeon. Captive breeding of the Houbara has long been touted, notably by people familiar with galliform birds, as the great solution to the falconers' needs, and enormously expensive facilities have consequently been established in various parts of the Arabian Peninsula. There is no evidence, however, that captive breeding is of any genuine relevance or value to this or any other member of the family.

Status and Conservation

Bustards are in general decline everywhere, retreating before the intensification of agriculture, hunting, and various kinds of modification of their habitat, including invasion by cattle, disturbance from roads and building, and the spread of overhead cabling.

The advent since around 1950 of mechanized cereal farming and pesticides has been particularly inimical, but the accumulating alterations in technique had all been contributing to declines in the Palearctic species ever since the industrial revolution. Nor is it simply a matter of intensification on existing farmland: it is also the spread of farming into areas not previously needed or considered viable. Cultivation in the Jamnagar District of Gujarat, in north-west India, a former stronghold of both Great Indian Bustard and Lesser Florican, grew from 40% in 1907 to over 70% in 1981, despite a small decline in the human population and a sharp decline in land needed to meet local food needs, owing to improved efficiency: the conversion of virgin land has been to cash-crops for export. Changes like this can be expected in the coming century throughout the lands on which bustards dwell.

All the other threats are more local or more targeted on individual species. Hunting is most focused in Islamic countries (see Relationship with Man). In the mid-1980's, this Arab interest fuelled a trade in some smaller African species which were used to train falcons prior to the winter hunting season; accordingly, all bustards became subject to trade controls, with the Houbara and Great Indian Bustards and the Bengal Florican being entered on Appendix I of CITES and the remainder on Appendix II. In some Islamic countries there have also been moves to encourage nomadic pastoralists to form permanent settlements: the resulting overgrazing has possibly irreversible consequences for the fragile semi-desert environments and the faunas they support. Power transmission cables and even telephone lines, crossing open terrain, connecting one town with another, and running to each farmstead, are a new and potentially serious hazard, known to affect larger species such as Great and Kori Bustards, although in some areas the attachment of large coloured balls to the wires has been effective.

Four species of bustard are currently treated as threatened with extinction: all three from the Indian Subcontinent and the Great Bustard. Four more, the Nubian, Blue, Little Brown and Little, are judged to be near-threatened. The Houbara is the next most obvious cause for concern and needs constant monitoring, while the four largest remaining species, Kori, Arabian, Australian and Denham's, are all showing signs of chronic decline and local extinction. Heuglin's and Hartlaub's need monitoring given

The Nubian Bustard occurs across northern Africa from Mauritania to Sudan. Bustard populations throughout the world are declining, with four species classified as threatened with extinction. They are birds particularly vulnerable to hunting and habitat changes. Unfortunately, the Nubian Bustard is under double pressure: the gradual desertification of the Sahel means suitable habitat areas are shrinking; and it is now also suffering from the attentions of Arab huntsmen. This species is very poorly known. While it is currently classed as near-threatened, there can be little doubt that survey work and research are urgently required in order to forestall the possibility of a calamitous decline.

[Neotis nuba, Sahara.
Photo: Alain Dragesco/ Planet Earth]

A male Lesser Florican leaps dramatically into the air in a display intended to attract a mate. He first squats down in a flat grassy site, then with neck inflated he springs into the air with accompanying shallow wingbeats, rising to a height of up to two metres. As he leaps, the wings make a loud rattling sound. The display lasts only a second, and may be repeated over 500 times a day. This charming species is considered to be the most threatened of all bustards, with the latest available estimates suggesting a total population of merely some 2200 birds.

[Sypheotides indica, Sailana, Madhya Pradesh, India. Photo: Joanna Van Gruisen/ Ardea]

the land-use pressures within their relatively restricted ranges within the Horn of Africa. The remaining members of the family, ten small African species, are least affected by status changes and are at present reasonably secure.

Much the most highly endangered is the exquisite Lesser Florican, which, with its unpredictable use of breeding areas in western India and its basically unknown movements outside the breeding season, is rendered extremely hard to conserve, especially when its grassland habitat is under such intense pressure from agriculture and pastoralism. In 1994 it was classified as Critically Endangered, the highest of the new IUCN threatened categories, and its future depends on small pockets of grassland, known as *vidis*, that are given strict protection as an insurance for cattle against drought.

The Bengal Florican and the Great Indian Bustard are both classified as Endangered, the second highest category of threat. In purely numerical terms, with perhaps as few as 300 birds left, and in view of its extremely fragmented range, the Bengal Florican is much the more precarious of the two, depending for its survival on India and Nepal's permanent commitment to the management and protection of half a dozen parks and reserves, Dudwa, Manas, Orang and Kaziranga in India, and Sukla Phanta, Bardia and perhaps Chitwan in Nepal. The Great Indian ranges much more widely and responds fairly well to management, but still musters perhaps only 1500 birds in total scattered mostly over unprotected terrain, and represents an immense long-term challenge.

The Great Bustard possesses possibly the widest range of any threatened species of bird, distributed as it is from close to the Atlantic seaboard in Iberia and Morocco across to the Pacific coast of China, a distance of very roughly 10,000 km. However, within this range it survives in small and ever-diminishing pockets, and has already become extinct in a series of European countries, and is about to do so in several more. Its future depends on farming within its range remaining at low intensity only. Given that European Commission funding of zones of such land is still awaited, there can be no guarantee of this, so the species qualifies as Vulnerable.

Of the species that come close to meeting the criteria for threatened status, the Little Bustard will share the same fate as the Great, with which it is largely sympatric. It is still, however, numerically strong in Iberia, Russia and Kazakhstan, but has suffered a catastrophic decline in Russia for reasons that remain only partly understood. Meanwhile, recent intensive hunting by Arab dignitaries in parts of the Nubian Bustard's range, coupled with the steady desertification of the Sahel, suggest that this species too could soon be threatened. The Little Brown Bustard has

a small range in a region where chronic warfare renders the future of its habitats unpredictable, and the Blue faces the danger of intensified farming within its even more restricted range.

The Houbara is the subject of a detailed recovery plan in the Canary Islands, and of various ecological and management studies elsewhere in its range. There is still a great deal of work to be done to obtain concrete data on population levels and recruitment and survival rates, so that some reasonable estimates of sustainable offtake levels can be determined. The hunting that so concerns many conservationists is conducted following agreement at the highest level, which thus overrides most national policies and laws. More dialogue between hunters and conservationists is needed to build consensus on the pattern and intensity of this hunting. The BirdLife Steppe and Grassland (formerly Bustard) Specialist Group has been a pioneer in this regard, as it has in many other bustard conservation issues.

In general, and for a variety of interrelating reasons, notably size, cost, pre-existing land-use patterns and the nomadism and migrations of the target species, it is clear that the kinds of area over which bustards range do not allow for conservation by the classic solution of protected areas. It is, of course, true that many national parks and other reserves, notably in the adjacent Sahel and savanna zones of Africa, and those at the foot of the Himalayas, play significant parts in bustard conservation, but they have all been created for other reasons. A few sanctuaries set up for the Great Indian Bustard are the only examples of protected areas targeted specifically at a member of the Otididae.

Far more important is the large-scale management of land at a level of intensity that permits bustards to remain on it as if it were unmodified. This has significant economic implications for local human communities that can only be addressed on a higher political and indeed philosophical plane; but it is increasingly being recognized that nature conservation cannot simply be relegated to reserves, but where possible must be integrated with other land uses. The bustards, being in such direct conflict with man over the use of the land, are one of the most significant challenges in this regard, and it falls in particular to India and Europe to take the lead to demonstrate that it is a challenge that can be met.

General Bibliography
Allan (1988), Collar (1979a, 1983b, 1985b), Downes (1975), Dunning (1993), Goriup (1985, 1987, 1992a), Goriup & Vardhan (1983), Hendrickson (1969), Hidalgo & Carranza (1990b), Johnsgard (1990, 1991b), Osborne *et al.* (1984), Peters (1934), Schulz & Schulz (1991), Sibley & Ahlquist (1990), Sibley & Monroe (1990), Wightman (1968).

♂

♀

1

2

ssp *stieberi*

ssp *arabs*

♀

♂

3

♂

4

♀

♂

5

♀

♂

ssp *macqueenii*

♀

♂

6

ssp *fuertaventurae*

ssp *undulata*

PLATE 23

inches 12

cm 30

Genus *OTIS* Linnaeus, 1758

1. **Great Bustard**

Otis tarda

French: Grande Outarde **German**: Großtrappe **Spanish**: Avutarda Euroasiática

Taxonomy. *Otis Tarda* Linnaeus, 1758, Poland.
Genus has frequently been merged with *Tetrax*, and sometimes also *Ardeotis* and *Neotis*, but nowadays species normally considered sufficiently distinct to merit generic isolation from these forms (see page 240). Birds of C Asia formerly awarded separate race *korejewi*, but extensive overlap with nominate *tarda*. Two subspecies recognized.
Subspecies and Distribution.
O. t. tarda Linnaeus, 1758 - N Morocco and Iberia, Germany and Hungary, and S Ukraine; remnant populations elsewhere in E Europe. Also breeds in Turkey and W Iran, and from SW Russia through Kazakhstan to Kyrgyzstan, wintering from S Turkey and Syria through S Azerbaijan and N Iran to Uzbekistan and Tadjikistan.
O. t. dybowskii Taczanowski, 1874 - SE Russia, Mongolia and NE China.

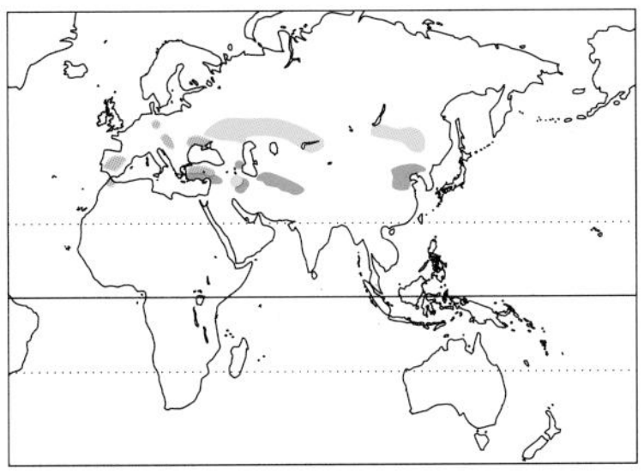

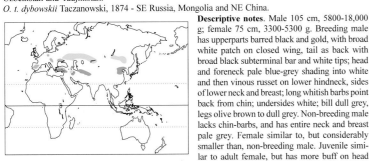

Descriptive notes. Male 105 cm, 5800-18,000 g; female 75 cm, 3300-5300 g. Breeding male has upperparts barred black and gold, with broad white patch on closed wing, tail as back with broad black subterminal bar and white tips; head and foreneck pale blue-grey shading into white and then vinous russet on lower hindneck, sides of lower neck and breast; long whitish barbs point back from chin; undersides white; bill dull grey, legs olive brown to dull grey. Non-breeding male lacks chin-barbs, and has entire neck and breast pale grey. Female similar to, but considerably smaller than, non-breeding male. Juvenile similar to adult female, but has more buff on head and neck, and upperparts less distinctly barred. Race *dybowskii* has head and neck slightly paler grey and upperparts more distinctly barred, but barely distinct from nominate and geographical limits unclear.
Habitat. Flat or rolling open short-grass plains, usually clear of trees, although uses cork oak (*Quercus suber*) "savanna" and olive groves in SW Iberia. Insect- and flower-rich grassland and pasture provide important habitat in spring and summer, fields of stubble are favoured in late summer and autumn, lucerne in winter, but a high diversity of low-intensity land use and lack of disturbance are generally important for year round needs.
Food and Feeding. Mainly plant material and invertebrates, although small mammals, amphibians and nestling birds sometimes taken. Key plant families include composites, legumes, crucifers and grasses, while chief animal food is Orthoptera and Coleoptera. High proportion of cultivated plants utilized from late summer through to winter, with green matter increasingly important from mid-winter into spring, and insects from spring into late summer.
Breeding. Laying in Apr-May, also Jun in colder NE parts of range. Nest on ground with or without scrape, occasionally with fragments of grass stems and crop stems as lining. Nearly always 2-3 eggs (1-4); incubation c. 25 days; chicks cinnamon-pink to pale buff, with sepia streaks and other markings; fledging period 30-35 days, although full size reached at 80-120 days, which is also probably the minimum period of dependency. First breeding at 5-6 years in male, 2-3 years in female.
Movements. Largely sedentary or dispersive in Iberia, C & E Europe to Ukraine, depending on severity of winter, and on age and sex, males appearing to move over shorter distances, probably related to degree of maturity. Migratory in Asia, where southward shifts occur, generally over limited distances, from Aug to early winter, with birds returning Mar-Apr.
Status and Conservation. VULNERABLE. CITES II. Total population unknown, but European populations may amount to 26,000-32,000 birds, with strongholds in Spain with 13,500-14,000 birds, Portugal 500-700, Hungary 1000-1200 and Russia 10,000-11,000; other important populations include Turkey 145-4000 birds and Ukraine 300-500 birds; in rest of Europe, populations remain only in Germany with 150, Austria 50-60, Slovakia 25-40, Romania 10-15, Czech Republic 10-13 and Moldova 2-3 birds. Significant declines in most areas, as in Hungary, from estimated total of 8557 birds in 1941, to 3000-3237 in mid-1970's, to 1000-1200 in 1991; in Austria, from estimated 700-800 birds in 1939/40, to c. 400 in 1958, to 200-230 in 1969-1972, to 110-120 in 1977, to 50-60 in 1993. In NW Morocco, population had declined to c. 100 birds by mid-1980's. Recently extinct in Poland, Bulgaria and Yugoslavia; last bred in England 1832, France 1863, and Sweden and Greece respectively middle and end of 19th century. Bred in Azerbaijan until 1940's or 1950's, and formerly wintered in considerable numbers with flocks of 150-200 birds recorded in 1930's; few sightings nowadays, and total wintering population may number only a few 10's to a few 100's. Throughout range, irrigation and agricultural intensification (the first promoting the second, and the second leading to sterilized monoculture) are chief threats; also pesticide use, electric cables, illegal hunting, overgrazing and disturbance. Destruction of nests and chicks during crop treatment and harvesting is substantial. Habitat management in Austria involves minimizing disturbance and maximizing the availability of various favoured food plants. Populations can only survive through the maintenance of low-intensity farming over large areas; in Europe this may be achieved through European Union Zonal Programmes under the Common Agricultural Policy.
Bibliography. Ali & Ripley (1980), Alonso, J.A. *et al.* (1995), Alonso, J.C. & Alonso (1990, 1992b), Alonso, J.C. *et al.* (1995), Anon. (1989a), Ardamatskaya (1992), Atta (1992), Berezovikov (1992), Block *et al.* (1993), Brazil (1991), Buzun & Golovach (1992), Carranza & Hidalgo (1993), Carranza *et al.* (1989), Coles & Collar (1979), Collar (1985a), Collar & Andrew (1988), Collar & Goriup (1980), Collar *et al.* (1994), Cornwallis (1983a), Cramp & Simmons (1980), Ding Tieming (1988), Ena & Martínez (1985, 1988), Ena, Lucio & Purroy (1985), Ena, Martínez & Thomas (1987), Étchécopar & Hüe (1964, 1978), Evans (1994), Faragó (1985, 1992, 1993), Fedorenko (1992), Flint & Mishchenko (1991), Flint *et al.* (1992), Garzón (1981), Gewalt (1959), Gewalt & Gewalt (1966), Golovach & Dikiy (1992), Goriup (1982b, 1992b, 1994c), Goriup & Parr (1983, 1985), Graczyk (1980), Hellmich (1991, 1992), Hidalgo (1990), Hidalgo & Carranza (1990a, 1991), Hüe & Étchécopar (1970), Hummel (1990), Isakov (1974), Kasparek (1989), de Knijff (1981), Knystautas (1993), Kollar (1988), Kollar & Seiter (1991), Litzbarski (1993), Lucio (1985), Lucio & Purroy (1985), Lukschanderl (1971), Martínez (1988, 1991a, 1991b), Osborne, L. (1985), Palacios *et al.* (1975), Patrikeev (1995), Paz (1987), Peris *et al.* (1992), Persson (1991), Ponomareva (1992), Potapov & Flint (1987), Razdan & Mansoori (1989), Roberts, T.J. (1991), Rogacheva (1992), Sanz-Zuasti & Sierra (1993), Shirihai (1996), Simeonov *et al.* (1990), Sjoberg (1991), Smythies (1986), Sonobe & Izawa (1987), Stepanov (1986), Sterbetz (1979, 1981), Urban *et al.* (1986), Yan Anhou (1982), Yu Changyun & Gao Wei (1983), Zhao Diansheng (1986).

Genus *ARDEOTIS* Le Mahout, 1853

2. **Arabian Bustard**

Ardeotis arabs

French: Outarde arabe **German**: Arabertrappe **Spanish**: Avutarda Árabe
Other common names: Sudan/Great Arabian Bustard

Taxonomy. *Otis arabs* Linnaeus, 1758, Yemen.
In past, genus frequently labelled *Choriotis*, but *Ardeotis* has priority; genus sometimes merged with *Otis*. Present species forms superspecies with *A. kori*. All four *Ardeotis* have occasionally been placed in same superspecies. Four subspecies recognized.
Subspecies and Distribution.
A. a. lynesi (Bannerman, 1930) - W Morocco (probably extinct).
A. a. stieberi (Neumann, 1907) - SW Mauritania and Senegambia E to NE Sudan.
A. a. butleri (Bannerman, 1930) - S Sudan; single record in NW Kenya.
A. a. arabs (Linnaeus, 1758) - Eritrea, Ethiopia, Djibouti and NW Somalia; SW Saudi Arabia and W Yemen.

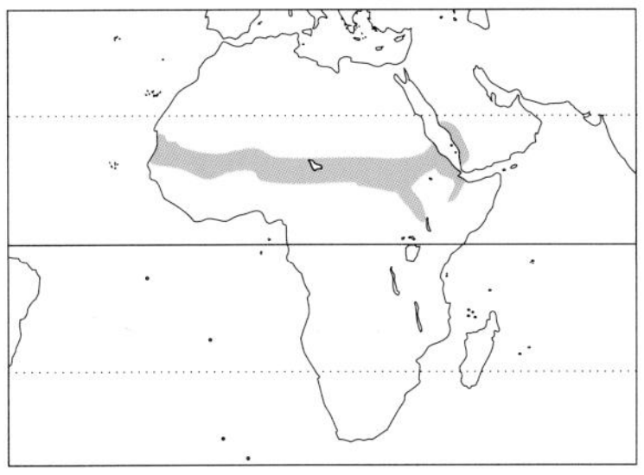

Descriptive notes. Male c. 100 cm, 5700-10,000 g; female c. 75 cm, 4500 g. Back, wings and central tail sandy brown with fine black markings, white flecking on folded wing; some broad black and white subterminal bands on outer feathers of tail, often concealed under uniform central tail feathers; head, neck and breast appear grey, being finely barred dark grey-brown on ashy white; crown black with pale grey centre, slight backwards crest, supercilium white; belly white; legs and eyes yellowish. Similar to *A. kori*, but somewhat smaller, and lacks black on base of neck and black flecking in wing. Female similar to male, but smaller and generally greyer above. Juvenile similar to female, but with less distinct pattern on wing. Racial variation based on differences in colour tones and size, with much less white flecking on closed wing in nominate *arabs* and *lynesi*; general coloration of upperparts varies considerably with colour of local substrate.
Habitat. Semi-desert and open grassy plains, arid bush country, savanna, *Acacia* parkland, and sometimes even in open woodland. Requirements in Djibouti appear to be a sandy substrate with either a good density of tall trees (chiefly *Acacia*) with sparse ground cover, or good ground cover with reduced tree density. In Yemen, found in cultivated areas, retreating in the hot hours into high crops of sorghum and millet.
Food and Feeding. Chiefly grasshoppers, but also locusts when swarming, and beetles, bugs, crickets, caterpillars and other invertebrates, as well as small vertebrates. Seeds, fruits of trees, succulent parts of plants and gum from *Acacia* are also taken.
Breeding. Season linked to warmer periods in Palearctic fringes, thus Apr-Jun in Morocco, Mauritania and Arabia, although display noted Oct-Nov in Yemen; wetter periods in Sahelian range Jul-Oct, possibly later. In Niger, solitary breeding females found every 2-3 km. Nest is a shallow scrape, sometimes lined with vegetation. 1-2 eggs. No further information available.
Movements. Unclear. In Sahel zone, migrates at 150-450 m above ground, in flocks, sometimes with *Neotis denhami*, moving N in Jun, S in Oct after breeding; presence in Sahel in dry season also reported, and species is resident in Senegal, only moving locally if conditions become severe. Rare dry season visitor to extreme N Ghana.
Status and Conservation. Not globally threatened. CITES II. Widespread in very poorly documented areas, so might still be common in many places; however, in more accessible and better monitored parts of its range species is now generally uncommon, having declined sharply owing to habitat destruction and hunting. Moreover, in W Africa, where abundant into 1960's, has become rare owing to hunting, at first by technical workers but in recent years by Arab falconers, whose activities extend throughout the Sahel; notable decline in numbers in N Nigeria due to hunting and trapping, and species now uncommon, limited mainly to NE. Race *lynesi* has not been reported for over 50 years, and may be extinct; more recent Moroccan records of the species may refer to stray *stieberi*. Population on Arabian Peninsula is very small and likely to be declining from hunting, habitat loss and effects of pesticides; still fairly common locally in Tihamah plain of W Yemen, at Wadi Mawr-Al-Zuhrah and Al-Murah, but intensification of agriculture may pose threat.
Bibliography. Ash (1989), Ash & Miskell (1983), Britton, P.L. (1980), Brooks *et al.* (1987), Cave & Macdonald (1955), Coverdale *et al.* (1991), Cramp & Simmons (1980), Dowsett & Forbes-Watson (1993), Elgood *et al.* (1994), Étchécopar & Hüe (1964), Gore (1990), Grimes (1987), Hollom *et al.* (1988), Lamarche (1988), Mackworth-Praed & Grant (1957, 1970), Morel, G.J. & Morel (1990), Morel, R. (1989), Newby (1979, 1990), Nikolaus (1987), Porter & Goriup (1985), Rahmani & Shobrak (1987, 1990), Rands *et al.* (1987), Shobrak (1988), Shobrak & Boug (1990), Shobrak & Rahmani (1991, 1993), Short *et al.* (1990), Turner (1982), Urban *et al.* (1986), Welch & Welch (1989).

3. **Kori Bustard**

Ardeotis kori

French: Outarde kori **German**: Riesentrappe **Spanish**: Avutarda Kori
Other common names: Large Bustard

Taxonomy. *Otis Kori* Burchell, 1822, confluence of Vaal and Orange Rivers.
In past, genus frequently labelled *Choriotis*, but *Ardeotis* has priority; genus sometimes merged with *Otis*. Present species forms superspecies with *A. arabs*. Sometimes alternatively considered to form

On following pages: 4. Great Indian Bustard (*Ardeotis nigriceps*); 5. Australian Bustard (*Ardeotis australis*); 6. Houbara Bustard (*Chlamydotis undulata*).

superspecies with *A. nigriceps* and *A. australis*; these three have even been lumped together in single species, *A. kori*. All four *Ardeotis* have occasionally been placed in same superspecies. Two subspecies recognized.

Subspecies and Distribution.

A. k. struthiunculus (Neumann, 1907) - NW Somalia and C Ethiopia through SE Sudan, NE Uganda and Kenya to N Tanzania.

A. k. kori (Burchell, 1822) - S Angola and Namibia E through Botswana to S Zimbabwe and S Mozambique, and S to South Africa.

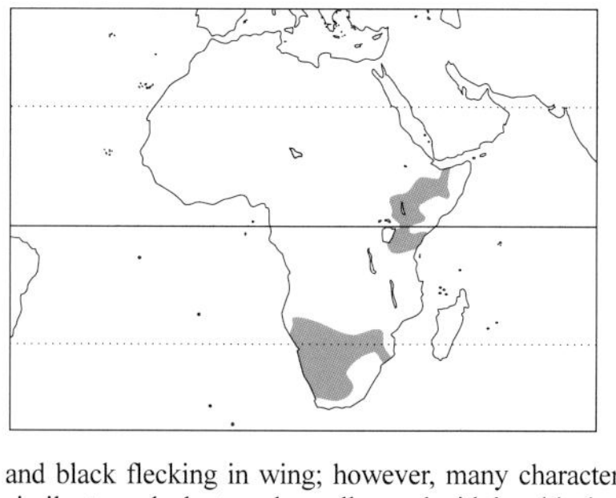

Descriptive notes. Male c. 120 cm, 10,900-19,000 g; female c. 90 cm, 5900 g. Back, wings and central tail brown with fine buff vermiculations, white panel with black spots on folded wing; two buffy white median bars on tail, often concealed; head, neck and breast appear grey, being finely barred dark grey-brown on ashy white, with often indistinct black band at shoulders and base of neck; crown black with pale grey centre, short straggling backwards crest, underlined by white supercilium; belly white; legs dull yellowish to greyish, bill grey, eyes orange-brown to yellow. Similar to *A. arabs*, but somewhat larger and with black on base of neck and black flecking in wing; however, many characters are variable for reasons not yet clear. Female similar to male, but much smaller, and with less black on crown. Juvenile lacks crest and is more spotted on mantle. Race *struthiunculus* slightly larger and less dusky, with more contrast in head pattern.

Habitat. Flat, arid, mostly open country, generally below 2000 m and usually with a short herb layer, e.g. grassland, karoo, bushveld, thornveld, scrubland and savanna, but also floodplains, duneland and fossil valleys; also man-modified habitats, such as wheat fields and recently burnt firebreaks. In the hot dry season in Kenya, many birds move into woodland, and use of closed-canopy miombo woodland is known from Zimbabwe. In one report, birds are commonest where grazing mammals are most plentiful.

Food and Feeding. Exploits a wide range of vegetable and animal resources: seeds, berries, bulbs, *Acacia* gum, snails, insects (chiefly Orthoptera), rodents, lizards and snakes (up to medium size), and birds (eggs and nestlings, also roadkills). Birds often gather in areas infested with locusts or caterpillars, or where fire is flushing small animals or has already scorched them. Importance of dung-dependent fauna in diet not clear, but possibly significant.

Breeding. Sept-Feb in S Africa, Dec-Aug (according to rains) in E Africa. Nests on ground often near a distinct feature, such as a grass clump or rocks, sometimes in partial tree shade; will breed in area just after herds have moved through the territory; nest is shallow scrape, sometimes with thin lining of grass. Usually 2 eggs, possibly 1 in drier years; incubation period c. 25 days; chicks have tawny down striped and mottled with dark brown. In E Africa, breeding success greater when wet season good.

Movements. Largely sedentary. In Kenya local movements, presumably on foot, occur into woodland habitat in the dry period, Jan-Mar, though possibly not by breeding birds.

Status and Conservation. Not globally threatened. CITES II. Where undisturbed, can still be common, as in parts of Botswana. Zimbabwe holds c. 5000 individuals, but the species is certainly declining there owing to habitat destruction, hunting pressure and disturbance; threatened in South Africa, where abundance has dropped since last century, although range thought not to have decreased, with same apparent causes of decline. Species suffers some mortality from collisions with electricity cables, vehicles and fences.

Bibliography. Allan & Davies (1995), Allen & Clifton (1972), Ash & Miskell (1983), Baker (1989), Britton, P.L. (1980), Brooke (1984a), Cave & Macdonald (1955), Chiweshe & Dale (1993), Dale (1990), Dowsett & Forbes-Watson (1993), Ginn *et al.* (1989), Hallager (1994), Hellmich (1988), Irwin (1981), Jubb (1981), Kok & Van Ee (1989), Lewis & Pomeroy (1989), Mackworth-Praed & Grant (1957, 1962), Maclean (1993), Maozeka (1993), Morgan-Davies (1965), Mwangi & Karanja (1989, 1992, 1993), Nikolaus (1987), Penry (1994), Pinto (1983), Pollard (1986), Prozesky (1977), Rockingham-Gill (1983, 1989), Schmidl (1982), Short *et al.* (1990), van Someren (1925-1935), Urban *et al.* (1986), Viljoen & Viljoen (1987).

4. Great Indian Bustard

Ardeotis nigriceps

French: Outarde à tête noire **German**: Hindutrappe **Spanish**: Avutarda India
Other common names: Indian Bustard

Taxonomy. *Otis nigriceps* Vigors, 1831, Himalayas.

In past, genus frequently labelled *Choriotis*, but *Ardeotis* has priority; genus sometimes merged with *Otis*. Present species forms superspecies with *A. australis*; these two sometimes separated from their two congeners in genus *Austrotis*, or, erroneously, in genus *Choriotis*, but type species of latter is *A. arabs*. Superspecies sometimes considered to include *A. kori*, as well as *A. australis*; all three have even been lumped into single species, *A. kori*. All four *Ardeotis* have occasionally been placed in same superspecies. Monotypic.

Distribution. W & C India, from Rajasthan S through Gujarat, Madhya Pradesh and Maharashtra to N Karnataka and W Andhra Pradesh; relict populations elsewhere.

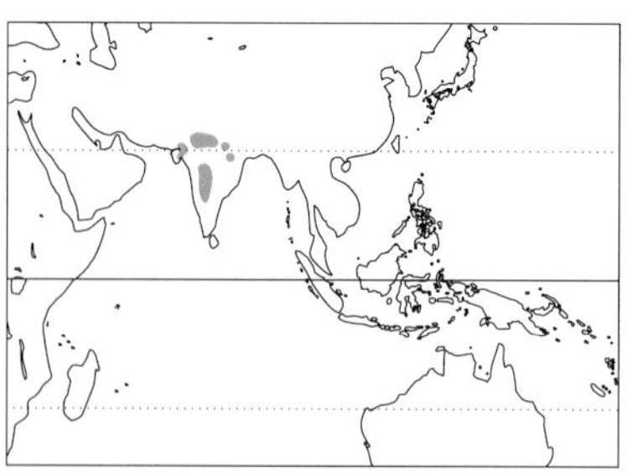

Descriptive notes. Male 120 cm, 8000-14,500 g; female 90 cm, 3500-6750 g. Often has extensive black crown; legs pale yellowish. Virtually identical to *A. australis*, but often with indistinct black breast band, some black on thighs, and either no distinct line behind eye or black cap descending through eye; tends to have less white on black wing patch. Female smaller, with greyer neck. Immature similar to female, but has buff spots on crown, hindneck and upper back.

Habitat. Optimally occurs in rolling grassland with vegetation 30-70 cm high, with or without scattered trees; but also found in open scrub, sandy semi-desert plains, broad pastures, marginal fields and lightly disturbed cultivation.

Food and Feeding. Opportunistic, exploiting local and seasonal abundance. Grain, shoots and berries, with a particular liking for the drupes of *Zizyphus rotundifolia* and the crops *Eruca sativa* and *Cicer arietinum*; also locusts, grasshoppers, beetles (including green blister beetles *Cantharis tenuicollis*), centipedes, lizards and small snakes and mammals.

Breeding. Occurs throughout year, varying with area and rainfall, e.g. chiefly Mar-Jun in N of range, Aug-Oct in W Deccan, Aug-Jan in E Deccan. Nest is a shallow, sometimes sparsely lined scrape, often with virtually no adjacent cover. Normally 1 egg, rarely 2; incubation period c. 27 days; chick has buff-coloured down with black markings on head and back; fledging takes 35-40 days, but young bird remains with female until start of next breeding season.

Movements. Sedentary or seasonally nomadic, or may follow both strategies; generally dispersing, or at least disappearing, at various periods depending probably on availability of water; possibly some birds migrate between the Thar Desert and the Deccan Tableland, profiting from the monsoon rains in each area.

Status and Conservation. ENDANGERED. CITES I. In 19th century ranged from E Pakistan, in Sind and Punjab, E to W Bengal, and S to C Tamil Nadu; in recent times, only rare vagrant to Pakistan. Total population now estimated to number 1500-2000 birds, mainly in Rajasthan with 500-1000 birds, remainder scattered mostly through parts of W India. Hunting considered chief cause of decline, but habitat loss and disturbance, probably underestimated in the past, are certainly key factors now, with nest failure commonly attributed to cattle trampling eggs or simply keeping female off nest; nests often predated by House Crows (*Corvus splendens*).

Bibliography. Ali & Rahmani (1982, 1985), Ali & Ripley (1980), Bhushan & Rahmani (1992), Chandra (1990), Collar & Andrew (1988), Collar *et al.* (1994), Cornwallis (1983b), Dharmakumarsinhji (1957, 1971, 1983), Goriup (1983a), Gupta (1975), Hasan (1983), Kapoor & Bhatia (1983), King (1978/79), Kulkarni (1981, 1983), Lal (1993), Manakadan & Rahmani (1986, 1989, 1990), Mathur (1983), Neginhal (1983a, 1983b), Prakash (1983), Rahmani (1984, 1986, 1987, 1988a, 1988b, 1989, 1991, 1992), Rahmani & Manakadan (1985, 1986, 1987, 1990), Rego (1983), Ripley (1982), Roberts, T.J. (1991), Sangha (1994), Saxena (1983), Shukla (1983), Sinha (1983), Vardhan (1985), Vyas *et al.* (1983).

5. Australian Bustard

Ardeotis australis

French: Outarde d'Australie **German**: Wammentrappe **Spanish**: Avutarda Australiana

Taxonomy. *Otis Australis* J. E. Gray, 1829, New South Wales.

In past, genus frequently labelled *Choriotis*, but *Ardeotis* has priority; genus sometimes merged with *Otis*. Present species forms superspecies with *A. nigriceps*; these two sometimes separated from congeners in genus *Austrotis*, or, erroneously, in genus *Choriotis*, but type species of latter is *A. arabs*. Superspecies sometimes considered to include *A. kori*, as well as *A. nigriceps*; all three have even been lumped into single species, *A. kori*. All four *Ardeotis* have occasionally been placed in same superspecies. Monotypic.

Distribution. Australia, in all states, but generally rarer or absent in S and especially in SE; also S Papua New Guinea in the Trans-Fly, ranging W into Irian Jaya.

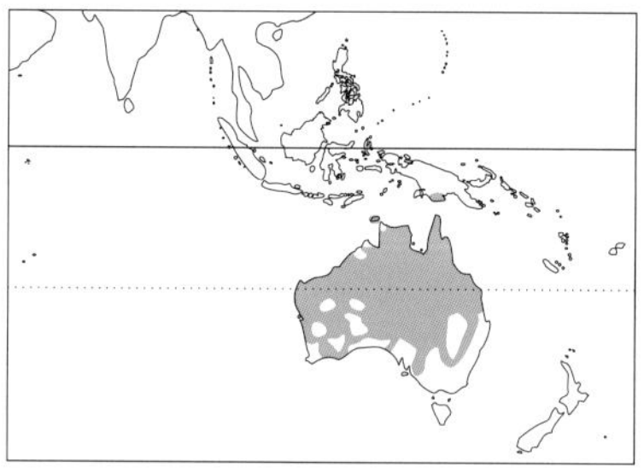

Descriptive notes. Male c. 120 cm, 5600-8200 g; female c. 90 cm, 2800-3200 g. Back, wings and central tail brown with fine dark vermiculations, black panel spotted with white on folded wing; outermost tail feathers chiefly black and white, but often concealed; head, neck and breast appear greyish white, being finely barred dark grey on white; black breast band often hidden; crown is black with slight backwards crest, underlined by white supercilium and a thin black line behind eye; belly white; legs and bill whitish, eye brown. Female smaller, with scattered dark blotches on upperparts, greyer neck and duller crown. Immature has pale grey and brown mottling on head, neck and upperparts.

Habitat. Mainly grassland dominated by tussocky forms, also in sparse low shrubland, savanna, open woodland and, in New Guinea, edges of swamps. Utilizes long grass areas in wet season, low open shrub plains in dry season. Often found in burnt or regenerating areas, sometimes in cultivated areas. Breeds mainly in ecotone between grassland and cover-yielding habitat such as hummock grassland, shrubland and woodland.

Food and Feeding. Shoots, roots, leaves, flowerheads, seeds and berries; molluscs, myriapods, arachnids, insects (especially grasshoppers, beetles and caterpillars), reptiles, young birds and small rodents. Often attracted to fire, taking live and dead prey; once recorded following a plough. In New Guinea, several birds may gather to feed in shallow water.

Breeding. Aseasonal in arid and semi-arid N regions, occurring in response to rainfall; Apr-Nov in S. Nests on bare ground, sometimes scraped clear of stones; on low sandy ridges usually with termite mounds and near gilgais. Normally 1-2 eggs, less commonly 3; incubation 23-24 days; chick has buff-coloured down, with darker brown stripes; fledging period apparently unrecorded.

Movements. Largely sedentary in parts of range, but may disperse nomadically in non-breeding season; in some areas shows small-scale seasonal displacements away from drying areas. Irrupts in response to inland droughts, regional rainfall and grasshopper and mouse plagues; also locally to bush fires. Report of migration between New Guinea and Australia requires substantiation.

Status and Conservation. Not globally threatened. CITES II. Range has contracted since European settlement, owing to heavy hunting for food and sport up to at least 1940, when formally protected; other main factors are habitat change and effects of introduced animals. Alteration of tussock grasslands by rabbits may be particularly important, as ranges of the two species are now largely mutually exclusive. Livestock may also have caused a decline; intensive land-use practices cause desertion of the areas affected. Locally common in Trans-Fly area of S New Guinea.

Bibliography. Anon. (1971b), Appayya (1982), Beehler *et al.* (1986), Blakers *et al.* (1984), Coates (1985), Fitzherbert (1978, 1983), Garnett (1993), Grice *et al.* (1986), Hoogerwerf (1964), Lindsey (1992), Lunt (1992), Macdonald (1988), Marchant & Higgins (1993), Mattingley (1929), Pizzey & Doyle (1980), Rand & Gilliard (1967), Roberts (1979), Schodde & Tidemann (1986), Simpson & Day (1994), Slater *et al.* (1989), White, D.M. (1985).

Genus *CHLAMYDOTIS* Lesson, 1839

6. Houbara Bustard

Chlamydotis undulata

French: Outarde houbara **German**: Kragentrappe **Spanish**: Avutarda Hubara
Other common names: Ruffed Bustard

Taxonomy. *Psophia undulata* Jacquin, 1784, captive bird from Tripoli.
Apparently close to *Neotis* (see page 240). Recent work suggests that race *macqueenii* might merit treatment as separate species. Three subspecies recognized.

Subspecies and Distribution.
C. u. fuertaventurae (Rothschild & Hartert, 1894) - E Canary Is.
C. u. undulata (Jacquin, 1784) - N Africa, E to NC Egypt.
C. u. macqueenii (J. E. Gray, 1832) - Middle East and Arabia E to Iran and extreme W Pakistan. Also breeds from NW Kazakhstan and NE Iran E to Mongolia and N China, wintering from Persian Gulf to Pakistan and NW India, and in C China.

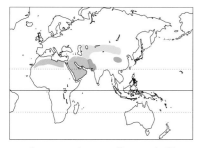

Descriptive notes. Male 65-75 cm, 1800-3200 g; female 55-65 cm, 1200-1700 g. Upperparts pale sandy buff, mottled and lined with darker brown, clear and paler on folded wing, tail with up to four bluish grey bars; crown buff with sometimes hidden central line of white erectile feathers, rest of head pale greyish buff with black line down side of neck composed of erectile filamentous plumes which turn white (usually hidden) on side of breast; underparts white; eye pale yellow; legs olive grey to pale straw yellow. Female similar but smaller, with filamentous neck plumes much reduced. Juvenile similar to female but ornamental plumes on head and neck scarcely present, plumage yellower and white areas of wing duller. Race *fuertaventurae* darker; *macqueenii* has black in white crown feathers, a blue-grey foreneck, and is larger; latter race and nominate both show much individual variation in size, with considerable overlap.

Habitat. Arid sandy semi-desert with tussock grass, flat bare stony plains dotted with xerophytic and halophytic scrub, wormwood steppe and sandy grasslands, often visiting marginal cultivation in non-breeding period.

Food and Feeding. Variable and opportunistic, with no clearly discernible seasonal or geographical pattern. Vegetable matter such as fruits, seeds, shoots, leaves and flowers; animal material chiefly Orthoptera and Coleoptera, but includes various invertebrates and small snakes and lizards.

Breeding. Nov-Jun, but chiefly Mar-Apr, in N Africa and Canaries; Mar-May in Syria; Apr-Jun in CIS; apparently Mar-Apr in Pakistan. Nest is a shallow unlined scrape on ground, sometimes in open but usually near some cover. Eggs 2-3, though up to 5 recorded in *macqueenii*; incubation usually 24 days, but on occasion up to 28 days; chicks have golden and buff down, with white, black and sepia markings; fledging period c. 35 days. Young stay with female parent into first autumn.

Movements. Sedentary and locally nomadic in Africa and Middle East. C Asian populations strongly migratory, leaving breeding grounds in Aug-Oct on trans-Himalayan migration, and arriving Sept-Nov in wintering grounds from Persian Gulf states to NW India, some occurring W to Egypt; abundance in given areas varies from year to year, apparently in response to rain-related condition of habitat; birds travel N again in Mar-Apr. Vagrant S to Sudan; expected to occur regularly in NW Sudan, but no records located.

Status and Conservation. Not globally threatened. CITES I. Although reportedly in decline in almost every range state this century, true status very difficult to gauge owing to birds' highly cryptic coloration, elusive behaviour, and remote and inhospitable habitat. Even in Canary Is, population hard to assess, with an estimated 400 birds on Lanzarote in 1993, where 15-20 birds were believed present in 1979, and 60 birds in 1991, indicating a remarkable capacity to hide, or to colonize areas rapidly, or to expand numbers in favourable conditions; however, tourist facilities, including the use of off-road vehicles, are rapidly affecting habitat in the Canaries. In Western Negev, Israel, population reckoned to number 185-355 birds. Species is in considerable decline throughout N Africa. Population in Kazakhstan estimated at 40,000-60,000 birds, with substantial numbers also in Uzbekistan and Iran. In Pakistan, hunted in thousands over three decades, but no clear evidence of decline: 4360 birds killed by local and visiting hunters in winter 1982/83, and 4955 in 1984/85; also some 2000 birds trapped there being sold to UAE in period 1986-1988; but total population wintering there each year anticipated at 20,000-25,000 birds. Threats include intensive agricultural practices, human disturbance, habitat degradation through livestock overgrazing, and hunting both by local people with guns and Arab dignitaries with falcons.

Bibliography. Alekseev (1985), Ali & Ripley (1980), Anegay (1994), Cao Yuping *et al*. (1989), Coles & Collar (1979), Collar (1979b, 1983a), Collar & Andrew (1988), Collins (1984, 1994), Cornwallis (1983a, 1983b), Cramp & Simmons (1980), Dharmakumarsinhji (1983), Domínguez (1989), Domínguez & Díaz (1985), Dowsett & Forbes-Watson (1993), Emmerson (1983), Étchécopar & Hüe (1964, 1978), Evans (1994), Fedorenko (1992), Flint *et al*. (1992), Gallagher & Woodcock (1980), Gaucher (1991), Gaucher *et al*. (1996), Géroudet (1974), Goodman *et al*. (1989), Goriup (1981, 1983b, 1983c, 1989, 1992a, 1994b), Gubin (1992), Haddane (1985), Hinz & Heiss (1989), Hüe & Étchécopar (1970), Knystautas (1993), Lack (1983), Launay & Loughland (1995), Launay & Paillat (1990), Lavee (1985, 1988, 1994), Ledant *et al*. (1981), Lorenzo & Emmerson (1993), Mackworth-Praed & Grant (1957), Malik (1985), Martín *et al*. (1996), Mendelssohn (1983), Mendelssohn *et al*. (1979, 1983), Mian (1984, 1985, 1986a, 1986b, 1988), Mian & Dasti (1985), Mian & Surahio (1983), Mukhina (1990), Osborne (1986, 1989), Patrikeev (1995), Paz (1987), Ponomareva (1983, 1985), Porter & Goriup (1985), Potapov & Flint (1987), Ramadan-Jaradi & Ramadan-Jaradi (1989), Razdan & Mansoori (1989), Renaud (1989), Roberts, T.J. (1991), Rogacheva (1992), Roshier (1995), Saleh (1989), Seddon (1995/96), Seddon & Gelinaud (1995), Shirihai (1996), de Smet (1989), Stepanov (1986), Surahio (1985), Thomsen & Jacobsen (1979), Urban *et al*. (1986).

ssp *stanleyi*

ssp *denhami*

♀

♂

8

♂

♂

♀

9

♂

♀

7

10

♀

♂

ssp *erlangeri*

ssp *mackenziei*

♀

♂

ssp *barrowii*

11

♀

♀

♂

ssp *senegalensis*

♂

12

ssp *vigorsii*

♂

♀

♂

13

ssp *namaqua*

♂

14

♀

♂

♀

15

PLATE 24

inches 12

cm 30

Genus *NEOTIS* Sharpe, 1893

7. Ludwig's Bustard

Neotis ludwigii

French: Outarde de Ludwig **German**: Ludwigtrappe **Spanish**: Avutarda de Namibia

Taxonomy. *Otis Ludwigii* Rüppell, 1837, South Africa.
Genus sometimes merged with *Otis*. Present species is most distinctive member of genus. Monotypic.
Distribution. Extreme SW Angola through W Namibia to S South Africa.

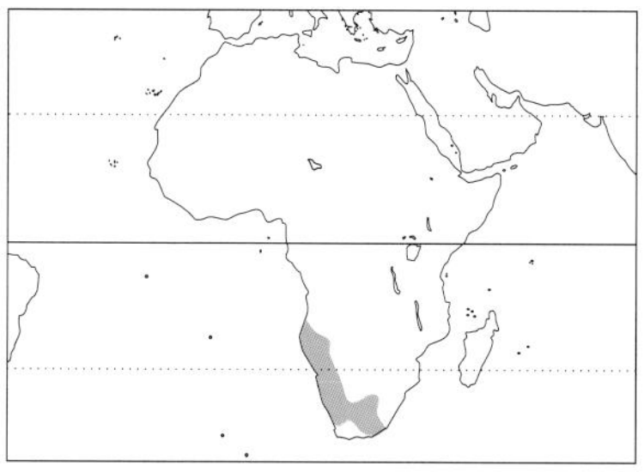

Descriptive notes. Male 85 cm, 4200-6000 g; female 2200-2500 g. Upperparts brown finely vermiculated with buff, tail similar with broad dark bars, white wing panel, usually concealed when wing folded; head, neck and breast dark brown to sooty brown, hindneck greyish white, base of hindneck dull orange, belly white; bill brown, legs yellowish. Female smaller than male, paler and more speckled on head and neck.
Habitat. Open lowland and upland plains with grass and light thornbush, sandy open shrub veld and semi-desert in the arid and semi-arid Namib and Karoo biomes.
Food and Feeding. Invertebrates, small vertebrates and vegetable matter have all been recorded, but strong evidence of movement with rains in pursuit of Orthoptera hatchings, although vegetation remains important and berries of *Lycium oxycladum* reported. Flocks (up to 70 recorded) may gather on cultivated areas or in natural vegetation after rain.
Breeding. Aug-Dec. Nest is a scrape on bare ground often among stones, on crest of low ridge or hill slope. Eggs 2; chick has reddish down streaked blackish.
Movements. Species is partial migrant towards SW from the more northerly and interior summer rainfall region (Nama Karoo), where present Nov-Apr, to the more southerly and coastal winter rainfall region (Succulent Karoo), for the period May-Oct.
Status and Conservation. Not globally threatened. CITES II. Total population size estimated at 56,000-81,000 birds. An assumed contraction of range, causing concern for its security in 1984, was based on birds that had in fact been *N. denhami*. However, snares set for mammals on farms, and electricity wires, appear to be two considerable threats to the species in some areas.
Bibliography. Allan (1993, 1994b), Allan & Davies (1995), Boobyer (1990), Brooke (1984a), Brown, C.J. (1993), Clancey (1967), Cyrus & Robson (1980), Dowsett & Forbes-Watson (1993), Earlé *et al*. (1988), Ginn *et al*. (1989), Herholdt (1987, 1988), Kok & Van Ee (1989), Mackworth-Praed & Grant (1962), Maclean (1993), van Niekerk (1993), Penry (1994), Pinto (1983), Sinclair (1987), Skead, C.J. (1967), Urban *et al*. (1986).

8. Denham's Bustard

Neotis denhami

French: Outarde de Denham **German**: Kafferntrappe **Spanish**: Avutarda Cafre
Other common names: Stanley Bustard; Burchell's Bustard ("*burchellii*")

Taxonomy. *Otis Denhami* Children, 1826, near Lake Chad.
Genus sometimes merged with *Otis*. Present species may form parapatric species pair with *N. heuglinii*. Normally considered to include form "*burchellii*" of uncertain status, known only by type specimen from E Sudan. In past, present species was at times known as *N. cafra*, but due to confusion in nomenclature with *Eupodotis senegalensis*, name *cafra* was officially suppressed. Three subspecies recognized.
Subspecies and Distribution.
N. d. denhami (Children, 1826) - SW Mauritania and Senegambia E to N Uganda and Ethiopia.
N. d. jacksoni Bannerman, 1930 - Kenya and W Tanzania S to Zambia, N Botswana and N Zimbabwe; S Congo and W Zaire; SW Angola.
N. d. stanleyi (J. E. Gray, 1831) - South Africa and Swaziland.

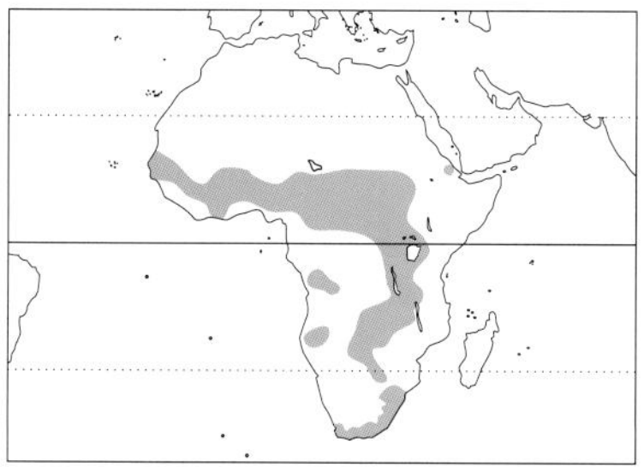

Descriptive notes. Male 100 cm, 9000-10,000 g; female 80 cm, 3000 g. Upperparts dull brown with fine black vermiculations, tail with several creamy bars; large panel on folded wing mottled white on black; crown grey bordered black, long white supercilium, black line through eye, chin white, cheeks, neck and breast grey, hindneck orange-brown, belly white; legs pale yellow, bill whitish horn with darker culmen and tip. Female smaller than male, with grey replaced by buff; more patterned upperparts and a finely barred foreneck. Immature similar to female; immature male generally rather variable, with neck almost black in form "*burchellii*". Race *jacksoni* slightly smaller, darker on hindneck (intermediates in SE Sudan); race *stanleyi* darker and more richly coloured on hindneck, paler on back, with foreneck white in breeding male.
Habitat. Grasslands including high plateau downland up to 3000 m, grassy *Acacia*-studded dunes, fairly dense shrubland, light woodland, farmland and crops, dried marsh and arid scrub plains; also grass-covered ironstone pans and burnt savanna woodland in NW Sierra Leone. In South Africa, a bird of high rainfall sour grassveld, and planted pastures and cereal croplands in fynbos, favouring natural vegetation in the breeding season and harvested cereal crop fields at other times.
Food and Feeding. Wide range of foods recorded, including many different arthropods (in places nymphal stages of invasive Orthoptera), small vertebrates and various parts of plants including flowerheads. Recorded defending active termite mound, pecking at animal droppings for arthropods, wading in pools apparently for frogs on emergent stems, and gathering in small numbers on recently burnt areas.
Breeding. Breeding schedule unclear in many areas, possibly reflecting opportunism based on rainfall; Jun-Oct in Sahel; nuptial display in Jan in Sierra Leone, Feb-Mar (dry season) in Ivory Coast; May in Nigeria; Dec-Feb in N Zaire, but in S Zaire nuptial display in Jun (dry season); Jan-Mar and Jul in E Africa; chiefly Oct-Jan (Aug-Apr) in C & S Africa. Nest is a shallow scrape on bare ground, usually amidst grass or on low prominence. Eggs 1-2; chick has buff down mottled and striped black.
Movements. Nominate *denhami* migrates N generally in May-Jun but as late as Aug; returns Sept-Oct or as late as Dec, following rains and usually, or at least sometimes, then breeding (but not in Senegal); only present in S Niger and Ivory Coast in dry season, but considered sedentary in Central African Republic. Movements of race *jacksoni* also unclear, but present May-Oct in SE Zaire, and Aug-May (mostly Dec-Apr) in Zimbabwe and Botswana, suggesting a N-S shift, though also present Aug-Jan in E Zaire; montane populations in E may move lower, Jun-Aug; records from S Congo and W Zaire are all of non-breeding birds. Race *stanleyi* also shows movements to lower regions in period Jun-Aug, with an apparently immigrant summer breeding population in coastal Zululand, South Africa, from Sept onwards.
Status and Conservation. Not globally threatened. CITES II. Common in Central African Republic and parts of Uganda, but decline in N of range in Sudan, and hunting widespread in Sahel zone; notable decline in numbers in Nigeria due to hunting and trapping. Threatened in Kenya, where range contraction well documented and population as low as 300-400 birds; also in South Africa, where total Transvaal breeding population only numbers c. 300 birds, and S Cape Province winter population an estimated 956 birds; in both countries decline related to competition with man for land.
Bibliography. Allan (1993), Allan & Davies (1995), Baker (1989), Benson & Benson (1975), Benson & Irwin (1972), Benson *et al*. (1971), Britton, P.L. (1980), Brooke (1984a), Carroll, R.W. (1988), Cave & Macdonald (1955), Cramp & Simmons (1980), Dowsett & Forbes-Watson (1993), Elgood *et al*. (1994), Ginn *et al*. (1989), Gore (1990), Grimes (1987), Herholdt (1988), Howells & Fynn (1979), Irwin (1981), Koster & Grettenberger (1983), Lewis & Pomeroy (1989), Lippens & Wille (1976), Mackworth-Praed & Grant (1957, 1962, 1970), Maclean (1993), Morel, G.J. & Morel (1990), Morel, R. (1989), Newby (1979), van Niekerk & Kotze (1993), Nikolaus (1987), Penry (1994), Pinto (1983), Pollard (1986), Prigogine (1971), Romig (1989), Short *et al*. (1990), Smith, M.J. (1987), Tarboton (1989), Tarboton, Kemp & Kemp (1987), Turner & Goriup (1989), Urban *et al*. (1986), Uys (1963), Wilson (1972).

9. Heuglin's Bustard

Neotis heuglinii

French: Outarde de Heuglin **German**: Heuglintrappe **Spanish**: Avutarda Somalí

Taxonomy. *Otis heuglinii* Hartlaub, 1859, near the wells of Thushha, between Zeila and Harar.
Genus sometimes merged with *Otis*. Present species considered to form parapatric species pair with *N. denhami*, but perhaps in reality closer to *N. nuba*. Monotypic.
Distribution. Eritrea, E & S Ethiopia, Djibouti, N & SC Somalia and N Kenya.

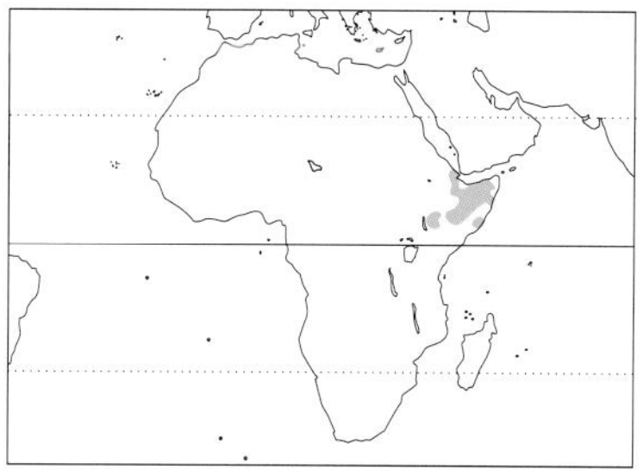

Descriptive notes. Male 75 cm, 4000-8000 g; female 2600-3000 g. Generally similar to *N. nuba*, but with smudged black face, crown paler shading backward to whitish, chestnut extending across breast and bordered below with a dark band, and upperparts more distinctly blotched and patterned. Female has much greyer head than male.
Habitat. Arid lowlands in open desert with annual grass, semi-desert savanna and tussocky grassland; 93% of range in Kenya lies within areas that receive less than 500 mm rainfall annually.
Food and Feeding. Little known. Orthoptera, small vertebrates, berries and other vegetable matter recorded.
Breeding. Apr-Jun in NE Africa, Jan and June in N Kenya, timed for when rains make grass tallest. Nest is a scrape on bare ground. Eggs 2. No further information available.
Movements. Sedentary and nomadic.
Status and Conservation. Not globally threatened. CITES II. Fairly common in N Kenya and N Somalia; uncommon in most of Ethiopia, rare in Eritrea. Species requires careful monitoring, given relatively restricted range; biology and ecology remain very poorly known.
Bibliography. Anon. (1995c), Archer & Godman (1937-1961), Ash (1989), Ash & Miskell (1983), Britton, P.L. (1980), Dowsett & Forbes-Watson (1993), Lewis & Pomeroy (1989), Mackworth-Praed & Grant (1957), Short *et al*. (1990), Urban *et al*. (1986).

10. Nubian Bustard

Neotis nuba

French: Outarde nubienne **German**: Nubiertrappe **Spanish**: Avutarda Núbica

Taxonomy. *Otis Nuba* Cretzschmar, 1826, Kurgos, near Shendi, Sudan.
Genus sometimes merged with *Otis*. Present species may be closely related to *N. heuglinii*. Claimed race *agaze* from Chad westwards is supposedly paler and smaller, but much more material needs examination to confirm that differences are not clinal or individual. Monotypic.
Distribution. Sahel zone from W Mauritania to E Sudan; distribution probably continuous, or at least with interbreeding populations, even though species very patchily recorded.
Descriptive notes. Male 70 cm, 5400 g; female 50 cm, no data on weight. Upperparts pale tawny buff, lightly vermiculated with black, tail similar but washed grey; crown as back, bordered by black line; face whitish, chin and throat black, neck pale grey, lower hindneck and sides of breast tawny buff; rest of underparts whitish; legs and bill pale yellow. Female smaller than male with much less black on chin and throat. Immature similar to adult, but black on head is browner, and amount of black on throat reduced to thin stripe.
Habitat. Arid and semi-arid scrub and savanna on desert fringes, penetrating further N into Sahara than other bustard species.
Food and Feeding. Invertebrates and vegetable matter: Orthoptera, Coleoptera, Hymenoptera, etc.; leaves and berries of desert plants, grass seeds and *Acacia* gum.

On following pages: 11. White-bellied Bustard (*Eupodotis senegalensis*); 12. Blue Bustard (*Eupodotis caerulescens*); 13. Karoo Bustard (*Eupodotis vigorsii*); 14. Rüppell's Bustard (*Eupodotis rueppellii*); 15. Little Brown Bustard (*Eupodotis humilis*).

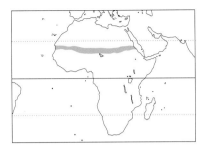

Breeding. Jul-Oct; the finding of 3 nests in one day in Aug suggests synchronized response to suitable conditions (as well as degree of local abundance). Nest situated on bare sand; one nest was between forks of a fallen branch. Eggs 2. No further information available.

Movements. Sedentary and almost certainly nomadic; in Mauritania, tends to move S in winter, returning N with rains.

Status and Conservation. Not globally threatened. CITES II. Currently considered near-threatened. Apparently still fairly common in many places, although hunting, more recently by Arab dignitaries, may now be causing substantial regression in parts of its vast, if latitudinally compressed, range. Only one record from Nigeria, a pair sighted in 1959. Rare and very little known in Sudan. Widespread in Mauritania, with groups of 15-20 birds recorded.

Bibliography. Beaman (1994), Cave & Macdonald (1955), Collar & Stuart (1985), Cramp & Simmons (1980), Dowsett & Forbes-Watson (1993), Elgood et al. (1994), Fairon (1975), Gee (1984), Giraudoux et al. (1988), Lamarche (1988), Mackworth-Praed & Grant (1957, 1970), Newby (1979, 1990), Newby et al. (1987), Nikolaus (1987), Salvan (1968), Urban et al. (1986), Vaurie (1961).

Genus *EUPODOTIS* Lesson, 1839

11. **White-bellied Bustard**

Eupodotis senegalensis

French: Outarde du Sénégal   **German**: Senegaltrappe   **Spanish**: Sisón Senegalés
Other common names: White-bellied Korhaan, Senegal Bustard

Taxonomy. *Otis Senegalensis* Vieillot, 1820, Senegal.
Populations of S Africa sometimes treated as separate species, *E. barrowii*; this form has alternatively been known as *E. cafra*, but due to confusion in nomenclature with *Neotis denhami*, name *cafra* was officially suppressed; slight differences from northern birds in plumage and voice probably do not justify treatment as separate species. Birds from Eritrea normally ascribed to nominate *senegalensis*, but more likely to belong to *canicollis*. Five subspecies normally recognized.

Subspecies and Distribution.
E. s. senegalensis (Vieillot, 1820) - SW Mauritania and Guinea E to Central African Republic, C Sudan and perhaps Eritrea.
E. s. canicollis (Reichenow, 1881) - Ethiopia S to NE Tanzania.
E. s. erlangeri (Reichenow, 1905) - S Kenya and W Tanzania.
E. s. mackenziei White, 1945 - E Gabon and C Congo to S & SE Zaire, E Angola and W Zambia; C & S Angola.
E. s. barrowii (J. E. Gray, 1829) - C & SE Botswana, E South Africa and Swaziland.

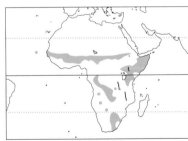

Descriptive notes. 50-60 cm, 1400-1500 g; female smaller. Upperparts tawny buff minutely vermiculated with brown, tail greyer with thin dark bars; crown black with grey centre, face whitish with black patch on throat, neck bluish grey, breast tawny buff, belly white; legs pale yellow, bill pinkish with dark culmen. Female similar to male, but lacks black on crown or throat; neck buff. Racial variation in size, shading, and degree and distribution of black on head or grey on neck or both.

Habitat. Open and relatively tall grassland and savanna, bushed or dwarf wooded grassland, clearings, cultivation, river plains; occurs up to 2000 m in E Africa. In interior W Africa, adapted to relatively dry conditions, penetrating well into desert in wet season, whereas in Central African Republic recorded from *Terminalia laxiflora* savanna woodland; in South Africa, prefers taller, denser grassland in more rolling country than *E. caerulescens*, although sometimes the two co-occur. In Sudan, present more on sandy than on cotton-soil areas. In Kenya, birds retreat to woodland areas in hot period of day.

Food and Feeding. Termites, locusts, caterpillars, beetles, spiders, scorpions, snails and lizards; also green herbage, grass seeds, bulbs, berries and flowers. Sometimes concentrates in areas recently burnt.

Breeding. Jul-Oct in W Africa; Jun and Aug-Oct in C Sahel; Mar-Jun in NE Africa; within the period Oct-May in various parts of E Africa; Sept-Oct in Angola; Dec in Zambia; Oct-Feb in South Africa. Probably monogamous, with group-territorialism; generally occurs in pairs or in groups presumed to consist of a mated pair and up to two offspring. Nest is a shallow scrape on bare ground or between grass tufts. Eggs 1-3; chick has pale sandy down, with heavy dark streaking.

Movements. Largely sedentary, but in Chad moves N in wet season, and in South Africa some birds winter at lower altitudes. Home ranges for family groups are around 40 ha.

Status and Conservation. Not globally threatened. CITES II. Apparently on decline in Sahel zone: only 3 recent records in Gambia, where was formerly commonest bustard species; apparently much rarer than in past in Ivory Coast; only one recent record in Niger; declining where formerly common in Nigeria; and formerly common but now uncommon in Sudan. Generally uncommon in E Africa, with a density estimated at 0·12-0·2/km², but frequent in Serengeti National Park, while a density of 3·0-4·6/km² was estimated in Nairobi National Park. In Ethiopia, Eritrea and Somalia rather common and widespread, with abundance increasing above 1500 m. Generally uncommon in C Africa; scarce in Zambia. Locally common in parts of South Africa, where outnumbered 4:1 by *E. caerulescens* when the two occur together.

Bibliography. Allan & Davies (1995), Ash (1989), Ash & Miskell (1983), Baker (1989), Benson et al. (1971), Britton, P.L. (1980), Carroll, R.W. (1988), Cave & Macdonald (1955), Dowsett & Dowsett-Lemaire (1993), Dowsett & Forbes-Watson (1993), Elgood et al. (1994), Ginn et al. (1989), Giraudoux et al. (1988), Gore (1990), Goriup (1987), Grimes (1987), Johst (1972), Kemp & Tarboton (1976), Kok & Van Ee (1989), Lewis & Pomeroy (1989), Mackworth-Praed & Grant (1957, 1962, 1970), Maclean (1993), Mwangi & Karanja (1989, 1992, 1993), Newby (1979), Nikolaus (1987), Pinto (1983), Short et al. (1990), Snow (1978), Tarboton, Kemp & Kemp (1987), Thiollay (1985), Urban et al. (1986).

12. **Blue Bustard**

Eupodotis caerulescens

French: Outarde plombée   **German**: Blautrappe   **Spanish**: Sisón Azulado
Other common names: Blue Korhaan

Taxonomy. *Otis Cærulesens* [sic] Vieillot, 1820, "Kaffraria" = eastern Cape Province.
In past, isolated by some authors in genus *Trachelotis*. Monotypic.
Distribution. South Africa in E Cape, Orange Free State, W Natal and S Transvaal (E & C Highveld); also Lesotho.

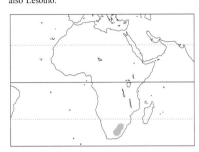

Descriptive notes. 55 cm; 1120-1612 g. Only bustard with blue-grey neck and underparts. Female has duller grey neck and buff ear-coverts. Immature has black and buff crown, black on upperwing-coverts and buff tips to flight-feathers.

Habitat. High grassveld, usually above 1500 m, with short-grazed grassland and termite mounds but no or few trees; old and fallow cropland, pastures and winter cultivation, usually in flat or undulating open Highveld grassland.

Food and Feeding. Caterpillars, grasshoppers, beetles, scorpions and small reptiles; also grass seeds, flowers and green leaves of various plants. In winter, often feeds on ploughed fields or land with crops such as turnips. Attracted to recently burnt grasslands.

Breeding. Aug-Apr, chiefly Oct-Nov. Nest situated on bare open ground, often in short, thick grass, also in old cropland. Eggs 1-3; incubation 24-28 days. Young may stay up to two years with parents, the breeding system appearing to involve group-territorialism.

Movements. Sedentary.

Status and Conservation. Not globally threatened. CITES II. Currently considered near-threatened. Reported decline in S and W of range unfounded, although now fairly scarce in lowland Lesotho owing to dense human settlement. Species remains generally common and locally plentiful with densities of c. 20 birds per 1000 ha in optimum habitat, in Transvaal, where the total population probably exceeds 10,000 birds. However, restricted range and the potential for intensified farming within it make this the small bustard of most concern in S Africa.

Bibliography. Allan & Davies (1995), Bonde (1993), Dowsett & Forbes-Watson (1993), Ginn et al. (1989), Kemp & Tarboton (1976), Kok & Van Ee (1989), Mackworth-Praed & Grant (1962), Maclean (1993), Maclean et al. (1983), Penry (1994), Sinclair (1987), Tarboton, Kemp & Kemp (1987), Urban et al. (1986), Vernon (1983a).

13. **Karoo Bustard**

Eupodotis vigorsii

French: Outarde de Vigors   **German**: Knarrtrappe   **Spanish**: Sisón del Karroo
Other common names: Black-throated/Vigors's Bustard/Korhaan, Karoo/Vaal Korhaan

Taxonomy. *Otis Vigorsii* A. Smith, 1831, South Africa.
Forms parapatric species pair with *E. rueppellii*, with which frequently considered conspecific; these two and *E. humilis* formerly placed in genus *Heterotetrax*. Two subspecies recognized.
Subspecies and Distribution.
E. v. namaqua (Roberts, 1932) - S Namibia and NW Cape Province.
E. v. vigorsii (A. Smith, 1831) - South Africa, in Orange Free State and S Cape Province.

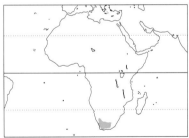

Descriptive notes. 60 cm; male 1600 g, female 1350 g. Head, neck and upperparts greyish brown with minute dark vermiculations, paling to pinkish white on belly; chin and throat black with thin white border, nuchal area black, tail with three thin bars. Has browner neck and different face pattern from *E. rueppellii*. Female smaller than male, with less black on throat, and more mottled wing-coverts. Race *namaqua* pinker and paler.

Habitat. Arid, flat gravel or sandy plains with scattered dwarf shrubs (karoo and scrub zones), ranging into veld with taller bushes, and annual rainfall of up to 250 mm. Prefers vegetation 10-50 cm high; occurs at highest densities (1·85 groups per km²) in areas of predictable winter rainfall of 250 mm per year, and at lowest densities (0·34 groups per km²) in areas of sporadic rainfall of 100 mm per year. Isolated population in SW Cape Province in karooid-like coastal fynbos in areas of cereal cultivation.

Food and Feeding. Chiefly plant matter, with flowers of Asteraceae, Brassicaceae and Mesembryanthemaceae dominant at certain times of year, but many annual ephemeral plants important along with fruit, leaves and corms. Insects, notably harvester termites, harvester ants and weevils, are important throughout the year. Visits pools to drink.

Breeding. Aug-Mar in South Africa. Nest is a slight scrape on bare ground. Normally 1 egg, possibly sometimes 2. Young birds stay several months with parents, and birds can be group-territorial, such groups consisting of a monogamous pair and offspring.

Movements. Sedentary and broadly site-faithful, with pairs defending a movable territory all year round; however, individuals range over many kilometres. Females disperse more readily than males.

Status and Conservation. Not globally threatened. CITES II. Generally common, and possibly even profiting from human agricultural activity, since it favours slightly degraded veld.

Bibliography. Allan & Davies (1995), Boobyer (1988, 1989), Boobyer & Hockey (1994), Dowsett & Dowsett-Lemaire (1993), Dowsett & Forbes-Watson (1993), Ginn et al. (1989), Hockey & Boobyer (1994), Kemp & Tarboton (1976), Kok & Van Ee (1989), Macdonald & Hall (1957), Mackworth-Praed & Grant (1962), Maclean (1993), Quinton (1948), Sinclair (1987), Snow (1978), Urban et al. (1986), Viljoen (1983).

14. **Rüppell's Bustard**

Eupodotis rueppellii

French: Outarde de Rüppell   **German**: Rüppelltrappe   **Spanish**: Sisón de Damaraland

Other common names: Rüppell's Korhaan

Taxonomy. *Otis Rüppelii* [sic] Wahlberg, 1856, Onanis, Damaraland.
Forms parapatric species pair with *E. vigorsii*, with which frequently considered conspecific; these two and *E. humilis* formerly placed in genus *Heterotetrax*. Two subspecies recognized.
Subspecies and Distribution.
E. r. rueppellii (Wahlberg, 1856) - coastal S Angola (N to Benguela) and NW Namibia.
E. r. fitzsimonsi (Roberts, 1937) - CW Namibia.

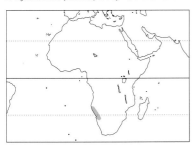

Descriptive notes. 60 cm; no data on weight. Differs from *E. vigorsii* in being pinker above with grey and white head pattern and black lines down front and back of neck. Female similar to male, but cheeks appear more mottled, and tail often has c. 2 faint bars. Immature similar to adult, but with more mottling on face, more dark markings on back and barring in tail. Race *fitzsimonsi* darker and greyer.
Habitat. Desert edge and subdesert, on flat dark basaltic gravel plains and barren flats with thin grass and sparse stunted scrub.
Food and Feeding. Very poorly known. Takes insects including termites, and small reptiles;

also vegetable matter including seeds.
Breeding. Probably at any time of year, depending on rainfall and food supply, but mostly Sept-Feb. Apparently monogamous. Nest situated on bare stony ground. Usually 1 egg, though possibly sometimes 2.
Movements. Sedentary.
Status and Conservation. Not globally threatened. CITES II. Very little information available on status. Species is frequent to common in habitat that is unlikely to be seriously modified by human development. Relatively common in coastal Angola. Biology and ecology remain poorly known.
Bibliography. Allan & Davies (1995), Dowsett & Dowsett-Lemaire (1993), Dowsett & Forbes-Watson (1993), Ginn *et al.* (1989), Mackworth-Praed & Grant (1962), Maclean (1993), Pinto (1983), Sinclair (1987), Snow (1978), Urban *et al.* (1986), Viljoen (1983).

15. **Little Brown Bustard**
Eupodotis humilis

French: Outarde somalienne   **German**: Somalitrappe   **Spanish**: Sisón Somalí
Other common names: Somali Black-throated/Brown Bustard

Taxonomy. *Sypheotides humilis* Blyth, 1856, Somaliland.
Formerly placed in genus *Heterotetrax*, along with *E. vigorsii* and *E. rueppellii*. Monotypic.
Distribution. E Ethiopia and N Somalia.

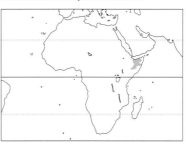

Descriptive notes. c. 40 cm; 700 g. Upperparts light orange-brown with pale grey clouding and minute black vermiculations, tail with 2-3 thin bars; head, neck and breast buffy with grey wash, clear grey on hindneck, black spot below nuchal crest, and black chin and throat with white spots; belly white; legs yellow, bill brown. Female similar to male, but lacks grey and black, and has upperparts coarsely blotched with buff; female *E. senegalensis canicollis* larger and darker, lacking this blotching on upperparts.
Habitat. Dry, sandy, grassland with bushes, light open thornbush and adjacent tussock grass plains.
Food and Feeding. Virtually no information

available. Known to take invertebrates and vegetable matter.
Breeding. Apr-Aug, chiefly May-Jun. Nest placed on sandy soil, usually without a scrape. Usually 2 eggs, but up to 3 recorded. No further information available.
Movements. Sedentary.
Status and Conservation. Not globally threatened. CITES II. Currently considered near-threatened. Fairly common in Ogaden, E Ethiopia, and common N of 7° N in Somalia. However, drought and warfare in the region may have caused a decline in this limited-range species, and current status is uncertain. Biology and ecology very poorly known; research and monitoring of populations highly desirable.
Bibliography. Archer & Godman (1937-1961), Ash (1977, 1989), Ash & Miskell (1983), Collar & Stuart (1985), Dowsett & Forbes-Watson (1993), Mackworth-Praed & Grant (1957), Urban *et al.* (1986).

ssp *damarensis*

ssp *afraoides*

ssp *etoschae*

PLATE 25

inches 11

cm 28

Genus *LOPHOTIS* Reichenbach, 1848

16. Savile's Bustard
Lophotis savilei

French: Outarde de Savile **German**: Saviletrappe **Spanish**: Sisón Moñudo de Saheliano
Other common names: Lynes's/Pygmy Bustard

Taxonomy. *Lophotis savilei* Lynes, 1920, Nahud, western Kordofan.
Genus frequently merged with *Eupodotis*. Present species forms superspecies with *L. gindiana* and *L. ruficrista*, but not known to perform their rocket-flight displays; all three often considered conspecific. Monotypic.
Distribution. SW Mauritania and Senegal through Mali, Burkina Faso, Ivory Coast, Niger, NE Nigeria and Chad to C Sudan.

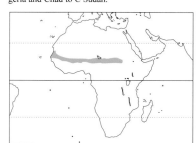

Descriptive notes. 42 cm; no data on weight. Smaller than *L. gindiana*, with more black on throat and less white on breast; more rufous sandy above with buff V-markings almost absent. Smaller than *L. ruficrista* with less grey on head. Female lacks grey on head and neck, which are tinged cinnamon.
Habitat. Bush and light woodland, thickets near dried pools and clearings, flat scrub with *Aristida* grass and *Acacia raddiana*.
Food and Feeding. No information available, but habits and food presumably similar to those of *L. ruficrista*.
Breeding. Sept-Oct in W of range; Jun-Aug (wet season) in Chad; Jul-Sept in Sudan. Nest details presumably similar to those of *L. ruficrista*.
Movements. Generally considered sedentary, but known to be a dry season (Dec-May) visitor to Park W in Niger, and may move N out of Nigeria during rains to breed.
Status and Conservation. Not globally threatened. CITES II. Little information available on status; species is said to be fairly common throughout its extensive range, but patchily so. Uncommon in Nigeria, where it is restricted to NE. Biology and ecology very poorly known, in part due to taxonomic confusion regarding present species and congeners.
Bibliography. Anon. (1995d), Cave & Macdonald (1955), Chappuis *et al.* (1979), Clancey (1977c), Dowsett & Dowsett-Lemaire (1993), Dowsett & Forbes-Watson (1993), Elgood *et al.* (1994), Koster & Grettenberger (1983), Lamarche (1988), Mackworth-Praed & Grant (1957, 1970), Morel & Chappuis (1992), Morel & Morel (1990), Newby (1979), Nikolaus (1987), Osborne (1989), Snow (1978), Urban *et al.* (1986).

17. Buff-crested Bustard
Lophotis gindiana

French: Outarde d'Oustalet **German**: Oustalettrappe **Spanish**: Sisón Moñudo Etíope

Taxonomy. *Eupodotis Gindiana* Oustalet, 1881, East Africa between Somalia and Zanzibar.
Genus frequently merged with *Eupodotis*. Present species forms superspecies with *L. ruficrista* and *L. savilei*; all three often considered conspecific. Birds of N & C Somalia formerly awarded separate race, *hilgerti*. Monotypic.
Distribution. SE Sudan, S Ethiopia, Djibouti and Somalia through Kenya to N & NC Tanzania.

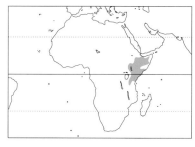

Descriptive notes. Male 50 cm, 675-900 g. Similar to *L. ruficrista* and *L. savilei*, but has black throat stripe extending to belly and more white on sides of breast; upperparts darker, tail unbarred. Female lacks grey on head and neck, replaced by brown; generally similar to female *L. ruficrista*, but has pale buff line down throat, breast more whitish, and upperparts darker, tail unbarred.
Habitat. A bird of arid and semi-arid bushland, like *L. ruficrista*, extending up to 1200 m in Ethiopia, and 1800 m in Kenya, but peripheral to highlands.
Food and Feeding. Very little information available. Known to take seeds, green herbage and insects; may subsist heavily on ants.
Breeding. Mar-Jun or later. Nest situated on bare ground. Eggs 1-2. No further information available.
Movements. Sedentary, although local migration claimed to occur in Kenya.
Status and Conservation. Not globally threatened. CITES II. Common throughout range, except in Sudan, where generally uncommon; an estimate of 25-40 females per 10,000 ha in suitable habitat. Biology and ecology very poorly known, in part due to taxonomic confusion regarding present species and congeners.
Bibliography. Ash (1989), Ash & Miskell (1983), Baker (1989), Britton, P.L. (1980), Brown & Britton (1980), Cave & Macdonald (1955), Chappuis *et al.* (1979), Clancey (1977c), Dowsett & Dowsett-Lemaire (1993), Dowsett & Forbes-Watson (1993), Goriup (1987), Goriup *et al.* (1989), Hallager (1994), Lewis & Pomeroy (1989), Mackworth-Praed & Grant (1957), Nikolaus (1987), Osborne (1989), Short *et al.* (1990), Snow (1978), van Someren (1925-1935), Urban *et al.* (1986).

18. Red-crested Bustard
Lophotis ruficrista

French: Outarde houppette **German**: Rotschopftrappe **Spanish**: Sisón Moñudo Austral
Other common names: Red-crested Korhaan, Buff-crested(!)/Crested/Bush Bustard

Taxonomy. *Otis ruficrista* A. Smith, 1836, near Latakoo (= Kuruman), Griqualand West, South Africa.
Genus frequently merged with *Eupodotis*. Present species forms superspecies with *L. gindiana* and *L. savilei*; all three often considered conspecific. Monotypic.
Distribution. S Angola and NE Namibia through Botswana, SW Zambia and Zimbabwe to S Mozambique, N South Africa and Swaziland.

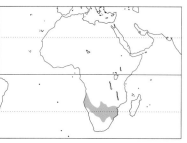

Descriptive notes. 50 cm; 680 g. Upperparts have distinctive cream V-marks giving mottled effect; grey on crown and lores, cream supercilium, indistinct pink nuchal crest (erectile in display), black on chin and throat, grey foreneck, buff hindneck and black belly; bill greyish, legs yellowish. Differs from *L. gindiana* and *L. savilei* in having more grey on head, especially on crown, and paler upperparts. Female similar to male, but grey areas on head and neck replaced with buff; cream V-marks on upperparts and absence of black on face distinguish from female *Afrotis afra*.
Habitat. Thorn country and other dry light woodland regions, bush savanna and riparian growth, often with long screening grass. In Botswana, commonest in *Acacia* and *Terminalia* savanna; occurs less commonly in more open habitat, where is generally replaced by *A. afraoides*. A population with different voice inhabits treeless grassy dunes in the S Kalahari.
Food and Feeding. Poorly known. Takes insects (beetles, grasshoppers, termites, ants) and other small arthropods; also berries, seeds and gum.
Breeding. Oct-Apr, with peak in Transvaal in Oct-Nov. Nest placed on ground, often near sapling or shrub. Eggs 1-2.
Movements. Sedentary.
Status and Conservation. Not globally threatened. CITES II. Common in much of range, with one calling male per 100 ha in C Transvaal; recorded as very common in 32% of squares in Botswana; still relatively common in Zimbabwe, where overgrazing may have caused a few local declines.
Bibliography. Allan & Davies (1995), Astley-Maberly (1967), Benson *et al.* (1971), Brown, C.J. (1993), Cassels & Elliott (1975), Chappuis *et al.* (1979), Clancey (1977c), Dowsett & Dowsett-Lemaire (1993), Dowsett & Forbes-Watson (1993), Ginn *et al.* (1989), Irwin (1981), Kemp & Tarboton (1976), Kok & Van Ee (1989), Mackworth-Praed & Grant (1962), Maclean (1993), Osborne (1989), Penry (1994), Pinto (1983), Rockingham-Gill (1989), Sinclair (1987), Sinclair & Whyte (1991), Snow (1978), Tarboton, Kemp & Kemp (1987), Urban *et al.* (1986).

Genus *AFROTIS* G. R. Gray, 1855

19. Black Bustard
Afrotis afra

French: Outarde korhaan **German**: Gackeltrappe **Spanish**: Sisón Negro Alioscuro
Other common names: Black Korhaan, Little Black Bustard

Taxonomy. *Otis afra* Linnaeus, 1758, Cape of Good Hope.
Genus frequently merged with *Eupodotis*. Present species forms parapatric species pair with *A. afraoides*, with which often considered conspecific. In past, species name commonly misspelt *atra*, the error originally arising probably from poorly printed text; scientific description has frequently been cited as Linnaeus, 1766, but pre-dated by valid 1758 description. Monotypic.
Distribution. South Africa in W & S Cape Province, from Little Namaqualand S to Cape Town, then E to Grahamstown.

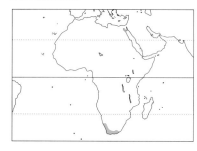

Descriptive notes. 50 cm; c. 700 g. Strongly marked, with back and lesser upperwing-coverts regularly barred dark brown on whitish, and broad white panel formed by greater and median upperwing-coverts; tail greyer with two broad black bars; rest of body black, with slightly crested hindcrown barred gold and brown and ringed in white, ear-coverts white, and broad white collar on lower hindneck; bill pinkish red, grey on culmen; legs strong yellow; eye orange-brown. Very similar to *A. afraoides*, but primaries all black, conspicuous in flight. Female is browner than male and more mottled on upperparts, extending onto head and neck; whitish breast and black belly.
Habitat. Coastal fynbos, semi-arid scrub, dunes with succulent vegetation, extending into renosterveld scrub in the semi-arid karoo. Frequently associated with cereal cropland both in the fynbos and parts of the karoo.
Food and Feeding. Very little information available. Known to include vegetable matter and insects in diet.
Breeding. Aug-Oct. Nest is a grass-lined scrape. 1-2 eggs. No further information.
Movements. Sedentary.
Status and Conservation. Not globally threatened. CITES II. No detailed information available, but species is apparently common within its restricted range. No threats known at present. Because until recently normally considered conspecific with more widespread *A. afraoides*, very little precise information is available on biology and ecology of present species; extensive research of these aspects is highly desirable, as is further investigation with a view to establishing a clearer picture of taxonomic relationship of these two forms.
Bibliography. Allan & Davies (1995), Brooke & Dowsett (1969), Clancey (1967, 1986, 1989), Crowe *et al.* (1994), Dowsett & Dowsett-Lemaire (1993), Dowsett & Forbes-Watson (1993), Frandsen (1982), Ginn *et al.* (1989), Kemp &

On following pages: 20. White-quilled Bustard (*Afrotis afraoides*); 21. Black-bellied Bustard (*Lissotis melanogaster*); 22. Hartlaub's Bustard (*Lissotis hartlaubii*); 23. Bengal Florican (*Houbaropsis bengalensis*); 24. Lesser Florican (*Sypheotides indica*); 25. Little Bustard (*Tetrax tetrax*).

Tarboton (1976), Mackworth-Praed & Grant (1962), Maclean (1993), Sinclair (1987), Snow (1978), Urban *et al.* (1986).

20. White-quilled Bustard

Afrotis afraoides

French: Outarde à miroir blanc   **German**: Weißflügeltrappe   **Spanish**: Sisón Negro Aliclaro
Other common names: White-quilled Korhaan

Taxonomy. *Otis Afraoïdes* A. Smith, 1831, flats near the Orange River.
Genus frequently merged with *Eupodotis*. Present species forms parapatric species pair with *A. afra*, with which often considered conspecific. Proposed races *mababiensis* (NW Botswana) and *kalaharica* (Kalahari Desert) nowadays included in *etoschae* and *damarensis* respectively. Three subspecies currently recognized.
Subspecies and Distribution.
A. a. etoschae (Grote, 1922) - NW Namibia and N Botswana
A. a. damarensis Roberts, 1926 - Namibia and C Botswana.
A. a. afraoides (A. Smith, 1831) - SE Botswana through N & NE South Africa (N Cape Province, W Transvaal, Orange Free State) to Lesotho.

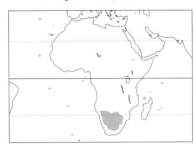

Descriptive notes. 50 cm; 700 g. Very similar to *A. afra*, but much white in primaries, conspicuous in flight. Female is browner than male and more mottled on upperparts, extending onto head and neck; white breast and black belly. Immature similar to female, but has pale tips to feathers of crown, back and wings. Race *etoschae* much paler; *damarensis* paler and more finely marked, with white extending round eye in male.
Habitat. Flat grassland with grass 50-100 cm high, open shrub veld, semi-desert scrub, grassy dunes and dry bush savanna, often in heavily grazed areas or those with patchy, sparse grass cover including old cropland. Males use vantage points such as rises and termite mounds to advertise presence.
Food and Feeding. Wide variety of plant and animal material, with latter taken twice as frequently. Diet dominated by Isoptera (particularly in May-Jun, when the harvester termite *Hodotermes mossambicus* is most active), curculionid beetles and grasshoppers. Plant material is mainly seeds, notably *Lycium tetrandum, Conyza bonariensis, Rhus lancea, Zea mays, Myrsine africana* and *Melilotus*, some of these indicating that human-disturbed areas are sometimes used for foraging.
Breeding. Most of year in Transvaal, where recorded Sept-Apr and Jul; elsewhere, records fall within the Sept-Apr period, although males are actively self-advertising throughout year. Nests on open bare ground, usually near a shrub. 1-2 eggs; incubation period 19-21 days in captivity; chick has pale tan down with darker brown markings.
Movements. Sedentary.
Status and Conservation. Not globally threatened. CITES II. Generally common throughout its range, with males being spaced at 300-500 m intervals in prime habitat.
Bibliography. Allan & Davies (1995), Bell (1970), Brown, C.J. (1993), Clancey (1967, 1986, 1989), Crowe *et al.* (1994), Dowsett & Dowsett-Lemaire (1993), Dowsett & Forbes-Watson (1993), Ginn *et al.* (1989), Gregson (1986), Kemp & Tarboton (1976), Kok & Earlé (1990), Mackworth-Praed & Grant (1962), Maclean (1993), Penry (1994), Sinclair (1987), Snow (1978), Tarboton, Kemp & Kemp (1987), Urban *et al.* (1986).

Genus *LISSOTIS*   Reichenbach, 1848

21. Black-bellied Bustard

Lissotis melanogaster

French: Outarde à ventre noir   **German**: Schwarzbauchtrappe   **Spanish**: Sisón Ventrinegro Común
Other common names: Black-bellied Korhaan

Taxonomy. *Otis melanogaster* Rüppell, 1835, Lake Tsana, Ethiopia.
Genus frequently merged with *Eupodotis*. Present species forms superspecies with *L. hartlaubii*. Two subspecies recognized.
Subspecies and Distribution.
L. m. melanogaster (Rüppell, 1835) - Africa S of Sahel S to R Zambezi and S Angola; absent from regions of heavy forest and from most of Horn of Africa.
L. m. notophila Oberholser, 1905 - Zimbabwe and Mozambique S of R Zambezi to extreme E South Africa and Swaziland.

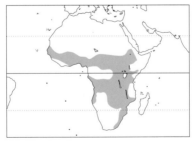

Descriptive notes. Male 60 cm, 1800-2700 g; female 60 cm, 1400 g. Upperparts tawny buff, with large dark arrow-shaped blotches, tail brown with four thin dark bars; face greyish white tinged buff on crown and cheeks, mottled black chin joining thin black line running back from eye to black nuchal crest; black line with white border down otherwise thin brown neck, merging in black of belly; much white in folded wing; legs and bill yellow. Generally browner than *L. hartlaubii*; coloration of rump and tail similar to that of back. Female has head and neck almost featureless pale buff, belly whitish. Immature similar to female, but has buff edges to wing feathers. Race *notophila* larger.
Habitat. Tall dense open grassland, grassland with bushes, and savanna woodland (including miombo woodland); also cultivation, pastures, fallow and old cropland and damper areas such as margins of vleis and dambos; also found in grass-covered ironstone pans and burnt savanna woodland in Sierra

Leone. Normally found close to water in both Gambia and parts of S Africa; occurs up to 2500 m. Termite mounds and other prominences are used for look-out and display.
Food and Feeding. Takes chiefly insects, apparently mostly beetles, but also grasshoppers, bugs, caterpillars and other terrestrial and stem-haunting arthropods; also seeds, flowerheads and vertebrate roadkills. In Kenya, old cultivation much frequented for certain green herbs.
Breeding. Jun-Sept in sub-Sahel, with evidence in Nigeria also for Dec-Jan; Apr and Sept in Ethiopia; Feb-Jun and Sept in E Africa; generally within period Oct-Mar in C & S Africa, although not necessarily in the rainy season. Nest is a shallow scrape on bare ground in grass, commonly near a feature such as an anthill, a bush or water. Eggs 1-2; chick has brown and black down.
Movements. Both sedentary and at least partially migratory. Situation in Ghana unclear, where resident in area of Accra but dry season breeding visitor 50 km to W, in Winneba; elsewhere in Ghana birds may move N after dry season breeding. In other parts of Sahel, birds move N to breed in rains in Jun; recorded in Sierra Leone only in period May-Oct, whereas in Central African Republic only Oct-Jun. Numbers increase in Jun in Ethiopian uplands. Local influx in one part of Kenya, Aug-Nov, and to parts of Tanzanian coast in dry season. Occasionally wanders outside normal range in South Africa.
Status and Conservation. Not globally threatened. CITES II. Decrease in Senegal and Gambia since 1980, but apparently still common in savanna zone of N Ivory Coast, Ghana, Nigeria and Sudan. The most widespread and numerous bustard in Uganda, Tanzania and Zambia, but likely to have declined in Zambia as consequence of hunting pressure; still fairly numerous in Zimbabwe, where a distinct decline is attributable to overgrazing by livestock; commonest bustard species in S Mozambique.
Bibliography. Allan & Davies (1995), Ash & Miskell (1983), Baker (1989), Benson & Benson (1975), Benson *et al.* (1971), Britton, P.L. (1980), Cave & Macdonald (1955), Chapin (1939), Clancey (1971a), Coverdale (1987), Dowsett & Forbes-Watson (1993), Elgood *et al.* (1994), Evans & Balmford (1992), Ginn *et al.* (1989), Gore (1990), Green (1983), Grimes (1987), Irwin (1981), Jensen & Kirkeby (1980), Kemp & Tarboton (1976), Lewis & Pomeroy (1989), Lippens & Wille (1976), Mackworth-Praed & Grant (1957, 1962, 1970), Maclean (1993), Newby (1979), Nikolaus (1987), Osborne (1989), Penry (1994), Pinto (1983), Rockingham-Gill, A. (1992), Rockingham-Gill, D. (1989), Schulz & Schulz (1986), Short *et al.* (1990), van Someren (1925-1935), Tarboton, Kemp & Kemp (1987), Thiollay (1985), Urban *et al.* (1986).

22. Hartlaub's Bustard

Lissotis hartlaubii

French: Outarde de Hartlaub   **German**: Hartlaubtrappe   **Spanish**: Sisón Ventrinegro de Hartlaub

Taxonomy. *Otis Hartlaubii* Heuglin, 1863, eastern Sennar, Sudan.
Genus frequently merged with *Eupodotis*. Present species forms superspecies with *L. melanogaster*. Monotypic.
Distribution. E Sudan through Ethiopia to NW & S Somalia, NE Uganda, NW & S Kenya and N Tanzania.

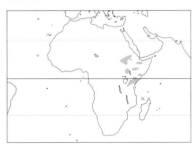

Descriptive notes. Male 60 cm, 1500-1600 g. Similar to *L. melanogaster* but greyer and more cleanly marked, with lower back, rump and tail blackish. Female has head and hindneck cream to buff with darker brown markings, belly whitish and tail paler than in male.
Habitat. Open, tall grassland with scattered *Acacia*, up to 1600 m. In Kenya, occurs in lower, drier habitat than *L. melanogaster*; in Ethiopia, may prefer *Acacia* short-grass savanna, which extends up to 2000 m, whereas *L. melanogaster* occupies tall-grass savanna, extending only up to 1500 m.
Food and Feeding. Little known. Invertebrates and vegetable matter recorded.
Breeding. Apr in Ethiopia; Jan and Jun in E Africa (in both rainy periods when grass tallest), with aerial display recorded in Nov. Chick has creamy buff down with pale and dark markings. No further information available.
Movements. Sedentary and nomadic, although considered a partial intra-African migrant based on records in Jan-Feb and Sept-Oct in Serengeti.
Status and Conservation. Not globally threatened. CITES II. Locally common in Kenya and Sudan, although rare and local at edge of range in Somalia, and uncommon in Ethiopia. Grazing by cattle can quickly destroy habitat, causing desertion of site. Species requires careful monitoring, given relatively restricted range.
Bibliography. Ash (1989), Ash & Miskell (1983), Baker (1989), Britton, P.L. (1980), Brown & Britton (1980), Cave & Macdonald (1955), Douthwaite & Miskell (1991), Dowsett & Forbes-Watson (1993), Fanshawe & Kelsey (1989), Lewis & Pomeroy (1989), Mackworth-Praed & Grant (1957), Nikolaus (1987), Schmidl (1982), Short *et al.* (1990), Urban & Brown (1971), Urban *et al.* (1986).

Genus *HOUBAROPSIS*   Sharpe, 1893

23. Bengal Florican

Houbaropsis bengalensis

French: Outarde du Bengale   **German**: Barttrappe   **Spanish**: Sisón Bengalí

Taxonomy. *Otis bengalensis* Gmelin, 1789, Bengal.
Genus sometimes merged with *Eupodotis*, but differs notably from all other bustards except *Sypheotides indica* in showing reversed sexual size dimorphism. Two subspecies recognized.
Subspecies and Distribution.
H. b. bengalensis (Gmelin, 1789) - patchily along border of S Nepal with India, and into lowland NE India.
H. b. blandini Delacour, 1928 - S Cambodia and S Vietnam (apparently non-breeding only; breeding grounds unknown).
Descriptive notes. Male 64 cm, 1250-1700 g; female 68 cm, 1700-2250 g. Upperparts and tail buffy brown, vermiculated and patterned black, with broad white panel on closed wing; slight crest, head, neck and underparts black, with elongated breast feathers; legs pale yellowish, bill dark horn to

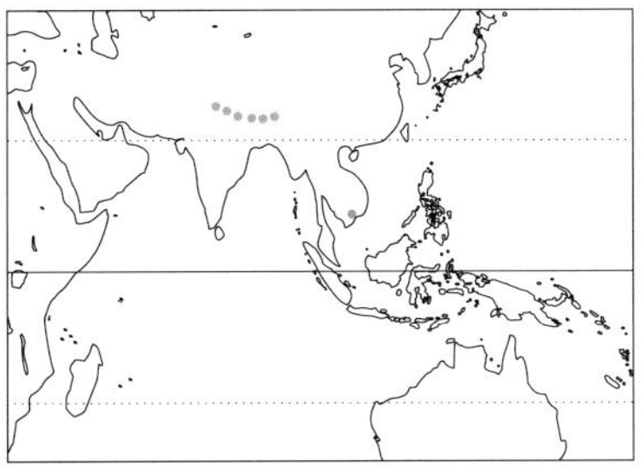

plumbeous brown with yellow lower mandible. Female has black of head and underparts replaced with buff, and has no white on wing; crown brown with buff central stripe. Immature similar to adult female; first spring male partially black, often reverting to female plumage in second autumn, but thereafter retains full adult male dress. Race *blandini* apparently larger.
Habitat. Flat, moist, open grasslands with scattered shrubs and bushes; often prefers areas of relatively short tussocky *Imperata* grass, recently burnt tracts, or long grass grazed down to c. 50 cm high, feeding in the shorter grass, and retreating in hotter parts of day to the longer. Birds also visit undisturbed mustard fields, and in some places use lightly wooded grassland and heavily grazed land.
Food and Feeding. Shoots, flowers, grasses, seeds and berries, but also insects such as locusts, grasshoppers, beetles, ants, and occasionally lizards and small snakes. Vegetable matter predominates in winter and spring, invertebrates becoming important or even exclusive later in the year.
Breeding. Mar-Jun. Nest is a scrape in thick grass cover. Eggs 1-2; incubation period c. 25-28 days; chick has rufous buff down marked with rufescent brown.
Movements. Nominate race dispersive, with males moving short distances from breeding territories in summer, and all birds seeming to disappear from late summer to mid-winter, Sept-Jan/Feb, when they are once more found in the grasslands where they breed. Race *blandini* known only from apparent winter quarters.
Status and Conservation. ENDANGERED. CITES I. Total population of nominate race may be as low as 300-400 birds, c. 100 of which are in Nepal. Population scattered widely among a handful of protected areas, but even here species cannot be considered secure: management of such areas is not necessarily optimal for the species, e.g. high grasses spreading through Chitwan National Park, Nepal; security is uncertain in some cases. Outside these reserves almost all habitat has been converted to agriculture. Race *blandini* is extremely poorly known, with as few as 4 birds recorded in recent years, in Vietnam, on land under development.
Bibliography. Ali & Ripley (1980), Anon. (1994c), Collar & Andrew (1988), Collar *et al.* (1994), Cornwallis (1983b), Goriup & Mundkur (1990), Hazarika (1981), Inskipp & Collar (1984), Inskipp & Inskipp (1983, 1985, 1991), Karim (1985), Lal (1993), Majumdar & Brahmachari (1988), Narayan (1990, 1992), Narayan & Rosalind (1990a, 1990b), Narayan *et al.* (1989), Rahmani (1988a), Rahmani & Sankaran (1988), Rahmani, Narayan, Rosalind & Sankaran (1990), Rahmani, Narayan, Rosalind, Sankaran & Ganguli-Lachungpa (1991), Rahmani, Narayan, Sankaran & Rosalind (1988), Ripley (1982), Sankaran (1990a, 1991), Vardhan (1985), Weaver (1990, 1991).

Genus *SYPHEOTIDES* Lesson, 1839

24. Lesser Florican

Sypheotides indica

French: Outarde passarage **German**: Flaggentrappe **Spanish**: Sisón de Penacho
Other common names: Leekh/Likh

Taxonomy. *Otis indica* J. F. Miller, 1782, India.
Genus occasionally merged with *Eupodotis*, but differs notably from all other bustards except *Houbaropsis bengalensis* in showing reversed sexual size dimorphism. Monotypic.
Distribution. NW India, mainly in Gujarat. In non-breeding season, moves to Deccan of C & S India; occasional records from Nepal.

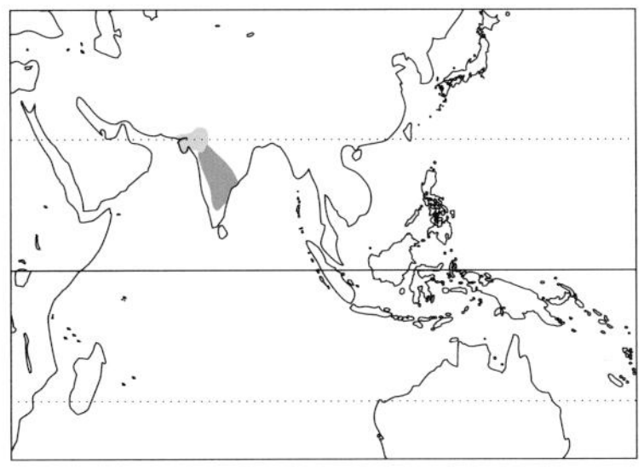

Descriptive notes. Male 46 cm, 450 g; female 51 cm. Unique among bustards in possessing c. 4-6 long, upcurving, spatulate black plumes projecting behind head; upperwing-coverts white, conspicuous in flight. Smaller than *Houbaropsis bengalensis*, with thinner neck, white band over shoulders, and distinctive head plumes. Non-breeding male is like female but white patch on wing much larger, visible on closed wing. Female has black areas replaced by buff and brown, extensively mottled and patterned with blackish markings; lacks ornamental head plumes of male; smaller and thinner-necked than female *H. bengalensis*. Immature similar to female, but more heavily mottled and lacks white on wing.
Habitat. Flat open grasslands, chiefly of *Sehima nervosum* and *Chrysopogon fulvus*, even patches smaller than 1 ha; also scrubland and crop fields, notably of soybean and groundnut; now chiefly in protected grasslands known as *vidis* or *rakhaals* that are set aside for fodder production.
Food and Feeding. Shoots, grass, herbs, seeds and berries; also grasshoppers, beetles (notably *Mylabris* blister beetles at certain times), centipedes, lizards and frogs.
Breeding. Jul-Sept, with exact timing depending on distribution and intensity of SW monsoon. Nest situated on bare ground in patch of grass or crops. Eggs 3-5; chick has dirty pale yellow down blotchily striped with blackish.
Movements. Leaves breeding region around Oct-Nov, apparently mostly dispersing south-eastwards, returning in Apr-May. Breeding area dependent on degree of rainfall, so birds commonly nomadic.
Status and Conservation. CRITICALLY ENDANGERED. CITES II. No longer visits W Pakistan or E India, a range contraction attributable to large-scale habitat loss and disturbance, with exceptionally high and ever-increasing grazing pressure from cattle; hunting is also a chronic problem. A decline of 80%, from 4374 birds in 1982 to 750 birds in 1989, is blamed on consecutive years of drought, but pesticides and loss of winter habitat also possibly implicated; however, reanalysis of data suggests 1989 total was really 1672 birds, and fieldwork in 1994 resulted in an estimate of 2206 birds.
Bibliography. Ali & Ripley (1980), Ali *et al.* (1986), Collar & Andrew (1988), Collar *et al.* (1994), Cornwallis (1983b), Dharmakumarsinhji (1950, 1983), Ganguli-Lachungpa & Rahmani (1990), Goriup & Karpowicz (1983a, 1983b, 1985), Hazarika (1981), Inskipp & Inskipp (1991), Lal (1993), Magrath *et al.* (1985), Majumdar & Brahmachari (1988), Narayan *et al.* (1989), Rahmani (1988a), Ridley *et al.* (1985), Ripley (1982), Roberts, T.J. (1991), Sankaran (1987, 1990b, 1991, 1993, 1994a, 1994b, 1995), Sankaran & Manakadan (1990), Sankaran & Rahmani (1986, 1990), Sankaran *et al.* (1992), Saxena & Meena (1985), Vardhan (1985), Yahya (1990).

Genus *TETRAX* T. Forster, 1817

25. Little Bustard

Tetrax tetrax

French: Outarde canepetière **German**: Zwergtrappe **Spanish**: Sisón Común

Taxonomy. *Otis Tetrax* Linnaeus, 1758, France.
In past, frequently placed in genus *Otis*, and considered to be closely related to *O. tarda* mainly on grounds of similar bill shape and extensive sympatry; nowadays almost universally awarded separate monotypic genus; may be more closely related to *Sypheotides* (see page 240). Eastern birds have been awarded separate race *orientalis*, on grounds of larger size and greyer, more heavily marked upperparts; but much individual variation and considerable overlap between populations, so not nowadays accepted. Monotypic.
Distribution. Morocco and Iberia to France, Sardinia and SE Italy; Ukraine and SW Russia through Kazakhstan to Kirgizia and extreme NW China; extreme N Iran. Winters from Mediterranean zone through Turkey and Caucasus to Iran, and erratically elsewhere in S Asia.

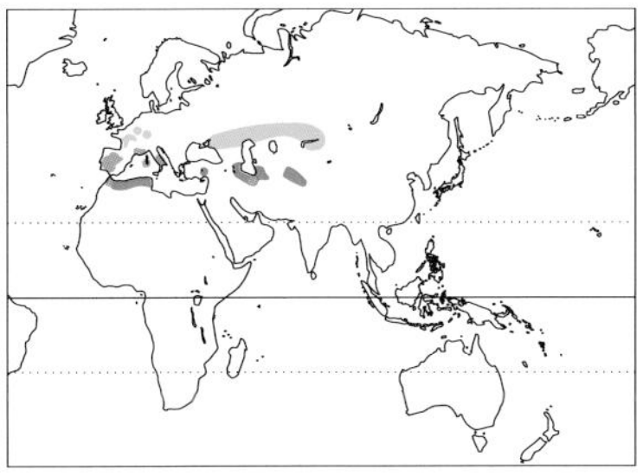

Descriptive notes. Male 43 cm, 794-975 g; female 43 cm, 680-945 g. Breeding male has streaked brown crown, blue-grey face shading to black on neck and breast, with broad white V across foreneck and broad white band across breast; upperparts buffy brown, lightly vermiculated with black; flight-feathers and greater wing-coverts white, tail white mottled brown with three bars; undersides white; legs greyish yellow, bill slate. Non-breeding male has buff face and neck, with buff breast streaked and barred. Female like non-breeding male, but uppersides more coarsely marked. Juvenile similar to adult female, but wing-coverts show more extensive buff with dark barring.
Habitat. Steppe and steppe-like landscapes, level or undulating short-grass plains, rich pastureland, fallow areas and certain kinds of cultivation, notably legume crops; preferably with vegetation over 20 cm high. Birds actively select areas with high diversity of plant species and high abundance of arthropods; hence, they prefer pasture to arable land, on both counts.
Food and Feeding. Beetles, grasshoppers and other terrestrial invertebrates; also much plant material such as shoots, leaves, flowerheads and seeds. Animals may predominate in the summer diet, plants in winter.
Breeding. Feb-Jun. Nest is a shallow scrape usually in dense short-grass cover. Eggs 2-6; incubation 20-22 days; chick has buff down with darker brown streaking and mottling; fledging period 25-30 days or possibly longer; young remain with female into first autumn.
Movements. Largely sedentary or dispersive in Iberia, Sardinia and Italy; migratory in France, with southward shift within the country in Sept-Oct, birds returning in Mar-Apr. Also migratory in Russia, Kazakhstan and rest of Asian range, where birds observe the same schedule when moving to and from Iran, Azerbaijan and, less regularly, other areas of S Asia.
Status and Conservation. Not globally threatened. CITES II. Currently considered near-threatened. Total breeding population probably numbers more than 100,000 individuals, with 50,000-70,000 birds in Spain, 10,000-20,000 in Portugal, 4000-5000 in France, 2000-2500 in Italy, 18,000-20,000 in Russia, and c. 20,000 in Kazakhstan. Declines noted in most countries; massive depletion in Russia over past century; now almost extinct in Ukraine, with only 8-10 birds recorded in 1978. In Azerbaijan, formerly wintered in huge numbers, with estimates of at least 200,000-300,000 birds in 1930's; current wintering numbers fluctuate at 10,000-40,000 individuals, with fewest birds in milder winters, but as many as 62,300 recorded in Kizil Agach Reserve in Dec 1971; most recent data include almost 30,000 birds counted in Mugan Steppe in Jan 1990. Extinct as breeder in much of C & E Europe, with last breeding records in 1907 in Germany, 1909 in Poland, 1921 in Austria, 1918 and 1952 in Hungary, 1948 in Serbia, and mid-20th century in Greece, Bulgaria and probably Azerbaijan. Formerly abundant breeder in Algeria and Tunisia, but now probably only irregular winter visitor. Agricultural intensification, mostly related to arable farming but also through overgrazing and disturbance, has been main factor in decline, at any rate in recent decades, and remains the chief threat. Nest predation by Rooks (*Corvus frugilegus*) and trampling by cattle cause breeding failure. Shooting may still be significant problem in some places, e.g. Sardinia; official records from 1930's of 40,000-50,000 birds shot annually in Azerbaijan, where poaching still remains a problem.
Bibliography. Ali & Ripley (1980), André (1985), Beaman (1994), Belik (1985, 1992), Boutin & Métais (1995), Brazil (1991), Collar & Andrew (1988), Cornwallis (1983a), Cramp & Simmons (1980), Étchécopar & Hüe (1964, 1978), Evans (1994), Fedorenko (1992), Ferguson-Lees (1967), Flint *et al.* (1992), von Frisch (1976), Goodman *et al.* (1989), Goriup (1994a), Goriup & Parr (1983, 1985), Hüe & Étchécopar (1970), Jolivet (1996), de Juana & Martínez (1996), Kasparek (1989), Knystautas (1993), Labitte (1955), Martínez (1994), Martínez & de Juana (1993, 1995), Moseykin (1992), Patrikeev (1995), Paz (1987), Petretti (1985), Potapov & Flint (1987), Razdan & Mansoori (1989), Roberts, T.J. (1991), Ryabov *et al.* (1984), Schenk & Aresu (1985), Schulz, H. (1980, 1985a, 1985b, 1985c, 1986a, 1986b), Shirihai (1995), Simeonov *et al.* (1990), Stepanov (1986), Thomsen & Jacobsen (1979), Urban *et al.* (1986), Vorobyova (1992).

Order CHARADRIIFORMES

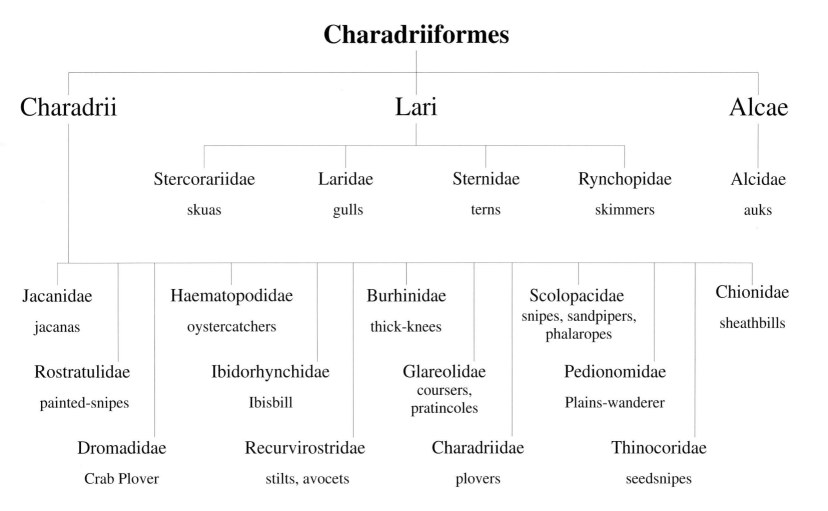

Class AVES
Order CHARADRIIFORMES
Suborder CHARADRII
Family JACANIDAE (JACANAS)

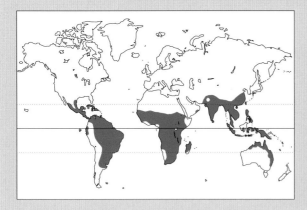

- Medium-sized, strikingly coloured waterbirds, with elongated legs, toes and claws.
- 15-58 cm.

- Pantropical, extending into subtropics.
- Shallow freshwater wetlands.
- 6 genera, 8 species, 17 taxa.
- No species threatened; none extinct since 1600.

Systematics

There is general agreement that the jacanas belong to the assemblage of shorebirds, or waders, but in the past there has been considerable confusion as to whether or not the jacanas are more closely related to the Charadriiformes or to the Gruiformes, specifically the Rallidae. This confusion has occurred in part because the shorebirds and the cranes and rails have many similarities, and because the jacanas, although distinct, superficially resemble rails, but careful analysis of a number of osteological characters and also recent biochemical analyses place the jacanas alongside the other shorebirds of the Charadriiformes. Behaviour, including that of the precocial young, also shows their affinity with the sandpiper family, Scolopacidae. They are most closely related to the painted-snipes of the family Rostratulidae, and, in fact, are commonly placed with them in the superfamily Jacanoidea, set apart from all other Charadrii.

The Charadriiformes apparently diverged from the Gruiformes in the late Cretaceous, but the jacanas appear to be much more recent in origin, with few fossils found to date. One large species, assigned to the extant genus *Jacana*, occurred in Florida during the middle Pliocene. Three other species, assigned to two extinct genera, including one species much larger than any existing species, came from an Oligocene formation in Egypt.

At the species level, the taxonomy generally seems pretty clear. There have been scattered records of possible hybridization between Northern Jacanas (*Jacana spinosa*) and Wattled Jacanas (*Jacana jacana*), where the two species come into contact in western Panama; indeed, their ranges used to overlap but no longer do so. This possible hybridization suggests that the two species might not be distinct, but the arguments that they constitute separate species are compelling. For instance, the local race *hypomelaena* of the Wattled Jacana is melanistic, and is easily the race that differs most in plumage from the Northern Jacana, suggesting the possibility of character displacement. With the exception of these two species, the jacanas have highly distinctive plumages.

Some systematists reduce the number of genera to two or three, and place the Lesser Jacana (*Micraparra capensis*), the African Jacana (*Actophilornis africanus*), the Madagascar Jacana (*Actophilornis albinucha*), the Comb-crested Jacana (*Irediparra gallinacea*) and the Bronze-winged Jacana (*Metopidius indicus*) all in the genus *Metopidius*; and the Pheasant-tailed Jacana (*Hydrophasianus chirurgus*) along with the Northern and Wat-

tled Jacanas in the genus *Jacana*. Others would keep the Pheasant-tailed Jacana in its own monotypic genus, *Hydrophasianus*. Still others retain *Micraparra* and *Hydrophasianus* as monotypic genera, but lump all the remaining forms in *Jacana*. Although these arrangements doubtless reflect relationships amongst the several species, there are no compelling arguments for combining the genera, and such lumping may actually do more towards obscuring relationships.

Despite the fact that the family is largely sedentary (see Movements), five of the eight living species show next to no geographical variation. Two species, the Comb-crested and

The jacanas constitute a very distinctive family of colourful, remarkably long-legged, long-toed waterbirds found around the world in the tropics. Madagascar boasts an endemic species which is very similar to the larger of the two African species, except that the crown, back and sides of neck are white, while the face and lower neck are black. There is no sexual plumage dimorphism in jacanas, but the female is generally larger than the male, sometimes much larger and heavier.

[Actophilornis albinucha, Lake Ampijoroa, Madagascar. Photo: Margaret Welby/ Planet Earth]

Northern Jacanas, each have three subspecies. The Comb-crested Jacana's races differ in the darkness of their plumage and in size, whereas the Northern Jacana varies primarily in size, and its different populations may really be ecotypes rather than genuine subspecies. The eighth species, the South American Wattled Jacana, is divided into six distinct subspecies that differ substantially in colour.

Morphological Aspects

Jacanas are small to medium-sized waterbirds. The Lesser Jacana measures only about 15-16 cm in overall length, whereas the Northern, Wattled and Comb-crested Jacanas are slightly larger at 17-24 cm. The remaining species are about 30 cm long, except for the Pheasant-tailed Jacana during the breeding season, when, because of the long tail characteristic of both sexes, its overall length approaches 58 cm.

The jacanas are characterized by having greatly elongated toes and claws that spread their weight out over a significant area, allowing them to walk on floating aquatic vegetation, especially lily pads, whence the popular name "lily trotters". Sometimes they walk on submerged vegetation, giving the distinct impression that they are walking on water. In adult Northern Jacanas, which weight roughly 90-160 g, the toes and claws of each foot splay out over an area approximately 12 x 15 cm, while the toes on each foot of the largest Comb-crested Jacana caught to date covered an area 15 x 20 cm. All jacanas have elongated tarsi, measuring 45-72 mm, and tibiae which are also mostly bare. The elongate legs and feet keep the birds' bodies well above the substrate, and make the jacanas appear relatively rather tall for their body size.

At all seasons adult females are significantly larger than the males. Jacanas show more extreme reversed sexual size dimorphism than any other bird or mammal species. Females of some species average 78% heavier than males, and some female Pheasant-tailed Jacanas may weigh more than twice as much as the males. Sexual differences in weight and linear measurements may actually be greater than the differences reported in the literature, because jacanas have monomorphic plumages and distinguishing between the sexes is difficult without dissection or observa-

tion of colour-marked birds during egg-laying or copulation. The size difference between the sexes is significantly less in the Lesser Jacana, in which females weigh only about 41 g.

Weights of individual jacanas fluctuate widely depending on season, amount of rain, food and an individual's ability to monopolize a territory. In the midst of a serious drought in northern Queensland, Australia, Comb-crested Jacanas were weighed at two locations: the first was a large artesian marsh that was serving as a refugium for several hundred jacanas; and the second was a small artificial impoundment, about 200 km distant, where some 12 birds were attempting to breed. At the first location adult females averaged 132 g and males 80 g, while at the second site the females averaged 153 g and the males 86 g; a biandrous female at the second site weighed 168 g, and the second largest female's weight increased from 145 to 158 g when she attempted to breed. In Northern and Comb-crested Jacanas, females that succeed in maintaining territories weigh significantly more than non-breeding females at the same locations.

Except for behavioural differences, and those in weight and measures, the sexes can not be distinguished in the field. In spite of their smaller body size, male Comb-crested Jacanas invariably have larger combs than those of females, and experienced observers can discriminate the sexes on the basis of the relationship of the size of the comb to the bill, the head and the rest of the body. The inability to distinguish the sexes has lead to much confusion in the literature, especially where parental behaviour has often been attributed to the female rather than to the male.

Coloration varies greatly amongst the species, but most are reddish or greenish brown to black above and below, although some are white below, one species has extensively white wings, and another a white nape and hindneck. Two species have yellowish flight-feathers. The Lesser Jacana is interesting in that it retains the juvenile plumage pattern throughout its adult life. Plumage is identical all year round, except in the Pheasant-tailed Jacana, which has a distinct breeding plumage including a much longer tail. All other jacanas have relatively short tails, and all have only ten tail feathers, compared to 12-28 in other shorebirds.

African Jacanas moult all their flight-feathers simultaneously and are flightless during this period. Other species, such as the Northern Jacana, moult their flight-feathers sequentially and never experience a flightless period, nor an interruption in their

The Lesser Jacana bears
a superficial resemblance
to the juvenile African
Jacana (Actophilornis
africanus), though a
careful examination shows
that the former has the bill
and legs shorter, a
chestnut crown and
supraloral patch, and a
darker back. The
confusion arises because
the two species are
sympatric and frequent
basically the same type of
habitat: extensive
freshwater wetlands with
floating vegetation.
However, the Lesser
Jacana does seem to
favour rather shallower
areas of sparse sedges
and aquatic grasses. It is
an uncommon species
and is difficult to see.

[Microparra capensis,
Chief Island, Okavango,
Botswana.
Photo: Jacques Gilliéron]

breeding activities in those areas where they breed all year round. Although moult in the jacanas is not well understood, the strategy of gradual moult appears to be an adaptation that allows the birds to breed at unpredictable times, whenever conditions are suitable, or at those locations where they can breed year round.

Adult jacanas of both sexes have conspicuous, bare, fleshy frontal shields, wattles or combs, except in the Pheasant-tailed Jacana, which has a strikingly visible white crown, and the Lesser Jacana, which either lacks the frontal shield or sometimes has a very small one. These head ornaments range from the small shields on the Lesser Jacana to large frontal shields that are continuous with the upper bill, to the distinctly flattened fleshy comb on the head of the Northern Jacana and the smaller, but more colourful, comb of the Wattled Jacana, which continues down to hang below the base of the bill in the form of conspicuous lappets or wattles. The most highly developed is the flattened, fleshy shield, with its well developed central comb, found in the Comb-crested Jacana. This entire structure may range from yellow, when the birds are relatively inactive, to bright red, when actively engaged in social interactions or other high stimulus situations; when the bird is excited, the comb also becomes engorged and fully erect, but at other times it may lie flat on the head.

Three species, the Pheasant-tailed, Northern and Wattled Jacanas, have sharp metacarpal spurs, while the Comb-crested and the Bronze-winged have hard, heavily cornified leading edges to the radii. Several species have conspicuously enlarged and flattened radii, which allow them to incubate their eggs and carry their young between the wings and the body.

Jacanas are weak fliers, and they typically fly only for relatively short distances. When they make short hovering display flights and in very short flights, their long feet dangle, but in prolonged flight their feet and toes trail behind the body and tail. Upon alighting, they extend their wings vertically over the body and hold this conspicuous position briefly before folding them. The sudden apparent decrease in size and the disappearance of the conspicuous wing patches in some species make them seem to disappear from view.

They are good swimmers, in spite of their having long, thin toes and tarsi. Presumably, their folded toes pass forward with ease and when the foot is pulled backwards the toes spread out clutching any submerged vegetation. Males and their chicks commonly swim through open water from one lily pad to the next while foraging or moving away from potential danger. Young birds, including very young chicks, take refuge under water when

danger threatens; they may stay submerged for long periods with only the tips of their bills above water, and may be hidden in the leaves of emergent vegetation or beneath a water-lily leaf. Adult jacanas can swim beneath the surface, and African Jacanas routinely use this technique to avoid potential predators during the flightless period.

Habitat

Jacanas occur in shallow freshwater wetlands throughout the tropics and subtropics. Breeding occurs on floating, floating-emergent and, less commonly, emergent vegetation, over water usually 0·5 to 2 m deep, although on some reservoirs with dense mats of floating vegetation they may nest over deep water.

Water-lilies (*Nymphaea*) are widely used wherever they occur, as are any other low profile floating aquatic plants, especially *Ludwigia*, *Salvinia*, *Potamogeton* and *Polygonum*. Jacanas also use dense mats of submerged species, such as *Myriophyllum*, for feeding from, but not for nesting on. Emergent plants, such as bulrushes, reeds, papyrus and robust stands of water hyacinth (*Eichhornia crassipes*), may be used for feeding and escape cover, but not for breeding. Jacanas may also feed in wet grasslands and other wetlands that are not suitable for breeding. They appear to use any plant community that has an extremely low profile of floating vegetation, but a few, dispersed emergents are acceptable and sometimes appear to be preferred. Small water hyacinths, when dispersed among other plant species, provide suitable breeding habitat, but dense, lush monocultures of this species do not. Non-breeding Comb-crested, Northern and Wattled Jacanas may also feed on short-grass uplands away from the water, especially where these are artificially maintained at a low profile by mowing or grazing. Likewise, Bronze-winged Jacanas sometimes feed in uplands and in croplands; even territory-holding individuals of these species, especially females, may leave their territories to feed on nearby uplands.

Throughout much of their tropical and subtropical distribution, suitable habitat for jacanas is widely dispersed. In some areas water levels remain fairly constant all year round, and jacanas may breed during any month. In areas with pronounced wet and dry seasons, however, habitat conditions may be extremely ephemeral and the birds may have suitable breeding habitat only during the wet season.

African Jacanas occupy more open areas over deeper water, while the sympatric Lesser Jacanas tend to occur over shallower water in areas with more emergent grasses, sedges and reeds. In Asia, the similarly sympatric Pheasant-tailed and Bronze-winged Jacanas both breed on large marshes, but the more widely distributed Pheasant-tailed also breeds on much smaller marshes and ponds than does the Bronze-winged.

General Habits

The jacanas exploit a unique niche. Their elongate toes and claws allow all members of the family to walk on floating aquatic vegetation where they glean food, establish territories, pair, nest, raise their young, fend off potential predators and sometimes fall prey to avian or aquatic predators. Although they spend much of their lives on floating water-lily leaves where they are conspicuously exposed, sometimes they can be extremely difficult to see. Their dark, or dark and white, coloration makes them inconspicuous in certain situations, for instance when wind or dropping water levels turn lily leaves on edge.

Jacanas frequently turn the head on its side and peer into the sky, apparently tracking aerial predators. They sometimes stand upright with the neck stretched forward at an angle of 60° above horizontal, the feathers on the back of the head raised and the bill pointed downward, as they peer into the water apparently looking at potential aquatic predators. Conspecific intruders and potential egg and chick predators on the substrate elicit similar upright postures but without the bird peering into the water. Northern Jacanas approach and partially or fully extend the wings laterally in a slightly crouched position, with the neck and head up, while they call raucously. This display exposes important fighting weapons, the bright yellow carpal spurs of some species and the cornified leading edge of the radii in others (see Morphological Aspects). Birds also extend their wings vertically as a visual signal in certain social situations and sometimes in response to territory invasion by jacanas and other species, or in response to potential threats in the water. Conspecific aerial intruders elicit raucous calling from one territorial bird after the other, as the intruders fly across their territories.

Outside the breeding seasons jacanas tend to be gregarious. It is not clear whether these are true social groups or whether the birds are simply aggregating on the few suitable sites available during the dry season. During times of severe drought in northern Queensland, Australia, Comb-crested Jacanas congregated in large numbers on a few permanent marshes. At one such site, some birds attempted to establish territories, but intraspecific competition for food and space was so great that most adults came to weigh only 75-80% of their breeding weight.

Voice

Jacanas are often noisy, and make calls variously described as thin, piping and squeaky, sharp and cackling or rattling, or a series of chittering or twittering notes. Calls given in response to predators, potential predators, or when the mate is not present are loud and raucous, but those uttered between mated jacanas that are close together are soft, as are those directed by a male at his chicks. Calls are highly variable within individuals and species and between species. They vary from hoarse-sounding notes that cover a wide range of frequencies to purer-toned whistled notes. Vocalizations have been studied only in the Comb-crested and Northern Jacanas, but descriptions in field guides and regional works suggest that other species are similar in this respect.

Jacanas have two distinct types of call. One is soft with a distinct stuttering cadence, composed of regularly repeated groups of 2-5 rapidly reiterated notes. These soft calls, which can be heard for only a few metres, are relatively stereotyped and often very long in duration, sometimes exceeding 600 notes. They are given by both sexes, but most often by males when accompanying chicks. Both sexes may give the calls during solicitations, mounting and copulation. Sometimes the calls are so soft that the repetitive movements of the bill or throat feathers can be seen, but no calls heard. Chicks often move closer to the male giving this call, but the function of the call between a mated pair is less obvious. In some species it is also given during flight.

The best known vocalizations are the louder, often raucous, calls that consist of anything from one to a few, but sometimes as many as 60 or more, similar notes. The regular unbroken cadence of these calls is completely different from the stuttering cadence of the soft calls. Within each call the notes are quite similar, but between calls there is much variation in volume, length of the individual notes, and number of notes comprising the call. When eggs, chicks, or territorial integrity are seriously threatened, these calls are louder and include more raucous, longer individual notes that are repeated more often. In less serious situations, the calls are quieter and consist of fewer notes that are individually shorter in duration. When these calls are persistent, the mate often approaches the vocalizing bird, but most of the time there is no overt response. The calls clearly advertise the presence of the caller and the level of danger it faces.

Food and Feeding

All species of jacana spend a significant part of every day foraging, sometimes simply walking in a normal upright position looking for food, but most often searching for food with the head and bill lowered toward the substrate and the back and neck angling down, while they walk quickly over the substrate.

Jacanas are small carnivores. Their primary food comprises insects, which they glean from floating vegetation; they also take a wide range of invertebrates by picking them from the root systems of small floating plants, such as *Salvinia*, which they grasp and flip upside down with their bills. From these upturned root masses they pick snails, crustaceans, insects and anything else that wiggles. Adults may also use their toes to grasp the edges of water-lily leaves and turn them over, at least partly, while they pick prey from the undersurface. They occasionally catch insects that fly by, especially flies and bees, and occasionally plunge the entire head beneath the surface of the water in pursuit of prey. Tiny fish, attempting to flee aquatic predators, sometimes slide up onto water-lily leaves where they may be eaten by

This juvenile Wattled Jacana has captured a water bug from among floating vegetation. In addition to insects and other invertebrates this species feeds on seeds, but most of the plant matter taken is thought to be ingested accidentally. Jacanas typically take most of their prey from the surface of the aquatic vegetation or from underneath, after turning it upside down. Note the incipient shield and wattles and the almost grotesquely long toes and claws.

[*Jacana jacana jacana*, Pantanal, Brazil. Photo: Hubert Klein/Bios]

jacanas. Birds may spend several minutes rapidly picking minute insects from the surface of the water, where they float after having been washed off water-lily leaves submerged by the weight of the foraging birds.

A female jacana spends an average of about 70-90% of her time foraging, except when one or more of her males has eggs or chicks. At such times, female Northern Jacanas spend a considerable amount of time resting and loafing near the chicks, where they can look out for potential predators. Male jacanas spend up to 90% of their time foraging unless they have eggs or chicks, when their foraging time drops to less than 50%. The precise amount of time spent foraging also depends on prey abundance and weather, and during cool, rainy periods males spend increased time with their eggs or chicks.

Jacanas commonly ingest at least small amounts of vegetation, especially when plucking prey from amongst mats of submerged algae and the upturned roots of plants. Whether all such material is taken incidentally, or whether some of it is taken intentionally, is not clear, with the possible exception of some reports that jacanas eat small seeds. In Guyana, 20% of the food taken by 30 Wattled Jacanas was composed of seeds. This sample came from an agricultural development, where the birds fed on flooded lawns and in shallow rice paddies and is probably atypical. In Costa Rica, Northern Jacanas frequently peck at the bases of water-lily blossoms and fruits that have been opened by Common Moorhens (*Gallinula chloropus*). Reports that jacanas in India are vegetarians are probably in error. It is unlikely that jacanas, especially chicks and juveniles, could survive, and even more unlikely that the females could lay replacement clutches so frequently, without a high protein and fat diet.

Jacanas sometimes associate with a variety of animals that stir up food while they swim or move through the water. They have also been reported picking ticks from capybaras (*Hydrochaeris hydrochaeris*) in Panama and standing on the backs of hippopotami (*Hippopotamus amphibius*) in Zimbabwe.

Adults never feed the precocial chicks, but lead young chicks to food and reportedly point to food with their bills. They accompany their chicks as they feed. Chicks feed at a significantly higher rate when in the presence of the adult, and are much more likely to feed at all when an adult feeds with them. Young chicks are more likely to sit quietly on the substrate rather than feed when unaccompanied than they are when the male is with them. Young chicks of the Northern Jacana die of starvation in the absence of the social facilitation of an adult male feeding with them, which may occur if their father disappears, or when he is preoccupied in interacting with a new female replacing or attempting to replace his mate.

Breeding

Little is known about the small, neotenic Lesser Jacana, but it differs from the other jacanas in being monogamous. In this species the sexes share, apparently equally, all the business of nest construction, incubation and care of the young.

All other jacanas exhibit sexual role reversal, with the males performing most or all nest building, all incubation and all brooding in most species, although in a few species females occasionally brood their chicks. In general, females perform some parental behaviour, such as predator defence, that does not involve direct interactions with the chicks. Female Northern Jacanas perform a disproportionate amount of maintenance behaviour, preening and resting in the general vicinity of the young, where they are able to look out for predators, when the male is feeding away from the chicks; only the male accompanies the young while they feed. Although the male sometimes feeds while accompanying his chicks, his feeding rate is slow and he must spend some time away from them, when he walks and pecks at a faster rate than when he is with them.

All these sexual role reversed species have polyandrous mating systems. The expression of polyandry occurs when ecological conditions allow a female to have access to two or more males either simultaneously or sequentially, and when a female is able to exclude other females from the males' territories. When the breeding habitat is so small that only one male can establish a territory; when the male's territory is extremely long and narrow, as along a narrow waterway; or where habitat quality is otherwise sub-optimal and male territories are unusually large, the female has no opportunity to monopolize more than one male, and mating is monogamous. An individual female may have up to four or more mates simultaneously, with an average of two or three, but sequentially she may have a higher number of mates.

Apart from the monogamous Lesser Jacana (Microparra capensis), *in all other jacanas the usual sexual order is reversed, with males undertaking nest building, incubation and rearing of the young. These species have complicated polyandrous mating systems, whereby a female has access to several mates simultaneously or sequentially and holds territories against other females. Where competition for males is fierce among females, some males may be sequentially polygynous, since new females may replace their previous mates. Courtship behaviour is not usually elaborate in the African Jacana. Both male and female solicit, often from a rudimentary nest platform, by walking round each other holding their heads low. The female assumes a copulatory position and the male pecks at her, beginning at the neck but usually ending near the vent. In only one in four cases do these preliminaries result in the male actually mounting the female, and even then cloacal contact is not frequent, although the male may remain mounted for more than a minute.*

[Above: *Actophilornis africanus,* Natal, South Africa. Photo: Nigel. J. Dennis/ NHPA.

Below: *Actophilornis africanus.* Photo: Richard T. Mills/ Aquila]

When competition for males is especially fierce among females a territorial male may find his mates being replaced one after the other during the season. The smaller male can have no influence on the interactions between the females, and, as there is no suitable, unoccupied habitat to move to, consequently he has no choice but to mate with the new female and become sequentially polygynous.

Female jacanas may exhibit sequential or simultaneous polyandry, but many authors are confused as to whether a female remains mated to her earlier males when she is involved in copulation and egg-laying with an additional, nearby male. Males are sexually inactive during the incubation period of up to 28 days, as well as for two to three months after hatching. If the male is successful in rearing his brood and the female is occupied with another male, or males, she may consort only rarely with her successful partner. She may return to his territory to help him repel potential predators or rival females attempting to pair with him. If a male loses his clutch, his partner typically resumes copulating with him and replaces the clutch, often within a few days. If his chicks disappear, he quickly becomes receptive and the female may start consorting with him again. Sometimes the female will persist with a current reproductive effort with another mate and not resume copulation with, and laying for, the first until she has completed a clutch for the other mate, but most often females lay replacement clutches before providing clutches for additional males. Only careful long-term observations of marked individuals in a breeding population can determine whether the relationships are sequential or simultaneous.

Considerable, conspicuous effort goes into the building of one to several platforms of floating aquatic vegetation, from which the birds solicit one another and where they copulate. The female almost always lays the clutch on one of these platforms. In spite of their flimsy appearance, these sodden masses of vegetation must be buoyant enough to support the two adults while they copulate, and repeated attempts to copulate on several sites may allow the female to select the most sturdy for egg-laying. Some of the nest-sites can not be distinguished from the surrounding floating vegetation, while others consist of a mat of stems and other pieces of aquatic vegetation. The upper surface of the nest sits barely above the water and sometimes the undersurfaces of the eggs are in contact with the water.

Males perform most of the nest building but after soliciting the male, or being mounted by him, females often perform nest building movements by picking up stems and pieces of vegetation and throwing them to the side or over the shoulder in the same way as the male does. These movements are performed as the female moves away from the nest-site and sometimes at a considerable distance from the nest, and may actually result in her moving vegetation away from the nest-site. Some of this behaviour must serve some function other than nest building, and it has been described as "substrate tossing" rather than nest building. Nest building behaviour by the male includes treading or pressing down on the nest itself, and involves building up a pad of vegetation. The bulk of the nest structure may be beneath the surface of the water, which would explain why so much nest building often results in such an inconspicuous nest. During incubation, the male frequently adds to the nest by reaching out in front or to the side, grasping plant material and pulling it up toward his breast, and by throwing additional stems toward the nest as he walks away from it.

In those species that have been studied closely, both members of a mated pair do a great deal of sexual solicitation of one another. Solicitations involve assuming the copulatory position with the male mimicking the female's posture, a procedure often referred to as courtship; these usually do not result in mounting, and may end with both sexes soliciting before one of them wanders off. A soliciting Comb-crested Jacana sometimes orientates itself towards its approaching mate and performs a ritualized "Bow Display" by gradually extending its wings laterally and rotating them so that the dorsal surface faces the approaching mate. A Comb-crested Jacana male extends his head and neck under the female's neck, and rubs her underneck with his head and comb. A male African Jacana prods at the soliciting female with his bill, sometimes starting as far forward as her neck, but usually ending near the vent.

Less than 1 in 3 solicitations in the Northern Jacana, and about 1 in 4 solicitations in the African Jacana, are followed by the male actually mounting the female. A high proportion of mounts end with the female straightening up and the male sliding off her back, or with the male simply dismounting, and only 1 in 4, to 1 in 5, mounts by male Northern Jacanas resulted in cloacal contact. Successful copulations lasted two seconds or less, but prior to cloacal contact males are mounted on the females for up to a minute or more. A male initially stands or crouches without moving, but then, while crouching, he begins shuffling his feet toward the female's tail, while waving the wings for balance. He eventually grasps the female's wings with his toes, as he lowers his posterior over one side, while wagging his tail from side to side. At the same time, the female raises her tail to the opposite side and rotates her vent area upward towards the male until cloacal contact is made.

Successful contact ends with the male moving forward over the female, and the two abdomens stretching until cloacal contact is lost. Successful contact is usually followed by the female remaining in the copulatory position at least briefly, and in the Northern Jacana she typically turns away from the male. She keeps her tail raised and the feathers around the vent spread away from it; the vent is alternately everted and inverted, alternately exposing its creamy interior, which contrasts conspicuously with the dark reddish feathers around it, and which then disappears only to reappear again. This cloacal winking at the male only follows successful copulations.

Females lay determinant clutches of four eggs, three in the Lesser Jacana, early in the morning, producing one egg every 24-25 hours. Reports of smaller clutches are fairly common, but these are probably the result of egg losses. There have been reports of very few larger clutches, but there is no satisfactory explanation of their causation. The posture of the female prior to egg-laying is conspicuous. She shuffles her feet apart, spreads her legs widely at the intertarsal joint, and holds her back up at an angle of about 30° with her vent area lowered between her legs. Sometimes she remains in this posture for several minutes, occasionally lowering herself so that she touches the nest or eggs with her breast feathers. Eventually she lowers the vent area, now swollen with the egg, between her legs and places the egg in the nest or drops it onto the nest platform from a height of a few centimetres. She then raises her body to a position near horizontal, as she shakes and resumes a normal posture and then walks away.

Jacana eggs are conspicuously glossy and shiny so that sunlight reflecting off them gives them the appearance of being wet and resembling the glossy surface of some aquatic vegetation. Pheasant-tailed Jacanas eggs are unmarked and uniformly brown in shades of yellowish, greenish or rufous. The eggs of all other jacanas are heavily, to very heavily, scrolled with dark brown or blackish markings; individual differences in markings and egg shape are consistent within and between clutches. Shell pores are plugged, but the significance of this is not clear. Jacanas lay extremely small eggs relative to their own body size. If egg weight is expressed as a percentage of the female's weight, jacanas lay eggs of about 25-50% of the relative weight of those laid by other shorebirds. The reasons for such small egg size are unknown. The hypothesis that small egg size is an adaptation allowing for production of multiple clutches appears invalid when jacanas are compared to high latitude shorebirds, but the tropical jacanas have a shorter period of daylight in which to feed.

While a male lowers himself onto his eggs to incubate, he rocks his body from side to side, slightly lifting first one leg then the other. He sits on the eggs with his legs closed together behind the abdomen, and with his tarsi and toes extending forward and laterally along the outside of the body and wings. While he rocks from side to side, he raises one wing and then the other very slightly from the body, lowering the edge of the wing down and under the eggs. At the same time, he reaches down and with the underside of the bill rolls the eggs up onto his wings. He ends up with the outside edges of his wings touching or almost touching in the middle, and with two eggs in a row held against his body on the inner surface of each wing. When he ends an incubation bout, the male rocks slightly, sliding the wings out from under the eggs, as he starts to stand. When startled, he jumps to his feet, then quickly flicks his wings to the side, so that two eggs fall from under each wing back onto the nest.

When a male returns to his nest, he often stops and leans forward over the eggs. In this position he raises and lowers each leg in what appears to be a slow, exaggerated dance as he circles the eggs compressing the nest material. He stops on the highest part of the rim and settles on the eggs, rolling them up to him as he tucks them under his wings.

Males occasionally move their clutches. When a nest platform begins to disintegrate, for example during rising water levels, a male may build a new nest, even several metres from the first, and move the eggs to it, one at a time. Sometimes he may simply move them to a new location with no apparent provocation, and without any nest building at the new site. He moves the eggs by backing up with an egg held against the breast with the undersurface of the chin and bill, or by simply backing up toward the new nest, dragging and rolling the egg over the vegetation and through the water with the underside of the bill. The male African Jacana may hold the eggs between his wings and body while he walks across the vegetation. He may set them

The Bronze-winged Jacana's nest, built by the male, is a typical construction of aquatic vegetation, mainly rushes or reeds twisted to form a circular pad. The male is alone responsible for incubating the eggs and caring for the chicks, while the polyandrous female defends her mates' territories against other females. The male sits on the nest with the tarsi and toes stretched forward alongside the body and wings. The bill of this heavily built species is very sturdy and the frontal shield briefly becomes bright red during courtship.

[Metopidius indicus, India. Photo: Belinda Wright/ DRK]

The Pheasant-tailed
Jacana's eggs are olive
brown, very glossy,
remarkably pyriform in
shape and, unlike other
jacana eggs, unmarked. A
chick may remain in the
egg for a day or more after
pipping, apparently in
order to facilitate
synchronous hatching.
Once the chick has
emerged, the male picks
up the shell and flies off
some 10 metres or so
before he drops it, a
behavioural trait shared
with the Northern Jacana
(Jacana spinosa), and
believed to guard
against predators being
attracted to the nest
by the empty shells.

[Hydrophasianus
chirurgus, Sri Lanka.
Photo: Joanna Van
Gruisen/Ardea]

down on a water-lily leaf rather than on a nest, and apparently may move them around to several different sites.

The initiation of incubation is not well known, but it typically starts with the laying of the third egg, or rarely late in the day of the second egg. It appears that some of this early incubation may not be effective, because the male appears to sit with the eggs outside his breast feathers rather than next to his brood patches. The inaccessibility of nests makes determination of the incubation period difficult, but it is reported to last roughly 22-28 days. Incubation constancy is highly variable and seems to be most influenced by ambient temperature and the amount of cloud cover. In general, males incubate for much longer periods, with shorter periods off the nest, in the early morning and late afternoon than during the middle of the day. Except in the Lesser Jacana, females are not known to incubate; however, at least in the Northern Jacana, females occasionally shade the eggs during the midday heat.

At midday males often stand over their eggs, shading them rather than incubating them, often sitting very briefly on them before again standing over them. Because of high ambient temperatures, some development of the first-laid eggs probably occurs before the male begins actively incubating them. It is highly unlikely that incubation begins with the laying of the first egg, as has been reported for some species. Because of the need for the male to accompany the chicks, in order to facilitate their feeding, it is adaptive for him to abandon any unhatched eggs within a day of first hatching. Synchronous hatching is therefore advantageous, and postponing the initiation of incubation until the clutch nears completion would be adaptive. The chicks themselves apparently help to co-ordinate hatching, for they begin calling in the egg a day or two before hatching, and the first to pip may remain in the egg for a day or more before emerging. Shortly after each egg hatches male Pheasant-tailed and Northern Jacanas pick up the empty shell and fly 10 m or more before dropping it, a behavioural pattern not reported in the other species, which is assumed to be an anti-predator adaptation, as is similar behaviour in gulls.

It is not clear how a simultaneously polyandrous female decides which one of two to four available males should receive her eggs. The problem is moot when the males are acquired sequentially, or when all but one are unavailable because they are incubating or caring for young less than 2-3 months old, but sometimes all her males are available to care for eggs simultaneously. Consorting with and copulating with each male on his individual territory may provide clues by which the female can compare their readiness to incubate and care for chicks, but just what these clues may be is unknown. As a female Northern Jacana becomes gravid, she spends increasing amounts of time with the male that will eventually receive the clutch. She copulates more frequently with him, and indeed may stop copulating with her other males. After laying each of the first three eggs, she copulates with the owner of the nest within a few minutes to an hour of laying. As the clutch nears completion, she copulates more frequently with any of her other males that are available, and, after laying the third or fourth egg, does not appear to copulate with the male as he becomes more involved with the clutch.

In some species, a female associates exclusively with one territorial male and seldom leaves his territory except to feed or chase other birds. She does not consort with other males until the clutch is complete, after which she pays little attention to him, and begins consorting with and copulating with an additional male. Such females appear to be sequentially polyandrous, but the probability of returning to the territories of earlier males probably depends on the need to help the males repel potential predators. These females return to lay replacement clutches when a clutch is lost. Incubating males do not copulate.

Males run some risk of cuckoldry, that is incubating eggs and raising young sired by other males. Because clutch loss is so high in the jacanas, females produce many more clutches than survive, and there is much replacement laying and much copulating with other males. Cuckoldry probably occurs in some situations. It is possible that males stand as reasonable a chance of cuckolding other males as of being cuckolded themselves which would result in reciprocal cuckoldry! However, recent research with other shorebirds shows that females can store sperm in their reproductive tracts for some time, and apparently select which insemination will be used for fertilization. The question of paternity in polyandrous jacanas remains unanswered. Sperm from earlier copulations will persist in the female tract, so there will always be the possibility that a male will receive one or more eggs fertilized by sperm from one of his female's earlier mates.

A close scrutiny of the tangle of legs protruding from this male Comb-crested Jacana's wings will reveal that he has at least two chicks on board! Jacana chicks are precocial, well able to swim and dive soon after hatching, sometimes even remaining under water with only the head or bill visible. At other times when danger threatens, the male parent may simply lead the chicks away or he may carry them under one or both of his wings and deposit them in a safer place.

[*Irediparra gallinacea novaehollandiae*, Kakadu National Park, Northern Territory, Australia. Photo: Belinda Wright/ DRK]

Confounding the issue is the fact that female jacanas usually copulate with the male that is receiving the clutch shortly after laying. Because ovulation occurs shortly after laying, copulation at this time might enhance the male's probability of fertilizing the next morning's egg.

Territoriality is very complex in polyandrous jacanas. One possibility is that males compete with one another for suitable breeding territories, and females compete with one another for ownership of one to several males and their territories, as appears to be the case where Northern Jacanas breed year round. Alternatively, females might compete for large territories which could be subdivided by males. Where jacanas breed seasonally, the initial territories established by males and females are quite large and the birds are often temporarily monogamous, but when the males start incubating their first clutches they defend much reduced areas. Additional males are able to establish themselves on more distant parts of the first males' original territories. The new male or males pair with and form bonds with the original female, which subsequently helps them to defend their territories against the first male, one another and neighbouring males. Thus, female jacanas help their individual males defend their territories even against their other mates. Following such interactions, females frequently visit each of their males on their territories and copulate with all that do not have clutches or young chicks.

Replacement of individuals within an established breeding population is straightforward. A female may defeat a neighbouring female and take over her male or males, or a previously non-breeding female may displace a territorial female and take over hers. Sometimes a new female appears to be unaware of how many males the previous female had, and neighbouring females take over one or more of them. In all species, non-territorial individuals appear to be available to take over any territory within a few hours of the disappearance of its owner. When a male Northern Jacana has a clutch of eggs from his previous female, the replacement female typically destroys the eggs by pecking at them until they break and then partially eating them. The new female, at least in Northern and Wattled Jacanas, may peck young chicks of the previous female to death, but she will not eat them. If the chicks are old enough to avoid the female's attack, they may be driven from the territory by her. Once the male is no longer involved in incubation or caring for the young of his previous mate, he soon becomes receptive to the new female and to the concern of caring for a new clutch.

Much of what has been called courtship behaviour in the literature is actually pre-copulatory behaviour between already paired or bonded birds. Courtship (in the sense of behaviour leading to the establishment of pair-bonds) at the beginning of the breeding season in seasonal populations differs from courtship of replacement individuals during the breeding season. At the beginning of the wet season, flocks of jacanas appear on the recently flooded wetlands and there is much aerial chasing. When a female and male succeed in excluding other jacanas from an area, the female charges the male, which crouches and shows subordinate behaviour rather than fleeing, and the two birds settle there and continue to consort with one another as a territorial pair. In an established breeding population, however, a territorial male, when he encounters a strange female that has succeeded in displacing his mate, responds by threatening and calling at her, behaviour that should attract his mate, but, of course, his displaced mate does not respond. In the meantime, the new female ignores him or behaves aggressively toward him. In response to her aggression, he may partially extend his wings while moving away, or he may crouch on the substrate or water and the female may peck at his back. By the second day, the new female typically assumes the copulatory posture and the male responds with upright postures, but he soon begins mounting her, and shortly thereafter aggression returns to a low level and he copulates with his new female. Because breeding habitat is limited and alternative territories are not available to him, the male has no choice. The seemingly endless calls of a male that has had its mate killed eventually attract a new female, and interactions between the two are identical with those following active displacement by a new female.

Compared to other shorebirds, the post-hatching rate of development in jacanas is extremely slow. It is also highly variable both between and within broods, with first flight occurring between six and twelve weeks of age. Chicks may disperse from their natal territory as early as at six weeks old, but more commonly associate with the male until 10-12 weeks old. In the Northern Jacana, juveniles may continue to reside on the male's territory until they complete their moult into adult plumage at about 12 months of age. Replacement females are more tolerant of older chicks than of younger ones.

Chicks are brooded almost continuously by the male for the first day or two, and for several weeks are brooded early and late in the day, whenever it is particularly cool, and when it rains. The male sits on the substrate with young chicks nestled between his wings and his body. The chicks' feet and legs grow quickly and within 1-2 weeks of their hatching the male crouches over them, and later stands to brood them while they stand on the substrate. The male often picks the chicks up off the substrate between his wings and body. In the Northern Jacana, chicks brooding between their father's wing and body sometimes stick their heads up through his plumage: they peer around for several seconds before withdrawing beneath the male's plumage again. In several species, most notably the African and Comb-crested Jacanas, the male walks about his territory while holding his chicks between his wings and his body, with the chicks' feet dangling beneath him. Chicks several weeks old may attempt to be brooded when only one of them can fit under each wing. An interesting parallel to the jacanas may be seen in male Sungrebes (*Heliornis fulica*), which brood one young chick in the depressions on each side of his body beneath the wings (see page 214).

Anti-predator defence by both males and females increases dramatically immediately after the chicks hatch. Potential predators that were ignored, except in the immediate vicinity of the nest, are suddenly not tolerated even in distant parts of the territory. Low levels of response to predators include the bird merely orientating itself towards the threat, followed by an upright alert posture that may include raising the crest. The male may simply lead his chicks away from less serious threats, or scoop them up under his wings and carry them off to safety. However, if the threat is significant, the alarmed jacana calls loudly, and very loud calls or screams usually attract the mate. Birds may threaten the potential predator by extending the wings laterally and charging, or they may make aerial attacks diving on and striking at the enemy with their feet. They may also attempt to lure the source of the threat away by making hunched "rabbit runs" away from it, or with a variety of distraction displays, ranging from lying on the substrate or water with the wings partly extended, sometimes flapping them as if trying to escape. They may drag one extended foot and leg, or circle it, as if it were caught on something.

Nesting success is very low in all species studied. During a dry year, all 16 African Jacana clutches laid at one study site were predated. One female laid 10 clutches at an average inter-clutch interval of only 9·8 days, but her male failed to hatch any of them. During a wet year, some clutches were lost to flooding and others to predators, but 15 clutches (38%) produced 30 young from the 145 eggs laid in 39 clutches. For all species, less than half the clutches survive until hatching. Except for the African Jacana, losses are probably greater than estimated in the literature because nests, eggs and incubating males are all inconspicuous and a significant number of clutches are lost during the laying period before they are ever discovered. In addition, predation itself is very seldom observed. Purple Swamphens (*Porphyrio porphyrio*) and American Purple Gallinules (*Porphyrio martinica*) do prey on eggs and chicks of African and Northern Jacanas respectively, but the lists of predators on jacanas are basically hypothetical. Many clutches are lost due to being upset or trampled by ungulates and large reptiles, and to the disintegration of nests, often aggravated by rapidly rising or falling water levels.

Movements

The Pheasant-tailed Jacana is migratory, at least in part. Its northernmost populations move southwards after breeding, and during the northern winter the species occurs south beyond its normal breeding range. However, very little is known about the migrations of this species, and both the origins of the birds turning up in the south and the destinations of those leaving the north remain uncertain.

All other species are basically sedentary, but may make extensive local movements, spreading out over seasonal wetlands during the wet season and retreating to permanent wetlands during the dry season. These irregular movements may actually extend over relatively large distances, up to several hundred kilometres in Africa, and may include large numbers of birds which move together. In Guanacaste Province, Costa Rica, Northern Jacanas sometimes frequent newly flooded sugar cane and

Two African Jacana chicks forage as they walk on floating vegetation in the company of the adult male. The downy chicks are white below and striped black and brown above. While growth in general is slow, already the legs and feet seem disproportionately large for the size of the body. The male does not feed them directly, but is reported to point food items out to them. In all jacana species the male's presence with the chicks is vital to their development as it activates them to forage: without him they may just sit passively, showing no inclination at all to feed.

[*Actophilornis africanus*, Masai Mara, Kenya. Photo: Ferrero & Labat/ Auscape]

In polyandrous jacanas territoriality is complex and to date imperfectly understood. Territories are maintained in the breeding season; where populations are dense, disputes are frequent. In general, a male holds his small territory on floating vegetation against intruders, whereas the female, facing pressure from other females, has the task of defending 1-4 males and their respective territories. In fights between two male Comb-crested Jacanas, wings and feet can become so entangled that a few well aimed pecks from the female are needed for them to extricate themselves and order to be restored!

[Irediparra gallinacea novaehollandiae, Kakadu National Park, Northern Territory, Australia. Photo: Jean-Paul Ferrero/ Auscape]

rice fields during the dry season. In Guyana, Wattled Jacanas may feed in adjacent rice fields while breeding on permanent waterways.

Relationship with Man

Most jacana species have long been well known to local fisherfolk. They are generally rather colourful birds and, as they can scarcely be seen as competitors to the fishermen, they have tended to suffer relatively little persecution, so they are often tame and confiding. This is all the more evident in that in many parts of the world they can be seen on artificial water bodies created or extensively modified by man, frequently in fairly close proximity to human habitation.

The name Jacana was derived from the Portuguese transliteration of a Brazilian Indian name for the Wattled Jacana. Although the name may be pronounced in a variety of ways, the original Portuguese spelling was Jaçaná.

Status and Conservation

None of the jacanas is considered to be threatened at present, but the Pheasant-tailed Jacana appears to be much less common than it was formerly in subtropical and south-eastern China. However, the species ranges extensively across southern Asia and is not known to be declining elsewhere in its immense range.

Like all birds that inhabit wetlands, jacanas are dependent on the maintenance of wetlands, in their case specifically extensive shallow wetlands that support water-lilies and other floating vegetation; draining of these areas, or their flooding to increase water storage are perpetual threats. In contrast, the creation of small ponds for livestock watering or irrigation purposes by damming or excavation provides many new sites for the birds, especially in semi-arid areas and those with distinct wet and dry seasons. Indeed, most of the studies of jacanas reported in the ornithological literature have been carried out on relatively small artificial impoundments of some sort. Lake Kariba, an immense impoundment in northern Zimbabwe, supports extensive floating mats of *Salvinia*, which in turn provide breeding habitat for a very large population of African Jacanas. Jacanas are quick to take advantage of shallow artificial wetlands created as water storage areas or botanical parks. One artificial impoundment in Costa Rica was made unsuitable for the jacanas that had bred there previously, when the water-lilies and other floating vegetation were removed to increase the open water area for aesthetic reasons, but when the floating vegetation was allowed to re-establish itself, the birds returned and began breeding again.

The destruction of wetlands is a significant factor: drainage of wetlands and overgrazing by livestock, especially during droughts, both destroy habitat. In some areas, introduced water hyacinth has displaced other floating vegetation and formed monocultures which are too tall and lush to provide suitable nest-sites for jacanas. Native water-lilies completely disappeared from Lake Naivasha, Kenya, in the late 1970's, in response to overgrazing by introduced coypus (*Myocastor coypus*) and a crayfish. However, large mats of the exotic water plant *Salvinia* replaced the native vegetation, and the jacanas utilize it as a feeding and breeding substrate. Overgrazing on floating and emergent vegetation by ungulates, especially horses and wild pigs, during severe drought years in Queensland, Australia, further reduced the limited amount of suitable habitat available. Likewise, destruction of aquatic vegetation by intentionally introduced herbivorous cichlid fishes causes habitat loss in parts of Africa.

It does not appear that jacanas are extensively pursued by humans for food, as pets or for other reasons anywhere in the world, although in Guyana children sometimes take their eggs. Their most serious threat is undoubtedly the filling or draining of their wetland habitat or its conversion for rice fields, aquaculture or other agricultural development. Pollution that kills insects or vegetation has also caused the loss of some habitat and could be, or become, a more serious problem.

General Bibliography
Björklund (1994), Board & Perrott (1979), Christian *et al.* (1992b), Chu (1995), Dunning (1993), Fry (1983a), Gochfeld *et al.* (1984), Hayman *et al.* (1986), Jehl (1968b), Jehl & Murray (1986), Jenni (1974, 1985), Johnsgard (1981), Lowe (1925, 1931), Miller, A.H. (1931), Miller, E.H. (1984), Peters (1934), Phillips (1989), Rosair & Cottridge (1995), Saether *et al.* (1986), Sibley & Ahlquist (1990), Sibley & Monroe (1990), Sibley *et al.* (1988), Strauch (1976, 1978).

PLATE 26

inches   6

cm   15

ssp *jacana*

ssp *scapularis*

ssp *intermedia*

ssp *hypomelaena*

Genus *MICROPARRA* Cabanis, 1877

1. Lesser Jacana
Microparra capensis

French: Jacana nain **German**: Zwergblatthühnchen **Spanish**: Jacana Chica
Other common names: Lesser African Jacana, Lesser Lily-trotter

Taxonomy. *Parra capensis* A. Smith, 1839, Algoa Bay, South Africa.
Genus occasionally lumped with *Actophilornis* and *Irediparra* in *Metopidius*, but this proposal not widely accepted. Species considered to represent a neotenic form of *Actophilornis africanus*. Monotypic.
Distribution. Mali to Sudan and Ethiopia, then S through Uganda and Kenya to Zambia, Zimbabwe, Mozambique and E South Africa, extending W to E Angola and E Namibia.

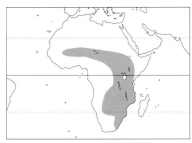

Descriptive notes. c. 15-16 cm; c. 41 g. Much smaller than other jacanas; frontal shield very small or lacking. Extended wings dark with conspicuous white trailing edges of inner primaries and secondaries; forehead golden rufous, crown cinnamon, hindneck and mantle darker, rest of back rufous to cinnamon; underparts white. Plumage superficially similar to that of juvenile *Actophilornis africanus*, but back darker. Sexes nearly identical, but female slightly larger; higher proportion of males are darker on the back and have black lateral margins to crown, but not reliable difference between sexes; subtle difference between mated birds makes it possible to distinguish them; most males and some females have violaceous black feathers on hindneck and mantle. Juvenile similar to adult except mantle, scapulars, back, rump and uppertail-coverts fringed buff.
Habitat. Shallow water around edges of permanent and seasonally flooded wetlands, especially areas of relatively sparse sedges and aquatic grasses; also uses less dense stands of floating vegetation, e.g. water-lily leaves. May appear in moderate numbers when pans that have been dry for five or more years are flooded in an unusually wet year.
Food and Feeding. Primarily insects; also reported to take bits of aquatic vegetation on occasion. Insects are gleaned from the substrate and from emergent vegetation, while bird walks at water level or climbs on stems of grasses; sometimes swims and picks food off the water like phalaropes (*Phalaropus*).
Breeding. Season highly variable throughout range, in response to wide range of wet seasons and availability of suitable habitat; May in Kenya; mainly Feb-Mar (-Aug) in Zambia; Jun, Sept, Oct in Malawi; mainly Mar-May (Feb-Oct) in Zimbabwe; Nov in South Africa. Differs from all other jacanas in being monogamous, both sexes sharing in nest building, incubation, care of young and defence of territory. Nest is a small mound of aquatic vegetation, often free-floating, with eggs up to 1 cm above the water level; nest building continues throughout incubation period. Normally 3 eggs, rarely 4; eggs relatively small; incubation 22-24 days, with constancy of over 80%, much higher than for other jacanas, perhaps because of very small egg size; chicks similar to those of *Actophilornis africanus* but smaller; accompany adult until at least half-grown. Very few nests found and nesting success unknown.
Movements. Poorly known. Species is permanent resident on permanent wetlands apparently throughout most of range; appears in reasonable numbers at beginning of wet season at seasonally flooded pans, even after years of absence during periods of drought. Vagrant to Sierra Leone.
Status and Conservation. Not globally threatened. Small size and secretive habits contribute to uncertainty as to precise distribution, especially in N of extensive range; for same reasons, local relative abundance poorly known, and true status not clear in most areas. Uncommon in N Nigeria; reported to be abundant at Okavango Delta; uncommon and local in E South Africa.
Bibliography. Bannerman (1953), Benson & Benson (1975), Britton, P. L. (1980), Brooke (1984a), Dowsett & Forbes-Watson (1993), Fry (1983a), Ginn *et al*. (1989), Irwin (1981), Lambert (1987), Lippens & Wille (1976), Mackworth-Praed & Grant (1957, 1962, 1970), Maclean (1993), Pinto (1983), Short *et al*. (1990), Snow (1978), Tarboton (1976), Tarboton & Fry (1986), Urban *et al*. (1986).

Genus *ACTOPHILORNIS* Oberholser, 1899

2. African Jacana
Actophilornis africanus

French: Jacana à poitrine dorée **German**: Blaustirn-Blatthühnchen **Spanish**: Jacana Africana
Other common names: Greater African Jacana, Lily-trotter

Taxonomy. *Parra africana* Gmelin, 1789, Ethiopia.
Genus occasionally lumped with *Microparra* and *Irediparra* in *Metopidius*, or alternatively with *Irediparra* and *Metopidius* in *Jacana*, but neither proposal widely accepted. Forms superspecies with *A. albinucha*. Monotypic.
Distribution. Wetlands throughout sub-Saharan Africa; largely absent from forest belts and arid zones.
Descriptive notes. 23-31 cm; male averages c. 137 g, female c. 261 g. Bill continuous with large frontal shield, both pale blue to grey-blue; rest of crown and hindneck black; sides of face, chin and throat white changing to golden yellow on upper breast; most of upperparts chestnut to rufous cinnamon, but rump, secondaries and underbody darker maroon chestnut; primaries black, but seen only during flight or display. Female similar to male, but larger. Immature has crown and hindneck blackish with some brown feathers; supercilium white, upperparts pale brown with glossy green, except for chestnut rump, secondaries and greater coverts; underparts white with weak yellowish breast band and chestnut on side of thighs.
Habitat. Permanent and seasonally flooded shallow freshwater wetlands, especially swamps and backwaters of slow-flowing rivers. Restricted to floating vegetation especially water-lilies, and floating-emergent vegetation, which provides more cover but does not appear to reduce predation. Occurs over deeper water with less emergent vegetation than extensively sympatric *Microparra capensis*. Seeks shelter in taller emergent vegetation near shore, but does not use this for nesting in. In Sierra Leone, during dry season, sometimes wanders onto river sandbanks, or even shallow streams with wooded banks.

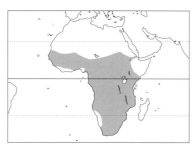

Food and Feeding. Mainly insects and worms, but also other arthropods, including spiders and crustaceans, and molluscs; seeds sometimes taken. Prey typically gleaned from surface of vegetation or water; also from roots of floating vegetation turned upside down by the feeding jacanas, and undersurfaces of lily leaves. Will also catch flies and other flying insects.
Breeding. Breeds year round in suitable permanent wetlands, but seasonally in seasonally flooded areas; most nests apparently Oct-Nov in Sierra Leone; Jun-Sept in Ghana; mainly Jun-Sept (Apr-Jan) in Nigeria; Jun-Aug/Sept in Ethiopia; mainly Mar-Apr (Nov-Jun) in Zambia; all months in Malawi and Zimbabwe, with peak Jan-Mar; Nov-Jul in South Africa. Polyandrous, but strategy highly variable; males hold nesting, breeding, feeding and chick rearing territories, while females, one to several adjacent males, hold their territories against other females; some males sequentially polygynous, because new females keep replacing their former mates. Sexual role reversal essentially complete, with male apparently performing most nest building, all incubation and all care of the precocial young. Cloacal contact occurs in only a small proportion of initiated courtship interactions. Nest is flimsy, mostly submerged pad of aquatic vegetation, extending to 2 cm above water surface; over deeper water, nest often placed on small floating islands; eggs sometimes laid on floating vegetation with no nest. Determinate layer, 4 eggs laid c. 24 hours apart, in early morning; male begins incubation after laying of 3rd egg, period c. 20-26 days; nest attentiveness varies with weather and temperature, but averages 52% in Transvaal; incubation much reduced during warm, sunny parts of day, when male may spend more time shading eggs than incubating them; sometimes carries eggs under wings to new nest site (see page 283); male celibate during incubation and for at least first several weeks of chick care. Female will lay replacement clutches, or clutches for additional males, every 4 days to 3 weeks (average c. 9 days). Downy chicks white below, with light and dark brownish striping above; young not fed by male, but he points out food to very young chicks, and accompanies chicks while they feed; broods chicks under wings, and may pick them up and carry them under wings, as in other jacanas; young birds stay with male 40-70 days; attain full adult plumage at c. 1 year, but age of first breeding unknown. Nest success very low, from 0% some years, to almost 50% in exceptionally good conditions, but averages c. 26%; brood survival much higher, up to c. 90%.
Movements. Not migratory, but extremely nomadic, often in connection with changing water levels; in wet years, birds may show up on pans from which species has been absent for several years. Birds may apparently move as much as several hundred kilometres, but non-breeding birds inconspicuous, so pattern of movements remains poorly known.
Status and Conservation. Not globally threatened. Generally common to abundant throughout most of extensive range, although few population figures available. Abundant on shallow freshwater wetlands in Sierra Leone, and also in Ghana and Nigeria except in brackish swamps along coast, where less common; common in Gambia and Malawi, on Zanzibar and Pemba, and locally in South Africa. May be locally threatened by habitat loss or deterioration through flooding of shallow wetlands for hydroelectric projects, draining of wetlands, or overgrazing; but, particularly in southern parts of its range, creation of stock watering ponds and small reservoirs has substantially increased amount of suitable habitat available. Introduced coypu (*Myocastor coypus*) destroyed water-lily habitat on L Naivasha, Kenya, during late 1970's, but present species switched to nesting on less stable mats of the exotic waterfern *Salvinia*.
Bibliography. Ash & Miskell (1983), Bannerman (1953), Benson (1961), Benson & Benson (1975), Britton, P. L. (1980), Cunningham-van Someren & Robinson (1962), Dowsett & Forbes-Watson (1993), Elgood *et al*. (1994), Every (1989), Fry (1983b), Ginn *et al*. (1989), Goodman & Goodman (1985), Gore (1990), Grimes (1987), Hodgson (1983), Hopcraft (1968), Irwin (1981), Mackworth-Praed & Grant (1957, 1962, 1970), Maclean (1993), Pakenham (1979), Pinto (1983), Pitman (1960), Postage (1984), Short *et al*. (1990), Simpson (1961), Steyn (1973), Tarboton (1976, 1992c, 1992d, 1993), Taylor & Harper (1988), Urban *et al*. (1986), Vernon (1973), Wilson (1974), Winterbottom (1961a).

3. Madagascar Jacana
Actophilornis albinucha

French: Jacana malgache **German**: Madagaskarblatthühnchen **Spanish**: Jacana Malgache
Other common names: Malagasy Jacana

Taxonomy. *Parra albinucha* I. Geoffroy Saint-Hilaire, 1832, Madagascar.
Genus occasionally lumped with *Microparra* and *Irediparra* in *Metopidius*, or alternatively with *Irediparra* and *Metopidius* in *Jacana*, but neither proposal widely accepted. Forms superspecies with *A. africanus*. Monotypic.
Distribution. Madagascar, except for highlands and shrub desert of S & SE of island.

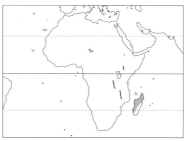

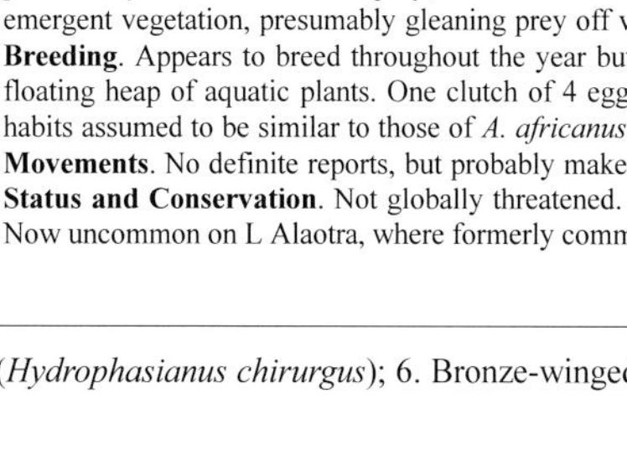

Descriptive notes. c. 30 cm; one female 139 g. Similar in size to *A. africanus*, to which identical except for crown, hindneck and sides of neck white, with golden yellow next to mantle; face and lower neck black; band of white sometimes from thighs across uppertail-coverts; tips of middle tail feathers black. Female slightly larger. Immature similar to immature *A. africanus*, but crown, hindneck and eyestripe blacker.
Habitat. Floating vegetation in freshwater marshes, on shallow lake margins, on ponds and along slow-flowing rivers. Occurs from sea-level up to 750 m.
Food and Feeding. Insects and their larvae, and presumably other invertebrate prey; also seeds of aquatic plants. Forages over floating or floating-emergent vegetation, presumably gleaning prey off vegetation or water.
Breeding. Appears to breed throughout the year but little studied; definite records Dec-Jun. Nest is floating heap of aquatic plants. One clutch of 4 eggs reported. Very little information available, but habits assumed to be similar to those of *A. africanus*.
Movements. No definite reports, but probably makes local movements as water conditions vary.
Status and Conservation. Not globally threatened. Abundant in N & W, but rare in E Madagascar. Now uncommon on L Alaotra, where formerly common; Alaotra, Madagascar's largest lake, has been

---

On following pages: 4. Comb-crested Jacana (*Irediparra gallinacea*); 5. Pheasant-tailed Jacana (*Hydrophasianus chirurgus*); 6. Bronze-winged Jacana (*Metopidius indicus*); 7. Northern Jacana (*Jacana spinosa*); 8. Wattled Jacana (*Jacana jacana*).

seriously degraded by siltation, agricultural development, drainage, overfishing and poaching. Species poorly known, but apparently secure at present.

Bibliography. Benson *et al*. (1976-1977), Dee (1986), Delacour (1932), Dowsett & Forbes-Watson (1993), Fry (1983b), Langrand (1990), Milon *et al*. (1973), Rand (1936).

Genus *IREDIPARRA* Mathews, 1911

4. Comb-crested Jacana

Irediparra gallinacea

French: Jacana à crête **German**: Kammblatthühnchen **Spanish**: Jacana Crestada
Other common names: Lotusbird, Lily-trotter, Christbird

Taxonomy. *Parra gallinacea* Temminck, 1828, Menado, Sulawesi.
Genus occasionally lumped with *Microparra* and *Actophilornis* in *Metopidius*, or alternatively with *Actophilornis* and *Metopidius* in *Jacana*, but neither proposal widely accepted. Validity of races uncertain and frequently challenged; there is apparently clinal increase in size from N to S, but considerable variation in size in any one population; supposed subspecific differences in tone of upperparts also seems variable; birds from Kai Is (SE Moluccas) may represent a racially mixed and possibly unstable population, although general characters perhaps closest to *novaeguinae*; species may be more appropriately considered monospecific, but further study required. Three subspecies currently recognized.
Subspecies and Distribution.
I. g. gallinacea (Temminck, 1828) - SE Borneo, Sulawesi, SE Philippines (Mindanao), Moluccas and Lesser Sundas.
I. g. novaeguinae (Ramsay, 1878) - N & C New Guinea, Misool I and Aru Is.
I. g. novaehollandiae (Salvadori, 1882) - S New Guinea, D'Entrecasteaux Is, N & E Australia S to Sydney.

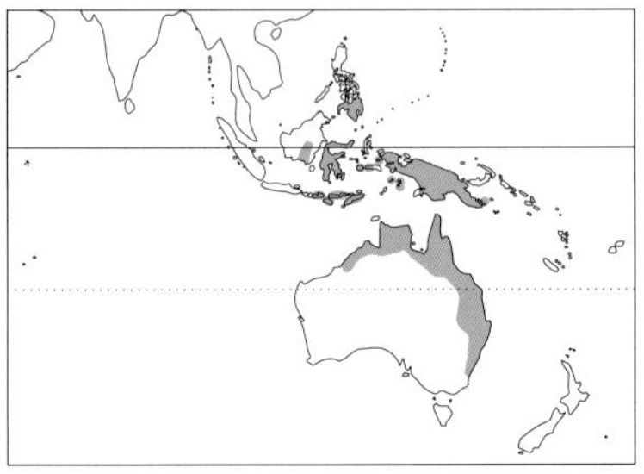

Descriptive notes. 21-24 cm; male c. 75-97 g, female c. 122-168 g. Mantle, back and upperwing-coverts brown, rest of plumage black except for white belly, undertail-coverts, face and upper neck; sides of neck bright golden yellow; bill pink to red, with black tip; bright pinkish red flat, fleshy shield up to 2 cm wide x 3 cm long, and a conspicuous comb rising up 1 cm or more in centre; shield and comb yellow to orangish in non-excited state becomes bright pinkish red with infusion of blood during breeding and other periods of excitement, but control of comb colour not understood; carpal knob (no carpal spur as reported in literature) has hard cornified leading edge along distal part of radius. Female similar to male, but considerably larger. Juvenile brown above, white below lacking black breast of adult; comb and wattle rudimentary; incomplete moult to immature plumage during first year, adult plumage at c. 1 year old. Racial differences somewhat masked by individual variation; *novaeguinae* has darkest upperparts; *novaehollandiae* largest, with palest upperparts.
Habitat. Floating, floating-emergent and emergent vegetation in freshwater wetlands, lagoons, billabongs, swamps, slow-moving rivers and lakes. Makes extensive use of artificial impoundments. Occasionally feeds on adjacent uplands with short vegetation.
Food and Feeding. Insects and other invertebrates; seeds also recorded. Prey gleaned from substrate and from just below surface of water, while bird walks on floating vegetation.
Breeding. Can breed year round when floating vegetation persists, but only during the wet season throughout most of range in Australia. Polyandrous with 1-3 (1-4) males per female; one very large female was able to monopolize 2 males in face of pressure from 4 other adult females. Males defend territory on floating vegetation, and females defend 1-4 adjacent males and their territories. In territorial fights males crouch, extend wings to the side and head and neck forward as they call loudly and lunge at one another; sometimes their feet and wings become entwined and they end up semi-submerged in water, whereupon female comes and pecks at the males until they separate. Either sex, but usually female, performs a unique pre-copulatory display: bird assumes copulatory position ("soliciting"); if the other bird approaches, displaying bird orientates self towards it and extends wings, while keeping tail high and head low, so wings nearly vertical; if second bird continues to approach, displaying bird folds wings and continues to hold copulatory position. Nest of stems and pieces of aquatic vegetation built primarily by male, but female does much vegetation tossing. Determinate layer, 4 eggs; female produces replacement clutches for her primary male as well as clutches for her other males; incubation 28 days; incubation and chick-care by male; chick striped above, white below; fledging c. 50-60 days.
Movements. Dispersive. Sedentary on permanent wetlands. Not known to be migratory anywhere within range; the few records reported from most of Wallacea have been taken by some authors as possible evidence of migration from Australia, although apparent subspecific differences do not support this. In Australia, birds moves considerable distances to occupy recently flooded wetlands at beginning of wet season, and disappear again when they dry.
Status and Conservation. Not globally threatened. Not known to be threatened anywhere within range, but degradation or loss of wetlands is a continual threat. Artificial impoundments have greatly increased the amount of breeding habitat in Australia. Few precise data available; Kakadu National Park in N Northern Territory, Australia, estimated to hold 1500 birds in 1987. Few records from most of Wallacea, but species recently found to be locally abundant on freshwater swamps in S Sulawesi.

Bibliography. Andrew & Holmes (1990), Baltzer (1990), Beehler *et al*. (1986), Blakers *et al*. (1984), Bowler & Taylor (1989), Coates (1985), Crawford (1979), Dickinson *et al*. (1991), Garnett (1985a), Hindwood, H. A. (1940), Lane (1994), Lindsey (1992), MacKinnon & Phillipps (1993), Marchant & Higgins (1993), Peckover & Filewood (1976), Perennou *et al*. (1994), Phillips (1989), Pizzey & Doyle (1980), Pringle (1987), Ramsay & Ramsay (1990), Rand & Gilliard (1967), Schodde & Tidemann (1986), Simpson & Day (1994), Slater *et al*. (1989), Smythies (1981), Trounson (1987), White & Bruce (1986).

Genus *HYDROPHASIANUS* Wagler, 1832

5. Pheasant-tailed Jacana

Hydrophasianus chirurgus

French: Jacana à longue queue **German**: Wasserfasan **Spanish**: Jacana Colilarga
Other common names: (Chinese) Water-pheasant

Taxonomy. *Tringa Chirurgus* Scopoli, 1786, Luzon.
Genus occasionally included within *Jacana*, but alternatively considered to be one of the forms most distant from that genus. Monotypic.
Distribution. Pakistan, Nepal, India and Sri Lanka through Myanmar to SE China and Taiwan, and S to SE Asia and Malay Peninsula, S Borneo and Phillippines. Winters sparsely S to Sumatra and Java, and also W to Oman and Yemen.

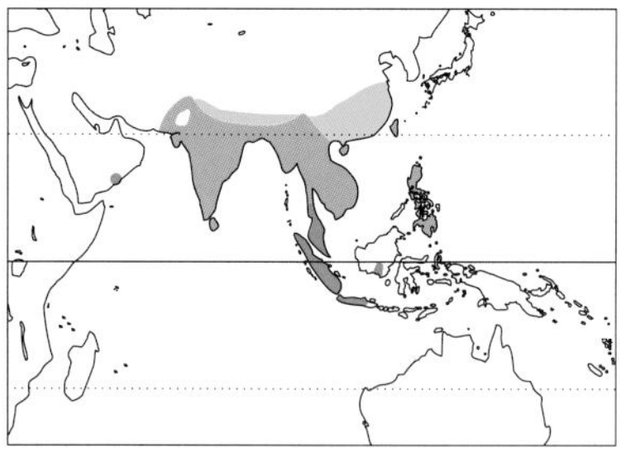

Descriptive notes. 39-58 cm (including 25-35 cm tail), in non-breeding plumage c. 31 cm; male c. 126 g, female c. 231 g. The only jacana with different breeding and non-breeding plumages. Conspicuous white wings, with black outermost primaries, and black tips to other primaries, outermost secondaries and greater primary coverts; sharp, pointed carpal spur. Breeding plumage: head and lower neck white, black patch at rear of crown continues as black line down each side of neck separating glossy golden yellow hindneck from white foreneck; body and tail feathers vary from blackish brown to paler brown, with greenish wash on back; tips of outer primaries with 2 cm spatulate extension; tail graduated with central two feathers greatly elongated, 19-38 cm. Non-breeding plumage: upperparts paler greenish brown extending onto outer parts of lesser and median coverts; crown and hindneck blackish, golden yellow on sides, with blackish brown eyestripe continuing down sides of neck and forming breast band; tail graduated but much shorter, 11-12 cm. Female similar to male, but significantly larger, although precise linear data lacking. Juvenile similar to non-breeding adult, but back paler, no yellow on sides of neck, and breast band indistinct.
Habitat. Extensive freshwater wetlands, including lakes, ponds and swampy ground; breeds on floating and floating-emergent aquatic vegetation, including water-lilies. Typically nests in wetlands cultivated for the edible seeds *Trapa* and corms of water chestnuts (*Eleocharis*), lotus (*Nelumbo*) and water-lilies. Winters in similar habitat, but may use more emergent vegetation.
Food and Feeding. Insects and invertebrates; reports that diet is vegetarian in India must be in error, but some aquatic vegetation ingested accidentally or incidentally, while seeds or ovules of lotus and lily may be taken intentionally. Prey gleaned from water surface and from surfaces and root systems of floating and emergent vegetation. Swims and feeds in open water more commonly than other jacanas.
Breeding. Season limited to summer months, Jun to early Sept at N limits, and to wet or monsoon months in India, Sri Lanka and SE Asia. Polyandrous, with female defending 3 males or more, and laying c. 10 clutches per year. Male reportedly remains mounted on female for up to 5 minutes before brief, 1-2 second, cloacal contact. Nest is a pad of stems and pieces of aquatic vegetation; construction primarily by male; some nests substantial, others disintegrate rapidly in rising water and sometimes eggs simply laid on floating leaf; male often moves clutch to new location. Clutch 4 eggs; replacement clutches laid every 6-15 days; male alone incubates and provides all direct parental care, but female aids in territory defence; downy chicks white below, striped with brown above; incubation and fledging periods unknown, but chicks may remain with male for up to 50-60 days. In N China, male becomes receptive to female much sooner after hatching a clutch than in other species: may consort and copulate with female when chicks only 2 weeks of age, and 1 clutch of 4 eggs laid for male with chicks only 19 days old. Breeding success unknown, but low. Age of maturity at least 1 year.
Movements. Makes local movements all year round, in response to changing water conditions throughout most of distribution. The only jacana with established migratory patterns, populations from China and high altitudes of Himalayas migrate S, but migration routes and behaviour unknown. Non-breeding birds occur throughout most of breeding range, and regularly in small numbers in Sumatra, Java, Oman and S Yemen; e.g. up to 50 recorded at Khawr Rawri, W Oman, in Feb. Probably breeds in SE Borneo, but no definite records. Single records in Bali and NW Australia; vagrant to S Japan.
Status and Conservation. Not globally threatened. Totally dependent on suitable wetlands; use of shallow water by human populations for growing seeds and corms causes much loss of nests and their contents. Conversion of wetlands to agricultural use, such as duck ponds and aquaculture, threatens birds on local levels. Common in Pakistan, with up to 150 birds wintering on single lake in S Sind; common resident and winter visitor in Thailand; uncommon in Peninsular Malaysia. Formerly bred as far N as Beijing, E China, but now apparently only S of R Yangtze; numbers apparently decreasing throughout E China. May have declined at major wintering site in S Sumatra: at Meggala (NC Lampung), generally common with 30+ birds on each swamp in 1976, but no birds recorded during surveys in 1992-1994.

Bibliography. Ali (1979), Ali & Ripley (1980), Anon. (1982), Bates & Lowther (1952), Betterton (1947), Biddulph (1954), Brazil (1991), Deignan (1945), Dickinson *et al*. (1991), Étchécopar & Hüe (1978), Gallagher & Woodcock (1980), Hoffmann (1949, 1950), Holmes & Rusila Noor (1995), Hüe & Étchécopar (1970), Indrawan (1991), Inskipp & Inskipp (1991), King *et al*. (1975), Kirkpatrick (1952), Kotagama & Fernando (1994), Lekagul & Round (1991), MacKinnon & Phillipps (1993), Marchant & Higgins (1993), van Marle & Voous (1988), Medway & Wells (1976), Meyer de Schauensee (1984), Neelakantan (1953b), Perennou *et al*. (1994), Phillips, T.J. (1961a, 1961b), Phillips, W.W.A. (1978), Ripley (1982), Roberts, T. J. (1991), Smythies (1981, 1986).

Genus *METOPIDIUS* Wagler, 1832

6. Bronze-winged Jacana

Metopidius indicus

French: Jacana bronzé **German**: Hindublatthühnchen **Spanish**: Jacana Bronceada

Taxonomy. *Parra indica* Latham, 1790, India.
Genus occasionally considered to include *Microparra*, *Actophilornis* and *Irediparra*, or alternatively lumped with *Actophilornis* and *Irediparra* in *Jacana*, but neither proposal widely accepted. Monotypic.
Distribution. India through SE Asia to S Sumatra and W Java.
Descriptive notes. 28-31 cm; 94-210 g. Glossy, black plumage with back, scapulars and upperwing-coverts greenish, tail and vent rufous; greenish yellow bill with yellow tip and red base, lappets and small frontal shield bluish, becoming all bright red during courtship; conspicuous white stripe extends from eye to nape; cornified carpal knob. Female similar to male, but larger. Juvenile has rufous cap and eyestripe, with small white supercilium; front of neck buff becoming yellowish buff on sides; rest of underparts white, upperparts dark.
Habitat. Floating and emergent vegetation on freshwater lakes, swamps, tanks, ponds, etc., especially in plains and in plateau country; also occurs in denser vegetation, wet grasslands, and overgrown paddyfields. On larger wetlands coincides with *Hydrophasianus chirurgus*, but latter not normally found on smaller ponds. Although present species sometimes dives when harassed, will also seek cover in vegetation away from wetlands.

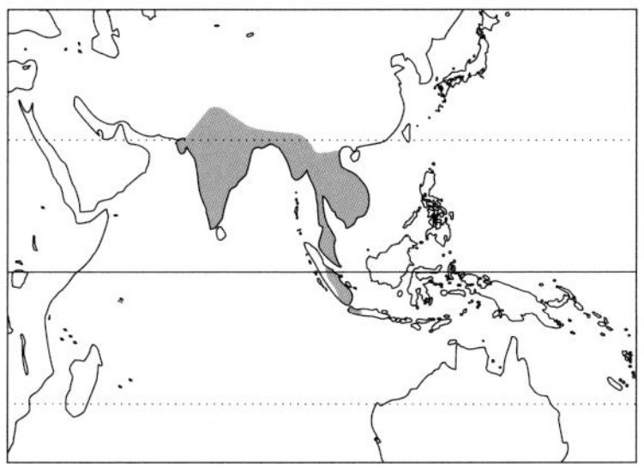

Food and Feeding. Reported to be chiefly vegetarian, but probably feeds extensively on insects, snails and other invertebrates. Food items taken from the water surface and aquatic vegetation. Apart from wetlands, in some areas probably forages often in grasslands and crop fields.
Breeding. Season during monsoons. Polyandrous; males vigorously defend territories against other males, females defend their mates' territories against other females. Scanty nest of aquatic vegetation on water-lily leaves or in emergent grasses, placed in denser vegetation than those of other jacanas; both sexes toss potential nest material, but it is not clear that female helps to build nest. Clutch 4 eggs, but 1 or more eggs sometimes lost; female has inter-clutch interval of c. 10 days; incubation c. 26 days; male alone incubates eggs and cares for chicks; male defends chicks aggressively, and in this is assisted by female. Unlike case of *Hydrophasianus chirurgus*, male does not resume sexual activity for over 2 months, reducing likelihood of his raising 2 broods during breeding season of c. 4 months. Fledging period, nesting success and age at sexual maturity unknown.
Movements. Sedentary, making local movements as necessary, in response to seasonal changes in water conditions; at Rawa Tenuk, S Sumatra, species appears to disperse throughout swamp during wet season, returning in dry season, presumably to breed.
Status and Conservation. Not globally threatened. Dependent on existence of wetlands, but apparently able to utilize some agricultural lands, e.g. wet grasslands, paddyfields. Apparently hunted in some areas, but elsewhere unmolested. Common in Thailand. Locally common in wetlands in lowland S Sumatra, especially at Rawa Tenuk; now very rare in Java, where formerly common.
Bibliography. Ali (1979), Ali & Ripley (1980), Baker (1929), Chattopadhyay (1980), Deignan (1945), Haensel (1991), Holmes & Rusila Noor (1995), Inskipp & Inskipp (1991), Kefford (1945), Khacher (1978), King *et al.* (1975), Lekagul & Round (1991), MacKinnon & Phillipps (1993), van Marle & Voous (1988), Mathew (1964), Medway & Wells (1976), Meyer de Schauensee (1984), Perennou *et al.* (1994), Ripley (1982), Roberts, T. J. (1991), Smythies (1986).

Genus *JACANA* Brisson, 1760

7. Northern Jacana

Jacana spinosa

French: Jacana du Mexique **German**: Gelbstirn-Blatthühnchen **Spanish**: Jacana Centroamericana
Other common names: (Middle) American Jacana

Taxonomy. *Fulica spinosa* Linnaeus, 1758, South America; error = western Panama.
Genus occasionally considered to include *Hydrophasianus*, or alternatively *Actophilornis*, *Irediaparra* and *Metopidius*, but neither proposal widely accepted. Forms superspecies with *J. jacana*, and considered conspecific by some authors, but evidence not convincing. Accepted races differ mainly in size, and may represent ecotypes rather than genuine races. Three subspecies normally recognized.
Subspecies and Distribution.
J. s. gymnostoma (Wagler, 1831) - Mexico, from SC Sinaloa and C Tamaulipas S to Chiapas, Yucatán and Cozumel I; rarely SE Texas (USA).
J. s. spinosa (Linnaeus, 1758) - Belize and Guatemala S to W Panama.
J. s. violacea (Cory, 1881) - Cuba, I of Pines, Jamaica and Hispaniola.

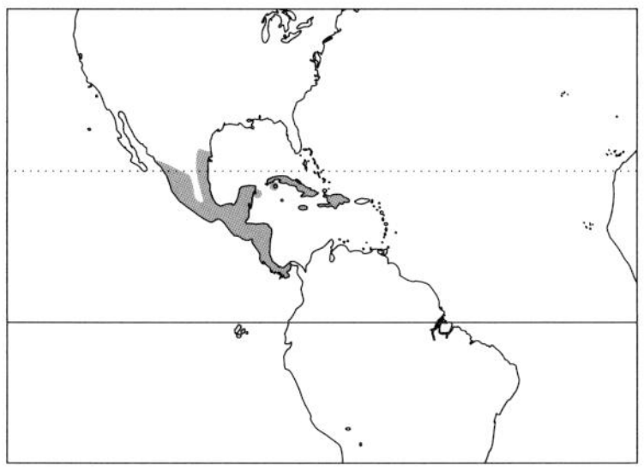

Descriptive notes. 17-23 cm; average of male 91 g, female 161 g. Head, neck, upper breast and upper mantle black; rest of upperparts, coverts, tertials and tail reddish to maroonish chestnut; rest of underparts maroon-chestnut; flight-feathers conspicuously yellow with pale greenish or chartreuse wash, tipped with brown which extends up outer margins of outer primaries and over primary coverts, alula and carpal area; bright yellow carpal spur contrasts conspicuously with dark plumage; bill yellow with pale blue to whitish base; conspicuous yellow soft, fleshy frontal shield tri-lobed, with central lobe larger; shield not continuous with bill as in other jacanas. Female similar to male but much larger. Juvenile has underparts white with pale buff breast; cap, hindneck, upper tail and rump dark brown, rest of upperparts pale brown; flight-feathers as in adult. Races very similar, differing slightly in size.
Habitat. Floating and floating-emergent vegetation in permanent and seasonally flooded shallow wetlands throughout range; in Mexico, even breeds on roadside ponds. Preferred territorial sites contain mixture of aquatic vegetation rather than monoculture of lily or hyacinth. Also occurs but does not breed in grassy marshes, nearby wetlands, and dry adjacent uplands; occurs up to c. 1500 m in Costa Rica.
Food and Feeding. Insects and other invertebrates; plant material apparently ingested incidentally, but species feeds actively on ovules or seeds of water-lilies opened by American Purple Gallinule (*Porphyrio martinica*); occasionally takes tiny fish. Feeds primarily by gleaning insects from the substrate, and picking invertebrates from root masses of floating vegetation which are systematically flipped upside down; occasionally plunges entire head beneath water in pursuit of prey.
Breeding. Virtually all year round in permanent wetlands. Polyandrous; females defend 1-4 (average 2·2) adjacent males and their territories; almost complete sex role reversal. In seasonally flooded sites, initial territories are large and additional males occupy sites on distant margins of territories as incubating males defend smaller areas closer to nests. Much of nest structure sits below water surface; nest material varies from virtually nothing to small pad of aquatic vegetation and stems; nest building movements performed by female primarily as part of interactions with male and not obviously related to nest building. Potential for cuckoldry highly variable, but female typically copulates preferably with male receiving eggs, especially shortly after egg-laying. Clutch 4 eggs; incubation 28 days; female highly variable in attention to nest and eggs, occasionally touching eggs with outside of breast feathers, but not known to incubate, and only male has brood patches; downy chicks white below with cinnamon to dark brown stripes above. Female performs vigilance behaviour near brood and attacks potential predators; both sexes spend much time attacking and chasing a variety of species from their territories. Chick-care normally by male alone; after two days of heavy rains, female sometimes broods chicks while male feeds; a monogamous female assumed care for a brood less than 2 weeks old while male incubated second clutch. Young stay with male up to 12 weeks, and may remain on his territory up to 12 months when adult plumage becomes complete. Normally male not receptive to female until chicks are 5-6 weeks old, and does not receive second clutch until later. In permanent habitats, individual females replaced by new females, which take over displaced female's territory and males; they commonly destroy any existing clutches and kill young broods, presumably bringing male into reproductive condition earlier than would occur if he were allowed to continue parental behaviour. Males replaced after 6-24 months' occupancy. Nesting success c. 30-40%, but 80+% of chicks survive. Does not breed until more than 1 year old, probably not until 2 or older.
Movements. Sedentary. Makes local movements between wetlands in areas with seasonal flooding. Immatures disperse along coast as much as 800-1000 km to N of northernmost breeding sites. Rarely wanders to S USA, where formerly bred and may still do so sporadically. Vagrant to Puerto Rico.
Status and Conservation. Not globally threatened. Common to fairly common throughout Mexican range; locally abundant in Costa Rica; common in W Panama. Creation of small artificial wetlands, including roadside ditches, has created new habitat, but economic development, drainage and development of rice production have reduced habitat elsewhere. Use of herbicides and insecticides sometimes eliminates prey and stunts plant growth. Large breeding colony near Houston, Texas, disappeared after poisoning of aquatic vegetation was followed by extreme freezing.
Bibliography. Anon. (1983a), Betts (1973), Betts & Jenni (1991), Biaggi (1983), Blake (1977), Fleetwood (1973), Hellmayr & Conover (1948), Howell & Webb (1995a), Jenni (1974, 1979, 1983), Jenni & Betts (1978), Jenni & Collier (1972), Jenni *et al.* (1975), Mace (1981), Miller (1931), Monroe (1968), Ridgely & Gwynne (1989), Rutgers & Norris (1970), Schaldach (1963), Slud (1964), Stephens (1982, 1984a, 1984b, 1984c, 1984d), Stiles & Skutch (1989), Wetmore (1965), Williams, S.O. (1987).

8. Wattled Jacana

Jacana jacana

French: Jacana noir **German**: Rotstirn-Blatthühnchen **Spanish**: Jacana Suramericana

Taxonomy. *Parra Jacana* Linnaeus, 1766, Surinam. Genus occasionally considered to include *Hydrophasianus*, or alternatively *Actophilornis*, *Irediaparra* and *Metopidius*, but neither proposal widely accepted. Forms superspecies with *J. spinosa*, but probably not conspecific as suggested by some authors. Range almost overlaps with that of *J. spinosa* in W Panama, and in past did so; local race *hypomelaena* of present species is the least similar to *J. spinosa*. Six subspecies recognized.
Subspecies and Distribution.
J. j. hypomelaena (G. R. Gray, 1846) - WC Panama (Veraguas) to N Colombia (Magdalena Valley).
J. j. melanopygia (P. L. Sclater, 1857) - W Colombia (Cauca Valley) to W Venezuela (L Maracaibo).
J. j. intermedia (P. L. Sclater, 1857) - N & C Venezuela.
J. j. jacana (Linnaeus, 1766) - SE Colombia E through S Venezuela to Trinidad and the Guianas, and S through most of Brazil to E Bolivia, N Argentina and Uruguay.
J. j. scapularis Chapman, 1922 - lowlands of W Ecuador and NW Peru.
J. j. peruviana Zimmer, 1930 - NE Peru (lower R Ucayali) and adjacent NW Brazil (upper R Amazon).

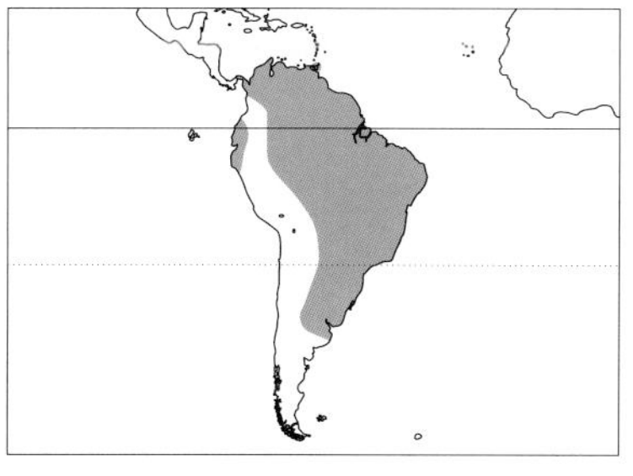

Descriptive notes. 21-25 cm; male 89-118 g, female 140-151 g. Red bi-lobed frontal comb or shield and conspicuous rictal lappets contrast with yellow bill and black head; blackish to reddish chestnut brown above; yellow to pale greenish yellow flight-feathers with dark brown to black tips, broader distally, and outermost edges of outermost primaries, primary coverts, alula and carpal area; bright yellow carpal spur. Female significantly larger and heavier than male, often with bluish caste along upper edge of comb. Juvenile very similar to that of *J. spinosa*, but has small frontal shield bi-lobed, rather than tri-lobed; lacks rictal wattles. Races vary from blackish above and below in *hypomelaena* to rich chestnut brown above and black below in *intermedia*, although some forms have chestnut flanks and vent, or black feathers mixed with chestnut in scapulars. Race *peruviana* resembles *J. spinosa* most closely, as is the least melanistic race. Immature *hypomelaena* differs from immatures of other races and that of *J. spinosa* in having darker brown back and black flanks, axillaries and underwing-coverts.
Habitat. Permanent and seasonally flooded freshwater wetlands with floating and floating-emergent vegetation. Also forages in shallow water and in adjacent cropland and grassland. In Guyana, nests in ditches, canals and small ponds, and regularly feeds on adjacent rice fields.
Food and Feeding. Primarily insects and other invertebrates; apart from seeds, most plant material may be ingested accidentally, but at a rice plantation in Guyana 20% of diet consisted of seeds. Prey gleaned from the surface of floating and emergent vegetation and picked from roots of floating plants upturned by bird.
Breeding. Polyandrous; females defend and breed with 1-3+ neighbouring, territorial males; number of mates highly variable and apparently depends on size of habitat and especially on quality, with more, smaller territories occurring in areas of dense, mixed species mats of floating vegetation. Females vigorously exclude other females and assist their mates to drive out intruders. Few details reported about breeding behaviour, but sex role reversal occurs and species is generally assumed to have similar behavioural traits and ecology to those of *J. spinosa*. Nest small, often partially submerged, collection of stems and aquatic vegetation. Clutch 4 eggs; incubation 28 days; incubation and chick-care by male; downy chicks white below with cinnamon and brown stripes above; male accompanies, broods and defends precocial chicks, but does not feed them; fledging age and age of sexual maturity assumed to be as in *J. spinosa*. Male does not copulate during incubation and for first several weeks of brood care; female lays replacement clutches and clutches for other males with as little as 8 days between clutches. Following removal of resident female, replacement females from nearby commonly kills chicks, especially those 3 weeks old or younger. In Guyana only 8 of 52 nests (15%) produced 1 or more young.
Movements. Sedentary, with local movements during dry season, when many marshes dry out. Occurs in flocks outside breeding season.
Status and Conservation. Not globally threatened. Dependent on preservation of suitable wetlands. Development of rice production, as in Guyana, can produce additional habitat or can cause its destruction, but invariably leads to greatly increased human disruption of breeding efforts. Development of grazing and pasture lands, and associated small reservoirs, has increased habitat in much of South America. Formation of L Gatun in Panama created immense amount of new habitat for local race *hypomelaena*. Attempts to drain wetlands constitute a threat in many areas, but, despite this, overall species not seriously threatened over most of distribution.
Bibliography. Anon. (1983a), Belton (1984), Betts (1973), Blake (1977), Canevari *et al.* (1991), Contreras *et al.* (1990), Emlen *et al.* (1989), Ferreira (1983), Fjeldså & Krabbe (1990), Haverschmidt (1968), Haverschmidt & Mees (1995), Hellmayr & Conover (1948), Hilty & Brown (1986), Marcus (1985), Meyer de Schauensee & Phelps (1978), Ortiz & Carrión (1991), Osborne, D. R. (1982, 1983), Osborne, D. R. & Beissinger (1979a), Osborne, D. R. & Bourne (1977), de la Peña (1992), Ridgely & Gwynne (1989), Sick (1985c, 1993), Snyder (1966), Tostain *et al.* (1992), Wetmore (1965).

Class AVES
Order CHARADRIIFORMES
Suborder CHARADRII
Family ROSTRATULIDAE (PAINTED-SNIPES)

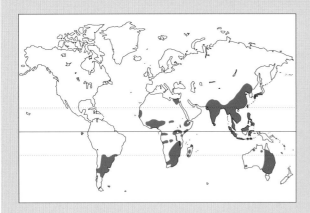

- Medium-sized waders, superficially resembling true snipes, with large eyes, long bill and relatively short, broad wings.
- 19-28 cm.

- All regions except Nearctic and Antarctic.
- Wetlands, especially swamps and wet grassland, normally at low altitude.
- 2 genera, 2 species, 3 taxa.
- No species threatened; none extinct since 1600.

Systematics

The family Rostratulidae is normally considered to comprise two well defined species, each in its own monospecific genus: the Greater Painted-snipe (*Rostratula benghalensis*), widely distributed throughout warmer parts of the Old World; and the South American Painted-snipe (*Nycticryphes semicollaris*), with a more restricted range in the southern half of South America. The relationship between them has long intrigued taxonomists, and the two have frequently been lumped together in the genus *Rostratula*. At the other extreme, the two commonly recognized races of the Greater Painted-snipe, nominate *benghalensis* of Africa and Asia east to Indonesia and *australis* of Australia, were formerly regarded as distinct species. However, they exhibit very limited morphological differences and are apparently similar in all aspects of their behaviour.

The recognition of two genera seems justified, as there are significant differences between *Rostratula* and *Nycticryphes*. For example, the Greater Painted-snipe shows notable reversed sexual dimorphism in plumage, while the sexes are virtually identical in the South American Painted-snipe. The latter species differs from the former in having the toes partially webbed, while the bill and tail shapes are markedly different in the two species. Most importantly, the female Greater Painted-snipe has an oesophageal crop unique among the Charadriiformes. It plays no part in the digestive process but instead has a role in courtship: the trachea is capable of considerable enlargement and the two act as a resonance chamber during the species' prolonged vocal displays (see Voice). A study of the feeding apparatus of the Greater Painted-snipe has revealed that the species possesses a simple adductor muscle, of a style not found in any other waders, in addition to a bill structure which is also unique within the order. Nonetheless, several of the painted-snipes' other anatomical characteristics, such as the lack of a complexus origin, are features which are shared with other waders that feed more or less wholly in aquatic environments.

As no fossilized remains of painted-snipes have yet been unearthed, their ancestral origins remain unclear. There are some skeletal and anatomical characters that are reminiscent of either rails (Rallidae) or cranes (Gruidae). The rather short, broad, rounded wings have been compared to those of *Rallus* rails and *Crex* crakes in appearance, but they are perhaps most closely akin to those of jacanas, and nowadays the Rostratulidae are generally agreed to belong with the waders, or shorebirds, in the order Charadriiformes. Within this order, superficial resemblances to the true snipes (*Gallinago*) have been viewed by most authorities as carrying no taxonomic significance, and the painted-snipes have traditionally been considered most closely related to the jacanas. There are important skeletal reasons for this, such as a similarly shaped sternum, with two notches on the rear border, a distinctive feature which is also found in cranes. Also, the two families differ from all other waders in having ten primaries, as opposed to eleven. The colour patterns of downy young were used by J. R. Jehl as the basis of an internal classification of the suborder Charadrii, involving the recognition of three superfamilies. The unfledged young of the painted-snipes have striking and complex down patterns with bold dorsal bands adorning the upperparts, as in young jacanas, thus emphasizing the similarity between these two families, as well as their distinctiveness from the more typical striped patterns exhibited by most other waders. Therefore, Jehl separated off the painted-snipes and the jacanas in the superfamily Jacanoidea, with a second superfamily for the Crab Plover (*Dromas ardeola*), and a third containing all the remaining wader families. This proposal has subsequently received widespread acceptance.

The hypothesis of a close relationship with the jacanas has recently received important additional support from the field of biochemical research. Work on DNA-DNA hybridization suggests that the painted-snipes' closest relatives may include the jacanas, the phalaropes (Phalaropodinae) and the *Tringa* and *Calidris* sandpipers. Other recent studies of charadriiform phylogeny, based upon character compatibility analysis, have viewed the painted-snipes as part of a monophyletic group which also includes the jacanas, the woodcocks (*Scolopax*) and the true snipes, as well as phalaropes and seedsnipes (Thinocoridae), and which is defined by a number of close similarities in skeletal make-up. Due to the fact that they possess basipterygoid processes, painted-snipes are clustered with the Scolopacidae in such work, in preference to the ideas of most earlier students of charadriifrom taxonomy and systematics.

Morphological Aspects

Painted-snipes are medium-sized waders, measuring up to 28 cm in overall length, with relatively long bills. Female Greater Painted-snipes weigh up to 200 g, but South American Painted-snipes usually weigh only 65-86 g, with females perhaps ave-

The painted-snipes bear a superficial resemblance to the true snipes of the family Scolopacidae. Their plumage, however, is more arresting, as can be seen in this female Greater Painted-snipe. The bill is shorter with the distal third distinctively swollen, while the legs are longer with very long, slender toes. Another feature typical of this family is the large eye, an adaptation to the birds' lifestyle, generally crepuscular, and even fully nocturnal on moonlit nights.

[*Rostratula benghalensis benghalensis*, Gambia. Photo: Mike McKavett/ Bruce Coleman]

raging slightly heavier. The race *australis* of the Greater Painted-snipe is distinctly longer-winged, with a shorter bill and tarsus than the nominate race.

As a consequence of their role reversal, the male Greater Painted-snipe is characteristically smaller and more cryptically plumaged than the brighter female: she initiates courtship, whilst he is primarily responsible for incubation and chick-care (see Breeding). In contrast, there is little, if any, evidence to suggest that the South American Painted-snipe is at all sexually dimorphic in respect of its plumage. This is presumably due to the fact that in this species the sexes undertake more normal roles, with the female responsible for incubating, and not taking the lead in courtship.

Structurally, painted-snipes bear a superficial resemblance to the true snipes, but they have brighter, more strikingly patterned plumage; shorter bills, with a markedly decurved and swollen distal third being especially noticeable in the South American Painted-snipe; broader, more rounded wings, with extensive yellowish spotting; shorter tails; and longer legs, which dangle down in flight, closely recalling rails. Both species have large eyes, set well forward on the head for binocular vision, and orientated towards the end of the bill; these are adapted for their crepuscular, and in the Greater Painted-snipe at least, semi-nocturnal lifestyle.

In plumage, the two species are broadly similar. As befits their name, the painted-snipes are striking and intricately patterned waders, with a conspicuous white or yellowish white orbital ring and streaks behind the eye, a white or golden scapular line and median crown stripe, and a whitish belly and flanks. Most of the head and breast are deep rufous brown, or sooty olive brown in the South American Painted-snipe; the mantle is greyish green, finely barred with dark brown, or dark brown with grey barring in the South American Painted-snipe; and the wing-coverts are dark olive green or dark brown with fine barring, except in males of the Greater Painted-snipe; whilst the flight-feathers are ash grey or brown, and either barred or spotted.

Male Greater Painted-snipes generally appear like duller versions of the female, except for their boldly patterned wing-coverts, which are greenish gold with striking pairs of golden buff spots near the tip of each feather. Better camouflaged than the bright females, they take most, if not all of the incubating duties. The South American Painted-snipe shows a few bold white spots on the wing-coverts, chiefly on the greater coverts. Although there is little evidence to suggest sexual plumage dimorphism in this species, some observers have conjectured that brighter individuals might be females.

Juveniles of the Greater Painted-snipe appear very similar to adults upon fledging. The South American Painted-snipe possesses a slightly more complex moulting pattern: juveniles lack the sooty olive brown coloration on the head and neck, and also show strongly patterned upperparts; in addition to the broad white "V" on the mantle, most mantle and wing feathers are broadly fringed with white or pale buff, producing a distinctly scaly appearance. Juvenile plumage is later replaced by a distinct subadult plumage, largely similar to that of the adult, as the bird gains both the sharp pattern on the head and neck and also the bold spots on the wing-coverts.

Within the Charadrii, the painted-snipes are, along with the jacanas, unique in possessing just ten primaries, as opposed to the eleven usual in other waders; there are around 15 secondaries. The tail consists of 14-16 feathers, and is rounded in the Greater Painted-snipe, but wedge-shaped or graduated in the South American species, which has the median rectrices tapered and soft at the tip.

Painted-snipes generally appear sluggish and weak in flight, although their wingbeats are quite deep and their movement buoyant, the fluttery, bat-like nature being accentuated by the dangling legs. In contrast to *Gallinago* snipes, the flight is usually direct, not zig-zagging, although the South American Painted-snipe, in particular, may occasionally perform a more erratic escape flight. Neither species, if flushed, will usually fly far, or much above about 10 m over the ground, the bird usually running on into deeper cover upon landing. In fact, both species are reluctant fliers, when alarmed preferring either to skulk in dense cover, like rails or crakes, or freeze in their adopted position, as in some herons (Ardeidae) and waders, particularly *Tringa* sandpipers and *Gallinago* snipes. Although both species have been reported to tower up and disappear some distance, such behaviour is apparently rare, but the South American Painted-snipe may at times fly around its breeding area for several minutes, and this species appears to have a much greater tendency to take flight. On alighting, Greater Painted-snipes

The South American
Painted-snipe and the
more widespread and
better known Greater
Painted-snipe (Rostratula
benghalensis) are usually
placed in separate genera
for a number of reasons.
The American species
shows no clear sexual
dimorphism and the
sexual roles are not
apparently reversed. It is
smaller, has darker
plumage and a different
shape of bill, more curved
and sharply kinked
towards the tip. The tail is
not rounded, but wedge-
shaped, with the central
rectrices tapered and soft
at the tip. In contrast,
other features, such as the
large eyes, the golden "V"
on the mantle and the long
greenish legs, are shared
by both species.

[Nycticryphes semicollaris,
Argentina.
Photo: R. Seitre/Bios]

may occasionally bob the rear body and tail, in a manner reminiscent of a Common Sandpiper (*Actitis hypoleucos*), but the head is bobbed only very rarely. Female Greater Painted-snipes characteristically perform low roding display flights during the breeding season (see Voice).

Both species have long legs, with the upper half of the tibia feathered, and the tarsus comparatively stout. The very long slender toes are adapted for the birds' life amidst a semi-aquatic environment. The middle toe of the Greater Painted-snipe can measure as much as 95% the length of the tarsus, and even the hind toe can measure up to nearly a third of the length of the central toe. The toes are unwebbed in the Greater, but the South American has basal webbing between the middle and outer toes. Both species have green or brownish legs and feet.

The South American Painted-snipe's bill is rather more markedly decurved and sharply kinked towards the tip, and is also more bulbous than its Old World counterpart, being much expanded and flattened on both the upper and the lower mandibles, but especially the latter; the bill is also pitted distally. The colour varies in this species, and is rarely uniform throughout its entire length, grading from yellow-brown and yellowish through green to reddish brown, and occasionally even approaching black on the nail or elsewhere on the distal half. The bill of the Greater Painted-snipe is usually brown, olive or even purplish, with a greyer brown base and dark or reddish brown tip. In this species, the nostrils are situated in deep, narrow grooves that extend over half way along the entire length of the upper mandible, a feature unique within the Charadriiformes.

Habitat

The two species have broadly similar habitat preferences. The South American Painted-snipe may show a greater willingness to utilize more open areas of wetland, including estuaries in Argentina and Uruguay, and wet meadows throughout its range, but the Greater Painted-snipe also inhabits rice fields, freshwater lakes with grassy islets for nesting, overgrown mudflats and dam-lakes, and it will move onto damp agricultural land, including ploughed areas, to feed at dawn or dusk. It has also been recorded from mangroves in Bangladesh. Both species live and feed primarily in swamps and marshes interspersed with fairly deep pools up to 30-50 cm deep, soft muddy areas and dense shrubbery or reedbeds. In Africa, the Greater Painted-snipe has also been recorded breeding in flooded waste ground with low scrub, and in thickly vegetated areas along the banks of rivers in both coastal and inland areas. However, it will also feed on the margins of pools, sewage tanks and irrigation channels, or wherever there is exposed mud in sufficiently close proximity to dense cover. Neither species exhibits any partiality for a particular habitat on a seasonal basis, but both seem to prefer recently flooded areas, and they will swiftly abandon sites where the water levels are either too high or too low.

Painted-snipes are only rarely recorded at high altitudes, being principally birds of the lowlands, although the Greater Painted-snipe is regularly encountered in the eastern and northern highlands of Madagascar up to 1500 m. The same species is also resident in Sumatra up to 800-900 m, where it has been recorded up to 1400 m; in Sri Lanka up to 1300 m; and in the Himalayas and Myanmar up to c. 1800 m. An exceptional record at the altitude of 5200 m in Tibet, in September, presumably corresponded to a vagrant, or perhaps a migrant. There is no evidence to suggest that the South American Painted-snipe will ever wander to truly montane areas, and its movements are usually confined to areas close to sea-level, although it has been recorded up to over 1000 m in Brazil.

General Habits

Both species are largely solitary, although the South American Painted-snipe breeds semi-colonially and, in conjunction with its polyandrous lifestyle, the Greater Painted-snipe also often nests in groups. Small groups consisting of two or more family units may congregate in the post-breeding season. Exceptional flocks of Greater Painted-snipes include one of 30 birds in Myanmar, and also one of 100 birds in Senegambia, where the species regularly forms flocks of up to 20 birds between March and May in the few remaining freshwater swamps in the dry season. However, even outside the breeding season, when feeding or loafing, most birds spend their time alone. A minimum individual distance spacing of at least 2 m is nearly always maintained be-

In accordance with the sexual role reversal, the plumage of the male Greater Painted-snipe is duller than his mate's. However, each median and greater upperwing-covert shows a striking pair of golden buff spots near the tip, making the bird particularly stunning when it performs the Spread-wing Display. This is a multi-purpose display, with different levels of intensity and several variants. It is carried out in heterosexual situations, females performing it after allopreening the male during courtship. It also forms part of the species' antagonistic behaviour, as territorial females use it to deter other females. Finally, it constitutes a basic element of the species' anti-predator strategy, since it is performed by birds of both sexes, and even small chicks only one week old, when confronting predators or human intruders. It is similarly used by males as a Distraction-threat Display when disturbed either at the nest or whilst accompanying the chicks.

[*Rostratula benghalensis australis*, swamps north of Sydney, Australia. Photo: Jean-Paul Ferrero/ Auscape]

tween birds outside the family grouping, although flocks can be observed flushing in close unison. Both species usually roost singly, by day or night, although parties of up to three birds have been encountered, either on dry ground under dense cover, or in shallow water under the overhang of emergent sedges or other vegetation.

The two painted-snipes are essentially crepuscular birds, although on moonlit nights they may be wholly nocturnal. The South American Painted-snipe is apparently only rarely active during the day. The Greater Painted-snipe, although typically confined to marshy or wetland areas, may visit nearby grassland, or even ploughed areas in order to feed at dawn or dusk. If undisturbed by humans or livestock, this species will also feed during the day at certain favoured, well vegetated sites.

Secretive and unobtrusive birds, painted-snipes are difficult to flush, preferring to freeze in their currently adopted position when disturbed, although they will on occasion scurry back to the safety of cover. They can hold their posture motionless for many minutes if necessary, staring fixedly at the object of danger throughout. Alarmed birds, unlike other Charadriiformes, do not appear to head-bob, but they regularly perform a tail-dipping action, like that of *Actitis* sandpipers, and presumably fulfilling a similar function. The South American Painted-snipe will lean towards the object of presumed danger with the bill virtually touching the ground, displaying almost the entire upperside, whilst otherwise remaining frozen in its alarmed posture; or it may just crouch flat against the ground, even if very close to an observer.

Even when surprised on the nest, the Greater Painted-snipe will typically slink away in the manner of a rail, as opposed to taking flight; it may then crouch in nearby vegetation until the danger has receded. However, the male may also run from the nest, then make a short flight before running forward again, in the manner of *Charadrius* plovers. Apparently, an incubating South American Painted-snipe will usually leave the nest several minutes ahead of approaching danger. When walking, this species always appears as if it is stooping or crouching, with the head and neck held in. When with eggs or small young, both species infrequently perform distraction displays in response to close approach by humans, in common with many other Charadriiformes. Juveniles of both species are capable of swimming some distance, when necessary, in order to escape danger, even though the Greater Painted-snipe has unwebbed toes. Both species will also swim across narrow deep channels whilst foraging. If flushed, neither species often flies far, its escape being direct, not zig-zagging like several of the true snipes, although the South American Painted-snipe will occasionally employ a stronger and more erratic, almost bat-like escape flight, alternatively flapping and then gliding on stiffened wings.

Voice

Painted-snipes are largely silent outside the breeding season. Both species are normally quiet when flushed, the South American Painted-snipe rarely, if ever, calling in flight. The Greater Painted-snipe will occasionally utter an explosive "kek", or a guttural croak when disturbed. A variety of deep, almost snake-like, alarm calls have been recorded from the latter species; when caught, both sexes are known to give a throaty hiss, and anxiety may also manifest itself as a low purring.

As with many other facets of its behaviour, the Greater Painted-snipe, apparently unlike its Neotropical counterpart, exhibits relatively strong sexual differences in vocalizations. The female is generally the more vocal and pugnacious of the sexes, being capable of stronger, more resonant calls than the male, due to her convoluted trachea, which actually measures twice the length of the neck. Folds of subcutaneous fat form in the neck, allowing the trachea great freedom of movement. Displaying females utter a series of soft, metallic drawn out hooting calls, occasionally over 80 notes long, likened by some to a human blowing across the top of an empty bottle, or a hiccough. These advertisement calls can be audible over a kilometre away. They are given from the ground, or alternatively as single notes during a low, woodcock-like roding flight. Such territorial displays gather momentum during the breeding season. In the Northern Hemisphere, they continue from March through to October, initially being confined to the twilight period, with daylight calling commencing in late April, although activity peaks in the hour immediately prior to dawn, and two to three hours after sunset. However, during the egg-laying and incubation periods, females can persist in display-calling almost continuously throughout the day and long into the night. A similarly mellow-sounding series of calls is used by females in a number of other situations: in response to human intruders; when combating rival females; and also to accompany the frontal "Spread-wing Display" (see Breeding) aimed at a prospective mate.

Male Greater Painted-snipes have, in contrast, few specific vocalizations, most of which are used around the nest. Indeed, males are known to call only comparatively rarely. Low calls are infrequently uttered when the male approaches the nest-site and he may make explosive or growling calls whilst performing the frontal Spread-wing Display in defence of his nest. The male will use "Assembly Calls" in order to summon his small young to follow him, and will also utter a short, sharp squeak call in response to courting females.

The South American Painted-snipe is known to utter a plaintive whistle on occasion during the breeding season, but otherwise it is virtually silent. Neither sex indulges in the prolonged nuptial roding flights and nocturnal "song" so characteristic of the female Greater Painted-snipe. Captive birds have been recorded as uttering a querulous, hoarse or hissing dual-noted whistle, when approached too closely either by humans or by conspecifics. It has been suggested that this call, used in varying degrees of intensity, may serve as a contact or warning note, as well as to accompany heterosexual or antagonistic displays.

Food and Feeding

Both species are omnivorous, feeding on both invertebrates and seeds. Invertebrates known to be taken by the Greater Painted-snipe include insects, particularly grasshoppers and crickets (Orthoptera); snails (Mollusca); earthworms (Annelida); and crustaceans. Crustaceans are also recorded in the diet of the South American Painted-snipe, as are a variety of aquatic insects and other invertebrates. Several grasses, including millet (*Panicum*) and rice (*Oryza*), have been reported as being eaten by both species; indeed, stomach analysis of ten Greater Painted-snipes in Japan found vegetable matter to be the predominant constituent. No other detailed food study of either species has been attempted. An adult Greater Painted-snipe kept in captivity in Australia was successfully fed on worms, insects and unspecified meat products.

The two species employ similar feeding techniques, largely involving shallow probing in the soft muddy margins of pools, marshes, rivers and other wetland areas where suitably dense cover is to be found nearby. Typically, they are crepuscular, emerging to feed in the early morning and towards dusk, although some feeding make take place at night, especially if there is sufficient moonlight. When feeding in shallow water, painted-snipes employ a scythe-like motion of the head and bill, sweeping from side to side in a short, semi-circular movement, keeping the bill tip permanently submerged, whilst the mandibles open and close, catching small molluscs and crustaceans. The South American Painted-snipe may, very rarely, fully immerse the head in water whilst feeding. In order to reach suitable feeding areas, both species will also swim short distances, for instance across narrow water courses, and the Greater Painted-snipe will occasionally travel to adjacent farmland in order to feed.

Breeding

As with so many aspects of the painted-snipes' life history, it is the better studied Greater Painted-snipe that furnishes most of the information currently available on breeding biology and behaviour. It is apparent that the two species adopt rather different

The painted-snipes are wetland birds, typically inhabiting swamps and marshes interspersed with fairly deep pools, and freshwater lakes with vegetated islets. The Greater Painted-snipe is largely solitary, but outside the breeding season it can form small groups, especially when suitable habitat is scarce; for example, during the dry season flocks of over 20 birds are occasionally recorded at the few freshwater swamps remaining in a particular area.

[*Rostratula benghalensis benghalensis*, India. Photo: Gertrud & Helmut Denzau]

systems, but as yet very little research has be carried out and little has been published on the breeding and nesting habits of the South American Painted-snipe.

The Greater Painted-snipe is well known for its polyandrous mating system, although in parts of its range where densities are low, such as southern Africa, it may occasionally practise monogamy. In contrast, its Neotropical counterpart appears to adopt a solely monogamous approach. Females of the former species will mate with at least two, and perhaps three to four males each year, the pair-bond surviving only until the point when the eggs are laid, whereupon the female seeks a new mate. The process is often rapid, with the second clutch often laid before the first has hatched. In Japan, a female was recorded to have completed one clutch and within twelve days to have commenced laying a second. Both species probably breed throughout much, or all, of the year, the key factor being the timing of the rainy season.

The displays of the Greater Painted-snipe have been comparatively well studied, considering that there is much concerning this species which remains wholly unknown. The "Spread-wing Display" is a multi-purpose display used in antagonistic, heterosexual and anti-predator situations; it is chiefly performed by the female, but sometimes by the male, mainly against predators. It is used in two degrees of intensity: in the lesser form, the near wing is extended, whilst the far wing is both raised and extended, and the tail is often fanned and depressed; in the full frontal version, the bird faces its opponent or prospective mate head-on, with both wings fully extended and arched slightly forward, the tail fanned and raised, and the whole body, including the bill, tilted downward and toward the object of display. On occasion, the bird will also fluff up its body feathers, or alternatively raise rather than lower its bill. Although females are intensively territorial, rival birds will actually go as far as fighting only in defence of an already established partner. Nonetheless, such aggression can be quite vicious, and captive individuals have been known to peck their human captors during such display.

During courtship the female Greater Painted-snipe will allopreen her prospective mate, before adopting the full frontal Spread-wing Display, and circling the male whilst calling softly, for approximately two minutes. She persists in displaying, even if the male is initially unresponsive. Once the pair have copulated, both sexes stand side by side calling, the female occasionally opening and lifting both wings straight upwards.

Painted-snipes are solitary nesters, with territories on average about 200 m wide, although due to the Greater Painted-snipe's polyandrous habits, its nests may be found grouped closer together, sometimes as little as 4-10 m apart, occasionally as much

as 200 m, but more usually 15-50 m apart. Individuals will utilize the same nest in successive years, if undisturbed or if the ground is relatively stable, but in any case they usually nest within a few metres of the previous year's site.

Nest building commences a few days prior to the laying of the first egg, and is usually completed by the time the second egg has been laid. During this period both parents remain in close proximity to each other and the nest for the vast majority of the time. Thereafter, the female spends a steadily decreasing proportion of time at the nest, and by the time the last egg is laid her visits have become minimal, and she usually seeks a new mate. On occasion, female Greater Painted-snipes may casually drop a single egg away from the nest-site.

The nest of both species is a shallow cup, lined with a few stems and leaves from available vegetation, and occasionally some small dead sticks. Sometimes this structure is elaborated and built up into a small platform, with the addition of more significant amounts of plant material. The South American Painted-snipe apparently shows a greater tendency to construct a nest platform, presumably as most nests described have been located in wet pasture or grazing marsh, situations where the water table can rise or fall dramatically in a short space of time. Nonetheless, this species will, just as likely, make use of a cow's hoofmark for its nest-site, or create its own shallow scrape. The site is usually concealed within dense vegetation, frequently on semi-floating water weeds and always in relatively close proximity to open water. The Greater Painted-snipe, at least, on occasion builds its nest atop the small bunds that enclose inundated paddyfields or lotus fields, provided these are vegetated; one nest of this species was found in a hollow under dead trees. However, it is probably unusual for the nest to be placed more than a couple of metres above the prevailing water level.

In the vast majority of cases in the Greater Painted-snipe, the male builds the nest, incubates the eggs and broods the young, and he is also responsible for rearing his offspring to fledging. He often remains with the juveniles for one or two months after fledging. Although the female usually takes a wholly passive role in chick-care, she may stay in close proximity to her mate, occasionally assisting in territorial defence of the nesting area, and even less regularly in nest construction and apparently also in sitting on eggs or small chicks; in South-east Asia, females have been flushed from chicks, and collected, whilst they were incubating eggs.

The eggs of painted-snipes are ovaloid or oblong, like those of sandgrouse, not high-topped like true snipe. They are slightly glossy, and are heavily marked with black or blackish brown blotches, streaks and spots on a pale buffy yellow background. In both species, but especially the South American, the background may instead be cream-coloured and occasionally the markings grey. Those of the Greater Painted-snipe average 36 x 26 mm and weigh approximately 13 g, or up to 9·5% of the female's body weight, a significant proportion, given that a typical clutch contains four eggs, and that females tend to lay two to four clutches per season, to be incubated by different males. Although the laying interval has not been accurately recorded, it is probably one day between each egg. The eggs of the South American Painted-snipe average very slightly smaller. Two eggs are the norm in this species, although clutches of three have been recorded. Females are monogamous, laying a single clutch and participating in the incubation of the eggs and care of the young. Their breeding and display habits have been little studied, and although it is probable that the species shows similarities to the Greater Painted-snipe in some aspects of its breeding biology and courtship behaviour, further research is required.

The incubation period lasts 15-21 days in the Greater Painted-snipe, the average probably being 18-19, with incubation only commencing once the last egg has been laid. Observations of nesting males in Japan suggest that the male usually leaves the nest on average just over once per hour, for a ten minute period, although he sometimes remains at the nest for several hours at a time, especially in the morning; occasionally, a male may leave the eggs for as long as 40 minutes. He characteristically spends approximately 50% of daylight hours on the nest, and 89% of the night.

The Greater Painted-snipe's downy young are precocial and nidifugous, leaving the nest virtually as soon as they are dry, so hatching is almost certainly near-synchronous; they are not known to return to the nest at any later stage. They wear a covering of pale buff down, with a bold pattern of dark lines on the upperparts and an orange-brown patch on the centre of the back. They are brooded for several days by the male, or occasionally by the female, and remain dependant upon the male for food for several days at least; in Nigeria, a small chick hand-reared for three days never learned to peck of its own volition, and had to be fed forcibly.

The young birds behave as a group, following the male closely, and crouching close together when threatened, until they are able to run away with ease. In one case, the members of a brood were observed to freeze in a crouching position with their heads all facing inwards. However, the chicks are soon able to give the full frontal Spread-wing Display towards intruders, sometimes at only one week old. Young of both species taken into captivity soon after hatching swiftly learn to imprint themselves on their human foster parents.

In a monogamous system, as has been observed in southern Africa, and which may presumably operate elsewhere, the female appears to remain as part of the family group. It is possible that, for instance, nest building and brooding by the female constitute normal behaviour in a monogamous pair relationship, and that observations of such family activity by females elsewhere in the species' range of the Greater Painted-snipe are also indicative of monogamy.

The fledging period is unknown in both species, as is the age of independence. Male Greater Painted-snipes are probably capable of breeding after a year, while females may take two years in order to reach sexual maturity.

Neither species' reproductive success has been accurately studied. Casual observations suggest that the male Greater Painted-snipe may raise up to four young to the stage of fledging: there are records from several Asian countries of males with three well grown young; and from South Africa with four fledglings.

Movements

In both species, the flight action appears slow and buoyant or, especially in the South American Painted-snipe, erratic, and they can resemble some of the larger species of rails or crakes. Notwithstanding this apparent feebleness, painted-snipes are actually capable of movements over considerable distances. In

northern India, for instance, a Greater Painted-snipe which was trapped and ringed at Bharatpur, Rajasthan, in December was later recovered 900 km away to the east, in Bihar. Vagrants of this species have been recorded from Afghanistan, Israel, Oman, Somalia, Zanzibar, Pemba and Tasmania, indicating certain mobility.

This species is largely resident in Egypt and throughout most of Asia, although the populations in northern China and northern Japan are migratory. However, African birds are partially nomadic and perhaps opportunistic, responding to local climatic conditions, and even undertaking more regular, but nonetheless relatively short distance, migrations in order to locate suitable breeding habitat. For example, in Chad the Greater Painted-snipe is recorded as a wet season visitor to the Sahel zone, where it arrives with the first rains in early July, returning south between September and November after breeding. The principle is the same but the pattern slightly different in Nigeria, where the species breeds in the south during the rainy season, before moving slowly northwards to spend the dry season in the remaining areas of marshland. In Zimbabwe, movements would, however, appear to be wholly random, as, of 134 birds trapped, none was recaptured in the same area in which it had been ringed. In much of Australia, the species behaves as a true nomad, appearing after good rains in areas where it has not been recorded for several years, sometimes even decades, and remaining temporarily to breed, before moving on in search of freshly flooded areas.

The South American Painted-snipe also performs regular seasonal movements in some parts of its range, for instance in the province of Buenos Aires, Argentina, and in parts of Brazil. Further south in Argentina, in northern Chubut and southern Río Negro, the species is known only as a non-breeding migrant.

After the breeding season is over, Greater Painted-snipes can gather in small flocks, or even, exceptionally, large ones, although in many areas, for example southern Africa, they are reported to remain essentially solitary or in pairs. Larger concentrations may form as a function of a lack of suitable habitat. South American Painted-snipes, however, seem to keep to themselves or in pairs, although they may sometimes be found in small, dispersed groups of fewer than ten individuals. It is unknown whether, or to what extent, movements outside the breeding season are influenced by factors other than climate. Both species exhibit a propensity for colonizing freshly flooded areas for breeding, and it would seem highly likely that climatic factors play a similarly important role in determining the movements in the non-breeding period.

Relationship with Man

In comparison to the true snipes, painted-snipes are largely silent upon flushing. This is reflected in the popular Portuguese name for the South American Painted-snipe, *Narceja-muda*, the "mute snipe". In Argentina it is known as the "sleepy-head", presumably largely in reference to its habit of roosting during the day, but perhaps also due to its generally quiet, unobtrusive habits, whilst in Chile its local names *Becasina pintada* and *Porotera pintada* reflect features such as its patterned plumage, its long bill and its typical habitat requirements. Amongst British sportsmen in India, the Greater Painted-snipe was colloquially referred to simply as the "Painter". In southern India it was called the "Peacock Snippet", a comment on the fine plumage, particularly of the female, over that of *Gallinago* snipes.

The Greater Painted-snipe was regarded as an easy shot for the competent sportsman in the Indian hill states, for instance in Kashmir, because of its relatively slow, heavy escape flight, added to which in some areas it was commoner than either the Common Snipe (*Gallinago gallinago*) or the Pintail Snipe (*Gallinago stenura*). Consequently the species was looked upon with some disfavour as being an unworthy bag for the true sportsman, although this did not necessarily prevent it from being hunted, sometimes in quite large numbers. In contrast, the flesh of the South American Painted-snipe is highly prized by hunters in Argentina and Chile, for its fine taste. Both species often live in relatively close proximity to man, utilizing partly flooded areas that also serve

The male Greater Painted-snipe's more cryptic plumage offers him better camouflage whilst incubating the eggs, a task which, like nest building, brooding and chick-care, is carried out virtually without help from the female. She remains with him only until she has completed the clutch, whereupon she normally goes off in search of a new mate. Incubation lasts an average of 18-19 days, during which time the male is reckoned to spend 50% of the daylight hours and 89% of the night on the nest. The eggs are pale buffy yellow, heavily marked with blackish brown blotches.

[*Rostratula benghalensis benghalensis*, Virunga National Park, Zaire.
Photo: M. R. Phicton/ Bruce Coleman]

as grazing land for livestock. Indeed, the Greater Painted-snipe, in addition to its traditional use of paddyfields and lotus fields, has also been able to adapt to life in other man-made habitats, such as sewage farms and the shores of dam-lakes. South American Painted-snipes will also breed in and around rice fields.

Not surprisingly, as with most Charadrii, neither species is commonly held in zoos or collections, although limited studies of both have been conducted using captive birds. Small chicks of both species easily become imprinted, closely following human feet. However, although adult birds can be easy to feed, the chicks will not peck at food instinctively, and have to be force-fed, making rearing more difficult.

Status and Conservation

There are few detailed population estimates available for either species, and their skulking and retiring habits make it very difficult to produce accurate assessments of their exact status and sometimes even their precise distribution. Nonetheless, at present, neither species is considered to be threatened. Both species remained unrecorded in certain areas now known to support them, until relatively recently. For instance, the South American Painted-snipe was known from Brazil by only a single specimen, taken in 1891, until the early 1960's, while in West Africa the Greater Painted-snipe, although long suspected to breed, was not conclusively shown to do so until the same decade.

The Greater Painted-snipe is generally regarded as uncommon, although it may be locally common in parts of its range in mainland Africa and Asia. Fluctuations in populations are undeniably hard to gauge, but in Egypt, for example, which boasts a wealth of historical data on its birds, and where recent standardized ornithological activity has been relatively intensive, the species is regarded as stable. During the period of British rule in India the species was quite commonly shot for sport, sometimes in comparatively large numbers. It is not known if such hunting pressure had serious effects, and the fact that the species is currently regarded as generally uncommon throughout the Indian Subcontinent might more probably be put down to habitat loss and deterioration, although judging from the evidence available it may only ever have been common locally. In contrast, in Ja-

pan, where the Greater Painted-snipe was apparently a common resident in the southern islands towards the end of the last century, it is now regarded as local and uncommon there. Habitat destruction and alteration have probably had a negative effect in many parts of its range, but the species is able to use semi-reclaimed wetland areas and has historically made use of rice and lotus paddies for both breeding and feeding, throughout extensive parts of South-east Asia. Indeed, this species also regularly visits reservoirs, sewage pools and other man-made wetlands throughout much of its range, provided that there is suitably thick vegetation close by, suggesting that it may be able to adapt quite readily to new conditions. The effects of long-term drought, a real problem in parts of its African range, are more or less unknown, but could theoretically be more damaging than either hunting or wetland reclamation, at any rate on a relatively localized scale. The race *australis* is generally considered to be rare throughout much of Australia, especially the drier western half, although even in the east it may be locally very rare, for example around Sydney, New South Wales.

There are very few population data available for the South American Painted-snipe. It is regarded as very local in Chile, but during the first half of the 1970's in central Argentina the species was not uncommon, and was even considered to be locally frequent, for instance in parts of Mendoza and Córdoba. Up-to-date information is not available, but given the decline in many species of drier grassland birds in both Argentina and many parts of Brazil, it would not be surprising if a similar decline were discovered in wet grassland birds, such as this species. Throughout its range, the species is highly prized by hunters for its flavoursome meat. Unfortunately, it is frequently shot during the breeding season, because it is a relatively early nester, the shooting season terminating on September 1st, well into the nesting period in many areas.

General Bibliography

Ahlquist (1974a), Beddard (1901), Björklund (1994), Burton (1974), Chu (1995), Dunning (1993), Gochfeld *et al.* (1984), Hayman *et al.* (1986), Jehl (1968), Johnsgard (1981), Lowe (1931), Niethammer (1966), Peters (1934), Prater *et al.* (1977), Richford (1985), Rosair & Cottridge (1995), Sibley & Ahlquist (1972, 1990), Sibley & Monroe (1990), Strauch (1976, 1978).

PLATE 27

inches 4
cm 10

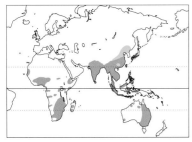

PLATE 27

Family ROSTRATULIDAE (PAINTED-SNIPES)
SPECIES ACCOUNTS

Genus *ROSTRATULA* Vieillot, 1816

1. Greater Painted-snipe
Rostratula benghalensis

French: Rhynchée peinte   **German**: Goldschnepfe   **Spanish**: Aguatero Bengalí

Taxonomy. *Rallus benghalensis* Linnaeus, 1758, Asia.
Races formerly regarded as separate species, but nowadays almost invariably lumped into one, as they differ so little in morphology and behaviour. Two subspecies normally recognized.
Subspecies and Distribution.
R. b. benghalensis (Linnaeus, 1758) - Africa and Madagascar; Pakistan E to NE China, extreme SE Russia (S Ussuriland) and Japan, and S through SE Asia, Greater Sundas and Philippines to Lesser Sundas (Lombok, Sumbawa, Flores).
R. b. australis (Gould, 1838) - Australia.

Descriptive notes. 23-28 cm; c. 90-200 g: wingspan 50-55 cm. Strong sexual dimorphism in plumage and also in size. Male has golden eyepatch, crown stripe and "V" on mantle; rest of head greyish brown, with ashy grey on neck, and throat streaked whitish; extensive golden buff on upperparts, especially upperwing-coverts; rest of underparts and underwing white. Female longer-winged, and brighter and more clearly patterned; head and neck mostly dark rufous, eye-patch clean white; most of upperparts, including wings, dark bronze green, barred finely with black. Both sexes differ from *Nycticryphes semicollaris* in larger size, straighter bill and many details of plumage; tail rounded. Juvenile similar to adult male, but initially lacks sharply separation between dark upper breast and white lower breast; wing-coverts greyer, with smaller, paler buff spots. Race *australis* averages considerably longer-winged; no significant plumage differences.
Habitat. Wetlands in tropical and subtropical lowlands, generally up to c. 1800 m in Himalayas, but usually much lower elsewhere; affects swamps, reedbeds, *jheels*, overgrown rice fields and muddy margins of pools, freshwater lakes with grassy islets, sewage pools, dam-lakes, even mudflats overgrown with marsh grass and mangroves. Habitat use governed by rains, and tends to favour recently flooded areas; in Kenya, usually absent from areas with less than 500 mm of rain annually; in S Africa, absent from large parts of the much drier western half. Occasionally feeds on more open grassland, adjacent to wetlands.
Food and Feeding. Omnivorous. Invertebrates taken include insects, snails, earthworms and crustaceans; also seeds, including a variety of grasses, rice and millet. May feed extensively on seeds, but few precise data on dietary preferences collected to date. In captivity, fed successfully on meat, earthworms and insects. Probes soft ground like true snipes (*Gallinago*); also uses scything action of bill and head in shallow water. Chiefly crepuscular, and may also feed at night. Usually solitary, occasionally in small parties, exceptionally large groups of up to 100.
Breeding. Mostly breeds during or immediately after rains in Africa, with laying mainly Mar-Jun in W Africa, Aug-Nov in S South Africa, but extensive local variation elsewhere, covering all months; also breeds throughout much of year in Asia, with eggs recorded in Nov-Apr in Sri Lanka, chiefly Jul-Sept in India, Jul-Aug in Myanmar, Oct-Dec in Philippines, Feb in Sumatra, and Jul on Flores; recorded in all months in Australia, but mainly Sept-Dec. Female normally polyandrous, but monogamous in some areas, e.g. in S Africa. Solitary nester, but nests may be grouped together due to polyandrous behaviour. Nests on ground, sometimes on low hummock or mound, normally concealed in thick, marshy vegetation; alternatively in more open aquatic environments, e.g. on dense mat of floating water weed; nest is shallow cup usually lined with leaves and stems, occasionally built up with interwoven plant material, but infrequently bare. Usually 4 eggs (2-5); female may lay up to 4 clutches in one season; incubation 15-21 days; downy chicks pale buff with bold pattern of lines on upperparts, greyish below; chicks precocial and nidifugous, brooded and dependent for first few days; fledging period unknown. First breeding probably occurs after 1 year in male, 2 years in female.
Movements. Mainly sedentary in Asia, and in Egypt. Short migrations reported from NE China, NW India (Kashmir) and Japan. Within Africa performs seasonal, but irregular, short distance movements, responding to feeding and breeding habitat requirements, principally in N tropics. Largely nomadic in Australia. Usually remains solitary in non-breeding season, but small, occasionally large, flocks may gather, probably due to scarcity of suitable habitat. Accidental in Afghanistan, Israel (where recently found breeding), Oman, Somalia, Pemba and Zanzibar, and Tibet and Tasmania; listed for Turkey, but probably erroneously.
Status and Conservation. Not globally threatened. Generally uncommon to frequent and even locally common. Few population estimates available, and population trends difficult to establish, due to inconspicuous habits; breeding not recorded in W Africa until 1960's. Perhaps declining in many areas due to drainage of wetlands and destruction of suitable habitat, although recorded in semi-reclaimed areas in Kashmir, and in rice paddies in many countries, e.g. Egypt and Ivory Coast; population considered stable in Egypt. In Japan, was considered a common resident in southern islands during 19th century, but now classed as uncommon and local. Generally rare in Australia, where apparently commoner in E than in drier W, although even in E is locally very rare in apparently suitable habitat, e.g. around Sydney, New South Wales. Uncommon in much of Africa; also in Nepal, China and over much of SE Asia. In past, was commonly hunted in India, although generally regarded as poor sport. Abnormally long periods of drought presumably have serious impact on populations, as breeding appears to hinge on availablity of suitable wetlands, especially in Africa, where species often dependent on seasonally flooded areas.
Bibliography. Ali & Ripley (1980), Anon. (1994b), Baird (1979), Baker (1911, 1921, 1935), Bates & Lowther (1952), Benson (1982), Benson & Benson (1975), Beste (1970), Beven (1913), Brazil (1991), Bright (1935b), Britton (1970), Broekhuysen & Stanford (1953), Clancey (1964b), Corrick (1981, 1982), Cramp & Simmons (1983), Deignan (1945), Dickinson *et al.* (1991), D'Ombrain (1944), Dowsett (1965), Dowsett & Forbes-Watson (1993), Elgood & Donald (1962), Elgood, Fry & Dowsett (1973), Elgood, Heigham *et al.* (1994), Étchécopar & Hüe (1978), Garnett (1992), Ginn *et al.* (1989), Goodman *et al.* (1989), Gore (1990), Grimes (1987), Harrison & Mulligan (1987), Hindwood (1960), Inglis (1940), Irwin (1981), Jaensch (1986, 1989), Kingston (1912), Knystautas (1993), Kobayashi (1948, 1954, 1955), Komeda (1983), Kumerloeve (1961), Lane & Davies (1987), Langrand (1990), Leach *et al.* (1987), Lekagul & Round (1991), Lewis & Pomeroy (1989), Lowe (1963, 1970), Mackworth-Praed & Grant (1957, 1962, 1970), Maclean (1993), Marchant & Higgins (1993), van Marle & Voous (1988), McClure (1974), McGilp (1934), Medway & Wells (1976), Milon *et al.* (1973), Muller (1975), Pakenham (1979), Paludan (1959), Paz (1987), Perennou *et al.* (1994), Phillips (1978), Pinto (1983), Pitman (1912), Rabor (1977), Robertsm, T. J. (1991), Salvan (1968), Schmidt (1961), Shirihai (1996), Skead (1977), Smythies (1986), Summers & Waltner (1979), Susanth *et al.* (1986), Urban *et al.* (1986), Vaurie (1972), Vincent (1945), Wesley (1986, 1990), Wheeler (1955), White & Bruce (1986), Wood-Mason (1878), Yudin (1965).

Genus *NYCTICRYPHES* Wetmore & J. L.Peters, 1923

2. South American Painted-snipe
Nycticryphes semicollaris

French: Rhynchée de Saint-Hilaire   **Spanish**: Aguatero Americano
German: Weißflecken-Goldschnepfe

Taxonomy. *Totanus semi-collaris* Vieillot, 1816, Paraguay.
Sometimes included in *Rostratula*, but exhibits marked differences in morphology and behaviour (see page 292). Monotypic.
Distribution. Paraguay E to SE Brazil and Uruguay, and S to C Chile and C Argentina.

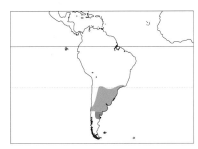

Descriptive notes. 19-23 cm; c. 65-86 g. Longish decurved bill; golden crown stripe, supercilium and "V" on mantle; head, neck and upper breast dark reddish brown; buff on lores and supercilium can be more extensive than depicted; upperparts mainly dark greyish brown and black, with variable white drops on scapulars and wing-coverts, and smaller buff spots on flight-feathers; rump and wedge-shaped tail greyish buff with narrow dark bars; belly white. Virtually no sexual dimorphism known, but female averages slightly larger; may also tend to be slightly brighter, although good evidence lacking. Differs from *Rostratula benghalensis* in generally darker plumage, more sharply decurved bill and distinctive white spots on scapulars and upperwing-coverts; large golden patch around eye reduced to supercilium; bill more bulbous at tip, due to expanded upper mandible, which is pitted towards base; tail distinctly wedge-shaped. Juvenile has drops on scapulars and wing-coverts creamy buff; buff spots on flight-feathers much reduced; throat and breast streaked white and dark brown.

Habitat. Tropical and subtropical lowlands, occurring in open swamps and marshes, along rivers and streams, and in rice fields and wet grassland. Generally favours more open areas than *R. benghalensis*, including estuaries in Argentina and Uruguay. Usually found close to sea-level, but recorded up to over 1000 m in parts of Brazil; unlike *R. benghalensis*, not recorded from montane areas.

Food and Feeding. Crustaceans, insects and their larvae, aquatic invertebrates in general, and seeds. In shallow water, takes shellfish using semi-circular sweeping action of bill, opening and shutting mandibles while tip remains submerged.

Breeding. Apparently breeds mainly during austral spring and summer, probably in all months Jul-Feb, depending on local conditions; also recorded in May, in Brazil; males with enlarged testes late Mar in Mendoza, WC Argentina; pairing may begin as early as middle to late winter. Monogamous; semi-colonial, with small groups of 5-6 nests often found in area of 1-1·5 ha, but no proof of polyandry. Simple ground nest of grasses and reed stems; situated in swamp, where often surrounded by water, or in dense vegetation in wet meadow, at edge of stream or open water, including estuaries. Usually 2 eggs, exceptionally 3; incubation and fledging periods unknown; chicks apparently cared for by both adults.

Movements. Mainly sedentary. Apparently regular seasonal movements recorded in some areas, e.g. in parts of Brazil and in Buenos Aires area, Argentina; regarded as non-breeding migrant to S Río Negro and N Chubut, C Argentina. Makes short distance movements in response to local conditions of drought or flooding, abandoning areas as soon as they become too dry. Largely solitary or in pairs, but outside breeding season may form small, dispersed flocks, of under 10 birds.

Status and Conservation. Not globally threatened. No precise information available on population levels or trends; secretive and nocturnal habits make species difficult to detect. Regarded as very local in Chile. Apparently not uncommon and even locally frequent in parts of C Argentina during 1970's. In Brazil, recorded only once prior to 1961, when discovered in state of Rio de Janeiro. In Argentina and Brazil, habitat alteration and destruction, often related to agricultural development, have caused declines in many birds of dry grasslands, and species of wet grasslands, such as present species, might be similarly affected. Species highly prized by hunters for its succulent flesh; frequently shot during breeding season, as tends to nest early, before local hunting seasons terminate.

Bibliography. Belton (1984), Blake (1977), Bucher & Nores (1988), Canevari *et al*. (1991), Contreras & Contreras (1990), Contreras *et al*. (1990), Cuello & Gergenstien (1962), Dubs (1992), Frisch (1981), Goodall *et al*. (1957), Gore & Gepp (1978), Höhn (1975), Hudson (1920), Johnson (1965b), Klimaitis & Moschione (1987), Meyer de Schauensee (1982), Narosky & Yzurieta (1987), Neithammer (1966), Nores & Yzurieta (1980), Olrog (1984), de la Peña (1992), Pinto (1964), Ruschi (1979), Scott & Carbonell (1986), Sick (1962, 1985c, 1993), Wetmore (1926).

Class AVES
Order CHARADRIIFORMES
Suborder CHARADRII
Family DROMADIDAE (CRAB PLOVER)

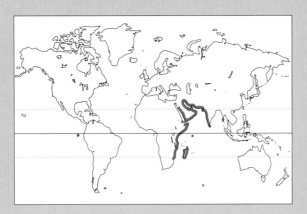

- Medium-sized, long-legged wading birds with thick, powerful bill and burrow-nesting habits.
- 38-41 cm.

- Indian Ocean coasts.
- Coastal sandbanks and tidal mudflats, sandflats and coral reefs.
- 1 genus, 1 species, 1 taxon.
- No species threatened; none extinct since 1600.

Systematics

The Crab Plover (*Dromas ardeola*) is a monotypic species found only on coasts of the Indian Ocean. Its relationship with other Charadriiformes is none too clear, but it is generally considered distinct enough to be awarded a family of its own, Dromadidae.

Although its evolutionary affinities are uncertain, the Crab Plover is usually classified as a wader. Frequently, because of similarities in skeletal characters and body shape, it is placed closest to the thick-knees (Burhinidae) or between the thick-knees and the pratincoles and coursers (Glareolidae); indeed, the results of studies using DNA suggest that it should actually be placed within Glareolidae, with only subfamily status. Then again, in plumage it closely resembles avocets (Recurvirostridae), although in terms of structure and behaviour it is quite different from them.

Some workers believe that the Crab Plover belongs elsewhere within the Charadriiformes. For instance, it is sometimes argued that it is most closely related to the auks (Alcidae), an idea originating from its burrow-nesting habit. Again, the Crab Plover's tarsal scutellation and also the countershaded, but unpatterned, grey down of its chicks are uncharacteristic of waders (Charadrii), and it has been suggested that the species may actually be more closely related to the gulls (Laridae).

With so many divergent opinions in vogue, it is probably most useful to stick to traditional usage for the mean time. A study of the patterns of downy chicks, published in 1968 by J. R. Jehl, proposed the division of all of the waders (Charadrii) into three groups, which may be recognized as superfamilies: the jacanas and painted-snipes (possible superfamily Jacanoidea); the Crab Plover (Dromadoidea); and all the remaining families in the suborder Charadrii (Charadrioidea). This division, which highlights the uniqueness of Dromadidae by awarding it a group or superfamily of its own, has received widespread acceptance and may be considered more or less the "standard" internal classification of the suborder Charadrii.

Morphological Aspects

The Crab Plover is a robust and highly distinctive black and white wader with a disproportionately heavy bill and head, and long legs. Its most conspicuous feature is the thick, relatively short, dagger-like bill, which is used for stabbing and breaking open crab shells. This large, black, laterally compressed bill has a pronounced gonys and an angled lower mandible, and is quite unlike that of any other wader, except perhaps those of the Great Thick-knee (*Esacus recurvirostris*) and the Beach Thick-knee (*Esacus magnirostris*). It may be no coincidence that these latter two species also feed extensively, perhaps almost exclusively, on crabs.

The plumage of the adult Crab Plover is predominantly white, with an obvious black saddle and flight-feathers, and a pale grey tail. In juveniles, the back and the lesser and median wing-coverts are grey, while the crown and hindneck are pale grey with darker streaks and spots. Some adults of both sexes also have darker streaks on the rear of the crown and the hindneck; it has been suggested that these variations are seasonal. In the field, males and females appear identical, the only known difference being that males tend to have slightly longer and heavier bills than females.

The Crab Plover's eye is large, presumably because of the species' crepuscular and nocturnal habits (see General Habits). Its size is emphasized further by black feathering immediately before and behind it. This combines with the down-turned gape of the large bill to give the Crab Plover a rather sad expression.

The legs are greyish blue, and the feet are similar in colour but a little darker. The powerful feet are partially webbed and have a well developed first toe, features which are probably connected with the species' habit of excavating nesting burrows. When walking, Crab Plovers tend to move slowly with a gait similar to that of *Charadrius* plovers. When pursuing crabs and other crustaceans, they adopt a more rapid, dashing walk, similar to that of avocets. During periods of inactivity, Crab Plovers regularly stand with their shoulders hunched, or rest squatting on their tarsi.

The Crab Plover's flight is perhaps slower than that of most other waders, and the wings are held quite stiffly, rather in the style of a thick-knee. In flight, the legs and feet extend beyond the tail, and the head and neck may be either sunk back into the shoulders or extended.

Habitat

A bird of subtropical and tropical Indian Ocean shorelines, the Crab Plover is rarely found more than a kilometre or so from the sea. Its foraging habits restrict it at all times of year to mudflats and sandflats, sandy beaches, estuaries, lagoons and exposed coral reefs. Roosting occurs in the vicinity, for instance typically on sand spits in Aldabra.

For breeding, the species is confined to coastlines and off-shore islands with relatively flat expanses of sand dunes, sand banks or sandy warrens. This restriction in breeding habitat ties in closely with the fact that, unique among waders, it nests in burrows (see Breeding).

General Habits

Crab Plovers are highly gregarious and noisy, whether breeding, on passage or at their wintering grounds. The species nests colonially in burrows (see Breeding), and this gives rise to a number of differences with other waders in terms of breeding biology and behaviour. For example, young Crab Plovers remain in the nest for several days after hatching, and food is brought to them by the adults.

When feeding, Crab Plovers can be seen in large flocks, and over 1000 have been seen together at non-breeding grounds in the Providence Group of Aldabra. Birds most often split up into small groups of 20 or more birds, although some individuals forage alone. When the tide is high, flocks concentrate from far around to roost communally, and birds within a radius of as much as 20 km may gather at traditional sites. In the Gulf of Kutch, up to 1200 birds have been recorded at a traditional roost-site on Bhaidar Island.

Both during and outside the breeding season, birds are most active at dusk and at night, but they also feed during the day. Crepuscular and nocturnal behaviour may be more accentuated during the breeding season, though it may cease on dark nights.

Voice

Crab Plovers are noisy, raucous birds. On the breeding grounds a constant chattering "tchuck-tchuck" can be heard, often well into the night. A shriller call, "tchuck-tchuck chuk-chuk-chuk", is given less frequently, but this call can carry up to 1·5 km. When a bird enters its nesting burrow at dawn, it will usually utter a rapid series of short and long notes, and, if disturbed by intruders, an incubating bird will hiss.

Outside the breeding season, Crab Plover flocks maintain a regular restless chattering, interspersed with far-carrying "ha-how" or "crow-ow-ow" notes and a musical "prooit". When alarmed, birds emit a loud sharp "kjep" or "kiep", repeated four or five times.

The calls of downy chicks resemble those of domestic hens. Half-grown young solicit food from their parents with a constant wheeze, resembling that produced by the young of *Larus* gulls. On migration and on their wintering grounds, young birds will beg for food from adults with a high, plaintive, twittering whistle, which rises in pitch.

Food and Feeding

As the bird's name suggests, crabs constitute the major component of the Crab Plover's diet. At any rate on Aldabra, and perhaps elsewhere, those crab species that burrow are particularly favoured. They are stalked and caught with a stab of the bill, and, if small, are swallowed whole. Larger crabs are shaken to dismember them of both claws and legs, and they are then broken into pieces by blows from the bird's powerful bill, before finally being consumed. Other crustaceans, small molluscs, marine worms and other intertidal invertebrates are also eaten, and

Even in flight, there are certain features that readily betray the identity of the Crab Plover, preventing confusion with any other waders of pied plumage. The massive bill, the conspicuously white head and neck and the long, pointed wings are all obvious. The white "V" on the lower back stands out against the black saddle, and the mostly black flight-feathers contrast strongly with the white wing lining. The length of the neck is not always apparent as it is often held hunched up into the shoulders. The wings are held rather stiffly and, as in avocets, the legs and toes trail well beyond the end of the short tail. Flight tends not to be as fast as in most other waders.

[*Dromas ardeola*, Malindi, Kenya. Photo: Paul Doherty/ Windrush Photos]

This sturdy, long-legged wader's most obvious peculiarity is its huge black bill, splendidly adapted for dealing with its main prey, crabs. These are either stabbed and swallowed whole, or are crushed first, all according to the size of the crab. The bird's head is also large, as are its eyes, the size of the latter being emphasized by dark smudges on both sides. In contrast, the neck is scarcely visible when the bird stands at rest with its shoulders hunched. The long, robust bluish grey legs have powerful partially webbed feet, effective tools when used in conjunction with the bill to excavate nesting burrows in sand dunes.

[Dromas ardeola, Barr al Hikman, Oman. Photo: Hanne & Jens Eriksen/Aquila]

the species has been seen feeding on mantis shrimps in the Andaman Islands and on mudskippers in Iraq.

Feeding is usually a restless, noisy and gregarious activity for Crab Plovers, which often gather in sizeable flocks to forage on mudflats, sandflats and exposed coral reefs, or elsewhere in shallow water. Flock members walk slowly in the same direction, often with a space of about two to five metres between individual birds. When a crab is spotted, a stalking bird advances rapidly in a short run, its partially webbed feet allowing it to move quickly even over silty mud. Prey items on the surface or in shallow water are stabbed with the bill, which may be held open during such strikes. Crab Plovers will also probe the substrate on occasion.

Young downy chicks are fed by their parents on pulped crab which has been brought back to the nest-burrow; older chicks are given whole live crabs to deal with.

Breeding

The Crab Plover is a colonial breeder, nesting at a small number of scattered coastal colonies. The largest colony for which an estimate of numbers has been made supports 1500 pairs, but most of the known colonies are considerably smaller. In and around the Arabian Peninsula, the breeding season begins in April and ends in June or July, with the first young seen in May and June. In Somalia, egg-laying does not take place until May or June.

It is assumed, but not known, that Crab Plovers are monogamous. Certainly, post-breeding behaviour is exhibited by groups of two adults and one juvenile, which arrive together on some wintering grounds and which are assumed to be family parties. However, groups of up to ten birds may attend nest-burrows; the precise implications of this are uncertain, but at the very least it

would seem to indicate that pairs may nest in very close proximity to one another.

Unique among waders, the Crab Plover nests in burrows. These are excavated, probably by both male and female, in relatively flat coastal sand dunes and other sandy substrates. The bird probably loosens the substrate with its bill, and then scratches the sand out using its powerful feet. Completed burrows are about 1 to 2·5 m long, about 20 cm in diameter, and slope downwards obliquely to a depth of about 50 cm. At this deepest point, the burrow rises slightly and opens out to form a chamber, in which a shallow, unlined hollow is created for the egg. Burrows may change direction several times along their length and it is possible that they are reused and extended in successive breeding seasons.

This habit of burrow-nesting is most likely to have originated as a mechanism for reducing nest predation. It is also postulated that, since the downy young are countershaded but unpatterned, the use of burrows may be a fairly recent adaptation for avoiding intense solar radiation. Indeed, if a chick is exposed to sunlight it instantly runs for shade.

The clutch almost always consists of a single egg, though occasionally two are laid. The egg itself is very large for the size of the bird, being 60-65 mm long and 43-47 mm wide, and weighing an estimated 45 g. Unlike the eggs of other wader species, which tend to be cryptically patterned, the Crab Plover's egg is pure white, a clear consequence of its burrow-nesting habit, which obviates the need for camouflaging the egg. The roles of sexes during incubation and chick rearing are not known, but eight adults that were collected from nests were all females. The presence of what are assumed to be family parties later in the year may suggest that both parents remain together throughout the breeding cycle and beyond.

Upon hatching, the young are unable to walk, and, again unlike any other waders, they remain in their nests for several days where they are dependent on the adults to bring them food. Older chicks may venture out to the burrow entrance to beg for food. Even when capable of leaving the burrow, young birds often remain there, and, once they have finally abandoned the nest, they still depend heavily on the adults for food. Frequent, persistent and sometimes indiscriminate begging for food by juveniles continues on the wintering grounds.

Movements

The Crab Plover is at least a partial migrant, and all individuals may well leave their breeding areas outside the breeding season. However, so little is known about the exact breeding range of the species that the full extent of its migration remains unclear.

It is thought that in August, after the breeding season, many adults and young move out of the Persian Gulf. These birds are thought to move southwards down the east coast of Africa or across the Indian Ocean. However, not all the birds move so far, and in the United Arab Emirates birds that breed in the colony on the island of Abu al Abyadh are thought to winter only about 250 km away at Khor al Beidah. The species is probably a passage migrant and winter visitor to southern Arabia. However, it has been recorded in all months of the year from Yemen, and it may breed on offshore islands in southern parts of the Red Sea, as indeed it does further north, off the Saudi Arabian coast.

In Africa, breeding has only been confirmed off Somalia, where the species is common from March to October. Nevertheless, the species is also suspected of breeding in Sudan and Eritrea. From September through until April, Crab Plovers are widespread along the coasts of Kenya and Tanzania, including Zanzibar, and also to a lesser extent those of Madagascar and the Seychelles; a few travel as far south as Natal. Small numbers remain throughout the northern summer on wintering grounds in the Indian Ocean, especially on Aldabra and down the East African coasts.

Lesser numbers of birds have been recorded moving along the coast of Pakistan after the breeding season, but a large concentration has been found to occur in winter nearby in the Gulf of Kutch. Crab Plovers also winter east to Sri Lanka and the Andaman Islands.

Little is known about how the birds migrate, but the limited evidence available suggests that they do so in flocks, flying low and fast over the water in tight formations, usually at night.

Relationship with Man

The coastal habitat requirements, especially the isolated sandy areas used for breeding, combined with the crepuscular and nocturnal habits of the Crab Plover, serve to ensure that the species has relatively little contact with man. A direct consequence of this is that the effects of human interference appear to be of minimal importance to this species (see Status and Conservation).

Crab Plovers are not shy, especially once they become more active towards dusk. One extraordinary story illustrates their boldness. When four individuals were shot by a collector from amongst a flock of 400, the remaining birds waded into the water and crowded round the corpses, pushing them along in the water and chattering loudly. Once the dead birds were retrieved, the flock followed the collector back onto dry land. Several other similar incidents have been reported.

Status and Conservation

The Crab Plover is endemic to the coastlines of the Indian Ocean region. The number of breeding colonies known is small, and they are situated in remote and isolated places. Consequently, little is known about population sizes, and even less about changes in numbers through time. Nevertheless, the Crab Plover is clearly sufficiently abundant to be at no immediate risk of global extinction. This said, if any of the large, densely packed breeding colonies were to be wiped out or severely threatened, the fortunes of the species might change dramatically.

The most comprehensive and thorough survey of sites important for the conservation of avifauna in the Middle East was carried out by BirdLife International and the Ornithological Society of the Middle East, in co-operation with the International Waterfowl and Wetlands Research Bureau between 1991 and 1994. The study highlighted the importance of the region for Crab Plovers.

In the non-breeding season the Crab Plover does occur singly on occasions, but it is essentially gregarious in all seasons. It forms large breeding colonies with the nest-burrows packed closely together; one colony is known to contain 1500 pairs, although most are much smaller. When feeding too it can be seen in large flocks which may disband into smaller groups to forage. Huge noisy gatherings are common on traditional roosting sites at high tide in winter.

[Dromas ardeola, Khor al Beidah, United Arab Emirates. Photo: Axel Halley]

The Crab Plover has highly unusual breeding habits. Alone among waders it excavates a nesting burrow, up to 2·5 m long with the nesting chamber at the end, where the single large pure white egg is laid. The chicks are altricial, unable to walk at hatching, and, unlike other wader young, they stay at the nest, in this case the burrow, for several days. They remain wholly dependent on their parents for food for a long time, and even in their winter quarters they may be observed begging insistently for food.

[Dromas ardeola, Barr al Hikman, Oman. Photo: Hanne & Jens Eriksen/Aquila]

Of the 391 sites identified as Important Bird Areas, 30 are of conservation value to Crab Plovers. These include all the known breeding colonies, apart from the one off the coast of Somalia.

Only nine breeding colonies are definitely known to exist, eight of which are in the Middle East. The largest is in Iran, with approximately 1500 pairs nesting on Ummal Karan Island, where the birds appear to be unprotected but not threatened. Also in Iran are two much smaller colonies, of 20 and two or more pairs, both of which fall within protected areas. At the southern end of the Persian Gulf, the United Arab Emirates supports two colonies: one, on Abu al Abyadh Island, supports about 280 pairs and is protected by the island's owner; the second is a smaller colony of 35-38 pairs at Umm Amin. Masirah Island, off Oman, has one colony of about 85 pairs, and may suffer low levels of exploitation. In Saudi Arabia there are two breeding colonies along the Red Sea coast at Al Wajh Bank, and in the Farasan Islands, where approximately 110 pairs nest; there may be a third colony at Qishran Bay. In Yemen, breeding is suspected at four different sites, but confirmation is still required. The species now appears to be present all year round in Kuwait and Iraq, but it is not thought to breed there. The only known breeding population outside the Middle East occurs on the islets of Zeyla Saad Din and Aibat, off Somalia, but the numbers present are not known. Breeding is also suspected on the coasts of Sudan and Eritrea.

The non-breeding distribution is much wider with birds turning up sporadically as far east as Thailand and Malaysia, north to the Mediterranean coast of Turkey and south to Natal. In India, one individual was recorded 100 km inland from the sea. Mostly, however, Crab Plovers remain on the coasts between southern Arabia, Madagascar and India; they are most numerous along the Kenyan and Tanzanian coastlines.

No threats to the Crab Plover are currently known to exist. The Persian Gulf suffers chronic oil pollution, especially at its north-western end, as, to a lesser extent, does the Red Sea. This could directly affect Crab Plovers foraging on polluted coastlines, and could have an indirect and possibly more damaging long-term effect on their food supply. However, data following the 1990/91 Gulf War suggest that the consequent oil pollution had only a minimal impact upon this species. In Kuwait, for example, during studies of the effects of oil pollution on waders, out of 35 Crab Plovers observed only four were oiled, and only one of these showed heavy oiling likely to result in death. Farther south along the Saudi Arabian coastline during the 1991 spring and autumn migration periods, no evidence of oiled Crab Plovers was found, even though oil pollution was much more severe, and other species of waders were suffering considerable losses.

The most likely potential threat to Crab Plovers is the destruction of breeding colonies. Considerable exploitation of both birds and eggs was reported from the breeding colonies of Iraq at the beginning of the present century. Up-to-date information of human impact on these populations is lacking, but recent data from breeding populations in Oman, the United Arab Emirates and Saudi Arabia show little evidence of human persecution. Indeed, significant exploitation is unlikely, given that these areas are mostly uninhabited and often largely inaccessible. It has been suggested that the offshore islet colonies in Somalia are exploited, and that the suspected breeding populations in Sudan and Eritrea may suffer some human impact, but none of this has yet been proved. Away from the breeding colonies exploitation is almost non-existent, though birds are occasionally catapulted on the East African coast and in the inner Seychelles. Human exploitation of breeding colonies probably continues to a small extent in some of these areas, but for the time being the level of exploitation is unlikely to be having a significant effect on the species as a whole.

PLATE 28

inches   5
cm   13

Family DROMADIDAE (CRAB PLOVER)
SPECIES ACCOUNTS   PLATE 28

Genus *DROMAS*   Paykull, 1805

Crab Plover

Dromas ardeola

French: Drome ardéole   **German**: Reiherläufer   **Spanish**: Dromas

Taxonomy. *Dromas Ardeola* Paykull, 1805, India.
Relationships uncertain; perhaps closest to Burhinidae and Glareolidae, but frequently awarded separate superfamily on its own, mainly on grounds of plumage of downy chicks; sometimes considered related to Laridae, or to Alcidae because of burrow-nesting habits. Monotypic.
Distribution. Coasts of Indian Ocean. Breeds on shores of NW Indian Ocean, Persian Gulf and Red Sea. Non-breeders regularly range S to Kenya, Tanzania and Madagascar, and E to W India, N Sri Lanka and Andaman Is; also small numbers to NE South Africa, and to single site in SW Thailand.
Descriptive notes. 38-41 cm; 230-325 g; wingspan 74-78 cm. Unmistakable black and white wader, with stout black bill and long bluish grey legs. Plumage white apart from black back, flight-feathers, primaries, and primary and greater coverts; tail greyish. Large dark eye. Sexes similar. Juvenile lacks distinctive adult pattern, which is replaced by grey-brown wing-coverts, blotchy black-brown crown and hindneck, silvery grey mantle and browner tail.
Habitat. Sandy coastlines and islands, intertidal sandflats and mudflats, estuaries, lagoons and exposed coral reefs. Also recorded on rocky shorelines.
Food and Feeding. Predominantly crabs, but also other crustaceans, small molluscs, marine worms and other intertidal invertebrates. Most often feeds in flocks on mudflats at low tide or in shallow water. Most active at dusk and at night. Feeds by picking and probing and slow stalking; crabs are stabbed with open bill, then crushed and eaten.
Breeding. Season Apr-Jul. Breeds colonially in burrows set close together, forming honeycomb effect in sandy areas. Nest is unlined chamber at end of burrow 100-250 cm long, in sandy substrate. Normally 1 egg, rarely 2; no data on incubation; chicks have plain grey down; nidiculous, fed by parents in

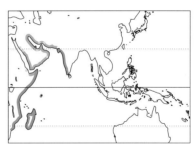

nest chamber; when older, fed at mouth of burrow; fledglings at least partially dependent on parents for several months.
Movements. Partially migratory, but extent of movement obscured by uncertainty of breeding range. Winters throughout breeding range in Persian Gulf, Red Sea, southern Arabia and Somalia, but many birds move S down coast of East Africa to Tanzania and Madagascar area, others E to India; also occurs on many Indian Ocean islands. Few birds S to Natal; rare but annual winter visitor to SW Thailand, also ranging S to Malaysia.
Status and Conservation. Not globally threatened. No overall population estimate available. Of 9 known breeding colonies, over 1500 pairs breed in Iran, at least 300 pairs in United Arab Emirates, 85 pairs in Oman, at least 110 pairs in Saudi Arabia and unknown numbers in Somalia; may also breed in Kuwait, Iraq, Yemen, Sudan and Eritrea. No evidence of changes in numbers; persecution probably only occurs on local scale. No specific threats known, partly because species inhabits relatively isolated areas and is primarily nocturnal. The small number of breeding colonies known implies species vulnerable to effects of oil pollution and human exploitation; also introduction of potential predators to breeding islands, which could have devastating effects.

Bibliography. Ali & Ripley (1980), Appert (1971), Archer & Godman (1937-1961), Benson (1960), Bharucha & Samant (1984), Björklund (1994), Bouwman (1987), Bregnballe *et al.* (1990), Brooks *et al.* (1987), Brown *et al.* (1991), Carp (1980), Cowan (1990), Cramp & Simmons (1983), Dowsett & Forbes-Watson (1993), Evans, M. I. (1988, 1994), Evans, M. I. & Keijl (1993), Feare (1985), Ginn *et al.* (1989), Gochfeld *et al.* (1984), Goodman *et al.* (1989), Hayman *et al.* (1986), Hollom *et al.* (1988), Jehl (1968b), Jennings (1981a, 1988), Johnsgard (1981), Langrand (1990), Mackworth-Praed & Grant (1957, 1962), Maclean (1993), Meinertzhagen (1954), Milon *et al.* (1973), Moore & Balzarotti (1983), Morris, R. P. (1992), Neelakantan *et al.* (1980), Pakenham (1979), Palmes & Briggs (1986), Phillips (1978), Pilcher & Sexton (1993), Rands *et al.* (1987), Richardson, C. (1990), Roberts, T. J. (1991), Sibley & Ahlquist (1985, 1990), Summers, Underhill, Pearson & Scott (1987), Swennen *et al.* (1987), Ticehurst, Buxton & Cheesman (1922), Ticehurst, Cox & Cheesman (1926), Urban *et al.* (1986), Verhage *et al.* (1990), Widgery (1982), Wright (1995).

Class AVES
Order CHARADRIIFORMES
Suborder CHARADRII
Family HAEMATOPODIDAE (OYSTERCATCHERS)

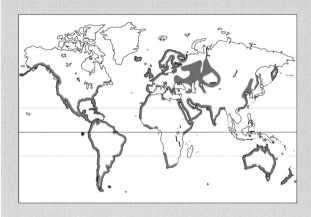

- Medium-sized shorebirds, with black or black and white plumage, pinkish legs and a long, dagger-like orange-red bill.
- 40-51 cm.

- Cosmopolitan, but absent from polar regions and marginal in tropical parts of Africa and Asia.
- Mainly coastal, but also inland in Palearctic and New Zealand.
- 1 genus, 11 species, 16 taxa.
- 2 species threatened; 1 of these probably extinct since 1600.

Systematics

Oystercatchers have a worldwide distribution and all taxa are either black or black and white, apart from the Variable Oystercatcher (*Haematopus unicolor*) of New Zealand, which can be either. Despite the large geographical range of the genus, there has been little morphological divergence between species. As a consequence, the group has a chequered taxonomic history. In general, in the past, discrete populations of black morphs have been treated as full species, Old World pied morphs have been treated as subspecies of the Eurasian Oystercatcher (*Haematopus ostralegus*), and New World pied morphs, with the exception of the Magellanic Oystercatcher (*Haematopus leucopodus*), have been treated as subspecies of the American Oystercatcher (*Haematopus palliatus*).

One of the problems underlying the classification of oystercatchers is the co-occurrence of species. In western South America, Australia and New Zealand, two oystercatcher species occur sympatrically. In all instances, one species is a black or polymorphic rocky shore specialist, while the other is a pied bird which typically forages on soft substrates. In southern South America, three species co-occur. The rocky shore niche is filled by the Blackish Oystercatcher (*Haematopus ater*) and the soft substrate niche by the American Oystercatcher. The third species, the Magellanic Oystercatcher, typically occupies marshy and inland habitats.

It was proposed in the 1950's that oystercatchers had evolved as dark-plumaged birds in Eurasia. Emigrants from this stock would have moved south during the Pliocene to establish themselves as isolated new species in Australia, New Zealand, southern Africa and South America. Following this southward movement, a mutation occurred in the north, with pied birds having a selective advantage over black morphs. Subsequently, there was a second southerly movement, of pied forms, during the Pleistocene. These birds settled in the south as "secondary immigrants", sometimes in areas where black forms were already established. The two species, however, were able to co-exist by virtue of evolved ecological differences.

Whilst this scenario may have some merit in that it does not require an explanation as to how sympatric speciation may have occurred, it seems flawed on several grounds. For example, it implicitly assumes that the southern black forms would have undergone niche contraction in the absence of a potential competitor. The initial premise, that prototypical oystercatchers were

black, may also be wrong. It seems likely that the pied Magellanic Oystercatcher, which is behaviourally unique among the oystercatchers in several respects, split off early from the main lineage. The Magellanic Oystercatcher also has a pale yellow eye-ring encircling a yellow eye, and secondaries that are virtually all white: these two features are unique among the oystercatchers. It is also the only New World oystercatcher to have black, not brown, dorsal coloration. Black dorsal coloration is common to all Old World species. Further evidence for the Magellanic Oystercatcher being a primitive species is that it shows several close affinities with the oldest known oystercatcher fossil, from Lower Pliocene deposits in North Carolina. Features of this species, in particular, call into question the validity of the "migration-mutation" explanation for oystercatcher distribution, as well as the initial assumption that the oystercatchers have a northern origin.

Chick coloration varies between species, but there are some consistent features of New and Old World taxa. The claws of New World chicks are dark at the base, whereas those of Old World taxa are pale. With the exception of the Magellanic Oystercatcher, the crown of New World chicks is unspotted or lightly spotted with black, while that of Old World taxa is prominently spotted and streaked with black. The crown patterning of Magellanic Oystercatcher resembles that of Old World taxa, further highlighting its enigmatic taxonomic status.

The majority of the world's oystercatchers occur in the Southern Hemisphere. Including the probably extinct Canarian Black Oystercatcher (*Haematopus meadewaldoi*), four species breed in the Northern Hemisphere compared with nine in the Southern Hemisphere. Two of the three surviving northern species are migratory, whereas no southern species migrates more than a few degrees of latitude between breeding and non-breeding grounds. These observations strongly suggest that the origins of the oystercatchers lie in Gondwanaland, and not in the Holarctic. Consistent differences between Old and New World forms in both dorsal plumage and eye colour suggest that these characters diverged following the separation of South America from the rest of Gondwanaland. If pied plumage is primitive, as indicated by the Magellanic Oystercatcher, then melanism arose independently in the two lineages. Recent studies have concluded that the oystercatchers and the avocets and stilts (Recurvirostridae) are closely related. If this is the case, the latter might be predicted to have a similar pattern of distribution to the oystercatchers. Although the Recurvirostridae are not as diverse as the Haematopodidae, six out of seven of the world's avocets

and stilts breed in the Southern Hemisphere whereas only three breed in the north. Also, 45% of the world's oystercatchers breed in Australasia, as do 57% of the world's avocets and stilts. It has been stated that the South Island Oystercatcher (*H. ostralegus finschi*) of New Zealand is a Palearctic element in the Australasian fauna. It is perhaps better to consider the three races of Eurasian Oystercatcher in the north as southern elements in the Palearctic fauna.

The internal taxonomy of the Haematopodidae still poses several problems regarding the recognition of full species. The South Island Oystercatcher, herein considered a race of the Eurasian Oystercatcher, has alternatively been treated as a full species, or a race of either the Australian Pied Oystercatcher (*Haematopus longirostris*) or the Variable Oystercatcher. However, as well as being morphologically similar to other races of the Eurasian Oystercatcher, it shares with them the inland breeding habit. Populations of both *H. o. ostralegus* and *H. o. finschi* have increased considerably this century as the inland breeding habit has become more prevalent.

The Sooty Oystercatcher (*Haematopus fuliginosus*) is usually considered to include the form *opthalmicus*, the Spectacled Oystercatcher, as a race. The two are phenetically similar, but the Spectacled differs from the Sooty in having a broader bill and a fleshy yellowish to orange orbital ring, that of the Sooty being bright orange-red. The ranges of the Sooty and the Spectacled do not overlap in the east of Australia, but there is a putative area of intergrading between Point Cloates and Shark Bay in the west. However, the specimen evidence for this intergrading is very slim, much of the literature in support of it is confused, and there is no field evidence for hybridization between the two; indeed, most authors give the range of the Spectacled as being limited merely to the Gulf of Carpentaria and the Cape York Peninsula, which would situate the putative zone of hybridization 2700 km west of the supposed western limit of this form! Unquestionably, further investigation is required, both in the field and in the laboratory, but the marked differences, especially in the bare parts, suggest that they may well prove to be separate species.

The pied form *galapagensis* of the Galapagos Islands is normally treated as a subspecies of the American Oystercatcher. It is geographically isolated from all other populations of this species, and differs in having markedly hypertrophied feet and often an irregular lower border to the black breast. The same foot character is found in the Chatham Oystercatcher (*Haematopus chathamensis*), and is one of the only features distinguishing this species from the pied morph of the Variable Oystercatcher; it also has an irregular lower breast border. The case for separating the Galapagos form from the American Oystercatcher may, in fact, be just as strong as that for separating the Chatham Oyster-

catcher from the Variable. However, in the absence of any other *a priori* compelling evidence for separating the two, *galapagensis* is for the time being probably best retained as a subspecies of the American Oystercatcher.

Morphological Aspects

The lack of morphological divergence among the oystercatchers is one of the main reasons why their systematics are so poorly understood. This statement holds true not only for body dimensions, but also for plumage. Apart from differences in eye and dorsal coloration between the New and Old Worlds (see Systematics), all pied taxa have dark upperparts, a black head, neck and upper breast, a white lower breast and belly, a black tail with white uppertail-coverts and a white bar in the upperwing. The Magellanic Oystercatcher is an exception in having white secondaries, and, on the underwing, showing wholly dark primaries and primary coverts. All black taxa have completely dark plumage. The Variable Oystercatcher is unique among oystercatchers, indeed among waders, in being strikingly polymorphic. The

Most oystercatchers are coastal breeders, favouring habitats ranging from rocky or stony shores to sandy, shingly beaches, and even salt-marshes. The African Black Oystercatcher, a scarce species with an estimated population of only about 5000 birds, breeds on both rocky shores and sandy beaches, often in dense colonies on offshore islands. Outside the breeding season it can occur in flocks in estuaries and lagoons. The sand dunes of the Namib-Naukluft Park provide a dramatic backdrop to this small flock taking off from the shoreline.

[Haematopus moquini, Namib-Naukluft Park, Namibia.
Photo: Thomas Dressler/ Planet Earth]

majority of the population (70%) is black, about 20% are pied, and the remainder are intermediate between the two extremes and are known colloquially as "smudgies". The black morph is most frequent in the south of the range.

Immature oystercatchers are characterized by having buffy margins to the dark feathering, giving them a slightly scaled appearance. They also have a much reduced, and dull-coloured, eye-ring. With the exception of the Blackish Oystercatcher, the legs of immatures are dusky grey and the bills are heavily suffused with brown: the adult bill colour develops from the base towards the tip. The bill and legs of the immature Blackish Oystercatcher are more of a horn colour.

In general, black morphs and the polymorphic Variable Oystercatcher are heavier than pied morphs. Of the taxa for which mensural data exist, the smallest birds are South Island Oystercatchers, in which males average 538 g and females 559 g, and Eurasian Oystercatchers, with males 594 g and females 608 g. The largest taxa are the African Black Oystercatcher (*Haematopus moquini*), with males 666 g and females 722 g, and the Variable Oystercatcher, which in the black morph has males of 678 g and females of 724 g, but in the pied morph males 717 g and females 779 g.

There is consistent sexual dimorphism in both body weight and bill length in all species: females are heavier and longer-billed than males. On average, the shortest bills belong to male African Black Oystercatchers, at 63 mm, and the longest to female Variable Oystercatchers of the intermediate morph, at 95 mm. Bill lengths of individual Eurasian Oystercatchers, and probably of other species too, vary seasonally depending on the choice of foraging habitat: bills tend to be longer when birds are foraging in soft substrates, such as fields, than when foraging on rocky shores, where the bill tip becomes abraded. Considering all oystercatcher species together, there are consistent differences in bill length between species that typically forage on soft substrates and those that forage on rocky shores, with means of 82±8 mm for males and 89±6 mm for females in the former, and 72±6 mm for males and 78±4 mm for females in the latter.

Within species, there is an overlap in bill length between the sexes. However, within pairs of African Black Oystercatchers, the female's bill is invariably longer than the male's. This consistent difference, which is linked to a difference in diet, may be related to minimizing territory size and thus the costs of territory defence.

The long bill of oystercatchers comprises an outer protective layer which is keratinized (the rhamphotheca) and an inner bony core which contains nerves and blood vessels. The rhamphotheca is thickest close to the bill tip, and is joined to the core by connective tissue containing many nerves and few blood vessels. The nerves of the core branch towards the bill tip, and the distal 15 mm of the bill, contain many Herbst's Corpuscles. These corpuscles are believed to act as mechano-receptors, which would come into play when the bird is foraging by touch rather than by sight, for instance in soft mud. Oystercatcher species which forage in soft sediments have more pointed, and presumably more sensitive, bills than those that feed on rocky shores. The blade-like bill, coupled with the bony core, is an excellent tool for capturing and handling shellfish. However, the highly sensory nature of the bill tip suggests that oystercatchers evolved from a tactile-foraging ancestor. This, in turn, suggests that use of rocky shores, and its link to black plumage, are derived rather than primitive features of oystercatchers, providing further support for a pied ancestor (see Systematics).

Being coastal birds that forage extensively along the seashore and feed mainly on marine creatures, oystercatchers have well developed salt glands, which are situated in the supra-orbital area. These enable the birds to drain off excess salt from the blood stream, if there is a build-up caused by their prey or imbibed sea water.

In keeping with other morphological characters, wing length is highly conservative within the group. Wing length averages 252-289 mm in males, and 252-285 mm in females. Despite these figures, females generally have longer wings than males, in keeping with their larger body size, but this is not a strict rule. For instance, the average wing lengths of male and female African Black Oystercatchers are identical, and the wings of male Sooty

Oystercatchers are longer than those of the females. There is no difference in the ratio of wing length to body weight in migratory and sedentary oystercatchers. The flight of oystercatchers is powerful, fast and direct, but they lack the manoeuvrability typically seen in members of Charadriidae and Scolopacidae.

They move freely about on land, and can run quite fast, although again they are probably somewhat less graceful than members of some of the other wader families. Relative to most other waders, the legs and feet are sturdy. Even so, African Black Oystercatchers foraging on rocky shores are regularly found to be missing one or more toes, or have toes that have been partially amputated. Such damage presumably occurs on sharp rocks or mussels. The unusually hypertrophied feet of the Galapagos race of the American Oystercatcher (see Systematics) are presumably an adaptation to minimize such damage: this species forages on shores of solidified lava, which are particularly sharp and jagged.

Oystercatchers normally have a complete post-breeding moult. Primary moult is descendant and, at least in the Eurasian Oystercatcher, secondary moult starts six to eight weeks after the beginning of primary moult. Post-breeding moult in some species, such as the Eurasian and African Black, usually starts while adults are still feeding young, and, in the case of the migratory Eurasian, often while they are still on the breeding grounds. The post-breeding moult of this species takes place mostly between June and November, with a tendency for more northerly breeders to start their moult later than southerly breeders. Post-breeding moult in the partially migratory South Island Oystercatcher starts in January, and is mostly completed by April, whereas in the more sedentary Australian Pied Oystercatcher it extends from January to May. In sedentary species, this moult tends to be more protracted than in migratory and partially migratory species. Thus in the Sooty Oystercatcher it lasts from January or February to June, in the Variable from December to July, and in the African Black from March to November. Eurasian Oystercatchers undergo a short, partial pre-breeding moult, mainly affecting the head and neck feathers, but whether all oystercatcher species do so is not known.

Habitat

Most oystercatchers are coastal breeders, nesting in a range of habitats from rocky shores to shingle and sand beaches, and salt-marshes. Some species, however, also breed inland. The central Palearctic race *longipes* of the Eurasian Oystercatcher has an entirely inland breeding distribution from the Black and Caspian Seas northwards, while portions of the populations of nominate *ostralegus* and the race *osculans*, respectively of the Western and Eastern Palearctic, also breed inland. In the south, Magellanic and South Island Oystercatchers breed inland, as do a few Australian Pied Oystercatchers. Extensive inland breeding by Western Palearctic Eurasian Oystercatchers and South Island Oystercatchers has evolved only during this century, concomitant with major population increases of both species. All of the species that breed away from the coast are species which habitually forage on soft substrates. This foraging behaviour is carried across to the inland breeding areas, where earth-dwelling arthropods dominate the diet. Most inland-breeding birds move to the coast outside the breeding season, including birds of central Palearctic *longipes*, which move south to the coasts of the Arabian Gulf and north-east Africa.

None of the rocky shore specialists, including all of the black taxa, breeds inland. Some of them do, however, undergo seasonal shifts in habitat choice. Those Eurasian Oystercatchers which forage on rocky shores during the breeding season move onto soft substrates, especially estuaries, during the winter. American Black Oystercatchers (*Haematopus bachmani*) and Sooty Oystercatchers also increase their use of soft substrates during the non-breeding season. In the case of American Black Oystercatchers, this seasonal shift is linked with avoidance of winter storms. The classification of oystercatchers as hard or soft substrate foragers is a useful one for ecological comparisons of the different species, but all species exhibit some plasticity in their habitat choice, indicating that they are not highly specialized at the species level. The lack of specialization at this level is presumably linked to the morphological conservatism of oystercatchers worldwide.

Oystercatchers have a highly developed system of displays used in various behavioural contexts, such as territory-holding, courtship and attention-distraction, most of them accompanied by varyied piping calls. The Magellanic Oystercatcher is remarkable for its cocked-tail display in the breeding season: as the bird bends forward, it raises its tail vertically, so as to reveal in startling fashion the pure white undertail-coverts. Notable features of this species are the yellow eye-ring and the almost completely white secondaries.

[*Haematopus leucopodus*, New Island, Falkland Islands. Photo: Kenneth W. Fink]

African Black Oystercatchers can be found on both sandy and rocky shores throughout the year, but during the breeding season part of the population moves away from mainland rocky shores onto sandy beaches and rocky offshore islands. This change in habitat use is probably not linked to either food supply or weather conditions, but is mediated by predation. Birds breeding on islands which are predator-free have much higher breeding success than mainland birds. Breeding success on the mainland may be higher on sandy beaches than on rocky shores, because predators are more easily detected on beaches. Incubating adults themselves are at considerable risk from nocturnal mammalian predators.

General Habits

All oystercatchers are territorial during the breeding season, and a proportion of the population of some species, including the Australian Pied, African Black and Chatham Oystercatchers, defend territories throughout the year. Many species form foraging flocks during the non-breeding season. In most cases these flocks are small, numbering less than 50 birds. There is a tendency for species which breed inland to form larger non-breeding flocks than coastal breeders. The Magellanic, Australian Pied and Eurasian Oystercatchers, the latter especially in its races *ostralegus* and *finschi*, all tend to gather in flocks which exceed 100 birds, and sometimes even 1000 birds. Black forms seldom form flocks of more than 10 birds, with the exception of the American Black Oystercatcher, which forms flocks of up to 50 birds in estuaries.

Several species form high tide roosts; these gatherings are usually larger than foraging flocks. Even in areas where African Black Oystercatchers are territorial throughout the non-breeding season, they still form such aggregations, both by day and by night. The function of high tide roosts probably varies between species. For African Black Oystercatchers, the primary function of roosts is predator avoidance, and roosts are usually sited on offshore rocks or on promontories with good all-round visibility. These roosts tend to contain more birds at night than during the day, as it is at night that the birds are at greatest risk from predators. African Black Oystercatchers suffer their highest mortalities

from predators during the breeding season, when adults are tied to the nest or chicks, and can not join such roosts. In the case of the Eurasian Oystercatcher, which mostly spends the non-breeding season in much colder climes, roosts probably also serve a thermoregulatory function: their roosts are much more tightly packed than are those of African Black Oystercatchers.

Both migratory and sedentary oystercatcher species are highly site-faithful. Migratory Eurasian Oystercatchers use the same breeding territories year after year, and also tend to return to the same area of the same estuary in each non-breeding season. Migration patterns have a very strong heritable component, and most oystercatchers exhibit long-term mate fidelity. Assortative mating should therefore produce offspring which exhibit very much the same patterns of site fidelity as their parents, and such fidelity has been clearly demonstrated for African Black and Eurasian Oystercatchers, young birds returning to breed at their natal sites, usually when three to five years old. They may have spent much of the intervening time several hundred kilometres away from the natal site.

Voice

Oystercatchers have loud, piercing, piping calls, most closely resembling those of the thick-knees (Burhinidae). Indeed, the call of the African Black Oystercatcher can be confused with that of the Water Dikkop (*Burhinus vermiculatus*) by the inexperienced ear.

At least nine different calls have been identified for Eurasian Oystercatchers in different behavioural contexts, ranging from contact calls to calls associated with "Butterfly Displays" and mobbing. The best known call is undoubtedly the piping call, which is the most complex and far-carrying call of the repertoire. It typically starts with an accelerating trill, evens out in pace and then gradually slows down. This call probably has similar functions in all oystercatcher species. Piping is primarily used in aggressive behaviour between pairs with adjacent breeding territories, and even among species which defend territories throughout the year, piping is most frequent during the breeding season. It is also given when mates meet one another on the territory, especially if one mate has just returned from elsewhere.

Among Eurasian Oystercatchers, the piping display is important in establishing and maintaining dominance hierarchies during the non-breeding season, but whether it plays this role in other oystercatchers is unknown. Piping calls are very similar to alarm calls, suggesting that they are a highly ritualized form of alarm calling.

Piping may also play a role in species recognition where two or three oystercatcher species occur sympatrically. In southern South America, the piping calls of American and Blackish Oystercatchers are very similar, and these two species hybridize where their ranges overlap, as do American Black and American Oystercatchers in their zone of overlap. The piping call of the Magellanic Oystercatcher, however, is markedly different: it has an extremely narrow band width, which is thought to be an adaptation for long distance sound propagation. There is only one putative instance of hybridization involving a Magellanic Oystercatcher.

Food and Feeding

Oystercatchers foraging inland eat mostly arthropods, especially earthworms and insect larvae. On the open coast and in estuaries they have a more varied diet. Bivalves, gastropods and polychaetes figure prominently, but they also eat amphipods, crabs, ascidians, echinoderms and, occasionally, fish. On rocky shores, the diet is usually dominated by molluscs, especially mussels, limpets, snails and chitons, whereas on soft substrates, bivalves and polychaetes are the dominant prey. In Panama, American Oystercatchers have been found to eat at least 30 different prey species. Elsewhere, 24 species have been recorded as prey for South Island and Variable Oystercatchers in New Zealand, and the Sooty Oystercatcher of Australia eats at least 24 species. Altogether 52 species have been recorded in the diet of African Black Oystercatcher.

Migratory oystercatchers are forced to change their diets seasonally as they move from one habitat to another. Seasonal changes in the diets of sedentary species have not been studied, but are probably far less pronounced. They may, however, occur in response to changing body condition of prey animals. For example, at Schiermonnikoog in the Netherlands, the im-

portance of the clam *Macoma balthica* in the diet of Eurasian Oystercatchers decreases towards late summer, as the meat content of the clams decreases. Prey behaviour is also important in diet choice. Eurasian Oystercatchers at Schiermonnikoog have a particularly high intake of *Nereis* worms during mid-summer, at the time when the burrowing depth of these worms is at a minimum.

Changes in prey selection can take place over much shorter time periods than seasons. The diet of the African Black Oystercatcher varies between day and night. Two important prey items for this species are mussels and the limpet *Patella granularis*; the proportion of mussels in the diet is maximal during the day but the proportion of limpets increases at night.

The American Black Oystercatcher frequents exposed shores and islands along the Pacific coast. It often feeds on rocks uncovered only at low tide where it finds a variety of food items, such as mussels and other bivalves, limpets and whelks, which it tackles with the appropriate technique of hammering, prising, probing or stabbing. Note the yellow eye, typical of the New World species and contrasting with the red iris of Old World taxa.

[Haematopus bachmani. Photo: Arthur Morris]

This difference can be explained by the foraging behaviour of the limpets themselves. During the day, they remain firmly attached to the rock because if they move about to forage they run the risk of desiccation. At night, however, the limpets forage at low tide, moving about over the rocks. When mobile they are much more easy to dislodge and become targets for hunting oystercatchers.

In addition to temporal and spatial influences on diet, the sex of the bird also plays a role. Although differences between the diets of males and females have been described for few species, the phenomenon is probably widespread because of consistent differences in bill structure between males and females of all species. The bill of the male is blunter and more robust than that of the female, and is usually shorter. Male Eurasian Oystercatchers in the Dutch Wadden Sea eat more large and thick-shelled molluscs than do females. In western England, mussels are the main prey of males, while the females select more of the smaller cockles. Both sexes of the African Black Oystercatcher eat mussels in approximately equal proportions, but the balance of the male's diet comprises mostly whelks and limpets, whereas that of the female is made up of polychaetes and small unshelled prey.

Worldwide, there is limited morphological variation among the different classes of prey taken, and there is also very limited morphological variation in the feeding apparatus of oystercatchers. For example, limpets and chitons are tightly attached to the rock and have to be knocked or levered off; bivalves must be prised or hammered open, and the flesh must either be pulled out of coiled gastropods or the shell must be broken. Whether an attack technique is effective will, in the main, be determined by prey size and shell strength. There are some small differences between oystercatchers in attack strategies. The African Black Oystercatcher almost invariably attacks only mussels that are themselves feeding. At this time the valves are gaping, and the oystercatchers stab between the valve margins to sever the posterior adductor muscle, which holds the valves together. Both Eurasian and Variable Oystercatchers use this technique, but also sometimes smash open mussel shells to reach the flesh. The African Black Oystercatcher preferentially attacks the posterior shell margins of limpets, whereas the Eura-

sian Oystercatcher directs most of its attacks at the anterior margins. At least among Eurasian Oystercatchers, there is cultural transmission of foraging techniques from adults to newly-independent young, but maturing birds may subsequently change their foraging techniques.

Considering any one prey species, the upper size limit eaten by oystercatchers is normally determined by the bird's ability either to dislodge the animal or to handle it. The lower size limit may be set either by dexterity or, probably more often, by profitability, in other words the amount of energy the bird will derive relative to the time and effort it must expend in obtaining that energy.

For oystercatchers that live on the coast, available foraging time is limited by two factors, the duration of tidal exposure and the digestive capacity of the bird. Even during the low tide period, oystercatchers rarely forage continuously. They are regularly forced to pause because the rate at which they capture prey is faster than the rate at which they can digest it.

Many intertidal molluscs and crustaceans are intermediate hosts to parasites, especially trematodes and cestodes, which use birds as their final host. It is in the interest of the parasite to try to ensure that the intermediate host is eaten by the definitive host, the bird, but it is in the interest of the birds not to eat parasitized prey. Birds carrying high parasite loads may be at a disadvantage, for example during periods of bad weather when prey is difficult to find. There is evidence from Western Europe and New Zealand that Eurasian Oystercatchers are partially successful in avoiding parasitized bivalves. This is not always the case, however. In England, the dogwhelk (*Nucella lapillus*) is the intermediate host to the castrating trematode parasite *Parorchis acanthus*. This parasite has a dual effect on the whelk. First, it produces gigantism, which makes the infected whelk attractive as prey. Second, it changes the whelk's behaviour: uninfected whelks form winter aggregations where they are free from predation by Eurasian Oystercatchers; although infected whelks do join these aggregations, they do so later than healthy individuals, and are thus at risk from being eaten by oystercatchers for a longer period. The oystercatchers appear unable to detect parasitized whelks and the parasite's "strategy" is thus successful.

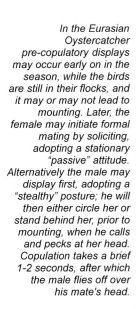

In the Eurasian Oystercatcher pre-copulatory displays may occur early on in the season, while the birds are still in their flocks, and it may or may not lead to mounting. Later, the female may initiate formal mating by soliciting, adopting a stationary "passive" attitude. Alternatively the male may display first, adopting a "stealthy" posture; he will then either circle her or stand behind her, prior to mounting, when he calls and pecks at her head. Copulation takes a brief 1-2 seconds, after which the male flies off over his mate's head.

[Haematopus ostralegus ostralegus, near Hermitage Castle, Scotland. Photo: R. Kunz]

Breeding

All oystercatchers are exclusively or predominantly monogamous: extra-pair copulations probably occur regularly in most or all species, but bigamy has been reported only for the Eurasian Oystercatcher. They are all territorial during the breeding season. Fidelity to mate and breeding site tend to be strong, and the same pair of Eurasian Oystercatchers may defend the same breeding territory for as long as 20 years. The only taxon studied for which this may not be true is the South Island Oystercatcher.

Breeding takes place during the summer months. There is a tendency for species which breed at high latitudes to have a shorter laying period than lower latitude breeders. In Eurasian Oystercatchers, the timing of egg-laying strongly influences reproductive success: birds that lay early in the season fledge more chicks than those that lay later. Whilst it is tempting to suggest that the latter are inexperienced birds, in at least three oystercatcher species the timing of egg-laying by individual females is correlated between years. This suggests that some factor other than experience influences laying date.

All oystercatchers are single-brooded, although replacement clutches are readily laid if nest contents are lost. Eggs are laid in a scrape made on the ground which may be lined or unlined. Nests are frequently placed adjacent to disruptive objects, and are often sited to provide good all-round visibility. Several scrapes are made before one is chosen: typically the male plays the dominant role in nest building, although the final choice of nest-site probably rests with the female.

As for waders in general, clutch size ranges between one and four eggs, rarely five in the Eurasian Oystercatcher. Among other charadriiforms, notably plovers, sandpipers and gulls, there is a marked pattern of clutch size decreasing towards the tropics, but this pattern is not evident in oystercatchers. All species which breed predominantly or exclusively in the Northern Hemisphere have a modal clutch of three eggs. In the south, the only taxa that normally lay three-egg clutches are the Variable and South Island Oystercatchers. All other southern species have a modal clutch of two. When oystercatchers are breeding at high densities, there is a tendency for the clutch to be smaller than when pairs are well spaced. This may be because resource availability, particularly food availability, for each pair and its offspring is reduced in high-density breeding areas.

The background colour of the eggs is usually grey-blue or grey-buff, with some variation. The eggs of all species are unevenly spotted and scrolled, and are very cryptic on a grainy background such as mussel shells or rock chips. The background colour of the eggs of the Magellanic Oystercatcher is darker and greener than those of other species, which provides a suitably cryptic colour for this species against the grassy background of its nest-site.

Incubation patterns have been studied in few species. The first-laid egg of Eurasian Oystercatchers is incubated discontinuously, which places it at high risk from predators. At Schiermonnikoog, 40% of first-laid eggs are lost before the second egg is laid. The American Oystercatcher, in turn, does not incubate the first egg at all before the second is laid. In this species, which normally lays three eggs, the second-laid egg is the largest. If the first-laid egg is at high risk, and the second and third eggs do not hatch synchronously, the second egg has the greatest chance of producing a fledged chick, so the female therefore places greatest investment in the egg with the highest chance of survival. The African Black Oystercatcher is highly susceptible to egg predation and starts incubation when the first egg is laid; there is no difference in the size of first- and second-laid eggs, or in their probability of being taken by predators. In all species, incubation is continuous once the clutch is completed.

The incubation period ranges from a minimum of 24 days, in the Eurasian, Chatham and American Black Oystercatchers, to 39 days in the African Black; for most species, the modal incubation period is 27-30 days. The chicks hatch with a covering of rather dull speckled greyish brown down, with belly colour pale or dark depending on the species. This pattern helps the chicks to blend into their habitat, so that a crouched chick may look like a small stone or a cluster of pebbles, a pattern closely similar to that found in the thick-knees.

During the breeding cycle there is some role differentiation between the sexes. In the pre-laying period, females spend more time foraging than males. Early in the breeding cycle, males generally commit more time to territorial defence than females, and females take a proportionally greater share of the incubation. The male's contribution to incubation increases gradually during the incubation period, as the investment value of the eggs increases and the opportunities for extra-pair copulations with other females decrease. In the American Oystercatcher, males provide more food to the chicks than females. Over the breeding cycle as a whole, however, energetic investment by both sexes is similar (as determined for American Oystercatchers), and there are no sex-linked differences in survival rates of adults.

In terms of chick-rearing, all birds fall somewhere along a gradient from fully precocial to fully altricial; that is from mobile, self-feeding young to defenceless young fed entirely by their parents until after fledging. Between these extremes, the oystercatchers occupy a unique position. They are the only birds with young that have full precocial mobility, most chicks leaving the nest within 24 hours of hatching, and yet receive all their food from their parents until well after fledging. A fully precocial strategy minimizes the risk of predation, because chicks can hide or run away, but at the cost of slow growth, because inexperienced young have to find their own food. A fully altricial strategy maximizes growth rate, because the young rely on experienced adults to provide food but at the cost of high predation risk because the young are confined to a nest and frequent visits by parents may attract predators to the nest. Oystercatchers have achieved the best of both worlds in a strategy known as "precocial 5", which maximizes benefits while minimizing risks.

Despite this apparent "super strategy", and the fact that both males and females feed the growing chicks, there is evidence that adult birds are energetically stressed during the chick-rearing period. Chicks of Eurasian, American, American Black and African Black Oystercatchers sometimes die due to starvation. In the case of the American Black Oystercatcher, a sibling hierarchy is established within broods, so that, if food shortage arises, it is the subordinate chick that dies first. In such cases of food becoming scarce, if the food supply is supplemented, either experimentally or due to change in invertebrate populations, breeding success increases.

The average breeding success of all oystercatchers is less than one fledged young per pair per year. Only among Eurasian and American Black Oystercatchers have average fledging successes of more than 0·5 chicks per pair per year been reported.

Most mortality occurs during incubation, rather than chick-rearing. Of 229 nests of American Oystercatchers monitored in Virginia, USA, eggs hatched in only 14%. Most chick mortality occurs when chicks are small: mortality rates of more than 60% for Eurasian Oystercatchers and more than 85% for African Black Oystercatchers have been reported in the first week after hatching. The main causes of egg and chick mortality are storms and predators. Generally, the former is the more important factor during the egg stage, and the latter during the chick stage.

The fledging period ranges from 33 days, the minimum for the Eurasian, to 49 days, the maximum for the Australian Pied, the Chatham and the Variable; reported fledging periods of 56 days for the Australian Pied are questionable. There is a tendency for the fledging period of migratory species to be longer than those of sedentary species.

After fledging, young oystercatchers are fed by their parents for varying lengths of time, and young may remain with their parents for up to six months. They are long-lived birds, and deferred maturity is the norm. Some female Eurasian and African Black Oystercatchers breed for the first time at three years old, and some males breed in their fourth year. Most, however, probably do not breed until they are older than this, and one male Eurasian Oystercatcher only bred for the first time at the age of 14! Young oystercatchers almost invariably breed close to where they themselves hatched, certainly within tens of kilometres. In one bay in South Africa, where African Black Oystercatchers breed at very high densities on three rocky islands, most young birds return to their natal islands to breed.

Movements

The only oystercatchers that are truly migratory are the four races of the Eurasian Oystercatcher. The three Palearctic races all move south during the boreal winter, and inland breeders move to the coast (see Habitat). The South Island Oystercatcher, an inland breeder on the South Island of New Zealand, moves to the coasts of both North and South Islands during the austral winter and it is thought that these birds fly directly between their breeding and non-breeding grounds, travelling in small flocks of 25-70 birds.

All oystercatchers rear a single brood, though replacement clutches may be laid when required. The nest is a simple scrape in the ground, in sand or gravel in the case of the American Oystercatcher, which may decorate its nest with a few shell fragments. On average the clutch consists of 3 eggs, and in all species the eggs are unevenly spotted or blotched, which helps to camouflage them. Incubation normally lasts up to 29 days and is carried out mainly by the female.

[*Haematopus palliatus palliatus*, Long Island, New York. Photo: Tom Vezo]

The Blackish Oystercatcher of South America sites its nest on the beach, just beyond the reach of the swell, among stones and pebbles. A shallow depression in the ground, it is lined on occasion with fragments of shell or rock. The clutch size is small, only 2 eggs, and this, together with the factor of heavy predation by gulls and skuas, results in a dismal rate of breeding success, well below the already low average for oystercatchers.

[Haematopus ater, Falkland Islands. Photo: David Hosking/ FLPA]

Migration occurs both by day and by night. Eurasian Oystercatchers breeding in Iceland fly 800 km non-stop across the North Atlantic to reach British non-breeding grounds, and these birds start their primary moult only once their migration is complete. The longest movements undertaken by this species are by the races *ostralegus* and *longipes*. The mid-points of the breeding and non-breeding ranges of these subspecies are separated by approximately 32° of latitude, about twice the distance moved by the eastern race *osculans*. Many long distance migrant waders lay down pre-migratory fuel reserves, which, in small species, may approach 100% of their lean body mass. There is no pronounced pre-migratory fattening of Eurasian Oystercatchers; indeed, birds in the Netherlands attain peak mass in mid-winter. This suggests that distances travelled between stop-overs are not great, and most flights probably cover less than 1000 km.

Eurasian Oystercatchers are strongly site-faithful to their non-breeding grounds, and spatial segregation of sub-populations occurs. Icelandic birds, for example, spend the non-breeding season on the coasts of Ireland and western Britain, while Norwegian birds are concentrated along the coasts of the North Sea.

The American Black and American Oystercatchers are migratory in the north of their ranges, moving south in the winter. There is also a slight northerly movement of Magellanic Oystercatchers during winter, but most of the population is non-migratory. None of the other species is migratory, although several undertake small-scale seasonal movements between different habitats (see Habitat). In winter, movements of Eurasian Oystercatchers also occur in response to severe weather conditions.

Relationship with Man

The genus *Haematopus* was erected by Linnaeus in 1758 for the Eurasian Oystercatcher. There is, however, earlier reference to at least one other species. In 1648, Étienne de Flacourt, the then Governor-general of Madagascar, visited the south-west coast of Africa and provided the first description of the African Black Oystercatcher: "There are birds like Blackbirds, with a very shrill and clear cry, as large as partridges, with a long sharp beak and red legs: they are very good to eat and when they are young they taste like Woodcock".

Other writers have been less impressed by the gastronomic potential of oystercatchers than by their appearance. In his *Birds of the West Coast*, of 1976, J. F. Lansdowne wrote of the American Black Oystercatcher: "Anyone seeing a Black Oystercatcher for the first time might be inclined to laugh at its grotesque and rather comic appearance. Its outsize red bill is impossibly bright, the eyes are red-ringed, and the pallid fleshy feet bring to mind a seaside bather who has taken off his shoes and socks. When the bird nods and utters a piercingly loud whinny, the observer is convinced that it is simple as well as strange looking"!

Being specialist predators of shellfish, oystercatchers have the potential to come into conflict with man at commercial shellfish farms. In western Europe, Eurasian Oystercatchers were thought for many years to be a major economic pest of commercial cockle fisheries. Recently, however, shore crabs (*Carcinus maenas*) were shown to eat twice the biomass and 25 times as many cockles as those eaten by the birds: the relative impact of oystercatchers had therefore probably been overestimated. In North America, American Oystercatchers prey on commercial oyster beds, especially during winter, but it is not known whether they have any economic impact, concentrating as they do on the smaller oysters.

Status and Conservation

Many oystercatcher species with predominantly mainland distributions are common, and there is no good evidence for population changes in either direction. There is a suggestion that the

In coastal areas, the feeding activity of Eurasian Oystercatchers is heavily dictated by tides, and birds typically roost or loaf around the period of high tide, when conditions are not ideal for foraging. Birds tend to roost communally, but off-duty breeders will remain on the territory, resting on elevated perches with good all-round visibility, such as rocky outcrops. This species is resilient in the face of inclement climatic conditions and it winters as far north as Iceland, so summer showers, which are not uncommon within its breeding range, need pose no great problem.

[*Haematopus ostralegus ostralegus*,
Foula, Shetland, Scotland.
Photo: Günter Ziesler]

American Oystercatcher is decreasing in abundance, as a breeding species, in the north of its range, but it has an extensive distribution in North, Central and South America and is not threatened.

The populations of two subspecies of Eurasian Oystercatcher, nominate *ostralegus* and *finschi*, have increased this century in parallel with an increased frequency of inland breeding. There has been a southerly extension of the breeding range of *ostralegus* over the past 60 years. The race *finschi* decreased in numbers from the late nineteenth century until the middle of the twentieth century, but it has undergone a spectacular irruption since 1940.

The world populations of five taxa number less than 5000 birds. These five include three species, the Chatham, the Variable and the African Black Oystercatchers; and two well marked subspecies, the Spectacled Oystercatcher and the Galapagos race of the American Oystercatcher, both of which may actually be good species.

The Chatham Oystercatcher is classified as Endangered, with a world population of only about 100-110 birds on the islands of Chatham, Pitt, Mangere and Rangatira (formerly South-east Island). Breeding is largely restricted to offshore islands and cliffs, because of predation by feral cats and Wekas (*Gallirallus australis*). The two most secure breeding islands of Mangere and Rangatira are protected reserves, and are free from introduced predators. There is some evidence for a slight recent increase in overall numbers, but, simply from the extremely low numbers, this species' status is precarious. Several conservation measures have been put into practice in recent years, including artificial incubation, with the aim of reducing egg loss due to predation or storm damage.

The Variable Oystercatcher is widely distributed in New Zealand, but has a total population of only about 3900 birds.

Whilst this species was not legally protected from shooting in the early part of the present century, it would appear that the effects of introduced predators combined with disturbance by humans may have been more serious. In recent years, some populations appear to be increasing, and conservation work appears to have achieved some successes, but, with its relatively low numbers, the species still may warrant monitoring.

The African Black Oystercatcher has a total population of about 4800 birds, of which 25% is supported on only ten islands, all of which are protected, with landing regulated by permit. The principal threat to the island populations is the introduction of mammalian predators. The connection of Marcus Island, in Western Cape Province, to the mainland by a causeway allowed access for several predators: in the space of four years, 25% of the island's adult oystercatchers were killed, and in three breeding seasons combined, the breeding population of about 60 pairs fledged only five chicks. On mainland coasts, however, the greatest threats to African Black Oystercatchers are development and associated disturbance, including an escalating use of off-road vehicles on beaches. The total population has probably decreased in the past 10 years and populations in the south-western Cape and Algoa Bay require monitoring.

The status and biology of the Spectacled Oystercatcher of northern Australia are very poorly known, but the total population probably numbers under 1000 individuals, and no major concentrations are known. This is one of the least known of all oystercatchers, together with the Chatham Oystercatcher and the Galapagos race of the American Oystercatcher, both of which are very rare too, and all three are amongst the priorities for conservation-related research within the family. All three taxa also constitute taxonomic enigmas (see Systematics), and further study in this field would be highly desirable, especially

American Oystercatcher chicks hatch with a rather drab coat of speckled greyish brown down, a cryptic pattern that helps them to escape detection. Oystercatcher young are fully precocial, but, strangely, they rely on their parents for food until after fledging, an advantageous strategy termed "precocial 5". Accordingly, the risk of predation is relatively small since the mobile chicks are able to run quickly for cover, while the growth rate is fast as the experienced adults provide all the food, thereby economizing on time. Despite all this, average breeding success in oystercatchers is less than one fledged young per pair per year.

[*Haematopus palliatus palliatus*, Long Island, New York. Photo: Tom Vezo]

When last counted in the late 1980's, the Chatham Oystercatcher's total population numbered only 100-110 birds. This species is found on five or so of the Chatham Islands, where the main threat it faces is in the form of predation by cats, rats and Wekas (Gallirallus australis), while grazing cattle and human disturbance are other negative factors. Conservation measures are currently being taken to safeguard the species and to encourage breeding. In the meanwhile it is classified as Endangered.

[*Haematopus chathamensis*, South East Island, Chatham Islands. Photo: J. Mills/Aquila]

with the use of molecular techniques. Like the Spectacled Oystercatcher, the Galapagos race *galapagensis* of the American Oystercatcher may warrant specific status. In view of this, the taxon requires urgent biological research and an accurate assessment of its distribution and abundance within the islands. The total population is estimated to be less than 100 pairs, with the introduction of predators considered to pose the biggest threat.

The presence of a black oystercatcher in the Canary Islands was first reported in the 1840's, although a specimen was not collected and described until 1888, while the last specimen was taken in 1913. This species probably became extinct early in the twentieth century. However, subsequent to 1960 there are two unsubstantiated sight records from Tenerife, outside the species' known range. Complete surveys of the west coasts of Fuerteventura and Lanzarote in June and July 1985 failed to find any sign of the bird. The only hope that a small, as yet undiscovered, population survives are two sightings, involving three birds, from the coast of Senegal in 1970 and 1975. These sightings were never ascribed to species, but it is highly unlikely that they refer to African Black Oystercatchers, which are sedentary and have never been reported north of Lobito, Angola.

Such a short time elapsed between the discovery and apparent extinction of the Canarian Black Oystercatcher that almost nothing is known of its biology, beyond the fact that it favoured rocky shores. The physical nature of the coastline in the eastern Canary Islands indicates that the population would always have been small. Its extinction was probably precipitated by increasing disturbance and competition with man for food. In the past few centuries there has been a progressive desertification of the eastern Canary Islands, accelerated recently by changing land-use practices. This has led in turn to an increasing dependence by the islanders on marine food resources, resulting in severe impacts on intertidal invertebrate populations over most of the species' historical range.

Only one wader species, the White-winged Sandpiper (*Prosobonia leucoptera*) of Tahiti and Moorea, has definitely become extinct in the past 200 years (see page 484). However, it seems very likely that the Canarian Black Oystercatcher and the Javanese Wattled Lapwing (*Vanellus macropterus*), which has not been seen since 1939 (see page 408), are now also extinct.

General Bibliography
Barbosa (1993), Björklund (1994), Burger (1984c), Burton (1974), Buxton (1985), Christian *et al*. (1992b), Chu (1995), Clay (1981), Dunning (1993), Evans *et al*. (1984), Gochfeld *et al*. (1984), Hayman *et al*. (1986), Heppleston (1973a, 1973b), Jehl (1968b), Johnsgard (1981), Larson (1957), Low (1923b), Maclean (1972a), Miller (1984), Murphy (1925), Nol (1984), Olson & Steadman (1979), Peters (1934), Prater *et al*. (1977), Rosair & Cottridge (1995), Rutgers & Norris (1970), Sibley & Ahlquist (1990), Sibley & Monroe (1990), Soothill & Soothill (1982), Strauch (1976, 1978), Webster (1943).

1

ssp *palliatus*

4

ssp *galapagensis*

2

3

5

6

ssp *ostralegus*

7

8

ssp *osculans*

ssp *finschi*

9

pied morph

dark morph

10

intermediate morph

ssp *fuliginosus*

11

ssp *opthalmicus*

PLATE 29

inches 9

cm 23

Genus *HAEMATOPUS* Linnaeus, 1758

1. **Magellanic Oystercatcher**

Haematopus leucopodus

French: Huîtrier de Garnot **German**: Magellanausternfischer **Spanish**: Ostrero Magallánico

Taxonomy. *Haematopus leucopodus* Garnot, 1826, Falkland Islands.
Distinctive species with taxonomic affiliations uncertain, as both adults and chicks show mixture of features which otherwise characterize taxa of Old World, rather than those of New World (see page 308). Monotypic.
Distribution. SC Chile (Chiloé I) and SC Argentina (Chubut) S to Cape Horn; Falkland Is.

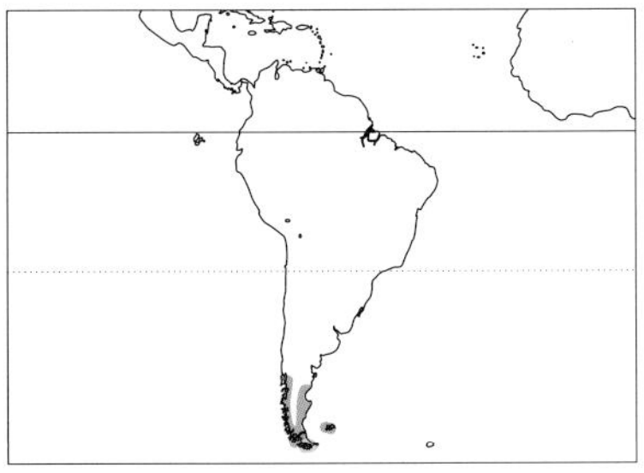

Descriptive notes. 42-46 cm; male 585-610 g, female 585-700 g. Unique amongst oystercatchers in having almost entirely white secondaries from above and below, and a yellow eye-ring. Eye yellow, as in all other New World oystercatchers; the only pied oystercatcher of New World with black dorsal coloration. Female very similar to male, but bill tends to be longer and shallower. Juvenile has browner upperparts with buff feather fringes, and duller bare part colours.
Habitat. Occurs on beaches, inland and upland grasslands and the margins of freshwater pools. Most birds move to the coast in winter, where large flocks may form, on rocky shores or soft substrates.
Food and Feeding. Feeds on mussels, limpets and crabs on rocky shores, marine polychaetes on coastal soft substrates. At inland sites eats mainly earthworms and insect larvae. All oystercatchers attack different prey types using variety of techniques, e.g. hammering, prising, probing, stabbing (see page 314).
Breeding. Laying starts in Oct-Nov in Tierra del Fuego. Cocked-tail display, with tail held vertically to display undertail pattern, is unique among oystercatchers. Nest often sited on a slightly raised grassy hillock. Clutch 1-2, usually 2; eggs have darker, greener background than those of other oystercatchers, providing cryptic aspect against a grassy background. Chick differs from those of other New World oystercatchers in having crown prominently marked with black; similar to chick of *H. ostralegus*, but differs in having dark bases to claws and dark upper breast. Incubation and fledging periods unknown.
Movements. Seasonal movement from inland breeding grounds to the coast. Breeders from extreme S of range move N in winter, but distances and destinations unknown.
Status and Conservation. Not globally threatened. Generally reckoned to be common to abundant, especially in southern parts of range. Fairly restricted range, but much of this supports very sparse human populations, with relatively limited human impact on natural environment. Extensive promotion of "adventure" tourism in recent years; and possible impact of increased human presence, recreational activities and general disturbance should be examined; nevertheless, species appears secure at present.
Bibliography. Blake (1977), Canevari *et al.* (1991), Clark (1986), Cobb (1910), Crawshay (1907), Fjeldså & Krabbe (1990), Hellmayr & Conover (1948), Humphrey *et al.* (1970), Jehl (1978), Jehl & Rumboll (1976), Jehl *et al.* (1973), Johnson (1965b), Maclean (1972a), Miller & Baker (1980), Olrog (1984), de la Peña (1981b, 1992), Scott & Carbonell (1986), Siegel-Causey (1991), Woods (1988).

2. **Blackish Oystercatcher**

Haematopus ater

French: Huîtrier noir **Spanish**: Ostrero Negro Suramericano
German: Südamerikanischer-Austernfischer
Other common names: Black Oystercatcher(!), South American Black Oystercatcher

Taxonomy. *Haematopus ater* Vieillot and Oudart, 1825, Straits of Magellan.
Some hybridization recorded with *H. palliatus* in zone of overlap. Monotypic.
Distribution. N Peru (Lambayeque) S through Chile to Tierra del Fuego and N up Atlantic coast to SC Argentina (Chubut); Falkland Is. Outside breeding season some birds move N to extreme N Peru, NE Argentina and probably Uruguay.

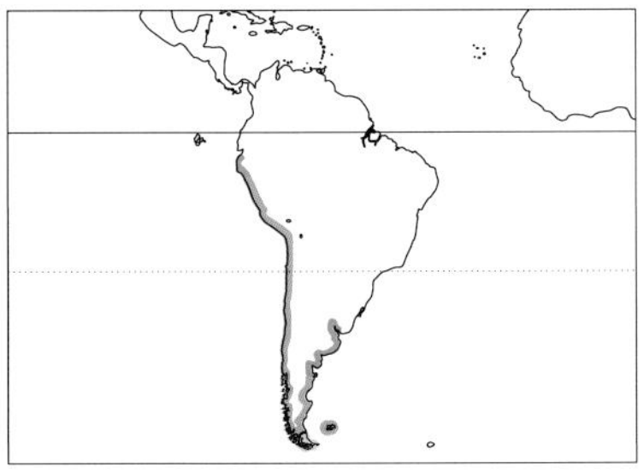

Descriptive notes. 43-45·5 cm; 585-708 g. Heavily built, all dark oystercatcher with dorsal plumage blackish brown; red eye-ring, yellow eye; deep, heavy bill orange-red, paler towards tip; legs pinkish horn. Almost identical to *H. bachmani*, but legs slightly paler, body slightly heavier and wings slightly longer; bill rather deeper, especially at gonys. Female very similar to male, but averages larger with larger bill; some white fringes to belly feathers in non-breeding plumage. Juvenile has plumage scaled with buff; bill dull, but may be yellowish at tip, whereas most juvenile oystercatchers have brown-tipped bill; legs pale.
Habitat. Breeds on pebble and shell beaches. Outside breeding season occurs on shingle and rocky shores.
Food and Feeding. Feeds mainly on mussels and limpets on rocky shores. All oystercatchers attack different prey types using variety of techniques, e.g. hammering, prising, probing, stabbing (see page 314).
Breeding. Laying mostly starts in Nov, in Tierra del Fuego; late Oct to Jan, in Falkland Is. Nest is scrape in ground placed as close to the high water mark as swells permit, sometimes on bare rock; nest depression is lined with shell fragments and rock chips. Clutch 1-2, usually 2. White ventral coloration of chick more extensive than in *H. bachmani*, but does not cover entire belly and flanks as in *H. palliatus*; buff tipping to down restricted to narrow strips on margins of dorsal and femoral stripes, resulting in greyish, rather than buffy, upperparts. Incubation and fledging periods unknown. Breeding success low due to predation by gulls and skuas; in one study only 1 chicks has reared from total of 20 nests.
Movements. Mainly sedentary. Birds breeding in extreme S (Tierra del Fuego) move an unknown distance N after breeding. Some birds occur N to extreme N Peru and also to NE Argentina and probably Uruguay, but origins of such birds unknown, and patterns of such movements unclear. Recorded in Juan Fernández Is, 800 km off Chilean coast.
Status and Conservation. Not globally threatened. Occurs at fairly low density throughout range, but range extensive and in many parts sparsely populated by humans. Densities may be depressed in areas where there is intensive exploitation of intertidal invertebrates by local people, e.g. in C Chile.
Bibliography. Baker & Miller (1978), Blake (1977), Canevari *et al.* (1991), Clark (1986), Cobb (1910), Crawshay (1907), Gewalt (1992), Hellmayr & Conover (1948), Humphrey *et al.* (1970), Jehl (1978), Jehl *et al.* (1973), Johnson (1965b), Koepcke (1970), Low (1923a), Miller & Baker (1980), Nol (1984), Olrog (1984), de la Peña (1981b, 1992), Scott & Carbonell (1986), Stresemann (1927), Woods (1988).

3. **American Black Oystercatcher**

Haematopus bachmani

French: Huîtrier de Bachman **Spanish**: Ostrero Negro Norteamericano
German: Klippenausternfischer
Other common names: Black Oystercatcher(!)

Taxonomy. *Haematopus Bachmani* Audubon, 1838, mouth of the Columbia River.
Occasionally included in expanded *H. ostralegus*. Name *H. frazari* may be invalid, referring to a hybrid swarm formed between present species and *H. palliatus* in Gulf of California and W Mexico; the hybridization in this overlap zone is limited. Monotypic.

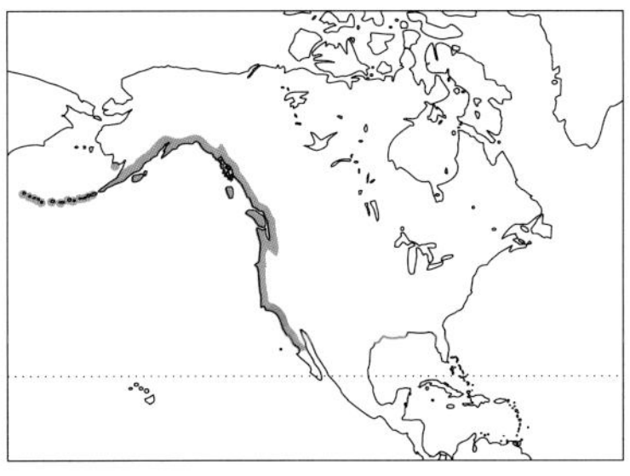

Distribution. W Aleutian Is (Kiska I) through S Alaska (including Round I), W Canada and W USA to NW Mexico (Los Coronados Is and Baja California). Outside breeding season, mostly concentrated between S British Columbia and Baja California.
Descriptive notes. 43-45 cm; male 555-648 g, female 618-750 g. All dark oystercatcher with yellow eye, orange-red eye-ring and pale pink legs; as in all other New World oystercatchers, except *H. leucopodus*, dorsal coloration is blackish brown. Very similar to *H. ater*, but wings slightly shorter, not extending to tail tip at rest; slightly less stcky, with slightly darker legs; bill roughly same length as that of *H. ater*, but not as deep, especially at the gonys. Female averages slightly larger, with longer, thinner bill. Juvenile has dull orange-brown eye-ring and bill, pinkish grey legs and buff-fringed feathers.
Habitat. Breeds on rocky shores and islands. Outside breeding season frequents mudflats and rocky shores.
Food and Feeding. Diet includes mussels, limpets, chitons, echinoderms, crustaceans, polychaetes, goose barnacles and, occasionally, fish. During breeding season on rocky shores around Vancouver I, W Canada, prey includes mussels (*Mytilus californianus*), gastropods (*Acmaea*, *Lottia*, *Tectura*, *Crepidula mummaria*), chitons (*Katharina truncata*, *Mopalia*), crabs (*Petrolisthes cinctipes*, *Oedignathous inermis*), isopods (*Idothea*, *Ligia*), nemertines and echinoderms. In winter these birds move to mudflats where they prey almost exclusively on the mussel *Mytilus edulis*. Approximately 600 km to S, birds foraging in winter on boulder field along coast ate large numbers of limpets, especially *Tectura scutum*, *Lottia pelta* and *L. digitalis*; less frequently taken were *T. persona* and *L. strigatella*. On rocky shores of coastal California, *L. digitalis* and *L. pelta* are frequent prey, while on sandstone shores *Collisella scabra* is rather commonly eaten. All oystercatchers attack different prey types using variety of techniques, e.g. hammering, prising, probing, stabbing (see page 314).
Breeding. Laying in May-Jun; breeding starts c. 2 weeks earlier in S than in N of range. Nest is a shallow scrape on ground, usually lined with rock chips and shell fragments; placed on gravel or turf, or in a rocky depression. Lays 1-4 eggs, but modal clutch 2 or 3, varying regionally; incubation 24-33 days. Chick has less extensive buffy tipping to down than that of sympatric *H. palliatus*, and sides and back of neck are blackish, not buffy. Fledging 40 days. Fledging success variable 0·19-1·10 young per pair per year. Age of first breeding 3 years.
Movements. Local movement away from rocky shores to estuaries during winter, probably due to avoidance of storms. Vagrant to Pribilof Is.
Status and Conservation. Not globally threatened. Fairly widely distributed, and much of range supports relatively sparse human populations, especially in N; very little precise information available regarding abundance and trends. Numbers have decreased steadily in parts of S California during present century. Population on San Nicolas I (off Los Angeles) started to increase rapidly in early 1980's for unknown reasons.
Bibliography. Andres (1994), Andres & Falxa (1995), Armstrong (1983), Bancroft (1927), Bent (1927-1929), Butler & Kirbyson (1979), Eley (1976), Falxa (1992), Frank (1981, 1982), Grinnell (1910), Groves (1978b, 1982, 1984), Hahn & Denny (1989), Hartwick (1973, 1974, 1976, 1978a, 1978b, 1981), Hartwick & Blaylock (1979), Helbing (1977), Hellmayr & Conover (1948), Howell & Webb (1995a), Jehl (1985), Kenyon (1949), Legg (1954), Leschner & Burrel (1977), L'Hyver (1985), L'Hyver & Miller (1991), Lindberg *et al.* (1987), Marsh (1986), Michael (1938), Morgan (1994), Morrell *et al.* (1979), Murphy (1925), Nol (1984), Nysewander (1974, 1977, 1978), Nysewander & Barbour (1979), Nysewander & Hoberg (1978), Nysewander & Knudtson (1977), Purdy (1985), Purdy & Miller (1988), Root (1988), Sorensen & Lindberg (1991), Stresemann (1927), Tulloch & Hartwick (1978), Vermeer, Ewins *et al.* (1991), Vermeer, Morgan & Smith (1992), Warheit *et al.* (1984), Webster (1941a, 1941b, 1942, 1951), Williams (1927).

On following pages: 4. American Oystercatcher (*Haematopus palliatus*); 5. Canarian Black Oystercatcher (*Haematopus meadewaldoi*); 6. African Black Oystercatcher (*Haematopus moquini*); 7. Eurasian Oystercatcher (*Haematopus ostralegus*); 8. Australian Pied Oystercatcher (*Haematopus longirostris*); 9. Chatham Oystercatcher (*Haematopus chathamensis*); 10. Variable Oystercatcher (*Haematopus unicolor*); 11. Sooty Oystercatcher (*Haematopus fuliginosus*).

4. American Oystercatcher

Haematopus palliatus

French: Huîtrier d'Amérique **Spanish**: Ostrero Pío Americano
German: Braunmantel-Austernfischer
Other common names: American Pied Oystercatcher

Taxonomy. *Haematopus palliatus* Temminck, 1820, Venezuela.
Sometimes considered conspecific with *H. ostralegus*. Name *H. frazari* may be invalid, referring to a hybrid swarm formed between present species and *H. bachmani* in Gulf of California and W Mexico; the hybridization in this overlap zone is limited, and some authorities retain *frazari* as race of present species. Present species also known to hybridize with *H. ater* in S South America. Some differences in adult morphology and plumage between nominate *palliatus* and race *galapagensis*, coupled with extreme isolation of latter and differences in chick coloration suggest that *galapagensis* may warrant separate species status (see page 309). Several proposed races probably insufficiently distinct to warrant recognition: *pitanay* of W South America, from Ecuador to SC Chile; *durnfordi* of E South America, from S Brazil to SC Argentina; and *prattii* of Bahamas. Two subspecies currently recognized.
Subspecies and Distribution.
H. p. palliatus Temminck, 1820 - coasts of North and South America, from Gulf of California to C Chile, and from Massachusetts to SC Argentina, including West Indies.
H. p. galapagensis Ridgway, 1886 - Galapagos Is.

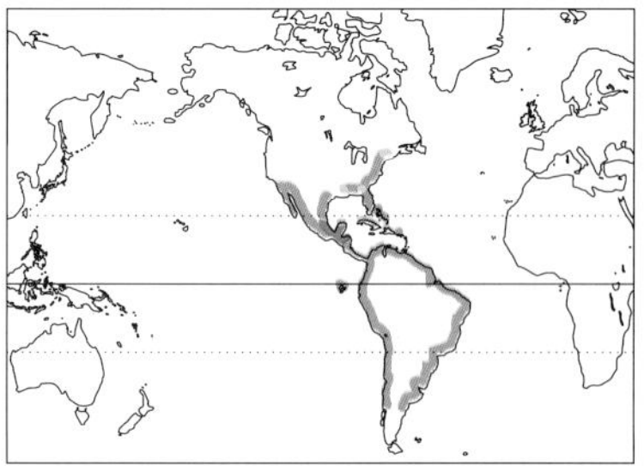

Descriptive notes. 40-44 cm; male averages 567 g, female 638 g. Head, neck, upper breast, flight-feathers and tail black; lower breast and belly white; the only "pied" oystercatcher species with blackish brown dorsal plumage; in flight, shows white greater secondary coverts and uppertail-coverts; eye yellow, eye-ring and bill orange-red, legs pinkish. Female averages slightly larger and longer-billed. Juvenile has buff edges to dark feathers; eye-ring, bill and legs dull. Race *galapagensis* slightly smaller, with shorter wings and bill, especially in female; black breast often has irregular lower border; legs shorter and heavier than in nominate race, and feet noticeably hypertrophied.
Habitat. Breeds in salt-marshes and on sandy and pebble beaches; many birds move to mudflats in winter. Regularly forages on rocky shores in Panama.
Food and Feeding. Feeds mainly on snails, limpets, crabs, oysters, mussels and clams. On soft substrates in Virginia, prey includes razor-clams (*Ensis directus*, *Solen viridis*), ribbed mussels (*Guekensia demissa*) and stout tagelus (*Tagelus plebeius*). On sandy beaches, birds take mole crabs (*Emerita*) and sand mussel (*Mesodesma donacium*), as well as other prey; also forage on commercial beds of the oyster *Crassostrea virginica*. In Panama, on rocky shores, molluscs (*Nerita scabricosta*, *N. funiculata*, *Siphonaria gigas*, *Fissurella*, *Thais melones*) make up more than 97% of diet. All oystercatchers attack different prey types using variety of techniques, e.g. hammering, prising, probing, stabbing (see page 314).
Breeding. Laying Apr-May in Virginia, Feb-Mar in Panama, Oct-Dec in Chile. Nest is shallow scrape on ground, usually placed on sand or gravel; depression usually unlined, but shell fragments sometimes placed around rim of nest. Clutch 1-4, usually 3; replacement clutches smaller, typically 2 eggs; incubation 24-29 days. Chick has drab upperparts with dark stripes down back and sides, and white underparts; that of race *galapagensis* has darker throat than nominate, and lacks buffy tipping on and near rectrices, having entire tail dense black. Fledging 35+ days. Fledging success (nominate *palliatus*) 0·24-0·39 young per pair per year; breeding failure most often due to predation and nest flooding during high tides or storms.
Movements. Resident throughout most of range, but most northerly breeders, especially in NE, move S in winter. Forms foraging flocks in winter. Race *galapagensis* is sedentary.
Status and Conservation. Not globally threatened. Beach development in North America has reduced nest-site availability and led to local changes in distribution, as well as a probable overall population decrease; however, distribution is extending northwards in NE of range. Race *galapagensis* is rare, with total population probably less than 100 pairs; numbers may be limited by availability of suitable feeding areas; potentially threatened by introduced predators, but distribution, biology and behaviour too poorly known to assess real conservation status.
Bibliography. Armistead (1978), Baker & Cadman (1980), Baldwin (1950), Belton (1984), Bent (1927-1929), Biaggi (1983), Blake (1977), Blus *et al.* (1978), Cadman (1979, 1980), Canevari *et al.* (1991), DeGange (1978), Dronen *et al.* (1988), Fjeldså & Krabbe (1990), Gibson (1978), Gifford (1913), Harris (1982), Hayes & Bennett (1985), Hellmayr & Conover (1948), Hilty & Brown (1986), Howell & Webb (1995a), Hoxie (1887), Humphrey (1988), Jehl (1985), Johnson (1965b), Kilham, L. (1979, 1980), Lauro & Burger (1989), Lauro *et al.* (1992), Lévêque (1964), Levings *et al.* (1986), Meyer de Schauensee & Phelps (1978), Miller & Baker (1980), Monroe (1968), Nol (1984, 1985, 1989), Nol & Humphrey (1994), Nol *et al.* (1984), de la Peña (1981b, 1992), Ridgely & Gwynne (1989), Ridgway (1886, 1897), Root (1988), Scott & Carbonell (1986), Sennet (1879), Shields & Parnell (1990), Sick (1985c, 1993), Siegel-Causey (1991), Slud (1964), Stiles & Skutch (1989), Toland (1992), Tomkins (1947), Venegas (1973), Wetmore (1965), Zarudsky (1985).

5. Canarian Black Oystercatcher

Haematopus meadewaldoi

French: Huîtrier des Canaries **Spanish**: Ostrero Negro Canario
German: Kanarischer Austernfischer
Other common names: Meade-Waldo's (Black)/Canarian Oystercatcher

Taxonomy. *Haematopus niger meade-waldoi* Bannerman, 1913, Jandía, Fuerteventura, eastern Canary Islands.
Validity of species has repeatedly been questioned, and scarcity of material limits scope of possible analyses; has been considered conspecific with *H. moquini* or *H. ostralegus*, or both. Monotypic.
Distribution. E Canary Is, especially Fuerteventura, Lanzarote and Graciosa, but also outlying islands including Montaña Clara and Roque del Este. Probably extinct.
Descriptive notes. c. 43 cm. All dark oystercatcher with red eye, orange-red eye-ring and bill, and pale pinkish red legs; in flight, when seen from below, primaries have pale bases, but this feature may be linked to feather wear. Differs from *H. moquini* in having shorter wings and longer bill; from New World black oystercatchers in having black, not blackish brown, dorsal coloration and a

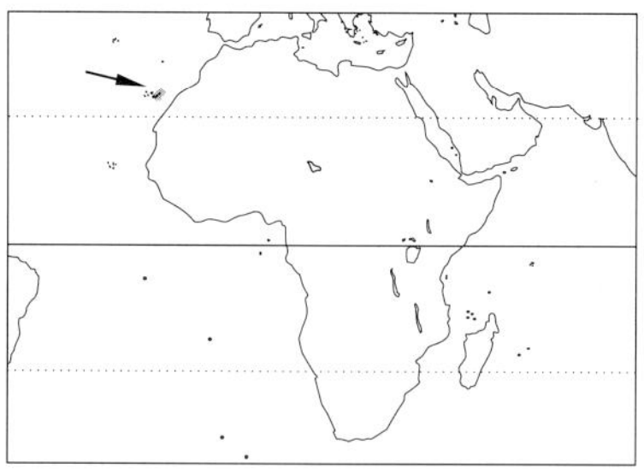

red, not yellow, eye; wing and tail shorter than in *H. fuliginosus*, and both bill and wing measurements average shorter than in black morph of *H. unicolor*. Juvenile unknown.
Habitat. Rocky and sandy shores. Probably predominantly a rocky shore species.
Food and Feeding. Unknown; probably mostly mussels and limpets. Likely prey species include limpets (*Patella candei*, *P. pipperata*, *P.* cf. *aspera*) and the mussel *Perna picta*; all of these species have been heavily exploited by man in E Canary Is. All oystercatchers attack different prey types using variety of techniques, e.g. hammering, prising, probing, stabbing (see page 314).
Breeding. Nest and eggs undescribed. A female "soon to lay" was collected in S Fuerteventura in early Apr 1888, and a pair in breeding condition collected on Graciosa in early Apr 1890. Clutch size probably 1-3.
Movements. Unknown, but very probably resident.
Status and Conservation. Almost certainly EXTINCT. Described as "not frequent" in mid-19th century. Last definite record was in 1913, although local fishermen and lighthouse keepers in 1970 estimated date of extinction as around 1940. Since 1965 there have been two unsubstantiated sight records from Tenerife. It is not known to which taxon 3 black oystercatchers seen on Senegal coast in 1970 and 1975 belonged: although movement from Canary Is to African mainland has been suggested in past, there is no evidence to support this; equally unlikely, however, that these birds were *H. moquini*, a species not recorded N of 12° S in Angola. Expeditions to Canary Is in 1956/57, 1970, 1985 and 1986 failed to find any trace of the bird.
Bibliography. Bannerman (1914, 1919-1920, 1922, 1963, 1969), Beaman (1994), Bolle (1854-1855, 1857), Collar & Andrew (1988), Collar *et al.* (1994), Collar & Stuart (1985), Cramp & Simmons (1983), Étchécopar & Hüe (1964), Godman (1872), Hockey (1982a, 1986a, 1986b, 1987), King (1978/79), Lovegrove (1971), Meade-Waldo (1889a, 1889b, 1890, 1893), Piersma (1986a), Stresemann (1927), von Thanner (1908).

6. African Black Oystercatcher

Haematopus moquini

French: Huîtrier de Moquin **Spanish**: Ostrero Negro Africano
German: Schwarzer Austernfischer
Other common names: African Oystercatcher, Black Oystercatcher(!)

Taxonomy. *Haematopus moquini* Bonaparte, 1856, Cape of Good Hope.
Has been considered conspecific with *H. meadewaldoi* or with *H. ostralegus*, or both. Monotypic.
Distribution. N Namibia S to Cape of Good Hope and E to E Cape Province, South Africa. Species recorded NE to KwaZulu-Natal and N to 12° S in Angola (Lobito), but only as vagrant.

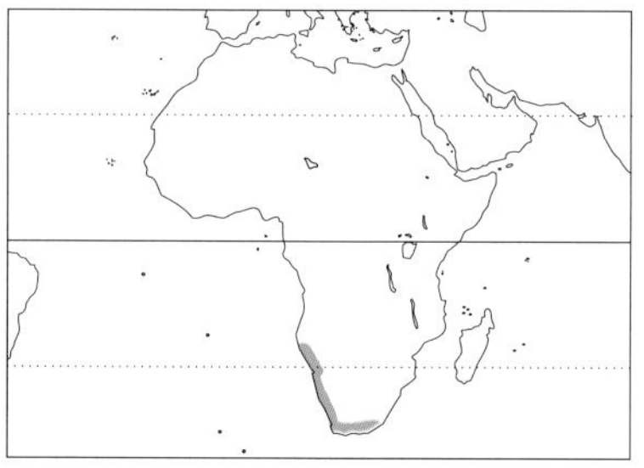

Descriptive notes. 42-45 cm; male 582-757 g, female 646-800 g. All dark oystercatcher with red eye, orange-red eye-ring and bill, and deep pinkish red legs. Has longer wings and shorter bill than *H. meadewaldoi*, but field separation of the two would be difficult; black dorsal coloration and red eye separate present species from New World black oystercatchers; bill is substantially shorter than that of any black oystercatcher in Australasia. Within pairs, males have blunter and shorter bills than females. Occasional plumage variants include birds with a small number of white feathers among flight-feathers, on breast or in axillaries; leucistic individuals rare, and no records of extensive albinism. Juvenile has dull eye, eye-ring, bill and legs; feathers fringed buffy-grey.
Habitat. Typically occurs on rocky and sandy shores, less frequent in estuaries and coastal lagoons. Offshore islands and sandy beaches favoured as breeding sites.
Food and Feeding. Diet includes limpets, mussels and other bivalves, polychaetes, whelks and crustaceans. On rocky shores important prey are polychaetes (*Pseudonereis variegata*, *Marphysa depressa*), mussels (*Choromytilus meridionalis*, *Perna perna*, *Aulacomya ater*, and introduced *Mytilus galloprovincialis*), limpets (*Patella cochlear*, *P. granularis*, *P. barbara*, *P. concolor*, *P. longicosta*, *P. granatina*, *P. oculus*) and whelks (*Burnupena catarrhacta*, *B. lagenaria*). On sandy shores diet dominated by sand mussels (*Donax serra*, *D. sordidus*). In estuaries the bivalves *Macoma* and *Solen* are eaten. All oystercatchers attack different prey types using variety of techniques, e.g. hammering, prising, probing, stabbing (see page 314).
Breeding. Laying Oct-Apr, mostly Dec-Feb; breeds slightly later in Namibia than in South Africa. Nest is scrape in sand or among shells; less often eggs laid on bare rock. Extent of nest lining variable, probably dependent on availability, and lining may include shell fragments and stone chips; nests on islands usually well lined, less so on mainland, perhaps influenced by abundance of Kelp Gulls (*Larus dominicanus*) on islands. Clutch 1-2, usually 2, rarely 3; incubation 27-39 days. Chick predominantly grey above, with black dorsal and femoral stripes; highly cryptic on granitic shores. Fledging 35-40 days. Fledging success 0·3-0·6 young per pair per year on predator-free offshore islands, lower on mainland: eggs and young vulnerable to terrestrial predators. Age of first breeding 3 years in females, probably 4 years in males. Longevity over 18 years.
Movements. Adults sedentary, although some undertake small-scale seasonal movements and habitat shifts. Most immatures do not disperse more than 150 km from their natal site, although maximum recorded of 600 km. Species is vagrant to KwaZulu-Natal and Angola.
Status and Conservation. Not globally threatened. Currently considered near-threatened. Uncommon, with total population of c. 5000 birds. Greatest concentrations: on mainland coasts of W Cape Province, with 1600 birds; islands off coast of Namibia, with 575 birds; and islands off W Cape, with 790 birds. Outside these areas, the key sites are: mainland shores around Lüderitz, Namibia, with 160 birds; St Francis Bay, E Cape Province, with 70; and Algoa Bay, E Cape with 125. Coastal development has undoubtedly caused population decreases in some areas, and off-road vehicles cause disturbance on sandy beaches. Most productive sector of population is on islands, amounting to c. 30% of total population; the major threat to these populations is introduction of terrestrial mammalian predators. There is evidence that breeding productivity has increased on W coast since 1980, following invasion of rocky shores by the alien Mediterranean mussel *Mytilus galloprovincialis*.

Bibliography. Avery (1977), Baker & Hockey (1984), Berry & Berry (1975), Blaker (1967), Bosman (1987), Bosman & Hockey (1988), Bosman *et al.* (1989), Braine (1987), Clancey (1964b), Cooper (1977a), Cooper *et al.* (1985), Dowsett & Forbes-Watson (1993), Elliott (1975), Ginn *et al.* (1989), Griffiths & Hockey (1987), Gurney (1872), Haagner (1948), Hall (1959c), Hockey (1980, 1981a, 1981b, 1982b, 1983a, 1983b, 1983c, 1984a, 1984b, 1985), Hockey & Bosman (1988), Hockey & Branch (1983, 1984), Hockey & Cooper (1980), Hockey & van Erkom Schurink (1992), Hockey & Underhill (1984), Jeffery (1987), de Kock & Randall (1984), Le Roux (1965), Mackworth-Praed & Grant (1962), Maclean (1993), Martin (1991), McLachlan *et al.* (1979), Pringle (1971), Rand (1949, 1950), Randall & Randall (1982), Robertshaw (1977), Rüppell (1845), Stresemann (1927), Summers & Cooper (1977), Urban *et al.* (1986), Ward (1990b, 1991, 1993), Watson & Kerley (1995).

7. Eurasian Oystercatcher

Haematopus ostralegus

French: Huîtrier pie **German**: Austernfischer **Spanish**: Ostrero Euroasiático
Other common names: Common/European/Northern Pied Oystercatcher, Sea Pie; South Island (Pied) Oystercatcher (*finschi*)

Taxonomy. *Haematopus Ostralegus* Linnaeus, 1758, Öland Island, Sweden.
At various times has been considered to include any or all of *H. palliatus*, *H. longirostris*, *H. chathamensis*, *H. unicolor*, *H. bachmani*, *H. moquini* and *H. meadewaldoi*. Taxonomic status of race *finschi* uncertain, and may be distinct species: frequently referred to *H. longirostris*, or occasionally to *H. unicolor* or even linked with *H. chathamensis*. Race *osculans* may also deserve treatment as separate species. Proposed races *malacophaga* of Iceland and Faeroes, *occidentalis* of British Is and *buturlini* of Turkmeniya and S Kazakhstan are probably insufficiently distinct to warrant recognition. Four subspecies normally recognized.
Subspecies and Distribution.
H. o. ostralegus Linnaeus, 1758 - Iceland and Scandinavia E to R Pechora, S through British Is to NW France, with isolated populations in Mediterranean from NE Spain and S France to Turkey; winters S to W Africa.
H. o. longipes Buturlin, 1910 - W & NC Russia (mouth of R Ob') S to Black, Caspian and Aral Seas and L Balkhash, and E to W Siberia; winters on coast from E Africa through Arabia to India.
H. o. osculans Swinhoe, 1871 - Kamchatka and W North Korea, and also suspected to breed from Amurland and Ussuriland through Manchuria to Hebei (NE China), and possibly in Kuril Is; winters in E China S to Guangdong.
H. o. finschi Martens, 1897 - South I, New Zealand; winters on coasts of South I and North I.

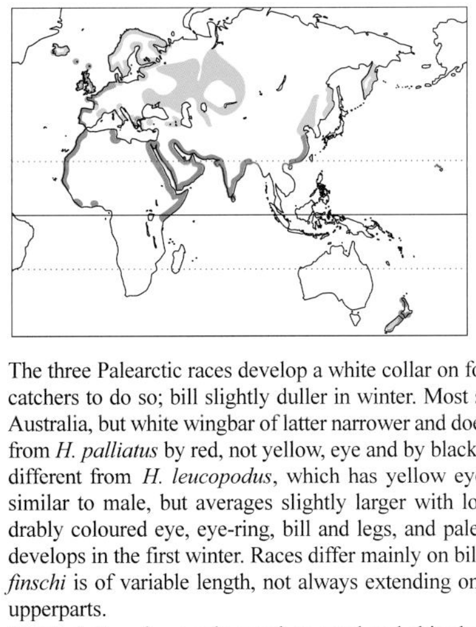

Descriptive notes. Nominate *ostralegus* 40-47·5 cm, male 425-805 g, female 445-820 g; race *finschi* c. 46 cm; male 518-615 g, female 538-622 g. Bill length of Palearctic races increases W to E: *ostralegus* male 76 mm, female 81 mm; *longipes* male 78 mm, female 89 mm; *osculans* (few data) male 99 mm, female 96 mm. Breeding adult has head, neck and upper breast all black; scapulars, upperwing-coverts and tail also black; broad white wingbar from inner secondaries to middle primaries, becoming narrower and more broken distally; middle and lower back, rump, uppertail-coverts, lower breast and belly white; eye and eye-ring red, bill orange-red, legs pink. The three Palearctic races develop a white collar on foreneck in non-breeding plumage, the only oystercatchers to do so; bill slightly duller in winter. Most similar in overall appearance to *H. longirostris* of Australia, but white wingbar of latter narrower and does not extent onto primaries; all races distinguished from *H. palliatus* by red, not yellow, eye and by black, not blackish brown, dorsal coloration; noticeably different from *H. leucopodus*, which has yellow eye and almost, wholly white secondaries. Female similar to male, but averages slightly larger with longer, thinner bill. Juvenile resembles adult with drably coloured eye, eye-ring, bill and legs, and pale margins to upperpart feathers; white neck collar develops in the first winter. Races differ mainly on bill length; also on extent of white wingbar, which in *finschi* is of variable length, not always extending onto inner primaries; *longipes* has slightly browner upperparts.
Habitat. Breeds on salt-marshes, sand and shingle beaches, less often on rocky coasts; also, especially in NW of range, breeds inland alongside water bodies and in agricultural land. In non-breeding season, mostly found on estuarine mudflats, but also salt-marshes and sandy and rocky shores. Race *finschi* breeds mostly inland on riverine shingle banks or in fields; outside breeding season, large flocks gather at major bays and estuaries.
Food and Feeding. Feeds on mussels and other bivalves, limpets, whelks, marine polychaetes, crabs, earthworms and insect larvae, rarely fish. When foraging on soft coastal substrates, important prey include bivalves (*Mytilus edulis*, *Cerastoderma edule*, *Macoma balthica*, *Mya arenaria*, *Scrobicularia plana*) and gastropods (*Littorina*). On coastal flats of W Africa, bloody cockle (*Anadara senilis*) taken. Polychaetes (*Nereis diversicolor*, *Arenicola marina*) eaten at estuaries, and crustaceans, including crabs (*Carcinus maenas*, *Uca tangeri*), also taken. Molluscs dominate diet on rocky shores, including mussels, limpets (*Patella*) and dogwhelk (*Nucella lapillus*). Inland prey includes earthworms, larvae of craneflies (*Tipula*) and caterpillars. All oystercatchers attack different prey types using variety of techniques, e.g. hammering, prising, probing, stabbing (see page 314).
Breeding. Laying (*ostralegus*) mostly Apr-May, with chicks mostly fledged by mid-Sept; *finschi* egg-laying mostly Sept-Nov. Nest is shallow scrape in ground, sometimes lined with shell and rock fragments, and, at inland sites, with small mammal droppings. Clutch size: *ostralegus* 2-5 (3), *longipes* and *osculans* 2-4 (3), *finschi* 2-3 (2). Incubation: *ostralegus* and *longipes* 24-35 days, *finschi* 24-28 days. Apart from striping common to oystercatcher chicks, upperparts and face of downy young are drab with sparse buffy tipping; crown heavily spotted black, as in *H. leucopodus*, but sooty brown throat markings do not extend onto breast, as in that species. Fledging: *ostralegus* c. 33 days, *finschi* c. 35 days. In *ostralegus*, age of first breeding 3 years in females, 4 years in males; longevity more than 40 years.
Movements. All races undertake seasonal movements and habitat shifts. Longest distance movements made by *ostralegus* and *longipes*. In nominate *ostralegus*, all inland breeders move to coast in winter; coastal populations between Norway, Gulf of Bothnia and White Sea move S; most birds spend winter in Europe, especially around the Wadden Sea and Irish Sea, with combined total of 500,000 birds; with exception of passage between Norway and Britain, North Sea acts as barrier to E-W migration; S limit to winter range of nominate *ostralegus* is normally Guinea. In races *longipes* and *osculans*, breeding and non-breeding ranges wholly disjunct. Race *longipes* winters on coast mainly from E Africa to India, but a few birds rarely penetrate as far S as South Africa. Race *osculans* occasionally winters on Anadyr estuary, Bering Is, Kuril Is and Sakhalin; also recorded in Myanmar and even Bangladesh. Birds are faithful to their non-breeding areas, but many do not return to breeding grounds for first time until their fourth year. Race *finschi* is short distance migrant, moving from inland breeding grounds to coasts of both North I and South I; several sightings of pied oystercatchers on Norfolk I and Lord Howe I, which have tentatively been attributed to *finschi* by some authors, could equally well refer to any of the other Australasian pied forms.
Status and Conservation. Not globally threatened. Both nominate *ostralegus* and *finschi* have increased during present century following on from decreases in 19th century; concomitantly, both taxa have increasingly spread to inland breeding habitats. Total breeding population of Europe reckoned at minimum of 200,000 pairs. Total population of *finschi* in early 1970's was estimated at 49,000 birds; in June 1984, 79,900 birds were counted. Numbers of race *longipes* have decreased this century, and this form is now rare in areas of Siberia where was once fairly common; reason for this decrease not known. Numbers of *osculans* have decreased since 1880's, when was described as locally abundant in parts of Japan, where is now a rare non-breeding visitor; may have bred in Japan during last century; breeding range of *osculans* poorly defined.
Bibliography. Ali & Ripley (1980), Altenburg *et al.* (1982), Anderson & Minton (1978), Baker, A. J. (1972, 1973a, 1974a, 1974b, 1974c, 1974d, 1975a, 1975b, 1975c, 1975d, 1977), Beser & von Helden-Sarnovski (1974), Blaszyk (1953), Boates (1988), Boates & Goss-Custard (1989), Briggs (1984a, 1984b), Brown & O'Connor (1974), Buxton (1939, 1957), Camphuysen & van Dijk (1983), Cayford (1988a, 1988b), Cayford & Goss-Custard (1990), Clancey (1971b), Cramp & Simmons (1983), Daan & Koene (1981), Dare (1966, 1970, 1977), Dare & Mercer (1973, 1974a, 1974b), Davidson, N.C. & Evans (1982), Davidson, P.E. (1967, 1968), Dewar (1922, 1940), Dijksen (1980), Dircksen (1932), Drinnan (1957, 1958a, 1958b), Durell & Goss-Custard (1984), Durell *et al.* (1993), Ens (1982, 1992), Ens & Goss-Custard (1984, 1986), Ens, Kersten *et al.* (1992), Ens, Safriel & Harris (1993), Feare (1971), Gloe & Busche (1974), Glutz von Blotzheim *et al.* (1975), Goede (1994), Goethe (1966, 1973), Goss-Custard (1996), Goss-Custard & Durell (1983, 1987a, 1987b, 1987c, 1988), Goss-Custard, Clarke & Durell (1984), Goss-Custard, Durell & Ens (1982), Goss-Custard, Durell, McGrorty & Reading (1982), Goss-Custard, Durell, McGrorty *et al.* (1981), Goss-Custard, Durell, Sitters & Swinfen (1982), Goss-Custard, McGrorty, Reading & Durell (1980), Grote (1951), Harris (1967, 1969, 1970c), Hausmann & Hausmann (1972, 1973a, 1973b), Heppleston (1968, 1970, 1971a, 1971b, 1971c, 1972), Heppleston & Kerridge (1970), Hockey & Cooper (1982), Holgersen (1962), Horlyk & Lind (1978), Horwood & Goss-Custard (1977), Hulscher (1971, 1973, 1974, 1975a, 1975b, 1976, 1977a, 1977b, 1982, 1985, 1988, 1989, 1990), Hulscher & Ens (1991, 1992), Jansen & Haase (1981), Jungfer (1954), Kersten & Brenninkmeijer (1995), Khrokov *et al.* (1980), Koene (1978), Koopman (1987, 1992), Lambeck (1991), Leopold *et al.* (1989), Lind (1965), Makkink (1942), Marchant & Higgins (1993), Marcström & Mascher (1979), Martínez-Vilalta *et al.* (1983), McKean (1978), Meininger, Blomert & Marteijn (1991), Meire & Kuyken (1984), Mercer (1968), Norton-Griffiths (1967a, 1967b, 1969), O'Connor & Brown (1977), Prater (1981a), Preuss (1961), Rafaelli *et al.* (1989), Richter (1967), Rittinghaus (1963), de Roos (1981), de Roos & Schaafsma (1981), Rosendahl & Skovgaard (1971), Safriel (1967, 1981, 1982, 1985), Safriel *et al.* (1984), Schnakenwinkel (1970), Sibson (1945, 1966), Speakman (1987), Stock, Herber & Geron (1989), Stock, Strotmann *et al.* (1987), Sutherland (1982a, 1982b, 1982c, 1982d), Sutherland & Ens (1987), Sutherland & Koene (1982), Swennen (1984, 1990), Swennen & de Bruijn (1980), Swennen & Duiven (1983), Swennen, de Bruijn *et al.* (1983), Swennen, Leopold & de Bruijn (1989), Thelle (1970), Thingstad (1978), Tinbergen & Norton-Griffiths (1964), Triplet (1989), Triplet *et al.* (1987), Urban *et al.* (1986), Väisänen (1977), von Vauk *et al.* (1989), Vines (1979, 1980), Wanink & Zwarts (1985), White & Gittins (1965), Williamson (1943, 1950, 1952), Wilson & Morrison (1981), Zwarts & Drent (1981), Zwarts & Wanink (1984), Zwarts *et al.* (1990).

8. Australian Pied Oystercatcher

Haematopus longirostris

French: Huîtrier à long bec **Spanish**: Ostrero Pío Australiano
German: Australischer Austernfischer
Other common names: Pied Oystercatcher

Taxonomy. *Haematopus longirostris* Vieillot, 1817, New South Wales.
Sometimes considered conspecific with *H. ostralegus*. Occasional hybridization recorded with *H. fuliginosus*. Form *H. ostralegus finschi* frequently considered to be race of present species. Monotypic.
Distribution. Coasts of Australia and Tasmania; Aru Is and Kai Is (SE Moluccas); also occurs locally on S coast of New Guinea, where probably only non-breeding visitor.

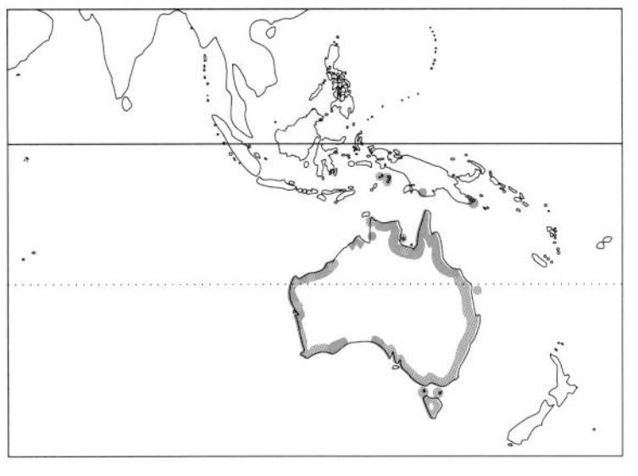

Descriptive notes. 48-51 cm; male averages 602-675 g (410-776), female 626-710 g (500-782). White of rump extends only onto lower back and ends rather squarely; white wingbar reduced; flight-feathers wholly blackish from below. Superficially resembles *H. ostralegus*, but markedly larger; latter has back extensively white, ending in sharp "V" between scapulars; no seasonal plumage change, unlike *H. ostralegus*. Separated from pied morph of *H. unicolor* and from *H. chathamensis* by crisp lower border to black breast; from *H. palliatus* by red, not yellow, eye and black, not blackish brown, dorsal coloration; *H. leucopodus* has yellow eye and mostly white secondaries. Female as male but averages somewhat larger with longer bill. Juvenile has brownish plumage and dull bare part colours.
Habitat. Breeds on salt-marshes, sandy and shingle beaches, dunes and pastures. Outside breeding season, typically occurs on estuarine mudflats and sandy beaches.
Food and Feeding. Prey includes marine and terrestrial polychaetes, gastropods (*Paphes striata*, *Anapella cycladea*) and bivalves (*Mytilus edulis*, *Codakia*, *Chione*), as well as crustaceans, insects and fish. All oystercatchers attack different prey types using variety of techniques, e.g. hammering, prising, probing, stabbing (see page 314).
Breeding. Breeding May-Sept in N, Aug-Jan in S. Nest is shallow scrape in ground, usually close to the high water mark. Usually 2 eggs (1-3), rarely 4; incubation 28-32 days. Downy chick pale speckled grey-brown with dark brown dorsal and femoral stripes; lower breast and belly white. Fledging 42-49 days, reportedly sometimes up to 56 days. Fledging success 0·27-0·89 young per pair per year. Young remain in parental territory for 1-6 months. Age of first breeding 4-6 years. Long-term mate and nest-site fidelity.
Movements. Forms non-breeding flocks, but no major movements recorded; may breed throughout range. Status in S New Guinea uncertain; may be only non-breeding visitor, but, if so, origin of such birds unknown.
Status and Conservation. Not globally threatened, although subject to disturbance from recreation, including use of off-road vehicles. By far the commonest oystercatcher in Australia; minimum population 10,000 birds. The most important 20 sites each support more than 100 birds, with a combined total of 5680 birds. Most abundant in large bays in Victoria, Tasmania and South Australia, but especially in stretch from Eyre Peninsula to Bass Strait.

Bibliography. Ashby (1991), Baker, A. J. (1975a, 1977), Beehler *et al*. (1986), Blakers *et al*. (1984), Christidis & Boles (1994), Coates (1985), Hewish (1990), Lane & Davies (1987), Lauro & Nol (1993), Marchant & Higgins (1993), Mathews (1913-1914), McFarland (1993), McKean (1978), Newman, O. M. G. (1982b, 1983, 1984, 1986, 1991, 1992a, 1992b), Newman & Park (1992a, 1992b, 1993), Pringle (1987), Rand & Gilliard (1967), Serventy & Whittel (1976), Slater (1987), Wakefield & Robertson (1988), White & Bruce (1986).

9. Chatham Oystercatcher

Haematopus chathamensis

French: Huîtrier des Chatham **German**: Chathamausternfischer **Spanish**: Ostrero de las Chatham

Taxonomy. *Haematopus ostralegus chathamensis* Hartert, 1927, Chatham Islands.
Has frequently been considered a race of *H. unicolor* or *H. ostralegus*; differentiation relatively weak, and species status questionable. Form *H. ostralegus finschi* has on occasion been associated with present species. Monotypic.
Distribution. Chatham Is, E of New Zealand, where restricted to coasts of Chatham, Mangere, Rangatira (formerly South-east I) and Pitt.

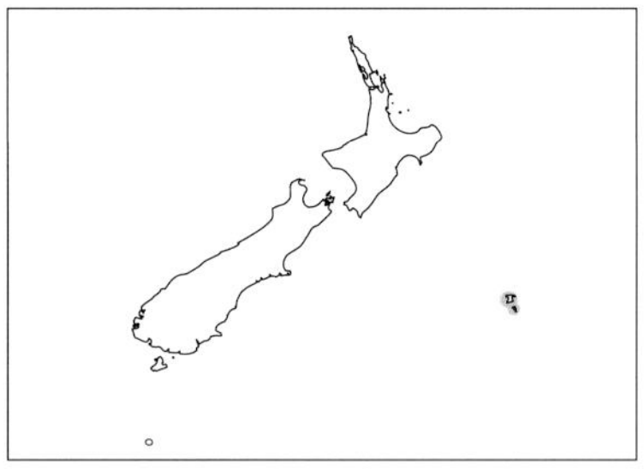

Descriptive notes. 47-49 cm; male averages 540 g, female 640 g. Black frontal coloration extends well down breast, and transition to the white lower breast is mottled, both features also found in pied morph of *H. unicolor*, but in no other Old World pied oystercatcher. Most closely resembles pied morph of *H. unicolor*, but averages slightly smaller with much shorter bill; legs and feet stockier; in flight, white uppertail-coverts less conspicuous. Distinguished from *H. palliatus* by red, not yellow, eye and black, not blackish brown, dorsal coloration; from *H. leucopodus* by red, not yellow, eye and mostly black secondaries. Female similar to male, but averages larger and longer-billed. Juvenile has brown fringes to feathers of upperparts, and dull bare part colours.
Habitat. Mostly found on rocky shores, less often on sandy or gravel beaches; sometimes nest in sites with some short vegetation.
Food and Feeding. Prey includes the anemone *Isactina tenebrosa*, an unusual prey type for oystercatchers; also polyplacophorans (*Chiton pelliserpentis*, *C. glaucus*), gastropods (*Haliotis australis*, *H. iris*, *Cellana chathamensis*, *Patelloidea corticata*, *Zelidoma digna* and several others), bivalves (*Aulacomya maoriana*, *Mytilus edulis*, *Xenostrobus pulex*), barnacles, isopods, echinoderms and ascidians. Rocky shores favoured for foraging. All oystercatchers attack different prey types using variety of techniques, e.g. hammering, prising, probing, stabbing (see page 314).
Breeding. Breeds Oct-Mar, with most laying Oct-Dec. Nest is scrape in ground, lined or unlined; often in sheltered site under overhanging rock or vegetation, sometimes in small cave or on cliff ledge. Clutch size 2-3; 3-egg clutches commonest early in breeding season; incubation c. 25 days. Chick has heavily speckled grey upperparts; tail with a conspicuous white subterminal band. Fledging period 46-49 days. Fledging success 0·20-0·85 (0·47) young per pair per year.
Movements. Mostly sedentary and territorial throughout the year; juvenile dispersal up to 40 km between islands.
Status and Conservation. ENDANGERED. Population increased from c. 50 birds in early 1970's to 100-110 birds in breeding season of 1987/88, including 44 pairs. Largest numbers on Chatham I, with 25 pairs, where population probably increasing; 9 pairs on Pitt, 8 on Rangatira, 2 on Mangere; possibly 1 pair on nearby Star Keys. Main threat is predation by introduced cats, rats and Wekas (*Gallirallus australis*); within range, only Rangatira I and Mangere I are predator-free, and both are nature reserves; in parts of range browsing mammals also have negative effects on species, while predation by Brown Skuas (*Catharacta antarctica*) may be another significant factor. Human disturbance is also a problem; access has been prohibited to a section of coast of Rangatira, in order to reduce level of disturbance. On Chatham I, some pairs nesting on sandy beaches are forced down towards seashore by introduced maram grass (*Ammophila arenaria*), where nest is more vulnerable to flooding during storms or high tides; since 1992, conservation efforts to avert this by moving nest further in from sea; artificial incubation of eggs, for return immediately prior to hatching, is probably contributing to reduce risk of predation.
Bibliography. Baker, A. J. (1972, 1973a, 1974a, 1974b, 1974d, 1975a, 1975d, 1977), Bell (1986), Collar & Andrew (1988), Falla (1939), Fleming (1939a), King (1978/79), Lindsay *et al*. (1959), Marchant & Higgins (1993), McKean (1978), Robertson (1985), Sibson (1982), Williams & Given (1981).

10. Variable Oystercatcher

Haematopus unicolor

French: Huîtrier variable **German**: Neuseeländischer Austernfischer **Spanish**: Ostrero Variable
Other common names: New Zealand Black/Sooty Oystercatcher; Northern Oystercatcher ("*reischeki*")

Taxonomy. *Haematopus unicolor* J. R. Forster, 1844, New Zealand.
Has been considered conspecific with *H. chathamensis* and sometimes also with *H. ostralegus*. The various different morphs have been considered separate races, or even distinct species, e.g. pied morph formerly labelled "*H. reischeki*"; in past, *H. ostralegus finschi* too was considered to be a pied morph of present species. Monotypic.
Distribution. New Zealand, on coasts of North I and South I and adjacent islands.
Descriptive notes. 47-49 cm. Polymorphic in plumage and size: in black morph, male averages 678 g, female 724 g; in pied morph male 717 g, female 750 g; in intermediate morph male 710 g, female 779 g. Culmen shortest in black morph, male 79 mm, female 89 mm; longest in intermediate morph, male 84 mm, female 95 mm. Black morph entirely black with red eye, eye-ring and bill; coloration almost identical to that of *H. fuliginosus*, but bill longer and tail does not project beyond wingtips at rest. Pied morph differs from other Old World pied oystercatchers, except *H. chathamensis*, in black frontal coloration extending further down breast, and ending with untidy lower border; lower breast and belly predominantly white, with a few dark feathers; lacks white shoulder patch of other pied species; in flight, white wingbar reduced, back and rump blackish, with white only on uppertail-coverts. Intermediate morphs range between black and pied extremes, generally being closer to former; they are also larger, longer-billed and longer-winged than other morphs. All morphs distinguished from *H. bachmani*, *H. ater* and *H. palliatus* by red, not yellow,

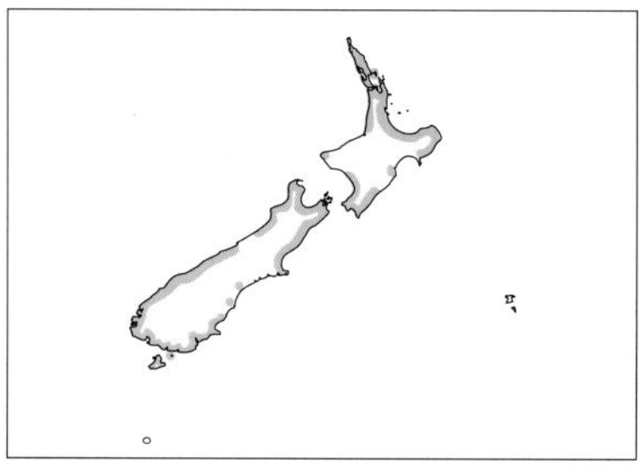

eye and black, not blackish brown, dorsal plumage; separated from *H. leucopodus* on eye colour and mostly black secondaries. Female similar to male, but averages larger and longer-billed. Juvenile has black areas browner, with some pale buff tips to scapulars and upperwing-coverts; bare parts duller.
Habitat. Breeds on sandy beaches and adjacent dunes. Outside breeding season, occupies sandy and rocky shores. On Stewart I, some pairs nest in small rocky bays with overhanging trees: chicks are hidden in caves if danger threatens.
Food and Feeding. Prey includes polychaetes (*Glycera americana*, *Perinereis nuntia*), polyplacophorans (*Chiton pelliserpentis*, *C. glaucus*), gastropods (*Haliotis iris*, *Cellana*), mussels (*Mytilus edulis*, *Aulacomya maoriana*, *Modiolus neozelandicus*), several other bivalve species, as well as isopods, amphipods and crabs. All oystercatchers attack different prey types using variety of techniques, e.g. hammering, prising, probing, stabbing (see page 314).
Breeding. Eggs usually laid Dec-Jan, sometimes as early as Sept. Nest is shallow scrape in sand or shingle, with minimal lining. Clutch size 2-3, usually 3; incubation 25-32 days (28). Chick patterning variable, depending on colour morph: that of black morph resembles that of *H. fuliginosus* in having dark underparts; pied morph chick has breast white, upperparts greyish brown, but less distinctly patterned than in *H. ostralegus finschi*. Fledging 42-49 days. Fledging success variable, 0·5 young per pair per year in protected sites, lower elsewhere. Longevity record 19 years 10 months.
Movements. Forms non-breeding flocks, but no major movements.
Status and Conservation. Not globally threatened. Generally uncommon, and less frequent on E coasts than elsewhere; total population estimated at 3900 birds, of which roughly 70% black morph, 20% pied morph and 10% intermediate morph; estimated c. 2600 birds on North I, c. 1150 birds on South I. Low breeding success has been linked to possible effects of human disturbance, in the form of off-road vehicles, dogs, etc.; introduced mammals have also caused many losses through predation of eggs and chicks. In recent years, several populations apparently increasing, especially on North I; conservation activity includes protection of nests from predators and disturbance.
Bibliography. Baker, A. J. (1972, 1973a, 1973b, 1974a, 1974b, 1974c, 1974d, 1975a, 1975d), Baker, A. J. *et al*. (1981), Blackburn (1968), Braithwaite (1950), Chambers (1989), Falla (1939), Falla *et al*. (1981), Fleming, C.A. & Falconer (1974), Fleming, P. (1990), Heather (1980), Hutton & Sloan (1993), Jones (1979), Mackereth (1992), Marchant & Higgins (1993), McKean (1978), Robertson (1985), Rothschild (1899), Scarlett (1980), Stidolph (1973), Stresemann (1927), Walter, D. M. (1984), Watt (1955).

11. Sooty Oystercatcher

Haematopus fuliginosus

French: Huîtrier fuligineux **German**: Rußausternfischer **Spanish**: Ostrero Negro Australiano
Other common names: Spectacled Oystercatcher (*opthalmicus*)

Taxonomy. *Haematopus fuliginosus* Gould, 1845, Tasmania.
Occasional hybridization recorded with *H. longirostris*. Form *opthalmicus* generally considered to be a race of present species, based on a putative region of intergrading with nominate *fuliginosus* in W Australia, where both taxa are rare, but no good evidence of interbreeding; also, some confusion regarding range limits of both forms, with *opthalmicus* usually said to be restricted to Gulf of Carpentaria and Cape York Peninsula; striking differences in eye-ring colour suggest that *opthalmicus* may well be a distinct species; field and laboratory research required, in order to clarify this case (see page 309); emendation of name to *ophthalmicus* is not justified. Two subspecies currently recognized.
Subspecies and Distribution.
H. f. opthalmicus Castelnau & Ramsay, 1877 - coast and islands of N Australia from Shark Bay (CW Western Australia) to Lady Elliot I (SE Queensland).
H. f. fuliginosus Gould, 1845 - coast and islands of Australia, from Houtman Abrolhos Is (CW Western Australia) round S coast and up E coast to about Brisbane (SE Queensland); Tasmania.

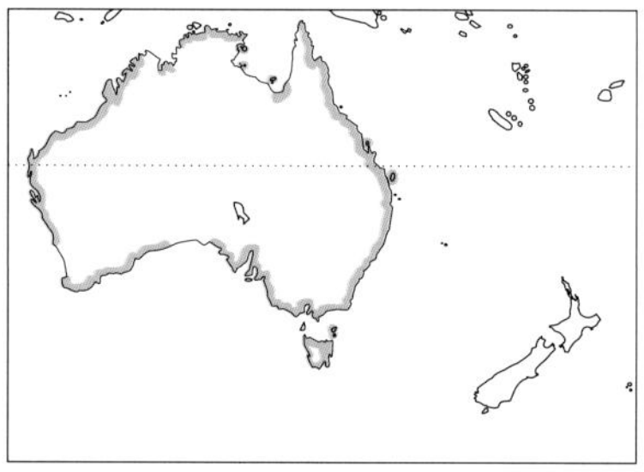

Descriptive notes. 46-49 cm; 550-774 g. Entirely sooty black oystercatcher with red eye, eye-ring and bill, and pink legs. Longer-tailed than other black oystercatchers; folded wings do not reach tail tip in present species, as they do in shorter-tailed, but otherwise very similar, black morph of *H. unicolor*. Differs from all New World black oystercatchers in having black dorsal coloration and red eye; wings and bill longer than in *H. moquini*, and eye-ring and bill redder. Female averages very slightly larger, with shorter wings and broader bill. Juvenile duller and browner, with pale buff or white tips to most of feathers; bare parts duller. Race *opthalmicus* differs from nominate race in having slightly shorter wings, a shorter, heavier bill, and a prominent fleshy yellowish to orange eye-ring; bill markedly shorter than in black morph of *H. unicolor*.
Habitat. Nominate *fuliginosus* breeds on sand and shingle beaches, and also on rocky shores, especially on islands; outside breeding season typically occurs on estuarine mudflats and sandy beaches. Race *opthalmicus* occurs more commonly on offshore islands with fringing coral reefs than on mainland shores.
Food and Feeding. Diet includes limpets, whelks, bivalves, chitons, crustaceans, echinoderms and ascidians, and also stranded fish. Commonly taken prey items include gastropods (*Cellana tramoserica*, *Clypidina rugosa*, *Patella peroni*, *Dicathais orbita*, *Nerita atramentosa*, *Turbo undulatus*); bivalves eaten include *Trichomya hirsuta*, *Xenostrobus pulex* and *Austromytilus rostratus*. Several species of polyplacophorans also eaten, most commonly *Ischnochiton australis*. Feeding habits of race *opthalmicus* undocumented. All oystercatchers attack different prey types using variety of techniques, e.g. hammering, prising, probing, stabbing (see page 314).
Breeding. Season Aug-Jan. Nest is scrape in ground, often among boulders, lined to varying extents with shell fragments. Usually 2 eggs (2-4); incubation and fledging periods unknown. As in other Old World oystercatchers, crown of chick is well marked with black; unusual among oystercatchers, however, the chick is an even, rusty colour and lacks white down on belly. No information available on breeding of race *opthalmicus*; chick undescribed.

Movements. Mostly sedentary. In area of Hobart (Tasmania), birds move very short distance from breeding islands to estuary of R Derwent in winter. Single record on Christmas I (Indian Ocean).

Status and Conservation. Not globally threatened. Total population probably under 4500 birds. Nominate *fuliginosus* is generally uncommon, and probably numbers less than 3500 birds; most abundant in SC & SE Australia, and also on Tasmania. The most important 20 localities together support a maximum of 2180 birds, including 1660 birds at only 7 localities; conservation action is considered necessary at these 7 main sites, in order to minimize habitat loss. Numbers in Hobart area decreased by c. 40% between early 1960's and early 1980's, but reasons for decrease unknown; over the same period, numbers of *H. longirostris* in the same area remained unchanged. Total population of race *opthalmicus* probably less than 1000 birds; precise distribution poorly known, but appears patchy; this and low abundance may be linked to apparent requirement of co-occurring islands and coral reefs, the latter being favoured feeding areas; no major concentrations of this form are known. Much scope for research.

Bibliography. Amiet (1957), Anderson, M. (1993), Ashby (1991), Baker, A. J. (1975a, 1977), Blakers *et al.* (1984), Chafer (1992a, 1992b), Considine (1979, 1982), Ford (1987), Hewish (1990), Lane & Davies (1987), Marchant & Higgins (1993), Mathews (1913-1914), McKean (1978), Newman (1982c), Newman & Fletcher (1982), Pringle (1987), Schulz (1989), Serventy & Whittel (1976), Slater (1987), Storr (1985), Thomas (1968), Wakefield & Robertson (1988).

Class AVES
Order CHARADRIIFORMES
Suborder CHARADRII
Family IBIDORHYNCHIDAE (IBISBILL)

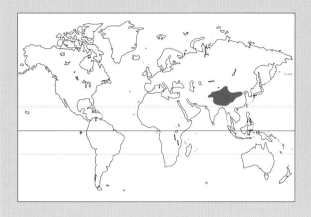

- Distinctive medium-sized wader, strongly built but elegant, with contrasting plumage, decurved bill and long legs.
- 39-41 cm.

- Mountain systems of Central Asia.
- Shingle-bed rivers.
- 1 genus, 1 species, 1 taxon.
- No species threatened; none extinct since 1600.

Systematics

The treatment most appropriate for the Ibisbill (*Ibidorhyncha struthersii*) has long been a matter of discussion amongst taxonomists. Whereas in early classifications it was often associated with the Scolopacidae and their allies, nowadays there is reasonable consensus that it is most closely related to three groups, the oystercatchers (Haematopodidae), the avocets and stilts (Recurvirostridae) and the lapwings and plovers (Charadriidae), although there is still considerable disagreement as to which of these groups contains its closest relatives.

Perhaps equally controversial is the question of precisely what level of taxonomic separation it requires from these other groups. On frequent occasions it has been argued that the peculiarities of the Ibisbill do not warrant its separation in its own monotypic family, and authors have frequently placed it within Recurvirostridae, while it has also been linked with Haematopodidae. It shows marked similarities with the oystercatchers in terms of general breeding behaviour and calls. On the other hand, there are many reasons for linking it with the avocets and stilts, not the least of which is DNA evidence, which suggests that these birds and the Ibisbill are very close relatives, sharing a single tribe in a subfamily that includes the oystercatchers as the only other tribe; the lapwings and plovers would make up the other subfamily in this expanded version of Charadriidae.

In contrast with these various points of proximity are the Ibisbill's distinctive morphology, also visible in young birds, together with its unique territorial behaviour. As the balance of the evidence rests at present, there is probably sufficient reason to justify classifying the Ibisbill in a family of its own, perhaps forming some sort of a link between Haematopodidae and Recurvirostridae. However, the debate will undoubtedly continue.

The origins of this highly specialized wader possibly date back to the early Tertiary, when the Charadriiformes were at their early stages of development. Study of morphological and anatomical features has, in fact, led to the conclusion that at present this species does not appear to have close relatives in any of the groups with which it is often associated. Very possibly, Recurvirostridae, Haematopodidae and Ibidorhynchidae separated from the main branch of Charadriiformes at different times and developed independently from each other.

On the other hand, a number of similarities in morphology and ecology between Ibidorhynchidae and Haematopodidae led to the theory that they had a common ancestor which developed on the shores of the ancient sea of Tethys in the heart of what is now Eurasia. Tethys started to disappear in the Tertiary, as the mountain systems of Central Asia began to form. Ibidorhynchidae may have developed ecological links with the newly forming habitats, whereas Haematopodidae continued to associate itself with the remains of the ancient sea. Earlier hypotheses argued that the ancestral form of the Ibisbill was an Arctic dweller, and that during recent glaciations it was pushed into Central Asian mountain refuges where it continued its development, but these hardly seem feasible, for it would surely have taken much longer for such a highly specialized form to develop.

Morphological Aspects

In appearance, the Ibisbill is one of the most distinctive of all the waders, or shorebirds. It is medium-sized and strongly built, normally weighing in the region of 270-320 g, with females slightly larger than males. Its very long, decurved bill and its rather strikingly contrasted plumage combine to make it unmistakable.

The bird's most notable feature is its crimson bill, which measures 68-82 mm, with a tendency to be slightly longer in the female than in the male. The bill would appear to have developed to enable the Ibisbill to forage in rocky mountain streams, by means of a number of specialized methods of feeding (see Food and Feeding).

For a bird that spends a good deal of time wading in a fair depth of water the tarsus is relatively short; it is reticulated throughout. There are three toes, with the outer and middle toes connected by a small, but deeply indented, web, but no webbing between the middle and inner toes. The legs are greyish purple in colour, quite different from that of the bill, although in museum collections they turn crimson after a short while and so look much the same colour as the bill. During the breeding season, Ibisbills run short distances, very much in the mode of *Charadrius* plovers, holding the head and bill down and standing upright only to look around and evaluate a given situation. They are good swimmers and will cross river channels by this means rather than by flying.

The Ibisbill's plumage is striking. The crown and forepart of the face are black or dark brownish black, with a white margin towards the rear. The nape, neck, mantle and upper back are bluish grey, while the lower back is brownish grey. The rump shows some faint greyish black bars, which become more pronounced closer to the tail, and on it, where they can be as much as 4 mm wide. The

The Ibisbill is usually seen feeding alone on slow-moving rivers in high mountain regions of Central Asia. Wholly dependent on aquatic invertebrates, it will often stand in quite deep water for long periods, plucking insects from the surface as they float by. Alternatively, as water temperatures influence insect activity, it may use its long, decurved bill to probe under stones or rake sideways through the water in order to find food. The white facial feathering shows that this bird is in non-breeding plumage.

[*Ibidorhyncha struthersii*, India. Photo: Markku Huhta-Koivisto]

belly is white with a broad, circular black breast band, above which is a narrow white band separating it from the grey upper breast. The bold grey, dark brown and white plumage provides remarkably effective camouflage in the surroundings, an asset which is particularly advantageous when a bird is incubating eggs or brooding chicks. Winter plumage is similar, except that there is a fair amount of scattered white feathering on the face.

The wings appear generally brownish grey, but the outer primaries and coverts are blackish. A dull white band across the inner primaries and outer secondaries is visible only in flight, when it appears rather conspicuous. The overall aspect of an Ibisbill in flight recalls that of an oystercatcher, although its wings are generally very square, and the plumage is, of course, totally dissimilar. Its flight is strong, with sharp but comparatively slow wingbeats.

The juvenile is distinctly browner than the adult, lacking the intense black markings on the head and breast, which are grey-brown. The mantle and wings are brown to brownish grey, with buff-orange fringes giving a scalloped effect. Bare parts too are duller, with the bill dark pinkish grey and the legs pink or greenish grey; the iris is pale yellowish red, as opposed to dark red in adults.

The moult pattern of the Ibisbill is little known, although it is thought to follow those of other Charadrii. Full moult usually starts at the end of June, whereas spring moult into breeding plumage reportedly occurs in March.

Unlike the cases of the oystercatchers, avocets and stilts, salt glands are nearly absent in the Ibisbill. This can, of course, be explained by the fact that water in the Ibisbill's habitat is almost totally devoid of salt, as it comes from snow melting in the mountains. Conversely, the other groups occur commonly in environments where water is high in salinity, whether on coasts or inland on saline lakes.

Habitat

The Ibisbill is closely associated with the bleak mountain environment, in particular shingle-bed rivers at 2000-4000 m. However, it has also been reported breeding at altitudes as high as 4400 m and as low as 500 m.

Even though the Ibisbill is widely distributed within the mountain systems of Central Asia, its habitat is very much the same throughout its range: a shingle-bed river valley varying from 100 m to 1500 m wide, covered with pebbles, cobbles and small boulders of varying sizes, usually interspersed with patches of sand and silt. Some of the longer valleys may accommodate several pairs of Ibisbills. Such areas normally contain more than one river channel and often hold a complicated network of small, shallow channels, islets and peninsulas which provide the main

feeding areas for the Ibisbill. These river valleys are usually treeless and indeed are generally fairly free of vegetation; they tend to have a slope of 5-15° or less, which ensures a relatively slow flow of water.

Ibisbills exhibit a very clear ecological preference for this particular type of habitat, since only here can they find suitable food supplies. Unlike other river specialists of the zone, such as the Brown Dipper (*Cinclus pallasii*), the White-capped Redstart (*Chaimarrornis leucocephalus*) and the Plumbeous Redstart (*Rhyacornis fuliginosus*), which are adapted to both the turbulent, boulder-strewn channels and slower-flowing waters of mountain rivers, the Ibisbill is restricted to areas of slow water flow. Hence, despite a comparatively expansive range, the high degree of specialization in the Ibisbill's feeding habits strictly limits it to the much more reduced areas of suitable habitat that are available.

General Habits

Ibisbills are solitary breeders, but the limited availability of suitable breeding sites sometimes creates the impression of loose colonies, despite individual territoriality. In autumn and winter, they are also generally solitary but are sometimes seen in pairs or in small groups of up to eight birds; flocks of up to 25 birds have also been reported. Outside the breeding season they sometimes roost together, for instance a group of seven birds was observed in early October in the Trans Ili Mountains of Kazakhstan, roosting together on a tiny islet. During winter months, birds tend to be fairly restful, but with the breeding season approaching they become much more active and vocal; at this time they become susceptible to disturbance.

Ibisbills feed during the day, most actively in the morning hours, when they are typically to be seen in short riverside grass, running a few steps and then stopping abruptly. They also have a characteristic habit of wading breast deep in the water, placing the whole head and neck under water in search of food. Birds will often spend long periods of time sitting motionless on the bank of a river or lake, when they may become virtually invisible against the surrounding landscape.

During the breeding season, Ibisbills tend to take flight more often, but otherwise they rarely fly unless disturbed, even apparently preferring to cross rivers by swimming. When disturbed, a bird usually moves its head up and down, sometimes as much as 18 times in one minute, in an apparent display of nervousness. Occasionally, an Ibisbill will run with its head turned to one side, giving the peculiar impression that the head is being carried loose, while the bird moves forward.

Voice

Outside the breeding season, Ibisbills generally tend to be silent, and it is only with the onset of breeding activity in spring that they start to become much more vocal.

Calls can be made in three main situations: when a bird is disturbed, in territorial displays with a neighbouring pair, or in courtship display. The call typically made during courtship display resembles that of the Eurasian Oystercatcher (*Haematopus ostralegus*), but it is louder, more melodious and silvery, consisting of up to 40 rather penetrating notes. The species also gives three or four loud "kleep" notes, the first two of which come close together, whereas the third and fourth are given after short pauses. Both types of call are reported to occur during territorial and agonistic behaviour, as well as during courtship displays.

Food and Feeding

The Ibisbill is a highly specialized species, entirely dependent upon a very harsh habitat for its food. Its diet consists of a variety of insects and their larvae, crustaceans and small fish. During the breeding season at higher altitudes, small fish are only taken occasionally, but their capture is much more frequent during the winter months at lower altitudes, where fish may comprise an important part of the diet.

A study of feeding behaviour during mid-April in Langtang Khola, Nepal, revealed that the food taken consisted mainly of aquatic insects. Faecal analyses revealed a diet of stonefly larvae (40%), mayfly larvae (34%) caddisfly larvae (8%), caddisfly adults (9%) and small fish (3%).

There are three main feeding methods: pecking, probing and raking. An Ibisbill will often peck drifting insects from the water surface, staying more or less at the same spot by the beginning or end of rapids; sometimes the entire foraging period of three or four hours is spent like this. However, normally birds peck while standing in the water at about belly depth and feeding singly, both members of a pair feeding together only occasionally. Probing is also carried out at about belly depth, the bill being inserted amongst all sizes of submerged stones, but the birds move about much more, taking roughly 15 minutes to cover 20 m of river edge. The third method, raking, involves tilting the head to one side and raking the bill sideways through the pebbles. When using this method, birds may dislodge invertebrates, which drift into view, enabling a bird to peck them up.

The cold, clear streams of the mountain systems of Central Asia present difficult feeding conditions. Yet the Ibisbill is very well adapted to the conditions and is able to switch its feeding method quickly in response to changing weather, as well as moving between aquatic and riparian feeding habitats. Fluctuating water temperatures affect the activity patterns of aquatic insects, which in turn affect the feeding behaviour of Ibisbills. Low water temperatures inhibit insect activity forcing the birds to feed by tactile probing, or by raking insects into view, whereas higher water temperatures permit the Ibisbills to feed on active or drifting insects.

Breeding

As with most other aspects of its biology, the breeding habits of the Ibisbill remain rather poorly known. It would appear to be monogamous, at any rate within one season, but detailed long-term studies are still required in order to clarify many points. Observations by Sálim Ali in Sikkim indicated that three adults seemed to be interested in the nest he was watching, but, while the implications of this could be many, to date there appear to be no further records of a similar sort.

The breeding season starts at slightly different times depending on the altitude, although the time delay is not as much as one might expect within a range as great as 500-4400 m. Pair formation takes place in March and early April, after which breeding territories are formed. In places where more than one pair of Ibisbills breed, territories vary in length from 90 m to 1000 m of river valley. There is also considerable variation in the width of a territory, with a minimum of over 100 m, but sometimes much more. Where there is a solitary breeding pair, for example in the delta of a mountain river, a territory may be well over 1 km², and birds move extensively around it. In the Trans Ili mountains of Kazakhstan, an area of about 1·3 km² supported three breeding pairs.

During courtship displays a male will call and move its head up and down. A female responds to this behaviour by moving slowly towards the male and then turning and standing motionless. The male then approaches rapidly and briefly simulates copulation. Eventually copulation takes place, after which both birds ruffle their feathers and start preening or foraging. Nest-site inspection involves the same initial behaviour, leading to the rapid circling of a potential nest-site.

The nest-site is situated on a bank, island or peninsula along the main river valley, sometimes as much as 100 m from the water. The nest itself is a simple pit, which in the Himalayas is about 30 cm wide and 6 cm deep, although nest bowls examined in Kazakhstan were somewhat smaller, at around 20 cm in diameter and about 2·5-3 cm deep. The nest is sometimes lined with small pebbles usually not exceeding 1 cm in size.

Laying takes place from the end of April to the first half of May. Eggs are laid daily, to produce a clutch of two to four eggs, most commonly four. The broadly oval eggs have a rather thin shell, but are fairly large for the size of the bird, on average measuring 51 x 37 mm and weighing around 37 g. They are drab grey to greenish grey with dark brown spots and speckles, mainly concentrated at the large end. If the first clutch is lost, birds may attempt a second.

The length of the incubation period has not yet been determined, but it is known that both parents take part. The female undertakes about two thirds of the daytime incubation, but the pattern at night is not clear. During the incubation period birds will not leave the nest unattended for more than 1-2 minutes at a time. Conditions can be harsh for incubating birds, and even in May snow is not a rarity in the mountains of Central Asia, so that a sitting bird may be almost covered with snow. An incubating bird often places its bill under the wing and in this posture is very difficult to detect. Approximately once an hour the duty bird will change its position, by up to 180°, but the eggs are turned less often. Observations at one nest-site showed that adults swapped duty about seven times a day. At the change over, the bird taking up incubation approaches the nest on foot. The departing bird moves away from the nest when its mate is still 10-15 m away. Both birds remain silent during the change over. This incubation pattern remains very much the same right up until the eggs hatch.

Hatching takes place from mid-May to late June. The newly-hatched chick is quite distinctive. Its brownish bill is about 18 mm long and shows slight decurvature only in its distal third. There are brown patches on the ear-coverts, while the upperparts are grey with blackish barring, the intervals increasing towards the tail, and this same pattern occurs on the wings. The belly is

There is no mistaking the identity of an Ibisbill: the long decurved deep crimson bill is the give-away feature. The black facial mask, crown and breast band add distinctive notes to the largely pale plumage. As the bird flies, with its head slightly raised and its neck stretched out, the white wing-flash and dark markings around the rump and tail also become conspicuous. The legs are rather short and do not protrude beyond the tail.

[*Ibidorhyncha struthersii*, Uttar Pradesh, India. Photo: Tim Loseby]

A bird of specialized feeding habits, the Ibisbill is restricted to high altitude, rather flat-bottomed river valleys, where the water flows fairly slowly through a network of channels forming banks and islets of shingle, pebbles and rounded boulders. Here it breeds, and only in autumn will it move down to a similar shingle-bed valley at a lower altitude in order to be able to feed in unfrozen waters. The nest-site is a depression hollowed out in the sandy shingle, sometimes lined with pebbles. The usual clutch consists of four greenish grey eggs speckled with brown. Both parents often face severe weather conditions, even snow, as they take turns in incubation, the length of which has not yet been ascertained. The newly hatched chick already has an 18-mm-long slightly decurved bill, mainly greyish down with dark barring and very large toes. Once dry, the chicks are led away from the nest and may be brooded by both parents for up to 23 days. The parents show great agitation and sometimes present an aggressive attitude towards an intruder, while the chicks remain "frozen" when danger threatens. Both parents and young birds will remain in the same general area until the onset of bad weather in the autumn obliges them to move downhill to milder climes.

[Ibidorhyncha struthersii, Trans Ili Range, Tien Shan, Kazakhstan. Photo: V. Morozov]

white and the throat greyish, while the sides of the neck and nape are ash grey, producing a whitish collar. The legs are greenish grey, and the chick has huge toes, the middle toe measuring around 25 mm. The iris is brown.

When the chicks are dry, the female immediately takes them away from the nest, at which point they are joined by the male, and the adults greet one another by bobbing their heads and necks. Studies at one nest-site showed that it may take an hour for the whole family to move 100 m away from the nest. During subsequent days, the family may remain roughly 100-200 m from the nest-site. Normally one adult attends the young while the other is feeding. In guarding the young, an adult usually stands somewhere higher, for example on a small rock, and will occasionally engage in preening. Both parents brood their chicks, sometimes for as long as 23 days after hatching. Young Ibisbills move about solitarily, but will stay within 50-60 m of an adult. They can fly when about 45-50 days old.

When disturbed, an incubating Ibisbill leaves the nest quickly and runs silently away. Only when an intruder has moved some 100-150 m away will the bird return to the nest. Once the chicks have hatched, this behaviour changes dramatically. Adults take to the air at a distance of about 300 m from an intruder and, emitting loud piping calls, will fly directly at the intruder, sometimes coming as close as 10-15 m before abruptly changing direction and flying on another 10-15 m. If the disturbance persists for more than half an hour, birds may disappear altogether for some time before starting to call again, usually from the ground. As the chicks grow, the adults become less active in showing alarm and attacking intruders. Occasionally, Ibisbills may perform an injury-feigning distraction display in an attempt to draw attention away from the chicks.

The chicks themselves react to danger by sitting motionless among pebbles where they may be almost invisible. On an alarm call of the parents, they can stay motionless with their eyes wide open for up to an hour. After the chicks have fledged, all members of the family stay in the same area until autumn, when they move off with the approach of the first spells of really cold weather. Family groups are sometimes joined by single adult birds.

Very few data have so far been collected on breeding success. Observations of two breeding attempts revealed that one and two chicks respectively were reared, and the young birds were seen with their parents up until the early autumn. In both cases one egg was infertile, and this caused one of the pairs to incubate for a longer period. One of the main threats to breeding Ibisbills may be grazing sheep, which sometimes use river valleys as passageways, trampling nests on the way. The red fox (*Vulpes vulpes*) occurs in the mountains of Tien Shan and may also pose a threat to nesting Ibisbills. Many nests are at permanent risk of flooding, since water levels in the mountain rivers change dramatically, as a result either of snow and ice melting or of a sudden increase in rainfall.

Movements

The Ibisbill is an altitudinal migrant, largely staying within its breeding range and rarely moving outside it. Normally birds stay on their breeding grounds until October before gradually moving down to shingle-bed river valleys at lower altitudes. During the late autumn and winter months, in the Himalayan *terai* they may descend to altitudes as low as 100 m, while in north-western parts of their range the lower limit seems to be about 500 m. The birds usually reappear on their breeding grounds in March.

Relationship with Man

The Ibisbill has no practical importance to man and is not normally hunted or persecuted. The fact that it breeds in such bleak mountainous areas, which tend to have rather thinly distributed human populations obviously has much to do with this, and generally people are not even aware of its presence.

In some areas of greater human impact, Ibisbills have been observed breeding alongside places where heavy tractors are working, but these birds eventually showed little concern as to the presence of the tractors, appearing to become used to disturbance quite readily.

The species takes its genus and common names from a certain resemblance to the ibises (Threskiornithidae), as it presents fairly similar overall structure, and, more specifically, has a very long, decurved bill.

Status and Conservation

To provide an estimate of the size of the total world population of Ibisbills is extremely difficult. The species still occurs in reasonable numbers in suitable and often inaccessible habitats across the mountain systems of Central Asia.

On a 6·5 km stretch of suitable habitat along the Langtang Khola River, in northern Nepal, 41 birds were counted in 1984, including 18 territorial pairs. Elsewhere, there are very few precise data available, but a survey was carried out in 1989 in south-east Kazakhstan, in the mountains of Trans Ili (Zailiy Alatau) and Kungey Alatau, both northern offshoots of the Tien Shan. This revealed that the upper reaches of the Chilik River held four breeding pairs, while the valley of the Chon Kemin River, which runs between the Trans Ili and Kungey and has massive gravel-covered valleys, had ten pairs; ten more pairs were found along the Kara Kara River in the Kungey range. A record from 1957 reported Ibisbills breeding on the Great Almaty Lake in the Trans Ili at an altitude of 2500 m, but there were no further records there until 1977, when one pair bred, and numbers subsequently increased to three pairs. Another pair is reported to breed in the valley of the Little Almaty River. With so few data to hand, it would be unwise to hazard a guess as to overall population trends in this zone, but monitoring of these known territories should prove very worthwhile.

A very rough estimate of the overall population of Ibisbills in the Commonwealth of Independent States (CIS) is 200 breeding pairs. There are, in fact, no clear data to show whether the population is decreasing as a result of human activities, but the species is red-listed in the CIS, which helps to draw attention to it, increase public awareness amongst local communities and schools, and to put pressure on any possible development which might place important breeding sites at risk. Very few data are available from the Chinese part of its breeding range.

Being a highly specialized bird adapted to a rather restricted habitat, the Ibisbill could become vulnerable in the face of the increasing human pressure that is apparent in some areas, especially if its habitat becomes seriously threatened. Shingle-bed river valleys are now used for gravel extraction in many parts of the Himalayas. Also, throughout the Himalayas, rivers that are currently ideal for Ibisbills are suffering considerable damage through increasing water abstraction, and through accelerated erosion which results in sediments covering large pebble-strewn valleys, while plans for the construction of hydro-electric power stations pose major threats. Sheep grazing too is a problem for breeding Ibisbills in that the sheep often use river valleys to move between their areas of pasture, which can easily result in nest destruction through trampling. Finally, increased human presence and activity in the form of tourism and recreation are also apparently becoming significant factors in some areas, with all of the concomitant forms of disturbance they imply.

Nevertheless, the Ibisbill's habitat remains largely intact in many parts of the CIS, and, although there is some destruction occurring locally, the pressure on its populations here is undoubtedly far less than in the Himalayas. Also, there are still areas in parts of the species' range that remain essentially inaccessible, and in which development or exploitation appear to be economically unviable, at any rate within the near future.

No special conservation measures have been taken to protect the Ibisbill, although it is afforded varying degrees of protection by its presence in several Himalayan national parks. A widespread survey of the main breeding sites, to ascertain the number of breeding birds and also the level of potential threats, would be the most effective first step towards ensuring the future of this spectacular bird. An important follow-up would then be the establishment of nature reserves on the major breeding grounds, as well as on some of the wintering grounds.

PLATE 30

inches 5

cm 13

Family IBIDORHYNCHIDAE (IBISBILL)
SPECIES ACCOUNTS

PLATE 30

Genus *IBIDORHYNCHA* Vigors, 1832

Ibisbill

Ibidorhyncha struthersii

French: Bec-d'ibis tibétain   **German**: Ibisschnabel   **Spanish**: Picoibis

Taxonomy. *Ibidorhyncha Struthersii* Vigors, 1832, Himalayas.
Sometimes placed within Recurvirostridae, usually in its own separate subfamily, Ibidorhynchinae; alternatively, on occasion, linked with Haematopodidae. Monotypic.
Distribution. SE Kazakhstan S to Kashmir and E through NW China, Tibet and NE India to EC & NE China. Occurs mainly in major mountain systems of C Asia, from Dzhungar Alatau S through Tien Shan, Pamir-Alay system, Hindu Kush and Karakoram to Himalayas, and E through Xinjiang, Kunlun Shan, Tibet-Qinghai Plateau, Sikkim and Arunachal Pradesh to SW Heilongjiang, Inner Mongolia, Hebei, Shanxi and Sichuan; main wintering range extends slightly further S of Himalayas.
Descriptive notes. 39-41 cm; c. 270-320 g; bill 68-82 mm. Unmistakable wader with long, decurved crimson bill and contrasting plumage; distinctive head pattern; legs greyish purple. Female similar to male, but marginally larger with slightly longer bill. Juvenile browner, with plumage pattern less clearly marked, and pale fringes on upperparts; bare part colours duller.
Habitat. Breeds in shingle-bed mountain river valleys usually devoid of any vegetation, at 500-4400 m. Occupies same habitat in winter, but at lower altitudes, occurring down to 100 m in places.
Food and Feeding. Mainly aquatic river invertebrates and fish; commonly recorded invertebrate prey include stoneflies (Plecoptera), larvae of mayflies (Ephemeroptera), caddisflies (Trichoptera), beetles (Carabidae) and crustaceans. Forages by pecking, probing and raking (see page 328), usually while wading in water roughly reaching up to belly; forages singly, rarely in pairs.
Breeding. Laying starts end of Apr and may continue for some time, with hatching mid-May to late Jun (Tien Shan, Himalayas, China). Monogamous and territorial. Nest is a shallow pit on the ground, sometimes with lining of pebbles. Usually 4 eggs, but completed clutches of 2 and 3 eggs recorded;

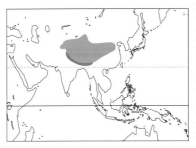

incubation by both sexes; chicks have greyish down with darker black and brown markings, and 18 mm long brownish bill; young start to fly when 45-50 days old, and stay with parents apparently until first winter.
Movements. Altitudinal migrant; birds tend to descend in winter, in Himalayan zone to as low as 100 m. Species remains more or less within breeding range all year round.
Status and Conservation. Not globally threatened. Occupies expansive range, mostly in zones with sparse human populations, but restricted to rather limited habitat. In Trans Ili and Kungey Alatau of N Tien Shan, Kazakhstan, 27 pairs counted in 1989. Breeds in several conservation areas in the Himalayas, including Langtang National Park in Nepal, where 41 birds counted on Langtang Khola R in 1984. In some parts of Tien Shan has apparently increased insignificantly over past 15 years, though reasons not clear; included in CIS Red Data Books as rare and declining, although no evidence of such a decline is documented. Main threat, especially in Himalayas, is habitat destruction, including water abstraction from rivers, industrial use of gravel and building of hydro-electric plants; nest trampling by sheep is also a problem; disturbance of nesting birds by humans probably becoming more frequent in some areas, due to growth of recreation and tourist activities. Species not known to survive in captivity, where species might be difficult to maintain due to specialized habitat and feeding requirements; no captive breeding programmes known to be in operation.

Bibliography. Ali & Ripley (1980), Andreenkov (1986), Annenkov (1988), Anon. (1978), Baker (1929, 1935), Bannikov (1978), Bates & Lowther (1952), Berezovikov (1980), Björklund (1994), Bub (1985b), Burton (1974), Chu (1995), Dementiev & Gladkov (1951b), Dolgushin (1962), Étchécopar & Hüe (1978), Flint *et al.* (1984), Gochfeld *et al.* (1984), Hayman *et al.* (1986), Inskipp & Inskipp (1991), Ivanov (1969), Ivanov *et al.* (1953), Jehl (1968b), Knystautas (1987, 1993), Kovshar (1980a, 1980b, 1982), Kozlova (1961a, 1961b), Phillips (1945), Pierce (1986c), Prater *et al.* (1977), Ripley (1982), Roberts, T. J. (1991), Simmons (1987), Smythies (1986), Soothill & Soothill (1982), Stepanjan (1979, 1990a), Strauch (1976, 1978).

Class AVES
Order CHARADRIIFORMES
Suborder CHARADRII
Family RECURVIROSTRIDAE (STILTS AND AVOCETS)

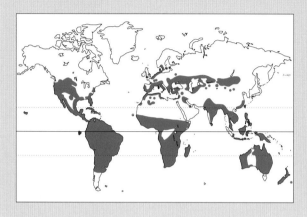

- Tall, elegant wading birds, with very long legs, longish and upcurved or medium-length and straight bill, and mostly pied plumage.
- 35-51 cm.

- Cosmopolitan, with greatest diversity in Australasian Region.
- Extensive open wetlands.
- 3 genera, 7 species, 11 taxa.
- 1 species threatened; none extinct since 1600.

Systematics

The distinctive recurvirostrid form is not common in the fossil record, but the group is known to have appeared by the early Cenozoic era. Over the years, the phylogenetic relationships of the Recurvirostridae have been determined primarily by morphological, molecular and behavioural comparisons. These indicate that stilts and avocets share a common ancestry with oystercatchers (Haematopodidae), the Ibisbill (Ibidorhynchidae), plovers (Charadriidae) and thick-knees (Burhinidae). Their closest relative would appear to be the Ibisbill (*Ibidorhyncha struthersii*), which has often been included within Recurvirostridae, usually with a subfamily of its own; indeed, on the evidence of DNA, it has even been included within the same tribe as the stilts and avocets.

Three genera are recognized within the Recurvirostridae. *Himantopus* and *Recurvirostra* are both near-cosmopolitan, the former containing two species of straight-billed stilt, and the latter four species of avocet, distinguished by their strongly upcurved bills. The third genus, *Cladorhynchus*, is monotypic and is confined to Australia. Its sole representative, the Banded Stilt (*Cladorhynchus leucocephalus*), combines some morphological and behavioural features of both *Himantopus* and *Recurvirostra*. Indeed, the relationships of *Cladorhynchus* have been questioned in light of morphological and behavioural similarities with flamingos (Phoenicopteridae; see Volume 1, page 508). However, these similarities are thought to be convergences rather than characters shared through common descent; recent DNA-DNA hybridization and protein electrophoresis analyses align *Cladorhynchus* with avocets and other stilts.

Of the three genera, *Himantopus* shows the most complex taxonomy. Most authors have preferred to accept only two species, the Black-winged Stilt (*Himantopus himantopus*) and the Black Stilt (*Himantopus novaezelandiae*), although some consider these two forms conspecific. However, the Black-winged Stilt is normally divided into five subspecies, and these forms are sometimes considered to constitute three to five separate species, with the recognition of: nominate *himantopus*, of Europe, Africa and Asia; *leucocephalus*, the Pied Stilt of Australasia; and *mexicanus*, the Black-necked Stilt of the Americas, which is often considered to include either or both of *melanurus*, the White-backed Stilt of more southerly distribution within South America, and *knudseni*, the Hawaiian Stilt of Hawaii. All these forms can be separated by plumage and biometrics, and they are geographically isolated, except for some overlap between *mexicanus* and *melanurus* in Peru, where hybridization does occur. Black-winged Stilts in South Africa and Sri Lanka have sometimes been accorded subspecific status, but this is generally considered to be unwarranted, as the plumage and size characteristics of these populations overlap closely with others of nominate *himantopus*. Nevertheless, this has led a few authors to list up to eight allospecies.

The Black Stilt is thought to be derived from an early invasion of New Zealand by stilts. It sometimes pairs with the Black-winged Stilt and the two forms hybridize. This indicates that the

The slender, strongly upcurved bill immediately betrays the generic identity of the Andean Avocet, the only member of Recurvirostra *to be found habitually at high altitudes. The highly specialized bill enables avocets to use a variety of feeding techniques and to find prey in various water depths. Compactly built, the Andean Avocet is much heavier in the body and appreciably shorter-legged than its congeners. The all-white head and body contrast strongly with the blackish wings and mantle to give the species its bold and attractive pied appearance.*

[*Recurvirostra andina*, Lauca National Park, Chile.
Photo: Luiz Claudio Marigo]

reproductive isolation of the Black Stilt was incomplete when the Black-winged Stilt invaded from Australia, probably during the nineteenth century. However, several factors are thought to promote reproductive isolation between the two species. For example, habitat choice, feeding behaviour and the extent of migratory behaviour differ between the two, as do various morphological characters, such as size, plumage, and bill and tarsal lengths. Furthermore, in areas where both forms occur, assortative mating is observed; in one study, in which Black Stilts comprised only 3% of all the stilts in the region, 70% of them were paired with other Black Stilts, the remainder being paired with hybrids (24%) or Black-winged Stilts (6%).

Morphological Aspects

Stilts and avocets are slim waders with very long flexible bills, long necks and especially long legs. These features enable them to exploit food resources in relatively deep water. The long neck and bill facilitate prey capture at the water surface, deep in the water column and in the upper layers of mud.

As reflected in the scientific name of their genus, avocets have highly specialized, upcurved bills, the curvature being strongest in the shorter-billed females. The bill is basally flattened and contains internal lamellae, which, during scything actions of the bird's bill and head, act as a filter for any small food items in the water or mud; the tongue is distinctively broad and fleshy. Avocets have bluish grey legs, strongly developed basal webbing of their three front toes, and vestigial hind toes.

Stilts of the genus *Himantopus* have straight or slightly upcurved bills which are associated with strong adductor muscles that facilitate rapid jaw actions and the gripping of prey. The tibia and tarsi are long and reddish pink, and the hind toe is absent.

The Banded Stilt combines features of both the avocets and the *Himantopus* stilts. As in avocets, the bill of the Banded Stilt is broad-based and lamellated, the tongue is enlarged, and basal webbing on the front three toes is strongly developed. However, like other stilts, the bill is straight or only slightly upcurved, the tibia and tarsi are long and orange-pink, and the hind toe is absent.

Stilts and avocets tend to be boldly pied. The Black-winged Stilt, the juvenile Black Stilt and the Andean Avocet (*Recurvirostra andina*) are generally blackish above and white below, whereas in the other species of avocets and the Banded Stilt, the black markings are more or less restricted to the primaries, the upperwing-coverts and the scapulars. Three species also have reddish brown plumage markings: the Banded Stilt has a chestnut breast band; the Red-necked Avocet (*Recurvirostra novaehollandiae*) has a dark chestnut head and neck; and the American Avocet (*Recurvirostra americana*) has the head, neck and breast orangish brown. The plumage of the adult Black Stilt, in contrast, appears almost entirely blackish. This apparent lack of a disruptive plumage pattern in the adult of this species may reflect the low levels of predation pressure that formerly prevailed in New Zealand.

Breeding and non-breeding plumages are generally similar in stilts and avocets. Exceptions to this are the chestnut breast band of the Banded Stilt, which is stronger in the breeding season, and the orange markings on the American Avocet, which are absent outside the breeding season.

Juvenile plumages are usually similar to those of adults, although pale fringes to the dark upperpart feathers give a scalloped effect. However, the juvenile Black Stilt has a markedly different plumage pattern from the adult, closely resembling that of the Black-winged Stilt; the typical all black adult plumage is not attained until 15-18 months of age.

In stilts and avocets, moult occurs twice annually, in the form of a complete post-breeding moult and a partial pre-breeding moult. In temperate areas moult is seasonal and is limited to short periods, whereas in the tropics the timing is variable. In general, adults begin the moult of their flight-feathers before their young have fledged. Concentrations of recurvirostrids frequently occur at some post-breeding moulting areas: for example, in the Jadebusen, in north-west Germany, up to 21,000 Pied Avocets (*Recurvirostra avosetta*) may collect in September before moving to more southerly winter quarters.

Habitat

Optimal feeding habitat for stilts and avocets is extensive shallow wetlands with abundant small invertebrate prey. In general, forested areas are avoided, and the highest densities of birds occur in areas of low rainfall, in treeless wetlands where there is adjacent open space for nesting and loafing.

Avocets and the Banded Stilt favour saline or hypersaline shallow inland lakes where tiny crustaceans, insects and other prey are abundant. Avocets occur in a range of coastal and inland sites, and they sometimes nest and feed at coastal estuaries,

A small group of Black-winged Stilts gives a theatrical high-leaping display with a parachute-like descent to the ground on wings spread wide; the significance of this performance is unclear. Other similarly unexplained aerial displays include the "Butterfly" flight, when an individual hovers 5-10 m above a particular spot, often flying on some 10 m or more to hover again. Another is the "Grouping-ceremony" or "Mob-display", in which a few birds come together and behave in a mildly aggressive fashion towards each other before dispersing, all for no apparent coherent reason.

[Himantopus himantopus himantopus, Aiguamolls de l'Empordà, Spain. Photo: Tono Folguera]

particularly in western Europe, in the case of the Pied Avocet, and on the Pacific coast of North America, in the case of the American Avocet. Usually, however, breeding takes place far inland and the birds undertake post-breeding movements to lowland and coastal wetlands, including estuarine and lagoon habitats. An exception to this is the Andean Avocet which occurs throughout the year at high altitude saline lakes, some of which are over 5000 m above sea-level; after the breeding season, some Andean Avocets descend to lower altitude lakes, but only rarely do they move to coastal tidal flats. In Asia, migrating Pied Avocets sometimes occur at altitudes of up to 5000 m.

The *Himantopus* stilts occur in the greatest variety of wetlands, with a wide range of salinity and altitude, and both lotic and lentic habitats, in other words those with fast-flowing and still water. Greatest habitat flexibility occurs in New Zealand, where both the Black-winged and Black Stilts regularly frequent the braided riverbeds that dominate the local landscape, a habitat that is similar to that frequented by the Ibisbill in central Asia. The stilts also occupy other freshwater, estuarine and artificial environments, such as irrigated fields and salt-works, and exhibit strong seasonal changes in habitat selection. In areas heavily modified by human activity, for example much of western Europe, recurvirostrids are increasingly coming to depend upon artificial wetlands, such as scrapes, salt-lakes, dams and sewage ponds, some of which are created for wildlife conservation.

All members of the Recurvirostridae are opportunistic in habitat selection. Avocets and the Banded Stilt often move long distances to take advantage of localized rains and temporarily rich food supplies, often within the same habitat type. In contrast, the Black Stilt exhibits great flexibility of habitat type over time, and is therefore able to remain relatively sedentary within smaller geographical areas.

General Habits

Stilts and avocets are considered to be mainly diurnal, although some species have been recorded feeding at night. Indeed, in estuarine areas outside the breeding season, feeding activity often follows a tidal cycle, slightly modified by a diurnal rhythm.

Nocturnal foraging reflects the versatility of recurvirostrid feeding methods, particularly the ability to switch between visual and tactile feeding methods (see Food and Feeding).

With the exception of the Black Stilt, which defends some form of territory throughout the year, all species tend to be gregarious. During the breeding season, colonies typically contain 5-100 pairs, which are usually moderately to closely spaced, and in the Black-winged Stilt pairs occasionally feed around the nest. Banded Stilt colonies, however, contain thousands of pairs packed together tightly, while the feeding grounds may be many kilometres away. The breeding territories of Black Stilts generally contain significant feeding areas.

Outside the breeding season all species tend to be more gregarious, or, in the case of the Black Stilt, more clumped, although this latter species will still defend its feeding territories. Recurvirostrids usually feed in flocks of up to several thousands of birds, which may be tightly packed together, though they sometimes defend individual distances. For loafing or roosting, they gather in dense flocks on nearby dry banks where a bird will stand on one leg or sit on the ground, with the head and neck retracted to the fold of the wing and bill tucked under the wing. Sometimes flocks will roost standing in water. Interspecific associations with other recurvirostrids or other species of wading bird occur rather frequently.

When alarmed, feeding and roosting birds often head-bob, which consists of a rapid extension of the neck, followed by its rapid retraction. Wing-stretching, indirect head-scratching and other comfort movements are similar among the few species studied in detail.

Voice

Recurvirostrids are noisy, particularly when breeding or when in flight. The commonest calls are repetitive monosyllabic or disyllabic barks or yelps, and these are usually given as contact and alarm calls. The calls of stilts of the genus *Himantopus* tend to be sharp and monosyllabic and are often rendered as "yep" or "kek". In contrast, avocet calls are inclined to be a disyllabic "kluit", "kluut" or "kleet", although when the bird is alarmed these become more monosyllabic and stilt-like. The Banded Stilt

Both the Black-winged Stilt and the American Avocet breed on shallow wetlands, the former mainly at freshwater sites the latter showing a preference for lowland saline lakes and lagoons. At times both are found on estuaries and tidal flats, and also at fresh water sites. The Black-winged Stilt's bill is the less sophisticated of the two, but, aided by strong head muscles, it provides for quick jaw movement and a firm grip on prey. Aquatic insects, the Black-winged Stilt's main food, are normally taken from or beneath the surface of the water by a quick pecking action. When feeding, this species often wades in water up to or above the "knee" joint and will sometimes use the "plunge" method of foraging, totally immersing the head and neck, but only rarely does it swim. The American Avocet's long, upcurved bill is a highly specialized, sensitive instrument equipped with filtering lamellae which allow the bird to retain only the small organisms that make up its food; these are flicked into the mouth by the fleshy tongue and then swallowed. It too feeds by pecking, but it is usually to be seen "scything", sweeping the bill from side to side through the water or the underlying soft slime, thus allowing food items to be filtered out by tactile means. This species feeds on a wide variety of aquatic insects, crustaceans and worms, at times freely swimming in deeper water to forage.

[Above: *Himantopus himantopus himantopus*, Al Ansab Lagoons, Oman. Photo: Hanne & Jens Eriksen/Aquila.

Below: *Recurvirostra americana*. Photo: Arthur Morris/ VIREO]

is, yet again, intermediate in character between the *Himantopus* stilts and the avocets in that its call, "chowk", is occasionally disyllabic. In all species, calling may sound continuous when the birds are in large flocks.

Detailed studies of the Black-winged Stilt, Black Stilt and Pied Avocet have revealed that each species has a variety of calls. The simplest contact calls are based around the monosyllabic or disyllabic "yep" or "kluit", but variations are used for the following situational calls: alert calls; alarm and mobbing calls, which include different calls for ground, human and aerial predators; intensive alarm or distress calls; bathing calls; parental calls; pre-copulatory calls; nest-site selection calls; and incubating calls. Among those species studied so far, remarkable similarities are apparent, such as the way in which alarm calls increase in rate and volume with the intensity of the alarm stimuli.

Age- and sex-related variation in calls has been noted. For instance male Black Stilts have higher-pitched calls than females. Juvenile Black-winged and Black Stilts give a soft, high-frequency piping call.

Food and Feeding

Recurvirostrids feed mainly on aquatic invertebrates and small vertebrates, and less often on vegetable matter and terrestrial prey. Most commonly, the avocets and the Banded Stilt consume crustaceans, whereas the *Himantopus* stilts tend to feed on insects; molluscs, crustaceans, polychaete worms, earthworms, small fish and water plants and their seeds are also taken. Most food is obtained in shallow water or on damp land, but all species, particularly the Banded Stilt and the avocets, swim to feed in deeper water.

An avocet has a long, strongly upcurved bill which contains a complex and highly specialized system of lamellae capable of filtering out small food items. Once filtered off, this food is subsequently flicked into the mouth by the large fleshy tongue. The bill of the Banded Stilt is slightly upcurved and also contains lamellae, while *Himantopus* stilts have straight or slightly upcurved bills that lack lamellae.

The range of feeding techniques used by stilts and avocets is varied; all species use both visual and tactile methods of prey detection and capture. The most widespread feeding method is a direct peck at visible prey on or in the water column or the ground. The prey is grasped by a slightly open bill and swallowed by means of a backward and forward jerk of the head, which also returns the head to its original search position. Larger prey, such as crabs, may have to be cut up by the bill into smaller pieces. Pied Avocets sometimes feed by sight on the siphons of the bivalve mollusc *Scrobicularia plana* in intertidal areas; peck rates are low but the success rate, as gauged by swallows, is high. Other visual methods commonly used by stilts and avocets are "plunging", an underwater form of pecking or probing in which the bill and head are totally immersed; and "snatching", which involves pecking at flying insects. "Bill-pursuit", in which the bird rapidly opens and closes its bill on the water surface to grasp abundant prey such as flies or pond skaters, is less frequent.

Tactile or non-visual methods of feeding include the characteristic avocet "scythe" in which the bill is swept sideways at a low angle through water or soft mud, and small food items are filtered out. Two types of scything strategies occur in Pied Avocets, a "normal feeding strategy" and a "worm-feeding strategy", both of which have been studied in detail on the estuary of the Tagus in Portugal. The normal feeding strategy involves the neck being stretched out, while the head and slightly opened bill are swept from side to side in a regular movement. This is repeated about 25-30 times a minute, with each sweep usually being followed by the visible swallowing of many small prey items. In the worm-feeding strategy, Pied Avocets hold their bills further open and have higher sweeping rates averaging 45 per minute. However, a lower frequency of swallowing indicates a lower success rate than with the normal feeding strategy. Sometimes the two scything styles are mixed. In the normal feeding strategy on the estuary of the Tagus, the main prey of Pied Avocets were spionid worms, tubificids, and small *Nereis diversicolor* and *Capitella capitata* polychaetes. Similarly, in California, the normal feeding strategy of American Avocets was found to capture primarily spionids, capitellids and oligochaetes.

When feeding at night, scything is commonly used by the Banded Stilt and by the Black and Black-winged Stilts in New Zealand. It is used less frequently by other races of Black-winged Stilts, but is probably most effective in the worm-feeding strategy, in which large prey such as oligochaetes and chironomids

Like all members of the family except the Black Stilt (Himantopus novaezelandiae), the Black-winged Stilt usually breeds in small, loose colonies of as many as 50 pairs. Sometimes the site may be shared with other species such as gulls, terns and waterfowl. The nest varies from a small mass of material to a fairly substantial, well lined construction made of twigs, stalks and any other available vegetation. It is normally built in the open, often amid grass and sedges and surrounded by shallow water. A normal clutch consists of four eggs, buff brown in ground colour and lightly spotted and blotched with black. Both parents share in the incubation which normally begins with the laying of the last egg, so that hatching is synchronous; if for any reason the eggs are lost a replacemant clutch is laid. The parent birds are noisy and aggressive when disturbed at the nest or with young, and various ploys are used when intruders approach too closely, among them distraction flights and injury-feigning. On occasion the whole colony may become alarmed and mob the intruder in a communal operation, creating a tremendous commotion as they screech and wheel around. Note the black hindneck characteristic of the northern American race, commonly known as the Black-necked Stilt.

[Himantopus himantopus mexicanus, Oregon, USA. Photo: John Gerlach/DRK]

As its first chick hatches, this Pied Avocet is removing a piece of eggshell from the nest. The remaining chicks are likely to emerge soon, as hatching is virtually synchronous, and all will have left the nest within more or less 24 hours. Avocets are colonial nesters, the size and density of the colony varying considerably. In most cases the nests are loosely grouped and sited on the ground in the open near shallow water, or occasionally in short vegetation but still near water. The eggs, normally 3-4 in number, are brownish buff with darker spots and blotches.

[*Recurvirostra avosetta*. Photo: Eric & David Hosking/FLPA]

are captured. Banded Stilts and avocets typically feed on smaller organisms when scything.

Another non-visual method of feeding employed by recurvirostrids is "filtering", in which the bill is rapidly dabbled and swept from side to side through surface weed or soft mud. Probing is also used, and involves the bill being inserted semi-vertically into a soft substrate, usually in search of large prey such as earthworms.

On braided riverbeds in New Zealand, the Black Stilt uses a specialist sideways "lateral probing" action to capture aquatic insect larvae sheltering beneath stones. This feeding behaviour is similar to that of the Wrybill (*Anarhynchus frontalis*), a species which shares this habitat with the stilt. An extension of this behaviour is "raking", a foraging method that combines both tactile and visual cues. The bill is swept through fine river shingle to dislodge and thus reveal prey items, which are then pecked at. The strong bill of the Black Stilt enables this species to maintain high rates of prey intake from riverbeds, even during periods of low prey availability, as can be caused by low water temperatures or high solar elevation. In contrast, the Black-winged Stilt in New Zealand is often unable to exploit prey in braided riverbeds during periods such as these, and as a result it switches habitats, for example moving to ponds. This habitat switching occurs most often in early morning on high altitude rivers, when the water temperature is less than 5°C, and in the middle of the day on all rivers in general, when solar insolation inhibits the activity of many larvae. Nevertheless, both species respond opportunistically to temporal changes of invertebrate abundance, such as those that can occur during periods of flooding or insect prey emergence. At these times, birds congregate along the main river channels and their prey intake increases above that of normal feeding conditions.

Weather patterns that can disrupt feeding include strong winds and heavy precipitation, and these can bring about total switching of feeding style, for instance from pecking to scything. At night too, tactile scything is commonly employed by *Himantopus* stilts, at least in New Zealand. Black-winged Stilts engaged in tactile feeding maintain individual distances that are considerably shorter than when the birds are feeding visually. In lentic habitats recurvirostrids respond, often in spectacular fashion, to changes in prey availability. In arid continental areas, such as in

Australia, birds congregate in response to sudden inundations of previously dry lake beds. In other areas sudden influxes of birds may occur if a sudden drop in water level creates a source of locally abundant prey.

Breeding

Although seasonal breeders for the most part, recurvirostrids tend to be opportunistic, and nesting is initiated only if local conditions are suitable. In this way, breeding can often be early, delayed or even abandoned. Furthermore, individuals and groups are not necessarily faithful to previous colony sites, and they often shift to new sites. Some species, particularly those in Australia, can move great distances, possibly in the order of hundreds of kilometres. The greatest opportunist of the family is the Banded Stilt, which breeds only in response to the appearance of ephemeral inland salt-lakes and the subsequent explosion in brine-shrimp abundance.

Stilts and avocets usually nest in colonies. Even the Black Stilt was once colonial, but its population is now so low that it tends to nest in solitary pairs. Colonial nesting is thought to enable the efficient exploitation of local and temporary abundance of food. It may also provide better anti-predator defences. Within colonies, nests are typically spaced 5-30 m apart, the exception being the Banded Stilt's, in which nest densities of up to 18 nests/m² have been recorded. The colonies of this species can be vast, and one was estimated to contain some 179,000 nests. Within the family, colonies are often of mixed-species composition. Avocets and stilts may nest together, and they have also been recorded nesting with plovers, pratincoles, sandpipers, gulls, terns, waterfowl and grebes.

In the species for which data are available, breeding birds are monogamous, although pair-bonds are not always maintained throughout the non-breeding season. In the Black Stilt pair-bonds are known to be lifelong. Among all species, pairing can take place *en route* to the breeding grounds or at them, and the tasks of nest-site selection and the lining of the nest are shared between the sexes.

Copulation in *Himantopus* stilts and avocets is similar. Pre-copulatory preening and bill-dipping often occur, followed by

A most attractive and fascinating Australian endemic, the Banded Stilt is the most opportunistic breeder of the Recurvirostridae: nesting depends totally on the advent of suitable climatic conditions. Where heavy rainfall has filled inland salt-lakes, and a resultant abundance of crustaceans, mainly brine-shrimps, occurs, the Banded Stilt may form huge, tightly packed colonies of many thousands of birds. Owing to the ephemeral nature of these sites a colony may be deserted at any time and the same sites can not be used every year. The species is therefore highly nomadic, whence the difficulty in locating breeding colonies, a problem aggravated by the extent of the species' range. The nests, usually sited on small islands within a lake, are saucer-shaped scrapes in the ground, sometimes sparsely lined with grass or stalks. The density of the nests varies according to the size of the colony and the availability of space, but can be as high as 18 nests/m². Average clutch size is 3-4 eggs, which can vary considerably in ground colour, but are mainly white with darker markings, though some eggs may be totally unstreaked. With predatory Silver Gulls (Larus novaehollandiae) usually in attendance at a colony, incubating Banded Stilts are loath to leave their nests even when provoked. Surprisingly little interaction among the incubating birds has been observed, though minor fighting bouts do occur. When the whole colony takes flight on being disturbed, temporary chaos may ensue until the nests are all reoccupied by their rightful owners.

[Cladorhynchus leucocephalus, Lake Ballard, Western Australia. Photos: Clive Minton]

The last of the brood to hatch, this Black-winged Stilt chick is still drying out, but will soon leave the nest. In this dry site the nest is a shallow, sparsely lined hollow in the sand amid glasswort (Salicornia). The outstanding feature visible on this chick is the already astonishing length of the legs and toes, which make it easier to understand that within a matter of a few hours it will be able to run and feed for itself, though always attended by its parents until it becomes fully independent 2-4 weeks after fledging.

[Himantopus himantopus himantopus, Camargue, France. Photo: Dominique Delfino/ Bios]

the female assuming a soliciting posture with her head lowered and her bill held more or less horizontal. The male then moves from side to side in a semi-circle behind the female several times, pausing at the side to perform a "Dip-shake-preen Display". If the ceremony proceeds, the male eventually remains at one side continuing the Dip-shake-preen Display, and then mounts the female, with copulation occurring quickly. On dismounting, the two typically cross bills and walk forward together, with their heads raised and one of the male's wings over the back of the female.

The similarity between the courtship and copulation behaviour of the avocets and the *Himantopus* stilts is such that successful interbreeding between Black-winged Stilts and American Avocets has occurred in captivity. In New Zealand, the Black Stilt and the Black-winged Stilt regularly interbreed and produce fertile offspring, which has resulted in areas of introgressive hybridization of these two species. Although the Black Stilt exhibits positive assortative mating, low productivity and the very scarcity of the species lead to unusual bond formation, such as trios, female-female pairs, and, most commonly, interspecific and hybrid pairings. The copulatory behaviour of the Banded Stilt has not been studied in detail, but it appears to be broadly similar to that of the other members of the family.

Egg-laying occurs at intervals of approximately 24 hours, occasionally 48 hours. Incubation usually begins after the laying of the third or fourth egg, or sometimes after the second. However, in areas where aerial predators pose a particular threat to unguarded eggs, sitting may begin with the first egg. Both sexes share in the incubation duties, with change-overs being frequent; for example, they can be approximately hourly in the *Himantopus* stilts. Both sexes also participate in nest defence, which can be carried out in decidedly aggressive fashion by some species. Anti-predator strategies are diverse and include sitting tight on the eggs or young in response to passing aerial predators, which may themselves be attacked and mobbed, and a variety of distraction displays that are usually directed towards predators on the ground. These include "Broken-wing Displays", in which a bird feigns injury on the ground; "Parachuting", which involves fluttering to the ground and giving distress calls; and "False Brooding", by which a bird gives the false impression that it is incubating or brooding in full view of a predator.

The normal clutch in the family is of 3-4 eggs; extremes of one egg and eight have been recorded, although the latter refers to two females laying in the same nest. Late nests may have smaller clutches. In general, the recurvirostrid egg has a yellow or brown background coloration, or, in the case of the Banded Stilt, white. The eggs are covered with darker spotting or blotching, or a combination of both. Average dimensions range from 44 x 31 mm in the Black-winged Stilt to 55 x 40 mm in the Banded Stilt. Incubation lasts 19-26 days, being shortest in the Banded Stilt. Hatching is synchronous in all recurvirostrids, and the chicks are precocial and nidifugous, generally leaving the nest within 24 hours of hatching.

Downy chicks are also disruptively marked, typically being buff, grey or fawn in background colour, with darker markings dorsally and on the sides of the head and on the thighs. The exception is again the chick of the Banded Stilt, which is unique amongst the whole suborder Charadrii in being white and completely lacking darker markings. Some camouflage may be afforded against the very pale salt-lake environment, or, alternatively, the large numbers of young produced by a colony and their subsequent crèche behaviour may reduce the effectiveness or need for a cryptic camouflage strategy.

Except in the case of the Banded Stilt, family parties remain discrete and the family group is maintained for a few weeks to several months after fledging. Black Stilt families remain together the longest, the young birds not being evicted until the beginning of the following breeding season. The Banded Stilt departs from the norm in that the downy chicks collect in large floating crèches to swim to the feeding grounds. At Lake Torrens, South Australia, one crèche covered a remarkable 130 km in only six days, in a wind-assisted movement.

Breeding success is highly variable interspecifically, and also intraspecifically between populations and seasons. The ephemeral nature of some habitats results in high fledging successes at times, but none at all at other times. For most species, a drop in water levels results in increased access for predatory mammals, as well as reduced food supplies. In Black Stilts, introduced mammalian predators such as feral cats, mustelids and brown rats account for most failed breeding attempts whilst native Pacific Marsh-harriers (*Circus approximans*) and gulls may also constitute threats on a local basis. In contrast, neighbouring Black-winged Stilts are better adapted to deal with the introduced predators through differences in nest-site selection, coloniality, fledgling period and distraction displays. In many parts of the world, gulls prey on nesting stilts and avocets, taking their eggs and chicks; a Great Black-backed Gull (*Larus marinus*) was even reported to take a juvenile avocet. In Australia, Silver Gulls (*Larus novaehollandiae*) and raptors are quick to respond to sudden local abundances of the Banded Stilt, and in such cases the predators tend to have a particularly heavy impact on any late-nesting stilts, with few young normally surviving from such nests.

Movements

Recurvirostrids occur in a wide variety of climates and habitats and, therefore, their seasonal patterns of movement are correspondingly diverse. Some populations are migratory, others dispersive, and yet others sedentary. Northern populations of the Black-winged Stilt, the Pied Avocet and the American Avocet are typically migratory, with regular and predictable seasonal movements between temperate and equatorial regions, sometimes with local moulting areas where they stage prior to long migrations. In maritime areas a proportion of birds from these northern populations may, however, winter nearer the breeding grounds, such as in western Europe, where about 500 Pied Avocets winter in England, up to 1000 in the Netherlands and over 20,000 in France and Iberia.

This pattern is mirrored in some Southern Hemisphere populations. For example, although many coastal breeding individuals are resident, Black-winged Stilts breeding in inland areas of South Island, New Zealand, migrate to estuaries on North Island. Similarly, in south-east Australia, inland movements occur regularly in late winter and early spring, as do coastal movements in summer, with all movements corresponding to the seasonal availability of wetlands. In New Zealand, the pattern of Black-winged Stilt movements has changed during the nineteenth and twentieth centuries. In the nineteenth century Black-winged Stilts were known mainly from central New Zealand, and there were very few records from the extensive tidal flats of northern New Zealand. However, by the 1940's the northern tidal flats were being utilized by thousands of post-breeding stilts, for in-

stance in the Firth of Thames and Kaipara Harbour, and this pattern has subsequently continued.

Stilts and avocets typically move in small parties along coastlines or river valleys, often at night. Migration occurs primarily during favourable weather conditions, and bad weather and opposing winds can delay passage for varying periods. Regular stopovers may be used for periods varying from only a matter of hours, in some cases, to several days, as in the case of the Pied Avocets that pause at the Banc d'Arguin, Mauritania.

In Australia any seasonal patterns are greatly affected by the availability of wetland habitat. Consequently, movements are often dispersive or erratic. Movements of the Red-necked Avocet and the Banded Stilt usually reflect recent heavy rainfall or the flooding of inland lakes, and birds may suddenly arrive or depart in their thousands. For example, in March 1989 the previously dry Lake Torrens was inundated by heavy rains. By late April about 100,000 Banded Stilts had collected to breed on islands in the newly formed lake; many of these birds had probably travelled hundreds of kilometres.

The least dispersive species are the Andean Avocet and the Black Stilt, although the former is little studied and might undertake significant altitudinal movements, and perhaps other local movements. The Black Stilt is known to be mainly sedentary, with most birds only undertaking short movements to different seasonal habitats within the same river systems. The wide feeding repertoire of the Black Stilt enables it to obtain its energy requirements under extremes of weather and climate in a relatively small area. Birds mated to Black-winged Stilts or hybrids often migrate to northern New Zealand.

Relationship with Man

Being noisy and conspicuous, stilts and avocets are well known to humans throughout their ranges, and, as a result, there are many local names for each species. For instance, at the Ebro Delta, in north-east Spain, the Pied Avocet is known as *Bec d'alena* or *Cusisacs*, meaning "sack-sewer", as its bill recalls the shape of traditional local darning needles used for mending sacks.

In most Western countries, recurvirostrids also enjoy a high and positive profile, and there are varying levels of effort to pro-

Three Banded Stilt chicks are being led at a brisk pace by one of their parents in order to join a crèche at the water's edge. The pure white downy chicks with their dark bills and eyes are unique in the suborder Charadrii in their totally white plumage without cryptic plumage. Even more remarkable is the organization of the chicks into large floating crèches often numbering several hundreds; they are attended by adults and swim to their feeding grounds, often covering considerable distances to do so. It is still not known for certain whether the adults ever feed their young, but chicks have been observed to feed themselves as soon as they reach water.

[Cladorhynchus leucocephalus, Lake Ballard, Western Australia. Photo: Clive Minton]

As Banded Stilts are
opportunistic breeders,
waiting for suitable
climatic conditions in order
to breed, they habitually
perform mass movements
when the time comes to
occupy habitat that has
just become suitable for
breeding. The social
behaviour of this species
has been little studied,
and virtually the only
information available is
based on observations
made at its huge breeding
colonies. Banded Stilts
are gregarious at all times
and seem to spend much
time resting on sandbars
and spits. If disturbed
when resting, flocks take
flight and wheel, dive and
turn in the air in a
markedly co-ordinated
fashion.

[Cladorhynchus
leucocephalus,
Australia.
Photo: M. P. Kahl/Auscape]

tect both the birds themselves and their habitats. Indeed, the level of interest in these species and the efforts afforded towards them can sometimes be disproportionate to their relative rarity, and are indicative of the impression that they are frequently considered very attractive birds. However, it should be remembered that this current period of favour was preceded by centuries during which these species were regularly collected both for the table and, latterly, as their rarity increased, as trophies.

However, one species in particular, the Pied Avocet, was at the centre of a successful conservation effort in western Europe earlier this century, and it was adopted as the symbol for the Royal Society for the Protection of Birds (RSPB). In this way, an image of the Pied Avocet was possibly the first to be used to symbolize the cause of ornithological conservation. More recently, the same society has used a more stylized logo, which features only the head and bill of the Pied Avocet, making powerful use of the distinctive form of the bird.

Status and Conservation

At the species level, all members of the Recurvirostridae have relatively secure, sometimes thriving, populations, with the exception of the Black Stilt. This can be attributed largely to the fact that the birds are no longer directly exploited by man, although it is probably also true to say that throughout their extensive range their habitats have not generally suffered the same critical depletions of some other habitat types. In parts of the world that have experienced major human impact only relatively recently, such as Australia, New Zealand and the Americas, the clearing of forested land for agriculture may have benefited some recurvirostrid species. All over their range, certain artificial wetlands, such as sewage ponds and salt-works, have also provided new habitat.

In western Europe, where pressures from human settlement are most marked, the two local recurvirostrid species appear to be making comebacks after declines in the nineteenth century. The Pied Avocet has increased spectacularly in the Netherlands, Germany and Britain, returning to breed in England in 1941 after a century's absence. The species has continued to increase to approximately 31,000 pairs in Europe. The Black-winged Stilt

population has also increased and is now reckoned to number some 21,000 pairs in Europe. Habitat improvement, protection of nesting areas, and perhaps climatic change, are generally credited with the population increases of the twentieth century.

The return of the Pied Avocet to breed in Britain is one of the heartening conservation success stories of the twentieth century. At Havergate Island and Minsmere, Suffolk, nesting pairs were carefully protected in their wetland reserves and new habitat created for their growing numbers. As the number of pairs increased, however, their productivity declined due largely to predation by gulls and other predators in a density-dependent relationship. Further increases in the Pied Avocet population in England are likely to occur only if new and suitable habitat is provided. Elsewhere in Europe artificial wetlands have proved beneficial in the continued survival of stilts and avocets in several heavily populated areas.

On the Hawaiian islands, the local form of the Black-winged Stilt, the Hawaiian Stilt, has come under pressure principally from the loss of natural wetlands. Urban development and the replacement of traditional crops, such as taro and rice, with other agriculture, such as sugar cane, has gradually depleted wetland areas over the past 150 years. To some extent this has been countered through creation of stock ponds, ditches, settling ponds, aquaculture and some golf course ponds, but remaining natural wetlands are still threatened by drainage and by introduced plants. Introduced predatory mammals, including feral cats, dogs and rats, as well as mongooses (Herpestes auropunctatus), have an undetermined impact on Black-winged Stilts in Hawaii, as do human disturbance and toxic chemical spills. However, active management and the creation of new nesting habitat on the islands of Maui and Oahu have enabled the number of birds there to increase steadily since 1982 to a total of about 1800 in 1988, and this accounts for about 80% of the total population of the Hawaiian form knudseni. The protection of a number of core nesting areas is of paramount importance to the survival of the Black-winged Stilt in Hawaii; beyond these core areas, productivity and survival are linked closely to climatic factors, particularly rainfall. This form currently occurs on all of the main Hawaiian Islands except Kahoolawe, although sightings on some islands, such as Lanai, correspond only to wet winters.

The single globally threatened member of the family is the Black Stilt, which had a total wild population of fewer than 100

birds in 1995. It was widespread and common in New Zealand in the middle of the nineteenth century but by the beginning of the twentieth it bred only on South Island. By the 1940's numbers had dropped to 500-1000 birds, and by 1960 to 50-100 birds.

The decline of the Black Stilt coincided with the introduction of carnivorous mammals, including feral cats, the rats *Rattus norvegicus* and *R. rattus*, and the three mustelid species *Mustela erminea*, *M. nivalis* and *M. furo*; native avian predators also increased, with greater availability of food. At the same time, Black-winged Stilts were also spreading, and major habitat changes were taking place, particularly with the drainage of wetlands fringing riverbeds. Nevertheless, introduced predators appear to have been sufficiently significant in their own right to bring about a decline in the population of the Black Stilt. One study showed that only about 1% of eggs succeeded in producing a fledgling and that these subsequently proved to have a relatively short life expectancy of less than 5 years. It is thought that certain features of the Black Stilt's life history render it vulnerable to predation: Black Stilts nest on dry banks, which are patrolled by hunting mammalian predators; they are solitary nesters; they have a long fledgling period; and they exhibit ineffective anti-predator behaviour. It is notable that these features are not shared by the Black-winged Stilt in New Zealand. A compounding problem, which increases in importance as population size decreases, is that those Black Stilts that do survive to maturity are not always able to find mates and often end up in unproductive groups, such as trios or lesbian pairs, or interbreeding either with Black-winged Stilts or with hybrids of the two species.

Since 1980, protective measures for Black Stilts have included a combination of anti-predator, captive rearing and habitat manipulation programmes. In the early 1980's the prime focus was on excluding predators from nesting areas, and this was attempted largely through trapping programmes, which either encircled a small nesting area or covered a large part of a river valley or delta. Two predator exclosures were also constructed around what were, at the time, dependable nesting areas. In both these exclosure areas and the trapping areas, as an additional level of protection, Black Stilt eggs were removed to an incubator and replaced with dummy eggs until the chicks were due to hatch. These anti-predator techniques succeeded in boosting productivity to fledging, but could not reduce post-fledging mortality rates.

The cross-fostering of Black Stilts to interbreeding pairs of stilts or hybrids was also attempted in the early 1980's. Eggs from the first breeding attempt of Black Stilts were removed, which also induced them to relay, while their first clutch was cross-fostered. However, imprinting and migration problems led to only 7% of cross-fostered fledglings being recruited into the Black Stilt breeding population, and this technique was discontinued.

A captive rearing programme for Black Stilts, centred at Twizel in southern central South Island, has ensured an annual production of juveniles which in some years has exceeded that of wild pairs. Many of these juveniles have been produced as a result of the removal of clutches from wild birds. Techniques for juvenile release have improved and released birds now have high survival rates, with some forming part of wild breeding pairs. This success is due partly to habitat enhancement programmes in local wetlands and river deltas, which include the removal of willows and lupins from potential and traditional breeding grounds. Current management focuses heavily on using dummy eggs in nests, captive rearing and release programmes, and habitat improvement, with localized predator control. A recovery plan for Black Stilts published in 1993, aims to increase mainland populations and explore the potential for island translocations.

All recurvirostrids live in habitats that are susceptible to environmental abuse and damage. Shallow wetlands are often the most modified and polluted habitats in regions inhabited by people. Problems that have resulted in stilt and avocet mortality and exodus have included organic pollution, PCB toxic loading, selenium pollution, lead poisoning from lead shot on lake beds, and the use of insecticides. Ultimately the continued survival of recurvirostrids and other wetland species depends on the collective abilities of national and international agencies to overcome these and other environmentally damaging effects.

General Bibliography

Barbosa (1993), Bickart (1990), Björklund (1994), Bub (1985a), Burton (1974), Christian *et al*. (1992b), Chu (1995), Dunning (1993), Gochfeld *et al*. (1984), Hale (1980), Harrison (1983a), Hayman *et al*. (1986), Jehl (1968b), Jehl & Murray (1986), Jessop (1987), Johnsgard (1981), Olson & Feduccia (1980), Peters (1934), Prater *et al*. (1977), Rosair & Cottridge (1995), Sibley & Ahlquist (1990), Sibley & Monroe (1990), Soothill & Soothill (1982), Strauch (1976, 1978).

ssp *himantopus*

ssp *leucocephalus*

ssp *mexicanus*

♂

♀

ssp *knudseni*

ssp *melanurus*

1

2

3

4

5

6

7

♂

♀

PLATE 31

inches   8

cm   20

Genus *HIMANTOPUS* Brisson, 1760

1. **Black-winged Stilt**

Himantopus himantopus

French: Échasse blanche **German**: Stelzenläufer **Spanish**: Cigüeñuela Común
Other common names: Common Stilt; Pied/White-headed Stilt (*leucocephalus*); Hawaiian Stilt (*knudseni*); Black-necked Stilt (*mexicanus*); White-backed Stilt (*melanurus*)

Taxonomy. *Charadrius Himantopus* Linnaeus, 1758, southern Europe.
Forms superspecies with *H. novaezelandiae*, with which known to hybridize and which is sometimes considered conspecific. Races often considered to warrant recognition of 2-5 distinct species (see page 332). Races can be split into three groups: nominate race; "pied" race, *leucocephalus*; and "black-necked" races *knudseni*, *mexicanus* and *melanurus*. Geographical variation also claimed in southern Africa and Sri Lanka, in forms *meridionalis* and *ceylonensis* respectively, but both show considerable overlap with other populations of nominate *himantopus*. Five subspecies normally recognized.
Subspecies and Distribution.
H. h. himantopus (Linnaeus, 1758) - France and Iberia S to sub-Saharan Africa and Madagascar, and E to C Asia and NC China, Indian Subcontinent, Indochina and Taiwan.
H. h. leucocephalus Gould, 1837 - Java E to New Guinea, and S to Australia and New Zealand; winters N to Philippines, Greater Sundas and Sulawesi.
H. h. knudseni Stejneger, 1887 - Hawaiian Is.
H. h. mexicanus (P. L. S. Müller, 1776) - W & S USA through Central America and West Indies to SW Peru, E Ecuador and NE Brazil.
H. h. melanurus Vieillot, 1817 - N Chile and EC Peru through Bolivia and Paraguay to SE Brazil, and S to SC Argentina.

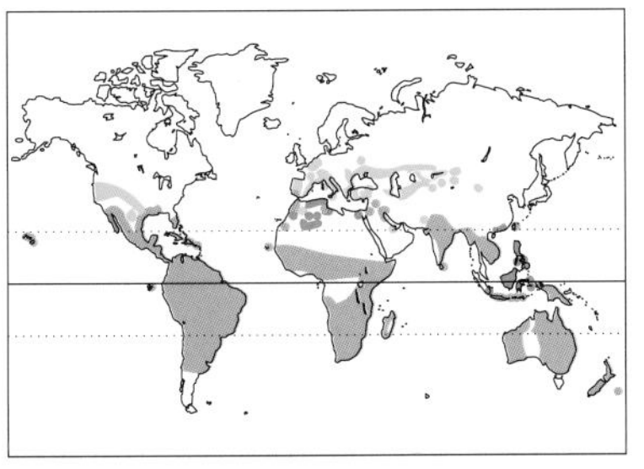

Descriptive notes. 35-40 cm; 166-205 g (mean of all races); tarsus 101-125 mm in male, shorter in female. Very long pink legs distinctive; thin black bill; wings and back black, often with greenish gloss; white below; tail white with variable grey banding. Female has upperparts duller brown, lacking greenish gloss. Some non-breeding birds of nominate race develop more extensive grey on crown, nape and hindneck. Juvenile similar to adult female. Races differ mainly in colouring and pattern of head and hindneck, varying from mainly white in nominate race to continuous black in *mexicanus* and especially *knudseni*, but nominate too sometimes shows limited amounts of greyish or blackish in these areas; races *leucocephalus* and *melanurus* intermediate; races *mexicanus* and *knudseni* show more pronounced sexual dimorphism in plumage; juvenile of *leucocephalus* lacks black of hindneck and nape, which may be white or grey. Hybrids of *leucocephalus* and *H. novaezelandiae* very variable, typically with black collar and some black markings on breast and belly.
Habitat. Shallow wetlands of tropical and temperate regions. Breeding habitats mainly at freshwater sites, including marshes and swamps, lake edges, riverbeds, sewage ponds and flooded fields, but also salt-pans and coastal salt-marshes; frequently found on alkaline lakes; sometimes occurs on lakes in mountainous areas, up to c. 2000 m in Turkey and 2500 m in C Mexico, but commonly at 2500-4200 m in *puna* zone of Peru, Bolivia and NW Argentina. After breeding, congregates mainly at estuarine coastal habitats and on large inland water bodies.
Food and Feeding. Carnivorous, preying on great variety of small, mainly aquatic, invertebrates and vertebrates, occasionally seeds. Main prey types are larvae and adults of aquatic insects, especially beetles (Coleoptera), mayflies (Ephemeroptera), caddisflies (Trichoptera), water-bugs (Hemiptera), dragonflies (Odonata), flies (Diptera), alderflies (Neuroptera), and butterflies and moths (Lepidoptera); also bivalves and gastropods (Mollusca), crustaceans, spiders (Araneae), oligochaete and polychaete worms (Annelida), and tadpoles, small fish and their eggs. Diet often strongly seasonal, depending on habitat; for example, shifting from varied but largely insectivorous diet on inland breeding grounds to diet of crustaceans, polychaete worms and molluscs on intertidal non-breeding areas. Captures prey by a variety of visual and tactile methods including scything in soft mud when prey not visible, e.g. at night. Males often feed in deeper water than females.
Breeding. Timing very variable over massive range: seasonal or after rain in tropical regions; in Palearctic, laying begins as early as late Mar in N Africa, later further N, and not until May in N parts of range; altitude also affects timing, e.g. in New Zealand, begins nesting late Jul to Aug at sea-level, but not until late Sept to Oct at altitudes over 700 m. Sometimes solitary but usually in colonies, typically of 2-50 pairs, rarely 100's. Nests widely spaced on ground, often amongst grasses and sedges; sometimes nest is floating mass of water weeds; usually well lined. Usually 4 eggs (3-6); incubation 22-26 days, by both sexes; downy young have crown and back olive brown to ochre dotted with parallel lines of black spots, larger on back, and with black lines on flanks, underparts off-white; chicks depart nest on day of hatching or next day; fledging 28-32 days (*himantopus*, and *leucocephalus* in Australia) or 30-37 days (*leucocephalus* in New Zealand); independent of parents 2-4 weeks after fledging (*himantopus*) or often after a few months (*leucocephalus*). Age of first breeding 1-2 years.
Movements. Sedentary in places, but local movements to long distance migration elsewhere. N populations of races *himantopus* and *mexicanus* migrate in Jul-Nov to Africa and Central and South America respectively, returning in Mar-May, usually over period of less than 1 month at any one site. Local movements recorded throughout most of tropics, but patterns poorly understood. In New Zealand, S and inland breeders of *leucocephalus* migrate to N New Zealand in Jan-Mar, returning in Aug-Sept, whereas lowland and N breeders mainly sedentary. Spring passage typically involves flocks of up to 15 birds.
Status and Conservation. Not globally threatened. Huge, near-cosmopolitan range and local abundance indicate species secure for present, but controversial taxonomy calls for analysis and monitoring at subspecific level; all races apparently secure, except Hawaiian *knudseni*; local populations in decline in many countries. In W Palearctic, nominate race declined during 19th century, but since then has recovered in several areas; current population estimated at minimum of c. 21,000 pairs, with stronghold in Spain (c. 10,500 pairs in 1989) which may be crucial as buffer to fluctuations in productivity and survival in other parts of Europe; local populations greatly affected by annual rainfall and habitat protection; population declines in E Europe, e.g. in Greece, Hungary and Bulgaria, attributed to loss of wetland habitat, but series of protected wetlands in W Europe providing secure breeding and feeding grounds; probably maximum of 500-600 pairs in Azerbaijan; widespread and locally very abundant throughout Africa; abundant in Pakistan. In Australia, extensive wetland habitats available, and population of *leucocephalus* estimated at 266,000 birds; in 19th century, colonized New Zealand, where current population 30,000 birds. Race *knudseni* is rarest form of present species, numbering only c. 1800 birds; survival depends on continued protection of its core nesting areas, as it breeds elsewhere only during very wet springs. Extensive wetland habitats in Americas suggest races *mexicanus* and *melanurus* remain relatively secure, but no population estimates available; within South America, *mexicanus* commonest in *llanos* of Colombia and Venezuela, *melanurus* in C Chile and N & C Argentina.
Bibliography. Abdulali (1951), Alberico (1993), Ali & Ripley (1980), Anon. (1985b, 1993a), Barbera *et al.* (1990), Belton (1984), Bent (1927-1929), Blake (1977), Bologna & Petretti (1978), Brazil (1991), Brouwer (1991), Burger, J. (1980b), Busching (1989), Casini (1986), Chapman *et al.* (1985), Child (1983), Coates (1985), Coleman (1981), Cramp & Simmons (1983), Cullen (1994), Dementiev & Gladkov (1951b), Dinsmore (1977), Dostine & Morton (1989b), Dowsett & Forbes-Watson (1993), Dubois (1992), van der Elst (1991a), Engilis & Pratt (1993), Espin *et al.* (1983), Finch (1982a), Fjeldså (1977), Fjeldså & Krabbe (1990), Fletcher & Fletcher (1989), Foster (1987), von Frisch (1961), Garcias (1991), Gollop (1989), González-Kirchner & Sainz (1990), Goodman *et al.* (1989), Goriup (1982a), Goutner (1989), Gubkin (1988), Hamilton (1969, 1975), Harvey (1971), Hilty & Brown (1986), Hirschfeld (1990), Howell & Webb (1995a), James (1991), Johnson, A.W. (1965b), Johnson, R. (1990), Joubert (1974), King (1978/79), Kitagawa (1988a, 1988b, 1989), Korzyakov & Petrovskeya (1988), Lane & Davies (1987), Langrand (1990), Lisetski & Gudina (1983), Marchant & Higgins (1993), van Marle & Voous (1988), McConkey (1971), McNeil & Robert (1988), Meininger (1991, 1993), Meininger & Schekkerman (1990), Mosansky (1977), de Naurois (1986), Palmer-Ball & Bennett (1993), Paton *et al.* (1985), Patrikeev (1995), Phillips (1978), Pierce (1982, 1983, 1984a, 1984b, 1985, 1986a, 1986b), Pringle (1987), Recorbet (1994), Robert & McNeil (1989), Roberts, T.J. (1991), Robinson (1975), Rohwer *et al.* (1979), Sagar & Pierce (1990), Schonert (1990), Schwartz & Schwartz (1951), Sériot (1989), Serrano *et al.* (1983), Shirihai (1996), Sick (1993), Slud (1964), Smythies (1986), Sordahl (1980, 1982, 1990, 1994), Stephens (1974), Tinarelli (1987a, 1990, 1992a, 1992b, 1993a), Tupiza & Gordillo (1978), Urban *et al.* (1986), Wetmore (1965), Williams, Hothem & Ohlendor (1989), Yen (1991), Zubakin (1979b).

2. **Black Stilt**

Himantopus novaezelandiae

French: Échasse noire **German**: Schwarzer Stelzenläufer **Spanish**: Cigüeñuela Negra

Taxonomy. *Himantopus novæ-zelandiæ* Gould, 1841, Port Nicholson, North Island, New Zealand.
Forms superspecies with *H. himantopus*, with which sometimes considered conspecific (see page 332); known to hybridize with *H. h. leucocephalus*, and the two species have very similar courtship and breeding behaviour. Monotypic.
Distribution. New Zealand: formerly widespread, but breeding now restricted to MacKenzie Basin, C South I; small numbers winter locally in North I.

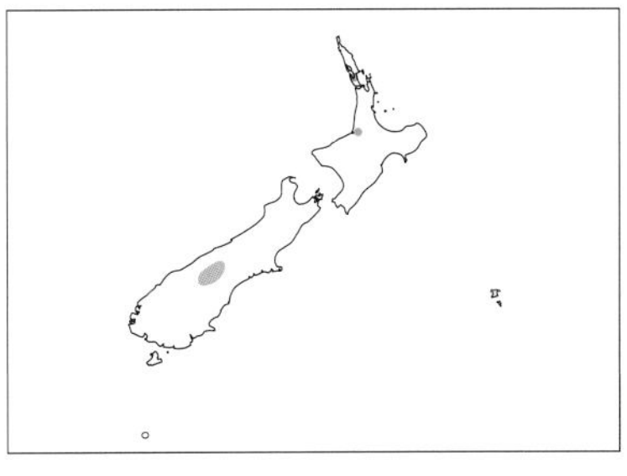

Descriptive notes. 37-40 cm; c. 220 g; tarsus mean 87 mm. Distinctive all black plumage with greenish gloss to back and wings; long pink legs. Differs structurally from *H. himantopus* in having shorter legs and longer bill. Female similar to male, but averages shorter-legged. Non-breeding adult can show greyish to whitish forehead and chin. Juvenile, at fledging, very similar to that of *H. himantopus*, mainly white below; however, soon develops variable greyish black markings on underparts in first winter; second summer plumage predominantly black with scattered white spots and streaks. Hybrids between present species and *H. h. leucocephalus* very variable, typically with black collar and some black markings on breast and belly.
Habitat. Braided riverbeds, lake shores, swamps and shallow ponds of MacKenzie Basin. Breeds beside streams with stable sides, or by main flood-prone river channels; also by well vegetated ponds and swamps. Outside breeding season, birds frequent ponds, river deltas and nearby lake edges, and a few visit coastal lagoons and estuaries.
Food and Feeding. Carnivorous, taking variety of invertebrates and small fish. On riverbed breeding grounds, feeds predominantly on aquatic insect larvae and adults, including mayflies (Ephemeroptera), caddisflies (Trichoptera), stoneflies (Plecoptera), and small fish (Galaxiidae, Eleotrididae); at other lentic breeding grounds also preys on damselfies (Odonata), various flies, especially midge larvae (Chironomidae, Diptera), various water-bugs (Hemiptera), also oligochaetes and molluscs. Post-breeding diet may include same groups. Few birds move to coastal habitats where diet is extended to include various crustaceans and polychaetes. Riverbed prey often obtained by probing beneath stones; also scythes and pecks; sometimes probes in fields.
Breeding. Seasonal, taking place in Sept-Jan. Usually solitary; defends territory against other congeners. Nest bowl usually well lined, and nest located near water. Usually 4 eggs (3-6); incubation 24-26 days, by both sexes; downy chick has pale brown upperparts speckled and spotted with black, with larger spots on back and in parallel lines, greyish black patch on thighs, off-white below; fledging 41-55 days; independent of parents after 9 months. In wild, most eggs and young are eaten by predators. First breeding at 2 years, or more usually 3 years of age. Known to have lived over 12 years in wild.
Movements. Sedentary in MacKenzie Basin with local movements of up to several kilometres, usually in autumn-winter to river delta of breeding valley, with birds returning to nesting area from late winter to early spring. A few birds spend autumn and winter at coastal lagoons, and especially estuaries, of North I; most of these are associated with, and may be paired with, individuals of *H. himantopus* or hybrids.
Status and Conservation. CRITICALLY ENDANGERED. Total population crashed from 1000 birds or more in 1950 to fewer than 100 birds by 1960, and currently remains at fewer than 100 birds. Habitat loss and predation of eggs, chicks and adults by introduced carnivorous mammals have greatly reduced the productivity of wild birds, and have further promoted interbreeding with increasingly abundant *H. himantopus*, which colonized New Zealand only in 19th century. Predator control and captive rearing and release began in early 1980's with mixed success, but overall at least halted decline. At

On following pages: 3. Banded Stilt (*Cladorhynchus leucocephalus*); 4. Pied Avocet (*Recurvirostra avosetta*); 5. American Avocet (*Recurvirostra americana*); 6. Red-necked Avocet (*Recurvirostra novaehollandiae*); 7. Andean Avocet (*Recurvirostra andina*).

present, New Zealand Department of Conservation is responsible for artificial incubation of most eggs, releasing numbers of captive-reared birds annually. See page 342.

Bibliography. Baker (1991), Buller (1878), Chambers (1989), Collar & Andrew (1988), Collar *et al.* (1994), Ellis (1975), Falla *et al.* (1981), Fleming (1962), Gray & Craig (1991), King (1978/79), Marchant & Higgins (1993), O'Donnell (1988), Pierce (1980b, 1982, 1983, 1984a, 1984b, 1985, 1986a, 1986b), Potts (1869, 1872), Reed (1986, 1994a, 1994b, 1995), Reed & Merton (1991), Reed, Murray & Butler (1993), Reed, Nilsson & Murray (1993), Sibson (1982), Soper (1967), Stead (1932), Williams & Given (1981).

Genus *CLADORHYNCHUS* G. R. Gray, 1840

3. Banded Stilt

Cladorhynchus leucocephalus

French: Échasse à tête blanche **German**: Schlammstelzer **Spanish**: Cigüeñuela Pechirroja

Taxonomy. *Recurvirostra leucocephala* Vieillot, 1816, Victoria.
Reported to show morphological and behavioural similarities to flamingos (Phoenicopteridae), but probably not significant (see page 332). Monotypic.

Distribution. Australia, mainly in S & C inland areas, particularly C Western Australia and South Australia.

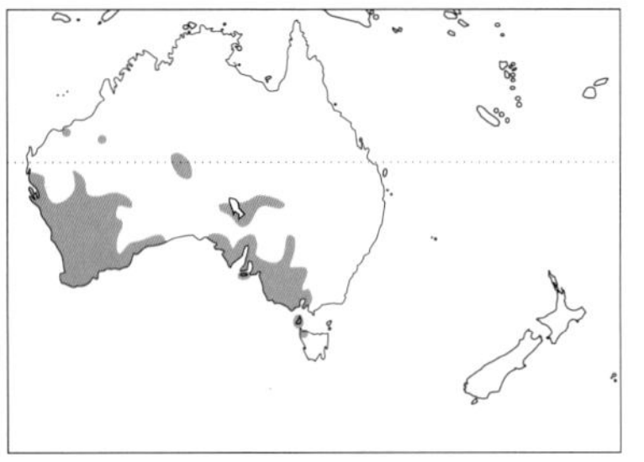

Descriptive notes. 35-43 cm; 220-260 g; tarsus mean 87 mm in male, and 80 mm in female. Distinctive, predominantly white stilt with mainly black scapulars and upperwing; broad chestnut breast band with narrow dark upper edge; bill slender and black; legs long and orange-pink; legs shorter than in *H. himantopus*. Sexes alike. Non-breeding adult has breast band reduced. Juvenile lacks breast band.

Habitat. Shallow saline or hypersaline waters inland and along coast, including ephemeral salt-lakes, salt-works ponds, salt-pans, saline lagoons, estuaries, bays and tidal flats, only occasionally on low-salinity waters. Highly opportunistic, breeding only in arid interior at large, shallow salt-lakes temporarily filled by rain or flood water.

Food and Feeding. Feeds on variety of small crustaceans, and also aquatic insects, molluscs, fish and vegetable matter. Staple prey are small crustaceans which become temporarily superabundant in saline lakes, including: brine-shrimps (Branchipoda); *Apus*, *Triops* (Notostraca); *Artemia*, *Parartemia* (Anostraca); ostracods; and isopods. Feeds by pecking, probing (including plunging) and scything. Forages in shallow water during day.

Breeding. Not well known, but timing sporadic and dependent on inundations of salt-lakes. Colonies may contain 10,000's of nests, and one contained 179,000; can occur at densities of up to 18 nests/m². At a given moment, different parts of a colony can be at markedly different stages; species may be double-brooded, or synchronized episodes of laying may occur. Nest-sites are islands of bare soil; nest bowl is a scrape in ground, or is patch of flat ground about which vegetation is collected. Usually 3-4 eggs (1-5); egg white with dark streaks, as opposed to yellow or brown with dark markings in other recurvirostrids; incubation 19-21 days, by both sexes; chick covered in white down, unique within suborder Charadrii (see page 340); nidifugous; mobile crèches of 100's of chicks attended by adults; fledging c. 50 days.

Movements. Dispersive, with movements dependent on rainfall: frequents coastal areas when arid inland zones are dry, returning inland after rain. Pre-breeding return inland occurs more rapidly than post-breeding exodus.

Status and Conservation. Not globally threatened. Total population reckoned to number normally over 200,000 birds, probably many more. Size of population probably fluctuates greatly from year to year, depending on suitability of habitat for breeding. Much of this habitat is either protected or unlikely to be significantly altered by man. Species may benefit from artificially increased salinity of many wetlands in western and eastern extremes of range.

Bibliography. Alcorn, M. & Alcorn (1990), Alcorn, R. (1985), Balogh (1989), Blakers *et al.* (1984), Burbidge & Fuller (1982), Carnaby (1946), Chandler (1995), Christidis & Boles (1994), Henderson (1982), Hewish (1989), Howe & Ross (1931), Jones (1945), Kolichis (1976), Lane & Davies (1987), Lindsey (1992), Macdonald (1988), Marchant & Higgins (1993), McGilp & Morgan (1931), Minton (1989), Minton, Lane & Pearson (1995), Minton, Pearson & Lane (1995), Pearson (1989), Pizzey & Doyle (1980), Pringle (1987), Robinson & Minton (1989), Schodde & Tidemann (1986), Simpson & Day (1994), Slater *et al.* (1989), Sonter (1987), Trounson (1987), Wall (1990), Wall & Harris (1978).

Genus *RECURVIROSTRA* Linnaeus, 1758

4. Pied Avocet

Recurvirostra avosetta

French: Avocette élégante **German**: Säbelschnäbler **Spanish**: Avoceta Común
Other common names: (Eurasian) Avocet

Taxonomy. *Recurvirostra Avosetta* Linnaeus, 1758, southern Europe = Italy.
Clinal increase in size from W Europe E across Asia. Monotypic.

Distribution. Europe through W & C Asia to SE Siberia and NE China, and locally through N Africa to E & S Africa; winters from W Europe and Africa through Middle East to NW India and SE China.

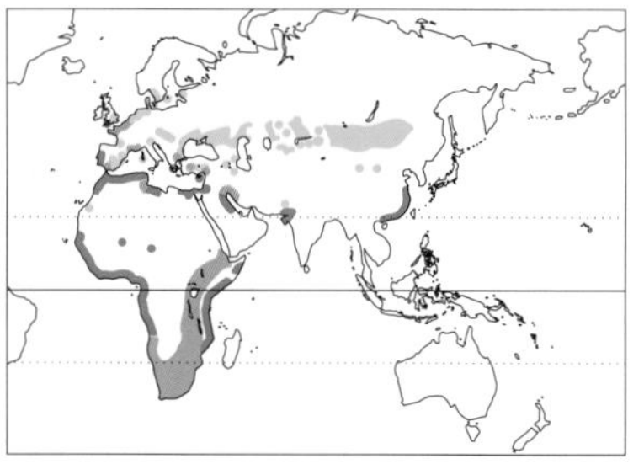

Descriptive notes. 42-45 cm; 225-397 g; tarsus 85-98 mm in male, 77-92 mm in female. Unmistakable; mainly white with black forehead, crown to below eyes, nape and upper hindneck; at rest, shows three distinctive black bands on mantle and scapulars, lesser and median upperwing-coverts, and outer 6 primaries; bill black and strongly upcurved, long legs blue-grey. Female tends to have shorter, more strongly curved bill. No seasonal variation. Juvenile similar to adult, but black less intense or tinged brownish, and white upperparts have mottling of sepia, grey-brown or buff.

Habitat. Breeds in flat, open areas typically at shallow saline lakes, lagoons, pools, salt-pans and estuaries with sparse vegetation; up to over 3000 m in Afghanistan. Outside breeding season also frequents muddy tidal flats; infrequently found on freshwater lakes and even rivers; sometimes found on agricultural land, particularly in Netherlands.

Food and Feeding. Carnivorous, taking great variety of mainly aquatic invertebrates 4-15 mm long, particularly aquatic insects, crustaceans and worms, rarely molluscs, fish and plant material. Winter diet known best from Portugal where spionid worms, tubificid worms, small *Nereis* and *Capitella* polychaetes comprise bulk of diet. Most often feeds by picking or by tactile scything of bill through water or mud; sometimes feeds communally.

Breeding. Apr-Aug in Eurasia. Usually nests in large colonies. Nest is typically a grass-lined scrape in open ground or amongst short vegetation. Usually 3-4 eggs (2-5); incubation normally 23-25 days, by both sexes; downy young silver-grey above grading to buff on sides of head, wing and sides of back, with small black spots on crown, two lines of larger parallel spots on back, and spots on thighs; chick nidifugous; fledging 35-42 days. Age of first breeding 2-3 years. Known to have lived over 24 years in wild.

Movements. Variable. N temperate birds mainly migrate Aug-Oct to tropical and warm temperate regions, staging *en route* in high numbers, e.g. in Netherlands. Roughly one third of Atlantic seaboard population migrates to sub-Saharan Africa, but average of over 10,000 birds each winter in both France and Iberian Peninsula, with up to 11,000 birds on Tagus Estuary, Portugal. Return movements in Mar-May, with many African migrants using Banc d'Arguin, Mauritania, as brief stopover. Some local overwintering elsewhere in W Europe. Patterns in Asia poorly documented, but wintering birds occupy Persian Gulf, NW India and SE China, presumably from C Asian breeding grounds. One-year-old migrant birds possibly remain on wintering grounds over following summer. E & S African birds sedentary or locally dispersive. Contrary to some reports, species is mere vagrant to Cape Verde Is, with only c. 3-4 records.

Status and Conservation. Not globally threatened. Extensive range, with over half of population reckoned to breed in Europe; locally abundant in several parts of Africa, often coinciding with presence of migrants from Palearctic. Europe reckoned to hold 31,000-56,000 breeding pairs, with largest numbers in Netherlands, Denmark, Spain (c. 4400 pairs in 1989) and Turkey; also minimum c. 37,000 birds in winter, with 14,000-16,000 in France, 7000-20,000 in Portugal, 7200-11,000 in Spain, 5000-10,000 in Italy, and 1760-6500 in Greece. After contraction of range in NW Europe in 19th century, species has increased since 1940's, recolonizing England and Sweden and extending breeding range to Belgium and Norway; numbers of breeders along coast of North Sea (including Sweden) increased from 1800 pairs in 1924/25 to c. 10,000 pairs in 1969, and 16,400-19,700 pairs in 1980's. Wetland breeding areas currently coming under increased pressure, and as this species is less opportunistic than most other recurvirostrids there is cause for concern in several regions; from E Europe to China, pressures have come about primarily through lack of protection of wetlands, both on inland breeding grounds and on wintering grounds of coastal China and Indian Subcontinent; similar problems exist in Mediterranean region, but protection and enhancement of wetlands in W Europe is believed to have assisted the recovery of populations in Britain, France, Belgium, Germany and Denmark. As with all wetland inhabitants, however, species susceptible to abuses of PCB, selenium, and lead pollution, and use of insecticides; similar problems also apply at several of African wintering areas. Over 80% of large Dutch population breeds on Wadden Sea, where depends on suitable management of salt-marsh habitat. As 90% of European winterers concentrated at 10 sites, protection of these sites is of paramount importance; over 15% of European winter population occurs at Tagus Estuary, Portugal, where threatened by mercury pollution, hunting and bridge building.

Bibliography. Adret (1982), Ali & Ripley (1980), Benson & Benson (1975), Bie & Zijlstra (1979), Blomert *et al.* (1990), Bouche (1991), Brazil (1991), Britton, P.L. (1980), Broekhuysen & Macleod (1948), Cadbury & Olney (1978), Cadbury *et al.* (1989), Casini (1986), Cramp & Simmons (1983), Dietrich & Hoetker (1991), Dowsett & Forbes-Watson (1993), Dubois & Maheo (1986), Elgood *et al.* (1994), Engelmoer & Blomert (1985), Étchécopar & Hüe (1964, 1978), Evans (1994), Fjeldså (1977), Flint *et al.* (1984), Géroudet & Juillard (1990), Girard & Yésou (1989, 1991), Goodman *et al.* (1989), Gore (1990), Goutner (1984, 1985), Heg (1991), Hill, D. (1988, 1989), Hill, D. & Carter (1991), Hill, D. & Player (1992), Hoetker & Dietrich (1992), Hüe & Étchécopar (1970), Knystautas (1993), Langrand (1990), Larousse (1995), Mackworth-Praed & Grant (1957, 1962, 1970), Maclean (1993), Makkink (1936), Moreira (1995a, 1995b), Morgan-Davies (1960a), Morris (1993), Olney (1970), Osieck (1994), Patrikeev (1995), Paz (1987), Perennou (1991), Perennou *et al.* (1994), Piersma (1986b), Piersma, Klaassen *et al.* (1990), Pinto (1983), Reay (1991, 1992), Roberts, T.J. (1991), Rogacheva (1992), Rutgers & Norris (1970), Rydzewski (1978), Shirihai (1996), Short *et al.* (1990), Smythies (1986), Sueur (1975, 1984), Summers, Underhill, Pearson & Scott (1987), Tinarelli (1987b), Tjallingii (1970), Urban *et al.* (1986), Watier & Fournier (1980), Wyndham (1942).

5. American Avocet

Recurvirostra americana

French: Avocette d'Amérique **German**: Braunhals-Säbelschnäbler **Spanish**: Avoceta Americana

Taxonomy. *Recurvirostra americana* Gmelin, 1789, North America.
Monotypic.

Distribution. SE British Columbia E to SW Ontario, and S to N Baja California E to C Texas; E USA; C Mexico. Winters from California and S Texas through Mexico to Guatemala and irregularly to N Honduras; SE USA and Bahamas to Cuba.

Descriptive notes. 41-51 cm; 302-461 g; tarsus 85-103 mm. Head, neck and breast orange-brown, becoming pinkish on upper mantle and upper belly, then shading into white; pattern of blackish dorsal markings resembles those of *R. avosetta* and *R. novaehollandiae*, but more extensive blackish on outerwing through dark primary and greater coverts; black bill strongly upcurved; long legs blue-grey. Female has shorter, more strongly curved bill. Non-breeding adult has crown, nape and hindneck pearly grey, rest of underparts white. Juvenile as adult, but crown pale brownish contrasting with dull chestnut nape and hindneck, merging into pinkish on upper mantle; whitish on inner primaries.

Habitat. Breeds around sparsely vegetated saline lakes and ponds, especially alkaline lakes, lagoons and marshes; also in estuaries; nests up to 2500 m in C Mexico. Outside breeding season, occurs in freshwater habitats and also coastal lagoons, estuaries and tidal flats.

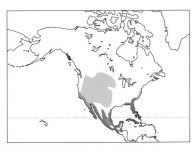

Food and Feeding. Mainly carnivorous, preying on wide range of mainly aquatic invertebrates including aquatic insects and their larvae, crustaceans, molluscs and worms. In inland areas, often extends diet to include seeds and terrestrial insects such as grasshoppers and crickets. On intertidal flats in California, diet comprises mainly spionid, capitellid and oligochaete worms. Usually feeds by scything, but also by pecking. Sometimes forages in dense flocks.

Breeding. Nests in spring and summer in N of range; Apr-Aug in NW Mexico, Mar-Aug in C Mexico. Usually nests in loose colonies, but sometimes in large, dense colonies. Nest is grass-lined depression in soil. Usually 4 eggs (3-5); occasionally clutches of up to 8 recorded, due to "dumping"; incubation 22-29 days, by both sexes; chicks have pale tan down with darker spots and stripes; both adults care for chicks; fledging 4-5 weeks; young not immediately independent.

Movements. Mostly migratory. Winters in S portion of breeding range in S & E USA and Mexico, S to Guatemala and rarely N Honduras, and also Bahamas and Cuba. N migration occurs in Apr-May; S migration in Aug-Nov.

Status and Conservation. Not globally threatened. Expansive range over North America, where many important sites are officially protected. In Mexico, fairly common to uncommon breeder, common to fairly common migrant and winter visitor.

Bibliography. Alberico (1993), Anon. (1983a), Armstrong (1983), Bent (1927-1929), Blake (1977), Boettcher *et al.* (1994), Brown & Engleman (1988), Bucher (1978), Burger & Gochfeld (1986a), Campbell, R.W. (1972), Cooke (1977), Cooper (1983), Davidson (1989), Dinsmore (1977), Dinzl (1990), Evans, T.J. (1988), Evans, T.J. & Harris (1994), Gibson (1971a, 1971b), Giroux (1985), Godfrey (1986), Gunderson *et al.* (1992), Hamilton (1969, 1975), Hellmayr & Conover (1948), Hill (1985), Hirsch & Fouchi (1984), Howell & Webb (1995a), Kondla (1977), Kondla & Pinel (1978), Kuyt (1989), Kuyt & Johns (1992), Mahoney & Jehl (1985b), Matthiessen (1994), Mayer & Ryan (1991a), McNair (1988), Monroe (1968), Osmundson (1989), Root (1988), Schaldach (1963), Scott & Carbonell (1986), Shipley (1984), Sidle & Arnold (1982), Smith (1994), Sordahl (1980, 1982, 1988a, 1988b, 1990, 1994), Urban (1959), Williams, Hothem & Ohlendor (1989).

6. Red-necked Avocet

Recurvirostra novaehollandiae

French: Avocette d'Australie   **German**: Rotkopf-Säbelschnäbler   **Spanish**: Avoceta Australiana
Other common names: Australian Avocet

Taxonomy. *Recurvirostra Novæ-Hollandiæ* Vieillot, 1816, Victoria.
Monotypic.
Distribution. Australia, occurring mainly in S, but widespread with scattered distribution.

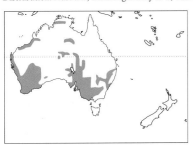

Descriptive notes. 40-48 cm; 270-390 g; tarsus 81-97 mm in male, 81-90 mm in female. Head and most of neck deep chestnut-red, sharply demarcated from white body; white eye-ring; pair of parallel blackish stripes on sides of back, extensive blackish on upperwing-coverts and outer 7 primaries blackish, pattern recalling that of *R. avosetta*; black bill strongly upcurved; legs pale blue-grey. Female has more steeply upcurved bill, although sexual dimorphism apparently somewhat less pronounced than in similar and closely related *R. avosetta* and *R. americana*. No seasonal variation. Juvenile similar, but head and neck paler brown; broad pale ring around base of bill.

Habitat. Breeds preferably at inland salt-lakes; also frequents, and commonly breeds at, variety of shallow, generally ephemeral, wetlands of wide salinity range, including hypersaline lakes, freshwater lakes, dams, lagoons, marshes, sewage ponds and shallow edges of rivers and estuaries.

Food and Feeding. Not studied in detail. Feeds on variety of aquatic invertebrates including annelid worms, molluscs, variety of crustaceans and insects; also seeds. Feeds by scything in lower water column or mud layer; sometimes also by pecking. Diurnal forager.

Breeding. Season Aug-Jan in some southern areas, elsewhere opportunistic, depending on wetlands being filled with floodwater. Breeds in solitary pairs or in colonies of up to 150 pairs, sometimes in company of *Himantopus himantopus* and other waterbirds; nests are minimum of 1·6 m apart, and comprise depression in ground, lined with vegetation. Usually 4 eggs (2-5); incubation probably at least c. 23-25 days; downy chicks buff above, white below, with dark brown eyestripe, dark brown spots on crown and large paired spots on back; chicks nidifugous, cared for by both parents. Hatching success 31% for 72 eggs.

Movements. Occurs mainly in S Australia, where dispersive in response to changing water levels. Seasonal pattern involving inland movement in winter and coastal movement in summer may be modified by inland drought, or rainfall and subsequent availability of food; prolonged or severe droughts cause dispersal into areas where species usually rare, e.g. E of Great Dividing Range. Possible movements into parts of N Australia also recorded. Vagrant to Tasmania and New Zealand.

Status and Conservation. Not globally threatened. Total population exceeds 100,000 birds; main site is L Eyre, with 95,000 birds in early 1980's. Gradual loss of wetlands in some areas possibly offset by creation of salt-works and sewage ponds where birds frequently occur. Species formerly present in New Zealand, where apparently became only tenuously established following irruption starting in 1859; present during latter half of 19th century, but now merely vagrant, with only 2 definite records from 20th century.

Bibliography. Alcorn (1989, 1990), Blakers *et al.* (1984), Brouwer (1991), Bryant (1947, 1948), Burnett (1985), Claridge & Johnson (1988), Kaigler (1968), Lane & Davies (1987), Lindsey (1992), Macdonald (1988), Marchant & Higgins (1993), Moore (1954), Pizzey & Doyle (1980), Pringle (1987), Saunders & de Rebeira (1986), Schodde & Tidemann (1986), Sibson (1982), Simpson & Day (1994), Slater *et al.* (1989), Sullivan (1988), Thomas (1989), Trounson (1987), Walter (1983), Weston & Rush (1992).

7. Andean Avocet

Recurvirostra andina

French: Avocette des Andes   **German**: Andensäbelschnäbler   **Spanish**: Avoceta Andina

Taxonomy. *Recurvirostra andina* Philippi and Landbeck, 1861, Laguna Parinacocha, Peru.
Monotypic.
Distribution. C Peru (Junín) S through W Bolivia to N Chile (NC Atacama) and NW Argentina (Catamarca).

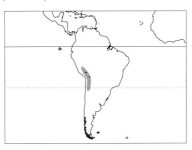

Descriptive notes. 43-48 cm; 315-410 g; tarsus 77-84 mm. Compact, heavy-bodied avocet, with relatively short legs compared to other members of family; stilt-like in plumage, but with typical avocet bill; differs from all other avocets in having orange iris and yellow eye-ring; head, neck, upper mantle, rump and underparts white, often stained ferruginous below; rest of mantle and wings blackish to very dark brown; bill black; long legs blue-grey. No sexual differences in plumage known. Juvenile has inconspicuous rusty feather edges on upperparts, but these soon wear off.

Habitat. Breeds at high altitudes, above 3100 m, typically in *puna* zone of Andes; generally occupies saline and alkaline lakes; also marshes, where occurs only in rather open parts, often on exposed alkaline flats; also seasonally flooded alkaline meadows; sometimes in and around small pools. Occasionally found on other wetlands, including even tidal flats along coast outside breeding season.

Food and Feeding. Little known. Apparently feeds on free-swimming invertebrates. Forages by scything in shallow water; sometimes swims and upends like other avocets. Often feeds in association with Chilean Flamingos (*Phoenicopterus chilensis*).

Breeding. Little known. Apparently breeds in local "summer", but timing of breeding may depend on local rainfall; eggs recorded in Sept and Oct, Jan and Feb, possibly representing two seasons per year, a practice which is regular for sympatric *Himantopus himantopus*. Usually 4 eggs; chick greyish white above with dark spotting, white below. No further information available.

Movements. Little known. Probably mainly sedentary. Some altitudinal movement to lower altitudes recorded in Apr-Jul, and species rarely wanders to coastal areas of N Chile and Peru, but in Jul still recorded up to 5000 m.

Status and Conservation. Not globally threatened. Status very poorly known, but species considered to be generally sparse; small parties of 15-20 birds may be regular. Population in C & SC Peru rather disjunct and isolated in Junín and Ayacucho. Massive desiccation of L Poopó, WC Bolivia, could represent serious loss of habitat, although species persists in small pools along dried up margins. Suitable habitat still fairly extensive; not known to suffer serious hunting pressure.

Bibliography. Blake (1977), Canevari *et al.* (1991), Fjeldså & Krabbe (1990), Hellmayr & Conover (1948), Hughes, R.A. (1984), Johnson (1965b), Koepcke (1970), Narosky & Yzurieta (1987), Olrog (1984), Parker *et al.* (1982), de la Peña (1992), Remsen & Traylor (1989), Scott & Carbonell (1986).

Class AVES
Order CHARADRIIFORMES
Suborder CHARADRII
Family BURHINIDAE (THICK-KNEES)

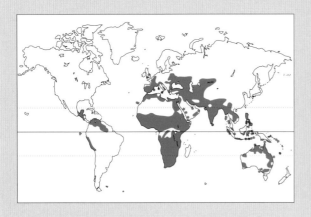

- Medium-sized terrestrial waders, with long legs, long wings and cryptic plumage; bill usually short, but large and heavy in some species.
- 32-59 cm.

- All regions except Antarctic, but mainly tropical; greatest diversity in Old World.
- Semi-arid to arid open areas, sometimes linked with water; one species strictly coastal.
- 2 genera, 9 species, 19 taxa.
- No species threatened; none extinct since 1600.

Systematics

As members of the Burhinidae superficially resemble some bustards (Otididae) the family was in the past sometimes classified alongside the bustards in the order Gruiformes. However, these similarities are nowadays agreed to be the product of convergent evolution of birds with somewhat similar terrestrial lifestyles occupying much the same biotopes. The combined weight of several skeletal, biochemical and parasitological characters, as well as the patterns of the downy young, suggests that this family is correctly placed in Charadriiformes.

Its closest relatives within this order are, however, quite uncertain, although there does at least appear to be general agreement that the family is allied to Charadriidae rather than to Scolopacidae. The Crab Plover (*Dromas ardeola*), with some structural, behavioural and dietary resemblance to the *Esacus* thick-knees, is sometimes suggested to be a close relative, although again the similarities adduced may well be attributable to parallel evolution. The peculiar Egyptian Plover (*Pluvianus aegyptius*), normally included within Glareolidae but on occasion awarded a family of its own, has been linked with Burhinidae on the basis of some shared osteological characters. Other studies back up a relationship with Glareolidae, but much of the evidence, such as the poorly developed salt glands and the structure of the nostrils and the palate, can yet again probably be considered to be the result of convergence within relatively similar arid habitats. In linear classifications Burhinidae has regularly been placed alongside Recurvirostridae and related families, and the evidence of work with DNA supports the idea that this group and the plover family Charadriidae may constitute the thick-knees' closest relatives.

One to three genera are recognized within Burhinidae, but most recent authors recognize two, with seven species in the semi-cosmopolitan *Burhinus* and two in the southern Asian and Australasian *Esacus*. Some authorities would lump all nine species in *Burhinus*, but there appear to be good reasons for maintaining two genera. The Great Thick-knee (*Esacus recurvirostris*) and the Beach Thick-knee (*Esacus magnirostris*) are clearly similar to each other in structure, size and plumage, and they also share ecological similarities, for instance in their food and habitat preferences. On the other hand, the typical *Burhinus* thick-knees are generally smaller and slimmer, with smaller bills and more mottled plumage patterns. They appear to form a close-knit group, clearly distinct from *Esacus*. The one exception that might be proposed within this group is the Bush Thick-knee (*Burhinus grallarius*) of Australia, which is actually as large as the two *Esacus* species, but in all respects this species can be considered simply a largish, long-legged, long-tailed, otherwise typical, member of *Burhinus*. Formerly, the two *Esacus* species were at times considered generically distinct, with the Beach Thick-knee being awarded the monotypic genus *Orthorhamphus*, but this treatment has now fallen into disfavour, in view of the marked similarities between the two.

There is a fairly general consensus as to species limits within the family, but the one case for dispute again concerns the two *Esacus* species. Some authors maintain that these two forms should be treated as conspecific, perhaps a somewhat surprising

Over the years generic treatment of the Beach Thick-knee has been rather varied. Formerly awarded the monotypic genus Orthorhamphus, *it is now usually placed in* Esacus *together with the Great Thick-knee (*Esacus recurvirostris*), although some authors prefer to lump all of the thick-knees in the genus* Burhinus. *However, these two heavily built species differ from the typical* Burhinus *species in a number of structural details, most notably the massive bill, while both feed extensively on crabs. The two are very closely related to one another, and indeed are still occasionally considered conspecific.*

[Esacus magnirostris, Lizard Island, Queensland, Australia. Photo: Jean-Paul Ferrero/ Auscape]

One of two Neotropical members of Burhinidae, the Double-striped Thick-knee is a fairly tall species, somewhat longer-legged and longer-necked than most other members of the family, with a large, broad head and large, staring yellow eyes that denote a mainly crepuscular or nocturnal lifestyle. The bill is darker and slightly heavier than in other Burhinus species, while the long greenish yellow legs, which suggest the mainly terrestrial nature of the bird, show the characteristic enlarged tibiotarsal or "knee" joint to which the birds owe their name of "thick-knees".
On the upperparts, upperwing-coverts and rump the dark brown centres of the feathers with their paler edges give this species a markedly streaked appearance overall, providing good camouflage. However, it is the head patterning, with the long whitish supercilium and the equally long, well defined dark lateral crown stripe, that constitutes the single most significant feature of this distinctive thick-knee, as its vernacular and scientific names underline.

[Burhinus bistriatus vocifer, Venezuela.
Photo: John Cancalosi/ Auscape]

Widely distributed over the African continent, the Spotted Dikkop is a dry country species that shows no particular liking for the vicinity of water. It is to be found in open savanna or grasslands but, unlike some thick-knees, also in bushy or sparsely wooded areas, where it seeks cover and shade in which to rest during the heat of the day. It does not seem to shun the proximity of man, and occurs at times in large parks, on playing fields and on sandy beaches. It has even been known to nest on occasions in suburban gardens.

[Burhinus capensis damarensis, Sandwich Harbour Bird Sanctuary, Namibia. Photo: Alberto Nardi/ NHPA]

suggestion, since until relatively recently many taxonomists regarded them as different enough to merit separate genera. Until new evidence appears to the contrary, the middle course is probably the most appropriate, namely to recognize two species in a single genus.

Several species show subspecific variation, but this is generally only to a rather limited degree, involving slight differences in size and colour tones, a tendency which is not altogether unexpected in a family that can, for the most part, be considered phenotypically rather homogeneous at the species level. Variation in the widespread Stone-curlew (*Burhinus oedicnemus*) is clinal in both size and coloration, but these characters vary in differing geographical directions so the establishment of racial identity is often difficult. Northern populations are migratory and may spend the winter months within the breeding ranges of southern ones, which has further complicated past understanding of geographical variation and subspeciation within this species. At present, six races are normally accepted, but the range of variation is such that several other races have been proposed.

Two thick-knee species have long been the source of much confusion due to problems of nomenclature. Until very recently, the scientific name of the Bush Thick-knee was almost invariably given as *Burhinus magnirostris*. This caused considerable problems when authors opted to include the Beach Thick-knee in the genus *Burhinus*, as it was frequently unclear whether the name *Burhinus magnirostris* was being applied to one species or the other. The Bush Thick-knee was originally described by J. Latham in 1801, when he named two "new species", *magnirostris* and *grallarius*, on the same page; unfortunately, both of them subsequently turned out to be the Bush Thick-knee! However, the International Code of Zoological Nomenclature covers such eventualities, and, following the principle of first reviser, J. Gould's adoption of the name *grallarius* for this species in 1845 now stands as definitive.

In the meantime, though, the Beach Thick-knee's valid species name has, in turn, been the source of much debate and several proposed name changes. It was suggested that L. P. Vieillot's 1818 name *magnirostris* was not applicable to this species, as it had become a junior secondary homonym due to the grouping of this species in the same genus as the Bush Thick-knee. J. Wagler's 1829 name *giganteus* was proposed, but it was argued that this

name was unidentifiable, and so should be replaced by G. M. Mathews's 1912 name *neglectus*. However, with the establishment of *grallarius* as the valid name for the Bush Thick-knee, the principle of homonymy does not come into play, so the correct species name for the Beach Thick-knee remains *magnirostris*, independent of whether it is placed in *Esacus* or *Burhinus*.

While the nomenclature should now be clear for future work, there can be no doubt that the confusion will persist with regard to many records in older literature, every time the name *Burhinus magnirostris* crops up, a situation not helped by the plethora of rather similar vernacular names that exist for both of the species involved. Scientific nomenclature is designed to clarify the identification of taxa by using unique names; this is a very clear case of the pandemonium that can result from the same name being applied to two species that are physically not even particularly similar!

Morphological Aspects

While thick-knees share some physical characteristics with similar-sized plovers and bustards, they remain a recognizably defined small group of species with distinctive traits of their own. They vary in overall length from about 32 cm in the Senegal Thick-knee (*Burhinus senegalensis*) to as much as 57 cm in the Beach Thick-knee and 59 cm in the Bush Thick-knee, although the latter is markedly slimmer, lankier and longer-tailed than both of the *Esacus* species. There are no differences between the sexes, apart from some very minor ones in plumage pattern in the Stone-curlew, and, equally, fledged juveniles are very similar to adults.

Species of the typical *Burhinus* group have rather stout but medium-short bills, with the bulbous tip tapering to a sharp point in a side view; from above or below, the bill is broad-based but compressed into a blade-like form towards the tip. Although short for a wading bird, the bill looks rather substantial in the field, more so than in plovers. In most species the bill is black with a variable amount of yellow at the base. The nostrils are long, slit-like openings perforated right through the bill, as, for example, in gulls (Laridae). The long legs are coloured pale ochre to vivid yellow, with an exposed tibia and a swollen tibiotarsal or "knee" joint, whence the name "thick-knee" given to the group, although ana-

Generally speaking, thick-knees are sociable birds, and outside the breeding season they gather in flocks of varying size, often frequenting traditional sites. A small group of Senegal Thick-knees is here seen resting during the daytime on the preferred habitat of a muddy river bank. Although sometimes occurring as solitary nesters, they mostly form loose breeding colonies and even closer nesting communities when space is at a premium, as, for example, on the flat roofs of houses, where they have occasionally been recorded as nesting.

[Burhinus senegalensis, Basse, Gambia. Photo: Alan Williams/ NHPA]

tomically this is a misnomer, as it is actually the "raised" ankle joint. The legs are markedly scaled, or reticulated. The hind toe is lacking, and the three forward-pointing toes are slightly webbed.

Apart from the stout bill, the large head is characterized by a broad, sometimes domed, crown. The shape of the head is the origin of the common name of both the Water Dikkop (*Burhinus vermiculatus*) and the Spotted Dikkop (*Burhinus capensis*), as the Afrikaans word *dikkop* means "thick head". In most species, the pale base of the bill may show more clearly than the pale eye at a distance, but at close range it is the eye that becomes the most arresting feature, always looking large, round and staring, an adaptation to a crepuscular or even predominantly nocturnal lifestyle. Further exaggerating the aspect of the eyes, the head is patterned with strong dark brown to black and creamy white stripes. In the four Eurasian and African species, a broad pale band continues the line of the pale base of the upper mandible as a sweeping, curved stripe underneath the eye.

The rest of the plumage is cryptically coloured, based on a pale, sandy brown ground with streaks, mottles and spots of cream, buff, brown and black. As is often the case with pale birds of open landscapes, the underside is paler still, using countershading as a means of cancelling out the effects of shadow cast by the sun or bright sky, so helping the bird to blend in with the background tone.

The closed wings have a more or less banded appearance, owing to the pale and dark rows of upperwing-coverts which create a succession of horizontal lines, an effect that is least marked on the two American species, the Double-striped Thick-knee (*Burhinus bistriatus*) and the Peruvian Thick-knee (*Burhinus superciliaris*). The latter is somewhat aberrant, having a much plainer and greyer plumage overall, although the head is boldly marked with a broad white supercilium bordered above by a conspicuous blackish stripe.

When a thick-knee takes flight, it reveals a much more striking and contrasted plumage and thus frequently becomes obvious for the first time to an observer who may have overlooked the bird as it remained motionless on the ground, relying on its camouflage to evade detection. The long wings are patterned with brownish, black and white, with a broad pale buff or greyish band across the inner upperwing-coverts. The black primaries have broad white patches, perhaps most noticeable in the

Bush Thick-knee, and remarkably obvious and eye-catching compared with the cryptic colours exhibited when the bird is at rest.

The wings are long, and are held rather straight and outstretched in active flight, with a long inner wing and a marked carpal angle; the outer wing is scarcely tapered, although the extreme tip of the wing can appear rather pointed. There are 11 primaries, with the outermost minute and concealed by the primary coverts, and 16-20 secondaries. The tail, made up of 12 feathers, is generally short and rounded, except in the cases of the Spotted Dikkop's medium-length tail and the Bush Thick-knee's longer, more tapered tail. In some species, notably the Double-striped Thick-knee, the legs and toes extend beyond the tail tip in direct flight.

The two *Esacus* species, the Great and Beach Thick-knees, are generally larger, considerably bulkier birds, in which sense they are reminiscent of miniature bustards; their deep-chested, broad-backed bodies, held horizontally on strong, thick legs, create a remarkably heavy, far less elegant, appearance compared with the *Burhinus* species. Indeed, both species are almost goose-like in their body shape and proportions when on the ground, while their strange, rather long bills and long legs give an improbable mixture of features very different from all other waders, except perhaps the Crab Plover. In addition to their heavy build, they are heavy-billed, which adds a grotesque note to their facial appearance, especially in the Beach Thick-knee, which has a particularly large, deep, boat-shaped bill, whereas that of the Great Thick-knee is a little more tapered and noticeably uptilted. In both species the bill is remarkably well adapted to the bird's feeding habits and diet: crabs and other invertebrates form a large proportion of their food, and the Great Thick-knee's heavy, upturned bill enables it to prise up stones as it searches for its prey, while the Beach Thick-knee dismembers or breaks crabs into small portions by hammering them on the ground with its massive bill before swallowing the bits. These large bills are mainly black with a restricted area of yellow at the base, and they combine effectively with the striking black and white head patterns.

These two species lack the fine streaking and mottling that characterize the plumage of most *Burhinus* species. They are more bustard-like in flight, with a protruding bill, head and neck, a stocky

body, long, broad, square-ended wings with more or less fingered primary tips and a particularly short, square tail. The wings have large white areas towards the tips and contrasting upperwing-covert patterns, while below the birds reveal large areas of pure white. The legs are pale, dull greenish yellow or yellowish, and the toes extend just beyond the tip of the tail in flight.

The long legs and three forward-pointing toes of the Burhinidae suggest that these birds are predominantly terrestrial in their lifestyle, as is indeed the case. Thick-knees have a measured, sedate walk, in which the head and body are held rather horizontally and maintain the same position relative to the ground, despite the long strides that the birds take. When necessary, the walk is easily accelerated into a smooth run, with the head frequently held farther forward while the legs are somewhat angled. The pale legs often appear much the same tone as the background earth or grasses and, from a distance, a thick-knee can look like simply a head and body moving smoothly, effortlessly and mysteriously forwards slightly off the ground.

Flight may be sudden or preceded by a quickening run, the long wings producing a fast, direct flight but relatively poor manoeuvrability. Landing may likewise extend into a short, forwards run before the bird settles into a walk or comes to a standstill. The Bush Thick-knee gains take-off speed with a short run and when alighting runs a short way, opens and closes its wings and then stalks away very slowly. Active flight is usually quite low, with regular, shallow wingbeats, recalling that of curlews (*Numenius*).

Adult thick-knees have a complete post-breeding moult, the primaries being shed in descendant sequence, and the whole process may take four or five months to complete. In the Stone-curlew, the moult of the outer primaries may be suspended and two or three old feathers retained during the winter, to be replaced the following spring, at which point the inner primaries may begin to moult again, so that the bird exhibits serially descendant moult. Normally, however, the pre-breeding moult is erratic and often restricted to the head and neck, sometimes extending over the body, but often apparently not undertaken at all. Juveniles have a post-fledging moult, involving the feathers of the head and body, some wing-coverts and the central tail feathers, which begins soon after fledging, but in the Stone-curlew this is suspended by late autumn. The Senegal Thick-knee exhibits a similar moult regime, with some individuals retaining some outer primaries during the winter and moulting them in the following spring.

Habitat

Although few in species, the thick-knees have representatives on all continents except Antarctica. Most live in the tropical or subtropical zones and are for the main part sedentary. Only one species, the Stone-curlew, breeds mostly in temperate climes and even then it is partly migratory in order to escape the northern winter.

Thick-knees are essentially birds of dry, open country, though several are more specific in their requirements and favour mainly waterside habitats. Most species tend to frequent a variety of exposed, largely low-lying, flat or rolling landscapes, and can breed in arid or semi-arid deserts with only a very limited amount of vegetation. They are entirely absent from all closed woodland and forest areas, but as they are essentially crepuscular and nocturnal in their principal activities they often seek the shade provided by bushes, trees, low vegetation or boulders, where they can rest inconspicuously during the heat of the day, relying heavily on the cryptic coloration of their plumage to escape detection.

The Stone-curlew is a typical member of the family in its requirements; indeed, its very name denotes the harsh, arid nature of the environment it ideally prefers to occupy. It needs open spaces with extensive visibility, dry and fairly even ground on which it can run easily, and a mixture of bare earth, shrubby or grassy vegetation. Unfortunately, in most European countries, the steppes, arid grasslands and heathlands that up to now have constituted the strongholds of the species are areas which are increasingly under threat, and, although the Stone-curlew has to some extent learnt to adapt to arable farmland conditions, its populations in several countries have suffered a marked decline (see Status and Conservation).

Although the ranges of certain species overlap, notably in Africa, it would seem that slight, but significant, differences in habitat requirement prevent their entering into competition with each other. Thus, in North Africa, where the Stone-curlew and Senegal Thick-knee co-occur, the latter, in general habits very similar to the Stone-curlew, nevertheless differs from it in avoiding open deserts. It is normally found within 2-3 km of water amd may be seen on the banks of rivers and even on rocks in mid-stream. In Africa south of the Sahara, the Senegal Thick-knee and the Spotted and Water Dikkops are all present, as is the Stone-curlew in certain restricted areas, in its winter quarters. Over this vast area, the Spotted Dikkop in general prefers dry open country and shows no marked preference for water, at least in the north of its range where it may coincide with the Senegal Thick-knee. The Water Dikkop, which is found mainly south of the equator, is, as its name suggests, closely tied to water, even more so than the Senegal Thick-knee; in addition, it is the only African thick-knee to occur in coastal areas, on the shores of creeks and islands.

In Australia, where both the Beach and the Bush Thick-knee are present, the former is a strictly coastal bird, never found inland, whereas the latter, although it is seen in coastal scrub, chiefly inhabits inland areas. The Great Thick-knee is partly sympatric with the Stone-curlew on the Indian Subcontinent, where the latter species is mainly sedentary. The Great Thick-knee is another species that favours waterside habitats, frequenting shingle banks along large rivers and the shores of freshwater lakes. It tends to visit grassland near water when the riverbanks may be flooded, but normally it stays close to its shingle sites.

Most of the Burhinidae are timid and wary of man, yet occasionally some of them can be observed in the vicinity of human habitation. The Stone-curlew is known to nest on the outskirts of villages and towns at some localities, while the Spotted Dikkop may perhaps even nest in suburban gardens. The Senegal Thick-knee does not shun humans, and apparently still nests on rooftops in the centre of Cairo, while the Bush Thick-knee, in the northern part of its range in Australia, will frequent wasteland in towns and villages.

General Habits

Thick-knees are mainly terrestrial. Most of their activities take place on the ground and, although they are capable of strong sustained flight, even when they know that danger is approaching, they nearly always prefer to walk or run away rather than fly. Only when they are suddenly surprised will they take to the wing immediately.

They are generally sociable birds, and outside the breeding season flocks of dozens or, where they are common, even hundreds, may gather, frequently using traditional sites that have been used at least for many decades. In Europe, Stone-curlew gatherings have been known to reach 300 birds, while up to 150 have been seen together in Tunisia and 100 in Morocco. Spotted Dikkops spend the daylight hours in loose flocks of up to 50 birds. Some species may even feed and display communally during the breeding season, although roosting parties generally scatter more widely to feed. Stone-curlew gatherings in Britain in autumn now rarely number more than 30-40 birds, as the species has declined, while parties of more than 100 Bush Thick-knees in New South Wales, Australia, are now described as a thing of the past, with 5-20 individuals more usual, after this species' long population decline; however, flocks of 30-40 birds remain more frequent in northern Australia.

All *Burhinus* species are largely nocturnal in their active behaviour, spending the day resting motionless and inconspicuously in the shade of low vegetation, or standing or sitting on some undisturbed patch of open ground. At dusk, the birds become more active and may fly some distance to a suitable feeding area, or, if they are within range, they simply walk to their feeding grounds. The Water Dikkop is more likely to be active and vocal by day than the other species, but it is still essentially a nocturnal species. Both feeding and social d'splays take place from late dusk onwards. This is one reason why displays are not all associated with display-flights and demonstrative behaviour, as with so many waders, but are instead centred more on loud and varied vocalizations. Of the two *Esacus* species, the Great Thick-knee is largely nocturnal, but the Beach Thick-knee is much less so, and can be seen feeding by day on beaches and islands, which in any case provide little daytime cover.

When resting, a bird may adopt a more upright pose than that assumed during active feeding, with the head hunched into the shoulders and tail tilted downwards. A typical resting posture involves sitting with the full length of the tarsus on the ground and the tibia upright. If alarmed, a thick-knee will suddenly bob its head up and down, making a corresponding movement with the tail as if the bird were swivelling, pivoting on the top of its legs. Unless immediately threatened, however, it generally prefers to run or to crouch stock-still, either freezing in a hunched stance or even lying flat on the ground to avoid being seen. Bush Thick-knees have several times been reported as allowing themselves to be picked up by observers who have detected them in this position. Downy chicks have the same habit of freezing, crouched to the ground, when a parent bird signals alarm.

Whatever they are doing, to a human observer thick-knees almost invariably have a furtive, secretive look. Water Dikkops and Senegal and Great Thick-knees prefer to remain still on the side of a stream, even when closely approached by a passing boat. Beach Thick-knees are described as shy in populated areas, but extremely inquisitive in remote areas where they seldom see humans.

Voice

All thick-knees are generally silent by day, but at dusk they start to become vocal. Their calls are penetrating and often far-carrying, and sound eerie to the human ear. The *Esacus* species have loud, rather harsh, wailing calls, with a more or less rising inflection, and weaker, more yapping alarm notes, but it is the *Burhinus* thick-knees which give the more remarkable vocal performances.

All thick-knee vocalizations have much the same quality, often described as wailing, whistling, mournful and plaintive, but several species have a wide variation of sounds. The Stone-curlew makes short, sharp notes recalling those of oystercatchers (Haematopodidae), and these are repeated in an accelerating series, which builds up to a more prolonged, curlew-like "cur-leee" and then dies away. The Senegal Thick-knee has a more nasal

quality to its calls, which ring around the buildings of African towns and villages after dark in a mysterious chorus. Double-striped Thick-knees, in turn, have shorter, but equally strident, calls. The Peruvian Thick-knee is locally named "Huerequeque" in an transliteration of its voice, and similarly the Aborigine name for the Bush Thick-knee is "Willaroo", an onomatopaeic approximation to its usual call, which is likened to a long-drawn, whistling scream. In this species, as in the Stone-curlew and Senegal Thick-knee, several individuals join in a prolonged chorus which gives the impression of excitement and urgency, increasingly so at the onset of the breeding season.

The precise role of thick-knee vocalizations is still poorly understood, owing to the difficulty of observing their behaviour when they are active, often very mobile, after dark. At least in the Stone-curlew, the best studied species, it is thought that groups are more vocal than pairs, so that voice may be more important in interactions between neighbouring pairs than in the relationships between a paired male and female. The members of a pair tend to be relatively silent when newly arrived in a breeding area in spring, but they become much more vocal around the pre-laying period, and quieter again thereafter, until the young are fledged, when they once again become noisier.

Daytime calling is most frequent from individuals establishing a territory, or from unpaired or non-breeding birds, which are more easily attracted to an imitation or recording of a call than are settled, territorial pairs. Normally, calls begin some 30 minutes after sunset, stimulated by a single individual which is then answered by its partner and other pairs. There is less calling during the middle of the night, and vocal activity ceases towards dawn.

Some of the calls are difficult to place into a particular context, or even to match closely with published descriptions, but a dozen or more call types have been described for adult Stone-curlews. These are related to aggression; to greetings between pairs and when groups of territory-holders meet; to specific behaviour such as nest-scraping and spring displays; to distraction displays, when adults defend nests with eggs or chicks from predators; and to the conversational notes used by adults when they are brooding newly-hatched chicks.

Food and Feeding

There is a certain uniformity about the food taken by *Burhinus* thick-knees, and the method of feeding is always much the same,

Unusually, a Stone-curlew
is caught drinking from a
pool in the daytime.
Normally Burhinus species
are nocturnal feeders;
they spend the day
resting, often in the shade,
and only become active
towards dusk when they
may either fly, sometimes
several kilometres, or walk
to a rich feeding area.
The diet of most thick-
knees is imperfectly
known. The Stone-curlew,
the most widespread and
best studied member of
the family, feeds on a
variety of insects and
small invertebrates, such
as lizards and frogs,
and will even take
other birds' eggs.

[Burhinus oedicnemus
oedicnemus,
La Serena, Spain.
Photo: Cristina Barros
Fuentes/Desert Photos]

involving the bird picking up items from the ground with the bill, as it walks forwards. Most food items are small animals, such as insects and other invertebrates, but a variety of small mammals, reptiles and birds' eggs are also taken.

The detailed food of most species is rather poorly known, but insects probably predominate in most cases, throughout the greater part of the year. For instance, Senegal Thick-knees take insects, particularly beetles, crickets and grasshoppers, but also crustaceans, molluscs, worms, rodents and frogs, which are found by foraging near water or as much as two or three kilometres away from it.

Beetles, earwigs, chafers, moths, snails and slugs, lizards, frogs, voles and mice, eggs and, much more rarely, shoots of low shrubs make up a varied fare for the Stone-curlew, and in Russia ants have been found to be more important in the diet. In a study of this species in southern Britain, nesting birds were found to feed on earthworms, woodlice, millipedes and beetles, and much of the food was associated with the dung of large grazing livestock. Feeding often took place close to the nest, but radio-tagged birds were followed as much as two kilometres away to feeding sites, such as grassland enclosures grazed by rabbits, outdoor enclosures with pigs, and arable fields; at these sites, the birds fed near the edges, around grassy margins, or even from heaps of animal manure.

While most other studies of food have relied on stomach contents, the British study used microscopic examination of faeces, in conjunction with the examination of the faeces of a captive individual, with known diet, which was used as a control to determine the validity of the method. Useful information is also to be gained from pellets of indigestible matter, such as bones and beetle wing cases, which can be found at daytime roosts.

The larger members of the Burhinidae can be quite formidable predators. Bush Thick-knees have been seen killing larger prey, such as frogs and rodents, by hitting them on the ground before swallowing them. The Great Thick-knee has a similar diet to the smaller thick-knee species, but it takes many crabs too, while the Beach Thick-knee is much more of a crab specialist, catching crabs and other marine invertebrates by day as it feeds on reefs and rocky shores.

When actively feeding, a thick-knee moves slowly, sometimes pausing and tilting forwards like a plover, picking up food from the ground ahead. Large food items may be spotted from several metres away, while more active, lively prey, such as grasshoppers and rodents, may induce a short, quick run or a more active lunge with the bill. Moths may be caught in the air, with short leaps from the ground to snatch them, while smaller insects and caterpillars are picked more deliberately from leaves and stems. The Beach Thick-knee forages along the shore, sometimes using a stop-start run and pause action, but often stalking prey more slowly and carefully, much in the style of a heron. Feeding parties of the smaller thick-knee species may number up to seven individuals.

Breeding

The breeding habits of the Stone-curlew, in particular, are fairly well documented, as the result of a considerable amount of investigation, but those of others, especially the two American species, the Double-striped and the Peruvian Thick-knees, have received very scant attention, so information about many aspects of their breeding cycle ranges from very limited to non-existent. However, as the biological and behavioural similarities between the members of this small family are great and the known details of their breeding cycles also mainly coincide, additional information gleaned from research on the Stone-curlew may well be applicable to other members of the family too. At the same time, though, it must be remembered that the Stone-curlew in temperate Eurasia is atypical in some respects, the most important of which is the fact that it is the only member of the family that is truly migratory, flying to temperate regions to breed in spring and returning to warmer climes in autumn to escape the rigours of the northern winter.

As all other thick-knees breed principally in the tropics or subtropics, their breeding season is much more variable than that of the Stone-curlew. The pattern is largely one of opportunism, matching the reproductive cycle to the availability of suitable nesting sites and food resources, and in many cases nesting during dry seasons. The Senegal Thick-knee, for example, which frequents waterside habitats, in some areas lays its eggs in the dry season, when the lower water levels in the rivers lay bare suitable sandy banks, where it can site its nest. Likewise, the Great Thick-knee, a species even more restricted to rivers and lake sides, in India nests from February to March, well before the monsoon rains begin. The Water Dikkop times its breeding for the dry season and the early rains in southern Africa, but in the drier spell before the October rains around Lake Victoria.

Most species are known to be monogamous. In Britain some Stone-curlews are clearly paired when they arrive in spring; they retain a monogamous relationship and remain faithful in a life-long bond, which appears to be reaffirmed and strengthened upon arrival each spring. Whether or not other thick-knees pair for life is not yet clear.

Most members of the Burhinidae seem to be solitary when nesting, although at times they will form loose groups where the species is common or the area of suitable habitat is restricted, at least in the Double-striped and Senegal Thick-knees. The latter species is known to nest semi-colonially in some places: 21 nests were once found on a flat roof in Egypt, and even today the species is still said to nest on rooftops in the centre of Cairo.

Courtship behaviour has been well studied in the Stone-curlew, but difficulties of interpretation arise because of the problems of distinguishing between the sexes, owing to their identical size and plumage. Display behaviour sometimes occurs in small groups, but it is generally rather ill-defined. Males have infrequently been seen to perform short runs, skips and leaps with open wings in front of a female; the black and white wing and tail patterns may be important in such brief displays. More obvious are simple visual and vocal contacts which the pair maintain throughout the breeding period.

In this species, the nest scrape is selected in a bowing performance, in which the members of the pair adopt a forward-leaning stance with head and neck pointing downwards and, in extreme examples, the bill tip touching the ground. The male's bill finally indicates a chosen spot, which the female then shuffles onto and scrapes. The birds then take turns to sit in the prospective scrape, shuffling and turning and using the bill to pick up stones and twigs, which are thrown backwards over one shoulder. Several sites are investigated in this way, not necessarily all in the area of the eventual nest-site. The male calls the female to a scrape, which she will then shuffle onto, kicking earth backwards with her feet. The pair may then sit together, inactive, close to the scrape for long periods.

Before the eggs are laid, the male and female Stone-curlew may greet each other at the scrape with a bowing performance, which develops into a more extreme posture, as the birds run towards each other and draw themselves gradually into a very upright stance, tails pointed downwards and necks steeply arched, so the head and bill point down to the ground. The arched pose quickly subsides and the two return to a normal, relaxed stance. This "Neck-arch" display seems to be a necessary preliminary to copulation, although it can be abbreviated considerably. Copulation may be most frequent during the early stages of nest selection, after which its frequency drops for a time before a further rise again immediately before the eggs are laid.

Far less information is available on the courtship behaviour of other thick-knees, but the above details are likely to be the basis of the general pattern, at least in the case of the *Burhinus* species. Bush Thick-knees have dramatic dancing displays, and their performances when calling during the breeding season have been more fully described. They stand erect, often with wings fully spread and twisted vertically to reveal the striking black and white patterns, with the underside clearly visible from in front of the bird. Meanwhile they "run on the spot" with high-stepping feet, producing repeated wails which increase in speed, before a final flourish of screams and trills. This sequence may be repeated many times over a period of an hour or so. The Beach Thick-knee, though poorly known, is said to indulge in acrobatic flights above the territory, as well as dancing and bowing displays on the ground.

The location of the nest-site would seem to vary with the species. For example, the Bush Thick-knee favours areas in the shade, under a bush or a tree or near tall vegetation. Other species are content to nest in very open sites with little or no cover to protect them, either from predators or from the glare of the sun. The cryptic coloration of their plumage, both in young and adult birds, and also of their eggs, is a powerful aid in avoiding detection. The eggs are laid into a simple scrape or depression in the ground, sometimes totally unadorned, but more often lined with variable quantities of stones or shells taken from the immediate environs. The Senegal Thick-knee may surround the eggs with small pieces of grit, straw, wood and shells. The Water Dikkop can have a little more lining in its nest, which is often close to a piece of driftwood or a tussock of vegetation. It sometimes lays its eggs on dried animal dung, such as the scattered droppings of elephants, whereas the Spotted Dikkop uses smaller animal droppings and pieces of vegetation to line its nest. The Double-striped Thick-knee is similarly said to prefer dried animal dung as a base for its nest.

Except in the case of the Beach Thick-knee, which lays a single egg, the normal clutch is two, much more rarely three. Cases of four eggs in a single Stone-curlew nest appear invariably to be the result of two females laying in the same scrape. The eggs are laid at intervals of two days. They vary in size and slightly in shape according to the species. The large Beach Thick-knee lays eggs of 65 x 45 mm, whereas in the Bush Thick-knee they average 58 x 39 mm, in the Stone-curlew 54 x 38 mm, and in the Senegal Thick-knee 49 x 32 mm. In general they are rather rounded ovals, smooth and slightly glossy, generally whitish or buffish with brown spots and mottles. This cryptic pattern is said to vary somewhat in the Bush Thick-knee according to the local colour of the soil. Usually a single brood is reared, but a replacement clutch may be laid after the loss of the first, or even after the death of small young in the first brood.

The largest member of the genus Burhinus, particularly long-legged though slim of body, the Bush Thick-knee will defend its territory courageously and adopt a variety of threat and distraction postures to deter and lure away any predator found in the vicinity of either its nest or its chicks. In the threat posture the wings are drooped until they almost touch the ground, forming a complete arc, and the tail is cocked and fanned. In this posture the apparent size of the bird is substantially increased and the effect of the threat intensified. If the intruder has not located the nest or chicks, the adult bird will attempt to distract it from its purpose by simply walking away from the sensitive danger zone with the intention of drawing the intruder away with it.

[Above:
Burhinus grallarius.
Photo: R. Russell/
ANT/NHPA.

Below:
Burhinus grallarius,
Queensland, Australia.
Photo: Brian J. Coates]

As far as is known, incubation is carried out by both parents and lasts around 24-27 days. It usually begins after the laying of the final egg, but it can start before the second egg is laid, and two eggs may hatch on the same day or on consecutive days. The broken eggshells are carried away from the nest by the parents.

The chicks are precocial and nidifugous, already active and moving from the nest when just a day old. They have long, stout legs and a thick covering of down. The parents guard them and collect food for them in the early stages, and may move them to favoured feeding areas considerable distances from the nest itself. The Bush Thick-knee has been seen to lift its chicks from the ground as it stands up to brood them under a wing, and Senegal Thick-knees are strongly suspected of carrying their young. When warned of danger by their parents, young thick-knees lie flat on the ground, adopting the prone position with head and neck outstretched, in which posture they are extremely difficult to spot.

Approaching predators may cause an incubating or brooding bird to leave the nest unobtrusively, but should the nest be more seriously threatened, distraction displays and aggressive behaviour may occur. The off-duty Stone-curlew is quick to spot danger and warns its sitting mate. Alarm is shown by a special upright, taut and thin posture. The sitting bird almost always walks away from the nest very furtively, then breaks into a run and only a little later a low, fast flight. Flight direct from the eggs or chicks is exceptional and seems to happen only when the bird is taken completely by surprise. The off-duty mate may fly in a different direction, but eventually turns to meet the other and both stand at a distance to watch developments. If the intruder leaves, the male bird follows until he is about 100 m from the nest, at which stage the female walks back cautiously. If the danger comes from a ground predator, the bird called from the nest by its mate will dive at the predator and attack it, or stand its ground and face the predator with the long wings opened and the neck thrust forwards. It will also stand very upright with the wings fanned and raised, or partly opened, and with the tail fanned, in an effort to drive off threatening animals, such as sheep, which sometimes trample eggs or chicks.

If an intruder discovers small chicks, but does not prey upon them, the parent bird will later lead them to a new-site. Adults have been seen to carry chicks in their bills for short distances, but this was probably after eggshells had recently been removed and may have been a continuance of such behaviour.

Injury-feigning appears to be rare, and some observers who have regularly handled small young have reported it only on exceptional occasions: an adult may lie on the ground, with one wing spread and the other flapping, perhaps then jumping up, or flying a few metres, to repeat the performance once more.

Senegal Thick-knees may be rather tame at the nest in the face of a human intruder, moving only 15 m away when the nest is examined, and returning again when the person moves away, even if he remains to watch from a distance of 15-20 m. Bush Thick-knees defend their territories boldly and are aggressive towards potential predators which approach the nest, adopting a threat posture with drooped wings. If a ground predator has not apparently discovered the nest or chicks, the adult moves away on foot to lure the predator from the vicinity.

The chicks quickly become independent, and generally fledge at about six or seven weeks old, depending on the species, slightly earlier in the Stone-curlew, slightly later, at 47-50 days, in the Bush Thick-knee. Although there are records of one-year-old Stone-curlews breeding, the normal age for first breeding in Burhinidae is probably two to three years.

Little is known about the rate of breeding success in most species of thick-knees, but precise figures are available yet again for the Stone-curlew in Britain. In one study, out of a total of 128 eggs, 73% hatched, with failures being attributed to destruction by farm machinery, predation and egg-collectors. In another British study, 105 eggs were located, of which 65·7% hatched; of 44 chicks, 77·3% survived until they were at least half-grown.

Movements

Most species perform no more than local movements and some individuals are likely to live their whole lives within a few kilometres of the site where they hatched. The Stone-curlew is the major exception to the rule, as some populations in the north of its range make long migrations to escape the continental or cool temperate winter conditions which prevail in these breeding areas.

In Australia, Bush Thick-knees gather into loose groups or "clans" after the breeding season, and these roam widely in search of food, but they do not undertake true migrations. Nevertheless, from an area of some 10-20 ha occupied during breeding, these groups may increase their ranges in winter to 100 km² or more.

As in other aspects, the American species are poorly known, but they rarely occur outside their known breeding ranges. In Africa, Senegal Thick-knees are mostly resident, but in northeast Zaire birds arrive after the rains in November and remain until April or May, while the species is present during and after the rains in Senegambia (December to March) and Ivory Coast (November to April), indicating a more organized and regular movement. Water and Spotted Dikkops, however, are strictly sedentary.

The Stone-curlews of Europe and Central Asia, however, are strongly migratory. Those breeding in Britain and France, eastwards to Italy, Greece, Turkey and beyond through the Caucasus

The Stone-curlew's nest is a scrape of variable depth often in stony ground, sometimes lined with dry grass and ringed with small stones and pieces of vegetation. Though generally a wary, timid bird, it will on occasion nest quite near human habitation, as in this case. The clutch normally consists of two eggs which are buff in ground colour with dark streaks and blotches. Incubation is carried out by both sexes and lasts roughly 26 days. Note the very big glaring yellow eye, the sharply defined bill coloration, and the distinctive pattern of the wing-coverts on this adult as it prepares to incubate.

[Burhinus oedicnemus oedicnemus, Loire Valley, France. Photo: Roger Powell/ Aquila]

and Transcaspia into western Siberia, move out in autumn, whereas Iberia is occupied all year round. Small numbers occasionally remain in winter in France, many more in Spain, but most northern birds move across the Mediterranean into Africa. Ringing recoveries have shown that some birds spend the winter north of the Mediterranean, while populations that move to zones south of the Sahara are difficult to relate to particular breeding areas, particularly given the complicated subspecific variation within this species (see Systematics). Nevertheless, those found in Senegambia include birds of nominate *oedicnemus* and perhaps also of the race *saharae*, of the Mediterranean and the Middle East; *oedicnemus* is also known to reach Sudan, Uganda and Kenya.

Birds begin to leave Britain in August although many linger late into October, and rarely even into November. Departures from Africa are noted in March, by which time early arrivals are reaching Britain. Farther east, European breeding ranges may not be reached until late April or May. Siberian populations, south to Afghanistan, are thought to winter farther south and on into parts of the Middle East, but the north-west Indian populations seem to be resident and apparently remain quite separate. Breeding populations in North Africa and the Middle East appear to be largely resident, and these areas are certainly occupied by Stone-curlews all year round, although there may be a withdrawal from higher ground in winter. In the Canary Islands birds move from island to island, but do not, as far as is known, leave the archipelago.

Relationship with Man

The chief impact that thick-knees have had on man originate from their typical habit of calling loudly, with often strange, wailing voices, at dusk and on through the night. This has led to a series of local names based on vocalizations. The vocal performances of displaying groups of Bush Thick-knees, involving screams and hysterical screeching, naturally caused unease among early white settlers, as well as amongst Aboriginal peoples, and there are many references to them in Australian literature. Folklore and local names, for instance "Weeloo" and "Willaroo", reflect these sounds. The fact that the birds are difficult to see at night and tend to "melt away" into the slightest cover of vegetation by day were additional grounds for fear and superstition.

On the other hand, the Great Thick-knee has been described as "an engaging pet". Similarly, the Double-striped Thick-knee is sometimes kept as a semi-captive, or semi-domestic, bird around South American farms and villages in order to keep insect pests under control.

Thick-knees have not figured very strongly in traditional folklore except as rather vague, disembodied voices of the night. However, in western Europe a medieval tradition, common to several species with yellow plumage, and in the case of the Stone-curlew relating to its striking yellow eyes and bill, was that such birds were efficacious in the treatment of jaundice!

Status and Conservation

Due in part to the secretive habits of the family, little is known about the status and population trends of the different species. Nevertheless, sufficient data are available to see that by and large they have suffered from human interference and pressure.

Nearly always the problems revolve around habitat loss and disturbance. In Australia, most populations are in steep decline; indeed, in many areas that formerly held thick-knees the birds are now altogether absent. The Bush Thick-knee was common in much of south-east Australia until the 1930's. It had already disppeared from Tasmania by about 1900, and gradually vanished from most settled areas, so that by the 1980's, although a few widely scattered pairs remained, the species had mostly gone from south-eastern Australia, even from rural parts. The causes of this decline include overgrazing and disturbance by livestock, and predation by introduced cats and foxes. Indeed, outbreaks of disease in local fox populations have been reflected in temporary increases in Bush Thick-knee numbers. Nevertheless, it is clear that the fox is not the only problem, or indeed even a major one in some areas even where foxes are common: in several other parts of Australia, Bush Thick-knee populations have persisted in the face of fox presence. Urban development, intense grazing pressure, burning and cultivation of hitherto semi-natural habitats have been more serious causes of decline.

Beach Thick-knees choose remote beaches with little disturbance. The increased human recreational use of beaches for a whole series of activities including a number of obviously dis-

A bemused sheep is confronted by a pair of Stone-curlews valiantly endeavouring to protect their nest-site from this lumbering great intruder by adopting spectacular threat postures. The bird on the left has raised and spread its wings, at the same time lowering its fanned tail, while the one on the right has drooped its wings, but cocked and fanned its tail. Unfortunately, it is not infrequent for cattle and sheep to trample Stone-curlews' eggs and chicks, although investigation indicates that more losses are actually caused by farm machinery.

[*Burhinus oedicnemus*. Photo: Chris Knights/ Survival Anglia/Oxford Scientific Films]

A solitary nester, the Stone-curlew normally lays two eggs and raises a single brood, although a replacement can be laid if eggs or even small chicks are lost. The downy chicks, buff-coloured with black streaks, are precocial and nidifugous. They are cared for by both parents and do not attain independence until fledging at about 6 weeks old. They will not begin breeding themselves until they are 2-3 years old.

[Burhinus oedicnemus oedicnemus, Bárdenas Reales, Spain. Photo: José Antonio Martínez]

ruptive beach and water sports has, not surprisingly, resulted in a contraction of range and a steady decline in this species.

In Africa, where thick-knees have generally shown either a healthy disregard for man or even a relatively positive relationship with people, their livestock and villages, thick-knees have generally fared well in the face of increasing human pressure. Senegal Thick-knees still nest on Cairo roofs and feed around the abundance of droppings of assorted cattle, goats, camels, horses and donkeys along the banks of the Nile. Spotted Dikkops adapt well to suburban areas, choosing to nest in many semi-developed areas with tracts of derelict or waste ground, and even feeding on football pitches.

Several thick-knees, including the two American species, draw benefits from human presence in some ways. Roads at night, cultivated fields, and other open areas near habitation offer opportunities for feeding, although they cause some losses too. Thick-knees suffer casualties on roads at night: a potential benefit suddenly turned into a death-trap. The long-term effects of such mortality are unknown.

It is the Stone-curlew in Europe that has, perhaps, suffered most from the advance of man. In Britain alone, there were 1000 pairs or more in 1930, but by 1994 just 145 pairs. This massive decline, followed by a shaky consolidation in numbers at this low level, has occurred despite great public and professional interest in conservation and years of expensive research into the needs of the species.

In Britain, the extent of suitable habitat available has been greatly reduced. There has been a movement away from semi-natural habitats of downland and lowland heath, where grazing by sheep and rabbits kept the vegetation short, to farmland. Reduced stocking of sheep has made the downland habitat less tenable, while heaths have been subject to extensive afforestation with conifers. However, the arable land alternatives are not good for Stone-curlews, as the crops are too tall and dense by the time the hatching period comes round, and changes in seeding and harvesting times have rendered Stone-curlews on farmland less productive, as eggs fail to hatch, are deserted when the crop becomes too tall, or are destroyed, as, like chicks, they fall foul of machinery. In parts of Britain, chick production is sufficient to maintain the population, but these levels are achieved only with wardening of nests and constant liaison with farmers.

British Stone-curlews now receive direct protection from illegal egg-collectors, and also from over-enthusiastic birdwatchers, who are guided to special hides at Stone-curlew reserves. Agricultural policies in important areas have, through lengthy debate and political lobbying, been altered to favour Stone-curlew conservation, necessitating some management of land by conservationists, payments to farmers to encourage sensitive land use and the increased use of set-aside agreements, in which land is taken out of

agricultural production. At the same time, individual threats, ranging from proposals to build golf courses and new roads to laying gas pipelines through breeding territories, have been fought in the planning process, while discussions with military authorities have been aimed at improving Stone-curlew productivity on army training grounds. Electric fences have been used to deter foxes from predating nests, newsletters have been published for farmers with Stone-curlews on their land, individual birds have been fitted with transmitters and radio-tracked, and pesticide usage and effects have been monitored. This is all expensive, labour-intensive and difficult work carried out by voluntary organizations, but the results have still been less than dramatic. The population decline appears to have been stabilized, but by the mid-1990's there is no clear sign of an increase. Nor has the range of the species in Britain been extended or returned to former dimensions. There is still, it seems, much to learn and much more to be done to ensure the Stone-curlew's future.

In other parts of Europe where Stone-curlew populations have been less studied and are for the most part totally unprotected, the species is under similar pressure. The main causes of death recorded in the Stone-curlew would seem to be collisions with fences and overhead wires, as well as hunting in southern Europe and Africa. There appears to be no evidence, however, that these threats are causing significant increases in the numbers of casualties. In southern countries, agriculture is changing rapidly, as European Union policies are having an effect. Semi-arid and other hitherto unproductive stony steppe-like areas are coming under the plough as farmers, with the aid of costly irrigation schemes, have been given incentives to produce cereal crops. In the last few years conservationists in Spain have launched a campaign to protect the "steppes" and their important avifauna, of which the Stone-curlew is only one of the threatened species. Coastal habitats, such as dunes and shingle, are under ever-increasing pressure, especially in Spain and France, as tourism and other recreational uses take a firm grip on the shoreline and its immediate hinterland. Farther east, agricultural development must also spell problems for Stone-curlew populations, as land-use trends follow those that have already caused declines in the west. There can be little doubt that the population trends of all species require regular monitoring, in order to ensure that any significant declines are detected before it is too late.

General Bibliography

Barbosa (1993), Björklund (1994), Christian *et al.* (1992b), Chu (1995), Gochfeld *et al.* (1984), Hayman *et al.* (1986), Jehl (1968b), Lowe (1931), Morgan (1985), Nol (1986), Peters (1934), Prater *et al.* (1977), Rosair & Cottridge (1995), Sibley & Ahlquist (1972, 1990), Sibley & Monroe (1990), Soothill & Soothill (1982), Strauch (1976, 1978), Wadewitz (1968).

ssp *oedicnemus*

1

ssp *indicus*

ssp *harterti*

2

ssp *capensis*

4

ssp *vermiculatus*

ssp *dodsoni*

3

ssp *buettikoferi*

ssp *bistriatus*

5

ssp *vocifer*

ssp *dominicensis*

6

7

rufous morph

8

grey morph

9

PLATE 32

inches
10

cm
25

Genus *BURHINUS* Illiger, 1811

1. Stone-curlew

Burhinus oedicnemus

French: Oedicnème criard **German**: Triel **Spanish**: Alcaraván Común
Other common names: (Northern/European) Stone-curlew, Common/Northern/Stone Thick-knee

Taxonomy. *Charadrius Oedicnemus* Linnaeus, 1758, England.
Non-parallel clines in size and coloration confuse subspecific definition (see page 350) and several other races proposed; possible races *jordansi* of Balearic Is and *astutus* of Afghanistan and Persian Gulf normally included within nominate race and race *saharae* respectively. Six subspecies recognized.
Subspecies and Distribution.
B. o. distinctus (Bannerman, 1914) - W Canary Is.
B. o. insularum (Sassi, 1908) - E Canary Is.
B. o. saharae (Reichenow, 1894) - N Africa, Mediterranean islands, Greece and Turkey to Middle East, E to Iraq and Iran.
B. o. oedicnemus (Linnaeus, 1758) - S Britain and Iberia E to N Balkans and Ukraine and Caucasus.
B. o. harterti Vaurie, 1963 - R Volga area E through Transcaspia and Turkestan to Zaysan basin, and S through C Iran to Pakistan and extreme NW India.
B. o. indicus (Salvadori, 1865) - India and Sri Lanka E to Indochina.
Winters in S of breeding range, and patchily in Sahel zone, E Africa and Arabia.

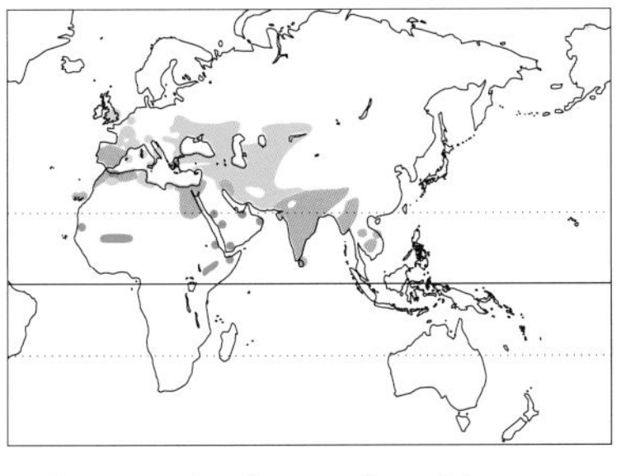

Descriptive notes. 40-44 cm; 338-535 g. Sandy brown with white belly and vent, upperparts streaked darker; head finely streaked dark, with whiter lores, line above eye and broad band from upper mandible beneath eye to rear cheek; dark malar stripe; white chin and throat; breast heavily streaked blackish; upperwing-coverts marked by parallel bands of dark brown and white, with black lower border; inner primaries have square white patch at base and fine white tips; outer primaries have white central patch; bill yellow with black tip; eyes yellow; legs pale yellow-buff. Juvenile very similar to adult but with bright rufous buff tips to scapulars and inner wing feathers. Races vary in colour tone from pinker to greyer types; variation in overall size and leg length, but much individual variation too, especially in race *saharae*.
Habitat. Semi-arid, arid and steppe grassland, heath, arable fields with bare, stony patches, coastal dunes and shingle; also short-grass plains and semi-desert. Requires open, level ground with sparse vegetation cover, where running is easy; not normally near water.
Food and Feeding. Mainly terrestrial invertebrates and small vertebrates: insects and their larvae, especially beetles, grasshoppers, crickets, ants, earwigs, caterpillars and flies; also earthworms, slugs, snails, small rodents and reptiles; occasionally some seeds. Mainly nocturnal and exclusively terrestrial feeder. Walks slowly along in search of prey, taking beetles, grasshoppers, earwigs, ants, small lizards and similar prey with bill; uses sudden, short run to capture prey, or a swift lunge, or simply picks less active prey from the ground with deft movement; also leaps to catch moths, and takes insects from vegetation. Forages singly, in pairs or small groups up to 6 birds.
Breeding. Breeds in spring in most of range, Mar-Jun in N Africa, Feb-Jun in Canary Is; starting from Apr in Britain and from late May in Siberia; in India, mainly Mar-Apr; in Sri Lanka, mainly Jun-Jul. Monogamous. Solitary, although pairs often nest within visual contact on restricted areas of habitat. Nest is scrape in ground, lined with a little grass or unlined, but often with a ring of stones or shells and pieces of vegetation around rim. Usually 2 eggs (1-3); single brood; incubation 24-26 days; downy chick pale with dark markings; fledging 36-42 days. Success varies according to habitat, predation and degree of protection: in Britain c. 0·65 young raised per pair; 77% of young hatched survive until half-grown. May breed at 1 year old, but normally at 3 years old.
Movements N European and C Asian populations migrate in autumn to S Europe, Middle East and beyond into Africa. Populations of Iberia, N Africa, India and SE Asia resident; N African breeders sometimes move S beyond Sahara, but normal extent of migration poorly known. Canary Is birds remain within the island group, but sometimes move from island to island
Status and Conservation. Not globally threatened. Widespread but restricted to small areas of suitable habitat, often widely separated. European population estimated at 41,000-160,000 pairs, but species has experienced considerable overall decline in recent decades: still numerous in Russia, probably with 10,000-100,000 pairs, although figures very uncertain; 22,000-30,000 pairs in Spain, but in decline; 5000-9000 pairs in France, where population stable; 1000-10,000 pairs in Portugal; probably 1000-5000 pairs in Turkey; in addition, several thousand pairs in Israel. Declines in many areas, sometimes substantial, e.g. in Britain, from 1000+ pairs in 1930's to 145 pairs in 1990's; marked decline in Poland since 1945. Pressure from habitat loss and disturbance, particularly associated with forestry, agricultural intensification, decline in sheep rearing in places, and human recreational pressure on coasts. Many birds shot and trapped on migration in Mediterranean region but numbers and effects on populations uncertain; collisions with overhead wires and fences, and predation by foxes also cause numerous losses. Conservation in Europe largely depends on future modifications of land-use policies, and also on mutual understanding with farmers. See page 359.
Bibliography. Ali & Ripley (1982), Amat (1986), Bannerman (1963), Barros (1991), Calvario *et al*. (1986), Christen (1980b, 1982), Cramp & Simmons (1983), Dementiev & Gladkov (1951b), Dentesani & Genero (1987), Dharmakumarsinhji (1965), Dowsett & Forbes-Watson (1993), Elgood *et al*. (1994), Étchécopar & Hüe (1964), Evans (1994), Flint *et al*. (1984), Gallagher & Price (1990), Glue & Morgan (1974), Goodman *et al*. (1989), Green (1988b), Green & Bowden (1986), Green & Tyler (1989), Heath (1994), Hempel & Rudolph (1991), Hüe & Étchécopar (1970), Knystautas (1993), Lekagul & Round (1991), Lewartowski (1983), Mackworth-Praed & Grant (1957, 1970), Malvaud (1985, 1993, 1995), Martin & Katzir (1994), Meschini (1991), Meschini & Fraschetti (1989), Mödlinger (1973-1974, 1978), Moreau (1972), Morel & Roux (1966), Nipkow (1989, 1990), Patrikeev (1995), Paz (1987), Perennou *et al*. (1994), Phillips (1978), Rathbone & Rathbone (1992), Reichholf (1989), Ripley (1982), Roberts, T.J. (1991), Rutgers & Norris (1970), Santharam (1980), Selous (1900, 1916), Sharrock (1976), Shirihai (1996), Short *et al*. (1990), Sierra (1993), Smythies (1986), Solís (1995), Solís & de Lope (1995), Uhlig & Baumgart (1995), Urban *et al*. (1986), Vaurie (1963), Wadewitz (1955), Walpole-Bond (1938), Westwood (1983), Yeatman (1976).

2. Senegal Thick-knee

Burhinus senegalensis

French: Oedicnème du Sénégal **German**: Senegaltriel **Spanish**: Alcaraván Senegalés
Other common names: Senegal Stone-curlew

Taxonomy. *Œdicnemus Senegalensis* Swainson, 1837, Senegal.
E populations sometimes separated as race *inornatus*, but differences rather slight and broad zone of intergradation through N Cameroon, Chad, Central African Republic and NE Zaire. Monotypic.
Distribution. Senegambia E through Nigeria and Central African Republic to Sudan, whence N to Egypt, E to Ethiopia and Somalia, and S to Kenya.

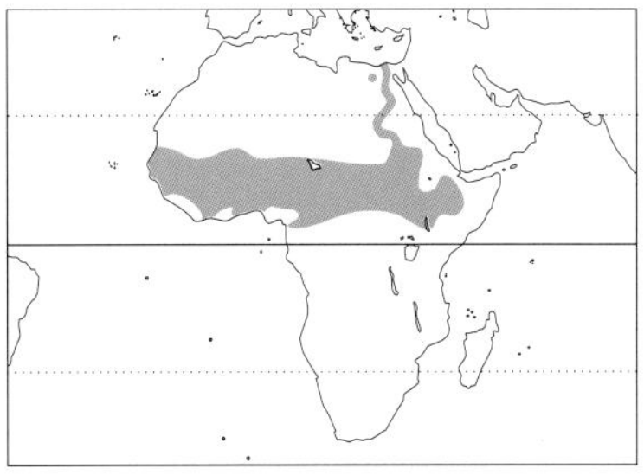

Descriptive notes. 32-38 cm. Very similar to both *B. oedicnemus* and *B. vermiculatus*, but somewhat smaller, and large, pale panel on median and greater upperwing-coverts lacks sharp white bar above; has slightly longer, heavier bill than *B. oedicnemus*, with less yellow at base, and shows rather more white on primaries, and, in flight, more rounded tip to shorter wing. Juvenile very similar to adult but with bright buff tips to median wing-coverts and tertials.
Habitat. Damp, muddy riversides to sandy ridges, extensive grassy flats beside rivers, irrigated fields, burnt woodland, and semi-arid grassland close to water. Also adapted to use urban and suburban areas with access to open ground and water margins.
Food and Feeding. Small invertebrates, reptiles, amphibians, molluscs and small rodents. Mainly nocturnal and exclusively terrestrial feeder. Forages by walking along, taking prey from ground with quick forward peck, or after short run and forward stoop. Forages singly or in small groups, up to 1 km from water.
Breeding. Season varies, but usually breeds before rains in areas with seasonal rainfall, when river levels are low, exposing suitable banks and islands: eggs in Apr (Mar-Jun) in Egypt, Apr-Aug in Senegambia, Apr in Sierra Leone, mostly Mar-Aug in Nigeria, May-Sept in Mali, Mar-Jun and Sept-Nov (wet seasons) in Kenya. Monogamous. Solitary and territorial or loosely colonial on riverbanks; but forms closer nesting groups in more restricted sites, e.g. on flat roofs of houses. Nest is shallow scrape, often ringed with grit, shells or pieces of twig. Normally 2 eggs; single brood; downy chick grey above with black speckles. No further information available.
Movements. Mostly sedentary but seasonal movements in parts of W Africa related to flooding and drought, both of which cause temporary exodus: species present Dec-Mar in Senegal, Nov-May in Zaire. Resident in Sierra Leone and Nigeria, with some local movements.
Status and Conservation. Not globally threatened. Generally common and shows ability to survive well in areas populated by man, although few solid data available. Common in Gambia and Nigeria; not uncommon in SE Ghana. Flocks along R Nile in Egypt frequently exceed 20 birds, and up to 60 birds have been recorded together.
Bibliography. Archer & Godman (1937-1961), Bannerman (1953), Britton, P.L. (1980), Cave & Macdonald (1955), Chapin (1939), Cramp & Simmons (1983), Dowsett & Forbes-Watson (1993), Elgood *et al*. (1994), Étchécopar & Hüe (1964), Glutz von Blotzheim *et al*. (1977), Goodman *et al*. (1989), Gore (1990), Grimes (1987), Mackworth-Praed & Grant (1957, 1970), Meinertzhagen (1930), Pinto (1983), Pitman (1931), Schönwetter (1967), Shirihai (1994), Short *et al*. (1990), Snow (1978), Symens & Werner (1994), Urban *et al*. (1986).

3. Water Dikkop

Burhinus vermiculatus

French: Oedicnème vermiculé **German**: Wassertriel **Spanish**: Alcaraván Acuático
Other common names: Water Thick-knee

Taxonomy. *Oedicnemus vermiculatus* Cabanis, 1868, Lake Jipe, near Taita, Kenya.
Two subspecies recognized.
Subspecies and Distribution.
B. v. buettikoferi (Reichenow, 1898) - Liberia to Nigeria and Gabon; sometimes claimed to occur E to Uganda.
B. v. vermiculatus (Cabanis, 1868) - Zaire E to SC Somalia, and S to E & S South Africa.

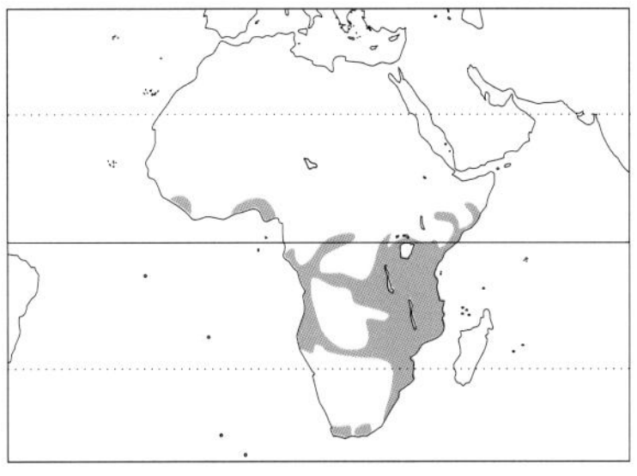

Descriptive notes 38-41 cm; 293-320 g. Similar to *B. oedicnemus* and *B. senegalensis*, but generally rather darker; broad, pale covert panel has thin white upper line on lesser coverts but lacks fine black lower edge; bill longer and rather heavier, with less yellow at base. Unlike other *Burhinus*, has fine vermiculated patterns on upperparts but only visible at close range; in flight, has rather broad, blunt wings and short tail, with feet projecting slightly beyond tip. Juvenile very similar to adult, but has buff spotting on grey upperwing-coverts, and more abundant vermiculations on upperparts and tail. Race *buettikoferi* rather darker and browner, less grey.
Habitat. Riverbanks and lake edges, estuaries and mangroves; also undisturbed, sheltered beaches; prefers areas with some bushes for cover. Light woodland or other cover provides the shade that is essential by day.
Food and Feeding. Feeds on insects, crustaceans and molluscs. Nocturnal and terrestrial feeder. Feeds by tilting forwards to grasp food in the bill. May forage more than 1 km from water.
Breeding. Season variable, but generally dry season and early rains in S Africa; Jan and Mar-Dec in Kenya; Nov in Tanzania; Aug-Dec in Zimbabwe and South Africa. Monogamous. Solitary. Nest is a

On following pages: 4. Spotted Dikkop (*Burhinus capensis*); 5. Double-striped Thick-knee (*Burhinus bistriatus*); 6. Peruvian Thick-knee (*Burhinus superciliaris*); 7. Bush Thick-knee (*Burhinus grallarius*); 8. Great Thick-knee (*Esacus recurvirostris*); 9. Beach Thick-knee (*Esacus magnirostris*).

scrape on ground, sometimes sparsely lined, often close to water and near a landmark, e.g. piece of driftwood or bush. Normally 2 eggs, rarely 1; single brood; incubation c. 24 days. No further information available.
Movements. Sedentary, apart from some local movements to avoid flooding; birds subsequently return to exposed riversides as water recedes.
Status and Conservation. Not globally threatened. Very little precise information available, partly due to secretive habits, and, in N of range, confusion with very similar *B. senegalensis*. Species still said to be locally abundant; locally common in southern Africa; common in Angola; probably uncommon in Nigeria. Precise distribution in W Africa still poorly known: status in Ghana uncertain, but probably very uncommon resident.
Bibliography. Ash & Miskell (1983), Benson & Benson (1975), Bregnballe *et al.* (1990), Britton, P.L. (1980), Brown & Britton (1980), Dowsett & Forbes-Watson (1993), Elgood *et al.* (1994), Gatter (1988), Ginn *et al.* (1989), Grimes (1987), Lewis & Pomeroy (1989), Lippens & Wille (1976), Louette (1981), Mackworth-Praed & Grant (1957, 1962, 1970), Maclean (1993), Newman, K. (1983), Pakenham (1979), Pinto (1983), Pitman (1928), Short *et al.* (1990), Sinclair *et al.* (1993), Urban *et al.* (1986).

4. Spotted Dikkop

Burhinus capensis

French: Oedicnème tachard **German**: Kaptriel **Spanish**: Alcaraván de El Cabo
Other common names: Spotted Thick-knee, Cape Dikkop/Thick-knee

Taxonomy. *Oedicnemus capensis* Lichtenstein, 1823, Cape of Good Hope.
Several other races proposed: doubtfully distinct are *ehrenbergi* of Dahlak I in Red Sea, and *affinis* on Red Sea coast of Ethiopia; also *psammochromus* included in *maculosus*, and *csongor* included in nominate *capensis*. Four subspecies normally recognized.
Subspecies and Distribution.
B. c. maculosus (Temminck, 1824) - Senegal E to Eritrea and Somalia, and S to Uganda and Kenya.
B. c. dodsoni (Ogilvie-Grant, 1899) - coastal Somalia and S Arabia.
B. c. capensis (Lichtenstein, 1823) - Kenya S to South Africa, and W from Zambia to Angola.
B. c. damarensis (Reichenow, 1905) - Namibia, Botswana and SW South Africa (Cape Province).

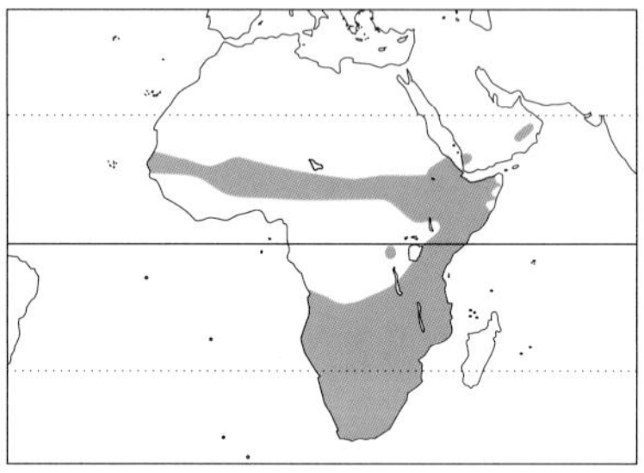

Descriptive notes. 37-44 cm; 375-610 g. Distinctive thick-knee, with upperparts clearly spotted, rather than streaked; upperpart feathers have basal bar and distal spot, rather than simple shaft-streak; face rather dark and poorly marked; wing-coverts more uniform with rest of upperparts than in other *Burhinus* species. Juvenile more streaked, less spotted; breast more finely streaked. Races vary according to general plumage hues, *damarensis* pale, *maculosus* more tawny; *dodsoni* more barred, less spotted than nominate race.
Habitat. Prefers arid areas, away from watersides; found in open woodland and savanna, grassland close to cover of bushes or trees; also fields, stony slopes and all kinds of eroded or waste ground; even large parks, playing fields and beaches. Prefers some daytime cover and shade, under trees or bushes or amongst boulders.
Food and Feeding. Main food probably insects, but also known to take small amphibians, molluscs, crustaceans and some seeds. Feeds mainly at night but also active on dull, cloudy days; terrestrial. Typical *Burhinus* feeding action, leaning forward to pick food from ground with bill, during pauses in steady forward walk, or after short run.
Breeding. Laying around end of dry season and beginning of wet season, or within the dry season. Monogamous. Solitary. Nest is a shallow scrape, lined with pieces of grass and leaves, small stones, pieces of earth and animal droppings; often sited next to small landmark, such as a stone, or in shade of a bush. Usually 2 eggs (1-3); incubation c. 24 days, beginning with 2nd egg; downy chick pale grey with black markings; captive young flew at 8 weeks old.
Movements. Resident and apparently wholly sedentary, although occasional records from sites outside normal breeding range suggest infrequent dispersal towards S Sahara and into Zaire.
Status and Conservation. Not globally threatened. Generally quite frequent, locally rather numerous; has benefited from ability to accept disturbed ground and occupy areas near presence of human activity. No precise details available on population sizes or trends.
Bibliography. Ash & Miskell (1983), Benson & Benson (1975), Bigalke (1933), Britton, P.L. (1980), Broekhuysen (1964), Dowsett & Forbes-Watson (1993), Elgood *et al.* (1994), Evans (1994), Gallagher & Price (1990), Gallagher & Woodcock (1980), Gichuki (1989), Ginn *et al.* (1989), Gore (1990), Grimes (1987), Hattingh (1993), Hollom *et al.* (1988), Koen (1983), Kok (1993), Mackworth-Praed & Grant (1957, 1962, 1970), Maclean (1966, 1993), Newby (1979), Newman, K. (1983), Perennou *et al.* (1994), Pinto (1983), Rands *et al.* (1987), Rutgers & Norris (1970), Short *et al.* (1990), Sinclair *et al.* (1993), Urban *et al.* (1986).

5. Double-striped Thick-knee

Burhinus bistriatus

French: Oedicnème bistrié **German**: Dominikanertriel **Spanish**: Alcaraván Venezolano
Other common names: Double-striped Stone-curlew, Mexican Thick-knee

Taxonomy. *Charadrius bistriatus* Wagler, 1829, Mexico.
Proposed race *vigilans* synonymous with nominate *bistriatus*. Four races recognized.
Subspecies and Distribution.
B. b. bistriatus (Wagler, 1829) - S Mexico S to NW Costa Rica.
B. b. dominicensis (Cory, 1883) - Hispaniola.
B. b. pediacus Wetmore & Borrero, 1964 - N Colombia.
B. b. vocifer (L'Herminier, 1837) - Venezuela, Guyana and extreme N Brazil.
Descriptive notes. 43-48 cm. Large thick-knee, with long neck and legs; long white supercilium bordered above by black line. Rather similar to *B. superciliaris*, but larger, darker and more heavily patterned above, with heavier bill and darker crown; more distinct contrast between dark breast and white belly; in flight, shows less contrasted wing pattern. Juvenile paler than adult, with head and neck tinged buff. Races separated mainly on measurements, with rather slight variations in overall colour tones: *dominicensis* smaller; *pediacus* palish and cinnamon; *vocifer* darker and browner, less grey, on breast.
Habitat. Open grassland and bushy savanna, mostly in semi-arid to arid areas; also farmland and ranchland with dry dirt tracks. Prefers flat landscape, with or without scattered trees and bushes, but essentially open in character.

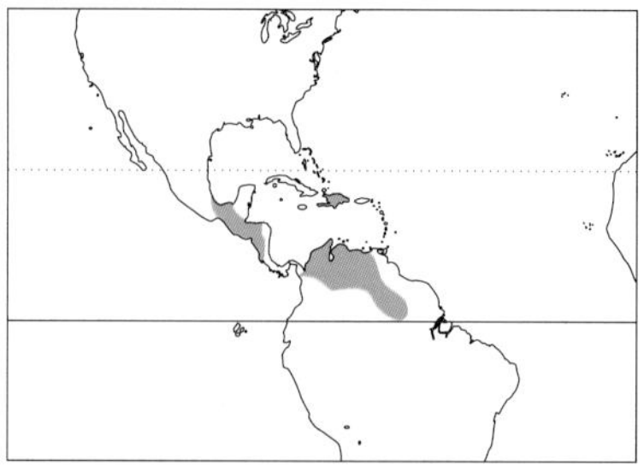

Food and Feeding. Poorly known. Feeds on small animals such as insects, worms, molluscs and occasionally lizards and small rodents. Feeds at or after dusk, often visiting open, unpaved tracks and roads where insects and small animal casualties can be found with ease. Picks prey from the ground, using typical plover-like walk with pause to tilt forward.
Breeding. Essentially breeds in dry season, e.g young in Apr and early May in Colombia. Solitary, but found breeding in loose groups where common. Nest is a scrape in ground, often among animal droppings. Lays 2 eggs; incubation 27-29 days (*dominicensis*), by both sexes but perhaps mainly by male. No further information available.
Movements. Sedentary, although with some exceptional occurrences beyond normal range, e.g. recorded in Texas, USA, in Dec 1961, and also in S Brazil in Nov.
Status and Conservation. Not globally threatened. Increasing locally as habitat changes open up new areas for colonization, especially deforestation, with forest giving way to pasture. Fairly common to common but local in S Mexico; in Guatemala and Costa Rica, more typically a bird of the W Pacific slope; uncommon on Hispaniola (1978), where formerly much more abundant, with decline attributed to hunting and habitat alteration; in Colombia, relatively common on Caribbean coast and E of Andes but much more infrequent and localized to W. Frequent victim of road traffic at night; long-term effects of such mortality could conceivably become more important. Sometimes semi-domesticated around ranches, where species is held to be a useful controller of insect pests and is kept on patios and in corrals of country houses. CITES III in Guatemala.
Bibliography. Anon. (1983a), Blake (1977), Bond (1985), Dickey & van Rossem (1938), Freese (1975), Friedmann & Smith (1955), Hellmayr & Conover (1948), Hilty & Brown (1986), Howell & Webb (1995a), Jones, T. (1987), Land (1970), Lowery & Dalquest (1951), Meyer de Schauensee & Phelps (1978), Monroe (1968), Pinto (1964), Ruschi (1979), Scott & Carbonell (1986), Sick (1985c, 1993), Slud (1964), Snyder (1966), Stiles & Skutch (1989), Stockton (1978), Verrill & Verrill (1909), Voous (1983), Wetmore & Borrero (1964).

6. Peruvian Thick-knee

Burhinus superciliaris

French: Oedicnème du Pérou **German**: Peruanertriel **Spanish**: Alcaraván Peruano

Taxonomy. *Oedicnenus* [sic] *superciliaris* Tschudi, 1843, coast of Peru.
Monotypic.
Distribution. Pacific coast, from extreme S Ecuador to S Peru.

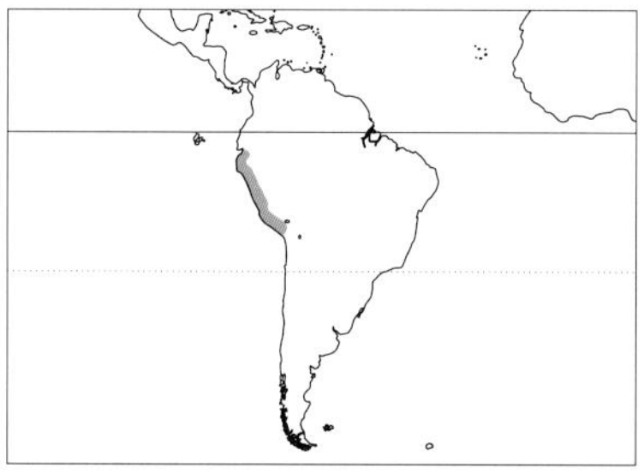

Descriptive notes. 38-43 cm. Fairly large thick-knee, with long neck and legs. Smaller and greyer than *B. bistriatus*, with which shares white supercilium with black upper border; bill smaller, with more pale yellowish green at base; less heavily streaked above; in flight, shows more contrasted, unmarked grey wing-coverts, which stand out much more clearly against dark flight-feathers. Juvenile has feathers of upperparts darker brown with warmer buff fringes.
Habitat. Typically found in dry agricultural land with open aspect, semi-desert and dry grassland; also in denser areas of bush in Andean foothills above coast.
Food and Feeding. Virtually nothing known. Species presumed to take small animals, such as insects and small lizards. Feed after dusk; terrestrial. Uses typical thick-knee feeding actions.
Breeding. Little known. Probably solitary, but, where common, small aggregations are likely to occur during breeding season. One nest found in Jun 1978, dry season, in NW Peru, contained 2 eggs; site was on a plateau c. 15 m above extensive plains, on a rocky slope with scattered clumps of low shrubs and cacti and sparse grasses; nest scrape was a slight depression, cleared of plant debris. No further information available.
Movements. Sedentary. One record from N Chile in 1851 may have referred to a vagrant, or perhaps to an extension, presumably temporary, of range as currently known.
Status and Conservation. Not globally threatened. Very limited range, so total numbers are likely to be relatively small, but species may be fairly frequent in N of range. Species was described as "very popular" with the local people, due to the mystique associated with its nocturnal habits and loud calls. No threats identified at present, but species requires monitoring; research into basic ecological requirements also highly desirable.
Bibliography. Blake (1977), Bolton (1993), Butler (1979), Dunning (1982), Hellmayr & Conover (1948), Howell & Webb (1995b), Johnson (1965b), Koepcke (1970), Meyer de Schauensee (1982), Ortiz & Carrión (1991), Parker *et al.* (1982), Scott & Carbonell (1986), Williams (1981).

7. Bush Thick-knee

Burhinus grallarius

French: Oedicnème bridé **German**: Langschwanztriel **Spanish**: Alcaraván Colilargo
Other common names: Bush Stone-curlew/Curlew, Southern Stone-curlew, Stone-plover, Australian Dikkop

Taxonomy. *Charadrius grallarius* Latham, 1801, New South Wales.
Considerable confusion concerning correct nomenclature: species name traditionally given as *magnirostris*, but this is replaced by *grallarius* as the valid name, due to principle of first reviser (see page 350). Sometimes divided into three races, with recognition of *rufescens* (NW & NC Australia) and *ramsayi* (N Queensland), but these forms are poorly marked and species probably more realistically treated as polymorphic. Monotypic.
Distribution. N & S Western Australia through Northern Territory to Queensland, then S to SE South Australia and Victoria; also Trans-Fly area of S New Guinea.
Descriptive notes. 54-59 cm; 625-670 g. Polymorphic, with rather similar grey and rufous morphs. Particularly long-legged, long-tailed thick-knee; slim and small-bodied, with proportions more akin to American than Eurasian and African congeners; streaked, cryptic plumage typical of genus, as well as large, pale eyes in big, round head, but bill rather fine, all dark; long wings have rather broad,

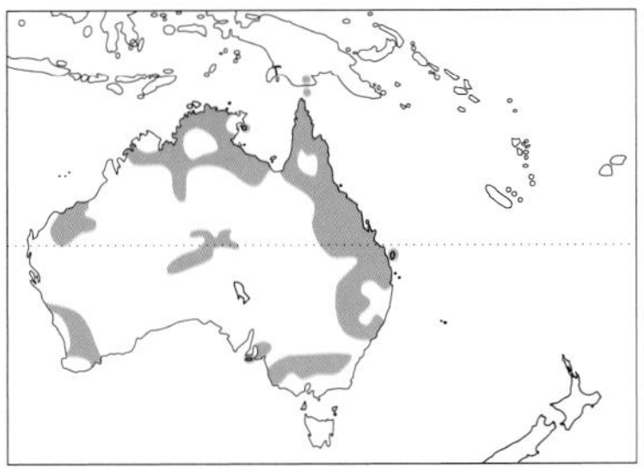

square, fingered tips; legs long, pale yellowish green, trailing well beyond tail tip in flight. Female similar to male but slightly smaller. Juvenile has eyes milky white, less yellow; more coarsely marked pale upperwing-coverts.
Habitat. Open forest and woodland with clearings; also cleared ground with mixed farmland and woodland fragments remaining, but lacking shrub or tall herb layer; dry grassland and cropland near cover; rarely swampy ground, mangroves or salt-marsh bordered by bushy cover or trees; avoids rain forest or other thick forest cover, preferring ground with scattering of fallen dead timber, or carpet of dead leaves, but otherwise open. Inland, associated with water courses and edges of lakes, but also sand dunes and shingle ridges.
Food and Feeding. Insects, molluscs, centipedes, crustaceans, spiders, amphibians, small reptiles and occasionally seeds. Nocturnal, but particularly active in bright moonlight. Takes food from ground and vegetation in tall grassland, from fallen, dead timber and also from among debris and stones along edges of water courses, by probing with bill. May feed on insects attracted by artificial lights. Typically forages for 20-30 minutes at one site, before moving on to another; may also change general feeding areas regularly, even each night.
Breeding. Breeds in spring, generally earlier in N than in S, e.g. laying Jun-Dec in Queensland, Aug-Jan in Victoria. Monogamous. Solitary. Nest on ground, often under trees in short or quite long grass, in open spots, averaging c. 12 m from nearest tree, with good visibility for 250+ m all round; more rarely nests on salt-marsh or beach; nest is bare scrape, often edged with animal dung; same site may be reused for many years. 2 eggs; incubation 25 days, by both sexes; chick has grey down with broad blackish longitudinal stripes; young brooded by both sexes, male perhaps taking greater share; young fly when 59 days old (perhaps as early as 47-50 days); cared for by parents for up to 138 days, but less if 2nd clutch laid. Success rather variable; some eggs destroyed by farming operations, flooding, or trampling by stock, and eggs and chicks taken by foxes.
Movements. Sedentary. No large-scale seasonal movements, but breeding territories break down after breeding season, when some local movements may occur and birds gather into flocks; apparent seasonal movements and changes in numbers probably always due to this flocking behaviour, producing ostensible erratic fluctuations. Accidental in Tasmania.
Status and Conservation. Not globally threatened. Species appears generally secure, but locally vulnerable. Total Australian population estimated at c. 15,000 birds; fairly common but local in Trans-Fly area, S New Guinea. Range has contracted especially in E & S Australia, owing to habitat changes; declines in many regions, withdrawals from traditional breeding areas and reduction in size of post-breeding flocks clearly evident. Losses normally attributed to predation by foxes, eating of poisoned bait put down for rabbits, illegal shooting and egg-collecting, but they principally reflect loss of habitat and increasing fragmentation of remaining populations.
Bibliography. Anderson (1991), Bedggood (1977), Beehler *et al.* (1986), Bigg (1988), Blakers *et al.* (1984), Bright (1935a), Christidis & Boles (1994), Coates (1985), Flegg & Madge (1995), Frith (1969), Garnett (1985b), Johnson & Baker-Gabb (1993), Lane & Davies (1987), Larkins (1989), Leach (1988), Lindgren (1971), Lindsey (1992), Macdonald (1988), Marchant & Higgins (1993), Pizzey & Doyle (1980), Pringle (1987), Schodde & Mason (1980), Schodde & Tidemann (1986), Simpson & Day (1994), Slater *et al.* (1989), Trounson (1987), Wilson (1989).

Genus *ESACUS* Lesson, 1831

8. Great Thick-knee
Esacus recurvirostris

French: Grand Oedicnème **German**: Krabbentriel **Spanish**: Alcaraván Picogrueso Indio
Other common names: Great Stone-plover/Stone-curlew

Taxonomy. *Œdicnemus recurvirostris* Cuvier, 1829, Nepal.
Genus sometimes merged into *Burhinus*. Forms superspecies with *E. magnirostris*, with which occasionally considered conspecific. Monotypic.
Distribution. SE Iran through Indian Subcontinent and Sri Lanka to Indochina and Hainan (S China).

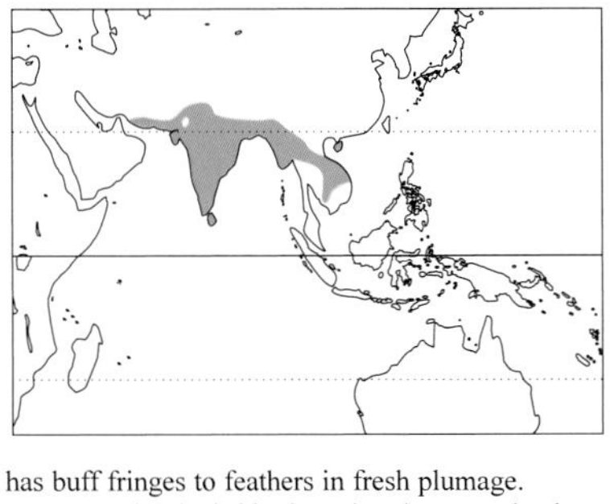

Descriptive notes. 49-54 cm; c. 790 g. Large, massive thick-knee with proportions somewhat recalling bustard; unstreaked greyish upperparts; face strongly patterned with white around and behind eye above black cheek patch and short malar stripe; bill massive, with more slender, uptilted tip and thick yellow base; in flight reveals largely black flight-feathers with striking white primary patches and broad pale grey band across median and greater upperwing-coverts. Differs from somewhat similar *E. magnirostris* in white forehead, black rather than pale grey secondaries, and slightly more slender and pointed bill. Juvenile very similar to adult, but has buff fringes to feathers in fresh plumage.
Habitat. Riverbed shingle and rocks, stony banks and mud (in preference to sand) around large lakes; sometimes visits nearby grassy flats when rivers flood. Infrequently on coastal beaches, sandy flats, tidal estuaries and salt-pans; inhabits coastal district of dry zone in Sri Lanka, but restricted to undisturbed beaches.
Food and Feeding. Feeds mainly on crabs and other crustaceans; also insects, and record of eggs of Kentish Plover (*Charadrius alexandrinus*). On oligotrophic reservoir, where crabs infrequent, young birds found to have eaten: young monitor lizard (*Varanus*) c. 21 cm long, intact but with head battered; whole shrew (*Suncus*) c. 6 cm long; and small fish c. 8 cm long; also winged termites. Mainly active after dusk, but sometimes feeds by day. Prises up stones with massive upcurved bill. Uses typical thick-knee feeding actions: wary and deliberate, walking slowly forward and tilting to take prey with large bill.
Breeding. Laying Feb-Jul in India, mainly Apr-Jul in Sri Lanka. Monogamous. Territorial; sometimes breeds in colony of River Tern (*Sterna aurantia*). Nest is scrape in ground on shingle bank, stony islet or on edge of lagoon in sparse grasses, usually close to water. 1-2 eggs; incubation by both sexes; chick has thick "pepper and salt" down with black speckles. No further information available.
Movements. Sedentary, apart from local movements forced by rising water levels in rivers and lakes, and temporary changes in feeding conditions.
Status and Conservation. Not globally threatened. Apparently still locally common, forming small parties after breeding. Scarce in Pakistan; no recent records from Thailand, where may have been extirpated. Tolerant of altered habitats and colonizes reservoir edges; however, is generally rather wary, and requires large undisturbed areas for breeding.
Bibliography. Ali & Ripley (1982), Deignan (1945), Étchécopar & Hüe (1978), Evans (1994), Henry (1971), Hollom *et al.* (1988), Hüe & Étchécopar (1970), Inskipp & Inskipp (1991), Kotagama & Fernando (1994), Lekagul & Round (1991), Meyer de Schauensee (1984), Mundkur (1991), Nameer (1992), Perennou *et al.* (1994), Phillips (1978), Ripley (1982), Roberts, T.J. (1991), Scott (1989), Smythies (1986), Wijesinghe (1994).

9. Beach Thick-knee
Esacus magnirostris

French: Oedicnème des récifs **German**: Rifftriel **Spanish**: Alcaraván Picogrueso Australiano
Other common names: Beach Stone-curlew/Curlew, Australian Stone-plover, Reef Thick-knee

Taxonomy. *Œdicnemus magnirostris* Vieillot, 1818, Depuch Island, Western Australia.
Formerly awarded monospecific genus *Orthorhamphus*; genus sometimes merged into *Burhinus*. Forms superspecies with *E. recurvirostris*, with which occasionally considered conspecific. Considerable confusion concerning correct nomenclature, resulting in recent proposals to adopt either *giganteus* or *neglectus* as valid species name, but *magnirostris* is the correct name (see page 350). Monotypic.
Distribution. Andaman Is and Malay Peninsula through Philippines, Indonesia and New Guinea to Australia and SW Pacific islands.

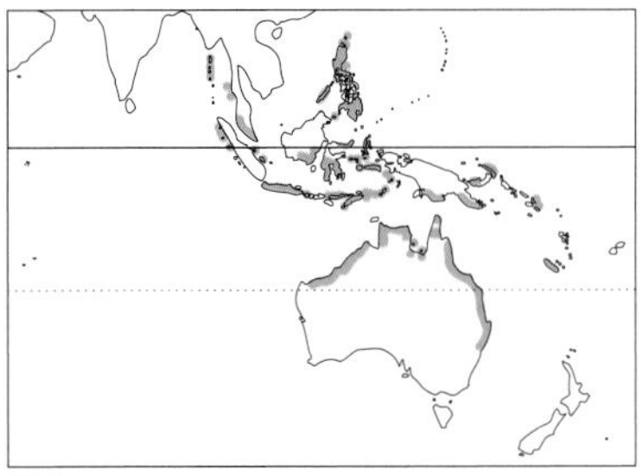

Descriptive notes. 53-57 cm; 870-1130 g. Massive, thick-set thick-knee with heavy head and stout bill; head boldly marked with black, white and grey-brown stripes; bill black, with yellow restricted to basal area; staring yellow eye; upperparts unstreaked; broad wings rather square-ended and deeply fingered in flight, enhancing somewhat bustard-like appearance; medium-long, sturdy legs. Differs from *E. recurvirostris* in bill shape and face pattern; on closed wing, blackish band across top edge of broad pale panel more marked; in flight, secondaries all grey, inner primaries uniform white. Juvenile has duller bare part colours; buff fringes to feathers of upperparts, especially upperwing-coverts.
Habitat. Exclusively coastal, on islands and mainland beaches. Adaptable, occupying beaches of sand, mud, stones and rock, both narrow and wide, sheltered or swept by surf; often at mouths of rivers, more rarely in tidal creeks. Frequents sandbars offshore and at mouths of estuaries; also on coral reefs and atolls; also prepared to use mangroves, readily entering mangroves 1·5 m high. Often flies out to sea when disturbed, before returning to beach; sometimes also found short distance inland on dunes, or around edges of coastal lagoons.
Food and Feeding. Probably feeds almost exclusively on crabs, where these are readily available; also takes other small crustaceans. Usually observed by day, when feeds actively at times, but true time preferences for feeding unknown. Forages on rocks and large intertidal areas of sand, mud or shingle. Feeds in manner recalling large *Ardea* heron, watching for prey then stalking it, or running forward with sudden, powerful forward lunge; also probes into mud, sand and even short grass, but does not usually wade. Crabs are dismembered or broken into small pieces by hammering with massive bill, before swallowing.
Breeding. Breeds Sept-Nov in temperate Australia, Jul-Nov farther N. Probably monogamous. Breeds in isolated pairs, at lower density than other shorebirds; pairs may be resident in the same area for several years; often associated with Little Terns (*Sterna albifrons*). Nest on sandbank, sand spit or island, at back of extensive beach, among mangroves or grass; shallow depression, unlined but sometimes ringed with dead leaves and twigs. 1 egg; incubation at least 30 days, roles of sexes unknown; young begins to grow feathers at 5 weeks; resembles adult at 7 weeks except for remnant down for 5 more weeks; cared for by both sexes; able to fly well at 12 weeks, but may not become independent for 7-12 months. Raptors, cats and dogs take eggs, which also suffer losses to high tides; also vulnerable to human disturbance.
Movements. Essentially sedentary, but some vagrants far S of usual range; some pairs observed on same area of beach for 10 years or more.
Status and Conservation. Not globally threatened. Very widespread, but generally rather sparsely distributed. Total population of Australia estimated at c. 1000 birds; rare and local on small islands off SW Thailand; only 2 recent records on Sulawesi; occurs sparingly on coasts of New Guinea. Species may be vulnerable due to loss of habitat, low reproductive rate, and widespread increase both in numbers of introduced predators and in human disturbance of beaches. Expansion southwards in mid-20th century probably occurred before disturbance became a serious factor; at present, holidaymakers and weekend visitors to beaches pose greatest potential threat in many areas.
Bibliography. Ali & Ripley (1982), Amiet (1957), Balmford (1990), Beehler *et al.* (1986), Blakers *et al.* (1984), Bregulla (1992), Bull (1948), Christidis & Boles (1994), Clancy (1986, 1987), Clancy & Christiansen (1980), Coates (1985), Condamin (1978), Crawford (1972), Dickinson *et al.* (1991), Garnett (1993), Gill (1970), van Helvoort (1985), Lane & Davies (1987), Lekagul & Round (1991), MacGillivray (1914, 1918), MacKinnon & Phillipps (1993), Marchant & Higgins (1993), van Marle & Voous (1988), Medway & Wells (1976), Morris (1975), Perennou *et al.* (1994), Pringle (1987), Ripley (1982), Rutgers & Norris (1970), Scott (1989), Silvius (1994), Smythies (1981, 1986), Wheeler (1959), White & Bruce (1986), Woodall & Woodall (1989).

Class AVES
Order CHARADRIIFORMES
Suborder CHARADRII
Family GLAREOLIDAE
(COURSERS AND PRATINCOLES)

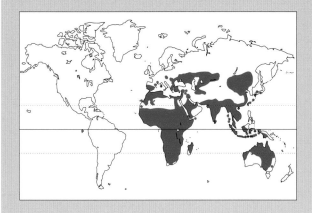

- Plover-like or tern-like waders, with long or very long wings, and long or relatively short legs.
- 17-29 cm.

- Old World tropics, with greatest diversity in Afrotropical Region.
- Desert to savanna, with some species usually adjacent to water; mostly at lower elevations, but sometimes up to 2000 m or higher.
- 6 genera, 17 species, 33 taxa.
- 1 species threatened; none extinct since 1600.

Systematics

While the glareolids are undoubtedly members of the order Charadriiformes, their exact position within the order and their relationships with other charadriiform families have been open to much debate. Even the internal relationships of some of the coursers with each other have not been fully resolved. On the basis of neonatal plumage patterns (those of the downy chicks), they have been placed close to the plovers (Charadriidae); however, this kind of evidence also placed the somewhat aberrant Inland Dotterel (*Peltohyas australis*) of Australia with the coursers, yet it has been shown to be an undoubted plover, very close to, if not in fact a member of, the genus *Charadrius* itself (see page 385). Neonatal plumage patterns among the coursers and the aberrant Australian Pratincole (*Stiltia isabella*) are highly variable, and in some cases rather unhelpful for indicating systematic relationships, especially within the genera *Smutsornis*, *Rhinoptilus* and *Stiltia*.

Osteological evidence points to the peculiar Magellanic Plover (*Pluvianellus socialis*), the sheathbills (Chionidae), the Crab Plover (*Dromas ardeola*) and the thick-knees (Burhinidae) as being the glareolids' closest relatives and sharing a common ancestor with them. On the other hand, the syringeal structure of the glareolids resembles very closely that of the plovers. Evidence from DNA-DNA hybridization advocates the glareolids' positioning in a superfamily consisting of two families, one for the gulls, terns, skimmers and auks, and the other for the coursers and pratincoles and also the Crab Plover, which is separated in its own subfamily. This relationship with the Laridae is supported by evidence derived from electrophoresis of proteins from liver and muscle tissue, which suggests that the Australian Pratincole is closer to the gulls and terns than it is to any of the other wader groups.

The family Glareolidae is divided into two well defined subfamilies, the coursers (Cursoriinae) and the pratincoles (Glareolinae), with the monotypic genus *Stiltia*, reserved for the Australian Pratincole, forming a link between the coursers and "typical" pratincoles. The Egyptian Plover (*Pluvianus aegyptius*) is very different from the other glareolids and may constitute its own family, Pluvianidae, or at least subfamily, Pluvianinae; on the basis of osteological evidence, it seems that it might be most closely related to the Burhinidae.

Fossils of the genus *Glareola* belonging to an extinct species, *Glareola neogena*, are known from the Middle Miocene of Europe, while of similar age is the extinct *Mioglareola gregaria*, also from European deposits. The oldest glareolid fossils are of the genus *Paractiornis* from the Lower Miocene of North America. On the basis of their present distribution, however, the Glareolidae appear to be of African origin, whence they probably spread later into Eurasia and Australasia. Alternatively, they might be the remnant of a more widespread Gondwanan ancestry. More recent remains of the Collared Pratincole (*Glareola pratincola*) have been found in Middle Pleistocene deposits in France.

Further evidence of an African origin for recent species can be concluded from the apparently close relationship between

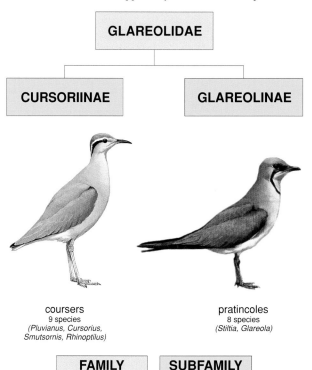

coursers
9 species
(*Pluvianus, Cursorius, Smutsornis, Rhinoptilus*)

pratincoles
8 species
(*Stiltia, Glareola*)

Subdivision of the Glareolidae.

[Figure: Hilary Burn]

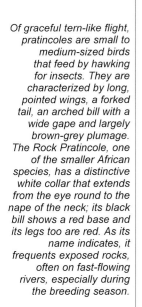

each of the Indian species of glareolid and their African equivalents. Temminck's (*Cursorius temminckii*) and the Bronze-winged Coursers (*Rhinoptilus chalcopterus*), like their Indian counterparts, the Indian (*Cursorius coromandelicus*) and Jerdon's Coursers (*Rhinoptilus bitorquatus*), are adapted to open savanna woodland; it seems likely that a vegetation corridor of this type connected Africa and India at some time in the past during a wetter period, perhaps in the Plio-Pleistocene, allowing the common ancestors of these closely related species pairs to spread from Africa to India. The Indian birds subsequently became isolated following climatic deterioration which destroyed the woodland corridor connecting Africa and India. The small riverine pratincoles, the Grey (*Glareola cinerea*) and Small Pratincoles (*Glareola lactea*), from Africa and Asia respectively, also form a species pair, sharing similar behaviour and habitat requirements.

Internal family relationships are also the subject of debate: on the evidence from feather lice (Mallophaga), which, because they are often highly species-specific, have been used as indicators of avian relationships, it has been suggested that the Double-banded Courser (*Smutsornis africanus*), host to the allegedly most primitive feather louse found among the coursers, is itself primitive; it also shows patterned plumage in the adult. More advanced species of feather louse, in order of their apparent evolution, parasitize respectively the Bronze-winged Courser, the Cream-coloured Courser (*Cursorius cursor*) and the Egyptian Plover. From this arises the possibility that the plain-backed genera of coursers, such as the Bronze-winged and Cream-coloured, are more advanced than those with patterned dorsal adult plumage, and that *Pluvianus* is the most advanced genus in the subfamily Cursoriinae. Certainly, the plumage patterns of the Egyptian Plover and the Double-banded Courser represent the extremes in appearance of this group. The argument is persuasive, though not necessarily supported by the morphological evidence, which places *Pluvianus* closer to the thick-knees than to the coursers. Only further evidence, perhaps from DNA-DNA hybridization, will help to establish the true relationships among glareolids in general, and coursers in particular.

It is, however, entirely possible that the evolutionary trend suggested by the feather-louse evidence is correct, indicating increasing specialization in bill morphology, from a generalized type in *Smutsornis* to the long, decurved bill shape of *Cursorius*, adapted for digging. Digging in sand, mainly for the purpose of covering its eggs and small chicks, is also a regular aspect of the Egyptian Plover's behaviour. Other behavioural characters, such as distraction displays of "False Nest-scraping" and "Mock-brooding", are shared by both the Egyptian Plover and the Cream-coloured Courser, supporting a close relationship of the Egyptian Plover with the coursers.

All the living species of courser are sometimes included in the single genus *Cursorius*, though a convenient split is usually made into the diurnal *Cursorius* and the largely crepuscular or nocturnal species of *Rhinoptilus* and *Smutsornis*, these last two frequently being considered congeneric.

There is also debate on the limits of the superspecies in the diurnal members of the genus *Cursorius*: although all four species are clearly closely related and are sometimes included in a single superspecies, as here, there is also a persuasive argument that *cursor* and *rufus* have been separate from *coromandelicus* and *temminckii* for some time as they are ecologically distinct, the former pair adapted to very arid savanna and semi-desert habitats, the latter pair preferring less arid regions such as open, dry woodland savanna. Indeed *temminckii* overlaps in range with both *cursor* and *rufus*, as does *coromandelicus* with *cursor*. It has also been proposed recently that the species limits within Cream-coloured and Burchell's Coursers (*Cursorius rufus*) be revised, with the East African races of *cursor* perhaps properly belonging with *rufus* on the basis of structure and wing pattern.

Within the pratincoles, in addition to the small riverine superspecies of the Grey and the Small, the large species of *Glareola*, namely the Collared, Oriental (*Glareola maldivarum*) and Black-winged Pratincoles (*Glareola nordmanni*), are all very closely related, though range overlap of the Black-winged with the Collared means that some authorities exclude the Black-winged from the superspecies.

Morphological Aspects

The Glareolidae are characterized by a short, arched bill with the nostrils at the base, not in a groove, and a nasal septum separating the nasal cavities. The tarsi have transverse scales on both

Much longer-legged than pratincoles, coursers are terrestrial birds rather similar to plovers in shape and size. The Indian Courser is a strikingly marked bird with black lores and eyestripe, and above them a distinctive white supercilium extending onto the nape; it has a warm cinnamon breast and upper belly, and white uppertail-coverts. It has the arched black bill typical of the Glareolidae, rather long in this case and well adapted for digging in soft soil for food. The long legs allow for swift running on the ground, where it spends much of its time, although, when the necessity arises, it can fly well, with rather jerky plover-like wingbeats.

[Cursorius coromandelicus, Karnataka, India. Photo: K. Ghani/NHPA]

the front and the back, except in the Egyptian Plover, which may belong to a family of its own (see Systematics), and has the tarsal scales arranged in two rows front and back. The hind toe is absent in the Egyptian Plover and the coursers, and reduced and elevated in the pratincoles; and the claw of the middle front toe is equipped with comb-like serrations, except in *Pluvianus* and *Stiltia*. In spite of its considerable differences from other glareolids, however, the jaw muscles of the Egyptian Plover generally resemble those of other members of the family.

Glareolids are small to medium-sized terrestrial birds with a range in length of 17-29 cm, and in weight from 37 g in the Small Pratincole to as much as 172 g in the Bronze-winged Courser. They have long and pointed wings, especially in the pratincoles; the wings of coursers tend to be proportionately shorter and somewhat more rounded, though still long in comparison with the wings of most other ground-dwelling birds. Coursers are long-legged terrestrial runners with short toes and square tails, whereas pratincoles are largely aerial feeders with very long wings, especially in *Stiltia*, relatively short legs, longish toes and forked tails, though in these latter respects *Stiltia* is an exception, with legs as long as those of the coursers and a square tail. The Egyptian Plover, at 73-92 g, is intermediate in weight between the generally lighter pratincoles and the heavier coursers.

The arched bill, unique among the Charadrii, characterizes all members of the family Glareolidae. In the pratincoles the bill is red at the base, often brighter in the male than in the female, and has a wide gape, presumably to facilitate the catching of flying insects on the wing. The bill of the coursers and the Egyptian Plover lacks the wide gape and is usually uniformly dark throughout, though yellow at the base in the Three-banded (*Rhinoptilus cinctus*) and Jerdon's Coursers and purplish red at the base in the Bronze-winged Courser; these three species appear to be closely related, on the basis not only of bill coloration, but also of plumage characteristics. In the genus *Cursorius* the bill is relatively long and is used for digging for food in soft sandy soils. The Egyptian Plover also uses its bill for digging, though mainly as a means of covering its eggs or chicks in sand when disturbed.

The long legs of coursers and the Australian Pratincole enable the birds to run at great speed on the ground, hence the

European names "courser", *courvite*, *Rennvogel*, *corredor* and so on. Species inhabiting open country, such as *Cursorius* and *Smutsornis*, are much faster runners than those of the woodland genus *Rhinoptilus*. Coursers have legs characteristically coloured white, yellow or red. Though much shorter-legged, pratincoles too may run on the ground like plovers. The *Rhinoptilus* coursers, especially the Bronze-winged Courser, have proportionately larger eyes, as befits their nocturnal activity.

The flight of pratincoles is particularly buoyant and free, with deep wingbeats and periods of agile gliding, and this allows them to exploit flying insects as their principal source of food. It also permits the larger species to undertake sometimes lengthy migrations, which, in the case of the Black-winged Pratincole, is apparently non-stop at high altitude. The flight of the Australian Pratincole, with its rather stiff, tern-like wingbeats, is very graceful, like that of the sometimes sympatric Oriental Pratincole, but it catches a higher proportion of its food on the ground. The flight of the smaller species, such as the Rock Pratincole (*Glareola nuchalis*), is more erratic.

Coursers tend to fly with more sustained, generally rather rapid, wingbeats, but most usually prefer to run away from danger rather than fly, unless hard pressed; some species have characteristic panels of contrasting white or rufous in the secondaries, and sometimes also the primary flight-feathers, allowing easy identification in the field. The flight of members of the genus *Cursorius* is characterized by quick, jerky wingbeats like those of a small plover, though the wingbeats of the Cream-coloured Courser appear leisurely but powerful when migrating, while the Indian Courser can easily evade capture in flight by a falcon. The Double-banded Courser tends to fly more buoyantly, rather like a lapwing, while members of the genus *Rhinoptilus* are altogether more sluggish birds, taking wing reluctantly and looking more like owls in flight. The flight of the Egyptian Plover is fast and low with flicking wingbeats; the black and white wing pattern is particularly striking, the birds often holding the wing open briefly on landing, usually as a display to the mate or young.

Adult plumage in the family, chiefly in shades of brown and buff, is generally cryptic when birds are on the ground, except in the boldly patterned, aberrant Egyptian Plover. However, in flight most species show striking wing or tail patterns, which suddenly disappear when they land. It is tempting to compare this strategy

A typical courser in most respects, the Double-banded possesses several distinctive features all its own. The head is relatively small and rather dove-like, and the black bill is short, thin and hardly decurved at all and is never used for digging. Whereas most adult coursers have plain buff or brown backs, the Double-banded, like the Three-banded (Rhinoptilus cinctus), is typified by having the upper body and crown strongly scaled; all feathers have dark brown centres and broad pale fringes, visible here to perfection at close quarters. The Double-banded further differs from other coursers in its bold double breast band, while on the open wing it shows a bright cinnamon band across the trailing edge of the flight-feathers. This species lives in dry, open habitats on mainly sandy or stony substrates where its scaly plumage provides excellent camouflage. Often when it senses the presence of an intruder it will simply turn its back, thereby becoming well-nigh invisible. Another singularity is the fact that as many as eight subspecies are normally recognized, each differing slightly in coloration according to the type of habitat and colour of soil.

[Smutsornis africanus traylori, Etosha National Park, Namibia. Photo: Günter Ziesler]

With its unique breeding habits and unmistakable plumage, the Egyptian Plover is an aberrant species very different from other glareolids. A bird of broad lowland tropical rivers with sandbars, it habitually covers its eggs with sand on leaving the nest and even young chicks are periodically buried in sand during their first 3-4 weeks. During the hottest hours of the day the parents soak their belly feathers every few minutes and use them to keep the eggs or chicks cool. This ploy is useful in times of danger as it permits the conspicuously plumaged parents to retreat to a safe distance, leaving the eggs or chicks both hidden and protected from the sun.

[*Pluvianus aegyptius*, Africa.
Photo: Mike Lane/Aquila]

with that of those cryptic grasshoppers which burst into colour when they spread their wings to fly, and just as suddenly disappear as soon as they land, confusing potential predators. Indeed, the Bronze-winged Courser sits tight until the last moment, getting up right under the feet of an approaching human, and only flying 30-40 m before landing again and again remaining absolutely motionless. The Double-banded Courser becomes all but invisible when it presents its back to the observer, its basic plumage colour varying according to the soil colour of the region, and the species is doubtless often overlooked. In immature plumages pratincoles and coursers are mottled above, presumably to aid in camouflaging the young; adult plumage is attained within a year after hatching. Collared Pratincole chicks in Malawi at first are almost black and crouch in hippo footprints in an area of black mud; later on, when they become mottled brown, they move to areas of dappled shade.

The unique purplish iridescence on the wing of the Bronze-winged Courser is unexplained, though it has been suggested that as the species is chiefly nocturnal it may be used in display to catch the moonlight; more mundanely, it may simply help to reduce abrasion.

Living in hot, dry climates means that the plumage of Burchell's and other coursers may bleach as it wears, resulting in considerable variation in colour tone according to the age of the feathers. Moult in Collared and Black-winged Pratincoles is undertaken after breeding, but before migrating, to ensure that the feathers are in good condition for the journey.

Habitat

Coursers are predominantly birds of dry regions where the rainfall is less than about 800 mm per year, from *Acacia* woodlands and semi-arid scrub to true desert. Most prefer relatively low altitudes, though Burchell's Courser can be found in the Afro-alpine regions of South Africa at 2000-3000 m above sea-level. Several species are adapted to overgrazed and recently burnt grasslands and semi-desert, and may have benefited to some extent from human activities; however, this is offset by their extreme vulnerability to disturbance, so that most species have suffered a considerable decline in numbers and a decrease in range.

Three-banded and Bronze-winged Coursers, and to a lesser extent Temminck's Courser, are more or less woodland species, seldom occurring in open country. Temminck's and Bronze-winged overlap in habitat and distribution almost throughout Africa south of the Sahara. They are separated partly by the more nocturnal habits of the Bronze-winged Courser, and partly by the greater preference of Temminck's Courser for burnt and overgrazed areas. The Three-banded Courser is almost entirely confined to mopane (*Colophospermum mopane*) woodland in the southern parts of its range, though it may also occur less often in other open woodland types; within its northern distribution it lives mainly in sparse *Acacia* thornbush. Jerdon's Courser, like its presumed close relative the Bronze-winged Courser, has a specific preference for dry "forest" and scrub.

The remaining species of courser are all birds of open habitats with little or no woody vegetation, apart perhaps from low shrubby growth. Cream-coloured and Burchell's Coursers favour the most arid country, followed closely by Double-banded and Indian Coursers. Within a given area, the degree of competition between species of courser is reduced by differences in habitat occupation: on the Wembere Steppe of East Africa, for example, the barest parts are occupied by the Double-banded Courser, the rather less bare parts by Temminck's Courser and the scrub zones by the Three-banded Courser.

Pratincoles and the Egyptian Plover are all more or less closely associated with inland waters or, more rarely, estuaries. Even the desert-nesting Australian Pratincole nests no more than 1-2 km from a water-filled pan or dam, as it needs to drink frequently. Most species are birds of riverine habitats, especially exposed rocks and sandbars. Sandbars are the preferred habitat of the Egyptian Plover and the Grey Pratincole, at least when breeding, when they may occur together; and the Small Pratincole of India is also an inhabitant of riverine sandbars. The Black-winged Pratincole is something of an exception among pratincoles in that it nests on the open steppes of central Eurasia and spends the non-breeding season in the steppes of sub-Saharan Africa, including the high open grasslands of the South African plateau region which approximate ecologically to a steppe habitat. However, it too frequents sandbanks along large African rivers, a habitat seldom used by Collared Pratincoles. On its breeding grounds, water may still be nearby, though it is not a prerequisite, and colonies may be as much as 10 km from the nearest wetland.

General Habits

Pratincoles are more or less gregarious at all times, and this includes when they are nesting, although solitary pairs are not unknown. Flocks of Black-winged Pratincoles formerly numbered tens of thousands of birds on the Russian steppes, even during breeding. As with most other pratincoles, the nests of this species are often deserted during the day while the birds repair to the nearest water to drink and bathe in numbers. The Australian Pratincole is also gregarious, but tends to nest in more widely scattered pairs 45-500 m apart on the open desert floor or on the shoreline of an inland lake.

Pratincoles are usually conspicuous birds, even when breeding. Members of a colony co-operate in defending their eggs and young against predators, attacking birds of prey with loud cries, and often successfully driving the raptor away. When approached by humans, the nesting birds perform elaborate injury-feigning displays, in which the striking black and white rump and tail patterns are flashed at the intruder.

Black-winged Pratincoles readily associate with other steppe species, especially the Northern Lapwing (*Vanellus vanellus*), and when nesting the Grey Pratincole may associate with skimmers and terns, as well as Egyptian Plovers. All species are highly sociable outside the breeding season, and flocks, sometimes numbering hundreds or thousands of birds, may join other gregarious waterbirds, such as terns, plovers and other charadriiforms. Collared Pratincoles sometimes mix with Black-winged or Oriental Pratincoles, while the latter species sometimes associates with Oriental Plovers (*Charadrius veredus*) in Australia, or, more rarely, with Australian Pratincoles. Rock and Grey Pratincoles occasionally feed together. When the rivers are in flood in West Africa, flocks of 300-500 Grey Pratincoles gather at Lake Chad and in coastal habitats near Lagos, in Nigeria; whereas their close relatives in India, Small Pratincoles, frequently feed at dusk in the company of swifts and bats.

Among the coursers, members of the genus *Cursorius* are somewhat gregarious, usually in flocks of fewer than 20 individuals, though the Cream-coloured Courser may occur in flocks of 25-30, while Temminck's Courser is said to form flocks of as many as 40 birds. Significantly, these are the species of the more arid habitats, and flocking may enable the birds to exploit patchy food resources more easily. In contrast, the *Smutsornis* and *Rhinoptilus* coursers are usually found singly, in pairs or in family groups of 3-4 birds, seldom of 5-6 birds. They are often highly cryptic and inconspicuous, especially by day. Unlike pratincoles, they seldom advertise their presence by flying about, and they lack elaborate distraction displays when nesting. The inconspicuousness of these coursers, especially those of woodland habitats, is further enhanced by their being largely crepuscular or nocturnal, birds remaining standing, but immobile, in the shelter of scrub during the heat of the day. The Bronze-winged Courser, if approached, will crouch facing the observer; it rests in the same area on successive days. Competition with lapwings (*Vanellus*) is avoided by the larger coursers by their adoption of largely nocturnal habits. Although coursers of open country are generally somewhat less secretive, they too show appropriate cryptic behaviour: for instance, the Cream-coloured Courser displays a natural curiosity and will crane its neck when curious, but when crouched it too becomes well camouflaged.

Many of the pratincoles are also more active at dawn and dusk, spending the heat of the day resting against an appropriate background: Grey and Small Pratincoles are superbly camouflaged when at rest on sandbanks, as too are the larger pratincoles on dried mud. Rock Pratincoles roost by day, huddled together on rocks, but in the early morning and late afternoon they swarm into the sky to feed on aerial insects. Similarly, the Small Pratincole is especially active towards dusk; when not feeding, it spends much time resting, either standing or sitting in habitual resting spots. A vagrant Oriental Pratincole in New Zealand adopted a typical daily regime, catching shore-flies on the ground between 07:00 and 08:20; later in the day most of its foraging was in the air, but it spent the middle of day roosting on mudflats. The Australian Pratincole regularly flies on moonlit nights, especially when migrating.

Birds living in these hot environments adopt a variety of strategies to survive the high temperatures. The adult Australian Pratincole never seeks shelter from the sun, even when the ambient shade temperature reaches 46°C, but because it drinks frequently it can afford to use water freely to promote heat loss through evaporation; it also pants when overheated. The chick can not drink but has active salt glands to allow for the excretion of excess salt with minimal fluid loss. The Double-banded Courser uses wing-spreading to lose heat, and more generally the long-legged coursers are able to lose heat through their legs, which can be particularly important during incubation (see Breeding).

The Australian Pratincole bobs its head and tail, and indulges in various forms of comfort behaviour, such as direct head-scratching, yawning, one-sided wing and leg stretching, preening and body-shaking.

Voice

Pratincoles are noisy birds, with sharp, rather tern-like chipperings, uttered in flight, as they commute back and forth to their breeding colonies, or as large flocks pass over on migration. The larger species, such as the Collared and Madagascar Pratincoles (*Glareola ocularis*), tend to produce harsher notes, while the smaller species generally have more musical voices.

Coursers have a singularly plover-like manner of seeking their prey by running fast over the ground, stopping abruptly to stoop and peck when a suitable morsel is found, then running on once more. The preferred prey item of Burchell's Courser is harvester termites. It takes food from the surface but may also use its long, curved bill to dig for insects in loose sandy soil.

[Cursorius rufus, Africa. Photo: David Hosking/ FLPA]

Calling to reinforce their protest, both members of a pair of breeding Collared Pratincoles adopt an unequivocally antagonistic attitude towards a Pied Avocet (Recurvirostra avosetta) that has strayed too close to their nest-site or chicks for comfort. When dealing with a human intruder, pratincoles are past-masters at the art of subterfuge and will lure the person away from a danger zone using a variety of display strategies, one of the most frequent being injury-feigning.

[Glareola pratincola pratincola, Doñana National Park, Spain. Photo: Günter Ziesler]

Grey Pratincoles are strongly vocal, communicating with liquid contact notes and a trilling song, as they wheel about in the air in noisy flocks. The Small Pratincole has a high-pitched rolled call, and the beautiful trilling song of the Rock Pratincole is usually uttered in flight, but also at times by birds standing on rocks. The flight call of the Australian Pratincole is a distinctive shrill sweet whistle. Pratincole alarm calls are loud and sharp.

Coursers are generally less vocal and have rather harsher and more grating calls. They often call in flight, especially the members of *Cursorius*, and the grating calls of these species can be heard at a great height as the birds migrate at night. Some courser calls have been likened to the sound of a rusty hinge and a soft rattle, and other notes are sandpiper-like. However, the calls of the Double-banded Courser, often heard on moonlit nights, are altogether more musical than those of other coursers, including a plaintive, mellow "peeu-wee" and a sharp "wik-wik" on take-off. The Bronze-winged and Three-banded Coursers are also vocal mainly at night, the "wicky-wicky-wicky-wick" song of the latter even having been confused with the song of a nightjar (*Caprimulgus*).

Food and Feeding

The coursers and the Egyptian Plover catch all their food on the ground, whereas the pratincoles take much of theirs while on the wing, whence they receive their alternative English name, little used today, of swallow-plover.

The food of all glareolids is principally insects, and larger insects such as locusts and beetles are especially favoured. Although pratincoles forage mostly in flight, they will catch insects on the ground as well. The Australian Pratincole is especially adept at this: it has a unique method of trapping ground prey by extending a wing to stop the prey from escaping, before catching it in the bill. The way in which pratincoles capitalize on swarms of locusts is well described in an early account, by A. Haagner and R. H. Ivy, of a flock of Black-winged Pratincoles feeding on these insects in South Africa in the first decade of the present century: "In January, 1906, at Brandfort, Orange River Colony, a large flock of these birds were busy making a morning meal off a swarm of locusts. The sun had not yet warmed the insects up to a proper degree of activity, and the birds had in consequence a fairly easy time of it. Flying in a crescent-shaped flock they would bear down on the insects and sweep over them with the effect of putting them on the wing. As soon as this was accomplished and the insects were about 2 or 3 feet [60-90 cm] from the ground, the flock of birds wheeled with the rapidity of thought, the outer edges of the crescent converging to the centre, and enclosing the insects in a living circle. The startled locusts, in their half lethargic condition, immediately settled again amidst a perfect hail of dropping wings, and the birds would repeat the manoeuvre."

Collared Pratincoles may occur in flocks of several thousand, accompanying herds of lechwe (*Kobus leche*) in Zambia, and feeding on insects disturbed by the grazing mammals. Similarly, Rock Pratincoles have been recorded feeding in hundreds around street lamps in the centre of Livingstone, Zambia, in October and November. Pratincoles are opportunists, taking advantage of temporary insect swarms, a favourite food being the winged termites which perform a mass emergence before rains. Pratincoles are often crepuscular feeders.

Coursers may add molluscs and seeds to their insect diet, although the ingestion of seeds may be fortuitous. They catch their food on the ground in a very plover-like fashion by running rapidly, stopping abruptly, pecking at the food item and running on again. The genus *Cursorius* is equipped with a longish, curved bill which is used for digging for insects, probably mainly larvae, in soft sandy soil. Differences in body size and in bill shape may determine the type of prey eaten, and therefore help to avoid competition in those species which occupy the same habitat. There are also differences in the timing of daily activity, some species being more nocturnal than others, and thus exploiting a different range of insect species.

Both pratincoles and coursers take relatively large insects, including locusts, large tenebrionid and dung beetles up to 25 mm and dragonflies up to 80 mm in body length, and even sometimes small lizards and scorpions. Chicks may be fed on insect larvae.

Pratincoles of all species drink frequently, though both they and coursers have functional nasal glands for the excretion of excess salt. This function is especially useful in coursers which are not known to drink and must obtain all their water require-

The Australian Pratincole is an enigmatic species thought to form a link between coursers and pratincoles. In general appearance and behaviour like a pratincole, it has some structural features in common with coursers, notably long legs and a short, unforked tail. It breeds in small, loose colonies in semi-desert habitats inland, but never very far from water, for it needs to drink frequently. No pretence of a nest is made: the 2-3 eggs are laid directly on the bare, often stony ground. More remarkably, though, the chicks may quite literally go to earth when danger threatens, by seeking refuge in a rabbit burrow; the adults are not recorded as ever joining them underground.

[*Stiltia isabella*, Australia. Photo: Hans & Judy Beste/ Animals Animals]

ments from their insect food, and must therefore be able to process the body fluids of their prey in order to extract the greatest amount of water.

Breeding

Although the nesting habits of some glareolids, such as the Egyptian Plover, the Double-banded Courser, the Collared Pratincole and the Rock Pratincole are very well known, those of most other species have been poorly studied.

Pratincoles all breed in loose colonies, sometimes of just a few pairs, at other times of hundreds of pairs, though the nests are usually several metres apart, and a small territory is defended. In the Australian Pratincole, intraspecific aggression is shown by territorial adults with a head-down threatening run toward an intruding bird. Coursers, on the other hand, are always solitary nesters.

The Rock Pratincole performs a display flight in which birds glide for several seconds with both wings raised high above the back. At dusk great numbers fly round low over the surface of the water, occasionally uttering a weak piping call. Greeting displays involve holding the collar flared to show the maximum expanse of chestnut for as long as 20 seconds; the head is also bobbed up and down, with the bill slightly open. Courtship in the Collared Pratincole includes a wings-spread, tail-up, head-bowed posture, and a stiff-winged display flight.

Courtship in coursers is not well known and appears to be rather simple. The Cream-coloured Courser has a poorly developed circular or gliding display flight in which the male flies diagonally up with shallow, rapid wingbeats, then planes down, uttering a warbling plover-like cry. Copulation is initiated by the female, as she crouches flat and is approached by the male with a pattering foot action and upright gait; he mounts the female, with his wings outspread and fluttering. Other displays of coursers have not been specifically linked with pair formation and need detailed study.

The glareolids appear to be typical waders in their nesting habits. The nest in all cases is on the ground, sometimes in a shallow scrape, or in a hollow on a rock. The clutch consists of 1-4 eggs, which are typically cryptic, having a dull whitish to yellowish or greyish ground colour, spotted, blotched and streaked more or less heavily in shades of black and grey. They tend to be rounded in shape, except in the case of the Three-banded Courser, which has rather elongate eggs. This species and the Egyptian Plover are unique in the family in incubating their eggs partially buried in the sand of the nest scrape. Perhaps the rounded shape of the exposed eggs of most species assists in their camouflage by making the eggs look very much like stones; this is certainly the case for those species of courser which nest on stony ground, as well as the Australian Pratincole. The very dark, heavily marked eggs of Burchell's and Temminck's Coursers confer excellent concealment when laid among tufts of burnt stubble or among sun-darkened antelope droppings.

Clutch size in the glareolids follows the pattern of other members of the Charadrii: those nesting at higher latitudes lay larger clutches than those nesting in the tropics, and those nesting in the most arid habitats lay the smallest clutches of all. For example, the Black-winged Pratincole, which nests in the steppes of southern Russia, as a rule lays 3-4 eggs, European-nesting Collared Pratincoles lay 3 eggs, while African-breeding populations of this species usually lay only 1 or 2 eggs. Coursers, most of which are birds of arid regions in tropical latitudes, seldom lay more than 2 eggs per clutch. The Double-banded Courser of Africa occupies some very arid regions indeed and lays only a single egg; however, it compensates for this small clutch size by raising at least 2-3 broods a year. This is probably a mechanism for keeping the population fairly sparse at any given time in a habitat of limited carrying capacity.

The roles of the sexes in incubation are known for most species, and appear to be about equal. The frequency of changeover at the nest depends to some extent on air temperatures: under very hot conditions, nest relief is relatively frequent, as often as every 15-20 minutes, but in milder conditions each parent may incubate the eggs for one to four hours at a time. The Cream-coloured Courser appears to be unusual in this regard, since an incubating parent may have to sit unrelieved for as long as six hours at a stretch. In mild conditions the eggs may even be left unattended, their camouflaged coloration giving them the necessary protection from predators. Nest-relief behaviour in coursers is similar to that of many other waders: the departing parent tosses small stones or other objects toward the nest scrape in a movement called side-throwing.

One of the main problems to be solved by those species nesting in hot environments is how to keep the eggs from overheating, which would kill the embryos. Adjustments of body posture in coursers help to regulate the temperature of the eggs. When the air temperature is well below normal body temperature, the eggs are incubated in the normal way, in contact with the brood patch and covered with the ventral feathers. As ambient temperatures rise to about 35°C, the incubating courser exposes its legs as areas for heat loss, and may merely crouch over the clutch to shade the eggs. When temperatures exceed about 36°C, the eggs may still only be shaded and the sitting bird will pant to keep cool. Above about 40°C, however, overheating of the egg becomes a real problem, and the incubating parent will again incubate the egg, panting as it does so, thereby shielding the eggs from direct radiation and withdrawing heat from the eggs by means of its own evaporative cooling mechanisms.

Pratincoles appear not to expose their legs or shade their eggs during incubation, as coursers do. This may have something to do with their shorter legs, but even the long-legged Australian Pratincole behaves in this regard just like other pratincoles. Off-duty pratincole parents do, however, use their legs as a heat loss centre, since they stand with the legs exposed to the air, but shaded by the body, during the midday hours, often on a raised stone or clod where the ambient temperature is 3-4°C lower than at ground level.

The purpose of covering the eggs with nesting material by the Egyptian Plover and the Three-banded Courser is not always clear: in most instances it appears to be for concealment only, but in the case of the Egyptian Plover there may be the secondary function of helping with temperature regulation of the eggs. When leaving the nest, the Egyptian Plover uses its bill to gather sand over the eggs until they are completely buried, with a 2-3 mm covering of sand on top; they are sometimes covered even while the adult is sitting on the nest, though it may at times scrape the sand from the tops of the eggs, using its feet. At night the eggs are uncovered for about two thirds of their volume and incubated continuously. During the hottest hours of the day, from about 10:00 hours to 16:00 hours, each incubating parent frequently soaks its belly feathers in the nearby river and returns to sit on the covered eggs, thereby keeping them surrounded by wet sand. In this way the eggs are kept at a mean temperature of around 37·5°C throughout the day, even when ambient temperatures reach 45°C or more.

The Egyptian Plover's chicks hatch under the sand and leave the nest scrape within a day of hatching. When danger threatens, the parents will cover chicks of up to the age of three weeks with sand, using the bill as in egg-covering. They may also wet the sand over the chicks with their soaked belly feathers. Although it has been claimed that the Egyptian Plover regurgitates water over the buried chicks, this appears not to be the case. Since adult Egyptian Plovers are highly conspicuously coloured, the covering and wetting of eggs and chicks allows them to be left concealed and protected from the sun for considerable periods of time in the face of danger, while the parents run or fly away to a safe distance.

Off-duty parents of Rock, Small and Collared Pratincoles may, like the Egyptian Plover, soak their belly feathers in water before flying back to relieve the incubating bird at the nest. Coursers do not do this, as they seldom have water nearby.

Egg-covering in the Three-banded Courser is also done with the bill. In all other Charadrii which cover their eggs, the feet are used for the task, so use of the bill is a glareolid feature, and points to the Egyptian Plover being a true glareolid. The eggs of the Three-banded Courser are incubated in a partly buried condition, usually with no more than a third of their volume showing above the sand of the nest scrape, which is filled by the parents, using a side-throwing action of the bill. Since this species usually nests under the shade of a small tree or bush, the function of egg-covering is probably more for concealment than for protection from the sun, but it is curious that this behaviour has not evolved in any other courser, possibly because most species of courser nest on hard soils, rather than sand.

Parental care in the glareolids is well developed. Injury-feigning behaviour at the nest or near young is developed only in the pratincoles, both *Glareola* and *Stiltia*, although some injury-feigning has also been noted in the Double-banded Courser. In such performances, the parent bird spreads its wings, collapses to the ground on bent legs, and often raises the wings or beats them noisily on the ground, either facing the intruder or moving away from the nest or young, at the same time exposing the conspicuous black and white rump and tail patterns so characteristic of pratincoles. This behaviour is extremely effective for luring predators away from the nest. False-sitting is also recorded in the Small Pratincole, in addition to the broken-wing display. Predator avoidance in those pratincoles that nest next to water, such as the Rock Pratincole, is further enhanced by the ability of the young to jump into the water and swim away. Even very tiny chicks of only 2-3 days of age do this, and may leap into the rushing waters of a powerful rapid. Once they reach the safety of a rock, they clamber out and crouch in a crevice until danger has passed.

Coursers usually simply run from the nest or young, keeping a safe distance of 50-100 m from the predator. Sometimes a parent will give agitated alarm calls, but injury-feigning is not part of the coursers' behavioural repertoire, even though many possess conspicuous rump or wing patterns. In the face of disturbance by non-predatory large mammals, however, most species of courser will defend the nest by approaching the mammals with wings and tail spread and often also with the bill open. Sometimes the incubating parent may simply threaten the intruder with open bill, and wrists slightly parted from the body. False Nest-scraping or Mock-brooding are also adopted by Cream-coloured and Burchell's Coursers, as well as by the Egyptian Plover.

Part of parental behaviour in all glareolids involves feeding the young for their first few days or weeks of life. The young birds often adopt a refuge, most notably in the Australian Pratincole, which may use a rabbit burrow in which to hide. Parental care of the young ensures enhanced survival of the chicks, and almost certainly compensates for the small size of the clutch in most members of the family. Reduction of clutch size in birds, especially if food resources are few or unpredictable, is a sound evolutionary economy measure, which has been adopted with great success by the coursers.

Movements

The long wings of pratincoles allow them not only to spend much time foraging in the air, but also to migrate long distances. The Black-winged Pratincole has probably the longest migration of any glareolid, from the steppes of southern Eurasia to Chad, Ethiopia and as far as South Africa, a maximum straight-line distance of about 10,000 km. Prior to migration, both Collared and Black-winged Pratincoles gather at moulting sites in late summer. The entire population of the latter spends the non-breeding season in Africa south of the Sahara, moving southward on a broad front through Iran, Iraq, Turkey and the northern parts of the Arabian Peninsula, probably entering Africa across the Red Sea. Non-breeding flocks of Black-winged Pratincoles may number up to 10,000 birds. The apparent absence of this species from parts of its route, such as the Middle East and central Africa is a result of its flying very high over inhospitable desert and forest regions. The first birds to return to the breeding grounds in Russia and Kazakhstan do so in late April, the main body arriving in May.

The Eurasian populations of the Collared Pratincole, by contrast, overwinter mainly along the southern edge of the Sahara between Senegal and Ethiopia, overlapping in parts of this range with the two resident or nomadic African subspecies. Birds returning to their breeding grounds in Europe do so around both ends of the Mediterranean, arriving in April and May.

The third member of this group, the Oriental Pratincole, also undertakes a long migration from north China south to Australia, while vagrants have appeared many thousands of kilometres out of range in several parts of the world. After breeding in Aus-

tralia, the rather aberrant Australian Pratincole moves in the opposite direction, to winter in Indonesia and northern Australia, north and north-west of its breeding range.

Within Africa, the Rock Pratincole migrates from equatorial regions to more southerly nesting grounds on the Zambezi River and its tributaries, but not all populations of this species are migrants. Non-breeding birds of the more southerly subspecies *nuchalis* may occur together with populations of the northern race *liberiae* in October in West Africa. As with many other intra-African migrants, the exact movements of the Rock Pratincole still need to be worked out, but it appears to be a true medium distance migrant, with highly seasonal arrivals and departures. The Madagascar Pratincole breeds only in Madagascar, but the entire population then migrates to East Africa when not breeding, following the same strategy as the Madagascar Pond-heron (*Ardeola idae*). Non-breeding pratincoles of several species tend to wander, often in response to rainfall, seeking out and exploiting temporary food gluts.

Coursers are not generally migratory, but most are highly nomadic, moving about according to rainfall and feeding conditions. The same applies to the Egyptian Plover, which performs strictly local movements that are determined by changing water levels in its riverine habitat. The absence of a regular migratory tendency among most coursers is reflected in the relatively large number of geographical races in those species with a fairly wide distribution, such as the Cream-coloured and Double-banded Coursers of Africa, which have five and eight subspecies respectively, though many of the more northerly populations of the Cream-coloured Courser do migrate. Temminck's and Bronze-winged Coursers appear also to have migratory populations, since regular seasonal fluctuations in numbers are documented, but these movements are poorly known. It appears that some populations of Temminck's Coursers may migrate from the Sahel to southern Africa, while the Bronze-winged Courser, in the extreme south of its range is essentially a non-breeding visitor and in the extreme north only a breeding visitor.

The daily movements of pratincoles when breeding often follow a pattern. For instance, on occasion on mild days there may be a complete absence of adult Australian Pratincoles from the breeding colony at certain times of the day, when birds gather at the nearest water.

Relationship with Man

Collared and Black-winged Pratincoles have in the past both had some economic value for man. In the case of the former, eggs were collected on a commercial scale in Hungary until some breeding colonies were eliminated altogether and others became too small to be viable. Even as recently as the 1970's, egg-collectors still took large numbers of pratincole eggs, ostensibly for scientific reasons, but in reality as part of a large illegal "oology industry". The loss of clutches of eggs is unavoidable when farm machinery and implements are used to work the land. Again in Hungary, for instance, camomile (*Matricaria recutita*) flowers are gathered by means of a box-like tool fitted with a set of long tines in front, which destroys large numbers of eggs of all ground-nesting birds, yet the camomile crop is of such significant financial importance that the practice is unlikely to be discontinued.

The Black-winged Pratincole used to occur in far greater numbers in the past and may have had a significant impact on locust swarms, especially in southern Africa. Now, however, numbers of this magnificent bird have dwindled to the point at which they probably have little, if any, noticeable effect on locust numbers in their non-breeding quarters, though they may still have some value as predators of insect pests on their Russian and Kazakh breeding grounds. Indeed, in Africa pratincoles are sometimes known as "locust birds", along with the European White Stork (*Ciconia ciconia*), the Wattled Starling (*Creatophora cinerea*) and others. Again, in Australia the Oriental Pratincole is popularly known as "grasshopper bird" or "swarmer" for the same reason.

Members of this family appear to be palatable, as the Cape Verde race *exsul* of the Cream-coloured Courser was first discovered by Boyd Alexander, who reported that it was by no means bad eating. According to Bannerman: "he was unaware he was enjoying an interesting new subspecies for his dinner, for it took another 23 years before it was described as such"! Both Oriental and Australian Pratincoles are hunted in Indonesia for food.

Both pratincoles and coursers have great aesthetic value, and birdwatchers tend to place them high on their lists of special birds to see in the regions where they occur. Many species are notoriously tame, including such diverse members of the family as the Egyptian Plover, Australian Pratincole, Grey Pratincole

Pratincoles are gregarious birds, usually breeding in loose colonies; even when nesting, during the day they often leave their nests to gather in numbers at the nearest water source to drink and bathe. After the breeding season Collared Pratincoles assemble in flocks to moult at riversides, coasts and lagoons. Whereas birds of the Eurasian population, once they have completed their moult, fly south to winter in Africa south of the Sahara, the movements of African populations, like these birds, are apparently mainly on a local basis, although at present they remain imperfectly understood.

[*Glareola pratincola fuelleborni*, Chobe National Park, Botswana. Photo: Rafi Ben-Shahar/ Oxford Scientific Films]

and Double-banded Courser, which only serves to enhance their appeal.

An interesting and curious story is that of the so-called "Crocodile Bird", which has its origins in the visit of Herodotus to Egypt in 459 BC. His account of a small bird picking food from the teeth of a gaping crocodile referred, it has been suggested, to the Egyptian Plover. Whether or not this is so, the tale was further romanticized by A. Brehm in the nineteenth century and R. Meinertzhagen in the twentieth century, both of whom stated that they had personally seen the Egyptian Plover picking the teeth of crocodiles on more than one occasion. Meinertzhagen also implicated the Spur-winged Lapwing (*Vanellus spinosus*) in this behaviour, but no reliable observer since then has seen either bird species acting as a crocodile toothpick. Brehm and Meinertzhagen were recalling observations from their distant past, and therefore the accuracy of their statements can not be relied on. However, the myth has been perpetuated in the literature and needs finally to be laid to rest, unless contrary proof can be found.

Status and Conservation

Human impact on populations of glareolids is usually negative, and though only a single species is threatened, many are undergoing long-term declines.

The only threatened member of the family is Jerdon's Courser of eastern India, which was considered extinct for much of the present century, until its rediscovery in 1986. Probably never very numerous, its small populations were pushed to the edge of extinction by disturbance and overgrazing, two human activities which have repeatedly acted against the welfare of the world's wildlife. Jerdon's Courser was first described in 1848, having been obtained by T. C. Jerdon in about that year from "hilly country above the Eastern Ghats...in rocky and undulating ground with thin forest jungle." It was recorded again in 1871 in Andhra Pradesh above the Godavari River in similar habitat. The last authentic sighting, in 1900, was in the Pennar River Valley near Anantapur, a linear distance of no more than 170 kilometres from the original site. A preliminary survey of this valley in June, July and October 1985 in the districts of Anantapur, Cuddapah

and Nellore revealed no trace of the species. However, a subsequent visit in January 1986 to the more easterly parts of the Pennar Valley was successful: a specimen of Jerdon's Courser was caught alive near Reddipalli just north of the Pennar River. After 86 years of presumed extinction, the species was rediscovered! A nocturnal survey in the same area that night revealed two more birds. Although not extinct, Jerdon's Courser must still rate as one of the world's rarest birds. Its occurrence in Anantapur in the upper reaches of the Pennar Valley rests on presumed sightings in the past, while the Nellore region downstream from Reddipalli is subject to much human disturbance and the chances of the future survival there of Jerdon's Courser must be slim. However, its nocturnal habits have undoubtedly contributed to the long period with no sightings. Rediscovery came just in time to divert an irrigation scheme planned to pass through the area. Subsequently, two reserves have been designated for the species with a third also proposed. It is hoped that further surveys may yet reveal the continued presence of the species in more than its tiny currently known range.

Though not yet a Red Data Book species, the Black-winged Pratincole is now ranked as near-threatened, primarily as a result of the conversion of steppes to arable agriculture and the increase of Rooks (*Corvus frugilegus*) and other corvids in the area. It urgently needs full legal protection in its breeding areas, while practical measures that might be adopted include the regulation of grazing at permanent colonies and the sheltering of individual nests with metal frames to prevent trampling and predation; also, where nesting on ploughed land, pratincole-friendly farming methods need to be encouraged; and Rook numbers may also need to be controlled in places. In Africa, too, locust control programmes may be having an adverse effect on this species.

The Collared Pratincole is declining, at least in Europe, again through loss of suitable habitat. It also shows poor breeding success because of high levels of disturbance from agricultural operations and other sources, while in its African wintering quarters water-management programmes in the Sahel are dramatically changing the structure of the original habitat, together with pesticide use on newly planted rice fields. Suitable habitat needs to be maintained in both the European breeding and African non-breeding ranges. In addition, it is to be hoped that pratincole-friendly farming methods might be adopted in western Europe under the new Agri-environment Regulation of the European Union, whereby farmers would receive financial help for adopting environmentally beneficial practices.

In eastern Europe, in years gone by, much of the former breeding habitat of this species was kept suitable by huge flocks of free-ranging long-horned cattle and sheep, which kept the vegetation short on the saline soils so favoured by the pratincoles. Since the sharp decline in the keeping of these traditional breeds and their replacement with more productive but less hardy stock, as well as the replacement of draught animals with mechanized farm machinery, the vegetation of saline steppes has been allowed to grow too tall. Furthermore, the steppes have increasingly been put under artificial fertilizers and irrigation, rendering them inhospitable for the pratincoles. In addition, the use of both insecticides and herbicides has reduced their insect food. All these factors, together with the formerly indiscriminate collection of eggs, have led to the disappearance of the Collared Pratincole from many of its east European breeding sites. Since the early 1970's, however, measures have been taken to declare nature reserves in parts of Austria and Hungary, such as the Hortobágy, where pratincoles and other ground-nesting birds like terns, plovers, lapwings, avocets, thick-knees and larks can breed successfully. The maintenance of these breeding places by the reintroduction of grazing ungulates is part of the management programme and gives hope for the future.

A major threat to certain river-dwelling pratincoles, and to a lesser extent the Egyptian Plover, is the damming of Africa's rivers. The main effects are the flooding of breeding habitats, such as exposed rocks and sandbars, above the dam, and unpredictable flooding regimes below the dam. Indeed, floods may threaten breeding colonies when water levels would under natural conditions be low; such effects are especially severe in narrow reaches of the rivers, where waters are deep and the water levels change most markedly. It is possibly for this reason that the Egyptian Plover has disappeared from Egypt, where formerly it was quite common in the upper reaches of the Nile; there seem to be no reliable sightings from this area for more than half a century.

A similar fate may befall the Rock Pratincole on the Zambezi and other large African rivers. Although it occurred formerly in the Kariba Basin of the Zambezi Valley, it no longer does so because of the damming of the river to form Lake Kariba. Two further dams are planned for the Zambezi, one upstream and one downstream of Lake Kariba: the Mupata Gorge Dam below Kariba will flood a section of the middle Zambezi River where about 73% of that zone's population of Rock Pratincoles breeds; while the Batoka Gorge Dam above Kariba will flood sites on the upper Zambezi below Victoria Falls, where some 6% of the population of the upper Zambezi nests. Most potential breeding sites on the Zambezi are therefore below Kariba. Conservation of high-density breeding sites is essential, since over 90% of Rock Pratincoles recorded on the upper and middle Zambezi occur along only about 17% of its length. The threat from direct human disturbance appears to be quite small because of the relatively low human population density in the Rock Pratincole's breeding areas.

In general, however, most coursers and pratincoles either seem to be able to adapt fairly well to man's activities, or else inhabit regions, such as deserts and remote woodlands, where human population densities are very low. Nevertheless, the game reserves and nature reserves of Africa are important refuges for the woodland species, notably Temminck's, Bronze-winged and Three-banded Coursers. Temminck's Courser is the most catholic in its choice of habitat, and therefore the least vulnerable. The Bronze-winged Courser's preference for *Acacia* and other types of wooded savanna brings it into some conflict with domestic livestock, notably cattle and goats, but it seems to be holding its own, while the mopane country favoured by the Three-banded Courser is usually very thinly populated by humans and their stock, which means that this courser is not in any immediate danger.

The western populations of Burchell's Courser appear to be maintaining their numbers in their very arid habitats, but in the

Sadly, many glareolid species are currently in a state of decline. However, the only one believed to be in imminent danger is Jerdon's Courser. This bird, inhabiting rocky hilly country in Andhra Pradesh, India, was thought to be extinct until rediscovered in 1986, after having remained unrecorded since 1900! Recent observations from six localities have confirmed its continued survival, but the present known range is of only 2000 km². It can only be hoped that further searches will discover the species in other similar areas. Meanwhile it must rank as one of the world's rarest birds.

[*Rhinoptilus bitorquatus*, Andhra Pradesh, India. Photo: S. Cook]

more easterly parts of their range their habitat has suffered from agricultural change, leading to a marked decline, especially in the last 30 years. One adverse effect in the high grasslands of South Africa is a change in livestock grazing regimes, which results in the animals being moved around more frequently than previously, causing increased disturbance to the birds, especially when they are nesting. A similar adverse impact is being experienced by cranes and other ground-nesting birds in these grasslands. Ironically, though, desertification caused by overgrazing by sheep and goats in the drier parts of southern Africa and in the Sahel has probably favoured the spread of the Double-banded Courser in the south and the Cream-coloured Courser in the north, though properly quantified information on these effects is, however, wanting. On the debit side, the population of Cream-coloured Coursers on Fuerteventura, in the Canary Islands, is under threat from disturbance by tourist development and military exercises, leading to habitat damage. Many sites holding glareolids are protected at the regional level, but in practice these are often poorly managed.

An interesting conservation measure adopted by some enlightened sugar farmers in the coastal regions of northern Natal is the ploughing of land immediately before the return of breeding flocks of Collared Pratincoles. The bare soil of such places provides suitable nesting substrate in a habitat so modified by the planting of sugar cane as to be otherwise totally uninhabitable by the birds. The ploughed land is then left unplanted until the birds have bred and their young are on the wing. It is to be hoped that in time such positive measures may be adopted elsewhere, for the benefit of wildlife, and also for those who delight in it.

General Bibliography

Ballmann (1979), Barbosa (1993), Björklund (1994), Bock (1964), Brown & Ward (1990), Burton (1974), Carroll, R.L. (1988), Christian *et al.* (1992b), Chu (1995), Clancey *et al.* (1991), Cooper (1984), Dunning (1993), Gochfeld *et al.* (1984), Hayman *et al.* (1986), Jehl (1968b), Maclean (1972a, 1974, 1975, 1985a, 1985b), Meinertzhagen (1927), Olson & Steadman (1979), Peters (1934), Reynolds (1975b), Rosair & Cottridge (1995), Rose & Scott (1994), Sibley & Ahlquist (1990), Sibley & Monroe (1990), Snow (1978), Strauch (1976, 1978), Timmermann (1954-1955), Yudin (1965).

1

ssp *cursor*

2

ssp *littoralis*

3

4

5

ssp *africanus*

ssp *traylori*

6

ssp *gracilis*

ssp *hartingi*

ssp *seebohmi*

7

ssp *cinctus*

8

9

PLATE 33

inches 5

cm 13

Subfamily CURSORIINAE

Genus *PLUVIANUS* Vieillot, 1816

1. Egyptian Plover

Pluvianus aegyptius

French: Pluvian fluviatile   **German**: Krokodilwächter   **Spanish**: Pluvial
Other common names: Crocodile-bird, Crocodile-plover, Egyptian Courser

Taxonomy. *Charadrius ægyptius* Linnaeus, 1758, Egypt.
Affinities uncertain: sometimes placed in its own family (Pluvianidae), or subfamily (Pluvianinae), or regarded as closer to subfamily Glareolinae. Birds from N Angola and Zaire somewhat smaller, sometimes regarded as race *angolae*, but variation is clinal and this form poorly defined, so not normally recognized as separate race. Monotypic.
Distribution. Sub-Saharan Africa from Senegal to Ethiopia, S to N Zaire and Uganda and narrowly into the lower basin of R Congo (Zaire) and extreme N Angola; formerly N along R Nile into Egypt, where now extinct.

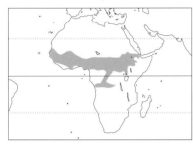

Descriptive notes. 19-21 cm; 73-92 g. Centre of back, crown, broad eyestripe and breast band black, edged with white; supercilium white; wing-coverts and tail blue-grey, latter tipped white; striking black and white wing pattern formed by white on coverts and flight-feathers, contrasting with black diagonal bar and black-tipped primaries; underwing brilliant white, also crossed by black diagonal bar; rest of underparts cream to tawny buff; bill black; legs and feet blue-grey. Sexes alike. Juvenile like adult, but lesser and median coverts rusty, and feathers of back edged brownish.
Habitat. Large lowland tropical rivers with sand and gravel bars; generally avoids heavily forested regions and also estuarine waters. Tame, often occurring around human settlements near rivers, e.g. at Tompari Ferry, Sierra Leone, in area without sandbanks feeds on slipway, dodging pedestrians quite unconcernedly.
Food and Feeding. Worms, molluscs, aquatic insects (both adults and larvae), small flies; said also to eat seeds and particles of scavenged fish. Food obtained by variety of methods, including surface-picking, catching flying insects on the run (these sometimes flushed by bird running with wings slightly spread), stalking insects, probing or foot-scratching in damp sand, turning over stones and occasionally bill-dipping in water. Occasionally seeks food on open ground away from water. Drinks water directly. No reliable evidence of assertion that species picks food from the jaws of crocodiles (see page 374).
Breeding. Jan to Apr or May N of equator when water levels low; season not recorded in S parts of range. Solitary nester. Eggs laid in deep scrape on exposed sandbank in riverbed. Usually 2-3 eggs (1-4); incubation 28-31 days, by both sexes; eggs partly or completely buried during incubation, covered by parents on departure, invariably using bill, and cooled during incubation by wetting sand with soaked belly feathers every few minutes in heat of day. Chick speckled black and buff above; broad black stripe through eye and down sides of hindneck; broad white band from above and behind each eye to join wide white patch on nape; black occipital stripe; white below and on wings; bill and legs as in adult; white nape patch very conspicuous when chick running; when danger threatens and chick crouches this recognition mark disappears. Chicks leave nest on first day, but may be buried with sand by parents while still in nest scrape or away from scrape until 3-4 weeks old; in heat of day buried chicks are cooled by wet belly plumage of brooding parent; chicks start feeding selves after c. 7 days; estimated age of fledging c. 30-35 days.
Movements. Local movements in response to changes of water levels are common, but longer distance migrations also recorded from Ethiopia to Sudan (600-800 km) and in Nigeria and Chad where birds make irregular northward movements during wet season, May-Oct, when rivers flood; similarly, no records in Sierra Leone from Jun to late Nov. Moves in flocks of up to 60 birds. During floods, birds may appear in unexpected habitats. Vagrant to Canary Is, Libya, Israel. Bird recorded in Poland in Oct-Nov 1991 presumed escape.
Status and Conservation. Not globally threatened. Appears to be common over most of range. In 19th century numerous everywhere along R Nile S of Cairo, Egypt, where it became extinct in early 20th century. Not uncommon in Ghana and Sierra Leone; in former, often occurs in flocks of 10 to 20 birds. Damming of rivers, causing change in habitat, is probably main threat.
Bibliography. Bannerman (1931, 1951), Beaman (1994), Britton, P. L. (1980), Butler (1931), Cramp & Simmons (1983), Dowsett & Forbes-Watson (1993), Elgood *et al.* (1994), Étchécopar & Hüe (1964), Goodman *et al.* (1989), Gore (1990), Grimes (1987), Howell (1978, 1979, 1983b, 1984), Hüe & Étchécopar (1970), Lippens & Wille (1976), Louette (1981), Mackworth-Praed & Grant (1957, 1962, 1970), Meinertzhagen (1959), Paz (1987), Pinto (1983), Reichenow (1900-1901), Richards & Boswall (1985), Rutgers & Norris (1970), Serle (1939a), Seymour & Ackerman (1980), Short *et al.* (1990), Steinbacher (1981), Tyrberg (1993), Urban *et al.* (1986), Zielinski (1992a, 1992b).

Genus *CURSORIUS* Latham, 1790

2. Cream-coloured Courser

Cursorius cursor

French: Courvite isabelle   **German**: Rennvogel   **Spanish**: Corredor Sahariano
Other common names: Desert Courser

Taxonomy. *Charadrius cursor* Latham, 1787, Kent, England.
Forms superspecies with *C. rufus*, *C. temminckii* and *C. coromandelicus*, although overlap in range of *C. temminckii* with present species and *C. rufus* indicates that *C. temminckii* and *C. coromandelicus* may represent a separate superspecies. Sometimes considered to include *C. rufus*. Smaller, darker races *somalensis* and *littoralis* of E Africa are more distinct and may actually belong to *C. rufus*. Some

intergradation between races *exsul*, *cursor* and *bogolubovi*. Canary Is population sometimes racially distinguished as *bannermani*, but separation from *cursor* dependent on size alone and probably not significant; proposed races *dahlakensis* and *meruensis* nowadays included in races *cursor* and *littoralis* respectively. Five subspecies normally recognized.
Subspecies and Distribution.
C. c. bogolubovi Zarudny, 1885 - SE Turkey through E Iran to SW Afghanistan, S Pakistan and NW India.
C. c. cursor (Latham, 1787) - Canary Is, N Africa, Arabian Peninsula and Socotra; winters S to Sahel, N Kenya and Saudi Arabia.
C. c. exsul Hartert, 1920 - Cape Verde Is.
C. c. somalensis Shelley, 1885 - Eritrea, E Ethiopia and Somalia.
C. c. littoralis Erlanger, 1905 - extreme SE Sudan, through N Kenya to S Somalia.

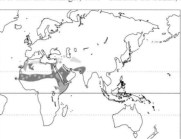

Descriptive notes. 19-22 cm; 115-156 g (*bogolubovi*), 102-119 g (*cursor*), 93-107 g (*littoralis*). Above pale sandy buff or sandy rufous with striking black stripe from behind eye to nape, bordered above by white stripe, with hindcrown blue-grey; below pale sandy, lower belly white; upperwing has black primaries and primary coverts, sharply contrasting with sandy secondary coverts and secondaries; underwing black with narrow white trailing edge to secondaries; bill black; legs and feet yellowish white. Plumage subject to bleaching and wear. Pale belly, lacking sharp contrast with rest of underparts, separates from other members of genus.
Juvenile finely mottled above and below with buff and black; head pattern inconspicuous; primaries tipped buff. Races distinguished on shades of difference in coloration, presence and extent of darker colouring on belly, and on size, though this last feature is clinal; *exsul* darker with reddish sand-coloured upperparts and breast. In size and structure, the smaller, duller E African races are closer to *C. rufus*, and they show same pale brown-grey underwing-coverts contrasting with black outer half of underwing, and broader white trailing edge to secondaries.
Habitat. Arid, open, usually fairly flat, warm to hot desert and semi-desert, both stony and sandy, including dune troughs, with or without low sparse vegetation; also short-grass and gravel plains, saltflats, semi-arid ground among sparse *Acacia*, semi-cultivated steppe and gravel roads. Usually occurs below 800 m. In Kenya, 87% of population occupies semi-arid areas with rainfall less than 500 mm a year. In N Kenya wintering nominate *cursor* found in sparsely vegetated or bare desert, whereas *littoralis* occurs in well vegetated thornbush savanna.
Food and Feeding. Mostly adult and larval insects, including beetles, grasshoppers, ants, flies; also molluscs, isopods, arachnids, seeds. Feeds by running over ground and stopping to pick up prey which is swallowed whole, even large insects up to 8 cm long. Sometimes catches locusts in flight. May dig for food using bill.
Breeding. Mar-Jun in N Africa, Mauritania, Israel and Iran, May-Jul in Turkmenistan, Apr in Pakistan, Apr-May in Jordan, Feb-May in Cape Verde Is, Dec-May in Senegal, Apr-Sept in Kenya; small chicks in NW India in Feb and Jul; possibly double-brooded. Nest is shallow unlined scrape on bare ground; in Kenya, eggs surrounded by antelope droppings. Usually 2 eggs; incubation 18-19 days, by both sexes. Chick finely mottled sandy rufous and white above; crown streaked dusky; below white, washed buff on breast. Adults recorded mock-brooding to distract observer from presence of chick; fledging c. 30 days. First breeding at one year old.
Movements. Nominate race makes extensive movements, much of N population apparently crossing Sahara for winter, when range extends to Sahel, Sudan and N Kenya; 30 birds of race *cursor* found in Jan-Feb 1987 along 165 km stretch of E shore of L Turkana, N Kenya; scarce in N Sahara at this season; main northward movement in Sahara in Mar-Apr, sometimes into Jun; movement of c. 1000 birds over front of a few kilometres reported in Mar in Tunisia. Winters in W Negev Desert, Israel, Dec and Jan; immigration into Saudi Arabia in winter, probably from Middle East, when numbers increase and birds spread into deserts of Nafud and Empty Quarter. Breeding birds arrive Jordan early Mar and depart late Jun; then late autumn arrival of small numbers of migrants. Race *littoralis* present in Kenya Sept-May. Race *bogolubovi* mainly winter visitor to Pakistan and NW India; occurs Aug-Apr from Baluchistan, Sind and Punjab to Rajasthan and Gujarat, in loose flocks of 6-10 birds, occasionally up to 30 or more. May occur in small flocks in most seasons; up to 45 birds together in Egypt, Aug-Sept. Has occurred widely in Europe as a vagrant, chiefly in autumn, including 10 birds seen together in Netherlands, Sept 1969.
Status and Conservation. Not globally threatened. Perhaps increasing in W Africa due to southward march of Sahel; increased grazing pressure may lead to desertification which may be of benefit to species; first recorded in N Nigeria, Jan 1988, in three flocks totalling 34 birds. Populations appear to be stable throughout most of range; however, reduced vagrancy in C Europe may indicate decrease since last century. In Cape Verde Is, race *exsul* occurs on all but two of the inhabited islands, with population 120-150 pairs. In Canary Is, known to breed only on Lanzarote and Fuerteventura, considered to have declined considerably in period 1970-1990; current population estimated at 200-250 pairs; in past, heavy egg-collecting pressure contributed to species' rarity; main threats now are destruction and alteration of habitat through development of tourist resorts, building of new roads and increase in off-road vehicles; need for site protection which would also benefit the endemic race of Houbara Bustard (*Chlamydotis undulata fuertaventurae*). Many hundreds of pairs of nominate *cursor* reported in Azraq Desert National Park, Jordan, and several hundred pairs in Israel; found breeding on Socotra in 1993. Noted at 23 localities in W Mauritania between 17° N and 18°20' N during breeding season in 1979 and 1980. Little information on numbers present in E Africa.
Bibliography. Ali & Ripley (1982), Archer & Godman (1937-1961), Argeloo & Stegeman (1988), Aspinall *et al.* (1994), Britton, P. L. (1980), Browne (1981), Bundy (1976), Cave & Macdonald (1955), Cramp & Reynolds (1972), Cramp & Simmons (1983), Curry & Sayer (1979), Dementiev & Gladkov (1951b), Dowsett & Dowsett-Lemaire (1993), Dowsett & Forbes-Watson (1993), Elgood *et al.* (1994), Étchécopar & Hüe (1964), Evans (1994), Flint *et al.* (1984), Glutz von Blotzheim *et al.* (1977), Goodman *et al.* (1989), Hazevoet (1988, 1995), Hüe & Étchécopar (1970), Jennings (1981b), Knystautas (1993), Lewis & Pomeroy (1989), Lorenzo (1994), Mackworth-Praed & Grant (1957, 1970), de Naurois (1983), Nelson (1973), Newby (1979), Paz (1987), Rahmani & Manakadan (1989), Ripley (1982), Roberts, T. J. (1991), Rodríguez *et al.* (1987), Schekkerman & van Wetten (1988), Sharma (1986), Shirihai (1996), Short *et al.* (1990), Smith (1957, 1965), Snow (1978), Stanford (1954), Triplet & Yésou (1994), Urban *et al.* (1986), Vangeluwe & Snethlage (1986).

3. Burchell's Courser

Cursorius rufus

French: Courvite de Burchell   **German**: Rostrennvogel   **Spanish**: Corredor Rufo

On following pages: 4. Temminck's Courser (*Cursorius temminckii*); 5. Indian Courser (*Cursorius coromandelicus*); 6. Double-banded Courser (*Smutsornis africanus*); 7. Three-banded Courser (*Rhinoptilus cinctus*); 8. Bronze-winged Courser (*Rhinoptilus chalcopterus*); 9. Jerdon's Courser (*Rhinoptilus bitorquatus*).

Taxonomy. *Cursorius rufus* Gould, 1837, islands in Indian Ocean; error = Potchefstroom, Transvaal, South Africa.
Forms superspecies with *C. cursor*, *C. temminckii* and *C. coromandelicus*, though last two taxa may represent a separate superspecies. Has been regarded as conspecific with *C. cursor*. E African races *somalensis* and *littoralis* of *C. cursor* may belong in present species. Proposed race *theresae* not generally recognized, as coloration too individually variable. Monotypic.
Distribution. S Africa, mainly in drier regions, from SW Angola through most of Namibia and Kalahari Basin of Botswana to W Cape, Karoo and high plateau of South Africa.

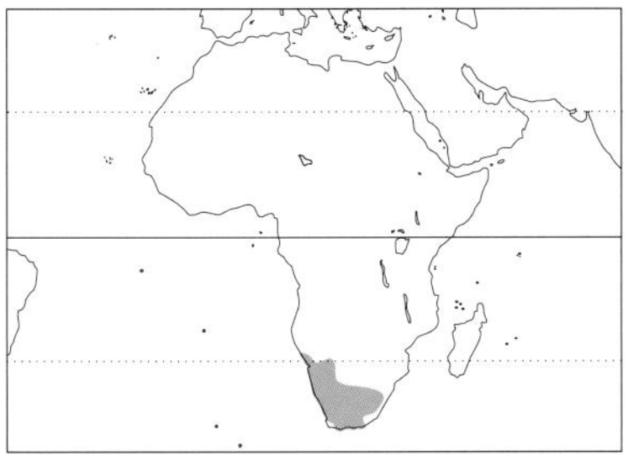

Descriptive notes. 20-22 cm; c. 75 g. Above mainly pale rufous brown, including upperwing-coverts; forecrown sandy rust, merging into blue-grey hindcrown, bordered below by black-white-black stripes behind eye, meeting in V on nape; throat and face whitish, merging to light rufous brown of breast bordered below by blackish brown band, sharply demarcated from white of lower belly; flight-feathers black, secondaries broadly tipped white; underwing black with grey-brown coverts and largely white secondaries; bill black; legs whitish grey. Shade of brown of upperparts highly variable individually and seasonally, though darker than in *C. cursor*; new feathers darker and more richly coloured than the old bleached plumage. Combination of dark belly patch, blue-grey hindcrown and extensively white secondaries separates from other members of genus. Juvenile mottled and barred with black and buff; lacks conspicuous black and white head markings.
Habitat. Open short-grass plains, sparse fallow fields, overgrazed and burnt grassland and pastures, bare or sparsely shrubby sandy or gravelly desert, salt-pans. Uncommon in pure sandy desert, such as Kalahari, where is localized on pans and exposed stony flats.
Food and Feeding. Insects, especially harvester termites (*Hodotermes mossambicus*). Takes prey on ground by running quickly, stopping and pecking; also digs for food with bill in soft windblown sand under bushes and grass tufts; may also eat seeds.
Breeding. Almost any month, but mostly Aug-Dec, in dry season just before rains; Feb in Namibia. Eggs laid on bare ground, sometimes among antelope droppings. Clutch 2 eggs; incubation and fledging periods unknown. Chick similar to that of *C. temminckii*.
Movements. Locally nomadic; no long distance migrations recorded. May occur in loose flocks of up to 10 birds.
Status and Conservation. Not globally threatened. Although fairly common in drier parts of range, numbers are declining in more southerly regions, probably as a result of poor grazing practices and disturbance by domestic stock. Conservation measures are needed in stock-farming areas of South Africa. Considerable decline reported in Orange Free State.
Bibliography. Anon. (1995h), Dixon (1975), Dowsett & Dowsett-Lemaire (1993), Dowsett & Forbes-Watson (1993), Ginn *et al*. (1989), Macdonald (1957), Mackworth-Praed & Grant (1962), Maclean (1967, 1993), Pinto (1983), du Plessis (1994), Snow (1978), Urban *et al*. (1986).

4. Temminck's Courser

Cursorius temminckii

French: Courvite de Temminck **German**: Temminckrennvogel **Spanish**: Corredor Etiópico
Taxonomy. *Cursorius Temminckii* Swainson, 1822, Senegal.
Forms superspecies with *C. cursor*, *C. rufus* and *C. coromandelicus*, although present species partly allopatric with the first two taxa, which may therefore represent a separate superspecies. Occasionally treated as a race of *C. coromandelicus*. Possible races *damarensis* from SW of range and *ruvanensis* from E of range poorly defined and not usually recognized, though slight differences in upperpart coloration and apparently different migration strategies may indicate their validity. Monotypic.
Distribution. Savannas of sub-Saharan Africa from S Mauritania and Senegal to Nigeria, discontinuously across Sahel to Ethiopia, and S through C Africa to N South Africa.

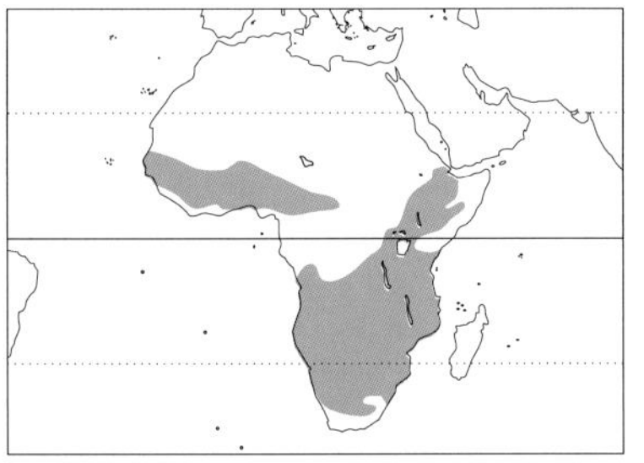

Descriptive notes. c. 20 cm; 64-80 g. Upperparts and breast light brown; crown bright rusty, black line through eye, white supercilia meet on nape; upper belly rufous, bordered below by large dark brown patch between legs; lower belly white; black flight-feathers above contrast with brown coverts, underwing all dark; bill dark, paler at base, legs whitish. Smaller and darker than *C. cursor* and *C. rufus*, with rufous crown and nape and all dark secondaries; latter feature also separates from *C. coromandelicus*. Juvenile has buff crown; dorsal feathers edged black giving mottled effect; breast pale rufous; belly blackish.
Habitat. Mostly in savanna on farmland, short-grass areas, especially on recently burnt ground and airfields; in Kenya 80% of population occurs in non-arid habitats, avoiding significant overlap with *C. cursor*. May appear on burnt grassland in savanna within hours of the fire. Where range overlaps with *C. rufus*, latter also occupies more arid areas. Nests up to 2000 m; on migration regularly occurs up to 3000 m.
Food and Feeding. Insects, harvester termites (*Hodotermes mossambicus*), molluscs and occasionally seeds. Feeds by running in bursts and stopping to peck at prey on ground.
Breeding. Mostly in dry season: all months except Sept and Oct in Senegal; nests Feb-Jul in Nigeria; Apr-Oct in Zaire; Jun-Oct in Zambia, with a peak in Aug-Sept; Jul-Nov in Zimbabwe; May-Jan in South Africa. No nest or just a shallow scrape, often among antelope droppings, usually on recently burnt ground. Clutch 2 eggs; incubation by both sexes, period unknown. Chick mottled black, buff and rufous above; chin and throat whitish, breast dull rufous; bill blackish, legs slaty grey. Young cared for by both parents; fledging period unknown.
Movements. Mostly nomadic, though some populations possibly intra-African migrants, depending on rainfall; southernmost populations in South Africa usually present only Feb-Aug; some birds from Sahel may migrate to S Africa Mar-Jul; in parts of Zaire, present only Mar-Jun, and in Malawi and Zambia Apr-Nov; departs from Zimbabwe at onset of rains in late Nov or early Dec, though remains in W of the country throughout rains, moving only very locally. Present in Cameroon savannas Nov-Mar, arriving at beginning of dry season to breed. Much local nomadism governed by burning of grassy understorey of savannas. On playing fields in Ghana, Jul-Nov, in flocks of up to 27 birds, moving to open burnt grassland Jan-Mar. In Gambia, 30-40 birds around Yundum Airport, Jan-Feb 1976. Vagrant to Sierra Leone.
Status and Conservation. Not globally threatened. Commonest and most widespread courser in sub-Saharan Africa; its wide habitat tolerance and generalized habits make it the most adaptable of the African coursers.
Bibliography. Bannerman (1931, 1951), Benson & Benson (1975), Britton, P. L. (1980), Clancey (1984), Dowsett & Forbes-Watson (1993), Elgood *et al*. (1994), Ginn (1991), Ginn *et al*. (1989), Gore (1990), Grimes (1987), Irwin (1981), Lewis & Pomeroy (1989), Lippens & Wille (1976), Louette (1981), Mackworth-Praed & Grant (1957, 1962, 1970), Maclean (1993), Maclean & Kemp (1973), Nuttall & de Swardt (1993), Pinto (1983), du Plessis (1994), Short *et al*. (1990), Snow (1978), Steyn (1965), Urban *et al*. (1986).

5. Indian Courser

Cursorius coromandelicus

French: Courvite de Coromandel **German**: Koromandelrennvogel **Spanish**: Corredor Indio

Taxonomy. *Charadrius coromandelicus* Gmelin, 1789, Coromandel Coast, India.
Forms superspecies with *C. cursor*, *C. rufus* and *C. temminckii*, although first two taxa may represent a separate superspecies. Occasionally considered to include *C. temminckii*. Monotypic.
Distribution. Pakistan and parts of Nepal through most of India to dry parts of NW Sri Lanka, from N of Puttalam to Jaffna Peninsula; no recent records in Bangladesh.

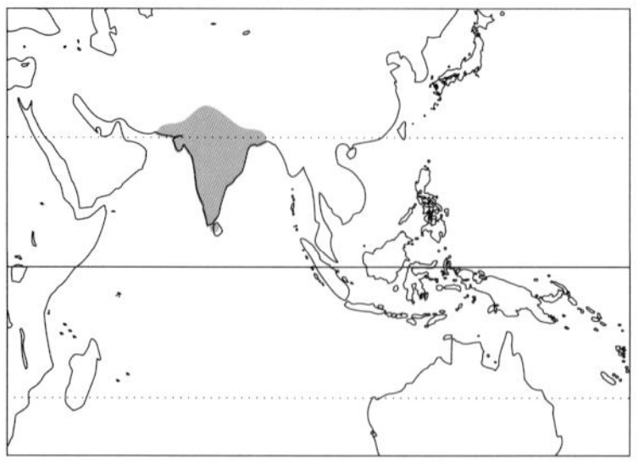

Descriptive notes. 23-26 cm. Above sandy greyish brown with white uppertail; crown bright rufous bordered below by white supercilia meeting in V on nape and black stripe through eye to bill; breast and upper belly cinnamon-chestnut, bordered below by blackish band on lower belly; undertail white; above black primaries and outer secondaries contrast with grey-brown coverts; underwing dark greyish brown, primaries black, narrow white trailing edge; bill black, legs white. Differs from other *Cursorius* by white uppertail and black lores. Juvenile strongly barred and blotched dark brown and buff above; crown dark brown, flecked buff.
Habitat. Dry stony plains, salty wastes, waste and fallow land with scattered scrub, ploughed fields, overgrazed areas and bare pastures around villages. Avoids areas of heavy rainfall.
Food and Feeding. Beetles and their larvae, especially tenebrionids; grasshoppers, crickets and other insects, such as ants; small molluscs. Catches insects by running in fast spurts, stopping and dipping forward to peck at ground.
Breeding. Mar-Aug; mainly May in Sri Lanka; in Lower Sind, peak egg-laying in third week of Apr. Nest is shallow unlined scrape on bare ground. Usually 2 eggs, sometimes 3; incubation mostly performed by female, period unknown. Chick mottled ginger, creamy white and black above; below creamy white with ginger breast; legs greyish. Chicks tended by both parents, but mostly by female; fledging period unrecorded.
Movements. Mainly resident, but locally nomadic. In Lower Sind overlaps with *C. cursor*. During Sept and Oct, after monsoon, gathers in small flocks of up to 10 birds; also c. 40 birds counted in Jul in bare fields near Delhi. No vagrancy outside Indian Subcontinent.
Status and Conservation. Not globally threatened. Apparently still fairly common; able to survive even in regions where grazing livestock, jackals, dogs and crows are plentiful, so unlikely to suffer severe decrease in numbers in short or medium term.
Bibliography. Ali (1953, 1979), Ali & Ripley (1982), Ganguli (1975), Harvey (1990), Henry (1971), Inskipp & Inskipp (1991), Kotagamana & Fernando (1994), Phillips (1942, 1978), Ripley (1982), Roberts, T. J. (1991), Whistler (1949), Wijesinghe (1994).

Genus *SMUTSORNIS* Roberts, 1922

6. Double-banded Courser

Smutsornis africanus

French: Courvite à double collier **Spanish**: Corredor Escamoso Chico
German: Doppelband-Rennvogel
Other common names: Two-banded Courser

Taxonomy. *Cursorius africanus* Temminck, 1807, Namaqualand. Often included in *Rhinoptilus*, sometimes in *Cursorius*, but probably merits its own monotypic genus. Alternatively, present species and *R. cinctus* have been placed in *Hemerodromus*. Birds from C Tanzania sometimes separated from *gracilis* as race *illustris*; race *sharpei sometimes* considered synonymous with nominate. Eight subspecies recognized.
Subspecies and Distribution.
S. a. raffertyi (Mearns, 1915) - E Ethiopia, Eritrea and Djibouti.
S. a. hartingi (Sharpe, 1893) - SE Ethiopia (Ogaden) and Somalia.
S. a. gracilis (Fischer & Reichenow, 1884) - Tanzania and Kenya.
S. a. bisignatus (Hartlaub, 1865) - SW Angola.
S. a. traylori (Irwin, 1963) - Etosha region of Namibia to Makgadikgadi system of Botswana.
S. a. sharpei (Erlanger, 1905) - C Namibia.
S. a. africanus (Temminck, 1807) - SW & C Kalahari, N Cape Province and S Namibia.
S. a. granti (W. L. Sclater, 1921) - W Cape Province and Karoo.

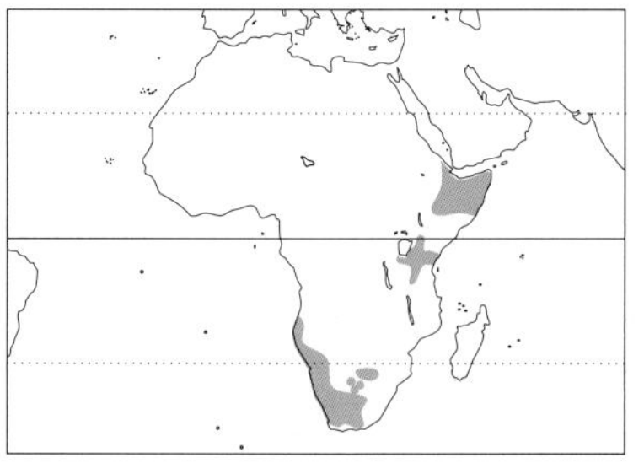

Descriptive notes. 20-24 cm; 69-104 g. Overall buff-brown; crown and back have boldly scaled appearance because of dark brown centres and broad pale fringes to all feathers; neck lightly streaked blackish; two well defined black breast bands round onto mantle; rest of underparts unstreaked, shading to whitish undertail; uppertail white; tail black; outer primaries black, inner primaries and all secondaries bright rusty cinnamon; short bill black; legs white. Plumage variable individually and seasonally. Differs from other coursers by double breast band, scaly upperparts and cinnamon flight-feathers. Juvenile similar to adult, but upperpart feathers have narrower fringes; lacks breastbands until 3 months old. Although basic coloration variable, races defined on basis of general darkness or paleness, with sandiest birds in N, through greyer, paler birds, to buffy brown birds in S of range; also slight size differences, central races smallest, southern largest.
Habitat. Stony and gravelly semi-desert with scattered low shrubs, overgrazed grassland and karoo, edges of dry clay-pans; patches of dry red sandy soils with low green vegetation and white grass tufts

c. 30 cm tall in Somalia; grassland and bushy grassland in E Africa, especially dry alkaline flats, sandy and short-grass plains. Generally uncommon or absent from sandy semi-desert, such as Kalahari, where confined to clay-pans and exposed stony ground. Occurs up to 1800 m in Tanzania and Kenya.

Food and Feeding. Insects, especially harvester termites (*Hodotermes mossambicus*). Feeds by pursuing prey during fast run, stopping and pecking at it on ground; does not dig. Largely nocturnal, also feeding at dawn and dusk.

Breeding. Feb-Jul in Somalia (mainly May-Jun); in E Africa, season varies with rainfall; all months in S Africa with peak in Oct-Nov; most nesting in dry months; usually 2-3 broods per year. No nest or just shallow scrape ringed with small stones, usually among antelope droppings, on bare ground in open semi-desert with good all-round visibility. Clutch 1 egg; incubation 26-27 days by both sexes. Chick mottled above with black and reddish brown, with pattern of white patches each bordered in black; below off-white, washed brownish in centre of breast; bill black; legs blue-grey. Young fed by both parents; fledging 5-6 weeks. Hatching success apparently high: in one study only 4 out of 56 eggs definitely failed to hatch.

Movements. Chiefly resident, but locally nomadic throughout range; movements governed by changes in vegetation: when ground cover too dense or too tall, or both, moves away to drier, more open areas.

Status and Conservation. Not globally threatened. Usually fairly common, but easily overlooked because of partly nocturnal habits; most populations probably stable. In South Africa, overgrazing by domestic stock may have allowed extension of range eastwards into grasslands; species adapts well to most livestock farming practices. Locally numerous in E Africa.

Bibliography. Archer & Godman (1937-1961), Beven & Chiazzari (1943), Britton, P. L. (1980), Dowsett & Dowsett-Lemaire (1993), Dowsett & Forbes-Watson (1993), Ginn *et al*. (1989), Lewis & Pomeroy (1989), Macdonald (1957), Mackworth-Praed & Grant (1957, 1962), Maclean (1967, 1970b, 1993), Pinto (1983), du Plessis (1994), Robertson, P. (1992), Short *et al*. (1990), Urban *et al*. (1986), Uys & Underhill (1977).

Genus *RHINOPTILUS* Strickland, 1852

7. Three-banded Courser
Rhinoptilus cinctus

French: Courvite à triple collier **German**: Bindenrennvogel **Spanish**: Corredor Escamoso Grande
Other common names: Heuglin's/Seebohm's/Treble-banded Courser

Taxonomy. *Hemerodromus cinctus* Heuglin, 1863, near Gondokoro, White Nile.
Sometimes placed in *Cursorius*; alternatively, along with *Smutsornis africanus* in *Hemerodromus*. Race *emini* may be better merged with nominate *cinctus*. Three subspecies recognized.

Subspecies and Distribution.
R. c. cinctus (Heuglin, 1863) - SE Sudan, E Ethiopia, Somalia and N Kenya.
R. c. emini Zedlitz, 1914 - S Kenya, Tanzania and N Zambia.
R. c. seebohmi Sharpe, 1893 - extreme S Angola and N Namibia to S Zambia, Zimbabwe and extreme N South Africa; possibly also N Malawi.

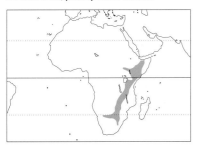

Descriptive notes. 25-28 cm; 122-142 g. Above dark brown, boldly scaled rich buff; broad pale supercilia, buff in front of eye, white behind eye, meet as V on nape; ear-coverts rufous; uppertail white; tail dark brown, outer feathers white with darker bars; underwing largely white with black tip; underparts white with elaborate pattern of stripes and bands: chestnut band extends from ear-coverts to upper breast; lower breast pale rufous, boldly streaked with black and bordered with black, white and chestnut bands below; black stripe down sides of hindneck meets on top of broad rufous breast band; bill black at tip, yellow at base; eye-ring yellow to whitish; legs pale yellow. Complex face and neck pattern, with patterned upperparts, immediately separate from similar species. Juvenile similar to adult, but bands on breast fainter or absent. Racial separation on size, from largest in S to smallest in N, and richness of coloration, especially of upperpart feathers.

Habitat. Open sandy clearings in dry *Acacia* scrub in Somalia and S Sudan; thorn-scrub, bushland and bushy grassland in E Africa, including miombo (*Brachystegia*) woodland; sparse mopane (*Colophospermum mopane*) woodland with bare ground in S Africa.

Food and Feeding. Very poorly known. Probably feeds entirely on insects caught during ground pursuit. Largely nocturnal.

Breeding. Mar-Jul in Somalia; Jan-Aug in Ethiopia; variable according to rainfall in rest of E Africa, mostly in dry season; May-Aug in Zambia; Mar-Nov (mainly Aug-Oct) in Zimbabwe; at least sometimes double-brooded. Nest is a deep scrape filled with sandy soil in which eggs almost completely buried, even during incubation; usually placed under shady tree or bush. Clutch 2 eggs; incubation c. 25-27 days. Chick mottled tan and pale grey above with sparse black blotches; below whitish; bill blackish; legs and feet grey. Fledging period unknown.

Movements. Largely resident; may undertake local movements, but is probably not long distance migrant. Absent from Zimbabwe Dec-Mar. Small influx to E Botswana in 1993/94 following wet summer. Occasional sightings outside main range.

Status and Conservation. Not globally threatened. Widespread and common in Kenya and Tanzania; abundant in open areas of *Acacia* in Sabi valley, Zimbabwe. Range in S Africa restricted to mopane woodland and therefore potentially in need of protection, though several game reserves in mopane country appear to offer sufficient protection at present.

Bibliography. Archer & Godman (1937-1961), Benson & Irwin (1967), Benson & Pitman (1964), Brewster (1994), Britton, P. L. (1980), Cassidy *et al*. (1984), Cave & Macdonald (1955), Dowsett & Dowsett-Lemaire (1993), Dowsett & Forbes-Watson (1993), Dowsett *et al*. (1977), Érard *et al*. (1993), Ginn *et al*. (1989), Irwin (1981), Kemp & Maclean (1973), Lewis & Pomeroy (1989), Mackworth-Praed & Grant (1957, 1962), Maclean (1993), Maclean & Kemp (1973), Medland (1989a), Pinto (1983), Short *et al*. (1990), Urban *et al*. (1986).

8. Bronze-winged Courser
Rhinoptilus chalcopterus

French: Courvite à ailes bronzées **German**: Amethystrennvogel **Spanish**: Corredor Patirrojo
Other common names: Violet-tipped Courser

Taxonomy. *Cursorius chalcopterus* Temminck, 1824, Senegal. Sometimes included in *Cursorius*. Probably closest to *R. bitorquatus* of India with which may form superspecies; shares similar lightly wooded habitat. Birds from Tanzania S to South Africa sometimes racially separated as *albofasciatus*. Monotypic.

Distribution. Senegal across Sahelian region to S Sudan and W Ethiopia, thence S to Kenya, Tanzania, S Zaire and Angola, and to N & E parts of South Africa.

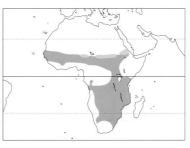

Descriptive notes. 25-29 cm; 117-172 g. Largest courser. Upper breast and upperparts dull greyish brown; white uppertail; tail dark brown fringed white; breast bordered below by black band; rest of underparts, forecrown, supercilium, line from behind eye, and sides of throat and upper neck cream or white; ear-coverts and lores dusky; primaries black, tipped iridescent purple to copper; underwing-coverts white, contrasting with black primaries and broad trailing edge to secondaries; bill black with purplish red base; large eye; eye-ring purplish red; legs dull red. Large size, plain dull upperparts, and distinctive head pattern separate from other coursers. Iridescent primary tips, visible only in flight, and hard to see; when flying away, superficially recalls lapwing (*Vanellus*). Juvenile duller; dorsal feathers tipped buff; black breast band narrower.

Habitat. Dry savanna woodland and thick bush, especially on recently burnt ground; occurs in less open situations than *R. cinctus*; more rarely in open grassland bordering wooded savanna. In Kenya, over 70% of records in rainfall range of dry sub-humid to semi-arid; mostly found at lower elevations.

Food and Feeding. Very little information available. Probably entirely insects, such as grasshoppers, caught on ground. Strictly nocturnal, feeding by night with plover-like action.

Breeding. Feb-Mar in Nigeria and Uganda; in E Africa variable according to rainfall; Jul-Dec, especially Sept-Oct, from Malawi to South Africa; mostly breeds in dry season. Usually makes no nest, but sometimes a bare scrape on ground. Clutch 2-3 eggs; incubation 25-27 days, by both sexes. Chick mottled black and rufous above with white nape; below white; bill black; legs dark grey. Chick cared for by both parents; fledging period unknown.

Movements. Probably an intra-African migrant that moves N after breeding. In Nigeria, undertakes seasonal movements, but not well understood; recorded in Ghana from Dec to mid-May; moves N in Sudan to breed before rainy season. In E Africa, movements not understood, but may include non-breeding visitors to Kenya from S tropics, mostly Dec-May; in Zaire, absent May-Jul in NE, present in S in dry season May-Nov, with marked passage in Apr and May. Present in Botswana Sept-Apr; influx to E Botswana Jan-Mar 1994, following wet summer. Influx to Zimbabwe between Apr and Jun after rains. Overwinters locally in South Africa. Sometimes in small parties, e.g. 10 together in Gambia in Dec 1975.

Status and Conservation. Not globally threatened. Nocturnal, so numbers often underestimated; probably fairly uncommon throughout range, but difficult to assess; most protection afforded by game and nature reserves in suitable habitat, because sensitive to human disturbance in farming areas. Often killed by traffic on dirt roads at night.

Bibliography. Bannerman (1931, 1951), Benson & Benson (1975), Brewster (1994), Britton, P. L. (1980), Crowe (1993), Dowsett & Dowsett-Lemaire (1980, 1993), Dowsett & Forbes-Watson (1993), Elgood *et al*. (1994), Freer (1981), Ginn *et al*. (1989), Gore (1990), Irwin (1981), Lewis & Pomeroy (1989), Lippens & Wille (1976), Macdonald (1957), Mackworth-Praed & Grant (1957, 1962, 1970), Maclean (1993), Pinto (1983), Pitman (1932a), Short *et al*. (1990), Snow (1978), Urban *et al*. (1986), Verschuren (1977), Wilson (1977).

9. Jerdon's Courser
Rhinoptilus bitorquatus

French: Courvite de Jerdon **German**: Godavarirennvogel **Spanish**: Corredor del Godavari
Other common names: Double-banded Courser(!)

Taxonomy. *Macrotarsius* [sic] *bitorquatus* Blyth, 1848, Eastern Ghats, Andhra Pradesh, India. Sometimes included in *Cursorius*. Probably most closely related to *R. chalcopterus* of Africa, with which may form superspecies; shares similar lightly wooded habitat. Monotypic.

Distribution. Limited to Pennar and, formerly, Godavari Valleys in Andhra Pradesh, EC India.

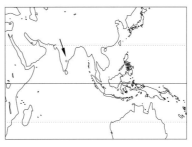

Descriptive notes. c. 27 cm. Crown and hindneck dark brown with whitish crown stripe; broad white supercilia sometimes meet as V on nape, tinged cream in front of eyes; rest of upperparts and broad breast band pinkish sandy brown; brown breast bordered above and below by narrow dusky band; chin and throat white with broad rufous patch on foreneck; white band across lower breast bordered below by narrow dusky band; rest of underparts mainly white; upperwing-coverts edged white; flight-feathers black with white patches at wingtips on outermost 3-4 primaries; underwing-coverts mainly creamy white, with patch of black and rufous at bend of wing; tail black with white base; bill black with yellow base; legs yellowish white. Only courser with white in wing tips; head and neck pattern distinctive. Juvenile plumage undescribed.

Habitat. Rocky undulating land with thin forest and scrub jungle. Prefers bare, grassless patches of open ground amidst scrub bushes, in zone between denser forests and areas of human impact. Never in areas of cultivation or near artesian wells. Hides among thorny *Carissa* bushes, about 50 cm tall.

Food and Feeding. Virtually nothing known. Feeds at night, presumably on insects.

Breeding. No authentic information available. Supposed clutch of 2 eggs claimed to have been taken in 1895.

Movements. Rather rounded wing suggests species is sedentary. However, according to local *shikari*, seen mainly during rainy season in flocks of 7-8 birds. Only ever recorded in two river valleys c. 400 km apart.

Status and Conservation. ENDANGERED. Until very recently, considered Extinct. Rediscovered in Jan 1986 after a year-long survey by Bombay Natural History Society: two surveys earlier this century in Eastern Ghats had drawn a blank. Perhaps one of the world's rarest birds and distinctly in danger of extinction; until its rediscovery, had not been seen since 1900, and prior to that only in c. 1848 and 1871; three living birds rediscovered at Reddipalli, near Cuddapah, in scrub forests below Lankamalai Hills in valley of R Sagileru, Pennar Valley, S Andhra Pradesh. Recent records now from 6 sites in vicinity of Lankamalai ranges. Total area of suitable habitat within known range only 2000 km². Species rediscovered just in time, as planned irrigation scheme passing through site was then diverted, following conservation pressure. Considerable progress made in protection of habitat: forest near Cuddapah where bird rediscovered designated as Sri Lankamalleswara Wildlife Sanctuary, and local tribespeople employed to warden sanctuary; a further reserve of 500 km² has been designated further S, and another of 1300 km² to SE also planned. Habitat under grazing pressure, though some grazing or other habitat management may be necessary to maintain scrub patches. Also threat from needs of local villagers; species apparently extremely sensitive to human disturbance. May still occur in Godavari Valley, N Andhra Pradesh; conceivably also awaits discovery in Maharashtra, Madhya Pradesh and Tamil Nadu.

Bibliography. Ali & Ripley (1982), Anon. (1986), Bhushan (1985, 1986a, 1986b, 1990, 1992a, 1992b), Collar & Andrew (1988), Collar *et al*. (1994), Ripley (1982), Ripley & Beehler (1989), Shuker (1993).

PLATE 34

inches 5
cm 10

10

11

12

13

14

15

ssp *nuchalis*

ssp *liberiae*

16

17

Subfamily GLAREOLINAE

Genus *STILTIA* G. R. Gray, 1855

10. **Australian Pratincole**

Stiltia isabella

French: Glaréole isabelle **German**: Stelzenbrachschwalbe **Spanish**: Canastera Patilarga
Other common names: Australian Courser, Long-legged/Isabelline Pratincole

Taxonomy. *Glareola isabella* Vieillot, 1816, "Australasie".
Forms apparent link between coursers and pratincoles. Sometimes included in genus *Glareola*, or at other extreme in its own subfamily Stiltiinae. Monotypic.
Distribution. Drier regions of N & E Australia, spreading further S in wetter years, but absent from SW; breeds sporadically throughout Australian range, but seldom N of 18° S; two breeding records in Trans-Fly, S New Guinea. Migrates to N Queensland and Northern Territory, New Guinea and E Indonesian archipelago as far NW as S Borneo.

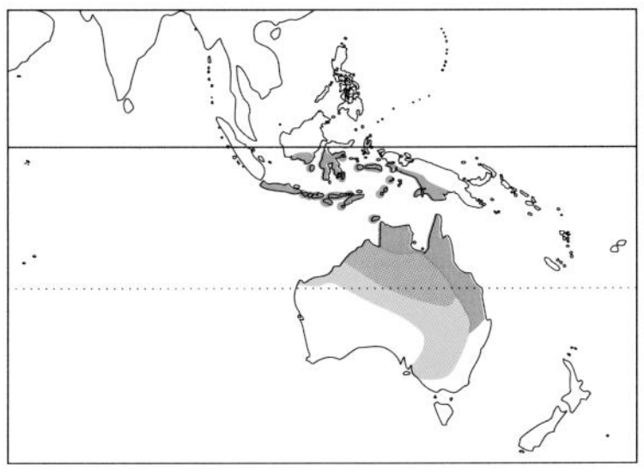

Descriptive notes. 21-24 cm; c. 65 g. Above light cinnamon brown, with white rump; black lores, throat whitish shading to pinkish cinnamon breast and deep chestnut across belly; vent and undertail white; tail square, white with large black central patch; underwing black with silvery grey secondaries and inner primaries; wings extremely long, slender and pointed, with black primaries, outermost elongated, extending well beyond tail when standing; bill scarlet with black tip; long legs greyish brown, extend well beyond tail in flight. Long wings and legs and short tail make this pratincole unmistakable. Non-breeding adult duller; lacks dark lores, and chestnut of belly divided. Juvenile has bill duller red, mantle feathers edged buff, outer primary not elongated. First non-breeding plumage darker above, neck and breast streaked brown.
Habitat. Rather bare areas: blacksoil country of Queensland with sparse grass, scrubby redsoil ridges, gravel plains, gibbers, open plains with limestone or ironstone pebbles and scattered low shrubs, airfields, open shorelines of lakes, lagoons and rivers. Seldom far from water. Also occurs in harvested or fallow rice fields, when not breeding. In Papua New Guinea, recorded from sea-level up to 1740 m.
Food and Feeding. Grasshoppers, beetles, dragonflies, termites and other large insects; also centipedes, spiders and seeds. Obtains most of prey on ground, but also forages in flight; runs swiftly on ground after insects, sometimes stopping prey with outstretched wing and quick forward lunge with bill; aerial prey may be hawked from ground, birds leaping or flying up to catch single items before returning to ground; also hawks high in air. Needs to drink frequently.
Breeding. Dependent on weather; Aug-Jan, but most breed Sept-Nov. Nests in small, loose colonies, nests spread thinly over as much as 2 km^2 of open ground. Nest on bare, stony ground; rarely a shallow scrape, site often ringed with small stones and dry plant material, usually within 2 km of water. Usually 2 eggs, occasionally 1-3; incubation 18-21 days, by both sexes. Chick weighs c. 5 g; clay-buff above with pattern of sooty black; faint tan stripe in centre of forehead and tan patches on wings; below pale honey-coloured, shading to white on belly; bill black with pink on lower mandible; legs pinkish grey. After hatching, young may use a rabbit burrow as refuge from danger, or shelter under shrub or tussock; young fed and brooded by both parents; broken-wing display by adults at nest; fledging c. 3-4 weeks, up to 5. Main cause of nesting failure is predation by ravens, introduced foxes, snakes and lizards.
Movements. Movements influenced by rainfall patterns, with reports of greatly increased numbers arriving in S Australia to breed in unusually wet years, when range extends further SW. Occurs in southern half of Australia mostly in austral spring and summer; most numerous in New South Wales in Oct-Feb. Only two breeding reports N of Australia, from Trans-Fly region of New Guinea. Migrates N as far as New Guinea, and W to Sulawesi, Borneo, Bali and Java; arrives at Darwin, Northern Territory, between Apr and Jun, and departs in Nov and Dec; in Papua New Guinea, occurs Mar-Dec, mostly May-Nov.
Status and Conservation. Not globally threatened. Common to abundant, but sporadic in occurrence; probably not under threat in any part of range; total Australian, and therefore world, population estimated in 1993 at 60,000 birds; also a report of 50,000 birds on Timor, E Indonesia, in Nov. Flocks of 700-800 birds commonly seen outside breeding season; many thousands noted in late dry season in R Bensbach area, Papua New Guinea; more than 12,000 recorded immediately inland from Gulf of Carpentaria, Northern Territory, in mid-May. Throughout Sept, flocks of up to 50 birds at a time arrive to breed, totalling about 1000 birds per day; New South Wales population estimated at 5000 birds. Most birds in N Australia, where human population sparse, so no immediate threat. Species may be hunted in Indonesia.
Bibliography. Andrews, M. (1991), Bailey (1935), Beehler *et al*. (1986), Bishop, K.D. (1985, 1988), Blakers *et al*. (1984), Bravery (1962), Bruce (1987), Campbell (1985), Chaffer (1949), Christian *et al*. (1992a), Coates (1985), Cumming (1981), Fergenbauer-Kimmel (1992), Hoogerwerf (1964), Hopkins (1976), Jaensch (1983a), Jesson & Maclean (1976), Judin (1981), Klapste (1977), Lane & Davies (1987), Liddy (1959), Macdonald (1988), MacGillivray (1924), MacKinnon & Phillipps (1993), Maclean (1973, 1976a), Marchant & Higgins (1996), North (1913-1914), Pringle (1987), Rand & Gilliard (1967), Smith, P. (1991), Smythies (1981), White & Bruce (1986).

Genus *GLAREOLA* Brisson, 1760

11. **Collared Pratincole**

Glareola pratincola

French: Glaréole à collier **German**: Rotflügel-Brachschwalbe **Spanish**: Canastera Común
Other common names: Red-winged/Common Pratincole, Swallow-plover

Taxonomy. *Hirundo Pratincola* Linnaeus, 1766, Austria.
Forms superspecies with *G. maldivarum* and *G. nordmanni*, although range overlap with latter leads some authorities to exclude that species from the superspecies. Formerly considered to include *G. maldivarum*, and even on occasion *G. nordmanni*, as races. Has hybridized with *G. nordmanni*. Possible race *boweni* of W Africa included in *fuelleborni*; form "*limbata*", described from Red Sea coasts, appears to be erroneous. Species has on occasion been regarded as monotypic. Three subspecies normally recognized.
Subspecies and Distribution.
G. p. pratincola (Linnaeus, 1766) - S Europe to Pakistan; winters in sub-Saharan Africa, N of 5° N.
G. p. erlangeri Neumann, 1920 - coastal plains of S Somalia and N Kenya.
G. p. fuelleborni Neumann, 1910 - Senegal E to S Kenya and S to Zaire, Namibia and E South Africa.

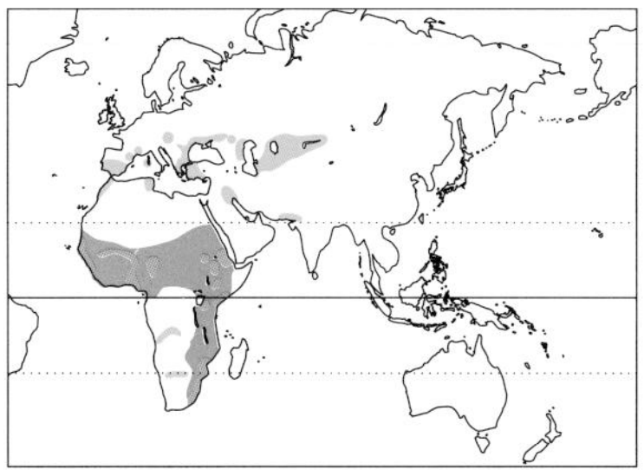

Descriptive notes. 22-25 cm; 60-95 g. Above brown, tinged olive, with white rump; long wingtips and deeply forked tail black; throat ochre yellow, bordered narrowly with black; breast brown shading to white belly; underwing-coverts and axillaries deep rich chestnut; narrow but distinct white trailing edge to secondaries; bill red with black tip, legs blackish. In non-breeding plumage black border to throat indistinct, lores paler and breast mottled grey-brown. Differs from *G. maldivarum* in longer tail, contrast from above between darker outer and paler inner wing, and white trailing edge; from *G. nordmanni* in last two features and also chestnut underwing. Juvenile mottled with black above and on breast; throat whitish without black collar. Races separated on small colour differences; African birds smaller and darker, not distinguishable in the field.
Habitat. Flat and open areas, fields, steppe plains in Eurasia, usually near water; in Africa open ground, often recently burned, overgrazed grassland, ploughed fields, alkaline flats or sandflats, usually near water, especially along larger rivers and estuaries. Feeds over water, rice fields or coastal scrub. On migration, occurs by water.
Food and Feeding. Locusts and grasshoppers, beetles, termites, flies and other, mainly large, insects; also some spiders and molluscs. Forages in flocks, chiefly on the wing, catching aerial insects in graceful flight, often at dawn and dusk, sometimes on moonlit nights; also chases prey with fast run on ground; leaps up to catch ephydrid flies along lake shoreline 10 cm above ground.
Breeding. May-Aug in Europe; May-Jun in Jordan; Apr-Jul Pakistan; in Africa, Mar-May in Sierra Leone, Apr-Jun in Nigeria, Apr-Sept (wet season) in Kenya, Uganda and NE Tanzania, Jun-Sept (dry season) elsewhere in Tanzania after floodplains have dried out, Apr-Jun in N Zaire, Jul-Nov in S Zaire and Zambia, Aug-Oct in Zimbabwe, Nov-Dec in Botswana, Aug-Dec in South Africa. Colonial nester in small groups of 10 or 20, up to 100 pairs, on dry mudflats or sandflats; sometimes forms mixed colonies with *G. nordmanni*. Nest is usually a shallow scrape or natural depression in ground, such as a hoofprint, in Africa often next to piece of driftwood or plant, sometimes lined with dry plant fragments; each pair defends small nesting territory within colony. Usually 3 eggs (2-4) in Eurasia, 1-2 eggs in Africa; incubation 17-19 days, by both sexes. Chick mottled above with charcoal and black; below white. Young leave nest at 2-3 days; fed by both parents by regurgitation or by presentation of food in bill tip, up to age of 7 days old; fledging 25-30 days. Comparison in Spain of breeding success in marshland and farmland found success much higher in former, despite equal amounts of insect food in both; however, egg losses during incubation much higher on farmland due to agricultural activities. Probably first breeding at one year old.
Movements. Nominate race migrates after breeding to savannas of Sahel, where probably overlaps with birds of race *fuelleborni* in N tropics. Southward passage migrant in Israel mainly in Aug and early Sept, moving N again in Apr and early May; common passage migrant through W Saudi Arabia, mainly around inland fresh waters; present in Pakistan Mar-Aug; some movement from Pakistan to W India, where species mingles with *G. maldivarum*; vagrancy recorded to most European countries N of breeding range. Many African populations nomadic, appearing and disappearing suddenly, often in response to changing water levels; may occur together with *G. nordmanni*; large numbers in Zambia in dry season, Apr-Nov. Flocks of 1000 or more birds regularly occur on migration; 30,000 birds noted moving N at Juba, S Sudan (4°52' N) in early Apr, 1983, though not clear whether these were all Palearctic breeders, as this race thought not to winter so far S.
Status and Conservation. Not globally threatened. Overall decline in range and numbers in Europe. Total of 6700-22,000 pairs breeding in Europe: largest populations are 1000-10,000 pairs in Russia, 500-1000 pairs in Greece, 500-5000 pairs in Turkey, c. 3800 pairs in Spain (fluctuating c. 3500-5000), and 250-1000 pairs in Portugal. As many as 10,000 pairs estimated in Guadalquivir Marshes, S Spain, as recently as early 1960's; use of insecticides and herbicides caused reduction in population to c. 2250 pairs in 1990, though this is still the most important site in Europe, current threats being changes in water levels and human disturbance. In SE Europe, many sites of former breeding colonies destroyed through ploughing of grasslands, artificial irrigation and fertilization, use of pesticides, change in traditional grazing regimes, and commercial collecting of eggs. In addition to habitat loss and degradation through agriculture and flood control measures, increasing urban encroachment is also a threat, especially through tourist pressure. Important colonies need protection, perhaps through establishment of reserves; measures also needed to reduce disturbance by agriculture and leisure activities. Decline in Ukraine from 3000 pairs in mid-1960's to 280-420 pairs in 1984; on N coast of Sea of Azov, Ukraine, colonization took place in 1950's, replacing *G. nordmanni*; numbers fell sharply in 1970's and early 1980's; breeding success very low owing to nests being trampled by cattle and preyed upon by Hooded Crows (*Corvus corone cornix*). Small numbers N of Caucasus; c. 500 pairs in Azerbaijan; range expansion further E in Chu Valley, Kyrgyzstan. Population of SW Asia numbers 10,000-100,000 pairs. Trends in E Palearctic not known. In N Africa, 200-300 pairs in Morocco, 200-250 pairs in Algeria, 1000-1500 pairs in Tunisia, and more than 1000 pairs in salt-marshes of Nile Delta, Egypt. Has become very uncommon in Israel, populations having declined by c. 90% since 1930's because of spraying with agricultural pesticides in species' nesting habitat of cultivated fields. Counts in sub-Saharan Africa include flocks of 3000 in Nigeria in Nov 1969; up to 100 together in S Somalia; 1500 in rice fields to N of L Maga, Cameroon, in 1991; 10,000 present along just 5 km (10%) of shore of L Ngami, NW Botswana, Nov 1989, some nesting; several thousand throughout Jun 1993 along R Chobe, Caprivi Strip, border of NE Namibia and N Botswana; up to 3000 wintering on R Baro, Sudan, along with *G. nordmanni*. Widespread decline of this and other insectivorous species through increased use of pesticides, both in Europe and in Sahelian wintering grounds; also, water management projects in Sahel are changing the habitat.
Bibliography. Ali & Ripley (1982), Ametov (1985), Arcamone *et al*. (1982), Ash & Miskell (1989), Banfield (1987), Bannerman (1931, 1951), Bekaert (1989), Benson & Benson (1975), Bowen (1980), Britton, P. L. (1980), Brooke (1984a), Calvo (1993a, 1993b, 1994a, 1994b), Calvo & Alberto (1990), Calvo & Furness (1995), Calvo *et al*. (1993), Canova & Saino (1983), Clancey (1979), Cramp & Simmons (1983), Dementiev & Gladkov (1951b), Dolz (1994),

On following pages: 12. Oriental Pratincole (*Glareola maldivarum*); 13. Black-winged Pratincole (*Glareola nordmanni*); 14. Madagascar Pratincole (*Glareola ocularis*); 15. Rock Pratincole (*Glareola nuchalis*); 16. Grey Pratincole (*Glareola cinerea*); 17. Small Pratincole (*Glareola lactea*).

Dolz *et al.* (1989), Dowsett & Forbes-Watson (1993), Dupuy (1977), Elgood *et al.* (1994), Étchécopar & Hüe (1964), Evans (1994), Flint *et al.* (1984), Francis (1991), von Frisch (1961), Ginn *et al.* (1989), Glutz von Blotzheim *et al.* (1977), Goodman *et al.* (1989), Grimes (1987), Hanmer (1988), Hayman (1956), Hüe & Étchécopar (1970), Jennings (1985), Kaverkina (1988), Knystautas (1993), Kobayashi (1960), Königstedt & Langbehn (1990), Lambert (1985), Lippens & Wille (1976), Longrigg (1992), Mackworth-Praed & Grant (1957, 1962, 1970), Maclean (1975, 1993), Makatsch (1952), Martínez-Vilalta (1991), Moreau (1972), Nadler (1969, 1983, 1990), Newby (1979), Patrikeev (1995), Paz (1987), Penry & Tarboton (1990), Perennou (1991), Pérez (1964), Phillips (1978), Pinto (1983), Randall (1994a), Reynolds (1977b), Ripley (1982), Roberts, T. J. (1991), Serle (1950), Shirihai (1996), Short *et al.* (1990), Snow (1978), Sterbetz (1974), Steyn (1992), Talpeanu (1963), Tomkovich (1992b), Tree (1987a, 1987b), Uhlig (1989, 1990d), Ullman (1994), Urban *et al.* (1986), Verschuren (1977), Volsøe (1950), Wittling (1984), Yeates (1948).

12. Oriental Pratincole

Glareola maldivarum

French: Glaréole orientale **German**: Orientbrachschwalbe **Spanish**: Canastera Oriental
Other common names: Eastern (Collared)/Large Indian Pratincole

Taxonomy. *Glareola (Pratincola) Maldivarum* J. R. Forster, 1795, open sea in the latitude of the Maldive Islands. Forms superspecies with *G. pratincola* and *G. nordmanni*, although some authorities exclude latter from the superspecies. Formerly included in *G. pratincola*. Monotypic.
Distribution. Extreme S Siberia, NE Mongolia and S Manchuria, S to N India, Sri Lanka, Thailand and SE Asia; also locally in W Japan and Ryukyu Is; has bred in Pakistan, Philippines and Borneo. Winters from India and SE Asia through Indonesia and New Guinea to Australia.

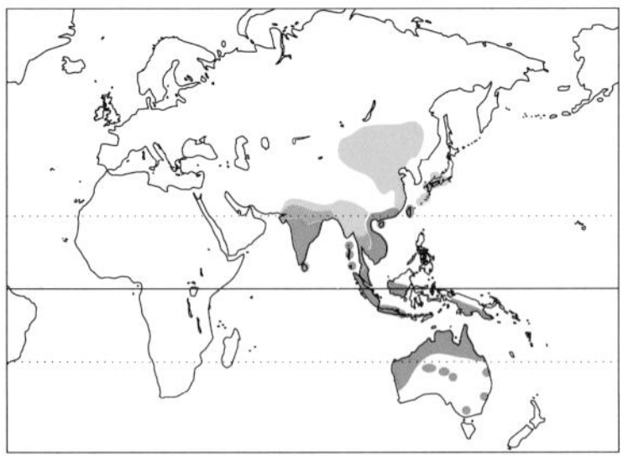

Descriptive notes. 23-24 cm; 87 g. Above olive brown, with white rump; throat ochre yellow, edged with narrow black collar; upper breast brown, shading to rufous and then white on belly and undertail; flight-feathers black, underwing chestnut; forked tail black, white at base; bill black with red gape; legs blackish. Collar indistinct in non-breeding plumage. Differs from *G. pratincola* in shorter tail, uniform upperwing lacking contrast between inner and outer wing, and lack of white trailing edge; from *G. nordmanni* by shorter tail and chestnut underwing-coverts. Juvenile mottled black and buff above.
Habitat. In Asia inhabits steppes, open grassland, dry floodplains, tidal mudflats, rice stubble, ploughed and fallow fields and open pastures, usually near water. In Australia, open grassy plains, clay-pans, muddy wetlands and airfields; occasionally found on beaches and intertidal mudflats.
Food and Feeding. Insects and other terrestrial arthropods, especially grasshoppers, crickets and beetles; also, in non-breeding quarters, winged termites which may emerge in large numbers before rain. Prey caught mainly in flight but some also on ground, e.g. shore-flies (Ephydridae); attracted to bush fires. Often crepuscular.
Breeding. Apr-Jun. Nests in colonies on open plains, often after recent grass fire; also on grassy islands in rivers with River Terns (*Sterna aurantia*). Nest is a shallow scrape or dried hoofprint. Clutch 2-3 eggs; incubation and fledging periods unknown, but probably similar to those of *G. pratincola*.
Movements. NE populations are long distance migrants S to winter Oct-Apr mainly in SE Asia, Indonesia and Australia; birds return N to breed in E Asia from May to about Aug. Most of Indian breeding population resident, locally nomadic, or short distance migrants. Rare but annual, Oct to late Mar, in New Guinea; birds overfly to N Australia Dec-Feb, when absent to N, therefore large portion of migratory population may be in Australia at this time. Late arrival in Australia: from Nov in Darwin area after local wet season starts; nomadic in Australian summer, following insect populations; departs from Darwin and NW Australia by first week in Apr. Common on migration in C & NE China, especially during S migration, Jul-Sept; passage Hong Kong Sept-Oct and again Mar-May. Up to 1500 birds recorded together, Malay Peninsula, on migration; arrives Thailand in Feb, most birds departing Aug-Sept, with few overwintering perhaps irregularly. Generally uncommon migrant to Japan, mostly in Aug-Sept, with maximum of 306 birds in 1984; now also breeds locally in W Japan. Uncommon visitor to W Micronesia. Vagrant to New Zealand, Seychelles and Mauritius, Arabian Peninsula, England, Cyprus and Attu I (Aleutians).
Status and Conservation. Not globally threatened. Numbers in winter in Indian Subcontinent in broad range of 25,000-1,000,000 birds; in rest of winter distribution, from SE Asia to Australia, population probably in range 100,000-1,000,000. Large numbers reported in Java; 300 in Bali, Nov-Dec 1983. Total of 50,000 winter in Australia, with several high counts from Western Australia including: 10,000 at Port Hedland Saltworks; 4000 on Pilbara Coast; flock N of De Grey River in Mar 1980, stretched for c. 300 km, at density of 10-50 birds/km along road at night. Largely crepuscular, sluggish by day, so numbers can be underestimated. Favours open grassy plains away from coast in N Australia so rarely counted; however, there is no immediate threat to this habitat. Appears to survive well even in areas of fairly heavy overgrazing by domestic stock, so unlikely to be threatened, though any intensive agricultural development over a wide area may have an impact. Probably declining in some areas; in NC Java large numbers are killed each year by hunters.
Bibliography. Ali & Ripley (1982), Beaman (1994), Beehler *et al.* (1986), Bharucha *et al.* (1988), Blakers *et al.* (1984), Brazil (1991), Burns (1993), Carruthers (1968), Coates (1985), Cooper (1964), Corben (1972), Deignan (1945), Dementiev & Gladkov (1951b), Dickinson *et al.* (1991), Endo *et al.* (1987), Étchécopar & Hüe (1978), Flint *et al.* (1984), Hobbs (1973a), Johnson, Lawler & Barter (1991), Johnson, Lawler, Noor & Barter (1992), Klapste (1977), Knystautas (1993), Lane & Davies (1987), Lekagul & Round (1991), Lewington *et al.* (1991), Lloyd & Lloyd (1991), MacKinnon & Phillipps (1993), Mann (1987), Marchant & Higgins (1996), van Marle & Voous (1988), Mason (1988), Medway & Wells (1976), Opie (1974), Penry & Tarboton (1990), Perennou *et al.* (1994), Phillips (1978), Pierce (1978), Pratt & Bruner (1981), Pringle (1987), Rand & Gilliard (1967), Rao & Mohapatra (1992), Ripley (1982), Roberts, T. J. (1991), Rowlands (1994), Smith, P. (1991), Smythies (1981, 1986), Temme (1991), Waugh (1988), White & Bruce (1986), Williams, M.D. (1986), Zheng Zuoxin (1955).

13. Black-winged Pratincole

Glareola nordmanni

French: Glaréole à ailes noires **Spanish**: Canastera Alinegra
German: Schwarzflügel-Brachschwalbe

Taxonomy. *Glareola Nordmanni* Fischer, 1842, steppes of southern Russia.
Forms superspecies with *G. maldivarum* and *G. pratincola*, though range overlap with latter causes some authorities to exclude present species from the superspecies. At one time erroneously regarded as colour morph of *G. pratincola*, with which has been known to hybridize; also, on occasion, considered a race of *G. pratincola*. Monotypic.
Distribution. Romania, E through Ukraine to SW Russia and N Kazakhstan. Winters in S Africa and, more irregularly, in W Africa.

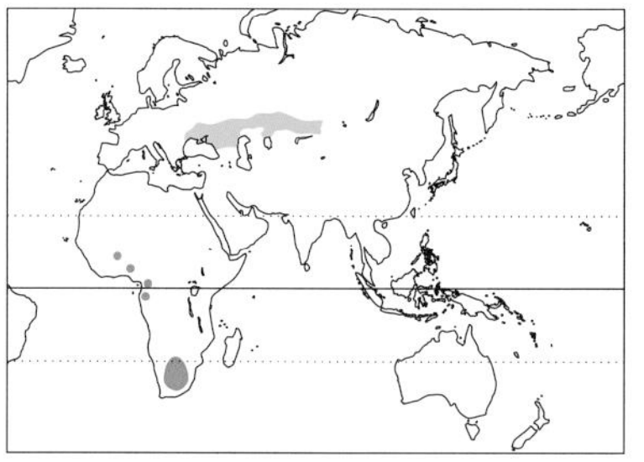

Descriptive notes. 23-26 cm; 84-105 g. Above brown with olive tinge, and white rump; flight-feathers and deeply forked tail black; throat ochre yellow with narrow black border; breast brown, shading to white belly; bill black with red at base, legs blackish. Black border to throat indistinct in non-breeding plumage. Separated from *G. pratincola* by black underwing-coverts, lack of white trailing edge to wing, darker, more uniform upperwing, and less red on bill; from *G. maldivarum* by black underwing-coverts, and longer tail. Juvenile mottled blackish above and on breast; throat dull whitish without black collar; may show few chestnut tips to underwing-coverts.
Habitat. In Eurasian breeding areas inhabits saline and alkaline steppes, grassland, ploughed and arable land, in river valleys and along shorelines of lakes or seas. Prefers saline soil with sparse vegetation; always with water or wet meadows nearby; tolerates taller and denser vegetation than *G. pratincola*. Non-breeding birds frequent open high altitude grassland or low-lying mudflats.
Food and Feeding. Locusts, grasshoppers, crickets and beetles, also flying ants, termites, wasps, bees, dragonflies, flies and other insects. Forages mainly on the wing, often in flocks of hundreds or even thousands of birds, especially when locusts are swarming; also feeds on ground by running swiftly after prey; usually hunts in early morning and late evening, often after dusk.
Breeding. May-Jul in Black Sea region. Nests in loose colonies of several tens or hundreds of pairs on open ground, usually near water, often with other Charadrii; occasionally several thousand in colony; sites may move from year to year, even when still apparently suitable. Nest is a simple scrape, sparsely lined with dry plant pieces. Clutch 3-4 eggs; incubation by both sexes, period unrecorded. Chick similar to that of *G. pratincola*, but somewhat darker. Young independent at 5-6 weeks. Breeding success has decreased with predation by Rooks (*Corvus frugilegus*) attracted by plantation of shelter-belts in steppe; in one study, grazing pressure resulted in destruction of 50% of chicks and 30% of nestlings; heavy rain and drought may also affect breeding success.
Movements. Long distance migrant from Eurasia to W & S Africa, chiefly South Africa, Namibia and Botswana, Sept-Apr; nomadic in winter range following swarming insect prey. On passage in Sudan, W Kenya, W Uganda, Zaire, Angola, W Zambia, but seldom in Malawi and Zimbabwe; thousands of birds pass southward through Zaire in Oct, and northward again in Mar. In W Africa, flocks of up to 200 birds in Nigeria, Sept and Dec-Apr. Arrival in breeding areas usually Apr-May, departure in Sept. Much migration at high altitude, so passage often not observed from ground. Rare passage migrant through Saudi Arabia, which species probably overflies; uncommon passage migrant through Israel along coastal plain, southward in Sept and Oct; also regular through Iran. Vagrant N and W to many European countries.
Status and Conservation. Not globally threatened. Has declined markedly and now considered near-threatened, requiring close monitoring of trends and numbers. Total world population now estimated at only 10,000-25,000 birds, and declining. Although non-breeding flocks may number hundreds of birds in S Africa, occurrence of large flocks in recent years sporadic: c. 10,000, with similar numbers of *G. pratincola*, at L Ngami, NW Botswana, in Nov 1989, along just 5 km of lake shoreline, largest recent documented count. On migration, flocks of 5000-10,000 noted in W Zambia in Oct-Nov 1966, and again in Mar 1967; up to 5000 birds with *G. pratincola* in 1970's in Dec and Jan on R Baro, Sudan; 400 Cyprus, Sept 1961; 230 in E Turkey, Sept 1968. In European breeding range population 6500-11,000 pairs, almost all now in European Russia, though still 40-100 pairs in Ukraine. In early 20th century flocks still numbered hundreds of thousands in Russian steppes. Sharp decline in numbers from 19th century in Romania and Ukraine. Has bred in Germany, occasionally in Hungary, and in Azerbaijan. Partial irrigation of dry steppes in Russia N of Caucasus may have allowed increased breeding numbers during second half of 20th century, reaching 5000-7000 pairs in mid-1980's, though by 1993 population had stabilized or started to decline. Population to E of R Volga appears to be fairly stable. Cause of overall decline appears to be cultivation of steppes in breeding areas; species may also be adversely affected by use of pesticides in Africa. Threatened not only by loss of steppe grassland, but also by agricultural operations such as harrowing and intensification of grazing, and predation by increasing numbers of corvids.
Bibliography. Ash (1977), Aspinwall (1977), Beaman (1994), Becker & Kollibay (1976), Belik, V. (1994a), Benson *et al.* (1971), van den Berg (1985), Britton, P. L. (1980), Cardno (1979), Coates (1978), Cramp & Simmons (1983), Dementiev & Gladkov (1951b), Dontschev (1975), Dowsett & Forbes-Watson (1993), Elgood *et al.* (1994), Étchécopar & Hüe (1964), Evans (1994), Flint *et al.* (1984), Ginn *et al.* (1989), Glutz von Blotzheim *et al.* (1977), Goodman *et al.* (1989), Gregory (1992), Grote (1932), Haagner & Ivy (1908), Hayman (1956), Heard (1994), Hüe & Étchécopar (1970), Khrokov (1983), Knystautas (1993), Lewington *et al.* (1991), Lewis & Pomeroy (1989), Lippens & Wille (1976), Mackworth-Praed & Grant (1957, 1962, 1970), Maclean (1993), Mauersberger (1990), Molodan (1988), Molodan & Pozhidayeva (1991), Moreau (1972), Nadler (1990), Newby (1979), Patrikeev (1995), Paz (1987), Penry & Tarboton (1990), Pinto (1983), du Plessis (1995), Robel (1982), Shirihai (1996), Short *et al.* (1990), Snow (1978), Somofalov (1986), Szabó (1975), Tomkovich (1992b), Uhlig (1990d), Urban *et al.* (1986), Walmsley (1970, 1976, 1988).

14. Madagascar Pratincole

Glareola ocularis

French: Glaréole malgache **German**: Madagaskarbrachschwalbe **Spanish**: Canastera Malgache

Taxonomy. *Glareola ocularis* J. Verreaux, 1833, Madagascar.
Monotypic.
Distribution. Madagascar, except extreme S & SW. Non-breeding visitor to E Africa from S Somalia to N Mozambique, mainly in coastal Kenya (dunes N of Malindi) and Tanzania.
Descriptive notes. 23-25 cm; 82-103 g. Above dark olive brown; forecrown dark chocolate brown; rump white; lores and ear-coverts blackish; short white line below and back from eye contrasts with dark crown; throat and breast brown, shading to dark rufous on upper belly and white on lower belly; flight-feathers black; shallowly forked tail mostly black with white sides; underwing-coverts pale chestnut with white spot near bend of wing; bill black with red base, legs greyish black. Differs from superficially similar *G. nuchalis* by much larger size, chestnut belly and underwing; darker than *G. pratincola*, especially on head, and shorter-tailed. Juvenile lightly scaled rufous above; paler below than adult, streaked rufous on breast; line under eye rufous.
Habitat. In Madagascar, breeds on rocky islets in permanent rivers and coastal waters. When not breeding, on African mainland, mainly coastal, on shores of lakes, sandbars in rivers and estuaries, short grasslands, estuarine flats, coastal dunes; forages over almost any habitat; often rests on offshore rocks or on open ground, including airfields.

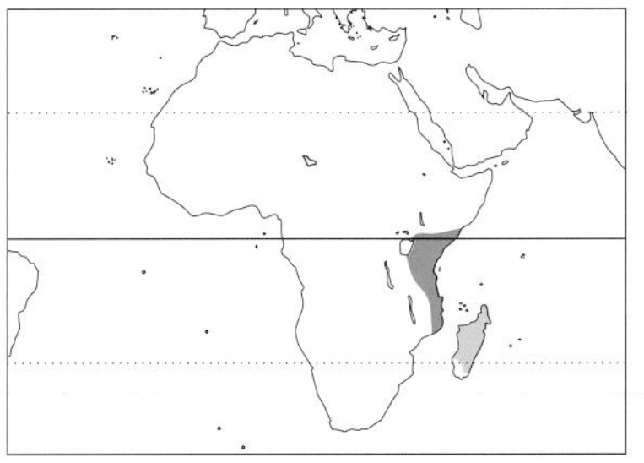

Food and Feeding. Mostly insects, including Hymenoptera, Neuroptera and beetles. Forages mostly in flight, in flocks, over grassland, beach, water or woodland; usually in late evening, but on overcast days, also during day.
Breeding. Poorly known. Early Nov. Small loose colonies on rocky islets in coastal waters and rivers. Nest is a hollow on the rock, sometimes lined with regurgitated insect exoskeletons. Clutch 2 eggs. No further information available.
Movements. After breeding, birds migrate to spend period Mar-Sept on E coast of Africa, from Mozambique N of R Zambezi to S Somalia; less often inland to L Victoria; S passage in Kenya most marked Aug-Sept; probably spends start of non-breeding season in Somalia before moving S along Kenya coast. Present in Madagascar mostly from Sept to Apr/May. Vagrant or scarce migrant to Mauritius, Reunion, Comores in Oct.
Status and Conservation. Not globally threatened. Fairly common, but poorly known. Non-breeding flocks on coast of Africa may number several hundred birds, but also flocks of 9000-10,000 birds on Kenya coast in Aug 1978, and 3000 S Somalia in May 1979 and Jul 1981. In Madagascar, flocks usually only of 10-50 birds, less often as many as 150 birds. Only apparently protected breeding sites are on granitic rocks off Special Reserve of Nosy Mangabe in NE Madagascar; other populations unprotected by legislation, but some security afforded by offshore inaccessibility.
Bibliography. Appert (1971), Ash (1977), Ash & Miskell (1989), Benson (1960, 1978), Benson *et al.* (1976-1977), Britton, P. L. (1977, 1980), Dee (1986), Dhondt (1975), Dowsett & Forbes-Watson (1993), Langrand (1990), Lewis & Pomeroy (1989), Louette (1981, 1988), Mackworth-Praed & Grant (1957, 1962), Milon *et al.* (1973), Nicoll & Langrand (1989), Short *et al.* (1990), Urban *et al.* (1986).

15. **Rock Pratincole**

Glareola nuchalis

French: Glaréole auréolée **German**: Halsband-Brachschwalbe **Spanish**: Canastera Sombría
Other common names: Collared Pratincole(!); Chestnut-collared/Rufous-collared Pratincole (*liberiae*); White-collared Pratincole (*nuchalis*)

Taxonomy. *Glareola nuchalis* G. R. Gray, 1849, Fifth Cataract of the Nile near Berber, Sudan. Sometimes placed in *Galachrysia* with *G. cinerea* and *G. lactea*. Race *liberiae* sometimes considered a megasubspecies. Two subspecies recognized.
Subspecies and Distribution.
G. n. liberiae Schlegel, 1881 - Sierra Leone to W Cameroon.
G. n. nuchalis G. R. Gray, 1849 - Chad E to Uganda, extreme W Kenya and Ethiopia, and S to R Zambezi in Zambia, NE Namibia, Zimbabwe and Mozambique.

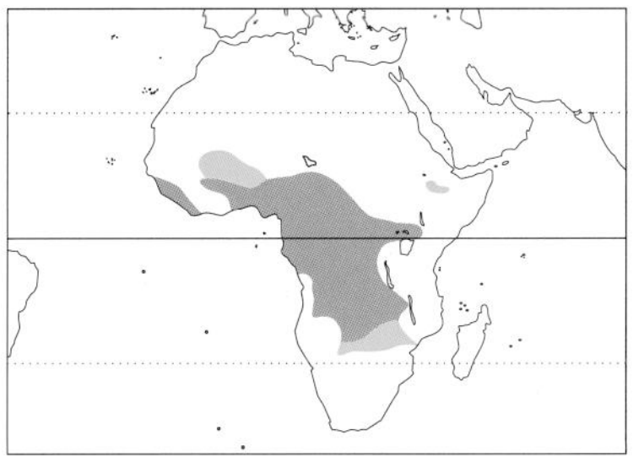

Descriptive notes. 18-19 cm; 43-52 g. Above dark brownish grey; white lines from behind each eye join to form white collar across nape; rump and base of tail white; below ash grey, shading to white on lower belly and undertail; underwing dark grey with white bar on inner wing; bill black, red at base; legs bright red. Differs from *G. ocularis* by much smaller size, collar, white underwing bar and red legs; much darker than *G. cinerea*, which also has striking wing pattern. Juvenile lacks pale collar and eyestripe; flecked buff above and below; legs more orangey. Race *liberiae* differs in having chestnut, not white, across nape; darker overall; intermediates occur in W Cameroon.
Habitat. Exposed rocks in larger rivers and streams, especially for breeding; may rest on sandbars; when rivers in flood moves to coastal localities or to other inland waters.
Food and Feeding. Flies, including tsetse flies (*Glossina*), ants, beetles and other insects. Strongly gregarious; forages mainly on the wing at dawn and dusk, catching insects over water or far from water 15-50 m above ground, sometimes very much higher; may enter towns at dusk to catch insects attracted to street lights.
Breeding. Feb-Apr in Sierra Leone, Apr-Jun in Nigeria at low water, Jul-Oct in Zaire, Sept-Oct in Zambia, Sept-Nov in Zimbabwe; breeding starts earlier where risk of flooding earlier, such as in narrow gorges with deep water. Breeding colonies usually small, up to c. 26 pairs. No nest; eggs laid on bare rock in river or lake, in depression or crack, or on ledge or under overhang. Usually 2 eggs (1-3); incubation 20 days, by both sexes. Chick mottled brownish grey and black above; smoky grey below. Chick fed by both parents on regurgitated insects; fledging c. 20-30 days. About 14% of young survive to fledging annually in Gabon; most losses of eggs and young result from predation, flooding and exposure.
Movements. May be resident at nesting sites in Nigeria, Cameroon, Zaire, Uganda and W Kenya, but much post-breeding dispersal during wet season to rivers further afield. On R Niger found only Mar-Sept; on Zambezi usually present only from about Jul/Aug to Jan/Feb during breeding season, migrating northward to more equatorial regions after breeding. Migrant *nuchalis* seen in Oct in Togo, in range of *liberiae*.
Status and Conservation. Not globally threatened. Nominate *nuchalis* quite common on suitable rivers where exposed rocks available; on R Zambezi c. 1·5 birds/km², but distribution patchy and confined to suitable habitat, usually near rapids; up to 300 birds may occur together; estimated total of more than 1000 birds in Victoria Falls area, including 700 birds in Batoka Gorge, over 105-km stretch of R Zambezi, in 1981. Not uncommon in Ghana in colonies of 20-30 birds, though L Volta has flooded some sites where species formerly common. In Sierra Leone, abundant in dry season on most rocky stretches of large rivers, e.g. 100 pairs on stretch of c. 3·2 km of R Moa, and 75 birds sitting on 3 small rocks on R Sewa close to women washing clothes. Species is vulnerable to unpredictable fluctuations in water levels of rivers on which dams have been built, especially where rivers are deep and narrow, and some sites lost permanently to dams; further dam building likely to be detrimental. Species is now only vagrant or rare visitor to Sudan, where first described.
Bibliography. Bannerman (1931, 1951), Benson & Irwin (1967), Benson & Pitman (1959), Britton, P. L. (1980), Brosset (1979), Cheke (1980, 1982), Chenaux-Repond (1975), Clancey (1981b), Dowsett & Forbes-Watson (1993), Elgood *et al.* (1994), Gatter & Hodgson (1987), Ginn *et al.* (1989), Grimes (1987), Irwin (1981), Johnston-Stewart *et al.* (1981), Jones, J. M. B. (1987), Lippens & Wille (1976), Louette (1981), Mackworth-Praed & Grant (1957, 1962, 1970), Maclean (1993), Penry (1979), Pinto (1983), Pollard (1982), Rand (1951a), Short *et al.* (1990), Urban *et al.* (1986), Williams, Coppinger & Maclean (1989).

16. **Grey Pratincole**

Glareola cinerea

French: Glaréole grise **German**: Graubrachschwalbe **Spanish**: Canastera Gris
Other common names: Cream-coloured Pratincole

Taxonomy. *Glareola cinerea* Fraser, 1843, mouth of River Niger. Sometimes placed in genus *Galachrysia* with *G. nuchalis* and *G. lactea*. Forms superspecies with *G. lactea*. Birds from upper R Niger, with more cinnamon on nape and breast, may merit subspecific separation as race *colorata*. Monotypic.
Distribution. Large rivers and coasts: Mali and Niger to Ghana, Cameroon, W Zaire and NW Angola.

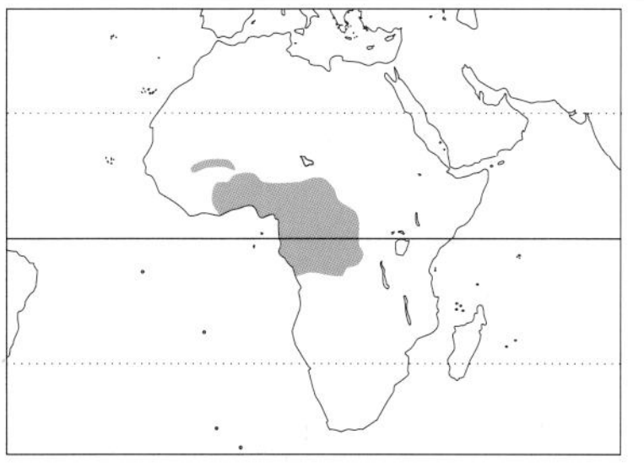

Descriptive notes. 18-20 cm. Above pale grey with pale chestnut nape and white rump; narrow black eyestripe curving down behind eye, and narrow white supercilium; tail black, with white sides and base, slightly forked; primaries black with white patch, secondaries white with black trailing edge; below white, washed buff on breast and upper belly; underwing largely white with black and white pattern on primaries; bill black, red at base; legs red. Differs from *G. lactea* by head pattern and largely white underwing. Juvenile scaled black and buff on upperparts; no black markings on face; tip of tail mottled black and buff.
Habitat. Sandbanks of larger slow-flowing rivers; during flood or high water also uses local reservoirs and coastal habitats, occasionally mangroves.
Food and Feeding. Flies, beetles, small grasshoppers and spiders. Catches prey mostly on the wing over water, mainly in evening; feeds socially.
Breeding. Mar-May in Niger, Mar-Jun in Nigeria, Feb in Gabon, Jun-Jul in Zaire when rivers at their lowest. Breeds in loose colonies, with nests a few metres apart. Nest is a shallow unlined scrape in sand of sandbar or on shingle, usually near water. Clutch 1-2 eggs; roles of parents, incubation and fledging periods unknown. Chick pale sandy grey above with fine black markings; below white.
Movements. Post-breeding dispersal in Nigeria and elsewhere, when rivers in flood, moving Jul-Sept to L Chad, and to smaller rivers and coastal localities.
Status and Conservation. Not globally threatened. Locally abundant and not under any immediate threat, except perhaps where relatively uncommon. In Nigeria, over 500 at L Chad in Sept, when rivers in spate; up to 300 on coast at Lagos, Jul-Nov. Not recorded since 1956 in Ghana, where creation of L Volta has removed much suitable habitat. Subject to human disturbance.
Bibliography. Bannerman (1931, 1951, 1953), Dowsett & Forbes-Watson (1993), Elgood *et al.* (1994), Grimes (1987), Lippens & Wille (1976), Louette (1981), Mackworth-Praed & Grant (1970), Pinto (1983), Snow (1978), Urban *et al.* (1986).

17. **Small Pratincole**

Glareola lactea

French: Glaréole lactée **German**: Sandbrachschwalbe **Spanish**: Canastera Chica
Other common names: Little/Small Indian/Milky Pratincole, Swallow-plover

Taxonomy. *Glareola lactea* Temminck, 1820, Bengal. Sometimes placed in *Galachrysia* with *G. cinerea* and *G. nuchalis*. Forms superspecies with *G. cinerea*. Monotypic.
Distribution. E Afghanistan and Pakistan, through India, Sri Lanka and Bangladesh to SC China (S Yunnan), and thence S & SE through Myanmar to Thailand, Laos and Cambodia.

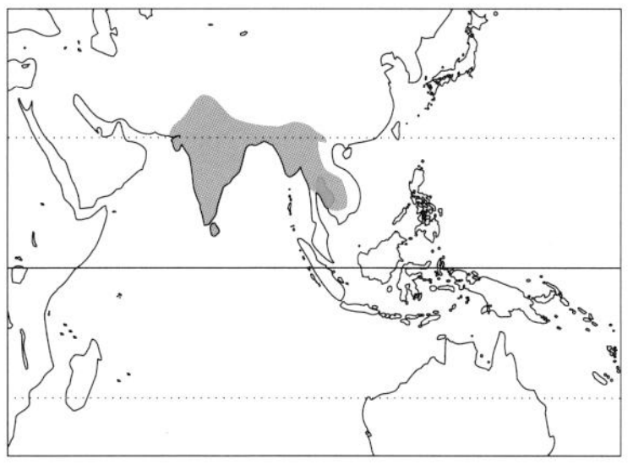

Descriptive notes. c. 17 cm; 37-38 g. Above pale sandy grey; forehead brownish; lores black; rump and base of tail white, with black subterminal band; primaries black, contrasting with pale coverts, secondaries white with black trailing edge; below pale rufous buff, shading to white on lower belly and undertail; underwing black with white bar across secondaries and inner primaries; bill black with small amount of red at base; legs dusky to black. Adult non-breeding duller, loses black lores. Differs from *G. cinerea* by plain head and darker underwing. Juvenile scaled and spotted buff above; spotted pale brown below.
Habitat. Large rivers and streams with exposed sandbars and shingle banks, up to c. 1800 m in Himalayas; also coastal marshes, estuaries; also large inland lakes when not breeding.
Food and Feeding. Beetles, bugs, termites, flies and other insects. Crepuscular; forages in large flocks on the wing, either high in air or low over water or ground; may also catch insects by running on ground like plover. When feeding may recall pipistrelle bat (*Pipistrellus*) with which often flies in twilight.
Breeding. Feb-Apr in India and Sri Lanka; from Mar in Pakistan; young in Jun in E Afghanistan. Nests colonially, often dozens of nests together, sometimes with River Terns (*Sterna aurantia*), Black-bellied Terns (*S. acuticauda*), or Indian Skimmers (*Rynchops albicollis*). Nest is a shallow scrape, or no nest at all; on sandbank in river, even up to water's edge. Clutch 2-3 eggs (2-4); incubation 17-18 days, by both sexes; during hot hours of day, attentive periods 25-35 minutes long; incoming parent often wets belly plumage before return to nest, to cool eggs. Chick finely mottled greyish white, pale buff and dusky above; narrow black line behind eye; below white. Chick fed by regurgitation; when threatened, mock-incubation and broken-wing distraction displays frequently performed by adults; fledging period not recorded. Unseasonal rains or snow melt may cause flooding of early clutches, but birds lay again soon after, even as late as Jun.
Movements. Locally migratory, depending on water levels of rivers. Present in many breeding areas only Apr-Aug; moves to lower levels in winter. Mainly summer breeding visitor to Pakistan, but up to 350 birds recorded in Jan; disappears from R Indus in mid-winter, though over 500 birds seen together on Indus in Mar. Vagrant W to Arabian Gulf and Oman, Nov-Mar; also S to Malay Peninsula in Nov and Jan.
Status and Conservation. Not globally threatened. Total population estimated to be in range 10,000-100,000 birds. Species seems able to survive adequately in large numbers throughout range. Flock of 2000 recorded at Chitwan, Nepal, Jan 1983; flocks of a few hundred birds often seen in S Nepal.
Bibliography. Ali (1953), Ali & Ripley (1982), Deignan (1945), Dharmakumarsinhji (1964), Gallagher & Woodcock (1980), Henry (1971), Hollom *et al.* (1988), Hüe & Étchécopar (1970), Inskipp & Inskipp (1991), King *et al.* (1975), Kotagamana & Fernando (1994), Lekagul & Round (1991), Maclean (1975), Medway & Wells (1976), Perennou *et al.* (1994), Phillips (1978), Ripley (1982), Roberts, T. J. (1991), Smythies (1986), Whistler (1949), Wijesinghe (1994).

Class AVES
Order CHARADRIIFORMES
Suborder CHARADRII

Family CHARADRIIDAE (PLOVERS)

- Small to medium-sized upright shorebirds, with round head, large eyes and short, pointed bill.
- 12-38 cm.

- All regions except Antarctic; almost all areas support several species.
- Open habitats, both wet and dry, including great variety of wetlands, coastal shoreline, grassland, tundra, steppe and semi-desert.
- 10 genera, 67 species, 106 taxa.
- 10 species threatened; 1 of these almost certainly extinct since 1600.

Systematics

Plovers are normally encountered in open wetlands, grassland and tundra and along seashores, habitats which they share with the sandpipers and their allies (Scolopacidae). The two families together comprise the great majority of the guild of shorebirds, or waders. The strong ecological congruence between plovers and sandpipers, and their overall morphological similarity has lead many scientists and most laypersons to infer a close evolutionary relationship between the Charadriidae and Scolopacidae. H. Gadow in the nineteenth century, and E. Mayr, D. Amadon, A. Wetmore and P. A. Johnsgard in the twentieth, regarded plovers and sandpipers as sister groups within the Charadriiformes. In contrast to this is the suggestion that plovers are more closely related to gulls (Laridae) and terns (Sternidae) than to sandpipers, a conclusion arising from several recent comparative stud-

ies of shorebirds and their allies using: morphology of bones, chromosomes, sperm and downy young; behaviour, for instance whether head-scratching is direct or, as in plovers, indirect; and biochemistry, of allozymes, DNA and some metabolic products. The same studies indicate that avocets and stilts (Recurvirostridae) and oystercatchers (Haematopodidae) may have evolved from plover-like ancestors. The intriguing proposal of A. Feduccia was that all of these families, and indeed most other avian taxa, are the result of a fantastic adaptive radiation emanating from a "transitional shorebird" that survived the wave of extinctions at the end of the Cretaceous, about 65 million years ago. During this episode the dinosaurs were wiped out completely, along with most bird species then alive. The "transitional shorebird" might well have looked like a plover, and might have behaved like one.

The modern plovers may have originated in the late Eocene, about 40 million years ago, but there are no known generally accepted fossil plover remains from that era. The first fossils assignable to two modern genera within the Charadriidae, a *Charadrius* species from Colorado and a *Vanellus* species from Belgian deposits, were retrieved from the middle Oligocene, dating back to 30 million years ago, the time when the first grasses appeared.

With the exception of the enigmatic Magellanic Plover (*Pluvianellus socialis*), biochemical evidence suggests the plover family to be holophyletic, in other words that all modern plovers, and no other taxa, share the same common ancestor. The morphological studies of skeletons by J. G. Strauch, corroborated by P. C. Chu and M. Björklund, confirm the idea of a common ancestor for the Charadriidae, but suggest that oystercatchers, avocets, stilts and the Ibisbill (*Ibidorhyncha struthersii*) have all evolved from early members of the plover family. Although the family is commonly divided into two subfamilies, the lapwings (Vanellinae) and the true plovers (Charadriinae), both the DNA-DNA hybridization studies of C. G. Sibley and J. E. Ahlquist and the protein electrophoretic studies by Canadian and Australian teams indicate that the four plovers of the genus *Pluvialis* may be an outgroup to the other two, having derived from a common ancestor early on. Perhaps, *Pluvialis* should not be included in the subfamily Charadriinae, but rather be awarded a subfamily of its own.

On several occasions it has been suggested that the plovers are a family that originated at low latitudes in the Southern Hemisphere, the region where most species are to be found today. The

Subdivision of the Charadriidae .

[Figure: Àngels Jutglar & Etel Vilaró]

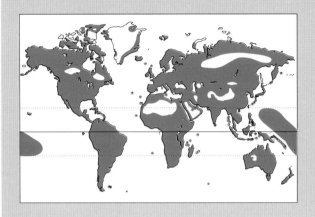

CHARADRIIDAE

VANELLINAE

PLUVIANELLINAE

CHARADRIINAE

lapwings
25 species
(Vanellus, Erythrogonys)

Magellanic Plover
1 species
(Pluvianellus)

plovers
41 species
(Pluvialis, Charadrius, Elseyornis, Peltohyas, Anarhynchus, Phegornis, Oreopholus)

FAMILY   SUBFAMILY

family would appear to have evolved under rather arid, semi-desertic conditions, specializing on small prey that are most active at night. Only the genus *Pluvialis*, of which all four species breed in tundra areas around the Arctic Ocean, may have its origin in the Northern Hemisphere. Nocturnal feeding on small invertebrates could have been the critical characteristic that allowed the similarly styled "transitional shorebird" to survive the period of relative cold and darkness at the end of the Cretaceous that wiped out most of the bigger beasts.

The lapwings, with 25 extant species in two genera, form a fairly close-knit group that would seem to be monophyletic on the basis of several morphological and biochemical studies, the latter including research on allozymes, DNA and the wax produced by the preen glands. Africa has the most species of lapwing, while North America has none. The tradition to split the lapwings into as many as 19 different genera, most of which contained only a single species, has generally been abandoned since the review of W. J. Bock in 1958. On the basis of morphological characteristics, two South American lapwings, the Southern Lapwing (*Vanellus chilensis*) and the Andean Lapwing (*Vanellus resplendens*) appear more closely related to one another than to any other lapwing species. They may descend from relatives of the Blacksmith Lapwing (*Vanellus armatus*) or the Spur-winged Lapwing (*Vanellus spinosus*). The Red-kneed Dotterel (*Erythrogonys cinctus*) was commonly placed in the genus *Charadrius* until allozyme studies of Australian plovers and lapwings by P. D. Christian and co-workers in 1992 showed that it is probably more appropriately considered a lapwing.

The subfamily Charadriinae with 37 species and seven genera, is somewhat more diverse than the Vanellinae. As well as *Charadrius* itself, it includes the distinctive genus *Pluvialis*, to which the Red-breasted Plover (*Charadrius obscurus*), endemic to New Zealand, was previously assigned. It also includes an aberrant plover with a side-ways curved bill from New Zealand, the Wrybill (*Anarhynchus frontalis*). Wrybills are *Charadrius*-like in all respects and would certainly have been placed in that genus were it not for their highly peculiar bill. Recently, it has been argued, on the basis of allozymes and behavioural characteristics, that two *Charadrius* species, the Hooded Plover (*Charadrius rubricollis*) of Australia and the Shore Plover (*Charadrius novaeseelandiae*) of New Zealand, should be placed in a distinct genus, *Thinornis*, although, with the limits of *Thinornis* still under discussion, for the time being it seems most prudent to retain these species in the genus *Charadrius*. This species pair may be most closely related to the Black-fronted

Dotterel (*Elseyornis melanops*), also an endemic of Australia and New Zealand. The desert-adapted Inland Dotterel (*Peltohyas australis*) was previously classified as a courser (Glareolidae), on the basis of overall resemblance and the colour pattern of its downy young. However, recent morphological studies and biochemical studies have suggested it to be a *Charadrius*, with which it shares an alternation of breeding and non-breeding plumages. Perhaps, instead of an ancient endemic, the Inland Dotterel is a quite newly arrived descendent from north-south migrant *Charadrius*-stock that has effectively adapted to the arid conditions of inland Australia.

In accordance with most recent authors, the genus *Eudromias* has been dropped herein and the Eurasian Dotterel (*Charadrius*

morinellus) assigned to the genus *Charadrius*, despite marked idiosyncrasies in both sexual dimorphism and breeding strategy (see Morphological Aspects, Breeding). Another species that was previously also assigned to *Eudromias* is the superficially similar Tawny-throated Dotterel (*Oreopholus ruficollis*) of the Andes and the arid coastal zones of South America; DNA-DNA hybridization studies place it firmly at the root of the plover lineage. Due to its relatively long and slightly down-curved bill, the Diademed Plover (*Phegornis mitchellii*), another Andean species, was sometimes thought to be a sandpiper, perhaps closely related to the peculiar Tuamotu Sandpiper (*Prosobonia cancellata*) of the Pacific islands. Studies of skeletal morphology confirm it to belong to the Charadriidae, however, and even suggest a closer relationship with the lapwings than with the true plovers. Modern studies of functional morphology and molecular genetics would surely help to elucidate the systematic position of this confusing wader species.

The Magellanic Plover is an unusual, grey-plumaged plover with turnstone-like morphological and behavioural features. It breeds around upland lakes in Tierra del Fuego and spends the non-breeding season several hundred kilometres away to the north in coastal Patagonia. For many reasons it is very doubtful whether this species really belongs in the Charadriidae, where it is often retained for convenience. Unlike the rest of the plover family, it has the habit of turning seaweed and stones to look for hidden prey, and it will dig into sand with its short legs to uncover buried prey items. Magellanic Plovers carry food to their chicks in the crop, a pouch which can also be distended in display. The osteological studies of J. G. Strauch, recently supported by P. C. Chu, place *Pluvianellus* in a single lineage with the sheathbills (*Chionis*), completely outside the plover family, and, consequently, many recent texts include the Magellanic Plover either in the Chionidae, or in a family of its own, Pluvianellidae.

At the species level, there has been rather little excitement over taxonomic issues regarding plovers in recent years. One development was the recognition of three species of golden plovers, where previously only two were accepted. In 1983, a thorough morphometric study by P. G. Connors confirmed the recognition of the Asian and the North American forms as full species: in an area of sympatry in western Alaska, Pacific Golden Plovers (*Pluvialis fulva*) and American Golden Plovers (*Pluvialis*

dominica) had distinct plumages and showed body size differences, while there was no evidence of interbreeding. Since then, field studies in western Alaska have demonstrated clear differences in nesting habitat and breeding vocalizations between the two plover species, and found that they mate strictly assortatively, thus confirming the biological importance of the differences in plumage and morphometrics.

Other cases are rather less clearly defined. For example, the St Helena Plover (*Charadrius sanctaehelenae*), restricted to a remote island in the South Atlantic, is clearly a close relative of Kittlitz's Plover (*Charadrius pecuarius*) of Africa and Madagascar, but whether or not it really merits separate species status is debatable; as the two are most unlikely to come into contact in the wild, the question is liable to remain academic. In contrast, another closely related species, the Black-banded Plover (*Charadrius thoracicus*), endemic to Madagascar, behaves as a separate species when in contact with Kittlitz's, although the phylogenetic proximity of the two species could prove to be the downfall of the threatened Black-banded (see Status and Conservation). Even more complicated is the case of the Kentish Plover (*Charadrius alexandrinus*) and its closest allies. At one extreme, the Javan Plover (*Charadrius javanicus*), the Red-capped Plover (*Charadrius ruficapillus*) and even the White-fronted Plover (*Charadrius marginatus*) have been considered conspecific with it, while, at the other, its races *nivosus* and *occidentalis* have been proposed to constitute two additional species. Once again, the treatment adopted is essentially a matter of personal preference.

One of the most recent taxonomic developments in the family came in 1994, when J. E. Dowding concluded that the allopatric populations of the Red-breasted Plover on Stewart Island and North Island were sufficiently distinct in respect of body size, plumage, eggs, ecology and habitat preference to warrant subspecific recognition.

Morphological Aspects

Although Charadriidae is a species-rich family, this does not go together with a proliferation of body forms, as in the other large shorebird family, the Scolopacidae. Plovers are rather uniform

The Eurasian Dotterel differs from all other plover species in that the female is the more brightly coloured sex, a phenomenon that is closely linked with the fact that the sex roles are reversed in this species. Here we see a rather drab-looking male sitting on the nest. Depending on local sex-ratios, females may have two or even three males incubating and raising young, although the males that receive the later clutches may receive some assistance from her. In breeding areas, when females are in excess males may mate with two or three, and some nests may contain the two to three clutches simultaneously.

[*Charadrius morinellus*, Cape Sterlikowa, Taymyr Peninsula, Siberia. Photo: Jan van de Kam]

in size, the largest species being only three times as long as the smallest; they have legs which are never very long nor very short, very small or vestigial hind toes, and a rather short, blunt bill that is swollen at the tip and narrower centrally. Perhaps most characteristically, they have relatively large eyes in a rounded head carried on a short, thick neck. The bill is usually straight, and no longer than the distance from the base of the bill itself to the back of the eye. The few exceptions are the Wrybill, with a sideways turned bill, and the Diademed Plover, with a rather long, decurved, sandpiper-like bill. The Magellanic Plover shares with the true plovers a rounded head and a short, stout bill, but otherwise reminds field observers of a turnstone rather than a plover. Its greyish coloration, relatively small eyes, hunched-back posture and flat-footed waddling gait are reminiscent of a small ground dove.

Now consider a mixed flock of Northern Lapwings (*Vanellus vanellus*) and Eurasian Golden Plovers (*Pluvialis apricaria*) foraging on a Western European field in winter. The feeding style and prey choice of the two plovers is similar; their foraging is typical for all Charadriidae. Then a raptor appears over the hedge. The plover flock flies up and splits into a loose, almost "dancing", group of rather slow-flying lapwings with broad wings, and a much denser group of straight- and fast-flying golden plovers with pointed wings. There, in the air, the two basic body forms and flight styles within the Charadriidae strike the eye.

All plovers are obligate visual foragers that catch their prey at boundary layers, usually picking small invertebrates from the surfaces of dry or wet substrates, or from low vegetation cover. Coming as close to probing as true plovers can, birds of the genus *Pluvialis* may sometimes pull invertebrates out of shallow holes. Plovers forage by making repeated runs, of up to a few metres at a time, interrupted by standstills, when the head is held high. Such pauses may also result in a peck, in order to capture a prey item detected on the surface. It is thought that these pauses allow plovers to detect prey at quite large distances, using a particularly acute form of monocular vision, and perhaps an auditory detection system as well. Whilst engaged in a run, a plover may be able to see and hear less acutely, but during the direct approach towards a detected prey item the plover may use binocular vision to judge the remaining distance. Field observations show that the bigger the plover species, the larger the distances run and the larger the prey items captured.

Not surprisingly perhaps, in the Magellanic Plover the archetypical run, stop and peck behaviour of plovers is absent. This bird waddles along the shore in a stoop-shouldered stance,

head low and eyes constantly peering at the ground. Except when disturbed, it rarely raises the head above the level of its back. Also unlike typical plovers, it does not peck perpendicularly to the ground but uses a slight twisting motion, so that the bill hits the ground at a sideways angle, resulting in a distinctive cock-headed feeding posture.

Plovers must also possess great visual acuity under poor light conditions, as they routinely feed at night as well as in daylight. This is made possible by specialized visual receptors. Compared with scolopacid waders, plovers have a higher retinal density of rods (useful for detection under poor light conditions), and also a greater ratio of rods and cones (the latter are for visual acuity in daylight and for colour discrimination). The bills of plovers

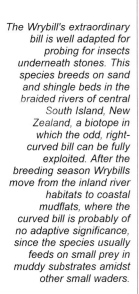

The differences between the two large subfamilies in the Charadriidae are amply illustrated by flying birds: the lapwings are larger, broad-winged species, generally with more attractive plumage and rather slower flight; the "true" plovers tend to be smaller, with longer and more pointed wings, duller, more uniform plumage and a swifter, more darting flight. The Pied Lapwing undoubtedly belongs to the first group, but it shows several similarities with Charadrius in details of plumage and physiology, and may perhaps form some sort of a link.

[Vanellus cayanus, Hato el Frío, Apure, Venezuela. Photo: Benjamín Busto]

are simple in their gross morphology: they do not have movable parts, apart from the Magellanic Plover, which can move the frontal part of the upper mandible independently, as can most sandpipers. The head anatomy aids rapid alignment towards a position indicated by a short-term cue, and appears tolerant of strong impacts on hard substrates. The jaw muscles of typical plovers are well developed but are unspecialized. Although plover-bills show quite high densities of touch-receptors, known as Herbst's Corpuscles, on both the inside and outside of the upper and the lower mandibles, these receptors are not arranged in the complicated ways known from probe-feeding scolopacid waders. It is likely that the touch-receptors are used for the inspection of captured prey items rather than for prey detection. The visual hunting style of plovers is correlated with the structure of the brain. The relative size of the optic lobe of plovers is almost twice that of probe-feeding sandpipers.

The Diademed Plover, an inhabitant of gravelly and grassy areas near freshwater lakes and streams in the high Andes, has a long and slender bill, only slightly swollen at the tip. Atypical of plovers, it uses its bill to make vertical probes, although it also commonly pecks at prey items on the surface. Nothing is known about the details of its bill structure and the arrangement of touch-receptors in the bill tip. The unique bill of the Wrybill, of which the distal quarter is laterally deflected to the right, has been subject to much more research. The Wrybill also breeds in highlands, in this case along the braided rivers of New Zealand's South Island, while it winters on intertidal mudflats on North Island. According to R. J. Pierce, the sideways curved bill is useful in capturing mayfly larvae typically clinging to the undersurface of stones. A Wrybill feeding in shallow water in shingle riverbeds tilts its head to the left, and pushes its bill under a stone so that the bill curvature fits closely. The bill is then moved forward and to the right. With a shorter, straight bill a plover would not be able to catch insects under stones; and with an upturned bill it would be impossible to open the mandibles between the undersurface of a stone and the stone beneath. On intertidal mudflats, Wrybills also feed by tilting the head to the left. They then make sideways sweeps with the bill, mostly from right to left, against the curvature of the bill, to sieve animals from water and the upper layer of mud. It is interesting that the Magellanic Plover of Patagonia preferentially pecks slightly sideways, with its head tilted in one direction. This is correlated with a slight lateral deflection of the tip of the horny covering of the bill, but not the bone; in 80% of examined specimens the twist was to the right.

Captured food items are processed in the gut. As in other birds, the digestive tract of plovers consists, from mouth to cloaca, of the oesophagus, the glandular stomach, the gizzard (muscular stomach), the small intestine and the large intestine. In all examined plovers, the glandular stomach is rather small compared to the gizzard, comprising about 10% of the total stomach mass. This means that plovers are not able to store much ingested food, nor can they achieve much digestion before the food has entered the gizzard. An exception is again provided by the Magellanic Plover, which has a well developed extensible crop, a strong-walled pouch that opens into the oesophagus on the right side of the neck. This crop serves as a storage organ and is also used for transporting food to the young, a form of behaviour otherwise unreported in the Charadriidae; the young are then fed by regurgitation. A crop may be particularly important for Magellanic Plovers in view of their reliance on clumped and small prey items, such as buried fly and chironomid larvae, that are only briefly available and must be gathered as the opportunity arises.

Plovers have gizzards of similar size, relative to body mass, to those of sandpipers, but species such as the Grey Plover (Pluvialis squatarola), which regularly ingest hard-shelled prey, have heavier, more muscular gizzards than those that feed on softer prey items, for instance the Eurasian Golden Plover. In contrast, the intestinal lengths of north temperate plovers is greater than that of co-occurring sandpipers with comparable diets. The caeca, a paired extension of the lower intestine that may have a function in the bacterial digestion of plant material, are also larger in plovers than in sandpipers; large caeca being typical of "primitive" birds, this has historically been interpreted to indicate that plovers are more primitive than sandpipers.

In the earlier morphological treatments of the Charadriidae, the width of bone between the eyes was used as a critical taxonomic character. In all plovers, and in many other avian taxa, this area on the forehead is also where the paired salt glands are found. When it turned out that plovers with larger salt glands had narrower bony rims between the eyes, and that the size of the salt gland was associated with the salinity of the chosen habitat within and between species, degree of ossification was discarded as a useful character in taxonomy. Salt glands are small, but powerful, glands that excrete excess salt directly from the blood plasma into the nasal cavity. Plovers of freshwater habitats, such as the lapwings, have rather small salt glands, whereas those frequenting estuarine and marine habitats have rather large salt glands. A careful allocation of energetically expensive tissue and a premium on being as lightly built as possible may prevent sea-

An African Wattled Lapwing on the look-out. The flat, open country that this species inhabits gives it little opportunity to survey its surroundings for rivals and predators, and consequently birds have been found to associate with termite mounds. In normal conditions, plovers are most unlikely to take up a position any higher than this. If at any stage they take advantage of the presence of trees, bushes or fence posts, it is almost always simply in order to stand in their shade during the hottest part of the day. In contrast to this, members of the Scolopacidae are more frequently observed making use of an elevated perch.

[*Vanellus senegallus lateralis*, KwaZulu-Natal, South Africa. Photo: Heinrich van den Berg/Bruce Coleman]

Tawny-throated Dotterels
live on overgrazed
grasslands or otherwise
essentially bare surfaces.
Some populations of the
nominate race live at
altitudes of up to 4600 m
in the Andes, and only
during migration can they
be found on grassy fields
and meadows in the
lowlands. Others,
including members of the
race pallidus, inhabit bare
coastal plains.
Interestingly, when
disturbed, this species
may turn its striped back
to the observer, offering a
highly effective disruptive
camouflage in
stony habitats.

[Oreopholus ruficollis
ruficollis,
Salar de Surire, Chile.
Photo: X. Ferrer &
A. de Sostoa]

shore plovers from having strongly ossified skullcaps. The strong, heavy membranes surrounding the salt glands provide a suitable replacement for the bone.

The ratio of leg to body length is relatively uniform in most plovers, although some of the Afrotropical and one Asian species of lapwing have rather long legs. Among these, the Long-toed Lapwing (*Vanellus crassirostris*) is the extreme. With its long legs and long toes it easily negotiates the floating vegetation in east African freshwater marshes. Long-toed Lapwings live like jacanas, show territorial interactions with jacanas and look like them as well, not only with respect to leg and toe length. The white head and foreneck in combination with a dark hindneck and back, and the rather uniformly coloured upperwing, provide a pattern that is more jacana-like than lapwing-like.

Lapwings have other features that set them apart from the remaining plovers. Of the 24 *Vanellus* species, 16 carry a crest or show facial wattles or sport wing-spurs, or have a combination of two of these features; no species has all three. In all lapwing species these showy characteristics are more prominent in males than in females, and their presence correlates with the aggressive nature of the genus, especially of the males. Wing-spurs are used in combat, and even in species that have no actual spur on the carpal joint, a bony knob is present beneath the skin, which makes blows with the leading edge of the wing more effective. Lapwings, and the Diademed Plover, are also characterized by their rounded wings. This is taken to an extreme by the Northern Lapwing, where the unfolded primaries almost form a semicircle. In this species, males have a spectacular flight display, during which they show much twisting and turning with great speed and agility. This display is even detectable at night by the quiet creaking of the wings with their large surface area. Although the Northern Lapwing is the most migratory species among the Vanellinae, it does not cover very long distances in single flights. Indeed, it does not have to, since suitable habitat is found along most of the routes between its breeding and wintering grounds, unbroken by large ecological barriers. Then again, it would not be able to anyway, since long distance flights require a different flight apparatus: long and pointed wings.

Most *Charadrius* and *Pluvialis* plovers have such slender wings, in which the outermost primary is the longest. Only sedentary species, such as the Black-banded Plover of south-west Madagascar, Kittlitz's Plover from much of Africa south of the Sahara, the St Helena Plover from the tiny island of St Helena, and the Shore Plover from one of the Chatham Islands of New Zealand, have more rounded wings. Birds with long, pointed wings are not the most manoeuvrable, but their flight is both rapid and energetically relatively cheap. Of course, such long distance flights need to be powered by strong pectoral muscles and must be fueled by large fat stores. The pectoral muscles of *Pluvialis* plovers form an even greater proportion (7-8%) of the total lean mass than those of sandpipers (5-6%), highly migratory birds too. The absolute size of these muscles in relation to the skeletal area of attachment is also larger in plovers than in sandpipers. At least in mid-winter, the fat stores that can be deposited by plovers is higher than that of most sandpipers. The genus *Pluvialis* and many *Charadrius* species thus seem particularly well equipped for undertaking long distance flights.

The plumage of plovers differs from that commonly found in the Scolopacidae in that it shows bold colour patterns in olive, brown, grey, black and white, but that it is nevertheless rather cryptic, owing to the disruptive effects of bands on the head, breast and tail. Species that nest on discontinuously coloured substrates tend to have breast bands. Species such as the Piping (*Charadrius melodus*), White-fronted, Kentish and Malaysian Plovers (*Charadrius peronii*) all nest in uniform beach habitats and have incomplete or no breast bands. A few large lapwing species do not show much crypsis. Due to their size, habits and nest-sites they can not hide effectively, and so they might as well advertise their presence. Although sexual differences in plumage are only slight in plovers, in many species males have a more intensely coloured plumage than females. Only in the Eurasian Dotterel is the breeding plumage of the females much more colourful than that of the males, a feature correlated with reversed sexual size dimorphism and also breeding role reversal, the female being the larger, competitive sex and the male caring for the eggs and chicks. The total mass of the contour feathers varies in direct proportion to body mass, accounting for about 7% of it. It is slightly higher in plovers wintering in cold temperate zones than in those in the tropics.

The facial markings and breast bands of many *Charadrius* species may have adaptive value for reasons of crypsis, but the counter-effect, conspicuousness, may also be important for reasons of display. In territorial aggressive interactions between the more brightly coloured males, threat displays are important. During such interactions the two contestants stand face to face and present the bold facial markings to each other. For this reason it may not be fortuitous that the black crown of 21 *Charadrius* species is restricted to the front edge of the crown and thereby maximally visible for a threatening opponent. Moreover, the black markings are most conspicuous during the courtship period. In Magellanic Plovers, it is iris coloration that features prominently in the complicated courtship and territorial displays. During these displays, the eye is opened widely and the pupil contracted, thus giving added prominence and brightness to an expanded coral iris; at these times the inner rim of the iris is yellow, which intensifies the contrast between eye and head.

Moult of the head feathers begins as soon as incubation has started. Yet, in rather few plover species is the seasonal change in plumage very pronounced. Several *Charadrius* plovers, however, especially those with rufous areas on the head, breast or belly, are more intensely coloured during the breeding season than during winter. The highly migratory *Pluvialis* plovers, seasonally commuting between Arctic or sub-Arctic and temperate to tropical habitats, show black underparts during the breeding period while these are whitish or grey during the rest of the year. That the black bellies, bordered by contrasting white edges, also combine the two functions of highly visible quality signals to attract mates and to impress competitors, without loosing the benefits of disruptive coloration, is suggested by the partial summer moult documented in Eurasian Golden Plovers. During the breeding season these plovers have part of their black breast and belly feathers replaced by much more cryptically coloured striped feathers. This makes the breeding plumage much less contrasting by the time that the pair-bond and territory are firmly established, and when most of the snow has melted, taking the starkest contrasts out of the landscape.

The juvenile plumage of plovers is not strikingly different from that of adults. All juveniles, and the freshly moulted adults of some species, show buff to rusty fringes on the contour feathers of the upperparts. Over the non-breeding season, as the contour feathers wear, the colour of these fringes fades, and after a few months young birds are generally indistinguishable from adults. Just before the breeding season, most plovers carry out a partial moult of the contour feathers only, especially with regard to the body parts that play a role in signalling. Depending on whether or not they make a breeding attempt as one year olds, young birds may or may not acquire this distinct breeding plumage. The Eurasian Golden Plover is an example of a species that breeds in its second calendar year after having acquired a full breeding plumage when only 9-10 months old.

In most plover species the complete moult takes place after the birds have arrived in their non-breeding quarters, and at this time the wing and tail feathers are renewed too. In some cases moult is started on the breeding grounds, or on staging areas during the post-breeding migration. During the moult of the flight-feathers, plovers start off by replacing some primaries. They start moulting the secondaries, the tertials and the tail feathers when the primaries are half completed. The primaries are moulted outwards from the "wrist", and the secondaries inwards. Wing moult is usually completed over a period of 3-5 months, but there are many cases in which wing moult is suspended and finished at a later date. An example is provided by the Grey Plover, a species that breeds in the high Arctic. The relatively long time that it takes these plovers to hatch a clutch and raise their chicks means that they only arrive late in the year in their temperate staging and wintering areas. As a consequence they often suspend wing moult after having completed the growth of 6-8 of the 10 primaries. Usually, primary moult is resumed when environmental conditions improve after the mid-winter. Regular yearly replacement is not the rule for the moult of secondaries in the genus *Pluvialis*, and perhaps in other plovers too. Each year only some of the secondaries are replaced, and the order in which this happens is rather chaotic. It may take 2-3 successive moulting seasons to replace them all. This contrasts with the annual and orderly replacement of all primaries, a difference that can be explained by the much heavier wear and tear to which primaries are exposed. Plovers that forego breeding in their second calendar year and which do not migrate to the breeding areas, capitalize on this free time by using the breeding period for a complete moult.

The plovers show an intriguing lack of size dimorphism between the sexes. Within a sample of Palearctic plovers, 10-20% of the species show some degree of dimorphy in wing, bill or tarsus length. This contrasts with scolopacid waders, of which more than 50% show dimorphism, often to a degree that is more extreme than in plovers. In many lapwing species the males tend to be slightly larger than the females. In the rest of the plover family, a few species show the opposite pattern, and in the Eurasian and Tawny-throated Dotterels and the Diademed Plover, the female is larger than the male. In the Eurasian Dotterel this is known to be correlated with a reproductive sex role reversal.

Habitat

A foraging style during which prey is detected by visual means and captured afoot provides adaptations for a life in open terrain

Most lapwing species are found at low latitudes with warm, dry climates. They inhabit a variety of open habitats, ranging from the edges of inland to coastal waters, and from dry savannas or steppes to cultivated land. Lapwings are not strongly migratory but may move erratically, following rain or fire or avoiding cold spells. The River Lapwing is largely confined to the margins of running water all year round, and is only rarely found near still or stagnant water. It breeds on shingle and sand banks where its contrasting plumage provides splendid camouflage. It sometimes feeds on cultivated land adjacent to the river.

[*Vanellus duvaucelii*, India. Photo: Getrud & Helmut Denzau]

Intraspecific territorial disputes are usually settled by means of threats in an upright posture, with the neck stretched out. On occasion, confrontations intensify and the carpal spurs, which are well developed in many lapwing species, may be used as effective weapons; in most cases, the spurs are brightly coloured red or yellow, and they tend to be longer in males. Like many of its congeners, the Southern Lapwing defends its territory with loud, persistent calls, and this has led to its employment as a sentinel on many ranches.

[Vanellus chilensis lampronotus, Pantanal, Brazil. Photo: Günter Ziesler]

with short vegetation or with completely barren ground. Plovers use inland habitats, including river and lake shores, marshes, dry plains and savannas, as much as the typical shorebird habitats along the coast. Most plover species avoid rocky shores, but the Shore Plover, an endemic of New Zealand's Chatham Islands, does not. Several other *Charadrius* species are beach dwellers in both breeding and non-breeding seasons. Only some of the highly migratory *Pluvialis* and *Charadrius* species show substantial habitat change in the course of the year, from tundra to coastal mudflats and inland grasslands.

Although the general features of plover habitats are easy to summarize, the details of habitats used by different plover species vary greatly and are finely tuned to their biology. To gain a feeling of what the habitats of a plover may look like in the course of a year, seasonal habitat use of a few will be examined in more detail. At one climatic extreme, Inland Dotterels occur year round on arid and sparsely vegetated plains and semi-desert in the tropical heat of Australia. At the other end of this spectrum, Eurasian Dotterels breed on cold and misty moorland and tundra in northern Europe and Asia, where they typically favour sparsely vegetated open flats with plenty of bare rock. During migration they are found on fallow and freshly ploughed fields and areas with short, heavily grazed or saline, vegetation. In North Africa and the Middle East, where Eurasian Dotterels spend the winter, they frequent stony steppe, semi-desert and marginal farmland.

The four *Pluvialis* species all breed in similar boreal and Arctic habitats to Eurasian Dotterels, but prefer the slightly more vegetated parts of upland moors and tundra. During migration and in winter the three golden plovers mainly occur on open fields and grassland. Eurasian Golden Plovers may feed on intertidal flats but most use cultivated fields and, especially, grassland. Within Europe, regional and seasonal differences in the use of these habitat types have been documented. This is unlike Grey Plovers that always and only feed on intertidal flats during migration, and wherever they spend the winter: from the north of Scotland to the deep south of South Africa or Tierra del Fuego. However, Grey Plovers wintering in Britain indicate a behavioural fine-tuning to habitat characteristics by establishing feeding territories only in intertidal areas with deep gullies, whereas they feed in loose flocks in other parts of the estuaries.

Common Ringed Plovers (*Charadrius hiaticula*), Semipalmated Plovers (*Charadrius semipalmatus*) and Long-billed Plovers (*Charadrius placidus*) are typical shoreline birds, usually occurring in areas where their distinct blotched plumage pattern has a disruptive effect. Ranging from north temperate to high Arctic latitudes, these species breed in well drained, gravelly and sparsely vegetated areas near a seashore, stream or pool. During the migration and winter periods they occur predominantly on wide sandy and shingle intertidal beaches. Similar shifts from inland to seaside shorelines is made by other species such as the Wrybill of New Zealand and the Magellanic Plover of Patagonia. The first moves from the upland braided riverbeds where it breeds to the estuarine intertidal areas where it winters. The second breeds along the open shorelines of pools and lakes on the south Patagonian steppe and winters further north on the wide beaches along the Atlantic coast of southern Argentina.

There are several *Charadrius* species that spend both the breeding and non-breeding seasons in salty beach-like habitats, a category that includes salt-lakes and salt-pans. Such habitats are the rule for south temperate resident species such as the Red-breasted, Red-capped and Hooded Plovers, north temperate migratory species such as Kentish and Piping Plovers, and tropical residents such as Wilson's (*Charadrius wilsonia*), White-fronted and Malaysian Plovers. Kentish Plovers not only breed along seashores, but also have an extensive inland distribution. They share the steppes and semi-deserts of Eurasia with the Greater Sandplover (*Charadrius leschenaultii*), a species also wintering along tropical seashores, and Caspian (*Charadrius asiaticus*) and Oriental Plovers (*Charadrius veredus*). The latter two species winter inland on the short dry grasslands of tropical Africa and Australia respectively. Greater Sandplovers spend the non-breeding season along the shores of the Indian Ocean, and are joined there by Lesser Sandplovers (*Charadrius mongolus*), a closely related species that breeds above the tree-line on elevated tundra and sparsely vegetated mountain steppes, thus showing many ecological similarities to Eurasian Dotterels.

The grassy Eurasian steppes are home to Sociable (*Vanellus gregarius*) and White-tailed Lapwings (*Vanellus leucurus*). The latter long-legged species usually nests close to water bodies, where it forages on the shallow margins. Both species are migratory, and winter in the region from north-east Africa to Pakistan, using habitats quite similar to those on the breeding grounds. Faithfulness to one habitat type is, in fact, typical of all lapwings, including the only two other north-south migrants, the Northern and Grey-headed Lapwings (*Vanellus cinereus*). The first is a grassland specialist, the second, with much longer legs than the first, an Asian marshland dweller.

Among the waders wintering on intertidal flats, plovers tend to forage at higher tidal levels than probing sandpiper-like shorebirds. Visual prey detection may allow plovers to feed profitably on the rather low densities of active and surface-living prey typical of high-lying and compact substrates. At the same time, plovers thus avoid areas with high densities of probing sandpipers which disturb their prey, since sandpipers usually concentrate foraging on lower and looser sediments.

Also in contrast to many scolopacid waders, plovers show relatively little tendency to make special movements between feeding and alternative roosting habitats. Many plovers simply roost on their feeding grounds. Some species, such as Eurasian Golden Plovers and Northern Lapwings, may regularly commute between grassland feeding areas and nearby arable fields or shore habitats to preen and roost. Such habitat shifts are the routine of American Golden Plovers and Tawny-throated Dotterels on Argentinian *pampas*. The two species come together in flocks in wetlands, to bathe and preen in the daytime and to roost at night. Plovers living on the coast are forced off the intertidal flats by the rising tide, and then coalesce into flocks on high-lying sandbanks, bare sandy patches between mangroves, or fields behind a dyke. However, in such cases plovers habitually keep their distance, roosting spread out and quite far away from the large, compact roosts of scolopacid waders, or at the most remaining along the fringes of such roosts.

Plovers rarely sit or stand on branches of shrubs or trees in tall vegetation. This is essentially a consequence of the hind toe being very short or vestigial, which means that they are unable to grasp a branch. In tropical coastal areas, the odd flock of Grey Plovers may spend the high water periods perched in a mangrove tree, but as a rule plovers do this less frequently than most of the co-occurring sandpiper species. Yet, plovers in the tropics do routinely use the sunshade of mangroves, or other stands of trees, to reduce the heat load at midday. Inland Dotterels in Australia roost in the shade of fenceposts, shrubs and tussocks when air temperatures reach over 45°C. In breeding areas, unlike the case with many scolopacid waders, one never encounters plovers that are vigilant or displaying in the top of a small tree or any other vertical structure. In wet grassland areas of Western Europe, where breeding waders reach high densities, one of the more typical sights is a shank, a snipe or a godwit on a fencepost, but never a Northern Lapwing.

General Habits

For most of the year the great majority of plovers operate in small flocks. These flocks are never very tightly packed and may comprise any number of birds up to a few thousand individuals. Plovers are rarely counted by the ten thousands, as can happen with several scolopacid waders. During peaks of southward migration in the Netherlands, a steady stream of flocks of Northern Lapwings, each containing several hundred to a few thousand individuals, may pass by. Even more spectacular sightings must have been made along the Gulf coast of Louisiana, USA, early in the last century. On a single day an estimated 48,000 American Golden Plovers were shot in one small area, indicating the simultaneous northward passage of even greater numbers.

During migration, plovers fly alone or in flocks comprising two to several hundred individuals. Grey Plovers migrate in flocks averaging about 30 birds. Especially upon departure on long distance flights, such as those between West Africa and the European Wadden Sea, such flocks are highly structured. They have the appearance of an echelon or a V. Migratory flocks are usually monospecific, but when flockmates are in short supply, outside the peak of the migration season for example, plovers may fly with like-minded shorebird species. When travelling to and from their Siberian breeding grounds, mixed flocks of Grey Plovers and Bar-tailed Godwits (*Limosa lapponica*), or Grey Plovers and Red Knots (*Calidris canutus*) occur regularly. In the last century, American Golden Plovers and Eskimo Curlews (*Numenius borealis*) often migrated together in flocks. During the breeding season most plover species are not gregarious, but split up in pairs or other small reproductive units, each of which usually defends a patch of ground, the breeding territory.

Territoriality is not limited to the breeding season, since many plover species also defend small feeding areas during migratory stopovers and on the wintering grounds. Such patches may be defended continuously for several months over an entire non-breeding season, or temporarily, for a few days at a suitable stopover site, or even for less than an hour when a clumped resource is monopolized by a bird in a feeding flock. Grey Plovers show long-term defence of feeding territories on intertidal mudflats in

Plovers usually roost in flocks. There is a good reason for this: a single bird roosting alone has to keep an eye on its surroundings constantly, in order to spot any approaching predator; with a roosting flock, however, the alarm can be given for the entire flock by a single bird detecting the predator, so each bird is able to repose more deeply. During the non-breeding season some Grey Plovers will defend a feeding territory to which they may return annually. Within such territories, birds often have a favoured loafing site, but even territorial birds tend to roost with the flock.

[*Pluvialis squatarola*, La Jolla, California, USA. Photo: A. & E. Morris/ Birds As Art]

The Killdeer is a characteristic species of agricultural land in North America. It is well known for the distinctive rufous rump and uppertail-coverts which it uses to stunning effect in several displays, most notably its distraction display. The other well known feature of this species is its distinctive call, "kill-dee", which is the source of its vernacular name, and more indirectly of its scientific name.

[*Charadrius vociferus vociferus*, southern USA. Photo: François Gohier/ Ardea]

many parts of their wintering range, at least from northern England to southern Africa. In fact, the same individual may return year after year to the same patch of mud once it has established itself as a young bird. Grey and Common Ringed Plovers feeding on polychaete worms in Moroccan estuaries during northward migration defend feeding territories over periods of up to several weeks. These territories show complete overlap between the two species and are only defended against conspecifics. Individual Eurasian Golden Plovers feeding in flocks on grassland, may occasionally and temporarily defend little patches of space against conspecifics. Territorial defence is much more outspoken in American Golden Plovers wintering on the *pampas* of Argentina. Most of these birds defend long-term territories during daytime in short-grass uplands and along streams, but come together at communal night-time roosts.

The behavioural components involved in territorial encounters in the non-breeding season are highly ritualized and are quite similar among different plover species. Normally the aggressor runs up to an encroaching neighbour in a head-down, tail-fanned posture. The two then walk parallel to each other virtually along the territory boundary, up to a metre apart, each with wings drooped towards the opponent, back feathers slightly raised and tail fanned. They may march repeatedly back and forth along the territory boundary in this posture. Contestants frequently show displacement feeding, and parallel walking is occasionally interrupted by bouts of posturing, during which the bird fans the tail and tilts it slightly, so that its upper surface projects towards the opponent. Simultaneously, the bird keeps the wing on the side of the opponent drooped and ready for a strike; it may crouch low or sit on the ground. Nevertheless, the behavioural repertoire involved in territory establishment and defence in non-breeding situations is impoverished relative to that used on the breeding grounds, where there is a larger aerial component to territorial displays, correlated with the fact that breeding territories are about an order of magnitude larger than the territories used exclusively for feeding.

Plovers may feed throughout day and night, but daily rhythms show marked variations depending on feeding conditions and the presence of predators. Northern Lapwings tend to feed by day and roost by night during most moon phases, but carry out all feeding by night for a few days around full moon. According to T. P. Milsom and co-workers, this lunar rhythm is clearest in mid-winter, except when the ground is frozen or covered in snow. During moonlit, but cloudy, nights the incidence of night feeding is also smaller, suggesting that light conditions play an important role. It is still unclear whether nocturnal foraging around full moon is a response to enhanced night-time feeding conditions, to decreased daytime feeding conditions, to changes in the relative predation risk for lapwings during day and night, or a combination of these factors. A good example of enhanced feeding conditions at night is provided by Grey Plovers in an English estuary that were studied by D. J. Townshend and colleagues. These plovers obtained high intake rates by eating large polychaete worms in an area that was not visited by day. A contrasting example of a diurnal pattern in a closely related species is provided by J. P. Myers' studies on American Golden Plovers on the *pampas* in northern Argentina. After feeding during the day, they assembled at communal roosts in shallow water during the night. Another contrast is provided by Wilson's Plovers in a mangrove area in Venezuela. These plovers roost in small flocks during much of the daylight period, while feeding solitarily at night, almost uniquely on small fiddler crabs. Because fiddler crabs are most available during the day, M. Thibault and R. McNeil interpret the nocturnal foraging habits of Wilson's Plovers as a strategy to avoid diurnal predation.

To avoid the claws of hunting raptors or the jaws of roaming jackals and foxes, plovers possess remarkable cognitive abilities and subtle behavioural adaptations. In a study of the Southern Lapwing in Venezuela and Long-toed and Blacksmith Lapwings in Kenya, J. R. Walters showed that the discriminative ability of these plovers of open savannas is quite sophisticated. Southern Lapwings have a specific call for reptiles that causes small chicks to move away. The lapwings' responses indicate that pigs, which are potential egg predators, are not classified with cows and horses. Vehicles are classified with hoofed herbivores, which is most appropriate since cars, cattle and horses pose the same threat of trampling the eggs upon close approach. Southern Lapwings ignore fish-eating raptors, but respond strongly to other large hawks. The African lapwing species have a similar ability to tell a dangerous raptor species, the Tawny Eagle (*Aquila rapax*), apart from the extremely similar looking vultures with which it often soars high in the air. In general, these lapwings appear to discriminate between various kinds of predators and non-predators, and give responses that reflect the type and degree of danger that each of them represents.

In breeding situations, plovers may show a great variety of behavioural responses, depending on the kind of threat and the stage of reproduction. For example, studies by I. Byrkjedal have shown that during incubation, Eurasian Golden Plovers either sneak away from the nest when a predator is still far off, or sit

tight, and leave the nest at the last moment to perform a distraction display, either in the air by showing impeded flight, or on the ground by walking away as if injured. Once the chicks hatch, the adults approach potential predators when they are still far away from chicks, and dog them whilst continuously giving loud alarm calls. The great wariness of lapwings and *Pluvialis* plovers may be capitalized on by other shorebird species that come to breed and feed in close association with these plovers and use them as sentinels. When a mammalian predator has been detected in a field where several lapwing pairs are breeding, the lapwings will assemble in a large mobbing flock over the intruder and try to scare it off with dive-bombing attacks. In non-breeding situations where a predator has been detected, behaviour may vary between flying up in flocks to move away, and crouching flat on the ground or in the water to get out of sight.

Diurnal feeding and roosting rhythms, the presence or absence of special communal roosts and the behavioural responses to potential threats will all be shaped by the energy and time demands of the plovers in combination with predation risks and feeding opportunities: a plover on its breeding grounds will find its movements constrained by the time for which it must incubate the eggs or tend the chicks; a plover in heavy wing moult will be constrained by high flight costs and low manoeuvrability; a plover in harsh winter weather will need much food per day to balance its energy budget; and a plover in the tropics will have to make behavioural adjustments to avoid overheating. All these demands will subtly affect the details of the habits that have been discussed here, and offer endless scope for future studies.

Voice

The melodious but mournful whistling songs of *Pluvialis* plovers, uttered most frequently in late spring and summer, but as briefer versions in other seasons too, provide very evocative sounds for the human ear. They are strong reminders of days spent in lonely moorland or tundra. Most *Charadrius* plovers have rather softer voices, and vocalize mainly on the breeding grounds. They have relatively low-pitched display calls and rather higher-pitched alarm calls. Lapwings, and their ecological equivalent in North America, the Killdeer (*Charadrius vociferus*), are characterized by louder and harsher sounds, especially when the birds are on their breeding territories. Magellanic Plovers have an unusually wide variety of calls by plover standards; many of

them are quite similar, and some appear to be used in more than one context. Overall, vocalizations of plovers have been rather poorly documented, with descriptions only being available for about 20 of the 67 species. For example, regarding the Vanellinae, detailed studies are available only for the Northern Lapwing, which in many respects is an atypical member of its genus.

Detailed studies of the communication behaviour of *Vanellus*, *Pluvialis* and *Charadrius* species usually come up with about 10 different vocalizations. These calls are categorized according to their sound and appearance on the sonagraph, and according to the behavioural context in which they appear. The tendency that the best studied species have the largest vocabularies underlines how rudimentary our present knowledge is. In the communication between adult plovers the following call types are usually recognized. The commonest call type heard when a human observer disturbs a plover on its territory is usually the general contact and alarm call, or "Warning-call". There may be up to eight distinct types in any one species, and these are given year round, but most commonly at the breeding grounds. The next category are the "Alarm-threat Calls", which are given during the breeding season in contexts where birds show ambiguity between approach and withdrawl. They usually sound somewhat harsher than the contact and alarm calls, and show a gradient in harshness towards real threat calls, which are given when birds in the reproductive phase are particularly excited, and sometimes during fights over feeding territories as well. Then there are a few vocal categories that are mainly used in sexual contexts, the most important of which is the "song", a conspicuous long-range signal that may be produced during highly choreographed song flights; especially in *Pluvialis* and *Vanellus*, quite complicated vocalizations (songs) may be produced. During advanced courtship and when making shifts during incubation, mates may approach each other with calls denominated as "Pair-contact Calls" (or "Tenderness Calls" and "Mating Calls"), which are much softer, short-range vocalizations. When making a nest scrape in a ritualized way, males, and rarely females, of some species may produce soft "Scraping Calls". The "Copulation-call" is usually attributed to the female and is given just before she is mounted by a male. A Eurasian Golden Plover settling on the nest for an incubation shift may produce a soft "Settling-call".

The final group of vocalizations given by adult birds are those that have a role in ensuring nest and chick survival. "Distraction Calls" are given when parents try to lure potential predators away from the nest and chicks, for instance by a "Broken-wing Display". The calls made towards chicks comprise those that warn the chicks of various kinds of threats, the sophistication of which we have only the faintest idea; those that summon the chicks out of a hiding place or a crouched position, the "All-clear" signals; and those signals that invite chicks to follow or to be brooded. The chicks themselves produce a graded series of vocalizations, starting with the soft peeps from a pipped egg that develop into the "Location Call", the juvenile version of adult contact call. Small chicks that have a decreased body temperature and need to be brooded to return to normal temperatures, make repeated series of this call. In some species, warm and contented chicks brooded by one of the parents convey this by a long, sustained and melodious "Contentment Call". Distress calls are made by older chicks, especially when they are frightened, for example when picked up by man.

One of the more spectacular and vocally accompanied behavioural displays given by any member of the Charadriidae is the song flight of male Northern Lapwings, a phenomenon studied in detail by T. Dabelsteen. Song flights may be made spontaneously, during interactions with other males, with females or with a predator, and sometimes when a male returns to an empty territory. More than half of all song flights are made during male-male interactions and are clearly meant to establish a territory. They are most commonly performed in the early morning, but otherwise continue throughout day and night during the breeding season, except in bad weather. They consist of fixed sequences of about eight different flight modes. The song phrases themselves are made when the bird makes a steep ascent or a vertical dive, thus accentuating his proficiency in flying. During the so-called "Alternating flight" phase of the song flight, during which the lapwing rolls from side to side, the bird does not vocalize but makes a thrumming sound with his wings: a strong and impressive signal. A quite similar phenomenon is shown by the Double-banded Plover (*Charadrius bicinctus*) when breeding in New Zealand. Males of this species produce loud "Wing-clicks", audible 100 m away; these are made at each beat of the wings during territorial flight displays that can be sustained for several minutes.

Food and Feeding

Plovers eat small invertebrate prey species that live close to the ground. Creepy and crawling arthropods and worms provide most of the diet of all plovers, always and everywhere. In terrestrial habitats, birds feed on earthworms, spiders and especially the larvae and adults of different insect groups, including flies, beetles, ants, chironomids and tipulids; these are sometimes supplemented with small berries, for instance of heather, and seeds. In riverine freshwater habitats, aquatic insects and small crustaceans make up the diet. In intertidal areas, plovers live on small crustaceans, including crabs, slow types of shrimp, amphipods and isopods, and also on worms, especially large polychaetes. In freshwater and marine habitats, small molluscs are sometimes preyed upon, but they never provide the bulk of the diet.

All members of the Charadriidae, except the Wrybill and the Magellanic Plover, forage by waiting for prey to reveal itself, either by coming to the surface of the ground, or, if already on the surface, by moving. The bird then runs rapidly to catch and swallow a detected prey item, before resuming a waiting position. It will move on to new waiting positions if no prey is detected. During the downward movement of the head, a further pause may occur, during which the bill is held close to the substrate before the plover finally grabs its prey. In such cases the prey is usually large and is captured by a relatively deep peck. Unsuccessful and aborted pecks are likely to result from misidentification of the prey rather than its escape. As the rate of prey detection increases, the pause rate increases too, and the average distance moved between pauses decreases. On rare occasions, plovers may wade in shallow water, making regular pecks on the water surface to capture small floating prey items.

The foraging style of typical plovers is thus highly stereotyped. It is well adapted for feeding on surface prey in flat compacted substrates that may be hard to penetrate with a long and sensitive bill. If prey is indeed detected mainly visually, as most

A Lesser Sandplover feeding at a coastal site during the non-breeding season. This polychaete worm was surprised when surfacing and is now being pulled out of its burrow. Swallowing such elongated prey needs some elaborate handling, and the risk that it will be snatched by neighbouring birds, either conspecifics or other kleptoparasitic species such as gulls, may be high. Migrant plovers appearing outside the breeding season in coastal habitats feed mainly on crustaceans, polycheates and molluscs, while insects are sometimes eaten. In the breeding areas the diet usually consists merely of insects.

[*Charadrius mongolus*, Changi Beach, Singapore. Photo: Morten Strange]

authors assume, then everything else being equal, feeding rates of plovers at night, relative to daylight performance, should be lower than those of tactile feeding sandpipers. Longer pause times, shorter sighting distances and lower peck rates in darkness have indeed been reported in several species. That plovers have a more southerly non-breeding distribution than sandpipers has thus been explained by the shorter daylight periods and the limited profitable feeding time available to plovers wintering further north. However, in several cases, prey reveals itself so much more at night by increases in surface activity, that a decreased detection efficiency during darkness is more than compensated for. In fact, intake rates may sometimes be higher at night than during the day. Several authors, with G. Lange as the strongest advocate, have argued that during prey detection plovers use auditory cues in addition to visual stimuli. In dry terrestrial habitats, plovers would be able to hear quite large invertebrates moving underground, thus enabling them to decipher the right location for a strike, but auditory detection is otherwise likely to be little used, even at night.

A recurring theme in studies of foraging plovers is the strong influence of prey activity and visibility on the plovers' feeding success and intake rate. For example, in a hayfield in Iceland, Eurasian Golden Plovers almost uniquely fed on lumbricid earthworms, but selected the more conspicuously coloured species over the cryptic one. The detailed research by M. W. Pienkowski and other scientists has shown that in intertidal areas Common Ringed and Grey Plovers have their highest intake rates during periods when prey is most active or visible, for example during incoming tides, with calm weather, at relatively high temperatures, and also on moonlit nights. At many of the intertidal sites where the diet and foraging of Grey Plovers has been studied, they indeed feed only on the active prey types, polychaete worms and surface-living crustaceans, even though such prey may comprise only a small fraction of the benthic communities at these sites. Bivalves are buried too deeply and snails may behave too sluggishly to be available for a group of birds that have specialized on actively moving prey. In terms of foraging, the most exceptional true plover is undoubtedly the Wrybill. Amazingly, it has adapted to catch invisible and static invertebrate prey under stones, in the braided rivers of New Zealand's South Island.

As a way of enhancing the availability of their active prey, most lapwing and plover species occasionally make tapping or trembling movements with one of their feet, usually alternating both legs. The movements disturb the invertebrates living on the surface, which then make themselves visible by moving away. To buried invertebrates, such as earthworms, the sounds or pressure ripples in the substrate produced by trembling of tapping plovers may signal "mole". As a consequence these animals creep towards the surface to escape from the putative mole, only to be captured by the plover waiting overhead. Foot-trembling is often shown by lapwings and smaller plovers feeding in grassland, but similar behaviour is displayed on intertidal mudflats, for example by Common Ringed Plovers and Lesser Sandplovers; it is rarely used by Grey Plovers. During foot-trembling one leg is lifted up slightly, while the toes vibrate the upper layer of sediment. Rather than stirring up the substrate, the trembling toes may elicit movements in small worms, such as nematodes, living close to the surface. It is likely that plovers are able to detect worms that are forced to move in this way much more easily than untriggered, stationary ones.

Typical plovers use foot-trembling to increase their capture success and intake rate, but Magellanic Plovers are unique in making prey items available by digging in sandy substrates with their strong feet. They dig by rapid backwards and sideways kicks, alternating the feet at a fast rate of about seven kicks per second, while small quantities of sand fly around; in this process, the birds look like tiny dogs digging up bones! At the same time, they pirouette rapidly over the shallow holes and peck rapidly, rather like a phalarope that picks tiny items from the water surface. According to J. R. Jehl, digging for food would be derived from nest building behaviour such as clearing a scrape, rather than from foot-trembling.

During the breeding season, plovers tend to forage individually, in the neighbourhood of the nest or young, within the breeding territory or slightly beyond. Non-breeding plovers do not usually forage alone, but nor do they do so in very tight aggregations. Plovers tend to feed dispersed. Foraging in groups is beneficial by reducing the chance for an individual plover to fall victim to birds of prey. This might be so for purely statistical reasons, such as finding safety in numbers by being one possible target among many others, or because in larger groups with an increased overall vigilance potential predators are detected ear-

lier, or both. Birds can also benefit from each other's experiences to find the best feeding locations. On the negative side, birds in tight flocks disturb each other's prey. Especially in plovers, birds that hunt for active prey crawling along the surface, the presence of other predators will disturb prey and depress its activity, hence lowering individual feeding success.

Interference during foraging is probably the reason that plovers usually spread themselves thinly over the feeding areas. An additional drawback of feeding in flocks is that high densities invite the stealing of prey, especially when food items are large and require long handling times. Such kleptoparasitism can be inflicted by conspecifics or by other species. An example of the latter is provided by Common Black-headed Gulls (*Larus ridibundus*) which steal earthworms from Northern Lapwings and Eurasian Golden Plovers in European grasslands. The presence of these gulls in a flock reduces the tendency of plovers to take large earthworms, and thus see their intake rate reduced. Common Black-headed Gulls are, however, highly vigilant, and this may partly compensate the cost of their kleptoparasitic behaviour. A contrasting observation from southern Africa is of Spur-winged Lapwings interfering with the courtship feeding of Grey-headed Gulls (*Larus cirrocephalus*). The lapwing chases away the female gull just when she has incited her male to regurgitate the content of his crop: delivery being under way, there is little that the excited male can do, thus presenting the lapwing with his offering!

A clear case of feeding dispersion and the avoidance of interference and prey depletion is the defence of feeding territories, areas exclusively exploited by a territory owner. Such birds may tolerate shorebirds of a different kind, though, and there are cases where Grey and Common Ringed Plovers, feeding on the same stock of polychaete worms, occupy completely overlapping territories. A feeding territory can be a small area of grassland defended during successive daytime periods, or an area of intertidal mudflat defended during successive low tide periods. Although territorial plovers spend 5-10% of the potential feeding time on the defence of their territories, the observations of J. K. Turpie on Grey Plovers in southern Africa show that their higher intake rates, when compared to nearby non-territorial birds, more than compensate for this time loss. Nevertheless, both territorial and non-territorial Grey Plovers have to feed during daytime and night-time low water periods in order to satisfy their daily energy requirements, a condition that has also been noted for north temperate feeding areas.

Most shorebirds, plovers as well as sandpipers, live in habitats where they are fully exposed to wind and rain. In the tropics,

Crabs can form a large proportion of the Grey Plover's diet. Only the soft parts are swallowed. First the crab is shaken vigorously in order to dismember it, after which the carapace is removed, revealing the digestable parts of the prey. The reward may be relatively high, but handling a crab is a tiresome task and foraging on soft-bodied prey, such as polycheate worms, may be more profitable. In order to assure their food supply, Pluvialis *plovers often hold feeding territories on their wintering grounds.*

[*Pluvialis squatarola*, Ceará, north-east Brazil. Photo: Luiz Claudio Marigo]

Plovers are frequently observed trembling with one foot, or tapping the ground alternately with each foot. In this way prey hidden just below the surface or taking shelter in the vegetation may be provoked into revealing itself. The Three-banded Plover is thought to feed by night, as well as by day. Nocturnally feeding waders have been shown to possess relatively more rods in the retina, thus gaining enhanced night-time vision. Nevertheless, the food intake rate is usually lower during the night.

[Charadrius tricollaris tricollaris.
Photo: M. C. Wilkes/Aquila]

air temperatures are such that no extra energy is required to maintain a high body temperature of 41°C, even in strong winds. In all other parts of the world, plovers face considerable heat loss and have a high energy requirement in order to keep up body temperature. High rates of energy expenditure not only require these plovers to eat relatively large quantities of food per day, but also force them to maintain a digestive system that is capable of processing so much food. In turn, sizeable processing machinery leads to a further increase in energy requirements, since the metabolically active tissue of which it consists needs to be maintained. For this reason plovers from the tropics that need to process less food, expend energy at lower rates than those from further north or south, even when both are asleep under thermoneutral conditions.

A low metabolism in the tropics has an additional advantage. The high solar radiation in combination with high air temperatures can load plovers with so much heat that they need to evaporate body water so as to maintain a core temperature of 41°C. In marine environments this is particularly problematic, since all ingested water, even the body water of prey, is saline. Birds need to get rid of the salt by way of their nasal salt glands, in order to produce osmotically free water for evapo-transpiration. Salt excretion is an intense metabolic process, during which yet more heat is produced, all of which leads to a chain of events that can easily result in overheating and death. Plovers in tropical environments often have relatively large salt glands, but they may additionally seek shade in the middle of the day, and preferentially feed on prey with low salt loads.

In general, however, plovers do not drink much. In most circumstances, they probably obtain sufficient water from the body fluids of their invertebrate prey. A plover drinks by inserting its bill horizontally in the water, then lifting its head and bill to swallow the water in the bill. An exception to this drinking style is, yet again, provided by Magellanic Plovers, which appear to drink by making sucking motions, just like doves and pigeons. In this way they may ingest a much higher quantity of water per unit time than typical plovers.

Apart from eating nutrient rich food items, at times plovers also ingest apparently indigestible items, such as little stones and pieces of shell. Grit and shells can be retrieved from gizzards of plovers, and are probably used to grind ingested nutritious food items. Common Ringed Plovers studied in Norway over an entire reproductive cycle by A. Moksnes, ate the valves of freshwater bivalves during the egg-laying phase only. In this case the plovers appeared to compensate a calcium deficit during egg-

shell production by the selective ingestion of calcareous material.

Reproduction affects food and feeding in other ways too. Plover chicks, which find food on their own and decide their movements quite independently from their parents, often have a different diet. For example, Northern Lapwing chicks feed on small surface-living beetles and fly larvae living in cow dung, at a time when the chief prey type of the parents is earthworms. The latter are partly obtained by foot-trampling, a technique that is not available to small, light-weight chicks. Probably typical of most boreal and Arctic breeding plovers, Eurasian Dotterel chicks ingest proportionally more soft-bodied types of insects than adults, while the adults may also feed on berries and seeds. Only during mass emergences of tipulids, when the parents and their young feed almost exclusively on this bumper crop, do the two age groups have perfectly similar diets.

Breeding

As in all birds, plovers breed during the time of the year when they are most likely to hatch eggs and raise chicks successfully. This usually means that plovers breed when arthropod food resources reach their peak: during summer in temperate, boreal and Arctic climates, and some time after the rains in the tropics. Latitudinal variations in seasonality also imply that the further north a plover breeds, the later in the year it starts, a relationship that holds good both within and between species. Species with a wide latitudinal breeding range, such as the Common Ringed Plover, delay laying the first egg by 1·6 days per degree of latitude. This means that southerly breeding populations at 56° N in north-east England are raising their first clutch before the Arctic breeders at 72° N in east Greenland have even started breeding. Although most species are single-brooded, plovers can produce additional clutches if the first fails. At higher latitudes the breeding season can be so short that there is little point in producing a replacement clutch if the first has been lost at a late stage of incubation.

In tropical lapwings and plovers, the timing of breeding is strongly influenced by the timing of the rainy and dry seasons, critical determinants of the abundance of insects available for parents and young. It is striking that most African lapwings breed in the dry season, whereas Australian plovers of arid environments breed immediately after the rains. If breeding grounds are otherwise available and open for settlement by competitors, for

Plovers feed mainly on small animals, especially arthropods and worms. One of the striking differences between them and the sandpipers and snipes of the family Scolopacidae is that the plovers essentially forage visually, taking their prey from or near the surface, as opposed to the tactile feeding typically used by members of Scolopacidae. In conjunction with this, almost all plovers have rather short, fairly stubby bills. Another consequence of their visual foraging is that they tend to feed some distance apart, as the close proximity of another feeding bird may disturb prey and drive it into hiding, or, quite simply, the prey item may be caught by the neighbouring bird. The Blacksmith Lapwing tends to forage along margins of water, or in ploughed fields or areas with short grass. It uses the typical plover technique of running along in swift bursts, pausing and perhaps pecking at a food item, and then following this with another quick run.

[Vanellus armatus. Photo: Heinrich van den Berg/Bruce Coleman]

example containing sufficient food and not covered by snow, plovers may establish their territory long before starting to breed. For example, male Northern Lapwings may defend their territories more than a month before clutches are laid. G. Högstedt showed that in southern Sweden the time between territory establishment and laying was a function of food availability; the higher the densities of earthworms, the shorter the interval. In the Netherlands, A. J. Beintema and associates have shown that between 1910 and 1970 Northern Lapwings started to breed about three weeks earlier. This represents a response to an advance in the seasonality of their earthworm prey, as a consequence of changed farming practices, such as increased gifts of fertilizer and reduced water tables, that stimulate an earlier growth of grass in spring.

The vast majority of plovers have a socially monogamous mating system, but as intensive studies on individually recognizable birds are tending to uncover more variability than initially reported, plovers may have some interesting surprises in store. For example, Northern Lapwings have long been thought of as monogamous birds. Yet, as a rule, a male Northern Lapwing will try to establish bonds with more than one female, even though most males remain monogamous in the end. Good percentages of bigynous and even trigynous males are now reported for some regions, and polygyny is also suspected in Eurasian Golden and Caspian Plovers. As another example, the Kentish Plover was long considered a monogamous species, but a recent flurry of detailed observational studies of individually colour-marked birds, initiated by C. M. Lessells, has revealed that sequential polyandry, whereby a female gains access to more than one male in the course of one season, and polygyny also occur quite regularly when females or males desert their partners soon after hatching, and turn up somewhere else with new partners. That mate change is not documented more frequently in Kentish Plovers may reflect the high degree of dispersal after desertion, rather than any rarity of the phenomenon. The considerable distances moved between breeding attempts can be illustrated by a pair of Kentish Plovers, which started a clutch in southern Sweden but left the area when the clutch was lost. In the meantime, the male had mated with a second female, but he deserted her with a full four-egg clutch to nest again with his first female 280 km to the south-west in Schleswig-Holstein, northern Germany; here the pair successfully hatched a brood, and returned a year later.

With respect to mating system, Kentish Plovers actually occupy an intermediate position. Mountain Plovers (*Charadrius montanus*), and perhaps Lesser Sandplovers too, have a rapid multiple-clutch system that may be accompanied by sequential polyandry, whereby the female leaves her first mate soon after the completion of "his" clutch, to start another by herself. In the Eurasian Dotterel, female reproductive investment usually ceases completely once a clutch is complete. The male is in charge of all parental care, during incubation as well as after hatching, so once a clutch is complete the female starts to search for a new male. In the Scottish Highlands, Eurasian Dotterel females, the larger and more colourful sex, compete for males on mating arenas. A female gains exclusive access to a male by isolating him from the rest of the flock, having to deter attacks from other females during courtship. In Norway, Eurasian Dotterels arrive back from their wintering areas already paired, so courtship must have taken place earlier in the season, perhaps at staging areas during northward migration. Males of this species try to ensure paternity of the clutch in which they invest so much, by controlling the copulations during the few days that they are accompanied by a female. In monogamous systems, incubation is usually shared fairly equally by the two sexes, but in general female plovers have a tendency to leave the chicks before fledging, while males continue to give parental care until, and even after, the young can fly. In an experimental study of Killdeers, D. H. Brunton showed that two adults were needed for successful breeding; lone males were able to hatch chicks while females were not, but no individual managed to raise offspring alone.

Although most plover species defend exclusive territories during the breeding season, there are several in which these territories are quite small and are clumped together. Especially when breeding territories are small, most feeding takes place outside the territory. Northern Lapwings and Kentish Plovers quite often breed "semi-colonially", although this pattern is most striking in Sociable Lapwings. These small lapwings live up to their name by nesting in scattered "neigbourhood groups" of up to 20 pairs, with several such aggregations of nests within an area of a few hectares. Aggregation allows birds to defend the area jointly against aerial and terrestrial predators. This benefit may explain why other wader species are attracted to breed close to concentrations of nesting Northern Lapwings.

Although both sexes may help in the defence of a breeding territory, males usually take on the larger share or indeed the

The "Broken-wing Display" is commonly performed by several ground-nesting species. In an attempt to distract attention from its nest, this Black-fronted Dotterel is fluttering its wings and fanning its tail, while moving away from the nest. Overall, eggs appear to have a better chance of survival than chicks. Eggs usually fail through predation, trampling or other dramatic events, such as flooding. During the chick phase factors such as weather and feeding conditions can become more critical.

[*Elseyornis melanops*, Australia. Photo: Wayne Lawler/ Auscape]

whole task on their own. In the Magellanic Plover territorial defence is peculiar, since it is often performed by both members of the pair acting together as a unit. In this respect its territorial behaviour differs notably from the territorial displays of typical plovers. It reminded J. R. Jehl of the piping displays of oystercatchers. When an intruder appears on a defended beach, the residents immediately run towards it, side by side with their heads held low and their bills pointed forward, calling aggressively.

Plovers do not build impressive nests. Although marsh-breeding lapwing species may pull together heaps of plant material to establish a nest on top of the mound, plover nests usually consist of a shallow scrape only. This scrape may be lined with small pebbles or shell fragments on the shore, with grass leaves in a meadow, or with pieces of lichen or moss on moorland and tundra. Several beach-breeding *Charadrius* species lay their eggs in a shallow depression in the sand.

Plovers lay their eggs at one or two day intervals. During actual egg-laying, a female stands on her "heels" in quite an upright manner, gaining additional support from slightly opened wings pressed firmly on the rim of the nest. Plover eggs have a pale ground colour that varies between whitish, beige and green, and are covered with dark spots and scribbles that vary in size and density. Clutch size varies between two and four eggs. Sometimes more than four eggs are encountered in a nest, but this always indicates that two females have laid there. Since the variation in colour and pattern of eggs, at least in Eurasian Dotterels, is more uniform within than between individual female plovers, eggs can often be told apart as issuing from different females.

Although four is the commonest modal clutch size in plovers, many species lay fewer eggs, usually three. Reviews by G. L. Maclean and J. R. Walters show that in northerly breeding species a clutch of four is commonest, while in the tropical and southern regions three eggs appear to be the rule. Also the Vanellinae tend to have larger clutches than the Charadriinae. Why restrict clutch size to three or four eggs? Does it represent a phylogenetic constraint, or has it functional significance today? The traditional explanation that food available to the laying female limits the clutch size is not well supported by the available data; Northern Lapwings can easily be induced to lay more than four eggs if the initial eggs are removed, and there are no indications that foraging time

is at a premium when eggs are being formed. The number of eggs that can be incubated successfully may be limited by the size of the brood patch; and the typical pear shape of plover eggs may allow an economically tight arrangement under a brooding plover, but only when there are three or four eggs. Small clutches may also be an adaptation to high rates of nest predation since larger clutches are exposed to the risk of predation for longer periods, and small clutches are replaced more easily if lost. Finally, there may be a limit to the number of chicks that can be successfully tended by the parent or parents. For the moment, the worldwide data set is too fragmentary to tell which of these functional hypotheses carries most of the truth.

Once the clutch is complete, plovers incubate for 21-30 days before the eggs hatch; small plovers require a shorter period than

Calling loudly and continuously, making a sound like a blacksmith's hammer hitting an anvil, a Blacksmith Lapwing shows itself to be quite undaunted by a sizeable warthog (Phacochoerus aethiopicus) *that is wandering too close to the lapwing's nest for comfort. Since many species of lapwings breed on open grassy fields where herds of cattle or wild ungulates commonly graze, a large proportion of clutches may be trampled.*

[Vanellus armatus.
Photo: Philip Perry/FLPA]

the large species. Compared to similarly-sized shorebirds of other families, these incubation periods are rather long. Long incubation times may have evolved to ensure that chicks hatch fully mature with respect to neural function, so that they are capable of detecting and capturing highly mobile insects from the start. For plovers breeding in temperate to Arctic climatic regions, the challenge is to keep the eggs warm. This is best achieved by incubating for a maximum of time, an activity shared by both parents in most species. Single incubators, such as male Eurasian Dotterels, indeed face difficulties in completing this task, even though they care for a three- rather than a four-egg clutch. Plovers in tropical and arid environments face the reverse problem, at least during the day: they have to ensure that the eggs do not become too warm. Again, the best way is to provide the eggs with a good thermal insulator or a shading device, such as the body of a living plover, during such stressful periods. If this does not suffice, or if the incubating birds become overheated themselves, lapwings breeding in hot environments may soak their belly feathers, and return to the nest to wet the eggs and the nest. Alternatively, the eggs can be buried under a layer of sand, a solution used by White-fronted Plovers. Egg-covering serves the dual function of concealment from predators and protection from the sun. In Wilson's Plover, also breeding on tropical shores, the eggs are incubated continuously: males incubate mainly at night and females during the day; relief takes place at low light intensities at dusk and dawn, perhaps to reduce the danger of nest predation.

After three or four weeks of incubation the eggs pip, and after another day the chick works its way out of the egg by cutting the shell open with the small egg tooth on the tip of its bill. As soon as the eggshell is free of the wet chick, it is carried away by the parent on duty. O. Moedt photographed Northern Lapwings flying off with eggshells that were then buried in the mud of a nearby ditch. The white insides of empty shells might attract the attention overflying predators, such as corvids, to the nest-site. As soon as all the eggs have hatched, usually within one or two days, both chicks and adults leave the immediate vicinity of the nest. Broods may wander over large areas, each day covering several 100 m or more. In arid regions, several families may come together in loose flocks at moist places. Due to confusion of nests, mixed broods of Common Ringed and Little Ringed Plovers (*Charadrius dubius*) occur in which the foreign young are apparently adopted and raised successfully.

The downy chicks of plovers, studied in detail by J. R. Jehl and J. Fjeldså, have proportionally large rounded heads, very short bills and strikingly large and strong legs and feet. The down is dense, woolly and short, with a pebbly colour pattern composed of finely stippled upperparts and a prominent black band bordering the white underparts. Some species have light coloured terminal "puffs" attached to the downy feathers, which gives them

Although disputes over territory ownership can lead to vigourous confrontations, like this one between two male Northern Lapwings, physical contact is rare. Once a male has established a territory he remains in permanent residence to fight off intruders and guard his mate, and he attempts to expand it at the expense of neighbouring lapwings. The female will help to defend the borders after she has laid the eggs. Territorial defence becomes increasingly directed towards potential predators rather than conspecifics.

[Vanellus vanellus, Warwickshire, England. Photo: M. C. Wilkes/ Aquila]

Plover nests are usually
no more than simple
shallow scrapes in the
ground. They are not lined
with insulating material as
in many other birds.
As plovers breed in open
habitats, without shelter
close by, the nests would
be very conspicuous if
lined with plant material.
Instead, some material
from the immediate vicinity
may be added to the nest
to improve the
camouflage, for example,
in the case of coastal
nesters, some shells or
pebbles. This beach-
nesting Red-capped
Plover relies heavily on
the camouflage of its eggs
and of its own plumage.

[Charadrius ruficapillus,
Australia.
Photo: Darran Leal/Auscape]

a densely stippled moss-like appearance. The dorsal markings are usually irregular and faint, but may form two parallel central dark bands, or one broader one, changing to an irregular row of U-shaped marks toward the rump. With few exceptions, the nape is white, heavily bordered by dark feathers from the crown, and this contrasting collar stands out when the chicks are active and move about with their necks erect. Independently and actively foraging plover chicks at a distance are best discovered by the collar, and signal their whereabouts to their vigilant parents in this way. When a chick crouches as a response to the alarm calls of its parents, it withdraws its neck tightly against the body so that the collar is hidden. The downy chicks of Magellanic Plovers have a colour and pattern unique among all waders (Charadrii). The head, face, back and upperwings are greenish grey, tinged with gold; the neck is greyish and the underparts white except for a golden patch on the breast. There is no dorsal pattern except for a short dark line on the head, and the upperparts show a sparse scattering of white-tipped feathers that are longer than average.

Plover chicks are precocial and feed for themselves, but parental care consumes considerable time. This time can be partitioned in three components. First, the chicks have to learn the dangers of their world, including raptorial birds, humans, other predatory mammals, cars and so on; plovers show a high level of vigilance and communication with their chicks which is maintained until they can fly. A substantial amount of time is also devoted to active parental behaviour, such as leading, following and gathering young. The gathering of chicks is usually the preamble to the third time cost activity, brooding. In open, sun-baked habitats, young birds run the risk of overheating, and parents may provide shade and a cooler thermal environment by brooding the chicks. In very cold weather, plover chicks need to be brooded at regular intervals so as to heat them up to normal body temperatures of about 40°C. This is because plover chicks are thermolabile. Over the first two to three weeks of their life they are not able to keep up their body temperature fully when foraging alone in the cold. In the course of the breeding season this may lead to bizarre scenes when three or four large chicks that have survived to almost three weeks of age and are close to fledging, want to be brooded by one of their parents. In such cases the adult is almost lifted off the ground! Although still competent

and active at body temperatures as low as 30°C, at a few degrees less the chicks become lethargic. The younger the chicks and the colder the weather, the longer they have to be brooded by a parent, and the less time there is for feeding. When young Northern Lapwings are not able to feed for periods longer than five hours per day, they can not sustain growth and eventually die from starvation.

Compared to those of sandpipers, plover chicks show an extended period of thermolability, combined with slow growth rates. Their lower metabolism has the benefit of considerably reducing the energy costs for growth, and it increases the capacity of chicks to survive temporary food shortages or inclement weather. It has the distinct disadvantage that chicks are dependent on parental care for such a long time, a factor that operates most severely in cold environments. If the plover family has indeed a tropical origin so that breeding at Arctic latitudes is a derived strategy, then relative growth rates may be "phylogenetically inert", that is not able to evolve into a pattern that is better suited to colder climatic conditions.

In the aberrant Magellanic Plover, clutch size is usually two eggs. Each egg comprises about 15% of the adult body mass, which is rather less than the 20-30% that is usual for typical plover eggs. The most striking characteristic of the small chicks is their general weakness; they are far less agile than chicks of typical plovers of the same age. The parents also feed the chicks, carrying the food in the extensible crop, a feature otherwise unknown in the Charadriidae. The growth rate of Magellanic Plovers is even slower than in other plovers and they can not fly until they are four weeks old. Even then the chicks remain associated with the parents, and may still be fed until they are 40 days old. Also unlike typical plovers, Magellanic Plovers show no distraction displays, either during incubation or when caring for chicks of any age.

In the nest, the daily survival rates of eggs are usually close to 99%. Over incubation periods of 25-30 days this yields overall nest survival rates of 70-75%. The daily survival rates of chicks are usually somewhat lower than those of eggs, an average of 96% per day leading to a chick survival of 25-30% over the 35 days from hatching to fledging. These values are just sufficient for Northern Lapwings in Western Europe to sustain their population sizes. It is interesting that in temperate as well as Arctic

Birds from the tropics
have to cope with
problems caused by high
temperatures. Moreover,
the open habitats where
plovers live do not offer
any protection from the
blazing midday sun.
Incubating the eggs or
leaving them in such
circumstances put the
fertility of the eggs at risk,
so, instead, the eggs must
be protected from the
sun's radiation by casting
some shade on them, as
demonstrated by this
Yellow-wattled Lapwing.
Some species may even
wet the eggs by
moistening their breast
feathers, thereby
enhancing heat loss
through evaporation.

[Vanellus malabaricus.
Photo: Vivek Sinha/
Survival Anglia/
Oxford Scientific Films]

regions, the population cycles exhibited by voles and lemmings influence breeding success of plovers. In years when vole and lemming populations reach a peak, potential mammalian predators such as ermines and foxes have high reproductive success, and show little interest in searching for plover eggs. During the subsequent breeding season, when voles or lemmings are almost absent, the then abundant mammalian predators are forced to switch to alternative prey types, and few shorebird eggs survive. This may be the reason why in the Netherlands egg survival of Northern Lapwings cycles in concert with vole populations, while in South Africa the years when large numbers of juvenile Grey Plovers arrive from the Siberian hatching grounds correspond with the years that the lemmings peak in Arctic Siberia.

Although small plovers may live for 10 years or more and large plovers for 20 years or more, most individual plovers that have survived to fledging do not reach such ages. The few studies of survival rates in plovers indicate considerable variability, partly due to methodological differences, with estimates ranging between 70% and 91%. During the first year, survival is always lower than later in life. A detailed study of Northern Lapwings by W. J. Peach and colleagues has shown that survival over the first year is 59·5%, whereas later in life 70·5% of the birds survive each year. In juveniles, as well as adults, survival is closely correlated with winter temperatures and rainfall: the warmer and wetter the winter, the higher the survival. Since 1960 adult survival rate has increased to 75·2% per year, a result of reduced hunting pressure in Europe. For this reason the average life expectancy of a Northern Lapwing has improved from 2·4 years during the first half of this century to 3·5 years in the second half. Recent declines in the British population must thus be due to poor breeding success, as a consequence of increasingly unfavourable agricultural practices. In the Netherlands, where lapwing populations appear stable, the increased survival apparently compensated for reduced reproductive rates.

The degree to which adult and juvenile plovers will return to the same breeding and wintering areas in successive years has attracted few comprehensive studies. Site-faithfulness will be a function of the environmental variability of the breeding and wintering areas, and the costs involved in making a move. Costs and benefits may differ between the sexes, territory-holding males usually being more site-faithful than females. Resident plovers, almost by definition, will tend to be more site-faithful than migratory ones. But some highly migratory species, such as Grey and Pacific Golden Plovers, are known to be very faithful to both breeding and wintering sites, in the latter case especially those birds that are territorial. Individual Grey Plovers on the Wash in eastern England may use the same high tide roost for several successive winters. Northern Lapwings mostly return to the previous breeding areas, and their natal sites too, but plover species in which there is less of a premium on meeting up with old partners in familiar areas are likely to show relaxed philopatry. Eurasian Dotterels may provide an example. In this species, large shifts in breeding area are the rule, and an individual has even been found changing from Norway to Scotland. In a population of Common Ringed Plovers on the Western Isles of Scotland, D. B. Jackson showed that adult site-fidelity is positively correlated with breeding success, and that birds nesting on unstable habitats show a tendency to move to habitats of equal or better quality in subsequent years.

Movements

The seasonal appearance of golden plovers on oceanic islands, at distances of 4000 km or more from the nearest landmass, provides excellent evidence that such plovers migrate over thousands of kilometres. In 1910, H. W. Henshaw published such observations for Pacific Golden Plovers on Hawaii. This was later followed by reports suggesting that even longer flights were made over the west Atlantic by American Golden Plovers migrating from North to South America. Golden plovers thus became celebrated cases in the literature on bird migration. In the early 1960's, E. G. F. Sauer made innovative tests on hand-raised Pacific Golden Plovers to show their orientation ability in the presence of different orientational cues, such as the sun and the stars. This intriguing research direction has not been followed up with plovers. A 1967 study by D. W. Johnston and R. W. MacFarlane on the fat content and metabolic rate of Pacific Golden Plovers on Wake Island, a lonely spot in the Pacific between the Hawaiian Archipelago and the Philippines, was one of the first that came up with estimates of the energy costs of transoceanic flights. This research was continued by O. W.

Johnson and co-workers who published detailed accounts on the ecology and physiology of Pacific Golden Plovers migrating between Hawaii and nearby Pacific islands and Alaska.

All these, and many other studies on different plover species, have confirmed the impression that the species belonging to the genus *Pluvialis* are the migratory champions among the Charadriidae. However, some smaller *Charadrius* species, such as Common Ringed Plovers, which also commute between tropical shorelines and high Arctic breeding areas, follow quite closely on their heels. At the opposite end of the spectrum are most members of the subfamily Vanellinae and some smaller plovers that live rather sedentary lives, often in the tropics and in isolated island habitats, or that carry out short altitudinal migrations. Most non-migratory plovers demonstrate this life history feature by the rounded shape of their wings: long, slender wings being favoured for cheap, fast forward flight. The round-winged Northern Lapwing provides something of an exception, as the northernmost breeders migrate quite far, although they cover the distance in short hops.

The long distance migrants within the Charadriidae all make seasonal north-south movements, radiating away from the extensive temperate, boreal and Arctic breeding areas in the Northern Hemisphere. With respect to the distances travelled, they are followed by several species in the Southern Hemisphere. Double-banded, Two-banded (*Charadrius falklandicus*) and Rufous-chested Plovers (*Charadrius modestus*), Tawny-throated Dotterels and Wrybills, for example, all migrate north of their breeding grounds in the austral winter, some birds moving up to several thousand kilometres; in the process, Double-banded Plovers cross the 1600-2000 km wide Tasman Sea between New Zealand and Australia.

Then there are the movements of equatorial and subtropical species of lapwings and plovers in South America, Africa and Australasia, migrations about which very little is known. In arid regions, these movements are probably mediated by the occurrence of regular or irregular cycles of rainfall and fires influencing plant growth, and thereby insect food abundance and nesting habitat. Recent studies in Australia, carried out by a large network of volunteers, have shown that only two of the four resident inland plover species studied, the Red-kneed Dotterel and the Red-capped Plover, make large-scale movements to and from regions with heavy rainfall. The other two, the Masked Lapwing (*Vanellus miles*) and the Black-fronted Dotterel, mostly appear to live sedentary lives in the more permanent wetland areas in eastern and central Australia, and are not affected by heavy rains elsewhere.

For some bird species, specific parts of the breeding grounds are connected with specific wintering areas, via the flight routes of individual birds. Grey and Pacific Golden Plovers have very extensive breeding and wintering ranges, but up to now the ringing efforts have failed to show much substructuring in the populations of these plovers. Grey Plovers breeding in Arctic Canada move southwards, to winter along the coastlines of Central and South America. These birds are separate from the Grey Plovers wintering along the shores of the east Atlantic, from Scotland to South Africa, which all appear to breed in Arctic Siberia, many of them on Taymyr Peninsula. Common Ringed Plovers wintering in West Africa share breeding origins as far apart as Greenland, Scandinavia and Siberia, whereas British breeding birds remain in Britain, migrating over short distances only. In Western Europe, Northern Lapwings and Eurasian Golden Plovers winter as far north as they possibly can, only moving south when pushed by the frost-line. Of the two, the somewhat smaller Eurasian Golden Plover is more sensitive to cold weather and departs southwards earlier.

In preparation for the flights to cover the long distances between suitable staging areas, along the route between the southern wintering and the Arctic breeding grounds, plovers must store considerable amounts of fuel before take-off, sometimes doubling in mass over a period of one to two months. Although a large proportion of the mass increase is fat, which contains eight times as much energy as proteinaceous muscle and organ tissue, there are changes in the size of the organs as well. During the refuelling phase, the digestive tract increases in size, and before take-off for long distance flights the breast muscles show hypertrophy. A detailed study of the compositional changes in Eurasian Golden Plovers, comparing the mass gains before the winter and the spring peaks in weight, indicated that most extra winter mass consists of fat, but that most of the mass gain in spring consists of fat-free tissue. Most of the fat is stored in a fairly homogeneous layer directly under the skin, as if wrapped around the body. Even in winter, such subcutaneous fat is unlikely to

The eggs require about three to four weeks of incubation before they hatch. Once the chick has left its egg, the remains of the shell are conspicuous with the white lining, a stark contrast with the well camouflaged outside of the shell. Therefore, the parent bird promptly removes the eggshells from the nest before they attract predators. There is even evidence of Northern Lapwings (Vanellus vanellus) *burying the shells in mud.*

[*Vanellus indicus aigneri*, Hafeet, Oman. Photo: Hanne & Jens Eriksen/Aquila]

Early on in life, chicks of precocial birds develop homoiothermia, the ability to keep the body temperature at a constant level. Nevertheless, as they still lack an insulating plumage, for a long period they remain dependent on their parents in order to maintain a high enough body temperature, and frequent solicit brooding by burrowing under an adult in the manner of these Eurasian Golden plover chicks. Young hatched at Arctic or temperate latitudes have to find good balance between the time spent being brooded by their parents and the time dedicated to feeding. During cold or wet spells brooding time may increase to a level that does not leave enough feeding time for the chicks to survive. In temperate regions this can be a crucial factor determining fledging success.

[*Pluvialis apricaria apricaria*.
Photo: John Hawkins/FLPA]

fulfill an insulatory function, since in air the insulative capacity of plumage is an order of magnitude larger than that of fat.

A successful migration, one that is survived by its participants, can lead to a successful reproductive season. Especially for high Arctic breeding plovers that experience a short summer season, a proper timing of different migratory activities such as fuelling, refuelling and flying, is of critical importance. The further the wintering areas are from the breeding grounds, the more difficult it may be to achieve an optimal timing of migration, but some individuals will have an easier time than others. In the case of Grey Plovers wintering in southern Africa, about 14,000 km away from their Siberian breeding grounds, territorial individuals preparing the northward flight achieve higher intake rates than non-territorial birds. For this reason, territorial Grey Plovers fuel faster and are the first to depart from South Africa, thereby building in some spare time for setbacks further along the route. Grey Plovers that defended a territory in South Africa are probably the earliest to arrive on the breeding grounds. However, non-territorial birds are quick to gain advantage of the departure of territory-holders, moving onto the vacated high quality feeding areas, and partially making up their time deficit regarding fuel storage.

Relationship with Man

The attitude of mankind towards plovers has mostly been of the exploitational kind. Only in the late twentieth century does a rather appreciative and even respectful attitude seem to be developing towards breeding shorebirds in general, and species like the Northern Lapwing in particular, in segments of the human population of some European countries. This respect is fed by the realization that these large bird populations are negatively affected by a growing pressure on natural environments in this part of the world, but provide something unique that is well worth preserving for future enjoyment.

In the agricultural province of Friesland in the northern Netherlands, the abundant Northern Lapwing, locally known as the "Ljip", is something of a regional symbol. Its flight displays are celebrated in Frisian folk songs, poems and expressions. Northern Lapwings have achieved this status after many centuries of regulated egg-collecting in early spring. The first egg of the season was traditionally presented to the Queen of the Netherlands, a ceremony now abandoned. Although the eggs are no longer brought onto the market either, the collection of lapwing eggs for local consumption is still allowed by law, on

Many plover species return to the same breeding grounds every year. The young, however, more often disperse to sites other than their natal breeding grounds. Of the many open habitats that members of the Charadriidae patronize, beaches are amongst the most typical. The Piping Plover of North America breeds on bare flats, on lake shores and on beaches along the Atlantic coast. The species is classed as Vulnerable, with only some 2000 breeding pairs remaining.

[*Charadrius melodus*, Silgo Beach, Long Island, New York. Photo: Arthur Morris]

the grounds that egg-collecting fosters another tradition, that of protecting wader nests from agricultural onslaughts, such as trampling by high densities of cattle and destruction by grass-harvesting machines. Nests are searched out and firm iron structures are put over them. This effectively prevents trampling by cattle and horses, and warns the mowing farmer of a nest. Breeding success of Northern Lapwings has been shown to improve markedly as a result. In 1994, volunteers protected breeding lapwings and other waders on 1220 km² of grassland, 860 km² of which were in Friesland, where this practice originated 40 years ago.

All lapwing species are exceptionally vigilant. They spot potential predators from distances of 100 m and more. This characteristic has been recognized by farmers in southern Argentina, who in the past kept tethered or wing-clipped Southern Lapwings as sentinels in their farmyards. These lapwings call "tero tero tero" in a loud barking way, as a response to approaches from large animals, humans included. Not surprisingly, a lapwing is onomatopoeically called "Tero" in much of Latin America.

Humans have a long tradition of exploiting plover populations. This varies from the sport hunting of Wrybills by the European settlers of New Zealand, the use of the colourful scapulars and back feathers of shot female Eurasian Dotterels for angling in Britain, and the collection and sale of over 100,000 lapwing eggs per spring season in the Netherlands, to the widespread hunting of the large plover species for fun and for the pot, which continues today in several parts of the world. The intense hunting of shorebirds and other waterfowl in eastern North America in the late nineteenth century almost exterminated the American Golden Plover. It was once very abundant, but by the early 1900's most authors were lamenting the disappearance or drastic decline in numbers of the species at all localities. According to A. C. Bent, the population reached a low point at about 1900, when large flights occurred no more and golden plovers were rarely seen in places where they once abounded. But changes in game laws occurred just in time, and American Golden Plovers showed a strong population increase when the artificially high mortality rate became reduced. Although hunted to a lesser extent, the Pacific Golden Plover did not entirely escape the onslaught. Having been taken as food for centuries by Pacific island natives, heavy sport gunning occurred in Hawaii well into the twentieth century.

In their attempts to shoot as many golden plovers as possible, the market hunters of eastern North America employed techniques that had been in use in Europe for centuries. They used little groups of decoys set out on a field, and tried to imitate the plovers' whistles to attract them close to their hides. Both of these aspects represent basic ingredients of a netting technique that has been used for catching Eurasian Golden Plovers in the Low Countries of Europe since the Middle Ages. This method, called "wilsternetting", is found on paintings of Dutch masters from the sixteenth century and has not been modified since. It involves a large net that, after an initial pull with a rope, is pushed by the wind towards flocks of plovers that have been tempted to land just behind the lying net. The temptation consists of a flock of realistic decoys in combination with one or two captive plovers that flap their wings. The captive birds sit on soft pads attached to a hook with a rope. If this rope is pulled by the catcher the birds are lifted from the ground and start to flap their wings. Flocks of golden plovers are called in from afar with loud imitations of their melodious whistle, made by the catchers on special flutes. The Eurasian Golden Plovers thus caught in the northern Netherlands in the first half of this century were sold to the big cities, notably Paris and London, for consumption. In late autumn and winter this hunt provided the income for a small but dedicated group of people that laboured on farms during the rest of the year. In contrast to the history of American Golden Plovers, neither wilsternetting, nor the shooting that still goes on in Denmark, France and Spain, have ever brought the Eurasian Golden Plover close to extinction; the southernmost breeding populations are now in sharp decline, but there may be other causes.

Market hunting of plovers and many other waterbirds is still an important economic activity, and hence a threat, in parts of the Middle East and Asia. The best information available is from Egypt, where surveys of the bird markets of Port Said and Damietta by P. L. Meininger, W. C. Mullié and their associates have documented the numbers of waterbirds killed each year at the Nile Delta. Plovers comprised only 2-3% of the 260,000-375,000 waterbirds taken annually between 1979 and 1986. However, an annual harvest of about 2000 Kentish Plovers, the plover species taken most, must surely represent a significant mortality factor. In addition, hunters cause much disturbance and thereby lower the carrying capacity of wetlands in subtle ways.

Al over the world man has been, and continues to be, responsible for the destruction or radical alteration of the habitats so often irreplaceable to particular plants and animals. Sometimes his modifications can actually provide new habitat for some other species. Few species may actually respond to these temporary opportunities, but those that do are often extremely successful. Common Ringed Plovers, for example, have adapted with a certain amount of success to breeding at artificial sites, such as gravel pits, reservoirs and playing fields.

[Charadrius hiaticula hiaticula, Lancashire, England. Photo: Mike McKavett/ Bruce Coleman]

Status and Conservation

The one recognized plover species that will fairly certainly not make it into the twenty-first century is the Javanese Wattled Lapwing (*Vanellus macropterus*), historically an endemic of the Indonesian Archipelago. It was last observed on the south-east coast of Java in 1939. Javanese Wattled Lapwings probably succumbed under the combined pressures of degradation of breeding habitat by intensified agricultural practices and hunting.

Other island populations of plovers are threatened with extinction too. The two populations of Red-breasted Plovers, living on Stewart Island and North Island, New Zealand, have shown drastic declines in numbers and range over the past 150 years, with some 65 birds surviving on the former and 1400 on the latter; as a result of predation by introduced rats and cats, the effective breeding population on Stewart Island is now reduced to 12 pairs. Another New Zealand endemic, the Shore Plover, living on a small island of only 2 km² in the Chatham group, is doing slightly better, with 40-50 breeding pairs. The total population remained stable between 1969 and 1993, and has probably been constrained by the availability of suitable habitat ever since Shore Plovers became extinct on North and South Islands more than 100 years ago. Habitat also seems the limiting factor for the third plover species classified as Endangered, the St Helena Plover, of which about 300 birds were counted during the last survey in 1993. An island dweller that is considered Vulnerable is the Black-banded Plover, a rare species limited to a small region of dry saline lowlands in southern Madagascar. It may be genetically swamped or outcompeted by its closest relative, the common Kittlitz's Plover.

Although plover populations living on islands may run the greatest risk of extinction due to their restricted distribution, there are several continental and more widespread plover species that give cause for concern as well. Sociable Lapwings once lived quite widespread on the steppes in southern Russia and Kazakhstan. They are now in sharp decline due to changes in land use for agricultural reasons, and, perhaps, desertification,

and the species is considered Vulnerable. In North America, two Vulnerable plover species are the Piping Plover, a bird of open, often saline, lowland habitats, and the Mountain Plover, which breeds and winters in short-grass prairies. In the last century both species were still very widespread, but they are now in steep decline, as a consequence of changes in land use and, perhaps, hunting. Also Vulnerable is the Hooded Plover, a southern Australian endemic shoreline species that is threatened by increased human use of beaches and nest predation by gulls and introduced mammals. The other Vulnerable plover is the Wrybill of New Zealand. Hunted until the 1940's for sport, the population of Wrybills subsequently expanded until the 1960's, when it stabilized at 5000-6000 birds. However, the entire population might be at risk if the breeding sites on braided rivers in the Canterbury and Mackenzie Basins of South Island were to be modified by the development of hydro-electric schemes.

There are a few widespread inland east Asian plover species about which precious little is known, but which might well be in the danger zone. One is the Grey-headed Lapwing of Manchuria and neighbouring areas of China and the Russian Far East. There are indications that the population of less than 20,000 birds is decreasing; land use changes and the application of pesticides and herbicides on the tropical south-east Asian wintering grounds could pose a serious threat for this species. The Long-billed Plover has a slightly larger but overlapping range, perhaps an even smaller world population of less than 10,000 birds, and very similar problems. In both species, the resident populations in Japan are of unknown but surely small size, but may be relatively safe. Grey-headed Lapwings and Long-billed Plovers require urgent attention, as does another resident species from south-east Asia, the coast-living Malaysian Plover. Its total population size is also under 10,000 birds, but only 410 individuals were counted during the most recent international Asian Waterfowl Census.

In South America, the Diademed Plover, a species restricted to the Andes, has an unknown but probably small population. It lives in areas of difficult access, and its status needs clarification. The Magellanic Plover, endemic to Patagonia, may have suffered badly from the introduction of sheep to Tierra del Fuego 100 years ago. Magellanic Plovers make no attempts to distract potential predators or herbivorous intruders from their nests or chicks. Since the shores of pools where they breed are paths for hordes of sheep, trampling is still an important cause of egg loss. With a total population of under 1500 individuals, this is a potentially vulnerable species. Certain management practices, for instance keeping sheep away from breeding sites during the nesting season, may be practical, and even critical, to safeguard this weird and wonderful species.

Some plover species are quite numerous. There are more than 250,000 Common Ringed Plovers and 168,000 Grey Plovers wintering along the east Atlantic. In Western Europe, Grey Plovers are on the increase. In Britain numbers have quadrupled over the last 25 years to more than 40,000 birds. Across the Atlantic, along the eastern seaboard of Canada and the USA, Grey Plovers have shown serious declines over the same period. In Europe, Eurasian Golden Plovers and Northern Lapwings are even more numerous than Grey Plovers, approaching a million birds or more each. During the last decades, Northern Lapwings have greatly increased their breeding range in Eurasia towards the north and east, apparently in response to climatic amelioration.

In spite of the fact that some species are very abundant, specific populations or races of the same species may not do so well. The nominate southern race *apricaria* of the Eurasian Golden Plover has become extinct in the southern part of its range, and is declining in Scotland and parts of southern Scandinavia; it may now be seriously threatened. On the basis of systematic interviews with old practitioners of wilsternetting, J. Jukema showed that a sizeable population of Pacific Golden Plovers must have wintered in Western Europe during the first half of the present century. Despite much better coverage than before, Pacific Golden Plovers have only very rarely been captured or sighted since 1950. The original population, probably breeding in western Siberia, may have gone extinct unnoticed.

Man-induced habitat modifications can also present plovers with opportunities. For example, the large populations of Northern Lapwings inhabiting parts of Europe and northern Asia owe their presence to the disappearance of forests and their conversion to cultivated land, a process that still goes on in Siberia. Also in Europe, the Little Ringed Plover has benefited from the many newly exacavated sand and shingle quarries that provide excellent breeding habitat.

That even an abundant species may be open to extinction is shown by the recent history of the American Golden Plover. A reduced annual survival rate due to intense seasonal hunting cer-

The St Helena Plover, endemic to the small, remote Atlantic island of the same name, is Endangered. In 1993, some 315 birds still remained, but numbers seemed to be declining, probably as a result of habitat loss due to housing development. Although the species would appear to be safe from extinction in the long run owing to some of its habitat appearing useless to people, caution is required. With such a small population, the species could be wiped off the map at one fell swoop, for instance by the unintentional introduction of an effective predator.

[Charadrius sanctaehelenae, Deadwood Plain, St Helena. Photo: Simon Bannister/ Aquila]

The world's coasts are increasingly being developed by money-makers for intensive human use. Many beach-living plover species, among them the Hooded Plover, have thus lost extensive tracts of potential breeding habitat. Its nests often fall victim to 4-wheel-drive vehicles using beaches as racing tracks, and chicks are sometimes killed while hiding in wheel ruts; the rate of predation of eggs and chicks also increases due to the expansion of scavengers, attracted by the humans.

[Charadrius rubricollis, Australia. Photo: D. Watts/ Nature Focus]

tainly brought this long distance migrant to the brink of extinction at the turn of the century. In Europe, hunting has been shown to decrease the annual survival rate of Northern Lapwings by 5% or more, to the extent that agriculture-induced declines in breeding success can not be compensated for. Large-scale changes in land use and agricultural practices will continue to pose threats to many plover species, including the presently abundant or widespread ones. Major declines are reported for coastal and inland breeding populations of Kentish Plovers over much of Europe between 1985 and 1995. Coastal species and those which depend on intertidal areas for part of the year, may be jeopardized by land reclamation, human disturbance of breeding sites, hunting, and the predicted fast rise in the water level of the oceans. Plovers need habitat, but so does man. It can only be hoped that an increased appreciation for members of the avian family that characterizes the only birds to survive the crash of a large meteorite at the end of the Cretaceous, the one that wiped out the dinosaurs, may help us to help them survive this time.

General Bibliography
Alcorn *et al.* (1994), Baker & Strauch (1988), Barbosa (1993), Barnard & Thompson (1985), Beintema & Visser (1989a, 1989b), Beintema, Moedt & Ellinger (1995), Beintema, Thissen *et al.* (1991), Beser & Helden-Sarnowski (1982), Björklund (1994), Bock (1958), Boere (1976), Bolze (1968), Boyd (1962), Burger & Olla (1984), Burton (1974), Christian *et al.* (1992b), Chu (1995), Davidson (1981), Eenshuistra (1973), Evans (1985), Evans & Pienkowski (1984), Evans *et al.* (1984), Feduccia (1995, 1996), Goede (1993), Graul (1973b), Hale (1980), Hayman *et al.* (1986), Hoerschelmann & Jacob (1992), Hunter *et al.* (1991), Jehl (1968b), Jehl & Murray (1986), Johnsgard (1981), Kersten & Piersma (1987), Lange (1968), Larson (1955, 1957), Maclean (1972a, 1972b, 1974), McNeil *et al.* (1992), Miller (1984, 1992, 1995), Morrison (1991), Myers *et al.* (1979a), Nethersole-Thompson & Nethersole-Thompson (1986), Nol (1986), Paulson & Erckmann (1993), Peters (1934), Pienkowski (1978/79, 1983a, 1983c, 1983d), Pienkowski & Evans (1985), Piersma, Beintema *et al.* (1987), Piersma, Koolhaas & Dekinga (1993), Piersma, Zwarts & Bruggemann (1990), Pitelka (1979), Portmann (1947), Prater (1981a, 1981b), Prater *et al.* (1977), Recher (1966), Rehfisch *et al.* (1996), Rosair & Cottridge (1995), Rundle (1982), Saether *et al.* (1986), Sibley & Ahlquist (1990), Sibley & Monroe (1990), Simmons (1957), Staaland (1967), Strauch (1976, 1978), Thompson (1983), Tomkovich & Soloviev (1994), Turpie (1994), Visser & Ricklefs (1993a, 1993b), Walters, J.R. (1982, 1984, 1990).

1 ♂ ♀

2

3

4

5

6 ssp *latifrons*

ssp *tectus*

7

8

9

10

11 ssp *coronatus*

ssp *demissus*

12 ssp *lateralis*

ssp *senegallus*

PLATE 35

inches 6

cm 15

Subfamily VANELLINAE

Genus *VANELLUS* Brisson, 1760

1. Northern Lapwing

Vanellus vanellus

French: Vanneau huppé **German**: Kiebitz **Spanish**: Avefría Europea
Other common names: Eurasian Lapwing, Peewit, Green Plover

Taxonomy. *Tringa Vanellus* Linnaeus, 1758, Europe, Africa; restricted to Sweden.
In past, genus *Vanellus* commonly considered to contain present species only. Monotypic.
Distribution. Europe, C Turkey and NW Iran through W Russia and Kazakhstan to S & E Siberia, Mongolia and N China. Winters from W Europe, E Atlantic islands and N Africa through Mediterranean, Middle East and Iraq across N India to SE China and S Japan.

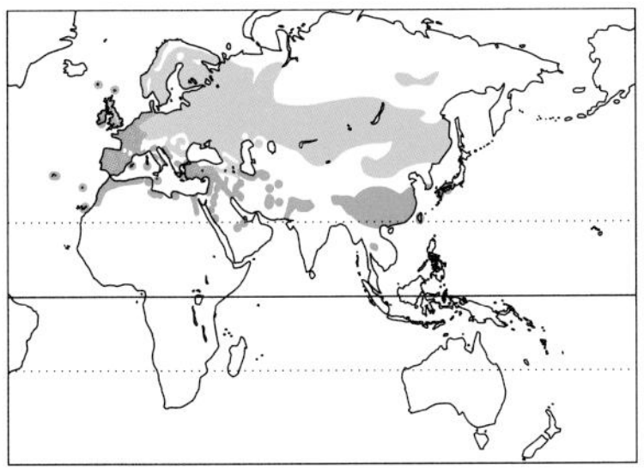

Descriptive notes. 28-31 cm; 128-330 g; wingspan 82-87 cm. Metallic glossy green upperparts, blackish crest and bronze scapulars; very broad wings, especially in breeding males. Female has less distinctive head pattern and white flecks on throat. Non-breeding adult has buff face, and white chin and throat; upperwing-coverts and scapulars have buff fringes. Juvenile similar to non-breeding adult, but has more extensive buff feather fringes, and narrower and browner breast band.
Habitat. Breeds in variety of wide open habitats with short vegetation or bare ground, including various wetlands, heaths, moors, arable fields, meadows and hay fields; in Europe mainly a farmland breeder. Outside breeding season also appears on harvested stubble and ploughed fields. Roosting flocks prefer spacious, old pastures and sometimes appear on mudflats.
Food and Feeding. Feeds on invertebrate prey, primarily earthworms and insects, including larvae and adults of beetles, ants, Diptera flies, moths and crickets; also spiders and snails. On arable fields, adults and chicks take mainly cranefly larvae and earthworms, but evidently not selectively. Sometimes feeds by foot-trembling. Diurnal and nocturnal; sometimes even primarily nocturnal on bright, moonlit nights.
Breeding. Laying late Mar to early Jun. Mostly seasonally monogamous, but sometimes polygamous. Territorial during incubation; solitary breeder, with average densities 0·6-1·8 pairs/ha, maximum 9 pairs/ha. High degree of site-faithfulness in males, and high degree of natal philopatry, usually nesting within 60 km of hatching site. Males perform dazzling aerial song flight display (see page 396), during which wingtips produce droning sound. Nest is shallow scrape, lined with some vegetation, situated in short grassy vegetation. Clutch 4 eggs, occasionally 3 or 2; clutch completed in 5 days; incubation 21-28 days, starting once last egg laid; downy chick pale brown or cinnamon, with black streaks and blotches and white nape; chicks tended by both parents, although brooding primarily by female; fledging 5-6 weeks. Agricultural activities may cause 36% of broods to fail, plus another 32% partial losses of clutches; rainy and cold weather can have deleterious effects during chick phase; other causes of failure are predation, especially by crows, trampling by cattle and flooding. Highest mortality of hatchlings during first 10 days. Fledging success varies with year and habitat, but averages 0·2-2·8 fledglings per pair. Age of first breeding mostly 1 year; annual mortality of adults c. 25-30%, first-year birds c. 35-40%. Oldest ringed bird 18 years, 11 months.
Movements. Migratory and resident. After breeding season gathers in flocks. Breeding areas left as early as beginning of summer, movements starting already in early Jun. Movements during summer are mainly westward. British and southernmost breeders partly sedentary; many British birds winter in Ireland. Migration towards SW takes place in Sept-Oct, and starts with cold spells. Wintering area bordered by 3°C isotherm, but exact S and W distribution depends on weather. Spring migration at peak in early Mar, but can start as early as Jan; males precede females.
Status and Conservation. Not globally threatened. Estimated 7,000,000 birds in Europe, with 1,000,000-1,200,000 breeding pairs in Europe (excluding Russia), of which 226,000-278,000 in Netherlands, 200,000-250,000 in Britain, 150,000 in Finland (1986), 120,000 in Sweden (1984), and high numbers in Norway, Germany, Denmark and Ireland. More than 25,000 birds winter in SW Asia, c. 20,000 birds winter in Iran, 10,000-25,000 birds winter in SC Asia; more than 25,000 birds in E & SE Asia, and this population on increase. Marked decreases in last decades in S Sweden, and in large areas of Britain, Netherlands, Germany and Czech Republic. In winter (Nov), 1,000,000-1,500,000 birds present in Netherlands and 100,000-200,000 in Denmark; in Jan, 275,000 in Britain. Breeding area expanding northwards throughout range, mainly following extensive, man-made water meadows. European population decreased in 19th and early 20th centuries, probably as result of intensification of land use, drainage and egg-collecting, and same now happening in many E parts of range; due to habitat shift to agricultural land, numbers thereafter increased, until last decades, when population of W Europe in decline again, apparently caused by intensifying and changing agricultural practices, resulting in reduced breeding productivity; on arable fields, clutch destruction during cultivation and poor chick survival can result in insufficient productivity to maintain a stable population.
Bibliography. Ali & Ripley (1980), Asensio (1992), Baines (1989, 1990), Bak & Ettrup (1982), Barnard & Stephens (1981), Beintema (1985, 1991a, 1994), Beintema & Müskens (1987), Beintema & Visser (1989b), Beintema *et al.* (1985), Berg (1991, 1993b), Berg *et al.* (1992), Beser (1983, 1987), Beser & Beser (1989), Beyerbach *et al.* (1988), Birrer & Schmid (1989), Blomqvist & Johansson (1994, 1995), Brazil (1991), Busche (1995), Cramp & Simmons (1983), Dabelsteen (1978), Dittberner & Dittberner (1991), Dowsett & Forbes-Watson (1993), Dubois & Maheo (1986), Elliot (1985), Étchécopar & Hüe (1964, 1978), Ettrup & Bak (1985), Evans (1994), Fjeldså (1977), Flint *et al.* (1984), Flodin *et al.* (1990), Fuller (1992), Futter (1989), Galbraith (1986, 1988a, 1988b, 1988c, 1988d, 1989a, 1989b), Galbraith & Watson (1991), Goodman *et al.* (1989), Gregory, R.D. (1987), Gristchenko & Serebryakov (1988), Högstedt (1974), Hötker (1989), Hüe & Étchécopar (1970), Imboden (1974), van Impe (1988), Källander (1977, 1988), Kirby & Lack (1993), Klemp (1993), Klomp (1954), Klomp & Speek (1971), Knystautas (1993), Kooiker (1984, 1987, 1990, 1993), Kraft (1993), Kramer (1994), Liker (1992), Mackworth-Praed & Grant (1957), Marchant *et al.* (1990), Marcström & Mascher (1979), Martínez *et al.* (1996), Matter (1982), Meltofte *et al.* (1994), Metcalfe (1985), Milsom (1984, 1990), Milsom, Holditch & Rochard (1985), Milsom, Rochard & Poole (1990), O'Brian & Smith (1992), O'Connor & Shrubb (1986), Onnen (1989), Patrikeev (1995), Paz (1987), Peach *et al.* (1994), Perennou *et al.* (1994), Redfern (1982, 1983), Ripley (1982), Roberts, T.J. (1991), Rogacheva (1992), Rutgers & Norris (1970), Scott (1989), Shirihai (1996), Shrubb (1988, 1990), Shrubb & Lack (1991), Smythies (1986), Thompson, D.B.A. & Barnard (1983, 1984), Thompson, P.S. *et al.* (1994), Tomkovich (1992b), Tucker *et al.* (1994), Urban *et al.* (1986), Weaver (1987), Weggler (1992), Williams, M.D. (1986), Zollner (1995).

2. Long-toed Lapwing

Vanellus crassirostris

French: Vanneau à ailes blanches **German**: Langzehenkiebitz **Spanish**: Avefría Palustre
Other common names: White-faced Lapwing, Long-toed/White-winged Plover

Taxonomy. *Chettusia crassirostris* Hartlaub, 1855, Nubia.
In past, commonly placed in monospecific genus *Hemiparra*. Races intergrade in Tanzania, SE Zaire and N Malawi, and these intermediate birds formerly separated as race *hybrida*. Two subspecies recognized.
Subspecies and distribution.
V. c. crassirostris (Hartlaub, 1855) - S Sudan through Uganda, E Zaire, W Kenya and Tanzania to N Malawi; W Angola; also NE Nigeria, where may not breed.
V. c. leucopterus Reichenow, 1889 - Tanzania, SE Zaire, Zambia and Malawi to E Angola, N Botswana and NE South Africa.

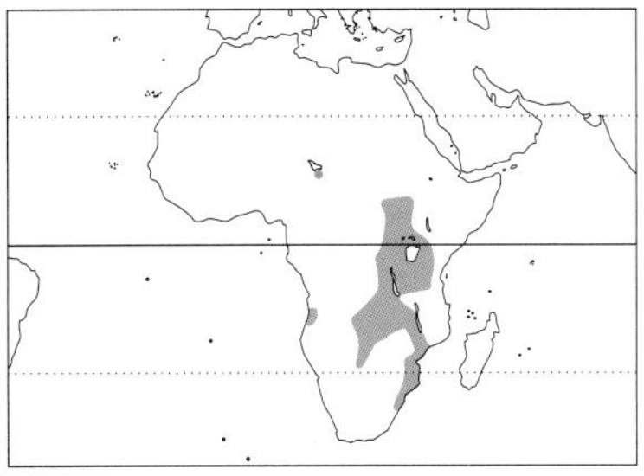

Descriptive notes. c. 31 cm; 162-225 g. Long-legged and unusually long-toed lapwing; nape, hindneck and breast black with bluish gloss, face and throat white; upperparts dark greyish brown; eye-ring red, heavy bill red with black tips; short wing-spurs; legs deep red. Sexes alike. No seasonal variation. Juvenile has black parts browner, with buff tips to feathers; upperparts mottled with brown and buff. Races differ in wing coloration: nominate has all flight-feathers black, while in *leucopterus* only outer primaries black, rest of primaries and secondaries white; some birds intermediate.
Habitat. Forages on surface of floating vegetation in stagnant water, e.g. lakes, pools and marshes; also occurs in swamps, rivers and floodplains. In dry season, feeds at muddy edges of pools and small waterways; in wet season, on inundated grassland and in flooded rice fields.
Food and Feeding. Feeds on aquatic insects, larvae, dragonfly nymphs, beetles, ants and small snails. Unlike any other *Vanellus* species, feeds mainly on surface of floating vegetation, like jacanas (Jacanidae), supported by its long toes. Associates with Spur-winged Goose (*Plectropterus gambensis*), profiting from the goose turning over dead vegetation.
Breeding. Laying probably mainly Dec-Mar in C Africa, Jun-Nov in S Africa, but breeding occurs year round throughout range. Monogamous. Rather small territory, aggressively defended against neighbouring conspecifics by attacking from the air; after chicks hatch, adults very aggressive against intruding birds of many other species, e.g. African Fish-eagle (*Haliaeetus vocifer*). Nest is shallow scrape lined with plant material on grassland or mud, up to 100 from water's edge; or cup made from plant material on floating vegetation; or 5-10 cm high platform of mosses, weeds and debris in swampy areas. Clutch 2-4 eggs; incubation c. 30 days; downy chick buff above with irregular black markings, white below with dark brown breast; fledging c. 2 months.
Movements. Mainly sedentary, unless habitat dries up. Some movements between habitats have been observed in Rwanda. Status uncertain in NE Nigeria on S shore of L Chad, where species occurs, but may not breed. Non-breeders occur seasonally in Upemba National Park, Zaire.
Status and Conservation. Not globally threatened. No population estimates available; frequent to common, with local aggregations due to restrictive habitat requirements. A concentration of nearly 100 birds noted on Kafue Flats, SW Zambia; fairly common in Malawi.
Bibliography. Benson & Benson (1975), Britton, P.L. (1980), Brown & Britton (1980), Dean (1986), Dowsett & Forbes-Watson (1993), Elgood *et al.* (1994), Ginn *et al.* (1989), Henderson & Harper (1992), Lippens & Wille (1976), Mackworth-Praed & Grant (1957, 1962, 1970), Maclean (1993), Nikolaus (1987), van Perlo (1995), Pinto (1983), Saunders (1970), Short *et al.* (1990), Snow (1978), Tree (1978), Urban *et al.* (1986), Walters, J.R. (1979).

3. Blacksmith Lapwing

Vanellus armatus

French: Vanneau armé **German**: Schmiedekiebitz **Spanish**: Avefría Armada
Other common names: Blacksmith Plover

Taxonomy. *Charadrius armatus* Burchell, 1822, Klaarwater (= Griquatown), South Africa.
Formerly placed in monospecific genus *Anitibyx*; sometimes included in *Hoplopterus*. Monotypic.
Distribution. Angola to C Tanzania and CS Kenya, and S to South Africa, except W coast of Namibia.
Descriptive notes. 28-31 cm; 114-213 g. Medium-sized lapwing with contrasting plumage colours; glossy black face, foreneck and back, white crown and hindneck, grey upperwing-coverts; black carpal spurs. Metallic alarm call "tink-tink" recalls blacksmith's hammer on anvil. Sexes alike; female has shorter wing-spurs. No seasonal variation. Juvenile has brownish crown, white chin and throat; black feathers between grey scapulars and upperwing-coverts and all black feathers with buff fringes.
Habitat. Dry areas near water, such as lagoons, lakes, rivers, dams, water-holes, sewage farms and marshes; also mudflats, sodaflats and floodplains. Often flies to open country to forage. Sometimes roosts in flocks on islets.
Food and Feeding. Feeds on molluscs, crustaceans, worms and insects in typical plover style. Also forages by foot-trembling, pecking from water surface while wading, and hunting for insects by turning over dung pats. Forages on ploughed land and agricultural fields and among cattle.
Breeding. Laying in all months throughout range; frequently at start of dry season. Monogamous. Territorial and solitarily, with nests at least 400 m apart (South Africa); intraspecific aggression rare.

On following pages: 4. Spur-winged Lapwing (*Vanellus spinosus*); 5. River Lapwing (*Vanellus duvaucelii*); 6. Black-headed Lapwing (*Vanellus tectus*); 7. Yellow-wattled Lapwing (*Vanellus malabaricus*); 8. White-headed Lapwing (*Vanellus albiceps*); 9. Lesser Black-winged Lapwing (*Vanellus lugubris*); 10. Greater Black-winged Lapwing (*Vanellus melanopterus*); 11. Crowned Lapwing (*Vanellus coronatus*); 12. African Wattled Lapwing (*Vanellus senegallus*).

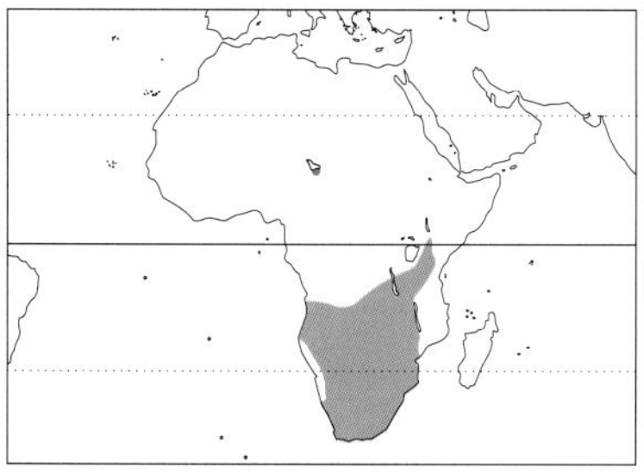

Courtship activity occurs in non-breeding flocks, often involving 3-5 birds. Nest is shallow scrape or depression, variably lined with pebbles, plant material and debris; located on ground or in short grass, very close to water. Clutch 3 eggs (1-4); double-brooded; incubation 23-31 days, by both sexes; chick has upperparts mixed brown and buff, underparts and collar white; fledging 41 days; chicks of first brood remain with adults until hatching of second brood. Main causes of egg and chick loss are flooding and predation.

Movements. Mainly sedentary. Occurs as non-breeding migrant in Zaire. Local movements occur due to flooding. Forms non-breeding flocks of up to 100 birds.

Status and Conservation. Not globally threatened. No population estimates available; generally common to locally abundant. In Zimbabwe, has benefited from increasing availability of artificial water supplies. Only recently found S of Orange R and Natal, but range now extending to coasts of SE Cape; reached W Cape in 1939, where first bred in 1947. Total of 2100 birds counted in South Africa in 1986, mostly in W & S Cape.

Bibliography. Benson & Benson (1975), Britton, P.L. (1980), Broekhuysen (1948), Brown (1972), Dowsett & Forbes-Watson (1993), Ginn *et al*. (1989), Hall (1959b, 1964), Henderson & Harper (1992), Kopij & Kok (1994), Kutilek (1974), Mackworth-Praed & Grant (1957, 1962, 1970), Maclean (1993), Nixon (1987), Penry (1980), Pinto (1983), Reynolds (1980, 1984), Rutgers & Norris (1970), Short *et al*. (1990), Thomas, D.H. (1983), Tucker (1979), Urban *et al*. (1986), Ward (1987, 1988, 1992).

4. Spur-winged Lapwing

Vanellus spinosus

French: Vanneau à éperons **German**: Spornkiebitz **Spanish**: Avefría Espinosa
Other common names: Spur-winged Plover

Taxonomy. *Charadrius spinosus* Linnaeus, 1758, Egypt.
Often placed in genus *Hoplopterus*. Forms superspecies with *V. duvaucelii*, with which sometimes considered conspecific. Monotypic.

Distribution. E Mediterranean and Middle East up R Nile to C & S Sudan, and S of Sahara from Senegal through Nigeria to Ethiopia, and S to Uganda and Kenya.

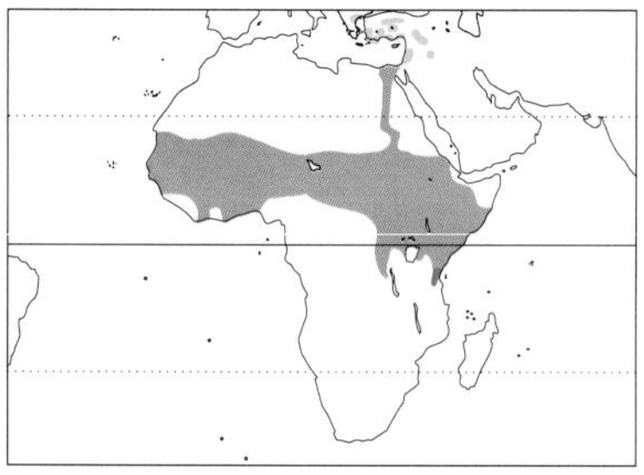

Descriptive notes. 25-28 cm; 127-177 g; wingspan 69-81 cm. Crown, forehead and throat black, cheeks and sides of neck white; slight crest not normally apparent; breast, upper belly and flanks black; dark red eyes, black spurs. Differs from *V. duvaucelii* most clearly by extensive black on underparts. Female as male, but spurs shorter. No seasonal variation. Juvenile has black parts of plumage brownish, speckled with white; feathers of upperparts have broad buff fringes.

Habitat. Usually on dry ground, but rarely far from water. Inhabits great variety of habitats, including cultivated fields or (burnt) grassland, near pools, lakes, rivers or lagoons, on mudflats, sandflats, sodaflats, rice fields, flooded fields, beaches and dunes. Sometimes in ponds and marshes.

Food and Feeding. Feeds mainly on insects and their larvae, especially beetles; also grasshoppers, flies, midges, termites, ants, spiders, myriapods; occasionally, crustaceans, molluscs, small lizards, tadpoles and adult frogs, fish and seeds. Takes few rapid steps followed by stabbing at prey; also flushes prey by foot-trembling.

Breeding. In tropical Africa, laying dates usually locally restricted, but great geographical variation; Israel Apr-Jul; Greece late Apr-May. Monogamous. Nests solitarily or in loose colonies. Territory aggressively defended against most other bird species, especially waders; conspecifics often tolerated in territory; territory sometimes occupied year round. Nest on bare, dry ground, usually a shallow scrape, unlined or lined with grass or other plant material and debris, or with a rim of earth, small shells or stones; alternatively, natural depression in rock lined with pebbles; nest on mud sometimes more substantial, with grass and reed stems. Lays 2-4 eggs (up to 5) at variable intervals of (1-) 2 days or more; often lays second clutch, and sometimes third; incubation 22-24 days (Europe); both parents incubate and tend chicks, but in case of second clutch, incubation by female while male tends chicks of first clutch; chick cinnamon-buff above, mottled grey and streaked black, with cheeks buff and hindneck white, lacks hind toe; fledging 7-8 weeks. Immatures independent soon after fledging, but sometimes stay with parents until next breeding season. Nests and eggs often trampled by cattle and ungulates. Fledging success in Israel c. 2 young per brood.

Movements. In Africa resident, locally making erratic movements; in places moves into drier areas during rainy season, but leaves driest areas; in general, not very sensitive to seasonal water level changes; local numbers can vary seasonally due to movements. Local migration in E Africa, with some birds occurring S to C Tanzania. Populations of Greece and Turkey migrate S in Oct, but main destinations unclear; some birds to Red Sea coast and presumably elsewhere in Africa. Middle East population probably dispersive or resident; Egyptian population resident. In non-breeding season occurs in flocks of up to 15 birds, maximum 200.

Status and Conservation. Not globally threatened. Probably 10,000-25,000 birds in SE Europe and SW Asia. No population estimate available for Africa, but thousands of pairs breed in Egypt; 1000-5000 birds in Sudan; a common bird in Israel, where 1550 birds, probably more, wintered between 1975 and 1983. Numbers have increased notably in Egypt and Israel since 1960's; at least in Israel, due to new irrigation fields, reservoirs, sewage farms and control of long vegetation bordering fish ponds. Species endangered in Europe; first noted breeding in Greece in 1959; but numbers decreased from 120-170 breeding pairs in 1970 to 32-45 pairs in 1993, due to loss of natural or semi-natural wetland habitat of salt-marshes. Population seems stable in Turkey at 1000-5000 pairs; 5000-15,000 birds occur in Egypt in winter. Locally exposed to hunting pressure.

Bibliography. Alessandria *et al*. (1990), Anon. (1995e), Ash & Miskell (1983), Britton, P.L. (1980), Caspers (1984), Cramp & Simmons (1983), Czackes-Rado & Yom-Tov (1987), Dowsett & Forbes-Watson (1993), Dragesco (1960), Elgood *et al*. (1994), Étchécopar & Hüe (1964), Evans (1994), Ferguson-Lees (1965), Glutz von Blotzheim *et al*. (1975), Goodman *et al*. (1989), Gore (1990), Grimes (1987), Hall (1965), Hasson (1991), von Helversen (1963), Hüe & Étchécopar (1970), Jerrentrup (1993, 1994), Keijl *et al*. (1992), Lewis (1990), Mackworth-Praed & Grant (1957, 1962, 1970), Makatsch (1962, 1969a), Mienis (1985), Paz (1987), Perennou *et al*. (1994), Reynolds (1980), Robin (1981), Rutgers & Norris (1970), Shirihai (1996), Short *et al*. (1990), Sims (1977), Urban *et al*. (1986), Van de Weghe & Monfort-Braham (1975), Ward (1992), Yawetz *et al*. (1993), Yogev & Yom-Tov (1994).

5. River Lapwing

Vanellus duvaucelii

French: Vanneau pie **German**: Flußkiebitz **Spanish**: Avefría Fluvial
Other common names: Indian/Asian Spur-winged Plover/Lapwing

Taxonomy. *Charadrius Duvaucelii* Lesson, 1826, Calcutta.
Often placed in genus *Hoplopterus*. Forms superspecies with *V. spinosus*, with which sometimes considered conspecific. Monotypic.

Distribution. NC India (Uttar Pradesh) and Nepal through EC & NE India to SC China (SW Yunnan) and Indochina; status unclear further E possibly to Hainan and to Hong Kong.

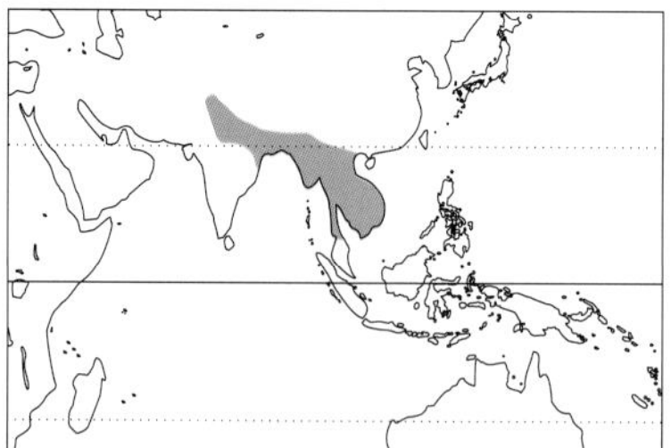

Descriptive notes. 29·5-31·5 cm; 143-185 g. Black-faced lapwing with dark red eyes; crown and nape feathers can be raised to form a crest; black carpal spurs. Differs from somewhat similar *V. spinosus* in greyish breast, pale grey sides of head and neck, and small black spot on belly. Sexes alike. No seasonal variation. Juvenile similar to adult, with buff fringes and brownish tips to black parts.

Habitat. Generally found near rivers, especially in cultivated land, and on sandbanks and shingle banks; rarely near stagnant water.

Food and Feeding. Mainly insects, worms, crustaceans and molluscs; also claimed to take frogs and tadpoles.

Breeding. Nesting Mar-Jun. Elaborate display by party of 4 birds has been described on 2 occasions. Nest is shallow scrape on exposed sandbar or shingle bank in river. Clutch 4 eggs (3-4); incubation apparently 22-24 days.

Movements. Sedentary; some seasonal nomadic movements.

Status and Conservation. Not globally threatened. Total population probably very small, unlikely to number more than 25,000 birds, and possibly no more than 15,000 birds. Annual Asian Waterfowl Census has never produced more than 500 birds. Uncommon in Thailand, apparently occurring mainly in NW.

Bibliography. Ali (1979), Ali & Ripley (1980), Bhunya & Mohanty (1990), Deignan (1945), Étchécopar & Hüe (1978), Harvey (1990), Hingston (1932), Inskipp & Inskipp (1991), Lekagul & Round (1991), Medway & Wells (1976), Perennou *et al*. (1994), Ripley (1982), Scott (1989), Smythies (1986).

6. Black-headed Lapwing

Vanellus tectus

French: Vanneau à tête noire **German**: Schwarzschopfkiebitz **Spanish**: Avefría Coletuda
Other common names: Black-headed/Blackhead/Crested Wattled Plover

Taxonomy. *Charadrius tectus* Boddaert, 1783, Senegal.
Sometimes placed in *Hoplopterus*, *Lobivanellus* or monospecific *Sarciophorus*. Two subspecies recognized.

Subspecies and Distribution.
V. t. tectus (Boddaert, 1783) - S Mauritania and Senegal to Ethiopia, Uganda and Kenya.
V. t. latifrons (Reichenow, 1881) - S Somalia to E Kenya.

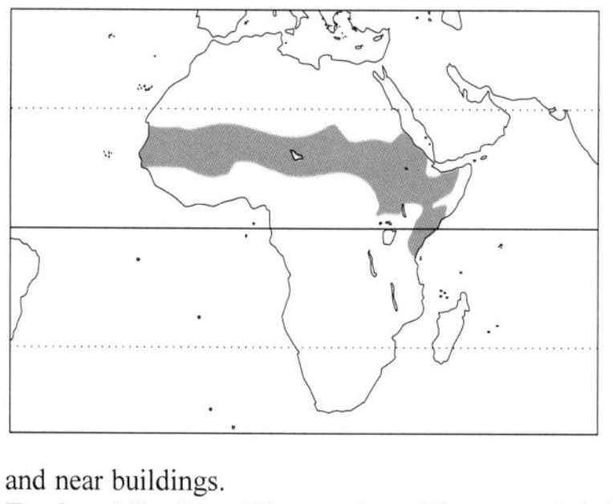

Descriptive notes. c. 25 cm; 99-120 g (*latifrons*). Crested lapwing with red wattles, black and white head, and pinkish red legs; vertical black streak on upper breast unique in *Vanellus*. Sexes alike. No seasonal variation. Juvenile like adult, but has buff edges to black and brown feathers; also shorter crest and smaller wattles. Race *latifrons* somewhat smaller, with broader white forehead band.

Habitat. Dry plains or desert, bare or with short grass; open bushland; open, bare areas in thornscrub; not necessarily near water. Also found near human settlement, e.g. airfields, football pitches, race courses, etc.; will nest in gardens and near buildings.

Food and Feeding. Diet consists of insects and their larvae and gastropods. Feeds mainly at night, resting in shade during the day.

Breeding. Laying dates locally restricted by seasons, but varying geographically, peaking either during dry or rainy seasons, depending on region; frequently Mar-May. Monogamous. Breeds singly or in loose colonies; in Chad, 14 pairs/ha; in Kenya, 7 nests within radius of 300 m. Colonial birds very aggressive, mobbing all intruders. Nest is shallow depression or scrape in sand or earth, unlined or variably lined with pebbles, gravel, plant material or debris. Lays 1-6 eggs (clutches of 5-6 probably involve 2 females) at interval of under 24 hours (but at least 28 hours in captivity); first eggs are covered before incubation starts; incubation 26 days; chick has upperparts spotted black and yellow, hindneck, cheeks and underparts white; fledging period less than 1 month (in captivity). Cattle cause nest losses.

Movements. Resident; local movements during rains noted in Mauritania, Mali and Nigeria; mainly dry season visitor to Ghana, Nov-May. In Ethiopia some groups move to higher altitudes, Nov-May. Groups of 6-10 birds (up to 40) gather outside breeding season.

Status and Conservation. Not globally threatened. No population estimates available; reported to be generally common throughout sizeable range. Widespread and common in Gambia; not uncommon in Nigeria; uncommon in Ghana. Tolerance of arid to desertic conditions, combined with apparent ability to adapt to man-made habitats suggest species secure at present.

Bibliography. Ash & Miskell (1983), Böhm (1987), Brown & Britton (1980), Dowsett & Forbes-Watson (1993), Elgood *et al*. (1994), Étchécopar & Morel (1960), Gore (1990), Greenham & Greenham (1975), Grimes (1987), Hüe & Étchécopar (1970), Jensen & Kirkeby (1980), Mackworth-Praed & Grant (1957, 1970), Morel & Morel (1990), Newby (1979), Nikolaus (1987), North (1936), van Perlo (1995), Rutgers & Norris (1970), Shirihai (1996), Short *et al*. (1990), Urban *et al*. (1986).

7. **Yellow-wattled Lapwing**

Vanellus malabaricus

French: Vanneau de Malabar **German**: Gelblappenkiebitz **Spanish**: Avefría Malabar
Other common names: Yellow-wattled Plover

Taxonomy. *Charadrius malarbaricus* [sic] Boddaert, 1783, Malabar Coast.
Formerly placed in monospecific genus *Lobipluvia*; occasionally included in *Hoplopterus*. Monotypic.
Distribution. S Pakistan, India, Bangladesh and Sri Lanka.

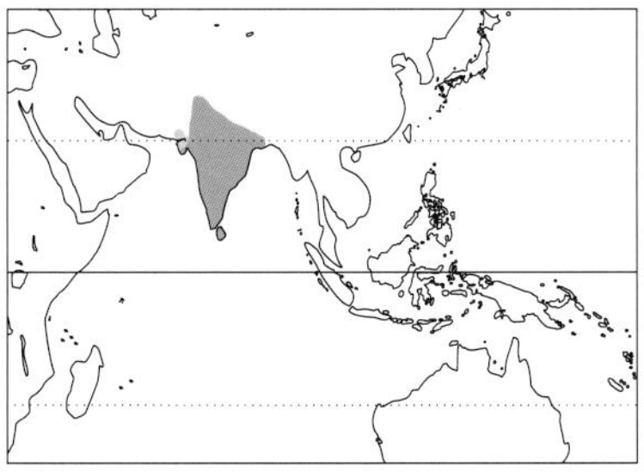

Descriptive notes. 24-28 cm; 108-203 g (3 specimens); wingspan 65-69 cm. Lapwing with yellow wattles and legs; cap black, bordered below by narrow white line; chin and throat blackish, breast and upperparts brown, belly white; white wingbar and rump, black flight-feathers; black bill with yellowish base; tiny yellow carpal spurs. When bird excited, black cap can be raised. Sexes alike. Non-breeding adult has all of black areas mottled with brown. Juvenile has brown crown, small pale wattles; dark subterminal bars and buff fringes on back feathers; chin and throat white. Clinal decrease in size from N to S.
Habitat. Dry and open habitats, including cultivated and fallow fields and wasteland; also on edges of wetlands, e.g. *jheels*, but not necessarily close to water.
Food and Feeding. Primarily insects and their larvae, including grasshoppers and beetles; also molluscs. Mainly feeds nocturnally.
Breeding. Breeds mainly Mar-Jul; season until Aug in Sri Lanka, from late Apr in Pakistan. Adults defend large territories where young and parents feed. Nest is shallow scrape, unlined, sometimes encircled by pebbles or mud pellets, situated on dry, open fallow or waste land. Clutch 4 eggs; on red laterite soil often has reddish eggs; incubation 26-29 days; chick buffy or fawn-grey, stippled black and rufous, with white hindneck collar; fledgling 32 days, or more.
Movements. Mainly sedentary; local movements to drier areas during monsoon. In lower Sind, Pakistan, present only in summer, when breeds; arrives late Feb-Mar and departs probably Aug-Sept. Outside breeding season sometimes occurs in small family groups.
Status and Conservation. Not globally threatened. No population estimates available; widely distributed, and apparently still rather common. No threats known; adaptation to rather dry areas, and tolerance of man-made habitats suggest species probably secure at present. Frequent in lower Sind, Pakistan.
Bibliography. Ali (1979), Ali & Ripley (1980), Bhunya & Mohanty (1990), Dhindsa (1983), George (1985), Harvey (1990), Henry (1971), Inskipp & Inskipp (1991), Jayakar & Spurway (1965a, 1965b, 1968), Johns & Thorpe (1981), Kotagama & Fernando (1994), Perennou *et al*. (1994), Phillips (1978), Phythian-Adams (1940), Ripley (1982), Roberts, T.J. (1991), Santharam (1980), Scott (1989), Tuljapurkar (1986), Vijayagopal & Chacko (1991), Wijesinghe (1994).

8. **White-headed Lapwing**

Vanellus albiceps

French: Vanneau à tête blanche **German**: Weißscheitelkiebitz **Spanish**: Avefría Coroniblanca
Other common names: White-headed/White-crowned/Black-shouldered (Wattled) Plover/Lapwing

Taxonomy. *Vanellus albiceps* Gould, 1834, Niger River or Fernando Po.
Sometimes placed in genus *Hoplopterus* or in monospecific *Xiphidiopterus*. Monotypic.
Distribution. Senegambia and Sierra Leone E to S Sudan, and S through W & C Zaire to NW Angola; SE Tanzania; R Zambezi and S Mozambique.

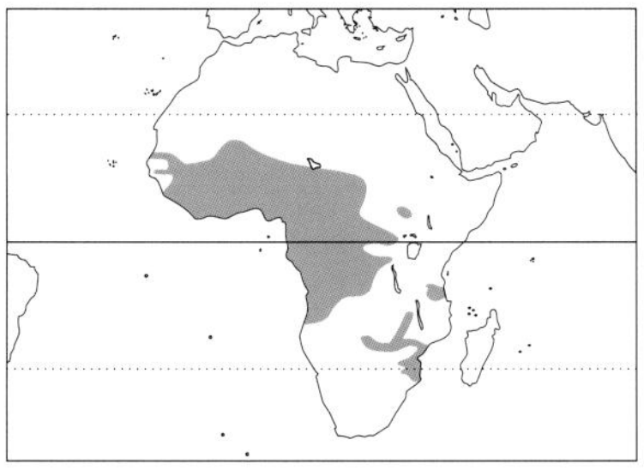

Descriptive notes. 28-32 cm; 201 g (1 adult). Lapwing with large yellow wattles, distinctive white crown band, and long black carpal spurs; wings extensively white, with outer primaries black, recalling race *leucopterus* of *V. crassirostris*, but median and greater coverts mostly black; almost entirely white from below in flight. Female has brown border to crown. No seasonal variation. Juvenile has smaller spurs and wattles, brownish white crown, upperwing-coverts fringed buff, and white and brown upperparts spotted with darker brown.
Habitat. Sandy riverbanks in open country and forests; prefers large rivers with sandbanks or islands; during floods also on small streams, pans and lagoons. Generally found in pairs or groups of 6-12 birds, maximum 30.
Food and Feeding. Takes insects, including beetles, ants, mantids and mutillid wasps; worms, molluscs, crustaceans and small fish; also some vegetable matter.
Breeding. Laying Jan-Mar (Dec-May) in W & C Africa; Jul-Oct (Nov) in E Africa; mainly during dry season. Monogamous. Solitary breeder; in Zaire, forms loose colonies; in Nigeria, nests at least 400 m apart; in South Africa, 1·46 pairs/km of river. Territory aggressively defended against conspecifics and also other bird species, especially after chicks hatch. Nests on sand or shingle in riverbeds when water level is low; nest is shallow scrape in sand or shingle, lined with small sticks and pebbles; rarely unlined. Clutch 2-4 eggs; when clutch is exposed to sun, has to be wetted frequently; incubation over 25 days; chick buff and black speckled upperparts, white underparts and hindneck collar. Parents sometimes cover eggs with plant matter, when leaving nest. Nests susceptible to trampling by crocodiles, hippopotami and ungulates.
Movements. In W Africa, migrates to drier areas when rivers flood, with movements recorded in Gambia, Sierra Leone, Niger, N Nigeria and elsewhere; sometimes moves outside breeding range. Populations S of equator only move during peak rains.
Status and Conservation. Not globally threatened. No population estimates available; said to be common in places, but range is rather limited, as restricted to certain rivers. Not uncommon seasonally in Nigeria; widespread but sparse in Sierra Leone; rare and irregular visitor to Gambia. Total of 50-75 birds known to breed on coast of Gabon.
Bibliography. Atkins, Johnston-Stewart, Atkins & Killick (1989), Bainbridge (1965), Begg & Maclean (1976), Britton, P.L. (1980), Brown & Britton (1980), Brooke (1984a), Dowsett & Forbes-Watson (1993), Elgood *et al*. (1994), Gatter (1988), Ginn *et al*. (1989), Gore (1989, 1990), Grimes (1987), Lippens & Wille (1976), Louette (1981), Mackworth-Praed & Grant (1957, 1962, 1970), Maclean (1993), Medland (1989b), Morel & Morel (1990), Nikolaus (1987), Pinto (1983), Reynolds (1968), Schepers & Marteijn (1993), Serle (1939a), Short *et al*. (1990), Tarboton & Nel (1980), Urban *et al*. (1986).

9. **Lesser Black-winged Lapwing**

Vanellus lugubris

French: Vanneau terne **German**: Trauerkiebitz **Spanish**: Avefría Lúgubre
Other common names: Senegal Plover/Lapwing, Lesser Black-winged Plover

Taxonomy. *Charadrius lugubris* Lesson, 1826, Senegal.
Sometimes placed in *Hoplopterus* or *Stephanibyx*. Has been proposed to form superspecies with *V. melanopterus*, but not supported by behavioural or morphological data. Monotypic.
Distribution. S Mali; N of forest zone in Guinea-Bissau and Ivory Coast; coast from Sierra Leone to SW Nigeria; Gabon, W Zaire and CW Angola E to Kenya, and S through Tanzania, NE Zambia, Malawi and Mozambique to E South Africa (Natal); Zanzibar, Latham and Mafia Is.

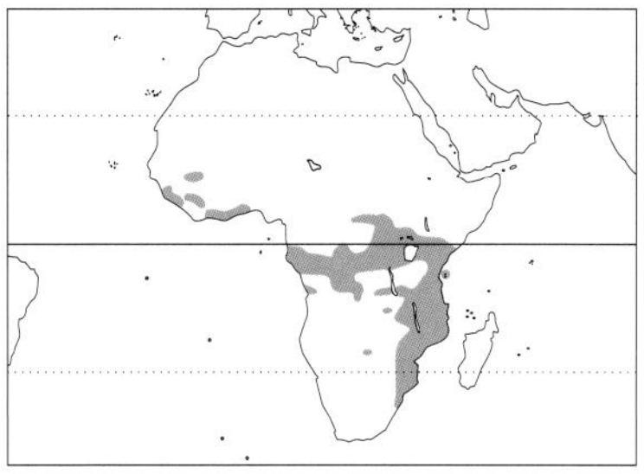

Descriptive notes. 22-26 cm; 107-120 g. Small, slender grey-headed plover. Slimmer than larger *V. melanopterus*; typically has smaller, more sharply defined white forehead patch; greener upperparts and shorter black bill; in flight, differs from *V. melanopterus* by white, not black, secondaries. Sexes alike. No seasonal variation. Juvenile has buff tips to feathers of white forehead and black breast band; buff-notched tertial edges.
Habitat. Dry, open habitats, sometimes with bushes, scrub and trees; prefers burnt grassland and newly grown grass; also cultivated ground, airfields, lake and river margins. In W Africa, occurs mainly in coastal savannas. Recorded at least once on seashore, on Zanzibar. In Sierra Leone, generally found on drier ground than *V. senegallus*, e.g. burnt laterite pans or grass ridges running into swamps. Occurs in flocks of 5-10 birds, up to 30 after breeding; sometimes loosely associated with *V. armatus*.
Food and Feeding. Small invertebrates, including insects and their larvae, especially beetles; also grass seeds. Sometimes feeds at night.
Breeding. Laying dates geographically very variable: Mar-May in Sierra Leone; Jun-Sept in coastal Gabon; Jun-Oct in S Africa; mainly dry season (Aug-Nov) in E Africa. Monogamous. Loosely colonial, with several pairs scattered over small area; territorial. Nests on burnt ground with new grass, also on bare patches in grassland or ploughed land; nest is scrape or depression on ground, lined with few stalks of dry grass; sometimes no nest at all. Clutch 3 eggs (2-4); incubation 18-20 days; chick has upperparts mottled yellow and blackish brown, white hindneck collar, greyish white below; nestlings stay with parents for c. 2 months.
Movements. Sedentary and intra-African migrant; movements possiby related to brush fires, resulting in new grass, conditions suitable for breeding. In Zaire, migrates in large flocks, with movement N recorded in Feb-Apr, and S in period Apr-Oct. Migratory in E Africa: high numbers occur in W Uganda, around L Victoria (Ugandan sector, Sept-May) and in coastal Tanzania (Jun-Aug) and Kenya (Apr-Jul). Regular seasonal presence in W Kenya in Jan-Mar (Nov-Jun), N Tanzania (Jan-Apr), Zimbabwe (Jul-Nov), South Africa (summer) and Zambia (Apr-Oct, but possibly year round). Some birds sedentary on Zanzibar, but numbers fluctuate, fewest birds present Oct-Dec. In Malawi, breeding birds dispersive Apr-Jun. Movements performed at night.
Status and Conservation. Not globally threatened. No population estimates available; at least regionally fairly common, but little information available. Locally common in Sierra Leone and Ghana; uncommon in SW Nigeria, where may have declined. Total of 300-350 birds on coast of Gabon outside breeding season.
Bibliography. Ash & Miskell (1983), Benson & Benson (1975), Benson *et al*. (1971), Britton, P.L. (1980), Brooke (1984a), Chapin (1939), Dowsett & Forbes-Watson (1993), Elgood *et al*. (1994), Ginn *et al*. (1989), Grimes (1987), Howells (1977), Irwin (1976), Mackworth-Praed & Grant (1957, 1962, 1970), Maclean (1993), Pakenham (1979), Philips (1988), Pinto (1983), Scott (1983), Short *et al*. (1990), Tree (1978), Urban *et al*. (1986), Vincent (1934), Ward (1987, 1989a, 1989b, 1989c, 1990a, 1992).

10. **Greater Black-winged Lapwing**

Vanellus melanopterus

French: Vanneau à ailes noires **German**: Schwarzflügelkiebitz **Spanish**: Avefría Lugubroide
Other common names: Black-winged Lapwing/Plover

Taxonomy. *Charadrius melanopterus* Cretzschmar, 1829, Djedda, Arabia.
Sometimes placed in *Hoplopterus* or *Stephanibyx*. Has been proposed to form superspecies with *V. lugubris*, but not supported by behavioural or morphological data. Two subspecies recognized.
Subspecies and Distribution.
V. m. melanopterus (Cretzschmar, 1829) - extreme E Sudan and Ethiopia; SW Kenya to CN Tanzania.
V. m. minor (Zedlitz, 1908) - NE Transvaal to E Cape Province (South Africa); winters on coast, from extreme S Mozambique to E Cape.

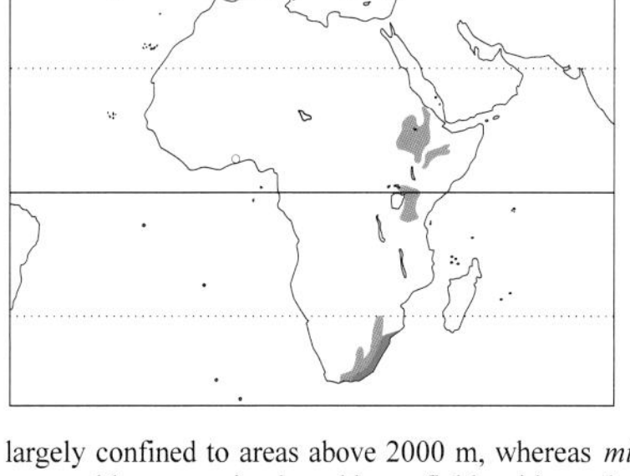

Descriptive notes. 26-27 cm; 163-170 g (3 adults, race *minor*). Very similar to *V. lugubris*, but larger, with legs averaging slightly shorter; shine on upperparts bronze to purplish, not greenish; generally larger, more diffuse white forehead patch; broader black breast band; in flight, secondaries black, not white. Sexes alike. No seasonal variation. Juvenile has grey areas of adult pale brown; feathers of upperparts have broad buff fringes. Races very similar, but *minor* somewhat smaller.
Habitat. Often occupies highland plains and grassland on high plateaux, mountain slopes, open plains and dry savanna; nominate race largely confined to areas above 2000 m, whereas *minor* often occurs at lower altitudes. Attracted to areas with game animals and burnt fields with newly grown grass. In winter, found at lower altitudes, when also occurs in wasteland, cultivated fields and coastal flats.

Food and Feeding. Molluscs, worms, adult and larval insects, such as beetles and flies, sometimes small fish. Often feeds in vicinity of wild or domestic animals. When foraging, runs quickly, freezes with body tilted forward and pointing at prey, and stabs 5-6 times.

Breeding. Laying Apr-Jul in Ethiopia; year round in Kenya and Tanzania, depending on rains, and avoiding wettest period; Jul-Oct in South Africa. Monogamous. Territorial. Solitary, but sometimes in small, loose colonies. Performs post-copulatory display consisting of side by side run, with wing on outside partly raised. Breeds in grassland, usually with very short grass; also on bare ground or ploughed land; nest is a scrape, lined with plant material and sometimes dung; eggs sometimes partly buried. Clutch 3 eggs (2-4).

Movements. Resident and intra-African migrant: migratory in most of E Africa, but sedentary in Ethiopia; migratory in South Africa. In Aug-Sept, after breeding, birds in Kenya migrate to lower altitudes, 1500-2000 m lower, returning in Jan-Apr. In South Africa most birds descend to coastal plains after breeding (Apr-Aug); occasional stragglers reach W Cape. Migrates both at night and during day. During non-breeding season, occurs in flocks of up to 50 birds, occasionally thousands, and possibly up to 10,000 prior to migration.

Status and Conservation. Not globally threatened. No population estimates available. Status of race *melanopterus* unknown, but pre-migratory flocks of several thousand birds recorded in W Kenya. Race *minor* is rather common to locally abundant. Type locality in Arabia may be erroneous, as no other records known.

Bibliography. Allan (1983), Britton, P.L. (1980), Cyrus (1982), Dowsett & Forbes-Watson (1993), Ginn *et al.* (1989), Mackworth-Praed & Grant (1957, 1962), Maclean (1972a, 1993), Sessions (1967), Short *et al.* (1990), Urban *et al.* (1986), Vincent (1945), Ward (1987, 1989a, 1989b, 1989c, 1990a, 1992), Ward & Maclean (1988).

11. Crowned Lapwing

Vanellus coronatus

French: Vanneau couronné   **German**: Kronenkiebitz   **Spanish**: Avefría Coronada
Other common names: Crowned Plover

Taxonomy. *Charadrius Coronatus* Boddaert, 1783, Cape of Good Hope.
Sometimes placed in genus *Hoplopterus* or *Stephanibyx*. Birds from SW Angola, Namibia, Botswana, W Zimbabwe and W Transvaal may be separated as third race *xerophilus*, but doubtfully distinct. Two subspecies recognized.

Subspecies and Distribution.
V. c. coronatus (Boddaert, 1783) - Ethiopia to South Africa; marginal in SW Somalia.
V. c. demissus (Friedmann, 1928) - Somalia.

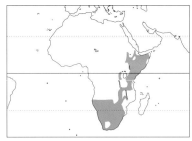

Descriptive notes. 20-34 cm; 126-200 g (*coronatus*). Very distinctive horizontal black and white bands surrounding black crown; pale brownish above and on breast, with darker lower breast ending in black line. Female smaller than male. No seasonal variation. Juvenile has less well defined white head band, buff brown at front; black head feathers tipped brown; feathers of upperparts fringed buff. Race *demissus* somewhat smaller, with paler, warmer brown on upperparts, wings and breast.

Habitat. Wide variety of dry, open habitats, treeless or sparsely wooded: savanna, open patches in thornbush or bushveld, cultivated land, fallow fields, airports, golf courses, open areas near towns and even desert and dunes. Attracted to recently burnt grasslands. Not associated with water, generally avoiding moist ground; however, large flocks may roost during the day near waterside or on small islands in lakes or rivers.

Food and Feeding. Food includes insects and their larvae, especially termites, beetles, grasshoppers, crickets and ants; possibly earthworms. Most active at dusk, and also active during moonlit nights; probably feeds mainly during late afternoon and night. Sometimes feeds near cattle. Take-off before flight to feeding ground is preceded by display.

Breeding. Breeds during dry season, when fires occur, but timing very variable geographically: year round in E Africa, but depending on rains; mostly Jun-Nov in S Africa. Monogamous. Non-territorial, semi-colonial nester; nests 25-50 m apart; occasionally noted defending territories when densities are high through space limitation; non-breeders often found close to breeding birds; highly demonstrative towards non-conspecific intruders after hatching. Prefers nesting among fresh grass on recently burnt fields; nest is scrape or depression in ground, lined with plant material and debris, which accumulates during incubation; often close to tree, providing shade for off-duty partner; location regularly reused during several years. Clutch 2-3 eggs, occasionally 4, with clutch of 5 from 2 females; laying interval 1 day; double-brooded; incubation 28-32 days; chick has upperparts deep buff blotched black, underparts and hindneck white; fledging takes over 1 month. Several families aggregate, even when young still unable to fly. Hatching success 54 % in Zimbabwe, 88% in South Africa; fledging success 31% in South Africa. Nests frequently destroyed by brush fires; young often taken by predators.

Movements. Commonly resident, but some erratic movements; in E Africa, some birds resident, others dispersive; mainly sedentary in South Africa. Movements related to habitat changes; birds follow dry season fires, and leave during peak rains or when grass grows too long. Occurs in pairs or flocks of 10-40, maximum 150 birds, especially just after breeding season; flocks are loosely associated and wide-ranging.

Status and Conservation. Not globally threatened. No population estimates available; rather common and widespread throughout extensive range. Common and widespread in Somalia. Numbers in the W Cape may have decreased, as *V. armatus* invades habitat of present species.

Bibliography. Ade (1976, 1979), Anderson & Kok (1990, 1991, 1992), Archer & Godman (1937-1961), Ash & Miskell (1983), Benson & Benson (1975), Britton, P.L. (1980), Dowsett & Forbes-Watson (1993), Ginn *et al.* (1989), Hanley (1983, 1988, 1990), Kok & Anderson (1989), Kopij & Kok (1994), Mackworth-Praed & Grant (1957, 1962, 1970), Maclean (1993), Moore & Vernon (1973), Pinto (1983), Short *et al.* (1990), Skead (1955), Symmes (1952), Tree (1981a), Urban *et al.* (1986), Ward (1987, 1989a, 1989b, 1989c, 1990a, 1992), Ward & Maclean (1988).

12. African Wattled Lapwing

Vanellus senegallus

French: Vanneau du Sénégal   **German**: Senegalkiebitz   **Spanish**: Avefría Senegalesa
Other common names: (Senegal) Wattled Plover/Lapwing

Taxonomy. *Parra senegalla* Linnaeus, 1766, Senegal.
Sometimes placed in monospecific genus *Afribyx*. Western population of race *lateralis* sometimes considered separate race, *solitaneus*. Race *major* not always accepted, as occurs at end of cline in size from W to E. Three subspecies normally recognized.

Subspecies and Distribution.
V. s. senegallus (Linnaeus, 1766) - SW Mauritania, Senegambia and NW Sierra Leone E to Sudan, NE Zaire and N Uganda.
V. s. major (Neumann, 1914) - W & C Ethiopia and Eritrea.
V. s. lateralis A. Smith, 1839 - S Congo and Angola E to S Uganda, and S through W Tanzania, S Zaire, Zambia and Malawi to Zimbabwe, S Mozambique and NE South Africa.

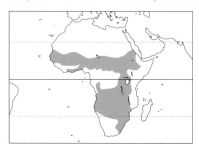

Descriptive notes. c. 34 cm; 197-277 g. Large yellow and red wattles; long yellow legs; yellow bill, with some black on culmen towards tip; black carpal spurs; plumage mainly brown, with white wingbar and black flight-feathers. Female has less black on throat. No seasonal variation. Juvenile has very small wattles; chin and throat whitish with black streaks; less white on forehead. Race *major* virtually identical to nominate, but usually larger; *lateralis* has blackish line on belly, in front of legs, and solid black bill tip.

Habitat. Wide variety of lowland habitats; in Ethiopia and rest of E Africa occurs up to 2200 m. Often near water, but also found in dry places; frequents marshes or areas of grass near lakes, ponds, rivers and streams; also savanna, fields with short grass (e.g. airports), cultivated land and wasteland, flooded rice fields, pools, burnt grassland. Has been found to associate with termite mounds, which are used as look-out posts. In Sierra Leone, shares wet grassland with *V. spinosus* and dry grassland with *V. lugubris*, without rivalry.

Food and Feeding. Chiefly insects, such as grasshoppers, locusts, beetles, crickets, termites and various aquatic insects; also worms and grass seeds. Regurgitated pellets contained insect remains and coarse grass. Does not normally forage in typical plover style; instead, walks slowly, pauses with one leg raised, takes one step or jumps, and grabs prey; also probes in base of grass tufts and uses foot-trembling.

Breeding. Laying dates geographically very variable, depending on rains; Mar-Jun in Nigeria; most frequently Jul-Dec in E & S Africa; Apr-Dec in Zaire and Rwanda; Mar-Jun in Ethiopia. Monogamous. Observed to be highly territorial, defending feeding territory against conspecifics, but also recorded breeding in small colony of 3-4 pairs. Nest usually on bare ground or in short grass within 100 m of water, frequently near roads or human settlements; shallow depression in ground, lined with grass stems, sticks, pebbles and bits of dry dung, which accumulate during incubation. Clutch 2-3 eggs in equatorial regions, 4 in S Africa; laying interval 1-2 days; incubation 30-32 days; chick speckled buff and black, with black patch on crown and back, white forehead and hindneck collar, and underparts yellowish white; chicks feed in adjacent feeding territory, continiously watched by adult, often from hillock; fledging c. 40 days. Young become independent after fledging.

Movements. Resident and dispersive, sometimes nomadic. Movements dependent on water levels and rains, but overall patterns none too clear. In parts of W Africa (Mali, Chad) moves N in wet season, but also southward migration in Nigeria. In E Africa and Rwanda apparently resident, with some local movements. Only seasonally present in some areas of SE Africa, but resident in others. May gather outside breeding season in newly available habitat.

Status and Conservation. Not globally threatened. No population estimates available; apparently common in much of extensive range, e.g. Gambia and Sierra Leone; not uncommon in Ghana and Nigeria; fairly common in Malawi; locally common in S Africa. High tolerance of humans and agricultural practices suggests species probably not threatened.

Bibliography. Beesley (1977), Benson & Benson (1975), Britton, P.L. (1980), Brooke (1967), Brown & Britton (1980), Dowsett & Forbes-Watson (1993), Elgood *et al.* (1994), Gatter (1988), Ginn *et al.* (1989), Gore (1990), Grimes (1987), Harpum (1978), Jensen & Kirkeby (1980), Lippens & Wille (1976), Little (1967), Louette (1981), Mackworth-Praed & Grant (1957, 1962, 1970), Maclean (1993), Morel & Morel (1990), Nikolaus (1987), Parnell (1968), Penry (1987), Pinto (1983), du Plessis (1987), Reynolds (1977a), Short *et al.* (1990), Urban *et al.* (1986), Van de Weghe & Monfort-Braham (1975), Ward (1987, 1992).

PLATE 36 ➤

PLATE 36

inches 6
cm 15

13

14

15

16

ssp *atronuchalis*

ssp *indicus*

17

18

19

ssp *novaehollandiae*

ssp *miles*

20

♂

♀

21

22

23

ssp *cayennensis*

24

ssp *lampronotus*

ssp *chilensis*

25

13. Spot-breasted Lapwing
Vanellus melanocephalus

French: Vanneau d'Abyssinie   **German**: Strichelbrustkiebitz   **Spanish**: Avefría Pechipinta
Other common names: Spot-breasted Plover

Taxonomy. *Lobivanellus melanocephalus* Rüppell, 1845, Mountains of Simien, Ethiopia.
Formerly placed in *Hoplopterus*, *Lobivanellus* or monospecific *Tylibyx*. Monotypic.
Distribution. Ethiopian Highlands.

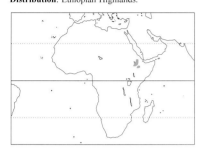

Descriptive notes. c. 34 cm; 2 adults 199 and 228 g. Ashy brown with yellow wattles and black crown, chin and throat; white supercilium; upperparts with greenish tinge; breast distinctly spotted black, even slightly striped, belly white; feathers of nape can be raised to form crest. In flight distinguished from *V. spinosus*, *V. melanopterus* and *V. senegallus* by narrower black tail band. Sexes alike. No seasonal variation. Juvenile not described.
Habitat. Damp grassland, moorland with giant lobelia, giant heath, *Alchemilla* and tussock grass; also marshes and near streams; often on pastures and near cattle. Generally found between 1800 and 4100 m.

Food and Feeding. Diet undescribed. Typically forages by means of a quick run, followed by a pause and a survey of ground. Very mobile during the day, often searching out cattle pastures.
Breeding. Season Apr in Bale Mts, Aug in Shewa district. Only one nest described, which was shallow scrape in patch of grass and moss, situated on tiny rocky island in shallow pool, in giant lobelia moorlands. This same nest contained 4 eggs. No further information available.
Movements. Sedentary, although some local movements probable: north of Gonder numbers increase during rainy season. Outside breeding season, often occurs in parties of 30-40 birds.
Status and Conservation. Not globally threatened. No population estimates available; locally frequent to common, but very restricted range makes species somewhat vulnerable. Like several sympatric endemics, species requires close monitoring; intensive survey would be highly desirable.
Bibliography. Dowsett & Dowsett-Lemaire (1993), Dowsett & Forbes-Watson (1993), Mackworth-Praed & Grant (1957), van Perlo (1995), Urban (1980), Urban, Brown *et al.* (1970), Urban, Fry & Keith (1986), Von Heuglin (1869-1873).

14. Brown-chested Lapwing
Vanellus superciliosus

French: Vanneau à poitrine châtaine   **German**: Rotbrustkiebitz   **Spanish**: Avefría Pechirrufa
Other common names: Brown-chested (Wattled) Plover

Taxonomy. *Lobivanellus superciliosus* Reichenow, 1886, Marungu, Zaire.
Formerly placed in monospecific genus *Anomalophrys*. Monotypic.
Distribution. Probably breeds from Togo to NE Zaire, but only definite records from Nigeria. Non-breeding records from E Ghana across C & N Cameroon and S Chad to most of Zaire (except CW), L Victoria and NW Tanzania. Limits of range poorly known.

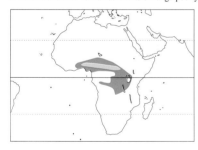

Descriptive notes. c. 23 cm; c. 150 g (estimated). Small lapwing, with black cap, narrow white eyeline, greenish brown upperparts and small yellow wattles; reddish chestnut forehead and breast. Sexes alike. No seasonal variation. Juvenile has no black on head, lacks wattles and has paler chestnut on forehead and breast; upperparts extensively fringed reddish chestnut.
Habitat. Open savanna with or without sparse covering of bushes or woods, with grass or bare ground, often near rivers and lakes; also football fields, lawns and recently burnt grassland. On migration in Zaire also sometimes found in cleared areas within forest.

Food and Feeding. Insects, such as ants. Pecks deep in loose soil. Also active at night, possibly feeding.
Breeding. Laying Jan-Feb in Nigeria; probably Dec-Jun in Zaire; breeding assumed to occur during dry season. Monogamous. Territorial. Breeds on newly burnt ground, often on rather stony red soil; nest is shallow depression in soil with rim, thickly lined with small stones and pieces of anthill, partly covering eggs. Clutch 2-4; many eggs are erythristic or reddish, closely matching lateritic soil on which laid; incubation by both parents, lasting at least 24 days, starting with last egg; chick buff and dark brown above, with dark patch on occiput and white patch on nape, underparts white with brown pectoral band. After fledging families gather in parties of up to 50 birds.
Movements. Intra-African migrant. Adults migrate through E & C Zaire in Nov-Dec, returning in Jul-Aug, then with immatures, suggesting migration to and from breeding grounds. Non-breeders in S Zaire, Rwanda and other parts of E Africa in Jul-Dec. Nigerian breeding birds have been shown to store fat before leaving breeding grounds. Outside breeding season, occurs in flocks of 30 birds, maximum 100.
Status and Conservation. Not globally threatened. Very poorly known, but apparently not particularly rare and reckoned to be secure; widespread though uncommon throughout much of Nigeria. Precise limits of breeding and non-breeding ranges very poorly known, e.g. status in Ghana could be anything from breeding visitor to vagrant, as only 1 record, and this coincides with breeding season in Nigeria; few records from Cameroon; considerable scope for extensive survey work and research.
Bibliography. Bowen (1979), Britton, P.L. (1980), Clarke (1936), Dowsett & Forbes-Watson (1993), Elgood *et al.* (1994), Grimes (1987), Heslop (1937), Lippens & Wille (1976), Louette (1981), Mackworth-Praed & Grant (1957, 1970), Serle (1956b), Short *et al.* (1990), Urban *et al.* (1986).

15. Grey-headed Lapwing
Vanellus cinereus

French: Vanneau à tête grise   **German**: Graukopfkiebitz   **Spanish**: Avefría Ceniza
Other common names: Grey-headed Plover

Taxonomy. *Pluvianus cinereus* Blyth, 1842, Calcutta.
Sometimes placed in genus *Hoplopterus* or, formerly, in monospecific *Microsarcops*. Monotypic.
Distribution. NE China, neighbouring parts of Russia and Japan; possibly C Manchuria and Inner Mongolia. Non-breeding in S Asia from Nepal, NE India and Bangladesh to SC China, N Indochina and Taiwan, occasionally further S.

Descriptive notes. 34-37 cm; 236-296 g. Large, rather plain lapwing with grey head, neck and upper breast, black breast band, brown upperparts and white belly; secondaries and greater upperwing-coverts white, primaries black; tail white with black tip; iris red, bill yellow with black tip, legs yellow. Sexes alike. Non-breeding adult has browner head and neck, black breast band partly obscured; chin and throat white, streaked brown. Juvenile has brown head and neck; breast band absent or obscure; extensively fringed buff on upperparts.
Habitat. Breeds in rather undisturbed areas in swamps, near rivers and rice fields. In winter also found in wet habitats, like marshes, riverbanks, wet grassland, rice stubble, *jheels*; also ploughed fields.

Food and Feeding. No information available; probably feeds on insects, worms and molluscs. Gregarious.
Breeding. Monogamous. Territorial. Breeds in undisturbed wetlands, e.g. river flats; but also in rice fields; nest is scrape, often lined with twigs. Clutch 4 eggs; incubation 28-29 days; chicks fledge mid-Jun, and families soon merge into flocks.
Movements. Mainly migratory, but sedentary in places. Breeding populations of NE China and SE Russia winter in SE Asia. Japanese population partly sendentary, with birds in N of range avoiding snow by migrating S. Outside breeding season occurs in flocks of 5-50 birds. Present in India from Sept/Oct to late Mar/Apr; returns to breeding grounds in mid-Feb.
Status and Conservation. Not globally threatened. Currently considered near-threatened. Population, excluding Japan, numbers less than 10,000-25,000 birds, and probably decreasing, with highest numbers wintering in India and Bangladesh; size of Japanese population unknown. On wintering grounds, possible problems through pesticides, especially herbicides on paddy fields, and through increased urbanization; in Japan, at S end of breeding range, increasing frequency of double-cropping, instead of single-cropping, in rice fields may negatively affect breeding opportunities.
Bibliography. Ali & Ripley (1980), Austin (1948), Austin & Kuroda (1953), Brazil (1991), Deignan (1945), Étchécopar & Hüe (1978), Grubh (1968), Harvey (1990), Inskipp & Inskipp (1991), Knystautas (1993), Lainer (1991), Lekagul & Round (1991), MacKinnon & Phillipps (1993), Meyer de Schauensee (1984), Okugawa *et al.* (1973), Perennou *et al.* (1994), Ripley (1982), Sakane (1957, 1958), Scott (1989), Smythies (1986), Subramanya (1987), Tanaka & Lida (1991), White & Bruce (1986), Williams, M.D. (1986), Won (1993), Yan Anhou (1986).

16. Red-wattled Lapwing
Vanellus indicus

French: Vanneau indien   **German**: Rotlappenkiebitz   **Spanish**: Avefría India
Other common names: Red-wattled Plover, Indian Decorated Lapwing

Taxonomy. *Tringa Indica* Boddaert, 1783, Goa.
Sometimes placed in *Hoplopterus* or *Lobivanellus*. Apart from *atronuchalis*, differences between races mostly clinal, involving depth of gloss, coloration of upperparts and size. Four subspecies normally recognized.
Subspecies and Distribution.
V. i. aigneri (Laubman, 1913) - SE Turkey, Iraq, Iran, S Transcaspia, E Arabia and Pakistan.
V. i. indicus (Boddaert, 1783) - E Pakistan, India, Nepal and Bangladesh.
V. i. lankae (Koelz, 1939) - Sri Lanka.
V. i. atronuchalis (Jerdon, 1864) - NE India (Assam) and Myanmar to N Malaysia and Vietnam.

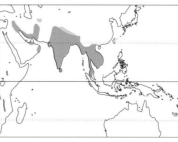

Descriptive notes. 32-35 cm; 110-230 g; wingspan 80-81 cm. Boldly patterned lapwing with black breast, red bill with black tip, small red wattles and long yellow legs. Sexes alike. Non-breeding adult, during wing moult, has brown tinged crown and white speckling on throat. Juvenile has generally duller plumage, with whitish throat; greyish brown breast and crown, latter with white speckles. Races generally differ noly rather slightly, mainly in amount of gloss, coloration of upperparts and size; *atronuchalis* has slender white hindneck collar, with white patch on ear-coverts isolated from white breast; other races very similar to nominate, with *aigneri* largest and palest, *lankae* smallest, darkest and glossiest.
Habitat. From lowlands up to c. 1800 m, in open areas near fresh or brackish water: *jheels*, rivers, mudbanks, wet grassland, pools, particularly on cultivated land, such as corn fields, grass fields and large gardens; also within open forests, and on waste, fallow and ploughed land; occasionally on grass along highways.
Food and Feeding. Beetles and other insects, including ants, butterfly and fly larvae, grasshoppers, crickets, bugs, earwigs and termites; also molluscs, worms and crustaceans. Feeds mostly at dawn and dusk, and during moonlit night.

On following pages: 17. Javanese Wattled Lapwing (*Vanellus macropterus*); 18. Banded Lapwing (*Vanellus tricolor*); 19. Masked Lapwing (*Vanellus miles*); 20. Sociable Lapwing (*Vanellus gregarius*); 21. White-tailed Lapwing (*Vanellus leucurus*); 22. Pied Lapwing (*Vanellus cayanus*); 23. Southern Lapwing (*Vanellus chilensis*); 24. Andean Lapwing (*Vanellus resplendens*); 25. Red-kneed Dotterel (*Erythrogonys cinctus*).

Breeding. Laying mid-Apr to late Jun in Iraq; race *indicus* breeds Mar-Aug/Sept; in Sri Lanka, breeds during SW monsoon, primarily Jun. Monogamous. Solitary and territorial. Nest is shallow scrape, unlined or lined with small stones and debris, usually situated near water. Clutch 3-4 eggs; possibly double-brooded; incubation c. 26-30 days; chick has upperparts grey-brown mottled with black, broad black collar from behind eye around occiput and a white collar below it, underparts whitish with black pectoral band; fledging 38 days.
Movements. Resident, dispersive and in places migratory. In winter, generally moves down from high altitudes. Resident to dispersive in Middle East, in Iraq leaving dried up places after breeding season. Breeding birds of S Turkmenistan migratory, probably wintering in Afghanistan or Pakistan, or both, arriving back in Turkmenistan in second half of Apr.
Status and Conservation. Not globally threatened. SW Asia holds in the order of 100,000 birds, SC Asia more than 100,000 birds, and unknown number in SE Asia. Occupies wide variety of niches, and also occurs in areas densely populated with humans. More than 5000 birds winter in Iran. Apparently in process of spreading up valley of R Tigris into SE Turkey, where first recorded in 1983; no recent reports on status, due to political turmoil in zone.
Bibliography. Ali & Ripley (1980), Cramp & Simmons (1983), Deignan (1945), Dementiev & Gladkov (1951b), Desai & Malhotra (1976), Étchécopar & Hüe (1978), Evans (1994), Flint *et al.* (1984), Green & Moorhouse (1995), Haefelin (1987), Hollom *et al.* (1988), Hüe & Étchécopar (1970), Inskipp & Inskipp (1991), Kalsi & Khera (1986, 1987, 1990, 1992), Khajuria (1970), Knystautas (1993), Lekagul & Round (1991), MacKinnon & Phillipps (1993), Madoc (1976), Medway & Wells (1976), Mian *et al.* (1994), Mukherjee (1975), Mundkur (1985), Naik *et al.* (1961), Perennou *et al.* (1994), Phillips (1978), Polozov *et al.* (1990), Richardson, C. (1990), Ripley (1982), Roberts, T.J. (1991), Roos & Schrijvershof (1993), Rutgers & Norris (1970), Samaraweera (1967), Scott (1989), Shirihai (1996), Smythies (1986), Sundararaman (1989), Tehsin & Lokhandwala (1982).

17. **Javanese Wattled Lapwing**

Vanellus macropterus

French: Vanneau hirondelle **German**: Javakiebitz **Spanish**: Avefría Javanesa
Other common names: Javanese Wattled Plover, Sunda/Black-thighed Wattled Lapwing

Taxonomy. *Charadrius macropterus* Wagler, 1827, Java.
Has also been placed in monospecific genus *Rogibyx*; *R. tricolor* is synonym. Monotypic.
Distribution. Java, possibly on Sumatra and Timor. Almost certainly extinct.

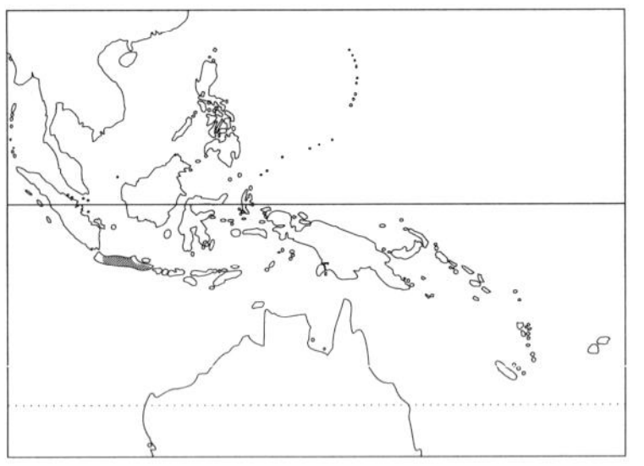

Descriptive notes. 27-29 cm; 325 g (estimated). Generally rather dark lapwing, with large yellow or white wattles; head, belly patch and flight-feathers deep black; upperparts, breast and upper belly dark brown; uppertail-coverts and vent white; curved black spurs; legs yellow-orange. Sexual and seasonal differences and juvenile plumage remain undescribed.
Habitat. Open areas near freshwater ponds; presumably also on agricultural land.
Food and Feeding. No information available.
Breeding. Breeding evidently occurred in May-Jun, in W Java.
Movements. Apparently resident. Some dubious reports suggest birds might have migrated to Sumatra or even Timor, though latter, in particular, generally treated with scepticism; one report of several birds perched on railing of ship off N coast of Java.
Status and Conservation. Almost certainly EXTINCT. Decrease caused by intensive agricultural and hunting activities within presumed range, with effects intensified by massive growth of human population. Some observations made on Java in late 19th century; in 1920's, collected from Citarum Delta and at Tangerang, W of Jakarta; not recorded since observation on S coast of E Java in 1939. Claimed to have bred in Sumatra, on grounds of single specimen and egg, although accuracy of collecting labels has been questioned. Traditionally listed as occurring on Timor, but origin of specimens thus labelled seems highly dubious.
Bibliography. Andrew, P. (1992), Collar & Andrew (1988), Collar *et al.* (1994), Hellebrekers & Hoogerwerf (1967), King (1978/79), Kooiman (1940), Kuroda (1936a), MacKinnon (1988), MacKinnon & Phillipps (1993), van Marle & Voous (1988), Temple (1979), White & Bruce (1986).

18. **Banded Lapwing**

Vanellus tricolor

French: Vanneau tricolore **German**: Schwarzbandkiebitz **Spanish**: Avefría Tricolor
Other common names: Black-breasted/Banded Plover

Taxonomy. *Charadrius tricolor* Vieillot, 1818, "Terres Australes" = New South Wales.
Formerly placed in *Lobivanellus* or in monospecific *Zonifer*. Monotypic.
Distribution. S Australia and Tasmania.

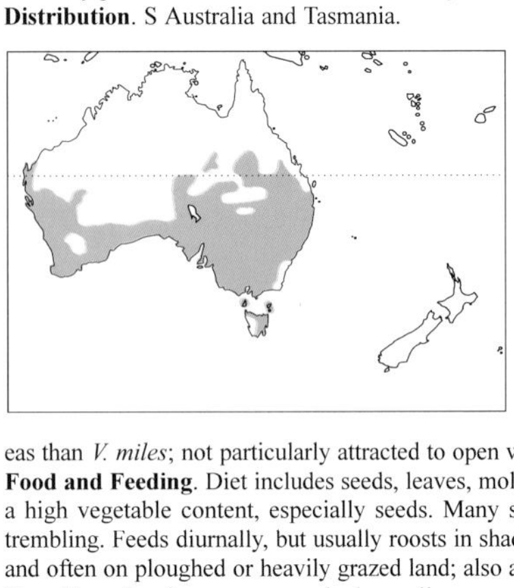

Descriptive notes. 25-29 cm; 150-200 g; wingspan 61-67 cm. Dark U-shaped breast band and clear white stripe behind eye; black and white head; upperparts dull purplish brown; small red wattle, fairly pale yellow bill and eye. Sexes alike. No seasonal variation. Juvenile like adult, but with dull yellowish brown bill and very small wattles; crown and breast band browner; brown feathers of upperparts have broad buff fringes.
Habitat. Prefers open, short grassland, including pastures, airfields and open savanna in semi-arid regions, and ploughed fields and salt-bush plains. Usually encountered inland, in drier areas than *V. miles*; not particularly attracted to open water.
Food and Feeding. Diet includes seeds, leaves, molluscs, worms, insects and spiders; seems to have a high vegetable content, especially seeds. Many stomachs contained grit. Often forages by foot-trembling. Feeds diurnally, but usually roosts in shade during very hot periods. Forages on grassland and often on ploughed or heavily grazed land; also at haystacks, where picks up seeds.
Breeding. Laying year round, depending on rains, but frequently Jun-Nov; often breeds opportunistically, e.g after rains; in Western Australia, pairs select territories within 2 weeks after rains. Monogamous. Solitary, rarely in loose colonies; highly territorial. Breeds on pastures, ploughed land, dry plains, salt-bush plains and airfields; nest is shallow scrape or depression in ground, unlined or lined with grass and other plant materials and debris. Clutch 4 eggs (3-5), laid at intervals of 24 hours, except last egg, which can take 4 days to be laid; incubation by both parents, 26-28 days, beginning after 3rd egg laid; chick has upperparts mottled buff, orange-buff and black-brown, hindneck and stripe behind eye white bordered above with dark brown stripe, underparts white; fledging c. 8 weeks, but young fully feathered at c. 5½ weeks. Nests may be lost due to flooding, predation or trampling by cattle. Reported fledging success ranges from 5·5% to 64%.
Movements. Generally resident with some erratic movements, apparently dependent on water and food conditions; sometimes moves over large distances. In inland areas, occurs in highest numbers after heavy rains and in lowest numbers (or absent) during drought, when higher numbers occur at coast. Moves by both day and night. Occurs in pairs and flocks of 3-20 birds, on occasion over 100.
Status and Conservation. Not globally threatened. Total population reckoned to number c. 27,000 individuals. Suitable habitat has increased due to cultivation of forest and scrubland. In some areas numbers have decreased due to termination of wheat farming and due to pasture vegetation having grown too tall.
Bibliography. Blakers *et al.* (1984), Bonnin (1982), Christian *et al.* (1992a), Dann (1981), Favaloro (1944), Flegg & Madge (1995), Frith (1969), Lane & Davies (1987), Lindsey (1992), Macdonald (1988), Marchant & Higgins (1993), Masters & Milhinch (1974), Pizzey & Doyle (1980), Pringle (1987), Rutgers & Norris (1970), Schodde & Tidemann (1986), Simpson & Day (1994), Slater *et al.* (1989), Trounson (1987).

19. **Masked Lapwing**

Vanellus miles

French: Vanneau soldat **German**: Maskenkiebitz **Spanish**: Avefría Militar
Other common names: Masked Plover, Spur-winged Plover/Lapwing

Taxonomy. *Tringa miles* Boddaert, 1783, Louisiana; error = Australia.
Sometimes placed in *Hoplopterus*, *Lobivanellus* or monospecific *Lobibyx*. Race *novaehollandiae* on occasion considered distinct species, but intergrades with nominate form in at least two areas of overlap, in N Queensland and in L Eyre catchment area. Birds of N Australia formerly awarded separate race, *personatus*. Two subspecies recognized.
Subspecies and Distribution.
V. m. miles (Boddaert, 1783) - NE & S New Guinea and Aru Is to N Australia; probably non-breeding visitor to SE Wallacea.
V. m. novaehollandiae (Stephens, 1819) - E & SE Australia, Tasmania and New Zealand.

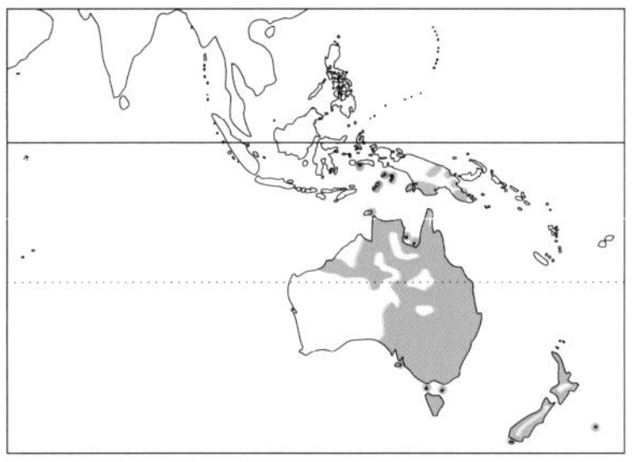

Descriptive notes. 30-37 cm; 230-440 g; wingspan 75-85 cm. Large lapwing with outsize yellow wattles and long yellow carpal spurs; crown black, upperparts plain olive brown, underparts white. Sexes alike. No seasonal variation. Juvenile has feathers on greyish upperparts fringed with buff; small wing spurs and wattles. Race *novaehollandiae* has somewhat smaller wattles; much more extensive black cap continuing down hindneck to black breast patches; forms intermediate between this race and nominate occur widely.
Habitat. Wide range of open habitats with, preferably, short grass, either natural or cultivated, including pastures, fallow fields, airfields and margins of various kinds of wetlands, ranging from temporary pools and water-holes to lakes and lagoons; usually close to water. Also found in sheltered coastal areas. Common within urban areas, including parks, playing fields and grassy roadsides.
Food and Feeding. Mainly insects, worms and spiders; also molluscs, crustaceans, seeds and leaves. Young seem to feed mainly on worms, beetles and beetle larvae. Apart from typical plover-style feeding, also feeds by foot-trembling. Usually forages in short grass, sometimes in gravel and mud. Possibly also feeds at night.
Breeding. Laying in all months in N Australia, Jun-Dec in S Australia, Jun to late Nov in New Zealand; breeding season covers 9-11 months. Monogamous on long-term basis; very faithful to breeding site. Piping-parties of up to 6-7 birds probably play role in pair formation. Breeds solitarily in territory, but may occasionally join nearby flocks. Usually nests in short grass, often near water; nest is depression in ground, unlined or lined with plant material, pebbles and debris. Clutch 4 eggs, sometimes 3; incubation 28-30 days; chick has upperparts pale brown speckled buff and mottled black, white hindneck collar, underparts mostly white; young can swim from early age; fledging usually 6-7 weeks (5-8); families from adjacent territories merge after fledging of young; young are dependent for up to 6 months; thereafter start associating with other birds, but often still with one or both parents nearby. One female observed breeding at end of 1 year old, others at 2. In Victoria, of 180 eggs laid, 45% hatched and 8·9% fledged; on North I, New Zealand, of 542 eggs, 74% hatched, c. 18% fledged. Large proportion of nests may fail through destruction by cattle, disturbance, mowing, predation and flooding. Longevity at least 12 years.
Movements. Resident and dispersive, responding to new food sources in recently constructed and temporary wetlands, leaving as soon as they dry out. Young more dispersive than adults. Numbers at Australian coastal areas seem to increase in autumn, when inland wetlands dry up. May fly as far as Christmas I (Indian Ocean) and Solomon Is, and from Australia to New Zealand. Status in Moluccas, Tanimbar and nearby islands unclear, but probably regular non-breeding visitor. In non-breeding season occurs in small flocks, sometimes of up to several hundreds; small flocks of non-breeders and failed breeders occur during breeding season.
Status and Conservation. Not globally threatened. Total population estimated at c. 287,000 birds, of which 258,000 in Australia. Breeding habitat has increased considerably due to cultivation of woodland. Rare on Tasmania until 1888, but now a common bird; has also increased numbers in C Australia. First reached New Zealand between 1886 and 1932; first breeding record in 1932 in Southland; population has increased and expanded since; first breeding record on North I 1970. Also in New Zealand, as species expands range, increasing number of collisions (or near-collisions) with aircraft; these caused 22% of all plane accidents in 1991, so species is extensively controlled on airfields, e.g. by destruction of nests, shooting of adults and maintenance of unsuitable habitat.
Bibliography. Alcorn (1990), Ashby (1991), Barlow (1972, 1978, 1988b), Barlow *et al.* (1972), Barter (1992d), Beehler *et al.* (1986), Blakers *et al.* (1984), Burger & Gochfeld (1985c), Chambers (1989), Chatto (1987), Christian *et al.* (1992a), Coates (1985), Dann (1977, 1981), Dowding & Murphy (1993b), Finch (1982c), Lane & Davies (1987), Luttrell (1991), Marchant & Higgins (1993), Morton *et al.* (1990), Pettigrew & Frost (1985), Pringle (1987), Rutgers & Norris (1970), Scott (1989), van Tets *et al.* (1967), Thomas (1969), Thomas & Dartnall (1971c), White & Bruce (1986).

20. Sociable Lapwing

Vanellus gregarius

French: Vanneau sociable **German**: Steppenkiebitz **Spanish**: Avefría Sociable
Other common names: Sociable Plover

Taxonomy. *Charadrius gregarius* Pallas, 1771, Volga, Jaiku and Samara.
Often placed in genus *Chettusia*. Monotypic.
Distribution. SC Russia and Kazakhstan. Winters in Sudan (formerly?) and Eritrea, Israel and Arabian Peninsula, Pakistan and NW India; possibly also Iraq.

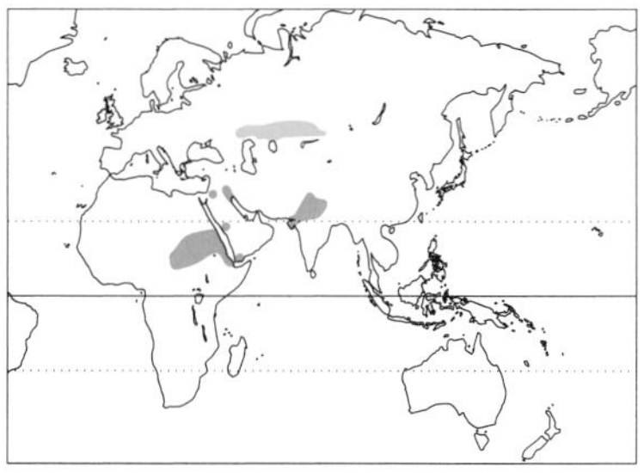

Descriptive notes. 27-30 cm; 150-260 g; wingspan 70-76 cm. Olive brown lapwing with bold, white supercilia meeting on forehead and nape; black crown and lores, thin dark line behind eye; belly black and chestnut; legs blackish. Differs from partially sympatric *V. leucurus* in dark belly, shorter dark legs, and contrasting head pattern. Female less intensely coloured than male, especially on belly. Non-breeding adult has buff wash to supercilia; pale belly. Juvenile similar to non-breeding adult, but with clear buff fringes and dark terminal lines to feathers of upperparts; breast heavily streaked brown.
Habitat. Breeding habitat mainly on transition zones of *Stipa* and *Artemisia* steppes; dry wasteland, cultivated, ploughed and stubble fields. During migration, found mainly on sandy plains with short grass, dry meadows, fallow land and cultivated fields. On wintering grounds, prefers burnt steppe and savanna, uncultivated wasteland, dump pastures and harvested millet fields; usually near water. In Arabia, often occurs in desert near coast.
Food and Feeding. Chiefly insects, such as grasshoppers, beetles, crickets and moth larvae; spiders; frequently small amounts of plant material (grains, leaves and flowers). Usually some small stones in stomach, occasionally remains of vertebrate bones and mollusc shells. Diet varies through breeding season; in winter, apparently chiefly grasshoppers and other insects. Diurnal.
Breeding. Laying mid Apr to late May or early Jun in N. Monogamous. Before start of breeding season, parties of 5-10 birds land on open field for display fights of males in front of females. Semi-colonial, with neighbouring parties 20-50 m apart, each consisting of 3-20 pairs; each pair is territorial; occasionally breeds alongside other wader species, e.g. Collared Pratincole (*Glareola pratincola*). Nests on bare saline patches or in short vegetation, near water; nest is scrape, unlined or lined with some plant material, pebbles and debris, but amount of lining material accumulates during incubation. Clutch 2-5 eggs; single brood, but replacement brood is laid after egg loss; incubation not more than 22 days, mainly by female; chick pale pinkish buff to creamy buff above with black speckles and stripes, cheeks plain cream, hindneck and underparts buffy white; fledging 35-40 days.
Movements. Migratory. Migrates from breeding grounds by Aug-Sept, varying between years. Disperses through Kyrgyzstan, Tadjikistan, Uzbekistan, Turkmenistan, Iran, Turkey and Israel; migrates through Middle East mostly Sept-Nov and Mar; reaches India and Pakistan by Sept-Oct, and, at least formerly, Sudan by late Oct; uncommon migrant, wintering in small numbers on Arabian Peninsula. Leaves wintering grounds in Mar or early Apr and arrives on breeding grounds mid Apr to early May. Migrating flocks are small, of 15-20 birds, rarely several hundreds. Vagrant to Sri Lanka, with only two records.
Status and Conservation. VULNERABLE. On steppes between R Volga and R Ural 1000-2100 pairs, but slowly decreasing; in Kazakhstan densities dropped from 13·2 birds/km^2 in 1930's to 0·12 birds/km^2 in 1992, and 0·08 birds/km^2 in 1993. In NE Africa and SW Asia less than 10,000 birds winter; numbers wintering in Indian Subcontinent probably do not exceed 1000; in total perhaps less than 10,000 mature individuals remain. Population has decreased throughout range due to rapid cultivation of steppe areas and high grazing pressure on remaining grasslands. Many nests are destroyed by cattle and agricultural activities. Change to drier climate in 20th century in breeding and wintering areas may have negatively influenced population too. Expansion of Rook (*Corvus frugilegus*), the main predator of its nests, may have had additional adverse effects. Breeding distribution reduced since 19th century; formerly in Ukraine, Crimea and Volga region. Numbers have dropped dramatically in N Kazakhstan since 1930, when post-breeding flocks consisted of 100's and 1000's of birds, but after 1970 only of 10's. Large wintering flocks (up to 270 birds) only recently seen in Eritrea and W Negev (Israel), but generally scarce in Eritrea and Oman; no records from Sudan since 1950; once a regular and fairly common wintering bird in Pakistan and NW India, but now rare. Contrary to earlier reports, may well not winter at all in Iraq; during period 1914-1918, huge flocks reported in C Iraq in Feb.
Bibliography. Ali & Ripley (1980), Bannikov (1978), Belik, V. (1994b), van den Berg (1984), Borodin *et al*. (1984), Calinin (1987), Chekmenev (1961), Collar & Andrew (1988), Collar *et al*. (1994), Cramp & Simmons (1983), Davygora *et al*. (1989), Dementiev & Gladkov (1951b), Dowsett & Forbes-Watson (1993), Étchécopar & Hüe (1964), Evans (1994), Flint *et al*. (1984), Goodman *et al*. (1989), Gordienko (1991), Grazhdankin (1985), Grisser (1983), Heredia & Máñez (1985), Hüe & Étchécopar (1970), Inskipp & Collins (1993), Kasparek (1992a), Khokhlov (1987), Khrokov (1978), Knystautas (1993), Kuchin & Chekcheev (1987a), Kürschner (1976), Mackworth-Praed & Grant (1957), Mawby (1988), Nikolaus (1987), Nikolaus & Hamed (1984), Paz (1987), Perennou *et al*. (1994), Phillips (1978), Riley & Rooke (1962), Ripley (1982), Roberts, T.J. (1991), Rogacheva (1992), Rutgers & Norris (1970), Sermet (1986), Shevchenko & Debelo (1991), Shirihai (1996), Solomatin (1973), Urban *et al*. (1986).

21. White-tailed Lapwing

Vanellus leucurus

French: Vanneau à queue blanche **German**: Weißschwanzkiebitz **Spanish**: Avefría Coliblanca
Other common names: White-tailed Plover

Taxonomy. *Charadrius leucurus* Lichtenstein, 1823, between the Kuwan and Ian Daria, Turkestan.
Often placed in genus *Chettusia*, in past sometimes in monospecific *Vanellochettusia*. Species name frequently misspelt *leucura*. Monotypic.
Distribution. C & SE Turkey and E Syria NE through Azerbaijan and Transcaspia to L Balkhash, and SE through Iraq and Iran to W Pakistan. Winters from Sudan through Iraq and Iran to C & E Pakistan and NW & NC India; also extreme SW Turkmenistan.
Descriptive notes. 26-29 cm; 99-198 g; wingspan 67-70 cm. Graceful, slim, long-legged lapwing, with pale, whitish face and all white tail; pinkish brown rest of head and back; grey breast, rosy-buff belly. Sexes alike. No seasonal variation. Juvenile has feathers of upperparts with dark centres and bright buff fringes; neck and breast mottled brown-grey.

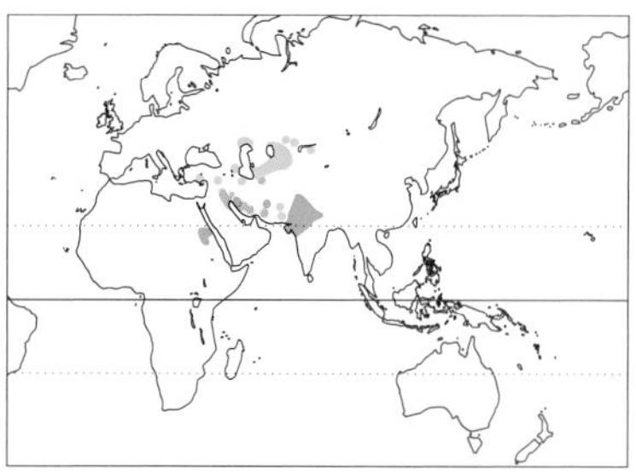

Habitat. Lake shores and river valleys; nearly always in vicinity of shallow standing or slow-flowing water with suitable bed for wading. Also flooded or recently dried out marshy meadows and salt-shrub terrain. Breeds in damp, vegetated areas near salt or fresh water; also small vegetated islets and swampy shores of brackish lakes. Small flock observed flying to dry ploughed field at dusk to roost, in Pakistan.
Food and Feeding. Diet probably consists mainly of insects, especially beetles and grasshoppers, but also caterpillars and fly larvae; also takes worms, molluscs and crustaceans, including freshwater shrimps. Usually feeds on dry land, but also by foot-dabbling in shallow water, and sometimes catches prey by probing in soft mud; in Africa also wades in deeper water. Diurnal.
Breeding. Laying mid-Apr to May. Monogamous. Often in loose colonies, sometimes of several hundred pairs (Iraq); frequently together with other colonial breeders, often pratincoles, Black-winged Stilts (*Himantopus himantopus*) and terns; occasionally solitary. Nest is shallow scrape with sparse lining of plant material, in the open, usually near water. Clutch 4 eggs, sometimes 3; single-brooded in Iraq; incubation 21-24 days, starting with last egg; chick has upperparts greyish buff with black streaks, rusty-red ring around eye, underparts buffy white; tended by both parents; fledging c. 30 days; stays with parents at natal site after fledging. Age of first breeding probably 1-2 years.
Movements. Sedentary in much of Middle East, partly migratory in C Asia. Departs from breeding grounds in C Asia Jul to mid-Sept. Present in N Iran Apr-Aug, and in Sudan Sept-Mar. Migratory flocks small, of 1-6 birds, but possibly augmented during passage; flocks in spring generally slightly larger, up to 100. Few birds winter in extreme SW Turkmenistan. Rare migrant and occasional winterer in Egypt, Israel and Arabia; probably migrates on broad front across Arabia. In Iraq, moves from breeding sites in summer when water bodies dry up, and makes local movements in winter, deserting flooded zones. Wintering birds in Sudan, Pakistan and India present Sept-Mar. Reaches breeding grounds in C Asia from mid-Mar. In winter usually found in flocks of 6-25 birds.
Status and Conservation. Not globally threatened. Population wintering in E Africa and SW Asia numbers 10,000-100,000 birds, with similar numbers in SC Asia; 500-1000 birds in Sudan; very common in marshes of Euphrates; c. 1400 birds in Iran; common wintering bird in Pakistan. Evidently rather abundant in CIS, within fairly restricted range. Probably recently expanded westward: in 1950's and 1960's a few pairs found breeding in Azerbaijan, where maximum 100 pairs now estimated; in 1970's discovered breeding in C & SE Turkey, coinciding with first records of spring migration across Cyprus, but no expansion noted after 1970's and now probably only a few pairs remain; in late 1970's started breeding on N Caspian coast. First breeding pair recorded in Pakistan in 1987; probably breeds in NE Afghanistan. Increasing numbers in deserts of C Asia, where has started breeding in cultivated areas.
Bibliography. Abdulali (1952), Ali & Ripley (1980), Ametov (1987), Bakaev (1979), Bauer (1990), Belik (1989), van Berkel & van Dijken (1985), Brandel (1976), Cramp & Simmons (1983), Ctyroký (1992, 1994), Dean *et al*. (1977), Dowsett & Forbes-Watson (1993), Étchécopar & Hüe (1964), Evans (1994), Flint *et al*. (1984), Glutz von Blotzheim *et al*. (1975), Goodman *et al*. (1989), Helbig (1985), Hüe & Étchécopar (1970), Karavaev (1977), Kashkarov & Ostapenko (1990), Kasparek (1992a), Khrokov *et al*. (1979), Knystautas (1993), Mackworth-Praed & Grant (1957), Nikolaus (1987), Patrikeev (1995), Paz (1987), Perennou *et al*. (1994), Pettet (1982), Radetzky (1976), Ramsay (1992), Ripley (1982), Roberts, T.J. (1985, 1991), Sagitov & Fundukchiev (1988), Scott (1989), Shirihai (1996), Tomkovich (1992b), Urban *et al*. (1986).

22. Pied Lapwing

Vanellus cayanus

French: Vanneau de Cayenne **German**: Cayennekiebitz **Spanish**: Avefría de Cayena
Other common names: (Three-toed) Cayenne/Pied/Little White-winged Plover/Lapwing

Taxonomy. *Charadrius cayanus* Latham, 1790, Cayenne.
Sometimes placed in monospecific *Hoploxypterus*. Shows several similarities with *Charadrius*, including plumage details and some physiological features. Monotypic.
Distribution. South America E of Andes, from E Colombia to mouth of R Amazon, then S to Paraguay, SE Brazil and extreme NE Argentina (Misiones).

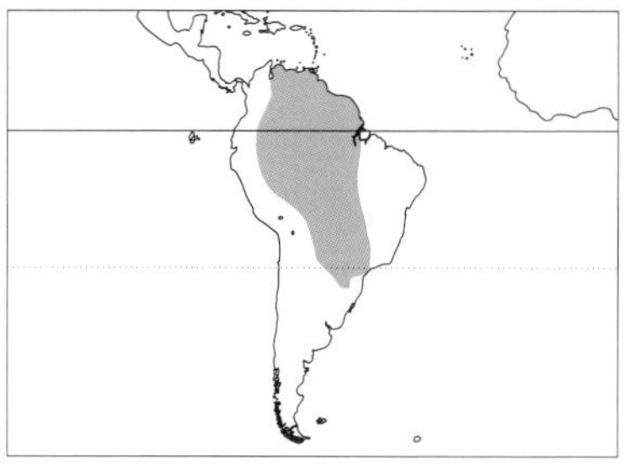

Descriptive notes. 21-24 cm; 55-84 g. Small lapwing, resembling *Charadrius* plovers in some aspects, but with long red legs and black carpal spurs; bold pattern in black, white and brownish grey; narrow white line encircles dark crown; forehead to nape deep black, sometimes with a little white on forehead; fairly narrow black breast band across otherwise white underparts; striking longitudinal black and white bar down scapulars; broad white wingbar stretches across most of secondaries and greater coverts to inner primary coverts. Sexes alike. No seasonal variation. Juvenile like adult, but with browner mask; smaller, dusky grey breast band; grey-brown with cinnamon-buff fringes on upperparts; less developed scapular markings.
Habitat. Mudflats and sandbanks of savanna ponds and rivers in forested zone; also along sea coast.
Food and Feeding. Poorly known. Items recorded mainly insects, including Hemiptera, Heteroptera, Hymenoptera, and Coleoptera, as well as Myriopoda; also snails.
Breeding. Display behaviour observed in May-Jul, and flightless young in Jun and Jul in NE Venezuela. Display included birds flying overhead, with peculiar undulating flight, while calling; also standing in front of each other with spread wings. Nest is slight depression in ground. One clutch comprised 2 eggs.
Movements. Sedentary.
Status and Conservation. Not globally threatened. No population estimates available; apparently very uncommon, although substantial numbers have been observed in savannas of Venezuela, with some 100 birds congregating around ponds. Uncommon and local in Colombia, where apparently restricted to sandy areas. Rare in Surinam and exceptional in French Guiana, with last record in latter in 1976; may be merely rare non-breeding visitor to the zone.
Bibliography. Blake (1977), Dubs (1992), Forrester (1993), Friedmann & Smith (1955), Haverschmidt (1968), Haverschmidt & Mees (1995), Hellmayr & Conover (1948), Hilty & Brown (1986), Meyer de Schauensee (1966, 1982), Meyer de Schauensee & Phelps (1978), de la Peña (1992), Pinto (1964), Remsen & Traylor (1989), Sargeant (1994), Scott & Carbonell (1986), Sick (1985c, 1993), Snyder (1966), Tostain *et al*. (1992), Zusi & Jehl (1970).

23. Southern Lapwing
Vanellus chilensis

French: Vanneau téro   **German**: Bronzekiebitz   **Spanish**: Avefría Tero
Other common names: Chilean Lapwing

Taxonomy. *Parra Chilensis* Molina, 1782, Chile.
Formerly placed in monospecific *Belonopterus*. Based on proportions and vocalization, might comprise two species, with separation of *cayennensis*, incorporating *lampronotus*; however, intergradation known at one locality. Race *fretensis* sometimes merged with nominate race. Four subspecies usually recognized.
Subspecies and Distribution.
V. c. cayennensis (Gmelin, 1789) - N South America, N of R Amazon.
V. c. lampronotus (Wagler, 1827) - R Amazon S through C, E & S Brazil to N Chile and N Argentina.
V. c. chilensis (Molina, 1782) - Argentina and Chile S to Chiloé I and Comodoro Rivadavia.
V. c. fretensis Brodkorb, 1934 - S Chile and S Argentina.

Descriptive notes. 32-38 cm; 1 male *cayennensis* 280 g, 1 adult *fretensis* c. 425 g. Large, crested lapwing with red carpal spurs, blackish breast band and bronze sheen on greyish brown upperparts. Sexes alike. No seasonal variation. Juvenile has crown feathers tipped buff, white facial band much reduced and infused buff, diffuse breast band, short crest and spurs; buff fringes and barring to feathers of upperparts. Race *fretensis* similar to nominate, but smaller; *cayennensis* has more white and less black on face, with rest of head and neck cinnamon brown; in *lampronotus*, head mainly intermediate brown-grey, with neat white line down face.

Habitat. Breeds in pastures, damp meadows, river plains and open boggy areas with short matted vegetation; has also been found breeding on ploughed land. During non-breeding season also occurs on inland wetlands and marshes, and tidal flats; occasionally open areas in woodland. Around ranch houses, or even in urban gardens; in Chile and Brazil, wing-clipped birds sometimes kept as sentinels.
Food and Feeding. Mainly insects, e.g. grasshoppers; also earthworms, and perhaps other terrestrial invertebrates; small fish and insect larvae disturbed by foot-trembling. Hatchlings mainly fed on earthworms.
Breeding. Season Apr-Jul in Venezuela; Mar in Colombia; in Chile, from Jul (nominate) and from Sept/Oct (*fretensis*); on Tierra del Fuego, eggs found in Oct and young birds observed late Nov and Dec. Monogamous, but co-operative breeding has been observed in Venezuela, with 2-3 adults or immatures helping in territory defence. Loosely colonial; territorial and highly aggressive, mobbing potential predators. Nest is shallow scrape, unlined or sparsely lined with grasses, usually on dry spot in, or very close to, wet area. Clutch 4 eggs, on occasion 3; incubation c. 27 days; chick variegated greyish cinnamon and black above with heavy black margins to white nape, underparts white with fuscous pectoral bar; fledging takes over 1 month.
Movements. Largely sedentary, with limited dispersion after breeding season. Populations of extreme S migrate to less cold areas in winter. Outside breeding season, occurs in small flocks, occasionally up to 200 birds.
Status and Conservation. Not globally threatened. No population estimates available; widespread and abundant throughout much of range. Apparently spreading due to forest clearance and cultivation; adaptability to use of some humanized habitats suggests species secure.
Bibliography. Belton (1984), Blake (1977), Canevari et al. (1991), Contreras et al. (1990), Fjeldså & Krabbe (1990), Gallegos (1984), Greer & Greer (1967), Haverschmidt (1968), Hayes & Fox (1991), Hellmayr & Conover (1948), Hilty & Brown (1986), Humphrey et al. (1970), Johnson (1965b), Maclean (1972a), Meyer de Schauensee (1966), Meyer de Schauensee & Phelps (1978), Myers (1978, 1980c), Naranjo (1991b), de Oliveira & Rech (1988), Oniki (1987), Ortega et al. (1988), de la Peña (1981a, 1987, 1992), Ridgely & Gwynne (1989), Scott & Carbonell (1986), Sick (1985c, 1993), Snyder (1966), Tostain et al. (1992), Walters & Walters (1980), Ward (1992), Wetmore (1926, 1965).

24. Andean Lapwing
Vanellus resplendens

French: Vanneau des Andes   **German**: Andenkiebitz   **Spanish**: Avefría Andina

Taxonomy. *Charadrius resplendens* Tschudi, 1843, Andes of Peru.
Formerly placed in monospecific *Ptiloscelys*. Monotypic.
Distribution. Andes from SW Colombia to N Chile and NW Argentina.
Descriptive notes. c. 33 cm; 193-230 g. Creamy grey head with dark brownish grey eye patch, bronzy green upperparts, purple patch on wing-coverts, and dark grey breast ending in sharp grey line; small red carpal spurs. Sexes alike. No seasonal variation. Juvenile like adult, but has brownish head and neck, breast mottled buff; pale buff fringes and dark green subterminal lines to feathers of upperparts.
Habitat. Breeds in open grassy areas, shore meadows, open parts of marshes, rushy pasture and boggy terrain of *páramo* and *puna* zones in Andes, at altitudes of 3000-4500 m, usually near lakes or rivers and often on partly inundated and hummocky ground; avoids saline water; sometimes in short grass of dry fields and hill sides. In southernmost portion of range, occurs down to 1500 m. During austral winter, found at lower altitudes and occasionally on coast.
Food and Feeding. No information available.
Breeding. Eggs found mainly Oct-Dec, occasionally later. One nest on barren ground was lined with plant material. Clutch 4 eggs (2 nests); chick mottled buff and black above, with thin, incomplete black demarcations of white nape. No further information available.

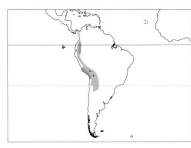

Olrog (1984), Parker et al. (1982), de la Peña (1992), Peris & Alaberce (1992), Remsen & Traylor (1989), Rocha & Peñaranda (1995), Scott & Carbonell (1986), Ward (1992).

Movements. Essentially resident, with only altitudinal migration, birds descending slopes during austral winter.
Status and Conservation. Not globally threatened. No population estimates available. Locally very common at 3000-4500 m. Occupation of bleak high altitude habitats with relatively low densities of humans suggests species probably secure at present.
Bibliography. Blake (1977), Canevari et al. (1991), Fjeldså & Krabbe (1990), Graves (1981), Hellmayr & Conover (1948), Hilty & Brown (1986), Hughes, R.A. (1984), Johnson (1965b), Koepcke (1970), Meyer de Schauensee (1966, 1982), Narosky & Yzurieta (1987),

Genus *ERYTHROGONYS* Gould, 1838

25. Red-kneed Dotterel
Erythrogonys cinctus

French: Pluvier ceinturé   **German**: Schwarzbrust-Regenpfeifer   **Spanish**: Chorlito Pechinegro

Taxonomy. *Erythrogonys cinctus* Gould, 1838, New South Wales.
Often placed in genus *Charadrius*, and traditionally grouped with other Australasian aberrant *Charadrius*-like genera; however, recently grouped in Vanellinae on basis of allozymes, patterning of wing and presence of hind toe. Monotypic.
Distribution. Extreme S New Guinea and Australia.

Descriptive notes. 17-19·5 cm; 35-77 g; wing-span 33-38 cm. Medium-sized, boldly patterned wader; black cap contrasts with white throat; black breast band and middle flanks, turning to chestnut towards rear; upper flanks white; long legs bicoloured, with tibiae and "knees" pinkish red, tarsi and feet grey; long, slender, very slightly decurved bill. Sexes similar. No seasonal variation. Juvenile as adult, but cap, nape and hindneck pale brown; back feathers have whitish buff fringes; mostly white underparts with brownish breast patches; duller red bill.
Habitat. Inland wetlands, including swamps, lakes, creeks, and various kinds of man-made water bodies and pools; prefers temporary or permanent freshwater wetlands, particularly when inundated by rain or floodwater. Habitat usually exposed, with scattered short emergent vegetation, shallow water and mud or clay; rarely in brackish or salt water; lacks supraorbital salt gland.
Food and Feeding. Snails, bivalves, crustaceans, spiders, all sorts of insects and their larvae, and seeds. Feeds diurnally, gleaning and probing along muddy edges of water, or wading in shallow water; occasionally swims in deeper water; also uses foot-trembling. Often in loose flocks of 10-100 birds, occasionally more; sometimes exhibiting many aggressive interactions.
Breeding. Lays in summer, autumn or early winter after heavy rains, usually Aug-Dec (Jan). Occurs in flocks before breeding; breeds solitarily or in loose colonies of up to 30 nests; territorial. Nests on sand, damp soil or mud, along shore or on small islet, often among dense vegetation; regularly in mixed colonies with Black-winged Stilts (*Himantopus himantopus*), Red-necked Avocets (*Recurvirostra novaehollandiae*) and Hoary-headed Grebes (*Poliocephalus poliocephalus*); nest is depression in ground, usually scantly lined, though in areas susceptible to flooding sometimes substantial; built of twigs, grass and other plant material and debris; may be located inder clumps of wetland plants. Usually 4 eggs (2-5), probably laid at daily intervals; both parents incubate, starting when clutch complete, period unrecorded; chick has golden brown upperparts with black patches, white underparts; tended by both parents; at alarm call of parents, chick wades or swims to nearest plant in water. Nest failure high, due to trampling by cattle, predation by Australian Ravens (*Corvus coronoides*) and introduced mammalian predators, or human disturbance.
Movements. Generally resident, showing erratic movements; probably reponds to availability of fresh water; during drought moves S and towards coastal regions; during wet season and after flooding, numbers inland increase. After successful inland breeding, seems to show northward movements. During movements and at flooded sites can appear in large flocks of several hundreds.
Status and Conservation. Not globally threatened. Widespread, with estimated population of at least c. 26,000, but probably more. Numbers have increased in SE coastal region since 1940's and 1950's. Status in S New Guinea uncertain, with several records from Trans-Fly; may breed locally.
Bibliography. Alcorn (1990), Barter (1992a), Beehler et al. (1986), Blakers et al. (1984), Christian et al. (1992a), Coates (1985), Finch (1982b), Flegg & Madge (1995), Lane & Davies (1987), Lindsey (1992), Macdonald (1988), Maclean (1977), Marchant & Higgins (1993), McGill (1944), Pizzey & Doyle (1980), Pringle (1987), Rand & Gilliard (1967), Rauzon (1988), Robertson & Dennison (1977), Schodde & Tidemann (1986), Schulz, M. (1986a), Scott (1989), Simpson & Day (1994), Slater (1987), Slater et al. (1989), Stranger (1991), Trounson (1987), Watkins (1993).

PLATE 37 ➤

PLATE 37

inches 5
cm 13

ssp *altifrons* ♂

♀

ssp *apricaria* ♂

26

27

28

♂ ♀

29

reddish individual

30 pale individual

ssp *hiaticula* ♀

♂

31

ssp *tundrae* ♂

♀

32

♂

33

ssp *curonicus* ♂

♀

ssp *dubius* ♂

34

♂

ssp *cinnamominus*

35

ssp *beldingi* ♂

♂

♀ ssp *wilsonia*

♀

♂

ssp *vociferus*

♀

36

bird with
extensive
breast band

♂

♀

37

♂

ssp *peruvianus*

38

39

bird with rufous supercilium

40

Subfamily CHARADRIINAE

Genus *PLUVIALIS* Brisson, 1760

26. **Eurasian Golden Plover**

Pluvialis apricaria

French: Pluvier doré **German**: Goldregenpfeifer **Spanish**: Chorlito Dorado Europeo
Other common names: (Greater/European) Golden Plover

Taxonomy. *Charadrius apricarius* Linnaeus, 1758, Lappland.
Validity of subspecific division regularly debated, due to considerable variation within local populations and no apparent differences in measurements. Birds of British Is to N Germany formerly considered separate race, *oreophilos*. Two subspecies normally recognized.
Subspecies and Distribution.
P. a. altifrons (C. L. Brehm, 1831) - EC Greenland, Iceland and Faeroes to N Fenno-Scandia, and thence E to Taymyr Peninsula.
P. a. apricaria (Linnaeus, 1758) - British Is, through W Germany, Denmark and S Fenno-Scandia to Baltic states.
Winters from British Is through Mediterranean to S Caspian Sea.

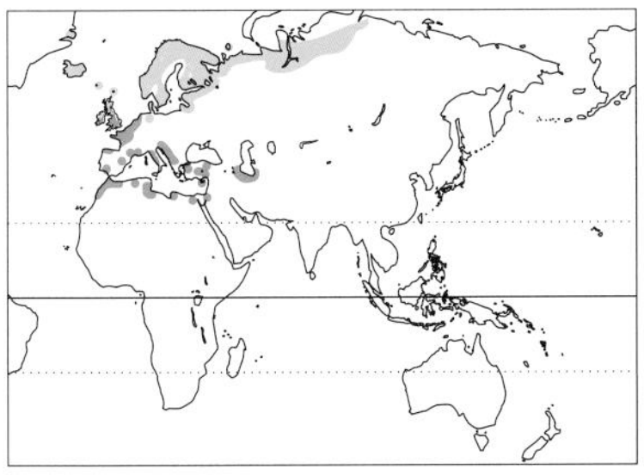

Descriptive notes. 26-29 cm; 157-312 g; wing-span 67-76 cm. Largest and bulkiest of golden plovers, with underwing white, as opposed to brownish grey; also differs in shape and plumage colour; wings equal in length to tail or slightly longer. Female less extensively black, with some brown markings below. Non-breeding adult lacks black on face and underparts; upperparts less distinctly spotted with yellow, can turn greyish. Juvenile as non-breeding adult, with faint grey fringes on flanks and belly. In race *altifrons* male more uniformly black below, whereas nominate male has cheeks, throat, breast and belly infused with white; female *altifrons* has yellowish cheeks with black marks, whereas nominate female very variable, can have very pale head, but sometimes virtually identical to male.
Habitat. Race *altifrons* breeds in humid moss, moss-and-lichen and hummock tundra, shrub tundra, open bogs in forest tundra and alpine tundra; nominate race breeds on highland heaths and peatlands. On migration and in winter, occurs on pastures and open agricultural land, such as stubble and fallow fields, and regularly feeds on intertidal flats. Often roosts on ploughed land or amongst low crops; sometimes roosts on flats and salt-marshes in shallow bays and estuaries.
Food and Feeding. Mainly invertebrate prey, especially beetles (including pupae and larvae) and earthworms; sometimes plant material, e.g. berries, seeds and grass; all kinds of insects and their larvae, spiders, millipedes and snails; on intertidal flats polychaete worms. Pecks from surface or probes for 1-2 cm; evidently also detects prey by sound. Sometimes feeds at night. Moves in flocks of 10's to 1000's; during breeding, flocks are smaller. During breeding season, Dunlins (*Calidris alpina*) often mix with off-duty birds, benefiting from vigilance of present species.
Breeding. Laying Apr to mid-May in Britain, mid-May to late Jul further N. Monogamous, with lifelong pair-bond. Solitary, with nests sometimes only few hundred metres apart; 1-4 pairs/km in linear survey, and 2-10·9 pairs/km² in Taymyr, but very variable between years; in Britain, up to 16 pairs/km² on fertile soil and 0·1-0·5 pairs/km² in montane zone; strong breeding-site fidelity and natal philopatry. Territorial; adults feed mostly outside territory. Breeds in flat and openly vegetated areas; nest is shallow scrape, lined with moss and plant material. Usually 4 eggs, occasionally 3 or 2, laid at intervals of 48-60 hours; incubation 28-31 days; chick has mottled black and bright yellow upperparts, whitish underparts; fledging 25-33 days; young independent soon after fledging. Hatching success 81% in Lappland. Many broods subject to predation. Breeds first at 2 years old. Oldest ringed bird 12 years, 2 months.
Movements. Migratory; only partially migratory in Britain and Ireland. Icelandic population leaves late Sept to early Nov, probably wintering mainly in Ireland, and in W Britain, W France and Iberia; birds from Scandinavia to Siberia winter from Britain and Netherlands to N Africa, but mainly in S Britain, France, Iberia and Maghreb; birds from Taymyr possibly fly across W Siberia and Kazakhstan and also S along R Yenisey across taiga, towards Caspian Sea and Mediterranean. Adults leave breeding areas late Jul to early Sept, juveniles Oct-Nov. N extremes of wintering distribution left as soon as frost starts, but soon reoccupied as weather improves. Ringing recoveries suggest more E route during return migration. In Netherlands and W Germany numbers grow in Apr and early May, and breeding areas reoccupied in May or early Jun on N tundra. In Britain, birds do not generally move far from breeding areas, which are abandoned Jul-Feb.
Status and Conservation. Not globally threatened. Breeding population of race *apricaria* estimated at 1,800,000 birds (1994), and is declining; no population estimates available for race *altifrons*, but range in Russia has been expanding in recent years. In W Europe c. 609,000 breeding pairs, with 300,000 in Iceland (1985), 130,000 in Norway (1981), 100,000 in Finland (1986) and 30,000 in Sweden (1984). Contraction of S limit of range in NW Europe since mid-19th century, mainly due to habitat changes, notably cultivation and afforestation of heathland: numbers have decreased in Ireland and Britain, with 22,600 pairs in 1987; breeders from former range of Belgium to Denmark to Poland have practically disappeared; in Norway recovered somewhat after decline in late 19th and early 20th centuries; in S Sweden decreased dramatically since mid-20th century, possibly due to climatic amelioration, but some recovery now in Sweden; major increase in Finland from 26,000 pairs in 1950's to 258,000 pairs in 1973-1976, but apparently followed by more recent decrease. Until 1950's, large numbers, probably up to 80,000 birds per year, caught in Netherlands by specialized plover-netting. Frequently taken by hunters on wintering grounds, especially in France. Counts of Dutch wintering birds suggest marked decrease in population since 1978; maximum numbers present in winter, up to 300,000 birds in Britain (85,000 in 1992), 400,000 in Netherlands (1978), 200,000 in Denmark, and 170,000 in Germany.
Bibliography. Ali & Ripley (1980), Alexandersson (1987), Beaman (1994), Bengtson & Rundgren (1978), Brown, A.F. (1993), Byrkjedal (1978a, 1978b, 1978c, 1980, 1985a, 1987a, 1989a), Byrkjedal & Kålås (1983, 1985), Catley & Hume (1994), Cramp & Simmons (1983), Crick (1992), Dittberner & Dittberner (1993), Dunn (1994), Edwards (1982), van Eerden & Key (1978), van Eerden *et al.* (1979), Étchécopar & Hüe (1964), Fjeldså (1977), Flint *et al.* (1984), Flore *et al.* (1994), Fuller & Lloyd (1981), Fuller & Youngman (1979), Goodman *et al.* (1989), Gregory, R.D. (1987), Henriksen (1985), Hüe & Étchécopar (1970), Jukema (1982, 1986, 1989, 1994), Jukema & Hulscher (1988), Jukema & Piersma (1987, 1992), Kirby & Lack (1993), Knystautas (1993), Kovács (1985), Kube *et al.* (1994), Meltofte *et al.* (1994), Nikolaev (1990), Osing (1993b), Parr (1980, 1992, 1993), Paz (1987), Piersma, Ott *et al.* (1991), Pulliainen & Saari (1993a), Ratcliffe (1976), Reicherzer (1986), Rogacheva (1992), Rutgers & Norris (1970), Shirihai (1996), Straka (1991), Thompson & Barnard (1983, 1984), Thompson & Lendrem (1985), Tomkovich (1992b), Urban *et al.* (1986), Yalden, D.W. (1986b, 1991), Yalden, D.W. & Yalden (1989a, 1989b, 1991), Yalden, P.E. & Yalden (1988, 1990).

27. **Pacific Golden Plover**

Pluvialis fulva

French: Pluvier fauvem **German**: Pazifischer Goldregenpfeifer **Spanish**: Chorlito Dorado Siberiano
Other common names: Asian/Asiatic/Eastern Golden Plover

Taxonomy. *Charadrius fulvus* Gmelin, 1789, Tahiti.
Forms superspecies with *P. dominica*, with which formerly considered conspecific (see page 386). Monotypic.
Distribution. NC & NE Russia, from Yamal Peninsula to Chukotskiy Peninsula and S across Koryakskiy highlands to N Kamchatka; W Alaska. Winters from E Africa through S Asia and Indonesia to Oceania, Australia and New Zealand; small numbers in S California.

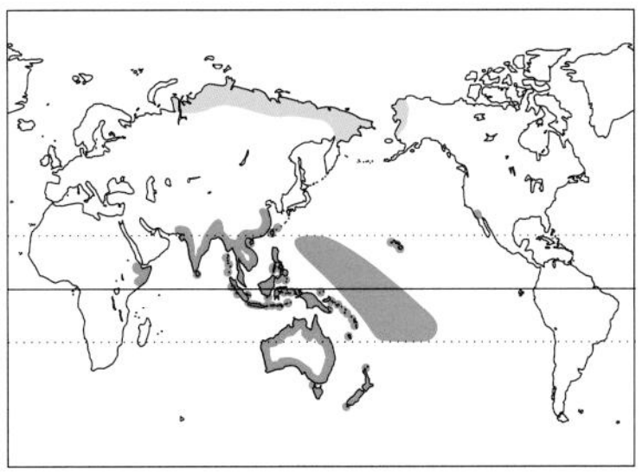

Descriptive notes. 23-26 cm; 100-192 g; wing-span 60-72 cm. Black underparts with narrow white flanking line; vent tends to be mostly white with scattering of black. Very similar to *P. apricaria* and *P. dominica*, but smaller; has longer legs and is yellower than *P. apricaria*, with brownish grey underwing, and wings clearly longer than tail. Female somewhat less black than male. Non-breeding adult has yellowish buff on breast, grading to whitish on belly and vent; golden spotting less prominent. Juvenile as non-breeding adult, but with brown barring on flank.
Habitat. Breeds in drier parts of typical tundra, but not on coastline; on shrub tundra, rarely forest tundra, and on stony well drained upland, with moss and lichens; montane tundra in Chukotskiy and Koryakskiy highlands. Winters in coastal areas, in fields with short grass, prairies, ploughed land, salt-marshes, beaches and open sandflats and mudflats; often on golf courses, playing fields, airfields, etc. Young birds occur more frequently on mud by inland waters and tidal flats. Roosts in same places used for feeding, but also near feeding areas on exposed sandy beaches or rocks; where such roosting sites are lacking, may roost on roofs of buildings.
Food and Feeding. Mainly insects, molluscs, worms, crustaceans and spiders; berries particularly important on tundra; occasionally seeds and leaves. Feeds in typical plover style; also gleans and probes in mud, sand and pastures. Feeds alone or in flocks of 100 birds or more. Some wintering birds occupy territories for entire season, returning each year.
Breeding. Breeds in N summer, with laying in Jun. Presumably monogamous. High degree of site fidelity, especially so for males; often breeding within 100 m of nest-site of previous year, and sometimes in same nest cup. Densities usually c. 1 pair/km², locally up to 6-7 pairs/km²; can vary considerably between years. Nest on dry spots, on hummock, lichen, *Dryas* or moss tundra; nest is shallow scrape, lined with lichens. Clutch 4 eggs; incubation 26 days, by both sexes; chick has black and bright yellow upperparts and white underparts; after hatching, chicks and parents move to moist shrubby or grassy tundra or patches with green moss; chick tended by both parents, or by male only if brood is late. Oldest ringed bird at least 6½ years.
Movements. Migratory. Appears in Siberian tundra in early Jun; Taymyr population migrates over middle taiga along R Yenisey in late May, stopping in parties of 3-7 birds at thawed patches in forest openings and near villages; departs late Aug or early Sept; some birds migrate E in broad front across taiga. Southward migration takes place in large flocks, and at night. Non-breeders leave 2-4 weeks before breeders, and young birds some weeks after adults. Some Alaskan breeders fly 4500 km non-stop across Pacific Ocean to Hawaiian Is; adults reach Hawaiian Is in Aug, juveniles in Sept; arrival in Fiji in early Sept, New Zealand in Oct. E Africa and E Asia probably reached by overland migration across W Siberia; Indian winterers cross Tibet. Highly faithful to wintering sites.
Status and Conservation. Not globally threatened. Population wintering in SW & SC Asia probably c. 100,000 birds, and in CE & SE Asia at least 100,000 birds; c. 9000 in Australia, 500 New Zealand. In past, was a favourite species of hunters in India, but current situation unknown. Small population apparently wintered in W Europe in first half of 20th century, but has now disappeared (see page 409).
Bibliography. Ali & Ripley (1980), Alström (1990), Ash (1980b), Aspinwall (1975), Barter (1988, 1989c), Beaman (1994), Beehler *et al.* (1986), Brazil (1991), Bregulla (1992), Catley & Hume (1994), Chambers (1989), Coates (1985), Connors (1983), Connors *et al.* (1993), Cramp & Simmons (1983), Deignan (1945), Dickinson *et al.* (1991), Dowsett & Forbes-Watson (1993), Dunn *et al.* (1987), Étchécopar & Hüe (1964, 1978), Evanich (1989), Flint *et al.* (1984), Glutz von Blotzheim *et al.* (1977), Golley & Stoddart (1991), Hansen (1986), Hewish (1988), Hindwood & Hoskin (1954), Hirschfeld (1995), Holyoak & Thibault (1984), Howell & Webb (1995a), Johnson, O.W. (1979, 1985, 1993), Johnson, O.W. & Connors (1996), Johnson, O.W. & Johnson (1983), Johnson, O.W., Connors *et al.* (1993), Johnson, O.W., Johnson & Bruner (1981a, 1981b), Johnson, O.W., Morton *et al.* (1989), Johnston & McFarlane (1967), Jukema (1987, 1988a, 1988b), Jukema & van der Veen (1992), Kinsky & Yaldwyn (1981), Knox (1987), Knystautas (1993), Lane & Davies (1987), Langrand (1990), Larsen & Ralph (1984), Lekagul & Round (1991), MacKinnon & Phillipps (1993), Mackworth-Praed & Grant (1957, 1962), Marchant & Higgins (1993), van Marle & Voous (1988), Mathiu *et al.* (1989), Medland (1991), Medway & Wells (1976), Perennou *et al.* (1994), Phillips (1978), Plumb (1978), Pym (1982), Rabor (1977), Ripley (1982), Roberts, T.J. (1991), Rogacheva (1992), Roselaar (1990), Sauer (1962, 1963), Scott (1989), Shirihai (1996), Short *et al.* (1990), Sikora (1986), Smythies (1981, 1986), Starks & Lane (1987), Thomas (1970), Underhill *et al.* (1993), Urban *et al.* (1986), White & Bruce (1986), Williams, M.D. (1986).

On following pages: 28. American Golden Plover (*Pluvialis dominica*); 29. Grey Plover (*Pluvialis squatarola*); 30. Red-breasted Plover (*Charadrius obscurus*); 31. Common Ringed Plover (*Charadrius hiaticula*); 32. Semipalmated Plover (*Charadrius semipalmatus*); 33. Long-billed Plover (*Charadrius placidus*); 34. Little Ringed Plover (*Charadrius dubius*); 35. Wilson's Plover (*Charadrius wilsonia*); 36. Killdeer (*Charadrius vociferus*); 37. Piping Plover (*Charadrius melodus*); 38. Black-banded Plover (*Charadrius thoracicus*); 39. Kittlitz's Plover (*Charadrius pecuarius*); 40. St Helena Plover (*Charadrius sanctaehelenae*).

28. American Golden Plover
Pluvialis dominica

French: Pluvier bronzé   **Spanish**: Chorlito Dorado Americano
          German: Amerikanischer Goldregenpfeifer
Other common names: Lesser Golden Plover

Taxonomy. *Charadrius Dominicus* P. L. S. Müller, 1776, Hispaniola.
Forms superspecies with *P. fulva*, with which formerly considered conspecific (see page 386). Monotypic.
Distribution. W Alaska E through N Canada to Baffin I. Winters in South America S to Tierra del Fuego.

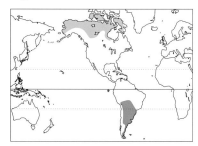

Descriptive notes. 24-28 cm; 122-194 g; wingspan 65-72 cm. Large white patches on sides of breast. Generally greyer, with paler flecks, than very similar *P. apricaria* and *P. fulva*; white flanks usually absent and vent mostly black; also differs from former in brownish grey underwing, and in wings being clearly longer than tail. Female somewhat whiter below. Non-breeding adult lacks black on underparts and breast; upperparts extensively grey, especially around head and neck; overall less yellow than *P. fulva*. Juvenile almost totally lacks golden colour, and has heavily marked greyish underparts.

Habitat. Breeds in Arctic and subarctic tundra beyond tree limit, in valleys and well drained uplands with short vegetation of moss and lichens. During northern winter, mostly inland on short-grass fields, prairies, ploughed land, wetlands and open sandflats or mudflats; young birds found more often on inland and tidal mudflats and saltings. Forms roosting flocks in salt-marshes and fields near lagoons or marshes, and occasionally on ocean beaches.
Food and Feeding. Insects, especially grasshoppers, crickets, beetles and caterpillars; also worms, spiders, molluscs, crustaceans; berries important on tundra; occasionally seeds and leaves. Feeds in typical plover style; also gleans and probes in mud, sand and pastures. Feeds alone or in flocks of 100 or more. Often defends feeding territory on wintering grounds.
Breeding. Laying Jun to mid-Jul. Monogamous, often for several years. Density c. 6 pairs/km². High degree of site fidelity. Nest is exposed, shallow scrape on dry patch amidst moss or lichen; lined with moss, lichen and dead leaves. Usually 4 eggs, sometimes 3, laid at intervals of 1-2 days; incubation c. 26 days, starting with 3rd egg; male incubates during day, female at night; chick mottled black and bright yellow above, with whitish cheeks and underparts; after hatching, chicks and parents move to moister areas; soon after fledging of young, adults collect in flocks on higher tundra during first half of Jul, just prior to migration; juveniles flock from mid-Aug. Hatching success c. 80% in Alaska.
Movements. Migratory, with elliptical migration pattern. Adults leave breeding grounds from early Aug, juveniles from mid-Aug; migrate across Canada to Hudson and James Bays, then SE, crossing W Atlantic to Lesser Antilles and N South America, and thence S, arriving in Argentina early Sept; regularly some birds S to region of Tierra del Fuego. May migrate without pause from James Bay to South America, if weather permits. During 19th century, may have followed route further E, as large numbers formerly used Nova Scotia as staging area. Return migration starts early Feb in Argentina, and follows route across interior South America, over Central America, across Gulf of Mexico and up Mississippi flyway; pauses on prairies of Texas in second half Mar, and on prairies of Canada in May, reoccupying Canadian breeding grounds late May to mid-Jun.
Status and Conservation. Not globally threatened. Total population 10,000-50,000 birds, apparently stable. Numbers dramatically reduced during 19th century, due to excessive hunting pressure in North and South America; exploitation similar to that of Eskimo Curlew (*Numenius borealis*), as both served as alternative game birds after Passenger Pigeon (*Ectopistes migratorius*) had been persecuted to extinction in second half of 19th century; records of 48,000 birds killed on single day; protection measures resulted in increasing numbers at beginning of 20th century. During 1980's numbers declined by 34-69% at one small staging site in NC Texas; might reflect population decline caused by degeneration of Cheyenne Bottoms staging site.
Bibliography. Alström (1990), Armstrong (1983), Baker, M.C. (1977), Beaman (1994), Belton (1984), Bent (1927-1929), Biaggi (1983), Blake (1977), Boland (1991), Byrkjedal (1987b, 1989c, 1989d, 1991), Canevari *et al.* (1991), Catley & Hume (1994), Connors (1983), Connors *et al.* (1993), Contreras *et al.* (1990), Cramp & Simmons (1983), Doughty & Carter (1977), Drury (1961), Dunn *et al.* (1987), Erickson (1991), Evanich (1989), Fjeldså & Krabbe (1990), Glutz von Blotzheim *et al.* (1977), Golley & Stoddart (1991), Hall (1992), Haverschmidt (1968), Haverschmidt & Mees (1995), Hilty & Brown (1986), Hirschfeld (1995), Howell & Webb (1995a), Johnson, A.W. (1965b), Johnson, O.W. (1985), Johnson, O.W. & Connors (1996), Johnson, S.R. & Herter (1989), Mayr & Short (1970), McClure & McClure (1983), Meyer de Schauensee & Phelps (1978), Myers (1980c), Myers & Myers (1979), Parmelee *et al.* (1967), Paulson & Lee (1992), de la Peña (1992), Pym (1982), Roselaar (1990), Sauer (1963), Scott & Carbonell (1986), Sick (1985c, 1993), Slud (1964), Snyder (1966), Stotz *et al.* (1992), Tostain *et al.* (1992), Wetmore (1965).

29. Grey Plover
Pluvialis squatarola

French: Pluvier argenté   **German**: Kiebitzregenpfeifer   **Spanish**: Chorlito Gris
Other common names: Black-bellied/Silver Plover

Taxonomy. *Tringa Squatarola* Linnaeus, 1758, Sweden.
Sometimes placed in monospecific genus *Squatarola*. Monotypic.
Distribution. Arctic Russia, from Kanin Peninsula to Chukotskiy Peninsula and Anadyrskaya; Alaska E to Melville Peninsula and Baffin I. Winters on coasts of North and South America, W Europe, Africa, S Asia, Indonesia and Australia.
Descriptive notes. 27-31 cm; 174-320 g; wingspan 71-83 cm. Sparkling silver upperparts with contrasting black underparts; black axillaries conspicuous in flight. Larger, chunkier and much greyer than congeners. Female has browner underparts than male, with pale flecking. Non-breeding adult lacks black of underparts; duller brownish grey above, dirty white below. Juvenile like non-breeding adult, but upperparts darker with pale yellow spots; faint streaking on breast and flanks.
Habitat. In Taymyr breeds from polar deserts to forest tundra, but commonest in Arctic tundra subzone. Typically found on dry hilly sites spotted with stony *Dryas* tundra; or on tundra with sedges, moss and lichens in both upland locations and river valleys. In non-breeding season, on intertidal mudflats and beaches; during migration, also frequents inland lakes and pools and more rarely grassland. Wintering birds roost in large flocks, of up to several thousand, in salt-marshes and on sandbanks and beaches.

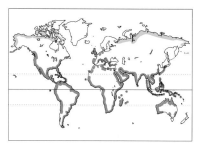

Food and Feeding. On tundra, mainly insects and their larvae, such as beetles and Diptera, and other invertebrates; occasionally some grass seeds and stems. In winter, takes marine polychaete worms, molluscs, crustaceans; occasional insects, such as grasshoppers and beetles, and earthworms; primarily feeds on intertidal flats at low tide. During foraging, sometimes exposes prey by making a sideways flick combined with a peck, sending a piece of mud in the air. Sometimes feeds at night. Most frequently alone or in small parties of up to 30 birds. In winter quarters, some birds defend feeding territories, to which they return yearly; similar pattern during spring migration.
Breeding. Laying late May to first half Jun. Monogamous, often for several years. Solitary, with nests not less than 400 m apart; breeds in densities of 0·3-3·6 birds/km²; shows high degree of site fidelity, sometimes nesting 30-100 m from previous year's nest-site. Nest is shallow scrape, lined with small stones, moss and lichens. Usually 4 eggs, sometimes 3, laid at intervals of 36-72 hours; incubation 26-27 days, by both sexes, sometimes perhaps starting before clutch is completed; single brood, replacement clutch laid only if first fails very early on; chick variegated sulphur yellow and black above, white below, with white collar and white cheeks bordered below by black stripe; chick tended in wet areas by both parents for 2-3 weeks, after which female usually leaves; fledging c. 23 days; young independent just before or just after fledging. Age of first breeding 2-3 years. In Alaska c. 80% of eggs hatch and in Canada 67%, producing 2·7 young per pair. Oldest ringed bird 20 years, 4 months.
Movements. Migratory. Departs from breeding grounds Jul-Sept; juveniles leave 5-6 weeks after adults; southward movements take place into Nov, and possibly later. Return migration starts Apr, and most N wintering birds do not leave until early Jun; first departures from South Africa in Feb. Returns to tundra late May to early Jun. Part of Russian population flies W, down W Palearctic coasts to W Africa; other birds migrate S along E Mediterranean flyway to E & S Africa, and to S Asia and Australia; regular migrant through Korea, Japan and NE China; birds in E Atlantic flyway come from all of Russia, but possibly also from E Canadian Arctic; birds depart from Taymyr in W & S directions. Nearctic population mainly winters on coasts of North and South America; flies N in broad front across S North America, up Atlantic and Pacific coasts and Mississippi Valley; on southward journey, route further E. In Old World, females winter further S than males; juveniles and other non-breeders stay in winter quarters or migrate part way N in their first summer. In autumn, usually migrates during morning and evening.
Status and Conservation. Not globally threatened. E Atlantic flyway population c. 170,000 individuals (1989), of which c. 103,000 birds winter in W Europe, 20,000 in Gulf of Gabès in Tunisia, 39,000 in Guinea-Bissau, and 14,500 in S Africa; 50,000 winter in E Africa and SW Asia, including 17,000-21,000 in Tanzania; c. 30,000 in SC Asia; probably 25,000-100,000 in E & SE Asia and Australia, including 12,000 in latter. Probably over 50,000 birds breed in North America, of which 27,500 winter in South America. Since 1930's, wintering population in British estuaries has increased, even by factor of 6 in period 1970-1992, to 47,600 birds in 1992; numbers in Wadden Sea increased too, indicating overall increase in wintering population of W Palearctic. Decline in numbers of 80-100% at small staging site in NC Texas during 1980's might indicate population decline, possibly caused by degeneration of Cheyenne Bottoms staging area; monitoring of numbers of staging birds on Atlantic coast in 1980's did not reveal decline, although the trend was real; it now seems clear that this population is decreasing. Almost entire W Palearctic population stages in Wadden Sea in late May, and probably during southward migration too, with maximum count of 140,000 birds.
Bibliography. Ali & Ripley (1980), Altenburg *et al.* (1982), Antas (1988), Baker, M.C. (1974), Bent (1927-1929), Blake (1977), Branson & Minton (1976), Brazil (1991), Burger *et al.* (1979), Chylarecki & Sikora (1990), Coates (1985), Cramp & Simmons (1983), Dierschke (1987), van Dijk, van Dijk *et al.* (1986), van Dijk, de Roder *et al.* (1990), Dowsett (1980), Dowsett & Forbes-Watson (1993), Dugan (1982), Dugan *et al.* (1981), Durell & Kelly (1990), Evans & Keijl (1993b), Fjeldså & Krabbe (1990), Flint & Kondratiev (1977), Glutz von Blotzheim *et al.* (1975), Goodman *et al.* (1989), Hewish (1987), Hilty & Brown (1986), Howe *et al.* (1989), Howell & Webb (1995a), Hussell & Page (1976), Johnson (1965b), Kalejta (1992, 1993), Kalejta & Hockey (1994), Kaufman (1995), Kersten & Piersma (1984), Langrand (1990), Maisonneuve *et al.* (1990), Marchant & Higgins (1993), van Marle & Voous (1988), Mayfield (1973), McCollough (1981), Meltofte *et al.* (1994), Michaud & Ferron (1986, 1990), Morrison *et al.* (1994), Moser (1988), Patrikeev (1995), Paulson (1990, 1995), Paulson & Erckmann (1985), Perennou *et al.* (1994), Pienkowski (1982), Piersma & Zegers (1983), Piersma, Klaassen *et al.* (1990), Prokosch (1988), Prys-Jones *et al.* (1994), Robert *et al.* (1989), Roberts, T.J. (1991), Rojas *et al.* (1993), Shirihai (1996), Sick (1993), Slud (1964), Smythies (1986), Stinson (1977), Summers & Waltner (1979), Townshend (1982, 1984, 1985), Townshend *et al.* (1984), Tubbs (1991), Turpie (1995), Turpie & Hockey (1993), Underhill *et al.* (1993), Urban *et al.* (1986), Wetmore (1965), Wong & Anderson (1990), Wood (1986), Wymenga *et al.* (1990), Zwarts (1988).

Genus *CHARADRIUS* Linnaeus, 1758

30. Red-breasted Plover
Charadrius obscurus

French: Pluvier roux   **German**: Maoriregenpfeifer   **Spanish**: Chorlito Maorí
Other common names: New Zealand/Red-breasted Dotterel

Taxonomy. *Charadrius obscurus* Gmelin, 1789, Dusky Sound, South Island, New Zealand.
Occasionally placed in *Pluvialis* or awarded monospecific genus *Pluviorhynchus*. Has alternatively been linked with *C. bicinctus*. Recently divided in two races, based on differences in morphometrics, plumage, ecology and behaviour. Two subspecies recognized.
Subspecies and Distribution.
C. o. aquilonius Dowding, 1994 - North I, New Zealand.
C. o. obscurus Gmelin, 1789 - Stewart I, New Zealand.
Descriptive notes. 26-28 cm; 128-179 g; wingspan 46-50 cm. Extent of reddish chestnut coloration on underparts very variable; bill often appears uptilted at tip. Sexes alike, male sometimes brighter. Non-breeding adult smudged grey-brown with white chin, throat and underparts, and whitish fringes to feathers of upperparts. Juvenile has darker upperparts, underparts washed pale orange-buff and dark marks on sides of breast. Races differ somewhat in plumage and size, male of nominate race usually dark brown above, rich chestnut below, whereas *aquilonius* tends to be paler and smaller.

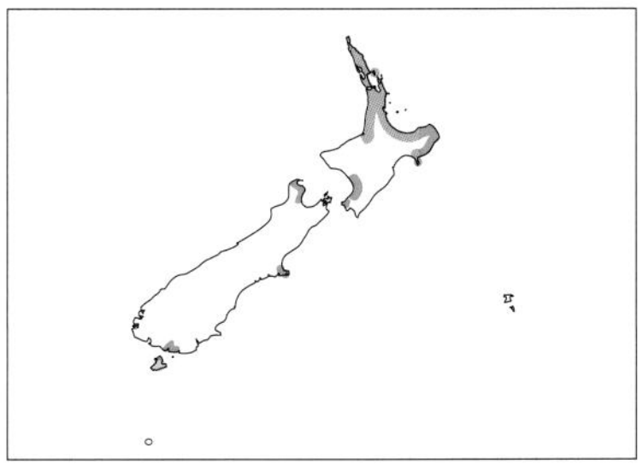

Habitat. Race *aquilonius* inhabits sandy beaches, sandbanks, shell banks, dunes; occasionally, stony beaches and short-grass pastures. Nominate breeds inland, on exposed hill tops above 300 m; winters coastally, in flocks of 20-60 birds, on sandy beaches and tidal mudflats. Formerly occurred on mountain slopes, foothills and plains of E South I.

Food and Feeding. Molluscs, insects, amphipods, crabs and fish, e.g. 1-2 cm flounder; nominate race also takes earthworms. Feeds in typical plover style; occasionally uses stand-wait-peck, sewing-machine technique and foot-trembling. Feeds by night and day.

Breeding. Laying late Aug to early Jan, usually late Aug to Sept, on North I; probably 1 month later on Stewart I. Monogamous on long-term basis, with pair-bond held year round. Solitary, occasionally in groups of 2-10 pairs; 0·6-10 pairs/ha or less, on North I; territorial, showing high degree of site fidelity. Nest (nominate race) in depression among cushion-plants or rocks, lined with leaves; nest of *aquilonius* is shallow depression in sand, unlined or lined with few shells or small pieces of seaweed. Usually 3 eggs, sometimes 2, laid over c. 7 days; single brood, but up to 3 replacement clutches may be laid; incubation by both parents 28-32 days, starting 1-2 days after completion of clutch; males probably incubate at night; chick buffy white, speckled and blotched black, brown and yellowish above, white on face and underparts; tended by both parents; fledging 28-52 days; young independent soon, or remain with parents for weeks or even months. Fledging success 0·1-0·6 per pair. Nests may be flooded or trampled by cattle, and eggs and young may be taken by (introduced) mammalian predators. First breeding in second year. Several birds reach 14-19 years old; oldest bird recorded 41 years, 1 month.

Movements. Sedentary in places, short distance migrant elsewhere. Race *aquilonius* essentially sedentary, moving only short distance between breeding territory and post-breeding flocking site, showing high degree of site fidelity in latter. Nominate race leaves inland breeding areas for coast; juveniles often dispersive, some wintering on S coast of South I; regularly recorded elsewhere in small numbers, e.g. NW South I. Post-breeding flocks form Jan-Feb; *aquilonius* returns to territory Apr-May, nominate Aug; some birds of race *aquilonius* do not leave territory.

Status and Conservation. ENDANGERED. Until 19th century, widespread in all of New Zealand, but has declined considerably in range and numbers during past 150 years. Two well separated breeding populations now remain: c. 1400 birds on North I, and c. 65 on Stewart I; based on old accounts of breeding habitat, a division between the two populations may already have existed for a long time, and was possibly situated in C North I. Annual adult mortality nearly three times higher on Stewart I than on North I. Only few males present in nominate population, where effective population size may be as low as 12 pairs, and therefore in serious danger of extinction. North I population threatened by developments of coastal regions and deterioration of habitat due to introduced weeds. Further threats come from introduced predators, i.e. cats and rats on Stewart I, cats, rats, stoats, possums and hedgehogs on North I.

Bibliography. Barlow (1993), Chambers (1989), Collar *et al*. (1994), Dowding (1989, 1993, 1994), Dowding & Chamberlin (1991), Dowding & Murphy (1993a), Edgar (1969), Falla *et al*. (1981), Foreman (1991), Gaza (1994), Graeme (1989), Habraken (1980), Heather (1980), Latham (1979), Latham & Parrish (1987), Marchant & Higgins (1993), McKenzie, H.R. (1978), McKenzie, M.E. *et al*. (1977), Phillips (1980), Powers (1971), Reed (1981), Robertson (1985), Searle (1984), Sibson (1967, 1982), Soper (1976), Williams (1975).

31. Common Ringed Plover
Charadrius hiaticula

French: Pluvier grand-gravelot **German**: Sandregenpfeifer **Spanish**: Chorlitejo Grande
Other common names: (Greater) Ringed Plover

Taxonomy. *Charadrius Hiaticula* Linnaeus, 1758, Sweden.
Probably forms superspecies with *C. semipalmatus*, with which sometimes considered conspecific; some hybridization on Baffin I. Distinction between subspecies based on moult; features changing clinally N-S, rather than E-W, make it impossible to draw dividing line in NW Europe. Populations from Canada to Faeroes formerly awarded race *psammodroma*, but based on extremely minor differences in average size, and not nowadays accepted. Two subspecies recognized.

Subspecies and Distribution.
C. h. hiaticula Linnaeus, 1758 - NE Canada through Greenland and Iceland to S Scandinavia, and S to NW France; winters from British Is S to Africa.
C. h. tundrae (Lowe, 1915) - N Scandinavia and N Russia; winters from Caspian Sea and SW Asia S to S Africa.

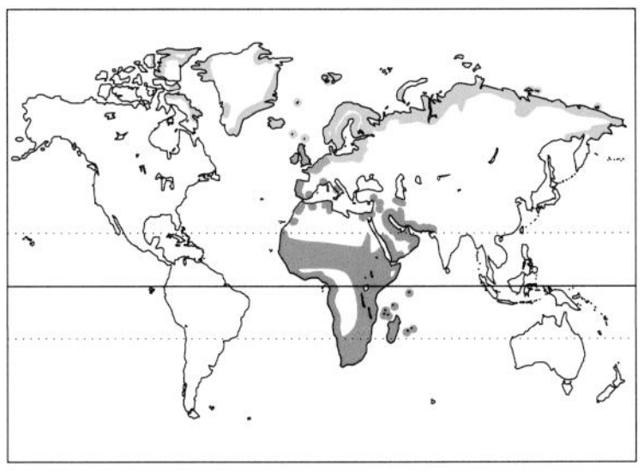

Descriptive notes. 18-20 cm; 42-78 g; wingspan 48-57 cm. More robust plover than *C. dubius*; very similar to *C. semipalmatus*, but lacks basal web between middle and inner toes, and has slightly broader breast band, larger white supercilium and clearer yellow eye-ring. Female has breast band and ear-coverts tinged brown on sides. Distinct non-breeding plumage absent in nominate race. Juvenile resembles pale adult with buffy fringes, but these soon lost; no black; narrow or broken frontal part of breast band. Race *tundrae* smaller, with darker, duller upperparts, often narrower white patch behind eye, and orange on bill often less extensive; in non-breeding plumage, black replaced by olive brown, bill duller.

Habitat. Along coast on sand or shingle beaches, sandbanks and mudflats, estuaries and, occasionally, rivers, lakes, lagoons, salt-marshes, short grassland, flooded fields and some artificial habitats, e.g. gravel pits, reservoirs, farmland and playing fields; also occurs on tundra. Prefers moist substrates, but rarely in shallow water; generally, at least during migration, race *tundrae* occurs on softer sediments than *hiaticula*. Roosts communally, close to feeding area, on exposed, bare ground, or that with short vegetation; usually on coast, above high water mark.

Food and Feeding. Small crustaceans, molluscs, polychaete worms, isopods, amphipods, various insects (e.g. ants, beetles, flies and their larvae) and millipedes. Sometimes uses foot-trembling. Typically in small flocks of up to 50, rarely 1200-1500 birds. Forages by day and night, often on tidal flats. In Morocco, Mar-Apr, may defend small feeding territories, overlapping with those of *Pluvialis squatarola*, on intertidal flats rich in ragworms (*Nereis diversicolor*).

Breeding. Laying Apr around North Sea, Jun to mid-Jul in Iceland, Jun in N Eurasia. Seasonally monogamous; pair-bond occasionally maintained over successive years. Solitary or in loose neighbourhood groups, with nests 5-100 m apart; in NE Greenland average 5-7 pairs/km² (maximum 16); densities in Taymyr 0·5-8 birds/km of shoreline, occasionally 50-80 birds/km², comparable to German Wadden Sea; high degree of site fidelity (90%) and natal philopatry (57%); often breeds in association with larger Charadriiformes species for protection; territorial, usually feeding outside territory; some birds pair up in special preliminary pairing territory. Participation of third bird in incubation and chick-rearing reported. Nest is shallow scrape, lined with pebbles, debris and pieces of vegetation. 3-4 eggs, usually 4, laid at intervals of 1-3 days; replacement clutch laid after loss; 2-3 broods, but only 1 in N of range; incubation 21-27 days, by both parents, starting with last or penultimate egg; chick pale buffy grey finely mottled with dusky and some cinnamon-buff above, white underparts, with blackish bordering band; fledging c. 24 days; young independent soon after. Hatching success 36%; fledging success 15%, but 65% of survivors may die in 1st year. In Britain 60-87% of clutches failed completely, due to predation, flooding and desertion. Age of first breeding 1 year. Annual mortality 18-42% and 61% in first-year birds; average longevity after 1st year 5·2 years; oldest ringed bird over 10 years.

Movements. Migratory. Northernmost birds migrate furthest S, while southernmost breeders are also northernmost winterers; some W European birds may remain close to their breeding grounds. Mainly winters in Africa, but also in Mediterranean Basin, Iberian Peninsula, Red Sea and Persian Gulf. Small numbers migrate through, or possibly winter in, China and Japan. Nearctic breeders all migrate across N Atlantic, in a single flight or via Greenland and Iceland, probably to winter in W Africa. Race *tundrae* migrates via Europe, but also crosses Eurasian and African landmasses in broad front, towards E & S Africa; possibly crosses Sahara. In Egypt arrives early Sept and departs late May, in South Africa Sept-Oct and Apr, in Morocco Aug-Nov and Apr-Jun. Returns to breeding grounds late Mar to May; Nearctic and N Eurasian populations arrive late May to mid-Jun. High degree of site fidelity during migration and wintering.

Status and Conservation. Not globally threatened. Population wintering in NW Africa and Europe c. 47,500 birds, of which 23,000 in Britain; in W & S Africa c. 195,000 birds, of which up to 30,000 in Guinea-Bissau, and possibly up to 30,000-50,000 more in Guinea; in E Africa and Asia at least 200,000 birds. Breeding population of race *hiaticula* 55,000-76,000 pairs in Arctic and subarctic W Europe, 12,500-13,800 in temperate W Europe (1986) and c. 25,000 pairs in Greenland and Ellesmere I (1985); race *tundrae* c. 36,500 pairs in Fenno-Scandia (1986). Numbers can fluctuate markedly: marked increase in Wadden Sea area during 1930-1950, but decreasing numbers since 1940 in other areas; apparently some decrease recently in Finland and E Germany, and some increase in W Germany, Britain and perhaps France and Netherlands. Decrease in Britain mainly due to disturbance. Number of inland breeders has decreased in Poland since 19th century, but has increased recently in Britain. Wintering numbers in W Europe have increased since 1970's.

Bibliography. Ali & Ripley (1980), Bateson & Barth (1957), Beaman (1994), Benson (1960), Benson & Benson (1975), Brazil (1991), Bregnballe *et al*. (1990), Briggs (1983), Broekhuysen & Stanford (1955), Bub (1962), Chandler (1987a), Clancey (1982a), Cramp & Simmons (1983), Dementiev & Gladkov (1951b), Dowsett & Forbes-Watson (1993), Dubois & Maheo (1986), Dunn (1993), Elgood *et al*. (1994), Étchécopar & Hüe (1964), Evans (1994), Figuerola & Martí (1994), Fjeldså (1977), Flint *et al*. (1984), van Gasteren (1984), Ginn *et al*. (1989), Glutz von Blotzheim (1972), Goodman *et al*. (1989), Grimes (1987), Hanssen (1980), Harz & Luge (1990), Henriksen (1991a), Herrmann & Holz (1988), Holz (1987a, 1987b), Hüe & Étchécopar (1970), Jackson (1994), Klaassen *et al*. (1990), Knystautas (1993), Kummer (1990), Langrand (1990), Lifjeld (1984), Mackworth-Praed & Grant (1957, 1962, 1970), Maclean (1993), Marchant, J.H. *et al*. (1990), Marchant, S. & Higgins (1993), Mayr & Short (1970), Meltofte *et al*. (1994), Moksnes (1987, 1988), Moser & Carrier (1983), Osborne, B.C. (1982), Pareigis (1989), Patrikeev (1995), Paz (1987), Perennou *et al*. (1994), Pienkowski (1982, 1983b, 1983e, 1984a, 1984b), Pienkowski & Pienkowski (1989), Piersma (1986b), Piersma, Klaassen *et al*. (1990), Pinto (1983), Prater (1974), Radford (1985), Riddiford (1983), Roberts, T.J. (1991), Rogacheva (1992), Schonert (1990), Schütz (1991), Shirihai (1996), Short *et al*. (1990), Siefke (1982, 1983), Smit & Piersma (1989), Smythies (1986), Taylor, R.C. (1974, 1978, 1980), Urban *et al*. (1986), Väisänen (1969, 1977), Volsøe (1950), Walters, J. (1984), Whitfield (1985), Wymenga *et al*. (1990), Zwarts *et al*. (1990).

32. Semipalmated Plover
Charadrius semipalmatus

French: Pluvier semipalmé **Spanish**: Chorlitejo Semipalmeado
German: Amerikanischer Sandregenpfeifer
Other common names: Semipalmated Ringed Plover

Taxonomy. *Charadrius semipalmatus* Bonaparte, 1825, coast of New Jersey.
Probably forms superspecies with *C. hiaticula*, with which sometimes considered conspecific; some hybridization on Baffin I. Monotypic.

Distribution. Alaska and N Canada, S to C British Columbia and S Nova Scotia. Winters on coasts of North and South America, from California to Chile, and from South Carolina to Patagonia; also Bermuda, West Indies, Galapagos.

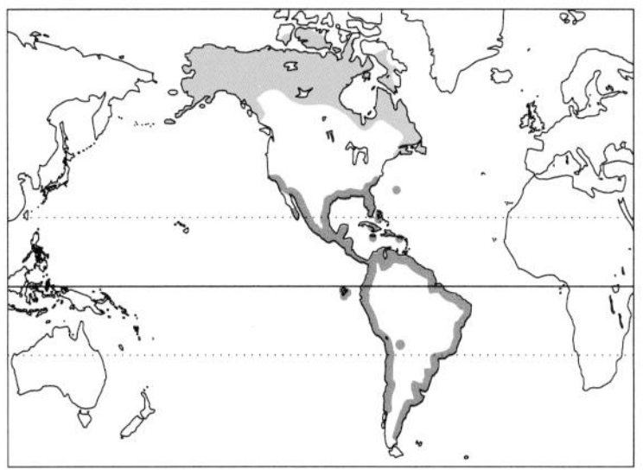

Descriptive notes. 17-19 cm; 28-69 g; wingspan 43-52 cm. Closely resembles *C. hiaticula*, but slightly smaller and less robust, with narrower breast band and smaller white supercillium; more extensive basal webbing between toes; black bands over forehead and bill until just behind eye. Female has brownish tinge to the black markings. Non-breeding adult paler, with black replaced by brown; bill blacker, breast band sometimes broken in centre. Juvenile like pale non-breeding adult; feathers of upperparts with buff fringes; breast band smaller, sometimes rather obscure; legs duller yellow-brownish.

Habitat. Freshwater and salt mudflat, intertidal mudflats and beaches, flat open margins of ponds, lakes and rivers, sparsely vegetated low gravel ridges, gravelly plains and dunes.

Food and Feeding. Primarily polychaete worms; also small gastropods, inarticulata, small crustaceans and insects, such as grasshoppers, beetles and ants. Frequently forages by foot-trembling. Feeds by sight; diurnal and nocturnal, and dependent on low water period during tidal cycle. Can be territorial during feeding.

Breeding. Laying early to late Jun. Solitary or in loose colonies. Density 0·4-1·3 pairs/ha. Nest is shallow depression in sparsely vegetated, sandy or gravelly area, lined with some debris. Clutch 3-4 eggs, completed within a week; incubation 24-25 days, by both parents, starting after laying of last or penultimate egg; chick similar to that of *C. hiaticula*; fledging 22-31 days; both parents tend young. Hatching success 29-100%, apparently higher at coast than inland.

Movements. Migratory. Winters on coasts of South and North America and all larger islands in the general zone; many birds remain in winter quarters during breeding season. Migrates mainly along coast, but also across interior Canada; breeding birds of C Arctic migrate N via interior USA, but S along coast; species probably crosses part of W Atlantic in autumn, but follows Atlantic coast in spring when 70% of population visits Delaware Bay to feed on eggs laid by horseshoe crabs (*Limulus polyphemus*). Departs from breeding grounds in Canada from early Jul; adults leave before juveniles; arrives in South America Sept to early Nov. Spring return starts Mar, reaching S of breeding range in late May, and N in early Jun. Many adults follow same migration route every year, at roughly same dates.

Status and Conservation. Not globally threatened. Total population probably numbers c. 50,000 birds, and seems stable; no threats identified. Approximately 84% of South American wintering population occurs in Surinam and French Guiana.

Bibliography. Armstrong, A.P. & Nol (1993), Armstrong, R.H. (1983), Baker, M.C. (1977), Baker, M.C. & Baker (1973), Beaman (1994), Bent (1927-1929), Biaggi (1983), Blake (1977), Bock (1959), Boland (1991), Burger *et al.* (1979), Canevari *et al.* (1991), Chandler (1987a), Cramp & Simmons (1983), Dunn (1993), Fjeldså & Krabbe (1990), Hallett *et al.* (1995), Haverschmidt (1968), Haverschmidt & Mees (1995), Hilty & Brown (1986), Howe *et al.* (1989), Howell & Webb (1995a), Ivey & Baars (1990), Ivey *et al.* (1988), Johnson (1965b), Loftin (1962), Mayr & Short (1970), McCollough (1981), Meyer de Schauensee & Phelps (1978), Michaud & Ferron (1986, 1990), Monroe (1968), Morrier & McNeil (1991), Napolitano *et al.* (1992), Peach (1981), de la Peña (1992), Ridgely & Gwynne (1989), Robert & McNeil (1989), Root (1988), Scott & Carbonell (1986), Sick (1985c, 1993), Slud (1964), Smith, N.G. (1969), Smith, P.W. & Houghton (1984), Snyder (1966), Stiles & Skutch (1989), Strauch & Abele (1979), Sutton & Parmelee (1955), Tostain *et al.* (1992), Wetmore (1965).

33. Long-billed Plover
Charadrius placidus

French: Pluvier à long bec **German**: Ussuriregenpfeifer **Spanish**: Chorlitejo Piquilargo
Other common names: Long-billed Ringed Plover

Taxonomy. *Charadrius placidus* J. E. and G. R. Gray, 1863, Nepal.
Has on occasion been considered a race of *C. hiaticula*; sometimes included within the *C. hiaticula* superspecies. Monotypic.
Distribution. Russian Far East, EC to NE China and Japan. Winters from E Nepal and NE India to N Indochina, S China, S Korea and Japan.

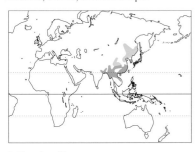

Descriptive notes. 19-21 cm; 41-70 g. Very similar to *C. hiaticula*, *C. semipalmatus* and *C. dubius*, but generally larger, with longer dark bill and longer tail; black breast band narrow; eyestripe brownish black. Sexes alike. Non-breeding adult has duller head and breast pattern, and brownish supercilium. Juvenile resembles non-breeding adult, but lacks blackish on forecrown; supercilium very pale; upperparts fringed with buff.
Habitat. Breeds in gravel, shingle or stony areas at edges of rivers and lakes. During non-breeding season, frequents shingle banks of large rivers and muddy areas, such as cut rice stubble fields and mudflats.

Food and Feeding. Very little information available. Diet apparently includes flies and beetles. Usually solitary feeder.
Breeding. Little known. Breeds from mid-Apr. Apparently lays 4 eggs. Nest is depression on sandy ground among pebbles and rocks on elevated riverbank.
Movements. Populations of Russia and China migratory, moving S to E Nepal, NE India, N Indochina, S China and S Korea. Japanese population appears to be mainly sedentary.
Status and Conservation. Not globally threatened. Currently considered near-threatened. Total continental wintering population probably numbers less than 10,000 birds; nowhere seen in large numbers; altogether, only a few records from Bangladesh, Myanmar, Malaysia and China; this population appears to be declining. Size and trends of sedentary Japanese population unknown.
Bibliography. Ali & Ripley (1980), Austin (1948), Austin & Kuroda (1953), Beaman (1994), Brazil (1991), Deignan (1945), Dementiev & Gladkov (1951b), Eck (1976b), Étchécopar & Hüe (1978), Flint *et al.* (1984), Knystautas (1993), Kolomijtsev (1988), MacKinnon & Phillipps (1993), Meeth & Meeth (1989), Meyer de Schauensee (1984), Panov (1963), Perennou *et al.* (1994), Ripley (1982), Scott (1989), de Silva & Perera (1993), Smythies (1986), Taylor, R.C. (1979), Won (1993).

34. Little Ringed Plover
Charadrius dubius

French: Pluvier petit-gravelot **German**: Flußregenpfeifer **Spanish**: Chorlitejo Chico

Taxonomy. *Charadrius dubius* Scopoli, 1786, Luzon.
In past, birds of S Japan and China erroneously attributed to nominate race, and those of New Guinea region erroneously placed in *jerdoni*. Three subspecies recognized.
Subspecies and Distribution
C. d. curonicus Gmelin, 1789 - Eurasia, from British Is, N Africa and Canary Is to Russian Far East, Korea, E China and Japan; winters in Africa S of Sahara, Arabia, E China and Indonesia.
C. d. jerdoni (Legge, 1880) - India and SE Asia.
C. d. dubius Scopoli, 1786 - Philippines S to New Guinea and Bismarck Archipelago.
Descriptive notes. 14-17 cm; 26-53 g; wingspan 42-48 cm. Eye-ring bright yellow. Smaller and less bulky than *C. hiaticula*, *C. semipalmatus* and *C. placidus*; also differs in having narrow white line behind black frontal bar, and in general shape of head pattern. Female has brown tinge to black parts and slightly narrower eye-ring. Non-breeding plumage of nominate race hardly differs from breeding plumage. Juvenile resembles non-breeding adult but olive brown upperparts have buff fringes. Races differ in size and bill coloration; in *curonicus*, non-breeding adult has reduced brownish breast band, and black on head brownish; *jerdoni*, like nominate, lacks markedly distinct non-breeding plumage.
Habitat. Mainly lowlands, up to 800 m; rarely coastal. On bare or sparsely vegetated flats of sand, shingle or silt; avoids rough terrain and tall or dense vegetation. Often in vicinity of standing or slow-flowing fresh water; sometimes saline inland pools and flats, or brackish lagoons and estuaries. Also found in artificial, often only temporarily suitable, habitats, such as gravel pits, sewage works and industrial wastelands. Habitat often unstable due to fast changing water level, growth of vegetation, etc.
Food and Feeding. Mainly insects, including beetles, flies, ants, mayfly and dragonfly larvae and crickets; spiders, shrimps and other invertebrates. Sometimes uses foot-trembling. Feeds on dry or moist surface, and occasionally in shallow water.
Breeding. Laying Apr-Jun in Europe, Mar-May in N Africa; breeding Dec-Jun, mainly Mar-May, in S India; nominate race breeds Feb-May. Monogamous for at least one brood, occasionally for several

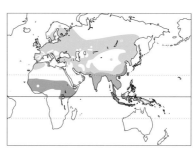

years; sometimes 3rd bird joins during breeding, but family relation of these "helpers" unknown. Solitary or in loose neighbourhood groups, 7-200 m apart; densities along R Yenisey 0·4-2 birds/km of shoreline. Low degree of natal philopatry, but high of site fidelity, usually breeding within few km of previous year's site. Territorial and highly aggressive, usually feeding outside territory; frequently breeds in vicinity of aggressive or demonstrative species, resulting in less egg loss due to predators; associations at least sometimes deliberately sought. Nest is shallow scrape, unlined or lined with some vegetation and stones, on bare ground or among low vegetation, in vicinity of water; often on small island. Usually 4 eggs, sometimes 3, laid at intervals of c. 36 hours; up to 3 replacement clutches laid; incubation 22-28 days, by both parents, beginning with last or penultimate egg; chick mottled cinnamon-orange, grey and dusky, with black band above whitish forehead, and underparts white with dark patches on sides of breast; chicks leave territory, tended by both parents, but female leaves family party before male in order to lay new clutch or to migrate; fledging 24-29 days; young independent 8-25 days thereafter. Hatching success 65-86%; fledging success 26-64%. Usually breeds for first time in second year. Annual mortality 35-55%, highest in first-year birds (53%). Oldest ringed bird 11 years.
Movements. Race *curonicus* migratory, but possibly resident in S breeding areas; W European population migrates across Sahara to tropics; leaves breeding areas Jun to early Jul, and migrates late Jul to early Sept, reaching tropical Africa late Aug to Sept; returns from late Feb, reaching NW Europe from mid-Mar, peaking Apr to early May, and a month later in NE; along R Yenisey, return migration peaks late May. Siberian and other Asian populations migrate to SE Asia and India, where they mix with resident *jerdoni*; cross Japan only on northward migration. Often migrates singly or in small flocks often of not more than 10 birds. Nominate race resident and locally nomadic in New Guinea; *jerdoni* resident, but moves about locally in response to water conditions. Race *curonicus* recently recorded regularly in small numbers in Australia.
Status and Conservation. Not globally threatened. Race *curonicus* in Europe and NW Africa numbers 100,000-1,000,000 birds, of which 17,000-28,000 breeding pairs in W & C Europe (1986); unknown numbers in rest of extensive range; races *jerdoni* and *dubius* number 25,000-100,000 birds each. Probably marked decrease from late 19th century in Europe, caused by habitat loss due to flood regulation; increasing numbers from 1930's in NW Europe, especially since late 1960's, linked to development of suitable man-made habitats like gravel and sand pits. Formerly common breeder on Mediterranean coast and along R Jordan, but pollution, especially from oil and tar, has had detrimental effects. In Russia, drainage and cultivation of riverine floodplains has created suitable new habitat; however, many such suitable sites are only temporary, because they will become overgrown or will be planted. Many breeding sites disturbed by recreational activities. Has recently expanded range N in Finland; first bred in Britain 1938 and has since spread: 608 pairs in 1984, and still increasing.
Bibliography. Albrecht (1992), Ali & Ripley (1980), Andrews, J. (1991), Baudraz & Guillaume (1993), Beehler *et al.* (1986), Beser (1977), Biondi *et al.* (1992), Brazil (1991), Chikina (1985), Christen (1980a), Coates (1985), Cramp & Simmons (1983), Deignan (1945), Dickinson *et al.* (1991), Dowsett & Forbes-Watson (1993), Dubois & Maheo (1986), Dvorsky & Dvorská (1980), Elgood *et al.* (1994), Étchécopar & Hüe (1964, 1978), Evans (1994), Finch (1983), Fjeldså (1977), Flint *et al.* (1984), Gatter (1971a, 1971b), Gavrilov & Bekbayev (1988), Glutz von Blotzheim (1972), Goodman *et al.* (1989), Grimes (1987), Grossler (1977), Hamann (1988), Hedenström (1985, 1987), Hölzinger (1975a, 1975b), Hölzinger & Schilhansl (1971, 1972), Hüe & Étchécopar (1970), Jacob & Fouarge (1992), Jaensch (1982), Khrokov (1973), Knystautas (1993), Krebs (1956), Kuhnapfel (1991), Lekagul & Round (1991), MacKinnon & Phillipps (1993), Mackworth-Praed & Grant (1957, 1970), Marchant & Higgins (1993), van Marle & Voous (1988), Medway & Wells (1976), Melde (1991), Osing (1992, 1993a), Parrinder, E.D. (1989), Parrinder, E.R. & Parrinder (1969, 1975), Patrikeev (1995), Paz (1987), Perennou *et al.* (1994), Phillips (1978), Rabor (1977), Raju (1978), Ranftl (1983), Ripley (1982), Roberts, T.J. (1991), Rogacheva (1992), Rodenko & Molodan (1990), Rutgers & Norris (1970), Schneider & Schneider (1970), Schönle (1983), Scott (1989), Shirihai (1996), Short *et al.* (1990), Simmons (1953a, 1953b, 1956), Smythies (1981, 1986), Truffi & Maranini (1989), Ulbricht (1979), Urban *et al.* (1986), Walters, J. (1984), Wang Haichang & Deng Minglu (1966), Werder & Gillieron (1978), White & Bruce (1986), Williams, M.D. (1986), Yurlov (1986).

35. Wilson's Plover
Charadrius wilsonia

French: Pluvier de Wilson **German**: Wilsonregenpfeifer **Spanish**: Chorlitejo Piquigrueso
Other common names: Thick-billed Plover

Taxonomy. *Charadrius wilsonia* Ord, 1814, shore of Cape May, New Jersey.
Birds breeding on Bahamas and Greater Antilles sometimes separated as fourth subspecies *rufinucha*. Three subspecies normally recognized.
Subspecies and Distribution.
C. w. wilsonia Ord, 1814 - E USA to E Mexico and Belize, Bahamas, Greater Antilles, and N Lesser Antilles; winters S to E Brazil.
C. w. beldingi (Ridgway, 1919) - Pacific coast from Baja California to Panama and Ecuador, ranging S to C Peru.
C. w. cinnamominus (Ridgway, 1919) - Colombia to French Guiana; also Netherlands Antilles, islands off Venezuela, Trinidad, Grenada and Mustique.

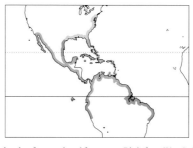

Descriptive notes. 16·5-20cm; c. 55 g. Distinctive plover with large, thick black bill. Female has black of breast band and forecrown replaced with brown. Non-breeding adult like breeding female, but lacks rufous tinges. Juvenile has breast band mottled buff and brown, sometimes broken; darker upperparts fringed buff. Races *beldingi* and *cinnamominus* darker above than nominate, with broader mask, shorter supercilium and more rufous on crown; in *beldingi*, male has black frontal bar, lores and breast band, female has breast band more rufous; in *cinnamominus*, male has crown, mask and breast band much more rufous, female has strongly rufous breast band, rufous mask and forecrown. Birds from West Indies like nominate, but with strongly rufous crown.
Habitat. Strictly coastal, occurring on barren or nearly barren sandy beaches and sandbars, preferring islands or edges of coastal lagoons. Outside breeding season, also on estuarine mudflats and near fresh water bodies that are only short distance inland.

Food and Feeding. Apparently mainly fiddler crabs, also blue crabs (*Callinectus*); insects and their larvae, e.g. Diptera; and isopods, amphipods, molluscs, shrimps and polychaete worms. Feeding action remarkably slow and deliberate; sometimes lunges at prey from up to 1 m away, and then runs to capture it. Feeds on intertidal flats and also on higher, drier part of beach. Feeds by day and by night, but in non-breeding season sometimes chiefly by night, probably to avoid predators. Usually feeds in small flocks or with other small plovers.
Breeding. Eggs found Apr to early Jul. Often nests in loose colonies, usually no nearer than 20 m apart, once at least 50 nests found on sandbank 800 m long. Breeds on open, unvegetated or sparsely vegetated sand; nest is shallow scrape, unlined or lined with shells, exposed or sheltered among open vegetation. Site fidelity 19-50% in males, much less in females and very low degree of natal philopatry. Usually 3 eggs (2-4), laid at intervals of 2 or more days; incubation 24-25 days, by both sexes, female performing larger share; chick creamy buff, mottled with black above and white below, with white bar on outer joint of wing; tended by both parents; fledging 21 days. In one study, less than 20% of nests raised at least 1 young. Nest failure caused by high tides and raccoons (*Procyon lotor*).
Movements. Partial migrant, with partially overlapping breeding and winter range. Nominate race migrates S to Brazil; Florida population sedentary. Some birds of race *beldingi* migrate S to C Peru; large numbers arrive alongside local breeders on beaches of Bay of Panama late Sept to mid-Oct, leaving during late Mar. Returns to breeding grounds mid-Mar to late Apr. Race *cinnamominus* essentially sedentary.
Status and Conservation. Not globally threatened. No population estimates available. Population of race *cinnamominus* seems to be stable. Locally common to fairly common in USA, Mexico, Panama and Colombia; very scarce and local breeder in French Guiana. In Panama, commoner on Pacific coast, where breeds locally; not yet known to breed on Caribbean coast, but may do so. Known to have bred S to Huacho, C Peru.
Bibliography. Bent (1927-1929), Bergstrom (1981, 1982, 1986, 1988a, 1988b, 1989), Bergstrom & Terwilliger (1987), Biaggi (1983), Blake (1977), Boland (1991), Dinsmore & Humphrey (1987), Duncan (1973), Eckert (1981), Fisk (1978a), Galindo (1987), Haverschmidt (1968), Haverschmidt & Mees (1995), Hellmayr & Conover (1948), Hilty & Brown (1986), Howell & Webb (1995a), Lee (1989), McMahon (1982), Meyer de Schauensee & Phelps (1978), Monroe (1968), Morrier & McNeil (1991), Ridgely & Gwynne (1989), Robert & McNeil (1989), Rodrigues & Lopes (1992), Root (1988), Scott & Carbonell (1986), Sick (1985c, 1993), Slud (1964), Snyder (1966), Stiles & Skutch (1989), Strauch & Abele (1979), Thibault & McNeil (1994, 1995a, 1995b), Tompkins (1944), Tostain *et al.* (1992), Wetmore (1965).

36. Killdeer
Charadrius vociferus

French: Pluvier kildir **German**: Keilschwanz-Regenpfeifer **Spanish**: Chorlitejo Culirrojo

Taxonomy. *Charadrius vociferus* Linnaeus, 1758, South Carolina.
Subspecies and Distribution.
C. v. vociferus Linnaeus, 1758 - Canada, USA and Mexico; winters S to NW South America.
C. v. ternominatus Bangs & Kennard, 1920 - Greater Antilles.
C. v. peruvianus (Chapman, 1920) - Peru and NW Chile.

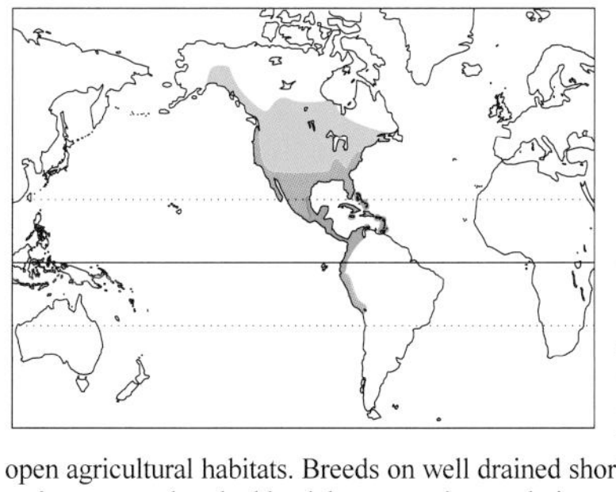

Descriptive notes. 23-26 cm; 72-93 g; wingspan 59-63 cm. Distinctive large plover with double blackish breast band and long tail; bright orange-brown rump and uppertail; brown upperparts with rufous fringes. Characteristic call "kill-dee" reflected in vernacular name. Female tends to have browner mask and breast bands. Non-breeding adult has rufous and buffish brown fringes to upperparts. Juvenile like dull non-breeding adult. Race *ternominatus* smaller, paler and greyer; *peruvianus* also smaller than nominate, and has more extensive rufous feather fringes.
Habitat. Open fields and flats with short vegetation, not necessarily near water. Exploits many open agricultural habitats. Breeds on well drained short-grass or sparsely vegetated savannas, meadows and pastures, ploughed land, bare gravel, gravel pits, golf courses, roadside ditches and wasteland; occasionally on gravelled roofs. After young fledge, birds move to moister areas in valleys, and on edges of rivers. In winter also found on beaches, mudflats, wet grassland and, rarely, salt-marshes.
Food and Feeding. Insects, mainly beetles and flies, also grasshoppers, crickets, caterpillars, dragonflies, etc.; millipedes, worms, snails, spiders, crustaceans and some seeds. Sometimes uses foot-trembling. Active day and night. Does not occur in big flocks.
Breeding. Eggs found Mar to early Jun in S, and mid-Apr to mid-Jul in N. Seasonally monogamous. Density 1-30 pairs/km²; territorial. Males show high degree of site fidelity, females less; very little natal philopatry. Nest is shallow scrape, unlined or lined with vegetation, stones and debris; in exposed, bare or sparsely vegetated site, often with gravelly or stony ground. Usually 4 eggs (3-5), laid at intervals of 24-48 hours; up to 3 replacement clutches laid; occasionally double-brooded; incubation 24-28 days, by both parents, starting with last egg; chick buffish and dusky above, white below and on forehead, neck and chin, with long downy tail; tended by both parents; fledging 31 days; fledged young sometimes stay with parents for up to 10 days. Total of 52-63% of nests fail; fledging success 27%. Breeds from 1 year old. Oldest ringed bird at least 6½ years.
Movements. Races *ternominatus* and *peruvianus* believed to be resident. Nominate migratory: winters from S of breeding range S to Central America, West Indies, Colombia, Ecuador and islands off Venezuela; departs breeding grounds from mid-Jul and gathers in flocks in wet valleys, along rivers and on coast; migration from late Aug to Nov, with peak in late Sept; flies along coast, but also in broad front over land; reaches S USA in Oct, some remaining till late Mar; returns to N & NE USA by Mar to early Apr. Late autumn storms may carry vagrants up Atlantic coast; possible cause of W European vagrants turning up Nov-Apr. Migrates at night.
Status and Conservation. Not globally threatened. No population estimates available; North American breeding population stable; this population was dramatically reduced, to local extinction, during second half of 19th century, especially in E of breeding range, due to excessive hunting; after protection measures taken, it partially reoccupied former breeding grounds in NE USA, in period 1910-1920. During second half of 20th century, has expanded range S in Florida, and NE towards Newfoundland. Quite tolerant of frequent disturbance during breeding. Common to fairly common in Mexico.
Bibliography. Anderson, E. (1993), Ankney & Hopkins (1985), Armstrong (1983), Baldassarre & Fischer (1984), Bent (1927-1929), Bergstrom (1989), Biaggi (1983), Blake (1977), Boland (1991), Brunton (1986, 1987, 1988a, 1988b, 1988c, 1990), Bunni (1959), Colwell & Oring (1989b), Costas (1990), Cramp & Simmons (1983), Cronan (1974), Culbert (1991), Demaree (1975), Fjeldså & Krabbe (1990), Furniss (1933), Hamas (1988), Hellmayr & Conover (1948), Hilty & Brown (1986), Howell & Webb (1995a), Johnson (1965b), Kull (1978), Lenington (1980), Lenington & Mace (1975), Mace (1978), Magyar (1988), Meyer de Schauensee & Phelps (1978), Monroe (1968), Mundahl (1982), Nickell (1943), Nol & Brooks (1982), Nol & Lambert (1984), Phillips (1972), Powell (1990, 1993), Powell & Cuthbert (1993), Ridgely & Gwynne (1989), Root (1988), Schardien, B.J. & Jackson (1979), Schardien, S. (1981), Scott & Carbonell (1986), Slud (1964), Stiles & Skutch (1989), Strauch (1971), Tamar (1983), Walbeck (1989), Wetmore (1965), Young (1991).

37. Piping Plover
Charadrius melodus

French: Pluvier siffleur **German**: Flötenregenpfeifer **Spanish**: Chorlitejo Silbador

Taxonomy. *Charadrius melodus* Ord, 1824, Great Egg Harbor, New Jersey.
In past, two subspecies recognized on basis of extent of breast band, with nominate (coastal nesters), and *circumcinctus* (Great Lakes and prairies); but subdivision rendered unsatisfactory due to considerable individual and seasonal variation. Monotypic.
Distribution. N Great Plains, Great Lakes and Atlantic coast from Newfoundland S to North Carolina. Winters on Atlantic coast of S USA, Gulf of Mexico, Bahamas and rather locally in Greater Antilles; also W Mexico.

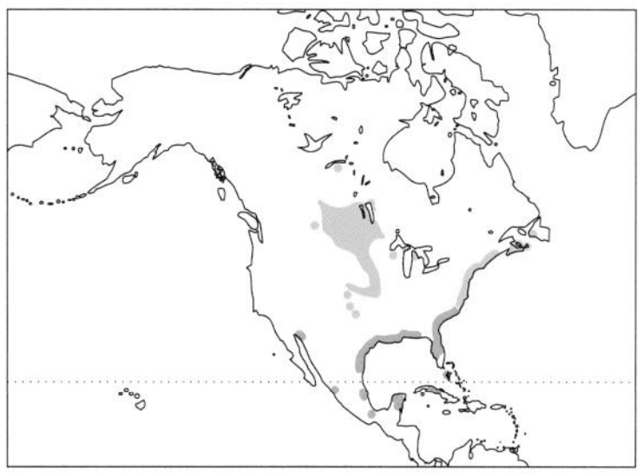

Descriptive notes. 17-18 cm; 43-64 g. Small, chubby plover; stubby orange bill with black tip; short bright orange legs; black frontal bar and breast band, latter often broken, especially in coastal breeders. Resembles *C. semipalmatus* and allies, but has much paler back and is somewhat bulkier. Female has black of forehead and breast browner; yellower bill. Non-breeding adult has greyish forehead and breast band, and often all black bill. Juvenile like adult non-breeding, but upperparts fringed pale buff; bill black.
Habitat. Coastal population breeds on sandy beaches; birds of Great Plains and Canadian prairie prefer muddy gravel, sand or gravel beaches of large alkaline lakes, or shores along prairie rivers, alkaline flats, sandflats and floodplains, favouring bare or scantily vegetated areas. In winter, occurs on coastal beaches and adjacent sandflats, sometimes intertidal mudflats. Sometimes makes scrape in sand to roost in.
Food and Feeding. Aquatic and terrestrial invertebrates, along with their larvae and eggs; polychaete worms, insects (e.g. midges, flies, grasshoppers and beetles), crustaceans and molluscs. Forages within several metres of water's edge, also on higher gravelly ground, small ponds and among detritus; also on drier ground near nest; during non-breeding season, on moist surface of muddy or sandy ground. Frequently uses foot-trembling. Forages day and night, alone or in small, loose flocks.
Breeding. Laying late Apr to early May. Seasonally monogamous, sometimes for longer; occasionally polyandrous. Solitary or in small, loose colonies; density up to 2·4 pairs/km of shoreline, 15-100 m apart. Territories include nesting and feeding sites; 25-70% return to previous year's breeding area, but degree of natal philopatry very low; regularly breeds in or near tern colonies (*Sterna antillarum*, *S. hirundo* and *S. paradisaea*). Nest is shallow scrape, unlined or lined with bits of shell and pebbles, well above high water mark, among sparse to moderately dense vegetation, often near clump of vegetation, large rock or log. Usually 4 eggs, sometimes 3, laid at intervals of 1-2 days; single-brooded, but up to 5 replacement clutches may be laid; incubation (mean) 25-28 days, by both parents, starting after clutch fully completed; chick brown-black above with creamy buff and greyish speckles, wings and thighs marked with brown spots, forehead buffish white and underparts white; tended by both parents, remaining within 150 m of nest; fledging 25-30 days. Eggs and nest suffer due to predation by mammals, including domestic dogs and cats, probably also avian predators, and flooding. Mean yearly fledging success 0·2-3 fledglings/pair; on remote, undisturbed site, hatching success 84%, fledging success 37%. Breeds at 1 year old. Annual adult mortality 34%; total of 13-28% reach age of 5 years; oldest ringed bird 14 years.
Movements. Inland breeders seem to undertake non-stop autumn migration to coast of Gulf of Mexico, as suggested by lack of sightings of migrating birds inland. Coastal breeders winter from North Carolina S to Florida and into Caribbean. Spring migration takes place late-Feb to early Apr, peaking in Mar; arrives on coastal breeding grounds along Atlantic mainly late Mar to Apr, and inland late Apr to mid-May. Departure from coastal breeding grounds in Aug, and southward movements noted into Oct; inland breeders may depart as early as Jun, especially when breeding fails, but otherwise Sept; females depart first, followed by unpaired males, males with fledglings, and finally juveniles; arrives on Texas coast in two peaks, early Jul to early Aug and Oct to early Nov. Shows high degree of fidelity to wintering site. Usually migrates in small flocks of 3-6 birds.
Status and Conservation. VULNERABLE. Came close to extinction around 1900, due to excessive hunting, with range decreasing considerably during second half of 19th century. Numbers now decreasing again, as result of expanding recreational use of beaches, increasing water levels and development of winter habitat. Total of 3535-4147 birds counted in breeding areas during 1977-1984; total of 2334 breeding pairs in 1991, with 500 pairs in Canadian prairie, 872 in Great Plains of USA, 16 in Great Lakes area, 245 on Atlantic coast of Canada, and 701 on Atlantic coast of USA. In Great Plains, numbers are decreasing by more than 7% annually, due to severe drought and inappropriate water management practices; also, in Great Lakes numbers are still decreasing; on Atlantic coast, numbers stable due to intense predator control and human management. Protection measures involve: closing nesting beaches to humans and restricting access of off-road vehicles; constructing predator exclosures around nests; avian and mammalian predator control; mitigation of water level policies; vegetation control; and creation of artificial habitat.
Bibliography. Bent (1927-1929), Bergstrom & Terwilliger (1987), Biaggi (1983), Blanco, P. *et al.* (1993), Boland (1991), Boyd (1991), Brown (1987), Burger, J. (1987c, 1991, 1994), Cairns, W.E. (1977, 1982), Cairns, W.E. & McLaren (1980), Collar & Andrew (1988), Collar, Crosby & Stattersfield (1994), Collar, Gonzaga *et al.* (1992), Desbrosse (1988), Dyer (1993), Dyer *et al.* (1988), Ehrlich *et al.* (1992), Faanes (1983), Flemming (1987, 1991, 1994), Flemming *et al.* (1988), Gaines (1986), Gaines & Ryan (1988), Goldin (1993), Goossen (1989, 1990a, 1990b), Haig (1985, 1986, 1987, 1991, 1992), Haig & Oring (1985, 1988a, 1988b, 1988c), Haig & Plissner (1993), Haig *et al.* (1988), Hecht (1995), Hoopes (1993), Howell (1993), Howell & Webb (1995a), Johnson, C.M. (1987), Johnson, C.M. & Baldassarre (1988), Kirkconnell *et al.* (1992), Kirsch (1993), Lambert & Ratcliff (1981), Loegering (1992), MacIvor (1990), MacIvor *et al.* (1990), Marchant (1956), Mayer (1991), Mayer & Ryan (1991a, 1991b), McNicholl (1985), Melvin, Griffin & MacIvor (1991), Melvin, Hecht & Griffin (1994), Midura *et al.* (1991), Millenbah (1995), Nelson (1993), Nicholls (1989), Nicholls & Baldassarre (1990a, 1990b), Niemi & Davis (1979), Nordstrom (1990), North (1986), Patterson *et al.* (1990, 1991), Powell (1993), Powell & Cuthbert (1992), Rimmer & Deblinger (1990), Root, B.G. *et al.* (1992), Root, T. (1988), Russell (1983), Ryan *et al.* (1993), Schaffer & Laporte (1994), Schwalbach (1988), Sidle & Kirsch (1993), Sidle, Carlson *et al.* (1992), Sidle, Mayne & McPhillips (1991), Smith *et al.* (1993), Staine & Burger (1994), Strauss (1990), Vaske *et al.* (1994), Weber & Martin (1991), Weseloh & Weseloh (1983), Whyte (1985), Wiens (1986), Wiens & Cuthbert (1988), Wilcox (1959), Woolfenden (1978), Ziewitz *et al.* (1992).

38. Black-banded Plover

Charadrius thoracicus

French: Pluvier à bandeau noir   **German**: Madagaskarregenpfeifer   **Spanish**: Chorlitejo Malgache
Other common names: Madagascar/Black-banded Sandplover/Plover

Taxonomy. *Ægialitis thoracica*, Richmond, 1896, Loholoka, east coast of Madagascar.
Probably best considered to form superspecies with *C. pecuarius* and *C. sanctaehelenae*. Monotypic.
Distribution. SW coast of Madagascar; occasionally reported from E coast.

Descriptive notes. 13-14 cm. Yellowish orange underparts, darkest on central belly; black breast band separates from otherwise very similar *C. pecuarius* and *C. sanctaehelenae*. Female like male, but may have slightly paler underparts. Non-breeding adult has much of black replaced with brown, and upperparts tinged orange. Juvenile like adult, but has greyish legs and greyish brown breast band; head pattern dull brown and pale buffish; upperpart feathers broadly fringed pale buff.
Habitat. Coastal grazed grasslands, often very dry; also edges of shallow brackish marshes and ponds, occasionally sandy beaches and sandy or muddy estuarine flats. Seems to prefer drier areas than *C. pecuarius* and to avoid flooded grassland.
Food and Feeding. Very poorly known, but habits apparently rather similar to *C. pecuarius*. Takes large and small insects. Commonly seen in company of other coastal plovers, such as *C. hiaticula* and *C. marginatus*.
Breeding. Evidently rather similar to *C. pecuarius*. Nesting probably mainly Nov-Jan; eggs reported in Nov and Jan, young in Dec and Aug. 2 clutches of 2 eggs each.
Movements. Sedentary. Almost all records from SW coast between Morondava and Androka; species originally described from E coast, where still reported very occasionally.
Status and Conservation. VULNERABLE. Declining, with possibly fewer than 1000 individuals remaining. Reported to be locally abundant at Lake Tsimanampetsotsa Nature Reserve in 1988, and occurring at two other protected areas; rather common in Morombe region, NW part of known range, in 1984; breeding range may not be yet fully described. Decline may be due to competition with relatively recently arrived *C. pecuarius* or by *C. marginatus*, or both; nowadays outnumbered by both of these species.
Bibliography. Appert (1971), Collar & Andrew (1988), Collar & Stuart (1985), Collar *et al.* (1994), Dee (1986), Delacour (1932), Dhondt (1975), Dowsett & Forbes-Watson (1993), Keith (1980), Langrand (1990), Milon (1948), Milon *et al.* (1973), Nicoll & Langrand (1989), Rand (1936), Salvan (1971).

39. Kittlitz's Plover

Charadrius pecuarius

French: Pluvier pâtre   **German**: Hirtenregenpfeifer   **Spanish**: Chorlitejo Pecuario
Other common names: Kittlitz's Sandplover

Taxonomy. *Charadrius pecuarius* Temminck, 1823, Cape of Good Hope.
Probably best considered to form superspecies with *C. thoracicus* and *C. sanctaehelenae*; often considered conspecific with latter (see page 406). Various races have been proposed: *allenbyi* (Egypt), *isabellinus* (Egypt to Zaire, Kenya), *tephricolor* (SW Africa and N Botswana); but variation is slight, overlapping and mainly clinal, and reported sample sizes are too small. Monotypic.
Distribution. NE Egypt; Africa S of Sahara; Madagascar.

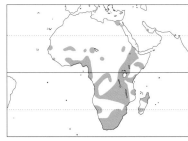

Descriptive notes. 12-14 cm; 26-54 g; wingspan 40-44 cm. Black eyestripe, white supercilium and dark brown upperparts with sandy rufous fringes; breast and belly sandy rufous. Resembles *C. thoracicus*, but lacks breast band, and has slightly longer legs; very similar to *C. sanctaehelenae*, but smaller with shorter legs, and more brightly coloured underparts. Female has slightly paler underparts and narrower black forecrown. Non-breeding adult has variable depth of colour; black on head browner, white parts of head may turn sandy brownish. Juvenile resembles non-breeding adult, but no black head lines, broader fringes on upperpart feathers and brownish lateral breast patches. Madagascan birds sometimes have orange-buff wash to supercilium.
Habitat. From coast to uplands; primarily inland in varied flat, open habitats with poor soil, usually close to water; often near margins of lakes, reservoirs, small, sometimes temporary, pools or flooded ground; also salt-pans, tidal mudflats and lagoons, salt-marshes, sandbanks and along sandy riverbeds. Avoids tall, dense closed vegetation and steep or broken terrain. Along coast, roosts at high water with other small *Charadrius* plovers.
Food and Feeding. Mainly terrestrial invertebrates, chiefly insects (e.g. beetles, flies, bugs, grasshoppers and butterfly and moth larvae) and spiders; also worms and molluscs. Sometimes uses foot-trembling. May feed during moonlit nights. Feeds singly or in flocks of 2-5 birds, rarely up to 50.
Breeding. Laying Apr in Egypt; very variable throughout rest of range, laying in 2-12 months of year. Monogamous. Solitary or in loose neighbourhood groups, nests mostly at least 20 m apart; territorial, feeding either in or out of territory; territory predominantly defended by male. Nest exposed, in sand or dry mud; shallow scrape, lined with plant material, pebbles and debris, sometimes unlined. Usually 2 eggs (1-3), laid at intervals of 1-2 days; 1-2 broods; incubation by both parents, female by day, male by night, 22-28 days, starting with last egg. Eggs totally covered with nest material and sand before disturbed bird leaves nest; bird stands up and runs around nest 2-3 times, making rapid inward-kicking movements ("Leaving-scuffle"), in total taking 3-6 seconds, but up to 90 seconds when ground damp or with high wind; hatchling sometimes covered in same way. Chick pale buff, mottled black above with dark centre line on back, but no dark band across nape; forehead and underparts white, buffish on flanks. Both parents care for young; fledging 26-32 days; young independent soon after; subsequently, young birds gather into flocks. Hatching success 19-77%, fledging success 0·5 to under 2 young/pair; mortality caused mainly by flooding, but also by motor vehicles and predators; birds will move eggs to new site after heavy rains, and possibly also as a anti-predator reaction. Some birds breed in first year.
Movements. Generally resident, but locally making seasonal movements, possibly related to seasonal rainfall and flooding; patterns poorly understood. Occasionally occurs in large numbers on shores of L Victoria; summer visitor to Botswana; dry season visitor to Sierra Leone (Dec-Apr), and to Zambia and Zimbabwe (Apr-Dec); presumably birds from Zimbabwe fly to Botswana, Namibia and Cape Province, to join sedentary coastal populations. Flocks of 100-200 birds reported during local movements.
Status and Conservation. Not globally threatened. No population estimates available; c. 2600 birds on South African coast, most in W Cape; 615-1170 birds, probably breeders, recorded on coast of Gabon. Locally common on L Mabesi, S Sierra Leone; locally not uncommon in Ghana and Nigeria; scarce in Egypt and Gambia.
Bibliography. Ash & Miskell (1983), Bennett (1992), Benson (1968b), Benson & Benson (1975), Britton, P.L. (1980), Clancey (1971c), Clark (1982a), Conway & Bell (1969), Cramp & Simmons (1983), Dowsett & Dowsett-Lemaire (1993), Dowsett & Forbes-Watson (1993), Elgood (1994), Étchécopar & Hüe (1964), Ginn *et al.* (1989), Goodman *et al.* (1989), Gore (1990), Grimes (1987), Hall (1958, 1959a, 1965), Hanmer (1994), Kutilek (1974), Langrand (1990), Mackworth-Praed & Grant (1957, 1962, 1970), Maclean (1993), Pinto (1983), Schepers & Marteijn (1993), Shirihai (1996), Shirihai & van den Berg (1987), Short *et al.* (1990), Slight (1966), Taylor, P.B. (1983), Took (1967), Tree (1973, 1980b), Urban *et al.* (1986), Winterbottom (1963).

40. St Helena Plover

Charadrius sanctaehelenae

French: Pluvier de Sainte-Hélène   **Spanish**: Chorlitejo de Santa Elena
German: St.-Helena-Regenpfeifer
Other common names: (St Helena) Wirebird, St Helena Sandplover

Taxonomy. *Ægialitis sanctæhelenæ* Harting, 1873, St Helena.
Often considered conspecific with *C. pecuarius* (see page 406); probably best considered to form superspecies with *C. pecuarius* and *C. thoracicus*. Monotypic.
Distribution. St Helena, S Atlantic Ocean.

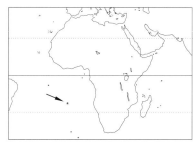

Descriptive notes. c. 15 cm. Resembles *C. pecuarius*, but larger, with longer bill and longer "wiry" legs; less buff on breast and on feather fringes of upperparts; black lines do not meet on nape. Sexes alike. No seasonal variation. Juvenile has dull brown head pattern, without black areas on head and neck; crown and upperpart feathers narrowly fringed pale buff.
Habitat. Widespread, particularly in flatter, more open upland habitats at medium elevations, and around edges of island. Forages on hot stony plains with wire-grass (*Cynodon dactylon*) and eroded areas of kaffir fig (*Carpobrotus edulis*); also upland pastures, especially when recently grazed by cattle, ploughed fields, and even large, remote vegetable gardens; never occurs on the shore. It has been suggested that, until deforestation at end of 19th century, species may have been woodland floor-dweller.
Food and Feeding. Very poorly known. Insects and snails recorded. Usually seen in pairs, rarely in groups of up to 6 birds.
Breeding. Breeds in drier part of year, late Sept to Jan, mainly Dec-Jan, possibly varying considerably between years, depending on conditions. Breeds on quite remote, open plains in N half of island. Probably solitary. Nest is simple scrape. 1-2 eggs (up to 3); possibly double-brooded; chick buff, streaked black, with grey tinge. Eggs and young occasionally taken by feral cats, introduced Indian Myna (*Acridotheres tristis*) and possibly rats, which occasionally form plagues on the island; *A. tristis* may also be competing for same food resources.
Movements. Sedentary.
Status and Conservation. ENDANGERED. Only occurs in northern, flatter parts of interior of St Helena; but distribution of species now shifting towards E, due to expansion of urban areas. All bird species on St Helena protected by law since 1894. Total population estimated at less than 100 pairs in 1952; in late 1960's, species thought to be commoner than that, a view supported in 1983 by an estimate of several hundred birds. In 1984, species seemed to be less numerous than 10 years before. Intensive survey in 1988/89 showed that c. 450 birds were present; recent censuses suggest continuous, steady decline from c. 375 birds in 1991, to c. 315 birds in 1993; numbers at a key area, Deadwood Plain, have halved since late 1980's. Several breeding areas now threatened by habitat changes; 11 separate breeding areas known in 1952. Species appears to be reasonably safe unless major habitat changes take place, especially if these affect important habitats, although ecological research still required in order to define precise requirements.
Bibliography. Anon. (1989b), Basilewsky (1970), Benson (1950), Collar & Andrew (1988), Collar & Stuart (1985), Collar *et al.* (1994), Dowsett & Dowsett-Lemaire (1993), Dowsett & Forbes-Watson (1993), Haydock (1954), McCulloch (1991, 1992), Pitman (1965b).

PLATE 38 ➤

ssp *bifrontatus*

41

ssp *tricollaris*

42

♀

43

ssp *marginatus*

♂

ssp *tenellus*

♂

ssp *seebohmi*

♀

ssp *nivosus*

44

♀

45

♂

♂

♂

ssp *alexandrinus*

♀

♀

ssp *venustus*

♀

ssp *pallidus*

48

♂

46

47

♂

♂

♀

51

♀

49

50

♂

52

♂

PLATE 38

inches 4

cm 10

41. Three-banded Plover

Charadrius tricollaris

French: Pluvier à triple collier **German**: Dreiband-Regenpfeifer **Spanish**: Chorlitejo Tricollar
Other common names: Treble-banded/Three-banded/Tri-collared Plover/Sandplover

Taxonomy. *Charadrius tricollaris* Vieillot, 1818, Cape Town.
Sometimes considered conspecific with *C. forbesi*; probably best considered to form superspecies. Two subspecies recognized.
Subspecies and Distribution.
C. t. tricollaris Vieillot, 1818 - Ethiopia to Tanzania and Gabon, and S to South Africa; non-breeding also around L Chad.
C. t. bifrontatus Cabanis, 1882 - Madagascar.

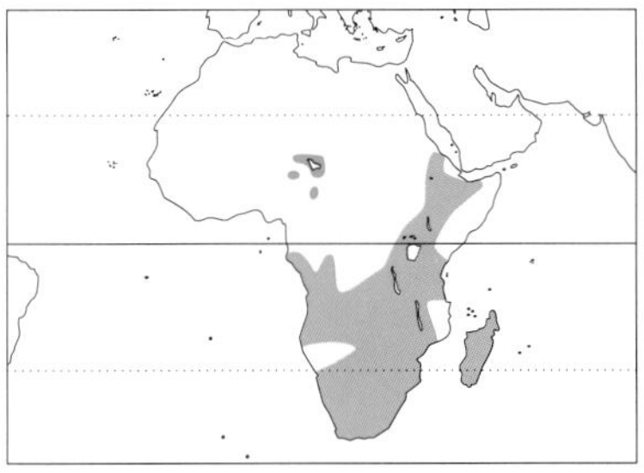

Descriptive notes. c. 18 cm; 25-43 g. Small, dark plover with red eye-ring, distinguished from *C. forbesi* by white forehead, paler upperparts and red bill with black tip. Sexes alike. No seasonal variation. Juvenile has narrow buff fringes on upperpart feathers, and pale brown forehead. Race *bifrontatus* has grey band between white forehead and bill; darker face and throat.
Habitat. Firm gravelly or sometimes muddy ground along edges of inland freshwater lakes, pools and rivers; occasionally at coastal lagoons and estuaries, when mostly uses the least saline areas; rarely on beaches and inland brackish water; also found at margins of some artificial water bodies, e.g. sewage tanks in Malawi. Roosts higher up shore, on gravelly or stony ground, in mixed flocks or solitarily.
Food and Feeding. Terrestrial and aquatic insects and their larvae, crustaceans, small molluscs and worms. Often feeds at water's edge, picking up food from surface, or just below; also uses foot-trembling. Probably feeds by night, as well as by day. Often solitary, but also mixes with other small waders; occasionally in loose flocks, rarely up to 40 birds.
Breeding. Breeds opportunistically, but mainly lays Apr-Sept in tropics, Jul-Dec further S, and Jul-Sept in Madagascar. Monogamous; solitary and territorial; territory usually along shoreline; sometimes 2 territories, 1 for nesting and 1 for feeding. Nest situated in sand or dry mud, close to water; sometimes on hard rock; simple scrape, lined with pieces of plants, pebbles and debris. Usually 2 eggs, sometimes 1, probably laid at interval of 2-4 days; frequently double-brooded, female starting second brood well before first brood fully-fledged; incubation 26-28 days, by both parents, probably starting when clutch complete; chick has sandy upperparts speckled black with black median stripe, white underparts; fledging 30-32 days; young sometimes remain with parents until 40-42 days old. Fledging success almost 2 young per pair in Botswana. Probably lives at least 10 years.
Movements. Essentially resident, showing some erratic movements, but movements poorly known; more widespread during non-breeding season, making use of temporary pools. Records of apparently non-breeding birds from Nigeria and Cameroon in dry season (Aug-Feb) suggest that longer movements occur; in Ethiopia, only present Mar-Apr and Jul-Dec; in E Zaire and Rwanda, numbers increase in Mar; in S Africa, movements complex, seeming to depend on rains.
Status and Conservation. Not globally threatened. No population estimates available. Total of c. 750 birds recorded on coasts of South Africa, with highest numbers in Cape Province.
Bibliography. Ash & Miskell (1983), Benson & Benson (1975), Blake (1977), Britton, P.L. (1980), Brown, A. (1992), Brown, L.H. & Britton (1980), Clancey (1981c), Clark (1982b), Dowsett & Forbes-Watson (1993), Elgood *et al.* (1994), Freeman (1970), Ginn *et al.* (1989), Langrand (1990), Lippens & Wille (1976), Louette (1981), Mackworth-Praed & Grant (1957, 1962, 1970), Maclean (1965, 1982, 1993), Martin (1971), Milon *et al.* (1973), Moreau (1946), Nikolaus (1987), van Perlo (1995), Pinto (1983), Short *et al.* (1990), Tree (1980b), Tyler (1978), Urban *et al.* (1986), Winterbottom (1963).

42. Forbes's Plover

Charadrius forbesi

French: Pluvier de Forbes **German**: Forbesregenpfeifer **Spanish**: Chorlitejo de Forbes
Other common names: Forbes's Banded Plover

Taxonomy. *Ægialitis forbesi* Shelley, 1883, Shonga, Niger River.
Has been considered conspecific with *C. tricollaris*; probably best considered to form superspecies. Monotypic.
Distribution. Ghana to SW Sudan, and S through Zaire and W Uganda locally to C & S Angola and extreme W Zambia. Recorded W to Senegal, but not known to breed W of Ghana.

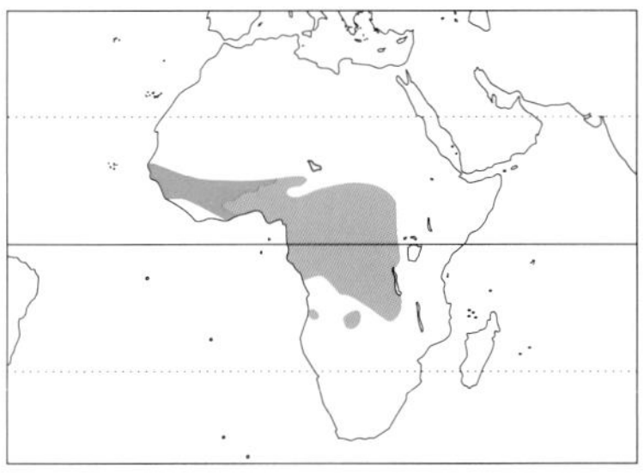

Descriptive notes. 20 cm; 46-49 g (4 specimens). Two black breast bands; red eye-ring. Resembles *C. tricollaris*, but larger, with darker upperparts; darker, browner head; dark brown bill with red at base of lower mandible. Sexes alike. In non-breeding adult, breast band can be dark brown; white on head is replaced with buff. Juvenile like non-breeding adult, but feathers of upperparts have narrow buff fringes.
Habitat. Not particularly attached to water. Breeds in rocky upland habitats with granite outcrops, in Nigeria sometimes on inselbergs. During dry, non-breeding season affects grassland habitats, even in open places within forests; also bare ground and recently burnt areas, and muddy areas near lakes and rivers; often close to habitation, on airfields or golf courses; occasionally at cultivated areas, pools or reservoirs.
Food and Feeding. Beetles, grasshoppers and other insects, and their larvae; also small molluscs, crustaceans and worms. Usually solitary, but sometimes in small flocks of 15-20 birds.
Breeding. Lays during rainy season, Jul-Aug in Ghana, Mar-Aug in Nigeria; during dry season in Gabon, Jun-Sept. Monogamous; solitary. Nest is scrape, lined with tiny pebbles, often on top of granite ourtcrop to avoid surface water run-off or in gravel stream bed; same nest-site may be used for several years. 2-3 eggs; possibly double-brooded; incubation at least 22 days, by both parents, starting probably after clutch completed; chick undescribed; tended by both parents; after fledging, young birds go to nearby cultivation, e.g. rice fields.
Movements. Migratory, at least on local basis; during dry season, breeding grounds deserted for nearby grassland habitats, but longer movements likely to occur too. Occurs in Sierra Leone and Ivory Coast only Nov-Apr. Vagrant to E Africa, recorded mainly Apr-Jul.
Status and Conservation. Not globally threatened. No population estimates available. Locally common to uncommon; not uncommon in Sierra Leone and Ghana; locally common in Nigeria; only 1 record in Gambia; apparently very uncommon in Angola, with very few records.
Bibliography. Brown (1948), Dowsett & Forbes-Watson (1993), Elgood *et al.* (1994), Gatter (1988), Grimes (1987), Herroelen (1987), Lippens & Wille (1976), Louette (1981), Mackworth-Praed & Grant (1957, 1962, 1970), Morel & Morel (1990), Nikolaus (1987), Pinto (1983), Serle (1956a), Short *et al.* (1990), Tree (1964), Urban *et al.* (1986).

43. White-fronted Plover

Charadrius marginatus

French: Pluvier à front blanc **German**: Weißstirn-Regenpfeifer **Spanish**: Chorlitejo Frentiblanco
Other common name: White-fronted Sandplover

Taxonomy *Charadrius marginatus* Vieillot, 1818, Cape Peninsula.
Forms superspecies with *C. alexandrinus*, *C. javanicus* and *C. ruficapillus*; all of these have on occasion been considered conspecific (see page 386). Some authors consider population from Sudan and Ethiopia to E Natal as belonging to race *tenellus*. Other races proposed: *hesperius* (W Africa to Central African Republic); *nigirius* (R Niger); *spatzi* (Rio de Oro); and *pons* (S Somalia); but evidence too scanty to support recognition of these possible forms. Four subspecies normally recognized.
Subspecies and Distribution.
C. m. mechowi (Cabanis, 1884) - locally in Africa S of Sahara to N Angola, Botswana, Zimbabwe and N Mozambique.
C. m. marginatus Vieillot, 1818 - S Angola to SW Cape.
C. m. arenaceus Clancey, 1971 - S Mozambique to SW Cape.
C. m. tenellus Hartlaub, 1861 - Madagascar.

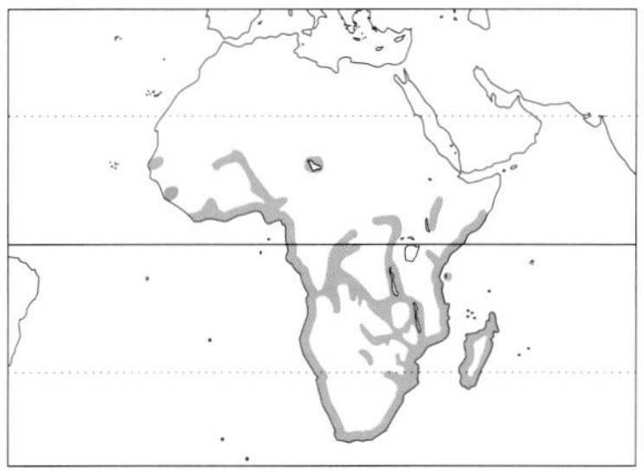

Descriptive notes. 18 cm; nominate 42-55 g, *mechowi* 27-40 g. Differs from similar species in always lacking well defined black or brown patches at sides of breast; conspicuous white forehead, with sharp black bar behind; narrow black eyestripe. Individually very variable: upperparts range from rufous to dull brown to brownish grey; underparts variably pure white to extensively creamy or rufous. Female like male, but black areas paler, and rufous on breast more often paler or lacking. Non-breeding male like breeding female, but black replaced by brown; non-breeding female sometimes loses black frontal bar. Juvenile lacks black frontal bar; brownish lores; underparts white; upperparts with buff fringes. Much racial variation in colour falls in range of individual variation: rufous breast patches may join to complete rufous breast band; *arenaceus* has slightly browner upperparts with cinnamon-buff, not off-white, fringes; race *mechowi* smaller; population of coastal E Africa often has rufous on upperparts; *tenellus* typically has rufous on neck and sides of breast.
Habitat. Sandy seashores and inland along sandy shores of larger rivers and lakes; also rocky coasts, coastal and inland mudflats, salt-pans and estuaries. Roosts higher up beach, in (mixed) flocks or solitarily.
Food and Feeding. Insects, such as sandflies, grasshoppers, termites, mosquito pupae and *Cheirocephalus* larvae; also gastropods, bivalves and bivalve siphons, small crustaceans, isopods and worms. Probes and jabs in wet sediment, or pecks; also uses foot-trembling, and occasionally hawks flying termites. Forages on sandy parts of mudflats or in shallow water, on upper levels of beaches, in intertidal areas mainly at low tide, and in damp areas between dunes; forages during daytime and on moonlit nights. Forages in pairs or small parties, in non-breeding season occasionally larger flocks of up to 375 birds.
Breeding. Laying Feb-Sept from Senegambia to Nigeria, mainly May-Jul in E Africa, and somewhat later further S, but all year round in S Africa with peak Jul-Sept and Jan in Namibia. Seasonally monogamous. Solitary; territorial, with separate territories for nesting and feeding; sedentary populations may have territories year round. Nest can be as close as 16 m; densities 1 pair/2 ha along R Zambezi, c. 7 birds/km of open shoreline in South Africa, and 0·4 birds/km shoreline in Gabon; strongly site-faithful. Nest is shallow scrape, often lined with pebbles, shell fragments, dried seaweed or twigs, in sand near high water mark, on dune, sandbar or occasionally in quarry. Normally 2 eggs (1-4), laid at intervals of 2-4 days; several replacement clutches may be laid; incubation 26-33 days, by both parents. Usually eggs partly covered with sand early in morning or when adult leaves nest, and uncovered at night; degree of cover increases as incubation proceeds, and probably serves for temperature regulation and camouflage. Chick grey above with black mottling forming lines down centre of head and back, white below; stay in dunes until almost fledged, moving to beaches thereafter; fledging 35-38 days. In S Africa, hatching success 38%, fledging success 0·08-1·4 young/pair; mortality caused by predators (mongooses), floods, high tides and motor vehicles. Average longevity 7·5 years, maximum 9+ years.
Movements. Sedentary, with some local seasonal movements of immatures. Inland populations of C & S Africa tend to be migratory, moving to E coast (S to E Cape) when rivers flood (Dec-May). In Nigeria, some movement related to changing water levels; in Mali, present all year, with higher numbers Dec-Jan; probably non-breeding visitor to Sierra Leone, where present Nov-May in small numbers.
Status and Conservation. Not globally threatened. No population estimates available. In N of range, uncommon to frequent (Ethiopia) to locally common (Somalia, Nigeria, Ghana, Gabon, Mali) to abundant (Kenyan and Tanzanian coasts). Total of 5000-6000 birds on Tanzanian coast in Feb; highest

On following pages: 44. Kentish Plover (*Charadrius alexandrinus*); 45. Javan Plover (*Charadrius javanicus*); 46. Red-capped Plover (*Charadrius ruficapillus*); 47. Malaysian Plover (*Charadrius peronii*); 48. Chestnut-banded Plover (*Charadrius pallidus*); 49. Collared Plover (*Charadrius collaris*); 50. Puna Plover (*Charadrius alticola*); 51. Two-banded Plover (*Charadrius falklandicus*); 52. Double-banded Plover (*Charadrius bicinctus*).

known densities inland at L Turkana and L Malawi; common on S African coasts with some 18,000 individuals recorded.

Bibliography. Ash & Miskell (1983), Atkins & Johnston-Stewart (1989), Benson & Benson (1975), Blaker (1966), Bregnballe *et al*. (1990), Britton, P.L. (1980), Clancey (1971d, 1975a), Crowe (1981, 1986), Crowe & Crowe (1984), Dowsett & Forbes-Watson (1993), Elgood *et al*. (1994), Ginn *et al*. (1989), Gore (1990), Grimes (1987), Kieser & Liversidge (1981), Langrand (1990), Liversidge (1965), Mackworth-Praed & Grant (1957, 1962, 1970), MacLachlan *et al*. (1980), Maclean (1993), Maclean & Moran (1965), Martin & Baird (1987), Medland (1988), van der Merwe (1987), van der Merwe *et al*. (1992, 1994), Milon *et al*. (1973), Pinto (1983), Reynolds (1977c), Roberts (1977), Shewell (1951), Short *et al*. (1990), Skead (1966), Steyn (1966), Summers & Hockey (1980, 1981), Taylor, P.B. (1982b, 1983), Tree (1980b), Urban *et al*. (1986), Watson (1992), Watson & Kerley (1995), Winterbottom (1963).

44. Kentish Plover

Charadrius alexandrinus

French: Pluvier à collier interrompu **German**: Seeregenpfeifer **Spanish**: Chorlitejo Patinegro
Other common names: Snowy Plover (New World races), Sandplover

Taxonomy. *Charadrius alexandrinus* Linnaeus, 1758, Egypt.
Forms superspecies with *C. marginatus*, *C. javanicus* and *C. ruficapillus*; all of these have on occasion been considered conspecific with present species, especially *C. javanicus* (see page 386); in contrast, races *nivosus* and *occidentalis* sometimes considered to constitute one or two additional distinct species. Part of population on Gulf of Mexico often separated as race *tenuirostris*, on basis of supposedly paler coloration, but many recent authors include it in *nivosus*. Five subspecies usually recognized.
Subspecies and Distribution.
C. a. alexandrinus Linnaeus, 1758 - W Europe, E Atlantic Is and N Africa (S to Senegal) E through Mediterranean, NE Africa, Middle East, SW & C Asia to Russian Far East and NE China; winters S to sub-Saharan Africa, S Asia and W Indonesia.
C. a. dealbatus (Swinhoe, 1870) - S Japan, Ryukyu Is and E & SE China; winters S to Philippines and Borneo.
C. a. seebohmi Hartert & Jackson, 1915 - SE India and Sri Lanka.
C. a. nivosus (Cassin, 1858) - W, C & SC USA, NW, C & E Mexico, Bahamas, Greater Antilles and Netherlands Antilles; winters S to Panama.
C. a. occidentalis (Cabanis, 1872) - coastal Peru to SC Chile.

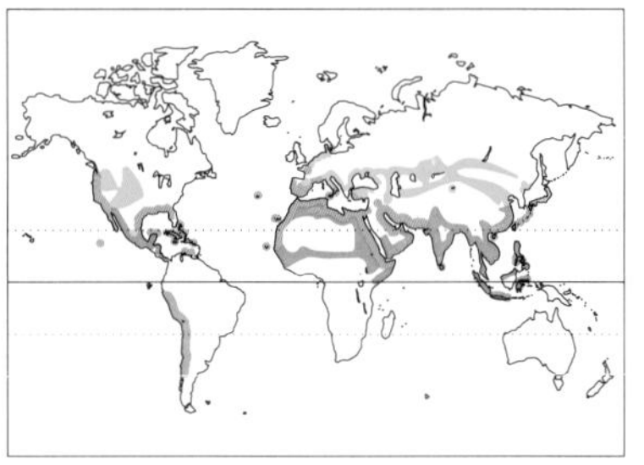

Descriptive notes. 15-17·5 cm; 32-56 g; wingspan 42-45 cm. Differs from most similar species by white collar on hindneck; black patches on sides of breast, black bar on forecrown, black eyeline; very variable rufous cap. Female has black areas replaced with brown to blackish brown. Non-breeding adult resembles breeding female. Juvenile like pale breeding female with buff fringes to upperparts. Racial variation fairly complex: *dealbatus* very similar to nominate, but has longer bill, and non-breeding male can have little rufous on cap; male of race *seebohmi* has no black bar on forecrown; most *seebohmi* and *occidentalis* and some *nivosus* have white lores and no rufous cap; *occidentalis* and *nivosus* have greyer, often much paler, upperparts, and are shorter-legged; in *occidentalis*, and sometimes in *nivosus*, sexes very similar.
Habitat. Chiefly sea coasts, but also open flats near brackish or saline lakes, lagoons, seasonal water courses, salt-works and depressions. Usually on sand, silt or dry mud with even surface, avoiding rocky or broken ground. Quickly invades newly created suitable habitats, such as gravel pits and reservoirs, although not in large numbers, nor far from possible areas of origin.
Food and Feeding. Inland takes mainly insects, such as beetles and flies, also crustaceans, molluscs and spiders; in brackish and salt water, chiefly crustaceans, polychaete worms and molluscs. Sometimes probes in wet sand and mud and frequently feeds by foot-trembling. Usually in small flocks of up to 20-30 birds.
Breeding. Laying mid-Apr to May in NW Europe; Mar-Jun in NW Africa; Feb-Jul in Ethiopia, Eritrea and Somalia; early Mar to mid-Jul in Iraq; from late Apr in interior W USA. Monogamous, occasionally over several years; polyandry and polygyny may occur if a parent deserts early in season, or if a parent hatches young or loses brood early. Solitary or in loose groups, with nests usually more than 20 m apart (0·8-80 m); site fidelity 60-70%, but may disperse long distance; very low degree of natal philopatry. Territorial; feeds in neutral area outside territory. Densities up to 96 pairs/ha in suitable habitat, but more often 0·5-2 pairs/ha. Nest often near water on bare or scantly vegetated ground; shallow scrape lined with small pebbles, shell fragments and vegetation. 3 eggs, occasionally 2, laid at intervals of c. 2 days; females single- to triple-brooded, males single- or double-brooded; replacement broods after egg loss; incubation 23-29 days, by both parents (female by day, male by night) starting with last egg; in some areas, eggs often partly buried in sand before adult leaves nest, probably for protection against sun; chick has pale grey crown and upperparts with buff tinge, finely speckled dull black and lacking distinct solid lines, underparts white; frequently, one parent, often female, deserts brood about 6 days (0-30) after hatching; fledging 27-31 days; young independent some time after fledging. Breeding success enhanced by associative breeding with more demonstrative and aggressive species. Main cause of breeding failure is predation. Hatching success 20-94%; 0·55 chicks/successful brood. Breeds first at 1 year; annual adult mortality 12-42%; oldest ringed bird at least 18 years.
Movements. Nominate race mainly migratory N of 40° N, dispersive and resident to S; winters in S Eurasia, Africa N of equator (where most birds occur on coast) to W Indonesia. W European breeders winter mainly in SW Europe; origin of large numbers of W African winterers not known. Dispersal from breeding grounds starts immediately after fledging of young from late Jun, and southward migration peaks in Sept; passage through Morocco in Sept, and largest numbers on Banc d'Arguin (Mauritania) in Oct, passage through E Mediterranean in Sept. NW African breeding grounds reoccupied Mar-Apr or May, and northernmost breeding areas in Kyrgyzstan from May. Race *dealbatus* has been reported wintering on Philippines and N Borneo. Race *nivosus* partly migratory, some birds wintering outside breeding range on W & E coasts of Mexico and S to Panama; inland breeders move to coast. Races *seebohmi* and *occidentalis* sedentary.
Status and Conservation. Not globally threatened. Nominate race: c. 67,000 birds winter on E Atlantic coasts, among which minimum 6400-9600 breeding pairs from W & C Europe (1986) and 5000 pairs from Tunisia (1983); 25,000-100,000 birds breed on Black Sea and E Mediterranean, c. 100,000 birds winter in SW Asia and NE Africa, with 15,000-20,000 in lakes of Nile Delta, and 25,000-100,000 birds winter in SC Asia. Population of *dealbatus* in order of 100,000 birds. Race *nivosus* has estimated 21,000 birds wintering in USA, of which 87% W of Rocky Mts; c. 18,500 birds estimated breeding in W USA, of which 2500 coastal. No estimates available for other races. Overall decline in NW & C Europe and Israel since 1950's, probably by 25-50% or more; southward retreat reported in Sweden; Sept counts on Sea of Azov showed decrease from 3000 to 1200 birds, from 1940 to 1970; probable decline by 20% in W North America from 1977/80 to 1988/89; main causes of declines are disturbance of mostly coastal habitats and habitat reduction and fragmentation through reclamation and urbanization. Small numbers of nominate *alexandrinus* formerly bred in S Britain and Norway.

Bibliography. Ali & Ripley (1980), Andell & Jönsson (1986), Ash & Miskell (1983), Bent (1927-1929), Biaggi (1983), Blake (1977), Boyd (1972), Brazil (1991), Buchanan *et al*. (1991), Cramp & Simmons (1983), Deignan (1945), van Dijk *et al*. (1986), Dowsett & Forbes-Watson (1993), Dubois & Maheo (1986), Dybro (1970), Ehrlich *et al*. (1992), Étchécopar & Hüe (1964, 1978), Evans (1994), Fjeldså (1977), Flint *et al*. (1984), Gavrilov, A.E. & Gavrilov (1990), Gavrilov, E.I. & Bekbayev (1988), Glutz von Blotzheim (1972), Goodman *et al*. (1989), Halpin & Paul (1989), Hazevoet (1995), Herman *et al*. (1988), Hill (1985), Hill & Talent (1990), Hilty & Brown (1986), Howell & Webb (1994, 1995a), Hu Yaoguang & Wang Jiao (1989), Hüe & Étchécopar (1970), Johnson (1965b), Jönsson (1983, 1986b, 1987c, 1989, 1991b, 1992, 1993, 1994, 1995), Knystautas (1993), Krebs (1956), Krey (1991), Lee (1989), Lessells (1984), Mackworth-Praed & Grant (1957, 1970), van Marle & Voous (1988), Marshall (1989), Mayr & Short (1970), Medway & Wells (1976), Meltofte *et al*. (1994), Meyer de Schauensee & Phelps (1978), Mullié & Meininger (1981), de Naurois (1986), Noszály & Székely (1993), Page & Ribic (1985), Page & Stenzel (1981), Page, Bidstrup *et al*. (1986), Page, Quinn & Warriner (1989), Page, Shuford & Bruce (1991), Page, Stenzel & Ribic (1985), Page, Stenzel, Shuford & Bruce (1991), Page, Stenzel, Winkler & Swarth (1983), Page, Stern & Paton (1995), Page, Warriner *et al*. (1995), Palacios *et al*. (1994), Paton (1994a, 1994b, 1995), Paton & Edwards (1990), Patrikeev (1995), Paz (1987), Perennou *et al*. (1994), Phillips (1978), Pineau (1993), Purdue (1976a, 1976b), Purdue & Haines (1977), Ripley (1982), Rittinghaus (1956, 1961), Roberts, T.J. (1991), Robiller & Borrmann (1988), Rogacheva (1992), Root (1988), Schulz & Stock (1993), Scott (1989), Scott & Carbonell (1986), Shirihai (1996), Shuford *et al*. (1995), Slud (1964), Smit & Piersma (1989), Smythies (1981, 1986), Stenzel *et al*. (1994), Székely (1991, 1992), Székely & Lessells (1993), Székely & Williams (1994), Székely, Karsai & Williams (1994), Székely, Kozma & Piti (1994), Tinarelli (1993b), Urban *et al*. (1986), Velasco & Alberto (1994), Walters, J. (1984), Warriner *et al*. (1986), White & Bruce (1986), Williams, M.D. (1986).

45. Javan Plover

Charadrius javanicus

French: Pluvier de Java **German**: Javaregenpfeifer **Spanish**: Chorlitejo Javanés
Other common names: Javan Sandplover

Taxonomy. *Charadrius javanicus* Chasen, 1938, Java.
Taxonomic status very unclear: may well not merit full species status, but various authors associate it with different species; most often treated as race of *C. alexandrinus*; alternatively linked with *C. ruficapillus* or with *C. peronii*, although structurally appears to be quite different from latter; very poorly known, and much more research needed. Tentatively treated as distinct species, forming superspecies with *C. marginatus*, *C. alexandrinus* and *C. ruficapillus*. Monotypic.
Distribution. Java and Kangean Is; possibly also Bali.

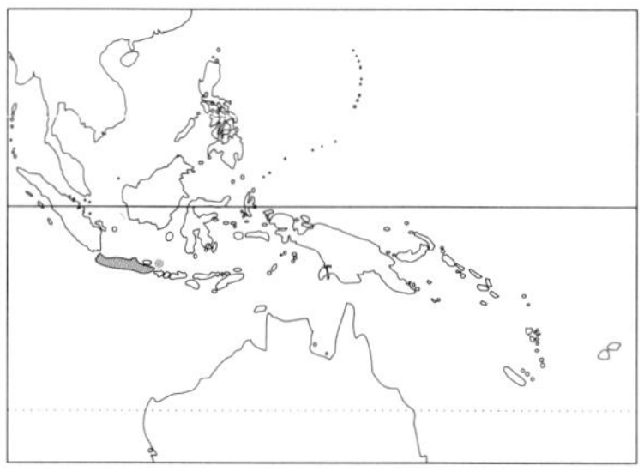

Descriptive notes. 15 cm. Differs from similar species by rufous-cinnamon extending from crown down hindneck onto sides of breast, with reduced dark brown to blackish brown patch below; black bar on forecrown; lores and eyeline mainly dark brown. Female has somewhat browner cap, and black areas replaced with drab brown. Non-breeding male resembles breeding female. No data available on juvenile plumage, but presumably similar to that of non-breeding adult.
Habitat. Coastal lowlands.
Food and Feeding. No information available. Probably similar to *C. alexandrinus*.
Breeding. Virtually no information available. Breeding recently recorded in Jun, W Java; also records of birds in breeding condition in May. Eggs much like those of *C. alexandrinus*.
Movements. Sedentary.
Status and Conservation. Not globally threatened. Currently considered near-threatened. No population estimates available; not encountered during Asian Waterfowl Censuses of 1987 to 1992; recently found to be common on S coast of Madura I (E Java). Very poorly known: confused taxonomic status, together with inaccurate descriptions, with result of very little definite information gathered. Considerable scope for research into biology and ecology; extensive surveys required in order to establish conservation status and potential threats; taxonomic reappraisal highly desirable, but much more field information required.

Bibliography. Andrew, P. (1992), Collar *et al*. (1994), Hellebrekers & Hoogerwerf (1967), Hoogerwerf (1936, 1949, 1966, 1969), Hoogerwerf & Siccama (1937), Kooiman (1940), MacKinnon (1988), MacKinnon & Phillipps (1993), Roselaar (1983), Sibley & Monroe (1990), White & Bruce (1986).

46. Red-capped Plover

Charadrius ruficapillus

French: Pluvier à tête rousse **German**: Rotkopf-Regenpfeifer **Spanish**: Chorlitejo Capelirrojo
Other common names: Red-capped Dotterel/Sandplover

Taxonomy. *Charadrius ruficapillus* Temminck, 1822, New South Wales.
Forms superspecies with *C. marginatus*, *C. alexandrinus* and *C. javanicus*; all of these have on occasion been considered conspecific (see page 386). Monotypic.
Distribution. Australia, mainly avoiding arid interior; Tasmania.
Descriptive notes. 14-16 cm; 27-54 g; wingspan 27-34 cm. Small, slim plover with short white supercilium and no white hindneck; black eyestripe, lores, frontal bar and breast patches; cap and nape rufous. Female has centre of crown pale grey-brown. Non-breeding adult has black and rufous head pattern mainly replaced with brown, but some tinges of rufous chestnut may remain; upperparts with buff fringes. Juvenile resembles non-breeding adult, but lacks traces of rufous chestnut; upperpart feathers have buff fringes; recalls juvenile *C. bicinctus*, but smaller, longer-legged and paler brown.
Habitat. Coastal habitats, especially sandy or shell beaches with muddy or sandy flats nearby, with preference for saline wetlands behind coast, such as salt-marshes and salt-pans; also bare areas at inland wetlands, preferring exposed inland salt-lakes, and artificial wetlands and watering points, including sewage ponds and salt-works.
Food and Feeding. Annelids, molluscs, small crustaceans, marine and terrestrial insects and their larvae, including ants and beetles, and some seeds and vegetation. Forages in typical *Charadrius* fashion, by sight. Feeds on sandy beaches and mudflats at sea shores, lakes, streams and inland wetlands,

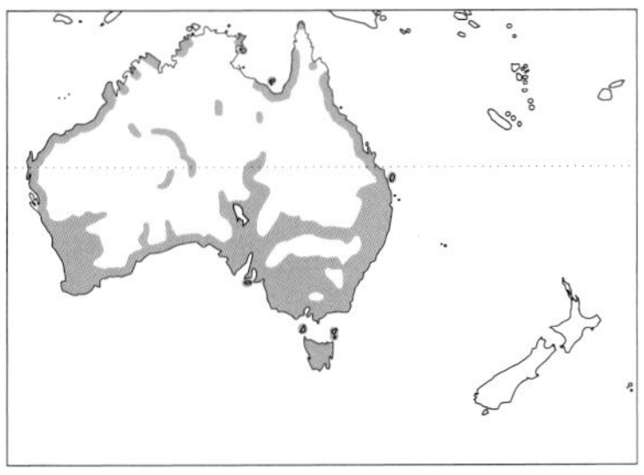

salt-marshes, pasture and gibber plains; often among beachcast seaweed and sparse vegetation. Usually in small parties, but in flocks of hundreds after breeding season.

Breeding. Laying seasonal at coast (Jul-Jan), but at inland wetlands occurs in response to unpredictable rainfall and flooding. Solitary on coast, and inland solitary or in loose colonies of 4-44 pairs (up to 100), usually 70-100 m apart; territorial. Mixed flocks of non-breeders and breeders occur next to nesting sites. Nests on sand, shell-grit, sandy mud, weed mats or beachcast seaweed, on bare or sparsely vegetated ground, usually not less than 40 m from water; shallow scrape, unlined or lined with some shell fragments, pebbles, vegetation and debris; nests on damp mud more substantial, built of water weed. Usually 2 eggs, rarely 3, laid at 1 day intervals, occasionally 2-3 days; single-brooded, but can lay perhaps up to 5 replacement clutches; incubation 30-31 days, starting when clutch complete, mostly by female; chick cream above, with black-brown blotches and speckles forming mid-dorsal line from mantle to rump, poorly defined whitish hindneck collar without broad black bordering, white underparts; tended by both parents. Fledging period and age of first breeding unknown. Nests can be flooded by irrigation works; breeding birds susceptible to disturbance, leaving nest when approached by people or dogs; eggs recorded being trampled by sheep. Hatching success 19-31%. Oldest ringed bird at least 6 years and 5 months.

Movements. Poorly known. Delimitation between breeding and non-breeding distribution very obscure. Birds move between inland wetlands and coast, and between inland wetlands, in response to flooding, drought and varying food availability. Present at all sites almost year round, but numbers can fluctuate without any apparent large-scale seasonal pattern; in some areas, changing numbers related to seasonality of rainfall; usually higher numbers on coast in summer, when inland wetlands are dried up. Probably moves at night in flocks of 8-50 birds.

Status and Conservation. Not globally threatened. Total population c. 95,000 birds; widespread throughout Australia and Tasmania. Vagrant to New Zealand, where small numbers even appear to have bred from 1950 to 1980. Coastal habitats may be threatened by low-density residential development.

Bibliography. Abensperg-Traun & Dickman (1989), Alcorn (1990), Ashby (1991), Blakers *et al.* (1984), Christian *et al.* (1992a), Davis (1980), Flegg & Madge (1995), Green (1956), Hobbs (1972), Hoogerwerf (1966), Hughey (1989), Jessop (1990), Lane & Davies (1987), Lane & Jessop (1983), Lindsey (1992), Macdonald (1988), Marchant & Higgins (1993), McKenzie (1980), Pizzey & Doyle (1980), Poore *et al.* (1979), Pringle (1987), Saunders & de Rebeira (1986), Schodde & Tidemann (1986), Simpson & Day (1994), Slater *et al.* (1989), Trounson (1987), Watkins (1993), White & Bruce (1986).

47. Malaysian Plover

Charadrius peronii

French: Pluvier de Péron **German**: Malaienregenpfeifer **Spanish**: Chorlitejo Malayo
Other common names: Malaysian/Malay Sandplover

Taxonomy *Charadrius peronii* Schlegel, 1865, Semao (= Samau), near Timor.
Has been linked with *C. javanicus* for biogeographical reasons, but structurally quite different. Proposed race *chaseni* is erroneous. Monotypic.
Distribution. S Thailand, Malay Peninsula and S Vietnam to Sumatra, Borneo, Philippines, Sulawesi and Bali to Timor.

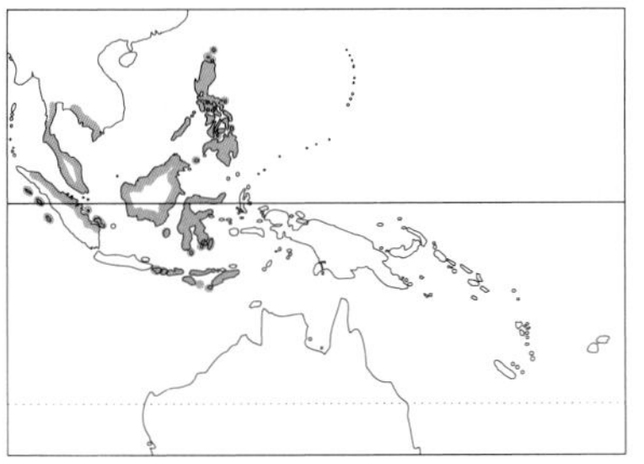

Descriptive notes. 14-16 cm; c. 42 g. Resembles *C. alexandrinus* but slightly smaller and chunkier, with black hind collar on upper back; upperparts with dark feather centres; chestnut crown, black frontal bar and eyeline; black breast patches sometimes almost forming complete band. Female has black parts of male rufous brown, sometimes with black flecking and less chestnut in crown; narrower white hindneck; rufous breast patches or breast band separate from female of *C. alexandrinus*. No seasonal variation. Juvenile like female, but never has black flecks in breast patches.

Habitat. Sandy beaches, especially small bays with coral sands, open dunes, either bare or with sparse, low vegetation, and artificial coastal sand-fills.

Food and Feeding. No information available on diet. Feeds among tide-wrack at low tide or on exposed flats; often close to water's edge. Typically found feeding in pairs, though may form communal roosts of up to 27 birds.

Breeding. Eggs found late Feb to Jul; May on Luzon (N Philippines). Chicks found mid-Mar to mid-Jun; downy young in Jun on Sumba. Solitary; occasionally nesting as close as 75 m from neighbour; density 0·5-4 pairs/km of shoreline. Nest is shallow, unlined depression, located high up beach, with little or no plant cover. Usually 3 eggs, sometimes 2. No further information available.

Movements. Essentially resident; minor dispersion along SW coast of Peninsular Malaysia mostly during non-breeding season.

Status and Conservation. Not globally threatened. Currently considered near-threatened. Total population may number less than 10,000 birds and possibly declining, but no good estimate available due to scarcity of data. Highest total in Asian Waterfowl Census was 410 birds in 1992. Recently colonized coastal sand-fill in Singapore, but habitat there is sure to degenerate; main cause of nest failure in Singapore is disturbance through beach recreation. Grass sowing and urban development of coastal habitats form major threats.

Bibliography. Andrew & Holmes (1990), Davidson *et al.* (1995), Dickinson *et al.* (1991), Duckworth & Kelsh (1988), Gibbs (1990), Holmes (1995), Hoogerwerf (1966), Lekagul & Round (1991), MacKinnon (1988), MacKinnon & Phillipps (1993), Madoc (1976), van Marle & Voous (1988), Mayr (1944), Medway & Wells (1976), Perennou *et al.* (1994), Scott (1989), Silvius *et al.* (1986), Smythies (1981, 1986), White & Bruce (1986).

48. Chestnut-banded Plover

Charadrius pallidus

French: Pluvier élégant **German**: Rotband-Regenpfeifer **Spanish**: Chorlitejo Pálido
Other common names: Chestnut-banded Sandplover

Taxonomy. *Charadrius pallidus*, Strickland, 1852, Walvis Bay.
Considerable confusion with nomenclature in past: name *C. pallidus* was considered synonymous with *C. (alexandrinus) marginatus*; present species was known as *C. venustus*, and S race as *C. v. rufocinctus*. Two subspecies recognized.
Subspecies and Distribution.
C. p. venustus Fischer & Reichenow, 1884 - Rift Valley soda-lakes on border of Kenya and Tanzania.
C. p. pallidus Strickland, 1852 - S Africa, on coast from SW Angola to Mozambique, and inland in N Namibia, N Botswana and CN South Africa.

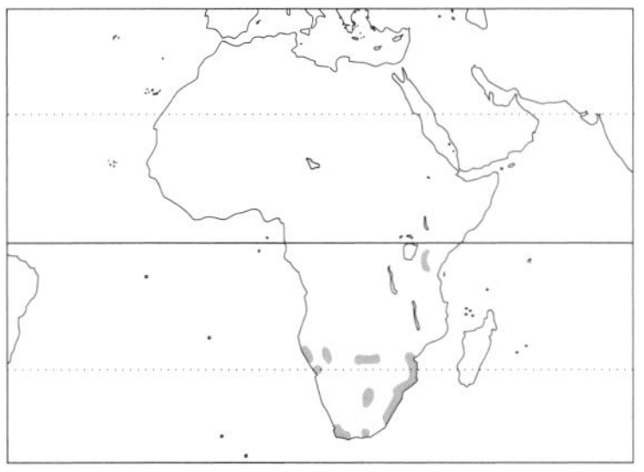

Descriptive notes. 15 cm; nominate 28-44 g, *venustus* 20-37 g. Proportionally long legs; black frontal bar, eyestripe and lores and chestnut band on forecrown joined to breast band; upper edge of breast band sometimes black. Female lacks black. No seasonal variation. Juvenile lacks chestnut and black; frontal bar and breast band greyish, latter usually broken; upperparts with whitish fringes. Race *venustus* smaller, with relatively larger bill and darker, browner upperparts.

Habitat. Prefers salt-pans, alkaline lakes and coastal lagoons and estuaries; habitat often of ephemeral nature; rarely occurs in freshwater habitats.

Food and Feeding. Feeds on insects and small crustaceans along the water's edge. Very active in early morning, in Kenya feeding until 09:00 hours, sometimes until 12:00 hours. Occurs singly, in pairs or in flocks of up to 50-60 birds.

Breeding. Laying Apr-Oct in E Africa, at end of rains and afterwards; Sept in Mozambique; Jul in Namibia; Mar-May and Sept-Jan, mostly Nov-Dec, in South Africa. Monogamous; solitary and territorial; 70 nests recorded along edges of single salt-pan. Nest situated on calcareous soil, mudflat or stony slope, within 50 m of water; shallow scrape, lined with small stones, grass, fish bones and small snail shells. Usually 2 eggs, sometimes 1, laid at 2-4 day intervals; possibly double-brooded; incubation by both parents, apparently by female during day and by male in evening, probably starting when clutch complete; incubation and fledging periods unknown. Chick has grey upperparts mixed with black markings and black lines down centre of crown and back; underparts white. Oldest bird recorded 11 years, 6 months.

Movements. Probably partial migrant and nomadic; makes local movements when breeding habitat dries up. In E Africa, moves up and down Rift Valley, with peak numbers in Jul-Sept at L Manyara. After breeding season, some inland birds disperse to coast to mix with sedentary coastal populations, e.g. in Namibia, where large numbers occur in Dec-Jan.

Status and Conservation. Not globally threatened. No population estimates available. Total of c. 5200 birds counted on coast of S Africa, mostly in Namibia; abundant to very abundant in E Africa; locally common to rare inland.

Bibliography. Blaker (1966), Britton, P.L. (1980), Brooke (1984a), Clancey (1962, 1985), Cunningham-van Someren (1971), Dowsett & Forbes-Watson (1993), Ellis (1971), Fraser (1969), Ginn *et al.* (1989), Harvey (1994), Jeffery & Liversidge (1951), Little (1966), Mackworth-Praed & Grant (1957, 1962), McLachlan & Jeffery (1949), Maclean (1993), Morgan-Davies (1960b), Perry (1975), Pinto (1983), Pollard (1980), Reynolds (1975a), Richards (1980), Robinson & Robinson (1951), Short *et al.* (1990), Snow (1978), van Someren (1956), Taylor, P.B. (1982b, 1983), Tree (1980a), Urban *et al.* (1986), Winterbottom (1963).

49. Collared Plover

Charadrius collaris

French: Pluvier d'Azara **German**: Schlankschnabel-Regenpfeifer **Spanish**: Chorlitejo de Azara
Other common names: Azara's Sandplover

Taxonomy *Charadrius collaris* Vieillot, 1818, Paraguay.
Shorter-winged population occurring from Mexico to N Brazil is by some authors considered subspecies *gracilis*. Monotypic.
Distribution. WC Mexico through Central America to W Colombia and W Ecuador, and E of Andes S to N Argentina; C Chile.

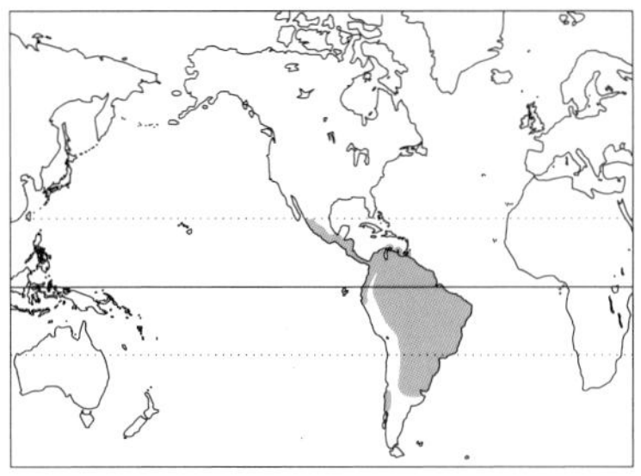

Descriptive notes. 14-15 cm; 26-31 g. Differs from most similar species by rather narrow black breast band; black frontal bar and lores; upperpart feathers have chestnut fringes; pale chestnut on central crown. Resembles *C. alexandrinus* but always lacks dark stripe behind eye; upperparts darker and browner; bill relatively long and thin; legs yellowish. Female generally very similar to male, but chestnut can be less extensive and black areas are sometimes brownish. No seasonal variation. Juvenile has no breast band, but has tawny brown lateral patches; no black on head; buff fringes on upperparts.

Habitat. Sandy coastal beaches, inland and estuarine wetlands, riverbanks and ponds; also open sandy savannas.

Food and Feeding. Little studied; (water) beetles and their larvae, dragonflies, fly larvae, ants; on intertidal flats, takes polychaete worms, small crustaceans, such as isopods, decapods and crabs, small gastropods; also seeds. Outside breeding season feeds solitarily, in pairs or in small loose flocks. Forages independent of tidal cycle, using intertidal flats at low tide, but beaches and nearby gravelly or short-grass areas at high tide.

Breeding. Breeding season varies with latitude: Nov-Dec in W Mexico; nest with eggs in Aug in S Colombia, another in Sept in Brazil; birds with young in Chile in Jan. Four nests reported, all with 2 eggs.

Movements. Sedentary. In Chile, said to be commoner Apr-Sept, outside breeding season, although no reports of movements. In South America, seems to be commoner on ocean beaches in austral winter than in summer. At Bay of Panama arrives on beaches in parties of 6 birds, from early to late Sept, departing middle to end of Feb.

Status and Conservation. Not globally threatened. No population estimates available, but apparently very common in E South America. Range is expanding on coast of Chile.

Bibliography. Belton (1984), Beltzer (1986b, 1991), Canevari *et al.* (1991), Contreras *et al.* (1990), Fjeldså & Krabbe (1990), Haverschmidt (1968), Haverschmidt & Mees (1995), Hayes & Fox (1991), Hilty & Brown (1986), Howell & Webb (1994, 1995a), Johnson (1965b), Klimaitis & Moschione (1984), Meyer de Schauensee & Phelps (1978), Monroe (1968), Oyarzo & Ruiz (1983), de la Peña (1981a, 1992), Ridgely & Gwynne (1989), Scott & Carbonell (1986), Sick (1985c, 1993), Slud (1964), Snyder (1966), Stiles & Skutch (1989), Strauch & Abele (1979), Tostain *et al.* (1992), Vilina & Droully (1990), Vooren & Chiaradia (1990), Wetmore (1965), Widrig (1980, 1983a), Yovanovich (1995).

50. **Puna Plover**

Charadrius alticola

French: Pluvier du puna **German**: Punaregenpfeifer **Spanish**: Chorlitejo Andino
Other common names: Puna Two-banded Plover

Taxonomy. *Ægialitis alticola* Berlepsch & Stolzmann, 1902, Ingapirca, Junín, Peru.
Sometimes considered a subspecies of *C. falklandicus*. Monotypic.
Distribution. *Puna* zone of high Andes, from C Peru through NE Chile and W Bolivia to NW Argentina.

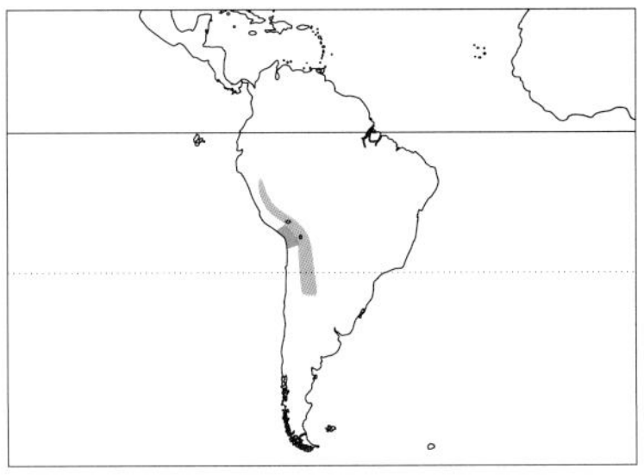

Descriptive notes. 16·5-17·5 cm. Compact plover with "neckless" appearance; black legs and bill, white face; large white forehead demarcated by black frontal bar joined to black lateral breast patches by thin black stripe behind eye; much of crown, hindneck and breast band pale chestnut. Female can be much duller; can have greyish breast band, and brownish patches in black areas. Non-breeding adult sometimes loses black and chestnut, and has obscure breast patches. Juvenile lacks black and chestnut; no lateral breast patches, and very faint breast band; less white-faced look. Birds from Catamarca, N Argentina, are pale and almost lack breast band.
Habitat. High plateau regions with wide expanses of rather firm clay or mud; partly flooded, strongly grazed grassland around salt and freshwater lakes; mainly at 3000-4500 m, but also occurs even higher.
Food and Feeding. Very little information available, but food includes small crustaceans. Outside breeding season usually feeds in loose parties.
Breeding. Laying mainly Sept-Oct, rarely Jan. Solitary. Nest situated on short, matted grass. Chick buffy white with black speckles above.
Movements. Probably mainly sedentary, but at least part of population regularly descends to Pacific coast, where reported from Ica and Tacna (S Peru), particularly in Jun-Oct; on coast observed in parties of up to 30 birds.
Status and Conservation. Not globally threatened. No population estimates available; rather common in S & C parts of range, e.g. on S shores of L Titicaca.
Bibliography. Blake (1977), Canevari *et al.* (1991), Fjeldså & Krabbe (1990), Graves (1981), Hellmayr & Conover (1948), Hoy (1967), Hughes, R.A. (1984), Johnson (1965b), Koepcke (1970), Meyer de Schauensee (1982), Narosky & Yzurieta (1987), Olrog (1984), Parker *et al.* (1982), de la Peña (1992), Remsen & Traylor (1989), Scott & Carbonell (1986).

51. **Two-banded Plover**

Charadrius falklandicus

French: Pluvier des Falkland **German**: Falkland-Regenpfeifer **Spanish**: Chorlitejo Malvinero
Other common names: Double-banded/Patagonian Two-banded Plover, Patagonian Sandplover

Taxonomy. *Charadrius falklandicus* Latham, 1790, Port Egmont, Falkland Islands.
Has been considered conspecific with *C. alticola*. Population of Falkland Is has been suggested as meriting a separate subspecies, on basis of high frequency of broken upper breast band. Monotypic.
Distribution. C & S Chile and Argentina; locally in S Brazil; Falkland Is. Winters N to N Chile, Uruguay and S Brazil.

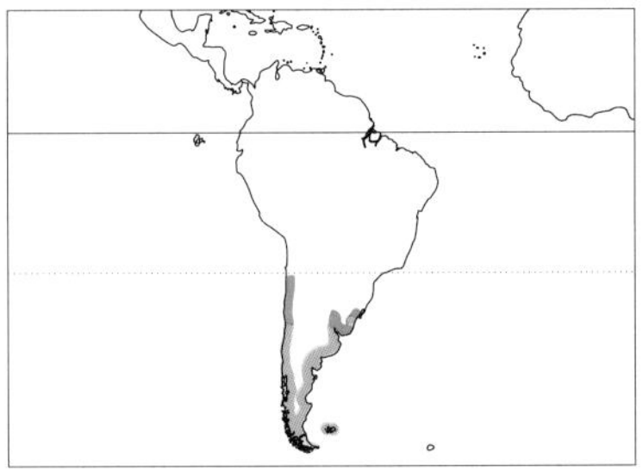

Descriptive notes. 17-18·5 cm; 62-72 g. Slightly larger and longer-billed than *C. alticola*; white forehead and lores, black frontal bar; crown and hindneck pale chestnut; two black breast bands, the upper one frequently broken, especially in Falkland Is birds. Female has rufous on head duller; black areas brownish; upper breast band flecked white. Non-breeding adult has black replaced by grey, and chestnut by grey-brown. Juvenile like non-breeding adult, but breast bands brown with buff fringes and face darker; clear buff fringes on upperpart feathers.
Habitat. Gravelly and stony sea shores; also sandy beaches, wet savannas and short-grass borders with patches of sand or gravel, near streams and freshwater or brackish ponds in lowlands. In non-breeding season, also occurs on intertidal mudflats. Mostly coastal, but breeds up to 1200 m on Andean foothills in Santa Cruz, S Argentina.
Food and Feeding. Known to take small invertebrates. Feeds along edges of surf, on beds of rotting kelp, on short grass and around edges of freshwater pools.
Breeding. Laying Sept-Dec, sometimes later in upland habitats. Solitary. 3 eggs. Very tame on breeding grounds. Chick pale buff with black speckles and lines above.
Movements. Most birds migrate N in non-breeding season, although some still found on most of breeding range except extreme S. On Pacific coast, reaches Antofagasta, N Chile; from Patagonia reaches Uruguay and Rio Grande do Sul, SE Brazil. Seems faithful to wintering sites. Falkland Is population sedentary, only moving short distance outside season. During non-breeding season loosely social, occasionally in flocks of 150 or more.
Status and Conservation. Not globally threatened. Population estimated at 10,000-100,000 birds. Numbers seem to be stable, but very little information available. In Rio Grande do Sul, SE Brazil, breeding on coast at Lagoa do Peixe suspected in 1972, proved in 1986.
Bibliography. Antas (1988), Belton (1984), Blake (1977), Canevari *et al.* (1991), Clark (1986), Fjeldså & Krabbe (1990), Forrester (1993), Hellmayr & Conover (1948), Humphrey *et al.* (1970), Johnson (1965b), Meyer de Schauensee (1982), Myers (1980c), Myers & Myers (1979), Narosky & Yzurieta (1987), Olrog (1984), de la Peña (1992), Pinto (1964), Resende & Leeuwenberg (1989), Ruschi (1979), Scott & Carbonell (1986), Sick (1985c, 1993), Vooren & Chiaradia (1990), Woods (1988).

52. **Double-banded Plover**

Charadrius bicinctus

French: Pluvier à double collier **Spanish**: Chorlitejo Bicinchado
German: Doppelband-Regenpfeifer
Other common names: Banded/Double-banded Dotterel

Taxonomy. *Charadrius bicinctus* Jardine and Selby, 1827, New South Wales.
Two subspecies recognized.
Subspecies and Distribution.
C. b. bicinctus Jardine & Selby, 1827 - New Zealand and Chatham Is; winters to S & E Australia, Tasmania, Norfolk I and Lord Howe I, New Caledonia, Vanuatu and Fiji.
C. b. exilis Falla, 1978 - Auckland Is.

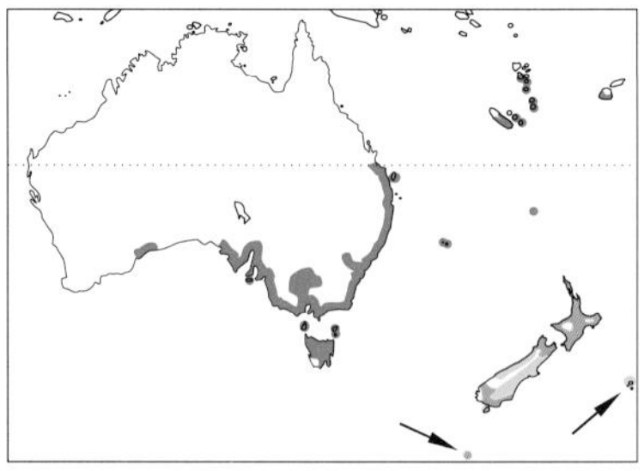

Descriptive notes. 18-21 cm; nominate 47-76 g, *exilis* 78-89 g (4 birds); wingspan 37-42 cm. Small, chubby, upright plover; narrow upper breast band black, broad lower breast band chestnut; thin black frontal bar above white forehead; white chin, throat and lower cheeks. Female can have black areas brownish, and lower breast band brown of variable intensity. Non-breeding adult lacks black and chestnut; breast bands reduced to grey lateral patches; clear buff supercilium. Juvenile like non-breeding adult, but has very obscure greyish breast bands; upperparts have whitish buff fringes; recalls juvenile *C. mongolus*, but smaller, less grey and with thinner bill. Race *exilis* plumper, heavier and longer-legged; female has warmer brown upperparts, but duller breast bands.
Habitat. Usually breeds inland on dry, open, firm banks of sand, gravel or shingle in wide rivers; at high altitudes in New Zealand, in dry montane habitats with short vegetation; also coastal beaches, pasture, ploughed land, gravel, quarries and moorland. Outside breeding season, on wide variety of coastal and freshwater wetlands, seldom far inland, for instance occurring on estuaries, lagoons, swamps, beaches, salt-lakes and salt-works; also salt-marshes, grassland and pasture. Outside breeding season roosts in flocks on traditional sites, especially in inaccessible areas at night, e.g. islets, headlands and protected beaches.
Food and Feeding. Molluscs, insects (e.g. larvae of chironomids and other flies and beetles, also caterpillars), crustaceans (e.g. isopods and small crabs), marine worms and spiders; sometimes seeds and berries, eaten especially by chicks. Feeds on vegetated shingle beds, mudflats, salt-marshes, closely cropped pasture, tilled ground; occasionally probes in soft ground. During breeding season, non-breeders and failed breeders feed in flocks on nearby pastures. Diurnal and nocturnal forager; outside breeding season sometimes forages in small loose groups, but others defend territories on wintering ground; breeding birds on Auckland Is move to beaches at night to feed.
Breeding. Laying Aug-Dec in lowlands; mid-Sept (or mid-Aug) to mid-Dec, mostly Oct, in higher areas. Seasonally monogamous, sometimes into second year. High nest-site fidelity and natal philopatry, especially in males. Male produces loud clicking sound with wings during territorial flight display. Solitary and territorial; sometimes clustered with nests mainly 100-150 m apart. Nest is scrape on bare ground with prostrate vegetation, almost unlined or lined with varying amounts of stones and pieces of vegetation and dung, which are also added during incubation. Usually 3 eggs (2-4), laid at intervals of under 60 to 120 hours; up to three replacement clutches; double-brooding rare; incubation 25-28 days, by both parents, female most of day and male possibly most of night. Chicks have two colour morphs, not related to geographical distribution or sex, rarely with intermediates: gold morph has crown and upperparts speckled buff and black-brown with some black-brown blotches, hindneck collar off-white to cream; grey morph has buff of gold morph replaced by grey. Fledging 5-6 weeks; young tended by both parents until 2 weeks after fledging. First breeding at 1 year old. Hatching success 10-44%; eggs and young can be taken by various predators, or trampled by sheep and cattle; predation severest after sudden decline in rabbit numbers or where stoats present; predation rates lowest on broad shingle fans and river islands. Oldest ringed bird over 12 years.
Movements. Nominate is partially migratory, the only plover that migrates from New Zealand to Australia; birds breeding inland or at high altitudes, above about 600 m, almost entirely migratory, migrating to N New Zealand, E & S Australia and Tasmania, or further afield; destination varies regionally. Coastal breeders mostly sedentary. In race *exilis*, probably only part of population makes local movements, moving to tidal shores of Enderby I in winter, while others may remain on territories. Migration starts Oct-Nov, when birds leave territories, and start flocking in Dec-Jan (-Apr), forming flocks of up to 150 birds; most departures for Australia occur Feb-Mar, usually from staging areas on E & S coasts of South I; birds moving to North I depart Jan-Mar. Highly site-faithful on wintering grounds, some birds defending feeding territories. Returns to breeding grounds Aug to early Sept; 1 year olds appear to return later than older birds.
Status and Conservation. Not globally threatened. Widespread in New Zealand; total population estimated at 50,000 birds, of which estimated 30,000 winter in Australia, and more than 4000 on Tasmania. Race *exilis* currently numbers 730 birds; population decreased in 19th century due to introduction of cats and pigs; numbers increasing since early 1970's, when total was 100-200 birds. Species is favoured by conversion of shrubland into pasture, but flood mitigation and planting of willows and other trees have decreased amount of available nesting habitat. Introduced predators prey on significant proportion of eggs and chicks.
Bibliography. Appleby (1992), Barlow (1988a), Barter (1989e, 1991c), Barter & Minton (1987), Bomford (1978, 1986, 1988), Chambers (1989), Christian *et al.* (1992a), Cunningham (1973), Dann (1991a, 1991b), Endersby (1994), Falla (1978), Falla *et al.* (1981), Lane & Davies (1987), Marchant & Higgins (1993), Minton, C.D.T. (1987a, 1987b), Minton, C.D.T. & Pierce (1986), Phillips (1980), Pierce (1980a, 1987, 1989), Pringle (1987), Robertson (1985), Sibson (1978), Soper (1976), Thomas (1972), Walker *et al.* (1991), Watkins (1993), Williams (1975).

PLATE 39 ➤

ssp *atrifrons*

♂

♂

53

♀

ssp *mongolus*

♀

ssp *leschenaultii*

54

ssp *columbinus*

♀

♀

55

♂

56

♂

57

♀

61

♂

58

59

60

♀

62

63

♂

64

65

66

67

PLATE 39

ssp *ruficollis*

ssp *pallidus*

inches   5

cm   13

53. Lesser Sandplover
Charadrius mongolus

French: Pluvier de Mongolie **German**: Mongolenregenpfeifer **Spanish**: Chorlitejo Mongol Chico
Other common names: Mongolian Plover/Sandplover/Dotterel/Sand-dotterel

Taxonomy. *Charadrius mongolus* Pallas, 1776, salt-lakes towards Mongolian border = Kulusutay, probably on Onon River, Siberia.
C Asian and Himalayan populations form megasubspecies, *atrifrons*. Five subspecies normally recognized.
Subspecies and Distribution.
C. m. pamirensis Richmond, 1896 - W Tien Shan, Pamirs and Karakoram to W Kunlun Shan; winters S & E Africa to W India.
C. m. atrifrons Wagler, 1829 - Himalayas and S Tibet; winters India to Sumatra.
C. m. schaeferi Meyer de Schauensee, 1938 - E Tibet N to S Mongolia; winters Thailand to Greater Sundas.
C. m. mongolus Pallas, 1776 - inland E Siberia and Russian Far East; winters Taiwan to Australia.
C. m. stegmanni Portenko, 1939 - Kolymskiy, Kamchatka, N Kuril Is and Commander Is N to Chukotskiy Peninsula; winters S Ryukyu Is and Taiwan to Australia.

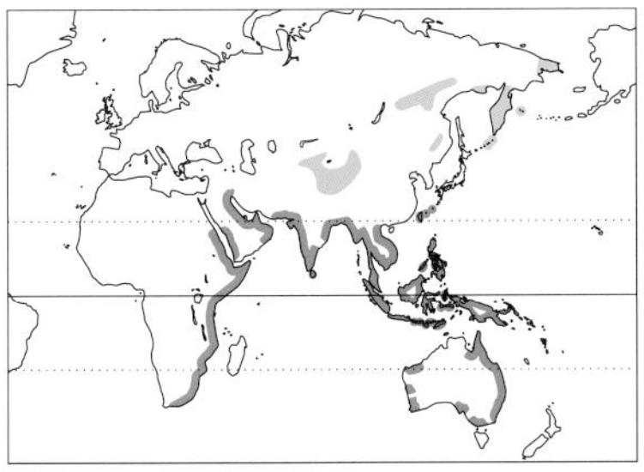

Descriptive notes. 18-21 cm; 39-110 g; wingspan 45-58 cm. Black eyepatch, broad rufous red breast band and hindneck collar; legs typically dark grey. Very similar to *C. leschenaultii* in all plumages, but smaller, with shorter legs, shorter and thinner bill and rounder head. Female like male but black on head browner, no black line on forehead, rufous parts duller, and no dark upper border to breast band. Non-breeding adult lacks black and chestnut; grey-brown upperparts with pale fringes; large grey lateral breast patches. Juvenile resembles non-breeding adult with buff fringes on upperparts; face, supercilium and breast patches with some buff. Nominate and race *stegmanni* have blackish upper border to breast band, and forehead white, bisected by thin black line; other races have forehead black, sometimes with a few white patches.
Habitat. In breeding season, occurs above or beyond tree-line, mainly in mountains at altitudes up to 5500 m in Ladakh and Sikkim; barren valleys and basins, elevated tundra and mountain steppes, mainly near water (e.g. bogs), on moist but well drained gravelly, rocky or sandy, sparsely vegetated surfaces, including salt-pans, patches of detritus, and in some areas dry edges of salt-marshes and places used by cattle herds; also at sea-level on sand dunes or on shingle, but at lower altitudes does not generally on cultivated or swampy terrain or lakesides until after breeding season. During non-breeding season strictly coastal, frequently tidal mudflats, sandy beaches and estuaries; occasionally airfields.
Food and Feeding. Rather few data available. In non-breeding habitats, takes insects; crustaceans, such as crabs and amphipods; molluscs, particularly bivalves; and polychaete worms. In breeding areas many beetles, and also fly larvae. Limbless bodies of crabs swallowed whole; stalks worms in their holes. May wade up to breast in water. Feeds solitarily or in scattered flocks, often mixed with other waders, including *C. leschenaultii*, on mudflats, salt-pans and salt-marsh, rarely at water's edge. Sometimes forages at night.
Breeding. Laying generally late May to mid-Jun, but from mid-May in *pamirensis*. Density of *pamirensis* c. 1 pair/km^2; rarely 3-12 nests only 100 m apart. Unique grating call or display song, "trit-it-it-it-turkhweeoo", lasting 1 second. Nest is scrape or cattle footprint in bare sand or shingle, sometimes besides bushes or big stones, in Far East among lichens and *Drias*; lining of vegetation, small stones and debris accumulates during incubation. Usually 3 eggs, sometimes 2; may lay replacement clutches; single-brooded; incubation 22-24 days, female often starts incubating first egg; chick grey-buff above, mottled with black on crown, grey-buff hindneck collar, underparts white, greyish buff at sides; fledging 30-35 days; in most cases only males tend chicks, but sometimes both parents. Foxes can apparently cause high mortality. Breeds first probably at 2 years old. Oldest ringed bird at least 20½ years.
Movements. Migratory. Four groups definable, migrating to different winter quarters, ranging from coasts of S Africa through S Asia to Australia, using staging areas in between on both ways, e.g. SE Asia and, on northward migration, Japan; occasional winterer in small numbers in Japan. Race *stegmanni* leaves breeding grounds late Jul to late Sept, females first, juveniles latest. Many E Siberian birds migrate coastally, but large numbers of *mongolus* pass overland through Transbaikalia and Manchuria; marked southward movement down E coast of Australia in Aug-Nov. C Asian populations probably migrate directly to S Asian coasts. In Siberia, flocks form early Jul and depart early Aug to early Sept, adults first; arrive in India, S Arabia and E Africa early Aug to mid-Sept. Race *atrifrons* starts moving N in late Feb; main departures Apr; northern breeding grounds reoccupied by mid-Apr to mid-May; *stegmanni* late May to early Jun. Some non-breeders remain on wintering grounds. Casual in NW Alaska, where has bred.
Status and Conservation. Not globally threatened. Population of *pamirensis* estimated to at minimum of 30,000 birds, with 28,000 estimated wintering along Saudi Arabian Gulf coast; *atrifrons* minimum 100,000 birds; and *schaeferi* 25,000-100,000 birds; in winter in E Asia and Australasia, probably 25,000-100,000 birds of races *mongolus* and *stegmanni*, of which c. 20,000 in Australia. In winter, is commonest wader on coasts of Pakistan and India; locally common to abundant from Ethiopia to Tanzania, with thousands in Kenya.
Bibliography. Alcorn (1986), Ali & Ripley (1980), Alström (1991), Balachandran & Natarajan (1992), Barter (1991b, 1991d), Barter & Davies (1991), Beehler *et al*. (1986), Berman & Dorogoy (1993), Bezzel (1986), Brazil (1991), Bregnballe *et al*. (1990), Britton (1982a), Chambers (1989), Coates (1985), Cramp & Simmons (1983), Dementiev & Gladkov (1951b), Dickinson *et al*. (1991), Dowsett & Dowsett-Lemaire (1976), Dowsett & Forbes-Watson (1993), Étchécopar & Hüe (1978), Evans (1994), Evans & Keijl (1993a, 1993b), Flint *et al*. (1984), Gebauer & Nadler (1992), Goodman *et al*. (1989), Heather & Robertson (1981), Hindwood & Hoskin (1954), Hüe & Étchécopar (1970), Kistchinski (1980), Knystautas (1993), Kydyraliyev (1990), Lane, B.A. (1986), Lane, B.A. & Davies (1987), Lane, B.A. & Jessop (1985), Lekagul & Round (1991), MacKinnon & Phillipps (1993), Mackworth-Praed & Grant (1957, 1962, 1970), Marchant & Higgins (1993), van Marle & Voous (1988), Mauersberger (1975), Medway & Wells (1976), Nadler & Königstedt (1986), Nielsen (1971), Perennou *et al*. (1994), Phillips (1978), Piersma (1985), Pook (1992), Ripley (1982), Roberts, T.J. (1991), Rogacheva (1992), Salter *et al*. (1986), Scott (1989), Short *et al*. (1990), Silvius *et al*. (1986), Sinclair & Nicholls (1980), Smythies (1981, 1986), Starks & Lane (1987), Taylor (1978, 1982a, 1982d), Urban *et al*. (1986), Watkins (1993), White & Bruce (1986), Williams, M.D. (1986).

54. Greater Sandplover
Charadrius leschenaultii

French: Pluvier de Leschenault **German**: Wüstenregenpfeifer **Spanish**: Chorlitejo Mongol Grande
Other common names: Great/Large/Large-billed/Geoffroy's (Sand) Plover/Dotterel

Taxonomy. *Charadrius Leschenaultii* Lesson, 1826, Pondicherry, India.
Three subspecies recognized.
Subspecies and Distribution.
C. l. columbinus Wagler, 1829 - Turkey, Syria, Jordan, Armenia, Azerbaijan and S Afghanistan; winters Red Sea, Gulf of Aden and SE Mediterranean.
C. l. crassirostris (Severtsov, 1873) - Transcaspia to SE Kazakhstan; winters in E & SE Africa.
C. l. leschenaultii Lesson, 1826 - W China (Dzungaria), S Mongolia (N Gobi Desert), S Siberia (Tuvinskaya) and Altai Mts; winters Australasia.

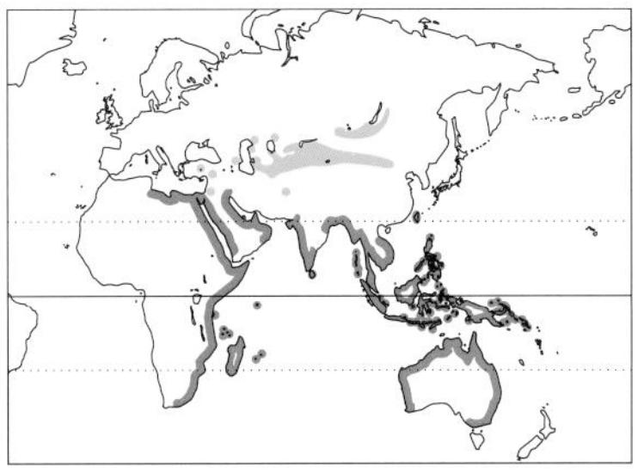

Descriptive notes. 22-25 cm; 55-121 g; wingspan 53-60 cm. Medium-sized plover; larger than *C. mongolus*, with larger, broader head, larger bill, longer legs and somewhat paler upperparts; legs usually paller greyish green, but rather variable. Male has narrower and more sharply demarcated rufous breast band than *C. mongolus*. Female has black on head dark grey-brown, no dark stripe on forehead, less extensive chestnut coloration on breast band. Plumages of non-breeding adult and juvenile very similar to those of *C. mongolus*. Races generally very similar, differing in bill shape and colour, both of breeding adult and of juvenile; *columbinus* extensively rufous on back and also on upper flanks.
Habitat. During breeding season predominantly found in deserts or semi-deserts, at lower altitudes than *C. mongolus*, although still up to 3000 m; in open, uncultivated and treeless areas with bare, dry surface, usually near water; in Turkey, also on heavily grazed saline steppe. During non-breeding season, mainly found on coast, on sheltered sandy, shelly or muddy beaches and estuaries, with large intertidal mudflats or sandbanks; also reefs, rocky islands and dunes; occasionally salt-lakes and brackish swamps; usually roosts on sandbanks and spits.
Food and Feeding. Mainly beetles, also molluscs (e.g. snails), worms, crustaceans (e.g. shrimps and crabs), other insects and their larvae (e.g. termites, midges and ants), and occasionally lizards. Recorded wading and foot-trembling. Feeds on mud or sand on intertidal mudflats, salt-marsh, shores of lakes and rivers and pastures. Often in feeding flocks of 2-50 birds, up to 1000 when roosting, commonly mixed with *C. mongolus*.
Breeding. Laying Apr-May in C Asia, late Apr to late May in Turkey; unfledged chicks in late Jun in Armenia. Solitary. Nest is shallow scrape in ground, variably lined with plant fragments, situated in the open or among low vegetation. Usually 3 eggs (2-4); single-brooded, but replacement clutches laid after egg loss; incubation by both parents for at least 24 days, probably starting with last egg; chick has crown, back and band down leg pale cream or straw yellow, marked with black spots and lines, eyeline, forehead and sides of head black, and hindneck collar and underparts white; tended by both parents, with brood often split between them; fledging at least 30 days; age of independence unknown. First breeds when 2 years old. Oldest ringed bird at least 10 years.
Movements. Migratory. Winters on shores of Australasia and Indian Ocean, but relation between breeding and non-breeding quarters poorly known. Probably migrates in broad front non-stop to non-breeding areas; some birds follow coast and occasionally large flocks are seen on passage, typically mixed with *C. mongolus*. Apparently, strong fidelity to non-breeding sites. Flocks form after breeding season between mid-Jul and early Aug, 1 month earlier in *columbinus*; abundant in S China and Hong Kong late Jul to Nov; arrives Australia mid-Aug, S Asia and Sudan to Tanzania late Aug to Sept, adults and immatures before juveniles. Body mass peaks in early Apr in Australia. Starts moving N from SE Asia in late Feb, peaking Mar to early Apr, and reaches breeding grounds from mid-Mar, most Apr-May. Departs E Africa and S Asia mid-Apr to early May. Some wintering birds, probably most non-adults, remain in wintering areas during breeding season.
Status and Conservation. Not globally threatened. Population of race *columbinus* probably numbers under 10,000 breeding birds, with 100-1000 pairs in Turkey and up to 150 in Jordan; *crassirostris* 65,000 birds, of which 10,000-25,000 in Sudan, 15,000 in Kenya and 5000-10,000 on Persian Gulf and in Baluchistan; race *leschenaultii* c. 99,000 birds wintering in E and SE Asia and Australia (74,000 birds), and probably 25,000-100,000 birds in SC Asia, with species abundant in India and Pakistan; c. 8000 birds estimated on Saudi Arabian Gulf coast. In Turkey, threatened by loss of wetlands and bordering fallow steppe through drainage and water extraction for irrigation. Status in Azerbaijan uncertain: species rarely recorded, but known to have bred.
Bibliography. Ali & Ripley (1980), Aspinwall (1973, 1975), Barter & Barter (1988), Beehler *et al*. (1986), Beijersbergen (1980), Benson (1960), Bottema (1987), Brazil (1991), Bregnballe *et al*. (1990), Brinkman (1980), Britton (1982a), Chambers (1989), Cheltsov-Bebutov (1976), Clancey (1982b), Coates (1985), Condamin (1987), Cramp & Simmons (1983), Dementiev & Gladkov (1951b), Dickinson *et al*. (1991), Dowsett (1969), Dowsett & Forbes-Watson (1993), Ellenbrook & Schekkerman (1985), Étchécopar & Hüe (1964, 1978), Evans (1994), Flint *et al*. (1984), Goodman *et al*. (1989), Harrison (1963), de Heer (1979), Hüe & Étchécopar (1970), Kaczmarek & Winjecki (1980), van Kalsbeek & Meijer (1986), Kashkarov & Ostapenko (1990), Keijl (1994a), Kitson *et al*. (1980), Knystautas (1993), Lane & Davies (1987), Langrand (1990), Lehmann (1969, 1971), Lekagul & Round (1991), MacKinnon & Phillipps (1993), Mackworth-Praed & Grant (1957, 1962), Marchant & Higgins (1993), van Marle & Voous (1988), Medway & Wells (1976), Meissner & Skakuj (1986), Nadler & Königstedt (1986), Newman & Vinicombe (1980), Nielsen (1971), Palfery (1988), Patrikeev (1995), Paz (1987), Perennou *et al*. (1994), Phillips (1978), Pook (1992), Ripley (1982), Robert (1983), Roberts, T.J. (1991), Scott (1989), Shaw & Webb (1991), Shirihai (1996), Short *et al*. (1990), Silvius *et al*. (1986), Sinclair & Nicholls (1980), Smythies (1981, 1986), Spence (1983), Taylor (1977, 1982a, 1982d), Tibor (1993), Urban *et al*. (1986), Watkins (1993), White & Bruce (1986), Williams, M.D. (1986).

On following pages: 55. Caspian Plover (*Charadrius asiaticus*); 56. Oriental Plover (*Charadrius veredus*); 57. Eurasian Dotterel (*Charadrius morinellus*); 58. Rufous-chested Plover (*Charadrius modestus*); 59. Mountain Plover (*Charadrius montanus*); 60. Hooded Plover (*Charadrius rubricollis*); 61. Shore Plover (*Charadrius novaeseelandiae*); 62. Black-fronted Dotterel (*Elseyornis melanops*); 63. Inland Dotterel (*Peltohyas australis*); 64. Wrybill (*Anarhynchus frontalis*); 65. Diademed Plover (*Phegornis mitchellii*); 66. Tawny-throated Dotterel (*Oreopholus ruficollis*); 67. Magellanic Plover (*Pluvianellus socialis*).

55. **Caspian Plover**

Charadrius asiaticus

French: Pluvier asiatique **German**: Wermutregenpfeifer **Spanish**: Chorlitejo asiático Chico
Other common names: Caspian Sandplover, Lesser Oriental Plover

Taxonomy. *Charadrius asiaticus* Pallas, 1773, salt-lakes of the South Tartar Steppes.
Sometimes placed in genus *Eupoda*. Forms superspecies with *C. veredus*, and possibly with *C. montanus*; formerly treated as conspecific with *C. veredus*. Monotypic.
Distribution. W, N & E Caspian Sea E to L Alakol and L Zaysan, E Kazakhstan, and extreme NW Xinjiang, NW China. Winters in E & S Africa.

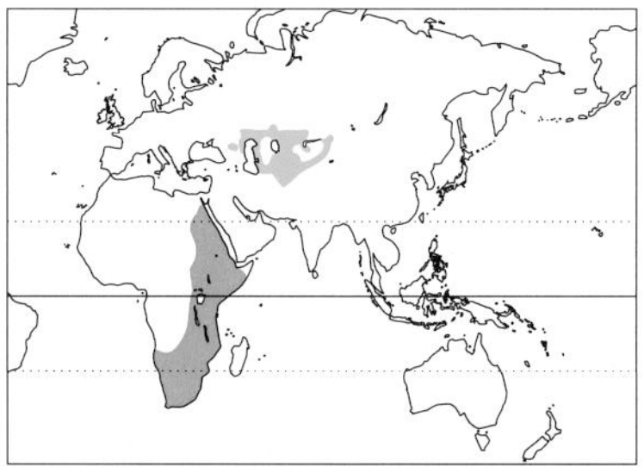

Descriptive notes. 18-20 cm; 60-91 g; wingspan 55-61 cm. Slim, upright plover, with clear white supercilium, forehead and throat; brown crown and upperparts; breast band rusty red or chestnut, with black line on border with white belly; white flashes on upperwing, underwing-coverts white; legs vary between pinkish yellow, greyish green and pale grey or brown. Resembles closely related *C. veredus*, but neck and legs slightly shorter, while *C. veredus* lacks white flashes on upperwing, and has underwing-coverts brown; taller and less compact than *C. mongolus* or *C. leschenaultii*. Female has breast grey-brown without black edge; sometimes has a few chestnut feathers tipped white; head and throat less white. Non-breeding adult has greyish brown breast band; face, forehead and throat pale buffish, upperparts with rufous-buff edges, when fresh. Juvenile like non-breeding adult, with clear rufous and buff fringes to upperpart feathers.
Habitat. Breeds in lowland desert and desert steppe, preferably in salt-pans and on saline soil, often subject to seasonal flooding, near water among sparse shrub vegetation. Concentrations after breeding on banks of lakes and rivers, and water-holes trampled by cattle. In Africa, occurs on recently burnt or heavily grazed grassland and dry floodplains, often far from water; sometimes on bare cultivated ground, coastal dunes (Somalia), airfields and golf courses; probably attracted by insects on animal droppings.
Food and Feeding. Few data available. Primarily insects and their larvae. In breeding season mainly takes beetles, also ants, grasshoppers, bugs, caterpillars and fly larvae; occasionally plant material, e.g. grass seeds. During non-breeding season, beetles, termites and grasshoppers, also small snails; observed hunting for insects in town garbage heaps and cow dung.
Breeding. Laying Apr to late Jun. Mating system uncertain, monogamous pair-bond reported. Song-flight may be heard until midnight on moonlit nights. Territorial, nesting singly or in small, loose groups of 10-25 pairs, at least 50-60 m apart. Adults will feed in small flocks outside territory, leaving eggs and (apparently) young unattended. Nest is shallow scrape, sparsely lined with plant material and debris, on ground in the open or among low vegetation. 3 eggs; probably single-brooded with replacements laid after egg loss; incubated by both parents, only female at night, period unknown; chick has crown, back and band down leg pale cream, marked with black spots, forming lines on crown, back and forewings, while forehead, sides of head, hindneck collar and underparts are white; tended by both parents; fledging at least 30 days; families with young tend to assemble in moist places or river bars; family groups possibly persist into non-breeding season. Age of first breeding probably 2 years.
Movements. Migratory. Usually moves in small flocks of 5-12 birds, sometimes up to 30. Flocks form after breeding, gradually merging for migration during Aug; migrates S Aug-Oct; return migration mid Mar to early May. Stop-over sites in Iran, Iraq, Arabian Peninsula, Red Sea, and perhaps Gulf of Aden, but probably overflies Middle East region during autumn migration; migrates in broad front to and from NE Africa; arrives NE Africa from middle to late Aug; main arrivals in non-breeding areas Sept-Oct, averaging later S of equator. On migration, common to very abundant in Ethiopia (peak Aug-Sept), Somalia and coasts of Kenya and Tanzania; while in Africa, gradually moves S in nomadic fashion following local dry seasons, in flocks of 5-20 birds, sometimes moving at night. Main wintering sites are upland plains of SW Kenya and N Tanzania, and Botswana, N & E Namibia and N South Africa. Departure from S Africa late Feb to early Mar, E & SE Africa late Mar to early Apr, arriving Turkmenistan and Kazakhstan from late Mar to early Apr. During non-breeding season, usually in small flocks of up to several hundreds.
Status and Conservation. Not globally threatened. Total population probably numbers 10,000-100,000 birds. Estimated 100-500 pairs in European Russia, where population reckoned to have declined considerably; populations in core of range thought to be fairly stable. Estimated 5000-10,000 winter in Sudan; locally very abundant in Kenya and Tanzania; common in Namibia, uncommon elsewhere in S Africa. Main threat is destruction of natural steppe and grassland, mainly due to overgrazing and conversion to intensive agricultural practices, especially within European part of range.
Bibliography. Ali & Ripley (1980), Ballot *et al.* (1981), Beaman (1994), Benson & Benson (1975), Campbell, L. (1972), Claassen & Claassen (1991), Cramp & Simmons (1983), Dowsett & Forbes-Watson (1993), Elliot (1956), Étchécopar & Hüe (1964, 1978), Evans (1994), Flint *et al.* (1984), Ginn *et al.* (1989), Goodman *et al.* (1989), Harvey (1972), Hüe & Étchécopar (1970), Kashkarov & Ostapenko (1990), Kazmierczak *et al.* (1992), Keijl (1994b), Knystautas (1993), Mackworth-Praed & Grant (1957, 1962, 1970), Maclean (1993), Nielsen (1971), Nielsen & Colston (1984), Oreel (1984, 1986), Paz (1987), Pellow (1990), Pinto (1983), Poslavsky (1978), Shirihai (1996), Short *et al.* (1990), Taylor, P.B. (1983), Urban *et al.* (1986).

56. **Oriental Plover**

Charadrius veredus

French: Pluvier oriental **German**: Steppenregenpfeifer **Spanish**: Chorlito Asiático Grande
Other common names: Asiatic/Eastern/Oriental Dotterel/Sandplover, Greater Oriental Plover

Taxonomy. *Charadrius veredus* Gould, 1848, northern Australia.
Sometimes placed in genus *Eupoda*. Formerly considered conspecific with *C. asiaticus*; probably best considered to form superspecies with *C. asiaticus*, and possibly with *C. montanus*. Monotypic.
Distribution. S Siberia (Tuvinskaya and S Transbaikalia) through W, N & E Mongolia to extreme NE China (N Inner Mongolia and NW Manchuria). Winters from Greater Sundas to NW & NC Australia, sparsely in S.
Descriptive notes. 22-25 cm; c. 95 g; wingspan 46-53 cm. Elegant plover, with creamy white head and neck, and brown hindcrown; rufous red breast band with black lower edge; legs yellowish or pinkish. Legs and neck relatively longer than in *C. asiaticus*. Female has pale brownish breast band without black border; more brown on head with whitish supercilium, forehead, chin and throat. Non-breeding adult resembles breeding female, but breast band more diffuse and face and neck more buff or pale brown; new feathers on upperparts show clear rufous or warm buff fringes. Juvenile as non-breeding adult, with larger and paler buff fringes on upperparts.

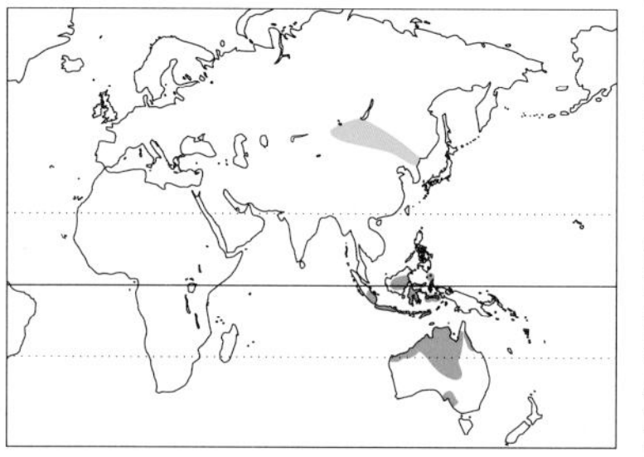

Habitat. Arid inland areas, especially stony flats and alongside rivers and salt or freshwater lakes. During non-breeding season, occurs on dry open grasslands and sparsely vegetated inland plains, interspersed with dry bare ground; also clay-pans, playing fields, lawns, cattle camps, recently burnt fields, bare margins of wetlands, mudflats and sandbanks; often far from water. May roost on beaches during the day.
Food and Feeding. Few data available. Mainly beetles, also other insects, such as termites, grasshoppers and bugs; snails and seeds. Feeds in loose, small parties or flocks of hundreds; often with other waders and waterbirds. At Eighty Mile Beach, NW Australia, feeds at night and roosts during day.
Breeding. Season Apr-Jul. Solitary breeder. Only females tend brood. No further information available.
Movements. Migratory. Departs from breeding grounds in Jul, males first. Main non-breeding grounds in NW & NC Australia; passage migrant in small numbers through Korea, Japan, Hong Kong, Philippines, Micronesia and SE Asia, Sept-Dec; migrant through E China Aug-Sept and Mar-Apr, where very abundant in Yangtze Valley; arrives Australia mid-Sept to Oct. Scarcity of records between China and non-breeding grounds suggests non-stop flights between these two zones; recorded rather rarely in Indonesia. In Australia, shows erratic movements, apparently moving in response to rainfall and temperature; occurrence in coastal areas often associated with droughts or heatwaves. Birds may depart for Asia directly from inland areas, without visiting coast; leaves NW Australia Feb-Apr, perhaps mostly mid-Mar; present C Mongolia, immediately S of breeding grounds, from late Apr.
Status and Conservation. Not globally threatened. Total population estimated at 44,000 birds, of which 40,000 winter in Australia, with important sites at: Port Hedland Saltworks, with maximum of 29,900 birds; Eighty Mile Beach with maximum of 18,400 birds; and Roebuck Bay maximum 8700 birds. Total of 14,000 birds counted on 12·5 km of Eighty Mile Beach in Mar 1993. In Australia, species not immediately threatened due to occupation of sparsely settled areas; no information on trends in breeding zone, but human pressure generally reckoned to be relatively low.
Bibliography. Ali & Ripley (1980), Beaman (1994), Bigg (1981), Brazil (1991), Christian *et al.* (1992a), Close (1982), Coates (1985), Cox (1988b), Edgar (1968), Étchécopar & Hüe (1978), Flint *et al.* (1984), Knystautas (1993), Kozlova (1975), Lane & Davies (1987), Larkins & McGill (1978), MacKinnon & Phillipps (1993), Marchant & Higgins (1993), van Marle & Voous (1988), McCrie (1984), McKenzie *et al.* (1956), Meyer de Schauensee (1984), Morton *et al.* (1990), Nielsen (1971), Ostapenko *et al.* (1980), Pedler (1982a), Scott (1989), Smythies (1981), Warakagoda (1994), Watkins (1993), White & Bruce (1986).

57. **Eurasian Dotterel**

Charadrius morinellus

French: Pluvier guignard **German**: Mornellregenpfeifer **Spanish**: Chorlito Carambolo
Other common names: Dotterel

Taxonomy. *Charadrius Morinellus* Linnaeus, 1758, Sweden.
Often placed in genus *Eudromias*, but possibly quite closely related to some or all of *C. asiaticus*, *C. veredus*, *C. modestus* and *C. montanus*. Monotypic.
Distribution. N Britain through Scandinavia and N Siberia to Chukotskiy Peninsula, and NE Kazakhstan and NW China (NW Xinjiang) E through S Siberia and N Mongolia to SE Russia; irregularly in Pyrenees, Alps, Carpathians, and also sporadically elsewhere in Europe, Caucasus and NW Alaska. Winters in N Africa and Middle East E to W Iran.

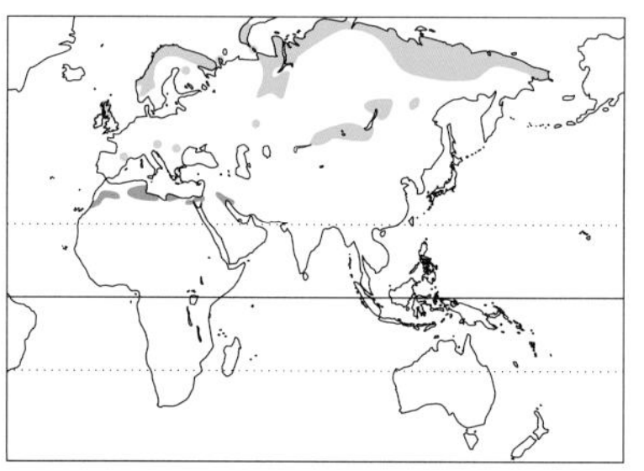

Descriptive notes. 20-22 cm; male 86-116 g, female 99-142 g; wingspan 57-64 cm. Bulky plover, with reversed sexual dimorphism in size and plumage; unmistakable in breeding dress; long white supercilia meet in "V" on nape; narrow white breast band separates grey throat and upperbreast from bright chestnut lower breast. Female more brightly coloured than male, with blacker crown and belly; breast band sharper than in male. Non-breeding adult lacks bright colours, and has supercilia brownish buff; upperparts fringed buff or sandy; pale white breast band, pale grey-brown breast with dull white bar; belly white. Juvenile shows greater contrast than non-breeding adult, with darker feathers and brighter fringes, and more buff on underparts.
Habitat. Breeds on extensive open, flat uplands, mountain ridges and plateaux, with sparse vegetation of moss, short grass or lichens and bare patches of rock, in Arctic tundra and Arctic-alpine zone; not particularly near water. On migration, stages in exposed areas with some short vegetation, heathland, fallow or ploughed land, often returning to same sites annually. Non-breeding grounds less known, but include stony steppe, ploughed farmlands, semi-desert, including marginal cultivation and shrubby steppe.
Food and Feeding. Insects, mostly beetles and Diptera larvae, also adult Diptera, larvae of butterflies and moths, grasshoppers, crickets, earwigs and ants, and spiders; occasionally snails, earthworms, especially in ploughed fields, and regularly some leaves, seeds, berries and flowers. Chicks have similar diet. Sometimes feeds by foot-trembling. May associate with cattle in some areas. Diurnal and nocturnal forager, primarily diurnal at southern breeding grounds.
Breeding. Laying mid-May to early Jul in Scotland, mid-May to early Jun in C Norway, from mid-Jun in Sweden, Finnmark and Taymyr. Seasonally monogamous, serially polyandrous and occasionally polygynous, depending on local sex ratios. Mating can take place on arenas. Sex roles reversed. No site fidelity apparent. Solitary, but where suitable habitat is restricted breeds in loose neighbourhood groups of 2-5 pairs; nests 200 m to several kilometres apart; density 4-6 birds/km² in NC Siberia, maximum density 8-10 pairs/km² and 17 pairs/km² recorded in Lappland. Usually feeds outside territory on neutral grounds; non-breeding and off-duty breeding birds often roost communally at night on feeding grounds. Nest in short vegetation or on bare gravel or soil; shallow scrape, lined with moss, lichens or leaves. 3 eggs, occasionally 2, laid at 30-36 hour intervals; in case of polyandry female produces second clutch c. 5-11 days or more after completion of first, and sometimes a third clutch; polygynous male usually has 2 mates simultaneously, occasionally 3, sometimes 2 clutches in 1 nest;

up to 2 replacement clutches. Incubation 23-29 days, starting with penultimate egg, (almost) entirely by male; in second or third clutches of polyandrous female, she participates more in incubation; chick blotched cinnamon, white and black, with off-white nape, broad supercilium and underparts; tended by male; fledging 25-30 days; young probably stay with male parent during migration and for some time in winter quarters. First breeding at 2 years old. Breeding success 162 fledglings per 427 breeding birds in N Scotland; hatching success 81% in Lappland; fledging success 72%. Important causes of failure are severe weather, especially sleet, snow and heavy rain, and predation.

Movements. Migratory. Migrates in broad front across Europe, staging at a few, often traditional, sites. Many birds probably migrate non-stop, especially in autumn. On autumn migration females usually precede juveniles and males by 2-4 weeks, and also tend to return first to breeding grounds. Birds depart from Scottish Highlands first half Aug, Siberia from late Aug to early Sept; passage W Europe mid-Aug to late Sept; some birds stage in Alps at altitude of 2000-3000 m or on crest of Jura Mts at 1600 m; many stage to moult in N Caspian region, migrating further S until early Nov; birds arrive in winter grounds from early Sept. Spring migration begins late Feb to Mar, passing W Europe mid-Apr to mid-May and Ukraine mid-Mar to late Apr; returns to breeding grounds in Scotland early May, S Scandinavia middle to late May, and Lappland and N Russia late May to mid-Jun. Despite vast and discontinuous breeding range no indication of subspeciation; this is in accordance both with limited faithfulness to breeding sites, which may be due to mixing in winter quarters, and with erratic breeding in Europe. During migration sometimes in flocks of 20-80 birds, but usually of 3-6.

Status and Conservation. Not globally threatened. Total breeding population in Europe 36,500 breeding pairs, with 28,000 in Norway (1981), 7500 in Sweden (1984), 800 in Finland (1986) and in excess of 550 pairs in Britain (1988), but decreasing; Asia 10,000-100,000 birds. In 19th century bred in Poland and Czech Republic and Slovakia. In Finland, significant decline in 1940's and since 1970's; cause for recent decline might be heavy persecution in N Africa; amelioration of climate in breeding area may also be significant factor. Numbers declined in Britain in late 19th century due to hunting and egg-collecting.

Bibliography. Armstrong (1983), Baumgart & Baumgart (1993), Brazil (1991), Brunner (1994), Burke & Thompson (1988), Burnier (1977), Byrkjedal (1987a, 1989a, 1989b), Byrkjedal & Kålås (1985), Cramp & Simmons (1983), Crozier & Argelich (1993), Dowsett & Forbes-Watson (1993), Étchécopar & Hüe (1964, 1978), Fjeldså (1977), Flint *et al*. (1984), Galbraith, Murray, Duncan *et al*. (1993), Galbraith, Murray, Rae *et al*. (1993), Goodman *et al*. (1989), Haas *et al*. (1988), Hüe & Étchécopar (1970), Ibáñez (1990), Kålås (1986, 1988), Kålås & Byrkjedal (1984), Kålås & Løfaldli (1987), Knystautas (1993), Kovács (1991), Mackworth-Praed & Grant (1957), Maumary & Duflon (1989), Nethersole-Thompson (1973), Nielsen (1975, 1986), Oring (1986), Owens, Burke & Thompson (1994), Owens, Dixon *et al*. (1995), Paz (1987), Perennou *et al*. (1994), Pulliainen (1970), Pulliainen & Saari (1992a, 1992b, 1993b, 1993c), Robel & Königstedt (1979), Rogacheva (1992), Sackl (1993), Shirihai (1996), Smith & Whitfield (1995), Thomas, C.J. *et al*. (1989), Thomson (1994), Tilba (1990), Urban *et al*. (1986), Vasilchenko & Unzhakov (1977), Watson (1988, 1989), Watson & Rae (1987), Wilkie (1981), Wozniak (1992).

58. **Rufous-chested Plover**

Charadrius modestus

French: Pluvier d'Urville **German**: Rotbrust-Regenpfeifer **Spanish**: Chorlito Chileno
Other common names: Rufous-chested Dotterel, Chilean/White/Winter Plover

Taxonomy. *Charadrius modestus* Lichtenstein, 1823, Montevideo, Uruguay.
Occasionally placed in genus *Zonibyx*. No subspecies recognized, although birds from Falkland Is have longer wings and tarsi. Monotypic.

Distribution. S South America in SC & S Chile and WC & S Argentina and Falkland Is. Winters N to N Chile and SE Brazil.

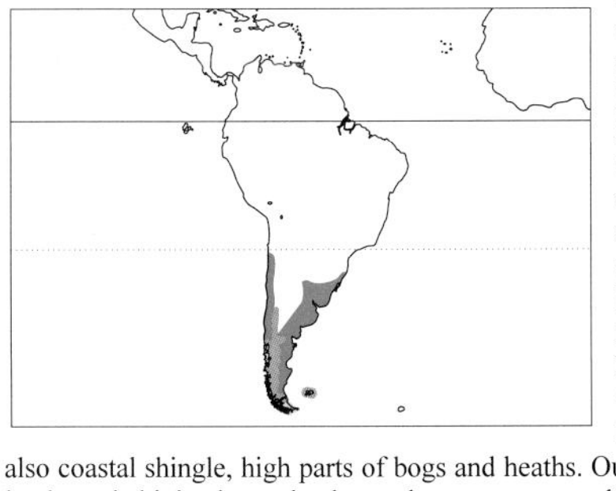

Descriptive notes. 19-22 cm; 71-94 g. Bright white supercilia meet on forehead; face, cheeks and throat ash grey, breast rufous red with broad black lower edge; belly white. Female tends to be slightly duller. In non-breeding adult, rufous and grey replaced with pale brown; feathers of upperparts with bright fringes and supercilia creamy. Juvenile as non-breeding adult, but upperparts and breast darker brown with clear buff fringes.

Habitat. Breeds mainly on inland short grassland, from coast up to altitude of 2000 m on windy inland foothills; sometimes boggy lowlands or dry stony areas around upland lakes; also coastal shingle, high parts of bogs and heaths. Outside breeding season occurs on flooded grassland, eroded inland grassland, marshes, streams, mudflats, beaches and rocky shores.

Food and Feeding. Insects, insect larvae, crustaceans, molluscs and some plant material (e.g. algae). Near water, forages at water's edge, where territory of 10-100 m often defended. Outside breeding season forages in small parties, of up to 100 birds or more; often together with *C. falklandicus*.

Breeding. Eggs Oct-Nov, rarely Jan; laying in Falkland Is late Sept to mid-Jan, with peak in Oct. Solitary. Nest placed in the open; in Falkland Is among stands of ferns and diddle-dee (*Empetrum*), providing cover. Usually 2 eggs, sometimes 3; incubated by both parents; chick golden buff, conspicuously marked with black dots and lines, nape rufous.

Movements. Migratory to resident; southernmost breeders migrate N in Mar-Apr and return Aug-Sept; some remain close to breeding grounds, even on Tierra del Fuego; most birds from Falkland Is migrate to mainland after breeding, but unknown proportion resident. Apparently faithful to wintering sites. Gathers in post-breeding flocks prior to northward migration.

Status and Conservation. Not globally threatened. Population size not known, but species generally reckoned to be not uncommon. Occupation of zones with relatively limited human impact suggests species likely to be secure at present; no threats identified.

Bibliography. Antas (1988), Belton (1984), Blake (1977), Canevari *et al*. (1991), Carstairs (1989), Clark (1986), Fjeldså & Krabbe (1990), Forrester (1993), Hellmayr & Conover (1948), Humphrey *et al*. (1970), Johnson (1965b), Meyer de Schauensee (1982), Narosky & Yzurieta (1987), Olrog (1984), de la Peña (1992), Pinto (1964), Scott & Carbonell (1986), Sick (1985c, 1993), Vooren & Chiaradia (1990), Woods (1988).

59. **Mountain Plover**

Charadrius montanus

French: Pluvier montagnard **German**: Bergregenpfeifer **Spanish**: Chorlito Llanero

Taxonomy. *Charadrius montanus* J. K. Townsend, 1837, central tableland of the Rocky Mountains = near Sweetwater River, Wyoming.
Sometimes placed in genus *Eupoda*. On occasion considered to belong to superspecies of *C. asiaticus* and *C. veredus*. Monotypic.

Distribution. Great Plains and plateau of E Colorado, in C North America. Winters from C California to Baja California and E to S Texas and NE Mexico.

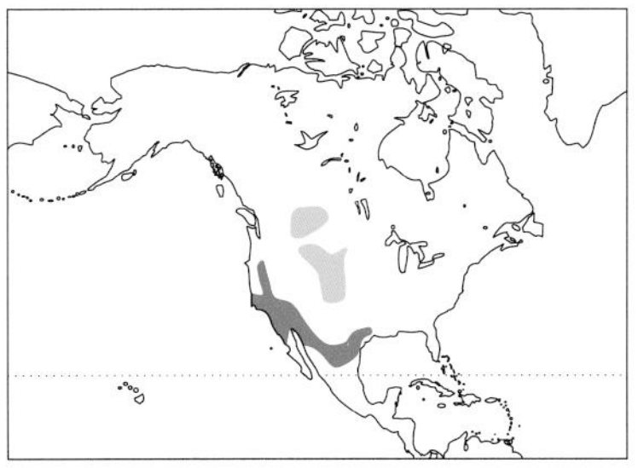

Descriptive notes. 21-23·5 cm; 67-112 g. Bright white forehead and supercilium, black frontal bar and black lores; never has black on breast; underparts white, washed buff on sides; relatively long pale yellowish brown legs. Somewhat similar to non-breeding *Pluvialis dominica*, alongside which sometimes occurs, but smaller, with less spotted plumage and white underwing. Sexes alike. Non-breeding adult has pale brown crown and lores, and darker breast patches, which may be connected; upperparts have rufous fringes. Juvenile like non-breeding adult, but upperparts and breast darker brown; buff supercilium; broader and brighter buff fringes on upperparts.

Habitat. Nests in disturbed upland short-grass prairie. After breeding season occurs in semi-desert and on dry agricultural land or heavily grazed rangelands; shows strong preference for alkaline flats, but these have almost disappeared from range. Often found in association with colonial fossorial mammals, e.g. kangaroo rats (*Dipodomys*) and prairie dogs (*Cynomys*). Often roosts on burnt fields at night; roost-site is commonly in shallow depression, typically hoofprint, with bird's eyes just above the surface. Despite scientific and vernacular names, not a mountain species.

Food and Feeding. Grassland insects, mainly grasshoppers, also crickets, beetles and flies. Feeds on disturbed insects in recently cultivated fields. During winter, typically remains only for few days at any site. Gregarious, in loose flocks of up to several hundred, especially in winter.

Breeding. Season late Apr to Jul. At least some males site-faithful, but virtually all young disperse to other areas. Monogamous, polyandrous and probably polygynous in different cases. Territorial, often feeding outside territory, in neutral area; on average, nests 140 m apart. Nests on short-grass prairies, particularly in association with blue grama grass communities; nest is shallow scrape on bare ground between plants in loamy soil, sometimes including plant material and debris, which are accumulated during incubation. Usually 3 eggs (2-4), laid at intervals of 1-6 days; incubation 28-31 days, starting when clutch complete, performed by male alone; female often leaves first clutch to male, and lays second clutch which she incubates herself, or, in case of polyandry, is incubated by a second male; female may start third clutch; chick creamy buff above with conspicuous black spots, underparts buffy white; fledging 33-36 days. 20-65% of nests successful; nests failure caused by predation, storms and trampling by cattle. Winter survival 95%.

Movements. Migratory. On breeding grounds, flocks form from mid-Jun onwards; present in inland wintering areas chiefly from early Nov to mid-Mar; main wintering area is Central Valley of California; arrives in flocks on breeding grounds in Colorado by late Mar to Apr, probably after non-stop flight from wintering areas; migratory routes unknown.

Status and Conservation. VULNERABLE. Proposed for Endangered status (1995). Population decreasing: before 1900 species was an abundant and important gamebird, but by c. 1970 numbers had fallen to 200,000-300,000 birds; between 1960 and 1991, dramatic decline of 63%; in 1994, population estimated at only 5000-10,000 birds. Much of breeding area lost due to increased vegetation height as a result of planting "tame" grasses and excessive declines in populations of grazers, especially bison (*Bison bison*) and prairie dogs; alternatively, lost to cereal production; wintering areas also suffer from lack of grazers; decline may be explained completely by disking, to control weeds, or planting during the nesting and early chick phases. Currently, two sites of major importance: Pawnee National Grassland, Colorado, and Charles M. Russell National Wildlife Refuge, Montana.

Bibliography. Bent (1927-1929), Boland (1991), Brazier (1991a), Clausen (1990), Collar *et al*. (1994), Davis & Knight (1989), Day (1994), Ehrlich *et al*. (1992), Fall (1988), Flowers (1985), Gallucci (1980), Graig *et al*. (1985), Graul (1973a, 1973c, 1974, 1975, 1976), Graul & Webster (1976), Hamas & Graul (1985), Howell & Webb (1995a), Janssen (1986), Johnson & Spicer (1981), Knopf (1994, 1996a, 1996b), Knopf & Miller (1994), Knopf & Rupert (1995, 1996a, 1996b), Knowles & Knowles (1984), Knowles *et al*. (1982), Mayr & Short (1970), McCaffery *et al*. (1984), Miller & Knopf (1993), Olson (1984, 1985a), Olson & Edge (1985), Olson-Edge & Edge (1987), Parrish *et al*. (1993), Prellwitz (1993), Ptacek & Schwilling (1983), Shackford (1991, 1995), Sordahl (1991), TenBrink (1993), Tolle (1976), Wallis (1986), Wallis & Wershler (1981), Wershler (1986), Wilds (1978).

60. **Hooded Plover**

Charadrius rubricollis

French: Pluvier à camail **German**: Kappenregenpfeifer **Spanish**: Chorlito Encapuchado
Other common names: Hooded Dotterel

Taxonomy. *Charadrius rubricollis* Gmelin, 1789, Adventure Bay, Tasmania.
Recently placed by some authors in genus *Thinornis* with *C. novaeseelandiae* (see page 385). Monotypic.

Distribution. S Australia and Tasmania.

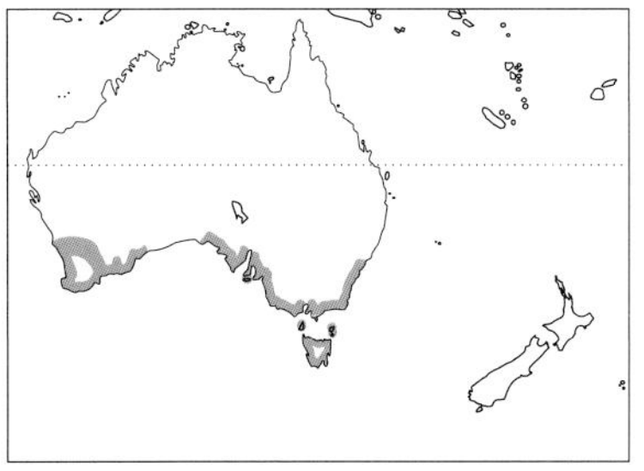

Descriptive notes. 19-23 cm; 79-110 g; wingspan 36-44 cm. Short-legged plover with neckless appearance; black head and broad white neck collar; upperparts grey bordered black on neck, extending into small black patch at side of breast; deep red eye-ring; bill orange-red at base, with black tip; dull orange-pink legs. Sexes alike. No seasonal variation. Juvenile as adult, but hindneck, crown and breast patches pale grey-brown mottled whitish buff; chin and throat whitish; upperparts pale brown-grey with pale fringes; bill blackish with flesh coloured base and eye-ring paler.

Habitat. Mainly found on broad, sandy ocean beaches, occasionally near rocky or sand-covered reefs, estuaries, inlets and saline and freshwater lakes and lagoons close to coast. Breeds in sparsely vegetated sand dunes backing onto beach, between high water mark and base of dunes, often with much seaweed spread around, or, especially in Western Australia, round margins of lakes.

Food and Feeding. Amphipods, isopods, polychaetes, bivalves, gastropods, crabs, insects (e.g. dragonflies, beetles and flies) and seeds. Feeds busily along water's edge on prey left behind by receding waves during low to mid-tide. At high tide forages among seaweed and debris of beachcast; on rocks, forages in wave-wash or spray zone; at lagoons and lakes, forages on dry or moist substrates or in

shallow water. Diurnal and nocturnal; feeding mostly tactile at night, involving continuous pecking. During non-breeding season forages in loose, small flocks of 10-40 birds, up to large flocks, occasionally of several hundred.
Breeding. Eggs found Aug-Mar, or later due to replacement and second clutches. Monogamous, often over several years. Solitary and territorial, with nests often kilometres apart, but also as little as 18 m apart; density 0·2-2 pairs/km; high degree of site fidelity; possible breeding association with Australian Pied Oystercatchers (*Haematopus longirostris*). Nests in sand, in the open; nest is scrape, unlined or lined with pebbles, seaweed, sticks and shell or stone fragments, and sometimes encircled with such material. 2-3 eggs, occasionally 4, probably laid at 1-4 day intervals; replacement clutch may be laid; incubation 27-31 days, by both parents, starting once clutch complete; chick has sandy brown upperparts mottled with black, white nape with black band extending to just below eye and white underparts; both parents tend chicks until fledging; fledging 32-36 days. May breed at 1 year old. Hatching success 17-31%; 0·1 young fledged per pair; causes of nest failure are flooding, human disturbance, destruction by vehicles, trampling by livestock and predation.
Movements. Essentially sedentary, showing erratic movements; inland breeders move to coastal lakes after breeding season; in SE Australia, some flocking occurs during non-breeding season, and at some breeding sites birds absent or sparse during Apr-Aug, suggesting at least local movements; also moves inland, e.g. to salt-lakes immediately behind beach, and may fly to offshore islands, c. 20-70 km away.
Status and Conservation. VULNERABLE. Population probably numbers at least 5000 individuals, of which 1730 on Tasmania. Small W population probably secure, but range contracting on coast and around salt-lakes in S Western Australia. In E Australia, human disturbance through recreational activities on beaches has probably contributed to decline of species; incubating birds readily leave eggs due to disturbance, and scavengers are attracted to human activities. Many nests may be crushed by 4-wheel-drive vehicles, e.g. 81% of nests at the Coorong in 1985-86; in some areas, predation by foxes and Silver Gulls (*Larus novaehollandiae*) and trampling of nests by livestock are major causes of nest failure; young can be killed by vehicles when hiding in wheel ruts.
Bibliography. Ashby (1991), Blakers *et al.* (1984), Bransbury (1983, 1988, 1990), Brouwer & Garnett (1990), Buick & Paton (1989), Chafer (1984), Christian *et al.* (1992a), Collar & Andrew (1988), Collar *et al.* (1994), Cooper, R. (1993), Garnett (1993), Heisler & Weston (1993), Holdsworth & Park (1993), Lane, B.A. (1981, 1982, 1991), Lane, B.A. & Davies (1987), Lane, S.G. (1985), Marchant & Higgins (1993), Morris (1989), Newman (1982d, 1992a), Newman & Park (1992a, 1993), Newman & Patterson (1984), Park (1993), Pringle (1987), Retallick & Bolitho (1993), Schulz, M. (1986b, 1987, 1988, 1992, 1993), Schulz, M. & Bamford (1987), Schulz, M. & Kristensen (1993), Schulz, M. & Lumsden (1983), Schulz, M. *et al.* (1984), Stewart (1989, 1991, 1993), Watkins (1993), Weston (1993).

61. Shore Plover

Charadrius novaeseelandiae

French: Pluvier de Nouvelle-Zélande **German**: Chathamregenpfeifer **Spanish**: Chorlitejo de las Chatham
Other common names: New Zealand/Shore Dotterel/Plover

Taxonomy. *Charadrius novæ-Seelandiæ* Gmelin, 1789, Queen Charlotte Sound, South Island, New Zealand. Often placed in genus *Thinornis*, in recent years increasingly with *C. rubricollis*, but limits and validity of genus *Thinornis* remain debatable, so both species probably best retained in *Charadrius* for present (see page 385). Monotypic.
Distribution. Rangatira I (South-east I) of Chatham Is.

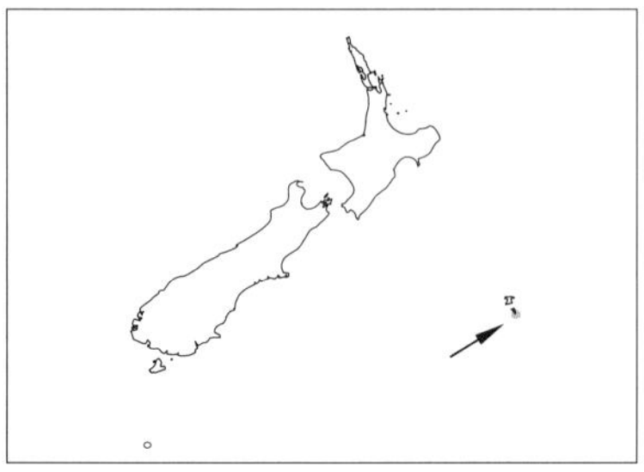

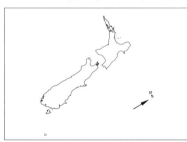

Descriptive notes. c. 20 cm; 52-69 g. Distinctive small, chubby plover, with proportions not unlike *Arenaria interpres*; black head, except for grey-brown crown encircled by white band; orbital ring orange to red; short, thick orange legs. Female similar to male, but black of head replaced with dusky brown; more black on bill tip. No seasonal variation. Juvenile has mainly white face with dark brown eyestripe and crown; brown lateral breast patches; upperparts more clearly scaled; bill mainly black, pale orbital ring and legs. Calls higher-pitched in females than in males, and in juveniles than in adults.
Habitat. Rocky shores with extensive wave-cut platforms containing shallow tidal pools, sometimes covered with barnacles, limpets or patches of algae; also adjacent boulder-strewn beaches and less often nearby barren salt-meadows with turf-like and halophytic vegetation. Formerly occurred on estuarine mudflats and sand-spits on mainland New Zealand. Breeds on beaches among high piles of boulders and on inland salt-meadows with mats of herbaceous plants or clumps of lignum.
Food and Feeding. Small crustaceans (e.g. copepods), spiders, gastropods, bivalves and insects of rocky shores; takes Hemiptera, caterpillars and larvae on salt-meadows. Sometimes feeds by foot-trembling. Active diurnally and nocturnally, depending on tide. Feeds at low tide, at edges of shallow tidal pools and on wet rocks, bare or with beds of barnacles or algae. Outside breeding season, often forages in small flocks of up to 15 birds.
Breeding. Laying mid-Oct to Dec; breeding synchronized amongst pairs in same area. Monogamous on long-term basis. Defends home range, including nest-site; also defends area for chick-rearing and, to varying extent, feeding area. Congregations form in suitable habitat, where nests may be only few metres apart; shows high degree of site fidelity. Nests in cavities among boulders or under rocks, logs, tree-roots, etc., on salt-meadows; nest is cup-shaped scrape in sand and grit, substantial in wetter sites, where made of roots and dead grass, lined with plant material, occasionally feathers, shells and pebbles. Some pairs may remain in breeding home range for most of year. 3 eggs, sometimes 2, laid at 1-2 day intervals; single-brooded, but replacement clutches are laid, incubation c. 28 days, by both parents, but more by female; chick has upperparts mottled with off-white, buff, pale brown and black-brown spots, lacks white hindneck collar, underparts tawny white; tended by both parents, but more intensively by female; fledging 29-63 days; young independent 4-36 days after fledging. Most birds breed first at 3 years old. Hatching success 83%, of which 7-43% fledge, i.e. 0·5-0·8 young/pair. Mass failure of beach-breeders may occur through storm surges, washing away eggs or chicks; other causes of failure include predation by Silver Gulls (*Larus novaehollandiae*) and Brown Skuas (*Catharacta antarctica*). Average longevity 6 years, maximum at least 17 years.
Movements. Sedentary; local movements of small flocks in non-breeding season. Juveniles very mobile immediately after independence, visiting other suitable habitats, but usually returning eventually to natal shore. Birds return to breeding territories May-Jul, females often preceding males.
Status and Conservation. ENDANGERED. Total population in 1993 was c. 130 birds, including 43-44 breeding pairs; numbers stable since 1969, probably constrained by shortage of suitable habitat. Formerly occurred on North I and South I and adjacent islands of New Zealand, but was already very rare, or even extinct, in 19th century; this decline was probably due to predation by introduced rodents and feral cats; no records on mainland New Zealand after 1888. Probably once occurred on all islands of Chatham group, but extirpated on Pitt I and Mangere I by introduced predators. Between 1890 and 1910, hundreds were collected on Rangatira I for sale as scientific specimens. Populations declined on Rangatira I after removal of sheep in 1958, resulting in deterioration of formerly suitable habitats, but numbers seem to have recovered and stabilized. In 1970 and 1971, adult and immature birds were unsuccessfully reintroduced to Mangere I, soon making their way back to Rangatira I. Very low numbers and tiny distribution make species extremely vulnerable to rapid extinction, e.g. if mammalian predators were to reach Rangatira.
Bibliography. Bell (1974), Chambers (1989), Collar & Andrew (1988), Collar *et al.* (1994), Davis (1987, 1994a, 1994b), Dowding & Kennedy (1993), Falla *et al.* (1981), Ferguson-Lees & Faull (1992), Flack (1976), Fleming (1939b), King (1978/79), Marchant & Higgins (1993), Phillips (1977, 1980), Robertson (1985), Rosair (1995d), Sibson (1982), Soper (1976), Williams (1975), Williams & Given (1981).

Genus *ELSEYORNIS* Mathews, 1914

62. Black-fronted Dotterel

Elseyornis melanops

French: Pluvier à face noire **German**: Schwarzstirn-Regenpfeifer **Spanish**: Chorlitejo Frentinegro
Other common names: Black-fronted Plover

Taxonomy. *Charadrius melanops* Vieillot, 1818, New South Wales.
Often included in genus *Charadrius*. Monotypic.
Distribution. Australia, Tasmania and New Zealand.

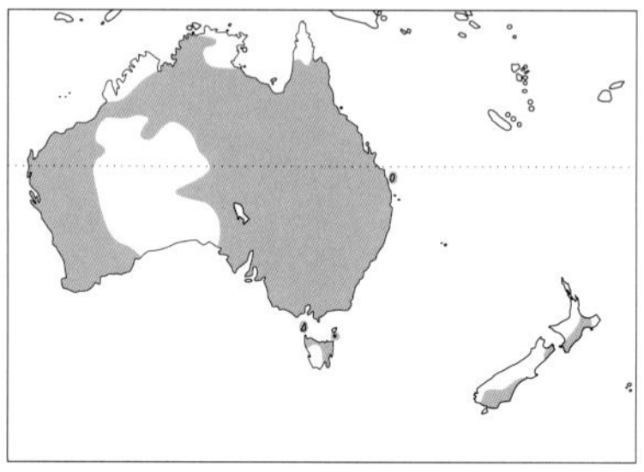

Descriptive notes. 16-18 cm; 27-42 g; wingspan 33-35 cm. Strikingly coloured, slim plover; black eyestripe and lores continuing onto forecrown; white supercilia join on nape; red bill with black tip; purplish patch on upper scapulars; black V-shaped breast band; rump and uppertail-coverts dark brown to chestnut with broad buff fringes; black stripes on undertail-coverts; pinkish or pale orange legs; in flight mainly white from below. Sexes alike. No seasonal variation. Juvenile has buffy cream forehead and crown, dark brown eyestripe and buff supercilium; upperparts with buff and brown fringes, no chestnut on rump; obscure breast band; bill brown to grey-black; orbital ring often absent; legs pink-brown.
Habitat. Bare or sparsely vegetated margins of wetlands, freshwater or sometimes brackish, on areas with mud, firm ground or gravel, including swamps, lakes, pools, water-holes, springs; also man-made habitats, including reservoirs, farm dams, tanks and even roadside ditches; often round receding floodwaters. In New Zealand, mainly on shingle or gravel beds of shallow, braided rivers, and on nearby farmland when rivers flood; also ditches beside roads and margins of wetlands; in arid regions, sometimes near saline water.
Food and Feeding. Water snails, crustaceans, earthworms and insects, such as crickets, grasshoppers, flies, ants, water beetles and larvae, occasionally seeds. Forages diurnally, on mud at edge of water; occasionally in shallow water. On hard substrates, taps and pecks. When foraging, usually solitary or in pairs, also in family groups.
Breeding. Season Sept-Feb in Australia, Aug-Mar in New Zealand, but can occur earlier or later owing to variable conditions, e.g. of rain and temperature. Monogamous, at least sometimes for more than one season. Solitary, with territory also used for feeding; site-faithful. Nest placed on open stony ground, often on banks of sand, gravel, pebbles or shingle, and sometimes besides or on gravel roads; nest is scrape or depression, unlined or lined with pebbles, plant material and debris. 3 eggs, sometimes 2, laid at intervals of 2 days; double-brooded and may lay up to two replacement clutches; incubation 22-26 days, by both parents; chick buff above, speckled and blotched black, with white collar and black along sides of back, underparts white; tended by both parents; fledging 23-40 days; young of first brood remain with parents until incubation of second brood starts, or until second brood hatched; young of second brood remain with parents for at least 8 weeks. Hatching success 61% in Australia, fledging success 32-67% in New Zealand. Broods may fail through predation by feral cats and foxes, human disturbance, flooding or trampling by cattle.
Movements. Poorly known in Australia, but apparently mainly sedentary; sedentary in New Zealand. Flocks of non-breeding birds at some sites in Australia suggest possible movements, but no large-scale movements apparent. In New Zealand, flocking occurs at favoured sites away from river, especially Apr-Jul, with flocks of up to 175 birds. Vagrant to India: single old record.
Status and Conservation. Not globally threatened. Has recently expanded range due to development of new suitable habitat resulting from construction of artificial wetlands, such as farm dams and sewage ponds. Now most widespread wader of Australia with total population of at least 19,000 birds, but almost certainly more. Colonized New Zealand from Australia, starting in Hawke's Bay in late 1950's, and has since expanded; in 1992, population of c. 1600 birds, but much suitable habitat on South I not yet occupied.
Bibliography. Andrew (1975), Barlow (1989), Barter (1991a), Blakers *et al.* (1984), Chambers (1989), Child (1982), Child & Child (1984), Christian *et al.* (1992a), Falla *et al.* (1981), Flegg & Madge (1995), Heather (1973, 1977), Lane & Davies (1987), Lindsey (1992), Macdonald (1988), Maclean (1977), Marchant & Higgins (1993), Phillips (1980), Pizzey & Doyle (1980), Pringle (1987), Robertson (1985), Schodde & Tidemann (1986), Schulz (1990), Sibson *et al.* (1972), Simpson & Day (1994), Slater (1987), Slater *et al.* (1989), Tarburton (1989), Trounson (1987).

Genus *PELTOHYAS* Sharpe, 1896

63. Inland Dotterel

Peltohyas australis

French: Pluvier australien **German**: Gürtelregenpfeifer **Spanish**: Chorlito Australiano

Other common names: Australian Dotterel/Courser, Desert Plover

Taxonomy. *Eudromias Australis* Gould, 1841, interior Australia.
Relationships uncertain, and somewhat controversial: formerly considered to belong to family Glareolidae, where was listed closest to genus *Rhinoptilus*; also in past, on occasion placed in genus *Eudromias*; recent biochemical studies suggest genus might possibly be merged with *Charadrius*. Race *whitlocki* has been proposed for birds in C & SW Australia, but doubtfully valid. Monotypic.
Distribution. SW, SC & EC Australia.

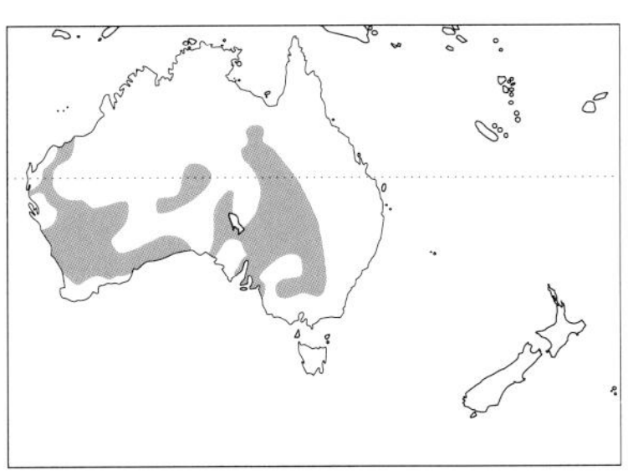

Descriptive notes. 19-23 cm; 64-107 g; wingspan 43-47 cm. Very distinctive black vertical eye-bar continuing onto crown; Y-shaped breast band continues onto hindneck; pale chestnut underparts, with dark chestnut lower edge and white lower belly; thin whitish eye-ring; underwing conspicuously rich rufous buff. Sexes alike. No seasonal variation. Juvenile like adult but generally duller, showing traces of dark face and collar.
Habitat. Mainly inland in flat, open, arid habitat with sparse growth of 20-40 cm tall salt-bush, blue-bush or samphire, often with bare patches of clay, including gibber plains, gravel flats, claypans and gilgais; at extremes of range, extends to coastal regions and into grasslands; often on gravel roads or airstrips at night; also heavily grazed pasture, and clearings opened in mallee vegetation for agriculture and ploughed land.
Food and Feeding. Seeds, leaves, insects (e.g. earwigs, crickets, beetles, termites, ants and larvae), and spiders. Mainly inactive during day, although very tolerant of high temperatures; feeds among shrubs in daytime; at night, feeds on dirt roads; tends to be herbivorous during day and insectivorous at night. Makes vigorous biting, pecking and pulling actions to procure pieces of plants up to 15 mm in diameter. Usually forages in small flocks of up to 20 birds, occasionally up to 50-400, but seems to feed solitarily at night.
Breeding. Not well known. Breeds at any time of year, responding to rains. Probably monogamous. Solitary or in small, loose colonies of up to 6 pairs. Nests on bare stony or sandy ground; nest is shallow scrape or depression, unlined or lined with small stones, plant material and debris. 3 eggs, sometimes 2, laid at daily intervals; incubation 26-30 days, probably by both parents, but mainly female; when leaving nest, e.g. if disturbed, adult rapidly covers eggs with soil and debris; chick has pale pinkish buff to cream upperparts with brown blotches, underparts off-white to cream; young tended by both parents. Fledging period and age of independence unknown. Eggs and young sometimes taken by foxes.
Movements. Little known. Dispersive, perhaps moving S in spring and N in summer; appears to be nomadic in Victoria. Movements probably dependent on rains and drought, and may be initiated by drought inland; recorded appearing before or after rains, but also during drought, and departing after heavy rains.
Status and Conservation. Not globally threatened. Total population estimated at 14,000 birds. No information available on population trends or impact of changes to vegetation caused by grazing in pastoral areas. Extensive distribution within many areas of relatively limited human impact suggests species likely to be fairly secure.
Bibliography. Blakers *et al.* (1984), Bock (1964), Bryant (1940a), Christian *et al.* (1992a), Emison *et al.* (1987), Flegg & Madge (1995), Lane & Davies (1987), Lindsey (1992), Macdonald (1988), Maclean (1973, 1976b), Marchant & Higgins (1993), McNamara (1980), Pizzey & Doyle (1980), Pringle (1987), Schodde & Tidemann (1986), Simpson & Day (1994), Slater *et al.* (1989), Trounson (1987).

Genus *ANARHYNCHUS*

Quoy & Gaimard, 1830

64. **Wrybill**

Anarhynchus frontalis

French: Pluvier anarhynque **German**: Schiefschnabel **Spanish**: Chorlitejo Piquituerto
Other common names: Wry-billed Plover

Taxonomy. *Anarhynchus frontalis*, Quoy and Gaimard, 1830, Hauraki Gulf, North Island, New Zealand.
Genus very close to *Charadrius*, and perhaps not justifiably distinct; species has been linked particularly with *C. bicinctus*. Monotypic.
Distribution. New Zealand: breeds in C South I; winters in N North I.

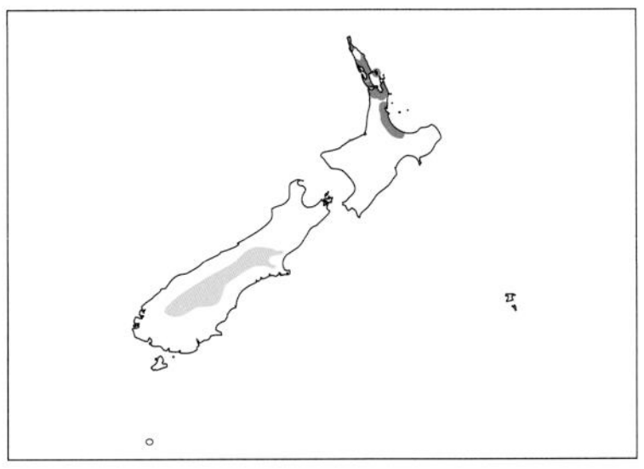

Descriptive notes. 20-21 cm; 43-71 g. Rather plump, greyish plover with conspicuous long bill curved to the right; male has black frontal bar and breast band. Female has duller, browner and narrower breast band and lacks black frontal bar. Non-breeding adult has breast band lacking or faint; no frontal bar. Juvenile as non-breeding adult, but has grey patches at sides of breast instead of breast band; feathers of upperparts have narrow dark subterminal bands, and narrow white fringes.
Habitat. Breeds inland on large braided rivers, occupying large bare beds of shingle and sand, with preference for large, glacier-fed rivers, fast-flowing water and dynamic shingle banks, which will not easily become overgrown with weeds; occasionally in smaller, less braided, slower-running rivers. Outside breeding season found in shallow estuaries, on sheltered coasts with large tidal mudflats, and lagoons with soft silty or muddy substrate. Occasionally in ploughed paddocks, reclaimed salt-marsh or muddy margins of small mountain lakes and ponds.
Food and Feeding. During breeding season takes aquatic invertebrates, including flatworms, annelids, gastropods, mites, spiders, and eggs, larvae, pupae and adults of various types of insect; also fish and their eggs. Uses curved bill to probe and sweep under stones, especially for catching mayflies (see page 388). In non-breeding areas, polychaete worms, small bivalves, crustaceans, beetles and Diptera larvae. During breeding season feeds at shallow riffles, pools and backwaters, on shingle banks and, when rivers flood, also among washed up debris; at non-breeding grounds pecks, probes and scythes on soft mud of mudflats, often at edge of receding tide. Diurnally active; in winter, night or day, depending on tide. Highly gregarious during non-breeding season, frequently in hundreds or thousands, often feeding together with other small waders.
Breeding. Laying late Aug to late Oct, with second clutch late Oct to late Dec. Monogamous on long-term basis. Solitary; holds vigorously defended territory in which nests and feeds, but also feeds in undefended areas; nests 400 m or more apart, rarely as close as 40 m. Highly site-faithful and high degree of natal philopatry in juveniles, immatures and adults. Nest in sand among shingle of large, smooth, rounded stones (often 1-2 cm in diameter) commonly sheltered by large stone or piece of wood; shallow scrape lined with small pebbles. 2 eggs, laid at intervals usually of less than 48 hours; double-brooded, and may lay replacement clutch; incubation 30-36 days, both parents, but more by female, starting once clutch complete; chick has pale, uniform, off-white to grey upperparts, with indistinct grey-black flecking, white underparts; tended by both parents; fledging 35-37 days; independent immediately after fledging. Breeds first at 2-3 years old. Hatching success 77%, fledging success 38%, i.e. 0·79 young/pair. 10% of laid eggs (47% of failed eggs) flooded, 1% of laid eggs (4%) predated. Average longevity 5·4 years; oldest recorded bird at least 12 years old.
Movements. Migratory. Moves from breeding grounds in C South I to mudflats of estuaries and harbours on N end of North I. Leaves rivers late Dec to early Feb; juveniles of first nest depart before parents finish second nest. Migrates via E coast of South I and W coast of North I, probably usually in single flight; juveniles arrive in winter quarters late Dec to early Jan, and most adults mid-Jan to Feb; highest numbers present on N coast May-Jul; adults show high degree of site fidelity to wintering and roosting sites. Most birds leave wintering sites in Aug; second-year non-breeders leave half way through breeding season and some, mainly first-year birds, spend summer in North I. Uses stopover sites on return migration, and arrives at river mouths late-Aug to Sept.
Status and Conservation. VULNERABLE. Hunted up to 1940; after hunting ceased, population increased, but stabilized by early 1960's, with c. 5000 birds. In 1994, total of 5111 birds counted. Now only breeds on 26 river beds E of Southern Alps, but only numerous on 10 of these. Nesting and roosting habitats, especially in lowlands, deteriorate through invasion of exotic weeds, such as broom (*Cytisus scoparius*) and whin or gorse (*Ulex europaeus*), caused by reduction of seasonal flushing of riverbeds as consequence of water abstraction. Further development, including hydro-electric schemes, threatens long-term survival of total population. Since floods are main causes of breeding failure, flood mitigation may have positive effects on breeding success; however, construction of dams also destroys nesting habitat, due to permanent flooding.
Bibliography. Burton (1972a), Chambers (1989), Child (1973), Collar *et al.* (1994), Davies (1991), Falla *et al.* (1981), Hay, J.R. (1984), Hughey (1985), Keeley (1985), Marchant & Higgins (1993), O'Donnell & Moore (1983), Pierce (1979, 1983), Riegen (1994), Robertson (1985), Robertson *et al.* (1983), Sibson (1963), Soper (1976), Turbott (1970, 1990).

Genus *PHEGORNIS*

G. R. Gray, 1846

65. **Diademed Plover**

Phegornis mitchellii

French: Pluvier des Andes **German**: Diademregenpfeifer **Spanish**: Chorlitejo Cordillerano
Other common names: (Diademed) Sandpiper-plover, Mitchell's Plover

Taxonomy. *Leptopus (Leptodactylus) Mitchellii* Fraser, 1845, Chile, probably in the province of Colchagua.
Affinities obscure. Monotypic.
Distribution. Andes from NC Peru through N Chile and W Bolivia to SC Chile and SC Argentina.

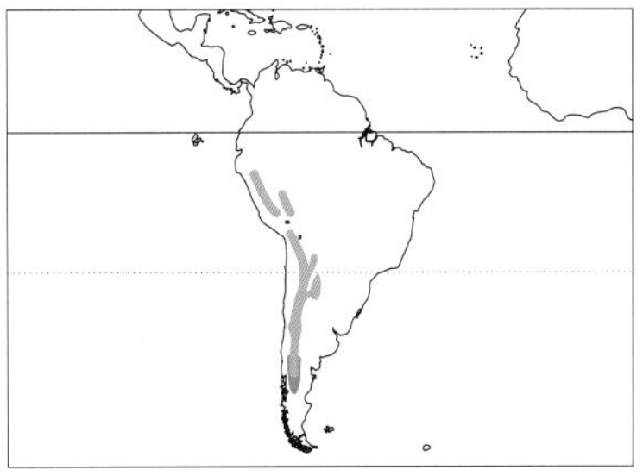

Descriptive notes. 16·5-19 cm; 28-46 g. Very distinctive small, compact plover with long, thin, slightly dropping bill, recalling those of *Calidris*; black head with white supercilia meeting on forecrown; grey upperparts, dark chestnut hindneck collar; underparts white with fine black bars; short, rounded wings; short, undulating flight, as in some passerine birds. Sexes alike. No seasonal variation. Juvenile has grey head with obscure supercilia; dark brown upperparts with dark buff fringes, paler underparts with less clear barring.
Habitat. *Puna* zone, on waterlogged mossy tundra and bogs with matted cushion-plant vegetation, especially *Distichia* bogs; also gravel or grass on river plains and near lakes. Breeds at altitude of 4000-5000 m; in S, descends to 2000 m in winter.
Food and Feeding. No information available on diet. Feeds in hidden spots, in eroded holes and creeks in bogs. Probes vertically with bill, and also picks prey off aquatic plants. Alone or in pairs, rarely more together.
Breeding. Laying Oct-Dec in Chile, Jan in Bolivia. Breeds in *puna* zone of high Andes, nesting at low densities. No further information available.
Movements. In southernmost parts of range, birds from highest ground descend to lower altitudes in Mar, after breeding season, but remains at relatively high altitudes; return to breeding areas in Oct. Possibly limited northward migration up Andes in austral autumn, and southward movement in spring.
Status and Conservation. Not globally threatened. Currently considered near-threatened. Very poorly known. Population size unknown. Uncommonly recorded, but easily overlooked. Occupation of bleak zone at high altitude suggests species may be relatively secure, at least in parts of range, but paucity of data calls for caution; nowhere known to be common, and may be rare and local throughout.
Bibliography. Blake (1977), Canevari *et al.* (1991), Fjeldså & Krabbe (1990), Hellmayr & Conover (1948), Howell & Webb (1995a, 1995b), Johnson (1964a, 1965b, 1972), Koepcke (1970), Meyer de Schauensee (1966, 1982), Narosky & Yzurieta (1987), Olrog (1984), Parker *et al.* (1982), de la Peña (1992), Pierce (1990b), Remsen & Traylor (1989), Rosair (1995a), Scott & Carbonell (1986), Zusi & Jehl (1970).

Genus OREOPHOLUS

Jardine & Selby, 1835

66. Tawny-throated Dotterel

Oreopholus ruficollis

French: Pluvier oréophile   **German**: Orangekehl-Regenpfeifer   **Spanish**: Chorlito Cabezón
Other common names: Slender-billed Plover

Taxonomy. *Charadrius ruficollis* Wagler, 1829, Canelones, Uruguay.
Sometimes placed in genus *Eudromias*. Two subspecies recognized.
Subspecies and Distribution.
O. r. pallidus Carriker, 1935 - coastal N Peru.
O. r. ruficollis (Wagler, 1829) - coastal C Peru S through W Bolivia, Chile and W & NC Argentina to Tierra del Fuego; non-breeding N to S Ecuador and E to E Argentina and SE Brazil.

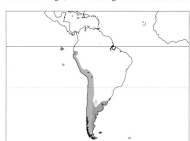

Descriptive notes. 25-29 cm; 120-154 g. Fairly upright plover with long, slender bill; striking plumage, mainly rich buff with heavily striped back, feathers with dark streaks and broad sandy to rufous fringes; chin white, throat orange-tawny, neck and breast grey; small, but prominent black patch on belly; legs dull pink;. in flight, underwing contrastingly white. Sexes alike. No seasonal variation. Juvenile has buff throat; feathers of upperparts have blackish centre and much narrower buff fringes; underparts paler and belly patch brown; legs grey. Race *pallidus* paler, and smaller than nominate.
Habitat. Mainly windy semi-arid ridges of open heathlands and overgrazed *puna* grassland up to 3500-4600 m, or sandy areas with sparse vegetation; seasonally on coastal plains and irrigated parts of the coastal desert in C Peru. On migration, also on fields and meadows in lowlands.
Food and Feeding. Very little known; one young bird had remains of beetles and grit in its stomach. Outside breeding season, often gathers in loose flocks of 10-30 birds, up to 100, for feeding; when disturbed, bird stands upright and turns striped back to observer, thereby presenting disruptive camouflage.
Breeding. Little known. Eggs Jun-Jan in race *pallidus*. Eggs apparently found generally Jun-Sept, but later towards S: two clutches Nov-Dec on island off NC Chile, where birds paired Sept-Nov; incubated nest found on Isla Grande, Tierra del Fuego, in Nov and a young bird in Dec. Race *pallidus* nests on sandy and nearly vegetation-free *lomas* zone near sea-level; one nest of nominate on top of clump of tussock grass, another surrounded by variegated pebbles arranged in concentric patterns. 4 eggs (4 nests); chick cinnamon, intricately patterned with black lines and zones of dense white "powderpuffs"; chicks of race *pallidus* very pale.
Movements. Poorly known; *pallidus* possibly resident in N Peru; nominate probably sedentary in parts of range, but migratory elsewhere. Birds breeding in high Andes migrate to lower altitudes after breeding season; those from southernmost areas mostly migrate N in Mar-Apr to Ecuador, and SE Brazil, Uruguay and E Argentina, returning late Aug to Sept. Absent from islands off NC Chile and adjacent mainland Feb-May.
Status and Conservation. Not globally threatened. No estimates of population, but species considered to be generally common in most parts of extensive range. Hunting in Chile and Argentina during autumn migration has apparently resulted in marked decreases, although no figures available.
Bibliography. Belton (1984), Blake (1977), Canevari *et al*. (1991), Clark (1986), Fjeldså & Krabbe (1990), Forrester (1993), Hellmayr & Conover (1948), Humphrey *et al*. (1970), Johnson (1965b), Klimaitis & Moschione (1987), Koepcke (1970), Meyer de Schauensee (1966, 1982), Myers (1980c), Narosky & Yzurieta (1987), Olrog (1984), Parker *et al*. (1982), de la Peña (1992), Remsen & Traylor (1989), Ruschi (1979), Scott & Carbonell (1986), Sick (1985c, 1993), Vilina & Teillier (1990).

Subfamily PLUVIANELLINAE
Genus *PLUVIANELLUS*

G. R. Gray, 1846

67. Magellanic Plover

Pluvianellus socialis

French: Pluvianelle magellanique   **German**: Magellanregenpfeifer   **Spanish**: Chorlito de Magallanes

Taxonomy. *Pluvianellus socialis* G. R. Gray, 1846, Straits of Magellan.
Relationships unclear and somewhat controversial: shows several unique features, and sometimes considered to form separate monospecific family, Pluvianellidae (see page 386); possibly related to sheathbills (Chionidae). Monotypic.
Distribution. Extreme S Chile and S Argentina. Winters N to Valdés Peninsula, SC Argentina.

Descriptive notes. 19·5-21·5 cm; male 79-102 g, female 70-87 g. Pale grey turnstone-like wader, with very short legs; soft grey upperparts and breast; lower breast with brown tinge; rest of underparts, throat and chin white; bill has pinkish patches at base of culmen and lower mandible, usually indistinct; pinkish red iris and legs. Sexes alike. No seasonal variation. Juvenile has upperparts spotted and fringed with white and buffish white; breast streaked; legs yellow, iris orange-grey.
Habitat. During breeding season, occurs in highlands, at open shores of freshwater or brackish lakes andalso at shallow pools in steppe-like regions. Outside breeding season, found on coast, mostly in sheltered bays, lagoons and river mouths.
Food and Feeding. During breeding season takes tiny arthropods; chironomid larvae apparently form staple food in winter. Pecks food from surface, turns over stones, shells and debris to find food, and may occasionally scratch or dig into sand for food using powerful legs, behaviour unique among waders; very active and fast-running. Outside breeding season, forages in small flocks.
Breeding. Laying probably early Sept to mid-Nov. Solitary, with strongly defended territories; additional feeding territory defended, sometimes well away from nest. Nests on wide clay or pebble shores of clear or clayey lakes with unstable water levels; nest is exposed scrape lined with gravel, situated very close to water. 2 eggs; incubated by both parents, period unknown; chick finely mottled ochraceous and dusky with some white down tips; newly-hatched chicks very weak, and fed by parents, apparently sometimes by their regurgitating food from their well developed crop, unique among waders (see page 388); fledging 28-30 days; young may be fed for 10 days more. The weaker chick, usually the second-hatched one, normally dies due to starvation.
Movements. Resident, dispersive and migratory. After breeding season, birds move to coast and some move relatively short distance N to Valdés Peninsula, SC Argentina. Small numbers may remain in wintering areas during breeding season. Generally arrives on breeding grounds by late Aug to early Sept.
Status and Conservation. Not globally threatened. Currently considered near-threatened. Total population may not exceed 1500 birds; estimate from 1990 suggests no more than 1000 birds in lowlands, where main breeding grounds in region of Straits of Magellan, with few birds in N & E Tierra del Fuego; a few hundred birds at 700-1200 m up to upland plateaux in inland Santa Cruz, S Argentina.
Bibliography. Blake (1977), Canevari *et al*. (1991), Clark (1986), Cracraft (1981), Fjeldså & Krabbe (1990), Hellmayr & Conover (1948), Humphrey *et al*. (1970), Jehl (1975a, 1975b), Johnson (1965b), Meyer de Schauensee (1966, 1982), Narosky & Yzurieta (1987), Narosky *et al*. (1993), Olrog (1984), de la Peña (1992), Pierce (1990a), Scott & Carbonell (1986).

Class AVES
Order CHARADRIIFORMES
Suborder CHARADRII
Family SCOLOPACIDAE (SNIPES, SANDPIPERS AND PHALAROPES)

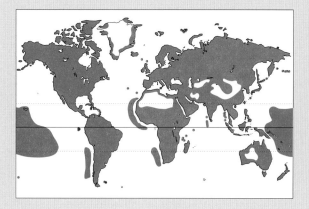

- Small to medium-sized waders with short to long legs; bill often long and may be straight, decurved or slightly recurved.
- 12-66 cm.

- All regions except Antarctic; most species breed in Northern Hemisphere and are highly migratory.
- Mainly coastal and on inland wetlands; breeds in open steppe, grassland, marsh, tundra, scrubland and even forest.
- 24 genera, 86 species, 134 taxa.
- 10 species threatened; 2 species and 1 subspecies extinct since 1600.

Systematics

The snipes, sandpipers and phalaropes of the Scolopacidae comprise a highly diverse family of birds that apparently arose in the early Tertiary, probably in the late Eocene, 40 million years ago. Their exact relationship with the plover family (Charadriidae) is still disputed, with most recent authors arguing that the two families are not sister groups, as has often been assumed in the past. Despite the great morphological and behavioural diversity within the Scolopacidae, modern morphological and biochemical evidence strongly suggests that the traditionally recognized members of this family do indeed derive from a common ancestor. This ancestor may also have given rise to the jacanas (Jacanidae) and the painted-snipes (Rostratulidae), according to the osteological studies of J. G. Strauch and the follow-up reanalyses of P. C. Chu and M. Björklund. Jacanas and painted-snipes may thus be derived sandpipers. This view is not corroborated by the DNA-DNA hybridization studies of C. G. Sibley and J. E. Ahlquist, which suggest that the jacanas along with the painted-snipes in one lineage, and the seedsnipes (Thinocoridae) in another, are the two most closely related outgroups to a monophyletic scolopacid family.

Snipes, sandpipers and phalaropes appear to be the result of an extraordinarily explosive evolution in the early Tertiary, after a great wave of extinctions at the end of the Cretaceous. This radiation is likely to have taken place in the late Eocene. From this period some fossil material of scolopacid waders is available, possibly representing the genera *Limosa* (godwits) and *Tringa* (shanks). If the Scolopacidae have diversified over a relatively short time period, there was little time between speciation events for neutral genetic changes to build up. For this reason it may be difficult or impossible, even with advanced molecular genetic techniques, to establish with any certainty the pattern of internal relationships within the family. However, using these same techniques, T. P. Birt and A. J. Baker have concluded that morphologically and behaviourally outlying taxa such as woodcocks (*Scolopax*), turnstones (*Arenaria*) and phalaropes (*Phalaropus*, *Steganopus*) appear to be unambiguously nested within the Scolopacidae. The phalaropes have frequently been placed in a separate family of their own.

The family Scolopacidae can usefully be divided into six subfamilies, with the recognition of Scolopacinae (woodcocks), Gallinagininae (snipes), Tringinae (shanks and allies), Arenariinae (turnstones), Calidrinae (sandpipers) and Phalaropodinae (phalaropes); in turn, Tringinae is usually further subdivided into three tribes, Numeniini (godwits and curlews), Tringini (shanks) and Prosoboniini (Polynesian sandpipers). Four of these subfamilies, Scolopacinae, Arenariinae, Calidrinae and Phalaropodinae, are almost certainly monophyletic. Apart from a possible merger of woodcocks and snipes into a single subfamily of snipe-like species (Gallinagininae), which would appear to be defensible on the basis of the latest biochemical evidence, the exact position of the three dowitchers (*Limnodromus*) remains unresolved. Most previous authors have listed them with the snipes, but others have placed them with the tringine sandpipers; there is something to be said for both views, but further study is unquestionably required. Tringinae is, in any case,

A notable difference between the Scolopacidae and the Charadriidae is that almost all members of the former have a hind toe, which enables them to perch in trees. Some members of the Tringinae will even nest in trees, in the wooded marshy habitats of the northern taiga belt, where they may make use of old thrush nests. Breeding tringines are very secretive, and finding their nests can be a major challenge; it is far easier to locate a vigilant breeder perched in the top of a conifer, like this Spotted Redshank.

[*Tringa erythropus.*
Photo: Gordon Langsbury/
Bruce Coleman]

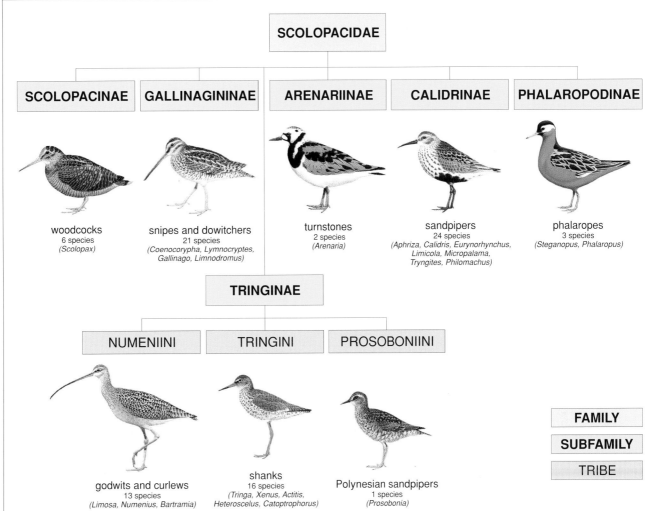

Subdivision of the Scolopacidae.

[Figure: Francesc Jutglar & Etel Vilaró]

most likely to be a polyphyletic assemblage. Recent work suggests that the "shank" genera *Tringa, Xenus, Heteroscelus, Actitis* and *Catoptrophorus* may be closely related to the phalaropes, and that this lineage may be a sister group to the woodcocks and snipes. The godwits (*Limosa*) and the curlews (*Numenius, Bartramia*) appear to be two independent taxa, quite unrelated to the rest of the Tringinae, possibly branching off at the base of the scolopacid family. The position of the Tuamotu Sandpiper (*Prosobonia cancellata*) and its two extinct relatives (see Status and Conservation) remains uncertain, particularly in view of a lack of modern phylogenetic studies. On the basis of the morphological studies by R. L. Zusi and J. R. Jehl, which suggested a closer relationship with the Tringini than with the curlews or calidrine sandpipers, *Prosobonia* is positioned as a separate tribe among the Tringinae.

Within the lineage of phalaropes, Wilson's Phalarope (*Steganopus tricolor*) appears to be the sister taxon to the closely related species pair of the Red-necked (*Phalaropus lobatus*) and Red Phalaropes (*Phalaropus fulicaria*). Within the Calidrinae, there is little doubt that the morphologically and behaviourally exceptional genera *Aphriza, Eurynorhynchus, Limicola, Micropalama, Tryngites* and *Philomachus* are all closely related to the "true" sandpipers of *Calidris*. In fact, some of these genera may be more closely related to many of the *Calidris* species, than some members of *Calidris* are to each other. If this suggestion were correct, *Calidris* would not be considered a monophyletic genus. For example, the Curlew Sandpiper (*Calidris ferruginea*), on the one hand, and the Great Knot (*Calidris tenuirostris*) and the Red Knot (*Calidris canutus*), on the other, may each provide lineages quite separate from the other calidrines. Modern molecular genetic studies have supported the suggestion of J. R. Jehl, based on morphological and natural history arguments, that the Surfbird (*Aphriza virgata*) is very closely related to the knots. It is retained in a monotypic genus because of its bill, which in contrast to all other calidrines is not rhynchokinetic, meaning that a Surfbird is unable to bend

the lower portion of its upper mandible. For the same reason, the Spoon-billed Sandpiper (*Eurynorhynchus pygmeus*) with a unique spoon-like bill, has a separate genus of its own despite a close overall resemblance to the Red-necked Stint (*Calidris ruficollis*). The systematics of sandpipers is ripe for a thorough revision, including the application of the latest biochemical and theoretical techniques.

The Long-billed (*Limnodromus scolopaceus*) and Short-billed Dowitchers (*Limnodromus griseus*) were considered conspecific until F. A. Pitelka showed in 1950 how different they actually are. Apart from differences in morphology and vocalizations, their habitat choices in the non-breeding season are very distinctive. Long-billed Dowitchers mainly use freshwater habitats, whereas Short-billed Dowitchers are confined to coastal, saltwater areas, a type of habitat that they have in common with Asian Dowitchers (*Limnodromus semipalmatus*). In spite of their close resemblance, the divergence of the mitochondrial DNA of the Long-billed and Short-billed Dowitchers is greater than that of many other avian species pairs. On the basis of widely used rates of hereditary change, or molecular clocks, J. C. Avise and R. M. Zink arrive at a crude estimate of the time since separation of 4 million years. This estimate can be compared with a figure of 4-6 million years for the separation of the lineage of Red Knots from the other calidrines estimated by A. J. Baker. These two estimates of the age of present day species can be contrasted with the supposed time of the original diversification of the Scolopacidae in the early Tertiary, almost 10 times as long ago. It would be exciting to use comprehensive information on molecular genetic divergence and calibrated molecular clocks to estimate periods of stasis and radiation in this fascinating and diverse family of birds.

In spite of the fact that most scolopacid waders nowadays breed in boreal to Arctic environments, the family seems to have evolved in the early Tertiary, when the world's climate was warm. The first cold period occurred about 10 million years ago, and

As a rule, shorebirds do not swim, but wade. The three phalarope species provide the exception to this rule, as this Red-necked Phalarope demonstrates. With their thick duck-like downy plumage they are able to remain on the water without becoming waterlogged. With their lobed toes and basally webbed feet, phalaropes are able to move rapidly on the water, twisting and turning. They feed on small planktonic prey items that occur near the water surface. These can be transported to the mouth in water droplets which move upwards between the lower and upper mandibles at great speed, due to capillary force.

[*Phalaropus lobatus*, Great Basin Desert, California, USA. Photo: Barbara Gerlach/ DRK]

from then onwards the region of cold moved south. By the end of the Pliocene, only 1·5 million years ago, the climate became similar to that of today, with polar ice caps and a circumpolar belt of tundra. Subsequently, during the Pleistocene epoch, there was an alternation of ice ages and interglacial periods, the first ice age reaching a peak about 500,000 years ago and the last about 18,000 years ago. With southward and northward invasions and retreats of the ice sheets, all the wader habitats continuously shifted dramatically in both geographical position and extent. Several authors, including S. Larson and W. G. Hale, have speculated on the role that these climate changes, through their effects on the distribution of suitable habitats, may have played in the evolution of species and subspecies of scolopacid waders, but these early attempts were strongly constrained by the absence of assays of genetic population structure and estimates of divergence times.

Until a few years ago, the only way to examine the genetic, subspecific, population structure of extant species was by the study, on the basis of museum material, of morphological characters, usually the size of external dimensions such as bill or wing length or the details of moult and plumage coloration. For example, in Rock Sandpipers (*Calidris ptilocnemis*), confined to the Bering Strait region during breeding, four subspecies were described in this way. In contrast, the closely related Purple Sandpiper (*Calidris maritima*) of the North American and European Arctic regions did not appear to show much substructuring, a finding that has now been backed up by allozyme studies. Reasonable congruence between classic museum studies and modern molecular genetic assays was also obtained by P. W. Wenink and associates for the population genetic structuring of the world's Dunlins (*Calidris alpina*). Of the six examined subspecies, five could be retraced in data of mitochondrial DNA variation. Time estimates of the origin of these groups based on sequence divergences suggest that there was repeated fragmentation of Dunlin populations during the late Pleistocene, from about 200,000 years ago onwards. The extant subspecies of Dunlins seem to originate from these old climatic events, a scenario that is quite different from that of the origin of five morphologically distinguished subspecies of Red Knots. Using the same methodology, these races are estimated to be in the order of 10,000 years old. If this were true, the present day world distribution and mi-

gration routes of Red Knots evolved from a small bottleneck population that survived during the retreat of the last great northern ice caps.

Recently there have been heated debates about the taxonomic status of a few aberrant *Calidris* individuals that were irregularly observed in Australia, and occasionally elsewhere. These birds, named Cox's Sandpiper ("*Calidris paramelanotos*") and Cooper's Sandpiper ("*Calidris cooperi*") by those that believed them to be distinct species, are now considered hybrids between the Curlew Sandpiper on the one hand, and respectively the Pectoral (*Calidris melanotos*) and Sharp-tailed Sandpipers (*Calidris acuminata*) on the other. In the case of a Cox's Sandpiper, molecular genetic analyses showed that the mitochondrial DNA was identical with that of Curlew Sandpipers. Since mitochondrial DNA is maternally inherited, the mother must have been a Curlew Sandpiper that most probably mated with a Pectoral Sandpiper male. Outside Australia, putative hybrids between other *Calidris* pairs have been reported: Curlew Sandpiper with White-rumped Sandpiper (*Calidris fuscicollis*); Dunlin with Sanderling (*Calidris alba*); Dunlin with Purple Sandpiper; Baird's Sandpiper (*Calidris bairdii*) with Buff-breasted Sandpiper (*Tryngites subruficollis*); and Little Stint (*Calidris minuta*) with Temminck's Stint (*Calidris temminckii*).

Considering the size and internal diversity of the family, there is relatively little disagreement as to which forms should be treated as species; this is clearly connected with the notable fact that of the total of 86 species as many as 64 are considered monotypic. The main area of doubt at the species level lies in the snipe genus *Gallinago*, which contains some of the least known of all scolopacids. Similarly, generic limits are almost universally agreed upon, although a few authors recognize slightly broader versions of the genera *Tringa* and *Calidris*. For many years the typical snipes were classified in the genus *Capella*, as opposed to *Gallinago*, but rather than a taxonomic issue this change reflects one of nomenclature: *Capella* Frenzel 1801 pre-dated *Gallinago* Koch 1816; however, the name *Gallinago* is actually attributable to Brisson 1760, and thus has priority.

The number of species recognized may be on the point of increasing! Until recently, the only species of woodcock known from the Philippines was the temperate breeding Eurasian Wood-

Compared with members of the plover family, the typical scolopacid wader is noted for its smaller eyes, more slender head, and longer, thinner bill. The bill tends to contain a very high density of tactile receptors towards the tip, these being closely linked with the more tactile, less visual, foraging style of the Scolopacidae. Body shape, size and general design are rather more varied in this family, and its members occupy a greater range of ecological niches than the Charadriidae, while it is also diverse in terms of reproductive systems. The sandpiper group, including all species but the snipes and woodcocks and the phalaropes, is a particularly varied assemblage. It contains small to large birds with legs ranging from medium length to very long. There is notable diversity in the bill, which ranges from short to extremely long and narrow, and may be slightly recurved or markedly decurved. This graceful Marsh Sandpiper shows the typical long legs after which the "shanks" are named, and the long, straight bill, characteristically needle-thin in this most attractive species.

[*Tringa stagnatilis*, Al Ansab Lagoons, Oman. Photo: Hanne & Jens Eriksen/Aquila]

Although most of these Common Redshanks roosting at high tide have their eyes covered with the white nictitating membrane, a few are keeping a watchful eye on their environment. They have good reason to do so, since many are taken by raptors during the non-breeding season. Juvenile and adult birds appear to make different habitat choices with regard to predation risk. Young Common Redshanks, outcompeted from musselbeds by adults, feed in high-risk areas of salt-marsh, where the food supply is, however, better. Only 10% of them survives the raptor predation throughout the winter.

[Tringa totanus, Little Eye Dee estuary, Britain. Photo: Alan Hartley/ Oxford Scientific Films]

cock (*Scolopax rusticola*), which turns up as a rare winter visitor in the north. However, on the southern island of Mindanao birds have recently been observed performing regular roding display flights, sure proof of breeding on the island. R. S. Kennedy is currently in the process of comparing specimens and vocalizations with the available material for the nearest populations of Eurasian Woodcocks in Japan, and also for the Sulawesi Woodcock (*Scolopax celebensis*). At the time of going to press the outcome is still uncertain, but it appears quite likely that this form will be described as a species new to science.

Morphological Aspects

The Scolopacidae are small to medium-sized birds. On dry land they can walk and run and on water they can swim, but many species are at their best when wading in shallow water. Compared to plovers (Charadriidae), they have smaller eyes and more slender heads. With their longer, thinner bills they are geared to a more tactile, less visual, foraging style than plovers. Their bill tips contain particularly high densities of tactile receptors. The Scolopacidae show a much greater variety of body forms and occupy a greater range of ecological niches than the Charadriidae. Three eco-morphological groups can roughly be distinguished: the snipe, sandpiper and phalarope groups.

The snipe group contains small to medium-sized birds with long legs and very long bills. These long bills have been the origin of vernacular names in many languages. For example, the English name "snipe" is derived from "snite" or "snout", later transformed into "snipe". All snipes, and the closely related woodcocks, are earthy brown with longitudinal brown or buffy stripes, which provides excellent camouflage in the bogs, marshes and forests where they live. The sandpiper group, containing all species except the snipes and their allies and the phalaropes, are small to large birds characterized by medium to very long legs and short to very long and narrow bills which may be slightly upcurved or prominently downcurved. All species show countershading, with darker browns and greys above and paler underparts; some species show rufous or black underparts during the breeding season. The third group, the pelagic-living phalaropes, are small, roundish but elegant birds with relatively

heavy duck-like plumages of the same general coloration as in the sandpipers, and with medium-length, narrow bills. Their legs are rather short, the tarsi laterally compressed, and the feet show small webs between "scalloped" toes. These coot-like feet with lobed toes have given them their name: the word *Phalaropus* is derived from the Greek words for "coot", *phalaris*, and "foot", *pous*. The Semipalmated (*Calidris pusilla*), Western (*Calidris mauri*) and Stilt Sandpipers (*Micropalama himantopus*), the Willet (*Catoptrophorus semipalmatus*), Nordmann's Greenshank (*Tringa guttifer*) and the Terek Sandpiper (*Xenus cinereus*), the dowitchers and the godwits all have partly webbed feet too, and the *Tringa* species have a small web between the outer toes, but the remaining scolopacid waders show no webs. Nearly all Scolopacidae have three long front toes and a small hind toe. As an adaptation to running on sandy beaches, which are firmer than most other substrates, Sanderlings differ from all other scolopacids in that they lack the hind toe.

Scolopacid waders show their greatest variability in the relative length and shape of their bills. Bill length relative to head length varies by a factor of seven, from more than 3 in the Far Eastern (*Numenius madagascariensis*) and Long-billed Curlews (*Numenius americanus*) to 0·45 in the Tuamotu Sandpiper, and bills may be straight, slightly upcurved or downcurved. With the Surfbird and the turnstones as clear exceptions, the tip of the bill of most scolopacids is slightly swollen and its horny sheath is internally honeycombed with hexagonal cells. These cavities are filled with tiny receptor organs, including Herbst's Corpuscles that measure pressure and Grandry's Corpuscles that measure shear, to which sensory fibres are attached. In addition, the brains of the Scolopacidae show an expansion of the frontal and brainstem area that is absent in the Charadriidae. This expansion is innervated by the receptor-rich bill tip. The neural modifications and enlargements make scolopacid waders very effective in the tactile detection of buried prey.

The great variation in bill types is not only interesting but also instructive, since the diversification in bill morphology goes hand in hand with the diversification of food resources and habitats used. Although a single species may show more than one feeding style, indicating the flexibility and scope for behavioural and morphological evolution, four general feeding styles can be distinguished; the first is pecking with occasional probing, mostly

As soon as food becomes a defensible resource and flock-feeding unnecessary, individual waders are liable to establish feeding territories. This tends to be the case particularly when the birds are foraging by means of visual techniques. These two non-breeding Black-tailed Godwits are involved in a "mandibular clash" over a profitable piece of wetland.

[*Limosa limosa*, India. Photo: David Hosking/ FLPA]

used by species that live in rather dry inland habitats and along fringe habitats, such as water-lines, including the genera *Bartramia, Actitis, Heteroscelus, Catoptrophorus*, some *Tringa, Arenaria* and probably *Prosobonia*; the second is probing of soft soils and intertidal flats, the common mode shown by all snipes and woodcocks and the majority of the sandpiper group; the third is running with the bill submerged chasing fish, a mode used by *Tringa*; and the fourth, rapid pecking of tiny prey from a water layer, is practised by the phalaropes and some *Calidris*. The motor arrangements of the skulls of scolopacid waders are sophisticated and include the capability of bending to bend the lower part of the upper mandible without opening the entire bill. This is called rhynchokinesis and allows a fine manipulation of the bill tip during deep probes and thus the capture of buried prey.

Once captured in the bill tip, prey items must be transported to the mouth. There are three possible ways to do so. Prey can be "glued" to the tongue and carried upward, as in most relatively short-billed sandpipers. In the longer-billed scolopacids, prey must be more extensively manipulated: capture is followed by throw and fetch movements that bring the prey higher in the bill until "glue" and tongue-carrying can take over to complete the movement towards the mouth. This method is used by species that have tongues shorter than their bills. Third, the feeding on tiny drifting invertebrate prey brings its own problems and solutions. Because water is incompressible, the movement of a bill tip through the water layer will displace water and with it the tiny prey items that a wader may have visually detected and aims to capture. Phalaropes, and probably many calidrine sandpipers too, have been shown by M. Rubega and B. S. Obst to solve this problem by "capturing" a small quantity of water that contains the tiny prey. Capillary forces then move the water droplet mouthwards between the mandibles as these are slightly opened. Transport is very rapid, sometimes taking as little as 1/100 second to complete. When the water droplet with the prey reaches the mouth, the jaws are abruptly closed so that the water is squeezed out and can be shaken off the bill. In this way the ingestion of osmotically stressful salt water is avoided.

It may seem impossible to bring such a great variety of scolopacid species under a common heading with regard to bill and skull morphology and feeding habits. However, their seemingly extravagant morphological and behavioural variability il-

lustrates a wide and rapid radiation that may well originate from a single basic design. According to the research by G. A. Zweers and co-workers, the whole trophic diversification, the whole range of current feeding mechanisms of the Scolopacidae, can be considered to represent varying degrees of specialization derived from a single common pecking mechanism originally displayed by a short-billed plover-like shorebird. This pecking mechanism has been modified to the different pecking, probing and prey-transport styles of snipes, sandpipers and phalaropes, changes that came along with morphological adjustments to maximize particular ways of penetration, detection, inspection and handling of prey items. This includes the evolution of sensory organs and brain capacity to detect buried cryptic prey items by remote-touch mechanisms. A common form of feeding behaviour, that of making pecks and shallow probes, is still shown by all members of the Scolopacidae, no matter their morphological and behavioural specializations. This is likely to be an only slightly modified version of that original pecking mechanism.

The decurved bills of curlews and Curlew Sandpipers and the slightly upcurved bills of godwits and Terek Sandpipers have generated considerable speculation and dispute in ornithological literature. A straight bill is more suitable mechanically for rapid thrusting in the substrate. This shape has the lightest construction, avoids local concentration of mechanical stress and requires minimal effort during penetration. When probing into small openings, in complex burrow systems, between stones or amongst branches, a decurved bill allows the bird to reach more of the space behind the entrance than a straight bill. A decurved bill is also advantageous for the intact removal of long and soft-bodied prey from mudflats, yields a larger touch-area when moved around in soft substrates and provides a better initial positioning to grasp a prey item from a surface. However, curvature weakens the construction, and decurved bills require structural reinforcements. These bony structures take up most of the bill cavity and require a great reduction in the size of the tongue. As a consequence, curlews must remove prey from the substrate before they can swallow it. It must be transported to the mouth by head-jerking and a co-ordinated opening and shutting of the mandibles. In contrast, snipes and woodcocks with long straight bills have an open bill cavity and a long tongue. By a combination of a rapid series of retractions of the rhynchokinetic upper jaw tip

Large mixed flocks are typical of the Scolopacidae, especially during migration and in winter. At all times of the year, but especially during migration, food supplies tend to be of paramount importance, and huge numbers of waders will gather at particularly high quality refuelling sites. These splendid Red Knots were photographed at one such site in Delaware Bay, USA, in the company of Ruddy Turnstones (Arenaria interpres) and Sanderlings (Calidris alba).

[Calidris canutus rufa, Reed's Beach, New Jersey, USA. Photo: Joe McDonald/ Animals Animals]

and by tongue action, they are able to transport prey inside the bill while it is still inserted in the substrate. Godwits show a certain degree of bill reinforcement and tongue reduction, and are only in some circumstances able to ingest prey without taking the bill from the substrate. In summary, shorebird species that predominantly forage by probing in small holes and crevices have the most curved bills, whereas species that probe in the firmest substrates will have relatively straight bills.

This is not, however, the whole story. There are scolopacid waders with bills that are out of the normal range by virtue of other characteristics than length or curvature, for example the turnstones. Superficially, their stout bills resemble those of plovers, and for this reason turnstones were in the past assigned to the Charadriidae. The turnstone bill is tough, deep at the base and strongly tapering. With this wedge-like instrument the birds can search for invertebrate prey by probing under, and then overturning, quite heavy stones and pieces of seaweed. This turning behaviour has also lead to an exceptionally strong neck musculature. Spoon-billed Sandpipers, small calidrine waders with plumage and external and internal morphology strongly reminiscent of Red-necked Stints, carry spatulate bills much like those of spoonbills (Platalea). The spoon-like expansion of the bill tip has enormously increased the number of Herbst's Corpuscles and also the size of the tactile surface applied to the sediment. This should greatly enhance the tactile detection of the tiny prey that Spoon-billed Sandpipers are known to feed on, and perhaps aid their capture. The spatulate bill may be most effective when the bird makes rapid sideways sweeps through the upper layer of the preferred soft sediments and shallow water with the mandibles slightly apart, just as in feeding spoonbills. The Broad-billed Sandpiper (Limicola falcinellus) has a bill that is broad over much of its length and is also packed with tactile receptor organs at the tip; it is used for sustained vertical probing rather than for pecking, and may be especially suited for the efficient capture and ingestion of quite large buried polychaete worms in soft sediments.

That visual prey detection is less important for most scolopacid waders than it is for plovers is reflected by other aspects of their respective morphologies as well. Not only are the eyes of scolopacid waders smaller than those of plovers, but the retinal density of rods (useful for detection under poor light conditions) is lower, and that of cones (for visual acuity in daylight and for colour discrimination) is relatively higher. In snipes and woodcocks the eyes are placed laterally and so high in the skull that the brain case is positioned below, rather than behind, the eyes. There is almost no skull structure in front or behind the

eyes, and, as a consequence, the ear openings are placed directly below the eyes. This arrangement gives the snipes comprehensive visual coverage of the hemisphere above them and total panoramic vision in a near horizontal plane, as shown in a detailed study of Eurasian Woodcocks by G. R. Martin. There is no blind area behind the head except at or below the horizontal. This panoramic vision is achieved at the expense of binocular depth vision, since the binocular field is only 12° at its widest, upwards from the head and perpendicular to the line of the bill. The binocular field is only 4° wide horizontally in the forward plane. That the bill tip falls just outside the visual field is no problem for birds that find their prey entirely by tactile and chemical cues. Like most other waders, snipes and woodcocks feed, roost and nest exclusively on the ground so that they are always vulnerable to both aerial and terrestrial predators. Freed from the constraint that vision is essential for prey location, their visual field appears primarily adapted for efficient and effective surveillance.

The guts of scolopacid waders are all quite uniform in relative size and shape. Moving towards the tail end of the bird, the oesophagus is followed by the glandular stomach or proventriculus, the "muscular stomach" or gizzard, the small intestine, and the large intestine. A pair of small caeca, possibly fulfilling a role in the bacterial digestion of fibrous material, can be found attached to the large intestine. Compared to the plovers of similar size and diet, the length of the intestine and the caeca is shorter. The glandular stomach of most scolopacid waders is also small, and can not contain much stored food. The gizzard shows quite large variations in relative size between species, much of which can be explained by the way in which it is used. Species that feed mainly on hard-shelled mollusc prey, such as Purple Sandpipers, Red and Great Knots and Surfbirds, have large muscular stomachs. These species ingest their prey whole and must crack and crush the food items before digestion in the intestine. In these species undigested shell fragments are discarded, compacted as firm and calcium-rich droppings, via the intestines. A closely related sandpiper species like the Dunlin feeds only infrequently on small bivalves, and ejects almost all shell fragments as regurgitated pellets. Pellets are routinely produced by many other species of Scolopacidae as well, especially when they feed on chitin-rich arthropods such as insects and crustaceans. A phenomenon that has received scant attention in the literature is the fact that several scolopacid waders eject the lining of their gizzards at particular times of the year. These linings, small yellowish bags, have been found in great numbers on roost-sites of northward migrating Whimbrels (Numenius phaeopus). In dissected shorebirds of a wide variety of species, linings are regularly separate from the muscular stomach wall. Such "moults" of the gizzard may prevent the build-up of stomach parasites.

Although mollusc-eating waders have relatively large gizzards, the size is not constant within a species or even within an individual bird. The gizzard varies depending on the work requirement, in other words the type and volume of food ingested. When eating soft arthropods that require no crushing, on Arctic tundra during the breeding season for example, gizzards of Red and Great Knots are greatly reduced in size. This flexibility is also paramount in other parts of a shorebird. For example, during fat storage in preparation for long distance flights, the size of the different organs involved in the digestion, absorption and internal transport of nutrients, namely the stomach, intestine, liver and kidneys, is temporarily increased considerably. Before take-off for the migratory journey these organs may again be broken down so that part of the released nutritional components can be used for a rapid build up over the last few days of the critical parts of a flight machine, the breast muscles and the heart.

In male waders on their way to the breeding grounds, the reproductive glands, the testes, have already increased in size at stopover areas. In contrast, the equivalent organs of females, the ovaries, usually begin full development after arrival on the breeding grounds, but then they become much heavier than the testes. Among calidrine sandpipers, monogamous species have a smaller testis size than non-monogamous species. Polygamous male sandpipers may be selected to mate with as many different females as possible, and this leads to sperm competition between males. A higher demand for sperm, a greater "work-load", will then select for larger organs, larger testicles, just as it does for any part of the shorebird body. The Ruff (*Philomachus pugnax*) in breeding condition has the biggest testes of all scolopacid waders, which contribute almost 5% to their body mass and thus weigh much more than their brains. The Scolopacidae differ from other shorebird families in their sperm. Whereas in the rest of the charadriiforms sperm cells are simple straight rods with tails, those of scolopacid waders are spiral in form. J. G. van Rhijn has suggested that this may also relate to sperm competition, with spiral sperm cells having higher motility and thus an edge over simpler forms during the race to reach the unfertilized egg first.

Particularly flexible little organs are the pair of salt glands, carried on the upper part of the head between the eyes. Salt glands excrete excess salt directly from the blood plasma as a concentrated saline fluid into the nasal cavity, from where it is discarded by fast sideways bill sweeps. Snipes and woodcocks, which occur almost exclusively in freshwater habitats, have no salt glands. The salt glands of sandpipers frequenting freshwater habitats are tiny. Scolopacids that live along the seashore generally show large salt glands, and the largest are found in bivalve-eating sandpipers that ingest their prey whole, such as Red Knots. These sandpipers can not avoid ingesting salt water since bivalve flesh is isotonic with seawater and since it is contained in pure form between the valves. For this reason the salt glands of Red Knots are relatively large, even larger than those of Wilson's Phalaropes that live on highly saline lakes. As discussed above, phalaropes squeeze out the salt water surrounding their planktonic prey before ingesting the prey. Yet, when Red Knots live without sea water for some time, as they do on their tundra breeding grounds, their salt glands become small. They are regrown upon a renewed encounter with sea water, during southward migration. In scolopacid waders occupying marine and saline habitats the size of the salt glands is thus finely tuned to the amount of ingested saltwater that needs to be processed, and to the volume of osmotically free (fresh) water that is required for evaporative, cooling, purposes.

Whereas the salt glands are the smallest functional organs of a scolopacid wader, the breast muscles are certainly the largest. The strong sternum has a prominent ventral keel, and on both sides lie a pair of muscles, the large flight muscle *pectoralis*, which generates the power for the downstroke, and the much smaller *supracoracoideus* muscle, which powers the upstroke of the wings. The breast muscles usually comprise about a quarter of the fat-free mass of shorebirds. This heavy flying gear is partly compensated for by the lightness of the bones. Although the dimensions of the skeletal attachment area of snipes and woodcocks is similar to that of the other scolopacid waders, the breast muscles are relatively heavy. This is correlated with the rather different wing morphology of woodcocks and snipes.

While the great majority of shorebirds are long distance migrants with long and pointed, high-speed, wings bearing a minimum of drag, the woodcocks, and to a lesser degree the snipes and the *Actitis* sandpipers, have more rounded wings. The rather elliptical shape of woodcock wings is designed for navigation

Once or twice a day, waders of the foreshore congregate on safe high-lying flats when the tides cover their intertidal feeding areas. At the period of high tide, waders can rest, preen and bathe, whereas all feeding has to be carried out at low tide. High tide is also the time when flocks aggregate, and there may be information exchange about the birds' inclination to migrate onwards or about the quality of different feeding locations.

[Elbe Estuary, Wadden Sea, Germany. Photo: Jan van de Kam]

and sex. As an example of the first phenomenon, the wing length of Common Redshanks (*Tringa totanus*) breeding in warmer climatic zones is shorter than that of conspecifics breeding in colder areas. This may be regarded as a nice example of Bergmann's Rule, which states that in colder climates warm-blooded animals should be larger in order to reduce relative heat loss by a smaller surface area/volume ratio. A weird contrasting congeneric pair of longitudinal size differences within a species is provided by Black-tailed (*Limosa limosa*) and Bar-tailed Godwits (*Limosa lapponica*): in this case, towards the east there is a cline of decreasing body size in Black-tailed Godwits, while there is one of increasing size in Bar-tailed Godwits. This has the confusing effect on worldwide birdwatchers that in western Europe Black-tailed Godwits are larger than Bar-tailed Godwits, but that in South-east Asia and Australia this is reversed. No easy explanatory "rule" is at hand here.

The Scolopacidae provide some of the best examples of pronounced sexual size dimorphism in birds. Indeed, the family contains some species in which males are larger, but also many in which the reverse is true. Male Ruffs are almost 25% larger than the females, called Reeves, in all linear dimensions. In other promiscuous sandpipers such as the Pectoral and Sharp-tailed Sandpipers, males are also quite considerably larger than females. In contrast, male knots, godwits, curlews and phalaropes are consistently smaller than the females. Amongst the woodcocks, snipes and tringines, the sexes are usually of equal size. Most published evolutionary interpretations of the sexual size dimorphism of scolopacid waders have emphasized the correlation with mating system and parental role division. In species that show a physically competitive lekking system the males are larger, with the notable exception of the Great Snipe (*Gallinago media*). In lekking species females carry full responsibility for breeding and rearing the chicks. Conversely, in species where females are larger, males take on the greater share of parental care. P. E. Jönsson and T. Alerstam have argued that a smaller body size is adaptive for the care-taking sex, since smaller individuals require less energy to maintain themselves. In addition, the short bills, with dimensions that mirror those of the chicks to an extent, are better adapted for foraging in typical chick-rearing habitats and are therefore advantageous when attending broods.

The flight-feathers and tail feathers of scolopacid waders are replaced once a year. Usually these feathers are moulted when the breeding plumage is also replaced. In most cases moult commences after arrival on the wintering grounds, but it can also occur earlier in the year. In this regard scolopacid waders seem quite flexible. In Dunlins there are breeding populations that already start flight-feather moult on the breeding grounds, while other populations only begin their moult after having arrived in their winter quarters. The primaries are moulted from the "wrist" outwards, the secondaries inwards. The moult of the secondaries, the tertials and the tail feathers starts when the primaries are half way done. Wing moult is usually completed in one continuous period of 2-4 months, but several inland-staging waders, such as Black-tailed Godwits and Ruffs, renew only the inner 3-6 flight-feathers in Europe and finish this moult later in the year on the African wintering areas. In scolopacid waders wintering along the eastern shores of the Atlantic Ocean, wing moult in northerly areas is completed faster and earlier in the year than in southerly areas. In western Europe shorebirds have completed their wing moult by late October, but the cline continues over the equator into southern Africa, where shorebirds in wing moult may be encountered into the month of February of the next calendar year.

During the non-breeding season the plumage of scolopacid waders is uniformly dull, usually with the belly paler and the back darker. In many of the species this changes during the breeding season, when the belly may turn from pale grey to dark rusty red or black, and when the back may be decorated with finely coloured scapulars with colours matching those of the breast and belly plumage. Red Knots, Curlew Sandpipers, Bar-tailed Godwits and Red Phalaropes develop rusty red bellies, brighter in males of the first three species, and in females of the last. In phalaropes, the males are the "choosing" sex that take care of all parental duties except, of course, egg-laying, and the duller plum-

Typically for "meadowbirds", this wary Upland Sandpiper uses a fence post to oversee its territory. A prairie grassland species, the Upland Sandiper experienced massive declines a century ago, due to the cultivation of its preferred habitat. It suffered even more when farmers started to lay down poison, killing large numbers, in the belief that the species ate their grain. In fact, these sandpipers consume wireworms, grasshoppers and other potential grassland pests.

[Bartramia longicauda, North Dakota, USA. Photo: Wayne Lynch/DRK]

among tree limbs. Most woodcock species do not carry out long distance migrations and lack the speed of shorebirds of open spaces. Instead, they have perfected a rocketing take-off in case of disturbance. Like little helicopters they can disappear straight up through the branches. The Common Sandpiper (*Actitis hypoleucos*) of the Old World and the Spotted Sandpiper (*Actitis macularia*) of the New, combine rounded wings with a special "buzzy" flight technique in which wingbeats are shallow and spasmodic. During level flight, usually low over the water, each wingbeat is curtailed just below the horizontal so that the wings do not get wet, and there are short glides on down-bowed wings between series of flickering shallow wingbeats. During their long migratory flights between their temperate breeding areas and tropical wintering areas, the rounded wings and peculiar flight style give Common and Spotted Sandpipers rather low flight speeds. These are in the order of 30-40 km/h rather than the 60-70 km/h of long-winged family members. The adaptive value of their wing morphology and wingstroke patterns only becomes apparent when potential predators, such as hawks, show up, upon which *Actitis* sandpipers immediately dive under water and swim with the help of the feet and wings to safety among rocks or vegetation along the shore. E. O. Willis has proposed that diving and swimming under water, starting from the buzzy flight low over the water, allow this genus to use water courses in closed habitats, such as tropical rivers and mangroves, to a much greater extent than other sandpipers. This author also suggests that their dives to safety provide a good analogy to the aerial glides of flying fish.

Scolopacid waders, much more than plovers, show intraspecific variation in size, with respect to both geography

Resting but wary at high tide, this Western Sandpiper is one of the several million that use the Copper River Delta as their major staging site on the way north to their breeding grounds in Alaska and on the Chukotskiy Peninsula. Unlike many other Calidris species, this sandpiper does not migrate in long, non-stop flights, but instead moves northward in rather short stretches of about 600 km from one stopover site to the next up the American Pacific coast. When sleeping, scolopacids typically stand on one leg, and tuck the head and bill into the feathers on the back; both of these habits are particularly useful in cold weather, as a great deal of heat can be lost through the extremities. Having once adopted this posture, birds appear loath to alter it, and can often be seen hopping about on one leg.

[Calidris mauri, Copper River Delta, Alaska. Photo: Kim Heacox/DRK]

A long decurved bill is a great asset when it comes to catching crabs, mudprawns and mudskippers buried in muddy and sandy substrates. It also comes in handy when feathers of the upperparts require preening, as this female Long-billed Curlew illustrates. At some 17 cm long, this bill is one of the very longest to be found in the family Scolopacidae.

[*Numenius americanus*, Coronado, California, USA. Photo: A. & E. Morris/ Birds As Art]

age may provide better camouflage, as is usually the case for females in other sandpiper species. In Great Knots, the back plumage during breeding resembles that of the closely related Red Knots, but the breast becomes blackish instead of rusty red. In another relative, the Surfbird, the plumage of the back shows a change very similar to that in the two knots, whereas the belly plumage becomes spotted, as in the Great Knot. Similarly, Spotted Sandpipers, Nordmann's Greenshanks and Slender-billed Curlews (*Numenius tenuirostris*) may develop dark spotted breasts in the breeding season. Among the smaller calidrines, only the Dunlin develops a real dark breast and belly patch, and the Rock Sandpiper a blackish brown patch. Most other calidrines show more intense hues on their backs and breasts only, with the exception of the male Pectoral Sandpiper which has a dark blackish brown throat and breast in breeding plumage. These longish dark feathers cover a breast sac, a prominent pendulous organ filled with fat and lymph. The sac is extended during display flights and with it the displaying male produces impressive hooting sounds.

The most bizarre and wonderful breeding plumage shown by any scolopacid wader is formed by the ruffs, tufts and scapulars of male Ruffs. A fully-grown ruff comprises a ring of long colourful feathers around the base of the head and neck and on the upper breast. It can be spread out as a wide, eye-catching collar but can also be carried, not quite invisibly, close to the skin. The head tufts consist of shorter feathers but these too can be erected. Together these specialized feathers, worn for about 2-3 months in late spring and summer, produce a very expressive aspect. Ruff- and tuft-feathers come in a range of hues, from white to red to brown to black, and a variety of patterns, from none, to specks and stripes to flecks. Their hues and patterns are combined in innumerable ways. As if this were not extravagant enough, males have the face bare and covered with yellow, orange or reddish wattles. In stark contrast, the Reeves are dull, brownish-plumaged, standard calidrine sandpipers. The adaptive significance of the impressive plumage variability of male Ruffs is not clear, although there exists one robust correlation with behaviour. Non-fighting males, those that do not defend little areas on an arena, have very pale or white tufts and ruffs. Another case of plumage variation is provided by the Ruddy Turnstone (*Arenaria interpres*), where males in particular have facial patterns which are especially striking during the breeding season. The pattern of the mask of an individual remains the same from year to year. On the basis of a series of ingenious experiments with fibreglass turnstone-decoys resembling territorial neighbours, D. P. Whitfield concluded that in Ruddy Turnstones plumage variation serves the function of individual recognition.

The intense coloration of some of the breeding plumages of scolopacid waders may, however, serve other functions too. Before their northward departure from West Africa to their Siberian breeding areas, Bar-tailed Godwits have more or less completed the moult into a rusty red breeding plumage. During their main stopover period in the Netherlands some of the Bar-tailed Godwits, males as well as females, nevertheless start a second contour feather moult. Moulting individuals are not only the ones with the brightest coloration, but also those that are heaviest at that time of year; during migration, fatter is better! Moulting individuals also carry fewer intestinal parasites and have a better blood profile, for instance with higher counts of red blood cells. Thus, individual Bar-tailed Godwits that can afford to upgrade their plumage during a stopover, in spite of the stress of rapid fuel storage, signal their own quality as healthy, well performing long distance migrants. Bright breeding plumages may therefore represent the products of sexual selection for quality traits. Incidentally, the bristles of Bristle-thighed Curlews (*Numenius tahitiensis*), which are actually barbless feather shafts, serve no known function, not even a sexual one.

The snipes have little to show in terms of sexual or seasonal body plumage variations, but they have something else: special tail feathers. Whereas most other scolopacids have 12 tail feathers, snipes commonly have as many as 16, with numbers ranging from 14 to 26 in different species. The outer tail feathers of snipes are different and of a stronger build than the inner tail feathers. With a narrow outer vane and a broader inner vane they look rather like outermost primaries. Connected to the body with special muscles, these feathers can be pointed outwards. During the plunge-dive of aerial displays, flight speed is high enough to make these feathers vibrate, thus producing the winnowing sounds that snipes are famous for. Any minor disarrangement of these specialized outer tail feathers can alter the sound of the bleat. When L. M. Tuck slightly clipped the tip of one of the outer rectrices, or notched its webbing, he could distinguish the bleating sound produced by that manipulated individual Common Snipe (*Gallinago gallinago*). During the dives the quivering of the wings interrupts the air flow, and this causes the tremulous quality of the bleating sound. In spite of their strong build, the outer tail feathers become so worn that they may be moulted twice each year. In this way the winnowing sound of a displaying snipe may be as much of a quality signal as the belly plumage colour of a Bar-tailed Godwit.

Like virtually all waders, Jack Snipes live in close contact with water. The uropygial gland, situated at the base of the tail feathers, produces oily waxes that are used in order to ensure the waterproofing of the plumage, a most important part of feather care. The oil is distributed over the feathers by means of rapid bill movements. The smallest of the snipes, this species is also the only one that lacks the characteristic central crown stripe, but it does have a well marked double supercilium.

[*Lymnocryptes minimus*, Al Ansab Lagoons, Oman. Photo: Hanne & Jens Eriksen/Aquila]

Great Snipes come together on ground-based leks and do not have the remarkable display flights shown by their congeners, but their tails nonetheless play a striking signalling role as well. The amount of white on the outer tail feathers is greater in males than in females. The white is displayed by males on the lek, where they fan out their tails in an upright posture. According to J. Höglund and co-workers, females prefer males with the whitest tails, including those with experimentally enlarged white areas. A large area of white on the tail feathers may act as a quality signal because white feather keratin is weaker than pigmented keratin and such tails are thus more difficult to maintain intact.

Another story connected with tails and signalling is the remarkable number of white rumps in scolopacid waders. These eye-catching white surfaces may be plain or broken by a dark mid-line or by transverse bars. T. Stawarczyk, who found that the aggression between shorebird species with dissimilar rump patterns was more frequent than between similarly rumped sandpipers, suggested that the colour pattern of the rump of sandpipers is a form of "social mimicry". White rumps would favour the formation and maintenance of multispecies feeding flocks during migration periods and in winter, and reduce the level of aggression between co-occurring individuals.

Hatchling scolopacid waders are characterized by very large legs. Their bills are still relatively small and show little of the eventual curvatures that can be so striking later in life. An exception is provided by hatchlings of the aberrant Spoon-billed Sandpipers. Their bills are dorsally flattened from the day of hatching. Although the bills of hatchlings are more rounded and shorter, at first sight they look like miniature versions of the spoon-like parental bills. The plumage of scolopacid chicks shows a great deal of variation between the taxa. The down of snipes is usually chestnut brown even on the underparts, with black bands on which complex patterns of "powder-puffs" are found. Powder-puffs are small, elongated white downy feathers with the appearance of minute snow flakes that may give excellent camouflage in particular habitats. The down of calidrine sandpipers and dowitchers is longer and looser, especially on the nape. It is whitish below and mainly greenish beige to rich brown above, with black notches and good numbers of powder-puffs. Powder-puffs are absent in woodcocks, turnstones, godwits, curlews, tringines and phalaropes, most of them breeding in more enclosed, marshy, scrubby or woody habitats than species with chicks that do have powder-puffs. Small chicks less than 10 days old have a bare patch on the neck where two thick blood vessels come close to the skin. Small wader chicks can not maintain a constant body temperature on their own and must be heated up regularly after spells of activity in the cold. The naked vascularized area functions as a heat exchanger which is pressed against the parents' naked brood patches during brooding sessions.

Habitat

The Scolopacidae live in an extremely wide range of habitats. They can be encountered in the form of a rare woodcock in the middle of a moist tropical forest, or of a Red or a Red-necked Phalarope far out on the open ocean. A great variety of sandpipers and similar species occur in grassland and scrubland, in taiga and tundra, and on mudflats and salinas. In spite of the variability, it is possible to recognize the common denominator of all these scolopacid habitats: their substrates are watery, wet or moist, and are usually penetrable by elongated sensitive bills. A few species, in particular Rock and Purple Sandpipers and Surfbirds, obey the wetness criterion but select hard substrates, rocky shores that carry good densities of marine invertebrate food items.

Overall, members of the Scolopacidae breed farther north than any other bird family, including the plovers. Most species breed in boreal, subarctic and Arctic regions, and only a few south of the temperate zone. In fact, only 11 of the 86 species breed at tropical latitudes, four of which are woodcock species living on forested islands, six are snipes, and the eleventh is the Tuamotu Sandpiper of the archipelago in the central Pacific of the same name. All the tropical species are residents, and most of them have very restricted ranges. Although travelling the world in the non-breeding season, several migrant calidrines also have fairly restricted breeding ranges. Spoon-billed Sandpipers breed in a small area of the Russian Far East. Western Sandpipers only breed around the Bering Strait, and Sharp-tailed Sandpipers breed on low Arctic tundra in easternmost Siberia. The Curlew Sandpiper occurs as a non-breeder over a very wide range, being commonly observed in much of Europe, Africa, Asia and Australia, yet the core of its breeding areas is limited to the Taymyr Peninsula and the New Siberian Islands, both in north-central Siberia. Scientists have no idea whether the small breeding ranges are a consequence of very precise habitat requirements during reproduction, requirements that are only fulfilled in small segments of the circumpolar tundra range, or whether these distributions reflect historical contingencies and constraints.

Almost all scolopacid waders breed in inland habitats, mostly in freshwater wetland systems. The clear exceptions are three north temperate breeding species of shank, the Common

Redshank, the Willet and Nordmann's Greenshank, all of which may breed on coastal salt-marshes and raise their chicks on the marsh and nearby intertidal flats. Considering that many scolopacid wader species are obligate coastal dwellers for the rest of the year, they not only fly large distances between breeding and wintering areas, but also show quite dramatic shifts in habitat and diet when moving towards and away from the breeding areas. A good example is provided by the Red Knot, a bird occurring worldwide, but only in coastal intertidal areas where it feeds in a probing manner on subsurface mollusc prey. Red Knots breed at the northernmost latitudes, on high Arctic tundra, where the frozen subsoil prevents seepage of the melted frosts to ensure the formation of ponds and pools. In spite of the many wet soils, Red Knots restrict foraging to moist or dry areas with sparse tundra vegetation, feeding on surface-dwelling arthropods and spiders detected by eye. Except just after arrival, during the breeding season Red Knots rarely probe. A complete ecological contrast is provided by the two *Actitis* sandpipers that migrate over quite large distances yet remain faithful to fairly similar, riparian habitats all year round, keeping to enclosed, forested waterways and ponds.

Shanks, several species of snipe and the western race of the Broad-billed Sandpiper, prefer wet wooded areas, especially during the breeding season. Many of them breed in the boreal and subarctic zones, in forested wetlands such as muskeg and taiga. Most calidrine sandpipers breed north of the taiga in the low to middle Arctic tundra zone, the majority thus remaining south of the breeding grounds of Red Knots, Sanderlings and Purple Sandpipers. These low and middle Arctic tundras are more productive than the tundra deserts of the high Arctic, and provide vast pastures of mosses, lichens, sedge grasses, sphagnum and dwarf willow. Snipes, dowitchers, godwits and curlews breed in marshes, and often also occur in man-made habitats such as meadows and cattle pastures at northern temperate latitudes. In all the northern wetlands mentioned, summer weather releases swarms of mosquitoes, flies, craneflies, caddisflies, aquatic midges, spiders and other small invertebrates. The migrating scolopacid waders take excellent reproductive advantage of the pronounced seasonal cycles of these animals.

During the northern winter, in the non-breeding season, many scolopacid waders are restricted to coastal intertidal habitats at tropical and both southern and northern temperate latitudes. Individuals of very few species, such as the Common Snipe, Eurasian Woodcock, Eurasian Curlew (*Numenius arquata*) and Green Sandpiper (*Tringa ochropus*), remain inland in the temperate zone during the northern winter. When the winter is severe, Eurasian Curlews move from the grasslands to the coast, and the others move south with the frost-line, each trying to keep to its own typical habitat type.

Many species, perhaps the majority, migrate south to winter in tropical non-tidal wetlands, including river deltas, floodplains, more permanent lake shores and lagoon areas close to the coast. An example of these important wintering habitats is provided by the floodplains and lagoon systems of West Africa. These areas depend on rainfall which is very seasonal and shows great variability from year to year. Normally, the main rains fall within the period March-July, followed by a short period of rains in September-November. In average years these wetlands are thus filled with water by the time the northern waders arrive in September-October. Since scolopacid waders exploit shallow water margins, the best habitat is available when the water tables drop during the course of the northern winter. Within such tropical lagoon systems, different species use different micro-habitats. In coastal lagoons in Ghana, for example, Little Stints, Ruddy Turnstones, and Common Sandpipers feed on the drying edges of the lagoons and the wet mudbanks. With their small body mass, only Little Stints can feed on algal beds that accumulate in stagnant lagoons or saline ponds. Curlew Sandpipers, Sanderlings and Wood Sandpipers (*Tringa glareola*) feed in the shallow water margins, and Marsh Sandpipers (*Tringa stagnatilis*), Common Greenshanks (*Tringa nebularia*), Spotted Redshanks (*Tringa erythropus*) and Black-tailed Godwits in slightly deeper water. The choice of water depth and substrate is a function of leg length and food availability. Deeper areas of the lagoon and recently flooded areas still devoid of prey items are not used by any scolopacid waders.

In Africa, species like the Ruff and the Black-tailed Godwit rely extensively on man-made habitats such as rice fields, where they feed on spilled rice and chironomid larvae. Seed- and insect-eating Ruffs also occur in dry grassland areas, as long as freshwater ponds are close by. Similar kinds of habitat are, or were, exploited by Buff-breasted Sandpipers and Eskimo Cur-

Away from their breeding areas Hudsonian Godwits are not very vocal, but "at home" in the North American Arctic, their loud and sustained alarm calls are used to confuse or scare away intruders, including humans.
Their calls are among the loudest of all sounds made by waders. In the past, in some areas shorebirds calling noisily to defend their territories sometimes irritated hunters to such an extent that they were rewarded with a barrelful of shot for their pains.

[*Limosa haemastica*, Churchill, Manitoba, Canada.
Photo: Arthur Morris/ Birds As Art]

lews (*Numenius borealis*) on the South American *pampas*, and by a close relative of the latter species, the Little Curlew (*Numenius minutus*), in New Guinea and northern Australia.

Coastal intertidal areas of sand and mudflats are frequented by a different assortment of scolopacid wader species than are the inland lagoon and grassland systems. Although some species, notably the Little Stint, Red-necked Stint, Sharp-tailed Sandpiper and Curlew Sandpiper appear as much at home on intertidal flats as in shallow lagoons, the tringine waders are relatively scarce in coastal areas. In contrast, Dunlins, Red and Great Knots, Bar-tailed Godwits, and a few selected shanks such as the Common Redshank and the Terek Sandpiper, are rarely seen off the coast. Intertidal areas derive their quality from the fact that at low water levels the sea bottom is exposed, and thereby all the marine organisms living there. Tidal flats are exposed on a regular basis, once or twice daily, in coastal regions where the tidal amplitude is larger than a few decimetres. However, along the shallow shores of enclosed seas such as the Baltic and the Black Sea, tidal amplitudes are minimal and flats only become exposed when wind drives the water away. In spite of their unpredictable availability, such wind-flats may harbour large densities of feeding *Calidris* and Broad-billed Sandpipers, especially in productive systems where there are alternative feeding areas depending on wind direction. The wind-flats of the Sivash in the Ukraine and the southern Baltic in Germany and Poland, with high polychaete and crustacean stocks, are intensively used as refuelling sites during northward and southward migration. A similar situation exists in shallow coastal lagoons in southern Brazil where wind exposes extensive flats used by Red Knots and Hudsonian Godwits (*Limosa haemastica*) during northward migration.

Depending on feeding style and prey choice, during low water periods different species prefer flats at different tidal heights and with different substrates. Asian and Short-billed Dowitchers, Broad-billed, Western and Semipalmated Sandpipers usually select muddy areas, whereas Bar-tailed and Hudsonian Godwits and Red Knots go for the more sandy parts of the intertidal flats. Species that hunt for crabs, notably the Whimbrel and the Terek Sandpiper, are traditionally found on the high parts of the intertidal zone since it is usually there that densities of burrowing crabs reach a peak.

Sandy substrates along the seashore, including various types of beaches, are the preferred habitat of Sanderlings. However, Sanderlings may also be found scavenging among the huts in shoreline fishing villages, a man-made habitat that they share with the scolopacid wader with the most catholic taste of all, the Ruddy Turnstone. Ruddy Turnstones may be found foraging in many other coastal habitat types, including beaches, salt-marshes, coastal meadows and rocky shores. Rock and Purple Sandpipers and Surfbirds almost uniquely occur on steep rocky shores. Along the Patagonian shores one finds an exceptional type of rocky habitat called *restinga*: this has the appearance of an intertidal mudflat but consists of flat areas of compacted siltstone. The patches of mussel on the *restinga* are harvested by scolopacid waders otherwise confined to soft intertidal substrates, especially White-rumped Sandpipers and Red Knots.

There exist clear differences in habitat selection between pairs of closely related species, and even between subspecies pairs. As an example of the first, of the two North American dowitcher species, the Short-billed lives in saltwater habitats, whereas the Long-billed inhabits freshwater marshes and avoids marine habitats. Bar-tailed Godwits live almost exclusively in coastal intertidal areas, in Europe as well as in Africa, whereas the Black-tailed Godwit in Africa only occurs inland, in rice fields, floodplains and freshwater lagoons. African-wintering Black-tailed Godwits belong to the subspecies *limosa*, which has a habitat choice that is quite different from that of the race *islandica* which breeds in Iceland; the latter winters on intertidal estuarine mudflats in western Europe. Such intraspecific variability also exists with respect to breeding habitats. Willets in north-western North America, for example, breed in coastal salt-marshes, whereas the population on the prairies occupies the shores of lakes and ponds with a wide range of salinities.

If the very strict habitat requirements shown by some species were known in sufficient detail, if such habitats were identifiable in the fossilized geomorphological record, and if reconstructions of past habitat distribution were carried out on sufficient scales, it would be possible to develop hypotheses of the past distribution of those species. Great efforts have been made to map the past distribution of ice-free tundra in the course of the Pleistocene climate cycles, and these habitat reconstructions have been used by ornithologists to speculate about the

To detect their buried prey, most scolopacids use a touch-sense located in their long bills. Several species have been shown to "feel" prey even at some distance from the bill tip. The Common Snipe is a typical example of such a tactile forager. Its bill tip is full of receptors, the so-called Herbst's Corpuscles, that can measure changes in pressure. These peripheral receptors are connected to specialized enlargements of the frontal brain area.

[Gallinago gallinago delicata, Colorado, USA. Photo: Wendy Shattil & Bob Rozinski/ Oxford Scientific Films]

evolution and past breeding areas of tundra-breeding waders, such as the Red Knot, a seemingly obligate high Arctic tundra breeder, which, according to molecular genetic data, underwent a recent population bottleneck 15,000-10,000 years ago. According to the distribution of high Arctic tundra around this time, Red Knots could have bred either in the North Sea basin or in the Bering Strait area. Additional studies of the past distribution of intertidal wintering habitats may allow an evaluation of hypotheses on past migration routes, the "paleoflyways".

Having talked in general terms about breeding habitats, and in more specific terms about the feeding habitats used during the nonbreeding season, it is important to remember that scolopacid waders need to fulfil more functions than feeding. Most importantly, birds need water for bathing and preening, and a safe or a sheltered place for resting and sleeping. In many non-tidal areas all micro-habitats can be used for all functions, but in dry grassland areas scolopacid waders need freshwater ponds. In intertidal areas birds are forced to come together on hightide roosts. Visually-hunting species may additionally congregate at nighttime roosts, usually in shallow water or in mangroves. Scolopacid waders show a wide variation in their readiness to accept tree perches as high tide roosts. For example, in tropical areas Red Knots will never roost in mangroves or in a baobab tree, but Bartailed Godwits, Whimbrels and Semipalmated Sandpipers accept such sites with no difficulty whatsoever.

General Habits

The maintenance of a balanced energy budget, the avoidance of predators and parasites, and sex, provide the main components of a functional framework in which most of the general habits of scolopacid waders can be explained. Species-specific behavioural characteristics such as the teetering of tails, the buzzy display flights or the zig-zag escape flights, and more generally the choice of feeding and roosting sites, the degree of flocking and territoriality, and the daily rhythms of shorebirds are all evolutionarily trimmed by these factors.

Outside the breeding areas some scolopacid waders such as dowitchers and knots customarily forage in compact groups, almost shoulder to shoulder. Since they feed by tactile means on

buried prey that have very limited means of escape once alarmed by the approaching avian predators, such shorebirds can afford to feed in dense flocks. At the other end of the spectrum are species like the Greater Yellowlegs (*Tringa melanoleuca*), Buff-breasted, Terek and Upland Sandpipers (*Bartramia longicauda*) that rely on eyesight for prey detection so that the presence of nearby conspecifics disturbs the prey and reduces intake rate. These waders scatter widely, or they may defend feeding territories. Several species, such as the Common Redshank, show considerable variation in the degree of flocking. When using visual stimuli to find prey they keep their distance and maintain territories, but when feeding on small buried gastropods, located by tactile means, they come together in flocks. Apart from woodcocks and snipes, flocking characterizes the majority of scolopacid waders during the non-breeding season. Phalaropes "dancing" on an ocean swell, sandpipers feeding on a mudflat, and shanks chasing fish in shallow water, all do it together in flocks.

As an example, in coastal lagoons in West Africa, most wintering scolopacid waders feed and roost in mixed-species flocks. Only Common Sandpipers live singly and mainly on their own, and a small proportion of the Wood Sandpiper population defends small, temporary feeding territories. Sizes of mixed-species flocks vary between two and almost 1000 individuals, with most birds feeding in flocks of 50 or more. Some flocks consist of dense aggregations of waders that all forage frantically, making seemingly orchestrated, synchronized movements together. In this way Common Greenshanks, Spotted Redshanks and Marsh Sandpipers drive shoals of fish to particularly shallow water, tire them out or confuse them, so that the catch is made easier.

Feeding in flocks may thus allow waders to enhance the catchability of fast-moving prey. Flocks may also serve the function of sharing information about good feeding sites. Although feeding flocks will always passively attract individual birds that have yet to find a good feeding location, scolopacid waders that make a living on cryptic and buried prey items "hidden" in "uninformative" habitats, may additionally employ active information sharing. A case in point is, again, the Red Knot, a species foraging in very large flocks in most coastal areas where it occurs. In the estuaries of western Europe, a wintering individual Red Knot experiences an average of several thousand flock-mates

For most scolopacids foraging on mudflats prey availability depends on the burrowing depth of benthic invertebrates, their own bill length and the height of the water covering the mudflat. Of course, the hungry wader must also show plenty of perseverance, as is exemplified by the frantic probing of this Marbled Godwit. The seasonal removal of large proportions of entire cohorts of prey species by migrating shorebirds is likely to leave its imprint on the life history strategies of the prey species. Thus, due to their own predation pressure, scolopacids may have lowered levels of prey availability, since the invertebrates concerned do their best to live out of reach of the waders.

[*Limosa fedoa fedoa,* San Diego, California, USA. Photo: Arthur Morris]

when feeding on buried bivalves and small gastropods. These prey occur patchily over intertidal flats that otherwise have a very uniform appearance, even at close range. To make it even more complicated for the predators, the availability of bivalves often changes. By burying themselves deeper or moving towards the surface of the sediment over a period of days, bivalve stocks can suddenly become unavailable or available. By living in large and wide-ranging flocks with many sensitive bills exploring the sediments, Red Knots are able efficiently to keep track of the best feeding sites.

Flocks also provide a defence mechanism against raptors and other potential predators. Even though some species such as snipes and woodcocks, Common and Spotted Sandpipers, and some tattlers are casual flockers at best, these species and most other scolopacid waders will cluster together in times of peril. A singular exception is provided by Solitary Sandpipers (*Tringa solitaria*). Living up to their name, even a group of Solitary Sandpipers will scatter upon taking flight. Flying together in flocks that make synchronized movements makes sense in most natural situations, since raptors seem daunted by the unity or just the plain bulk of a tight flock in the air. At many coastal sites all over the world, the appearance of a Peregrine Falcon (*Falco peregrinus*) will bring sandpipers together in a dense flock. Such flocks may ascend to heights of several hundred metres, outflying the raptor that is no longer able to make its impressive groundward stoops on the waders.

That thousands of birds flying together at high speeds are able to execute abrupt manoeuvres with precise co-ordination is a miracle in itself. By analysing high-speed film recordings of Dunlin flocks, W. K. Potts was able to demonstrate that a single bird may initiate the manoeuvre that spreads itself through the flock in a wave. The propagation of this wave begins rather slowly, but then increases to speeds that are three times higher than would be possible if the sandpipers were simply reacting to their immediate neighbours. This speed of propagation appears to be achieved in much the same way as in human chorus lines and in organized "waves" at North American sporting events. Individuals take note of the approaching wave and ensure that their own manoeuvre coincides with its arrival.

Feeding in flocks also has an element of information sharing in relation to predation. On the ground many watchful eyes help the detection of approaching raptors and ground predators; flock-feeding provides an early warning system. In Eurasian Curlews feeding on inland grassland, birds in larger flocks look up less often and have a greater food intake per unit foraging time. Studies by N. B. Metcalfe of Ruddy Turnstones and Purple Sandpipers feeding together on a Scottish rocky shore, show that vigilance increases when their view is obscured by boulders, even though they are better camouflaged in such places. Vigilance is reduced when birds can see a conspecific or an individual of a similar-sized species, but it is not shared with much larger species. In spring, before departure to the breeding grounds, adult Ruddy Turnstones have reduced levels of vigilance, but non-migratory juveniles have not. During this period the adults feed hard to store fuel fast, and for this reason appear to accept the increased risk of predation which results from a decrease in vigilance. A similar kind of trade-off between feeding rate and risk of predation is apparent in the choice that Common Redshanks, studied also in Scotland by W. Cresswell, have to make between a high-risk/high-intake area of salt-marsh and a low-risk/low-intake musselbed. The adult birds opt for the relatively unprofitable musselbed and evict juveniles to the dangerous salt-marsh, where over 90% are killed over a winter. Along beaches in California, Sanderlings give up their linear beach territories in winters when Merlins (*Falco columbarius*) are around. During such winters they forage only together, in the relative safety of flocks.

Several studies have proved that being in a flock is indeed safer for an individual wader. For example, feeding in flocks reduces the probability that an individual Common Redshank be killed by Sparrowhawks (*Accipiter nisus*) or Peregrines. Although raptors are more inclined to attack larger than smaller feeding flocks, attacks on small flocks are usually more successful. Larger flocks are safer because there is increased common vigilance, a greater degree of predator confusion and, quite simply, safety in numbers. Depending on the geography of the area, scolopacid waders run the highest risk of raptorial predation either at roosts or on the feeding grounds. On the Banc d'Arguin in Mauritania, where waders disperse widely over extensive tidal flats, three co-occurring species of falcon are most active at high tide, trying to catch the roosting waders by surprise. In habitats with smaller spatial scales, such as small enclosed estuaries, foraging waders can also be taken by sur-

Some types of prey are
not only hard to find, but
are even harder to ingest
in one piece. Active,
crawly polychaetes require
specialized handling
techniques and a
considerable amount of
patience in order to
end up with successful
swallowing. The broad,
flat bill of the aptly named
Broad-billed Sandpiper
could well be an
adaptation designed for
the effective capture and
ingestion of large
polychaete worms.

[Limicola falcinellus sibirica,
Australia.
Photo: Darran Leal/
Auscape]

prise during low water. At such sites hawks and falcons may kill up to 50% of the initial wintering population of scolopacid waders.

The question remains whether wader flocks are anonymous assemblages of individuals that just happen to group together in different ways on different days, or whether individuals in a flock know each other. Along Pacific beaches in California, J. P. Myers could only find random associations among the 700 wintering Sanderlings. He concluded that "Sanderlings have no friends". As a clear contrast, Ruddy Turnstones on a European wintering area have high site fidelity and forage regularly with as few as 50 other individuals in small flocks. In spite of the fact that they regularly come together in large roosting aggregations of several hundred birds, these Ruddy Turnstones show a clear social structure. That not all individual scolopacid waders knowing each other would necessarily regard themselves as "friends", is suggested by the discovery that wintering Ruddy Turnstones maintain rather strict dominance relationships on the feeding areas. Individuals low in rank pay a price by not being able to use the most profitable feeding techniques. The establishment of dominance hierarchies may involve much fighting, and unlike other scolopacid waders, Ruddy Turnstones have been known to kill each other.

Most of the small *Tringa* and the *Actitis* sandpipers routinely make frequent, restless up and down movements with the tail end of the body when they are standing "still". This nodding and bobbing is called teetering or tipping, and is also shown by dippers and wagtails, passerines that likewise often feed along water margins enclosed by high vegetation. The striking parallel of habit and habitat in species so unrelated has led to the suggestion that teetering makes shoreline birds blend into the lapping wavelets of river and pond and the play of light and shadow thus created on the shore. Since small shanks also teeter when the sun does not shine, this hypothesis is not very convincing. Teetering may be analogous to the tail-flicking behaviour of rails (see page 116). It may improve visual acuity, a better perception of distant prey or predators. Interestingly, such marsh-living birds have been noted to increase the rate of tail-flicking as they go further from protective cover, and also when they are orientated away from conspecifics or when predators are present. It has been suggested that by making themselves more conspicuous, teetering birds tell their potential predators that a profitable surprise attack is out of the question. No scolopacid wader species has yet been studied to see whether teetering could safely be interpreted as what is called a "pursuit-deterrent signal".

An alternative to signalling one's presence is for individual birds to stay out of sight. By flattening themselves against the ground, shorebirds are able to decrease or eliminate the shadow that could give them away, an effect which is enhanced when the wings are slightly spread so that the body tapers imperceptibly into the surroundings. Species such as the Pectoral, White-rumped and Least (*Calidris minutilla*) Sandpipers will crouch down on their tarsi behind reed stumps or lumps of mud. A disturbed Wandering Tattler (*Heteroscelus incanus*) has been seen to act much like a crocodile, disappearing completely into shallow water on a tidal mudflat; only its eyes and nostrils remained above the water surface. Snipes and woodcocks are famous for lying still until the final moment when they burst away from a dangerous intruder. Upon disturbance, Green and Solitary Sandpipers and especially snipes will fly up and move away in a zig-zag escape flight. This behaviour is shared with some other species of inland grassy mudflats such as Least and Pectoral Sandpipers, that will also zig-zag away, if flushed when alone.

During sleep, scolopacid waders usually stand on one leg with the head laid on the back pointing tailwards. The bill, where much heat is lost, may be tucked away among the scapular feathers. The frequent observation that roosting birds will hop one-legged for considerable distances when they are lightly disturbed on a roost, suggests that the one-legged stance is quite relaxing. Dunlins observed on particularly food-rich feeding areas in coastal Morocco, habitually hopped around feeding on one leg. Waders may roost during high water periods, spread out throughout the day or just at night. This depends on their feeding method, the pattern of prey availability and predator abundance. The roost-site may be an area of shallow water behind a reedbed, a high beach or sand spit, an open patch of sand or mud among tropical woodlands, or even the branches of mangroves. When not attached to a breeding territory, most of the migratory scolopacid waders have the habit of congregating on communal roosts at regular times. Roosting together may be a consequence of a limited supply of safe roosting sites but may also serve biological functions comparable to those of feeding and flying flocks. High densities of birds shield each other from wind and cold, offer safety in numbers, enable the exchange of information about good feeding areas and, more generally, help the synchronization of daily and seasonal behaviour on the basis of information accumulated and shared by many different individuals.

In intertidal areas the feeding grounds are only available when the tide goes out. Scolopacid waders must use the low water periods to feed, and preen and sleep in the period around high water. Feeding may take place during day and night, but daylight feeding is preferred by most species. In a detailed study of the time budgets of waders on the Banc d'Arguin, Mauritania, in spring, A. M. Blomert and colleagues showed that even tactile feeders may spend less time foraging during night-time low waters than during daytime. They also demonstrated that scolopacid waders increase the fraction of total time spent feeding during the 4-6 weeks before their northward departure to the breeding grounds. This is accomplished by foraging throughout neap tides, when relatively unprofitable feeding areas remain available during high water periods, and by foraging more at night. In non-tidal coastal lagoons in Ghana, nocturnal feeding is common in many scolopacids. It is mostly used by species that detect their prey by touch. Visual surface-foragers feeding on small prey items, such as Wood and Common Sandpipers, spend over 75% of the daytime foraging. Several larger species including the Eurasian Curlew, Black-tailed Godwit and Common Greenshank, forage for less than 40% of the day. These and several other studies have shown that the fraction of time spent foraging is related to body size, with small waders spending far more time foraging than bigger birds. An additional factor is prey size, with species that eat small prey spending much more time feeding than species eating large prey, for example fish.

On the breeding grounds at the northernmost latitudes, the daily rhythms of scolopacid waders are quite different from those in the north and south temperate and tropical wintering areas. When the scolopacid waders are present in the Arctic, daylight is continuous. Upon arrival, exhausted after very long flights, they may sleep for half a day or so, but in the 6-8 weeks thereafter there is little time for rest. Incubating birds may take a nap, but overall, activity levels during the breeding period are extremely high. The details of daily rhythms vary with species and with the phase of the reproductive cycle. At temperate breeding grounds, diurnal rhythms of waders come closest to a "normal" 24 hour periodicity. For example, snipes show most display during twilight periods. Their bleating flights can best be heard during the early morning and the early evening, especially when the weather is clear.

Lumbricid earthworms commonly dominate the diet of the Eurasian Woodcock, since it generally resorts to other food items only when the soil is frozen and can not be penetrated by its long, pointed bill, or when the earthworms have crept out of reach in dry ground. Remarkably, this species is capable of consuming twice its own body weight in earthworms during a 24-hour period. While foraging is typically carried out by means of probing, the bird may also peck at the ground surface or rummage in the dead leaves.

[*Scolopax rusticola*, Bavaria, Germany. Photo: Alfred Limbrunner]

Voice

In contrast to the tail-bleats of snipes, real wader songs sung during display-flights can be very melodious. A good example is the fluting of an Upland Sandpiper as it drifts over a sunny meadow in spring: first one hears some notes resembling the gurgling of water from a large bottle, then the loud "whip-whel-ee-you", long drawn out and weirdly thrilling. Then there is the "poor-me poor-me" of Red Knots ringing over snowfields and tundra, of which many authors have written that it is one of the loveliest of shorebird songs.

But the sounds of scolopacid waders have not always been appreciated by human observers. Black-tailed and Hudsonian Godwits with chicks, for example, have the habit of maddening human intruders to their territories with their loud, sustained alarm calling. Similarly, Lesser Yellowlegs (*Tringa flavipes*) respond to the presence of people with loud calls, chuckles, screams and yodels. Their larger relatives, Greater Yellowlegs, are so noisy that A. C. Bent reported that "many a yellowleg has been shot by an angry gunner as a reward for its exasperating loquacity". In the past, the Black Turnstone (*Arenaria melanocephala*), a noisy sentinel of the Pacific coast of North America, was often silenced for the same offence by hunters of sea otters.

There is a great difference between the vocal repertoire of woodcocks and snipes on the one hand, and that of the most other Scolopacidae on the other. Among the subfamily of snipes, Common Snipes advertise their presence from an elevation in the territory by a rapid "jick-jack" called "yakking". Except for the Great Snipe, all *Gallinago* species also display in the air during courtship, though aerial display is not restricted to the breeding season. Display-flights are accompanied by hooting, bleating, neighing or winnowing sounds that are widely believed to be non-vocal but made by the quivering tail feathers during high-speed aerial descents, but some of the sounds made during snipe display-flights may have a vocal origin. For instance, the courtship flights of Giant Snipes (*Gallinago undulata*) are like those of their smaller congeners but accompanied by trisyllabic sounds that are probably vocal. During their aerial display, Pintail Snipes (*Gallinago stenura*) combine the fizzing sounds of the tail feathers with several different vocal elements. The small Jack Snipe (*Lymnocryptes minimus*) makes distinctive sounds as it precipi-

tously plunges downward from high in the sky. These sounds are reminiscent of the clopping made by galloping horses on hard ground, and since they are given from the ground as well as from the air, they are presumably vocal at least in part. Woodcock species make vocal beeps and purrs as they patrol their woodland territories during tree-top flights. However, during song flight American Woodcocks (*Scolopax minor*) additionally make twitterings that are produced by air passing between the three special attenuated outer primaries. In the sex-role reversed phalaropes, the number of vocalizations is relatively limited compared to most other scolopacid species. Phalaropes have no elaborate flight displays and songs. Among the sandpipers, the lekking Ruff and Buff-breasted Sandpiper must be reckoned the least vocal, even during the mating season. The highly decorated male Ruffs sometimes make indistinct nasal grumbling sounds on leks, in foraging flocks and during arrival at nocturnal roosts. Male Buff-breasted Sandpipers may utter similarly soft purrs as females fly over or leave a display area. Their quietness may help to avoid giving away the lek's position to ground-dwelling predators.

In order to advertise their presence and attract females, the males of the great majority of scolopacid waders perform aerial displays that are accompanied by vocalizations in the form of song. These displays usually have a complement enacted on the ground. Aspects of the ground displays, and the songs that go along with them, are carried out as pre-copulatory behaviour. In general, songs seem to be aimed to emphasize and enhance the visual signals made during aerial and ground displays. Even though the songs and vocalizations of many scolopacid waders remain undescribed to this day, the variation and complexity of known vocalizations is so great and so relatively poorly analysed, that for the present it defies an adequate summary description at the family level. Instead, it may be instructive to examine one fairly typical example of song flight of scolopacid waders in general and of calidrine sandpipers in particular, that of Broad-billed Sandpipers studied in the mosquito-ridden bogs of northern Sweden by B. W. Svensson. Males defend territories and attract mates by aerial display-flights at heights of 15-20 m. These consist of repeated alternations of brief episodes of wing-fluttering, and long descents during which the wings are held increasingly high above the body as the glide becomes steeper,

Members of the tribe Tringini do not usually catch their prey by probing, but instead use more visual techniques and, like plovers, run and snatch prey as soon as it comes into sight. When trying to catch small fish gathered in shoals in shallow water, several tringine waders show social foraging, during which they concentrate the prey into a small area by walking up together in rows. The Lesser Yellowlegs, however, is no communal fisher, each individual tending to chase its fish singly.

[*Tringa flavipes*, Long Island, New York, USA. Photo: Tom Vezo]

followed by rapid ascending flights. The staccato-like song during the glide is introduced by a brief chattering and followed by rhythmically repeated calls during the ascent and the horizontal early phase of the glide.

Aerial vocalizations are taken to an impressive extreme by Pectoral Sandpipers. The sounds and displays are described by J. P. Myers and were published in 1982 by *American Birds* as a unique combination of a sound-disk and a written article. Male Pectoral Sandpipers carry a breast-sac that is inflated during display flights low over the tundra. The sac is pumped up and down in the rhythm of the wingbeat, producing loud hooting, resonant, owl-like reverberations sounding like "oó-ah oó-ah oó-ah". Each syllable is separated by a moment's silence and is repeated 2-3 times per second for 10-15 seconds during a shallow descent towards a female standing on the tundra. After several such "bombing flights" low over the female, the male starts to approach her on the ground, making series of brief muted growls once every 1-2 seconds; these are sustained for several minutes if necessary. He then runs to her side, tail cocked, and if she stays he droops his wings, the breast-sac balloons down and starts to bounce, and with an escalated voice he utters a muted version of the aerial hoot against a background of growls. A copulation may follow shortly afterwards.

The singing of migratory waders may start in the staging areas, several days before take-off on the several thousand kilometre long flight to the breeding grounds. Such pre-departure vocal displays have been noticed in species as varied as the Short-billed Dowitcher, Bar-tailed Godwit, Western and Least Sandpipers, Dunlin and Red Knot. In several instances the vocalizations are accompanied by complete acts of ground or aerial display. Since it is likely that most long distance migrating wader species only pair up after arrival on the breeding territories, the functional significance of such early displays is unclear. It may be an uncontrolled expression of rising sexuality or it may function as a means of synchronizing the migratory behaviour of flocks.

At the start of long distance migration flights, waders assembling in flocks on the ground, or sorting out their initial flight formation in the air, may show intense calling. Some of the vocalizations refer to those made during flight displays, others are more reminiscent of contact calls. Although vocal intensity usually drops after the flight formation, often a V-formation or an echelon of 50-100 individuals, has been established, many species continue to make contact calls during their entire migration. On the basis of such calls, nocturnal migration intensity has been studied at various locations, for example on the island of Helgoland in the German Bight.

There are many other vocalizations that are important to scolopacid waders. Several are used in the subtle signalling that goes on between mates during the final stages of pair formation, before copulation and during nest-relief. There are special calls made during distraction displays, and there is an entire vocabulary of soft contact and loud alarm calls for the communication between parents and their chicks and vice versa. Within the parent-chick repertoire, a particular vocalization is made when the attending parent discovers a predator, nearby or still very far off. This makes chicks freeze on the spot, and this lasts until another call is made which signals that all is clear. When chicks are very young and still thermolabile, parent sandpipers make chuckling calls to collect them under the brood patch for warming-up. Similar soft and short contact calls are made by the foraging adults of many species that habitually feed in flocks, especially calidrine sandpipers. Another category of vocalizations consists of the harsh notes made during intra- and interspecific aggressive interactions. This includes frightening rattles uttered by Ruddy Turnstones during their hot aerial pursuits of intruders of their breeding territories. Similar rattles are made during interactions on the ground, and indeed during the rest of the year as well.

A final category of vocalization is the short calls commonly made by many scolopacid waders in the presence of hunting predators, especially on the non-breeding grounds. Such alarm calls may serve a function as warning signals to neighbouring relatives, as pursuit-deterrent signals that persuade hunting predators to move on, or as calls that incite and co-ordinate flocking. Waders feeding in close-knit flocks have softer alarm calls than species that tend to feed more widely dispersed. A detailed study of Common Redshanks indicated that their loud alarm calls are mainly directed at conspecifics, are used most in visually obstructed habitats, and that they result in the formation of flocks. In a tight flock the calling individual finds safety from hunting raptors, especially since callers are not more likely to be attacked than silent birds. Common Redshanks are less likely to give an alarm on attack by a Peregrine Falcon than by a Sparrowhawk:

This Ruddy Turnstone lives up to its name. With its wedge-like bill it lifts up stones and may also bulldoze away seaweed in its search for hiding invertebrates. This feeding technique requires not only a strong bill, but also strong muscles in the neck. Although specifically adapted to rocky shore life, Ruddy Turnstones are well known for their highly opportunistic foraging habits, which frequently involve scavenging. Given half a chance, they will eat almost anything, including even soap washed up on the beach.

[*Arenaria interpres interpres*, Lake Constance, Vorarlberg, Austria. Photo: R. Kunz]

this makes sense since staying put is the best strategy to avoid the claws of falcons rather than hawks. Territory-holding adult Common Redshanks may incur long-term benefits by calling more than juveniles in the presence of resident Sparrowhawks, since calling birds reduce the profitability for the hawk of the territory area where the hawks' potential prey are repeatedly alarmed. That scolopacid waders subtly tailor both their vocal signals and their responses to the conditions they are in is also suggested by a study on Western Sandpipers that were exposed experimentally to alarm calls. Birds feeding closest to the salt-marsh, whence hunting raptors would be expected to start their surprise attacks, were most likely to fly away upon an alarm, even though they were farthest removed from the loudspeaker.

Food and Feeding

The great morphological radiation within the Scolopacidae reflects the fact that different species use different habitats and food types (see Morphological Aspects). In the course of evolutionary history over the last 40 million years each clade has pursued its favoured sort of excellence. Indeed, the very strict habitat requirements shown by some scolopacid wader species today are correlated with different sensory specializations that allow profitable and efficient exploitation of particular kinds of food. As a consequence the Scolopacidae, and the trophic resources on which they rely, have diversified to such an extent that it is difficult to see that an American Woodcock probing the turf of a thicket for lumbricid worms, Sanderlings on a beach in search of crustaceans exposed by the retreating surf and Red-necked Phalaropes darting and fluttering undaunted at the crests of breaking ocean waves, share a common ancestor, not even so very long ago.

Turnstones, with the stout tapering bills and strong neck musculature that make them expert overturners of stones and seaweed, sometimes seem to have turned into specialists of opportunistic foraging. Ruddy Turnstones will eat almost anything, and the list of things they have been observed to prey upon varies from soap, via gull excrements to human carcasses. So great is the variety that R. E. Gill wondered "what won't turnstones eat?" His feeding trials demonstrate that they indeed go for al-

most any edible item, but when a variety of foods is put on offer they have a preference for fresh fish and crustaceans. Ruddy Turnstones are also reputable egg predators, especially in colonies of Common (*Sterna hirundo*) and Arctic Terns (*Sterna paradisaea*) and Mew Gulls (*Larus canus*). In such sites they can additionally make off with food brought to the surviving larid hatchlings. The fact that turnstones have raided nests of Red Phalaropes suggests that even dispersed wader nests are not completely safe from them. In seabird colonies on small Pacific islands, Bristle-thighed Curlews may sneak eggs from beneath albatrosses as the latter briefly stand up to shuffle their feathers and resettle.

A Red Phalarope has once been seen to eat carrion in New York City, a form of behaviour that mirrors picking skin-lice and other crustaceans off surfaced whales, but phalaropes routinely obtain their food by a subtle scooping of small zooplanktonic animals from the upper layer of water. With swift pecks prey are captured within a water droplet, which is transported mouthwards by surface tension (see Morphological Aspects). During feeding, phalaropes often spin around rapidly, probably to bring deep prey closer to the water surface. During the breeding season, they feed on a great variety of arthropods, notably chironomid midges and spiders, which are collected from shallow water, or sometimes picked from relatively dry marsh or tundra. Non-breeding phalaropes congregate in productive water basins. These may be saline lakes with enormous blooms of brine-shrimps, areas of oceanic upwelling where high stocks of zooplankton are found, and areas of sea with surface swarms of euphausiid shrimps. Indeed, any oceanographic phenomenon that will concentrate zooplankton at the ocean surface will attract them. For example, Red and Red-necked Phalaropes like ocean slicks, lines of debris, algae and other floating objects accumulated on the zone of convergence between surface currents.

The phalaropes' way of transporting tiny prey items towards the mouth by moving water droplets may also be used by several small sandpiper species, for instance Western and Semipalmated Sandpipers. Outside the breeding season these birds feed on mudflats with soft upper layers of sediment. They feed by stitching, making rapid sewing movements with the bill, and do not take the bill out of the substrate to ingest individual prey items. Although the diet of most small sandpipers has hitherto eluded

Ingestion of hard-shelled prey items requires a strong muscular gizzard to crush the shells; the shell remains may then either be regurgitated as pellets or flushed through the intestine and voided as calcium-rich droppings. Some species are specialized mollusc-eaters, and go for shellfish as a rule. Others will take shellfish on occasion but are also well adapted to eating polychaetes and crustaceans. The Marbled Godwit, for example, has a varied diet combining bivalves with crustaceans, insects, annelids and leeches.

[Limosa fedoa, California, USA. Photo: Tom Vezo]

detailed description, the fact that amphipods, oligochaetes and small polychaete worms usually occur in high densities where small sandpipers concentrate their feeding suggests that these meiobenthic prey provide the bulk.

Small tringines, such as the Common, Spotted, Wood, Green and Solitary Sandpipers, are called sandpipers although they belong to the Tringinae. They are built as shanks, but their diet converges to a fair degree with that of small sandpipers. Small tringines eat a great taxonomic variety of small prey that are captured at the surface of water, wet sediments or shallow vegetation. Quite similar feeding habits are shown, but somewhat larger prey are taken, by Common Redshanks, Willets and probably Tuamotu Sandpipers. The large tringines such as the yellowlegs, Marsh Sandpiper, Common Greenshank and Spotted Redshank, and perhaps the rare Asian Nordmann's Greenshank too, provide the other extreme. They may feed on small invertebrates picked from surfaces, but during migration and on the wintering grounds they are also prone to operate in large flocks that make fairly synchronized movements to drive together, and feed on, pelagic schools of small fish in shallow water.

One tringine species is truly aberrant. This is the Terek Sandpiper that during migration and on the wintering grounds specializes in catching and eating small burrowing crabs. Since these crabs tend to be burrowed, for good reasons, at greater depths than where the slightly upcurved bill of Terek Sandpipers can reach, the crabs, when showing on the surface in order to feed or to court, can only be captured by surprise after short sprints on the part of the bird. In many coastal non-breeding areas, different species of curlew, notably the Whimbrel and Far Eastern Curlew, also concentrate their feeding on burrowing crabs. The profitable size of sentinel crabs fed upon by Far Eastern Curlews is much larger than the size of sand-bubbling crabs eaten by Terek Sandpipers, so much so, in fact, that in coastal areas of Southeast Asia and Australia where the three species occur together, Far Eastern Curlews do not even take notice of the small crabs favoured by Tereks, even though their relatively shallow burrows make them readily accessible to the curlews. A small curlew species like the Little Curlew lives mainly on arthropods other than crabs. Little Curlews, and Eskimo Curlews in the past, feed on the surface-living insect life of pastures, steppes and

grasslands in their wintering areas in Australasia and South America respectively. Another curlew, the gravely threatened Slender-billed Curlew, may depend on the arthropods of temperate and Mediterranean steppe-like grasslands, but it can also feed on estuarine fauna.

Eurasian Curlews wintering on temperate and subtropical coastal wetlands in western Europe and West Africa, where crabs are not so abundant as in some tropical areas, feed on small bivalves and large polychaetes, in addition to the occasional shorecrab. Such a mixed diet is also typical of all the coastal wintering populations of godwits, whether the Marbled Godwits (*Limosa fedoa*) along the Pacific shorelines of California, the Hudsonian Godwits along the southern Atlantic shores in Patagonia, the Bar-tailed Godwits at the opposite side of the Atlantic in tropical West Africa, and in north-west Australia, or the Black-tailed Godwits in western Europe. Molluscs, especially bivalves and to a lesser extent the harder-shelled gastropods, dominate the diets of the clade of knots, including Surfbirds, Great Knots and Red Knots, and a few species of northerly wintering sandpiper, Rock Sandpipers in the Pacific Northwest and Purple Sandpipers in the Atlantic region. The two sandpipers and the Surfbirds have a preference for rocky shores, on which the small sandpipers also find much crustacean food between the mussel and algal beds. Red and Great Knots show a preference for bivalves buried in soft sediments.

The beach-combing Sanderlings make a living on small sandcrabs and similar crustaceans that live buried in sand in the wave-washed zone. These sandcrabs feed on small particles of organic material carried in the receding waves by sticking their antennae into the waves. Once the wave has washed back, the crabs withdraw their antennae and retreat beneath the surface. At the tail end of retreating waves just before the crabs retract, but when the water is shallow enough for access, they are most easily captured. This explains the Sanderlings' incessant running up and down in front of the waves. Sanderlings also take other invertebrates from sandy beaches, including isopods, amphipods, polychaete worms, and small bivalve molluscs. They also respond opportunistically to rich food resources such as fish drying in coastal villages. Another example is provided by the large quantities of eggs that horseshoe crabs (*Limulus polyphemus*) deposit on the shores of Delaware Bay in May. This occurs just as Sanderlings, Red Knots and Ruddy Turnstones are on their way north to the breeding grounds, and all three come together in great numbers to feed on this superabundant but temporary food resource, and store nutrients for further flight.

To detect small polychaetes and crustaceans buried in the sand, Sanderlings and related *Calidris* sandpipers possess a form of "remote sense". With the array of sensory receptors in the bill tips, Sanderlings have been shown to detect the vibrations of small polychaetes moving in the sand at distances of 2 cm from the bill tip. Red and Great Knots forage on soft intertidal sediments, and the hard-shelled molluscs that they are after do not usually move. Even so, Red Knots, with equally sophisticated sensory equipment in their bill tips, seem to have some sort of remote sense as well. Perhaps they detect the hard-shelled objects in soft sediments from the direction in which counter-pressure builds up as they push their bills in the substrate.

In coastal habitats, non-breeding Asian and Short-billed Dowitchers and Broad-billed Sandpipers constitute the typical polychaete-eaters; members of the ragworm family (Nereidae) are especially favoured. A different group of annelid worms fed upon by scolopacid waders are the lumbricids that provide much of the diet of woodcocks and snipes. Lumbricid worms are supplemented by insect larvae and adults, particularly beetles, which are captured by the birds' long rhynchokinetic bills on or in soft soils. American and Eurasian Woodcocks, and probably the other woodcock species too, habitually try to lure worms upward by trampling the ground with their feet, thus creating shallow funnel-shaped depressions. In difficult environmental conditions, for example when soils are frozen or covered with snow, woodcocks and snipes may rely to some degree on plant material such as seeds, buds and shoots.

Few scolopacid waders subsist on a purely vegetarian diet, but in southern Europe and tropical West Africa Ruffs and Black-tailed Godwits periodically eat only rice, mostly the grains spilled during the harvest; Ruffs may also take corn grains and ground nuts. On small dykes bordering rice fields in Guinea-Bissau, individual Black-tailed Godwits defend temporary feeding territories against conspecifics at heaps of harvested rice grains. In view of these rice-eating habits, in some Sahel countries Ruffs and Black-tailed Godwits are customarily considered pest species. Hudsonian Godwits are known to feed on aquatic vegetation in ponds along the coastlines of Hudson Bay and James Bay, and in the prairie provinces of Canada.

During late spring and early summer, when long distance migrating sandpipers arrive on their high Arctic tundra breeding grounds, where snow is just beginning to clear away and the summer cycle is just getting under way, the birds find themselves faced with rather lean feeding conditions. At this time many species that otherwise eat only animal food, may temporarily supplement their diet with seeds and shoots. It should be noted, however, that the stomach content analyses on which many diet studies of breeding waders are based must be biased in favour of plant food, simply because plant material is more difficult to digest and thus more likely to be encountered in stomachs; the most nutritious foods, the ones that are easiest to digest, do not show up. Nevertheless, even stubborn mollusc-eaters like Red Knots that turn to spiders and insects on the tundra, have been observed to pick and eat seeds and fresh horsetail shoots. Juvenile Red Knots were observed stripping seeds from grass stems using sideways sweeps of the bill during a short period in late summer on Ellesmere Island, Canada. Another example is provided by the rather similar Great Knot. In the summers of 1994 and 1995, P. S. Tomkovich discovered in north-eastern Siberia that adults, as well as large chicks, feed extensively on heather berries. Great Knots also eat the hard-shelled nuts of dwarf pine (*Pinus pumila*), which the birds find in the soil where they have been buried by Spotted Nutcrackers (*Nucifraga caryocatactes*); the nuts are crushed in the muscular stomachs of the Great Knots. Berries have also been the staple food of Eskimo Curlews during breeding, and especially during refuelling stops in Labrador, before their long flights south over the western Atlantic Ocean to South America. Similarly, southward migrating Whimbrels on Kamchatka and Sakhalin are called "berriers" by local hunters in view of their appetite for heather berries.

On the breeding grounds, the diet of adults of different species shows extensive overlap, which hints at relaxed competition in an environment that offers abundant resources during this time of year. Adults and their chicks both live on the spiders and insects that emerge over the summer, and their diet is fairly similar too. In most scolopacids, chicks gather their own food, and are merely brooded and guarded by one or both of their parents. The exception is provided by woodcocks and snipes, where parents bring lumbricid worms to their chicks. But even in these cases, the precocial young catch most of the food themselves, mainly in the form of small insects and worms. Before their first southward migration, scolopacid chicks are left on their own. How the ontogenetic development of food and habitat choice is steered by trial-and-error learning in combination with endogenously programmed instructions is a subject area that has not yet been studied in any wader species.

Whatever the developmental or ecological reasons behind it, there are sometimes clear-cut and repeatable differences between categories of a particular scolopacid species with regard to feeding techniques and diet. As an example, in Bar-tailed Godwits where the females are significantly larger than the males, females follow the waterline where they have highest success in catching polychaete worms. Males only forage on the exposed intertidal flats. This sexual segregation of feeding habitat has been observed in European estuaries and also in West Africa. The Ruddy Turnstone is the only scolopacid in which individuals have been observed to specialize in the use of particular feeding techniques. On a rocky shore in south-east Scotland wintering Ruddy Turnstones employ six different feeding techniques: flicking and bulldozing seaweed aside; probing; stone-turning; hammer-probing; digging; and surface-pecking. Females are more liable than males to turn over stones. Strikingly, high status birds resort more to the most profitable technique, flicking and bulldozing, than do birds with a low dominance status. Experimental temporary removal of dominant individuals suggests that the relative "weaklings" are in fact actively prevented by the "bullies" from using the best feeding techniques.

Successfully foraging scolopacid waders are predicted to select prey items that are profitable. Profitability is defined as the nutritional or energy equivalent divided by the time required for handling a prey item; "handling" refers to the time between prey detection and ingestion. If a discovered prey item has a profitability that is below the current intake rate, a bird would lower its long-term intake rate by accepting it. If waders are not threatened by starvation, they do best by eating only food items with profitabilities above the average, long-term intake rate. Depending on the size of the shorebird and its feeding style, profitability will vary with the taxon, size, body condition, quality and behaviour of the prey. In a comparative study of four scolopacid waders feeding on mudshrimps (*Corophium volutator*), Least and Semipalmated Sandpipers were predicted to select shrimps longer than 2·5 mm, Common Redshanks to select shrimps longer than 4·5 mm, and Bar-tailed Godwits to eat shrimps with a body length over 7 mm. As a matter of fact, all four predator species obliged. Obeying the profitability principle, the two small sandpipers ate the smallest mudshrimps and the godwits the largest. When different waders eat different size and age classes of the same prey species, the waders may indirectly compete for food. In European estuaries Red Knots may deplete small, up to one year old, bivalves to an extent that subsequently, when the remaining bivalves are older and larger and profitable for Eurasian Curlews and Eurasian Oystercatchers (*Haematopus ostralegus*), their densities are below the threshold where they can be economically harvested by the large waders.

Another issue is the relative digestibility of the prey. Invertebrates such as crabs and molluscs carry a good deal of indigestible calcareous matter and are unprofitable for this reason. Some tropical crabs escape wader predation by becoming so salty and unpalatable that they can walk in hordes on exposed sandflats without being captured and eaten by the Whimbrels and Terek Sandpipers roaming around in like fashion. Then there are other criteria which are not so easily measured as nutritional value. Prey carrying parasites that use scolopacids as intermediate hosts,

The Scolopacidae show a great and exciting variety of mating systems, including males mate with several females (polygyny), females laying eggs for several males (polyandry), and also social monogamy. A few species use a lekking system in which males display on an arena with the aim of being chosen by passing females. Once such lekking species is the Buff-breasted Sandpiper, which breeds from the Chukotskiy Peninsula east into northern Canada. In this species, the males do not fight among one another in order to gain ascendancy, but limit themselves to showing off their strikingly outlined white underwings to the females present on the lek-site.

[*Tryngites subruficollis*, Alaska, USA. Photo: Kevin T. Karlson]

are best avoided, even though the parasites may try hard to turn infected prey into effective extensions of their phenotype, by making them nicely available and highly profitable. Although this topic has hitherto scarcely been addressed by wader ecologists (see page 314), the fact that two genera of tapeworm are found only in shorebirds suggests the biological relevance of the interactions between waders and their parasites.

In stark contrast, scolopacid waders have featured prominently in classic studies on feeding dispersion and territoriality in relation to prey availability, competitor densities and other constraints, especially those by L. Zwarts, J. D. Goss-Custard, J. P. Myers and their respective research teams. For example, the problem of feeding territories of wintering Eurasian Curlews and Sanderlings was tackled in populations in which many individuals were colour-ringed. The system of linear beach territories maintained by Californian Sanderlings in winter proved particularly accessible for study. At very low food densities there are not enough buried crustaceans to make defence worthwhile. However, at high densities there are so many Sanderlings trying to feed, that defence would not be feasible because of high intruder densities. Along parts of the beach where food conditions are intermediate Sanderlings do maintain territories of which the size varies inversely with prey density: the higher the intrusion rate the smaller the length of beach that can be kept free of competitors. This suggests that feeding territories are not aimed to prevent absolute prey depletion by conspecifics, but rather to enhance temporarily food availability and feeding rate by reducing the disturbance of prey. A clear example of short-term benefits of feeding territories is provided by Dunlins that take up the defence of human foot prints against nearby flock members as soon as prints are made in soft mud. In such depressions polychaete worms have lost cover and can very easily be captured. Some Eurasian Curlews feeding on intertidal flats, especially long-billed females, may defend territories over the entire winter season and return to these sites from year to year. Such territories may serve the dual function of preventing long-term depletion and reducing interference. Interference effects may work through the short-term depression of prey availability as a consequence of the presence of many predators, or through direct aggressive and indirect evasive behaviour of co-occurring foragers.

The most important variable determining the abundance and dispersion of feeding waders is the availability of prey. As we have seen, availability is related to prey size, composition and behaviour, but availability can also be a direct or indirect function of substrate characteristics. For example, Dunlins find it easier to locate buried polychaetes and crustaceans in sediments that are soft and that are covered by a film of water. Most probing waders have difficulty in foraging in sediments that are either unsorted, with lots of small stones or shell fragments, or in sediments that are stuffed with the sandgrain tubes of tube-living polychaetes. Indirectly, sediment characteristics affect the amount of detrital organic material and thus the growth of the invertebrate food organisms, as well as affecting the depth of living of burrowing creatures in other ways. For example, the North Atlantic intertidal bivalve *Macoma balthica* lives deeper in sandy than in muddy sediments, and is therefore easiest to obtain on the muddy foreshore. In addition, there will be seasonal variation in prey availability owing to depth differences and growth. In a remarkable megastudy sustained over a full seven years, L. Zwarts and his team measured the availability parameters of a whole intertidal macrobenthic community on a site in the Wadden Sea, in the Netherlands, and managed to combine this with studies of the presence and the diet of waders. Apart from a wealth of insight about predator-prey relationships on tidal flats, they come to the conclusion that despite the abundance of waders on intertidal flats, such areas provide them with a poor and unpredictable dinner table, especially in winter.

Perhaps, a poorly laid table is exactly what one would expect if scolopacid waders and their prey have been evolutionarily exposed to each other for long periods of time. In all predator-prey relationships, for the prey their lives are at stake, but for the predators only their meals. Thus, prey species exposed to particular predation pressures should have evolved the traits to mini-

mize the risk of dying because of those pressures. If scolopacid waders are a regular and important component of the communities in which they live, rather than a transient phenomenon that takes what is given at any one time, the continuing evolutionary arms race will ensure relative scarcity. Predatory roles can sometimes be dramatically reversed when bivalves damage or kill bivalve eaters, by closing their valves around part of a foot or around a bill. Mussels and cockles can hold their valves clasped tight for long periods, and are frequently reported to have wrecked Dunlins and Red Knots.

Another layer of complication can be added by the realization that food scarcity is not only related to food availability, but also to the predators' nutritional and energetic demands. A small sandpiper requires 3-4 times as much food at temperatures below 5°C than above 20°C. In the tropics the energy demands of scolopacid waders are thus much lower than in temperate climates, especially in winter. In sheltered habitats where there is no wind, energy requirements are reduced relative to exposed shorelines and mudflats, particularly when it is cold. Finally, during fuel storage before long distance flights the required intake also goes up by a factor of two to four. Higher energy demands imply that the lower thresholds of available prey densities that can be accepted go up too: in cold weather and during migration waders should become more choosy.

The size of organs in scolopacids is rather flexible (see Morphological Aspects), a characteristic that comes into play in the course of their annual cycles. When lower demands no longer necessitate large machinery to keep the food processed and the body going, the birds reduce the size of parts of that machinery, the organs. Smaller metabolic machinery has the added benefit of being cheaper to maintain, thereby further reducing the food requirement and the choosiness with regard to suitable habitat. The energy that is necessary to maintain a body can be measured as the basal metabolic rate. This is the rate of oxygen consumption of thoroughly resting waders at congenial air temperatures. Scolopacid waders have relatively low basal metabolic rates during their stay in the tropics, but the same species have high levels when wintering at temperate latitudes. Similarly, woodcocks living in sheltered forests have a lower basal metabolic rate than equal-sized waders living exposed on intertidal flats at the same latitude.

In most conditions, a diet of animal matter suffices. However, during the pre-breeding period, the normal diet of scolopacids may not yield enough calcium for egg-formation. S. F. MacLean found many lemming teeth and bones in the stomachs of pre-laying females and growing chicks of four tundra-breeding sandpiper species in northern Alaska, and no such skeletal remains in males, fully-grown chicks or non-laying females. As an alternative to eating calcium-rich bone fragments to enhance their laying performance, female sandpipers might also store labile calcium in their own skeletons before egg-laying. Evidence for this has recently been obtained for Red Knots.

Breeding

The observations by E. Selous on the breeding displays of Ruffs published in 1906 and 1907 report the first modern ethological studies of reproductive behaviour in birds. His observations on breeding scolopacid waders were soon followed up by two of the founding fathers of modern evolutionary biology and ethology. J. S. Huxley studied the display behaviour of Common Redshanks and Black-tailed Godwits, while N. Tinbergen published a long paper on breeding Red-necked Phalaropes in Greenland. In recent decades, scolopacid waders have been widely recognized as an interesting group showing an especially wide variation in reproductive strategies. This has led to detailed comparative studies of causal and functional aspects of the various and variable breeding patterns.

Many of the Scolopacidae have a reproductive strategy that most of us take for granted as being the basic, "normal" strategy: they form monogamous pairs. Monogamy is the rule for Jack Snipes, Common Snipes, Common Redshanks, Black-tailed Godwits, Long-billed and Eurasian Curlews and many other spe-

Woodcocks provide an exception to the rule that scolopacid waders live in open habitats. This roding Eurasian Woodcock patrols its territory in deciduous woodland with plenty of undergrowth and moist soils. The woodcocks show specific adaptations for life in a woodland setting: the eyes are located high in the skull and allow the bird a complete view of the sky, facilitating detection of approaching predators; the elliptically shaped wings provide the means for a "rocketing" take-off amidst a dense tangle of twigs and small branches, in case a predator should approach too close for comfort; and the basal metabolic rate is relatively low, constituting an energy-saving adjustment to a sheltered life in the woods.

[Scolopax rusticola. Photo: A. Christiansen/ FLPA]

cies. However, this common arrangement belies the great flexibility of the reproductive systems of scolopacid waders, even within species where most individuals do establish monogamous pair-bonds. For example, female Sanderlings can produce one, two or three clutches per summer season. In this species monogamy prevails, but females may also mate sequentially with different males, the first clutch being sired by one male, the second by another and so forth. Having laid two clutches, the female often departs from the breeding site shortly after the males have started incubation, and males are thus fully responsible for all parental care. Alternatively, females may lay twice and assume full care of the second clutch themselves. When a single individual of one sex reproductively claims more than one individual of the other sex, the system is called polygamous. Systems in which females pair up with more than one male, as in the Sanderling example, called called polyandrous. When males pair with more than one female, the system is called polygynous. At the extreme end are polygynous systems in which the only thing that one of the sexes contributes is sperm. This happens in promiscuous lek-breeding waders where males compete with one another for access to fertile females, but otherwise do not contribute reproductively.

In phalaropes male parental care is the rule, and it is the colourful females that defend the territory and display. Females will try to produce clutches for more than one male, and so they court,

harry and pursue the males. They do so to the extent that male Wilson's Phalaropes have developed a special wing-fluttering display that signals to females that they are unavailable as mates. Such a polyandrous system with an exchange of "normal" sex roles is shared with Spotted Sandpipers and perhaps a few other scolopacid wader species, such as Upland Sandpipers and Spotted Redshanks. J. R. Jehl recently uncovered an explanation for the polyandry of Wilson's Phalaropes. It was published in 1923 in a respectable scientific magazine and tells an interesting tale about the reproductive attitudes of human society in some places around that time. The large numbers of female phalaropes seen in summer on the Great Salt Lake in Utah were considered to represent non-breeders, rather than the post-breeding birds in moult that they are now known to be. The atrophied, non-functional ovaries found in dissected females were taken as proof of a venereal disease that was thought to have its origin in the "strange excess of libido which has brought the females of the species to their musky perfection of size and power". With so few healthy females around on the breeding areas, the poor phalarope males were thus forced to accept at least one rival male partner if they were to breed at all.

The bewildering diversity of parental care and reproductive social systems within and among the species of Scolopacidae can be explained with respect to intricate webs of interactions between ecological conditions, fitness advantages and sexual

Ruffs are easily the most variable of waders and they are also perhaps the weirdest. Males are some 25% larger than females, which are known as Reeves. The reproductive process is all rather complicated and extremely spectacular, involving groups of males competing for potential matings on leks. With their colourful and endlessly variable ruffs, head-tufts and wattles for display, and with their wings and strong legs as armour and weapons, individual males defend small parts of a lek. Males come in two behavioural categories: the "residents" or "independent males" that defend an area on the lek; and the "satellites" that do not defend their own court but which are tolerated in the arena and can then "steal" matings. Satellite males are somewhat smaller than residents and usually show white or light-coloured ruffs and tufts. The group of extravagantly displaying males has often been said to bring to mind a medieval court full of strutting dandies.

[Philomachus pugnax, Workumer Waard, Netherlands. Photos: Günter Ziesler/ Bruce Coleman]

selection. For example, in conditions of much food, low costs of living and few predators, a single parent will be able to raise a brood, so that females can afford to leave their mates after clutch delivery, start another clutch with a second male, or breed on their own. In populations where some females are polyandrous, there will be competition between females for males, and this may open the way for the evolution of competitive traits such as intense coloration and increased size, as in female phalaropes.

Relatively congenial ecological conditions would also allow for male emancipation from breeding activities, as occurs in lekking species like Ruffs and non-lekkers like Curlew Sandpipers and White-rumped Sandpipers.

Over the last 20 years, an ecological framework for the evolution of social organization in calidrine sandpipers, all of which breed in the Arctic, has been developed by F. A. Pitelka, P. S. Tomkovich and their respective associates. A distinction is made

The rival males adopt a series of stereotyped postures, such as the "Upright-posture", the "Forward-posture" and the "Tiptoe-posture", which have certain slight variants, and may be combined with actions such as "Bill-thrusting", "Tail-trembling", "Wing-lifting" and a "Strut-walk" display. Upon the arrival of females, or other males, the males will perform "Wing-fluttering", in which the wings are opened, raised and lifted backwards, as can be seen in some of these birds. Higher intensity forms of this greeting ceremony are "Flutter-jumps" in which the bird spreads its wings more fully and jumps into the air, and a "Hovering-display" whereby the bird may rise a few metres into the air, although at the cost of its white underwing being less visible; both of these variants are also visible here. Except on very small arenas, actual fighting is generally rare; it involves birds jumping at each other, often striking out with the claws towards the opponent's bare facial skin, and sometimes drawing blood. The females visit the leks for the purpose of mating. Once they have received the sperm, they take on the entire responsibility of caring for the eggs and chicks without help from any male. The intriguing behaviour of male Ruffs at the lek has invited much detailed research, and has now been shown to have some genetic basis.

[Philomachus pugnax, Workumer Waard, Netherlands. Photos: Günter Ziesler]

between "conservative species" that show monogamy, high site fidelity in males, the defence of overdispersed breeding territories, and minor population fluctuations from year to year, and "opportunistic species" that show polygamy and promiscuity, low site fidelity, a pattern of clumped dispersion, and large year-to-year fluctuations in abundance. The latter species concentrate in areas where environmental conditions happen to be favourable in a particular year. In this view, reproductive strategies of sand-

pipers primarily reflect variations in amount and dependability of food resources in the Arctic modified by intensity of nest predation.

The fact is that those sandpiper species in which one of the partners departs early from the breeding grounds, and also those that deviate from monogamy, migrate farther than biparental monogamous species, which suggests that the relative investments made by males and females do not depend merely on eco-

Not all shorebirds copulate in silence. Female Willets have been heard making rather soft grunted exclamations during copulation, and the male emits a sort of jaunty clicking, said to be reminiscent of a man snapping his fingers. The intimacy of the occasion can sometimes end abruptly, when the female throws off the male, forward over her shoulders, whereafter the irritated male may attempt to continue in a rougher manner.

[*Catoptrophorus semipalmatus inornatus*, Inyo County, California, USA. Photo: John Gerlach/DRK]

logical circumstances in the breeding areas. Sex role division may also depend on factors like the distance to and from the wintering areas, which may differ between the sexes, and the extent to which mates are engaged in sexual selection games. Long distance migration, as well as the development of extravagant secondary sexual characters and display, divert nutrients away from reproduction proper, and thus set additional constraints on the way parental roles must be shared or can be divided. In addition, evolutionary explanations for any specific reproductive system have to take historical constraints into consideration. For example, J. G. van Rhijn has argued that the ancestral state of birds is pure male parental care. This system can evolve into biparental care with identical roles for the two sexes, via uniparental care where females take over if males desert, or via double-clutching. The latter system, nowadays seen in Temminck's and Little Stints and Sanderlings, is perhaps the original pattern in scolopacid waders. Lek systems where females perform all the parental care may have evolved from double-clutching systems where there is intense competition between males.

Of the three ground-lekking scolopacid wader species, the Great Snipe, the Buff-breasted Sandpiper and the Ruff, the last species is the most extreme and has been studied in greatest detail. Male Ruffs not only come in innumerable different plumage colours, but also in two distinct behavioural types. "Independent" males defend lek mating courts against other independents, whereas "satellites" are non-territorial males that move between, are recruited to, and share the courts of independent males. Satellites are slightly smaller in size and have pale coloured or white tufts and ruffs, whereas independents are more pigmented. By carrying out cross-breeding experiments between the two forms in captivity, D. B. Lank, C. M. Smith and colleagues showed that environmental factors can not alter a chick's development into a satellite or an independent male. Instead, the two plumage-linked reproductive behavioural strategies of Ruffs have a simple genetic basis. That independent males clearly display their sex, whereas satellites seem to mimic female behaviour, has led to the suggestion that the alternative strategies may have derived from a double-clutching system where females select males with good care qualities (later becoming the satellites) for the first clutch, and males with other good genetic properties (independ-

ent males) for the second clutch. In contrast to Ruffs, Buff-breasted Sandpipers are monomorphic and males do not engage in the courtship battles so typical for Ruffs. When females arrive near a lek, all resident males start flashing their white underwings against the tundra's brown background. The rest of the courtship of Buff-breasted Sandpipers involves much fluttering and the stretching and turning of open wings.

The fact that many sandpipers arrive unpaired on the breeding grounds and begin nesting within a few days after arrival may indicate that there is selection for rapid pair formation, possibly in view of the short northern breeding season. Apart from the three ground-lekking species, in the many scolopacid waders that breed in open habitats where there is a definite lack of elevated perches, the competing sex tries to attract the choosing mate to the territory through persistent flight singing, which is followed by ground displays associated with nest-site selection. Temminck's Stints and several other species often use perches, provided by dwarf willow and alder, for singing, whereas Dunlins use mossy hummocks. In addition to attracting females, aerial courtship flights and perch-singing also help to establish the boundaries of territories. Aerial courtship varies from the rather discrete butterfly flights low over the female's head in Baird's Sandpiper to the wild pursuit flights of Curlew Sandpipers; during the only two weeks of the year that males of the latter show up on the breeding grounds, they relentlessly, even in small groups, pursue single females until copulation. Display flights are lacking in turnstones.

It is difficult to think of a greater contrast with these systems than that provided by the Subantarctic (*Coenocorypha aucklandica*) and Chatham Snipes (*Coenocorypha pusilla*), species that live on oceanic islands off New Zealand. The islands are free of predators and in this stable environment the snipe populations are limited by intense competition for food. Instead of making costly aerobatic display-flights, the male displays his quality by bringing food to the female as part of the courtship ritual. Both sexes take part in incubation and the care for chicks; *Coenocorypha* chicks are fed over a period of at least 40 days and take even longer to fledge.

Coition usually takes place on the ground, though Eurasian Curlews have been observed to attempt aerial mating. Waders may copulate several times a day over a period of several days in some

species, and only once or twice in others, though little information has been collected on this aspect. In polyandrous species, such as the Spotted Sandpiper, copulation rates are high, presumably because males compete to fertilize the female's eggs. In view of the possibility of extra-pair copulations, even males of monogamous species can not be completely sure that all hatched chicks are theirs. As a means to ensure paternity, males must try to inseminate their female partners around the time of ovulation, a few days before the eggs are laid, and prevent other males having access to their fertile partners. Again, in Spotted Sandpipers this is a particularly relevant problem since not only does a female try to monopolize more than one male, but the males are also subsequently responsible for all parental tasks. L. W. Oring and associates found that copulation rates of Spotted Sandpipers peak on the day before the eggs start to be laid, and that males engaged with females that are often absent from the territory mate most frequently. That males show little evidence of mate-guarding during egg-laying may relate to the discovery, using DNA fingerprinting, that males pairing early in the season cuckold their females' later partners by means of their stored sperm.

Most shorebird nests are nothing more than a vague depression or scrape in the open ground, scantily lined with soft pieces of vegetation, and barely deep enough to hold four eggs. A large species like the Marbled Godwit merely stamps the grass flat and sits down. In contrast, Baird's Sandpipers have been found to make nice nest cups in thick cushions of *Dryas* plants, whereas Nordmann's Greenshanks build large nests from twigs and bearded lichens in larch trees. Scolopacids may thus use a wide variety of nest-sites, even in the far north where the rather uniform habitats seem to offer limited choice. Several species such as the Little Stint and the Curlew Sandpiper like wet marshy ground, while others nest on nearby dry uplands, including bare stony tundra. Sanderlings, Red Knots and Ruddy Turnstones prefer the latter, although in Finland and Sweden Ruddy Turnstones nest almost exclusively in colonies of gulls and terns. Surfbirds inhabit rock slides, Wandering Tattlers like gravel bars in mountain river beds above the tree-line, Spotted Sandpipers nest among vegetation in the vicinity of fresh water, and American Woodcocks nest in forests on soft ground not far from the base of a tree or shrub. Species that nest in grassland are at pains to bend grasses over the nest so that they become invisible from above.

Wood Sandpipers have a tendency to nest on raised tussocks in dense vegetation and may occasionally even nest in an old thrush nest in a tree. Solitary and Green Sandpipers and Grey-tailed Tattlers (*Heteroscelus brevipes*) as a rule make use of nests left by thrushes or other species in spruce or other dense trees. These exceptional species regularly breed at heights of more than 10 m, and only occasionally on the ground among tree roots.

Scolopacid eggs are pear-shaped, so that the pointed ends of three or four of them neatly fit together in the centre of a nest scrape. Pyriform eggs also have the advantage of rolling in circles and never far away. The ground colour of shorebird eggs may vary from buff and pale green to red or purple. In most species eggs are blotched earthy brown at the blunt end and scratchily marked elsewhere. These random streaks and squiggles break up their outline. Unlike in thrushes, the eggs of tree-nesting Solitary and Green Sandpipers have cryptic markings too. The coloration and pattern of sandpiper eggs is very variable even within species, but is rather constant for individual females.

Scolopacid waders share with other shorebirds the habit of not laying more than four eggs per clutch. Fewer are laid by the dowitchers, and the snipes and woodcocks of temperate and tropical latitudes. The smallest clutch size is reached by the *Coenocorypha* snipes that lay two relatively large eggs that take a long time to incubate and hatch. The size of the clutch of scolopacids is fixed, and is not adjusted in response to external conditions. Nutritional constraints during egg formation have traditionally been invoked to explain why scolopacids only lay two, three or four eggs, and this may indeed partially account for the two-egg clutches of *Coenocorypha* snipes. It has also been suggested that brood patch size limits the number of eggs and chicks that can be successfully brooded, to a maximum of four. Small clutches might be adaptive when the rates of nest predation are high, since larger clutches are exposed to the risk of predation for longer periods, and small clutches are replaced more easily when lost.

Full incubation starts only when the clutch of 2-4 eggs has been completed. During the first week of incubation eggs can still survive periods of serious cooling. In monogamous biparental care systems, both partners share incubation duties usually fairly equally. The duration of uninterrupted incuba-

As with this Short-billed Dowitcher, all scolopacid waders lay clutches of four eggs, never more.
The formation of eggs requires a great deal of calcium, and this may be a limiting nutritional component in birds engaged in the business of egg-laying. Some female sandpipers breeding in the Arctic appear to overcome this problem by ingesting lemming teeth and bones found loose on the tundra, but they may also store calcium in advance of egg-formation, perhaps accumulating it within their own skeletons.

[Limnodromus griseus hendersoni,
Churchill, Manitoba,
Canada.
Photo: Ralph A. Reinhold/ Animals Animals]

tion bouts is variable between species and breeding areas. Some of the high Arctic nesters may remain on the nest for periods of 15-18 hours per session. Single incubators like female Curlew Sandpipers and male phalaropes regularly leave the nest to feed. Also incubating alone, female White-rumped Sandpipers increase the time spent on the nest early and late in the day, and make most feeding trips in the middle of the day when air temperatures are highest.

Many of the Arctic breeding scolopacids are not afraid of humans. For example, Western Sandpipers and Little Stints may crawl under a hat placed on their nests, while female White-rumped Sandpipers may attack an approaching hand. Some well camouflaged species sit extremely tight when approached by potential predators, whereas others leave early, either discretely or calling loudly. Nice contrasts are provided by three species breeding in high Arctic Canada. Ruddy Turnstones tend to leave the nest when an approaching human or fox is still very far away. Disturbed birds will approach the intruder and give intense alarm calls. The abandonment of the nest by Baird's Sandpipers is very discrete, and these birds may not be seen leaving at all. Red Knots commonly remain tight on the nest until they are almost stepped upon. Even repeated nest visits make them no more wary; they have complete trust in their excellent camouflage. Red Knots share with Great Knots, Surfbirds, White-rumped Sandpipers, Long-billed Dowitchers and Willets the technique of sitting close to the final second, then to "explode" in the face of the intruder. The Alaskan breeding range of the Surfbird overlaps extensively with that of Dall mountain sheep. The first nest ever found in 1926 was within a metre of one of their trails. The pair of Surfbirds at this nest kept exploding at the sheep at very regular intervals. Large species, such as Long-billed and Bristle-thighed Curlews and Marbled Godwits, sit very tight as well but do not explode upon disturbance; instead, they hurriedly fly away, calling loudly.

Certain tundra-nesters, when disturbed by potential nest robbers such as Arctic foxes (*Alopex lagopus*), Snowy Owls (*Nyctea scandiaca*) and humans, react with a true distraction display called the "Rodent Run". Purple Sandpipers are the acknowledged masters of this behaviour. They jump into view 1-2 m from the nest and zig-zag away, feathers fluffed like fur and squeaking like a mammal; the black line that splits the white rump of many *Calidris* species even resembles the dorsal stripe of a fleeing lemming. Some species such as Sanderlings and Red Knots do not usually run like rodents but reveal themselves fully with loud squeaks when they are some distance away from the nest. They spread the tail, and feign injury by drooping their wings and flapping them on the ground. They also show "False Brooding".

Skuas, crows and hawks, dangerous intruders of the neighbourhood of nests or chicks, are pursued in the air by some of the larger species, in what is called predator-mobbing. Among the *Calidris* sandpipers this is shown only by Red Knots, but also by godwits, curlews, large tringines, and, of course, the turnstones. Ruddy Turnstones are suspected of boring their bills into the anal openings of these predatory birds. This would explain why victims scream so loudly and disappear so swiftly after aerial encounters with turnstones.

After about three weeks of incubation, somewhat shorter in the small species and a few days longer in the large species, the eggs pip and all four chicks hatch within about a day. To ensure that the strikingly white insides of the eggshell do not attract the unwanted attention of predators, the empty shell is carried away by one of the parents as soon as the wet chick has left it. Wader chicks are highly precocial and are able to walk and pick up food items within a few hours of hatching; indeed, a Spotted Sandpiper chick was seen teetering 31 minutes after hatching! The chicks usually lose some weight during the first day of life when they catabolize the little yolk that remains in their belly cavity at hatching. Their precociality means that scolopacid chicks grow 3-4 times slower than altricial passerine birds, since fast-growing tissue can not do much work or generate heat. In spite of this, small chicks are still thermolabile. They are not able to keep up their core temperature of about 40°C for very long at low air temperatures. After periods foraging in cold conditions, the body temperature of small chicks drops below 30°C, so that the chicks must return to the parent before they become lethargic. Under the father or mother the chicks are heated up with their necks pressed against the brood patch. Thermolability means that in colder weather conditions chicks must be brooded more often, have less time to feed, and thus grow slower. Chicks of small calidrines may take almost two weeks to become thermally independent, whereas those of the large species such as godwits and curlews reach this point within a week. Species differ considerably in the susceptibility of their chicks to cold. Young of high Arctic breeding species still grow at fast rates in weather conditions during which temperate wader chicks would surely die. Depending on adult body size, after two weeks of growth in small species, to five weeks in large species, the young bird is ready to fly, even though its flight-feathers take a few more days to complete growth fully.

The care-taking parent guards the chicks and gives them alarm calls warning them to hide and stay immobile when predators are in the vicinity. The parent also broods the chicks when their body temperatures have dropped too low. In scolopacids nesting in open habitats such as tundra and grassland, the families move around over large areas, perhaps as an adaptation to avoid "stationary" predators such as Rough-legged Buzzards (*Buteo lagopus*) or Arctic foxes that may re-search areas where they previously had success. Only in woodcocks and snipes are chicks fed by their parents. Snipe broods are usually split up, the parents separately taking care of half of the brood each. The recurring suggestion that the American Woodcock and its relatives routinely carry their chicks in flight is believed to be a myth by some specialists; wildlife biologists who observe and ring hundreds of broods apparently never see it. If it does occur in any of the woodcocks or snipes, it is probably accidental and quite unusual.

As soon as chicks are old and mature enough no longer to require brooding, the broods of different parents and even of different species may come together in crèches. This has been described for several tundra-breeding long distance migrating scolopacid species such as the Least Sandpiper, Bar-tailed and Hudsonian Godwits, Whimbrel, Bristle-thighed Curlew and perhaps Ruddy Turnstone and Red Knot. In the Bristle-thighed Curlew in Alaska, chicks quite often come together with other locally breeding wader species, especially Bar-tailed Godwits and Whimbrels. Regularly, one or both of the parents leave their chicks, which then remain attended by another curlew, usually a male. The formation of such wader crèches is probably no "accidental" response to highly localized food, but seems to serve the function of predator defence by means of more effective detection and shared mobbing. The formation of brood amalgamations also allows some adults, enforced by severe nutritional depletion, to desert their young early.

At fledging or immediately afterwards, young scolopacids are left alone by the last of their attendants. Most adults have departed on southward migration before the young have stored sufficient fuel to embark on the same trip. Brood amalgamation thus also helps the young to establish flocks with which to migrate to the distant non-breeding areas, thus minimizing energy expenditure and enhancing orientation. For Spotted Sandpipers there is evidence that siblings remain associated for at least part of their first year. In spite of the fact that young migrate by themselves, the southward flights can still be very rapid. On the *pampas* of Argentina, Pectoral Sandpipers still carrying yellow natal down on the head were seen by the end of August, no more than a month after they could have fledged in northern Canada. The chicks do not become imprinted on their attendants as happens in the equally precocial chicks of geese, where families stay together over the whole winter. K. Lorenz reports that chicks of the Eurasian Curlew can not be brought to respond to their keeper in any way other than attempted escape, even when they are hatched artificially and have never seen any other living creature.

In most scolopacids, less than half of the fledglings survive the first year. In some species, Common Sandpipers and Little Stints for example, the survivors return northwards to breed as one-year-olds. In many other species, juveniles remain on the southern wintering areas or make incomplete northward migrations, to return "home" only when they are two or three years old. In most species where this has been examined, juveniles

Spot the Sanderling! With its perfectly mottled plumage, this incubating bird merges most effectively into the Greenland tundra, and indeed it relies fully on camouflage to remain undiscovered by predators. Highly gregarious outside the breeding season, Sanderlings lead a lonely life on the vast open spaces of the Arctic tundra while they are breeding. In fact, even in their winter flocks they may have no "friends", since these flocks appear to be composed of randomly associated individuals.

[*Calidris alba*, Greenland. Photo: Hubert Klein/Bios]

Scolopacids commence incubation only once the clutch has been completed, so that the nidifugous chicks all hatch in a brief period and are all ready to leave the nest at about the same time.
The duration of incubation is approximately three weeks, a little more or less depending on the species. In the Stilt Sandpiper the period has been found to be 19·5-21 days, the male sitting during the day and the female at night.
This species shows a high degree of fidelity, both to partner and to breeding site, with about 15% of the birds reusing the nest scrape from the previous year.

[Micropalama himantopus. Photo: Tom Vezo]

show rather little natal philopatry or hatch-site fidelity, although Rock Sandpipers and some populations of Dunlins show it quite strongly. A return, year after year, to the same breeding site may be beneficial in view of the enhanced familiarity with local environmental factors such as food, cover and predators, enhanced familiarity with local conspecifics and enhanced competitive ability as a consequence of local dominance. Since chicks have not had the chance to build up much of this sort of experience, it makes sense that they are not as faithful to the natal area as adults are to the previous breeding territory. This will be especially the case for males of what we have earlier described as conservative, monogamous species, which usually show high breeding site fidelity. In contrast, species that are not strongly site faithful are characterized by uniparental care and little territorial behaviour. As is true for most birds, females are much less site faithful than males. Since males and females are unlikely to return to a previous territory, they can not form long-term pair-bonds, which are indeed never reported in scolopacid waders.

In 1979, C. S. Roselaar published a short paper in Dutch in which he pointed out that the numbers of Curlew Sandpipers observed in autumn in the Netherlands peaked approximately every three years. He proposed a functional link with the famous three-year Arctic lemming cycles. A couple of years later the idea was corroborated by R. W. Summers and L. G. Underhill, who demonstrated correlations between rough indices of lemming abundance in Arctic Siberia and juvenile proportions of wintering populations of Brent Geese (*Branta bernicla*) in western Europe, and Curlew Sandpipers, Sanderlings and Red Knots in southern Africa. They suggested that densities of predators such as skuas, gulls, Snowy Owls and Arctic foxes build up during lemming peak years. During the following summer, after the collapse of the lemming populations, these predators would be forced to switch to more unprofitable prey: the eggs and chicks of waders and geese. This hypothesis has since received empirical underpinning from studies on the Siberian breeding grounds, where indeed few eggs and chicks survive the onslaught of hungry predators in seasons following lemming peak years. Variable recruitment at the population level may even be a feature of temperate breeding wader populations. In the Netherlands, chick survival of grassland-breeding scolopacids is lower in years with small vole

densities, a phenomenon that is also attributed to the vole-eating predators switching to eggs and chicks.

Scolopacid waders are comparable in that almost all species have a clutch of four eggs, that they start breeding when 1-2 years old, and that they live quite long. Aspects of their population dynamics have been studied at many locations during different phases of their annual cycle, including a 27 year long study of the breeding biology of Common Greenshanks in Scotland, but science can boast about rather few comprehensive analyses of scolopacid demography. The team of L. W. Oring has studied the breeding and population biology of several scolopacids, and spent 17 summer seasons following a population of polyandrous Spotted Sandpipers on Little Pelican Island in Leech Lake, Minnesota. In this species, males as well as females live up to nine years, but females have more mates, eggs, chicks, fledged young, and young returning in subsequent years than do males. Females produce an average of 5·2 fledglings over an average of 3·0 reproductive seasons; for males the values are 3·3 young over 2·8 seasons. Reproductive lifespan and the proportion of chicks that fledge determine their lifetime reproductive success. Compared to other scolopacids, the Spotted Sandpiper can be considered a pioneering species that quickly and frequently colonizes new sites in response to reproductive failure at a previous breeding site, breeds first at an early age, lives a relatively short time, lays many eggs per female and has low nesting success. The Common Sandpiper of Eurasia shares most of these characteristics. In the only study on lifetime reproductive success of scolopacids in the Western Palearctic, female Common Sandpipers in England were shown to rear on average about 3·5 fledglings per lifetime. This is just enough to balance mortality in this population. As in their spotted congener, the longer a female lives, the more fledglings she produces. Over half of the fledglings were produced by just 14% of the females.

Compared to temperate breeding songbirds and other birds of similar size and with similarly high rates of energy expenditure, scolopacid sandpipers reach rather advanced ages, most species easily showing longevity of 10 years. This characteristic is shared with other charadriiform birds and is interpreted by A. A. Goede to be a consequence of the high levels of selenium-rich enzymes found in the bodies of species belonging to this group. Such enzymes can "catch" free radicals that otherwise damage DNA, the carrier of genetic information, and thus slow down the process of ageing. For some years the longevity record for the Scolopacidae was of a 17-year-old male Least Sandpiper, ringed as a two-year old on migration in 1970, that was recaptured on its nest on Sable Island, Nova Scotia, in 1975 and 1976 and captured again on the same nesting site in 1985. This record has since been beaten a few times, most recently by a Red Knot that was ringed as a first-year bird in Langebaan Lagoon in South Africa, and was shot in the Bay of Cadiz, Spain, in May 1995, at the age of 22. It was on its way back to Siberia, probably for the 21st time. This bird not only convincingly demonstrates the fact that free-living scolopacid waders can reach considerable ages, but also impresses one with the distances flown by these birds over a lifetime. If the Red Knot migrated back and forth to Langebaan Lagoon during its whole life, it covered over 700,000 km. This little creature thereby covered the distance to the moon, and made it back again!

Movements

Four of the six subfamilies of Scolopacidae, and 58 of their 59 extant species, breed at moderate to high latitudes in the Northern Hemisphere. Almost all these species show extensive southward movements in autumn to escape the stress and vagaries of northern winters. The Tuamotu Sandpiper, restricted to a handful of tropical Pacific islands, stands out as the grand exception. In the woodcock and snipe subfamilies, inhabitants of tropical regions and isolated islands are also resident, but the temperate breeding species migrate. The southernmost breeding populations of two snipes in South America, the Fuegian Snipe (*Gallinago stricklandii*) and the South American Snipe (*Gallinago paraguaiae*) in southern Patagonia and Tierra del Fuego, show south-north rather than north-south directed post-breeding mi-

grations. Although little is known about the details of their movements, the South American Snipe apparently migrates a few thousand kilometres northward into northern Argentina and Uruguay. Even in the otherwise highly migratory calidrine sandpipers, some restricted populations may opt for a sedentary lifestyle. This is demonstrated by Rock Sandpipers breeding in coastal regions of the North Pacific, where strictly coastal birds in the southern part of the range do not migrate. More northerly and inland breeding Rock Sandpipers do travel up to a few thousand kilometres south along the Pacific shores of North America, leap-frogging over their resident conspecifics.

For the typical north-south migrating scolopacids, life is definitely one of great hurry. To prove this point with a little narrative, let us start in the tropics, or even further away from the Arctic, where birds spend the northern winter season. After having arrived between August and November, the waders go through a complete moult of flight- and body contour feathers. Those that winter within 10,000 km of their breeding areas usually then have time to do "nothing": no moult, no nutrient storage, just survival. But soon, from early February onwards, waders must start preparations for breeding. They do so by growing a new breeding plumage, and by storing the fat and protein needed for the first of a series of long northward flights. Some birds cover the distance in a few very long flights, others do it in a longer series of much shorter flights, visiting many refuelling sites *en route*. Depending on wintering latitude, northward migration may take up most of March, April and May. Especially for the high Arctic breeders, the short summer season dictates that they arrive as early as possible, as soon as the first tundra vegetation is uncovered by the melting snow. The "early" timing implies that the northernmost staging areas, areas that can be used after breeding, are still covered with snow and ice. The waders have thus to embark for the Arctic from refuelling areas in the temperate zone, which are often at a distance of 3000 km, and sometimes over

Even though the plumage of this American Woodcock mirrors the different shades of brown found in the leaves on the surrounding ground, nesting remains a risky business in a wood full of ground-dwelling predators. The visual world of a woodcock is almost entirely monocular, but its field of vision is huge and the incubating bird has no blind spots from which potential enemies might suddenly creep up on it unseen. Woodcocks have been claimed to be capable of carrying their chicks between their feet in flight, but extensive observation by scientists has yielded no corroboration; if it occurs at all, it is likely to be very rare and accidental.

*[Scolopax minor, USA.
Photo: R. Austing/FLPA]*

Breeding in the high Arctic is energetically costly. During mid-summer snowfalls, arthropod prey availability is reduced and the surrounding world becomes even colder than normal, as experienced by this Red Knot incubating its eggs in late June. At such high latitudes shorebirds expend energy at maximum rates for about 15% of the days. The birds can save 10% of their daily energy expenditure by choosing a relatively sheltered nest site.

[*Calidris canutus canutus*, Sterlegova Cape, Taymyr Peninsula, Siberia. Photo: Jan van de Kam]

5000 km. Once they have arrived in the taiga or the tundra, they need to find a suitable partner, a process that may involve the establishment of a good territory and intense behavioural escapades, and select a nest-site. Within one or two weeks of arrival, the first eggs are usually laid and "romance" is over. In some of the species one of the partners takes the rest of the breeding season for granted and migrates southwards straight away. Reproductively successful birds spend three weeks incubating and then a further three weeks caring for chicks, but then also leave southwards as quickly as they can. By that time in late July most of the northern arthropod peaks are over, snow may start to fall in the northernmost parts of the range, and food availability is already on the decline in temperate staging areas. Although more of the northerly sites are suitable for refuelling than in spring, overall southward migration is just as stressful, and many birds succumb during the trip. Those that make it to tropical wintering areas, often arrive exhausted; occasionally they can be picked up by hand there at this time of the year. Then, after a year of intense use in flight, the worn wing feathers urgently need renewal, and the birds also change their colourful breeding dress into the cryptic plumage of winter. An annual cycle is complete.

This was the story of a typical long distance migrating scolopacid, and at this point it will not surprise any reader that there are many intriguing variations to this theme, some of which will be discussed below. That we now know so much about the details of the migration of many species in all parts of the world is to a considerable extent due to the creativity, infectious enthusiasm and pushing-power of a single person, C. D. T. Minton. An industrial manager by profession, he made his first attempts to catch large numbers of waders in the 1960's by firing nets over roosting flocks at high tides in Britain. He and his friends not only developed the cannon net, and a special vocabulary with which to make it operational, they also established groups of enthusiastic amateurs in different parts of Britain that go out at weekends and during holidays to catch, ring, and measure the size, mass and moult of waders. Among these groups, the Wash Wader Ringing Group always has, and continues to handle the largest numbers of waders, many thousands per year. The activities in Britain were soon followed up by British-based ringing expeditions overseas, initially to Iceland, Mauritania, Morocco,

and countries in western Europe where the seeds of enthusiasm, and sets of catching equipment, were left.

This surge in wader migration studies also began to receive academic involvement, and led in 1970 to the establishment of the international Wader Study Group. Initially based in Britain, but now worldwide, this highly active, politically low-profiled, research network of amateurs and professionals, has done much to further the research on scolopacids and other wader families, by arranging meetings and by co-ordinating fruitful international collaborative volunteer research programmes. For Minton the work was not over by the time he left Britain in the late 1970's for a career in Australia. Together with his Australian colleagues, he started another surge in wader migration studies, now along the west Pacific rim. Many thousands of scolopacids are captured each year in Australasia, even in rather remote places. Worldwide, the web of wader workers leaves its mark on their favourite birds: in many wader populations, a notable proportion of the individuals now carry rings, and these continue to inform us about their worldwide movements.

Especially in the early years of large-scale ringing, great strides were made in the delineation of the movements of different breeding populations. In many cases, birds of a single species from different segments of a circumpolar breeding range were found to winter in different parts of the world, with populations usually, but not always, moving to areas roughly south of their breeding grounds. The discovery that there is reasonable congruence between the movements of populations of different species breeding in the same areas or staging at the same refuelling sites, led to the recognition of different wader "flyways", a concept borrowed from North American waterfowl biologists. About eight different north-south flyways are now recognized around the world. These are (following sunrise): the East Asian/Australasian; the Siberian/Indian; the East African/West Asian; the Mediterranean; the East Atlantic; the West Atlantic; the Interior American; and the East Pacific. Obviously, the flyways provide only approximate descriptions of seasonal wader movements in different parts of the world. There are five flyways that converge in northern Eurasia and three that do so in northernmost America; different species make the migratory divides in different ways. Some species do not obey the flyway definitions given here. For example, Pectoral Sandpipers and

Long-billed Dowitchers from the Taymyr Peninsula in central Siberia migrate to South America! Several species also show the tendency to use one flyway during southward, and another during northward migration. Such species carry out "loop migrations". For example, of the Curlew Sandpipers breeding in Arctic Siberia, a certain proportion travels via western Europe and northwest Africa to wintering areas in West and southern Africa. In spring, however, most of these birds take a more easterly route, the great majority then following the Mediterranean flyway northwards. Another loop migrant, the Eskimo Curlew, first migrates eastward from breeding areas in the Canadian Arctic, then overflies the western Atlantic Ocean in southern directions to end up on the South American *pampas*. Eskimo Curlews migrate northward via a more coastal route along the Andes, then over the Central American land-bridge and along the northern shores of the Gulf of Mexico, and finally following the Interior American flyway northwards into the Arctic.

Species with atypical ecological requirements are also hard to fit against the crude and linear flyways. For example, Red Phalaropes avoid continental routes, and migrate from the circumpolar Arctic breeding areas to the tropical oceans over the open sea, not following the chains of wetlands that comprise the main wader flyways. Red-necked Phalaropes do show extensive overland migrations, however, the most spectacular of which is the south-eastward migration from Arctic Europe and west Siberia, via lakes in Kazakhstan, to the Indian Ocean. Prairie-breeding Wilson's Phalaropes migrate west and south along the Rocky Mountains, travelling from mountain lake to mountain lake, before a short Pacific sea crossing and the arrival at wintering lakes high in the Andes. Using alpine tundra rather than mountain lakes for feeding, a rather similar route is followed by Baird's and Pectoral Sandpipers migrating from the Nearctic to southernmost South America. A peculiar migration is also shown by the Sharp-tailed Sandpiper, the adults of which migrate transcontinentally in a straight line from the east Siberian breeding grounds to the Australian wintering grounds, but the young of which migrate southwards down the Pacific coast.

Although it might be expected that species breeding furthest south also winter furthest south, and that, within the same species, the southernmost breeding populations winter furthest south too, this type of "chain migration" appears to be rather rare among scolopacid waders. In comparisons between species, it is clear that the reverse is more usual, with northernmost breeders often wintering furthest south. For example, temperate breeding Willets and Common Redshanks winter much further north than Arctic breeding Hudsonian and Bar-tailed Godwits. Such "leap-frog migration" patterns also hold widely for comparisons within scolopacid genera and subfamilies. Some of the clearest avian examples of intraspecific leap-frog migration are also provided by scolopacids. For example, the northerly breeding populations of Common Snipes, Dunlins, Bar-tailed Godwits and Rock Sandpipers overfly the more southerly populations, and thus combine a more extreme breeding climate with a longer migration and a more contrasting, warmer, wintering climate. The migration system of Purple Sandpipers, some of which remain north of the Arctic Circle in mid-winter, is a composite of chain and leap-frog patterns.

Of course, these patterns, and especially leap-frogging, invite explanation. T. Alerstam and G. Högstedt start their reasoning by assuming that intraspecific competition for resources is an important factor for wintering shorebirds, and that birds distribute themselves so that on an annual basis the mean suitability of sites in different parts of the winter range is similar for all birds. Leap-frog migration would then be explained by the strong selection on temperate breeding birds to remain close to their breeding sites, so that they can respond quickly to the onset of favourable conditions, the timing of which varies markedly from year to year. Arctic breeding waders would obtain no extra advantages from wintering close to their breeding sites, since outside the polar climatic zone spring progress in the Arctic can not be detected anyhow. Alternative hypotheses are based on the general argument that, for many different reasons, shorter migration distances are favourable, and invoke the existence of differences in size and dominance between northern and southern winterers. Dominant or large southerly breeders would displace sub-dominant or small birds attempting to winter in the north. It is now widely understood that there is a host of rather confusing factors that influence the evolutionary shaping of migration patterns. The time of unidimensional explanatory hypotheses is behind us.

Recent studies have attempted to measure the energetic costs and benefits of long distance migration in scolopacids. In a comparison between Siberian breeding Red Knots that winter in tropical West Africa and Nearctic breeding Red Knots that winter in north temperate Europe, the African winterers were shown to expend only half as much energy over the non-breeding season as the European winterers, even when the extra energy costs of flight incurred by the Africans were included. This large difference is due to the enormous effect of climatic conditions on energy expenditure of relatively small birds living in open and exposed intertidal habitats. Though the Red Knots wintering in Africa expend little energy in winters with high air temperatures, much sunshine and calm winds, nevertheless, given the scarcity of their mollusc food at these sites, they would not be able to expend much more. A real contrast with these tropical winterers is provided by the Canadian breeding population of Red Knots that flies all the way to the frigid southern point of South America. These birds' high rates of energy expenditure are probably compensated for by the rich feeding grounds that they encounter on the underexploited tidal flats of Tierra del Fuego. Northerly wintering not only leads to high costs of sustaining a body temperature of 41°C, but also entails a substantial risk of starvation when mudflats freeze over or are covered with ice. Common Redshanks appear particularly prone to die in severe weather. For example, during a single spell of freezing weather in February 1992, almost 50% of the 4000 Common Redshanks wintering on the Wash in eastern England died.

Good timing of long distance migrations, as carried out by most scolopacids, includes well timed starts of moult and fuelling activities, and puts high demands on the birds' abilities to organize an annual cycle properly. In spring, good scheduling is particularly critical, since the profitable time window for arriving on the breeding grounds, especially at Arctic latitudes, is short, both for ecological reasons and because of intrasexual competition. In northern resident birds, changes in day length are known to trigger seasonal activities. Ruddy Turnstones, Red Knots and Dunlins maintain appropriate seasonal cycles of body mass and moult when kept outdoors under conditions of constant food availability. However, the fact that so many scolopacids spend the non-breeding season in the tropics or even further south, where photoperiodic changes are either small or show a reversed cycle, suggests that they have an internal chronometer quite in-dependent of external stimuli. Scolopacids have not been well studied in this respect, but the single study on Red Knots kept under constant climatic and photoperiodic conditions, confirms the possibility of an "endogenous circannual clock".

The preparations for the breeding season include a moult of part of the contour feathers into a fresh and sometimes colourful breeding plumage, and the storage of fuel to keep the birds in the air until the next suitable stopover site. Recent studies on scolopacid waders have clearly shown that long distance migrants not only store fat, but increase the size of the flight muscles as well. At intermediate stopover sites the picture is even more complicated, as waders may have catabolized part of the metabolic machinery that they need for rapid refuelling. In Bar-tailed Godwits and Red Knots arriving on a stopover site, the birds first grow a large digestive apparatus, of which the protein is turned into breast muscle in the last few days before take-off on the next flight. In the meantime they may have doubled their body mass. In waders that are ready to fly, fat can make up 50% of total body mass. Subcutaneous fat envelopes the body in a thick white layer. Until late last century, Eskimo Curlews provided abundant examples of such light-coloured fat migrants. Before take-off on their transoceanic flights from north-east America, their thin skins were stretched so taut with fat that when they were shot and fell from the sky, the fat would sometimes burst out of the skin when they struck the ground. For this reason, Eskimo Curlews were called "dough-birds" in New England. Before departure on their transoceanic flights to the Guianas in northern South America, Semipalmated Sandpipers in the Bay of Fundy, Canada, can be so fat that they have difficulty in getting airborne and remaining so. When such sandpipers are harassed by raptors, they can fall on the beach and burst out of their skins, as if they were small dough-birds.

Of course, the actual timing of migratory flights is not only a function of appropriate physiological and behavioural changes. The external ecological conditions must also be good enough to enable the storage of fuel and the moult into breeding plumage. A nice example of food availability constraining the timing of departure from the wintering grounds is provided by the Whimbrels on the Banc d'Arguin, Mauritania. Whimbrels feed

Growing shorebirds, like these Whimbrel hatchlings, face an energetic dilemma. Being brooded by one of the parents saves them important energy, but their energy gains amount to zero since they are not fed by their parents. During feeding bouts to catch surface-living insects, however, small wader chicks lose body heat faster than they can generate it, and thus they quickly cool off. This problem is most marked in the smallest species, which may therefore avoid the coldest breeding areas. Each of these small chicks still has an egg tooth at the bill tip.

[Numenius phaeopus phaeopus, Fokstummyra, Norway. Photo: Allan G. Potts/ Bruce Coleman]

on crabs, especially fiddler crabs (*Uca tangeri*). In winter fiddler crabs are in short supply, since they keep to the safety of their deep burrows most of time. In spring, however, the males come to the surface to display and attract mates. The timing of these reproductive activities is entrained on the lunar rhythm, so that a new moon early in the period from 10th March to 10th April leads to an early start of enhanced fiddler crab availability, and thus to an early start of maximal nutrient storage. In years when the new moon is early, the Whimbrels pass Europe at earlier dates than in years when it is late. Thus, more than 4000 km further north and several weeks later, the timing of migration of this species attests the extent to which moonlight influences the reproductive activities of tropical fiddler crabs.

During long distance migration, scolopacids fly in flocks. Such flocks usually contain 10-60 conspecific individuals, with the larger species occurring in larger flocks. A small percentage of flocks may contain more than one species, although in such cases the co-occurring species are of roughly the same size. During peak migration and at high tides, the moments when the greatest numbers of conspecifics are available, departing flocks are largest. Starting flocks usually assemble from clusters into V-formations or echelons, and ascend to flight heights of several hundred to several thousand metres with climb rates of approximately half a metre per second. In coastal areas, wader departures bear no uniform relationship with the timing and the height of the tides, but at all study sites most flocks leave just before sunset. With such a departure timing, birds can maximize the use of multiple orientational cues such as skylight polarization patterns and the position of both the setting sun and the stars, and also fly under the calmer wind conditions of the night. For many species the night is also a better period to fly because foraging is less profitable than during the day.

The flock, with its cumulative sense of direction, prevents individuals from straying off into wrong directions, while formation-flying may be important in reducing flight costs. The ability of Ruddy Turnstones and Bristle-thighed Curlews to navigate reliably to the same lonely islands in the Pacific year after year, bears witness to the immense navigational capacities that the birds must possess, but that have never been studied. It pro-

vides an area of research where the technologies of the late twentieth century could do wonders: for instance, terrific insights could be gained from the use of micro-satellite-transmitters attached to Bristle-thighed Curlews, following them through their entire transoceanic migrations!

Transmitter techniques may also help to clarify the energetics of long distance flights, as has been demonstrated in recent studies, by G. C. Iverson and associates, of Western Sandpipers during their northward migration up the Pacific coast of North America. Although body mass proved a poor predictor of subsequent flight range, accurate measurements of individual travel speeds and staging times were obtained. Hitherto, studies on flight costs in migrating scolopacids were limited to longitudinal studies of the average individual in populations showing synchronized migrations. Estimates of average values of mass loss and fat depletion during specific flights, divided by the roughly estimated lengths of these flights, give just an approximation of the costs of travel. Using such data for the northward migration of Bar-tailed Godwits from West Africa to western Europe, on their way to Arctic Siberia, T. Piersma and J. Jukema were able to suggest that without the help of tailwinds *en route*, these godwits would not be able to cover the 4500 km separating the Banc d'Arguin from the Wadden Sea in a single flight. In order to encounter these tailwinds, godwits have to fly at altitudes of several thousand metres along the north-west African coast, and somewhat lower when overflying southern Europe. Such altitudes are commonly reached by the species that overfly the 5000-8000 m high Himalayan mountain chain, and should provide no major difficulties in spite of greatly reduced oxygen pressure and air temperatures of 20-30°C below zero. Red Knots travel the same route as Bar-tailed Godwits, and have been shown to overfly French stopover sites during their migration to the Wadden Sea only in years when high altitude winds are favourable.

Flying high has its risks, of course, an important one being the possibility of being blown off course. High altitude winds are often much stronger than the flight speeds of 60-70 km per hour attained by long distance migrating scolopacids. Especially when clouds obscure the view of the landscape below, it must be

Thermoregulatory capacities not only depend on the age and size of an individual bird, but also differ between species. Purple Sandpipers are the only sandpipers that overwinter along Arctic seashores where days are short and temperatures low. As they winter relatively close to the tundra regions where they breed, and where they in their turn hatched, their migration flights are short, and their departure from the breeding grounds occurs later than in any other calidrine sandpiper.

[Calidris maritima, Spitsbergen, Svalbard. Photo: Hubert Klein/Bios]

When Bar-tailed Godwits arrive on the Wadden Sea in May, flying in from their West African wintering grounds, they already wear their rufous breeding plumage, as in this flock of males. Nevertheless, during the stopover some birds start to moult again, replacing even more breast feathers with bright rusty red ones. Individuals that do so carry more fat, have better blood profiles and carry fewer intestinal parasites than non-moulting birds. With only these birds able to overcome the nutritional stress of migration and afford to become so brightly coloured, breeding plumages may thus reliably signal "migratory quality" and be used as a cue in mate choice decisions.

[Limosa lapponica lapponica, Wadden Sea, Germany. Photo: Jan van de Kam]

hard to keep to the optimal track. With regard to the strong winds at great heights, it is easy to imagine that some Red Knots might reach the point of exhaustion above Switzerland, where there is no suitable habitat for them. Inland and coastal waders may also be blown offshore, a mechanism that may explain an observation of a flock of nearly 1000 Willets resting on the Atlantic Ocean east of Newfoundland in May 1907. These Willets had overshot their breeding destination by about 1000 km. While many species can rest on a water surface if necessary, they can not survive long if the sea is rough. P. Matthiessen has suggested that whales and turtles may have provided resting points when they were still abundant throughout the tropical seas, and Red Phalaropes have been seen to use both of these types of animal in this manner, but the reported sensitivity of the whales' skin may make them quite unsuitable as dependable floats.

Avoidance of inhospitable areas, dependence on particular suitable staging sites, and the use of favourable wind streams all provide factors that may explain why some species do not fly the shortest routes between breeding and wintering areas, but sometimes deviate substantially. For example, Red Knots and Bar-tailed Godwits travel via West Africa and western Europe to Siberia instead of taking a straight route over the Middle East, a substantial detour of almost 3000 km, one way. According to some accounts the Buff-breasted Sandpipers breeding in northern Canada fly a real zig-zag course to Argentina. First they go east from the breeding grounds towards Hudson Bay and somewhat beyond, then they fly south-west following the Appalachians to Central America, and then south-east again until they reach the Argentinian *pampas*.

Every single wader must establish its own lifetime track. How do young birds select a wintering area, and how do they subsequently select a breeding site? Experimental fieldwork with Sanderlings in California demonstrates that young birds captured shortly after their arrival on wintering grounds can be "transplanted" to other wintering sites. If juveniles are transported to other sites before January, none of them returns to its capture site. A year later, about 50% of the transplanted Sanderlings are seen again along the beaches where they were released. Juvenile Dunlins, transported between Italian wintering sites in December, fly back to the catching sites just as frequently as site faithful adults. This means that they have developed a certain

attachment to the wintering site by the time they are four months old. Scolopacids that have a certain degree of faithfulness to their breeding sites, may use part of the first full summer in the north to reconnoitre the potential breeding range. A study on individually marked Spotted Sandpipers showed the presence of transient birds on a high density breeding island. Such birds are mostly young, and several facts suggest that transient birds are searching for good future breeding sites. Strong intrasexual competition makes this information more important for females than for males in this polyandrous species, but it is likely that the reverse will hold for the majority of waders with monogamous or polygynous mating systems.

As already mentioned, flocks of migrating waders may be blown off course at times, but observations of single shorebirds at unusual localities are much commoner. Records of such vagrancy suggest that wader species common on the coast and making long transoceanic migrations, such as Semipalmated Sandpipers, cross the Atlantic Ocean far less often than species with a more inland distribution, for example Buff-breasted and Upland Sandpipers. Another observation is that species that breed in the western Nearctic, such as the Long-billed Dowitcher, wander more frequently to Europe than similar species breeding further east, such as the Short-billed Dowitcher. In Britain, the Pectoral Sandpiper is observed about eight times more often than Baird's Sandpiper, a species that breeds much closer in northeastern Canada and actually overlaps with several scolopacid species that winter in Britain, notably Ruddy Turnstones and Red Knots. It has been hypothesized that waders from western North America which habitually first fly east before striking south are more apt to carry on eastwards to Europe than species which set out on a southerly course straight away.

Relationship with Man

Few birds are so closely associated with folklore as the Common Snipe. In the Middle Ages, snipes were often associated with the supernatural. In parts of France, for some reason, female Common Snipes were believed to represent the devil's wife. Most omens, however, were related to the first appearance of the birds in spring. The time and place at which a farmer in northern

Germany hears his first Common Snipe gives him a prognosis of certain events of the year. In parts of Newfoundland fishermen have long associated Common Snipes with the arrival of lobsters inshore: "when the snipe bawls, the lobster crawls". In New England, the arrival of Common Snipes was associated with good river catches of a commercial fish, the alewife. In Delaware the arrival of Common Snipes in spring coincided with the appearance of an inshore commercial fish, the shad.

In their vernacular naming, the Nunamiat Eskimos of Alaska compared the bleating of the Common Snipe to the blowing sound made by the walrus. They also believed that killing a Common Snipe would bring bad weather, and alternatively called the bird "weather maker". In many parts of Europe the presence of snipes is also associated with storms and rain. In parts of northern Germany the bleating of Common Snipe at twilight was believed to be made by the god Donar's team of goats, as they drew his chariot across the heavens. The Faeroese say that its bleating predicts rain, or snow if heard before 25th March. Forecasting rain by the intense bleating of snipe is not very difficult. According to L. M. Tuck, in Newfoundland snipes are inclined to display intensely during the approach of high pressure areas. The erratic bleating at low levels during the day thus nearly always precedes rain. The departure of Eurasian Curlews from a given place is supposed to occur just prior to a storm, and in the old days in England the curlew's cry boded good to no man. In northern England, Eurasian Curlews and Whimbrels were called "Gabriel's hounds"; the name Whimbrel comes from "whimpernel" which in the Durham Household Book of 1530 refers to a habit attributed to it of hound-like whisperings. Both species were known as harbingers of death.

As part of initiation ceremonies, members of an Aborigine tribe in north-central Arnhem Land in Australia carry out "sandpiper dances". The dancers dress up as sandpipers and godwits, and look very realistic, with excellent jizz! In this part of the world the return of the migratory waders coincides with the first rains of the wet season. This is the first supply of fresh water after the long hot and dusty dry season during which water-holes either dry up or the water becomes undrinkable. Shorebirds are thus associated with good health. In other parts of the world, specific shorebirds may be associated with *machismo* and sexual appetite. The lekking behaviour of Ruffs so impressed the indigenous people of Chukchi Peninsula in The Russian Far East, that they celebrate it with an imitative dance.

As symbols of low, wet countryside more than as economic icons, in 1977 the Central Bank of the Netherlands issued bank notes of 100 guilders that feature a Common Snipe on one side, and a Great Snipe on the other. Unfortunately, the depiction of the latter species was rather an inappropriate choice, as Great Snipes are very rare in the Netherlands. Going for a very common wader instead, in 1996 the same bank issued new notes, of 1000 guilders, depicting a Northern Lapwing (*Vanellus vanellus*) and its egg.

Over the ages, however, man's relationship to scolopacid waders has usually been one of more severe economic exploitation. In the Middle Ages, Ruffs, and perhaps Red Knots too, were captured alive in late summer in the countries bordering the North Sea in Europe. The birds were kept in caged flocks and fed wasted grain to make them fat before they were consumed later in winter. The Red Knot may have gained both its common name and its scientific name, *canutus*, from King Canute's love of knot meat, although alternative derivations come from the tendency of Red Knots to stand "Canute-like" on the edge of the sea and from their characteristic "cnut" contact calls. The Rock Sandpiper of the north Pacific has the unfortunate habit of gathering on top of boulders. The Aleuts made good use of this behaviour by knocking them off these rocks with well aimed sticks, often in large numbers. Further north, in Arctic Alaska, Red-necked Phalaropes are so tame that they are hunted commonly and with great success by very young Eskimo children.

But the real slaughter of scolopacid waders came with the arrival of European immigrants in North America. The habit of many waders of bunching together in the air when disturbed, was very convenient for the market gunners in North America in the nineteenth century. Marbled Godwits came in huge flocks to coastal estuaries, and together with Long-billed Dowitchers they were harvested by the wagon load in the basin of the Columbia River. If early success by the hunters filled the wagons too quickly, they were emptied on the ground and the slaughter began anew. The abundance of the now nearly extinct Eskimo Curlew in North America has been compared to the great flights of the definitely extinct Passenger Pigeon (*Ectopistes migratorius*). From earliest colonial times onwards these small curlews were hunted in spring and autumn together with American Golden Plovers (*Pluvialis dominica*). Only in the last part of the nineteenth century, when the Passenger Pigeon had been hunted to oblivion and market hunters turned their attention towards shorebirds and waterfowl, did Eskimo Curlew populations begin their steep decline. By the turn of the century they had become a rare commodity. In 1954 a novel was published on the plight of the Eskimo Curlew. This book, *Last of the Curlews*, was written by F. Bodsworth and stunningly illustrated by T. Shortt. It was translated into Dutch, Spanish, Portuguese, Italian, French, German, Japanese and six other languages, and sold over 3 million copies! Hanna-Barbara Productions made the story into a one hour animation movie that was shown on television and in schools, and that won the 1973 Emmy award for children's broadcasting.

Not only were waders trapped and shot in enormous numbers, large numbers of Red Knots and other species were also taken by "fire-lighting", a nocturnal practice on Long Island and elsewhere in north-eastern USA. Resting flocks were blinded by bright beams so that they stayed put while the market hunters captured them by hand and wrung their necks. Barrel loads of the birds were sent to the Boston markets for sale. Scolopacids larger than Red Knots suffered much more heavily from hunting than smaller species, but even Least Sandpipers were gunned when the large species were in short supply. According to one account, 97 of these diminutive sandpipers were killed in one shot.

Snipes and woodcocks, of course, have long been a popular worldwide hunting quarry. The word "sniper" was doubtlessly used first to describe a man skilled in shooting these erratic zigzag fliers. One such gentleman was James J. Pringle from Louisiana who, from 1867 to 1887, kept careful records and indicated a personal bag of 69,087 snipes, plus several thousand other waders "killed accidentally". Since many hunters consider snipes the most diffi-

cult of all gamebirds to bring down, these figures bear stern witness to both Pringle's prowess and snipe prosperity.

Although wader eggs may have been collected for local consumption since time immemorable, egg collecting only became something of a gentleman's sport in Europe late last century. In 1875, Henry Seebohm, a successful Sheffield steel manufacturer and an amateur ornithologist of great repute, set out for the Pechora Valley in northern Russia in search of the nests and eggs of waders that he only knew from their British wintering grounds. So successful was his first trip that he made a second one in 1877 to the Yenisey River, further east in Siberia. His journeys were great tales of bird and egg collecting, even though some dearly wanted scolopacid waders still escaped him and the others that followed his lead. An ultimate "pipe-dream wader" was the Red Knot. Red Knot eggs were found first on the New Siberian Islands in 1886, and in Taymyr eggs were first collected in 1901. North America had to wait until 1909 when the first clutch was found in northernmost Ellesmere Island, Canada, by a member of the team of Admiral Peary as they journeyed southward from "discovering" the North Pole. In oological circles this discovery was scarcely less momentous than the possibility that Peary had reached the pole, since the nest of the Red Knot had been searched for assiduously by westerners for half a century. Many hunters of Red Knot eggs, even when they had reached the extremely remote breeding grounds, mistakenly interpreted the presence of Red Knots near tundra pools as indicating that the nests must lie in nearby grass, instead of the dry barren tundra and rocky shales where the perfectly camouflaged nests are usually found.

Nests of other scolopacid waders proved difficult to find too. The first nests of the Wandering Tattler and the Surfbird were found in the mountains of Alaska in 1912 and 1926 respectively. Grey-tailed Tattler nests escaped discovery in eastern Siberia until 1960, but the most recent of all is Nordmann's Greenshank, for which the first nests were found in 1976 on Sakhalin. The first nest of the Bristle-thighed Curlew was located only in 1948 on upland tundra inland near the Yukon River, western Alaska, nearly two centuries after the species was made known to science by the crew of Captain James Cook. The Solitary Sandpiper confused nest seekers for nearly a century, until in 1903 a settler in what is now Alberta discovered the sandpiper flying to the nest of an American Robin (*Turdus migratorius*), five metres up in a tree. The first nest of a Great Knot was found in 1914, and the second only in 1976. The first nests of the Critically Endangered Slender-billed Curlew were found early this century on large bogs in south-west Siberia but the current breeding grounds still remain to be found, possibly somewhere in the steppes of Kazakhstan and Siberia.

Upland Sandpipers nested widely on the plains of North America cleared by the colonists, and together with the great migrating clouds of plovers, curlews and other shorebirds, they provided the farmers excellent service by eating grasshoppers, cutworms, wireworms and their likes. Yet their role as insect-destructors was so little appreciated that in the nineteenth century they were poisoned in the belief that they ate grain. On the other hand, scolopacids breeding in temperate grasslands have built up a reputation as conservation symbols in some parts of the world. For example, Black-tailed Godwits concentrate most of their breeding in the grasslands and meadowlands of the Netherlands, which thus harbours the great majority of the European population in spite of its small land surface. The Netherlands recognizes its responsibility for this species by setting aside specially managed land, and by subsidizing farmers for godwit-friendly management practices. In spite of these efforts, the greatest part of suitable grassland habitat is now too intensely managed to accomodate the large numbers of Black-tailed Godwits and other species of breeding waders of the twentieth century.

Status and Conservation

Although the status of no fewer than 21, or almost a quarter, of all extant scolopacids gives reasons for concern, only two species are known to have become extinct over the past few centuries. Both are members of the tringine genus *Prosobonia*, and until 1991 they were lumped together as a single species. The White-winged Sandpiper (*Prosobonia leucoptera*) and Ellis's Sandpiper (*Prosobonia ellisi*) lived in the Society Archipelago, on the adjacent islands of Tahiti and Moorea respectively. Based on a few skins and several drawings, the two sandpipers were different with respect to several plumage characteristics and in the shape of the bill. If they

According to the reckoning of BirdLife International, there is a 50% chance that no Slender-billed Curlews will survive the next five years. Less than 100 individuals persist on the Mediterranean wintering grounds of this Critically Endangered species. The decline of the Slender-billed Curlew is probably due to uncontrolled hunting, a factor that has also caused the near-extinction of the Eskimo Curlew (Numenius borealis) in the Americas. Extensive habitat modifications severely damaging the species' breeding grounds have probably aggravated the plight of the Slender-billed Curlew.

[Numenius tenuirostris, Merja Zerga, Morocco. Photo: Hans Gebuis/ Aquila]

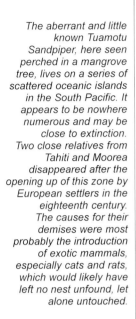

The aberrant and little known Tuamotu Sandpiper, here seen perched in a mangrove tree, lives on a series of scattered oceanic islands in the South Pacific. It appears to be nowhere numerous and may be close to extinction. Two close relatives from Tahiti and Moorea disappeared after the opening up of this zone by European settlers in the eighteenth century. The causes for their demises were most probably the introduction of exotic mammals, especially cats and rats, which would likely have left no nest unfound, let alone untouched.

[*Prosobonia cancellata*, Tuamotu Islands. Photo: R. Seitre/Bios]

indeed lived as residents along mountain streams, it is quite likely that the two populations were geographically isolated in spite of their proximity. The sandpipers of Tahiti and Moorea passed away unnoticed in the late eighteenth century, perhaps as a consequence of the introduction of goats, pigs and rats on the islands. A close relative, the Tuamotu Sandpiper is still distributed widely but thinly over a 3700 km area of ocean within the Tuamotu Archipelago, east of Tahiti in French Polynesia. It is considered Endangered, being judged to have a 20% chance of going extinct in the next 20 years. Several hundred individuals live scattered over two groups of islands, all of which are isolated and rarely visited, and all of which have no rats.

A similar status has been fixed for the migratory Nordmann's Greenshank, breeding at the edge of peatmoss-larch bog forests near coastal salt-marshes around the Sea of Okhotsk in the Russian Far East, and wintering in coastal sites in south Asia. With a world population of less than 1000 birds, Nordmann's Greenshank is threatened by habitat loss in breeding and non-breeding areas and by hunting. Its decline may have been advanced by its popularity as a noisy decoy bird with hunters in the Shanghai region, who used it to attract other wader species to their clap-nets. Two other migratory species, both of them curlews, are in even graver danger and are considered Critically Endangered, with a 50% chance of going extinct within five years. The Eskimo Curlew was hunted close to extinction in the last century (see Relationship with Man), and was not seen for several decades until two birds were encountered in Texas in 1945. Eskimo Curlews were reported in 24 of the next 40 years, but the numbers observed were never greater than 23 individuals. Still, the Eskimo Curlew may linger on to this very day as suggested by the sporadic sightings. The reasons behind the slump of the Slender-billed Curlew certainly include heavy hunting pressure on its Mediterranean wintering grounds, but this process may have been aggravated by serious habitat loss both on the breeding grounds, now thought to be the heavily developed steppe-land of the Kazakhstan region, and in the winter range. Although the species is observed every winter in very small numbers, it is now likely to number fewer than 100 individuals.

The category Vulnerable has a purported 10% chance of going extinct in the next 100 years and includes the peculiar long distance migrating Spoon-billed Sandpiper, as well as the Bris-tle-thighed Curlew, which breeds in Alaska and winters on islands spread out over the Pacific, and four species of essentially sedentary snipes and woodcocks. The populations of the sandpiper and the curlew both number several to many thousand individuals. The Moluccan Woodcock (*Scolopax rochussenii*) is restricted to the small islands of Obi and Bacan in the Moluccas, Indonesia. Only known from eight specimens, the most recent of which was collected in 1980, the species may still occur on Obi, where its description appears to coincide with the reports of a local guide. The Amami Woodcock (*Scolopax mira*), restricted to broadleaf forest on several small islands in the Ryukyu chain, off southern Japan, is probably less rare and may number several thousand birds. It is nevertheless seriously threatened by deforestation, and also predation by newly released mongooses. A thousand pairs of Chatham Snipe are confined to two small predator-free islands in the Chatham group, New Zealand. The Wood Snipe (*Gallinago nemoricola*) is a bird of alpine meadows with scattered scrubs and streams. With an unknown population size, it is confined to the Himalayan region, escaping the harsh winters by a short southward migration to the lowlands of southern Asia. Another snipe of high slopes close to the tree-line, the Imperial Snipe (*Gallinago imperialis*), was thought to be extinct for over 100 years until it was discovered in 1967 in the Andean highlands of Peru, about 2000 km south of the locality from which it was originally known.

Several species confined to the Asian and Australasian regions which were considered quite rare for a long time have been found in considerable numbers during recent extensive surveys. Asian Dowitchers are not as rare as previously supposed, and 13,000 were counted in south-east Sumatra in November 1988. Great Knots were also thought to be rather rare, the world population numbering fewer than 20,000 individuals, until the Australians began to count their remote shores. Along Eighty Mile Beach in north-west Australia, aerial and ground surveys have registered up to 160,000 Great Knots, out of a total population of 270,000 birds. This has turned them into the second most abundant wader of Australia. Also, recent work by Russian scientists in the 1990's has shown them to be more common on alpine tundra in the Russian Far East than previously supposed. Similarly, the Little Curlew was considered a rare species with a restricted and fragmented breeding distribution, and it was included in the Red Data Book of the USSR. Since the early 1980's new studies have indicated a more extensive breeding range, while counts in the Australian wintering grounds have shown a minimum wintering population of 180,000 birds. That the waders breeding in the immense territory of the former Soviet Union are still rather poorly known comes as no surprise if one realizes that the average density of ornithologists is one knowledgeable person per 22,000 km² of land area, with many of them concentrated in the Moscow area.

In the Americas similar discoveries have been made as a result of several counting efforts, including continent-wide surveys. The most epic is the circumnavigation of the South American continent in small aeroplanes by R. I. G. Morrison, R. K. Ross and collaborators. In January and February 1982-1986 they covered some 28,000 km of the South American coastline, including nearly all parts of the coast thought to contain significant habitat for shorebirds. More than 2,900,000 shorebirds were counted, and among the discoveries was that of the wintering grounds of Hudsonian Godwits in Tierra del Fuego and southern Chile. As recently as the 1940's this species was thought to be on the verge of extinction, since rather small numbers were seen during passage on the east coast of North America. During the aerial surveys, over 45,000 godwits were seen.

The recent increases in knowledge about scolopacid species are part of a general recent upsurge in the enthusiasm for shorebirds, especially the migratory species, for other than economic reasons. This has not only led to several research projects in different parts of the world, but has simultaneously stimulated several conservation initiatives. In the early 1960's the International Waterfowl Research Bureau (IWRB) was established as the first conservation organization devoted to waterbird and wetland conservation. Its foundation and early growth was certainly to an extent inspired by migratory shorebirds. Working alongside IWRB since 1982, the Working Group for International Wader and Waterfowl Research (WIWO) from the Netherlands aims to stimulate and facilitate the research expeditions and related activities of volunteers, focused on waders and wetlands especially in Europe, Africa and the Middle East. In 1983 the East Asia/Pacific shorebird study programme Interwader began to carry out conservation-relevant studies of migratory wader and waterbird populations in South-east Asia and nearby regions. Interwader quickly grew larger, and was soon transformed into a more widely and politically orientated conservation organization, the Asian Wetland Bureau, based in Kuala Lumpur, Malaysia. In the meantime Interwader had made an impressive series of wader and wetland surveys, and, in 1989, produced an unrivalled and very stimulating guide to baseline wader studies, the *Shorebird Studies Manual*. On the other side of the Pacific, shorebird workers in the Americas established the Western Hemisphere Shorebird Reserve Network (WHSRN) in 1985. By networking activities between sites and through designations of sites of national, international or hemispheric importance, WHSRN aimed to achieve the protection of entire flyways. Following a rather similar ontogeny as the other groups, WHSRN showed steep growth and soon developed into an organization with a wider working remit, covering not only shorebirds but whole wetland ecosystems and called Wetlands for the Americas. Not surprisingly, IWRB had broadened its scope too, and was meanwhile rechristened the International Waterfowl and Wetlands Research Bureau. From 1996, the three organizations will join forces as Wetlands International, with the three founding bureaux taking care of, respectively, the African-Eurasian, Australasian and American flyway systems.

The multiplication of politically conscious non-governmental waterbird and wetland organizations brought with it the development, jointly with national governments, of a host of international conventions and agreements aimed at protection of the wetlands of the world and the waders and waterbirds that depend on them and link them. The best known, and most widely signed, is the Ramsar Convention of 1975, but several others have followed. The extent to which these conventions have helped to safeguard scolopacid populations and their habitats is hard to evaluate at present, but their existence has certainly brought the birds into focus as an important aspect of the world's heritage, as

sensitive indicators of the ecological health of wetland ecosystems, and as interesting phenomena in their own right.

The increased efforts in determining the abundance of scolopacids makes it possible to evaluate their fates and fortunes over several different time scales. In North America some shorebird species were much commoner two centuries ago than they are now, the Eskimo Curlew being a clear example. Whimbrels are now on the increase and may gradually be occupying the territory that the smaller curlew has left. Grassland-breeders such as the Upland Sandpiper may have profited initially from the coming of the white man to North America, since the area of open country was increased enormously by the clearing of primeval forests. On the Eurasian scolopacid breeding grounds similar changes are taking place. During this century, Marsh Sandpipers have expanded northwards and eastwards into Siberia, partly in response to forest clearance. In contrast, the Great Snipe has greatly declined in numbers. Around the turn of the century Russian hunters quite often used to bag several hundred per autumn, but by the 1950's and 1960's the maximum bag for a specialized hunter was only 30 Great Snipes per autumn season. The Great Snipe is now rare in European Russia, and further east its range seems to have fragmented, possibly due to drainage and deforestation. Ruff populations declined in European Russia but expanded in the east, possibly as a consequence of better feeding conditions during migration and in winter, since birds began to use the spilled grain and rice in south-eastern Russia and adjacent countries.

In North America and Europe Long-billed and Eurasian Curlews, respectively, are adapting to breed in modern farmland, thereby slightly expanding their ranges. Marbled Godwits, rare through the early part of the century, may have increased in recent decades as a consequence of similar adjustments. In the lowlands of western Europe, several species of scolopacid have benefited from the drainage of marshland and the application of fertilizers. In the Netherlands, populations of the meadow-breeding bird community, including Black-tailed Godwits, Ruffs, Common Redshanks and Common Snipes peaked during the first half of this century. Continued drainage has now led to a decrease in the availability of arthropod food for chicks. Early mowing with fast machinery has also reduced to almost nil the chance of small chicks surviving. Over the last 20 years, the Dutch population of Black-tailed Godwits has declined by a third. Other, even more sensitive species such as the Common Redshank, Common Snipe and Ruff, have decreased by 50-90%; in an international context these declines are less of a tragedy since these species are not confined to the Netherlands.

Given the minor role that humans still play in the polar regions, it is reasonable to suppose that scolopacids breeding on the tundra have not been affected as much by habitat modification. That hunting pressure has recently been the key factor responsible for early declines is suggested by the fact that when viewed over a century, most coastal scolopacids in North America have shown positive population trends. Data collected in the collaborative International and Maritimes Shorebird Surveys in north-eastern North America, however, suggest that the general upward swing in shorebird numbers has now reversed. Significant declines are reported for Least and Semipalmated Sandpipers, Sanderlings, Red Knots, Short-billed Dowitchers and Whimbrels, most of the decreases occurring during the latter part of the 1970's. In Europe, wintering Red Knots showed a steep decline during the same period too, but they have partially recovered since. Other wader species showed variable fortunes, but few show sustained increases. The wintering areas in Mauritania and Guinea-Bissau are numerically very important but have been covered by complete surveys only once or twice around 1980. Partial surveys of the Banc d'Arguin made in the early 1990's suggest that many species have dramatically decreased in number, some by more than half over 10 years. These are very drastic numerical changes in an area that could previously boast of holding a third of all coastal waders wintering along the East Atlantic flyway.

Such dramatic population declines should perhaps not surprise us. Long distance migrating waders in particular have life history characteristics that make them rather susceptible to changes in their

As vulnerable as a wader chick is the status of this highly specialized species, the Spoon-billed Sandpiper. The total population is currently estimated at 2000-2800 pairs, but the main wintering sites remain largely unknown. Its extraordinary spoon-like bill may help in the capture of surface-living arthropods when the species is on its Arctic tundra breeding grounds, and also during prey-detection when foraging in soft mud on the coastal non-breeding areas. This hatchling already shows an incipient version of the characteristic broad, rounded bill.

[Eurynorhynchus pygmeus, Kolyuchinskaya Bay, Chukotskiy Peninsula, Siberia. Photo: Pavel S. Tomkovich]

environments. First of all, their habit of migrating long distances along chains of critical sites brings them together at particular times. At such sites and times they are all at risk at once, a characteristic that violates the basic assumption of conservation biology that being common means being safe. Long distance migration is nutritionally and behaviourally highly demanding and is constrained in time by the seasons, adding to the fragility of the system. A maximum clutch of four eggs is indicative of relatively low reproductive rates and hence a limited capacity to recover from population declines. Finally, for many scolopacid species there is evidence of strong sexual selection pressures. Sustained sexual selection may compromise adaptations with respect to other components of fitness. Thus, sexually dimorphic species may allocate less energy to adaptations that reflect selection pressures arising from interspecific competition, environmental change, and co-evolutionary responses to parasites and prey. Consequently, strongly sexually selected populations may be especially vulnerable to extinction, a factor that could be aggravated in scolopacid populations by the reduced levels of genetic heterogeneity resulting from past population bottlenecks.

These ecological and biological characteristics are played out in a world where scolopacids compete with humans for critical habitats, especially in tropical regions and at temperate staging areas close to large human populations. Worldwide, the application of pesticides in agriculture may interfere with migratory competence. On the oceans an increase in particle pollution may affect fuel deposition in phalaropes: birds do not get fat from eating plastics! The pressure of sport hunting has perhaps slightly decreased over the last 100 years, but can not be discounted as an unimportant factor, especially in view of possible synergisms with other ecological pressures. Apart from adding a mortality factor, hunting clearly lowers the quality of a habitat for waders. Hunting is therefore basically similar to other forms of habitat degradation and habitat loss. The effects that rapid climate change, with its influence on sea-level and weather systems, may have on breeding, staging and wintering habitats and profitable flight routes are far beyond present comprehension. Growing numbers of scientists are involved in the development of theoretical models to investigate and simulate the consequences of habitat changes on migratory populations of waterbirds. Until now, the biological features of scolopacid waders have proved

too complicated to make such exercises a success with respect to prediction, and in their possible role as sentinels for a caring human society. The wonderfully diverse Scolopacidae provide a great vehicle for ecological and biological understanding on vast spatial and temporal scales. They enrich our lives, and the webs of migration that they spin around the world tell us about global connections, global causality and global responsibility.

General Bibliography

Ahlquist (1974b), Alerstam (1990), Alerstam & Högstedt (1980, 1982, 1985), Baker, A.J. & Strauch (1988), Baker, M.C. (1979), Barbosa (1993), Beintema, Moedt & Ellinger (1995), Beintema, Thissen *et al.* (1991), Bergman (1946), Björklund (1994), Boere (1976), Boland (1990), Bolze (1968), Boyd (1962), Burger & Olla (1984), Burton (1974, 1986), Cartar (1985), Castro *et al.* (1992), Christian *et al.* (1992b), Chu (1995), Colwell & Oring (1988c, 1988e, 1990), Cresswell & Whitfield (1994), Davidson & Pienkowski (1987), Davies (1992), Drent & Piersma (1990), Ens, Piersma & Drent (1994), Ens, Piersma, Wolff & Zwarts (1990), Evans (1976, 1979, 1991), Evans & Davidson (1990), Evans & Pienkowski (1984), Evans *et al.* (1984), Gerritsen (1988), Goede (1993), Goss-Custard (1970a, 1977a, 1985, 1993), Goss-Custard *et al.* (1994), Hale (1980, 1985), Harrap & Fisher (1994), Hayman *et al.* (1986), Hötker (1991), Howes & Bakewell (1989), Hunter *et al.* (1991), Jehl (1968b, 1968c), Jehl & Murray (1986), Johnsgard (1981), Jönsson & Alerstam (1990), Kersten & Piersma (1987), Kube (1994), Lange (1968), Lank (1989), Larson (1957), Maclean (1972a, 1972b, 1974), Matthiessen (1994), McNeil *et al.* (1992), Meltofte (1993), Metcalfe (1984a, 1984b), Metcalfe & Furness (1984), Miller (1984, 1992, 1995), Morrison (1977, 1991), Myers (1981b), Nethersole-Thompson & Nethersole-Thompson (1986), Nol (1986), Paulson & Erckmann (1993), Peters (1934), Pettigrew & Frost (1985), Pienkowski & Evans (1985), Pienkowski & Greenwood (1979), Piersma (1987), Piersma & Beukema (1993), Piersma & Ntiamoa-Baidu (1995), Piersma, van Gils *et al.* (1995), Piersma, Koolhaas & Dekinga (1993), Pitelka (1979), Pitelka *et al.* (1974), Prater (1981a, 1981b), Prater *et al.* (1977), Reynolds (1985), van Rhijn (1990), Rosair & Cottridge (1995), Rubega & Obst (1993), Saether *et al.* (1986), Sibley & Ahlquist (1990), Sibley & Monroe (1990), Smit & Piersma (1989), Sordahl (1981), Stawarczyk (1984), Strauch (1976, 1978), Visser & Ricklefs (1993a, 1993b), Vuilleumier *et al.* (1992), Walters, J.R. (1984), Wenink *et al.* (1993, 1994), Whitfield (1987), Zwarts (1974), Zweers (1991).

PLATE 40

inches 5
cm 13

1

2

ssp *saturata*

3

4

5

ssp *rosenbergii*

6

7

ssp *aucklandica*

8

ssp *huegeli*

9

10

11

12

13

14

Subfamily SCOLOPACINAE

Genus *SCOLOPAX* Linnaeus, 1758

1. Eurasian Woodcock

Scolopax rusticola

French: Bécasse des bois **German**: Waldschnepfe **Spanish**: Chocha Perdiz
Other common names: (European) Woodcock

Taxonomy. *Scolopax Rusticola* Linnaeus, 1758, Sweden.
Forms superspecies with *S. mira*, with which often considered conspecific. Traditionally considered rare winter visitor to Philippines, where recorded on Luzon; however, recent work indicates presence of probably new, as yet undescribed, species on Mindanao (see page 448), so occurrence of present species in Philippines probably requires reviewing. Monotypic.
Distribution. Azores, Madeira, Canary Is and British Is through N & C Europe and C Asia to Sakhalin and Japan; also Caucasus, NW China and N India. Winters from W & S Europe and N Africa to SE Asia.

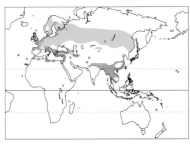

Descriptive notes. 33-35 cm; 144-420 g; wingspan 56-60 cm. Bill long and straight, but relatively shorter than congeners; thick transverse bars on crown, typical for all woodcock species; mainly rufous brown and reddish above providing good camouflage; broad wings, in flight recalling owl. Plumage somewhat variable; individuals with bill half normal length have been recorded in W Europe, especially since 1970, possibly related to pesticide contamination. Differs from very similar, possibly conspecific, *S. mira* in having area of whitish feathering around eye, rather than bare skin; rounder head; dark subterminal band on tail; narrower wings and shorter tarsi. Sexes alike. No seasonal variation. Juvenile very similar to adult, but forehead more spotted.
Habitat. During breeding season occurs in moist forests, where favours mosaic habitats, and extensive woodland covered by undergrowth of scrub, e.g. of brambles, holly, whin or gorse and bracken; avoids warm and dry areas. Often feeds along streams or springs, or in damp and swampy patches. Non-breeding habitat similar to breeding habitat during daytime, but less restricted, e.g. also occupies young conifer plantations; avoids habitat with coppice less than 7, or more than 20, years old, or that which lacks coppice; often gathers for roosting and feeding in earthworm-rich permanent grasslands at night.
Food and Feeding. Mainly animals, with some plant matter. Animals include earthworms, insects and their larvae, particularly beetles, but also earwigs; millipedes, spiders, crustaceans, slugs, leeches and ribbonworms. Plant material comprises seeds, fruits, oats, maize grain and roots and blades of various grasses. Earthworms often dominate diet, but relatively less common on harder soil. Composition of diet and use of habitat may differ between sexes. Feeds by probing in puddles or damp ground, or by pecking at ground surface, or under leaf litter and twigs; may use foot-trembling. Mostly feeds at night, especially outside breeding season, when earthworms taken on pasture land may predominate.
Breeding. Lays from early Mar to mid-Apr, late nests to mid-Jul. Polygynous mating system; male performs self-advertising display flight (roding flight) around dusk and dawn. Nest is a shallow depression in ground concealed by shrubs. Clutch 4 eggs (2-6), laid at interval of 24-48 hours; normally single brood, sometimes two; incubation 22 days (21-24), by female only; chick pale pinkish buff with large, ferruginous brown and chestnut brown blotches and bands above; fledging 15-20 days; female alone cares for young, and occasionally claimed to carry young chicks between feet and belly during flight (see page 475). On average 2·3 hatchlings per nest. Males start roding in 1st year. Annual adult survival 0·39-0·63. Apparently, 9-year cycle exists in numbers of W European wintering birds, peaks coinciding with high proportion of juveniles in population; this might be result of an 8-year cyclical abundance of a major predator or of this predator's main prey.
Movements. Mostly migratory. Fenno-Scandian and some W Russian birds winter in W & S Europe and N Africa; breeding birds of British Is and France mainly resident. Asian breeders winter in Iraq, Iran, Azerbaijan, Afghanistan and India through Indochina to SE China, and occasionally S to Brunei; few records in Luzon (N Philippines) perhaps require reconfirmation. Timing of autumn departure related to onset of frosts (Oct-Nov); return to breeding grounds, Mar to mid-May, also closely related to temperature. Females migrate first, at least in some areas. Both young and parents often return to previous nesting areas. Migrates nocturnally.
Status and Conservation. Not globally threatened. African and European post-breeding population estimated at 15,000,000-37,000,000 birds (1982); 310,000 pairs estimated breeding in Fenno-Scandia (1986); population of Asia unknown. Small increases in NW Europe from 1930 to 1970, probably due to climatic changes and population shift from E to W; however, in Azores and on Madeira populations decreased. From 1970's onwards, substantial decline in large wintering population in France, probably due to excessive hunting on migration and wintering grounds. Up to 3,700,000 individuals hunted annually in Europe, with 1,500,000 in Italy, 1,300,000 in France, 400,000 in W USSR and 200,000 in Britain. No clear trend in European breeding population; numbers wintering in Morocco seem stable since 1950's; numbers declining in several regions of Russia, with 3-6 fold decreases locally during last 10-15 years; formerly occurred in summer in Azerbaijan, presumably breeding, and might still breed there. Increased fragmentation of woodlands might explain decline in some areas in Britain and C & N Europe. Disappearance of permanent grasslands is a threat to wintering birds; in France, this involves 160,000 ha per year. Appearance in recent years of short-billed individuals, which sometimes also show malformations, may be caused by some pesticides having teratogenic effect.
Bibliography. Alexander (1947), Ali & Ripley (1980), Baillie *et al*. (1986), Berlich & Kalchreuter (1983a), Brazil (1991), Burlando *et al*. (1994), Carballo (1995), Clausager (1974), Cramp & Simmons (1983), Creutz (1983), Deignan (1945), Devort (1988), Dickinson *et al*. (1991), Étchécopar & Hüe (1964, 1978), Evans (1994), Fadat (1994a, 1994b, 1995), Ferrand (1983, 1988), Ferrand & Gossmann (1988), Fincher (1985), Fjeldså (1977), Flint *et al*. (1984), Gibbons

et al. (1993), Goodman *et al*. (1989), Gossmann *et al*. (1994), Granval (1988a, 1988b), Granval & Muys (1992), Harradine (1988), Henderson *et al*. (1993), Hirons (1980, 1982, 1983, 1988), Hirons & Bickford-Smith (1983), Hirons & Johnson (1987), Hirons & Linsey (1989), Hoodless (1993, 1994), Hoodless & Coulson (1994), Hüe & Étchécopar (1970), Imbert (1988), Ingram (1978), Kalchreuter (1983), Kiss *et al*. (1988), Knystautas (1993), Kuzyakin (1994), Lucio *et al*. (1994), MacKinnon & Phillipps (1993), Marchant *et al*. (1990), Marcström (1988), Morgan & Shorten (1974), Nyenhuis (1990), Patrikeev (1995), Paz (1987), Piersma (1986b), Potts & Hirons (1983), Puzovic (1994), Ripley (1982), Roberts, T.J. (1991), Rogacheva (1992), Shirihai (1996), Shorten (1974), Smythies (1986), Stronach (1983), Tikhonov & Fokin (1980), Urban *et al*. (1986), Wadsack & Alaoui (1994), Williams, M.D. (1986), Wilson, H.J. (1982), Wilson, J. (1983), Yeatman-Berthelot (1991).

2. Amami Woodcock

Scolopax mira

French: Bécasse d'Amami **German**: Amamischnepfe **Spanish**: Chocha de Amami

Taxonomy. *Scolopax rusticola mira* Hartert, 1916, Amami-O-shima.
Forms superspecies with *S. rusticola*, of which often considered a subspecies. Monotypic.
Distribution. Amami-O-shima, Tokuno-shima, Okinawa and Tokashiki Is (C Ryukyu Is).

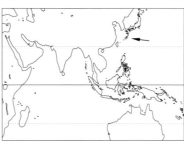

Descriptive notes. 34-36 cm. Plumage variable, can be rather dark, but equally can be paler than *S. rusticola*. Differs from very similar *S. rusticola* by broader wings, longer tarsi, flatter forehead and crown, deeper base of bill and pinkish bare skin around eye (not present in all individuals); generally less rufous brown, more olive brown and more uniform in general coloration, with far fewer contrasting dark and grey areas on wings and mantle; first crown bar slightly narrower than second; lacks dark subterminal band in tail. Sex and seasonal differences and juvenile undescribed.
Habitat. Occupies broadleaf evergreen hill forests; possibly also adjacent fields, including sugar cane plantations, although this might refer to *S. rusticola*.
Food and Feeding. Nothing known of diet. Probes in soft earth and short vegetation on forest floor, along road edges and mud of roadside banks.
Breeding. Laying mid-Mar to early May. No aerial display recorded; single males observed displaying on the ground in vicinity of single females, with quivering, hanging wings and gently bobbing head, uttering strong "gu" calls and softer "ku" calls. 2-4 eggs. No further information available.
Movements. Sedentary.
Status and Conservation. VULNERABLE. No precise information available, but population does not exceed 10,000 individuals. Locally common on Amami, but less numerous on the other islands. In some parts of range, threatened by habitat loss through deforestation; may be hunted locally. Another cause for concern is predation by mongooses, which have been introduced to Amami and Okinawa in order to control poisonous snakes. This seems to have caused population decline already in part of Amami. Census work on species complicated by presence of very similar, easily confusable, *S. rusticola* as winter vistor to the islands.
Bibliography. Austin & Kuroda (1953), Beaman (1994), Brazil (1991), Brazil & Ikenaga (1987), Collar *et al*. (1994), Hachisuka (1952), Perennou *et al*. (1994), Sonobe (1982).

3. Rufous Woodcock

Scolopax saturata

French: Bécasse de Java **German**: Malaienschnepfe **Spanish**: Chocha Oscura
Other common names: Javanese/East Indian/Dusky Woodcock; Horsfield's Woodcock (*saturata*); Rosenberg's Woodcock (*rosenbergii*)

Taxonomy. *Scolopax saturata* Horsfield, 1821, Mount Perahu, Java.
Races sometimes treated as two separate species. Two subspecies recognized.
Subspecies and Distribution.
S. s. saturata Horsfield, 1821 - mountains of N & SC Sumatra and W Java.
S. s. rosenbergii Schlegel, 1871 - mountains of New Guinea.

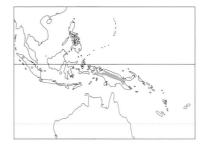

Descriptive notes. 29-31 cm; 220 g (1 female *rosenbergii*). Smallish, rather dark woodcock with long bill; breast and most of belly brownish, chin buff; pale area on upper belly separates from all congeners. Sex and seasonal differences and juvenile undescribed. Race *rosenbergii* normally has more contrasted plumage; has whiter chin and cheeks, usually white spot above lores, much more white on belly and more conspicuous brown barring of underparts.
Habitat. Remnants of montane primary rain forest with moderate or dense understorey, at 1500-3000 m. Not found in secondary forest; often in little patches of forest in alpine grasslands.
Food and Feeding. Two stomach analyses yielded caterpillars and moth pupae. Feeds nocturnally.
Breeding. Breeds during wet season, Feb-Apr, in Java; chicks in mid-May in Sumatra; in E New Guinea roding observed during Aug-Sept. Performs roding display at dawn and dusk, particulary around clearings. Nest consists of a bed of moss in between ferns, slightly raised above forest floor. Probably lays 2 eggs.
Movements. Apparently sedentary.
Status and Conservation. Not globally threatened. No precise information available. Not uncommon in New Guinea, but inconspicuous so infrequently recorded. Surveys required, especially in Sumatra, in order to establish limits of distribution.

On following pages: 4. Sulawesi Woodcock (*Scolopax celebensis*); 5. Moluccan Woodcock (*Scolopax rochussenii*); 6. American Woodcock (*Scolopax minor*); 7. Chatham Snipe (*Coenocorypha pusilla*); 8. Subantarctic Snipe (*Coenocorypha aucklandica*); 9. Jack Snipe (*Lymnocryptes minimus*); 10. Solitary Snipe (*Gallinago solitaria*); 11. Latham's Snipe (*Gallinago hardwickii*); 12. Wood Snipe (*Gallinago nemoricola*); 13. Pintail Snipe (*Gallinago stenura*); 14. Swinhoe's Snipe (*Gallinago megala*).

Bibliography. Andrew, P. (1985b, 1992), Beehler (1978), Beehler *et al.* (1986), Coates (1985), Diamond (1972b), Gregory (1995a), Hellebrekers & Hoogerwerf (1967), MacKinnon (1988), MacKinnon & Phillipps (1993), Majnep & Bulmer (1977), van Marle & Voous (1988), Mayr & Rand (1937), Meyer de Schauensee & Ripley (1940), Perennou *et al.* (1994), Rand (1942), Rand & Gilliard (1967), Ripley (1964).

4. Sulawesi Woodcock

Scolopax celebensis

French: Bécasse des Célèbes **German**: Celebesschnepfe **Spanish**: Chocha de Célebes
Other common names: Celebes/Indonesian Woodcock

Taxonomy. *Scolopax celebensis* Riley, 1921, Rano Rano, Sulawesi.
Forms superspecies with *S. rochussenii*, with which sometimes considered conspecific. Race *heinrichi* proposed for N Sulawesi, based on somewhat smaller bill of only three specimens. Form recently discovered breeding on Mindanao (SE Philippines) might be attributable to present species, but probably constitutes new, as yet undescribed, species (see page 448). Monotypic.
Distribution. NE & C Sulawesi.

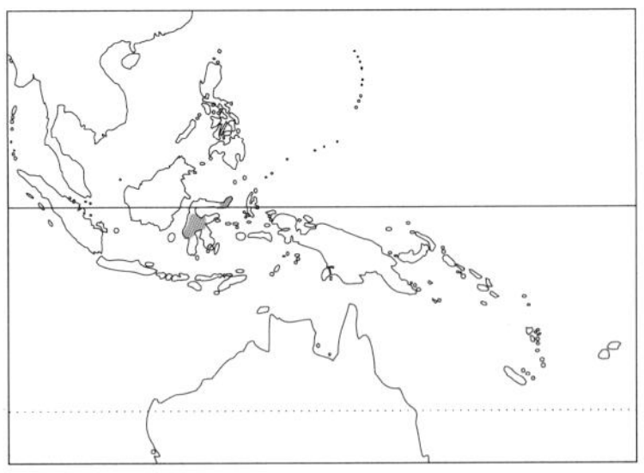

Descriptive notes. 30-35 cm. Large woodcock with shortish, rounded wings; upperparts blackish with red-brown markings; underparts almost unbarred ochre-buff. Pattern somewhat similar to that of *S. rusticola* and *S. mira*, but darker above, with much brighter, almost unbarred underparts; bill and tarsi longer and much darker. Sex and seasonal differences and juvenile undescribed.
Habitat. Dense, mature montane forest at 1100-2500 m; hides in thick undergrowth, running when disturbed; requires some wet, open patches with little undergrowth for foraging.
Food and Feeding. Feeds in wet spots; has been seen in puddles of water in hollows made by wild pigs.
Breeding. No information available.
Movements. Apparently sedentery.
Status and Conservation. Not globally threatened. Currently considered near-threatened. Very poorly known; no precise information available; inconspicuous so infrequently recorded.

Bibliography. Andrew, P. (1992), Collar & Andrew (1988), Collar *et al.* (1994), Perennou *et al.* (1994), Scott (1989), Stresemann (1932, 1941), White & Bruce (1986), Whitten *et al.* (1987).

5. Moluccan Woodcock

Scolopax rochussenii

French: Bécasse des Moluques **German**: Obischnepfe **Spanish**: Chocha Moluqueña
Other common names: Obi/Maluku/Indonesian Woodcock

Taxonomy. *Scolopax Rochussenii* Schlegel, 1866, Obi.
Forms superspecies with *S. celebensis*, with which sometimes considered conspecific. Monotypic.
Distribution. Obi and Bacan (N Moluccas). Also claimed to occur on Ternate and Halmahera, but probably erroneously, due perhaps to inaccurate museum labels and misidentification.

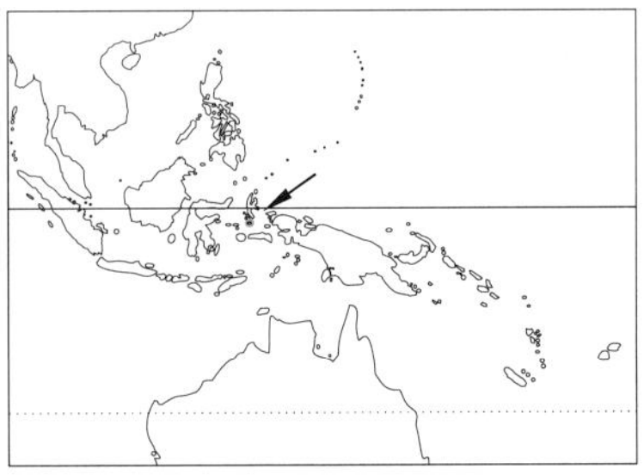

Descriptive notes. 32-40 cm. Largest woodcock, c. 25% bulkier than *S. rusticola*; fairly long, heavy, dark bill; large, contrasting ochre-buff spots on black upperparts; bright ochre-buff underparts with only faint traces of barring. Larger and much brighter than *S. celebensis*; spots on upperparts larger and yellower. Sex and seasonal differences and juvenile undescribed.
Habitat. Apparently a bird of dense, moist montane forest; maximum altitude of Obi is c. 1550 m.
Food and Feeding. No information available.
Breeding. No information available.
Movements. Probably sedentary.
Status and Conservation. VULNERABLE. Last definite record was a specimen collected in 1980; in total, only 8 specimens have been collected, probably all from Obi and Bacan. No birds located during surveys of Obi and Bacan in 1991 and 1992; however, a local guide on Obi was familiar with birds apparently of present species, which he occasionally encountered in forests on ridge tops above c. 500 m during dry periods; birds apparently fairly tame, flushing at very close range and flying only short distances. The areas of hill forest on Obi and Bacan are small, but have official protection.

Bibliography. Andrew, P. (1992), Collar & Andrew (1988), Collar *et al.* (1994), Hartert (1903), Lambert (1994), Perennou *et al.* (1994), White & Bruce (1986).

6. American Woodcock

Scolopax minor

French: Bécasse d'Amérique **German**: Kanadaschnepfe **Spanish**: Chocha Americana

Taxonomy. *Scolopax minor* Gmelin, 1789, New York.
In past sometimes placed in genus *Philohela*. Monotypic.
Distribution. S Manitoba through Ontario and Quebec to New Brunswick and SW Newfoundland, and S through Great Plains and E USA to EC Texas, Gulf states and Florida. Winters in SE USA, on Atlantic and Gulf coastal plains from S Texas to S Florida.
Descriptive notes. 25-31 cm; male 116-219 g, female 151-279 g. Smallest woodcock, with unbarred orange-buff underparts and underwing-coverts; silverly grey "V" along edges of mantle, and another (less obvious in flight) on scapulars; outer three primaries greatly reduced in size, producing broad, square-ended wings in flight. Female slightly larger than male. No seasonal variation. Juvenile very similar; on middle four secondaries, clear pale tips and dark brown subterminal zone.
Habitat. Mixed or deciduous moist woodlands with scattered openings (40% of surface area seems to be minimum). Preferably in young forest and abandoned farmland mixed with forest; often areas with herbaceous ground cover; mainly crepuscular and nocturnal, especially in winter. During non-breeding season occurs in similar habitat, with preference for shrubland, particularly bottomland hardwoods and pine hardwoods; also found in pine uplands and even gardens.

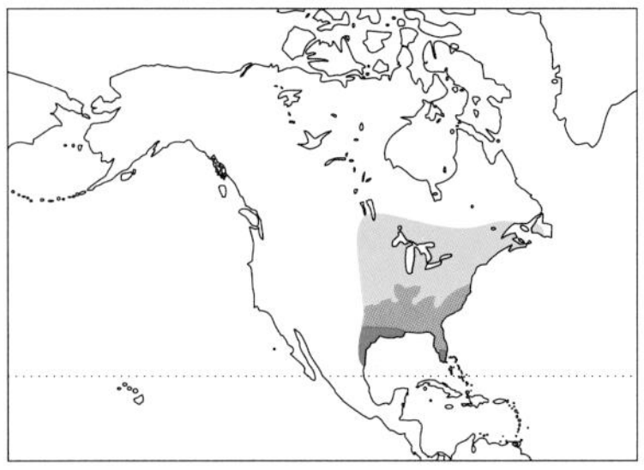

Food and Feeding. Earthworms form 68-86% of diet; when available, also Diptera, beetles, Hymenoptera, Lepidoptera, snails, millipedes, centipedes and spiders; plant material rarely eaten. Variety of diet may increase in early spring due to frost, and in summer if soil moisture low, as earthworms may be unavailable in such conditions. Constant rocking motion during feeding; probes deeply into moist soil or picks from surface; forages in damp fields and marshes in non-breeding season.
Breeding. Lays from Jan (S USA) to late Apr (N USA and Canada). Male performs display flight above bare, open ground, often in forest clearing. Males apparently promiscuous, and take no share in parental care. Nest has rather rudimentary structure and often close to tree, bush or bushy field edge. 4 eggs, sometimes 3; when renesting, unsuccessful females lay 3 eggs (2-4); incubation c. 21 days (20-22); chick pale grey and pale brown, with darker brown markings; young can fly at 14-15 days, nearly fully-grown after 4 weeks; females claimed to carry young chicks between feet and belly during flight (see page 475). Hatching success (considering all nests) 50-89%. Maximum recorded longevity 8 years.
Movements. N breeders migratory, leaving area from Sept to mid-Nov; start and progress of migration considerably influenced by weather; cold fronts appear to prompt heavy flights S; earliest autumn movements precede decrease in food availability. Birds return Jan to mid-Apr. Migrants probably follow coastline in E and broad river valleys in Midwest. Birds from NE USA and most of Canada E of Ontario move into S Atlantic states, from Virginia southward; birds from W of Appalachian Mts and also from Quebec and Ontario probably follow Mississippi R and major tributaries into Gulf states; Gulf states receive migrants from NW, NC & NE of range. S breeders probably mostly sedentary, but some early hatched young might join northward migrations. Vagrant W to Montana and Colorado.
Status and Conservation. Not globally threatened. No population estimate available. At present, c. 2,000,000 birds shot annually by c. 700,000 hunters. In period 1963-1973, no clear trend in population; numbers have declined recently, particularly in E of range. Decline probably due to natural succession and man-induced loss of forest; however, no evidence that overall range has shrunk. Uneven-aged stands, favoured by forest management, do not provide suitable large areas of shrubland and young forest required by species for successful breeding, and this will result in further decline in numbers. Nevertheless, extensive use of N coniferous forests that are being opened up by large-scale timber harvesting suggests that species may be extending distribution northward. Introduced to California, apparently unsuccessfully.

Bibliography. Anon. (1990), Bent (1927-1929), Boggus & Whiting (1982), Bourgeois (1977), Britt (1971), Butts (1994), Causey *et al.* (1987), Connors & Doerr (1982), Coon, Caldwell & Storm (1976), Coon, Dwyer & Artmann (1977), Coon, Williams *et al.* (1982), Couture *et al.* (1993), Cushwa *et al.* (1977), Davis (1970), Derleth & Sepik (1990), Diefenbach *et al.* (1990), Docherty *et al.* (1994), Dunford & Owen (1973), Dwyer & Nichols (1982), Dwyer, Derleth & McAuley (1982), Dwyer, Sepik *et al.* (1988), Dyer (1976), Dyer & Hamilton (1974), Ellingwood *et al.* (1993), Glasgow (1958), Gregory, J.F. (1987), Gutzwiller *et al.* (1983), Haasch (1979), Hervieux (1987), Horton & Causey (1979, 1982), Hounsell (1992), Keppie & Redmond (1985, 1988), Keppie & Whiting (1994), Krementz & Pendleton (1994), Krementz, Seginak & Pendleton (1994), Krementz, Seginak & Smith (1994), Krohn (1970, 1971), Marshall (1982), Matthiessen (1994), McAuley *et al.* (1990, 1993), Miller & Causey (1985), Modafferi (1967), Murphy & Thompson (1993), Nero (1977, 1986), Owen & Galbraith (1989), Owen & Krohn (1973), Owen & Moran (1975), Pace (1980), Pace & Wood (1993), Pitelka (1943), Rabe, Prince & Beaver (1983), Rabe, Prince & Goodman (1983), Redmond (1983), Redmond & Keppie (1988), Reynolds *et al.* (1977), Roberts, T.H. (1980, 1993), Root (1988), Rushing (1980), Samual & Beightol (1973), Sauer & Bortner (1991), Sepik & Derleth (1993a, 1993b), Sepik *et al.* (1993), Sheldon (1967), Shissler (1981), Smith & Barclay (1978), Stamps & Doerr (1977), Straw (1993), Stribling & Doerr (1985), Vander Haegen (1992), Vander Haegen, Krohn & Owen (1993), Vander Haegen, Owen & Krohn (1993, 1994), Weir & Graves (1982), Whiting & Boggus (1982), Williams (1969), Wishart & Bider (1976).

Subfamily GALLINAGININAE

Genus *COENOCORYPHA* G. R. Gray, 1855

7. Chatham Snipe

Coenocorypha pusilla

French: Bécassine des Chatham **German**: Chathamschnepfe **Spanish**: Chochita de las Chatham
Other common names: Chatham Subantarctic Snipe

Taxonomy. *Gallinago pusilla* Buller, 1869, small rocky islet off Chatham Island.
Forms superspecies with *C. aucklandica*, of which sometimes considered a race. Monotypic.
Distribution. Chatham Is, occurring only on islands of Rangatira (South-east), Mangere, Little Mangere and Star Keys.
Descriptive notes. 19-20 cm; 61-110 g, wingspan 28-30 cm. Small, compact, short-legged snipe; creamy white lower breast and belly. Smaller than very similar *C. aucklandica*; paler below even than palest races of latter, with less barring and blotching on underparts; bill smaller and shorter. Female paler and less brightly patterned above. Juvenile has less well defined upperpart markings, greyish legs and base of bill.
Habitat. Mainly in areas with substantial bush cover and remnant forest, especially among *Carex* sedges; less often among damp grasses and mosses in more open habitats.
Food and Feeding. Diet includes earthworms, amphipods, beetles and insect larvae and pupae. Feeds by probing in leaf-mould or moist grassland soils; probes to full length of bill. Most prey swallowed without bill being withdrawn from soil.
Breeding. Laying Sept-Mar. Monogamous. Male probably performs nocturnal drumming display flight and shows courtship feeding. Solitary and territorial; in relatively high densities, up to 5·6 pairs/ha. Nest placed in between sedges or grasses under canopy, preferably *Carex*; nest filled with leaves, or unlined scrape. 2 eggs, sometimes 3; incubation period more than 19 days; sexes share incubation, and

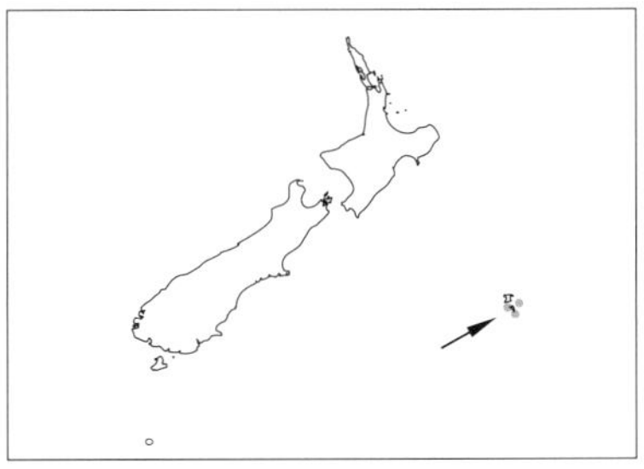

brood divided between parents; chick similar to those of *Gallinago*, but only dimly patterned, with inconspicuous white powder-puff tips; chick develops relatively slowly, and fed entirely by parents for first 2-3 weeks; able to fly after 21 days; independent at c. 41 days. Pair-bond often re-formed after chicks independent. On average, c. 1·7 hatchlings per nest, c. 1·9 per successful nest.

Movements. Sedentary, although inter-island movements within Chatham Is have occurred. All ringing recoveries within 200 m of ringing site.

Status and Conservation. VULNERABLE. Total population estimated at 900-1050 pairs, with Rangatira I holding 700-800 pairs, Mangere I holding 200-250 pairs, and Little Mangere I and Star Keys less than 50 pairs. Population stable but in danger of rapid extinction if island refuges colonized by rats, cats, pigs or Wekas (*Gallirallus australis*), which are all present on nearby islands. Formerly occurred throughout Chatham group, but became confined to Rangatira I when the other populations were exterminated by introduced predators (feral cats on Pitt, Mangere and Little Mangere). Successfully reintroduced to Mangere I in 1970, after feral cats had died out. Scarce on Rangatira I before removal of livestock in 1961, probably as result of loss of ground cover through overgrazing and burning.

Bibliography. Chambers (1989), Collar & Andrew (1988), Collar *et al.* (1994), Falla *et al.* (1981), King (1978/79), Lowe (1915), Marchant & Higgins (1996), Miskelly (1987, 1990a, 1990c), Robertson (1985), Soper (1976), Tuck (1972).

8. Subantarctic Snipe
Coenocorypha aucklandica

French: Bécassine d'Auckland **German**: Aucklandschnepfe **Spanish**: Chochita de las Auckland
Other common names: New Zealand/Auckland Snipe

Taxonomy. *Gallinago aucklandica* G. R. Gray, 1845, Auckland Islands.
Forms superspecies with *C. pusilla*, with which sometimes considered conspecific, especially in past. Race *barrierensis* of Little Barrier I known from single specimen taken in 1870; presumably extinct. Four extant subspecies recognized.

Subspecies and Distribution.
C. a. iredalei Rothschild, 1921 - Little Moggy I, Big South Cape I and other small islands off Stewart I.
C. a. huegeli (Tristram, 1893) - Snares Is (North-east, Broughton and Alert Stack).
C. a. aucklandica (G. R. Gray, 1845) - Auckland Is (Disappointment, Ewing, Adams, Figure of Eight, Rose, Enderby, Ocean and Dundas).
C. a. meinertzhagenae Rothschild, 1927 - Antipodes Is (Antipodes, Bollans, Archway and Inner Windward).

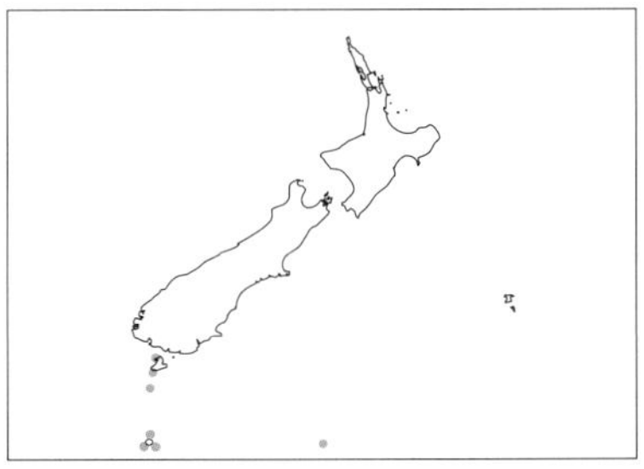

Descriptive notes. 21-24 cm; 82-131 g; wingspan 30-35 cm. Small, compact snipe with very short legs and long, slightly drooping bill. Nominate is largest and palest race, with almost unbarred, pale buff belly, so rather similar to *C. pusilla*, but separated by longer, slightly decurved bill. Female slightly larger than male. Juvenile very similar to adult, but black markings and streaking on upper breast and throat are less distinct. Racial variation considerable: *meinertzhagenae* tends to be darkest, with yellowest underparts; *huegeli* has totally barred underparts; *iredalei* is the most rufous form, with barred flanks and belly and spotted throat. Juvenile *huegeli* greyer above than juvenile nominate, with bill base greyer.

Habitat. Cool temperate and subantarctic islands, occurring in tussock grassland on cliff tops, and in moist open woodlands with mosaic of dense undergrowth, including grass tussocks, mat-forming herbs, sedges and shield ferns; also herb fields and scrubland.

Food and Feeding. Mainly soil-dwelling invertebrates, such as earthworms, amphipods, adult beetles, and larvae and pupae of flies and beetles. Probes soil and bases of tussocks, to full length of bill, evidently feeling for insect movements; rarely pecks prey from surface. Most prey swallowed while probing; only large items are removed from soil and manipulated before swallowing. Diurnally and nocturnally active, feeding in more open areas at night.

Breeding. Based mostly on information from *huegeli*. Lays mid-Aug (*meinertzhagenae*) to Apr. Monogamous (95%), sometimes polygynous. Male performs nocturnal drumming flight and courtship feeding. Solitary in territory; nests at relatively high densities, up to 4 pairs/ha. Nest often under shield ferns; nest is natural depression or bowl in plant detritus. 2 eggs, with laying interval of 3 days; single-brooded, though pairs renest after failure; incubation for pairs 22 days by both parents, but with polygyny 37-39 days for mated female; brood divided between parents; chick similar to those of *Gallinago*, but only dimly patterned, with inconspicuous white powder-puff tips; chick develops relatively slowly, and fed entirely by parents for first 2-3 weeks; able to fly after 30 days; fully independent only after 65 days. Pair-bond often re-formed after chicks independent. Each pair produces c. 0·6 fledglings/year. Adult annual survival 83%; longevity probably exceeds 20 years; oldest ringed bird more than 14 years old.

Movements. Presumably sedentary, even within island groups. Occasional sightings on Enderby, Rose, Ocean and Dundas Is may represent dispersal from Ewing I, 1·7-5 km away, although these islands may all have undiscovered resident populations.

Status and Conservation. Not globally threatened. Currently considered near-threatened. Total population estimated at 34,000 birds, with Auckland Is probably holding more than two thirds of total, mostly on Adams I, Disappointment I and Ewing I; race *aucklandica* numbers c. 25,000 birds, *meinertzhagenae* c. 8000 birds and *heuegeli* c. 1100 birds; no recent information on race *iredalei*. Current populations stable, but in danger of rapid extinction if islands colonized by new predators. One or two subspecies were recently exterminated by feral cats and black rats (*Rattus rattus*): race *barrierensis* only known from single specimen from Little Barrier I, taken in 1870; introduced Wekas (*Gallirallus australis scotti*) probably eliminated population of race *iredalei* on Jacky Lee I. Race *iredalei* formerly bred on at least 9 islands off Stewart I, and may still survive on Big South Cape I, Little Moggy I and some other islands, although definite information lacking. Population of *huegeli*, confined to Snares Is, is so small that risk of extermination if rats introduced is a major concern. Race *meinertzhagenae* is surviving on Antipodes I in presence of introduced house mice (*Mus musculus*).

Bibliography. Anderson (1968), Bell (1975), Chambers (1989), Collar & Andrew (1988), Falla *et al.* (1981), Galbreath & Miskelly (1988), King (1978/79), Marchant & Higgins (1996), Miskelly (1987, 1988, 1989, 1990a, 1990b, 1990c), Robertson (1985), Sibson (1982), Soper (1976), Tuck (1972), Warham & Bell (1979).

Genus *LYMNOCRYPTES* Boie, 1826

9. Jack Snipe
Lymnocryptes minimus

French: Bécassine sourde **German**: Zwergschnepfe **Spanish**: Agachadiza Chica
Other common names: Half-snipe

Taxonomy. *Scolopax minima* Brünnich, 1764, Christiansø Islands, off Bornholm, Denmark.
Monotypic.

Distribution. Subarctic, boreal and sub-boreal zones from NE Scandinavia to E Siberia; isolated populations in S Sweden, N Poland, N Belarus and Baltic states. Winters from British Is S through W Europe and Mediterranean to N Afrotropics, and E through Asia Minor, N Middle East, Azerbaijan, Iran, Afghanistan and India to S China and Vietnam.

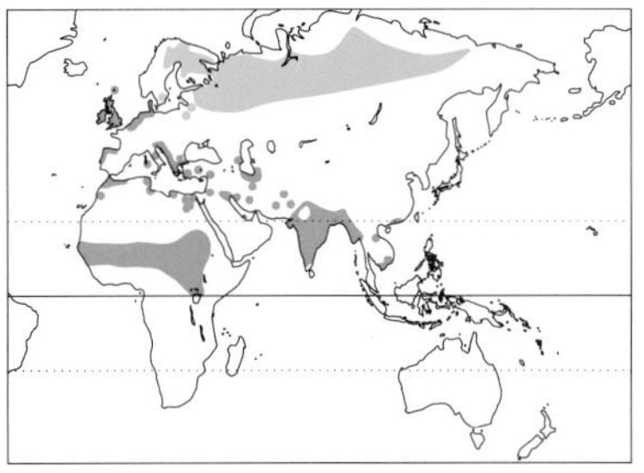

Descriptive notes. 17-19 cm; 28-106 g; wingspan 38-42 cm. Smallest snipe; large head, relatively short bill; narrow wings with white trailing edge. Differs from all other snipes by wedge-shaped tail, which lacks white; also lacks central stripe on crown and has purple and green gloss on black upperparts. Sexes alike. Juvenile very similar to adult, but has white undertail-coverts with smaller and paler brown stripes.

Habitat. Breeds in open marshes, floodplains and bogs, in forest tundra and northern taiga. In winter, found in various brackish and freshwater habitats, often a mosaic of moist and waterlogged mudflats with tussocks of vegetation; prefers soft silty mud. During cold spells often along margins of rivers, streams and inland spring-fed meadows.

Food and Feeding. Diet includes adult and larval insects, annelids, small freshwater and terrestrial gastropods and sometimes seeds. Moves body rhythmically up and down when probing in mud; also pecks prey items from surface. Chiefly nocturnal or crepuscular. Usually feeds singly, sometimes in groups of up to c. 5 birds.

Breeding. Nests May to early Sept. Probably monogamous; male performs switchback display flight, typically at dawn and dusk, but sometimes throughout day. Nest often on floating bogs, but sometimes on drier ground among bushes; lined with pieces of grass or leaves. 4 eggs, sometimes 3; possibly double-brooded; incubation at least 21-24 days; chick mahogany red, slightly paler below, with black and white bands on face and black areas with small white down tips on crown, nape, wing-pads and upperparts; brood care apparently only by female. No further information available.

Movements. Migratory. Both adults and young remain in, or close to, breeding area during moult, Aug-Sept. SW movements over broad front across Europe from mid-Sept to mid-Nov, with arrival in non-breeding areas from Oct onwards, in tropics mainly from Nov. Migrates across C Russia Sept-Oct; reaches Egypt in Oct-Nov and India in Oct; sometimes winters in Iceland. High degree of site fidelity to staging areas. Birds wintering in Asia and E Africa originate from Siberia; uncommon migrant in Azerbaijan, but small numbers overwinter. Departs from wintering grounds Mar to mid-Apr; returns to breeding grounds mid-Apr to mid-May, up to end May in Siberia.

Status and Conservation. Not globally threatened. European breeding population may number several 100,000's of birds; estimated 28,000 pairs in Finland and Sweden (1986); up to 10,000 birds may winter in Sudan; sizes of Russian breeding and Asian wintering populations not known, but species apparently fairly common in parts of S Asia. Due to substantial loss and degradation of wetlands, breeding population believed to have declined during 19th and 20th centuries; although breeding population may now have stabilized, wintering population in Denmark and Britain declined between 1970 and 1990; now up to 100,000 winter in Britain and Ireland. Major threats are wetland drainage for agricultural intensification, afforestation and peat extraction. Hunting is another reason for concern: during autumn migration, 5% of European population is believed to be shot. Apparently rather rare in Russia, particularly E of Urals.

Bibliography. Ali & Ripley (1980), Beere (1981), Bochenski & Tomek (1991), Boyd (1956), Brazil (1991), Bruster (1990), Cramp & Simmons (1983), Devort (1993), Dowsett & Forbes-Watson (1993), Étchécopar & Hüe (1964, 1978), Evans (1994), Fearnside (1990), Fjeldså (1977), Flint *et al.* (1984), Glutz von Blotzheim *et al.* (1977), Goodman *et al.* (1989), Hermenau & Pannach (1993), Hollyer (1984), Hüe & Étchécopar (1970), Kliebe (1974), Knystautas (1993), Kozlova (1961a), Mackworth-Praed & Grant (1957, 1962, 1970), Massoli-Novelli (1988b), Mjelstad & Saetersdal (1986), Nilsson & Nilsson (1978), Okulewicz & Witkowski (1979), Paz (1987), Pedersen (1989a, 1989b, 1990, 1991, 1992, 1994, 1995), Perennou *et al.* (1994), Phillips (1978), Piersma (1986b), Prys-Jones & Wilson (1986), Ripley (1982), Roberts, T.J. (1991), Rogacheva (1992), Sack (1961), Schönn & Schiller (1979), Shirihai (1996), Short *et al.* (1990), Smythies (1986), Sutton (1981), Taylor, P.B. (1988), Urban *et al.* (1986), Veiga (1985, 1988), Zonfrillo (1981).

Genus *GALLINAGO* Brisson, 1760

10. Solitary Snipe
Gallinago solitaria

French: Bécassine solitaire **German**: Einsiedlerbekassine **Spanish**: Agachadiza Solitaria
Other common names: Tibet/Hermit Snipe

Taxonomy. *Gallinago solitaria* Hodgson, 1831, Nepal.
Genus formerly named *Capella*, as this name erroneously considered to pre-date *Gallinago* (see page 446). Validity of races uncertain. Two subspecies normally recognized.

Subspecies and Distribution.
G. s. solitaria Hodgson, 1831 - high mountains of C Asia, from SC Siberia through Altai, Tien Shan and Pamirs to Himalayas and probably S Tibet; winters S to E Pakistan and N India, and E to Myanmar.
G. s. japonica (Bonaparte, 1856) - mountains of Sakhalin and NE China (Heilongjiang), and probably also from Stanovoy Mts through Dzhugdzhur and Kolymskiy Mts to Kamchatka, and S to Sikhote Alin; winters from Amurland and Sakhalin to Kamchatka, and in Korea, Japan and E China.

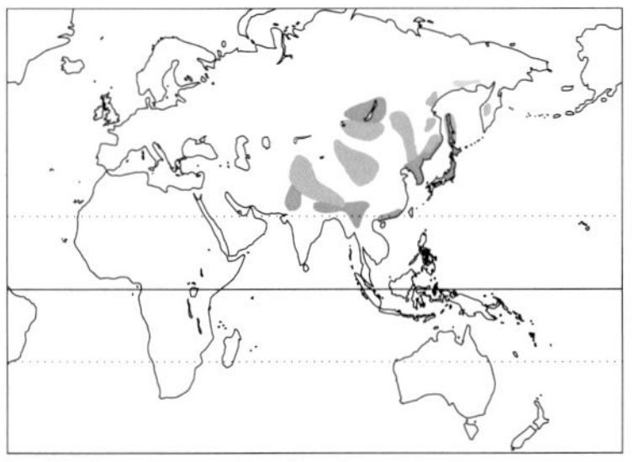

Descriptive notes. 29-31 cm; 126-227 g; wingspan 51-56 cm. Largest of Palearctic snipes, except for *G. nemoricola*; large and heavy, with rather long bill; typically with distinctive gingery brown breast and vermiculated upperparts, although plumage somewhat variable; head greyish white; crown stripe thin, sometimes broken; white fringes to mantle and scapulars; long wings, tertials and tail; prominent chestnut on tail. Female slightly larger than male. No seasonal variation. Juvenile very similar to adult. Race *japonica* may have more red and less white on upperparts.
Habitat. Almost exclusively found at high altitudes, 1500-5000 m, well above tree-line; river valleys, grassy swamps and mountain bogs, often near running water. Outside breeding season, occurs at lower altitudes in similar habitat, at unfrozen water bodies in foothills and adjoining plains, along mountain streams, in paddyfields and marshes, and even on coast.
Food and Feeding. Diet includes small snails, worms, beetles, insect larvae, flies. Feeds by probing in wet grass and mud. Whole body bobs up and down while feeding. Feeds solitarily.
Breeding. Breeds late Jun to Aug. Nest is a well concealed depression in shrubs, sparsely surrounded or lined with dead rushes, grass or moss. 4 eggs. No further information available.
Movements. Partial migrant; generally flies only short distances. Some birds essentially sedentary, being driven to lower altitudes by cold spells. Others migratory, wintering S to foothills of Himalayas, in N India and Pakistan, and also sometimes in NE Iran; E birds winter S to Korea, Japan and E China.
Status and Conservation. Not globally threatened. Included in Russian Red Data Book, in category "insufficiently studied species". Numbers generally appear to be low, and species only locally common in SC Siberia. Less than 10,000 birds winter in Japan; rather scarce in S & E Asia; in 1992, total of 74 birds counted in Assam (NE India), and 82 birds counted in China. Occupation of bleak, high altitude habitats in extensive, but rather poorly studied, zones suggests species may be relatively secure at present.
Bibliography. Ali & Ripley (1980), Brazil (1991), Dementiev & Gladkov (1951b), Étchécopar & Hüe (1978), Flint *et al.* (1984), Hollom *et al.* (1988), Hüe & Étchécopar (1970), Inskipp & Inskipp (1991), Irisov (1976), Knystautas (1993), Kozlova (1961a), Lobkov (1989), Meyer de Schauensee (1984), Perennou *et al.* (1994), Ripley (1982), Roberts, T.J. (1991), Rogacheva (1992), Scott (1989), Shcherbakov (1980), Smetanin & Belikovich (1987), Smythies (1986), Sutton (1981), Tuck (1972), Vinokurov (1976a), Zubarovskij (1976).

11. Latham's Snipe

Gallinago hardwickii

French: Bécassine du Japon **German**: Japanbekassine **Spanish**: Agachadiza Japonesa
Other common names: Japanese/Australian Snipe

Taxonomy. *Scolopax Hardwickii* J. E. Gray, 1831, Tasmania.
Genus formerly named *Capella*, as this name erroneously considered to pre-date *Gallinago* (see page 446). Monotypic.
Distribution. E Primorskiy, S Sakhalin and S Kuril Is S to Hokkaido and N & C Honshu, and possibly Kyushu (S Japan). Winters in E Australia and Tasmania; perhaps also small numbers in New Guinea.

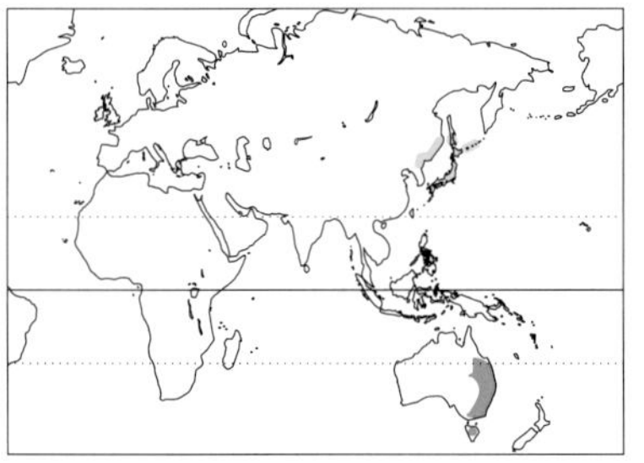

Descriptive notes. 23-33 cm; 95-277 g; wingspan 48-54 cm. Extremely similar to *G. megala* and *G. stenura*, but larger, with proportionately long tail and wings forming smoothly attenuated rear end at rest; in flight, toes do not project beyond tip of tail; differs in primary-tail and primary-tertials projections; only 18 tail feathers, as opposed to 20-22 in *G. megala*, and 26 in *G. stenura*; outer tail feathers fairly broad; structure and colour of tail feathers not visible in field. Differs from *G. gallinago* and *G. paraguaiae* by supercilium broader than eyestripe and crown stripe at base of bill; pale panel across median upperwing-coverts, evident in flight, with white trailing edge virtually absent. Sexes similar. No seasonal variation. Juvenile has pale buff, not brown-buff, fringed wing-coverts; primaries with clearer white fringes.
Habitat. Breeding habitat consists of farmland, such as meadows, pastures, fallow fields, and areas of firing and reafforestation, from coast up to 1400 m; also natural grassland, hillock bogs, river valleys with low herbaceous cover. Outside breeding season, found in variety of permanent or ephemeral freshwater wetlands, generally with dense cover, including meadows, bogs, swamps, edges of creeks and rivers, flooded areas and rice paddies. On migration, rarely on beaches and other saline or brackish habitats.
Food and Feeding. Mainly earthworms, also beetles, cranefly larvae and pupae, spiders and freshly fallen seeds; occasionally molluscs, centipedes and isopods. Diet varies with locality and month. Feeds by probing bill into soft soil. Occurs singly or in small loose groups; mainly crepuscular.
Breeding. Laying May to early Jun. Courtship flights performed alone or in groups of 4-7 birds. Nests in scattered, single pairs. Nest is shallow depression filled with stems and leaves, placed against tussock or under bush, in dry site near bog; rarely on hillock close to water. 4 eggs (2-5); single brood; apparently only female incubates.
Movements. Strongly migratory. Migration route is still a mystery; presumably flies from Japan to E Australia in few days, non-stop or stopping only at few staging sites, e.g. New Guinea and N Australia. Leaves breeding grounds late Jul to early Aug, concentrating in wet lowlands, then departing Sept to early Oct; arrival in Australia from late Jul to Oct. Erratic movements in non-breeding quarters, probably in response to rainfall and food availability. S Australia vacated in late Feb, and birds move gradually to N Australia; Japan reached early Apr to May, Primorskiy late Apr to mid-May, Sakhalin from late Apr. Fair numbers visit New Guinea, but few, if any, overwinter; species rarely spends N winter in NW Australia; vagrant in New Zealand. Most first-year birds put on fat in winter quarters, and migrate N. Species said to move at night; weather might influence timing and use of stopover sites.
Status and Conservation. Not globally threatened. Currently considered near-threatened. Total population c. 36,000 birds; estimated 27,400 birds breed on Hokkaido (1985), over 500 pairs on Sakhalin (1989); non-breeding population in Victoria, South Australia and Tasmania estimated at 15,000 birds, but hard to assess; small numbers may winter in New Guinea. During 1950's and 1960's, species expanded range from Japan to Sakhalin and Primorskiy, perhaps filling new niches in anthropogenic landscape; range in Primorskiy has recently expanded further. Adversely affected by drainage, modification of wetlands or creation of less suitable artificial wetlands, e.g. farm dams and hydro-electric impoundments; also sensitive to disturbance by humans and grazing cattle, although sometimes inhabits wetlands prone to disturbance, e.g. near factories, along roads, airfields, railways and school grounds. Industrialization in Japan gives cause for concern. Declined in Tasmania, coastal and N New South Wales and Victoria in early 1900's, 1930's, 1960's and 1970's; decline also noted in Japan during present century. Formerly shot in most Australian states, with up to 10,000 birds killed annually; in Japan c. 2,000 were killed each year; no hunting in Japan since 1974; after termination of hunting in Victoria (1984) and Tasmania (1983), slight, but not significant, increase recorded; moratorium on snipe shooting now in force throughout Australia.
Bibliography. Austin & Kuroda (1953), Baker *et al.* (1986), Beehler *et al.* (1986), Blakers *et al.* (1984), Brazil (1991), Bywater & McKean (1987), Coates (1985), Elsukov & Labzyuk (1981), Endo & Hirano (1986), Étchécopar & Hüe (1978), Frith *et al.* (1977), Fujimaki (1994), Fujimaki & Skira (1984), Garnett (1993), Hoogerwerf (1964), Iida (1991), Knystautas (1993), Lane, B.A. & Davies (1987), Lane, B.A. & Forest (1984), Lane, S.G. (1978), Leach & Hines (1992), Lida (1991), Marchant & Higgins (1996), Miskelly *et al.* (1985), Murobushi (1986), Naarding (1986), Nakamura & Shigemori (1990), Nechaev (1994), Nitta & Fujimaki (1985), Ohata (1988), Pook (1992), Scott (1989), Sutton (1981), Tuck (1972), Wolfe (1954).

12. Wood Snipe

Gallinago nemoricola

French: Bécassine des bois **German**: Nepalbekassine **Spanish**: Agachadiza del Himalaya
Other common names: Himalayan Snipe

Taxonomy. *Gallinago nemoricola* Hodgson, 1836, Nepal.
Genus formerly named *Capella*, as this name erroneously considered to pre-date *Gallinago* (see page 446). Monotypic.
Distribution. Himalayas, from NW India (Himachal Pradesh) through S & E Tibet, Nepal, Bhutan and NE India (Arunachal Pradesh and extreme NE Assam) to N Myanmar and probably SC China (W Sichuan); possibly also Pakistan. Winters in India, Bangladesh, Myanmar, N Laos, N Vietnam and rarely N Thailand.

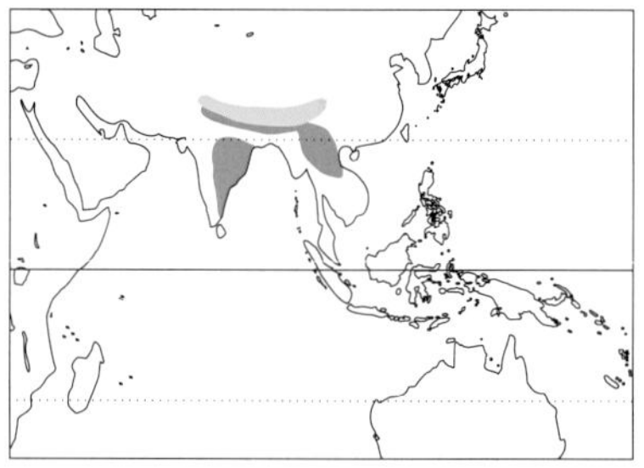

Descriptive notes. 28-32 cm; 142-198 g. Large, dark, woodcock-like snipe with broad, rounded wings and barred underparts, extending to belly; plumage somewhat variable; narrow pale crown stripe and blackish upperparts with dull buff-grey fringes; bill broad at base. Juvenile very similar to adult but has narrower fringes to feathers of mantle and scapulars, giving scaly appearance.
Habitat. Woodlands and dense tall herbage, especially at relatively high altitude around tree-line, at 1200-4000 m. In China, breeds in alpine meadows with scattered bushes and a few streams, and in dwarf scrub in barren, boulder-strewn areas, at 3000-5000 m. After breeding, occurs at lower altitudes, usually in densely vegetated marshes or swamps, and along streams, under waist-high grass and scrubs.
Food and Feeding. Poorly known. Worms, small aquatic insects and their larvae and seeds. Usually feeds singly.
Breeding. Virtually unknown. Lays Jun. Male performs aerial drumming display.
Movements. Probably partly sedentary, although many birds move down to lower altitudes after breeding season. Some are migratory and winter to S in hill ranges of India; only rather occasionally recorded in Indochina; vagrant to Singapore and Sri Lanka.
Status and Conservation. VULNERABLE. One of least known of all snipes; believed to be very rare, with total population probably not more than 10,000 birds. Population declining locally in Nepal; since breeding habitat seems to be secure, this decline is thought to be caused by loss of wintering habitat. Might occur in Pakistan, but only single dubious record from 1887.
Bibliography. Ali & Ripley (1980), Buckton & Morris (1993), Clive (1928), Collar & Andrew (1988), Collar *et al.* (1994), Deignan (1945), Étchécopar & Hüe (1978), Hackney (1940), Inskipp & Inskipp (1991), King *et al.* (1975), Lekagul & Round (1991), Meyer de Schauensee (1984), Perennou *et al.* (1994), Phillips (1978), Phythian-Adams (1934), Ripley (1982), Roberts, T.J. (1991), Smythies (1986), Suter (1950), Sutton (1981), Tuck (1972).

13. Pintail Snipe

Gallinago stenura

French: Bécassine à queue pointue **German**: Spießbekassine **Spanish**: Agachadiza Colirrara
Other common names: Pin-tailed/Asiatic Snipe

Taxonomy. *Scolopax stenura* Bonaparte, 1830, Sunda Islands.
Genus formerly named *Capella*, as this name erroneously considered to pre-date *Gallinago* (see page 446). Monotypic.
Distribution. NC & E Russia, from Ural Mts through Siberia and Transbaikalia to Sea of Okhotsk. Winters from Indian Subcontinent and Maldives through Indochina to SE China and Taiwan, and S to Philippines and W Indonesia; also found irregularly in small numbers in Saudi Arabia, E Africa and Aldabra Is.
Descriptive notes. 25-27 cm; 84-170 g; wingspan 44-47 cm. Medium-sized snipe, very similar to *G. hardwickii* and *G. megala* but primaries normally only just longer than tertials, and tail projects only slightly beyond primaries; wing-coverts have brown-buff spots at tip; has short tail, with distinctive pin-shaped outer tail feathers, not usually visible in the field; in flight, toes project beyong tail tip notably more than in *G. megala*. Differs from *G. gallinago* and *G. paraguaiae* by supercilium broader than eyestripe and crown stripe at base of bill; pale panel across median upperwing-coverts, evident in flight, with white trailing edge virtually absent. Female very similar to male, but bill averages slightly longer. No seasonal variation. Juvenile very similar to adult, but with pale buff fringes on wing-coverts and narrower fringes on upperparts.
Habitat. During and outside breeding season occurs in slightly drier areas than those favoured by *G. gallinago*. Breeds in Arctic and boreal wetlands, damp meadows and shrub tundra with patches

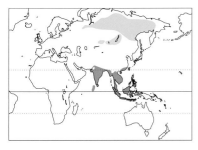

of dwarf birch (*Betula nana*); up to 2500 m, along tree-line. Reports of species in grassy swamps and sphagnum bogs possibly erroneous, referring to *G. gallinago*. After breeding, found in wide variety of wetland habitats, e.g. flooded paddyfields, wet grassland, seepage swamps and marshland. Often feeds on muddy shorelines and stream banks.

Food and Feeding. Diet includes molluscs, insects and their larvae, earthworms, occasionally crustaceans, seeds and other plant matter. Feeds by probing in soft ground, or pecking from surface. Crepuscular, nocturnal and, when undisturbed, diurnal.

Breeding. Lays late May to mid-Jun. Presumably monogamous. Dazzling communal aerial display (called "tok"), in which flock of up to 15 males suddenly plunges sideways, or each male glides and falls downwards, turning from side to side, whilst uttering frequent cries and producing sounds with modified tail feathers. Densities highly variable, locally up to 0·34 birds/ha, especially in forest clearcuts. Nest is shallow depression lined with vegetation, usually well concealed by dense cover. 4 eggs, sometimes 3, laid at intervals of 24 hours; single brood; incubation 20 days; role of sexes in incubation and brood care unclear; chick yellowish brown or dark brown with white or pale buff-tipped down; independent after 2 months.

Movements. Migratory. Moves overland in broad front; crosses Pakistan and Iran, C Asia, Mongolia, Tibet, N China, NE Bo Hai (Gulf of Chihli), Hong Kong and Taiwan; birds in W breeding range cross Himalayas to India; common on passage in Borneo (spring and autumn); uncommonly recorded in Korea. Arrives in winter quarters late Aug to Oct, and remains till Mar to early May. Many birds winter in S & NE Indian Subcontinent. Probably also some movement over Middle East and across Indian Ocean towards E Africa (Kenya), where species occurs in small numbers at least in some years; recently reported from Benin and Gabon. Migrates in small flocks of 5-10 birds.

Status and Conservation. Not globally threatened. Number in wintering grounds in Indian Subcontinent in order of 25,000-1,000,000 birds, and similar numbers in E & SE Asia. On Russian breeding grounds fairly rare, though actual population size hard to assess. At favourable breeding sites density generally high. Anthropogenic forest changes, especially creation of forest clear-cuts, lead to increase in numbers and range; breeding range expanding slightly westwards. Commonest snipe in zone from India through Indochina to Sumatra. Subject to some hunting pressure.

Bibliography. Ali & Ripley (1980), Baccetti (1987), Backhurst (1969), Berman & Kuz'min (1965), Brazil (1991), Bundy (1983), Byrkjedal (1990), Cramp & Simmons (1983), Deignan (1945), Dementiev & Gladkov (1951b), Dickinson *et al*. (1991), Étchécopar & Hüe (1978), Flint *et al*. (1984), Hirschfeld (1992), Hüe & Étchécopar (1970), Jaensch (1990), Knystautas (1993), Kozlova (1961a), Lekagul & Round (1991), MacKinnon & Phillipps (1993), Madge (1977), Madoc (1976), Malkov *et al*. (1983), van Marle & Voous (1988), Medway & Wells (1976), Meissner & Skakuj (1988), Morozov (1993b), Olsson (1987), Pearson (1984b), Perennou *et al*. (1994), Phillips (1978), Prys-Jones & Wilson (1986), Ripley (1982), Roberts, T.J. (1991), Rogacheva (1992), Scott (1989), Shcherbakov (1979), Shirihai (1988), Short *et al*. (1990), Smythies (1981, 1986), Sutton (1981), Taylor, P.B. (1984b, 1988), Tuck (1972), Urban *et al*. (1986), White & Bruce (1986), Williams, M.D. (1986).

14. Swinhoe's Snipe

Gallinago megala

French: Bécassine de Swinhoe　　**German**: Waldbekassine　　**Spanish**: Agachadiza del Baikal
Other common names: Chinese/Forest/Marsh Snipe

Taxonomy. *Gallinago megala* Swinhoe, 1861, between Takoo and Beijing, north China.

Genus formerly named *Capella*, as this name erroneously considered to pre-date *Gallinago* (see page 446). Monotypic.

Distribution. CS Siberia and N Mongolia; Amurland and Ussuriland. Winters from S & E India to E & S China and Taiwan, and S through Malay Peninsula, Philippines and Indonesia to New Guinea and N Australia.

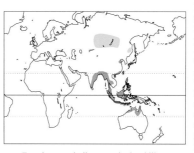

Descriptive notes. 27-29 cm; 82-164 g; wingspan 38-44 cm. Medium-sized snipe, very similar to *G. stenura* and *G. hardwickii*; primaries project beyond tertials slightly more than in *G. stenura*; tail projects beyond primaries slightly more than in *G. stenura*, but less than in *G. hardwickii*; paired buffish white spots on tips of upperwing-coverts more clearly marked than in the other two species; in flight, toes project only slightly beyond tail tip. Differs from *G. gallinago* and *G. paraguaiae* by supercilium broader than eyestripe and crown stripe at base of bill; pale panel across median upperwing-coverts, evident in flight, with white trailing edge virtually absent. Female very similar to male, but bill averages slightly longer. No seasonal variation. Juvenile very like adult, but wing-coverts and tertials narrowly fringed whitish buff; tertials have buff barring.

Habitat. In, or at margins of, deciduous or mixed open woodland, river valleys, and grassy localities near marshes and streams; usually favours drier and more enclosed sites than *G. gallinago*; sometimes on alpine meadows at tree-line. During non-breeding period, found at edges of wetlands, including marshy areas, paddyfields, sewage farms and freshwater streams. Often feeds among hummocks or on mudflats around seepage areas.

Food and Feeding. Diet includes earthworms, glow-worms, adult and larval insects, such as beetles and ants, terrestrial gastropods and seeds. Crepuscular and nocturnal; mainly solitary.

Breeding. Laying May-Jul. Monogamous. Flight display usually solitary, but can apparently be performed by flock, flying in large circles above forest. Scattered solitary pairs at highly variable densities, 2-63 pairs/km²; highest concentrations in industrial clear-cuts in boreal mountain forests. Nest placed among bushes, in meadows, often on slight elevations; simple scrape, sparsely lined with grass. Usually 4 eggs (2-5); single brood; males do not participate in incubation; chick overall tawny chestnut with white-tipped down on back and sides of head; male probably shares in care of chicks; fledging 18-20 days.

Movements. Strongly migratory. Post-breeding movement through Russia chiefly towards SE, then apparently via E Mongolia, China (late Jul to Aug), Taiwan and Philippines, occasionally through Japan, rarely Korea; present in Australia mainly Nov-Feb, late birds up to mid-Apr. Birds moving N from Philippines may follow coast of China from early Mar, until they move inland near Bo Hai (Gulf of Chihli).

Status and Conservation. Not globally threatened. Status uncertain due to confusion with other extremely similar species and secretive behaviour; total population probably numbers 25,000-100,000 birds. In 1992, total of 146 birds counted wintering in China; uncommon but regular visitor to India and Pakistan; in some seasons very abundant in rice fields in Philippines. At beginning of 20th century, considered extremely abundant in forest-steppe and sub-taiga areas of C Siberia; nowadays, species is locally distributed in this area, and has become rare in forest-steppe zones; still rather numerous in sub-taiga zone.

Bibliography. Abdulali (1970), Ali & Ripley (1980), Beehler *et al*. (1986), Blakers *et al*. (1984), Brazil (1991), Coates (1985), Dementiev & Gladkov (1951b), Dickinson *et al*. (1991), Étchécopar & Hüe (1978), Ey (1984), Flint *et al*. (1984), Hoogerwerf (1964), Knystautas (1993), Königstedt (1986), Kozlova (1961a), MacKinnon & Phillipps (1993), Madge (1989a, 1989b), Madoc (1976), Marchant & Higgins (1996), Medway & Wells (1976), Meissner & Skakuj (1988), Meyer de Schauensee (1984), Naumov (1962), Perennou *et al*. (1994), Poslavsky & Sokolov (1980), Prys-Jones & Wilson (1986), Rabor (1977), Ripley (1982), Rogacheva (1992), Scott (1989), Smythies (1981, 1986), Sutton (1981), Tuck (1972), Wallace (1989), White & Bruce (1986).

15

16

17

ssp *gallinago*

18

ssp *delicata*

ssp *paraguaiae*

19

ssp *magellanica*

ssp *andina*

20

21

22

23

24

25

ssp *griseus*

ssp *hendersoni*

26

27

♂

♀

PLATE 41

inches   5

cm   13

15. **African Snipe**

Gallinago nigripennis

French: Bécassine africaine **German**: Afrikanische Bekassine **Spanish**: Agachadiza Africana
Other common names: Ethiopian Snipe

Taxonomy. *Gallinago nigripennis* Bonaparte, 1839, Cape of Good Hope.
Genus formerly named *Capella*, as this name erroneously considered to pre-date *Gallinago* (see page 446). May form superspecies with *G. gallinago* and *G. paraguaiae*, and all three sometimes treated as conspecific. Species sometimes considered monotypic. Three subspecies recognized.
Subspecies and Distribution.
G. n. aequatorialis Rüppell, 1845 - Ethiopia through Uganda, E Zaire, Kenya and Tanzania to Malawi, E Zimbabwe and N Mozambique.
G. n. angolensis Bocage, 1868 - Angola and Namibia through Botswana to Zambia and W Zimbabwe.
G. n. nigripennis Bonaparte, 1839 - S Mozambique and South Africa.

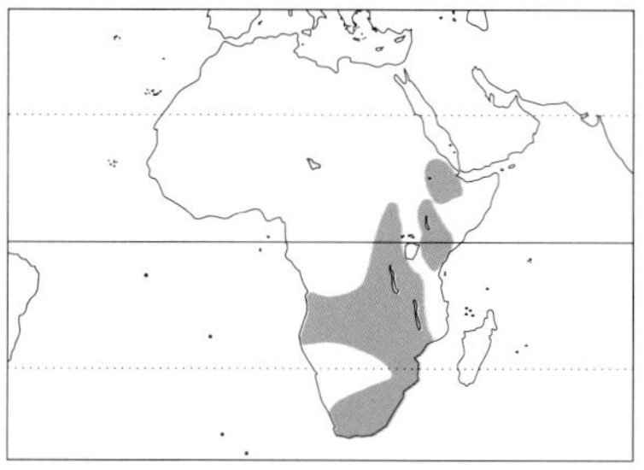

Descriptive notes. 25-29 cm; 93-164 g. Resembles *G. gallinago* and other close relatives, but larger, and has darker upperparts contrasting with white belly; bill often longer; white trailing edge to wing; more white on outer tail feathers, noticeable in flight. Female very similar to male, but bill averages slightly longer. No seasonal variation. Juvenile has mantle, scapulars and wing-coverts more narrowly fringed. Races rather similar: *aequatorialis* somewhat blacker above; *angolensis* averages longer-billed.
Habitat. Breeds in highland bogs, swampy lake edges and ditches, seasonally flooded grassland and wet moorland; in Ethiopia and E Africa occurs at altitudes above 1500 m, occasionally up to 4000 m; during breeding season typically at 1800-2700 m. After breeding, found at lower altitudes, even down to coastal lowlands. Feeds in muddy areas with scattered low vegetation.
Food and Feeding. Mainly larvae of beetles, dragonflies, and flies, annelids, small crustaceans and molluscs, sometimes seeds. Chiefly crepuscular or nocturnal feeder, usually in small numbers and somewhat scattered groups.
Breeding. In tropics, laying irregular, Mar-Nov, during or just after rains; in S Africa, mainly Apr and Jun-Oct. Monogamous. Solitary, or several pairs clustered. Nest is pad of grass leaves, hidden in tussock, surrounded by flooded or moist ground. 2-3 eggs; chick has rich tawny down. No further information available.
Movements. No regular migration, but may move erratically several hundred kilometres from nesting grounds, often associated with drying of temporary floods. In E Africa, descends somewhat from higher areas after breeding.
Status and Conservation. Not globally threatened. Limits of breeding range very poorly known. Locally common (e.g. in South Africa) to abundant, but, like most snipes, true status hard to judge; no population estimates available.
Bibliography. Benson & Benson (1975), Britton, P.L. (1980), Brown & Britton (1980), Clancey (1967), Dowsett & Dowsett-Lemaire (1980, 1993), Dowsett & Forbes-Watson (1993), Ginn *et al.* (1989), Hockey & Douie (1995), Lippens & Wille (1976), Mackworth-Praed & Grant (1957, 1962, 1970), Maclean (1993), van Perlo (1995), Pinto (1983), Pirow (1981), Short *et al.* (1990), Sinclair & Davidson (1995), Sinclair *et al.* (1993), Snow (1978), Sutton (1981), Taylor, P.B. (1980a), Tuck (1972), Urban *et al.* (1986).

16. **Madagascar Snipe**

Gallinago macrodactyla

French: Bécassine malgache **German**: Madagaskarbekassine **Spanish**: Agachadiza Malgache
Other common names: Malagasy/Madagascan Snipe

Taxonomy. *Gallinago macrodactyla* Bonaparte, 1839, Madagascar.
Genus formerly named *Capella*, as this name erroneously considered to pre-date *Gallinago* (see page 446). Has been treated as conspecific with *G. gallinago* and *G. nobilis*, and might form part of *G. gallinago* superspecies. Monotypic.
Distribution. Madagascar, mainly in C & E.

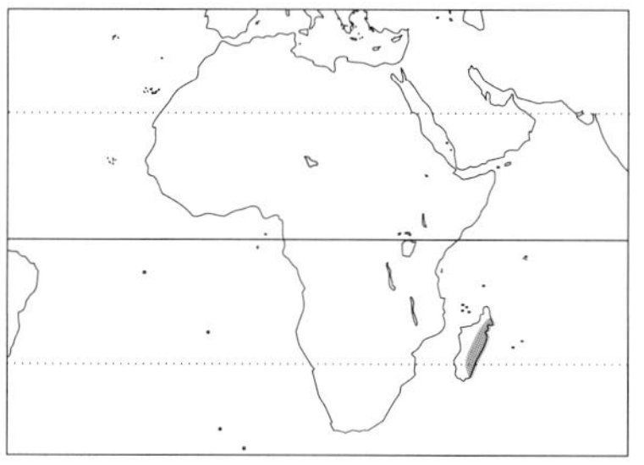

Descriptive notes. 29-32 cm; 216 g (1 female). Large, heavy, long-billed snipe. Structurally similar to *G. nigripennis*, but with less contrast between upperparts and underparts; outer rectrices greyer brown; similar to *G. gallinago* and other close relatives, but long bill and legs dark; only narrow greyish trailing edge to secondaries, darker underwings and wing-coverts with warm olive-buff fringes. Adult has cold olive-brown spots on tips of wing coverts. Female very similar to male, but bill averages slightly longer. No seasonal variation. Juvenile has narrower and paler warm olive-buff fringes to scapulars and mantle feathers.
Habitat. Grassy and sedge-covered marshes and swamps, margins of water courses, and rice paddies, from sea-level up to elevations of 2700 m; prefers presence of dense vegetation and muddy areas.
Food and Feeding. Invertebrates, seeds and other plant matter recorded. Probes deeply into mud; normally feeds in muddy areas or shallow water. Outside breeding season, frequently forages in small groups of 4-8 birds.
Breeding. Very poorly known. Laying probably Jul-Jan. Nest is depression on dry hummock, scantily lined with grass. 3 eggs (2-4). No further information available.
Movements. Apparently sedentary.
Status and Conservation. Not globally threatened. No population estimate available; apparently uncommon within restricted breeding range, but, as with other snipes, secretive habits probably mean species under-recorded. Threatened by habitat transformation, particularly with spread of paddyfields; hunting pressure may also be significant.
Bibliography. Albignac (1970), Benson (1981), Benson *et al.* (1976-1977), Dee (1986), Delacour (1932), Dowsett & Forbes-Watson (1993), Langrand (1990), Milon *et al.* (1973), Rand (1936), Salvan (1970, 1972b), van Someren (1947), Sutton (1981), Tuck (1972).

17. **Great Snipe**

Gallinago media

French: Bécassine double **German**: Doppelschnepfe **Spanish**: Agachadiza Real
Other common names: Double Snipe

Taxonomy. *Scolopax Media* Latham, 1787, England.
Genus formerly named *Capella*, as this name erroneously considered to pre-date *Gallinago* (see page 446). Monotypic.
Distribution. Scandinavia E through Baltic states, Poland and W Russia to R Yenisey. Winters in sub-Saharan Africa.

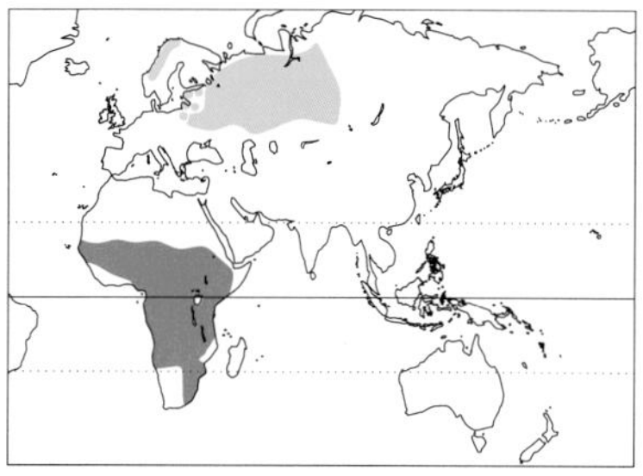

Descriptive notes. 27-29 cm; 140-260 g; wingspan 47-50 cm. Medium-sized, bulky snipe; differs from similar species by bold white tips on wing-coverts, bold dark barring on white underparts, and unbarred white corners to tail; distal half of bill has slight droop. Female very similar to male, but averages slightly larger. Non-breeding adult has duller and darker upperparts. Juvenile like breeding adult, but duskier and less well marked; brown bands on white tail corners; white on wing-coverts obscure; belly often more fully and regularly barred.
Habitat. Selects habitats rich with sub-surface invertebrates and medium scrub cover for breeding, usually in wide river valleys; floodplain meadows, tussock meadows, peatland, tundra with scattered bushes, and sometimes drier woodlands adjacent to marshes or bogs. After breeding, occurs in marshland, in short grass or sedges on lake edges or flooded fields, tracks in wooded areas; usually drier habitat than that preferred by *G. gallinago*.
Food and Feeding. Mainly earthworms, but also gastropods and larvae and adults of terrestrial insects, such as beetles and tipulids; also seeds, mainly of marsh plants. Probes in soil for earthworms, but also pecks from surface and feeds in very shallow water. Feeds singly or in small numbers. Crepuscular and nocturnal feeder.
Breeding. Lays mid-May to early Jul. Polygamous. The only *Gallinago* with no aerial nuptial display in which distinctive sounds made by tail feathers; instead, has complex lekking system, with males gathering after sunset on traditional display grounds (leks); performs elaborate display on top of small mound in which white outer tail feathers are distinctly advertised; female alone builds nest, incubates, and cares for young. Solitary breeder. Nest is shallow depression in ground, filled with some moss or grass; in thick vegetation, usually completely concealed, but sometimes more open. 4 eggs (3-5); incubation 22-24 days; chick cinnamon-buff or densely mottled ferruginous brown above with brown median zone bordered black with dense buffish white down tips, distinctly marked head with brown and black bands and cinnamon- or ochraceous-buff underparts grading to nearly white on central belly; fledging 21-28 days; young independent immediately after fledging.
Movements. Migratory. Departure from breeding grounds from early Aug onwards, and wintering on flooded grasslands in African regions just after rainy season. Migrates across Turkey and down R Nile to Ethiopian plateau, arriving Aug-Sept; only rare passage visitor in Egypt, late Aug to late Oct and early Mar to mid-Apr. In Ethiopia, large numbers stay until grasslands dry up in Oct, whereafter they move S & SW, following the rains; recorded in Kenya, SW Tanzania, Malawi, Zambia, Zaire, Zimbabwe, Namibia and South Africa from mid-Oct; 5000-10,000 birds have been counted in Mali, in Nov. High numbers probably migrate to wetlands along Gulf of Guinea where they stay Aug-Dec; as wetlands dry up, these birds migrate to other, undetermined areas in Africa; moult data suggest that these birds constitute separate population. Northward migration occurs in broad front over Africa Mar-Apr, and probably orientated more to W, crossing Mediterranean, but northward migration passes largely unnoticed; males arrive in Ukraine before females; arrives on R Yenisey in early Jun. Irregularly, some birds winter in NW Europe and S Scandinavia.
Status and Conservation. Not globally threatened. Currently considered near-threatened. Has declined enormously over entire breeding range this century; extinct as breeder in Germany and Denmark, primarily due to loss and deterioration of floodplain meadows and marshlands. In Russia, however, decrease started at end of 19th century, before beginning of land reclamation. Breeding in meadows is probably a secondary development; damp tussocky bogs are preferred. Also, excessive hunting and climatic change have been suggested as relevant factors; still hunted in E Europe. In USSR, was seen in large flocks until 1940's. World population estimated at 170,000-290,000 "pairs": Scandinavian breeding population has stabilized at 6000-17,000 "pairs"; breeding population in Poland 400-500 "pairs", Estonia 50-100, Lithuania 30-50, Belarus 12,000-20,000, Ukraine 400-500 and Russia 150,000-250,000 "pairs". Numbers still decreasing and breeding range contracting and fragmenting in some parts at western and southern limits. In Scandinavia, decreased grazing intensity in low alpine areas causes further decline. Ethiopian wintering population seems stable or even increasing since 1913, but this may be due to degradation of formerly used wintering areas; local densities in Ethiopian Highlands may reach 1300 birds/km^2 in Aug-Oct.
Bibliography. Albrecht (1986), Ali & Ripley (1980), Avery & Sherwood (1982), Benson & Benson (1975), Berlijn & Luijendijk (1995), Blankert (1980), Borkowski (1990), Cramp & Simmons (1983), Devort (1993), Devort & Paloc (1994), Dowsett & Forbes-Watson (1993), Elgood *et al.* (1994), Elveland & Tjernberg (1984), Étchécopar & Hüe (1964), Evans (1994), Ferdinand (1966), Ferdinand & Gensbøl (1966), Fiske & Kålås (1995), Fiske *et al.* (1994), Fjeldså (1977), Flint *et al.* (1984), Gantz (1985), Ginn *et al.* (1989), Glutz von Blotzheim *et al.* (1977), Goodman *et al.* (1989), Höglund (1989a, 1989b), Höglund & Alatalo (1995), Höglund & Lundberg (1987), Höglund & Robertson (1990a, 1990b), Höglund, Eriksson & Lindell (1990), Höglund, Kålås & Fiske (1992), Höglund, Kålås & Løfaldi (1990), Hüe & Étchécopar (1970), Kålås, Fiske & Saether (1995), Kålås, Løfaldli & Fiske (1989), Kirwan (1992), Knystautas (1993), Kube (1991), Lemnell (1978), Løfaldli (1985), Løfaldli *et al.* (1990, 1992), Mackworth-Praed &

On following pages: 18. Common Snipe (*Gallinago gallinago*); 19. South American Snipe (*Gallinago paraguaiae*); 20. Noble Snipe (*Gallinago nobilis*); 21. Giant Snipe (*Gallinago undulata*); 22. Fuegian Snipe (*Gallinago stricklandii*); 23. Andean Snipe (*Gallinago jamesoni*); 24. Imperial Snipe (*Gallinago imperialis*); 25. Short-billed Dowitcher (*Limnodromus griseus*); 26. Long-billed Dowitcher (*Limnodromus scolopaceus*); 27. Asian Dowitcher (*Limnodromus semipalmatus*).

Grant (1957, 1962, 1970), Maclean (1993), Massoli-Novelli (1987, 1988a, 1988b), Meissner & Skakuj (1988), Morozov (1994), Müller (1988b), Müller & Königstedt (1987, 1989, 1990), Nikiforov & Hybet (1981), Palmgren (1983), Piersma (1986b), Pinto (1983), Prys-Jones & Wilson (1986), Rogacheva (1992), Saether (1994), Saether *et al.* (1994), Shirihai (1996), Short *et al.* (1990), van Spanje *et al.* (1995), Swanberg (1965), Taylor, P.B. (1980a, 1981a), Tomkovich (1992b), Tuck (1972), Urban *et al.* (1986), Wallace (1977).

18. **Common Snipe**

Gallinago gallinago

French: Bécassine des marais **German**: Bekassine **Spanish**: Agachadiza Común
Other common names: Fantail/Wilson Snipe

Taxonomy. *Scolopax Gallinago* Linnaeus, 1758, Sweden.
Genus formerly named *Capella*, as this name erroneously considered to pre-date *Gallinago* (see page 446). Forms superspecies with *G. paraguaiae* and perhaps *G. nigripennis*, which are sometimes included as subspecies of present species, but differences in size, outer tail feathers and quality of aerial "winnowing" suggest separate species status; *G. macrodactyla* may also belong to superspecies. Race *delicata* may constitute separate species; has 16 tail feathers, as opposed to usually 14 (sometimes 12, 16 or 18) in nominate; both forms breed nearby in Aleutians. Three subspecies currently recognized.
Subspecies and Distribution.
G. g. faeroeensis (C. L. Brehm, 1831) - Iceland, Faeroes, Orkney and Shetland; winters in British Is.
G. g. gallinago (Linnaeus, 1758) - British Is, Scandinavia and W Europe through NC Eurasia to Kamchatka and W Aleutians, with isolated population from NE Afghanistan to N India; winters from W Europe, Mediterranean and equatorial Africa through Middle East, Arabia and Indian Subcontinent to E China, S Korea, S Japan, Philippines and W Indonesia.
G. g. delicata (Ord, 1825) - E Aleutians and Alaska E through Canada to Newfoundland, and S to C California, New Mexico, C Iowa and New Jersey; winters from NW & C USA through Central America and Greater Antilles to N South America.

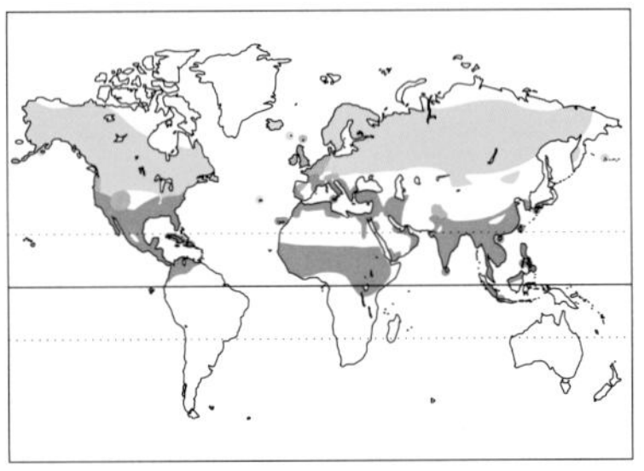

Descriptive notes. 25-27 cm; 72-181 g; wingspan 44-47 cm. Small to medium-sized snipe, with rather long bill and white belly; plumage variable, and melanistic morph occurs (e.g. in Ireland); flight faster and more erratic than other snipes of similar size. Differs from very similar *G. paraguaiae* normally by neck, breast and flanks more heavily marked, and, in flight, wings more pointed; from *G. stenura*, *G. hardwickii* and *G. megala* by prominent white trailing edge to wing, and supercilium narrower than eyestripe at base of bill. Sexes alike. No seasonal variation. Juvenile very similar to adult, but wing-coverts more neatly fringed pale buff. Race *faeroeensis* darker and more rufous above, with narrower, less contrasting, back stripes; *delicata* darker than *faeroeensis*, generally less rufous than nominate with heavier barring on flanks, and usually has darker underwing.
Habitat. Open fresh or brackish marshland with rich or tussocky vegetation, grassy or marshy edges of lakes and rivers, wet hay fields, swampy meadows and marshy tundra, in forest tundra and extreme northern taiga zones; in general, found in areas providing combination of grassy cover and moist soils, rich in organic matter. Outside breeding season, generally occupies similar habitats, with more use of man-made habitats, e.g. sewage farms and rice fields; also upper reaches of estuaries, sometimes on coastal meadows.
Food and Feeding. Diet includes larval insects (10-80%), adult insects, earthworms, small crustaceans, small gastropods and spiders; plant fibres and seeds consumed in smaller quantities. Feeds by vertical, rhythmic probing in substrate, often without removing bill from soil. Feeds typically in small groups; essentially crepuscular.
Breeding. Laying Apr-Jun. Monogamous, but both sexes show high degree of promiscuity. Territorial; densities up to 10-38 (even 110) pairs/km². Nest usually on dry spot, covered by grasses, rushes, sedges or sphagnum. 4 eggs (2-5), with laying interval 1 day; lays replacement clutches; incubation 17-20 days, by female alone; chick mahogany red, more hazel brown or tawny on sides of head and underparts, with black and white bands on head; both parents care for young, but male entices oldest 1 or 2 from nest to tend; young initially fed bill-to-bill; fledging 19-20 days. Success 2·2 hatchlings per nest, 3·5 per successful nest. High proportion of eggs may be predated or trampled by cattle. Mean annual mortality 52%.
Movements. Mostly migratory, wintering S to N tropics; some populations sedentary or partially migratory, e.g. British Is, W & C USA. Moves quickly from breeding grounds to moulting areas, and after few weeks quickly migrates to wintering grounds. High degree of site fidelity at staging sites. Birds wintering in Afrotropics presumably from Russia, crossing Sahara on broad front. European and Atlantic birds move to S & W Europe; species seems to have shifted main moulting grounds from continental (particularly Netherlands) to Britain since late 1950's. Nearctic population mainly migratory, and birds from Canadian Maritime Provinces perform transoceanic passage to Neotropics. Autumn passage from late Jul to Nov, with arrival in N Africa mainly late Sept to early Oct, S of Sahara mainly Oct to early Nov, South America from Jul; most birds leave South America and Africa in Mar; crosses Europe Mar to early May, males typically arriving on breeding grounds 10-14 days earlier than females.
Status and Conservation. Not globally threatened. Total North American population probably numbers in low millions; in Europe 530,000 pairs (1986) and 100,000's of pairs in W Russia; in W Siberia at least 1,000,000 breeding birds; possibly more than 1,000,000 birds winter in SW & SC Asia, and 100,000's in E & SE Asia. Total of 300,000 pairs (*faroeensis*) breed in Iceland, 30,000 pairs in Britain, 100,000 pairs in Fenno-Scandia, c. 20,000 pairs in Germany, 20,000-30,000 in Estonia (1994) and 13,000-15,000 pairs in Poland. Common to very abundant on African wintering grounds (c. 1,500,000 in Sudan). Decline noted in breeding populations of Europe, W Siberia and C & E Canada, probably chiefly due to habitat changes, especially drainage; in Schleswig-Holstein, N Germany, decline from 13,000 pairs in 1970 to 1500 in 1992; 99-100% decline after improvement of marginal grasslands in N England. Low water levels shorten period of food availability in pastures, due to lower penetrability of soil, and thereby strongly influence length of breeding season; careful manipulation of water levels may allow improvement of breeding success. Estimated 1,500,000 birds hunted annually in Europe (notably France) and 500,000 in North America.
Bibliography. Ali & Ripley (1980), Arango (1986), Armstrong (1983), Asensio & Carrascal (1987), Baines (1988), Beintema (1985, 1986a), Beintema & Müskens (1983), Bent (1927-1929), Blake (1977), Boyd (1956), Brazil (1991), Carey (1993), Chadwick (1991), Cramp & Simmons (1983), Devort (1988, 1993, 1994, 1995), Dowsett & Forbes-Watson (1993), Dubois & Maheo (1986), Étchécopar & Hüe (1978), Fjeldså (1977), Fjeldså & Krabbe (1990), Flint *et al.* (1984), Fog (1978), Forristal (1991), Fritzell *et al.* (1979), Goodman *et al.* (1989), Granval *et al.* (1993), Green, R.E. (1984, 1985, 1988a, 1991), Green, R.E., Hirons & Cresswell (1990), Grisser (1988), Henderson *et al.* (1993), Hilty & Brown (1986), Hötker (1991), Howell & Webb (1995a), Hüe & Étchécopar (1970), Kålås (1980), Knystautas (1993), Marchant *et al.* (1990), Mason & Macdonald (1976), Massoli-Novelli (1988b), McKibben & Hofmann (1985), Meissner & Skakuj (1988), Müller & Königstedt (1990), Münster (1975), Olsson (1987), Pang Bingzhang (1981), Patrikeev (1995), Pedersen (1991), Perennou *et al.* (1994), Piersma (1986b), Pörner (1987, 1989), Prys-Jones & Wilson (1986), Reddig (1981), Ripley (1982), Roberts, T.J. (1991), Rogacheva (1992), Rufino & Neves (1991), Rutschke (1976), Scott (1989), Senner & Mickelson (1979), Shirihai (1996), Slud (1964), Smythies (1986), Spence (1988), Strandgaard (1988), Sutton (1981), Taylor, P.B. (1980a, 1981a), Tuck (1972), Urban *et al.* (1986), Veiga (1986, 1988), Weggler (1992).

19. **South American Snipe**

Gallinago paraguaiae

French: Bécassine de Magellan **German**: Magellanbekassine **Spanish**: Agachadiza Suramericana
Other common names: Magellan/Paraguayan Snipe; Puna/Andean Snipe (*andina*); Chilean Puna Snipe ("*innotata*")

Taxonomy. *Scolopax Paraguaiæ* Vieillot, 1816, Paraguay.
Genus formerly named *Capella*, as this name erroneously considered to pre-date *Gallinago* (see page 446). Forms superspecies with *G. gallinago* and perhaps *G. nigripennis*, and all three occasionally considered conspecific. Race *andina* has often been regarded as full species, and *magellanica* too may be close to separate species status. Possible race *innotata*, from R Loa, N Chile, proposed on basis of densely barred underwing-coverts; on occasion, this form has even been considered separate species. Three subspecies recognized.
Subspecies and Distribution.
G. p. paraguaiae (Vieillot, 1816) - E Colombia through Venezuela to the Guianas, and S through E Peru and W, C & S Brazil to N Argentina and Uruguay; Trinidad and possibly Tobago.
G. p. andina (Taczanowski, 1875) - S Peru, W Bolivia, N Chile and NW Argentina.
G. p. magellanica (King, 1828) - C Chile and C Argentina S to Tierra del Fuego; Falkland Is.

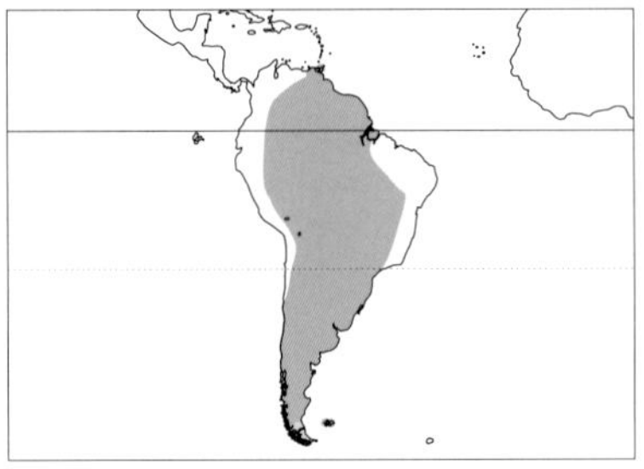

Descriptive notes. 22-29 cm; 1 nominate bird 136 g, *andina* 65-105 g. Small snipe, very similar to *G. gallinago* and *G. nigripennis*, but normally differs in having paler face and fainter markings on neck, breast and flanks; outer tail feathers narrower and whiter, underwing normally slightly paler. Separated from *G. stenura*, *G. hardwickii* and *G. megala* by prominent white trailing edge to wing, and supercilium narrower than eyestripe at base of bill. Female very similar to male, but slightly larger. No seasonal variation. Juvenile very similar to adult, but wing-coverts more neatly fringed pale buff. Race *magellanica* more buff tinted and generally warmer coloration with fainter markings on breast and flanks; longer wings. Race *andina* smallest, with shortest bill and dull yellow legs, (greenish grey in other races); more contrasting plumage, especially blackish mantle, primaries and primary coverts.
Habitat. Habitats quite different between races. Widespread *paraguaiae* typically occurs in wet grassy savannas. High altitude *andina* found along boggy rivers high in *puna* zone of Andes, up to 4500 m; occupies boggy ground with cushion-plants, but also areas of rushes, reeds and grassland. Race *magellanica* occurs in peat bogs and grass-covered *pampas* and steppes; also sometimes open, swampy woods; in S Patagonia, often in areas with tussock grass.
Food and Feeding. Said to feed mainly on invertebrates, e.g. insect larvae and earthworms. Feeds by probing in mud, in style similar to that used by *G. gallinago*.
Breeding. Race *paraguaiae* probably nests from late Nov onwards, and eggs found in May in Uruguay considered atypical; *andina* mainly Oct-Dec in C Peru, Sept in N Chile; eggs of *magellanica* found Aug and Nov. One nest in tussock of tall grass. Race *magellanica* typically lays 2 eggs and *paraguaiae* 4, but very few data available.
Movements. Nominate *paraguaiae* essentially sedentary, in some areas performing short seasonal movements to permanent marshland during austral winter. Race *andina* moves to lower altitudes, e.g. reaching Argentinian *pampas*. Race *magellanica* more migratory, especially on Tierra del Fuego, birds moving N to N Argentina and Uruguay in Apr-Jul; in past mostly summer visitor to Falkland Is, but no recent evidence of migration and some birds certainly overwinter.
Status and Conservation. Not globally threatened. No population estimates available, but numbers thought to be relatively stable and range huge. Race *andina* widespread and apparently common in *puna*, though least so in more arid S parts of range. Race *magellanica* common in all low valleys of S Andes, and in lake district around Valdivia, SC Chile; on migration, not uncommon on upland plateaux of Patagonian steppe.
Bibliography. Arango (1986), Barlow (1967), Belton (1984), Blake (1977), Clark (1986), Contreras, J.F. (1980), Contreras, J.R. *et al.* (1990), Dubs (1992), Fjeldså & Krabbe (1990), Forrester (1993), Haverschmidt (1968, 1976), Haverschmidt & Mees (1995), Hellmayr & Conover (1948), Hilty & Brown (1986), Howell & Webb (1995b), Humphrey *et al.* (1970), Johnson (1965b), Klimaitis & Moschione (1987), Meyer de Schauensee & Phelps (1978), Navas & Bo (1993), Parker *et al.* (1982), de la Peña (1981, 1992), Remsen & Traylor (1989), Scott & Carbonell (1986), Sick (1985c, 1993), Snyder (1966), Sutton (1981), Tostain *et al.* (1992), Tuck (1972), Wetmore (1926).

20. **Noble Snipe**

Gallinago nobilis

French: Bécassine noble **German**: Nobelbekassine **Spanish**: Agachadiza Noble
Other common names: Paramo Snipe

Taxonomy. *Gallinago nobilis* P. L. Sclater, 1856, Bogotá, Colombia.
Genus formerly named *Capella*, as this name erroneously considered to pre-date *Gallinago* (see page 446). Monotypic.
Distribution. N Andes, from NW Venezuela through C Colombia to Ecuador.
Descriptive notes. 30-33 cm; 188-197 g. Medium-sized, bulky snipe with disproportionately long, two-toned bill; underwing relatively dark; wings rather broad and rounded; tail virtually without white; toes project beyong tail tip. Larger and usually darker than *G. paraguaiae*, with broader wings which lack white trailing edge. Differs from *G. jamesoni* by white belly and larger white throat patch. Rather similar to *G. macrodactyla*, but breast warmer buff, and bill base pale. Female similar but bill longer. No seasonal variation. Juvenile very similar to adult, but has narrow buff edges on wing-coverts.

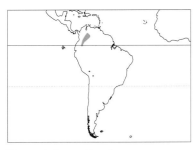

Habitat. Montane grassy wetlands, swamps and bogs, wet savannas, rushy pasture and reed-marsh adjoining eutrophic lakes; mainly at 2500-3900 m, but sometimes up to 4000 m and down to 2000 m; above and just below tree-line, typically in *páramo* zone.

Food and Feeding. No information available.

Breeding. Season Mar-Sept. Circling aerial display; may perform lek behaviour. Nest is depression on dry hummock of grasses and mosses; composed of grasses and fragments of other plants. Probably only 2 eggs; chick rich chestnut with black pattern and rows of white spots. No further information available.

Movements. Presumably sedentary.

Status and Conservation. Not globally threatened. No population estimates available; locally fairly common in Colombia. Very poorly known; research required.

Bibliography. Arango (1986), Blake (1977), Butler (1979), Fjeldså & Krabbe (1990), Hellmayr & Conover (1948), Hilty & Brown (1986), Meyer de Schauensee (1966), Meyer de Schauensee & Phelps (1978), Ortiz & Carrión (1991), Scott & Carbonell (1986), Sutton (1981), Tuck (1972), Varty *et al.* (1986).

21. Giant Snipe
Gallinago undulata

French: Bécassine géante   **German**: Riesenbekassine   **Spanish**: Agachadiza Gigante
Other common names: Guianan Giant Snipe

Taxonomy. *Scolopax undulata* Boddaert, 1783, Cayenne.
Genus formerly named *Capella*, as this name erroneously considered to pre-date *Gallinago* (see page 446). Some authors suggest that race *gigantea* may merit treatment as separate species. Two subspecies recognized.

Subspecies and Distribution.
G. u. undulata (Boddaert, 1783) - W & E Colombia; Venezuela to extreme N Brazil and probably E to the Guianas.
G. u. gigantea (Temminck, 1826) - E Bolivia, Paraguay and SE Brazil; probably also Uruguay and NE Argentina.

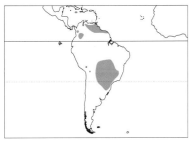

Descriptive notes. 40-47 cm; *undulata* 270-362 g, *gigantea* 420-500 g. Largest snipe, with flat-headed profile, and bill very long with broad base; bold blackish and cinnamon markings contrast with whitish ground colour; unlike any other snipe, has barred flight-feathers; in flight, shows broad, rounded wings and no white in tail. Race *gigantea* larger, and usually has more boldly marked plumage and broader cinnamon edging on upperparts.

Habitat. In swamps with tall vegetation, marshy pastures and flooded grasslands, from tropical zone up to 2200 m; sometimes in dense herbage of dry savannas, but possibly only for roosting.

Food and Feeding. Virtually nothing known; diet said to include frogs. Probably rather solitary, but possibly more gregarious during non-breeding season. May feed only at night.

Breeding. Very poorly known. Calls during display flight very different from those of *G. gallinago*: 2-5 sonorous cries with a human timbre, and loud buzz lasting c. 4 seconds. Nests found in Sept in Brazil, and from Nov to early Jan. Often nests on small hillock among swamps. 2-4 eggs; chick black, finely spotted white.

Movements. Virtually nothing known; arrives at some sites seasonally, apparently after rain.

Status and Conservation. Not globally threatened. No population estimates available, but Brazil may be main centre of population. Species nowhere common, but nocturnal habits, together with extreme wariness towards approaching humans, may exaggerate impression of scarcity. Local and uncommon in Colombia; rare in French Guiana, where reported to suffer severe hunting pressure. First definite record for Bolivia recently established by means of tape-recording of nocturnal display calls; surveys may show range to be more extensive in other areas. Population of race *gigantea* seems to be declining; apparently easier to shoot than some other sympatric snipes.

Bibliography. Abramson (1977), Arango (1986), Belton (1984), Blake (1977), Dubs (1992), Forrester (1993), Haverschmidt (1968, 1974b), Haverschmidt & Mees (1995), Hellmayr & Conover (1948), Hilty & Brown (1986), Mayer (1995), Meyer de Schauensee (1966), Meyer de Schauensee & Phelps (1978), Pearman (1995a), Pinto (1964), Scott & Carbonell (1986), Sick (1985c, 1993), Snyder (1966), Sutton (1981), Teixeira *et al.* (1983), Tostain *et al.* (1992), Tuck (1972).

22. Fuegian Snipe
Gallinago stricklandii

French: Bécassine de Strickland   **German**: Kordillerenbekassine   **Spanish**: Agachadiza Fueguina
Other common names: (Southern/Strickland's) Cordilleran Snipe

Taxonomy. *Gallinago stricklandii* G. R. Gray, 1845, Hermit Island, Cape Horn.

Formerly placed in genus *Chubbia*. Forms superspecies with *G. jamesoni*, with which often considered conspecific. Monotypic.

Distribution. SC Chile and SC Argentina S to Tierra del Fuego.

Descriptive notes. 29-30 cm. Dark and rufous woodcock-like snipe, with broad, rounded wings; small, unmarked throat patch; central belly unbarred buff. Like *G. jamesoni* and *G. imperialis*, lacks clear pale stripes on head and upperparts typical of other snipes; lacks white on wings and tail. Very similar to *G. jamesoni*, but underparts richer buff. Sexes alike. No seasonal variation. Juvenile very similar to adult, but feathers of mantle and scapulars narrowly edged pale buff.

Habitat. Grassy or forested boggy areas with low scrub or rushes; often mosaic of grassy bog, bamboo and lichen-clad dwarf forest, sometimes cushion-plant bogs; occurs from sea-level, in fjordland habitat and on small islands, up to more than 3000 m.

Food and Feeding. Virtually nothing known, but diet includes beetles. Apparently largely nocturnal.

Breeding. Not well known. Nest and chicks found in Dec. Nest sited on elevated ground among short, sparse grasses and rushes. Normally 2 eggs; chick like that of *G. jamesoni*, but brighter, with white spots in pale zones.

Movements. Mostly sedentary, but extreme S including Tierra del Fuego vacated during winter. Rarely occurs on Falkland Is.

Status and Conservation. Not globally threatened. Currently considered near-threatened. No population estimates available; highly secretive habits make possible census work very difficult. Status extremely uncertain; species reported to be common on islands around Cape Horn, but decreasing in numbers towards N.

Bibliography. Blake (1977), Clark (1986), Fjeldså & Krabbe (1990), Hellmayr & Conover (1948), Humphrey *et al.* (1970), Johnson (1965b), Meyer de Schauensee (1966), Narosky & Yzurieta (1987), de la Peña (1992), Reynolds (1935), Scott & Carbonell (1986), Sutton (1981), Tuck (1972), Woods (1988).

23. Andean Snipe
Gallinago jamesoni

French: Bécassine des paramos   **German**: Andenbekassine   **Spanish**: Agachadiza Andina
Other common names: Northern Cordilleran/Jameson's Snipe

Taxonomy. *Xylocota jamesoni*. Bonaparte, 1855, high Andes of Quito, Ecuador.
Formerly placed in genus *Chubbia*. Forms superspecies with *G. stricklandii*, with which often considered conspecific. Monotypic.

Distribution. Santa Marta Mts (N Colombia) and Andes from W Venezuela S to WC Bolivia.

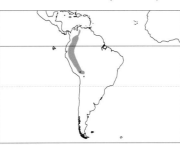

Descriptive notes. 29-30 cm; 140-224 g. Bulky, woodcock-like snipe. Like *G. stricklandii* and *G. imperialis*, lacks clear pale stripes on head and upperparts typical of other snipes; lacks white on wings and tail. Very similar to *G. stricklandii*, but bill deep at base, tapering and often drooping slightly towards tip; larger unmarked throat patch; underparts colder buff, whiter on belly and more heavily barred; in flight, wings slightly longer and narrower. Sexes alike. No seasonal variation. Juvenile very similar to adult, but wing-coverts warmer buff and less clearly barred, but notched with dark brown and tipped pale tawny buff.

Habitat. Found in variety of habitats from open swampy forest to coastal moorland with dwarf shrubs and miry parts; also in grassy marshland above tree-line, at 2100-3800 m, occasionally 4300 m; typically found on open slopes of *páramo*, especially grassy areas with *Espeletia*.

Food and Feeding. No information available.

Breeding. Gonads of few specimens suggest egg-laying from Mar to early Apr, but species also nests in May and Aug-Nov; display recorded at dusk in mid-Sept, Colombia. Nest is delicate saucer of grass on dry slope, at some distance from bog. Normally 2 eggs; chick tawny buff with bold fuscous pattern and some buff-white stripes on head and back.

Movements. Probably sedentary. In Santa Marta Mts, records at lowest altitudes were at end of dry season.

Status and Conservation. Not globally threatened. No population estimates available; status extremely uncertain, but species probably not rare. Uncommon and perhaps local in Colombia.

Bibliography. Arango (1986), Blake (1977), Butler (1979), Fjeldså & Krabbe (1990), Hellmayr & Conover (1948), Hilty & Brown (1986), Koepcke (1970), Meyer de Schauensee (1966), Meyer de Schauensee & Phelps (1978), Ortiz & Carrión (1991), Parker *et al.* (1982), Remsen & Traylor (1989), Scott & Carbonell (1986), Sutton (1981), Tuck (1972), Vuilleumier (1969).

24. Imperial Snipe
Gallinago imperialis

French: Bécassine impériale   **German**: Kaiserbekassine   **Spanish**: Agachadiza Imperial
Other common names: Banded/Bogota Snipe

Taxonomy. *Gallinago imperialis* P. L. Sclater and Salvin, 1869, Bogotá, Colombia.
Formerly placed in genus *Chubbia*. Monotypic.

Distribution. Isolated sites in Peru, in Piura, Amazonas, La Libertad and Cuzco.

Descriptive notes. 29-31 cm. Large, dark rufous woodcock-like snipe, with very broad, rounded wings and slightly drooping bill; lacks pale stripes on head and upperparts; upperparts barred dark rufous chestnut and black; breast mottled chestnut and dark brown; belly, flanks and undertail-coverts strongly banded dark brown on whitish background; at rest, primaries concealed by tertials. Perhaps more similar to *Scolopax saturata* than to other snipes. Juvenile undescribed, as are any possible sexual and seasonal differences.

Habitat. Occurs in zone around tree-line at 2745-3500 m, where probably mainly restricted to bogs and damp elfin forest intermixed with tree-ferns and tall grass; also glades fringed by bamboo with extensive covering of *Sphagnum* mosses.

Food and Feeding. No information available. Thought to feed on worms and arthropods by probing in layer of thick mosses.

Breeding. Virtually nothing known. Crepuscular aerial display often continues well into darkness; observed in Jul-Aug.

Movements. Probably sedentary.

Status and Conservation. Not globally threatened. Currently considered near-threatened. No population estimate available, and biology virtually unknown; species apparently occurs at very low densities; population apparently very small and localized, although species is difficult to find. Known only from a few specimens; thought to be extinct for over a century, but rediscovered in 1967, since when has been found at several localities. Survey work and research required to establish limits of range and approximate size of population. Original specimen labelled "Bogotá", but probably not from Colombia; at the time, this was commonly given as locality for birds collected over vast areas of South America.

Bibliography. Arango (1986), Blake (1977), Fjeldså & Krabbe (1990), Hellmayr & Conover (1948), Hilty & Brown (1986), Meyer de Schauensee (1966), Ortiz & Carrión (1991), Parker *et al.* (1982), Rasmussen *et al.* (1996), Sutton (1981), Terborgh & Weske (1972), Tuck (1972).

Genus *LIMNODROMUS* Wied, 1833

25. Short-billed Dowitcher

Limnodromus griseus

French: Bécassin roux **German**: Kleiner Schlammläufer **Spanish**: Agujeta Gris
Other common names: Common Dowitcher

Taxonomy. *Scolopax grisea* Gmelin, 1789, Long Island, New York.
Forms superspecies with *L. scolopaceus*, with which formerly considered conspecific. Three subspecies recognized.
Subspecies and Distribution.
L. g. caurinus Pitelka, 1950 - S Alaska and S Yukon; winters on Pacific coast from C USA to S Peru.
L. g. hendersoni Rowan, 1932 - EC British Columbia to SE Keewatin and C Manitoba; winters from SE USA to Panama.
L. g. griseus (Gmelin, 1789) - C Quebec and W Labrador; winters on Atlantic coast from S USA to Brazil.

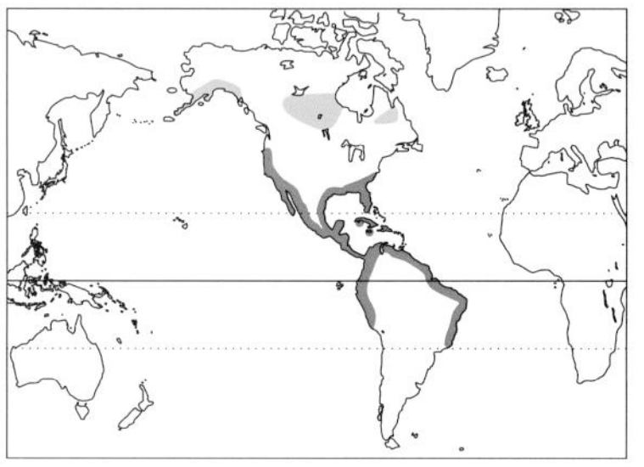

Descriptive notes. 25-29 cm; 65-154 g; wingspan 45-51 cm. Snipe-like bill, godwit-like plumage. Very similar to *L. scolopaceus*, but bill tends to be shorter; foreneck with few or no spots; tail pattern variable, but white bars normally broader than black ones; best separated by call, mellow "tu-tu-tu". Female slightly larger than male. Non-breeding adult has plain grey upperparts and breast, pale supercilium, dark eyestripe and whitish underparts. Juvenile has crown, upperparts and tertials with broad chestnut-buff edges; face, foreneck and breast buffish and white towards rear. Races differ mainly in breeding plumage and size, latter decreasing eastwards; race *caurinus* has very variable underparts, male generally brighter than female, with fewer spots; *hendersoni* lacks white on centre of belly, being uniform rufous below with sparse brown markings on flanks and undertail.

Habitat. Muskegs, wet sedge meadows and bogs with low vegetation, also swampy coastal tundra. On migration, found on both inland and coastal wetlands. In winter, mainly on intertidal mudflats bordered with mangroves and sandy shores; also borders of shallow pools on salt-marshes.

Food and Feeding. On breeding grounds chiefly larvae and pupae of Diptera, also snails, beetles and adult insects and sometimes plant material, particularly seeds. On coast, feeds on marine polychaetes, molluscs and crustaceans. Feeds by rapid, vertical probing, often in water, submerging head. In wintering areas often feeds in large flocks. Diurnal and nocturnal forager.

Breeding. Nests late May to Jul. Monogamous. Nest well hidden in soggy grass or sedge cover, near standing water. Usually 4 eggs (3-5); incubation 19-21 days, by both sexes; care of young mainly by male.

Movements. Long distance migrant. Race *caurinus* moves down Pacific coast, some birds inland through W USA, wintering on coast from California to Peru; *hendersoni* passes E Great Plains, valley of R Mississippi and E coast of USA, S of New York and New Jersey, and winters from the Carolinas round Gulf coast and down both coasts of Central America to Panama; *griseus* moves down Atlantic coast to North Carolina and S through Caribbean to N Brazil, with highest numbers wintering in Surinam. Small number of non-breeders spend N summer on wintering grounds. Females leave breeding grounds from early Jul, before males, and juveniles from late Jul; birds reach N South America from mid-Aug to early Oct. Spring migration early Mar to early Jun.

Status and Conservation. Not globally threatened. Total population exceeds 100,000 birds, possibly several 100,000's; no estimates available for populations of different races. Declining trends evident for races *caurinus* and *griseus*, while population of *hendersoni* seems stable; between 1972 and 1983, numbers staging on Atlantic coast of USA decreased by 46%, and by almost 8% annually in E Canada. No significant trend in numbers in E Canada during period 1986-1991.

Bibliography. Armstrong (1983), Avise & Zink (1988), Bent (1927-1929), Biaggi (1983), Blake (1977), Burton (1972b), Byrkjedal (1987b), Cramp & Simmons (1983), Fjeldså & Krabbe (1990), Haverschmidt (1968), Haverschmidt & Mees (1995), Hicklin & Smith (1979), Hilty & Brown (1986), Howe *et al.* (1989), Howell & Webb (1995a), Jaramillo & Henshaw (1995), Jaramillo *et al.* (1991), Jehl (1963), Jehl & Hussell (1966), Jehl & Smith (1970), Maisonneuve (1993), Mallory & Schneider (1979), Matthiessen (1994), McCollough (1981), McNair (1991), McNeil & Burton (1973), Meyer de Schauensee & Phelps (1978), Miller, Gunn & Harris (1983), Miller, Gunn, Myers & Veprintsev (1984), Monroe (1968), Morrison *et al.* (1994), Mullarney (1988), Napolitano *et al.* (1992), Nehls (1989), Pfister *et al.* (1992), Pitelka (1950), Pittaway (1992), Ridgely & Gwynne (1989), Robert & McNeil (1989), Root (1988), Rowan (1927, 1932), Schneider (1992), Scott & Carbonell (1986), Sick (1985c, 1993), Slud (1964), Snyder (1966), Stiles & Skutch (1989), Tostain *et al.* (1992), Wetmore (1965), Wilds & Newton (1983), Yésou (1982).

26. Long-billed Dowitcher

Limnodromus scolopaceus

French: Bécassin à long bec **German**: Großer Schlammläufer **Spanish**: Agujeta Escolopácea

Taxonomy. *Limosa scolopacea* Say, 1823, Council Bluffs, Iowa.
Forms superspecies with *L. griseus*, with which formerly considered conspecific. Monotypic.
Distribution. NE Siberia (R Yana E to Chukotskiy Peninsula), St Lawrence I and coastal W Alaska; N Inuvik and probably also N Yukon. Winters from W & S USA to Guatemala, and uncommonly to El Salvador; also rare S to Panama and French Guiana.

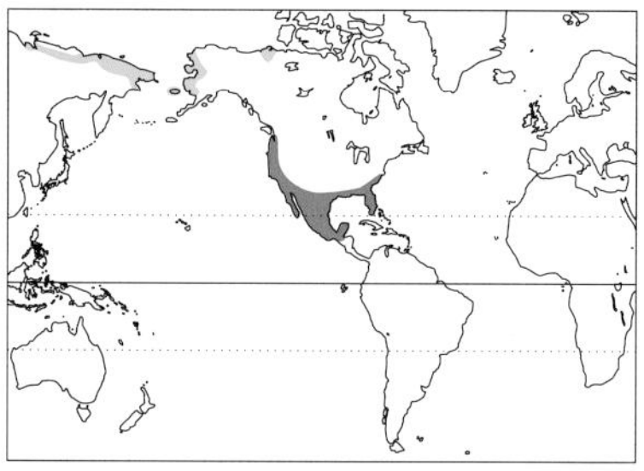

Descriptive notes. 24-30 cm; 90-135 g; wingspan 46-52 cm. Very similar to *L. griseus*, but bill and tarsi generally longer; breeding plumage darker red below with stronger breast and flank barring and no pale belly; on tail, black bands broader than white ones; best separated by call, high-pitched "keek", given 1-6 times. Female averages larger, more so than in *L. griseus*. Non-breeding adult mostly grey, virtually identical to *L. griseus*, but clearer separation between grey breast and white belly. Juvenile darker grey with narrower edges to upperparts.

Habitat. Grassy or sedgy marshes and swamps on Arctic tundra, often on shores of shallow lakes, mainly in floodplains; also moist tundra. On migration and in winter, mainly found at freshwater sites, such as marshes and drying lake shores; also saltmarshes and mudflats.

Food and Feeding. Diptera larvae, beetles, small gastropods, crustaceans, seeds and even mosses or plant fibres, less frequently polychaete worms. Probes in mud while wading, sometimes immersing head entirely. Usually in smaller flocks than *L. griseus*.

Breeding. Nests late May to Aug. Monogamous. Density up to 7-14 pairs/km². Nest usually located in small clump of sedges, typically damp at the bottom. 4 eggs; incubation 20-21 days, initially by both sexes, but later only by male; it has been suggested that only male cares for brood.

Movements. Migratory. Southward migration through North America in Jul-Oct; moves down Pacific coast, though many birds cross interior and along Atlantic coast up to New England; few birds follow W Pacific route and occur in Japan on passage. Juveniles migrate later than adults; females leave breeding area before males. Northward migration in Apr-May; more westerly than autumn route, mainly W of Mississippi and staging in Cheyenne Bottoms (Kansas). Some non-breeders spend summer in USA and Mexico. Regularly sighted in Britain and Ireland, mainly juveniles.

Status and Conservation. Not globally threatened. Total population numbers 50,000-100,000 birds. Breeding range has expanded considerably since 1920; towards W, now stretching beyond Yana Delta; in E Siberia, spreading S into Koryak Highlands; westward expansion may still be continuing. Very high numbers use Cheyenne Bottoms as a staging site during northbound migration.

Bibliography. Armstrong (1983), Avise & Zink (1988), Beaman (1994), Bent (1927-1929), Blake (1977), Brazil (1991), Burton (1972b), Conover (1941), Cramp & Simmons (1983), Elvers (1988), Foster & Greaves (1986), de Groot (1993), Hilty & Brown (1986), Howell & Webb (1995a), Jaramillo & Henshaw (1995), Jehl (1963), Knystautas (1993), Matthiessen (1994), Miller *et al.* (1984), Minton & Campbell (1995), Nehls (1989), de la Peña (1992), Pitelka (1950), Ridgely & Gwynne (1989), Robbins *et al.* (1983), Rogacheva (1992), Root (1988), Slud (1964), Stiles & Skutch (1989), Tomkins (1964), Tomkovich (1992b), Ulrich (1984), Wetmore (1965), White & Mitchell (1990), Wilds & Newton (1983), Wills (1958), Yésou (1982).

27. Asian Dowitcher

Limnodromus semipalmatus

French: Bécassin d'Asie **German**: Steppenschlammläufer **Spanish**: Agujeta Asiática
Other common names: Asiatic/Snipe-billed Dowitcher

Taxonomy. *Macrorhamphus semipalmatus* Blyth, 1848, Calcutta.
Formerly placed in genus *Pseudoscolopax*. Separation of W & E breeding populations, with different migration routes and wintering areas, may warrant subspecific status. Monotypic.
Distribution. Disjunct populations from W to E Siberian steppe regions, S into Mongolia and N Manchuria; the eastern areas may be continuous. Winters from E India through SE Asia, SE Sumatra and Java to N Australia.

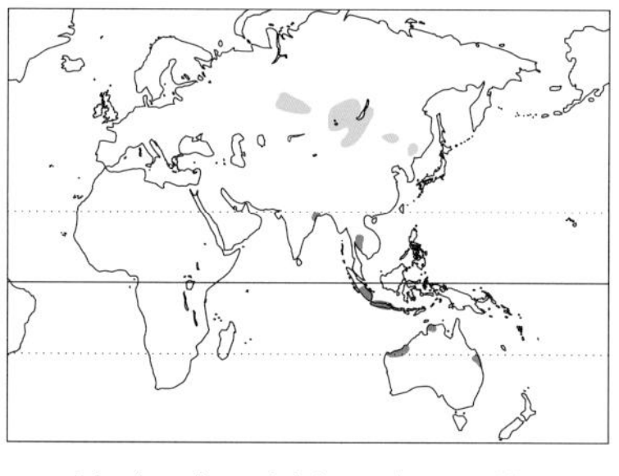

Descriptive notes. 33-36 cm; 127-245 g; wingspan 59 cm. Face, neck and breast chestnut-red, lower belly and flanks mainly white; upperparts blackish broadly fringed pale brown and chestnut, streaked rather than mottled. Noticeably larger than congeners, with fewer dark markings on neck and breast. Similar in plumage to *Limosa lapponica*, but smaller, with bill straighter, not tapering, differently shaped and mostly black; rump is barred (unlike *Limosa l. lapponica* and *L. l. menzbieri*) and underwing mostly white with fine black streaking; bill normally held at lower angle. Female somewhat duller than male with more white in chestnut areas. Non-breeding adult has pale supercilium, darkish grey-brown upperparts, grey-brown mottled breast and whitish underparts. Juvenile has streaks on buff neck and breast; upperparts black with narrow pale buff fringes.

Habitat. Breeding in extensive freshwater wetlands on lake shores or in deltas and flooded areas of rivers, e.g. flooded meadows and grassy bogs, in steppe and forest-steppe zone, with short vegetation of grasses and sedges; observed feeding in rice fields. During non-breeding season, occurs in sheltered coastal environments, primarily estuarine and intertidal mudflats, muddy lagoons, tidal creeks and salt-works. Roosts, often with *Limosa*, on sandy beaches or in shallow lagoons.

Food and Feeding. Poorly known. On breeding grounds, takes small fish, insect larvae and oligochaetes. Away from breeding grounds feeds on polychaetes, insect larvae and molluscs, following edge of receding or incoming tide. Feeds on damp ground or in shallow water by walking and repeatedly probing deeply into mud, sometimes fully submerging head; feeds with stiff neck and typical wooden "sewing-machine" action; large prey is pulled up slowly with tremendous effort, small prey can be taken quickly. Gregarious, usually in pairs or small flocks, sometimes in large flocks of over 100 birds at roosts and favoured feeding sites.

Breeding. Lays late May to early Jun; timing and location of breeding may vary considerably, depending on water levels. Breeds in small colonies of 6-20 pairs, with nests 4-350 m apart, often mixed with White-winged Terns (*Chlidonias leucopterus*); territorial. Nests in sparsely vegetated parts of breeding area; nest is shallow depression on bare ground or in vegetation, lined with grass, sometimes 8-12 cm above water that is up to 25 cm deep. 2 eggs, rarely 3; single brood; incubation c. 22 days, by both parents; both parents tend chicks. Nests may fail due to flooding (occasionally 75% or more) and trampling by cattle.

Movements. Not well known. On migration occurs in small numbers in Japan, China, Hong Kong, Thailand, Malaysia, Philippines, E Kazakhstan, Uzbekistan, Mongolia and NE India; migration may occur across interior of C Asia and along SE Asian coast. Largest wintering populations are probably those of E & SE Sumatra and N Java; smaller numbers occur in NW Australia (no more than 500). Westernmost population may, in fact, migrate SW, to winter in Persian Gulf and on coast of Arabian Sea; presumed vagrants have turned up in Arabia, and even in Kenya. Present in wintering areas from early Sept to late Apr. Departs from wintering grounds from Mar, mostly Apr; arrives on breeding grounds early to late May. Small groups remain in winter quarters during boreal summer.

Status and Conservation. Not globally threatened. Currently considered near-threatened. Recent work in Indonesia, mostly in Sumatra, has shown that world population comprises at least 20,000 birds; previously considered rare. Important wintering sites are Banyuasin Delta (Sumatra), where up to 13,000 birds estimated in 1988, and Ujung Pangkah (E Java); significant numbers have been counted in Philippines, India and Thailand; during migration significant numbers occur at Hutan Bakau Pantai Timor and Tanjung Jabung (E Sumatra), Gulf of Thailand and Sheyang Salt-works (Jiangsu, China). During severe droughts in Mongolia and China, large numbers appear in N parts of breeding range, e.g. c. 6000 were breeding at Selenga Delta, L Baikal, in late 1970's. At present reckoned not to be in immediate danger, although dependent on rather a small number of wetlands; drainage or drying out of wetlands reduces

area of suitable breeding habitat. Poorly studied; listed as endangered in Russian Red Data Book. Population density everywhere small; numbers difficult to estimate, as typically flocks together with very similar *Limosa lapponica*, hampering counts and easily causing present species to be overlooked.

Bibliography. Ali & Ripley (1980), Barthel (1988), Beehler *et al.* (1986), Blakers *et al.* (1984), Brazil (1991), Brouwer & Garnett (1990), Collar & Andrew (1988), Dementiev & Gladkov (1951b), Dickinson *et al.* (1991), Étchécopar & Hüe (1978), Evans (1994), Fennell *et al.* (1985), Fiebig & Jander (1985), Finch (1981), Garnett (1993), Glustchenko & Shibnev (1979), Heron (1977), Howes & Parish (1989), Jaensch (1983b), King (1978/79), Knystautas (1993), Kuchin & Chekcheev (1987b), Lane & Davies (1987), Lekagul & Round (1991), Leonovitch (1976a), Liedel (1982, 1987), MacKinnon & Phillipps (1993), Marchant & Higgins (1996), van Marle & Voous (1988), Mauersberger *et al.* (1982), Medway & Wells (1976), Melnikov, Y.I. (1985, 1988, 1990a, 1990b, 1991a, 1991b, 1994), Melville & Round (1982), Mikhalkin & Bascakov (1987), Osipova (1986), Paige (1965), Perennou *et al.* (1994), Pitelka (1948), Ripley (1982), Rogacheva (1992), Scott (1989), Silvius (1986, 1988), Silvius & Erftenmeijer (1989), Smart & Forbes-Watson (1971), Smith (1974), Smythies (1986), Sueur *et al.* (1990), Tipper (1993), Tolchin & Melnikov (1977), Urban *et al.* (1986), Verheugt (1988), Verheugt, Danielsen *et al.* (1990), Verheugt, Skov & Danielsen (1993), Williams, M.D. (1986), Yurlov (1981).

ssp *melanuroides*

♂

28

♂

ssp *limosa*

29

♀

30

♀

♂

31

♂

32

33

ssp *phaeopus*

34

35

36

ssp *hudsonicus*

40

37

38

39

PLATE 42

inches 7

cm 18

Subfamily TRINGINAE

Tribe NUMENIINI

Genus *LIMOSA* Brisson, 1760

28. **Black-tailed Godwit**

Limosa limosa

French: Barge à queue noire **German**: Uferschnepfe **Spanish**: Aguja Colinegra

Taxonomy. *Scolopax Limosa* Linnaeus, 1758, Sweden.
Forms superspecies with *L. haemastica*, with which sometimes considered conspecific. Three subspecies recognized.
Subspecies and Distribution.
L. l. islandica C. L. Brehm, 1831 - Iceland, Faeroes, Shetland and Lofoten Is; winters in Ireland, Britain, W France, Spain and Portugal.
L. l. limosa (Linnaeus, 1758) - W & C Europe and Russia E to upper R Yenisey; winters in Mediterranean and sub-Saharan Africa, and E through Middle East to W India.
L. l. melanuroides Gould, 1846 - disjunct populations in Siberia E of R Yenisey, E Mongolia, NE China and Russian Far East; winters from India, Indochina, Taiwan and Philippines S to Indonesia, New Guinea and Australia.

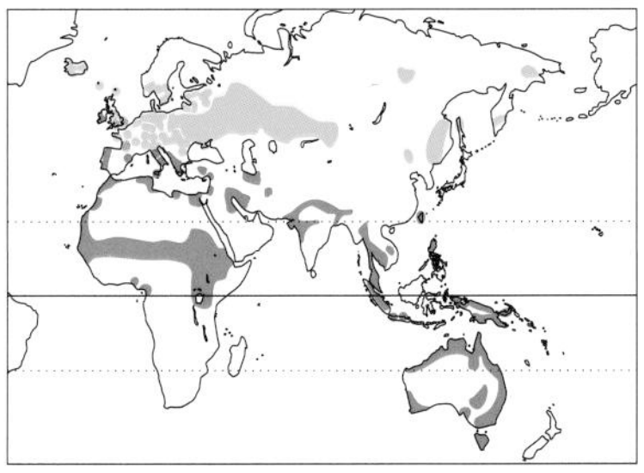

Descriptive notes. 36-44 cm; male 160-440 g, female 244-500 g; wingspan 70-82 cm. Tall, elegant godwit with chestnut breast and upper belly; dark brown barring on belly, with lower belly white; mantle and scapulars blotched pale red, black and grey; long, straightish bill orange pink at base; long legs. Variable numbers of brownish grey feathers in upperparts give untidy, half-moulted look. Combination of distinctive black tail and white uppertail-coverts and wingbar separates from *L. lapponica* and *L. fedoa*, and white underwing separates from *L. haemastica*. Female paler and less red than male, with less barring on underparts; bill averages longer. Non-breeding adult pale grey-brown above, greyish white below, with pale greyish supercilium; lacks chestnut; base of bill fleshy pink. Juvenile as non-breeding adult but upperparts dark grey-brown, with pale chestnut and buff fringes; neck and breast pale cinnamon, more richly coloured in race *islandica*; no barring on white underparts. Races *islandica* smaller than nominate, *melanuroides* smaller still; both are darker red and have shorter bills than nominate; non-breeding *melanuroides* has darker upperparts and breast.
Habitat. Wet grassland with moderately high grass and soft soil, in lowlands; also grassy marshland, raised bogs and moorland, reclaimed areas and damp grassy depressions in steppe. Winters in sheltered estuaries and lagoons with large intertidal mudflats, sandy beaches, salt-marshes, salt-flats, and inland wetlands, such as swampy lake shores, river pools, flooded grassland and irrigated rice fields. Race *limosa* winters mainly in freshwater habitats; *islandica* and *melanuroides* mainly in estuarine habitats.
Food and Feeding. Chiefly invertebrates, most frequently insects and their larvae (especially beetles), annelids, molluscs, ragworms, crustaceans, spiders, fish eggs, and spawn and tadpoles of frogs; also plant material, such as berries and seeds, especially of rice. In winter quarters, race *limosa* feeds mainly on plant material, in parts of W Africa almost 100% rice; also takes chironomid larvae and snails. Feeds by picking and by forward-angled, prolonged probes. Locates food by touch or sight; recorded foot-trembling to disturb prey; sometimes washes food. Usually feeds gregariously in winter and on migration, using communal night-time roosts in shallow water. Chicks on pastures feed very actively on mobile prey in quite tall vegetation.
Breeding. Laying Apr to mid-Jun. Monogamous on long-term basis. Often in loose, semi-colonial groups, up to 3 pairs/ha. High degree of site fidelity, low degree of natal philopatry. Nest in short vegetation, open to rather concealed, lined with thick mat of vegetation. 4 eggs (3-5), with laying interval 1-2 days; single brood, but replacement clutches laid; incubation 22-24 days, by both sexes; chick light pinkish cinnamon with fuscous bands and mottles on back, wing-pads and thighs; both sexes care for young, although brooding primarily by female; fledging 28-34 days. Including failed nests, 49% of eggs hatch; c. 26% of nests in meadows and c. 62% in pastures produce at least 1 hatchling; production on agricultural grasslands c. 0·4 fledglings per breeding pair, but half of these fledglings die without becoming adults; mortality may increase dramatically during cold spells, especially in combination with rain; trampling by cattle, predation and agricultural activities, notably mowing, may cause high losses. Annual adult mortality c. 20%; 1st-year mortality c. 40%. Age of first breeding 1 year, sometimes older.
Movements. Migration on broad front, often overland, characterized by long distance flights between relatively few staging sites and wintering areas. S migration late Jun to Oct, return passage Feb-Apr. Many 1-year-olds spend summer in winter quarters. Race *islandica* migrates via Ireland to coasts of British Is, France, Spain and Portugal, and some to Morocco. Main body of *limosa* population winters in W Africa S of Sahara, Sept-Mar, flying through France and Iberia, and pausing in N Morocco to moult; may have more easterly route back to breeding grounds; populations from C & E Europe and Russia winter in sub-Saharan Africa from Mali and L Chad eastwards; they fly in broad front between Balkans and Black Sea; breeding birds from Kazakhstan winter in India. Origin of wintering birds in E Spain and Tunisia unknown. Race *melanuroides* migrates through Mongolia, Ussuriland, Manchuria, Korea, Japan, Taiwan, Philippines, Hainan and China, some passing through Indochina, SE Asia and Malay Peninsula; staging areas in SE Sumatra used on S migration towards Australia. During N migration, may roost in concentrations of up to 12,000 birds in moist pastures, in Netherlands.
Status and Conservation. Not globally threatened. Total population estimated at 140,000-270,000 pairs, of which over two thirds breed in Europe, with 85,000-100,000 pairs breeding in Netherlands alone; 110,000-120,000 winter in rice fields in Guinea-Bissau (1986) and of 10,000's in Senegambia and Niger inundation zone; minimum of 25,000 winter in SW Asia and minimum 100,000 in SC Asia, with high numbers in Pakistan; Australasian wintering population estimated at 162,000 birds, of which 81,000 in Australia, with SE Gulf of Carpentaria and NE Arnhem Land being most important sites; abundant in Indonesia. Race *islandica* numbers c. 65,000 birds (1989), possibly less, but numbers increasing. Up to 1970's marked increase in W European countries, including Iceland; colonized Finland and Norway, and recolonized Britain during present century. Increase mainly due to ability to adapt to man-made habitats, e.g. fertilized meadows. However, substantial decline occurred in 1970-1990, mainly due to effects of agricultural intensification, e.g. drainage, and earlier and rotary mowing; drought in W African wintering grounds may also have been factor. Numbers in SC Asian wintering grounds are increasing. Preservation of wet grassland in lowlands and regulation of disturbance from certain farming activities are main conservation measures necessary.
Bibliography. Ali & Ripley (1980), Altenburg & van der Kamp (1985), Altenburg *et al*. (1985), van Balen (1959), Beehler *et al*. (1986), Beintema (1985, 1986b, 1991a, 1991b, 1991c, 1994), Beintema & Drost (1986), Beintema & Müskens (1987), Beintema & Visser (1989a, 1989b), Beintema, Beintema-Hietbrink & Müskens (1985), Beintema, Thissen *et al*. (1991), Blakers *et al*. (1984), Brager & Meissner (1990), Brazier (1991b), Brazil (1991), Buker & Groen (1989), Byrkjedal (1985b), Chambers (1989), Coates (1985), Cramp & Simmons (1983), Danielsen & Skov (1988), Dementiev & Gladkov (1951b), Dickinson *et al*. (1991), van Dijk (1980), Dowsett & Forbes-Watson (1993), Dubois & Maheo (1986), Elgood *et al*. (1994), Étchécopar & Hüe (1964, 1978), Evans (1994), Fjeldså (1977), Gerritsen (1990), Glutz von Blotzheim *et al*. (1977), Golovina (1988), Goodman *et al*. (1989), Gore (1990), Green, Cadbury & Williams (1987), Green, Hirons & Kirby (1990), Groen (1991, 1993), Haverschmidt (1963b), Hoogerwerf (1964), Hötker (1991), Hüe & Étchécopar (1970), Kirby & Green (1991), Kirchner (1969), Knystautas (1993), Lane & Davies (1987), Lekagul & Round (1991), Lind (1961), MacKinnon & Phillipps (1993), Mackworth-Praed & Grant (1957, 1962, 1970), Marchant & Higgins (1996), van Marle & Voous (1988), Meadows (1977), Medway & Wells (1976), Moreira (1994), Morel & Roux (1966), Mulder (1972), Palsson (1992), Patrikeev (1995), Paz (1987), Perennou (1991), Perennou *et al*. (1994), Phillips (1978), Piersma (1983, 1986b), Prater (1975), Rahmani & Shobrak (1992), Rands *et al*. (1987), Ripley (1982), Roberts, T.J. (1991), Rogacheva (1992), Roselaar & Gerritsen (1991), Rutgers & Norris (1970), van Scheepen & Oreel (1995), Scott (1989), Serra & Baccetti (1991), Shirihai (1996), Short *et al*. (1990), Smythies (1986), Tolchin & Melnikov (1974), Tomialojc (1994b), Tréca (1984), Urban *et al*. (1986), Watkins (1993), White & Bruce (1986), Williams, M.D. (1986), Witt (1992), Wymenga & Altenburg (1989).

29. **Hudsonian Godwit**

Limosa haemastica

French: Barge hudsonienne **German**: Hudsonschnepfe **Spanish**: Aguja Café

Taxonomy. *Scolopax Hæmastica* Linnaeus, 1758, Hudson Bay.
Forms superspecies with *L. limosa*, of which sometimes considered a subspecies. Monotypic.
Distribution. Locally from NW & S Alaska to Hudson Bay. Winters on Atlantic coast of S South America; also Chiloé I, SC Chile.

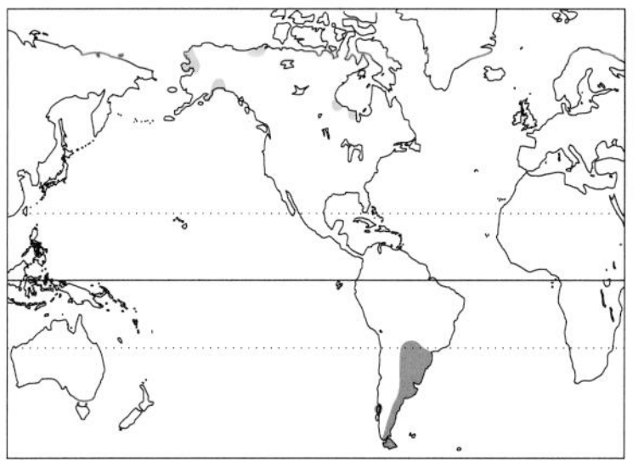

Descriptive notes. 36-42 cm; male 196-266 g, female 246-358 g; wingspan 66 cm. Darkish godwit with slightly uptilted bill; face and throat whitish; breast, belly and undertail-coverts deep chestnut, irregularly barred; upperparts dark brown with variable buff or cinnamon fringes and notches; in flight, narrow white wingbar and very dark underwing. Structure intermediate between *L. limosa* and *L. lapponica*; extent of barring on underparts variable, but always more than in *L. lapponica*. Female less reddish chestnut; paler on mantle; heavily blotched white below, frequently barred. Non-breeding adult dark, plain grey-brown on breast and upperparts, white on lower belly; white supercilium; bill base brownish. Juvenile has dark upperparts, fringed with buff; neck and breast washed brownish buff; lower belly whitish.
Habitat. Sedgy marshland near tree-line in lowlands, close to coast or river. In winter and on migration, occurs in muddy estuaries, tidal pools, coastal lagoons, flooded grassland, shallow freshwater lakes, rice paddies and salt-works; less often on sandy beaches.
Food and Feeding. On breeding gounds mainly Diptera larvae; also snails, beetles, adult insects and seeds. Diet on wintering grounds not well known; includes worms, insects, molluscs, crustaceans and other small invertebrates; polychaete worms predominate on intertidal mudflats of Tierra del Fuego; sometimes plant tubers in N of range. Feeding behaviour rather similar to that of *L. limosa*; often wades in water 10-15 cm deep. Mostly feeds gregariously.
Breeding. Nests late May to Jul. Nest typically placed on dry hummock at edge of dwarf birch, usually well hidden; saucer-shaped depression in or under edge of prostrate dwarf birches or on top of dry hummock in sedge marsh. Usually 4 eggs; incubation 22-25 days, by female during day, male at night; chick pale buff-grey to buffy brown, with brownish black dorsal stripes and blotches, brownish black crown patch and greyish white underparts; both sexes care for young until just before fledging; fledging c. 30 days.
Movements. Long distance migrant. During late Aug, much of population gathers along S Hudson Bay and James Bay and at certain sites in Saskatchewan and Alberta; crosses W Atlantic and arrives at unknown locations in N South America and stages at Amazon basin, then possibly passes through W Brazil on way to S Argentina; apparently young depart after adults. Birds wintering around Chiloé I may originate from Alaska, and follow different route. N migration probably very rapid, using few or no staging sites in South America; passage through USA more westerly, with many birds crossing Great Plains, Apr-May; rarely on Pacific coast of Guatemala and Costa Rica. Main wintering sites are Tierra del Fuego and areas around Chiloé I in SC Chile.
Status and Conservation. Not globally threatened. Currently considered near-threatened. Total population c. 50,000 birds or perhaps more; on South American wintering grounds 45,500 birds counted (1989), with 19,400 in Bahía de San Sebastian and 10,500 in Bahía Lomas (Tierra del Fuego), and over 12,600 in Chiloé area. Until 1960, species was considered threatened, largely as result of being very poorly known; now considered to be locally common in breeding range. Population thought to be stable.
Bibliography. Armstrong (1983), Baker, M.C. (1977), Belton (1984), Bent (1927-1929), Blake (1977), Brown & Engleman (1986), Contreras *et al*. (1990), Cox (1990), Fjeldså & Krabbe (1990), Grieve (1987), Hagar (1966, 1983),

On following pages: 30. Bar-tailed Godwit (*Limosa lapponica*); 31. Marbled Godwit (*Limosa fedoa*); 32. Little Curlew (*Numenius minutus*); 33. Eskimo Curlew (*Numenius borealis*); 34. Whimbrel (*Numenius phaeopus*); 35. Bristle-thighed Curlew (*Numenius tahitiensis*); 36. Slender-billed Curlew (*Numenius tenuirostris*); 37. Eurasian Curlew (*Numenius arquata*); 38. Far Eastern Curlew (*Numenius madagascariensis*); 39. Long-billed Curlew (*Numenius americanus*); 40. Upland Sandpiper (*Bartramia longicauda*).

Harrington *et al.* (1993), Hayes (1995), Hayes & Fox (1991), Hilty & Brown (1986), Howell & Webb (1995a), Jehl & Smith (1970), Johnson (1965b), Martin, A.P. & Martin (1988), Martin, P. & Martin (1987), Matthiessen (1994), Meyer de Schauensee & Phelps (1978), Morris (1991), Patterson *et al.* (1994), de la Peña (1992), Ridgely & Gwynne (1989), Ryan & Graham (1989), Scott & Carbonell (1986), Seppi (1995), Sick (1985c, 1993), Skinner & Langham (1981), Stiles & Skutch (1989), Sutton (1968b), Tostain *et al.* (1992), Wetmore (1926), Williamson & Smith (1964), Wiltraut (1991), Wright (1987).

30. **Bar-tailed Godwit**

Limosa lapponica

French: Barge rousse **German**: Pfuhlschnepfe **Spanish**: Aguja Colipinta

Taxonomy. *Scolopax lapponica* Linnaeus, 1758, Lappland.
Race *menzbieri* sometimes included within race *baueri*. Three subspecies recognized.
Subspecies and Distribution.
L. l. lapponica (Linnaeus, 1758) - Lappland W through Kola and Kanin Peninsulas to Taymyr; winters from North Sea, W Iberia and NW Africa S to W South Africa, and E to Persian Gulf and W India.
L. l. menzbieri Portenko, 1936 - N Siberia, between R Khatanga and Kolyma Delta; winters from SE Asia to NW Australia, and possibly E Australia.
L. l. baueri Naumann, 1836 - NE Siberia, E of R Kolyma, to W Alaska; winters from China to New Zealand and some Pacific Is.

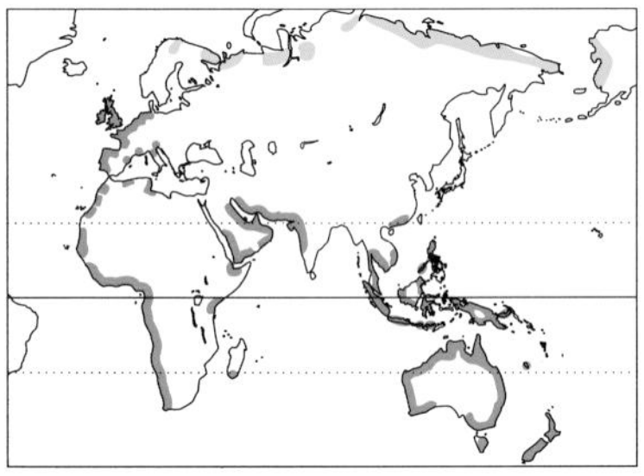

Descriptive notes. 37-41 cm; male 190-400 g, female 262-630 g; wingspan 70-80 cm. Medium-sized godwit with slightly upcurved bill and barred tail; in flight, lacks white wingbar and has white underwing; virtually no barring on underparts; upperparts fringed chestnut; shorter legs and bill, and less upright stance than other godwits. Less white on rufous underparts than *L. limosa*. Female larger with longer bill; much paler. Non-breeding adult has upperparts pale grey-brown, partly edged whitish; breast turns grey, with fine dark streaking; underparts white. Juvenile has neck and breast washed buff with scattered streaks; upperparts dark, with bright buff fringes; belly whitish; bill darker. Rump and uppertail-coverts white in nominate, but heavily barred brown in *baueri*; race *menzbieri* intermediate in plumage between nominate and *baueri*, with lower back and rump fairly strongly barred; bill and tarsus shortest in nominate; *baueri* has relatively long wings and tail.
Habitat. Lowland scrub tundra, forest tundra, rolling uplands, wet river valleys and open larch woodland close to water bodies. After breeding, mainly in intertidal areas, preferably sandy parts of estuaries, inlets, mangrove-fringed lagoons, sheltered bays. Locally at inland wetlands and short-grass meadows.
Food and Feeding. Diet on breeding grounds mainly comprises insects, annelids, molluscs, occasionally seeds and berries. Non-breeding diet mainly *Nereis* and *Arenicola*, and smaller annelids, bivalves, crustaceans in intertidal areas, cranefly larvae and lumbricids in grassland; occasionally tadpoles, small fish and fruits. Feeds by pecking, stitching or probing. Longer-billed females tend to feed in deeper water. Outside breeding season, feeds in flocks, e.g. along edge of tide.
Breeding. Lays late May to Jun. Monogamous. Densities 0·1-1·0 pairs/km². Nest usually on dry, elevated sites, often between clumps of grass; depression lined with bits of vegetation and lichens. 4 eggs (2-5); single brood; incubation 20-21 days, by female at night and male during day; chick pale vinaceous cinnamon to pinkish cinnamon to nearly white on belly, brownish cap and dark brown bands and mottles on back, wing-pads and thighs; both parents tend young, or possibly only male; fledging c. 28 days; adults depart soon after young fledge. Annual mortality 40%. Age of first breeding 2 years.
Movements. Long distance migrant. Race *lapponica* wintering in Europe originates from N Europe and Russia E to Yamal Peninsula; birds breeding further E (to Taymyr) winter in W Africa, Sept-Apr, staging at W European intertidal areas during mid-Apr to May and mid-Jul to Aug; females winter further S than males. Major migration passes through North Sea basin and Baltic, only some through Caspian Sea area, presumably birds wintering in S Africa; inland records suggest continental crossing by SW African wintering birds. In Apr-May, many birds gather in Wadden Sea to moult and fatten. In E Asia, *baueri* and *menzbieri*, commonly migrate through W Kamchatka, Sakhalin, Japan and Korea; probably also use trans-Pacific route, between Korea, Japan and SE China and Australia. Wintering birds in NW Australia are likely to be of race *menzbieri*, while SE Australian birds possibly originate from Alaska. Alaskan birds move down Bering Sea coast and through Pribilof and Aleutian Is. High degree of site fidelity on non-breeding grounds; many non-breeders remain S all year.
Status and Conservation. Not globally threatened. European wintering population fluctuates, but estimated at 115,000 birds (1989), with up to 57,000 in Britain; numbers in Britain and Portugal decreased during 1980's, but may now be increasing; up to 341,000 birds counted staging in Wadden Sea; W & S African wintering population estimated at minimum 700,000 birds (1989); at least 100,000 *lapponica* winter in E Africa and SW Asia. Of race *baueri* and *menzbieri* c. 165,000 birds winter in Australia, with 65,000 in Roebuck Bay and 34,000 on Eighty Mile Beach, 102,000 in New Zealand (1988) and 125,000 in E & SE Asia; numbers increasing in some areas. Species vulnerable due to concentration at a few wetlands in non-breeding season. Land reclamation, pollution and human disturbance have detrimental effects on feeding conditions. Important staging and wintering areas in France, Portugal and Guinea-Bissau are not yet protected. Other important wintering areas may include sites in Oman, Saudi Arabia and Sumatra.
Bibliography. Ali & Ripley (1980), Altenburg *et al.* (1982), Armstrong (1983), Barter (1989a, 1989b), Barter & Wang Tianhou (1990), Beehler *et al.* (1986), Bent (1927-1929), Blakers *et al.* (1984), Brader (1991), Brazil (1991), Bregulla (1992), Byrkjedal *et al.* (1989), Chambers (1989), Coates (1985), Cramp & Simmons (1983), Danielsen & Skov (1988), Dementiev & Gladkov (1951b), Dickinson *et al.* (1991), Dowsett & Forbes-Watson (1993), Étchécopar & Hüe (1964, 1978), Evans, M.I. (1994), Evans, M.I. & Keijl (1993b), Evans, P.R. & Smith (1975), Fjeldså (1977), Ginn *et al.* (1989), Goodman *et al.* (1989), Gore (1990), Hockey & Douie (1995), Hoogerwerf (1964), Hüe & Étchécopar (1970), Knystautas (1993), Lane & Davies (1987), Langrand (1990), Larsen (1993), Larsen & Moldsvor (1992), Lekagul & Round (1991), MacKinnon & Phillipps (1993), Mackworth-Praed & Grant (1957, 1962, 1970), Maclean (1993), Marchant & Higgins (1996), van Marle & Voous (1988), Medway & Wells (1976), Mercier *et al.* (1987), Milon *et al.* (1973), Mjelstad & Saetersdal (1986), Perennou *et al.* (1994), Phillips (1978), Pierre (1994), Piersma (1986b, 1989b), Piersma & Jukema (1990, 1993), Piersma, Klaassen *et al.* (1990), Pinto (1983), Prokosch (1988), Radamaker & Ludden (1993), Rands *et al.* (1987), Ripley (1982), Roberts, T.J. (1991), Rogacheva (1992), Schiefart *et al.* (1993), Scott (1989), Shirihai (1996), Short *et al.* (1990), Smit (1994), Smit & Piersma (1989), Smith & Evans (1973, 1975), Smythies (1981), Thompson (1990), Tulp *et al.* (1994), Urban *et al.* (1986), White & Bruce (1986), Williams, M.D. (1986), Yésou *et al.* (1992), Zwarts (1985, 1988).

31. **Marbled Godwit**

Limosa fedoa

French: Barge marbrée **German**: Marmorschnepfe **Spanish**: Aguja Canela

Taxonomy. *Scolopax Fedoa* Linnaeus, 1758, Hudson Bay.
Two subspecies recognized.
Subspecies and Distribution.
L. f. beringiae Gibson & Kessel, 1989 - Alaska Peninsula; winters on Pacific coast of USA from S Washington to C California.
L. f. fedoa (Linnaeus, 1758) - C Alberta and SW Manitoba to SC Montana and W Minnesota, also SW James Bay; winters from California and the Carolinas S to Panama, occasionally occurring S to N Chile, Colombia and Venezuela.

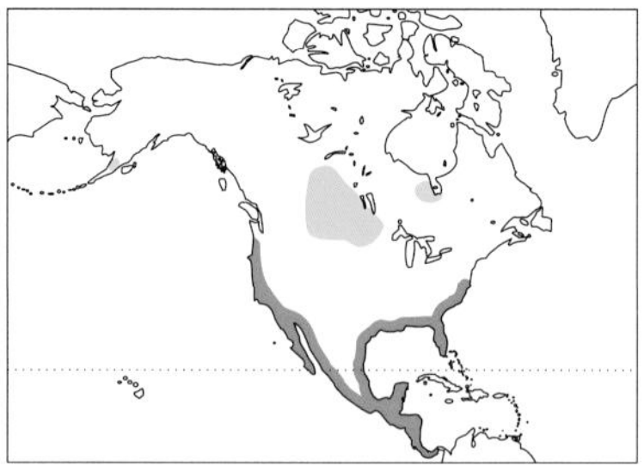

Descriptive notes. 42-48 cm; male 278-365 g, female 312-510 g. Fairly large cinnamon-buff godwit, with cinnamon wingbar and underwing; buff underparts irregularly streaked brown; upperparts with sooty black and reddish buff spotting and barring. Female more sparsely barred than male. Non-breeding adult paler and plainer above; few individuals can turn as pale as *L. lapponica*, but always has longer bill and legs. Juvenile as non-breeding adult, but with buff fringes to upperparts, underparts cinnamon-buff with only a little streaking. Race *beringiae* has shorter bill, wing and tarsus, but appears to be slightly heavier than nominate.
Habitat. Wet meadows and grassland near pools on prairies and coastal marshland. After breeding, largely coastal, occurring in muddy bays and estuaries, coastal pools and salt-marshes, preferably with adjoining wet savannas or grassy borders.
Food and Feeding. Mainly insects, also bivalves. In non-breeding range, takes small molluscs, crustaceans, insects, worms and leeches. Feeding style involves calm pecking and probing. Feeds in flocks on intertidal mudflats.
Breeding. Lays early May to Jun. Often in semi-colonial groups, up to 27 pairs/km². 4 eggs, sometimes 5, with laying interval 1-3 days; incubation 21-23 days, by both sexes; both parents tend chicks; fledging c. 3 weeks. Annual survival c. 87%; oldest ringed bird at least 25 years, 9 months.
Movements. Relatively short distance migrant. Movements in broad front over coast and interior; *beringiae* probably crosses Gulf of Alaska. Birds wintering on Pacific coast of USA (mainly Washington and Oregon) are probably *beringiae*, while *fedoa* presumably moves via W Montana, Idaho and E Oregon to Sacramento/San Joaquin Delta or San Francisco Bay area, and along Pacific coast southwards. During northward migration, high numbers stage at Cheyenne Bottoms (Kansas). High degree of wintering site fidelity. N migration of *beringiae* mainly late Apr and early May, some throughout May; southward Jul-Oct. Casual in West Indies. Traditionally said to winter S to N Chile, but only three records up to 1986, with first in 1852 and second not till 1977; only one record up to 1986 in Colombia, where probably occurs sporadically; also said to occur in Venezuela.
Status and Conservation. Not globally threatened. Total of c. 100,000 birds on Pacific flyway. Numbers apparently stable. Range has contracted considerably in recent decades, but species still moderately common in large part of breeding area; in 1967, total of 37,000 pairs were breeding in North Dakota. Decline at least partly caused by hunting and conversion for agriculture of prairie breeding grounds, on which species is fully dependent.
Bibliography. Argabrite (1988), Armstrong (1983), Bent (1927-1929), Blake (1977), Colwell *et al.* (1995), Cook (1986), Edwards (1989), Gibson & Kessel (1989), Heller (1991), Higgins *et al.* (1979), Hilty & Brown (1986), Horn (1990), Howell & Webb (1995a, 1995b), Igou (1986), Kelly & Cogswell (1979), Knopf (1994), Luckner (1992), Matthiessen (1994), McNeil *et al.* (1985), Mercier *et al.* (1987), Meretsy (1988), Monroe (1968), Nowicki (1973), Ridgely & Gwynne (1989), Root (1988), Ryan (1982), Ryan *et al.* (1984), Schaldach (1963), Slud (1964), Stiles & Skutch (1989), Ulrich (1984), Wetmore (1965), Whittle (1992), Wilbur (1987), Wishart & Spencer (1980).

Genus *NUMENIUS* Brisson, 1760

32. **Little Curlew**

Numenius minutus

French: Courlis nain **German**: Zwergbrachvogel **Spanish**: Zarapito Chico
Other common names: Little Whimbrel

Taxonomy. *Numenius minutus* Gould, 1841, New South Wales.
Forms superspecies with *N. borealis*, with which formerly considered conspecific. Monotypic.
Distribution. N & C Yakutia, from S slopes of Putorana Mts E to R Anabar, and Verkhoyansk and Cherski Mts on upper R Yana and R Indigirka as far E as R Anyuy, along Siberian coast. Winters in New Guinea and Australia.

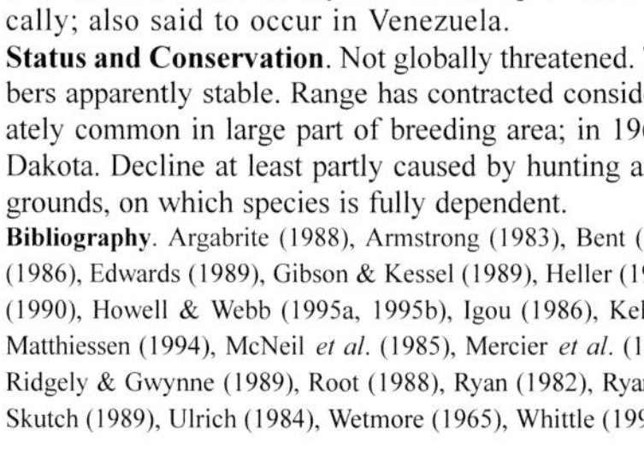

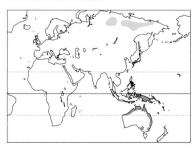

Descriptive notes. 28-32 cm; 118-221 g; wingspan 68-71 cm. Smallest curlew, with short bill only slightly and evenly decurved; rounded head and large eye, somewhat reminiscent of *Bartramia longicauda*; head strongly patterned with dark eyestripe, brown crown stripe and buffish supercilium; buffish brown rump and back. Very similar to *N. borealis*, but paler buff rather than cinnamon-coloured, less streaked on flanks and whiter on belly; shorter-winged, and at rest lacks distinct primary projection. Female averages slightly larger. No seasonal variation. Juvenile very similar to adult, but with pale buff spots and fringes on scapulars, and brown coverts broadly edged with buff; less streaking on flanks and breast.

Habitat. Breeds on N montane taiga, often in river valleys; preferably with secondary vegetation, such as fire-damaged areas, or grassy clearings in sparse larch or dwarf birch woodland. In non-breeding zone, found in dry, inland grassland, blacksoil plains, bare cultivation, often on artificial short-grass flats; always near fresh water, such as swamps, pools, lakes or flooded ground; rare on coast.
Food and Feeding. Mainly insects, including grasshoppers, crickets, weevils, beetles, caterpillars and ants; also spiders and vegetable matter, including seeds, rice husks and berries. Feeds mostly by picking and shallow probing. In winter quarters, occurs in dense flocks of several hundreds, sometimes thousands. Feeds in morning, and gathers near water to roost during warmest part of day, to resume foraging at mid-afternoon; forms roosting flocks again before night.
Breeding. Breeds late May to early Aug. Forms loose colonies. Nest is shallow depression lined with grass, in open ground. 4 eggs, sometimes 3; single brood; incubation 22-23 days, by both parents; fledging 5 weeks.
Movements. Migratory; primarily continental. Occurs on passage (mid-Aug to Oct) in S Siberia, Mongolia, Japan, China and E Indonesia and New Guinea; presumably moves in narrow front to and down coasts of Yellow and East China Seas; route S of China lies E of Borneo; presumably non-stop from China to S New Guinea and N Australia, and same route back. Main winter quarters, S New Guinea and N Australia, are reached in early Sept. Erratic movements within Australia depending on rainfall; once dry grassland becomes wet at start of monsoon (Nov-Dec), moves further inland, being most abundant on Barkly Tableland (Northern Territory) during main wet season (Jan to early Apr); in some years, reaches S Australia and Tasmania, rarely New Zealand. Flocks move N from early Apr, primarily through unflooded grasslands near Broome (CN Western Australia) and Karumba (NW Queensland). Departs N Australia late Mar to late Apr, probably non-stop to China. Moves in flocks of up to 1000 birds. 1st-year birds presumably leave Australia during non-breeding season.
Status and Conservation. Not globally threatened. CITES I. Total population c. 200,000 birds; abundant in N Australia, with 180,000 birds; 250,000 birds recorded at Humpty Doo, near Darwin, N Australia, in 1966, but possibly an overestimate; important areas are Alligator Rivers area with c. 180,000 birds, Roebuck Plains with c. 50,000, and Anna Plains with c. 12,000. In 1992, total of 324 birds reported to be wintering in China. No threats in wintering area, as favoured habitat is very extensive in N Australia. In Australia, has benefited from provision of watering points and large areas of grassland for livestock, and maybe from control of numbers of feral water buffalo (*Bubalus bubalis*), though in some areas this has led to denser vegetation cover, leaving less suitable habitat for shorebirds. Agricultural intensification and pesticides could affect population. Species formerly considered rare, but breeding range is much more extensive than formerly believed. Listed by CITES due to very similar appearance to Critically Endangered *N. borealis*.
Bibliography. Andersson, G. (1971), Artyukhov (1988), Bamford (1989, 1990), Barter (1992c), Beaman (1994), Beehler *et al*. (1986), Blakers *et al*. (1984), Boswall & Veprintsev (1985), Brazil (1991), Butyev (1983), Coates (1985), Cramp & Simmons (1983), Crawford, D.N. (1978), Dementiev & Gladkov (1951b), Dickinson *et al*. (1991), Étchécopar & Hüe (1978), Farrand (1977), Garnett & Minton (1985), Hicks & Burrows (1994), Hoogerwerf (1964), Jaensch (1994), Knystautas (1993), Labutin *et al*. (1982), Lane & Davies (1987), MacKinnon & Phillipps (1993), Marchant & Higgins (1996), McGill (1960), McKean *et al*. (1986), Moon (1983), Park (1986), Rogacheva (1992), Scott (1989), Veprintsev & Zablotskaya (1982), Vinokurov (1976b), Volkov (1986), Walker & Gregory (1987), Watkins (1993), White & Bruce (1986), Williams, M.D. (1986).

33. Eskimo Curlew

Numenius borealis

French: Courlis esquimau **German**: Eskimobrachvogel **Spanish**: Zarapito Esquimal

Taxonomy. *Scolopax borealis* J. R. Forster, 1772, Fort Albany, Hudson Bay.
Forms superspecies with *N. minutus*, with which formerly regarded as conspecific. Monotypic.
Distribution. CN Canada, on S shore and inland of Amundsen Gulf along Coppermine R to Point L; possibly also N Alaska. Winters in Uruguay and Argentina and possibly also in Chile.

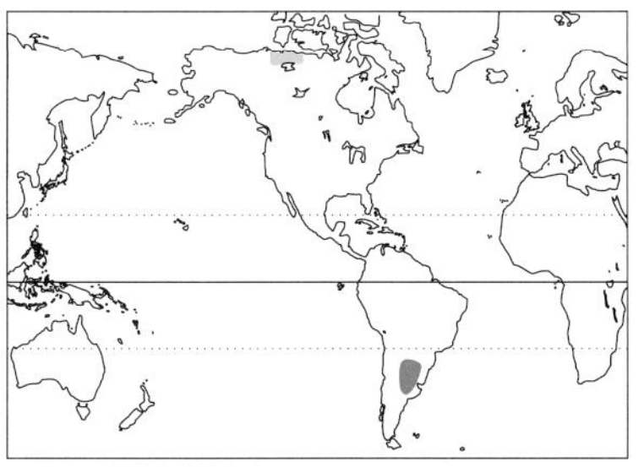

Descriptive notes. 29-34 cm. Tiny curlew with rather short bill and legs; dark eyestripe and black crown streaked with pale buff; upperparts with brown-buff notches; underparts buff-cinnamon with streaks on breast and Y-shaped marks on flanks. Somewhat larger and more cinnamon-coloured than *N. minutus*; more heavily marked below; wings longer and more pointed; bill longer and more decurved. Female averages slightly larger. No seasonal variation. Juvenile as adult, but underparts more buff and upperparts with neat pale buff fringes and spotting.
Habitat. Barren Arctic tundra, just N of tree-line and lowlands along coast. In Maritime Provinces of Canada, frequents areas covered in ripening bushes of crowberry (*Empetrum nigrum*) on tundra hillsides; these were on occasion called "curlew-berry" as a consequence. On migration, occurs on prairies and coastal grassland; winters on *pampas* grassland.
Food and Feeding. On breeding grounds, takes ants, grubs and freshwater insects; also large proportions of crowberries. On southward migration, feeds mainly on field crickets and grasshoppers and also other insects, snails and worms; on northward migration apparently chiefly grasshopper egg pods. In past, was highly gregarious in foraging.
Breeding. Not well known. Laying probably in Jun, and birds seen on nesting grounds from late May to early Aug. Nest is mere hollow in barren ground, lined with few leaves. 3-4 eggs, with highly variable camouflage pattern; hatching peaks from late Jun to mid-Jul; downy chicks undescribed.
Movements. Migratory; leaves breeding grounds late Jul to early Aug; moves via Canadian Maritime Provinces and New England; departs from Labrador and Newfoundland on a direct oceanic flight to N South America, a distance of 4000-5000 km, late Aug to early Sept; some birds follow route along W shores of Hudson and James Bays, SE across Quebec and then down over WC Atlantic. Chief wintering grounds probably in Uruguay and Argentina, and possibly also in Paraguay and Chile; may occur S to S Argentina. Return migration starts late Feb to early Mar, and follows route farther W, moving through Yucatán across Gulf of Mexico to Texas coast, and continuing N along W Mississippi Basin and Prairie Provinces of Canada to breeding grounds. Arrives on breeding grounds from mid-May.
Status and Conservation. CRITICALLY ENDANGERED. CITES I. World population estimated at 50 birds in 1992. Apparently very abundant before 1850, although perhaps not as abundant as often suggested; subsequently, serious decline due to excessive shooting on Atlantic seaboard and along R Mississippi; there is no evidence for suggested shooting on wintering grounds. Habitat loss on Argentinian *pampas* and at stopover sites on North American prairies may have been significant factors in decline. However, many wintering areas in Argentina and Uruguay still provide excellent shorebird habitat. As population never recovered after hunting stopped, some important ecological factor may have been operating. Species now very close to extinction and only occasionally reported: 18 times between 1982 and 1987. Report of a nest in Canada in 1992 now considered likely to have been referable to *N. phaeopus*, as thorough searches have revealed no further sightings. In 1987 a recovery plan was devised, and in 1990 an advisory group was formed. Species is legally protected in USA, Canada, Argentina and Mexico.
Bibliography. Anon. (1995k, 1995l, 1995m), Banks (1977), Bent (1927-1929), Blanco, D.E. *et al*. (1993), Blake (1977), Canevari & Blanco (1994), Chebez (1994), Collar & Andrew (1988), Collar, Crosby & Stattersfield (1994), Collar, Gonzaga *et al*. (1992), Daniels (1972), Dinsmore (1988), Emanuel (1962), Eubanks & Collins (1993), Faanes (1990a), Faanes & Senner (1991), Farrand (1977), Gollop (1988), Gollop *et al*. (1986), Hagar & Anderson (1977), Hayes (1995), Howell & Webb (1995a), Iversen (1976, 1989a, 1989b, 1995), Johnson (1965b), King (1978/79), Lahrman (1972), MacKay (1996), Matthiessen (1994), Michelutti (1991), de la Peña (1992), Sick (1993), Tostain *et al*. (1992), Wege & Long (1995), Weston & Williams (1965), Williams (1988).

34. Whimbrel

Numenius phaeopus

French: Courlis corlieu **German**: Regenbrachvogel **Spanish**: Zarapito Trinador

Taxonomy. *Scolopax phœopus* Linnaeus, 1758, Sweden.
Four subspecies recognized.
Subspecies and Distribution.
N. p. phaeopus (Linnaeus, 1758) - Iceland, Faeroes and N Scotland through Scandinavia to R Yenisey and SW Taymyr; winters from extreme SW Europe and Africa through Middle East to W India, Sri Lanka and Andaman and Nicobar Is.
N. p. alboaxillaris Lowe, 1921 - steppes N of Caspian Sea; winters on islands and coasts of W Indian Ocean.
N. p. variegatus (Scopoli, 1786) - NE Siberia, from Verkhoyansk Mts, and perhaps SE Taymyr, to basins of R Kolyma and R Anadyr; winters from E India to Taiwan, and S through Philippines and Indonesia to Australasia.
N. p. hudsonicus Latham, 1790 - W & N Alaska, E to W Yukon and NW Mackenzie, and also W Hudson Bay; winters from S USA to S South America.

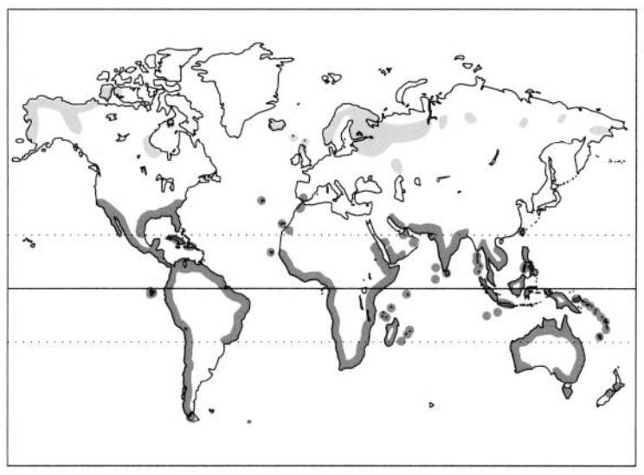

Descriptive notes. 40-46 cm; male 268-550 g, female 315-600 g; wingspan 76-89 cm. Medium-sized curlew showing blackish brown crown with pale central stripe, conspicuous pale supercilium and medium-sized bill; upperparts greyish brown with pale spotting; neck and breast finely streaked. Generally darker and greyer above than other *Numenius*; differs from larger curlews and generally paler *N. tenuirostris* by dark loral stripes and crown stripe; from very similar *N. tahitiensis* by smaller, paler markings on upperparts, more extensive markings on underparts, and different colour of rump and uppertail-coverts. Female averages slightly larger. No seasonal variation. Juvenile as adult, but upperparts brown with buff fringes and spots and underparts more buff; juvenile *hudsonicus* browner above and more buff below. Race *alboaxillaris*, like nominate, has unbarred white lower back and rump, and white underwing, which is almost unbarred in paler *alboaxillaris*; *variegatus* and *hudsonicus* have underwing brown; *hudsonicus* richer buff overall, with lower back and rump brown.
Habitat. Boreal, subarctic and subalpine moorland, birch forest and tundra near tree-line, open montane forest and river valleys. On migration, occurs in wetlands, on tidal flats and dry to wet grassland; in spring, prefers heathland with crowberries (*Empetrum*) and farmland; during migration often visits inland grassland to feed. In winter, essentially coastal, occupying exposed reefs, muddy, rocky or sandy beaches, tidal mudflats and mangrove swamps. Roosts communally in mangroves; may perch high up in mangrove trees; uses night-time communal roosts in shallow water during migration.
Food and Feeding. Inland diet includes insects (beetles and Orthoptera, and cranefly larvae), spiders, millipedes, earthworms, snails and slugs; on arrival at breeding grounds, also berries; on southward migration, also seeds and leaves. On coast, diet includes crabs and other crustaceans, molluscs, large polychaetes and rarely fish, reptiles and birds. Usually feeds more by pecking than by probing; feeds on crabs by probing in burrows. Generally forages in small groups or singly; individuals may defend feeding territory on wintering grounds.
Breeding. Laying May to mid-Jun. Monogamous and solitary, in densities of 1-11 pairs/km². Nest is depression filled with fragments of vegetation, usually in exposed location. 4 eggs (2-5); single brood; incubation 22-28 days, by both sexes, but more by female; chick warm buff above clouded with blackish brown, dark crown with buff mid-line, and creamy buff belly; both parents care for young; fledging 35-40 days. In NE Lapland, 60% of eggs hatched, 74% in Shetland, 67% in race *hudsonicus*. Annual mortality may be as high as 31%. Age of first breeding usually 2 years.
Movements. Migratory. Moves over broad front, in spring with relatively few staging areas, often inland, e.g. in Hungary and Netherlands; in autumn no concentrated staging. Most N European and NW Russian *phaeopus* migrate to coastal W Africa; return migration sometimes involves long diagonal Sahara crossing from W African coast and some transcontinental migration in S Africa. Icelandic birds fly over W Britain and some make long flights over water, directly to Africa. Birds in E & SE Africa include *alboaxillaris*, which migrate via Middle East. Race *variegatus* moves through Japan, coastal China, Korea, Hong Kong and Taiwan to wintering grounds in SE Asia and Australasia. Alaskan *hudsonicus* migrates down Pacific coast; Canadian populations over broad inland front to Canadian Maritime Provinces and New England and then S down coast, mainly to N & W South America. Migrates through NW Europe early Jul to late Aug, and late Apr to late May; arrives in Africa and E Australia late Jul to early Oct and departs from Apr. Many non-breeders remain in winter quarters all year, and all 1-year-olds probably do so.
Status and Conservation. Not globally threatened. E Atlantic flyway population numbers 600,000-700,000 birds, although figure of only 83,000 was estimated from counts in wintering areas; high numbers probably feed within mangroves where they are overlooked, or perhaps major wintering sites have yet to be found; numbers of W Siberian breeders and SE African winterers unknown; breeding population of Fenno-Scandia estimated at 62,500-123,000 pairs in 1993, and that of Iceland at 200,000 pairs in 1985; species is not generally numerous in Russia, although locally abundant in C Siberia. Wintering population of race *phaeopus* in SW Asia exceeds 25,000 birds; in SE Asia and Australasia 40,000 birds of race *variegatus*, of which 10,000 in Australia in 1993. Population size of race *alboaxillaris* unknown. Race *hudsonicus* comprises 25,000-100,000 birds; numbers apparently declined by 61% on Atlantic staging sites between 1972 and 1983. Probably the most abundant curlew, due to extremely extensive breeding range.
Bibliography. Ali & Ripley (1980), Armstrong (1983), Ash (1981), Beehler *et al*. (1986), Bent (1927-1929), Blake (1977), Brazil (1991), Bregnballe *et al*. (1990), Bregulla (1992), Chambers (1989), Clancey (1964a), Coates (1985),

Cramp & Simmons (1983), Dann (1993a, 1993b), Dickinson *et al.* (1991), van Dijk (1976), Dowsett & Forbes-Watson (1993), Elgood *et al.* (1994), Étchécopar & Hüe (1964, 1978), Evans (1994), Fjeldså (1977), Fjeldså & Krabbe (1990), Ginn *et al.* (1989), Goodman *et al.* (1989), Gore (1990), Grant (1991a, 1991b, 1992), Grant *et al.* (1992a, 1992b), Grimes (1987), Handel & Dau (1988), Haverschmidt (1968), Haverschmidt & Mees (1995), Hazevoet (1995), Hilty & Brown (1986), Hockey & Douie (1995), Howe *et al.* (1989), Howell & Webb (1995a), Hüe & Étchécopar (1970), Johnson (1965b), Kasparek (1990), Knystautas (1993), Kumari (1977), Lane & Davies (1987), Langrand (1990), Larsen & Moldsvor (1992), Lekagul & Round (1991), MacKinnon & Phillipps (1993), Mackworth-Praed & Grant (1957, 1962, 1970), Maclean (1993), Madoc (1976), Mallory (1982), Marchant & Higgins (1996), van Marle & Voous (1988), Medway & Wells (1976), Meeus *et al.* (1985), Meyer de Schauensee & Phelps (1978), Milon *et al.* (1973), Monroe (1968), Morozov (1993a), Nikolaev (1990), Pakenham (1979), Patrikeev (1995), de la Peña (1992), Perennou *et al.* (1994), Phillips (1978), Piersma (1986b), Pinto (1983), Pulliainen & Saari (1993d), Rands *et al.* (1987), Richardson, M.G. (1990), Ridgely & Gwynne (1989), Ripley (1982), Roberts, T.J. (1991), Rogacheva (1992), Root (1988), Rose (1994), Scott (1989), Scott & Carbonell (1986), Shirihai (1996), Short *et al.* (1990), Sick (1985c, 1993), Skeel (1976, 1978, 1982, 1983), Skeel & Mallory (1996), Slud (1964), Smythies (1981, 1986), Snyder (1966), Stiles & Skutch (1989), Tostain *et al.* (1992), Turpie & Hockey (1993), Uhlig (1990b), Urban *et al.* (1986), Velásquez & Navarro (1993), Watkins (1993), Wetmore (1965), White & Bruce (1986), Williams, M.D. (1986), Williamson (1946), Zwarts (1990), Zwarts & Blomert (1990), Zwarts & Dirksen (1990).

35. Bristle-thighed Curlew

Numenius tahitiensis

French: Courlis d'Alaska **German**: Borstenbrachvogel **Spanish**: Zarapito del Pacífico

Taxonomy. *Scolopax tahitiensis* Gmelin, 1789, Tahiti.
Monotypic.
Distribution. W Alaska, from Seward Peninsula to Yukon Delta. Winters from Marshall and Hawaiian Is, S to Santa Cruz, Fiji, Tonga, Samoa, Marquesas, Tuamotu Is and Pitcairn I.

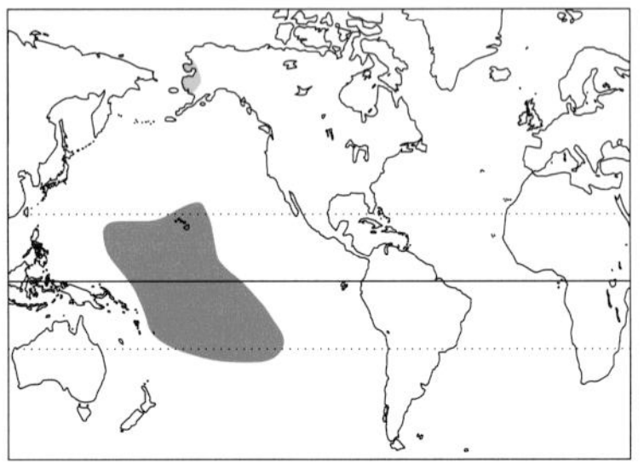

Descriptive notes. 40-44 cm; male 254-553 g, female 372-796 g; wingspan 82-90 cm. Medium-sized curlew with broadly striped head; cinnamon-buff spotted upperparts; dark underwing; bristle-like extensions on some flank and thigh feathers, rarely visible in field. Differs from very similar *N. phaeopus* by generally warmer buff and more cinnamon plumage; head characteristically appears more flattened; less densely streaked below, with undertail-coverts unmarked; in flight, conspicuous unmarked cinnamon patch on rump and uppertail. Female averages heavier, with longer wings and shorter bill. No seasonal variation. Juvenile, as adult but upperparts have bold, large, cinnamon-buff spots; more buffish breast lightly streaked.
Habitat. Exposed montane shrub-meadow tundra and shrub-tussock tundra. Winters exclusively on oceanic islands, where most birds prefer vegetated interior of island, while some birds use beaches; also tidal mudflats, exposed reefs, salt-pans, grassy fields, narrow channels between islets and in and around seabird colonies.
Food and Feeding. Diet in breeding range not well known, but known at least to include berries. Highly opportunistic on wintering grounds, taking vegetable matter, crustaceans, insects, spiders, gastropods, and even scorpions; also seabird carrion and fish regurgitated by seabirds and lizards; occasionally takes eggs of various seabirds, opening them with bill or by dropping them on hard surfaces, some birds even using stone tools. Usually feeds singly or in small groups.
Breeding. Probably starts laying in late May, and eggs have been found in Jun. Nest is simple, almost bare, depression in mossy vegetation. 4 eggs; both sexes incubate and tend young, but most females desert brood before young fledge; hatchlings and parents often move to wet sedge meadows to feed. Just after fledging several broods (c. 11) merge into groups tended by 1-5 adults; attending birds are, at least occasionally, non-parental adults. Age of first breeding at least 3 years. Annual survival 85-90%, and over 90% for non-migrating subadults once they have arrived at wintering grounds. Oldest ringed bird at least 23 years, 10 months.
Movements. Makes long distance, non-stop migrations of at least 4000 km over open ocean. After breeding, adults and juveniles gather on Alaskan coast prior to migration; juveniles migrate unaccompanied by adults. Occurs on passage on Pribilof, Aleutian, Hawaiian and Marquesas Is. Failed breeders start migrating S from late Jun, successful breeders and juveniles from early Aug; adults and juveniles arrive in wintering areas late Aug to early Sept, and adults depart early May. During moult on wintering grounds c. 50% of adults become flightless for c. 2 weeks. Immature birds spend all of their pre-breeding years on wintering grounds. Migrates in small flocks. Shows no diurnal pattern in timing of departures. Possibly birds wintering in C & S Pacific overfly Hawaiian Is on both migrations, flying distances of over 6000 km, relying on aid of tailwinds.
Status and Conservation. VULNERABLE. Total population 10,000 birds; breeding population 7000 birds (1992), and possibly decreasing. Designated a "Category 2" candidate by US Fish & Wildlife Service: species is rare and presumed to be in danger, but little is known. Low numbers and restricted breeding range are reasons for concern. Only two continental breeding areas known, at Seward Peninsula and floodplain of Yukon and Kuskokwim Deltas; other breeding grounds may yet await discovery; few birds may breed on Chukotskiy Peninsula, at least intermittently. Owing to moult-induced flightlessness on wintering grounds, numbers have probably declined through predation by introduced cats and dogs and possibly pigs. Potential threats on breeding grounds are off-road hunting and gold-mining activities; nest may suffer predation by Arctic Skuas (*Stercorarius parasiticus*), Common Ravens (*Corvus corax*) and foxes. On Tuamotu Is, species has traditionally been trapped for food; as possesion and use of firearms in Tuamotu Is is now restricted, greatest threat comes from introduced predators.
Bibliography. Allen & Kyllingstad (1949), Armstrong (1983), Bent (1927-1929), Brazil (1991), Collar & Andrew (1988), Collar *et al.* (1994), Ehrlich *et al.* (1992), Gill & Redmond (1992), Gill, Lanctot *et al.* (1991), Gill, McCaffery & Tobish (1988), Handel & Dau (1988), Holyoak & Thibault (1984), Konyukhov & McCaffery (1993), Kyllingstad (1948), Lanctot *et al.* (1995), Marks (1992, 1993), Marks & Hall (1992), Marks & Redmond (1994a, 1994b), Marks & Underhill (1994), Marks *et al.* (1990), Matthiessen (1994), McCaffery & Gill (1992), McCaffery & Peltola (1986), Meijer (1995), Pratt *et al.* (1987), Pyle (1991), Rosair (1995b), Tobish & Isleib (1992), Veitch (1974), Vilina *et al.* (1992), Widrig (1983b).

36. Slender-billed Curlew

Numenius tenuirostris

French: Courlis à bec grêle **German**: Dünnschnabel-Brachvogel **Spanish**: Zarapito Fino

Taxonomy. *Numenius tenuirostris* Vieillot, 1817, Egypt.
Monotypic.
Distribution. SW Siberia and N Kazakhstan, precise breeding range virtually unknown. Winters in NW Africa, and probably also Iraq.

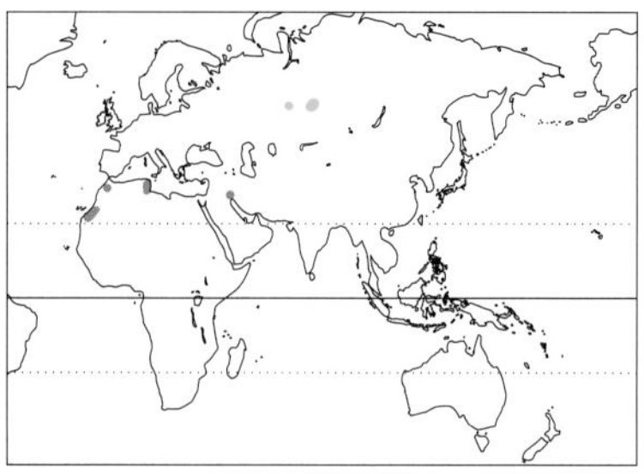

Descriptive notes. 36-41 cm; 255-360 g; wingspan 80-92 cm. Very pale curlew, with shortish, slim, pointed bill; white or pale buff ground colour of head, neck and breast; lower back, rump, undertail and underwing white; uppertail-coverts white with sparse brown markings; typically has rounded or heart-shaped dark markings on breast and flanks. Similar to *N. phaeopus*, but paler; lacks dark crown stripe. Female averages larger with longer bill. Non-breeding adult has fewer marks on flanks. Juvenile like adult, but flanks streaked brown.
Habitat. Breeds in extensive peat bogs with some small willow (*Salix*) and birch (*Betula*) trees, in habitat transitional from bog to forest. On migration, occurs in coastal lagoons and adjoining salt-marshes, estuaries, inland soda- or salt-lakes or (drained) fishponds in steppe area. Winters in coastal bays and lagoons with salt-marshes and temporary inland marshes. Few birds observed in Morocco appear to be habitat generalists, occurring on seashore, in saline and brackish lagoons and estuaries, in temporary and permanent lakes with adjoining marshes, on mudflats, and in sandy grassland and arable fields.
Food and Feeding. Outside breeding season, takes annelids, molluscs, snails, crustaceans and small insects, such as grasshoppers, earwigs and beetles. Probes in soft mud and soil or pecks from surface; observed taking insects from scrubby bushes.
Breeding. Very little known. Eggs found in May; may apparently breed in small colonies, with nests 2-3 m apart, up to 10-15 m apart; nest in dense growth on dry areas within bogs, constructed of dry grass. 4 eggs (variation unknown).
Movements. SW-WSW migration towards Mediterranean, mainly ending up in Atlantic Morocco and in Tunisia; chiefly via Turkmenistan, Caspian steppes, Ukraine, Bulgaria, Romania, former Yugoslavia, S Hungary, Greece and Italy; a second migration route may lead from breeding grounds to Middle East, where winters in Iraq and also reported to occur in Iran, Saudi Arabia and Oman. Records from Morocco mainly Nov-Mar; formerly irregular migrant in NE Africa late Jul to Aug and Apr-May. Status in Turkey uncertain, as many records of *N. arquata orientalis* have been erroneously attributed to present species; 2 skins exist of birds thought to have been shot in Istanbul area in late 19th or early 20th century. Status in Azerbaijan also uncertain; definite record of bird shot in Aug 1988, and species said to pass through regularly in very small numbers. Reported to have been seen in Argentina, but these reports now discounted.
Status and Conservation. CRITICALLY ENDANGERED. CITES I. Population estimated at 50-270 birds in 1994. Has only been recorded breeding in Tara region N of Omsk in SW Siberia, but no breeding records since 1925. Until early 1890's probably very abundant in Morocco, Algeria and Tunisia, but since then numbers have declined dramatically and probably still dropping, so species seriously threatened; only regularly used wintering site is Merja Zerga, NW Morocco. In 1964, as many as 600-900 birds were counted in SW Morocco, but almost all recent sightings in entire non-breeding range usually involve only 1-3 birds; in S Italy, c. 20 birds reported to be seen regularly during Jan-Mar 1995; surprising report of 50 birds from Iran in 1994. Species used to stage in steppes, and its decline may be due to massive loss of this particular habitat; also hunting, particularly on migration, and drainage of staging areas may have been significant. Breakdown of social behaviour patterns in a species which formerly migrated in large flocks may also constrain recovery. It has recently been suggested that the main breeding areas may not have been located in W Siberia but in steppe zone, which has been cultivated on large scale, thus perhaps explaining rapid decline of species. Area N of Caspian Sea, between R Volga and R Ural has been suggested as potential breeding location.
Bibliography. Albrecht (1989), Allport (1995), Anon. (1989c, 1993b), Baccetti (1991, 1995), Belik, V.P. (1994), Beretzk *et al.* (1959), van den Berg (1988a, 1988b, 1990), Brosselin (1968), Bruns (1991), Collar & Andrew (1988), Collar *et al.* (1994), Cramp & Simmons (1983), Czikeli (1976), Étchécopar & Hüe (1964), Evans (1994), Ewins (1989), Goodman *et al.* (1989), Goutner & Handrinos (1990), Gretton (1990, 1991, 1994, 1995), Hüe & Étchécopar (1970), van Impe (1995), Kistyakovski (1980), Knystautas (1993), Marchant (1984), Nankinov (1991), Patrikeev (1995), Perennou *et al.* (1994), Semmler (1983), Serra *et al.* (1995), Smith (1963), Thévenot (1989), Urban *et al.* (1986), von Volker (1994), Wymenga & van Dijk (1985).

37. Eurasian Curlew

Numenius arquata

French: Courlis cendré **German**: Großer Brachvogel **Spanish**: Zarapito Real
Other common names: Common Curlew

Taxonomy. *Scolopax Arquata* Linnaeus, 1758, Sweden.
Racial variation clinal; W populations of *orientalis* have on occasion been separated as race *sushkini*. Two subspecies recognized.
Subspecies and Distribution.
N. a. arquata (Linnaeus, 1758) - British Is and France across W Europe (N to Arctic Circle) and E to R Volga and Urals; winters from Iceland and British Is S to Mediterranean and NW Africa, and E to Persian Gulf and W India.
N. a. orientalis C. L. Brehm, 1831 - R Volga and Urals E through C Russia and N Kazakhstan to C Manchuria; winters in W, E & S Africa, and from S Caspian Sea S to Persian Gulf and E through S Asia to E China and S Japan, and S to Philippines and Greater Sundas.

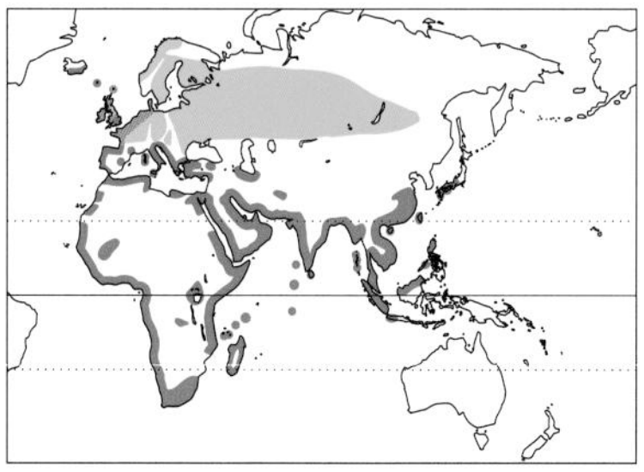

Descriptive notes. 50-60 cm; male 410-1010 g, female 475-1360 g; wingspan 80-100 cm. Large greyish brown curlew with long bill and plain head pattern; head, neck, breast and upperparts buffy brown with dark streaking, although plumage variable; pale underwing, white rump and lower back; belly white, flanks streaked. Most similar to *N. madagascariensis*, but bill less massive and normally shorter; underparts whiter. Female averages larger, especially with longer bill. Non-breeding adult has breast and upperparts grey-brown and underparts whiter. Juvenile has breast more buff and flanks less streaked; upperparts with buff spotting and fringes. Race *orientalis* usually paler, with underwing-coverts and axillaries largely unmarked; lower rump may be more barred and inner wing paler, but considerable overlap.

Habitat. Breeds on peat bogs, fens, upland moors, damp grassland, grassy or boggy open areas in forest, extensive farmland, swampy and dry heathland, dune valleys and coastal marshes; increasing numbers breed in meadows. In non-breeding period, chiefly on muddy coasts, bays and estuaries; also regularly on muddy shores of inland lakes and rivers. During migration, also found on wet grassland and arable fields. Males are more likely to feed in inland grassland than females.

Food and Feeding. Throughout year, diet includes annelids, arthropods, crustaceans, molluscs, berries and seeds; occasionally vertebrates, including small fish, amphibians, lizards, young birds (and possibly eggs), small rodents; chiefly terrestrial insects and earthworms, especially in summer. Feeds by pecking, jabbing or deep probing in mud or damp soil. Occasionally takes food from conspecifics or other wader species. Some birds territorial on wintering grounds, others feed gregariously. Long-billed females tend to forage more on intertidal flats, feeding on molluscs, crabs and polychaetes, while shorter-billed males tend to feed more on lumbricids on cultivated grassland.

Breeding. Lays Apr to early Jul. Monogamous. High degree of site fidelity. Densities of up to 10 pairs/km². Nest typically in open, often in grass or sedge cover. 4 eggs (2-5), with laying interval 1-2 days; single brood; incubation 27-29 days, by both sexes; chick pale ochraceous buff above clouded with blackish brown, black crown and creamy buff on belly; both parents care for young; fledging 32-38 days. Including unsuccessful clutches, production c. 1·7 hatchlings/pair, and 0·25-1·4 fledlings/pair; reproductive success is higher in semi-natural habitats than in farmland, and lowest on intensively cultivated land; on farmland, nest failure caused by predation and farming practices; fledging survival until maturity c. 30%. Annual mortality 66% in 1st year, deceasing to 18% until 3rd year. Age of first breeding 2 years. Oldest ringed birds at least 32 years.

Movements. Mostly migratory; some birds resident in W of range, especially in British Is and Ireland. Small numbers regularly winter in Iceland and Faeroes. Scandinavian and Baltic populations move SW to W European coast. The subspecies mix in Balkans after breeding, and probably in winter quarters from Mediterranean to W India. Nominate *arquata* presumably winters as far S as Banc d'Arguin (Mauritania), Morocco, Algeria and Italy, with *orientalis* occupying rest of African wintering grounds, e.g. birds wintering in Guinea-Bissau originate from C Siberia. Some transcontinental migration in Africa, e.g. across Sahara. Most birds winter at moulting grounds, with little evidence of post-moulting movements. High fidelity to wintering grounds. Southward migration Jun-Nov, starting with non-breeders and adult females; return starts Feb, but mainly Mar-Apr; migration to Fenno-Scandian and Russian breeding grounds mainly mid-Apr to early May. Many 1st-year birds remain in winter quarters all year.

Status and Conservation. Not globally threatened. E Atlantic wintering population estimated at 348,000 birds, plus probably c. 80,000 birds inland (1989), with c. 250,000 birds wintering in Europe; up to 227,000 birds have been counted on Wadden Sea. Breeding population of Europe, excluding Russia, comprises 125,000-147,000 pairs (1986-1993), mostly in Scandinavia and British Is; has occasionally bred in Spain, e.g. in 1993. Most European breeding populations have declined, except in Russia, Finland and Britain; numbers of wintering populations have dropped even more. Numbers of *orientalis* wintering in SW Asia and E Africa exceed 28,000 birds; 15,000-20,000 counted in Iran in 1970's; SC, SE & E Asia hold c. 25,000 birds each. Decline of nominate race probably due mainly to loss of breeding habitat and loss and fragmentation of grassland, caused by agricultural intensification, e.g heavy egg and chick mortality occurs if grassland is cut, and predation is high in agriculturally improved habitats; "improvement" of marginal grassland shown to reduce breeding population. In Ireland, afforestation of moorlands has led to decline in breeding pairs. Wintering populations affected by disturbance and building developments on high tide roosts, by pollution, and locally by intensive hunting. Recommended conservation measures are protection of wintering sites and reductions in intensive farming.

Bibliography. Abramson (1979), Ali & Ripley (1980), Bainbridge & Minton (1978), Baines (1988), Berg (1991, 1992a, 1992b, 1993a, 1994), van den Berg (1989), Berndt (1986), Boschert & Rupp (1993), Braaksma (1960), Brazil (1991), Bregnballe *et al.* (1990), Broyer & Roché (1991), Cramp & Simmons (1983), Davidson *et al.* (1986), Dementiev & Gladkov (1951b), Desender (1983), Dickinson *et al.* (1991), Dowsett & Forbes-Watson (1993), Dubois & Maheo (1986), Ens & Zwarts (1980), Ens, Esselink & Zwarts (1990), Étchécopar & Hüe (1964, 1978), Evans (1994), Evans & Keijl (1993b), Ferns & Siman (1994), Fjeldså (1977), von Frisch (1956), Ginn *et al.* (1989), Glutz von Blotzheim *et al.* (1977), Goodman *et al.* (1989), Goss-Custard & Jones (1976), Grimes (1987), Henriksen (1991b), Hockey & Douie (1995), Hötker (1991), Hüe & Étchécopar (1970), Kipp (1991), Knystautas (1993), Lekagul & Round (1991), Luge (1992), MacKinnon & Phillipps (1993), Mackworth-Praed & Grant (1957, 1962, 1970), Madoc (1976), Marchant *et al.* (1990), van Marle & Voous (1988), Medway & Wells (1976), Meltofte (1986, 1987), Mulder & Swaan (1992), Norrdahl *et al.* (1995), Owens (1984), Pakenham (1979), Patrikeev (1995), Perennou *et al.* (1994), Phillips (1978), Piersma (1986b), Piersma, Klaassen *et al.* (1990), Pinto (1983), Poslavsky (1969), Rands *et al.* (1987), Ripley (1982), Roberts, T.J. (1991), Robertson & Berg (1992), Rogacheva (1992), Rutgers & Norris (1970), Schuster (1994), Scott (1989), Shirihai (1996), Short *et al.* (1990), Slotta-Bachmayr (1992), Smythies (1986), Tomialojc (1994c), Tuellinhoff & Bergmann (1993), Urban *et al.* (1986), White & Bruce (1986), Whitfield (1985), Williams, M.D. (1986), Wymenga *et al.* (1990), Ylimaunu *et al.* (1987), Zwarts (1988), Zwarts & Esselink (1989), Zwarts & Wanink (1984).

38. **Far Eastern Curlew**

Numenius madagascariensis

French: Courlis de Sibérie **German**: Isabellbrachvogel **Spanish**: Zarapito Siberiano

Other common names: Eastern/Australian/Long-billed/Red-rumped Curlew

Taxonomy. *Scolopax madagascariensis* Linnaeus, 1766, Madagascar; error = Macassar, Sulawesi. Monotypic.

Distribution. E Siberia, from upper reaches of R Nizhnyaya Tunguska E through Verkhoyansk Mts to Kamchatka, and S to NE Mongolia, Manchuria and Ussuriland. Winters in Taiwan, Indonesia and New Guinea, but most birds migrate to Australia and a few reach New Zealand. Never recorded in Madagascar.

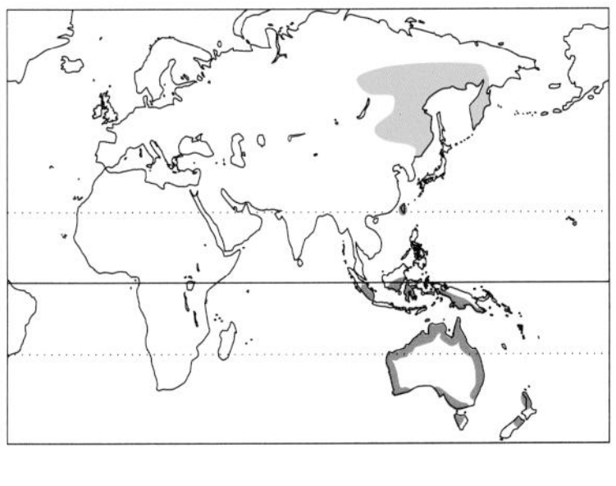

Descriptive notes. 53-66 cm; 390-1350 g, male averaging 110 g lighter than female; wingspan 110 cm. Largest curlew with very long, heavy bill; female has longest bill of any wader (184 mm). Plain head pattern; upperparts have dark feather centres and buff notches and fringes; breast and flanks finely streaked; underwing densely barred brown. Differs from *N. arquata* in dark rump, back and underwing; longer, heavier bill. Female averages larger, especially with longer bill. Non-breeding adult lacks rufous tinge on upperparts. Juvenile has more extensive whitish edging on upperparts when plumage fresh; streaking on underparts finer.

Habitat. Breeds in open mossy or transitional bogs, moss-lichen bogs and wet meadows, and on swampy shores of small lakes. In non-breeding season essentially coastal, occurring at estuaries, mangrove swamps, salt-marshes, intertidal mudflats or sandflats, particularly those with extensive seagrass (*Zosteraceae*) meadows; sometimes on beaches; very rarely inland near large wetlands. Often roosts in salt-marshes behind mangroves, or on sandy beaches.

Food and Feeding. Diet on breeding grounds includes insects, such as larvae of beetles and flies, and amphipods. During autumn migration berries also consumed. In non-breeding areas, marine invertebrates, mainly crabs and small molluscs, but also other crustaceans and polychaete worms. Probes bill down burrows, or pecks from surface, detecting prey by sight or touch; prefers soft-sediment intertidal mudflats. Feeding action slow and deliberate. Manipulates large prey, swallowing it piece by piece; sometimes washes prey. Sexual differences in length of bill can lead to corresponding differences in diet: females feed solitarily on burrow-living shrimps and defend feeding territory; males feed in loose flocks (up to 100's) on crabs. Diurnal and nocturnal.

Breeding. Nests early May to late Jun. Often in small colonies of 2-3 pairs. Nest lined with dry grass and twigs, on small mound in swampy ground, often close to areas with wild berries growing. Usually 4 eggs. Probably delays maturity longer than most shorebirds, perhaps not breeding until 3-4 years old.

Movements. Long distance migrant; moves down coasts of Kuril Is, Sakhalin, Ussuriland, Korea, Japan, parts of Philippines, E Sumatra and Borneo; less common in transit in E China, Hong Kong and New Guinea. Fewer birds appear in continental Asia in autumn than in spring, vice versa in Japan. NW & E Australia reached as early as Jun, but mainly in late Aug, followed by gradual southward movement; most birds reach S Australia in Nov. Northbound migration up coast of E Australia occurs mainly Feb-Apr, but birds from SE Australia seem to bypass E coast sites. More females seem to migrate farther S. Non-breeding birds spend boreal summer in N & NW Australia and Victoria, and possibly do so until late in their 3rd year.

Status and Conservation. Not globally threatened. Currently considered near-threatened. At present, world population reckoned to number 21,000 birds at most, with Australia holding 19,000 birds in boreal winter; in Philippines, 457 birds counted in 1992, and 75 in 1993; up to c. 370 recorded in Sumatra. Small numbers apparently wintering in China in recent years, with 64 birds counted in 1992, and 10 in 1993. Has declined mainly through loss of habitat and disturbance, and possibly persecution (Tasmania) and decrease of available food through pollution (South Korea); hunting may also have been significant at breeding grounds, on migration and in S Australia. Easily disturbed at feeding and roosting sites. Potential threat may be that females probably tend to migrate farther S, to S Australian wetlands, which are more at threat than those in N Australia. Over last 30-60 years, numbers have fallen significantly in some areas in Australia, Tasmania and New Zealand; this may be due to population decline or to change in non-breeding range. In Western Port Bay, SC Victoria, dramatic loss of seagrasses on intertidal mudflats caused substantial decline in mid-1970's, but population now seems to be recovering.

Bibliography. Alcorn (1988), Barter (1990), Beehler *et al.* (1986), Blakers *et al.* (1984), Brazil (1991), Bregulla (1992), Brouwer & Garnett (1990), Chambers (1989), Close & Newman (1984), Coates (1985), Congdon & Catterall (1994), Dickinson *et al.* (1991), Étchécopar & Hüe (1978), Garnett (1993), Knystautas (1993), Kragh *et al.* (1986), Lane & Davies (1987), MacKinnon & Phillipps (1993), Marchant & Higgins (1996), van Marle & Voous (1988), Medway & Wells (1976), Meyer de Schauensee (1984), Minton (1993), Parish & Howes (1989), Perennou *et al.* (1994), Piersma (1986e), Pook (1992), Rogacheva (1992), Rogers, K.G. (1982, 1995), Scott (1989), Silvius (1986), Starks & Lane (1987), Tolchin (1980), Vinter (1980), Watkins (1993), White & Bruce (1986), Williams, M.D. (1986), Yi *et al.* (1994).

39. **Long-billed Curlew**

Numenius americanus

French: Courlis à long bec **German**: Rostbrachvogel **Spanish**: Zarapito Americano

Taxonomy. *Numenius americanus* Bechstein, 1812, New York.

Race *parvus* formerly labelled *occidentalis*; type specimen of latter lost. Two subspecies recognized.

Subspecies and Distribution.

N. a. parvus Bishop, 1910 - SC British Columbia E to S Manitoba, and S to California and South Dakota; winters from California and Louisiana S to Mexico.

N. a. americanus Bechstein, 1812 - Nevada E to South Dakota and S through Utah and NW Oklahoma to N Texas; winters from California, and Texas S to Mexico and Guatemala.

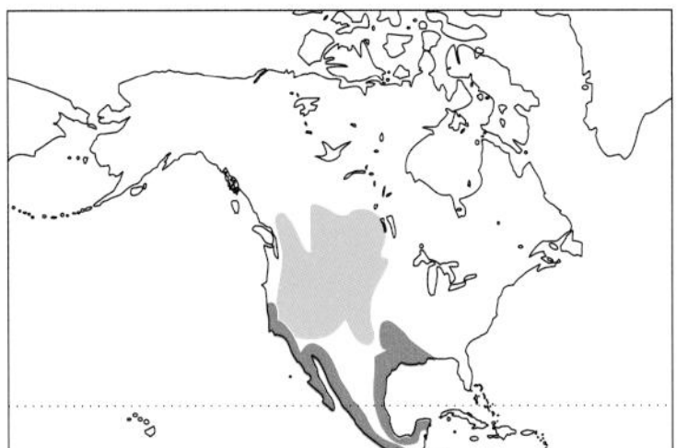

Descriptive notes. 50-65 cm; males 445-792 g, females 630-951 g. Large cinnamon-coloured curlew with droplet-shaped bill tip; fairly large eye; upperparts speckled black and cinnamon-buff; strong barring on tertials; mostly unstreaked cinnamon underparts. Much more richly coloured than congeners, including rich cinnamon underwing. Female averages larger, especially with longer bill. Non-breeding adult has duller upperparts. Juvenile almost identical to adult, but upperparts buffer, especially wing-coverts. Race *parvus* smaller.

Habitat. Prairies, including damp meadowland, grain fields, grazed mixed grass and drier short-grass areas, especially on gravelly soils in rolling terrain. After breeding, occurs in moist upland environments, shallow estuaries, inland waters and open parts of marshes; some move to farmland.

Food and Feeding. Adult and larval insects. During non-breeding season often feeds on burrow-dwelling crustaceans (e.g. mud crabs and shrimps), also on molluscs, worms, toads, adult and larval insects, and sometimes berries. Occasionally preys on nesting birds. Feeds by pecking and probing, striding rapidly over substrate; in non-breeding habitat, often feeds in flocks.

Breeding. Laying Apr-May. Density 0·6-2·4 pairs/km², up to 9 pairs/40 ha. Low degree of natal philopatry, only 4%. Nest sited in flat area, with short grass cover and well spaced grass clumps, often close to object such as rock or dried cow dung. 4 eggs (3-5), laying interval 1-2 days; incubation 27-28 days, by both parents; during first weeks young cared for by both parents, later only by male; fledging 41-45 days. Nest success 44-69%, 28-44% of young survive till fledging; 10-16% of nests destroyed by mammalian and avian predators; productivity adversely affected by grazing and dragging. Age of first breeding unknown, but some birds return to breeding grounds as 1-year-olds.

Movements. Relatively short distance migrant, which arrives on breeding grounds early, mid-Mar, and departs by mid-Aug. Mostly moves across interior W half of USA, and also fairly common to uncommon across inland Mexico. Most non-breeders spend all year in winter range. Rarely winters S to N South America.

Status and Conservation. Not globally threatened. Population size of race *americanus* unknown; that of *parvus* numbers c. 6500 birds (1992) and apparently in continuing decline. Formerly bred in several states of Midwest, but breeding range has contracted westwards during present century, due to constant loss of open prairies to agriculture. Was heavily hunted in late 19th and early 20th centuries. Species now benefits from full protection and overall numbers may now be stable.

Bibliography. Allen (1980), Bayer (1994), Bent (1927-1929), Bicak (1977), Blake (1977), Cochran & Anderson (1987), Fitzner (1978), Forsythe (1970, 1972, 1973), Goater & Bush (1986, 1988), Graul (1971), Grinnell (1921), Hardee (1988), Hertzel (1990), Howell & Webb (1995a), Knopf (1994), Krych (1992), Matthiessen (1994), Monroe (1968), Pampush & Anthony (1993), Paton & Dalton (1994), Redmond (1986), Redmond & Jenni (1982, 1986), Redmond *et al.* (1981), Ridgely & Gwynne (1989), Ritchie (1990), Root (1988), Salder & Maher (1976), Schon (1988), Shackford (1994), Silcock (1991), de Smet (1992), Stenzel *et al.* (1976), Stiles & Skutch (1989), Wilson (1988).

Genus *BARTRAMIA* Lesson, 1831

40. Upland Sandpiper

Bartramia longicauda

French: Maubèche des champs **German**: Prärieläufer **Spanish**: Correlimos Batitú
Other common names: Bartram's Sandpiper, Upland Plover

Taxonomy. *Tringa longicauda* Bechstein, 1812, North America. Monotypic.
Distribution. C Alaska, Yukon and S Mackenzie; British Columbia and Alberta E through Great Plains to S Quebec and New Brunswick, and S to NE Oregon, NC Texas, C Missouri, West Virginia and Maryland. Winters in Surinam and from Paraguay and S Brazil to C Argentina.
Descriptive notes. 26-32 cm; 98-226 g; wingspan 64-68 cm. Curious sandpiper, reminiscent of small curlews; elegant, with short yellow bill, large dark eye, long neck and small, rounded head; upperparts olive brown with extensive dark barring and pale buff fringes; neck and breast pale buff with dark streaking, rest of underparts white; in flight, conspicuous black rump. Recalls *Numenius minutus* but has shorter, much straighter bill, yellowish legs and longer tail; paler than *N. borealis*, with whitish underwing and axillaries densely barred blackish. Female averages slightly longer in wings and tail. No seasonal variation. Juvenile has dark brown scapulars and upperparts with pale buff fringes; flanks less streaked.
Habitat. Inland, on primary or restored prairie grasslands, locally extensive tracts of wet meadows, domestic hay fields, retired croplands and marginal habitats. In non-breeding season uses similar habitats in *pampas*, frequenting alfalfa fields, pastures, rough grassland, areas of short grass including golf courses and airfields, even suburban lawns, and sometimes wet shorelines; vegetated sand banks in Amazon zone. Commonly perches on posts or even in trees.

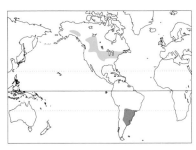

Food and Feeding. Diet chiefly consists of terrestrial insects such as grasshoppers, crickets and weevils, larvae of beetles and Lepidoptera, also centipedes, millipedes, spiders, snails, earthworms and seeds. Feeding style is sometimes plover-like, alternating short runs with sudden stops; forages singly or in small groups.
Breeding. Laying May-Jun. Density 5-22 pairs/km², but 25-75 pairs/km² reported in 1930's; sometimes in loose colonial groups. Nest usually well hidden in tussock 5-20 cm high. 4 eggs (2-5), laid at intervals of c. 26 hours; incubation 24 days (21-28), by both sexes; chick brownish above with buffy feather tips; roles of sexes in tending chicks not clear; fledging 32-34 days. 41-74% of nests successful; major cause of nest failure is predation.
Movements. Long distance migrant. Main wintering areas seem to be located in Argentina and Uruguay. Migrates through Great Plains, Mexico, Central America, across Gulf of Mexico and most of South America E of Andes; some movement across W Atlantic; no evidence of Atlantic crossing during northward migration. Leaves breeding areas late Aug to early Sept, arriving in non-breeding areas late Sept to Oct; return passage starts mid-Feb, birds reaching breeding grounds early Apr to Jun.
Status and Conservation. Not globally threatened. Total population size unknown; estimated c. 2000 birds in Canada. Enormous numbers once bred on grasslands in Great Plains. After eastward expansion following deforestation, numbers declined dramatically due to hunting and cultivation of prairies during late 19th and early 20th centuries. Still fairly abundant in some parts of breeding range, although part of range has contracted. Numbers breeding on grasslands increased by 3·5% annually during period 1961-1991, although species declining locally. In Pacific Northwest, only tiny relict populations remain; these are in real danger of extinction. Species is a good indicator species for undisturbed grasslands.

Bibliography. Ailes (1976, 1980), Ailes & Toepfer (1977), Amos (1991), Armstrong (1983), Belton (1984), Bent (1927-1929), Blake (1977), Bowen, B.S. & Kruse (1993), Bowen, D.E. (1977), Buhnerkempe & Westemeier (1988), Contreras *et al.* (1990), Cramp & Simmons (1983), Dorio & Grewe (1979), van den Driessche *et al.* (1994), Fjeldså & Krabbe (1990), Haverschmidt (1966, 1968), Haverschmidt & Mees (1995), Hayes (1995), Hayes & Fox (1991), Higgins & Kirsch (1975), Hilty & Brown (1986), Howell & Webb (1995a), Johnson (1965b), Kirsch & Higgins (1976), Knopf (1994), Matthiessen (1994), Meyer de Schauensee & Phelps (1978), Monroe (1968), de la Peña (1992), Reel (1989), Ridgely & Gwynne (1989), Robbins *et al.* (1983), Scott & Carbonell (1986), Sick (1985c, 1993), Slud (1964), Snyder, D.E. (1966), Snyder, D.L. *et al.* (1989), Tostain *et al.* (1992), Van *et al.* (1994), Wetmore (1965), White, C.M. (1983), White, R.P. (1988).

PLATE 43 ➤

41

42

ssp *totanus*

43

ssp *ussuriensis*

45

46

44

47

PLATE 43

inches 5

cm 13

48

49

53

52

50

51

54

55

56

57

♀

♂ 58

59

60

Tribe TRINGINI

Genus *TRINGA* Linnaeus, 1758

41. Spotted Redshank
Tringa erythropus

French: Chevalier arlequin   **German**: Dunkler Wasserläufer   **Spanish**: Archibebe Oscuro
Other common names: Dusky Redshank

Taxonomy. *Scolopax erythropus* Pallas, 1764, the Netherlands.
Monotypic.
Distribution. N Scandinavia and NW Russia across N Siberia to Chukotskiy Peninsula. Winters from W Europe through Mediterranean to equatorial Africa, and E through Persian Gulf and India to SE Asia, SE China and Taiwan.

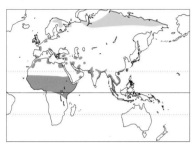

Descriptive notes. 29-32 cm; 97-230 g; wingspan 61-67 cm. Elegant wader, with long neck, legs and bill; entirely black, with white dots on upperparts, and often variable amounts of whitish on underparts; in flight, shows white wedge on back and white underwing. Female slightly larger and generally paler, with white tips on crown feathers and more white fringes on underparts. Non-breeding adult has contrasting dark eyestripe and white supercilium, ash grey upperparts with white fringes, plain grey breast and white underparts; rather similar to *T. totanus*, but has longer darker red legs; longer, finer bill, lower mandible basally red; white above lores. Juvenile darker than non-breeding adult; upperparts, head and breast brownish with dense white marks; underparts paler, densely barred.
Habitat. Open wooded tundra, swampy pine or birch forest near tree-line, and also more open areas such as heathland and shrub tundra. After breeding, occurs in variety of freshwater or brackish wetlands, including sewage farms, irrigated rice fields, brackish lagoons, salt-marshes, salt-pans and sheltered muddy shores along coast.
Food and Feeding. Chiefly aquatic insects and their larvae, terrestrial flying insects, small crustaceans, molluscs, polychaete worms, fish and amphibians, rarely up to 6-7 cm length. When feeding on fish, may forage socially in dense flock of conspecifics or mixed with other tringines, moving erratically while pecking at prey or running synchronously in one direction, while each bird sweeps bill through water. Often found in water, and occasionally swims while feeding in deep water; may immerse head and neck completely. Pecks, probes, jabs or sweeps bill through water from side to side. Mostly in small flocks, occasionally up to several 100's, sometimes singly. Diurnal and nocturnal feeder.
Breeding. Laying mid-May to late Jun. Monogamous; apparently sometimes polyandrous. Rather patchy dispersion, in densities of 2-3 pairs/km² (maximum 15). Nest usually in grass tussocks or moss, sparsely lined with plant material. 4 eggs (3-5); laying interval and incubation period unknown; chick pale drab grey finely marked with fuscous black above, dark cap and dirty white on chin and belly; fledging 28 days; male undertakes most of incubation and tends brood largely on his own; most females often leave before eggs hatch (mid-Jun). Oldest ringed bird 6 years 1 month.
Movements. Migratory. Passage overland on broad front, although also important route down W coast of Europe. Movements characterized by long flights between staging areas, such as Wadden Sea, Dutch delta region, S Hungary, SE Greece, C Turkey, Black and Caspian Seas, C Kazakhstan, L Baikal, Chang L (Ussuriland), C Yakutia, Sakhalin, Japan and Korea. Birds wintering in Sahel and N savanna zones evidently cross Sahara, e.g. to Mali, Nigeria and Chad. Adults moult in staging areas before moving to wintering grounds. Present in tropics mainly Oct-Apr. Migrates N along European coast late Apr to mid-May; females move S from early Jun, males during Jul, and juveniles in Aug-Sept. Few birds oversummer in tropics, but most non-breeders spend summer just S of breeding grounds.
Status and Conservation. Not globally threatened. European and W African population numbers 75,000-150,000 birds (1994); 23,000-40,000 birds breed in Fenno-Scandia (1993); further E, in Russia, breeds in fairly high numbers. Total of c. 25,000 birds winter in Egypt, E Africa and SW Asia, 10,000-25,000 birds in SC Asia and similar number in SE & E Asia. Number of wintering birds in NW Europe was fairly stable over period 1971-1977.
Bibliography. Ali & Ripley (1980), Brazil (1991), Byrkjedal *et al.* (1988), Carter & Sudbury (1993), Clark (1978), Cooper & Tove (1989), Cramp & Simmons (1983), Dementiev & Gladkov (1951b), Dowsett & Forbes-Watson (1993), Elgood *et al.* (1994), Étchécopar & Hüe (1964, 1978), Evans (1994), Fjeldså (1977), Goodman *et al.* (1989), Grimes (1969, 1987), Grimm (1991), Hildén (1979a), Holthuijzen (1979), Hüe & Étchécopar (1970), Kitazawa & Watanabe (1992), Knystautas (1993), Lekagul & Round (1991), MacKinnon & Phillipps (1993), Mackworth-Praed & Grant (1957, 1962, 1970), Medway & Wells (1976), Mjelstad & Saetersdal (1986, 1987), Nebelung (1993), Patrikeev (1995), Paz (1987), Perennou *et al.* (1994), Piersma (1986b), Pinto (1983), Rands *et al.* (1987), Raner (1972), Ripley (1982), Roberts, T.J. (1991), Rogacheva (1992), Schmidt (1988), Scott (1989), Shirihai (1996), Short *et al.* (1990), Skeen (1991), Smith, M.R. (1990), Smythies (1986), Taverner (1982), Urban *et al.* (1986), Williams, M.D. (1986).

42. Common Redshank
Tringa totanus

French: Chevalier gambette   **German**: Rotschenkel   **Spanish**: Archibebe Común
Other common names: Redshank

Taxonomy. *Scolopax Totanus* Linnaeus, 1758, Sweden.

Increasing evidence for separation of population of British Is and Netherlands as race *britannica*, as was earlier suggested. Birds from S portions of European range have sometimes been awarded race *bewickii*. Six subspecies currently recognized.
Subspecies and Distribution.
T. t. robusta (Schiøler, 1919) - Iceland, Faeroes and possibly Scotland; winters in British Is and W Europe.
T. t. totanus (Linnaeus, 1758) - Orkney, Shetland and N Scandinavia S to Iberian Peninsula, N Italy, Tunisia and Turkey, and E to W Siberia; winters from Mediterranean to tropical Africa, India and Indonesia.
T. t. ussuriensis Buturlin, 1934 - S Siberia and Mongolia E to N Manchuria and Russian Far East; winters from E Mediterranean and E Africa through Red Sea, Persian Gulf and Arabia to W India, and probably also farther E.
T. t. terrignotae R. & A. C. Meinertzhagen, 1926 - S Manchuria; winters in SE & E Asia.
T. t. craggi Hale, 1971 - NW Xinjiang (NW China); wintering grounds unknown, but probably in E China.
T. t. eurhinus (Oberholser, 1900) - Pamirs, N India and C & S Tibet; winters in India.

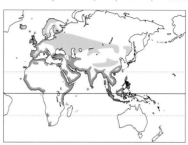

Descriptive notes. 27-29 cm; 85-155 g; wingspan 59-66 cm. Ashy brown upperparts, head and breast, streaked and spotted with black and dark brown; white secondaries conspicuous in flight. Differs from non-breeding *T. erythropus* by shorter, orange-red legs, shorter bill, indistinct supercilium and redder bill. Female often has paler upperparts than male, at least in race *totanus*. Non-breeding adult has greyer upperparts, without streaks or spots, but some narrow white fringes; underparts paler, breast finely streaked. Juvenile has warm brown upperparts with buff fringes and bill dull red at base. Races generally vary only in small details of plumage and size; *robusta* and *ussuriensis* more cinnamon.
Habitat. Wide diversity of coastal and inland wetlands, including coastal salt-marshes, inland wet grasslands, grassy marshes and swampy heathlands. After breeding, chiefly in coastal habitats including rocky, muddy and sandy shorelines, salt-marshes and open mudflats, salt-lakes, freshwater lagoons, salt-works and sewage farms; sometimes at inland waters or flooded grasslands.
Food and Feeding. Insects, spiders and annelids; non-breeders also consume molluscs and crustaceans, particularly amphipod *Corophium volutator*; on occasion, feeds on small fish or tadpoles. Like diet, feeding method varies seasonally; uses typical brisk walk while pecking; occasionally probes, jabs or sweeps bill through water; often wades, and occasionally swims. When feeding on fish, may forage socially in dense flock, often mixed with other tringines: birds move erratically while pecking at prey or running synchronously in one direction, ploughing or scything bills through water. Feeds diurnally and nocturnally. Mostly in small flocks, occasionally many 100's, sometimes singly. May defend feeding territory.
Breeding. Laying Apr-Jun. Monogamous. Moderate degree of natal philopatry and, especially in experienced and successful breeders, of site faithfulness and mate fidelity. Solitary or in loose colonies; on coast up to 100-300 pairs/km², but inland usually below 10 pairs/km². Nest typically at base of tall clump of grass, with leaves covering overhead. 4 eggs (3-5), laying interval 38 hours (35-43); replacement clutches laid; incubation 23-24 days, by both sexes; chick has creamy or greyish buff upperparts with black-brown lines, buff suffused breast and whitish underparts; both parents initially tend young; but later on often only male, and brood sometimes split up between sexes; fledging 23-35 days. Hatching success c. 14%; from hatching to fledging 20-50%; mortality may increase dramatically during cold spells, especially in combination with rain; other important causes of nest loss are trampling by cattle, predation and agricultural activities, notably mowing. Mortality of 1st-year birds 55%, of adults c. 30%. Age of first breeding 1-2 years. Oldest ringed bird 17 years.
Movements. Chiefly migratory, although some birds in Iceland and W Europe virtually resident. Much overlap between subspecies in winter range, but in general smallest birds (N Scandinavia) winter farthest S (typically W Africa), while largest (Iceland) winter on average farthest N (Iceland to North Sea). Migration through Europe is SW-SSW, except for Atlantic Is; presumably on broad front over land and along coast; birds wintering in W Africa may cross Sahara on passage. In Asia, movements noted through Japan, Mongolia, E China (Chihli Plains), Hong Kong and Korea (scarce); breeders of Altai and Novosibirsk area and probably C Siberia winter in India. A few birds remain in winter quarters all year. Occurs annually in small numbers in NW & N Australia. In nominate race, W African winterers migrate N from late Apr to May, when S breeders already incubating; these S birds migrate S in Jul (adults) and mid-Jul to early Aug (juveniles); N breeding birds of races *totanus* and *robusta* migrate S in Jul (adults) and mid-Aug to early Sept (juveniles).
Status and Conservation. Not globally threatened. W Palearctic breeding population has declined since 1970, and estimated at 50,000-100,000 pairs of race *robusta* (1993) and 145,000-185,000 pairs of race *totanus* (1986-1993). Counts along E Atlantic flyway yield estimates of 177,000 birds of race *totanus* and 109,000 of *robusta* (1989), with highest numbers in British Is, Guinea-Bissau and Mauritania; considering breeding numbers, these must be underestimates. In Egypt 8000-10,000 birds, in SW Asia (mainly *ussuriensis*) c. 55,000 birds, in SC Asia (*ussuriensis* and *eurhinus*) probably c. 100,000 birds, and in SE & E Asia (mainly *terrignotae*) also in order of 100,000 birds; no figures available for race *craggi*. Decline of W Palearctic population mainly due to loss of winter and breeding habitats, agricultural intensification, wetland drainage, flood control, afforestation, land reclamation, industrial development and encroachment of *Spartina* on mudflats; severe cold spells on W European wintering grounds may also have had disastrous effects. Improvement of marginal grassland may result in declining density of breeding pairs by up to 80%. Currently, winter population of E Atlantic flyway seems rather stable.
Bibliography. Ali & Ripley (1980), Atkinson (1976), Baines (1988), Beintema (1985, 1991a, 1994), Beintema & Müskens (1987), Beintema & Visser (1989a, 1989b), Beintema *et al.* (1991), den Blanken *et al.* (1981), Brazil (1991), Bregnballe (1986), Cramp & Simmons (1983), Cresswell (1994a, 1994b, 1994c), Davidson (1982), Davidson & Evans (1982), Dowsett & Forbes-Watson (1993), Dubois & Maheo (1986), Étchécopar & Hüe (1964, 1978), Fjeldså (1977), Glutz von Blotzheim *et al.* (1977), Goodman *et al.* (1989), Goss-Custard (1969, 1970b, 1976, 1977b), Goss-Custard & Jones (1976), Grosskopf (1958, 1959, 1963), Hale (1971, 1973, 1974), Hale & Ashcroft (1982, 1983), Hötker (1991), Hüe & Étchécopar (1970), Jackson (1994), de Jong (1993), Knystautas (1993), Mackworth-Praed & Grant (1957, 1970), Marchant *et al.* (1990), van Marle & Voous (1988), Meltofte (1987), Morozov (1988), Ogilvie (1963), Patrikeev

---

On following pages: 43. Marsh Sandpiper (*Tringa stagnatilis*); 44. Common Greenshank (*Tringa nebularia*); 45. Nordmann's Greenshank (*Tringa guttifer*); 46. Greater Yellowlegs (*Tringa melanoleuca*); 47. Lesser Yellowlegs (*Tringa flavipes*); 48. Green Sandpiper (*Tringa ochropus*); 49. Solitary Sandpiper (*Tringa solitaria*); 50. Wood Sandpiper (*Tringa glareola*); 51. Terek Sandpiper (*Xenus cinereus*); 52. Common Sandpiper (*Actitis hypoleucos*); 53. Spotted Sandpiper (*Actitis macularia*); 54. Grey-tailed Tattler (*Heteroscelus brevipes*); 55. Wandering Tattler (*Heteroscelus incanus*); 56. Willet (*Catoptrophorus semipalmatus*); 57. Tuamotu Sandpiper (*Prosobonia cancellata*); 58. Ruddy Turnstone (*Arenaria interpres*); 59. Black Turnstone (*Arenaria melanocephala*); 60. Surfbird (*Aphriza virgata*).

(1995), Perennou *et al.* (1994), Piersma (1986b, 1989c), Rezanov & Khrokov (1988a, 1988b), Ripley (1982), Roberts, T.J. (1991), Rogacheva (1992), Roselaar (1993), Rutgers & Norris (1970), Scott (1989), Selman & Goss-Custard (1988), Shirihai (1996), Smythies (1986), Speakman (1987), Speakman & Bryant (1993), Stiefel & Schleufer (1984), Summers & Underhill (1991), Summers, Nicoll *et al.* (1988), Summers, Underhill, Pearson & Scott (1987), Thompson, D.B.A. *et al.* (1988), Thompson, P.S. & Hale (1989, 1991, 1993), Thompson, P.S. *et al.* (1990), Urban *et al.* (1986), Voous (1993), Walker & Chandler (1985), Whitfield (1985, 1988b), Williams, M.D. (1986), Winkelman (1994), Witt (1992), Zhmud, M.E. (1988), Zhmud, M.Y. (1992).

43. Marsh Sandpiper

Tringa stagnatilis

French: Chevalier stagnatile **German**: Teichwasserläufer **Spanish**: Archibebe Fino

Taxonomy. *Totanus stagnatilis* Bechstein, 1803, Germany.
Monotypic.
Distribution. W Russia and E Ukraine to EC Siberia; isolated populations in Ussuriland and W Heilongjiang (NE China). Winters from Mediterranean and sub-Saharan Africa through Persian Gulf and S Asia to Indonesia and Australia.

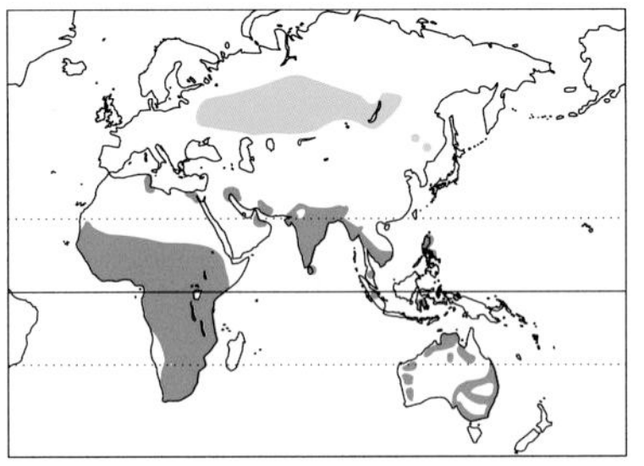

Descriptive notes. 22-26 cm; 43-120 g; wingspan 55-59 cm. Small body, long legs and straightish, needle-like bill; looks like small, fine *T. nebularia*; wings dark, rump and back white, face pale; upperparts strongly spotted and blotched with greyish cinnamon and black-brown; foreneck, breast and flanks with black markings. Female averages slightly larger. Non-breeding adult has plain grey upperparts with narrow white fringes and contrasting dark wing-coverts; face and underparts white. Juvenile as non-breeding, but upperparts browner with buff spots and fringes.
Habitat. Steppe and boreal wetlands, deep inland, preferably in open marshland with fresh grassy cover; brackish shallow marshes; less frequently around salt-lakes. Outside breeding season, occurs typically at margins of inland fresh to brackish wetlands, including paddyfields, swamps, salt-pans, salt-marshes, sewage farms, estuaries, lagoons and intertidal mudflats; avoids open beaches. On migration often feeds alongside *T. nebularia*.
Food and Feeding. Diet not well known, but includes at least small fish, crustaceans, molluscs and many insects, mostly aquatic, sometimes terrestrial; occasionally plant material. Often feeds in shallow water, pecking from water surface, while walking steadily and briskly; may glean from vegetation; sometimes probes, jabs or sweeps bill through water; rarely swims. When feeding on fish, may forage socially in dense flock of conspecifics or mixed with other tringines, moving erratically while pecking at prey or running synchronously in one direction while ploughing or scything bill through water; also recorded following ducks, egrets and other waders, feeding on prey disturbed by activity of other birds. Feeds singly or in flocks of up to several 100's.
Breeding. Laying late Apr to Jun. Probably monogamous. Solitary or in loose colonies; frequently together with marsh terns (*Chlidonias*), *T. totanus*, *Vanellus vanellus* or *Limosa limosa*. Nest placed on mound, in short vegetation, close to water; usually filled with dry grass. 4 eggs (3-5); both sexes incubate and tend brood; chick creamy buff above with blackish brown markings, face, chin and belly almost white. Age of first breeding 1 year or older.
Movements. Migratory. Generally scarce at stopover sites and many birds fly long distances overland on broad front. Main passage from USSR occurs E of Black Sea, through Kazakhstan and Middle East towards E & S Africa; few birds cross Slovakia, Hungary, Balkans, Italy and E Mediterranean; less commonly, though regularly, through W Europe. Nile Valley in Sudan frequently used as stopover, whereafter Sahara is crossed diagonally to W & WC African wintering grounds, where species present Sept to mid-Apr. In E Asia, passes through C Mongolia, C, NE & coastal China (Yellow R Delta), Korea (only on S migration), Japan, Hong Kong, Myanmar, Malaysia and Sumatra. In E Australia, may move away from coast after rains, and, as in C Australia, disperse among temporary inland wetlands. Most non-breeders stay in winter quarters or at intermediate sites during N summer.
Status and Conservation. Not globally threatened. Population of W African and Palearctic winterers c. 100,000 birds; in E Africa and SW Asia 25,000-100,000 birds; SC Asia in order of 100,000 birds, with important sites in SW India and Sri Lanka; E & SE Asia c. 90,000 birds; estimated 9000 birds in Australia, where SE Gulf of Carpentaria is the most important site, with 1150 birds. Little known about population trends, but breeding range in W Palearctic has shrunk, and species has even disappeared as breeding bird in E Europe, Belarus and Moldova, as result of losses of steppe habitat due to agricultural intensification; egg-collecting might also have played a role. Since 1960's, northward expansion of breeding range in Russia, although recently some Russian breeding populations declining in Caspian and Aral Sea regions, e.g. around Volga-Kama confluence and Orenburg. In E Russia, breeding range has expanded S as result of agricultural development. In Kharkov, NE Ukraine, amount of rain in spring affects numbers of breeding birds.
Bibliography. Ali & Ripley (1980), Autorowe (1992), Battley (1991), Baumanis (1989), Beck (1985), Beehler *et al.* (1986), Blakers *et al.* (1984), Brazil (1991), Coates (1985), Cramp & Simmons (1983), Dementiev & Gladkov (1951b), Dickinson *et al.* (1991), Dowsett & Forbes-Watson (1993), Elgood *et al.* (1994), Étchécopar & Hüe (1964, 1978), Evans (1994), Gavrilov (1986), Ginn *et al.* (1989), Girard (1992), Golovina (1988), Goodman *et al.* (1989), Grimes (1987), Hockey & Douie (1995), Hoogerwerf (1964), Hötker (1990), Hüe & Étchécopar (1970), Kieser & Kieser (1982), Knystautas (1993), Kuzniak & Pugacewicz (1992), Lane & Davies (1987), Lekagul & Round (1991), Luttik & Wassink (1980), MacKinnon & Phillipps (1993), Mackworth-Praed & Grant (1957, 1962, 1970), Maclean (1993), Marchant & Higgins (1996), van Marle & Voous (1988), Medway & Wells (1976), Morozov (1988), Olioso (1992), Patrikeev (1995), Paz (1987), Pearson (1974), Perennou *et al.* (1994), Phillips (1978), Pinto (1983), Rands *et al.* (1987), Ripley (1982), Roberts, T.J. (1991), Rogacheva (1992), Scott (1989), Shirihai (1996), Short *et al.* (1990), Smythies (1986), Tolchin (1976), Tomkovich (1992b), Urban *et al.* (1986), Velasco (1992b), Watkins (1993), White & Bruce (1986), Williams, M.D. (1986), Zhukov (1988).

44. Common Greenshank

Tringa nebularia

French: Chevalier aboyeur **German**: Grünschenkel **Spanish**: Archibebe Claro
Other common names: (Greater) Greenshank

Taxonomy. *Scolopax nebularia* Gunnerus, 1767, district of Trondheim, Norway.
Possible race *glottoides* proposed for E populations, on grounds of larger size range and details of non-breeding plumage. Monotypic.
Distribution. N Scotland and Scandinavia E through C Asia to E Siberia and Kamchatka. Winters from W Europe through Mediterranean to Africa, and E through Middle East to S Asia, Indonesia and Australasia.

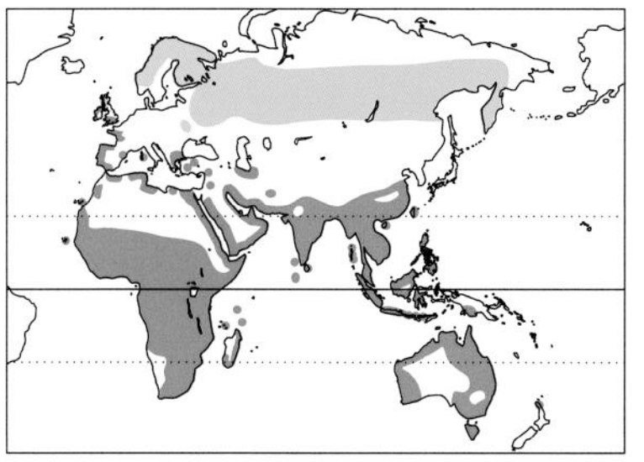

Descriptive notes. 30-35 cm; 125-290 g; wingspan 68-70 cm. Largest *Tringa* with long, robust, slightly uptilted bill and dull green legs; upperparts spotted and streaked black-brown, lesser wing-coverts browner; head, neck and upper-breast streaked brown-black; in flight, shows dark wings, white back and rump. Paler above than *T. guttifer* and *T. melanoleuca*, with longer legs than former. Female averages slightly larger. Non-breeding adult has feathers of upperparts rather uniform grey, without dark markings; breast, foreneck and face white; stronger contrasting dark wing-coverts. Juvenile resembles non-breeding adult, but upperparts browner with buff fringes and neck and breast somewhat more streaked.
Habitat. Taiga zone, in forest clearings, woody moorland or open bogs and marshes, including blanket bog; characteristic of northern and middle taiga. On migration, occurs at inland flooded meadows, dried-up lakes, sandbars and marshes. Winters in variety of freshwater and marine wetlands, including estuaries, sandy or muddy coastal flats, salt-marshes, mangroves, swamps and lakes; also on artificial wetlands, such as sewage farms, salt-works and inundated rice crops; less often on open coast, sometimes along quiet stretches of rivers.
Food and Feeding. Chiefly insects and their larvae, especially beetles, but also crustaceans, annelids, molluscs, amphibians and small fish; reported also rodents. Usually pecks and probes in shallow water walking with steady pass, sometimes running with erratic changes of direction; when feeding on fish may forage socially in dense flocks of conspecifics or mixed with other tringines, moving erratically while pecking at prey or running synchronously in one direction, ploughing or scything bill through water. Singly, or in small to large flocks of up to 100's. Feeds diurnally and nocturnally.
Breeding. Lays late Apr to Jun. Usually monogamous, though some males bigynous. High degree of site fidelity, but no natal philopatry. Densities 1·4-10 birds/km of riverbed (R Yenisey). Nest is shallow scrape lined with some plant material, on ground in the open, typically placed next to piece of dead wood. 4 eggs (3-5), with laying interval of 30-72 hours; single brood; incubation 24 days (22-26), by both sexes, but males with two mates normally do little incubation; chick pale grey marked above with fuscous black, white belly; often one parent leaves brood before fledging; fledging 25-31 days. On average, 74% of eggs hatch, 32% of hatchlings fledge. Age of first breeding unknown, but some return to breeding grounds as 1-year-olds. Oldest ringed bird 11 years, 11 months.
Movements. Mostly migratory, though some populations move only short distances. Migrates overland on broad front, but largest numbers pass through coastal sites. Movements over Europe mainly SSW-SW. Wadden Sea used by many Fenno-Scandian birds as stopover and moulting site from late Apr to mid-May; some move to Morocco. Most Palearctic birds are trans-Saharan migrants. Some non-breeders remain S all year. Spring migration more direct, without large coastal concentrations. Birds from Russia wintering in Africa are presumed to cross E & S Europe. In E Asia, passes through Kuril Is, Commander Is, Korea, Japan, NE China and New Guinea, mainly to coastal N Australia. Females start S migration in late Jun, but most adults arrive in Wadden Sea in Jul, followed by juveniles in Aug. Arrives in S Africa and Australia Aug-Sept, and begins N migration as early as Mar; arrival in W Australia may perhaps be followed by movement towards E & S; numbers in SE Australia continue to increase until Mar.
Status and Conservation. Not globally threatened. In Europe and W Africa probably several 100,000's of birds, although only 25,000 actually counted in coastal Europe and W Africa; in E Africa and SW Asia probably c. 100,000 birds; in SC Asia probably c. 25,000 birds; in E & SE Asia and Australasia c. 20,000 birds each. Scotland holds 400-900 breeding pairs; Fenno-Scandia 50,000-90,000 pairs (1993); locally abundant on Russian breeding grounds. Overall population considered secure due to extensive breeding range.
Bibliography. Alcorn (1988), Ali & Ripley (1980), Beehler *et al.* (1986), Benson & Benson (1975), Blakers *et al.* (1984), Brazil (1991), Bregnballe *et al.* (1990), Chandler, R.J. (1990), Clancey (1995), Coates (1985), Cramp & Simmons (1983), Deignan (1945), Dickinson *et al.* (1991), Dowsett & Forbes-Watson (1993), Elgood *et al.* (1994), Étchécopar & Hüe (1964, 1978), Evans (1994), Fjeldså (1977), Ginn *et al.* (1989), Goodman *et al.* (1989), Gore (1990), Grimes (1987), Hazevoet (1995), Hockey & Douie (1995), Hoogerwerf (1964), Hüe & Étchécopar (1970), Kieser & Kieser (1982), Kiis (1984), Knystautas (1993), Lane & Davies (1987), Langrand (1990), Lekagul & Round (1991), MacKinnon & Phillipps (1993), Mackworth-Praed & Grant (1957, 1962, 1970), Maclean (1993), Manakadan (1991), Marchant & Higgins (1996), van Marle & Voous (1988), Medway & Wells (1976), Milon *et al.* (1973), Nethersole-Thompson & Nethersole-Thompson (1979), Pakenham (1979), Paz (1987), Pearson (1974), Perennou *et al.* (1994), Phillips (1978), Piersma (1986b), Pinto (1983), Rands *et al.* (1987), Ripley (1982), Roberts, T.J. (1991), Rogacheva (1992), Scott (1989), Shirihai (1996), Short *et al.* (1990), Smythies (1986), Summers & Waltner (1979), Swennen (1971), Thompson, D.B.A. *et al.* (1986, 1988), Thompson, P.S. & Thompson (1991), Tree (1979, 1982, 1987c), Urban *et al.* (1986), Watkins (1993), White & Bruce (1986), Williams, M.D. (1986), Zwarts (1988).

45. Nordmann's Greenshank

Tringa guttifer

French: Chevalier tacheté **German**: Tüpfelgrünschenkel **Spanish**: Archibebe Moteado
Other common names: Spotted Greenshank

Taxonomy. *Totanus guttifer* Nordmann, 1835, Okhotsk.
Formerly separated in monospecific genus *Pseudototanus*. Monotypic.
Distribution. Sakhalin and W Sea of Okhotsk; possibly also N Sea of Okhotsk and Kamchatka. Winters in NE India, Bangladesh, Myanmar and Hainan S to Malay Peninsula; may also be regular in South Korea, perhaps E Sumatra and elsewhere.
Descriptive notes. 29-32 cm; 136-158 g. Heavily built *Tringa*; dark brown upperparts with whitish spots and fringes; head and neck densely spotted and streaked dark brown; breast and flanks spotted blackish. Very similar to *T. nebularia*, but legs short and yellowish; bill almost straight and two-toned. Sexes alike. Non-breeding adult has dull grey upperparts with whitish fringes, contrasting dark brown lesser wing-coverts; head and neck much paler; breast and flanks lack spots. Juvenile as non-breeding, but crown and upperparts browner, with buff spots and streaks; wing-coverts have pale buff fringes; breast with brown wash.
Habitat. On breeding grounds, occupies coastal lowland swamps and sparse larch forests around marshy pools, close to shallow bays. After breeding, mostly at large, coastal mudflats or sandflats, deltas, shallow lagoons, occasionally with mangroves or beds of seagrass; also swamps, willow beds, mossy meadows near streams, salt-pans and rice paddies.

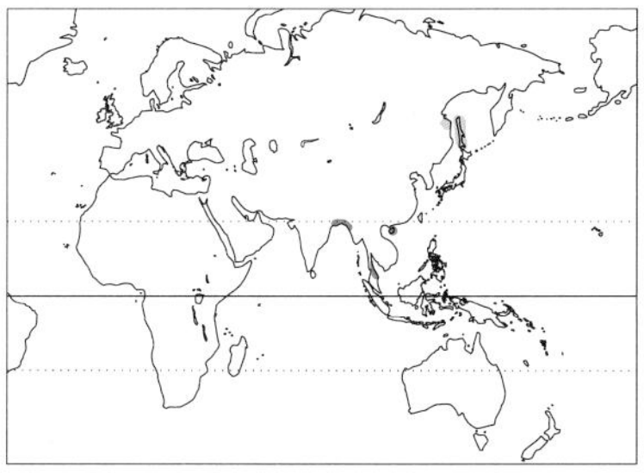

Food and Feeding. On breeding grounds takes small fish, especially sticklebacks; also polychaetes, small crustaceans and insects, especially aquatic beetles. Outside breeding areas, shows preference for crabs, but also other aquatic invertebrates, molluscs, insect larvae and small fish. Large crabs shaken until legs come off, and body and legs swallowed separately; small crabs swallowed whole. Takes multiple and single pecks with slightly opened bill, moving head from side to side; also runs after prey with bill held low, probably chasing fish. Feeds during low tide on tidal flats, prefering the tide-line. Roosts at high tide, preferably in shallow water.
Breeding. Laying in Jun. Monogamous; nests in scattered single pairs or in colonies of 3-10 pairs. Nest placed in low larch tree at height of 2·3-4·5 m; formed of larch twigs, lichen and moss; unlike other *Tringa*, nest is built by the birds themselves; both female and male birds collect material from the ground and pull twigs from trees. 4 eggs; single brood; both sexes incubate. Reported predators include Carrion Crow (*Corvus corone*) and foxes.
Movements. Not well known; has been recorded widely as a migrant or winter vistor in Ussuriland, Japan, North and South Korea, China, Taiwan, Hong Kong, Vietnam, Thailand, Sumatra, Philippines and S India. Adults leave Sakhalin breeding grounds late Jul to mid-Aug, juveniles from late Aug to mid-Sept; species migrates through Japan and Korea in Sept. Returns to breeding grounds from mid-May.
Status and Conservation. ENDANGERED. CITES I. Total population comprises perhaps c. 1000 birds (1989), but both breeding and winter distributions poorly known. Breeding population on Sakhalin (Chaivo Bay and Dogy Bay) estimated at 30-40 pairs (1985-1988); urbanization, increased crow predation, human disturbance and increased hunting pressure are major threats for this population. At least 36 pairs counted in bays of W Sea of Okhotsk in 1990/91. Main wintering grounds seem to be located in Bangladesh (Nijhum Dweep and Maulavir Char), Thailand (Krabi Bay) and perhaps also in South Korea, where over 50 birds may occur; c. 300 birds reported from Bangladesh in winter 1988/89; up to 27 birds staging in Sheyang Saltworks, Jiangsu, CE China, in Aug-Sept 1991. Winter distribution still very poorly known, and may regularly include E Sumatra, where flock of 21 birds seen in 1988; total of 25 birds in Karnataka, S India, in 1992. In general, rarely seen and not well known; apparently in process of disappearing from its highly restricted range.
Bibliography. Ali & Ripley (1980), Austin & Kuroda (1953), Bijlsma & de Roder (1986), Borodin *et al.* (1984), Brazil (1991), Collar & Andrew (1988), Collar *et al.* (1994), Dickinson *et al.* (1991), Étchécopar & Hüe (1978), Howes (1988), Howes & Lambert (1987), Howes & Parish (1989), Kennerley & Bakewell (1987, 1991), King (1978/79), Knystautas (1993), Kuroda (1936b), Lekagul & Round (1991), Lim Kimseng (1994), MacKinnon & Phillipps (1993), van Marle & Voous (1988), Medway & Wells (1976), Nechaev (1978, 1982, 1989), Neufeldt & Vietinghoff-Scheel (1983), Perennou *et al.* (1994), Ripley (1982), Scott (1989), de Silva (1992), Silvius (1986), Smythies (1986), Swennen & Park (1991), Verheugt *et al.* (1993), Wang Hui (1992).

46. Greater Yellowlegs
Tringa melanoleuca

French: Grand Chevalier **German**: Großer Gelbschenkel **Spanish**: Archibebe Patigualdo Grande

Taxonomy. *Scolopax melanoleuca* Gmelin, 1789, Chateaux Bay, Labrador.
Monotypic.
Distribution. S Alaska and British Columbia E to Labrador, Newfoundland I, Anticosti I and NE Nova Scotia. Winters from British Columbia and the Carolinas through Mexico, Central America and West Indies to South America, S to Tierra del Fuego.

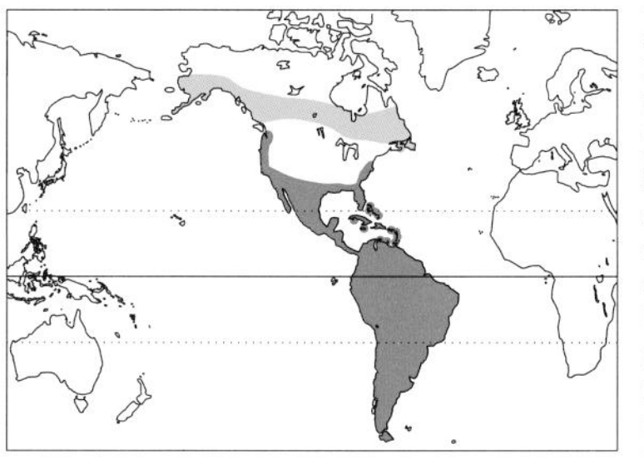

Descriptive notes. 29-33 cm; 111-235 g; wingspan 70-74 cm. Large *Tringa* with long legs and longish bill; head and neck heavily streaked dark brown; breast, flanks and upper belly with blackish spots; white rump, dark back. Larger and heavier than *T. flavipes*, with longer, stout, straight or slightly uptilted bill; more heavily marked below; dark secondaries fringed whitish. Sexes alike. Non-breeding adult has grey-brown upperparts with white spots and fringes, and grey streaking on breast and flanks. Juvenile as non-breeding, but has buff spots and brown on breast usually forming a breast band.
Habitat. Muskeg forest with low and sparse undergrowth, scattered trees, marshy ponds and open areas; also on hills near swamps, subarctic tundra and subalpine scrub; generally in fairly flat terrain. After breeding, occurs at freshwater or brackish wetlands, especially ponds with emergent vegetation, flooded rice fields and rain pools; also mangrove stands, muddy coasts, salt-marshes, intertidal flats and man-made reservoirs. On wintering grounds, most abundant on intertidal flats and lagoons. On occasion, found in dry areas such as pastures and dunes, and small numbers at streams and pools at medium to high altitudes, up to 4600 m.
Food and Feeding. Diet includes small crustaceans, fish, worms, aquatic insects and their larvae, also terrestrial insects, such as small grasshoppers, ants and flies. Feeding techniques include skimming water surface for food, picking, and dashing through shallow water after small fish; often wades and sometimes swims. Outside breeding season, feeds singly or in small flocks; often defends feeding territory. Diurnal and nocturnal forager, at night scything (side-sweeping with bill through water) to catching small fish.
Breeding. Poorly known. Season starts May. Nest is usually next to branch or log, on dry hard substrate on ridge, close to water. 4 eggs (variation unknown); incubation 23 days; chick-care, and presumably also incubation, by both parents.
Movements. Migration through interior North America and along coasts, on both passages. Few birds overfly W Atlantic between Canadian Maritime Provinces and Lesser Antilles, but most birds on E coast pass along Atlantic seaboard, or from Florida across Great Antilles to South America. Spring return flight presumably non-stop from the Guianas to USA, some via Lesser Antilles, then majority across C North America and up Atlantic coast. Largest winter numbers recorded in Surinam and, to lesser extent, in Guyana and French Guiana. Possibly faithful to wintering sites. Many non-breeders, presumably immatures, remain S all year.
Status and Conservation. Not globally threatened. Total population reckoned at c. 20,000 birds in 1994, but very few precise data available; population seems to be stable.
Bibliography. Achtermann (1992), Amos (1991), Armstrong (1983), Barthel (1992), Belton (1984), Bent (1927-1929), Biaggi (1983), Blake (1977), Brazil (1991), Brooks (1967), Buchanan (1988), Contreras *et al.* (1990), Cramp & Simmons (1983), Dott (1985), Fjeldså & Krabbe (1990), Glustchenko & Dorogoi (1986), Haverschmidt (1968), Haverschmidt & Mees (1995), Hayes (1995), Hayes & Fox (1991), Hilty & Brown (1986), Howell & Webb (1995a), Johnson (1965b), Key (1991), Kwater (1992), Matthiessen (1994), McNeil (1970), Meissner *et al.* (1989), Meyer de Schauensee & Phelps (1978), Monroe (1968), de la Peña (1992), Ridgely & Gwynne (1989), Robbins *et al.* (1983), Robert & McNeil (1989), Rojas *et al.* (1993), Root (1988), Scott & Carbonell (1986), Sick (1985c, 1993), Slud (1964), Snyder (1966), Stiles & Skutch (1989), Tostain *et al.* (1992), Tree (1981b), Ulrich (1984), Urban *et al.* (1986), Wetmore (1965), Whoriskey & Fitzgerald (1985), Wilds (1982), Zusi (1968).

47. Lesser Yellowlegs
Tringa flavipes

French: Petit Chevalier **German**: Kleiner Gelbschenkel **Spanish**: Archibebe Patigualdo Chico
Other common names: Yellowshank

Taxonomy. *Scolopax flavipes* Gmelin, 1789, New York.
Monotypic.
Distribution. Alaska to SC Canada, E to James Bay. Winters from S USA through Mexico, Central America and West Indies to South America, S to Tierra del Fuego.

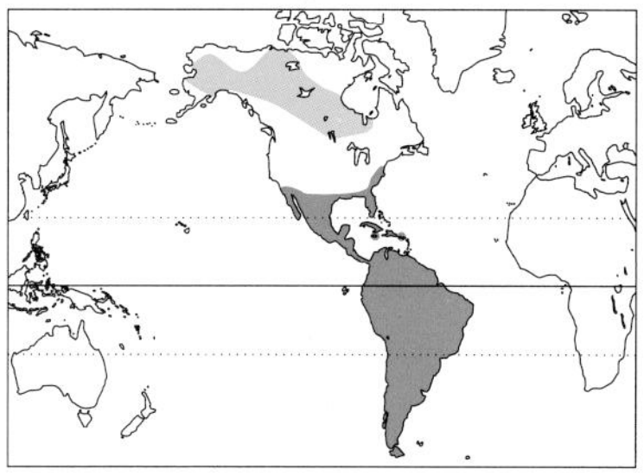

Descriptive notes. 23-25 cm; 48-114 g; wingspan 59-64 cm. Slim, medium-sized *Tringa* with relatively short, straight, thin, pointed bill; blackish upperparts with white spots and grey-brown wing-coverts; head, neck and breast heavy blackish streaked. Very similar to *T. melanoleuca*, but smaller with shorter bill; sparser dark markings on underparts; dark secondaries unmarked. Female averages slightly longer-winged. Non-breeding adult paler grey with pale spots on inner greater coverts and tertials. Juvenile as non-breeding, but upperparts brown with buff spots; breast washed brownish grey with little streaking.
Habitat. Swampy muskeg habitat, clearings within tall, open woodland with sparse undergrowth, sometimes close to marshy or grassy ponds, grassy meadows and bogs; usually drier and more sheltered than breeding habitat of *T. melanoleuca*. Outside breeding season occurs in variety of inland and coastal wetlands, usually with emergent vegetation, including inundated farmland and grassland, mangrove stands, sewage beds, shallow prairie sloughs, man-made reservoirs, marshes, lagoons, mudflats and salt-marshes. On wintering grounds, most abundant on intertidal flats and in lagoons.
Food and Feeding. On breeding grounds, takes cranefly larvae, beetles, Diptera eggs and larvae, snails and spiders. Non-breeding diet includes variety of terrestrial and aquatic insects and their larvae (Diptera, beetles), worms, crustaceans, gastropods and small fish. Often wades in shallow, belly-deep water, and also walks on floating water weeds; pecks from water or mud surface, rarely probes, skims, or dashes after prey like *T. melanoleuca*. In wintering range, often defends feeding territory. Diurnal and nocturnal forager, using sweeping technique at night.
Breeding. Breeds May-Aug. Often up to 3-4 pairs/km². Nest often on ridge, at base of tree stump under bush, usually situated close to water. 4 eggs (3-5); incubation 22-23 days; both sexes incubate and care for chicks; fledging probably 23-25 days. Oldest ringed bird 5 years, 11 months.
Movements. Migratory. Moves through E Canada, E of breeding range, and (mid-Jul to mid-Sept) interior USA between Rocky and Allegheny Mts; also down Atlantic coast, S of Gulf of St Lawrence. Some may fly direct, or via Bermuda, to Lesser Antilles and N South America; others move S down Atlantic seaboard; commonly stages at W Amazonian lakes and rivers. Uncommon transient in Central America. Few birds winter on W coast USA, more in S USA, majority in West Indies and N South America, where most abundant in Surinam, and high numbers in Guyana and French Guiana. Fair numbers remain S in N summer. In spring, return migration across W Caribbean and Gulf of Mexico, and North America; in USA, most birds move through interior, fewer up Atlantic coast.
Status and Conservation. Not globally threatened. Total population comprises at least 100,000 birds; 91,000 yellowlegs counted during aerial survey of South American coasts, with large proportion probably of present species. Few precise data available, but numbers are apparently declining.
Bibliography. Achtermann (1992), Amos (1991), Armstrong (1983), Baker, M.C. (1977), Baker, M.C. & Baker (1973), Baldassarre & Fischer (1984), Barthel (1992), Belton (1984), Beltzer (1991), Bent (1927-1929), Biaggi (1983), Blake (1977), Bolster & Robinson (1990), Brazil (1991), Brooks (1967), Contreras *et al.* (1990), Cramp & Simmons (1983), Fjeldså & Krabbe (1990), Harmsen (1989), Haverschmidt (1968), Haverschmidt & Mees (1995), Hayes (1995), Heiser (1992), Hilty & Brown (1986), Howell & Webb (1995a), Johnson (1965b), Kwater (1992), Matthiessen (1994), McNeil (1970), Meyer de Schauensee & Phelps (1978), Michaud & Ferron (1986, 1990), Monroe (1968), de la Peña (1992), Ridgely & Gwynne (1989), Robert & McNeil (1989), Root (1988), Schwarhoff (1992), Scott & Carbonell (1986), Sick (1985c, 1993), Slud (1964), Snyder (1966), Spaans (1978), van der Spek & van der Spek (1992), Stiles & Skutch (1989), Street (1923), Taylor, P.B. (1980b), Tostain *et al.* (1992), Tree (1981b), Tree & Kieser (1982), Urban *et al.* (1986), Wetmore (1965), Whoriskey & Fitzgerald (1985), Wilds (1982).

48. Green Sandpiper
Tringa ochropus

French: Chevalier cul-blanc **German**: Waldwasserläufer **Spanish**: Andarríos Grande

Taxonomy. *Tringa Ocrophus* [sic] Linnaeus, 1758, Sweden.
Monotypic.
Distribution. Scandinavia and E Europe through C Asia to E Siberia; isolated population in Kyrgyzstan and NW Xinjiang. Winters in Mediterannean and tropical Africa, and from Turkey through Middle East and Indian Subcontinent to S Japan, E China, Philippines and N Borneo; small wintering populations in W & WC Europe, and in sheltered valleys of Tien Shan zone.
Descriptive notes. 21-24 cm; 53-119 g; wingspan 57-61 cm. Medium-sized, dark sandpiper; foreneck, breast and upper flanks streaked grey-brown, underparts white; rump white, tail white with thick black bars. Very similar to *T. solitaria*, but larger and darker; head greyer, spots on upperparts whiter and more distinct, white rump; bill generally heavier and longer, wings broader. Resembles *Actitus hypoleucos* and *T. glareola*, but larger; generally darker above, with dark underwing. Female averages larger. Non-breeding adult has less spotted upperparts and face, foreneck and centre of breast whiter, and no streaking on flanks. Juvenile like breeding adult, with buff spots on upperparts, paler breast and no streaks on flanks; white eye-ring very distinct.

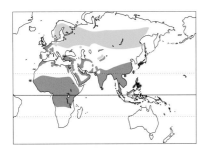

Habitat. Damp wooded areas, in old, swampy woodland and montane forest; preferably pine woods, but also in spruce or alder, in vicinity of rivers, streams, swamps or lakes. Outside breeding season less attracted to vicinity of trees, in variety of inland fresh waters, such as marshes, riverbanks, sewage farms, small ponds and narrow ditches, often with protective vegetation. Scarce in intertidal areas, and then only in channels of salt-marshes.

Food and Feeding. Feeds on aquatic and terrestrial insects, mainly adults and larvae of beetles, Diptera and Trichoptera, but also dragonfly larvae, ants, water-bugs and moth larvae; annelids, small crustaceans, spiders, fish and plant fragments. Mainly pecks food from shallow water and from surface of ground and plants; rarely probes; sometimes uses trampling to stir up food. Sometimes wades or swims, and even dives, while feeding. Normally feeds singly, sometimes in small, scattered groups of up to 30 birds.

Breeding. Laying late Apr to Jun. Monogamous. Densities normally 1-8 birds/km², but 11-19 birds/km² recorded and under 0·5 birds/km² in extreme N taiga. Usually uses old tree nests of other bird species, especially thrushes (*Turdus*) or Common Woodpigeon (*Columba palumbus*), normally with little modification; sometimes on natural platform; up to 20 m high; occasionally nests on ground. 4 eggs, sometimes 3; incubation 20-23 days, by both sexes, but mainly female; chick pale drab grey marked fuscous black, with dark line across and along crown and long tail; both sexes tend chicks at first, but female may leave before fledging; fledging c. 28 days. Oldest ringed bird 9 years, 8 months.

Movements. Moves overland on broad front, generally in low concentrations on passage and at stopover sites; many passage records at Saharan oases. N European population probably moves S & SW to wintering grounds. In mild winters some birds stay in S Scandinavia. Southward movements from Jun to early Nov; species present in N and equatorial Africa late Aug to early Apr and in S Africa Oct-Mar; return passage late Feb to mid-May. At least locally very faithful to wintering areas. Few birds remain in wintering areas during breeding season.

Status and Conservation. Not globally threatened. Possibly more than 1,000,000 breeding birds in Europe; numbers wintering in E Africa and SW Asia unknown; in S Asia and E & SE Asia probably 100,000 to several 100,000's of birds. Breeding range in Poland has probably decreased, although species colonized Denmark in 1950's and recent northward expansion in Finland. Fenno-Scandian breeding population estimated at 123,000 pairs in 1986. Breeding population of Ukraine has declined due to habitat changes.

Bibliography. Ali & Ripley (1980), Benson & Benson (1975), Bonisch *et al.* (1991), Brazil (1991), Cramp & Simmons (1983), Deignan (1945), Dickinson *et al.* (1991), Dowsett & Forbes-Watson (1993), Elgood *et al.* (1994), Étchécopar & Hüe (1964, 1978), Evans (1994), Fjeldså (1977), Ginn *et al.* (1989), Goodman *et al.* (1989), Gore (1990), Gunther & Gunther (1987), Heg (1988), Hoelzinger *et al.* (1973), Hoogerwerf (1964), Hüe & Étchécopar (1970), King *et al.* (1980), Kirchner, H. (1972), Kirchner, K. (1978), Kittle (1975), Knystautas (1993), Kraatz & Beyer (1982, 1984), Landmann (1979), Lekagul & Round (1991), MacKinnon & Phillipps (1993), Mackworth-Praed & Grant (1957, 1962, 1970), van Marle & Voous (1988), Medway & Wells (1976), Müller (1988a), Münster (1989a), Oring (1968), Ormerod & Tyler (1988), Patrikeev (1995), Paz (1987), Perennou *et al.* (1994), Phillips (1978), Piersma (1986b), Pinto (1983), Pourreau & Guennec (1992), Raju (1978), Rands *et al.* (1987), Ripley (1982), Roberts, T.J. (1991), Rogacheva (1992), Rutgers & Norris (1970), Scott (1989), Shirihai (1996), Short *et al.* (1990), Slator & Worwood (1995), Smith, Reed & Trevis (1992), Smythies (1981, 1986), Tree (1979), Tyler & Ormerod (1987), Urban *et al.* (1986), Williams, M.D. (1986).

49. Solitary Sandpiper
Tringa solitaria

French: Chevalier solitaire   **German**: Einsamer Wasserläufer   **Spanish**: Andarríos Solitario

Taxonomy. *Tringa solitaria* Wilson, 1813, Pocono Mountains, Pennsylvania.
Formerly considered conspecific with *T. ochropus*. Two subspecies recognized.
Subspecies and Distribution.
T. s. cinnamomea (Brewster, 1890) - C & S Alaska through W Northwest Territories and N British Columbia to NE Manitoba; winters from N South America S to C Argentina.
T. s. solitaria Wilson, 1813 - E British Columbia through SC Canada to Quebec and Labrador; winters from Central America and West Indies to South America S to Argentina, and occasionally in S USA.

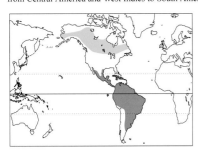

Descriptive notes. 18-21 cm; 38-69 g; wingspan 55-59 cm. Adult has dark upperparts with pale spots; head and breast finely streaked dark brown; the only *Tringa* with combination of dark rump and underwing. Closely resembles *T. ochropus*, but smaller and appears more slender; bill generally shorter and finer; at rest, primaries clearly longer than tail; rump dark. Female averages slightly larger. Non-breeding adult has head, neck and upperparts greyer; upperparts less spotted; clear white eye-ring. Juvenile has pale spots on upperparts; breast washed dark, often forming lateral patches; clear white eye-ring. Race *cinnamomea* averages slightly larger, with slightly paler, warmer brown spotting on upperparts; juvenile has upperparts dotted buff, rather than whitish.

Habitat. Wet boreal muskeg forest, usually in rather open terrain with scattered trees. Outside breeding season, most abundant in savannas, in enclosed inland fresh waters, often in isolated ditches and temporary tiny stagnant pools; also man-made reservoirs, wet meadows, quiet streams and swamps in woodlands; often found near human settlements; rare at coast.

Food and Feeding. Diet includes aquatic insects and their larvae, small crustaceans, spiders, terrestrial insects (e.g. grasshoppers) and even small frogs. Often wades in shallow water, vibrating leading foot to disturb and catch aquatic invertebrates. On wintering grounds defends feeding territory.

Breeding. Often uses old tree nests of passerines, such as thrushes (*Turdus*) up to 12 m high, usually in coniferous trees; also on ground in areas above tree-line. 4 eggs; probably both sexes incubate; incubation and fledging periods unknown.

Movements. Migratory, overland on broad fronts, extending right across North America, but main passage E of Rocky Mts. Race *cinnamomea* migrates mainly through region from mountains of W USA E to Montana and Colorado, on occasion E to Mississippi Valley; race *solitaria* moves through region from Montana and Utah E to Atlantic states of USA. In autumn, some birds apparently pass over W Atlantic, directly from Canadian Maritime Provinces to N South America. Races mix in

winter quarters; species is common migrant and short-term resident along lakes and rivers in W Amazon area. Seldom migrates in flocks. Some birds oversummer in Neotropics.

Status and Conservation. Not globally threatened. Population of *cinnamomea* numbers less than 10,000 birds; no figures available for nominate race. Thought to have suffered little from hunting, probably due to solitary habits; cutting of boreal forests may be threat in some areas. Commonest shorebird in inland Brazil, occurring on almost all water bodies.

Bibliography. Amos (1991), Armstrong (1983), Aspinwall *et al.* (1995), Belton (1984), Bent (1927-1929), Biaggi (1983), Blake (1977), Conover, H.B. (1944), Contreras *et al.* (1990), Cramp & Simmons (1983), Fjeldså & Krabbe (1990), Haverschmidt (1968), Haverschmidt & Mees (1995), Hayes (1995), Hayes & Fox (1991), Hilty & Brown (1986), Howell & Webb (1995a), Lethaby (1995), Matthiessen (1994), Meyer de Schauensee & Phelps (1978), Monroe (1968), Moskoff (1995), Navas & Bo (1993), Oring (1968, 1973), de la Peña (1992), Ridgely & Gwynne (1989), Root (1988), Scott & Carbonell (1986), Shelley (1933), Sick (1985c, 1993), Slud (1964), Snyder (1966), Stiles & Skutch (1989), Street (1923), Tallman & Tallman (1986), Tostain *et al.* (1992), Webber (1968), Wetmore (1965).

50. Wood Sandpiper
Tringa glareola

French: Chevalier sylvain   **German**: Bruchwasserläufer   **Spanish**: Andarríos Bastardo

Taxonomy. *Tringa Glareola* Linnaeus, 1758, Sweden. Monotypic.
Distribution. N Europe through C Siberia to Anadyrland, Kamchatka and Commander Is; occasionally Aleutian Is. Winters mainly in tropical and subtropical Africa, across S Asia to S China, Philippines, Indonesia and Australia.

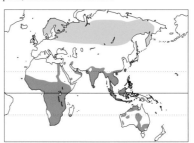

Descriptive notes. 19-23 cm; 34-98 g; wingspan 34-37 cm. Small, graceful sandpiper; head, neck and breast finely streaked grey-brown; supercilium and throat white; upperparts blackbrown with white spots, underparts white. Similar to *T. ochropus*, but paler, less bulky and longer-legged; underwing much paler. Has longer neck and legs than more uniform *Actitis hypoleucos*. Female averages slightly larger. Non-breeding adult has browner and less spotted upperparts; breast washed grey and less streaked; supercilium more distinct. Juvenile like non-breeding adult, but warmer brown above with buff spots; breast washed greybrown, finely streaked brown.

Habitat. Peatlands, open swampy areas in boreal forest, especially scrubland between tundra and coniferous forest, wet heathlands with or without scattered conifers, and marshlands with deciduous bushes. Outside breeding season, generally not associated with woodlands; found in more open areas than those favoured by *T. ochropus*, including open margins of inland fresh waters, muddy marshes, grassy stream banks, sewage farms, wet paddyfields, tiny temporary pools and streams; only rarely in coastal habitats, such as channels of salt-marshes and mangrove swamps.

Food and Feeding. On breeding grounds chiefly takes small, especially aquatic, insects, up to 2 cm long, e.g. beetles, Hemiptera, larvae of Diptera. Elsewhere, aquatic and terrestrial insects and their larvae, worms, spiders, crustaceans, molluscs, small fish (up to 2 cm) and even frogs; sometimes plant matter (seeds). Gleans, pecks, probes or sweeps bill through water; also able to catch flying insects from air. Feeds in shallow water or on mud; occasionally swims. Often feeds singly, but also in pairs or scattered groups. May defend feeding territories.

Breeding. Lays May to mid-Jul. Monogamous. Solitary; normally 1-10 pairs/km², but up to 50 birds/km² in forest tundra. Nest is scrape lined with moss, stems and leaves, on ground among dense cover; also frequently in trees, in old nests of other species. 4 eggs, sometimes 3, with laying interval 1-2 days; single brood; incubation 22-23 days, by both sexes; chick pale buff to pale cream marked fuscous black and mottled greyish brown to cinnamon on upper back, with wide dark cap and white belly; from 7-10 days after hatching, care of young usually only by male; fledging 28-30 days. Annual adult mortality 46%, 1st-year mortality 83-88%. Oldest ringed bird 9 years, 2 months. Age of first breeding 1 year.

Movements. Migratory. Many birds move to sub-Saharan Africa and India, few to Australia. On migration, scarce in W Europe, especially during N migration in May, commoner Aug to mid-Sept. Migration across Europe and Middle East overland on broad front, predominantly S-SSW; scarce in Britain and Ireland; many stop over in N Mediterranean, especially France (Camargue) and Italy, whereafter they overfly Sahara, chiefly in SW direction to W Africa; common on passage through C Chad. Spring migration probably more easterly, with briefer pauses. Birds wintering in E & S Africa originate from former USSR; birds wintering in India from breeding zone in Siberia between Tyumen and R Kolyma. Many E Siberian breeders pass through S Ussuriland, Japan, Korea, Taiwan, E China and Hong Kong to SE Asian wintering grounds, with only small fraction continuing to Australia, where mainly in NW; also movements through N China and Tibet. In spring, large numbers pass W Aleutians.

Status and Conservation. Not globally threatened. European breeding population estimated at up to 1,400,000 pairs, representing probably around one fifth to quarter of total world population (1994). Possibly over 1,000,000 birds wintering in SW Asia and E & C Africa, where 250,000-500,000 in Sudan, 30,000 on W shore of L Edward, Zaire; 100,000's in SC Asia and in E & SE Asia. Australian non-breeding population estimated at 6000 birds; has benefited from irrigation schemes and construction of open sewage ponds. Breeding population has declined in some European countries, especially Finland, where currently 200,000-300,000 pairs; decline mainly due to exploitation, destruction or drainage of peatlands for forestry and agriculture; decline noted in S Sweden, Germany and Poland, possibly due to climatic changes. Populations in Sweden, Norway and European Russia currently fairly stable; status of population E of Urals poorly known.

Bibliography. Akriotis (1991), Ali & Ripley (1980), Amos & Wingate (1983), Armstrong (1983), Beehler *et al.* (1986), Benson & Benson (1975), Blakers *et al.* (1984), Blitzblau (1990), Boyd (1962), Brazil (1991), Chattopadhyay & Chattopadhyay (1988), Chattopadhyay *et al.* (1994), Chojnacki & Stawarczyk (1988), Coates (1985), Cramp & Simmons (1983), Deignan (1945), Dickinson *et al.* (1991), Dowsett & Forbes-Watson (1993), Elgood *et al.* (1994), Étchécopar & Hüe (1964, 1978), Evans (1994), Ferguson-Lees (1971), Fjeldså (1977), Galbraith & Thompson (1981, 1982), Gavrilov (1988), Ginn *et al.* (1989), Glutz von Blotzheim *et al.* (1977), Goodman *et al.* (1989), Gore (1990), Grimes (1987), Hoath (1994), Hockey & Douie (1995), Hoffmann (1957), Hoogerwerf (1964), Hüe & Étchécopar (1970), Kirchner (1978), Knystautas (1993), Kolmodin & Risberg (1994), Lambert (1984), Lane & Davies (1987), Lekagul & Round (1991), Leuzinger & Jenni (1993), MacKinnon & Phillipps (1993), Mackworth-Praed & Grant (1957, 1962, 1970), Maclean (1993), Madoc (1976), Marchant & Higgins (1996), van Marle & Voous (1988), Medway & Wells (1976), Neill (1987), Ostergaard (1986), Pakenham (1979), Patrikeev (1995), Paz (1987), Pearson (1974), Perennou *et al.* (1994), Phillips (1978), Piersma (1986b), Pinto (1983), Pulliainen & Saari (1991), Raju (1978), Rands *et al.* (1987), Ripley (1982), Roberts, T.J. (1991), Rogacheva (1992), Sampath (1990), Scott (1989), Shirihai (1996), Short *et al.* (1990), Smythies (1981, 1986), Tree & Kieser (1982), Urban *et al.* (1986), Watkins (1993), Weggler (1992), White, C.M. *et al.* (1974), White, C.M.N. & Bruce (1986), Williams, M.D. (1986).

Genus *XENUS* Kaup, 1829

51. **Terek Sandpiper**

Xenus cinereus

French: Chevalier bargette **German**: Terekwasserläufer **Spanish**: Andarríos del Terek

Taxonomy. *Scolopax cinerea* Güldenstädt, 1774, Terek River, Caspian Sea.
Often placed in *Tringa*; *Tringa terek* is synonym. In past, occasionally split into two subspecies, with recognition of *australis*; based on differences noted at winter quarters, but variation poorly understood. Monotypic.
Distribution. S Finland; NW Russia and Ukraine E through C Siberia to Anadyrland, mainly in boreal taiga zone, extending N into subarctic tundra and S to steppe fringes. Winters from SW, S & E Africa through Middle East, S Asia and Indonesia to N & W Australia.

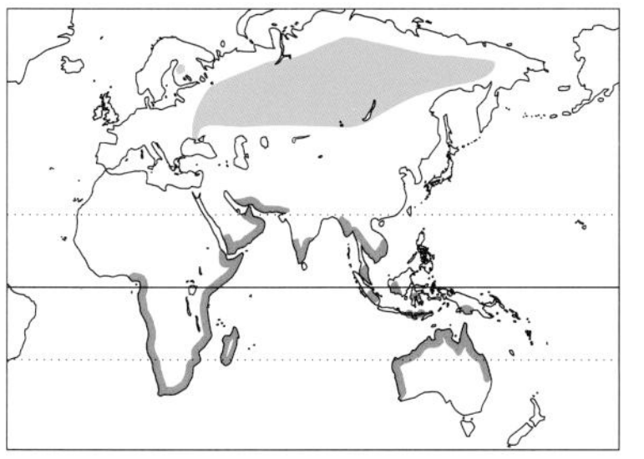

Descriptive notes. 22-25 cm; 50-126 g; wingspan 57-59 cm. Distinctive, rather small sandpiper with long upcurved bill and short orange to greenish yellow legs; grey-brown upperparts with almost black centres to feathers, particularly distinct on scapulars; streaked crown, hindneck, cheeks and sides of breast; broad white trailing edge to wings. Some birds have shorter bills, not very obviously upcurved. Female averages slightly larger. Non-breeding adult plainer; brownish grey above with pale fringes; paler head. Juvenile as breeding adult, but upperparts darker and browner with narrow buff fringes; black scapular lines less prominent.
Habitat. Breeds in lowland valleys, especially on floodplains with alternation of tall grasses and scrub willows; most typical on northern taiga and forest tundra. Outside breeding season, on tropical coasts, especially open intertidal mudflats and estuaries, also coral reefs, sandy beaches, sandbars or mudflats at mouths of rivers, and coastal swamps and salt-pans; sometimes up to 10 km inland, around brackish pools and riverbeds. Often roosts communally on branches of mangroves. During migration, occasionally inland on freshwater wetlands.
Food and Feeding. On breeding grounds, diet consists mainly of adult and larval midges, as well as seeds. Elsewhere, variety of insects, small molluscs, crustaceans including crabs, spiders and annelid worms. Rapid feeding action, with abrupt changes of direction; often teeters; pecks at sand or water surface; chases mobile prey on surface, also uses avocet-like sideways sweeping action; frequently probes; often washes prey in water's edge. Usually feeds during low tide, but may also feed during high tide around embedded seaweed high on beach. Scattered when feeding, in groups of 5-25 birds.
Breeding. Breeds May-Jul. Semi-colonial. Nest is shallow depression sparsely lined with grass and debris, in open or short vegetation, close to water. 4 eggs (2-5), with laying interval 1-2 days; single brood; incubation 23-24 days, starting with 3rd egg; role of sexes unclear; chick greyish brown or rusty grey above finely stippled and mottled dusky, with black mid-line across crown and back and white chin, throat and underparts; fledging 15 days. Oldest ringed bird at least 14 years, 11 months.
Movements. Migratory. Moves S from late Jul to Oct, N in Apr-May. In E Asia migrates along coasts of Ussuriland, Japan, Korea, NE China, Taiwan, Hong Kong, Philippines and W Micronesia. Birds wintering in N Australia and E Indonesia probably breed farther N than those wintering in SE Asia and W Indonesia. On E coast of Australia two southbound waves of migration occur, one in Sept, the other in Nov. Return passage probably non-stop from NW Australia to Philippines or Taiwan. In W Asia birds pass S through Caspian region and Middle East to Africa; Finnish birds fly across E Europe, probably crossing Mediterranean and Sahara non-stop. Strong site tenacity. Many non-breeders spend N summer on wintering grounds.
Status and Conservation. Not globally threatened. In Africa and SW Asia minimum 44,000 wintering birds (1991); in SC Asia probably c. 25,000 birds; in E & SE Asia in order of 100,000 birds, with highest concentrations on W coast of Peninsular Malaysia and in Banyuasin Delta of SE Sumatra; Australian non-breeding population estimated at 18,000, with most important sites at Eighty Mile Beach with 6100 birds, SE Gulf of Carpenteria with 2800, and Great Sandy Strait with 2494. Finnish breeding population comprises only c. 20 pairs; on Russian nesting grounds, common to abundant. Common to abundant in Pakistan. Increasingly sighted in W Europe, W Africa and New Zealand. In tropical Australia no immediate threats to habitat.
Bibliography. Ali & Ripley (1980), Andreeva (1991), Baumanis (1989), Beehler *et al*. (1986), Bijlsma & Roder (1991), Blakers *et al*. (1984), Brazil (1991), Bregnballe *et al*. (1990), Chambers (1989), Coates (1985), Cramp & Simmons (1983), Dickinson *et al*. (1991), Dowsett & Forbes-Watson (1993), Étchécopar & Hüe (1964, 1978), Evans & Keijl (1993a, 1993b), Fry (1990), Ginn *et al*. (1989), Goodman *et al*. (1989), Hockey & Douie (1995), Hüe & Étchécopar (1970), Klimov & Sarychev (1987), Knystautas (1993), Lane & Davies (1987), Langrand (1990), Lekagul & Round (1991), MacKinnon & Phillipps (1993), Mackworth-Praed & Grant (1957, 1962, 1970), Maclean (1993), Marchant & Higgins (1996), van Marle & Voous (1988), Martin (1983), Mauer & van Ijzendoorn (1987), Medway & Wells (1976), Milon *et al*. (1973), Monroe (1989), Nikiforov *et al*. (1991), Pakenham (1979), Patrikeev (1995), Perennou *et al*. (1994), Phillips (1978), Piersma (1986c), Pinto (1983), Pook (1992), Rands *et al*. (1987), Ripley (1982), Roberts, T.J. (1991), Rogacheva (1992), Schulz (1989a), Scott (1989), Shirihai (1996), Short *et al*. (1990), Smythies (1986), Sueur *et al*. (1990), Uhlig (1990c), Urban *et al*. (1986), Waltner & Sinclair (1981), Smythies (1981), Watkins (1993), White & Bruce (1986), Williams, M.D. (1986), Wilson & Harriman (1989), Winkler (1980).

Genus *ACTITIS* Illiger, 1811

52. **Common Sandpiper**

Actitis hypoleucos

French: Chevalier guignette **German**: Flußuferläufer **Spanish**: Andarríos Chico
Other common names: Eurasian Sandpiper

Taxonomy. *Tringa Hypoleucos* Linnaeus, 1758, Sweden.
Sometimes placed in genus *Tringa*. Occasionally considered conspecific with *A. macularia*. Monotypic.
Distribution. Europe E across C Asia to Kamchatka, Sakhalin and Japan. Winters from W Europe and Africa through Middle East and S Asia to Indonesia and Australia; irregularly on islands of W Pacific.

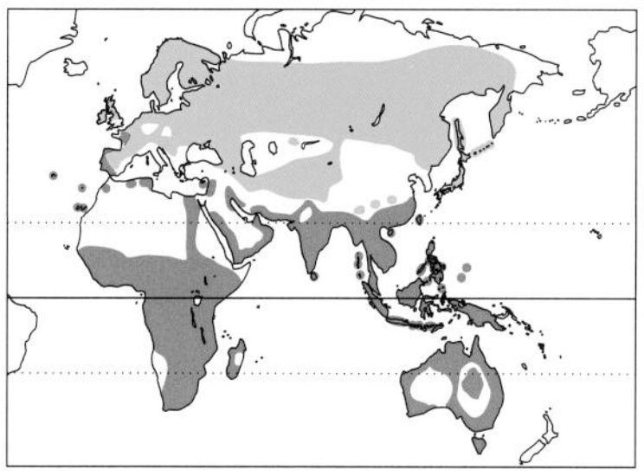

Descriptive notes. 19-21 cm; 33-84 g; wingspan 38-41 cm. Small, short-legged sandpiper, with pale eye-ring; greenish brown upperparts, white underparts with dark lateral breast patches; dark brown streaks and marks on upperparts; in flight, shows dark rump and white wingbar. Resembles non-breeding *A. macularia*, but slightly larger, with more obvious wingbar in flight; at rest, tail much longer than wings; legs normally greener or greyer, less yellow. Female averages slightly larger than male. Non-breeding adult has faintly barred olive brown upperparts; less streaking on head. Juvenile resembles non-breeding adult, but feathers of upperparts have buff tips and bars; more heavily buff and sepia barred wing-coverts.
Habitat. Prefers margins of water bodies, mostly riverbanks, preferably with pebbles, sand or rocks and patches of dry meadows; also small ponds, lake shores, sheltered sea coasts. Outside breeding season, in wide variety of habitats, such as coastal shores, estuaries, salt-marshes, inland wetlands, riverbanks, pools and tidal creeks in mangroves; sometimes on grassland, along roadsides or in urbanized areas; large coastal mudflats are not favoured.
Food and Feeding. Adult and larval insects (e.g. beetles, Diptera), spiders, molluscs, crustaceans and annelids, sometimes frogs, tadpoles or small fish; occasionally plant material. During breeding season, adults and young chicks frequently feed on grassland. Prey located visually; feeds mainly by pecking and stabbing, free stalking and dashing, rarely by probing; runs quickly, frequently pausing with tail moving up and down and head bobbing; insects often caught from surface, or pulled out from rocks or mud; sometimes washes prey before eating it. Mostly forages singly, defending feeding territory, but sometimes in small parties. Mainly diurnal forager; forming night-time roosts occasionally of over 100 birds.
Breeding. Laying May-Jun. Monogamous. In scattered single pairs, in optimal habitat 60-70 m apart. High degree of site fidelity and low degree of natal philopatry. Nest in sheltered depression, sometimes among shrubs and trees. 4 eggs (3-5), with laying interval 1-2 days; incubation 21-22 days, by both sexes; chick greyish brown, above faintly stippled dusky and with fuscous black mid-line on crown and back, and narrow eyeline; brood tended by both sexes, but one parent, often female, usually leaves before young fledge; fledging 22-28 days. Around 85% of eggs hatch, but lifetime reproduction may be as low as 1·5-3·5 fledglings/female; 1st-year survival 21%, annual adult survival 75-79% but much lower during adverse spring weather. Age of first breeding 1 year or older. Oldest ringed bird 12 years.
Movements. Migratory. Many move to S wintering areas, though some stay in N maritime climatic zone (British Is, Mediterranean, Japan). Moves overland on broad fronts, even across deserts and mountains, usually singly or in small flocks. European population mainly winters in W Africa, and basically moves SSW-SW from mid-Jul to Aug, juveniles following one month later; moves N from late Mar to Apr. Many Norwegian birds cross Britain, Swedish birds cross W Germany, Finnish cross E Germany. Wintering populations in E, C & S Africa presumably originate from CIS. E Asian birds move through Korea, Japan (especially during S migration), Hong Kong (both migrations), Peninsular Malaysia, Wallacea and New Guinea. Many immatures remain in N wintering quarters all year. Migrates at night.
Status and Conservation. Not globally threatened. European breeding population comprises 885,000 pairs (1986), of which 96% found in Fenno-Scandia, the rest mainly in Britain and Ireland (22,000-25,000 pairs); this should yield more than 2,000,000 African wintering birds; 100,000's winter in SC Asia and similarly in E & SE Asia and Australasia (1991), with mangroves in W Peninsular Malaysia holding large numbers; numbers wintering in E Africa and SW Asia unknown. Numbers declined in C Europe, Britain and Ireland, particularly in 1930's and 1950's; European population currently believed to be declining. Numbers greatly underestimated in wintering areas, possibly due to habit of frequenting inaccessible mangroves.
Bibliography. Ali & Ripley (1980), Baccetti *et al*. (1992), Bauer (1989), Beehler *et al*. (1986), Benson & Benson (1975), Blakers *et al*. (1984), Brazil (1991), Bregnballe *et al*. (1990), Bregulla (1992), Brown (1973), Coates (1985), Cramp & Simmons (1983), Deignan (1945), Dickinson *et al*. (1991), Dowsett & Forbes-Watson (1993), Dubois & Maheo (1986), Elgood *et al*. (1994), Erhart (1994), Étchécopar & Hüe (1964, 1978), Evans (1994), Fjeldså (1977), Ginn *et al*. (1989), Glutz von Blotzheim *et al*. (1977), Goodman *et al*. (1989), Gore (1990), Grimes (1987), Hazevoet (1995), Henderson & Harper (1992), Hockey & Douie (1995), Holland & Yalden (1983, 1991a, 1991b, 1994), Holland *et al*. (1982), Hüe & Étchécopar (1970), Knystautas (1993), Lane & Davies (1987), Langrand (1990), Lawrence (1993), Lekagul & Round (1991), Løfaldli (1981), MacKinnon & Phillipps (1993), Mackworth-Praed & Grant (1957, 1962, 1970), Maclean (1993), Madoc (1976), Marchant, J. *et al*. (1993), Marchant, J.H. *et al*. (1990), Marchant, S. & Higgins (1996), van Marle & Voous (1988), Mauersberger (1978), Medway & Wells (1976), Milon *et al*. (1973), Nicoll & Kemp (1983), Pakenham (1979), Patrikeev (1995), Paz (1987), Pearson (1977), Perennou *et al*. (1994), Pfeifer (1993), Phillips (1978), Piersma (1986b), Pinto (1983), Poulsen (1950), Rabor (1977), Rands *et al*. (1987), Ripley (1982), Roberts, T.J. (1991), Roché (1988), Roché & Frochot (1993), Rogacheva (1992), Rutgers & Norris (1970), Scott (1989), Serasinghe (1992), Shirihai (1996), Short *et al*. (1990), Simmons (1951), Smythies (1981, 1986), Stein (1926, 1928), Tatner & Bryant (1993), Theiss *et al*. (1992), Urban *et al*. (1986), Wadewitz (1952, 1957), Wang Haichang (1984), White & Bruce (1986), Williams, M.D. (1986), Willis (1994), Yalden (1986a, 1986c, 1992), Yalden & Dougall (1994), Yalden & Holland (1992).

53. **Spotted Sandpiper**

Actitis macularia

French: Chevalier grivelé **German**: Drosseluferläufer **Spanish**: Andarríos Maculado

Taxonomy. *Tringa macularia* Linnaeus, 1766, Pennsylvania.
Sometimes placed in genus *Tringa*. Occasionally considered conspecific with *A. hypoleucos*. Some authors have recognized two subspecies, with *rava* (W North America) and nominate (E North America), but generally considered invalid. Monotypic.
Distribution. Alaska across Canada to Newfoundland, S to SC California, N Texas and North Carolina. Winters from S USA through Central America and West Indies to South America S to S Brazil; in most years, also Galapagos.
Descriptive notes. 18-20 cm; 19-64 g; wingspan 37-40 cm. Smallish size and neatly spotted underparts distinctive; greenish brown upperparts with dark barring; bill pink to orange with black tip, legs often pinkish. Female averages slightly larger; usually has larger, blacker spots on underparts. Non-breeding adult has plainer upperparts and lack spots on underparts; bill mostly dark brown but paler at base; similar to *A. hypoleucos*, but smaller, with greyer upperparts and normally yellowish legs; white wingbar less obvious. Juvenile as non-breeding adult, but upperparts greyish with narrow buff fringes; wing-coverts with distinct buff and brown fringes.

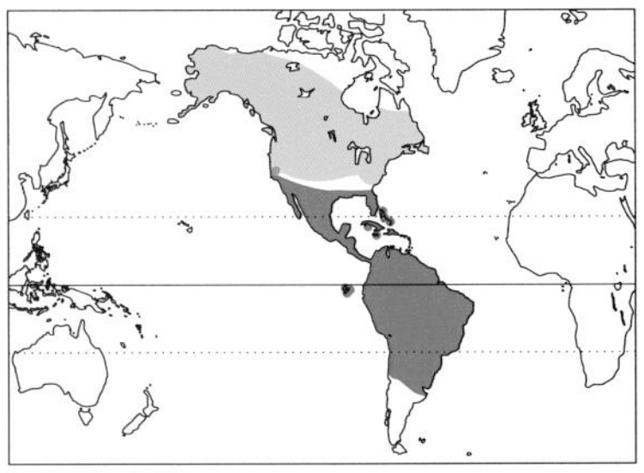

Habitat. Nesting habitat similar to that of *A. hypoleucos*, in wide variety of habitats, preferably in open terrain with freshwater pools, lakes, streams, rivers, marshes and impoundments, from sea-level up to over 2000 m. Outside breeding season occupies similar habitats, and also found along coast, e.g. sandy beaches, muddy edges, lagoons and mangroves.

Food and Feeding. Mainly aquatic and terrestrial insects, e.g. adult, larval and pupal Diptera, mayflies, Orthoptera, beetles and caterpillars; also spiders, annelids, small crustaceans, molluscs and even small fish (e.g. trout fry). Typically feeds at water margin rather than by wading, with rapid downward pecking movements; also by slow approach followed by quick forward thrust of head. Sometimes washes prey before swallowing. Mainly feeds solitarily; often defends feeding territory on migration and in winter.

Breeding. Laying mid-May to Jun. Sex role reversed, with female larger and socially dominant over male. Yearling sequentially resource-defence polyandrous; 2-year-old primarily simultaneously resource-defence and mate-access polyandrous; older females primarily simultaneously resource-defence polyandrous and c. 26% monogamous; female mates with up to 3 (rarely 4) males per season. Females can store sperm for long periods, cuckolding later mates. High degree of site fidelity in successful breeders and of natal philopatry, with siblings from same nest returning more frequently. Solitary, sometimes nests clustered, especially on small islands. Nest-site on ground, usually in sparse vegetation; nest is shallow depression lined with plant material. 4 eggs (3-5), with laying interval of 1 day, occasionally 2; several clutches laid over short periods; incubation 19-24 days; chick pale drab grey, finely mottled and stippled dusky with black eyeline and mid-line on crown and back, white underparts; fledging 18-21 days. Male incubates and broods young; female never broods, but helps males in rearing chicks, primarily playing defence role; female helps last mate of season more than others, but may also help earlier mates until she goes on to another mate. Of 119 eggs laid, 62% of eggs hatched, with mean 3·36 young per nest. Mice, mustelids and birds are nest predators.

Movements. Migrates on broad fronts all across North America, after breeding presumably moving SE down Atlantic states, though some may use direct transoceanic passage from New England to E South America, including W Amazonian rivers. Females precede males and juveniles southwards, and also arrive first at breeding territories. In Venezuela, unlike many other wader species, more numerous in N spring than in autumn. N migration from South America more westerly, suggesting more use of interior route through USA and absence of transoceanic movement then. Usually migrates singly. Not infrequent vagrant to Europe, and has nested in Scotland.

Status and Conservation. Not globally threatened. No population estimate available; most widely distributed breeding scolopacid in North America, with more than 50,000 birds in Canada, at least. Roosts of up to 1000 birds occur at mouth of R Amazon. Population apparently stable. Overall abundance was not severely affected by hunting around turn of present century, basically because species is usually solitary, which prevented hunters from killing large numbers with single shot. Current tendency to turn estuaries into shrimp ponds in Central and South America represents serious threat to species.

Bibliography. Alberico *et al.* (1991, 1992), Amos (1991), Armstrong (1983), Belton (1984), Bent (1927-1929), Biaggi (1983), Blake (1977), Brown (1987), Colwell & Oring (1989a), Contreras *et al.* (1990), Cramp & Simmons (1983), David (1991), Fivizzani *et al.* (1987), Fjeldså & Krabbe (1990), Gochfeld (1971a), Haverschmidt (1968), Haverschmidt & Mees (1995), Hayes (1995), Hayes & Fox (1991), Hays (1972), Heidemann & Oring (1976), Helbig *et al.* (1991), Hilty & Brown (1986), Johnson (1965b), Kuenzel & Wiegert (1973), Lawrence (1993), Lissak & Willy (1991), Matthiessen (1994), Maxson & Oring (1980), Meyer de Schauensee & Phelps (1978), Miller & Miller (1948), Monroe (1968), Murray (1991), Oring (1988), Oring & Knudson (1972), Oring & Lank (1982), Oring, Colwell & Reed (1991), Oring, Fleischer *et al.* (1992), Oring, Lank & Maxson (1983), Oring, Reed & Alberico (1994), Oring, Reed, Colwell *et al.* (1991), Oring, Reed & Maxson (1994), de la Peña (1992), Pickett *et al.* (1988), Reed & Oring (1992, 1993), Ridgely & Gwynne (1989), Root (1988), Rowan (1927), Schmolz (1991), Scott & Carbonell (1986), Sick (1985c, 1993), Slud (1964), Snyder (1966), Stiles & Skutch (1989), Tostain *et al.* (1992), Varty *et al.* (1986), Wetmore (1965), Willis (1994), Wilson (1976).

Genus *HETEROSCELUS* Baird, 1858

54. Grey-tailed Tattler

Heteroscelus brevipes

French: Chevalier de Sibérie **German**: Grauschwanz-Wasserläufer **Spanish**: Playero Siberiano
Other common names: Grey-rumped/Grey-tailed Sandpiper, Polynesian/Siberian Tattler

Taxonomy. *Totanus brevipes* Vieillot, 1816, Timor.
Sometimes placed in genus *Tringa*. Forms superspecies with *H. incanus*, with which sometimes considered conspecific. Monotypic.

Distribution. NC & NE Siberia in Putorana Mts, and from Verkhoyansk Mts and Transbaikalia E to Anadyrland; probably also Kamchatka and N Kuril Is. Winters from Taiwan, Malay Peninsula and Philippines through Indonesia, New Guinea and Solomon Is to Australia, a few reaching New Zealand; also Fiji and Tuvalu.

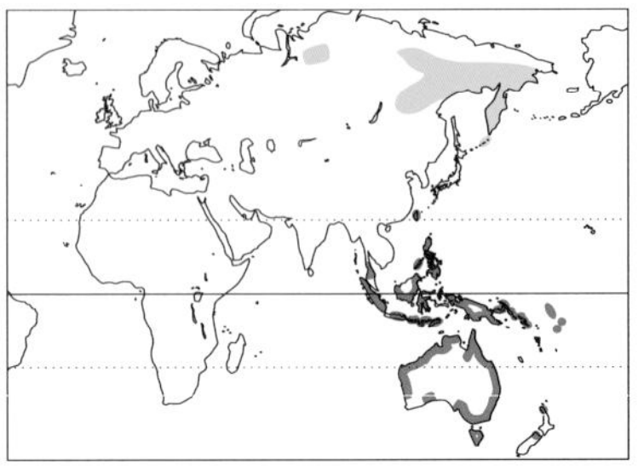

Descriptive notes. 23-27 cm; 80-162 g; wingspan 51 cm. Short yellow legs and darkish grey upperparts. Very similar to *H. incanus*, but slightly paler and shorter-winged; barred paler grey on neck, breast and flanks, with more white on belly and vent; shorter nasal groove and scutellated rear edge to tarsus; best identified by flight call, a whistle of two notes. Female averages larger. Non-breeding adult has greyish white flanks. Juvenile like non-breeding adult, but with whitish spots on upperparts.

Habitat. Breeds in N montane taiga and forest tundra, along rivers and streams and on stone or pebble shorelines of lakes. In non-breeding season found on sheltered coasts with reefs and rock platforms or with intertidal mudflats; also shores of rock, shingle, gravel or shells; often roosts in mangroves, and may perch for roosting; prefers areas with dense beds of seagrass. On migration may occur at inland wetlands, such as paddyfields; exclusively coastal in Australia. Frequents a wider range of environments than *H. incanus*.

Food and Feeding. Food on breeding grounds includes insects, e.g. beetles, mosquitoes, springtails and aquatic larvae of flies. Crabs form large part of non-breeding diet; also other crustaceans, polychaetes, molluscs, insects and occasionally fish. Often teeters and runs during feeding; mostly pecks, sometimes probes in shallow water; large prey detected visually. Crabs often washed on water's edge. Usually forages singly or in loose groups.

Breeding. Breeds late May to late Aug. Nest is shallow depression, often on stony riverbed; sometimes in deserted nests in trees. Usually 4 eggs; sexes share care of young.

Movements. Migratory. Migration mainly coastal, but sometimes on inland wetlands. On passage, occurs in W Aleutian Is, Kuril Is, Korea, Japan, NE China, Hong Kong and Philippines; some birds cross Mongolia and C China; also some movement across SW Pacific; probably two migration routes into Australia, on either side of New Guinea. Migrates in Jul-Oct and Mar-May. Some birds estimated to be capable of flying non-stop from NW Australia to Philippines or S China. Most departures from N Australia late Mar to late Apr. Most 1st-year birds remain S during N summer.

Status and Conservation. Not globally threatened. Total population maximum 100,000 birds. Wintering population in Australia estimated at 36,000 birds; in 1989, total of 22,052 individuals recorded at Moreton Bay, SE Queensland; high numbers occur on Eighty Mile Beach and in Great Sandy Strait. Some 100's winter in Philippines. Species apparently in no danger at present.

Bibliography. Andreev (1980a), Beaman (1994), Beehler *et al.* (1986), Blakers *et al.* (1984), Brazil (1991), Bregulla (1992), Chambers (1989), Coates (1985), Dementiev & Gladkov (1951b), Dickinson *et al.* (1991), Étchécopar & Hüe (1978), Haward & Barter (1991), Keast (1949), Knystautas (1993), Lane & Davies (1987), Leonovitch & Kretzschmar (1966), MacKinnon & Phillipps (1993), Marchant & Higgins (1996), Medway & Wells (1976), Melville (1977), Neufeldt *et al.* (1961), Paulson (1986), Perennou *et al.* (1994), Piersma (1985), Pook (1992), Prater & Marchant (1975), Rogacheva (1992), Scott (1989), Smythies (1981), Stenning & Hirst (1994), Watkins (1993), White & Bruce (1986), Williams, M.D. (1986).

55. Wandering Tattler

Heteroscelus incanus

French: Chevalier errant **German**: Wanderwasserläufer **Spanish**: Playero de Alaska
Other common names: American Grey-rumped Sandpiper

Taxonomy. *Scolopax incana* Gmelin, 1789, Moorea (Eimeo), Society Group, Pacific Ocean.
Sometimes placed in genus *Tringa*. Forms superspecies with *H. brevipes*, with which sometimes considered conspecific. Monotypic.

Distribution. Extreme NE Siberia and S Alaska E to Yukon R and NW British Columbia. Winters in SW USA and W Mexico, Ecuador and Galapagos Is; also Hawaiian Is, C & S Pacific Is to E New Guinea and NE Australia.

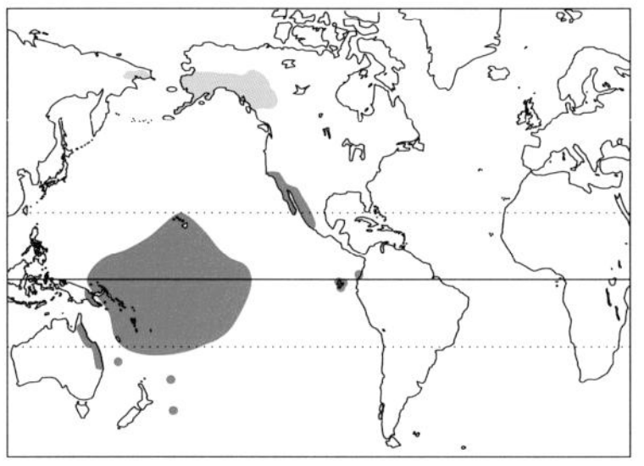

Descriptive notes. 26-29 cm; 72-213 g; wingspan 54 cm. Short yellow legs and dark grey upperparts. Very similar to *H. brevipes*, but slightly darker, with longer wings; broader, more extensive dark barring on underparts including central undertail-coverts; distinctive flight call is rippling trill of ten notes. Female averages larger. Non-breeding adult has plain dark grey upperparts, neck, breast and flanks; supercilium only clear above lores. Juvenile as non-breeding adult, but with pale fringes to feathers of upperparts.

Habitat. Similar to that of *H. brevipes*, but variety of wintering habitat narrower. Breeding habitat restricted to alpine zone, along often fast-flowing mountain streams. Outside breeding season found on coral reefs or rocky coast with platforms and piers, and on offshore islands. One of most typical waders of isolated oceanic islands. Incidentaly occurs on adjacent beaches or inland freshwater pools, only on migration; rarely on estuarine mudflats.

Food and Feeding. Breeding season diet mainly aquatic insects and their larvae. In winter and on migration, feeds on crustaceans, polychaete worms, molluscs, insects and fish. When feeding, bobs and teeters almost continuously; moves rapidly over rocky substrates, probing into mats of mussels, barnacles and algae, or picking prey from surface. Usually singly or in small groups.

Breeding. Present in breeding area from late May to Aug, with incubation starting around mid-Jun. Nest is simple depression on gravel shores of mountain streams, or compact structure of twigs and roots. Usually 4 eggs; single brood; incubation 23-25 days, by both parents; both parents tend young. Fledging period unknown, but parents return to rocky ocean shores soon after young fledge.

Movements. Migratory. Passage oceanic towards Hawaiian Is, but many birds move along outer coast and islands of British Columbia and Washington; some birds pass Kuril Is, Japan and Korea on migration, but probably most reach Australia directly across Pacific, some via New Guinea; stragglers reach N New Zealand. 1st-year birds often remain S during breeding months. Spring migration Apr-May; autumn migration mid-Jul to mid-Oct. Probably high fidelity to breeding site.

Status and Conservation. Not globally threatened. Total population estimated at maximum of 25,000 birds. No immediate threats identified, although status very poorly known.

Bibliography. Armstrong (1983), Beehler *et al.* (1986), Bent (1927-1929), Blaber (1993), Blake (1977), Blakers *et al.* (1984), Brazil (1991), Bregulla (1992), Chambers (1989), Coates (1985), Dixon (1933), Doyle *et al.* (1985), Étchécopar & Hüe (1978), Fjeldså & Krabbe (1990), Hilty & Brown (1986), Holyoak & Thibault (1984), Howell & Webb (1995a), Knystautas (1993), Lane & Davies (1987), Marchant & Higgins (1996), Matthiessen (1994), Monroe (1968), Murie (1924), Paulson (1986), Prater & Marchant (1975), Ridgely & Gwynne (1989), Robbins *et al.* (1983), Root (1988), Sibson (1965), Stiles & Skutch (1989), Weeden (1959, 1965), Wizeman (1972).

Genus *CATOPTROPHORUS* Bonaparte, 1827

56. Willet

Catoptrophorus semipalmatus

French: Chevalier semipalmé **German**: Schlammtreter **Spanish**: Playero Aliblanco

Taxonomy. *Scolopax semipalmata* Gmelin, 1789, New York.
Two subspecies recognized.
Subspecies and Distribution.
C. s. inornatus (Brewster, 1887) - C Alberta and SW Manitoba S to N Colorado and W Nebraska; winters from coastal S USA to N South America, mainly on Pacific coast, S to N Chile.
C. s. semipalmatus (Gmelin, 1789) - S New Brunswick, Atlantic and Gulf coasts of USA, and West Indies; winters from Atlantic and Gulf coasts of USA and Mexico through Central America and West Indies S to S Brazil.

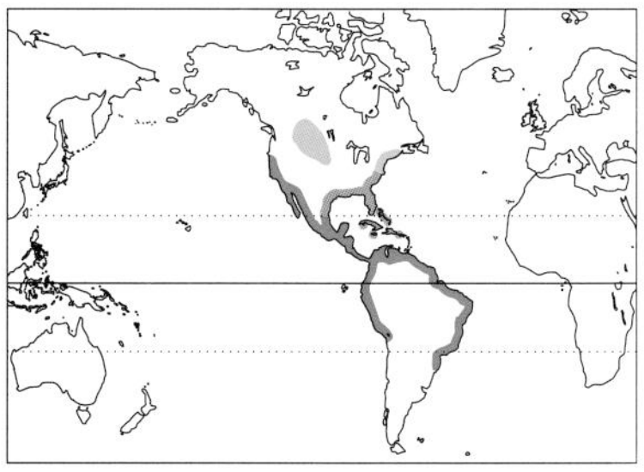

Descriptive notes. 33-41 cm; 173-375 g. Medium-sized, tall wader resembling *Tringa*; heavy bill, long legs; pale eye-ring, white above lores; in flight, striking black and white patterns on both upperwing and underwing. Female averages larger. Non-breeding adult has brownish grey upperparts with narrow white fringes; head, throat, neck and breast washed grey. Juvenile as non-breeding, but upperparts grey-brown with dark barring and broad buff fringes. Race *inornatus* paler, with more sparsely streaked and barred neck, breast and flanks.
Habitat. Races differ in habitat preferences: *inornatus* associated with prairie marshes; *semipalmatus* mainly coastal, in salt-marshes with short vegetation. Around temporary pools and lakes of wide range of salinities, preferably more alkaline. In non-breeding season, near seashore, on salt-marshes, intertidal mudflats especially when bordered with mangroves, and sandy or rocky beaches.
Food and Feeding. While breeding, feeds on small molluscs, fish fry, marine worms and aquatic insects. Outside breeding season often takes small crabs, especially fiddler crabs; also small fish, molluscs, marine annelids, isopods and aquatic insects. Pecks or probes, and stalks larger prey in water; also runs while ploughing bill through water or while scything (continuously moving bill from side to side) to catch fish. May defend feeding territory on wintering grounds. Feeds singly or in flocks. Diurnal and nocturnal forager.
Breeding. Laying Apr-Jun. Probably monogamous. Often in loose colonies. Nest usually well concealed in heavy grass, sometimes placed on open sand and almost completely exposed. 4 eggs, with laying interval 1-4 days; incubation 21-29 days, mainly by female, male taking over at night; both parents tend young; fledging period unknown. Age of first breeding 2 years.
Movements. Race *inornatus* strongly migratory, but nominate fairly sedentary around Gulf of Mexico and in Caribbean. Race *inornatus* moves S in three main directions: almost due E to Atlantic coast of New York and New England; SE & S to Atlantic and Gulf coasts, with some moving into Caribbean and reaching Surinam; fairly small numbers migrate SW to Pacific coast, from Oregon to N Peru, scarcely S to N Chile; regular migrant to Galapagos in small numbers. Nominate race moves S down Atlantic coast into Caribbean and to N South America, where occurs mainly in NC Brazil and Surinam.
Status and Conservation. Not globally threatened. No population estimate available, but W Pacific flyway supports at least 70,000 birds; in South America 44,400 counted on aerial surveys in 1989. Population of race *inornatus* declined due to conversion of wetlands and grassland to small grain and row crops, but no notable change in numbers since 1970. In 1967, estimated 41,000 pairs bred in North Dakota. Still moderately abundant over much of original range, perhaps because of considerable tolerance for human activities such as modification and burning of marshes. Numbers of both races apparently fairly stable at present.
Bibliography. Bent (1927-1929), Biaggi (1983), Blake (1977), Burger & Shisler (1978a), Custer & Mitchell (1991), Fjeldså & Krabbe (1990), Haverschmidt (1968), Haverschmidt & Mees (1995), Higgins *et al*. (1979), Hilty & Brown (1986), Howe (1974, 1982), Howell & Webb (1995a, 1995b), Johnson (1965b), Kelly & Cogswell (1979), Llinas & Galindo (1990), Matthiessen (1994), McNeil & Rodríguez (1990), McNeil & Rompré (1995), Meyer de Schauensee & Phelps (1978), Monroe (1968), Ridgely & Gwynne (1989), Rompré & McNeil (1994), Root (1988), Ryan & Renken (1987), Scott & Carbonell (1986), Sick (1985c, 1993), Slud (1964), Snyder (1966), Sordahl (1979), Stenzel *et al*. (1976), Stiles & Skutch (1989), Tomkins (1965), Tostain *et al*. (1992), Wells & Vickery (1990), Wetmore (1965), Wilcox (1980).

Tribe PROSOBONIINI

Genus *PROSOBONIA* Bonaparte, 1850

57. **Tuamotu Sandpiper**

Prosobonia cancellata

French: Chevalier des Touamotou **German**: Südseeläufer **Spanish**: Andarríos de Tuamotu

Taxonomy. *Tringa cancellata* Gmelin, 1789, Kiritimati (Christmas Island), Line Islands, Pacific Ocean. Formerly placed in genus *Aechmorhynchus*. May have formed superspecies with extinct *P. leucoptera* and *P. ellisi* (see page 484). Population of Tuamotu sometimes separated as *parvirostris*, awarded subspecies or even species status; in latter arrangement, extant birds would become *P. parvirostris* and name *P. cancellata* restricted to extinct form of Kiritimati; however, available information probably too scanty to enable firm conclusions. Monotypic.
Distribution. Tuamotu Is (French Polynesia).
Descriptive notes. 15-17 cm; 32-44 g. Small, very dark brown wader with very short, thin bill; ashy white supercilium; upperparts have extensive buff spots and feather edges; breast, flanks and undertail spotted or barred brown; legs yellowish brown to greyish; in flight, very rounded wings. Sexual and seasonal differences and juvenile undescribed.
Habitat. Tiny atolls, mainly in habitats such as open coastal shoreline, lagoon beaches and areas of bare gravel or open shingle; also among vegetation.
Food and Feeding. Very poorly known. Mainly insects: at least 4 species of ant, leafhoppers and a wasp were found in stomach contents. Plant matter also consumed.
Breeding. Breeding season quite prolonged; on one island breeding in Aug, on another in May; unclear whether season is synchronized on different islands. Nest constructed from bits of shell, coral debris and plant fragments; on shoreline, usually on pebbly rather than sandy substrate. One nest contained 2 eggs. No further information available.

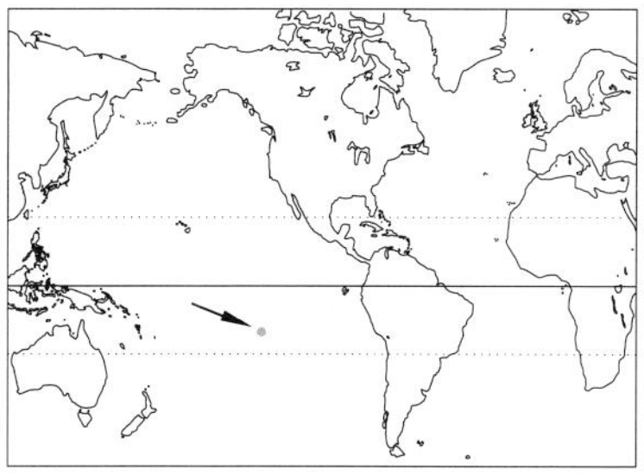

Movements. Probably sedentary as a rule, although recent records on Nakutavaké and Rangiroa presumably represent visitors from other islands.
Status and Conservation. ENDANGERED. Population currently in decline. On Morane 150-200 birds (1990), on Anuanu Raro 30-40 birds (1990) and on Tahanea 12-15 birds (1989). Former range spanned 3700 km of C Pacific. Since c. 1965 reported from 11-12 islands, while c. 26 atolls have not yet been surveyed. Decline probably due to introduction of mammalian predators, particularly rats and cats; populations do best on islands free of introduced predators, and without permanent human populations. Species now in severe danger of extinction, but at present no conservation measures have been taken; proposed measures include total protection of atolls on which species still known to occur, with special efforts recommended to prevent introduction of cats and rats.
Bibliography. Bruner (1972), Collar & Andrew (1988), Collar *et al*. (1994), Ferguson-Lees & Faull (1992), Greenway (1967), Hay, R. (1984, 1986), Holyoak (1973), Holyoak & Thibault (1984), King (1978/79), Lacan & Mougin (1974), Lovegrove *et al*. (1989), Pratt *et al*. (1987), Rosair (1995e), Seitre & Seitre (1991), Thibault (1973, 1988), Walters (1993), Wragg & Weisler (1994), Zusi & Jehl (1970).

Subfamily ARENARIINAE

Genus *ARENARIA* Brisson, 1760

58. **Ruddy Turnstone**

Arenaria interpres

French: Tournepierre à collier **German**: Steinwälzer **Spanish**: Vuelvepiedras Común
Other common names: Turnstone

Taxonomy. *Tringa Interpres* Linnaeus, 1758, Gotland, Sweden.
Two subspecies recognized.
Subspecies and Distribution.
A. i. interpres (Linnaeus, 1758) - Axel Heiberg I and Ellesmere I (N Canadian Arctic), Greenland, N Eurasia and NW Alaska; winters on coasts of W Europe, Africa, S Asia, Australasia and S Pacific islands, with some also on Pacific coast of North America, from California to at least Mexico.
A. i. morinella (Linnaeus, 1766) - NE Alaska and most of Arctic Canada; winters from South Carolina and Gulf of Mexico to SC Chile and N Argentina.

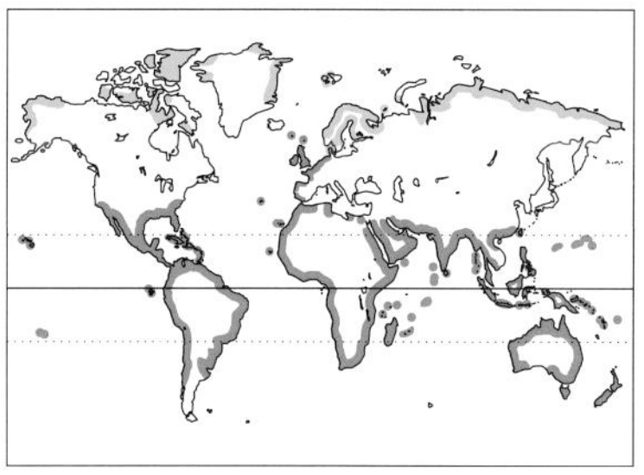

Descriptive notes. 21-26 cm; 84-190 g; wingspan 50-57 cm. Robust shorebird with short legs; black and white head, throat, neck and breast; upperparts rufous-chestnut with black-brown patches; underparts white; distinctive pattern in flight, with white back, rump, uppertail-coverts, wingbar and patch on inner wing contrasting with otherwise dark upperparts. Female has more extensive streaking on crown; brownish nape; somewhat duller upperparts; some pale flecking on breast patch. Non-breeding adult much duller, with upperparts dark greyish brown and blackish; head mostly dark grey-brown; black areas of neck and breast replaced with dark grey-brown. Juvenile like adult non-breeding, but browner above with buff fringes and paler on head. Race *morinella* slightly smaller, with less dark streaking on crown; more extensive deep chestnut-red on scapulars and upperwing-coverts.
Habitat. Stony coastal plains, marshy slopes and flats in lowlands, and tundra; always close to areas that remain moist until late summer. Outside breeding season, chiefly coastal; occurs inland only on migration, on short-grass salt-marshes and along dykes; rocky, shingly, and stony shores and breakwaters, sandy beaches with washed-up seaweed, sheltered inlets, estuaries, mangrove stands, exposed reefs and mudflats, preferably with beds of mussels or cockles; also lake shores.
Food and Feeding. In breeding season, mainly Diptera (especially adult and larval midges), also Lepidoptera larvae, Hymenoptera, beetles and spiders; some vegetable matter taken early in season; probing and jabbing are main techniques during breeding. Non-breeding diet diverse, including insects, crustaceans, molluscs, annelids, echinoderms, small fish, carrion such as dead fish or mammals, discarded human food, and birds' eggs. On staging areas in E USA, takes large quantities of horseshoe crab (*Limulus polyphemus*) eggs. Flips over objects such as stones, shells and seaweed with quick jerking movements; prey underneath is pecked at or chased; sometimes pushes larger object with breast; frequently scavenges, occasionally even for bread from people. Age-related differences in foraging rate, and individuals may specialize. Often in rather close flocks, especially on tidal roosts, of 10-100+ birds.
Breeding. Laying mid-May to early Jul, primarily mid-Jun in Canada. Monogamous and solitary. In Taymyr 0·1-12·5 birds/km², in high Arctic Greenland up to 3·8 pairs/km². Nest placed in wet or dry hummocky sites; may be concealed in or under vegetation, or in fully open sites; nest is slight depression lined with various amounts of plant material. 4 eggs (2-4), with laying interval of 1 day, sometimes 2; incubation 22-24 days (22-27), by both sexes, although male much less; chick has buffish grey to cinnamon-buff upperparts, faintly striped and mottled grey or blackish and lacking white tips to down, with face and underparts pale grey; chicks cared for by both sexes for 1-2 weeks, whereafter female leaves; fledging 19-21 days; male departs soon after chicks fledge. 26-88% of eggs hatch, 50-74% of chicks fledge; 1st-year annual mortality 42-55%; adult annual mortality 22-34%. Age of first breeding 2 years. Oldest ringed bird 19 years, 8 months.
Movements. Migratory. Breeding range divisible into 5 populations: (1) birds of Axel Heiberg I, Ellesmere I and Greenland move to W Europe, mainly from Irish and North Seas to Iberia, with vagrants S to Mauritania; direct trans-Atlantic crossing or stopover in Iceland or SW Norway; (2) Fenno-

Scandian and W Russian birds move along coastlines of Baltic and W Europe (May and mid-Jul to mid-Sept) to Morocco and W Africa; (3) birds breeding from White Sea to C Siberia probably move through Kazakhstan lakes and Caspian and Black Seas to winter in E Mediterranean, Red Sea, Persian Gulf, coasts of Indian Ocean and S Africa; on southward migration locally frequent inland in Africa; (4) birds from E Siberia and W Alaska, wintering in SE Asia, Australia, W Pacific and locally on W coast of Mexico and California; possibly two routes to Australia, first with movement to E Australia and New Zealand across Pacific, returning N via E coast of Asia, and second with movement to and from W Australia along E Asian coasts; arrives Australia Aug-Nov and departs Mar-Jun; (5) race *morinella* moves to Pacific and Atlantic coasts of Central and South America, staging in large numbers in Delaware Bay on northward migration, and with highest numbers wintering in N South America. Most immature birds spend summer S of breeding grounds. High fidelity to wintering sites. Juveniles migrate S c. 1 month later than adults. i.e. mid-Aug to early Sept. Migrates in flocks of 10's of birds.

Status and Conservation. Not globally threatened. Estimated numbers of wintering birds: 67,000 in Europe, including estimated 50,000 in Britain, but excluding Iceland, S Norway and Ireland, all important sites; 43,000 birds in W Africa (1988) and 34,000 in S Africa (1989); 50,000-100,000 birds in E Africa and SW Asia; 10,000-100,000 birds in SC Asia; probably 25,000-100,000 birds in E & SE Asia and Australasia, of which 14,000 in Australia; 30,000-100,000 birds in America, with significant proportion wintering on N coast of Brazil and significant numbers staging at Delaware Bay on northward migration. At least 15,000-30,000 pairs breed in Fenno-Scandia (1993) and c. 25,000 pairs in high Arctic Greenland and Ellesmere I (1985). European wintering population probably increased slightly during 1970's and 1980's. Winter populations in W Palearctic, W & S Africa and America considered stable.

Bibliography. Alerstam *et al.* (1990), Ali & Ripley (1980), Altevogt & Davis (1980), Anderson & Bellin (1988), Armstrong (1983), Azevedo-Junior (1988), Barrantes & Pereira (1992), Bent (1927-1929), Bergman (1946), Beven & England (1977), Blake (1977), Boertmann *et al.* (1991), Botton *et al.* (1994), Bradley & Bradley (1973), Branson *et al.* (1978, 1979), Brazil (1991), Brearey (1979), Brearey & Hildén (1985), Burger *et al.* (1979), Cadée (1994), Clark *et al.* (1993), Coates (1985), Cramp & Simmons (1983), Crossin & Huber (1970), Crossland (1995), Dowsett & Forbes-Watson (1993), Ens, Duiven *et al.* (1990), Estafiev (1989), Evans & Keijl (1993b), Ferns (1978), Fjeldså (1977), Fjeldså & Krabbe (1990), Fleischer (1983), Gill (1986), Goodman *et al.* (1989), Groves (1978a), Gudmundsson (1993), Gudmundsson *et al.* (1991), Harris (1979), Hedenström & Alerstam (1994), Hilty & Brown (1986), Hockey & Douie (1995), Holyoak & Thibault (1984), Houston & Barter (1990), Howell & Webb (1995a), Johnson (1965b), Jones (1975), Kalejta *et al.* (1994), Kasparek (1992b), Klaassen *et al.* (1990), Lane & Davies (1987), Langrand (1990), Loftin & Sutton (1979), MacDonald & Parmelee (1962), Mackworth-Praed & Grant (1957, 1962, 1970), Marchant & Higgins (1996), van Marle & Voous (1988), McKee (1982), McNair (1991), Meltofte (1985), Metcalfe (1986, 1989), Metcalfe & Furness (1985, 1987), Meyer de Schauensee & Phelps (1978), Morris & Wiggins (1986), Morrison (1975), Nettleship (1973), Norman (1994), Parkes *et al.* (1971), Perennou *et al.* (1994), Petersen (1992), Piersma (1986b), Piersma & Morrison (1994), Prys-Jones *et al.* (1992), Roberts, T.J. (1991), Rogacheva (1992), Rutgers & Norris (1970), Shirihai (1996), Sick (1985c, 1993), Slud (1964), Smith & King (1988), Smythies (1986), Summers *et al.* (1989), Thompson (1973), Underhill *et al.* (1993), Urban *et al.* (1986), Vuolanto (1968), Watkins (1993), Wetmore (1965), Whitfield (1985, 1986, 1988a, 1988b, 1990a).

59. Black Turnstone
Arenaria melanocephala

French: Tournepierre noir   **German**: Schwarzkopf-Steinwälzer   **Spanish**: Vuelvepiedras Oscuro

Taxonomy. *Strepsilas melanocephalus* Vigors, 1829, north-west coast of North America. Monotypic.
Distribution. W & S Alaska. Winters from SE Alaska to NW Mexico.

Descriptive notes. 22-25 cm; 98-148 g. Large white spot at base of bill; small white spotting on crown, sides of neck, breast and greater coverts; dark spotting on flanks. Always darker than *A. interpres*, with dark chin and all dark breast; greyer legs; in flight, shows similar pattern on upperparts. Female averages slightly larger; has smaller white spot at base of bill. Non-breeding adult lacks spotting on head, nape and breast; flanks less marked. Juvenile as non-breeding, but dark feathers browner and upperparts with buffish fringes.
Habitat. Salt grass, graminoid and dwarf shrub meadows; also tidal marshes; mostly within 2 km of coast. In non-breeding season on rocky coasts, jetties, isolated rocky outcrops, and barnacle-covered reefs, especially those on offshore islands; sometimes on adjacent sandy beaches or mudflats.
Food and Feeding. Diet on breeding grounds not studied, but probably similar to that of *A. interpres*. Non-breeding diet primarily crustaceans (especially barnacles) and molluscs (especially limpets); also herring eggs in Prince William Sound, on N migration. Turns up patches of seaweed, sometimes follows receding breakers, or gleans from surface; moves slowly and steadily over rocks. Opens shells by inserting bill into gap, or by hammering at shell; only swallows soft part. In small flocks of up to few dozen birds.

Breeding. Lays May-Jun. Solitary or semi-colonial; densities of 40-111 birds/km², highest in coastal salt grass meadows. Nest usually quite close to water; simple depression in dead grass, or sometimes in bare mud, sparsely lined. 4 eggs; incubation 21 days, by both sexes. No further information available.
Movements. Less migratory than *A. interpres*. Migrates down Pacific coast, as far S as Sonora, W Mexico. Vagrant to inland areas of coastal provinces and states. Some non-breeders remain S all year.
Status and Conservation. Not globally threatened. Total breeding population estimated at 76,000-114,000 birds (1991) of which 85% nest on C floodplain of Yukon and Kuskokwim Deltas, SW Alaska. Decline noted in recent years in population wintering in S British Columbia and NW USA.
Bibliography. Anderson & Bellin (1988), Armstrong (1983), Bent (1927-1929), Brandt (1943), Campbell (1975), Connors (1977), Conover (1926), Denny (1992), Edwards (1989), Gill & Handel (1990), Gill *et al.* (1983), Handel (1982), Handel & Gill (1992a), Howell & Webb (1995a), Matthiessen (1994), Norton *et al.* (1990), Paulson & Erckmann (1993), Roe (1990), Root (1988), Wilbur (1987).

Subfamily CALIDRINAE
Genus *APHRIZA*   Audubon, 1839

60. Surfbird
Aphriza virgata

French: Bécasseau du ressac   **German**: Gischtläufer   **Spanish**: Correlimos de Rompientes

Taxonomy. *Tringa virgata* Gmelin, 1789, Prince William Sound, Alaska. Formerly classified within subfamily Arenariinae, with superficially similar turnstones, but clearly belongs very close to genus *Calidris*, in which occasionally placed (see page 445). Monotypic.
Distribution. C & S Alaska and C Yukon. Winters on Pacific coast of America, from Alexander Archipelago (SE Alaska) S to Straits of Magellan.

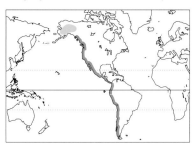

Descriptive notes. 23-26 cm; 121-193 g. Large sandpiper, recalling *Arenaria* but also reminiscent of *Calidris tenuirostris*; strongly streaked head, neck and upperparts, bold markings on lower breast and flanks; largest scapulars are bright buff with bold black marks. Sexes apparently similar. Non-breeding adult has plain brownish grey upperparts, head, neck and breast; chin whitish; flanks with some spots. Juvenile like non-breeding, but buff fringes on both upperparts and brownish breast.
Habitat. Rocky ridges in mountains, alpine tundra, typically with vegetation of moss, avens and heather, interspersed with mosses and lichens. Non-breeding habitat includes seaweed-covered rocky coasts, and jetties; sometimes on adjacent sandy beaches, rarely on mudflats; often together with *Arenaria interpres*, *A. melanocephala* or *Calidris ptilocnemis*.
Food and Feeding. On breeding grounds, takes insects, mainly Diptera, also beetles; caught by stealth or by active chase. In winter quarters and on migration, feeds on barnacles, bivalves (e.g. mussels), periwinkles and limpets, normally under 12 mm long; also herring eggs in Prince William Sound on northward migration, and decopods on sandy beaches. Tugs or hammers on prey; pecks from surface. Shells are crushed in gizzard. Gregarious feeder, in flocks of 20-100 birds.
Breeding. Not well documented. Lays late May to early Jun. Probably monogamous. Nest is natural depression lined with few bits of lichen and moss. 4 eggs, sometimes 3; both sexes probably incubate; fledging period under 1 month.
Movements. Strongly migratory; mainly along coast, but few birds may overfly W USA during northward movement from head of Gulf of California; main wintering areas located in Chile and Peru. Non-breeders may remain in some parts of wintering range all year.
Status and Conservation. Not globally threatened. Breeding population 50,000-70,000 birds. Large proportion of total population may stop in Prince William Sound, SC Alaska, during spring migration, with over 18,000 staging in Rocky Bay. Vulnerable to oil spills.
Bibliography. Armstrong (1983), Bent (1927-1929), Blake (1977), Connors (1977), Dixon (1927), Frisch (1978), Howell & Webb (1995a), Jehl (1968a), Johnson (1965b), Marsh (1984, 1986b), Matthiessen (1994), Meese (1993), Miller, Gunn & MacLean (1987), Miller, Gunn & Veprintsev (1988), Murie (1924), Navarro *et al.* (1989), Norton *et al.* (1990), Paulson (1989), Pearman (1995b), de la Peña (1992), Ridgely & Gwynne (1989), Root (1988), Slud (1964), Stiles & Skutch (1989), Wetmore (1965).

PLATE 44 ➤

61

62

ssp *canutus*

ssp *rufa*

64

65

pallid individual

63

bright individual

66

67

68

69

70

71

72

♀

73

74

♀

75

76

♂

♂

♂

ssp *pacifica*

♂

ssp *arctica*

ssp *couesi*

ssp *alpina*

78

77

♀

♂

ssp *ptilocnemis*

ssp *hudsonia*

PLATE 44

inches   4

cm   10

Genus *CALIDRIS* Merrem, 1804

61. **Great Knot**

Calidris tenuirostris

French: Bécasseau de l'Anadyr **German**: Großer Knutt **Spanish**: Correlimos Grande
Other common names: Eastern/Greater Knot, Great Sandpiper

Taxonomy. *Totanus tenuirostris* Horsfield, 1821, Java.
In past, genus *Calidris* was on occasion reserved for present species and *C. canutus* only. Monotypic.
Distribution. NE Siberia, from Verkhoyansk Mts E to Magadan, Koryak Highlands and S Chukotskiy Peninsula; distribution poorly known. Winters mainly in SE Asia and Australia; also in Arabia, Pakistan, NW & NE India and Bangladesh.

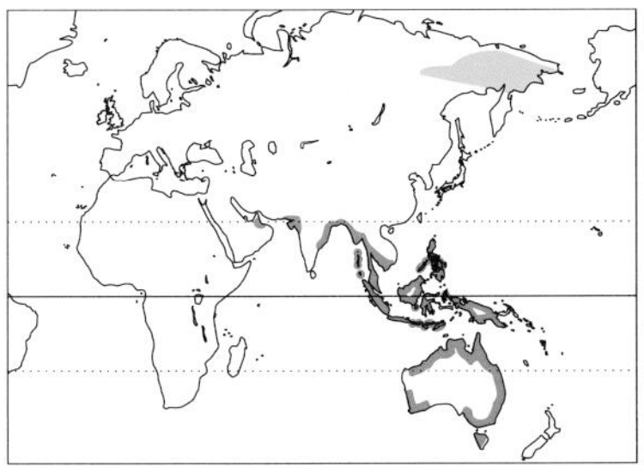

Descriptive notes. 26-28 cm; 115-248 g; wingspan 58 cm. Largest *Calidris*; breast and flanks heavily spotted black; scapulars with large chestnut spots and blackish tips; uppertail-coverts mostly white. Different proportions from *Aphriza virgata*, especially longer bill. Female averages larger, with less chestnut in scapulars. Non-breeding adult has paler grey upperparts and breast; upperparts, head and neck finely streaked dark grey; breast streaked, flanks lightly streaked; faint white wingbar; white rump and uppertail-coverts; similar in shape to *C. canutus* but larger, with longer bill, and at rest wings project beyond tail. Juvenile like non-breeding, but darker and browner; upperparts with narrow pale fringes; dark crown and breast suffused with brown-buff.
Habitat. Breeds in subarctic, on plateaux or gentle slopes with montane tundra at 300-1600 m, in habitats ranging from gravelly areas covered by lichens and patches of herbs and heather to areas with a continuous thick layer of lichen and scattered depressed larch (*Larix*) or dwarf pine (*Pinus pumila*), or both. Non-breeding habitat includes sheltered coasts with large intertidal mudflats and sandflats, e.g. in inlets, bays, harbours, estuaries and lagoons; also on ocean beaches; rarely on inland swamps and lakes or at river mouths.
Food and Feeding. During breeding season primarily plant material, mainly berries, also kernels of dwarf pine trees; only small chicks feed exclusively on insects, such as Diptera larvae, beetles, and spiders. Contrary to previous reports, does not feed in bogs. In non-breeding season feeds mainly on bivalves, up to 36 mm long, buried in soft sediment; also gastropods, crustaceans, annelids and sea cucumbers. Searches mainly by probing in mud, also by pecking and gleaning. Feeds in large flocks of c. 100 to 1000's, often in company of *C. canutus*, *Limosa lapponica* or *Heteroscelus brevipes*. Nocturnal and diurnal forager.
Breeding. Lays late May to late Jun. Monogamous. Territorial; density 13 pairs on 9·5 km^2 of suitable habitat; highly faithful to site. 4 eggs (sometimes 3), laid over 5 days; single brood; incubation 21 days, by both parents; female leaves area after hatching, leaving male to care for chicks; chick similar to that of *C. canutus*; fledging 20-25 days, varying between years depending on weather; young independent several days after fledging. 2·3-2·5 fledglings per brood; chick survival till fledging at least 47%. Oldest ringed bird at least 10 years.
Movements. Long distance migrant, mainly along coast, probably with few stopovers. Females leave breeding grounds early Jul, males and young late Jul. N & S migration routes quite different. Most birds migrate via coast of Sea of Okhotsk (only on S migration), Ussuriland, South Korea (especially N migration), and E China (stopover, at least in N migration); straggler to New Zealand. Arrival in NW Australia late Aug and early Sept, 1st-year birds in Oct; Gulf of Carpentaria not reached until Dec; N migration occurs in Mar-Apr, and departure from NE Australia occurs late Mar to mid-Apr; probably flies non-stop to S China; arrival on breeding grounds late May to early Jun. Small numbers, with highest count 1193 birds, winter in or pass through Arabia, particularly Oman, United Arab Emirates and Saudi Arabia; birds wintering in Pakistan and India may cross Tibetan Plateau. Some 1st-years spend first boreal summer, and maybe longer, in non-breeding range, others migrate at least N to Sakhalin.
Status and Conservation. Not globally threatened. Australian wintering population estimated at 270,000 birds; in E & SE Asia 50,000 birds; less than 10,000 birds wintering in SW & SC Asia. Common on Borneo before 1940, but has declined since. Currently one of most abundant shorebirds in Australia, although species was considered rare, endangered or uncommon till 1970's, as world population was estimated at 10,000-20,000 birds. Important sites in Australia are Eighty Mile Beach, Roebuck Bay, NE Arnhem Land, Roper R area, and SW & SE Gulf of Carpentaria. Hunting and habitat loss in stopover zone in China may constitute major threats. Australasian wintering population seems to be in decline, but no immediate threats evident.
Bibliography. Ali & Ripley (1980), Andreev (1980b), Aspinall (1993), Bamford (1992), Barter (1986c, 1987a), Barter & Wang Tianhou (1990), Beehler *et al*. (1986), Blakers *et al*. (1984), Blomqvist (1983a), Brazil (1991), Brown (1980), Coates (1985), Cramp & Simmons (1983), Dickinson *et al*. (1991), Eigenhuis (1992), Ellis (1992), Étchécopar & Hüe (1978), Evans (1994), Flint *et al*. (1980), Gerasimov (1980), Hoogerwerf (1964), King & Gallagher (1983), Knystautas (1993), Lane & Davies (1987), Lekagul & Round (1991), Lethaby & Gilligan (1991, 1992), Lister (1981), MacKinnon & Phillipps (1993), Marchant, J.H. (1986), Marchant, S. & Higgins (1996), van Marle & Voous (1988), Medway & Wells (1976), Myers *et al*. (1982), Nehls & Schmeckebier (1988), Perennou *et al*. (1994), Piersma & Barter (1991), Portenko (1933), Ripley (1982), Roberts, T.J. (1991), Safford (1992), Schekkerman (1986), Scott (1989), Smythies (1981), Tipper (1993), Tomkovich (1994c, 1995a, 1995b, 1996), Tulp & de Goeij (1991, 1994), Tulp *et al*. (1994, 1995), Wang Tianhou & Qian Gouzhen (1988), Wang Tianhou & Tong Sixian (1991), Watkins (1993), White & Bruce (1986), Williams, M.D. (1986).

62. **Red Knot**

Calidris canutus

French: Bécasseau maubèche **German**: Knutt **Spanish**: Correlimos Gordo
Other common names: (Lesser/European) Knot

Taxonomy. *Tringa Canutus* Linnaeus, 1758, Sweden.
In past, genus *Calidris* was on occasion reserved for present species and *C. tenuirostris* only. Races *islandica*, *rogersi* and, until recently, *roselaari* formerly included within nominate *canutus*. Five subspecies currently recognized.
Subspecies and Distribution.
C. c. canutus (Linnaeus, 1758) - CN Siberia, in Taymyr Peninsula, New Siberian Is and possibly Yakutia; winters in W & S Africa and probably Australasia.
C. c. rogersi (Mathews, 1913) - Chukotskiy Peninsula and possibly areas farther W; winters in Australasia.
C. c. roselaari Tomkovich, 1990 - Wrangel I and NW Alaska; probably winters in Florida, S Panama and N Venezuela.
C. c. rufa (Wilson, 1813) - Canadian low Arctic; winters in NE & S South America.
C. c. islandica (Linnaeus, 1767) - islands of Canadian high Arctic and N Greenland; winters in W Europe.

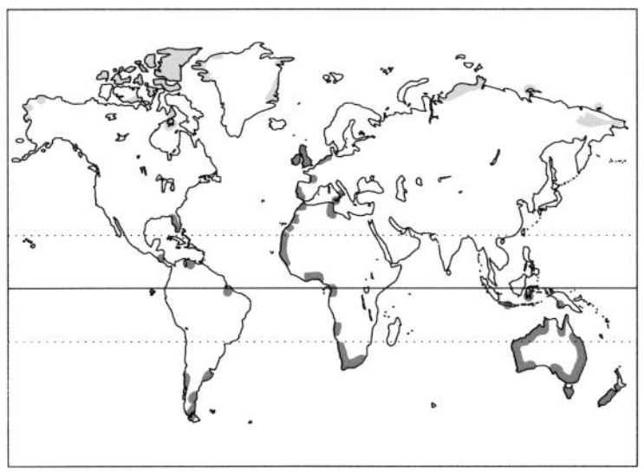

Descriptive notes. 23-25 cm; 85-220 g; wingspan 45-54 cm. Distinctive large *Calidris*, with rich rusty chestnut underparts; upperparts mainly blackish mixed with pale to rufous chestnut. Female has underpart coloration broken with white feathers; more white on rear belly. Non-breeding adult plain grey above with narrow white fringes on larger feathers; underparts white, with grey barring on breast and flanks; recalls larger *C. tenuirostris*, but rump white barred grey appearing uniform grey with rest of upperparts, and white wingbar more marked. Juvenile like non-breeding adult, but breast washed buffish, upperparts brownish grey and wing-coverts and scapulars with buff fringes and dark subterminal bars. Race *islandica* paler below with yellowish fringes on upperparts; *rogersi* similarly paler, with more white on rear belly; *rufa* palest below with most white on rear belly; *roselaari* has more richly coloured belly and undertail-coverts.
Habitat. High Arctic, occupying tundra and upland glacial gravel, marshy slopes and flats in foothills, close to streams or ponds, usually near coast. In non-breeding range, strictly coastal; rarely inland on migration, in W Africa; prefers large tidal mudflats or sandflats; also on sandy beaches of sheltered coasts, rock shelves, bays, lagoons and harbours; occasionally on ocean beaches and saline wetlands near coast.
Food and Feeding. Insects, mainly adult and larval Diptera, also Lepidoptera, Trichoptera, beetles and bees; spiders, small crustaceans, snails and worms. Away from breeding grounds, feeds on small range of intertidal invertebrates, chiefly bivalve and gastropod molluscs, less frequent crustaceans, annelids and insects, rarely fish and seeds. During N migration on staging areas in E USA, feeds primarily on horseshoe crab (*Limulus polyphemus*) eggs. Probes in soft sediment; sometimes pecks. Highly gregarious, often in dense flocks of 300-10,000 birds. Diurnal and nocturnal feeder.
Breeding. Lays Jun. Monogamous. Solitary, territory not important for feeding; normally c. 1 pair/km^2. Nest on open vegetated tundra or stone ridge, often close to clump of vegetation. 3-4 eggs, with laying interval 1-2 days; incubation 21-22 days, by both sexes; chick mottled dull blackish brown above with some buff and with rows of white or cinnamon-buff tips to down, underparts white to buffish white; females depart immediately after hatching, leaving male to tend young alone; fledging 18-20 days. In one sample of 26 eggs, 54% hatched, 27% fledged; annual adult mortality 32%. Age of first breeding probably 2-3 years. Oldest ringed bird 16 years, 1 month.
Movements. Long distance migrant, with relatively few stopover sites. Race *islandica*, from Canada and W Greenland, crosses Greenland icecap, N Atlantic, often Iceland (probably not used by birds from E Greenland), to NW Europe; some move down SW Norway and Denmark, mainly juveniles, only in autumn; spring migration more synchronized, passing through Iceland and N Norway. Race *canutus* probably has 3 migration routes: birds from Yakutia perhaps move overland to Gulf of Finland, through Baltic and W Europe to W Africa (mainly Banc d'Arguin, Mauritania) and S Africa; Taymyr population presumably halts in W Europe; N migration of both groups along same route, many also stopping over in W France; birds from New Siberian Is probably move down E coast of Asia to Australasia. Most *rufa* cross W Atlantic from NE North America to coast of the Guianas, whereafter most continue to Patagonia and Tierra del Fuego; birds wintering in Florida traditionally ascribed to this race, but probably referable to *roselaari*; on way N, most birds stage at Delaware Bay. Race *rogersi* may perform loop migration to Australasia, moving S non-stop across W Pacific, via Sea of Okhotsk, and down E Asian coast (Shanghai and Korea); arrives in N Australia from late Aug, in New Zealand arrives from late Sept, and departs late Mar to early Apr; possibly flies non-stop from NW & SE Australia to SE China. Migration route of *roselaari* not clear, but assumed to winter in W Florida, S Panama and N Venezuela. Adults depart breeding grounds before young. Degree of site fidelity to wintering grounds unclear. Many immatures remain in winter quarters all year.
Status and Conservation. Not globally threatened. Population estimates: *islandica* 345,000-500,000 birds (1989), of which 253,000 winter in the British Is; *canutus* 520,000 birds (1989), of which c. 362,000 winter on Banc d'Arguin, Mauritania, and c. 144,000 in Archipélago dos Bijagós, Guinea-Bissau, in 1992, although only 31,000 estimated in 1992/93; *rogersi* 255,000 birds (1993), including c. 153,000 birds wintering in Australia and 88,000 in New Zealand, with most important wintering sites at Eighty Mile Beach and SE Gulf of Carpentaria, and Farewell Spit and Firth of Thames; *roselaari* at least 20,000 birds; *rufa* 100,000-150,000 birds, of which 53,000 winter in Tierra de Fuego (1989), mostly in Bahía Lomas, while 10,000 birds in Florida are, in fact, probably referable to *roselaari*. Population of *rufa* declined in 1972-1983, possibly due to cold breeding seasons; *islandica* declined from 609,000 birds in early 1970's, perhaps due to severe weather in Arctic; *canutus*, *islandica* and *rufa* currently considered to be stable. Vulnerable to extensive land reclamation projects, encroaching on relatively few staging areas, especially in W Europe, where virtually the entire adult population of race *canutus* and most of population of *islandica* stage in Wadden Sea, where up to 433,000 birds counted at one time; significant numbers of *rufa* (c. 80% of population) stage in Delaware Bay on N migration. Human overexploitation of shellfish stocks in the Wadden Sea directly leads to reduction of food supply and indirectly to alterations in sediment characteristics, which reduce prey availability. Disturbance outside breeding season from recreational activities and overflying aircrafts reduces size of foraging areas. In New Zealand, some illegal shooting persists.

On following pages: 63. Sanderling (*Calidris alba*); 64. Semipalmated Sandpiper (*Calidris pusilla*); 65. Western Sandpiper (*Calidris mauri*); 66. Red-necked Stint (*Calidris ruficollis*); 67. Little Stint (*Calidris minuta*); 68. Temminck's Stint (*Calidris temminckii*); 69. Long-toed Stint (*Calidris subminuta*); 70. Least Sandpiper (*Calidris minutilla*); 71. White-rumped Sandpiper (*Calidris fuscicollis*); 72. Baird's Sandpiper (*Calidris bairdii*); 73. Pectoral Sandpiper (*Calidris melanotos*); 74. Sharp-tailed Sandpiper (*Calidris acuminata*); 75. Curlew Sandpiper (*Calidris ferruginea*); 76. Purple Sandpiper (*Calidris maritima*); 77. Rock Sandpiper (*Calidris ptilocnemis*); 78. Dunlin (*Calidris alpina*).

Bibliography. Alerstam, Gudmundsson & Johannesson (1992), Alerstam, Gudmundsson, Jönsson *et al.* (1990), Ali & Ripley (1980), Armstrong (1983), Baker *et al.* (1994), Barter (1989d, 1992e), Barter *et al.* (1988a, 1988b), Belton (1984), Bent (1927-1929), Blake (1977), Blanco *et al.* (1992), Blomqvist (1983a), Blomqvist & Lindström (1992), Botton *et al.* (1994), Boyd (1992), Brazil (1991), Clancey (1965), Clark *et al.* (1993), Cramp & Simmons (1983), Davidson (1994), Davidson & Evans (1986), Davidson & Morrison (1992), Davidson & Piersma (1992), Davidson & Wilson (1992), Dekinga & Piersma (1993), Dick (1979), Dick *et al.* (1976), Dorogoy (1982), Dowsett & Forbes-Watson (1993), Fjeldså & Krabbe (1990), Frikke & Laursen (1992), Gerasimov (1980), Godfrey (1992), Goodman *et al.* (1989), Green *et al.* (1977), Gromadzka (1992), Gudmundsson (1993, 1994), Gudmundsson & Alerstam (1992), Gudmundsson & Gardarsson (1992), Gudmundsson *et al.* (1991), Harrington, B.A. (1983, 1996), Harrington, B.A. *et al.* (1988), Hedenström & Alerstam (1994), Hewish (1987), Hilty & Brown (1986), Hobson (1972), Hockey & Douie (1995), Howe *et al.* (1989), Howell & Webb (1995a), Johnson (1965b), Knystautas (1993), Koolhaas *et al.* (1993), Lane & Davies (1987), Mackworth-Praed & Grant (1962, 1970), Marchant & Higgins (1996), Meissner (1992), Meltofte (1985), Miller *et al.* (1988), Morrison (1975, 1992), Morrison & Harrington (1992), Morrison & Wilson (1992), Nettleship (1974b), Ntiamoa-Baidu (1993), Pfister *et al.* (1992), Piersma (1989a, 1994), Piersma & Davidson (1992a, 1992b), Piersma, Bruinzeel *et al.* (1996), Piersma, Cadée & Daan (1995), Piersma, Drent & Wiersma (1991), Piersma, van Gils *et al.* (1995), Piersma, de Goeij & Tulp (1993), Piersma, Hoekstra *et al.* (1993), Piersma, Koolhaas *et al.* (1993), Piersma, Prokosch & Bredin (1992), Piersma, Tulp *et al.* (1991), Piersma, Verkuil & Tulp (1994), Prater (1972), Prokosch (1988), Prys-Jones *et al.* (1994), Rogacheva (1992), Schekkerman *et al.* (1992), Shepherd (1992), Shirihai (1996), Sick (1985c, 1993), Slud (1964), Strann (1992), Summers & Waltner (1979), Swennen (1992), Tiedemann (1992), Tomkovich (1990, 1992a), Tomkovich & Soloviev (1994), Tulp & de Goeij (1991), Underhill (1990), Underhill & Summers (1992), Underhill, Prys-Jones *et al.* (1993), Underhill, Waltner & Summers (1989), Urban *et al.* (1986), Verboven & Piersma (1995), Watkins (1993), Wetmore (1965), Whitfield (1985), Whitfield & Brade (1991), Wiersma & Piersma (1994), Wiersma *et al.* (1993), Wilson & Morrison (1992), Zwarts & Blomert (1992), Zwarts *et al.* (1992).

63. Sanderling
Calidris alba

French: Bécasseau sanderling **German**: Sanderling **Spanish**: Correlimos Tridáctilo

Taxonomy. *Tringa alba* Pallas, 1764, coast of North Sea.
Formerly placed in monospecific genus *Crocethia*. Monotypic.
Distribution. Canadian Arctic, Greenland and Svalbard to Severnaya Zemlya Is, Taymyr Peninsula, Lena Delta and New Siberian Is; small numbers in N Alaska. Winters on coast from C North to S South America, and from W & S Europe and Africa through S Asia to Australasia and some tropical Pacific islands.

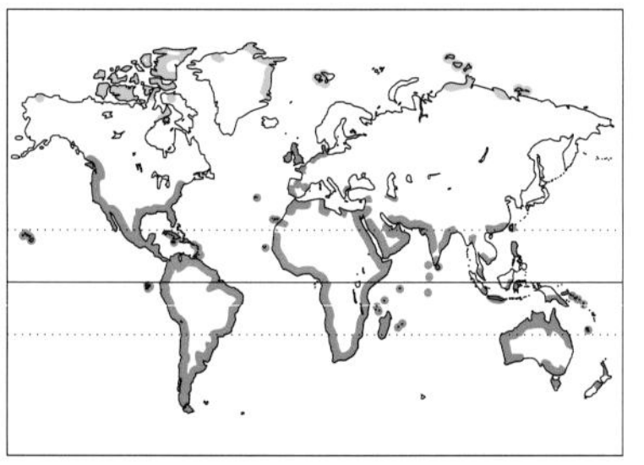

Descriptive notes. 20-21 cm; 33-110 g; wingspan 35-39 cm. Chunky, medium-sized *Calidris* with shortish, thickish bill; intensity of coloration variable, with head, upperparts and breast mostly pale buff to chestnut; dark streaks on head and breast and bold black marks and white spots on upperparts; underparts white; in flight, striking white wingbar in all plumages. Female averages slightly larger and paler, with less chestnut. Non-breeding adult very white; pale grey above with white face and underparts; lesser wing-coverts darker. Juvenile has buffy white head and breast; streaked crown and sides of breast; upperparts marked black and grey with almost black shoulder patch.
Habitat. High Arctic barren stony tundra supporting scant vegetation with well drained ridges and sparse growth of willow and saxifrage; access to shores of neighbouring waters is important requirement for young. Outside breeding season, on open sandy beaches exposed to swell of open sea, and sandy outer reaches of estuaries; also rocky or muddy shores, less frequently on mudflats. On migration, occasionally at inland waters; few birds winter at inland saline lakes.
Food and Feeding. On breeding grounds, insects, mainly adult and larval Diptera, occasionally beetles and Lepidoptera; also spiders and crustaceans and vegetable matter (seeds, saxifrage buds, moss and algae). On migration and in winter, small molluscs, crustaceans, polychaete worms, adult, larval and pupal insects (Diptera, beetles, Lepidoptera, Hemiptera, Hymenoptera); occasionally fish, medusae and larger molluscs and crustaceans taken as carrion; on outer beaches in North and South America, mostly hippid crabs (*Emerita*); on N migration up E coast of USA, primarily eggs of horseshoe crabs (*Limulus polyphemus*); observed scavenging bread from people, often in company of *Arenaria interpres*. Mostly feeds by rapid probing or pecking. Typically, close to water's edge, following retreating waves. Touch, smell and probably taste important for locating prey, and sometimes vision initially. Feeds in small flocks, or very large ones, especially on staging sites. Some birds defend winter feeding territories. Diurnal and nocturnal forager.
Breeding. Laying Jun to mid-Jul. Monogamous; occasionally polyandrous. High degree of breeding site fidelity. Solitary; density up to 13·7 pairs/km². Nest is exposed depression, frequently on bare earth or stones, often lined with dry leaves and lichens. 4 eggs, sometimes 3, with laying interval 26-29 hours; incubation 24-32 days, by both sexes; often 2 clutches, each incubated by one parent; perhaps occasionally 3rd clutch, with different male; chick cinnamon-buff to ochraceous above with fine black down tips and black bands with rows of white down tips, pale buff-yellow face and throat and white underparts; fledging 17 days; when both parents incubate, both probably care for chicks, at least initially; parents depart soon after fledging. Annual adult mortality c. 44%, 1st-years c. 62%. Age of first breeding unknown, but many return to breeding grounds as 1-year-olds. Oldest ringed bird 11 years.
Movements. Long distance migrant. Seems to be restricted to few stopover sites along flyways; highly faithful to wintering sites. Migration largely offshore and coastal, but locally frequent inland across Africa and North America; also occurs on many small oceanic islands. Birds from Greenland and Siberia (E to Taymyr) pass through British Is, some staying there, but most winter down continental coasts from Europe S to S Africa; evidently loop migration, as in spring some birds from W Africa cross Sahara to C Mediterranean. Siberian birds E of Taymyr move down E Russian coast or overland, to Indian Ocean and SW Pacific; in E Asia, common migrant through Korea, E China and Japan, and also through Vietnam and Cambodia. Birds wintering in SE Asia and Australia probably originate from New Siberian Is. Nearctic birds move along Pacific and Atlantic coasts and via prairies and Texas coast; most abundant on Pacific coast of South America, whence N migration mainly via inland and Atlantic routes; high numbers staging at Delaware Bay, probably mostly from Brazil; Pacific North American winterers migrate along Pacific coast. Many 1-year-olds apparently return to breeding grounds, but some remain S all year.
Status and Conservation. Not globally threatened. North American winter population comprises probably 100,000-200,000 birds; most numerous small shorebird on beaches of South American Pacific coast; in 1952, population on Banks I estimated at 65,000 birds; in 1958, population on Prince of Wales I at 70,000; in 1970, c. 450,000 birds claimed overwintering at Puerto Viejo, NC Chile (presumably overestimated). E Atlantic winter population estimated at c. 123,000 birds (1989), with large numbers in W & S Africa; 17,000 pairs estimated breeding in high Arctic Greenland and Ellesmere I (1985); major portion of E Atlantic flyway population stages in Wadden Sea, where numbers considered stable. E Africa and SW Asia hold c. 120,000 birds (1991); SC Asia probably 25,000-100,000 birds; E & SE Asia and Australasia c. 25,000 birds, with c. 8000 in Australia. Numbers staging in E North America declined by 80% from 1972 to 1983; in Pacific North America, winter populations have fluctuated in recent years, but no apparent overall decline. Species sensitive to disturbance on beaches, moving to other sites if disturbance becomes too intense.
Bibliography. Ali & Ripley (1980), Armstrong (1983), Azevedo-Junior (1988), Belton (1984), Bent (1927-1929), Blake (1977), Blomqvist (1983a), Botton *et al.* (1994), Brazil (1991), Burger & Gochfeld (1991e), Burger *et al.* (1979), Castro & Myers (1989, 1990), Castro, Myers & Place (1989), Castro, Myers & Ricklefs (1992), Clark *et al.* (1993), Coates (1985), Connors *et al.* (1981), Cramp & Simmons (1983), Crowe (1981, 1986), Dowsett (1980), Dowsett & Forbes-Watson (1993), Estelle (1991), Evans, M.I. & Keijl (1993b), Evans, P.R. *et al.* (1980), Fjeldså & Krabbe (1990), Gerritsen & van Heezik (1985), Gerritsen & Meiboom (1986), Green *et al.* (1977), Goodman *et al.* (1989), Gudmundsson & Lindström (1992), Gudmundsson *et al.* (1991), Hayes & Fox (1991), Heezik *et al.* (1983), Hilty & Brown (1986), Hockey & Douie (1995), Holyoak & Thibault (1984), Howe *et al.* (1989), Howell & Webb (1995a), Jessop (1992), Johnson (1965b), Kaufman (1996), Knystautas (1993), Lane & Davies (1987), Langrand (1990), Mackworth-Praed & Grant (1957, 1962, 1970), Marchant & Higgins (1996), van Marle & Voous (1988), Maron & Myers (1984, 1985), McGill (1951), Meltofte (1985), Miller *et al.* (1988), Morrison *et al.* (1987), Myers (1980a, 1981a, 1983, 1988), Myers, Connors & Pitelka (1979a, 1979b, 1980), Myers, Maron & Sallaberry (1985), Myers, Sallaberry *et al.* (1990), Myers, Schick & Castro (1988), Myers, Schick & Hohenberger (1984), Myers, Williams & Pitelka (1980), Parmelee (1970), Parmelee & Payne (1973), Perennou *et al.* (1994), Pienkowski & Green (1976), Roberts, G. (1991), Roberts, G. & Evans (1993), Roberts, T.J. (1991), Rogacheva (1992), Sallaberry (1991), Shirihai (1996), Sick (1985c, 1993), Slud (1964), Smit & van Spanje (1989), Spaans (1980), Summers & Waltner (1979), Summers, Underhill, Waltner & Whitelaw (1987), Tomkovich & Soloviev (1994), Underhill (1991), Underhill *et al.* (1993), Urban *et al.* (1986), Wetmore (1965), Wood (1987).

64. Semipalmated Sandpiper
Calidris pusilla

French: Bécasseau semipalmé **German**: Sandstrandläufer **Spanish**: Correlimos Semipalmeado

Taxonomy. *Tringa pusilla* Linnaeus, 1766, Santo Domingo.
Formerly placed in genus *Ereunetes* with *C. mauri*. Monotypic.
Distribution. W & N Alaska and N Canada. Winters on Pacific coast from S Mexico to S Peru, and on Atlantic coast from Yucatán and West Indies to C Argentina.

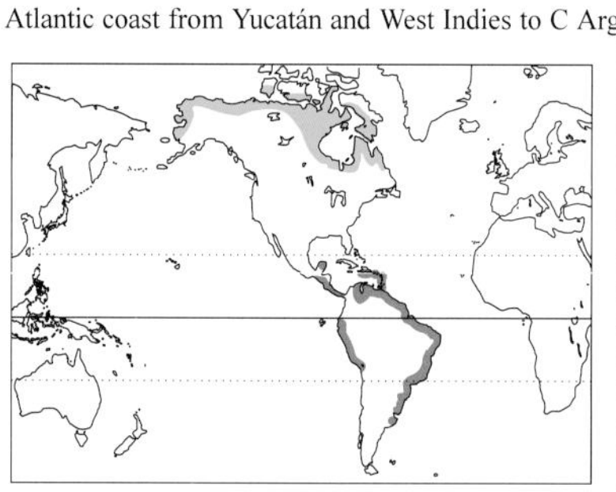

Descriptive notes. 13-15 cm; 20-41 g; wingspan 34-37 cm. Breeding plumage duller than in most congeners; brownish grey upperparts with dark centres to scapulars; breast and flanks with dark streaks; toes partly webbed. Resembles *C. mauri*, but bill averages broader at base and shorter, with rounded or droplet-like tip; legs shorter. Female averages larger. Non-breeding adult plain grey-brown above; dark crown and eyestripe; face, breast and flanks white; faint lateral breast patches. Juvenile has varying amounts of rufous on scapulars and mantle.
Habitat. High and low Arctic and subarctic wet sedge or heath tundra, often near pools, rivers and lakes; river deltas in dry shrubby areas; sandy areas along rivers. Non-breeding habitat mainly coastal, on sandy beaches and intertidal mudflats, also in shallow lagoons with dead mangroves, sometimes salt-marsh; on migration, also at inland wetlands, edges of lakes, junctions of short-grass marshes and tidal flats.
Food and Feeding. During breeding season mainly chironomid larvae; also spiders, snails, larvae of other Diptera and beetles, and seeds; prey items usually 2-5 mm long. During migration, small aquatic and marine invertebrates, including small arthropods, especially amphipod *Corophium volutator*, various larvae, snails, molluscs and polychaetes, some terrestrial invertebrates such as insects (Diptera larvae) and spiders; on N migration up E USA, feeds on horseshoe crab (*Limulus polyphemus*) eggs. Pecks (visual) and probes (tactile); compared to *C. mauri*, probes less often and less deeply. Highly gregarious; occasionally, when food scarce and patchy, defends feeding territory.
Breeding. Lays Jun to early Jul. Monogamous. Territorial; density 11-100 pair/km². Low degree of natal philopatry (5%). Nest is mere depression filled with plant matter, often on top of small island or hill, under willow bush or small birch tree, or in tussock. 4 eggs, sometimes 3, with laying interval 24-32 hours; single brood; incubation 20-22 days, by both sexes; female usually leaves brood 0-11 days after hatching, occasionally (9%) male deserts family first; fledging 16-19 days. Nest success, in nests where at least 1 chick hatched, 7-100%; egg survival 25-59%; chick survival c. 50%; 0·3-1·2 young fledged per pair, 1·5-1·7 per successful pair; adult annual survival 70%. Age of first breeding 1 year. Oldest known individual 12 years.
Movements. Long distance migrant; non-stop flights of up to 4000 km; flocks of up to 350,000 birds may gather at key stopover sites. Few move to S Florida, most to West Indies and N South America, mainly Surinam and French Guiana. Alaskan birds move across Great Plains, sometimes farther E, especially on way S. C population migrates by James Bay, upper Bay of Fundy and W Atlantic; return migration across Gulf of Mexico and Great Plains. E Canadian population crosses W Atlantic to West Indies, with return migration up Atlantic coast. About two thirds of all juveniles spend summer on wintering grounds. High fidelity to staging areas and breeding grounds, but unknown for wintering grounds.
Status and Conservation. Not globally threatened. Total population estimated at 3,200,000-3,900,000 birds (1993); up to 1,000,000 breeding birds in E Canadian Arctic. Total winter population in South America estimated at 2,142,000 birds (1989), of which about 80% wintering on coast of Surinam. Flocks of up to 350,000 appear in upper Bay of Fundy and 1,122,000-2,200,000 estimated to stage there during S migration. Numbers migrating in E Canada declined significantly from 1974 to 1991, possibly in part due to cold breeding seasons in 1970's; numbers staging in Delaware Bay on N migration, have declined since 1986. Destruction and manipulation of coastal and inland wetlands, and perhaps pollution, are major threats to populations.
Bibliography. Amos (1991), Armstrong (1983), Ashkenazie & Safriel (1979a, 1979b), Ashmole (1970), Azevedo-Junior (1988), Bent (1927-1929), Biaggi (1983), Blake (1977), Blomqvist (1983a), Boates & Smith (1989), Brock (1990), Cartar (1984), Clark *et al.* (1993), Cramp & Simmons (1983), Driedzic *et al.* (1993), Dunn *et al.* (1988), Gilliland (1992), Grant, P.J. (1981), Gratto (1983, 1988, 1991, 1992), Gratto & Cooke (1987), Gratto & Dickson (1994), Gratto & Morrison (1981), Gratto, Cooke & Morrison (1983), Gratto, Morrison & Cooke (1985), Harrington (1982), Harrington & Groves (1977), Harrington & Morrison (1979), Harrington & Taylor (1982), Haverschmidt

(1968), Haverschmidt & Mees (1995), Hayes & Fox (1991), Hicklin (1983), Hicklin & Smith (1984), Hilty & Brown (1986), Holloway (1995), Holmes & Pitelka (1968), Howe *et al.* (1989), Howell & Webb (1995a), Johnson (1965b), Knystautas (1993), Lank (1983), Leger (1982), Manseau & Ferron (1991), Matthews *et al.* (1992), Matthiessen (1994), Mawhinney *et al.* (1993), McCollough (1981), Meyer de Schauensee & Phelps (1978), Michaud & Ferron (1986, 1990), Miller (1983c), Monroe (1968), Morrison & Ross (1989), Norton (1972), Page & Bradstreet (1968), Page & Middleton (1972), Page & Salvadori (1969), de la Peña (1992), Petursson (1992), Phillips (1975), Ridgely & Gwynne (1989), Root (1988), Safriel (1980), Scott & Carbonell (1986), Sick (1985c, 1993), Skagen & Knopf (1994), Slud (1964), Snyder (1966), Steeves & Holohan (1994), Stevenson (1975), Stiles & Skutch (1989), Tostain *et al.* (1992), Votier (1992), Wallace (1979), Wetmore (1965), White, L.M. (1985), Wilson (1990).

65. **Western Sandpiper**

Calidris mauri

French: Bécasseau d'Alaska **German**: Bergstrandläufer **Spanish**: Correlimos de Alaska

Taxonomy. *Ereunetes Mauri* Cabanis, 1857, South Carolina.
Formerly placed in genus *Ereunetes* with *C. pusilla*. Monotypic.
Distribution. E Chukotskiy Peninsula and W & N Alaska. Winters on Pacific coast from N California to N Peru, and locally down Atlantic coast from S New Jersey through Gulf of Mexico and West Indies to Surinam.

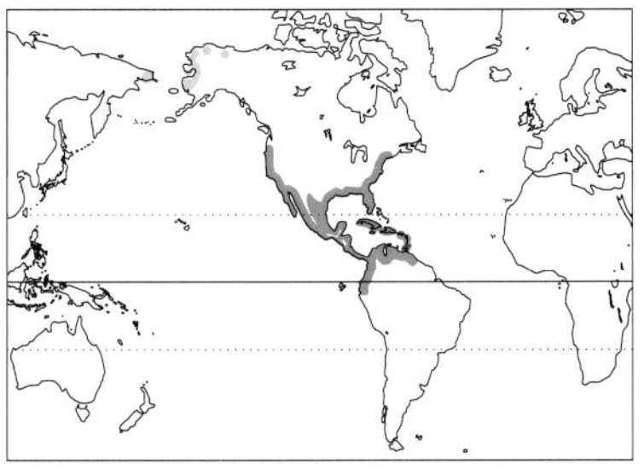

Descriptive notes. 14-17 cm; 18-42 g; wingspan 28-37 cm. Distinctive with rufous chestnut on crown and ear-coverts; chestnut and black scapulars with pale fringes; neck, breast and flanks heavily streaked dark brown; toes partly webbed. Resembles *C. pusilla*, but bill normally longer and more pointed, with drooping tip; legs longer. Female averages larger; tends to have longer bill, with more drooping tip. Non-breeding adult plain brownish grey above; head, neck and sides of breast finely streaked grey; rest of underparts white. Juvenile has rufous on upper scapulars and grey on lower scapulars; crown buff-grey and streaked; mantle blackish, fringed rufous and white; underparts white with breast washed orange-buff and finely streaked.
Habitat. For breeding, occupies tundra of low Arctic and subarctic, preferably dominated by dwarf birch, dwarf willow, crowberry and various shrubs; elevated areas required for nesting, wet areas for feeding; generally drier than breeding habitat of *C. pusilla*. In winter and on migration, preferably on estuarine mudflats and sandy beaches; also wide variety of other coastal or near-coastal wetlands, such as margins of lakes and ponds.
Food and Feeding. During breeding, mainly insects (larvae, pupae and some adults), especially Muscidae and chironomids, also craneflies and beetles; also spiders and small crustaceans; young mainly eat surface-dwelling insects, but later diet identical to adults'. On migration, amphipods, bivalves, polychaetes, fly larvae, beetles, ants, snails, spiders and occasionally seeds. Pecks or probes; feeds more in water and probes more than *C. pusilla*. Recently suggested that planktonic food may be taken, using a filtering system in bill. Highly gregarious.
Breeding. Lays late May to late Jun. Monogamous. Territorial; nests sometimes strongly clustered; density up to 490 pairs/km² (W Alaska), c. 30 pairs/km² (Siberia and N Alaska). Nest is depression in tundra, usually under dwarf birch, sometimes among grasses; filled with plant material. 4 eggs (3-5), with laying interval 23-28 hours; single-brooded, but may renest after clutch failure; incubation 21 days, by both sexes; fledging 18-21 days; in Alaska both parents tend young until fledging, although sometimes female deserts family earlier; in Siberia often female, but sometimes male, abandons mate during incubation, whereas latter may depart prior to fledging. Adult annual survival c. 70%. Age of first breeding probably 1 year. Oldest known individual 9 years, 2 months.
Movements. Unlike other small *Calidris*, migration appears as series of shorter flights; flight range c. 600 km. E Siberian birds join Nearctic population on migration. Most migrate down Pacific coast, although significant numbers move through interior North America, with Cheyenne Bottoms as most important interior stopover site, during both spring and autumn. During N migration Copper R Delta functions as a key staging site, used by more than 90% of total population; other major spring stopover sites are San Francisco Bay, Grays Harbor, Fraser Delta, Chesterman Beach, Tofino mudflats and Stikine Delta; southbound, Yukon Delta, Kuskokwim Bay and Boundary Bay. On Atlantic coast, common autumn migrant to Puerto Rico. Males winter, on average, closer to breeding grounds, and predominate at start of N migration. In autumn, departure occurs Jul to early Aug; adults precede juveniles, and females slightly precede males. Migrates in huge flocks. Many immatures stay in non-breeding range all year. Arrival on breeding grounds May to mid-Jun.
Status and Conservation. Not globally threatened. Total world population estimated at 2,000,000-3,000,000 birds (1994); other estimates have claimed 6,500,000 individuals, but unlikely; virtually entire population passes through Copper R Delta each spring, and numbers passing through British Columbia each autumn have been estimated at 2,400,000 birds. Stopover and wintering areas in need of protection, though some stopover sites are already listed as "Hemispherically Significant", including Cheyenne Bottoms, San Francisco Bay, Grays Harbor and Copper R Delta; oil spill from Exxon Valdez in Mar 1989, which just missed Copper R Delta, demonstrated vulnerability of even such a huge population.
Bibliography. Armstrong (1983), Ashmole (1970), Bardon (1991), Bent (1927-1929), Biaggi (1983), Blake (1977), Blomqvist (1983a), Brazil (1991), Brown (1962), Butler & Kaiser (1988), Butler *et al.* (1987), Cartar (1984), Colston (1975), Colwell (1993), Colwell & Landrum (1993), Cramp & Simmons (1983), Gill & Handel (1990), Harrington & Haase (1994), Haverschmidt (1968), Haverschmidt & Mees (1995), Hilty & Brown (1986), Holmes (1971a, 1972, 1973), Holmes & Pitelka (1968), Howell & Webb (1995a), Isleib (1979), Iverson *et al.* (1996), Knystautas (1993), Matthiessen (1994), Meyer de Schauensee & Phelps (1978), Monroe (1968), Morrison & Myers (1989), Mullarney (1992), Myers, Hildén & Tomkovich (1982), Myers, Morrison *et al.* (1987), Naranjo *et al.* (1994), Nisbet (1963), Norton (1972), Ouellet *et al.* (1973), Palindant *et al.* (1973), Rattner *et al.* (1995), Ridgely & Gwynne (1989), Root (1988), Scott & Carbonell (1986), Senner (1979), Senner & Martínez (1982), Senner, Norton & West (1989), Senner, West & Norton (1981), Slud (1964), Snyder (1966), Spaans (1978), Stevenson (1975), Stiles & Skutch (1989), Tomkovich (1996), Tomkovich & Morozov (1980, 1994), Tostain *et al.* (1992), Warnock & Takekawa (1996), Wetmore (1965), Wilson, W.H. (1993, 1994a, 1994b).

66. **Red-necked Stint**

Calidris ruficollis

French: Bécasseau à col roux **German**: Rotkehl-Strandläufer **Spanish**: Correlimos Cuellirrojo
Other common names: Rufous-necked Stint/Sandpiper, Eastern Little Stint

Taxonomy. *Trynga* [sic] *ruficollis* Pallas, 1776, Kulussutai, southern Transbaikalia.
Formerly placed in genus *Erolia*. May form superspecies with *C. minuta*. Monotypic.
Distribution. C & E Taymyr; Kharaulakh Mts and area around Lena Delta; R Kolyma to Chukotskiy Peninsula and S to extreme N Kamchatka; sporadically W & N Alaska. Winters in SE Asia, from E India, Myanmar, S China and Taiwan through Philippines and Indonesia to Solomon Is, Australia and New Zealand.

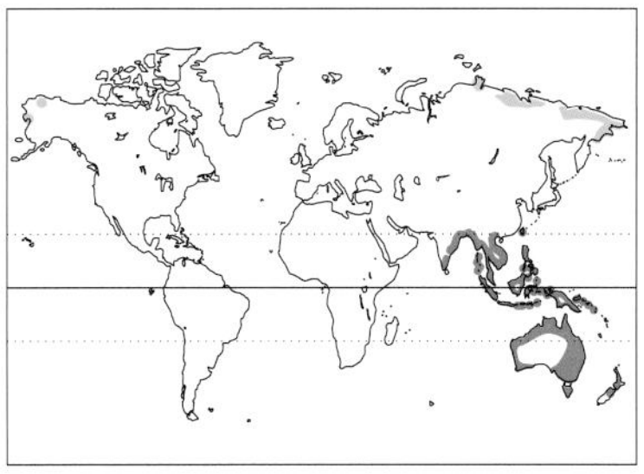

Descriptive notes. 13-16 cm, 18-51 g, wingspan 29-33 cm. Chestnut lower face, throat and upper breast; white around bill base and on part of supercilium; crown and upperparts have chestnut, black and white markings contrasting with grey upperwing; underparts white. Resembles *C. minuta*, but slightly larger; slightly shorter legs and rather longer wings; bill shorter and thicker. Female averages slightly larger in wing and bill. Non-breeding adult has crown streaked; grey lateral breast patches; usually indistinguishable from *C. minuta* in field. Juvenile has back buff and grey with pale edges; crown streaked buff and black, ear-coverts greyish; breast with ochre wash and faint streaks on sides of breast; very similar to *C. minuta* and *C. pusilla*.
Habitat. Low altitude montane tundra in subalpine belt, on mossy and scrubby tundra, usually in rather dry and raised areas. During non-breeding season, mostly coastal, on intertidal mudflats, sheltered inlets, bays and lagoons, but also commonly on wide variety of freshwater, brackish and saltwater wetlands; occasionally on sandy beaches and rocky shorelines.
Food and Feeding. On breeding grounds takes beetles, insect larvae, Hymenoptera and tiny seeds; may forage far from nest in wet habitat. Outside breeding season, small invertebrates, such as polychaete worms, crustaceans, insects and molluscs; also seeds. Constant pecking motion, like *C. minuta*; probes in sediment to depth of 20 mm, or jabs; also gleans. Feeds in dense flocks; birds spread out during feeding, but come together when flushed.
Breeding. Laying Jun. Monogamous. Densities 4-6 pairs/km², up to 28 pairs/km². Low degree of site fidelity. Nest is shallow depression lined with leaves and grass. 4 eggs, sometimes 3; single brood, but replacement clutches laid; incubation 20·5-22 days, by both parents; female leaves soon after hatching (especially in late breeders), and male usually tends chicks up to fledging; fledging 16-17 days. Annual survival estimated at 80%; longevity up to 10-15 years; oldest ringed bird at least 11 years, 1 month.
Movements. Migratory. Probably moves in large flocks. Uses several stopovers, mostly on coasts of Japan, Korea, SE China, Taiwan, Hong Kong, Vietnam, Malaysia, Indonesia, New Guinea, Philippines and W Micronesia; migrating flocks crossing Pacific often stage on islands. Some Siberian birds move overland and cross Krasnoyarsk, Irkutsk and Buryatskaya regions; some cross Mongolia, Manchuria and Ussuriland; others W to E Kazakhstan. Most of population breeding in Alaska appears to pass through Aleutian and Pribilof Is to migrate with Siberian population; some spend boreal winter in the Americas. Australia reached by late Aug and arrivals continue until Nov; juveniles arrive latest and may use different route; departure mainly Mar-Apr. Immatures usually remain in non-breeding range throughout 1st year, often moving inland after rains fill wetlands. Adults show high fidelity between years to non-breeding sites.
Status and Conservation. Not globally threatened. Australasian population estimated at 471,000 birds, with 353,000 wintering in Australia (1993); numbers apparently declining. In SE Asia, concentrations occur in Philippines and W Peninsular Malaysia. Locally common in breeding areas; in non-breeding areas often abundant. Populations in Tasmania have declined since mid-1980's; New Zealand populations have increased significantly since late 1950's. Most important Australian sites are Coorong and Eighty Mile Beach, but many also move to SE Australia, where human population is densest; in Victoria, birds seem not to be greatly disturbed by boating traffic and pedestrians. Hundreds died round L Forrestdale, Perth, Western Australia, after spraying with pesticides.
Bibliography. Alcorn (1988), Ali & Ripley (1980), Alström & Olsson (1989), Anders & Andersson (1990), Armstrong (1983), Barter (1984b, 1992b), Beehler *et al.* (1986), Berg (1987), Blakers *et al.* (1984), Blomqvist (1983a), Brazil (1991), Bregulla (1992), Breife & Alind (1990), Chambers (1989), Clancey (1964c), Coates (1985), Cramp & Simmons (1983), Dickinson *et al.* (1991), Dowsett & Forbes-Watson (1993), Étchécopar & Hüe (1978), Evans, P.R. (1975), Flint (1980b), Flohart (1995), Gladkov (1957), Knystautas (1993), Lane & Davies (1987), Lekagul & Round (1991), MacKinnon & Phillipps (1993), Marchant & Higgins (1996), van Marle & Voous (1988), Medway & Wells (1976), Melville (1981), Miller *et al.* (1988), Morozov & Tomkovich (1984, 1986, 1988), Morris, A. (1986), Myers *et al.* (1982), Newman *et al.* (1985), van Ommen & van Ijzendoorn (1988), Paton & Wykes (1978), Perennou *et al.* (1994), Rabor (1977), Richards (1989), Ripley (1982), Rogacheva (1992), Schwarze & Schwarze (1981), Scott (1989), Sinclair & Nicholls (1976), Smythies (1981, 1986), Taylor (1981b), Thomas, D.G. (1987), Thomas, D.G. & Dartnall (1970, 1971a, 1971b), Tomkovich, P.S. (1986, 1996), Tomkovich, P.S. & Morozov (1994), Urban *et al.* (1986), Veit (1988), Veit & Petersen (1982), Wallace (1979), Watkins (1993), White & Bruce (1986), Williams, M.D. (1986).

67. **Little Stint**

Calidris minuta

French: Bécasseau minute **German**: Zwergstrandläufer **Spanish**: Correlimos Menudo
Other common names: Lesser Stint

Taxonomy. *Tringa minuta* Leisler, 1812, Hanau am Main, Germany.
Formerly placed in genus *Erolia*. May form superspecies with *C. ruficollis*. Monotypic.
Distribution. N Scandinavia through S Novaya Zemlya and NW & NC Siberia to New Siberian Is and R Yana. Winters from Mediterranean and Africa through Arabian Peninsula and Persian Gulf E to Indian Subcontinent and Myanmar; small numbers in SE Britain and Madagascar.

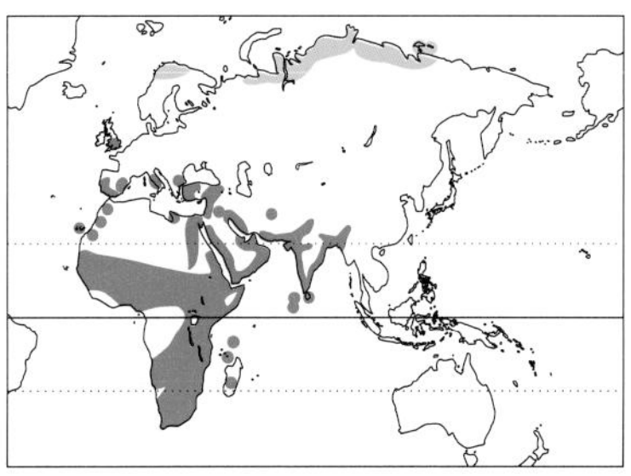

Descriptive notes. 12-14 cm; 17-44 g; wingspan 28-31 cm. Tiny, compact stint with short bill; feathers of upperparts have dark brown centres and pale rufous fringes or tips; mantle with yellowish edges forming distinct "V"; head, neck and breast rufous buff with brown streaks; rest of underparts, throat and chin white. Differs from *C. ruficollis* by slightly longer bill and legs; white throat, dark streaks on sides of neck and breast. Female averages larger. Non-breeding adult has brownish grey upperparts mottled dark and fringed pale; crown grey, streaked dark; eyestripe and sides of breast dull grey; rest of face and underparts white. Juvenile has tertials, lower scapulars and wing-coverts with dark brown centres and rufous and white edges; white edges of mantle form distinct "V"; head and breast suffused pale buff; pale grey crown, neck and broad eyestripe with fine streaking; whitish supercilium.

Habitat. Tundra of high Arctic, chiefly on dry ground at lower altitude, often among dwarf willows, near swampy areas or salt-marshes; avoids areas with more than 250 mm annual rainfall. On migration found at small inland waters and riverbanks, or coastal, on mudflats and seashore. In winter quarters mainly coastal, at estuarine mudflats, enclosed lagoons, tidal creeks; also at inland fresh waters, such as open pools in marshes, paddyfields, *jheels*.

Food and Feeding. Chiefly invertebrates; during breeding season primarily larval and adult Diptera and small beetles; after breeding also ants, Hymenoptera, water-bugs, annelids, small molluscs, crustaceans, freshwater mites and plant material. Feeds by rapid pecking actions, sometimes probes; detects prey by sight. Gregarious, in small to large flocks, up to several thousand birds; sometimes defends feeding territory.

Breeding. Lays late Jun to early Jul. Monogamous, polygynous or polyandrous. Loosely territorial, with no clearly defined area defended; little or no fidelity to breeding site. Density of up to 5 pairs/ha, more often c. 10 nests/km²; very variable between years. Nest on ground, exposed, but sometimes covered by vegetation, and lined with leaves and pieces of grass. 4 eggs, sometimes 3; incubation 20-21 days, by both parents, but in cases of polygamy by male or female only; polyandrous females may incubate a second clutch; chick orange to tawny, mottled above with black bands and dense rows of white or pale down tips, white underparts; chick-care by one parent; fledging period unknown; fledged young start migrating S after several days. Age of first breeding unknown, but at least some return to breeding grounds as 1-year-olds. Oldest ringed bird 8 years, 10 months.

Movements. Migratory; in broad front across much of W Palearctic; movements S-SW in Jul-Nov, birds returning mid-May to early Jun. Juveniles probably migrate farther W than adults, due to weather displacement. Finnish and Swedish population crosses C Europe, Italy, Mediterranean, France and Tunisia; also major routes between C Mediterranean and Black Sea, and via Caspian Sea and Kazakhstan lakes to and from E & S Africa, apparently following route via Rift Valley lakes; W & C Siberian breeders presumably winter in India, passing through Kazakhstan and also N through Mongolia and Tuva. In Britain, commoner in autumn than in spring, with few birds passing winter. Small numbers may migrate along E Asian coasts, including Hong Kong and Philippines. Many immatures remain S all year. Typical migrating flocks comprise 20-30 birds.

Status and Conservation. Not globally threatened. Population wintering in coastal W Africa and Europe considered to be stable and estimated at 211,000 birds (1989); of these, up to 123,000 in Guinea-Bissau, which was earlier estimated to hold 350,000 but only 60,000 in 1992/93, with numbers perhaps varying due to exchange with inland habitats; numbers inland evidently exceed those at coastal wetlands; wintering population in S Africa 23,000 birds; more than 1,000,000 birds estimated in NE & E Africa and SW Asia, with 250,000-500,000 in Sudan, some 100,000's along freshwater and soda lakes in Ethiopia and E Africa and over 100,000 in Egypt; in SC Asia at least 200,000 birds, with high numbers in India, Pakistan and Sri Lanka. In Norway, no overall change in breeding numbers since 19th century.

Bibliography. Ali & Ripley (1980), Barber (1986), Beehler *et al.* (1986), Bengtson & Svensson (1968), Benson & Benson (1975), Blomqvist (1983a), Brazil (1991), Bregnballe *et al.* (1990), Carter *et al.* (1992), Chafer (1989), Chernyaev (1986), Cox (1988a), Cramp & Simmons (1983), Dean (1977a), Dowsett & Forbes-Watson (1993), Elgood *et al.* (1994), Étchécopar & Hüe (1964, 1978), Evans (1994), Evans & Keijl (1993b), Gavrilov (1991), Gavrilov *et al.* (1988), Ginn *et al.* (1989), Goodman *et al.* (1989), Gore (1990), Grazhulyavichius & Machalov (1988), Grimes (1987), Hazevoet (1995), Hildén (1983), Hockey & Douie (1995), Hüe & Étchécopar (1970), Johnson, J. (1987), Keijl *et al.* (1992), Kennerley (1987), Knystautas (1993), Lambert (1983), Mackworth-Praed & Grant (1957, 1962, 1970), Maclean (1993), Middlemiss (1961), Morrison (1980), Mullié & Meininger (1981), Nightingale (1986), Patrikeev (1995), Paz (1987), Pearson (1984a, 1987), Perennou *et al.* (1994), Perry (1992), Phillips (1978), Piersma (1986b), Pinto (1983), Raju (1978), Rands *et al.* (1987), Ripley (1982), Roberts, T.J. (1991), Rogacheva (1992), Schmidt & Barthel (1993), Scott (1989), Shirihai (1996), Short *et al.* (1990), Smythies (1986), Summers, Underhill, Pearson & Scott (1987), Thomas, D.G. (1987), Tomkovich (1980a, 1996), Tree (1974), Underhill *et al.* (1993), Urban *et al.* (1986), Zwarts (1985, 1988).

68. Temminck's Stint

Calidris temminckii

French: Bécasseau de Temminck **Spanish**: Correlimos de Temminck
German: Temminckstrandläufer

Taxonomy. *Tringa Temminckii* Leisler, 1812, Hanau am Main, Germany.
Formerly placed in genus *Erolia*. Monotypic.

Distribution. Scandinavia through NW Russia and N Siberia E to Chukotskiy Peninsula and Anadyrland; irregularly in Britain. Winters from Mediterranean, N tropical Africa and Middle East through Indian Subcontinent and Indochina to S China, Taiwan and S Ryukyu Is, and S to Peninsular Malaysia and Borneo; occasionally to Philippines.

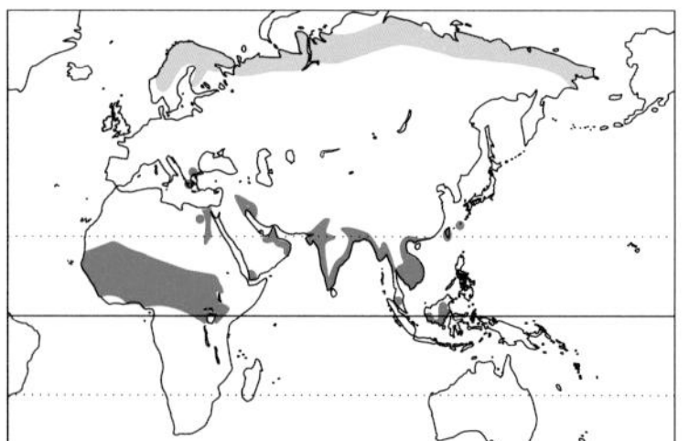

Descriptive notes. 13-15 cm; 15-36 g; wingspan 34-37 cm. Small, short-legged stint with broad white sides of tail and rump, unique amongst *Calidris*; upperparts range from dull grey to olive brown, with variable patches of black-brown, dull rufous and grey; head and breast grey-brown; breast heavily streaked brown; white on chin, throat and belly. Female averages slightly larger. Non-breeding adult has plain dark grey upperparts and head; breast uniform pale grey-brown; chin and throat white. Juvenile like non-breeding, but upperpart feathers brown-grey with dark subterminal band and buff fringes.

Habitat. Typical (southern) tundra, shrub tundra and along floodplains in forest tundra; on flat ground clear of vegetation, or covered with short grass interspersed with patches of shrubs; also near inlets, fjords, deltas and streams; upland and inland, at sheltered sites on shrubland fringes, around human habitation; avoids severe Arctic conditions. Outside breeding season, variety of wetland types, preferably inland freshwater sites, e.g. floodlands, irrigated fields, sewage farms and more or less densely vegetated wetlands; more rarely on tidal mudflats and coastal lagoons; avoids open coast.

Food and Feeding. At breeding grounds and inland, primarily insects and their larvae, especially beetles and Diptera, occasionally plant material; on coast, mainly annelids, crustaceans and small molluscs. Pecks prey from surface, rarely probes. Singly or in small groups of up to 30 birds.

Breeding. Lays late May to early Jul. Successive bigamy by both sexes, occasionally with third clutch. Territorial; up to 6-7 "pairs"/km², but on C Siberian tundra locally 25-40 (52) birds/km². Site fidelity c. 50% and some natal philopatry. Nest on ground, in open or low vegetation, lined with plant stems and leaves. 4 eggs (2-4); 2nd clutch started 2-9 days after 1st; each nest cared for by one parent, 1st by male; in case of 3 clutches, 2nd cared for by another male, 3rd cared for by female; incubation 21-22 days; chick obscurely mottled cinnamon-buff to ochraceous above with blackish band and white to buff down tips, buff-yellow face and throat, and white underparts; fledging 15-18 days. Nesting failure mainly caused by flooding and predation; c. 56% egg mortality; 3·5 hatchlings per succesful clutch; 1st-year mortality c. 50%; annual adult mortality 19%. Age of first breeding 1 year and older. Oldest ringed bird 11 years.

Movements. Migratory. Broad front migration spans towards N Africa and S Asia. Arrival in N Africa late Jul to mid-Sept or mid-Oct, reaching Mali Aug-Oct, Eritrea Sept to early Oct, and tropics mainly from Oct. Departs wintering grounds mainly late Mar to Apr, some as late as May. Small numbers winter in Europe, occasionally as far N as Britain. Scandinavian birds move S-SW in autumn. Usually migrates in small flocks, up to 250 individuals.

Status and Conservation. Not globally threatened. Wintering population in SW Asia unknown, but up to 10,000 have been counted in Iran; in SC Asia probably 25,000-100,000 birds, with high numbers in India and Pakistan; E & SE Asia probably up to 100,000 birds; no estimates available for populations wintering in Africa, and irregularly in Europe. Evidence for southward expansion of breeding range in Norway, and also, with irregular breeding, in Britain. Increases and decreases noted locally in Fenno-Scandia; breeding population estimated at 25,000 pairs, of which 20,000 in Sweden (1976).

Bibliography. Ali & Ripley (1980), Blomqvist (1983a), Brazil (1991), Breiehagen (1989), Brogger-Jensen (1977), Cramp & Simmons (1983), Deignan (1945), Dowsett & Forbes-Watson (1993), Elgood *et al.* (1994), van der Elst (1991b), Étchécopar & Hüe (1964, 1978), Fjeldså (1977), Goodman *et al.* (1989), Harrap (1990), Hildén (1975, 1978, 1979b), Hüe & Étchécopar (1970), Kautesk *et al.* (1983), Knystautas (1993), Lekagul & Round (1991), MacKinnon & Phillipps (1993), Mackworth-Praed & Grant (1957, 1970), Medway & Wells (1976), Moksnes (1987, 1988), Onnen (1985), Paz (1987), Perennou *et al.* (1994), Phillips (1978), Piersma (1986b), Rands *et al.* (1987), Ripley (1982), Roberts, T.J. (1991), Robiller (1983), Rogacheva (1992), Scott (1989), Shirihai (1996), Short *et al.* (1990), Smythies (1986), Southern & Lewis (1938), Tomkovich (1988b), Tomkovich & Fokin (1983, 1984), Urban *et al.* (1986), Velasco (1992a), Williams, M.D. (1986).

69. Long-toed Stint

Calidris subminuta

French: Bécasseau à longs doigts **Spanish**: Correlimos Dedilargo
German: Langzehen-Strandläufer

Taxonomy. *Tringa subminuta* Middendorff, 1853, Stanovoye Mountains, Russia.
Formerly placed in genus *Erolia*. Forms superspecies with *C. minutilla*, with which in past considered conspecific. Monotypic.

Distribution. Disjunct populations from forest zone of SW Siberia to S tundra of Koryak Mts; also Commander Is and N Kuril Is. Winters from E India and Indochina to Taiwan, and S through Philippines and Indonesia to W & SE Australia.

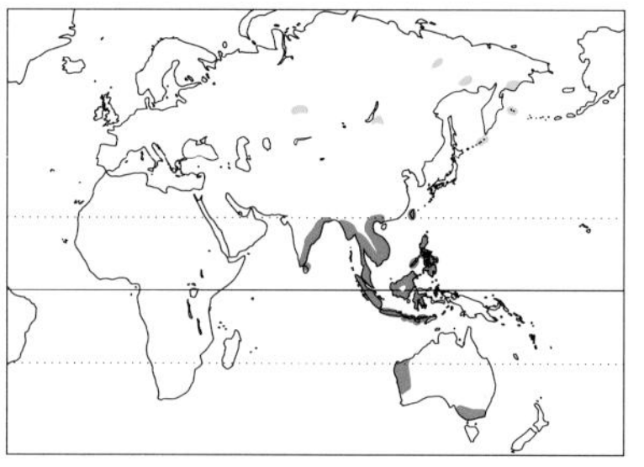

Descriptive notes. 13-16 cm, 20-37 g, wingspan 26-31 cm. Small, slim stint with relatively long neck, legs and toes; short bill; rufous crown and ear-coverts, with dark streaks; prominent whitish supercilium and narrow dark loral stripe; nape pale rufous and neck, flanks and rufous-tinged breast finely streaked dark brown; upperpart feathers have dark brown centres and rufous and pale buff fringes. Female averages slightly larger. Non-breeding adult has upperpart feathers with black-brown centres and grey edges; crown, neck and ear-coverts grey, finely streaked; breast suffused grey-brown with faint streaks on sides and flanks. Juvenile similar to breeding adult but streaking on breast finer, and more contrasting pattern on mantle and scapulars; rufous crown contrasts with white supercilium; head, neck and breast streaked.

Habitat. Breeds in wide variety of subarctic and boreal open habitats, often in open bogs or mountain tundra in taiga zone. In non-breeding season prefers inland wetlands, especially rice fields; also muddy or vegetated edges of coastal and sub-coastal shallow freshwater and brackish wetlands, sewage farms, salt-works and salt-marshes; less frequent on intertidal flats. Sometimes hides in depressions in mud.

Food and Feeding. Diet poorly known, but includes insects (carabid beetles), small gastropod molluscs, crustaceans and seeds. Usually feeds among vegetation at water's edge; often pecks prey items from mud or water surface; pecks more, probes less than *C. minutilla*. Feeds singly or in small flocks; possibly defends feeding territory in non-breeding period.

Breeding. Nests early Jun to Jul. Probably monogamous. In scattered single pairs, often very close together. High degree of site fidelity. Nest is shallow depression filled with leaves, well hidden. 4 eggs, sometimes 3; both parents incubate, only male tends brood. No further information available.

Movements. Migratory. Probably two main routes, which converge in China: down E coast of Asia, through Ussuriland, Manchuria, Japan and Korea; and overland on broad front through continental Asia, where locally abundant in Tuva; some indications of weak migration through Middle East. In Australia movements dispersive, between temporary wetlands. Most birds winter in SE Asia and Philippines; very few in Australia, though small numbers visit every year and their moult pattern suggests that they are different to SE Asian birds. S passage of adults, females first, starts early Jul and peaks Aug-Sept; N migration Apr-May. Only mildly gregarious, and seldom in large flocks.

Status and Conservation. Not globally threatened. Total wintering population probably 25,000-100,000 birds. Regular migrant to freshwater wetlands in Australia; annual maximum of 277 birds counted during austral summer shorebird counts in period 1981-1985. No specific threats identified, and species appears in no immediate danger, but poorly known.

Bibliography. Ali & Ripley (1980), Alström & Olsson (1989), Beaman (1994), Beehler *et al.* (1986), Blakers *et al.* (1984), Blomqvist (1983a), Brazil (1991), Coates (1985), Cramp & Simmons (1983), Curry (1984), Deignan (1945), Dickinson *et al.* (1991), Doherty (1991), Dunnett (1992), Étchécopar & Hüe (1978), Hirschfeld (1991), Hutton (1992), Jaensch (1988), Knystautas (1993), Lekagul & Round (1991), Leonovitch (1973), MacKinnon & Phillipps (1993), Marchant & Higgins (1996), van Marle & Voous (1988), Medway & Wells (1976), Miller *et al.* (1988), Myers *et al.* (1982), Perennou *et al.* (1994), Phillips (1978), Ripley (1982), Rogacheva (1992), Scott (1989), Short *et al.* (1990), Smythies (1981, 1986), Tomkovich (1980b, 1989, 1996), Urban *et al.* (1986), White & Bruce (1986), Williams, M.D. (1986).

70. Least Sandpiper

Calidris minutilla

French: Bécasseau minuscule **German**: Wiesenstrandläufer **Spanish**: Correlimos Menudillo
Other common names: American/Least Stint

Taxonomy. *Tringa minutilla* Vieillot, 1819, Halifax, Nova Scotia.
Formerly placed in genus *Erolia*. Forms superspecies with *C. subminuta*, with which in past considered conspecific. Monotypic.

Distribution. Alaska through NW & NC Canada to Quebec, Newfoundland and Nova Scotia. Winters from S USA through Central America and West Indies to N Chile and CE Brazil.

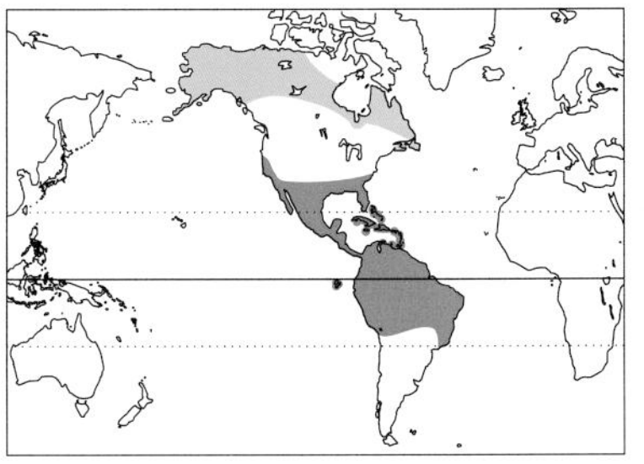

Descriptive notes. 13-15 cm; male 17-33 g, female 20-33 g. Smallest of all shorebirds, with needle-like bill; dark brown upperparts with chestnut and grey fringes; head dark with indistinct supercilium. Differs from *C. subminuta* by more compact build, shorter legs and slightly bill length; darker lores; breast washed brown, with dense streaking; darker, more uniform upperparts. Female averages slightly larger, especially in longer bill. Non-breeding adult has brown-grey upperparts with paler fringes; throat and breast washed and streaked grey brown. Juvenile has rufous cap and black-brown upperparts with chestnut and whitish fringes, forming thin "V" on mantle; breast suffused buff-grey with streaking at sides.

Habitat. Breeds from subarctic tundra to far N boreal forest, farther S than other Nearctic *Calidris*; on treeless vegetated bogs with nearby muddy areas, near fresh and brackish ponds, pools, lakes and brackish lagoons with vegetated sand dunes; tussock-heath ridges and valley bottoms; ditches near intertidal cobble and mudflats. During migration, on muddy margins of inland lakes, ponds, sloughs, riverbanks, ditches, bogs and marshes, and intertidal mudflats, mainly at upper edges of small creeks; also wet meadows and flooded fields; on coast, roosts in adjacent salt-marshes and wet pastures. In winter quarters, on muddy parts of similar variety of inland and coastal wetlands.

Food and Feeding. Benthic and terrestrial invertebrates smaller than 6 mm, such as small amphipods, particularly *Corophium*, gastropods, isopods, ostracods, adults, larvae and pupae of Diptera, beetles, worms and also eggs of horseshoe crabs (*Limulus polyphemus*). Probes in moist mud or pecks from surface; during brood-rearing, also in drier habitats; pecking rates very high. During non-breeding season, occurs in compact to scattered flocks; some may defend feeding territories. Diurnal and nocturnal.

Breeding. Laying mid-May to early Jun. Monogamous, for one season or longer. Territorial, with maximum reported density of 90 pairs in 111 ha; birds feed outside territory; males very faithful to sites; at least some natal philopatry. Nests in short grass or sedge on damp ground; where very wet, on drier rise or hummock; nest is depression in ground cover, sparsely lined with bits of dead vegetation. 4 eggs, laid at intervals of c. 30 hours; single brood; replacement clutches laid; incubation 19·5-23 days (starting with 4th egg), by both parents, but females briefer and mainly in evening; chick black and yellowish to golden or chocolate brown above with white-tipped down on middle of back, while hind crown and nape orange-buff mottled black, underparts whitish and face, neck and breast whitish with buff or brown tinge; both parents tend young; female deserts brood 1-2 weeks before male; fledging 14-20 days; young independent few days later. 11-40% of clutches predated, and also subject to trampling by cattle; 86-93% of eggs in successful clutches hatch; hatchling mortality 38-67%. Significant predation by falcons outside breeding season. Age of first breeding 1 year, possibly later in N. Oldest ringed bird 17 years old.

Movements. Migratory. Migrates in broad front over interior North America to S USA, Greater Antilles, Gulf of Mexico and NW South America; E population crosses Atlantic Ocean from NE North America to Lesser Antilles and NE South America, but returns N through S North America or up coast; part of W population migrates down Pacific coast to NW South America. Some fidelity to wintering and staging sites. Adults precede juveniles during S migration, departing respectively from late Jun and mid-Jul, and adult females precede males; arrives N wintering grounds late Jun to Jul, in Surinam mostly Aug but juveniles mid-Aug to Oct; in California most birds disperse S in Nov. Migrates N across USA and Canada in May, up E USA coast mid-Apr to mid-May, 1-2 weeks earlier on W coast; males arrive on breeding grounds c. 7 days earlier than females. Migrates in flocks of 10's to 100's.

Status and Conservation. Not globally threatened. Total population over 100,000 birds; Canadian breeding population estimated at 50,000-100,000 birds. Numbers apparently increased after hunting stopped in early 20th century. No significant trend in numbers staging on Atlantic coast in period 1972-1983. Numbers migrating through E Canada declined between 1974 and 1991, especially during late 1970's perhaps due to cold breeding seasons. Species is difficult to count, due to scattered distribution in wintering areas and mixing with other small *Calidris* species. Not threatened at breeding areas, but wetlands used for wintering and staging are threatened with destruction and irrigation.

Bibliography. Amos (1991), Armstrong (1983), Baker, M.C. (1977), Baker, M.C. & Baker (1973), Baldassarre & Fischer (1984), Bent (1927-1929), Biaggi (1983), Blake (1977), Blomqvist (1983a), Brooks (1967), Butler & Kaiser (1995), Colwell & Landrum (1993), Cooper, J.M. (1993, 1994), Cooper, J.M. & Miller (1992), Cramp & Simmons (1983), Doherty (1991), Fjeldså & Krabbe (1990), Gratto *et al*. (1984), Haverschmidt (1968), Haverschmidt & Mees (1995), Hayes (1995), Hilty & Brown (1986), Howell & Webb (1995a), Jehl (1970), Jonsson & Grant (1984), Matthiessen (1994), Meyer de Schauensee & Phelps (1978), Miller (1977, 1979a, 1979b, 1983a, 1983b, 1985, 1986), Monroe (1968), Page (1974b), Page & Bradstreet (1968), Page & Salvadori (1969), Page & Whiteacre (1975), Ridgely & Gwynne (1989), Root (1988), Scott & Carbonell (1986), Sick (1985c, 1993), Slud (1964), Snyder (1966), Spaans (1976), Stiles & Skutch (1989), Tostain *et al*. (1992), Wetmore (1965), Yarbrough (1970).

71. White-rumped Sandpiper

Calidris fuscicollis

French: Bécasseau à croupion blanc **Spanish**: Correlimos Culiblanco
German: Weißbürzel-Strandläufer
Other common names: Bonaparte's Sandpiper

Taxonomy. *Tringa fuscicollis* Vieillot, 1819, Paraguay.
Formerly placed in genus *Erolia*. Monotypic.

Distribution. NE Alaska and N Canada E to S Baffin I. Winters in SE South America, from CE Brazil to Tierra del Fuego.

Descriptive notes. 15-18 cm; 30-60 g; wingspan 36-38 cm. White uppertail-coverts contrast with dark rump and tail; yellow base to lower mandible; crown, cheeks, mantle and scapulars centred dark brown and edged rufous pink and grey; wing-coverts paler; sides of neck, breast and flanks spotted and streaked brown; at rest, wings project beyond tail tip. Male has inflatable throat; female averages slightly larger, with smaller white throat. Non-breeding adult has head and upperparts plain ashy brown with faint streaks and paler fringes; breast pale ashy brown with faint dark streaks. Juvenile like breeding adult, but upperparts more brightly coloured, and with more white tips; breast streaked and washed buff-grey.

Habitat. Breeds in low areas on marshy, hummocky tundra, well vegetated with mosses, grasses, sedges or shrubs. On migration in N South America, occurs on sea beaches, riverbanks, open fields and marshes. On wintering grounds, on intertidal mudflats, salt-marshes, flood fields, marshes, ponds and lagoons.

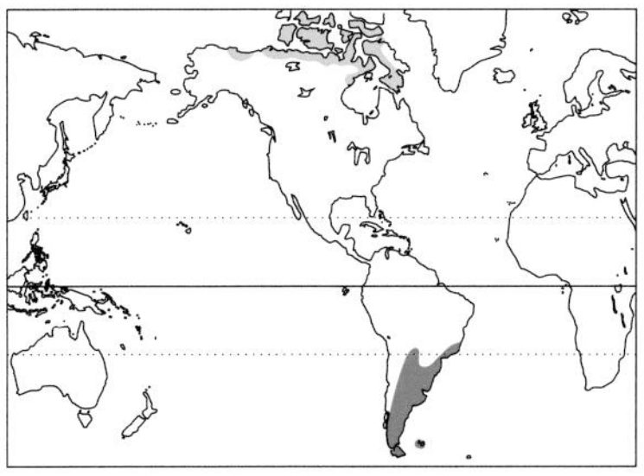

Food and Feeding. Invertebrates, including adult and larval insects, such as grasshoppers, beetles and craneflies, also spiders, small molluscs, crustaceans, leeches, polychaete worms and earthworms; some seeds. On breeding grounds, probes in moss and wet vegetation; during non-breeding season probes in muddy substrates at edge of water and picks prey from surface. May defend feeding territories on wintering grounds.

Breeding. Laying early to mid-Jun. Polygynous. Solitary; territory vigorously defended by male during egg-laying; birds often foraging outside territory; highest local density c. 1 bird/ha; nests usually widely spaced, but sometimes as close as 12 m. Male extends highly inflatable throat while performing aerial display. Nests near ponds, lakes or streams; well hidden, shallow scrape with lining of willow leaves and bits of moss and lichens. 4 eggs; females single-brooded, some males multiple-brooded; replacement clutches not reported; incubation 22 days (1 observation); male deserts female soon after egg-laying; chick mottled grey-brown or tawny and black above with white spots, face, throat and breast buffish, nape buff, grey and dusky, underparts greyish white; fledging 16-17 days. Nest predation by Arctic Skuas (*Stercorarius parasiticus*), other avian predators and Arctic foxes (*Alopex lagopus*); skuas also take young on Canadian coast in autumn. Age of first breeding presumably 1 year.

Movements. Migratory. Migrates in few, non-stop jumps of up to 4000 km; flies from NE North America over W Atlantic directly to N South America, whence continues with short hops down coast, then moving inland at mouth of R Amazon, reaching wintering grounds 1 month later; shows some degree of site fidelity. During N migration flies across Central America, Caribbean and inland North America, staging in Great Plains; little information on other staging areas. Departs from winter quarters Mar to mid-Apr, arriving N South America late Apr to mid-May, and on breeding grounds early Jun. Leaves breeding grounds up to early Aug; arrives at Canadian coast Aug to early Sept, N South America late Aug, and S Brazil and Argentina mid-Nov to Dec.

Status and Conservation. Not globally threatened. Population 50,000-100,000 birds, with 25,000 on Banks I (1959), 15,000 on Prince of Wales I and adjacent islands (1961), only rather irregularly in N Alaska; up to 30,000-40,000 birds at Decatur (Alabama) and Cheyenne Bottoms (Kansas) in spring. In past, large numbers were shot for human consumption. Preservation of wetlands in Great Plains and in Latin America is critical to secure areas of migratory fattening along migration route, but many of these areas are drying out due to irrigation for agricultural purposes.

Bibliography. Alström (1985, 1987), Alström *et al*. (1989), Armstrong (1983), Barthel (1989), Belton (1984), Beltzer (1986a, 1991), Bent (1927-1929), Biaggi (1983), Blake (1977), Blomqvist (1983a), de Bruin & Dietzen (1995), Cartar & Montgomerie (1985, 1987), Contreras *et al*. (1990), Cramp & Simmons (1983), Drury (1961), Dufourny & Lebailly (1991), Fjeldså & Krabbe (1990), Godfrey (1986), Harrington *et al*. (1991), Haverschmidt (1968), Haverschmidt & Mees (1995), Hayes (1995), Hayes & Fox (1991), Hilty & Brown (1986), Holmes & Pitelka (1962), Howell & Webb (1995a), Humphrey *et al*. (1970), Johnson (1965b), Maisonneuve *et al*. (1990), Matthiessen (1994), McCaffery (1983), Meyer de Schauensee & Phelps (1978), Miller (1983c), Miller *et al*. (1988), Monroe (1968), Myers & Myers (1979), Parmelee (1992), Parmelee, Greiner & Graul (1968), Parmelee, Schwilling & Stephens (1969), Parmelee, Stephens & Schmidt (1967), de la Peña (1992), Scott & Carbonell (1986), Sick (1985c, 1993), Skagen & Knopf (1994), Skagen *et al*. (1993), Snyder (1966), Spaans (1978), Stotz *et al*. (1992), Thomas, B.T. (1987), Tostain *et al*. (1992), Urban *et al*. (1986), Weber (1989), Wetmore (1965).

72. Baird's Sandpiper

Calidris bairdii

French: Bécasseau de Baird **German**: Bairdstrandläufer **Spanish**: Correlimos de Baird

Taxonomy. *Actodromus Bairdii* Coues, 1861, Great Slave Lake, Canada.
Formerly placed in genus *Erolia* or alternatively in *Pisobia*. Monotypic.

Distribution. Wrangel I and Chukotskiy Peninsula E across N Alaska and N Canada to Ellesmere I, N Baffin I and NW Greenland. Winters in W & S South America.

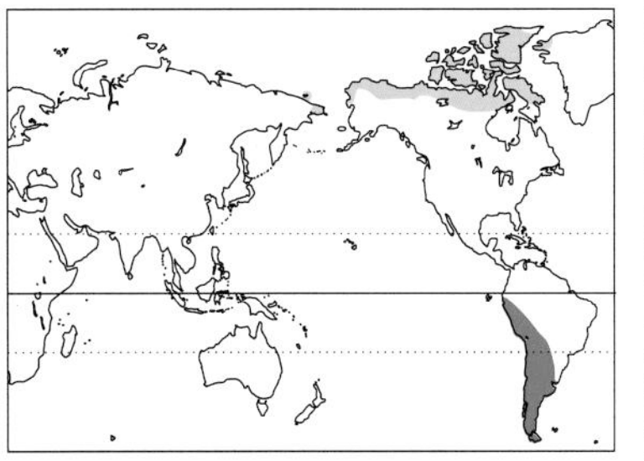

Descriptive notes. 14-17 cm; 32-63 g; wingspan 36-40 cm. Small sandpiper with long wings and short legs; black-brown crown, nape, mantle and scapulars with broad buff and brown fringes; ear-coverts and breast buff with brown streaks; lower back, rump and uppertail dark; at rest, wings project beyond tail. Very similar to *C. fuscicollis*, but complete breast band sharply cut off from white underparts; thin, pointed bill all dark; uppertail-coverts dark, with only narrow white edges. Female averages slightly larger. Non-breeding adult has more subdued coloration, becoming mainly dull greyish brown above. Juvenile like breeding adult, but with narrower, white fringes.

Habitat. Low mountain tops, river terraces and coastal barren areas and bluffs in high Arctic tundra; dry, high-lying lichen tundra and stony ridges. On migration and in winter, inland wetlands to coastal habitats, including grassland, ditches, irrigated or rain-soaked fields, pools in desert, sand dunes; occasionally in upper littoral zone of estuaries, mudflats and beaches; usually on higher parts of shore or dry fringes of wetland sites, often among vegetation. Locally abundant staging and in winter in high Andes along alpine lakes and on grasslands at altitudes of 2500-4700 m.

Food and Feeding. During breeding, mainly insects, such as chironomid and cranefly larvae and adults, and beetles; also spiders. On migration, adult and larval beetles, larval Diptera. Feeding action brisk; pecks up prey with quick bill jabs, less frequently probes. Less gregarious than most other calidrines; in winter, in flocks of 20-30 birds; some individuals defend feeding territory.

Breeding. Laying Jun. Monogamous. Density 5-8 pairs/km², up to 18 pairs/km² (Nearctic), c. 0·2 pairs/km² (Chukotskiy Peninsula). Nest is relatively exposed; simple, shallow depression in bare ground, or amid short vegetation, filled with bits of lichens or other vegetation. 4 eggs, sometimes 3, with laying interval of 1 day; incubation 19-21 days, by both parents; chick tawny above with bold black bands and clear rows of white down tips, face, throat and underparts white; both parents tend chicks, but female often leaves earlier, and females from late nest may even leave at or prior to hatching; fledging 19-20 days.

Movements. Migratory. Many migrate inland, across North American prairies, Rockies and N Andes, often staging at high altitude lakes. Funnel through Canada W of Hudson Bay, then stopover in prairies of S Canada and N USA, especially Cheyenne Bottoms (Kansas), whereafter non-stop journey to Andes by mid-Aug, bypassing Central America off W coast. Adults depart early Jul, females slightly preceding males; juveniles migrate later from breeding grounds, from late Jul, in more leisurely fashion, and over broader front, from Pacific states to Atlantic; unlike adults, many juveniles move into SW USA; juveniles reach Patagonia mainly early Oct. N migration largely along same route.

Status and Conservation. Not globally threatened. Total population estimated at 50,000-100,000 birds, and thought to be relatively stable; remote, high latitude breeding grounds probably relatively secure at present, as is much of winter habitat. Cheyenne Bottoms is a very important staging site during northward migration.

Bibliography. Alström (1985, 1987), Alström *et al.* (1989), Andersson & Breife (1986), Armstrong (1983), Baldassarre & Fischer (1984), Bent (1927-1929), Blake (1977), Blomqvist (1983a), Brazil (1991), Contreras & Contreras (1994), Contreras *et al.* (1990), Cramp & Simmons (1983), Dixon (1917), Dott (1985), Drury (1961), Finch (1986b), Fjeldså & Krabbe (1990), Hayes (1995), Hilty & Brown (1986), Holmes & Pitelka (1968), Howell & Webb (1995a), Jehl (1979), Johnson (1965b), Knystautas (1993), Matthiessen (1994), Meyer de Schauensee & Phelps (1978), Miller *et al.* (1988), Murphy (1991), Myers *et al.* (1982), Norton (1972), Page (1978), Parmelee *et al.* (1967), Paulson (1983), de la Peña (1992), Prainsson (1995), Reid & Montgomerie (1985), Schiefer & Hodges (1987), Scott & Carbonell (1986), Sick (1985c, 1993), Slud (1964), Smith, F.T.H. (1987), Snell (1988), Stiles & Skutch (1989), Tomkovich (1985b, 1996), Urban *et al.* (1986), Wetmore (1965).

73. Pectoral Sandpiper
Calidris melanotos

French: Bécasseau à poitrine cendrée **Spanish**: Correlimos Pectoral
German: Graubrust-Strandläufer

Taxonomy. *Tringa melanotos* Vieillot, 1819, Paraguay.
Formerly placed in genus *Erolia*. Recently discovered Cox's Sandpiper "*C. paramelanotos*" shown to be hybrid between *C. ferruginea* and, most probably, present species (see page 446). Monotypic.

Distribution. Taymyr E through Chukotskiy Peninsula to W & N Alaska, NC Canada and W Hudson Bay; recent records from Yamal Peninsula, NW Siberia. Winters from S Bolivia, Paraguay and N Argentina to S Argentina; much smaller population in SE Australia, Tasmania and New Zealand.

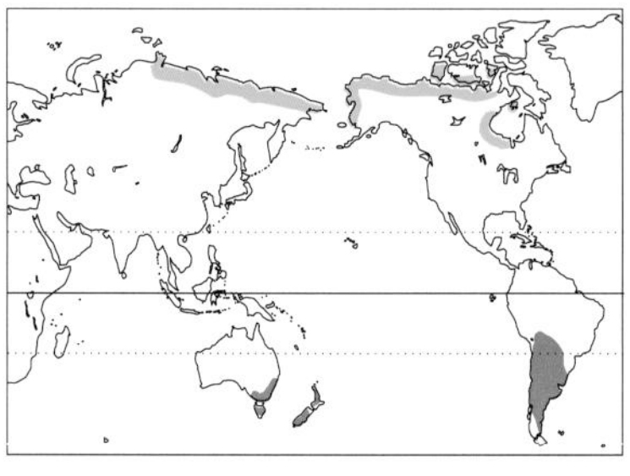

Descriptive notes. 19-23 cm; male 45-126 g, female 31-97 g; wingspan 37-45 cm. Medium-sized sandpiper with heavily streaked buff breast sharply demarcated from white belly; black-brown mantle and scapulars with buff and chestnut fringes and whitish tips, wing-coverts paler; crown black-brown; crown, neck, face, breast and upper flanks streaked; legs yellow to greenish or brownish. Female smaller, with paler breast. Non-breeding adult duller. Juvenile like breeding adult, but upperparts have paler, narrower fringes, producing clear "V" across mantle and scapulars; finer streaking on breast.

Habitat. Breeds on Arctic tundra, usually in wet and well vegetated habitats, such as bog and tundra complexes with vegetation of moss or *Eriophorum*, bogs of *Polygonum*, and moss-lichen tundra lining water bodies. Outside breeding season, in variety of freshwater and brackish wetlands, both coastal and inland, including upland plateaux and *puna* zone at 3500-4500 m, in salt-marshes, swamps, lakes, floodplains, wet grasslands, sewage farms, commercial salt-works, coastal lagoons and bays. Usually feeds on drier, vegetated patches away from water's edge.

Food and Feeding. In breeding area, variety of insects, especially larvae and adults of craneflies, chironomids and Diptera; also beetles; spiders. On migration, often grasshoppers and crickets; diet outside breeding range includes annelids, molluscs, crustaceans, spiders, insects, algae and seeds. Feeding action leisurely, with steady walking; very similar to that of *C. acuminata*, combined pecking with rapid shallow probing. Often feeds in pairs or small flocks; some defend feeding territory.

Breeding. Lays Jun-Jul. Monogamous, sometimes polygamous; males mate several times within territory, while females may visit territories of other males. Densities 0·5-6 birds/km² (Siberia) and over 10 nests/km² (Alaska), but numbers may vary considerably between years. Nest-site well drained and covered by sedges and grasses. Male guards mate, does not incubate, and often leaves area before hatching, to gather in pre-migratory flocks, although some males participate in brood defence. 4 eggs; incubation 21-23 days; fledging c. 3 weeks.

Movements. Siberian and North American birds migrate to South America, down Atlantic and Pacific coasts and through highlands of Colombia and Ecuador, and lakes in W Amazonia. Small fraction of Siberian population winters in Australasia and passes through Magadan, Commander Is, Kuril Is, Sakhalin, Ussuriland, Japan and Korea; on SE Asian coast, not recorded farther S than China, Taiwan and Hong Kong. Males start S migration late Jun; females to early Aug; juveniles migrate over broader range of North America early Aug and Oct. N migration Mar to early Jun, farther W via interior North America, but avoiding W USA; high numbers stage at Cheyenne Bottoms (Kansas). Regular on passage on Hawaiian, Phoenix and Line Is. Many 1st-years probably migrate N to breeding grounds in boreal spring.

Status and Conservation. Not globally threatened. Population spending boreal winter in South America estimated at 25,000-100,000 birds; no estimate available for Australasian wintering population. Extensive range and moderately high breeding densities attained in favorable habitats suggest that total population must be substantial. Possible westward expansion of breeding range recently noted, with birds recorded breeding on Yamal Peninsula.

Bibliography. Amos (1991), Armstrong (1983), Beehler *et al.* (1986), Beel (1991), Belton (1984), Bent (1927-1929), Biaggi (1983), Blake (1977), Blomqvist (1983a), Brazil (1991), Brooks (1967), Chambers (1989), Coates (1985), Contreras *et al.* (1990), Cramp & Simmons (1983), Eckert (1967), Fjeldså & Krabbe (1990), Flint & Tomkovich (1982), Garrod (1991), Hamilton (1959), Haverschmidt (1968), Haverschmidt & Mees (1995), Hayes (1995), Hilty & Brown (1986), Holmes & Pitelka (1968), Howell & Webb (1995a), Jaensch (1988), Johnson (1965b), Kaufman (1987), Kieser & Smith (1982), Kistchinski (1974), Knystautas (1993), Marchant & Higgins (1996), Matthiessen (1994), Meyer de Schauensee & Phelps (1978), Miller *et al.* (1988), Monroe (1968), Myers (1982), Norton (1972), de la Peña (1992), Pitelka (1959), Ridgely & Gwynne (1989), Rogacheva (1992), Scott (1989), Scott & Carbonell (1986), Shirihai (1996), Sick (1985c, 1993), Slud (1964), Snyder (1966), Stiles & Skutch (1989), Stotz *et al.* (1992), Taylor, P.B. (1980b), Tostain *et al.* (1992), Urban *et al.* (1986), Veling (1977), Wetmore (1965).

74. Sharp-tailed Sandpiper
Calidris acuminata

French: Bécasseau à queue pointue **Spanish**: Correlimos Acuminado
German: Spitzschwanz-Strandläufer
Other common names: Siberian Pectoral Sandpiper

Taxonomy. *Totanus acuminatus* Horsfield, 1821, Java.
Formerly placed in genus *Erolia*. Cooper's Sandpiper "*C. (Pisobia) cooperi*" was probably hybrid between *C. ferruginea* and present species (see page 446). Monotypic.

Distribution. NC & NE Siberia from Lena Delta to R Kolyma. Winters from New Guinea through Melanesia to New Caledonia and Tonga, and S to Australia and New Zealand.

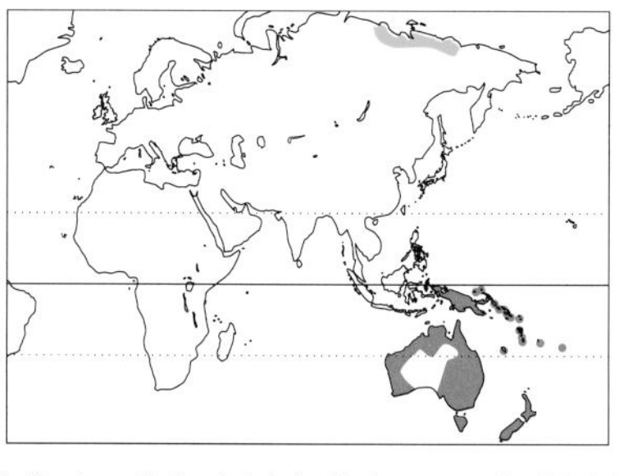

Descriptive notes. 17-22 cm; male 53-114 g, female 39-105 g; wingspan 36-43 cm. Medium-sized sandpiper with rufous cap; dark brown upperparts with chestnut and whitish buff fringes; neck and breast heavily streaked; lower breast, upper belly and flanks have heavy blackish chevrons; legs yellowish to greenish or brownish. Differs from *C. melanotos* by lack of sharp demarcation of breast from belly; more distinct ginger cap; bolder white supercilium and prominent eye-ring. Female smaller, especially with shorter wing. Non-breeding adult lacks warm coloration; breast greyish with faint streaks, indistinctly demarcated from white belly. Juvenile has bright buff, chestnut and whitish fringes on upperparts, rufous crown and conspicuous white supercilium; breast bright buff, sometimes with faint streaks forming narrow gorget; flanks washed buff.

Habitat. Tundra of low Arctic and subarctic, especially damp hillock tundra and moss-sedge bogs with drier, shrub-covered hummocks; more specialized in habitat than *C. melanotos*. During non-breeding season, wide variety of coastal and inland wetlands (many ephemeral), including coastal salt-marshes, intertidal mudflats, shallow brackish lagoons, flooded grassland, river mouths; often feeds amongst vegetation, on drier margins.

Food and Feeding. Diet highly variable, including insects and their larvae, bivalves, snails, crustaceans, polychaete worms and seeds. Feeds at water's edge; uses combined pecking and jabbing with rapid, shallow probing. Often in large flocks of 100's to 1000's, fragmented into scattered groups for feeding.

Breeding. Laying early Jun. Polygynous or promiscuous. Up to 20 birds/km². Large breast sac important in flight display, producing dry, crackling warble unlike any other calidrine vocalization. Nest well hidden, shallow depression filled with grass and leaves. 4 eggs, sometimes 3; single brood; only female incubates and cares for young; males leave during incubation period. Oldest ringed bird at least 5 years, 9 months.

Movements. Migratory. Leaves breeding grounds Jul-Sept. Main flyway via Transbaikalia, E of L Baikal, with smaller numbers in broad front from E Kazakhstan to Sea of Okhotsk; continues over E Mongolia and China, including Manchuria, to Japan, Korea, Philippines and New Guinea; probably overflies New Guinea during N migration. Juveniles on passage also occur regularly down Pacific coast and even into Alaska. Arrival in Australia Aug-Nov, and 25,000 birds arrived in single night, mid-Sept 1984; birds leave S Australia early, mid-Feb to early Mar, undertaking rather prolonged N migration to breeding grounds, with series of short flights. Movements within Australia seem to be dispersive, with birds leaving when wetlands dry. Most of population migrates to Australia, mainly SE; few 1st-year birds spend N summer in winter quarters.

Status and Conservation. Not globally threatened. Total population numbers c. 166,000 birds. Although using a variety of wetlands, and therefore probably relatively able to adapt to changes in wetlands brought about by human activities, most of world population winters in SE Australia, where human population density is high; therefore, suitable management of coastal and inland wetlands in this region is essential for survival of species. Most important wintering sites are Coorong (South Australia), and area of Port Hedland Saltworks, Eighty Mile Beach and Anna Plains wetlands (Western Australia).

Bibliography. Ali & Ripley (1980), Ameels *et al.* (1989), Armstrong (1983), Beehler *et al.* (1986), Bekaert (1991), Blakers *et al.* (1984), Blomqvist (1983a), Brazil (1991), Bregulla (1992), Britton, D. (1980), Catley (1984), Chambers (1989), Coates (1985), Contreras (1988), Cramp & Simmons (1983), Dann (1983), Dementiev & Gladkov (1951b), Dennison (1979), Dickinson *et al.* (1991), Étchécopar & Hüe (1978), Flint & Kistchinski (1973), Flint & Tomkovich (1982), Fröbel (1982), Granberg (1978), Holyoak & Thibault (1984), Kaufman (1987), Kent (1991), Knystautas (1993), Kozlova (1966), Lane & Davies (1987), Lowe (1976), MacKinnon & Phillipps (1993), Mantlik (1986), Marchant & Higgins (1996), Myers *et al.* (1982), Perennou *et al.* (1994), Petersen (1989), Rogacheva (1992), Rosenband (1982), Scott (1989), Starks & Lane (1987), Tomkovich (1982c), Veling (1977), Watkins (1993), Webb & Conry (1979), White & Bruce (1986), Willi (1983), Williams, M.D. (1986), Wren (1988).

75. Curlew Sandpiper
Calidris ferruginea

French: Bécasseau cocorli **German**: Sichelstrandläufer **Spanish**: Correlimos Zarapitín

Taxonomy. *Tringa Ferrugineus* Pontoppidan, 1763, Christiansø Islands, Denmark.
Formerly placed in genus *Erolia*. Species name *testacea* formerly used, but pre-dated by *ferruginea*. Recently discovered Cox's Sandpiper "*C. paramelanotos*" shown to be hybrid between present species and, most probably, *C. melanotos*; Cooper's Sandpiper "*C. (Pisobia) cooperi*" was probably hybrid between present species and *C. acuminata* (see page 446). Monotypic.

Distribution. Arctic Siberia from Yamal Peninsula to Kolyuchinskaya Gulf (N Chukotskiy Peninsula). Winters from sub-Saharan Africa through S Asia to Australasia.

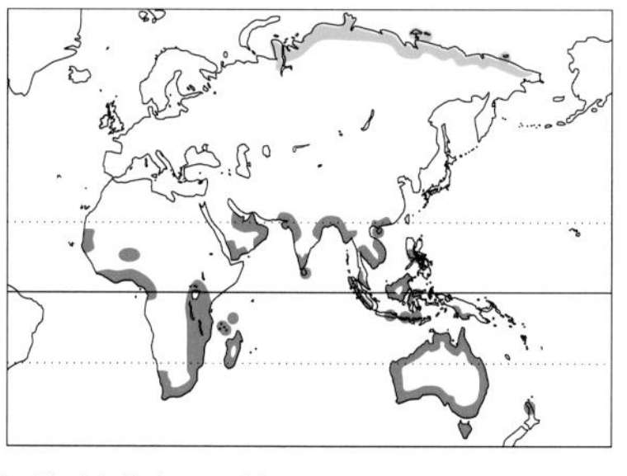

Descriptive notes. 18-23 cm; 44-117 g; wingspan 38-41 cm. Medium-sized sandpiper with longish neck and legs and long, decurved bill; head, neck and all underparts rusty rufous to deep chestnut-red, with dark streaks on crown; mantle and scapulars dark brown with chestnut and whitish fringes; wing-coverts greyer. Female normally has longer bill; somewhat paler, with greater tendency to have white barring on underparts. Non-breeding adult plain grey above, white below; contrasting white supercilium; sides of breast washed grey. Juvenile like non-breeding adult, but upperparts brownish with whitish fringes; breast washed buff with little streaking.

Habitat. Breeds on lowlands of high Arctic, along coast and on islands in Arctic Ocean, on open tundra with marshy depressions and pools. In winter, chiefly on coast, on muddy or sandy surface of tidal flats, coastal lagoons, estuaries and salt-marshes; also inland, at muddy edges of marshes, large rivers, lakes, salt-pans, irrigation schemes and flooded areas.

Food and Feeding. On breeding grounds, mainly insects, including adults, pupae and larvae, especially of Diptera and beetles; also bugs and leeches. Feeds by pecking and probing in wet marsh and peat. Outside breeding season, mainly polychaete worms, molluscs, crustaceans, such as amphipods, shrimps and copepods, and sometimes insects; occasionally seeds. Picks prey from mud or sand surface or probes in mud, regularly wading in shallow water; worms usually washed before being eaten. Diurnal and nocturnal. Gregarious outside breeding season, in flocks of up to several thousand.
Breeding. Nests Jun-Jul. Density 2·3 nests/km², but may exceed 50 birds/km²; nests sometimes 200-300 m apart. Nest on margins of marshes and pools, on slopes of hummocky tundra or dry patches in *Polygonum* tundra. Average clutch size 3·8, with laying interval of 1 day; incubation 19-20 days, by female only; chick-care by female; fledging 14-16 days. Breeding success highly dependent on lemming (*Lemmus sibiricus*, *Dicrostonyx torquatus*) abundance, with considerable predation by Arctic foxes (*Alopex lagopus*) during low lemming years, which occur once every 3-4 years. Age of first breeding 1 year or older. Oldest ringed bird at least 11 years.
Movements. Migratory. In W Palearctic three major routes: to White Sea, down W European coasts to W Africa; across E Europe via Black Sea and Tunisia to W Africa, following N African coast or flying via Mali; and via Black and Caspian Seas and across Middle East and Rift Valley lakes to E & S Africa. Route through W Europe little used during N migration; instead, many fly via Tunisia and Sivash (N Crimea); birds passing S through Sivash winter in E , C & S Africa and probably migrate N via Caspian Sea. Other routes are across Siberia to India, where some continue through SE Asia to Australia, but many winter in S India and Sri Lanka; also overland to E Asia and via Chinese coast to Australia, a route used more on N migration. Migrates long distances non-stop. Males show high degree of site faithfulness. During autumn migration adults precede juveniles and adult males depart early Jul, 3-4 weeks before females; more males than females migrate farther S. On S migration, crosses Europe in Jul, reaching Africa from mid-Jul in N and mainly Sept in S; arrives Australia late Aug to early Sept; juveniles follow 4-6 weeks later. N migration late Apr to May; arrives on breeding grounds from early Jun. Many 1st-year birds remain on wintering grounds while other non-breeding birds apparently remain just S of breeding grounds, in C Siberia.
Status and Conservation. Not globally threatened. Population wintering in W Africa and SW Europe estimated at 436,000 birds, of which 340,000 in Guinea-Bissau, but possibly up to 50,000 more in Guinea; E Africa and SW Asia 310,000, and species is typically most abundant wader on E African coast, with 90,000-120,000 in Tanzania; SC Asia at least 100,000 birds, with high numbers in SE India and Sri Lanka; E & SE Asia 60,000; and Australia 188,000. Australasian population possibly declining. Species has bred in N Alaska, apparently only irregularly, between 1962 and 1972.
Bibliography. Ali & Ripley (1980), Armstrong (1983), Atkinson *et al*. (1981b), Barter (1984a, 1985, 1986a, 1986b, 1987b), Beehler *et al*. (1986), Benson & Benson (1975), Blakers *et al*. (1984), Blomqvist (1983a), Blomqvist *et al*. (1987), Brazil (1991), Bregnballe *et al*. (1990), Chambers (1989), Coates (1985), Cramp & Simmons (1983), Dean (1977b), Dickinson *et al*. (1991), Dowsett & Forbes-Watson (1993), Elgood *et al*. (1994), Elliott *et al*. (1976), Étchécopar & Hüe (1964, 1978), Evans (1994), Frodin *et al*. (1994), Ginn *et al*. (1989), Goodman *et al*. (1989), Gore (1990), Grimes (1987), Gromadzka (1985a), Harris, J.G.K. (1984), Hazevoet (1995), Hockey & Douie (1995), Holmes & Pitelka (1964), Hüe & Étchécopar (1970), Kalejta (1992, 1993), Kalejta & Hockey (1994), Knystautas (1993), Lane & Davies (1987), Langrand (1990), Lekagul & Round (1991), Lifjeld (1984), MacKinnon & Phillipps (1993), Mackworth-Praed & Grant (1957, 1962, 1970), Maclean (1993), Marchant & Higgins (1996), van Marle & Voous (1988), Medway & Wells (1976), Meltofte *et al*. (1994), Melville (1981), Miller *et al*. (1988), Milon *et al*. (1973), Minton (1983), Newman (1982a), Newman *et al*. (1985), Pakenham (1979), Parish & Wells (1984), Paton *et al*. (1982), Patrikeev (1995), Patterson (1989a), Pearson *et al*. (1970), Perennou *et al*. (1994), Phillips (1978), Pinto (1983), Pook (1992), Portenko (1959), Puttick (1978, 1979, 1980, 1981), Rands *et al*. (1987), Ripley (1982), Roberts, T.J. (1991), Rogacheva (1992), Roselaar (1979), Schekkerman & van Roomen (1995), Scott (1989), Shirihai (1996), Short *et al*. (1990), Smit & Piersma (1989), Smythies (1981, 1986), Stanley & Minton (1972), Starks & Lane (1987), Summers (1978), Summers & Waltner (1979), Thomas & Dartnall (1971a, 1971c), Tomkovich (1988a, 1995c), Tomkovich *et al*. (1994), Underhill (1987, 1990), Underhill *et al*. (1993), Urban *et al*. (1986), Watkins (1993), White & Bruce (1986), Williams, M.D. (1986), Wilson *et al*. (1980), Wymenga *et al*. (1990), Zwarts *et al*. (1990).

76. Purple Sandpiper

Calidris maritima

French: Bécasseau violet **German**: Meerstrandläufer **Spanish**: Correlimos Oscuro

Taxonomy. *Tringa Maritima* Brünnich, 1764, Christiansø Islands, off Bornholm, Denmark.
Formerly placed in genus *Erolia*. Forms superspecies with *C. ptilocnemis*, with which sometimes considered conspecific. Considerable geographical variation in size may warrant recognition of at least two subspecies. Monotypic.
Distribution. Arctic and subarctic, from NE Canada through Greenland, Iceland, Svalbard and Franz Josef Land to NW Siberia; also N temperate regions of Fenno-Scandia. Winters on coasts of E North America and NW Europe.

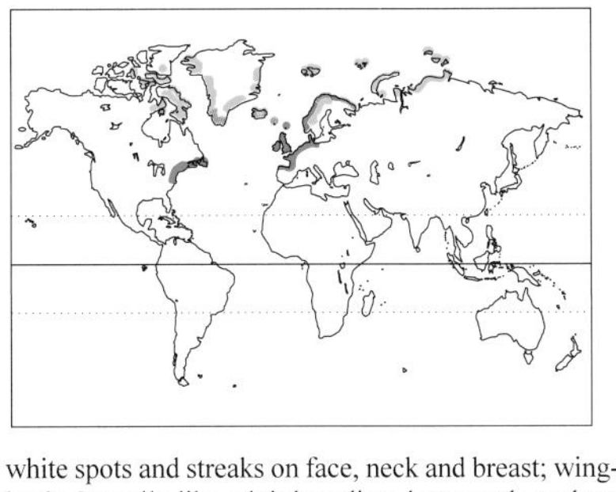

Descriptive notes. 20-22 cm; male 52-94 g, female 60-105 g; wingspan 42-26 cm. Medium-sized sandpiper with yellow legs and yellow base to bill; black-brown crown, mantle and scapulars with chestnut, pale buff and whitish fringes; whitish supercilium; neck, breast and flanks heavy streaked brown. Very similar to all but nominate race of *C. ptilocnemis*; normally has finer streaks on underparts, although some birds can have similar dark smudges; white wingbar normally fainter. Female averages slightly larger, especially with longer bill. Non-breeding adult has black-brown head and upperparts with pink or buff tips to crown, mantle and scapulars, and white spots and streaks on face, neck and breast; wing-coverts with whitish fringes; purplish gloss over back. Juvenile like adult breeding, but mantle and scapulars with pale chestnut fringes, wing-coverts and tertials with pale fringes; breast washed brown-grey and distinctly spotted.
Habitat. In high Arctic breeds from sea-level up to c. 300 m, in low Arctic and subarctic also on inland uplands, close to fringes of snow and ice; also on rocky islands and islets; on wet tundra with cover of mosses, and on barren, rocky upland tundra with patches of lichens and vegetation; shingle beaches, among boulders near streams; on Svalbard, before and after breeding, mainly on mudflats, shingle beaches and coastal lagoons. Outside breeding season, on wave-beaten tidal rocky shores with nearby high tide rocky roosting place; also on breakwaters, jetties and piers.
Food and Feeding. During breeding season, invertebrates, including insects such as springtails, adults, pupae and larvae of dipteran flies, ichneumons and aphids, spiders, gastropods and annelid worms; also plant material, such as leaves, buds, berries and seeds. During migration and winter, many gastropods, especially *Littorina* and bivalves, e.g. mussels (*Mytilus edulus*); also insects, including beetles and dipteran flies, small crustaceans (e.g. amphipods), annelid worms and some algae (e.g. *Enteromorpha*). Runs over seaweed and rocks in littoral zone, sometimes almost into waves, picking prey from between rocks, mussels or barnacles or turning over seaweed or debris; also picks from tundra surface and rarely probes in soil; swims well. Probably mainly diurnal feeder, although nocturnal feeding observed. Gregarious, often also during breeding season, usually in small flocks but sometimes up to 250 birds; in Scotland, 40-100 birds/km of rocky shore.
Breeding. Laying from mid-May in Faeroes and Iceland, late Jun in Svalbard, mid-Jun to mid-Jul in Russia. Monogamous. Solitary and territorial; also feeds outside territory. Densities low, 0·04-11 nests/km²; high degree of site faithfulness. Nests in tundra moss, in the open; nest is small scrape, lined with plant material. 4 eggs, sometimes 3, laid at 24-48 hour intervals; single brood; incubation 21-22 days, starting with last egg, by both parents equally, though during first 2 weeks males less during day; chick extensively black above, mottled with cinnamon and with white specks, much black on face, underparts pale greyish or off-white; young tended by male, female deserting just before or after hatching; fledging 21-24 days. On Svalbard, 35% of hatchlings survived to 35 days old. Breeds first at 2 years old, sometimes 1 year old; oldest ringed bird 8 years, 1 month.
Movements. Migratory and sometimes partially migratory, but movements in various low Arctic and N temperate regions unclear. Non-breeding range extends further N than in other *Calidris*, to just below ice, e.g. SW Greenland, Finnmark and Murmansk, and S to Maryland (USA) and W France. Northernmost breeders fully migratory. Easternmost breeders migrate W to Murmansk or beyond. Unclear whether breeders at S of range are replaced by N breeders or N breeders show leap-frog migration, wintering S of S breeders. E Greenland breeders believed to winter in Iceland. Birds breeding in W Greenland winter in W & S Greenland. Ringing recoveries indicate migration between W Europe and Iceland, Greenland, Newfoundland and Baffin I, and between Norway and E Britain. Post-breeding migration later than in other *Calidris* species; females depart breeding grounds in advance of males and young, from Iceland in late Jun; males in Iceland until late Aug, and on Arctic islands from late Aug to mid-Sept. Arrival in North Sea and Iceland Oct-Nov. N movement Apr-May, and arrival in N breeding grounds mid-May to mid-Jun.
Status and Conservation. Not globally threatened. Altogether c. 66,000 breeding pairs in NW Europe, with some 50,000 pairs in Iceland (1985), 10,500 pairs in Norway (1981), 2000-4000 in Svalbard (1981) and 2000 in Sweden (1984). Eurasian population, wintering on E Atlantic coasts, estimated at 50,000 birds (1989) and considered to be stable; in winter 10,000's on Icelandic and Norwegian coasts, and c. 20,000 in Britain. Nearctic population comprises c. 10,000 birds.
Bibliography. Atkinson, Davies & Prater (1978), Atkinson, Summers *et al*. (1981a), Bengtson (1970, 1975a, 1975b), Bent (1927-1929), Blomqvist (1983a), Boere *et al*. (1984), Burcar (1992), Cane (1980), Cramp & Simmons (1983), Cresswell & Summers (1988), Davidson (1991), Dierschke (1993, 1994), Dunn (1994), Feare (1966), Feare & Summers (1985), Fjeldså (1977), Gerritsen & van Heezik (1985), Gerritsen & Sevenster (1985), Harrap (1993), Hoffman & Hoffman (1992), Knystautas (1993), Korducki (1992), Leinaas & Ambrose (1992), Maranini *et al*. (1991), Matthiessen (1994), McKee (1982), Metcalfe (1989), Morrison (1976), Nicoll, Rae *et al*. (1991), Nicoll, Summers *et al*. (1988), Piersma (1986b), Rogacheva (1992), de Roos (1992), Root (1988), Soulen (1991), Strann & Summers (1990), Summers (1994), Summers & Rogers (1991), Summers, Corse *et al*. (1988), Summers, Ellis & Johnstone (1988), Summers, Smith *et al*. (1990), Summers, Strann *et al*. (1990), Summers, Underhill *et al*. (1992), Tessen (1991), Tomkovich (1985a), Urban *et al*. (1986), Whitfield (1985), Wood (1991).

77. Rock Sandpiper

Calidris ptilocnemis

French: Bécasseau des Aléoutiennes **German**: Beringstrandläufer **Spanish**: Correlimos Roquero
Other common names: Aleutian/Pribilof Sandpiper

Taxonomy. *Tringa ptilocnemis* Coues, 1873, St George Island, Pribilof Islands.
Formerly placed in genus *Erolia*. Forms superspecies with *C. maritima*, with which sometimes considered conspecific. Birds from Kuril Is have on occasion been awarded separate race *kurilensis*. Four subspecies normally recognized.
Subspecies and Distribution.
C. p. quarta (Hartert, 1920) - Kuril Is, S Kamchatka and Commander Is.
C. p. tschuktschorum Portenko, 1937 - E Chukotskiy Peninsula, St Lawrence I, Nunivak I and W Alaska; winters in NW North America and locally in E Japan.
C. p. ptilocnemis (Coues, 1873) - St Matthew and Hall Is and Pribilof Is; winters on Alaska Peninsula.
C. p. couesi (Ridgway, 1880) - Aleutian Is and Alaska Peninsula.

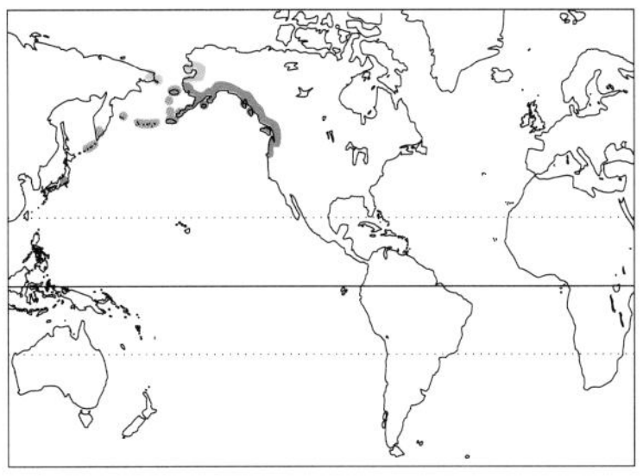

Descriptive notes. 20-23 cm; male 80-132, female 118-135 g. Chunky, medium-sized sandpiper. Adult nominate (and many *tschuktschorum*) very pale on head, neck and breast with dark patches on lores, ear-coverts and lower breast; rich buff fringes to upperparts; underwing extensively white; recalls *C. alpina*, but different shape and face pattern. Other races virtually identical to *C. maritima*, but generally darker chestnut fringes above; broader streaks below create variable blackish patch on breast and sometimes belly; white wingbar typically bolder. Female averages larger, especially with longer bill. Non-breeding adult of nominate has grey upperparts and pale grey breast, with rest of underparts mainly white; all other races like *C. maritima*. Juvenile nominate similar to that of *C. maritima*, but scapulars fringed pale chestnut and buff, and breast washed buff; other races very similar to *C. maritima*. In addition to plumage, races differ in size, with nominate largest, *couesi* smallest.
Habitat. Nests in upland tundra in coastal regions, probably at lower altitudes than *C. maritima*, in areas with cover of lichens, mosses and sometimes dwarf willows on rolling plains and in low mountains; also on exposed hills, along stream beds and on grassy wet tundra. Outside breeding season, occurs on rocky shores and stony beaches; on large boulders and rocky shelves covered with seaweed; also tidal mudflats. Often with *Aphriza virgata*. Roosts on rocks near feeding grounds just above high tide spray.
Food and Feeding. Molluscs (including snails), marine worms, crustaceans, icebound sea lice, sandfleas, flies, beetles and gammarids; some algae. Picks prey from mussel and barnacle beds, and especially from mats of foliose algae, while walking slowly; often feeds up to breast in water, and swims readily; on Pribilof Is, often probes in muddy and sandy areas. Can form rather large flocks in winter.
Breeding. Laying early May to late Jun, mainly early Jun. Monogamous, often for several years. Up to 12 breeding pairs/km²; high degree of site fidelity. Nests often among dense cover of reindeer moss, or among *Hyphnum* mosses and dwarf willow; also in debris on beach gravel. 4 eggs, laid at intervals of 1-3 days; replacement clutches can be laid; incubation probably c. 20 days, by both parents; chicks tended by male; immediately after fledging, young move to beach, later joined by adults, forming

flocks of over 100 birds. Breeding success may be strongly affected by Arctic foxes (*Alopex lagopus*) and other predators.

Movements. Partly migratory; leap-frog migration, with northernmost breeders winter S of more S breeding populations. Race *quarta* possibly only moves short distance to C Kuril Is; *tschuktschorum* migrates to Alaska and farther S, regularly to Tokyo region in Japan, and Oregon and N California; nominate moves to Alaska Peninsula; *couesi* thought to be resident, possibly moving as far as Kodiak I in winter. Late autumn migrant. Returns to breeding grounds early, from mid-Apr, and adults start autumn migration early Jul, followed by juveniles in late Jul to early Aug. Occurs on N Vancouver I from mid-Sept and in Oregon from mid-Oct, remaining till early May.

Status and Conservation. Not globally threatened. No population estimates available; numbers thought to be low; 4000 counted on Nelson Lagoon, Alaska Peninsula, in 1979, of which maximum of several hundred were breeding pairs. Winter counts from periphery of wintering distribution, in NW America, show numbers decreasing since 1970's; although the actual numbers counted were very low, this might suggest overall decreasing numbers or contraction of wintering range in S.

Bibliography. Armstrong (1983), Beaman (1994), Bent (1927-1929), Blomqvist (1983a), Boland (1990), Brazil (1991), Conover, B. (1944), Gabrielson & Lincoln (1959), Gill & Handel (1981, 1990), Hanna (1921), Matthiessen (1994), Miller *et al.* (1988), Murie (1959), Myers *et al.* (1982), Paulson & Erckmann (1993), Portenko (1972), Root (1988), Tomkovich (1982a, 1982b, 1994b, 1996).

78. Dunlin
Calidris alpina

French: Bécasseau variable   **German**: Alpenstrandläufer   **Spanish**: Correlimos Común
Other common names: Red-backed Sandpiper

Taxonomy. *Tringa alpina* Linnaeus, 1758, Lappland.
Formerly placed in genus *Erolia*. During recent years 5-13 races have been recognized, but validity of some obscure: suggested race *centralis* included in *alpina*; race *hudsonia* sometimes included in *pacifica*, and *pacifica* sometimes included in either *sakhalina* or *arcticola*. Nine subspecies recognized.

Subspecies and Distribution.
C. a. arctica (Schioler, 1922) - NE Greenland; winters mainly in NW Africa.
C. a. schinzii (C. L. Brehm, 1822) - SE Greenland and Iceland through Faeroes and British Is to Baltic and S Scandinavia; winters in S Europe and NW Africa.
C. a. alpina (Linnaeus, 1758) - N Scandinavia and N Russia E to R Kolyma; winters from W Europe and Mediterranean to NW India, and sparsely to Bangladesh.
C. a. sakhalina (Vieillot, 1816) - R Kolyma to Chukotskiy Peninsula and Anadyrland; winters in E China, Korea, Japan and Taiwan, and perhaps in small numbers in W North America.
C. a. actites Nechaev & Tomkovich, 1988 - N Sakhalin; wintering grounds unknown.
C. a. kistchinskii Tomkovich, 1986 - N Sea of Okhotsk and Koryak Mts through Kamchatka to Kuril Is; wintering grounds unknown.
C. a. arcticola (Todd, 1953) - NW Alaska N of Seward Peninsula, and NW Canada; winters in E China, Korea and Japan.
C. a. pacifica (Coues, 1861) - SW Alaska S of Seward Peninsula; winters in W USA and W Mexico.
C. a. hudsonia (Todd, 1953) - C Canada; winters in SE USA and probably E Mexico.

Descriptive notes. 16-22 cm; 33-85 g; wingspan 33-40 cm. Smallish, short-necked sandpiper with hunched posture; rufous upperparts, black belly; longish bill noticeably decurved, especially towards tip. Female averages larger and longer-billed; often has browner, less contrasting hindneck. Non-breeding adult has plain grey head, breast and upperparts; white chin, throat and lower underparts. Juvenile has pale buff, streaked breast; flanks and sides of white belly with lines of bold brownish spots. Races differ mainly in size, bill length, coloration of upperparts and extent of black on belly: *pacifica* and *hudsonia* largest and brightest, with longest bills; *arctica* smallest and dullest, with shortest bill; fringes of upperparts rusty-red in *alpina*, yellower in *schinzii*, reddish yellow in *arctica*.

Habitat. Utilizes wide variety of breeding habitats, primarily on moist, boggy ground, interspersed with surface water, including tussock tundra and peat-hummock tundra in Arctic, and wet coastal grassland, salt-marshes and wet upland moorland. Outside breeding season, mainly at estuarine mudflats, but also at wide variety of freshwater and brackish wetlands, both coastal and inland, including lagoons, muddy freshwater shores, tidal rivers, flooded fields, sewage farms, salt-works; sometimes on sandy coasts.

Food and Feeding. During breeding, diet includes insects, primarily adults and larvae of Diptera, craneflies, beetles, caddisflies, wasps, sawflies and mayflies; also spiders, mites, earthworms, snails,

slugs and plant material. Non-breeding diet chiefly polychaete worms and small gastropods; also insects, crustaceans, bivalves, occasionally small fish and plant matter. Feeds mainly by probing, in quick manner, often interspersed with short runs; also by "sewing", lunging and pecking. Most prey swallowed as bill extracted from mud; worms often washed before swallowed; when ingesting molluscs, ejects shell fragments by regurgitation. Diurnal and nocturnal forager. In non-breeding range highly gregarious.

Breeding. Lays Jun to early Jul in Arctic, late Apr to May in S. Monogamous. Solitary; locally up to 100 pairs/km², more often 3-30 birds/km²; parents feed within territory. Nest concealed in vegetation, usually on top of tussock; nest cup filled with grass and leaves. 4 eggs, sometimes 3, with laying interval 24-36 hours; single brood, rarely second is started; often starts replacement clutch after failure; incubation 20-24 days; both sexes incubate and tend brood, female usually leaving first; chick ochraceous tawny to orange-cinnamon above mottled with black bands and dense rows of white down tips, ochraceous face and dirty white underparts; fledging 18-24 days. Number of hatchlings per nest 0·83-1·72, but 0·3-0·4 in a declining *schinzii* population. 1st-year mortality 62-75%; adult annual mortality 25-39% (Europe). Age of first breeding 1 year or older. Oldest recorded bird 24 years.

Movements. Migratory. Variety of migration strategies, from short coastal flights to long, non-stop flights overland on broad front. Race *arctica* moves from Greenland through Iceland, Britain and W France to Morocco and W Africa, primarily to Banc d'Arguin, Mauritania; arrives in Africa from late Jul and departs mainly Mar to early Apr; return migration farther W up W Britain, probably overflying Iceland. Race *schinzii* passes through Britain, France and Portugal to NW Africa; few may winter in SW England; continental birds move N up continental coasts, when fewer reach Britain than after breeding. Race *alpina* winters in Europe and NW Africa; easternmost birds migrate farthest; many moult in Wadden Sea or Wash, arriving from Jul, followed by W movements in Oct-Nov to British Is; birds wintering in E Mediterranean make long distance, flights overland across E Europe. At least 3 races move down E Asian coast, where passage recorded through Ussuriland, Korea, Japan, Hong Kong and coastal China. Race *arcticola* stages in W Alaska, and crosses Bering Strait to E Asian winter quarters. Almost entire population of *pacifica* uses Copper R Delta, SE Alaska, as spring staging site. Some 1-year-old birds remain in non-breeding range all year.

Status and Conservation. Not globally threatened. Total population of *arctica* estimated at 15,000 birds (1989); *schinzii* 821,000 birds (1989), virtually all breeding in Iceland, with c. 10,000 pairs in temperate Europe (1986); *alpina* 1,373,000 birds (1989), possibly few 100,000's more, with 55,000 pairs breeding in Scandinavia (1986); *sakhalina* probably c. 100,000 birds; *pacifica* 450,000-600,000 birds (1992); *hudsonia* more than 100,000 birds. Total European wintering population c. 1,000,000 birds, of which up to 566,000 in British Is; this European population has declined considerably since 1970, especially in Britain, France, Belgium and Portugal, but seems to have stabilized now or even recovering somewhat; on migration, c. 900,000 pass NW Europe and up to 1,200,000 birds have been counted in Wadden Sea; up to 800,000 on Banc d'Arguin; over 100,000 in Egypt; c. 150,000 birds winter in E Africa and SW Asia, where very common in Oman, Saudi Arabia and Iran; 25,000-100,000 birds in SC Asia. Populations of races *arctica* and *schinzii* considered stable. In winter, species restricted to small number of estuaries, making it vulnerable to changes in this restricted habitat; such sites under pressure from land reclamation, pollution incidents, and in Britain from spread of *Spartina anglica* on mudflats resulting in decreased feeding area. Palearctic breeding populations at N latitudes stable; at temperate latitudes declining (*schinzii* in Britain, Finland, Denmark and Estonia), chiefly due to changes in land use; Scottish breeding population has declined by 17% due to afforestation of moorland. Race *hudsonia* shows (non-significant) declining trend over last decades. Rarer and poorly known races should be monitored.

Bibliography. Ali & Ripley (1980), Anon. (1971a, 1992b), Baccetti *et al.* (1995), Baker (1982), Bengtson & Svensson (1968), Bent (1927-1929), Blomqvist, D. & Johansson (1991), Blomqvist, S. (1983a), Blomqvist, S. *et al.* (1987), Boyd (1962), Brazil (1991), Brennan *et al.* (1990), Brenning (1989), Browning (1977, 1991), Buchanan *et al.* (1988), Byrkjedal & Kålås (1983), Clark (1983, 1984, 1994), Cramp & Simmons (1983), Durell & Kelly (1990), Ens, Wintermans & Smit (1993), Evans (1986), Ferns (1981), Ferns & Green (1979), Ferns & Worrall (1984), Fjeldså (1977), Fry (1980), Gerritsen (1992), Gerritsen & van Heezik (1985), Goede & Nieboer (1983), Goede *et al.* (1990), Goodman *et al.* (1989), Goss-Custard & Moser (1988), Greenwood (1979, 1983, 1984, 1986), Gromadzka (1983, 1985b, 1986, 1989), Gromadzka & Przystupa (1984), Handel & Gill (1992b), van der Have *et al.* (1984), Heezik *et al.* (1983), Holmes (1966a, 1966b, 1971b), Holmes & Pitelka (1968), Holmgren *et al.* (1993a, 1993b), Howell & Webb (1995a), Jackson (1994), Jönsson (1986a, 1987a, 1987b, 1988, 1990, 1991a), Kania (1990), Kelsey & Hassall (1989), Kirby *et al.* (1991), Krey (1991), Król (1985), Kus *et al.* (1984), Mascher & Marcström (1976), Meltofte (1985, 1991), Miller *et al.* (1988), Morrison *et al.* (1994), Mouritsen (1992, 1993, 1994), Mouritsen & Jensen (1992), Mullié & Meininger (1981), Nechaev & Tomkovich (1987, 1988), Nehls & Tiedemann (1993), Norton (1972), Ogilvie (1963), Onnen (1991), Page (1974a), Page & Gill (1994), Patrikeev (1995), Pienkowski & Dick (1975), Pienkowski & Pienkowski (1983), Pienkowski *et al.* (1979), Piersma (1986b), Prys-Jones *et al.* (1994), Redpath (1988), Roberts, T.J. (1991), Rogacheva (1992), Rösner (1990), Ruiz *et al.* (1989), Senner, Norton & West (1989), Senner, West & Norton (1981), Shi Ming & Lu Jianjian (1990), Shirihai (1996), Soikkeli (1966, 1967, 1970a, 1970b, 1974), Sterbetz (1992), Stiefel & Scheufler (1989), Stolt *et al.* (1992), Tomkovich (1994b), Tubbs *et al.* (1992), Underhill *et al.* (1993), Urban *et al.* (1986), Warnock (1994), Warnock & Gill (1996), Warnock *et al.* (1995), Wenink *et al.* (1996), Wetmore (1965), Worrall (1984), Yalden & Yalden (1988).

PLATE 45 ➤

ssp *sibirica*

ssp *falcinellus*

80

81

82

79

83

various plumages ♂

♀ grey bird

♀ rufous bird

84

♂

♀

86

♂

85

♂

♀

PLATE 45

inches 4

cm 10

Genus *EURYNORHYNCHUS* Nilsson, 1821

79. Spoon-billed Sandpiper

Eurynorhynchus pygmeus

French: Bécasseau spatule **German**: Löffelstrandläufer **Spanish**: Correlimos Cuchareta
Other common names: Spoonbill Sandpiper

Taxonomy. *Platalea pygmea* Linnaeus, 1758, Surinam = eastern Asia.
Often placed in genus *Calidris*. Monotypic.
Distribution. Chukotskiy Peninsula S to N Kamchatka. Winters locally from SE India and Sri Lanka to Indochina and S China, and S to Singapore.

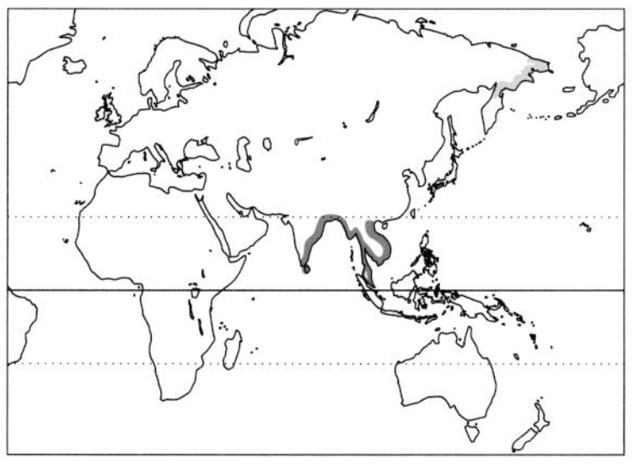

Descriptive notes. 14-16 cm; male averages 29·5 g, one female 34 g. Small wader closely resembling *Calidris*, but with spatulate bill; red-brown head, neck and breast with dark brown streaks; upperparts blackish with buff and pale rufous fringes. Resembles *Calidris ruficollis*, but very different bill. Female averages slightly larger. Non-breeding adult lacks reddish coloration, but has pale brownish grey upperparts with whitish fringes on wing-coverts; supercilium and underparts white. Juvenile has blackish upperparts with white and buff fringes; wing-coverts paler; underparts white with buff on breast; crown and broad eyestripe brown, supercilium white.
Habitat. Nests on sea coasts with sparsely vegetated sandy ridges near lakes and marshes, often near a river mouth, lagoon or sandy spit; also stream-deposited gravel strips alternating with marshy sections on dry and gravelly tundra. During non-breeding season, apparently on muddy coasts and mudflats in coastal lagoons.
Food and Feeding. Terrestrial insects, including beetles, Hymenoptera and Diptera, small seeds, larvae of beetles and small aquatic amphipods; possibly larval crustaceans, juvenile polychaetes and juvenile molluscs. On breeding grounds usually feeds around freshwater pools. Feeds in shallow water and soft, wet mud by sweeping bill from side to side, while moving forward slowly, much like Eurasian Spoonbills (*Platalea leucorodia*); also picks at food items from water and mud surface; drill-like action with bill tip in mud, bill held slightly open; also observed foot-trembling. Feeds alone or in small flocks and often associates with small calidrines.
Breeding. Nests Jun-Jul. Monogamous, usually for more than one season; parents feed in territory, but also in communal feeding areas. Site faithful, with c. 65% of adults returning each year, and males establishing territories in same places. Two nests found in area of mosses, sedges and creeping osiers; one lined with dwarf willow leaves. 4 eggs, usually 3 in replacement clutches; incubation probably 18-20 days, by both parents; chicks initially tended by both parents, but female abandons when they are 4·5-6 days old, or immediately after hatching in late broods; males leave when chicks are 15-20 days old. Adults aggressive towards conspecifics. Breeds successfully only when lemmings (*Dicrostonyx groenlandicus*) present in moderate or high numbers, as predators alternatively feed on eggs and chicks when lemmings not available. Males do not breed before 2 years of age. Oldest ringed bird more than 10 years.
Movements. Migratory. Migrates along coasts of E Asia. During non-breeding season occurs at scattered localities on coasts of E, SE & SC Asia. Migrates N through E Russia from late May to early Jun; after breeding season, adults migrate Jul to late Aug, females first, and juveniles early Aug to mid-Oct. Most frequented stopover areas are S Sakhalin and W Kamchatka. Occurs on passage in North and South Korea, Japan, Taiwan, Hong Kong and E China, chiefly in late Apr to May and Sept; small numbers recorded wintering in Vietnam, Thailand, Peninsular Malaysia, Singapore, Myanmar, Bangladesh, E India and Sri Lanka; large numbers observed only in Bangladesh; vagrant to Alaska and Canada. Main wintering area or areas still undiscovered.
Status and Conservation. VULNERABLE. Total population estimated at 2000-2800 pairs. Stopover sites holding 10's to 100's of birds are mouth of R Moroshechnaya (WC Kamchatka) and Lososey Harbour (S Sakhalin); in addition, Terpeniya Bay (SC Sakhalin), coasts of Tatarski Strait and S Primorskiy area may prove important, as may other sites. In winter quarters, highest number counted is 257 birds on islands in Bay of Bengal in Bangladesh (1989); also regularly found in Maulavir Char (50 birds), Dhal Char and Urir Char in SE Bangladesh (1987-1991); 48 birds in Orissa, EC India, in 1992. In 1993, only 3 birds encountered during Asian Waterfowl Census. Wintering sites of rest of population remain unknown. Breeding habitat is limited to suitable patches distributed along narrow coastal zone. Combination of small population, specialized breeding habitat requirements and high risk of nest predation makes species vulnerable.
Bibliography. Ali & Ripley (1980), Bent (1927-1929), Burton (1971), Cha Meiwah & Young (1990), Collar & Andrew (1988), Collar *et al.* (1994), Dixon (1918), Étchécopar & Hüe (1978), Fujimaki & Haneda (1976), Gerasimov (1988), Howes & Parish (1989), Inskipp & Collins (1993), Knystautas (1993), Lim Kimseng (1994), MacKinnon & Phillipps (1993), McWhirter (1987), Medway & Wells (1976), Perennou *et al.* (1994), Piersma (1986d), Portenko (1957, 1972), Rosair (1995c), Sauppe *et al.* (1978), Scott (1989), Smythies (1986), Sugathan (1985), Swennen & Marteijn (1988), Thompson *et al.* (1993), Tomkovich (1991a, 1991b, 1991c, 1992c, 1992d, 1994a, 1996), Voronov (1980).

Genus *LIMICOLA* Koch, 1816

80. Broad-billed Sandpiper

Limicola falcinellus

French: Bécasseau falcinelle **German**: Sumpfläufer **Spanish**: Correlimos Falcinelo

Taxonomy. *Scolopax Falcinellus* Pontoppidan, 1763, Denmark.
Occasionally included in *Calidris*. Two subspecies recognized.
Subspecies and Distribution.
L. f. falcinellus (Pontoppidan, 1763) - Scandinavia and NW Russia; winters from E & S Africa through Arabia to W & S India and Sri Lanka.
L. f. sibirica Dresser, 1876 - Taymyr, and R Lena E to R Kolyma; winters from NE India through SE Asia, Philippines and Indonesia to Australia.

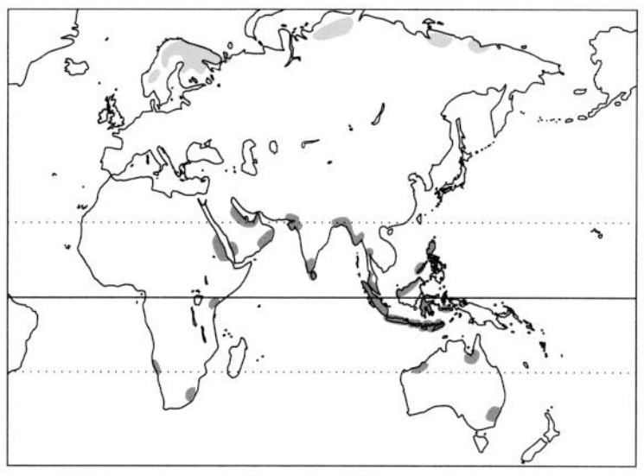

Descriptive notes. 16-18 cm; 28-68 g; wingspan 34-37 cm. Small sandpiper with long, broad bill decurved at tip; distinctive split supercilium; short legs; black mantle and scapulars with whitish fringes in fresh plumage, and whitish lines down edges; wing-coverts grey-brown with whitish fringes. Female averages larger. Non-breeding adult has grey-brown upperparts with dark streaks or feather centres and white fringes; underparts white, but breast with faint grey-brown streaks; resembles *Calidris alpina*, but supercilium remains apparent. Juvenile like breeding adult, but with chestnut and whitish fringes on upperparts; wing-coverts pale brown with pale buff fringes; breast washed buff-brown with faint brown streaks. Race *sibirica* has brighter rufous fringes to feathers of upperparts; also distinguished by broader "lower" supercilium and narrower "upper" supercilium.
Habitat. Race *falcinellus* breeds in subarctic montane and lowland zone, usually at altitudes of above 200 m, possibly up to northernmost taiga, in wet bogs and on open peatland; race *sibirica* breeds in wet Arctic tundra. During migration, species occurs in soft muddy areas on shores of ponds and lakes; also found on windflats, shallow freshwater to saline, occasionally hypersaline, lagoons, overgrazed meadows, temporary small swampy patches, inlets of fjords, harbours, flooded rice fields, and farther S also riverine sandbanks. Winters mainly on large, soft intertidal mudflats, in brackish lagoons and also saltpans.
Food and Feeding. Mainly marine worms, including nereids; also small bivalves and snails, crustaceans (e.g. amphipods), adult and larval insects, including beetles, flies, grasshoppers and ants; also seeds. While feeding, walks slowly, picking from side to side and occasionally drilling and probing, often with head at typical sideways angle; may make short runs; feeds on soft mud or wet sand and occasionally wades in shallow water. Singly or in small flocks, sometimes mingling with other waders. In Namibia, recorded holding a feeding territory along a beach.
Breeding. Laying early to late Jun in Fenno-Scandia, mid-Jun to early Jul in Russia. Monogamous. Breeds in loose colonies, of 2-10 pairs, 80-100 m apart, minimum 9 m; densities of up to 20 pairs/km^2 locally in Finland; males aggressively territorial. Nest is cup lined with vegetation, often on top of tussock. 4 eggs, sometimes 3; single brood; no evidence of replacement clutches; incubation 21-22 days (2 records); chick has chestnut or hazel brown upperparts, with bold black bands and lines of powder-puff, contrasting white underparts and buff tinged breast; young initially tended by both parents, but female deserts before fledging; fledging period unknown. Oldest ringed bird at least 10 years.
Movements. Adults depart breeding grounds in Fenno-Scandia Jul, juveniles Aug; migrates in broad front SE across Europe; substantial numbers stage in Sivash, S Ukraine, in late May; also Middle East coasts, Caspian Sea and Sivash in Jul (adults) and Aug (juveniles), and Bulgarian seaboard in Sept; evidently some cross Sahara from Mediterranean and some pass E Mediterranean, from late Apr to late May and in early Oct. Present in Africa mainly from Sept to early Apr, early adults from Aug; in Sind, Pakistan, adults arrive late Jul to early Aug, juveniles late Aug to early Sept. In E, probably flies across taiga in broad front, concentrating in S to cross the mountains; at least some birds apparently migrate via Minusinsk depression and Tuva (SC Siberia) and Transaltai Gobi (Mongolia) in autumn; migrates through Hong Kong, along E Chinese coast, Taiwan and Japan in Apr-May and Sept-Oct, taking a more westerly route northward; large numbers pass Jiangsu, NE China, in Aug. Present in NW Australia mainly from late Oct. Return migration mid-Apr to early Jun, reaching breeding grounds in Fenno-Scandia mid-May to mid-Jun. A few remain at wintering sites. Migrates singly or in small parties, but on spring migration flocks of up to several hundred.
Status and Conservation. Not globally threatened. Total population of nominate 13,000-22,000 pairs, with 200-1000 pairs in Norway (1990), 3000-5000 pairs in Sweden (1987), 10,000-15,000 pairs in Finland (1992), and 100-1000 pairs in NW Russia, but all numbers uncertain, especially those in Russia; 25,000 estimated to winter in E Africa and SW Asia, with possibly up to 6000 on Saudi Arabian Gulf coast. Race *sibirica* has population estimated at c. 16,000 birds. Breeding range poorly known, due to inaccessibility of habitat and skulking habits; Swedish population decreasing since 1970's, and range has probably contracted, especially towards E. Local extinctions in Norway, partly due to habitat changes, but also some new breeding areas dicovered in S Norway in 1970's; now probably stable. Reported common on coast of Pakistan. Much of breeding habitat probably too wet for afforestation, perhaps safeguarding it for future. In Finland some peatland areas have been flooded to create artificial lakes. Most important site for European population during migration is Sivash, S Ukraine, with 6000-8000 birds estimated staging in spring; up to 600 birds stage in Bulgaria in Sept. Important wintering sites are Bahrein with 1500-2000 winterers, Barr al Hikman in Oman, As-Sayhat Bay and lagoons in Tarout Bay in Saudi Arabia, and Khor Dubai in Dubai, with up to 1000 wintering birds each (in Barr al Hikman 1648 birds in 1989/90). 7 sites in SE Asia hold more than 100 birds each, with up to 400 in Samut Sakhon in Gulf of Thailand; c. 8000 birds winter in Australia, with Port Hedland Saltworks holding up to 6000 birds and SE Gulf of Carpentaria up to 1740 birds.
Bibliography. Ali & Ripley (1980), Ash (1978a), Barthel (1989), Becker *et al.* (1974), Beehler *et al.* (1986), Blakers *et al.* (1984), Blomqvist (1983a), Brazil (1991), Buckley (1980), Chernichko, Chernichko *et al.* (1993), Chernichko, Grinchenko & Siokhin (1991), Coates (1985), Cramp & Simmons (1983), Dementiev & Gladkov (1951b), Dickinson *et al.* (1991), Dowsett (1980), Dowsett & Forbes-Watson (1993), Étchécopar & Hüe (1964, 1978), Evans (1994), Fjeldså (1977), Flint (1973b), Fry (1989), Gavrilov & Beresovski (1988), Goodman *et al.* (1989), Hackett & Hackett (1988), Herremans (1984), Hoogerwerf (1964), Hopson & Hopson (1972), Hüe & Étchécopar (1970), Karpov (1994), Kliebe & Kliebe (1985), Knystautas (1993), Koskimies (1994), Lane & Davies (1987), Lekagul & Round (1991), MacKinnon & Phillipps (1993), Mackworth-Praed & Grant (1970), Marchant & Higgins (1996), van Marle & Voous (1988), Medway & Wells (1976), Minton, C. (1987), Nankinov (1985), Nielsen (1991), Nisbet (1961), Perennou *et al.* (1994), Phillips (1978), Piersma (1986b), Pook (1992), Rands *et al.* (1987), Rapin & Versel (1988), Ripley (1982), Roberts, T.J. (1991), Rogacheva (1992), Scott (1989), Shirihai (1996), Short *et al.* (1990), Smythies (1986), Sotnikov & Litun (1988), Svensson (1987), Tremauville (1984), Uhlig (1990a), Urban *et al.* (1986), Uttley *et al.* (1988), Verkuil,

On following pages: 81. Stilt Sandpiper (*Micropalama himantopus*); 82. Buff-breasted Sandpiper (*Tryngites subruficollis*); 83. Ruff (*Philomachus pugnax*); 84. Wilson's Phalarope (*Steganopus tricolor*); 85. Red-necked Phalarope (*Phalaropus lobatus*); 86. Red Phalarope (*Phalaropus fulicaria*).

Koolhaas & van der Winden (1993), Verkuil, van de Sant *et al.* (1993), Wagner (1980), White & Bruce (1986), Williams, M.D. (1986), van der Winden *et al.* (1993).

Genus *MICROPALAMA* Baird, 1858

81. **Stilt Sandpiper**

Micropalama himantopus

French: Bécasseau à échasses **German**: Bindenstrandläufer **Spanish**: Correlimos Zancolín

Taxonomy. *Tringa himantopus* Bonaparte, 1826, Long Branch, New Jersey.
Should perhaps be included in genus *Calidris*, but more research required. Monotypic.
Distribution. N Alaska E to S Victoria I; W & S Hudson Bay. Winters from N Chile, Bolivia and SC Brazil to N Argentina and Uruguay; small numbers locally in S USA.

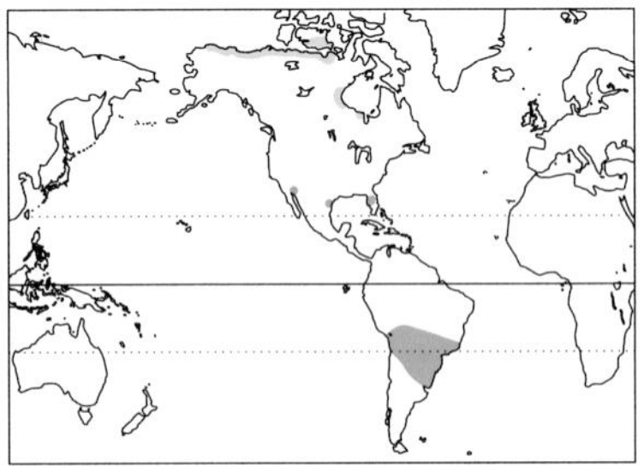

Descriptive notes. 18-23 cm; 40-68 g; wingspan 38-41 cm. Medium-sized wader resembling *Calidris*, but with long, slightly decurved bill and long legs; chestnut stripe across side of head, broad white supercilium; dark upperparts fringed with rufous and whitish; neck and upper breast with dark brown streaks; rest of underparts barred. Female averages slightly larger in wing and bill. Non-breeding adult has brown-grey upperparts with white-fringed wing-coverts; distinct white supercilium; underparts white with grey streaking on lower neck, breast and flanks. Juvenile has dark brown upperparts fringed rufous or whitish buff; wing-coverts greyer with buff fringes; foreneck and breast washed buff and streaked; belly white.
Habitat. Breeds mainly in subarctic, on sedge tundra near water, moist tundra with willow growth and high, dry slopes; often near wooded borders of taiga. During non-breeding season, in freshwater wetlands; flooded fields, shallow ponds and pools, sewage lagoons and freshwater or brackish marshes; rarely along coast, on intertidal mudflats and beaches.
Food and Feeding. Adults and larvae of aquatic and terrestrial beetles, adult Diptera, other larval insects, snails and also seeds; young birds often eat larval midges. Diet similar throughout year. Feeds by probing, often with rapid "stitching" action, moving forward slowly; in open water, often belly-deep with head frequently submerged; rarely in soft, wet mud or sand. Occasionally picks up insects from water's surface. Usually feeds singly or in small groups, regularly associating with *Tringa flavipes* and dowitchers (*Limnodromus*).
Breeding. Laying early Jun in Victoria. Monogamous, often for several years. High degree of site fidelity; 15% of birds reuse nest cup from previous year. Territorial, but feeding outside territory. In Alaska breeds at low densities; in Manitoba 5-25 pairs/km². Nest on relatively open dry tundra, especially on top of sedge hummock or on low, well drained gravel ridge that crosses sedge meadow, but sometimes in wet tundra habitat; nest is unlined scrape. 4 eggs, laid at average interval of 36 hours; incubation 19·5-21 days, starting with final egg, by male during day and female at night; parents accompany hatchlings to wetter areas; fledging 17-18 days; both parents desert brood before fledging, female after 1 week and male 1 week later; fledglings congregate near inland waters. Hatching success c. 80% in Alaska. Age of first breeding unknown.
Movements. Migrates through interior North and Central America to C South America, but during autumn also down Atlantic coast to N South America, where fairly large numbers occur in Surinam Aug-Sept; small numbers winter locally in S USA. Females migrate S from 2nd week of Jul, males 1 week later, and juveniles from mid-Aug; in Manitoba young and adults move at same time. On return, overflies West Indies and Gulf of Mexico from coast of Colombia and Venezuela, reaching USA mainly Apr; migrates N along rivers to Arctic coast; arrives at breeding grounds from late May, males c. 2 days earlier than females. Some remain in winter quarters during breeding season. Migrating flocks can total up to hundreds of birds.
Status and Conservation. Not globally threatened. Total population estimated at 50,000-100,000 birds; few precise data available, but no major threats identified, and numbers seem to be stable. May also breed locally farther S in Canada, at border of taiga.
Bibliography. Amos (1991), Armstrong (1983), Baker, M.C. (1977), Baldassarre & Fischer (1984), Belton (1984), Bent (1927-1929), Biaggi (1983), Blake (1977), Bolster & Robinson (1990), Brazil (1991), Burton (1972b), Contreras *et al.* (1990), Cramp & Simmons (1983), Fjeldså & Krabbe (1990), Haverschmidt (1968), Haverschmidt & Mees (1995), Hayes (1995), Hayes & Fox (1991), Hilty & Brown (1986), Howell & Webb (1995a), Jehl (1970, 1973a), Johnson (1965b), Matthiessen (1994), Meyer de Schauensee & Phelps (1978), Miller (1983c), Miller *et al.* (1988), Monroe (1968), Parmelee *et al.* (1967), de la Peña (1992), Ricklefs (1987), Root (1988), Scott & Carbonell (1986), Sick (1985c, 1993), Smith, F.T.H. (1992), Stiles & Skutch (1989), Tejedor (1986), Tostain *et al.* (1992), Wetmore (1965).

Genus *TRYNGITES* Cabanis, 1857

82. **Buff-breasted Sandpiper**

Tryngites subruficollis

French: Bécasseau roussâtre **German**: Grasläufer **Spanish**: Correlimos Canelo

Taxonomy. *Tringa subruficollis* Vieillot, 1819, Paraguay.
Genetically close to *Calidris*; also suggested to be intermediate between *Calidris* and *Philomachus*. Monotypic.
Distribution. Wrangel I and Ayon I E to R Ekvyvatan and N coast of Chukotskiy Peninsula; Barrow area (N Alaska) E to Boothia Peninsula, and irregularly N to Devon I. Winters from SE Bolivia, Paraguay and S Brazil to Uruguay and NE Argentina.

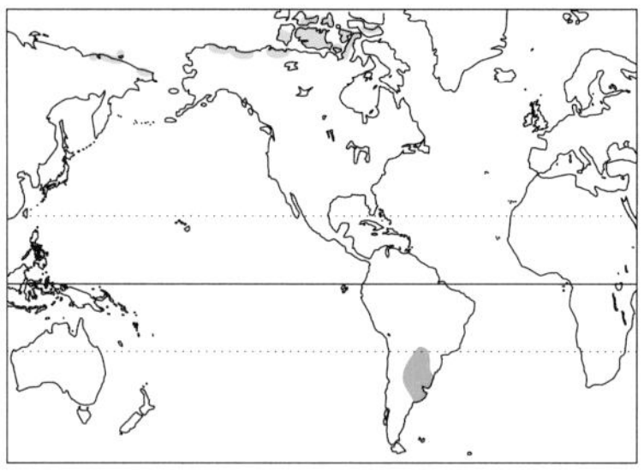

Descriptive notes. 18-20 cm; male 53-117 g; female 46-81 g; wingspan 43-47 cm. Medium-sized wader with small, round head, fairly long neck and warm buff face and underparts; dark brown centres to feathers of upperparts and blackish spots on crown, hindneck and mantle; belly white towards rear; underwing mostly silvery white with black band on coverts. Resembles juvenile *Philomachus pugnax*, but smaller and more compact, with noticeably shorter legs. Female smaller than male. Non-breeding adult has broader, browner fringes to feathers of upperparts. Juvenile like adult, but paler below, especially towards vent, and with narrower fringes and dark subterminal line to feathers of upperparts.
Habitat. Breeds in high Arctic on well drained sandy tundra with tussocks and scant vegetation, or with vegetation of mosses, willows and grass, or on moist meadows with sedges and grass; not often near sea, and avoids marshes; favoured sites for leks, though not for nests, are well vegetated hummocky ground around marshy ponds; during brood-rearing, does not move to wet lowland areas. During migration, on short-grass prairies, meadows, golf courses, airfields, pastures, burnt grassland, stubble, ploughed fields, inundated barren land and margins of freshwater wetlands; in Venezuela, also recorded on rain forest riverbanks, marshes and seashores. Winters primarily on flooded *pampas* and grazed grasslands; also in short vegetation near wetlands.
Food and Feeding. During migration, takes terrestrial invertebrates, especially adults, larvae and pupae of beetles and Diptera, and craneflies; spiders, copepods and gammarid crustaceans; also seeds. Forages while walking steadily; occasionally runs and stops like a plover. On migration, often forages in short, sparse grass or dry stubble, close to water's edge. Gregarious outside breeding season, in flocks of 5-6 birds, although frequently defends small territories on staging and wintering grounds. Often associates with *Pluvialis dominica*.
Breeding. Laying early to late Jun. Polygynous; uses lekking system, where 2-10 males in relatively large territories attract females with typical "Wing-flash" display; males also perform solitary displays away from lek. Copulation may take place before reaching breeding grounds; males do not participate in nesting activities; 8 of 32 broods had multiple-paternity. Densities vary considerably between years, 0-14 and 1-19 birds/km² at some sites; 0-3·3 nests/km² in Alaska. Little or no site fidelity and no natal philopatry. Nest on moist, grassy or "black" lichen tundra, usually close to stream; shallow scrape lined with lichens and plant material. 4 eggs; single brood; no records of replacement clutches; incubation 23-25 days, starting fully with 3-4 eggs; chick brownish grey above with blackish brown mottling and white down tips, dark crown patch and whitish below; fledging 18-20 days. 50-65% of nests lost in N Alaska due to predation; of remaining eggs 42-43% hatch; minimum 7-18% fledge; another Alaskan study reports hatching success of 80%. Presumably breeds first at 1 year old.
Movements. Migrates, probably non-stop, through interior North America, mainly Canadian prairies and C USA, across Gulf of Mexico to N South America; on S migration, some pass W Hudson Bay and Great Lakes, probably crossing W Atlantic to N South America; flies through interior South America to wintering grounds. Migrates S in broad front, and reverse route N on much narrower front. Stages at traditional stopover sites. Departs from breeding grounds late Jul to early Sept, adults before juveniles; males and non-breeding or failed-breeding females leave mid-Jun to early Jul, crossing USA Aug-Sept to arrive at wintering grounds from late Aug, but mainly mid-Sept to mid-Oct. Departure from wintering grounds from late Jan, mainly early Feb, to late Mar (mainly females); arrives S North America mid-Apr to early May, S edge of breeding grounds late May, and farther N until mid-Jun. Probably nocturnal migrant. Extremely tame during migration.
Status and Conservation. Not globally threatened. Total population estimated at maximum of 25,000 birds; 5000 to over 10,000 birds in Canada, with c. 2000 breeding birds on Banks I; not more than several 10's of birds on Wrangel I, and sporadic distributional pattern on Chukotskiy Peninsula. Close to extinction by early 1920's due to excessive hunting, especially around turn of century, when population may have numbered millions. Numbers declined by 65-100% at small staging site in NC Texas during 1980's; similar decline in numbers of birds staging in Canada; population decline, thus indicated, possibly caused by degeneration of staging areas, especially Cheyenne Bottoms, and South American wintering grounds. Surveys in Argentina no longer indicate declining numbers. Flocks of 100's to 1000's found near Houston (Texas), York County (Nebraska), Beaverhills L (Alberta) and Saskatoon (Saskatchewan). Considering distances involved, a staging area in N South America is to be expected, but none known. Estimated 2000 birds wintering on 11,000 ha ranch of Estancia Medaland in Buenos Aires Province, Argentina (1973).
Bibliography. Abbott (1982), Alberghetti *et al.* (1992), Ali & Ripley (1980), Antas (1983), Armstrong (1983), Arthur (1987), Beehler & Forster (1988), Belton (1984), Bent (1927-1929), Beser (1986), Blake (1977), Blanco & Canevari (1992), Bolster & Robinson (1990), Brazil (1991), Campbell & Gregory (1976), Cartar & Lyon (1988), Castan (1964), Contreras *et al.* (1990), Cramp & Simmons (1983), Dorogoy (1983), Driessens & van Rossum (1988), Fjeldså & Krabbe (1990), Haverschmidt (1968, 1972b), Haverschmidt & Mees (1995), Hayes (1995), Hayes & Fox (1991), Hayes *et al.* (1990), Hilty & Brown (1986), Hobcroft (1987), Hopson & Hopson (1974), Howell & Webb (1995a), Hubaut (1984), Knolle & Balten (1993), Knystautas (1993), Lanctot (1994, 1995), Lanctot & Laredo (1994), Matthiessen (1994), Meyer de Schauensee & Phelps (1978), Miller *et al.* (1988), Monroe (1968), Myers (1979, 1980b, 1981b), Myers & Myers (1979), Oring (1964), Palmer (1967), Parmelee *et al.* (1967), Paulson & Erckmann (1985, 1993), de la Peña (1992), Pitelka *et al.* (1974), Prevett & Barr (1976), Pruett-Jones (1988), Ridgely & Gwynne (1989), Scott & Carbonell (1986), Sick (1985c, 1993), Slud (1964), Sorensen (1990), Stiles & Skutch (1989), Stishov (1989, 1994), Strauss (1991), Sutton (1967), Trawoger & Kurz (1986), Urban *et al.* (1986), Wetmore (1965).

Genus *PHILOMACHUS* Merrem, 1804

83. **Ruff**

Philomachus pugnax

French: Combattant varié **German**: Kampfläufer **Spanish**: Combatiente
Other common names: Reeve (female)

Taxonomy. *Tringa Pugnax* Linnaeus, 1758, Sweden.
Has been proposed for inclusion in *Calidris*. Monotypic.
Distribution. NW Europe through Siberia to Chukotskiy Peninsula and Sea of Okhotsk. Winters from Mediterranean and sub-Saharan Africa through Middle East to Indian Subcontinent.

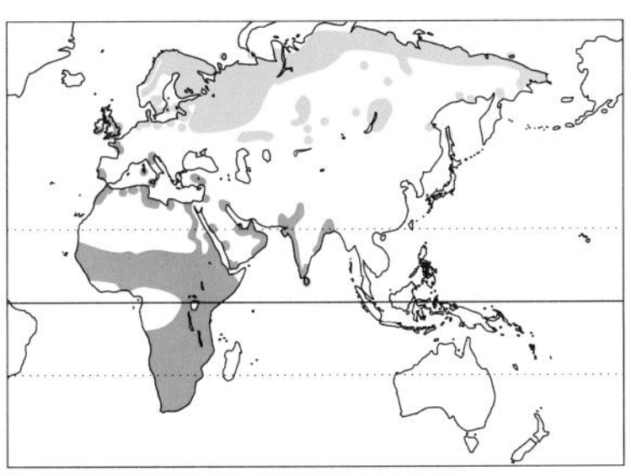

Descriptive notes. Male 26-32 cm, 130-254 g, wingspan 54-58 cm; female 20-25 cm, 70-170 g, wingspan 48-52 cm. Extreme sexual dimorphism. Male has head-tufts and ruff variably coloured buff, chestnut, dark purple, black or white, often barred or flecked; white coloration of tufts and ruff associated with satellite behavioural role (see page 472); mantle and scapulars vary from black to brown, buff, chestnut, ochre or white; yellow to brown facial warts; underparts usually dark, lower belly and undertail white; bill brown to dull orange and legs yellow-green to dark orange. Female considerably smaller than male, with overall colour rather variable; lacks specialized head plumage of male; dark upperparts with buff to rufous fringes and black blotches on breast and flanks; bill black, legs pinkish orange to green or grey. Non-breeding adult like breeding female, but paler grey-brown above with whiter lower face and dusky buff on breast; bill dark, legs duller; some males retain much white on head and neck. Juvenile has buff-fringed dark brown upperparts and rufous buff foreneck, breast and belly; face mainly buff with pale throat; bill and legs as in breeding female.

Habitat. Breeds in Arctic and subarctic, and S to temperate zones in Europe; requires habitat with adjacent feeding, lekking and nesting areas; coastal tundra to forest tundra, near small lakes, in marshes and deltas with shallow water margins, variably covered with vegetation, and with dry mounds and slopes with some low scrub for leks; in W Europe, damp to swampy meadows, often with shallow pools or ditches, and patches of birch, willow scrub and short grass or bare ground. Outside breeding season, prefers muddy margins of lakes, pools, ponds, rivers, marshes and flooded areas, including brackish, saline or alkaline waters; in India, large numbers on tidal mudflats and lagoons, but not commonly on seashore elsewhere; W African wintering sites include flooded or dry plains, marshes and grass, wheat or rice fields, not always close to water; observed picking up spilled grains from road. During migration commoner along shores and in freshly mown or short-grazed grasslands in W Europe. Uses night-time roosts on shallow water along lake edges.

Food and Feeding. During breeding season, mainly terrestrial and aquatic insects, including adults and larvae particularly of beetles and dipteran flies; outside breeding season diet more varied, including caddisflies, water-bugs, mayflies and grasshoppers, small crustaceans, spiders, small molluscs, annelid worms, frogs and small fish; birds wintering in Sahel zone often feed on rice seeds and other cereals, sedges, grasses and aquatic plants. Probes in mud or soil and picks up prey from surface or plants; sometimes follows ploughs; sometimes wades in shallow water. Nocturnal and diurnal feeder.

Breeding. Laying from early May in NW Europe, mid-May in Sweden and early Jun in Finnmark. Polygynous, with no true pair-bond; mating primarily takes place at traditional leks where males gather to display and females visit. Three types of males appear on arena: (1) residents, possesing small territories ("courts"); (2) marginals, without territory; and (3) satellites, occurring on periphery of arena and mating opportunistically; satellites are generally white tufted and ruffed. Many females may copulate during migration. No site fidelity and natal philopatry. Nests solitary or semi-colonial, in densities of 0·1-2·5 nests/ha, occasionally only several metres apart and sometimes near lek; non-territorial. Nest concealed in marsh plants or meadow grass; shallow scrape lined with grass, leaves and stems. 4 eggs, sometimes 3, laid at 24-36 hour intervals; incubation 20-23 days, starting with last egg; incubation and brood rearing by female only; chick ochre-orange above, with black and brown streaks and lines of "powder-puffs", of which two along crown, underparts entirely buff; fledging 25-28 days; female leaves chicks at or some days before fledging. Hatching success 93% (only one study). Age of first breeding 2 years, probably later in males; annual mortality 48%; oldest ringed bird 10 years, 11 months.

Movements. Migratory. Chief winter quarters in Africa; huge concentrations in Sahel zone, e.g. Senegal Delta, Niger inundation zone in Mali, Sokoto region in Nigeria, Yobe Delta in Niger and Nigeria, Nile system in Sudan. In autumn, flies in broad front SW across Europe, following route farther E in spring; Scandinavian breeders probably virtually all stage in Wadden Sea region from late Apr to mid-May; W movement of E breeders in autumn towards Europe; E & S African winterers come from Siberia, migrating via Caspian and Black Seas; smaller numbers fly across easternmost Asia. Autumn migration starts late Jun to early Jul (males), mid-Jul (females) and late Jul to Aug (juveniles), crossing temperate Europe mainly late Jul to mid-Sept, and S Asia Sept; at least in Britain juvenile females precede juvenile males; important staging and moulting areas lie around North Sea, W Germany and N Caspian Sea; arrives Senegal from mid-Jul (earliest males) and tropics mainly late Aug to Sept. Females winter farther S than males and juveniles move S gradually. Spring migration starts Mar, but mainly Mar to mid-May, males starting a month earlier than females; some non-breeders remain in winter quarters; breeding grounds reoccupied from mid-Apr in W Europe, but progressively later to N & E, mid-May to Jun in Siberia. Migrates in large groups, of hundreds or thousands.

Status and Conservation. Not globally threatened. Total population possibly over 2,000,000 birds, of which over 1,000,000 winter in W Africa, up to 1,000,000 in E Africa and SW Asia; up to 1,000,000 birds counted within a 25 km radius of Senegal Delta in 1972, 180,000-200,000 in 1991 and 1992; less than 10,000 birds in Atlantic Europe and Mediterranean; c. 100,000 in SC Asia, with 113,000 in India in 1992. In Norway and Sweden, 60,000-95,000 breeding "pairs" and 30,000-50,000 in Finland, where earlier estimated at 196,000 in 1973-1976 and 150,000 in 1986. Numbers declining at W African wintering sites. W breeding range has contracted considerably during last 200 years, especially in S, as result of drainage of wetlands; in Netherlands decline of 90% since 1950's. In Norway and Finland, has expanded range S since 1940's. In recent years breeding range and numbers have increased in E Russia; small British population has increased since late 1960's.

Bibliography. Ali & Ripley (1980), Andersen (1944, 1948, 1951), Anderson, K.R. (1974), Armstrong (1983), Banerjee & Banerjee (1977), Batten *et al.* (1990), Beehler *et al.* (1986), Beintema (1985), Beintema & Müskens (1987), Beintema *et al.* (1991), Benson & Benson (1975), Bradbury (1981), Brazil (1991), Busche (1995), Chandler, R.J. (1987b, 1990), Coates (1985), Cramp & Simmons (1983), Dickinson *et al.* (1991), van Dinteren (1989), Dowsett & Forbes-Watson (1993), Drenckhahn (1968), Dubois & Maheo (1986), Dunn (1994), Elgood *et al.* (1994), Étchécopar & Hüe (1964, 1978), Evans (1994), Fjeldså (1977), Gavrilov & Keskpaik (1992), Ginn *et al.* (1989), Goodman *et al.* (1989), Gore (1990), Hill (1991), Hockey & Douie (1995), Hogan-Warburg (1966, 1992), Höglund & Alatalo (1995), Höglund & Lundberg (1989), Höglund *et al.* (1993), Hötker (1985), Hüe & Étchécopar (1970), Ivanova (1973), Jukema *et al.* (1995), Kepp *et al.* (1991), Khlebosolov (1989), Knystautas (1993), Koopman (1986), Lank & Smith (1987, 1992), Lank *et al.* (1995), Lifjeld (1984), Mackworth-Praed & Grant (1957, 1962), Maclean (1993), Marchant & Higgins (1996), van Marle & Voous (1988), Melter (1995), Morel & Roux (1966), Münster (1989b, 1990, 1991), Patrikeev (1995), Paz (1987), Pearson (1981), Perennou (1991), Perennou *et al.* (1994), Phillips (1978), Piersma (1986b, 1995), Pinto (1983), Prater (1982), Rands *et al.* (1987), van Rhijn (1973, 1983, 1985a, 1991), Ripley (1982), Roberts, T.J. (1991), Rogacheva (1992), Rutgers & Norris (1970), Schleufler & Stiefel (1985), Schmitt & Whitehouse (1976), Scott (1989), Serra & Baccetti (1991), Serra *et al.* (1990), Shepard (1976), Shirihai (1996), Short *et al.* (1990), Tolchin (1983), Tomkovich (1992b), Tréca (1983, 1993), Trolliet & Girard (1991), Trolliet *et al.* (1992), Urban *et al.* (1986).

Subfamily PHALAROPODINAE

Genus *STEGANOPUS* Vieillot, 1818

84. Wilson's Phalarope

Steganopus tricolor

French: Phalarope de Wilson **German**: Wilsonwassertreter **Spanish**: Falaropo Tricolor

Taxonomy. *Steganopus tricolor* Vieillot, 1819, Paraguay.
Commonly placed in genus *Phalaropus*, but genetically distinct; apparently quite close to *Tringa*. Monotypic.

Distribution. N Alberta and EC California E to Great Lakes area, with scattered small outlying populations. Winters from N Peru to Uruguay and S to Tierra del Fuego.

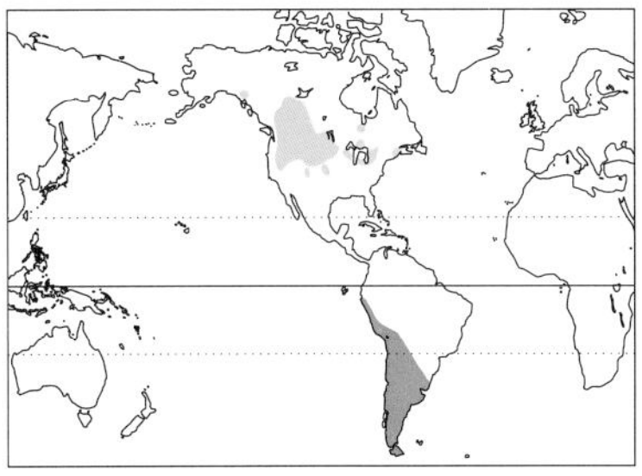

Descriptive notes. 22-24 cm; male 30-110 g, female 52-128 g; wingspan 35-38 cm. Largest phalarope, with longest legs and bill; legs grey to black; toes lobed, but less so than in *Phalaropus*. Reversed sexual dimorphism. Female has greyish white cap and nape, black band from bill through eye to side of breast; blue-grey mantle and wing-coverts, reddish chestnut edge to mantle and scapulars; foreneck and upper breast rich orange. Male much darker and generally duller above. Non-breeding adult uniform pale grey above and white below; white forehead and supercilium; white uppertail-coverts conspicuous in flight; legs yellow. Juvenile has dark brown upperparts with buff fringes, producing somewhat scaled aspect; sides of breast washed buff; legs yellow.

Habitat. Breeds mostly in wetlands in prairie region, up to taiga region, on grassy plains, often grazed or cultivated, peppered with small potholes; hay meadows and pastures, in vicinity of water; near marshy grassland and marshes with open grassy fringes; only occasionally near lakes. After breeding, all adults stage at large, shallow, hypersaline lakes in W North America; not common at coast, although sometimes in sheltered tidal pools, lagoons and estuaries. Unlike other phalaropes, not pelagic in winter; chief wintering habitats are mudflats and shallow, open water of saline lakes in highlands of Andes in Peru, Chile, W Bolivia and NW Argentina; sparsely at freshwater wetlands in *pampas* and on alkaline ponds.

Food and Feeding. Small, mostly aquatic, invertebrates, especially dipteran flies, bugs, beetles and their larvae, crustaceans, spiders and some seeds. At breeding areas feeds on open water and flooded meadows; females more aquatic than males. At staging sites, females feed on brine-shrimps (*Artemia*) and brine-flies (*Aphydra*) from water's surface, while males and juveniles feed more terrestrially on brine-flies, later becoming fully aquatic too. At salt-lakes in wintering sites, recorded taking brine-shrimps, copepods, chironomid midges and brine-flies. When swimming, spins less than other phalaropes; usually pecks prey from water or mud surface, also upends, lunges at prey, probes in soft mud, and in shallows scythes with bill through water.

Breeding. Laying early May to late Jun. Usually monogamous; 0-11% of females polyandrous when males in excess, or in extended breeding season. Sex roles reversed. Densities up to 1·1 nests/ha; nests average 60 m apart, sometimes less than 5 m; not territorial; low degree of natal philopatry and site fidelity. Nest in fairly tall, dense vegetation, within 100 m of water; scrape lined, during egg-laying, with plant material. 4 eggs, laid at 24-27 hour intervals; single or double brood; up to 3 replacement clutches laid; incubation 18-27 days, starting regularly with 3rd egg, by male; female deserts male 0-18 days after clutch completed, and courts other males, which may still be incubating; chick has tawny and fulvous breast band and upperparts, latter with some black spots and black line on back, pale buff or greyish white underparts; young tended by male; fledging period and timing of independence unknown. Many clutches may be lost due to predation by birds, mammals or reptiles, and incubating males occasionally taken; also disturbance by cattle and humans. Hatching success 12-50%; in some years, local fledging success close to 0%. Age of first breeding 1 year.

Movements. Migratory. After breeding, adults migrate to large hypersaline lakes in W North America to moult and to fatten up, attracted to abundance of food; up to 600,000 recorded on Great Salt L. Females depart from breeding areas and arrive at staging sites by mid-Jun, followed by males and finally juveniles. Adults migrate across Pacific to coastal W South America and thence S through Andes; females depart late Jul to late Aug, males 2 weeks later; juveniles migrate after males, overland on broad front to N South America; adults arrive in South America from early Aug, juveniles late Aug, and at wintering sites late Sept to early Nov, occurring on lakes in concentrations of up to 500,000. Main wintering areas in Bolivia, Chile and Argentina. On spring migration crosses highlands of South America in mid-Mar, then Central America or Gulf of Mexico and interior USA; arrives at breeding areas from late Apr to early May. Migrates nocturnally in large flocks. A dead specimen found at Alexander I (71° S) is most southerly wader record.

Status and Conservation. Not globally threatened. Total population estimated at 1,500,000 during autumn 1988, but not over 1,000,000 in 1994. Numbers likely to have decreased as consequence of substantial habitat loss of prairie wetlands until middle of present century. During last few decades breeding range has expanded enormously in all directions. Population may have declined since mid-1980's, probably as result of drought, but now considered stable. Movements indicate eastward shift since 1920's, possibly due to drought in breeding areas. Recreational use of water and reclamation projects in W North American staging areas present threats.

Bibliography. Baldassarre & Fischer (1984), Belton (1984), Bent (1927-1929), Blake (1977), Blomqvist (1983b), Bomberger (1984), Bousfield *et al.* (1986), Burger & Howe (1975), Colwell (1986, 1987, 1991, 1992), Colwell & Jehl (1994), Colwell & Oring (1988a, 1988b, 1988c, 1988d, 1988e, 1988f, 1990), Contreras *et al.* (1990), Cramp & Simmons (1983), Delehanty (1991), Delehanty & Oring (1993), Disher (1990), Dittmann & Zink (1991), Dittmann *et al.* (1989), Dott (1985), Einemann (1991), Ellis & Jehl (1991), Fevold *et al.* (1973), Fivizzani, Oring & El Halawani (1987), Fivizzani, Oring, El Halawani & Schlinger (1990), Fjeldså & Krabbe (1990), Garcher & Carroll (1991), Hayes (1995), Hedley *et al.* (1986), Hilty & Brown (1986), Höhn (1965, 1967), Höhn & Barron (1963), Howe (1975a, 1975b), Howell & Webb (1995a), Hurlbert *et al.* (1984), Jehl (1987a, 1987c, 1988, 1990, 1994b), Johns (1969), Johnson (1965b), Kagarise (1979), Mahoney & Jehl (1985b), Matthiessen (1994), McAlpine *et al.* (1988), McNeil *et al.* (1987), Monroe (1968), Morrison & Manning (1976), Murphy, W.L. *et al.* (1991), Murray (1983), Oring *et al.* (1988), de la Peña (1992), Reynolds *et al.* (1986), Rubega (1991), Schiemann (1980), Schlinger *et al.* (1989), Scott & Carbonell (1986), Sick (1985c, 1993), Siegfried & Batt (1972), Sinclair & Hockey (1980), Skagen & Knopf (1993), Spaans &

Autar (1982), Stiles & Skutch (1989), Urban *et al.* (1986), Viet & Peterson (1993), Wetmore (1965), Wiens *et al.* (1993), Wilson, M.A. (1993).

Genus *PHALAROPUS* Brisson, 1760

85. **Red-necked Phalarope**

Phalaropus lobatus

French: Phalarope à bec étroit **German**: Odinshühnchen **Spanish**: Falaropo Picofino
Other common names: Northern Phalarope

Taxonomy. *Tringa tobata* [sic] Linnaeus, 1758, Hudson Bay.
Sometimes placed in monospecific genus *Lobipes*. Monotypic.
Distribution. Circumpolar, in coastal regions of Arctic Ocean, S to Aleutians and NW Britain. Winters pelagically off CW South America, in Arabian Sea and from C Indonesia to W Melanesia.

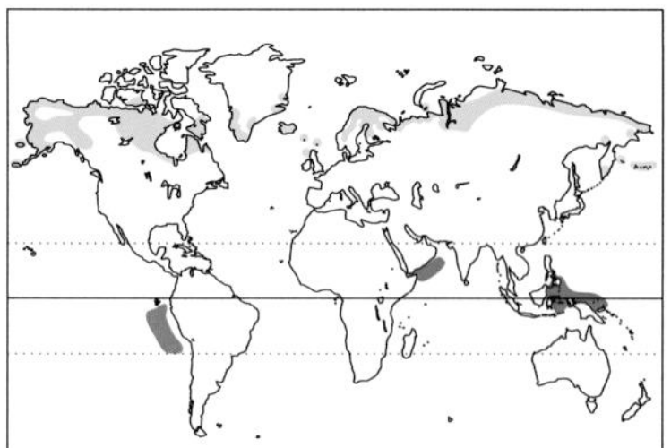

Descriptive notes. 18-19 cm; 20-48 g; wingspan 31-34 cm. Smallest phalarope, with needle-like bill and slender neck; toes lobed. Reversed sexual dimorphism. Female has slate-grey head, neck and sides of breast with bright orange-red horseshoe collar and white throat; golden buff fringes on upperparts form lines on sides of mantle. Male much duller, with browner head, neck and upperparts; white above eye often spreads out to form narrow supercilium. Non-breeding adult has dull blue-grey upperparts with white fringes; head mainly white with black patch through and behind eye; underparts white with faint streaks on lower flanks. Juvenile has brown crown, hindneck and eye-patch; upperparts black-brown with bright buff fringes; breast washed buff, rest of underparts white.
Habitat. Breeds from coast to interior of Arctic, to lower latitudes than *P. fulicaria*; on tundra, forest tundra and Scandinavian alpine tundra, at or near lakes and pools with marshy margins, often overgrown with grass, sedges and moss; sparsely vegetated lava deserts in Iceland; coastal moorland; often in floodplains of large rivers or on islets; also *Polygonum* bogs. During migration, uses inland saline and hypersaline lakes. Winters at sea, in upwelling zones and ocean slicks with high availability of plankton.
Food and Feeding. During breeding season, chiefly insects, especially dipteran flies and their larvae, as well as beetles, caddisflies, ants and bugs; also other small invertebrates, including snails, crustaceans and annelid worms; some seeds. On saline lakes brine-flies (*Ephydra*), mostly larval. During pelagic non-breeding period, mainly euphausiids and calanoid copepods, and small amounts of various other floating particles. Forages by swimming, wading and walking; pecks at prey at water surface, from vegetation or mud, rapidly lunges at prey just below water surface, upends, seizes flying insects, and often spins around in water, anti-clockwise, slightly faster than *P. fulicaria*. Makes use of surface tension to transport prey from bill to mouth. Associates with other feeding birds, probably to benefit from the higher prey availability brought about by disturbance; at sea, reported to be found near whales and shoals of fish, where profits from high local plankton densities; also at floating seaweed; in flocks of 20-100.
Breeding. Laying Jun in Fenno-Scandia. Monogamous, but sometimes polyandrous when males in excess; sex roles reversed. Solitary or loosely colonial where habitat restricted, with up to 50 nests at 1 site; densities in N Siberia 0·3-6 pairs/ha, and 0·6-32 birds/km² in S, varying greatly between years; not territorial. Low degree of site fidelity and natal philopatry. Nest on bare ground or among sparse vegetation, close to water; scrape, lined with leaves and stems. 4 eggs, occasionally 3, laid at intervals of 24-30 hours; usually single-brooded, but in case of polyandry double-brooded; replacement clutches may be laid; incubation 17-21 days, by male only, starting fully with 4th egg; chick cinnamon-buff to whitish with black bands, crown and eyestripe black and three black bands down back, underparts white, greyish and buff; chicks tended by male; fledging 18-21 days; young independent at c. 14 days. Females depart soon after hatching of 1st clutches and males c. 2 weeks later, before young fledge. Breeding success can be high: 80% of nests reported to hatch at least 1 egg. Breeds first as 1-year-old. Oldest ringed bird at least 5 years old.
Movements. Migrates over land more than *P. fulicaria* and spends non-breeding season pelagically. Nearctic population winters mainly at edges of Humboldt Current off W South America; large numbers off Peru in Oct-Mar and few off Chile indicate more N distribution than *P. fulicaria*; migrates S across N Canada and W USA, where occurs on saline lakes, with 10,000's on Mono L, Great Salt L and L Albert; thence S over sea. In NW Atlantic, birds migrating S possibly include some from Nearctic, Greenland and Iceland; huge numbers, up to 2,000,000 (Aug 1977) aggregate at Bay of Fundy in May and Aug, but winter quarters of these birds unknown; it seems unlikely that they fly farther S crossing Caribbean and Central America towards Pacific, since rarely observed in these zones, but no wintering sites known in Atlantic Ocean. W Eurasian population winters in Arabian Sea; migrates on broad front, but many via Caspian Sea and lakes in Kazakhstan, Aug-Sept and Apr-May, with 600,000 at L Tengiz in May 1959; enter and leave Arabian Sea via Gulf of Oman. Arrive at breeding grounds late-May to mid-Jun, 3-4 weeks earlier at temperate latitudes, and females often earlier than males; females depart from end Jun, followed by adult males late Jul, and juveniles in Aug. E Siberian population winters among East Indies, migrating across land and sea. Gregarious in winter and on spring migration.
Status and Conservation. Not globally threatened. Total breeding population in Eurasia estimated at 500,000-1,000,000+ birds; Nearctic population exceeds 2,000,000 birds; Iceland 50,000-100,000 breeding pairs (1985), Norway 9500 pairs (1981), Sweden 50,000 pairs (1984) and Finland 15,000 pairs (1986). Numbers in Bay of Fundy have decreased dramatically during recent years, but cause unknown. Numbers may be decreasing at S of range; those in Britain and Ireland decreased in 19th century probably due to egg-collection; 28-32 pairs in 1985; still breeds irregularly in Ireland. More than 1,000,000 birds winter in Arabian Sea.
Bibliography. Ali & Ripley (1980), Armstrong (1983), Ash & Ashford (1977), Baker, M.C. (1977), Beehler *et al.* (1986), Bent (1927-1929), Blake (1977), Blomqvist (1983b), Bourne (1991), Brazil (1991), Briggs, Dettman *et al.* (1984), Briggs, Tyler *et al.* (1987), Brown, P.P. & Harris (1988), Brown, R.G.B. (1979), Brown, R.G.B. & Gaskin (1988), Bruijns & Bruijns (1957), Chernyaev (1986), Coates (1985), Cramp & Simmons (1983), Dickinson *et al.* (1991), Dittmann & Zink (1991), Dittmann *et al.* (1989), Dowsett & Forbes-Watson (1993), Duncan (1995), Ellis & Jehl (1991), Étchécopar & Hüe (1964, 1978), Evans (1994), Fevold *et al.* (1973), Fivizzani *et al.* (1990), Fjeldså (1977), Gavrilov & Bekbayev (1988), Gavrilov, Beresovski *et al.* (1982), Gavrilov, Jerochov *et al.* (1983), Goodman *et al.* (1989), Gratto, Fivizzani *et al.* (1990), Gratto, Oring *et al.* (1990), Haney (1985), Hildén & Vuolanto (1972), Hilty & Brown (1986), Höhn (1965, 1968, 1971), Hoogerwerf (1964), Howell & Webb (1995a), Hüe & Étchécopar (1970), Jehl (1986), Knystautas (1993), Mackworth-Praed & Grant (1957), Mercier (1985), Monroe (1968), Nechaev (1988), Orr *et al.* (1982), Orsini (1980), Patrikeev (1995), de la Peña (1992), Perennou *et al.* (1994), Piersma (1986b), Pocock (1962), Pringle & Pringle (1971), Raner (1972), Reynolds (1987), Reynolds & Cooke (1988), Reynolds *et al.* (1986), Ridgely & Gwynne (1989), Ripley (1982), Roberts, T.J. (1991), Rogacheva (1992), Rubega (1993a, 1993b), Rubega & Inouye (1994), Rubega & Obst (1993), Ryabitsev (1985), Schamel & Tracy (1988, 1991), Schiemann (1985, 1986, 1989, 1992), Shirihai (1996), Short *et al.* (1990), Shubin (1988), Slud (1964), Smythies (1981), Stiles & Skutch (1989), Tinbergen (1935), Urban *et al.* (1986), Wetmore (1965), White & Bruce (1986), Whitfield (1989, 1990b).

86. **Red Phalarope**

Phalaropus fulicaria

French: Phalarope à bec large **German**: Thorshühnchen **Spanish**: Falaropo Picogrueso
Other common names: Grey Phalarope

Taxonomy. *Tringa Fulicaria* Linnaeus, 1758, Hudson Bay.
Genus sometimes broadened to include *Steganopus tricolor*, or conversely narrowed to exclude *P. lobatus*. Species name often erroneously spelt *fulicarius*. Monotypic.
Distribution. Circumpolar, on coasts of Arctic Ocean. Winters pelagically mainly off W South America and W & SW Africa.

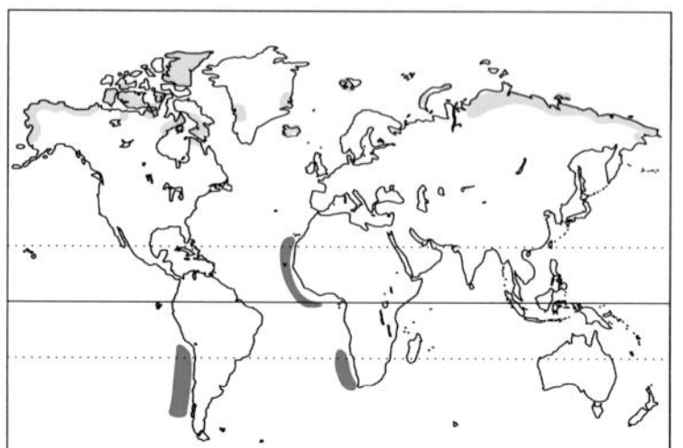

Descriptive notes. 20-22 cm; 37-77 g; wingspan 37-40 cm. Larger and chunkier than *P. lobatus*, with broader, heavier mainly yellow bill. Reversed sexual dimorphism. Female mainly chestnut-red with blackish brown crown and front of face; grey centre of nape, white at side of face; upperparts blackish brown with cinnamon and buff fringes. Male duller, with streaked crown and mantle; white on face less pure; duller underparts often mixed with white. Non-breeding adult pale blue-grey above, white below; dark crown-patch, black eye-patch. Juvenile has upperparts like breeding male and head pattern as non-breeding adult, but browner; face, neck and sides of breast pink-buff; belly white.
Habitat. Most pelagic of phalaropes. Breeds near coast, on marshy tundra with small pools, boggy meadows with moss and grass, marshy river valleys or islets in fjords. Outside breeding season pelagic, in tropical and subtropical upwelling zones where plankton occurs at high concentrations of over 50,000 organisms/litre. Regularly seen ashore during gales.
Food and Feeding. During breeding season takes invertebrates, including insects and their larvae, such as dipteran flies, caddisflies, beetles and bugs, also molluscs, crustaceans, annelids, spiders and mites, and occasionally plant material, mainly seeds, especially when food is limited; feeds in or around small pools or lagoons or on *Fucus* seaweed washed ashore; also often at sea; forages by swimming, wading and walking, and typically spins around fast pecking at or just below water surface; also quickly lunges forward at prey, or upends, tilting body forward and immersing bill only or part of head, or seizing flying insects. Outside breeding season feeds at sea on plankton, including amphipods less than 2 mm long, Hydrozoa and small fish, from water surface or just below, using exceptionally broad bill; reported to be found near whales or schools of fish that bring plankton to surface and even recorded picking parasites from whale's back; formerly used by whalers to locate their prey; recorded feeding and resting on floating mats of seaweed. Large quantities of floating plastic particles may be ingested. Outside breeding season in small flocks of c. 20, occasionally several thousand together.
Breeding. Laying mid-Jun to mid-Jul in Iceland, early Jun to early Jul in Russia. Usually monogamous, but, when excess of males, polyandrous, with females starting 2nd clutch several hundred metres from 1st; female usually leaves male after clutch completed. Sex roles reversed. Breeds in loose groups when habitat is limited; 0·02-2 pairs/ha, up to 7-10 in patchy habitat, but very variable between years; no territorial behaviour; breeding males have their own feeding flocks and females, failed breeders and non-breeders also feed together in small parties; low degree of site faithfulness; may nest in colony of aggressive seabirds, e.g. Arctic Terns (*Sterna paradisaea*), thus reducing risk of predation. Nest in short vegetation, usually close to or surrounded by water; shallow scrape, which male lines with plant material. 4 eggs, sometimes 3, laid at 24-26 hour intervals; sometimes double-brooded and 1 replacement clutch can be laid; incubation 18-20 days, by male, starting once clutch complete; chick has cinnamon-buff upperparts with white patches and black streaks, 3 black streaks on back, underparts pale violet-grey with some buff on flanks and white on breast; tended by male; fledging 16-20 days; independent at or just before fledging; soon after fledging young move to larger lakes in large flocks. Fledging success almost 2 young/pair in Iceland, 0·1-0·2 young/pair in poor year in E Siberia. Many non-breeders present over summer in coastal waters near breeding grounds. Age of first breeding 1 year.
Movements. Migrates almost exclusively via sea routes; observed migrating 80-160 km offshore. Non-breeding birds disperse from late Jun, adult females leave early Jun and adult males and juveniles late Jul to Aug, adult males on average earlier; few birds S of equator before late Aug, but most present at non-breeding quarters by end Nov. Chief non-breeding areas off coast of W & SW Africa, in upwellings of Guinea and Canary Currents, especially off Mauritania, and also Benguela Current off Namibia and South Africa, and W South America, especially Humboldt Current off Chile; suggested wintering areas in SW Atlantic and Arabian Sea uncertain. Nearctic breeders do not move down W Atlantic coast but winter off Africa, uncertain how many Nearctic breeders winter in Pacific; sightings in C Pacific and lack of them in SE Asia suggest that Siberian breeders winter in Humboldt Current. Evidently departs South African and Chilean seas in Mar, and W & SW African seas in Apr. Migrates along Arctic coasts and reoccupies breeding grounds late May to mid-Jun, C Siberia from early Jun; females on average first, often after waiting at sea for 2-3 weeks for ground to thaw.
Status and Conservation. Not globally threatened. Population size 100,000-1,000,000 birds. On Svalbard 150-300 pairs (1981), Iceland probably 50-60 pairs and low numbers in Greenland and on Ellesmere I. Few precise data available; as with *P. lobatus*, pelagic wintering habit makes counts of non-breeding birds rather difficult.
Bibliography. Ali & Ripley (1980), Armstrong (1983), Aston (1993), Bengtson (1968), Bent (1927-1929), Blake (1977), Blomqvist (1983b), Bond, S.I. (1971), Brazil (1991), Briggs, Dettman *et al.* (1984), Briggs, Tyler *et al.* (1987), Brown & Gaskin (1988), Connors & Smith (1982), Cramp & Simmons (1983), Dittmann & Zink (1991), Dittmann *et al.* (1989), Dodson & Egger (1980), Dowsett & Forbes-Watson (1993), Étchécopar & Hüe (1964), Fivizzani *et al.*

(1990), Ginn *et al*. (1989), Goodman *et al*. (1989), Grebmeier & Harrison (1992), Haney & Stone (1988), Harrison *et al*. (1990), Hilty & Brown (1986), Hockey & Douie (1995), Höhn (1965, 1971), Howell & Webb (1995a), Hüe & Étchécopar (1970), Johnson (1965b), Kistchinski (1975), Knystautas (1993), Mackworth-Praed & Grant (1962, 1970), Maclean (1993), Martin & Martin (1992), Mayfield (1978a, 1978b), Mehlum (1991), Moser & Lee (1992), Myers (1981a), Obst & Hunt (1990), Orr *et al*. (1982), Penrith (1992), de la Peña (1992), Ridley (1980), Rogacheva (1992), Ryan & Rose (1989), Schamel & Tracy (1977, 1987, 1991), Schiemann (1991, 1992), Schneider, Harrison & Hunt (1990), Senior (1987), Shirihai (1996), Stanford (1953), Stiles & Skutch (1989), Tracy & Schamel (1988), Urban *et al*. (1986), Wander (1981), Wetmore (1965).

Class AVES
Order CHARADRIIFORMES
Suborder CHARADRII
Family PEDIONOMIDAE (PLAINS-WANDERER)

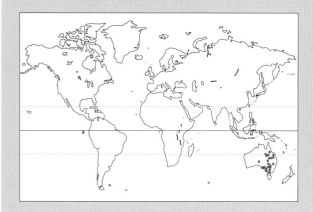

- Small, quail-like terrestrial birds, with slim bill and very short tail; unlike Turnicidae, hind toe present.
- 15-19 cm.

- Australia.
- Sparse native grasslands.
- 1 genus, 1 species, 1 taxon.
- 1 species threatened; none extinct since 1600.

Systematics

The Plains-wanderer (*Pedionomus torquatus*) is of great scientific interest, as the sole representative of a family of birds found only in eastern Australia. The fact that the female is both larger and more colourful than the male led John Gould to describe them as two separate species in the early 1840's.

Through the years, this singular species has almost invariably been classified alongside the buttonquails (Turnicidae), these two groups usually sharing a suborder, Turnices, in the order Gruiformes. The main taxonomic issue was whether *Pedionomus* merited a family of its own or only subfamily status within the Turnicidae. However, osteological studies published by S. L. Olson and D. W. Steadman in 1981 switched the focus elsewhere, as their results strongly suggested that this species belonged in the Charadriiformes. Further studies of the anatomy and behaviour of the Plains-wanderer, together with those based on DNA-DNA hybridization, support the conclusion that Pedionomidae is probably more aptly placed in the Charadriiformes, and that it is related to the seedsnipes (Thinocoridae) of South America. In this case, it may be that the Plains-wanderer is an ancient member of Australia's avifauna, with origins dating back to when Australia was part of the Gondwanan supercontinent and connected to South America via the Antarctic land bridge. This ancient link remains hypothetical because the fossil records of both Pedionomidae and Thinocoridae consist entirely of Quaternary specimens of genera that are still extant.

A detailed analysis of the anatomy and osteology of the Plains-wanderer has revealed that the formula of the thigh muscles, the configuration of the carotid arteries, the morphology of the liver, the nature of the brachial nerve plexus, the presence of the hind toe, the diastataxic condition of the secondaries, and 22 osteological characters all combine to support its removal from the Gruiformes and its placement in the Charadriiformes. In common with some waders, but not the buttonquails, the Plains-wanderer has pointed, rather than oval, eggs; spotted, rather than striped, downy young; two long brood patches, rather than one; and a noticeable wingbar in flight. The gait of the Plains-wanderer is free, and typical of a wader. When alarmed, the bird will often run a short distance, stop and stand tall, with its head bobbing, and then repeat this behaviour several times, again as some waders do. Unlike buttonquails, Plains-wanderers never occur in coveys, but are solitary, except when breeding; at that time only, the members of a pair or a male with its dependent young may be seen together.

Morphological Aspects

The Plains-wanderer is a small ground-dwelling bird, similar in size and shape to the *Coturnix* quails, but it has a finer bill, longer legs and neck, and a lankier appearance. With its slim bill, it takes both seeds and insects, while its walks about and stretches up to its full height from time to time (see General Habits). In flight, it is more ponderous than a quail, and the tips of its feet trail beyond the end of its short tail. It has a fluttering descent and will land in an open area, this behaviour contrasting with the characteristic dive of quails into cover. It is reluctant to fly, but its longer, high-stepping legs carry it much more quickly than quails enable it to run.

The adult male Plains-wanderer is pale brown with dark brown and white scallops on the sides of the neck, upper breast and flanks. The bare parts are cream to pale yellow and the sides of the head, chin and throat are pale buff. Although the adult female has a similarly coloured body, unlike the male she sports a distinctive broad black collar, spotted white, and a rufous gorget on the upper breast, while the bare parts are a brighter yellow than those of the male. This reversal of sexual dimorphism in plumage ties in with the different roles taken by the sexes in the reproductive cycle (see Breeding).

Prior to moult, the juvenile is similar to the adult male, but shows dark brown spotting, rather than scallops, on the breast and flanks. The species' well camouflaged plumage and cryptic behaviour mean that, though diurnal, it is seldom seen, even in the few remaining areas where it is common.

Adults undergo one complete (pre-basic) moult a year, probably in the post-breeding season, as most individuals are in body moult from February to May, although there are records as early as October and as late as June. Primary moult is gradual, interruption is not uncommon, and the sequence of moult may be similar to that of seedsnipes, in which the outer three primaries are moulted before a complex moult sequence of the inner primaries takes place. The post-juvenile body moult begins between the fifth and thirteenth weeks, and is complete by 22 weeks of age.

Habitat

The lowland native grasslands of eastern Australia form the natural habitat of the Plains-wanderer. The species is more or less restricted to those areas with only a very sparse covering of vegetation. Permanent water does not seem to be a requirement, as the bird gleans droplets of dew and rain from blades of grass.

The Plains-wanderer has traditionally been linked with the buttonquails (Turnicidae), but recent work suggests that it may belong close to the seedsnipes (Thinocoridae) in the shorebird order Charadriiformes. Like the buttonquails, it shows reversed sexual dimorphism, the female wearing the brighter plumage, but it differs from them in possessing a hind toe. This splendid female illustrates an upright stance rather typical of the species.

[Pedionomus torquatus. Photo: Christo Baars/ Foto Natura]

The Plains-wanderer is not present in dense pastures formed of introduced species, nor is it found in treed areas, even when the ground layer is similar to that of its favoured habitat. Similarly, large expanses of bare ground are avoided, whilst areas preferred seem to be where the topsoil has been eroded to expose a red clay subsoil, which does not support dense vegetation under any seasonal conditions, but rather low-growing herbs, such as salt-bushes (chenopods). Such areas contain about 50% bare ground, where fallen litter covers a further 10%. The more robust plants in the flora are generally spaced 10-20 cm apart and rarely exceed 30 cm in height. The bulk (94%) of the vegetation is less than 5 cm tall, but the small proportion that is over this height is important for the bird's concealment. As the Plains-wanderer stands about 15 cm tall when on tiptoe, in areas with thinnish grass cover it can see over the vegetation, move freely when foraging and running away from terrestrial predators, and at the same time avoid detection from the air.

Breeding, foraging and roosting all take place in sparse native grasslands which may be grazed by flocks of domestic animals. Changes to the preferred habitat brought about by cultivation, pasture improvement and weed invasions can cause populations of Plains-wanderers to become locally extinct. Overgrazing during droughts and burning can lead to widespread displacements of the birds, but, in contrast, light to moderate grazing pressure from domestic stock during droughts can change the structure of grasslands and enable birds to occupy areas that are normally too dense for them.

The Plains-wanderer is occasionally found in cereal stubble and some low crop fields. These are similar in structure to the sparse grasslands, but offer the bird only a temporary refuge until they are cultivated again. Areas of habitat suitable for the species can be indicated by the presence of more conspicuous species, such as the Banded Lapwing (*Vanellus tricolor*) in the Riverina region of New South Wales, and Inland Dotterels (*Peltohyas australis*) in south-west Queensland. However, when overgrazing temporarily eliminates Plains-wanderers from an area, these two other species sometimes remain.

General Habits

The Plains-wanderer is typically seen walking between tussocks in the sparse open grasslands that it frequents, periodically standing on tiptoe to keep a look-out for potential predators.

If threatened by a terrestrial predator, Plains-wanderers will run through the thin grass in a crouching posture. Birds sometimes lie flat on the ground, relying on their cryptic plumage to conceal them from any predators that may be in the vicinity. When such threats are present, Plains-wanderers do not seek dense cover, as quails do, nor do they usually "explode" into flight when discovered. On the contrary, birds that are hiding can sometimes be picked up by a human or a dog, or they will run when flushed, and only fly when hard pressed. They are probably vulnerable to raptors when in the air, particularly on their fluttering descent flights. Like waders, such as coursers (Glareolidae), alert or disturbed Plains-wanderers may stand on tiptoe with the head bobbing, as they scan the surrounding open country for intruders.

Because the birds are so seldom seen, they were once assumed to be nocturnal, but studies of both captive and wild radio-tracked birds prove that they are diurnal and crepuscular. Captive birds spend over a third of their day walking and foraging, a similar amount standing on tiptoe scanning their surroundings, and most of the rest in comfort behaviour, such as preening, stretching, standing hunched, sitting and dust-bathing. They have rarely been seen drinking but they avidly peck up droplets of water that accumulate at the tips of blades of grass after rain has fallen. The dominant, more colourful females spend significantly more time than males standing on tiptoe, on tufts of grass, with the head bobbing conspicuously. This behaviour, which is typical of the bird in the wild when alarmed, could attract predators and may in part account for the ratio of two to one in favour of males that has been recorded in field studies.

At night, Plains-wanderers roost solitarily on the ground in sparse grass, and accumulations of faeces indicate that the same site may be used for many nights. If disturbed with a spotlight, roosting birds seem reluctant to fly away, although some birds may walk away from the danger.

The species is usually solitary, especially outside the breeding season. At times during the breeding season, members of a pair may be 1-3 m apart, or a breeding male may be found in sole charge of two to four young. During droughts, up to ten birds may be found in an area normally occupied by one or two pairs in wetter years, but they never form flocks. Home ranges of breeding birds may cover 7-21 ha, but they average 12 ha in extent. There tends to be a considerable overlap between birds of the opposite sex, but there is none with birds of the same sex, unless the female takes a second mate.

Voice

Outside the breeding season Plains-wanderers are usually silent. When the birds are vocal, the most obvious call is a repeated low-pitched resonant "oo", which sometimes sounds dove-like, though at other times it appears bovine. It is associated with the establishment and maintenance of the pair-bond, and may be given only by the female. The male makes a quiet "irr-irr" call in response to the chicks' staccato "chip-chip-chip" distress calls. He also utters a piping drawn out "pie-pie-pie" to summon to him lost chicks which are giving a weak "peep" call.

Food and Feeding

The Plains-wanderer is omnivorous, and a wide variety of seeds and insects have been recorded in its diet. In all seasons insects comprise about 40% of the diet, except in spring, when their proportion is slightly higher. Ants, and beetles up to 15 mm long, constitute the major portion of the insect foods that are eaten throughout the year. Sucking bugs and caterpillars, the next most important insect foods, are taken mainly in summer and autumn. Grass, chenopods and other plants provide seeds that comprise about 58% of the remainder of the annual diet. Whereas in summer grass seeds make up the main part of the seed intake, in autumn the predominance shifts to seeds of chenopods and other plants. Native plants provide the majority of the seeds while introduced plant species make only a minor contribution to the Plains-wanderer's diet. It is rare for the Plains-wanderer to eat plant parts other than seeds.

Foraging takes place during the day and also at dusk. Birds feed by pecking up seeds and insects from the ground, and rarely by gleaning seeds off standing inflorescences. They will also hammer compacted soil with the bill in order to expose arthropods.

Breeding

The Plains-wanderer probably practises serial polyandry, a strategy also known in the charadriiform families Rostratulidae, Jacanidae and Scolopacidae (Phalaropodinae). In Pedionomidae, both sexes may incubate, but the male takes the dominant role and he assumes the sole responsibility of rearing the chicks, leaving the female free to pair with another male.

Though eggs have been found in all months except March and April, the main breeding season in the south-east of the continent commences with pairing and the females calling during winter, in June and July. Prior to copulation, the female walks about, calling, with her wings drooped. First clutches are laid in late winter and spring, from late August to November. If summer rains fall, second clutches may be laid in the summer months of January and February. North of the Tropic of Capricorn Plains-wanderers tend to breed in autumn and early winter, from March to June.

Most nests are in sparse native grassland rather than crops, often with a sheltering plant alongside or above them. Sometimes grasses are pulled together to form a concealing cone above the nest. The nest hollow is 6-8 cm wide and 2-4 cm deep. It is scratched in the ground by the female and lined with grass. Anything from two to five pyriform eggs may be laid, though clutch size is normally four. The eggs are ground-coloured and well covered with brown specks and splotches, measuring 32·8 x 23·6 mm on average. Incubation lasts 23 days, and is undertaken mostly by the male, even though the female remains on the territory.

Chicks are mustard-coloured with dark brown spots. They are precocial and nidifugous, attaining full independence about two months after hatching. The male feeds in the company of the chicks, but has not been seen to provide food for them. When danger threatens, the male is a stout defender of the young and may place himself with wings outstretched between a human intruder and the chicks; he may also call the chicks until they are all gathered out of sight beneath him.

Neighbouring pairs are usually 250-400 m apart. After the first clutch has hatched the female may pair with a second male and lay a second clutch, generally about 40 m from the first nest-site.

Virtually nothing is known about breeding success, but recently independent young captured and ringed during surveys were found to outnumber adults by a ratio of three to two. Torrential rains can flood nests and cause widespread breeding failure. Nevertheless, the species has the ability to recover quickly from population slumps following droughts, and birds can breed when they are only one year old. It is not known how long birds may survive in the wild, but in captivity they have been known to live for at least eight years.

Movements

Plains-wanderers are sedentary unless displaced by changes to their habitat, such as overgrazing during droughts, cultivation or burning. Birds that have been forced to disperse may move long distances, as evidenced by sporadic records in unusual localities, but whether most of them successfully settle elsewhere or die is not known. While overgrazing can force birds away, after rain and the regrowth of the grass and herbs suitable habitat may be reoccupied by newly arrived birds. Conversely, when unusually heavy rains promote dense growth of introduced grasses and weeds in the native pastures, Plains-wanderers can be forced to move to other areas in search of better feeding opportunities.

Most recaptures of ringed birds have been within 200 m of the ringing site, even though in some cases many months had elapsed. Radio-tracked birds also remain close to their release site, so in normal circumstances the birds would appear to carry out all of their foraging, breeding and roosting activities in the same area.

Relationship with Man

Being small, cryptic both in plumage and behaviour, and uncommon into the bargain, it is hardly surprising that the Plains-wanderer has made little impact on man. The fact that the sexes were originally described as two distinct species is proof enough of how poorly known the bird was, at least in the early years of the nine-teenth century, when Australia was even more sparsely populated than it is today, and the native grasslands survived intact.

Although Plains-wanderers have suffered to some extent from the activities of hunters (see Status and Conservation), at the same time it would seem that it has partly been through hunters that the Plains-wanderer's presence and habits have been brought to the public notice, as this typical report of Plains-wanderer escape behaviour from an early shooter testifies: "Whilst quail shooting in 1892 our dog which was a remarkably good worker made a decided set, but before either of us got within shot he started off for about 20 yards, and again set. This was repeated again and again until we had traversed the greater part of a 50 acre paddock in a zig-zag fashion. At last we saw a Plains-wanderer running like a rat through the grass. During the time occupied in following the dog we must have walked nearly half a mile. The same tactics were followed for about an hour, during which three more birds were shot. On several other occasions I have known them to lie motionless when set by the dog, and continue in that position until caught".

Status and Conservation

Lowland native grasslands are among the most depleted ecosystems in eastern Australia, and threatened grassland fauna have undergone a marked decline. There are now possibly fewer than 11,000 Plains-wanderers left in the wild, and in drought years, when overgrazing of habitat occurs, the population may be halved. These threats to the habitat remain constant, and the species is currently listed as globally Vulnerable.

The Plains-wanderer has been unable to adapt to the many changes that have taken place in these grasslands, changes brought about by the gradual influx of European settlers and the spread of their agricultural and pastoral activities. The species can not survive where sparse native grasslands are converted to crops or dense pastures formed of introduced plants, nor where the grasslands are dominated by weeds. Incapable of modifying its dietary requirements, it has become extinct in many areas where before it was not uncommon, and its numbers overall have dwindled alarmingly.

Conservation work for the Plains-wanderer and its threatened habitat took a major step forward with a study of the biology and management requirements of the species during the period 1984-1987. This study showed that on large inland grazing properties, the relatively small areas that are to be managed for Plains-wanderers need to be fenced off, in order to enable the intermittent removal of domestic animals. Grazing animals should be removed for the duration of the Plains-wanderer's breeding season, and reintroduced after this only if sufficient rain has fallen to prevent overgrazing.

The study identified the need for surveys to locate and rank areas with Plains-wanderers in order of priority, and for further work with landowners. These surveys have now commenced and have confirmed the threatened status of the species and the lack of large populations in any reserve. However, funds have been allocated for the reservation of the one remaining highly significant property, located during surveys of north Victoria. This 1400 ha property contains at least 150 Plains-wanderers and ten species of threatened plant, including one, *Leptorhynchos medius*, which was previously thought to be extinct. Also of importance is Willandra National Park in New South Wales, which contains perhaps some 50 Plains-wanderers, and a new reserve in south-west Queensland supports at least 150 Plains-wanderers, as well as threatened marsupials, such as the greater bilby (*Macrotis lagotis*). Despite this progress in the conservation of the species' habitat, much has still to be done with landowners, because it is on private land that the future of the Plains-wanderer rests. The fact that the species can readily be bred in captivity may yet prove significant.

The extent of the pressure that shooting may have had on the species is not clear. In the past, quail shooters killed many Plains-wanderers, and a few of these legally protected birds are still shot by mistake. In addition, introduced predators, such as the red fox (*Vulpes vulpes*), and pesticide spraying against locusts are further causes of some mortality amongst Plains-wanderers. However, there is no evidence that any of these three factors may be limiting populations to a degree remotely comparable with the dire effects of habitat alteration.

PLATE 46

inches 3
cm 8

Family PEDIONOMIDAE (PLAINS-WANDERER)
SPECIES ACCOUNTS

PLATE 46

Genus *PEDIONOMUS* Gould, 1841

Plains-wanderer

Pedionomus torquatus

French: Pédionome errant **German**: Steppenläufer **Spanish**: Llanero
Other common names: Plain Wanderer, Collared Plains-wanderer/Hemipode, Turkey Quail

Taxonomy. *Pedionomus torquatus* Gould, 1841, plains near Adelaide, South Australia.
Traditionally placed in Gruiformes, in close association with Turnicidae, but evidence currently available suggests link with Thinocoridae (see page 538). Populations in New South Wales were proposed as separate race, *goulburni*, but no genuine geographical variation detectable. Monotypic.
Distribution. E Australia.
Descriptive notes. 15-19 cm; male 40-80 g, female 55-95 g. Resembles *Coturnix* quails, but bill finer, neck and legs longer, and overall appearance lankier. Male has throat grey-white, breast buff, with pattern of dark brown or black crescents on side of neck, upper breast and flanks. Female larger and more brightly coloured than male; distinctive broad collar, black with white spots; yellow-buff or rufous breast band. Juvenile similar to male, but with dark brown spots, rather than crescents, on underparts.
Habitat. Sparse lowland native grasslands with low-growing herbs; rarely in cereal stubble. Avoids trees, woodland, scrub, dense pasture of introduced plants, and large bare areas. Breeding, feeding and roosting all occur in sparse native grasslands, usually without permanent water.
Food and Feeding. Omnivorous. Insects comprise nearly half annual diet; seeds of grass, chenopods and other plants make up remainder. Insects and seeds taken from ground; water droplets pecked from leaf tips after rain. Roughly one third of day is spent foraging.
Breeding. In SE, first clutches from late Aug to Nov, second clutches in Jan-Feb if summer rains fall; further north breeding occurs Mar-Jun. Solitary and probably serially polyandrous. Nest is shallow scrape in ground, lined with grass. Usually 4 eggs (2-5). Incubation 23 days, mainly by male; chicks

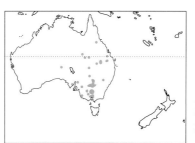

mustard-coloured with dark brown spots; chick-care solely by male, lasting c. 2 months. Sexual maturity at 1 year. After breeding season, independent young outnumber adults 3:2.
Movements. Sedentary, unless displaced by changes to habitat, e.g. cultivation, burning, overgrazing during droughts.
Status and Conservation. VULNERABLE. CITES II. Fewer than 11,000 birds and in drought years this number may be halved. Massive conversion of native grasslands to crops and dense pastures of introduced plants with weeds has brought about marked decline in total numbers. Regional extinctions across very large tracts of coastal and sub-coastal E Australia in all four states where species occurs. Recent surveys of Victoria, where species perhaps once most numerous, indicate possibly as few as 1000 birds; these birds mainly confined to small remnant islands of native grassland in a sea of cropland and introduced pastureland; future of many of these populations is not assured. Further inland, cultivation is not widespread, but overgrazing during droughts causes displacement, and decline in local populations. Key inland region is SW Queensland and NE South Australia, with combined population of c. 4500 birds. Recent conservation work has led to establishment of three widely separated reserves supporting c. 350 birds. Vast majority of overall population found on privately owned land, and much more joint work required with landowners. Alteration of habitat constitutes by far the major threat; additional dangers include hunting, introduced predators and pesticide spraying against locusts.
Bibliography. Baker-Gabb (1987, 1988, 1989, 1990a, 1990b, 1993), Baker-Gabb *et al.* (1990), Bennett (1983), Blakers *et al.* (1984), Bock & McEvey (1969), Bonnin & Angove (1989), Brouwer & Garnett (1990), Collar & Andrew (1988), Collar *et al.* (1994), Crome & Rushton (1975), D'Ombrain (1926), Frith (1969, 1985), Garnett (1993), Gochfeld *et al.* (1984), Harrington, G. N. *et al.* (1988), Johnsgard (1991b), Keartland (1901), Llewellyn (1975), Maher & Baker-Gabb (1994), Marchant & Higgins (1993), North (1913-1914), Olson & Steadman (1981), Ridley (1985), Rutgers & Norris (1970), Sibley & Ahlquist (1990), Taylor, P. W. (1988).

Class AVES
Order CHARADRIIFORMES
Suborder CHARADRII
Family THINOCORIDAE (SEEDSNIPES)

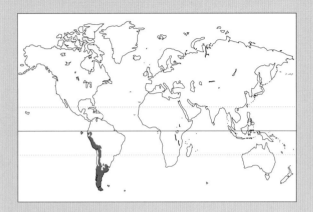

- Small to medium-sized birds with short legs and bills, resembling quails or partridges, but with snipe-like flight.
- 16-30 cm.

- Neotropical Region.
- Alpine vegetation, steppe and semi-desert, from sea-level up to 5500 m.
- 2 genera, 4 species, 10 taxa.
- No species threatened; none extinct since 1600.

Systematics

The seedsnipes are endemic to the Neotropical Region, where they inhabit Patagonia and the Andean zone. There is no paleontological record of them, apart from Pleistocene subfossils within the current range. However, their distinctive appearance and the DNA divergence data available indicate that the lineage dates well back into the Tertiary.

The seedsnipes differ strongly in overall impression and shape from the majority of charadriiform birds, but not more so than the sandgrouse (Pteroclidae), which are frequently considered to be close to Charadriiformes, and indeed are even sometimes included in this order. Although early systematists recognized that seedsnipes resembled the shorebirds, or waders, in a number of anatomical characters, they also noted that they showed some similarities with passerine birds, sandgrouse and gamebirds. All this resulted in confusing statements about their relationships with other birds. The cranial anatomy is superficially similar to that of passerine birds, with the aegithognathous palate, and seedsnipes differ from most other shorebirds by having a crop, a gizzard and long intestinal caeca; also, the legs are short, and a hind toe is present. However, with only two exceptions, all classifications of birds proposed over the last 100 years have included the seedsnipes in the order Charadriiformes, which was previously known as Limicolae. Their aberrant characters have thus been accepted as a result of their vegetarian diet.

A detailed analysis of skeletal characters by J. G. Strauch, published in 1978, placed the seedsnipes on the same main charadriiform branch as the snipes. However, in 1981 S. L. Olson and D. W. Steadman provided strong evidence that the nearest relative of the seedsnipes may be the Plains-wanderer (*Pedionomus torquatus*), an enigmatic Australian bird which had previously been regarded as an aberrant buttonquail (see page 534). The Plains-wanderer and the seedsnipes could be relicts of an ancient group of grassland charadriiforms which might have dispersed across the Antarctic continent before it was covered by ice in the Upper Miocene period, 10-15 million years ago.

Several earlier anatomical studies had shown that *Pedionomus* differed notably from the buttonquails. Its placement alongside them might be considered an historical accident which can be traced back to the influence of H. von Gadow in the 1890's, and which remained unchallenged because later students simply did not compare *Pedionomus* skeletons with those of other bird groups. Thus, Olson and Steadman were the first taxonomists to

put forward the view that the *Pedionomus* skeleton was quite typical for charadriiform birds, and particularly close to that of the small *Thinocorus* seedsnipes. The most striking similarities are the broad, two-notched sternum and the broad pelvis. A close relationship between the seedsnipes and the Plains-wanderer, as well as a more distant relationship of these two groups with the Scolopacidae, has subsequently been supported by the DNA-DNA hybridization data collected by C. G. Sibley and J. E. Ahlquist.

It may be added here that the Magellanic Plover (*Pluvianellus socialis*), a species of controversial taxonomy that is traditionally placed in the plover family, Charadriidae (see page 386), resembles *Thinocorus* seedsnipes not only in shape, but also by having a crop and in fine details of the juvenile and natal plumages. However, the anatomical characters provide conflicting evidence, and DNA data are lacking.

Morphological Aspects

The external appearance of seedsnipes resembles that of quails or grouse, except for the wings, which are long and pointed. The tail is fairly short and wedge-shaped. When the birds are flushed, their erratic, zig-zagging flight recalls that of snipes or calidrine sandpipers, and the small *Thinocorus* species may at first glance be confused with Pectoral Sandpipers (*Calidris melanotos*), which commonly winter within their range.

The *Thinocorus* species range in size roughly from that of a sparrow to that of a snipe, and they are shaped much like the Old World sandgrouse. The two *Attagis* species are much larger, resembling ptarmigans (*Lagopus*) in size, shape and, to some extent, coloration; however, in flight they differ clearly from these gallinaceous birds by having longer, pointed wings.

The seedsnipe's head is small, while the bill is short and thick, with the nostrils protected by a large shield-like corneaceous flap. The legs are short, but the toes are relatively long and strong; indeed, the middle toe is as long or longer than the tarsus, while the hind toe too is well developed.

Studies of the jaw muscles of *Thinocorus* indicate that the bill is primarily adapted for high-precision browsing, as the birds bite off leaf tips, buds and other tiny plant parts (see Food and Feeding). A strong tendon, originating from the postorbital and zygomatic processes, and connecting the lower mandible with the postorbital region of the skull, is ossified along much of its length, restricting the mobility of the lower mandible. Apparently, then, the birds bite mainly by using the muscles of the palate, protracting the upper mandible and depressing its tip. Small plant parts are torn off by moving the bill towards the breast with a quick movement. Kinetic movements of the upper mandible are also of fundamental importance in many sandpipers, although the precise feeding mechanism varies somewhat. The *Attagis* skull differs from that of *Thinocorus* in many respects, but the functional implications of this are unknown.

Seedsnipes are cryptically coloured, the upperparts being intricately mottled and scalloped with black, brown, rufous, buff and whitish, the breast scalloped or speckled. The nominate southern race of the Rufous-bellied Seedsnipe (*Attagis gayi*) is adapted to Arctic-style desert, and has a finely vermiculated and stippled pattern, giving a "frost-bitten" appearance, as is also seen in some races of the Rock Ptarmigan (*Lagopus mutus*).

Males, but not females, of the two small seedsnipes have the face, neck and breast dove grey, but apart from this sexual dimorphism is very minor. Juveniles resemble adults, but the dorsal feathers are usually more finely vermiculated or obscurely spotted, and the primaries often pale-tipped. Juvenile Least Seedsnipes (*Thinocorus rumicivorus*) have much weaker breast stripes than those exhibited by the adult females.

Newly-hatched young are covered with dense down. However, *Attagis* and *Thinocorus* chicks look quite different. Those of *Attagis* are rich buff with a complicated pattern of black speckles. A second generation of uniform plumbeous grey down emerges, pushing out the initial down, just before the appearance of the contour feathers. This sequence is remarkably similar to that found in sheathbill (Chionidae) chicks. The chicks of *Thinocorus* are drab grey to hazel brown, with a more simple pattern of blackish spots and bands on the back, and a dense stippling of white tips to the down. Unlike the white "powder-puffs" which dot the natal plumage in many snipes, these are composed of dense brushes of barbules on just one side of each barb. However, similar brushes are also found in chicks of a few other aberrant shorebirds, such as the Magellanic Plover.

Examination of Least Seedsnipes collected in late February, towards the end of the austral summer, indicates that the juvenile plumage which replaces the natal down may, in turn, be replaced rapidly, through a partial moult, by feathers rather similar to those of adults. The pattern of replacement may be complex, or perhaps just quite variable between individuals. Primary moult

in adult seedsnipes progresses with the outer three primaries moulted first, after which the inner primaries follow in a complicated sequence.

Habitat

Within their exclusively South American range, seedsnipes inhabit grassland, semi-desert and alpine habitats in Patagonia, in the Andes and along the coast of Peru. They are found in some of the most inhospitable parts of the continent.

The White-bellied Seedsnipe (*Attagis malouinus*) inhabits the windswept top ridges of the crowberry (*Empetrum*) moorlands of Tierra del Fuego and the islands south to Cape Horn. The Rufous-bellied Seedsnipe occurs in almost barren Arctic-style desert near the snow-line in the Andes, locally ranging up to 5500 m, but at altitudes as low as 2000 m in southern Chile. Both species seem to feed mainly in places with spongy cushion-plants (*Azorella*, *Pycnophyllum*, *Plantago rigida*) and a very sparse covering of grass. They are sympatric in the Andes of southern Chile and Argentina, and are apparently segregated ecologically, with the White-bellied mainly occurring on desolate moorland plateaux and the Rufous-bellied associated with well watered places fed by melting snow. The White-bellied Seedsnipe leaves its upper ridge habitat in February or March to appear on adjacent foothills and lowland flats, where it seems to favour areas with boulders and gravel in dry riverbeds. In contrast, the Rufous-bellied Seedsnipe remains at high altitudes, descending only a few hundred metres during the worst winter storms.

The Grey-breasted Seedsnipe (*Thinocorus orbignyianus*) is associated with Andean grass steppes, from Patagonia to Peru. Within this ecoregion, its most typical habitats are rather open vegetation with low cushion-plants, scattered *Tetraglochin* scrub, a matted vegetation of very short grass and herbs, or boggy habitat near the snow-line.

The Least Seedsnipe is associated much more with sandy areas in the southern lowlands and on the upland plateaux just east of the Patagonian Cordillera. It is common in areas which are heavily overgrazed by sheep. This habitat is characterized by widely scattered tussocks of bunch-grass, as well as small cushion-plants and low scrub. Another important habitat for this species comprises clay-pans, which are filled with water from

With its plump body, short legs and short, thick bill, a seedsnipe bears a superficial resemblance to the gallinaceous birds, but it has long, pointed wings and flies in a fast, erratic fashion, often zig-zagging, like the true snipes of the family Scolopacidae. Among the most peculiar physical features of the Thinocoridae are the shield-like cornaceous flaps that cover the nostrils, as can be seen on this Rufous-bellied Seedsnipe. These flaps may provide protection during the dust storms that frequently occur in arid seedsnipe habitats.

[Attagis gayi simonsi, Salar de Surire, Chile. Photo: A. de Sostoa & X. Ferrer]

melting snow in spring, but which dry up during the summer. Rather dry, sandy grassland is also favoured on the major wintering grounds in the Argentinian *pampas*. The Peruvian population of this species inhabits areas with short, scattered "mist vegetation" of tiny annuals in the coastal desert.

Seedsnipes spend most of their time on the ground, feeding mainly in places with a prostrate vegetation. However, singing males often use elevated posts such as rocks. In the sheep-ranching districts of Patagonia, the Least Seedsnipe sings mainly from fence posts; large heaps of their droppings can be found below some such posts, demonstrating that territorial males may use the same favourite post for long periods of time.

General Habits

The *Attagis* species are extremely poorly known. Most Andean ornithologists know them only from brief encounters, when a group of birds is suddenly flushed from a small bog, and flies away rapidly, accompanied by loud calls. However, birds actually tend to be quite approachable and can sometimes be watched at close range while feeding; at other times they are shy.

The smaller (*Thinocorus*) species are generally easier to observe, but there is very little information published on their habits. They usually feed quietly in a low, crouched attitude, looking quite flat-backed. When alerted, they often freeze in a low crouching attitude, relying on their perfect camouflage to enable them to escape detection. However, they may also walk away with the head raised, sometimes showing distinctive bobbing movements, like plovers. When flushed, they dash off with zig-zagging flight, sometimes dropping to the ground again rather quickly.

Seedsnipes roost on the ground, making shallow scrapes in which they lie. The birds are most often found in pairs or in small groups, which may be family parties. Territorial males spend long periods of time on or near their look-out posts, which are ascended promptly when the song of a conspecific, or a human imitation of it, is heard. Song activity is highest at night. In the early part of the breeding season males make aerial song flights almost throughout the night, but are quiet for much of the day.

Small flocks are often seen outside the breeding season. Up to 80 Rufous-bellied Seedsnipes have been observed in one flock, which is noteworthy considering the low density of birds generally in the Arctic-like environment frequented by this species. White-bellied Seedsnipes sometimes pack together in large numbers when the snow is deep. In Patagonia, Least Seedsnipes aggregate in large numbers in February, towards the end of the austral summer. Hundreds of individuals may forage in loose flocks on lake shores, where they feed on the low herbaceous vegetation which develops as the shallow lakes dry up around that time of the year.

Voice

The calls of seedsnipes are distinctive. In fact, the easiest way for an observer to locate the two smaller species is by imitating their territorial songs and listening for a reply. Often, a territorial male will quickly mount his traditional song post and begin to sing.

During the day, most songs are given from a rock, although the Least Seedsnipe often sings from a thick bush, a tall weed or a fence post. Song can also be given while birds are flying in wide circles. In such cases, variations in the relative direction of the flight give the impression of variations in the strength and pitch of the song, due to the Doppler effect. Aerial songs are mainly given at night. On the windy Patagonian plains, singing activity is often fairly intense during calm periods around midnight.

The song of the Grey-breasted Seedsnipe is an easily imitated soft cooing, which can be repeated monotonously for several minutes, "pooko-pooko-pooko-pooko..." (see Relationship with Man); up to 850 "pookos" have been recorded in one song. Individual birds may differ slightly in song quality, some individuals giving a more grating version, "pooráak pooráak pooráak pooráak..."

The Least Seedsnipe has a similar but less melodic and much more variable song, as illustrated by some of the different versions transcribed during fieldwork as "krii-oko", "kroo", "krro...pucui pucui-pucui" from song posts, and "vut-vut-vut-vut...", "puc-curr puc-curr puc-curr...", "pehooy pehooy pehooy...", or accelerating "tjupo-cooo tjupo-cooo..." during song flight. Aerial songs may also be more snipe-like "djek-djek-djuk-djuk" or alternate with series of low "puc-puckepuck", and may fade out during the "parachuting" final part of the display, as "phu-phrr, phu-phrr..."

When at ease, the members of a group of *Thinocorus* seedsnipes may call to one another continually, using a two note call, and feeding birds may also give low "dyurr" or "dyuc" calls. When flushed, Grey-breasted Seedsnipes make a grating snipe-like "chrp" or "bzzep", while the Least Seedsnipe gives a short snipe-like "djuc" or "djiric", or low grunts. In both species, this is often followed by a rapid series of deeper and more melodic calls, "tuc-tucketuck..."

Rufous-bellied Seedsnipes give a characteristic loud melodic "gly-gly-gly-gly..." or "cul-cul-cul-cul..." (see Relationship with Man). This can be heard, as a song, throughout the morning, and is also given continously in flight. Alerted birds may start calling before they fly, while running on the ground, and this rises to a bewildered chorus as all birds call together in flight, their calls being echoed back from the surrounding hills. The voice of this species has also been described as a rasping "tchaa", similar to the call of a Fuegian Snipe (*Gallinago stricklandii*) but even

The grey breast with a black anchor-shaped pattern identifies the male Least Seedsnipe. This species differs from other seedsnipes by its stronger preference for sandy areas, where many seeds are to be found, and it appears to live up to the name "seedsnipe" better than the rest of the family, as it may take a higher proportion of seeds.

[*Thinocorus rumicivorus rumicivorus*, Cabo Dos Bahías, Chubut, Argentina. Photo: A. de Sostoa & X. Ferrer]

louder; this description certainly differs from the impression of the present author.

The flight call of the White-bellied Seedsnipe has been described as an excited "tu-whít tu-whít..." recalling the flight call of the Grey Plover (*Pluvialis squatarola*); this voice is given as long as the bird is on the wing.

Food and Feeding

The name seedsnipe is rather misleading, as careful field observations reveal that the members of this family usually feed by browsing, biting off tiny bits of plants, such as buds, leaf tips and small green leaves. This is done while a bird is walking slowly in a low, crouching attitude, by means of rapid snapping movements. The plant fragments are swallowed whole. Most often the birds feed in areas with short, prostrate vegetation, such as cushion-plants or low succulent plants. They may also stretch up a little to bite off the tops of grasses, or to browse on taller herbs (*Polygonum*, *Trifolium*) or dwarf shrubs (*Margarocarpus*, *Tetraglochin*). However, aside from these generalizations, it should be noted that detailed studies of stomach contents identified to species level are still lacking, and consequently the more precise feeding habits of this family remain largely unknown.

The Least Seedsnipe, which often feeds in sandy places, may possibly take more seeds than the other species. In the Peruvian Desert it is often encountered in habitats influenced by seasonal fog, where tiny green herbs exist for only a short period each year. Because of the climatic oscillations related to El Niño (see Volume 1, page 341), a lush cover of herbs develops in certain years, indicating that large numbers of seeds must usually lie "dormant" in the desert sand. However, scattered observations indicate that even the Least Seedsnipe browses in most situations, and succulent leaves may make up a considerable part of its diet. Indeed, in its arid habitat, such leaves may represent the only source of water. No seedsnipes are known to drink in natural conditions, although they may do so in captivity.

Breeding

As with most other aspects of their biology, the breeding habits of seedsnipes remain very poorly known, and offer considerable scope for intensive study. Judging from rather unsystematic observations and anecdotal evidence, seedsnipes appear to be monogamous and territorial; for instance, males often fight and chase each other, and spend much time on or near traditional watch posts. For much of the year seedsnipes are to be seen in pairs or in small parties which may represent family groups.

Males of the two *Thinocorus* species often sing for long periods from their vantage posts, standing with the swollen neck upright or sloping slightly forwards. In suitable habitat, territory centres can be as little as 50 m apart. During the night, aerial song flights may last for several hours with only short interruptions. Song flights are also often seen by day, as a bird will fly around in wide circles while singing, and on windy days singing birds often sing from a "hanging hover", using updraught winds. Song flights terminate with a parachute-like descent with the wings downcurved or partly folded, the bird often landing on its usual vantage post; during the final horizontal glide, the Least Seedsnipe keeps the tail raised vertically.

In southern Patagonia, eggs of Least Seedsnipes can be found from August to February, suggesting that females may lay several clutches per season. The Grey-breasted Seedsnipe nests in November and again in January and February. Some Least Seedsnipes collected in Patagonia in February, at the end of the austral summer, had enlarged gonads and plumages which would seem to contain a mixture of juvenile and adult-type feathers. Although most birds were aggregating in post-breeding flocks at this time, others were displaying, and nests with eggs were also found. This could indicate a very rapid sexual maturation, as is known to occur in *Coturnix* quails, where young birds may nest towards the end of the season in which they have hatched. However, such observations need to be followed up by more thorough studies, both in Patagonia and in the Peruvian Desert. Adaptations for opportunistic breeding and for maximizing population growth could be expected especially in the latter area, where the climatic oscillations related to El Niño cause marked vegetational changes in certain years (see Food and Feeding).

In the Andean *puna* zone, the principal nesting season may be at the beginning of the rainy season, in November. However, seedsnipe nests may also be found at other times, even in the dry "winter" season.

The nests of seedsnipes are crude scrapes in the ground, often lined with some mosses and plant debris, and placed close to a stone, a bunch-grass tussock or a dense dwarf shrub. Many nests are placed in dry horse dung. All seedsnipes generally lay four eggs, or sometimes three, and these resemble those of snipes in being strongly pear-shaped, with a polished surface and cryptic spotting. *Thinocorus* eggs are usually creamy to pink or greenish white, profusely spotted with dark brown, often as a halo or cluster around the larger pole. Eggs of the Rufous-bellied

There are no published
records of seedsnipes
drinking in the wild, and,
despite the highly
suggestive photo, this
Grey-breasted Seedsnipe
male was not definitely
recorded as doing so.
As is often the case with
birds inhabiting rather arid
areas, the grasses and
succulent plants which
make up the diet
apparently provide all the
water that the birds need.
Nevertheless, seedsnipes
are known to drink once in
a while in captivity, and
further observations might
yet show that they can do
so in the wild too, at least
occasionally.

[*Thinocorus orbignyianus
ingae*,
Ayacucho, Peru.
Photo: Günter Ziesler]

Seedsnipe are normally olive-buff with spots in various shades
of brown and purplish grey, while the eggs of the White-bellied
Seedsnipe have been described as olive-citrine with brown spots.

In the *Thinocorus* species, at least, only the females incubate, and the same may possibly apply in *Attagis* too. The male
spends much time on a perch near the nest, where he acts as a
look-out, giving a warning call and running away, together with
the female, as soon as danger is sighted. The female invariably
covers the eggs completely with plant debris or soil whenever
the nest is left, whether this be to feed or because of disturbance.
This egg-covering is performed rapidly, using sideways kicks of
the feet and can result in the nest resembling a completely random accumulation of plant debris. In the case of the Rufous-
bellied Seedsnipe, the supply of nest material may be too scarce
to allow egg-covering. An incubating female will leave the nest
to feed for about an hour in the morning, and again in the late
afternoon.

If the female is disturbed suddenly on the nest, and especially if there was not time to cover the eggs, she performs an
elaborate injury-feigning distraction display, running with drooping and partly spread wings and tail, or fluttering away low over
the ground.

The incubation period of the Least Seedsnipe is about 26
days, but no precise data exist for the other species. The young
are highly precocial, and are led away from the nest by both
parents as soon as they are dry after hatching. However, it is the
female alone that broods them. From the start the young chicks
feed by themselves and do not need to be shown food by their
parents. If disturbed with young, both parents may perform distraction displays, but those of the male usually consist only of
the "rodent-run" typical of shorebirds. The young may fly at about
seven weeks of age.

Movements

Southern populations of the Least Seedsnipe are partially migratory, wintering on sandy grassland as far north as Buenos Aires
and Uruguay. The species may vacate the Magellanic zone and
Patagonian uplands in winter, but this is poorly documented in
the literature and remains to be demonstrated. White-bellied

Seedsnipes probably leave their inhospitable upland habitats in
late February and March, at the first snowfall. They turn up at
this time in the foothills and are found on lowland flats during
periods of heavy snowfall. Similarly, Grey-breasted Seedsnipes
vacate Tierra del Fuego and the high parts of the Patagonian
Andes, and appear in winter in low mountain ranges east of the
Cordillera and also in the coastal hills of Chile. There are several
records of Least Seedsnipes and two of White-bellied Seedsnipe
on the Falkland Islands.

In the *puna* zone of Bolivia and Peru, Grey-breasted
Seedsnipes are often found in low parts of the terrain in the dry
season, including *Tetraglochin* heaths, cultivated areas, river
plains and shore meadows. In the rainy season they usually disappear from these parts and are instead found on high hills, in
places with low cushion-plants or densely matted short vegetation, and along the edges of highland bogs, sometimes as high as
5000 m. The race *bolivianus* of the Least Seedsnipe, which breeds
in the arid *puna* of western Bolivia and adjacent parts of Chile,
has been found in high densities in the non-breeding season, from
May to September, on gravelly moraine plains up to 4500 m in
the Eastern Cordillera of La Paz.

The Peruvian population of the Least Seedsnipe may show
seasonal or nomadic movements, judging from observations of
flocks in some places where the species was unrecorded during
other visits. There is no documentation of local or altitudinal movements in connection with the climatic oscillations related to El Niño.

To date there are no published observations which indicate
significant migrations in the Rufous-bellied Seedsnipe. Observations in the Peruvian part of the range seem to indicate that the
species is present near the glaciers at all seasons, in flocks in the
dry season and mainly in pairs during the rainy season. However, many birds can sometimes assemble in boggy valley bottoms or in the corrals near shepherds' huts. In Chile, birds are
said to withdraw briefly a few hundred metres downhill during
the severest storms.

Relationship with Man

The vocalizations of seedsnipes are well known by local peasants in the Peruvian and Bolivian highlands, as reflected by the

Quechua names "Puco-puco", "Pucu-pucu", "Tuco-tuco" or "Pucpush" for the *Thinocorus* species, and "Kulle-kulle" or "Kuli" for the Rufous-bellied Seedsnipe. Despite this familiarity, nothing appears to have been recorded about the role of seedsnipes in legends or folklore.

Similarly, little is known about their economic use. Since most peasants and pastoralists kill highland tinamous (*Nothoprocta*, *Nothura*) with sling-shots or by throwing stones, one would imagine that seedsnipes are also likely to be killed in this way sometimes. The *Thinocorus* species may be too small to represent attractive prey, but they are sometimes hunted in Chile and Argentina on their wintering grounds, where they appear in large flocks. The larger Rufous-bellied Seedsnipe is regarded as excellent game. It is easy to shoot and its populations have been devastated in some mining districts in Peru, but fortunately in most parts of its range the local people lack guns. Furthermore, most Rufous-bellied Seedsnipe habitats are very sparsely inhabited and utilized by man, so the impact of hunting is presumably slight.

Status and Conservation

Over a long time perspective, human activities have probably led to an increase of seedsnipe habitat. There is growing evidence that most of the Andean highlands, up to the level of true alpine vegetation, were once dominated by dispersed woodland vegetation (*Polylepis*) and shrub-steppe (*Lepidophyllum*), with tall grasses and rushes on the floodplains. After the last glacial period, however, early human hunters and gatherers colonized the highlands as soon as the ice retreated. There was probably some use of firewood, but the main human impact in the period about 10,000-7500 years ago may have been in the form of the use of fire during hunting. Even occasional fires may have had a severe impact on the fragile high Andean ecosystems. After the establishment of permanent centres of settlement 7500-4500 years ago, fire was also used to clear pasture areas for the domesticated camelids, the llama and the alpaca. However, burning was probably kept under some control, since camelids do not like the grasses favoured by frequent burning. At the same time, many flat-bottomed mountain valleys were dammed to increase the areas of bogs favoured by camelids. All these changes would increase the habitat available for seedsnipes.

There is some debate about the relative importance of climatic changes, cutting of firewood and introduction of ecologically unsound agricultural methods after the arrival of the Spanish 500 years ago. However, there is little doubt that the sheep-grazing and the incessant burning practised today, either to stimulate the development of bunch-grass or for no clear purpose, have

caused a change now which is less favourable for seedsnipes. Nevertheless, the Least Seedsnipe is still extremely abundant on those parts of the Patagonian steppes which are most strongly overgrazed by sheep. It can also be found on cultivated land in the Peruvian Desert, and may be positively affected by the irrigation schemes here. Both *Thinocorus* species may feed on cultivated areas, as long as the crop plants remain low.

With the current knowledge about seedsnipes, no realistic population estimates can be made. The *Thinocorus* species are generally common, with huge populations in certain parts of their ranges, and the Least Seedsnipe is one of the commonest birds on the windy plains of southern Patagonia. Although the population levels may change locally or in time, in response to changing land use, there is no reason for concern about the future survival of either of these species.

There are very few published records of the Least Seedsnipe on the Altiplano, where it is represented by the subspecies *bolivianus*. However, it has been found to be abundant in certain places in north-eastern Chile, and it is known to winter at considerable density on the moraine plains of the Eastern Cordillera of La Paz, in Bolivia.

The *Attagis* species undoubtedly have populations that amount to more modest numbers, which is quite natural in view of their inhospitable and unproductive environments, and the restricted extension of this high altitude habitat. As a simple consequence of the very small area available, the population of the Ecuadorian race *latreilli* of the Rufous-bellied Seedsnipe is unlikely to number more than a few hundred pairs; the total area above 4000 m in Ecuador is less than 5000 km², and only a small fraction of this is suitable habitat for the species. According to N. Krabbe, the species occurs only on the volcanoes Pichincha, Iliniza, Chimborazo, Cayambe, Antisana, Cotopaxi and Tungurahua, with an estimated total for Ecuador of 200 pairs. A careful study of the status of the Rufous-bellied Seedsnipe in Ecuador would be highly relevant and opportune.

Fortunately for the Rufous-bellied Seedsnipe, the habitats it frequents are generally little used by man. In most areas the only human activity is some pastoralism, mainly with llamas and alpacas. It is even more fortunate that many of the areas of mountain wilderness inhabited by this species have received formal protection. Thus, four of the seven Ecuadorian populations are to be found in protected areas, the Cotopaxi National Park, the Cayambe-Coca Ecological Reserve, the Chimborazo Production Reserve and the Pichincha Protection Forest Reserve. The species is protected in Peru in the large Huascarán Biosphere Reserve and in the Salinas y Aguada Blanca National Reserve. Some of the best habitats along the border between Bolivia and Chile are included in Lauca and Volcán Isluga National Parks and Las Vicuñas National Reserve in Chile, and Sajama National Park and the Eduardo Avaroa National Reserve in Bolivia. A number of protected areas are also found in the jagged Andean Cordillera along the border between Argentina and Chile. Finally, a substantial portion of the distribution range of the White-bellied Seedsnipe lies within areas where resource conservation is required by law.

Clearly, these two larger species have an advantage in inhabiting landscapes which modern man regards as beautiful and awe-inspiring. Very locally this may lead to some disturbance because of the increasing popularity and promotion of ski-ing, hiking and mountain climbing, but the only serious threat to the *Attagis* species at present seems to be from mining activities. Large areas in the Western Cordillera in Peru and Bolivia have been severely scarred and polluted by mining, and the existence of mining communities may also lead to severe hunting pressure. With this in mind, some attention should certainly be given to the conservation status of seedsnipes in mining areas.

General Bibliography
Björklund (1994), Campbell (1976, 1979), Chu (1995), Cuello (1994), Fjeldså (1988), Gochfeld *et al.* (1984), Hayman *et al.* (1986), Hellmayr & Conover (1948), Jacob (1978), Jehl (1968b, 1975b), Lowe (1923), Maclean (1969, 1970a, 1985c), Olson & Steadman (1981), Peters (1934), Sibley & Ahlquist (1990), Sibley & Monroe (1990), Sibley *et al.* (1968), Strauch (1976, 1978).

*Seedsnipes are apparently monogamous and territorial and, especially during the breeding season, are mostly found in pairs. Their overall resemblance to gallinaceous birds, and to ptarmigans (*Lagopus*) in particular, is especially evident in the case of the White-bellied Seedsnipe, the similarity being reinforced by the desolate moorland habitats this species occupies.*

[Attagis malouinus, Baribaldi Pass, Tierra del Fuego, Argentina. Photo: A. Greensmith/ Ardea]

PLATE 47

inches 5
cm 13

PLATE 47

Genus *ATTAGIS*

I. Geoffroy Saint-Hilaire & Lesson, 1831

1. Rufous-bellied Seedsnipe

Attagis gayi

French: Attagis de Gay   **German**: Rotbauch-Höhenläufer   **Spanish**: Agachona Grande
Other common names: Gay's Seedsnipe

Taxonomy. *Attagis Gayi* I. Geoffroy Saint-Hilaire and Lesson, 1831, Santiago, Chile.
Three subspecies recognized.
Subspecies and Distribution.
A. g. latreillii Lesson, 1831 - N Ecuador.
A. g. simonsi Chubb, 1918 - C Peru (Lima) through N Chile and W Bolivia to NW Argentina (Jujuy).
A. g. gayi I. Geoffroy Saint-Hilaire & Lesson, 1831 - Andes of Chile and Argentina, from Antofagasta and Salta S to Tierra del Fuego.
Descriptive notes. 27-30 cm; 300-400 g. Cryptically coloured, intricately mottled rufous brown, dorsal feathers with concentric dusky lines giving scalloped effect, underparts pale pinkish cinnamon. In flight, appears uniform cinnamon brown, with no pattern on wings or tail; wing linings coloured like underside of body. Juvenile similar to adult, but with more finely mottled pattern above. Races differ mainly in general tone of coloration, with underparts deep cinnamon rufous in *latreillii*, pinkish cinnamon in *simonsi*.

Habitat. Rocky slopes, scree, and other bleak alpine terrain in Andean Cordilleras. Often stays close to snow-line, but when feeding usually descends to nearest bog or other areas with cushion-plants or low matted vegetation. In Ecuador, occurs in highest *páramos*. Typically found at 4000-5500 m in N half of range; further S occurs above 2000 m, and in extreme S of range above 1000 m.
Food and Feeding. Fragments of thorny and succulent plants recorded. No further information available.
Breeding. Egg-laying in Sept-Oct in Chile; young found in Oct in Ecuador. Monogamous and solitary. Nest is a shallow scrape. Clutch 4 eggs; chicks buff densely streaked and spotted black, but this coat soon replaced by grey down, then by feathers. No further information available.
Movements. Apparently moves only on a very local scale.
Status and Conservation. Not globally threatened. Status of species poorly known because of its harsh and inaccessible habitat. Generally fairly common within its narrow altitudinal zone near the snow-line, but strongly persecuted in some mining areas. Race *latreilli*, inhabiting seven Ecuadorian volcanoes, may not number more than c. 200 pairs; four of these populations occur in protected areas, in Cotopaxi National Park, Cayambe-Coca Ecological Reserve, Chimborazo Production Reserve and Pichincha Protection Forest Reserve. Species also occurs in protected areas elsewhere in range (see page 543).

Bibliography. Blake (1977), Butler (1979), Canevari *et al*. (1991), Dunning (1982), Fjeldså & Krabbe (1990), Humphrey *et al*. (1970), Johnson (1965b, 1972), Koepcke, H.W. & Koepcke (1971), Koepcke, M. (1970), Meyer de Schauensee (1982), Olrog (1984), Ortiz & Carrión (1991), Parker *et al*. (1982), de la Peña (1992), Remsen & Traylor (1989).

2. White-bellied Seedsnipe

Attagis malouinus

French: Attagis de Magellan **German**: Weißbauch-Höhenläufer **Spanish**: Agachona Patagona

Taxonomy. *Tetrao Malouinus* Boddaert, 1783, Falkland Islands.
Northern birds have on occasion been separated as subspecies *cheeputi*, recognized by darker rump, but doubtfully valid. Monotypic.
Distribution. S Chile and Argentina, from Magellanes and Río Negro to islands off Cape Horn.

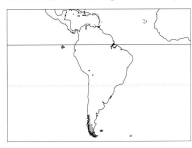

Descriptive notes. 26·5-29 cm. Cryptically coloured, resembling Northern Hemisphere ptarmigan (*Lagopus*) in general appearance. Above and on most of foreparts densely speckled and scalloped black, buff and cinnamon; this contrasts with white chin and belly. In flight, shows white greater and median underwing-coverts and axillaries. Female tends to have demarcation between scalloped breast and white lower underparts somewhat less sharp; little or no sexual size dimorphism. Juvenile similar to adult, but appears slightly paler and more heavily scalloped.
Habitat. Occurs mainly on windswept ridges with scree or in moorland, especially in places with crowberry heath (*Empetrum*) and *Azorella* cushion-plants; breeds from 650 m up to 2000 m. Outside breeding season, found mainly on stony parts of Patagonian steppe, e.g. along dry riverbeds or wide shores of partly dry lakes.
Food and Feeding. Crowberry and other plant material recorded. No further information available.
Breeding. Eggs known from Jan. Nest is depression lined with plant matter, e.g. short stems, moss and lichen. Lays 4 eggs; downy chicks slightly warmer buff and less densely spotted than those of *A. gayi*. No further information available.
Movements. Descends in winter to adjacent lowland plains. Two records from Falkland Is.
Status and Conservation. Not globally threatened. Generally occurs at low densities, but largely protected from human interference by occupation of harsh and inaccessible habitat. Large portions of range in Chile are within areas which have received some form of legal protection.
Bibliography. Blake (1977), Canevari *et al.* (1991), Clark (1986), Dunning (1982), Fjeldså & Krabbe (1990), Humphrey *et al.* (1970), Johnson (1965b), Meyer de Schauensee (1982), Olrog (1984), de la Peña (1992), Williams (1995b), Woods (1988).

Genus *THINOCORUS* Eschscholtz, 1829

3. Grey-breasted Seedsnipe

Thinocorus orbignyianus

French: Thinocore d'Orbigny **German**: Graubrust-Höhenläufer **Spanish**: Agachona Mediana
Other common names: D'Orbigny's Seedsnipe

Taxonomy. *Tinochorus* [sic] *Orbignyianus* I. Geoffroy Saint-Hilaire and Lesson, 1831, Santiago, Chile.
Racial differentiation appears to be rather weak. Two subspecies normally recognized.
Subspecies and Distribution.
T. o. ingae Tschudi, 1843 - Andes from N Peru through W Bolivia to N Chile (Tarapacá) and NW Argentina (Catamarca).
T. o. orbignyianus I. Geoffroy Saint-Hilaire & Lesson, 1831 - Andes from NC Chile (Antofagasta) and NC Argentina (La Rioja) S to Tierra del Fuego.

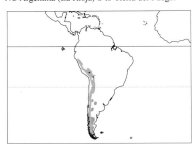

Descriptive notes. 19-24 cm; 110-140 g. Cryptically coloured, with the upperparts scalloped and vermiculated with cinnamon-buff. In flight, shows narrow white wingbar above, broad white wingbar below, and contrasting black or dark brown wing linings. Male has uniform grey neck and breast with black border to white throat; also tends to have narrow black border to white lower breast and belly. Female has head and breast pale buff with heavy dark streaking. Juvenile similar to female, but more obscurely patterned. Race *ingae* has smaller wings and tarsi on average.
Habitat. *Puna* grassland, sometimes on bunchgrass steppe, but most frequent in areas with low and matted vegetation of cushion-plants and tiny herbs, or on short grass bordering highland bogs. Common at 3400-5000 m in Peru; in S of range, breeds above 1000 m, but normally much lower down during winter.

Food and Feeding. Mainly buds and leaf tips of herbs and succulent plants. No further information available.
Breeding. Eggs in Oct-Nov, but also at other times of year, e.g. Jan-Feb. Breeds in solitary pairs. Nest is placed in grass or clump of vegetation, usually near water. Clutch usually 4 eggs; chick has pale vinaceous to cinnamon drab grey down, marked with complex pattern of black bands and dense white tips to down feathers. No further information available.
Movements. Poorly known. Most populations may show seasonal altitudinal shifts. Tierra del Fuego is vacated in winter.
Status and Conservation. Not globally threatened. Generally common throughout range, even in quite heavily overgrazed highlands. Much of habitat is at high altitude where, being remote or inhospitable, seems relatively secure; species appears reasonably well adapted to limited human impact in these zones.
Bibliography. Blake (1977), Canevari *et al.* (1991), Clark (1986), Dunning (1982), Fjeldså & Krabbe (1990), Humphrey *et al.* (1970), Johnson (1965b, 1972), Koepcke, H. W. & Koepcke (1971), Koepcke, M. (1970), Maclean (1969, 1970a), Meyer de Schauensee (1982), Olrog (1984), Parker *et al.* (1982), de la Peña (1992), Remsen & Traylor (1989), Rocha & Peñaranda (1995).

4. Least Seedsnipe

Thinocorus rumicivorus

French: Thinocore de Patagonie **German**: Zwerghöhenläufer **Spanish**: Agachona Chica
Other common names: Patagonian/Pygmy Seedsnipe

Taxonomy. *Thinocorus rumicivorus* Eschscholtz, 1829, Concepción, Chile.
Southernmost populations formerly awarded separate race, *patagonicus*, but not normally accepted nowadays. Four subspecies currently recognized.
Subspecies and Distribution.
T. r. pallidus Salvadori & Festa, 1910 - lowlands of SW Ecuador and extreme NW Peru.
T. r. cuneicauda (Peale, 1848) - Peruvian Desert.
T. r. bolivianus Lowe, 1921 - Altiplano from extreme S Peru through N Chile and W Bolivia to NW Argentina (Jujuy).
T. r. rumicivorus Eschscholtz, 1829 - Patagonian steppe S to N Tierra del Fuego; migrates to C Chile and plains of NE Argentina and Uruguay.

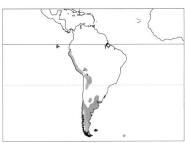

Descriptive notes. 16-19 cm; 50-60 g. Cryptically coloured, with upperparts more distinctly spotted and finely scalloped than in *T. orbignyianus*, to which shows similar wing pattern in flight, but tail more distinctly wedge-shaped. Male has uniform grey face, neck and breast with the black borders of white throat and lower underparts connected by black line down centre. Female has grey of head, neck and breast replaced by pale buff with diffuse darker markings; dark border to white throat. Juvenile similar to female but lacks distinct dark border to white throat. Races differ in size and overall tone of coloration, with smallest, palest birds in N; race *bolivianus* largest and, with upperparts distinctly scalloped warm buff, female recalls that of *T. orbignyianus*.
Habitat. Mainly semi-desert with rather scattered grass, low herbs or succulent plants. Race *bolivianus* inhabits Altiplano at 3700-4600 m; other races occur in lowlands, with *cuneicauda* found up to over 1000 m, and nominate below 1200 m. In Bolivia, inhabits highland semi-desert to desert *puna*; in Peru, occurs in sparse fog vegetation in the coastal desert. On Patagonian steppe frequents roads, wide gravelly shores and areas with tiny annual herbs around partly dry clay-pan lakes. Often found on cultivated land.
Food and Feeding. Mainly buds and leaf tips of succulent herbs and some seeds; may take more seeds than other species (see page 541).
Breeding. Eggs recorded Aug-Feb in Patagonia, probably with several successive broods. Breeds in solitary pairs. Nest is scrape in sandy soil, sometimes lined with animal dung. Clutch 4 eggs; incubation c. 26 days; chick has pale vinaceous to cinnamon drab grey down, marked with some black bands and speckles, and dense white tips to down feathers forming two bands down back; fledging 7 weeks. Young birds may possibly start breeding towards the end of their first summer.
Movements. Most Patagonian birds migrate in winter, possibly vacating S part of range. Observations of large flocks in other parts of the range may suggest seasonal or opportunistic movements, or long daily feeding excursions. Race *bolivianus*, which breeds in desert *puna*, winters on moraine plains in Eastern Cordillera of La Paz, Bolivia.
Status and Conservation. Not globally threatened. Generally common throughout extensive range, even in parts of Patagonia which are strongly degraded by sheep-grazing. Much of habitat is remote or inhospitable and seems to be relatively secure; species appears reasonably well adapted to limited human impact in these zones, e.g. possibly favoured by irrigation schemes enabling cultivation in Peruvian Desert. Status in Falkland Is uncertain: may be very rare breeder, but few records.
Bibliography. Blake (1977), Butler (1979), Cabot (1988), Canevari *et al.* (1991), Carp (1991), Clark (1986), Dunning (1982), Fjeldså & Krabbe (1990), Humphrey *et al.* (1970), Johnson (1965b, 1972), Koepcke (1970), Maclean (1969, 1970a), Meyer de Schauensee (1982), Olrog (1984), Ortiz & Carrión (1991), Parker *et al.* (1982), de la Peña (1992), Remsen & Traylor (1989), Sick (1993), Woods (1988).

Class AVES
Order CHARADRIIFORMES
Suborder CHARADRII
Family CHIONIDAE (SHEATHBILLS)

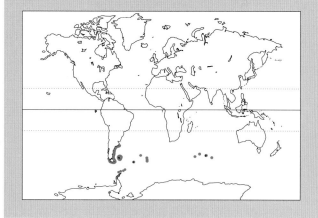

- Chunky, pigeon-like shorebirds with stout legs and distinctive bill sheaths.
- 34-41 cm.

- Antarctic Peninsula and subantarctic islands of Atlantic and Indian Oceans.
- Terrestrial and intertidal.
- 1 genus, 2 species, 5 taxa.
- No species threatened; none extinct since 1600.

Systematics

Sheathbills constitute the only bird family with a breeding range that falls entirely within the Antarctic and subantarctic. In this harsh environment, with an avifauna dominated by seabirds, they are the only common and widespread land-based birds. Sheathbills probably evolved from plover-like birds, in the subantarctic tip of South America. Today, as predators and scavengers, they are strongly dependent for food on colonial seabirds, particularly penguins, and they almost certainly evolved in association with penguins.

Their inclusion in the Charadriiformes is not in doubt, but their affinities within this order have been subject to much speculation. Various morphological, behavioural and biochemical studies have produced conflicting results, showing links with seedsnipes (Thinocoridae), the Magellanic Plover (*Pluvianellus socialis*), the plover family (Charadriidae) and even skuas (Stercorariidae). Results of DNA-DNA hybridization suggest that sheathbills are offshoots of a lineage which includes seedsnipes, the Crab Plover (Dromadidae), coursers and pratincoles (Glareolidae) and oystercatchers (Haematopodidae), but that they also have affinities with gulls and their allies.

The family has commonly been called Chionididae, but current policy on nomenclature urges the use of the shorter Chionidae. The single genus includes two species, different in appearance but very similar in habits, with non-overlapping ranges. The Pale-faced Sheathbill (*Chionis alba*) breeds on the Antarctic Peninsula and subantarctic islands of the Scotia Arc, and many birds migrate to Patagonia, Tierra del Fuego and the Falkland Islands in winter. The Black-faced Sheathbill (*Chionis minor*) is a year round resident on four widely separated island groups close to the Antarctic Convergence in the southern Indian Ocean. These four populations are usually regarded as subspecies. They have probably been genetically isolated for about 10,000 years, since the last ice age ended and the pack ice "bridge" linking the islands retreated southwards.

Morphological Aspects

Sheathbills display several adaptations for the rigorous Antarctic and subantarctic environment. They are sturdily built, with stout legs and feet. They have dense, pure white plumage, with a thick grey layer of underdown. Lacking webbed feet and other adapta-

tions for aquatic life, they are restricted to foraging on land, although the bulk of their food actually comes from the sea.

Both species have diagnostic bill sheaths and facial caruncles. The sheath is greenish and the caruncles pink in the Pale-faced Sheathbill, whereas the bill and facial features are all black in the Black-faced Sheathbill. Both species have thick, fleshy eye-rings. The sheath and facial features are smaller and less obvious in juveniles and one year old birds, and are useful for ageing birds. It has been suggested that the sheath is used as a hook to carry eggs, but modern studies do not support this idea. The sheath and facial features contrast with the all white plumage and probably evolved to enhance social signals, in which the head plays a prominent part. Social dominance in wintering flocks of Pale-faced Sheathbills was found to correlate with the size of the bill, and this is likely to apply in the other species too. Adults also develop blunt, black carpal spurs which are used to batter opponents in the rare and brief bouts of territorial fighting. The bill is conical and stout and is used for ripping flesh off carcasses, pecking open eggs, scooping up krill dropped by penguins, scraping algae off intertidal rocks, probing and uprooting boggy vegetation to search for terrestrial invertebrates, and picking up insects.

Sheathbills' flight is strong and direct, usually with a continuous succession of wingbeats, but with occasional gliding. Their flying capacity is clearly considerable, for the migration of Pale-faced Sheathbills takes them over hundreds of kilometres of open sea, which they evidently cover without alighting on the water. When foraging, they seldom fly unless commuting to and from roosts, or threatened by predatory skuas. On the ground, their gait is purposeful and chicken-like, and they can run rapidly. They use their feet to hold down bits of bone or skin while pecking at the flesh, but they do not scratch for food. They often tuck one leg into their dorsal feathers for long periods of time, and will even hop about on one leg while feeding. Sheathbills sometimes wade, but they avoid deep water, and do not voluntarily swim.

Sexes are alike but in both species the males average about 15% heavier than the females, and have larger bills and sheaths, although these weights and body dimensions overlap somewhat. Body masses vary through the year and tend to be lowest in immatures and those wintering adults which have no access to penguin colonies.

Moult occurs once a year and is relatively protracted, with the replacement of the primaries taking 70 days. Adults moult after breeding, in late March, but immatures and non-breeding adults start earlier, in January.

It is not clear whether the white plumage is an adaptive coloration. It confers camouflage in the snow, but sheathbills ordinarily spend little time on clean snow, and their plumage makes them very conspicuous on the shoreline or in penguin colonies. One possibility is that it evolved to facilitate territorial advertisement in these colonies.

Habitat

Sheathbills inhabit coastal regions from the Antarctic Peninsula north to the subantarctic islands and southern South America. Their lives are strongly intertwined with those of penguins, and, to a much lesser extent, other colonial seabirds, notably cormorants and albatrosses, and seals. Breeding territories of both species of sheathbill almost always include parts of a penguin colony and the nest itself is often in a cavity surrounded by penguins. The sheathbills patrol among the penguins looking for food, and their breeding chronology is linked with that of the penguins. Cormorant colonies support a few breeding sheathbills in the same manner, while albatrosses and petrels are usually exploited opportunistically. An exception to this occurs in the Kerguelen Islands, where many Black-faced Sheathbills breed without access to seabirds; at this locality, the sheathbills have become true shorebirds, foraging all year round on extensive rocky intertidal areas.

Outside these colonies sheathbills forage along the shoreline on both sandy and rocky beaches and among the rotting piles of kelp wrack. On some islands many sheathbills forage extensively for invertebrates on the lowland bogs, meadows and tussock grass, sometimes wandering more than 1 km from the shore. They are common visitors to Antarctic and subantarctic research stations where they live off kitchen scraps and other refuse. In the past, many were attracted to shore-based whaling or sealing operations. The Pale-faced Sheathbill can also be found among the pack ice, particularly during the pupping season of the Weddell Seal (*Leptonychotes weddelli*).

General Habits

Sheathbills are the smallest members of the subantarctic predator-scavenger guild which also includes giant petrels (*Macronectes*), skuas and Kelp Gulls (*Larus dominicanus*). Their small size restricts their predatory capability to the smallest chicks of penguins or cormorants, but it also allows them to move more freely among the breeding penguins than the larger birds, without incurring the same antagonism shown to larger birds by the penguins. They are adept at stealing unguarded eggs and small chicks, and most breeding adults have perfected the art of robbing penguins and other seabirds while they are in the midst of regurgitating food to their chicks (see Food and Feeding).

In both species one finds a fascinating range of social behaviour. Breeding adults establish strongly defended territories, and, with a few exceptions, these foraging territories include parts of a penguin or cormorant colony. The nest is placed within the feeding territory if the terrain is suitable. The preferred hosts are Adelie (*Pygoscelis adeliae*) and Chinstrap (*Pygoscelis antarctica*) Penguins in the Pale-faced Sheathbill, and Rockhopper (*Eudyptes chrysocome*) and Macaroni (*Eudyptes chrysolophus*) Penguins in the Black-faced Sheathbill. The larger King Penguins (*Aptenodytes patagonicus*) are also exploited, particularly in winter, but very large colonies of these birds support few breeding sheathbills, probably because the flat terrain on which they occur provides few cavities for sheathbill nests. This limitation also applies to very dense colonies of Macaroni Penguins on flat ground.

Detailed studies at Marion Island and the Crozet Islands have revealed interesting variations and flexibility in the social and foraging behaviour of Black-faced Sheathbills, dependant on the

Sheathbills are distinct oddities in the world of the Antarctic and subantarctic to which they are restricted. In no way adapted to an aquatic lifestyle, they form the only terrestrial bird family in an environment teeming with seabirds. They are, nonetheless, built to withstand the rigours of a hostile climate: the body is plump and sturdy, the legs and feet strong, and the white plumage dense, with a thick layer of underdown. The Pale-faced Sheathbill, seen here, has a greenish bill sheath and pink facial caruncles. The bill is stout and conical, well suited for the bird's multifarious scavenging habits. Sheathbills seem averse to water and reluctant to fly; they are most often seen walking or scampering along the shore in much the same fashion as a domestic fowl.

[Chionis alba, Gosling Island, South Orkneys. Photo: Pete Oxford/ Planet Earth]

type of penguin being exploited. The crested penguins (Rockhopper and Macaroni) are the preferred hosts during the summer, but these penguins leave the islands after breeding and moulting, and little food is available to sheathbills at their colonies through the six months of winter. Most sheathbills breeding here abandon their territories in winter. Some forage nearby on the shore or on inland vegetated areas, solitarily or in flocks. Many move to nearby King Penguin colonies, where they may establish temporary winter territories, and even temporary pair-bonds with birds which were not their previous mates. These territories and pair-bonds are abandoned in spring when the sheathbills move back to their former breeding territories as the crested penguins return. In contrast, pairs with breeding territories within King Penguin colonies remain territorial and paired all year, and they allow their chicks to overwinter within their territories, thereby giving them access to more reliable, high-quality food. A preliminary study has shown that the non-breeding territoriality is achieved without elevated levels of testosterone, the male hormone which is usually associated with territoriality in many birds. It appears to be a behavioural response to the availability of high-quality, defendable food resources in the winter.

Wintering birds which feed on the shore or in inland vegetated areas tend to form flocks of 2-50 birds, and they also roost communally at night on shoreline platforms. A study at Marion Island showed that 83% of the sheathbills which foraged in inland areas occurred in flocks, and 98% roosted communally. By feeding and roosting in flocks, the wintering sheathbills were improving their chances of finding profitable foraging areas in bog and tussock vegetation. Compared to single birds, those in flocks had higher rates of food intake, spent more time eating and less time looking around or being alert, and were less vulnerable to predation from skuas.

Within the same populations, therefore, one can find a complete range of social behaviour, including solitary foraging, year round or seasonal territoriality, flocking and communal roosting. This fascinating flexibility of social and foraging behaviour is a key to the year round survival of Black-faced Sheathbills in very isolated, sometimes inhospitable islands. Pale-faced Sheathbills avoid the more severe winter conditions at their breeding grounds by migrating, but this option is not available to the Black-faced Sheathbills living on more remote islands.

Boundary disputes between neighbours are rare and involve ritualized movements and redirected aggression. The disputing neighbours crouch low with wings slightly opened and jab with their bills at the air, the ground or bits of debris; this is interspersed with bill-wiping. These encounters usually end peacefully, with the protagonists wandering off or performing the "Bowing Ceremony" (see Breeding) with their respective mates, but fights can erupt. Fights involve pecking and grabbing the opponent with the bill, while vigorously battering with the wings and carpal spurs. Between bouts, protagonists also face each other in "Upright" postures with the wings slightly open to expose the black carpal spurs. Fights usually last just a few seconds and result in bedraggled plumage but no injuries, and "Bowing Ceremonies" often follow fights. Fighting occasionally occurs outside territories in conflicts over carcasses.

Sheathbills spend most of the daylight hours foraging, but also spend an hour or two preening and resting. In general, they spend considerable time bathing and preening, which is essential for maintaining insulation in a muddy, wet and windy environment. Territorial adults preen and rest on a conspicuous perch within their territories and frequently have to threaten or chase off intruders. In contrast, non-territorial birds gather in flocks, sometimes numbering 300 birds or more, at the edges of seabird colonies or on the shoreline in order to preen and rest.

Nocturnal roosting behaviour varies through the year. Breeding adults roost within their nest cavities in summer, but non-breeders and all wintering birds roost communally on shoreline rock platforms, sometimes forming flocks of several hundred birds. These night roosts are usually close to foraging sites but the birds will fly several kilometres, sometimes crossing open water, to reach suitable roosts which offer favourable micro-climates near the sea. A few sheathbills roost in inland caves which offer the same protection. Communal night roosts might also act as information centres in winter for birds foraging in flocks on widely distributed patches of food: those birds lacking knowledge of profitable patches can follow the flocks to these patches at dawn.

Skuas are sheathbills' main predators, but predation rates are relatively low, and juveniles and weakened birds are the usual victims of skua attacks. Nevertheless, all sheathbills are wary of skuas, and will avoid open beaches or meadows if skuas are present. Birds foraging on inland bogs or meadows usually fly to the shore if a skua approaches, and at Marion Island sheathbills could be found further inland during the winter months, when skuas were absent, than in summer. Other predators include Peregrine Falcons (*Falco peregrinus*), which sometimes kill sheathbills wintering in the Falkland Islands. There is also a low level of intraspecific predation among sheathbills, mainly of eggs and chicks, but also occasionally of wintering juveniles.

Voice

Sheathbills utter harsh, high-pitched, strident calls, which are audible above the hubbub of penguin colonies. Most calls are associated with defence or advertising of territories, and non-territorial birds tend to be silent.

In the Black-faced Sheathbill "Forward" threat displays and "Bowing Ceremonies" are often accompanied by series of loud, staccato "kek, kek, kek, kek..." calls, which can be given by either sex. The alarm call is a single sharp call usually given in response to a skua overhead. Short series of calls and single clucks are heard when flocks take off or land. Chicks and newly-fledged juveniles solicit food with shrill cheeping calls. The calls of the Pale-faced Sheathbill are not well known, but consist of harsh, throaty caws and muttering.

There appears to be variation in voice between the different island populations of the Black-faced Sheathbill, and this might have significant taxonomic implications, but no detailed studies have yet been carried out.

Food and Feeding

Although sheathbills themselves are restricted to land, most of the food they eat comes from the ocean. They are omnivorous and extremely opportunistic, and will attempt to eat any form of animal matter and some types of algae. This generalist diet appears to be a key to their survival in harsh, seasonally variable environments where each food type is often available only for a short period. Penguins provide the bulk of the food for both species, and access to seabird colonies is usually essential for breeding success. Detailed studies of energetics and time budgets of the Black-faced Sheathbill on Marion Island support this idea: the rate of food intake from the shoreline or from terrestrial invertebrates is simply inadequate to sustain breeding on this island. In contrast, the exceptionally large intertidal areas in the Kerguelen Islands provide large amounts of low-quality food, which are sufficient to support breeding in this unusual population, albeit with lower reproductive success than elsewhere.

Eggs are an important, briefly available, food item, particularly for sheathbills nesting in association with Macaroni or Rockhopper Penguins, which do not guard their first-laid eggs very well. Predated eggs are often carried to the proximity of the nest cavity, which can be surrounded by a conspicuous cluster of white eggshells. Small chicks are snatched from beneath unwary penguins or cormorants and dragged away to be eaten. Eggs and chicks are also sometimes taken from petrel burrows. Carrion is an important source of food, and sheathbills will spend hours picking tiny scraps of blubber and flesh off the skin and skeletons of carcasses discarded by larger predatory or scavenging birds. Within penguin colonies, sheathbills also eat faeces, feather-shafts shed by moulting birds and any invertebrates living in the muddy ooze.

Sheathbills are extreme examples of opportunistic feeders, the real "dustbin" birds of the Antarctic. They leave nothing remotely edible untouched, which probably explains their success in a harsh environment where feeding opportunities on land tend to be rather fleeting. Penguins play a major role in the lives of sheathbills, for in one way or another they provide them with most of their food. Limited by their size as to the type of predation they can practise, sheathbills take penguin eggs and small chicks with impunity and feed on all kinds of carrion. Both species are adept kleptoparasites; they will steal food from penguins and other bird species, such as albatrosses and cormorants, when these are in the act of regurgitating food for their young. In a King Penguin (Aptenodytes patagonicus) colony a Black-faced Sheathbill has located a chick on the point of receiving food from its parent; with beady eye, it calculates the exact moment when intervention will reap its reward. Given the powerful bill of the parent King Penguin, the success of such a daring operation depends on spot-on timing and a quick get-away!

[Above:
Chionis minor crozettensis,
Crozet Islands.
Photo: D. Parer &
E. Parer-Cook/Auscape.

Below:
Chionis minor crozettensis,
Crozet Islands.
Photo: R. Seitre/Bios]

Sheathbills of both species are highly successful kleptoparasites. They steal food from penguins, and sometimes from albatrosses and cormorants, by fluttering or leaping against these birds while they are in the act of regurgitating a bolus of food to their chicks. The sheathbills occasionally strike small penguins with sufficient force to knock them over. Any food spilled during this disruption is then scooped up by the sheathbill. Mated pairs sometimes work together to harass and rob a penguin in this manner. On Marion Island, 90% of the food delivered to sheathbill chicks within colonies of Rockhopper Penguins comprised marine crustaceans obtained by means of kleptoparasitism. Although it was essential to the sheathbills, the loss of food had little impact on the penguin hosts and amounted to only about 1% of the food coming into the colonies. The penguins threaten and lunge, but are unable to drive off the nimble sheathbills. Larger penguins, however, such as King Penguins, are less easily robbed. Such piracy involves careful timing, skill and daring and is almost never attempted by juveniles.

Sheathbills gather at rookeries and haul-outs of seals, particularly when the seals are pupping. Weddell Seals and Southern Elephant Seals (*Mirounga leonina*) are preferred by Pale-faced, and Elephant Seals by Black-faced Sheathbills. Here, too, the sheathbills will try eating almost anything available, including carrion, placentae, faeces, blood picked from scabs and wounds, and nasal mucous. Any seal with an open wound is relentlessly tormented by sheathbills. They will even take milk by inserting the bill between the pup's mouth and its mother's nipple.

Leafy algae, primarily *Porphyra*, scraped off intertidal rocks are the main food taken by sheathbills foraging along the shore. They also eat limpets, mussels, amphipods and other intertidal invertebrates. Piles of rotting kelp wrack provide profitable supplies of the larvae and adults of kelp flies, and plankton washed ashore on beaches is also eaten. Stormy seas and ice often restrict shoreline foraging in winter.

Terrestrial invertebrates are important food for Black-faced Sheathbills at some islands, particularly in winter. Any invertebrates larger than 1 mm long are eaten. Earthworms make up most of the intake, but larvae and adults of flightless moths, weevils, flightless flies and other insects, as well as spiders, snails and slugs are also eaten. These prey types are obtained by uprooting or flipping over moss and grass tussocks, or by probing the bill into soft substrates. Bogs and meadows that have been intensively foraged by flocks of sheathbills have a ploughed-over appearance. At Marion Island the terrestrial invertebrates supported one third of the 3500 sheathbills during winter, when preferred food from penguin and seal colonies was less abundant. These sheathbills showed acute habitat discrimination and foraged predominantly in those vegetation types in which invertebrates were most abundant and accessible. Snow cover greatly restricts inland foraging and prolonged periods of snow can lead to starvation, usually of immature birds.

Breeding

Detailed studies of Pale-faced Sheathbills at Signy Island, in the South Shetland Islands, and of Black-faced Sheathbills at Marion Island and also at Île de la Possession, in the Crozet group, show remarkable similarities in the breeding biology of the two species. The timing of breeding in sheathbills is closely tied with that of the penguins and other seabirds on which they depend. Sheathbills begin to occupy their territories in October, often before the host penguins have arrived. Ovogenesis occurs at the time that eggs are available from penguins, and by the time the sheathbill chicks hatch the penguins are already feeding small chicks. Laying occurs in middle to late December, and the chicks hatch in middle to late January, fledging at the end of March.

The age of first breeding is three to five years old, but most three year olds are unsuccessful. At all three study areas many adults were unable to gain access to territories, suggesting that there was an excess of potential breeders. At Île de la Possession, this floater population comprised 30-40% of all adults.

Breeding territories contained 40-300 *Eudyptes* or *Pygoscelis* penguins or 200-400 King Penguins.

Sheathbills show strong fidelity to their territories, nest-sites and previous mates. Divorce is rare and usually follows breeding failure. The most common ritualized display in both species is the "Bowing Ceremony", also called a "Bob-call" display. In this display, both members of the pair bow their heads rapidly up and down, while uttering a series of staccato calls. The display is usually given within the territory and can be initiated by either sex. It is used as a greeting display or given in response to intruders or other disturbances. Both sexes defend the territory, but males tend to be more active and aggressive. Territorial intruders are warned off with loud calls and a "Forward" threat posture similar to that of gulls. If that fails, the intruder is evicted by chasing, which involves running, flying or a flapping run.

Nests are simple cups on top of untidy, smelly piles of tussock grass, moss, algae, feathers or old bones. They are hidden from view within crevices, behind rock overhangs, in small caves and occasionally in petrel burrows; sheathbills do not dig their own cavities. Protection from skuas and inclement weather are probably the critical factors in nest-site selection. Where possible, nesting among penguins appears to provide some additional protection against skuas.

Clutch size in both species is typically of two or three eggs, but ranges from one to four. Eggs are pyriform, or pear-shaped, and have a creamy white base colour, speckled with grey or brown. At Marion Island, eggs were laid at intervals averaging four days, with a range of three to six days apart. Incubation commences soon after the first egg has been laid, and is undertaken by both sexes. Incubation shifts in males are longer than those in females, with means of 172 and 90 minutes respectively. The off-duty bird forages within the territory or rests on a vantage point near the nest cavity. Incubation takes 28-32 days. Egg survival varies within and between populations, with a range of 60-84%. Egg failure can be due to infertility, predation by skuas and other sheathbills, flooding of nests, accidental breakage or eggs rolling out of nests.

Hatching is asynchronous. At Marion Island the first chick hatched one day before the second (range 0-7 days), and the second three days before the third (range 0-4 days). Asynchronous hatching facilitates brood reduction by rapid elimination of younger chicks, when food is limited, so that the older chicks have improved chances of survival. The first-hatched chicks are always heavier than their siblings and have higher survival rates. Chicks may die as a result of starvation, predation by skuas and possibly by other sheathbills, and trampling by penguins. Most pairs succeed in rearing one chick per season. Production averaged 1·6, 1·8 and 1·9 fledglings per pair in three studies of Pale-faced Sheathbills, and 1·1, 1·2 and 1·4 fledglings per pair in three studies of Black-faced Sheathbills. The type of penguin exploited does not appear to affect breeding success. At Kerguelen, pairs with no access to seabirds showed lower productivity (0·7 fledglings per pair) than those breeding in seabird colonies (1·1 fledglings per pair).

The chicks are semi-precocial and nidicolous. They hatch with dense brown down, which is replaced by mottled grey mesoptile down at 7-14 days. White contour plumage appears from day 12 and covers the chicks by day 50. Chicks are able to move about the nest within hours of hatching but are brooded by a parent, continuously for the first two weeks and thereafter progressively less. About 30 days after hatching the chicks begin to wander away from the nest, and by 55-60 days they forage independently, although they often still follow their parents and solicit food for up to six months. Chick growth is slower and fledging occurs later, at 65-70 days, in pairs that nest in the intertidal zone in the Kerguelens.

Parents deliver food by the billful to the chicks at the nest, but they do not regurgitate it. Males and females spend similar amounts of time and effort in brooding and feeding the chicks. Chicks receive the same food as adults, but crustaceans, particularly krill and pelagic amphipods, and other marine food stolen from penguins are generally more important than carrion or invertebrates as food for chicks.

Penguins are not alone in suffering the attentions of sheathbills; seals too are often the victims of their indelicate attacks. Sheathbills will gather at seal rookeries and haul-outs, especially around the time of pupping, when the spoils are greatest. There, they will attempt to eat anything available, including umbilical cords, placentae, faeces and carrion. Nothing is disdained and no conduct is too demeaning. They will torment seals with open wounds in order to feed on their blood, and they have even acquired the remarkable skill of drinking a seal's milk by interposing the bill between the pup's mouth and the mother's nipple.

[Above:
Chionis alba, Photo: Mike Tracey/Survival Anglia/ Oxford Scientific Films.

Below:
Chionis minor crozettensis, Crozet Islands. Photo: D. Parer & E. Parer-Cook/Auscape]

Movements

Pale-faced Sheathbills are partial migrants. Some birds remain near nesting sites or at other subantarctic locations through the winter, but most migrate to the southern extremes of South America. The post-breeding northward movements occur from late March to July, with most birds gone from their breeding sites in late May. At Signy Island, breeding birds tend to return to nesting areas throughout October and early November.

Migratory routes are poorly charted, but birds have been reported flying over the sea 600-700 km from land. They probably cross the 800 km or so of the Drake Passage in a single flight, but in Antarctic waters migrants stop over on icebergs and pack ice where they forage opportunistically among seals or penguins. Ship-assisted passages have been documented on numerous occasions, and account for the appearance of this species in such unlikely places as Brazil, St Helena, South Africa and even England (after the Falklands war).

The behaviour, diets and movements of Pale-faced Sheathbills on their wintering grounds are very poorly known. Most birds appear to winter on the coasts of the Falkland Islands, Tierra del Fuego, and Patagonia, but vagrants have been reported further north on both the Pacific and Atlantic coasts. Some non-breeders remain on the Falkland Islands through the summer, instead of returning to the breeding grounds in the south.

Black-faced Sheathbills are resident all year round. There is, however, some intra- and inter-island movement within an archipelago, generally associated with birds moving to a King Penguin colony in winter. On the western islands of the Crozet group, hundreds of sheathbills cross 30 km from Île des Pingouins, or 15 km from Île des Apôtres, to winter in the large King Penguin colonies on Île aux Cochons. There are no similar movements among the eastern islands of the group, even those 20 km apart, because food is available on these islands all year. Similarly, movements between Marion and Prince Edward Islands, 22 km apart, are very rare.

Immatures and non-breeding adults wander more than breeders. On Marion Island, colour-ringed breeding adults were always within 1 km of their nesting sites, whereas almost half the subadults and a third of juveniles were seen 1 km or more from their ringing sites. Daily commuting flights between feeding grounds and night roosts may cover several kilometres, and at Heard Island include stretches of open water.

Relationship with Man

Most populations of sheathbills have been affected very little by humans, except through the alien mammals they have introduced (see Status and Conservation). Unless molested, sheathbills are unafraid of people, and they are intensely curious and bold. They will steal unguarded food and even pencils from field biologists, or peck at one's boots to test their edibility. They are attracted to weather stations and research camps, where they live on kitchen scraps and other waste, loitering around like flocks of small white chickens, and they will even occasionally wander indoors in search of food. The availability of this food has caused some Pale-faced Sheathbills to overwinter in places not normally used in winter, including Signy Island and South Georgia.

Sheathbills were hunted for food in the past. Norwegian whalers on South Georgia in the early twentieth century referred to them as "ptarmigan" and found them to be good eating, despite their unpleasant feeding habits. Intensive hunting was reported to have reduced this population by 1913, but hunting is no longer a problem at the breeding sites of either species. Interactions between humans and Pale-faced Sheathbills wintering in South America are less well documented, but there does not appear to be any significant hunting or other persecution. In the Falklands, many sheathbills aggregate in harbours and coastal settlements, where they presumably benefit from having extra sources of food.

Status and Conservation

The breeding population of Pale-faced Sheathbills is unlikely to exceed 10,000 pairs, scattered over about 400 sites on the Antarctic Peninsula and islands of the Scotia arc, and about half of

The breeding of sheathbills is intimately linked with that of penguins. In the first place, the timing coincides. Then the sheathbill's nest is often situated within or at least near a penguin colony. The Black-faced Sheathbill here has its nest under a boulder, hidden from sight to avoid predation from skuas. Normally, by the time the eggs hatch the penguins are already feeding their young, thereby providing the sheathbill parents with a reliable source of food on which to feed their chicks, in turn. Both parents bring food to the nest, but they do not regurgitate it. Although young sheathbills leave the nest after 30 days and are able to forage independently after two months, they are prone to solicit their parents for food for up to six months.

[*Chionis minor marionensis*, Marion Island. Photo: Alan E. Burger]

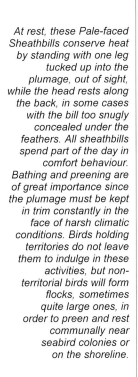

At rest, these Pale-faced Sheathbills conserve heat by standing with one leg tucked up into the plumage, out of sight, while the head rests along the back, in some cases with the bill too snugly concealed under the feathers. All sheathbills spend part of the day in comfort behaviour. Bathing and preening are of great importance since the plumage must be kept in trim constantly in the face of harsh climatic conditions. Birds holding territories do not leave them to indulge in these activities, but non-territorial birds will form flocks, sometimes quite large ones, in order to preen and rest communally near seabird colonies or on the shoreline.

[*Chionis alba*, Falkland Islands. Photo: Stan Osolinski/ Oxford Scientific Films]

these birds are to be found on the South Orkney Islands. The population of Black-faced Sheathbills is in the range of 6400-10,000 pairs, with more than half breeding in the Kerguelen Islands. There are insufficient data to determine population trends, and many island populations have never been adequately censused, notably Heard Island and Kerguelen. Most local populations of both species are relatively small, with less than 1000 pairs, and Black-faced Sheathbill populations are very isolated, making them vulnerable to introductions of mammals and viral or bacterial disease. The practice of keeping domestic chickens, which might carry diseases that affect sheathbills, at some of the French bases in the Crozet and Kerguelen groups should be discouraged for this reason.

Studies on Marion Island and Île de la Possession provide some basis for understanding the population dynamics of the Black-faced Sheathbill. Annual survival rates are high in breeding adults (88% on Marion, 85% on Possession), but lower in non-breeding adults (75% on Possession), subadults (49% on Marion, 63% on Possession) and juveniles (37% on Marion, 40% on Possession). Most mortality occurs in winter and can usually be attributed to the combined effects of starvation and inclement weather, and, to a lesser extent, predation by skuas. Most birds die during cold, snowy weather which inhibits foraging and raises thermal stress. Juveniles and subadults are most frequently found starved.

Both species of sheathbill have life history traits normally associated with stable, saturated populations, including: delayed breeding, at the age of three years or more; low annual reproductive output, with an average of less than two fledglings per pair; high adult survival, of 85-88%; territories centred on food resources; and high fidelity to territory, mate and nest-site. Research at Signy Island, Marion Island and Île de la Possession showed floating populations of adults unable to secure territories; on Possession, an increase in the population of penguins coincided with a similar increase in the numbers of sheathbill pairs breeding. Overall, these data suggest that populations of sheathbills are limited by the availability of breeding territories, and that their breeding numbers are thus strongly correlated with the populations of suitable penguin species that provide their food. Future changes in penguin populations, perhaps caused by human exploitation of krill, will likely also affect sheathbills.

Introduced mammals are the greatest threat to sheathbills. Pale-faced Sheathbills are apparently not affected at their breeding sites, but feral cats have effects on Black-faced Sheathbill populations, although their impact has differed in different islands. At Marion Island, prior to their extermination in 1990, feral cats appeared to have had little impact on sheathbills, as the cats preyed primarily on small petrels, with sheathbills comprising less than 1% of their prey. In an interesting twist, the eradication of cats might actually be detrimental to sheathbills, because an increasing population of introduced house mice appears to be reducing densities of terrestrial invertebrates, an important source of winter food for sheathbills.

At Île aux Cochons, in the Crozet Islands, feral cats have severely depleted the population of Black-faced Sheathbills. Sheathbills are rare here despite a huge King Penguin colony and thousands of Rockhopper Penguins; this is the only island in the Crozets that has cats. Likewise, cats appear to be having a negative impact on sheathbills on parts of the main island of Kerguelen where petrels are rare. Quantitative studies of the impact of cats on sheathbills are required in both the Crozet and Kerguelen groups.

General Bibliography

Björklund (1994), Cracraft (1981), Dunning (1993), Furness (1987a), Harrison (1985, 1987), Jehl & Murray (1986), Meise (1968b), Peters (1934), Sibley & Ahlquist (1990), Sibley & Monroe (1990), Stonehouse (1985), Tuck & Heinzel (1978).

PLATE 48

inches 5
cm 13

ssp *minor*

2

1

ssp *marionensis*

Family CHIONIDAE (SHEATHBILLS)

PLATE 48
SPECIES ACCOUNTS

Genus *CHIONIS* J. R. Forster, 1788

1. Pale-faced Sheathbill
Chionis alba

French: Chionis blanc   **Spanish**: Picovaina de Malvinas
                    German: Weißgesicht-Scheidenschnabel
Other common names: Wattled/Snowy/American/Greater Sheathbill, Snowy Paddy

Taxonomy. *Vaginalis alba* Gmelin, 1789, New Zealand; error = Falkland Islands.
Genus *Chionis* described by diagnosis, but no species included; thus, description of genus pre-dates those of both species. Monotypic.
Distribution. Breeds on Antarctic Peninsula, and along Scotia Arc on South Shetland Is, Elephant I, South Orkney Is and South Georgia; probably also South Sandwich Is, where breeding not confirmed. Non-breeding migrant to Falkland Is, Tierra del Fuego and Patagonia, with some birds wandering further N.
Descriptive notes. 34-41 cm; 460-780 g; wingspan 75-80 cm. No obvious seasonal variations in plumage or soft parts. Facial features more colourful and bill sheath less conspicuous than in *C. minor*. Female smaller than male, but similar in external appearance. Juvenile similar to adult, but sheath and facial wattles smaller; fledglings may have traces of grey down.
Habitat. Coastal, frequently occurring on islands. Typically found in seabird colonies, especially of penguins, but occasionally cormorants or albatrosses; also seal rookeries and haul-outs, and rocky and sandy shoreline. Sometimes near human settlements, e.g. in Falklands. Migrating birds sometimes stop off on icebergs.
Food and Feeding. Omnivorous. Krill, fish, squid and other marine prey stolen from penguins; also takes eggs and small chicks, mainly from penguins; carrion, faeces of birds and seals, intertidal algae and invertebrates, seal placentae and blood, and human refuse.

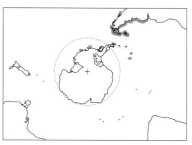

Breeding. Arrives at breeding sites Oct-Nov, lays Dec-Jan, chicks hatching Jan-Feb and fledging Mar. Monogamous, with high fidelity to territory, mate and nest-site; sexes have similar roles in all phases of breeding. Strongly territorial when breeding; territories invariably include colonies of penguins or, rarely, cormorants, which provide food. Nest is cup in pile of debris, within cavity, in or near feeding territory. Usually 2-3 eggs (1-4); incubation 28-32 days; chicks have dense brown down, followed shortly by coat of mottled grey down; fledging 50-60 days. Average success varies with sites, 1·5-1·9 fledglings per pair.
Movements. Most birds leave breeding sites late Apr to Jun, a few leaving later, in Jul, and some overwintering in breeding sites or other subantarctic locations if food is available; return Oct-Nov. Migratory routes poorly known. Main wintering grounds on shores of Falkland Is, Tierra del Fuego and S Patagonia. Some birds wander further N, e.g. to Uruguay. Ship-assisted vagrants in Brazil, South Africa, St Helena and even Europe.
Status and Conservation. Not globally threatened. Total population numbers c. 10,000 pairs widely distributed through breeding range: Antarctic Peninsula has 17+ sites, with 200 pairs; South Shetland Is 26 sites, 650 pairs; Elephant I 152 sites, c. 1450 pairs; South Orkney Is 6 sites, 5500 pairs; South Georgia c. 200 sites, c. 2000 pairs. Censuses incomplete. No serious threats from humans, and populations generally considered to be fairly healthy and stable. Poisoning from human chemical waste products may have caused some deaths in past, e.g. near Signy I.
Bibliography. Blake (1977), Burger, A.E. (1979, 1980b, 1981a), Canevari *et al.* (1991), Clark (1986), Cohen (1992), Croxall, Prince *et al.* (1984), Favero (1993a, 1993b, 1995, 1996), Favero *et al.* (1991), Furse (1979), Humphrey *et al.* (1970), Jablonski (1986), Jchl *et al.* (1979), Johnson (1965a), Jones (1963), Kaiser (1986), Loveridge (1969), Marchant & Higgins (1993), Montalti & Coria (1993), Murphy (1936), Olrog (1984), de la Peña (1992), Peter *et al.* (1988), Rossouw (1992), Schmidt & Schmidt (1991), Shaw (1986), Sick (1993), Tucker (1982), Watson (1975), Woods (1988).

2. **Black-faced Sheathbill**

Chionis minor

French: Petit Chionis   **Spanish**: Picovaina de las Kerguelen
German: Schwarzgesicht-Scheidenschnabel
Other common names: Lesser Sheathbill, Paddy

Taxonomy. *Chionis minor* Hartlaub, 1841, no locality = Kerguelen Islands.
There is no genetic mixing among subspecies, except in rare cases of ship-assisted vagrants. Four subspecies usually recognized.
Subspecies and Distribution.
C. m. marionensis Reichenow, 1908 - Marion and Prince Edward Is.
C. m. crozettensis (Sharpe, 1896) - Crozet Is.
C. m. minor Hartlaub, 1841 - Kerguelen Is.
C. m. nasicornis Reichenow, 1904 - Heard I and McDonald Is.
Descriptive notes. 38-41 cm; 450-760 g; wingspan 74-79 cm. Bill, bill sheath and facial caruncles all black, eye-ring pink; leg colour variable among and within populations, ranging from pink to purplish black. Small races are generally slightly smaller than most *C. alba*. Sexes alike, but male averages c. 15% larger than female. Bill sheath and eye-ring smaller in juvenile, a useful aging character; legs darker in immatures. Races form two groups, and differ slightly in overall size, in size of bill sheath, and, somewhat irregularly, in leg colour; race *nasicornis* very similar to nominate, with facial features and bill sheath perhaps slightly larger; races *marionensis* and *crozettensis* slightly smaller, with smaller bill sheath and more prominent and extensive caruncles.
Habitat. In summer, nearly all birds occur in colonies of penguins, particularly those of Rockhopper (*Eudyptes chrysocome*) and Macaroni (*Eudyptes chrysolophus*) Penguins; King Penguin (*Aptenodytes patagonicus*) colonies more important in winter. Also feeds among cormorants and albatrosses, at seal rookeries and haul-outs, in rocky and sandy intertidal zone, inland bogs, meadows and tussock grass within 1 km of shore, and around human settlements.
Food and Feeding. Omnivorous. Krill, fish, squid and other marine prey stolen from penguins; also eggs and small chicks, especially of penguins, carrion, faeces of birds and seals, intertidal algae and invertebrates, seal placentae and blood, and human refuse. Habits generally very similar to those of *C.*

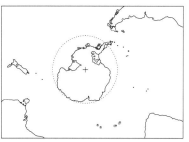

alba, but terrestrial invertebrates (e.g. earthworms, insects, spiders), taken from inland vegetated areas, are important as winter food.
Breeding. All pairs nest in association with penguins or other colonial seabirds, except in parts of Kerguelen (see page 547); some birds in King Penguin colonies remain in nesting territories all year; others reoccupy territories in Rockhopper or Macaroni Penguin colonies in Oct-Nov; eggs laid Dec-Jan, chicks hatching in Jan-Feb and fledging from late Mar to Apr. Normally 2-3 eggs (1-4); no replacement clutches; incubation averages 28 days (27-33); chicks have dense brown down, followed shortly by coat of mottled grey down; brooded continuously for first 14 days and less thereafter; fledging 55-60 days. Some chicks remain with parents through winter in King Penguin colonies. Fledging success varies with parents' age and quality of territory, average 1·1 fledglings per pair on Marion I, 1·4 in Crozets and 1·2 in Kerguelen. Age of first breeding 3-5 years. Successful breeders return to same territory and mate each season.
Movements. Sedentary. Some intra- and inter-island movement within an archipelago, in response to food availability. Adults usually stay within 1 km of breeding territory all year; non-breeders and immatures wander more widely, sometimes 10's of km from natal site.
Status and Conservation. Not globally threatened. Total population 6500-10,000 breeding pairs: 3000-6000 pairs in Kerguelen Is; 1400 on Marion and Prince Edward Is; c. 1000 on Crozet Is; size of population on Heard I not known, but probably numbers more than 1000 pairs. Feral cats reported to have depleted breeding population severely on Île aux Cochons, in Crozet Is, and causing declines in parts of Kerguelen. Rising numbers of house mice on Marion I might affect sheathbills by depleting terrestrial invertebrates, an important winter food. Population of sheathbills on I de la Possession, in Crozets, increasing slightly, in response to rising penguin populations.
Bibliography. Blankley (1981), Burger, A.E. (1978, 1979, 1980a, 1980b, 1980c, 1981a, 1981b, 1982, 1984, 1991), Burger, A.E. & Millar (1980), Derenne *et al.* (1976), Despin *et al.* (1972), Downes *et al.* (1959), Ealey (1954a, 1954b), Jouventin *et al.* (1988), Marchant & Higgins (1993), Paulian (1953), Prévost & Mougin (1970), Verheyden (1988), Verheyden & Jouventin (1991), Watson (1975), Williams *et al.* (1979).

Class AVES

Order CHARADRIIFORMES

Suborder LARI

Family STERCORARIIDAE (SKUAS)

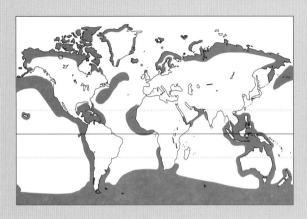

- Medium-sized to large gull-like piratical and predatory seabirds, with strong bill and plumage generally brown, or brown and white.
- 41-64 cm.

- Cosmopolitan in all oceans, but mainly at high latitudes.
- Predominantly marine, but also inhabits tundra.
- 2 genera, 7 species, 10 taxa.
- No species threatened; none extinct since 1600.

Systematics

The skuas (Stercorariidae) are thought to have diverged from their closest relatives, the gulls (Laridae), about 10 million years ago, towards the end of the Miocene. However, there are very few fossil skuas. One of these, named *Stercorarius shufeldti*, and looking like a rather small *Catharacta* skua, was found in Pleistocene deposits of Oregon, USA, consistent with the view that skuas, together with gulls and auks, originated in the Northern Hemisphere. However, while gulls and auks radiated into large numbers of species with most remaining in the north, skuas evolved into only seven species, with almost equal representation in the two hemispheres.

The three small skuas, the Pomarine Skua (*Stercorarius pomarinus*), the Arctic Skua (*Stercorarius parasiticus*) and the Long-tailed Skua (*Stercorarius longicaudus*), share many features of plumage, morphology, distribution and ecology, that separate them from the large skuas of the genus *Catharacta*, which lack the white-bellied morph found in small skuas, have only marginally elongated central tail feathers, and lack the distinctive barred plumage of juvenile small skuas. Thus it appears that there was an early split into the small skuas of the genus *Stercorarius* and the large skuas of the genus *Catharacta*, with the small skuas evolving in the Northern Hemisphere but the large skuas colonizing the Southern Hemisphere and more recently radiating there into three species. It has generally been supposed that the one Northern Hemisphere large skua, the Great Skua (*Catharacta skua*), recolonized the North Atlantic from the Southern Hemisphere, no ancestor of the large skuas having remained continuously in the Northern Hemisphere. This has led to much speculation as to the taxonomic affinities of the North Atlantic Great Skua with the various large skua taxa in the Antarctic and subantarctic.

Molecular data now provide some indications of the evolutionary relationships. In the mitochondrial cytochrome *b* gene of gulls and skuas there are about 70 differences in 1000 base pairs between present day gulls and skuas and the most likely reconstructed sequence of their common ancestor, whereas Arctic and Long-tailed Skuas and *Catharacta* taxa differ from their most likely common ancestral sequence by about 50 in 1000 base pairs. The molecular data would suggest that the split between the small and large skuas into two genera occurred closer to the date of separation of skuas from gulls than to the present day. The sequences of the Chilean (*Catharacta chilensis*), South Polar

(*Catharacta maccormicki*) and Brown (*Catharacta antarctica*) Skuas differ from their putative ancestor by only 3 to 10 bases in 1000, indicating that these taxa are only very recently diverged, but the Southern Hemisphere taxa and Great Skuas differ from their ancestral sequence by about 6 to 12 bases in 1000, suggesting that the Great Skua diverged from the Southern Hemisphere skua before the separation of the southern stock into three species.

Most surprisingly, the molecular data show the mitochondrial sequences of Great Skuas and Pomarine Skuas to be extremely similar, differing from each other by only 8 bases in 1000. Since mitochondrial DNA is clonally maternally inherited, the most plausible explanation seems to be hybridization between female Great Skuas and male *Stercorarius*, resulting in Pomarine Skuas carrying the mitochondrial sequence from Great Skuas but nuclear genes from both Great Skuas and the *Stercorarius* parent. The molecular data seem to have uncovered a most unexpected event: hybridization between a female Great Skua and a male Arctic Skua or Long-tailed Skua, leading to the evolution of the Pomarine Skua; or possibly hybridization between Pomarine Skuas and female Great Skuas, leading to the replacement of the Pomarine Skua mitochondrial DNA by Great Skua mitochondrial DNA. While such events seem unlikely to a natural historian, no other molecular explanations for the sequence data have yet been forthcoming. However, although Pomarine Skuas are generally thought to belong in the genus *Stercorarius* because of their many similarities with Arctic and Long-tailed Skuas, there are aspects of their biology that suggest strong affinities with the Great Skua. The Pomarine is the only small skua to share the characteristic "Wing-raising Display" with the "Long Call" shown by all *Catharacta* (see Voice), and multivariate analysis of skeletal measurements and characters has shown the Pomarine Skua to be closer to the Great Skua than to the Arctic or the Long-tailed Skua. All this is consistent with the idea that Great Skua genes recently entered the Pomarine Skua population through hybridization.

With Chilean, South Polar and Brown Skuas differing only by a few bases per thousand in mitochondrial cytochrome *b* sequences, one might be tempted to view these taxa as subspecies rather than full species. However, the separation into three full species has been based on a careful and thorough analysis by P. Devillers. He emphasized their tendency not to hybridize extensively in areas of overlapping breeding range, and for there to be few hybrids in the population, suggesting both behavioural avoidance of hybridization and reduced hybrid viability or fertility. The three species differ in behaviour as well as in plumage and measurements, according to Devillers more than Arctic and Pomarine Skuas differ from each other! For example, South Polar Skuas are transequatorial migrants, while Brown and Chilean Skuas winter close to their breeding areas. Even juvenile plumages of the three Southern Hemisphere species are clearly distinguishable.

Taxonomic views have varied over the years, and in the past all four *Catharacta* skuas were sometimes lumped in a single species; indeed, the genus *Catharacta* is still frequently merged into *Stercorarius*, by some authors. With the current widely agreed separation of the southern forms of *Catharacta* into three species, it would seem odd to lump the Great Skua with one of the southern species, as some authors have advocated, since it seems to have diverged more from the southern forms than they have from each other. Therefore, the Great Skua is probably best treated as a distinct, monotypic species; this treatment diverges from most previous versions, but seems the only logical arrangement given the new molecular data. Under the present arrangement, the Brown Skua is divided into three races, with nominate *antarctica* in the Falklands, *hamiltoni* on Tristan da Cunha and Gough, and *lonnbergi* on other subantarctic islands and the Antarctic Peninsula.

Amongst the small species, Arctic and Pomarine Skuas are monotypic, despite their wide breeding ranges, while the Long-tailed Skua is usually split into two subspecies, with nominate *longicaudus* breeding in Europe and western Siberia, and *pallescens* breeding in Greenland, North America and eastern Siberia.

Morphological Aspects

Although closely related to gulls, skuas show many differences from gulls that can be associated with their more piratical and predatory way of life and to breeding at high latitudes.

As in terrestrial birds of prey, females are larger than males. Though the difference in size between the sexes averages only about 3% for linear dimensions and 12% for weight, it is usually evident when looking at a breeding pair standing together. As with birds of prey, this reversed sexual size dimorphism is associated with differences in the behavioural roles of the sexes during breeding (see Breeding).

Although the sexes differ in size, they differ only very slightly in shape, the most consistent tendency being for males to have relatively longer tails and central tail streamers than females. Longer tails may allow males to perform better in the aerial display flights of the small skuas and may enhance their success in piracy, but the longer central tail streamers of males are probably a sexual signal rather than any aid to flight performance. Indeed, the Pomarine Skua may bite off its large and spoon-shaped, twisted central tail feather projections after breeding has begun, as they increase drag in flight and so have a significant energetic cost. The striking differences in central tail feather projections of the three small skuas probably aid in species recognition, but may also signal quality of the individual. Central tail feather projections become longer with age and it seems likely that birds with longer projections will gain a partner more readily, as has been shown with several other species with tail projections. The small skuas all moult the central tail feathers in spring as part of their limited pre-breeding moult, and this occurs just as the post-breeding moult has been completed, so the birds may have difficulty in finding the sulphur-containing amino acids and time needed to renew the central tail feathers between the end of the post-breeding moult and the start of breeding; these feathers take about 40 days to grow. In many immature small skuas the central tail feathers are not renewed, and other traces of immature plumage are retained into their first breeding season, strongly suggesting difficulty in carrying out this moult. Then birds with particularly long tail projections may be signalling particularly high quality.

Among the large skuas there is a complete moult of the flight-feathers each autumn/winter, but many body feathers and coverts are retained for more than a year. In particular, back feathers seem not to be renewed for many years, and, as a result, these wear and fade dramatically, even giving a good indication of the status of the individual as a young, middle-aged or old adult. Also, the older birds with more faded and worn feathers look conspicuously paler than young birds with fresh plumage. Whether these signals are intended to convey information to conspecifics is not clear, but it seems likely that they do, even if

Polymorphism occurs in four of the seven skua species. Intermediate colour morphs are sometimes found, rendering accurate identification at times extremely tricky and more dependent on structure than on plumage. This pair of Arctic Skuas presents a clear-cut case of a pale and a dark morph side by side. The distinction is not one of sex, despite the tendency among Arctic Skuas for the dark morph birds to be predominantly males. Interestingly, the incidence of dark morph birds decreases the farther north one goes until on the far northern Arctic tundra the majority of Arctic Skuas are pale birds.

[Stercorarius parasiticus, Foula, Shetland, Scotland. Photo: Günter Ziesler]

All four species of the genus Catharacta *show the same characteristic build; they are large, bulky birds that can appear heavy, even clumsy, on land, although all are capable of agile, speedy flight. Note the powerful hooked bill of this Chilean Skua, an admirable instrument for tearing food. The short, sturdy legs and feet end in long, sharp claws, a feature not found in any other web-footed birds.*

[Catharacta chilensis, Argentina. Photo: Conrad Greaves/ Aquila]

the reason for the pattern is to do with costs of feather renewal rather than status signalling.

Juvenile skuas are generally darker in tone than adults, and have shorter, more rounded wings and lack the elongations of the central tail feathers. Juvenile small skuas have heavily barred underparts and flanks, and well marked back feathers with pale edgings. Juveniles of the larger skuas lack barring, but have more uniformly coloured underparts than adults. The legs of juveniles are usually blue, but darken to black within a few weeks in large skuas, or over several years in small skuas. Immature birds pass through a series of plumages, slowly developing from the juvenile to the adult pattern.

In all skuas, flight is powerful and the ability to accelerate is well developed by comparison with gulls. Skuas not only have large pectoral muscles, but also have higher concentrations of mitochondria and of aerobic enzymes associated with energy metabolism, so that they are able to chase other seabirds more effectively than gulls can. The short wings of *Catharacta* allow a faster wingbeat than that of gulls, giving the birds enhanced ability to accelerate, while, compared with gulls, both *Catharacta* and *Stercorarius* skuas have relatively larger areas of the wing given to primaries and thus can generate greater forward thrust.

The powerful, hooked bill of skuas allows them to tear food more effectively than gulls can, and the long and sharp claws, unique among web-footed birds, and the heavily scuted and hard legs are probably also adaptations to a predatory way of life, though skuas are unable to hold prey with their feet in the manner of terrestrial birds of prey. This limits their ability to handle carrion and prey, and reduces their hunting success in some situations (see Food and Feeding), though they possess short and thick, heavily muscled necks that probably help to permit them to tear prey. Heavily armoured legs and feet also tend to limit heat loss, and this may be advantageous in the cold climates inhabited by most skuas, though they may reduce the ability of heat-stressed birds to dump excess heat too. The caeca of skuas are very much larger than those of gulls, though the reasons for this are unclear.

The generally dark coloration of skuas is thought to be an example of aggressive camouflage, allowing the skua to approach closer to a potential victim of kleptoparasitism than it could if it was light in colour. This idea is consistent with the fact that the populations of Arctic Skuas that most use kleptoparasitism when breeding are those at the southern end of the breeding range, and where the dark colour morph is most frequent. However, on the Arctic tundra, most Arctic Skuas are pale morph birds. Plumage

polymorphism is best known in the Arctic Skua, which shows a clinal increase in pale morph birds with breeding latitude, but also exists in the Pomarine Skua, where about 5-20% of each population are dark morph, regardless of geographical location. In the Long-tailed Skua a dark morph occurs but only extremely rarely and only in the population in Greenland. The South Polar Skua also has pale and dark colour morphs, dark birds predominating in the Atlantic parts of Antarctica and pale morph birds predominating in the Pacific parts of Antarctica. In Arctic Skuas and South Polar Skuas there is a tendency for males to be darker than females, with the dark morph being more frequent among males, but the colour morphs are thought to be controlled by a single autosomal gene with two alleles. Although Brown and Great Skuas can not readily be classified into two distinct colour morphs, they show a great deal of individual variation in colour and tone. Great Skua fledglings in particular seem to fall into pale (cinnamon) and dark (brown) types, and this may be an expression of the colour morph gene, since Arctic Skua chicks can readily be classified into pale and dark morphs. In Shetland, dark morph male Arctic Skuas have been found to be preferred by females and so, when forming a new partnership, achieve slightly higher breeding success through breeding earlier in the season. However, pale morph males tend to start breeding on average at an earlier age than dark males. Observations of the success of chases by pale and dark morph Arctic Skuas in Shetland found no differences in success rates of the two morphs. This does not necessarily disprove the "aggressive camouflage" hypothesis, since pale morph birds are much less common than dark morph birds in Shetland, and it is possible that the pale morph birds gain a balancing advantage through their relative scarcity. Atlantic Puffins (*Fratercula arctica*), terns and other victims may recognize the common colour morph, the dark, as a threat but be less responsive to the rarer, but less cryptic, form.

In addition to having short and well insulated legs, all skuas also have particularly dense body and head plumage, giving them especially good insulation from cold. This undoubtedly helps where they sometimes have to incubate underneath a cover of fresh snow, through Antarctic blizzards or in Arctic sub-zero conditions. However, combined with a high metabolic rate due to their high density of mitochondria and enzyme activity, skuas maintain a particularly high core body temperature for non-passerine birds, and may have difficulties in shedding excess heat in sunny or warm conditions. It is possible that the lower latitude limits of their breeding distributions may be set by the maximum temperatures and rates of solar energy irradiation that they can tolerate while breeding. Certainly, skuas nesting in Scotland resort to rapid panting when incubating under (rather rare) warm and sunny conditions, and the numbers bathing in freshwater pools are considerably higher on warmer afternoons.

Habitat

Skuas use the full range of marine habitats: Long-tailed Skuas are the most pelagic, spending the winter far out to sea, whereas Great Skuas prefer to remain out of sight of land but over the continental shelf, and Arctic Skuas migrate and winter close to the coastline, often entering estuaries and bays to associate with local aggregations of gulls and terns. Chilean Skuas winter in the channels, straits and fjords of southern South America, even using the rocky shore and intertidal habitat. Skua winter habitats range from subantarctic ocean, for the Long-tailed and Brown Skuas, to tropical ocean, in the Pomarine Skua. While most species spend the winter at sea, some birds in populations of Brown Skua that breed on subantarctic oceanic islands, where there are huge populations of nocturnal burrow-nesting petrels, are able to remain on their island throughout the year without the need to exploit marine habitats and foods at all. This is made possible by the presence of certain winter-breeding seabirds and by the behaviour of prions (*Pachyptila*), a major prey of many Brown Skua populations. Although prions breed during the summer, they continue to visit their burrows throughout the year, and so provide a food supply for skuas on the island even in mid-winter. This means that, at least in principle, some Brown Skuas in the

Undoubtedly the most graceful of the skuas in both flight and silhouette, the Long-tailed Skua is also the smallest, its long, slender tail streamers accounting for almost half its total length. The flight action has a light, buoyant, effortless quality that is distinctly tern-like. The bird soars easily with great agility in order to hawk for insects. It hunts lemmings, its main source of food on the tundra, by hovering and then swooping down on its prey, a feat that neither of its heavier congeners is capable of performing. Outside the breeding season its diet is little known; it is reputed to be less piratical than other skuas, but will take fish and scavenge on carrion. Little observed once migration begins in the northern autumn, it is thought to be the most pelagic of the three Stercorarius species, and to spend the winter entirely in the Southern Hemisphere.

[Stercorarius logicaudus pallescens, Rowley Island, Northwest Territories, Canada. Photo: Jan van de Kam]

Chatham Islands and other colonies near New Zealand, and at Gough Island and Tristan da Cunha, are able to remain continuously on their respective islands without the need to feed at sea at all. In practice, it seems likely that these birds will at least use the marine habitat from time to time during winter, and probably all fledglings will disperse to sea. However, it is established that some skuas are present on these islands whenever visits have been made in winter.

During the breeding season skuas use a wider variety of habitats. The three small *Stercorarius* skuas breed predominantly on tundra. The Long-tailed Skua not only inhabits coastal Arctic tundra, preferring drier ground, but also nests on alpine tundra in the mountains of Sweden and Norway and far inland in Alaska, Canada and Russia. Pomarine Skuas inhabit mainly low-lying flat, wet tundra along the coast, while Arctic Skuas prefer drier conditions than the Pomarine, but extend less far inland than Long-tailed Skuas and remain at lower altitudes. Arctic Skuas also inhabit many moorland or grassland habitats close to major seabird colonies where they can feed by kleptoparasitism, rather than on the terrestrial prey they take in tundra habitats. When nesting in association with seabird colonies in temperate areas, Arctic Skuas prefer to nest on ground that is well drained and with relatively short vegetation. They avoid grass or heather more than 10 cm high, apparently because they need to have a good view of any approaching predators while incubating. Nesting habitat tends to be on islands and away from human disturbance where possible, although Arctic Skuas are less intolerant of humans than are Great Skuas.

Great, Brown and Chilean Skuas all tend to nest on islands in grassy habitat, avoiding tall grass or bracken, shrubby areas, steeply sloping ground and areas of human activity. The exception to this last is furnished by those pairs that have learned to nest close to scientific bases or weather stations where they receive food scraps; for example, on Gough Island the weather station kitchen is fiercely defended as a core area of the territory

of a particularly aggressive pair of skuas. In Iceland, Great Skuas nest mainly on the *sandur*, huge areas of very flat ground created by the deposition of gravel from braided melt-water rivers that criss-cross the plain between the upland glaciers and the sea.

The South Polar Skua is well named in that it has been recorded closer to the South Pole than any other wild animal, and small numbers nest inland at relatively snow-free mountain sites where there are breeding Antarctic Petrels (*Thalassoica antarctica*) and Snow Petrels (*Pagodroma nivea*). However, most South Polar Skuas nest in the same habitat as is chosen by Adelie Penguins (*Pygoscelis adeliae*), namely relatively flat coastal areas of snow-free ground. These sites generally lack vegetation so that the birds nest on bare rock, on moss or lichen, or on scrapes in the gravel. It had been supposed that the skuas chose this nesting habitat in order to hold territories that included penguins, so that they could defend a food supply of penguin eggs and chicks. In fact, only a small proportion of South Polar Skuas exploit penguins as a food supply, and many skuas hold territories that include sections of penguin rookery but make no use of this potential feeding opportunity. The close association between South Polar Skua and Adelie Penguin nesting habitats seems to be primarily due to both species seeking a very limited nesting resource: flat coastal snow-free ground close to open ice-free sea.

General Habits

Skuas are not particularly social. At sea they usually travel and forage individually, though the larger species will join mixed-species flocks over shoals of fish or at fishing boats, and Pomarine Skuas do seem habitually to travel in small groups. Co-operative hunting will occasionally occur, but is unusual. Even when groups of skuas chase a single victim, this is generally a result of a shortage of potential victims resulting in scramble competition, rather

One of the skuas' most characteristic displays is the "Long Call", which can be used to proclaim ownership of a territory, to repel intruders, or to greet the mate. In the four Catharacta species and also the Pomarine Skua (Stercorarius pomarinus), the call is typically accompanied by a "Wing-raising Display", in which the large white flashes around the bases of the primaries stand out most effectively. The Brown Skua is chiefly a coastal species, to be found on and around subantarctic islands that are heavily populated by penguins and burrow-nesting seabirds on which it relies heavily for its food. Where the environmental conditions are not too severe and prey is plentiful, it may not disperse out to sea at all, remaining resident on its breeding grounds throughout the year.

[Catharacta antarctica lonnbergi, Antarctica. Photo: Philip Shaw/Aquila]

Skuas are infamous for their attacks on other seabirds but they do not always rely on such tactics for obtaining food. In Shetland, for example, even though there are huge numbers of seabirds available for exploitation, Great Skuas tend to feed mainly on sandeels (Ammodytes) when shoals are present near the surface, and they also relish the discards of fishing boats. At such locations of temporary plenty, large numbers of skuas can gather together, often in the company of other seabird species. Squabbles may break out even on the water, birds displaying aggressively and lunging out at each other.

[Catharacta skua, Foula, Shetland, Scotland. Photo: Günter Ziesler]

than collaboration for mutual benefit. Territorial defence by breeding skuas is very strong. While skuas often nest in colonies, they can also nest as isolated pairs, and colonial nesting seems to be a consequence of shortage of nesting habitat or highly aggregated distribution of food resources.

Many skua colonies have traditional freshwater bathing sites within or adjacent to the colony, and both breeding and non-breeding birds attend these frequently. The largest bathing pool on Foula, Shetland, can have up to 200 Great Skuas on it on a warm summer afternoon. Here the birds drink, bathe and interact vigorously with frequent displays and fights. While bathing, they exhibit a number of apparently highly ritualized exaggerated bathing postures. After bathing, the birds rest in groups beside the pools, preening thoroughly or just sleeping. The functions of this communal bathing are unclear. Drinking fresh water will reduce energy costs of salt excretion, and drinking and bathing may reduce energy costs of keeping cool on warm sunny days; certainly the numbers bathing are higher on days when it is warmer. Perhaps the communal activity allows dominance relationships to be maintained or information transfer. Since absence from the territory does increase the risk of chicks being killed by neighbouring skuas, there would seem to be some good reason for birds joining bathing flocks, as breeders apparently do almost daily.

On the territory, skuas tend to have a traditional spot where they sit or stand when thet are not otherwise occupied. As a consequence of the trampling, but more especially the manuring, these patches develop distinct vegetation; in Shetland, Great Skua patches are clearly visible as bright green swards of short grass looking like tiny golf greens within a matrix of longer coarse grass or heather. Similar, but much larger, patches, fully the size of a real golf green, are created by non-breeding skuas loafing on their traditional "club" sites. These nutrient enriched areas of sweet grass are very attractive to sheep, and so tend to be closely grazed, despite the aggression of breeding skuas towards sheep that approach their nest or chicks.

Male and female skuas differ in breeding role to a variable extent among species. Female Great Skuas at Shetland tend to

remain in the territory guarding the eggs or chicks, and are provisioned by the male. Arctic Skuas in Shetland show much less pronounced division of duties though again the larger females spend longer guarding, and less time foraging, than the males do. On the tundra, differences in behaviour between the sexes seem less evident. Given the larger size of female skuas, the female is probably better able to defend the eggs and chicks from potential predators, so such a division of duties is not unexpected.

Voice

Unlike the gulls, skuas tend not to be particularly vocal birds, and they are normally silent at sea. Indeed, even when they are on their breeding grounds their vocalizations are fairly limited.

Although registering a clamorous protest, the otherwise defenceless Gentoo Penguin (Pygoscelis papua) parent can do little more than stand and watch as its hapless chick is snatched away by a Brown Skua. This skua species is heavily predatory on penguins, regularly plundering their eggs and young, and scavenging the corpses of adults too.

[Catharacta antarctica antarctica, Falkland Islands. Photo: Francisco J. Erize/ Bruce Coleman]

All *Catharacta* and the Pomarine Skua have a "Long Call", a series of 4-12 "laughs" lasting 0·2 seconds each, which they give to indicate territory ownership to intruders or to greet the mate. This call is usually accompanied by the "Wing-raising Display", which shows off the white flashes in the proximal parts of the primaries. Long-tailed and Arctic Skuas have similar "Long Calls", given with the head lifted and neck stretched, but without the "Wing-raising Display".

Long-tailed and Arctic Skuas both perform noisy display flights, often with adults from elsewhere joining in over the territory. The cries of Arctic Skuas are often described as "cat-like". Sharper and less melodic cries are made when birds are chasing intruding skuas. Female skuas give a characteristic soft panting call when soliciting food or copulation. Chicks, in turn, have a shrill food-begging call.

Great Skuas, when nervous, give a repeated soft "quack", so human visitors to Great Skua colonies are continuously accompanied by this call; I have never heard this call given by Brown Skuas or South Polar Skuas, and these species mostly give a harsh cry as they swoop at a human intruder to their territory. This harsh cry is given by only a very small percentage of Great Skuas, those few most aggressive individuals in breeding colonies that regularly strike human intruders. The voice of the Chilean Skua is said to be much higher-pitched and more nasal than that of the Brown Skua. The South Polar Skua also has a much harsher and higher-pitched voice than the Brown Skua, with the Great Skua being least raucous.

Food and Feeding

Skuas use a wide range of feeding behaviour, though they are notorious as pirates and predators. Piracy, or kleptoparasitism, is carried out by threatening other birds with physical attack or injury, in order to cause them to drop or regurgitate food that the skua can recover and swallow. Arctic Skuas often attack terns, puffins and small gulls, while Great Skuas tend to attack larger seabirds, such as Common Murres (*Uria aalge*), gulls and Northern Gannets (*Sula bassana*). Attacks can involve stooping from great height like a Peregrine Falcon (*Falco peregrinus*), in order to startle an auk to drop a fish, or may involve prolonged chases of slower-flying and less manoeuvrable seabirds. Terns often drop fish when chased by Arctic Skuas apparently to avoid physical attack, but gannets chased by Great Skuas can be repeatedly caught by the wingtip and tipped into the sea. Although Great Skuas appear to be intimidated by the gannet's powerful bill and do not attack birds they have pulled down onto the sea, the gannet may often regurgitate food, apparently to allow it to get away from the skua's attentions.

Tundra-nesting skuas feed on small mammals, but also on insects, berries, small birds, eggs and carrion. The three *Stercorarius* species differ in their abilities to exploit these different foods, owing to the greater flight agility of the Long-tailed Skua, but greater muscular digging and tearing power of the Pomarine Skua. Long-tailed Skuas pounce on lemmings (*Lemmus*) from above, whereas Pomarine Skuas lack the agility to do this and tend to dig the lemmings out from within their tunnels. In winter, Arctic Skuas feed largely by kleptoparasitism, but Long-tailed Skuas do not, and probably catch food for themselves, while Pomarine Skuas appear to be the most predatory, killing phalaropes and other small seabirds at sea.

Catharacta skuas are great opportunists, learning new feeding opportunities quickly. They will feed as predators but can often obtain food more easily, or with less risk of injury, by other means. South Polar Skuas generally fish for themselves at sea, catching Antarctic silverfish (*Pleuragramma antarcticum*), but they will take Adelie Penguin eggs or small chicks, especially if feeding conditions at sea are poor. Brown Skuas are much more predatory, and, where sympatric with South Polar Skuas, the larger Brown Skuas feed predominantly on penguins and rarely on fish. Great Skuas on St Kilda, off north-west Scotland, feed mainly on seabirds during breeding, especially on Black-legged Kittiwakes (*Rissa tridactyla*), Atlantic Puffins and storm-petrels. Some of these they find dead at the colony or at sea, simply because there are such large numbers of seabirds at these colonies, but some they kill by catching hold of them in mid-air, and dragging them to the sea surface and then drowning them. By contrast, Great Skuas breeding in Shetland kill or scavenge very few seabirds, though plenty are available; in Shetland they prefer to catch sandeels (*Ammodytes*), when shoals are available at the sea surface, and to scavenge on small whiting (*Merlangius merlangus*) and haddock (*Melanogrammus aeglefinus*) discarded from fishing boats. They catch sandeels by joining mixed species flocks of Northern Gannets, gulls and Northern Fulmars (*Fulmarus glacialis*) above dense shoals of sandeels and splash-diving onto the masses of fish. Discards are taken from behind fishing boats in direct competition with gannets, fulmars and large gulls, sometimes by stealing fish from these other species, but more often by simply picking discarded fish directly from the sea. Neither of these options is normally available at St Kilda.

Breeding skuas of most species are diurnally active and sleep during the night. Great Skuas in Shetland are essentially inactive from 22:00 to 04:00 hours, despite it being moderately light through the night in mid-summer. However, Brown Skuas nesting on islands with burrow-nesting petrels are essentially inactive throughout the day, and forage entirely at night by walking around until they find a petrel, then jumping on it and killing it.

Some skuas, certainly including several or all of the *Catharacta* taxa, have a very poor sense of taste. This may be adaptive for birds that often feed on carrion, but it is striking to see the large skuas happily eat meat laced with hot chilli sauce or with bitter tasting alphachloralose narcotic. Experiments presenting meat buried in snow to South Polar Skuas also showed that they have little or no sense of smell; unlike the petrels, skuas' brains have only small olfactory bulbs and they are unable to locate prey by scent.

Within skua colonies individual birds will learn particular feeding specialities. A few Great Skuas at Foula specialize on stealing eggs from Northern Fulmars without being spat on and covered in oil. One bird specialized in killing Black Guillemots (*Cepphus grylle*) by sitting on a boulder above the guillemot nest and pouncing on the emerging adult; this behaviour led to the desertion of an entire Black Guillemot colony. One bird learned to walk into the Arctic Tern (*Sterna paradisaea*) colony to pick up chicks, rather than fly in causing terns to attack in force. A few birds learn to scavenge on sheep afterbirth, and some go on from this to learn to attack lambing ewes and newborn lambs. At Hermaness, Shetland, a few Great Skuas take many Black-legged Kittiwake chicks from nests, whereas at Foula they never do, but they do kill many kittiwake fledglings. Several years of shortage of sandeels in Shetland led to the development of widespread cannibalism, Great Skuas eating chicks from other territories. Although sandeel stocks have since recovered, many Great Skua chicks are still being killed each year, apparently because this habit has been retained.

Breeding

Skuas are generally monogamous and pair for life, showing strong territory site fidelity. There are two major exceptions to this generalization. One is the Pomarine Skua, which shows an element of nomadism, and forms new partnerships as a result. This behaviour is in response to the fluctuations in lemming abundance which cause this specialist predator to seek areas of high lemming numbers before settling to breed. The other exception is the bizarre habit of Brown Skuas at some colonies to nest in communal groups, which always consist of a single adult female and two or more males; such polyandry is unusual among birds, although it has now been recorded in a number of families. It could arise if one male was unable to provision a mate and chick, in which case a second male could permit higher breeding success to be achieved. In the Chatham Islands this is clearly not the case as the breeding success of pairs, trios and larger groups is uniformly very high. In fact, groups have marginally lower breeding success because the confusion among adults leads to a slight loss of egg viability through irregular incubation. Nor can kin selection be invoked as an explanation,

The Brown Skua is probably the most piratical of all the Stercorariidae. In these photos, two skuas collaborate to force a Southern Giant Petrel (Macronectes giganteus) off its nest, while another has already successfully got hold of a Gentoo Penguin (Pygoscelis papua) egg. Some Brown Skuas never leave the islands on which they breed, as the presence of large seabird colonies assures them of an easy living all year round.

[Above: Catharacta antarctica lonnbergi, Macquarie Island. Photo: G. Robertson/ Auscape.

Below: Catharacta antarctica antarctica, Falkland Islands. Photo: Wayne Lynch/DRK]

On their territories skuas are notoriously aggressive towards all intruders, birds and mammals alike, including humans. Their usual method of attack, and a most effective one, is a blow to the head, delivered with either bill or feet. This sheep and its lamb have strayed too close to an Arctic Skua's nest-site and are receiving a timely warning.

[*Stercorarius parasiticus*. Photo: Tim Loseby]

since the males in groups are normally not closely related. On the few small uninhabited islands in the Chathams where skuas nest, much of the island is covered with dense scrubby woodland, bracken, flax and tree ferns, excluding skuas from holding territories. Most territories are on the edge of the island, often on rocky areas on the edge of the sea. This limited nesting habitat may encourage group formation, allowing males to hold a territory that they might lose to another male if they tried to defend it alone. The habit of winter residency seems to correlate with formation of groups, and it may be that low levels of territorial defence in winter permit the establishment of groups that carry on into breeding seasons. Whatever the reason, groups are remarkably stable: some trios and groups of up to seven birds on territories on Rangatira Island, in the Chathams, have remained intact for seven or more consecutive breeding seasons. DNA fingerprinting has shown that chicks in group territories may be fathered by any male in the group, but that extra-group copulations either do not occur or do not fertilize eggs. Bonds within groups appear every bit as strong as within pairs.

Established breeding pairs of skuas usually re-establish the pair-bond by meeting on the territory used in the previous year. Limited courtship ceremony is needed and, with high adult survival rates, most neighbouring territories are likely to contain the same adults as in the previous year too, so territorial boundaries are already established. Birds that have lost a partner soon accept a new mate; experimental removal of one bird early in the season often leads to a replacement partner entering the territory within 48 hours. Occasionally birds will force their way in to replace an existing adult. This can sometimes be achieved by dive-bombing the bird on the territory or by physical attack and fighting; broken wings or other serious injuries are not uncommon when these conflicts escalate, though usually the owner is successful in retaining its status. New pairs of inexperienced birds often form on club sites and sometimes attempt to breed on a small territory on the fringe of the club. This is usually unsuccessful due to disturbance from other club birds, and the eggs are usually lost, but some such pairs later manage to expand their territory into the colony proper.

Formation of the nest scrape is usually carried out by both adults together, following circular parading displays and much squeaking. Often several scrapes are made before one is selected for the eggs. Most clutches are of two eggs, but about 5-10% may consist of only one. Clutches of more than two eggs are very unusual, though a few females lay three eggs consistently, year after year. These larger than normal clutches usually fail to hatch because all eggs at some times fail to receive adequate warming. Skuas have only two brood patches to warm the eggs, and incubate with one egg on each foot to insulate them from the ground since nests have little or no lining material. The webs

provide good insulation but have very little blood flow through them so do not transfer significant heat to the eggs. The habit presumably allows skuas to avoid making a conspicuous nest, so that predators such as Arctic foxes (*Alopex lagopus*), or indeed other skuas, will be less likely to notice a skua clutch on the tundra. The lack of material to raise eggs off the ground can lead to loss of large numbers of eggs through chilling if heavy rainstorms occur during the incubation period.

Eggs are laid at intervals usually of 48 hours, but sometimes of 24 or 72 hours. Incubation begins with the laying of the first egg, so that hatching is asynchronous, though usually with a gap smaller than that between the laying of the two eggs, since the second egg is slightly smaller and so develops faster, and incubation temperature is usually rather lower over the first day or two than for the rest of the incubation period. When food is short, the larger and older chick will attack the younger one, preventing it from getting much of the meal regurgitated by the parent. In the South Polar Skua this almost invariably leads to the death of the second chick, but in other skuas the second chick has a good chance of surviving, except in unusually poor seasons. In view of the hostile behaviour between siblings, it is not surprising that skua chicks have a habit of wandering, leaving the nest a day or two after hatching, but often returning for periods of brooding until too big to fit under the adult. However, even in skua populations where sibling conflict is not induced by food shortage, and in single-chick broods, chicks wander some distance from the nest but seem to learn the limits of the territory. Approaching danger leads to chicks crouching motionless, often behind a stone or clump of vegetation, until danger has passed. Surprisingly, chick wandering can lead to adoption by an adjacent pair. On Foula, while sandeels were scarce and Great Skua breeding success was very low because chicks were starving or being eaten by neighbouring adults when parents were away foraging, several starving chicks tried to beg from adults returning to a nearby territory to feed their own chicks, and at least some of these were accepted into the new family. Perhaps attempting to be adopted by a more successful adult, with its attendant risk of being killed, is a viable alternative to staying at home and starving to death.

Breeding success is high in most skuas. If eggs are lost during incubation a replacement clutch may be laid about 10 days after the loss. Though clutches lost towards the end of incubation are rarely replaced, egg loss is most frequent early in incubation. Only the South Polar Skua normally has low breeding success, apparently due to difficulties in catching enough fish to keep chicks alive, as well as added losses caused by sporadic harsh weather conditions. In Long-tailed Skuas, breeding success varies considerably with variations in food supply. This is true also of other skuas, but food supply is not so variable for Arctic Skuas, and is uniformly high for most Brown

Skuas, giving them consistently the highest chick production among skua taxa.

Hybridization among skuas tends to be of a predictable nature. Where pairs of species breed side by side, assortative mating is strong, with hybridization rare. The few hybrids that do arise on the Antarctic Peninsula are of male South Polar Skuas with female Brown Skuas, because the Brown Skua returns to establish territories and pairs first. When male South Polar Skuas return there are already some unpaired female Brown Skuas with which they can pair, whereas female South Polar Skuas have not yet arrived. A female Brown Skua accepted by a male South Polar Skua is likely to be able to repel any female South Polar Skua trying to enter the territory because Brown Skuas are so much larger. However, although there are suggestions that hybridization between these two species may have increased with recent range expansion, few hybrids can be identified in the adult population, suggesting that the viability of hybrids may be low.

Skuas are long-lived, and the larger species especially so. The oldest recorded ringed bird is a 34 year old Great Skua trapped on its nest on Foula. Colour ringing indicates a survival rate of breeding adults of 89% per annum at present on Foula, where food has been in short supply in recent years, while the survival rate at Handa, north-west Scotland, where food supply seems to be better, is 94% per annum. Brown Skuas in the Chatham Islands have an average adult survival rate of over 94% per annum.

Movements

The family includes species that are transequatorial migrants through to species in which some populations are predominantly resident or show only local winter dispersal. The South Polar Skua holds the record amongst all birds for the longest movement recorded by ringing: a bird ringed as a chick on the Antarctic Peninsula shot north of the Arctic Circle in Greenland six months later.

Young skuas tend to migrate further than adults, and are more likely to be driven off course by bad weather. "Wrecks" of skuas may occur in Europe in autumn when there are strong onshore storms that carry inexperienced birds over land. Such conditions have led to recoveries of Great Skuas, ringed a few months ear-lier as chicks in Scotland, on motorways, lakes and farmyards in Austria, Switzerland, Poland and southern Germany.

Transequatorially migrating skuas pass rapidly through the tropics, but movements within temperate regions tend to be slow, the birds taking advantage of feeding opportunities that arise. In general, autumn migrations tend to be more leisurely than those in spring, and the concentrated spring migration can lead to spectacular numbers of skuas passing within view of Irish and Scottish coastal seawatching sites, if onshore winds deflect the birds from their preferred paths further offshore.

The extent to which skuas deliberately migrate over land is unclear. It seems likely that some Arctic and Pomarine Skuas nesting on the tundra of north Russia or Canada migrate over land rather than taking the much longer northern coastal route to the Atlantic or Pacific, but the highly pelagic Long-tailed Skua is rarely encountered inland and perhaps avoids these overland routes.

Many juvenile and some immature skuas remain in the wintering area through the following summer, rather than returning to the breeding range, while some immature birds migrate beyond the breeding area to explore. Subadult Great Skuas ringed as chicks in Scotland have been recovered from as far beyond their natal area as west Greenland, Svalbard and north Russia while others from the same cohort summer off Brazil or the Cape Verde Islands.

Relationship with Man

Because of their tendency to breed at high latitudes, skuas were little known to ornithologists before the nineteenth century. During the seventeenth and eighteenth centuries, the leading European ornithologists obtained some specimens of skuas shot during migration through Europe, and expeditions to the Faeroes, northern Scandinavia, Greenland and Spitsbergen returned with some skuas collected at their breeding areas. This limited material resulted in enormous confusion, compounded by the variety of colour morphs and juvenile and subadult plumages. As a result, by 1876, the review by H. Saunders, the leading expert on skuas in the nineteenth century, contained no mention of the South Polar Skua, but listed, for example, 18 different post-Linnaean scientific

Less colonially inclined than most other skuas but strongly territorial, the Pomarine Skua breeds in widely dispersed pairs on marshy tundra at high northern latitudes. Choice of the general breeding area is heavily dependent on the presence of rodents, especially lemmings, which are important food for its young. It prefers low mossy tundra and will often site the nest in hummocky grass alongside a bog or a freshwater pool. In a bad lemming year it may not breed at all, instead migrating early, but in a good year even birds in immature plumage have been known to breed.

[Stercorarius pomarinus, Canada. Photo: Brian Hawkes/ Aquila]

As a general rule, skuas tend to be rather successful breeders, the only notable exception being the South Polar Skua. Fish supplies sometimes prove too scanty for the second chick to stand any chance of survival, and sudden severe storms can also cause mortality among the young. Note the chick's sturdy legs and pale soft, woolly down with erect silky spikes; the egg tooth is still present on the already robust bill.

[Catharacta maccormicki, Ross Island, Antarctica. Photo: Rich Kirchner/ NHPA]

names for the Long-tailed Skua, and 23 for the Arctic Skua. He pointed out that the name Linnaeus gave to a small skua, *Larus parasiticus*, from which we now derive the scientific name of the Arctic Skua, was given to a bird which the description of Linnaeus shows clearly to have been a Long-tailed Skua! Similarly, the name *Catharacta*, now used for the genus of large skuas, was a name originally given by Aristotle to a bird mistakenly thought to be a great skua by eighteenth century ornithologists, but clearly from Aristotle's description a juvenile Northern Gannet!

Though ornithologists did not know skuas well, local peoples in certain remote areas did. In Iceland, the Faeroes and Shetland, skua eggs and chicks were a valuable food resource, easily collected from the ground nesting areas. In the Faeroes, in particular, skua chicks were tethered to prevent them from wandering, and harvested as food shortly before their due fledging date. However, the Faeroese Great Skuas were considered a mixed blessing, as they attacked cliff-nesting seabirds that were also harvested, and so skuas were on the list of "vermin" for the heads of which a bounty was paid. In Shetland, the Great Skua was a highly prized, but very rare, bird during the eighteenth century, owing to its habit of chasing away White-tailed Sea-eagles (*Haliaeetus albicilla*), and so preventing the eagles from attacking sheep and lambs. However, with the increase in numbers of Great Skuas in Shetland during the early nineteenth century, and the decrease in eagle numbers, the balance of favour shifted towards harvesting skuas as food. Especially at Foula, Great Skua eggs were harvested around mid-May, causing the birds to lay a replacement clutch about ten days later. The replacement clutch was also harvested, then the smaller number of pairs producing another replacement clutch were usually allowed to breed unmolested.

Harvesting probably had rather little effect on skua numbers, but during the late nineteenth century many "sportsmen" and taxidermists visited skua colonies to shoot adults for museums and private collectors. Many colonies were exterminated, and Great Skua numbers were reduced to only about four pairs in the Faeroes and a couple of dozen pairs in Shetland around 1890-1900. Then strict protection, including wardening of colonies in Shetland, resulted in a sustained population increase, continued in Scotland until very recently, with considerable colonization of new areas on the southern fringe of the breeding range and dramatic northward

expansion of the range into Svalbard, Norway and Russia. Population growth in the Faeroes was less dramatic, partly due to greater illegal persecution there, but also because Faeroese populations did not receive the benefits of increased food supply that were provided in Scotland. In particular, Scottish Great Skuas have taken advantage of the huge quantities of undersized haddock, whiting and other fish discarded from fishing boats, and this has formed a large part of their breeding season diet, and has undoubtedly contributed to their high breeding success and population growth. Association with fishing boats is not entirely beneficial though, as a few birds swallow baited hooks and are killed as a result, and some become entangled and drown in fishing nets, especially in the wintering areas.

Although Great Skuas are often denounced for attacking sheep, it is not clear that they are, on balance, damaging to the interests of crofters and their sheep. Sheep tend to congregate on the "club" sites used by non-breeding skuas, and this is probably because the skuas' droppings add large amounts of nitrogen and phosphorus to the vegetation and so stimulate the growth of nutrient rich grass. These areas frequented by skuas are thus the best areas for sheep to graze. This improvement to the grazing by skuas has not been generally recognized by crofters, but it may well more than counterbalance the amount of damage that skuas do by very occasionally killing lambs and by chasing sheep away from their nests or chicks.

Status and Conservation

Several skua taxa have small populations, notably the South Polar Skua with 5000-8000 pairs, the Brown Skua with 13,000-14,000 pairs, the Great Skua with 13,600 pairs, and the Chilean Skua with unknown but probably similar numbers. However, none of the species is threatened or declining significantly in range or numbers.

Indeed, generally skuas can be considered a considerable conservation success story. Great Skuas in Scotland and the Faeroes were rescued from the verge of local extinction (see Relationship with Man), despite a prevailing view in 1870-1900 that their loss from the British and Faeroese avifaunas was almost inevitable. Although there were hundreds of Brown Skuas on

The Arctic Skua breeds colonially at seabird sites where its food supply is assured, yet it is also found nesting widely dispersed over moorland and tundra. The chicks, normally two in number, are able to leave the nest, a simple depression in the ground, 1-2 days after hatching and they usually separate to hide in vegetation nearby, the cryptic dark brown down affording them a certain measure of protection against predators.

[Stercorarius parasiticus, Spitzbergen, Svalbard. Photo: Michel Gunther/ Bios]

Amsterdam Island, in the southern Indian Ocean, in the 1870's, the population was reduced to only a single breeding pair after humans introduced agriculture, feral cattle, pigs, rats, goats, dogs and cats. However, with the help of several recent conservation measures, skua numbers have increased again to 19 pairs.

Nevertheless, as these same successes illustrate, the past history of skuas confirms that populations are potentially vulnerable to persecution. Increases to the normally low adult mortality rate can lead to rapid decreases in numbers and whole colonies can easily be driven to extinction through persecution of adults, so current and recent cases of persecution require vigilance. Great and Arctic Skuas in Scotland have suffered from some illegal persecution, which has kept numbers down in a few particular areas. Brown Skuas in the Falklands have probably also suffered from some persecution by sheep farmers, though in that case the skuas gain some support for their habit of attacking the local sheldgeese (*Chloephaga*), which farmers consider to be a greater threat through their competition for grazing. Brown Skua numbers have been reduced where they nest near farms, as on Tristan da Cunha and in the Chatham Islands. Again, numbers near Antarctic bases have changed as a result of human activities, some increasing as a result of new feeding opportunities and some decreasing as a result of increased disturbance.

As top predators in several ecosystems, skuas tend to accumulate high levels of pollutants that are amplified through the food chain. These include all lipid-soluble pollutants, such as organochlorine pesticides, PCB's and organic mercury. Skuas that feed on prey which concentrate pollutants that are not lipid-soluble into particular tissues can also acquire high concentrations. For example, Brown Skuas eating prion and petrel livers and kidneys accumulate high levels of cadmium. Despite the high concentrations produced, there is little evidence of any toxic effects, but individuals with particular predatory specializations may be at risk.

Oil and chemical pollution threats to skuas seem to be relatively minor, but changes to fishery practices might have profound effects on Great Skua numbers if discarding were to cease. Locally, Arctic Skua numbers may be adversely affected by increases in Great Skua colonies and consequent predation and competition for territories, but such effects seem to be minor and result in movement, rather than extermination, of Arctic Skua colonies.

Perhaps the most important conservation issue is in the impact of skua predation on other seabird populations. Some petrel populations have been severely reduced in size by introduced alien mammals or habitat change, and the remnants of these may be vulnerable to skuas. Fortunately, the extremely rare Magenta Petrel (*Pterodroma magentae*), endemic to the Chatham Islands, nests well away from skua colonies, but on Rangatira Island, also in the Chathams, skuas nest over the burrows of the Chatham Petrel (*Pterodroma axillaris*), a Vulnerable species now reduced to only about 300 individuals. Though apparently they do not eat it, the skuas kill a high proportion of the similar and sympatric Black-winged Petrel (*Pterodroma nigripennis*), and killed the only Juan Fernandez Petrels (*Pterodroma externa*) occupying burrows in New Zealand and may have prevented a new colonization by that species! On Gough Island, the endemic Atlantic Petrel (*Pterodroma incerta*) is eaten by skuas, but currently it is still a relatively abundant bird, and the skuas also have plentiful supplies of prions, Soft-plumaged Petrels (*Pterodroma mollis*) and storm-petrels, so their impact on the Atlantic Petrel population is slight.

Since the numbers of Great Skuas seem now to be artificially high as a result of the provision of discards from fishing boats, any sudden reduction in the supply of discarded fish in northern Scotland could result in Great Skuas switching to predation in order to meet their food requirements, and this could have a major effect on populations of smaller seabirds, especially storm-petrels, Black-legged Kittiwakes and Atlantic Puffins, and perhaps Red-throated Divers (*Gavia stellata*), Arctic Skuas, Eurasian Oystercatchers (*Haematopus ostralegus*) and Common Eiders (*Somateria mollissima*). That situation requires monitoring in view of the current concern to abolish discarding within the European Union Common Fisheries Policy.

General Bibliography

Barton (1982), Björklund (1994), Blechschmidt *et al.* (1993), Burger, J. (1980d), Burger, J., Olla & Winn (1980), Croxall (1987), Croxall *et al.* (1984), Dunning (1993), Furness (1985, 1987b), Furness & Monaghan (1987), Harrison (1985, 1987), Jehl & Murray (1986), Löfgren (1984), Nelson (1980), Olsen (1989b), Parmelee (1988a), Peters (1934), Schnell (1970), Sibley & Ahlquist (1990), Sibley & Monroe (1990), Sick (1993), Trivelpiece *et al.* (1990), Tuck & Heinzel (1978), Webb *et al.* (1990).

PLATE 49

inches 10
cm 25

1

pale morph

2

dark morph

ssp *lonnbergi*

ssp *antarctica*

ssp *hamiltoni*

3

4

6

intermediate morph

pale morph

pale morph

5

dark morph

dark morph

pale morph

ssp *longicaudus*

7

dark morph

ssp *pallescens*

Genus *CATHARACTA* Brünnich, 1764

1. **Chilean Skua**
Catharacta chilensis

French: Labbe du Chili **German**: Chileskua **Spanish**: Págalo Chileno

Taxonomy. *Stercorarius antarcticus* b. *chilensis* Bonaparte, 1857, Chile.
Sometimes considered conspecific with all three congeners, and all four probably form superspecies; genus frequently merged into *Stercorarius*. Occasional hybridization with *C. a. antarctica* reported. Monotypic.
Distribution. Coasts of S South America, from SC Chile (Concepción) and S Argentina (Deseado) to S Tierra del Fuego. Apparently winters mainly along coasts of Chile and Argentina, extending N to S Peru and possibly E to W Falkland Is.

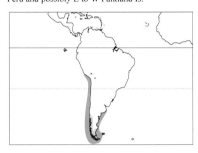

Descriptive notes. 53-58 cm; 1100-1700 g; wingspan 130-138 cm. Brown dorsal plumage with bright cinnamon underparts in many but not all individuals; lesser and median underwing-coverts usually bright cinnamon. All ages have a dark brown or blackish cap ending just below the eye; in adults, this contrasts strongly with a straw-coloured streaked collar and ear-coverts. Unlike other *Catharacta* species, which have black bills, in this species bill is pale blue with dark tip. Cinnamon underparts are most pronounced in juvenile birds, apparently becoming duller in immatures; in juveniles the straw streaking is not evident; unique among skuas in having gull-like strongly edged or barred feathers on the backs of juveniles.

Habitat. Marine, apparently predominantly coastal, and occurring especially in channels and straits. Breeds on islands and remote mainland coastal areas of Chile and Argentina.
Food and Feeding. Largely unknown. Dense gull-like colonial nesting suggests feeding may be more gull-like than skua-like. Species will visit bird colonies, presumably as a predator on eggs and young, and will scavenge on Patagonian rubbish dumps; may feed intertidally alongside Kelp Gull (*Larus dominicanus*).
Breeding. Starts Nov. Colonial, sometimes at high nesting density similar to large gulls and unlike all other skuas. Nest scrape usually lined with dead grass. Usually 2 eggs, but occasionally only 1; incubation 28-32 days; chick has uniformly coloured light pink-grey-brown down. Unlike other *Catharacta*, adults generally do not attack humans entering their territory.
Movements. Little known, but apparently disperses northwards along the coasts of Argentina and Chile to S Peru in Apr, returning to breeding areas in Oct.
Status and Conservation. Not globally threatened. Total population unknown but probably numbers several thousands of pairs. No information available on population trends or changes in extent of breeding range. Census data are required for this rather poorly known species. Threats unknown but it is likely that eggs and chicks are harvested for food.
Bibliography. Blake (1977), Clark (1986), Devillers (1977c, 1978b), Humphrey *et al.* (1970), Jehl (1973b), Johnson (1965b), Koepcke (1970), Meyer de Schauensee (1982), Moynihan (1962), Murphy (1936), de la Peña (1992), Pinto (1964), Sick (1985c, 1993), Wetmore (1926, 1965), Woods (1988).

2. **South Polar Skua**
Catharacta maccormicki

French: Labbe de MacCormick **German**: Antarktikskua **Spanish**: Págalo Polar
Other common names: MacCormick's/Antarctic Skua

Taxonomy. *Stercorarius maccormicki* Saunders, 1893, Victoria Land, Antarctica.
Sometimes considered conspecific with all three congeners, and all four probably form superspecies; genus frequently merged into *Stercorarius*. Occasional hybridization with *C. antarctica lonnbergi* reported. Monotypic.
Distribution. Antarctic Continent and Peninsula, especially in Ross Sea area. Winters as far N as Alaska and Greenland, though distribution in North Atlantic confused by presence of *C. skua*, and difficulties of field identification.

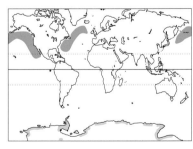

Descriptive notes. 50-55 cm; 900-1600 g; wingspan 130-140 cm. Two colour morphs: pale birds show strong contrast between pale golden brown to smoke grey body plumage and dark brown wings, back and tail; dark morph birds have dark brownish olive body, head and neck, and very similar sepia wings and back, so appear less "two-tone" and can be more easily confused with *C. skua* or *C. antarctica*. Buffy-yellow hackles on the neck are larger on pale morph birds. Birds become paler with age, and amongst adults plumage fades to a lighter tone through the breeding season. Pale morph birds predominate in Ross Sea area, while dark morph birds predominate

on Antarctic Peninsula; in all regions, males in breeding pairs are almost invariably darker in colour than their larger mates. Compared with other *Catharacta*, present species has slighter body, thinner bill, smaller head and narrower wings, and lacks the capped and rufous appearance of juvenile *C. skua*. As a long distance migrant, primary moult is more intense than in congeners, several primaries often being renewed at the same time in May-Aug.
Habitat. Marine, apparently being pelagic in winter and feeding predominantly at sea while breeding. Breeds on relatively snow-free areas in Antarctica; sometimes associated with penguin rookeries or inland petrel colonies, though perhaps due to shared need for snow-free nesting habitat more than to a

custom of exploiting other seabirds for food. Predominantly coastal, but forms small colonies inland in snow-free mountain areas.
Food and Feeding. Mostly feeds on fish, especially Antarctic silverfish (*Pleuragramma antarcticum*), caught at sea some distance from the breeding colony. Predation on eggs and chicks of penguins is of variable importance to particular pairs or at particular colonies, but is generally secondary to catching fish. Winter diet not known, but probably made up of fish actively caught, complemented by some scavenging.
Breeding. Starts Nov. Loosely colonial, highly territorial. Nest scrape usually unlined. Usually 2 eggs but only 1 laid by some inexperienced birds; incubation 28-31 days; chick has uniformly coloured pale grey-brown down; leaves nest 1-2 days after hatching; fledging 36-45 days. Older chick usually kills younger one, and breeding success characteristically low. Sexual maturity at 6+ years; adult survival 90-95 %.
Movements. Transequatorial migrant, departing from breeding grounds in Mar and returning Oct-Nov. Many Northern Hemisphere specimens are of immature birds, as far north as Greenland, Japan and British Columbia. Wintering areas thought to be throughout North Pacific and North Atlantic, perhaps with clockwise loop migrations. Commonest *Catharacta* in May-Aug on Grand Banks of Newfoundland. Records from E North Atlantic few, and confused by presence of *C. skua*.
Status and Conservation. Not globally threatened. Total population 5000-8000 pairs; 2000-6000 pairs in Ross Sea area, c. 800 pairs in Wilkes Land, 650 pairs on Antarctic Peninsula, 80 pairs in Adelie Land, 10 pairs in South Shetlands, 10 pairs in South Orkneys. Breeding success is almost invariably low, but is further reduced by harsh weather affecting chick survival or adult foraging. Hazards to adults at sea on passage or in winter unknown, but any species with low reproductive output and high adult survival is necessarily vulnerable to factors increasing adult mortality. Population trends unclear and more data needed.
Bibliography. Ainley, Morrell & Wood (1986), Ainley, O'Connor & Boekelheide (1984), Ainley, Ribic & Wood (1990), Ainley, Spear & Wood (1985), Ali & Ripley (1982), Beaman (1994), Bourne & Curtis (1994), Bourne & Lee (1994), Brazil (1991), Brook & Beck (1972), Brooke (1978), Caughley (1960), Croxall, Prince *et al.* (1984), Devillers (1977c), Eklund (1961), Goodman *et al.* (1989), Hemmings (1984), Howell & Webb (1995a), Ilicev & Zubakin (1988), Johnson (1965b), Jouventin & Guillotin (1979), Lansdown (1993), Maher (1984), Marchant & Higgins (1996), van Marle & Voous (1988), Morvan *et al.* (1967), Müller-Schwarze *et al.* (1975), Norman & Ward (1990), Norman *et al.* (1994), Olmos *et al.* (1995), Parmelee (1985), Pascoe (1984), Perkins (1992), Peter *et al.* (1990), Pietz (1985, 1986, 1987), Pietz & Parmelee (1994), Proctor (1975), Reid (1966), Salomonsen (1976), Shirihai (1996), Sick (1985c, 1993), Spear & Ainley (1993), Spellerberg (1970, 1971a, 1971b), Trillmich (1978), Trivelpiece & Volkman (1982), Urban *et al.* (1986), Veit (1978), Wahl (1977), Wang & Norman (1993), Woehler & Johnstone (1991), Wood (1971, 1972), Young (1963a, 1963b, 1972, 1990, 1994).

3. **Brown Skua**
Catharacta antarctica

French: Labbe antarctique **German**: Subantarktikskua **Spanish**: Págalo Subantártico
Other common names: Southern (Great)/Subantarctic/Falkland Skua; Lönnberg's Skua (*lonnbergi*)

Taxonomy. *Lestris antarcticus* Lesson, 1831, Falkland Islands.
Sometimes considered conspecific with all three congeners, and all four probably form superspecies; genus frequently merged into *Stercorarius*. Often considered conspecific with *C. skua*, but differs more from *C. skua* than from *C. maccormicki* and *C. chilensis* (see page 557). Occasional hybridization reported with *C. maccormicki* and with *C. chilensis*, but hybrids very rare. Race *hamiltoni* differs only slightly from nominate *antarctica*. Race *lonnbergi* has been considered a separate species. Proposed races *clarkei* and *intercedens* invalid, and nowadays included in *lonnbergi*. Name *lonnbergi* sometimes erroneously spelt *loennbergi*, but removal of Scandinavian umlaut does not justify addition of "e". Three subspecies currently recognized.
Subspecies and Distribution.
C. a. antarctica (Lesson, 1831) - Falkland Is and SE Argentina; winters off SE South America.
C. a. hamiltoni (Hagen, 1952) - Tristan da Cunha and Gough I; winters near breeding areas.
C. a. lonnbergi Mathews, 1912 - Antarctic Peninsula, subantarctic islands of Atlantic, Indian and Pacific Oceans; winters near or slightly dispersed from breeding areas.

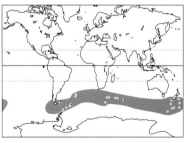

Descriptive notes. 52-64 cm; 1200-2100 g; wingspan 126-160 cm. Brown plumage, but highly variable from uniformly dark brown to light brown with pale flecking; relatively large bill, and bulky body. Lacks distinct capped appearance of *C. skua* and *C. chilensis*; has dark lesser and median underwing-coverts. In all races, juveniles darker and more uniform in colour with more chestnut in body plumage and with less distinct white wing flashes than in adults. Race *hamiltoni* has less white or golden flecking, and little rufous on body, so appears uniformly dark with few markings on head and little

contrast between head and collar; larger than nominate race in all linear measurements. Race *lonnbergi* much larger than either of the other subspecies, especially around New Zealand, showing less pale flecking than nominate race but more than *hamiltoni*.
Habitat. Marine, or on and around subantarctic islands populated by burrow-nesting seabirds or penguins. Nests mainly on islands free from human disturbance, though can be attracted to scientific bases that provide scavenging opportunities. May use territory just for breeding, or for breeding and all feeding needs, or may hold separate feeding territories. Breeding territories may be on grass, gravel or bare rock.
Food and Feeding. Highly predatory, feeding mainly on burrow-nesting prions, gadfly-petrels, storm-petrels, shearwaters and penguins, and scavenging on penguin eggs, chicks and adults, afterbirth and carcasses of seals. Will also scavenge around fishing boats and ships, and feed at sea, but some populations are essentially resident with seabird prey available all year round, and so rarely venture to sea. Burrow-nesting seabirds are mainly caught at night on the ground as they seek burrows, and remains are often put onto a "midden", a characteristic prey storage site within the territory.
Breeding. Starts Oct-Nov. Loosely colonial, highly territorial. May breed in trios or larger groups, with several males but only one female per territory; communal breeding associated with all year round residency, and may occur in more than 30% of territories at some New Zealand colonies. Nest scrape unlined or scantily lined with dead grass. Usually 2 eggs, but only 1 laid by some inexperienced

On following pages: 4. Great Skua (*Catharacta skua*); 5. Pomarine Skua (*Stercorarius pomarinus*); 6. Arctic Skua (*Stercorarius parasiticus*); 7. Long-tailed Skua (*Stercorarius longicaudus*).

birds; incubation 28-32 days; chick has uniformly coloured light pinkish brown down; leaves nest 1-2 days after hatching; fledging 40-50 days. Breeding success usually high. Sexual maturity at 6+ years; adult survival 90-96 %.

Movements Some birds at colonies in New Zealand, Tristan da Cunha and Gough I remain resident throughout year, with others dispersing to sea locally. In harsher environments all birds leave colony during winter and disperse at sea. Probably does not normally reach Northern Hemisphere, and several earlier northern records now reassigned to *C. maccormicki*. Usually breeds close to birthplace, facilitating racial divergences.

Status and Conservation. Not globally threatened. Total population c. 13,000-14,000 pairs: 3000-5000 pairs of nominate race, in Falklands and Argentina; 2500 pairs of *hamiltoni*, predominantly on Gough I with c. 200 pairs on Tristan da Cunha; and c. 7000 pairs of *lonnbergi*, with 1000-2000 pairs in Kerguelen Is, 1000 pairs on South Georgia, 550 pairs on Macquarie I, 460 pairs on Marion and Prince Edward Is, 400-1000 pairs in Crozet Is, 420 pairs in South Shetlands, 300 pairs in South Orkneys, 190 pairs on Elephant I, 100's of pairs at South Sandwich Is and Heard I, 150 pairs on Antarctic Peninsula, 105 pairs in Chatham Is, 100 pairs on Auckland I, c. 50 pairs each on Snares, Campbell and Antipodes Is, and a few pairs on Stewart I, Bouvetøya and Amsterdam I. Numbers have been greatly reduced by human persecution in Chathams and Tristan da Cunha, and possibly in parts of Falklands, but increases and range expansion on Antarctic Peninsula may be partly due to provision of increased feeding opportunities at Antarctic research bases, with skuas benefiting from refuse and disturbed seabird colonies. Many populations would be adversely affected by declines in numbers of prions, gadfly-petrels and storm-petrels breeding on islands, but populations of those long-lived birds are normally very stable.

Bibliography. Ali & Ripley (1982), Barré (1976), Barton (1982), Beaman (1994), Blake (1977), Bourne & Curtis (1994), Bruemmer (1993), Burton (1968a, 1968b), Court & Davis (1990), Croxall, McInnes & Prince (1984), Croxall, Prince *et al.* (1984), Devillers (1977c, 1978b), Fraser (1984), Hagen (1952), Hamilton (1934), Hemmings (1989, 1990), Johnson (1965b), Jones & Skira (1979), Jouventin (1994), Lamey (1992, 1995), Langrand (1990), Marchant & Higgins (1996), Millar, Anthony *et al.* (1994), Millar, Lambert *et al.* (1992), Milon *et al.* (1973), Moors (1980), Osborne, B.C. (1985), Parmelee (1985), Parmelee & Pietz (1987), Peter *et al.* (1990), Pietz (1985, 1986, 1987), Richardson (1984), Ryan & Moloney (1991), Sick (1985c, 1993), de Silva (1991), Sinclair (1980), Skira (1984), Stonehouse (1956), Swales (1965), Trivelpiece & Volkman (1982), Trivelpiece *et al.* (1980), Urban *et al.* (1986), Williams (1980a, 1980b, 1980c), Woehler (1991), Young (1977, 1978).

4. Great Skua

Catharacta skua

French: Grand Labbe   **German**: Skua   **Spanish**: Págalo Grande
Other common names: Bonxie, Northern Skua

Taxonomy. *Catharacta Skua* Brünnich, 1764, Faeroes.
Sometimes considered conspecific with all three congeners, and all four probably form superspecies; genus frequently merged into *Stercorarius*. Has often been grouped in single species with *C. antarctica*, but range, mitochondrial DNA, plumage and biometrics all indicate specific status for both forms. Monotypic.
Distribution. Iceland, Faeroes, N Scotland, and recently a few sites in Svalbard, Bear I, Norway, Jan Mayen and Veshnjak I, Kola Peninsula (NW Russia). Winters predominantly off Iberia, with young birds moving as far S as Cape Verde Is and Brazil; small numbers winter on Grand Banks of Newfoundland.

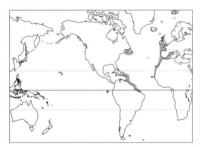

Descriptive notes. 53-58 cm; 1100-1700 g; wingspan 132-140 cm. Generally brown plumage but with much white, yellow, ginger and black flecking, individually very variable; birds tend to become paler with age, partly due to retention of back feathers for many years and these fading with wear and exposure, but also due to increased white feathers especially on head. Brown plumage reminiscent of dark juvenile *Larus* gulls, but distinguished by white wing panels towards bases of primaries; flight much more powerful than that of gulls, with more rapid and stiffer wingbeats; wings shorter and broader than gulls and tail relatively short. Compared to Southern Hemisphere *Catharacta*, present species has distinctly dark cap, conspicuous straw yellow hackles, and much rufous streaking, but little contrast between body and wing coloration or tone. Juvenile has much darker and more uniformly coloured plumage, but with general body colour varying from chestnut to brown; white wing flashes, or panels, less evident in juveniles.

Habitat. Marine. Avoids land during migration and winter, so can often be found in unexpectedly large numbers a few km offshore from coastal seawatching sites where it is only rarely seen. Aggregates in winter in areas where it can scavenge from fisheries, e.g. Bay of Biscay and W Mediterranean. Breeds on islands, usually avoiding areas frequented by humans, preferring flat ground with some vegetation cover, but less than 20 cm tall. Often breeds near other seabird colonies which provide opportunities for kleptoparasitism and scavenging or predation.

Food and Feeding. A highly opportunistic feeder, but also frequently showing individual specializations in diet and feeding, with some colony-specific learning. In Shetland, feeds chicks mainly on sandeels (*Ammodytes*) caught by surface-plunging, or on small whiting (*Merlangius merlangus*), haddock (*Melanogrammus aeglefinus*) and pout (*Trisopterus esmarkii*) discarded from trawlers. Will scavenge on goose-barnacles or dead seabirds, rob Northern Gannets (*Sula bassana*) and auks of fish, or kill birds, especially Black-legged Kittiwakes (*Rissa tridactyla*) and Atlantic Puffins (*Fratercula arctica*). In Iceland and NW Scotland, diet is more varied including some squid and more seabirds. Winter diet includes waste from fishing boats, scavenging, and fish caught or stolen.

Breeding. Starts May. Loosely colonial, highly territorial. Nest scrape usually lined with dead grass. Usually 2 eggs, but only 1 laid by some inexperienced birds; incubation 28-32 days; chick has uniformly coloured light pink-grey-brown down; leaves nest 1-2 days after hatching; fledging 40-50 days. Sexual maturity on average at 8 years (5-12); adult survival 90 % (Shetland).

Movements. Migrates, wintering mainly off Iberia; younger birds travel further, some reaching Cape Verde Is and Brazil. Leaves breeding areas in Aug-Sept and moves slowly S. Young birds often driven inland by autumn storms, but otherwise species avoids coasts and can be more numerous offshore than coastal records indicate. Northward migration in Mar-Apr; immatures may stay south or visit high latitudes in summer. Few cross to W Atlantic and these are probably birds from Iceland, as UK ring recoveries in W Atlantic are very rare. Most birds breed within 1 km of birthplace, but ringed birds from Shetland founded colonies in Norway, Svalbard and Russia.

Status and Conservation. Not globally threatened. Total breeding population is only 13,600 pairs: 7900 pairs in Scotland; 5400 pairs in Iceland; 250 pairs in Faeroes; 60 pairs on Svalbard; and less than 10 pairs each in Norway, Jan Mayen and Russia. Numbers have increased enormously since 1900

when Scottish and Faeroese populations were close to extinction (see page 566). Recent range expansion to Svalbard, Norway, Jan Mayen and Russia is continuing, and numbers are likely to increase there. Recent reductions in sandeel stocks at Shetland have led to declines in breeding success and decreases in numbers at the largest colonies, but increases continue further south in Scotland; however, discards from fisheries provide more than half the summer diet at Shetland, so that changes in fishing practices could drastically affect numbers. Some colonies have been limited in size by human persecution (often illegal). As a top predator, pollutant burdens can be high but there is little evidence of toxic effects. Some birds drowned in fishing nests or caught on hooks, especially in wintering areas. Harvesting for food has now almost ceased.

Bibliography. Andersson (1976c), Barrett & Mehlum (1989), Bayes, Dawson, Joensen & Potts (1964), Bayes, Dawson & Potts (1964), Beaman (1994), Boulinier (1988), Bourne & Curtis (1994), Cramp & Simmons (1983), Darling (1991), Devillers (1977c), Dittberner & Otto (1986), Dunn (1994), Evans (1984b), Ewins *et al.* (1988), Furness, R.W. (1977, 1978a, 1978b, 1979, 1981, 1983, 1984, 1987a), Furness, R.W. & Hislop (1981), Goodman *et al.* (1989), Hamer & Furness (1991a, 1991b, 1993), Hamer *et al.* (1991), Heubeck (1992), Hill & Hamer (1994), Howell & Webb (1995a), Hudson & Furness (1988), Ilicev & Zubakin (1988), Kahl (1989), Klomp & Furness (1990, 1992a, 1992b), Lansdown (1993), Lloyd *et al.* (1991), Lund-Hansen & Lange (1991), Meek *et al.* (1994), Paterson (1986), Perdeck (1960), Perkins (1992), Rennie (1988), Richards (1990), Shirihai (1996), Sick (1985c, 1993), Tasker, Jones *et al.* (1985), Tasker, Webb *et al.* (1987), Thompson *et al.* (1991), Tyrberg & Hernández (1995), Urban *et al.* (1986), Vader (1980), Webb *et al.* (1990).

Genus *STERCORARIUS* Brisson, 1760

5. Pomarine Skua

Stercorarius pomarinus

French: Labbe pomarin   **German**: Spatelraubmöwe   **Spanish**: Págalo Pomarino
Other common names: Pomarine/Pomatarhine Jaeger

Taxonomy. *Lestris pomarinus* Temminck, 1815, Arctic regions of Europe.
May actually be more closely related to *Catharacta skua*, than to either of congeners (see page 556). Monotypic.
Distribution. Tundra of N Russia, N Alaska and N Canada. Winters at sea close to coasts, mainly between Tropic of Cancer and equator, and around Australia.

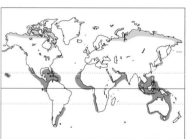

Descriptive notes. 46-51 cm (including central tail streamers of up to 11 cm); 550-850 g; wingspan 125-138 cm. Striking white wing panels more like *Catharacta* than smaller skuas. Adults occur in pale and dark morphs, as in *S. parasiticus*, but dark morph occurs at frequency of c. 5-20% in all populations. Moult leads to heavy barring appearance of underparts from late autumn, but vent area and flanks often barred even in summer plumage, similar to subadult *S. parasiticus*. Tail streamers often lost during summer. Compared to *S. parasiticus*, has heavy bill, large head, large, stout body and broad wings. Juvenile and immature rather variable in plumage but distinguished from smaller *S. parasiticus* by

heavier and more powerful flight, broader wings, heavier body, stouter bill, conspicuous white wing panels and more strikingly barred plumage with paler rump.

Habitat. Marine outside breeding season, remaining somewhat coastal, especially in upwelling regions of the tropics and subtropics. Breeds on Arctic tundra, only in areas where lemming (*Lemmus*) numbers are high; prefers low-lying moss tundra with pools, and hummocky areas in moist bogs.

Food and Feeding. While breeding, species is a specialist lemming predator, catching rodents mainly from the ground, and often digging open their burrows. Lemmings frequently constitute over 90% of diet in breeding season. Will also take birds' eggs, young waders and gamebirds, some carrion and fish. In winter, feeds on fish, sometimes by kleptoparasitism; also kills small seabirds, including phalaropes (*Phalaropus*), and scavenges on carrion.

Breeding. Starts Jun. Widely scattered over tundra, highly territorial. Nest scrape unlined and inconspicuous. Usually 2 eggs; incubation 25-27 days; chick has dark grey-brown down; leaves nest 2-4 days after hatching, but wanders less than other skua chicks; fledging 31-35 days. Sexual maturity at 3+ years; in good lemming years may breed in immature plumage.

Movements. Migrates to winter in low latitude seas, chiefly N of equator, apparently including extensive migration over land. Departs from breeding areas mainly in Sept, with peak migration through temperate North Atlantic in Oct, rather later than other congeners. Return migration in May, usually in small flocks. Immatures remain in temperate regions through summer.

Status and Conservation. Not globally threatened. Total population is unknown, but probably several 10,000's of pairs in Russia, Alaska and Canada. There is no evidence of changes in range or numbers but data are very poor. Breeding success depends on lemming abundance. Some eggs and chicks are lost to Arctic foxes (*Alopex lagopus*) and Snowy Owls (*Nyctea scandiaca*), but relatively few as this skua is large enough to drive off nest predators. Hazards to adults in winter are unknown.

Bibliography. Ali & Ripley (1982), Andersson (1973), van Balen (1991), Barton (1982), Blake (1977), Brazil (1991), Breife (1989), Britton & Britton (1974), Broome (1987), Camphuysen & van Ijzendoorn (1988), Coates (1985), Cramp & Simmons (1983), Custer & Pitelka (1987), Davenport (1982, 1987), Egnell & Elmberg (1990), Escalante (1972), Fox & Aspinall (1987), Goodman *et al.* (1989), Harrop *et al.* (1993), Howell & Webb (1995a), Ilicev & Zubakin (1988), Kemp (1984), Maher (1970a, 1974, 1984), Mann (1974), Marchant & Higgins (1996), van Marle & Voous (1988), Meininger & Sørensen (1986), Olsen (1989a), Richards (1990), Roberts, T. J. (1991), Schnell (1970), Shirihai (1996), Sick (1985c, 1993), Slud (1964), Smythies (1986), Southern (1944), Spear & Ainley (1993), Tasker *et al.* (1987), Taylor (1993b), Urban *et al.* (1986), Webb *et al.* (1990), Wetmore (1965), Wood (1989), Yosef (1995).

6. Arctic Skua

Stercorarius parasiticus

French: Labbe parasite   **German**: Schmarotzerraubmöwe   **Spanish**: Págalo Parásito
Other common names: Parasitic Jaeger

Taxonomy. *Larus parasiticus* Linnaeus, 1758, Sweden.
Monotypic.

Distribution. Circumpolar in coastal tundra, mainly within the band 57°-80° N. Winters in oceans of Southern Hemisphere, especially close to coasts of South America, S Africa, S Australia and New Zealand.

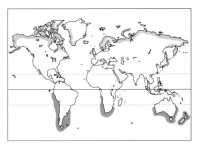

Descriptive notes. 41-46 cm; 330-610 g; wing-span 110-125 cm. Two colour morphs strikingly different: dark morph, common at S end of breeding range, uniformly sooty brown; heterozygotes, often called intermediates, are almost identical to dark morph, but with paler cheeks and often slightly paler belly; pale morph, commoner further N and almost 100% of population above 75° N, with straw yellow ear-coverts and side of neck, and may have a pale brown pectoral band. Pale morph is very variable and can be quite dusky: such birds are often called "intermediates", but are in fact still homozygous for the light morph allele. Adult plumage becomes barred through feather wear and when birds moult in autumn. Pale panels evident on underwing, but not very distinct on upperwing, at proximal parts of primaries, whereas in *S. longicaudus* both surfaces are uniform, and in *S. pomarinus* pale panels are obvious on both surfaces. Juveniles can be assigned to colour morph fairly accurately, dark birds having dark brown, brown and grey barred plumage, while pale morph juveniles have brown, golden brown and cream barring. Legs blue in juveniles, but darken to black by adult plumage, at three years old or more; central tail feather projection increases to adult age. Immature and juvenile differ from *S. pomarinus* in lighter build, smaller bill, less obvious barring, darker rump and less powerful flight.

Habitat. Marine, and predominantly coastal, in winter often aggregating at coastal sites such as estuaries frequented by large numbers of terns or small gulls. Not uncommonly migrates over land. Breeds on tundra or moorland or grassland, either in association with coastal seabird colonies where it can rob other species of food, or at low nesting densities on tundra where it can obtain food from the terrestrial ecosystem.

Food and Feeding. When nesting close to other seabird colonies, will obtain most or all of food by kleptoparasitism, especially stealing fish from Arctic Terns (*Sterna paradisaea*), Black-legged Kittiwakes (*Rissa tridactyla*), Atlantic Puffins (*Fratercula arctica*) and Black Guillemots (*Cepphus grylle*). In tundra habitats, microtine rodents are often not a major prey item, in contrast with *S. pomarinus* and *S. longicaudus*; adult and fledgling passerines, wader chicks, bird's eggs, insects and berries are all exploited. Present species appears to be less able to catch insects or to pounce onto lemmings (*Lemmus*) than *S. longicaudus*, and less able to dig out lemmings than *S. pomarinus*. In winter and on migration, present species often associates with aggregations of terns or small gulls, and feeds mainly by kleptoparasitism.

Breeding. Starts May or Jun, later in N than in S. Colonial at seabird sites or widely scattered over tundra; territorial. Nest scrape unlined and inconspicuous. Usually 2 eggs, but only 1 laid by some inexperienced birds; incubation 26-27 days; chick has dark brown down; leaves nest 1-2 days after hatching; fledging 26-30 days. Sexual maturity at 3+ years; adult survival 84 % (Shetland).

Movements. Mainly transequatorial migrant, with very small numbers wintering in Northern Hemisphere. Leaves breeding areas in Aug, and moves slowly S down coasts associating with small gulls and terns during passage. Some migration over land. Winters coastally, especially in Coral and Tasman Seas, and around Humboldt and Benguela Currents. Rapid northward migration in Apr-May. Some immatures remain in south.

Status and Conservation. Not globally threatened. The most numerous skua, with total population in 100,000's of pairs: 8000 pairs in Norway; 4000 pairs in Iceland; 1000-10,000 pairs in Greenland and Svalbard; 3350 pairs in Scotland; 1300 pairs in Faeroes; 10,000-100,000 pairs each in Alaska and Canada; and perhaps 100,000 pairs in Russia. These last three, the largest populations, are not censused, and estimates are very approximate. No evidence of significant changes in numbers or distribution, though clearly has increased in Scotland in the last 30 years. Human persecution is a very local problem in Scotland, Faeroes, Iceland and Scandinavia. Increasing numbers of *Catharacta skua* have displaced some colonies in Scotland. Arctic fox (*Alopex lagopus*) is major predator of eggs and chicks at higher latitudes, and Snowy Owls (*Nyctea scandiaca*) can also take many chicks.

Bibliography. Ali & Ripley (1982), Arnason (1978), Arnason & Grant (1978), van Balen (1991), Barton (1982), Berry & Davis (1970), Blake (1977), Brazil (1991), Caldow & Furness (1991), Coates (1985), Cramp & Simmons (1983), Davenport (1987), Davis (1976), Davis & O'Donald (1976), Elmberg (1992), Evans (1984a, 1984b), Ewins *et al.* (1988), Furness, B.L. (1980, 1983), Furness, R.W. (1977, 1978a), Goodman *et al.* (1989), Götmark & Andersson (1980), Götmark *et al.* (1981), Grant (1971), Herroelen (1983), Hildén (1971), Howell & Webb (1995a), van Ijzendoorn (1981), Ilicev & Zubakin (1988), Johnson (1965b), Langrand (1990), Lloyd *et al.* (1991), Maher (1974, 1984), Marchant & Higgins (1996), Martin & Berry (1978), Meininger & Sørensen (1986), O'Donald (1983), O'Donald & Davis (1975), O'Donald *et al.* (1974), Olsen (1989a), Perdeck (1963), Richards (1990), Roberts, T. J. (1991), Ryan & Avery (1990),

Shirihai (1996), Sick (1985c, 1993), Tasker *et al.* (1987), Taylor, I.R. (1979), Taylor, P. (1993b), Urban *et al.* (1986), Vooren & Chiaradia (1989), Webb *et al.* (1990), Wetmore (1965), Wood (1989), Wuorinen (1992), Yosef (1995).

7. **Long-tailed Skua**

Stercorarius longicaudus

French: Labbe à longue queue **German**: Falkenraubmöwe **Spanish**: Págalo Rabero
Other common names: Long-tailed Jaeger

Taxonomy. *Stercorarius longicaudus* Vieillot, 1819, northern Europe.
Individuals with plumage characteristics of *pallescens* occasionally occur in nominate race. Two subspecies recognized.
Subspecies and Distribution.
S. l. longicaudus Vieillot, 1819 - Arctic and subarctic uplands of Scandinavia and Russia E to delta of R Lena; winters in subantarctic and offshore S South America and S Africa.
S. l. pallescens Løppenthin, 1932 - Arctic Greenland, North America and Siberia E of delta of R Lena; winters in subantarctic and offshore S South America and S Africa.

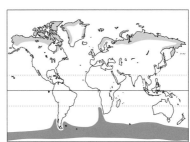

Descriptive notes. 48-53 cm (including central tail streamers of up to 22 cm); 230-350 g; wing-span 105-117 cm. Smallest, most buoyant and graceful skua; extremely long tail, uniform dark underwing with only bases of innermost two primaries white at base, and greyish tinge to upperparts also distinctive. Wholly sooty grey dark morph, known only from Greenland, is extremely rare. Moult and wear create barring pattern so underparts and tail-coverts, and form a dark pectoral band so that winter plumage of adults (3 years or more) is much more similar to that of *S. parasiticus* than is breeding plumage, though most confusion occurs in identification of juveniles and immatures; key features of subadult *S. longicaudus* are agile flight, small bill and head, narrow wings and long tail, pale barred rump, and grey rather than brown coloration. Race *pallescens* has whiter underparts than nominate.

Habitat. Marine and highly pelagic, seldom occurring within sight of land except when breeding. Nests on Arctic and subarctic or montane tundra, up to 1300 m in Scandinavia. Prefers dry ground, often occurring further inland than *S. parasiticus*.

Food and Feeding. Mainly lemmings (*Lemmus*) during summer, caught by pouncing on them on the tundra surface, after hovering 10-20 m above ground. When microtine rodents are scarce, will take shrews, many insects, berries and small birds, including adult and fledgling passerines and shorebird chicks. Winter diet is largely unknown, but probably includes marine insects and fish, some scavenging and kleptoparasitism. Usually solitary feeder, though will share tearing up prey with mate.

Breeding. Starts Jun. Widely scattered over tundra, highly territorial. Nest scrape unlined and inconspicuous. Usually 2 eggs, but only 1 laid by some inexperienced birds, or when food in short supply; incubation 24 days; chick has light grey-brown down; leaves nest 1-2 days after hatching; fledging 24-27 days. Sexual maturity at 4+ years.

Movements. Transequatorial migrant, but highly pelagic so routes and winter distribution poorly known. Rare vagrant inland. Moves S in Aug-Oct, returning to Northern Hemisphere in Apr-May. Rarely seen during coastal seawatches except with strong onshore winds.

Status and Conservation. Not globally threatened. Total population probably many 10,000's or several 100,000's of pairs. At least 13,000 pairs in Europe; 10,000 in Sweden, several thousand in Greenland and Norway, 1000 in Finland; at least several 10,000's of pairs each in Russia, Alaska and Canada. No evidence of any changes in numbers or distribution, but more information on populations required. Arctic fox (*Alopex lagopus*) is a major predator of eggs and young. Breeding success is closely linked with lemming abundance.

Bibliography. Andersson, M. (1971, 1976a, 1976b, 1981), van Balen (1991), Blake (1977), Blomqvist & Elander (1988), Brady (1994), Brazil (1991), Chang Jiachuan (1989), Cramp & Simmons (1983), Davenport (1982, 1991), Dunn & Hirschfeld (1991), van der Elst (1987), Evans (1984a, 1984b), Goodman *et al.* (1989), Hansen (1984), Howell & Webb (1995a), Huang Zhengyi & Tang Ziying (1984), van Ijzendoorn (1981), Ilicev & Zubakin (1988), Johnson (1965b), Kampp (1982), de Korte (1977, 1984, 1985, 1986), de Korte & Wattel (1988), Lambert (1980), Lewis, M. (1991), Maher (1970b, 1974, 1984), Marchant & Higgins (1996), McGeehan (1995), Meininger & Sørensen (1986), Melville (1985), Moore (1981), Olsen (1989a), Olsen & Christensen (1984), Price (1973), Richards (1990), Robel (1991), de Roo & van Damme (1970), Roseveare & Allen (1991), Ryan (1989), Shirihai (1996), Sick (1985c, 1993), Taylor (1993b), Urban *et al.* (1986), Veit (1985), Vooren & Chiaradia (1989), Wetmore (1965), Wood (1989), Yosef (1995).

Class AVES
Order CHARADRIIFORMES
Suborder LARI
Family LARIDAE (GULLS)

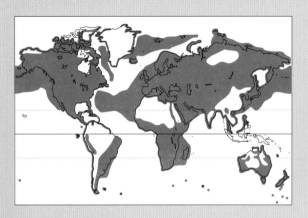

- Fairly small to large, heavy-bodied, long-winged seabirds, with stout bill, webbed feet and generally rounded tail; most species white below with pale grey to black back and wings, some with dark hood when breeding.
- 25-79 cm.

- Cosmopolitan.
- Mainly coastal, but also inland in wide variety of habitats, typically near water.
- 7 genera, 51 species, 78 taxa.
- 5 species threatened; none extinct since 1600.

Systematics

The gulls (Laridae) form a worldwide family of about 50 species, with greatest diversity in temperate latitudes of both the north and the south. Herein, the gulls and the terns (Sternidae) are considered to form distinct families, as are the skuas (Stercorariidae) and the skimmers (Rynchopidae). The division of all these taxa into four separate families was suggested by J. Dwight in 1925, but since then many authorities have preferred to combine gulls and terns as subfamilies (Larinae, Sterninae) of the Laridae, or even as tribes (Larini, Sternini) of a much expanded family that also includes the skuas and the skimmers, even though such treatments tend to obscure the obviously close relationships between species within each of the four taxa. Nevertheless, all authors agree that there are four distinct groups, and these differing treatments simply reflect individual perceptions of the degrees of differentiation that may warrant familial status, or a rigorous attempt to match the taxonomic hierarchy to evolved differences in DNA. Although gulls and terns are similar in many respects, they also exhibit significant morphological and ecological differences which probably warrant their treatment as separate families; the skuas and the skimmers are generally agreed to be more distinct.

In most parts of the world, the fossil record of gulls is meagre. Gulls are believed to have diverged from other charadriiform groups as early as the Paleocene, but the earliest gull-like fossils found so far date to the Oligocene. *Halcyornis toliapicus* of the Upper Paleocene, although long thought to have been a gull, is no longer considered so. The fossil species *Rupelornis definitus* of the Middle Oligocene, about 30 million years ago, was described on the basis of a tibiotarsus from the Repelian Sands of Belgium. While it may indeed be a gull, the first true gulls come from the Lower Miocene, with both *Larus elegans* and *Larus totanoides* very common in the Aquitanian Formation in France. The most interesting species from this period is the unique *Gaviota niobrara* from Nebraska, USA. The Pliocene gravel of Florida yielded a right humerus of a species that was named *Larus elmorei*.

Several paleospecies and modern species are known from the Pleistocene, less than 2 million years ago, including a rich representation from the Fossil Lake Formation of Oregon, USA. Both the Mew Gull (*Larus canus*) and the Herring Gull (*Larus argentatus*) are known from the Pleistocene, only in Europe, and appear in recent deposits and middens in the Western Hemisphere,

perhaps indicating a spread eastwards from Asia through Alaska. At least nine neospecies are known from the Pleistocene and 13 from the post-Pleistocene, especially from Alaska. The dearth of fossils from eastern North America, Australia and New Zealand may reflect the overall poor fossil fauna, rather than a relatively recent invasion by gulls.

Various researchers have used different criteria, such as behavioural, anatomical and biochemical characteristics, to examine relationships between gulls and the closely related families Sternidae, Rynchopidae and Stercorariidae. J. Dwight recognized several natural subgroups among the gulls, most species of which he assigned either to the large white-headed tribe or the small dark-hooded tribe. He classified the gulls in nine genera, whereas M. Moynihan, on behavioural grounds and emphasizing the commonality of display patterns, placed all gulls in the genus *Larus*. Others have recognized from five to 12 genera.

Apart from the unique Swallow-tailed Gull (*Creagrus furcatus*) of the Galapagos, the other species usually placed in separate genera are the high Arctic Ross's Gull (*Rhodostethia rosea*), Ivory Gull (*Pagophila eburnea*) and Sabine's Gull (*Xema sabini*), plus the two kittiwakes (*Rissa*). Less often separated are the south temperate Pacific Gull (*Larus pacificus*) and Dolphin Gull (*Leucophaeus scoresbii*), both of which have sometimes been placed in *Gabianus*; on a combination of behavioural and plumage characteristics, it seems appropriate to retain monotypic *Leucophaeus*, but not *Gabianus* which is distinguished essentially by its stout bill. Of all, the Swallow-tailed and Ivory Gulls show the greatest divergence in behaviour, plumage and soft part colours, and the most marked breeding adaptations.

Among the "hooded gulls", three primarily Central Asian species are of uncertain relationships. The Mediterranean Gull (*Larus melanocephalus*) has unique variations of display, the Relict Gull (*Larus relictus*) has display patterns similar to those of some primitive "white-headed gulls", and the Great Black-headed Gull (*Larus ichthyaetus*) differs from the rest in size and bill colour.

Among the "white-headed gulls", excluding Audouin's (*Larus audouinii*) and the Slender-billed (*Larus genei*), there is a remarkable uniformity in behaviour and in bill colour, the latter being yellow with a red gonydeal spot. The Herring Gull complex includes its close relatives the Lesser Black-backed (*Larus fuscus*), Slaty-backed (*Larus schistisagus*), Armenian (*Larus armenicus*) and Yellow-legged Gulls (*Larus cachinnans*), as well as nine others; the Mew or Common Gull and the Ring-billed

Gull (*Larus delawarensis*) are more distantly related. Probably no group of birds has done more to challenge the biological species concept than the Herring Gull and its relatives. For more than 70 years, systematists have applied different approaches to understanding relationships, mainly among the Herring, Lesser Black-backed and Yellow-legged Gulls, but inevitably extending to include Iceland (*Larus glaucoides*), Thayer's (*Larus thayeri*), Glaucous-winged Gulls (*Larus glaucescens*), and virtually all of the large white-headed species. One study shows that Herring and Yellow-legged Gulls do not interbreed in France, but do so comfortably in other parts of Europe, while another reveals that their genetic distance is equivalent to that between most gull species, and indeed that Yellow-legged is closer to Lesser Black-backed than to Herring. There is no entirely satisfactory and definitive relationship that can describe their mosaic evolution.

While species limits among many species pairs in the Herring Gull complex are controversial, two taxa have been particularly troublesome. The Asiatic form *heuglini* has variously been assigned to the Herring Gull or the Lesser Black-backed Gull; it is here treated as a race of the latter, but additional studies may reveal that it deserves elevation to species status. The high Arctic *thayeri* has likewise been assigned to either the Herring or the Iceland Gull, but has recently been treated as a full species. Several authors have recommended that it again be treated as a subspecies of the Iceland Gull, based on mixed pairs of *thayeri* x *L. g. kumlieni* observed at one site, and considerable plumage variation; very few intermediate or "hybrid" birds were found at the site, however, and one could equally argue that this shows post-mating isolation. Hybridization between Thayer's Gull and this race, known as Kumlien's Gull, is probably no greater than that between Herring and Glaucous Gulls (*Larus hyperboreus*) in Alaska or between Western (*Larus occidentalis*) and Glaucous-winged Gulls in the north-west USA. It, therefore, seems best to retain Thayer's Gull as a full species, pending further study in this contact zone.

Several radiations in the evolution of gulls can be identified. An early radiation may have arisen in Central Asia, where certain primitive species still occur. More recent radiations have involved the Herring Gull types which have diversified separately and relatively recently at temperate latitudes and in the Arctic, and an American radiation of hooded gulls producing Laughing (*Larus atricilla*) and Franklin's Gulls (*Larus pipixcan*). In the Southern Hemisphere, speciation has been slower. The Kelp Gull (*Larus dominicanus*), present on all southern continents, has differentiated so little that many authors consider it monotypic. The Australian Silver Gull (*Larus novaehollandiae*) is represented in New Zealand by the Red-billed Gull (*Larus scopulinus*) and in southern Africa by Hartlaub's Gull (*Larus hartlaubii*), and many authors still treat these three as a single species. Similarly, the Grey-headed Gull (*Larus cirrocephalus*) occurs in both South America and Africa, where it has differentiated only at the subspecies level.

In general, the genus *Larus* comprises two main groups: the large, white-headed gulls and the small, dark-hooded gulls, the latter including the so-called "masked" gulls. They differ not only in appearance, but also in behaviour. Nevertheless, the Sooty (*Larus hemprichii*) and White-eyed Gulls (*Larus leucophthalmus*) of the northern Indian Ocean and Middle East show behaviour like that of the white-headed gulls, despite their dark heads. Conversely, the Slender-billed, Hartlaub's, Silver, Red-billed and Black-billed Gulls (*Larus bulleri*) are, in terms of behaviour, "hooded" gulls without hoods.

Both M. Moynihan and N. Tinbergen provided classifications of the gulls based on behaviour, arguing that displays, being less directly adaptive to the external environment, are not so likely to show evolutionary convergence as are morphological features. Moynihan assigned all but the Ivory Gull to either the hooded or the white-headed groups, with the former group further divided into several subgroups. Primitive hooded gulls are mostly moderate-sized, with the bill either light or heavy and usually reddish, and they have a black or brown hood; these birds

The taxonomy of the large gulls has long been the focus of much debate, never more so than in recent decades. The Herring Gull (Larus argentatus) complex has been the cause of heated argument among taxonomists, some of whom still maintain that the Armenian Gull is no more than a subspecies of the Herring Gull. The more popular view nowadays is that it is in fact a distinct species, but research may yet modify this approach when more is known about other gulls in this complex of forms.

[Larus armenicus, Israel. Photo: Roger Tidman/ NHPA]

have elaborate hostile and courtship repertoires. Some have quite restricted and possibly relict ranges in the tropics.

Morphological Aspects

Gulls are rather uniform in shape, with heavy bodies, long wings, medium-length necks, moderately long tarsi, and fully webbed feet. They have 11 primaries, the outermost vestigial, and 12 rectrices. The tail is slightly rounded in all but Sabine's and the Swallow-tailed Gulls, in which it is forked, and Ross's Gull, which has a strongly wedge-shaped tail.

The bill is generally stout and slightly hooked, but there are variations. The larger-bodied gulls have a larger, thicker bill with a marked gonydeal angle, and they use this stout, hooked instrument to pry open shells. The smaller species have a thinner, more delicate and more pointed bill, with a less pronounced gonydeal angle, the smaller bill reflecting their smaller food items. Bill colour is an important variable among gulls. Most of the white-headed gulls, such as the Herring Gull, have a yellow bill, often with a bright red dot on the mandible that is used by young chicks as a stimulus to initiate feeding. Many of the hooded gulls have the bill bright red, dark red or black.

The wings are long, moderately broad, and slightly rounded. Again, there are differences among species, but in general the larger gulls have more rounded wings, while the smaller species have proportionately longer wings, producing a lighter flight with much more manoeuvrability. The legs are longer than those of terns, and the feet are webbed.

In most aspects gulls are generalists. Among seabirds they are the least specialized with regard to foraging method, food type, or nesting habitat, and are adapted to occupy a variety of habitats from the high Arctic and Antarctica to sea coasts and interior deserts. They are also more agile on land than most other seabirds. Their generalized body shape makes them equally adept at flying, walking and swimming. Most species walk with a slight side-to-side movement, which is often exaggerated for display purposes. Gulls can hover over objects, or duck under them. The smaller gulls are more manoeuvrable on the ground, and are able to avoid moving objects more readily than the larger gulls; at rubbish dumps, they are able to walk much closer to moving bulldozers while obtaining food, whereas the less agile larger species can sometimes be buried by moving refuse. All species can perch on objects, the size of the perch depending on the size and weight of the gull: smaller species, such as Franklin's and Little Gulls (*Larus minutus*), will perch on wires and thin vegetation, while the larger species perch more on posts, tree branches and boats. All gulls swim well, bathe frequently, and alight on the water without hesitation. They can land in small patches of open water, and require only a little space in which to take off.

Gulls range in weight from as little as 100 g in the case of the Little Gull to over 2000 g in the Great Black-backed Gull (*Larus marinus*). They exhibit no sexual dimorphism in plumage patterns, but females are slightly smaller than males, which in some species show a heavier, thicker neck and bill. Males are presumably larger because they defend the territories and engage in high levels of aggression. In general, within any of the major groups of gulls, the larger species live in the colder zones and the smaller ones in more temperate and tropical regions.

Gulls are generally white-bodied, with a darker mantle varying from pale silvery grey to black; the sole exception is the all-white Ivory Gull. During the breeding season they have either a dark hood, which can be rather obscure in some species, or an all-white head. In non-breeding plumage, the hood is lost or replaced by a variable dark ear-spot, while many white-headed species then have a streaked head. The wingtips of almost all species are black, offering resistance to wear, but they have a complex pattern of white "windows" and "mirrors" on the black

A distinctive feature of several gulls in breeding plumage is the dark hood, often with prominent white eye-crescents and a red bill. It is not unusual for some species to breed while still not fully adult. This second-summer Mediterranean Gull, identical to an adult apart from the black on its wings, is displaying to a first-summer bird, which has only a few dark markings on its head and some patches of greyish brown on its wing-coverts.

[*Larus melanocephalus*, near Tuz Gölü, Turkey. Photo: Alfred Limbrunner]

primaries which may differ among closely related species, and are of diagnostic importance.

Among the hooded gulls, some, for example the White-eyed, Sooty, Laughing, Franklin's, Lava (*Larus fuliginosus*), Great Black-headed and Mediterranean Gulls, have a complete dark hood which extends down the nape, with white crescents above and below the eyes. On others, such as Bonaparte's (*Larus philadelphia*), Common Black-headed (*Larus ridibundus*), Grey-headed, Andean (*Larus serranus*), Brown-headed (*Larus brunnicephalus*) and Brown-hooded (*Larus maculipennis*), the black, grey or brown covers the face and the top of the head, but not the back of the head or neck. Swallow-tailed and Sabine's Gulls have a complete hood, but without white "eyebrows". Heermann's Gull (*Larus heermanni*) and the Grey Gull (*Larus modestus*) have a white hood in nuptial plumage, contrasting with the dark neck and body. The Black-billed Gull has only the hint of a mask remaining.

Juvenile plumage is generally brown, with buff or black speckles produced by pale or dark tips to most contour feathers, and with the flight-feathers brownish black. After 2-4 months, the young birds moult into a first-winter plumage. This may resemble the juvenile or the adult plumage; in the latter case it is usually mottled with brown, and includes unmarked, brownish black primaries and a black tail band.

Gulls vary in their plumage cycles. The smaller hooded gulls reach adult plumage in two years, while the larger species have 3-4 distinct plumage classes and may not acquire full adult plumage until their fifth year.

Adults have one complete moult annually, starting immediately after the breeding season in most species and after migration in a few. Sabine's Gull, however, moults completely before breeding; at this time most species have only a partial moult, involving the head and some of the body. Franklin's Gull is the exception, with two complete moults each year. This may be

because it migrates farther than any other gull, from the northern prairie regions of North America to southern South America, although Sabine's Gull migrates nearly as far.

Albinism and leucism are reported frequently among gulls. These conditions, however, are not only difficult to detect in birds that are largely white, but also pose problems in identification: white Herring Gulls could easily be confused with Glaucous Gulls, while leucistic individuals of any of the small gulls might be confused with the Ivory Gull at a distance. The proportion of leucistic birds is certainly very small, much less than 0·001%, but, owing to the abundance of gulls in many places, such birds are reported occasionally. On the other hand, melanism is inexplicably rare, with only one published record, involving a Bonaparte's Gull.

Overall, adult gulls exhibit the general pattern of seabirds that feed on underwater prey from above the surface. The white ventral coloration presumably functions as camouflage against the pale sky. Moreover, white adult gulls gathering over food are more visible to distant conspecifics, and this is believed to function in social attraction to favourable feeding areas. Like terns, gulls also have a relatively high percentage of orange and red oil droplets in their eyes, which allows them to see long distances through the atmospheric haze that often occurs over estuaries and over the ocean. They can therefore see the white of active gulls from a long way off, and can join foraging groups following ships or feeding over schools of fish. In many species, the dark-plumaged juveniles and immatures are generally less adept at diving, and employ this feeding strategy less often than adult gulls.

Gulls have functioning salt glands which enable them to live in marine habitats. Those of young birds are activated by exposure to salt loading. In Franklin's Gulls nesting in interior prairie regions, however, the salt gland is small during their months on their freshwater breeding grounds, but enlarges and begins to

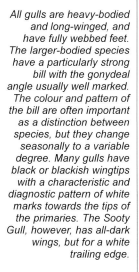

All gulls are heavy-bodied and long-winged, and have fully webbed feet. The larger-bodied species have a particularly strong bill with the gonydeal angle usually well marked. The colour and pattern of the bill are often important as a distinction between species, but they change seasonally to a variable degree. Many gulls have black or blackish wingtips with a characteristic and diagnostic pattern of white marks towards the tips of the primaries. The Sooty Gull, however, has all-dark wings, but for a white trailing edge.

[Larus hemprichii, Shinzi Island, Oman. Photo: Hanne & Jens Eriksen/Aquila]

function in early October, before they have reached salt water on their migration to the Pacific. Thus, the salt glands are turned on by external factors, perhaps decreasing light or hormone levels, rather than a change in salt loading.

Gulls living on salt-lakes, such as Mono Lake, where the salt concentration is 2½ times that of sea water, require special behavioural adaptations to handle the salt load. California Gulls (*Larus californicus*), for example, take in very little lake water with their invertebrate food; they visit freshwater sources along the shore, and feed on prey with dilute body fluids and high body-water content.

Habitat

Gulls occur throughout the world, and breed on all continents, including the margins of Antarctica, where the Kelp Gull nests, and the very high Arctic, the breeding grounds of the Ivory Gull. Most species typically occur around sea-level, but the Andean Gull is regularly found above 4000 m in the high Andes, where it ranges up to about 5300 m.

Habitat preferences vary widely, during both the breeding and non-breeding seasons. Gull colonies can be found in coastal or inland habitats, the birds showing a strong preference for islands. A few species, such as the Brown-hooded and Franklin's, nest mainly on inland lakes or marshes, whereas Lava and Swallow-tailed Gulls nest on remote oceanic islands. On migration, gulls usually travel directly to coastal and estuarine habitats, although they may do so in leisurely fashion, and regularly travel overland. During winter, they generally remain along coasts or at larger inland lakes, but some species can be found as far out as the edge of the continental shelf and others regularly feed on inland fields far from water.

Nesting gulls occupy a greater variety of habitats than most other colonial species. They utilize sandy or rocky islets or beaches, with or without vegetation, sandbars on rivers or lakes, wind-swept sand dunes and steep cliffs, coastal and inland marshes, trees, and even built-up areas. One species, the Grey Gull, breeds in the interior montane deserts of Chile, far from water. More than 40 species sometimes or always nest on the ground. Although most colonies are generally located in places secure from mammalian predators, some are in terrestrial habitats exposed to predation. Roof-nesting is now regularly reported for a number of species, including Herring, Yellow-legged, Great Black-backed and Mew Gulls and Black-legged Kittiwakes (*Rissa tridactyla*), and, less often, in Hartlaub's and Kelp Gulls.

Some gulls are specialists, nesting only in one habitat. These include Franklin's and Brown-hooded Gulls, which nest almost exclusively in marshes, the other regular marsh-nesters being Grey-headed, Common Black-headed, Mediterranean, Laughing and Little Gulls. Kittiwakes nest only on cliff ledges, although increasing numbers are now turning to ledges of buildings, while Bonaparte's Gulls normally nest in trees. Other species are generalists, using nearly all the possible habitat types. Herring Gulls nest on the ground on sand or gravel, or among rocks, but they also nest on cliffs, in trees, and even on buildings; during their expansion southwards into New Jersey, USA, in the early 1950's, they adapted to nesting on the higher areas of salt-marsh rather than on rocky or sandy islands. Mew Gulls nest in a variety of different marsh and dryland colonies, and Kelp Gulls in southern Africa nest on sandy cliffs, sand dunes, rocky or grassy islands, and rock ledges. In general, the large species are more habitat generalists than the small ones.

N. Tinbergen proposed that the ancestral gull was a ground-nesting species, and that all other nesting habits evolved from this generalized larid form. In terms of displays and vocalizations, however, the most primitive gulls are the small hooded gulls, and several of these are primarily marsh-nesting.

The distribution of gulls during the non-breeding season is controlled largely by food availability, and, since gulls eat a wide variety of foods, they can be found in nearly all aquatic habitats at virtually all ice-free latitudes. Even some high latitude species, including the Ivory and Ross's Gulls, move only far enough to find open water, although Sabine's Gull is a transequatorial migrant, like the prairie-nesting Franklin's Gull. Open fields in lowland areas are regularly used for feeding by, among others, the Common Black-headed Gull, which is one of several species, such as the Silver Gull, that commonly frequent urban areas. A large number of species, in particular the Herring Gull and its close relatives, also visit rubbish dumps.

General Habits

Gulls are highly gregarious birds that breed, roost, feed and migrate in groups, often of thousands. Generally, they are diurnal, performing most of their breeding and foraging activities during the day. The only species that are primarily nocturnal during the breeding season are the Swallow-tailed and Grey Gulls. Both members of a Swallow-tailed Gull pair spend the daytime at the nest-site, sleeping or preening, courting or sharing in incubation; they leave at night to feed at sea, returning to feed the chick before or shortly after dawn. They have large, specially adapted eyes to facilitate nocturnal feeding.

Although gulls are mostly diurnal, several species are known to fly and feed on moonlit nights or under artificial light. This behaviour has seldom been studied, but gulls seem to be more active at night during the breeding season, when the constraints of incubation impose additional feeding pressures, than during the non-breeding season. Except on bright moonlit nights, however, gull colonies are remarkably quiet after dark.

Many colony sites have been in use for many years, or even centuries. Once individual gulls have started to breed, they will return to the same colony, and even to the same nesting territory, for many seasons; many will do so throughout life, unless social or environmental conditions change, or they are unsuccessful because of predation, weather, flooding or human disturbance. The Common Black-headed Gull colony at Ravenglass, England, has been occupied since the 1600's, and some Black-legged Kittiwake colonies for more than a century. Records for these colonies are available only because their eggs have been har-

Their great adaptability has enabled the gulls to conquer virtually all of the world's varied habitats. They frequently nest beside water, but also far from it, and even in dry deserts. Some have adapted to built-up areas, while others breed in places remote from human civilization. The Glaucous Gull is one of a number of species with populations breeding mainly or solely in the high Arctic, far removed from the dangers of man, though it often seeks out human settlements, or colonies of geese or other gulls. With its varied diet, so typical of the Laridae, it has no problem in raising its young in these inhospitable parts of the Northern Hemisphere. Many gulls remain in this bitterly cold climate throughout the winter, but others move varying distances southwards. The extremes in habitat preferences within the gull family, between the species inhabiting the polar regions and those nesting in hot, dry steppe or montane desert, are quite extraordinary.

[Larus hyperboreus hyperboreus, Monaco Glacier, Liefdefjord, Spitsbergen, Svalbard. Photo: Tui De Roy/ Auscape]

During the day, gulls often sit around in large or small groups, preening, resting or just watching the scenery, waiting for the tide to turn before they resume feeding, or simply conserving their energy. Gulls living in high latitudes, such as Red-legged Kittiwakes, cope with the cold partly by reducing the levels of their activity, and hence minimizing their energy expenditure. During the non-breeding season, most gull species form flocks, the size of which depends on the species and the activity.

[Rissa brevirostris, St George, Pribilof Islands, Alaska. Photo: Richard Coomber/ Planet Earth]

vested by humans over this period, and it was important for local inhabitants to track the timing of egg-laying, population levels and productivity.

Since most gulls breed in temperate or Arctic regions, where conditions may shift quickly from hot and sunny to cold and rainy, parental care and chick behaviour must be adapted to these extremes. For some, however, such as Grey Gulls breeding in Chile or Western Gulls on the southern Californian coast, thermoregulation in extreme heat is the main problem. Some Western Gulls even nest in linear colonies along the water's edge, allowing all colony members access to water, which they visit periodically to cool themselves, and to wet their breast feathers so as to be able to cool their eggs. Further observations of some little studied Asian species may show similar patterns.

Grey Gulls experience the most extreme thermal conditions of any gull. They nest in deserts where there is no rain for many years, and hence no fresh water. This imposes severe constraints, for they must travel 30-100 km to reach the coast. The gulls maintain temporary courting territories on the coast in order to avoid extensive courtship activities at their inland territories. Grey Gulls are partly nocturnal, at least in the early stages of the breeding cycle, when they can perform functions such as courtship, copulation and territorial aggression at night. Once incubation begins, they shade their eggs during the hottest part of the day, and they exchange incubation duties only once every 24 hours, usually at night. Most chick feeding also occurs at night, when the off-duty adult arrives from the coast. The dark pigmentation of the feathers may be an adaptation to avoid excessive heat loading from solar radiation, by allowing the outer surface to absorb heat, and then to lose it by convection during the winds of the late afternoon.

Extreme cold stress is faced by Kelp Gulls breeding in Antarctica and by Ivory Gulls at the other end of the globe. They cope with the cold partly by remaining relatively inactive on their territories during most of the breeding cycle. Presumably, their time budget allows the gulls to reduce energy expenditure, while providing protection for the eggs and chicks.

During the non-breeding season, gulls tend to rest, forage and roost in groups, the size of which depends on the species and the activity. Franklin's Gull migrates and overwinters in flocks of up to a million birds, as recorded during migration through the central and southern USA, and in the boreal winter along the Peruvian coasts. In general, the smaller species form larger and denser passage and wintering flocks than the larger species.

Voice

Most gulls are noisy during most of their activities, including breeding, feeding and migration. Only when alone, in small groups, or flying determinedly, are they silent. A few species such as the Andean Gull are quite silent when breeding, presumably to avoid attracting predators. Being highly social birds, gulls have well developed systems of communication, involving both visual and vocal displays. There are notable differences in voice at both the interspecific and intraspecific levels, yet there are many homologous vocalizations among those species that have been studied. In general, gulls have a remarkable diversity of threat displays and vocalizations, with a relatively low number of calls and displays used in non-aggressive situations.

Most calls are variations of harsh croaking and screaming notes. The majority of species utter a variant of "kek-kek" when alarmed at the colony, and a harsh, loud scream when threatening an intruder at the colony or on the feeding grounds. Long calls and mewing notes are characteristic of many species.

Gulls have a number of generalized calls. Contact calls, often a variant of "kek-kek", are used between separated individuals. Food calls are given when a new food source is discovered. Alarm calls warn off conspecifics or perhaps threaten intruders. Long calls are used in a variety of aggressive, courtship and other family interactions. In addition, various other calls are uttered primarily during courtship or at the breeding colonies. Some species, such as the Black-billed Gull, will give a contact call when they leave the colony, the function in this case being to attract other gulls to follow them; this is believed to allow unsuccessful foragers to find food by accompanying successful individuals (see Food and Feeding).

During courtship and pair-bond maintenance, and while nesting, gulls give a number of calls that usually accompany ritualized visual displays. Long calls are used in a variety of situations, such as soliciting a mate, calling the mate or chicks, soliciting courtship feeding, and defending the territory. The most familiar of gull calls, in some species it is termed a "Laughing Call" and originally gave rise to the vernacular name Laughing Gull, and the scientific names *ridibundus* and *cachinnans*. It begins with a short "kah" note, followed by a series of high-pitched and then descending long "keaaaah" notes, and then by a series of shorter "Head-toss Calls", usually as the bird raises its head and points its bill skywards or even backwards over its shoulder. For some species, the long call does not end with head-toss notes.

The "Landing Call" resembles the long call, but has a shorter series of notes. It is given when a gull lands at its nest or at a temporary territory, such as a pier or rock used for courting. When an approaching bird gives a landing call, the mate sometimes responds with a long call, a head-toss call or a "Mew Call". This last call is one of several vocalizations used during the breeding season. The mew call, or "Crooning", is given in courtship, during chick feeding, or at nest-relief. "Choking" is a call given to mates during courtship or when showing a potential nest-site, and the copulation call is a series of short "ka-ka-ka-ka" notes that accompanies copulation and "Wing-flagging". Some species give a "Charge-call" during rapid "Swoop-and-soar" aerial displays, aimed at driving off intruders.

Although not all calls given to mates are individually recognizable, many are, including the long call, mew call and landing call. Individual distinctiveness, which can be demonstrated by sound spectrographs, allows mates and neighbours, and parents and chicks, to recognize each other. Gulls learn the calls of their neighbours at the breeding colony, reducing the need for overt territorial defence. Chicks also learn to recognize the calls of their parents, usually from the time they begin to wander from the nest.

Food and Feeding

More than any other group of seabirds, gulls exploit a wide variety of food types, and have evolved highly diversified foraging methods and habitats. This is demonstrated both in the family as a whole and within each species, and at all times of the year. There is no gull species that is specialized to feed on just one food source, using only one method, in only one habitat, although the little known Olrog's Gull (*Larus atlanticus*) does specialize on crabs in the intertidal zone. At any one locality, however, a single food type may dominate the diet in most years, or for a period of weeks: for example, euphausiid shrimps in the case of breeding Red-billed and wintering Bonaparte's Gulls, and mole crabs (*Eremita analoga*) for Grey Gulls.

Gulls are thus adaptable, opportunistic and omnivorous. They take living, moribund or dead fish and invertebrates from the water, intertidal zone or shoreline, and arthropods, rodents, eggs and chicks of birds, amphibians and reptiles on land. They also scavenge for offal, carrion and refuse, as well as feeding on sewage items and marine mammal prey, placentae and dung, and they can be aggressive predators and pirates. Great Black-backed Gulls will even kill and eat adult seabirds, such as Manx Shearwaters (*Puffinus puffinus*) and Atlantic Puffins (*Fratercula arctica*). Not only does their diet cover a wide variety of animal organisms, such as insects, squid, crustaceans, molluscs, earthworms, small mammals, fish and so on, but it also includes seeds and fruits. Indigestible material is regurgitated as pellets.

More seeds, fruits, insects, earthworms and small mammals are consumed during the breeding season than at other times of

Almost all gulls are essentially diurnal, but there are two major exceptions. The Grey Gull is one of these. Its breeding habitat is in the arid, rainless Chilean desert, devoid of any freshwater sources, and subjecting it to the most intense thermal conditions of any gull. It must therefore travel up to 100 km to reach the coast, where individuals maintain temporary courting territories. In this way it avoids energy-sapping courtship activities in the harsh climate of its inland nesting territories, although some courtship takes place at the breeding site at night, when temperatures are much cooler.

[Larus modestus, near La Serena, Chile. Photo: Günter Ziesler]

the year. Seeds and fruit are not preferred food items, but are usually eaten when superabundant or when other foods are scarce. Franklin's Gulls will eat sunflower seeds and other grain when they arrive at the snow-covered breeding grounds in early spring, before insects become active; Ring-billed Gulls will feed on dates and other fruits; and Herring Gulls will eat grain, grasses and berries. Being highly opportunistic, gulls will make extensive use of food that suddenly becomes available, such as the multitudes of pelagic red crabs (*Pleuroncodes planipes*) that are sometimes stranded on Pacific coast beaches during occurrences of El Niño (see Volume 1, page 341).

In the non-breeding season, gulls spend more time on large bodies of water, along coasts or on the open ocean, resulting in an increase in the presence of fish and marine invertebrates in their diet. Some species also increase their use of human refuse dramatically during this season, feeding almost exclusively on refuse from landfills or offal from fishing vessels. Landfills provide a dependable, though less nutritious, food source at all times of the year.

Gulls forage in a wide range of natural habitats, including the open ocean, the surf zone, intertidal mudflats, rocks and jetties, estuaries, bays, harbours, lakes, reservoirs and rivers, wet meadows and farm fields. They are an integral part of coastal and estuarine habitats, and many species are particularly characteristic of the intertidal zone.

For many people, however, the most familiar feeding habitats are man-influenced sites, such as landfills and rubbish dumps, sewage outfalls, city parks, picnic sites and fish-processing plants, and also behind boats and ploughs. In populated areas, many species become habituated to human beings and approach them for "hand-outs". In general, the habitat used for foraging by any species of gull depends on what is available, and most species use a variety of habitats opportunistically throughout the year.

Gulls feed by a variety of methods, on items obtained from the air, water and land, as well as by piracy. They capture insects in the air by flying in circles at sites where there are recent insect emergences, often over water or wet fields. The hooded gulls that nest in marshes or over inland lakes and rivers specialize in aerial hawking for insects. In the early spring, when the first large emergences of midges (Chironomidae) occur, big flocks of Franklin's and Brown-hooded Gulls fly gracefully above the water through dense swarms of insects, or glide along the surface, snatching them as they emerge; they thus gather enough food to courtship-feed mates or to provision young chicks. When winged ants emerge on sultry days in summer, Common Black-headed Gulls regularly soar high up among these insects, snatching them from the air. The intermediate-sized gulls, such as the Ring-billed, will also hawk for insects, but the larger species seldom do so.

From an aerial position, gulls also pluck food items from the surface of water or land, or plunge-dive. They will also swim on the water to pick up items, or dip into the water to snare them. Surface-seizing involves grasping individual prey while on the water. Some species even foot-paddle to stir up invertebrates just below the surface, or swim in tight circles, almost like phalaropes (*Phalaropus*), to pick up swimming arthropods or small fish. When dipping, gulls pick up prey from just above or just below the surface while in flight. The smaller gulls, more buoyant in flight and considerably more manoeuvrable than the larger species, frequently hover-dip over schools of small fish. In high winds, feeding over water becomes impossible.

The small and intermediate-sized gulls engage in foot-paddling when feeding in shallow water. This behaviour is particularly common among Franklin's, Bonaparte's and Laughing Gulls. Franklin's Gulls food-paddle in shallow water to "scare up" small aquatic insects; Bonaparte's in shallow bays, estuaries and the edges of the Great Lakes to draw up small fish; and Laughing Gulls in estuaries and bays when feeding on small insects, small fish, or the eggs of horseshoe crabs (*Limulus polyphemus*). Mew and Herring Gulls, and no doubt some other species, occasionally foot-paddle on inland fields, presumably to bring earthworms to the surface.

Gulls also walk on the ground, picking up live food items or scavenging along the shore. They sometimes obtain food by digging in the sand or mud, or among rubbish. Along the Peruvian shore, Grey Gulls probe the wet sand behind retreating waves for mole crabs. In total, over half of the foraging done by gulls

Despite their general adaptability, gulls are nevertheless also creatures of habit. Many return to traditional colony locations year after year, some colonies having been in existence for hundreds of years. Each spring, at the start of the breeding season, most of the world population of Heermann's Gull arrives at the same island in the northern Gulf of California; this pair is indulging in a somewhat frenzied bout of courtship feeding. Following breeding, this species loses the striking white plumage of its head, which then becomes more uniform in colour with the rest of its body plumage.

[*Larus heermanni*, Baja California, Mexico. Photo: Ramón Torres Valdivia]

At its breeding sites, the remarkable Swallow-tailed Gull is almost entirely nocturnal in behaviour. Both pair members remain at the nest-site during the day, sharing incubation duties. At night the non-incubating adult flies out to sea to forage for the abundant squid that are one of its preferred foods; since the bird does not return until around dawn, the single chick has a long wait before it receives a feed. The species' abnormally large eyes betray its nocturnal habits. Apart from its behaviour and breeding adaptations, this gull is also unique in several other aspects, including its plumage and bare-part features. Once fledged, the young do not return to their natal colony to breed.

[*Creagrus furcatus*, Galapagos. Photo: Hans Reinhard/ Bruce Coleman]

takes place on the ground. The smaller species, however, tend to be more aerial in their foraging methods than the larger gulls, both during and outside the breeding season.

One foraging method almost unique to gulls is the dropping of hard-shelled items onto hard surfaces to break them open. Even with their strong bills, gulls can not open certain prey such as clams and mussels. They solve this problem by rising vertically in the air to 10 m or more, and then dropping the shell on to a surface such as rocks, a road or car park, a jetty, driftwood, an abandoned boat, or a beach-house roof. Gulls which indulge in this habit include Kelp, Mew, Herring, Glaucous-winged and Western Gulls. Age-related differences exist, and young gulls must learn which food items to drop, where to drop them, and from what height.

Some species of gulls frequently engage in piracy from their own or other species, and this can be an important foraging method, particularly during the breeding season. At breeding colonies, piracy can be the end result of an aerial chase, or involve the stealing of food from other adults that are feeding chicks, or from chicks that are trying to swallow large food items. Large chicks will even try to pirate food from smaller neighbouring chicks, making it particularly important for parents to feed their chicks items that they can swallow quickly and easily. For some species, such as Audouin's Gull, kleptoparasitic attacks, in this case by adult Yellow-legged Gulls, are the most frequent kind of disturbance at colonies. Several species, including Laughing and Common Black-headed Gulls, sometimes engage in piracy at terneries. Both the Laughing Gull in the Caribbean and Heermann's Gull on the Pacific coast specialize in piracy on Brown Pelicans (*Pelecanus occidentalis*): they land on or near a pelican surfacing after a dive, and wait to

snatch escaping food items as the pelican empties water from its bill.

Piracy also occurs in the non-breeding season: over schools of fish, behind boats, at garbage dumps, and at other sites where there are dense flocks of gulls and abundant food. This foraging method is often more prevalent among adults than among young, perhaps because it requires skill in selecting victims and in pursuing them. Most studies also show that adults are victimized less often than young, and that success rates of piracy attempts directed at adults are lower than for those directed at immatures.

In mixed-species flocks, the larger gulls are the pirates more often, and the victims less often, than are the smaller species. For example, at a garbage dump in New Jersey, USA, Great Black-backed Gulls were seldom victims, while Ring-billed and Laughing Gulls were more often victims than the larger species. Up to 32% of the fish obtained by gulls when following fishing boats can be lost to pirates, but the larger species such as the Great Black-backed lose far less in this way.

Gulls follow boats to obtain food items, both offal that is thrown overboard during processing operations and fish brought to the surface by the churning action of the boat itself. Dense throngs of noisy gulls accompany fishing boats in to port while the fishermen clean their catch and throw the waste overboard. The white plumage of the swirling, diving gulls over the open ocean acts as a signal to other birds, resulting in multi-species foraging aggregations.

Although Herring Gulls often plunge-dive in the surf, where edible matter is exposed by the turbulence, gulls have only a limited ability to dive for fish and to pursue them underwater. To exploit fish below the surface, some species frequently associate with diving seabirds, with marine mammals, or with

predatory fish that drive other fish to the surface. Bonaparte's Gulls will feed with Hooded Mergansers (*Mergus cucullatus*), which "churn up" fish. Kelp Gulls exploit food items exposed by right whales (*Eubalaena glacialis*) off the Argentine coast in winter, and Black-legged Kittiwakes and Herring Gulls in the North Atlantic forage with humpback whales (*Megaptera novaeangliae*) or pilot whales (*Globicephala melaena*). Sea lions (*Zalophus*, *Eumetopias*) off California are often accompanied by flocks of gulls, including Bonaparte's, Heermann's, Glaucous-winged and Western Gulls and Black-legged Kittiwakes; interestingly, Western Gulls that forage in assemblages with sea lions have higher feeding success than those which feed only with other seabirds. Similar associations involving different species of gulls and mammals have been observed from Alaska to Peru.

At coastal or inland localities, some gulls take advantage of food stirred up by the movements of other species. One example is that of Slender-billed Gulls in the French Camargue and elsewhere: the gulls frequently accompany Greater Flamingos (*Phoenicopterus ruber*) and feed on brine-shrimps (*Artemia*) disturbed by the larger birds.

The exploitation of rubbish dumps has played a major role in the dramatic increases of many gull populations during the twentieth century. In less than one hour at a dump, gulls can usually obtain enough food to sustain their daily needs. Rubbish dumps can provide food for juveniles in the critical months immediately after fledging. The previously high mortality during this period has been drastically reduced by the availability of superabundant refuse; thus, many more gulls survive their first year of life, contributing to the population increases experienced by several species that have become pests. Conversely, with the increased practice in the 1980's of covering and even closing over landfills, a number of gull populations have stabilized, and some, such as the Herring Gull in eastern North America, are even declining.

Even at rubbish dumps, immatures are less able to compete for the best foraging sites. Immature Herring Gulls in Britain are often forced to the secondary dumping sites, rather than being able to feed on the primary dumping face. Direct competition with adults influences the extent to which juveniles can feed on the high-quality patches of food. The amount of food varies tem-

porally and spatially at dumps, and the numbers of gulls and the timing of their arrival at dumps vary in relation to the amount of available food. Gulls have learned that most dumps do not operate on Sundays, and they seek alternative food sources every seventh day; but they are confused by public holidays, and wait for hours in vain!

There is disagreement over the proportion of refuse used as a source of food for growing chicks. In some cases, parents appear to feed chicks a large amount of such food, while other species avoid feeding it to their chicks, even though they themselves may eat refuse during the breeding season. Silver Gulls use landfills all year, but less so during the breeding season. Western Gulls feed heavily on refuse in the early part of the season, but switch to small fish when the chicks hatch; the very act of hatching appears to trigger this change for each individual pair.

Diversity in food items, foraging habitats and foraging methods does not increase with the age of the individual gull, nor with the age of maturity for individual species. Young gulls feed on as many different food items, in as many different habitats, and using as many different methods, as do adults. The time given to each habitat and each method, and the success in gaining food, do change, however, as a function of age. Younger birds generally acquire less food per unit of time than do adults.

Age-related differences in foraging success have been found in nearly every species of gull examined, and for nearly every method. Young birds are less efficient and must spend more time searching for and manipulating prey. They make fewer capture attempts, have a lower capture rate, and are more likely to attempt to eat inappropriate prey, including inedible items. Young birds must therefore devote more time to foraging than adults. Differences among age-classes are less marked where food is more readily available, as at refuse tips and when feeding on offal. Proportionately more young feed at the sites where their foraging success rates most closely approach those of adults; immatures can thus partially compensate for their generally lower feeding success by selecting their foraging sites.

Foraging efficiency generally increases with age. This fact has been suggested as a possible cause of delayed maturation in some species of gulls. If sub-optimal foraging efficiency is a cause of delayed breeding, then species that wait the longest before

The foraging methods of gulls are highly diverse, reflecting their omnivorous diet and unmatched opportunism. Many are inveterate scavengers, exploiting almost any habitat, from coastal waters, intertidal shingle and mudflats to inland fields and rubbish dumps, and grabbing any food that happens to be available. Some species conform more to the popular idea of a gull, and forage almost exclusively along the coast or at sea. Audouin's Gull, for instance, forages mainly over the sea, where it often joins other seabirds to exploit shoals of fish swimming near the surface. Its normal hunting method, used frequently, is a specialized form of contact-dipping: it quarters back and forth just offshore, flying very slowly and very close above the water; on sighting a fish just below the surface, it gives a quick downward and sideways turn of its head and bill, snatches the prey from the water, and then continues its flight with hardly a pause. Like many other gulls, it also readily exploits fish offal thrown overboard by fishing boats, and this has recently been found to be a particularly important source of food for this very localized Mediterranean species. If its normal food sources diminish for any reason, it may resort to feeding at non-marine sites such as rice fields and even occasionally rubbish dumps.

[*Larus audouinii*, Ebro Delta, Spain. Photos: Jacob González-Solís]

nesting for the first time should exhibit the greatest difference between juveniles and adults in foraging success rate. This is indeed the case: the disparity between age-classes, as shown by success rates and inter-food intervals, is less for species such as the Laughing Gull, which reach sexual maturity at 2-3 years of age, than it is for those such as the Herring Gull, which are sexually mature at 4-5 years of age.

This difference between species could arise because the foraging methods of gulls that do not breed until 4-5 years are more difficult than those of gulls breeding at 2-3 years; or because young of the former have more difficulty learning the foraging methods; or because their food supply is either more ephemeral or more patchily distributed. It may equally be due to a combination of all of these factors. A final possibility is that the young of the smaller gulls maintain closer contact with their parents after the breeding season, permitting easier location of the feeding grounds and a higher potential for imitative learning. These aspects remain to be studied for most species.

The degree to which colonies serve as information centres for food finding by gulls has been widely debated. One suggestion is that unsuccessful foragers would follow successful individuals from the colony. This requires that they watch within the colony for gulls which, on returning, immediately begin to feed chicks, and that they then follow these successful individuals when they leave on another foraging trip. Although this information centre hypothesis is attractive, there are few quantitative data to support it. Common Black-headed Gulls that nest in dense colonies might be expected to have information transfer within the colony, but no evidence has been found.

Laughing Gulls may sometimes follow others from the colony, as probably happened in New Jersey, USA, when a group of 13 neighbours in one area of a 5000-pair colony fed on the eggs of estuarine turtles. Obtaining turtle eggs is a difficult task: the gull has to locate a female turtle that is excavating a nest, wait for her to begin laying, peck at her shell until she departs, and then pull out the exposed eggs. It is highly likely, therefore, that these neighbouring birds had left the colony together and were seeking food in a flock when the turtle was encountered. The Black-billed Gull and some other species will make a contact call when leaving the colony, the purpose in this context apparently being to encourage others to follow, thus allowing foraging groups to form. Presumably, for some species, there are reciprocal advantages to foraging in groups, in terms of food finding and making use of food resources.

Breeding

In all gull species, pair-bonds are overwhelmingly heterosexual and monogamous, with a relatively high degree of mate fidelity from year to year. The mating systems of gulls have received considerable attention because of the relatively recent recognition of female-female pairs or trios in Ring-billed, Herring, Western, Red-billed and California Gulls. Female-female pairs constitute at least 10% of the total in some Western Gull colonies, and 6% of Red-billed Gull pairs. They can be identified initially from the occurrence of supernormal clutches of five or six eggs, sometimes with two distinct colour patterns. Other species for which such clutches have been reported in the literature or located in museum collections, and which might indicate female-female pairing, include Laughing, Common Black-headed, Mew, Glaucous-winged, Glaucous and Great Black-backed Gulls. Clutches of four eggs have been reported for Black-billed and Silver Gulls and for Black-legged Kittiwakes, species that normally lay two-egg clutches.

Female-female pairs apparently result from a shortage of breeding males, which may be a consequence of differential survival rates. In an experimental study of Ring-billed and California Gulls, removal of males resulted in an increase in female-female pairings compared with control colonies. In addition, a DDT-induced feminization of male embryos, associated with inability to breed as adults, may explain the highly skewed sex ratios and reduced number of male gulls in some populations (see Status and Conservation). Mature females faced with a shortage of males may nest with subadult males. Alternatively, some gulls form polygynous trios.

One or both members of a female-female pair may mate and produce fertile eggs, but, although some young are raised, reproductive success rates are generally far lower than in male-female pairs. For example, research indicated that the hatching rate of Ring-billed Gulls nesting in Quebec averaged nearly 70% for heterosexual pairs, whereas it was only 38% in female-female pairs and 33% in trios; in Michigan, it averaged 61-77% for male-female pairs and 30-34% for female-female pairs. The lower hatching success is due to a higher infertility rate of eggs in female-female pairs. Nonetheless, female-female pairing is a strategy whereby surplus females can produce some young themselves.

Some promiscuity occurs among gulls, both sexes copulating with birds other than their mates. For example, male Western Gulls on Santa Barbara Island participate in considerable promiscuous activity with unmated females.

Pairing for life is characteristic of gulls that have been studied, so long as both members return to the colony. Divorce occurs, however, when pairs are unable to work out incubation and brooding activities, or when they are unsuccessful at raising offspring. Individuals that remain together lay earlier, and raise more young, than those that have found new mates. Moreover, the effect of divorce persists for more than one year. Long-term studies indicate that there is strong selection pressure for monogamy in gulls.

In their role as predators, gulls take large numbers of chicks and eggs of other birds. In North America, American White Pelicans (Pelecanus erythrorhynchos), despite their far greater size, are a frequent target of several gull species, which exploit them in a number of ways. Some pelicans, as here, lose their eggs and newly hatched young to California Gulls. There are populations of this large gull that specialize on bird eggs, while others take substantial quantities of grain; in parts of its breeding range the species appears to subsist largely on refuse.
The California Gull's diet also includes crabs, rodents and a variety of insects, as well as fruit and carrion; it is best known, however, for consuming vast numbers of crickets and grasshoppers.

[Larus californicus californicus, Bowdoin Lake National Wildlife Refuge, Montana, USA. Photo: Charles Palek/ Animals Animals]

Hybridization between gull species is not rare. Western Gulls interbreed with Glaucous-winged Gulls regularly where their ranges overlap in Washington and Oregon. Herring Gulls interbreed with Glaucous, and Thayer's with Iceland. Common Black-headed Gulls interbreed with Brown-headed Gulls in Asia and with Mediterranean Gulls in Europe, and within this group of hooded gulls interbreeding has also been reported for Black-billed x Red-billed and Hartlaub's x Grey-headed.

Gulls nest almost exclusively in colonies. One advantage of this is that it facilitates early warning and anti-predator behaviour. Most gull colonies are noisy, and at the first sign of a predator alarm calls are given; active defence, including communal mobbing and attacks, is generally pronounced. The Andean Gull, however, is an exception: when predators or humans approach, the gulls silently leave their nests and disappear from the vicinity, making it difficult to locate the colony in the vast, barren landscape of the Altiplano. This may be the Andean Gull's only defence in a habitat that has been heavily occupied by people for many centuries. Gulls in general have no nocturnal anti-predator defences, and will desert their nests for hours at a time; repeated nocturnal intrusions, as by owls or foxes, may cause them to desert the colony, even abandoning eggs or chicks.

Most gulls breed in colonies of a few to several hundred pairs, although some, such as Bonaparte's and Herring Gulls, will occasionally breed solitarily, while single pairs of Band-tailed Gulls (*Larus belcheri*) will nest beside other seabirds. Conversely, certain species, such as the Black-legged Kittiwake, form colonies of tens of thousands of pairs, and Franklin's Gulls breed in dense colonies of up to 150,000 pairs in freshwater marshes. The degree of coloniality increases with foraging range and unpredictability of food sources, in accordance with the information centre hypothesis (see Food and Feeding).

Differences in coloniality and nesting density also relate to body size: larger species have an easier time with defending their territory, eggs and young, making it possible to nest in small colonies or solitarily. Spacing of nests may be influenced by the risk of chicks being killed by aggressive conspecifics. Some of the smaller gulls, including Relict and Heermann's, can nest very densely as an anti-predator strategy, since adults seldom attack chicks of neighbouring pairs. Bonaparte's Gull is unique in that it never nests in large or dense colonies, but instead in very small groups of well dispersed pairs: 5-20 pairs may nest in a loose colony that extends over a square kilometre or two, each pair in the top of a spruce tree, in visual contact with colony members only when they are in the air mobbing a predator.

Although some species breed in monospecific colonies, many nest in mixed colonies with other gulls, or with other species such as terns, grebes, gannets, cormorants, herons, ducks, skuas, auks and even penguins. Sometimes the gulls are intermingled with other species, as in most Herring and Lesser Black-backed Gull colonies, or when Laughing Gulls nest with Common Terns (*Sterna hirundo*), but often they form discrete, monospecific clumps within the matrix of other nesting species, as Brown-hooded Gulls do within heron and ibis colonies in reedbeds in Argentina. They may also form discrete subcolonies adjacent to colonies of another species, as with the Black-billed Gull and Kelp Gulls on shingle islands in braided rivers of New Zealand. In some cases, the different species begin nesting at the same time. In others, the gulls act as a magnet, drawing the other species to their colonies. Ducks, grebes and some herons nest preferentially in gull colonies, apparently because they derive anti-predator advantages. Large species such as herons and egrets can defend their young from the gulls, and can enjoy increased reproductive success by nesting in gull colonies. Grebes often nest with those gull species that do not prey on their young, and they, too, have higher breeding success than they do when nesting without gulls.

Of special note is the relationship between gulls and ducks that nest within gull colonies. By nesting close to a gull nest,

Dead fish represent an important food source for many species, including the Pacific Gull. Such food, when it is not immediately obvious to the scavenger's eye, is often found by walking along beaches searching the intertidal area. Pacific Gulls are also among those species which habitually drop hard-shelled items such as gastropods onto hard surfaces in order to break them open and get at the contents. This species has the deepest, heaviest bill of any gull, and a distinctive tail and underwing pattern. Its numbers have decreased in eastern parts of its range, where it suffers from competition with the recently established Kelp Gull (Larus dominicanus).

[Larus pacificus, southern Australia. Photo: Darran Leal/ Auscape]

the duck derives the advantages of early warning of and protection against predators, but at the risk of the gull preying upon the ducklings once they hatch. In some cases the ducks have been found to benefit, but in others their reproductive success in gull colonies approaches zero. This has been labelled an "ecological trap".

All gulls are territorial, the size of territory depending on the size of the species, the number of pairs in the colony, and the structure and availability of nesting habitat. Herring Gulls may exclude neighbours from encroaching within a 5 m radius of the nest, while kittiwakes may defend only a narrow cliff ledge.

The small gulls generally nest in denser colonies than the larger gulls, with nests in some cases as close together as 50 cm. Intermediate-sized gulls, such as the Ring-billed, and larger species, such as Olrog's, may also nest in very dense colonies with small inter-nest distances. The large gulls, however, usually nest in more open colonies, with larger territories. This pattern results partly from the degree of aggression or cannibalism exhibited towards neighbouring chicks by each species. Cannibalism is common among the large gulls and, when territories are not sufficiently large, the wandering young are regularly killed or eaten by neighbours. Territory size, therefore, often increases during the fledging period. With Great Black-backed Gulls, over half of the territories may be increased in size after hatching; in densely occupied nesting sites of this species, where territories can not be enlarged, cannibalism is a significant cause of mortality, and reproductive success is lower than in less dense areas. In some gulls, such as the Slaty-backed, males feed more chicks of their own species to their brood than do females. Cannibalism is far rarer among the smaller gulls, and has not been reported for well studied species such as Franklin's, Laughing and Brown-hooded Gulls.

Most gulls have a twelve-month annual cycle, with a predictable nesting period that usually lasts from three months for the smaller species to five months for the larger ones. The exception is the Swallow-tailed Gull of the Galapagos, which breeds in all months of the year; even within a colony there is asynchrony among pairs, and timing varies from island to island. Individual Swallow-tailed Gulls have a breeding cycle of 9-10 months' duration. With no clear environmental cues to initiate breeding, individual gulls are absent from the colony for up to ten months between the end of one breeding cycle and the start of the next. Even so, there are peaks in this species' breeding activities in May-June and in February.

The age of first breeding varies, from two years for some smaller species to five years of age for some large ones. Even within a species, however, there is some variation. For example,

Marine fish and invertebrates form a considerable part of the diet of many gull species. Very few marine animals are considered unsuitable, whether they be small insects or larger items such as starfish.
For species which live all their lives in coastal areas, such as the Western Gull, the tide-line is an important feeding habitat; predation on other seabirds is also common, and these gulls often associate with marine mammals and eat seal placenta.

[Larus occidentalis, Point Pinos, Monterey, California, USA.
Photo: A. & E. Morris/ Birds As Art]

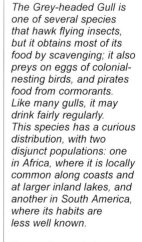

The Grey-headed Gull is one of several species that hawk flying insects, but it obtains most of its food by scavenging; it also preys on eggs of colonial-nesting birds, and pirates food from cormorants. Like many gulls, it may drink fairly regularly.
This species has a curious distribution, with two disjunct populations: one in Africa, where it is locally common along coasts and at larger inland lakes, and another in South America, where its habits are less well known.

[Larus cirrocephalus poiocephalus, southern Africa.
Photo: Heinrich van den Berg/Bruce Coleman]

in exceptional circumstances Herring Gulls may breed at three years of age, although most breed at four or five, and some delay breeding until they are six years old. Factors that influence age of breeding within a species include availability of mates, of nesting sites and of nesting materials, body condition, weather conditions, and food availability. In newly established colonies, there is often a preponderance of young birds breeding that have not yet attained full adult plumage. Once they reach breeding age, most gulls breed every year.

In a normal breeding season, the sequence of events is as follows: arrival in the colony vicinity a few weeks before occupation; colony occupation for a few weeks, before the start of nest building and egg-laying; territorial defence and courtship; a copulation period of a few days to two weeks; an egg-laying period of 1-3 weeks; an incubation period of 24-30 days, resulting in incubation activities in the colony over about 6-8 weeks; and a pre-fledging phase of 4-6 weeks. These time periods are slightly shorter for the small gulls, and slightly longer for the large gulls.

Environmental constraints such as low food supply or poor weather impose synchrony on the breeding cycle. For example, species that breed at high latitudes spend less time on the breeding grounds prior to egg-laying, and the laying period may be highly synchronized. Franklin's Gulls usually arrive on their prairie marshes when snow is still on the ground and the marshes frozen; they do not occupy the colony until conditions moderate, and this can result in highly synchronous nesting. Unusually bad conditions can result in no breeding in a given year: for example, in 1986, Black-legged Kittiwakes occupied their colony on Bylot Island, off the north coast of Baffin Island, north-east Canada, but did not breed because of the slow snow-melt, harsh weather, and poor food supply. Even for species nesting in temperate climates, low food supply or excessive storms can delay the onset of colony occupation or egg-laying, resulting in synchrony of egg-laying in that year.

Breeding synchrony is often imposed on a population by environmental factors and migration constraints, but it can also be caused by social factors. In 1938, F. Fraser Darling suggested, on the basis of his studies of Herring and Lesser Black-backed Gulls, that the social facilitation that results from the displays of colony members leads to increased synchrony within colo-

nies. Larger colonies, with more birds, and more frequent and intense displays, have greater synchrony. That is, a higher proportion of the birds initiate egg-laying in a shorter period of time, and the egg-laying period is generally shorter than in less synchronous aggregations. He proposed that this was one advantage of colonial nesting. Higher breeding synchrony leads

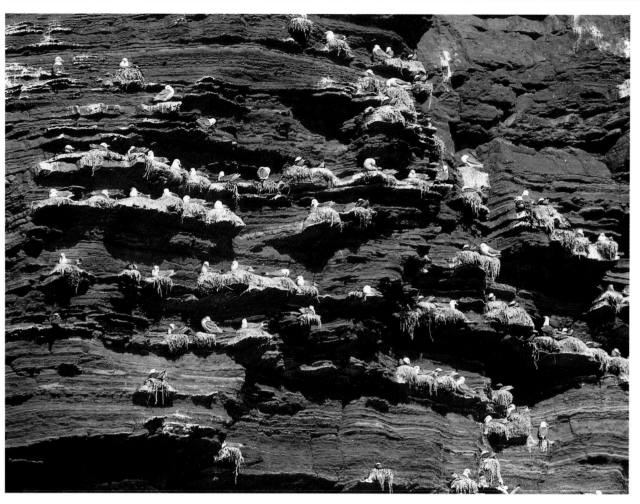

Gull colonies may be on the ground or in a more elevated position. Among the cliff-nesters, the largest colonies are formed by Black-legged Kittiwakes, and the noise emanating from them is a most characteristic and unforgettable sound as tens of thousands of birds utter their unmistakable call. Even in colonies, individual pairs defend a territory immediately around the nest.
For kittiwakes, nesting on narrow cliff ledges, the territory size is determined by the size of the ledge. Moreover, whereas chicks of most gull species learn to recognize their parents' calls at about one week, when they begin to wander from the nest, voice recognition is less important for kittiwakes; the precarious nest-site prevents chicks from wandering.

[Rissa tridactyla tridactyla, Helgoland, Germany. Photo: Günter Ziesler]

to predator "swamping": the predators take a smaller proportion of the eggs or chicks, because these are available for a shorter time.

The relationship between breeding synchrony, predation and breeding success has been studied in a large number of gull species. In general, larger colonies are more synchronous up to a point, and have higher breeding success. There seems, however, to be a threshold of 100-300 pairs; above that, any increase in the number of pairs is not associated with an increase in breeding synchrony or reproductive success. It may be that social facilitation increases only up to a certain group size, and thereafter a rise in the number of birds does not lead to more social stimulation.

Early in the breeding cycle, gulls begin to gather at "clubs" on their nesting colonies, where they solicit for mates or re-establish pair-bonds. They gradually spread out over the colony to delimit and defend nesting territories. Unmated males defend territories and court potential mates, while mated pairs defend the territory together and engage in pair-bond maintenance. During this phase, gulls use long calls, mew calls or crooning to attract mates, and mew calls and head-toss calls to continue pair-bonding. They use aggressive long calls and ground and aerial attacks to repel intruders of both sexes.

Gulls are very vocal at all phases of the breeding cycle, from territory acquisition to the fledging of chicks. They call when flying, before landing, on landing, and when on their territories. Whereas almost all gull colonies are noisy, some, including those of Franklin's and Laughing Gulls, are particularly so. There are two exceptions: Bonaparte's Gulls, which nest in very loose colonies, and Andean Gulls, which nest in small colonies at remote Andean ponds, are relatively silent as part of their nest defence.

The visual displays of gulls are usually accompanied by calls. They are quite stereotyped, and are recognizable from species to species. The most frequent display observed at breeding colonies is the "Long Call", which is given in a variety of contexts, both from the ground and while flying. The bird raises its head above the horizontal, and gradually lowers it while giving a series of long notes. The long call is frequently followed by a series of "Head-tosses", when the gull flings its head up over its back while giving a plaintive note.

Once pairs have formed, they may spend hours every day engaging in displays and calling, alternating with courtship feeding. Within a few days, the pair begins to select a nest-site, and each partner shows the other its choice with a "Choking" display that becomes more intense and more frequent as the time of nest building approaches. The gull presses its cheek towards the ground until it nearly touches it, and then utters a low sound as if it were choking or trying to regurgitate; all the while the bird moves rhythmically up and down, with breast feathers puffed out and neck withdrawn. Each member of the pair "Chokes" at its chosen spot, and then watches while its partner "Chokes" at its favoured nest-site; this continues until the two agree on the same site, and both "Choke" there in tandem. "Choking" displays can go on for several minutes.

Nest building is an integral part of pair formation and pair maintenance for some species, and is less important for others, depending upon physical constraints. All gulls construct a nest, and use vegetation to form a nest cup. Typical nests are large bulky structures of grass and herbaceous vegetation plucked from the area around the nest. Marsh-nesting species begin building soon after selecting territories, because they must construct a nest platform for displaying to potential mates and for re-establishment of pair-bonds. For these species, such as Franklin's and Brown-hooded Gulls, both sexes gather material, but the male may make more trips while the female does more of the arranging of material. For species that nest in tidal marshes, such as the Laughing Gull and some Common Black-headed Gulls, nest construction is essential to provide a dry place for breeding activities. For cliff-nesting species such as the kittiwakes, for which nest material is very limited, provisioning of material plays an important role in maintaining the pair-bond.

Males of most gull species courtship-feed their mates in the period prior to egg-laying, although to a lesser degree than in the terns. Nonetheless, courtship feeding can provide the female with a substantial percentage of her energy requirements. Courtship feeding is usually associated with copulation.

Over a period of 7-10 days before egg-laying, pairs engage in copulation, which increases in frequency and duration as the time of laying approaches. Copulation is always accompanied by a staccato, repetitive copulation call and by "Wing-flagging", which is visible far across the colony and leads to contagious copulation by neighbouring pairs. This social facilitation is believed to lead to greater breeding synchrony both within subcolonies and within the colony as a whole. Bouts of copulation are longer and more frequent in the early morning than later in the day.

Since, in many species of gulls, both members of the pair are on their territory for much of the day, territorial defence is strong, and territories tend to be relatively large during courtship and the pre-incubation period. Intruders have a difficult time inserting themselves into occupied parts of the colony. Species that nest on the ground or on water can determine territory boundaries based on social interactions. On water, however, emergent vegetation is required for anchoring the nest, and this limits the placement of nests as well as the size of territories. For species that nest on cliff ledges or in trees, territory size is often determined by the size of the ledge, the closeness of trees, or the space on the tree that can support a gull nest.

Most gulls have a clutch size of three eggs, although some, such as Hartlaub's, Black-billed and Silver Gulls and the kittiwakes, usually lay only two, and Swallow-tailed Gulls lay only one. Eggs are normally laid at two-day intervals. Generally, the first and second eggs are similar in size and shape, while third eggs are usually smaller, in particular narrower, and sometimes distinctly paler. Most gulls' eggs are pale tan to dark brown, or an olive greenish, with dark brown to black splotches and scrawls. They are thus camouflaged, and difficult to see on most surfaces, which effectively reduces predation, especially in species where nests are not close together. Some predators, however, including human beings, can form a "search image" and readily find the cryptic eggs.

Virtually all species raise only a single brood, although most will lay at least one replacement clutch, and sometimes more, if they lose their eggs or chicks. In general, replacement clutches average about one egg fewer than the initial clutch.

Both sexes incubate. For most species the incubation period averages 22-26 days, or more if the birds are frequently disturbed. The territory is defended by both members of the pair during this period, but its size may shrink slightly because the first priority is protecting the eggs. Some species, particularly those that nest densely, use a staccato "gakkering" call to defend the nest against neighbours and intruders, including those of other species: a bird remains sitting, stretches its neck forward, and opens its bill, sometimes "gakkering" for several minutes. Incubation sometimes begins with the first egg, but becomes continuous only after the second egg is laid. In most species, incubation bouts usually range from one to four hours during daylight, with one member of the pair sitting throughout the night, when the other normally also stays on the territory.

A clutch of three eggs normally takes 4-6 days to complete, while the hatching interval is usually under two days. The first two chicks hatch within a few hours of one another, but the third may hatch a day or two later, giving it a distinct disadvantage. The cryptic downy chicks are usually pale tan or greyish, variously spotted or streaked with small, discrete or irregular blackish marks. They are brooded until 1-2 weeks old, and are usually guarded by one or both parents until they fledge.

Both parents feed the chicks. During the first week the male provides more food, while the female remains on the territory and broods and guards the chicks. After the first week or two, the parents take turns in foraging and chick-guarding. Unless disturbed by storms, flooding or human beings, chicks remain near the nest-site throughout the fledging period. At this time, territories may be enlarged slightly, encompassing space abandoned by unsuccessful pairs or currently unoccupied. The larger territories provide room for the young to walk about without clashing with neighbours. Territorial conflicts can result in injury or death, quite apart from cannibalistic attacks. In some species, for example Black-billed and Western Gulls, the older chicks form a loose crèche when the parents are away feeding.

Gull colonies are usually noisy places, but those of the Andean Gull are an exception. This species breeds in small colonies at remote lakes in the Altiplano of the Andes, at altitudes from 4000 m to above 5000 m, where it nests on small islets or builds a floating nest anchored to emergent vegetation. At the approach of an intruder, the nesting gulls, rather than giving alarm calls and actively defending the colony by communal mobbing, all leave the area in complete silence; this presumably makes it difficult for the colony to be located by a predator in the vast and rather uniform, barren landscape, and would appear to have evolved as an efficient anti-predator strategy in an area which has long been occupied by man.

[Larus serranus, Lauca National Park, north Chile. Photo: Günter Ziesler]

The inland montane deserts of north Chile where the Grey Gull breeds are so barren and arid that the birds have to visit the coast every day to feed, a round trip of up to 200 km. The non-incubating mates leave after dark and return just before dawn. They feed along sandy beaches, mainly on mole crabs (Eremita analoga), *which they obtain during a brief period before and after low tide, by probing the wet sand behind retreating waves. They make one feeding trip daily, bringing back mostly fish to feed to the chicks. As soon as the young fledge, at around 40 days, they, too, fly to the coast. Like several other seabirds, the Grey Gull may not breed in years when its food sources and foraging efficiency are adversely affected by El Niño.*

[*Larus modestus*, near La Serena, Chile. Photo: Günter Ziesler]

Chicks learn to recognize their parents' calls at about the time they begin to wander from the nest. In ground-nesting gulls this is by 6-8 days of age, although in marsh-nesting Franklin's Gulls it is not apparent at 15 days of age, and in the cliff-nesting kittiwakes not even by 28 days of age. In the last two cases, however, early recognition is not necessary, since chicks do not wander from the nest: kittiwakes because they nest on cliff ledges, and Franklin's because the nest is surrounded by water.

When disturbed by floods or human activities, gulls may move their chicks to higher ground or to other places where there is more vegetation and less disturbance. For example, if floods threaten Black-billed Gulls nesting on ephemeral islands in the middle of potentially raging rivers, the adults move their chicks to higher ground or to other islands soon after they hatch; and Herring and Laughing Gulls nesting in salt-marshes move their chicks to higher ground during excessively high storm tides. By contrast, Western Gulls exposed to excessive heat will move their chicks closer to water.

The fledging period for gulls ranges from four to seven weeks, depending on body size. For most species, at least one parent remains at the nest to protect the chicks from predators or conspecifics until they are able to fly. Young gulls usually spend a week or two learning to fly before leaving their nest-site, although they may exercise their wings much earlier. Once capable of flying, some species leave the colony and disperse or begin migration. Others, such as Herring Gulls, may continue to occupy the colony site as a family for up to 45 days, while the young learn to forage; during this time, the young may return to the territory only once a day, and the parents continue to feed them, either at the nest-site or in the vicinity of the colony. In Western Gulls, too, post-fledging care may extend beyond a month after the young can fly. The full extent of post-fledging parental care has not been established for most gulls, but for some it clearly continues for several weeks after fledging.

Parental effort has been examined for a number of species, and in general, averaged over the entire season, the two sexes contribute an approximately equal effort. Males often provide more of the initial territory defence than females, perform all of the courtship feeding, and may provide the bulk of territorial defence during incubation, as occurs in Western and Ring-billed Gulls. Females sometimes undertake more of the incubation and chick defence than males. In territorial clashes, if both sexes are present on the territory, males tend to defend against males and females against females. When the time and energy devoted to territory defence, incubation, chick feeding and chick protection are examined over the entire breeding cycle, however, the sexes generally have equal investment.

Herring Gull pairs with equal parental investment during incubation raise more young that those with unequal investment. Contrary to some sociobiological theories, equal investment and increased productivity may result when each pair member is trying to maximize rather than minimize investment, resulting in the chicks receiving maximum care. Species such as gulls, for which food is often abundant, have sufficient time to devote to breeding activities, and conflict between pair members over parental duties may be minimal compared with that of some other seabirds which travel many hundreds of kilometres to find food.

Gulls have provided important models for studying the role of conflict between parents, between parents and young, and between siblings. Their abundance, accessibility and density make it possible to follow investment, behaviour and conflicts, and the breeding cycle is short enough that both parent and young gulls can easily be marked and followed.

Conflict between parents over breeding activities clearly occurs: sometimes both parents attempt to incubate at once, or to feed the chicks at the same time, or both attack an intruder. This is contrary to traditional sociobiological theories, which state that each parent should minimize its own effort so that the other parent contributes more than 50% to current reproduction, thereby saving energy and reducing its own vulnerability, so as to protect its future breeding efforts. As mentioned above, however, when breeding activities and investments are considered for the entire breeding cycle, the sexes generally have equal investment. Moreover, Herring Gull pairs that have a relatively equal distri-

For a week to 10 days before egg-laying, gulls engage in copulation, the frequency and duration of which increase as the time of laying approaches. Bouts of copulation are also more frequent and of longer duration in the early morning than later in the day. The act of copulation itself is frequently preceded by the male courtship-feeding his mate; it is always accompanied by a repetitive copulation call, a series of short, staccato "ka-ka-ka-ka" notes, and by "Wing-flagging". The latter action, which can be seen by other gulls across the colony, appears to stimulate neighbouring pairs to copulate. This social facilitation may lead to increased synchrony in the breeding timetable within subcolonies, and also within the colony as a whole, but this is not always borne out in studies. In southern South America, for example, the Dolphin Gull nests in small, dense colonies, generally of up to 25 pairs, but the breeding timetable within colonies has been found to be highly asynchronous.

[*Leucophaeus scoresbii*, Patagonia. Photo: Jen & Des Bartlett/ Bruce Coleman]

The Black-billed Gull of
New Zealand breeds
almost solely inland,
on rocky islands in
fast-flowing rivers and
along lake shores,
sometimes near colonies
of Kelp Gulls (Larus
dominicanus). Such
habitats may on occasion
be threatened by sudden
raging floodwaters, which
the gulls counter by
moving their chicks to
higher ground. The normal
gull clutch size is three
eggs, although the
Swallow-tailed Gull
(Creagrus furcatus) lays
only one egg and a few
species, including the
Black-billed, usually two.
The eggs are a light tan to
dark brown or olive green,
with darker splotches and
scrawls, a camouflage
which helps to reduce
predation, especially
where nests are
widely spaced.

[Larus bulleri,
bed of Eglinton River,
Fiordland National Park,
New Zealand.
Photo: Frances Furlong/
Survival Anglia/
Oxford Scientific Films]

bution of incubation and brooding effort between the sexes raise more young than pairs with an unequal distribution of such duties. Minimizing short-term parental investment is clearly disadvantageous.

In theory, parent-young conflict usually relates to chicks seeking more and longer parental care, while parents attempt to protect their own survival and future investment by limiting the number of feeding trips and shortening the duration of care. Evidence for this conflict comes from observations of the squabbles that occur at the nest-site when chicks beg for food from parents that do not feed them. In California Gulls, the amount of time parents withheld food from offspring increased through the nestling period, but older, presumably more experienced, parents were less likely than younger ones to withhold food and they offered longer periods of parental care. In some species, such as Herring Gulls, this conflict may be as to when, rather than whether, to provide care. Moreover, Herring Gull parents remain on the territory long after the young fledge, and feed them as soon as they return. Thus, gull studies partly refute the traditional understanding of parent-young conflict.

There may be conflict among siblings. Although siblicide is rare, older chicks beg more vigorously and may outcompete late-hatched siblings for food, thereby hastening the latter's demise. At least in Herring Gulls, parents may compensate, with each one providing food almost simultaneously in different parts of the territory, allowing all chicks to obtain food.

Conflicts between different generations have also been described, and not only within a family. Gulls may either adopt strange chicks that wander into their territory or they may attack and kill them. Adoptions have been reported for several species, including Western, Herring, Ring-billed, Mew, Lesser Black-backed, Laughing, Franklin's and Sabine's Gulls, although it may occur in most ground-nesting gulls with chicks that can move between nests. Adoptions have even been reported in a Black-legged Kittiwake colony where movement between nests was possible, although only 8% of the chicks that moved were adopted. When examining this phenomenon, it is important to

be certain that events occur naturally, rather than as a result of human interference. For example, adoptions detected among Franklin's Gulls were due mainly to human disturbance causing chicks to swim from their nests; in normal circumstances, young Franklin's Gulls never leave their floating nest platforms, and adoptions would not occur.

Since recognition both of chicks by parents and of parents by chicks becomes well developed in ground-nesting gulls after several days, it is not clear why adoptions occur, as parents will then be investing time and energy in offspring that are not their own. Hypotheses proposed to explain why adoptions occur regularly at some colonies include reciprocal or weak altruism, mistakes by parents in high-density sites, and that adoption is a chick strategy to increase its own survival. Chicks that are not receiving adequate parental care may abandon their nests and seek care from other, unrelated adults. Their behaviour is aimed at promoting adoption by thwarting aggression from both adults and future "siblings". Chicks seek adoption in broods with slightly younger and smaller chicks.

In several species, 20-30% of the chicks that abandoned their natal territories were successfully adopted by foster parents, while a similar proportion were killed by conspecific adults. The adopted chicks, however, were often fed at lower rates than the adult's own offspring. Considerable research is needed to establish the role of adoptions in the reproductive strategies of different species of gulls.

Reproductive success usually increases over the first few years of breeding, and remains relatively high, decreasing only in very old birds. This basic pattern has been observed for all species for which there are adequate data, including Black-legged Kittiwakes and Herring, Glaucous-winged, Red-billed and California Gulls. Age-related increases in fledging success are correlated with increased adult mortality, at least for California Gulls.

Measures of reproductive success for gulls have traditionally included egg size, clutch size, hatching rates, fledging rates (young per pair), chick weight and, more recently, recruitment rates to the breeding population. Gulls normally lay two or three

Typical gull nests are bulky structures of grass and herbaceous vegetation gathered from the immediate surroundings. In marsh-nesting species, which have to construct a nest platform for display purposes, building starts soon after territory selection, both sexes gathering material, but the female doing more of the arranging. For those species nesting in tidal marshes, which include some Common Black-headed Gulls (Larus ridibundus) and Laughing Gulls (Larus atricilla), a solid nest construction is needed to provide a dry site for breeding; for cliff-nesting species such as kittiwakes (Rissa), the provisioning of nest material, which is limited in availability, is important in pair-bond maintenance. Franklin's Gull breeds in exceptionally noisy colonies, containing up to 150,000 pairs, exclusively at inland lakes and marshes. Although some of its nests may be free-floating, most are placed on emergent vegetation over water about 1 m deep, and require daily maintenance to prevent them from sinking. The chicks normally remain on their floating nest platforms unless seriously threatened, when they may swim into nearby reeds. During incubation, some gulls, but particularly those that nest at high densities, utter a staccato threat call when confronted by intruders, including those of other species: with neck stretched forward, they give a "gakkering" call, which can persist for some minutes.

[Larus pipixcan, Kaysville, Utah, USA. Photo: R. J. Erwin/DRK]

Incubation is performed by both sexes, and for most species lasts an average of 22-26 days, being extended if there are frequent disturbances during this period. At the same time both sexes defend the territory, but their main priority is to protect the eggs; the territory size may therefore be somewhat reduced during the incubation period. During the day an incubation stint generally lasts for one to four hours; at night, one member of the pair sits throughout, while its mate normally remains close by on the territory.

[*Xema sabini sabini*, Rowley Island, Foxe Basin, Northwest Territories, Canada. Photo: Jan van de Kam/ Bruce Coleman]

eggs, and fledging rates for most of those that fledge any young range from one to two chicks. The availability of supplementary food from refuse has enabled Herring Gulls successfully to rear all three chicks, and no doubt contributed to their population explosion. It is becoming clear, however, that survival to fledging or independence is not always predictive of recruitment into the breeding population. This is partly because other factors have a major influence on the survival of young after they leave the breeding grounds. At least in Western Gulls, recruitment into the breeding population is more reliably predicted by survival of young to one year of age.

Several long-term studies have followed individuals throughout their reproductive years. In a 29-year study, 81 male and 66 female Red-billed Gulls showed considerable variation in the total numbers of young raised to fledging. Depending on the year cohort, 45-100% of the male and 66-100% of the female fledglings died before they could breed; and, of those that did return to breed, nearly 40% fledged no young in their lifetime. Thus, during their entire reproductive careers, only 17% of breeding males and 24% of females produced young that successfully bred in the colony. Frequency of breeding, longevity and laying date were the most important sources of variation in lifetime productivity. Gulls laying earlier in the season were more successful.

Current reproductive effort may affect future survival. For example, in California Gulls, increasing effort with age was associated with reduced survivorship. Reproductively induced mortality resulted from the cumulative effects over the entire breeding season. Younger adults fledged fewer offspring but had high survival rates, while old gulls tended to fledge more offspring but had low survival. Old gulls that fledged few offspring, however, survived as well as young gulls.

Movements

Typically, gulls leave the breeding grounds following the fledging of their chicks, remain with the juveniles for a few weeks, and then migrate or disperse for a variable distance to wintering grounds.

Most gull species are migratory, moving to warmer regions for the winter. Movement patterns vary with age, young often moving farther than adults. Migration of large flocks usually occurs at night, although gulls will also migrate during the early morning and late afternoon, when hundreds or thousands may be seen streaming over land or along coasts or waterways.

Many species, including the Black-legged Kittiwake and Sabine's, Laughing, Common Black-headed and Brown-headed Gulls, show directed migration to lower latitudes for the winter. Remarkably, however, some of the high latitude species do not show this trend. Ivory, Iceland and Glaucous Gulls disperse only to the edge of the ice and open water. Ross's Gull migrates in large numbers eastwards past Point Barrow, Alaska, in autumn, and, since no return spring migration has been documented, it may have a complete circumpolar movement or may return far from shore over the ice. The Mediterranean Gull likewise migrates across longitudes, mainly from the Black Sea to the western Mediterranean.

Some gulls are long distance migrants, flying many thousands of kilometres from Arctic or north temperate breeding grounds to South America, Africa or southern Asia. The small gulls migrate longer distances than the large gulls, several being transequatorial migrants. Franklin's Gull migrates farther than any other, some reaching extreme southern South America from breeding grounds in Canada. Other small gulls, such as Sabine's and Common Black-headed, also have long transequatorial migrations. The small gulls that breed in interior South America and Africa, however, do not migrate so far, and some of their movements are nomadic rather than truly migratory. Brown-hooded Gulls leave their breeding marshes of northern Argentina and roam the coasts of Argentina and Brazil, but do not show directed migration towards the tropics. Similarly, Black-billed Gulls breeding on riverine shingle in New Zealand move only to the coasts during winter. Many Heermann's Gulls disperse northwards along the Pacific coast after breeding.

In three-egg clutches, the first two chicks hatch within a few hours of one another; the third may hatch up to 48 hours later, and so starts off with a distinct size disadvantage. The downy chicks of gulls are usually pale grey or tan brown, with irregular dark markings on the dorsal surface, giving them very good camouflage. They are fed by both parents, the male providing more food during the first week, while the female broods and guards the chicks. The large red spot on the mandible of many large white-headed gulls, such as the Great Black-backed Gull, serves as a stimulus to the young chicks to initiate feeding.

[*Larus marinus*, Unst, Shetland, Scotland. Photo: C. Reddick/Aquila]

Many large species of temperate and subarctic regions migrate only a few hundred kilometres, and others simply disperse along nearby coasts to favourable feeding grounds. Thus, Herring, Ring-billed and California Gulls spread out along the coasts of North America. In the Old World, however, many Herring Gulls breeding in the Baltic winter in the southern North Sea and Britain, while Baltic Lesser Black-backed Gulls migrate to the Black Sea and the eastern Mediterranean, many even continuing into Africa. Some species, such as the Western Gull, are essentially sedentary, remaining in nearby coastal areas or moving south only short distances in the non-breeding season.

The smaller species usually migrate in large, dense flocks, while this is less true for the larger gulls. Huge aggregations sometimes remain intact during the winter. In 1994, flocks of up to half a million Franklin's Gulls migrated through the southern USA, and up to a million have been observed together in Peru in winter.

Vagrancy among gulls is by no means uncommon. For instance, Nearctic species occur annually in western Europe, and of particular interest is the Ring-billed Gull. This species was unknown in Britain until 1973, when it was reported in Wales; subsequently, the number of annual records increased dramatically, and this gull has become regular in many parts of Britain and can be seen at all times of the year. These events are no doubt linked to the species' huge increase in eastern North America. Ring-billed Gulls have now been recorded in many countries of Europe, as far east as Sweden and Poland, and frequently south to Spain.

Relationship with Man

Unlike many seabirds, most gulls spend their entire lives along coasts, and some breed inland. Gulls have therefore been an integral part of the natural world around coastal human settlements, establishing a level of commensalism, and they have been exploited for thousands of years.

Throughout history, gulls have provided man with food in the form of eggs, chicks, and even adults, and their feathers have been used in the fashion industry. Since gulls are primarily coastal, the first sighting of flocks of gulls was used by ancient mariners as a welcome sign that land was near. Fishermen today recognize that flocks of gulls can help them locate fish.

Bird eggs can provide an important and free, although seasonal, source of food for man. Collecting eggs for food, or "egging", has a long and continuous history in Europe, the tropics, the Arctic, and other parts of the world. In many places, colonies of gulls and other seabirds were "managed". Particular colonies or parts of them belonged to specific families or clans, and individuals and their descendants were responsible for maintaining the colony for the use of future generations. Eggs were collected only early in the season, and pairs were then allowed to raise young. In other cases, only a part of the colony was egged each year, and the areas egged varied from year to year. In some cultures, elaborate records were kept of the areas egged, the timing of egging, and the number of eggs taken. At Ravenglass in northwest England, records of continuous, yearly egging date back to the 1600's; this colony of Common Black-headed Gulls had an annual yield of 30,000 eggs, and was protected from overexploitation by careful local regulation. There are similar histories of egging of Black-legged Kittiwake colonies in many regions, although often only the lower areas of cliff were accessible. Even today, gull and other seabird eggs remain an important food source for many people.

In parts of Europe, gulls were often featured at banquets. During the seventeenth century chicks were collected soon after hatching, and were fattened in gull houses on country estates for special feasts. Fashionable ladies sent gulls as gifts to neighbours, much as we might send cakes or flowers today.

The early European settlers in North America brought with them a predilection for bird eggs. Unlike those in Europe and the Arctic, however, North American colonies were not owned by particular families, protection was non-existent, and overexploitation occurred. By the nineteenth century gull numbers had decreased along the Atlantic coast, but legal protection in the early twentieth century, and artificial sources of food, dramatically reversed this process (see Status and Conservation).

Recently, some species have become pests in places. Gulls have caused problems at landfills and airports, and in agricultural areas or suburban communities, where they occur in high concentrations. Gull control has become a controversial issue, involving a mixture of scientific information, conservationists' pleas, public perception, political pressures, and legal constraints.

Most major airports located in coastal areas experience problems with gulls, particularly during migration, involving species such as Ring-billed, Herring and Laughing Gulls in North America, Silver Gulls in Australia, and Black-headed and Mew Gulls in Europe. Elaborate control measures have been introduced to decrease the likelihood of collisions between aeroplanes and birds, referred to as bird strikes, most of which occur near airports while planes are landing or taking off. Control measures include scaring with shell crackers, bangers, and blank and live artillery shells; playing recordings of gull distress calls; flying captive falcons; installing monofilament lines over loafing areas; preventing nesting near airports; and shooting of adults. One effective method of preventing accidents on take-off or landing is to use vehicles to clear gulls off the runway before their use by aircraft. In 1979, Laughing Gulls began breeding in a marsh at the end of a runway at J. F. Kennedy Airport, New York, and this colony grew exponentially to thousands of pairs; from the early 1990's thousands of the gulls and other species were shot at the airport, despite substantial public objection.

In North America, the Great Lakes' Ring-billed Gull population has increased dramatically, from 27,000 breeding pairs in the 1940's and 1950's to 710,000 pairs in 1990. This increase has been associated with concerns for airline flight safety, human health, and agricultural and horticultural damage. Gulls nest on urban roofs and sometimes interfere with industrial operations, while expanding populations may preempt colony sites of other species such as Common Terns. Control of Ring-billed Gulls has involved scaring them, excluding gulls from areas by wires or other devices, removing or modifying attractive habitat, and re-

ducing or preventing their reproduction. Yet the gull numbers are still growing. Even with constant vigilance, humans have been able to halt the population explosions only so long as the control measures continue.

Similar problems are caused by Glaucous-winged, Herring, Yellow-legged, Common Black-headed and Silver Gulls, which have adapted to urban environments and learned to take advantage of food at landfills and from marine processing activities. They have all increased dramatically this century. While the problems are acute and potentially lethal around airports, gulls are no less of a nuisance in agricultural, suburban and urban environments. In Europe, the expansion of Herring Gulls has provided additional problems for fish and shellfish aquaculture, and has been linked with the possible spread of harmful pathogens.

Gulls also compete directly or indirectly with other native species for breeding places, and they prey on other birds. When their populations were in balance with those of other species, their habits were not harmful. With increased numbers and consequent range expansions, however, they now compete directly with smaller species, which in some cases have been extirpated from their traditional nesting islands by large gulls. Management of gulls can be a major problem at some nature reserves. Attempts have therefore been made to control their populations or even eliminate certain colonies to facilitate the recovery of terns and other seabirds. In the north-eastern USA, for example, some efforts have been made to control populations of Herring and Great Black-backed Gulls, so that Common and Roseate Terns (*Sterna dougallii*) can re-establish nesting on some islands.

On a more positive note, gulls are now serving man as bioindicators of environmental problems. The feminization of embryos as a result of DDT exposure was first noted in gulls in the early 1980's, and was our first warning of the subtle but pervasive effects of environmental oestrogens or endocrine disruptors, now being examined as a cause of widespread developmental and reproductive problems in vertebrates.

In North America, colonial fish-eating seabirds such as Herring Gulls are being used to study the effects of chronic exposure to complex mixtures of persistent environmental contaminants,

Young gulls are guarded by one or both of their parents throughout the fledging period, the family remaining at or near the nest-site. The threat of predators is ever present, and in many gull colonies conspecifics will attack and kill young of other pairs, especially if chicks wander out of their parents' individual territory. Here, an Andean Gull on its remote high altitude breeding lake is giving a threat display and call to other Andean Gulls flying past. As a further safeguard to protect their chicks, many breeding gulls will enlarge their territory during the fledging period, enabling chicks to walk around without risk of attack from neighbours.

[*Larus serranus*, Salar de Surire, north Chile. Photo: Günter Ziesler]

In parts of the Arctic, the Ivory Gull breeds on inaccessible cliffs. The chicks take at least four to five weeks to fledge, and, as with most gulls, at least one parent stays with them until they can fly sufficiently well to have a reasonably good chance of surviving on their own. Unlike most gulls, in which juveniles and early immatures are heavily patterned with dark markings, juvenile Ivory Gulls look very white, having only small, sparse blackish spots, a "dirty" face and a narrow blackish tail band. This most beautiful of gulls spends its entire life in Arctic waters, and is very rarely seen south of the ice limit.

[Pagophila eburnea, Spitsbergen, Svalbard. Photo: Rinie van Meurs/ Bruce Coleman]

particularly the lipophilic chlorinated hydrocarbons such as DDT and PCB's, within the entire Great Lakes ecosystem. Birds are being used as models to determine large-scale environmental effects, and in places contaminants have been suspected to have significant effects on gull populations (see Status and Conservation). The capacity of gulls to provide early warning of environmental problems is particularly important when indicators are required to assess ecosystem health.

Status and Conservation

The world populations of gull species range from a few hundred pairs to more than a million pairs. Ironically, some gulls with global populations of under 50,000 pairs, such as the Yellow-footed Gull (*Larus livens*) and the Western Gull, are considered serious pests and, paradoxically, attempts may be made to reduce their numbers in order to protect other species on which they prey or with which they compete, even when the latter are much more abundant than the gulls themselves.

Several species have limited or highly restricted breeding distributions, but, for the most part, gulls have wide ranges and enjoy stable or even increasing populations. Because many gulls breed in places which are readily accessible to humans, their nesting colonies are vulnerable to direct human exploitation, disturbance and habitat loss. Nonetheless, only five species are currently listed as globally threatened. These are Olrog's and the Lava Gulls in the Neotropics, the White-eyed Gull in the Middle East, Saunders's Gull (*Larus saundersi*) of eastern China, and the Nearctic Red-legged Kittiwake (*Rissa brevirostris*).

Olrog's Gull was recognized as a species distinct from the Band-tailed Gull only in 1958, and it was not named until 1977, at which time only one colony was known. With a very limited breeding range, restricted to the Argentine coast, its numbers do not exceed 1400 pairs, and the few known colonies suffer disturbance, destruction and egg-collecting for food. It is certainly threatened.

The Lava Gull has the smallest world population of any gull, with only about 300-400 pairs. It is currently well protected, but, with increasing human colonization of the Galapagos, the National Park itself may be in jeopardy and the gull's future is by no means assured.

The White-eyed Gull breeds only in the Gulf of Aden and on Red Sea islands, with a total population probably of around 4000-5000 pairs. It is at risk from the effects of oil pollution and various human pressures, including disturbance, the taking of eggs and young from breeding colonies, and development of its nesting habitat.

Saunders's Gull similarly has a limited distribution, on the east coast of China, where about 3000 pairs survive. Having already lost most of its salt-marsh breeding habitat, it is now Endangered owing to further coastal development, along with disturbance, hunting and pollution. All seven known colony sites are either being developed or are planned for development for agriculture or aquaculture. Unfortunately, it is not treated as an endangered species by the Chinese authorities, yet protection of its breeding grounds is of critical importance.

The seven known colonies of the Red-legged Kittiwake are all in the Bering Sea. Although there has been some increase in numbers at some of these in the last two decades, the two colonies in the Pribilof Islands have experienced a 50% decline, apparently a result of food shortage. The species is considered Vulnerable.

The Relict Gull, which breeds at a few sites in Kazakhstan, Russia, Mongolia and China, is one of three near-threatened gull species. Its world population is uncertain, but may perhaps be no more than 2000 pairs, although the existence of as yet undiscovered breeding sites is possible. The Relict Gull has declined seriously in Kazakhstan, and its nesting colony on Lake Alakol is nearly gone. The cause of this is obscure, for this remote species has rarely been studied. Nevertheless, its eggs and chicks are known to suffer serious predation from Yellow-legged Gulls, and the species is extraordinarily susceptible to adverse weather and to human and other disturbances, both of which factors can lead to the elimination of entire colonies.

The other two near-threatened species are Heermann's Gull and the Pacific Gull. The former is still numerous, but 90% or more of all its pairs nest in a single colony on Mexico's Isla Rasa, in the northern Gulf of California. The Pacific Gull is Australia's only endemic gull, restricted to remote coasts and islands of the south, where it may now be subject to competition with the successful Kelp Gull, which has recently colonized this zone. Although still numerous and not listed as threatened, the Black-billed Gull, a New Zealand endemic which nests mainly on ephemeral river shingle bars, is vulnerable to a loss of habitat caused by invading exotic vegetation; it requires habitat management.

A recent, well documented conservation success story is that of Audouin's Gull, a species endemic to the Mediterranean zone. Very few breeding sites exist, and 90% of the total population breeds along the Spanish coast. Its colonies suffered serious disturbance from fishermen and visitors, and also from military activities, and, in view of the precarious situation, in 1987 the Spanish government initiated a co-ordinated conservation programme for the species. This involved constant protection of all the breeding colonies, as well as additional measures, such as the culling of Yellow-legged Gulls at two island sites and the elimination of rats from one of them, vegetation management at another site, the protection of some of the principal stopover sites, and thorough research of the parameters dictating the species' biology.

These measures have enabled a marked increase from the total of 800-1000 pairs estimated in 1966, when the species was considered one of the rarest of all gulls, to 15,600 pairs in 1993. Much of this overall increase is due to the growth of the colony at the Ebro Delta, which was first occupied only in 1981, but by 1995 had grown to hold 10,300 pairs, or 60% of the world population. Remarkably, this colony has increased at an annual average of 40%, and in the first years at a staggering average of 350%, figures which can only be explained by mass immigration of breeding birds in the early years, together with very high productivity of up to 2 chicks per pair per year.

The recent studies have shown that this species has a rather specialized diet, based on pelagic clupeid fish, for which it depends on the discards of the local fishing fleet. The existence of this highly predictable, superabundant source of food has certainly played a major part in the observed population growth, especially in the main colony at the Ebro Delta. Therefore, the maintenance of this food supply, coupled with continued protection of the breeding colonies, must be seen as key factors for the continuing survival of this species. Audouin's Gull is currently classified as Conservation Dependent, which means that due to specific active conservation measures it is not listed as a globally threatened species, but that it would be considered so if the measures were to cease.

Gulls have been profoundly influenced by man, perhaps more so than any other group of seabirds except for the auks and penguins, which were used extensively for their oil. Most of these influences have been negative, affecting reproductive success and population levels. The taking of gull eggs and whole birds for food and for the millinery trade had the potential to decimate their populations, but by the early twentieth century protective laws and treaties in several countries halted this wholesale exploitation.

Although eggers have lived in relative harmony with colonial-nesting gulls for most of the history of their co-existence, seabird populations began to suffer in the seventeenth and eighteenth centuries, because of expanding human populations and a breakdown in individual responsibility for colonies. Well into the nineteenth century, Black-legged Kittiwakes were still taken in large numbers by New England fishermen for food and bait; the small gulls were lured to boats by cod liver or other bait, and were captured by hand, nets or hooks. In England, Norway and other parts of Europe, Black-legged Kittiwakes were slaughtered on their breeding grounds. A century ago, harvesting at colonies in the USA was totally unregulated; during this period, the Great Black-backed Gull disappeared as a breeding bird from the Maine coast, breeding populations of Herring Gulls were pushed farther north, and Western Gull numbers on the Farallon Islands were seriously reduced.

During the late nineteenth century, bird hunting or market-gunning became serious business in North America, and birds were shot both for food and for fashion. White was a fashionable colour for the millinery trade, and the feathers of gulls, as well as those of herons, egrets and terns, were eagerly sought (see Volume 1, page 396). Entire wings of gulls often festooned fashionable hats in New England.

With the cessation of the killing of gulls for food and fashion, populations slowly began to rebound, and to reclaim former nesting grounds. Several species increased greatly, especially during the 1950's, and have become real or potential problems in some areas. In many cases, these increases are directly attributable to the availability of superabundant food at rubbish dumps, sewage outfalls, and fish-processing boats and factories.

The growth of gull populations during the present century is well known, most notably the enormous increases of Herring Gulls in both Europe and North America, of Silver Gulls in Australia, of Ring-billed Gulls in interior North America, and of Common Black-headed Gulls throughout Europe. Some of these expansions have slowed or stabilized, but through the 1980's Laughing Gulls have undergone almost a doubling of population levels in New Jersey, with a northward expansion into New York, where they bred prior to their elimination in the 1880's.

The Herring Gull provides an excellent example of a gull that has undergone extensive range expansions and a population explosion. At the end of the last century, the Herring Gull was largely a species of the low Arctic, in both the Western and the Eastern Hemispheres, with colonies in southern Canada and northern Europe. At the turn of the century, Herring Gulls began to increase in numbers and to spread southwards. From Canada, they spread into Maine, taking over islands once used by cormorants, puffins and terns; within a few years, small colonies grew into colonies of hundreds or thousands of pairs. In the first third of the twentieth century, they began to move into Massachusetts, taking over rocky and sandy islands used by terns and other species. Herring Gulls then moved into New York state, nesting on sandy beaches, grassy knolls and rocky islands, and by the 1950's they were firmly established in both Massachusetts and New York. The number of breeding pairs in New York peaked at about 25,000 in the mid-1980's, but has since decreased to about 15,000 pairs.

In 1948 the first Herring Gulls nested in New Jersey, and by the 1960's there were nearly 2000 pairs. With few sandy islands available for nesting, and no rocky islands, the gulls moved onto salt-marsh islands. By the 1980's there were nearly 4000 pairs in New Jersey, and they have displaced terns, skimmers and the smaller Laughing Gulls from many islands. Not only do they compete with these species for nesting places, but they also prey on their eggs and chicks. By the early 1990's there were nearly 6500 pairs nest-

Saunders's Gull is restricted as a breeding species to the east coast of China, where most of its salt-marsh breeding habitat has already been destroyed. Development is currently taking place at, or is planned for, the very few remaining colony sites, and disturbance, hunting and pollution are additional threats to its survival. It is now classified as Endangered, with only some 3000 pairs left. Protection of its breeding grounds is vital.

[Larus saundersi, Deep Bay, Hong Kong. Photo: Sue Earle/ Planet Earth]

Although a not unfamiliar bird in the Red Sea and the Gulf of Aden, the White-eyed Gull occurs nowhere else in the world. Its total population probably numbers about 4000-5000 pairs. Its status is not well known, but it is considered to be Vulnerable. It is at permanent risk from the effects of pollution by beached and floating oil, and is subject to various other human pressures, including increasing disturbance from tourism-related activities. Its colonies are robbed of both eggs and chicks, and its nesting habitats are threatened with further development.

[Larus leucophthalmus, Red Sea coast, Egypt. Photo: Oriol Alamany]

ing in New Jersey, but their numbers have now stabilized. Herring Gulls now nest regularly as far south as North Carolina.

Similar expansions can be described for Europe, where Herring Gulls have also displaced terns and the smaller Common Black-headed Gull from their nesting colonies. Attempts to control their numbers by shooting or harrassment, or by destroying their eggs have generally failed. Only the closure of rubbish dumps has been at all successful. Their populations do eventually stabilize, but at what is probably an artificially high level.

Not all of the commoner gulls, however, benefit from the activities of modern man. Franklin's Gull provides a good example of a gull that is particularly vulnerable to habitat loss. It requires large, undisturbed prairie marshes for nesting, and will not use small marshes that are near human activities. Its preferred sites are vulnerable to natural variations in the water-cycle, as well as to draining by man. When such marshes become unsuitable, whole colonies of upwards of 50,000 birds may leave in search of suitable sites. When these are not available, the gulls do not breed. A succession of drought years can result in a drastic reduction in the entire population of Franklin's Gull, to only 10% of its former level. Presumably, the drainage of large prairie marshes by man, added to the effects of natural drought cycles, could threaten this species. A similar plight exists for the Brown-hooded Gull in South America, and its populations should be monitored. Common Black-headed Gulls in Europe also use marshes traditionally, but they have adapted to nesting on dunes and beach habitats.

Contaminants are another cause of changes in gull populations. Although eggshell thinning was not a serious problem among gull populations in the 1960's, high levels of DDT have been responsible for the feminization of gull embryos, resulting in the inability of males to breed and contributing to skewed sex ratios.

On the Great Lakes, high mortality of embryos and chicks was reported among Herring Gulls as early as 1964, and by the early 1970's reproductive success was at best 10% of normal. Hatchlings exhibited impaired growth, congenital malformations, enlarged livers, and subcutaneous oedemata. Lower hatching rates appeared to be due to both intrinsic and extrinsic factors. Great Lakes parents did not incubate as effectively as gulls elsewhere; they applied less heat and were less attentive. The problem was a result both of egg quality and of parental

quality: birds at "clean" sites elsewhere were unable to hatch "contaminated" eggs, and birds from "contaminated" colonies were unable to hatch eggs from "clean" colonies, where hatching rate was otherwise normal. Furthermore, more eggs disappeared from Great Lakes nests, a result of a lower level of parental attendance. The total organochlorine content of eggs from Lake Ontario was negatively correlated with the total time the eggs were attended.

This example clearly indicates that environmental pollutants can affect parental behaviour, embryo quality, and eventually reproductive success. It suggests that toxins, when present at lower levels, may also be affecting subtle aspects of behaviour and physiology that have a bearing on reproductive success. In the milieu of other factors that cause decreases in productivity, toxins may fail to be identified as a cause of reproductive problems until breeding success has decreased precipitously.

General Bibliography

Ayers (1982), Barnard & Thompson (1985), Beer (1975, 1976, 1980), Bergman (1982a), Björklund (1994), Blokpoel & Spaans (1991), Bossley & Boord (1992), Brodkorb (1953), Burger, J. (1980d, 1981e, 1983b, 1984a, 1987b, 1988a, 1988b, 1988c), Burger, J. & Gochfeld (1981d, 1983a, 1984b), Burger, J., Olla & Winn (1980), Cane (1994), Carrera (1987), Chapman & Parker (1985), Chernichko (1985), Christian *et al.* (1992b), Conover (1984a), Conover & Hunt (1984a, 1984b), Coulson (1968), Croxall (1987, 1991), Croxall & Rothery (1991), Croxall, Evans & Schreiber (1984), Devillers (1985), Drent *et al.* (1992), Dunning (1993), Dwight (1925), Fox *et al.* (1991), Fry & Toone (1981), Furness & Monaghan (1987), Furness *et al.* (1988), Götmark (1989), Graham (1982), Grant (1986), Hackett (1989), Hand (1981a, 1985), Hand *et al.* (1981), Haney & Lee (1994), Harrison (1985, 1987), Hébert (1988), Hiom *et al.* (1991), Hoerschelmann & Jacob (1992), Hoffman (1984), Hudson *et al.* (1969), Kharitonov (1983), Löfgren (1984), Lythgoe (1979), McNicholl (1975), Miller & Sibley (1941), Moynihan (1959), Nelson (1980), Nettleship *et al.* (1994), Olson (1985b), Peters (1934), Pierotti (1988a, 1988b), Pierotti & Murphy (1987), Salzman (1982), Schnell (1970), Shufeldt (1892), Shuntov (1972), Sibley & Ahlquist (1990), Sibley & Monroe (1990, 1993), Simmons (1972), Southern & Southern (1978), Spaans (1992), Spaans & Blokpoel (1991), Stewart *et al.* (1984), Tinbergen (1953, 1956, 1959, 1960, 1964), Tinbergen *et al.* (1967), Tuck & Heinzel (1978), Veen (1987), Zubakin (1975a, 1976, 1982b, 1983, 1985).

ssp *canus*

ssp *kamtschatschensis*

PLATE 50

inches   8

cm   20

Genus *LEUCOPHAEUS* Bruch, 1853

1. Dolphin Gull
Leucophaeus scoresbii

French: Goéland de Scoresby **German**: Blutschnabelmöwe **Spanish**: Gaviota Patagona
Other common names: Scoresby's Gull

Taxonomy. *Larus Scoresbii* Traill, 1823, South Shetland Islands (probably = Falkland Islands).
Recently placed in *Larus* by many authors. Sometimes combined with *Larus pacificus* in genus *Gabianus* on basis of strongly hooked bill, but unique behaviour, plumage and chick pattern advocate placement in monospecific genus. Probably most closely related to *L. belcheri* and *L. atlanticus*, or to *L. heermanni*. Monotypic.
Distribution. S South America, from SC Chile (Chiloé I) and SC Argentina (Punta Tombo, Chubut) to Tierra del Fuego; also Falkland Is. Outside breeding season, occurs slightly further N on both mainland coasts.

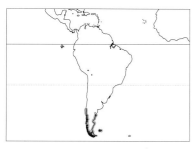

Descriptive notes. 40-46 cm; 524 g; wingspan 104-110 cm. Uniquely plumaged gull, with uniform grey suffusion on head and underbody, dark mantle and black primaries, the latter with no white windows, and broad white triangular trailing edge to secondaries and inner primaries; tail white; heavy bill and shortish legs startlingly bright red; iris white, with conspicuous red orbital ring. Distinguished from *Larus belcheri*, which shares some of the same features, by smaller size, lack of black tail band, and noticeably different bare part colours. Non-breeding adult and second-winter bird have a darker grey-mottled hood. Juvenile unique among gulls, uniform dark brown with whitish belly and slaty-brown wing-coverts.
Habitat. Rocky coasts; breeds on low sea cliffs, sand or gravel beaches, marshy depressions, or headlands; often near fresh water or on ridges over sea (Falklands); usually found in vicinity of seabird colonies, marine mammals, slaughterhouses, sewers or farmyards. Non-breeders also frequent harbours.
Food and Feeding. Mainly carrion, offal, bird eggs and chicks; marine invertebrates, and other natural food. Scavenges around marine mammals for dead fish, placentae, and particularly faeces; natural foods are taken mostly early in season, before bird eggs available. Exploits human intrusion into seabird colonies by preying on unguarded eggs and chicks. Occasionally steals food being delivered to cormorant (*Phalacrocorax*) and penguin chicks, and pirates stolen penguin eggs from *Larus dominicanus*. Chicks fed mainly on fish scavenged from around penguin nests. Probes in seaweed; captures swarming beach flies; picks mussels, which are then dropped onto rocks. Does not frequent rubbish dumps, but sometimes feeds at sewage outlets.
Breeding. Attends colonies from Sept, laying sometimes in early Nov (Tierra del Fuego) or late Nov (Punta Tombo), but mostly in Dec; highly asynchronous. Changes location from year to year. Small, dense colonies (1-1·6 pairs/m²) of up to 25 pairs; maximum 210 pairs. Nest of kelp and vegetation, lined with grass; among boulders, or on bare volcanic rock (Punta Tombo), often sheltered by tussock grass. Lays 2-3 eggs (mean 1·9-2·0 Punta Tombo); incubation 24-27 days; tolerates intruders within 1 m of nest, but once flushed will attack; chick is the most boldly marked in any gull, with discrete black spots and streaks forming long bars from gape to below eye, on very pale ground colour; mean hatching weight 41 g; at 2-5 days follows parents from nest; older chicks may form crèche. Hatching success c. 50%; remainder of eggs presumably lost to predators.
Movements. Falklands population resident, but adults and young disperse widely around the islands. Populations from mainland South America move N, Chilean birds as far as Santa María I; Punta Tombo birds attend sea lion colonies 200 km to N, on Valdés Peninsula.
Status and Conservation. Not globally threatened. Many small colonies on South American coast, but size of total population unknown, although probably in low 10,000's. Species considered common in S Chile and on much of Tierra del Fuego. Most Patagonian colonies support fewer than 25 pairs (maximum 210 pairs); Punta Tombo colony holds only 17-24 pairs. In Falklands 85% of colonies contain fewer than 100 pairs, and overall population estimated at only c. 1000 pairs.
Bibliography. Blake (1977), Canevari *et al*. (1991), Castellanos (1935), Cawkill & Hamilton (1961), Clark (1986), Croxall, McInnes & Prince (1984), Devillers (1977b), Hellmayr & Conover (1948), Humphrey *et al*. (1970), Johnson (1967), Kury & Gochfeld (1975), Murphy (1936), Meyer de Schauensee (1982), Moynihan (1962), Olrog (1984), de la Peña (1992), Pettingill (1960), Philippi *et al*. (1954), Reynolds (1935), Woods (1988), Yorio *et al*. (1994), Zapata (1965, 1967).

Genus *LARUS* Linnaeus, 1758

2. Pacific Gull
Larus pacificus

French: Goéland austral **German**: Dickschnabelmöwe **Spanish**: Gaviota Tasmania
Other common names: Large-billed/Australian Gull

Taxonomy. *Larus pacificus* Latham, 1801, New South Wales.
Often placed in separate genus *Gabianus*, either alone or with *Leucophaeus scoresbii*. Considered monotypic by some authors. Two subspecies currently recognized.

Subspecies and Distribution.
L. p. georgii P. P. King, 1827 - Western Australia (Shark Bay) S and E to South Australia (Kangaroo I).
L. p. pacificus Latham, 1801 - Tasmania and Victoria; post-breeding visitor to New South Wales, rarely N to Queensland.

Descriptive notes. 58-65 cm; 900-1185 g; wingspan 137-157 cm. White head and underbody, with blackish mantle and wings, the latter with white trailing edge but lacking white windows on primaries; tail white with narrow black subterminal band; bill very deep and heavy (the heaviest of any gull), yellow, with red spot at tip; nostrils oval rather than slit-like; legs and feet yellowish. Eyes whitish, with orbital ring pinkish or yellowish. Larger than *L. dominicanus*, from which it differs also in darker mantle, black tail band, and heavier bill. Immature paler below and on rump. Juvenile dark brown, with dark bare parts. Races differ minimally.
Habitat. Coastal; rarely occurs inland. Breeds on elevated offshore islands; rarely on headlands in SE of range.
Food and Feeding. Fish, squid, and intertidal molluscs, echinoderms and crabs; fish offal, carrion and refuse; eats many gastropods (*Turbo undulatus*). At colony on Green I (Tasmania), feeds mainly on crabs (*Ovalipes australiensis*, *Paragrapsus gaimardii*) and chitons, as well as fish waste. Takes bird eggs and young, and occasionally adult birds, e.g. White-faced Storm-petrel (*Pelagodroma marina*). Feeds by walking along beaches and intertidal zone, and also by plunge-diving; opens gastropods by dropping them on rocks or on other hard surfaces.
Breeding. Sept-Jan. Most colonies small and open, but 400 pairs at Wilson's Point (S Victoria); nests a few metres apart; often solitary. Builds sturdy nest of grass and seaweed; situated on ground among rocks, grass, shells. Lays 3 eggs (1-3); incubation 23-26 days. Very few other data available.
Movements. Most populations relatively sedentary, but young disperse up to 200 km. Post-breeding movement from Tasmania, N to Victoria and New South Wales coasts, uncommonly as far as Queensland. Accidental in interior and N Australia.
Status and Conservation. Not globally threatened. Currently considered near-threatened. Although not at serious risk at present, species is nowhere common. About 100 breeding colonies known, but total population probably under 10,000 pairs. Expanded in early 20th century, and bred N to S Queensland. Range now shrinking somewhat in E, where it has suffered from competition with recently established and rapidly increasing population of *L. dominicanus*. In Tasmania, populations have been culled to protect other seabirds.
Bibliography. Barker & Vestjens (1989), Blakers *et al*. (1984), Boehm (1961), Brouwer & Garnett (1990), Coulson & Coulson (1993), Flegg & Magde (1995), Fleming (1987), Garnett (1993), James (1995), Lindsey (1992), Macdonald (1988), Marchant & Higgins (1996), McGill (1955), Pizzey & Doyle (1980), Schodde & Tidemann (1986), Serventy & Whittell (1976), Serventy *et al*. (1971), Simpson & Day (1994), Slater *et al*. (1989), Sutton (1935), van Tets & Fullagar (1984), Wheeler (1946), Woodbury & Knight (1951).

3. Belcher's Gull
Larus belcheri

French: Goéland siméon **German**: Schwanzbandmöwe **Spanish**: Gaviota Simeón
Other common names: Simeon's/Band-tailed Gull

Taxonomy. *Larus Belcheri* Vigors, 1829, no locality (presumably Peru).
Formerly treated as polytypic, with *L. atlanticus* as a subspecies. Monotypic.
Distribution. Humboldt Current area, between N Peru (Libertad) and N Chile (Tarapacá). Disperses N to N Ecuador and S to C Chile (around Valparaíso).

Descriptive notes. 48-52 cm; wingspan 120 cm. White, with blackish brown mantle and upperwings, and broad black subterminal tail band; nape washed grey; bill yellow, with blackish subterminal ring and red tip; legs yellow; eyes dark, with red orbital ring. Very similar to *L. atlanticus*, but with slightly shorter wings and bill, grey wash on nape, brown tinge to mantle, and differently shaped tail band; bill slighter, with less pronounced gonydeal angle, while at tip the black is less extensive and the red paler. Non-breeding adult has a brownish hood extending below eyes, with a broad white eye-surround. Juvenile, with dark brown head, scaled greyish brown mantle, and brownish underwing with dark primaries, resembles *L. hemprichii*; tail black, with whitish base.
Habitat. Rocky shores and inshore guano islands.
Food and Feeding. Fish, crabs and shellfish, carrion; seabird eggs and young important during breeding season. Feeds along beaches and around bird colonies; scavenges in intertidal zone; at sea does not usually follow ships.
Breeding. From Dec. Scattered colonies, mostly of under 100 pairs, but occasionally exceeding 1000. Nest-site in hollow among rocks or on sand on shore, close to high tide line, or on steep rocky slope; often no nest built. Usually 3 eggs (1-3); darker olive brown than those of *L. dominicanus*. No information available on incubation and fledging periods, or appearance of chick.
Movements. Not studied. Most birds apparently remain close to breeding colonies, but some disperse N and S within Humboldt Current region; accidental to Panama. Three records from Florida may involve spontaneous occurrence.
Status and Conservation. Not globally threatened. Endemic to Humboldt Current region, with few known breeding sites. Total population certainly under 100,000 pairs, with centre of abundance at San Gallán I (C Peru). Relatively common in Peru, where more abundant than *L. dominicanus* in S; generally scarce and much less common than latter species in Chile. From early 1900's to 1960's, thousands of adults, eggs and chicks periodically killed to protect guano-producing species; however, destruction

On following pages: 4. Olrog's Gull (*Larus atlanticus*); 5. Black-tailed Gull (*Larus crassirostris*); 6. Grey Gull (*Larus modestus*); 7. Heermann's Gull (*Larus heermanni*); 8. White-eyed Gull (*Larus leucophthalmus*); 9. Sooty Gull (*Larus hemprichii*); 10. Mew Gull (*Larus canus*); 11. Audouin's Gull (*Larus audouinii*); 12. Ring-billed Gull (*Larus delawarensis*); 13. California Gull (*Larus californicus*); 14. Great Black-backed Gull (*Larus marinus*).

of 7000 eggs and young on San Gallán I did not effectively reduce population. Vulnerable to effects of El Niño (see Volume 1, page 341).

Bibliography. Blake (1977), Duffy (1983), Duffy *et al.* (1984), Hellmayr & Conover (1948), Johnson (1967), Koepcke, H.W. & Koepcke (1971), Koepcke, M. (1970), Meyer de Schauensee (1982), Moynihan (1962), Murphy (1936), Olson (1976), Olson (1985b), Parker *et al.* (1987), Ridgely & Gwynne (1989), Tovar (1965, 1968, 1974).

4. **Olrog's Gull**

Larus atlanticus

French: Goéland d'Olrog **German**: Olrogmöwe **Spanish**: Gaviota Cangrejera
Other common names: Simeon's/Band-tailed Gull

Taxonomy. *Larus belcheri atlanticus* Olrog, 1958, Mar del Plata, Argentina.
Originally described as a race of *L. belcheri*, but now almost universally considered a distinct species. Monotypic.
Distribution. SE Uruguay (R de la Plata) to Argentina (Puerto Deseado), but breeding known only in Argentina (Buenos Aires, Chubut).

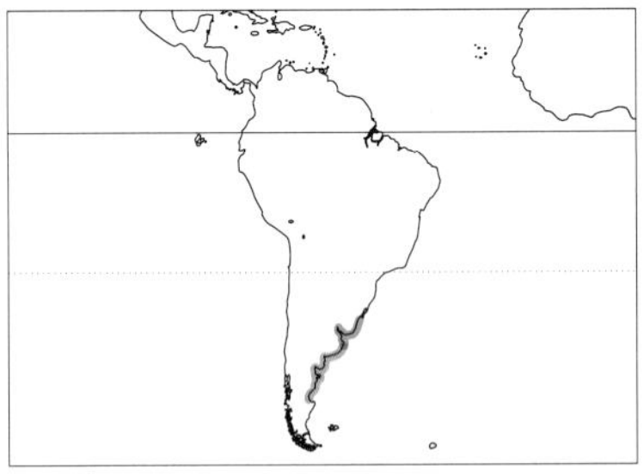

Descriptive notes. 50-56 cm; 900-960 g; wingspan 130-140 cm. White, with black mantle and wings; broad black tail band, except on outermost rectrices, with narrow white terminal band; bill yellow, with red and black tip; legs and feet yellow; iris blackish brown, with red orbital ring. Very like *L. belcheri*, but with slightly longer wings and bill, no grey wash on nape, no brown tinge to mantle, and differently shaped tail band; bill heavier, with sharper gonydeal angle, and at tip has the black more extensive and the red duskier.
Habitat. Coasts and estuaries, breeding on flat sandy islands. Non-breeders frequent sea coasts and riverbanks.
Food and Feeding. Specializes on crabs (*Chasmagnathus granulatus*, *Cyrtograpsus*, *Uca*), and on mussels; also takes fish and offal. Near breeding colony patrols along shores or swims among reeds, picking food items from surface; often hovers over water and then drops to surface. Much less predatory than *L. belcheri*. In Uruguay, feeds in large numbers on exposed mudflats or along rocky shorelines; does not associate with *L. maculipennis* or *L. dominicanus* near sewers or sea lion carcasses.
Breeding. From Sept, with large chicks in Nov. Colonies of 12-400 pairs, in subcolonies c. 50 m apart, at edge of large colonies of *L. dominicanus*; in beds of glasswort (*Salicornia*), among grass tussocks, or on bare ground, often far (100 m or more) from high tide line. Nest variable in form, ranging from flat scrape lined with vegetation to elevated platform of twigs and *Salicornia*; nests very densely crowded together, some even touching. 2-3 eggs. No further breeding details documented.
Movements. Post-breeding dispersal from colonies, S to Río Negro and Chubut, and N to Uruguay. Accidental in S Brazil and Tierra del Fuego.
Status and Conservation. VULNERABLE. Species appears to breed in very low numbers, and should perhaps be considered Endangered. Total known breeding population numbered under 1200 pairs in 1975-1977, and was estimated at 1239±127 pairs in 1992. Breeding distribution not fully documented, and only 6 colonies known, the largest with fewer than 400 pairs. Recent discovery of the Chubut breeding population, however, is very encouraging, and other colonies might still await discovery. Colonies vulnerable to disturbance and destruction through development of tourism, increased fishing, and petroleum exploitation; its eggs are regularly collected for food (e.g. at Bahía San Blas). Existing colonies require full protection and extensive study.

Bibliography. Belton (1984), Blake (1977), Canevari *et al.* (1991), Collar & Andrew (1988), Collar, Crosby & Stattersfield (1994), Collar, Gonzaga *et al.* (1992), Contreras (1978), Daguerre (1933), Devillers (1977a), Escalante (1966), Gore & Gepp (1978), Harris & Yorio (1996), Hellmayr & Conover (1948), Klimaitis & Moschione (1987), Meyer de Schauensee (1982), Moynihan (1962), Murphy (1936), Olrog (1958, 1967, 1984), de la Peña (1992), Wege & Long (1995).

5. **Black-tailed Gull**

Larus crassirostris

French: Goéland à queue noire **German**: Japanmöwe **Spanish**: Gaviota Japonesa
Other common names: Temminck's Gull (Russia)

Taxonomy. *Larus crassirostris* Vieillot, 1818, Nagasaki, Japan.
Relationships unclear; some analyses place present species closest to *L. hemprichii*, others to *L. heermanni*. Monotypic.
Distribution. SE Russia (S Kuril Is, Sakhalin, Popov I, Moneron I, Peter the Great Bay), Japan, Korea and E China (Shandong). More widespread in winter, occurring S to N East China Sea.

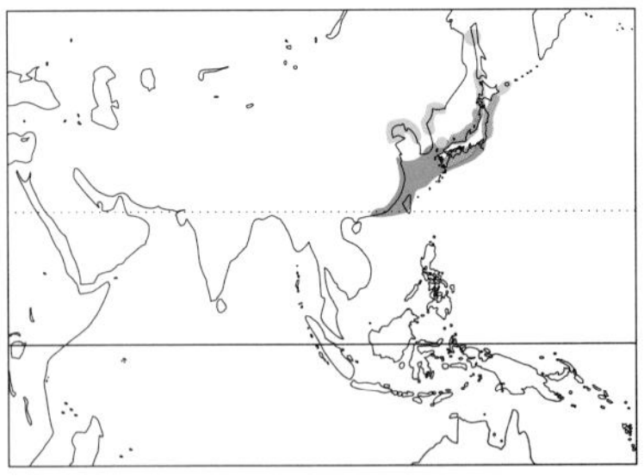

Descriptive notes. 44-47 cm; 436-640 g; wingspan 126-128 cm. Fairly distinctive gull, with white head and underparts, slaty mantle and upperwing, black primaries with white windows, and white tail with broad, even, black subterminal band; bill yellow, with red spot at tip and black subterminal ring, the latter with or without a red spot behind on lower mandible; legs greenish-yellowish. Juvenile dark brown, with whitish rump and belly, black primaries and tail tip, and black-tipped flesh-coloured bill; as adult after 4 years.
Habitat. Coasts, bays and estuaries; breeds on sandy or rocky seashores, sea cliffs, and rocky islets.
Food and Feeding. Diet varies locally and annually. Mainly small fish, crustaceans, insects and offal; also molluscs and polychaetes. In winter feeds heavily on commercial fish offal. In Hokkaido relied mainly on sardines (*Sardinops melanosticta*), but switched to sandeels (*Ammodytes personatus*) after former crashed in mid-1980's. Often follows fishing boats. Steals food from other seabirds, especially auks, gulls and terns. Visits rubbish dumps. Feeds by surface-seizing, occasionally immersing; also plucks prey from surface, and drops hard-shelled items onto hard surfaces to break them open.
Breeding. Colonies form mid-Apr, with laying May-Jun (Siberia). Many colonies hold over 10,000 pairs. Rough nest of dry grass; on sandy or rocky substrate. 2-3 eggs; incubation 24-25 days, rarely 27 days; chick greyish ochre to reddish ochre, spotted brown-black above and on throat; hatching weight 36-44·5 g; fledging 35-40 days. Predation highest near edge of colony. Fledgling survival 63-70%; main mortality due to neighbouring adults attacking wandering chicks.
Movements. Post-breeding dispersal to areas rich in food. 1st-year birds from Peter the Great Bay move to the maritime coast and the Tatar Straits. Birds from NW Honshu fly to the Pacific coast of Honshu, Hokkaido and S Sea of Okhotsk, while those from Yellow Sea spread N and S along its coast. Main wintering areas in Sea of Japan and N East China Sea, but particularly in Korea Strait; smaller numbers further S off Chinese coast, and on Pacific coast of Japan.
Status and Conservation. Not globally threatened. Total population estimated to be below 350,000 pairs, of which c. 100,000 in Russia (96% in Peter the Great Bay, including c. 80,000 on Furugelma I), and c. 150,000 in Japan. Colonies suffer some predation, mainly from corvids, and occasionally gulls; at some colonies many chicks taken by *L. schistisagus*, particularly late in season; feral cats may also take heavy toll. The commonest gull in Japan.

Bibliography. Armstrong (1983), Austin (1948), Austin & Kuroda (1953), Brazil (1991), Cheng Zhaoqin (1990), Étchécopar & Hüe (1978), Flint *et al.* (1984), Hasegawa (1984), Howell & Webb (1995a), Ilicev & Zubakin (1988), Knystautas (1993), Lekagul & Round (1991), Litvinenko (1980, 1986), Litvinenko & Shibaev (1991), Meyer de Schauensee (1984), Monroe (1955), Narita (1994), Perennou *et al.* (1994), Turton (1993), Wang (1991), Watanuki (1982, 1990, 1992, 1994), Williams, M.D. (1986), Yamashina (1961).

6. **Grey Gull**

Larus modestus

French: Goéland gris **German**: Graumöwe **Spanish**: Gaviota Garuma

Taxonomy. *Larus modestus* Tshudi, 1843, Lurin, south of Lima, Peru.
Most closely related to *L. heermanni*. Monotypic.
Distribution. Inland deserts (mainly Atacama) of N Chile and probably S Peru; feeding birds and non-breeders range along coast from Ecuador (Manta, virtually on equator) S to SC Chile (Valdivia).

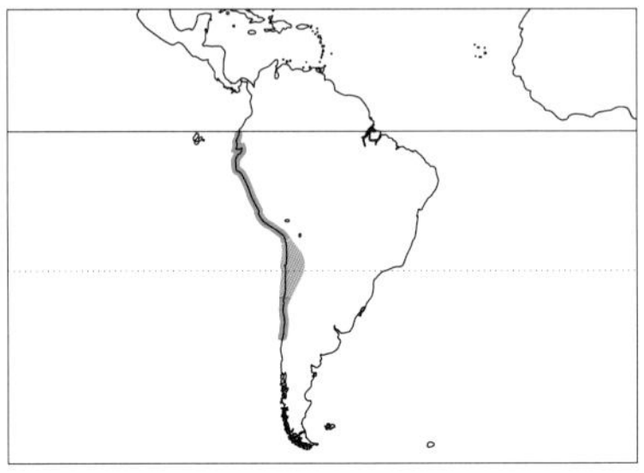

Descriptive notes. c. 45 cm; 360-400 g. Unmistakable within range. Distinctive medium-sized, dull grey gull, with whitish head and black wingtips; darker above than below; pale trailing edge to wing; bill and legs black; iris brown. Differs from *L. heermanni* in somewhat smaller all black bill, and in overall plumage tone.
Habitat. Barren montane deserts, lacking vegetation and fresh water, 35-100 km inland. Feeds along sandy coastal beaches, eschewing rocky areas.
Food and Feeding. Mainly and sometimes exclusively mole crabs (*Eremita analoga*); also fish, nereid worms and offal. Mostly fish fed to young (only one feeding trip per day). Feeds in rather sandpiper-like fashion in wave-washed littoral zone, taking mole crabs from 1 hour before low tide to 2 hours after; surface-plunges for fish and nereid worms. Scavenges in harbours; follows fishing boats.
Breeding. Nov-Jan; eggs from mid-Dec. Does not breed in years with severe occurrence of El Niño. Colony of c. 60,000 nests in 5·5 km², with density of c. 1/m². Nest is a scrape in sand, usually near a rock. 1-3 eggs, usually 2 (mean 1·55, the lowest for any *Larus*); notably pale, sometimes white, with extremely low water-vapour conductance; incubation c. 29-31 days; one adult attends nest during day, while mate forages on coast; chick pale grey (occasionally buffy), with obscure black spots on sides of head, throat, back and flanks; hatching weight c. 31-38 g; brooded for several days, growth slower than in any other gull. Young fly to coast at c. 40 days.
Movements. During breeding season, daily movement of off-duty birds from coast to colony after dark, with mates returning shortly before dawn. No true migration, but non-breeding birds disperse N as far as Ecuador.
Status and Conservation. Not globally threatened. Abundant along Pacific coast, but generally less conspicuous inland. Total population exceeds 100,000 pairs. Egg-collecting can on occasion be serious, with up to 30,000 eggs recorded as being taken from a single colony; vast, uninhabited areas suitable for nesting remain, however, so some colonies should escape plunder. Breeding birds vulnerable to food shortage.

Bibliography. Blake (1977), Cikutovic *et al.* (1988), Devillers & Terschuren (1976a), Duffy (1983), Fitzpatrick *et al.* (1989), Fjeldså & Krabbe (1990), Goodall *et al.* (1945), Guerra & Cikutovic (1983a, 1983b), Guerra & Fitzpatrick (1987), Guerra, Aguilar & Fitzpatrick (1988), Guerra, Fitzpatrick & Aguilar (1988), Guerra, Fitzpatrick, Aguilar & Luna (1988), Guerra, Fitzpatrick, Aguilar & Venables (1988), Hellmayr & Conover (1948), Hilty & Brown (1986), Howell (1983a), Howell *et al.* (1974), Johnson (1967), Koepcke & Koepcke (1971), Moynihan (1962), Murphy (1936), Stiles & Skutch (1989), Tovar (1965, 1968), Wetmore (1965), Woods (1988).

7. **Heermann's Gull**

Larus heermanni

French: Goéland de Heermann **German**: Heermannmöwe **Spanish**: Gaviota Mexicana

Taxonomy. *Larus Heermanni* Cassin, 1852, San Diego, California.
Monotypic.
Distribution. Breeds in Gulf of California (particularly Isla Rasa) S to Nayarit; also Baja California (from San Benito Is off Pacific coast) and N very sparsely in S California, occasionally and irregularly to San Francisco Bay.
Descriptive notes. 43-49 cm; 371-643 g; wingspan 117-124 cm. Distinctive medium-sized gull, with dark body and white head; grey-brown above, pale grey below, with pale grey rump and conspicuous white tips to tail and secondaries; bill bright red, often tipped with black; legs black; iris dark brown, with bright red orbital ring. Non-breeding adult has greyish or brownish streaks on head. Immature entirely dark brown, with pale base to bill; acquires adult plumage at 3 years.
Habitat. Wide range of coastal and estuarine areas; breeds on remote rocky coasts and islets with sparse vegetation.
Food and Feeding. Mainly fish in breeding season; also lizards, insects and other invertebrates. Associates with feeding sea lions to seize scraps of food; specializes on stealing fish from surfacing Brown Pelicans (*Pelecanus occidentalis*). Feeds mainly on beaches, estuaries and riverine marshes, by surface-plunging and surface-dipping.
Breeding. Egg-laying in late Apr; hatching from mid-May. Most colonies hold fewer than 100 pairs, one huge (Isla Rasa); species sometimes breeds among *L. occidentalis*, including solitary pair at Alcatraz I (San Francisco Bay), and 2 pairs at colony in San Luis Obispo County. On Isla Rasa, average nest

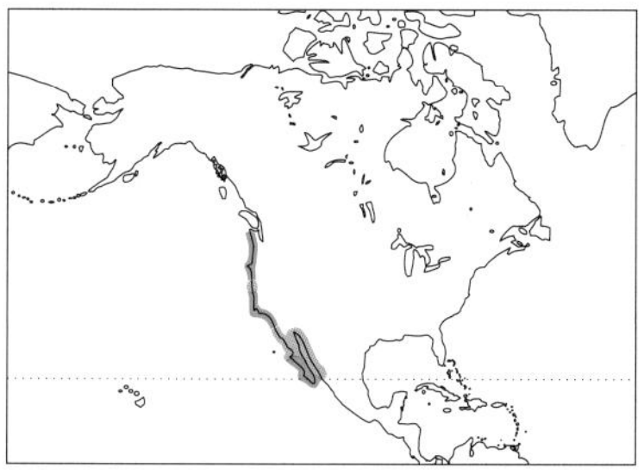

density 13·7/100 m² (range 8·2-20·5), densest in rock-free, flat-bottomed valleys; also on rocky slopes and in sparse vegetation (*Suaeda*) close to high tide line. 1-2 eggs, uncommonly 3 (mean 1·5-2·1); chick hatching weight 35-40 g; fledging 45 days. During food shortage, parents selectively feed one chick, and may attack third chicks. First breeding at 4 years, sometimes 3 years.

Movements. Post-breeding dispersal commonly to C California, and in smaller numbers N to British Columbia and S to Guatemala.

Status and Conservation. Not globally threatened. Currently considered near-threatened. Only eight colonies known, four of which are in Gulf of California. Total population 150,000 pairs or fewer; essentially stable since late 1960's. Species must be at risk, however, since 90% of total population nest on Isla Rasa, where estimates have varied alarmingly from 55,000 pairs in 1975 to 150,000 in 1990's. *L. livens*, if its population expands, could pose a serious threat through predation at this colony. Elsewhere in Gulf of California: 150 pairs on George I, 500 on Cholluda, and 4000 on Partida. Californian colonies small, and variable from year to year. Evaluating census data is difficult, because of different estimates of size of islands, variation in numbers of birds present at different times of year, and presence of non-breeding birds at some times.

Bibliography. Anderson (1983), Bartholomew & Dawson (1979), Blake (1977), Boswall (1978), Boswall & Barrett (1978), Cassidy (1990), Drury (1984), Everett & Anderson (1991), Howell, J. *et al*. (1983), Howell, S.N.G. & Webb (1995a), Jehl (1976), Land (1970), Rahn & Dawson (1979), Richards (1990), Root (1988), Schaldach (1963), Urrutia & Drummond (1990), Velarde (1992, 1993), Velarde & Anderson (1994), Wilbur (1987).

8. White-eyed Gull

Larus leucophthalmus

French: Goéland à iris blanc **German**: Weißaugenmöwe **Spanish**: Gaviota Ojiblanca

Taxonomy. *Larus leucophthalmus* Temminck, 1825, Red Sea coasts.
Morphometrically closest to *L. hemprichii*. Monotypic.

Distribution. Red Sea from Gulf of Suez and Gulf of Aqaba (Tiran) S into Gulf of Aden.

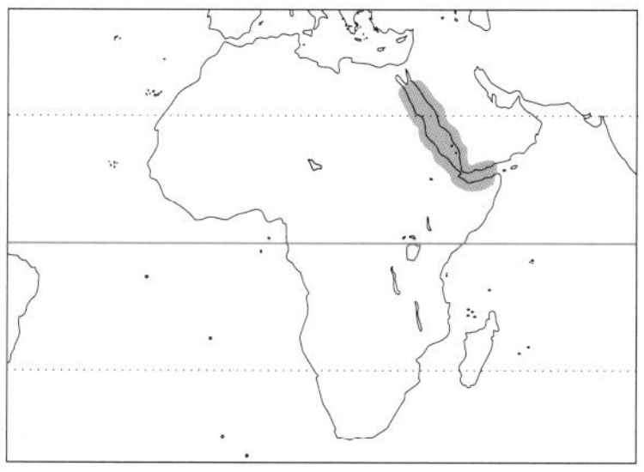

Descriptive notes. 39-43 cm; 275-415 g; wingspan 110-115 cm. Dark-backed gull, characterized by black head and upper breast with thin, slightly drooped bill; conspicuous white crescents above and below eye; dark grey underwing; legs bright yellow; iris dark brown, with red orbital ring. Separated from *L. hemprichii* by slender red bill with black tip, white eye-crescents, and paler upper breast sharply demarcated from hood. Juvenile dark grey-brown, very similar to juvenile *L. hemprichii*, but has large eye-crescents, paler head with streaked hindneck, heavily spotted throat, and slender drooping bill.

Habitat. Coastal, breeding especially on inshore islands, where occupies bare rock and sandflats. Less closely linked with fishing boats and harbours than *L. hemprichii*, thus often occurs further out to sea. Roosts on rocks, coral reefs, piers and fishing vessels.

Food and Feeding. Mainly fish; also some crabs, molluscs and annelids; even some fruits (*Nitraria retusa*). Feeds mainly by plunge-diving from surface. Less of a scavenger than *L. hemprichii*, but occasionally scavenges in harbours. Forages offshore in non-breeding season; usually in small groups, but sometimes gathers in flocks of hundreds or even thousands.

Breeding. Lays mainly in Jul; hatching complete by late Aug. Loosely colonial, in groups of about a dozen to hundreds; most colonies under 25 pairs. Nest on bare rock, sand, or exposed flats near sea; shallow scrape, lined with seaweed and debris. 2-3 eggs; chick greyish buff above with dark spots and streaks; incubation and fledging periods not documented.

Movements. Mostly sedentary; some dispersal and wandering, both N and S. Adults tend to remain along Red Sea coast. Small numbers seen throughout year at Elat, N Gulf of Aqaba. Accidental in E Africa.

Status and Conservation. VULNERABLE. Status poorly known. Total population estimated at 4000-6500 pairs in 1985. Most important sites in Egypt, at mouth of Gulf of Suez, where 1000-2000 pairs breed; elsewhere in Egypt, a few colonies with up to c. 50 pairs each; 350 at 10 sites in C Red Sea, mostly in colonies of less than 25 pairs. Colonies are subject to egging and collecting of chicks. Species is at permanent risk from effects of oil, both floating and beached; also from increasing human pressure of tourism and related activities, and from activities related to oil exploration.

Bibliography. Archer & Godman (1937-1961), Bednall & Williams (1989), Britton, P.L. (1980), Clapham (1964), Collar & Andrew (1988), Collar *et al*. (1994), Cowley (1981), Cramp & Simmons (1983), Dowsett & Forbes-Watson (1993), Étchécopar & Hüe (1964), Gallagher & Woodcock (1980), Gallagher *et al*. (1984), Goodman *et al*. (1989), Goodman & Storer (1987), Hollom *et al*. (1988), Hüe & Étchécopar (1970), Jennings *et al*. (1985), Mackworth-Praed & Grant (1957, 1962), Paz (1987), Perennou *et al*. (1994), Shirihai (1996), Symens (1991), Urban *et al*. (1986).

9. Sooty Gull

Larus hemprichii

French: Goéland de Hemprich **German**: Hemprichmöwe **Spanish**: Gaviota Cejiblanca
Other common names: Hemprich's/Aden Gull

Taxonomy. *Larus* (*Adelarus*) *hemprichii* Bruch, 1853, Red Sea.
Morphometrically linked with *L. modestus* and *L. leucophthalmus*. Monotypic.

Distribution. Red Sea and Gulf of Aden, and Persian Gulf and Gulf of Oman, E to S Pakistan, and S to N Kenya (Kiunga Is).

Descriptive notes. 43-48 cm; 400-510 g; wingspan 105-118 cm. Distinctive dark gull, with brown head and breast, white collar and greyish brown back and wings; short white eyebrow; heavy bill yellowish green, with red tip (extreme tip yellow) bordered at rear by black ring; legs dull yellowish olive; iris brown, orbital ring red. In all plumages (and especially immature) similar to *L. leucophthalmus*, but appears larger-bodied, longer-winged and stouter-billed. Non-breeding adult has head and foreneck pale brown, mottled with white, and no collar. Immature whitish-scaled pale brown above, with pale

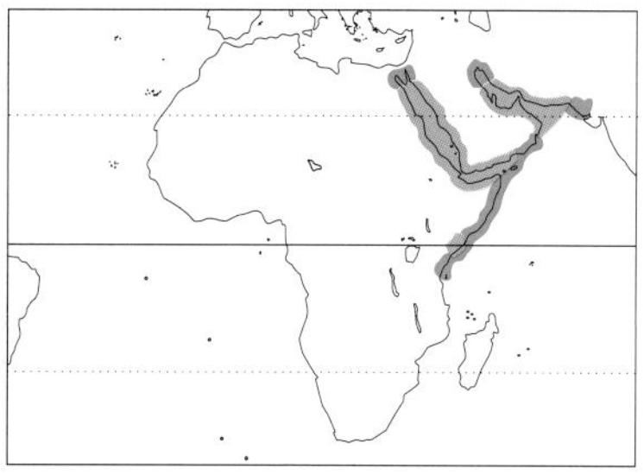

rump, brownish tail with broad brown subterminal band, black iris, dark-tipped greenish grey bill, and greyish legs.

Habitat. Maritime, mainly occurring and breeding along coasts and at islands; hardly ever seen inland. Commonly associates with fishermen, following boats and frequenting harbours, or even sizeable ports, e.g. Karachi; sometimes feeds on mudflats. Frequently rests on piers, buoys and fishing boats.

Food and Feeding. Mainly dead fish and offal; also tern eggs and chicks, and turtle hatchlings. Opportunistic; scavenges along shoreline, usually alone, but highly gregarious at times. Kleptoparasitic on conspecifics and other species; serious predator of other seabirds, including near-threatened Socotra Cormorant (*Phalacrocorax nigrogularis*); takes advantage of human intrusions to steal eggs; takes prawns or dead fish from nets (Pakistan). Rarely seen plunge-diving for fish. Feeds mainly inshore and in intertidal zone, occasionally up to 140 km offshore; follows ships.

Breeding. Summer breeder, laying in Jun at Hurghada (NW Red Sea), Jun-Sept in Pakistan, Jul-Oct in Kenya. Colonial, occasionally solitary; in Kiunga Is (Kenya), 1-3 pairs on each island among hundreds of terns. Nest a slight depression with scant vegetation lining, on bare coral (Kiunga Is), often under bush or overhanging coral, or sheltered by tuft of vegetation. 1-3 eggs; incubation c. 25 days; fledging period not documented, but some birds fledge in Nov.

Movements. Many remain in Red Sea throughout year. Post-breeding dispersal mainly S, sometimes as far as N Mozambique. Common winter visitor to Kenya, less common in Zanzibar. Mainly summer visitor to Pakistan; common in Karachi Port May-Jun, before dispersing to breed.

Status and Conservation. Not globally threatened. Size of total population essentially undocumented, but probably numbers 50,000-100,000 pairs. Two colonies off Arabia hold 5000 pairs each. Species uncommon in Persian Gulf; numbers breeding down coast of E Africa now much reduced, with perhaps only 50-100 pairs remaining. Numbers of non-breeding birds in Kenya increased between 1950's and 1970's. Main predation pressure comes from humans; most important colony in Pakistan (Astola I) is regularly robbed of eggs. Many colonies are vulnerable to oil spills.

Bibliography. Ali & Ripley (1982), Archer & Godman (1937-1961), Baha el Din & Saleh (1983), Bailey (1966), Britton, P.L. (1980), Cramp & Simmons (1983), Dowsett & Forbes-Watson (1993), Étchécopar & Hüe (1964), Fogden (1964), Gallagher & Woodcock (1980), Gallagher *et al*. (1984), Goodman & Storer (1987), Goodman *et al*. (1989), Hollom *et al*. (1988), Hüe & Étchécopar (1970), Jennings (1981a), Jennings *et al*. (1985), Mackworth-Praed & Grant (1957), Pakenham (1979), Paz (1987), Perennou *et al*. (1994), Rands *et al*. (1987), Richardson, C. (1990), Roberts, T.J. (1991), Shirihai (1996), Symens (1991), Urban *et al*. (1986).

10. Mew Gull

Larus canus

French: Goéland cendré **German**: Sturmmöwe **Spanish**: Gaviota Cana
Other common names: Common Gull (Eurasia); Short-billed Gull (*brachyrhynchus*)

Taxonomy. *Larus canus* Linnaeus, 1758, Sweden.
Sometimes considered to form a superspecies with *L. delawarensis*, but morphometric analysis links it instead with *L. melanocephalus*. *L. glaucus* is a synonym. Race *kamtschatschensis* sometimes treated as a separate species, but interbreeds with *heinei* in Siberia. Four subspecies recognized.

Subspecies and Distribution.
L. c. canus Linnaeus, 1758 - Iceland and British Is E to White Sea; winters from Europe to N Africa and Persian Gulf.
L. c. heinei Homeyer, 1853 - Russia, from Kanin Peninsula and Moscow area E to NC Siberia (R Lena); winters in SE Europe and at Black and Caspian Seas.
L. c. kamtschatschensis (Bonaparte, 1857) - NE Siberia; winters SE Asia.
L. c. brachyrhynchus Richardson, 1831 - N Alaska and N Mackenzie S to S British Columbia and N Saskatchewan; winters S to California.

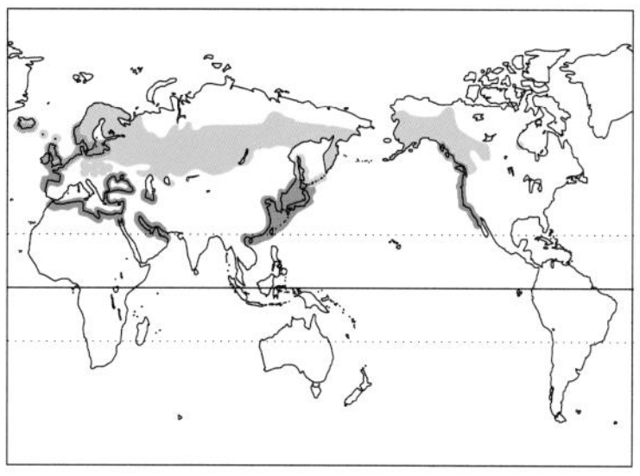

Descriptive notes. 40-46 cm; 290-552 g, but *kamtschatschensis* 394-586 g; wingspan of *canus* 110-125 cm, of *brachyrhynchus* 96-102 cm. Typical white-headed gull, with white body and tail, and pale grey mantle and upperwing; outer 2 primaries black with large white subterminal patch, remainder grey with broad black areas and white tips; bill and legs greenish yellow; iris brownish. Much smaller than *L. argentatus*, and slightly smaller than *L. delawarensis*, with more slender, unmarked bill. Non-breeding adult has dusky streaks on head and neck, and bare parts duller; bill sometimes marked with black. Juvenile brown, mottled with buff; bill dark, with pinkish base. 1st-winter has rump, tail base, outer rectrices and underwing-coverts pale (*canus*) to dark (*brachyrhynchus*), and iris yellow (*kamtschatschensis*) to brown (*canus*). Achieves adult plumage at c. 27 months. Races differ in size and colour tone of upperparts, *kamtschatschensis* largest, adult *heinei* darkest.

Habitat. Coasts, tidal estuaries, agricultural land, reservoirs; breeds on coastal cliffs and islands, in beaches, bogs, marshes and meadows, not necessarily close to wetlands.

Food and Feeding. Earthworms, insects, aquatic and terrestrial invertebrates, small fish; grain (in spring); occasionally kills birds and small mammals. In Baltic, 73% fish. In British Columbia, takes euphausiids (*Thysanoessa raschii*) in winter. Follows plough, feeds on new-mown fields; foot-paddles on water and on soft ground. Exploits fish-processing areas; visits rubbish dumps less than some sympatric congeners, e.g. *L. ridibundus*. Occasionally kleptoparasitic; also occasionally uses aerial foraging, rarely hover-gleaning; swim-dipping and surface-dipping have been recorded. Drops molluscs from air onto hard surfaces.

Breeding. Lays usually in May. Typically breeds in small colonies; in Sweden mostly 2-10 pairs; in Britain largest 320 pairs; often solitary. Site tenacity lower in colonies, although colonies tend to be stable. In Sweden, colonial breeders experience lower nest predation than solitary nesters. Nesting substrates include grass, rock, sand, earth, floating vegetation, bogs, trees, dykes, roofs. Nest is a shallow cup of vegetation (larger at wet sites), often with some vegetative cover. Usually 3 eggs (1-3); incubation mostly 24-26 days (22-28); chick buff with heavy dark spots above, pale below; hatching weight c. 37 g; fledging 30-35 days, independent soon thereafter. Some adults give distraction display when flushed; pairs with vigorous anti-predator defence raise more young. First breeding usually at 3 years, occasionally 2, but normally no recruitment results from pairs younger than 5 years old. Recorded longevity of 24 years.

Movements. Fairly migratory. E Siberian birds winter from S Ussuriland coast and S Japan to SE Asia. C Russian breeders winter in Baltic, Black and Caspian Seas and in Middle East, some moving to S Asia. Those breeding in Finland winter from Denmark to Britain, while other European birds winter from Baltic to Brittany, with few reaching Mediterranean. Birds wintering in Scotland undergo synchronous emigration to Scandinavia in Apr. Alaskan birds winter along Pacific coast to Baja California.

Status and Conservation. Not globally threatened. Total population may exceed 1,000,000 pairs. Increasing and spreading in Europe, where in 20th century has colonized many new areas, including Iceland; breeds in Poland and Austria mainly since 1950's. Probably 72,000 pairs in Britain and Ireland, 60,000 in Denmark, 400,000 in Fenno-Scandia, and 50,000 in E Europe. Rapidly expanding populations have been controlled in some areas, e.g. E Germany. In Alaska, coastal survey counted 1700 pairs at 44 colonies, but at least 3 times that number breed inland along rivers, and total population probably over 10,000 pairs. Species suffers some predation at colonies, mainly from crows (*Corvus*), large owls (*Bubo*), large gulls, foxes and mustelids.

Bibliography. Armstrong (1983), Barth (1955, 1967a, 1967b), Beaman (1994), Bergman (1986), Bianki (1967), Bourne & Patterson (1962), Brazil (1991), Burger & Gochfeld (1987b, 1988a), Cramp & Simmons (1983), Dowsett & Forbes-Watson (1993), Drury (1984), Étchécopar & Hüe (1978), Evans (1984b), Goodman *et al*. (1989), Götmark (1982), Götmark & Andersson (1980, 1984), von Haartman (1980), Howell & Webb (1995a), Ilicev & Zubakin (1988), Johansen (1961), de Juana (1986), Kilpi (1992), Kilpi & Saurola (1985), Knystautas (1993), Koerkamp (1987), Koskimies (1952), Kumari (1976), Kuyt & Johns (1992), Lauro & Spencer (1980), Lensink (1984), Lloyd *et al*. (1991), Nehls (1973), Onno (1965), Patrikeev (1995), Paz (1987), Pennie (1946), Perennou *et al*. (1994), Rattiste & Lilleleht (1987, 1990), Richards (1990), Roberts, T.J. (1991), Rogacheva (1992), Root (1988), Ruttledge (1962), Shirihai (1996), Soikkeli (1990), Spencer & Lauro (1984), Strang, G.L. (1974), Tasker, M. (1994), Tasker, M.L. *et al*. (1987), Tima (1961), Tove (1993), Urban *et al*. (1986), Vermeer & Devito (1986, 1987), Vermeer, Szabo & Greisman (1987), Vernon (1970, 1972), Walters (1978), Weidmann (1955), Yésou (1985), Ytreberg (1960).

11. Audouin's Gull

Larus audouinii

French: Goéland d'Audouin **German**: Korallenmöwe **Spanish**: Gaviota de Audouin

Taxonomy. *Larus audouinii* Payraudeau, 1826, Sardinia and Corsica.
Probably closest to *L. canus*. Monotypic.

Distribution. Mediterranean coasts, with main breeding areas at Ebro Delta (NE Spain) and Chafarinas Is (off NE Morocco), scattered colonies E to Tunisia, Aegean Sea, S Turkey and Cyprus. Winters S to Senegambia.

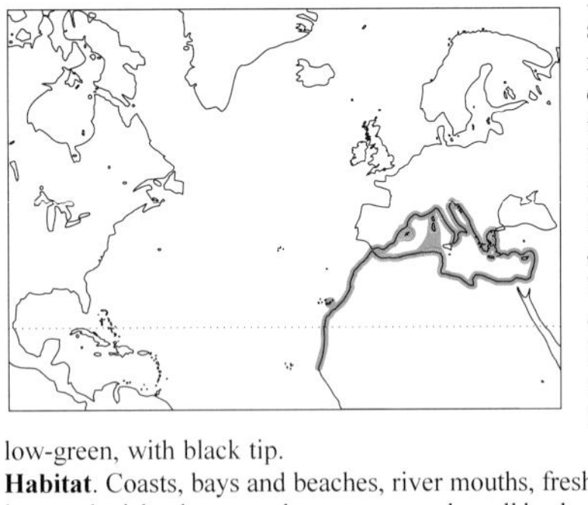

Descriptive notes. 48-52 cm; 580-770 g; wingspan 125-138 cm. White-headed, white-bodied marine gull, with grey mantle and upperwings; characteristic profile, with elongated sloping forehead and a deep hooked bill; bill red, with black subterminal ring and narrow yellow tip (a few show a double black mark); legs dark greyish olive to blackish; iris dark, with crimson orbital ring. Paler than *L. cachinnans*, with more black on outer wings and reduced white windows; different bare part colours. Immature pale-backed, with dark outer wing. Juvenile has unform grey-brown face, with mottled back; black tail with broad white rump; bill dull yellow-green, with black tip.

Habitat. Coasts, bays and beaches, river mouths, fresh water beside coast; breeds mainly on offshore low, rocky islands among large stones and small bushes, on sandy beaches, or in low xerophytic scrub. Sometimes feeds over rice fields.

Food and Feeding. Relies mainly on fish, in particular clupeiforms, especially sardines; also insects and aquatic invertebrates, small birds, voles, plant matter (olives, peanuts and grain reported as locally important early in season); small passerines (particularly flycatchers), occasionally lizards and mice. Forages mainly at sea, sometimes quartering back and forth just offshore; joins other seabirds exploiting surface shoals of fish. Skims close to water and seizes fish from just below surface, without pausing. Readily exploits trawler discards (see page 598); during a moratorium on trawling, species shifted to feeding in marshes and rice fields, and also occasionally in rubbish dumps.

Breeding. Returns to colonies late Feb to mid-Apr; lays from late Apr; peak hatching late May. Colony size up to over 10,000 pairs (Ebro Delta, NE Spain); colonies usually monospecific, although sometimes breeds close to *L. cachinnans*; some colonies quite dense, up to 1 nest/m^2. Nest among rocks and vegetation, a scrape lined with debris. Usually 3 eggs (1-4, mean 1·9-2·8); incubation 26-33 days; chick pale grey-buff above, mottled dark brown, with marks forming stripes; hatching weight 46 g; fledging c. 35-40 days, with independence delayed to 3-4 months. Productivity sometimes very low.

Movements. Partially migratory, and dispersive. Disperses around coasts of Mediterranean; virtually all young birds and some adults pass Gibraltar to winter on coast of NW Africa, occurring S to Senegambia.

Status and Conservation. Not globally threatened. Conservation Dependent. Formerly considered Endangered, but now increasing slowly under protection. Colonies recently discovered in Aegean Sea and in Spain and Italy may have been newly established or overlooked. Inadequately known in 1981, this species is currently the most thoroughly censused of all gulls. As recently as 1966, total population was estimated at 800-1000 pairs, but in 1993 total estimated at 15,600 pairs in 30 colonies. It remains one of the most threatened seabirds, and a species of special concern; c. 72% of population breeds in two colonies: Ebro Delta, NE Spain, where no pairs at all in 1980, but 10,300 pairs in 1995; and in Chafarinas Is (off NE Morocco) with c. 2000 pairs in 1986, and 3500 in 1993; also c. 350 pairs in Italy, 210 pairs in Greece, and c. 500 pairs in Turkey. Species still threatened in E of range. Egging has a significant impact in some areas. Another threat at some colonies is from increasing *L. cachinnans* population, which pre-empts nest-sites and kills chicks, and rarely even adults; more chicks, however, are killed by conspecific adults. Predation by Peregrine Falcons (*Falco peregrinus*) is significant at some colonies, but probably has only minor effect on overall population. Extensive research and conservation work carried out in Spain in recent years (see page 598).

Bibliography. Álvarez (1994), Baillon (1989), Beaubrun (1983), Bournonville (1964), Bradley (1986), Brosset & Olier (1966), Castilla (1995), Castilla & Pérez (1995), Collar & Andrew (1988), Collar *et al*. (1994), Cramp & Simmons (1983), Demartis (1986), Dowsett & Forbes-Watson (1993), Evans (1984b), Fasola (1986), Fernández-Cruz (1974), Goodman *et al*. (1989), Hoogendoorn (1995a, 1995b), Hoogendoorn & Mackrill (1987), Jacob & Courbet (1980), de Juana (1984, 1986, 1994), de Juana & Varela (1987, 1993), de Juana, Bradley *et al*. (1987), de Juana, Bueno *et al*. (1979), de Juana, Varela & Witt (1984), King, J. & Shirihai (1996), King, W.B. (1978/79), Lambertini (1993, 1995), Mackrill (1989), Makatsch (1968, 1969b), Martínez & Motis (1982), Mayol (1978), Meschini *et al*. (1979), Monbailliu & Torre (1986), del Nevo *et al*. (1994), Oró (1995, 1996), Oró & Martínez-Vilalta (1992, 1994), Papacotsia *et al*. (1980), Paterson *et al*. (1992), Paz (1987), Pechuán (1974, 1975), Richards (1990), Ruiz *et al*. (1996), Shirihai (1996), Urban *et al*. (1986), Varela & de Juana (1987), Varela *et al*. (1980), Voous (1968a), Wallace (1969), Watson (1973), Witt (1974b, 1975, 1976, 1977a, 1977b), Witt, Crespo *et al*. (1981), Witt, Stempel *et al*. (1982).

12. Ring-billed Gull

Larus delawarensis

French: Goéland à bec cerclé **German**: Ringschnabelmöwe **Spanish**: Gaviota de Delaware

Taxonomy. *Larus Delawarensis* Ord, 1815, Philadelphia.
Morphometric analysis links it most closely with *L. californicus*. W population significantly larger and possibly subspecifically distinct. Monotypic.

Distribution. N California, E Washington and interior British Columbia across prairie provinces and N mountain and plains states; Great Lakes to Maritime Provinces. Winters in S portion of breeding range S to Gulf Coast, Central America and Greater Antilles, increasingly ranging to Lesser Antilles.

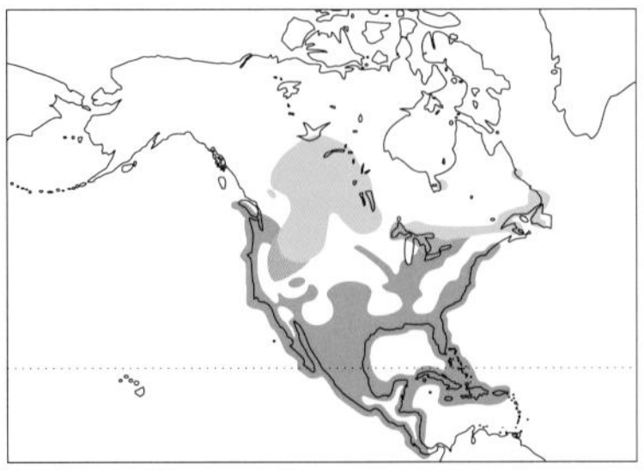

Descriptive notes. 46-54 cm; 400-590 g; wingspan 121-127 cm. White head, body and tail, grey mantle and wings; slender yellow bill, with black subterminal ring in adults; iris bright yellow, with red orbital ring; legs yellow-green. Male averages 7% larger, with longer, deeper bill. Paler and slightly bigger than *L. canus*, with less white at wingtip. Non-breeding adult has heavily streaked head. Juvenile has pinkish legs, and black-tipped pinkish bill; attains adult plumage in 3rd winter.

Habitat. Coasts, rivers and estuaries, reservoirs, rubbish dumps; breeds on low-lying islands in freshwater lakes, on wet meadows, rarely on rivers.

Food and Feeding. Fish, insects, earthworms, other invertebrates, refuse and offal; also swarming ants, fiddler crabs, dates, fish eggs, grain, rodents and birds. On tidal flats in Maine species preferentially selected ragworms (*Nereis virens*). Highly opportunistic. Garbage used mainly in winter, in spring, and after young fledge. Also feeds behind plough, and on wet lawns; some nocturnal feeding on night-surfacing fish. Most food picked up from ground. Captures fish by plunge-diving, rarely by skimming along surface. Kleptoparasitism reported.

Breeding. Lays late Apr to May; in N of range often delayed by snow cover. Colonies often very large. Large, bulky nest, often beside rock, driftwood or vegetation; often within 1 m of neighbour; nest-sites reused year after year, often by same pair. 3 eggs (mean 2·7-2·9); incubation 25-28 days; chick semi-precocial, hatches with eyes closed, remains in nest 24-48 hours, leaves nest-site by 4th day; small crèches may be formed in some colonies; fledging c. 37 days; departs from colony at c. 45 days.

Movements. Wanders N to Alaska and Yukon. Winters from S part of breeding range S to Greater Antilles; becoming commoner in Central America, both in the interior and along coasts; also occurs increasingly in Lesser Antilles; first recorded in Florida in 1930, now common in winter. E population migrates to Atlantic coast and S to Gulf Coast, few reaching West Indies and Central America. Birds of plains and mountain states move to Pacific coast. Large numbers remain on Great Lakes until freeze-up. Most Great Lakes birds return to the lake where they hatched, but not necessarily to same colony. Since mid-1970's has become regular vagrant to W Palearctic (see page 595), especially in British Is, where records span all months of the year; massive influx of over 400 individuals in first half of 1980's has led to species becoming a virtual resident in some coastal areas.

Status and Conservation. Not globally threatened. Population now estimated at c. 1,500,000-2,000,000 pairs. Declined dramatically during late 19th century, and fears were expressed for its future. In recent decades, however, an enormous increase has occurred. Now an abundant species, particularly on the Great Lakes, where its population has grown exponentially throughout 20th century to nearly 500,000 pairs, and where it is now considered a serious pest to other breeding birds. On Little Galloo I, L Ontario, increase from: c. 20,000 pairs in 1950; to 45,000 in 1955; 63,000 in 1961; 85,000 in 1968; and stabilized at c. 74,000 pairs from 1981, suggesting saturation. On L Huron and L Michigan, 27,000 pairs in 1960 increased to 150,000 by 1974. Range expanded greatly in mid-20th century. First bred in New York in 1936, California in 1940, and British Columbia in 1974.

Bibliography. Allan (1978), Ambrose (1986), Bayer (1980), Bent (1921), Blokpoel & Courtenay (1980), Blokpoel & Haymes (1979a, 1979b), Blokpoel & Scharf (1991a, 1991b), Blokpoel & Tessier (1986), Blokpoel, Blancher & Fetterolf (1985), Blokpoel, Weller *et al*. (1990), Boersma & Ryder (1983), Broun (1941), Brown & Morris (1994), Burger & Gochfeld (1979, 1983b, 1984b), Burger, J. & Staine (1993), Burger, Fitch *et al*. (1980), Cade (1982), Chardine & Morris (1983), Chudzik *et al*. (1994), Conover (1983b, 1984b, 1987), Conover & Conover (1981), Conover & Hunt (1984a, 1984b), Conover & Miller (1978, 1979, 1980), Conover, Miller & Hunt (1979), Conover, Thompson *et al*. (1979), Cramp & Simmons (1983), Dawson *et al*. (1976), Delude, Baron & McNeil (1987), Delude, McNeil & Baron (1988), Dexheimer & Southern (1974), Dowsett & Forbes-Watson (1993), Drury (1984), Dubois & Frémont (1996), Elston & Southern (1983), Emlen (1956), Emlen & Miller (1969), Emlen *et al*. (1966), Evans, R.M. (1970a, 1973, 1975, 1977, 1980), Evans, R.M. & Welham (1985), Evans, R.M. *et al*. (1994), Fetterolf (1979, 1983a, 1983b, 1984a, 1984b, 1984c), Fox & Boersma (1983), Freitag & Ryder (1973), Grace (1980), Grant (1979), Haymes & Blokpoel (1978a, 1980), Hayward *et al*. (1982), Howell & Webb (1995a), Howells (1968), Jarvis & Southern (1976), Johnston, D.W. & Foster (1954), Johnston, V.H. & Ryder (1987), Kinkel & Southern (1978), Kirkham & Morris (1979), Kovacs & Ryder (1981, 1983), Lagrenade & Mousseau (1983), Lauro & Spencer (1980), Leck (1971), Lock (1988), Ludwig (1974), MacLean (1986), Maxwell & Smith (1983), Meathrel & Ryder (1987a, 1987b), Miller & Conover (1979), Miller & Emlen (1975), Nol & Blokpoel (1983), Patton & Southern (1978), Richards (1990), Ryder, J.P. (1975, 1983, 1993), Ryder, J.P. & Somppi (1977, 1979), Ryder, J.P. *et al*. (1977), Ryder, P.L. & Ryder (1981), Shugart (1976), Southern, L.K. (1981), Southern, L.K. & Southern (1980, 1982, 1983), Southern, L.K. *et al*. (1982), Southern, W.E. (1967, 1974, 1977, 1980), Southern, W.E. & Southern (1982), Spencer & Lauro (1984), Tolonen (1970), Tove (1993), Urban *et al*. (1986), Vermeer (1969, 1973b), Welham (1987), Weseloh & Myers (1981), Weseloh *et al*. (1983), Wetmore (1965), Yésou (1985).

13. California Gull

Larus californicus

French: Goéland de Californie **German**: Kaliforniermöwe **Spanish**: Gaviota Californiana

Taxonomy. *Larus Californicus* Lawrence, 1854, Stockton, California.
Fossil from late Pleistocene of Oregon. The races, formerly disjunct, have recently come together in N plains, where a zone of secondary contact is forming; genetic studies have shown little divergence between them. Two subspecies currently recognized.

Subspecies and Distribution.
L. c. albertaensis Jehl, 1987- S Mackenzie (Great Slake L), Alberta and W Manitoba to South Dakota.
L. c. californicus Lawrence, 1854 - E Washington and Great Basin to C Montana and Wyoming.
Winters mainly from SW Canada to SW Mexico.

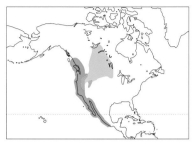

Descriptive notes. 51-58 cm; *californicus* 432-885 g, *albertaensis* 568-1045 g; wingspan 122-140 cm. Typical white-headed gull; bill yellow, with red gonydeal spot edged in black; legs yellowish; iris dark brown, with red orbital ring. Male averages 6% larger than female, with head and bill c. 8% larger. Non-breeding adult has heavy brown streaking on head and neck. Juvenile dusky brown with creamy buff edges, all black primaries, all brown tail, and bill with sharply defined black tip. Race *albertaensis* larger, with paler mantle.

Habitat. Coasts, estuaries, bays, mudflats, marshes, freshwater wetlands, lawns, agricultural fields; breeds in open habitats in arid interior, usually on low rocky islands in both freshwater and hypersaline lakes.

Food and Feeding. Insects and grubs (especially Orthoptera), bird eggs and young, earthworms, crabs, rodents, carrion, rubbish, fruit and grain; locusts are commonest animal matter, although bird eggs the highest volume. Renowned for destruction of crickets, grasshoppers. In British Columbia, fed mainly on grain at one colony, rubbish at a second, and insects at a third. Some populations specialize on bird eggs; capable of killing chicks of Canada Goose (*Branta canadensis*); may almost eliminate duck production on some lakes. Eats carcasses of adult birds killed by botulism, as well as road-killed animals. Takes rodents when these are abundant, particularly when flooded out of their burrows. Can be a serious pest at cherry and strawberry farms. Feeds mainly by picking; also surface-plunges, e.g. for crabs.

Breeding. Returns to colonies in early Mar; lays late Apr to May; hatching mostly from early Jun (mid-May). Mated pairs tend to be of same age, probably because of long-term monogamy. Upper Critical Density (UCD) of colonies c. 50 pairs/100 m², but no depression of productivity even at 77 pairs/100 m²; centrally located sites with protective shrubs support high density nesting, and are more productive; in years of high density, territorial aggression increases adult mortality through injury. Lays 3 eggs in most of range (over 80% of clutches in British Columbia), but normally 2 in Great Basin (e.g. Mono L); at Mono L, 2-chick broods more successful than those of 1 or 3; incubation 26-28 days; chick whitish, with buff band across with breast, mottled dark brown blotches above, blacker and more sharply defined on head; fledging c. 40 days. Chicks of older parents grew more rapidly and were more likely to fledge. Productivity from 0·12/nest for 1-egg clutches to 0·35/nest for 2-egg clutches.

Movements. Wanders to SE Alaska. Winters mostly along Pacific coast to S Baja California and Colima, and locally elsewhere in Mexico. Saskatchewan breeders migrate W to coastal British Columbia, then disperse S as far as Sinaloa.

Status and Conservation. Not globally threatened. Total population approaching 200,000 pairs at over 100 colony sites. Numbers were seriously reduced by commercial egging in late 19th century, but from early 20th century species was protected, and even esteemed, for its role in destroying crickets. In mid-1930's, however, reported as an agricultural pest on cherries, and more recently recognized as a serious predator on ducks. USA population grew at 2% per year, from c. 50,000 pairs in 1930 to nearly 140,000 in 1980, while number of colonies increased from 15 to 80. There were at least 17,000 pairs at known colonies in Canada. Largest colonies are at Great Salt L and Mono L. Population increase has been accompanied by range expansion.

Bibliography. Ainley & Hunt (1991), Armstrong (1983), Behle & Goates (1957), Bent (1921), Clapp *et al.* (1982), Conover (1983b, 1984b), Conover & Conover (1981), Conover & Hunt (1984b), Conover & Miller (1980), Conover, Miller & Hunt (1979), Conover, Thompson *et al.* (1979), Drury (1984), Greenhalgh (1952), Hayward *et al.* (1982), Howell & Webb (1995a), Jehl (1987b, 1989, 1994a), Jehl & Chase (1987), Jehl & Mahoney (1987), Jehl, Babb & Power (1984, 1988), Jehl, Francine & Bond (1990), Johnston (1956a, 1956b), Karl *et al.* (1987), Mahoney & Jehl (1985a), Nur (1984), Pugesek (1981, 1983, 1984, 1987, 1990, 1993), Pugesek & Diem (1983, 1986, 1990), Richards (1990), Root (1988), Schnell *et al.* (1985), Smith & Diem (1972), Southern (1980), Vermeer (1969), Wahl (1977), Winkler (1985), Winkler & Shuford (1988), Young (1952), Zink & Winkler (1983).

14. **Great Black-backed Gull**

Larus marinus

French: Goéland marin   **German**: Mantelmöwe   **Spanish**: Gavión Atlántico

Taxonomy. *Larus marinus* Linnaeus, 1758, Gotland, Sweden.
Monotypic.

Distribution. Great Lakes, E Canada and USA to North Carolina; S Greenland; Iceland, Faeroes, British Is, NW France and Scandinavia E to at least White Sea, including Bear I and Spitsbergen. Winters S to West Indies and Iberia, occasionally reaching Morocco.

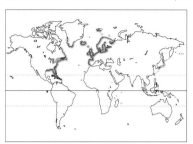

Descriptive notes. 68-79 cm; 1435-2272 g; wingspan 152-167 cm. Largest gull; large-winged, with massive head and bill, particularly in male; white head, underbody and tail, with slaty black back and upperwings; bill yellow, with red gonydeal spot; legs pink; iris yellow, with red orbital ring. Juvenile heavily mottled white and pale brown, with all dark bill. Immature similar, but with distinctive whitish head and breast; black subterminal tail band; bill pale, with dark tip.

Habitat. Rocky or sandy coasts, estuaries and open sea; locally larger inland waters, fields and moorland; breeds on vegetated islands, dunes, flat-topped stacks, sometimes salt-marsh islands among bushes, and locally on buildings.

Food and Feeding. Omnivorous and opportunistic. Fish, adult and young birds, bird eggs, mammals, marine invertebrates, insects, carrion, rubbish, offal and berries. Fish include e.g. cod (*Gadus morhua*), herring (*Clupea harengus*), capelin (*Mallotus villosus*). Aggressive predator, particularly on eggs and chicks of *L. argentatus*, *Rissa tridactyla*, ducks, seabirds, and other species. Can kill adult birds: has major impact on alcid populations in Scotland, but perhaps not in Newfoundland; seriously impairs Common Eider (*Somateria mollissima*) productivity; takes large numbers of Manx Shearwaters (*Puffinus puffinus*). Eats rodents, rabbits, lemmings, rats and mice; occasionally young lambs (Iceland); sometimes fruits. Cracks molluscs and goose eggs by dropping them on hard surfaces; kills young birds in same way. Scavenges on shore, also at rubbish dumps. Some reports of kleptoparasitism.

Breeding. Lays from early Apr in S to mid-May in N. Usually small colonies, near or intermingled with *L. argentatus*, and often solitary pairs among other species; few large colonies (e.g. 700 pairs at Placentia Bay, Newfoundland); chick mortality increases with number of neighbouring territories and frequency of agonistic encounters; normally uses open sandy, grassy or rocky substrate. Bulky nest of dry grass, moss and seaweed, often next to rock or vegetation; nearest-neighbour distance in colonies 5-20 m; shows nest-site tenacity. Adults more aggressive to non-neighbouring intruders than to neighbours. Usually 3 eggs (1-3); incubation c. 26-28 days; chick pale grey with large black spots; hatching weight 80-90 g; fledging c. 7-8 weeks. Productivity often high. First breeding at 4-5 years.

Movements. Variable. High Arctic birds migrate S, while southern breeders disperse shorter distances. Most Icelandic birds disperse around the island, but some juveniles reach Britain. Complex pattern, since Norwegian birds move mainly W and SW to North Sea and Britain, while Swedish and Finnish breeders move mainly E and S into Baltic. North American recoveries were all within 800 km of breeding colony, but numbers reaching Gulf Coast are increasing, and a few reach West Indies.

Status and Conservation. Not globally threatened. Total population at least 200,000 pairs, with c. 30% in Norway. Population of W Palearctic under 200,000 pairs, including 23,000 in British Is in 1987. Greenland c. 10,000 pairs; E North America tallied 17,415 pairs in 1983. Has increased and extended range S between 1930's and 1975, as well as spreading N to Spitsbergen, but breeding populations appear to have stabilized since then, perhaps related to closing of landfills. Increased greatly in Iceland in 20th century, and now the commonest large gull there. In Nearctic, range has extended S considerably since mid-20th century; first bred in Maine in 1928, Massachusetts in 1931, New York in 1940, Great Lakes in 1954, and New Jersey in 1966; New England population increased from 30 pairs in 1930 to 12,400 in 1972. Species is considered a threat to other bird species, particularly eiders, and control measures were advocated as early as 1945.

Bibliography. Addy (1945), Ali & Ripley (1982), Ambrose (1986), Barth (1967a, 1967b), Beaman (1978), Bent (1921), Bergman (1982b), Blokpoel & Scharf (1991b), Bourget (1973), Brown & Nettleship (1984b), Buckley & Buckley (1984b), Burger, J. (1978b, 1983a, 1983b), Burger, J. & Gochfeld (1981b, 1983a, 1984a), Butler & Janes-Butler (1982, 1983), Butler & Trivelpiece (1981), Clapp *et al.* (1982), Cleghorn (1942), Cobb (1957), Cramp & Simmons (1983), Dowsett & Forbes-Watson (1993), Dunn (1994), Eaton (1931), Erwin (1971), Evans (1984a, 1984b), Foxall (1979), Good (1992), Götmark (1982), Götmark & Ahlund (1988), Gross (1945), Guðmundsson (1954), Harllee (1933), Harris (1964), Heg (1991), Howell & Webb (1995a), Ilicev & Zubakin (1988), Ingolfsson (1970a, 1976), Jackson & Allan (1932), de Juana (1986), Kilpi & Saurola (1984a), Knystautas (1993), Kuerzi (1936), Lien (1975), Lloyd *et al.* (1991), Parnell & Soots (1975), Paz (1987), Peakall (1967), Perennou *et al.* (1994), Pierotti (1983), Richards (1990), Roberts, T.J. (1991), Root (1988), Shirihai (1996), Southern (1980), Tasker *et al.* (1987), Taylor, K. (1985), Transue & Burger (1989), Urban *et al.* (1986), Vandenbuicke (1989), Verbeek (1979b), Walters (1978), Wilcox (1944).

15

16

ssp *occidentalis*

17

ssp *wymani*

18

19

ssp *glaucoides*

20

21

ssp *kumlieni*

22

ssp *argentatus*

23

ssp *atlantis*

ssp *cachinnans*

ssp *vegae*

ssp *argenteus*

24

PLATE 51

inches   10
cm   25

25

ssp *fuscus*

26

ssp *graellsii*   ssp *heuglini*

15. **Kelp Gull**

Larus dominicanus

French: Goéland dominicain **German**: Dominikanermöwe **Spanish**: Gaviota Cocinera
Other common names: Dominican Gull (New Zealand), Southern Black-backed Gull (Africa, Australia)

Taxonomy. *Larus dominicanus* Lichtenstein, 1823, coasts of Brazil.
South Shetlands population formerly separated as *austrinus*, but matched by birds elsewhere in S of range. Some authors give subspecific status to South African population, race *vetula*, based mainly on its mottled brown iris. Monotypic.
Distribution. S Africa, from Namibia (Cape Cross) to Cape Province (Algoa Bay), and S Madagascar; S Australia and New Zealand; N Peru and S Brazil (São Paulo) S to Tierra del Fuego, and Falkland Is; subantarctic islands and Antarctica.

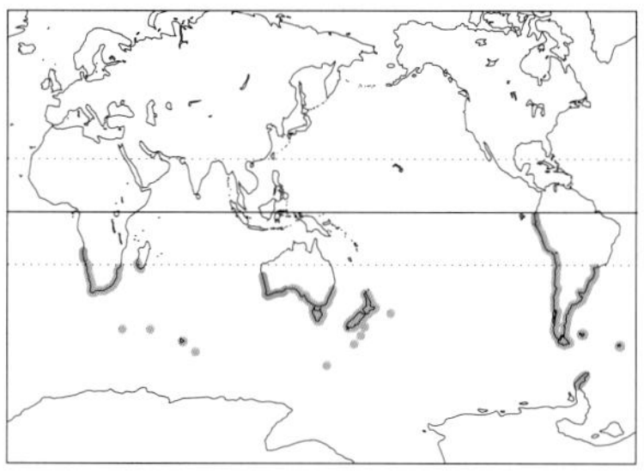

Descriptive notes. 54-65 cm; 900-1335 g; wingspan 128-142. Typical large, white-headed, black-mantled gull, with white tail; black upperwings with white trailing edge and white windows at tips; bill yellow, with red gonydeal spot; legs greenish yellow, greyer in Africa; iris yellow, with red to orange-red orbital ring. Similar to *L. pacificus*, but lacks black tail band and has thinner bill. In Africa, distinguished from *L. fuscus* by greyish rather than yellow legs, and heavier bill and body. Non-breeding adult has some brown mottling on head and neck. Juvenile dark brown, speckled with buff and whitish on head, neck, back and underparts; flight- and tail feathers dark brown with buff edges, secondaries and scapulars tipped with white. Immature has much white on rump and tail; 3rd-year similar to non-breeding adult; full adult plumage achieved in 4th year.
Habitat. Mainly coastal regions, exclusively so in S Africa, but elsewhere often visits large inland lakes (e.g. in Andes of Argentina), and feeds or roosts at lakes (including mountain tarns in New Zealand), reservoirs, estuaries and rivers, and on lawns and farmland; breeds on oceanic and offshore islands, headlands, sea cliffs, beaches, pastures, lava fields, rocky islands in rivers and urban areas.
Food and Feeding. Very varied. Molluscs, fish, echinoderms, worms, arthropods, reptiles, amphibians, small mammals, birds and occasionally swarming termites (*Microhodotermes viator*); scavenges rubbish, fish offal, sewage and carrion; steals food from terns. Occasionally takes sickly lambs and young poultry; may attack and kill adult birds as big as geese. In Antarctica main food is Antarctic limpet (*Nacella concinna*). At Valdés Peninsula, SC Argentina, associates with right whales (*Eubalaena glacialis*), capturing stirred-up invertebrates; also lands on whales and eats living flesh. Frequents slaughterhouses and also fish and seafood factories; sometimes at sewage outfalls; follows boats at sea. Feeds by plunge-diving, dabbling in water and picking from ground; also opens shellfish by dropping them onto hard surfaces.
Breeding. Oct in S Africa, Sept-Dec in Australia, mid-Oct to Jan in New Zealand, mid-Nov on subantarctic islands, Dec in Falklands; mainly Oct-Dec in South America, but on guano islands at any time (cycle adjusted to seabird breeding). Usually in colonies of dozens (particularly at edges of range) to 100's of pairs, occasionally solitary; nest density 20-106 nests/ha. On sandy or rocky substrates, often well vegetated; bulky nest of dried plants or seaweed, often at base of bush, tree, rock or other vertical structure. 3 eggs; incubation 24-30 days; fledging c. 7 weeks.
Movements. In S Africa, non-breeding visitor as far as Mozambique. In Australia, non-breeding birds disperse N to Queensland, and along S coast; accidental on N coast and in interior. Some N movement of New Zealand birds, but many remain near breeding grounds. Falklands birds are resident, but disperse widely around the islands, while some of those from S South America migrate N to winter with their subtropical counterparts. Birds remain in Antarctica throughout year, frequenting open water away from pack ice.
Status and Conservation. Not globally threatened. Common and conspicuous over much of range. Over 1,000,000 pairs in New Zealand, perhaps 50,000 in South America and Falklands, 15,000 in S Africa, and 10,000-20,000 in Antarctica and subantarctic; only a few hundred pairs (but increasing) in Australia, where first seen in 1943, first bred in 1958, and now breeds from S Western Australia E around coast to Tasmania and New South Wales. Has increased throughout range with expansion of agriculture and fisheries.
Bibliography. Appleton & Randall (1986), Belton (1984), Bernstein (1983), Berutti *et al*. (1979), Blake (1977), Blankley (1981), Brooke (1976), Brooke & Cooper (1979a, 1979b), Brooke *et al*. (1982), Burger & Gochfeld (1981a, 1981e), Canevari *et al*. (1991), Chambers (1989), Cooper (1977b), Cooper *et al*. (1984), Coulson & Coulson (1993), Crawford *et al*. (1982), Donnelly (1966), Dowsett & Forbes-Watson (1993), Duffy (1983), Escalante (1991), Favero *et al*. (1991), Fjeldså & Krabbe (1990), Fordham (1963, 1964a, 1964b, 1967, 1968, 1970), Ginn *et al*. (1989), Hockey (1980), Hockey, Ryan & Bosman (1989), Howell & Webb (1995a), James (1995), Johnson (1967), Kinsky (1963), Klimaitis & Moschione (1987), Koepcke & Koepcke (1971), Langrand (1990), Mackworth-Praed & Grant (1962), Maclean (1993), Marchant & Higgins (1996), Maxson & Bernstein (1980, 1984), Merilees (1969), Milon *et al*. (1973), Moynihan (1962), Murphy (1936), de la Peña (1992), Pinto (1983), Shaughnessy (1980), Sick (1985c, 1993), Siegfried (1977), Steele (1992a), Steele & Hockey (1990), Summers (1977), Taylor & Wodzicki (1958), Thomas (1988), Urban *et al*. (1986), Verheyden (1993), Ward (1991), Williams (1977a), Williams *et al*. (1984), Zuquim (1991).

16. **Glaucous-winged Gull**

Larus glaucescens

French: Goéland à ailes grises **German**: Beringmöwe **Spanish**: Gaviota de Bering

Taxonomy. *Larus glaucescens* J. F. Naumann, 1840, North America.
Fossil from late Pleistocene, prehistoric specimens from Alaska and California. Closely linked with *L. hyperboreus* and *L. argentatus*, and hybridizes with both. Hybridizes freely with *L. occidentalis* from S British Columbia to Oregon, and by some authors treated as conspecific. Monotypic.
Distribution. Commander Is E through Aleutians, Pribilofs and S Bering Sea to S Alaska, then SE to N Oregon. Winters from Bering Sea to N Japan and Baja California.
Descriptive notes. 61-68 cm; 900-1250 g; wingspan 132-137 cm. Head, body and tail white; thick bill yellow, with red gonydeal spot; legs flesh-coloured; iris dark brown, with dull red orbital ring. Like *L. argentatus*, but bulkier, with paler grey mantle, and pale grey rather than black primaries. Non-breeding adult has head and neck streaked with brownish grey; in autumn the red gonydeal spot becomes obscured with black in c. 90% of adults. Immature pale greyish with pale mottling; tail ashy grey; bill blackish. Hybrids with *L. hyperboreus* and *L. argentatus* (S Alaska) often have dark iris (*L. glaucescens* trait); hybrids with *L. argentatus* may have dark grey (but not black) primaries (*L. argentatus* trait), but back-crosses can resemble either parental species, as well as *L. thayeri*. Hybrids with *L. occidentalis* (which in some areas outnumber both parental types) have intermediate mantle colour and primaries, and are similar to *L. argentatus*; difficult to identify outside their normal range.

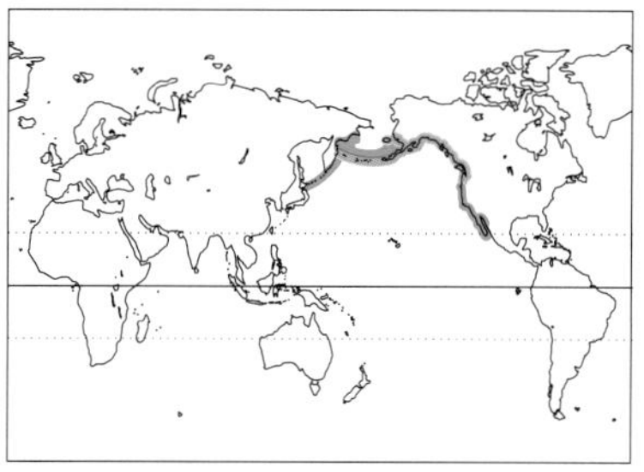

Habitat. Coastal areas and shelf waters; breeds on barren, rocky or vegetated islands, bays and estuaries, grassy meadows, cliffs, inland lakes (Alaska), city parks, breakwaters and buildings (on roofs), showing preference for smaller, flatter, and less forested islands with more bare rock and low herbaceous cover.
Food and Feeding. Fish, various marine invertebrates (e.g. mussels, barnacles, crabs, starfish, sea urchins), carrion, offal, bird eggs and small mammals. In breeding season, predominant foods vary from invertebrates to fish, to birds; at Cape Thompson (Alaska), fed mainly on murre (*Uria*) eggs; on W coast of Vancouver ate gooseneck barnacles (*Pollicipes polymerus*), and fed sandeels (*Ammodytes hexapterus*), herring (*Clupea harengus*) and sauries (*Colalabis saira*) to chicks. Cannibalistic in colonies. Swims in rivers and plucks salmon roe; feeds on remains of bear-killed or dying fish during spawning runs; exploits raptors for their catches. Feeding habitats vary with local conditions and competitors; favours intertidal zones near some colonies, avoids them elsewhere. Variety of feeding methods including plunge-diving, diving from the surface, walking etc.; drops shellfish on rocks. Makes daily round trips of up to 140 km to feeding grounds (e.g. Vancouver).
Breeding. Arrives back at colonies in Feb-Mar; lays from early May in Washington, early Jun in Alaska. Older birds breed earlier in season; 95% retain mates between years. Usually colonial (up to 2000 pairs), often solitary, including nests on some artificial structures. Nests on various substrates, often in the open, but shifts to denser colonies when Bald Eagles (*Haliaeetus leucocephalus*) are present, the eagles taking adult gulls, as well as chicks. Mean territory size 5-20 m². Usually 2-3 eggs (1-6, mean 2·82); incubation 26-28 days; chick grey-brown, tinged yellowish below, with blackish blotches; fledging c. 45 days. Breeding success often rather low; c.45% of chick mortality inflicted by neighbouring adults, with mortality heaviest in 1st week. Average age of first breeding 5·4 years, with no difference between sexes.
Movements. Some birds remain on territory all winter, but most move S; some wander S of Bering Sea into open N Pacific. Alaskan birds move S ahead of ice margin. 1st-year birds migrate further (up to 2000 km), some reaching Baja California. Stragglers reach coast of China.
Status and Conservation. Not globally threatened. Total population probably c. 250,000-300,000 pairs. In Alaska 135,000 pairs at over 600 sites, and increasing; marginal in Commander Is, with few thousand pairs. Has expanded S and N, leading to increased hybridization with *L. occidentalis* in Washington and with *L. hyperboreus* in Alaska. Is now becoming a nuisance in cities, and a safety risk at airports. Foxes cause this gull to desert some breeding islands.
Bibliography. Amlaner & Stout (1978), Armstrong (1983), Baird (1990), Barash *et al*. (1975), Beaman (1994), Brazil (1991), Butler *et al*. (1980), Drury (1984), Firsova (1983), Galusha & Stout (1977), Gillett *et al*. (1975), Hoffman *et al*. (1978), Hooper (1988), Howell & Webb (1995a), Hughes, M.R. (1984), Ilicev & Zubakin (1988), Irons (1987), Irons *et al*. (1986), James-Veitch & Booth (1954), Jyrkkanen (1975), Knystautas (1993), Kvitek (1991), Lensink (1984), Merilees (1974), Morgan *et al*. (1978), Mossman (1958), Moyle (1966), Murphy, Day *et al*. (1984), Murphy, Hoover-Miller *et al*. (1992), Patten & Weisbrod (1974), Pearse (1946), Reid (1987a, 1987b, 1988a, 1988b, 1988c), Richards (1990), Roberts, B. (1985), Rockwell (1982), Rodway (1991), Root (1988), Salzer & Larkin (1990), Scott (1971), Searcy (1978), Southern (1980), Sprout (1937), Stout (1975), Stout & Brass (1969), Stout *et al*. (1969), Trapp (1979), Verbeek (1979a, 1984, 1986, 1988, 1993), Vermeer (1963, 1982), Vermeer & Devito (1987), Vermeer & Irons (1991), Vermeer & Sealy (1984), Vermeer, Morgan & Smith (1992), Vermeer, Morgan, Smith & York (1991), Vermeer, Power & Smith (1988), Weber & Fitzner (1986), Williamson & Peyton (1963).

17. **Western Gull**

Larus occidentalis

French: Goéland d'Audubon **German**: Westmöwe **Spanish**: Gaviota Occidental

Taxonomy. *Larus occidentalis* Audubon, 1839, Cape Disappointment, Washington.
Interbreeds freely with *L. glaucescens* at N end of range. Two subspecies recognized.
Subspecies and Distribution.
L. o. occidentalis Audubon, 1839 - NW Washington (Destruction I) to C California (Farallon Is).
L. o. wymani Dickey & Van Rossem, 1925 - C California (Monterey Bay) to C Baja California (Guadalupe I).

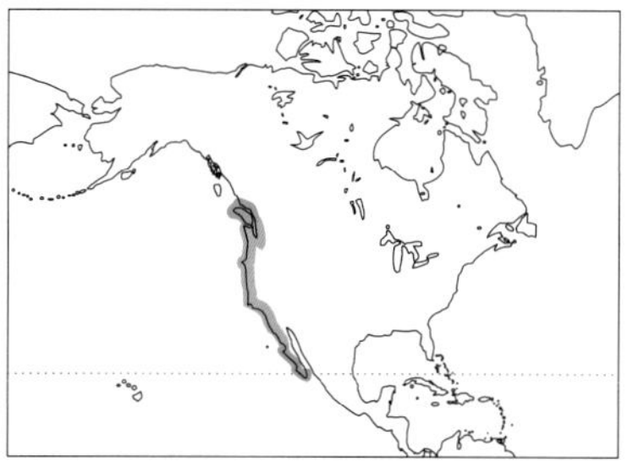

Descriptive notes. 54-66 cm; 800-1190 g; wingspan 132-142 cm. Typical large, white-headed gull with dark mantle; bill bright yellow, with red gonydeal spot; legs and feet pink; iris amber-yellow, with orange-yellow to pinkish yellow orbital ring. Larger than *L. fuscus*, with more sloping head, and longer, heavier bill; iris darker than in *L. argentatus* and *L. fuscus*; gonydeal spot smaller and rounder than in other dark-mantled gulls. Non-breeding adult has moderately streaked head. Juvenile mottled dark brown, with pale-barred rump, blackish flight-feathers, and black bill. Immature has pale head and underparts, grey back, and flesh-coloured bill base. Races differ in mantle colour, slaty in *occidentalis*, blacker in *wymani*; non-breeding adult *wymani* has less head streaking.
Habitat. Essentially confined to the coast, generally straying only a few kilometres inland; breeds on rocky islets with some herbaceous cover and gravelly beaches, often near California sea-lions (*Zalophus californianus*).

On following pages: 18. Yellow-footed Gull (*Larus livens*); 19. Glaucous Gull (*Larus hyperboreus*); 20. Iceland Gull (*Larus glaucoides*); 21. Thayer's Gull (*Larus thayeri*); 22. Herring Gull (*Larus argentatus*); 23. Yellow-legged Gull (*Larus cachinnans*); 24. Armenian Gull (*Larus armenicus*); 25. Slaty-backed Gull (*Larus schistisagus*); 26. Lesser Black-backed Gull (*Larus fuscus*).

Food and Feeding. Very varied. Marine fish and invertebrates; eggs, chicks and adults of seabirds; carrion; occasionally moves up rivers to exploit spawning salmon. At Farallon Is, takes rockfish (*Sebastes jordani*). Predation on seabirds increases when other foods scarce. Associates with seals, and eat placentae; may attack and kill newborn pups. A few individuals, mainly males, establish feeding territories in alcid or cormorant colonies, feeding mainly by predation, piracy and scavenging; these specialists occupy same territory year after year. Much food obtained by scavenging. Drops shellfish onto rocks to break them.

Breeding. Lays late Apr to early May, later in N. Colonial, with inter-nest distances ranging from 1·75 m in centre to over 30 m at periphery; killing of neighbouring chicks more serious in dense areas. Sites on ridges of islands preferred. Nest on barren substrate, surrounded by stones, guano and feathers. Usually 3 eggs (1-5, mean usually 2·3-2·7); in some colonies 4- and 5-egg clutches common (from female-female pairs), but these have lower hatching success, and eggshells thinner; incubation 23-28 days; chicks under 10 days attended 97% of time, fed by both parents; in one study, males made equal number of feedings but provided lower-quality food; fledging c. 6 weeks, but parental care continues until at least 70 days. Hatching success 55-80%. Young chicks are vulnerable to heat stress, and heatwaves cause mass mortality, particularly in microhabitats with low wind velocity. Age at first breeding 4·8 years for males, 6·2 years for females; average number of breeding seasons 6·2 years for males, 5·2 for females.

Movements. Post-breeding movement to British Columbia and accidentally to peninsular Alaska, also S to the tip of Baja California and occasionally to Sonora coast of Mexico. Birds from S colonies disperse, those from N colonies migrate S. Migration distance correlated with latitude, and young birds move further than adults. Farallon Is birds are mainly sedentary, adults maintaining breeding territories most of year. Young birds disperse N to areas of high oceanic productivity in summer, and move S to San Francisco Bay in winter. Dispersal of young varies from year to year, depending on food availability, but adults tend to return to the same site each winter.

Status and Conservation. Not globally threatened. Common in most of its range, but total population only c. 32,000 pairs (certainly less than 50,000); the rarest gull in North America. Altogether 13,000 pairs (c. 40% of population) breed on Southeast Farallon I, which lies in a major shipping channel. Subject to effects of pesticides, oil pollution, and consequences of El Niño (see Volume 1, page 341); also to human disturbance, which lowers productivity. Hybridization with *L. glaucescens* is an adverse factor in the maintenance of the species. Is frequently subjected to control measures of wildlife managers, seeking to protect other species of waterfowl and seabirds which may actually be far more numerous.

Bibliography. Ainley & Hunt (1991), Annett & Pierotti (1989), Aurioles & Llinas (1987), Bayer (1983), Bent (1921), Carter & Spear (1986), Clapp *et al.* (1982), Coulter (1970, 1975, 1977), DeSante & Ainley (1980), Drury (1984), Everett & Anderson (1991), Ewald *et al.* (1980), Hand (1980, 1981b, 1986), Hand *et al.* (1981), Harper (1971), Hoffman *et al.* (1978), Howell & Webb (1995a), Hunt & Hunt (1973, 1975, 1976a, 1976b, 1977), Hunt *et al.* (1980), Maron (1982), McCaskie (1983), Pearse (1946), Pierotti (1981), Pierotti & Annett (1995), Pierotti & Bellrose (1986), Pyle *et al.* (1991), Robert & Ralph (1975), Richards (1990), Root (1988), Salzman (1982), Sayce & Hunt (1987), Schreiber (1970), Scott (1971), Southern (1980), Spear (1980, 1988, 1993), Spear & Nur (1994), Spear, Henderson & Ainley (1986), Spear, Penniman *et al.* (1987), Spear, Sydeman & Pyle (1995), Sydeman & Emslie (1992), Sydeman *et al.* (1991).

18. **Yellow-footed Gull**

Larus livens

French: Goéland de Cortez **German**: Gelbfußmöwe **Spanish**: Gaviota de Cortés

Taxonomy. *Larus occidentalis livens* Dwight, 1919, San José Island, Baja California.
Until recently treated as a race of *L. occidentalis*, but differs in vocal repertoire, particularly its lower-pitched long call. Some authorities consider it more closely related to, and perhaps derived from, *L. dominicanus*. Monotypic.

Distribution. NW Mexico, in Gulf of California; rare in S California, USA.

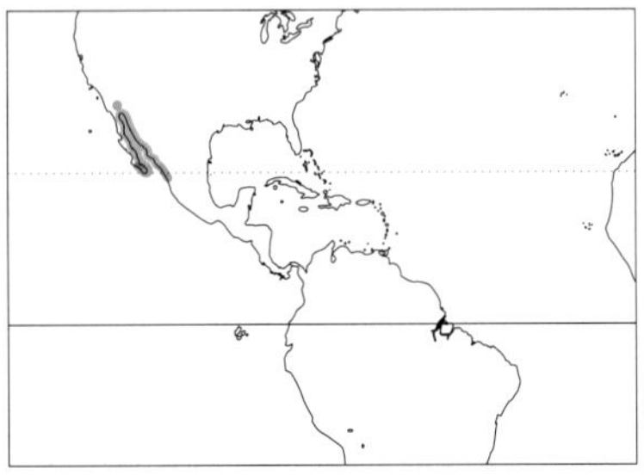

Descriptive notes. 60-67 cm; 1110-1400 g; wingspan 142-155 cm. Typical white headed, dark-mantled gull; iris yellow. Separated from *L. occidentalis* most clearly by yellow legs; also slightly larger size, and heavier bill. Juvenile differs from juvenile *L. occidentalis* in whiter underparts and rump, and bolder spotting on back; head dark, intermediate between *L. occidentalis* and *L. argentatus*.

Habitat. Sandy and rocky islands, usually with little or no vegetation.

Food and Feeding. Fish, invertebrates, carcasses of marine mammals, and offal; takes small seabirds (petrels), pelican eggs, crabs, fish and food scraps. Preys on eggs and young of *L. heermanni* and Elegant Tern (*Thalasseus elegans*), and is a serious threat at some colonies.

Breeding. Essentially undescribed. Egg-laying in early Apr. Most colonies under 100 pairs; occasionally solitary. To reduce heat stress, nests are distributed in linear form, parallel to high tide line, allowing unimpeded access to water. Mean nearest-neighbour distance in 9 colonies 594-1070 cm.

Movements. Some post-breeding dispersal N to Salton Sea, and rarely to Californian coast; disperses S to Sonora, and rarely to Guerrero.

Status and Conservation. Not globally threatened. Probably requires reclassification as Vulnerable, due to very low numbers and small range. Population possibly as low as 3600 pairs in 11 documented colonies, ranging from 200 to 600 pairs each. Shows some local increases which may jeopardize other seabirds. One of the least studied and least known of all gull species, and also clearly one of the least numerous; extensive research needed on biology, ecology, status, trends, and conservation requirements.

Bibliography. Anderson (1983), Devillers *et al.* (1971), Drury (1984), Dunning (1988), Dwight (1919), Everett & Anderson (1991), Hand (1981b), Howell & Webb (1995a), McCaskie (1983), Penniman *et al.* (1990), Richards (1990), Rodríguez-Estrella *et al.* (1995), Spear & Anderson (1989), Velarde (1992), Velarde & Anderson (1994), Wilbur (1987).

19. **Glaucous Gull**

Larus hyperboreus

French: Goéland bourgmestre **German**: Eismöwe **Spanish**: Gavión Hiperbóreo

Taxonomy. *Larus hyperboreus* Gunnerus, 1767, northern Norway.
Variously considered monotypic or polytypic; subspecific distinctions subtle. Race *leuceretes* sometimes merged into nominate race. *Larus glaucus* is a synonym for *L. canus*. Four subspecies normally recognized.

Subspecies and Distribution.
L. h. hyperboreus Gunnerus, 1767 - Jan Mayen and Spitsbergen E to Taymyr Peninsula.
L. h. pallidissimus Portenko, 1939 - Taymyr Peninsula E to Bering Sea, including Pribilof Is.
L. h. barrovianus Ridgway, 1886 - Alaska to W Canada (NW Mackenzie region).
L. h. leuceretes Schleep, 1819 - E Mackenzie region through N Canadian archipelago to Greenland and Iceland.
Winters S to CW Europe, Japan and CW & CE USA.

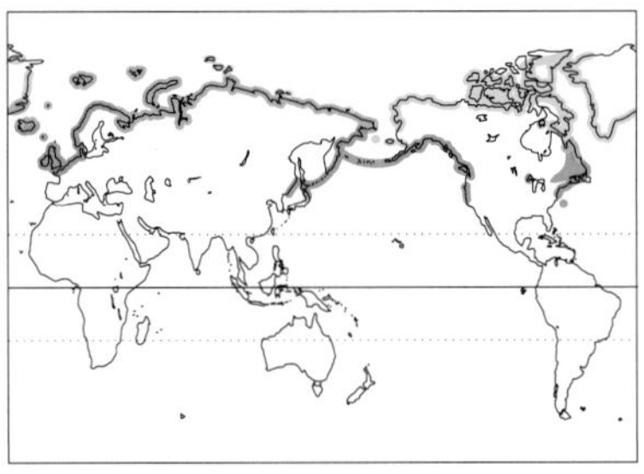

Descriptive notes. 64-77 cm; 1070-1820 g; wingspan 132-142 cm. One of the largest gulls; plumage all white, except for pale grey mantle and upperwings; all flight-feathers tipped white; bill yellow, with red gonydeal spot; legs pinkish; iris pale yellow, with red orbital ring. Similar to *L. glaucoides* but larger; appears heavier-bodied and proportionately shorter-winged. Has shorter wing, heavier bill and paler mantle than *L. argentatus*, and lacks dark markings on primary tips. Non-breeding adult streaked brown from head to upper breast. Juvenile pale brown below, and white above with variable and extensive pale brown scaling; wingtips whitish to pale tan. 1st-winter mottled greyish-buff; bill pink, with well defined black tip. Older immature nearly immaculate white, with some dusky brown flecks and bars. Races differ in size and in tone of mantle, but much individual variation; *barrovianus* smallest and darkest. Hybrids with *L. glaucescens* common in W Alaska (in Seward Peninsula, over 50% of birds), showing dark iris and grey on primary tips. Many birds in S Iceland appear to be hybrids with *L. argentatus*, although opinions on this differ.

Habitat. Coasts, bays, harbours, landfill sites and fishing wharves; rarely large inland lakes. Breeds on cliffs in Arctic and subarctic, mainly coastal or a few kilometres inland, particularly near human settlements, and often near gull or goose colonies; also on islands offshore or in lakes.

Food and Feeding. Fish, molluscs, crustaceans, rodents, birds, eggs and young of birds (especially ducks, auks, shorebirds), insects, berries, carrion, refuse and offal. In Iceland, consumes blue mussel (*Mytilus edulis*), *Littorina palliata*, crabs (*Hyas*), sea-urchins and sandeels (*Ammodytes*). At Barrow, Alaska, feeds on fish, on minute crustaceans in surf, and on offal and refuse; gathers at whale corpses. Inland breeders rely heavily on birds, but also take fish from rivers. In winter, southernmost birds feed mainly at rubbish dumps, behind ships, at sewage outfalls, and on fish offal; also exploit spawning squid, pelagic crabs, mammal carcasses, and occasionally faeces of marine mammals. Piratic on other gulls and skuas. Scavenges in intertidal zone.

Breeding. Synchronous laying mid-May to mid-Jun, depending on latitude and ice conditions; strong selection for early nesting because of short season. Solitary or in small colonies. Many non-breeders around nesting areas in W Alaska. Nest is a pile of seaweed and debris, often lined; usually on edge of cliff, rock pinnacle, sometimes on slope. 2-3 eggs (mean 2·88 in W Alaska); incubation 26-30 days; chick similar to that of *L. marinus*, but paler, greyer, with markings more obscure; chick phase 40 days (fledging reported as c. 49 days in Spitsbergen); most young apparently independent by early Sept.

Movements. Partially migratory. Winters from edge of ice to N USA, N Europe and Japan, casually further S. W Palearctic birds remain in breeding range, moving S ahead of ice. E Siberian birds winter on coasts of E Asia S to Japan. Alaskan breeders winter from Aleutians to California. Those breeding in E Canada winter sparingly to Middle Atlantic States. Adults leave Greenland in early Sept, while young linger until freeze-up. In some winters, occurs in S in larger numbers than usual.

Status and Conservation. Not globally threatened. Total population probably over 100,000 pairs. W Palearctic holds c. 20,000 pairs, with 50% on Spitsbergen; E Palearctic 10,000-50,000 pairs. Estimated Alaskan population at least 15,000 pairs at thousands of sites; abundant at Barrow. Greenland holds at least 10,000 and possibly closer to 100,000 pairs. Is being displaced by *L. argentatus* in some areas, e.g. S Iceland; decreasing in Greenland.

Bibliography. Andresen & Thomas (1986), Armstrong (1983), Brazil (1991), Cramp & Simmons (1983), Drury (1984), Étchécopar & Hüe (1978), Evans (1984a, 1984b), Gaston (1991), Guömundsson (1955), Helms (1926), Howell & Webb (1995a), Hume (1975), Ilicev & Zubakin (1988), Ingolfsson (1970a, 1970b, 1976), Jacob & Lardinois (1982), Kay (1947), Knystautas (1993), Kondratiev (1991), Lensink (1984), Parmelee & MacDonald (1960), Perennou *et al.* (1994), Richards (1990), Rogacheva (1992), Root (1988), Salomonsen (1967b), Spear (1987), Stempniewicz (1983), Strang, C.A. (1974, 1977), Tasker *et al.* (1987), Urban *et al.* (1986).

20. **Iceland Gull**

Larus glaucoides

French: Goéland arctique **German**: Polarmöwe **Spanish**: Gaviota Groenlandesa
Other common names: Greenland Gull; Kumlien's Gull (*kumlieni*)

Taxonomy. *Larus glaucoides* B. Meyer, 1822, Iceland.
Formerly listed as *L. leucopterus*. Closely related to *L. argentatus*, and sometimes treated as conspecific. Form *kumlieni* sometimes considered a separate species, as birds with grey wingtips occur alongside those with white wingtips in Nearctic. E-W cline apparent, from pale *glaucoides* to slightly darker *kumlieni* to darker *L. thayeri*. Increasing tendency to lump *L. thayeri* with *L. glaucoides* refuted, as such treatment would make the species undiagnosable; yet *kumlieni* hybridizes with *L. thayeri*, and may be closer to latter than to *L. g. glaucoides*. Two subspecies provsionally recognized.

Subspecies and Distribution.
L. g. kumlieni Brewster, 1883 - NE Canada, on Baffin I and NW Ungava; winters from Labrador S to E Great Lakes and Virginia.
L. g. glaucoides B. Meyer, 1822 - S & W Greenland; winters S to N Europe.

Descriptive notes. 55-64 cm; 557-863 g; wingspan 125-130 cm. Medium-large, long-winged gull, all white but for pale grey mantle, upperwing-coverts and flight-feather bases; bill yellow, with red gonydeal spot; legs pink; iris yellow, with red orbital ring. Plumage pattern similar to that of larger *L. hyperboreus*, but bill shorter and more slender; at rest, wingtips extend well past tail; has more buoyant flight. Smaller than many *L. argentatus* (though size range overlaps), generally more gracile, and lacks black on primaries. Non-breeding adult streaked brownish on head to upper breast. Juvenile and 1st-winter plumage very pale, more uniform than in *L. hyperboreus*, head sometimes dusky, and tail with pale grey terminal band; bill dusky brownish to brownish horn (may seem black at distance), and usually paler at base than distal half, though not so sharply demarcated as in *L. hyperboreus*. Slightly larger-billed race *kumlieni*, with darker red orbital ring and dark iris, has pale grey outer webs to outer primaries 10 and 9, as well as grey tips to primaries 8 and 7, but highly variable (some individuals in

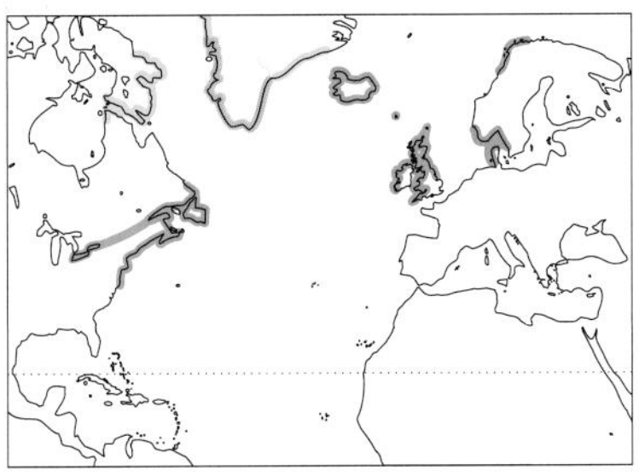

kumlieni colonies have all white wingtips, some have nearly uniform pale grey primaries); immature shows darker primaries and is less barred than in nominate race. Hybrid *L. argentatus* x *L. hyperboreus* (formerly identified as "*L. nelsoni*") very similar to *kumlieni*, but larger, with heavier bill.

Habitat. Rocky coasts and fjords of low Arctic, breeding on steep cliffs, offshore stacks, sometimes undisturbed low islands. In winter also occurs in harbours, occasionally rubbish dumps, and rarely inland reservoirs, but normally shuns fresh water.

Food and Feeding. Mainly small fish, e.g. salmon (*Salmo*), sprat (*Sprattus*), herring (*Clupea*), as well as marine invertebrates; eggs and chicks of various birds; seeds and fruits sometimes important. Scavenges in intertidal zone; feeds on stranded carcasses. Some individuals specialize on *Rissa tridactyla* colonies, hunting for unguarded eggs and chicks. Wintering birds likely to exploit rubbish dumps and sewage outfalls. Feeds mainly from the water surface, but also by plunge-diving; picks from ground.

Breeding. Lays mid-May to mid-Jun in Greenland. Solitary or in small colonies. On cliff ledge, occasionally on ground. Prefers steep cliffs over 100 m in height. In mixed colonies with *R. tridactyla*, tends to nest higher on cliffs, preferring broader ledges; in Greenland often nests with *L. hyperboreus*. Cliff-nesting individuals reported to behave more like *Rissa*, ground-nesters more like *L. argentatus*. Nest of seaweed and dry grass. 2-3 eggs; incubation and fledging periods not documented; chick undescribed. Chicks preferentially do not face cliff wall; not recognized by adults until c. 19 days. Chicks from cliff nests do not run or jump when disturbed, while those from ground nests run. Young fledge in late Jul, and move with adults to coastal feeding areas.

Movements. Northernmost populations migratory; populations of S Greenland resident. Post-breeding birds linger around colony areas into Aug or Sept. Young disperse more widely than adults. Birds from E Greenland more migratory than those in W Greenland, the latter moving mainly from inland fjords to coast after breeding, and dispersing mainly along coast in winter. Some Greenland birds disperse to North America, most to Iceland and Faeroes, fewer to NW Europe. Those from E Greenland move mainly to Iceland, where species is very common in winter. Birds from Baffin I move S to Hudson Bay, and thence to the Maritime Provinces, wintering sparsely from Labrador to E Greak Lakes and Virginia. Most birds reaching New England, Middle Atlantic states and N & NW Europe are juveniles; they usually associate with *L. argentatus* in harbours and at rubbish dumps. Numbers reaching S areas vary anually.

Status and Conservation. Not globally threatened. Population figures insufficiently known. Greenland population estimated at 10,000-100,000 pairs, but world total (including *kumlieni*) may number under 100,000 pairs. Only a minute portion of the population filters down to Europe and North America, where ornithologists might assess trends. No adequate studies on breeding grounds. No reason to assume that numbers are declining, although increased non-native predators pose a hazard to many Arctic and subarctic species. In Greenland the local inhabitants hunt present species extensively, and may harvest 23% of population annually.

Bibliography. Alström & Olsson (1985), Andresen & Thomas (1986), Beaman (1994), Brazil (1991), Cassidy (1990), Cramp & Simmons (1983), Dubois (1994b), Evans (1984a), Fjeldså & Jensen (1985), Gaston (1991), Gaston & Decker (1985), Gaston & Elliot (1990), Howell & Webb (1995a), Hume (1975), Ilicev & Zubakin (1988), Kay (1950), Millington (1993), Richards (1990), Salomonsen (1967b), Smith (1966a, 1966b), Snell (1989, 1991a), Sutton (1968a), Zimmer (1991).

21. Thayer's Gull

Larus thayeri

French: Goéland de Thayer **German**: Thayermöwe **Spanish**: Gaviota Esquimal

Taxonomy. *Larus thayeri* W. S. Brooks, 1915, Banks Island.

A highly controversial and variable taxon, alternatively treated as a race of *L. argentatus* or of *L. glaucoides*. Interbreeds with *L. g. kumlieni* in N Hudson Bay and E Baffin I, prompting some to treat it as a race of *L. glaucoides*. Although seemingly random pairing occurred in N Hudson Bay, a deficit of intermediate plumages suggested that post-mating isolation may exist. Pending further hybridization studies, *thayeri* is best treated as a discrete species. Merging it with *L. glaucoides* would make latter species undefinable; moreover, other species frequently hybridize in some localities (e.g. *L. occidentalis* and *L. glaucescens*), and consistency would demand that they also be merged. Monotypic.

Distribution. N Canada, from Banks I E to N Hudson Bay and N Baffin I (E to vicinity of Home Bay), N through Ellesmere I to W Greenland (near Thule). Winters on Pacific coast, from British Columbia to Baja California.

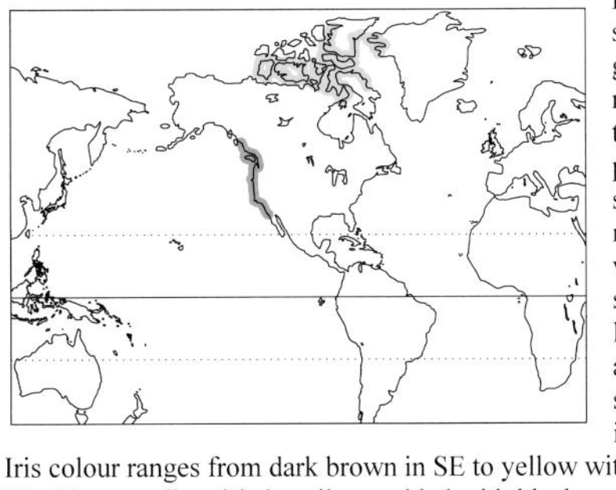

Descriptive notes. 56-63 cm; 846-1152 g; wingspan 130-140 cm. White-headed gull with pale grey mantle and upperwings; bill yellow, with red gonydeal spot; legs pinkish; iris dark brown to yellow, with purplish orbital ring. In all plumages very similar to *L. argentatus*, but slightly smaller, and usually with slaty black rather than black on upper surface of primaries; wingtips usually mostly white below, with slightly greyer "tongues"; mantle sometimes lighter, but on many birds somewhat darker; feet a deeper pink, sometimes purplish; bill more slender than in *L. argentatus*, with gently curving culmen and less prominent gonydeal angle. Iris colour ranges from dark brown in SE to yellow with brown flecks in far N. Specimens from Bylot I had ivory-yellow iris heavily speckled with black, and mottled yellow-and-pink eyelids; olive-ochre bill, becoming olive-buff at tip. Very difficult to distinguish from some *L. glaucescens* or *L. argentatus*, however, and from the more numerous hybrids that winter on Pacific coast of North America. Most constant features are rounded head, and bill shape.

Habitat. Coasts of rocky islands, feeding also around fishing piers, rubbish dumps, and settlements; breeds mainly on coastal cliffs.

Food and Feeding. Diverse diet. Inadequately studied on breeding grounds; non-breeders feed on refuse and scraps, offal, and animal debris around settlements. In winter, takes fish, marine invertebrates and offal; follows fishing boats with other gulls.

Breeding. Essentially unrecorded. Lays in early Jun. Small colonies of up to a few dozen pairs. Mainly on cliffs, usually with *L. hyperboreus*, nesting below the larger species; requires ledges about 3 x larger (mean 920 cm²) than those used by *R. tridactyla*; rarely on ground. Gathers nest material away from colony; guards nest-site aggressively before laying. Reported to build larger nest cup than ground-nesting gulls, but does not incorporate mud; many first eggs roll off ledges. Usual clutch size unknown, probably 2-3 eggs; incubation and fledging periods not documented; chick said to be darker and greyer than *L. argentatus*, with finer spotting, and more white on underparts, but probably just as variable as latter, and indistinguishable. Chicks preferentially do not face cliff wall; reported not to pump head while begging; not recognized by adults until c. 19 days. Chicks of cliff-nesting pairs do not run or jump when disturbed, while those from ground nests run.

Movements. Migrates S and W, some reaching North Slope and Pacific coast at Alaska, others (mainly juveniles) moving into Chukchi Sea, then moving S. Winters from British Columbia to Baja California, with birds arriving in Oct; 1st-year birds move further S. Numbers detected along Pacific coast, however, are hardly sufficient to account for the large numbers which may breed in Arctic Canada. Species very rare in the Maritime Provinces and NE USA, being accidental in most states. Presumably still overlooked in many areas.

Status and Conservation. Not globally threatened. Status and trends insufficiently known, but species probably secure. Very few breeding sites have been studied. Christmas Bird Counts locate c. 20,000 individuals, mainly along Pacific coast. Apparently widely distributed in NE Canadian Arctic, nesting in small colonies on cliffs.

Bibliography. Armstrong (1983), Brazil (1991), Brooks (1915), Drury (1960, 1984), Dubois (1994b), Evans (1984a), Gaston (1991), Gaston & Decker (1985), Gosselin & David (1975), Howell & Webb (1995a), Jehl (1974), Lehman (1980), Macpherson (1961), Manning *et al.* (1956), Parmelee & MacDonald (1960), Richards (1990), Salomonsen (1967b), Smith, N.G. (1966a, 1966b, 1991), Snell (1989, 1991a), Sutton (1968a), Sutton & Parmelee (1978), Thing (1976), Van Tyne & Drury (1959), Wilbur (1987).

22. Herring Gull

Larus argentatus

French: Goéland argenté **German**: Silbermöwe **Spanish**: Gaviota Argéntea

Taxonomy. *Larus Argentatus* Pontoppidan, 1763, Denmark.

Systematics of present species and its close relatives represent one of the most complex challenges in ornithology, and typify the discord between evolution, biogeography, reproductive isolation, and taxonomy. The closely related taxa were often treated as a ring of subtle races, until the two extremes (*L. argentatus*, *L. fuscus*) met in W Europe and did not freely interbreed. Many forms are now treated as separate species, since it is uncertain how to apply the biological species concept to the complex pattern of variation and interbreeding. Present species is reported to hybridize extensively with *L. hyperboreus* in Iceland (but this disputed), with *L. glaucescens* in Alaska, but rarely with *L. fuscus* in Europe. Confusion prevails over the species boundaries of *L. argentatus*, *L. cachinnans* and *L. fuscus*, with many of the identifiable races assigned at one time or another to 2 or even 3 of these species. The most extreme lumping has included *L. glaucoides*, *L. fuscus* and even *L. californicus* within *L. argentatus*; a more traditional treatment includes *L. cachinnans* and *L. armenicus*. Owing to sympatry without hybridization in W France, *L. cachinnans* is now seen as a distinct species, further supported by molecular evidence. Much controversy surrounds the form "*omissus*" of the N Baltic region, with pink-legged individuals in a (formerly) predominantly yellow-legged population: it has been treated as a race either of *L. argentatus* or of *L. cachinnans*, but it is probably simply a morph of *L. argentatus* (based mainly on voice and primary pattern). Bluish-legged birds of Russian Arctic islands included in *vegae*, but sometimes separated as *birulae*. See also *L. cachinnans*, *L. armenicus*, *L. fuscus*. Four subspecies recognized.

Subspecies and Distribution.

L. a. smithsonianus Coues, 1862 - North America; winters S to Central America.

L. a. argenteus C. L. Brehm, 1822 - Iceland, Faeroes, British Is and W France to W Germany; winters S to N Iberia.

L. a. argentatus Pontoppidan, 1763 - Denmark and Fenno-Scandia, to E Kola Peninsula; winters mostly in N & W Europe.

L. a. vegae Palmén, 1887 - NE Siberia; winters S to China.

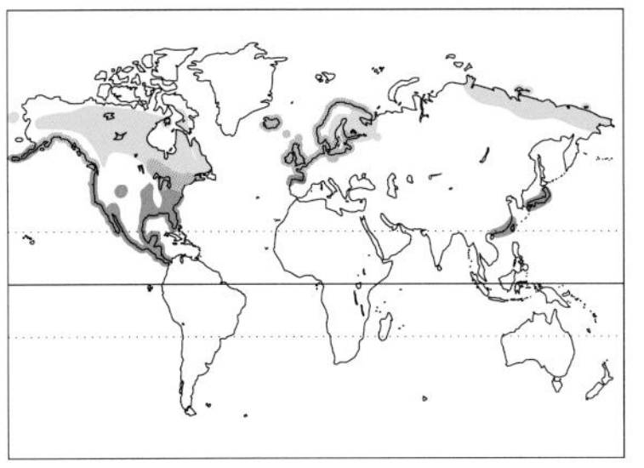

Descriptive notes. 55-67 cm; 720-1500 g; wingspan 135-145 cm. Large gull with powerful bill; white head, underparts and tail, with grey upperwings and mantle (varying from pale to dark grey), and black wingtips with a white-spotted pattern; bill yellow, with red gonydeal spot; legs and feet pink (yellowish on some N Baltic birds); iris pale yellow, with orange to yellowish red orbital ring. Differs from *L. cachinnans* in pink legs. Non-breeding adult has dark-streaked head and neck, and duller bill and orbital ring. Juvenile varies with race, but basically grey-brown with pale spots, and blackish primaries and tail feathers; full adult plumage not achieved until 4 years. Races differ mainly in size, in tone of mantle and upperwing, and in exact pattern of primary tips, but quite variable; even within Netherlands (*argenteus*) mantle colour varies among colonies from light to dark grey, and the darkest-mantled birds from Norway (nominate *argentatus*) are comparable to the lightest-mantled *L. fuscus graellsii* from Britain; NE Asian *vegae* is large, heavy-billed, with a darker mantle, and a heavily spotted head in winter; *argenteus* generally smallest and palest, *smithsonianus* intermediate between *argenteus* and nominate. Minimal hybridization with *L. fuscus*; offspring have lower survival than either parental type.

Habitat. Mainly coastal and near-coastal areas; also inland, at large lakes and reservoirs, on fields and at rubbish dumps; sometimes at sea. Breeding habitats very varied: coastal cliffs and stacks, rocky and grassy islands, sandy beaches, gravel bars, salt-marshes, limestone outcrops, and buildings; exploits man-altered habitats such as clay pits.

Food and Feeding. Omnivorous and highly opportunistic, exploiting superabundant food when available; spans the full range of gull dietary items and feeding behaviour; powerful predator. Feeds extensively on fish, earthworms, crabs, and other marine invertebrates (molluscs, starfish), taken alive or found dead; fish and molluscs can comprise 60-70% of diet. On tidal flats in Maine (NE USA), preferentially selected large ragworms (*Nereis virens*) over smaller worms, and blue mussels (*Mytilus edulis*) and crabs (*Cancer maenas*, *C. irroratus*). Huge numbers scavenge at rubbish dumps, fishing wharves and sewage outfalls; frequently follows fishing boats. Preys on birds, bird eggs and young, and rodents, some individuals specializing on these items; flocks sometimes prey on fatigued migrant passerines, particularly those struggling to land into a wind. Takes insects, including ants; sometimes gorges on berries, even bayberry (*Myrica pennsylvanica*), or on turnips. Feeding methods very varied, include walking on mudflats, plunge-diving and surface-dipping; less likely than the smaller gulls to engage in aerial hawking; occasionally foot-paddles on mud, grass or in shallow water. Routinely drops bivalves onto hard surface to crack them; immatures do so less often, and less successfully. Catches small mammals and birds by stalking and ambushing them.

Breeding. Lays from early May to early Jun (rarely late Apr) in NE USA and NW Europe; early May in Murmansk; average dates earlier as colonies age. Colonies of dozens to thousands of pairs; occasionally solitary, or as single pairs on edge of other seabird colonies. With increased population, density in some colonies rose from 30 pairs/ha to 100 pairs/ha, and aggression and cannibalism increased. In Newfoundland, rocky marine terraces had highest density and highest productivity, while nests in grassy meadows suffered higher predation. Nearest-neighbour distances range from 0·6 to 10 m, but usually over 2 m. Shows high philopatry to natal colonies. Bulky nest of grass and vines, on ground, cliff ledge or roof, usually sheltered in vegetation. Usually 2-3 eggs (1-5, mean 1·7-2·8); incubation 28-30 days; chick buff-grey above with large blackish spots, well defined on head, buffy white below, with black throat spot; hatching weight c. 49-66 g (Barents Sea); fledging c. 40-45 days, independent c. 1-2 weeks later. Chick growth rate declined as population density increased. Pairs in which mates contribute equally have greater success. Main egg and chick losses due to predation by conspecifics and other gulls. First breeding at 3-7 years, usually 5 years. Recorded longevity of 32 years.

Movements N birds are migratory, and may leapfrog over S breeders. Winters as far S as West Indies and Central America, but in Palearctic usually only to Iberia. Finnish breeders move short distances, most remaining in Baltic; many N European birds winter in S North Sea. Some of those breeding in NE Asia remain well N in winter, but many migrate, wintering as far S as coasts of South China Sea; some post-breeding wandering to N Alaskan coast.

Status and Conservation. Not globally threatened. One of the most abundant coastal birds in North America and Europe. Centre of abundance is in Norway. At least 1,000,000 pairs breed in the Palearctic, including 206,000 in British Is; over 150,000 in E North America. With the enforcement of protection from persecution and egging, and aided by the availability of refuse and other food items to diminish juvenile mortality, a massive and dramatic growth in numbers has taken place throughout its range. Populations expanded greatly from 1910 to 1975, but have stabilized in most places, or the rate of increase has slowed down. Species colonized Iceland only in 1925, and increased steadily until 1940. In Britain, population grew at annual rate of 12·8% during period 1930-1978, with colonization of moorlands and development of roof-nesting. In Nearctic, New England population increased from 11,000 to 90,000 pairs from 1901 to 1972. On Long I, New York, numbers peaked in mid-1970's with 20,000 pairs, and have actually declined since with 14,800 pairs in 1983; egging has increased to serious proportions. Pollutant levels in eggs at Great Lakes declined steadily until early 1980's, before levelling off. Species is regarded as a pest and a threat to many other colonial species, as it usurps their habitat and preys upon their eggs and young; preventative measures are frequently taken. Often considered hazardous at airports, and control efforts are frequently introduced.

Bibliography. Amlaner & McFarland (1981), Andersson (1970), Baerends & Drent (1970), Barth (1966, 1967a, 1967b, 1968, 1975), Becker & Erdelen (1982), Becker et al. (1980), Belant et al. (1993), Bergman (1982b), Blake (1977), Blodget (1988), Blokpoel & Scharf (1991b), Blösch (1971), Bourget (1973), Brazil (1991), Brouwer et al. (1995), Brown (1967a, 1967b), Buckley & Buckley (1984b), Burger, J. (1977a, 1977b, 1979a, 1979b, 1980a, 1980c, 1981a, 1981b, 1981c, 1981d, 1984b, 1987a), Burger, J. & Gochfeld (1981b, 1981c, 1983a, 1988b, 1994a), Burger, J. & Lesser (1980), Burger, J. & Shisler (1978b, 1979, 1980a), Cederroth (1995), Chabrzyk & Coulson (1976), Chudzik et al. (1994), Coulson (1991), Coulson & Butterfield (1985, 1986), Coulson et al. (1982), Cramp & Simmons (1983), Darling (1938), Davis (1975a, 1975b), Dowsett & Forbes-Watson (1993), Drost & Schilling (1951, 1952), Drury (1984), Drury & Kadlec (1974), Drury & Smith (1968), Dumas & Witman (1993), Duncan (1978), Dunn (1976), Dunn & Brisbin (1980), Dwight (1920), Elkowe & Payne (1979), Emlen (1964), Erwin (1971), Evans et al. (1995), Fitch & Shugart (1983), Fox et al. (1990), Goethe (1937, 1963), Götmark (1982, 1984), Grieg et al. (1983), Hackl & Burger (1988), Hario (1984, 1994), Hario et al. (1991), Harris (1964, 1965, 1970, 1971), Harris et al. (1978), Haycock & Threlfall (1975), Hébert & Barclay (1986), Holley (1984), Howell & Webb (1995a), Hunt (1972), Ilicev & Zubakin (1988), Ingolfsson (1970b), Kadlec & Drury (1968), Kadlec et al. (1969), Keith (1966), Kilpi (1989, 1990, 1992, 1995a, 1995b), Kilpi & Byholm (1995a, 1995b), Kilpi & Hario (1986), Kilpi & Saurola (1983, 1984a), Kilpi et al. (1996), Ludwig & Tomoff (1966), Maccarone et al. (1993), MacRoberts, B.R. & MacRoberts (1972), MacRoberts, M.H. & MacRoberts (1972), Marion et al. (1985), McCleery & Sibly (1986), McGill-Harelstad (1985), Mierauskas et al. (1991), Monaghan (1979, 1980), Monaghan et al. (1986), Morris (1987), Morris & Bidochka (1983), Morris & Chardine (1985), Mudge & Ferns (1982), Nicolau-Guillaumet (1977), Nisbet & Drury (1972b), Noordhuis & Spaans (1992), Noseworthy & Lien (1976), Paludan (1951), Parnell & Soots (1975), Parsons (1970, 1971, 1972, 1975a, 1975b, 1976a, 1976b), Patten & Weisbrod (1974), Paynter (1949), Paz (1987), Peakall et al. (1980), Pierotti (1982, 1987), Pierotti & Annett (1991), Pierotti & Good (1994), Poor (1946), Richards (1990), Rutgers & Norris (1970), Shirihai (1996), Shugart (1980), Sibly & McCleery (1983, 1985), Snell (1991b), Southern (1980), Spaans (1971), Spaans, Coulson et al. (1991), Spaans, de Wit & van Vlaardingen (1987), Spear (1987), Stegmann (1934, 1960), Stresemann & Timofeeff (1947), Stromar (1967/68), Tinbergen (1953), Transue & Burger (1989), Urban et al. (1986), Verbeek (1977a, 1977b), Vercruijsse (1995), Vermeer (1973a, 1973b), Vinicombe et al. (1995), Voous (1959, 1961a), Weaver (1970), Wetmore (1965), Williamson & Peyton (1963), Wink et al. (1994), de Wit & Spaans (1984), Witt et al. (1981), Yésou (1991), Zykova (1983).

23. Yellow-legged Gull

Larus cachinnans

French: Goéland leucophée   **German**: Weißkopfmöwe   **Spanish**: Gaviota Patiamarilla

Taxonomy. *Larus cachinnans* Pallas, 1811, Caspian Sea.
All subspecies listed below have often been treated under *L. argentatus*. Some earlier authors emphasized the view that *L. cachinnans* was a separate species; now widely accepted as such, based on sympatry with *L. argentatus* in W France, and on behaviour and morphology. Molecular data also show it to be a distinct species, closer to *L. fuscus*, suggesting that the three species may have diverged during the Pleistocene. The form "*ponticus*" of the Caspian Sea is a synonym of nominate *cachinnans*. See also *L. argentatus*. Five subspecies recognized.

Subspecies and Distribution.
L. c. atlantis Dwight, 1922 - Azores to Madeira and Canary Is.
L. c. michahellis J. F. Naumann, 1840 - W & S Europe and NW Africa E through Mediterranean.
L. c. cachinnans Pallas, 1811 - Black Sea to Caspian Sea and E Kazakhstan; winters S to SW Asia, Middle East and NE Africa.
L. c. barabensis Johansen, 1960 - C Asian steppes; winters mostly in SW Asia.
L. c. mongolicus Sushkin, 1925 - SE Altai and L Baikal to Mongolia; winters mostly in S Asia.

Descriptive notes. 58-68 cm; 800-1500 g; wingspan 140-155 cm. Large white-headed, white-bodied gull, with grey mantle and upperwings, and black and white wingtips; bill deep yellow, with large bright red gonydeal spot; legs yellow; iris pale yellow, with conspicuous red orbital ring. Distinguished from *L. argentatus* by yellow legs, vermilion orbital ring, blacker primaries, and slightly darker mantle. Non-breeding adult has unstreaked white head, unlike *L. argentatus* and *L. fuscus*. In some *L. cachinnans* populations (NW Spain), however, 5-10% of birds have pink or partly pink legs, despite the claim that yellow leg colour is a universal characteristic of this species. 1st-winter bird usually paler below and on head than that of *L. argentatus*; immature has a black subterminal mark on

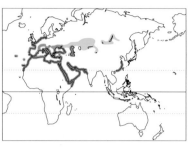

the bill, which occasionally persists in adult plumage. Races differ in size, in tone of mantle, and in amount of black in primaries, but variable; race *atlantis* smaller, with darker mantle.
Habitat. Coasts and inland habitats. In W Europe, largely confined to coastal regions, but locally also rivers and inland lakes; in C Asia inhabits lakes in steppe and semi-desert. Also feeds at rubbish dumps, fields, and various other terrestrial habitats. Breeds on rocky and sandy islands, beaches, cliffs, spits, and grassy or shrubby river islands; in flooded areas may nest on bushes; at Black and Caspian Seas nests mainly on islands, ranging from barren to well vegetated.

Food and Feeding. Mostly fish, invertebrates, mammals, refuse, scraps, offal, bird eggs and chicks, and insects. Off Morocco, breeding birds fed on refuse, fish, insects, molluscs and a lizard, but fed their chicks mainly fish. At Caspian Sea sometimes feeds chicks mainly on mole-crickets (*Gryllotalpa*). In some Caspian Sea colonies, main prey is susliks (*Spermophilus*, up to 140 g) and other small rodents, obtained in surrounding steppes; also insects (particularly beetles), with fish only 7% of food items. In Crimea mostly susliks and voles (*Microtus*), but in some colonies mainly fish and crustaceans, and in others preys heavily on eggs and chicks of gulls (conspecifics, as well as *L. melanocephalus*, *L. genei* and even *L. ichthyaetus*). Exploits human intrusion, seizing eggs when incubating birds flushed. Some adults obtain food mainly by following fishing boats and taking offal. In Selvagen Is (N of Canary Is) flies inland to feed on grasshoppers and moths. Kleptoparasitic on *L. audouinii*, particularly when fishing vessels not active. Forages mostly by wading in intertidal zone, plunge-diving, and following ships; also follows plough.

Breeding. Similar to *L. argentatus*. In some colonies, territorial throughout winter; lays from mid-Mar. Colonies of up to c. 8000 pairs (Medes Is, NE Spain); forms monospecific clusters, even when nesting beside other gulls; sometimes on high ground, hundreds of metres from water. Nests preferentially close to or under bushes, sometimes in bushes or dense copses of osier (*Cornus*); on rooftops in several cities, e.g. Barcelona (Spain). Density 20-140 nests/ha, usually a few metres apart. Nest made of nearby vegetation, feathers, debris and old carcasses; often builds or lines nest with eelgrass (*Zostera marina*). Usually 2-3 eggs (1-4, mean 2·68 at Volga Delta); incubation averages 26-29 days; chick similar to that of *L. argentatus*; hatching weight c. 60 g; swims at c. 10 days, when partly feathered; fledging c. 6-7 weeks.

Movements. Many populations sedentary or slightly dispersive. E population (*mongolicus*) migrates to China and India. Birds from Balkans disperse locally as far as R Danube. French and Spanish breeders disperse overland to Atlantic and E along Mediterranean. Birds from N Africa disperse around Mediterranean. In recent years, increasing numbers of birds breeding in SW Europe and the Mediterranean have moved N after breeding, fair numbers now spending the winter in SE England and S coasts of North Sea.

Status and Conservation. Not globally threatened. Overall status uncertain, owing to treatment as conspecific with *L. argentatus* until relatively recently. Mediterranean populations have increased during 20th century, but still number under 100,000 pairs. On Chafarinas Is (off NE Morocco) one colony increased from 250 pairs in 1976 to 850 pairs in 1985, while a second totalled 3000 pairs. Over 6500 pairs of race *atlantis* breed in Macaronesia. In Black Sea area many nests were destroyed and adults shot during 1940's, to reduce their predation on the "beneficial" *L. melanocephalus*. Culling is also considered to protect *L. audouinii* from expanding *L. cachinnans* populations; has taken place in parts of Spain. A frequent victim of oil pollution in some areas (e.g. Azerbaijan). Many colonies, especially in E of range, are regularly robbed of eggs by local human communities.

Bibliography. Ali & Ripley (1982), Antoniazza (1995), Bauer (1953), Beaman (1994), Beaubrun (1993), Blondel (1963), Borodulina (1960), Brazil (1983, 1991), Buzun & Mierauskas (1988), Carrera & García (1986), Carrera, Monbailliu & Torre (1993), Carrera, Nebot & Vilagrasa (1981), Cederroth (1995), Cezilly & Quenette (1988), Coverley (1931), Cramp & Simmons (1983), Demartis (1986), Dennis (1995), Dowsett & Forbes-Watson (1993), Eigenhuis (1991), Étchécopar & Hüe (1978), Faggio (1991), Fasola (1986), Fasola & Canova (1992), Fasola, Bogliani et al. (1989), Fasola, Goutner & Walmsley (1989), Géroudet (1968), Goethe (1963), Goodman et al. (1989), le Grand et al. (1984), Gruber (1995), Isenmann (1976a), de Juana (1984, 1986), de Juana et al. (1984), Kiselev (1951), Klimenko (1950), Kist (1961), Knystautas (1993), Kozlova (1938), Lönnberg (1933), Mackworth-Praed & Grant (1970), Marion et al. (1985), Mierauskas & Buzun (1991), Mierauskas & Greimas (1992), Mierauskas et al. (1991), Monbailliu & Torre (1986), Moore (1996), Nicolau-Guillaumet (1977), Oró & Martínez-Vilalta (1994), Oró et al. (1995), Paz (1987), Perennou et al. (1994), Richards (1990), Roberts, T.J. (1991), Shirihai (1996), Spitzer (1978), Stegmann (1934, 1960), Stresemann & Timofeeff (1947), Teyssèdre (1984), Urban et al. (1986), Varela & de Juana (1986), Vercruijsse (1995), Vinicombe (1995), Vinicombe et al. (1995), Voipio (1968, 1972), Voous (1959), Wilds & Czaplak (1994), Wink et al. (1994), Witt (1974a), Witt et al. (1981), Yésou (1991), Zikova & Panov (1983).

24. Armenian Gull

Larus armenicus

French: Goéland d'Arménie   **German**: Armenienmöwe   **Spanish**: Gaviota Armenia

Taxonomy. *Larus armenicus* Buturlin, 1934, Lake Sevan, Armenia.
Historically treated as a race of *L. argentatus*, but smaller, with shorter bill; black band across both mandibles diagnostic, but not mentioned in original description. Also has a delayed moult. Monotypic.
Distribution. Caucasus through Armenia to E Turkey and NW Iran. Winters in SE Black Sea, E Mediterranean and N Red Sea.

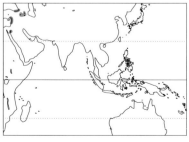

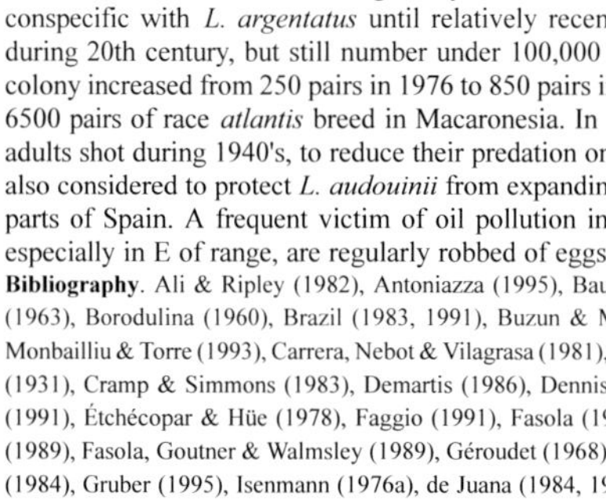

Descriptive notes. 57-60 cm; 950-1050 g; wingspan c. 140 cm. White-headed gull with grey mantle and upperwings; bill deep yellow, with narrow subterminal black band, and red spot near gonys; legs yellow to orange-yellow, brighter than in *L. cachinnans*; iris mainly yellowish to brown, with red orbital ring. Upperparts slightly paler than in *L. fuscus heuglini*, but darker than in *L. argentatus argenteus*. Distinguished from *L. argentatus* by wing pattern, bill, yellow legs, and darker eyes. Compared with both *L. argentatus* and *L. cachinnans*, has more extensive black at wingtips, with a large triangle from outer primary to primary 7, and more extensive black as far as primary 3; primaries have small white tips, with a small white subterminal window on outer primary. Despite much individual variation, present species and *L. cachinnans* show subtle differences in size and appearance: present species is smaller, more slender, with a shorter, stubbier bill, and more rounded forecrown and hindcrown (*L. cachinnans* has flatter, more angular head); grey base to secondaries forms a subterminal band on underwing. Post-breeding adult has a smudged appearance to bill, often with both red and black markings ill-defined; by winter, bill is deep yellow, with a sharp black subterminal band that covers the red spot, and creamy yellow tip; some non-breeding adults have fine streaking on crown and sides of head, and coarser streaking on nape, which is more extensive than in *L. cachinnans*, but less than in *L. argentatus* or *L. f. heuglini*. Juvenile and 1st-winter birds have all black bill. 2nd-winter has white head with faint streaking on face, and stronger markings on hindneck which may suggest a faint collar; bill sometimes all black, but usually with distal half dark and base pale (sometimes yellow). By 3rd winter, head is white with dark markings on hindneck.

Habitat. Inland and coastal waters. Breeds only at mountain lakes, using reedbeds, beaches, and agricultural fields; at L Sevan (Armenia), at altitude of 1900 m, now confined to small islands.

Food and Feeding. Very inadequately studied. Presumably feeds on fish, invertebrates and offal.

Breeding. Lays from late Apr. Only 2 colonies known, with nests 1-2 m apart in densest areas; among stones and grass or under bushes. Species is quite tolerant of intruders. Long-call display usually accompanied by complete upward head-toss, as in *L. fuscus*; frequently displays with wings held slightly outwards and lowered. Usual clutch 3 eggs. No further information available.

Movements. Some birds remain in the breeding area all year, but many migrate short distances. Winters in Black Sea, and in E Mediterranean from Turkey to Israel, where it co-occurs with *L. cachinnans*; many winter S at least to Tel Aviv, with few reaching N Red Sea. Only a vagrant to Persian Gulf.

Status and Conservation. Not globally threatened. Probably requires reclassification as Vulnerable, due to very low numbers and minute range. No published censuses available; possibly numbers fewer than 10,000 pairs. Very few studies have been carried out on present species, presumably in part because until recently it was widely regarded as merely a subspecies of *L. argentatus*. Severe decrease from 1930's to 1960's, when gulls were persecuted because of damage to fisheries, and eggs were harvested for food. At L Sevan only 60-100 pairs in 1970's, but 4000 pairs in 1990; this area now forms Sevan National Park. The other known Armenian colony is at Arpilich L, where more than 4000 pairs breed.

Bibliography. Beaman (1994), Bertault *et al*. (1988), Bourne, W.R.P. (1993a), Buturlin (1934), Buzun (1993), Cramp & Simmons (1983), Dubois (1985), Filchagov (1993), Géroudet (1982), Ginn *et al*. (1989), Hollom *et al*. (1988), Hüe & Étchécopar (1970), Madge (1990), Richardson, C. (1990), Satat & Laird (1992), Voous (1959).

25. Slaty-backed Gull

Larus schistisagus

French: Goéland à manteau ardoisé **German**: Kamtschatkamöwe **Spanish**: Gaviota de Kamchatka
Other common names: Pacific Gull, Kamchatka Gull

Taxonomy. *Larus schistisagus* Stejneger, 1884, Kamchatka.
Considered closely related to *L. genei* by some authors, to *L. argentatus* (with which it occasionally hybridizes) by others, but appears to be a distinctive N Pacific species. Monotypic.

Distribution. NE Siberia, from Cape Navarin and Kamchatka S to Hokkaido, NE Honshu and Vladivostok. Winters S to Taiwan.

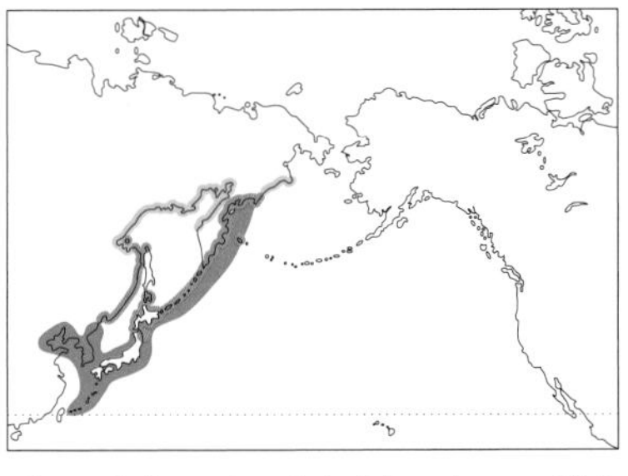

Descriptive notes. 55-67 cm; 1050-1695 g; wingspan 132-148 cm. Typical large, white-headed, dark-mantled species, with slightly greater sexual size dimorphism than in most gulls; head heavy, with peak well behind eye, giving a flat sloping forehead and crown, and a steeply sloping hindcrown; usual mantle colour dark slaty grey, somewhat paler than in *L. marinus*, but highly variable, ranging all the way to pale grey; primaries black, with very extensive white windows and tips in outer primaries; underwing with extensively slaty, black-tipped primaries, contrasting with pale underwing-coverts; relatively short but stout bill yellow, with red gonydeal spot; legs dark pink to almost reddish pink; iris yellow, with pink to purple orbital ring. Distinguished by its angular head, bright pink legs, and dark primaries below, with heavy bill proportionately deeper than in *L. argentatus*. Non-breeding adult has dusky streaking on head and neck. Immature very similar to that of *L. argentatus*.

Habitat. Inshore coastal waters; breeds on low sea cliffs, rocky islets, sandy shores, or rocky tops of sea cliffs.

Food and Feeding. Varies from year to year, depending on availability. Mainly fish and invertebrates (e.g. crabs, sea urchins), also carrion, refuse, offal, bird eggs and chicks; occasionally voles and insects. During salmon-spawning, flies upriver to feed on fish and roe; takes leftovers from bear-kills; eats berries in late summer; in winter, exploits waste from fisheries and slaughterhouses. Some Hokkaido males specialize on predation, piracy and scavenging in seabird colonies, taking adult and young alcids and *L. crassirostris* chicks, but they feed their chicks mostly fish (80%); on Teuri I (N Japan) has heavy impact on *L. crassirostris*, particularly late in season. Foods utilized varied from colony to colony on Hokkaido, with sardines (*Sardinops melanosticta*), rock fish (*Sebastes*), sandeels (*Ammodytes*) and seabirds in different proportions, depending on year; with crash of sardine stocks, took more birds, sandeels and refuse. In Sea of Okhotsk eats mainly adult seabirds, eggs and chicks, taking disproportionate numbers of murrelets (*Brachyramphus*), *Rissa tridactyla*, and Parakeet Auklets (*Cyclorrhynchus psittacula*). Uses variety of foraging methods, including plunge-diving and surface-plunging.

Breeding. Arrives Apr in S, early Jun in Sea of Okhotsk; lays from late May in S to early Jun in N. Colonies of dozens to 1500 pairs on low riverine islands, sloping clifftops, and cliff ledges; density often 2 nests/m², but more sparse on slopes. Nest of grass, seaweed and feathers, often placed in dense vegetation or among boulders, frequently close to cliff face. Usually 3 eggs (1-4); incubation 28-30 days, on Kuril Is 31-33 days; chick grey-brown, spotted black above, on breast, and more distinctly on head, with white belly; fed by parents for 40-45 days. Productivity greater among pairs exploiting seabird chicks to feed their young.

Movements. Many populations non-migratory, dispersing into Bering Sea and Sea of Japan; some migrate S towards coast of China. Non-breeding and wintering birds reach Alaska. Winters from Bering Sea to Japan and Taiwan; occurs casually on coasts of China in winter.

Status and Conservation. Not globally threatened. Total population c. 100,000 pairs. Estimates for Kamchatka population range from 47,000 pairs in more than 200 colonies, to 110,000 pairs. Largest colony (1500 pairs) on Ptichem I, off Karaginskiy I (NE Kamchatka). Hokkaido population small, but increasing by perhaps as much as 19% per year in some colonies.

Bibliography. Armstrong (1983), Austin & Kuroda (1953), Beaman (1994), Brazil (1991), Drury (1984), Étchécopar & Hüe (1978), Firsova (1986), Firsova *et al*. (1982), Flint *et al*. (1984), Goetz *et al*. (1986), Gustafson & Peterjohn (1994), Hasegawa (1984), Hashimoto (1977), Ilicev & Zubakin (1988), Knystautas (1993), Kondratiev (1991), Kondratyva (1994), Litvinenko (1986), Perennou *et al*. (1994), Portenko (1963), Velizhanin (1977), Vyatkin (1986), Watanuki (1982, 1983, 1988a, 1988b, 1989, 1992), Watanuki *et al*. (1988).

26. Lesser Black-backed Gull

Larus fuscus

French: Goéland brun **German**: Heringsmöwe **Spanish**: Gaviota Sombría

Taxonomy. *Larus fuscus* Linnaeus, 1758, Sweden.
Closely related to *L. argentatus*, and sometimes considered conspecific, but in most areas of sympatry the two are reproductively isolated; molecular evidence separates present species from *L. argentatus* and *L. cachinnans*. Very complex systematics involving several of the races. Some evidence that *heuglini* overlaps nominate *fuscus*, perhaps without interbreeding; may merit specific status as *L. heuglini*, which may even include *L. a vegae*. Form described as "*antelius*" (W Siberia) is a synonym of *heuglini*; "*taimyrensis*" (Yenisey and Taymyr Peninsula) considered not separable from *heuglini*. See also *L. argentatus*. Four subspecies recognized.

Subspecies and Distribution.
L. f. graellsii A. E. Brehm, 1857 - Iceland, Faeroes, British Is, France and Iberia; winters from SW Europe to W Africa.
L. f. fuscus Linnaeus, 1758 - Sweden and N Norway E to White Sea; winters mostly in Africa and SW Asia.
L. f. intermedius Schiøler, 1922 - Netherlands, Denmark and S Norway, with isolated population in NE Spain (Ebro Delta); winters mostly in W Europe and W Africa.
L. f. heuglini Bree, 1876 - N Siberia, from S Kola Peninsula E to Taymyr Peninsula; winters from Middle East S to E Africa, and E to NW India.

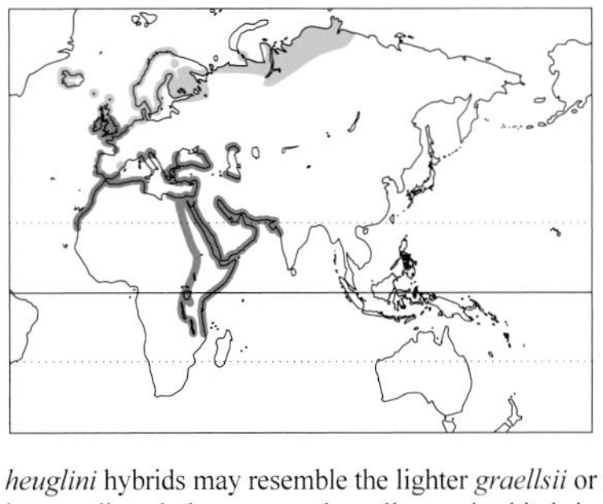

Descriptive notes. 51-61 cm; 550-1200 g; wingspan 124-127 cm. Medium-sized, dark-mantled, yellow-legged gull; bill yellow, with red gonydeal spot; iris yellow, with red orbital ring. Much smaller than *L. marinus*, which has pink legs. Non-breeding adult has head less heavily streaked than *L. argentatus*. Juvenile and immature similar to *L. argentatus*, but somewhat darker and more contrastingly patterned. Races differ mainly in size, proportions, and degree of darkness of upperparts: nominate *fuscus* darkest (black), *graellsii* dark neutral grey, *heuglini* variable; S and W races have much heavier head streaking in non-adult plumages. Nominate *fuscus* x *heuglini* hybrids may resemble the lighter *graellsii* or *intermedius*. Rare hybrids with *L. argentatus* have intermediate dark grey mantle, yellow-red orbital ring, and pink legs tinged with yellow.

Habitat. Coastal and inland waters, estuaries, harbours, tropical lagoons, rubbish dumps, fields; breeds mainly on sandy, rocky or grassy sea coasts, rocky islands, islands of lakes and rivers, buildings, moorland, sea cliffs (*heuglini*), but tends to avoid cliffs favoured by *L. argentatus*.

Food and Feeding. Small fish, aquatic invertebrates, nestlings and eggs of birds, carrion, offal, rodents and berries. Baltic herring (*Clupea harengus*) important in diet. In Mediterranean, prefers trawler discards, but during trawling moratorium fed at rubbish dumps, olive groves and rice fields. With increasing competition from *L. argentatus* since 1960's, proportion of marine invertebrates in diet has increased; also more of fish are freshwater species. In one study, took smaller pieces of offal than congeners. Little or no cannibalism. Methods include contact-dipping and surface-plunging; nominate race tends to avoid sites frequented by *L. marinus*, *L. argentatus* and *L. canus*, and forages in deeper water, mainly by plunge-diving. In intertidal zone, more likely to peck at visible food items than to rummage in seaweed or under stones.

Breeding. Arrives at colony in Mar, lays mostly from May (late Apr) to mid-Jun. Colonies usually small in Russia, but large in Britain. Sites include grassy shores, dunes, clifftops, ledges of cliffs or buildings, rooftops; usually well vegetated, nest-sites with denser vegetation than *L. argentatus* in same colony; sometimes under pine trees. Nest of dry stalks, grass, lichens and feathers. 2-3 eggs; eggs and clutch size smaller in years when food scarce; chicks from larger eggs have greater survival; incubation 24-28 days; chick similar to that of *L. argentatus*; fledging c. 30-40 days. In Finland, chick mortality up to 70%, apparently due to (unidentified) disease. First breeding at 4 years. Recorded longevity of 26 years.

Movements. Migratory in most of range. Shows leapfrog migration, with N populations moving farther to winter in tropics, some covering 7500 km to equatorial Africa; many winter in Mediterranean, Red Sea and Persian Gulf, S to Africa. N European breeders move to W & E Africa and Arabia, some wintering on Black and Caspian Seas. Birds from W Europe and W Scandinavia move SW, some move SE, though numbers wintering in breeding area have increased; British birds winter mainly off Iberia and Morocco, a few reaching Senegal coast. Siberian race *heuglini* winters from Middle East and Red Sea E to Pakistan and India, with some reaching the coast of E Africa. Species is now regular though rare in E North America, also wandering accidentally to Pacific coast.

Status and Conservation. Not globally threatened. Total population probably 250,000-300,000 pairs. At least 175,000 pairs in W Palearctic, including 88,700 in British Is. Has increased greatly since 1940's. May be invading North America, where first recorded in 1940's, reaching Hudson Bay in 1969, Florida and Colorado in 1970's, and California in 1978; increasing numbers recorded from Massachusetts to New Jersey, where species now regular but rare. In Netherlands is competing favourably with *L. argentatus*, and has experienced relatively greater growth in numbers. Some colonies of nominate *fuscus*, however, seriously affected by *L. argentatus* predation. Populations in Shetland, Norway and Finland have declined significantly owing to decreasing food availability caused by change in fishing practices, and to competition with *L. argentatus* and *L. marinus*, perhaps abetted by contaminants and by exploitation on W African wintering grounds.

Bibliography. Ali & Ripley (1982), Barnes (1952), Barth (1966, 1967a, 1967b, 1968, 1975), Beaman (1994), Bergman (1982b, 1982c), Binford (1978), Bolton (1991), Bourne, W.R.P. (1993a), Britton, P.L. (1980), Brooke (1976), Brown (1967a, 1967b, 1967c), Coulson (1991), Cramp & Simmons (1983), Darling (1938), Davis & Dunn (1976), Donnelly (1974), Dowsett & Forbes-Watson (1993), Dunn (1994), Evans (1984b), Filchagov & Semashko (1987), Filchagov *et al*. (1992), Ginn *et al*. (1989), Goethe (1963), Gómez-Tejedor & De Lope (1995), Goodman *et al*. (1989), Götmark (1982, 1984), Greenhalgh & Greenwood (1976), Hario (1984, 1990, 1992, 1994), Harris (1962a, 1962b, 1964, 1970), Harris & Plumb (1965), Harris *et al*. (1978), Hosey & Goodridge (1980), Houston *et al*. (1983), Howell & Webb (1995a), Ilicev & Zubakin (1988), de Juana (1986), Kilpi & Saurola (1984a), Kist (1961), Knystautas (1993), Koskimies (1952), Lloyd *et al*. (1991), Mackworth-Praed & Grant (1957, 1962, 1970), Maclean (1993), MacRoberts, B.R. & MacRoberts (1972), MacRoberts, M.H. (1973), MacRoberts, M.H. & MacRoberts (1972), Noordhuis & Spaans (1992), Paludan (1951), Paz (1987), Perennou (1991), Pinto (1983), Post & Lewis (1995a, 1995b), Richards (1990), Ridgely & Gwynne (1989), Roberts, T.J. (1991), Rogacheva (1992), Root (1988), Ryttman *et al*. (1978), Shirihai (1996), Stegmann (1960), Strann & Vader (1992), Stresemann & Timofeeff (1947), Tasker *et al*. (1987), Tostain & Dujardin (1989), Tostain *et al*. (1992), Urban *et al*. (1986), Verbeek (1977b), Vinicombe *et al*. (1995), Wink *et al*. (1994), Yésou (1991).

PLATE 52

inches 8

cm 20

27

28

29

30

31

32

33

34

35

36

37

38

39

40

41

42

43

44

45

27. Great Black-headed Gull

Larus ichthyaetus

French: Goéland ichthyaète **German**: Fischmöwe **Spanish**: Gavión Cabecinegro

Taxonomy. *Larus Ichthyaetus* Pallas, 1773, Caspian Sea.
Despite large size, behavioural repertoire typical of hooded gulls, although behaviour considered distinctive by some. Possibly a link between the hooded and the white-headed gulls. Monotypic.
Distribution. Breeds in a few very small, scattered localities from Black Sea (Crimea) E to L Balkhash and spottily to NW Mongolia; possibly also N China (Gansu, Qinghai) and Tibet. Winters on coasts of E Mediterranean, Red Sea, S Caspian Sea and N Indian Ocean E to Myanmar; SC Ethiopia.

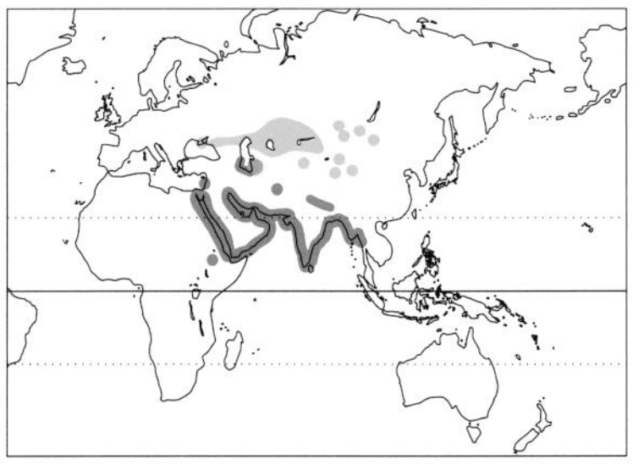

Descriptive notes. 60-72 cm; 900-2000 g; wingspan 155-170 cm. One of the largest gulls, averaging nearly as large as *L. marinus*, sometimes larger; typical hooded appearance, black from face and throat to nape, with conspicuous white eye-crescents; mantle pearl grey; upperwing-coverts very pale grey; flight-feathers mostly white, primaries with conspicuous black subterminal marks and white tips; bill large, orange-yellow, becoming reddish distally, with subterminal black band and yellow tip; legs greenish yellow, with orange webs: iris brown, with thin red orbital ring. Non-breeding adult has white head with dusky area around eye, over ear-coverts and hindcrown. Immature similar to non-breeding adult, but with dark brown flight-feathers and black tail band; bill yellowish with dark subterminal band. Juvenile dark brown above, with prominent pale fringes, very pale below; bill greyish, with diffuse black tip.
Habitat. Coasts and major rivers, harbours, fish ponds, rubbish dumps; breeds on barren islands in fresh and saline lakes and inland seas in generally arid areas, preferring saline soils.
Food and Feeding. Chiefly fish (particularly dead fish) and crustaceans, as well as insects, small mammals, birds, eggs and reptiles. In Volga Delta 88% of diet was fish, including bream (*Abramis brama*) and carp (*Cyprinus carpio*) up to 500 g; also insects and ground squirrels. On Kitai I, rodents (mainly *Spermophilus pygmaeus*) comprised 78% of diet. In cooler weather eats seeds. Frequently piratical on a variety of species. Follows fishing boats; takes fish offal in harbours; one of most solitary gulls. Often flies long distances from colonies to feed aerially on swarming insects.
Breeding. Returns to colonies in early Mar; lays from early Apr. Distinctive courtship displays include raising back feathers, and a howling long call. Colonies of 70-3000 pairs, rarely fewer than 10 pairs; sometimes near but not among *L. argentatus*; single pairs always nest with other gull species, not solitarily. In largest colonies tends to form subgroups of up to 200 nests; small aggregations often linear, parallel to shoreline. Colonies often dense, with nest rims 40 cm apart, especially in centre of colony; at periphery 1-4·5 m apart. Use of breeding areas dependent on fluctuating water levels. Nest of dried aquatic plants and feathers, often on bare rock substrate, sometimes among reeds or other vegetation, or vegetated sand dunes. Very little aggression between neighbours, although gakkering sometimes observed. Normally 2 eggs (1-3); incubation c. 25 days, female sitting for longer spells than male; chick creamy buff or silvery white; recognized by parents by 5th day; may leave territory after c. 5 days; chicks form dense crèche at 7+ days when parents absent or colony disturbed. First breeding usually not until 4 or 5 years.
Movements. Generally migratory, but few details. Migration recorded through NW & C China (Xinjiang, Sichuan). Locally fairly common migrant and winter visitor in Nepal. Recently found to migrate through Red Sea to islands and Ethiopian Rift Valley. Some movement W to Middle East and E Mediterranean (Israel), where apparently much scarcer now than 50 years ago. Immatures may remain in wintering range. Winters mainly on S Caspian Sea, with smaller numbers in Israel (rare), Ethiopia (32-111 birds in mid-1970's), Persian Gulf, S Iran, Pakistan, India and Myanmar. Occasional inland on large lakes and rivers, e.g. c. 100 at Hamun-i-Puzak, SW Afghanistan. Increasingly recorded in Europe, mostly inland; single report from E Atlantic, in Canary Is (Mar 1995).
Status and Conservation. Not globally threatened. Total population unknown, but c. 25,000 pairs in former USSR. Numerous on and N of Caspian Sea, with smaller numbers in Kazakhstan. Bred in Azerbaijan until early or middle 20th century. Apparently stable, but in some colonies expanding populations of *L. cachinnans* cause increased predation. Agricultural benefits from its destruction of insects and rodents considered to outweigh depredation on commercial fish, but still persecuted in some regions. Eggs and young sometimes taken by mammals, e.g. wild boar (*Sus scrofa*), and colonies subject to flooding following storms.
Bibliography. Ali & Ripley (1982), Androsenko (1981), Ash & Ashford (1977), Barthel (1994), Borodulina (1960), Brazil (1991), Britton, P.L. (1980), Cramp & Simmons (1983), Delgushin (1962), Dementiev & Gladkov (1951b), Dowsett & Forbes-Watson (1993), Étchécopar & Hüe (1978), Flint *et al.* (1984), Gladkov (1949), Goodman *et al.* (1989), Ilicev & Zubakin (1988), Knystautas (1993), Kostin & Panov (1982), Lekagul & Round (1991), Mackworth-Praed & Grant (1957), Mierauskas & Buzun (1991), Morris, P. (1992), Panov & Zikova (1982, 1987), Panov *et al.* (1980), Patrikeev (1995), Paz (1987), Perennou *et al.* (1994), Robel & Beschow (1994), Roberts, T.J. (1991), Rogacheva (1992), Samorodov, A.V. & Samorodov (1968), Samorodov, Y.A. (1971), Samorodov, Y.A. & Ryabov (1969, 1971a, 1971b), Shirihai (1996), Smythies (1986), Urban *et al.* (1986), Vinicombe & Hopkin (1993), Zubakin (1975b, 1976, 1982b).

28. Brown-headed Gull

Larus brunnicephalus

French: Mouette du Tibet **German**: Braunkopfmöwe **Spanish**: Gaviota Centroasiática
Other common names: Indian Black-headed Gull

Taxonomy. *Larus brunnicephalus* Jerdon, 1840, west coast of Indian Peninsula.
Sometimes treated as race of *L. ridibundus*, the Pamir population showing intermediate characteristics. Monotypic.
Distribution. Mountains of SC Asia, between 3000 m and at least 4500 m: Turkestan and W Xinjiang E to SE Gansu, and S to Pamirs (L Kara-Kul), Ladakh and Tibet. Winters on coasts of India, N Sri Lanka and SE Asia, sparingly W to Arabian Peninsula.

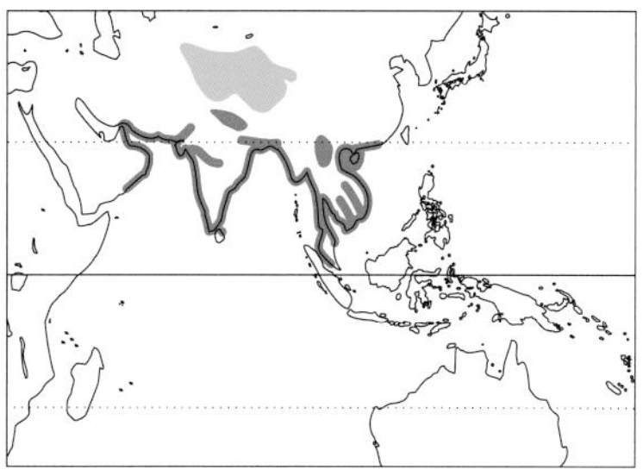

Descriptive notes. 41-45 cm; 450-714 g. Hood pale brown, becoming blackish at nape, forming an indistinct collar reminiscent of *L. cirrocephalus*; narrow white eye-crescents towards rear; mantle, back and inner part of wing grey, outer wing-coverts white; primaries white at base, broadly black distally, with white windows on outer 2; bill bright red, with dusky tip; legs bright to dark red; iris pale yellow or greyish, with narrow red orbital ring. Distinguished by wingtip pattern, recalling that of *L. delawarensis*, very different from *L. ridibundus* and *L. maculipennis*, which have largely white outer primaries. Non-breeding adult has pale grey head with grey-brown marks around eye, on ear-coverts, and often across crown; in winter crown becomes pale grey, cheeks and throat white. Immature resembles young *L. ridibundus*, but with sooty brown primaries that are white at the base; bill yellowish, with dusky tip; legs orange.
Habitat. Breeds on islands in large, cold high altitude lakes of varying salinity, or in adjacent marshes; frequents coasts and rivers outside breeding season.
Food and Feeding. Fish, shrimps, offal; also insects, grubs, slugs, earthworms, sewage, potatoes, rodents and plant shoots; occasionally winged termites. Fish, where present, form main diet. On L Kara-Kul, where there are few fish, feeds mainly on invertebrates, particularly adult caddisflies (*Astratus alaicus*) and amphipods. In winter, associates with fishing boats and consumes refuse. Often feeds in shallow water, by immersing head and neck. Catches termites by aerial hawking.
Breeding. Returns to colonies in May; lays from end of May, mainly in early Jun, even when lakes still frozen. Colonies of c. 50 pairs, but reports of several thousand pairs (Tibet); often near Common Terns (*Sterna hirundo*). Nests usually close together, made of masses of plant stems; large, bulky nests built in marshes, smaller nests on land. Usually 3 eggs (1-4, mean 2·4 in Pamirs); incubation and fledging periods unknown (former possibly c. 24 days); chick very pale grey, spotted dark above; mean hatching weight c. 33 g; brooded for most of time up to c. 10th day, only at night until 14th. Even older young may perish in heavy overnight frosts.
Movements. Migrates over mountains to coasts of S Asia; fairly common in Nepal, where some remain to winter. Known to migrate through Hebei, Shanxi and Inner Mongolia also to India, Gulf of Thailand and SE Asia, where often common close inshore and inland. Abundant in winter on Sambhar L (Rajasthan). Less numerous on large rivers.
Status and Conservation. Not globally threatened. Status insufficiently known, but species probably not rare. Virtually nothing known of numbers over most of breeding range, and virtually unstudied except in Pamirs (Tadjikistan), where c. 1000 pairs nest. In winter, large flocks of several hundred birds noted in many parts of India and SE Asia; common in N Sri Lanka.
Bibliography. Ali & Ripley (1982), van den Berg *et al.* (1991), Baker (1935), Bourne & Bundy (1990, 1993), Bradshaw (1993a), Étchécopar & Hüe (1966, 1978), Hazevoet (1987), Hoogendoorn (1991a, 1991b), Hoogendoor *et al.* (1991), Ilicev & Zubakin (1988), Inskipp & Inskipp (1991), Knystautas (1993), Lekagul & Round (1991), Liao Yanfa & Wang Xia (1983), MacKinnon & Phillipps (1993), Mackworth-Praed & Grant (1957), van Marle & Voous (1988), Medway & Wells (1976), Meyer de Schauensee (1984), Neufeldt & Wunderlich (1986), Oreel (1976), Perennou *et al.* (1994), Phillips (1978), Potapov (1966), Roberts, T.J. (1991), Shaw (1936), Smythies (1986), Stegmann (1935), Xian Yaohua (1983), Zubakin (1982a).

29. Grey-headed Gull

Larus cirrocephalus

French: Mouette à tête grise **German**: Graukopfmöwe **Spanish**: Gaviota Cabecigrís
Other common names: Grey-hooded Gull

Taxonomy. *Larus cirrocephalus* Vieillot, 1818, Brazil.
Morphometric analysis links it with *L. novaehollandiae* and *L. serranus*. Two subspecies recognized.
Subspecies and Distribution.
L. c. cirrocephalus Vieillot, 1818 - coastal Ecuador and Peru; coastal C Brazil to Argentina (S Buenos Aires), and up Paraguay and Paraná basins inland to Santa Fé (Laguna de Melincué).
L. c. poiocephalus Swainson, 1837 - coasts and inland rivers of W Africa; widely scattered localities from Ethiopia to Malawi and S Africa, including Rift Valley lakes (Naivasha, Manyara, Elmenteita, Nakuru, Turkana).

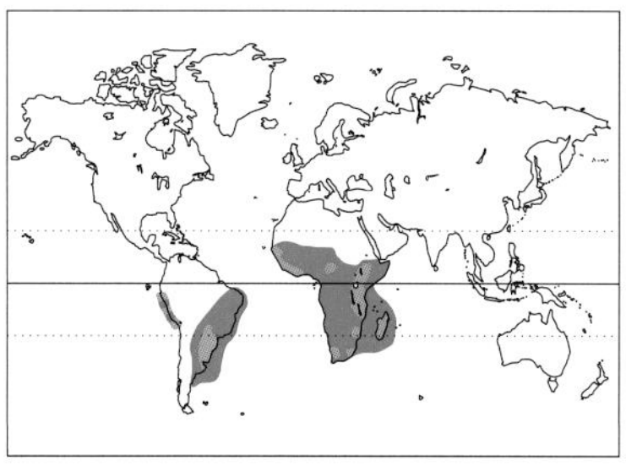

Descriptive notes. 38-43 cm; 250-335 g; wingspan 100-105. Tall, lanky gull with long bill, neck and legs; crown, face and throat grey, bordered with a narrow black line from hindcrown to lower throat; neck, tail and underparts white, a few birds faintly tinged pink below in spring; mantle and wings grey; underwing-coverts dusky; primaries mainly black, with small white windows; bill red, tipped black; legs bright pinkish red; iris yellowish white, with bright red orbital ring. Slightly larger than *L. ridibundus*, and has darker underwing and different wingtip pattern. Non-breeding adult has hint of grey head pattern, without black border; bill duller red, with more extensive black tip. Immature like that of *L. brunnicephalus*, but with darker underwing and narrower dark tail band. Races differ minimally, nominate *cirrocephalus* being c. 2% larger.
Habitat. Tropical and subtropical coasts, offshore islands, and inland lakes and rivers. Breeds on rocky islands, earthen dykes, rarely on coastal dunes; in Argentina mainly in marshes. In Africa, estuaries, harbours, fresh and alkaline lakes; non-breeders also frequent settlements, cattle pens and fishing harbours; remains mainly along shores.
Food and Feeding. Mainly fish and invertebrates, occasionally termites; scavenges broken flamingo eggs and dead fish. In Mauritania preys on eggs of herons and cormorants. Kleptoparasitic on cormorants in Zaire. In winter, scavenges refuse, dead fish and fish scraps. Habits in South America inadequately known. Feeds by plunge-diving; seizes small surface invertebrates while swimming; takes insects by aerial hawking.

On following pages: 30. Hartlaub's Gull (*Larus hartlaubii*); 31. Silver Gull (*Larus novaehollandiae*); 32. Red-billed Gull (*Larus scopulinus*); 33. Black-billed Gull (*Larus bulleri*); 34. Brown-hooded Gull (*Larus maculipennis*); 35. Common Black-headed Gull (*Larus ridibundus*); 36. Slender-billed Gull (*Larus genei*); 37. Bonaparte's Gull (*Larus philadelphia*); 38. Saunders's Gull (*Larus saundersi*); 39. Andean Gull (*Larus serranus*); 40. Mediterranean Gull (*Larus melanocephalus*); 41. Relict Gull (*Larus relictus*); 42. Lava Gull (*Larus fuliginosus*); 43. Laughing Gull (*Larus atricilla*); 44. Franklin's Gull (*Larus pipixcan*); 45. Little Gull (*Larus minutus*).

Breeding. Lays in Apr-May in W Africa (before rainy season), early May in Peru. Colonial; nearest-neighbour distance less than 1 m to a few metres, in Mauritania up to 100 m. Nest on bare ground, in clumps of reeds or papyrus, or on floating vegetation; in Mauritania in tufts of glasswort (*Salicornia*); shallow scrape lined with dry grass and bits of vegetation, to well built cup of rushes and grasses. 3 eggs in South America, 2-3 in Africa (mean 2·4 in E Africa); incubation and fledging periods undocumented; chick buffy yellow, spotted black on head and upperparts, forming irregular linear pattern.
Movements. Many populations are permanent residents or disperse short distances, with many inland breeders moving to coast. Birds from Natal move up to 2000 km N along Atlantic or Indian Ocean coasts. Dispersal apparent along coasts of W Africa and Argentina. In Peru, occurs as far S as Mollendo between Jul and Sept. Vagrants recorded N to Panama, and to Spain and N Red Sea.
Status and Conservation. Not globally threatened. Status inadequately known, but world population reckoned to be under 50,000 pairs. Centre of abundance in equatorial Africa, with several colonies greater than 2000 pairs in Senegal, Kenya and Tanzania; common seasonally at L Chad; abundant breeder (1000's) at Massambwa (L Victoria); c. 200 pairs in S Africa. Suffers serious problems from egging in some areas, e.g. W Africa. Neotropical population uncensused, but few known nesting areas. In E South America probably under 10,000 pairs; rare on Brazilian coast, and very rare in Uruguay; considered fairly abundant in Entre Ríos (NE Argentina), but breeding not specified. On Pacific coast has become common only since 1920's, and was not recorded there by earlier expeditions; first discovered nesting W of Andes in 1967, in Peru at Laguna Grande (Ica); only a few known breeding sites, but probably c. 1000 pairs in Peru.
Bibliography. Belton (1984), Benson & Benson (1975), Blake (1977), Bourne & Bundy (1990), Britton, P.L. (1980), Canevari *et al.* (1991), Cramp & Simmons (1983), Dowsett & Forbes-Watson (1993), Duffy & Atkins (1979), Durnford (1877), Elgood *et al.* (1994), Ginn *et al.* (1989), Gore (1990), Hellmayr & Conover (1948), Hughes (1968), Johnson (1972), Johnstone (1982), Klimaitis & Moschione (1987), Langrand (1990), Mackworth-Praed & Grant (1957, 1962, 1970), Maclean (1993), McLachlan (1955), Miller (1951), Milon *et al.* (1973), Murphy (1936), de la Peña (1992), Perennou (1991), Pereyra (1923), Pinto (1983), Quäbicker (1939), Randall & Hosten (1983), Ridgely & Wilcove (1979), Ruschi (1979), Serié & Smyth (1923), Shirihai (1992), Sick (1985c, 1993), Sinclair (1977b), Tovar & Ashmole (1970), Urban *et al.* (1986), Williams, A.J. (1989), Winterbottom (1961b), Zoutendyk & Feely (1953), Zuquim (1991).

30. Hartlaub's Gull

Larus hartlaubii

French: Mouette de Hartlaub **German**: Hartlaubmöwe **Spanish**: Gaviota Plateada Surafricana

Taxonomy. *Larus* (*Gavia*) *Hartlaubii* Bruch, 1853, Cape of Good Hope.
Little known and requiring substantial study. Forms superspecies with *L. novaehollandiae* and *L. scopulinus*; often treated as a race of the former, but now usually considered a separate species, closely related also to *L. cirrocephalus* and *L. ridibundus*. Monotypic.
Distribution. Coastal SW Africa, mainly from C Namibia (Swakopmund) to SW Cape Province (Dyer I).

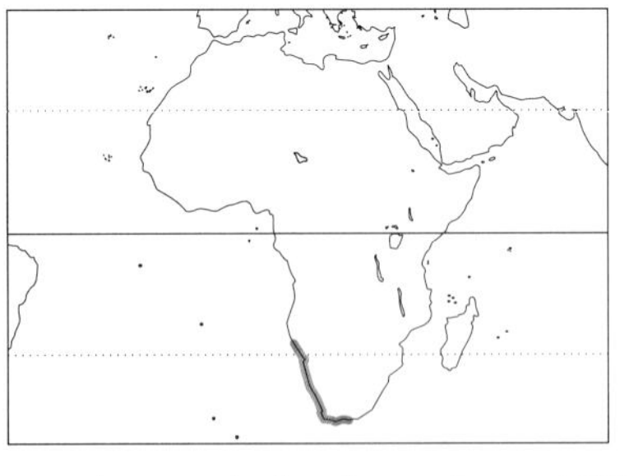

Descriptive notes. 37-39 cm; 235-340 g; wingspan 89-92 cm. White-bodied, with grey mantle; often a suggestion of a faint lavender-grey hood with darker border; outer primaries black, with small white windows; bill and legs deep red; eye brown. "Hooded" birds very like a pale version of *L. cirrocephalus*, but eye is dark, not white. Non-breeding adult fully white-headed. Juvenile has white head and body, no dark ear spot; back and wings brown, marked with pale buff.
Habitat. Coasts, harbours, wet lawns, rubbish dumps and slaughterhouses. Breeds on low, flat islands, including artificial islands and dykes in sewage lagoons and salt-works; sometimes on buildings.
Food and Feeding. Marine invertebrates, small fish, earthworms, insects, offal and refuse. Occasionally feeds on emerging kelp-flies and flying termites, and behind ploughs. Feeds by plunge-diving, swimming, and aerially; also scavenges.
Breeding. Much conflicting information, and laying variously listed as Feb or Apr to Sept, or peaking Apr-Jun; begins breeding in Nov in N, Jan in S; at Swakopmund, breeds throughout year. Frequently nests with Greater Crested Terns (*Thalasseus bergii*), and may be displaced by them. Colonies of 10-1000 pairs, with inter-nest distance usually 1-2 m. Prefers bare or slightly vegetated ground; sometimes roofs. Nest a slight hollow with variable lining material, occasionally 50 cm up on shrubs. Usually 1-3 eggs (1-5, mean 1·8); shell comstitiutes 11·6% of fresh weight, greater than in almost all other gull species; many eggs lost, replacement clutches having lower survival; incubation c. 25 days; incubating gulls responded to human intrusion at distance of 5 m, returning quickly to nest after intrusion; chick buff with black spots, pale on belly; average hatching weight 28 g, by 5th day 68 g; fledging c. 40 days. Productivity often very low. First breeding at 3 years.
Movements. Non-migratory. Disperses to mainland coast in both directions; wanders N on Atlantic coast, and rarely E to Natal.
Status and Conservation. Not globally threatened. Total population estimated at c. 31,000 individuals in 1990, based on 12,000 pairs now breeding at 31 localities; species may be vulnerable. Declining in Namibia, but increasing in Cape Province; 28% of population at Robben I. High rate of breeding failure from both man-induced and natural causes; 60% mortality documented around fledging period, mainly from predation; roof-nesting hazardous, as chicks run off the edge. Main cause of egg mortality was displacement of incubating gulls by *Thalasseus bergii*; displaced gulls usually renest, but replacement clutches average smaller and survival lower than in initial nests. Some advocate that control of *T. bergii* could benefit present species. *L. dominicanus* takes eggs, chicks, and occasionally adults; Sacred Ibises (*Threskiornis aethiopicus*) and Cattle Egrets (*Bubulcus ibis*) eat eggs and chicks. Mongooses (*Herpestes*) are also major predators.
Bibliography. Allanson (1953), Betham (1931), Braine & Loutit (1987), Broekhuysen & Elliott (1974), Brown, A. (1977, 1990), Cooper (1976a, 1977b), Cooper & Pringle (1977), Cooper *et al.* (1977), Crawford (1995), Dowsett & Forbes-Watson (1993), Ginn *et al.* (1989), Graham & Brooke (1985), Hofmeyr (1991), Mackworth-Praed & Grant (1962), Maclean (1993), Robertson & Wooller (1981), Ryan (1987), Simon (1977), Sinclair (1977b), Steele (1989, 1992a, 1992b), Tinbergen & Broekhuysen (1954), Underhill & Underhill (1986), Urban *et al.* (1986), Walter, C.B. (1984), Williams, A.J. (1977b, 1989, 1990), Williams *et al.* (1990), Winterbottom (1971), Zoutendyk & Feely (1953).

31. Silver Gull

Larus novaehollandiae

French: Mouette argentée **German**: Silberkopfmöwe **Spanish**: Gaviota Plateada Australiana

Taxonomy. *Larus Novæ-Hollandiæ* Stephens, 1826, New South Wales.
Forms superspecies with *L. hartlaubii* and *L. scopulinus*, and all three sometimes treated as a single species. Morphometric analysis of skeletal characters links prtesent species consistently with *L. maculipennis*, *L. serranus* and *L. cirrocephalus*. Tasmanian birds sometimes separated as race *gunni*, but variation only clinal. Two subspecies recognized.
Subspecies and Distribution.
L. n. forsteri Mathews, 1912 - N Australia; New Caledonia and Loyalty Is.
L. n. novaehollandiae Stephens, 1826 - S Australia and Tasmania.

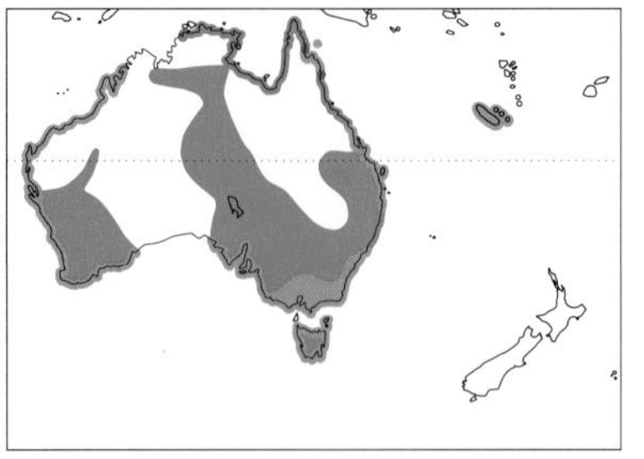

Descriptive notes. 38-43 cm; 260-350 g; wingspan 91-96 cm. White head, body and tail, blending into grey mantle, back and wings; outer primaries mostly black, with white subterminal spots on outer 3, inners white at bases; bill entirely bright red; legs dull red; iris whitish, with narrow fleshy red orbital ring. Bare-part colours duller in W than in E. Sexes differ in bill depth, male over 11 mm and female under 11 mm. Juvenile has brown markings on head, brown-mottled mantle, scapulars and upperwing-coverts, and a dark brown subterminal band on the tail; bill, iris and orbital ring dark; legs vary from flesh to blackish. Moults into adult plumage at c. 12 months. Race *forsteri* differs in being slightly larger.
Habitat. Both coastal and inland locations, frequenting sandy and rocky shores, parks, beaches and rubbish dumps, as well as inland fields; some birds frequent slaughterhouses and livestock pens. Breeds on small islands and points, mainly with low vegetation, mainly offshore, but also on freshwater and brackish lakes; off South Australia mostly on marine islands, but also on islands in lakes, on breakwaters, and on causeways in salt-pans.
Food and Feeding. Very varied. Refuse, fish, fish offal, marine and terrestrial invertebrates, berries, seeds and insects. Has been observed on water's surface 30 km offshore, eating pelagic amphipods (*Hyperia gaudichaudi*); inland flocks feed similarly on brine-shrimps. Patrols the edge of seabird colonies. In some disturbed colonies, opportunistically takes eggs of conspecifics. Occasionally steals food from terns and pelicans. At Sydney, refuse is an important constituent of diet during breeding season for 85% of adults, while 5-25% feed mainly on natural foods; amount of natural food increased as chicks hatch. Scavenges along shore. Often seen hawking flying ants; kelp-fly larvae and locust swarms attract large flocks. Feeding in ploughed fields is a relatively recent occurrence, but now common. Frequent visitor at picnic sites.
Breeding. Covers all months. Lays from Mar to Nov in W Australia, some pairs raising 2 broods per year; from Jul in S; "winter" breeder in N. Older birds nest earlier, and produce more young. Often chooses same territory and mate in successive years. Colonial, occasionally solitary. May nest close to terneries, particularly of Greater Crested Tern (*Thalasseus bergii*), as does *L. hartlaubii* in Africa. In tropical areas colonies tend to be small (3-25 pairs); up to 3000 pairs in South Australia; colony size limited by immediate food availability. In Capricorn Group in Great Barrier Reef, nests mostly on ground (on sand, low vegetation, rocks), under trees and shrubs, sometimes in bushes up to 2·5 m up; closer than random to trees, with greater vegetation cover, but less grass around nest. Nests vulnerable to flooding. Nest a shallow cup. Usually 3 eggs (1-5); eggs and clutch sizes smaller in drought years; incubation 21-27 days; chicks remain in colony until c. 4 weeks, when led away by parents; parental care ceases at c. 6 weeks. First breeding usually at 4 years, sometimes 3; c. 24% of ringed chicks returned to colony at 2 years, but less than 1% produced young. Reproductive life c. 11 seasons.
Movements. May wander widely outside breeding season. Some populations move short distances, mainly from colony to nearby coastlines. S populations more likely to migrate N; general movement in E Australia is N, but in W Australia is S. Some W movement also takes place along S coast.
Status and Conservation. Not globally threatened. Abundant and increasing, especially in S of range. Over 500,000 pairs at c. 200 colony sites in Australia. Occasionally a pest at airports, and at colonies of other seabird species. Status in New Caledonia unclear.
Bibliography. Beehler *et al.* (1986), Blakers *et al.* (1984), Bregulla (1992), Burger & Gochfeld (1987a), Carrick & Murray (1964), Carrick *et al.* (1957), Coates (1985), Domm & Recher (1973), Gibson, J.D. (1979), Hannecart & Létocart (1980), Hulsman (1984), Johnstone (1982), Marchant & Higgins (1996), Meathrel *et al.* (1991), Murray & Carrick (1964), Nichols (1974), Ottaway *et al.* (1984, 1985, 1988), Rand & Gilliard (1967), Serventy *et al.* (1971), Smith, G.C. (1991b, 1992b), Smith, G.C. & Carlile (1992a, 1992b, 1993), Smith, G.C., Carlile & Louwerse (1991), Smith, G.C., Carlile & Tully (1992a, 1992b), Walker (1988), Wheeler & Watson (1963), Wooller & Dunlop (1979, 1981a, 1981b).

32. Red-billed Gull

Larus scopulinus

French: Mouette scopuline **German**: Rotschnabelmöwe **Spanish**: Gaviota Plateada Neozelandesa

Taxonomy. *Larus scopulinus* J. R. Forster, 1844, Dusky Sound, South Island, New Zealand.
Forms superspecies with *L. hartlaubii* and *L. novaehollandiae*, and usually considered a race of latter. Exceptional mixed pairs with *L. bulleri*, producing fertile hybrids, but the two appear behaviourally isolated. Monotypic.
Distribution. New Zealand, breeding mainly on E coasts of North I and South I, and inland at L Rotorua (North I); also Stewart I, Chathams, Bounties, Snares, Aucklands and Campbell I.

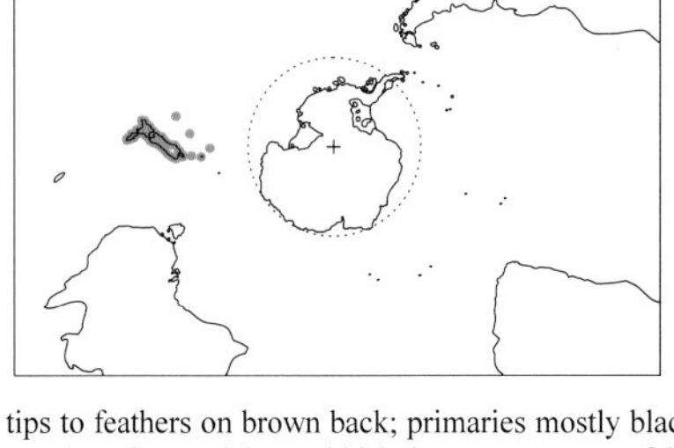

Descriptive notes. 37 cm; 245-360 g; wingspan 91-96 cm. Head, body and tail white; mantle and wing-coverts pale grey; outer primaries black, tipped white, with large white mirrors; inner primaries (6-3) mainly white with narrow black tips, producing conspicuous white wing patch in flight; bill and feet scarlet; iris yellowish white, with narrow red orbital ring. Female slightly smaller and slighter-billed. Differs from *L. novaehollandiae* in slightly smaller size, slightly darker upperparts and relatively deeper bill. Non-breeding adult similar to breeding, but with bill and feet duller red. Immature like adult, but with brown patches on secondaries and buffy tips to feathers on brown back; primaries mostly black; iris, bill and legs dark brown.
Habitat. Coasts, lakes, rubbish dumps, sewage outfalls, fishing piers, wet lawns, and fields. Breeds on rocky beaches, islands, and stacks, rarely on inland lakes.

Food and Feeding. In breeding season, mainly euphausiid krill (*Nyctiphanes australis*) and other planktonic crustaceans, but also earthworms, insects and small fish; at other times diet more varied, including more fish and refuse. Kleptoparasitism on other seabirds and waders common. Feeds behind plough; sometimes eats berries.

Breeding. Most data from 29-year study of Kaikoura colony (NE South I). Begins nesting Jul; prolonged egg-laying (late Sept to Dec), with peak in Oct (mid-Nov on subantarctic islands). Colonies very dense on the main islands; small groups or even solitary on subantarctic islands. Almost all birds, particularly males, return to natal colony; retain mates from year to year; early pairs take central territories. Large number of non-breeders frequent colony. Territory defended for long period; nest building begins 2-3 weeks prior to laying; courtship feeding rare until c. 3 weeks before laying; mounting begins about same time, often following feeding. Normally 2 eggs (1-5); older females lay larger eggs; egg and clutch sizes reduced when less food available; incubation 22-26 days; fledging 28-35 days. Productivity low: c. 33% of adults never fledge young in their lifetime, and only 17% of males and 24% of females recruited young into population. Some birds breed at 2 years, most not until 4-5 years; males breed at younger age than females.

Movements. Leaves breeding areas in mid-Jan. Most adults remain within 380 km of colony, while juveniles disperse further N. Adults ringed at Kaikoura have reached North I (Auckland).

Status and Conservation. Not globally threatened. Total population probably over 500,000 pairs. As with many gulls, this species has increased dramatically through most of 20th century, benefiting from supplementary winter food at fish-processing plants and rubbish dumps. Legislation limiting discharge of offal has been followed by a decline in numbers of present species. Colonization of inland area of L Rotorua (North I) was facilitated by agricultural practices making food available. Eggs are subject to predation by stoats (*Mustela erminea*).

Bibliography. Chambers (1989), Cunningham (1946), Fleming (1946), Gurr (1967), Gurr & Kinsky (1965), Marchant & Higgins (1996), Mills (1969, 1970, 1971, 1973b, 1979, 1989, 1991), Morris (1976), Reid & Reid (1965), Robertson (1985), Stidolph (1947), Tasker & Mills (1981), Williams (1975), Wooller & Dunlop (1981b).

33. **Black-billed Gull**
Larus bulleri

French: Mouette de Buller   **German**: Maorimöwe   **Spanish**: Gaviota Maorí

Taxonomy. *Larus bulleri* Hutton, 1871, New Zealand.
Rarely hybridizes with *L. scopulinus*, even where breeding alongside (L Rotorua). Morphometric analysis links it with *L. ridibundus* or *L. genei*. Monotypic.
Distribution. New Zealand, on South I and at a few sites on North I (Rotorua, Gisborne, Clive, Porangahau). Winters mainly on S North I and N South I, some straggling to Stewart I and Snares Is.

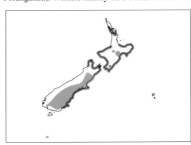

Descriptive notes. 35-38 cm; 190-270 g; wingspan c. 90 cm. Very pale gull, distinguished by mainly white wingtip with narrow black trailing border, and long, slender black bill; head, body and tail white; mantle and upperwings, including secondaries and inner primaries, very pale grey; outer 2 primaries white, edged black, with subterminal black bar and white tip; decreasing amounts of black on remaining primaries; bill black, with red-orange gape; legs reddish black, with some brick-orange colour on toes; iris white. Non-breeding adult has black eyelids, and blackish feet marked with orange. Immature similar to adult, with buffy tips to feathers of crown, back and upperwing (by 6 months tips worn away); more black on primaries, and brown patches on secondaries; tail may have partial black marks; iris dark brown; bill pinkish, with black tip; legs flesh, with black markings on feet.

Habitat. Coasts, rivers, lakes, parks, wet lawns, sheep pastures, ploughed fields; breeds almost exclusively inland, mainly on rocky islands in fast-flowing braided rivers and along lake shores, rarely attempting to breed at coastal sites.

Food and Feeding. Mainly earthworms, insects, small fish and aquatic invertebrates; sometimes refuse. Gregarious forager; flocks follow plough, and feed on freshly tilled fields, wet grass and sheep pastures. Most feeding sites suitable for only 1 day, so food highly patchy in time and space; birds leaving colony give a contact call that recruits followers, presumably due to benefits of group foraging. Mean feeding distance from colony 4·7 km. Adept at surface-dipping; hawks aerial insects.

Breeding. Courtship begins in Aug, along coast; colonies occupied by mid-Sept; often deserted early in season when food supply poor. Flocks engage in noisy swoop-and-soar displays. Pairs tend to occupy same nest-site in successive years. Synchronous nest building from early Oct; nest is a deep depression of small sticks, lined with grass. Usually 2 eggs (1-3); incubation 20-24 days, by both sexes, eggs never left unattended; in disturbed colonies families abandon nest within 1 day of hatching; remain longer in undisturbed colonies. When disturbed, chicks flock together and run or swim from intruders, often forming dense rafts attended by a few adults; chicks recognize parents' mew calls; fledging c. 26 days. Can breed at 2 years, but usually at 3-4 years.

Movements. After fledging period, adults and young move mainly to coastal habitats, with some movement N; some reach North I.

Status and Conservation. Not globally threatened. Many colonies vulnerable. Total population c. 100,000 pairs. Present species has increased since colonial times, aided by agricultural practices (ploughing) increasing the availability of insects and worms; plays an important role in controlling insect pests. Breeding habitat is limited, and threatened by vegetation overgrowth with exotic lupins (*Lupinus*). Middens reveal that this species was formerly eaten as food by Maori people.

Bibliography. Allen (1984), Beer (1965, 1966), Black (1955), Burger & Gochfeld (1996), Chambers (1989), Cooper (1991), Daniel (1963), Dawson (1958), Drake (1980), Evans (1970b, 1982a, 1982b, 1982c, 1982d, 1983), Gleeson *et al.* (1972), Gurr (1967), Marchant & Higgins (1996), Reid & Reid (1965), Robertson (1985).

34. **Brown-hooded Gull**
Larus maculipennis

French: Mouette de Patagonie   **German**: Patagonienmöwe   **Spanish**: Gaviota Cahuil
Other common names: Pink-breasted Gull

Taxonomy. *Larus maculipennis* Lichtenstein, 1823, Montevideo.
Sometimes treated as a race of *L. ridibundus*. Morphometric analysis links it most closely with *L. brunnicephalus* or *L. novaehollandiae*. Monotypic

Distribution. SC Chile and Uruguay S to Tierra del Fuego and Falkland Is; probably also SE Brazil (Rio Grande do Sul). Winters N to N Chile and CE Brazil.

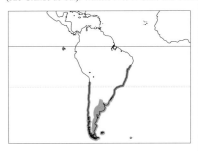

Descriptive notes. 35-37 cm; 290-361 g. Frontal hood chocolate brown to dark brown, darker at rear, forming blackish margin; white crescents behind eye; neck white; underparts white, commonly suffused with pink; back and upperwings grey; outer primaries white, all but outermost primaries tipped black; undersurface of primaries black, with broad white triangle at wingtip (pattern visible at a distance); tail white; bill dark red, blackish distally; legs orange-red; eye brown. Compared with *L. brunnicephalus*, has darker and more uniform head, with less well demarcated black margin. Non-breeding adult (from mid-Feb) has white head with few dark spots behind eye; moults back to breeding plumage in Jun-Jul. Juvenile mottled brown on back, wings and head, with narrow black trailing edge to wing, and narrow black subterminal tail bar; bill dull orange, with black tip; legs brownish. Back and wing-coverts become greyish in 1st winter. 1st-summer birds have a partial dark hood.

Habitat. Sea coasts, rivers, lakes and marshes; in winter also frequents sewage outfalls, slaughterhouses, harbours and fields. Breeds mainly on freshwater or alkaline lakes and *esteros* (marshes) among emergent vegetation (*Scirpus*), but also on rocky peninsulas or high shingle beaches; in Chile among rushes at lakes or rivers close to the sea; in Falklands up to 5 km inland, and in Argentina far inland.

Food and Feeding. Largely insectivorous, but in Chile breeding birds feed mainly on small fish; takes offal and carrion when available. Forages over marshes, damp fields or pastures, and agricultural land; frequently feeds behind plough. Occasionally hawks flying insects. In Tierra del Fuego mainly a scavenger.

Breeding. Lays Nov-Dec in Chile, from late Oct to early Jan in Argentina, from Dec in Falklands. Sometimes solitary, but usually in colonies of 5-50 nests, occasionally over 500 nests. In Argentina nests with White-faced Ibis (*Plegadis chihi*) and grebes; in Falklands with South American Terns (*Sterna hirundinacea*) and *Leucophaeus scoresbii*. Nests close together, particularly where plant stems reduce visibility of neighbours. Usurps grebe nest, or may assemble floating nest platform; on dry ground builds bulky grass nest, with cup 25 cm across. Usually 2-3 eggs (1-4; mean 2·6); mobs various intruders, including shorebirds and caracaras; incubation and fledging periods not documented. Chicks remain on nest platform if not disturbed. Solitary breeders sometimes more successful than colonial birds, suffering lower predation by grebes and caracaras. First breeding at 3 years.

Movements. Relatively sedentary, dispersing to large rivers and coastal areas after breeding.

Status and Conservation. Not globally threatened. Status poorly known. Total population probably 50,000-100,000 pairs; c. 600 pairs in Falklands. Common in Chile; usually considered common in E Argentina. Breeding status in Tierra del Fuego unclear.

Bibliography. Aravena (1927), Belton (1984), Blake (1977), Burger (1974b), Canevari *et al.* (1991), Clark (1986), Contreras *et al.* (1990), Croxall, McInnes & Prince (1984), Dubs (1992), Escalante (1970c, 1991), Fjeldså & Krabbe (1990), Hellmayr & Conover (1948), Hudson (1920), Johnson (1967), Klimaitis & Moschione (1987), Meyer de Schauensee (1982), Moynihan (1962), Murphy (1936), Naroski (1969), Olrog (1984), de la Peña (1992), Philippi *et al.* (1954), Pinto (1964), Plotnick (1951), Ruschi (1979), Sick (1985c, 1993), Vooren & Chiaradia (1990), Woods (1988), Zotta (1934), Zuquim (1991).

35. **Common Black-headed Gull**
Larus ridibundus

French: Mouette rieuse   **German**: Lachmöwe   **Spanish**: Gaviota Reidora
Other common names: Black-headed Gull

Taxonomy. *Larus ridibundus* Linnaeus, 1766, England.
Morphometric analyses link it to various other hooded gulls, with no consistent pattern. Some authors recognize possible race *sibiricus* (NE Siberia). Monotypic.
Distribution. S Greenland and Iceland through most of Europe and C Asia to Kamchatka, extreme SE Russia (Ussuriland) and NE China (Heilongjiang); marginal in NE North America. Winters S to W & E Africa, India, Malaysia and Philippines.

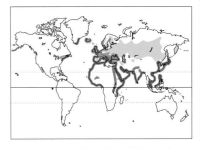

Descriptive notes. 37-43 cm; 195-325 g; wingspan 94-110 cm. Frontal hood dark chocolate brown to dusky blackish, with blackish border; white eye-crescents, mainly behind eye; neck white; underparts white, but in some populations (e.g. in Norway) up to 50% of arriving adults have pink bloom on underparts; back, upperwing-coverts, secondaries and inner primaries grey, secondaries with white tips; outer primaries white, edged and tipped black; tail white; bill and legs dark red; eye dark brown. Distinguished from slightly larger but very similar *L. brunnicephalus* by largely white leading edge to wing, lacking black wingtip with white subterminal spots. Differs from slightly smaller but almost identical *L. maculipennis* in having black tips to outermost primaries. Non-breeding adult has white head, but retains dusky spot on ear-coverts and some blackish clouding on nape. Juvenile has extensive rich buff to darker brown markings on upperparts and upperwing-coverts; black terminal band to tail; bare parts duller.

Habitat. Temperate zone to edge of boreal forests of Palearctic; mainly at low altitudes, and generally near calm, shallow water of coastal or inland waters, including rivers and their estuaries. In winter, tends to occur far more in coastal habitats, but also inland at relatively low elevations. Chiefly inland breeder, with much breeding habitat created by rising water levels, and colonies eventually abandoned when water levels fall and leave dry basin; in many places, however, nests on relatively dry sites, e.g. moors, sand dunes and beaches. Overall, most colonies on freshwater lakes and marshes, but invading certain coastal areas (e.g. coasts of Baltic and North Seas) in huge numbers; in Scandinavia, has recently adapted to colonize salt-marshes, settling ponds, clay pits and coastal dunes and offshore islands. In very wet years may nest in low trees. Often found on sewage farms or near canals.

Food and Feeding. Relies heavily on aquatic and terrestrial insects, earthworms and marine invertebrates, and to lesser extent on fish; also variety of grains. In Baltic, 93% of stomachs contained insects, 5% molluscs, and 3% each oligochaetes (May only) and fish. Feeds by swimming and seizing objects from surface, or dipping head under surface; along coast, by walking on mudflats and probing for shrimps and marine worms; sometimes by foot-stirring and foot-paddling. Also follows fishing boats and ferries that churn up food items, and may feed at night. Rarely takes berries and acorns from trees. Occasionally kleptoparasitic on terns and other birds, and takes eggs but not chicks of Sandwich Terns (*Thalasseus sandvicensis*). In non-breeding season, also relies heavily on various artificial food sources provided by man, especially in W Europe.

Breeding. Returns to colonies from late Feb to late Mar; lays in late Apr and May. Most colonies 11-100 pairs, a few exceeding 10,000 pairs; inter-nest distances often average 1 m, and large, bulky nests often touch; solitary nesting generally rare, except in Sweden. Shows strong preference for nesting near vegetation, but some colonies deserted because of vegetation overgrowth; very variable substrate, including sand, vegetation, rocks and marshes. 1-3 eggs (mean 2·6-2·78); incubation 22-26 days; chick warm buff, boldly spotted with irregular black blotches on back and wings and smaller, rounder, sparser black spots on head; mean hatching weight declines from 26 g to 23 g during season; adults and chicks recognize each other by 4th day; fledging by 35 days. Young birds likely to return to breed in natal colony; few breed at 2 years. Recorded longevity of 32 years.

Movements. N populations migratory, while lower latitude birds tend to be resident or dispersive. Most birds breeding in Switzerland migrate to W Mediterranean; Scandinavian breeders migrate to Britain and many follow Atlantic coast down to W Africa, but most birds wintering in Britain originate in Baltic republics. Abundant in N Africa especially Egypt in winter; small numbers ascend R Nile; common visitor to Red Sea; uncommon along Rift Valley and E African coast, winter range having extended to tropical Africa fairly recently. Asian birds winter S to India, Malaysia and Philippines; fairly common migrant and winter visitor to Nepal.

Status and Conservation. Not globally threatened. World population close to or perhaps exceeding 2,000,000 pairs, with recent estimates for W Europe of 1,500,000-1,800,000 pairs; as many as c. 300,000 pairs estimated in Sweden alone, and over 200,000 in British Is. Spread and increase impressive 1950-1980, after which slower increase or stability, or even slight decline (e.g. Sweden). Species on increase in Norway and Iceland owing to availability of refuse, but declining in Denmark due to egging and interference by *L. argentatus*. At one site in Netherlands, eggs were collected until 1963 in order to protect colonies of *Thalasseus sandvicensis*; when collecting ceased, population rebounded, increasing from 170 pairs to 6000 pairs in 10 years. Species colonized Ebro Delta, NE Spain, in late 1950's. Range spreading to W: colonized Iceland in about 1910, and Greenland in 1969; numbers have increased in E North America since 1950's, and first bred in E Canada in 1977; now 4 breeding sites known in Canada and New England, but fewer than 20 breeding pairs. In Czech and Slovak colonies, congenital defects numerous, affecting 3-5% of eggs, and particularly common in single-egg clutches; attributed in part to chemical pollutants.

Bibliography. Ali & Ripley (1982), Andersson *et al*. (1981), Aubrey (1984), Baerends & van Rhijhn (1975), Beer (1961, 1962, 1963a, 1963b), Beklova (1991), Borodulina (1960), Brandl & Gorke (1988), Brazil (1991), Bremond & Aubin (1992), Britton, P.L. (1980), Bukacinska & Bukacinski (1993), Burger (1976a, 1977a), Coates (1985), Cramp & Simmons (1983), Curtis & Thompson (1985), Dowsett & Forbes-Watson (1993), Erskine (1963), Evans (1984b), Fasola (1986), Fasola & Canova (1992), Flegg & Cox (1972, 1975), Fuchs (1977a, 1977b), Ginn *et al*. (1989), Goethe (1969), Goodbody (1955), Goodman *et al*. (1989), Gosling *et al*. (1990), Götmark (1982), Groothuis (1989, 1992), Groothuis & Mulekom (1991), Guthova (1993), Horton *et al*. (1984), Howell & Webb (1995a), Hutson (1977a, 1977b), Huxley & Fisher (1940), Ilicev & Zubakin (1988), Ilyenko & Burov (1985), Isenmann (1977a, 1977b), Isenmann *et al*. (1991), Jones (1980), de Juana (1986), Kharitonov (1978, 1981a, 1981b, 1993), Kirkman (1937, 1940), Kruuk (1964), Landry (1978), Lebreton & Isenmann (1976), Lebreton & Landry (1979), Lundberg & Vaisanen (1979), MacKinnon & Coulson (1987), Mackworth-Praed & Grant (1957, 1970), Manley (1960a, 1960b), Montevecchi *et al*. (1987), Moynihan (1955), Patterson (1965), Paz (1987), Ptaszyk (1981), van Rhijn (1981, 1985b), van Rhijn & Groothius (1985, 1987), Richards (1990), Ritter & Fuchs (1980), Roberts, T.J. (1991), Rothschild (1962), Shirihai (1996), Smythies (1986), Stamm (1969), Storkersen (1986), Tasker *et al*. (1987), Tima (1961), Tinbergen (1967), Tinbergen & Moynihan (1952), Tinbergen, Broekhuysen *et al*. (1962), Tinbergen, Kruuk & Paillette (1962), Tostain & Dujardin (1989), Ulfstrand (1979), Ulfvens (1993), Urban *et al*. (1986), Veen (1977), Vernon (1970, 1972), Viksne (1961, 1968a, 1968b, 1968c, 1980, 1985), Viksne & Janaus (1980, 1990), Vine & Sergeant (1948), Weidmann, R. & Weidmann (1958), Weidmann, U. (1956), Weseloh & Mineau (1986), Ytreberg (1956, 1960), Zubakin & Kharitonov (1981).

36. Slender-billed Gull

Larus genei

French: Goéland railleur **German**: Dünnschnabelmöwe **Spanish**: Gaviota Picofina

Taxonomy. *Larus Geneï* Brème, 1839, Sardinia.
Nearest relative uncertain: although white-headed, has display repertoire more like that of the hooded gulls, and possibly closest to *L. bulleri*. Formerly listed as *L. gelastes*. Monotypic.

Distribution. Widely scattered, isolated localities from Senegal, Mauritania, S & E Iberia through Mediterranean, Black Sea, Asia Minor and Middle East to E Kazakhstan, Afghanistan, Pakistan and NW India. Winters S to Horn of Africa.

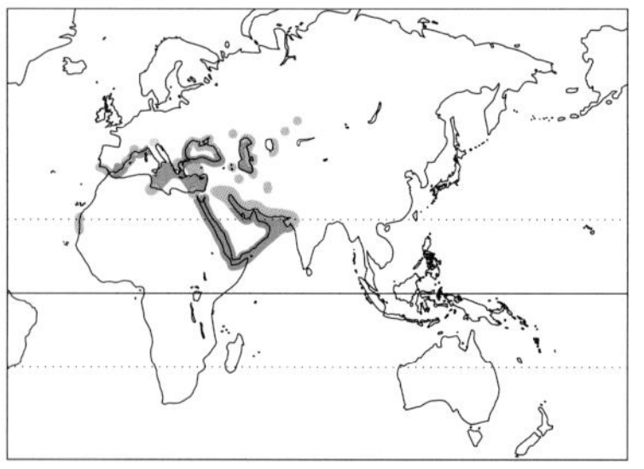

Descriptive notes. 42-44 cm; 220-350 g; wingspan 102-110 cm. Distinctive shape, with long sloping forehead, long, slightly drooping bill, and long legs; head, neck, rump and tail white; back and upperwings grey; conspicuous white leading edge to wing, as outer 5 primaries mainly white, with black tips; underparts white, with rosy bloom on breast and belly in fresh plumage; bill and legs dark red to blackish red; iris yellowish white, with red eye-ring. Non-breeding adult similar, but some show a small dusky auricular spot. Readily distinguished from *L. ridibundus* by more angular profile, with smaller head, longer bill and flat-sloping forehead. Juvenile has buff-grey marks on head, including ear spot and vague partial hood. Immature differs from non-breeding adult in having dark flight-feathers, though primaries with much white, and dusky band on upperwing-coverts; bill bright red to pinkish orange, with small dark tip; legs pale orange or pinkish orange.

Habitat. Almost entirely coastal outside breeding season, feeding in shallow inshore waters and at salt-pans; tends to avoid harbours, but exploits them in Africa. Breeds on coasts of Mediterranean, Black and Caspian Seas and Persian Gulf, and at inland seas and steppe lakes in E Europe to C Asia; utilizes islands, sand spits and beaches, or meadows, grassland, brackish or freshwater marshes of broad river deltas, occasionally in the marine littoral zone.

Food and Feeding. Mainly fish, insects and marine invertebrates, captured alive and scavenged. Fish make up c. 50% of diet; vegetable matter also important. One bird had 3400 bloodworms in its crop. Engages in aerial dipping to surface, plunging from about 1 m, surface-dipping and upending; feeds in intertidal zone, probing in mud with bill; aerial foraging on swarming insects noted. Scavenges far less than most gulls, hence usually does not congregate near villages, but in winter joins other gulls at sewage outfalls.

Breeding. Returns to colonies in late Mar; lays in late Mar to May. Forms colonies of tens to thousands of pairs, often with terns. Preferentially selects open mud, but some birds nest in *Salsola* or *Salicornia*. Nests closely packed; inter-nest distances 20-300 cm (average 42 cm). Some colony-site tenacity, but also shifts colonies between years. 2-3 eggs; eggs much paler than those of most other gulls; incubation 22 days; chick pale grey to pale buff, variably patterned with dark brown or black spots on head and upperparts, with whitish breast and belly; mean hatching weight 28·8 g; adults recognize chicks by 4th day; chicks form crèches, which adults lead towards sea; fledging 30-37 days. First breeding at 2-3 years. Recorded longevity of 23 years 4 months.

Movements. Populations from W Africa, Iberia, Persian Gulf and Pakistan not highly migratory, but generally some dispersal to nearby areas. Birds breeding in C Asia migrate, and mix with the more southerly birds in the Persian Gulf and along Arabian coasts. Most Black Sea birds winter in the Mediterranean, many off Egypt and Tunisia. Regular winter visitor to Red Sea, where some disperse S; may even reach E Africa. Small numbers winter inland, on Black and Caspian Seas.

Status and Conservation. Not globally threatened. Population in W Europe, but recently increasing. World population 75,000-125,000 pairs, with stronghold in Black Sea. Breeding numbers irregular in Spain (10-1000 pairs); also in France, with up to 60 pairs at Camargue, but steady increase to 850 pairs in 1995; 2000 pairs in Italy. Has declined in Romania since 19th century and is now rare. Total European population (excluding former USSR) 2000-3000 pairs. Black Sea population variable and poorly documented; up to 50,000 pairs in some years. On Caspian Sea, currently 450-550 pairs in Azerbaijan. Total of 6000-7000 pairs in Senegal/Mauritania, 3000 pairs in Turkey, and up to c. 5688 nests (1990) in N Egypt. Eggs and chicks preyed upon by *L. cachinnans* and *L. melanocephalus*, particularly when colonies are disturbed by human intruders. Adverse weather not uncommonly causes nests to be flooded; young may perish in cold, wet weather. Contamination by oil can be a problem in Caspian Sea.

Bibliography. Ali & Ripley (1982), Barthel & Königstedt (1993), Borodulina (1960), Brazil (1991), Britton, P.L. (1980), Cramp & Simmons (1983), Dowsett & Forbes-Watson (1993), Dragesco (1961), Étchécopar & Hüe (1964, 1978), Fasola (1986), Fasola & Canova (1992), Fasola, Bogliani *et al*. (1989), Fasola, Goutner & Walmsley (1989), Goodman *et al*. (1989), Gowthorpe (1979), Harber (1962), Hollom *et al*. (1988), Hüe & Étchécopar (1970), Ilicev & Zubakin (1988), Isenmann (1976b), Isenmann & Goutner (1993), Jones (1980), de Juana (1986), Kennerly & Hoogendoorn (1991), Knystautas (1993), Lekagul & Round (1991), Mackworth-Praed & Grant (1957, 1970), Patrikeev (1995), Paz (1987), Perennou (1991), Perennou *et al*. (1994), Reeber (1995), Richards (1990), Roberts, T.J. (1991), Shirihai (1996), Taylor (1982c), Urban *et al*. (1986), Wallace (1964), Watson (1971), Zikova *et al*. (1986), Zubakin (1976, 1982b).

37. Bonaparte's Gull

Larus philadelphia

French: Mouette de Bonaparte **German**: Bonapartemöwe **Spanish**: Gaviota de Bonaparte

Taxonomy. *Sterna Philadelphia* Ord, 1815, Philadelphia, Pennsylvania.
Monotypic.

Distribution. W Alaska and S British Columbia E to E Quebec, and possibly N Maine. Winters along Pacific coast S to Mexico (Sinaloa) and on Atlantic coast to Florida and Greater Antilles; in mild winters from Great Lakes to Gulf of Mexico.

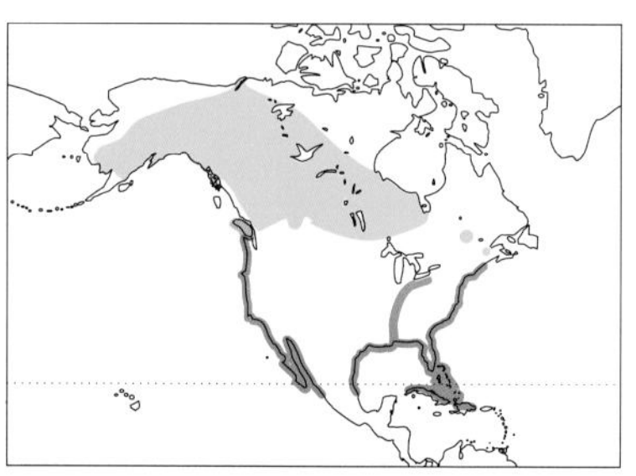

Descriptive notes. 28-30 cm; 170-230 g; wingspan 78-84 cm. Hood black, with white eye-crescents; neck and underparts white; back and upperwing, including inner primaries, grey; outer primaries white, tipped black; tail white; bill black; legs orange-red; iris black, with narrow red orbital ring. Non-breeding adult has white head with dark auricular spot, regaining black hood by Apr-May. In all plumages very like *L. ridibundus*, but noticeably smaller, with smaller, black bill. 1st-winter bird very similar, but with darker diagonal bar across upperwing-coverts.

Habitat. Breeds at ponds or muskeg in coastal and inland areas of taiga zone, nesting mainly in spruce (*Picea*) and tamaracks (*Larix*) close to or over water, mostly at low elevation but up to 600 m in Alaska (Denali Park); arrives before snow-melt. Winters on Great Lakes and in coastal estuaries, moving S ahead of freeze-up.

Food and Feeding. Small fish, euphausiids, amphipods, and insects. In British Columbia, euphausiids comprised at least 93% of biomass in spring. On Long I, New York, feeds almost exclusively on small invertebrates, mainly sand-fleas (Amphipoda: Gammaridae). Forages mainly 1-3 m above the water, in flocks of dozens to thousands of birds. Feeds mainly by surface-seizing (51% of attempts) and diving (46%), and by dipping to the surface; occasionally takes swarming insects by aerial hawking. In San Francisco Bay feeds like a phalarope, circling and darting to pick up abundant swarming sand-fleas; also captures them by probing exposed aquatic vegetation. Characteristic feeding pattern is to drift with the surface current, plucking food items from the water, then fly upwind to the front of the flock, land and begin to drift again; birds plunge-diving fly upwind, diving when prey sighted, then veer to the side, fly quickly downwind to the end of the flock, then return upwind over the food source. Concentrates in flocks exceeding 2000 birds over incoming tide. Also feeds at sewage outfalls, particularly at low tide.

Breeding. Arrives in early May; lays late May. Non-colonial, but nests often clumped, with a few pairs in 1 km². Nests in coniferous trees, usually in a muskeg lake or bog pond. Courtship and copulation mainly in trees; copulation often preceded by delivery of nest material. Flat nest c. 25 cm across, c. 3-10 m above ground, built of leaves and twigs bound together by stringy grasses, and lined with grass and moss. Group mobbing occurs where nests are clumped. 3 eggs (1-3); incubation 22-25 days; chick vinaceous cinnamon, spotted with irregular brownish black blotches, with black line through each eye, and unmarked pinkish cinnamon below; may leave nest at a few days old; fledging period not documented. Some breed at 2 years.

Movements. Leaves breeding grounds in Aug in loose flocks, coalescing into larger groups on reaching the coast or the Great Lakes. Alberta breeders migrate to Pacific, those from Saskatchewan to the Mississippi flyway or Great Lakes. E birds migrate SE to R St Lawrence, some moving E to Bay of Fundy, others S across New York to Long I, and others W to L Erie and valley of Mississippi. Winter aggregations of more than 30,000 occur in Bay of Fundy, and more than 100,000 sometimes occur on Niagara R in Nov and L Erie in Dec, prior to freeze-up. Birds move quickly down Maine coast in Sept, and in Oct reach Massachusetts, where they linger until Dec. On Long I numbers peak in mid-Nov, but some remain throughout winter, particularly in mild years. Accidental in Europe and Japan.

Status and Conservation. Not globally threatened. Estimated world population 85,000-175,000 pairs based on averages of Christmas Bird Counts, with 19% migrating to the Pacific, 21% along the Atlantic, and 60% along the Mississippi flyway. Alaskan population estimated to number several 10,000's, and stable.

Bibliography. Armstrong (1983), Beardslee (1944), Bohlen (1993), Braune (1987a, 1987b, 1989), Braune & Gaskin (1982, 1987a, 1987b), Brazil (1991), Burger (1967), Burger & Brownstein (1968a), Cramp & Simmons (1983), Drury (1984), Grow (1978), Howell & Webb (1995a), Imai *et al.* (1986), Koonz (1986), Lauro (1980), Lensink (1984), MacLean (1986), Richards (1990), Ridgely & Gwynne (1989), Root (1988), Stedman & Stedman (1989), Stiles & Skutch (1989), Taylor (1993a), Twomey (1934), Vermeer, Szabo & Greisman (1987), Wilbur (1987), Wolf & Gill (1961).

38. Saunders's Gull

Larus saundersi

French: Mouette de Saunders **German**: Saundersmöwe **Spanish**: Gaviota de Saunders
Other common names: Chinese Black-headed Gull

Taxonomy. *Chroicocephalus saundersi* Swinhoe, 1871, Fujian, China.
Quite similar to *Larus maculipennis*; sometimes placed in monotypic subgenus *Saundersia*, based on its compressed bill, its long, slender tarsi, and its incised webs between the long toes. Monotypic.
Distribution. Coastal E China from Liaoning through Hebei and Shandong to Jiangsu. Winters from South Korea and S Japan S to N Vietnam.

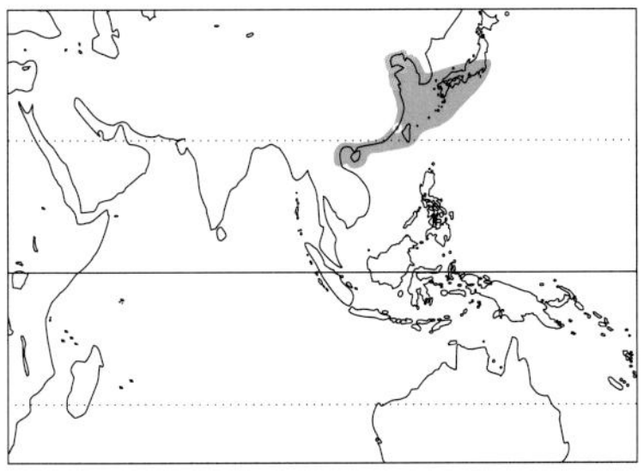

Descriptive notes. 29-32 cm. Head and nape black, with white crescents above and below rear of eye; back and upperwing-coverts blue-grey; outer primaries white, tipped black; inner primaries mainly black, forming diagnostic black patch on underwing beyond "wrist"; secondaries mainly white; bill black; legs and feet reddish; iris dark brown. Non-breeding adult has white head, with grey marks on neck and black spot before and behind eye. Superficially similar to *L. minutus*, but larger, with different upperwing and underwing patterns. Wing pattern similar to that of *L. ridibundus*, but differs in short, heavy, black bill. Resembles *L. philadelphia*, but with disproportionately heavy bill.
Habitat. Mainly along coast, occasionally on bodies of fresh water near coast. Breeds at coastal wetlands, rather than inland lakes as originally reported.
Food and Feeding. Essentially unstudied. Main feeding areas are coastal mudflats, where species presumably feeds on intertidal organisms; also crustaceans and small fish in coastal lagoons.
Breeding. Virtually unstudied. All known colonies are in coastal salt-marshes. Normally 3 eggs (1-6); clutches of 5 and 6 eggs suggest female-female pairing. No published information on other aspects of breeding.
Movements. Poorly known. Birds move S and E off coast of E China, and in winter recorded in South Korea, S Japan, and from E China and Taiwan to Hong Kong, Hainan and N Vietnam. Main wintering areas appear to be S Japan, Hong Kong and N Vietnam. Up to 200 have been recorded at delta of Song koi (Red R) near Hanoi, and up to 90 in Taiwan.
Status and Conservation. ENDANGERED. Total population estimated at below 5000, and probably closer to 3000 individuals, and all 7 known colony sites are either being developed or planned for development for agriculture or aquaculture (particularly for shrimps). The breeding grounds of this poorly known species were not discovered until 1984. It breeds only in four Chinese provinces: Liaoning, with c. 600-700 pairs; Hebei, with c. 25 pairs; Shandong, with c. 200 pairs at 2 colonies; and Jiangsu, with 300-750 pairs at 2 colonies. Oil exploration also destroys the species' salt-marsh habitat and displaces the gulls. Fishermen collect eggs for food. Delayed breeding subjects vulnerable young to late-summer typhoons. Colonies are close to fishing villages, and the frequent human disturbance causes low reproductive success or even desertion. The coastal cities are undergoing industrial development, and this contributes to pollution from coastal sewage and industrial waste. Female-female pairing possibly a consequence of contamination by chemical agents. Extinction very likely by about the year 2010 if breeding habitat is not protected very soon.
Bibliography. Anon. (1988, 1994e), Austin (1948), Austin & Kuroda (1953), Brazil (1991), Brazil & Moores (1993), Collar & Andrew (1988), Collar *et al.* (1994), Étchécopar & Hüe (1978), Ilicev & Zubakin (1988), Melville (1984, 1990), Meyer de Schauensee (1984), Perennou *et al.* (1994), Rose & Scott (1994), Shi Zerong *et al.* (1988), Swinhoe (1871), Takeshita *et al.* (1993), Williams, M.D. (1986), Williams, M.D. *et al.* (1986), Wong (1994), Xu Weishu & Melville (1994).

39. Andean Gull

Larus serranus

French: Mouette des Andes **German**: Andenmöwe **Spanish**: Gaviota Andina

Taxonomy. *Larus serranus* Tschudi, 1844, Jauja Valley, Junín, Peru.
Monotypic.
Distribution. Andean lakes, from N Ecuador to N Chile, W Bolivia and N Argentina (Tucumán). In winter extends to Pacific coast, S to SC Chile (Aisén).

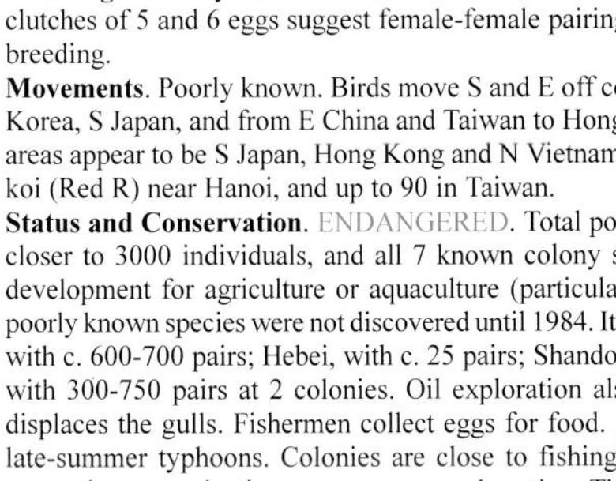

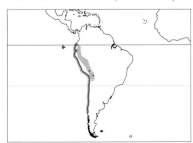

Descriptive notes. 44-48 cm; 478 g. Glossy black hood, with white rear eye-crescents; neck white; back and upperwing grey; unique wing pattern, with broad dark band across middle of black-tipped white primaries, creating a white-black-white-black pattern; from below, distal half of wing is mainly blackish, with large white mirrors on outer 3 primaries; underparts white, sometimes suffused with pink; bill, legs and feet blackish brown, tinged reddish; iris brown. Non-breeding adult lacks black head and has blackish legs, similar in plumage to smaller *L. maculipennis*. 1st-year bird more likely to be confused with *L. cirrocephalus*; has a complex black and white pattern on upper primaries and secondaries, partially dark head, and black subterminal tail band.
Habitat. Lakes, river mouths, marshes and fields; breeds on riverbanks, or on small islets in Altiplano lakes, usually at altitudes of 4000-5300 m, occasionally lower.
Food and Feeding. Earthworms, insects, amphibians, small fish, and sometimes eggs and chicks of various waterbirds. Outside breeding season, takes offal, marine invertebrates and fish.
Breeding. Nests mainly Jul-Aug, but variable, depending on climate. Breeding biology largely unknown. Usually in small colonies, which are remarkably silent; sometimes solitary. Birds leave when intruders approach. Nest among tall grasses and rocks on vegetated islands, or builds floating nest anchored to emergent vegetation, up to 1 m above water. Nests 1-3 m apart (mean 1·3 m), usually at base of rock or vegetation. Usually 2-3 eggs (1-4); eggshell has reduced pores and lower water-vapour conductance than those of gulls breeding at sea-level, but water loss is greater because of increased gaseous diffusion and lower barometric pressure at high altitude; reported to leave eggs unattended for long periods while feeding, but this seems unlikely. Attains adult plumage by 2 years old, but age of first breeding not known.
Movements. Many birds remain on Altiplano lakes and marshes throughout year, but most descend to congregate at river mouths on the Pacific coast; occasionally reaches the Atlantic coastal plain, where may be overlooked.
Status and Conservation. Not globally threatened. Total population unknown, but may be fewer than 50,000 pairs; species probably vulnerable, with no large populations. Centre of abundance in S Peru and N Chile. Most breeding areas are in remote high altitude lakes, but many are increasingly subject to agricultural pressure and human disturbance.
Bibliography. Blake (1977), Burger & Gochfeld (1985a), Butler (1979), Canevari *et al.* (1991), Carey *et al.* (1987), Fjeldså & Krabbe (1990), Galván (1974), Harris (1981), Hellmayr & Conover (1948), Johnson (1967), Koepcke & Koepcke (1971), Matos (1974), Meyer de Schauensee (1982), Moynihan (1962), Murphy (1936), Olrog (1984), Ortiz & Carrión (1991), Parker *et al.* (1987), de la Peña (1992), Rocha & Peñaranda (1995).

40. Mediterranean Gull

Larus melanocephalus

French: Mouette mélanocéphale **German**: Schwarzkopfmöwe **Spanish**: Gaviota Cabecinegra
Other common names: Mediterranean Black-headed Gull

Taxonomy. *Larus melanocephalus* Temminck, 1820, coasts of the Adriatic Sea.
Formerly often considered to include *L. relictus*. Monotypic.
Distribution. Mainly on Black Sea coasts of Ukraine, with recent spread to N Caucasian Plains and Azerbaijan (Baku archipelago); also at scattered localities throughout Europe, with large numbers recently in Netherlands, S France (Camargue), Italy, Greece and Turkey; also limited breeding in S England, Belgium, NE Germany, NE Spain and C Europe. Winters in Mediterranean, Black Sea, NW Europe and NW Africa.

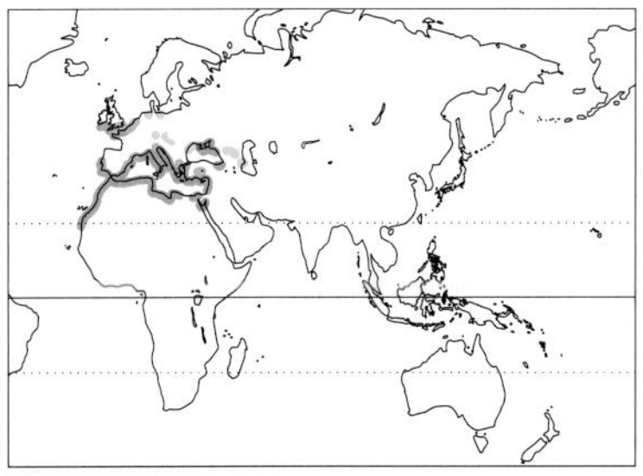

Descriptive notes. 36-38 cm; 215-350 g; wingspan 98-105 cm. Head black, with prominent white eye-crescents; neck white; upperparts very pale grey; flight-feathers white, with outer web of outer primary black; tail white; underparts white; bill scarlet, with variable dark subterminal band, often mainly on lower mandible, and often with yellow tip; legs bright red; iris blackish brown, with red orbital ring. Differs from *L. ridibundus* in full black hood covering most of nape; bulkier body, larger head, heavier bill, paler general appearance, lack of black at wingtip, and more buoyant flight. Non-breeding adult very pale, with head white but for distinct dark ear-coverts and dark streaks across nape, looking all white at a distance; bare parts deep red to blackish red. Immature like non-breeding adult, but with variable small black marks at wingtips. Juvenile has streaky cap, pale collar, upperparts mottled brown and buff, strongly patterned upperwing with pale grey greater coverts and inner primaries, and white tail with broad blackish subterminal band; bare parts blackish.
Habitat. Coasts, estuaries, harbours, marshes, inland lakes, fields and grasslands. Breeds on Mediterranean coasts, coastal lagoons, steppe lakes and marshes in open lowland areas, favouring sparse vegetation, but generally avoiding barren sand; sometimes on coastal salt-marshes (NW Europe). Appears able to adapt more readily than many other species to new habitats, both breeding and wintering; in recent years has successfully colonized areas which differ markedly from its original habitats in e.g. climate and vegetation.
Food and Feeding. In breeding season, mainly terrestrial and aquatic insects; also gastropods (Greece), and small numbers of fish, rodents and worms. Flocks descend on agricultural fields when abundant insect pests are detected. Obtains beetle larvae behind plough. May fly up to 80 km from colony to feed on grassland. On Russian steppes, sometimes feeds in large flocks on Orthoptera. In some colonies, preys on chicks of *Larus genei* and of Sandwich Tern (*Thalasseus sandvicensis*); unmated birds within colony reported to eat eggs of breeding pairs. On migration and in winter, when shifts to coasts and harbours, consumes fish, molluscs and offal, occasionally sewage and refuse. Feeds by aerial hawking, surface-plunging, contact-dipping, and picking from water surface while swimming. Walks and runs after prey on ground. Scavenges.
Breeding. Returns to colonies in early Apr, most laying first half of May. Highly synchronous, with egg-laying spanning only 10 days. Colonies usually under 1000 pairs; occasionally single pairs in colonies of other species. Often breeds near, but not among, *Thalasseus sandvicensis*; may intermingle with *L. ridibundus*, with which sometimes hybridizes. Nest on sparsely vegetated sites, or thickets or reedbeds, a shallow depression lined with grass. Nests dense, with nest rims as close as 8 cm; average nearest-neighbour distance 63 cm. Usually 2-3 eggs (1-5); incubation 23-26 days, and hatching relatively synchronous; chick spotted brown, grey and buff on head, with 2-3 broad brown bands on buffish back, and pale greyish to pinkish buff underparts; fledging 35-40 days. Productivity often very low. First breeding at 2-3 years. Recorded longevity of 15 years, but no doubt lives longer.
Movements. Mostly migratory, with main wintering areas in the Mediterranean, mainly in Spain. Some birds remain in Black Sea, mostly around N & E coasts, but most move W to Mediterranean. Small numbers reach extreme N of Red Sea in Gulfs of Suez and Aqaba. Also winters along NW African coasts S to Mauritania, rarely to Senegal and Gambia, and off Iberia. Few in NW Europe, mainly in S British Is and W france. Main migration route is coastal.
Status and Conservation. Not globally threatened. Total population c. 300,000-370,000 pairs, with 99% in former USSR, including 90% in Tendrovsky Bay of Black Sea. Tendrovsky Bay population has increased markedly, from c. 93,500 pairs in 1961 to at least 170,000 in 1977 and 330,000 in 1982. In 1989 range spread E, and species bred for first time on Caspian Sea, in Azerbaijan (28 nests). Has expanded W in past 50 years, but still very few pairs breeding from Britain to Italy. Since nesting in Hungary in 1960's, species has bred at least once in most European countries. Recent increase noted in W Europe, with over 125 pairs in Netherlands in 1990, up to 370 pairs in S France (Camargue) in 1995, and 1218 pairs in N Italy in 1988. Main enemies are *L. cachinnans*, corvids and harriers (*Circus*). Extremely susceptible to disturbance, often returning to nest only after some time; this can result in heavy losses and desertion, with instances of up to 98% of nests in colony failing.

Bibliography. Borodulina (1960), Britton, P.L. (1980), Buzun & Mierauskas (1987), Carrera & García (1986), Cramp & Simmons (1983), Dowsett & Forbes-Watson (1993), Dunn (1994), Fasola (1986), Fasola & Canova (1992), Fasola, Bogliani *et al.* (1989), Fasola, Goutner & Walmsley (1989), Goodman *et al.* (1989), Goutner (1986, 1987), Goutner & Isenmann (1993), Grant & Scott (1967), Hoogendoorn *et al.* (1992), Hüppop (1996), Ilicev & Zubakin (1988), Isenmann (1975b), Jansen & Remeeus (1978), Johnson & Isenmann (1971), de Juana (1986), Klimenko (1950), Knystautas (1993), Mainardi (1988), Mayaud (1954, 1956a), Meininger, Berrevoets *et al.* (1991), Modesto (1943), Olsen (1995), Patrikeev (1995), Paz (1987), Richards (1990), Shirihai (1996), Siokhin (1981), Taverner (1976), Urban *et al.* (1986), Zubakin (1982b).

41. Relict Gull

Larus relictus

French: Mouette relique **German**: Reliktmöwe **Spanish**: Gaviota Relicta
Other common names: Central Asian Gull

Taxonomy. *Larus melanocephalus relictus* Lönnberg, 1931, Inner Mongolia.
Originally described as race of *L. melanocephalus*, known only from 1 specimen; then suspected of being an aberrant *L. brunnicephalus* or a hybrid *L. brunnicephalus* x *L. ichthyaetus*. Since breeding colonies discovered in 1970, almost universally considered a distinct species. Monotypic.
Distribution. L Alakol' in NE Kazakhstan; L Barun-Torey in Chita, S Transbaikalia; Tatsain Tsagaan Nuur, C Mongolia; on edge of Edsin Gol, N Gansu, NC China; and Taolimiao-Alashan Nur in C Ordos Highlands, Inner Mongolia. Winter quarters still essentially unknown: probably in SE Asia (Vietnam) and perhaps also in South Korea.

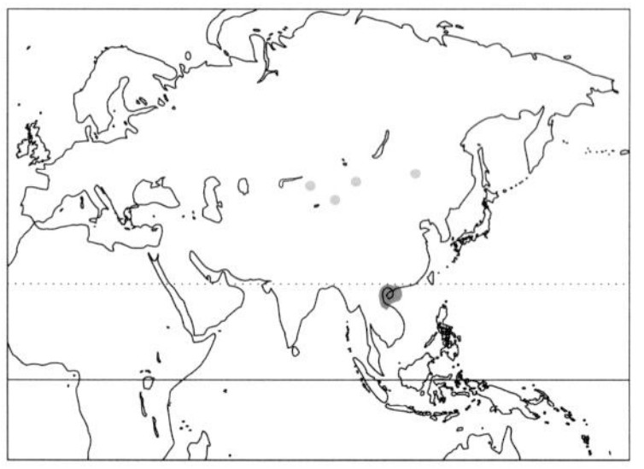

Descriptive notes. 44 cm; 420-665 g. Hood black, grading to pale brown between eye and bill; broad white eyelids, often meeting behind eye; neck, underparts, rump and tail white; mantle, back and upperwing-coverts very pale grey; wingtip pattern distinctive, with outer 5-6 primaries largely white with pale grey base and black subterminal mark, outermost 2-3 having black outer web and primary 9 with broad black patch at tip; stout bill dark red; legs red. Prior to 1970, was probably often misidentified as *L. brunnicephalus*, but is larger, with conspicuous eye-crescents and very different wingtip pattern. Primary pattern similar to that of *L. ichthyaetus*, but latter is considerably bigger. Non-breeding adult loses dark hood, and has dark ear patch and streaking on crown and hindneck. Juvenile has upperparts scaled brown and white, with dark tail band and black outer primaries; bill dark brown, legs dark grey. 1st-winter has head white apart from dark brown mottling on crown and nape; upperwing-coverts extensively marked brown; black subterminal tail band; dark bare parts.
Habitat. Breeds on shores or small islands of arid, usually saline, montane lakes, either on low-lying pebbly or clay rubble islands or spits; usually on islands at least 100 m from shore. Tends to avoid farms or fishing areas.
Food and Feeding. Mainly insects, beetles, small fish and crustaceans; sometimes small birds and mammals (e.g. *Microtus*); occasionally eggs and young of birds. In Inner Mongolia feeds on insects and plant matter, with 90% of food items chironomid larvae. Forages in the surf zone of large lakes and in nearby grassy fields, within 5 km of colony.
Breeding. Highly gregarious. Returns to colonies early Apr to mid-May; lays from early May. Mating reported to occur outside the colony, and also on nest. Frequently changes colony locations. Colonies of 15-2000 pairs, often in discrete subcolonies. Generally beside Gull-billed Terns (*Gelochelidon nilotica*) and Caspian Terns (*Hydroprogne caspia*); sometimes with *L. cachinnans*. Density higher than in any other gull species, with median inter-nest distance of 45 cm. Nest is a scrape surrounded by small stones, usually with small branches and grasses, and feathers. 2-3 eggs (mean 2·4-2·8); incubation 24-26 days; hatching from early Jun (Inner Mongolia); chick pale silvery grey, with fine dark grey spots on back and wings, pure white below; hatching weight 35-43 g; adults attack and often kill intruding chicks of other pairs; young tend to form crèche when alarmed. Chick mortality often high. First breeding at 3 years.
Movements. Migratory, but routes not well documented. Young birds show post-breeding dispersal around colony, before beginning migration in Sept. Has been recorded from over 30 localities, mostly in China; a few records in Hong Kong, Japan and Korea. Part of population migrates through E Gobi; reported from Yellow Sea shores in Apr. Probably winters in SE Asia, e.g. Vietnam, but some may winter in South Korea.
Status and Conservation. Not globally threatened. CITES I. Currently considered near-threatened, but may require reclassification as Vulnerable, due to very low numbers and small range currently known. Total population may be under 2000 pairs. Declining severely in Kazakhstan. In Inner Mongolia, c. 600 pairs nest at the one known colony in Ordos Highlands. Single pair bred at L Balkhash (Kazakhstan) in 1984. Colonies suffer high chick mortality due to adverse weather and predation; *L. cachinnans* may eliminate entire colonies. Extremely sensitive to disturbance in any form. Much research carried out in recent years; much more still needed, especially survey work to establish limits of range, and population size and trends, as well as ecological requirements.
Bibliography. Auzzov (1970, 1971, 1974, 1975, 1977), Auzzov *et al.* (1981), Bakewell *et al.* (1989), Bannikov (1978), Beaman (1994), Borodin *et al.* (1984), Brazil (1991), Collar & Andrew (1988), Delgushin (1962), Dementiev & Gladkov (1951b), Duff *et al.* (1991), Fisher (1985, 1989), Golovushkin (1988), Golovushkin & Ossipova (1989), Grant (1988), He Fenqi *et al.* (1992), Ilicev & Zubakin (1988), Isenmann (1977c), King (1978/79), Kitson (1980), Knystautas (1993), Kovshar (1974), Larionov & Cheltsov-Bebutov (1972), Lönnberg (1931), Melville (1984), Neufeldt & Wunderlich (1980), Ossipova (1987a, 1987b), Perennou *et al.* (1994), Shuker (1993), Stubbe & Bolod (1971), Vaurie (1962), Zhang Yinsun (1991), Zhang & He (1991), Zhang Yinsun, Ding Wenning *et al.* (1992), Zhang Yinsun, Liu Changjiang *et al.* (1991), Zhuravlev (1975), Zubakin (1979a), Zubakin & Flint (1980).

42. Lava Gull

Larus fuliginosus

French: Mouette obscure **German**: Lavamöwe **Spanish**: Gaviota Fuliginosa
Other common names: Dusky Gull

Taxonomy. *Larus fuliginosus* Gould, 1841, Santiago (James) Island, Galapagos.
Not closely related to other dark-bodied gulls, possibly relatively recently derived from *L. atricilla*. Monotypic.
Distribution. Galapagos Is.

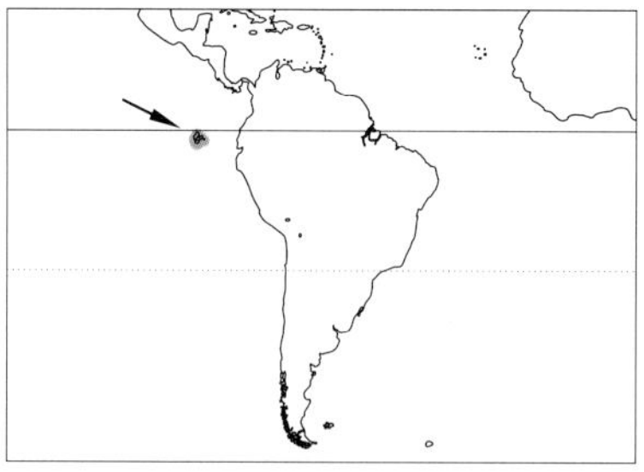

Descriptive notes. 51-55 cm. Highly distinctive: head sooty brown to blackish, with white eyelids; body and wings sooty grey, becoming paler grey on belly, with whitish uppertail- and undertail-coverts; tail pale grey, with dark grey centre; bill blackish, sometimes with red towards tip; legs and feet brownish, or purplish black; iris dark, with variable red orbital ring. Juvenile mainly sooty brown, unmarked. 1st-year birds show dark hood, and grey tinge to mantle.
Habitat. Mainly sandy and gravelly beaches on desert islands; also frequents harbours, and associates with boats. Largest numbers seen in Academy Bay, Santa Cruz.
Food and Feeding. Seabird eggs, baby marine iguanas (*Amblyrhynchus cristatus*), small fish, crustaceans, offal and scraps. Mainly a scavenger at tide line, around fishing boats, and at human settlements. Feeds almost exclusively along shore, flying at 3-5 m while scanning for food; rarely settles on sea, but perches on rocks, piers and boats. Associates with sea lions, eating placentae and fish fragments. Hovers over surface of water to snatch floating offal. Pirates crabs from Green-backed (Lava) Herons (*Butorides striatus sundevalli*).
Breeding. Nests throughout year, with peak May-Oct. Solitary nester with large territory, usually on a sandy beach or low outcrop close to water; not on cliffs. First nest found only in 1960; only 6 known by 1970, mostly near saline lagoons. Lays 2 heavily blotched olive eggs in a scrape; incubation 33 days; fledging period uncertain, may be 60 days, but parental care continues subsequently for nearly 3 weeks. Adults very wary at nest, leaving when intruder is still as much as 1 km away.
Movements. Non-migratory, but disperses up to 25 km from nest-site.
Status and Conservation. VULNERABLE. The world's rarest gull. Total population under 400 pairs. Considered globally threatened because of very low numbers, even though its entire habitat is currently protected in the Galapagos National Park system, where it is widely but sparsely distributed; the park is vulnerable to various forms of exploitation and human intrusion, and these pressures are increasing.
Bibliography. Bailey (1961, 1962), Cepeda & Cruz (1994), Collar *et al.* (1994), Coulter (1984), Hailman (1963), Harris (1982), Moynihan (1962), Ortiz & Carrión (1991), Snow & Snow (1969).

43. Laughing Gull

Larus atricilla

French: Mouette atricille **German**: Aztekenmöwe **Spanish**: Gaviota Guanaguanare

Taxonomy. *Larus Atricilla* Linnaeus, 1758, Bahamas.
Considered an excellent "structural ancestor" of all other hooded gulls. Two subspecies recognized.
Subspecies and Distribution.
L. a. megalopterus Bruch, 1855 - SE California to W Mexico (Jalisco), and Nova Scotia to Florida and Texas, locally through E Central America; winters S to S Peru.
L. a. atricilla Linnaeus, 1758 - West Indies to Trinidad and islands off Venezuela; winters S to N Brazil.

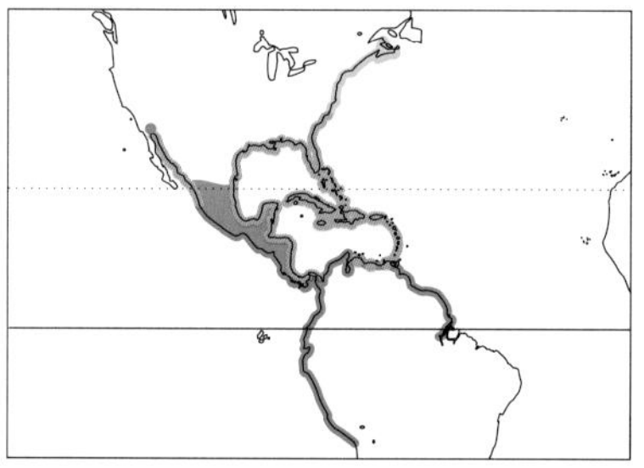

Descriptive notes. 39-46 cm; 240-400 g; wingspan 102-107 cm. Hood black, with white eye-crescents; neck, rump, tail and underparts white; mantle, back and upperwings dark slaty grey, with black wingtips, upperwing having a narrow white trailing edge; bill dull red; legs dull red to blackish; iris brown, with red orbital ring. Distinguished from *L. pipixcan* by larger size, heavier bill, more pointed wings, and lack of white in wingtip. Non-breeding adult has white head with light greyish nape band; lacks partial hood of non-breeding *L. pipixcan*, although may, rarely, retain or moult again into a nuptial plumage; bill and legs blackish. Juvenile light brownish above, with feathers edged pale, black on primaries and secondaries, white on throat and belly, and with broad black band on white tail; bare parts blackish. Immature has whiter head, grey back, and dusky breast. Races differ minimally, *megalopterus* having more black in primaries.
Habitat. Strictly coastal. Breeds on vegetated sandy beaches or islands and salt-marshes (Long I to Virginia), and on tops of rocky islands (West Indies). Moves from tidal flats to protected lagoons on rising tide, or during high winds. Visits rubbish dumps, sewage outfalls, beaches, harbours and parks.
Food and Feeding. Aquatic invertebrates and insects (beetles, grasshoppers, ants); also fish, particularly in winter, scraps and refuse. Kleptoparasitic on Brown Pelicans (*Pelecanus occidentalis*), alighting on head of surfacing bird and seizing fish from edge of pouch. In summer (Jun) feeds on superabundant eggs of horseshoe crab (*Limulus polyphemus*) in Delaware Bay, but these have relatively low nutritive value. Scavenges; picks food from surface. Frequently follows tractors; follows fishing boats. Adept at surface-dipping and contact-dipping; hawks flying insects.
Breeding. Lays from mid- to late May in N, in late Apr in Florida. Colonies of dozens to 10,000 pairs; high turnover rate. In West Indies nests under vegetation, but usually near open spaces. Nest of seaweed or grasses on sand or on marsh vegetation. 2-3 eggs (mean 2·6 in Texas); incubation 24-28 days (20 days reported in error); adults remove eggshells, but drop them close to nest; chick hatches weighing 25-35 g; undisturbed chicks remain at nest 1-5 days; chicks recognize parents by day 6; fledging 35-42 days. Nests often subject to flooding; renesting rare unless flooding occurs in early incubation or before.
Movements. Post-breeding dispersal N, followed by movement S. Those breeding in Florida and West Indies largely resident, but N birds migrate as far as South America. In autumn most ringing recoveries are between Cape Cod and North Carolina, but by Feb most birds are in Central and South America. Most ringed birds recovered as adults were within 50 km (but usually N of) natal colony. Winters from Mexico to S Peru, and from North Carolina through Caribbean to Brazil (Amazon). First recorded in Chile in 1990's. Vagrant to Pacific Is, including Hawaii and Galapagos, and regularly to Europe.
Status and Conservation. Not globally threatened. Total population probably c. 400,000 pairs. Abundant and increasing breeder along most of E and S coasts of USA in mid-19th century, but eliminated from much of its breeding range by 1900. With protection from 1913, populations recovered. N population (Nova Scotia to New England), however, which nested mainly on rocky islands, declined again in 1950's owing to competition from *L. argentatus* as latter moved S; marsh-nesting populations from New Jersey and S fared better, and were large enough to tolerate *L. argentatus*. Colonies near airports

considered to constitute a hazard. In Texas, breeding impaired by organophosphates, but not by organochlorine pesticides.

Bibliography. Beer (1969, 1970a, 1970b, 1979), Belant & Dolbeer (1993a, 1993b), Bent (1921), Biaggi (1983), Blake (1977), Blom (1990), Bongiorno (1968, 1970), Bottom (1984), Buckley & Buckley (1984b), Buckley *et al.* (1978), Burger, J. (1976b, 1978a, 1979a, 1981c, 1983a), Burger, J. & Beer (1975), Burger, J. & Galli (1987), Burger, J. & Gochfeld (1983c, 1985b, 1991b), Burger, J. & Shisler (1978b, 1980b), Burger, J. & Staine (1993), Burger, J. & Wagner (1995), Burger, J. *et al.* (1982), Cavanagh & Griffin (1993), Cramp & Simmons (1983), Dinsmore & Schreiber (1974), Dolbeer *et al.* (1989), Dowsett & Forbes-Watson (1993), Drury (1984), Érard *et al.* (1984), Evans *et al.* (1993), Fjeldså & Krabbe (1990), Frohring & Kushlan (1986), Gochfeld & Burger (1981), Hahn (1981), Hailman (1961, 1968b), Hailman & Reed (1982), Hanners & Patton (1985), Hatch (1975), Haverschmidt (1968), Haverschmidt & Mees (1995), Herrmann (1977), Hilty & Brown (1986), Holyoak & Thibault (1984), Hoogendorn (1993), Howell & Webb (1995a), Impekoven (1971, 1973), Jackson & Key (1992), Margolis *et al.* (1987), Monroe (1968), Montevecchi (1975, 1976, 1977, 1978, 1979), Murphy (1936), Nisbet (1971, 1976), Noble & Lehrman (1940), Noble & Wurm (1943), Norton (1986), Post & Riepe (1980), Richards (1990), Ricklefs *et al.* (1978), Ridgely & Gwynne (1989), Root (1988), Schreiber, E.A. & Schreiber (1980), Schreiber, E.A. *et al.* (1979), Schreiber, R.W. & Schreiber (1979), Slud (1964), Snodderly (1978), Southern (1980), Stiles & Skutch (1989), Sullivan (1984), Telfer & Shisler (1981), Tolonen (1970), Tostain *et al.* (1992), Tuck (1968), Urban *et al.* (1986), Wetmore (1965), White *et al.* (1983).

44. Franklin's Gull

Larus pipixcan

French: Mouette de Franklin **German**: Präriemöwe **Spanish**: Gaviota Pipizcan

Taxonomy. *Larus Pipixcan* Wagler, 1831, Mexico.
Considered closely related to *L. atricilla*, with an almost equally unspecialized display repertoire. Monotypic.

Distribution. Inland North America, from British Columbia to Alberta and from Montana to Minnesota, with scattered populations in N Rocky Mts and Great Basin. Winters mainly off South America, S to Chile.

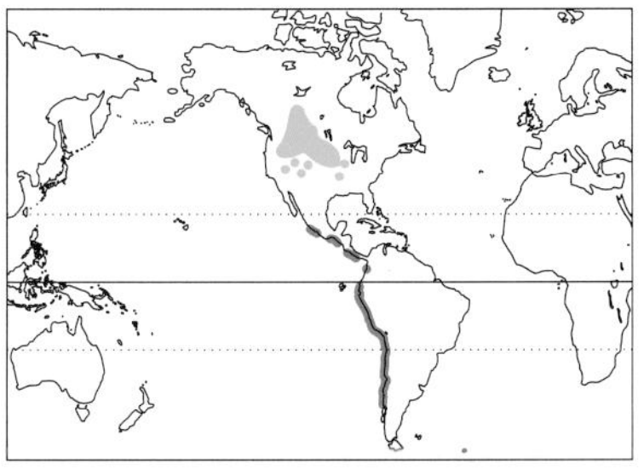

Descriptive notes. 32-38 cm; 220-335 g; wingspan 87-91 cm. Smallish, somewhat dove-like gull with black hood, bold white crescents above and below eye, and medium-grey mantle and upperwings; secondaries and inner primaries tipped white; outer 5 primaries black subterminally, tipped white, and with white proximal band, producing pale contrast between grey inner wing and black wingtip; tail very pale grey, with white outer feathers; neck and underparts white, latter with pink bloom early in breeding season; bill dull red; legs brick orange to blackish. Non-breeding adult has partial dark hood on rear head, and retains white eye-crescents; bare parts blackish. Distinguished from adults of other gulls by combination of smallish size, dark upperparts, and wingtip pattern. Subadult as adult, but wingtip often with more black and less white. Immature has brownish mantle, all black primaries, a broad greyish brown hood over sides of face and top of head and hindcrown, with a white forehead; unlike *L. atricilla*, black tail band does not reach outer feathers, and underparts white without grey breast band.

Habitat. Coasts, lakes, marshes, fields and rubbish dumps. Breeds exclusively at inland lakes and marshes, over water preferably c. 1 m deep; requires emergent vegetation, although some nests float freely; also nests in dense cat-tails (*Typha*).

Food and Feeding. In breeding season, almost exclusively earthworms or emerging chironomids; also aquatic invertebrates, grasshoppers, and incidentally small rodents and small fish; early arrivals may rely on grain or sunflower seeds before insects become available. Feeds mainly in agricultural fields near colonies. In winter small fish make up an important part of diet, as do fish offal and refuse; feeds along coast, fishing in the surf, and exploits fish factories, sewage outfalls and rubbish dumps. In Peru, feeds on mole crabs (*Eremita analoga*) by walking behind receding waves. Foraging methods include much aerial hawking for insects; follows plough.

Breeding. Highly synchronous; arrives near colonies in mid-Apr, laying mainly in mid- to late May. Pairing occurs just before arrival. Highly gregarious, with most colonies of 100's, and several greater than 10,000 pairs. Low colony-site tenacity due to fluctuating water conditions. Nest of marsh vegetation; requires daily maintenance, as tends to sink. Normally 3 eggs (1-3); incubation 23-26 days; chicks remain on nest platform unless seriously threatened, then swim into nearby reeds; fledging c. 35 days. First breeding at 3 years.

Movements. Most birds migrate through interior USA to Gulf Coast, then across Mexico to Pacific coast, eventually reaching Peru (Sept) and Chile (Oct), where they remain to early May. Very common visitor to sandy beaches, river mouths and cultivated fields along coast from Ecuador to C Chile, rarely to Tierra del Fuego; occasionally visits Altiplano lakes, e.g. Titicaca; scattered records in Argentina from Córdoba to Chubut. Accidental on Pacific islands, and in Europe and W Africa.

Status and Conservation. Not globally threatened. Total population c. 350,000 pairs in more than 25 colonies. Was rare at the turn of the century, becoming more common after 1915; has recently expanded its range westwards. Each individual colony is vulnerable to vagaries of local water levels, and draining of marshes or drought can eliminate colonies completely. Sensitive to human disturbance early in the breeding cycle, when may completely desert colonies; intrusion during hatching stage can have particularly severe impact. Some mortality from agricultural chemicals, and likely to be vulnerable to effects of El Niño (see Volume 1, page 341) on wintering grounds; protection of breeding habitat is the most important requirement.

Bibliography. Armstrong (1983), Bent (1921), Blake (1977), Blokpoel *et al.* (1992), Brazil (1991), Burger (1971, 1972a, 1972b, 1973a, 1973b, 1974a), Burger & Gochfeld (1984c, 1994b, 1995), Canevari *et al.* (1991), Cikutovic & Guerra (1983), Clapp *et al.* (1982), Collias & Collias (1957), Cramp & Simmons (1983), Dowsett & Forbes-Watson (1993), Drury (1984), DuMont (1940), Easterla & Damman (1977), Érard *et al.* (1984), Fjeldså & Krabbe (1990), Ginn *et al.* (1989), Guay (1968), Hilty & Brown (1986), Hochbaum & Ball (1978), Holyoak & Thibault (1984), Howell & Webb (1995a), Hughes (1977), Johnson (1967), Kopachena (1987), Kopachena & Evans (1990), Littlefield & Thompson (1981), Maclean (1993), McColl & Burger (1976), Monroe (1968), Murphy (1936), Nicholls (1988), de la Peña (1992), Richards (1990), Ridgely & Gwynne (1989), Rivadeneira (1987), Roberts (1900), Root (1988), Slud (1964), Southern (1980), Stiles & Skutch (1989), Swales & Murphy (1965), Tostain & Dujardin (1989), Tostain *et al.* (1992), Urban *et al.* (1986), Weseloh (1981), Wetmore (1965), White & Kolbe (1985).

45. Little Gull

Larus minutus

French: Mouette pygmée **German**: Zwergmöwe **Spanish**: Gaviota Enana

Taxonomy. *Larus minutus* Pallas, 1776, rivers of Siberia.
Apparently most similar to *Rhodostethia rosea* and *Xema sabini*, although both of these highly divergent from the hooded gulls. Sometimes placed in separate genus *Hydrocoloeus*. Despite disjunct nature of breeding distribution, geographical variation insufficient to warrant subspecific division. Monotypic.

Distribution. N Scandinavia, Baltic republics and W Russia to W Siberia (between R Ural and R Ob'); E Siberia (E from Lena basin and L Baikal); also sporadically in W & C Europe, and casually in North America. Winters mostly S and W of breeding range.

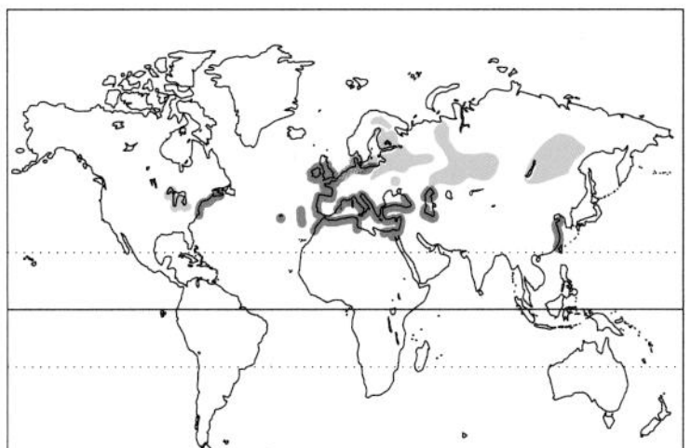

Descriptive notes. 25-30 cm; 88-162 g; wingspan 70-78 cm. Smallest gull, with broad rounded wings, adult with characteristic blackish underwing; flight recalls that of *Chlidonias* terns; head black, with no white eye-crescents; neck, tail and underparts white, breast often with pink flush; mantle, back and upperwings pale grey, wings with white trailing edge; primaries paler grey with white tips, lacking all black; underwing blackish, with white trailing edge; bill dark red to reddish black; legs red. Non-breeding adult has white head with dark cap and ear spot. Immature similar to juvenile, but with grey back. Juvenile blackish on crown, ear-coverts and upperparts, with black outer primaries and black diagonal band across coverts to rear scapulars, forming zig-zag pattern; black tail band; underwing pale; resembles young *Rissa tridactyla*, but smaller, and has weaker flight.

Habitat. Coastal areas, lagoons, sandy beaches, mouths of streams and rivers. Breeds mainly inland, from subarctic to temperate forest and steppe zone, at freshwater lakes, river valleys, marshes and bogs with abundant vegetation; locally at coastal lagoons; nests on sandbanks, in reedbeds and in marsh vegetation.

Food and Feeding. Varied; mostly invertebrates, e.g. dragonflies, beetles and midges. Mainly insectivorous when breeding and on migration; presumably eats mainly small fish and invertebrates in winter. In Baltic, all stomachs contained insects, while only 4% contained fish. Feeds by walking, and swimming; hovers in air and foot-patters on surface. Also feeds tern-like by surface-dipping, flying into wind and dropping to seize insects from surface of water. Occasionally plunge-dives.

Breeding. Lays from late Jun. Older adults return to colony already paired. Readily colonizes new wetlands and abandons old sites. Breeds in small colonies or subcolonies, or as scattered individuals; occasionally up to 1000 pairs. Often nests with other species. Inter-nest distances c. 1-1·5 m. Nest a shallow depression with added grass or reeds, sited on ground in wet vegetation on or adjacent to water, or floating at edge of emergent vegetation (e.g. Ontario); in marshes, incubating adults often obscured by vegetation. Usually 2-3 eggs (1-3); incubation 23-25 days; chick grey-buff, spotted black on crown and back, unmarked whitish below; mean hatching weight 15·1 (Moscow); fledging 21-24 days, with independence a few weeks later. 1st-summer birds often associate with colony, but first breeding not until 2-3 years.

Movements. Poorly documented. After breeding usually gathers in small flocks, occasionally in large groups of thousands, often associating with *L. ridibundus* and Black Terns (*Chlidonias niger*). W population winters along coast, and slightly offshore, from Irish Sea and the Baltic to Mediterranean, Black and Caspian Seas, and off NW Africa (Morocco); large numbers at Nile Delta. Rarely winters inland (e.g. L Turkana, Kenya). Peak migration past Calais (N France) in early Nov. In Netherlands up to 10,000 birds, mainly immatures, present in autumn. W Siberian population migrates through Aral and Caspian Seas to the Mediterranean, where some overlap with more westerly breeders. Movements of easternmost population uncertain; probably migrates to E China, since birds have been recorded in N China in winter. Origin of New World birds uncertain, and may be endogenous breeders or transatlantic migrants; usually seen singly among flocks of other species, particularly *L. philadelphia*, but along Niagara frontier up to 10 noted in Sept and up to 25 in winter.

Status and Conservation. Not globally threatened. Main breeding range in C Asia, hence global population unknown. Marginal and sporadic breeder in most of Europe; up to 21 pairs in Netherlands and 75 pairs in Denmark; under 100 pairs in Sweden and 200 pairs in Finland; 1000-2000 pairs in Latvia. In British Is, substantial increase in passage records occurred in 1970's, apparently involving Baltic breeders. In North America, first bred in Canada in 1962 and in USA in 1975; breeding now documented in Ontario, Quebec, Manitoba, Michigan and Wisconsin.

Bibliography. Ali & Ripley (1982), Bannon (1983), Blokpoel & Scharf (1991b), Borodulina (1960), Brazil (1991), Brindley & del Nevo (1994a), Britton, P.L. (1980), Burger & Brownstein (1968b), Carrera & García (1986), Cramp & Simmons (1983), Dowsett & Forbes-Watson (1993), Étchécopar & Hüe (1978), Goodman *et al.* (1989), Howell & Webb (1995a), Hutchinson & Neath (1978), Ilicev & Zubakin (1988), de Juana (1986), Knystautas (1993), Kokhanov (1993), Mackworth-Praed & Grant (1957), McRae (1984), Meininger (1995), Patrikeev (1995), Paz (1987), Perennou *et al.* (1994), Richards (1990), Reeber (1996), Rogacheva (1992), Root (1988), Scott (1963), Shirihai (1996), Smith, P.H. (1975), Tasker *et al.* (1987), Tima (1961), Urban *et al.* (1986), Veen (1980, 1985), Veen & Piersma (1986).

PLATE 53

inches 7
cm 18

PLATE 53

Genus *PAGOPHILA* Kaup, 1829

46. Ivory Gull
Pagophila eburnea

French: Mouette blanche   **German**: Elfenbeinmöwe   **Spanish**: Gaviota Marfileña

Taxonomy. *Larus Eburneus* Phipps, 1774, Spitsbergen.
Osteologically quite distinct from *Larus*; considered by some intermediate with the skuas (Stercorariidae). Morphometric analysis shows no consistent link with any other species. Has very different display repertoire. Strong rationale for retaining *Pagophila*, though species sometimes placed in *Larus*. Monotypic.
Distribution. Almost circumpolar in Arctic seas and pack ice, breeding from N Canada (Queen Elizabeth Is, N Baffin I) through Greenland, Svalbard, Franz Josef Land, Novaya Zemlya and Severnaya Zemlya to Herald I (New Siberian Is).

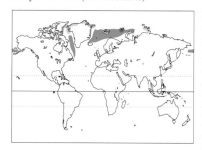

Descriptive notes. 44-48 cm; 520-700 g; wingspan 106-118 cm. Very distinctive gull, pure white, with black legs and yellow-tipped blue-grey bill. Immature white, with dusky blackish face and throat, sparse brownish black spots on body and tips of flight-feathers, and narrow dark subterminal tail band. Wing moult apparent in Jun on breeding grounds.
Habitat. Breeds mainly on inaccessible cliffs (W Spitsbergen), on broken icefields and inland cliffs (Ellesmere I), and on low rocks or flat shoreline. Outside breeding season associated with pack ice, favouring areas with 70-90% ice cover near the ice edge.

Food and Feeding. Mainly fish, shrimps, shellfish, algae, carrion, offal and animal faeces. In winter swallows large pieces of frozen food. Since part of its winter range is in continuous darkness, species must feed at night; some stomachs contained only the nocturnal lantern-fish (Myctophidae). Birds wintering at lower latitudes mainly scavenge dead fish. Regularly follows polar bears (*Thalarctos maritimus*), and feeds on scraps from their kills and on bear and seal excrement; eats seal placentae. Associates with human hunters to exploit carcasses. Often reluctant to alight on water, perhaps due to risk of icing. At Spitsbergen, takes marine crustaceans by surface-dipping in flight. Usually tolerant of humans, and even exploits food around camp-sites.
Breeding. Arrives late Mar at Spitsbergen, Apr at Franz Josef Land, and late May in Canadian Arctic and N Greenland; breeds in brief period from late Jun to Aug; most birds do not lay until early Jul. Occasionally does not breed when food conditions are unfavourable. Most colonies of 5-60 pairs,

rarely more than 100, with inter-nest distances usually 1-20 m, occasionally over 100 m; rarely solitary. Nest of moss, straw and debris, lined with dry grass and feathers, on bare snow-free rock behind some shelter. 2 eggs; incubation period probably 24-26 days; chick very pale grey above, with indistinct darker grey streaks on wings, white below with pale grey belly patch; fledging at least 4-5 weeks.
Movements. Spends most of year along ice edge, most birds dispersing only as far as edge of pack ice; in summer may even wander N of breeding range. Outside breeding season, most of the breeding population concentrates in Labrador Sea along ice edge of Davis Strait (between Greenland and Baffin I), where largest numbers gather in spring in hooded seal (*Pagophilus groenlandicus*) whelping area; some winter in Bering Sea, also concentrated along ice edge. Odd individuals winter casually S to N Europe and N USA, accidentally as far S as North Carolina; at least one New Jersey record involved a ship-assisted individual.
Status and Conservation. Not globally threatened. Current status essentially unknown. Species may have declined as a result of glacier recession. Documented world population c. 9000 pairs, but true figure must be closer to 25,000 pairs if estimate of up to 35,000 in Davis Strait in Mar 1978 is correct. Status in former USSR largely undocumented. Recent estimate of 1000 pairs on Demahini I in Severnaya Zemlya; also large colony on Tronoy, and c. 250 pairs in NE Greenland; rest of Greenland holds between 100-1000 pairs, and E Canadian Arctic perhaps as many as 1500 pairs. 2000-2500 pairs estimated on Graham Bell I (Franz Josef Land), and up to 1000 on Svalbard. Only 5 Svalbard colonies have been visited twice, and 4 have declined or disappeared; unknown whether this reflects a widespread population decline, or a shift in colony sites.
Bibliography. Armstrong (1983), Bateson & Plowright (1959a, 1959b), Beaman (1978), Birkenmajer (1969), Birkenmajer & Skreslet (1963), Blomqvist & Elander (1981), Brazil (1991), Brown, R.G.B. (1976a), Brown, R.G.B. *et al.* (1974), Camphuysen (1991b, 1994), Clarke (1898), Cramp & Simmons (1983), Dalgety (1932), Divoky (1976), Drury (1984), Evans (1984a), Frisch & Morgan (1979), Hakala (1975), Haney (1993), Haney & MacDonald (1995), Hjort (1976), Hjort *et al.* (1983), Ilicev & Zubakin (1988), Knystautas (1993), de Korte & Volkov (1993), Kurotshkin (1970), Laybourne (1978), Løvenskiold (1964), MacDonald & Macpherson (1962), Orr & Parsons (1982), Perennou *et al.* (1994), Renaud & MacLaren (1982), Richards (1990), Rogacheva (1992), Ryan (1955), Salomonsen (1950, 1961, 1967b), Striberny (1981), Tomkovich, P.C. (1986), Vuilleumier (1995), Wright & Matthews (1980).

Genus *RHODOSTETHIA* MacGillivray, 1842

47. Ross's Gull
Rhodostethia rosea

French: Mouette rosée   **German**: Rosenmöwe   **Spanish**: Gaviota Rosada
Other common names: Rosy Gull

Taxonomy. *Larus roseus* MacGillivray, 1824, Melville Peninsula, Canada.

Relationships rather obscure. Resembles *Larus minutus* in size and plumage sequence, but with very different adult plumage. Morphometric analysis suggests it is an early derivative of a primitive larid or of a hooded larid. Monotypic.

Distribution. NE Siberia, from Taymyr Peninsula E to R Kolyma; also locally in Greenland, and irregularly in Canada. Winters mainly in Arctic. Limits of distribution very poorly known for all seasons.

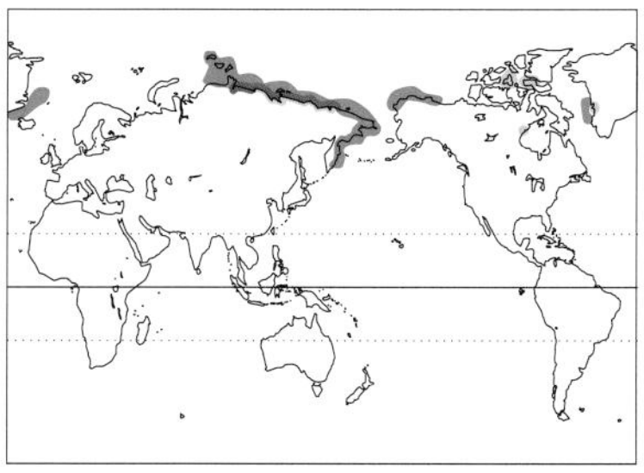

Descriptive notes. 29-32 cm; 120-250 g; wingspan 82-92 cm. Dove-like or tern-like, with a buoyant tern-like flight, and unique combination of wedge-shaped tail (not always apparent), grey underwing and black nuchal collar; in fresh breeding plumage, head, neck, underparts and tail rosy-white; rose colour strongest on breast and belly, more intense than on any other larid, but fades with wear, although still visible on some birds in early Oct; narrow black collar completely encircling head; outer web of outer primary black; white trailing margin to secondaries; bill black; legs bright red to reddish orange; iris dark, with red orbital ring. In flight, characteristic dark grey underwing-coverts with broad white trailing edge to wing. Non-breeding adult lacks black collar and rosy hue, has pale greyish crown, indistinct dusky black flecks around eye, and small black auricular spot. *L. minutus* has more rounded wings, and blacker underwing with narrower white margin. Immature has black outer primaries and broad black diagonal band across inner wing, enclosing broad white triangle on rear upperwing, and broad black tail band.

Habitat. Very few nesting colonies found. Breeds in boggy terrain of the upper taiga and tundra, preferring marshy tundra in river deltas or small ponds with stunted alders (*Alnus*) and willows (*Salix*). Often associates with Arctic Terns (*Sterna paradisaea*) and waders. In non-breeding season, found in open seas and at edge of pack ice.

Food and Feeding. Little information. On breeding grounds chiefly insectivorous; on migration and in winter, mainly marine invertebrates (plankton, crustaceans, molluscs, and even priapulids) and small fish. Reported feeding on wave-washed "scum" on the beach, presumably plankton. Occasionally feeds on walrus (*Odobenus rosmarus*) dung. Forages in small loose flocks or solitarily; may join *Xema sabini* or phalaropes. Often follows ships through ice, capturing organisms on undersurface of disturbed ice. Often feeds by aerial dipping; sometimes by walking, also by surface-dipping. Flocks sometimes gather around dead mammals.

Breeding. Lays in early to mid-Jun. Loose colonies of 2-10 pairs, rarely 18, in tussocks on islands in tundra or taiga pools, often with *Sterna paradisaea*; a nearly unique feature of colonies is their "invisibility". Nest built of dry grass, sedge and moss, often damp, lined with dry grass, sedges and reindeer moss. Nearest-nest distances averaged 43 m, sometimes as much as 100 m, rarely less than 5 m. Social interactions among neighbours very rare; change-overs quiet and unobtrusive. Normally 3 eggs (1-3); incubation 19-22 days; incubating bird flies up at call of incoming mate, which lands and goes to exposed nest; non-incubating mate does not remain on territory; intruders do not elicit alarm calls; chick yellowish to rusty-brown, with dark spots and lines on crown, back and wings, and breast and central belly unmarked whitish; hatching weight 15 g; parental defence aggressive, and also with well developed distraction displays including "rodent-run", "false feeding" and "impeded flight"; adults may lead brood away from colony; at 7 days, chicks left unattended and form groups at water's edge; extremely short fledging period reported to be 3 weeks or less. Fledging rate low, usually less than 33%; hypothermia a frequent cause of chick mortality.

Movements. Post-breeding movement started by late Jul, N to Arctic Ocean, and then migrating E or W along the coast or edge of pack ice; arrives back at breeding grounds in late May, depending on snow and ice conditions. Winter distribution poorly known, but presumably along edge of pack ice. Very rare even in the Bering Sea after winter. Sept-Oct records around Wrangel I and in Chukchi and Beaufort Seas, with birds often flying NE ahead of westerly winds; presumably these birds continue past Barrow, Alaska, where birds first seen in early Aug, with notable movements from late Sept to early Oct when thousands pass NE to feed in Beaufort Sea; many or most return W in Oct-Nov to their unknown wintering grounds. No corresponding spring movement. From Siberia, birds disperse W in Aug-Sept, eventually reaching Franz Josef Land and Spitsbergen. Ocean transect from E Greenland to Franz Josef Land recorded 1000 birds, mainly in groups of 2-16, 90% in adult plumage. Rare visitor to Europe, and accidental in USA in winter.

Status and Conservation. Not globally threatened. Information inadequate to assess true status. Very few breeding localities known, and none regularly monitored. Total population may be as low as 10,000 pairs, but probably closer to 25,000 pairs; even suggested as probably no fewer than 50,000. At least 20,000 (up to 38,000) individuals move past Point Barrow in autumn. Canadian and Greenland populations very small: breeding recorded at 4 sites in N & W Greenland, although permanence of these sites uncertain; all known Canadian colonies have contained fewer than 6 pairs, and indeed entire North American population may not be permanent. Adverse factors on species' numbers include predation on chicks by gulls, skuas and Peregrine Falcons (*Falco peregrinus*). In Canada, nests at Churchill fail frequently owing to human disturbance. Some harvesting of subadults and adults continues at Barrow, and migrants are still shot for food by Alaskan eskimos. Oil development in Beaufort Sea a potential threat.

Bibliography. Andreev & Kondratiev (1981), Armstrong (1983), Bailey (1948), Beaman (1978), Bent (1929), Bledsoe & Sibley (1985), Blomqvist & Elander (1981), Brazil (1991), Brown & Nettleship (1984b), Buturlin (1906), Chartier & Cooke (1980), Cramp & Simmons (1983), Degtyaryev (1991), Dementiev & Gladkov (1951b), Densley (1977a, 1977b, 1979, 1991), Divoky (1976), Divoky *et al.* (1988), Drury (1984), Étchécopar & Hüe (1978), Evans (1984a), Hjort (1980), Hjort *et al.* (1983), Ilicev & Zubakin (1988), Kampp & Kristensen (1980), Knystautas (1993), MacDonald (1979), Meltofte *et al.* (1981), Meeth (1969), Moerbeek (1993), Palmer (1897), Perennou *et al.* (1994), Petersen (1928), Pleske (1928), Richards (1990), Rogacheva (1992), Salomonsen (1950, 1967b), Ticehurst (1933), Williams (1941), Zubakin & Avdanin (1983).

Genus *XEMA* Leach, 1819

48. Sabine's Gull

Xema sabini

French: Mouette de Sabine **German**: Schwalbenmöwe **Spanish**: Gaviota de Sabine

Taxonomy. *Larus Sabini* J. Sabine, 1819, Sabine Islands, near Melville Bay, west coast of Greenland.

Subspecific variation poorly marked, and species often considered monotypic. Four subspecies currently recognized.

Subspecies and Distribution.

X. s. palaearctica Stegman, 1934 - Spitsbergen E to Taymyr Peninsula and Lena Delta.
X. s. tschuktschorum Portenko, 1939 - Chukchi Peninsula.
X. s. woznesenskii Portenko, 1939 - NE Siberia (Anadyr Gulf) to Alaska.
X. s. sabini (J. Sabine, 1819) - Arctic Canada to W Greenland.
Winters in SE Atlantic off SW Africa, and in E Pacific off NW South America.

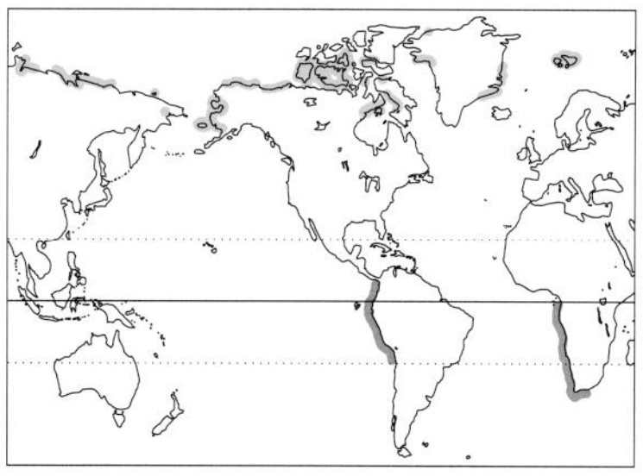

Descriptive notes. 27-33 cm; 135-225 g; wingspan 81-87 cm. Highly distinctive, with slightly forked tail, unique upperwing pattern, and delicate, buoyant tern-like flight; hood dark slaty grey, narrowly bordered black at rear; neck, rump and tail white; mantle and back dark grey; inner wing from carpal to scapulars dark grey (as back), outer primaries white-tipped black, leaving contrasting white triangle in between; underparts white, sometimes tinged pink early in breeding season; underwing whitish, outer primaries with black subterminal marks; bill black, with yellow tip; legs blackish grey; iris blackish brown, with bright red orbital ring. By Oct non-breeding adult has white head, with grey hindcrown and nape. Juvenile grey-brown from crown to lower back and on upperwing-coverts (same basic pattern of triangles on wing as in adult); black tail band. Races differ little, becoming darker from E Canada E to Alaska; *woznesenskii* darkest, with extreme slaty upperparts and very restricted white tips to primaries.

Habitat. Arctic tundra, breeding at wetlands with mosses and sedges; on Southampton I, Canada, breeds mainly in narrow band of brackish water habitat just above summer high tide line. Pelagic in winter.

Food and Feeding. Invertebrates and small fish; occasionally small birds, eggs of Arctic Tern (*Sterna paradisaea*) and of conspecifics; carrion. Breeding birds feed mainly on terrestrial prey in marshes; when breeding sites snow-covered at time of arrival, takes Collembola and Arachnida, as well as seeds and plant matter. Non-breeders mainly marine. Swoops low over water and snatches prey from surface; sometimes swims, or feeds on land; feeds plover-like on mud. Rarely hawks insects in the air. In South Africa in winter, adults feed at Cape Town sewage outfall.

Breeding. Returns to colonies in late May to early Jun, when tundra still snow-covered; lays mainly from Jun, depending on latitude and snow cover. Colony size usually 6-15 nests, occasionally up to 60 nests, usually at low density, but nests occasionally only 1 m apart; also nests solitarily. Usually breeds with *Sterna paradisaea*, often as single pairs. Nest of grass, placed on rocky or bare ground with grass or moss cover, near water's edge. Usually 2 eggs (1-3); incubation 23-25 days; chick golden brown above, spotted and streaked, especially on crown and lower back, and brown below with whitish breast and belly; mean hatching weight c. 16·2 g; leaves nest within 3 days, and led by parents to edge of water; adults give distraction display, landing 10-20 m away, and adopting a hunched posture similar to "rodent-run", also injury-feigning.

Movements. Migrates in flocks of few to hundreds of birds, mostly offshore; winters in smaller flocks. Siberian and Alaskan birds migrate through the Bering Sea and Bering Strait, past the Californian coast to W South America, where they frequent Humboldt Current region off Peru. Flocks of dozens regularly seen in Oct off Monterey, California, but most birds probably migrate further offshore. Large numbers of adults from E Canada and Greenland migrate SE through the Atlantic to winter off SW Africa (mostly Namibia and Cape Province), where many adults but very few young are recorded in the Benguela Current region; rarely moves E to Mozambique. Some Canadian birds migrate overland, where recorded from Rocky Mts to Great Lakes, usually solitarily. Autumn storms may drive many birds onto mainland coasts, e.g. in W Europe (over 2000 in W France in autumn 1993, and 850 there in Sept 1995).

Status and Conservation. Not globally threatened. Total population unknown, but probably under 100,000 pairs. Alaskan population reckoned to number several tens of thousands and to be stable. Greenland holds between dozens and a few hundred pairs.

Bibliography. Abraham & Ankney (1984), Andrew (1985a), Armstrong (1983), Beaman (1994), Bierman (1966), Blake (1977), Blomqvist & Elander (1981), Brazil (1991), Brown *et al.* (1967), Campbell (1970), Chapman (1969), Cochrane (1978), Cramp & Simmons (1983), Desmots & Yésou (1994, 1996), Dorogoy (1984), Dowsett & Forbes-Watson (1993), Drury (1984), Evans (1984a), Forchammer & Maagaard (1991), Furness & Furness (1982), Gaston (1991), Ginn *et al.* (1989), Hilty & Brown (1986), Hjort *et al.* (1983), Howell & Webb (1995a), Ilicev & Zubakin (1988), Kondratiev & Kondratieva (1984), Knystautas (1993), Lambert (1967, 1975), Lensink (1984), Liversidge & Courtenay-Latimer (1963), Mackworth-Praed & Grant (1962, 1970), Maclean (1993), Mayaud (1961, 1965), Meeth (1969), Nikolskii (1987), Paz (1987), Perennou *et al.* (1994), Pinto (1983), Portenko (1939), Post (1971), Richards (1990), Ridgely & Gwynne (1989), Rogacheva (1992), Roux (1961), Salomonsen (1967b), Shirihai (1996), Stiles & Skutch (1989), Strang, G.L. (1974), Urban *et al.* (1986), Vinicombe (1971), Wetmore (1965), Zoutendyk (1965, 1968).

Genus *CREAGRUS* Bonaparte, 1854

49. Swallow-tailed Gull

Creagrus furcatus

French: Mouette à queue fourchue **German**: Gabelschwanzmöwe **Spanish**: Gaviota Tijereta

Taxonomy. *Larus furcatus* Néboux, 1846, Monterey, California (error = Galapagos).

Morphometric analysis consistently shows this to be a particularly distinctive species. Monotypic.

Distribution. Galapagos, mainly in E half of archipelago; also Malpelo I, off W Colombia.

Descriptive notes. 51-57 cm; 610-780 g. Very distinctive, strikingly patterned gull with deeply forked tail; breeding adult has dark grey head, becoming paler on upper neck and breast; white patch above base of bill; mantle, back and wings grey; rump and tail white; underbody white; bill blackish, with pale tip; legs and feet dull pinkish red; iris dark brown, with broad crimson eye-ring. In flight, shows a broad triangular white patch in centre of wing.

On following page: 50. Black-legged Kittiwake (*Rissa tridactyla*); 51. Red-legged Kittiwake (*Rissa brevirostris*).

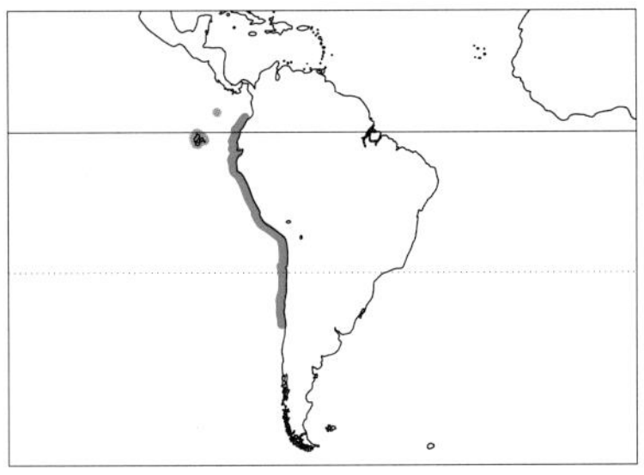

Habitat. Virtually endemic to Galapagos Is, where nests on all major and several minor islands, but avoids the colder waters around E Fernandina and W Isabela. Breeds mainly on steep slopes or broken cliffs, often on broad clifftop ledges, but also just above the wave zone; also on gravelly beaches and under vegetation. Many nests readily accessible to humans. Fairly pelagic, and quite often observed feeding 500 km from nearest land.

Food and Feeding. Feeds mostly at night, but also by day; most nocturnal of all gulls, with characteristic large eye. Exploits squid heavily at night, when latter more readily available near surface; also takes clupeid fishes. Regurgitated samples included *Sardinops*, as well as squid (*Symplectoteuthis oualaniensis*). Appears to suffer from periodic food shortages.

Breeding. Breeds throughout year; very asynchronous across Galapagos, but individual subcolonies are synchronized by social interactions. Breeding cycle generally lasts c. 6 months, but 9-10 months for individual pairs. Forms loose colonies with large inter-nest distances; densest colony contained 30 pairs in 200 m²; often solitary. Nests on dirt, bare lava, or gravel, often under rocks and bushes; most nests close to sea. Slight hollow, lined with pebbles, feathers or bones; adults may swallow pebbles and regurgitate them at the nest. Lays 1 egg; incubation 33-35 days, by both sexes, with shift sometimes lasting c. 24 hours; eggshells not removed; chick brooded continuously for first 48 hours, and remains close to nest for several weeks; both parents almost invariably attend nest during daylight; fledging 58-65 days, but young remain near colony and dependent on parents until 90-140 days.

Movements. Adults leave colony after breeding, but return in 4-5 months, often to their previous nest-site; young never return to the same colony. From Galapagos main movement is E. Highly pelagic during non-breeding season, but often seen off South American coast from Ecuador to C Peru, occasionally to C Chile. Accidental in Panama; recorded once in USA (California), presumably a ship-assisted bird.

Status and Conservation. Not globally threatened. Total population c. 10,000-15,000 pairs in more than 50 colonies on all major islands; 50 pairs on Malpelo I, Colombia. Currently protected by Galapagos National Park, but increasing human population and a burgeoning fishery are causes for concern.

Bibliography. Bailey (1961), Blake (1977), Burger & Gochfeld (1993b), Cepeda & Cruz (1994), Coulter (1984), Gifford (1913), Hailman (1964a, 1964b, 1965, 1968a), Harris (1970b, 1982), Hilty & Brown (1986), Lévêque (1964), Moynihan (1962), Murphy (1936), Nelson (1968a, 1968b), de Roy (1984), Snow, B.K. & Snow (1968), Snow, D.W. (1966), Snow, D.W. & Snow (1967), Wetmore (1965).

Genus *RISSA* Stephens, 1826

50. **Black-legged Kittiwake**

Rissa tridactyla

French: Mouette tridactyle **German**: Dreizehenmöwe **Spanish**: Gaviota Tridáctila
Other common names: Kittiwake

Taxonomy. *Larus tridactylus* Linnaeus, 1758, Great Britain.
Morphometric analysis links it with the white-headed gulls. Two subspecies recognized.

Subspecies and Distribution.
R. t. tridactyla (Linnaeus, 1758) - N Atlantic, from NC Canada and NE USA E through Greenland to W & N Europe, and on to N Taymyr Peninsula and Severnaya Zemlya; winters S to Sargasso Sea and W Africa.
R. t. pollicaris Ridgway, 1884 - N Pacific, from NE Siberia, Kamchatka, Sea of Okhotsk and Kuril Is through Bering Sea to Alaska; winters S to East China Sea and NW Mexico.

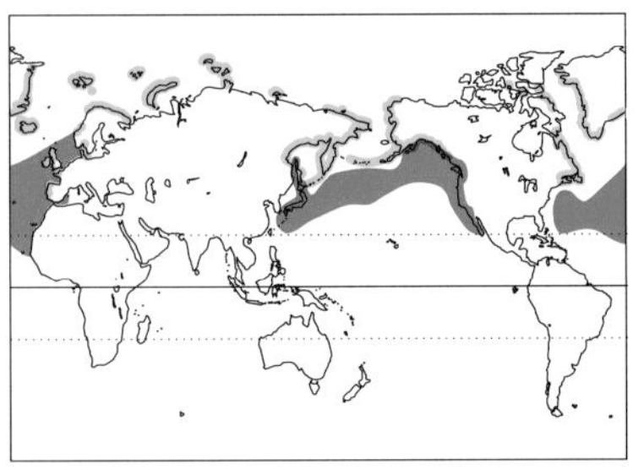

Descriptive notes. 38-40 cm; 305-512 g; wingspan 91-97 cm. Typical white-headed gull, but with short legs; mantle and upperwing-coverts blue-grey; outer wing slightly paler, with sharply defined, triangular, all black wingtip; bill yellow; legs blackish, very rarely reddish; iris dark brown, with narrow red eye-ring. Distinguished from *R. brevirostris* by paler primary bases contrasting more strongly with grey wing-coverts and black wingtips; also, almost always, by leg colour. Non-breeding adult has dusky grey crown band and nape, usually a darker band across hindcrown, and dark marks around eye. Juvenile and immature have a black zig-zag pattern across the upperwings, a black nuchal band and a black subterminal tail band; resemble young *Larus minutus*, but larger and stockier, with stronger flight. Race *pollicaris* larger, with more extensively black primaries.

Habitat. Arctic and temperate waters. Breeds on coasts as far N as open water occurs, preferring high, steep cliffs with narrow ledges; nests on glacier or snowbank face when it covers traditional cliff sites. In Europe nests also on buildings and piers, and occasionally even on flat rocky or sandy sites, rarely up to 20 km inland. Access to fresh water important. Highly pelagic in non-breeding season, when usually not in sight of land; usually remains on wing, but in severe weather may alight on sea and ride out storms.

Food and Feeding. Mainly marine invertebrates and fish. Outside breeding season also takes planktonic invertebrates, and has recently begun to exploit sewage outfalls and fishing vessels, and to take other offal in estuaries; wintering birds in California ate squid, fish and shrimps. Many species of fish recorded in diet, but sandeels (*Ammodytes*), capelin (*Mallotus villosus*) and herring (*Clupea harengus*) particularly important; also Gadidae (e.g. *Pollachius virens*). Rarely takes bird eggs. More frequently scavenges offal and carcasses. Sometimes feeds on intertidal molluscs and crustaceans, earthworms and small mammals, and on vegetation, e.g. aquatic plants, potatoes and grain. Main fishing methods are surface-dipping with or without foot-pattering, and plunge-diving to c. 1 m below surface; also feeds on surface. Occasionally pirates food from alcids, terns and seals, but is frequently itself a victim of skua piracy. Breeding birds feed mainly within 50 km of colony.

Breeding. Some colonies occupied as early as Jan, and regularly by Feb; lays from mid-May to mid-Jun, depending on latitude; later after cold springs, when many birds do not remain at colony. Usually breeds in huge colonies, many exceeding 10,000 pairs, occasionally over 100,000 pairs, sometimes with other species, especially alcids. Nest-site on narrow cliff ledge, or on ledge or windowsill of building or factory; most courtship, including copulation, takes place on ledge, which is defended most of the year, except in mid-winter. Elaborate nest, incorporating grass and feathers. Usually 2 eggs (1-3); incubation c. 24-28 days; downy chick not cryptic, white with greyish back and wings; remains still on ledge, and begs from 3rd day; guarded continuously for 4 weeks, intermittently thereafter; fledging period variable, c. 5-7 weeks. Poor reproductive success in Newfoundland due to increasing gull predation. Annual adult survival estimated at 95% in Alaska, but only 81% in Britain. First breeding usually at 4 years.

Movements. Post-breeding dispersal from colonies to open ocean, usually well away from coast, and perhaps concentrating at continental shelf or other areas of upwelling. Birds from Greenland remain in Davis Strait until Nov, returning in Mar. Subadults are relatively pelagic. Species is found across entire N Atlantic and N Pacific in winter, and many birds congregate at rich fishing banks off Nova Scotia. Very few ever reach the tropics.

Status and Conservation. Not globally threatened. Has generally increased and expanded its range during 20th century. By far the most abundant gull. Overall world population c. 6,000,000-7,000,000 pairs. Centre of abundance in E Kamchatka, with up to 1,600,000 pairs; also major population in Alaska, where over 1,250,000 pairs estimated in 1977, though only 650,000 pairs in 1990's, with S Alaskan population seriously affected by 1989 Exxon Valdez oil spill (see Volume 1, page 572). About 300,000 in E Canada and New England, and figures ranging from 140,000 to 1,100,000 for Greenland. Old World population exceeds 3,500,000 pairs, including over 500,000 pairs each in British Is, Norway, Iceland and Spitsbergen. In Britain, where was the first species to be protected from slaughter in the 19th century, it has increased and expanded in the 20th century, with annual growth of 2% during period 1969-1979, although populations have now stabilized. Now decreasing in the Faeroes and Iceland but increasing at Bear I, where now more than 200,000 pairs. In S Norway increased by 6-8·5% per year from 1967 to 1975 and by 4-5% per year from 1977 to 1983, but in N Norway only by 1%/year. Few threats, but hunted extensively in Greenland. Gyrfalcons (*Falco rusticolus*) and skuas (*Stercorarius*) prey on adults and young, and Great Skuas (*Catharacta skua*) and *Larus marinus* prey on fledglings.

Bibliography. Aebischer & Coulson (1990), Armstrong (1983), Baird (1994), Barrett (1978a, 1978b, 1980), Barrett & Runde (1980), Beaman (1978), Bech *et al.* (1984), Belopol'skii *et al.* (1976), Braune & Hunt (1983), Brazil (1991), Brent *et al.* (1983), Brown & Nettleship (1984b), Burger & Gochfeld (1984a), Chapdelaine & Brousseau (1989), Chardine (1987), Coulson (1958, 1959, 1961, 1963, 1966, 1968, 1983), Coulson & MacDonald (1962), Coulson & Nève de Mévergnies (1992), Coulson & Porter (1985), Coulson & Thomas (1980, 1983, 1985), Coulson & White (1956, 1958a, 1958b, 1959, 1960, 1961), Coulson & Wooller (1976, 1984), Cramp & Simmons (1983), Cramp *et al.* (1974), Cullen, E. (1957), Danchin (1987, 1988a, 1988b), Danchin & Monnat (1992), Danchin & Nelson (1991), Daniels *et al.* (1984), Docampo & Velando (1994), Dowsett & Forbes-Watson (1993), Drury (1984), Evans (1984a, 1984b), Fairweather & Coulson (1995), Firsova (1978), Ginn *et al.* (1989), Goodman *et al.* (1989), Haase (1993), Hatch *et al.* (1993), Hodges (1969, 1974), Howell & Webb (1995a), Ilicev & Zubakin (1988), Irons (1988), de Juana (1986), Kaufman (1989), Knystautas (1993), Kosinski & Podolsky (1979), Lensink (1984), Mackworth-Praed & Grant (1970), Maunder & Threlfall (1972), McLannahan (1973), Murphy, E.C. *et al.* (1991), O'Connor (1974), Paludan (1955), Paz (1987), Perennou *et al.* (1994), Poluszynski (1979), Porter (1988), Porter & Coulson (1987), Richards (1990), Roberts & Hatch (1994), Rodríguez & Días (1975), Rogacheva (1992), Root (1988), Runde & Barrett (1981), Shirihai (1996), Sluys (1982), Tasker *et al.* (1987), Thomas, C.S. (1983), Thomas, C.S. & Coulson (1988), Urban *et al.* (1986), Vyatkin (1986), Wooller (1978, 1979), Wooller & Coulson (1977).

51. **Red-legged Kittiwake**

Rissa brevirostris

French: Mouette des brumes **German**: Klippenmöwe **Spanish**: Gaviota Piquicorta

Taxonomy. *Larus* (*Rissa*) *brevirostris* Bruch, 1853, north-western North America.
Closely related to and partially sympatric with *R. tridactyla*, but no interbreeding known. Bones found in deposits on Kodiak I. Monotypic.

Distribution. Bering Sea, in Commander Is, Pribilof Is (St Paul I, St George I) and Aleutians (Buldir I, Bogoslof I). Winters widely over N Pacific.

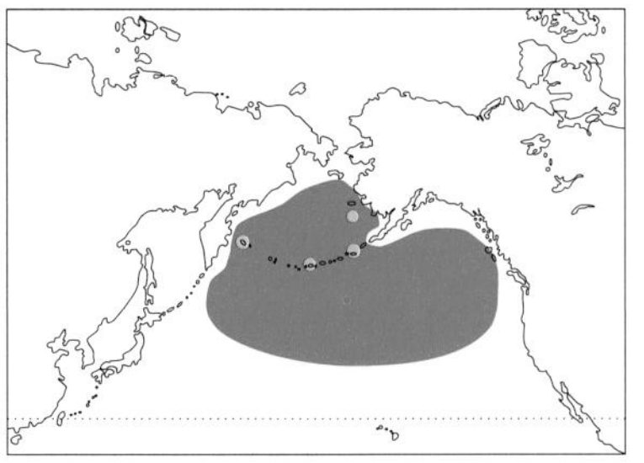

Descriptive notes. 36-38 cm; 340-450 g; wingspan c. 90 cm. Plumage white, apart from dark grey mantle, back and upperwing, grey underwing, and black wingtips; bill yellow; legs and feet bright orange-red to scarlet; iris dark brown, with scarlet orbital ring. Very like *R. tridactyla*, but smaller in all measurements, with shorter, paler bill and steeper forehead; distinguished by darker grey back and upperwing and darker underwing, producing very conspicuous white trailing edge to wing; differs in leg colour, but *R. tridactyla* may rarely have pinkish to reddish legs. Non-breeding adult has dusky grey markings on head and neck. Juvenile and immature have more black on outer primaries, white on inner primaries and secondaries, and black nuchal collar, but lack the black carpal bar and tail band of *R. tridactyla*.

Habitat. Arctic seas. Breeds on vertical sea cliffs on remote islands with other seabirds, including *R. tridactyla*.

Food and Feeding. Fish, squid, and other small marine animals. More than 50% of recorded food items are northern lampfish (*Stenobrachius leucopsarus*); also walleye pollock (*Theragra chalcogramma*, 20%) and various squid and amphipods. Research showed that reliance on squid varied between years from 14% to 82%. Forages both day and night, over deep water along a front of upwellings at the continental shelf. Feeds mainly by pursuit-plunging or dipping. Sometimes forms feeding frenzies over dense schools of fish. Only a single record of kleptoparasitism. Frequent reproductive failures attributed to fluctuating food supplies.

Breeding. Arrives at Pribilof Is in Apr. Apparently, some degree of mate-retention and nest-site fidelity; over 90% of marked birds resighted at Buldir I were within 10 m of marking location. Nest building from May; at Pribilofs, lays from mid-Jun to mid-Jul, with peak hatching in Jul, and peak fledgling departure early to mid-Sept. Nests interspersed with those of *R. tridactyla*, but present species prefers, or is restricted by latter to, narrower ledges averaging 12 cm wide. Nest of mud and vegetation, stamped into a platform, with a shallow cup. Average distance of nearest conspecific neighbour 53 cm. Clutch almost always 1 egg; very sparse data suggest incubation 25-32 days, perhaps averaging slightly longer than in *R. tridactyla*; downy chick has white head, breast and belly, and buffy brown or grey back; hatches with eyes closed and lies still until 2 days old (longer than in most gulls); brooded constantly until at least 2 weeks old; fledging c. 37 days, but returns to nest-site to be fed for several weeks. Smaller clutch size, longer incubation, less frequent feeding intervals, and slower growth rate are associated with more pelagic feeding habitat compared with *R. tridactyla*.

Movements. Little studied. Birds move S in winter, some keeping just ahead of advancing ice, others dispersing widely over ocean. Many presumably leave Bering Sea; most probably spread over N Pacific E as far as Gulf of Alaska, where recorded in winter; several have been seen S to N Japan. Accidental inland in Alaska and Yukon and Nevada, and as far S as Oregon.

Status and Conservation. VULNERABLE. Endemic to Bering Sea and Aleutians, with only 6-7 currently active breeding sites. Total population formerly c. 120,000-150,000 pairs, but now probably closer to 100,000 pairs. Most breed at St George I in Pribilofs, where recent estimates of c. 57,000 pairs. Commander Is population has apparently increased, from 5000 pairs in 1978 to c. 17,000 pairs in 1992; slight increase at Buldir I, with c. 6600 birds; only 200 at Bogoslof I. In 20th century numbers have declined, and colonies have been abandoned. In Pribilofs, c. 222,000 individuals estimated in 1970's, but reduced by c. 50% since then; attributed mainly to diminishing food supply and increasing fox populations. Clutch size has apparently decreased in past 50 years, as formerly said to be 2-3 eggs. Not all nesting females lay (sometimes only 14% do so), and in some years no eggs at all hatch, or all chicks die. Chicks tolerate human disturbance and overflying aircraft without leaving nests, but foxes and gulls occasionally take chicks from accessible ledges. Some harvesting of adults, chicks and eggs occurs at Pribilofs; enough to prevent population increase at St Paul, but trivial impact estimated at St George. Great increase in commercial trawling may have contributed partially to depletion of food supply. A protective buffer zone around nesting islands is recommended. In Commander Is, nesting areas are protected from access; not formally protected in USA, despite significant decline.

Bibliography. Armstrong (1983), Balch (1980), Beaman (1978), Brazil (1991), Byrd (1978), Byrd & Tobish (1978), Byrd & Williams (1993a), Collar et al. (1994), Drury (1984), Firsova (1978), Flint et al. (1984), Gabrielson (1933), Hatch et al. (1993), Ilicev & Zubakin (1988), Kaufman (1989), Knystautas (1993), Kondratiev (1991), Lensink (1984), Perennou et al. (1994), Siegel-Causey & Meehan (1981), Squibb & Hunt (1983), Squibb & Pitts (1982), Storer (1987).

Class AVES
Order CHARADRIIFORMES
Suborder LARI
Family STERNIDAE (TERNS)

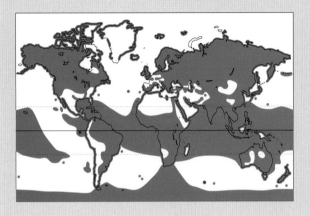

- Small to medium-sized slender, graceful seabirds, with long forked tail; most species grey above with black crown, white below.
- 20-56 cm.

- Cosmopolitan.
- Typically marine, coastal or pelagic; some species on inland waters..
- 10 genera, 44 species, 123 taxa.
- 5 species threatened; none extinct since 1600.

Systematics

The terns are a cosmopolitan, highly homogeneous group, closely allied to the gulls (Laridae), and often treated as a subfamily or even a tribe in expanded versions of Laridae. However, there are good reasons for treating the terns as a separate family (see page 572), recognizing the distinctive features which set them apart from all of the gulls. Regardless of the taxonomic level assigned, there is general agreement that the terns are more closely related to the gulls than either is to the skimmers (Rynchopidae) or the skuas (Stercorariidae), although certain authorities argue that some tern species have skimmer-like behavioural attributes, while one morphometric analysis also linked terns and skimmers. On the basis of behaviour, the terns are derived from gull-like ancestors, but they have adopted a more specialized aerial form of feeding and, furthermore, aerial displays play a more prominent role in the courtship of all tern species.

Although terns may have evolved from a primitive larid-like bird as early as the Paleocene, there is no reliable fossil record to provide clues either as to their affiliations with other birds or to the relationships of groups within the tern family. Several species of tern described from the Tertiary were probably misidentified, but a bird from the Miocene of Maryland, USA, originally regarded as a diminutive *Stercorarius* skua, is now considered more tern-like, and may have been a primitive noddy.

Herein, 44 species of terns are recognized in ten genera, although they have been variously classified by other authorities in anything from three to ten genera. A third of the species are "typical" black-capped terns of the genus *Sterna*. They occur throughout the world, but are poorly represented in the tropics. Often referred to as "sea-swallows" because of the long, forked tail, they have grey upperparts, a black cap and whitish underparts, and most have a reddish or black bill and legs; in non-breeding plumage, the soft parts tend to become darker and the forecrown lighter. Several very small *Sterna* terns, once placed in a separate genus *Sternula* and comprising the widespread Little Tern (*Sterna albifrons*) superspecies, are small versions of the typical terns, but with the tail short and notched rather than long and forked; with the exception of the Damara Tern (*Sterna balaenarum*), these "small terns" have a yellow bill with or without a black tip. Three *Sterna* species form the "brown-winged" group: the Sooty Tern (*Sterna fuscata*), the Bridled Tern (*Sterna anaethetus*) and the Grey-backed Tern (*Sterna lunata*) have dark

upperparts and a black bill. All three are tropical oceanic species, the first two being pantropical.

The six "crested terns" (*Thalasseus*) are also black-capped, but all are larger than any typical *Sterna* and have elongated crest feathers and most have a bright yellow or orange to orange-red bill. They have characteristic display patterns and breed in very dense colonies, with the nests often arranged in an hexagonal pattern and incubating adults about a body length apart. The chicks of these species tend to form a crèche, particularly when disturbed, a characteristic not found in any other tern except the Sooty Tern. The Chinese Crested Tern (*Thalasseus bernsteini*) is assumed to exhibit the behavioural traits of the genus, although its breeding grounds have never been found. Most recent authors have merged the crested terns into *Sterna*, but they probably form a sufficiently distinct group to warrant generic separation. The Roseate Tern (*Sterna dougallii*) shows a ritualized swaying in its ground displays, which places it between the Common Tern (*Sterna hirundo*) on the one hand and *Thalasseus* on the other.

There are three atypical black-capped terns, each of which is placed in a monotypic genus, although several recent authors differ in their generic treatment of these species. The heavy-billed Gull-billed Tern (*Gelochelidon nilotica*) and the very large and massive-billed Caspian Tern (*Hydroprogne caspia*) both occur on most continents, while the Large-billed Tern (*Phaetusa simplex*), conversely, breeds only on rivers of South America.

The three "marsh terns" (*Chlidonias*) have a short, slightly forked tail and are extensively black or dark grey in breeding plumage. Apart from M. Moynihan (see below), most authors agree that they represent a separate genus. The Black-fronted Tern (*Sterna albostriata*) might be considered to form some sort of a link between *Sterna* and *Chlidonias*, as it is occasionally included in the latter genus.

The noddy group includes 5-7 species in three genera: the typical dark-coloured genus *Anous*, the all white *Gygis*, and the blue and grey *Procelsterna*. The status of closely related forms or species pairs in each of these genera requires further study. The specific status of the Brown Noddy (*Anous stolidus*) is not disputed. The Black Noddy (*Anous minutus*) and the Lesser Noddy (*Anous tenuirostris*), however, with allopatric distributions, are sometimes treated as conspecific, although on present evidence it seems reasonable to treat them as distinct species. A similar case is that of the Blue Noddy (*Procelsterna cerulea*) and the Grey Noddy (*Procelsterna albivitta*) which are herein treated as specifically distinct. In the White Tern (*Gygis alba*), current research does not favour the separation of the form *microrhyncha*: the two taxa are closely similar in appearance and behaviour, and there is evidence of their interbreeding in the Marquesas.

The monotypic genus *Larosterna* has been recognized by all authors for the Inca Tern (*Larosterna inca*), because of its remarkable plumage pattern and its distinctive breeding behaviour, as this Humboldt Current endemic nests in deep crevices and small caves; a tendency towards this habit is demonstrated by some Roseate and Bridled Terns which nest under boulders.

G. D. Schnell compared different statistical approaches to analysing skeletal and external characters of the terns and their allies, grouping birds on the basis of their similarities. Although there are many inconsistencies, several constant morphological patterns emerge which support the use of separate genera for several species. For example, *Gelochelidon* does not link closely with the typical terns, in many respects showing closer similarity to the crested terns. *Hydroprogne* sometimes links with *Thalasseus*, on the basis of size, but in other analyses it is distantly related to both *Sterna* and *Thalasseus*. *Phaetusa* is most similar to the larger crested terns, but does not consistently link with the smaller-billed ones.

Within the crested terns, Schnell found that the Great Crested Tern (*Thalasseus bergii*) and the Royal Tern (*Thalasseus maximus*) consistently show close affiliations with each other, although not always with the other members of *Thalasseus*, which likewise form a consistently linked group. Interestingly, the "Cayenne" form *eurygnatha* of the Sandwich Tern (*Thalasseus sandvicensis*) emerges as more similar to the Elegant Tern (*Thalasseus elegans*) than to the Sandwich Tern, suggesting that their assumed relationship at the species level warrants closer study.

The Roseate and Black-naped (*Sterna sumatrana*) Terns consistently form a species pair, and Forster's Tern (*Sterna forsteri*) and Trudeau's Tern (*Sterna trudeaui*) another, both of which associations have been suggested on other grounds by many field observers. Black and Lesser Noddies are the most closely similar of any species pair, even when they are not closely linked to Brown Noddy because of size differences. *Procelsterna* (treated by Schnell as a single species) shows morphological similarities to *Chlidonias*, rather than to *Anous*. As expected, *Larosterna* often appeared as a sister group to the remaining terns, although in some analyses it is linked with the noddies on account of its dark plumage.

In his 1959 taxonomic revision of gulls and terns, based on a comparative analysis of behaviour, M. Moynihan noted the uniformity of behaviour among the terns, and, as a consequence, he divided the family into just three genera. He placed the dark and the white noddies in the genus *Anous*, retained *Larosterna* for the Inca Tern, and placed all others, including the marsh terns, in the genus *Sterna*. No other authority has opted for such extensive generic lumping. Moynihan thought that, on behavioural grounds, the Large-billed Tern was closely related to the small terns, while the distinctiveness of the latter led him to conclude that this might justify their generic separation. Other authors differ as to which genera they retain: most recognize *Chlidonias*, *Procelsterna*, *Gygis*, *Larosterna* and *Phaetusa*, but lump all others in *Sterna*; some accept *Gelochelidon* but not *Hydroprogne*, and others the reverse.

More recently, in 1990, C. G. Sibley and B. L. Monroe listed 45 species of terns in seven genera. In addition to *Sterna*, they included *Chlidonias*, *Phaetusa*, *Anous*, *Procelsterna*, *Gygis* and *Larosterna*, while the Gull-billed, Caspian and crested terns were grouped in *Sterna*. The decision as to where exactly the line is drawn ultimately comes down to the extent to which one is a generic lumper or splitter. Herein, contrary to most recent authors, *Gelochelidon*, *Hydroprogne* and *Thalasseus* are retained, as much to emphasize the remarkable uniformity among the remaining typical terns as to stress the distinctiveness of these forms.

Morphological Aspects

Compared with gulls, terns are more specialized in terms of nesting habitat, diet and foraging methods, and their morphology reflects these specializations from a generalized larid ancestor. There is little doubt that the terns have a monophyletic origin. In general, terns forage by plunge-diving for fish or swooping to seize items at the water's surface, and the streamlined body and long, pointed wings and bill are well suited to such foraging methods.

Terns are small to medium-sized birds, ranging from 20 cm to 56 cm in length. There are no sexual differences in plumage patterns, and only slight size dimorphism, with males about 2-5% larger than females; dimorphism in bill size tends to be greater than that in body size. All species have very slender, elongated bodies, unlike the robust rounded shape of gulls, and they have relatively shorter legs, longer and narrower wings and longer bills. Most typical terns have elongated outer tail feathers or streamers, giving them a deeply forked tail, while in almost all other tern species the tail is at least notched. All these structural features produce a style of flight that is swift and graceful, with the distinctive shape giving an almost aircraft-like appearance: the aerial "high-flights" of terns (see Breeding) are among the most spectacular avian phenomena of coastal habitats in spring.

Although a few species are all dark or all white, most terns are pale below and grey above, with a black crown in nuptial plumage. Their white or light grey underparts reduce their con-

Taxonomists have divided the Sternidae into anything from three to nine or ten genera. The noddy genus *Procelsterna*, morphologically closer to *Chlidonias* than to *Anous*, is recognized as valid by most authors, but disagreement continues over whether it contains one, two or even three species. The Grey Noddy is still sometimes considered no more than a pale morph of the Blue Noddy (*Procelsterna cerulea*).

[*Procelsterna albivitta albivitta*, Lord Howe Island, Australia. Photo: Fred Bruemmer/DRK]

Despite its initially aberrant appearance, the Inca Tern still possesses the characteristic structural features of the Sternidae, including a rather elongated and slender body, relatively narrow wings, a forked tail, short legs and a long bill. Because of its unique plumage pattern and remarkable breeding behaviour, however, it is placed in its own monotypic genus Larosterna. It is endemic to the Humboldt Current region, where it nests in deep crevices and small caves, quite unlike most typical terns, although one or two Sterna species show a certain tendency towards similar nesting sites.

[Larosterna inca, Paracas, Peru. Photo: Günter Ziesler]

spicuousness to underwater prey when they are foraging over-head; this applies to juvenile terns as well, whereas juveniles of most gull species are dark grey or brown below, reflecting less plunge-diving activity. Like gulls, terns have a relatively high percentage of red and orange oil droplets in their eyes, allowing them to see through atmospheric haze above the ocean and to see fish in water to the depths to which they normally plunge. Terns that are dark-bodied engage in less aerial plunge-diving, and more surface- or hover-dipping, than those having a white frontal aspect.

Although short-legged, all terns walk well on the ground, but they are less likely than gulls to engage in running attacks during aggressive encounters. Many terns land on the water to bathe, and a few actually feed from the surface, but for a family with webbed feet, so closely tied to water, swimming is remarkably unusual and uncommon. Nevertheless, chicks in waterside colonies, when disturbed by intruders, often jump into the water and swim skilfully. Sooty Terns, however, do not have water-repellent plumage and quickly become waterlogged if they land on water.

With regard to overall body size, Caspian, Royal, Great Crested and Sandwich Terns are large and weigh over 250 g. Most of the rest are intermediate-sized, weighing about 100-180 g, while the small terns, 80 g or less in weight, include the Fairy (*Sterna nereis*), the Little, Saunders's (*Sterna saundersi*), the Least (*Sterna antillarum*), the Damara, the Yellow-billed (*Sterna superciliaris*) and the Peruvian (*Sterna lorata*) Terns. While there is almost complete overlap in size between males and females of a given species, within pairs the males are often slightly larger than their mates. In some species, such as the Common Tern, males have longer, deeper and wider bills than do females.

The plumage patterns of terns vary as a function of age. The downy chicks of most species are a tan or grey colour with dark speckles or splotches which provide them with camouflage, although in a few species the chicks are uniformly pale grey or black. At fledging, the juvenile plumage is often scaly or speck-led above, with a head pattern similar to that of the adult winter plumage. During the summer of their first year, terns normally have a white forehead. Full adult plumage is usually developed by two or three years of age. Melanism has not been reported among terns, and albinism would be difficult to detect in a pri-marily white family. Leucism has been reported in Black Nod-dies, and occurs with a frequency of less than 0·01% in juvenile Sooty Terns.

Moult patterns vary among species. The typical and crested terns often begin their body moult during the breeding season, and even incubating birds, particularly those which have relaid, can show white foreheads, while Least and Little Terns begin primary moult during incubation. Those breeding in north tem-perate environments mostly undergo a partial moult on the win-tering grounds prior to migration north. Noddies have protracted moults which extend into the breeding season, as in the Brown Noddy, or they interrupt their moult to breed, as is the case with the White Tern.

Habitat

Terns occur throughout the world and breed on all continents, including Antarctica, where there are colonies of Antarctic Terns (*Sterna vittata*). They exploit a variety of breeding habitats, oc-cupying inland marshes and rivers, coastal marshes and estua-ries, sandy or rocky beaches, rocky cliffs, and oceanic islands. Only 11 species regularly breed inland. Historical data from Eu-rope show that there is a "tern zone", located in the lower middle reaches of large rivers, used extensively by nesting Common Terns. Least and Little Terns have populations breeding on in-land rivers of North America and Europe respectively, and the closely related Yellow-billed Tern is strictly a riverine species, as is the Large-billed Tern with which it nests, as well as the Black-fronted Tern of New Zealand's South Island. The three marsh terns, Trudeau's Tern and some populations of Forster's Tern nest on inland marshes. A similar number of species, 11, breed on oceanic islands. These are the dark-winged *Sterna*, namely the Sooty, Bridled and Grey-backed Terns, the six spe-cies of noddies, and the Antarctic and Kerguelen (*Sterna virgata*) Terns. Some populations of Roseate Terns also nest on oceanic islands. The remaining members of the family breed on rocky and sandy coasts, estuarine and barrier islands, and inshore ar-chipelagos.

During migration most inland breeders move to coastal ar-eas, and outside the breeding season most species of terns re-

The Sooty Tern exhibits all the classic tern features: a slender, streamlined body, long, narrow, pointed wings, and a deeply forked tail with elongated outer feathers, giving an elegant appearance very different from that of the heavier and more robust Laridae. In all aspects of their life terns are far more aerial than the latter, their structure being designed to produce a swift, buoyant and graceful flight in which their shape is quite distinctive. A very common foraging method of terns involves plunge-diving for fish from a height of several metres, a method for which the long, pointed bill and general streamlined shape are ideally suited; the white or pale grey underparts of most tern species reduce their conspicuousness to underwater prey when they are foraging overhead. The Sooty Tern, however, is one of the species that feed mainly by dipping to the water's surface. Oddly, its plumage is not water-repellent, and the bird rapidly becomes waterlogged and unable to fly properly if it settles on water. It therefore spends all of its life in the air apart from periods at the breeding site. Sooty Terns have never been seen to swim or to sleep on water, and are assumed to sleep on the wing. They feed at night, on fish which come to the surface only after dark. The graceful soaring flight of Sooty Terns as they head out to the open ocean to feed is a glorious sight to behold.

[Sterna fuscata nubilosa, Glorieuse Islands, western Indian Ocean. Photo: R. Seitre/Bios]

In terns, patterns of daily activity are frequently affected by tidal regimes, but the busiest times tend to be early and late in the day. This is especially true in tropical climes, where birds are likely to spend the hottest hours of the day loafing in flocks at favoured sites. During such periods of rest, individuals may perform different kinds of comfort behaviour; some birds bathe, which they may follow with a session of preening. While one of these River Terns is busying itself in feather-care, the other looks on and indulges in a little wing- and leg-stretching.

[Sterna aurantia, Ramnagar, north India. Photo: Tim Loseby]

main along coasts, a few venturing out to the edge of the continental shelf. In the Southern Hemisphere, Arctic Terns (*Sterna paradisaea*), which spend the northern winter in Antarctica, often wander through the pack ice along the edge of that continent. The more highly marine species either stay close to their breeding islands or become entirely pelagic, and the wintering areas of these species, as well as of the Aleutian Tern (*Sterna aleutica*) and several populations of the Roseate Tern, are largely unknown.

Sooty Terns maintain a strictly oceanic existence from the moment they fledge from the nesting colonies until, at about five years of age, they return to land to breed for the first time. One of the great ornithological mysteries is how this species, which lacks water-repellent plumage and soon becomes waterlogged if it lands on the sea, spends these five years; healthy juveniles have never been found on land, apart from a few that return to the nesting areas a year before they actually breed, nor on flotsam, where Bridled Terns often rest. Do these young Sooties remain on the wing for the entire five years between fledging and returning to their natal colonies?

Many terns seek inaccessible nesting places, on islands on barrier beaches, in rivers or on lakes, in marshes, on long extended sand spits, or on remote oceanic islands. On the last of these, several species nest on trees or cliffs. These anti-predator strategies deter most mammalian predators, although rats, cats, foxes and mustelids exact a toll on some inshore islands. Nesting substrates include sand, fine or coarse gravel, shell, dry mud, mats of floating or prostrate terrestrial vegetation, pockets of coral or coral rubble as well as concrete and concrete rubble, and artificial surfaces such as gravel roofs, dykes and other man-made features of the landscape. Some species, including Common and Little Terns, exhibit wide variation in their choice of colony sites and nest-sites, embracing most of the above choices in one part of their range or another. For example, Common Terns will nest on sandy or rocky beaches, in heavily or sparsely vegetated areas, on bare sand, on wrack, mud or bent-over grasses in salt-marshes, on sand or vegetation in freshwater marshes, on rock or rubble beaches, and on man-made structures such as wooden platforms. They may even use several of these different substrates in one local area.

Other species have different habitat preferences in different parts of their geographical range. Sooty Terns often prefer to nest under tall, dense vegetation on some Caribbean islands, but nest on bare or sparsely vegetated sand on many Pacific islands. Even when bare areas are created within vegetated colonies in Culebra, Puerto Rico, Sooties still choose nest-sites under dense cover. Roseate Terns in north-west Europe and north-east North America generally nest under vegetation or in rock crevices, but on the Caribbean islands their nests are exposed on coral rocks, while in Australia they often nest on bare sand with no vegetation cover.

Some terns exhibit a narrower range of habitat preferences. For example, Black Terns (*Chlidonias niger*) usually nest on floating vegetation in marshes, colony sites varying only in the percentage of vegetation cover and its dispersion pattern and in the water depth. In the same habitats Forster's Terns exhibit more variability, nesting on floating vegetation or boards, and on muskrat (*Ondatra zibethicus*) houses. Coastal Forster's nest on exposed mud or wrack on salt-marshes.

Still other species will nest in habitats that seem very different, but are structurally similar. Black Noddies nest either in trees or on cliffs, in both cases elevated sites that prevent the access of ground predators. These habitats also have limited space for nesting, which both increases competition for nest-sites and reduces the level of interspecific interactions. The White Tern is unique in making no nest, instead balancing its single egg on a narrow tree limb or cliff ledge. Many eggs and chicks are lost from such vulnerable sites, and the terns have adapted to more secure perches, including tap or faucet handles where the lip retains the egg even in winds.

The marine distribution of terns is influenced by the availability of food. Most species frequent continental coasts, concentrating particularly in areas of upwelling, at coral reefs, or near estuaries and river mouths: places where aquatic productivity is high. The distribution of pelagic species is little known, but, like most seabirds, they must track patchily distributed foods. Current research, combining satellite tracking of individual birds with acquisition of physical and biological oceanographic data, will greatly increase our understanding of the complex movement patterns of oceanic birds, including those of the terns.

General Habits

Terns are highly gregarious species. They generally breed, forage and migrate in flocks that can range from a few individuals

to many thousands or even, in the case of Sooty Tern, millions. Most species are diurnal, and a typical day begins at first light when the birds leave their overnight roost or breeding colony to search for food. Whereas many social bird species leave their roost synchronously in large flocks, terns move out from their roosting or breeding colonies solitarily or in small groups. During the breeding season, an individual tern which is not incubating often rests on its territory near its mate. Sooty Terns, and probably other species, feed at night, when bottom-dwelling prey rise to the surface. Foraging terns disperse far and wide, searching for prey either singly or in flocks, or in association with other marine vertebrates. A few feed frequently over land, but only in the Gull-billed Tern is this the usual foraging method.

The activity patterns of terns are affected by a number of factors, including tides, breeding activities, weather conditions, social facilitation and time of day. Terns are often most active in the early morning and late afternoon, whether they are feeding or courting, but the daily activity patterns of coastal-nesting species are often influenced by tidal cycles. Inclement weather can dampen the frequency of courtship and display behaviour, while social facilitation can increase these activities.

Terns are usually short distance foragers over shoals of fish. Within a few hours they can obtain enough food for themselves, and they then return to resting flocks or the breeding colony for a few hours. Those hunting at sea, however, where food is very unevenly distributed, may spend hours simply locating a feeding area. In these circumstances, a bird returning to the breeding site relieves its mate, which then goes out to forage. These incubation bouts range from 20 minutes to more than 20 hours, in Common Terns typically 1-4 hours, after which the mate returns and another change-over occurs. A courting male or a bird with chicks may take slightly longer on a foraging trip, because he must first feed himself, and then catch a large fish to bring to his female or an appropriate-sized fish for his chicks. There is often an increase in foraging activity of both breeding and non-breeding terns in the hour or two before dusk, as they obtain sufficient food for the night; a peak in chick-feeding is generally evident too during late afternoon and at dusk.

Although the tern family breeds from tropical and equatorial regions to both polar areas, most species nest in only one climatic region, which narrows the range of adaptations required.

Some, however, such as Little, Least, Common, Gull-billed and particularly Roseate Terns, have both a temperate and a tropical distribution, making their adaptations to thermal stress especially interesting. The Sandwich Tern spans about 100° of latitude, from north Britain and the Baltic to southern South America, while its "Cayenne" race alone spans 60° from the Greater Antilles to Patagonia. Adaptations to heat stress include nesting near rocks or vegetation, as well as gular-fluttering and panting, and behavioural mechanisms such as feather-fluffing and wing-drooping. Some species wet their bellies to reduce heat stress, and return directly to their nests, depositing water on eggs or chicks.

A particularly fascinating and somewhat obscure form of behaviour is sometimes seen at terneries, when some or all of the birds suddenly leave in a dense mass and fly low and silently towards the sea. After a very short time they start to call, and then return singly or in small groups to the colony. These sudden "panics" or "dreads", which seem to be spontaneous, appear to have no obvious cause, but they are thought possibly to be connected with aerial predators. They are most intense in species with the densest nest dispersion.

Voice

The voices of many terns are harsh in quality, and a single call may convey different messages depending more on its context than on its structure. Most terns are noisy, whether on the breeding grounds, while foraging, or while migrating. In the non-breeding season, vocalizations are limited to those associated with flock formation, foraging behaviour and predator avoidance. Even on migration, vocalizations help terns to maintain flock coherence and to find food.

Noise levels in breeding colonies can be very loud, particularly in dense colonies where many adults are mobbing intruders. On the other hand, those species that nest solitarily, in small colonies, or in colonies with widely scattered nests are often very quiet, partly as an anti-predator adaptation. Even species that are noisy when in dense colonies are relatively quiet when they nest in very small colonies or solitarily. For example, Forster's Terns breeding in colonies of 100-150 pairs on salt-marsh islands in New Jersey are quite vocal, but those nesting solitarily in fresh-

water marshes in Minnesota are usually silent; even those dispersed within Franklin's Gull (*Larus pipixcan*) colonies are usually silent unless an intruder comes within a few metres of their nests.

Terns have a wide variety of vocalizations that are used during the breeding season: when defending territories, soliciting mates, engaging in courtship behaviour, maintaining the pair-bond, exchanging incubation duties, and communicating with their chicks. Although interspecific variations exist in the nature of the calls, most terns have variants of some common call types. When flying around the colony or arriving with fish they often give a "che-wick" or "kiewick". In aggressive interactions they will give a "keek, keek, keek" or a "keow, keow", both to conspecifics and to other intruders. During high-intensity interactions this call is shortened to a frantic "kek k k k k k". The "Rattle" call too is used to repel conspecific intruders.

Vocalizations are an integral part of courtship, again with interspecific differences. For those species that have fish-flights

(see Breeding), the first bird to depart, usually the male, may utter a "kearr, kearr, keari" call, the partner will give a "ki ki ki ki ki", and the male will answer with a "kor kor kor korrrrr". All terns have a copulation call: the male gives a repetitive "kuk kuk kuk", undulating in quality, and repeated for the duration of copulation.

Food and Feeding

Although terns are generalists with regard to nesting habitat, they are more specialized foragers than are gulls. They are not, however, complete specialists: there is no species of tern that feeds by only one method, in only one habitat zone, or on only one prey. Apart from the Gull-billed Tern, which feeds over terrestrial habitats, most terns obtain most of their food from aquatic habitats, either freshwater, estuarine or oceanic. The Kerguelen Tern feeds largely on insects over uplands during the breeding season, but on aquatic prey during the rest of the year. During the breeding season some of the marsh terns specialize in foraging over freshwater lakes or marshes or over coastal marshes; they search for prey over open or sparsely vegetated water, although they sometimes capture aerial insects over marshland. Terns feed on a large variety of small, usually schooling, fish, and congregate when large shoals are discovered. Hence, when two or more tern species occur together, they are likely to exploit the same food resources, as these are temporally and spatially patchy.

Coastal breeders usually forage from tidal creeks and estuaries to ocean waters, usually close inshore, but occasionally ranging across the continental shelf. Most species prefer to fish in sheltered bays and lagoons, since rough water depresses their success. Those nesting on oceanic islands either forage along the fringe of the island, or travel far offshore to forage in the open ocean. Sooty Terns often do not hunt near the colony, but may fly up to 100 km or more over the open ocean.

All the foraging methods used by terns involve skill, grace and agility in flight. A dense flock of Common Terns or Black Noddies foraging over a compact school of fish forced to the surface by larger predatory fish is one of the most aesthetic of coastal spectacles, and the graceful swooping and soaring flight of Sooty Terns as they head out to the open ocean is equally breathtaking. In inland marshes, the dark silhouette of a Black Tern swooping through a brilliant blue sky to the still waters of a pool surrounded by gently waving cat-tails or reeds is riveting.

Although typical and crested terns generally feed by plunge-diving for fish over water, most are capable of using a variety of

One way in which some terns counter heat stress in very hot climates is to moisten their belly feathers and then return directly to their nests, where they are able to wet the eggs or chicks and thus cool them down. Terns not infrequently alight on the water to bathe, but swimming is a remarkably uncommon occurrence among this family of web-footed birds.

[*Sterna antillarum*. Photo: Mike Wilkes/Aquila]

It is very important for all birds to keep their plumage in excellent condition, as their success and survival frequently depend directly on it. This is particularly true of such aerial birds as terns. Despite their very short legs, terns are able to walk well on land, although they are noticeably less mobile than gulls. Note the darkish grey upperparts of this preening Greater Crested Tern, one of the main features of geographical variation in this species.

[*Thalasseus bergii velox*, Nafoon, Oman. Photo: Hanne & Jens Eriksen/Aquila]

methods. These include contact-dipping, aerial-dipping, hover-dipping, surface-dipping, aerial hawking for insects, and piracy from their own or other species. Some species, such as the Sooty Tern, do not plunge-dive.

Plunge-diving involves quartering back and forth at a height of 3-15 m while searching for prey below the water's surface, hovering over the prey to fix its location, and plunging directly into the water, sometimes after a stall or even a brief upward movement. The tern generally submerges completely, although sometimes, if prey are near the surface, only the bill and head will be immersed. Terns sometimes even pursue their prey for a short distance under water, where their swimming movements resemble those used in flight. In most cases, however, they submerge, pick up the fish with the bill, and immediately leave the water and rise up into the air. This foraging method requires great skill and agility, since birds must compensate for refractive properties of the air-water interface, while they and their prey are both in motion.

Contact-dipping involves flying closer to the water, swooping down, and plunging the bill alone beneath the surface. It is particularly appropriate when there are many food items near the surface, since a tern can contact-dip repeatedly with no interruption in feeding, while plunge-diving is necessary for fish more than a few centimetres below the surface. Aerial-dipping is the same as contact-dipping, but without any contact being made with the water.

Hover-dipping entails hovering about 1-2 m above the water, and dropping down to seize items from the surface. Sometimes this method is combined with foot-paddling to stir up prey items.

Surface-dipping, unusual for most terns, involves sitting or swimming on the water and picking up items from the surface or from just below it. Some terns sometimes forage on mudflats by walking, gull-like, and stabbing at prey.

In aerial pursuit or hawking, a tern wheels and circles in the air to catch insects which have just emerged in vast numbers, often over freshwater marshes. Forster's, Black and Common Terns regularly engage in this type of foraging, and many others use it less frequently.

Many tern species forage in association with other marine organisms, such as porpoises (Phocoena) and predatory fish which drive schools of small fish and concentrate them near the surface. Examples include Common and Roseate Terns over bluefish (Pomatomus saltatrix) in the Atlantic; noddies, Great Crested, Lesser Crested (Thalasseus bengalensis), Roseate and Bridled Terns over tuna (Neothunnus macropterus) and bonito

(Euthunnus affinis) in Australian waters; and Black-naped and Roseate Terns foraging over schools being pursued by Spanish mackerel (Scomberomorus commersoni) off Africa. In the northern tropical Pacific, Sooty Terns, noddies and White Terns feed together with the combined schools of tuna and dolphins, while in the southern tropical Pacific mostly single-species flocks of Sooty Terns feed over small tuna only seldom accompanied by dolphins.

Piracy is another common foraging method, usually practised at breeding colonies, where a steady stream of fish is brought in by males courtship-feeding their mates, or by parents feeding chicks. Terns pirate fish from their own species as well as from others. Conversely, they are often victimized by larger birds, particularly gulls and skuas. Some tern species are extensively targeted by other pirates: Arctic Skuas (Stercorarius parasiticus), for example, rely heavily on piracy of terns, and may accompany Arctic Terns on migration so as to continue to exploit them.

Terns also exhibit a variety of unusual foraging methods. Common Terns wintering off Peru aerial-dip towards wet sand to pick up mole crabs (Eremita analoga) behind receding waves. Bridled Terns in Japan and Kerguelen Terns will forage for small fish and invertebrates associated with drifting seaweed. Several species follow the plough, although this feeding method is not nearly so important as it is for gulls. Least Terns will pick up fish from a fisherman's bucket, and several species follow fishing boats or patrol the shoreline to pick up offal discarded by fishermen. Roseate Terns and Brown Noddies feed in association with Brown Pelicans (Pelecanus occidentalis), hovering over a pelican as it emerges and snatching fish that fall from its bill.

Except for the mainly insectivorous and lizard-eating Gull-billed Tern, all species rely primarily on aquatic organisms, mainly fish, for their food. Many terns also eat crustaceans, and some freshwater species opportunistically take frogs and tadpoles. Gull-billed Terns forage extensively over agricultural fields, and grasshoppers often constitute an important part of their diet; this species also eats frogs and crabs.

The size of prey taken is determined largely by the size and width of the tern species' bill: larger terns, with a larger bill and wider gape, can consume larger fish. It also varies according to prey availability, breeding phenology, and the prevalence of pirates; larger fish are more vulnerable to piratic attempts. The species composition and size of fish present vary seasonally, and birds must sample from the available pool or travel further to find more adequate prey.

Age-related differences in foraging ability have been found in nearly all terns for which this aspect has been examined. Birds of the year are less efficient at locating feeding sites, at attempting to catch prey, and at actually catching prey once they make an attempt. Presumably, the difficulties of learning to forage account for delayed first breeding. Sooty Terns, which sometimes do not breed until they are 6-10 years old, have to be capable of finding very patchily distributed prey in the open ocean.

Breeding

Terns are normally monogamous, although other mating systems have been recorded. Trios or female-female pairs, or both, have been observed only in the Caspian, Roseate and Common Terns, although supernormal clutches have been used as an index of female-female pairs. Such clutches have been reported in the literature and from museum collections for Gull-billed, Caspian, Elegant, Sandwich, Royal, Roseate, Black-naped, Common, Arctic, Forster's, Least, Sooty, Black-fronted and Black Terns and Brown Noddy. However, these data must be interpreted carefully, because: egg-collectors may have prized large clutches, leading to bias in the frequency of supernormal clutches in museum collections; in colonies with small distances between nests, eggs can be rolled into other nests; and in marsh colonies, eggs flooded out of one nest can be retrieved into another by nearby nest-owners. This last phenomenon has been documented at nests of Common and Forster's Terns, where marked eggs were checked before and after floods.

Terns are among the
noisiest of birds, their
voices in most cases
being very harsh and
grating. One of the loudest
and harshest of all
vocalizations is the
rasping call of the Caspian
Tern. The vocal repertoire
of terns is widest during
the breeding season, with
different sounds being
used in relation to
mate-soliciting, courtship
and pair-bonding
activities, territorial
defence, change-overs
at the nest, and
communication with
chicks. Some call types
are common to most
species, with relatively
minor variations. A single
call can convey different
messages, depending on
the context in which
it is given.

[Hydroprogne caspia,
Sweden.
Photo: Bengt Lundberg/
Bios]

Hybridization is rare among terns, but has been recorded between Roseate and Common Terns in Europe and North America. Mixed pairings have also been found in Europe involving Sandwich x Lesser Crested, Sandwich x Elegant, the latter a presumed vagrant, and Black x White-winged (*Chlidonias leucopterus*) Terns.

Most terns exhibit an annual cycle, in which they breed once annually, at approximately the same time of year. The breeding season may last 2½-3 months for Arctic species, 3-4 months for temperate species, and 3-5 months for tropical species. It is extremely rare for a pair of terns to raise more than one brood in a single cycle.

In a few tern populations with an annual cycle, breeding is not synchronous among colony members, while some tropical terns, notably the Sooty, do not exhibit an annual breeding cycle at all. In both cases, some breeding may occur in all months of the year at a given colony, as on some tropical islands. On Christmas Island in the Pacific Ocean, the breeding cycle of White Terns lasts up to 10½ months for successful birds, but is shorter for unsuccessful ones; moult always takes 5½-7 months, so failed breeders nest out of synchrony. The so-called "Wideawake Fairs" or mass breedings of Sooty Terns occur at intervals of about 9·6 months on Ascension Island and at intervals of 6 or 7 months on Christmas Island, although in the Caribbean the species has an annual cycle. On Ascension Island, there are Sooty Terns and Black Noddies breeding at all times of the year. For most Bridled Terns there is a well defined annual breeding cycle at the same time each year, but in the Seychelles the breeding cycle lasts 7-8 months.

Documentation of age at first breeding benefits from long-term ringing studies, which have so far involved relatively few species. Although some individuals of the small and intermediate-sized terns first breed when they are two years old, most do not breed until three years and some not until four. Some species, such as the Bridled Tern, regularly breed only when they are four years old, although individuals come back to the colony at two and three years of age. The larger species do not breed until they are three, four or five years of age, and some species do not regularly breed until they are still older. Sooty Terns at Johnston Atoll breed at four years, but some wait until they are six to eight or even ten years old. Presumably, this delay is because young terns must master the difficult foraging and feeding techniques. Some studies show evidence of assortative mating by age, young birds tending to pair with birds of a similar age, but whether this reflects a true preference or simply the age distribution of available mates requires study.

In the vast majority of cases terns are colonial, sometimes forming huge agglomerations. Many species occupy the same colony site for many years, whereas some others, such as Little and Least Terns, often change sites after only one or a few seasons. Colonies are abandoned when the site becomes unsuitable because of habitat change, frequent human disturbance, predation, or weather stresses such as severe storms or floods. In general, the sites that have been used for the longest periods of time are isolated coastal or inland islands or remote oceanic islands, where the threat from predators and human visitors is low. Sooty Terns have apparently occupied certain oceanic islands for several centuries.

Faithfulness to a nesting site, or philopatry, varies according to habitat stability. Species that nest on cliffs and remote oceanic islands can occupy the same colony site for years, since the habitat is stable. Habitats that change from year to year, such as freshwater marshes, riverine sandbars and coastal sand spits, may be used for only a few years or even a single year. Terns return to their previous site, assess its suitability, and then either occupy the site or move elsewhere. Those which normally nest in unstable environments often exhibit group adherence: the members of the group, subcolony or small colony remain together, even though they may shift colony sites.

Terneries range in size from a few pairs to many thousands. In the colonies of some species, such as the Damara Tern, the nests are so widely spaced that they can be considered solitary, but the distribution of pairs is nonetheless clumped. Some true solitary nesting does occur, and, moreover, a single pair of one species will nest in a colony of other terns or gulls. Species such as the Black-bellied Tern (*Sterna acuticauda*) and the Yellow-billed Tern nest in small colonies of only a few to a dozen pairs, with inter-nest distances ranging up to 1000 m. Interme-

In keeping with their social habits, terns are often seen foraging in flocks. Common Terns frequently gather in large numbers to exploit food sources, and are quick to spot any shoals of small fish that may appear in inshore waters. The feeding method perhaps most closely associated with terns is plunge-diving, and this is indeed the commonest method employed by most of the typical Sterna terns and by the "crested terns" of the genus Thalasseus. Virtually all terns do, however, use a variety of tactics for capturing food, all of which call for great agility and skill in flight. Besides plunge-diving, they frequently indulge in contact-dipping, in which they swoop down towards the water and catch food items by dipping the bill just below the surface, without making any other contact with the water; surface-dipping, involving swimming on the water and picking items from on or just below the surface, is far less common. In addition, several species, among them the Common Tern, are highly skilled at hawking aerial insects, and they also steal food from other terns.

[Sterna hirundo hirundo, Norfolk, England. Photo: Roger Tidman/ NHPA]

With very few exceptions, terns obtain most of their food from freshwater or saltwater habitats. Fish and aquatic invertebrates form the bulk of the diet of many species. Having seized an item following a plunge-dive, which generally involves complete, though brief, submersion, the tern immediately leaves the water and rises into the air. The strike rate has been found to be higher among adult terns than among immatures, which have to learn the skills required for efficient foraging.

[*Sterna hirundo*.
Photo: Áke Lindau/Ardea]

diate-sized terns generally nest in colonies of tens or twenties to several hundred pairs. An exception is the Sooty Tern, which occupies colonies containing several hundred to several thousand pairs, and occasionally up to two million pairs. Colonies of crested terns normally hold hundreds and occasionally thousands of pairs.

Nesting dispersion also varies. Sooty Tern and various crested terns regularly breed in very dense colonies only a body length apart, while other species nest in very loose colonies. Unlike the situation with gulls, inter-nest distance in terneries decreases with increasing size of the tern species. The larger species, such as the Caspian, Royal, Great Crested and Sandwich, form very dense colonies, where an incubating bird can almost reach its neighbour. Colonies of the intermediate-sized terns, such as Common, Roseate, Arctic, Forster's and the noddies, are fairly dense, with nests 1-5 m apart. The small terns often nest in fairly loose colonies in which distances between nests may be 5-100 m or more. All tern species are territorial, although the size of the territory and the intensity with which it is defended vary. Territory size determines the pattern of nest dispersion within colonies, which is itself partly a function of competition and anti-predator strategy.

When taking occupation of the site, the larger species can displace nesting gulls from parts of their colony by entering *en masse* and setting up territories; even the larger gulls soon abandon their eggs when faced with so many large terns. In this way Caspian Terns displace nesting Herring Gulls (*Larus argentatus*) in the Great Lakes of North America, Royal or Sandwich Terns displace Laughing Gulls (*Larus atricilla*) along the Atlantic coast of North America, Sandwich Terns displace Black-headed Gulls (*Larus ridibundus*) in Europe, and Elegant Terns displace Heermann's Gulls (*Larus heermanni*) in the Gulf of California.

In Puerto Rico, Royal and Sandwich Terns, two species which regularly associate with each other, often nest in adjacent, but dense colonies. Late-arriving potential competitors for nesting space find it difficult to enter such a dense colony of large terns, and are relegated to nesting on the edge. Colonies thus expand in size during a breeding season.

The larger terns also rely on their nesting pattern to prevent aerial predators from getting within the colony. With the dense packing and noisy commotion of a Caspian, Royal or Sandwich Tern colony, aerial predators can not find a suitable place to land, and it is difficult to enter from the edge.

Intermediate-sized terns and some of the small terns, however, rely on behaviour such as mobbing and aerial attacks to repel predators. They repeatedly swoop low overhead, one after the other, often striking with the bill, and sometimes even killing predators. Even casual human intruders are discouraged by such mobbing, although it is ineffective against eggers or other determined humans. These terns also rely on the cryptic coloration of their eggs and chicks to reduce the likelihood of predation, a strategy that is most successful if the eggs or chicks are not close together; this is, indeed, the case, since the nests of these terns are well spaced.

Peruvian and Damara Terns nest in very small colonies in which pairs are often 100 m or more apart, the cryptic coloration of their chicks and eggs helping to prevent ground or aerial predators from finding their nests. They do, however, nest close enough to be in vocal communication, which allows for early warning and mobbing of predators.

Predation pressures can affect nesting dispersion. In a Least Tern colony in New Jersey, USA, inter-nest distances increased dramatically following intense fox (*Vulpes fulva*) predation. The nests remained widely spaced for several years while the predators were still present, and coalesced into a denser colony only after the foxes were controlled.

Although some terns breed in monospecific colonies, many nest with other species of terns, as well as with gulls, skimmers, boobies, alcids, ducks, and even sea turtles. In some instances the terns select the colony site after the other species is already nesting, but in many cases the latter is attracted to the terneries, gaining benefit from the terns' aggressive mobbing. For example, Forster's and Black Terns often select nest-sites and begin egg-laying within Franklin's Gull colonies only after the gulls have laid. In this case, the tern species are smaller than the gulls but derive protection from them, as the gulls mob and attack aerial predators such as hawks. The terns, present in small numbers, also benefit from a "swamping" effect, since they are thus only a few among many thousands of colony members.

Terns will also nest beside colonies of albatrosses, cormorants, and any other seabirds that nest within their range. In many of these cases, however, the terns are not choosing to nest with the other species, but rather both species are selecting the same remote, suitable breeding site. Often, such sites are in limited availability.

Terns usually spend a few weeks in the vicinity of the colony before taking up residence. During this time they may fly over

Terneries vary in size and in density. Colonies of the larger Thalasseus *"crested terns" contain hundreds and not uncommonly thousands of pairs, which are normally very densely packed together. In contrast to the pattern in gulls, the inter-nest distance decreases with increasing size of the tern species. Royal Terns, for example, form colonies that are often very large and almost always very dense, with up to 8 nests/m². Such a dense assembly of birds makes it difficult for a predator to land within the colony.*

[Thalasseus maximus maximus, Baja California. Photo: Ramón Torres Valdivia]

the colony during the day, or stand in clubs or courting groups. Attendance at the colony gradually increases, and the birds then begin to establish territories. The normal phenology of temperate zone species is to select territories, defend them, solicit mates or re-establish pair-bonds with mates from the previous year, engage in courtship and courtship feeding for a few days or weeks, followed by an egg-laying period of a few days to two or three weeks, an incubation period of 21-28 days, and a chick-rearing phase or fledging period of about four weeks. Depending on the degree of synchrony within a colony, egg-laying may extend over a period of two months, with later laying due to failures or the influx of new, usually young, birds. These time periods may be slightly shorter for the smaller terns, and slightly longer for the larger ones. This schedule basically applies to temperate- and Arctic-nesting species, with activities generally more synchronous at high latitudes. Tropical terns, however, have adapted to the lower food availability by prolonging each phase.

The detailed activities during each of these phases vary with species and locality, and are greatly influenced by food availability and weather. Common Terns provide a basic example. Early in the breeding cycle, they gather in small groups on the colony, mainly at night, sometimes huddled against the cold; they may be absent during the day, or a few distant notes may be heard from birds flying high overhead. Gradually the terns spend time on the colony during the day, at first landing for a few minutes and then staying for longer periods. They select territories, and spread out in the available habitat. Factors determining their territory selection include both physical features of the habitat, such as vegetation structure and density, and social factors, such as the presence of conspecifics or other species. Unmated males defend their territories while they solicit for mates, and mated pairs defend their territories and engage in re-establishing pair-bonds. Some unmated males shift their territories from one place to another within the colony, hoping to attract females, while others fly above the colony, searching for mated females that they can steal from other males or unmated females that they can court.

Normal territorial defence against conspecifics involves walking or flying towards opponents, aerial chases, "upward flutter flights" and ground and aerial fights, as well as a number of displays, including "Oblique", "Crouch" and "Gape" displays. In an aggressive encounter, a tern may initially give a "Head-toss", followed by "Up-erect" with head-turning for insecure birds, and

by "Down-erect" for secure birds. In appeasement, a bird may give a "Head-nod", "Head-tilt" or "Head-turning", all equivalent to "Facing-away" in gulls.

Normal courtship and pair-bonding involve a variety of highly ritualized displays, performed on the ground and in the air. In many species, courtship sequences are initiated when the male brings back a fish; he may offer this to the female, and she may either swallow it immediately or keep it in her bill during the display.

During this courtship period, both mated and unmated birds engage in aerial "high-flight" displays or "fish-flights". These typically begin when a male brings back a fish to a female; almost immediately after he lands, both take off and fly high in the air, in tandem, often alternating with gliding on rigid wings. One or two other birds frequently join in these fish-flights. Most terns have a high-flight, although some do not have so elaborate or so ritualized a fish-flight as do the Common, Roseate, Least or Arctic Terns. In some the high-flight is similar to the fish-flight, and in others the two displays differ. The Caspian Tern's high-flight differs from that of both the crested terns and the typical terns, supporting its separate generic status.

Once pairs have formed, the frequency and intensity of courtship displays accelerates, with the addition of courtship feeding. During this period the female often remains on the territory, defending it against intruders, while the male spends all day bringing back fish to feed her. When pairs are firmly established, either the male departs immediately after giving her the fish, or copulation follows fish-transfer without the intense and prolonged courtship displays.

Prior to copulation, courting pairs circle around each other, often with wings slightly drooped and bill pointed downwards. The male points the bill up in a full "Upright" display similar to that of gulls, while calling softly. For several minutes the two may dance around each other, calling softly, with their wings drooped. Copulation often follows such displays. A receptive female crouches, and the male hops onto her back. This copulatory stance may occur several times before cloacal contact is achieved, and birds sometimes maintain this position for many minutes. At the time of contact, the male raises his wings in "copulatory wing-flagging" to achieve balance and lowers his tail to one side, the female simultaneously raising hers to the other side. Cloacal contact lasts a few seconds, and is usually followed by the male dismounting. A pair may mate many times in a day

Courtship feeding is an integral part of the breeding ritual of terns, serving the important function of reinforcing the pair-bond. It may continue for some days or even weeks before egg-laying begins, and the male may appear to spend most of his time during this period bringing fish to the female. Although most tern species usually carry back only one fish at a time in the bill, whether for courtship feeding or to provision the chicks, White Terns regularly return with three or more fish lined up in the bill. If the male offers the fish to the female, as in the case of these Forster's Terns in the second photo, she may either swallow it or hold it in her bill. In the early stages of courtship, the next step can be a "high-flight" or "fish-flight" display, in which both birds fly high in the air, intermittently gliding, and often being joined by one or two other individuals. Once pairs are firmly established, either the male leaves immediately after presenting the fish, or copulation follows. The amount of courtship feeding is thought to help the female to judge the quality of her mate; if he seems to be a poor provider, she may leave him early in the breeding cycle and mate with a "better" male.

[Above:
Gygis alba candida.
Photo: David Hosking/
FLPA].

Below:
Sterna forsteri,
Cape May, New Jersey,
USA.
Photo: A. & E. Morris/
Birds As Art]

A receptive female Common Tern crouches and the male hops on, but several attempts may be required before cloacal contact is achieved; terns sometimes maintain this position for some minutes. The male balances by raising his wings and lowering his tail to one side, the female raising her tail to the other side; cloacal contact is very brief, before the male dismounts. A pair of terns may mate many times in a day. Copulation is often preceded by the two birds circling around each other with wings drooped and bill pointed down. As with gulls, this display and "wing-flagging" during copulation may act as signals to other pairs in the colony, leading to synchronous mating.

[*Sterna hirundo hirundo*, Long Island, New York, USA. Photo: Tom Vezo]

prior to egg-laying. The pre-copulatory circling display and the wing-flagging often appear to serve as a signal to other pairs, and there is evidence of synchronous matings in several species.

During courtship through to incubation, a male Common Tern will bring back up to five or six fish an hour for his mate. The amount of courtship feeding is believed to help the female to judge the quality of her mate, and early in the cycle a female may leave a mate which shows signs of being a poor provider. The frequency of feeding declines somewhat during incubation, as the female does more fishing on her own. At this time, piracy increases in frequency and intensity, and males must balance the rewards of bringing back particularly large fish against the increased risk of piracy. The rates of both attempted and successful piracy increase with the size of the fish; as the fish are carried in the tern's bill they are visible, and pirates can therefore choose to pursue terns carrying large fish.

Nest-site selection occurs during the period immediately before laying, since most terns except tree-nesting noddies and marsh-nesting species make little or no nest. Both members of the pair engage in scrape-making, and species with relatively large territories may make several scrapes before agreeing on a given location. In the densest terneries the nest-site is determined by its position in relation to neighbours. The "Scrape" and "Bent" displays are amongst the pair-maintenance displays.

Marsh-nesting terns, such as Forster's, Trudeau's, the Black, Whiskered (*Chlidonias hybridus*) and White-winged, must construct a floating nest out of the available vegetation. During courtship and territory acquisition they must find a suitable platform for displaying, and this often amounts to only a few stems matted together from winter storms. During the territory defence phase, both sexes may add material until it becomes a sturdy nest platform. They then begin to fashion a cup by swaying and settling their bodies in the vegetation, in much the same way as beach-nesting terns fashion a cup in the sand.

Tree-nesting species, such as the White Tern, must select a particularly stable branch for the egg and chick, and Black and Lesser Noddies must select a place where they can build a nest of twigs, feathers and excreta. By not building a nest, White Terns may reduce the parasite load for their chicks, but the loss of wind-blown eggs and chicks is great. Cliff- or ledge-nesting species, such as Brown Noddies, often move the small coral rubble to the edge of the cliff, providing a smooth surface for the eggs and chicks, and a slight lip to prevent the egg from rolling off.

Clutch size varies among species. For instance, Royal, Elegant, White-fronted (*Sterna striata*) and Sooty Terns and Brown and Black Noddies lay one egg; Caspian, Roseate, Arctic, Sandwich and Least Terns lay two; and Gull-billed and Common lay three eggs. For species that normally lay two or three eggs, clutch size is dependent on food supply. When this is low, it can reduce the average clutch size to one or two eggs, and can also increase the laying interval between eggs. In bad food years, Roseate Terns will lay only one egg and Common Terns only two. Species that lay only one egg have the option in bad food years of not laying, or of delaying breeding, or they may lay smaller eggs; smaller eggs, however, produce smaller chicks, which in general have lower survival rates. By contrast, clutch size can be increased in good food years, as apparently happened with Arctic Terns in the Baltic in 1989 and 1990. In species laying more than one egg, average clutch size normally decreases through the season, and replacement clutches are often smaller. As with gulls, supernormal clutches of five or more eggs are often the result of more than one female at a nest, in the form of trios or female-female pairs. In dense colonies, however, a bird may roll neighbouring eggs into its own nest, particularly if the eggs have been displaced by flooding.

Both members of the pair engage in territory defence and incubation, and both brood, feed and defend the chicks. In most species studied in detail, females perform somewhat more than half of the incubation, and males do more of the chick-feeding in the week following hatching. Aggression peaks during the hatching period, when the small chicks are most vulnerable, remains high when the chicks are small, and gradually decreases as they approach fledging. By that time the colony thins out, as early or failed pairs leave.

Territories of ground- and marsh-nesting species may shrink slightly during incubation, as the efforts of the pair are directed towards protecting the eggs. Nonetheless, both members of the pair will defend against intruders that are still searching for territories, although neighbours are often ignored. For cliff- and tree-nesting terns the territory is often limited to the ledge or area immediately around the nest, since it is difficult for intruders to land close by. However, species such as noddies that nest in denselimbed trees, often have a number of close neighbours, and territorial squabbles may be frequent, both between neighbours and with intruders that are trying to claim a new nest-site. These tree-nesting species show no evidence of recognizing their own eggs or chicks.

Most terneries are subject to breezy or windy conditions, and there is a strong tendency for all incubating birds to face the same direction, into the wind. Incubation can involve sitting on the eggs 100% of the time in Arctic and temperate environments. In tropical regions, terns incubate during the night and early morning, stand to shade the egg in the hot part of the day, and incubate again in the late afternoon and evening. In extremely hot environments, they may resort to flying to nearby waters to wet their bellies, and may return to the nest to wet the eggs or chicks to reduce heat stress.

For most terns incubation usually lasts 21-28 days, although for some tropical species it is more prolonged. The length of incubation bouts depends on how far adults must travel for food and its availability once they get there. At some colonies, Sooty Terns may travel over 100 km to feeding areas, and incubation stints often exceed 24 hours, reaching six days at Ascension Island. Stints of 1-3 hours are typical of most species, although Black Terns and Least Terns may make two or more change-overs per hour when feeding close to the colony.

The hatching process generally takes more than a day, and during this time parents are particularly protective of their eggs, increasing their mobbing activities. Chicks hatch using an egg tooth on the upper or both mandibles, and gradually lose this by day 5. Terns that lay three eggs usually start incubating after the second egg is laid, so the first two eggs hatch within a few hours of one another. The third egg may hatch a day or two later, giving the chick a decided disadvantage in terms of size, weight and strength when competing with its siblings for food; moreover, the third egg is usually smaller than the others, adding to its size disadvantage. In general, chicks hatching from larger eggs do better, primarily because of the higher protein content, which influences vigour and survival. Consequently, survival to fledging is usually lower in third-hatched chicks. One method third chicks have of combating competition with their siblings is to seek adoption in nearby broods; in such cases they are more likely to be successful if they join one- or two-chick broods, and if they are older than the youngest chick in the adoptive brood.

Young chicks spend more than 80% of their time inactive, usually crouched in the nest or in nearby shelter, waiting for the parents to arrive with food. Better-fed, faster-growing chicks spend more time preening, walking, and attacking neighbouring

chicks. In most high latitude terns, and in some tropical species, the chicks are fed several times a day or even several times an hour. The parent brings back fish, shrimps or other invertebrates in its bill, and extends it to the chicks. A chick seizes the food at a point near the parent's bill, and, with a series of upward jerks of its body and head, manipulates the fish until the head is in its gullet; it then jerks its head again until the fish is swallowed. With relatively large fish, a tiny chick must heave itself backwards with all its strength, and if it pauses to rest it may lose its fish to an alert pirate or a larger sibling. In broods of two or three chicks there is competition for the food, and fights often occur.

The young of some tropical terns are fed less regularly, and their growth rate reflects this difference in the adults' foraging pattern. The chicks of inshore foragers generally grow faster than those of more pelagic species, the latter being limited by the ability of their parents to transport prey from the foraging grounds to the breeding colonies. This is true for chicks of inshore-feeding Black-naped Terns breeding on islands in the Great Barrier Reef: their growth rate is faster than that of the more pelagic-feeding Great Crested Terns nesting on the same islands.

Although most tern species usually bring back one fish per trip, making many trips a day, Roseate and Common Terns occasionally bring several fish at a time, the record being eight. White Terns regularly return with three or more fish lined up in their bills. Sooty, Bridled and Grey-backed Terns and the dark noddies, however, are not known to carry fish in the bill, but they bring back several fish in the stomach and crop and regurgitate these directly into the chick's bill; in this way they may transport many fish and make far fewer trips per day. Interestingly, since the adult swallows these fish head-first and regurgitates them tail-first, the chicks swallow them tail-first. Some studies have shown a tendency for the size of fish brought to chicks to increase as the chicks grow, but this may reflect prey availability rather than selection.

As with gulls, the onset of parent-young recognition is associated with chick mobility. Chicks of most ground-nesting species begin to move out of the nest at 2-4 days of age, while those of marsh-nesters will stay in the nest for two weeks, and tree and cliff nesters until fledging. Forster's Tern chicks raised in dry land colonies exhibit mobility at the same age as ground-nesting species, despite the fact that most Forster's Terns nest in marshes.

As chicks grow older, there are two patterns of behaviour: crèching and non-crèching. Crèches are characteristic of all crested terns and the Sooty Tern. If their colonies are disturbed, the chicks leave their nests early and form crèches a week or more before they would do so in undisturbed colonies. The

Most terns nest on the ground, selecting the nest-site just before the egg-laying phase.
The nest itself is no more than a shallow, unlined scrape in the ground. Clutch size varies, but for many, including the White-cheeked Tern, it normally consists of two or three eggs. When the species' food supply is poor, however, it has the option of reducing the number of eggs it lays.

[*Sterna repressa.*
Photo: G. K. Brown/Ardea]

crèche is a large, dense group of chicks, a tight herd attended by only a few adults. The entire crèche moves away from intruders as a unit, creating the illusion of a giant amoeboid creature. During this period, both parents are normally away from the colony on foraging trips, and when they return they call their chicks from the crèche for feeding. Crèching evolved as an anti-predator strategy for times when the parents are not present to defend their young; the chicks derive early warning, and benefit from a swamping effect through being in a large dense mass of birds.

Most typical species of ground-nesting terns, such as Common, Roseate, Arctic, Least and Little Terns, do not form crèches. Instead, the chicks remain at the nest-site or on their natal territory, and are normally guarded by one or both parents throughout the brooding phase. As they grow, they begin to defend their territory against intruding chicks or even adults. If disturbed, they may run or be led by their parents to secure areas outside the colony.

In terns that form crèches, and in species where the chicks wander away from the territory, parents are able to recognize their own eggs and chicks. Even when a crèche has formed, they feed only their own offspring. For some species, such as the Caspian Tern, recognition is at least partly by down colour and pattern; in others, voice plays a role. Parental recognition of chicks usually develops at the time when chicks begin to move away from the nest; chicks learn to recognize their parents at about the same age. Tree-nesting noddies do not recognize their young if they are out of the nest.

Food piracy, although not recorded for several species, occurs regularly at Common, Arctic, Roseate and Least Tern colonies. Much of this piracy involves conspecifics. Depending upon the nesting assemblage at the colony site, terns can be either the pirates or the victims, or they can be both. In temperate and Arctic regions gulls are often the pirates, and are usually successful against the smaller terns. In tropical colonies the pirates are usually frigatebirds, and on Caribbean islands Laughing Gulls.

Piracy rates vary during the breeding season, being highest during courtship feeding and the brooding phase, when the terns are bringing the most fish back to the colony. Pirates preferentially chase, and are also more successful against, terns carrying large fish. Thus, in colonies with intense piracy pressure, terns try to reduce the risks by bringing back slightly smaller fish and flying lower over the colony, making piracy more difficult.

Both adults and neighbouring chicks will try to pirate fish during the transfer from parent to young, and while chicks are trying to swallow particularly large fish. In some species, par-

ents feed small fish to small chicks, gradually increasing the fish size as chicks grow and are able to swallow the larger meal quickly.

A notable feature of many terneries is their active defence against predators. This includes early warning by vocalizations, mobbing and harassment of predators, and direct attacks on predators. Terns will also mob and attack human beings entering their colonies. In general, the frequency of mobbing is highest at hatching and when the chicks are small, and decreases thereafter. It is common among terns that do not form crèches, such as Common, Arctic, Roseate, Little, Least, Bridled, Black-naped and Sooty, as well as in Great Crested Terns, although the intensity of actual attacks varies.

At some colonies, the larger species, such as Caspian, Royal, Great Crested and Sandwich Terns, defend their eggs and chicks by sitting tightly on them. Adults then threaten predators with open bill and erect feathers, and by uttering an aggressive "gak gak gak" or a screaming call. The difference in defence between species of terns relates to the threat the potential predator poses to the adults themselves: smaller terns are more vulnerable than larger terns, and usually do not remain on the nest when predators are near. Peruvian Terns leave when an intruder is still very far off, and do not mob. Predators themselves can use mobbing intensity as a clue to a nest's location. Least Terns occasionally give a very weak distraction display, landing a short distance from the nest, making short, weak hopping flights, and even collapsing for a moment, but these are nothing like the distraction displays of many shorebirds.

The territory and colony site are usually abandoned only a few days after the chicks fledge, but in some species, such as the Common Tern, the family may continue to use the nest-site, returning there for the purpose of feeding fledglings. Terns typically disperse with their young to surrounding areas, and in many cases they show a brief dispersal in the direction opposite to that of migration, for example in the Northern Hemisphere moving some distance northward. Within a few weeks they leave the vicinity of the colony and migrate to wintering grounds. The juveniles may remain with their parents for many weeks or months, their dependence on them for food slowly decreasing. After a few months on the wintering grounds, the terns migrate back to the vicinity of the breeding colony, before beginning to settle for another breeding attempt.

Measures of productivity, such as clutch size, hatching rate and fledging rate, are often related to colony size. Birds in large colonies do better than those in small ones, and this is even true of Gull-billed Terns, which usually breed in colonies of fewer

Young tern chicks spend most of their time crouched in or near the nest, awaiting their parents' arrival with food. In three-egg clutches, the third egg is usually smaller; since incubation begins with the laying of the second egg, the hatching of the third may also be delayed by a day or two. The third chick is therefore at a great disadvantage when competing for food with its larger and stronger siblings, and survival to fledging is generally lower for third-hatched chicks.

[Chlidonias niger niger. Photo: Oene Moedt/ Foto Natura]

than 100 individuals. Other factors that affect reproductive rate include initial egg size, parental performance, predation, human disturbance, tick infestations, age and experience of the female, timing of laying, food availability, and weather. Older, experienced females do better, though their productivity declines after 12-14 years of age, and early or mid-season nests achieve the best success. Not surprisingly, prolonged rains chill chicks and impair the adults' feeding, while hurricanes and wind-driven waves and storm tides wash out nests and even whole colonies.

Terns are long-lived seabirds. Indeed, they outlive their rings, so true longevity estimates are lacking for most species. An Arctic Tern reached 34 years and a Sooty Tern 32, while Caspian, Sandwich, Great Crested, Common and Least Terns have all exceeded 20 years. Many other species have records of around 17 years, which are certainly lower than the true figure, although in most studies the life expectancy of a bird that has returned to breed is about 7-10 nesting seasons.

Movements

Most terns are migratory, although some tropical species are nomadic during the non-breeding season. Most of those breeding in the north temperate region winter in the tropics or the Southern Hemisphere, while the south temperate breeders have much more varied and less well understood movement patterns. This mirrors the migration of landbirds as well, presumably reflecting ancient climatic conditions. Species such as the Arctic Tern remain at their breeding grounds for the minimum time necessary to mate, nest, and fledge their young. At lower latitudes, species such as the Common Tern may be present for a month before nesting, and may stop off near their breeding grounds for several weeks before migrating. Some pelagic species, for example Grey Noddies, are present near their colonies throughout the year, whereas others, such as Sooty Terns, may be absent for several to many months. Much migration of large flocks occurs at night, although flocks can be seen moving in the early morning and late afternoon. The steady migration of Bridled Terns past Sri Lanka continues for many days, within a few hundred metres of the shore. In Ghana, radar revealed a much heavier autumn than spring passage, with up to 30,000 terns (of five species) present on a single day.

Several species show a distinct post-breeding dispersal to higher latitudes while the young are still partially dependent. This takes them to richer feeding areas, where they can learn feeding techniques prior to migration to the tropics.

Some species are long distance migrants, travelling from north temperate or Arctic breeding grounds to winter in the Southern Hemisphere. Others travel shorter distances. In general, many of the intermediate-sized terns breeding in temperate and Arctic regions migrate farther than the larger terns. The Arctic Tern has the longest transequatorial migration of any bird, travelling to the Antarctic from its Arctic breeding grounds. Arctic Terns from the eastern Canadian and European Arctic migrate through the eastern South Atlantic and then split, most continuing along the African coast, some passing through the mid-Atlantic and some crossing the Atlantic to move southwards off Brazil and the Argentine coast; the first group reach South Africa by October and then continue east-south-east ahead of trade winds to the edge of the pack ice, where they remain for 3-4 months. Other species, such as Nearctic populations of the Common and the Roseate, migrate from north temperate regions to the northern and central coasts of South America. Sooty Terns from the Dry Tortugas migrate east across the Atlantic and south down the coast of Africa, returning north in the West Atlantic. The movements of some species are less well known: the Aleutian Tern, for instance, leaves its breeding colonies in the North Pacific but its wintering areas are not known, although a few have been found in the Philippines.

Some tropical species, including some Sooty Tern populations, move great distances during the non-breeding period, but they move around the globe ahead of the trade winds in tropical regions, rather than in a north-south direction. Little is known of the migration of most Southern Hemisphere species.

Vagrancy occasionally occurs among terns. There are several records of Nearctic species in Europe, and a number of West Palearctic terns have made the reverse journey. Perhaps the most extraordinary record of all, however, is that of the Aleutian Tern which appeared in Britain in May 1979, far distant from its breeding range in the northern Pacific.

Relationship with Man

Many terns breed along coasts and inland waterways, and they have thus had a long history of interactions with man. Over much of this mutual history, terns have been exploited for food, fashion and information. Eggs, chicks and adults have been used for food, and feathers and whole birds have been utilized for capes, hats and other apparel. Since terns often feed over dense schools of fish forced to the surface by large, predatory fish, fishermen have long searched for these frenzied flocks, beneath which large bluefish, tuna or other food-fish can be caught.

The Sooty Tern is one of several pelagic species that do not carry prey in the bill. It returns to the colony with several fish or squid in the crop, and regurgitates them directly into the chick's bill. This enables it to transport a greater number of items and make far fewer trips each day to the feeding grounds, which are often far from the colony. It is interesting to note that, since the adult swallows fish head-first and regurgitates them tail-first, the chick swallows them tail-first; with soft-bodied squid, such details are likely to be less significant.

[Sterna fuscata serrata, Lord Howe Island, Australia. Photo: Jean-Paul Ferrero/ Ardea]

Throughout history, bird eggs have provided an easily acquired, high-protein, low-cost food source. Exploitation of tern eggs has been recorded for most species, and for most areas of the world. Even terns nesting on remote oceanic islands were exploited by early mariners, who regularly stopped at these islands to load up on eggs. Since the breeding season of many tropical terns, as well as other seabirds, is often prolonged and may extend over much of the year, eggs were readily available. When they were not, large chicks were present to be taken.

Even today, and despite legal restrictions, egging is a problem for many tern species, because colonies are often in places that are hard to monitor and eggs are often highly prized. In some places, tern eggs are sought as an aphrodisiac. Such qualities are attributed to Roseate and Sooty Tern eggs by people in the West Indies, who collect their eggs while those of more common species are ignored. Egging for hotels and restaurants persists in some European and South American countries. Managed egging of Sooty Terns in the Seychelles has been successful in maintaining a stable population, and has been proposed in Jamaica and elsewhere. Similar controls have been shown to be effective in parts of Europe.

For centuries, the feathers of birds have been used to decorate clothing and ceremonial paraphernalia. During the second half of the nineteenth century, however, terns were exploited even more heavily by the European millinery trade. White was a favourite colour for ladies' hats and capes, and terns provided an easy source of white feathers. Towards the end of the craze, entire wings and whole terns were used on hats in fashionable circles.

Recently, terns have been used as bioindicators of environmental contamination. Population size, reproductive success and the incidence of developmental defects have been monitored as indicators of potential exposure; behavioural and morphological abnormalities have been examined as indicators of toxins; and levels of organochlorines and heavy metals in eggs and dead birds have been used as indicators of environmental pollution. Thus, humans are currently exploiting terns as providers of early warnings of potential human health problems, as well as monitors of environmental quality.

Status and Conservation

Although terns have a worldwide distribution, most individual species have more restricted ranges, and several taxa are threatened, while for other very rare taxa information remains inad-

equate. Surprisingly, the Gull-billed Tern is the most cosmopolitan, occurring on all continents except Antarctica, although it is nowhere numerous. The Roseate Tern is nearly as widespread, although it barely breeds in South America. Several other species, such as Arctic, Caspian and Common Terns, have Holarctic ranges; Sooty and Bridled have pantropical ranges; and the Antarctic Tern is widespread in the Southern Ocean. Other terns are confined to relatively narrow breeding ranges: the Damara to southern Africa, the Black-fronted to New Zealand's South Island, Saunders's and the White-cheeked (*Sterna repressa*) to the northern Indian Ocean, and the Kerguelen to three archipelagos in the southern Indian Ocean.

The global population sizes of the various species of tern vary considerably, ranging from only a few thousand pairs of Fairy and Kerguelen Terns to several tens of millions of Sooty Terns. The Elegant and Damara Terns are near-threatened. The Californian and interior populations of the Least Tern number only a few hundred pairs, and the Easter Island race of the Grey Noddy is close to extinction, if not already extinct. The Roseate Tern is listed as endangered in North America and Europe, is threatened in the Caribbean, and is uncommon to common elsewhere.

Virtually nothing was known of the Chinese Crested Tern until 21 birds were collected on the Shantung coast in 1937. It was long considered extinct, none having been collected in the 60 years since then, but a few recent reliable sight records from wintering grounds indicate that small numbers survive somewhere. It is the only tern of which the breeding grounds have never yet been found.

The Kerguelen Tern probably has the smallest total population of any tern species: under 3000 pairs, almost all at Kerguelen Island, where it is threatened by cats. It avoids competition with the Antarctic Tern by breeding earlier and exploiting upland insects when the fish-eating Antarctic Tern is present. The Fairy Tern of Australasia may number no more than the Kerguelen Tern.

New Zealand's Black-fronted Tern also has a small global population, and hydro-electric projects proposed for some South Island rivers could dramatically alter its habitat, which is already being greatly reduced by proliferating lupins (*Lupinus*), which grow in profusion on the rocky and sandy islands in the braided rivers which are this tern's main breeding grounds. In southern Asia, the Black-bellied Tern is thought to number fewer than 10,000 individuals; it is threatened by habitat destruction and flooding of nests, and its eggs are also collected for food.

The populations of Peruvian and Damara Terns are difficult to determine, as these species nest solitarily or in very open colonies of only 3-10 pairs on remote parts of beaches. Both are markedly uncommon, even where their beaches have not been highly developed. Throughout the world, tern populations have declined, and there is serious concern that several species might not survive. The Damara Tern was formerly considered endangered, but recent counts of 5000 birds provide some cause for optimism. More than 1000 km of Namibia's "Diamond Coast" is off-limits to the public and could afford protected habitat for this species. Its status there is inadequately known, however, and increasing mining developments in the area may jeopardize even this habitat.

The combination of egging, hunting and exploitation for feathers (see Relationship with Man) resulted in massive declines in most terns nesting along the coasts of North America and parts of Europe during the latter part of the nineteenth century, and many nesting populations were completely eliminated. It was when the protective laws for migratory birds were enacted in the twentieth century that tern populations began to recover. Their recovery, however, was dampened and halted in some regions because of habitat loss and competition with gulls.

During the present century, tern populations have suffered serious declines in many regions of the world because of competition with gulls. When human persecution of gulls ceased at the turn of the century, and when refuse became more available, gulls began to increase their populations and expand their ranges, often settling on traditional terneries, rendering them unsuitable for the terns when they arrived weeks later. Terns were forced to shift to sub-optimum nesting habitats. Gulls also prey directly on the eggs and chicks of terns. Since gulls normally arrive on the breeding colonies 2-3 months before the terns, and are up to four times larger depending on species, the terns are at a decided disadvantage. Although there is widespread agreement that gulls have had a direct impact upon tern populations, there are exceptions. In Germany, Little and Common Terns began to decline in the 1950's and 1960's, when gull populations were slowly increasing, but in the 1970's both species increased rapidly. Terns have been eliminated by gulls from many of their breeding colonies in parts of North America, Europe and Australia. Gull-control measures are required in many places before tern colonies can be re-established. This is a continuous problem, and in some areas the terns will need constant protection from the gulls if their colonies are to survive.

Terns often suffer heavy predation from predators introduced by man, or with populations that have increased because of human activities. Dogs, cats and rats introduced accidentally or deliberately are major predators, even on remote oceanic islands. Foxes and raccoons (*Procyon lotor*) were very rare on barrier beaches and coastal islands of the north-east USA, until man provided food for them to survive over the winter; they are now able to prey on the terns when they arrive. Humans have also introduced rabbits, goats and pigs on remote islands, resulting in serious habitat degradation. On a worldwide basis, cats are probably the most serious mammalian threat to island-nesting seabirds, including terns; they are both formidable predators and difficult to control or eradicate from islands. Avian predators include gulls, which take eggs, chicks and even adults; herons, which prey on chicks; and owls and raptors, which take adults.

Today, terns benefit from some human activities, for instance by foraging behind ploughs or boats or around fishing nets. However, otherwise they suffer from the impacts of man, such as overfishing, chemical pollution, human disturbance, and habitat loss and degradation of traditional nesting areas. The usurpation of their coastal nesting habitat by recreational, residential and commercial development was already recognized by conservationists in the 1950's and has continued despite conservation efforts. With beach stabilization and the control of mosquitos, coastal areas have been extensively developed, often reducing the habitat available to nesting terns. Both young and adults of coastal species often die from becoming entangled in fishing line and plastic items.

Terns have suffered at the hand of man as, in many parts of the world, overfishing has eliminated the fish for both terns and, eventually, the fishing industry itself. The northern isles of Britain, Orkney and Shetland, hold particularly high densities of breeding Arctic Terns, which feed almost exclusively on sandeels (*Ammodytes*). When sandeel stocks collapsed in the 1980's, virtually no tern chicks fledged in any Shetland colony during 1984-1990; breeding numbers fell from 31,000 pairs in 1980 to 8000 pairs in 1990. Although the local sandeel fishery may have caused the crisis, there was little scientific evidence for this, and the low recruitment of sandeels was possibly related to oceanographic factors. The fishery was closed in 1991, and sandeel recruitment in that year was excellent, for the first time since 1983. The once-largest Shetland colony had been reduced to 115 pairs in 1990, but in 1991 over 1000 pairs

Some studies have shown that the size of fish brought to chicks tends to increase as the chicks grow. As this photograph demonstrates, however, this may reflect prey availability rather than selection; this very young Caspian Tern would have an extremely hard time dealing with a fish of this size! All terns run the risk of food being pirated during the food transfer, and especially while chicks are trying to swallow particularly large fish. When taking food, the chick jerks its body and head until the fish's head is in its gullet, then jerks its head again until the food is swallowed; if it stops to rest, its fish may be stolen.

[*Hydroprogne caspia*. Photo: Geoff Moon/FLPA]

Some tree-nesting species, such as the Black Noddy, build a nest of twigs and leaves cemented together with excreta; nest-site selection therefore takes place earlier than in most other species, which make a small nest or none at all. On some islands Black Noddies nest in *Pisonia* trees, as here, and the young may become trapped by the sticky seeds, which can form dense mats in some years. It is most unusual to see two Black Noddy chicks in one nest, as this species normally lays only one egg. Noddies appear not to be able to recognize their own chicks; one of these two has presumably dropped out of another nest.

[*Anous minutus minutus*, Heron Island, Great Barrier Reef, Australia. Photo: Gary Bell/ Planet Earth]

nested, many of which had been ringed there as chicks in the period 1979-1983; they reared 0·67 chicks per pair. Since then, however, breeding numbers have not recovered further, probably as a consequence of the long period of breeding failure.

Tern populations can also be seriously affected by pollutants. Forster's Terns nesting in Green Bay, Michigan, have suffered low reproductive success over a number of years; hatching success of artificially incubated eggs was 52% that of nearby uncontaminated colonies. No tern pairs in the Green Bay colonies fledged young, compared with a 55% fledging rate for colonies inland from the polluted bay. Egg-exchange experiments confirmed that both intrinsic and extrinsic factors contributed to the poor hatching success. Embryos from the Green Bay colonies weighed less, had increased liver weights and had shorter femurs compared with the inland colonies, and some had deformities. These abnormalities were similar to those reported for other fish-eating colonial birds from the Great Lakes, and were directly attributed to high levels and complex mixtures of lipophilic environmental contaminants.

The simultaneous decline of the Roseate Tern in Europe and North America is at least partially attributable to harvesting on the wintering grounds in West Africa and northern South America, where large numbers of birds are taken. A metapopulation study of the population of the north-eastern USA showed low annual adult survival of only 75%, compared with values greater than 85% for most other seabirds studied.

Although many tern populations are declining, some are increasing and expanding their ranges, while others are subject to great fluctuations. The populations of the Sandwich Tern in northern Europe fluctuate widely, but in eastern North America the species has been on the increase in recent decades, and its "Cayenne" race is extending northwards in the Caribbean. Forster's Tern has increased in many parts of the Great Lakes, while other species have declined in the same area. Arctic Tern populations in Scandinavia have increased, probably owing to the elimination of egging. There are many accounts in the literature of one or a few pairs of terns pioneering in new locations since 1970.

Declining species benefit from conservation management. Many tern populations already nest on protected reserves, but other important sites need protection. Acquiring private land can be a major first step, but habitats have to be secured and man-

aged. Formerly, terns had abundant choices once a traditional site became unsuitable. Now they may have nowhere to turn to.

Stabilization of sandy islands, creation of artificial nesting platforms, removal of vegetation, and maintenance of water levels in marshes can all play major parts in habitat management. Removal of predators, particularly feral cats, and elimination of rats are time-consuming but important processes. Cats, if their current petrel prey became scarce, could quickly eradicate the Kerguelen Tern population on that island.

There are many reports on the effects of pollutants, but the magnitude of any impact on tern populations needs to be studied. Efforts must be made to limit pollution discharges, particularly the release of oil in intracoastal waterways. A combination of habitat protection, predator elimination and the use of decoys can successfully attract terns to suitable sites, and allow the reestablishment of thriving colonies. Terneries must then be signposted, fenced, or even wardened to exclude human activities which might jeopardize tern reproduction. In tropical regions, the conservation efforts are at an earlier stage, for egging is still widespread, even where terns are ostensibly protected by law.

General Bibliography
Ainley *et al.* (1984), Ashmole (1968b, 1971), Au & Pitman (1988), Ayers (1982), Becker (1987), Becker & Erdelen (1987), Beer (1980), Beyerbach & Heidmann (1990), Björklund (1994), Burger, J. (1980d, 1988c), Burger, J. & Gochfeld (1988d, 1988e, 1988f, 1991a, 1991d, 1994c), Burger, J., Olla & Winn (1980), Burger, J., Shealer & Gochfeld (1993), Chandler, R.M. (1990), Christian *et al.* (1992b), Coulter (1980), Crowell & Crowell (1946), Croxall (1987, 1991), Croxall & Rothery (1991), Croxall, Evans & Schreiber (1984), Cullen (1960a), Diamond (1978), Drent *et al.* (1992), Drury (1965), Dunn (1973a, 1975, 1985), Dunning (1993), Dwight (1925), Erwin (1978), Fletcher (1989), Fry (1992), Furness & Monaghan (1987), Gochfeld (1975b), Harrison (1985, 1987), Hoffman (1984), Hudson *et al.* (1969), Hulsman (1981), van Iersel & Bot (1958), Kaverkina (1986a, 1989), Klaassen *et al.* (1992), Koskimies (1957), Lind (1963b), Löfgren (1984), Lythgoe (1979), McNicholl (1975), Moynihan (1959), Nelson (1980), Nettleship *et al.* (1994), Nisbet (1975, 1983b, 1994), Peters (1934), Rahn *et al.* (1976), Ricklefs (1983), Roché (1993), Roschevski & Laukhina (1980), Schnell (1970), Sibley & Ahlquist (1990), Sibley & Monroe (1990), Simmons (1972), Spaans (1992), Tasker (1988), Tuck & Heinzel (1978), Veen (1987), White *et al.* (1976), Wuorinen (1992).

1

2

3

4

ssp *bengalensis*

ssp *torresii*

ssp *sandvicensis*

ssp *eurygnatha*

5

6

7

9

8

ssp *bergii*

ssp *enigma*

ssp *velox*

PLATE 54

inches   6

cm   16

Genus *GELOCHELIDON* C. L. Brehm, 1830

1. **Gull-billed Tern**

Gelochelidon nilotica

French: Sterne hansel   **German**: Lachseeschwalbe   **Spanish**: Pagaza Piconegra

Taxonomy. *Sterna nilotica* Gmelin, 1789, Egypt.
Along with *Hydroprogne* and *Thalasseus*, genus often merged with *Sterna*; behaviour intermediate between typical terns and crested terns, and unique combination of characters supports separate generic treatment. Listed as *G. anglica* in many older works. Proposed race *affinis* for birds of E Asia and SE China is not separable. Six subspecies recognized.

Subspecies and Distribution.
G. n. nilotica (Gmelin, 1789) - Europe S to Mauritania and Tunisia, and E through Middle East, Kazakhstan and Indian Subcontinent to NW China; winters from tropical Africa through Persian Gulf to India.
G. n. addenda Mathews, 1912 - Transbaikalia, Manchuria and E China (Fuzhou to Hainan); winters mainly SE Asia.
G. n. macrotarsa (Gould, 1837) - Australia.
G. n. aranea (Wilson, 1814) - New Jersey (rarely New York) S to Texas, Cuba, Bahamas and Puerto Rico, and sparsely along Mexican coast to Yucatán; winters along Central American coasts and S to Brazil and Peru.
G. n. vanrossemi Bancroft, 1929 - California (coastal plain and Salton Sea) to N Baja California and Sinaloa (and probably S to Gulf of Tehuantepec), with isolated breeding recorded in Alaska (Copper R Delta); winters S to Ecuador.
G. n. groenvoldi Mathews, 1912 - coast and river valleys from French Guiana (Cayenne) to NE Argentina (Buenos Aires); Ecuador and N Peru breeders may be this race or *vanrossemi*, or an undescribed race.

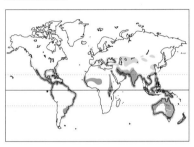

Descriptive notes. 33-43 cm; 130-300 g (*nilotica* 190-290 g, *aranea* 160-185 g); wingspan 85-103 cm. Unique heavy-billed, long-legged tern with slightly forked tail, broad wings and very pale body; all black bill has sharp gonydeal angle, but no terminal hook, resembling that of small gull; eye dark brown; crown and nape black, upperparts including rump pale grey, primaries slightly darker but wingtips whitish to pale grey; tail and underparts white. Non-breeding adult nearly pure white with some dark streaking on hindcrown, and dark patch behind eye. Juvenile has scapulars and upperwing-coverts variably splotched with brown; head white with fine dark speckling. Races differ mainly in size, especially of bill, and also in colour tone of upperparts; *macrotarsa* is largest race, especially in bill and feet.

Habitat. Breeds on barrier beaches and dunes, salt-marshes, salt-works, man-made islands, and rivers and freshwater lagoons; far more along coastal plains than in continental interiors, but also breeds on hypersaline lakes; race *aranea* strictly coastal. Often feeds in large numbers on emerging insects over lakes, fields and grassland, and in Azerbaijan even over semi-desert; migrants typically feed over salt-ponds, coastal lagoons and mudflats, as well as marshes and wet fields. Winters on estuaries, lakes and salt-pans.

Food and Feeding. Opportunistic: more insectivorous than most other terns, prey including mainly grasshoppers, dragonflies, moths and grubs; also takes spiders, earthworms, small reptiles and frogs, small fish (mainly 6-9 cm) and aquatic invertebrates; rarely voles and small birds. More varied diet and larger items in N Europe than in S Europe. In Italy, 67% of food items were reptiles in one study, mostly insects in another. In Russian steppes, 80% Orthoptera. Hawks for insects over estuaries, mudflats, coastal lagoons and agricultural fields and pastures. Flies slowly and then darts swiftly down to seize prey item from surface of ground, water or vegetation; does not feed by surface-dipping, and plunge-dives only exceptionally. Occasionally pirates food from other terns. In Italy, most birds foraged within 2 km of colony, occasionally up to 11 km.

Breeding. Lays May-Jun in North America and Europe, Apr-May in India, Oct-Dec in Australia. Loosely to densely colonial, usually 5-50 pairs, but up to 1000 pairs; often 1-2 pairs nest in colonies of other terns or Common Black-headed Gulls (*Larus ridibundus*). Low to moderate colony site tenacity, e.g. turnover 0·38 in Italy; larger clutches and higher productivity in larger colonies; coloniality deters gull predation. Prefers vegetated nest-sites in Italy, but often nests on barren beaches in E USA; nests on sand, shell bars, dry mud, dykes, seawrack, floating vegetation, waterfowl nests; prefers elevated ridges or objects, and recorded nesting on roofs. Nearest-neighbour distance ranges from 20 m in small colonies to 0·3 m in large colonies. 2-3 eggs (1-5), with average 2·5 in Denmark and North Carolina, but 2·2 in S California; incubation 22-23 days; chick white, usually unspotted; hatching weight 24 g; fledging c. 28-30 days; parents attend young for 3 months. Productivity often low in USA. Returns to colony at 4 years old, but first breeding at 5 years. Recorded longevity of 15 years 9 months.

Movements. European birds disperse in all directions after breeding, then migrate across Spain, Italy and N Africa to W Africa, Rift Valley and coastal E Africa; others of nominate race winter E to India, and occasionally Indonesia, while E Asian breeders winter mostly in SE Asia. E North American birds migrate to SE USA and Gulf of Mexico; some cross to Pacific; some winter along Costa Rican coast, others reach even Brazil and Peru. Birds of W North America winter from W Mexico to Ecuador; vagrant to West Indies. In E Australia, species nomadic; may wander to remote lakes in interior after rains, and remain to breed.

Status and Conservation. Not globally threatened. Nowhere abundant, and considerable decline noted in recent years in Europe. World population estimated at up to 55,000 pairs centred mainly in CIS, which holds up to 40,000 pairs, including 2000 on L Alakol'. Estimated 6800-16,000 pairs in Europe, with 1800-5000 pairs in Russia, 1869 pairs in Spain (in 1989), and perhaps 2000-7000 pairs in Turkey; also 3000 pairs in E North America, and 2000+ pairs in W Africa. As with most terns, numbers seriously depleted in late 19th century by millinery trade, with slow recovery in 20th century, until confronted with major problems of habitat loss, human disturbance and pesticides; many populations have

declined since 1960's. In E USA, c. 2700 pairs in 83 colonies in 1977, but only 1500 pairs in 1984. Main causes of decline in Europe are deterioration and loss of habitat, caused by: wetland drainage; agricultural intensification; pesticides and other chemicals, causing death of prey species or of birds themselves; changing water levels, causing flooding or facilitating access to colonies for predators.

Bibliography. Ali & Ripley (1982), Ash & Miskell (1983), Beehler *et al*. (1986), Belton (1984), Bent (1921), Biaggi (1983), Biber (1993, 1994), Blake (1977), Blus & Stafford (1980), Bogliani *et al*. (1990), Borodulina (1960), Bourke *et al*. (1973), Bregnballe *et al*. (1990), Browne (1981), Buckley & Buckley (1984b), Canevari *et al*. (1991), Coates (1985), Cramp (1985), Davies (1988), Dementiev & Galdkov (1951b), Densmore (1990), Dickinson *et al*. (1991), Dowsett & Forbes-Watson (1993), Eminov (1974), Étchécopar & Hüe (1964, 1978), Evans (1994), Everhart *et al*. (1980), Fasola (1986), Fasola & Bogliani (1990), Fasola & Canova (1992), Fasola & Saino (1990), Foschi (1986), Goodman *et al*. (1989), Goutner (1987), Grant (1978), Grant *et al*. (1984), Harrison (1984a), Haverschmidt (1968), Haverschmidt & Mees (1995), Hilty & Brown (1986), Howell & Webb (1995a), Hüe & Étchécopar (1970), Ilicev & Zubakin (1988), de Juana (1986), Knystautas (1993), Lekagul & Round (1991), Lind (1963a, 1963b), MacKinnon & Phillipps (1993), Mackworth-Praed & Grant (1957, 1970), Marchant & Higgins (1996), van Marle & Voous (1988), Medway & Wells (1976), Meininger (1988), Meyer de Schauensee & Phelps (1978), Møller (1975a, 1975b, 1975c, 1978a, 1978b, 1981, 1982), Monroe (1968), Olsen & Larssen (1995b), Parnell *et al*. (1995), Patrikeev (1995), de la Peña (1992), Perennou (1991), Perennou *et al*. (1994), Phillips (1978), Pinto (1983), Quinn & Wiggins (1990), Richards (1990), Ridgely & Gwynne (1989), Ripley (1982), Roberts, T.J. (1991), Rohwer & Woolfenden (1968), Saino & Fasola (1990), Sánchez *et al*. (1991), Sears (1978, 1981), Serventy *et al*. (1971), Shirihai (1996), Short *et al*. (1990), Sick (1985c, 1993), Slud (1964), Smythies (1981, 1986), Snyder (1966), Stiles & Skutch (1989), Teague (1955), Tostain *et al*. (1992), Urban *et al*. (1986), Wetmore (1965), White & Bruce (1986), Zubakin (1975c).

Genus *HYDROPROGNE* Kaup, 1829

2. **Caspian Tern**

Hydroprogne caspia

French: Sterne caspienne   **German**: Raubseeschwalbe   **Spanish**: Pagaza Piquirroja

Taxonomy. *Sterna caspia* Pallas, 1770, Caspian Sea.
Along with *Gelochelidon* and *Thalasseus*, genus often merged with *Sterna*, based primarily on ethological evidence; differs from all other terns, however, in massive, heavy bill. Species name often given as *H. tschegrava*, particularly in recent Russian works, both names dating from same year; to avoid further confusion, name *tschegrava* officially suppressed in 1970. Australian and New Zealand birds sometimes separated as race *strenua*, but characters matched by many individuals of other populations. Monotypic.

Distribution. North America, N Europe (Baltic), Africa, Madagascar, C & S Asia, Australia (coastal and sparsely inland), New Zealand; everywhere very local. Probably bred in British Columbia (1984); recent fledglings observed in delta of R Copper suggests breeding in Alaska. Disperses more widely in winter.

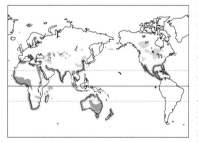

Descriptive notes. 48-56 cm; 574-782 g; wingspan 127-140 cm. Largest tern; large, stout blood red bill with variable black tip, and slightly forked tail; also distinguished by black undersurface of primaries, conspicuous in flight; eye dark brown, legs black. Non-breeding adult has forehead and crown whitish with dark spotting. Confusable only with *Thalasseus maximus* and *T. bergii*, which have orange or yellowish bill and paler under primaries, but is much more gull-like than either and never becomes as white-headed as is *T. maximus* for most of year. Juvenile grey above with brown bars, strongest on scapulars and inner secondaries; crown mainly white; tail and primaries dark grey; bill red-orange with blackish tip.

Habitat. Locally along coasts, as well as on large inland lakes and reservoirs, breeding on sand, shell or rocky islands, rarely on salt-marsh (New Jersey, USA). Feeds at freshwater lakes, inland seas, and coastal estuaries; rarely pelagic. Winter roosts at large lakes and estuaries on sandbars, mudflats, shell banks.

Food and Feeding. Mainly small to medium-sized fish; occasionally eggs and young of other birds, and carrion. Takes larger fish (usually over 9 cm and up to 25 cm) than smaller terns with which it associates. In Scandinavia, main prey roach (*Rutilus rutilus*) and herring (*Clupea harengus*). In Ukraine, cyprinoids comprise 80% of diet. In USA, at L Michigan main prey alewife (*Alosa pseudoharengus*) and smelt (*Osmerus mordax*); in Elkorn Slough, California, birds fed mainly on northern anchovy (*Engraulis mordax*, 49%), shiner perch (*Cymatogaster aggregata*, 29%), topsmelt (*Atherinops affinis*, 19%), and Pacific staghorn sculpin (*Leptocottus armatus*, 3%); in Washington, northern anchovy ranged from 0% in 1975 to 44% in 1976. Often feeds in loose flocks, but occasionally exhibits feeding territoriality. Hovers and plunge-dives, and occasionally uses surface-dipping; also pirates food from other terns and gulls. Feeds up to 60 km from colony.

Breeding. Apr-Jun in N Hemisphere, Sept-Dec in S Hemisphere, but nearly year round in N Australia. Densely colonial to solitary: in Europe, most breed as single pairs in gull or tern colonies; solitary pairs exclude conspecifics from the colony. 25% of pairs remained mated in second year of a study. Colony site tenacity high if previous breeding attempt successful; some colonies have been occupied for 100 years. Very sensitive to disturbance early in cycle and entire colony will desert. Nest a depression in sand, gravel, shell, or even ground vegetation; in colonies, nests 0·7-4 m apart. Clutch 2-3 eggs, fewer at lower latitudes: averages more than 2·5 in Great Lakes (USA) and Finland, 2·5 in Washington (USA) and 1·9 in Texas (USA); larger clutches (4+ eggs) may be due to female-female pairing in some colonies. Incubation 26-28 days (earlier reports of 20-21 days erroneous); chicks dimorphic, pale creamy whitish with faint or no spots, white throat, yellowish skin, and orange feet, or greyish brown with dark spots, sooty throat, dark skin, and olive feet (a few intermediate); hatching weight 70 g; adults rely at least partly on down colour for chick recognition; chicks remain in nest 3 days; fledging c. 35-45 days; prolonged parental care continues, at least occasionally, even in winter quarters. Productivity 1·5 chicks/

On following pages: 3. Elegant Tern (*Thalasseus elegans*); 4. Lesser Crested Tern (*Thalasseus bengalensis*); 5. Sandwich Tern (*Thalasseus sandvicensis*); 6. Chinese Crested Tern (*Thalasseus bernsteini*); 7. Royal Tern (*Thalasseus maximus*); 8. Greater Crested Tern (*Thalasseus bergii*); 9. River Tern (*Sterna aurantia*).

pair in Finland. Some 2-year-old birds return to colonies and may breed, but most wait until 3 or 4 years. Annual adult mortality 9-15% (Finland), 11% (California). Longevity of 26+ years recorded.

Movements. North American and European birds show brief post-breeding dispersal, then migrate slowly S. Great Lakes birds move S and E to Gulf and Atlantic coast to winter in SE USA and Caribbean, rarely reaching Panama and Trinidad; those from W USA winter from C California to Mexico. Baltic birds pass through C Mediterranean and E Europe en route to tropical W Africa (particularly Mali) and C Africa (approximately to equator), and Middle East. In Australia, juveniles disperse widely; Tasmanian birds winter in New South Wales; Queensland birds may disperse S as well as N. Juveniles wintering S move further than adults; most 2nd-years remain in wintering area in spring. Spring migration usually rapid.

Status and Conservation. Not globally threatened. Many vulnerable populations, and recent decline in some areas. World population probably c. 50,000 pairs: 15,000 in CIS, 12,000 in North America, 3000 in Europe, c. 5000 in W Africa, and 500 in S Africa; fewer than 5000 in New Zealand, but many thousands in Australia. Californian population grew by 70% from 1960 to 1980, reaching 6000 pairs. Declining in Baltic, and fewer than 500 pairs in Sweden in 1994. Nearly eliminated from most E North American and C European colonies in late 19th century, with gradual recovery in mid-20th century. Listed as threatened in Canada, where some colonies subject to vandalism. In E North America, rapid plant succession on dredge-spoil islands limits habitat. Reliance on relatively large fish increases exposure to bioaccumulated contaminants such as chlorinated hydrocarbons and methyl mercury. Some local evidence of organochlorines causing eggshell thinning and hatching failure.

Bibliography. Alcorn (1958), Ali & Ripley (1982), Baltz *et al.* (1979), Becker (1976), Bent (1921), Bergman (1953, 1956, 1980), Bijlsma (1985), Blake (1977), Blokpoel (1977, 1981), Blokpoel & Scharf (1991b), Borodulina (1960), Brooke (1984a), Chaniot (1970), Chodkov (1979), Clinning (1978a), Coates (1985), Conover (1983a), Cooper *et al.* (1992), Cramp (1985), Cuthbert (1985a, 1985b, 1988), Cyrus & MacLean (1994), DeGroot (1931), Diamond (1984), Dobrowolski (1970), Dowsett & Forbes-Watson (1993), Eminov (1964b), Gill & Mewaldt (1983), Goodman *et al.* (1989), Harrison (1984a), Hayward (1935), Hilty & Brown (1986), Hockey & Hockey (1980), Howell & Webb (1995a), Ilicev & Zubakin (1988), Isenmann (1975a), Józefik (1969), de Juana (1986), Khodkov & Totunov (1979), Kilpi & Saurola (1984b), Koli & Soikkeli (1974), Koonz (1982), L'Arrivee & Blokpoel (1988), Langrand (1990), Ludwig, F.E. (1942), Ludwig, J.P. (1965, 1979, 1981), Mackworth-Praed & Grant (1957, 1962, 1970), Maclean (1993), Marchant & Higgins (1996), van Marle & Voous (1988), Martínez & Muntaner (1979), Martini (1964), Mayaud (1956b), McDaniel & Beckett (1971), McNicholl (1990), Meininger (1988), Miller (1943), Mitchell & Custer (1986), Ohlendorf, Custer *et al.* (1988), Ohlendorf, Schaffner *et al.* (1985), Olsen & Larssen (1995b), Paul (1995), Penland (1981, 1984), Pierce (1984c), Pulliainen & Marjakangas (1980), Quinn (1985, 1990), Quinn & Morris (1986), Richards (1990), Roberts, T.J. (1991), Schew *et al.* (1994), Schreiber & Dinsmore (1972), Serventy *et al.* (1971), Shebareva (1962), Shirihai (1996), Shugart (1977, 1990), Shugart *et al.* (1979), Smith, G.A. (1987), Smythies (1986), Soikkeli (1970c, 1973a, 1973b), Staav (1977, 1979), Struger & Weseloh (1985), Tomialojc (1994d), Tomkins (1963), Tye (1983), Urban *et al.* (1986), Väisänen (1973), Wetmore (1965).

Genus *THALASSEUS* Boie, 1822

3. Elegant Tern
Thalasseus elegans

French: Sterne élégante   **German**: Schmuckseeschwalbe   **Spanish**: Charrán Elegante

Taxonomy. *Sterna elegans* Gambel, 1849, Mazatlan, Sinaloa, Mexico.
Genus often merged with *Sterna*, but the six species here placed within *Thalasseus* do share certain common features of morphology which set them apart from other terns. Forms superspecies with *T. bengalensis* and *T. sandvicensis*, and perhaps *T. bernsteini*, and subspecific status has even been suggested. Monotypic.

Distribution. Pacific coast of North America, with very restricted breeding range from S California to C Baja California and from Gulf of California to Nayarit.

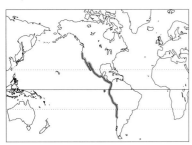

Descriptive notes. 39-43 cm; 217-300 g (breeding), 186-246 g (winter, Peru); wingspan 76-81 cm. Typical crested tern with black cap and long crest, white body, and grey mantle and wings; underparts white, often suffused with rosy; bill long and very slender, varying from yellow-orange to bright orange-red; ratio of bill length to depth greater than 5:1; legs and feet black, but 10% have orange legs and feet. Crest longer and usually more extensively black than in *T. maximus*. Differs from *T. bengalensis* in having rump and tail white, rather than pale grey. Non-breeding adult has white forehead and crown. Juvenile strongly mottled dark above. Immatures have darker grey secondaries, upperwing-coverts and tail feathers, and variable soft-part coloration; bill usually yellow.

Habitat. Sandy beaches and low-lying islands along coast and estuaries. Migrants feed in harbours, estuaries, salt-ponds and lagoons, resting in tight flocks on mudflats and sandbars.

Food and Feeding. Small fish. Preferred food is northern anchovy (*Engraulis mordax*). Flies at height of 1-3 m, then plunge-dives. Non-breeders feed in lagoons and bays, avoiding rough waters. In winter in Peru, plunge-dives beyond surf, mainly for small fish, and does not feed with other terns and gulls on abundant mole crabs (*Eremita analoga*) on wave-washed beach. In Peru, present species is favoured victim of piratical attacks by Arctic Skuas (*Stercorarius parasiticus*).

Breeding. Relatively few studies. Laying Apr-May. Dense nesting aggregations with hexagonal packing of nests (9-10 nests/m²), forming highly synchronous subcolonies. 1 egg (less than 2% of nests have 2 eggs); adults recognize own eggs; incubation c. 25 days; fledging 30-35 days; prolonged parental care continues until Nov. Colonies suffer predation by Heermann's (*Larus heermanni*), Western (*L. occidentalis*) and Yellow-footed Gulls (*L. livens*).

Movements. Post-breeding dispersal northward to N California and rarely to British Columbia. Uncommon migrant off Pacific coast of Costa Rica. Winters on Pacific coast from Guatemala to C Chile, mostly in Peru and N Chile. Accidental in Texas. Odd records from Netherlands, Ireland, Spain and France (including hybridization with *T. sandvicensis*), but provenance of such birds in question, as species virtually unrecorded anywhere in North America away from Pacific coast; probably attributable to escapes from shipments of exotic seabirds from wintering grounds in W South America.

Status and Conservation. Not globally threatened. Currently considered near-threatened. Global population probably 30,000-50,000 pairs. Much of population vulnerable. Sometimes 90% of entire population nests on Isla Rasa (Gulf of California), where there have been drastic changes in numbers. First documented flocks in USA were in 1950's, and first nesting in 1970's. About 800 pairs nest in San Diego Bay (California). Colony at Bolsa Chica (California), where first nested only in 1987, has grown to 4000 pairs. Several former colonies in Mexico have been abandoned. Nearly eliminated from Isla Rasa by eggers, until the island was declared a sanctuary in 1964; estimated population there was 80,000 in early 1980's, but only 22,500 a decade later. Human disturbance from ecotourism is a threat.

Bibliography. Blake (1977), Blokpoel *et al.* (1989), Boesman (1992), Boswall & Barrett (1978), Cassidy (1990), Collins *et al.* (1991), Devillers & Terschuren (1977), Dubois (1994a), Edwards (1989), Everett & Anderson (1991), Harrison (1984a), Hilty & Brown (1986), Howell & Webb (1995a), Hudon & Brush (1990), Johnson (1967), Koepcke (1970), Land (1970), Monroe (1956, 1968), Olsen & Larssen (1995b), Peterson (1995), Ridgely & Gwynne (1989), Root (1988), Schaffner (1986, 1990), Stiles & Skutch (1989), Terres (1982).

4. Lesser Crested Tern
Thalasseus bengalensis

French: Sterne voyageuse   **German**: Rüppellseeschwalbe   **Spanish**: Charrán Bengalí
Other common names: Crested Tern

Taxonomy. *Sterna bengalensis* Lesson, 1831, coasts of India.
Genus often merged with *Sterna*. Forms superspecies with *T. elegans* and *T. sandvicensis*, and perhaps *T. bernsteini*, and subspecific status has even been suggested. Often treated as monotypic, but described races based on subtle variation in plumage tone of upperparts and size: much overlap and intergradation, however, as well as intermediate populations, and distributions of races are confused; racial divisions require revision. Mediterranean and Red Sea birds sometimes classified together as race *par*; *emigrata* may be synonymous with *torresii*, although biogeographically allogical. Three subspecies normally recognized.

Subspecies and Distribution.
T. b. emigrata (Neumann, 1934) - Libya; most winter off W African coast.
T. b. bengalensis (Lesson, 1831) - Red Sea, and presumed to be this race in Pakistan, Laccadives and Maldives; winters S to S Africa and Sri Lanka.
T. b. torresii Gould, 1843 - Persian Gulf, and from Sulawesi to New Guinea and N Australia; in winter extends into N Indian and SW Pacific Oceans.

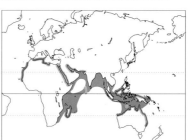

Descriptive notes. 35-43 cm; 185-242 g; wingspan 88-105 cm. Cap and crest black; upperparts uniform grey; bill orange to orange-yellow with yellow distal area, and slight droop towards tip; legs and feet black with yellow webs; iris brown. Underparts white, apparently less often tinged with pink than in *T. elegans* or *T. sandvicensis*; similar in size and appearance to *T. sandvicensis*, but bill colour differs; resembles *T. bergii*, but smaller, with proportionately longer, slimmer, orange (not dull yellow) bill; differs from all similar species in having rump and tail grey, not white. Non-breeding adult has white on forehead and crown and yellower bill. Juvenile paler than that of *T. bergii*, like *T. sandvicensis* but less heavily spotted and with darker flight-feathers; dusky grey band across upperwing-coverts. Conflicting evidence as regards racial variation, but most *torresii* from Australia are darker above than nominate; Mediterranean race *emigrata* larger and very slightly paler, said to be virtually identical to some *torresii*; many birds breeding in N Indian Ocean from Red Sea to Pakistan intermediate between these and nominate race.

Habitat. Tropical and subtropical coasts. Often associates with *T. bergii*, but tends to be more pelagic in Kenya and India. Breeds on low-lying sandy and coral islands and coral flats. Forages in surf and ranges offshore.

Food and Feeding. Mainly fish and shrimps. Feeds mostly on herrings (Clupeidae) in Sri Lanka, extensively on prawns in Pakistan. Quarters c. 5 m above water, turning, hovering and plunge-diving, often submerging; also surface-dips. Often feeds in large mixed tern flocks. Suffers heavy piracy from Silver Gulls (*Larus novaehollandiae*) on Great Barrier Reef, Australia, with loss of up to 23% of fish.

Breeding. May-Jun in Persian Gulf; Jul-Aug in Libya; Aug in Somalia; in Australia, breeds Sept-Dec in E, Mar-Jun in N and both seasons in W. Forms large, dense colonies (up to 20,000 pairs) on offshore islands, sandbanks and coral cays; shifts sites frequently. Often nests with *Sterna dougallii* or *T. bergii*; vagrants in Europe have produced hybrid young with *T. sandvicensis*. Average density 2·76 nests/m², but in high-density areas nests touch and may reach 9-10/m². Makes shallow unlined scrape in sand or shells, usually selecting ridges or bare areas surrounded by vegetation. 1 egg, rarely 2; incubation 21-26 days, occasionally 30 days; downy chick very pale to almost white above, with black spots on crown, back and wings forming fine lines, pure white below, with bill olive-yellow or black; led from nest at 2-4 days, and fed outside colony; from day 7 chicks of mixed ages form crèche, protected by adults; fledging 30-35 days; parental care to age of 5 months. Productivity not studied. Age of first breeding presumably 2 years.

Movements. Inadequately known owing to lack of ringing studies. Migratory in Mediterranean, with post-breeding movement to Morocco and Senegambia, but only partly migratory in most of range. Middle East birds pass E coast of Africa to Natal. N Indian Ocean populations partly migratory. Vagrant inland.

Status and Conservation. Not globally threatened. World population c. 225,000 pairs, more than half in Australia; c. 10,000 pairs in S Pacific; 8000 in Indonesia; 10,000 in E Africa; 50,000-60,000 in Middle East, with 24,500 pairs found on islands off Abu Dhabi in 1994, also c. 24,250 pairs off Saudi Arabia in early 1990's, and many 1000's in Iran; 10,000 in N Africa. Non-breeders common along coasts of S Asia, from Persian Gulf and both coasts of India to Indonesia. The commonest tern of Karachi.

Bibliography. Al-Hussaini (1939), Ali & Ripley (1982), Ash & Miskell (1983), Beehler *et al.* (1986), Bregnballe *et al.* (1990), Brichetti & Foschi (1985, 1987), Clapham (1964), Coates (1985), Cramp (1985), Domm & Recher (1973), Dowsett & Forbes-Watson (1993), Étchécopar & Hüe (1964), Evans (1994), Frith, H.J. (1976), Gallagher *et al.* (1984), Géroudet & Landenbergue (1977), Ginn *et al.* (1989), Goodman *et al.* (1989), Gore (1990), Hüe & Étchécopar (1970), Hulsman (1974, 1977, 1987), Hurford (1989), de Juana (1986), Langrand (1990), MacKinnon & Phillipps (1993), Mackworth-Praed & Grant (1957, 1962), Maclean (1993), Marchant & Higgins (1996), van Marle & Voous (1988), Medway & Wells (1976), Meininger (1988), Meininger *et al.* (1994), Milon *et al.* (1973), Moore & Balzarotti (1983), Olsen & Larssen (1995b), Paz (1987), Perennou *et al.* (1994), Petit (1976), Phillips (1978), Ripley (1982), Roberts, T.J. (1991), Serventy *et al.* (1971), Shirihai (1996), Short *et al.* (1990), Smythies (1981), Symens & Evans (1993), Urban *et al.* (1986), White & Bruce (1986).

5. Sandwich Tern

Thalasseus sandvicensis

French: Sterne caugek **German**: Brandseeschwalbe **Spanish**: Charrán Patinegro
Other common names: Yellow-nibbed Tern; Cabot's Tern (*acuflavidus*); Cayenne Tern (*eurygnatha*)

Taxonomy. *Sterna Sandvicensis* Latham, 1787, Sandwich, Kent, England.
Genus often merged with *Sterna*. Forms superspecies with *T. elegans* and *T. bengalensis*, and perhaps also *T. bernsteini*, and it has been suggested that all may even be conspecific. Form *eurygnatha*, Cayenne Tern, generally considered separate species until work in S Caribbean showed it to be race or possibly morph of *T. sandvicensis*, and that all but northernmost New World populations have at least small percentage of "Cayenne"-type birds. Races *acuflavidus* and *eurygnatha* interbreed freely in S Caribbean, and mixed pairs occur also in Patagonia and Puerto Rico; possibility of assortative mating deserves further study. In Curaçao typical *acuflavidus* make up 20% of population, while in French Guiana they comprise less than 1%. Three subspecies currently recognized.
Subspecies and Distribution.
T. s. sandvicensis (Latham, 1787) - Europe E to Caspian Sea; winters from Caspian, Black and Mediterranean Seas to coasts of W & S Africa, and from S Red Sea to NW India and Sri Lanka.
T. s. acuflavidus (Cabot, 1848) - E North America (Virginia locally to Campeche Bank and Belize), and through Antilles to S Caribbean; winters from Caribbean S to S Peru and Uruguay.
T. s. eurygnatha (Saunders, 1876) - highly local breeder in Caribbean, off Venezuela and French Guiana (Cayenne), and from E Brazil to S Argentina (Buenos Aires, and Patagonia from Chubut to Santa Cruz).

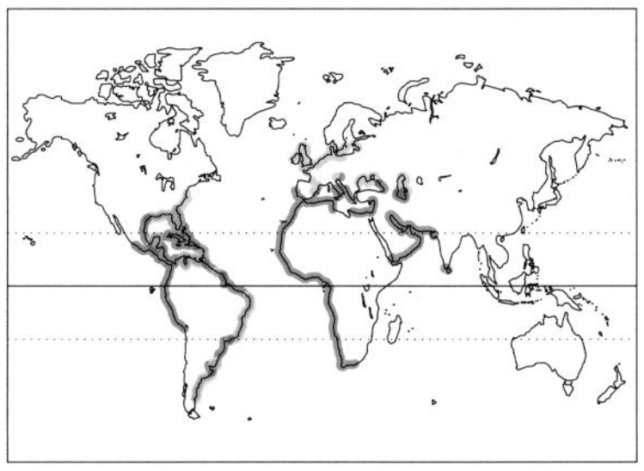

Descriptive notes. 36-46 cm; 130-311 g (*sandvicensis* 130-285 g; *acuflavidus* mostly 175-202 g; *eurygnatha* 170-210 g in Caribbean, 250-300 g in Uruguay); wingspan 86-105 cm. Medium-sized pale tern with black cap and crest, long slender bill, long pointed wings and moderately long, forked tail; back and upperwings pale ash-grey; rump and tail white; underparts white, sometimes tinged with pink; primaries with white inner webs and silvery outer webs; bill varies from black with yellow tip (Europe and North America) to mainly or wholly yellow (South America); legs black, occasionally yellow. Similar in size to *Gelochelidon nilotica*, but has more slender bill and distinctive calls; usually differs from similar *Thalasseus* species in having dark bill. Non-breeding adult has white forehead and forecrown. Juvenile spotted dark above, with dark tip to tail. Races differ only slightly: *acuflavidus* slightly smaller, with outer tips of outer primaries grey rather than white; *eurygnatha* is mainly yellow-billed, but often with dark bill base; legs sometimes partly yellow, rarely all yellow.
Habitat. Strictly coastal and mainly a warm-water species. Favoured breeding sites are low-lying, and subject to inundation, wind-blown sand, erosion and human intrusion: prefers open, unvegetated sandy, muddy or gravelly or bare coral substrates, nesting on highest open area available; late breeders forced to nest closer to high tide line. Outside breeding season frequents sandy or rocky beach fronts, mangrove flats, estuaries and harbours. At Curaçao feeds mainly along seashore, sporadically in bays. Feeds in inlets over water 1·5-2 m deep and at sea, very rarely over fresh water.
Food and Feeding. Almost entirely fish, mostly 9-15 cm long, particularly menhaden (*Brevoortia*) and anchovies (*Anchoviella*) in USA, and sardines (*Sardinella*) in W Africa; flying-fish in Caribbean; occasionally small shrimps. Also swoops to pick up marine worms from mudflats, and takes shorebird chicks, including Pied Avocets (*Recurvirostra avosetta*) in E Europe. Plunge-dives for small fish, from greater heights than *Sterna hirundo*, up to 10 m. Feeds over fishing nets; scavenges over sea-lions and sometimes feeds over porpoise pods. May fish with *T. bengalensis*. Occasional intraspecific kleptoparasitism. In Italy, most forage 10-15 km from colony; up to 70 km in Scotland. May defend feeding territories along shore.
Breeding. May-Jun in Europe, mid-May in Curaçao, Jun in C Brazil, Dec in Argentina. Colonies rarely monospecific; usually nests next to other terns or Common Black-headed Gulls (*Larus ridibundus*) in Europe, or with *T. maximus* in Americas. Late-arriving terns displace *L. ridibundus* from centre of colony. Forms dense colonies: eggs sometimes only 20 cm apart; sometimes only 2 nest/m², but usually 5-7 (maximum 9). In Europe colonies contain up to 4000 pairs, mean 853, but one Dutch colony reached 35,000 pairs prior to 1960; 20,000 pairs in a Louisiana colony in 1970's; 1300 nests, mostly *eurygnatha*, in Curaçao in 1958. At some sites forms synchronous subcolonies of 5-25 pairs, but larger groups more synchronous than small ones. Frequent changes in colony site, particularly if predators become established early in breeding cycle, but tolerant of disturbance after egg-laying; prefers nesting far from upright vegetation, and abandons colonies when vegetation encroaches. Nest a shallow scrape rimmed with excreta. 1-2 eggs (1-3), with average 1·66; larger clutches in larger colonies and for older birds (5-year-olds average 1·81, 3-year-olds 1·33), with highest mean 2·07 in large Scandinavian colonies; 1·7 in Argentina. Incubation 21-29 days, average 25 days; chick whitish to buff, grey or brown, with few or heavy black speckles; hatching weight 22-24 g; in some colonies, young form crèche at 1-2 weeks; fledging 28-35 days; prolonged parental care into 1st winter. Productivity very variable, c. 0·6/pair, higher in larger colonies. Average hatching success 47-81%, lower in high-density areas, and for late eggs (0-60%). Fledging success usually 80-90%. Older early breeders more successful. Some birds breed at age 3, most not until 4. Oldest recorded bird 23 years 7 months.
Movements. Post-breeding movement both N and S to favourable feeding grounds, until S migration begins in mid-Sept. European birds move S along W coast of Africa, to winter mostly in tropics, a few remaining in W Europe; up to 35,000 off Mauritania in Dec. Adults move further S than young, the latter spending their 2nd year in Africa. Many Black Sea birds winter in the Mediterranean or Black Seas; rarely reach W Africa. Caspian Sea birds winter in the N Indian Ocean from S Red Sea to Pakistan, including Persian Gulf, but some remain in the Caspian and a few reach S India and Sri Lanka; irregular winter visitor E Africa (Kenya, Tanzania). North American birds move S through Caribbean and along both coasts of Central America to South America; some linger in SE USA and Caribbean, others reach Uruguay and W South America; sometimes numerous on C coast of Peru. Race *eurygnatha* winters in S Caribbean and along Atlantic coast of South America to Argentina; some post-breeding wandering in Gulf Stream N to North Carolina; few sightings from Colombia, including one on Pacific Coast. In Uruguay, *eurygnatha* is uncommon along coast in breeding season, while typical *acuflavidus* appears in winter from North America.
Status and Conservation. Not globally threatened. World population at least 100,000 pairs, including c. 45,000 in E USA and 40,000 in Europe; but estimate of c. 40,000 pairs at Caspian Sea alone in 1985, and of 75,000-80,000 for whole of former USSR. Total *eurygnatha* population may be under 20,000 pairs. Significant decline in NW Europe (Wadden Sea) attributed in part to organochlorines, and in W Europe due to human disturbance on breeding grounds and human predation on wintering grounds. Fluctuating population levels obscure trends. UK populations rebounded in first half of 20th century to 15,000+ pairs. Netherlands population increased to 40,000 pairs in 1950's, declined to 12,000 in 1961 and only 650 in 1965, apparently due to pesticides; then increased to 6000 in late 1970's. First bred in Sweden in 1911, and in Norway in 1974. In USA, has increased slightly during present century in Middle Atlantic States. Race *acuflavidus* extending SE since the 1970's, and now meets and interbreeds with *eurygnatha*; latter extending N, first noted in Curaçao in 1952, Virgin Is in 1970's, and Culebra (Puerto Rico) in 1986. Few colony sites known from E South America. First discovered breeding in Argentina in 1964. Colonies vulnerable to human disturbance or heavy predation, particularly early in season, and birds sometimes abandon eggs en masse. Suffers heavy predation from Laughing Gulls (*Larus atricilla*) in Curaçao. Egging a serious threat throughout tropics, and capture of wintering birds in W Africa potentially significant. Responds favourably to habitat management, such as clearing of vegetation and site protection, and in Europe and Caribbean readily attracted to suitable nesting habitat by use of decoys.
Bibliography. Ali & Ripley (1982), Ansingh *et al.* (1960), Becker & Erdelen (1987), Bent (1921), Blake (1977), Borodulina (1960), Bourne & Smith (1974), Brichetti (1986), Brindley & del Nevo (1994b), Buckley & Buckley (1984a), Campbell (1971), Campredon (1978), Chestney (1970), Clancey (1977a), Clapp & Buckley (1984), Cochrane *et al.* (1991), Cramp (1985), Daciuk (1976), Dircksen (1932), Dowsett & Forbes-Watson (1993), Drent *et al.* (1992), Dujardin & Tostain (1990), Dunn (1972), Escalante (1970a, 1973), Fasola (1986), Fasola & Bogliani (1990), Fasola & Canova (1992), Fasola & Saino (1990), ffrench & Collins (1965), Fuchs (1977a, 1977b, 1977c), Furniss (1983), Gauzer, M.E. (1981a, 1981b), Gauzer, M.E. & Vassiliev (1979), Gauzer, M.Y. (1989), Gochfeld & Burger (1982), Götmark (1990), Grant, G.S. (1981), van Halewijn (1990), van Halewijn & Norton (1984), Hilty & Brown (1986), Howell & Webb (1995a), Hutchison *et al.* (1968), Ilicev & Zubakin (1988), Isenmann (1972), de Juana (1986), Junge & Voous (1955), Kaverkina (1989), Kaverkina & Babitsch (1987), King (1973), Koeman (1972), Langham (1971, 1972, 1974, 1983), Lanier (1990), LeCroy (1976), Lind (1963b), Mackworth-Praed & Grant (1957, 1962, 1970), Marples & Marples (1934), Mathiasson (1980), McGuigan (1990), Meininger (1988), Mueller (1959), Nehls (1969), Norton (1984), Olmos *et al.* (1995), Olsen & Larssen (1995b), Petit (1976), Poslavsky & Krivonosov (1976), Richards (1990), Roberts, T.J. (1991), Rodgers, Smith & Paul (1996), Rooth (1989), Rooth & Jonkers (1972), Saino & Fasola (1990), Shealer & Burger (1995), Shirihai (1996), Sick (1985c, 1993), Sick & Leao (1965), Smith, A.J.M. (1975), Steinbacher (1931), Taverner (1965, 1969), Taylor, I.R. (1983), Teague (1955), Thomas, G.J. *et al.* (1989), Thompson (1943), Urban *et al.* (1986), Veen (1977), Voous (1968b), Wetmore (1965), Zapata (1965).

6. Chinese Crested Tern

Thalasseus bernsteini

French: Sterne d'Orient **German**: Bernsteinseeschwalbe **Spanish**: Charrán Chino

Taxonomy. *Sterna bernsteini*, Schlegel, 1863, China.
Genus often merged with *Sterna*. Species closely related to *T. bengalensis*; may belong to *T. sandvicensis* superspecies. Formerly known as *T. zimmermanni*. Monotypic.
Distribution. Breeding areas unknown, possibly on coast of N China in Shandong: on islands near Qingdao and on islet of Mukuantao, or at delta of Huang Ho (Yellow R). Winter records from E China S to Indonesia.

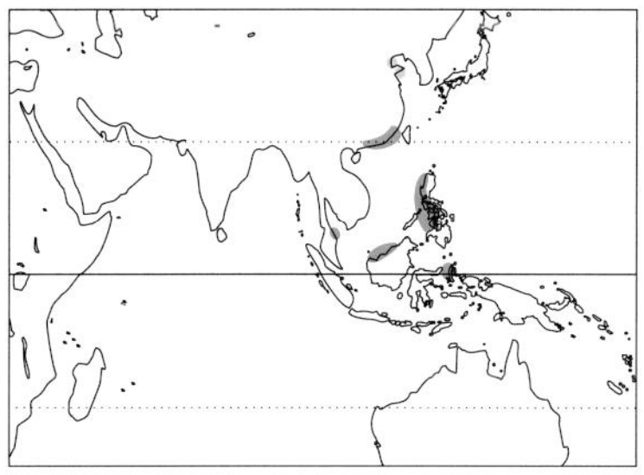

Descriptive notes. 42 cm. Similar to *T. bengalensis*, but bill stouter, with more pronounced gonydeal angle, orange-yellow with broad black tip; back paler grey.
Habitat. Presumably coastal estuaries.
Food and Feeding. Unknown. Presumably fish.
Breeding. Presumably May-Jul, but breeding sites have never been found. Nothing known.
Movements. Appears to migrate to tropics, where recorded from E China (Fujian, Guangdong), Philippines, NW Borneo (Sarawak), S Thailand and Halmahera.
Status and Conservation. CRITICALLY ENDANGERED. Virtually unknown, and possibly even extinct, but several recent sight records suggest species may survive. Last collected at Tsangkow near Qingdao (Tsingtao), and on Mukuantao islet off Shandong coast, where 21 specimens taken in 1937, some in breeding condition; long feared extinct. Most recent record is of 10 birds near Libong, S Thailand, in Jul 1980, but 3 terns probably of this species reported in Huang Ho Delta in Sept 1991. May be overlooked among flocks of *T. bergii*. Survey work urgently required.
Bibliography. Andrew, P. (1992), Collar & Andrew (1988), Collar *et al.* (1994), Dickinson & Eck (1984), Dickinson *et al.* (1991), Étchécopar & Hüe (1978), King (1978/79), LaTouche (1931), Lekagul & Round (1991), MacKinnon & Phillipps (1993), Mann (1990), Medway & Wells (1976), Mees (1975), Melville (1984), Meyer de Schauensee (1984), Perennou *et al.* (1994), Smythies (1981), Stepanjan (1990b), Wang *et al.* (1991), White & Bruce (1986), Xu Weishu & Melville (1994).

7. Royal Tern

Thalasseus maximus

French: Sterne royale **German**: Königsseeschwalbe **Spanish**: Charrán Real

Taxonomy. *Sterna maxima* Boddaert, 1783, Cayenne.
Genus often merged with *Sterna*. Sometimes considered to form superspecies with *T. bergii*. Racial variation questionable. Two subspecies normally recognized.
Subspecies and Distribution.
T. m. albididorsalis (Hartert, 1921) - Mauritania to Guinea, occasionally further S; winters S to Namibia.
T. m. maximus (Boddaert, 1783) - S California to Sinaloa, and Maryland (rarely New Jersey) to Texas, and through West Indies to the Guianas and possibly Brazil, with disjunct breeding populations on Yucatán, and in S Brazil, Uruguay and N Patagonia; winters S to Peru and to Uruguay and Argentina.
Descriptive notes. 45-51 cm; 320-500 g (*maximus* 380-500 g; *albididorsalis* 320-440 g, mean 367 g); wingspan 100-135 cm. Crown and elongated nape feathers black; mantle and upperwing very pale pearl grey; bill bright orange, rarely red; legs and feet black. Slightly smaller than *Hydroprogne caspia*, with more slender bill, and primaries pale grey below, not blackish. Similar to *T. bergii*, but paler above and heavier-billed. Non-breeding adult has mostly white forehead, white crown streaked with black, and black extending from nape forwards to eye; moult begins early, so that forehead and even forecrown often white while still incubating. Juvenile has greyish hindcrown, and white mantle feathers with brown subterminal chevrons and grey tips; flight-feathers grey, also with brown and grey markings; most wing-coverts pale grey, lesser coverts darker; bill and feet yellowish; less brown and black on upperparts than juvenile *T. bergii*. Immature resembles winter adult. Races very similar, *albididorsalis* with smaller wing-bill ratio; if races valid, Patagonian birds need to be examined, as they are more similar to *albididorsalis*.

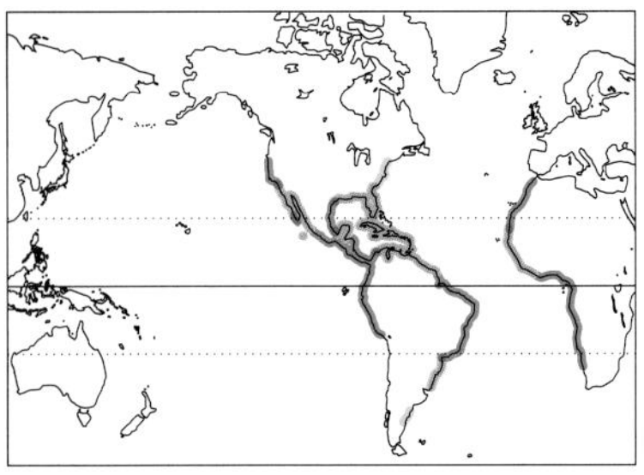

Habitat. Subtropical and tropical coasts. Breeds on barren sandy barrier beaches, salt-marsh islands, shell bars, dredge spoil, and coral islands. Shuns vegetation. Many colony sites vulnerable to flooding. Breeding colonies typified by inaccessibility, high visibility, absence of mammalian predators, and surrounded by shallow waters near the mouth of bays. Feeds along estuaries, lagoons and mangroves. Outside breeding season, frequents coasts, estuaries, harbours and river mouths, sometimes penetrating a short distance up broad rivers.

Food and Feeding. Mainly small fish (3-18 cm, average 6·7 cm), also squid, shrimps and crabs. In Africa, mainly Clupeidae, Mugilidae, Pomadasyidae, Carangidae, Ephippidae. In Virginia, mainly *Menidia*, *Fundulus*, *Anchoviella*, *Brevoortia*; in Florida *Brevoortia*, *Micropogonias*; in California, relies on Pacific sardine (*Sardinops sagax*). Usually feeds singly or in small flocks, despite gregarious roosting. Flies 5-10 m above water and plunge-dives, but does not submerge; also performs aerial skimming and surface-dipping for offal. Occasionally piratic on conspecifics. Forages mostly within 100 m of shore, but feeds up to 40 km from colony.

Breeding. Lays Apr-Jul in W Africa, Apr in Texas, May from Florida to Maryland, Jun in Cayenne, Nov in Patagonia. Breeds in dense, often very large colonies, often near Laughing Gulls (*Larus atricilla*) and/or *T. sandvicensis*; estimates of 11,000 nests on Cape Romain, South Carolina, in 1947 and 10,000 at Saloum, Senegambia; most colonies 100-4000 pairs. Nests show classical hexagonal packing, with 5-8 nests/m². Occasionally nests singly among other tern species, usually at margin of range. Nest a mere scrape in substrate, occasionally on roofs (Florida). 1 egg (1-10% lay 2), although adults have two brood patches; incubation 25-31 days; chick greyish or buffy, with or without dark spots, soft parts very variable; 45-55 g at hatching; chicks form crèche when disturbed; fledge at c. 30 days; parental care to 5-8 months. Productivity highly variable. First breeding at age 3 or, more typically, 4. Recorded longevity of 17 years certainly an underestimate.

Movements. Post-breeding dispersal N, followed by S migration. In America, winters from South Carolina and Gulf Coast to Argentina, very rare along Peruvian coast. Chicks ringed in South Carolina colonies recovered mainly along Gulf Coast, in Florida and West Indies, but 1 in California; those ringed in Virginia found mainly in Greater Antilles. W African birds disperse N to Morocco, where flocks of up to 200 in Aug 1995; most then move S to winter from Senegal to Angola, with smaller numbers S to Namibia.

Status and Conservation. Not globally threatened. Population declining in several areas. In SE USA, numbers increased in early 1900's and species slowly colonized northwards, breeding as far N as Maryland and rarely New Jersey. E coast population c. 34,000 pairs; Caribbean under 1000 pairs; French Guiana (Cayenne) 1000 pairs, but remainder of South American population not known. Numbers in California have crashed in past 25 years along with virtual disappearance of species' staple food, the Pacific sardine; c. 8500 pairs on Isla Rasa (Gulf of California). About 25,000 pairs in Africa. Colonies subject to flooding; also to egging, formerly in USA, and still in Caribbean. Pesticides potentially important because of large prey size. In South Carolina, sand crabs (*Ocypoda arenaria*) destroyed many eggs. Common Black-headed Gulls (*Larus ridibundus*) take both eggs and chicks; Laughing Gulls take eggs only.

Bibliography. Ashmole & Tovar (1968), Barbour (1978), Belton (1984), Bent (1921), Biaggi (1983), Blake (1977), Buckley, F.G. & Buckley (1972, 1974), Buckley, P.A. & Buckley (1970, 1972, 1977, 1984b), Buckley & Hailman (1970), Canevari *et al.* (1991), Clancey (1975b), Clapp & Buckley (1984), Clapp *et al.* (1982), Cramp (1985), Dowsett & Forbes-Watson (1993), Dragesco (1961), Dujardin & Tostain (1990), Egensteiner *et al.* (1996), Elgood *et al.* (1994), Erwin (1977a), Escalante (1962, 1968, 1970c, 1985), Étchécopar & Hüe (1964), Everett & Anderson (1991), Gibson (1920), Gore (1990), Grant, G.S. (1981), Grant, P.J. *et al.* (1971), Grimes (1987), van Halewijn & Norton (1984), Harrison (1984a), Haverschmidt (1968), Haverschmidt & Mees (1995), Hilty & Brown (1986), Howell & Webb (1995a), de Juana (1986), Kale *et al.* (1965), Kilham (1981), King *et al.* (1983), LeCroy (1976), Loftin (1982), Loftin & Sutton (1979), Mackworth-Praed & Grant (1962, 1970), Meyer de Schauensee & Phelps (1978), Meininger (1988), Monroe (1968), de Naurois (1969), Olmos *et al.* (1995), Olsen & Larssen (1995b), de la Peña (1992), Pinto (1983), Portnoy (1977), Richards (1990), Ridgely & Gwynne (1989), Root (1988), Schaffner (1985), Sick (1985c, 1993), Slud (1964), Stiles & Skutch (1989), Teague (1955), Toland & Gilbert (1987), Tomkins (1963), Tostain *et al.* (1992), Urban *et al.* (1986), van Velzen & Benedict (1972), Voous (1963), Wetmore (1965), Wheeler (1989).

8. Greater Crested Tern

Thalasseus bergii

French: Sterne huppée **German**: Eilseeschwalbe **Spanish**: Charrán Piquigualdo
Other common names: Crested Tern, Swift Tern (Africa)

Taxonomy. *Sterna Bergii* Lichtenstein, 1823, Cape of Good Hope.
Genus often merged with *Sterna*. Sometimes considered to form superspecies with *T. maximus*. Subspecific taxonomy unusually confusing, with many other races proposed, e.g. *bakeri*, *edwardsi*, *halodramus*, *pelecanoides*, *poliocercua*; race *gwendolenae* may not be valid. Six subspecies currently recognized.

Subspecies and Distribution.
T. b. bergii (Lichtenstein, 1823) - Namibia to South Africa; some non-breeders move to S Mozambique.
T. b. enigma (Clancey, 1979) - Zambezi Delta, believed to nest on islands off Mozambique and Madagascar.
T. b. thalassinus (Stresemann, 1914) - Tanzania, Seychelles, Aldabra and Rodrigues I, and possibly this race in NW Madagascar; wanders to S Somalia.
T. b. velox (Cretzschmar, 1827) - Red Sea and NW Somalia E to Myanmar, Maldives and Sri Lanka; W populations winter S to Kenya.
T. b. cristatus (Stephens, 1826) - Malaysia to Philippines and Ryukyu Is, and E Australia to Society Is.
T. b. gwendolenae (Mathews, 1912) - W & NW Australia.

Descriptive notes. 43-53 cm; 320-400 g (*velox* 340-400 g, *thalassinus* 320-350 g, *cristata* 325-383 g); wingspan 100-130 cm. Large tern with white forehead in breeding plumage, when has a glossy black cap and long crest; neck, underparts and secondaries white, latter contrasting with otherwise grey back and upperwing; bill chrome yellow, sometimes tinged greenish at base, or entirely greenish yellow with irregular black blotches; feet black. Differs from *T. bengalensis*, with which often cooccurs, in larger size and longer, yellower bill. Similar to *T. maximus*, but with darker upperparts, slimmer body, and more slender, cold yellow (not orange) bill with steeper gonydeal angle. Non-breeding adult has white crown with some dark spotting, but retains black on hindcrown. Juvenile has crown feathers tipped brownish; upperparts and upperwing very heavily mottled or barred with brown; primaries dark brown, with white on inner webs; secondaries ashy brown with white tips; bill greenish; feet brownish black. Immature resembles non-breeding adult, but has browner crown with pale spots, and brown markings on neck, back and wing-coverts. Races vary mainly in colour tone of upperparts and amount of white on forehead: *enigma* palest, nominate *bergii* with least white on forehead; *velox*, *thalassinus* and *cristatus* very dark above, *velox* with heaviest bill and body, *thalassinus* with broader white band on forehead.

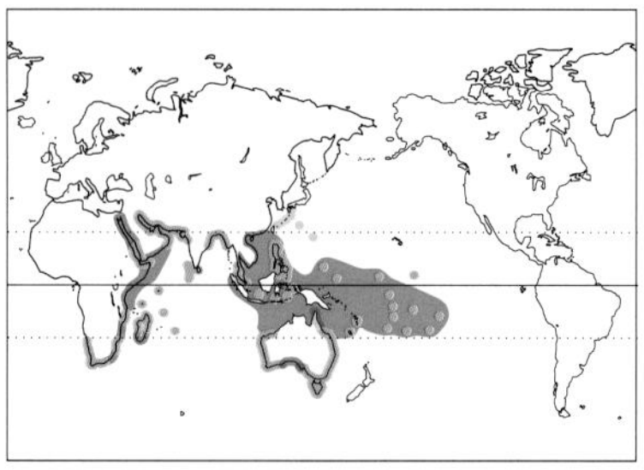

Habitat. Tropical and subtropical coasts and oceanic islands. More marine than *T. maximus*. Nests on offshore islands, low-lying coral, sandy or rocky islets, coastal spits, lagoons, and recently on artificial islets in salt-pans and sewage works within 3 km of coast (S Africa). Forages in shallow waters of lagoons and barrier reefs, in estuaries, along beaches, and also well out to sea. Rests on buoys or on rocks and sandbars, often with other terns and gulls.

Food and Feeding. Feeds mainly on fish (10-15 cm long); also opportunistically on squid, crabs, insects, baby turtles and other aquatic prey. In South Africa 86% of fish is Cape anchovy (*Engraulis capensis*), but 20 fish species represented in 1311 prey items. In W Australia mainly clupeids. Along Great Barrier Reef, 7 fish families represented in diet, mainly clupeids. Usually forages in small groups, flying c. 3-6 m above water and plunge-diving or contact-dipping; juvenile feeds by contact-dipping. Occasionally engages in piracy, but more often a victim, with up to 12% of fish stolen (Australia). Forages mostly within 3 km of colony.

Breeding. Apr-Jun in Indian Ocean, May-Jun in Sudan and S Africa, Aug in Somalia, Sept-Dec in E Australia, Dec-Jan in tropical Australia, Oct in Kenya, Nov in Tanzania; two peaks in Aldabra (Jan and Jul) and in SW Australia (Apr-May and Oct-Nov), but each individual nests only once yearly. Forms large dense colonies (mainly Australia), or very small subcolonies, often fewer than 10 pairs, among gulls, especially Silver Gull (*Larus novaehollandiae*) and Hartlaub's Gull (*L. hartlaubii*). Nest a shallow scrape in bare sand, rock or coral; nests close together (33-44 cm apart), rims often touching. Lays 1 egg in Australia, otherwise 1-2, rarely 3 in Indian Ocean probably result of 2 females laying in same nest; incubation 25-30 days; chick whitish with fine, sparse, black speckles; leaves nest at c. 2 days; fledging c. 38-40 days; dependent at least until 4 months. First breeding usually at age 3, although one record of breeding attempt at 1 year. Productivity 0-0·6/nest. Oldest ringed bird 20 years.

Movements. Movement patterns mostly unknown, and many populations more or less resident around breeding areas. Australian birds disperse several hundred kilometres around colony. Race *velox* disperses mainly within its breeding range, but Middle East birds move S to E African coast after breeding, and winter mainly from Egypt to Kenya, overlapping with *thalassinus*. Non-breeding birds of nominate race overlap with *enigma*.

Status and Conservation. Not globally threatened. Locally vulnerable owing to propensity for nesting in just a few, large, dense colonies. More than 500,000 pairs in Australia, and c. 50,000 pairs elsewhere; c. 33,000 pairs in Middle East including minimum 4000 pairs off Oman, c. 3500 pairs on islands off Saudi Arabia in early 1990's, also 1256 pairs off Abu Dhabi in 1994, and many 1000's in Iran. Race *bergii* has about 5000 pairs in 6-10 colonies, but c. 95% of these in 2 colonies; largest, on Marcus I (NW Pacific), is in a fairly well protected reserve. Many colonies subject to egging and to predation by gulls and ibises, particularly when incubating terns are flushed by raptors or human intruders. Apparently declining in Indonesia owing to egging, but population difficult to assess. Formerly bred in Gulf of Thailand, but not recently.

Bibliography. Ali & Ripley (1982), Ash & Miskell (1983), Beehler *et al.* (1986), Blaber & Wassenberg (1989), Brazil (1991), Bregnballe *et al.* (1990), Bregulla (1992), Britton & Osborne (1976), Carrick *et al.* (1957), Clancey (1975b), Coates (1985), Cooper & Pringle (1977), Cooper, Crawford *et al.* (1990), Cooper, Shaughnessy & Clinning (1977), Cramp (1985), Crawford & Dyer (1995), Davies & Carrick (1962), Dickinson *et al.* (1991), Domm & Recher (1973), Dowsett & Forbes-Watson (1993), Duffy (1987), Dunlop (1985a, 1985b, 1986), Étchécopar & Hüe (1964, 1978), Evans (1994), Feare (1975), Gallagher *et al.* (1984), Gibson (1956), Ginn *et al.* (1989), Goodman *et al.* (1989), Holyoak & Thibault (1984), Hüe & Étchécopar (1970), Hulsman (1976, 1977, 1984, 1987, 1988), Hulsman *et al.* (1989), Komen *et al.* (1986), Langham (1983, 1986), Langham & Hulsman (1986), Langrand (1990), Lekagul & Round (1991), MacKinnon & Phillipps (1993), Mackworth-Praed & Grant (1957, 1962), Maclean (1993), Marchant & Higgins (1996), van Marle & Voous (1988), Medway & Wells (1976), Milon *et al.* (1973), Moore & Balzarotti (1983), Oberholser (1915), Olsen & Larssen (1995b), Pakenham (1979), Perennou *et al.* (1994), Phillips (1978), Purchase (1973), Ripley (1982), Roberts, T.J. (1991), Serventy & Whittell (1976), Serventy *et al.* (1971), Shirihai (1996), Short *et al.* (1990), Smith, G.C. (1992a, 1993), Smythies (1981, 1986), Symens & Evans (1993), Urban *et al.* (1986), Uys (1978), Walker (1992), Walter, C.B. (1984), Walter, Cooper & Suter (1987), Walter, Duffy *et al.* (1987), White & Bruce (1986), Woehler *et al.* (1991).

Genus *STERNA* Linnaeus, 1758

9. River Tern

Sterna aurantia

French: Sterne de rivière **German**: Hinduseeschwalbe **Spanish**: Charrán Indio
Other common names: Indian River Tern

Taxonomy. *Sterna aurantia* J. E. Gray, 1831, India. Monotypic.

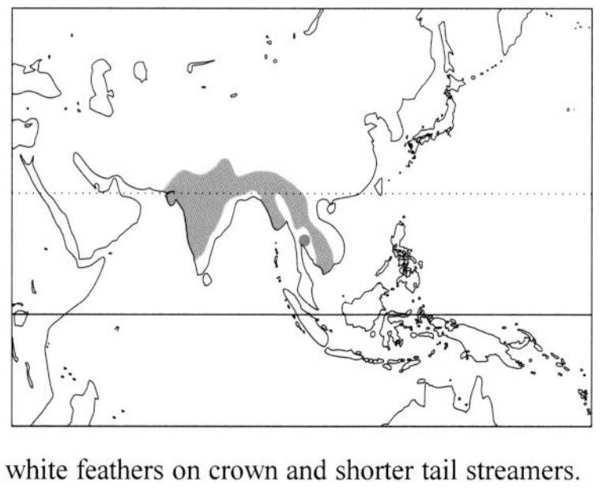

Distribution. E Pakistan to S India and E through Nepal to SW China (Yunnan) and Mekong Delta.

Descriptive notes. 38-46 cm; wingspan 80-85 cm. Typical tern, with black crown and lores and deeply forked tail; darkish grey upperparts; bill somewhat stout, bright yellow; iris dark brown; legs red. Non-breeding adult has whitish forehead and forecrown, with black marks around eye to nape; bill dull yellow with dusky tip. Immature grey above, flecked with buffy white and boldly marked with black chevrons; forehead and broad eyeline white; bill dull ochre. 1st-summer very similar to adult, but with a few white feathers on crown and shorter tail streamers.

Habitat. Breeds on sandy islands in freshwater lakes and rivers, and rarely estuaries; shuns mainland sites. Feeds mainly over fresh water. Rare along the coast, where feeds in estuaries and over mudflats. Occurs up to 600 m in Nepal.

Food and Feeding. Mainly fish, small crustaceans and insects. Usually feeds by plunge-diving.

Breeding. One of least studied terns. Breeds mainly Feb-May in dry season, but extreme dates Nov-Jun. First nests often flooded out, and re-laying occurs. Nests colonially, often with other terns, skimmers and Little Pratincoles (*Glareola lactea*); colonies generally contain fewer than 20 pairs. Readily mobs intruders, including hawks and corvids. Nest a shallow scrape on bare sand. Usual clutch 3, rarely 4; incubation reported as 18-19 days, but probably longer; young independent by 3 weeks after fledging. Some nest at 1 year of age.

Movements. Mainly a permanent resident, with some short nomadic movements. A few birds winter on seashores of S Asia.

Status and Conservation. Not globally threatened. Widely distributed in small colonies, but overall status poorly known. No evidence to suggest that species is threatened at present, but many nesting areas are vulnerable to flooding, predation and human disturbance. Now very rare in Thailand, where once not uncommon. Uncommon in S India, and rare along the coast; locally common resident in Nepal.

Bibliography. Ali (1979), Ali & Ripley (1982), Bharucha *et al*. (1988), Deignan (1945), Harvey (1990), Lekagul & Round (1991), Lowther (1949), Meyer de Schauensee (1984), Mundkur (1990, 1992), Neelakantan (1953a, 1990), Perennou *et al*. (1994), Ripley (1982), Roberts, T.J. (1991), Saxena (1991), Smythies (1986).

PLATE 55

inches 7

cm 18

with all-red bill

10

11

12

ssp *hirundo*

13

14

ssp *longipennis*

15

16

17

18

19

10. **Roseate Tern**

Sterna dougallii

French: Sterne de Dougall **German**: Rosenseeschwalbe **Spanish**: Charrán Rosado

Taxonomy. *Sterna Dougallii* Montagu, 1813, Firth of Clyde, Scotland.
In some respects intermediate between *Sterna* and *Thalasseus*. Internal taxonomy in need of revision, as subspecific boundaries confused: racial allocation of birds breeding on islets off E Africa requires study, perhaps closer to *bangsi* than to *dougallii*, although included in latter; *arideensis* may not be distinct from *bangsi*; variation of nominate *dougallii* encompasses almost entire range of variation of species. Five subspecies currently recognized.
Subspecies and Distribution.
S. d. dougallii Montagu, 1813 - Nova Scotia to New York and Florida, S through Gulf of Honduras and West Indies to islands off N Venezuela, and also Azores, NW Europe, and E & S Africa from S Somalia to Tanzania and in S Cape Province; American populations may winter mainly in mid-Atlantic, E Atlantic birds winter on coasts of tropical W Africa.
S. d. arideensis Mathews, 1912 - Seychelles S to Madagascar and E to Rodrigues I.
S. d. korustes (Hume, 1874) - Sri Lanka, Andaman Is and Mergui Archipelago (SW Myanmar).
S. d. bangsi Mathews, 1912 - Arabian Sea, Ryukyu Is, coastal China and Taiwan S to Greater Sundas and E to S New Guinea, Solomons, New Caledonia and possibly Fiji; presumably this race on Cocos (Keeling) Is.
S. d. gracilis Gould, 1845 - Moluccas and Australia.

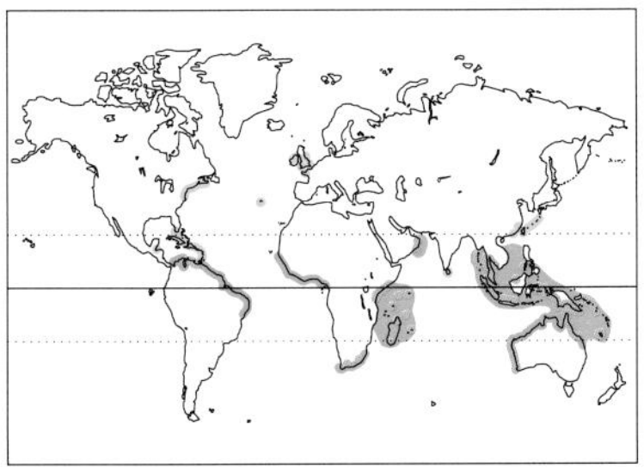

Descriptive notes. 33-43 cm; 90-125 g (average 110 g, New York); wingspan 72-80 cm. Very pale typical tern with very long tail streamers; forehead to nape black; mantle and upperwing very pale grey; tail entirely white and deeply forked; black outer webs on 3 outer primaries only; immaculate white below, tinged pink early in breeding season (pink reduced or absent in tropical populations, and in South Africa appears only during chick phase); legs and feet dull to bright red. Changes in bill colour vary geographically: in N latitudes and in Somalia, bill black with slight red at base at start of breeding, red increasing steadily throughout season until bill half or mostly red as migration begins; Caribbean birds arrive with all black bill, but basal two thirds red by time of egg-laying; in Seychelles, bill all black prior to breeding, fully red at end of cycle. Species differs from *S. hirundo* in shorter wings and longer tail, with faster, shallower wingbeats, different bill pattern, paler plumage, and distinctive rasping "aaask" calls and sharp, high-pitched "chew-ik". Non-breeding adult has forecrown mottled black and white, no pink below, faint dusky bar on lesser coverts, and all black bill. Juvenile heavily barred with black and/or brown crescents on mantle, mottled brownish grey on back and rump; bill and legs dark. Subadult like non-breeding adult, but with white forehead and hindneck, speckled with brownish, and sooty brown mark across crown and ear-coverts to nape; legs usually darker. Races differentiated by wing length, and bill length and colour, but these parameters vary with latitude; apart from *korustes*, which has both shorter wing and bill and greyer upperparts, all racial differences covered by variation within nominate *dougallii*.
Habitat. Breeds on sandy, rocky or coral islands, often with dense vegetation in temperate areas, or barren islets in tropics; rarely breeds on salt-marsh. Off Kenya, nests on mushroom-shaped blocks of coral up to 18 m above sea. On Long I, New York, some birds nest under boulders. Feeds along tide-rips, in estuaries and several kilometres offshore.
Food and Feeding. Diet much less varied than that of *S. hirundo*, with which it often nests: almost exclusively small fish, rarely insects and marine invertebrates. Strong preference for sandeels (*Ammodytes*) and various clupeids in N latitudes. In South Africa 11 species of fish recorded, mainly ratfish (*Gonorhynchus gonorhynchus*, mean length 8 cm). In W Africa often snatches sardines (*Sardinella*) from beach. Often feeds in flocks with other species. Plunge-dives from greater heights and submerges more deeply (up to 50 cm) than *S. hirundo*. Also feeds by aerial-dipping for small fish driven to surface by predators, and contact-dips for small fish and invertebrates over shoals of bonito (*Sarda*), tuna (*Thunnus*) and bluefish (*Pomatomus saltatrix*). Scavenges behind fishing boats. Sometimes piratical.
Breeding. Apr in W Australia, India, Sri Lanka and Madagascar, May-Jun in NE USA and Europe, Jun in Somalia, Jul-Aug in Kenya and Seychelles, Jun-Oct in South Africa; lays earlier in good food years. Usually in mixed colonies, but monospecific colonies of up to 4000 pairs in Madagascar and 8000 pairs on Kiunga Is, Kenya. Colonies often very dense, with inter-nest distances 40 cm, particularly in Africa; less dense in temperate regions. In North America and Europe almost always nests with *S. hirundo*, and occasionally interbreeds; in India and E Australia usually with *S. sumatrana* and often *Thalasseus bergii*. Nest usually a bare scrape in sand or on coral rubble or bare rock; sometimes on vegetation, often without nest material; in NE USA and Europe nest usually beside or under vegetation, rocks or wood, so eggs barely visible from above, but in Caribbean and Australia often fully exposed on bare substrate. Usually 2 eggs, with tendency towards 1 in poor food years or in tropics; average 1·4 in Kenya, 1·3 in South Africa, but only 1 in Seychelles. Incubation 22-26 days; chick mottled dark, with dark grey chin and throat and white to buffy white underparts, not speckled like most *Sterna*; average hatching weight 14·8-16·0 g; hides in vegetation near nest, until fledging at 23-30 days. Productivity often 1-1·5 young raised/nest, but in West Indies less than 1 largely as a result of crab predation on hatchlings; in South Africa 0·1-0·4/nest.
Movements. Palearctic birds winter W Africa, mainly between Guinea and Gabon; usually remain in tropics in 2nd and even 3rd years. Wintering grounds of American populations inadequately known, though some apparently winter on N coast of South America. Birds from NE USA gather in large post-breeding flocks in Aug-Sept, moving N to rich fishing areas on Maine coast; then migrate S, passing offshore, and species is very rare visitor to the Carolinas; common migrant off Trinidad and the Guianas, but winters further S or at sea. Essentially absent from Caribbean Oct-Apr, but wintering grounds uncertain; some recoveries from Guyana suggest wintering somewhere in South America, perhaps mixed with NE birds; a juvenile ringed Long I, New York, recovered on Pacific coast of Colombia. Few sightings in Caribbean Colombia, perhaps of birds from Venezuelan colonies. Adults from NE USA have lingered in Puerto Rico during breeding season, but do not mix with resident *S. dougallii*. E African birds mostly absent Nov-May, may move to S Africa. Winter quarters of most other populations (e.g. of Great Barrier Reef) unknown.
Status and Conservation. Not globally threatened. NE North American and European populations much reduced, and considered endangered; Caribbean population threatened. World population c. 50,000 pairs. In North America numbers peaked before 1950's, declining steadily to mid-1980's, but now stable at c. 3000 pairs. European population declined drastically, and reduced in UK to 57 pairs in 13 colonies by 1991; 1995 was good year in Europe, with over 1700 pairs breeding, mainly in Ireland and Azores. Egging is continual threat and significant cause of mortality in Caribbean and E Africa. In NE South America and W Africa, wintering adults are captured for food by netting, baited hooks, or snaring; this may account for population decline, at least in part. Colonies of *arideensis* have disappeared in Seychelles, and the surviving colony on Aride has declined from 4000 pairs in 1975 to 1000 in 1988, perhaps due to increased long-line fishing. Compared with *S. hirundo*, adults, if trapped for ringing early in incubation, are more likely to abandon nests, and in certain colonies some do not return for hours after release. In Puerto Rico, land crabs (*Gecarcinus*, *Coenobita*) cause heavy chick mortality. On Long I, New York, ants enter pipping eggs and kill hatchlings. Tick infestation sometimes causes abandonment in Seychelles and perhaps E Africa.
Bibliography. Ali & Ripley (1982), Ash & Karani (1981), Austin (1940, 1944), Avery, M.I. *et al.* (1995), Bent (1921), Blake (1977), Braune & Gaskin (1982), Brazil (1991), Britton & Brown (1974), Brooke (1984a), Buckley, F.G. & Buckley (1982), Buckley, P.A. & Buckley (1980, 1981, 1984b), Burger & Gochfeld (1988c, 1988e, 1991d), Burger, Nisbet, Safina & Gochfeld (1995), Burger, Nisbet, Zingo *et al.* (1995), Burggraeve (1977), Coates (1985), Collins & LeCroy (1972), Cooper *et al.* (1970), Cormons (1976), Cramp (1985), Cramp *et al.* (1974), Custer *et al.* (1983), Diamond (1994), Donaldson (1968), Dowsett & Forbes-Watson (1993), Duffy (1986), Dunn (1973b), Dunn & Mead (1982), Gochfeld (1983a), Gochfeld & Burger (1987), Grant & Scott (1969), Guichard (1955), van Halewijn & Norton (1984), Hamilton (1981), Harlow (1971), Hatch (1970), Hays (1975, 1993), Howell & Webb (1995a), Hulsman (1977, 1987), de Juana (1986), Kirkham & Nettleship (1987), Kirkham & Nisbet (1987), Kress *et al.* (1983), Langham (1983), Langrand (1990), LeCroy (1972), LeCroy & Collins (1972), Leroux & Thomas (1989), Maclean (1993), Marchant & Higgins (1996), van Marle & Voous (1988), Marples & Marples (1934), Meininger (1988), del Nevo (1994), Nisbet (1972, 1978a, 1980, 1981a, 1981b, 1984, 1989), Nisbet & Cohen (1975), Nisbet & Drury (1972a), Nisbet, Burger *et al.* (1990), Nisbet, Spendelow & Hatfield (1995), Norton (1988), Olsen & Larssen (1995b), Ramos & del Nevo (1995), Randall & Randall (1978, 1980, 1981), Richards (1990), Robbins (1974), Robertson (1964), Safina (1990a, 1990b), Safina, Burger & Gochfeld (1994), Safina, Burger, Gochfeld & Wagner (1988), Safina, Wagner *et al.* (1990), Serventy, D.L. & Whittell (1976), Serventy, D.L. *et al.* (1971), Serventy, V. & White (1951), Shealer & Burger (1992, 1993, 1995), Shealer & Kress (1994), Shealer & Saliva (1992), Shealer & Zurovchak (1995), Smith, G.C. (1991a), Smith, H.T. (1996), Smythies (1986), Spendelow (1982, 1991), Spendelow & Nichols (1989), Spendelow, Burger *et al.* (1994), Spendelow, Nichols *et al.* (1995), Takeshita (1994), Thomas & Elliott (1973), Trull (1988), Urban *et al.* (1986), Voous (1983), Wagner & Safina (1989), Warman (1979).

11. **White-fronted Tern**

Sterna striata

French: Sterne tara **German**: Weißstirn-Seeschwalbe **Spanish**: Charrán Maorí

Taxonomy. *Sterna striata* Gmelin, 1789, New Zealand.
Sometimes considered monotypic, and validity of races requires study. Three subspecies currently recognized.
Subspecies and Distribution.
S. s. incerta Mathews, 1912 - Flinders I and Cape Barren I, off NE Tasmania.
S. s. striata Gmelin, 1789 - North I, South I and Stewart I (New Zealand).
S. s. aucklandorna Mathews, 1929 - Chatham Is, Auckland Is, and possibly Snares Is.

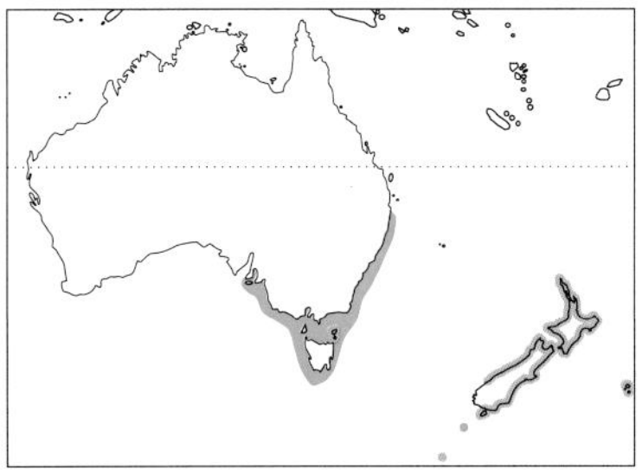

Descriptive notes. 39-42 cm. Crown black, with narrow white forehead and lores; upperparts pale grey, including long tail which extends beyond folded wingtips; underparts white, sometimes with faint pink or rusty tinge to breast; iris brown; bill black; legs dark brownish. Non-breeding adult has more extensive white forehead and white spotting on crown, with black spot before eye; resembles non-breeding *S. hirundo*. Juvenile has brown mottling on upperparts, white streaking on dark nape, blackish outer wing and large black triangular patch on inner forewing. Races differ little in appearance.
Habitat. Coastal areas, nesting on rocky or sandy beaches and shingle islands in rivers, also on coastal cliffs and deserted barges, often close to the surf. Feeds along shore and in bays. In winter, also oceanic.
Food and Feeding. Almost exclusively fish; also shrimps. Feeds in surf zone or several kilometres out to sea, often in flocks. Plunge-dives from 7-10 m, with or without hovering; also feeds by contact-dipping. Frequently victimized by skuas.
Breeding. Laying Oct-Dec. Most colonies contain 100-500 pairs, but solitary pairs reported at margin of range. Some colonies stable for many years, but on Bass Strait islands (*incerta*) frequently changes sites from year to year. Forms a hollow in sand or small rocks, sometimes assembling large nest of plant stems. 1-2 eggs, average 1·54 in Tasmania; incubation unrecorded; chick whitish to brownish, and speckled; brooded for 4-6 days, then may form crèche; fledging 29-35 days; remains dependent for 3-6 months. Storms cause high winter mortality of adults. First breeding at 2 years. Recorded longevity of 20 years.
Movements. Winter visitor to E Australia, from S Queensland to Tasmania and W to South Australia. Some northward dispersal in New Zealand. Race *aucklandorna* recorded as straggler to Campbell I.
Status and Conservation. Not globally threatened. About 500,000 pairs breed in New Zealand. The Bass Strait form, putatively considered a separate subspecies, is rare; its breeding sites were not discovered until 1979, although historical records of eggs from SE Tasmania date back to 1888.
Bibliography. Blakers *et al.* (1984), Chambers (1989), Davis & Mykytowycz (1982), Flegg & Madge (1995), Hindwood (1946), Hitchcock & Favaloro (1951), Imber & Crockett (1970), Lindsey (1992), Macdonald (1988), Marchant & Higgins (1996), Napier (1982), Oliver (1974), Pizzey & Doyle (1980), Robertson (1985), Schodde & Tidemann (1986), Serventy *et al.* (1971), Simpson & Day (1994), Slater *et al.* (1989), Soper (1976), Trounson (1987), Whinray (1980, 1982).

12. **Black-naped Tern**

Sterna sumatrana

French: Sterne diamant **German**: Schwarznacken-Seeschwalbe **Spanish**: Charrán de Sumatra

Taxonomy. *Sterna Sumatrana* Raffles, 1822, Sumatra.

On following pages: 13. South American Tern (*Sterna hirundinacea*); 14. Common Tern (*Sterna hirundo*); 15. Arctic Tern (*Sterna paradisaea*); 16. Antarctic Tern (*Sterna vittata*); 17. Kerguelen Tern (*Sterna virgata*); 18. Forster's Tern (*Sterna forsteri*); 19. Trudeau's Tern (*Sterna trudeaui*).

Thought to be closely related to *S. dougallii*, with which sometimes nests, but chick pattern very different. Sometimes considered monotypic, but divided into races on basis of shape. Two subspecies recognized.

Subspecies and Distribution.

S. s. sumatrana Raffles, 1822 - Andaman and Nicobar Is E to S Japan and China, and S through Malaysia, Philippines, Indonesia and New Guinea to NE & E Australia and Pacific islands (Yap, Marshall Is, Ponapé, Micronesia), with breeding also suspected (at least formerly) in Bengal, Bangladesh and S Myanmar; birds from Japan and China winter to S.

S. s. mathewsi Stresemann, 1914 - Aldabra, Amirante, Chagos and Maldive Is, W Indian Ocean.

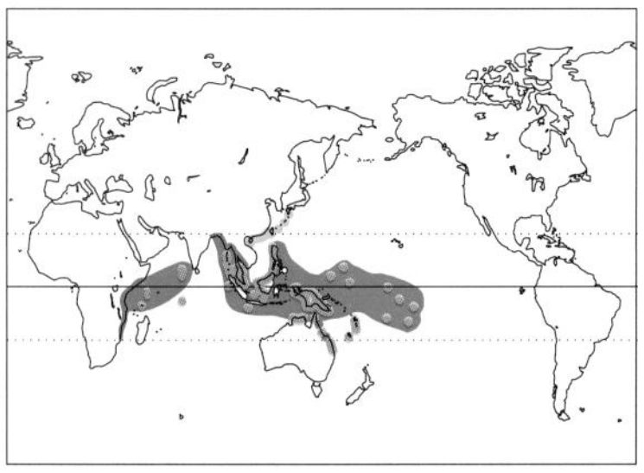

Descriptive notes. 34-35 cm; 98-100 g. Forehead and crown white; black band from eyes around nape, in side view appearing to sweep sharply down back of neck, setting off white crown; upperparts very pale grey; tail white with grey centre, deeply forked; outer web of outermost primary black; underparts white, often with rosy tinge; bill black, occasionally with slight yellow tip; legs black. Non-breeding adult similar, but nuchal band reduced. Juvenile has buffy head mottled with grey or black, black nape, and pale grey upperparts with blackish chevrons; lacks pink tinge below. Race *mathewsi* has shorter wing and longer bill.

Habitat. Frequents small rocky, coral and sandy offshore islands, reefs, sand spits and rocky cays. Feeds in atoll lagoons and close inshore over breakers, but sometimes at sea.

Food and Feeding. Feeds mainly on small fish, 4-8 cm long: Engraulidae, Exocoetidae, Atherinidae, Clupeidae, and secondarily other families (Mugiloididae, Blennidae, Hemiramphidae, Scombridae, Pomacentridae). Almost always forages singly, occasionally in company of *Anous minutus* over predatory fish. Feeds mainly by shallow plunge-diving, also by surface-dipping and occasionally swim-dipping. In N Great Barrier Reef feeds mainly inshore over reef flats; 80% of feeding trips within 2 km of colony.

Breeding. May in India and Polynesia, Sept-Nov in Indian Ocean, Sept in tropical NE Australia, and Nov-Dec on S Great Barrier Reef. Usually forms small colonies of 5-20 pairs, sometimes up to 200 pairs; colonies often monospecific, but may be associated with *S. dougallii* or *S. anaethetus*; not highly synchronous. Nest an unlined depression in sand (Australia) or in gravel or pockets on coral banks (Maldives), close to high tide line, sometimes demarcated with shell or with fragments of coral; sometimes on or next to vegetation. May also nest on artificial structures. 2-3 eggs on Andaman Is, but usually only 1-2 in Indian Ocean and 1 at Cook Is, average 1·5 on Great Barrier Reef; incubation 21-23 days; chick white to yellow-buff, usually with large blackish marks on body and fine blackish spots on head (sometimes unmarked), and reddish orange bill and legs; brooded or shaded for 7 days; adults mob predators and also give plover-like "ungulate" display with upright posture and spread wings. Many nests lost to flooding; typically, 1-20% of eggs result in fledged young.

Movements. Resident around some colonies and disperses to sea from others. Migration routes, if any, not documented. Straggler to Line Is (C Pacific); vagrant to S Africa (*mathewsi*).

Status and Conservation. Not globally threatened. Total population not well known. Thousands nest throughout SW Pacific, which appears to be stronghold of species, but most archipelagos hold only small numbers, and species apparently absent from central islands of S Pacific. Has declined in Malaysian waters, where population now under 2000 pairs. One of commonest seabirds in Indonesia, where c. 50 known nesting sites, each with up to 100 pairs. Species is probably secure because of its many small colonies.

Bibliography. Ali & Ripley (1982), Baker & Boswell (1989), Beehler *et al.* (1986), Brazil (1991), Bregulla (1992), Coates (1985), Diamond (1984), Dickinson *et al.* (1991), Dowsett & Forbes-Watson (1993), Étchécopar & Hüe (1978), Feare (1979b), Hawkins, F. (1993), Holyoak & Thibault (1984), Hulsman (1976, 1977, 1987, 1988), Hulsman & Smith (1988), Langham (1983), Lekagul & Round (1991), MacKinnon & Phillipps (1993), Madoc (1976), Marchant & Higgins (1996), van Marle & Voous (1988), Medway & Wells (1976), Ripley (1982), Serventy *et al.* (1971), Sinclair (1977a), Smith, G.C. (1990, 1991b, 1993), Smythies (1981, 1986), Urban *et al.* (1986), Vesey-Fitzgerald (1941), Walker (1986), Wallace (1966), White & Bruce (1986).

13. South American Tern

Sterna hirundinacea

French: Sterne hirundinacée **German**: Falklandseeschwalbe **Spanish**: Charrán Suramericano

Taxonomy. *Sterna hirundinacea* Lesson, 1831, Santa Catarina, Brazil.
Monotypic.

Distribution. Coasts of S Peru and Espírito Santo (CE Brazil) S to Tierra del Fuego, including Falkland Is. In austral winter extends N to Ecuador and Bahia (CE Brazil).

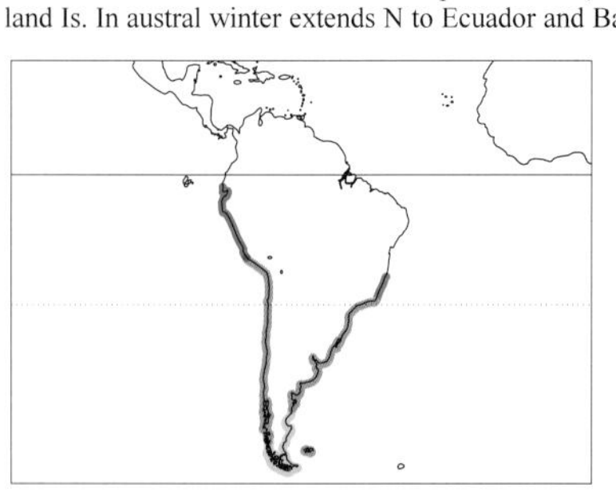

Descriptive notes. 41-43 cm; 172-196 g; wingspan 84-86 cm. A typical *Sterna*, with black cap and pale grey upperparts; underparts pale grey, contrasting somewhat with white cheeks and white undertail-coverts; bill and legs all red. Very similar to *S. hirundo*, but larger, roughly size of *Thalasseus sandvicensis eurygnatha*; has longer bill and tail, and greyer underparts. Non-breeding adult has white forehead and forecrown. Juvenile has creamy white crown with dark mottling; blackish barring on upperparts, particularly on upperwing-coverts; dark grey primaries; whitish tail feathers with dark outer webs; black bill and dirty yellow feet.

Habitat. Almost exclusively coastal. Breeds on sandy and rocky beaches, tops of cliffs, and often on small islands. Non-breeders frequent coastal waters, beaches, estuaries and harbours.

Food and Feeding. Small fish and crustaceans; probably also takes insects. Feeds mostly by plunge-diving. Often follows schools of porpoises or predatory fish.

Breeding. Lays Apr-Jun in Brazil (Espírito Santo to Santa Catarina), early Nov in N Argentina and Uruguay, and early Dec in S Argentina. Forms colonies of dozens to 10,000's of pairs; in dense areas, 3 nests/m². Changes colony site frequently. Forms nest scrape in sand or fine gravel, sometimes surrounded by small shells; often on sandy or gravel spit or beach ridge, occasionally with dense vegetation, but also uses artificial structures. 2-3 eggs; incubation 21-23 days; incubating adults usually not aggressive to human intruders in remote colonies, but mob vigorously in more disturbed colonies; chick very variable, from olive-buff to grey, mottled dark, with black throat and dirty white underparts; fledging 27 days. Hatching success 73%; fledging success 0-58 chicks/pair.

Movements. Present in Tierra del Fuego Nov-Apr, where a few birds remain all year. After breeding, however, most move N along coast to Uruguay, where this is commonest tern; common also in Chubut, S Argentina. In austral winter, ranges N to S Ecuador on Pacific coast and to Bahia, Brazil, on Atlantic coast.

Status and Conservation. Not globally threatened. Total population inadequately documented, and many colonies vulnerable to human disturbance. Abundant breeder on Argentine coast of Chubut, with "tens of thousands of pairs" nesting at Punta Tomba in 1969, compared with estimate of 67,500 nests in 1877. More recent survey data required, particularly because of greatly increased ecotourism. Colony exceeding 1000 pairs rediscovered in S Peru in 1995.

Bibliography. Antas (1991), Bege & Pauli (1988), Belton (1984), Blake (1977), Canevari *et al.* (1991), Clark (1986), Daciuk (1973), Escalante (1970c, 1991), Fjeldså & Krabbe (1990), Hellmayr & Conover (1948), Humphrey *et al.* (1970), Johnson (1967), Koepcke (1970), Murphy (1936), Narosky & Yzurieta (1987), Olmos *et al.* (1995), Olrog (1984), de la Peña (1992), Pinto (1964), Scolaro *et al.* (1996), Sick (1985c, 1993), Tovar (1968), Vooren & Chiaradia (1990), Woods (1988).

14. Common Tern

Sterna hirundo

French: Sterne pierregarin **German**: Flußseeschwalbe **Spanish**: Charrán Común

Taxonomy. *Sterna Hirundo* Linnaeus, 1758, Sweden.
In North America, genetic studies of populations in Minnesota and Wisconsin and ringing studies in NE USA reveal high degree of gene flow, despite colony site tenacity. C Asian *minussensis* often considered to be no more than a hybrid form between nominate *hirundo* and *longipennis*. Four subspecies normally recognized.

Subspecies and Distribution.

S. h. hirundo Linnaeus, 1758 - North America to N South America, Atlantic islands, Europe, N Africa (Tunisia) and W Africa (Mauritania, Senegal, erratically Nigeria), through Middle East and Black and Caspian Seas to Yenisey Valley; winters S of Tropic of Cancer.

S. h. minussensis Sushkin, 1925 - C Asia through Transbaikalia to N Mongolia and S Tibet; winters mainly N Indian Ocean.

S. h. tibetana Saunders, 1876 - W Mongolia S to Kashmir, Tibet and Sichuan, at high altitudes; winters mostly E Indian Ocean.

S. h. longipennis Nordmann, 1835 - NE Siberia S to NE China (C Heilongjiang to Inner Mongolia and Shanxi); winters SE Asia to Australia.

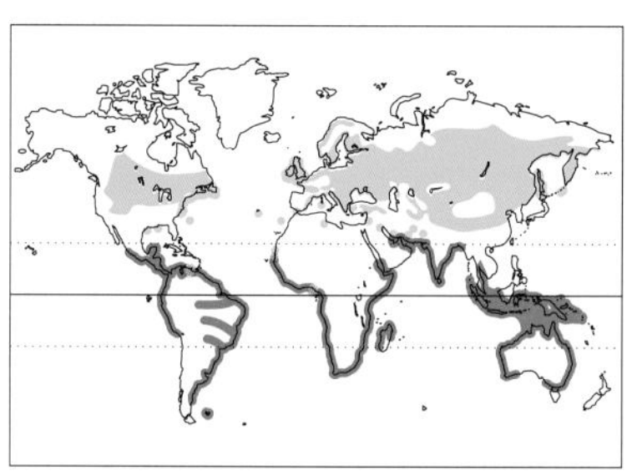

Descriptive notes. 32-39 cm; 97-146 g (average 120-135 g in breeding season, 102 g in winter); wingspan 72-83 cm. Typical tern; forehead and crown black; back and upperwings grey; tail white, with grey outer web to outer rectrices; underparts white with greyish wash, sometimes faintly suffused with pink early in breeding season; bill red with black tip; legs red; long, forked tail reaches wingtips at rest. In all plumages, but especially in summer and autumn, outer 5 primaries have conspicuous dark outer webs, compared with uniform grey upperwing surface of *S. paradisaea*. Non-breeding adult has forehead white, crown black with white streaks, and prominent dark bar on lesser coverts; underparts greyish; bill blackish, with red only at base; legs duller red to blackish red. Juvenile grey above, barred with dark grey or brown; blackish carpal bar on wing (darker than in *S. paradisaea*), and dark secondary bar; bill orange at base, soon becoming dusky grey-brown. In winter, nearly half of birds seen off W Africa are in "*portlandica*" (1st-summer) plumage, with white forehead and black mid-crown and hindcrown, and very worn, dark outer primaries and secondaries. Montane race *tibetana* slightly darker above and below, with shorter bill; *longipennis* has black bill and red-brown to blackish brown legs, but racial identification difficult when mixed with black-billed wintering birds.

Habitat. Breeds in both coastal and inland areas, from sea-level to 4000+ m. Wide variety of habitats including sandy barrier beaches; vegetated inter-dune areas; sandy, rocky, shell or well vegetated islands in estuaries, lakes and rivers; grassy plateaux atop sea cliffs (Madeira). Where co-occurs with *S. paradisaea*, present species uses grassier areas. Adapts to artificial nesting substrates. In Europe, occupies middle reaches or confluences of rivers. Winters mainly on coastal estuaries and up large rivers. Frequents harbours, jetties, piers and beaches.

Food and Feeding. Mainly small fish, particularly *Ammodytes*, *Menidia*, *Fundulus*, *Tautogolabrus*, *Clupea*, *Brevoortia*, *Scomber*; in W Africa mainly *Engraulis*. Occasionally crustaceans, insects and fish offal. Prey availability varies greatly within and between seasons, and this species more opportunistic than *S. dougallii*; when preferred prey (*Ammodytes*) fails, readily switches to other fish. In Italy 91% of fish 6-15 cm. In Ukraine, 83% of regurgitations and stomachs contained fish, and 27% insects. Wintering flocks in C Peru feed mainly over planktonic crustacea; in S Peru mainly by aerial-dipping in wave-washed zone on abundant mole crabs (*Eremita analoga*); in North Carolina, occasionally switches to *Eremita talpoida* when these become superabundant. In NE South America, where food limited (body weights average 99-104 g), relies on human fishing activities for food, and in turn is harvested commercially using small fish as bait. Feeds in dense flocks over ocean, but some maintain individual feeding territories along shorelines. Most forage 5-10 km from colony, but some feed at sea over 15 km from shore. Feeds mainly by plunge-diving, also by contact-dipping and aerial-dipping, and occasionally aerial hawking. Kleptoparasitism common in some colonies or in conditions when food availability limited; often victimized by skuas.

Breeding. Laying mainly Apr-Jun. Mainly colonial, often in thousands, but sometimes solitary. Inland colonies smaller than coastal ones; at N edge of British range, colonies hold fewer than 20 pairs; many colonies of 100-1000 pairs, but up to 6000 pairs; average 263 pairs in Britain, 95 in Virginia, USA; Dutch colonies on Griend held 25,000 pairs until 1955; race *tibetana* usually in small, widely dispersed colonies. Nest spacing ranges from 40 cm (or less with visual barrier) to 5 m; mortality and piracy higher in dense areas. Favours edges of bare sand among moderate vegetation, rocks, or logs, but also uses open substrates with little or no vegetation; on beaches shows preference for nesting beside open area on margin of vegetation, and in marshes prefers edges of mats of dead vegetation, but occasionally on muskrat houses or on floating cattail (*Typha*) mats; on rocky islets, prefers grassy to rocky substrates; readily nests on artificial rafts. Forms shallow depression, sometimes lined and/or with rim of stones, debris, etc., occasionally roofed over with vegetation; often placed near some vertical object such as rock, shell, plant or artifact, which may later provide shelter for chicks and may facilitate nest identification. Clutch and egg sizes depend on food availability; at higher latitudes normally 3 eggs, but usually 2 in poor food years, or at lower latitudes or after heavy storms; average clutch in temperate regions 1·7-2·7, depending on food availability; in W Africa mean 1·5-2·7; in Cuba mean 1·1; older adults lay earlier and larger clutches, and have higher productivity in good food year; chicks from larger eggs have higher survival. Incubation 22-28 days, depending on disturbance; on extremely hot days, adults wet belly feathers to cool eggs; chick buffy brown above with bold black spots (0·5% are immaculate buffy), black chin, and white below, lacking grey cast of *S. paradisaea* chicks; mean hatching weight 14·8 g in New York, 18-21·4 g in Poland; by day 6 chick recognizes parental landing call; fledging 24-28 days. Productivity very variable, from 0 to 2 young/nest; usually higher on beaches, mostly 1·1-1·5/ nest, than on marshes, which are subject to flooding. Annual adult mortality 7-17% in different studies, but sometimes much higher due to viral epizootics in Africa; 8-14% of fledged young are recruited as breeders. Adults tend to return to same colony and subcolony where previously successful; chicks often settle in another colony. Very few breed at 2 years, few at 3, and most at 4. Recorded longevity of 25 years.

Movements. Palearctic birds move S late Aug to Oct, returning in Mar-Apr. European birds pass quickly down NW African coast to winter in W & S Africa; a few may remain off Iberia. Northernmost breeders winter further S. Abundant migrant in NE Africa, mainly from E Europe, with some inland migration through Rift Valley. Birds from Black Sea have been recovered in Somalia. Nominate race common in winter along W coast of S Africa, and a few also reach W Australia. C Asian birds winter mostly on coasts of Indian Subcontinent, and SC Asian *tibetana* winters from E India to Malaysia, a few reaching Natal. Chinese breeders migrate to coasts of China and SE Asia, and NE Asian birds move through Japan and Philippines to New Guinea, Indonesia and Australia. North American birds migrate along Atlantic coast, through West Indies, reaching the Guianas in late Oct, and wintering mostly from Brazil to Argentina; others move to Pacific coast of C America and S to S Peru, some wintering as far N as Gulf of California. Nearctic breeders do occasionally cross the Atlantic: one ringed on Long I, New York, was recovered in W Africa.

Status and Conservation. Not globally threatened. World population at least 250,000, possibly 500,000 pairs: c. 35,000 pairs in E North America, plus 140,000 in Europe; possibly several 100,000's pairs in former USSR. Very sparse breeder in tropical America. Stable in Europe, spreading in some areas and decreasing in others from 1960's through 1980's. Populations greatly reduced in 19th century by egging, hunting and millinery trade, and human development of coastal habitat has eliminated colonies from 19th century to present. Populations recovered with protection, but began to decline again in late 20th century, with loss of many colonies due only partly to habitat development. Many factors implicated in different locations. In parts of W Africa, human predation results in only 12% of chicks fledging. Many colonies jeopardized by flooding, vegetation overgrowth, gull colonization, human disturbance and off-road vehicles, while quarrying of shingle islands reported in Italy. Flooding sometimes leads to complete failures; spring floods often eliminate early nesters. Oiling affected 50% of birds wintering in Trinidad, but did not always result in poor body condition. Pollutants cause eggshell thinning, but are usually not a major contributor to hatching failure. Rat predation on eggs often significant; unusual egg predators include garter snakes (*Thamnophis sirtalis*) and migrating Ruddy Turnstones (*Arenaria interpres*); nocturnal mammalian and avian predators often cause adults to leave, and in addition to predation, some chicks die of chilling. Artificial nesting rafts have proved effective in places where suitable habitat is lacking, or where human disturbance is a problem.

Bibliography. Ali & Ripley (1982), Álvarez & Canet (1983), Austin (1942, 1945, 1947, 1949, 1951, 1953), Becker, P.H. (1984, 1991, 1995), Becker, P.H. & Anlauf (1988a, 1988b), Becker, P.H. & Finck (1985, 1986), Becker, P.H. & Specht (1991), Becker, P.H., Finck & Anlauf (1985), Becker, P.H., Frank & Sudmann (1992), Bergman (1980), Blokpoel, Boersma *et al.* (1989), Blokpoel, Morris & Tessier (1984), Boecker (1967, 1969), Bogliani & Barbieri (1982), Bollinger (1994), Bollinger *et al.* (1990), Borodulina (1953a), Buckley & Buckley (1982), Burger, J. (1982b), Burger, J. & Gochfeld (1985d, 1988e, 1991c, 1991d), Burger, J. & Lesser (1977, 1978, 1979), Burger, J. *et al.* (1988), Burness *et al.* (1994), Butkauskas (1981), Cavanagh & Griffin (1993), Chapdelaine *et al.* (1985), Chestney (1970), Cooper *et al.* (1970), Coulter (1986), Courtney & Blokpoel (1980, 1983), Cramp (1985), Debout & Debout (1988), DiCostanzo (1980), Duffy (1986), Dunlop *et al.* (1991), Erwin (1977a, 1979), Erwin & Smith (1985), Erwin *et al.* (1986), Everhart *et al.* (1980), Fasola (1986), Fasola & Bogliani (1984), Frank (1992), Frank & Becker (1992), Gauzer & Ter-Mikhaelyan (1987), Gemperle & Preston (1955), Gochfeld (1971b, 1975a, 1977a, 1978a, 1978b, 1979c, 1979d, 1981b), Gochfeld & Burger (1987), Gochfeld & Ford (1974), Greenhalgh (1974), Haymes & Blokpoel (1978b), Hays (1975, 1978), Hays & LeCroy (1971), Hays & Parkes (1993), Hilty & Brown (1986), Hoffman (1990), Holt (1994), Hopkins & Wiley (1972), Hume & Grant (1974), Ilicev & Zubakin (1988), Källander (1991), Kasparek (1982), Kirkham & Nisbet (1987), Klaassen (1994), Klaassen *et al.* (1994), Kress *et al.* (1983), Langham (1972), LeCroy & Collins (1972), LeCroy & LeCroy (1974), Lemmetyinen (1971, 1973b, 1973c, 1974, 1976), Lobkov & Golovina (1978), Marchant & Higgins (1996), Massias & Becker (1990), Maxwell & Smith (1983), Melnikov & Sadkov (1977), Mes *et al.* (1978), Mlody & Becker (1991), Morris, R.D. (1986), Morris, R.D. & Hunter (1976), Morris, R.D. & Wiggins (1986), Morris, R.D., Blokpoel & Tessier (1992), Morris, R.D., Kirkham & Chardine (1980), Morris, R.D., Woufle & Wichert (1991), Muselet (1983), Neubauer (1990), Nisbet (1973b, 1978a, 1978b, 1981a, 1983a), Nisbet & Cohen (1975), Nisbet & Drury (1972a), Nisbet & Welton (1984), Nisbet *et al.* (1984), Olsen & Larssen (1995b), Onno (1965), Palmer (1941), Post & Gochfeld (1978), Richards & Morris (1984), Ricklefs & White (1981), Roberts, T.J. (1991), Rowan (1962), Safina (1990a, 1990b), Safina & Burger (1985, 1988, 1989), Safina, Burger, Gochfeld & Wagner (1988), Safina, Wagner *et al.* (1990), Safina, Witting & Smith (1989), Saino & Fasola (1993), Sellin (1983), Severinghaus (1982), Storey (1987a, 1987b), Stromar (1967/68), Switzer *et al.* (1971), Taylor, I.R. (1983), Tinbergen (1931, 1938, 1940), Urban *et al.* (1986), Walters, J. (1979, 1985), Waltz (1987), Wiggins (1989), Wiggins & Morris (1986, 1987, 1988), Wiggins *et al.* (1984), Yuan (1993).

15. **Arctic Tern**

Sterna paradisaea

French: Sterne arctique **German**: Küstenseeschwalbe **Spanish**: Charrán Artico

Taxonomy. *Sterna Paradisaea* Pontoppidan, 1763, Christiansø Islands, Denmark.
Listed as *S. macrura* in many older works. Monotypic.

Distribution. Iceland, Britain and Netherlands through Scandinavia, and across Asia, almost exclusively N of Arctic Circle, to Bering Strait, with isolated breeding sites in Kamchatka, and northernmost breeding area in Franz Josef Land; Aleutians and N Alaska across to NW & NE Greenland, and S to British Columbia and New York, with isolated colony in NW Washington. Migrates to Antarctica, where spends much of N winter in pack ice zone.

Descriptive notes. 33-36 cm; 86-127 g; wingspan 76-85 cm. Forehead and crown black; rest of plumage rather uniform grey, including underparts, but with narrow white cheeks and white rump and tail, latter with very long streamers; underparts slightly duller grey, extending onto throat and setting off white cheek; outer primaries have inner webs grey, with narrow black line along tips; more pale on secondaries, resulting in a translucent "window" in flight; bill usually completely bright red, but rarely with dark tip; legs red. Very similar to *S. hirundo*, but darker below, with narrower wings and longer tail streamers, shorter legs and shorter bill; lacks dark "wedge" on primaries shown by *S. hirundo*. Similar to *S. vittata*, but is not in breeding plumage when they co-occur. Plumage pattern intermediate between *S. hirundo* and *S. repressa*, and pale cheek can also suggest differently structured

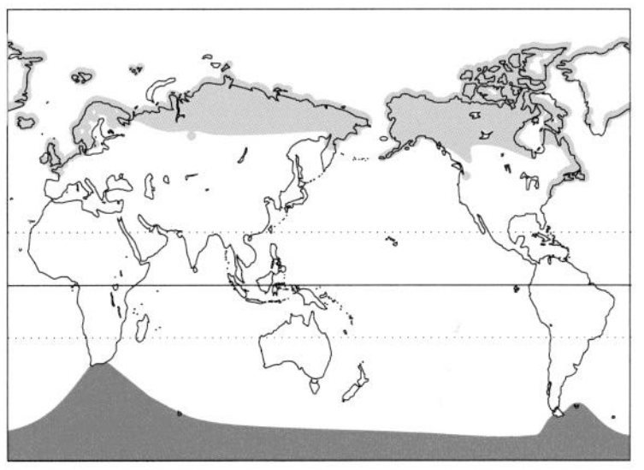

Chlidonias hybridus. Non-breeding adult has white forehead, and sometimes shows dark carpal bar like *S. hirundo*; bill and legs blackish. Juvenile has dark mantle and upperwing (including greater coverts), with broad white area on secondaries and inner primaries; carpal bar paler and greyer than in *S. hirundo*; bill blackish with pinkish base, becoming all blackish by time birds migrate.

Habitat. Temperate to high Arctic regions, mainly coastal, but also far inland. Nests on shingle beaches, gravel ridges (preferring sandy pockets), earth dykes, bog hummocks, tundra, lichen-covered rocks, barren fields, peat moss, grassy meadows, and islands in lakes and coastal lagoons; also on inland heath or pasture. Vegetation cover ranges from less than 5% to 40%. Prefers more barren areas than *S. hirundo*, and where both occur together it occupies rocky shore more than grassy heath. Fishes in ice-filled bays and offshore, and over wet tundra and ponds. In winter more pelagic than *S. hirundo*, ranging from open sea to pack ice zone. Often seen resting on flotsam.

Food and Feeding. Mainly small fish; also crustaceans, molluscs and insects; amphipods and euphausiids important in certain areas. In early spring occasionally feeds on berries; readily accepts fish offal and even bread; also takes caterpillars off grass, or lands to pick up earthworms. In Finland increasingly reliant on chironomids, which are now increasing in number owing to eutrophication. Many studies indicate diverse diet, with fish predominating. In E North America, chicks fed mainly sandeels (*Ammodytes*) up to 9 cm long and capelin (*Mallotus villosus*), but at Petit Manan (Maine) main fish fed to chicks were various clupeids. In Iceland and N Europe, chicks fed mainly sticklebacks (*Gasterosteus aculeatus*), but also locally crustaceans (*Gammarus*, *Thysanoessa*). In Britain, at Farne Is, 95% fish, mainly sandeels and herring (*Clupea harengus*), while at Coquet I clupeids became more important as season advanced. In Murmansk, adults had more varied diet (only 50% fish) than chicks (88% fish). When preferred prey (*Ammodytes*) fails, does not readily switch to alternative prey. Very varied foraging methods: hovers and plunge-dives for fish, and hover-dips for fish fry; takes chironomids by flying at height of c. 2 m and dipping to water surface, catching up to 20 prey/minute. Also feeds from perch near water or by surface-dipping. Kleptoparasitism infrequent, but pirates from Atlantic Puffins (*Fratercula arctica*) on Faeroes; often a victim of piracy from skuas and *S. hirundo*. Has daily feeding cycles, even in continuous daylight; some feeding occurs at night when prey close to surface. Feeds mainly within 3 km of colony, but up to 20 km and occasionally 50 km from colony.

Breeding. Laying May-Jun in S of range, Jul in N; varies also with temperature and food availability. Colonies range from few pairs to 300, mostly 5-25; occasionally solitary, but in Baltic 10% of nests solitary; fewer than 2% of colonies exceed 1000 pairs. Often changes sites from year to year, but some colonies persist many years; some birds have strong territory fidelity. Will nest on artificial structures. Forms a shallow scrape, often unlined; nests often more than 10 m apart, but occasionally less than 1 m. 2-3 eggs, average 1·4-2·9, lower on offshore islands and in high Arctic, and in years with food scarcity; incubation 22-27 days; chick usually brownish (oceanic coasts) or usually grey (Baltic), with greyish cast to belly, compared with immaculate white underparts of downy *S. hirundo*; hatching weight 14 g; fledging 21-24 days. Chick survival influenced mainly by hatching sequence and number of siblings, and also by egg size and hatching weight. Productivity reports variable, c. 0·23-1·25 young/pair; productivity increases until age c. 9, then declines. First breeding usually at 4 years, rarely 3 or 5; 3-year-olds unsuccessful. 1st-year survival 80·5%, adult 87-88%. Recorded longevity of 34 years.

Movements. Renowned for exceptionally long and unparalleled migrations between high Arctic breeding sites and Antarctic wintering grounds. Birds from Finnish archipelago depart in Jul; high Arctic birds may linger until mid-Sept. Most migration well offshore. From Siberia and W North America, moves S through E Pacific. Southbound migrants in Atlantic move SE, and juveniles reach W Africa by Aug; some remain off equatorial Africa through winter. Reaches S Africa by Oct, and many continue ESE to edge of pack ice in Nov. Crossing of Antarctic sea aided by westerly winds which drift some birds E in Southern Ocean. Many winter in Antarctic pack ice between Magnet Bay and Oates Land, with some reaching W to Weddell Sea. Accidental in S South America and New Zealand. Return migration mostly in W Atlantic, but mainly offshore. Rare in West Indies and Gulf of Mexico. Common migrant off S Africa (Oct-Nov and May), including both Nearctic and Palearctic birds.

Status and Conservation. Not globally threatened. Widespread colonies at high latitudes in North America and Eurasia, and species common along most of Greenland coast, but many populations have apparently declined. Has increased in many parts of Scandinavia, however, partly due to reduction in egging. Total population may be 500,000 pairs, including several 100,000's in former USSR, 100,000 in Iceland, 20,000 in Norway, c. 44,000 in Britain (of which c. 66% in Orkney and Shetland) and 2500 in Ireland. Nearctic population not censused: Alaskan coastal population estimated at 12,500, but inland population may be much greater. Species remains vulnerable because of dietary habits, and there are some episodes of mortality from red tide. Recent massive declines in N Britain attributed to collapse of stocks of sandeels, the terns' staple food there (see page 642). On N shore of Gulf of St Lawrence, populations of both this species and *S. hirundo* experienced 5·7% growth from 1977 to 1982, but only 0·4% growth over the next 6 years. In N Atlantic, Svalbard population may be vulnerable to oil, particularly in post-breeding period.

Bibliography. Abraham & Ankney (1984), Ali & Ripley (1982), Andersen (1959), Anzigitova & Zubakin (1975), Austin (1940), Avery *et al.* (1992), Belopol'skii *et al.* (1977), Bengtson (1971), Bergman (1980), Bianki (1967), Blake (1977), Boecker (1967), Borodulina (1960), Braune & Gaskin (1982), Buckley & Buckley (1984b), Bullock & Gomersall (1981), Burton & Thurston (1959), Busse, K. & Busse (1977), Busse, K.V. (1983), Camphuysen (1991a), Chapdelaine *et al.* (1985), Coulson (1987), Coulson & Horobin (1976), Craik & Becker (1992), Craik & Harvey (1984), Cramp (1985), Cramp *et al.* (1974), Cullen, J.M. (1957, 1960b), Debout & Debout (1988), Dementiev & Gladkov (1951b), Devillers (1978a), Dircksen (1932), Dowsett & Forbes-Watson (1993), Drent *et al.* (1992), Drury (1960), Evans, P.G.H. (1984a), Evans, R.M. & McKnicholl (1972), Ewins (1985b), Fairall (1995), Feare (1969), Finnlund *et al.* (1985), Fjeldså (1975), Grant & Scott (1969), Grant *et al.* (1971), von Haartman (1982), Harrison (1984a), Hawksley (1957), Hopkins & Wiley (1972), Howell & Webb (1995a), Hume & Grant (1974), Ilicev & Zubakin (1988), Johnson (1967), de Juana (1986), Källander (1991), Kaverkina (1983, 1984, 1986a, 1989), Kaverkina & Roschevski (1984), Kilpi *et al.* (1992), Kirkham & Nisbet (1987), Klaasen (1994), Klaassen & Bech (1992), Klaassen, Bech, Masman & Slagsvold (1989), Klaassen, Bech & Slagsvold (1989), Klaassen, Habekotte *et al.* (1994), Langham (1972, 1983), Lee & Cardiff (1993), Lemmetyinen (1971, 1972, 1973a, 1973b, 1973c, 1974, 1976), Lemmetyinen *et al.* (1974), Manuwal *et al.* (1979), Marchant & Higgins (1996), Marples & Marples (1934), Monaghan, Uttley & Burns (1988, 1992), Monaghan, Uttley & Okill (1989), Murphy (1938), Norderhaug (1964), Olsen & Larssen (1995b), Onno (1965), Parmelee & MacDonald (1960), Pettingill (1939), Quine & Cullen (1964), Radford (1985), Richards (1990), Salomonsen (1967a, 1967b), Serventy *et al.* (1971), Sick (1993), Skipnes & Slagsvold (1984), Urban *et al.* (1986), Uttley (1992), Uttley, Monaghan & White (1989), Uttley, Tatner & Monaghan (1994), Villaseñor & Phillips (1994), Volet (1994), Wuorinen (1992).

16. **Antarctic Tern**

Sterna vittata

French: Sterna couronnée **German**: Antarktikseeschwalbe **Spanish**: Charrán Antártico

Taxonomy. *Sterna vittata*, Gmelin, 1789, Kerguelen Island.
Birds of St Paul and Amsterdam Is sometimes included in nominate *vittata*; further study required. Six subspecies recognized.
Subspecies and Distribution.
S. v. tristanensis Murphy, 1938 - Tristan da Cunha, Gough, and possibly Amsterdam and St Paul; single breeding report from South Africa questioned, but based on a ringing recovery.
S. v. georgiae Reichenow, 1904 - South Georgia; birds of South Orkney Is, South Sandwich Is and Bouvetøya I possibly of this race.
S. v. gaini Murphy, 1938 - South Shetland Is; presumably this race breeds S to Marguerite Bay on Antarctic Peninsula.
S. v. vittata Gmelin, 1789 - Prince Edward I, Marion I, Crozet Is, Kerguelen Is, and (probably this race) Heard I.
S. v. bethunei Buller, 1896 - Stewart I, and Snares Is, Auckland Is, Bounty Is, Antipodes Is and Campbell I.
S. v. macquariensis Falla, 1937 - Macquarie I.
Sometimes said to breed (*vittata*) on Ascension and St Helena, but almost certainly erroneous.

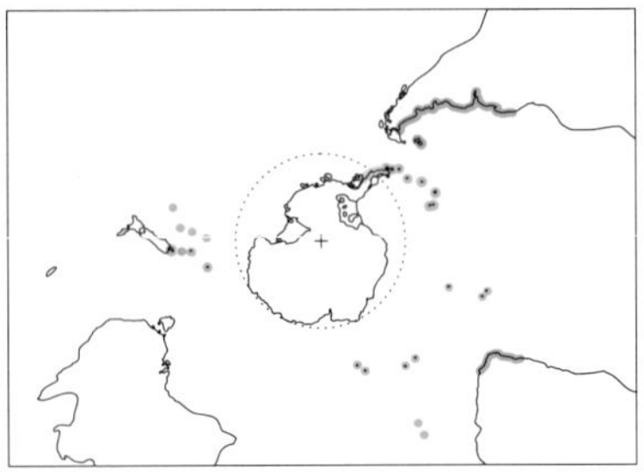

Descriptive notes. 35-40 cm; 150-180 g (average summer 167-170, winter 197-205 g; *bethunei*, Campbell I, 114-171 g); wingspan 74-79 cm. Forehead to nape black; upperparts pale grey, with contrasting white rump and forked tail; variably grey to black outer web to outer primary; grey-white below, with white undertail-coverts; eye brownish black; bill and legs red. Distinguished from *S. paradisaea* (which, in same region, is normally in winter plumage) by longer legs, and shorter tail with paler webs to outer feathers. Separated from *S. virgata* by white, rather than smoky grey, uppertail-coverts and underwing. Non-breeding adult similar, but forehead white, crown streaked with white, and underparts white; bill and legs variable, from reddish black to dull red. Juvenile has white forecrown streaked with black, and dark brownish grey to blackish hindcrown; grey above, with heavy black and buff bars; white below with finer barring; bill and legs black. Scaly dark tips to feathers wear quickly, hence juvenile plumage changes without moult. 1st-years have white forehead, whiter underparts and dull reddish black bill. Races vary in size and plumage tone: *gaini* largest, followed by *tristanensis*, with *georgiae* smallest but long-winged; upperparts darkest on Kerguelen I (nominate *vittata*) and palest in Antarctica (*gaini*).
Habitat. Rocky islets, with or without vegetation. Often near other seabirds. Often nests on cliffs, but also gravel and rocky beaches, and on Auckland Is sometimes in sparse scrub. Formerly sandy beaches on Tristan da Cunha, but after rats introduced shifted to ledges on offshore stacks. In Bounty and Snares Is nests solitarily on cliff ledges, since sea lions pre-empt flat areas; on Amsterdam I, 200 pairs breed on coastal cliffs inaccessible to cats. Outside breeding season, seeks ice edges in Antarctica, and in South Africa frequents rocky headlands and beaches.
Food and Feeding. Diet almost exclusively small fish (particularly nototheniids) in some places; polychaetes and limpets at Heard I; mainly crustaceans at Kerguelen and Campbell; fish and euphausiids in Antarctica; fish, euphausiids and amphipods at Snares. Occasionally takes insects, scavenges in intertidal zone, or follows boats for offal. Forages mainly in inshore waters, singly or in flocks. Obtains food mainly by plunge-diving. May defend good feeding grounds. Feeding significantly impaired by high wind or seas; plunge-dives over calm water, but switches to contact-dipping in rougher water.
Breeding. Mainly Nov-Dec, with some variation depending on climate and food availability: Oct-Nov in Snares, Nov-Jan on Campbell, Nov in Antarctica, Dec-Feb on Marion and Crozets, Feb-Mar in Antipodes; on Kerguelen I nests Dec-Feb, whereas *S. virgata* nests Oct-Dec. Forms loose colonies of 5-20 pairs, occasionally 40, often solitary, but in S Shetlands several colonies exceed 1000 pairs. Nest a depression or scrape in rock, cliff ledge, soil, sand or vegetation mat, often with pits of pebble or shell. 1-2 eggs (1 on Kerguelen, 2 in Antarctica); incubation 23-25 days; chick buffy with heavy black spots above, greyish white below, throat dark grey, bill flesh to blackish, and feet pale flesh to reddish black; fledging 27-32 days; some post-fledging parental feeding. Productivity low on Heard I; inadequately studied elsewhere. Skuas kill adults, and many chicks die from exposure to harsh weather. Some eggs lost to gulls and skuas, and sometimes destroyed by conspecifics.
Movements. Adults and young leave nesting area shortly after young fledge. Some populations remain close to breeding grounds (e.g. Snares, Anvers I). In some places 1st-year birds found near colony. Post-breeding flocks may migrate long distances from S part of range, being absent Apr-Oct. Race *georgiae* common non-breeding visitor to South America; arrives mid-Apr and moults, then leaves mid-Oct. Birds from Antarctica moult on breeding grounds. Race *tristanensis* also winters in South Africa, where *vittata* vagrant. Vagrant to Australia.
Status and Conservation. Not globally threatened. Total population unknown, but must be c. 50,000 pairs, including: 35,000 in South Shetlands, with one colony of c. 9000 pairs at Livingston I; 3000 in South Orkneys; and 2500 on South Georgia. Some archipelagos have tiny populations. Endemic race on Macquarie I, estimated at 40 pairs, must be considered endangered owing to frequent reproductive failures due to human disturbance and domestic and feral cats.
Bibliography. Bailey & Sorensen (1962), Berrutti & Harris (1976), Blake (1977), Brooke (1984a), Chambers (1989), Cooper (1976b), Courtenay-Latimer (1957), Croxall, Prince *et al.* (1984), Dowsett & Forbes-Watson (1993), Escalante (1970c), Favero *et al.* (1991), Garnett (1993), Ginn *et al.* (1989), Johnson (1967), Jouventin (1994), Kaiser (1995, 1996), Liversidge (1957), Mackworth-Praed & Grant (1962), Maclean (1993), Marchant & Higgins (1996), Murphy (1936, 1938), Obst (1985), Parmelee (1988b), Parmelee & Maxson (1975), de la Peña (1992), Rounsevell & Brothers (1984), Sadleir *et al.* (1986), Sagar (1978, 1991), Sagar & Sagar (1989), Sick (1993), Stahl & Weimerskirch (1982), Teague (1955), Urban *et al.* (1986), Watson (1975), Williams *et al.* (1979).

17. **Kerguelen Tern**

Sterna virgata

French: Sterne de Kerguelen **German**: Kerguelenseeschwalbe **Spanish**: Charrán de las Kerguelen

Taxonomy. *Sterna virgata* Cabanis, 1875, Kerguelen Island.
Some authors have separated Crozet birds as race *mercuri*, based on more restricted grey forehead in non-breeders and subtle soft-part distinctions. Monotypic.
Distribution. S Indian Ocean close to Antarctic Convergence at Kerguelen Is, Prince Edward and Marion Is, and Crozet Is; reported breeding on Heard I erroneous; sympatric with *S. vittata*, but different phenology and feeding niche. Non-breeders remain close to breeding areas throughout year.

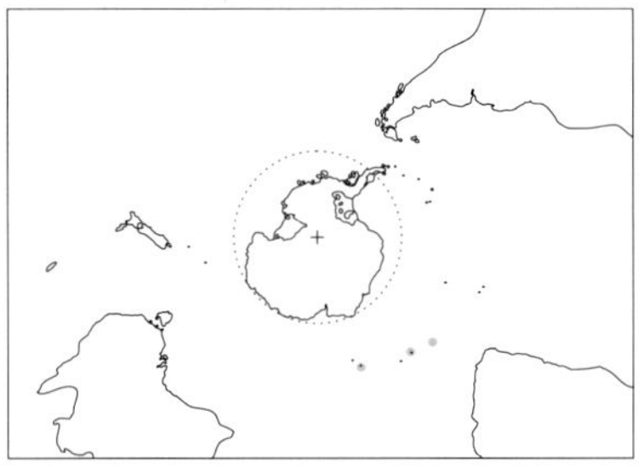

Descriptive notes. 33 cm; wingspan 71 cm. Forehead to nape black; upperparts, including uppertail-coverts, smoky grey, with contrasting white rump; outer tail streamers grey, tail greyish; smoky grey below, becoming white on undertail-coverts; white cheek and moustachial area contrasts strongly with grey chin and throat; grey underwing-lining diagnostic, and narrow black trailing edge of primaries; at rest tail does not extend beyond folded wing; bill deep red; feet bright orange (Crozet Is) to dull red (Kerguelen). Separated from *S. vittata* by slightly smaller size, with shorter bill and wings, darker plumage, and grey, rather than white, uppertail and underwing-coverts. Non-breeding adult has bill dull reddish (Crozets) to black (Kerguelen); birds acquire white forehead by Feb, moult beginning during incubation. Juvenile like that of *S. vittata*, finely vermiculated grey, brown and buff, with broad pale and dark bars.
Habitat. Rocky, volcanic islands. Breeds on sparsely vegetated flat ground, either cliff tops or river flats, occasionally close to beach. Non-breeders feed mainly in inshore waters around islands.
Food and Feeding. Fish, crustaceans, molluscs, earthworms, insects and spiders. Diet changes seasonally from mainly crustaceans in Sept, fish in Nov, insects in Dec, to fish in Jan-Feb. In courtship feeding, small fish 50%, crustaceans 14%, insects 36%. Chicks fed mainly on spiders, insects, crustaceans, molluscs and earthworms, at period when *S. vittata* has arrived and is feeding mainly on fish. Feeds alone, or in flocks of up to 20 or more. Fish caught by aerial contact-dipping (83%) and plunge-diving, in inshore waters and around kelp (*Macrocystis*); sometimes walks on kelp to capture invertebrates. Amphipods taken by wading in tide pools. Inland flocks of up to 50 birds feed on insects snatched from vegetation in flight (90%), or by walking. High winds frequently interfere with feeding.
Breeding. Virtually unstudied. Returns to colony in Sept, and begins laying mid-Oct, continuing until Jan; peak breeding early Nov to mid-Dec, 2 months before *S. vittata* nests. Small colonies of up to 30 pairs (mean 8·1), with some solitary pairs, usually more than 200 m from sea. Nests widely scattered; mean nearest-neighbour distance 36 m. Aggressive to intruding skuas. Display repertoire similar to that of *S. hirundo* and *S. vittata*. Nests on moss or grass, assembling stones and twigs, sometimes near high tide line, but often on slopes above beach, occasionally well inland; scrape often lined with plant material. 1 egg on Crozets, 1-2 on Marion, 2 on Kerguelen; incubation 24 days; chick tan with irregular black spots above, buffy below with dark brown chin; brooded for 5 days, then hides in rocks or vegetation near nest; fledging 31-39 days (shorter for earlier chicks), followed by 20 days of dependence. Hatching success in 3 years 73-88%. High mortality of late-hatching chicks through starvation.
Movements. Sedentary. Remains around breeding sites. Movement away from islands not documented.
Status and Conservation. VULNERABLE. One of the most threatened tern species, with no truly secure colony. World population probably not more than 2400 pairs, unless there is an as yet unknown breeding area. About 50 pairs on Prince Edward I, 75 on Marion I, 150-200 in Crozet Is, and up to 2000 in Kerguelen Is. Large population of feral cats on Kerguelen is main potential threat. Salmonid fish introduced into Kerguelen rivers should assist by providing additional food supply. Species requires study and management.
Bibliography. Berruti & Harris (1976), Brooke (1984a), Collar & Andrew (1988), Collar *et al.* (1994), Despin *et al.* (1972), Falla (1937), Jouventin *et al.* (1988), Milon & Jouanin (1953), Murphy (1938), Paulian (1953), Prévost & Mougin (1970), Sagar (1991), Stahl & Weimerskirch (1982), Thomas, T. (1983), Watson (1975), Weimerskirch & Stahl (1988), Weimerskirch *et al.* (1989), Williams *et al.* (1979).

18. **Forster's Tern**

Sterna forsteri

French: Sterne de Forster **German**: Forsterseeschwalbe **Spanish**: Charrán de Forster

Taxonomy. *Sterna Forsteri* Nuttall, 1834, Saskatchewan River.
Monotypic.
Distribution. British Columbia S to C Californian coast and E to S Ontario, Great Lakes and N Indiana; New York (Long I) to North Carolina; Gulf Coast, from Alabama to Tamaulipas, NE Mexico. Winters from S California to Panama, and from North Carolina to Gulf of Honduras.

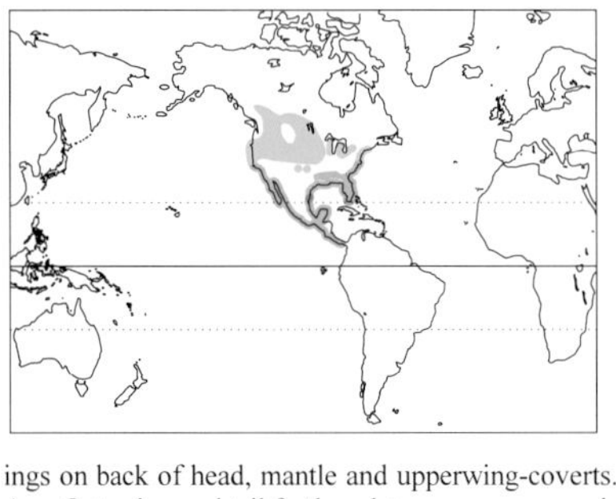

Descriptive notes. 33-36 cm; 127-193 g; wingspan 73-82. Forehead to nape black; upperparts pale grey, underparts white; bill usually distinctly orange-red, not vermilion, and with black tip; legs orange-red; in flight, upper primaries notably pale, silvery-white, contrasting with wing-coverts. Differs from *S. hirundo* in slightly shorter wings and rather paler plumage, especially primaries, which lack dark "wedge" of *S. hirundo*; most easily recognized by its more nasal, lower-pitched calls. Non-breeding adult distinctive: white head and hindneck, with bold black ear patch and dusky nape, and black bill. Juvenile greyish brown, with pale brown markings on back of head, mantle and upperwing-coverts. Head and body moult into 1st-winter plumage Aug-Oct, wing and tail feathers later; appears very similar to non-breeding adult, except for pale grey nape and dark tip to outer tail feathers.
Habitat. Wetlands. Breeds mainly at freshwater lakes, potholes, inland and coastal marshes and salt-pond dykes, rarely on sand, mud or rocky islets. Nests among floating and emergent vegetation, optimal habitat being dense mats at least 5 m across in at least 30 cm of water. Feeds over lakes, streams and estuaries, favouring water less than 1 m deep.
Food and Feeding. Mainly small fish (5-7 cm), also aquatic insects and crustaceans. On Californian coast, mainly shiner perch (*Cymatogaster aggregata*) and northern anchovy (*Engraulis mordax*) up to 10 cm. In South Carolina in winter, mainly menhaden (*Brevoortia tyrannus*) and anchovy (*Stolephorus*). Feeds mainly by plunge-diving or dipping to surface. Sometimes dives from a perch, kingfisher-like, which has twice the energy return of plunge-diving, but is not always an available method. Feeding efficiency enhanced under light wind conditions, rather than dead calm. Sometimes maintains feeding territories.
Breeding. Apr-May on Gulf Coast, to late May elsewhere. Forms loose colonies of 5-250 pairs, rarely more; sometimes solitary. Fairly high turnover rates. Nest a depression in floating vegetation; 98% of

nests on large muskrat (*Ondatra zibethica*) lodges where these are available; also on boards, infrequently (but increasingly) on dredge spoil, sand or fine shell, and occasionally on coarse gravel islands (Washington). May assemble a nest of grass and sedge or horsetail on dry mud or grassy hummocks; uses higher, dryer and larger sites than *Chlidonias niger* in same marsh; in salt-marshes relies mainly on wrack, building taller nests on lower sites than *S. hirundo*, but re-laying sooner, with larger clutches and higher hatching success, if initial nest flooded. Nests sometimes widely spaced, depending on available surfaces; usually 3-20 m apart, but on muskrat houses as close as 20 cm and on salt-marsh 50 cm apart. Adults recognize nest-site rather than eggs. Mean clutch size 2·8; incubation 23-26 days; chick similar to that of *S. hirundo*, but with darker, more discrete black spots. Nest losses due mainly to flooding, and to mink (*Mustela vison*) predation, muskrat activity, and spawning carp (*Carassius*); 12-36% of nests successful in one study. Aggressive reactions of Yellow-headed Blackbirds (*Xanthocephalus xanthocephalus*) help terns deter predators. Productivity very variable, from total failure to c. 1·4 young/nest. In one study, 58% of chicks survived at least 5 days. Colonies on Great Lakes have much lower hatching success, negligible productivity, and more developmental defects than nearby inland colonies.

Movements. Following northward post-breeding dispersal, migrates S. Birds breeding on Pacific coast winter from S California to Costa Rica and Panama. Great Plains birds migrate mainly overland, and winter mostly on Gulf Coast. Atlantic coast breeders winter from S Virginia to Costa Rica and in Caribbean; occasionally found N to New England in winter.

Status and Conservation. Not globally threatened. USA population exceeds 14,000 pairs, but numbers in Canada and Mexico not known. Atlantic coast population totals c. 6000 pairs; Gulf Coast population centred on Louisiana, where colonies of nearly 3000 pairs have been found; W and Great Plains population has not been censused. Species has extended range northwards in recent decades: in 1950's, bred N only to Virginia, but is now an uncommon breeder in a few colonies in S New Jersey, and a marginal breeder in New York, where first recorded nesting in 1981. In Great Lakes, number of nests at L St Clair and L Huron increased in early 1980's from 100 to 850. With loss of coastal marsh habitat, some birds have shifted to dredge-spoil islands. Reproductive failure in Great Lakes attributed in part to contamination by PCB's (see page 643).

Bibliography. Baltz *et al.* (1979), Bent (1921), Bergman *et al.* (1970), Blake (1977), Blokpoel & Scharf (1991b), Buckley & Buckley (1984b), Cave (1982), Clapp & Buckley (1984), Cramp (1985), Fox *et al.* (1991), Goossen *et al.* (1982), Hall (1988, 1989), Hall & Miller (1991), Harrison (1984a), Howell & Webb (1995a), Kubiak *et al.* (1989), Martin & Zwank (1986), McNicholl (1979, 1981, 1982, 1983), Monroe (1968), Neuchterlein (1981), Ohlendorf *et al.* (1988), Olsen & Larssen (1995b), Portnoy (1977), Reed (1985), Reed & Ha (1983), Reed *et al.* (1982), Richards (1990), Ridgely & Gwynne (1989), Root (1988), Salt & Willard (1971), Scharf & Shugart (1984), Schwartz & Satlling (1991), Stiles & Skutch (1989), Storey (1987b).

19. Trudeau's Tern
Sterna trudeaui

French: Sterne de Trudeau **German**: Weißscheitel-Seeschwalbe **Spanish**: Charrán Coroniblanco
Other common names: Snowy-crowned Tern

Taxonomy. *Sterna Trudeaui* Audubon, 1838, Great Egg Harbor, New Jersey (probably in error). Monotypic.

Distribution. Coast and interior of South America, breeding from SE Brazil and Uruguay to Patagonia, rarely to Santa Cruz, and in Chile (Aconcagua to Llanquihue).

Descriptive notes. 35 cm; 146-160 g; wingspan 76-78 cm. Head and upper neck white, with black spot in front of eye and dark band behind; upperparts and upperwings pale grey, with whitish rump and uppertail-coverts; underparts greyish white; iris dark brown; bill yellow, with broad subterminal black band; feet reddish orange. Like non-breeding *S. forsteri*, but latter has all black bill and dusky nape. Non-breeding adult similar, but with stripe on side of head greyer. Juvenile has back and scapulars patterned with dark and white markings, dark carpal bar, tail feathers with dark subterminal mark, bill black, and legs dark with yellowish webs. Immature creamy white.

Habitat. Fresh and saline wetlands, both inland and coastal. Breeds on vegetated lagoons of *pampas* and Patagonia, mainly in marshes, but also on dykes and islands in saline lagoons. Feeds at wetland edges, and also over fields.

Food and Feeding. Small fish and insects. In Chile, feeds mainly on pejerrey (*Austromenidia laticlavia*). Forages over shallow clear water on edges of lagoons, rivers and estuaries, but also over ploughed fields. Plunge-dives for fish.

Breeding. Virtually no data published. Recorded Oct in N, Nov in Buenos Aires, Dec in Chubut. One colony in a lagoon held 30-40 nests. Often nests with Brown-hooded Gulls (*Larus maculipennis*), in densely vegetated marshes. Builds floating platform of plant stems, free or anchored to emergent vegetation, in water 10-150 cm deep. 3 eggs (2-4); adults vigorously attack and even strike intruders. Productivity not studied, but one report of 55 adults accompanied by 37 juveniles in Dec.

Movements. Outside breeding season, ranges N on Pacific coast to S Peru, and on Atlantic coast to Rio de Janeiro region. Some linger as far S as Chubut into Jul. Accidental in Straits of Magellan. Considered abundant on coast of Uruguay and at mouth of R de la Plata in Mar; numerous on Buenos Aires *pampas* in Sept-Feb, but less common during austral winter.

Status and Conservation. Not globally threatened. Status not well known, and no trends documented. In Brazil no colonies known, although breeding activities observed in Rio Grande do Sul, and species common in lagoons along coast. Does not nest on small lakes, so maintenance of largest freshwater wetlands essential. Loss of wetland habitat and lack of protection of existing wetlands are potential major problems. In Chile, uncommon from Aconcagua to Llanquihue.

Bibliography. Antas (1991), Belton (1984), Blake (1977), Canevari *et al.* (1991), Clark (1986), Contreras *et al.* (1990), Donahue & Petersen (1980), Escalante (1970c, 1991), Gibson (1920), Hellmayr & Conover (1948), Johnson (1967), Klimaitis & Moschione (1987), Meyer de Schauensee (1982), Murphy (1936), Narosky & Yzurieta (1987), Olmos *et al.* (1995), Olrog (1984), de la Peña (1992), Pinto (1964), Sick (1985c, 1993), Teague (1955), Vooren & Chiaradia (1990).

PLATE 56

inches 6

cm 15

20. **Little Tern**

Sterna albifrons

French: Sterne naine **German**: Zwergseeschwalbe **Spanish**: Charrancito Común

Taxonomy. *Sterna albifrons* Pallas, 1764, Netherlands.
Forms nearly cosmopolitan superspecies with *S. saundersi*, *S. antillarum*, *S. superciliaris*, *S. lorata* and probably also *S. balaenarum*, all of which formerly placed in separate genus *Sternula*. Some works treat *S. antillarum*, and sometimes *S. saundersi*, as conspecific with *S. albifrons*. Validity of races *innominata* and *placens* questionable. Apparent hybridization with *S. nereis* in S Australia indicates close relationship; long-term study of relationships required. Six subspecies recognized.

Subspecies and Distribution.
S. a. albifrons Pallas, 1764 - Europe through W Asia E to Nepal, and presumably this race also in Kenya (breeding at L Turkana), and in W Indian Ocean (Seychelles and Comoro Is, where resident, but breeding not confirmed); winters on coasts from Africa E to W India.
S. a. guineae Bannerman, 1931 - Ghana to Gabon, with marginal population in Mauritania and Senegal which may be this race or nominate.
S. a. innominata Zarudny & Loudon, 1902 - islands in Persian Gulf.
S. a. pusilla Temminck, 1840 - NE India and Myanmar, islands off Sumatra and Java, and probably this race in Sri Lanka.
S. a. sinensis Gmelin, 1789 - SE Russia, China, Japan, SE Asia, Philippines and New Guinea; recent colonist to Micronesia (Saipan) E to Hawaii most likely this race, and possibly also some birds in Australia, New Britain and nearby waters; N populations mostly winter in Malaysia.
S. a. placens Gould, 1871 - E Australia and E Tasmania.

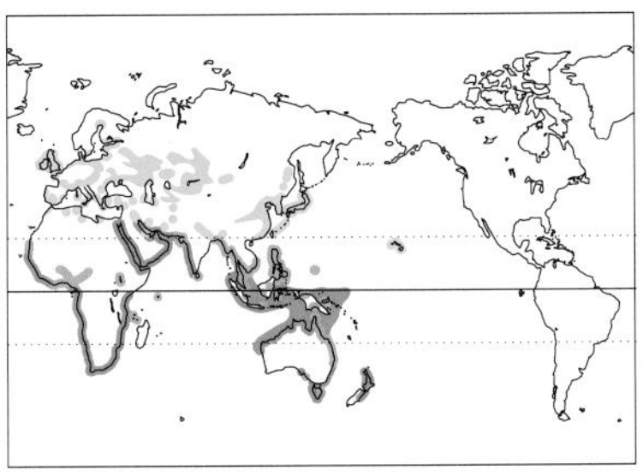

Descriptive notes. 22-28 cm; 47-63 g (average 50 g, Ukraine); wingspan 47-55 cm. Archetypical small tern: small, with white forehead, black cap and lores, grey back and wings, white rump, and white underparts; bill bright yellow with small dark tip; legs and feet orange-yellow to yellow. Differs from *S. saundersi* in white of forehead reaching behind eye, less black on primaries, and usually brighter yellow legs. Separated from *S. nereis* mainly by black, not white, lores (black from eye to bill base), and by black tip to bill; apparent hybrids have black on lores reaching almost to bill, and very small black bill tip. Non-breeding adult has pale-streaked forecrown, white lores with black spot before eye, dark lesser coverts, and blackish bill and legs. Juvenile has black chevrons on mantle; paler secondaries and inner primaries contrast with darker wing-coverts and outer primaries. 1st-winter plumage acquired Oct, when similar to non-breeding adult. Races differ little; shafts of outer 3 primaries dark brown to brownish white in nominate, but white in *pusilla* and *sinensis*.
Habitat. Subtropical to temperate regions, reaching altitude of 2000 m in Armenia. Continental populations mainly coastal, but also inland along rivers; also on oceanic islands. Breeds on barren or sparsely vegetated sandy, shell, rocky and coral islands, shingle beaches, spits in estuaries and lakes, salt-marshes, salt-pans and rivers, and on reefs. Occasionally in grassy areas or on bare mud. Outside breeding season, frequents tidal creeks, coastal lagoons and salt-pans; sometimes feeds far out to sea.
Food and Feeding. Mainly small fish and crustaceans (3-6 cm), also insects, annelids and molluscs. Main fish sandeels (*Ammodytes*), roach (*Rutilus rutilus*), rudd (*Scardinius erythrophthalmus*), carp (*Cyprinus carpio*), perch (*Perca fluviatilis*). Insects mainly Orthoptera, Odonata, Diptera, Coleoptera. In Crimea 91% of birds had eaten fish, but in neighbouring Sivash (Ukraine) 99% had eaten insects and only 54% fish. Some studies show 90% crustaceans brought to young (S England). Forages by quartering back and forth over water; specializes in prolonged hovering and plunge-diving into shallow water, often at edge of advancing tide. Groups of birds may dive synchronously. Takes insects from vegetation and water surface by aerial-dipping. Also hawks for small flying insects over water. In Italy, most birds foraged within 3 km of colony.
Breeding. Apr in W Africa, May-Jun in Europe and India, May-Aug in Sri Lanka. Usually in small to medium-sized colonies; 42% of 1-5 pairs, only 5% of 40+ pairs; rarely over 100 pairs. Forms synchronous subcolonies, usually monospecific. Vegetation cover usually less than 15%, though occasionally nests in shelter of bushes; sometimes on floating objects, e.g. buoys, abandoned concrete structures, also on roofs in some areas. Nest usually bare, but in marshes builds on platforms of shell or vegetation. Distance between nests usually over 2 m, often much more, but sometimes only 0·6-1 m. Clutch 2-3 eggs (1-4); incubation 21-24 days; chick creamy-grey or white with sparse or dense black spots; hatching weight 6·5 g; reported to recognize parents' voices on day 1; up to 63 feeds/day recorded: fledging 20-24 days. Average age of first breeding 3 years, occasionally 2. Recorded longevity of 21 years.
Movements. N breeders migrate S from late Aug. Those from W & C Europe spend Nov-Mar on African coasts, mainly in Gulf of Guinea area, but ranging to South Africa and even Kenya. Birds from E Europe and SW Asia migrate to Red Sea and Arabian Sea to E Africa, thousands congregating on passage in inlets in SW Caspian Sea when fish fry abundant. Breeders from Caspian Sea region move to Persian Gulf and W India, while E Asian birds migrate S to SE Asia and winter in the seas of Malaysia to Philippines. Some of those nesting in Australia winter in waters around Indonesia and New Guinea.
Status and Conservation. Not globally threatened. World population c. 70,000-100,000 pairs, but many local populations declining. In former USSR c. 50,000, increasing in E but decreasing in W; in Europe c. 11,000 and decreasing, with large numbers in Italy and Netherlands, and estimated c. 5500-6000 pairs in Spain and 2430 pairs in Britain; few 100's of pairs in W Africa (Mauritania, Senegal); 800-1150 pairs in Iran. Faces many adversities: many coastal beaches have been developed, and mainland breeding sites vulnerable to human disturbance, rats and cats; direct damage and disturbance by humans are main factors accounting for recorded decline. Human intrusion, including birdwatchers, causes nest failures. Many predators in colonies, especially various gulls, corvids, and even *S. hirundo*. Marked declines in Britain and W Europe due to human impact on beaches; range contracting in C Europe, but less change in Scandinavia. In Italy 20% of colonies have suffered human disturbance, and in Crimea many nests lost to destructive children, cattle and gulls. Some apparent range extensions: colonized South Australia in late 1960's; in 1988, discovered nesting in Saipan and Hawaii.
Bibliography. Ali & Ripley (1982), Baker (1928a), Beaman (1994), Beehler *et al.* (1986), Beijersbergen (1991), Bogliani & Barbieri (1982), Borodulina (1960), Brazil (1991), Bregnballe *et al.* (1990), Briain & Farrelly (1990), Calado (1996), Chambers (1989), Chandler & Wilds (1994), Clancey (1982c), Clapp (1989), Coates (1985), Conant *et al.* (1991), Cooper (1971), Cox & Close (1977), Cramp (1985), Cramp *et al.* (1974), Davies (1981), Deignan (1945), Dementiev & Gladkov (1951b), Dickinson *et al.* (1991), Dowsett & Dowsett-Lemaire (1993), Dowsett & Forbes-Watson (1993), Eckert (1970), Elgood *et al.* (1994), Eminov (1964a), Étchécopar & Hüe (1964, 1978), Evans (1994), Everett (1980), Fasola (1986), Fasola & Bogliani (1984, 1990), Fasola & Canova (1992), Fasola & Saino (1990), Fasola, Bogliani *et al.* (1989), Fasola, Goutner & Walmsley (1989), Feare & Bourne (1978), Garnett (1993), Ginn *et al.* (1989), Glutz von Blotzheim & Bauer (1982), Goodman *et al.* (1989), Gore (1990), Goutner (1990), Grimes (1977, 1987), Haddon & Knight (1983), Hitchcock (1959), Holloway (1993), Hüe & Étchécopar (1970), Ilicev & Zubakin (1988), de Juana (1986), Kanai & Isobe (1990), Knystautas (1993), LaTour (1973), Lekagul & Round (1991), Lloyd, C. *et al.* (1991), Lloyd, C.S. *et al.* (1975), MacKinnon & Phillipps (1993), Mackworth-Praed & Grant (1957, 1962, 1970), Maclean (1993), Madoc (1976), Marchant & Higgins (1996), van Marle & Voous (1988), Marples & Marples (1934), Massey (1976), Mead (1973), Medway & Wells (1976), Meininger (1988), Muselet (1983, 1985, 1990), Norman (1992), Olsen & Larssen (1995a, 1995b), Ortali (1977), Patrikeev (1995), Paz (1987), Perennou (1991), Perennou *et al.* (1994), Phillips (1978), Pitman (1967), Reichel *et al.* (1989), Richards (1990), Ripley (1982), Rittinghaus (1964), Roberts, T.J. (1991), Saino & Fasola (1990, 1993), Schonert (1961), Serventy *et al.* (1971), Sharland (1938), Shirihai (1996), Short *et al.* (1990), Smythies (1981, 1986), Soikkeli (1962), Thomas, G.J. (1980), Thomas, G.J. *et al.* (1989), Toba (1989), Tomialojc (1994e), Urban *et al.* (1986), White & Bruce (1986).

21. **Saunders's Tern**

Sterna saundersi

French: Sterne de Saunders **German**: Orientseeschwalbe **Spanish**: Charrancito de Saunders
Other common names: Black-shafted Tern

Taxonomy. *Sterna Saundersi* Hume, 1877, Karachi. Forms a superspecies with *S. albifrons*, *S. antillarum*, *S. superciliaris* and *S. lorata*. Sometimes considered conspecific with *S. albifrons*. Monotypic.
Distribution. Breeds in Red Sea (N to at least Yanbu) S to Socotra and S Somalia and off Saudi Arabia and Oman, along coasts of Persian Gulf and locally E to NW India; Sri Lanka, mainly in NW & E; large numbers throughout year at Addu Atoll (Maldives), where probably breeds in Apr with other terns, and probably also on Amirantes and possibly Seychelles. Winters from Red Sea S to Tanzania and Madagascar and E to India, and probably in Seychelles and off Malaysian Peninsula.

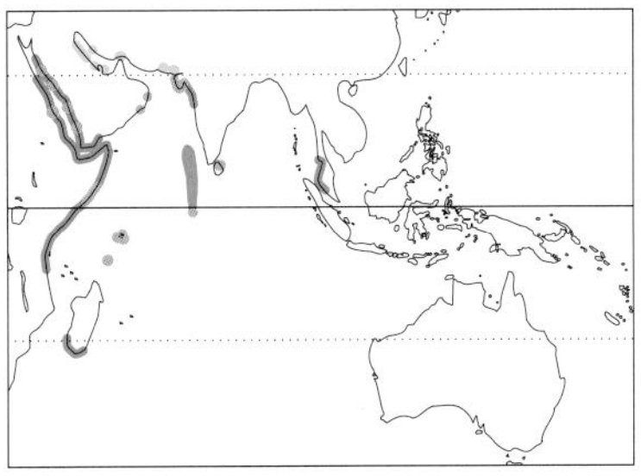

Descriptive notes. 20-28 cm; 40-45 g; wingspan 50-55 cm. Extremely similar to *S. albifrons*, from which distinguished by: straight upper border to white forehead (white does not reach behind eye); slightly paler grey upperparts, contrasting more with blackish outer primaries; grey rump same colour as mantle, whereas usually much paler in *S. albifrons*; legs and feet dusky yellow-olive, rather than orange-yellow; 3-4 outer primaries black, with black shafts, whereas *S. albifrons* usually has only 2 outer primaries dark, brownish to grey-black, with 2-3 brownish shafts. Non-breeding adult darker above, often darker than *S. albifrons*, otherwise very similar. Juvenile virtually identical to that of *S. albifrons*, but may have darker bar on secondaries.
Habitat. Coasts, estuaries, and tidal lagoons; rare inland.
Food and Feeding. Small fish, crustaceans and molluscs; also various insects. Feeds mainly by plunge-diving, often preceded by long bouts of hovering.
Breeding. Very few data available. Season May in Karachi and Sri Lanka. Forms small, sparse colonies; nests 20-100 m apart. Nest-site above high tide line, or on mudflats; prefers small mounds of wind-blown sand around a plant or other object. Nest is a hollow or an animal footprint, bare or lined with shall fragments and small pebbles. Lays 2 pale eggs. No further information available.
Movements. Movements not well understood. Non-breeders seen in Red Sea N to Gulf of Aqaba, and S along E African coast to N Tanzania, as well as Madagascar and along W coast of India, in Gujarat, Bombay, also Laccadives and Maldives; probably this species also in Seychelles. Uncommon to very rare non-breeding visitor to S Thailand, Malay Peninsula and Straits of Malacca. Research needed.
Status and Conservation. Not globally threatened. Not at all well known: population figures unknown, and even colony inventory not available; Iran thought to hold 130-150 pairs. Species probably frequently overlooked, due to considerable difficulties in identification. Stated to be abundant in Karachi area. Colonies vulnerable to most of same adversities as those facing *S. albifrons*.
Bibliography. Ali & Ripley (1982), Ash & Miskell (1983), Beaman (1994), Bregnballe *et al.* (1990), Chandler & Wilds (1994), Cramp (1985), Dowsett & Dowsett-Lemaire (1993), Dowsett & Forbes-Watson (1993), Evans (1994), Feare (1979a), Gallagher *et al.* (1984), Goodman *et al.* (1989), Harrison (1983b), Hüe & Étchécopar (1970), Langrand (1990), Mackworth-Praed & Grant (1957), Medway & Wells (1976), Milon *et al.* (1973), Olsen & Larssen (1995a, 1995b), Perennou *et al.* (1994), Phillips (1978), Rands *et al.* (1987), Richards (1990), Ripley (1982), Roberts, T.J. (1991), Shirihai (1996), Short *et al.* (1990), Smythies (1986), Ticehurst (1924), Urban *et al.* (1986).

22. **Least Tern**

Sterna antillarum

French: Petite Sterne **German**: Amerikanische Zwergseeschwalbe **Spanish**: Charrancito Americano

Taxonomy. *Sternula antillarum* Lesson, 1847, Guadeloupe, Lesser Antilles.
Forms superspecies with *S. albifrons*, *S. saundersi*, *S. superciliaris* and *S. lorata*. Long considered a race of *S. albifrons*, but recently separated mainly on basis of voice. Currently accepted polytypic arrangement disputed by findings of morphometric and biochemical analyses. Proposed form *mexicana* for birds of Pacific coast of Mexico is not separable. Three subspecies recognized.
Subspecies and Distribution.
S. a. browni Mearns, 1916 - C California (San Francisco Bay) to Baja California and W Mexico; winters mostly in Central America.
S. a. athalassos Burleigh & Lowery, 1942 - inland rivers in C North America, from N Great Plains to N Louisiana and Texas; winters to N Brazil.
S. a. antillarum (Lesson, 1847) - Bermuda, and Maine S to Texas (including lower Rio Grande Valley) and Honduras, and on through Caribbean to N Venezuela; winters to N Brazil.
Descriptive notes. 22-24 cm; 39-52 g (New York 44-52 g, average 47·4 g); wingspan 51 cm. Very similar to *S. albifrons*, with white forehead, black cap, grey upperparts and white underparts; differs marginally in greyer rump and tail, and more clearly inflected disyllabic contact call. Bill bright yellow with black tip; legs yellow to orange, sometimes with greyish or pinkish tinge. Non-breeding adult and juvenile much as *S. albifrons*, but adult has grey rump and tail, and juvenile has stronger brown scaling

On following pages: 23. Yellow-billed Tern (*Sterna superciliaris*); 24. Peruvian Tern (*Sterna lorata*); 25. Fairy Tern (*Sterna nereis*); 26. Damara Tern (*Sterna balaenarum*); 27. White-cheeked Tern (*Sterna repressa*); 28. Black-bellied Tern (*Sterna acuticauda*); 29. Aleutian Tern (*Sterna aleutica*); 30. Grey-backed Tern (*Sterna lunata*); 31. Bridled Tern (*Sterna anaethetus*); 32. Sooty Tern (*Sterna fuscata*); 33. Black-fronted Tern (*Sterna albostriata*).

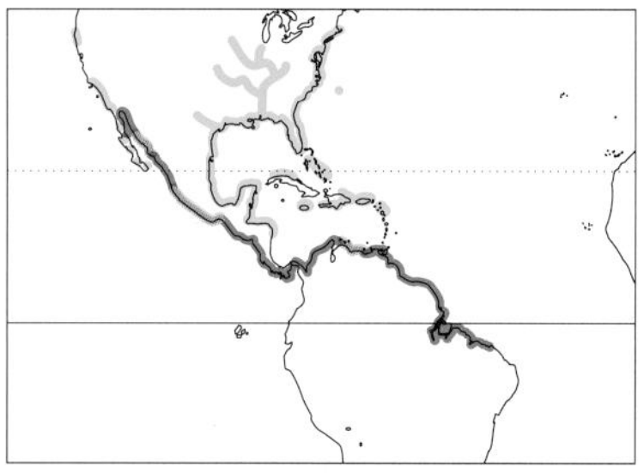

on upperparts and bolder lesser-covert bar. 1st-summer birds have conspicuous dark carpal bar, and either black bill, white forecrown and black eyestripe and nape ("*portlandica*"), or yellowish bill and white flecking on blackish crown ("*pikei*"). Races poorly differentiated; *browni* deeper grey above, greyish white below, and frequently lacks black tip to bill.

Habitat. Lakes, rivers and estuaries; Californian and E populations generally strictly coastal, though some nest inland in Florida. Breeds on barren or sparsely vegetated sandy beaches or islands, gravel, sand or shell bars, dry mudflats, dredge-spoil islands, dykes, parking lots; also roof tops, now predominant site in Florida; more recently, in sandpits inland. Forages over quiet waters of lagoons, marshes and estuaries; occasionally beyond surf zone.

Food and Feeding. Small fish fry on breeding grounds. Also shrimps, marine worms, and occasionally flying ants and other insects. Feeds mainly by plunge-diving from up to 10 m, often preceded by prolonged hovering. Occasionally performs surface-dipping and aerial hawking. Often feeds within few hundred metres of colony.

Breeding. Apr in Florida and Texas, May in West Indies and California, May-Jun in NE USA, May-Jul in S Caribbean; mid-Jun in interior (when floodwaters recede). Usually in monospecific colony or subcolony of 5-200 pairs, but up to 1500 on Long I and 3000+ in Mississippi. Nests 3-20 m apart, occasionally less than 1 m; in interior often more than 100+ m, or even solitary. Prefers sand mixed with shell or gravel, and slightly elevated ridges; on vegetated beaches nests further from vegetation than random, but converse true when cover less than 5%. Slight scrape, often in bare sand, occasionally near object such as a shell, rock or stick. Clutch 1-3 eggs, (1-3), usually 2 in tropics; average 1·6-2·2 in New York, 2·1-2·5 in Mississippi and interior USA, 1·7-2·2 in California, 1·6 in Cuba. Incubation 19-24 days (report of 14-16 days erroneous), eggs unattended 11% of time in undisturbed colonies; chick greyish white or buffy (66% buffy, Mississippi), and immaculate (less than 15%, New York; 37%, Mississippi) to heavily spotted; fledging 17-21 days. Productivity very variable, 0·2-1·5 per pair; many total failures through flooding. Average adult annual survival 85-92%; adults have c. 9·5 breeding seasons. First breeding at 2 or 3 years. Longevity 21 years.

Movements. Highly migratory. Pacific breeders arrive late Apr, and return in Aug to coasts of W Mexico and Central America. Interior and E birds migrate to Caribbean and N South America, wintering mainly off Brazil. Substantial inter-colony exchange from year to year, even when original colony persists. Nominate race accidental inland.

Status and Conservation. Not globally threatened. All races vulnerable. Due to taxonomic split from *S. albifrons*, status should be re-examined. Race *browni* (800 pairs, 1994) and *athalassos* (under 1000 pairs) considered endangered. Nominate *antillarum* population in E USA estimated at 21,500 pairs in 300 colonies, with 3000-3600 pairs on Long I (New York) in mid-1980's; but has declined greatly in many areas owing to beach development and severe recreational pressure; intensive protection and management have stabilized some populations. Vulnerable to disturbance by trapping (for ringing and patagial tagging). Many avian and mammalian predators documented; ants and ghost crabs (*Ocypode quadrata*) kill chicks, and Fish Crows (*Corvus ossifragus*) eliminate all chicks in some colonies. Mississippi coastal population thriving, however, since mid-1970's, with up to 7000 pairs. Many natural habitats are being lost, while in Florida changing roof surfaces from gravel to plastic threatens established colonies. Decoys effective in attracting adults to protected beaches. Chick-shelters both protect against and facilitate predation, and must be studied at each colony prior to use. Intensive site-protection, management and wardening has increased New Jersey population. Interior population has suffered habitat loss through managed water levels connecting islands to mainland, or through flooding; many sandbars degraded, but birds now shifting to sandpits when available; current productivity in Mississippi River Valley sufficient to maintain population. Protection of habitat essential.

Bibliography. Ainley & Hunt (1991), Alleng & Whyte-Alleng (1993), Altman & Gano (1984), Álvarez & Canet (1983), Armistead (1985, 1989), Atwood (1986), Atwood & Kelly (1984), Atwood & Massey (1982, 1988), Atwood & Minsky (1983), Avery, M.L. *et al.* (1995), Bent (1921), Biaggi (1983), Blake (1977), Blodget (1978), Blus & Prouty (1979), Boyd & Thompson (1985), Buckley & Buckley (1984b), Burger, J. (1984d, 1988d, 1989), Burger, J. & Gochfeld (1990a), Burger, J. *et al.* (1994), Butchko (1990), Caravacho *et al.* (1989), Cardiff & Remsen (1994), Carreker (1985), Chandler & Wilds (1994), Clapp & Buckley (1984), Colón (1982), Cowgill (1989), Davis (1974), Densmore (1990), Downing (1973), Ehrlich *et al.* (1992), Engstrom *et al.* (1990), Everett & Anderson (1991), Faanes (1983), Fisk (1978a, 1978b), Gochfeld (1973b, 1977b, 1983b), Gore (1991, 1996), Gore & Kinnison (1991), Grover & Knopf (1982), Hagar (1937), van Halewijn & Norton (1984), Hardy (1957), Harrison (1984a), Haverschmidt (1968), Haverschmidt & Mees (1995), Hill (1985), Hill & Talent (1990), Hilty & Brown (1986), Howell & Webb (1995a), Jackson (1976), Jackson & Jackson (1985), Jackson & Key (1992), Jenks-Jay (1980), King (1978/79), Kotliar & Burger (1984, 1986), LeCroy (1976), Linz *et al.* (1990), MacLean *et al.* (1991), Massey (1974, 1976, 1977), Massey & Atwood (1978, 1981), Massey & Fancher (1989), Massey, Bradley & Atwood (1992), Massey, Keane & Bordman (1988), Meyer de Schauensee & Phelps (1978), Monroe (1968), Moseley (1979), Nisbet (1973a), Olsen & Larssen (1995b), Palacios & Mellink (1996), de la Peña (1992), Renken & Smith (1995a, 1995b), Richards (1990), Ridgely & Gwynne (1989), Schwalbach (1988), Schulenberg *et al.* (1987), Sick (1985c, 1993), Sidle & Kirsch (1993), Sidle *et al.* (1992), Slud (1964), Smith & Renken (1991, 1993), Snyder (1966), Stiles & Skutch (1989), Swickard (1972), Thompson & Slack (1982, 1984), Thompson *et al.* (1992), Tomkins (1942, 1959), Tostain *et al.* (1992), Voous (1963), Wetmore (1965), Whitman (1988), Wilbur (1974a), Wolk (1974).

23. **Yellow-billed Tern**

Sterna superciliaris

French: Sterne argentée **German**: Amazonasseeschwalbe **Spanish**: Charrancito Amazónico
Other common names: Amazon Tern

Taxonomy. *Sterna superciliaris* Vieillot, 1819, Paraguay.
Forms superspecies with *S. albifrons*, *S. saundersi*, *S. antillarum* and *S. lorata*. Monotypic.
Distribution. E Colombia E to the Guianas and S to NE Peru and on to C Argentina (Buenos Aires).
Descriptive notes. 23 cm; 40-57 g. Very similar to *S. antillarum*, but with stouter, entirely yellow bill, lacking dark tip. Subadult has yellowish bill with dark horn-brown tip, and greyish crown with black streaks, whereas subadult *S. antillarum* usually has wholly black bill and conspicuous blackish carpal band. Juvenile has ochraceous forehead, lores and crown, with dark streaking and dark auricular area; upperparts greyish, with pale buffy markings, and with dark subterminal marks on each feather; dark carpal bar.
Habitat. Broad rivers. Breeds mainly on riverine sandbars and lake beaches, in mixed colonies with Black Skimmers (*Rynchops niger*) and *Phaetusa simplex*; more restricted to large rivers than *Phaetusa*; feeds mainly over shallow shoals on large rivers, often concentrating at tributary mouths. In Brazil, breeds mainly along inland rivers and lakes, sparingly at river mouths on coast; in Argentina along R Uruguay, R Paraná and R Pilcomayo to NE Buenos Aires; in Uruguay commonly on lakes and rivers, uncommonly along coast. Non-breeders mainly on coast and estuaries, also various water bodies, from rice fields to brackish lagoons.

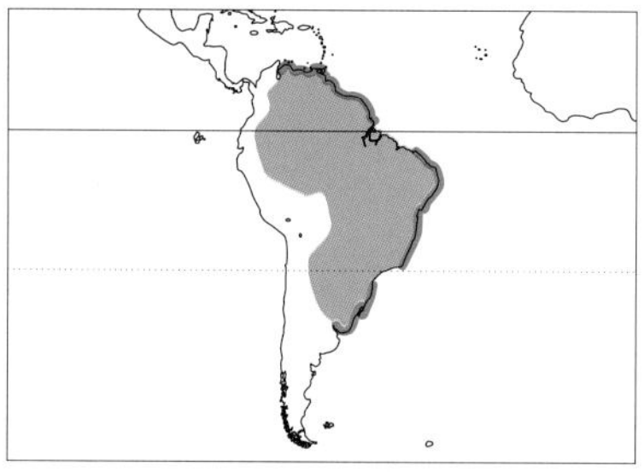

Food and Feeding. Small fish (7-45 mm), shrimps and insects; sometimes predominantly insects (Peru). Often feeds by hovering and plunge-diving from 3-8 m into shallow water, usually close to shore. Usually feeds alone.
Breeding. Virtually unstudied. Nov in Surinam, Dec in Uruguay, Jul in Peru; timing dependent on exposure of riverine sandbars in dry season. Colonies of up to 20 pairs, more often 3-10; nests widely spaced, often more than 50 m apart, frequently solitary. 2-3 eggs, average 1·94. Productivity 1·04/nest; flooding is main cause of egg loss.
Movements. Unknown. Main movement is apparently along river valleys to coasts, where non-breeders congregate.
Status and Conservation. Not globally threatened. No population figures available, and status and trends virtually unknown. Main threats are flooding and human disturbance, latter significant on some beaches.

Bibliography. Antas (1991), Belton (1984), Blake (1977), Canevari *et al.* (1991), Contreras *et al.* (1990), Davis (1935), Escalante (1970b, 1970c, 1991), Groom (1992), Haverschmidt (1968, 1972a), Haverschmidt & Mees (1995), Hayes (1995), Hellmayr & Conover (1948), Herklots (1961), Hilty & Brown (1986), Klimaitis & Moschione (1984), Krannitz (1989), Meyer de Schauensee & Phelps (1978), Murphy (1936), Olmos *et al.* (1995), de la Peña (1992), Preston (1962), Remsen (1990), Ridgely & Gwynne (1989), Sick (1985c, 1993), Snyder (1966), Teague (1955), Tostain *et al.* (1992), Vooren & Chiaradia (1990), Willard (1985).

24. **Peruvian Tern**

Sterna lorata

French: Sterne du Pérou **German**: Peruseeschwalbe **Spanish**: Charrancito Peruano

Taxonomy. *Sterna lorata* Philippi and Landbeck, 1861, Arica, Chile.
Forms superspecies with *S. albifrons*, *S. saundersi*, *S. antillarum* and *S. superciliaris*. Monotypic.
Distribution. Humboldt Current zone, from C Ecuador (Guayaquil) to N Chile (Tarapacá).

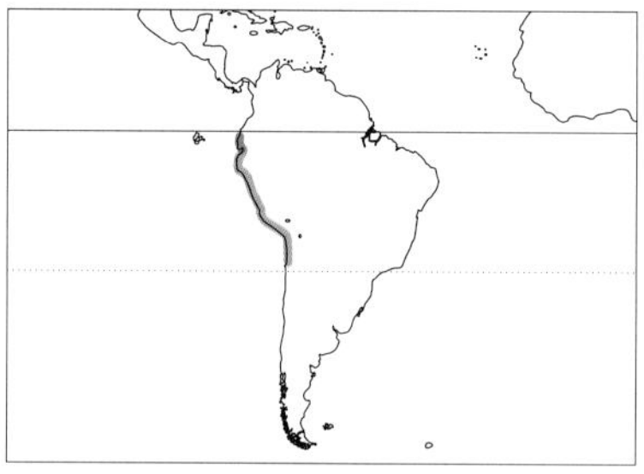

Descriptive notes. 22-24 cm. Typical small tern: white forehead extending over eye, contrasting with black cap and lores; pale grey upperparts; dark outer primaries; pale greyish white sides of neck and underparts; yellow bill tipped black, dark yellow legs. Non-breeding adult has crown streaked with white. Juvenile has broad dark brown face mask from lores to ear-coverts; buffy underparts; beige upperparts with bold black chevrons on lesser coverts, less pronounced on greater coverts; blackish primaries; dark-tipped flesh-coloured bill and flesh-coloured legs.
Habitat. Coastal. Breeds on broad sandy beaches and sand dunes, often more than 1000 m from tide-line; and on barren stony desert several kilometres inland.
Food and Feeding. Mainly small fish, particularly anchovetta (*Engraulis ringens*); c. 10% of diet is krill (*Euphausia*). Feeding methods similar to those of allospecies.
Breeding. Oct-Jan (mainly Nov); full-grown juveniles in mid-Feb. Semi-colonial to solitary; nests more than 50 m apart in sparse colonies of 2-15 pairs on back beaches and on desert plains. Scrape on unvegetated flats, usually near some object such as stone, shell, bone, stick. 1-2 eggs; incubation 22-23 days; chick pale grey, finely spotted black on head and back; hatching weight 6-7 g. Many eggs disappear; usually only 1 chick raised. May skip nesting in El Niño years.
Movements. Unknown, but returns to colony sites in mid-Oct.
Status and Conservation. Not globally threatened. Status very poorly known; species probably rather rare. Estimated maximum population in Peru 5000 pairs. Potential predators include Peregrine Falcon (*Falco peregrinus*), grey fox (*Dusicyon culpaeus*), and skunk (*Conepaetus rex*). Vulnerable to egg loss. Unattended nests may quickly be buried by sand.

Bibliography. Blake (1977), Devillers & Terschuren (1976b), Duffy & Hurtado (1984), Duffy *et al.* (1984), Hellmayr & Conover (1948), Johnson (1967), Koepcke (1970), Meyer de Schauensee (1982), Minaya (1968), Murphy (1936), Parker *et al.* (1982).

25. **Fairy Tern**

Sterna nereis

French: Sterne néréis **German**: Australseeschwalbe **Spanish**: Charrancito Australiano
Other common names: Nereis/Australian Fairy Tern

Taxonomy. *Sternula nereis* Gould, 1843, Bass Strait.
Overlaps in SE Australia with *S. albifrons*, and occasionally hybridizes. Four subspecies recognized.
Subspecies and Distribution.
S. n. horni Mathews, 1912 - Western Australia.
S. n. nereis (Gould, 1843) - South Australia, Victoria and Tasmania.
S. n. exsul (Mathews, 1912) - New Caledonia.
S. n. davisae (Mathews & Iredale, 1913) - N North I, New Zealand.
Descriptive notes. 22-27 cm; 57 g; wingspan 45-51 cm. Forehead and lores white, white not extending behind eye; crown and nape black, extending just forward of eye as dark spot on rear lores; upperparts and upperwing pale grey, rump paler than back; forked tail pale grey, with inner feathers white; neck and underparts whitish; bill bright yellow, usually without black tip; legs orange to orange-yellow. Very like *S. albifrons*, but latter has black tip to yellower bill, and black lores. Non-breeding adult has white extending as streaks over crown, and broad black band across nape from eye to eye; lacks dark carpal bar of *S. albifrons*, and has less contrasting primaries; bill has black tip, and often small black basal region. Subadult has wing-coverts grey-brown, and bill and legs dark brownish or black.
Habitat. Coasts, occasionally inland. Breeds on sandy or coral islands and extensive coastal dunes. Forages mainly in bays and estuaries, occasionally beyond surf.
Food and Feeding. Mainly small fish, also gastropods and crustaceans. Chicks seen to eat plant matter and small arthropods in seaweed. Feeds in shallow water by plunge-diving, or hovering and contact-dipping.
Breeding. Early Sept in N to late Sept in S; from mid-Nov in New Zealand. Colonial in Australia; often solitary or widely spaced in New Zealand, nests sometimes 20 m apart, usually further. In SE Australia sometimes in *S. albifrons* colonies, occasionally interbreeding. Prefers raised ridges or mounds.

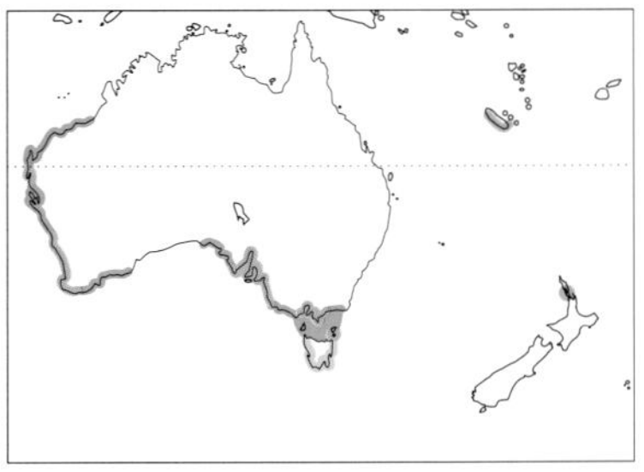

Nest a hollow in sand or shell, sometimes surrounded by shells on barren beach or spit. 1-2 eggs, with 20% 1 egg, average in New Zealand 1·77; incubation 20-25 days; adults leave early when intruders approach (small New Zealand colonies), or vigorously mob (large Australian colonies); chick very pale buff-white with very faint black dots or grey streaking, pinkish bill and legs; remains by nest for several days; fledging 22-23 days; dependent up to 50 days. Productivity in protected New Zealand colonies averaged 0·7 young/pair.

Movements. Tasmanian breeders and some from S Australia migrate N. Some from W Australia sedentary, others move N to NW Australia. New Zealand birds leave colony site, returning in Aug.

Status and Conservation. VULNERABLE. Australian population currently estimated at no more than c. 2000 pairs. New Zealand race *davisae* endangered; formerly common on both islands, but now confined to N North I, where only 4 pairs in 1983, when protection began; increased to 10 breeding pairs in 1994; main threats are human disturbance and intrusion, to which breeding birds are very vulnerable, and predation by rats and cats. Formerly common in Western Australia, where flocks of up to 15,000 birds recorded, but population greatly reduced; in Victoria, many colonies lost as offshore islands have become more accessible to humans; may also suffer from competition with *S. albifrons*, which is extending its range. Status of New Caledonian race *exsul* unknown. In all areas, nests are lost through flooding.

Bibliography. Blakers *et al*. (1984), Bransbury (1992), Brouwer & Garnett (1990), Chamberlin & Dowding (1985), Chambers (1989), Collar *et al*. (1994), Cooper (1971), Cox & Close (1977), Flegg & Madge (1995), Frith, H.J. (1976), Garnett (1993), Hannecart & Létocart (1983), Hitchcock (1959), Lindsey (1992), Macdonald (1988), Marchant & Higgins (1996), Parrish & Pulham (1995a, 1995b), Pizzey & Doyle (1980), Robertson (1985), Schodde & Tidemann (1986), Serventy & Whittell (1976), Serventy *et al*. (1971), Sharland (1938), Sibson (1982), Simpson & Day (1994), Slater *et al*. (1989), Trounson (1987).

26. Damara Tern

Sterna balaenarum

French: Sterne des baleiniers **German**: Damaraseeschwalbe **Spanish**: Charrancito de Damara

Taxonomy. *Sternula balænarum* Strickland, 1852, Damaraland.
Sometimes included in *S. albifrons* superspecies. Monotypic.

Distribution. Namibia to Cape Province; recorded N to Cabinda (N Angola) during breeding season. Migrates as far as Nigeria.

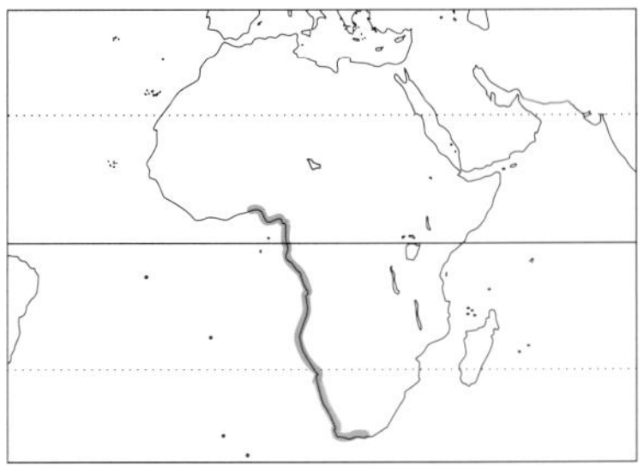

Descriptive notes. 23 cm; 46 g; wingspan 51 cm. Typical small tern, but all black bill, black forehead and lores; legs yellowish to dusky. Non-breeding adult has white forehead, and crown mottled grey and blackish. Juvenile has buffy crown, dark band through eye and across nape, grey flight-feathers, and brown wing-coverts with dark edging. 1st-winter as non-breeding adult, but darker primaries and faint carpal bar.

Habitat. Breeds on gravel and stony plains and dunes, up to 3 km inland; shuns outer beach frequented by predators. Feeds in inshore waters of bays, estuaries, lagoons and salt-pans, and in surf zone.

Food and Feeding. Mainly small fish, including mullet (*Mugil richardsonii*) and anchovy (*Engraulis japonica*), as well as small squid. Chicks fed fish 1·5-12 cm long, and up to 30 g. Forages by hovering followed by plunge-diving.

Breeding. Late Oct to mid-Nov, with new clutches into Feb. Groups of 1-10 pairs, occasionally 50; nests widely spaced, average distance 57-185 m; no territorial interactions observed. Prefers unvegetated troughs between dunes, with scattered shells and stones; often only 1 pair per trough. Barely visible scrape, with few pieces of shell or none. 1 egg, very rarely 2; adults weakly mob intruders; incubation 18-22 days; chick white below, fawn above finely speckled with black, matching lichen-flecked rocks; leaves nest at 2 days, crouches motionless among gravel; fledging 20 days; dependent for 2·5 months after fledging. Productivity 0·16-0·35 young/pair.

Movements. Disperses N after breeding season, reaching as far N as Nigeria, where present at Lagos Apr-Jan and most numerous Jul-Oct.

Status and Conservation. Not globally threatened. Currently considered near-threatened. Estimated population 1000-2000 pairs in 1982, but recent observations of 5000 in NW Namibia result in minimum total population of 5755 individuals. Although species is protected by ordinances in both Namibia and South Africa, its breeding areas are not protected. Restricted access to c. 1000 km of Diamond Coast between Swakopmund and Oranjemund incidentally protects some breeding habitat from human disturbance, but only a few pairs known to nest in that area; mining development near breeding areas may threaten even these. Off-road vehicles threaten colonies; land reclamation, dredging and hotel construction impact on feeding areas. Direct effect of human disturbance unknown, but has caused some nests to be abandoned. Nesting in widely scattered, loose colonies, far behind outer beaches, helps to reduce predation risk, particularly from black-backed jackal (*Canis mesomelas*).

Bibliography. Braby *et al*. (1992), Brooke (1984a), Clinning (1978b), Collar & Andrew (1988), Collar & Stuart (1985), Crawford (1995), De Villiers & Simmons (1994), Dowsett & Forbes-Watson (1993), Elgood *et al*. (1994), Feare & Bourne (1978), Frost & Shaughnessy (1976), Ginn *et al*. (1989), Grimes (1987), Johnson, P. (1979), Johnson, P. & Frost (1978), King (1978/79), Mackworth-Praed & Grant (1962, 1970), Maclean (1993), Pinto (1983), Randall & McLachlan (1982), Siegfried & Johnson (1977), Simmons (1993a, 1993b), Simmons & Braine (1994), Urban *et al*. (1986), Watson & Kerley (1995).

27. White-cheeked Tern

Sterna repressa

French: Sterne à joues blanches **German**: Weißwangen-Seeschwalbe **Spanish**: Charrán Arábigo

Taxonomy. *Sterna repressa* Hartert, 1916, Al Faw, south Iraq, Persian Gulf. Monotypic.

Distribution. Red Sea S to Somalia and Kenya, and E through Persian Gulf and Oman to W India (Bombay). Winters on coasts of NE Africa and Arabian Sea to SW India and Laccadives.

Descriptive notes. 32-35 cm; 113-142 g; wingspan 73-83 cm. Darker than all other typical *Sterna* terns, in breeding plumage recalling *Chlidonias hybridus*: black forehead to nape, with white cheeks set off by ash grey underparts; dark ashy grey above, including upperwing, rump and tail; bill dark red

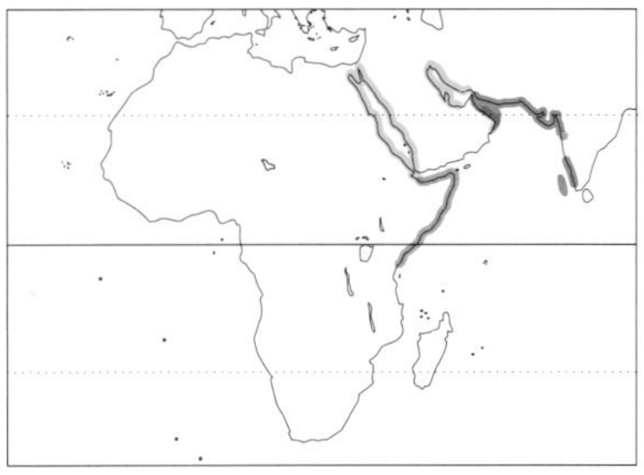

at base with black tip, but variable, and sometimes all black; legs bright red to dark brownish red. Very similar to *S. hirundo* and *S. paradisaea*, especially in winter, but smaller, with shorter wings and legs, and chunkier appearance in flight. Non-breeding adult has head white, with black or dark brown areas around eye, and from ear-coverts across nape, with pale nuchal collar; often shows patchy grey and white underparts. Juvenile brownish above, with pale brown scaling on coverts, and dark grey primaries; upper mandible and tip of bill blackish.

Habitat. A tropical coastal species, often found at sea, but very rare inland. Nests on rock, sand, gravel or coral islands, often more than 100 m from sea. Forages mainly within 3 km of land, mainly over coral reefs; in Kenya regularly 5-10 km offshore.

Food and Feeding. Small fish (average 5 cm) and invertebrates. In Egypt, mainly silverside (*Atherinomorus lacunosus*) and clupeids (*Spratelloides*). Feeds by plunge-diving, but more often by contact-dipping. Often lands on water, or walks in shallow water. Associates with predatory fish and marine mammals; follows fishing boats.

Breeding. May-Jun in Sudan and Oman, Jul-Sept in Egypt, Somalia and Kenya. In mixed colonies with other terns, e.g. *Thalasseus bengalensis*, *T. bergii*, *S. dougallii*, *S. anaethetus*, *S. fuscata*; usually in scattered colonies of 10-200 pairs, but up to 900 pairs (Egypt). Forms discrete, synchronous subcolonies on barren or sparsely vegetated areas. Nearest-neighbour distance from as little as 46 cm, but average up to 4·6 m; 0·5-3 nests/m². Shallow scrape, often unlined. 2-3 eggs (1-3); incubation and fledging not documented, but chick dependent on parents for weeks after fledging; chick buffy above with black spots, whitish below with black chin, and buffy tinge to belly; fledglings may form crèche at water's edge. Productivity not recorded, but avian predators are serious threat in some colonies.

Movements. Present Red Sea Apr-Sept, Egypt Apr-Nov, E Africa throughout year (peak Mar-Jun), Persian Gulf mainly Sept-Apr. Common on Sind coast of Pakistan Mar-May, but does not breed. Egyptian birds may disperse N after breeding, making stopover near Hurghada, before migrating out of Red Sea; probably winter along E African and Indian coasts. Common spring migrant along coasts ofPakistan and Kenya, but corresponding autumn migration probably offshore.

Status and Conservation. Not globally threatened. Total population variously estimated at 20,000-70,000 birds. Colony of 21,000+ pairs discovered off Abu Dhabi in 1994; c. 10,400 pairs off Saudi Arabia in early 1990's; minimum 2000 pairs in Oman, but flock estimated at 70,000 birds roosting at Masirah I in 1979. In 1972, reported 300,000 pairs in 60 ha on Sheedvar I (Iran), but by 1976/77 only 25,000-50,000 pairs recorded, with decline attributed to massive egg-collecting by local islanders. Subject to egging in many areas, and suffers losses to avian predators; at Kiunga Is (Kenya), latter include Intermediate Egret (*Egretta intermedia*), Sacred Ibis (*Threskiornis aethiopicus*) and Yellow-billed Stork (*Mycteria ibis*).

Bibliography. Ali & Ripley (1982), Ash & Miskell (1983), Britton (1971, 1982b), Britton & Brown (1974), Brown & Britton (1980), Bundy (1988), Cramp (1985), Dowsett & Forbes-Watson (1993), Étchécopar & Hüe (1964), Evans (1994), Gallagher *et al*. (1984), Goodman *et al*. (1989), Hüe & Étchécopar (1970), Mackworth-Praed & Grant (1957), Moore & Balzarotti (1983), Olsen & Larssen (1995b), Paz (1987), Perennou *et al*. (1994), Rands *et al*. (1987), Ripley (1982), Roberts, T.J. (1991), Shirihai (1996), Short *et al*. (1990), Symens (1991), Symens & Evans (1993), Urban *et al*. (1986), Walker & Turley (1989).

28. Black-bellied Tern

Sterna acuticauda

French: Sterne à ventre noir **German**: Schwarzbauch-Seeschwalbe **Spanish**: Charrán Ventrinegro

Taxonomy. *Sterna acuticauda* J. E. Gray, 1832, Kanpur, India.
In past, commonly listed as *S. melanogaster*, but name *melanogaster* was preoccupied. Monotypic.

Distribution. Pakistan (R Indus), Nepal and most of India E to SW China (W Yunnan), and S through Myanmar, N Thailand, Laos, Cambodia and S Vietnam.

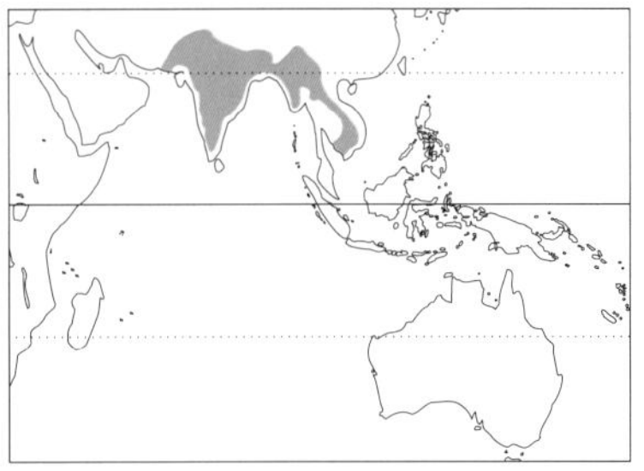

Descriptive notes. 32-35 cm. Typical tern from above, with black cap and grey back and wings, latter long and pointed; throat white, breast pale grey shading into deep black and brownish black belly and undertail-coverts; dark underparts contrast with white underwing, latter with darker band across secondaries; bill yellow-orange; legs reddish orange. Non-breeding adult has white forecrown streaked with black, black band behind eye, whitish underparts mottled black on belly, and black tip to bill. Juvenile has red at base of lower mandible and blackish feet; can be confused with "*portlandica*" plumage of *S. hirundo*, but darker.

Habitat. Inland lakes and rivers, preferring broad, barren, featureless flats, sand spits and sandy islands in rivers. Feeds along rivers and lakes, and over paddies, ditches and village ponds. Occurs up to 700 m in Nepal.

Food and Feeding. Insects and small fish. Plunge-dives for fish, and aerial-dips for insects over water and land. Despite non-colonial breeding, occasionally feeds in flocks.

Breeding. Feb-Apr. Early nests sometimes flooded. Often breeds with *S. aurantia*, skimmers and pratincoles, but not colonial; nests very widely spaced, often over 1 km and essentially solitary. Shallow, unlined scrape in bare sand, sometimes near a small object; usually more than 200 m from water's edge. Clutch 3 eggs, sometimes 2, rarely 4; incubation and fledging not studied, and reports of 15-16 days and 8 weeks, respectively, certainly erroneous; parents shade eggs and chicks, and also sprinkle water from belly feathers; adults mob intruding birds and predators. Productivity: one report of 0·7 young/nest.

Movements. Not migratory. Virtually unknown away from breeding sites.

Status and Conservation. VULNERABLE. Total population believed to number fewer than 10,000 individuals, and in continuing decline. Now very rare, possibly extinct, in Thailand; disappearing from Laos and Cambodia; no more than 25 pairs in Myanmar. Said to be common resident in Nepal, and fairly common in N & C India, but virtually unstudied. Destruction of breeding habitats is a major threat; eggs widely collected for food; and nests subject to flooding. Wide nest dispersion presumably an adaptation to heavy pressure from terrestrial predators, including man.

Bibliography. Ali & Ripley (1982), Collar *et al*. (1994), Deignan (1945), Étchécopar & Hüe (1978), Harvey (1990), Inskipp & Inskipp (1991), Lekagul & Round (1991), Lowe (1933), Lowther (1949), Meyer de Schauensee (1984), Mundkur (1988), Neelakantan (1953a), Perennou *et al*. (1994), Ripley (1982), Roberts, T.J. (1991), Rose & Scott (1994), Smythies (1986).

29. Aleutian Tern

Sterna aleutica

French: Sterne des Aléoutiennes **German**: Aleutenseeschwalbe **Spanish**: Charrán Aleutiano
Other common names: Kamchatka Tern

Taxonomy. *Sterna aleutica* Baird, 1869, Kodiak Island, Alaska.
Listed as *S. camtschatica* by many authors, particularly in Russia. Monotypic.
Distribution. Sakhalin through Sea of Okhotsk to Kamchatka and perhaps other sites in Bering Sea; Alaska, on Bering and Pacific coasts, from Chukchi Sea and Kotzebue Sound S to Aleutian Is, and E to delta of Copper R and Dry Bay; has bred in Japan (Hokkaido). Main wintering area unknown, although some birds in Philippines.

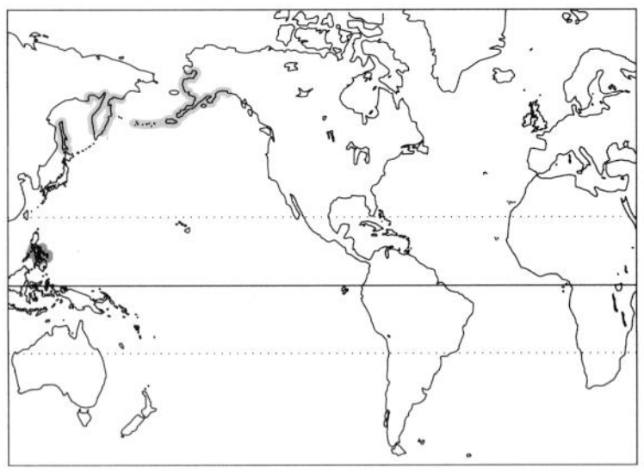

Descriptive notes. 32-34 cm; 83-140 g; wingspan 75-80 cm. White forehead, black cap and lores, mid-grey back and wings, white rump and tail, and darkish grey underparts; underwing whitish, with dark-tipped primaries and dark bar on secondaries; bill and legs black. Distinguished from *S. paradisaea*, even when forehead and soft parts not seen, by darker plumage, slower wingbeats, more floating flight, and by distinctive call, a squeaky 3-note whistle. Non-breeding adult similar to non-breeding *S. paradisaea*, but with dark secondaries. Juvenile has smoky brown crown and upperparts, latter with sandy feather edges, and often yellow-brown sides of breast.
Habitat. Arctic and subarctic coastal plains, mainly around Bering Sea. Partially vegetated sandy and shell beaches and grassy meadows, mossy flats, bogs and marshes on isolated rocky islands or along coasts, often near river mouths; occasionally in bogs 20 km inland. In Kamchatka and Sakhalin prefers grassy areas. Usually more coastal than either *S. paradisaea* or *S. hirundo*, with which often nests. In Kamchatka feeds mainly at river mouths, estuaries and along seashore, rarely over marshes. Pelagic when not breeding.
Food and Feeding. Mainly small fish. On Sakhalin primarily sticklebacks (*Pungitus pungitus*, *Gasterosteus aculeatus*). Feeds both at sea and over inland water bodies. Only contact- and surface-dipping observed, even in places where other species seen plunge-diving. Not reported to engage in kleptoparasitism. On Sakhalin, fed up to 40 km from colony.
Breeding. Laying mainly Jun. Usually small, monospecific colonies of 4-150 pairs, but up to 700 pairs on Sakhalin; occasionally solitary, or as single pairs in *S. paradisaea* colonies. Monospecific colonies often uniquely quiet; disturbed adults leave quickly and do not mob. Nearest-neighbour distance 2-16 m, but mean of 31 m reported in one colony; 4-24 m in Sakhalin, with average 17·7 m; nests more widely spaced in monospecific colonies. Nest-site sometimes among tall grasses and sedges, or in berry bushes. Scrape in sand, pebbles, among rocks, mosses, or on matted grass, even on bog hummocks; often assembles grassy nest, sometimes raised above wet substrates, but also lays directly on sand with no scrape. 2 eggs (1-4), average 1·3 (Kamchatka) to 1·84 (Sakhalin); incubation c. 22-27 days; chick has down feathers dark at base and pale grey or tan at tip, creating grizzled appearance similar to *S. dougallii*; hatching weight reported as low as 11·2 g; chick remains in nest 1-4 days, then hides in nearby vegetation; fledging 26-28 days; dependent young remain at colony for 2 weeks. Hatching success low: only 21% (Sakhalin) to 50% (Kamchatka); most eggs lost to predators; chick mortality also high.
Movements. Little information. Arrives in breeding areas mid-May and leaves by mid-Sept. Non-breeders presumably pelagic, dispersing into Bering Sea and N Pacific. No Nearctic records outside Alaska, and only accidental in Commander Is and Japan. Winter records from Philippines, and recorded as migrant Hong Kong, but main wintering areas still unknown. One extraordinary record of vagrancy: an adult in Britain in May 1979.
Status and Conservation. Not globally threatened. Virtually endemic to Bering Sea, with total population possibly below 15,000 pairs; relatively few known breeding areas. Occupies a sparsely studied area of the world. Alaskan census in mid-1970's found 850 pairs in 28 colonies, resulting in an estimated population of 5000-10,000 pairs. Copper Delta holds at least 1000 pairs. Kamchatka (where first found breeding in 1973) holds 500 pairs in at least 14 colonies; Sea of Okhotsk 1000 pairs; Sakhalin 2100 pairs. Predation by corvids and gulls on eggs, and by foxes and mustelids on chicks and adults, locally significant; predation by river otter (*Lutra canadensis*) on adults reported. Food apparently a limiting factor, as young chicks experienced slower growth and higher mortality than *S. paradisaea* in same colony.
Bibliography. Anon. (1993c, 1994f), Armstrong (1983), Baird & Moe (1978a), Bent (1921), Brazil (1991), Buckley & Buckley (1979), Cramp (1985), Davidova & Korotitskaya (1977), Dementiev & Gladkov (1951b), Duffy (1995), Gabrielson & Lincoln (1959), Haney, Andrew & Lee (1991), Harrison (1984a), Kaverkina (1979, 1982, 1986b, 1989, 1990), Kennerley *et al.* (1993), Kessel & Gibson (1978), Knystautas (1993), Kovalev *et al.* (1980), Lee (1992), Lensink (1984), Leonovitch (1976b), Litvinenko (1986), Litvinenko & Shibaev (1991), Lobkov (1976), Lobkov & Golovina (1978), Lobkov & Nechaev (1986), Nechaev (1977, 1981), Olsen & Larssen (1995b), Sowl (1979), Sowls *et al.* (1978), Stepanjan (1990b), Voronov & Eremin (1982).

30. Grey-backed Tern

Sterna lunata

French: Sterne à dos gris **German**: Brillenseeschwalbe **Spanish**: Charrán Lunado
Other common names: Spectacled Tern

Taxonomy. *Sterna lunata* Peale, 1848, Tuamotu Islands.
Formerly united with *S. fuscata* and *S. anaethetus* in separate genus *Haliplana* or *Onychoprion*. Monotypic.
Distribution. Northern Mariana Is E through Wake I and N Marshall Is to Hawaiian Is, and S through Phoenix and Line Is to Fiji, then E to Austral and Tuamotu Is; also Easter I (at least formerly); possibly also Samoa and Society Is. Wanders irregularly W to N Moluccas.
Descriptive notes. 38 cm; 115-177 g; wingspan 73-76 cm. Somewhat reminiscent of *S. fuscata*, but with grey upperparts and upperwings; white forehead patch smaller, but extends further back over eye; relatively short-winged, with very short inner wing. Non-breeding adult has forecrown faintly streaked white. Juvenile has less clear-cut head pattern, and buff scalloping on upperparts; sides of breast dusky.
Habitat. Oceanic islands of tropical Pacific, breeding on low sea cliffs, sandy beaches or bare ground on coral or rocky islands. Pelagic outside breeding season.
Food and Feeding. Mainly small fish, e.g. clupeids and flying-fish (Exocoetidae), and squid; one of the few terns occasionally to take lizards (at Enderbury I, Phoenix Is). Feeds mainly inshore, often with other terns. Takes tiny fish by plunge-diving. Often contact-dips or hover-dips over schools of tuna. Seizes lizards from vegetation by swooping down in flight.

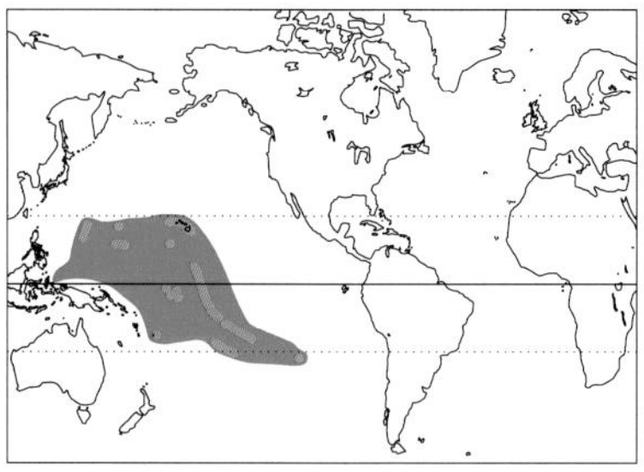

Breeding. Long breeding period Feb-Sept, with peak Mar-Jul; breeds c. 1-2 months earlier than *S. fuscata* and *Anous stolidus* occupying same colonies. Nest-site on rocky ledge, cliff, or on ground under vegetation, also on piers; usually higher on slopes than *S. fuscata*; also in shallow cavity and ledge on cliff, and hollow in rocks. 1 egg; incubation 24-35 (usually 29-30) days; fledging 7 weeks. Oldest ringed bird 16 years, but no doubt lives longer.
Movements. After breeding, abandons colony in Aug and presumably "winters" pelagically in Pacific. Non-breeders recorded from Palau Is and Yap I (Caroline Is), and also infrequently W to Halmahera (N Moluccas).
Status and Conservation. Not globally threatened. Line Is and Phoenix Is each hold 10,000's of pairs. Said to be common formerly on Easter I, but current status there uncertain. Rare in Micronesia. Wide disparity in estimates from Hawaii Is, from 18,000 to 51,000 pairs. Subject to heavy rat predation on Midway, Kure and other islands. Suffers high chick mortality from later-arriving *S. fuscata* which settle on its colony. On some islands, many nests lost to high tides.
Bibliography. Amerson (1971), Amerson & Shelton (1976), Brazil (1991), Clapp & Kridler (1977), Clapp, Klimkiewicz & Kennard (1982), Clapp, Kridler & Fleet (1977), Coates (1985), Fefer *et al.* (1984), Harrison, C. S. (1984a, 1990), Harrison, C. S., Hida & Seki (1983), Harrison, C. S., Naughton & Fefer (1984), Holyoak & Thibault (1984), Howell & Webb (1995a), Johnson (1967), Muse & Muse (1982), Munro (1960), Niethammer *et al.* (1992), Pratt *et al.* (1987), Roger (1976), White & Bruce (1986), Whittow (1984), Whittow *et al.* (1985).

31. Bridled Tern

Sterna anaethetus

French: Sterne bridée **German**: Zügelseeschwalbe **Spanish**: Charrán Embridado
Other common names: Brown-winged Tern

Taxonomy. *Sterna Anaethetus* Scopoli, 1786, Panay, Philippines.
Formerly united with *S. fuscata* and *S. lunata* in separate genus *Haliplana* or *Onychoprion*. Geographical variation subtle, and subspecific divisions probably exaggerated; taxonomy in need of revision; validity of forms named as *novaehollandiae* (Queensland to S Australia) and *rogersi* (N Western Australia) requires further study. Six subspecies currently recognized.
Subspecies and Distribution.
S. a. melanoptera Swainson, 1837 - W Africa.
S. a. fuligula Lichtenstein, 1844 - Red Sea and E Africa through Persian Gulf and Arabian Sea to W India.
S. a. antarctica Lesson, 1831 - Madagascar, Aldabra, Seychelles and Mascarenes through Maldives to Andaman Is.
S. a. anaethetus Scopoli, 1786 - extreme S Japan (S Ryukyu Is) and Taiwan S through Philippines and Indonesia to Australia, including Lord Howe I and Norfolk I.
S. a. nelsoni Ridgway, 1919 - W coast of Mexico and Central America.
S. a. recognita (Mathews, 1912) - West Indies, Belize and islands off N Venezuela.

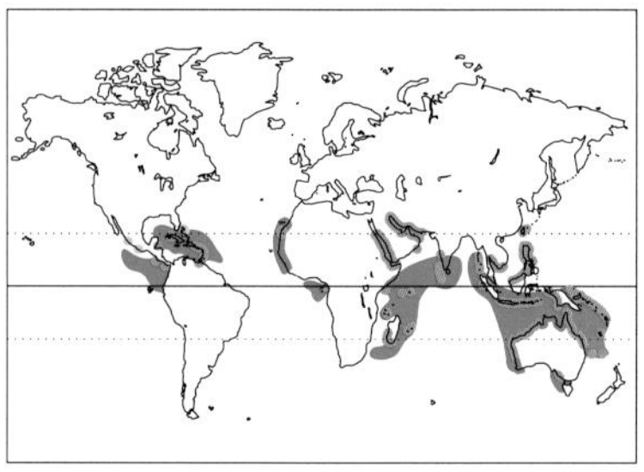

Descriptive notes. 35-38 cm; 95-150 g (Great Barrier Reef 125-135, average 131); wingspan 76-81 cm. Semi-pelagic tern with long, deeply forked tail and long, narrow wings; forehead patch white and triangular, extending short way behind eye; crown and nape black, occasionally with narrow paler hindneck collar; upperparts dark grey-brown, paler on rump and tail, with white outer tail feathers; upperwing dark grey-brown, with conspicuous pale leading edge; whitish below, with grey breast; bill and legs black. Shorter-winged than than *S. fuscata*, and 10% smaller, with paler upperparts contrasting with black crown, and narrow white eyebrow extending further behind eye; unlike *S. fuscata*, bill tomia not serrated, and webbing of toes more deeply incised which may facilitate perching on vegetation. Non-breeding adult somewhat paler, crown and nape with whitish and brownish streaks, reducing conspicuousness of white eyebrow. Juvenile has white forehead and supercilium and blackish brown hindneck, with crown and nape streaked grey and white; dark brown above, with broad whitish scaling, dark brown flight-feathers. Immature paler brown, with white-edged feathers, crown brown and speckled with grey, black head pattern more obscure. Races differ mainly in darkness of plumage, amount of white in outer tail, and size; *melanoptera* somewhat paler above, with greyish collar between nape and upperparts.
Habitat. Pantropical, occurring on tropical and subtropical coasts. Breeds on coral beaches and rocky and sandy slopes. Forages inshore and offshore, up to 50 km from land; mostly within 15 km, hence less pelagic than *S. fuscata*. Often perches on floating objects and on trees at night; roosts on sandbanks or rocky beaches, also in trees (Seychelles); reports of roosting on sea not corroborated.
Food and Feeding. Mainly surface-schooling fish (93%) and squid; 97% of fish less than 6 cm; also crustaceans; occasionally aquatic insects. Prefers various flying-fish at Los Roques (Venezuela) and in Ryukyu Is, filefish at Puerto Rico, Mullidae in Seychelles (90%), anchovy (*Engraulis australis*) and monocanthids on Great Barrier Reef, and marine insects (*Halobates*) in Sri Lanka. Flocks feed over shoals of small fish; only occasionally with *Anous* over schools of predatory fish. Feeds by plunge-diving without submerging, or contact-dipping from 1 m; also by surface-dipping or aerial-dipping, often over drifting seaweed. Sometimes forages up to 28 km from colony.
Breeding. May-Jun in S Caribbean and W Africa, Jun-Aug in E Africa, Jul-Aug in Madagascar, Oct-Dec in Australia. Most populations breed annually; 7·6-month cycle in Seychelles, with nesting in any month. Usually associates with *S. fuscata*, sometimes with *Thalasseus bergii*. Colonies of 3-20 pairs, up to 400 pairs, but 500-2000 pairs in W Australia; often not synchronous. Nests often distributed in vegetation, rock or rubble around rim of island, rather than clustered; spacing dictated by nest-site availability, usually 1-5 m, minimum 30 cm; 70% of birds retain nest-site from year to year, even with different mates. Nest contents normally concealed under rock or vegetation, reducing predation; reported to give broken-wing display to humans near nest. 1 egg, 2-egg clutches believed to be product of 2 females; incubation 28-30 days; chick finely mottled (not spotted), resembles that of *S. dougallii*; hatching weight 16-20 g; young do not form crèches; fledging 50-65 days; dependent young remain around colony a further 30-35 days. Productivity often high: 90% of eggs hatch and 77% of chicks fledge. May visit colony late in breeding season at 3 years, but first breeding usually at 4 years. Recorded longevity of 17 years 11 months; doubtless lives longer.
Movements. Virtually unknown for most areas. Widespread at sea. Birds from West Indies and Atlantic probably move E to upwellings off W Africa. Some Seychelles birds appear on E coast of Africa.

Australian breeders leave colonies in Mar, but movements unknown. Heavy southward autumn movement past Colombo, Sri Lanka, with estimate of 125,000 migrating S in Aug 1974, and possibly twice that number in 1978. Rare visitor to coasts of USA and Europe, usually after hurricanes.

Status and Conservation. Not globally threatened. Population figures unknown, but world total probably exceeds 200,000 pairs. Centre of abundance probably in Persian Gulf, where over 40,000 pairs counted off Abu Dhabi in 1994, also c. 34,400 pairs off Saudi Arabia in early 1990's, and 25,000-27,000 pairs in Iran; also minimum of 31,000 pairs off Oman. Usually nests with or close to *S. fuscata*, but almost always much less numerous. Predation by Yellow-crowned Night-herons (*Nycticorax violaceus*) observed at Los Roques, Venezuela. Jackals take young and adults in W Africa. Human predation low, owing to hidden nests; but human intrusion to colonies causes some damage.

Bibliography. Ali & Ripley (1982), Ash & Miskell (1983), van den Berg *et al.* (1982), Biaggi (1983), Blake (1977), Brazil (1991), Bregulla (1992), Britton & Brown (1974), Coates (1985), Cooper (1948), Cramp (1985), Diamond (1976, 1984), Dickinson *et al.* (1991), Domm & Recher (1973), Dowsett & Forbes-Watson (1993), Dunlop & Jenkins (1992), Dunlop *et al.* (1988), Étchécopar & Hüe (1964, 1978), Evans (1994), Feare (1979a), Gallagher *et al.* (1984), Goodman *et al.* (1989), van Halewijn & Norton (1984), Hilty & Brown (1986), Hoffman *et al.* (1993), Howell & Webb (1995a), Howell *et al.* (1990), Hüe & Étchécopar (1970), Hulsman (1974, 1977, 1987), Hulsman & Langham (1985), Kohno & Kishimoto (1991), Langham (1983, 1986), Langrand (1990), LeCroy (1976), Lekagul & Round (1991), Loftin (1991), MacKinnon & Phillipps (1993), Mackworth-Praed & Grant (1957, 1970), Marchant & Higgins (1996), van Marle & Voous (1988), Medway & Wells (1976), Meininger (1988), Meyer de Schauensee & Phelps (1978), Milon *et al.* (1973), Moore & Balzarotti (1983), Nicholls (1977), Olsen & Larssen (1995b), Paz (1987), Phillips (1978), Ridgely & Gwynne (1989), Ripley (1982), Roberts, T.J. (1991), Serventy *et al.* (1971), Shirihai (1996), Short *et al.* (1990), Slud (1964), Smaby-Stone (1991), Smythies (1981, 1986), Stiles & Skutch (1989), Symens & Evans (1993), Tunnicliffe & Langlands (1990), Urban *et al.* (1986), Voous (1963), Warham (1958), Wetmore (1965), White & Bruce (1986).

32. Sooty Tern

Sterna fuscata

French: Sterne fuligineuse **German**: Rußseeschwalbe **Spanish**: Charrán Sombrío
Other common names: Wideawake (Tern)

Taxonomy. *Sterna fuscata* Linnaeus, 1766, Santo Domingo.
Formerly united with *S. anaethetus* and *S. lunata* in separate genus *Haliplana* or *Onychoprion*. Geographical variation subtle: separation of races *crissalis*, *infuscata* and *serrata* probably not warranted; validity of proposed form *somaliensis*, possibly endemic to Mait I (Gulf of Aden), requires study. Eight subspecies currently recognized.

Subspecies and Distribution.
S. f. fuscata Linnaeus, 1766 - Gulf of Mexico, including West Indies and E Mexico, with sporadic isolated nesting attempts in the Carolinas and Florida, more regularly in Louisiana and Texas; also islands in Gulf of Guinea and in S Atlantic.
S. f. nubilosa Sparrman, 1788 - S Red Sea, Gulf of Aden and Indian Ocean E to Ryukyu Is and Philippines.
S. f. infuscata Lichtenstein, 1823 - C Indonesia (range uncertain).
S. f. serrata Wagler, 1830 - New Guinea, Australia and New Caledonia.
S. f. kermadeci (Mathews, 1916) - Kermadec Is.
S. f. oahuensis Bloxham, 1826 - Bonin Is to Hawaii and S through Pacific.
S. f. crissalis (Lawrence, 1872) - islands off W Mexico and Central America S to Galapagos.
S. f. luctuosa Philippi & Landbeck, 1866 - Juan Fernández Is (Chile).

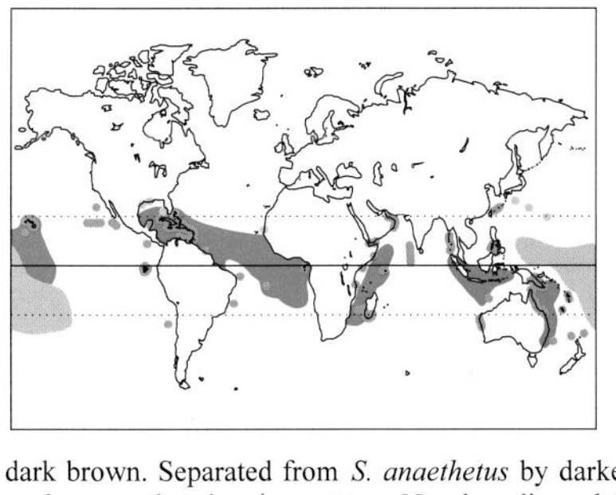

Descriptive notes. 36-45 cm; 147-240 g, average 173 g in Australia and on Kiritimati I (Christmas I, Pacific), 175 g on Ascension I, 189 g in Dry Tortugas; wingspan 82-94 cm. Distinctive black and white tern, with long wings and long tail; very noisy, with yelping "wide-a-wake" call at breeding colony; black above, sometimes with brownish cast, white below (in flight, often reflecting pale blue from water), and with white forehead with black line from bill to eye; deeply forked tail black, except for white outer rectrices; underwing blackish grey, with contrasting white coverts; bill and legs black, bill with tomia serrated; iris dark brown. Separated from *S. anaethetus* by darker and more uniform upperparts, lack of white eyebrow, and underwing pattern. Non-breeding adult has variable white feather fringes above. Juvenile blackish brown above, finely vermiculated and spotted with white, and grey-brown below, becoming paler from lower belly downwards. Races differ only slightly; *nubilosa* has pale grey tinge to belly and underwing-coverts; *oahuensis* and *kermadeci* are larger-billed.

Habitat. Pantropical, in tropical and subtropical waters; largely absent from cold-current areas; mainly productive waters rich in plankton and conducive to fish and squid abundance. Breeds on oceanic and barrier islands of sand, coral or rock, including artificial islands; usually flat, open and with sparse vegetation, but often heavily vegetated, e.g. Culebra (Puerto Rico); eschews islands with terrestrial predators. Highly pelagic outside breeding season; vagrants occur inland after hurricanes.

Food and Feeding. Mainly fish and squid, also crustaceans; occasionally insects and offal. At Kiritimati, squid comprise more than half the diet by volume, and both fish and squid regurgitated at most feeds. In Hawaii, fish and squid about equal in diet; fish mainly 6-8 cm, but up to 18 cm, with 21 families, of which flying-fish (Exocoetidae) and Scombridae predominant; most common prey was yellowfin (*Neothunnus macropterus*). Feeds mainly by aerial-dipping or contact-dipping; occasionally by plunge-diving; flying-fish caught in air. Unable to swim and very rarely seen to rest on water, as becomes waterlogged. Feeds at night on bathypelagic fish which come to surface only in darkness. At Ascension I feeds far at sea, possibly over 500 km from colony, but in Tortugas mainly within 80 km.

Breeding. Breeds all year round in some places, but seasonal in others; cycle on Ascension 9·6 months. Dec in Laccadives, Feb at Kermadecs and in Brazil; at Oahu (Hawaiian Is) lays Apr-May on Manana I, but 15 km away on Moku Manu some nest in Nov; Apr-May in Dry Tortugas, May in Greater Antilles, Jun-Jul in Seychelles, Nov in Tanzania. In many areas all first layings harvested, artificially retarding breeding by c. 1 month. Normally large to huge colonies; occasionally single pairs colonize new areas (e.g. one pair in *S. dougallii* colony on Madeira in 1982, first W Palearctic breeding record). Courtship and copulation often synchronous. Most nest-sites flat, open sand, shell or coral with sparse vegetation, but many are heavily vegetated (e.g. Culebra). Prefers vegetative cover where available, usually selecting the tallest, yet in Ryukyu Is tall grass succession excluded terns from former nesting area. Lays on bare areas, sometimes making slight depression. Nests dense, c. 50 cm apart; 3·38 nests/m² at Bird I (Seychelles); clusters of pairs may be constant from year to year. 1 egg, rarely 2; incubation 26-33 days, mainly 28-30; chick buffy brown, sparsely and obscurely splotched dark brown; grows more slowly than typical *Sterna*, fledging c. 2 months. In unvegetated colonies some chicks succumb to heat exposure. Productivity: 70% of eggs produce chicks at Tortugas except in hurricane years, but only 2-20% on Ascension I; up to 75% of chicks fledged at Manana. Occasionally subject to mass starvation and breeding failure, e.g. Ascension in Jan 1959. A few attempt nesting as early as 4 years, some not until 10, but first breeding usually at 6-8 years. Recorded longevity of 32 years.

Movements. Rarely seen on water and believed to sleep on the wing. Once chicks fledge (or die), all birds leave colonies. Adults return after 2-3 months at sea, and settle only at night for 2-3 months prior to initiating new breeding cycle. Adults from West Indies disperse into Gulf of Mexico and Caribbean where some winter; juveniles cross Atlantic and move S down African coast. Little information on Indian Ocean population, which probably disperses widely over Indian Ocean. Pacific adults disperse away from colony Jun-Oct and begin to return to area in late Nov, occupying colony in Feb, but not laying until Apr (Johnston Atoll).

Status and Conservation. Not globally threatened. One of most abundant seabirds, with several colonies of 1,000,000+ pairs. Total world population probably exceeds 25,000,000 pairs. Huge numbers in S Pacific, with over 10,000,000 in Line Is and over 1,000,000 each in Phoenix Is and Marquesas. About 1,500,000 breed in Hawaii, and a further 5,000,000 birds may breed from Indian Ocean to W Australia. Many marginal populations, however, are vulnerable. Conversely, new breeding attempts, often by single pairs, indicate range expansion, though these are often unproductive and impermanent. Most remote oceanic islands are free from terrestrial predators, but some colonies subject to rat and cat predation; at Ascension I, population has declined from 500,000 pairs (1954) to under 200,000 pairs (1994), largely due to cat predation. Many avian predators take eggs and chicks, which can significantly reduce productivity in some colonies. Hurricanes may completely eliminate productivity. Eggs sometimes harvested, such activities being partly managed in Seychelles and Jamaica. Tick infestation and arthropod-borne viruses have caused abandonment and abnormal chick development in Seychelles. Species also vulnerable to oil pollution from tankers and spills. Total hatching failure attributed to repeated low-flying by jet planes, although this has not been proven.

Bibliography. Abe *et al.* (1986), Ainley *et al.* (1986), Ali & Ripley (1982), Amerson (1966), Amerson & Shelton (1976), Ash & Karani (1981), Ashmole (1963a, 1963b, 1965, 1968b), Ashmole & Ashmole (1967), Ashmole *et al.* (1994), Bailey *et al.* (1987), Blake (1977), Bourne *et al.* (1977), Brazil (1991), Britton & Brown (1974), Brown, W.Y. (1975a, 1975b, 1976a, 1976c, 1976d, 1977), Burger & Gochfeld (1986b), Chapin (1954b), Chapin & Wing (1959), Clancey (1977a, 1977b), Clapp *et al.* (1983), Coates (1985), Converse *et al.* (1975), Cramp (1985), Crossin & Huber (1970), Dinsmore (1972), Dowsett & Forbes-Watson (1993), Dujardin & Tostain (1990), Dunlop & Jenkins (1992), Dunlop *et al.* (1988), Feare (1975, 1976a, 1976b, 1976c, 1979a, 1984), Feare *et al.* (1995), Fefer *et al.* (1984), Flint (1991), Flint & Nagy (1984), Gould (1967, 1974), van Halewijn & Norton (1984), Harrington (1974), Harrison (1984a), Harrison *et al.* (1983), Holyoak & Thibault (1984), Howell, S.N.G. & Webb (1995a), Howell, S.N.G. *et al.* (1990), Howell, T.R. & Bartholmew (1962), Hughes (1991), Johnson (1967), Johnson *et al.* (1970), Johnston (1979), Kohno *et al.* (1986), Lane, S.G. (1986), Langrand (1990), LeCroy (1976), Mackworth-Praed & Grant (1957, 1962, 1970), MacMillen *et al.* (1977), Marchant & Higgins (1996), van Marle & Voous (1988), Mathiu (1994), Merton (1970), Morris (1984), Murphy (1936), de Naurois (1969), Niethammer *et al.* (1992), Olsen & Larssen (1995b), Pitman (1967), Rahn *et al.* (1976), Richardson & Fisher (1950), Ricklefs & White (1981), Robertson (1964, 1969), Robertson & Robertson (1996), Saliva & Burger (1989), Schodde *et al.* (1983), Schreiber & Ashmole (1970), Schreiber & Schreiber (1984), Serventy *et al.* (1971), Sick (1985c, 1993), Slud (1964), Sprunt (1948a), Taylor, R.H. (1979), Urban *et al.* (1986), Vesey-Fitzgerald (1941), Walmsley (1991), Watson (1908), Webster *et al.* (1990), Wetmore (1965), White *et al.* (1976), Whittow (1984, 1985), Whittow *et al.* (1992), Woodward (1972).

33. Black-fronted Tern

Sterna albostriata

French: Guifette des galets **German**: Graubauch-Seeschwalbe **Spanish**: Charrán Fumarel
Other common names: Tara (Maori)

Taxonomy. *Hydrochelidon albostriata* G. R. Gray, 1845, New Zealand.
Sometimes placed in *Chlidonias* even as race of *C. hybridus*, but is a typical *Sterna*. Species name sometimes misspelt *albistriata*. Monotypic.

Distribution. New Zealand, breeding in interior South I. Post-breeding visitor to North I, where formerly bred.

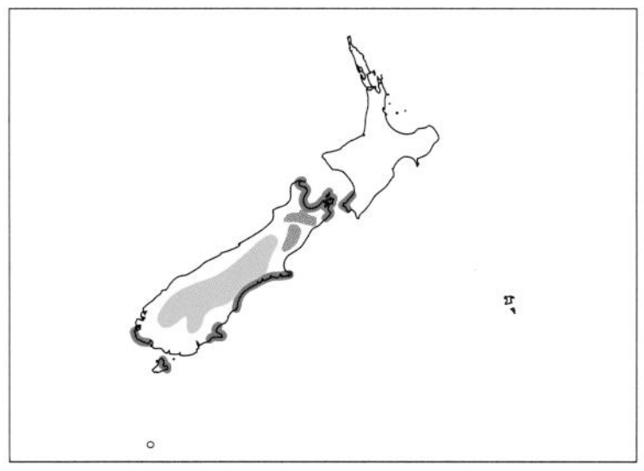

Descriptive notes. 30 cm; 88-96 g. Forehead to nape black, back and wings grey, with darker grey primaries, and underparts pale grey; uppertail- and undertail-coverts and rump white; tail pale grey with darker tips; outer primary has dark leading edge and white shaft; eye black; bill and feet bright yellow-orange. In breeding plumage Jun to late Nov, then undergoes complete moult from mid-Dec to May. Non-breeding adult has grey head with black patch around nape from eye to eye, and black-flecked crown. Juvenile has greyish brown crown and nape, mottled with black, and black ear-coverts and lores; mantle, back and wing-coverts brown, margined with buff; breast and belly grey, throat and undertail-coverts white; bill dark brown with orange base, feet orange. Immature similar to non-breeding adult, with grey body, black-mottled grey crown, and black patch on ear-coverts and nape; wings and tail brownish, with darker tips; bill dark brown, often with reddish orange base; legs and feet orange.

Habitat. Breeds mainly on gravel and sandy bars in fast-flowing braided rivers; also on lake beaches. Forages over lakes and farm fields. In winter, coastal harbours and estuaries, roosting on tidal flats and islands; seldom ventures more than 10 km offshore.

Food and Feeding. Small fish (up to 10 cm long), insects, beetles, grubs, earthworms and lizards; in winter, mainly crustaceans and fish. Feeds commonly by aerial-dipping to surface of rivers or lakes, but may also plunge-dive for fish; also by aerial hawking for swarming insects. Follows ploughs.

Breeding. Mid-Oct to late Nov, occasionally to Jan. Colonies from under 10 pairs up to 75; nearest-neighbour distance usually 5-20 m. Nest a vague depression in gravel at base of rock or bush, very difficult to find. 2 eggs; incubation 21-23 days; chick grey-brown to olive with dark speckles, dark patch on cheeks and lores, dark throat, white breast and belly, black-tipped dull chrome bill, orange feet; leaves nest within 4 days; adults very aggressive, attack intruders. Productivity usually low.

Movements. After breeding, birds move to coast of South I and to S North I and Stewart I. Vagrant to Snares and Chatham Is.

Status and Conservation. VULNERABLE. Total population estimated at 1000-5000 pairs in 1982, alternatively 10,000 pairs, but all figures no more than speculative. Although there are many colonies, most contain only a few to c. 25 pairs. Breeding habitat, rocky islets in rivers, dry river beds and lake shores, is threatened by encroachment of exotic plants, particularly lupins (*Lupinus*), and by tree-planting; also by proposed development of hydro-electric plants on rivers, and by introduced predators. Many nests or broods are lost to predation by cats and mustelids, trampling by sheep, and flooding.

Bibliography. Chambers (1989), Child (1986), Collar & Andrew (1988), Collar *et al.* (1994), Falla *et al.* (1981), Lalas (1979), Lalas & Heather (1980), Latham (1981), Marchant & Higgins (1996), Robertson (1985), Sibson (1982), Soper (1976), Williams (1975).

34

35

36

37

38

39

ssp *melanops*

40

ssp *tenuirostris*

ssp *cerulea*

41

ssp *teretirostris*

ssp *alba*

42

43

ssp *candida*

ssp *microrhyncha*

44

PLATE 57

inches   5

cm   13

Genus *CHLIDONIAS* Rafinesque, 1822

34. Whiskered Tern
Chlidonias hybridus

French: Guifette moustac **German**: Weißbart-Seeschwalbe **Spanish**: Fumarel Cariblanco

Taxonomy. *Sterna hybrida* Pallas, 1811, southern Volga, Russia.
Genus sometimes merged into *Sterna*. *Sterna albostriata* sometimes considered a race of *C. hybridus*, but morphology and ecology more typical of *Sterna*. Race *swinhoei* may be inseparable from *javanicus*; proposed race *leggei* included in latter. All Eurasian populations often lumped in nominate *hybridus*. Six subspecies normally recognized.
Subspecies and Distribution.
C. h. hybridus (Pallas, 1811) - SW & C Europe through W Russia, Middle East and Transcaspia to SC & E Kazakhstan; winters mainly in Africa and also SW Asia.
C. h. swinhoei (Mathews, 1912) - Transbaikalia, E China and Taiwan.
C. h. indicus (Stephens, 1826) - E Iran and Pakistan to N India.
C. h. javanicus (Horsfield, 1821) - NE India and probably Sri Lanka; winters Malaysia to Indonesia.
C. h. sclateri (Mathews & Iredale, 1912) - Kenya to South Africa and Madagascar.
C. h. fluviatilis (Gould, 1843) - Australia; migrates to New Guinea and Moluccas.

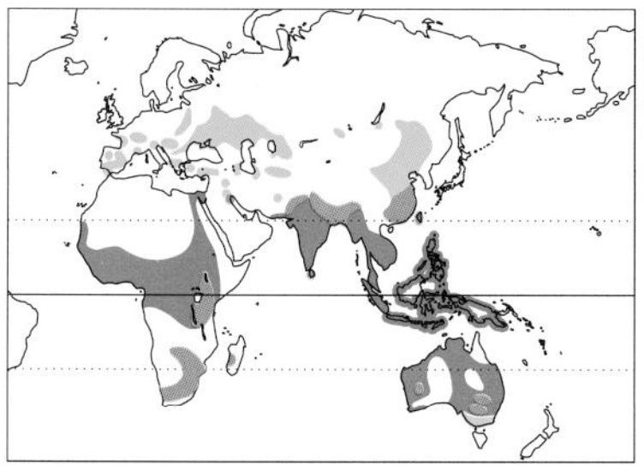

Descriptive notes. 23-29 cm; 60-101 g (average 84 g); wingspan 64-70 cm. Slender, medium-small tern, with wings more rounded than in typical *Sterna*; shortish tail with only slight fork; forehead to nape black, with contrasting white cheeks; upperparts, including rump and tail, mid-grey; underparts grey, darker on belly, with contrasting pale grey underwing and white undertail-coverts; iris dark brown; bill dark reddish, legs red. Superficially resembles *Sterna paradisaea* and *S. repressa*, but darker below, with much shorter tail. Non-breeding adult very pale above and below, with dark-flecked pale crown, black patch behind eye merging into dark band across nape, and black bill; crown pattern less contrasting than in *C. niger*, but more complete than in *C. leucopterus*. Female significantly smaller than male in all dimensions. Juvenile has head pattern similar to non-breeding adult, but with face washed buff and hindneck tipped dark grey; mantle, scapulars and tertials contrastingly darker, with buff tips. Races differ somewhat in coloration of breeding plumage, but only slightly in size; *delalandii* darkest, with white cheek stripe narrower.
Habitat. Breeds on vegetated inland lakes, marshes and rivers, mainly in lowlands, but up to 2000 m in Armenia; in Italy prefers artificial fish ponds and drainage ponds covered with water-lilies; in Africa opportunistically seeks pans after heavy rains. In Australia mainly coastal, breeding in arid interior in very wet years. Feeds over lakes, marshes, and rice fields, but also over sprouted farm fields, and coastal lagoons, tidal mudflats and estuaries.
Food and Feeding. Terrestrial and aquatic insects, e.g. water beetles (Dytiscidae), Odonata and their larvae, grasshoppers, flying ants, spiders; also tadpoles and frogs, small crabs, small fish. In N Australia, 55 stomachs revealed c. 32% Coleoptera, 18% Odonata, 9% Hemiptera, and 9% spiders; fish made up 13% of items but 45% of weight, and frogs 2% of items and 6% of weight; larger males took more fish and fewer insects, and had more diverse diet. Flies back and forth or flutters 2-6 m above water, then swoops (aerial-dipping) or drops (hover-dipping) to pick up small surface items; infrequently engages in plunge-diving. Often hawks insects over fields and lake margins; sometimes feeds behind plough in Spain. Generally forages within 1 km of colony, occasionally up to 9 km.
Breeding. May-Jun in Europe, Nov-Dec in Australia, Dec in Tanzania. Forms synchronous subcolonies, usually in monospecific colonies of 10-100 pairs. Broad but flimsy nest of stems or decaying rushes, placed on floating or emergent vegetation over water, usually 60-80 cm deep; in very shallow water, nest may rest on bottom; alternatively nest of dry grass on water-lily leaves; may usurp grebe nest. Nests 1-5 m apart. 2-3 eggs; incubation 18-20 days; chick black-spotted buff, with black forehead, creamy breast, black bill and pink legs; can leave nest within 1 day and swim to vegetation; fledging 23 days; fed for few weeks after. Hatching success 66% in Australia. Many breed first at 2 years.
Movements. From W Europe migrates to W Africa; E European birds winter mostly in E Africa, with a few in S Middle East; those from Caspian and Turkestan zone winter from Iran to Pakistan and Sri Lanka, and possibly also E Africa. Migration of race *swinhoei* poorly known, but small numbers winter in Thailand; *indicus* is irregular migrant in Nepal, usually in small numbers. Australian birds mainly nomadic, but those from S Australia migrate N.
Status and Conservation. Not globally threatened. In much of W & C Europe breeding is occasional and irregular, and species may have declined; however, apparently abundant in Andalucia (S Spain), where possibly 100,000 pairs breed; perhaps an additional 25,000 pairs elsewhere in Europe. Probably several 10,000's of pairs in former USSR. Formerly bred in N Africa, from Morocco to Tunisia. In sub-Saharan Africa, breeds in small, scattered, often non-permanent colonies. In India, large quantities of eggs are collected for sale and for local consumption, causing population decline in certain areas of Kashmir. In Ukraine, fishermen collect eggs. Many nests lost to adverse weather, e.g. high winds and waves.
Bibliography. Ali & Ripley (1982), Beehler *et al*. (1986), Benson & Benson (1975), Borodulina (1960), Bourke (1956), Brazil (1991), Coates (1985), Craig (1974), Cramp (1985), Crawford (1977), Dean & Skead (1979a), Deignan (1945), Dementiev & Gladkov (1951b), Dickinson *et al*. (1991), Dostine & Morton (1989a), Dowsett & Forbes-Watson (1993), Elgood *et al*. (1994), Elwell (1976), Étchécopar & Hüe (1964, 1978), Evans (1994), Fasola (1986), Fuggles-Couchman (1962), Ginn *et al*. (1989), Glutz von Blotzheim & Bauer (1982), Goodman *et al*. (1989), Hüe & Étchécopar (1970), Ilicev & Zubakin (1988), Knystautas (1993), Langrand (1990), Lekagul & Round (1991), Liang (1989), MacKinnon & Phillipps (1993), Mackworth-Praed & Grant (1957, 1962, 1970), Maclean (1993), Marchant & Higgins (1996), van Marle & Voous (1988), Medway & Wells (1976), Mees (1977), Meininger (1988), Milon (1947), Milon *et al*. (1973), Olsen & Larssen (1995b), Patrikeev (1995), Paz (1987), Peero *et al*. (1985), Perennou (1991), Perennou *et al*. (1994), Phillips (1978), Pinto (1983), Rabor (1977), Richards (1990), Ripley (1982), Roberts, T.J. (1991), Serventy *et al*. (1971), Shirihai (1996), Short *et al*. (1990), Smythies (1981, 1986), Spina (1982, 1986), Steyn (1960), Swift (1960), Talposh (1977), Tomialojc (1994f), Trotignon (1994), Tucker (1973), Urban *et al*. (1986), Wehner (1966), White & Bruce (1986), Williams, M.D. (1986), Williamson (1960).

35. White-winged Tern
Chlidonias leucopterus

French: Guifette leucoptère **German**: Weißflügel-Seeschwalbe **Spanish**: Fumarel Aliblanco
Other common names: White-winged Black Tern

Taxonomy. *Sterna leucoptera* Temminck, 1815, Mediterranean coasts.
Genus sometimes merged into *Sterna*. More similar to *C. niger* than to *C. hybridus*, but closely related to both; has apparently hybridized with *C. niger*. Monotypic.
Distribution. NW Italy and C & E Europe E through Siberia, Transbaikalia and N Mongolia to Amurland; has bred in New Zealand. Winters in Africa, and from S Asia to Australia and New Zealand.

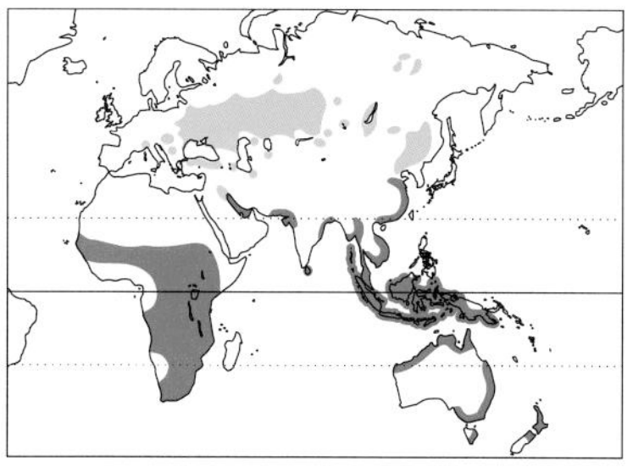

Descriptive notes. 23-27 cm; 42-79 g (average 66 g in Ukraine, 54 g in winter in Transvaal); wingspan 58-67 cm. Very distinctive, appearing markedly black and white: head, body and scapulars black, with contrasting white rump, tail and undertail-coverts; upperwing grey, with white lesser and median coverts; underwing pale grey, with all coverts contrastingly black; bill reddish black; legs bright to dull red. Non-breeding adult pale grey above, white below, and head white, with dusky crown and auricular patch; very like non-breeding *C. hybridus*, but dark of crown and ear-coverts usually separated by white supercilium, usually shows darker grey band across lesser coverts, and often diagnostic black bar on underwing. Moults back into breeding plumage in mid-Mar. Juvenile has blackish brown saddle and silver-grey wings, contrasting with white rump and collar.
Habitat. Breeds mainly inland, on vegetated freshwater lakes and swamps, and rice fields (Italy), from boreal forest to Mediterranean; up to 2000 m in Armenia. On passage and in winter occurs in variety of habitats, from inland lakes to rocky coasts, rivers, impoundments, lagoons and mangrove swamps. Often roosts on emergent branches of drowned trees or on pilings.
Food and Feeding. Mainly aquatic insects (especially Diptera, Odonata, Coleoptera), also terrestrial insects; occasionally small fish or tadpoles. Rarely fish may predominate, e.g. sardines (*Limnothrissa miodon*) in South Africa. In dry season in Africa, feeds on fish trapped in residual pools. Opportunistic; will congregate at outbreaks of caterpillars, e.g. of army moth (*Laphygma exempta*) in Uganda. Forages in variety of wetland habitats, including wet fields, and also over dry farmland and steppe; in New Zealand feeds along rocky riverbeds. Species is accomplished aerial feeder; uses contact-dipping, also hover-dipping, and hawks flying insects; does not plunge-dive.
Breeding. Apr-Aug, mainly Jun. May skip breeding in drought years. Breeds in small colonies of 3-100 pairs, mostly 20-40, occasionally over 100 pairs; usually monospecific, sometimes with other terns or with Little Gulls (*Larus minutus*) or Black-necked Grebes (*Podiceps nigricollis*); low colony site fidelity. Nest of water weed with shallow cup, built on mat of floating vegetation in water 30-120 cm deep, occasionally on dry shore or resting on bottom; nests widely spaced (10-30 m), but occasionally as close as 2·5 m. 2-3 eggs (average 2·8); incubation 18-22 days; chick buffy above, streaked with black, paler below with few dark spots, and pale patch surrounding eye; fledging 20-25 days. First breeding at 2 years.
Movements. Migratory. European and W Asian populations leave breeding grounds from late Jul to late Aug, wintering mostly in Africa; large flocks on E side of Sea of Azov in late Aug, and passing through E Mediterranean in Aug-Sept; negligible movement off W coasts, but species numerous in Senegal in Sept. A few occasionally winter on Black Sea. Common migrant through E Africa, mainly inland, occasionally on coast. In spring, large flocks pass through E Mediterranean, and massive numbers recorded at N Red Sea; at N Gulf of Aqaba, c. 20,000 in one afternoon in 1984, and total of 81,000 in 5-day period in 1990. C & E Asian breeders winter from Burma and SE China, S through Indonesia and Indochina to Australia and New Zealand; wintering birds in Persian Gulf, Pakistan, Sri Lanka and elsewhere in N Indian Ocean may come from these populations.
Status and Conservation. Not globally threatened. True status not known over most of its range. Many populations probably vulnerable. Very scarce in C Europe, where breeds rarely or sporadically, but fairly common in parts of E Europe and C & E Asia; very common in steppes of Kazakhstan; perhaps several 100,000's of pairs in former USSR. Formerly bred in Algeria, and has bred once in New Zealand.
Bibliography. Ali & Ripley (1982), Ash & Miskell (1983), Beehler *et al*. (1986), Begg (1973), Benson & Benson (1975), Borodulina (1960), Brazil (1991), Bundy (1982), Coates (1985), Cramp (1985), Crawford (1977), Dementiev & Gladkov (1951b), Dickinson *et al*. (1991), Dowsett & Forbes-Watson (1993), Elgood *et al*. (1994), Étchécopar & Hüe (1964, 1978), Evans (1994), Ginn *et al*. (1989), Goodman *et al*. (1989), Gore (1990), Hockey (1982c), Hüe & Étchécopar (1970), Ilicev & Zubakin (1988), Knystautas (1993), Langrand (1990), Lekagul & Round (1991), MacKinnon & Phillipps (1993), Mackworth-Praed & Grant (1957, 1962, 1970), Maclean (1993), Marchant & Higgins (1996), van Marle & Voous (1988), Medway & Wells (1976), Meininger (1988), Milon *et al*. (1973), Olsen & Larssen (1995b), Patrikeev (1995), Paz (1987), Peero *et al*. (1985), Perennou (1991), Perennou *et al*. (1994), Phillips (1978), Pierce (1974), Pinto (1983), Pulcher (1986b), Richards (1990), Ripley (1982), Roberts, T.J. (1991), Rogacheva (1992), Roslyakov (1979), Schmitt *et al*. (1973), Serventy *et al*. (1971), Shirihai (1996), Short *et al*. (1990), Sinclair (1981), Smythies (1981), Tucker (1973), Urban *et al*. (1986), Vinicombe (1980), Wehner (1966), White & Bruce (1986), Williams, M.D. (1986), Williamson (1960).

36. Black Tern
Chlidonias niger

French: Guifette noire **German**: Trauerseeschwalbe **Spanish**: Fumarel Común

Taxonomy. *Sterna nigra* Linnaeus, 1758, near Uppsala, Sweden.
Genus sometimes merged into *Sterna*. Two subspecies recognized.
Subspecies and Distribution.
C. n. niger (Linnaeus, 1758) - S Scandinavia S to S Spain, and E through E Europe and W Asia to L Balkhash and Altai; winters in Africa.
C. n. surinamensis (Gmelin, 1789) - Great Slave L, S Mackenzie and C Manitoba S to California, and E to Great Lakes, NW Pennsylvania and NW New York, with disjunct populations in Kansas, Indiana and N Vermont; winters in Central America and N South America.

On following pages: 37. Large-billed Tern (*Phaetusa simplex*); 38. Brown Noddy (*Anous stolidus*); 39. Black Noddy (*Anous minutus*); 40. Lesser Noddy (*Anous tenuirostris*); 41. Blue Noddy (*Procelsterna cerulea*); 42. Grey Noddy (*Procelsterna albivitta*); 43. White Tern (*Gygis alba*); 44. Inca Tern (*Larosterna inca*).

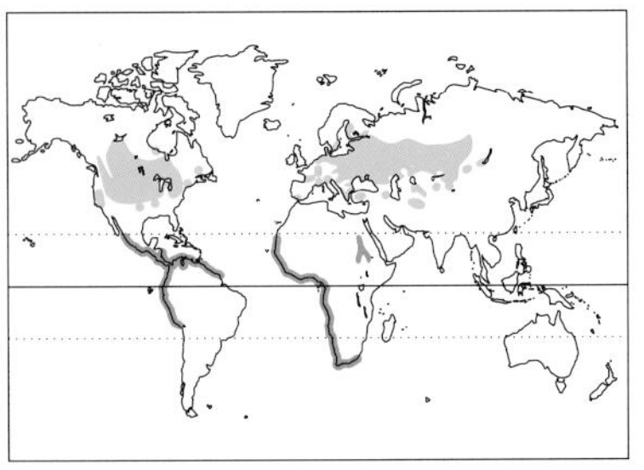

Descriptive notes. 23-28 cm; 60-74 g (average 64 g); wingspan 57-65 cm. Distinctive small dark tern; head, neck and breast black, becoming more dark slaty grey on back and belly, with grey upperwing and tail; vent and undertail-coverts white; underwing grey; bill black; legs blackish-red. Shows slight sexual plumage dimorphism, probably the only tern to do so: breeding female greyer, with dull black on head restricted to crown. Non-breeding adult pale grey above, white below with characteristic dark patch on side of breast; head white, with contrasting dusky blackish central crown that meets black patch behind eye, and with dark spot in front of eye. Juvenile as non-breeding adult, but with pale brown wash on forehead, and back and scapulars grey-brown with pale buffish fringes. Race *surinamensis* smaller and darker; non-breeding adult and juvenile differ from nominate in having pale streaks on the dark crown, and more extensive dark patch on side of breast.

Habitat. Breeds on well vegetated inland pools, lakes, peat bogs and marshes, rice fields (Italy), and brackish marshes, with water usually 1-2 m deep; prefers sparse, open vegetation of bulrush and cat-tail (*Typha*) and other emergents, or floating water-lilies. Generally avoids marshes under 4 ha in extent. Forages over wetlands, but also in drier areas. On passage occurs on coasts and estuaries, but also at virtually any wetland, including even small ponds and ditches. Often roosts on emergent branches of drowned trees or on pilings. In winter found on estuaries, coasts and coastal lagoons.

Food and Feeding. Aquatic insects (particularly Coleoptera), small fish, snails, tadpoles and frogs. In breeding season mainly insects, including chironomids, Odonata, Ephemeridae; in analysis of 270 stomachs, fish formed 19% of diet. Insects comprise over 85-90% of nestling food. Usually feeds by aerial hawking and contact-dipping, occasionally hover-dipping, and more rarely plunge-diving. May feed 2-5 km from colony. Migrants feed in estuarine and coastal habitats, and flocks coalesce over schools of predatory fish; in Mediterranean, reported feeding in flocks over dolphins and tuna. Usually does not feed at night.

Breeding. May-Jun in Europe and North America. Some assortative mating, larger males mating with larger females. Most colonies contain fewer than 20 pairs, rarely more than 100; predation highest in small colonies. Usually nests over water, at least 50 cm deep; also on muskrat (*Ondatra zibethicus*) houses, boards, or old grebe or coot nests; prefers smaller, lower and wetter sites than *Sterna forsteri* in North America. Assembles mass of floating vegetation, or selects clump of dead reeds or cat-tail rootstalks. Nests usually more than 3 m apart in USA; sometimes 1·5-2 m in Ukraine, but often 20-100 m. Clutch 2-3 eggs, average 2·2-2·6; incubation 20-23 days (reports of under 20 days probably erroneous); adults leave nest early when intruders approach, and do not mob; chick similar to that of *C. leucopterus*, but paler, with dark chin and throat; fed within 2 hours after hatching; fledging 25 days. Nest success 20-40%; hatching success 52-70%; fledging success 1·3-2·1 chicks/pair. Recorded longevity of 17 years.

Movements. North American birds migrate to both Pacific and Atlantic coasts, wintering from Mexico (rarely) and Panama S to Peru, and from the Gulf Coast to N South America; accidental in Chile and Argentina. Many non-breeding birds, failed breeders or early migrants reach the coast by mid-summer; fairly common (formerly abundant) migrant off both coasts of Costa Rica; 1st-years summer along Pacific coast. Arrives back on breeding grounds in Apr. Palearctic birds often disperse N after breeding, with sometimes very large concentrations e.g. in S North Sea; migrates in huge numbers through Mediterranean, and also across N Africa (even over deserts), to main wintering grounds on tropical W African coasts from Mauritania to Namibia, some reaching South Africa; some winter in Nile Valley. Adults begin southbound migration by Aug, juveniles about a month later. Occasional birds linger over winter on Black and Caspian Seas.

Status and Conservation. Not globally threatened. World population may be of order of 500,000 pairs, including several 100,000's in former USSR (43,000 in Belarus), 25,000 in W Europe, and possibly 100,000 in North America. Many local populations vulnerable and declining; decreasing severely in many areas owing to wetland reclamation, with some local increases due to protection. Serious decline in E USA, and now rare or absent in coastal areas where flocks of 100's or 1000's seen in migration prior to 1970; along upper Niagara R (New York) typical numbers were 2000-5000 in 1965, but only 30-60 in 1987. Many nests are lost through storms and wave action, muskrat activity or predators; also when falling water level allows access to animals, including pigs. Main long-term cause of decline is loss of freshwater marsh habitat for agriculture, or through overgrowth of cat-tail, and human disturbance. Herbicide treatment of cat-tail has provided both open water and mats of dead vegetation, attracting nesting terns; but some suitable marshes are now unoccupied as well. Pesticides believed to have played some role in species' decline, either through direct poisoning or by eliminating aquatic prey and vegetation. Introduction of peacock bass (*Cichla ocellaris*) to Gatun L, Panama, eliminated the silverside (*Melaniris chagresi*) used for food by this tern, forcing it to winter elsewhere.

Bibliography. Ali & Ripley (1982), Ash (1970), Baggerman *et al.* (1956), Bent (1921), Bergman *et al.* (1970), Biaggi (1983), Blake (1977), Borodulina (1953b, 1960), Brazil (1991), Carroll, J.R. (1988), Chapman & Forbes (1984), Contreras *et al.* (1990), Cramp (1985), Cuthbert (1954), Davis & Ackerman (1985), Dementiev & Gladkov (1951b), Dowsett & Forbes-Watson (1993), Dunn (1979), Dunn & Agro (1995), Ehrlich *et al.* (1992), Elgood *et al.* (1994), Étchécopar & Hüe (1964, 1978), Fasola (1986), Finch (1986a), Ginn *et al.* (1989), Glutz von Blotzheim & Bauer (1982), Goodman *et al.* (1989), Gore (1990), Grant *et al.* (1971), Grimes (1987), Harrison (1984a), Haverschmidt (1933, 1944, 1968), Haverschmidt & Mees (1995), Hilty & Brown (1986), Hoffman (1927), Howell & Webb (1995a), Hüe & Étchécopar (1970), Ilicev & Zubakin (1988), Isenmann (1976c), Karpovitch *et al.* (1958), Knutson (1991), Knystautas (1993), Linz *et al.* (1994), Loftin (1991), Macikunas (1981, 1990, 1993), Mackworth-Praed & Grant (1957, 1970), Maclean (1993), Meininger (1988), Meyer de Schauensee & Phelps (1978), Monroe (1968), Olsen & Larssen (1995b), de la Peña (1992), Perennou (1991), Pinto (1983), Pulcher (1986a), Richards (1990), Richardson (1967), Ridgely & Gwynne (1989), Rogacheva (1992), Samorodov, A.V. & Samorodov (1972), Samorodov, Y.A. (1971), Schmitt *et al.* (1973), Schroeder & Zockler (1992), Shirihai (1996), Sirois & Fournier (1993), Slud (1964), Spillner (1975), Stern & Jarvis (1991), Stiles & Skutch (1989), Tomialojc (1994g), Tordoff (1962), Tostain *et al.* (1992), Trotignon (1994), Urban *et al.* (1986), Vinicombe (1980), Welham & Ydenberg (1993), Wetmore (1965), Williamson (1960).

Genus *PHAETUSA* Wagler, 1832

37. **Large-billed Tern**

Phaetusa simplex

French: Sterne à gros bec **German**: Großschnabel-Seeschwalbe **Spanish**: Charrán Picudo

Taxonomy. *Sterna simplex* Gmelin, 1789, Cayenne.
Morphometric analysis does not provide clear evidence of relationship to other terns or gulls, but apparently most similar to *Thalasseus*. Two subspecies recognized.

Subspecies and Distribution.
P. s. simplex (Gmelin, 1789) - E Colombia E to Trinidad, and S through Amazonia; W Ecuador.
P. s. chloropoda (Vieillot, 1819) - basins of R Paraguay and R Paraná SW to NC Argentina (Santiago del Estero, very rarely Cordoba); non-breeding visitor to Uruguay.

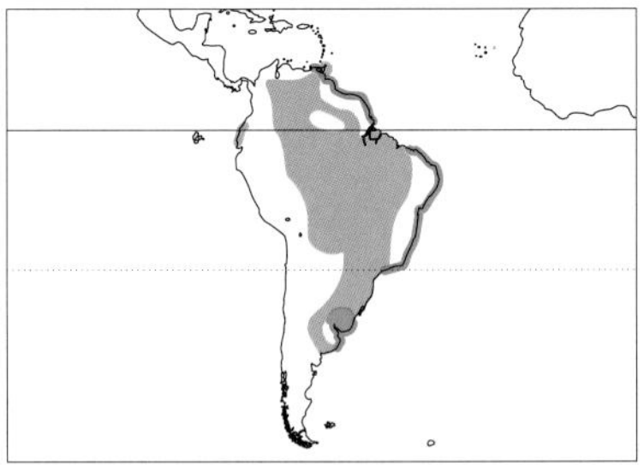

Descriptive notes. 38 cm; 208-247 g. Unmistakable large, relatively short-tailed tern, with very heavy yellow bill, and striking wing pattern; crown to ear-coverts black; upperparts medium grey (darker than in most terns), but secondaries and greater wing-coverts white; lores and underparts white, sides of flanks tinged grey; iris blackish brown; legs and feet yellow. Conspicuous pattern in flight: black primaries, grey back, and triangular white patch on secondaries and coverts, reminiscent of Sabine's Gull (*Xema sabini*). Non-breeding adult has crown and forehead paler. Juvenile has less black on crown; back and wings mottled with brown; bill duller. Race *chloropoda* has slightly paler upperparts and brighter bill.

Habitat. Occupies broad (and occasionally narrow) inland rivers and lakes, breeding on beaches and sandbars; has bred once on coast (Rio Grande do Sul). Non-breeders also frequent coastal mangroves, beaches and estuaries.

Food and Feeding. Fish 4-12 cm long; also insects. Feeds mainly by plunge-diving from 6-11 m; also by contact-dipping (swooping about 2 m over water), hover-dipping, and occasionally skimming. Performs aerial hawking over mudflats, and follows plough (Surinam) to capture insects. Occasionally pirates food from conspecifics.

Breeding. May-Jun and Oct-Dec in N of range, Aug-Sept in Argentina. Nests singly or in groups of up to 100 pairs, mainly on sandbars with Black Skimmers (*Rynchops niger*), *Sterna superciliaris* and Sand-coloured Nighthawk (*Chordeiles rupestris*). Changes nest-sites from year to year. Usually no nest material. Up to 3 eggs (average 2·3). Few other published data. Productivity 1·66 young/nest. In Peru 68% of nests successful.

Movements. Winters on rivers and on coast. Common throughout year on Guyanan coast, with lower numbers May-Aug when breeding. Accidental in West Indies, Bermuda, Panama, and North America (Illinois, Ohio, New Jersey).

Status and Conservation. Not globally threatened. Very widespread E of Andes, and common along the length of R Orinoco, but population figures not known. Breeding beaches are frequently inundated, or subject to disturbance from humans or ungulates. Egg-collecting occurs, but unpredictability of colony locations and of breeding phenology mean that species is not currently threatened. Most nest failures are apparently due to flooding; adults and young sometimes eaten by boas (*Constrictor constrictor*).

Bibliography. Belton (1984), Blake (1977), Canevari *et al.* (1991), Chubb (1916), Contreras *et al.* (1990), Davis (1935), Escalante (1962), Fjeldså & Krabbe (1990), Groom (1992), Hartert & Venturi (1909), Hayes (1995), Haverschmidt (1968), Haverschmidt & Mees (1995), Hellmayr & Conover (1948), Hilty & Brown (1986), Kane *et al.* (1989), Krannitz (1989), Meyer de Schauensee & Phelps (1978), Murphy (1936), Olmos *et al.* (1995), de la Peña (1992), Preston (1962), Remsen (1990), Ridgely & Gwynne (1989), Sick (1985c, 1993), Snyder (1966), Teague (1955), Tostain *et al.* (1992), Vooren & Chiaradia (1990), Willard (1985).

Genus *ANOUS* Stephens, 1826

38. **Brown Noddy**

Anous stolidus

French: Noddi brun **German**: Noddi **Spanish**: Tiñosa Boba
Other common names: Common Noddy, Noddy Tern

Taxonomy. *Sterna stolida* Linnaeus, 1758, Jamaica, West Indies.
Race *plumbeigularis* possibly inseparable from *pileatus*. Racial separation of birds from Madagascar is not warranted. Birds from Desaventurados Is (Chile) may represent an undescribed race. Five subspecies currently recognized.

Subspecies and Distribution.
A. s. plumbeigularis Sharpe, 1879 - S Red Sea and Gulf of Aden.
A. s. pileatus (Scopoli, 1786) - Seychelles and Madagascar E to N Australia, Polynesia, Hawaii, and Easter I, and possibly this race in Desaventurados Is.
A. s. galapagensis Sharpe, 1879 - Galapagos.
A. s. ridgwayi Anthony, 1898 - W Mexico (including Socorro I, Tres Marias and Isabella, Nayarit) and W Central America (including Cocos I).
A. s. stolidus (Linnaeus, 1758) - Caribbean and S Atlantic islands (including Trinidade, Ascension, St Helena, Tristan da Cunha, Inaccessible), and Gulf of Guinea to Cameroon.

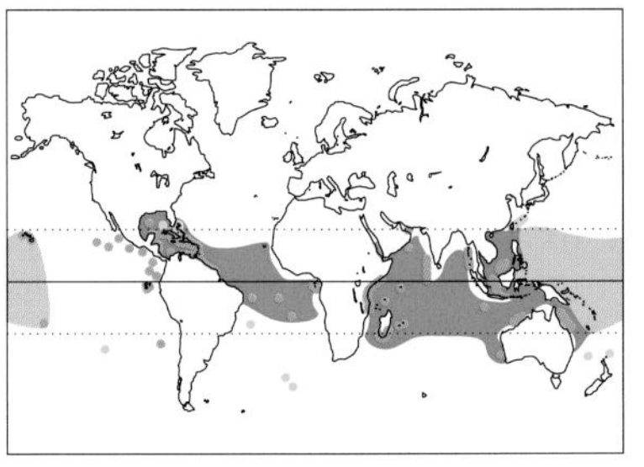

Descriptive notes. 38-45 cm; 150-272 g (average 173 g Pacific, 186 g West Indies); wingspan 75-86 cm. Dark chocolate brown noddy, with pale grey crown, sometimes almost white on forehead; narrow incomplete white eye-ring; upperwing shows slightly paler band across greater coverts; primaries black, and long wedge-shaped tail blackish; iris dark brown; bill, legs and feet black or blackish brown. Resembles *A. minutus*, but is not so dark and has shorter but thicker bill; also utters unique low, growling notes, and feeding flocks give sharp "eyeak" notes. Female significantly smaller and lighter in weight than male. Non-breeding adult similar; long period of moult continues into breeeding season. Juvenile similar to adult, but with brown crown and pale fringes to upperpart feathers. Races differ in size and in general colour tone; *galapagensis* darkest, almost blackish, with more or less distinct pale grey superloral stripe; *pileatus* has forehead and crown bluish grey rather than ashy white; *ridgwayi* similar to latter, but slightly darker.

Habitat. Pantropical and subtropical islands, often with small populations dispersed throughout many inshore and oceanic islands. Almost inaccessible islands and coral reefs (off Somalia). Nests on cliffs, and offshore stacks (Ascension, Culebra); sometimes on ground or in tree. When resting, settles on buoys, flotsam, ships and even on the sea.

Food and Feeding. Small fish and squid. At Kiritimati (Christmas I, Pacific), about half of food in volume was fish (7-16 cm), mainly Exocoetidae and Scombridae. In Hawaii, 354 food samples contained 50 prey species. In some studies, squid comprise c. 38% of diet. Feeds mainly by hover-dipping and contact-dipping; regularly foot-patters at surface, rather than swooping; usually does not plunge-dive. Captures flying-fish in air. In Galapagos steals fish from Brown Pelicans (*Pelecanus occidentalis*). Often associates with other birds over schools of predatory fish. Forages on moonlit nights. Feeds up to 50 km from colony.

Breeding. Nests all months in Galapagos, but fewest eggs Aug-Oct; may breed at less than annual intervals (Galapagos, Ascension); aseasonal in Hawaii, but mainly Jan-Feb; Feb in Laccadives, Feb-Mar in Trinidad, Apr-May in Dry Tortugas, Apr-Aug in Seychelles; May-Jun in NE South America, Jun-Jul in Polynesia, Oct-Apr on Great Barrier Reef, Nov in Tanzania, Dec on Ponapé. In Seychelles, breeding highly synchronous on Aride and Cousin, but not on Bird I. Colonies very dense or more open, depending on available ledges; occasionally nearly solitary; few colonies of 1000's. Nest-site variable, from flat beaches to cliffs, from bare ground to low bushes and tall trees: on Dry Tortugas from 10 cm to 10 m above ground, usually not directly on ground; in Indian Ocean, on rock shelf, bare shingle and in coconut palm (*Cocos*) or *Pandanus*; in Seychelles, almost exclusively in planted coconut palms, and formerly in *Scaevola* and *Tournefortia* bushes. Nest flimsy or bulky, of seaweed and/or twigs or sticks; sometimes no material, or just small layer of debris; at Los Roques (Venezuela), bulky stick nest 1-8 m up in mangroves. 1 egg; incubation 28-37 days (mean 35-36 days); chick white or charcoal grey, with few intermediates, proportion of morphs varying among colonies (35% white Dry Tortugas, 44% Culebra); fledging c. 8 weeks. Recorded longevity of 25 years.

Movements. Poorly known. Seldom seen on or close to shore away from breeding colony. Present most of year at most tropical colonies, but seasonally absent at subtropical ones. Disperses to sea after breeding. No known directed movement.

Status and Conservation. Not globally threatened. Innumerable small to medium-sized colonies, with few exceeding 1000 pairs. World population 300,000-500,000 pairs. About 93,000 pairs in Hawaiian Is, including 30,000 on Nihoa. Caribbean population estimated at 28,000 pairs, plus possibly 50,000 in Bahamas. At least 100,000 pairs in Australian waters, including c. 76,000 in Pelsart Is (W Australia) in 1986. Very large concentrations in Phoenix and Society Is, with 10,000-100,000 in each. Some populations are increasing under protection (e.g. Dry Tortugas), and some range expansions; recently nested in New Zealand (1991). Some populations, however, are vulnerable; dwindling 500-pair colony on Ascension I is threatened by rats and cats. Christmas I (Indian Ocean) population stable, estimated at 5500 birds.

Bibliography. Ali & Ripley (1982), Amerson & Shelton (1976), Amerson *et al*. (1974), Ash (1980a), Ash & Miskell (1983), Ashmole (1968b), Ashmole & Ashmole (1967), Beehler *et al*. (1986), Biaggi (1983), Blake (1977), Brazil (1991), Bregnballe *et al*. (1990), Bregulla (1992), Brown, W.Y. (1975a, 1975b, 1976a, 1976b, 1976d, 1977), Brown, W.Y. & Robertson (1975), Chardine & Morris (1989, 1996), Clapp & Kridler (1977), Clapp *et al*. (1983), Coates (1985), Collias (1988), Cramp (1985), Dickinson *et al*. (1991), Dorward & Ashmole (1963), Dowsett & Forbes-Watson (1993), Dujardin & Tostain (1990), van der Elst & Pr s-Jones (1987), Étchécopar & Hüe (1978), Evans (1994), Feare (1979a), ffrench (1990), Gallagher *et al*. (1984), Gibson-Hill (1947), van Halewijn & Norton (1984), Harrison (1984a), Harrison & Stoneburner (1981), Harrison *et al*. (1983), Hayes & Baker (1989), Hilty & Brown (1986), Holyoak & Thibault (1984), Howell (1990), Howell & Webb (1995a), Johnson (1967), Johnson *et al*. (1970), Kohno & Kishimoto (1991), Langrand (1990), LeCroy (1976), Lekagul & Round (1991), MacKinnon & Phillipps (1993), Mackworth-Praed & Grant (1957, 1962, 1970), Marchant & Higgins (1996), van Marle & Voous (1988), Mathiu *et al*. (1991), Matsunaga *et al*. (1989), Medway & Wells (1976), Meyer de Schauensee & Phelps (1978), Milon *et al*. (1973), Monroe (1968), Moore & Balzarotti (1983), Morris (1984), Morris & Chardine (1990, 1992), Moynihan (1962), Niethammer *et al*. (1992), Olsen & Larssen (1995b), Pakenham (1979), Pettit & Whittow (1983), Rahn *et al*. (1976), Ricklefs & White-Schuler (1978), Ridgely & Gwynne (1989), Ripley (1982), Riska (1984, 1986a, 1986b), Robertson (1964, 1978, 1996), Schodde *et al*. (1983), Serventy *et al*. (1971), Short *et al*. (1990), Sick (1985c, 1993), Smythies (1981, 1986), Sprunt (1948a), Stiles & Skutch (1989), Stokes (1988), Tostain *et al*. (1992), Urban *et al*. (1986), Watson (1908), Wetmore (1965), White, C.M.N. & Bruce (1986), White, S.C. *et al*. (1976), Woodward (1972).

39. **Black Noddy**

Anous minutus

French: Noddi noir **German**: Weißkopfnoddi **Spanish**: Tiñosa Menuda
Other common names: White-capped Noddy

Taxonomy. *Anous minutus* Boie, 1844, Raine Island, Australia.
Forms superspecies with *A. tenuirostris*, with which sometimes considered conspecific. Seven subspecies recognized.

Subspecies and Distribution.
A. m. worcesteri McGregor, 1911 - Cavilli I and Tubbataha Reef (Sulu Sea).
A. m. minutus Boie, 1844 - NE Australia and New Guinea to Tuamotu Is.
A. m. marcusi (Bryan, 1903) - Marcus I and Wake I through Micronesia to Caroline Is.
A. m. melanogenys G. R. Gray, 1846 - Hawaiian Is.
A. m. diamesus (Heller & Snodgrass, 1901) - EC Pacific at Cocos I and Clipperton Is.
A. m. americanus (Mathews, 1912) - Central America and Venezuelan islands; recently found and possibly nesting off Yucatán, Mexico, and in Lesser Antilles.
A. m. atlanticus (Mathews, 1912) - Atlantic islands (St Paul, Fernando de Noronha, Ascension, St Helena, formerly Inaccessible) N & E to Gulf of Guinea.

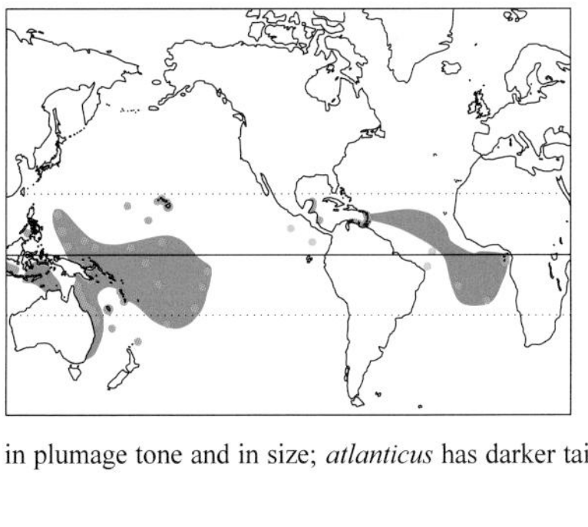

Descriptive notes. 35-39 cm; 98-144 g; wingspan 66-72 cm. Very dark noddy with pale crown; iris brown, bill black, legs brown. Smaller and slimmer than *A. stolidus*, with subtly blacker body and greyer tail; head with more extensive white, and proportionately longer, more slender bill. Distinguished from *A. tenuirostris* by darker sooty black body, and more abruptly demarcated white forehead and pale crown. Voice also distinctive, "tik-tikoree" and staccato rattle. Non-breeding adult identical to breeding adult. Juvenile has more obvious white on head than juvenile *A. stolidus*, but more obscure pale fringes above. Races differ only slightly, mainly in plumage tone and in size; *atlanticus* has darker tail; *melanogenys* has dull yellowish orange legs.

Habitat. Oceanic and offshore islands. Breeds on sea cliffs, e.g. at Ascension and Hawaii; also on trees and bushes, e.g. in Pacific and Australia.

Food and Feeding. Almost exclusively fish, particularly small Atherinidae; lesser amounts of squid, and small amounts of crustaceans. At Ascension predominantly fish (mostly Blennidae, Holocentridae, Exocoetidae), with squid present in 12% of regurgitation samples. In Hawaii 90% fish (of 18 families), and 10% squid; mainly Synodontidae and Mullidae and squid (Ommastrephidae) in NW Hawaii. In Australia mainly anchovy (*Engraulis australis*). Feeds by hover-dipping and contact-dipping; foot-patters. Flocks of 5000 and more gather quickly over shoals of fish. May feed up to 80 km from breeding colony.

Breeding. Mostly annual cycle: Mar-May in Hawaii, May in Venezuela, Jun-Jul at Ascension, Oct-Nov in Australia; but in Fiji Jun in some years, Sept in others (possibly a secondary peak of failed breeders). Colonies often dense. Nest in trees and bushes where available, usually a platform of seaweed and/or twigs and leaves cemented by excrement, quite distinct from bulky stick nest of *A. stolidus*; collects nest material in flight by contact-dipping. In Australia nests up to 15 m up in *Pisonia grandis*, but favours *Ficus* and *Celtis* when available; in *Cecropia* on Cocos I (Costa Rica); in Belize and in Los Roques (Venezuela), 4-10 m up in mangroves. Larger trees hold proportionately more nests, but species shuns largest trees. Where no trees, nests on ledges on sea cliffs (e.g. Ascension, main islands of Hawaii). 1 egg; prolonged incubation 30-37 days; chick blackish with whitish forehead; fledging c. 48-60 days; returns to nest to be fed for several weeks; chicks that fall from nest are abandoned. In French Frigate Shoals (Hawaii) regularly double-brooded, laying second egg while feeding first fledgling at nest; successful in c. 50% of cases.

Movements. Poorly known. Permanent resident around some islands (e.g. Hawaii, Ascension). Partial dispersal from others; from Fiji, some birds disperse up to 2900 km W through Solomon Is. High degree of racial variation suggests species is generally sedentary, with isolated populations.

Status and Conservation. Not globally threatened. Total population over 200,000 pairs, including 10,000 on Ascension I and 20,000 in Hawaii. Largest concentrations in Line Is and Phoenix Is, with 10,000-100,000 pairs in each. In Australia, logarithmic growth at Heron I (Capricorn Group) since first nests in 1920, to 40,000 in 1985. Many local populations, however, vulnerable; extirpated from Malden I (Line Is) due to destruction of vegetation by goats. Cyclones occasionally interfere with parental feeding, causing chick starvation; occasionally subject to massive starvation, as at Ascension I in Jul-Oct 1958, when many young died. On some islands, young birds are trapped by sticky seeds of *Pisonia*, which form dense mats in some years.

Bibliography. Amerson (1971), Amerson & Shelton (1976), Ashmole (1962, 1968b), Ashmole & Ashmole (1967), Ashmole *et al*. (1994), Barnes & Hill (1989), Beehler *et al*. (1986), Blake (1977), Bond & Ripley (1960), Bregulla (1992), Buttemer & Astheimer (1990), Coates (1985), Congdon (1990, 1991), Cullen & Ashmole (1963), Dale *et al*. (1984), Danchin & Nelson (1991), Dickinson *et al*. (1991), Dowsett & Dowsett-Lemaire (1993), Dowsett & Forbes-Watson (1993), van Halewijn & Norton (1984), Harrison (1984a), Harrison *et al*. (1984), Hill & Rosier (1989), Holyoak & Thibault (1984), Houston (1979), Howell & Webb (1995a), Howell *et al*. (1990), Hulsman (1987, 1988), Hulsman *et al*. (1984), Langham (1983, 1986), LeCroy (1976), Mackworth-Praed & Grant (1962, 1970), Marchant & Higgins (1996), van Marle & Voous (1988), Merton (1970), Meyer de Schauensee & Phelps (1978), Moynihan (1962), Niethammer *et al*. (1992), Norton (1989), Ogden (1979, 1993), Olsen & Larssen (1995b), Pettit & Whittow (1983), Pettit *et al*. (1984), Rahn *et al*. (1976), Robertson *et al*. (1961), Schodde *et al*. (1983), Schreiber & Ashmole (1970), Seki & Harrison (1989), Serventy *et al*. (1971), Smythies (1981), Soper (1969a), Stiles & Skutch (1989), Tarburton (1987), Urban *et al*. (1986), White & Bruce (1986), Whittow (1980).

40. **Lesser Noddy**

Anous tenuirostris

French: Noddi marianne **German**: Schlankschnabelnoddi **Spanish**: Tiñosa Picofina

Taxonomy. *Sterna tenuirostris* Temminck, 1823, Senegal; error = Seychelles.
Forms superspecies with *A. minutus*; further study may even show the two to be conspecific. Two subspecies recognized.

Subspecies and Distribution.
A. t. tenuirostris (Temminck, 1823) - Seychelles, Mascarene Is, and probably Maldives, with possible breeding attempts having taken place in Somalia; non-breeders visit Arabia, Madagascar and rarely Tanzanian coast.
A. t. melanops Gould, 1846 - Houtman Abrolhos Is (Western Australia), and formerly Indonesia.

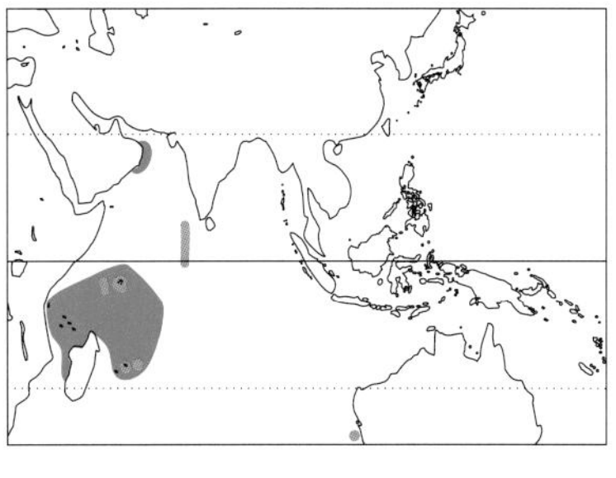

Descriptive notes. 30-34 cm; 97-120 g; wingspan 58-63 cm. Blackish brown, with whitish forehead and crown blending into more ashy grey hindcrown and nape; lores whitish; sides of neck and throat sooty; iris dark brown, bill black, legs brownish black. Very similar to *A. minutus*, but smaller and paler, with pale (not dark) lores; pale of head blends more evenly into dark of neck. Juvenile paler brown, but also has white cap. Race *melanops* similar to nominate, but with blackish stripe above eye extending onto lores.

Habitat. Oceanic islets. Nests in trees, occasionally in bushes.

Food and Feeding. Small fish and invertebrates. Feeds by hovering and aerial- or contact-dipping. Associates with *A. stolidus*.

Breeding. Aug-Oct. Sometimes congregates in large colonies; 5000 pairs on Lizard I (Mauritius), up to 30,000 pairs in Pelsart Group (Houtman Abrolhos). Some colonies stable, others shift from year to year. On Cousin and Aride (Seychelles), builds bulky nests 5 m apart in tall trees, occasionally in low bushes. In Houtman Abrolhos, substantial platform of brown algae and excreta on mangroves; nests often close together, only 30 cm apart. 1 egg; incubation and fledging periods not documented, but incubation probably c. 35 days; incubating adult tolerates close approach; chicks that fall from nest are not fed.

Movements. Permanent resident around Pelsart Group. Other movements not known, but species occurs fairly regularly outside breeding season off E Africa.

Status and Conservation. Not globally threatened. Few colonies have been discovered to date. Abundant in Western Australia until about 1900, then unexplained disappearance of large colonies; recovery in mid-20th century, and now apparently stable, with estimates of 27,000 nests in late 1960's and 30,000 in 1986. Size of Indian Ocean populations not known. Some colonies are apparently vulnerable.

Bibliography. Ali & Ripley (1982), Ash (1980a), Ash & Miskell (1983), Bullock (1990), Burbidge & Fuller (1989), Dowsett & Dowsett-Lemaire (1993), Dowsett & Forbes-Watson (1993), Evans (1994), Feare (1979b), Garnett (1993), Langrand (1990), Marchant & Higgins (1996), Milon *et al*. (1973), Penny (1974), Serventy & Whittell (1976), Serventy *et al*. (1971), Short *et al*. (1990), Surman & Wooller (1995), Urban *et al*. (1986), Vesey-Fitzgerald (1941).

Genus *PROCELSTERNA* Lafresnaye, 1842

41. **Blue Noddy**

Procelsterna cerulea

French: Noddi bleu **German**: Blaunoddi **Spanish**: Tiñosa Azulada
Other common names: Blue Ternlet; Blue-grey Noddy/Ternlet (superspecies)

Taxonomy. *Sterna Cerulea* F. D. Bennett, 1840, Kiritimati (Christmas) Island, Pacific Ocean.
Forms superspecies with *P. albivitta*, with which often considered conspecific, but significant differences in size, coloration and geographical range; the two are sometimes incorrectly treated as pale and dark morphs of same species; some authors have claimed that races *skottsbergii* and *imitatrix* of *P. albivitta* belong to present species, but specimen evidence refutes this. Internal taxonomy confused at present, with much overlap of forms, e.g. birds from Society Is significantly darker than those from Tuamotu Is, and might not be referable to same race; validity of races and their distributions require careful systematic revision based on known breeding specimens, but these are lacking from various parts of its range. Emendation of species name to *caerulea* is unjustified. Five subspecies currently recognized.
Subspecies and Distribution.
P. c. saxatilis W. K. Fisher, 1903 - Marcus I and N Marshall Is E to NW Hawaiian Is.
P. c. nebouxi Mathews, 1912 - Tuvalu (Ellice Is) E to Phoenix Is and S to Fiji and Western Samoa.
P. c. cerulea (F. D. Bennett, 1840) - Kiritimati (Christmas) I in Line Is, and also Marquesas Is.
P. c. teretirostris (Lafresnaye, 1841) - Tuamotu Is, and probably this race likewise in Cook, Austral and Society Is.
P. c. murphyi Mougin & de Naurois, 1981 - Gambier Is.

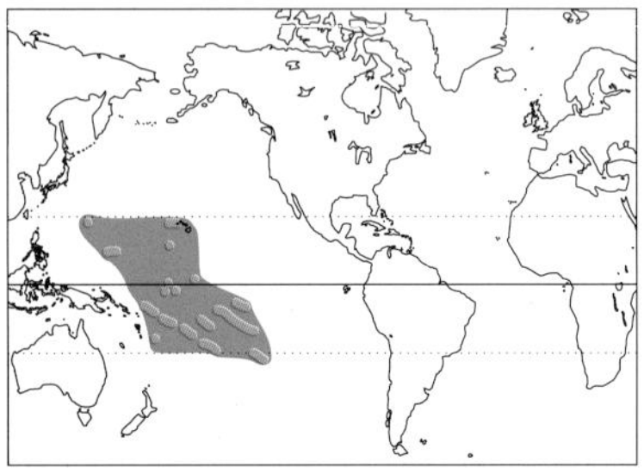

Descriptive notes. 25-28 cm; 41-69 g (average 45·4 g, but non-breeders significantly lighter); wingspan 46-60 cm. Distinctive pale noddy, with relatively short, slender black bill and short, slightly forked tail; all-grey head and body, with only slightly paler underparts; white partial spectacle behind eye and small black spot in front; upperwing has slightly darker grey or brown-tinged coverts, and blackish primaries; below, shows little contrast between primaries and underwing-coverts; eye brownish black; bill and legs black. Smaller than *P. albivitta*, which is also paler grey above, and white below and on head. Races differ mainly in plumage tone, but some confusion exists; nominate *cerulea*, at least in Marquesas, apparently darkest; *teretirostris* has paler head and underparts, but is significantly paler in Tuamotu Is than in Society Is.
Habitat. Tropical oceanic islands. Breeds on cliffs or rocky areas. Forages over lagoons and inshore waters.
Food and Feeding. Has narrowest gape of any tern, and takes tiniest fish (average length 17 mm; mainly larval Synodontidae, Exocoetidae, Mullidae, Bothidae), squid, crustaceans, and pelagic sea striders (*Halobates sericeus*, *H. micans*); proportions vary seasonally and geographically. Fish present in 97% of samples, and squid in 50%. At Kiritimati over 50% of food items (75% of food volume) fish, with squid and crustaceans equally represented. At sea, species is the only primarily insectivorous pelagic tern. Usually feeds in small groups close inshore at breeding islands. Flies low over water with quick shallow wingbeats, dipping to surface to snatch tiny prey; often hovers low, foot-pattering on surface. Adults do not carry fish in bill.
Breeding. In Hawaii reported to breed throughout year, with laying peak Feb-Mar, few nests in May, Aug, Nov, hence probably an asynchronous spring breeder, rather than truly aseasonal; Aug-Nov at Kiritimati, and Jun-Aug in Phoenix Is. Loose colonies of up to 100 pairs on islets in lagoons. Nests on rocky substrate using crevice, ledge or concavity in cliffs or rock crops, or on gravel or coral rubble, usually on slopes; also under coral slabs or vegetation, seldom fully concealed; nest generally inaccessible to most predators. Usually no material, but may assemble a few shells, bones, feathers or stems around egg. Clutch 1 egg; incubation period not known; chick uniform whitish, with black bill and eye; hatching weight under 10 g; fed by regurgitation, and brooded continuously for 2-3 weeks. Productivity estimated at 0·5 young/pair on Nihoa (Hawaii); some eggs predated by Nihoa Finch (*Telespyza ultima*). Age of first breeding not reported, but some may breed at 1 year where nest-sites not limiting. Recorded longevity of 11 years.
Movements. Not known. Usually remains close to breeding colonies.
Status and Conservation. Not globally threatened. Censuses in small part of range gave at least 30,000 pairs, and overall total for species may be closer to 100,000 pairs. In NW Hawaii, 4000 pairs plus 8000 non-breeders. Up to 10,000 pairs each in Line and Phoenix Is; up to 1000 in Gambier Is, 2000 on Kiritimati. Difficult to census owing to inaccessible sea-cliff nesting sites, which protect species from egging and predators in most places. Cliff nesting habitat is a limiting factor. The colony on Kaula I (Palmyra, Line Is) was eliminated when the island was used for a bombing range.
Bibliography. Amerson (1971), Ashmole (1968b), Ashmole & Ashmole (1967), Cheng & Harrison (1983), Clapp & Kridler (1977), Clapp *et al*. (1977), Fefer *et al*. (1984), Fisher (1903), Garnett (1984), Harrison, C. S. (1984a, 1990), Harrison, C. S. *et al*. (1984), Holyoak & Thibault (1984), Mougin & de Naurois (1981), Munro (1960), Murphy (1936), Muse & Muse (1982), Pratt *et al*. (1987), Rauzon *et al*. (1984).

42. **Grey Noddy**

Procelsterna albivitta

French: Noddi gris **German**: Graunoddi **Spanish**: Tiñosa Gris

Taxonomy. *Procelsterna albivitta* Bonaparte, 1856, Lord Howe Island.
Temperate and subtropical counterpart of *P. cerulea*, with which it forms a superspecies; sometimes considered conspecific. Some authors have claimed that races of SE Pacific belong to *P. cerulea*, but specimen evidence refutes this. Three subspecies recognized.
Subspecies and Distribution.
P. a. albivitta Bonaparte, 1856 - Lord Howe I, Norfolk I, Kermadec Is and Tonga.
P. a. skottsbergii Lönnberg, 1921 - Henderson I, and Easter and Sala y Gómez Is.
P. a. imitatrix Mathews, 1912 - San Ambrosio and San Félix (Desaventurados Is), off C Chile.
Descriptive notes. 28-31 cm; wingspan 46-60 cm. Small, relatively long-legged noddy, with grey back, darker grey wings and tail, and pale greyish to whitish head and underparts; white or pale

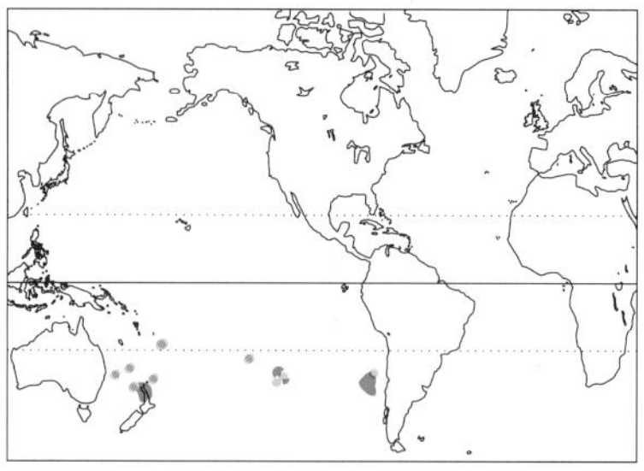

underwing-coverts; eye with narrow black semicircle at front, white behind; iris brown, bill black; legs and feet blackish brown, with pinkish yellow webs; mouth-lining yellow. Distinguished from slightly smaller *P. cerulea* by paler plumage, with much whiter head and underparts. Juvenile tinged brownish above, but uniform, without scaling or barring. Races differ mainly in plumage tone; underparts whitest on *skottsbergii* and *imitatrix*.
Habitat. Temperate and subtropical oceanic islands. Breeding birds occur around coasts of rocky islands, nesting on cliffs up to 600 m high, or on ground. Forages in inshore waters.
Food and Feeding. At Desaventurados Is (Chile) takes tiny crustaceans, and also fish and squid; small crustaceans at Kermadec Is and Lord Howe I. Feeds by fluttering or hovering low over water, and repeatedly dipping; does not foot-patter. Seen to face upwind, and at end of food patch circle back to beginning.
Breeding. Aug-Nov in SW Pacific; at Easter I present in Dec, but not nesting. Reported to be only passively colonial. Nest in cliff crevice or ledge, or on ground under rocks, on bare rock, or under vegetation such as tussock grass (Kermadecs). 1 egg; incubation period unknown; chick uniform smoky grey or chocolate brown, unspeckled, with dark felted forecrown, and paler belly, nape and face; pin feathers appear c. day 17; fledging 32-45 days. Some may be double-brooded.
Movements. Non-migratory; disperses around breeding colony, but rarely reaches continental waters. Uncommon visitor to N New Zealand, with flocks of 1000 in Jan 1970; non-breeders reported in many parts of S Pacific. Straggler to E Australia.
Status and Conservation. Not globally threatened. Total population probably under 25,000 pairs, most in SW Pacific. Norfolk I holds several thousand pairs, possibly up to 10,000; under 10,000 pairs in Kermadecs, where said to be common, with several thousand pairs on Herald Islets; fewer than 1000 pairs on Lord Howe I. Status not at all well known, and species possibly rare. The two SE Pacific subspecies are probably endangered: Easter I population is threatened by cats; only about 40 birds documented on Desaventurados, but no recent data. Cliff-nesting assures some survival, even on predator-infested islands.
Bibliography. Eller (1989), Falla (1970), Falla *et al*. (1981), Flegg & Madge (1995), Hermes (1985), Holyoak & Thibault (1984), Johnson (1967), Lindsey (1992), Marchant & Higgins (1996), Merton (1970), Morris (1972), Mougin & de Narois (1981), Murphy (1936), Oliver (1974), Pizzey & Doyle (1980), Robertson (1985), Schodde *et al*. (1983), Simpson & Day (1994), Slater *et al*. (1989), Soper (1969a, 1976), Tarburton (1981), Trounson (1987).

Genus *GYGIS* Wagler, 1832

43. **White Tern**

Gygis alba

French: Gygis blanche **German**: Feenseeschwalbe **Spanish**: Charrán Blanco
Other common names: Fairy Tern(!); Common White Tern (*alba*); Little White Tern (*microrhyncha*)

Taxonomy. *Sterna alba* Sparrman, 1786, Ascension Island.
Placed in a monotypic genus, owing to unique plumage and bill. Race *microrhyncha* sometimes separated as distinct species, but apparently interbreeds with *G. alba* in Kiribati. Internal taxonomy extremely confusing, with correct subspecific allocations and limits frequently unclear and disputed; some authors have preferred to recognize several additional races, including *royana* of Norfolk I and Kermadec Is, *pacifica* of Caroline Is, Melanesia and other islands of S Pacific, and *rothschildi* of Hawaii, all of which herein included in nominate race, but all are sometimes referred instead to race *candida*. Birds of Seychelles and Mascarenes described as *monte*, but not separable from *candida*. Four subspecies currently recognized.
Subspecies and Distribution.
G. a. alba (Sparrman 1786) - Caroline Is through Melanesia to Norfolk I and Kermadec Is; Hawaii; W Mexico (Clipperton), Costa Rica (Cocos I) and probably Colombia (Malpelo); S Atlantic islands (Fernando de Noronha, Trinidade, Ascension, St Helena).
G. a. candida (Gmelin, 1789) - Seychelles and Mascarenes through Indian Ocean to SC Pacific, including Marquesas Is (Hatutu).
G. a. microrhyncha Saunders, 1876 - Marquesas Is (Eiao to Fatu Hiva) and apparently also Phoenix and Line Is.
G. a. leucopes Holyoak & Thibault, 1976 - Henderson I and Pitcairn I (SE Pacific).

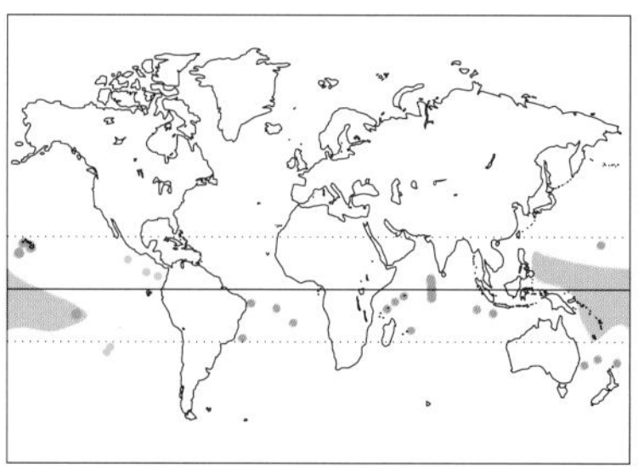

Descriptive notes. 25-30 cm; 92-139 g; wingspan 76-80 cm. Most ethereal of seabirds; entire plumage immaculate white, with black ring around eye and dusky flight-feather shafts; unique black bill slightly upcurved, and tapering to point; legs blackish to dull bluish; short tail with slight fork; buoyant and erratic flight with deep, slow wingbeats. Juvenile white, with black mark behind eye, grey hindneck, brownish grey back and scapulars, and some black edges to remiges. Races differ mainly in colour of remex shafts, and soft parts: *alba* and *microrhyncha* have slimmer, straighter, all black bill and paler primary shafts; *microrhyncha* also has paler legs and feet; *candida* has blue-grey base to noticeably up-angled bill, and dark primary shafts; *leucopes* often has creamy white legs.
Habitat. Coral islands, usually with vegetation. Nests in trees and bushes, and on rocky slopes and cliffs; also on artificial substrates.
Food and Feeding. Mainly small fish, occasionally squid and crustaceans. At Kiritimati (Christmas I, Pacific), fish and squid taken equally, and 22 fish families represented; adults ate mainly Blennidae, mostly smaller than 2 cm, but fed chicks mainly halfbeaks (Hemiramphidae) 1-8 cm long. In Hawaii c. 85% fish and 14% squid. Carries 1-6 fish neatly arranged in bill to young. Catches prey by diving to water surface.

Breeding. Mar-Sept with peak Apr-May in Hawaii, May-Aug at Kiritimati and Chagos Is; in Maldives intermittently throughout year; in Seychelles, throughout year on Cousin I but apparently absent after Jan on Bird I. Nest-spacing varies with nest-site availability; in Seychelles 1 nest/180 m². Unique nesting habit: lays single egg on bare branch, usually in slight depression at a fork or on midrib of palm frond or banana leaf. Nest height 0-20 m; branch width 8-25 cm. On Bird I, only on *Casuarina* trees or on buildings (former site secure from rats, latter subject to heavy predation on eggs and chicks). On Ascension 10% nest in cliffs. Where sites scarce (Ascension), successive pairs occupy same site. In other cases the same pair re-lays after losing egg. On most islands no ground predators apparent. Tree-nesters sit tighter, not flushing until observer within 2 m; those on rock flush sooner. Eggs and chicks often blown from nest, particularly from smooth-limbed *Casuarina*. Clutch 1 egg; incubation 30-41 days (average 34-36); chick white, with strong claws with which it clings to branch. Hatching success 35-45%. Recorded longevity of 17 years.

Movements. Resident all year round on some islands, seasonal visitor on others. Outside breeding season lives at sea, but movement patterns not known.

Status and Conservation. Not globally threatened. World population unknown, but exceeds 100,000 pairs. A very widespread species on tropical islands, although absent from many apparently suitable islands. Largest concentrations in Western Samoa, Tokelau, Line Is and Phoenix Is, each with more than 10,000 pairs.

Bibliography. Ali & Ripley (1982), Ashmole (1968a, 1968b), Ashmole & Ashmole (1967), Ashmole *et al.* (1994), Beehler *et al.* (1986), Bourne *et al.* (1977), Brazil (1991), Bregulla (1992), Clapp & Kridler (1977), Clapp *et al.* (1977), Coates (1985), Diamond (1984), Dorward (1963), Dowsett & Forbes-Watson (1993), Étchécopar & Hüe (1978), Fefer *et al.* (1984), Harrison, C. S. (1984a, 1990), Harrison, C. S. *et al.* (1984), Holyoak & Thibault (1976, 1984), Houston (1979), Howell & Webb (1995a), Johnson (1967), Langrand (1990), MacKinnon & Phillipps (1993), Mackworth-Praed & Grant (1962), Marks & Hendricks (1989), van Marle & Voous (1988), Miles (1986), Milon *et al.* (1973), Moynihan (1962), Murphy (1936), Niethammer *et al.* (1992), Pettit, Grant & Whittow (1984), Pettit, Grant, Whittow *et al.* (1981), Rahn *et al.* (1976), Rauzon & Kenyon (1984), Schodde *et al.* (1983), Sick (1985c, 1993), Stiles & Skutch (1989), Tarburton (1984), Vesey-Fitzgerald (1941), Woodward (1972).

Genus *LAROSTERNA* Blyth, 1852

44. Inca Tern
Larosterna inca

French: Sterne inca   **German**: Inkaseeschwalbe   **Spanish**: Charrán Inca

Taxonomy. *Sterna Inca* Lesson, 1827, Lima, Peru.
Unique among terns in morphology, appearance, habitats and habits, and unquestionably warrants segregation in monospecific genus. Monotypic.

Distribution. Humboldt Current region from N Peru (Lobos de Tierra I) S to C Chile (S at least to R Aconcagua).

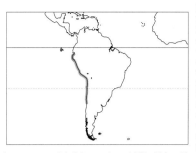

Descriptive notes. 39-42 cm; 180-210 g (in captivity, average 189 g). Unique and unmistakable; body dark slate, paler on throat and underwing-coverts; white stripe curling back and downwards from gape to side of neck, where it fans out into long satiny feathers; trailing edge of wing white, and white edges to four outer primaries; iris brown, bill and legs dark red; yellow bare area at base of bill; wing shape rounded, and tail moderately forked; has characteristic fluttering flight, with rapid wingbeats; serrated flange on middle toe unique among terns. Juvenile uniform blackish, with small grey tufts at base of bill. Subadult has brown cast, and dark horn-coloured bill which reddens with age; curling gape plumes dull brownish.

Habitat. Mainly found on inshore "guano islands", but also 67 km offshore on Hormigas de Afuera I; typically along rocky coasts, or where sandy beaches are backed by cliffs. Nests on rocky sea cliffs and guano islands, also in artificial structures.

Food and Feeding. Mainly small anchovetta (*Engraulis ringens*); also planktonic crustaceans; offal and scraps. Associates with fishing boats; large flocks (average 100+ in C Peru) attend fishing activities, including dynamiting. Rapidly detects a surfacing sea lion, and is the most numerous species associating with these mammals. Feeding flocks number up to 5000. Forages mainly by plunge-diving, and contact- and surface-dipping; scavenges for scraps left by sea lions and avian predators.

Breeding. Probably aseasonal. Eggs found Apr-Jul and Oct-Dec; young found mid-Jul. Nests in fissures, burrows and small caves, in troughs in guano or sand, and at base of or under rocks and boulders on island slopes; in abandoned petrel burrows or at entrance of penguin burrows; also on ledges in and under buildings and piers. Many nest on abandoned dredges and barges in harbours. Often with Peruvian Diving-petrel (*Pelecanoides garnotii*) or Red-legged Cormorant (*Phalacrocorax gaimardi*). Where vultures present, nests more hidden; sometimes forced to abandon breeding attempt when other seabirds begin nesting. 2 eggs, sometimes 1, usually well hidden in tunnel or crevice; incubation period not reported; chick dark grey above, paler grey below, with faint speckling on head; fledging c. 4 weeks; fully dependent for at least 1 month further, during which practises foraging techniques.

Movements. Permanently resident, with no systematic migration. Non-breeders move opportunistically to follow food. Some disperse N to Ecuador.

Status and Conservation. Not globally threatened. Numbers fluctuate from year to year, depending on food availability in relation to El Niño (see Volume 1, page 341); populations decline greatly during severe occurrences of El Niño, but rebound quickly, suggesting mass emigration rather than mass starvation; total population estimated to vary around c. 50,000 pairs. Main abundance on C coast of Peru among inshore guano islands, particularly Chinchas, Pescadores and Asia Is. Formerly considered present in enormous numbers, but neither as abundant, nor as vulnerable, as the typical guano species. Main nesting habitat is not limited. Formerly confined to coastal Peru; first bred in Chile during late 1930's, and is now common S to Valparaíso.

Bibliography. Anon. (1994h), Ashmole & Tovar (1968), Blake (1977), Bruning & Clare (1977), Duffy (1983), Duffy *et al.* (1984), Duquet (1995), Guillen (1988), Hellmayr & Conover (1948), Hilty & Brown (1986), Johnson (1967), Koepcke (1970), Meyer de Schauensee (1982), Moynihan (1962), Murphy (1936), Parker *et al.* (1982), Ridgely & Gwynne (1989), Rivadeneira *et al.* (1986), Schlatter (1984), Tovar (1968).

Class AVES
Order CHARADRIIFORMES
Suborder LARI
Family RYNCHOPIDAE (SKIMMERS)

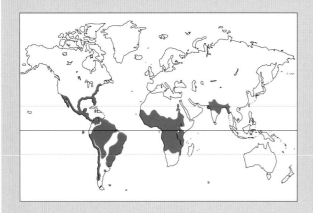

- Medium-sized rather aerial waterbirds, with long, pointed wings and short legs; unique bill structure, with very narrow lower mandible much longer than upper.
- 36-46 cm.

- Pantropical, extending to subtropics and marginally into temperate zone.
- Large rivers and other water bodies, mainly inland.
- 1 genus, 3 species, 5 taxa.
- 1 species threatened; none extinct since 1600.

Systematics

In the absence of any known fossil of Rynchopidae, estimates of the phylogenetic history of the skimmers are based entirely on the comparative anatomy, behaviour and molecular make-up of extant species. Anatomists of the nineteenth and early twentieth centuries established the skimmers within the order Charadriiformes and the suborder Lari, which also includes the skuas, gulls and terns. The three extant species of Rynchopidae are included in a single genus, *Rynchops*, because all share a unique foraging behaviour and its associated structural adaptations, and they closely resemble each other in plumage pattern.

Recent publications that are based on myology, osteology, behaviour and molecular data, and analysed by phylogenetic methods, agree that the gulls (Laridae) and the terns (Sternidae) are more closely related to each other than either group is to the skimmers. However, questions about the relationships among terns have been raised, and one author concluded that the noddies (*Anous, Procelsterna*) are more closely related to skimmers than to "true" terns; in addition, there are some who disagree about the precise placement of the skuas within the suborder Lari. To date, studies of the Lari have been incomplete in their coverage of genera, and have differed somewhat in the taxa covered. Until we have corroborative results from different kinds of data covering all of the genera, such problems must remain unsolved.

Several fossils have been referred to Sternidae and Laridae, but all those identified as terns are suspect. Since the oldest of the gull-like fossils are from the Eo-Oligocene deposits of France, we may infer that the origin of the skimmer and larid lines occurred at an earlier stage, perhaps in the early Eocene.

The family covers a wide geographical area, with the Indian Skimmer (*Rynchops albicollis*) occurring in southern Asia, the African Skimmer (*Rynchops flavirostris*) throughout much of Africa, and the Black Skimmer (*Rynchops niger*) in North, Central and South America. The South American races *cinerascens* and *intercedens* have on occasion been considered to constitute two additional species, but current opinion suggests that the New World forms should be treated as a single species with three subspecies. More information is required from the northern part of the Santa Fé Province, Argentina, where the races *cinerascens* and *intercedens* appear to meet without intergradation.

The birds of South America and Asia are mainly restricted to large rivers and estuaries, and those of Africa to large rivers and lakes. North American birds are atypical in their dependence on sandy coasts and barrier islands. Nevertheless, most of our knowledge of the biology of skimmers applies to the North American Black Skimmer. Studies on African Skimmers and the few data available for the Indian Skimmer suggest that their biology and behaviour closely match those of the Black Skimmer except for some details related to their distinctive environments.

Morphological Aspects

Skimmers compare in size with medium-sized to large terns, or medium to small gulls, and they have a wingspan ranging from 102 to 127 cm. Size designations are complicated by pronounced sexual dimorphism, with males notably larger than females in the American and Asian species, while the African Skimmer is the smallest and least dimorphic of the three.

Adult skimmers are striking and conspicuous. The plumage is largely blackish above and pure white below, the bill mainly orange-red, and the feet red. Seasonal changes are minor apart from the acquisition of a white collar during the non-breeding season in the Black and African Skimmers. Young birds are much less conspicuous and handsome than the adults, as juvenile plumage is brown above, mottled or scalloped with buff or whitish. The well camouflaged downy chicks are sand-coloured, flecked with black.

Adult birds undergo two moults yearly, a complete moult after breeding and a body moult prior to breeding. Moult of the flight-feathers is protracted and may overlap the pre-breeding moult to some extent. Birds of the year resemble adults in most respects within about six months of fledging, but juvenile wing-coverts and brownish crown feathers take longer to be replaced.

Skimmers seem front-heavy because of the long, deep bill and large head, and a tail that is not correspondingly enlarged. The appearance in flight or on the ground is distinctive and not particularly gull-like or tern-like, while their foraging behaviour is unique (see Food and Feeding). When foraging they fly low over the water with the mouth open and lower mandible partially submerged, whence the name "skimmer". A skimmer's flight is usually relaxed and graceful, and the long, pointed wings beat slowly for the size of the bird. Wingbeats during skimming are shallower and more rapid, but in a favourable wind the birds may glide for considerable distances with the wings raised about 40° above horizontal. The proportionally long outer primaries extend far beyond the tip of the tail when the wings are folded.

The three skimmer species are unmistakable birds that seem somehow strangely proportioned on account of the very long, pointed wings, the heavy head and the long bill. By far the most arresting feature is the oddly shaped mainly bright red bill, the lower mandible of which is much longer than the upper and extremely thin towards the tip, both specialized developments related to the remarkable method of foraging. The slightly smaller size, the colour of the bill tip, and the lack of a white collar in breeding plumage are the best features for differentiating the African Skimmer from its two allopatric congeners.

[*Rynchops flavirostris*, Okavango, Botswana. Photo: Wendy Dennis/ Planet Earth]

The legs are intermediate in length between those of terns and gulls, and the three front toes are connected by incised webs. The webbing on the toes may help to support the bird when it is standing on soft sand or mud, and it probably also assists in some forms of thermoregulation behaviour (see General Habits). Skimmers sometimes wade, but they do not swim, dive or plunge into water.

The most curious feature of a skimmer is its bill, in which the mandibles are strikingly different in size and shape. Both are streamlined to plough through water with little resistance. The upper mandible is laterally compressed toward the tip, but more inflated and oval in transverse section near its base; overall, it is slightly down-curved, and is pointed at the tip. Its ventral, or lower, surface is very narrow, but broadens abruptly towards the mouth. The lower mandible, after a similar widening for the mouth, becomes even more compressed into a vertical, knife-like blade, and this extends forward approximately 1-3 cm beyond the tip of the upper mandible. When seen from above or below it is extremely thin, but from the side it appears deep and blunt-tipped. Many low, parallel ridges obliquely cross each side of the mandibular blade. The mouth opening is broad, while the tongue is short and does not extend to the streamlined mandibles. When the jaws are closed the knife-edge of the lower mandible fits into a narrow groove on the upper, but a greater curvature of the upper tomia often leaves a slight gap near the middle of the closed bill in lateral view. Despite the protruding rhamphotheca, or horny covering, of the lower jaw, its bony core is only slightly longer than that of the upper jaw. Interestingly, the laterally compressed mandibles of the unfledged chick are of nearly equal length, and both are pointed. The significance of the skimmer's odd bill structure is closely related to its remarkable method of foraging (see Food and Feeding).

Unlike most through gulls and terns, skimmers are active at night, often flying and calling in flocks, and feeding from dusk until dawn. Correspondingly, the skimmer's eye has an unusually large maximum pupillary opening. In order to protect the retina in the brilliant daylight reflected by white sand beaches and their aquatic environs, the circular pupil closes to a narrow, vertical slit, a unique adaptation among birds. The slit provides a greater reduction of the pupil than is possible with a circular sphincter.

Habitat

Skimmers frequent the edges of salt, brackish or fresh water in tropical to temperate zones, mostly at altitudes from sea-level up to about 450 m on larger rivers, but sometimes much higher on lakes. In the non-breeding season, their lives consist largely of alternating periods of foraging and resting. Most foraging is done in calm, shallow water without emergent vegetation; because skimmers forage most effectively where prey are concentrated, such habitat must be extensive to guarantee location of suitable foraging conditions daily. Isolated, open beaches, sandbars and mudflats are preferred for both roosting and breeding, although some Black Skimmers also breed on flat mats of vegetation in salt-marshes. Such habitats and conditions are found mainly on coasts with barrier islands, on large rivers that experience extensive periods of high and low water, and on some inland lakes. Man-made habitats may also be used (see Status and Conservation).

In coastal areas, tides influence fish concentrations. During flood tide, myriads of fish crowd along the edge of the advancing water to gain access to marshy areas left dry at low tide, and the Black Skimmer forages regularly in salt-marsh channels. The ebbing tide leaves shallow, temporary or permanent tidal pools, in which fish and shrimps are trapped. Different studies have found peak skimming activity to occur at different tidal stages, but middle and low tides are apparently favoured.

Skimmers sometimes feed in deeper water on schools of fish, such as mullet (*Mugil*), that are near the surface. They also catch fish in the thin sheet of water spread on the beach by breaking waves, while skimming along the beach edge for considerable distances.

Except in North America, skimmers' annual cycles are governed largely by the alternation of rainy and dry seasons, and the concomitant rise and fall of water levels of the large rivers. At flood stage, the water may rise many metres, often breaching the riverbanks, and in some areas flooding vast areas of forest. At low water, silt is deposited and sandbars are formed. These seasonal changes are somewhat analogous to the tides: concentrations of fish are stranded in pools and small lakes left by the receding water, and fish are also concentrated in the shallows of the reduced river channel. Skimmers tend to leave the rivers when the waters run high, but find suitable breeding and roosting conditions at low water.

General Habits

Skimmers are social birds, breeding in colonies and roosting in tight groups, usually in the company of terns and other species. Foraging, however, is carried out independently of other species and may be solitary, in pairs, in family groups, or sometimes in moderate to large flocks. Groups of skimmers are more likely to maintain a tight flock in flight than are terns or gulls, sometimes performing turns and other manoeuvres with considerable synchrony, and, even when skimming, pairs or small groups may fly in formation.

When not otherwise occupied, skimmers sleep, rest or perform maintenance or comfort behaviour. They usually sleep with the head turned to one side and the bill tucked into the scapular feathers. Most birds on the periphery of large roosting flocks turn their heads toward the outside to be alert to any possible approaching danger. At the colony, one member of a pair typically stands beside its incubating mate but usually faces in the opposite direction, again maximizing their combined vigilance. All birds, both in the colony and when roosting, orientate their bodies to face into strong winds. Sometimes they lie prone on their bellies and rest the bill on the ground, and when incubating birds do this they leave a radiating pattern of lines in the sand around the nest, from the sharp, lower edge of the bill, indicating the directions in which they have faced.

Skimmers bathe in shallow water, and preen by nibbling the oil-gland and stroking the feathers between the mandibles. They yawn by opening the mouth for one or two seconds, presumably to clear the eustachian tubes. Stretching occurs with the legs flexed, the head lowered and the folded wings raised. Relief from extreme heat is typically achieved by fluttering the gular region, raising the body feathers and holding the folded wings slightly away from the body, but cooling can also be effected by dragging the webbed feet and breast feathers through water in flight.

An adult skimmer's bill can not be used effectively for pecking or grasping at the tip, although the bird can grasp objects on the ground if it first turns its lowered head sideways. This limited dexterity with the bill may explain the lack of nest building in this family. In contrast to the adults, chicks are able to peck effectively almost until they fledge (see Breeding).

Voice

Although skimmers are not raucously vocal, their calls may be heard at dusk and at night, as well as during the day. They are most vocal in the colony during aggressive interactions or upon taking flight after disturbance. The larger species give single or repeated, short calls that have been likened to the distant barking of hounds, but these barks become longer and harsher under stress; although the sexes have similar calls, those of males are lower in pitch. Calls of the slightly smaller African species are sharper, more strident and higher-pitched.

In the colony, birds call to each other at the time of nest relief, and they utter soft, liquid notes when settling on their eggs. Adults bringing fish attract the attention of small chicks by calling softly, and chicks utter soft calls when begging for food. Vocalizations of the skimmer in the colony continue through the night, when other species are silent. A chick captured in the hand or by a predator emits a shrill alarm note that usually causes other chicks crouched nearby to run away.

Food and Feeding

The foraging method of all skimmers is highly stereotyped and is unique among birds. It consists of flying along ploughing the water with the lower mandible more or less at random, in order to locate concentrations of fish and to grasp individual prey items following chance collisions. Birds typically skim a stretch of about 50-100 m, before flying up and round and skimming the same stretch again. Skimming proves to be an effective feeding method in habitats that provide consistently high densities of fish or shrimps, in shallow water or near the surface of deeper water. Because skimming is more tactile than visual it permits crepuscular and nocturnal feeding, and skimmers are known to feed intensively at dusk and even on the darkest of nights. The combined influences of nocturnal and tidal cycles on feeding activity are complicated and poorly understood.

Skimmers are sociable birds that breed in loose colonies and roost in tight huddles on sandbanks, often along with terns and other species. When feeding, they may fly in ones and twos, or perhaps in small flocks. Much of the time is spent loafing on beaches or indulging in preening or bathing activities, again communally. At rest they will always point head and body to face into the wind. Unlike gulls and terns, when flying in flocks they synchronize their movements, wheeling and turning gracefully in unison. The dark bill tip is the most obvious feature indicating that these birds are Black Skimmers.

[Rynchops niger niger, Long Island, New York. Photo: Tom Vezo]

The skimmer's upper and lower mandibles are different in length and shape, both compressed laterally to form a thin, streamlined instrument that enables the bird to catch prey as it flies along with the bill open and the lower jaw ploughing through the water surface. Fish are hardly ever scooped up on the lower jaw, but rather the head and the top of the neck are drooped so that the upper jaw can fasten onto the catch. When a larger fish is encountered, the head is twisted backwards under the bird, enabling both jaws to snap shut on the prey, which is then swallowed either in flight or once the bird lands. Note the very slight wake created by the skimming action of this Black Skimmer.

[*Rynchops niger.* Photo: Kevin T. Karlson]

Skimmers eat almost exclusively fish, but shrimps may be important too, particularly on the south-eastern and Gulf coasts of North America. Among the fish most important to the North American Black Skimmer are the tidewater silverside (*Menidia peninsulae*), sheepshead minnow (*Cyprinodon variegatus*), and several species of killifish (*Fundulus*) and of mullet. The prey taken are typically 4-12 cm in length, or exceptionally up to 20 cm long. Elsewhere in the world, the precise prey species of skimmers have not been well documented.

Skimmers are structurally and behaviourally adapted as "skimming machines". Newly fledged chicks instinctively attempt to skim sand dunes and beach edges as well as water, resulting in sharp downward jerks of the head. They soon learn to skim only in water, and suitable foraging habitats are learned while they accompany their parents. Skimming water does not require a disproportionately long lower jaw, but it is facilitated by the lateral compression of the mandibles. Unfledged chicks have laterally compressed upper and lower mandibles of roughly equal length, and those of newly fledged young are only moderately disparate in length. The bill reaches adult proportions within about three months of fledging. The rhamphotheca of a skimmer's lower jaw grows continuously faster than that of the upper, and this is kept in check by wear against the sandy or muddy bottom when skimming in shallow water, and by breakage upon hitting obstructions. The length and shape of the lower mandible is correspondingly variable among individuals, and over time, within individuals.

The chance of catching a fish while skimming with the tip of the lower mandible would be reduced if the upper mandible also ploughed the water. Such is usually not the case because the bird raises its upper jaw as much as 45° above the closed position by bending it at its base, a capacity of movement greater than that found in gulls and terns. If fish are to be found deeper in the water, however, the bird may submerge the entire lower jaw and part or all of the upper.

How does the bird grasp a fish if it is struck beyond the reach of the upper jaw? It is often stated that fish slide up the edge of the lower mandible during skimming. In almost every case, however, the head and the upper segment of the neck bend downward, doubling under the body in such a way that the upper mandible can reach the prey. Larger fish are withdrawn from the water with the head facing backwards, but this action is not readily observed in the field because the time to catch a fish and return the head to normal position is only a fraction of a second. Flight is uninterrupted while catching a fish, except for an extra wingbeat and a downward flick of the tail.

Fish are held crosswise in the bill, and are swallowed in flight or after landing; those intended for a mate or chick at the colony may be carried for several kilometres. The knife-edge of the lower mandible and the extremely narrow upper jaw provide little stability for carrying a flopping fish, but the grip is powerful and the mandibles dig into the fish, sometimes almost severing it in two. Additional stability is provided by the slightly decurved tomia of the upper mandible which prevent the grasped fish from sliding forward. Nevertheless, fish are occasionally dropped because of an insecure grip, or because of harrassment by gulls.

The long bill and relatively long neck permit the bird to maintain its body in position about 5 cm above the surface of the water while in the skimming posture. The wave created in the wake of the submerged mandible is not high enough to wet the bird's neck or belly, and the height of this wave may be influenced by the series of ridges on the mandible. Although the wingbeat is restricted to an arc of about 45°, the skimmer compensates by its relatively low wing-loading and by an aerodynamic surface effect that increases lift and reduces drag when birds fly within a few centimetres of the substrate. Friction between the bill and the water is not a significant factor because hydrodynamic drag is almost nil for the highly streamlined mandibles. In fact, skimming is often accomplished while gliding or with intermittent wingbeats. Flight speed during skimming is typically 16-32 km/h, but in strong headwinds it may be much slower.

Crepuscular and nocturnal feeding are regularly practised by all species of skimmer. Benefits of nocturnal foraging might be that some species of fish come closer to the surface and strong daytime winds often diminish. Tactile feeding at night provides ecological segregation from diurnal fish-eaters, and even during the day it enables skimmers to forage in opaque, silt-laden water where fish are less available to visual predators.

The average skimming time required to catch a fish is extremely variable depending on the size of the prey, its density and the depth at which it is situated. Measured rates vary from

Black Skimmers typically start to assemble at a colony a week or so before nesting begins in earnest. During this time there is great deal of activity, as groups and pairs indulge in aerial displays and chases with much calling, as partnership bonds are established, although some birds may already be paired when they arrive at the colony. Colonies tend to be situated on coastal islands and isolated beaches.
If breeding is successful at a given site one season, the same site is normally occupied and used again the following year.

[Rynchops niger niger, Long Island, New York. Photo: Tom Vezo]

one catch per minute to one per seven minutes. An exceptional rate occurred at a small pond near the coast of Texas, at which several Black Skimmers fished actively all night, skimming in the central portion of the pond. Just before sunrise myriads of small fish congregated at the surface and formed a dense border that was clearly visible around the pond. Birds then skimmed only through this concentration, where they averaged one fish caught per three seconds of skimming time. It is not uncommon for skimmers in any situation to direct their skimming towards surface disturbances made by schools of fish.

How did skimming behaviour and its associated structural modifications evolve? If we assume that extant gulls and terns are less modified than skimmers from the common ancestor of all three, then we might ask whether extant, unspecialized larids are capable of skimming. In fact, Laughing Gulls (*Larus atricilla*) have been observed repeatedly skimming stretches of up to two metres at a time with the distal third of the lower mandible immersed in turbid water. The birds always flew directly into the wind while skimming, and fish-catching was not observed. Terns also skim on occasion, perhaps to drink, but observations of Royal Terns (*Thalasseus maximus*) revealed that birds catching small crabs by plunging usually skimmed briefly after a catch, presumably to clean the bill; the birds actually caught fish, perhaps inadvertently, during three among hundreds of such observations of skimming.

Probably extreme streamlining of the bill evolved rapidly under strong selection after skimming became an important feeding method of the ancestral skimmer. Other refinements in bill structure, proportions of the skeleto-muscular system, wings and eyes could then evolve gradually and individually because each would improve the efficiency of skimming, and hence the bird's fitness, in its own way. Other ancestral feeding methods would eventually become difficult or impossible as the specialization for skimming approached its present level.

Breeding

Most breeding in South America, Africa and southern Asia takes place between April and November, during what tends to be the period of low water in major rivers, but the dates vary locally

and from year to year, depending on the termination of the rainy season in the headwaters. In North America, breeding is more strictly seasonal, usually from April to July, although this can be extended to early September in the event of renesting.

Although the three species are colonial nesters, colonies sometimes consist of only a few pairs, and even single pairs may breed successfully. Skimmers either join terns, and sometimes gulls, plovers and other species, or they form pure colonies. Colonies usually number less than 200 pairs, and most actually support less than 100, although exceptionally several thousand pairs may congregate, without counting the associated species.

Preferred colony sites for North American skimmers are the more isolated tracts of suitable habitat, particularly coastal islands and beaches, but birds also nest with terns on mats of dead vegetation deposited in salt-marshes by winter tides. When selecting a breeding site in any given year, an individual bird may simply return to its previous breeding location, or it may be at-

A pair of Black Skimmers vigorously defend the nest-site as an intruder appears, in this case a Common Tern (Sterna hirundo). Skimmers frequently form nesting colonies with other species, in particular with Common Terns, which are more aggressive and provide the skimmers with some extra protection from predation by gulls. However, there are limits to the behaviour one can tolerate from one's neighbours!

[Rynchops niger niger, Cedar Beach, New York. Photo: A. & E. Morris/ Birds As Art]

tracted to other birds nesting in a new location, rather than favouring specific physical features of the environment. Skimmers are not bound by tradition when conditions are unfavourable, and they will renest in a different place in the same year if the first attempt is unsuccessful. A study in New Jersey, USA, showed that Black Skimmers are more likely to choose a new colony site in the succeeding year if the previous year's colony was destroyed by predators than if it was flooded, probably because predators are likely to return to the site year after year whereas floods are unpredictable. Such flexibility is important to the birds of South America, Africa and southern Asia, where colonies on riverine sandbars or beaches are subject to flooding when local rains cause sudden fluctuations in water level.

Black Skimmers accumulate at the colony site for about a week before most breeding activities begin. Pairs or groups of birds engage in aerial chases during pair formation, but some birds are already paired, and courtship feeding may occur within packed groups, which gradually give way to more evenly spaced pairs. Although skimmers usually breed in the company of terns, they tend to cluster near the middle of the colony.

The skimmer's nest is formed by the bird kicking sand backwards while it rests on its belly and turns slowly in concentric circles. Later, the chicks use a similar technique to bury themselves partially in the sand for protection. The finished nest cup is about 20-30 cm in diameter and 2-4 cm deep. Several such scrapes are made in the territory but only one is chosen for laying. Even a bare cup serves to shield the eggs and young from extremes of temperature and to make them less conspicuous; it also prevents the eggs from being scattered by the wind. Copulation occurs at the nest-site after a male offers the female a fish, which she often holds during mounting, and eats following copulation.

The size of the defended area around the nest varies inversely with the size of the colony, and according to the stage of breeding activities. Territories are smallest during the incubation period, when activity is at a minimum, but larger before and during egg-laying, when the pair must repel intruders attempting to find nest-sites, or to steal fish brought by the male for courtship feeding or held by a female during copulation. Males aggressively defend their mates from other males attempting to interrupt or steal copulations. Defence and aggression increase again once

the chicks begin to wander away from the nest cup; neighbouring birds usually stab at such chicks, sometimes killing them. At this time, females are especially aggressive toward intruders of both sexes. A parent may attempt to recover its wandering chick by carrying it in the bill, but more often it tries to drive away the menacing neighbour. Skimmers have a variety of aggressive displays, one of the commonest being the "Aggressive Upright", in which the neck is extended vertically and the bill held horizontally or raised about 45° at highest intensity; the bill may be opened or closed and the wings are held slightly away from the body. This display usually precedes an attack on the ground or in flight. The Black Skimmer's bark also indicates aggression, when it becomes shorter and sharper if uttered from the ground, or longer and harsher if given in flight. Unlike terns and gulls, skimmers often perform a distraction display consisting of spreading or dragging the wings, lowering the head and body, and stumbling movements, when gulls, other skimmers or large mammals, including humans, approach their young.

Skimmers' eggs are pale grey, sandy, buff or olive with bold brown and purplish blotches and lines, ranging in size from 4·5 x 3·3 cm in the Black Skimmer to 3·9 x 2·8 cm in the African Skimmer. Clutch size usually numbers 2-6 eggs, and typically averages either 3-4 or 2-3 eggs; a gradient from 4 to 2-3 eggs may occur from north-west India to Burma. Second and third clutches, following nest failure, are generally smaller than the first.

In the Black Skimmer, the period of egg-laying lasts 4-8 days, whereas that of incubation is 21-26 days. Both sexes incubate, and alternation of incubation becomes critical, and more frequent, when ambient temperatures exceed the incubation temperature of 35·6°C, requiring frequent cooling, not only of the eggs but also of the parents. Under these conditions a bird relieved from incubation flies directly over water, patters its feet, and ploughs the surface with its breast feathers, which serves not only to cool the bird but also to wet and cool the eggs upon its return to the nest. Such exchanges are frequent during the heat of the day, when shade temperatures at ground level may exceed 50°C, but in more moderate temperatures changes at the nest mainly coincide with foraging activity.

Because incubation begins with the first egg, the chicks hatch asynchronously over about four days. Studies differ as to whether

the first chick hatched dominates the others and survives at their expense, or whether most or all chicks survive. Such differences may depend on the abundance of food in a given year or locality. While feeding young, adults bring single small fish to the colony from foraging areas that may be 2-8 km away. Black Skimmers less than six days old were fed fish less than 5 cm long at a rate of 3-4 fish per 10-20 minute period, followed by several hours of inactivity. Undigested material is regurgitated in the form of a pellet. Sometimes chicks peck at fresh pellets, giving rise to the statement that they are fed by regurgitation, but in fact they take fish directly from the parent's bill, or if dropped, from the ground. A fish too large to be swallowed by a chick may be softened by parental mandibulation.

Apart from sibling rivalry for food, the chick's life is precarious in several ways, as it depends on both parents for shelter from heat and rain, protection from neighbouring skimmers and terns, and protection from predators. The chick's behaviour also contributes to its survival in aspects such as the recognition of its own parents, competition for fish held in the adult's bill, crouching in the scrape or digging into the sand for camouflage, seeking shade in vegetation to avoid heat stress, and running rapidly when necessary. After fledging, which takes about four weeks in the Black Skimmer, young birds soon accompany their parents on foraging excursions, but they continue to be fed for at least two weeks more. Adults and young congregate in open areas prior to final departure from the colony.

Hatching success is highly variable, mainly because of flooding or predation, either of which may destroy a colony. Renesting may occur once or twice in a season, but in the absence of catastrophe nesting occurs only once, and hatching success may be as high as 85%. Fledging success is typically lower, ranging from 0 to 1·4, or occasionally 2, young per pair, and one factor is that chicks 7-15 days old that are no longer brooded rarely survive periods of heavy rain lasting two or three days. Some of the more important predators of eggs and young include small to medium-sized carnivores, crows, gulls, raptors, snakes and large lizards. Skimmers benefit from intense mobbing of such predators by terns, and sometimes they participate in this behaviour, particularly when terns are less numerous. A hazard beyond the control of African Skimmers is the trampling of eggs and young by hippos, elephants and cattle, which may all use sandbars as walkways.

Movements

The daily cycle of movements is mainly between feeding grounds and resting areas or the breeding colony. Some movements are also related to tidal cycles, when most resting occurs during high tide. In Florida, Black Skimmers may fly 70 km inland each night to feed at lakes.

Post-breeding dispersal of North American Black Skimmers involves mostly immature birds, but both immatures and adults have been recorded far inland in the USA and Mexico. Some, but not all, of these were presumably storm-blown, and records from Newfoundland have been linked to hurricanes, which often move north-eastwards up the Atlantic coast.

Both young and adult birds migrate and flock together. Populations that breed in north-eastern North America shift south to Florida and the Gulf coast, while many of the more southern breeders winter on both coasts of Central America, south to Panama. On the great rivers of South America, Africa and southern Asia, birds migrate between their breeding grounds up-river and the non-breeding grounds near the river's mouth or on the coast; the distances involved may amount to hundreds, or even thousands, of kilometres. In Africa, many birds leave the main rivers to spend the non-breeding season at Lake Chad, the Rift Valley lakes or other inland sites.

An intriguing question in South America is the origin of the Black Skimmer populations of the race *cinerascens*, which winter along the Pacific coast from Ecuador to southern Chile. Except for a breeding population in the Gulf of Guayaquil, this subspecies breeds mainly east of the Andes on the Orinoco, Amazon and Paraná Rivers and their major tributaries, as far west as eastern Colombia and eastern Peru, almost to the Andes. Do some of these birds move westwards over the Andes to reach the coast? If so, they probably represent the populations breeding in the western Amazon Basin, as their non-breeding period coincides with the appearance of birds on the west coast; more northerly birds apparently breed later and probably migrate to the north coast of South America and Trinidad. Non-breeding birds have been recorded on the Bolivian shores of Lake Titicaca, at an altitude of 3800 m, indicating that skimmers are certainly capable of traversing high mountainous zones.

Relationship with Man

Although skimmers are unique and distinctive in appearance and behaviour, they do not appear to have played an important role in folklore, ritual or pictorial representation of the indigenous peoples within their range. Extensive use of plumes and whole birds, such as terns, for millinery and other forms of decoration in the nineteenth and early twentieth centuries in North America and Europe brought some terns and herons nearly to extinction (see Volume 1, page 396), but skimmers were not in great demand for this trade.

The eggs of all species of skimmers are used regularly for food by native and immigrant peoples, and they are especially valued for their large size. In North America, eggs are still taken for this purpose despite their protection under Federal and State Laws. In the past, egg-collectors took large series of skimmer eggs in order to represent the striking variation in markings and background colours.

Status and Conservation

Due to the fact that skimmers tend to have a rather scattered distribution, often at low densities, their numbers are often difficult to estimate with any real degree of certainty. A few incomplete censuses of the Black Skimmer, mostly from the 1950's-1970's indicated about 68,000 breeding birds on the Atlantic and Gulf coasts of the USA, with most of these birds in Louisiana and Texas. The largest recorded wintering flocks were 10,000 birds in North Carolina in 1935 and again in 1964. There are few data from the Neotropics: on the rivers of South America they are usually sighted in small flocks, and the few colonies for

The Black Skimmer may prepare several nests by kicking sand backwards while it pivots round in circles on its belly, but only one will be used for laying. The cup-shaped depression thus formed is usually 2-4 cm deep and will hold 2-6 eggs, pale in ground colour with heavy brown and purplish blotches. The sexes take turns in incubating, which may last up to 26 days. When temperatures soar, the bird leaving the nest often flies to water to wet both the feet and the breast feathers. Once it has refreshed itself, it may return to the nest where the eggs are then wetted and cooled to help maintain them at a constant incubation temperature.

[Rynchops niger. Photo: Steven C. Kaufman/Bruce Coleman]

which numbers have been reported are also small, in the range of 5-50 pairs, although admittedly such flocks and colonies may go unrecorded along hundreds or thousands of kilometres of river. The entire populations of African and Indian Skimmers are each estimated at something in the region of 10,000 birds, but the latter species is now considered globally threatened.

Even for the best-censused taxon, the North American Black Skimmer, it is difficult to say whether populations have remained stable, increased or declined during the twentieth century. Censuses performed in different years are often at different localities, or taken in different ways, and are thus not comparable. Apparent differences in local populations or numbers of colonies occupied between years may simply reflect a local shift in colony sites. During a given decade, skimmer populations may increase in one area and decrease in another, with no net change. Although populations of North American skimmers appear to be stable, it is doubtful that their numbers have recovered from the intense egging and hunting for food, including commercial exploitation, that occurred in the nineteenth century.

How vulnerable are skimmer populations to human predation, disturbance and environmental manipulation? All three species are adapted to endure natural disasters and heavy predation at colonies by a readiness to renest and change the colony site. The Black Skimmer uses structures such as dredge deposition islands, levees, causeways and gravel roofs for breeding. In marsh habitats on the north Gulf coast, dredge deposition from recent oil exploration has provided new colony sites for skimmers, and, indeed, a significant proportion of all nesting in the USA now takes place on dredge islands comprised largely of sand and shell. Nevertheless, plant succession makes much of the dredge habitat unsuitable within a few years, and breeding on gravel roofs is almost entirely unsuccessful. To a large extent, use of artificial habitats by skimmers results from their displacement from natural beach and barrier islands because of recreational use, commercial development, and predation by dogs, cats, rats and humans.

Black Skimmers are adaptable in their use of feeding sites, accepting man-made ponds, ditches and shipping channels if fish are abundant. However, they are specialized in their basic needs, namely open, calm water with high concentrations of fish either in shallows or near the surface of deeper water. Thus, they are vulnerable to any major threat to fish populations, such as coastal oil spills and chemical pollution of estuaries from various industries and agricultural run-off. Another danger is in the form of toxic water pollutants deposited in fish tissues, including organochlorines, such as DDE and PCB's, used for insect control related to public health or agriculture, and heavy metals and selenium from industry. Black Skimmers are known to accumulate organochlorines in their eggs and heavy metals in their feathers, but the extent to which current levels of such toxins affect reproduction or adult viability is not well known.

We lack information about the prey species of South American skimmers at their different localities, and it is therefore difficult to predict the long-term effects of various land use and fishing practices on skimmer populations. The birds breed along nutrient poor clear-water and black-water rivers, as well as nutrient rich white-water rivers. Fish faunas in the latter are sustained by phytoplankton and zooplankton, while those in clear- and dark-water rivers depend heavily on fruits, seeds and insects that fall from the flooded forest at periods of high water. Cutting of riverine forest would thus seriously deplete the fish stocks in nutrient poor rivers. Riverine breeding habitat in the Amazon, Orinoco, Paraná and lesser drainage basins is admittedly vastly extensive, but rivers are also the focus of human settlement and agriculture, which proceed at a particularly rapid pace with the construction of new roads. A hope for the future is that large stretches of river and adjacent forest will be preserved to protect local fishing industries, a development that would certainly benefit the skimmers. Human predation on skimmer eggs is already a serious threat in the Neotropics, and increased use of beach habitat will displace colonies there, as it has done in North America.

Non-breeding birds migrate in part to estuaries, which are also focal points for large human populations; other birds spread along the coasts where human impact on their environment has been little studied outside North America.

The Indian Skimmer is judged to be at risk, and is currently classified as Vulnerable. The entire population may not number more than 10,000 birds. While little is known of former population sizes to help estimate the amplitude of the apparent decline, it is obvious that, as a species of broad rivers and estuaries, its habitat is coming under increasing pressure. Huge human populations continue to grow, while at the same time dam and irrigation projects, and the ever more frequent use of sandbars for agriculture, are also contributing to reduce the amount of suitable habitat available to the species.

*[Rynchops albicollis, India.
Photo: Goran Ekström/
Windrush]*

The future of the African Skimmer will also depend on the preservation of sufficient riverine breeding habitat, free from excessive human disturbance. Construction of dams and river bar agriculture have removed extensive areas of breeding habitat. In addition, conditions also need to remain favourable on the large lakes where many birds spend the non-breeding season. Some of the Rift Valley lakes are particularly vulnerable to environmental perturbation by pollution because of their extremely low rates of water turn-over. Their remarkably diverse faunas of cichlid fishes are subject to reduction or annihilation by introduced predatory fish, as has already happened in Lake Victoria with the Nile perch (*Lates niloticus*), introduced in the 1960's.

The Indian Skimmer is currently classified as Vulnerable. It is a bird of large rivers and estuaries, and has to contend with massive human populations along rivers, especially the Ganges, as well as extensive pollution in some areas, large hydro-electric and irrigation projects, and cultivation of sandbars during the season of low water. Little is known about its former and present populations, but comparison of early anecdotal accounts and recent censuses suggests a marked decline throughout its range in recent years, a pattern mirrored by a large number of Asian waterbird species. There is no doubt that the plight of this species requires careful monitoring in the years to come.

Despite the skimmers' resilience to moderate levels of human disturbance, we must be concerned about their ability to withstand interference from increasing human populations and modification of their habitat. Major breeding colonies are protected from human access to some extent in the USA, but recommendations for management of dredge islands to maintain suitable habitat have been largely ignored. Preservation of the natural environment along extensive portions of the major tropical rivers of the world may prove to be necessary for the long-term survival of Asian, African, and South American skimmers.

General Bibliography
Burger, J. (1980d), Burger, T., Olla & Winn (1980), Croxall, Evans & Schreiber (1984), Dunning (1993), Furness & Monaghan (1987), Goulding (1980), Hackett (1989), Harrison (1985, 1987), Hoffman (1984), Hudson *et al.* (1969), Löfgren (1984), Moynihan (1959), Nelson (1980), Olson (1985b), Peters (1934), Schnell (1970), Sears *et al.* (1976), Sibley & Ahlquist (1990), Sibley & Monroe (1990), Tuck & Heinzel (1978), Zusi (1985).

PLATE 58

inches 7
cm 18

ssp *niger*

1

ssp *cinerascens*

2

3

Family RYNCHOPIDAE (SKIMMERS)
SPECIES ACCOUNTS

PLATE 59

Genus *RYNCHOPS* Linnaeus, 1758

1. Black Skimmer
Rynchops niger

French: Bec-en-ciseaux noir **Spanish**: Rayador Americano
German: Amerikanischer Scherenschnabel
Other common names: American Skimmer

Taxonomy. *Rynchops nigra* Linnaeus, 1758, America = coast of South Carolina.
Forms superspecies with *R. flavirostris* and *R. albicollis*; some authorities have suggested that all three might be conspecific, but good evidence apparently lacking. Species name changed from *nigra* to *niger*, when all genera ending in -*ops* were ruled as being of masculine gender. Races *cinerascens* and *intercedens* formerly considered to constitute two further species, on account of white, as opposed to dusky, on wing linings and tail, and amount of white edging on secondaries; however, variability of these characters is more consistent with subspecific differentiation. Dubious race *intermedia* (W South America) normally included within *cinerascens*; proposed race *melanura* is synonymous with *cinerascens*. Three subspecies normally recognized.
Subspecies and Distribution.
R. n. niger Linnaeus, 1758 - coasts of USA (S California; Massachusetts to Texas) and Mexico (Sonora to Nayarit; Tamaulipas to Yucatán Peninsula); winters from California and North Carolina S to both coasts of Panama.
R. n. cinerascens Spix, 1825 - coasts of Colombia to mouth of R Amazon and W Ecuador (Gulf of Guayaquil), and large river systems (especially Orinoco and Amazon) S to Bolivia and NW Argentina; winters on coasts, from Ecuador to S Chile, and from Panama to Trinidad and NC Brazil.
R. n. intercedens Saunders, 1895 - large rivers of E Brazil (W to Maranhão and E Mato Grosso), E Paraguay, Uruguay and NE Argentina (S to Bahía Blanca); winters mainly on coast.
Descriptive notes. 41-46 cm; male 308-374 g, culmen 64-74 mm; female 232-295 g, culmen 52-65 mm; wingspan 107-127 cm. Unmistakable within range. Differs from *R. flavirostris* in larger size and

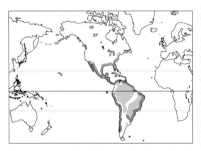

dark bill tip; from *R. albicollis* by black hindneck in breeding plumage, and dark bill tip. Wing lining white in nominate race, with secondaries and inner primaries broadly edged white, and tail white with dark central streak. Non-breeding adult has white nuchal collar and somewhat browner upperparts. Female similar to male in plumage, but smaller. Immature similar to non-breeding adult, but generally browner above, with some streaking, scaling and mottling, and duller bill. Race *cinerascens* has longer wings and bill than nominate *niger*, wing lining grey (whiter in immatures), narrow white edging on secondaries, and tail sooty; race *intercedens* resembles *cinerascens* in size, with wing lining white or greyish, white on secondaries variable, and tail grey (intermediate between *cinerascens* and *niger*).
Habitat. Mainland coast or barrier islands on sandy beaches, sandbars, shell banks, dredge islands and mudflats; tidal pools, inlets and creeks; salt-marsh wrack and creeks; ponds, lagoons and estuaries. In South America, frequents larger rivers at low water, coastal beaches and lagoons, islands and estuaries; breeds on sandbars and beaches of large rivers during season of low water. Recorded up to 3800 m on Bolivian shore of L Titicaca.
Food and Feeding. Mainly fish, e.g. in USA, silversides (*Menidia*), killifish (*Fundulus*), minnows (*Cyprinodon*), mullet (*Mugil*), anchovy (*Anchoa*), menhaden (*Brevoortia*), mollies (*Poecilia*); also some crustaceans, especially shrimps (*Palaeomonetes, Penaeus*). Food caught exclusively by skimming the water in flight with mouth open and lower mandible submerged; prey items touched by mandible are grasped while head doubles back under body; prey swallowed in flight or after landing.
Breeding. Birds of nominate race arrive at breeding grounds from mid-Mar to early May, laying from late May, or as late as Sept when renesting; season mainly May-Oct in upper basin of R Amazon; Oct-Mar in N Brazil, N Venezuela, N Colombia; season of race *intercedens* not well documented, but Sept-Nov on Rio Uruguay (Entre Ríos, Argentina). Colonial, with few to over 1000 pairs, but sometimes single; usually nests in company of terns, in Brazil commonly alongside Large-billed Terns (*Phaetusa simplex*). Nests on sand or shell beach; in USA, also on island of dredged material, sometimes on marsh wrack or gravel roof; nest is simple depression in substrate. Clutch usually 3-4 (mean 3·6) on

Atlantic coast, 2-3 on Gulf coast and in Colombia and Brazil; incubation 21-26 days, starting with first egg; semi-precocial chick has greyish buff down, irregularly and sparsely spotted black; leaves nest after about a week; brooded and fed by both parents; fledging 28-30 days. Fledging success in USA 0-2·77 young/pair, but often less than 1. Natural predators at colonies include foxes (*Vulpes*, *Urocyon*), weasels (*Mustela*), and racoon (*Procyon*). Age at first breeding not well established, but probably 1-3 years; maximum lifespan in wild at least 20 years.

Movements. Migratory. Northernmost breeding zones vacated Nov-Mar, birds wintering scantily S from North Carolina, and in greater number S from South Carolina to Florida, and down Gulf coast and both coasts of Mexico to Panama; sometimes carried far afield by storms, e.g. to Newfoundland, inland USA and Mexico, West Indies and Venezuela. Non-breeding *cinerascens* arrive in Chile in Oct, leaving in May; present in Trinidad May-Nov. Non-breeding *intercedens* on coast and estuaries mainly Dec-May, but poorly documented.

Status and Conservation. Not globally threatened. Population estimates unavailable for most of extensive range; in late 1970's, estimated total population of USA was c. 68,000 birds, with c. 70% in Louisiana and Texas. In USA, preferred breeding site of sandy beaches conflicts with increasing human use for recreation and commercial development; most colonies already displaced to dredge islands; Florida breeding sites reduced in number because of boating and other human disturbance. Chemical pollution also of concern; organochlorines (DDE, PCB) in eggs and heavy metals and selenium in body tissues and eggs potentially detrimental to reproduction; sample eggs from nests where none of remainder hatched showed higher concentrations of DDE (mean 5·9 ppm) than those from nests where all others hatched (mean 1·9 ppm). Oiling of plumage is not a common problem. Predators associated with humans, notably dogs, cats and rats, damage some colonies. Numbers in Mexico and wintering along Pacific coast of South America apparently much reduced since mid-19th century; pre-migration flocks of 1000-1500 birds near Valparaiso, C Chile, in 1960's. Reported to be common during early to middle 20th century at Gulf of Guayaquil in Ecuador, along lower R Magdalena in Colombia, and at several localities in Venezuela. Common breeder at Manu National Park, Peru, in 1980's-1990's.

Bibliography. Arthur (1921), Bales (1919), Below (1979), Belton (1984), Bent (1921), Black & Harris (1981, 1983), Blake, E.R. (1977), Blake, R.W. (1985), Blus & Stafford (1980), Buckley, F.G. & Buckley (1972), Buckley, P.A. & Buckley (1984b), Burger, J. (1981f, 1981g, 1982a, 1982b), Burger, J. & Gochfeld (1990b, 1992a, 1992b, 1993a), Burger, J. *et al.* (1994), Chaney *et al.* (1978), Clapp *et al.* (1983), Custer & Mitchell (1987), Davis (1951), Downing (1973), Duffy (1977), Erwin (1977a, 1977b, 1979, 1980, 1990), Erwin *et al.* (1981), Fisk (1978a), Fjeldså & Krabbe (1990), Garrett & Dunn (1981), Gochfeld (1973a, 1976, 1978c, 1979a, 1979b, 1980, 1981a, 1981b), Gochfeld & Burger (1994), Gochfeld *et al.* (1991), Gore (1987, 1991), Grant (1978), Grant & Hogg (1976), Grant *et al.* (1984), Groom (1992), Groves (1977), Hailman & Reed (1982), Halkin (1983), Harrison (1984b), Hartman (1961), Hays (1970), Hilty & Brown (1986), Howell & Webb (1995a), Jackson *et al.* (1982), Johnson (1967), Kale & Loftin (1982), King (1989), King & Cromartie (1986), Klimaitis & Moschione (1984), Krannitz (1989), Langridge & Hunter (1986), Leavitt (1957), Loftin (1982), McCaskie *et al.* (1974), Murphy (1936), Nicholson (1948), Palacios & Alfaro (1992), Pettingill (1937), Portnoy (1978), Preston (1962), Quinn (1988, 1989, 1990), Quinn *et al.* (1994), Richards (1990), Robinson (1981), Safina & Burger (1983), Schew & Collins (1990), Schreiber & Schreiber (1978), Sharp (1995), Sick (1985c, 1993), Smith (1985), Stone (1937), Tomkins (1933, 1941, 1951), Tuck (1968), Wetmore (1944, 1965), White *et al.* (1984), Williams, B. *et al.* (1993), Williams, S.O. (1982), Withers & Timko (1977), Wolk (1959), Zusi (1958, 1959, 1962), Zusi & Bridge (1981).

2. African Skimmer

Rynchops flavirostris

French: Bec-en-ciseaux d'Afrique **Spanish**: Rayador Africano **German**: Afrikanischer Scherenschnabel
Other common names: Scissorbill

Taxonomy. *Rhynchops* [sic] *flavirostris* Vieillot, 1816, "Australasie"; error = Senegal.

Forms superspecies with *R. niger* and *R. albicollis*; some authorities have suggested that all three might be conspecific, but good evidence apparently lacking. Monotypic.

Distribution. Major rivers and lakes of Africa S of Sahara, from Senegal E to Sudan and SW Ethiopia, and S to extreme N Namibia (R Kunene), N Botswana, basin of R Zambezi and S Mozambique; may have bred on L Nasser, Egypt, in 1987. Non-breeding visitor NW to R Gambia and Egyptian stretches of R Nile.

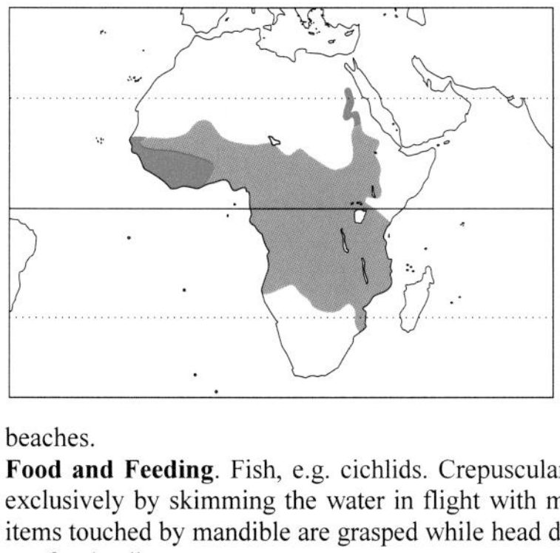

Descriptive notes. 36-42 cm; 111-204 g; wingspan c. 106 cm; culmen of male 61-70 mm, of female 51-62 mm. Unmistakable within range. Smaller than congeners; differs from *niger* by pale whitish yellow tip to bill; from *albicollis* by black hindneck in breeding plumage. Non-breeding adult has white nuchal collar and somewhat browner upperparts. Female similar to male. Immature similar to non-breeding adult, but generally browner above, with buff fringing and mottling, and paler bill.

Habitat. Rivers at low water, coastal lagoons, salt-pans, open marshes, lakes; less common along coast. Rests and breeds on sandbars and beaches.

Food and Feeding. Fish, e.g. cichlids. Crepuscular and nocturnal, as well as diurnal. Food caught exclusively by skimming the water in flight with mouth open and lower mandible submerged; prey items touched by mandible are grasped while head doubles back under body; prey swallowed in flight or after landing.

Breeding. Laying generally Mar-Jun in W & E Africa, mainly Jul-Nov S of equator; season varies locally depending on local dry season and period of low water in river. Colonial, often with terns, plovers, pratincoles and other species; birds chase one another noisily day and night on arrival at colony. Nests on sandy beaches and sandbars in rivers and islands in lakes; nest is unlined scrape in sand. Clutch 2-3 (mean 2·6), rarely 4, laid over several days; incubation c. 21 days, by both sexes, but mainly by female; chick has buffy white down, with irregular peppering of small black dots; tended and fed fish by both parents; stays in nest scrape for 2 days; fledging c. 4 weeks. Rising river water may destroy colony; eggs may be trampled by hippopotami and elephants; predators include raptors and other birds, mammals, lizards and snakes; parents will mob some species even away from nest, others only when near nest.

Movements. Migrates up and down larger rivers, and to and from inland lakes. Uncommon on coast, but outside breeding season may congregate in estuaries, e.g. well over 200 birds together off Bonthe, Sierra Leone, in Jan.

Status and Conservation. Not globally threatened. Total population estimated at less than 10,000 birds; largest colony supports only 50 pairs. Census on 1550 km of upper and middle R Zambezi yielded 1428 birds; largest recorded flocks of non-breeders include 1000 birds in Kenya and 1500 in Tanzania. South African populations decreasing; species no longer breeds in Natal. Dams flood habitats upstream and alter flow downstream producing unsuitable breeding conditions; DDT spraying for malaria and against tsetse fly and agricultural pests is dangerous for fish-eaters. Egg-collecting routinely practised, and this is facilitated by fact that incubating adults tend to be conspicuous; in addition, disturbance of colony by humans and cattle during hottest season is often fatal to eggs and chicks. Pollution, overfishing and decimation of native fish faunas by introduced predatory fish is a potential problem in many lakes.

Bibliography. Atkins, Johnston-Stewart & Killick (1989), Attwell (1959), Bannerman (1931), Benson *et al.* (1971), Beven (1944), Britton, P. L. (1980), Britton, P. L. & Brown (1974), Brooke (1984a), Brown & Britton (1980), Chapin (1939), Coppinger *et al.* (1988), Couto & Couto (1994), Cramp (1985), Curry-Lindahl (1981), Dowsett (1975), Dowsett & Forbes-Watson (1993), Elgood, Fry & Dowsett (1973), Elgood, Heigham *et al.* (1994), Étchécopar & Hüe (1964), Fryer (1972), Gardiner (1975), Ginn *et al.* (1989), Goodman *et al.* (1989), Gore (1990), Grimes (1987), Hanmer (1982, 1989), Harvey (1973), Hawksley (1974), Livingstone & Melack (1984), Mackworth-Praed & Grant (1957, 1962, 1970), Maclean (1993), van Meurs (1989), Modha & Coe (1969), Perennou (1991), Pitman (1932b), Randall (1994b), Roberts (1976), Shirihai (1996), Short *et al.* (1990), Taylor, P.B. (1979), Turner & Gerhart (1971), Urban *et al.* (1986), Verschuren (1978), Williams, A.J. (1986).

3. Indian Skimmer

Rynchops albicollis

French: Bec-en-ciseaux à collier **German**: Indischer Scherenschnabel **Spanish**: Rayador Indio
Other common names: Scissorbill

Taxonomy. *Rhynchops* [sic] *albicollis* Swainson, 1838, India.

Forms superspecies with *R. niger* and *R. flavirostris*; some authorities have suggested that all three might be conspecific, but good evidence apparently lacking. Monotypic.

Distribution. E Pakistan (R Indus) through N & EC India (E to Assam) to Bangladesh and W Myanmar (R Irrawaddy); also Cambodia (R Mekong). Current distribution uncertain: might also breed in Nepal and S Laos; possibly only winter visitor to Bangladesh.

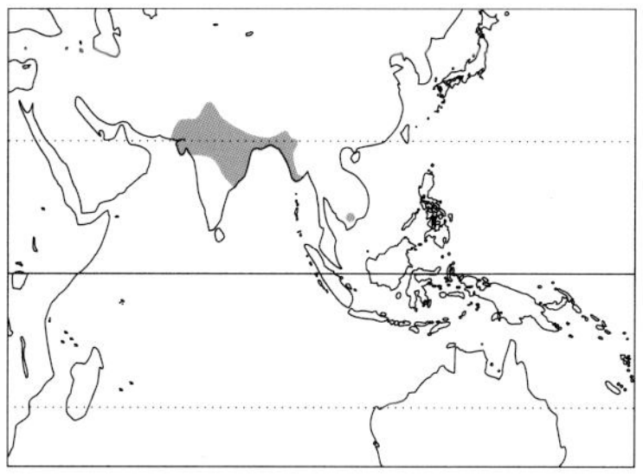

Descriptive notes. 38-43 cm; wingspan 102-114 cm; culmen 58-75 mm. Unmistakable within range. Differs from *R. niger* and *R. flavirostris* by having white collar in adult breeding plumage; tail white with inconspicuous dark centre stripe. Non-breeding adult has somewhat duller, browner upperparts. Female similar to male, but somewhat smaller. Immature similar to non-breeding adult, but generally browner above, with buff scaling, and duller bill.

Habitat. Largely restricted to major rivers, particularly along calm stretches with sandbars; rare or vagrant to estuaries, inshore coastal waters and freshwater tanks.

Food and Feeding. Fish and shrimps. Crepuscular and nocturnal, as well as diurnal, sometimes foraging on moonlit nights. Food caught exclusively by skimming the water in flight with mouth open and lower mandible submerged; prey items touched by mandible are grasped while head doubles back under body; prey swallowed in flight or after landing.

Breeding. Generally mid-Feb to Jun, with local variations. Colonial, often with terns and pratincoles. Nests on sandbanks of larger rivers during season of low water; nest is an unlined scrape in sand. Clutch usually 4 eggs in NW India, 2-3 eggs further E; incubation c. 21 days, by both sexes but mainly by female; chick has greyish or sand-coloured down with scattered dark brown spots. Predators on eggs and young include Pallas's Fish-eagle (*Haliaeetus leucoryphus*), crows, kites and jackals.

Movements. Moves upriver during season of low water, and down during period of floods. Occasionally visits lakes. Vagrant to SE China, Thailand and Vietnam.

Status and Conservation. VULNERABLE. Total population estimated at c. 10,000 birds, but status very poorly documented throughout most of range. In India, still fairly common locally but only 18 birds recorded in mid-winter counts, 1991. In Pakistan, has apparently declined over last 50-60 years; in latter part of 19th century was tolerably common all along R Indus, but by mid-1960's no birds at all seen except during monsoon season; main cause of decline is probably habitat loss, as result of damming of major rivers, which reduces risk of flooding, and encourages human populations to move in and cultivate river islands and sandbars. In Nepal, species is uncommon and irregular winter visitor near Indian border; may have bred. In Bangladesh, no recent breeding records; local winter visitor to coast and major rivers, where c. 3000 birds counted in 1988/89, and 602 birds in 1991. No recent records from Bhutan. Formerly common locally in Myanmar, but now rare. Rare or merely vagrant to other parts of SE Asia, but may breed in Cambodia. Human disturbance and habitat modification are probably the greatest threats throughout range.

Bibliography. Ali & Ripley (1982), Baker (1929), Cheng Tsohsin (1987), Collar *et al.* (1994), Harvey (1990), Himmatsinhji (1968), Hume (1890), Inskipp & Inskipp (1991, 1994), Lekagul & Round (1991), Lowther (1941, 1949), Majumdar & Roy (1993), Perennou *et al.* (1994), Ripley (1982), Roberts, T. J. (1991), Rose & Scott (1994), Smythies (1986), Stairmand (1970).

Class AVES
Order CHARADRIIFORMES
Suborder ALCAE
Family ALCIDAE (AUKS)

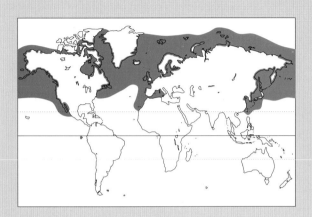

- Small to medium-sized marine, wing-propelled diving birds with stocky body, short wings and tail, mainly black or dark grey above and white below, and legs placed far back for swimming.
- 12-43 cm.

- Circumpolar.
- Exclusively marine, neritic and pelagic.
- 11 genera, 22 species, 45 taxa.
- 1 species threatened; 1 species extinct since 1600.

Systematics

The fossil record of birds (Aves) *per se* is poor, significantly less than its mammalian counterpart. Current paleontology of the Alcidae, or auk family, tells us little about the first appearance and evolution of this major taxon. However, with the information that does exist, it appears that the principal radiation of modern genera of Alcidae took place by the late Miocene (6 million years ago) or Pliocene (5-3 million years ago), regardless of how long the family may have been around prior to these times. This broad diversification by the late Miocene does, however, indicate that the auk family was of considerable age by that time and doubtless its roots extend back 40-30 million years earlier or more.

Geological history suggests that the northern Pacific Ocean was the centre of origin for most or all of the modern Alcidae, based largely upon differential stability of the land masses and ocean basins at the time: at the beginning of the Tertiary, some 60 million years ago, the Pacific Ocean was similar in size and shape to its current state, whereas the Atlantic was still a young ocean, very unlike its present form. The genus *Hydrotherikornis* is the earliest alcid group known, from the late Eocene, found in the eastern Pacific. Little is known for the next 40-50 million years until the late Miocene and early Pliocene (6-5 million years ago) when the next Pacific alcids, belonging close to the *Fratercula* puffins, were recorded in deposits from California and Baja California. Pacific species of the genera *Uria* (murres) and *Cepphus* (guillemots) have been documented in the late Miocene, whereas they are unknown in the Atlantic until much later, the Pleistocene (less than 3 million years ago), suggesting a Pacific origin for both genera.

The fossil record for the Alcidae in the Atlantic is richer than that for the Pacific. However, the earliest Atlantic auk is *Miocepphus mcclungi* from the middle Miocene (about 17-15 million years ago), found in Maryland and North Carolina. This, and numerous subsequent fossil finds, indicate a much more recent appearance of alcids in the Atlantic than the Pacific. It seems that the first ones arrived in the Atlantic after the early Eocene, probably much later. The recent fossil record shows only a small number of auks in the middle Miocene in the western mid-Atlantic, with a subsequent rapid and diverse radiation of the family there by the early Pliocene, including *Alca*, *Australca* and *Pinguinus*, and perhaps *Alle* and some undescribed genera. Although *Fratercula* (puffins) is considered to be of Pacific origin,

there were two Atlantic species in the early Pliocene, with dispersal from the Pacific to the Atlantic in the late Miocene. Most interchange of marine animals between the two oceans is believed to have occurred during this short time interval, with most species moving from the Pacific to the Atlantic. There is little evidence to support an Atlantic to Pacific movement, with the possible exception of *Alca* which may have entered the Pacific in the late Miocene and subsequently perished. Overall, the fossil evidence indicates an evolutionary origin in the North Pacific followed mainly by a spread to the North Atlantic via the Arctic Ocean. The fact that 18 of the 22 living species breed in the Pacific, with two species common to the Pacific and the Atlantic, also supports the view of a Pacific origin. But future studies may prove this summary to be oversimplified as there remains much more to be learnt about the origin and radiation or dispersal of the Alcidae.

During the last 160 years the Alcidae have been linked with the penguins (Spheniscidae), the divers or loons (Gaviidae), the grebes (Podicipedidae), and the diving-petrels (Pelecanoididae). Although now believed to be members of the order Charadriiformes, their relationships to other charadriiform groups remain uncertain. Evidence of close affinities with both the Lari and the Charadrii has given support for a shared shorebird-like common ancestor of alcids and larids. The current consensus is that Alcidae are charadriiform seabirds placed in a separate suborder, Alcae.

The living Alcidae comprise 22 species in 11 genera that separate easily into eight distinct species groups. The first contains a single small species, the Dovekie (*Alle alle*), which is black above and white below and short-billed; it is largely restricted to the Atlantic and is the only exclusively plankton-feeding alcid in that ocean. The second group comprises three large species, the Common (*Uria aalge*) and Thick-billed Murres (*Uria lomvia*) and the Razorbill (*Alca torda*), which are all blackish above and white below and long-billed; the murres occur in both Atlantic and Pacific, while the Razorbill is restricted to the Atlantic. The third holds three medium-sized species, the Black Guillemot (*Cepphus grylle*), the Pigeon Guillemot (*Cepphus columba*) and the Spectacled Guillemot (*Cepphus carbo*), which are mostly all black in summer; the Pigeon and Spectacled Guillemots are found in the Pacific and the Black Guillemot in the Atlantic. The fourth group numbers two small species, the Marbled (*Brachyramphus marmoratus*) and Kittlitz's Murrelets (*Brachyramphus brevirostris*), which are chiefly darkish brown in summer, scaled or barred; both are restricted to the Pacific. In the fifth group are four small species, Xantus's (*Synthliboramphus hypoleucus*), Craveri's (*Synthliboramphus craveri*), the Ancient (*Synthliboramphus antiquus*) and the Japanese Murrelets (*Synthliboramphus wumizusume*), which are all mainly dark above and white below, short-billed and with precocial young; all are Pacific species. The sixth group contains five small species, Cassin's (*Ptychoramphus aleuticus*), the Parakeet (*Cyclorrhynchus psittacula*), the Crested (*Aethia cristatella*), the Whiskered (*Aethia pygmaea*) and the Least Auklets (*Aethia pusilla*), which are darkish grey above and white to grey below, sometimes scaled or barred, with ornamental plumes and short-billed; all are Pacific species. Alone in the seventh group comes a medium-sized species, the Rhinoceros Auklet (*Cerorhinca moncerata*), greyish black above and grey-barred white below, with ornamental head plumes and a robust bill; this is another Pacific species. Finally, in the eighth group are three medium-sized species, the Atlantic (*Fratercula arctica*), Horned (*Fratercula corniculata*) and Tufted Puffins (*Fratercula cirrhata*), which are all black above with white cheeks, white (Atlantic, Horned) or black (Tufted) below, and with large, laterally compressed triangular bills which are brightly coloured during breeding; the first species occurs essentially in the Atlantic, the other two in the Pacific. The extinct Great Auk (*Pinguinus impennis*), the only recent flightless alcid, was black above and white below, and occupied boreal latitudes across the North Atlantic; it shared close affinities with the Razorbill, so strong that it is sometimes included within the genus *Alca*.

Morphological Aspects

The family Alcidae is made up of a highly specialized and ecologically diverse group of marine, wing-propelled pursuit-diving birds. The present day auks are small to medium-sized birds with small wings and short tails, with plumage that is mainly black or dark grey above and white below. They are rather elongated or torpedo-shaped in overall appearance with an orange size range of 12-43 cm long and 140-1100 g in body mass.

The smallest forms are found in the Pacific, the Least and Whiskered Auklets weighing 85-116 g, and Craveri's and Xantus's Murrelets 128-167 g, while the smallest Atlantic form is the Dovekie at 163 g. Intermediate in size are the *Cepphus* guillemots at 400-450 g and the puffins at 375-550 g, while the largest species are those of the genera *Alca* and *Uria*, which weigh 625-750 g and roughly 800-1100 g respectively. The largest recent member of the family, the extinct Great Auk of the Atlantic, probably weighed 5500-8000 g. The rather slight sexual dimorphism in auks is largely limited to body size differences, females tending to be smaller and lighter than males except in Xantus's Murrelet, in which females are larger.

The family shows a circumpolar distribution in an almost unbroken arc mainly in the cold waters of the Northern Hemisphere from eastern Canada through the North Atlantic and eastern shores of the Arctic Ocean to the Bering Sea and North Pacific. Auks are the ecological counterparts of the Southern Hemisphere's penguins, although they are much smaller in size, with the murres barely reaching the size of the smallest member of Spheniscidae, the Little Penguin (*Eudyptula minor*), at 1000 g. Both groups have undergone structural modifications suited for their marine existence, including greatly reduced wings which they use to swim under water in pursuit of prey. While the penguins lost the ability of aerial flight in order to maximize their underwater swimming efficiency, the alcids retained a wing size capable of allowing them to "fly" in both air and water, with the exception of the Great Auk, the last northern member of a succession of flightless alcids that arose in the North Pacific sometime after the Cretaceous. The remarkable underwater propulsion abilities displayed by these two groups are convergent and both groups have undergone somewhat similar and extensive morphological and ethological radiation. Owing to their reduced, or lost, flying proficiency, both are very susceptible to mammalian land predators and have become restricted for breeding to certain locations, normally predator-free islands or inaccessible, sheer sea cliffs within range of an adequate food supply for rearing young. Sites meeting these requirements are rare, and this has led to the formation of large, often immense, single-species or mixed-species colonies. Pen-

Perched photogenically on a cliff, this mixed bunch of alcids is composed of Crested, Parakeet and Least Auklets. Despite size and plumage differences, they show many morphological features in common. Alcids have rather elongated, sturdy bodies; the tail, legs and neck are all short and the head is relatively large. The legs are set far back on the body, while the feet are webbed and the claws adapted to gripping well on uneven surfaces. The rather stubby, narrow wings seem better adapted for diving than for flying. Some species have ornamental crests and plumes, and several have brightly coloured bills.

[Aethia cristatella, Cyclorrhynchus psittacula, Aethia pusilla, St George, Pribilof Islands, Alaska, USA. Photo: Richard Coomber/ Planet Earth]

guins and auks also share certain other life history characteristics that menace their survival: they are long-lived, reach sexual maturity slowly, and have low reproductive rates with correspondingly slow recovery rates. With their 5000 km wide and hemispheric spatial separation, the auks and penguins are true ecological counterparts.

Although the present day auks are less modified in structure for their marine existence than are the penguins, there are many morphological and behavioural features that characterize the family as a whole and each of its member species. Overall, the alcids have elongated and robust bodies with large heads, short necks, short, narrow and generally pointed wings, and short tails. The shortened wing and reduced surface area improves underwater propulsion immensely, but restricts aerial flight by high wing-loading, making it direct, rapid and energetically expensive with limited manoeuvrability once airborne. Take-off is difficult, especially in the medium-sized to large species such as the puffins and murres.

The legs are short, placed well back on the body, and laterally compressed, though not to the same extent as in the foot-propelled diving grebes and divers (loons). The tarsi are fully scutellated, covered in front by transverse scales. The feet are palmate, the first toe being absent or vestigial, and the other three digits fully webbed with the middle one comparatively elongated. Generally, claws are well developed and are used for grasping onto uneven or vertical rocky and rough surfaces, with the second toe in Atlantic and Tufted Puffins particularly strong for excavating underground burrows. All of these features enhance the swimming, diving and overall movement efficiency of the birds in water, in the air, and on land. Under water, the wings propel the bird forward, whereas the feet are used for steering and braking, as they are in aerial flying. Movement on the ground and posture vary between species groups related to the position of the legs. Murres and the Razorbill walk on their tarsal bones and are most limited and upright, whereas puffins walk on their toes, as do most other alcids, and show intermediate mobility on land. The *Cepphus* guillemots and Dovekies display the highest proficiency for ground movement, along with most of the small auklets and murrelets. The post-acetabular part of the pelvis in *Fratercula*, *Cepphus* and *Aethia* is broad enabling these birds to run and use their feet for digging; in addition, the pectorals in *Cepphus* are attached farther forward than in other alcids, maximizing their locomotory abilities on land and permitting more rapid take-off.

Some species, usually colonial breeders, have ornamental crests or plumes, and brightly coloured bills, mouth linings, legs and feet; breeding plumage can be strikingly attractive. Others may be cryptic, particularly species nesting as solitary or widely scattered pairs, such as the Marbled and Kittlitz's Murrelets. Bill shapes and sizes vary greatly, ranging from short and stubby in the murrelets, auklets and Dovekie to fairly long and pointed in the murres and *Cepphus* guillemots, or long and laterally compressed in the Razorbill and the Great Auk. The most impressive are the massive, laterally compressed, broad mandibles of puffins, with brightly coloured ornamental horny plates which are shed during the post-breeding moult. The facial and head ornaments, including the large and colourful bills of puffins, play important roles in pair formation and maintenance, courtship, and agonistic behaviour.

Morphology of the mouth parts varies markedly between species, differences that are associated with food habits and feeding technique. Plankton-feeders have wide bills and a palate densely covered with denticles, as well as a soft, flexible tongue that in six species is combined with a specialized gular throat pouch (sublingual diverticulum) for transporting food to the young over long distances; these species are the five small Pacific auklets and the Dovekie. In contrast, those that are almost exclusively fish-eaters, such as the Razorbill, the Common Murre and the *Brachyramphus* murrelets, have relatively narrow bills and high tongue cornification to press prey against evenly-spaced but less dense palatal denticles. Intermediate between these extremes are the more generalist feeders on fish and plankton, such as the puffins, the Thick-billed Murre and the Rhinoceros Auklet.

The plumage of auks is uniformly thick and heavy with remarkably high insulating qualities. The feathers are short and dense, with numerous feather tracts and down covering the entire body, reaching a density almost twice that found in Laridae. The nostrils are normally covered with feathers from the loral region except in puffins where they are exposed. The uropygial gland at the base of the upper spine is crowned with feathers. The contour feathers have aftershafts, and the apteria are narrow and down-covered, as are the pterylae. There are 11 primaries, the eleventh being reduced and non-functional, and the tenth the longest; the 15-19 secondaries are generally shorter, while the greater secondary and primary coverts are lengthened. The tail is short and normally rounded to wedge-shaped, with 12 rectrices in all genera except *Fratercula*, which has 16, and *Cepphus* with 12-14.

Adults are usually darkish brown to grey and black above and uniformly white to pale white below, both in summer and winter, except for some Pacific species which are more or less darkish brown or grey, sometimes mottled, as in *Aethia* and *Cerorhinca*, or black all over, as in the Tufted Puffin. Other notable exceptions are the *Brachyramphus* murrelets, with their cryptic brown-grey summer plumage and more conventional black-grey above and white below winter plumage, and the *Cepphus* guillemots, with their predominantly black summer and white winter plumages. Sexes are alike in plumage. Juvenile plumage colours are similar to those of winter adults except in the Dovekie and the Razorbill, in which they resemble summer adults; adult plumages are normally attained at 3-15 months, but the horny bill sheaths and plates in several species do not reach adult size until much later, for example at two and four years respectively in *Aethia* and *Fratercula*.

Moult is poorly known. The absence of complete records of plumage condition through the birds' annual cycle, combined with the complexity inherent within a family made up of species with extensive geographical ranges and deferred sexual maturity, make a thorough study of moult pattern and plumage succession extremely difficult. However, all species have one complete and at least one partial moult annually. The post-breeding moult, which occurs in most species soon after breeding is over, is complete, involving all contour and flight-feathers, with the primaries usually shed simultaneously, but gradually in some small auklets. Head and facial ornaments, including crests and plumes, but also ceres, bill plates, eye-rings and fleshy horns, are also lost, accompanied by shrinkage and general fading of other brightly coloured parts like the rictal rosette of puffins, and by colour changes in the legs, in puffins from bright orange to dull yellow, and in *Cepphus* guillemots from brilliant vermilion to pale red, almost pinkish. In spring, the pre-breeding partial moult is slight, usually limited to head, throat area and upper breast, although feather growth can be more extensive in some cases, for example in *Cepphus*. Most species become flightless for a period of up to 45-50 days during the autumn moult, when the flight-feathers are lost and replaced simultaneously; the exceptions are the five small auklets that moult their flight-feathers gradually, which allows them to retain the ability to fly.

In summary, Alcidae as a whole constitute a well defined family with many morphological and anatomical characteristics common to all member species, mostly adaptations for a wing-propelled diving existence. These principal traits and associated functions define alcids as a group and include: efficient wing-propelled underwater swimming and diving; reduced wing size, due to the shortening of the forearm (the antebrachium, the area supported by the radius and ulna), which is always shorter than the carpals and humerus, increasing propulsion efficiency in water; the extended crest of the sternum along its entire length and the enlarged triosseal canal provide enhanced muscle attachments for wings used under water; the thoracic vertebrae are all unfused and thus free, with well developed hypapophyses on the anterior ones for superior attachment of the neck muscles, which combine to facilitate body movement and manoeuvrability under water; and a skeleton which, in order to reduce buoyancy when diving, is virtually non-pneumatic, limited to only the coracoids and scapulae in certain species. Other traits that dis-

This Tufted Puffin in flight reveals a stocky, torpedo-shaped all black body, and rather short, narrow wings, which, though ideal for underwater swimming, make flying rather laboured and take-off from water difficult. It must run, often some considerable distance across the water, before it becomes airborne. In breeding plumage, among the unmistakable features of this puffin are the white face and the yellow straw-like tufts that sprout from behind the eyes and hang down the nape, but most eye-catching of all is the huge, parrot-like salmon red and olive bill.

[Fratercula cirrhata, Talan Island, Russia. Photo: Hanne & Jens Eriksen/Aquila]

tinguish the group from most foot-propelled diving waterbirds including divers (loons), grebes and cormorants are: the sternum longer than the synsacrum; the synsacrum broad at the acetabulum; the tarso-metatarsus short and not as laterally compressed; foot area small, relative to body mass; 15 cervical vertebrae; large supraorbital salt glands; the manus or first finger absent; and feather structures including 10 functional primaries, 15-19 secondaries, and 12-16 rectrices. Together, these characteristics also distinguish the Alcidae from other Charadriiformes.

Habitat

Seabirds, defined as those species which spend long periods away from land and obtain all or most of their food from the sea while flying, swimming or diving, occupy all of the world's oceans. This informal group comprises four orders, with all members of Sphenisciformes and Procellariiformes and several of Pelecaniformes and Charadriiformes, including 13 families and in the region of 280 species, all with evolutionary histories that have been principally marine.

Alcidae, one of the most marine of all bird families, is restricted mainly to the colder waters of the Northern Hemisphere, and well reflects the general characteristics of the seabird group. All 22 alcid species have distinct marine evolutionary backgrounds in one or more of the three northern oceans: 16 are restricted to the Pacific and adjacent seas; four to the Arctic and Atlantic; and two occur in both marine regions. Some of the auks are inshore feeders, for instance the *Cepphus* guillemots, while most others feed offshore, foraging over regions of deep water to the edge of the continental shelf, with only a few, notably the Tufted Puffin, extending into the outermost pelagic zone of the open ocean. Regardless of the water region the individual species occupy outside the breeding season, they live continuously at sea and are independent of land for both feeding and resting, usually remaining out of sight of it for much of the year. In general, auks are almost exclusively marine, with most species breeding along sea coasts, on headlands and offshore islands, and wintering mainly in continental shelf waters.

Marine ornithologists have known for some time that the numbers, species composition, and movements of auks in any water region are largely determined by the physical and biological characteristics of the surface waters. The physical features of sea surface temperature, salinity and ice cover in the upper water layers, less than 25 m down, affect the overall pattern of distribution of the birds. Superimposed over these coarse-grained features come the fine-tuned, and often predictable, attributes of water masses, such as special current systems, notably converging and convection currents, areas of upwelling and gyres, the overall interactions and convergences of which lead to high marine productivity. Correlations between the densities of macroplankton and birds are well known and have been instructive when combined with other measures of ocean waters to define distinctive water types and their occurrence worldwide. The northern oceans have been subdivided by oceanographers into four major oceanic zones (restricted to the upper waters), using combined temperature-salinity relationships and distribution patterns of marine invertebrates: the first is the high Arctic, which contains unmixed water of polar origin with surface layers close to freezing (0-3°C) even in August, the warmest month, and salinity usually below 31‰; the second is the low Arctic, which includes mixed high Arctic and boreal water, where the upper water temperatures in August are 4-10°C, with salinities 31-34‰; third the boreal, comprising a broad band with August temperatures of 10-19°C, and salinities of 31-35‰, which overlap with those of the low Arctic zone; and, fourth, the cool subtropical, the waters immediately south of the boreal zone, where August surface temperatures are usually 19-23°C and salinity is over 35‰. The Alcidae breed almost exclusively in boreal, low and high Arctic water zones; only the two southernmost auk species, Craveri's and Xantus's Murrelets, nest on islands in cool subtropical waters of the North Pacific.

The marine environment occupied by the auk family and other seabirds divides easily into two parts: neritic and oceanic waters. The neritic zone encompasses the waters over the continental shelf, normally to the edge, corresponding roughly to the 200 m depth contour. Waters seaward of this, including those of the continental slope, form the oceanic zone. Most auks remain within neritic waters throughout the year, varying the selection and use of foraging area and habitat according to the phase of their annual cycle. This restriction of marine habitat use relates directly to marine productivity. Neritic waters generally have higher primary and secondary production culminating in a richer and more predictable food supply than oceanic waters. Vertical mixing of waters over the shelf area from tidal flow and seafloor irregularities, resulting in high nutrient recycling combined with local upwellings close to shore and the input of land-based nutrients through drainage, culminate in unusually high productivity.

Although neritic waters are more productive overall, concentrations of zooplankton and associated foraging fish are not uniformly distributed, causing the birds to disperse in relation to areas of known and predictable high food abundance, or to scatter widely looking for lower-density food patches. During the non-breeding period, many species exploit the full span of neritic shelf waters, using physical characteristics of the surface water layers to identify regions of potentially high prey density. Common and Thick-billed Murres are found offshore to the shelf edge and along sea coasts and in bays where concentrations of their winter fish and invertebrate foods are aggregated, moving in relation to changes in prey abundance. Factors that concentrate their foods such as fronts, converging currents, eddies at headlands and islands, and other fixed oceanographic features are very predictable and therefore attended continuously by large numbers of foraging birds for periods ranging from weeks to months. Other coastal and offshore habitats often contain prey, but at lower densities and for shorter time intervals. Certain species, such as the inshore *Cepphus* guillemots and offshore puffins, exploit these habitat types by dispersing widely to reduce competition with conspecifics and feeding solitarily or in small groups; they are also opportunistic, as short-term food patches are found. Between these two extremes lie a myriad of feeding regimes that have evolved amongst auk species to exploit a limited food supply distributed in a non-random manner over a vast area of ocean. Although significant advances have been made since the early 1970's in understanding the links between the abundance of alcids and their prey and the oceanographic factors responsible, the current insufficiency of knowledge about prey abundance or availability, both temporally and spatially, will limit our ability to identify and define the determinants of alcid foraging niches and their oceanographic correlates. Only through a continued long-term research effort focused on gathering oceanographic and alcid data simultaneously will we be able accurately to define the marine pelagic habitats important to auks.

Alcids also display a marked non-random pattern of distribution in their marine environment during the breeding season. They return to land only to reproduce, often forming immense single-species or mixed-species colonies, like those of the Dovekie or certain *Aethia* auklets. Most species breed in small to large colonies, but some in loose aggregations or scattered pairs, rarely as isolated or solitary pairs. Virtually all breeding sites represent compromises between the oceanographic conditions that provide an adequate and predictable marine food supply and land sites within range of this food source with available nesting sites and few ground predators. Locations meeting these requirements are rare. Even the *Synthliboramphus* murrelets, with precocial young that are taken to sea soon after hatching, are limited to sites where suitable foraging habitats are within easy swimming distance of the colony. Overall, most auk species breed at a considerable distance from their food supply, though obviously not beyond the foraging range that permits them to rear their young successfully.

Together, these severe limiting factors have led to low reproductive rates in most alcid species, normally a single chick each year. Species with two-egg clutches have typically overcome the food factor by either feeding inshore near the colony in shallow waters on benthic prey, as in the case of the *Cepphus* guillemots, or by producing precocial chicks that are taken to sea soon after hatching, as with the *Synthliboramphus* murrelets. In northern regions, ice cover and patterns of break-up also strongly influence the decision of where to breed. In addition to an adequate

food supply to feed the young, the surrounding waters must be ice-free early enough in summer to fit in a full breeding season, a period ranging from 60 days in the Thick-billed Murre, for example, to 80-85 days in the Atlantic and Horned Puffins. This means that choice of colony site is crucial, and that many cliffs, islets and islands along sea coasts are likely to lack one or more of the essential requirements for breeding.

Micro-requirements at the breeding site can also be limiting. For species nesting in crevices in rock talus or scree slopes, such as the Dovekie and numerous small auklets, the cavity must not only be accessible and available, but also dry, of the correct size, with certain features of drainage and snow melt that satisfy minimum requirements for incubating an egg and rearing young. Needs of subterranean burrow-nesters like Atlantic and Tufted Puffins are equally demanding, namely a soil type suitable for excavation as well as a vegetative complex that stabilizes and maintains the integrity of the breeding habitat. For surface-breeders such as Thick-billed and Common Murres, the fine-scale features of the bare rocky ledge are of great importance for successful incubation and chick-rearing, and include general characteristics such as height above the sea, steepness of cliff-face, and site-specific details like angle of slope, sides and cover. The same holds for the family's two lowest-density breeders. The Marbled Murrelet searches out moss- and lichen-covered branches of large old-growth coniferous trees that are suitable for using as platforms for nests, and safe from aerial and ground predators; it sometimes nests on open ground. Kittlitz's Murrelet nests alone on the ground in tundra vegetation or on rocky mountain slopes. Both species often breed considerable distances inland from the sea coast. This micro-habitat selection of the actual breeding site is a major determinant of the life-time reproductive performance of individual breeding pairs, probably second in importance only to the general location of the colony or breeding site.

Taken together, all species require suitable land-based habitat for breeding, free from ground predators and in close proximity to an adequate food supply. In Alcidae, the high degree of coloniality, with birds of most species concentrated at a small number of locations, indicates that places to breed possessing all basic ecological requirements for successful reproduction are few. Marine productivity also shapes the dispersion after breeding causing most species to be aggregated in space and time. Such clumped concentrations throughout the annual cycle make most alcids highly vulnerable to human activity and disturbance in marine waters.

General Habits

Alcids are highly social, with most species breeding in colonies, and only a few in loose aggregations or nesting solitarily. Some colonies may be enormous and contain over a million birds, such as those of the Dovekie, or in the hundreds of thousands, as in Crested and Least Auklets. Nineteen of the 22 species can be found in medium to large colonies, although most of these also occur in small groups, infrequently as loose aggregations or scattered pairs, as in the Dovekie and the Black and Pigeon Guillemots, or rarely solitarily, as in the Black and Spectacled Guillemots and the Rhinoceros Auklet. Only one species, Kittlitz's Murrelet, is truly non-colonial, breeding in solitary pairs. Craveri's Murrelet probably occurs most often in loose aggregations and scattered pairs, whereas the Marbled Murrelet seems to breed mainly in loose aggregations, only occasionally as isolated pairs. In summary, most alcids are colonial, with 14 of the 22 living species truly colonial; six intermediate, either loosely colonial or forming colonies at least occasionally; one in loose aggregations and sometimes in isolated pairs; and one solitary.

This high level of sociality within the family has led to many special forms of behaviour and habits. It has generated considerable interest in the group from biologists, particularly evolutionary and behavioural ecologists, regarding the evolution of colonial breeding and the development of social signals and intraspecific characteristics that allow auk species to reproduce successfully in large, often dense, single- and mixed-species colonies. Although the factors responsible for the evolution of coloniality in

the auks remain unclear, as they do for most birds living in groups, there is a clear association between degree of clumping in alcid species for breeding and the distribution of their prey. Colonial species tend to feed offshore on schooling fish or zooplankton that occur in "patches" which are unpredictable in space and time owing to their mobility, whereas loosely colonial or solitary species feed inshore on prey which are more evenly dispersed and predictable.

The assumption that colonies are located where the potential for food is high and vulnerability to predators is low seems reasonable. One obvious advantage of breeding in a colony is finding food. If prey is clumped, mobile and unpredictable, though generally abundant, current information on the whereabouts of good feeding locations can be obtained from other colony members. At small colonies, incoming food-carrying neighbours can be used by other birds either by flying off in the direction from which they have arrived or by waiting until they depart and following them out to sea. Large colonies offer even greater opportunities for finding food because the stream of birds with food flying in towards the colony is normally so dense and compact that food-rich sites can be located by simply following the "highway" of incoming birds to its source. Observations of many alcids support this information-centre hypothesis. For example, detailed studies of Thick-billed Murres, Common Murres and Atlantic Puffins all show that individual birds do not leave the colony at random, but depart in relation to the arrival or departure of conspecifics that have recently delivered food. Organized streams of auks moving between feeding areas and their colonies are known for Pacific and Atlantic colonial species, such as the Dovekie, murres, *Aethia* auklets and puffins, at both high and low latitudes, making their appearance a characteristic feature of a large alcid colony. Such behaviour can be considered essential to attaining a high performance in reproduction at a large alcid colony.

Many alcids breed in colonies with other auk species and seabirds. The immense mixed colonies of *Aethia* auklets and other alcids on the Yamskie Islands in the northern Sea of Okhotsk, probably comprise the largest and most diverse concentration of colonially-breeding alcids anywhere. The 6,000,000 Least Auklets, 300,000-400,000 Crested Auklets and 150,000-200,000 Parakeet Auklets, along with tens of thousands each of both murre

species and Horned Puffins and lesser numbers of Tufted Puffins and Spectacled Guillemots, make the location very special. Single-species colonies appear to be rare, and colonies supporting 2-4 alcid species are the commonest. In general, mixed-species colonies are likely to be a consequence of paucity of suitable breeding sites (see Habitat) within range of an adequate food supply. This means that species will typically come together where oceanographic and terrestrial conditions dictate, with final species composition and numbers mainly determined by differences in the availability of species-specific breeding habitats. Competition between species for nesting space and food resources appears limited, as requirements for breeding differ, even amongst congeneric species like the murres and the small *Aethia* auklets. There may even be advantages in mixed colonies such as increased effectiveness in detection of predators and in food-finding. But, overall, most of the advantages of coloniality occur regardless of the number of auk species in the colony.

The development of social signals, their diversity and functions are intertwined with the degree of coloniality of the species. Alcid species that breed in large, dense aggregations have a larger repertoire of signals and typically a more complex array of social behaviour and relationships than those breeding in loose groups at relatively low densities. The need to communicate with mate and neighbours with clarity and speed is probably higher when breeding occurs at densities exceeding 20 pairs/m^2, as in Common Murres, than in Dovekies and puffins where nest densities are normally below 1/m^2. Behaviour within Alcidae is less ritualized than in other colonial seabird groups like the gannets and boobies, the cormorants and the gulls. A greater diversity in body size and life-history pattern in alcids may well explain the differences. Many displays exhibited in larids and sulids occur in each of the species in the family, whereas few displays are common to all auk species. Behaviour and signals of all species serve as communication pathways between individuals for exchange of information.

Social signals in alcids can be divided into sexual and agonistic behaviour. Sexual behaviour functions in pair formation, maintenance of the pair-bond, and reproduction. Since all alcids are monogamous and show high mate fidelity, behavioural processes involved with mate selection and maintenance are critical to life-time reproductive success and they are probably complex. Although descriptions of the social signals used by most auk species have been made, their origins, functions and contributions to overall patterns of social behaviour are largely unknown. What is known is that considerable time is spent performing displays at or near the breeding site. Greeting displays, often in the form of mutual billing or fencing between pair members, and ceremonies are common in most species ranging from the clashing of open bills and loud calling in Common Murres and vigorous bill-vibrating and billing of Razorbills to the elaborate hunch-whistle posture and billing of the Black Guillemot. The conspicuous billing ceremony in the Atlantic Puffin, almost always initiated by the male, functions in pair maintenance but not as a greeting display. Many forms of behaviour within the pair also occur on the sea near the colony, often at the base of the cliffs where the birds have their breeding site, as is the case in Razorbills, *Cepphus* guillemots and puffins. Allopreening is highly developed in the three large alcids, most frequent in the Common Murre which breeds at the highest density, and less common in the medium to small-sized auks, such as puffins, *Cepphus* guillemots and the Dovekie. Behaviour patterns and courtship signals associated with copulation are highly developed and diverse, often intense and almost ritualized, and most intricate in the auklets. These and other displays centred at the breeding site are all important in pair-bonding, copulation and defence of the site, all critical to successful reproduction.

In contrast to this, are the agonistic behaviour and displays related to territorial defence and site-ownership. These contain elements of aggression directed towards intruders or competitors for limited resources, such as quality breeding sites and mates. The territory may be the small ledge-space occupied by a pair of murres or the area at the entrance of a puffin burrow or guillemot crevice. Breeding sites are defended by both members of a pair using threat displays and fighting. Aggressive encounters are most frequent in high density breeders like the murres, but these interactions are normally of short duration and offset by highly developed appeasement displays and signals. Most confrontations between intruders and resident birds begin with ownership displays or lunges by the owner and end in retreat or presentation of an appeasement signal or posture by the intruder. Actual fighting is rare in all auks, but when it does occur it is unritualized and usually consists of spearing or grabbing the opponent with the bill, followed by twisting and turning, or strong wing-beating, and in some species such as puffins and *Cepphus* guillemots, also involves slashing with the sharp claws. Physical combat occurs when threat displays have failed or where the aggressive action arrives too quickly to permit an averting display. Fights are usually short, though some may go on for several minutes. Competition and fighting for breeding sites can result in regular fighting bouts between individuals over periods of days and weeks, rarely months.

Most threat displays in alcids are unritualized, but some may be ritualized, particularly those associated with site-ownership. For example, in the Atlantic Puffin there is a step-wise progression of events from low- to high-intensity threat displays, culminating in fighting. The progression in response to the approach of an intruding bird proceeds thus: sitting at the burrow entrance, with a low threat advertising ownership; then a neck stretch and slow head waving; standing and head waving; higher-intensity bill displays, holding the closed bill in profile towards the intruder; followed by head-flicking with the bill closed; then, finally, head-flicking with the gape and head-flick, while the bird is frozen in an upright position with maximum bill gape, the most aggressive display in the repertoire of the species, which may be followed, if necessary, by actual attack and physical combat. Display of the bill to maximize its size and potential for fighting is most important, and most interactions end before head-flicking with the open bill.

There are also numerous post-landing and ritualized walking postures in auks, including those of puffins as they land within the nesting space, a low-profile wings-raised posture that is held for 5-10 seconds before the bird moves. Where landing has been inaccurate, and the distance the bird must walk to reach its burrow is lengthy, it will often adopt a hunched low-profile posture,

similar to the landing position except with the wings down, as it walks through areas of the colony occupied by breeding birds. Both these ritualized displays have an appeasement function, motivated to reduce aggression from neighbouring birds by signalling the displaying bird's presence and non-aggressive intent. Each auk species has its own set of appeasement displays and signals, but the largest repertoire occurs in the highest-density breeders, the murres, which suggests that the evolution of inter-pair appeasement signals has been closely related to breeding density.

To a lesser degree, those species in small, loosely aggregated colonies, or those breeding as isolated pairs, also display features deserving of special attention. For example, Kittlitz's Murrelet, breeding widely dispersed and solitarily on mountain scree and rocky ground, and the Marbled Murrelet, occurring as isolated or scattered pairs mainly in old-growth coniferous forests, both considerable distances inland from the sea, offer a great challenge to alcid observers. What are the principal determinants of their selection of habitat for nesting, and what factors in the marine environment are important to chick-rearing and post-fledging survival? And what behavioural patterns are associated with successful reproductive performance and how are they inter-related to those of other alcids? Knowledge of the reproductive ecology of these low-density breeders may provide considerable insight into the evolution and diversity of alcid coloniality.

Voice

The name "auk" originates from the Scandinavian root "ālka", the old Norse word describing the vocalizations or noises of some Alcidae. In general, little is known about vocalizations outside the breeding season, but the information that does exist suggests that the birds tend to be mostly silent. However, during the breeding season most alcids are vocal, with calls that can be loud and very obvious, though not highly specialized in structure or form. At breeding colonies, vocal displays are usually associated with breeding behaviour, most often as threat displays during agonistic encounters with conspecifics or potential predators, but also as integral parts of courtship and social rituals or communication between parents and offspring. Calls range from delicate soft whistles in *Cepphus* guillemots and *Aethia* auklets to loud, raucous growls and groans in murres and puffins.

Vocalizations tend to be simple in construction and diversity, separating into three broad categories: sharp single notes representing warning or distress; trilling calls involved with pair communication and bonding; and hoarse, unmelodious calls, taking the form of clucks, snarls, growls and extended series of quivering, gargling calls during aggressive encounters, varying in intensity, frequency and amplitude according to the degree of involvement. Studies of voice in auk species are limited, but males seem to be more vocal than females, probably related to the male's dominant function in the acquisition and defence of the breeding site. The groans of two male puffins, with bills locked together, pulling and twisting, in a dispute over ownership of a burrow or the high-pitched growls of two murres in combat, spearing and sparring with their long and pointed bills, for possession of a small space on a rock ledge, leave little doubt as to their threat-aggression component. In contrast are the soothing and melodious whistles of Black and Pigeon Guillemots sitting at the entrance to their rocky nest crevice early in the breeding season or the trilling calls of Dovekies performed at the colony by flying or sitting birds, often involving the simultaneous participation of large numbers of birds. The social functions of these mass vocal displays are poorly understood.

Characteristic calls are produced between breeding birds and their chicks, some unique and distinct to facilitate parent-chick recognition, others to communicate immediate needs such as brooding and feeding. Chicks generally make plaintive, high-pitched, monotonous calls when soliciting food, apparently most pronounced in cavity- and burrow-nesting species where parent-chick recognition is limited or absent and where there is no parental care after fledging, for instance in puffins and *Cepphus*

guillemots. The loud, distinctive calls of adult murres searching for their chick after becoming separated on a crowded ledge or at sea after fledging, and the corresponding wailing distress cry of a lost chick, underline the significance of vocalizations that are individual-specific and easily identified at a distance. These calls function to reunite separated family members and enhance chick survival and productivity of breeding pairs; they are found in species breeding at high densities where parents and young can become separated and where there is prolonged parental care after fledging, for example murres, the Razorbill and *Synthliboramphus* murrelets.

Overall, auks are highly vocal during the summer at the colony, mostly when on land but also to a lesser extent on the water and in flight. The degree of vocalization and extent of repertoire are highly variable between species, but are generally most pronounced and developed amongst species breeding in large colonies, notably the Dovekie, *Aethia* auklets and murres. Certain species are less vocal than others during breeding and have a smaller number of calls, for example puffins; some appear to be mostly silent, for example *Brachyramphus* murrelets. The magnitude and functions of calls are imperfectly known for all species. Although quantitative data and details of vocal repertoire are unavailable for any single species, partial quantitative analyses have been made of some species including the Dovekie, Common Murre, Razorbill, *Cepphus* guillemots and Atlantic Puffin.

Food and Feeding

Feeding habits are extremely diverse among the Alcidae. Diets span all the trophic levels between plankton-feeding and exclusively fish-eating, and foraging occurs over the entire neritic zone, from near-shore to offshore in the deep ocean, and at variable depths from middle upper waters to on, or close to, the sea floor. Members of the family show impressive ecological segregation and dominate other species-groups within their range in relation to number of species and biomass. Other co-existing marine groups, especially shearwaters and petrels, gulls and terns, and to a lesser extent gannets, cormorants and pelicans, are either surface-feeders (which auks are not), or so markedly different in body form and specialization that the potential for interactive, competitive relationships is minimal. The auks stand out from other marine bird groups in the Northern Hemisphere by the adaptive radiation they have achieved within the broad and ecologically diverse sub-surface water zone of the northern oceans, which makes their study both exciting and stimulating, particularly in relation to food and feeding.

Auks obtain all their food from the sea, by diving from the surface and propelling themselves under water with their wings, in pursuit of prey. They are all solitary feeders, capturing and swallowing their relatively small prey individually, mainly while swimming in the water chasing mobile prey, but sometimes at the sea bottom in the case of *Cepphus* guillemots. Individual alcid species are plankton-feeding specialists, fish-feeding specialists, or intermediate generalists feeding on both plankton and fish. Apart from the conspicuous gradation in body size, from small in plankton-feeders to large in fish-eaters, which corresponds to increasing prey size, the size and shape of bills also differ according to feeding adaptation. The small plankton-feeders have short, stubby bills whereas those of the fish-eaters are generally longer and larger. In addition, the six true plankton-feeders have gular throat pouches used for storing and carrying food to their young, a specialization for long distance foraging.

The true plankton-feeders comprise the Dovekie, Cassin's and the Parakeet Auklets, and the *Aethia* auklets, all of which are known to feed throughout the year on planktonic herbivorous crustaceans, particularly the calanoid copepods *Calanus* and *Neocalanus*, the euphausiids *Thysanoessa*, and amphipods *Parathemisto*. The five auklets share this niche in the North Pacific, with ranges that overlap in boreal waters, but only one of these species, Cassin's Auklet, has a range that extends south into cool subtropical waters. The ecological equivalent of the five Pacific auklets is limited to a single species in the Atlantic, the Dovekie. This difference in number of plankton-feeding alcids between oceans corresponds with the greater diversity and total biomass of macroplankton in the Pacific, as does the diversity of plankton-feeding whales and other marine vertebrate groups.

The bill and tongue are variable and distinct in each of the three feeding groups. The plankton-feeders, which prey mainly on small, soft-bodied crustaceans, have a relatively wide bill, a broad tongue that is thick and fleshy, and a broad palate covered with numerous denticles. The flexible and muscular characteristics of the tongue allow small food items to be handled with ease after capture, and held in place against the upper palate until the bird is ready to push them into the gular food pouch; only the soft, strong, flexible tongue shown by all *Aethia* auklets could accomplish this. The fish-eaters, on the other hand, normally prey on hard-bodied, fast-swimming pelagic fish that must be caught and manipulated with speed and precision. To achieve this, the fish-eating auks have a narrow, sharp-tipped bill with a long, partially cornified and rigid tongue that is encased in a deep trough formed by the horny sides of the lower mandible, and a narrow palate with sharp regularly spaced denticles for pinning prey effectively. Together, these features ensure robust, vice-like leverage of the tongue onto the roof of the mouth when holding large, mobile prey, a tendency most pronounced in the Common Murre and the Razorbill, but also well displayed by *Cepphus* guillemots. Between these two extremes lie the more generalized fish- and plankton-feeders, the puffins, the Rhinoceros Auklet, and the murrelets. These species show characters of the bill and tongue that are intermediate, though variable between species, but all with relatively broader bills and tongues than the species feeding almost exclusively on fish, and with the distribution pattern and density of palatal denticles mid-way between those of the fish- and plankton-feeding alcids.

Although the family exhibits trends in body size and structure of the bill and tongue that seem to be food-related and important to ecological theory, its relatively high species diversity and close interspecific relationships indicate a reasonably high degree of overlap in food habits. Since most information about diet comes from studies of food delivered to chicks during the breeding season, knowledge of what adults eat is generally limited, as is true of the winter diets of all age groups. We know little about actual foraging ranges of pelagic auks, and even less about their behaviour once they have discovered prey. To what depths do individual species normally dive and feed, for what durations of time, and at what energetic costs? Is segregation achieved between the three broad feeding groups and among closely related species within each group by differences in niche exploitation in time and space? Are species mainly separated by position in the water column rather than by prey type? These and numerous other questions abound, many that will remain unanswered, simply because the ocean is vast and our abilities to observe auks at sea are very limited. While these gaps in information seem enormous, particularly when compared with what is known about feeding relationships in terrestrial avian communities, great advances have been made over the past 20-30 years. Doubtless much more information is required to answer the cutting questions of adaptive radiation in Alcidae, but an examination of some of the highlights of what is known of the feeding and foraging habits of the Alcidae may be revealing.

Auks do not find their food at sea by random search. Oceanographers have known for decades that plankton is not uniformly abundant over all parts of the sea, nor are the standing stocks of macroplankton and nekton in the upper surface waters. High primary and secondary production are associated with zones of intense mixing of water masses, and it is in these regions of upwelling and convergences, as well as "downstream" from them, that phytoplankton and zooplankton become especially concentrated at convergent fronts and tidal rips of dissimilar water types. This patchy distribution of prey, makes it necessary for the birds to reside in or close to these food-rich areas throughout the year, in winter for self-maintenance and survival, and in summer to meet the extra demands of reproduction. These places may be widely separated, often by thousands of kilometres, making it necessary for staging areas between the two to enable successful migratory movements in spring and autumn. Requirements for

breeding are particularly demanding, making it necessary to have sufficient food of the correct quantity and quality available at the right time and place for egg formation, incubation and chick-rearing. Choice of place is especially important for the true plankton-feeding alcids that can only feed effectively where their prey occurs at high concentrations. This perhaps accounts for the enormous colonies of such plankton-eaters, like Cassin's, Crested and Least Auklets in the Pacific and the Dovekie in the Atlantic.

Concentrations of alcids are almost always found in association with major areas of upwelling, systems that are often patchily distributed in space and well offshore away from breeding locations. In many regions of convergent fronts and current rips there are distinct water masses with steep temperature differences causing opposing water movements and sinking. All of these physical properties and temperature gradients at or near the sea surface contribute to high concentrations of zooplankton and fish. At high latitudes in Arctic regions, massive local concentrations of plankton often form in places that show vertical mixing of waters with differing salinities, such as the enormous dilution produced by the introduction of glacier melt-water into surrounding seas. One example is the Devon Ice Cap at the northern entrance to Lancaster Sound, Canada, where millions of Dovekies from colonies in north-west Greenland occur each spring and early summer to exploit the high-density zooplankton patches that cover an area about 110 km long by 24 km wide along the south-east coast of Devon Island. This area of water, roughly 400 km distant from the Dovekie colonies, seems an important if not essential food source for most of the 30,000,000 pairs of Dovekies during their energy-demanding period of egg formation and initiation of breeding in late May and June; it is also used later in the season, particularly in August during chick-rearing and fledging. Similar "hot spots" have been noted elsewhere in low and high Arctic waters, as they have been too at lower latitudes around convergences and upwellings of cold and warm water masses. But only more detailed oceanographical studies of the regions known to have large concentrations of colonially-breeding auks will reveal the general correspondence and biological significance of these dynamic water systems and details of their exploitation by local breeding populations of Alcidae.

The main prey of the plankton-feeders comprises planktonic crustaceans, principally copepods, euphausiids and amphipods. Seasonal changes occur in the diets of most species, often reflecting differences in availability over time and, in some cases, availability and the relative nutritional values of individual prey species. In the high Arctic, Dovekies feed mainly on copepods early in spring during May and June, but switch largely to amphipods and larval fish when rearing young in July and August. In north-west Greenland the change coincides with the increased availability of larger stages of the free-swimming *Parathemisto*, amphipods with a caloric value significantly higher than the copepods. The summer diets of all the *Aethia* auklets and Cassin's Auklet also comprise planktonic crustaceans. Crested Auklets feed mainly on *Thysanoessa* euphausiids with lesser amounts of amphipods and large copepods, and Whiskered and Least Auklets concentrate on *Neocalanus* and *Calanus* copepods supplemented by some euphausiids, the latter often dominating the winter diet of all three auklet species. Cassin's Auklets feed heavily on euphausiids, amphipods and copepods alike, in proportions varying with time and location, and they appear to select large copepods (*Neocalanus cristatus*) over smaller ones (*N. plumchrus*, *Eucalanus bungii*) when both types are present; they also take some squid and fish, such as sandlance or sandeels (*Ammodytes*) and sculpin. Parakeet Auklets have a more diverse diet than the *Aethia* and *Ptychoramphus* auklets, feeding largely on hyperiid amphipods (*Parathemisto*) and euphausiids (*Thysanoessa*) early in the season, and copepods (*N. cristatus*) later, supplemented by numerous decapod larvae, gelatinous zooplankton (ctenophores, jellyfish), immature fish such as sandeels and walleye pollock, and fish eggs. This broad diet with considerable exploitation of fish larvae and eggs is believed to explain why the species is so abundant in the south-eastern Bering Sea and along the shallow coastal inner shelf regions where primary production and zooplankton biomass are normally low. After breeding, the euphausiid *T. inermis* becomes the principal

The Horned Puffin, the Pacific counterpart of the Atlantic Puffin (Fratercula arctica), *is very similar to the latter in both appearance and general habits. More abundant at the higher latitudes of its breeding range, it is largely sympatric with the Tufted Puffin, with which it may compete for nest-sites. Like the majority of the alcids it forms vast breeding colonies at times, the size depending on the availability of nesting sites, which are typically in crevices and cracks in rocks and scree and under boulders, and less often in burrows on grassy slopes. In its social behaviour, displays are various: "Head-jerking" on the part of the male may take place before copulation, but is also performed on other occasions, rarely by both members of a pair. "Billing" occurs throughout the breeding season and indicates pair-bonding: in the Horned Puffin it frequently follows a bird's landing near its mate at the nest-site. The two birds slap the lateral surfaces of their bills together, such displays lasting perhaps 2-3 minutes. The main threat display is "Bill-gaping" when the bill is pointed towards the opponent wide open, while in the "Landing Display" the wings are held high and the tail cocked, probably to show appeasement by signalling lack of aggressive intention when a bird is landing or walking through the colony.*

[Fratercula corniculata, Alaska, USA. Photo: J. J. Alcalay/Bios]

food of many auklet species during autumn and winter, best exemplified by the Whiskered Auklet with a winter diet containing at least 90% *T. inermis*.

Most auks have a varied diet, even though invertebrates or fish alone are predominantly eaten for much of the year or at certain times. For example, only Whiskered and Least Auklets can be described as almost exclusively planktivorous, as small or larval fish do occasionally appear in the diets of adults or chicks of Dovekies and Cassin's, Parakeet and Crested Auklets. The other species are either primarily fish-eaters or species that consume significant quantities of both fish and zooplankton. Although the Thick-billed Murre, Razorbill, *Cepphus* guillemots, Rhinoceros Auklet, Atlantic and Horned Puffins feed mostly on fish throughout the year, euphausiids and other crustaceans, squid or polychaete worms normally supplement the birds' diets during the non-breeding season. The Common Murre comes closest to being an exclusive fish-eater, but even in this species the winter diet regularly includes small quantities of crustaceans. The dominant summer foods of the piscivores vary between species and water type. In the Arctic, Thick-billed Murres take demersal species like Arctic cod (*Boreogadus saida*), the dominant small fish in high Arctic waters, supplemented by sculpins (Cottidae) and blennies (Pholidae, Strichaeidae, Zoarcidae), and a wider variety of prey farther south including pelagic capelin (*Mallotus villosus*). The other large auks, the Common Murre and the Razorbill, along with the medium-sized Rhinoceros Auklet and puffins, feed principally on pelagic shoaling fish such as clupeids, sandeels and capelin. The *Cepphus* guillemots feed mostly on sculpins and blennies in the near-shore coastal waters.

The murrelets, in turn, display summer diets encompassing zooplankton and fish. Both Marbled and Kittlitz's Murrelets take euphausiid crustaceans (*Thysanoessa spinifera*) from late winter to early summer, with mostly sandeels (*Ammodytes hexapterus*) and smaller amounts of herring (*Clupea harengus*), capelin and shiner perch (*Cymatogaster aggregata*) and certain smelt (Osmeridae) through the remainder of the breeding season. Xantus's and Craveri's Murrelets are predominantly fish-eaters, usually foraging over deep water rather than in shallow coastal regions. Xantus's appears to feed mainly on larval northern anchovies (*Engraulis mordax*) supplemented by Pacific saury (*Cololabis saira*) and rockfish (*Sebastes*), while Craveri's feeds largely on larval rockfish and herring, as well as adult lanternfish (*Benthosema panamense*), euphausiids and squid. The remaining two *Synthliboramphus* species, the Ancient and Japanese Murrelets, feed on roughly equal amounts of euphausiid crustaceans and small larval fish. The Japanese Murrelet takes mainly crangonid shrimps (*Sabinea*, *Sclerocrangon*) and herring and saury (*Hypoptychus dybowskii*), sandeels, smelt and sculpin (*Triglops*). Ancient Murrelet diet varies between regions, but mainly comprises euphausiids (*Thysanoessa spinifera*, *T. pacifica*, *T. inermis*) with lesser amounts of fish including small sandeels, shiner perch, rockfish, capelin, walleye pollock (*Theragra chalcogramma*), smelt and sculpin.

Little is known about the diving depths to which alcids regularly descend in search of prey. Measurements of time intervals between initiating a dive and reappearance at the surface provide some indication of potential maximum depths attained, but these rely on assumptions of speed of descent and proportions of total time under water spent diving and foraging at a constant depth. A combination of incidental drownings of auks in fishing gear at known depths and small depth gauges attached to free-living birds have provided valuable insights into actual maximum depths. These findings also show a close correspondence between diving depth and bird body size, larger birds diving deeper and more often than smaller species. The murres are the deepest divers, probably attaining depths greater than of 100 m regularly, whereas the Razorbill and medium-sized auks, puffins and Rhinoceros Auklet likely forage mostly at depths of 20-40 m, and the smaller plankton-feeders normally above 20 m, rarely deeper than 30 m. The Black Guillemot, though restricted to shallow inshore habitat when breeding, probably dives to considerable depths when farther offshore in winter. The amount of time spent foraging at different depths is poorly known for all species, as are the cues used by the birds to assess the food potential

of any given water area. We do know, however, that the larger auks dive for longer periods and beat their wings at a higher rate than other species, which is probably reflected in both rate of descent and depths achieved. The *Cepphus* species are unusual in that they use their feet as well as their wings when swimming along the sea floor; this is most likely an adaptation for their bottom-feeding habits, enhancing their ability to maintain a position and probe the benthos effectively.

The foraging distances of breeding auks vary over a wide range. The murres, Dovekie, *Synthliboramphus* murrelets and *Aethia* auklets may travel lengthy distances for food, 50 km or more, with the Razorbill, Rhinoceros Auklet and puffins also flying similar distances but more often feeding closer inshore. Although the coastal *Cepphus* guillemots may forage close to shore, they can travel long distances to bays and other sites where food is abundant. The inland-breeding *Brachyramphus* murrelets often fly long distances over land from their nests to reach the sea, most flights covering about 20 km, but sometimes as much as 75 km; however, they usually feed within 1-10 km of the shore in shallow waters adjacent to their nesting site.

The manner of carrying and delivering food to the young shows remarkable variation. In the true plankton-feeders, like the Dovekie and Least Auklet, both parents feed their young on small crustaceans, mainly calanoid copepods, transported from often distant feeding areas back to the colony in their specialized distensible gular throat pouch. Food items in a meal may be 1-17 mm long and are given to the chick as a mucous-covered package or "soup" typically containing 400-600 individual prey items weighing a total of 3-8 g. About 5-8 meals are delivered to a chick each day, with no differences in frequency of feeding or meal size carried by male and female parents.

In contrast are the fish-eating murres, Razorbill and puffins. On each journey, Common and Thick-billed Murres feed their chick a single fish which they carry back to the colony lengthwise in the bill with the head deep inside the mouth and tail forward, which may allow partial digestion of the bony head before it is given to the chick. The number of chick meals delivered daily by a pair of Common Murres varies at 3-8, the total weight averaging 28 g of pelagic schooling fish like capelin, sandeels or sprat (*Sprattus sprattus*), and each fish about 100-140 mm long. Thick-billed Murres at high latitudes feed their young predominantly Arctic cod in a manner and at rates similar to those of Common Murres, but the total daily amount of fish consumed is higher, at about 58 g. Razorbills and puffins usually carry two or more immature fish crosswise in the bill, mostly capelin, sandeels, herring or sprat depending upon geographic region, with the number of fish per meal decreasing with size of fish caught. Daily provisioning rates to chicks by both parents equally are of 2-9 meals, with average total amounts of food delivered daily varying from 20-25 g in the Razorbill, to 43-62 g in the Atlantic Puffin, 24-72 g in the Horned Puffin and 16-80 g in the Tufted Puffin. When more than one of these fish-eating species is rearing young on the same prey at one colony, average sizes and numbers of fish taken usually vary between the species: for example, Common Murres deliver one large item, Razorbills a few medium-sized ones, and Atlantic Puffins many small ones. The *Cepphus* guillemots specialize on small, benthic fish such as sandeels, gunnels (Pholidae), pricklebacks (Stichaeidae), eelpouts (Zoarcidae), sculpins and rockfish. All three species take similar-sized fish which both parents deliver to their 1-2 chicks, normally one fish at a time held crosswise in the bill, with 3-15 meals daily.

Little is known about the feeding habits of the Great Auk, and there are obviously limited prospects of learning more about this unusual, large flightless alcid, now extinct for over 150 years. However, examinations of bill measurements in relation to today's fish-eating alcids, especially the Great Auk's closest extant relative the Razorbill, suggests maximum and preferred prey weights of at least 100-150 g and 30-40 g respectively for this species. Detailed observations of the Great Auk at sea, given in the *English Pilot* of 1767, indicate a typical offshore feeder, probably foraging most often on benthic fish prey in waters of 75 m or less, sometimes at greater depths. It probably had a foraging range stretching at least 60-70 km from the colony,

Outside the breeding season alcids tend to be rather silent. During breeding most vocal displays are associated with some aspect of breeding behaviour, though many are still of uncertain interpretation, maybe used in threat displays to deter rivals or intruders, forming a part of courtship and pair-bonding, or purely a means of general social communication. In the breeding season, the Parakeet Auklet has been noted as being very vocal close to its nest-site. It has a call uttered from land or water which may be provoked by the approach of danger, or can be given before the bird takes flight. One observer remarked that a mated bird would land near the nest and utter a trilled song until its partner arrived, when a duet would ensue. At other times a single bird, sex unspecified, gives voice from a perch as in the case of this Parakeet Auklet. During this vocalization, the significance of which is again unknown, the neck is stretched somewhat, the bill is opened, and the head tilted up briefly.

[*Cyclorrhynchus psittacula*, Alaska, USA. Photo: Winfried Wisniewski/FLPA]

possibly even as much as 110 km based on comparisons with the similar-sized Macaroni Penguin (*Eudyptes chrysolophus*), and normally fed inside the continental shelf or shelf slope areas. Some support for these proposals comes from the direct evidence that remains of the Great Auk's diet, the food content of birds collected in south-west Greenland around 1770; this comprised short-horn sculpins (*Myoxocephalus scorpius*) and lumpsuckers (*Cyclopterus lumpus*), both largely bottom-dwelling fish.

It has recently been suggested that young Great Auks were fed mainly planktonic crustaceans carried back to the colony by the parent in the gullet and regurgitated. But the morphology of the Great Auk's mouth and bill, combined with its overall body size and structure, suggest instead feeding habits similar to the other large Alcidae. It seems more likely that this flightless 5500-8000 g alcid probably fed on both pelagic schooling fish and those on or close to the sea floor by diving, possibly transporting large fish catches back to the colony within its greatly expandable proventriculus, much in the manner of penguins and gannets. Unfortunately, of necessity this all remains highly speculative, as this remarkable species has been lost for ever.

Breeding

Most alcid species breed in colonies on islands and sea cliffs along rocky coasts. Colonies vary in size, from a few scattered pairs like the low-density breeding inshore *Cepphus* guillemots to more than a million birds like the gregarious Dovekie or Least Auklet. Two species, Kittlitz's and the Marbled Murrelet, are non-colonial, both nesting considerable distances inland, up to 75 km from the sea coast. Kittlitz's nests on rocky mountain slopes, the Marbled usually high above the ground on branches in the upper canopy in old-growth coniferous forests. The other 20 species occur in small to large aggregations in single- or mixed-species colonies on offshore islands, almost always facing the sea or in close proximity, in a wide range of terrestrial habitats free of mammalian predators. Generally, most colonial alcids breed either on or in rocky substrates, earthy burrows, or in holes and cavities in sandy loam, exposed tree roots and logs.

Nest descriptions exist for all species, even though the reasons and processes involved in their selection are poorly understood for many species. In a few species only a small number of nests have been found, for example in Marbled, Kittlitz's, Xantus's and Craveri's Murrelets.

The range of breeding habitats used by Alcidae is considerable, and some species have very specific habitat requirements for breeding while others are more adaptable. The *Cepphus* Guillemots normally choose fissures or crevices in rocky cliffs or boulder fields, but also make use of abandoned burrows of other species, and cavities provided by human artifacts such as discarded barrels or other abandoned structures. In contrast, the largest species, the Thick-billed and Common Murres and the Razorbill, breed mainly on rocky cliff ledges, murres mostly in the open but sometimes in crevices or caves, and Razorbills usually under partial cover; all three also occur on expansive rock areas and on flat, low-lying isolated islands, Razorbills most often in boulder fields and rubble. Ledges occupied by the Thick-billed Murre have been found to show very specific site characteristics including width and slope. Puffins and the Rhinoceros Auklet nest in burrows that they excavate in the ground on maritime slopes, likewise showing highly specific habitat requirements; Atlantic and Tufted Puffins normally select grassy maritime slopes where the ground has certain characteristics of texture, integrity and angle of slope. The Horned Puffin commonly nests in rock crevices or fissures on sea cliffs or slopes, and the other three species do so less frequently, while the Rhinoceros Auklet will also use the bare forest floor of thickly forested islands. The four colonial small murrelets use cavities and hollows around root systems of trees, logs or rock crevices for breeding sites, while the Ancient and Japanese Murrelets also excavate holes in soft ground. Dovekies and most of the small auklets nest most often in sea-facing scree slopes and boulder fields, Dovekies also often on precipitous cliffs and auklets in rock rubble along coastal beaches; again, detailed examinations of the scree slopes chosen reveal numerous species-specific microhabitat preferences, as is the case for most auk species. Selection of breeding habitat is critical in all alcid species, and there is a gradient of quality within a species' range. Where examined, for instance in the Atlantic Puffin, high quality habitats where breeding performance is highest are usually occupied by the largest males, but not females, which suggests a competitive advantage related to male body size, probably important to success in aggressive encounters and breeding site acquisition.

All auk species are marine, coming to land only to breed, being otherwise totally independent of it for feeding, resting and sleeping. Certain other features are common to all members of Alcidae: they are long-lived, many of the medium-sized to large species like the Common Murre and Tufted Puffin reaching ages well over 20 years; they reach sexual maturity slowly, most at around 4-5 years of age, for instance the murres, Razorbill and puffins, but others like the *Cepphus* guillemots at 3 years; and they have low reproductive rates, normally with a single-egg clutch except in *Cepphus* guillemots and *Synthliboramphus* murrelets which usually lay two eggs, and correspondingly slow recovery rates. These life history characteristics make all auks vulnerable to natural or man-induced disturbances that reduce their numbers owing to their relatively low fecundity. For example, a 50% population reduction in a cormorant (Phalacrocoracidae) might show complete recovery within 4-5 years, whereas an auk might require 20-25 years to do so, everything else remaining equal.

Adult annual survival is known for 10 of the 22 alcid species. Estimates range from 75% for Least Auklets and 77% for Ancient Murrelets, both relatively small species, to 89-95% in the larger murres, Razorbill and Atlantic Puffin. Most species probably breed once annually, though Cassin's Auklet sometimes lays a second clutch after successfully fledging the first chick, and only about 50% of Spectacled Guillemots seem to reproduce each year. In general, adult life history characteristics are incompletely known and require additional study.

Most alcids return to their colonies several weeks, sometimes months in boreal water regions, before initiating egg-laying. This pre-laying period is used to make the transition from a sea existence to one that is land-based, the birds performing activities that include repossession and occupancy of breeding sites, re-establishment of pair-bonds, mating and preparation of the site

for an egg, which for burrow- and crevice-nesters can be demanding work. The time available for completing these tasks is shortest in northern regions where the whole area may remain covered with ice and snow until late spring or early summer. In temperate regions, birds may spend 4-8 weeks on or near the colony before the first egg is laid, some species even longer, like the Common Murre which at certain British colonies reappears 4-5 months before breeding, or Cassin's Auklet in southern parts of its range where night-time visits to the colony occur throughout the non-breeding period. But 3-5 weeks is the norm, and colonial birds typically display a cyclical and normally synchronous pattern of colony attendance during this period, with all birds present for 3-5 days followed by an equal time period when the colony is deserted. Although features of this attendance pattern vary between species, its occurrence is conspicuous among all colonial auks. It is believed to be associated on the one hand with the need for the re-establishment of individuals at the colony in the presence of conspecifics, for site occupancy, defence and pairing, and on the other with a distant supply of food early in the season, birds typically fasting when together at the colony during this settlement period.

Fidelity to colony and breeding site are high. Results of ringing studies show that most alcids return not only to the same colony year after year, but also to the same breeding site. At one British colony, 96% of Common Murres ringed as breeders returned the following year, and of those that did, 90% used the same breeding site. Similar strong attachments to the colony and site have been recorded for Razorbills, Black Guillemots, Xantus's Murrelets, Least Auklets and Atlantic Puffins, with other species likely to show the same levels of fidelity to colony and breeding site.

Mate fidelity, or monogamy, is also the rule in all auks, birds remaining together as pairs through their entire breeding life. Not all species have been studied, but those that have indicate high mate fidelity with a corresponding low divorce rate, about 7% in Black Guillemots and Atlantic Puffins, though somewhat higher in Crested Auklets at 24%. Divorce seems to be associated with low or failed breeding performance. Co-operation between male and female partners in producing and raising offspring successfully seems likely, and in Cassin's Auklet and other species mate retention has been demonstrated to have a highly positive influence on breeding performance by enhancing both hatching and fledging success. Some species, however, may exhibit distinctly non-monogamous forms of behaviour such as extra-pair copulations in Common Murres and puffins, usually males attempting to mate with any unattended female nearby. Mate guarding is therefore prevalent in most species, each male staying close to his female during her fertile period and vigorously attacking any intruding male. Although such defence is effective most of the time, successful rapes do occur, particularly among species that mate on exposed breeding sites at high density.

Copulation usually takes place at or near the breeding site, in the open, as in Dovekies, murres, Razorbills, *Cepphus* guillemots and murrelets, less often on the sea, as in *Aethia* auklets and puffins. Mating takes place quickly, lasting only 15-30 seconds, but occurs frequently each day during the pre-laying period. In Atlantic Puffins, intense courtship displays occur on land near the burrow entrance, mostly involving repeated bouts of billing initiated by the male, and often developing into ritualized head-flicking and sky-pointing by the male. Attempts by the male to mount at this point may occur, but are invariably rejected by the female, and usually the partners simply depart together for the sea at the base of the cliffs where they copulate before returning to the colony. Some small auklets show elaborate courtship displays prior to copulation. In Least Auklets this includes a high-intensity rodent-run display, the male running in a circle round the female while in a low-hunched posture, continuously emitting a "chattering" vocalization. Copulation in Dovekies is always preceded by numerous bouts of head-wagging and billing. This period before laying is, in most colonial species, a frenzy of site defence and mating activity.

Timing of breeding is crucial to success in reproduction among the auks. For birds with a low reproductive rate, producing a single clutch of only 1-2 eggs each year, the time of laying

A flock of flying Dovekies fills the sky dramatically near a breeding colony on Spitsbergen. Such colonies can be immense, in some cases containing more than a million individuals. The Dovekie is estimated to be the most abundant auk in the Atlantic, with most colonies sited in the remote far north on mountain scree slopes that offer abundant nesting sites, where nearby offshore waters provide an abundant plankton-rich food supply, and where ground predation is minimal. One of the great advantages of living in a large colony is that information regarding the location of good feeding areas is readily available. The constant dense stream of birds flying into a colony carrying food serves to indicate to others bent on seeking food the general direction in which they might go. They have only to fly in the opposite direction to the incoming "traffic" in order to find where it originates. Studies of certain alcids confirm that birds do not leave the colony on a random search, but that their departure is related to others that have either recently arrived with food or have just departed in search of it. It is this incessant toing and froing of masses of birds between the colony and feeding sites, with all the attendant hubbub, that makes a really large auk colony such an impressive spectacle.

[Alle alle alle, Hambergbukta, Spitsbergen, Svalbard. Photo: Tui De Roy/ Auscape]

The Common Murre feeds
extensively on fish,
although it also takes
some invertebrates. When
searching for food it dips
its head just below the
surface and, once prey
has been located, dives
down after it directly from
the surface. Normally it
dives only to depths of
10-30 m, but dives to
60-70 m are known to
occur regularly, while
exceptionally the species
has been recorded down
to 180 m. Food brought to
the chicks consists almost
exclusively of fish,
especially capelin, herring,
sprat and sandeels. Only
one fish is carried at a
time, held head-first and
lengthwise in the bill.

[Uria aalge californica,
Neah Bay, Strait of Juan
de Fuca, Washington,
USA.
Photo: A. & E. Morris/
Birds As Art]

is all-important. The general rule is to time egg-laying so that young are reared when food is most abundantly available for them. Most alcid species do appear to lay eggs in relation to the average seasonal peak of food availability. This is most pronounced in cold water systems where prey diversity is low, which provides better opportunities for examining links between timing and prey abundance. One of the clearest examples is the Atlantic Puffin in the low Arctic and boreal waters of the north-west Atlantic. Here, laying (and therefore hatching 42 days later) by puffins in the Gulf of Maine takes place about 4 weeks earlier than at colonies in south-east Newfoundland and 8 weeks before those in southern Labrador. Examination of the timing of arrival of the principal fish that breeding puffins feed to their chicks in each of these areas shows it to correspond with peak hatching. Puffins in Newfoundland and Labrador time their breeding schedule with the influx of capelin inshore into coastal upper waters for spawning, which occurs 4 weeks later in Labrador than Newfoundland, whereas Gulf of Maine puffins focus on herring movements which occur 4-8 weeks earlier. The influence of food on timing of breeding in auks, fish- and plankton-feeders alike, is well established for many species, as are the consequences of not rearing young when food is most abundant. Young hatched at peak of food availability normally grow faster, fledge earlier and in superior condition (heavier, with maximum feather development) than chicks hatched late which usually depart prematurely in poor condition, if they survive to fledge. Although food is probably the ultimate factor controlling the timing of laying in auks, the close correspondence between sea surface temperatures and time of breeding in all alcid species suggests that sea temperature affects timing of food availability and probably serves as an important proximal cue for the birds, either alone or in combination with others such as day length.

Auk eggs are large for the size of the birds, ranging in weight from 18 g in the Least Auklet to 100 g in the Thick-billed and Common Murres, which represents 10-20% of female body mass. The largest eggs in relation to adult body size, at 22-23%, are those produced by the *Synthliboramphus* murrelets, species which have precocial chicks. The eggs range in shape from pyriform to ovoid with colours and markings that are highly variable between species, from mainly dull white with light markings in subterranean nesters, like puffins, to the strikingly bright green and blue to buff and white with conspicuous dark blotches and intricate scribbles, as in murres. Those of the two non-colonial nesters, Kittlitz's and Marbled Murrelets, are cryptic pale olive green to greenish yellow with light and dark brown spots and small blotches, to hide them in their exposed locations on the ground or, in the case of Marbled Murrelets, more frequently on lichen-covered branches. Eggs are laid on bare rock ledges in murres and the Razorbill; in rough shallow scrapes inside crevices and holes or on open gravelly substrate in the Dovekie, Razorbill, *Cepphus* guillemots, most murrelets and auklets; or on imperfect nest platforms made of grasses, twigs and feathers in the Ancient Murrelet, Rhinocerous Auklet and puffins, or of moss and lichens in the Marbled Murrelet. The usual clutch is one egg, except for species that feed inshore (*Cepphus*) or have precocial young (*Synthliboramphus*), which lay two eggs.

The incubation period is highly variable, at 41-46 days in the puffins, 32-39 days in the auklets, 32-36 in the large auks, 31-34 days in *Synthliboramphus*, 27-29 in *Alle*, *Cepphus* and *Brachyramphus*. Both parents share incubation duties, with bouts lasting from only a few hours in *Cepphus* guillemots to several days in *Synthliboramphus* murrelets. The length of time spent incubating by an individual probably also reflects the amount of time required by the off-duty bird to locate and consume food. Egg-care or attentiveness is another obvious feature during incubation. Species such as murres and the Razorbill which lay their eggs in the open rarely leave them unattended, whereas eggs under cover in burrows and crevices, or cryptically coloured, are often deserted for periods of time ranging from less than a day in the Dovekie, *Cepphus*, *Brachyramphus* and puffins, to several days in Xantus's and the Ancient Murrelets. Such behaviour lengthens the incubation period but shortens the total amount of time spent incubating by an individual bird, adaptations that may be important to energy budgets of adults, particularly by allowing more time for foraging, or as a mechanism to regulate the timing of hatching, or both. Egg neglect, the act of leaving eggs unattended, is known in at least nine alcid species and may well reflect "care" rather than "neglect" if the egg eventually hatches closer to the optimal time for rearing young than it would do otherwise. In species with two-egg clutches, incubation normally only starts after the second egg is laid to ensure that the eggs hatch at about the same time.

The Atlantic Puffin is mainly a fish-eater, but in winter the diet is supplemented with small crustaceans. It catches its prey by pursuing it under water, using the wings to propel itself forwards. If several fish are caught in a single dive and intended for the young, the puffin will stack them crosswise in its bill for easy transportation back to the nest. This species takes most of its prey fairly near the surface, and it appears that dives do not normally exceed depths of 15-20 m, although the capture of crustaceans may necessitate much deeper diving. Prey is usually obtained from waters within a few kilometres of the colony, but much more lengthy journeys may be necessary.

[*Fratercula arctica*. Photo: Henry Ausloos/ Bios]

Hatching success, the proportion of eggs laid that hatch, is generally high in Alcidae, averaging above 70% for most species examined. Ancient Murrelets and Whiskered Auklets have the highest rates at 91% and 86% respectively, and Xantus's Murrelet the lowest at 33%, among the 19 species that have been studied. Most egg losses are caused by mammalian and avian predation. For example, the island-nesting Xantus's Murrelet loses most of its eggs to introduced black rats (*Rattus rattus*) and deer mice (*Peromyscus maniculatus*). Other factors include infertility, embryonic mortality, accidental breakage and exposure. In species breeding on cliff ledges, mostly the murres, eggs are lost as the result of parental mishandling of the egg at laying or during change-overs, causing the egg to roll off the ledge. Clutches lost early in the season are replaced in most auk species, normally within 10-20 days, though re-laying is uncommon in the three *Aethia* auklets and rare or non-existent in Ancient Murrelets and probably also in the other *Synthliboramphus* species. Replacement eggs generally have a lower rate of hatching success than those of first clutches.

Most newly hatched alcid chicks are semi-precocial, covered with thick down, and brooded by their parents until they become homoiothermic, which takes 2-10 days. Once able to regulate their body temperature, chicks are normally left alone, as both parents are away finding food for the young, except in Thick-billed and Common Murres and Razorbills, where one parent must remain at the breeding site to brood and guard the chick continuously from predators such as gulls. Chicks are usually fed by both their parents at the colony or nesting site for periods ranging from 15-23 days in the large auks to 40-55 days in Cassin's and the Rhinoceros Auklet and puffins, with the genera *Alle*, *Cepphus*, *Brachyramphus*, *Aethia* and *Cyclorrhynchus* all intermediate. The four *Synthliboramphus* species alone have a highly precocial post-hatching development pattern whereby the chicks are taken to sea unfed 1-2 days after hatching. Alcidae is unique among bird families in the diversity of its patterns of chick growth and development.

Alcid species can be divided into three groups based upon their chick development patterns. The commonest pattern is that of the semi-precocial group, which contains the Dovekie, *Cepphus* guillemots, auklets, *Brachyramphus* murrelets and puffins. All use enclosed breeding sites or have cryptically coloured eggs, and hatch open-eyed downy young that are capable of eating. The young are fed by the parents at the breeding site for 27-55 days, by which time they are well grown, at 61-111% of the adult mass; they become independent of their parents at fledging. In contrast is the precocial group containing Xantus's, Craveri's, Ancient and Japanese Murrelets, all of which are small, nocturnal species that lay two-egg clutches in enclosed sites and hatch well developed downy young with legs and feet almost adult size. The young are capable of going to sea within 1-2 days after hatching, when they are only 12-14% of adult size, but they are accompanied by their parents which guard and feed them away from land until they are fully grown. Eggs of this second group each weigh about 22-23% of an adult female, amongst the largest eggs produced by any birds relative to adult size. Species in the third group, the murres and Razorbill, are intermediate. They are diurnal and breed on exposed rocky sites where they hatch and feed their single chick for 15-23 days; at this time the chick leaves the colony for the sea, flightless and only partially grown at 20-30% adult size, but with the male parent which cares for it for the next 4-8 weeks.

These developmental patterns have evolved in relation to the availability of food resources during the chick-rearing period and the ability of the birds to exploit them. Parents with semi-precocial young can find sufficient food near the breeding site to rear them to full size, whereas those that are intermediate have food supplies that are predictable in the early stages, but likely to diminish in certainty and quantity later on, which has resulted in an early-departure strategy. Unlike these two patterns, species with precocial young are free of the colony attachment soon after their young hatch, which allows them to take the young to the food supply and move as a family group in relation to it through the period of chick growth to independence. This approach may save parents energy by eliminating the cost of flying between the food supply and breeding site. It has also allowed them to rear two chicks, something that among the other auks only the inshore-feeding *Cepphus* guillemots have accomplished. The evolution of precociality within the family and the interplay of feeding and behavioural ecological adaptations for breeding that have led to three distinct pathways to accomplish the same goal, the production of surviving progeny, are impressive. This wide range of developmental patterns of the young in Alcidae is truly remarkable in both evolutionary and ecological contexts.

The process of departure of the young from the breeding site varies between species and developmental groups. Some species like *Cepphus* guillemots, auklets and puffins leave at night, fully developed and unaccompanied by parents. They normally fly out to sea a short distance under cover of darkness, from evening twilight to early morning, to reduce the risk of predation by gulls, both at the time of departure and later when dispersing away from the colony. Several days to a week or more before fledging, the chicks spend considerable time exercising their flight muscles by flapping their wings vigorously, either inside the burrow or nest crevice where space permits or outside close to nest-site entrance. When ready to depart, most young climb to vantage points from which they can fly off into the air or make short flights down the maritime slopes to the cliff edge where they take flight.

The murres and Razorbills, on the other hand, are flightless when they leave the colony with their male parent. Departures are usually synchronous, concentrated during the evening twilight period at which time the colonies, when large, ring with the continuous roar of the raucous calls and cries of anxious parents and young, followed by the spectacular "parachute" fluttering descents of chicks from cliff ledges, often 200-300 m high, with parents following close behind trying to maintain contact with their chick in order to avoid becoming separated and permit a quick departure from the colony immediately the chick reaches the water. Predation by gulls, and sometimes foxes, is high during departure, and unattended chicks, alone on the water or beach, are highly vulnerable. The din and commotion are no less on low-lying islands where streams of pairs of father and young move over the rocky flats and shelves descending towards the sea. Recognition of individual calls between parent and young is critical during the evening exodus where parents and young can easily become separated owing to the enormous numbers and density of birds that are involved, often thousands or tens of thousands in the case of Thick-billed and Common Murres.

In the precocial murrelets, family groups depart at night, usually a few hours after sunset, once the off-duty adult has returned. After many vocalizations by chicks and adults inside the nest, the adults emerge calling and make movements toward the sea, waiting for the two chicks to appear. Once the chicks begin their walk to the water, often scrambling or tumbling down steep hillsides and cliffy slopes, as they follow their parents, the adults fly off and land on the sea calling continuously. Chicks call as soon as they reach the sea and families reunite through mutual recognition of calls. Once together again on the water, parents and chicks immediately swim away from the colony, apparently moving several kilometres offshore before sunrise and achieving distances of 40-50 km within 18 hours after departure.

The survival of chicks to fledging varies from 66% in Crested Auklets to over 90% in Razorbills, Ancient Murrelets and Whiskered Auklets. Mortality of young after hatching is typically below that for eggs in most alcids. Major causes of chick loss prior to fledging include predation by gulls, mammals and reptiles, and food shortages causing starvation, as well as injury from conspecific adults, nest habitat destruction, and inclement weather. Post-fledging survival is difficult to measure accurately, but ringing results indicate immature survival to be low, from 15-36% for Atlantic Puffins and 30-34% in the murres and Razorbill to about 50% in Ancient Murrelets and 65% in Cassin's Auklet, the latter two both small species.

Overall, all alcids have a low reproductive rate with relatively high rates of hatching and fledging success, but a low rate of recruitment of young into the population. Although a great deal is now known about the breeding biology of the Atlantic auks and most Pacific species, it remains obvious that we lack sufficient information on variation of reproductive performance within single species and intrapopulation differences, as well as that required to make meaningful comparisons between species. All of this is required to permit better understanding of the adaptive significance of the diversity of reproductive strategies displayed by this complex and exciting family of marine birds.

Movements

Alcid migration patterns in the three northern oceans show wide divergences in movements of populations of the same species and between species and species groups or guilds. Patterns range from largely sedentary to heavily dispersive, with some lengthy and complex migrations. Pronounced differences between age cohorts of the same populations often exist, with younger birds normally moving farther south than adults away from the breeding areas into warmer waters. Many species, however, move relatively short distances away from where they breed and remain largely within their breeding ranges. At high latitudes, particularly in the northern Sea of Okhotsk, the Bering Sea and high and low Arctic water regions of the Arctic and North Atlantic Oceans, populations undergo some migratory movements after breeding owing to the development of heavy ice cover. In these cases, a general southward dispersal occurs from breeding areas to where waters remain ice-free. These autumn movements vary from comparatively slow ones, with birds concentrated at the edge of the ice where they are pushed southwards in relation to the expansion of ice cover during winter, to a rapid exodus and complete desertion of a region until the following spring. Even when lengthy, movements are normally restricted to continental shelf waters with few species moving beyond the southern limit of the boreal oceanic zone. Overall, alcid population movements tend to constitute post-breeding dispersal of adults and immatures rather than a "true" migration as performed by many other seabird groups like shearwaters, petrels, sulids and terns that travel enormous distances, often transequatorially.

Although the forms, directions and magnitude of movement within and between species populations do differ greatly within Alcidae, they all share certain features. First, post-breeding dispersal movements, whether short or long, generally tend to take birds to regions where food is more abundant or accessible, such as the Kuroshio and Oyashio Currents, the Gulf of Alaska, the California Current, the Bay of Biscay, the North Sea, the Newfoundland Grand Banks, the Scotian Shelf and Georges and Brown's Banks; for the northernmost species they also take them away from areas that become ice-covered in winter, notably the Chukchi and north Bering Seas, the Sea of Okhotsk, Baffin Bay, the Greenland and east Barents Seas, and the east and central Baltic. Second, where birds do undergo more than short distance movements, the distances travelled by young birds, especially those of the year, usually exceed those of adults. And third, the pattern of dispersal from breeding areas by most species, regardless of chick developmental type, is "downstream", following prevailing currents to wintering quarters.

Reasons for these common characteristics are simple. Changes in location due to seasonal alterations in the food supply or access to it seem straightforward: the high survival value of movements away from areas with low potential for meeting winter nutritional requirements to those known to be adequate. Differences in extent of movement between age cohorts may simply reflect differences in nutritional needs and prey composition (type and quality) or advantages gained by growing and learning necessary foraging skills in a warmer environment largely free of competition with older, more experienced birds, or both. Advantages gained by adults in remaining as close as possible to breeding areas may be related to enhanced success in re-occupation of their breeding sites, pairing, and timing of breeding. Benefits of the use of current flow patterns by almost all birds seem self-evident: reduced energy expenditure in reaching a preferred wintering area through actual physical transport by the water, and the likelihood of moving with important prey concentrations that are also being transported "downstream" from areas of high water mixing, as well as the overall associated potential for increased food availability. All auks share the need to move and forage economically, and they tend to exploit all physical and biological processes that help achieve that goal.

Patterns of movement and migration among Alcidae can be roughly divided into three basic groups. The first comprises inshore fish-feeding species that occupy distinct near-shore shallow water feeding niches and do not normally display long distance movements offshore; these are the *Cepphus* guillemots

Alone among the alcids of the Atlantic in preferring shallow coastal waters to the open ocean, the Black Guillemot is an inshore bottom-feeder, finding prey on or near the sea floor in waters of little depth. An opportunistic feeder, it takes a wide variety of fish and invertebrates. Fish are caught by surface-diving, mainly to depths of 1-8 m, although the bird may cover some distance and remain underwater for up to a minute. The chicks are fed largely on fish which the adult takes to the nest singly, held crosswise in the bill.

[*Cepphus grylle arcticus*, Norway. Photo: Uwe Walz/ Bruce Coleman]

and *Brachyramphus* murrelets. At the other extreme are the off-shore fish- and plankton-feeding species that undergo relatively long distance movements or migrations and inhabit deep waters, including two planktivores, the Dovekie and the Parakeet Auklet, and seven piscivores, the Thick-billed and Common Murres, Razorbill, Rhinoceros Auklet and puffins. The third group, made up of the *Synthliboramphus* murrelets, Cassin's and *Aethia* auklets, is intermediate. Most *Synthliboramphus* murrelets move away from their colonies, some such as Craveri's Murrelet mostly remaining within their general breeding range, but distances moved by all species tend to be short and rather limited, whether they be to offshore continental shelf waters as in the Ancient and Japanese Murrelets, or along the coast as, for example, in Xantus's Murrelet. The remaining four small, planktivorous auklets winter mainly offshore, but normally near or within the limits of their breeding area, except where waters become ice-covered.

Special cases of extreme long distance movement and pattern complexity are exemplified by Dovekies and Thick-billed Murres in the Atlantic Ocean and adjacent seas. Dovekies undertake migratory movements of considerable length. Two principal patterns dominate, one that brings most of the enormous population from north-west Greenland to waters off Newfoundland and south-west to the Scotian Shelf, and a south-westerly movement from the European high Arctic into the north-east Atlantic with some birds eventually reaching south-west Greenland. In the north-west Atlantic, Greenland birds move 3500 km after breeding is over in late August and occupy the Labrador Shelf, Grand Banks and Scotian Shelf from late October right through the winter. Movements are timed to coincide with ice-edges and concentrations of food. They move first into the ice-covered waters of western Baffin Bay where they feed at rich ice-edges, then go south with the East Baffin Current to the juncture of the Davis and Hudson Straits, where there is another rich source of epontic food and a late zooplankton bloom. Movement out of the Hudson Strait region occurs slowly, but the birds reach southern Labrador and Newfoundland from October to December. The Grand Banks are the principal winter quarters, an area where plankton is exceptionally abundant and where blooms of copepods begin as early as February. The birds concentrate at the shelf edges where existing fronts and upwellings result in high-density zooplankton patches. They begin to move

north in April, appearing back at their colonies in north-west Greenland in mid-May. This 7000 km round trip is made up of a series of journeys from one food-rich water area to another, as are the movements displayed by the European Arctic Dovekies in the north-east Atlantic.

Movements of Thick-billed Murres in the Atlantic are even more complex. Like Dovekies, there are two main pathways from northern breeding locations to wintering areas, both associated with major current flow patterns. In the north-west Atlantic, birds from colonies in the eastern Canadian Arctic and west Greenland move south via the East Baffin and Labrador Currents to eastern Newfoundland, where most birds winter on the Grand Banks, whereas those from the European Arctic move south-west using the East Greenland Current towards south-west Greenland. However, not only do the birds from the different regions arrive at different times and spend different amounts of time in south-west Greenland and Newfoundland waters, but the timing of the appearance of adults and immatures differs. Although there is some overlap, of birds coming from Arctic Canada and Greenland many more young birds than adults arrive in south Labrador and east Newfoundland in September and October, whereas adults normally appear in November. The numbers of birds from the Barents Sea region (Bear Island, Murmansk coast, Novaya Zemlya) and from other east Atlantic colonies (Spitsbergen, Iceland, east Greenland) that reach south-west Greenland are unknown, but the majority of European murres are believed to winter in the east Atlantic. At least a few disperse as far as Greenland, some of these moving still farther south-west to east Newfoundland waters where recoveries of birds ringed in Spitsbergen and east Greenland show that at least some east Atlantic murres winter on the Eastern Grand Bank. Thick-billed Murres initiate their northern and north-eastern movements away from the Grand Banks and south-west Greenland in March. Only a long-term ringing programme at a representative number of the major North Atlantic colonies will permit any possibility of clarifying this complex set of population movements and migratory patterns.

Movements elsewhere are usually less complex, even where information is incomplete. For example, in the North Pacific, Thick-billed Murres and several other northern auks, for instance the *Aethia* auklets, remain relatively close to their breeding locations except where ice conditions interfere. Some murres overwinter in the east Chukchi Sea, north to Cape Thompson and Point Hope, others move out of the north Bering Sea due to ice into the central and south Bering Sea, along with Crested and Least Auklets and other alcid species. Farther south, the degree of migratory movements are variable. Xantus's Murrelets move away from their south California colonies offshore, moving westwards over the shelf area and north as far as southern British Columbia and northern Washington, whereas Craveri's Murrelets remain rather sedentary showing only local, short distance movements north and south of their breeding sites. In contrast are the Pacific puffins, both species wintering far offshore, with the Tufted Puffin moving farther, often off the continental shelf into deep mid-Pacific waters.

The key message derived from any examination of movements of alcids throughout the oceans they inhabit year round is how little is known. Explanations and interpretations presented for the movements of single species or general patterns of movement of Alcidae as a whole in either the Atlantic or Pacific Oceans are little more than best guesses. Considerably more detailed work is required to unravel the complexities of present day movements of existing species, particularly interpopulation differences within the same species, to say nothing about their evolutionary origin and current biological significance.

Relationship with Man

The history of interactions between alcids and humans is a long one. It goes back as far as humans have been a species living and depending upon the sea for at least part of its sustenance. In recent times, man has become enamoured by certain auk species like the puffins, particularly the Atlantic Puffin, because of their exotic appearance, overall beauty, and often "human" antics; their upright posture on land, as they strut to and fro at colonies, displaying many of our own "comic" forms of behaviour ranging from affection to bickering and fighting, has endeared them to many people. The clearest evidence of this lies in the enormous numbers of people that flock to sites where they can see puffins and other auks at their colonies, and by the legislation enacted to conserve and protect them from harmful human activities. But this attitude towards Alcidae is new, a reflection of technological man and his move away from subsistence and recreational hunting in many parts of the developed world, although not everywhere for example in Canada, Greenland, the Faeroes, Iceland, Norway and Russia. In the recent past, however, the relationship was exclusively man the predator and auks the prey, a story of extreme human exploitation and destruction.

Alcids have been hunted by humans for food, feathers and oil for thousands of years. The presence of auk bones of many species, including the Dovekie, Great Auk, murres, auklets and puffins, in archeological middens throughout the family's range from eastern Asia through western and eastern North America to Scotland, Norway and Russia dating back to at least 3000 BC attests to the widespread use of Alcidae. The magnitude of early human exploitation and its impact on auk colonies and populations are unknown, but traditional hunting was probably only of local importance, given the small sizes of human populations and their limited distribution and hunting methods. Utilization by early coastal peoples was likely as a secondary food source, restricted mainly to the collection of birds and their eggs at colonies during summer, with fish and marine mammals comprising the principal part of their diet year round. But by the turn of the nineteenth century, the extent of the pressure from humans increased dramatically and impacts became obvious. Human populations expanded rapidly in size and range, particularly along accessible coastlines in north-western Europe, southern Britain, eastern Canada and the north-eastern USA, causing the extinction of many colonies.

Continued human population growth from the mid-nineteenth to early twentieth centuries, combined with the technological development of more efficient fire-arms and boats, resulted in still further pressure on auks. In temperate regions where people were concentrated, the demand for food and land was high, and many coastal island colonies were destroyed by habitat altera-tion through the construction of buildings, introductions of alien predators or domestic animals, or direct overexploitation for food. For example, Common Murres and Atlantic Puffins were once numerous and widespread in Atlantic Canada and New England (north-east USA), but lengthy persecution by egging, shooting and netting during the second half of the nineteenth century brought both species close to extinction throughout the region by the early 1900's. Part of this massive reduction came from commercial egging enterprises that were initiated in the mid-nineteenth century at murre colonies along the North Shore of the Gulf of St Lawrence and Labrador, to supply southern markets in Halifax and Boston with exotic foods. About 500,000-750,000 Common Murre eggs were collected each year by schooner fleets until the murre populations collapsed in the late 1880's. Puffin populations in the region also declined during the same period of time, but mainly from excessive hunting of breeding birds and destruction of the nesting habitat, activities that continued through to the 1920's even after widespread local extinctions had taken place. Similar declines of the large auks occurred in Western Europe through the same period. In Britain and Ireland, major decreases took place from the late eighteenth century to early in the present century, especially on accessible islands along the west coasts. Populations in northern Spain and France, the North and Baltic Seas, and parts of the Barents Sea were also severely reduced by human activity, particularly egging, hunting and netting during the breeding season.

Generally, alcids breeding in large, dense colonies have been vulnerable to human persecution wherever they have been accessible. Even colonies in remote and relatively inaccessible regions such as the Arctic became targets as northern exploration exploded through the nineteenth century. This meant the removal of "buffer" refuges that partially offset the destruction taking place farther south of certain species like the murres. Once the resources of the immense Arctic populations became exposed, heavy human exploitation quickly followed by sailors and whalers looking for sources of fresh meat, and commercial developers searching for new products to sell.

Large-scale alcid harvesting operations have been common in the Atlantic and Pacific Oceans in the past and this century. For example, Thick-billed Murres in the Atlantic have been intensively hunted at their colonies and wintering areas for at least 130 years. In Greenland, where records of population changes are best known, heavy shooting at west coast colonies since the 1880's has resulted in drastic declines of the species. Many colonies have been extirpated, and those that have survived are much reduced in size. Since 1930, the murre population has fallen by at least 35-50% to a current level (1990) of about 535,000 breeding birds. This dramatic decline has been caused by the combined impact of: summer and winter hunting in Greenland, with an annual kill estimated at 200,000 birds in the late 1940's, and 300,000-400,000 birds in 1988-89; massive drownings in offshore salmon gill-nets, with 250,000-500,000 birds perishing annually from the 1960's to 1976, when the fishery was closed; and additional large-scale unregulated winter hunting in Newfoundland and Labrador. Birds shot in Greenland are sold at local settlements, and until recently were also sent to freezer processing plants for export to Danish markets.

Other Atlantic entrepreneurial developments have also taken place. A project initiated in 1927 to collect Thick-billed Murre eggs and young at the large colony on Novaya Zemlya in the eastern Barents Sea was so intensive that it caused the murre population to decrease from 1,600,000 birds in 1933 to only 290,000 in 1948, a decline of about 82% over 21 years, from which the birds have yet to recover. Similar unregulated actions have occurred where large concentrations of breeding auks existed. In the Faeroe Islands, overharvesting of Common Murres resulted in population declines from the late 1950's to the 1980's, aggravated by shortages in the birds' food supply due to commercial fishing. However, one of the most serious recent assaults on alcids anywhere has been the winter hunt of murres in Newfoundland-Labrador, where traditional low-volume subsistence hunting of the 1940's has changed to a massive "black-market" and recreational sport hunt without bag limits: birds are sold illegally, and residents of the province can legally shoot as many

Common Murres are social birds at all times of the year and they form breeding colonies that vary in size from small to huge, with densities that can reach 20 pairs/m². It would seem that the birds prefer such densely packed areas to less crowded ones, and close physical contact is widely tolerated among neighbouring pairs. The colonies are situated on rocky coasts with high, perpendicular cliffs and on the tops of isolated stacks, though more low-lying coasts may be used, provided they are remote, undisturbed and free from predators. The birds lay on broad or narrow ledges, less frequently in rock crevices or caves, or under boulders. There is no nest; the single large egg, very variable in ground colour and markings, is laid directly on the bare rock, where its remarkably pyriform shape helps to stop it rolling over the edge. Losses are mainly due to eggs falling off ledges and also to predation. Gulls, ravens and crows frequently act more as scavengers than as predators, but when the whole colony is disturbed or the adult bird is not in attendance, there is ample opportunity for them to take eggs and chicks.

[*Uria aalge.* Photo: Oene Moedt/ Foto Natura]

murres as they wish between 1st September and 31st March. This has resulted in annual kill tolls of 500,000-1,000,000 birds from the 1960's to the present time (1995/96) involving mostly Thick-billed Murres from the eastern Canadian Arctic, West Greenland, Spitsbergen and Iceland. The expansion of the Newfoundland hunt was caused by economic growth in the province and the introduction of high-powered fire-arms and speedboats, combined with the relocation of most of the human population from rural to urban situations, resulting in a market for selling birds to people who no longer have easy access to the birds. Regulations have recently been established (1994/95), but these new rules are virtually unenforceable owing to the size and remoteness of coastal Newfoundland-Labrador. This hunt is almost certainly responsible for much of the 30% decline of Thick-billed Murres observed in eastern Canada between the 1950's and early 1980's, as well as possibly being a major contributor to murre declines in west Greenland and those reported for other alcid species that are mistakenly shot for murres, namely Razorbills and Atlantic Puffins. The killing of murres in the north-west Atlantic is one of the most pressing seabird conservation issues in the Northern Hemisphere today.

Human exploitation of auks in the Pacific Ocean came later, but has been just as severe. The entire Bering Sea area and adjacent regions of the North Pacific have suffered serious impact from human activities since the mid-eighteenth century. From this early period of exploration and expansion of human populations to the 1950's, there was uncontrolled and widespread exploitation of alcids and other seabird species, mainly by shooting adults and large-scale collecting of eggs and chicks at colonies. However, introductions of alien animals, such as Arctic foxes (*Alopex lagopus*), red foxes (*Vulpes vulpes*), rats (*Rattus norvegicus*), ground squirrels (*Spermophilus undulatus*), domestic livestock and game animals, to seabird islands have had the most drastic consequences on auk populations. Although fox farming in eastern Russia and Alaska was begun in the eighteenth century by Russian fox trappers, it was not until the early 1880's, when the government of the USA leased Alaskan islands for the propagation of foxes, that the industry grew, particularly through the early 1900's in response to the demand for fox furs by the fashion trade. Arctic and red foxes were deliberately released on islands with large and accessible alcid populations which were viewed as inexpensive sources of fox food. Rodents were also introduced as food for the foxes, especially ground squirrels, voles (*Microtus*) and mice (*Mus*), but that only compounded the predation pressure on the alcids. During this period, alien foxes mainly ate seabirds including enormous numbers of alcids estimated at certain island colonies to exceed 40,000 annually. Large breeding colonies of Ancient Murrelets and Cassin's, Crested and Whiskered Auklets were extirpated from the 1900's to the 1930's, with other species like Common Murres and Tufted Puffins also markedly reduced or eliminated. By 1945, foxes had been introduced to over 450 islands from south-east Alaska to Attu Island, at the western end of the Aleutian Islands, at an immense cost to alcid populations through the destruction of hundreds of breeding colonies. Fortunately, the demand for fox furs has declined steadily since the 1930's, and island fox-farming has therefore diminished in Alaska and many parts of eastern Russia. However, many introduced fox populations continue to thrive on former and active auk colonies, and eradication programmes on certain islands are under way or being considered, albeit slowly owing to limits placed on the use of control toxicants and the high costs of fox removal programmes. Alien foxes now remain on only 48 islands in Alaska. In contrast, in the north-west Pacific, where despite very low profits from fox-farming and enormous damage to breeding auks and other seabirds, recommendations for new introductions of Arctic foxes to the Kuril Islands and nearby regions have recently been made. Some sites important for alcids have recently received special protective status, for example Moneron Island and Sakhalin, but removal of introduced predators from such nature reserves remains at the discussion stage.

Predation by introduced mammals has been the principal cause of the reduction or extinction of alcid populations and their island colonies throughout northern regions of the North Pacific. But in more temperate coastal regions of western North America and eastern Asia, damage from introduced domestic livestock (sheep, goats, pigs) and pets (feral cats and dogs) has been as devastating to seabird colonies as that of alien predators. Rats introduced to islands by human visitors have had serious impacts on breeding seabirds almost everywhere. Next to rats are mink (*Mustela vison*) and raccoons (*Procyon lotor*), both of which have historically been introduced to seabird islands, and most recently on the Queen Charlotte Islands, British Columbia, where they pose a major threat to Ancient Murrelets and other auks. South of British Columbia, along both Pacific coasts to Japan in the west and Baja California in the east the impact of human activity on seabird colonies has been longer and more varied than in the northern regions. Problems have ranged from predation by feral dogs and cats in Craveri's and Japanese Murrelets, by rats in the Pigeon Guillemot, Ancient Murrelet, Cassin's and Rhinoceros Auklets and Tufted Puffin, and by other small rodents like voles and deer mice in Xantus's Murrelet, to trampling and erosion of the breeding habitat of subterranean nesters by grazing herbivores such as sheep in Rhinoceros Auklets, and European rabbits (*Oryctolagus cuniculus*) in Rhinoceros Auklets and Tufted Puffins. Feral cats and dogs remain a serious problem on islands in the Sea of Okhotsk, particularly on Sakhalin and in the Kuril Islands.

Direct human exploitation of auks on a commercial scale has also taken place on both sides of the Pacific Ocean. In the north-west, alongside fur-farming enterprises was the development of commercial fisheries during the 1920's and 1930's. One outgrowth of this new industry was the systematic destruction of seabird colonies in areas considered important for the fisheries. Seabirds were regarded as serious competitors for the available fish which led to a programme in the mid-1950's to eradicate cormorants, gulls and alcids breeding in the Sakhalin and Kuril Islands area by egging, shooting, netting and poisoning. The Common Murre was targeted and an uncontrolled programme launched to take 200,000 eggs, 420 t of meat, and 2100 m² of murre-skins for commercial use. Murre numbers at the largest colony on Tyulenii Island rapidly declined, from about 650,000 birds when the programme began to about 140,000 by 1960 and 100,000 in 1976. Although this destructive initiative has ceased and certain island and water areas have received protective status under new legislation, significant egg-collecting and shooting of birds at colonies continues within most locations where commercial fisheries occur and law enforcement is absent.

In the north-east Pacific, large-scale commercial egg-collecting of alcids is known only from the Farallon Islands, California, dating back to the 1850's. Excessive collecting of Common Murre eggs at Farallon colonies caused the murre population to decrease from about 400,000 birds in 1850 to only a few hundred by the 1920's. Some recovery took place over the next 25-30 years with numbers reaching 6000 birds in 1950, but population growth was slow, owing to additional pressure from introduced predators. Once these aliens were removed, the murres increased to over 80,000 by 1982, but the population has fallen once again, apparently due to high mortality in the gill-nets of newly established commercial fisheries.

Perhaps the true nature of Alcidae and human interactions is best exemplified by the history of the extinct Great Auk, the only alcid species exterminated in recent times. This large and flightless auk, the "penguin" of the Northern Hemisphere, and the first species to be called Penguin, had a widespread distribution in boreal and low Arctic waters of the North Atlantic, probably breeding in large numbers on coastal islands free of predators within suitable distance of an adequate supply of fish. While it had become extremely well adapted for underwater swimming and diving with its small flipper-like wings and streamlined body, those same features made for a clumsy and defenceless existence when on land, to which it had to return to for egg-laying and incubation. Upon the arrival of man the predator in coastal regions, safe sites for breeding diminished as colonies close to land were exploited and probably extirpated in a short time after their discovery; the kitchen middens of ancient peoples reveal the efficiency of these early bird hunters.

The Ancient Murrelet, a small alcid of the temperate north Pacific, breeds on islands that are often densely vegetated. Nocturnal at the breeding colony, it nests chiefly in burrows excavated in the soil, favouring areas with dense growth of matted grass, but also in natural cavities under trees and rocks, usually on slopes within 300 m of the sea. The two eggs are laid at night at the end of the short burrow in a scrape lined with grass, leaves and twigs. Both sexes incubate, nearly always in complete darkness, for periods lasting some 72 hours, the longest incubation shift known among alcids. As incubation begins after the laying of the second egg, hatching is synchronous. The highly precocial newly hatched chicks remain in the nest unfed for 1-3 days until they depart seawards at night, usually escorted by both parents. The family group then swims away from the colony, often covering a considerable distance in a short time. The parents care for and feed the young until they are fully grown at 4-5 weeks. Nesting success at undisturbed sites is high, with most losses attributable to desertion of nests prior to the start of incubation rather than to predation.

[Synthliboramphus antiquus, Chilbal Island, Yellow Sea, Korea. Photo: Moo-Boo Yoon]

By historical times, most of the easily accessible Great Auk colonies were gone, and remnant populations were probably restricted to remote and inaccessible locations for breeding, mainly predator-free offshore islands associated with biologically productive water systems such as those in eastern Canada and Iceland. As man's sea-faring abilities increased, so did the vulnerability of surviving Great Auk colonies to further human predation. By the early seventeenth century, the last large breeding site on Funk Island, a small rocky islet 60 km off the east coast of Newfoundland, was a regular stop-off site for sailors, fishermen and merchants for restocking their fresh meat supply after an arduous trans-Atlantic voyage from the Old World. Before long, commercial ventures began at the Funk Island colony, first as a source for eggs, meat and oil to sell, and then feathers for the lucrative mattress trade. Teams of men went ashore each summer to corral and boil Great Auks, a practice that continued for more than 100 years before the species became exterminated on Funk Island by 1800. In order to have withstood such a lengthy and continuous persecution, bird numbers must have been enormous on the island, and indeed have been estimated to have been at least 100,000 pairs, based upon bird size and island area. At that time, the status of the Great Auk became known to the scientific community as a rare species on the verge of extinction, prompting a rush by collectors on behalf of science museums and private individuals to obtain specimens before it was too late. This activity sealed the fate of the Great Auk, and the last known breeding pair was collected for a museum from Eldey, a small island off Iceland, on 2nd June 1844.

Has anything been learned from the Great Auk experience? Over 150 years have passed since the last pair were killed for their skins at Eldey, but human attitudes towards wildlife in general, and threatened species in particular, seem largely unchanged. In rural areas and developing countries, the hunting culture remains intact, believing that all living things on earth are mere resources for the use and benefit of mankind. In the developed world, little conservation concern and action is expressed until a species is endangered globally. The skills of early identification of species with problems, factors responsible, and conservation actions necessary to safeguard the population before it becomes threatened or endangered defines today's conservation requirement. Are we any better than the three Icelandic fishermen who caught and strangled the two Great Auks and sold their dead "booty" to a museum dealer in 1844? As we look around and see the relentless destruction of marine ecosystems in all the oceans of the world through human overexploitation and pollution, the answer becomes obvious. No, we still have a long way to go in our own development if we expect to reverse the "extinction inevitable" principle so deeply engrained in the make-up of *Homo sapiens* towards both itself and the wealth of other living things in the biosphere.

However, the loss of the Great Auk did consolidate public opinion in Britain after the 1850's. Once it was realized that this remarkable bird was gone for ever, conservationists of the day were able to lobby for protection of other threatened seabird species like the Northern Gannet (*Sula bassana*) and Southern Hemisphere penguins, both of which were being overexploited for their oils. In 1869 the British Seabird Protection Act was enacted, the earliest piece of legislation passed to protect seabirds anywhere in the world. It set a benchmark for other nations to follow and emulate. But it took another 40 years of brutal persecution of most marine species and the conspicuous disappearance of many populations of cormorants, gulls, terns and auks to move governments of other countries. Since the turn of this century, attempts to curb the human assault on auks have been many. Protective legislation to control and limit human activity believed harmful to alcid populations now exists for most regions of the North Atlantic, North Pacific and Arctic Oceans. However, effective observation of these laws is spotty and mainly limited to Britain, Ireland, Canada (except Newfoundland-Labrador), the USA, Mexico and Japan. Some countries provide special protection to certain species when problems arise (Faeroe Islands, Iceland, Norway) or enact legislation and regulations that can not be enforced (Canada, Denmark, Greenland, Norway, Russia, Spitsbergen). The conservation task is formidable and solutions few.

In eastern North America the plight of colonial alcids, and seabirds generally, was extremely serious with numerous species close to extinction by the early 1900's. As a consequence of this, a pioneering international treaty, the Migratory Birds Convention, was signed between Canada and the USA in 1916, prohibiting the killing of almost all migratory birds and their eggs in most regions in North America including coastal waters of the three oceans bounding the two countries. This initiative was negotiated because of public pressure, spearheaded by a small group of concerned scientists, that demanded the enactment of the treaty's primary objective of "saving from indiscriminate slaughter and ensuring the preservation of such migratory birds as are either useful to man or are harmless". Thus, an international system of uniform protection over a vast geographical region was established, the first of its kind ever. However, seabirds and some other species could still be hunted by native peoples in certain regions of Canada, a provision that was expanded to include the legal hunting of Common and Thick-billed Murres (between 1st September and 31st March) by all residents of Newfoundland-Labrador soon after the province had joined Canada in 1949. But overall, this major North American conservation accomplishment, combined with the earlier British legislation to protect seabird colonies from disturbance, and regulations prohibiting the hunting of all alcid species in Britain and Ireland throughout the year, provided a solid base for the recovery of many alcid species in the North Atlantic and eastern Pacific. Most auk populations did respond positively to protection and showed some growth during the next few decades.

However, human exploitation of auks continues today at a high level in Russia, Norway, Spitsbergen, Bear Island, the Faeroes, Iceland and Greenland, involving the taking of eggs and killing of adults and young by shooting, snaring and netting, and winter hunting of murres in Newfoundland-Labrador. But certain conservation measures have been put in place recently even where alcids are exploited. For example, in Norway, where all auk species may be hunted from 21st August to 1st March, the dramatic decline of murres and Razorbills prompted the government in 1979 to ban hunting them except in Spitsbergen and Bear Island. In the Faeroes, a law limiting the overexploitation of Common Murres was enacted in 1980, protecting the birds from eggers and hunters from 1st June to 15th August, owing to observed declines in the murre population. Some areas have regulations to protect alcid populations, but enforcement is difficult or impossible. For example, in Greenland, regulations to protect seabirds were first enacted by the Greenland Provincial Council in 1977 and later revised by the Assembly of the Greenland Home Rule Authority in 1988. But hunting restrictions on Thick-billed Murres, the most threatened alcid in Greenland, remained legal outside the breeding season with little likelihood of enforcing the summer ban or winter quotas, and subsequently conservation rules were relaxed (1989-1992) causing an expanded hunt and further reduction of the murre population. Similar situations exist throughout remote regions of eastern Russia where regulations to protect alcids have been only recently established and means of enforcement are absent. In Atlantic Canada, the previously unregulated winter hunt of murres now has rules and regulations, put in place in 1994/95, but it remains to be seen if they can be enforced or have a positive effect on the massive and unsustainable annual kill of 500,000-1,000,000 birds that has taken place in the past.

The significance of other man-induced mortality of auks is also seriously high. Commercial fishing activities have expanded tremendously this century, becoming so widespread and highly developed in capture technology that overfishing and the subsequent collapse of exploited fish populations are commonplace. The impacts on alcids have been extreme and in two forms. Massive commercial gill-net fisheries in the Atlantic and Pacific have caught and drowned millions of auks since the 1960's. The coastal gill-net fishery in California, for example, killed at least 70,000 to 75,000 Common Murres between 1980 and 1986, the principal cause of the 52% decline of the breeding population in central California recorded during that period, one of dramatic increase in fishing effort in the region; significant numbers of other alcid species also drowned including Pigeon Guillemots

The Atlantic Puffin, a highly social species, breeds on grassy slopes along rocky coasts in the North Atlantic, and it forms colonies which are sometimes large and densely packed. Puffins nest in burrows 1-2 m long that they excavate themselves, using both the feet and the bill; the feet serve to dig at ground level and the bill higher up. Alternatively, they may take over an already made burrow from another puffin, a rabbit or a shearwater. In either case burrows are reused in subsequent seasons, the males spending more time on their defence and maintenance than the females. The prime, most successful burrows are those in seaward-facing slopes that are too steep for most predators to reach and where landing sites are nearby so that gulls have less chance of snatching food from adults returning to the burrow to feed the young. The single mainly white egg is laid at the end of the burrow and incubated by both adults, often for spells of more than 30 hours. They feed the chicks and care for them until they finally abandon them in their last days as nestlings. Driven by hunger to leave their burrows, most young fly or walk down to the sea at night and begin to fend for themselves unaccompanied.

[Above:
Fratercula arctica grabae,
Shetland, Scotland.
Photo: Dominique Halleux/
Bios.

Below:
Fratercula arctica.
Photo: Ian Beames/Ardea]

and Marbled Murrelets. Estimates of losses of auks in other coastal and high sea gill-net fisheries in the North Pacific suggest high kill tolls wherever the birds and fisheries co-exist, and local populations in many regions are vulnerable, particularly those of Common Murres and Marbled and Japanese Murrelets. Incidental kills of auks in Atlantic fisheries are equally high. The worst recorded case was the Danish salmon gill-net fishery in west Greenland that killed at least 500,000 Thick-billed Murres each year from 1968 to 1975, after which the fishery was closed by regulation. Mortality by accidental drowning in fishing gear occurs where gill-net fisheries occur, inshore and offshore, and such activities are widespread throughout the range of Alcidae involving most member species.

However, direct competition for the same species of fish is perhaps potentially even more lethal to alcid populations. Originally, commercial fisheries were directed at the larger fish species, like cod and herring. But by the 1960's, as commercial stocks were depleted, fishing fleets diversified and redirected their attention to the smaller species, such as capelin, sandeels, herring and sprat, pelagic species often lower in the food chain and central to food webs, such as capelin in both the North Atlantic and Pacific Oceans. These small fish are critical to alcids, and their removal or reduction by human fisheries can have catastrophic consequences for most auk species. Collapses of these small pelagic fish populations have occurred in low Arctic and boreal waters in the Atlantic and Pacific, and overfishing has played a role in most. In many cases, these collapses are accompanied by reproductive failure in colonial seabirds, particularly the auks. The best examples are from the North Atlantic, where fisheries in west-central Norway, the Barents Sea and Newfoundland have had major impacts on alcid populations. In Norway, the collapse of the herring stock in the late 1960's has caused almost total breeding failure of Atlantic Puffins since 1969 with virtually all young produced starving to death before they could fledge, followed by a consequent major decline in the breeding population. Similar food shortages and high chick mortality have been recorded at Atlantic Puffin colonies in east Newfoundland since 1972, when an international commercial capelin fishery began.

This fishery underwent a huge expansion until it collapsed for the first time in 1978, reopened in 1982 and then closed again in 1992 when almost no capelin appeared inshore to spawn. Not unexpectedly, the North American Atlantic Puffin breeding population, which is centred in Newfoundland, has decreased by about 30% since 1972. Events in the Barents Sea have been equally catastrophic. On Bear Island, more than 280,000 adult Common Murres, over 60% of the total breeding population, died from food shortages during a single winter (1986/87) due to a collapse of capelin. Fisheries aimed towards these small pelagic "keystone" fish species pose serious threats to Alcidae, perhaps comprising the single most important factor influencing the future welfare of fish-eating auks.

Many auks have also been destroyed by oil pollution, particularly during the past 50 years. The global transportation of oil has resulted in thousands of accidental spills killing millions of marine birds. Auks are particularly vulnerable to oil fouling owing to the unusually large amount of time they spend on or in the water. The large tanker spills in coastal boreal waters have caused the greatest known mortality of alcids and other seabirds. For example, at least 250,000 birds were estimated to have been killed by the 1989 Exxon Valdez oil spill in Prince William Sound, Alaska (see Volume 1, page 572), of which 74% were murres, the highest level of alcid mortality ever reported from a single acute oil spill. The populations of other auks, the Pigeon Guillemot and Marbled Murrelet, were also seriously affected with projections of 50-100 years before recovery of the alcid breeding community. But chronic oil pollution, the small spills from transfer operations, bilge pumping and tank cleaning at sea, probably causes greater mortality of birds overall, as evidenced by the regular beaching of dead oiled birds along coastlines associated with oil tanker traffic, for instance in Belgium, Britain, the Netherlands and Norway, as well as Newfoundland, Nova Scotia, British Columbia, Washington and California.

Apart from direct mortality caused by external oiling on plumage, there are also many sublethal toxic effects of ingested petroleum oils including impaired breeding performance with high embryonic mortality, in addition to developmental and osmoregulatory problems, and haemolytic anaemia. Overall, oil-related mortality has adversely affected alcid populations regionally such as Common Murres, Razorbills and Atlantic Puffins in the North Atlantic and Common Murres in the northeast Pacific, particularly in winter. Species most at risk are those with small total populations that occupy restricted areas like Xantus's, Craveri's and Japanese Murrelets. Although long-term effects of oiling on auk populations are difficult to determine, heavy mortality can be expected to continue in the future in relation to increased tanker traffic and further deep water drilling offshore, often in waters important for wintering alcids and where the likelihood of accidents is high, for instance Hibernia on the Newfoundland Grand Banks and developments in the Sea of Okhotsk, off Sakhalin.

Concentrations of toxic chemicals, essentially chlorinated hydrocarbons and heavy metals, in alcid species are relatively low. Advances in pollution control since the early 1970's, especially on the uses and discharges of persistent organochlorine pesticides and polychlorinated biphenels (PCB's), has resulted in a gradual decline of these pollutants in the marine environment. Residue levels are generally highest in birds associated with industrialized areas such as the Baltic and Irish Seas, the Gulf of St Lawrence and the Southern California Bight. However, no population declines observed in alcids can be attributed directly to toxic chemical poisoning. Despite this fact, sublethal effects of these chemicals on auks are very poorly known, and populations close to sources of industrial and agricultural discharges should be monitored closely.

Overall, human exploitation and disturbance, either directly or indirectly, remain the most important threats to alcid populations in the Pacific, Atlantic and Arctic Oceans and adjacent seas. First and foremost is the continued uncontrolled destruction of alcid populations by egging and hunting in the north-west Pacific, largely by the east Russian fishing fleets, and by summer and winter hunting of Thick-billed and Common Murres, Razorbills and Atlantic Puffins in the North Atlantic,

The Thick-billed Murre accepts narrower cliff ledges for its nest-site than does the Common Murre (Uria aalge). The single large egg is laid on the bare rock. Very variable in colour, the egg is markedly pyriform in shape, which helps to prevent it from rolling over the edge. A bird preparing to incubate will settle in a nearly upright position over the egg with its back to the sea, its breast pushed up against the cliff face, and the egg resting on the tarsi. The chick is fed and cared for by both parents until fledging, when it jumps off the ledge and glides in a hazardous journey down to the sea, closely followed by one of the parents. Chick and parent join up again on the sea through mutual calling, and then swim out to sea together.

[Uria lomvia arra, St Paul, Pribilof Islands, Alaska, USA. Photo: William M. Smithey/Planet Earth]

A fairly common small dark North American species, Cassin's Auklet breeds in dense communities of roughly 500-1,000,000 birds. Strictly nocturnal at its colony, its nest-site is in a crevice or cave, or in a burrow excavated in soft soil by both adults. Only one egg is laid, which both partners incubate, relieving each other every 24 hours. The semi-precocial chick is fed by both parents only at night until, after about 43 days, it departs for the sea, alone and usually at night.

[*Ptychoramphus aleuticus aleuticus*, Prince Islet, Channel Islands, California, USA. Photo: Herbert Clarke]

particularly in west Greenland and Atlantic Canada (Newfoundland and Labrador), but also in the Faeroes and Iceland. Disturbance and predation from introduced alien animals (foxes, small rodents, livestock) at colonies continues to be a dominant limiting factor on some alcid populations, particularly in the North Pacific. However, the single most potentially damaging activity to Alcidae, in both the short and long terms, is commercial fishing. The depletion of small pelagic fish populations, essential to many auk species for reproduction and survival, combined with direct mortality from entanglement and drowning in fishing gear, pose an enormous threat to alcid populations throughout their range, a pressure that can only be expected to increase as the demand for human food escalates over time. Oil spills, small and large, and industrial pollutant discharges continue to contaminate marine systems and their living occupants including alcids. Exposure to these toxic pollutants will likely remain high or increase, as petroleum developments and transport expand with human population growth, as will run-off of chemicals from agricultural activity and industrial effluents. Ultimately, the oceans are the final repository for most of these persistent compounds. If such human activities are allowed to continue or increase, the future of Alcidae can be considered very grave indeed and man's relationship with the family no better than that with the Great Auk 150 years ago.

Status and Conservation

Alcidae has a widespread distribution in the Northern Hemisphere largely coinciding with human populations. Sharing ecological roles as top trophic feeders, auks and people naturally came together in search of a common food source, fish, sometimes in direct competition, but more often perhaps as species co-existing in a marine-based system. The correspondence of both populations in food-rich areas, whether as early human colonizers of Arctic lands or more recently in low Arctic and boreal to cool subtropical water regions, seems self-evident. Places of high biological productivity and activity are not distributed at random, but are concentrated in space and time, and it is that feature of marine waters that doubtlessly brought man and bird together in search for food. Historically, humans occupying marine ecosys-

tems focused on fish as their principal prey, less often on marine mammals except for certain northern peoples. However, large aggregations of seabirds at specific locations and times, whether at sea or on land, offered a substantial supplementary food source to exploit. As a consequence, humans have eaten colonial auks and their eggs for thousands of years. The historical relationship was man as predator, utilizing auks principally for food, but also for fish-bait, with fat to use in oil lamps, and feathers for insulation in clothing and decoration. The tendency of human populations to expand in size and range more recently, within the last 500 years, has resulted in a switch of man from a casual local predator to a diligent destroyer by direct overexploitation for food, alteration and destruction of marine and terrestrial habitats vital to Alcidae, and physical displacement from coastal islands formerly used by the birds for breeding. Man the low-volume auk-predator of historical times is now man the potential exterminator of the Alcidae, directly or indirectly, through human activities in coastal and offshore marine waters of the northern oceans.

Virtually all extant alcid species have undergone widespread decreases in population size and range during the first half of the present century, reductions that began during the eighteenth and nineteenth centuries. Some of these declines continue today. The fate of the recently extinct Great Auk (see Relationship with Man) should serve as a warning to all of how rapid and final the disappearance of a species can be. Presently, there are four species at serious risk: one, the Japanese Murrelet, is globally threatened, with no more than 6000 breeding birds remaining; and three are classed as near-threatened species, the Marbled, Xantus's and Craveri's Murrelets, the latter two with populations of under 10,000 individuals, and both very likely soon to be reclassified as globally threatened. Of equal concern is the increasing vulnerability of several other species including the Razorbill, Black Guillemot, Ancient Murrelet and Whiskered Auklet, all with relatively small populations and in various states of decline over their world ranges. In the short term, the prognosis is far from encouraging as, where sufficient information is available, almost all species indicate declining numbers with only certain regional or local populations in equilibrium or showing slight increases. The family is very vulnerable to man-induced perturbations, either directly or indirectly, clearly exemplified by the recent status of its present 22 member species: 12 species (54·5%) are known to be decreasing in numbers, including the four species (18%) that are globally threatened or near-threatened; nine species (41%) vary between stable to decreasing through their range; and only one species (4·5%), the Dovekie, is believed to be relatively stable at present.

That widespread decreases have occurred in population sizes of most auk species should come as no surprise. Top trophic feeders in a food chain are always vulnerable to environmental change and disturbance. In marine ecosystems, seabirds, marine mammals, and humans occupy this position. All three groups share certain features that endanger them: they are long-lived with high adult survivorship, reach sexual maturity slowly, and have low reproductive rates, often rearing only a single offspring annually. The consequences of these demographic characteristics is that recovery from environmental disturbances is slow and that increases in adult mortality have a much greater impact on the population than it does on a species with a high reproductive rate and high adult mortality. For example, a species with high fecundity and a short lifespan, such as a small songbird, may be able to recover from a 50% decrease in population within one or two years, whereas recovery of an alcid species may require 20 years. Thus, high longevity associated with low productivity places a species at considerable risk, features shown by most seabirds.

Like many other marine birds, alcids are especially vulnerable to factors that reduce their numbers, as most auk species have single-egg clutches, breed for the first time at 3-5 years, and display low juvenile survivorship with only some 30% surviving to breed, and a correspondingly high adult survival rate of about 90%. In addition, they tend to have, on the one hand, specialized diets, usually with just 1-2 prey species predominating, and, on the other, mostly clumped patterns of distribution throughout the year, with a high proportion of the total breeding population at only a small number of colonies and the concentration of wintering birds at only a few oceanic areas; together all these factors combine to make most auk species particularly vulnerable to human activities.

Specialists like alcids live a precarious life at the best of times, and, although they long ago adapted to natural variations in their marine environment, they do not adjust easily to changes brought about by man-induced factors, such as depletion of important prey by overfishing or by an oiling incident. The consequences of activities such as these can be severe and rapid. Perhaps the most dramatic example, the collapse of the capelin population in the Barents Sea in 1986, believed to have been caused by overfishing, resulted in the loss at Bear Island of over 400,000 Common Murres (more than 80% of the breeding population) during the winter of 1986/87 owing to food shortages, as well as causing declines of murres and other auk species at colonies in northern Norway. Results can be equally catastrophic when human disturbance from more than one source occurs simultaneously with natural negative events. In California, mortality of Common Murres from oil pollution and drowning in gill-nets combined with prey shortages, partially due to the Southern Oscillation of El Niño (see Volume 1, page 341) in the early 1980's, resulted in a 47% decrease of the murre population on the Farallon Islands. Not only can alcid populations decrease significantly over short periods of time due to human activity, but the impact of such losses can have widespread implications for distant breeding populations. For example, the collapse of the capelin population on the Grand Banks of Newfoundland in 1992 from excessive commercial fishing over the previous 20 years is not only adversely affecting auk populations that breed in the area, but also those species that winter there in large numbers from breeding colonies as far away as the eastern Canadian high Arctic, west and east Greenland, and even Iceland and Spitsbergen. Consequences of present day human disturbance to marine systems can be severe to alcid species.

In the Atlantic, all alcid species except the Dovekie declined during the first half of this century, reductions that began over much of their range by at least the middle of the nineteenth century. Information on the Dovekie is too sketchy to determine what changes in population size and status have occurred for the species as a whole, except for the localized declines known to have taken place this century in Iceland and south-western Greenland. The general impression derived from recent studies at certain colonies in west Greenland and Spitsbergen since the early 1970's suggest a relatively stable population in those regions. Declines have continued to the present time, however, for the Common Murre, Razorbill and Atlantic Puffin, especially in the southern parts of their ranges, and for Thick-billed Murre in the north-west Atlantic. Changes in Common Murre and Razorbill populations have been similar overall, decreases over much of their range at first followed by reductions mainly in southern regions, with numbers stabilizing or showing slight increases at some colonies through the late 1960's and 1970's, and decreases or stable populations thereafter. Large declines of Thick-billed Murres have occurred in many Atlantic locations including the eastern Canadian Arctic since at least the mid-1950's and west Greenland and Novaya Zemlya from the 1920's and 1930's to the present. Atlantic Puffins declined through most of their range until the early 1970's, after which numbers stabilized or increased slightly to the mid-1980's when declines, some marked, began again, continuing now in most regions. The scattered breeding distribution of the Black Guillemot makes it more difficult to examine, but numbers appear to be decreasing in certain northern boreal water parts of its range and remaining relatively stable in the south, the reverse pattern to that shown by Common Murre and Razorbill; nothing is known of status changes of Black Guillemots in Arctic regions.

Causes of the declines are rather straightforward. Human persecution by direct exploitation early on, through egging and hunting, followed by oil contamination and heavy mortality from commercial fisheries, first by large-scale drowning in gill-nets as in Thick-billed Murres in west Greenland, and then by food shortages caused by overexploitation of small pelagic fish as in the Common Murre, Razorbill and Atlantic Puffin. Human predation remains a significant contributor to certain auk declines in eastern Canada, Greenland, Iceland, the Faeroes and parts of Norway and western Russia, the most notable of which is Thick-billed Murre in the north-west Atlantic from largely unregulated hunting in Greenland and Atlantic Canada (see Relationship with Man). Alien predators such as rats and mink have had a significant impact on certain populations, especially in southern regions on both sides of the Atlantic, as have introductions to breeding islands of domesticated livestock, particularly sheep, goats, pigs and rabbits. Disturbance at major breeding colonies by human visitors has increased dramatically over the last 20 years, even in regions recently believed to be remote and relatively inaccessible such as the Arctic. Demands for access to major alcid colonies are frequent and vary in form: tourist developments, often encouraged and initiated by governments for socio-economic purposes; places for university and government biologists to work and for land-use managers to perform their assignments; and subjects for film-makers and naturalists interested in wild places and adventure seekers to have fun. All these activities place extra stress on already hard-pressed breeding populations of colonial alcids. Moreover, these pressures are likely to increase still further in the future as human populations continue to grow and seek additional outlets for their recreational interests.

In summary, over the last two centuries in the Atlantic and adjacent seas, negative influences of humans in the form of direct human exploitation, habitat disturbance and destruction, introduced predators, mismanaged commercial fisheries and incidental kills in fishing nets, oil pollution and chemical poisoning, have resulted in the extermination of one species, the Great Auk, and marked reductions in population size and range of five of the remaining species comprising the North Atlantic alcid community. Two of the five species presently decreasing in numbers have small populations and should be considered vulnerable to further human disturbance and persecution: the Razorbill and Black Guillemot. The future of the Thick-billed Murre in the north-west Atlantic is also precarious, with a 35-50% reduction in the breeding population of Greenland having taken place since the 1930's, including the extinction of numerous major colonies, and major declines elsewhere on both sides

The heavy-billed, starkly black and white Razorbill breeds in habitats similar to those of the Common Murre (Uria aalge), often forming mixed colonies with it and with other seabird species. Flexible as to nest-sites, its choice ranges from crevices in large rock and boulder fields, cracks in rocky cliff faces or exposed ledges, though it shows a preference for somewhat more protected and concealed sites than the open ledges used by murres. There is no nest, the single egg being laid in a slight hollow in the bare rock. The semi-precocial chick is covered in short thick down with silky tips, mainly darkish brown above, but much lighter on the head and breast. Cared for and fed by both parents until it fledges, it then departs for the sea, escorted by the adult male which will remain with it for at least three weeks.

[Alca torda. Photo: Andre Fatras/Bios]

of the Atlantic, notably the eastern Canadian Arctic and the eastern Barents Sea. If unrestricted shooting continues at colonies in west Greenland during the breeding season and during the winter in both south-west Greenland and Newfoundland-Labrador where many of the Greenland birds overwinter, the consequences for the Greenland murre population may be very grave. Overfishing and the subsequent collapse throughout the Atlantic of "keystone" forage species such as capelin and herring, small fish critical as food to all Atlantic auks except the Dovekie, pose the greatest threat to Atlantic Alcidae.

Conditions in the North Pacific are no better, perhaps worse. Alcid populations throughout the North Pacific range have been subjected to a lengthy persecution by humans, even in the remote northern regions believed by most people to have gone largely undisturbed until recent times. Nothing could be farther from the truth. Although most northern islands and sea coasts remained relatively uninhabited compared to areas farther south along both west and east coasts, most islands and their resident seabirds were heavily affected by the introduction of foxes, rats, ground squirrels, other rodents and numerous varieties of domesticated cattle and game animals. Insular fox farming, by far the most destructive human activity in northern regions, began in the mid-eighteenth century, peaked early in the present century and continued as an intensive industry into the 1940's, both in Russia and Alaska. By this time irreparable damage had been done, particularly to colonial breeding auks that had evolved on the hundreds of islands free of mammalian predators and therefore lacking defences against alien predators like foxes when they appeared. On island after island, breeding populations of auklets, puffins and other seabirds disappeared or became drastically reduced because of introduced foxes that were deliberately released on colonies by fur trappers to exploit the auks as fox food. Foxes, combined with other introductions such as rats,

squirrels, mink, raccoons and other rodents, devastated auk populations for at least a century and a half. Farther south along both west and east Pacific coasts, human disturbance of alcid colonies came in the form of direct exploitation through egging and hunting for food, feathers and oil, and the introduction of alien rats, domestic livestock and feral pets. The history of human impact on alcids throughout the North Pacific is lengthy and documents severe widespread persecution (see Relationship with Man).

The current status of the offshore fish-feeding auks in the North Pacific, the Common and Thick-billed Murres, Rhinoceros Auklet, Tufted and Horned Puffins, is unsettling. The murres have declined markedly through most of this century, declines that have continued over the last 25 years in much of the Bering Sea area, north-west Pacific and parts of the west coast of the USA with populations in certain regions stable or showing increases, though remaining far below recent historical levels. Information on the Rhinoceros Auklet and puffins is poor, but available data indicate major declines overall in all three species, with some parts of the population of the Horned Puffin and Rhinoceros Auklet stabilizing or increasing, respectively, since the early 1970's. The size and status of the four inshore fish-feeding alcid populations in the North Pacific are more difficult to determine, owing to their more dispersed breeding patterns. Generally, the two resident *Cepphus* guillemots have declined this century, mainly due to introduced predators. The Pigeon Guillemot has undergone marked declines in northern and southern parts of its range, in the Pribilof and Farallon Islands respectively, as has the Spectacled Guillemot at colonies in northern Japan, with a 93% decline between 1963 and 1987, and eastern Russia, with a 53% decline since 1979. The total population of the Spectacled Guillemot numbers less than 75,000 pairs, is concentrated and is declining, which together clearly indicate a ma-

The Japanese Murrelet, an attractive little species, is the rarest of all alcids. It is restricted to five small breeding areas on islands of south-east Japan. With a total population estimated at only some 5000-6000 birds in 1995, it is considered globally threatened and is currently classified as Vulnerable. Biro Island probably holds at least half of the total population. One or two days after hatching, the chicks leave the nest at night with their parents and go to sea where they will feed for the first time.

[*Synthliboramphus wumizusume*, Biro Island, Kyushu, Japan. Photo: Koji Ono]

jor problem probably warranting globally near-threatened status. Disturbance by alien predators, illegal hunting, and oil developments offshore in the Sea of Okhotsk all pose major threats to this species. Both *Brachyramphus* murrelets appear to be experiencing declines. Destruction of old-growth forests from southeast Alaska to California and in the Sea of Okhotsk poses a serious threat to the future of Marbled Murrelet populations. Major declines in bird numbers have already occurred, partly due to continued removal of nesting habitat, but also undoubtedly from the chronic problem of birds drowning in commercial gill-nets, and mortality from oil spills along the entire west coast of North America. Although the status of Kittlitz's Murrelet is uncertain, either stable or decreasing, considerable numbers were killed in the Exxon Valdez oil spill in 1989 which has raised serious concern.

The *Synthliboramphus* murrelets and the auklets occur around the rim of the North Pacific and adjacent seas. Although their general distributions are well known, sizes of populations within many regions are poorly known and they are all difficult to census owing to their nocturnal activity patterns in the case of murrelets and Cassin's Auklet, or subterranean and often inaccessible nest locations in the *Aethia* auklets. The Ancient Murrelet and Cassin's Auklet range widely from northern boreal to cool subtropical waters. Both species were decimated by foxes in the Aleutian Islands and northern Gulf of Alaska during the lengthy fox farming era, and significantly reduced in numbers elsewhere by other alien introductions, notably rats, cats and raccoons, and also by human disturbance. The other three murrelet species, Xantus's, Craveri's and the Japanese, have restricted mostly cool subtropical distributions and are all threatened to near-threatened species. The Japanese Murrelet is probably the rarest alcid in the world with a maximum of 6000 individuals, its numbers reduced by human disturbance and introduced predators this century to its present critical low level and globally threatened status. Xantus's and Craveri's Murrelets also have extremely small and restricted populations that are designated globally near-threatened. Feral cats, rats, deer mice and livestock introductions, combined with other human disturbance at breeding colonies, have been responsible for the decline of both species. Removal of cats and other alien mammals from Xantus's Murrelet colonies in the Channel Islands, California, has had positive results; additional predator eradication programmes are required at other breeding

sites in southern California and the outer coast of Baja California for Xantus's, and in the Sea of Cortez for Craveri's.

The Parakeet Auklet and three *Aethia* auklets all breed predominantly in low Arctic and northern boreal waters in the Bering Sea and Sea of Okhotsk, showing only a little overlap with murrelets and Cassin's Auklet. Although they have not been surveyed thoroughly because of deficient census methods, certain trends seem clear. All four species have been seriously affected by introduced mammalian predators and human exploitation and disturbance from the late nineteenth to the middle of the twentieth century. The Whiskered Auklet has the smallest population and most restricted distribution of the *Aethia* auklets, making it highly vulnerable to human activity. Alien rats and foxes at colonies, combined with recent high mortality from oil pollution and fatal attraction to ships' lights suggest the species may be declining in parts of its range. Current trends of Crested and Least Auklets are uncertain: in both species, some populations appear relatively stable while others are decreasing. Crested Auklets underwent drastic reductions throughout their range due to fox farming, and present numbers are only a small fraction of what they were before foxes were introduced. For example, the large colony at Yukon Harbor in the Pribilof Islands fell from a high of 300,000 birds in the early 1900's to 30,000 by the mid-1970's, and only 6000 in the mid-1980's. The removal of foxes from some island colonies in 1985/86 in Alaska has resulted in populations becoming stable or even increasing slightly, but declines continue at other locations due to human disturbance, alien predators and oil pollution. The Least Auklet is the most abundant auklet in the Bering Sea and Sea of Okhotsk, but it too has decreased in numbers in recent times. Qualitative assessments suggest a declining population overall with marked decreases at Pribilof and Aleutian colonies, as well as serious reductions from human disturbance and introduced predators at colonies in the Sea of Okhotsk. The Parakeet Auklet population has also probably undergone a major reduction in size and numbers of colonies since the turn of this century for the same causes. Today, introduced predators, commercial fisheries and marine pollution, through both oiling and the ingestion of plastics, pose serious threats, as they do to the other auklets and murrelets.

Overall, human exploitation and disturbance at alcid breeding colonies in the North Pacific during the last 150 years or more have had severe and disastrous consequences for the birds. Hundreds, if not thousands, of auk colonies have been destroyed and even greater numbers of islands have undergone permanent damage from direct human habitat alteration and occupation, as well as introductions of alien animals. More recent assaults from intensive commercial fisheries, offshore petroleum developments and transport, and widespread removal of old-growth coniferous forests along both Pacific coasts have added to the impact on the auk community. Consequences have been marked. Almost all 18 alcid species are in a state of disequilibrium, with populations either known or suspected to be decreasing in size and range. The Japanese Murrelet is classed as Vulnerable, with extinction in the near future a distinct possibility. Three other species, the Marbled, Xantus's and Craveri's Murrelets, are globally near-threatened, and an additional three should be so designated, namely the Spectacled Guillemot, Kittlitz's Murrelet and the Whiskered Auklet. Human disturbance and exploitation, followed by introduced mammalian predators, oil pollution and commercial fisheries, remain the greatest threats to alcid populations in the North Pacific.

To conclude, the future of the 22 species of Alcidae distributed in the North Pacific, North Atlantic and Arctic Oceans must be considered precarious, particularly as human disturbance is likely to be even greater in the future. Direct exploitation of alcids for food, oil and feathers, though now much reduced over the family's world range if compared with the first half of this century, remains significant and at unsustainable levels in eastern Russia and certain parts of the North Atlantic, notably Russia, Norway, the Faeroes, Iceland, Greenland and Canada. The most serious threats to auks come from the indirect effects of other human activity: drowning in fish nets and oiling, when the birds are at sea; and, when they come ashore to breed, alien predators, artificial increases in natural predators, human disturbance and tourism; also, indirectly, by reducing the quality and quantity of their food supply through fishery developments, overfishing, and toxic chemical contamination. The present conservation needs for Alcidae require the total protection of the most important breeding colonies, including the land and adjacent waters, and key feeding areas both inside and outside the breeding season. Sites used for reproduction require protection from the many sources of human disturbance, both direct and indirect. An international system of enforcement must be developed to ensure that regulations are respected and effective in the attainment of management and conservation objectives. But can these conservation goals be attained, and if they can, what general approaches to management and research need to be implemented and followed?

Solutions to these problems are by no means clear. To be effective, a management strategy must comprise a careful co-ordination of effort on a regional, national and international basis, to permit an adequate assessment of threats to be made and solutions developed. Conservation biologists must not limit thoughts to a single colony or species, or even to a small area of ocean, but instead collectively agree to standardize protocol and co-ordinate activities, and to sample entire ranges of individual species and oceans. Only in this way can we expect to succeed in the formulation of a meaningful conservation policy and the identification of processes and actions by which alcid diversity and abundance can be protected and maintained. The overall conservation plan required for auks today must satisfy a suite of general requirements.

First, it is essential to regulate the impact of general and specific environmental stresses on alcids and their marine and terrestrial habitats including: offshore petroleum developments, operations and transport systems; national and international fisheries directed towards forage prey species (fish and invertebrates) important to alcids throughout their annual cycle; and forestry developments and operations targeting critical nesting habitat, such as old-growth forests.

The second requirement is the mitigation and removal of current man-induced disturbances known to be adversely affecting individual species populations with: the cessation of human predation, particularly in eastern Russia, Norway, the Faeroes, Iceland, eastern Canada and Greenland; the eradication of introduced alien predators from important extant alcid colonies and former breeding sites; the elimination and control at key breeding colonies and nesting sites of human disturbance, including habitat alteration and destruction, the presence of domesticated animals, tourism, and other unnecessary human activity; and restrictions and control of commercial fisheries within areas of important colonies.

The third point is to establish programmes to protect, preserve and restore important breeding colonies and marine and terrestrial habitats on regional, national and international levels.

Fourth, it is essential to maintain or establish monitoring systems capable of measuring key population parameters of individual species that will produce statistically meaningful results to determine current status at major colonies, predict changes, and identify cause-and-effect relationships.

Fifth, a global database for Alcidae should be developed, to bring regional and national data sets together to provide a baseline for the assessment of species population changes on a wide range, a system capable of examining whole ranges of species and entire oceans.

And finally, a multinational site classification system should be established to facilitate easy identification of alcid sites (colonies and marine water areas) of national and international importance to be designated "significant" and worthy of protection; this approach will allow international designation to be given to individual sites and force national owners to accept the "special site" status and provide the protection necessary under national laws and international treaties.

In the end, it is critical to remember that successful conservation of auks is dependent upon long-term compliance of conservation policy which can only be attained through education and understanding. Biologists and managers must therefore devise better communication pathways and networks to inform people of conservation needs and explain why wildlife laws and regulations are required. It is essential that both ecological and human factors, and their interactions, are considered in the formulation of policy. This is particularly important in regions where subsistence hunting was, or remains, part of the traditional culture. In these cases, increased education aimed at all age groups, but particularly at children and their parents, is essential to the adjustment of traditional mores and to reinforce alcids and other marine wildlife as part of their culture. This approach may be the best defence for many alcid colonies and habitats. Clearly, conservation goals can only be attained by a combined effort through public education, public pressure, and the enactment of suitable legislation, all of which requires public awareness and support. The management of alcids and other seabirds will remain largely at the ecosystem level: protect the island or mainland site and its nearby waters, and those marine areas known to be important outside the breeding season, and manage them for alcid species and communities. By managing auk populations successfully, we will prevent large-scale destruction of a rich group of marine animals, and contribute to maintaining the health of the world's oceans on which most living things depend.

General Bibliography
Ashmole (1971), Bartonek & Nettleship (1979), Bédard (1969c), Bengtson (1984), Birkhead (1985a, 1994), Birkhead & Nettleship (1984), Bourne, W.R.P. (1976, 1993b), Bureau (1879), Burger, J. (1980d), Burger, J., Olla & Winn (1980), Coues (1868), Croxall (1987, 1991), Croxall, Evans & Schreiber (1984), Duffy & Nettleship (1992), Dunning (1993), Feduccia (1980), Fisher & Lockley (1954), Freethy (1987), Furness & Monaghan (1987), Furness & Nettleship (1991), Gaston et al. (1985), Grieve (1885), Harris, M.P. (1984), Harrison (1985, 1987), Hobson & Montevecchi (1991), Hoerschelmann & Jacob (1992), Hudson et al. (1969), Judin (1965), Kaftanovskii (1951), Kuroda (1954, 1955), Lack (1968), Löfgren (1984), Lucas (1890), Nelson (1980), Nettleship (1991a), Nettleship & Birkhead (1985), Nettleship & Duffy (1992), Nettleship & Hunt (1988), Nettleship, Burger & Gochfeld (1994), Nettleship, Sanger & Springer (1984), Olson (1985b), Peters (1934), Salomonsen (1944), Sealy (1990), Sibley & Ahlquist (1990), Sibley & Monroe (1990), Spring (1968, 1971), Storer (1945, 1960), Strauch (1978, 1985), Swartz (1966), Tuck, G.S. & Heinzel (1978), Tuck, L.M. (1961), Udvardy (1963), Verheyen (1958).

bridled form

1

2

ssp *aalge*

ssp *albionis*

3

4

bird with
all-black wings

ssp *grylle*

5

6

ssp *columba*

ssp *mandtii*

ssp *snowi*

ssp *islandicus*

7

8

9

ssp *marmoratus*

ssp *perdix*

PLATE 59

inches   6

cm   15

Genus *ALLE*   Link, 1806

1. **Dovekie**
Alle alle

French: Mergule nain   **German**: Krabbentaucher   **Spanish**: Mérgulo Atlántico
Other common names: Little Auk

Taxonomy. *Alca Alle* Linnaeus, 1758, Scotland.
In past, species was commonly placed in monotypic genus *Plautus*, but this name was deemed una-vailable, giving way to *Alle*. Normally treated as polytypic, but evidence incomplete and requires further examination; subspecific status of populations breeding Severnaya Zemlya, New Siberian Is and Bering Sea uncertain. Two subspecies normally recognized.
Subspecies and Distribution.
A. a. alle (Linnaeus, 1758) - E Baffin I through Greenland and Iceland to Jan Mayen, Spitsbergen, Bear I and Novaya Zemlya.
A. a. polaris Stenhouse, 1930 - Franz Josef Land, and possibly this race in region from Severnaya Zemlya E to Bering Sea (St Lawrence I, Little Diomede).
Winters mainly in low Arctic waters from Grand Banks of Newfoundland E across N Atlantic to N Norway; also regularly in boreal zone S over Scotian Shelf and Gulf of Maine E to N Scotland and North Sea, rarely farther S.

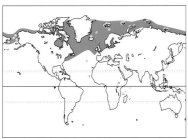

Descriptive notes. 17-19 cm; 163 g (140-192 g); wingspan 40-48 cm. Rather distinctive small, compact, chubby auk with short, stubby black bill and black iris; glossy black head, neck and upperparts, with browner-toned face and upper breast, contrasting with white underparts; white-streaked scapulars and white-tipped secondaries; legs and feet blackish grey. In winter, chin, throat, upper breast and ear-coverts white. Juvenile resembles summer adult, but generally paler and browner. Races rather similar, based upon size differences only; *polaris* larger overall, including longer bill and wing.
Habitat. Mainly high Arctic, breeding in large colonies on sea coasts, usually in crevices in rock scree of maritime slopes. Mostly pelagic during winter, mainly in low Arctic waters, often associated with edge of pack ice and in boreal zone; rarely farther S. Winter distribution corresponds with regions of greatest abundance of oceanic zooplankton.
Food and Feeding. Feeds mainly on small invertebrates, especially copepods, amphipods and euphausiids, less frequently decapods and gastropods; also fish larvae. Chick diet mainly comprises planktonic crustaceans, *Calanus* copepods and amphipods; parents deliver c. 5-8 meals/day, each amounting to 3·0-3·8 g. Species is opportunistic feeder, usually foraging within 100 km of colony, often much closer; food transported in gular pouch. Dives normally last 30 seconds or less, probably most to depths of less than 20 m, though rarely to 30 m. Winter diet poorly known, but planktonic crustaceans and other zooplankton are presumably important.
Breeding. Spring arrival at colony is variable, from late Feb to early Mar at Franz Josef Land, early Apr in Spitsbergen, and early May in NW Greenland; laying occurs in late Jun, and fledging complete by end Aug. Forms immense colonies at selected sites in high Arctic, breeding in scree slopes on coastal cliffs; egg often laid on bed of small pebbles lined with fragments of vegetation. 1 egg; incubation averages 29 days (28-31), by both sexes equally, with c. 4 change-overs each day; downy chick blackish brown, with paler belly, c. 21 g, semi-precocial; chick-rearing usually 27-30 days, with care and feeding by both parents; chick apparently becomes independent at fledging, when flies out to sea alone. Breeding success variable, with average of c. 50-52% of eggs laid producing fledglings; most losses during incubation are due to neglect, accidental breakage, and predation by Arctic foxes (*Alopex lagopus*), gulls, and infrequently even polar bears (*Thalarctos maritimus*). Survival rates and age of first breeding unknown.
Movements. Most northerly of the Atlantic auks. Mobile, undertaking migrations of substantial length. Abandons colonies end Aug. In winter, commonest in W Atlantic on S Grand Banks and shelf edge E of Nova Scotia, but scarce farther S, with distribution limits in E Atlantic less well defined. Two principal migratory patterns known: NW Greenland birds winter off Newfoundland; many from Euro-pean Arctic winter off SW & (less frequently) SE Greenland, with massive westerly movement past NW Russia in Oct and return in Apr, presumably of birds from Novaya Zemlya, possibly from Severnaya Zemlya. Unlike others, Franz Josef Land birds appear to winter in NE Barents Sea, close to the breed-ing archipelago.
Status and Conservation. Not globally threatened. Believed to be the most abundant Atlantic auk, with most colonies situated in remote and inaccessible regions at high latitudes. Total breeding population estimated to number c. 12,000,000 pairs (8,000,000-18,000,000), with main concentra-tions located in: NW Greenland, with c. 10,000,000 in Thule region; E Greenland, with c. 500,000 in Scoresby Sound and Liverpool Land; W Spitsbergen with c. 1,000,000; Jan Mayen with c. 50,000; Franz Josef Land with 250,000; and NW Novaya Zemlya with c. 50,000. Human predation and disturbance at colonies is localized, and not thought to be serious at present; human exploitation worst in NW Greenland. Disturbance from offshore oil developments and transport gives some cause for concern, particularly developments on Newfoundland Grand Banks scheduled for 1997 (Hibernia and Terra Nova fields) and also continuing activity in Greenland, Svalbard region and Barents Sea. Widespread distribution of species reduces immediate risk from man-induced distur-bance of marine ecosystems.

Bibliography. Armstrong (1983), Bédard (1985), Birkhead (1985b), Birkhead & Harris (1985), Bradstreet (1982), Bradstreet & Brown (1985), Breckenridge (1966), Brown, R.G.B. (1976b, 1985), Cramp (1985), Day *et al.* (1988), Evans (1981, 1984a, 1984b), Evans & Nettleship (1985), Flint *et al.* (1984), Follestad (1990), Gabrielsen *et al.* (1991), Gaston (1985c), Harris & Birkhead (1985), Hudson (1985), Knystautas (1993), Manuwal (1984), Mehlum & Bakken (1994), Mehlum & Gabrielsen (1993), Nettleship & Evans (1985), Norderhaug (1967, 1970, 1980), Norderhaug *et al.* (1977), Richards (1990), Roby *et al.* (1981), Rogacheva (1992), Salomonsen (1944, 1967b, 1979a, 1979b), Stempniewicz (1980, 1981, 1982, 1983, 1986, 1990, 1993), Stempniewicz & Jezierski (1987), Stempniewicz & Weslawski (1992), Stenhouse (1930), Tasker *et al.* (1987), Urban *et al.* (1986), Wetmore & Watson (1969).

Genus *URIA*   Brisson, 1760

2. **Common Murre**
Uria aalge

French: Guillemot marmette   **German**: Trottellumme   **Spanish**: Arao Común
Other common names: (Common) Guillemot, Thin-billed Murre

Taxonomy. *Colymbus aalge* Pontoppidan, 1763, Iceland.
Birds of Faeroes sometimes separated as race *spiloptera*. Proposed race *intermedia*, for populations of small islands in S Baltic, probably invalid, as claimed differences probably reflect individual variation. Five subspecies recognized.
Subspecies and Distribution.
U. a. aalge (Pontoppidan, 1763) - E North America, Greenland and Iceland, through Faeroes and Scotland to S Norway and Baltic Sea.
U. a. albionis Witherby, 1923 - Ireland and S Britain through Brittany to W Iberia; Helgoland.
U. a. hyperborea Salomonsen, 1932 - Svalbard through N Norway and Murmansk to Novaya Zemlya.
U. a. inornata Salomonsen, 1932 - E Korea and Japan (N Hokkaido) N through Sakhalin to Kamchatka, whence E through Bering Sea, Aleutians and W Alaska to NW British Columbia.
U. a. californica (H. Bryant, 1861) - N Washington S to California.
Winters mainly in boreal waters, S to Georges Bank and W Mediterranean, and to S Japan and S California.

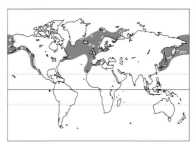

Descriptive notes. 38-43 cm; mean 945-1044 g; wingspan 64-71 cm. Long, pointed, slender black bill with yellow mouth-lining, and dark brown iris; black to brownish head and upper-parts, white underparts; white-tipped secondar-ies; legs and feet greyish black, with yellowish tinge beneath. Bridled or ringed morph has white eye-ring and post-ocular stripe; restricted to At-lantic, and most prevalent in N populations. Dif-fers from *U. lomvia* in thinner bill which lacks white stripe. In winter, cheeks and underside of head and foreneck white, with dark spur behind eye; bill and feet paler. Juvenile similar to adult, but one third of size, with darker head. Second most differentiated alcid species, with races based largely on differences in plumage colour, degree of streaking, bill length, wing length and overall body size.
Habitat. Exclusively marine, occurring along sea coasts on rocky cliffs and offshore islands. Breeds mainly on steep sea cliffs and low, flat islands. Mostly offshore during winter, along edge of continen-tal shelf and shallow banks, marine coasts and bays, generally in boreal waters but with some birds in cool subtropical zone; winter distribution largely determined by concentrations of schooling fish.
Food and Feeding. Mostly fish throughout year, supplemented to small degree by invertebrates: crus-taceans, molluscs, polychaetes and fish eggs; daily intake 25-33% of adult body weight. Chicks fed almost exclusively fish except late in rearing period, when invertebrates may appear; 2-6 meals/day, averaging daily total of 20-32 g of fish, usually species high in fat and calorific value, e.g. capelin (*Mallotus*), herring (*Clupeus*), sprat (*Sprattus*) and sandeels (*Ammodytes*). Food usually obtained within 10-20 km of colony, infrequently up to 50 km away. Dives normally last under 60 seconds and to depths of 10-30 m, but 60-70 m recorded regularly, with maximum of 180 m exceptional.
Breeding. Spring arrival and start of laying variable, with relatively lengthy pre-laying period, longest in extreme S, shortest towards extreme N, determined largely by water temperature and ice; laying normally mid-May to early Jun, fledging mostly by late Jul to mid-Aug. Monogamous, with high mate and site fidelity. Highly colonial, in small to immense aggregations, usually at high density, reaching average of 20 pairs/m² on flat, rocky areas. Lays on broad or narrow cliff ledges and low, flat islands, and less commonly in crevices, under boulders and in caves; no nest, egg sitting on bare rock. 1 egg; incubation averages 32·5 days, by both sexes for periods of 12-24 hours; early egg losses replaced after 14-16 days; downy chick blackish brown above, white below, 55-95 g, semi-precocial; chick-rearing averages 20-22 days (16-30), with care and feeding by both parents until fledging, when adult male accompanies chick to sea; post-fledging parental care c. 4 weeks; female remains at breeding site for up to 2 weeks after chick departure. Breeding success variable within and between colonies, overall average usually 72-80% eggs laid producing fledglings; success greatly influenced by breeding den-sity and synchrony, with performance highest where density and synchrony are high; age, experience and timing also important. Most egg and chick losses due to mishandling by adults, e.g. rolling or falling off ledge, and separation during fledging; also from gull predation. Adult survival 87-90%; survival of fledglings to breeding age variable, 17-41%. First breeding usually at 5 years, sometimes 4.
Movements. Winters offshore at sea, mostly within breeding range and some birds close to colonies; extends S to W Mediterranean and Gulf of Maine (casually to Virginia) in Atlantic, and to Korea, N Japan and S California (rarely to Baja California) in Pacific; N limits normally determined by ice conditions. Post-breeding dispersal highly variable: birds from Newfoundland, Irish Sea, Helgoland, Baltic and N Norway relatively sedentary, whereas those from N Britain, Faeroes and possibly Iceland move to W Norway and North Sea; no trans-Atlantic migrations known, though some Icelandic birds suspected to reach Greenland and E Grand Banks of Newfoundland. Pacific populations winter off-shore near breeding colonies, except for N birds that move S after breeding, distance determined by weather and ice patterns. Most birds return to colonies Mar-Apr, rarely May in Labrador owing to ice break-up. In general, dispersal patterns often complex, requiring further examination, especially in N Atlantic.
Status and Conservation. Not globally threatened. Population sizes and trends relatively well known. Total population estimated at c. 9,000,000 pairs, with c. 4,000,000 (3,000,000-4,500,000) in Atlantic and c. 5,000,000 (4,000,000-5,500,000) in Pacific; c. 70% of total in S low Arctic zone, including large colonies in E Newfoundland, Iceland, Bear I and Alaska. High concentrations during and outside breeding season make species highly vulnerable to disturbance by human activities. Historically, world population severely reduced through 19th and early 20th centuries, mainly through egging and shoot-ing at colonies, and introduced alien predators; species extirpated in many regions, particularly in S parts of range, during expansion in size and range of human population; some populations on verge of extinction, e.g. in NW Spain only 6-10 pairs in 1991. Slow recovery occurred over much of Atlantic

On following pages: 3. Thick-billed Murre (*Uria lomvia*); 4. Razorbill (*Alca torda*); 5. Black Guillemot (*Cepphus grylle*); 6. Pigeon Guillemot (*Cepphus columba*); 7. Spectacled Guillemot (*Cepphus carbo*); 8. Marbled Murrelet (*Brachyramphus marmoratus*); 9. Kittlitz's Murrelet (*Brachyramphus brevirostris*).

breeding range up to early 1970's with enactment of bird protection laws, except in N Norway, Faeroes and probably Iceland; little known of population size and status of birds in Pacific prior to early 1970's. Current status of entire population complex and variable; where long-term data exist, including W & E North America, N Europe and W Pacific, generally appears to be decreasing in most regions, in fewer instances stable. Since early 1980's, marked declines in C & N zones of California Current, stable numbers in Gulf of Alaska, and decreases in E Bering Sea. Major threats are unregulated hunting in Faeroes, Greenland and Newfoundland, overfishing of important forage species e.g. capelin, herring, cod and sandeels in N Atlantic (Barents Sea, Iceland, E Newfoundland and Grand Banks, Scotian Shelf and Gulf of Maine) and N Pacific, uncontrolled gill-net fisheries in NE Atlantic and N Pacific, and oil pollution and offshore petroleum developments in both oceans, e.g. Barents and North Seas, Greenland, E Newfoundland and Grand Banks, Alaska S to California. Changes in breeding numbers can be dramatic, e.g. Bear I population decreased by 85% from 250,000 to 36,000 pairs between 1986 and 1987, owing to collapse of Barents Sea capelin stock, and has since failed to recover. Detailed monitoring therefore required at major colonies, including Iceland, where status of largest Atlantic population is poorly known.

Bibliography. Ainley & Hunt (1991), Ainley *et al*. (1994), Armstrong (1983), Bárcena *et al*. (1984), Bayer *et al*. (1991), Bédard (1985), Belopol'skii (1957), Bent (1919), Birkhead (1976, 1977, 1978, 1985b), Birkhead & Harris (1985), Birkhead & Hudson (1977), Birkhead & Nettleship (1980, 1985, 1987a, 1987b, 1987c), Birkhead *et al*. (1985), Bradstreet & Brown (1985), Bräger (1995), Brazil (1991), Briggs, Ainley *et al*. (1987), Brown (1985), Brown & Nettleship (1984a, 1984b), Burger & Piatt (1990), Burger & Simpson (1986), Byrd *et al*. (1993), Cairns *et al*. (1987, 1990), Cramp (1985), Croll (1990), Durinck *et al*. (1991), Étchécopar & Hüe (1978), Evans (1984a, 1984b), Evans & Nettleship (1985), Flint *et al*. (1984), Gaston (1985c), Golovkin (1963), Harris & Bailey (1992), Harris & Birkhead (1985), Harris & Wanless (1988, 1989, 1995a, 1995b), Harris, Halley & Swann (1994), Harris, Webb & Tasker (1991), Hasegawa (1984), Hatch (1983), Hatchwell & Birkhead (1991), Hedgren (1976, 1980), Heubeck *et al*. (1991), Howell & Webb (1995a), Hudson (1985), Joiris (1978), Knystautas (1993), Kondratiev (1991), Lensink (1984), Litvinenko & Shibaev (1991), Lloyd *et al*. (1991), Manuwal (1984), McGeehan (1996), Mehlum & Bakken (1994), Nettleship & Evans (1985), Ogi & Shiomi (1991), Page *et al*. (1990), Piatt (1990), Piatt & Nettleship (1985, 1987), Piatt, Lensink *et al*. (1990), Piatt, Nettleship & Threlfall (1984), Piatt, Carter & Nettleship (1991), Richards (1990), Rodway (1991), Scott (1973), Skov *et al*. (1992), Speich & Wahl (1989), Spring (1971), Stettenheim (1959), Storer (1952), Swartz (1966), Swennen & Duiven (1977), Takekawa *et al*. (1990), Tasker *et al*. (1987), Tuck (1961), Urban *et al*. (1986), Uspenski (1956), Vader *et al*. (1990), Verspoor *et al*. (1987).

3. **Thick-billed Murre**

Uria lomvia

French: Guillemot de Brünnich **German**: Dickschnabellumme **Spanish**: Arao de Brünnich
Other common names: Brünnich's Guillemot/Murre

Taxonomy. *Alca Lomvia* Linnaeus, 1758, Greenland.

Considerable geographical variation through circumpolar range; biometric variation in general quasi-clinal, but high colour variation more difficult to interpret. Four subspecies recognized.

Subspecies and Distribution.

U. l. lomvia (Linnaeus, 1758) - NE Canada S to Gulf of St Lawrence, and Greenland E to Franz Josef Land, Novaya Zemlya and Severnaya Zemlya.

U. l. eleonorae Portenko, 1937 - E Taymyr Peninsula E to New Siberian Is.

U. l. heckeri Portenko, 1944 - Wrangel I, Herald I and N Chukotskiy Peninsula.

U. l. arra (Pallas, 1811) - N Pacific, from NW Alaska S to N Japan, Aleutians and SE Alaska.

Winters offshore and along sea coasts mainly in low Arctic waters, but some in N part of boreal zone S to Gulf of Maine, North Sea, Sea of Japan and Gulf of Alaska.

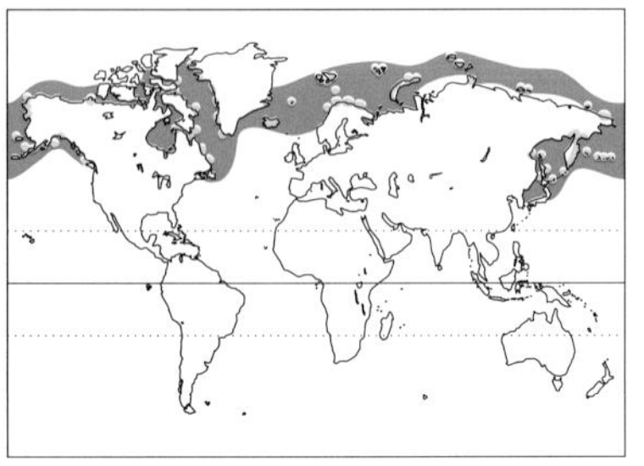

Descriptive notes. 39-43 cm; mean 810-1080 g; wingspan 65-73 cm. Largest extant alcid; blackish head and upperparts, white underparts; white-tipped secondaries; legs and feet greyish black, tinged yellowish beneath. Similar to *U. aalge*, but slightly larger in body size, with longer wings, shorter, heavier bill, and thicker head and neck (adult); differs in whitish line along cutting edge of upper mandible near gape, and the more acute-angled peak of white extending from upper fore-breast into neck-throat region; has no bridled or ringed morph. In winter, chin and throat white, producing dark-headed, almost capped appearance which separates from winter-plumaged *U. aalge* and *Alca torda*. Juvenile normally similar to winter adult, but about one third of size, with slightly darker chin, throat and underbody; some similar to breeding adult, with black throat and chin. Races based on differences in length of wing and tarsus, and length and depth of bill, averaging larger in E of breeding range; Pacific *arra* averages darker.

Habitat. Exclusively marine, occurring offshore and along sea coasts. Breeds on coastal cliffs and islands, and almost completely restricted to high and low Arctic zones with open water and adequate summer food supply; over 70% of population breeds in N parts of low Arctic water zone; colony locations usually associated with dynamic water systems, e.g. fronts, upwellings and converging currents, where primary and secondary productivity high. Winters mostly offshore to edge of continental shelf, and along sea coasts and in bays where concentrations of fish and invertebrates occur. At sea found in flocks, often large, likely related to non-random distribution of winter prey.

Food and Feeding. Chiefly fish, squid and crustaceans throughout year, supplemented by polychaetes and molluscs; invertebrates more significant than for *U. aalge*, particularly outside breeding season. Fish predominate during summer, main species varying with location: Arctic cod (*Boreogadus saida*) at high Arctic colonies (N Baffin Bay), and mix of Arctic and Atlantic cod (*Gadus morhua*) in low Arctic (Hudson Strait, Murmansk, Novaya Zemlya), often supplemented by other species including sculpins (Cottidae), pricklebacks (Gasterosteidae), capelin (*Mallotus villosus*) and infrequently Atlantic herring (*Clupea harengus*) and sandeels (*Ammodytes*). Daily intake c. 20-25% adult body weight. Chick diet almost entirely fish, with Arctic cod dominant (78-100%) at all high Arctic colonies, supplemented by sculpins (*Triglops*) and *Gammarus* amphipods and, to lesser extent, *Parathemisto* amphipods, *Gonatus* squid and *Harmothoe* polychaetes; invertebrates always under 7% of food. In low Arctic, Arctic cod still important, but less so than in high Arctic: 51% (Digges I, Hudson Bay; Novaya Zemlya) and 35% (Akpatok I, Ungava Bay) in N of zone, but only 2% at S location (Gannet Is, Labrador), where capelin, blennies and other benthic species predominate; also significant were blennies and sculpins (Akpatok), Atlantic cod and herring (Novaya Zemlya), and herring, capelin and daubed shanny (Jan Mayen). Chick feeding rates variable, generally c. 4-5 meals/day (1-8) with average daily intake of c. 58 g of fish (Prince Leopold I: chicks 3-20 days old). Food obtained close to colony, usually within 30-50 km, but often as far away as 100 km or more; distance determined by prey density and movements, as well as ice cover. Average dive times vary with location: 40-50 seconds (Novaya Zemlya), 29 seconds (Lancaster Sound and Baffin Bay: maximum 75), 83 seconds (Lancaster Sound: maximum 192). Dives under 60 seconds to depths of 10-30 m, but 50-70 m probably not unusual, with 100 m or more exceptional; prevalence of benthic fish indicates regular visits to sea floor area, often at considerable depths.

Breeding. Spring arrival and start of laying variable, usually related to sea temperatures, with laying latest where temperatures lowest; in mixed *Uria* colonies, timing similar between species. Median laying dates in both Arctic zones similar, usually late Jun to early Jul, slightly earlier towards S edge of low Arctic water: in E Canada, late Jun to early Jul in high Arctic (Prince Leopold I, Coburg I, and Cape Hay, Bylot I), end Jun in N low Arctic (E Digges I), and late Jun in S low Arctic (Gannet Is, Labrador); earlier towards S limit of low Arctic water and in N boreal waters, late May to early Jun (e.g. E Murmansk and Novaya Zemlya). Fledging mostly peaks by mid- to late Aug, earlier in S low Arctic and boreal zones. Highly colonial, usually in immense aggregations and at high densities on steep sea cliffs, but normally at densities below those of *U. aalge*. Lays on narrow ledges; no nest, egg laid on bare rock. 1 egg; incubation averages 32-33 days, by both sexes, for stints of 12-24 hours, infrequently 48 hours; most early eggs losses replaced, usually after 14 days (11-17); downy chick blackish brown, white on belly, with white-streaked head, 65-70 g, semi-precocial; chick-rearing averages 21 days (16-30), with brooding, guarding and feeding by both parents until fledging, when male parent accompanies chick to sea; post-fledging parental care at least 4 weeks, probably up to 8-12 weeks; female remains at breeding site for 2 weeks or more after chick departure. Breeding success variable between years and colonies, normal average c. 70-80% of eggs laid producing fledglings, early breeders more successful than later breeders. Most failures due to egg loss, largely from mishandling by adults at laying or during change-overs, causing egg to fall off ledge; eggs and some chicks also lost to predators, e.g. Glaucous Gull (*Larus hyperboreus*), Common Raven (*Corvus corax*), arctic fox (*Alopex lagopus*). Adult survival c. 91%; survival of fledglings from departure to wintering grounds c. 40%, to breeding age 24-37%. First breeding normally at 5 years, infrequently 3 or 4 when colony small and expanding.

Movements. Winters mostly offshore at sea, mainly in low Arctic waters, but some in N of boreal zone S to North Sea and N Europe (occasionally to Britain and Netherlands, rarely France), Gulf of Maine (to Long I, infrequently to South Carolina), Gulf of Alaska and British Columbia (casually Washington S to California), and Sea of Japan (Hokkaido); dispersal determined largely by ice conditions and food availability. In Atlantic two major migratory pathways, associated with Labrador Current and E to W Greenland Currents: birds from Arctic Canada and W Greenland move S to E Newfoundland (shelf and Grand Banks) and Nova Scotia; those from European Arctic move SW towards W Greenland, including Spitsbergen birds that reach both SW Greenland and Newfoundland waters and remain until Mar. In N Pacific, birds likely remain close to breeding areas except where ice conditions interfere, with most wintering in C & S Bering Sea and fewer in Gulf of Alaska or Seas of Okhotsk and Japan; some regularly winter in E Chukchi Sea N to Cape Thompson and Point Hope, but most birds probably move SW to Bering Sea. Return begins in Mar, most birds back at colonies between mid-Apr and late May, sometimes later owing to late break-up of sea ice. Dispersal patterns poorly known in many regions, especially European Arctic and many parts of N Pacific.

Status and Conservation. Not globally threatened. Total breeding population estimated at c. 11,000,000 pairs, with c. 6,500,000 (4,900,000-7,500,000) in N Atlantic and 4,500,000 (3,500,000-6,000,000) in N Pacific and Chukchi Sea. In Atlantic, c. 25% of population in NW, with especially large colonies in E Canadian Arctic (Hudson Strait, Lancaster and Jones Sounds) and NW Greenland; remainder in NE Atlantic, concentrated in Iceland, Bear I, Spitsbergen, Franz Josef Land and Novaya Zemlya. Almost 80% of Pacific population in NE, particularly E Bering Sea, e.g. Pribilofs, St Lawrence I, St Matthew I; NW portion largely in W Bering Sea (554,000 pairs), with smaller numbers in Sea of Okhotsk (c. 210,000 pairs, with major colonies on Matykyl and Talan Is) and W Chukchi Sea (c. 140,000 pairs). Most colonies in Bering and Okhotsk Seas mixed with *U. aalge*, as are some in Chukchi Sea. High aggregations during and outside breeding season make species highly vulnerable to human activities. Information on population sizes from 19th century is both scarce and qualitative; since early 1900's, population severely reduced due to human exploitation and disturbance. In Atlantic, information since 1930's clearly indicates major declines in many parts of range, notably: E Canadian Arctic, where probably 20-40% decline mid-1950's to late 1970's; W Greenland, 35-50% decline 1930-1990 and continuing, with many colony extinctions occurring or imminent; and Novaya Zemlya, reductions by 40-50% from 1930 to late 1940's; decreases at other sites suspected, e.g. Iceland, Jan Mayen. E Canadian population apparently now stable, as seems the case at Novaya Zemlya, albeit at markedly reduced levels. Data for N Pacific and Chukchi Sea sparse before mid-1970's, since when trends indicate declines in E Bering Sea (e.g. Cape Pierce, Pribilofs) and relative stability elsewhere following large declines through human activity (commercial egging, hunting, cliff habitat alteration) from late 1940's to 1960 (Sea of Okhotsk); trends for Chukchi Sea variable, both declines (Cape Thompson, 1960-1979) and slight increases (Cape Lisburne, 1976-1987) recorded, but all populations there now believed to be stable. Main threats to world population during first half of 20th century were direct and indirect human exploitation: egging, hunting, disturbance, and introduction of mammalian predators (N Pacific). Current threats remain man-induced: unregulated hunting in Newfoundland and Labrador (winter) and Greenland (summer and winter); incidental kills in fishing nets; competition with commercial fisheries, notably in Barents Sea, Iceland, E Newfoundland and Grand Banks, Bering Sea, Gulf of Alaska, Sea of Okhotsk; introduced predators, N Pacific; and oil pollution and offshore oil developments in many areas, e.g. Barents Sea, North Sea, Greenland, E Newfoundland and Grand Banks, Scotian Shelf, Alaska S to California, W Bering Sea, Sea of Okhotsk. Immediate conservation requirements include: enhanced monitoring of major colonies, particularly in Greenland, Iceland, Spitsbergen, Russian Arctic and Alaska, where population size and status inadequately known; further development and refinement of census methods to deal with separation of species at large mixed *Uria* colonies, especially in N Pacific; regulation of hunting in E Canada and Greenland; detailed assessment of impacts of overfishing by commercial fisheries in both oceans, particularly of capelin, cod, herring and sandeels in Barents Sea, Iceland, E Newfoundland and Grand Banks, and Bering Sea; continuation and expansion of assessment of by-catch in gill-net fisheries, particularly in NE Atlantic and N Pacific; development of tighter legislation and penalties (national and international) associated with oil pollution from offshore developments and transport, as well as expansion and refinement of monitoring schemes to assess bird mortality; and eradication of alien predators, especially foxes at N Pacific Alaskan and Russian colonies. Population problems and conservation needs similar to *U. aalge*. Overall, main need is rapid reduction of human activities that seriously threaten future of species and health of marine ecosystems.

Bibliography. Armstrong (1983), Bailey (1993a, 1993b), Bédard (1985), Bent (1919), Birkhead (1985b), Birkhead & Harris (1985), Birkhead & Nettleship (1980, 1981, 1982, 1987a, 1987b, 1987c), Bradstreet (1980), Bradstreet & Brown (1985), Brazil (1991), Brown (1985), Brown & Nettleship (1981, 1984a, 1984b), Byrd *et al*. (1993), Cairns & Schneider (1990), Cramp (1985), Croll, Gaston, Burger & Konnoff (1992), Croll, Gaston & Noble (1991), DeGange & Day (1991), Elliot, Collins *et al*. (1991), Elliot, Ryan & Lidster (1990), Evans (1984a, 1984b), Evans & Nettleship (1985), Falk & Durinck (1991, 1992, 1993), Flint *et al*. (1984), Gaston (1980, 1985a, 1985b, 1985c, 1991), Gaston & Bradstreet (1993), Gaston & Elliot (1991), Gaston & Nettleship (1981, 1982), Gaston, Cairns *et al*. (1985), Gaston, de Forest, Donaldson & Noble (1994), Gaston, de Forest, Gilchrist & Nettleship (1993), Golovkin (1984), Harris & Birkhead (1985), Harrison (1982), Hatch (1983), Hudson (1985), Hunt, Burgeson & Sanger (1981), Hunt, Eppley & Schneider (1986), Johnson & Herter (1989), Kampp (1990), Kampp *et al*. (1994), Kessel (1989), Knystautas (1993),

Kondratiev (1991), Kondratiev *et al.* (1993), Lensink (1984), Litvinenko & Shibaev (1991), Manuwal (1984), McGeehan (1996), Mehlum & Bakken (1994), Mehlum & Gabrielsen (1993), Nettleship (1977a, 1977b, 1991a), Nettleship & Evans (1985), Nettleship & Gaston (1978), Ogi *et al.* (1985), Piatt, Hatch *et al.* (1988), Piatt, Lensink *et al.* (1990), Richards (1990), Rodway (1991), Rogacheva (1992), Shuntov (1986), Sowls *et al.* (1978), Spring (1971), Storer (1952), Swartz (1966), Tuck (1961), Uspenski (1956), Vader *et al.* (1990), Vyatkin (1986).

Genus *ALCA* Linnaeus, 1758

4. **Razorbill**

Alca torda

French: Petit Pingouin **German**: Tordalk **Spanish**: Alca Común
Other common names: Razor-billed Auk

Taxonomy. *Alca Torda* Linnaeus, 1758, Stora Karlsö, Baltic Sea.
Populations of E Canada, W Greenland, Norway and Murmansk described as race *pica*, having additional furrow on upper mandible, but not valid as this characteristic now known to be age-related. Two subspecies recognized.
Subspecies and Distribution.
A. t. torda Linnaeus, 1758 - E North America (Digges Sound and SE Baffin S to Gulf of Maine), Greenland and E to Bear I, Norway, Denmark, Baltic Sea region, Murmansk and White Sea.
A. t. islandica C. L. Brehm, 1831 - Iceland, Faeroes, Britain, Ireland E to Helgoland, Channel Is and NW France (Brittany).
Winters mostly offshore and along sea coasts in N part of boreal water zone, S in W Atlantic to Long I (New York), casually to South Carolina and Florida; in E Atlantic, from S Norway and Baltic to W Mediterranean.

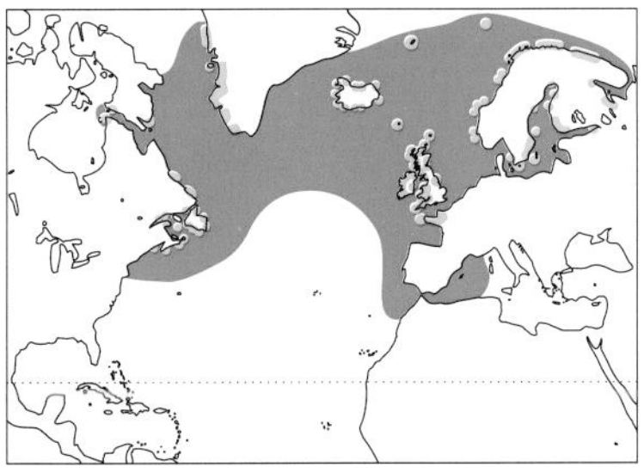

Descriptive notes. 37-39 cm; 524-890 g; wingspan 63-66 cm. Similar to *Uria*, but body and wings average slightly smaller, with head and bill larger, appearing distinctly rectangular; coloration also similar, but normally upperparts darker, dark extends farther onto breast, and thicker bill shows diagnostic markings: broken transverse white line across both mandibles, with prominent white line extending from base of culmen to eye; bill otherwise mostly black, with pronounced transverse ridges or furrows on upper mandible (older birds have more ridges); legs and feet blackish grey, with black claws. Female averages slightly smaller. In winter, throat, cheeks and ear-coverts white; white line between eye and bill absent. Juvenile similar to winter adult, but cheeks, ear-coverts, throat and sides of breast with darkish streaking; transverse white line across bill less distinct. Races based on differences in body size, bill length and depth, and wing length; *islandica* smaller.
Habitat. Marine, occurring offshore and along sea coasts in boreal or low Arctic waters. Breeds in rocky coastal regions on steep mainland cliffs and rocky offshore islands. Winters offshore from breeding areas, often at considerable distances, but normally only to edge of continental shelf, and extending farther S into warmer waters (N cool subtropical zone) than *Uria* species in both W & E Atlantic; in flocks at sea, often mixed with *Uria*, probably owing to similarity of winter diets and patchiness of prey distribution.
Food and Feeding. Mainly fish and crustaceans throughout year. Considerable geographical and temporal variation in principal prey during summer: in Labrador, initially almost 100% fish, mainly capelin (*Mallotus villosus*), whereas during chick-rearing sculpins (*Myxocephalus*) and euphausiids dominate; in Murmansk, diet mainly fish, i.e. (in descending importance) Atlantic herring (*Clupea harengus*), Atlantic cod (*Gadus morhua*), sandeels (*Ammodytes*) and capelin, with small amounts of crustaceans and polychaetes; in White Sea sandeels predominate, followed by capelin and some Atlantic herring. In winter, diet variable, largely fish in Baltic (clupeids, gobies, and fewer garfish, gadids and sticklebacks, 20% crustaceans) and crustaceans in Newfoundland. Chick fed almost exclusively fish, average 2-5 meals/day, usually totalling 20-25 g, generally of species with highest calorific value: in low Arctic waters normally sandeels, with capelin of secondary importance (Labrador, Gulf of St Lawrence, White Sea); at boreal locations mainly sprat (*Sprattus sprattus*), supplemented by young herring and rarely sandeels (Irish Sea, Baltic). Food normally obtained near colony, usually within 15 km, sometimes as close as 2 km, with fish carried crosswise in bill on return flight. Dives normally under 60 seconds to shallow depths, usually 5-7 m, but regularly to 10-15 m, with maximum of 120 m exceptional.
Breeding. Timing variable, with laying earliest at S extremes of range, e.g. Wales from early May; later at higher latitudes where waters colder, e.g. Murmansk mostly early Jun, Labrador mid- to late Jun; timing related more to surface-water temperature than to latitude. Monogamous, with high mate and breeding site fidelity. Loosely colonial, in small to large groups from a few pairs to 100's, infrequently 1000's, usually mixed with other colonial seabird species; normally at relatively low densities owing to nature of breeding habitat. Lays mostly in crevices in boulder fields and rock rubble, but often in rock crevices on cliff faces or exposed ledges; no nest, egg sometimes laid in a rough. 1 egg; incubation averages 35-37 days, by both sexes probably for bouts of c. 12-24 hours; eggs lost early may be replaced after c. 14 days; downy chick mottled brown and buff above, white below with brown-mottled flanks, with much white on head, c. 60 g, semi-precocial; chick-rearing averages c. 18 days (17-19), with care and feeding by both parents until fledging, when adult male accompanies chick to sea; post-fledging parental care at least 3 weeks. Breeding success variable, 62-85% eggs laid producing fledglings, average probably c. 70%, with egg loss greater than chick mortality; timing of breeding, quality of breeding site, and age of female parent all affect success. Adult survival 89-92%; survival of fledglings to breeding age 16-33%. First breeding at 4-5 years.
Movements. Winters mostly offshore at sea, in W Atlantic off E Newfoundland as far as Flemish Cap (c. 700 km offshore), off S Nova Scotia S regularly to North Carolina, and common on Georges Bank off New England. In E Atlantic, movements outside breeding season roughly similar to those of *Uria aalge*, but extends farther S. Overall, N populations move S or SW: Greenland and Labrador birds to offshore E Newfoundland and SW to Gulf of Maine and farther S, those from Barents and White Seas to Skagerrak, like Baltic breeders. N British birds first move to SW Norway and North Sea (young birds later to Bay of Biscay), whereas those from Irish Sea move S to Bay of Biscay and W Mediterranean. Most birds return to colonies from mid-Apr to early May in W Atlantic, except where ice persists longer (e.g. Labrador), and between early Mar and mid-Apr in E Atlantic, though some colonies reoccupied by late Feb or earlier. Dispersal patterns complex, requiring further study of birds at sea outside breeding season on both sides of Atlantic.
Status and Conservation. Not globally threatened. Total breeding population estimated at c. 700,000 pairs (300,000-1,200,000), with roughly 70% in Iceland, 20% in Britain and Ireland, and remainder divided between E (7%) and W (3%) Atlantic. Population sizes and recent changes relatively well known in NW Atlantic, Britain and Ireland and N Europe, less so at centre of breeding range in Iceland. Widespread declines known to have taken place throughout N Atlantic since early 1900's, probably starting in 19th century through human disturbance, particularly egging and hunting. In general, reductions continue in S range, particularly Gulf of St Lawrence, E Newfoundland and Labrador, Greenland, Norway and France, except in British Is, where appears to have increased between 1969/70 and 1985-1987; present status in Iceland and Faeroes uncertain, though decline of 60-75% may have occurred in Faeroes between 1960 and early 1980's. Major threats now are: unregulated hunting, in Labrador, Gulf of St Lawrence, Newfoundland, Greenland, Faeroes and Norway; uncontrolled gill-net fisheries in summer in most of breeding range, and gill-netting of birds on wintering grounds in Kattegat and Iberia; overfishing of important prey species and alteration of marine ecosystems, in Gulf of St Lawrence, E Newfoundland and Grand Banks, Georges Bank, North Sea, Barents Sea; and oil pollution and offshore petroleum developments on both sides of Atlantic, in Barents and North Seas, Greenland, E Newfoundland and Grand Banks, Scotian Shelf. Also vulnerable as 70% of world population concentrated in one area, Iceland; relatively small total population. Most important conservation need is rapid establishment of integrated international monitoring system to measure changes in population size and status in Iceland, British Is, Norway and E North America.
Bibliography. Ashcroft (1976), Bédard (1969c, 1985), Belopol'skii (1957), Bent (1919), Bianki (1967), Birkhead (1985b), Birkhead & Harris (1985), Birkhead & Nettleship (1985), Bradstreet & Brown (1985), Bräger (1995), Brown (1985), Buckley & Buckley (1984b), Cramp (1985), Cramp *et al.* (1974), Dunn (1994), Evans (1984a, 1984b), Evans & Nettleship (1985), Flint *et al.* (1984), Gaston (1985c), Harris & Birkhead (1985), Hudson (1985), Knystautas (1993), Lloyd *et al.* (1991), McGeehan (1996), Nettleship (1977b), Nettleship & Evans (1985), Piatt & Nettleship (1985), Richards (1990), Tasker *et al.* (1987), Urban *et al.* (1986).

Genus *CEPPHUS* Pallas, 1769

5. **Black Guillemot**

Cepphus grylle

French: Guillemot à miroir **German**: Gryllteiste **Spanish**: Arao Aliblanco
Other common names: Tystie

Taxonomy. *Alca Grylle* Linnaeus, 1758, Baltic Sea.
Forms superspecies with *C. columba*. Considerable geographical variation throughout range, with subspecific limits uncertain. Five subspecies recognized.
Subspecies and Distribution.
C. g. mandtii (Mandt, 1822) - Arctic E North America S to Labrador and N Newfoundland, W & E Greenland, Jan Mayen and Svalbard E through E Siberia to N Alaska.
C. g. arcticus (C. L. Brehm, 1824) - North America (S of *mandtii*) and S Greenland to British Is, Norway, SW Sweden, Denmark, Murmansk and White Sea.
C. g. islandicus Hørring, 1937 - Iceland.
C. g. faeroeensis (C. L. Brehm, 1831) - Faeroes.
C. g. grylle (Linnaeus, 1758) - Baltic Sea.
Winters close to breeding area except where water frozen over; casual S to Long I and New Jersey and to N France.

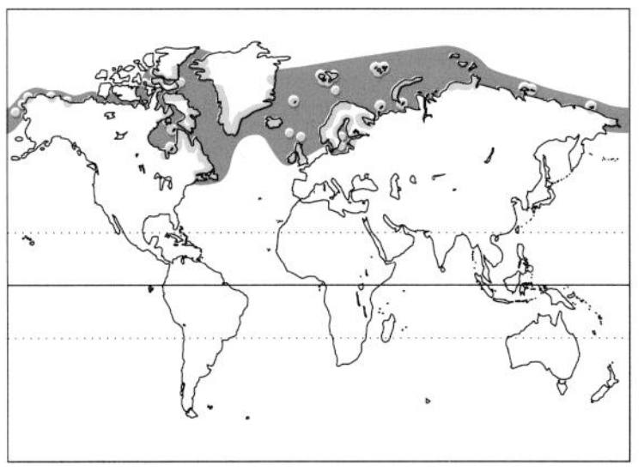

Descriptive notes. 30-32 cm; 450-550 g; wingspan 52-58 cm. Slender, pointed black bill with red mouth-lining; plumage entirely black, except for white upperwing patch and white underwing-coverts; bright vermilion legs and feet; occasional individuals lack white wing patch. Distinguished from *C. columba*, by lack of dark bands in upperwing patch and by whiter underwing. In winter, head and underparts mostly white, with upperparts speckled greyish brown and white. Juvenile resembles winter adult, but has mottled upperwing patch, with brown-tipped coverts. Races based on complex differences in morphometric characters, often quasi-clinal, involving wing length, bill length and depth, and plumage, including amount of white in upperwing.
Habitat. Exclusively marine, rarely in brackish water, along rocky sea cliffs and shores. Breeds in all marine waters N of cool subtropical zone, usually close to areas of shallow water, often at considerable height on cliffs. Mostly pelagic in winter, close to breeding area (except N populations, which are influenced by ice cover), with movements inshore to sheltered waters; some individuals overwinter at high latitudes in polynyas and leads in ice.
Food and Feeding. High diversity of benthic fish and invertebrates, found on or near sea floor in shallow water. Mostly small demersal and pelagic fish, young of larger fish, and vast variety of invertebrates including: polychaetes, pteropods, jellyfish, lamellibranchs, sponges and ctenophores and crustaceans (copepods, amphipods, decapods, euphausiids, isopods and mysids). Winter diet poorly known, probably higher proportion of invertebrates (crustaceans, polychaetes, molluscs) than fish overall. Chick diet largely fish, except in high Arctic regions, where crustaceans can comprise 25-30% (by weight) of diet: normally, blennies (Pholidae, Strichaeidae, Zoarcidae), gobies (Gobiidae), sculpins (Cottidae), Arctic cod (*Boreogadus saida*) and sea snails (Cyclopteridae) predominate in Arctic regions, and sandeels (*Ammodytes*) at boreal locations, less frequently clupeids, osmerids, rockfish (Scorpaenidae), flatfish (Pleuronectidae) and wrasse (Labridae). Chick-feeding rates widely variable, from averages of 3 meals/day (Barents Sea) to 7-15 (White Sea), 5·3-14 (SW Finland) to 15 (Iceland) and 12·4 (Gulf of St Lawrence). Feeds mainly inshore, during summer usually within 4 km of breeding site, sometimes farther. Diving times average 25-40 seconds, with maxima of 75-146 seconds exceptional, to depths of normally less than 20 m.
Breeding. Median laying usually between late May and mid-Jun, sometimes earlier (N Norway) or later (Spitsbergen, Franz Josef Land, Novaya Zemlya) owing to water characteristics; fledging mostly Aug. Monogamous, with high mate and site fidelity; annual divorce rate 5-7%. Normally breeds at low density in small scattered groups of 5-100 pairs, or singly; in N of range some groups large, exceeding

1000 pairs. Lays in rough scrape at back of crevices and cavities in cliff face, scree slopes and boulder fields; often at considerable height on cliffs. 2 eggs, sometimes 1; incubation averages 28-32 days (1st eggs 31 days, 2nd eggs 28 days), by both sexes for shifts of several hours; early egg losses may be replaced after c. 15 days; downy chick blackish brown, slightly paler below, c. 40 g, semi-precocial; chick-rearing averages 34-39 days (30-40), with care and food provisioning shared by parents until fledging, when chicks fly out to sea unaccompanied. Breeding success variable within and between breeding locations, overall averages 66% for hatching and 68% for fledging; mean annual productivity (fledged young/pair) varies from 0-0·6 (Finland, Denmark) to 0·7-0·9 (Bay of Fundy, Gulf of St Lawrence, Prince Leopold I) and 1·2-1·6 (Iceland, White Sea). Main causes of egg and chick loss are predation, mostly by introduced mink (*Mustela vison*) and rats (*Rattus*), adverse weather and flooding of breeding sites, and starvation. Adult survival 81-87%; survival of fledglings to breeding age 16-32%. First breeding usually at 4 years, sometimes 2 or 3.

Movements. Resident and mostly sedentary except in N regions, where movement to adjacent ice-free waters occurs. In general, winter distribution of adults essentially as breeding, with concentrations at traditional locations to moult, usually in sheltered waters near colony, where they spend winter. Fledglings often move considerable distances from natal sites, usually in direction of prevailing sea currents; reasons for their long distance dispersal unclear. Overall, dispersal patterns of the various populations poorly known, particularly in remote and inaccessible regions; better known in S of range, e.g. N Britain.

Status and Conservation. Not globally threatened. Breeding population size unknown, but conservative estimate in 1985 of 270,000 pairs (200,000-350,000) with largest numbers in N, including 50,000 in E Canadian Arctic, 40,000 in Greenland and 50,000 in Iceland. Most breeding groups small, but large colonies known in high Arctic, e.g. 4000 pairs on Prince Leopold I and 10,000 pairs at Skruis Point (Devon I). Population sizes and trends only poorly known. Species relatively difficult to census owing to low breeding density and colony-attendance patterns; inter-year count comparisons therefore difficult, and often unreliable. Current status in Arctic regions unknown; farther S, declines recorded in W Norway and E Canada since mid-1930's, though stable or increasing at S edge of range in British Is (Irish Sea, Firth of Clyde) and NE USA (New England). Wide distribution and dispersal patterns safeguard the species from human disturbance, but local impacts from introduced predators (e.g. mink, rats), oil spills, and commercial gill-net fishing can be serious.

Bibliography. Andersen-Harild (1969), Armstrong (1983), Asbirk (1979), Bédard (1985), Belopol'skii (1957), Bent (1919), Bergman (1971, 1978), Bianki (1967), Birkhead (1985b), Birkhead & Harris (1985), Bradstreet (1976, 1977, 1980), Bradstreet & Brown (1985), Bräger (1995), Brown (1985), Buckley & Buckley (1984b), Cairns, D.K. (1978, 1980, 1981, 1982, 1987a, 1987b), Cramp (1985), Divoky *et al.* (1974), Drury (1973-1974), Evans (1984a, 1984b), Evans & Nettleship (1985), Ewins (1985a, 1986, 1988a, 1988b, 1990, 1992), Ewins & Kirk (1988), Ewins & Tasker (1985), Flint *et al.* (1984), Gaston (1985c, 1991), Gaston & McLaren (1990), Greenwood (1987), Harris & Birkhead (1985), Hudson (1985), Knystautas (1993), Kondratiev (1991), Lensink (1984), Lloyd *et al.* (1991), MacLean & Verbeek (1968), Manuwal (1984), Mayr & Short (1970), Nettleship (1974a), Nettleship & Evans (1985), Nettleship & Smith (1975), Petersen (1979, 1981, 1994), Piatt & Nettleship (1985), Preston (1968), Richards (1990), Rogacheva (1992), Salomonsen (1944, 1979a, 1979b), Storer (1952), Tasker *et al.* (1987), Winn (1950).

6. Pigeon Guillemot
Cepphus columba

French: Guillemot colombin   **German**: Taubenteiste   **Spanish**: Arao Colombino
Other common names: Sea Pigeon

Taxonomy. *Cepphus Columba* Pallas, 1811, Kamchatka and Bering Strait.
Forms superspecies with *C. grylle*. Race *snowi* sometimes considered a megasubspecies. Five subspecies recognized.
Subspecies and Distribution.
C. c. columba Pallas, 1811 - Kamchatka N to Bering Strait and W Alaska.
C. c. snowi Stejneger, 1897 - Kuril Is.
C. c. kaiurka Portenko, 1937 - Commander Is to WC Aleutian Is.
C. c. adianta Storer, 1950 - C Aleutian Is S to Washington.
C. c. eureka Storer, 1950 - Oregon and California.
Winters mostly at sea and along coasts, from S Bering Sea and S Alaska S to Japan and S California.

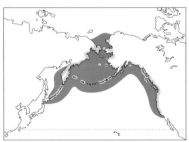

Descriptive notes. 30-37 cm; 450-550 g. Bill long, straight and pointed, black with bright red mouth-lining; dark blackish brown plumage, with dark brown wedge in white upperwing patch, and dusky grey underwing; legs and feet vermilion, claws black. In winter, upperparts greyish with white barring, underparts mostly white. Juvenile similar to winter adult, with white wing patch often obscured. Races based largely on trends in morphometric characters, with culmen and wing lengths decreasing from S to N (except in Bering Sea and Siberia) and white in outer primary and underwing-coverts increasing; *snowi* commonly has white in upperwing reduced or absent.

Habitat. In summer along rocky coastlines, breeding on sea cliffs and slopes close to regions of shallow water usually less than 50 m deep. Along rocky sea coasts in winter, often in sheltered coves; leads and openings in ice used regularly in Bering Sea and S Alaska.
Food and Feeding. Wide variety of small benthic fish and invertebrates (shrimp, crabs, sometimes polychaetes, gastropods, bivalve molluscs) throughout year; winter diet more diverse. Chicks usually fed fish, predominantly sandeels (*Ammodytes*), herring (Clupeidae), gadids, gunnels/pricklebacks (Xiphisteridae, Lumpenidae), eelpouts (Zoarcidae), sculpin (Cottidae), rockfish (Scorpaenidae), and flatfish (Bothidae, Pleuronectidae), usually obtained within 1 km of colony; provisioning rate varies with brood size and age, average 0·7-1·9 fish/hour/nest in Alaska and British Columbia. Dive times 10-144 seconds, optimal efficiency in water depths of 10-20 m.
Breeding. Normally arrives early Mar in California, Apr in British Columbia, 40-50 days before first eggs; peak laying mid-May to mid-Jun in California and British Columbia, 1-2 weeks later in Alaska. Monogamous, with high mate (probably) and site fidelity. Usually in small colonies of under 50 birds, sometimes as single pairs; concentrations of over 1000 birds exceptional. Nests in crevices and cavities on cliffs, talus slopes and rock rubble, sometimes excavating burrow. Usually 2 eggs; incubation averages 29 days (29-32) for 1st and single eggs, 27 days (26-32) for 2nd eggs, by both sexes in shifts of 2-4 hours (up to 17); downy chick blackish brown, c. 38 g, semi-precocial; chick-rearing averages c. 38 days (30-53), with care and feeding by both parents; chicks independent at fledging, when they fly to sea alone. Breeding success and annual productivity highly variable between years, 0·2-1·5 fledglings/pair. Adult survival averages 80% (76-89%); survival of fledglings to breeding age c. 40%. First breeding usually at 4 years, sometimes 3, rarely earlier.

Movements. Spring and autumn migrations poorly known, as are details of winter range. Generally winters at sea and along coast from Pribilofs and Aleutians (Bering Sea) S to N Japan (Hokkaido) and S California. Most birds from British Columbia, Washington, Oregon and Kuril Is remain near breeding grounds during winter; those from California and Alaska move N and S, respectively. Main migration periods likely Oct and Mar.
Status and Conservation. Not globally threatened. Population size estimated at c. 235,000 birds (1993), with largest numbers on Farallon Is (California) and Chukotskiy Peninsula. Local populations vulnerable to oil pollution, drowning in gill-nets, and introduction of mammalian predators to colonies; widespread distribution believed to offset local threats. Vulnerability to oil considered high, but impact on population size and breeding unclear. Numbers reduced in parts of California by oil pollution and human disturbance, also by food shortages in warm-water years in California and Oregon; relatively stable elsewhere, except for Prince William Sound, Alaska, where steady decline in breeding birds has occurred since 1972 from unknown causes but also from Exxon Valdez oil spill in 1989. Inshore gill-net fisheries can cause significant local mortality, as can introduced mammalian predators on islands. Status of NW Pacific population unknown.
Bibliography. Ainley & Boekelheide (1990), Ainley & Lewis (1972, 1974), Armstrong (1983), Bent (1919), Brazil (1991), Drent (1965), Emms (1987), Emms & Morgan (1989), Emms & Verbeek (1989, 1991), Ewins (1993), Ewins *et al.* (1993), Follet & Ainley (1976), Gould *et al.* (1982), Hodder & Graybill (1985), King (1984), King & Sanger (1979), Knystautas (1993), Koelink (1972), Kondratiev (1991), Lehnhausen (1980), Lensink (1984), Litvinenko & Shibaev (1991), Manuwal (1984), Mayr & Short (1970), Nelson (1982, 1987, 1991), Oakley (1981), Page *et al.* (1990), Piatt, Lensink *et al.* (1990), Richards (1990), Rodway (1991), Sowls *et al.* (1978), Storer (1950, 1952), Thoresen (1989), Thoresen & Booth (1958), Trapp (1985), Vermeer, Briggs *et al.* (1993), Vermeer, Morgan & Smith (1993a, 1993b).

7. Spectacled Guillemot
Cepphus carbo

French: Guillemot à lunettes   **German**: Brillenteiste   **Spanish**: Arao de Anteojos
Other common names: Sooty/Bridled Guillemot

Taxonomy. *Cepphus Carbo* Pallas, 1811, Kuril Islands.
Monotypic.
Distribution. Coasts and islands of NW Pacific, from Kamchatka and Sea of Okhotsk S to NE Korea, Kuril Is, and N Japan (Hokkaido, N Honshu). In winter, pelagic and coastal, usually near breeding locations and somewhat farther S.

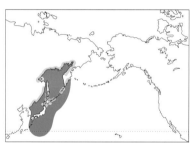

Descriptive notes. c. 38 cm; 490 g; wingspan 65·5-69 cm. Largest of *Cepphus* guillemots, plump and grebe-like, with long, thick neck and relatively short, robust, pointed black bill; dull sooty blackish brown, with conspicuous white "spectacle" patch around eye and small whitish area at base of bill; legs and feet red. In winter, crown mottled grey and white and underparts mostly white. Juvenile similar to non-breeding adult, but with brownish black cross-bars on underparts.
Habitat. Exclusively marine; near-shore, breeding along rocky mainland coasts in cliffs or on slopes and boulder fields, or in more accessible sites on predator-free islands; most breeding sites close to shallow water suitable for foraging in food-rich areas of vegetated or rocky benthos. In winter mostly pelagic, along coasts.
Food and Feeding. Chick diet largely fish, with wide diversity of benthic species, sardines (*Sardinops*) and herring (Clupeidae), plus a few invertebrates. Adult diet probably similar; winter diet of adults and juveniles little known. Feeds mainly inshore along coast, usually close to breeding area; in summer, adults forage in shallow water (15-20 m) and tidal rifts and races, usually within 6 km of breeding site.
Breeding. Less known than any other alcid species. Timing uncertain: most birds probably arrive Apr-May; laying probably begins mid-May, with hatching mid-Jun to early Jul; fledglings not seen at sea before 2nd week of Aug. Believed monogamous, with mate and site fidelity similar to other *Cepphus*. Breeds usually in groups of 10-20 pairs, sometimes as single pairs, and rarely in large colonies of 200-300 pairs. Lays in cliff crevices, in holes and cavities in scree slopes and boulder fields, or in more accessible sites on predator-free islands; in S Ussuriland many nests found among boulders 1·5-20 m above high water line, with fewer in cliff crevices or under shrubs and tree roots up to 120 m from sea, whereas at Teuri I over 60% of nests more than 20 m above sea-level. Normally 2 eggs, sometimes 1; incubation averages c. 28 days (possibly 30-33), by both sexes, length of shifts unknown; chick c. 40 g, semi-precocial; chick-rearing period uncertain, but 1 chick fledged at 33 days. Breeding performance and annual productivity not known, probably low. Eggs and small chicks taken by Large-billed Crows (*Corvus macrorhynchos*), Common Ravens (*Corvus corax*) and Slaty-backed Gulls (*Larus schistisagus*), adults sometimes by Northern Eagle-owls (*Bubo bubo*) and Peregrine Falcons (*Falco peregrinus*); introduced predators, especially foxes (*Alopex lagopus*, *Vulpes vulpes*), sable (*Martes zibellina*, *Lamprogale flavigula*, *Kolnocus sibirica*), and rats (*Rattus*) can cause colony to be abandoned. Survival rates and age at first breeding unknown.
Movements. Resident and mostly sedentary, remaining in vicinity of colony, except in N areas. Pronounced movement from Peter the Great Bay in Aug and Sept (to moulting areas?), and most Sea of Okhotsk birds are forced S by ice formation, usually by early Dec; influx into Sea of Japan in early Sept believed to be related to N exodus. Also S movement along coasts of Japan in winter, probably mostly juveniles. In spring, reverse movement of adults probably complete by late Apr, with immatures arriving later. Winter distribution and movements little known.
Status and Conservation. Not globally threatened. Approaching near-threatened status. Conservative rough estimate in 1993 gives total breeding population of 71,000-74,000 pairs, with 89% in Sea of Okhotsk and remainder in Sea of Japan. Largest known concentrations at Shantarsky Is (18,000-20,000 pairs), Peter the Great Bay (c. 5500 pairs), and Matykyl I (c. 4000 pairs). Limits of breeding range reasonably well known, but in numerous parts of Sea of Okhotsk and W Kamchatka breeding is only suspected and requires confirmation. Overall, the least numerous inshore-feeding alcid in N Pacific. Population decreasing, and marked declines recorded recently at several locations: 10-20% annual reductions at colonies around Hokkaido; 93% decline at Teuri I in period 1963-1987; and 53% decrease on Furugelm I since 1979. Causes of declines uncertain, but introduced mammalian predators (foxes, sable, rats) and reductions in forage fish stocks seem likely factors; human disturbance of breeding habitat and illegal hunting may also be involved. Offshore oil developments in Sea of Okhotsk pose additional threat. Immediate conservation needs: systematic surveys early in season (pre-breeding) to assess distribution and size of breeding populations; post-breeding surveys to identify locations of moult concentrations of flightless birds; and initiation of colony and at-sea studies to determine species' ecological requirements throughout year.

Bibliography. Austin (1948), Brazil (1991), Dementiev & Gladkov (1951b), Elsukov (1984), Étchécopar & Hüe (1978), Ewins *et al.* (1993), Flint *et al.* (1984), Gizenko (1955), Hasegawa (1984), Knystautas (1993), Kondratiev (1991), Kozlova (1957), Litvinenko & Shibaev (1991), Nazarov & Labzyuk (1972), Nechaev (1986), Roslyakov (1986), Shibaev (1987), Shuntov (1986), Storer (1952), Thoresen (1984), Udvardy (1963), Velizhanin (1969, 1975, 1977), Vyatkin (1986), Vyshkvartsev & Lebedev (1986), Watanuki *et al.* (1988).

Genus *BRACHYRAMPHUS* M. Brandt, 1837

8. Marbled Murrelet

Brachyramphus marmoratus

French: Guillemot marbré **German**: Marmelalk **Spanish**: Mérgulo Jaspeado
Other common names: Long-billed Murrelet

Taxonomy. *Colymbus marmoratus* Gmelin, 1789, Prince William Sound, Alaska.
Recent work suggests race *perdix* may be distinct species, but evidence incomplete and further examination required. Two subspecies recognized.
Subspecies and Distribution.
B. m. perdix (Pallas, 1811) - Kamchatka and Sea of Okhotsk S to N Japan (Hokkaido).
B. m. marmoratus (Gmelin, 1789) - W Aleutians (Attu I) to Barren Is and SE Alaska, S to C California (Santa Cruz Mts).
Winters mainly offshore and along coasts near and somewhat S of breeding grounds.

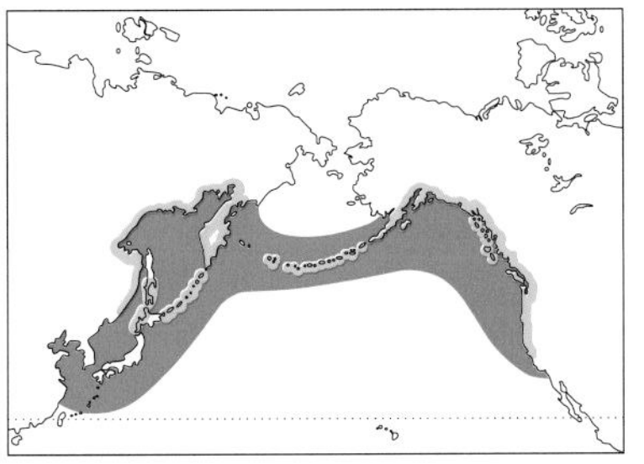

Descriptive notes. 24-26 cm; 220 g (196-269 g). Chunky alcid with slender, pointed blackish bill, and blackish brown iris; dusky dark brown crown and upperparts, back feathers tipped with rusty brown; entire underparts mottled brown and white, sometimes forming indistinct brownish breast band; legs and feet flesh-coloured, with darker webs. Distinguished from *B. brevirostris* by longer bill, more uniform upperparts and darker belly. Winter adult blackish above, with black cap extending below eye (unlike *B. brevirostris*), narrow white band from cheeks around nape, white scapular patches; underparts mainly white. Immature similar to winter adult, but white underparts finely streaked dusky brown. Race *perdix* larger (c. 50-70 g heavier), with markedly longer bill and wing; in summer plumage, lacks rusty brown tones above, and outermost rectrix has narrow white marginal stripe (lacking in nominate race).
Habitat. Pelagic and along sea coasts, in summer usually offshore from coniferous forests along mainland coast and islands. Breeds in old-growth and late successional coniferous forests, usually within 60 km of coast, with western hemlock (*Tsuga heterophylla*), Sitka spruce (*Picea sitchensis*) and Douglas fir (*Pseudotsuga menziesii*) the most important nest trees; less frequently on bare ground, usually on inland slopes, in boreal tundra regions along sea coasts (e.g. NW Gulf of Alaska). At sea, found inshore to offshore as widely spaced pairs or in flocks associated with ocean processes such as upwellings, converging currents and river plumes. In winter, mostly inshore in sheltered and productive coastal waters within or adjacent to breeding range; also uses coastal lakes year round.
Food and Feeding. Adult diet normally invertebrates, especially euphausiid crustaceans (*Thysanoessa spinifera*), from Mar to early Jun, with fish predominating through rest of breeding season, primarily sandeels (*Ammodytes hexapterus*) supplemented by herring (*Clupea harengus*), capelin (*Mallotus villosus*), shiner perch (*Cymatogaster aggregata*) and small quantities of other Osmeridae, Scorpaenidae and Stichaeidae; autumn and winter diet poorly known, but crustaceans probably dominate through winter, with fish (including rockfish, herring, sandeels) of secondary importance. Chick fed almost exclusively fish, principally sandeels, sometimes herring, capelin and anchovy; 1-8 meals/day (mean 3·2), mostly at low-light dawn and dusk periods. Food usually obtained singly or in pairs, rarely in groups, usually close to breeding site (up to 10 km offshore) in shallow waters at depths of less than 30 m.
Breeding. Breeding season longer and less synchronous than in other alcid species, with laying and incubation in North America from late Mar to late Aug, and chick-rearing from late Apr to 3rd week Sept; breeding season length increases N to S, c. 110 days in Alaska to c. 180 days in California. Probably monogamous, with high breeding site and mate fidelity. Non-colonial; single pairs at low density in mature forests. Usually lays on platform of moss- and lichen-covered branches or limbs of old-growth conifers at variable heights in lower canopy, less frequently (under 5%) on ground; infrequently on bare ground in tundra regions, usually on inland slopes. 1 egg; incubation 27-30 days, by both sexes for 24-hour periods, with change-overs immediately before sunrise, rarely at dusk; downy chick yellowish with dark brown-black spots above, pale grey on belly, 33 g, semi-precocial; chick-rearing period 27-40 days, with parental care and feeding by both sexes until fledging, when chick flies directly from nest to sea unaccompanied. Breeding success relatively low, c. 30%, with unusually high chick mortality. Survival rates, longevity, and age of first breeding unknown.
Movements. Seasonal post-breeding movements poorly known. Most birds move from exposed coasts into sheltered productive inshore waters, usually near breeding area, where they often occur in large aggregations. Important wintering areas include Kodiak Archipelago, Strait of Georgia, E Puget Sound and Grays Harbor channel; little known of movements or winter concentrations along coastal Oregon and California. Russian population appears more migratory, deserting breeding areas in Sept and Oct, moving into S parts of Sea of Okhotsk during winter; some may overwinter off Sakhalin, but most migrate S to Japan (Hokkaido, Honshu), returning to breeding sites early to late May.
Status and Conservation. Not globally threatened. Currently considered near-threatened. Total breeding populations estimated at c. 300,000 individuals in North America, 85% of which along coasts of Gulf of Alaska and in Prince William Sound, and probably 50,000-100,000 birds in E Russia (based on limited quantitative at-sea observations). Most serious threat is rapid removal of old-growth forest habitat throughout breeding range; also known to incur substantial mortality at sea by drowning in gill-nets and from oil pollution. Population size small and vulnerable, with declines recorded or suspected throughout range (presently c. 3-5% per annum in Alaska and British Columbia), with possible 50% decrease in Alaska in period 1972-1992. Cumulative effects of logging of breeding habitat, gill-netting and oil pollution probably prime causes of reduction; impact of declining forage-fish populations in Gulf of Alaska and elsewhere may also be involved. Forming of large aggregations during winter, often in regions with high oil-tanker traffic, places species at considerable risk. Management plans proposed by Marbled Murrelet Conservation Assessment Core Team must be implemented immediately in order to: ensure adequate nesting habitat; eliminate human activities responsible for current high adult mortality; and minimize loss of nest contents to predators.
Bibliography. Ainley & Hunt (1991), Ainley *et al.* (1995), Armstrong (1983), Bent (1919), Binford *et al.* (1975), Brazil (1991), Burger (1995), Carter (1984), Carter & Erickson (1992), Carter & Morrison (1992), Carter & Sealy (1986, 1987, 1990), Day *et al.* (1983), DeSanto & Nelson (1995), Ehrlich *et al.* (1992), Étchécopar & Hüe (1978), Flint *et al.* (1984), Ford & Brown (1995), Hamer & Cummins (1995), Hasegawa (1984), Hobson (1990), Irvine (1996), Johnsgard (1987), Johnson & Carter (1985), Kaiser *et al.* (1994), Kiff (1981), Knystautas (1993), Kondratiev (1991), Konyukhov & Kitaysky (1995), Lensink (1984), Leschner & Cummins (1992), Litvinenko & Shibaev (1991), Manuwal (1984), Mendenhall (1992), Naslund (1993), Nelson & Hamer (1995), Nelson *et al.* (1992), Page *et al.* (1990), Paton *et al.* (1992), Piatt & Ford (1993), Piatt & Naslund (1995), Quinlan & Hughes (1990, 1992), Ralph (1994), Ralph *et al.* (1995), Rodway (1991), Rodway, Carter *et al.* (1992), Rodway, Regehr & Savard (1993), Sealy (1975a, 1975b), Sealy & Carter (1984), Sealy *et al.* (1991), Simons (1980), Singer *et al.* (1991), Speich & Wahl (1995), Speich *et al.* (1992), Thoresen (1989).

9. Kittlitz's Murrelet

Brachyramphus brevirostris

French: Guillemot de Kittlitz **German**: Kurzschnabelalk **Spanish**: Mérgulo Piquicorto
Other common names: Short-billed Murrelet

Taxonomy. *Uria brevirostris* Vigors, 1829, San Blas, Mexico; error = North Pacific.
Monotypic.
Distribution. Bering Sea coasts N into Chukchi Sea and S to Gulf of Alaska: in Russia probably limited to E Chukotskiy Peninsula in Chukchi Sea W to Cape Schmidta and S to Anadyr Gulf, as well as Shelekhov Bay in N Sea of Okhotsk; in Alaska from just E of Cape Lisburne S to Aleutians and E to Glacier Bay and Stileine R (Gulf of Alaska). Winters mainly offshore near breeding area, from E Siberia and Kuril Is S to N Japan (Hokkaido), and from Aleutians E to Glacier Bay.

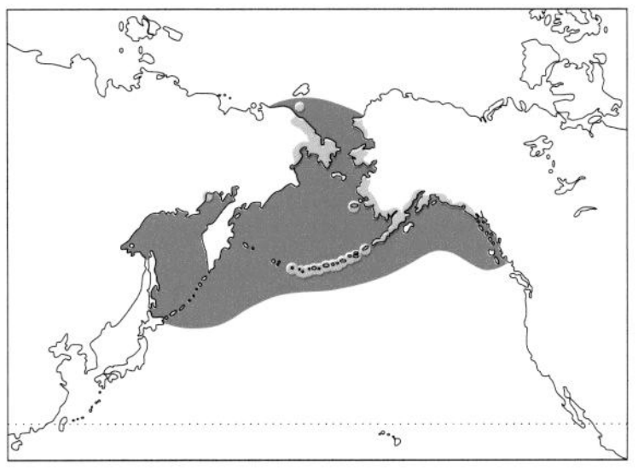

Descriptive notes. 22-23 cm; 224 g. Small alcid with short brownish bill, and darkish brown iris; brown to darkish brown upperparts mottled buff and white (cryptic sandy brown), merging into largely white belly; dark brown to black tail, with outer edges of feathers white; legs and feet brownish. In winter, largely blackish grey above, with black cap which ends well above eye (unlike *B. marmoratus*); white-fringed scapulars; face, throat and underparts mainly white, with dark patch in front of eye. Juvenile similar to winter adult, but with fine barring on face, neck, underparts and tail.
Habitat. Neritic, usually along rocky sea coasts. In summer, associated with coastal (sometimes inland) mountains and slopes in alpine tundra, glaciers and glacial moraines, breeding on mountain scree slopes, often 0·5-75 km (average c. 16 km) from coast. Winter habitats poorly known, but species thought to winter usually offshore from S parts of breeding range, particularly over banks and along coasts from SE Siberia S to Kuril Is and in SE Alaska.
Food and Feeding. In summer feeds primarily on sandeels (*Ammodytes hexapterus*), capelin (*Mallotus villosus*), herring (*Clupea harengus*), smelt (Osmeridae) and Pacific sandfish (*Trichodon trichodon*), supplemented by euphausiids, gammarid amphipods, and shrimps. Chick diet unknown, probably similar to that of adult in summer. Food habits in winter poorly known, probably planktonic crustaceans and small fish; displays patchy distribution, and concentrates in large flocks of up to 500 birds at food-rich locations, e.g. gatherings over Fairweather Bank (SE Alaska) in Apr totalling 1000's of birds. In summer, forages mainly inshore, in bays and inlets, often concentrated at glacier outfalls and heads of fjords; in Chukchi Sea, up to c. 60 km offshore once ice recedes.
Breeding. Information extremely limited, only 22 nests known (1995). Timing of breeding varies markedly through range, with start of laying c. 1 month later at northernmost locations than those in S: mid-May to mid-Jun in SE Alaska, late May to mid-Jun in S coastal Alaska, early to mid-Jun in Aleutians and Sea of Okhotsk, mid-Jun in Bering Sea, and mid-Jun to late Jun in Chukchi Sea; fledging from mid-Jul to early Aug (SE Alaska) to mid-Aug (Chukchi Sea). Probably monogamous, with behaviour and reproductive patterns similar to *B. marmoratus*; site fidelity possibly high, mate retention unknown. Non-colonial; usually isolated pairs at low densities on unvegetated mountain scree slopes, often at high elevations (mean 570 m). Lays on rock ledge, in crevice, or usually in depression on bare gravelly substrate at base of moderately sized rock (0·3-0·5 m diameter), near top of ridge or summit. 1 egg; incubation period unknown, probably c. 30 days; downy chick buffy-yellow with black spotting above, grey breast and pale grey belly, semi-precocial; chick-rearing 24 days (only 1 record), with both parents at nest delivering food; most fledglings fly directly from breeding site to sea, with post-fledging parental care unlikely. Productivity, survival rates and age of first breeding unknown.
Movements. Post-breeding dispersal into bays and fjords of Prince William Sound occurs late Jul and Aug. Migratory movements limited, most birds in Bering Sea and E Pacific remaining within breeding range; only small numbers from N regions (Chukchi Sea, N Bering Sea) move SW past Kamchatka Peninsula to N Kuril Is and SE to Gulf of Alaska, with few stragglers to N Japan and California. Winter distribution poorly known, but spring influx and initiation of breeding in Chukchi Sea area by mid-Jun is c. 4 weeks later than at S & SE Alaskan coastal locations; some birds push N in leads in ice by late Apr, most later, but normally on site and displaying at Cape Lisburne by Jun.
Status and Conservation. Not globally threatened. Total population size poorly known, but believed to be much smaller than that of *B. marmoratus* (based on summer pelagic count statistics); probably 30,000-130,000 birds, of which at least 70% in Alaska. Information on present status very limited, though small population size alone makes species highly vulnerable to marine pollution and activities of commercial fisheries. Alaskan numbers believed relatively stable up to early 1980's (based upon qualitative indicators), uncertain thereafter owing to possibility of significant mortality from oil spills (Exxon Valdez), commercial gill-net fisheries, and offshore oil developments. Threats at sea similar to those for *B. marmoratus*. Much additional research and survey effort required, particularly along W Pacific coast, to delineate breeding range in NE Russia, and during autumn and winter to identify biological "hot spots". Census methods need to be developed and a monitoring system established to assess population trends throughout range, as well as a major study programme to determine species' basic ecological characteristics and requirements.
Bibliography. Armstrong (1983), Bailey (1973), Bent (1919), Brazil (1991), Day (1995, 1996), Day *et al.* (1983), DeGange *et al.* (1993), Dementiev & Gladkov (1951b), Ewins *et al.* (1993), Flint *et al.* (1984), Forsell & Gould (1981), Fox & Hall (1982), Gabrielson & Lincoln (1959), Gould *et al.* (1982), Harrison (1978), Johnsgard (1987), King & Sanger (1979), Knystautas (1993), Kondratiev (1986, 1991), Kozlova (1957), Lensink (1984), Manuwal (1984), Naslund *et al.* (1994), Piatt, Naslund & van Pelt (1994), Piatt, Lensink *et al.* (1990), Piatt, Wells *et al.* (1991), Portenko (1972), Sanger (1986, 1987), Sowls *et al.* (1978).

ssp *scrippsi*

ssp *hypoleucus*

10

11

12

13

14

15

16

17

18

19

20

21

22

PLATE 60

inches 5
cm 13

Genus *SYNTHLIBORAMPHUS* M. Brandt, 1837

10. **Xantus's Murrelet**

Synthliboramphus hypoleucus

French: Guillemot de Xantus **German**: Lummenalk **Spanish**: Mérgulo Californiano Aliclaro
Other common names: Scripps's Murrelet (*scrippsi*)

Taxonomy. *Brachyramphus hypoleucus* Xántus de Vesey, 1860, Cape San Lucas, Baja California.
Sometimes placed in *Brachyramphus*. Both races sympatric with closely related *S. craveri* at San Benito Is (Baja California), where further study required to determine degree of mixing and gene exchange; may be conspecific with *S. craveri*. Race *scrippsi* sometimes considered a separate species. Two subspecies recognized.
Subspecies and Distribution.
S. h. scrippsi Green & Arnold, 1939 - S Californian Channel Is and islands off W coast of Baja California S to at least San Benito Is.
S. h. hypoleucus (Xántus de Vesey, 1860) - NW Baja California (San Benito Is, Guadalupe I); status uncertain on Santa Barbara I, Channel Is, in S California.
Winters from area of breeding colonies N up Pacific coast to S British Columbia and S to S tip of Baja California, mainly inshore.

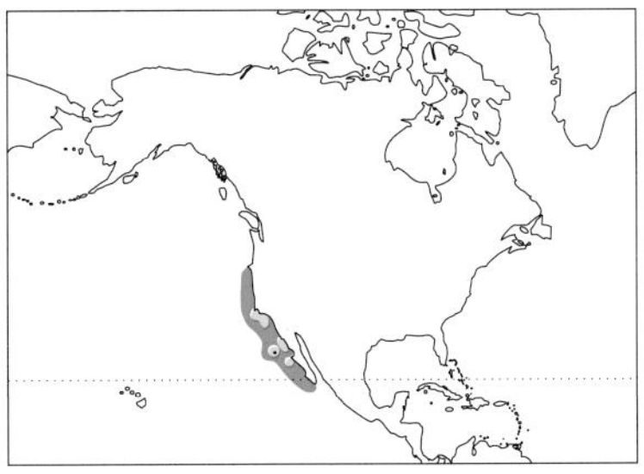

Descriptive notes. 23-25 cm; mean 148-167 g (130-215 g); wingspan c. 40 cm. Small auk with short, slender black bill; black upperparts with faint greyish cast, including top of head, neck, back, wings and tail; prominent white crescents above and below eye, meeting white of throat; mostly snowy white underparts, with flanks varying from white to mottled grey and white; legs and feet bluish grey, with black webs and claws. Female usually significantly larger than male in culmen, wing chord and weight (averages 11 g heavier), but not bill depth or tarsus length. In winter, often paler greyish black above due to feather wear. Juvenile similar to adult, but with scattered dark barring along flanks. Race *scrippsi* differs in having eye-crescents only very indistinct; suspected clinal variation in bill size, shorter and deeper in N.
Habitat. Offshore and along sea coasts, occupying warmer waters than all alcids except *S. craveri*. Breeds on steep sea cliffs, slopes and canyons on islands. Winters primarily well offshore, with most of population in warm pelagic waters of California Current (14-16°C, off Washington and Oregon), rarely seen inshore where colder waters occur; major concentrations found 20-100 km offshore, usually over deep water, though regularly in small numbers up to 200 km offshore. Pelagic distribution probably determined by relative abundance of small pelagic schooling fish.
Food and Feeding. Mainly larval fish and other small prey. During breeding, mainly larval fish, especially northern anchovies (*Engraulis mordax*) on Santa Barbara I, and also Pacific saury (*Cololabis saira*) and rockfish (*Sebastes*); also sandeels (*Ammodytes*) and crustaceans. Feeds usually within 2-14 km of colony island, with highest numbers over shelf waters (40-100 m deep). Chicks precocial, not fed at nest but fed at sea; diet unknown, likely small fish similar to those eaten by adults. In non-breeding season, occurs in warm waters in association with schooling fish, especially Pacific saury and albacore tuna (*Thunnus alalunga*).
Breeding. Appears on sea near colonies mid- to late Dec, first landing mid-Feb, c. 3 weeks before first laying. Nocturnal at colony; laying asynchronous and variable between years, late Feb to mid-Jun, usual peak from late Mar to mid-Apr (Santa Barbara I), slightly later farther S (Guadalupe I); most hatching late Apr to mid-May. Probably monogamous, with high mate and nest-site fidelity. Breeds mostly in small colonies and at low densities, possibly determined by patchy distribution of suitable nesting habitat: rock crevices, caves, burrows and shrubs. Lays in back of small (usually under 1 m long) dark cave or crevice in cliff, or under boulder, rarely at shallow depth or exposed; sometimes on bare ground under dense vegetation, especially on maritime sandy slopes. 2 eggs, with laying interval 8 days (5-12); incubation from 2nd egg, averages 34 days (27-44), by both sexes equally with shifts averaging 3 days (1-6); hatching synchronous; downy chick c. 25 g, black above and white below (adult pattern), with foot almost as large as adult's; chick mobile soon after hatching, brooded but not fed for 1-2 days, then taken by parents at night to sea, where family immediately swims away from colony, often 10 km or more offshore; young can undergo partial hypothermia during at least 1st week of life, but details of parental care at sea and time to independence not known. Breeding effort and performance lower when anchovy abundance low. Nesting success (nests fledging at least 1 young) averaged 57% (27-75%) at Santa Barbara I (1983-1993), with annual productivity 0·72 chicks fledged/clutch (0·3-1·36). Prime cause of egg loss is predation by deer mice (*Peromyscus maniculatus*). Survival and age of first breeding unknown, probably similar to congeners.
Movements. Post-breeding dispersal from nesting islands Apr or May (sometimes late Mar or Jul), largely offshore to W, and to N; individual pairs and their flightless offspring swim on water. Movement to wintering areas probably slow, with arrival Jun to early Jul (peak numbers Jul-Aug) off C Californian coast, where large numbers remain on outer continental shelf and fewer in similar habitats N to Washington and S British Columbia until late Nov or early Dec. Return to breeding locations probably Nov-Jan.
Status and Conservation. Not globally threatened. Currently considered near-threatened, but probably merits Vulnerable status. Total population c. 5600 breeding birds, concentrated at 4 major colonies: Santa Barbara I (1500) and Los Coronados (750) in S California and N Baja California, and San Benito (c. 1000) and Guadalupe (2400-3500) farther S. Population has undergone marked declines, including numerous colony extinctions, largely due to introduced predators such as black rats (*Rattus rattus*) and feral cats. Limited breeding range and concentration of remnant population at only a few colonies make species highly vulnerable to other human activity, including: oil pollution, as Santa Barbara colony is 80-100 km from offshore oil wells and within 20 km of major Los Angeles oil-tanker lane, indeed oil spills from either source could easily extirpate species from S California Bight; commercial fisheries, with drowning in offshore drift gill-nets; disturbance at nesting grounds, with high desertion rate noted during laying and incubation; and possible chemical poisoning. Immediate management needs are: control and eradication of introduced predators on extant and recently extirpated breeding islands; careful regulation of tourism on islands of Baja California; expanded fisheries observer programmes for better assessment of impact of gill-net fisheries; and establishment of system of protection of all major colonies, and monitoring programme to measure population size and status with precision.
Bibliography. Bancroft (1930), Bent (1919), Boswall (1978), Briggs, Tyler, Lewis & Carlson (1987), Briggs, Tyler, Lewis & Dettman (1983), Carter *et al*. (1992), Collins (1979), Cowan & Martin (1954), Drost & Lewis (1995), Eppley (1984), Everett & Anderson (1991), Feinstein (1958), Howell & Webb (1995a), Hunt & Butler (1980), Hunt, Pitman *et al*. (1981), Jehl (1984), Jehl & Bond (1975), Jehl & Everett (1985), Manuwal (1984), Murray (1980), Murray, Winnett-Murray, Eppley *et al*. (1983), Murray, Winnett-Murray & Hunt (1980), Page *et al*. (1990), Scott *et al*. (1971), Sealy (1975c), Sowls *et al*. (1980), Springer *et al*. (1993), Wilbur (1987).

11. **Craveri's Murrelet**

Synthliboramphus craveri

French: Guillemot de Craveri **German**: Craverialk **Spanish**: Mérgulo Californiano Alioscuro

Taxonomy. *Uria Craveri* Salvadori, 1865, Raza Island, Gulf of California.
Sometimes placed in *Brachyramphus*. May be conspecific with *S. hypoleucus*, but little evidence of hybridization in San Benito Is, where both breed. Monotypic.
Distribution. Numerous islands in Gulf of California (N to Consag Rock), and probably islands along Pacific coast of Baja California N to San Benito. Winters at sea in Gulf of California and along coasts N to S California (Monterey Bay) and S to Sonora.

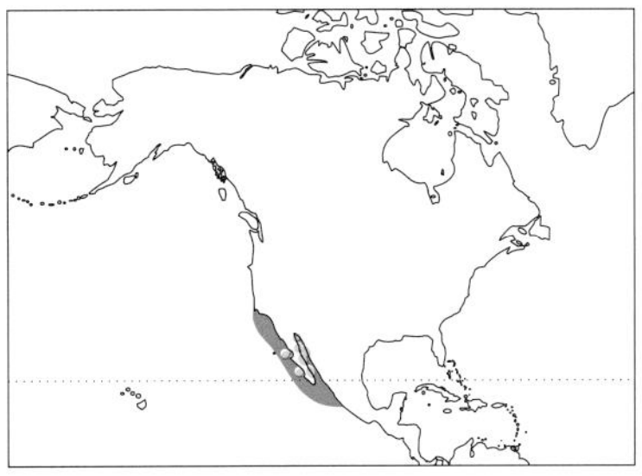

Descriptive notes. c. 21 cm; 128-149 g. Small alcid with short, slender black bill; brownish black upperparts, with black cap extending to bottom edge of lower mandible; white throat and lower sides of face; white underparts, with narrow black wedge on side of breast, and blackish on flanks extending back over body; legs and feet bluish grey, with black claws. Bill slightly longer, but less robust, than in *S. hypoleucus*; black of cap reaches farther below eye and extends to bottom of lower mandible; more elongated black patch on side of breast, and darker dusky grey underwing-coverts. No seasonal variation. Juvenile similar, but with slightly shorter bill, darker upperparts, and fine blackish bars or spots on sides of breast and belly.
Habitat. Offshore and along sea coasts; has southernmost and most restricted range of any alcid, and occupies warmest waters. Breeds on steep sea cliffs and maritime slopes of islands. In winter, occurs mostly offshore close or adjacent to breeding range, often at considerable distances from shore in relatively warm pelagic waters of California Current (probably similar to S winter population of *S. hypoleucus*).
Food and Feeding. Studies lacking, but limited collections during nesting period and early post-breeding dispersal indicate mainly small-sized larval fish (largest 40-70 mm), especially rockfish (*Sebastes*), herring (Clupeidae) and lanternfish (*Benthosema panamense*), but also small Pacific mackerel (*Scomber japonicus*), shrimps and squid; northern anchovy (*Engraulis mordax*) and Pacific saury (*Cololabis saira*) may also be important. Appears to forage in pairs or alone, often in small groups widely scattered, rarely associated with other seabird species. Probably feeds relatively close to colony during nesting season, at or near surface over deep water. Precocial young taken to sea at 1-2 days and fed small pelagic fish.
Breeding. Appears in waters off breeding sites in late Dec and Jan, occupying sites early Feb; peak laying 2nd half of Feb and early Mar, but breeding synchrony low, and nesting period extends to early Apr; most families depart Apr to early May. Mating system poorly known; probably monogamous, with high mate and site fidelity. Nests in small groups at low density, largely determined by availability of suitable sites; nocturnal at colony. Lays usually in scrape on bare rock or soft substrate at end of rock cavity or crevice, but also in ground burrows, under dense shrubs and boulders. 2 eggs; incubation from 2nd egg, probably averages 31-33 days, shared by both sexes equally; hatching synchronous; downy chick c. 25 g, mostly dark brown-black above and white below (adult pattern, including sooty underwing), precocial and mobile, not fed at nest, which abandoned after 1-2 days when entire family goes to sea at night; family undertakes migration by swimming away from colony; parents protect and feed chicks at sea, but time to independence not known. Nesting success probably variable, sometimes high (75%), though chick survival during first month at sea appears low (30-35%). Most egg losses due to introduced predators (small rodents). Survival rates, recruitment and age of first breeding unknown.
Movements. Post-breeding dispersal begins Jun-Jul; most birds remain within breeding range, with general movement N in Aug-Oct off Pacific Baja California N to S California (Monterey) and some S to Sonora (W Mexico), and offshore W to Guadalupe I. Numbers increase in Gulf of California during Dec-Jan, with reoccupation of breeding sites starting early Feb. Pelagic distribution during autumn and winter uncertain due to confusion with *S. hypoleucus*.
Status and Conservation. Not globally threatened. Currently considered near-threatened, but probably merits Vulnerable status. Total population estimated at 6000-10,000 breeding birds, with 90% at 3 locations (Partida, Rasa, Tiburón) in Gulf of California, and remainder scattered elsewhere in Gulf and on Pacific coast of Baja California. Population small and extremely vulnerable to human activities during and outside breeding season. Major threats are: disturbance at breeding locations, including introduced predators (mice, rats, cats), human disturbance (predation, tourism developments) and habitat alteration; and disturbance at sea, including commercial fisheries (competition for food, drowning in gill-nets), oil spills from offshore drilling and tanker traffic, and chronic disturbance caused by increase in ship traffic in Gulf of California. Population known to have declined recently, with several colonies extirpated and others severely reduced and threatened (e.g. Tiburón), mostly by introduced predators. Management needs similar to those for *S. hypoleucus*; immediate conservation action required.
Bibliography. Anderson (1983), Anderson *et al*. (1976), Anon. (1983a), Bancroft (1930), Bent (1919), Breese *et al*. (1993), DeWeese & Anderson (1976), Dunning (1984), Everett & Anderson (1991), Howell & Webb (1995a), Hunt, Pitman *et al*. (1981), Jehl (1984), Jehl & Bond (1975), Johnsgard (1987), Manuwal (1984), Springer *et al*. (1993), Velarde & Anderson (1994), Velarde *et al*. (1985), Violani & Boano (1990), Wilbur (1987).

12. **Ancient Murrelet**

Synthliboramphus antiquus

French: Guillemot à cou blanc **German**: Silberalk **Spanish**: Mérgulo Antiguo
Other common names: Black-throated/Grey-headed Murrelet

On following pages: 13. Japanese Murrelet (*Synthliboramphus wumizusume*); 14. Cassin's Auklet (*Ptychoramphus aleuticus*); 15. Parakeet Auklet (*Cyclorrhynchus psittacula*); 16. Crested Auklet (*Aethia cristatella*); 17. Whiskered Auklet (*Aethia pygmaea*); 18. Least Auklet (*Aethia pusilla*); 19. Rhinoceros Auklet (*Cerorhinca monocerata*); 20. Atlantic Puffin (*Fratercula arctica*); 21. Horned Puffin (*Fratercula corniculata*); 22. Tufted Puffin (*Fratercula cirrhata*).

Taxonomy. *Alca antiqua* Gmelin, 1789, Bering Sea.
Racial subdivision recently revived, and requires additional examination. Two subspecies provisionally recognized.
Subspecies and Distribution.
S. a. antiquus (Gmelin, 1789) - Yellow Sea and Sea of Japan (Peter the Great Bay) N through Sakhalin, Kuril Is and N Sea of Okhotsk (Talan I) to Kamchatka, then E through Aleutians to S Alaska (St Lazaria I, Forrester I, Kodiak I, Semidi Is, Shumigan Is, Sandman Reefs), and then S to Queen Charlotte Is.
S. a. microrhynchos Stepanyan, 1972 - Mednyi I, Commander Is.
Winters mostly offshore on continental shelf, with widespread distribution from Pribilofs and Aleutians S to Taiwan, and in America S regularly to N California, rarely to N Baja California.

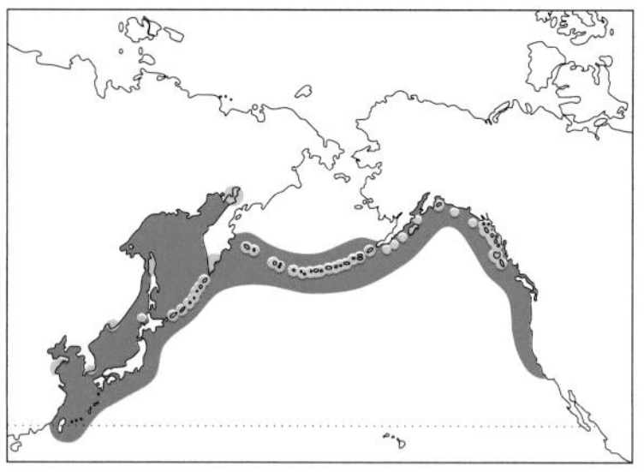

Descriptive notes. 24-27 cm; c. 206 g (177-249 g). Small, stocky alcid; thick, rather short horn-coloured bill with blackish culmen; dark brown iris; black head, nape and throat, with white stripe (filamentous plumes) over eye to nape; bluish grey upperparts; snowy white underparts, with greyish brown line separating underwing and belly; legs and feet pale pinkish grey, with dusky joints and blackish webs. Separated from *S. hypoleucus*, S. craveri, *Brachyramphus marmoratus* and *Ptychoramphus aleuticus* by contrasting black throat bib. In winter, lacks white head plumes, has less or no black on throat, and white from underparts extends high up on sides of neck. Juvenile similar to winter adult, but bill darker, shorter and less robust, and black of head extends down only to gape, not to chin and lower face as in adult. Race *microrhynchos* said to have smaller bill and less speckling on side of neck.
Habitat. Offshore and along rocky sea coasts. Breeds on islands, often with dense vegetation of trees, shrubs and grassy hummocks, normally on soft slopes, sometimes near trees or rocks; often in association with other alcids. Forages mainly in offshore waters to edge of continental shelf, but sometimes inshore where oceanographic processes (e.g. tidal upwellings) concentrate food near sea surface. Winters well offshore, often off the shelf break, but also inshore in regions of strong tidal currents and upwellings. Distribution determined largely by concentrations of planktonic crustaceans and small fish.
Food and Feeding. During early nesting in British Columbia mostly planktonic crustaceans, especially euphausiids (mainly *Thysanoessa spinifera*, with smaller numbers of *T. pacifica*), small larval fish later comprising juvenile sandeels (*Ammodytes hexapterus*), shiner perch (*Cymatogaster aggregata*), and rockfish (*Sebastes*). Diets similar elsewhere, largely mixed crustaceans and fish: in Gulf of Alaska, euphausiid *T. inermis* dominant, with lesser amounts of fish, i.e. capelin (*Mallotus villosus*) and walleye pollock (*Theragra chalcogramma*); in Sea of Okhotsk, crangonid shrimps (*Sabinea*, *Sclerocrangon*) and sandeels, rainbow smelt (*Osmerus mordax*) and sculpin (*Triglops*) dominated; in Peter the Great Bay (Sea of Japan), some chicks fed Pacific herring (*Clupea harengus*), Pacific saury (*Hypoptychus dybowskii*) and small cancroids. Variation in diet due to intraseasonal changes in available prey and differences in prey types between water types and systems. Winter diets poorly known, but mainly *Euphausia pacifica* (12-24 mm long) off Vancouver I (British Columbia), varying from 30% in Nov (60% *Clupea harengus*) and 82% in Dec to 92% in Jan and 100% in Feb. Forages mainly over continental shelf and shelf breaks, usually in small flocks sometimes up to 50 birds, rarely solitarily. Diving times under 45 seconds, indicating depths of c. 10-20 m.
Breeding. Arrives in vicinity of colonies a month before laying, with first landing c. 2-3 weeks before first egg laid; median clutch completion mid-Apr to early May in British Columbia, end Apr to mid-May in SE Alaska, first half Jun in Aleutians, and from mid-Mar in China to late Jun or early Jul in Sea of Okhotsk and Kamchatka; most hatching late May to mid-Jul. Probably monogamous, with mate and site fidelity high; no definite divorces recorded. Colonial, at relatively low densities (under 1 pair/10 m^2 in British Columbia), often in association with other alcids, e.g. *Ptychoramphus aleuticus* and *Cerorhinca monocerata* (British Columbia), and *Aethia* auklets, *Fratercula corniculata* and *F. cirrhata* (Alaska). Nocturnal at colony. Nests primarily in burrows excavated in soil, but also in rock crevices and cavities, occasionally in holes dug by other subterranean nesters, usually on slopes less than 300 m from sea. Lays at night in nest chamber at end of short burrow (60-150 cm, rarely 2 m), in scrape lined with grass, leaves and twigs; laying fairly synchronous, usually spanning c. 45 days, with 50% of clutches initiated within 10 days. 2 eggs, laying interval 7-8 days (6-10); incubation averages 32-33 days (29-37), by both sexes equally in shifts usually lasting c. 3 days (1-6); hatching synchronous, usually within 2-3 hours, occasionally up to 36 hours; downy chick mostly bluish grey on back with black head, white below, c. 33 g, precocial and mobile; chicks remain in burrow unfed for 1-3 (maximum 4) days before departing for sea usually with both parents at night, and family immediately swims away, often 40-50 km from colony within 12-20 hours of departure; parents guard and feed chicks until fully grown, at least 4-5 weeks. Hatching success normally high (c. 96%) at undisturbed nests, with c. 92% of pairs taking 2 chicks to sea; most losses due to desertion, usually before start of incubation, less frequently to predation of eggs and chicks by deer mice (*Peromyscus*). Adult mortality from natural predators such as Bald Eagle (*Haliaeetus leucocephalus*), Peregrine Falcon (*Falco peregrinus*) and Common Raven (*Corvus corax*) can be high, but heaviest predation from introduced rats (*Rattus norvegicus*) and raccoons (*Procyon lotor*). Adult annual survival averages 77%, with estimated life expectancy of breeders c. 4·5 years (Reef I, British Columbia). Age of first breeding 2-4 years.
Movements. Post-breeding dispersal somewhat limited, some birds remaining within breeding range. Rapid exodus from N British Columbia Jul-Sept, with marked S movement in Oct in both W and E Pacific, S to California (arrives late Oct) and to Japan and Korea (high numbers present Dec-Mar). Dispersal generally limited to short distances except in Sea of Okhotsk, where birds forced out by winter ice. Returns to breeding areas at least a month before laying begins. Details of winter distribution and movements are lacking throughout range.
Status and Conservation. Not globally threatened. Total population estimated at 1,500,000 birds (1,000,000-2,000,000). Vulnerable in many areas, and population much reduced throughout breeding range owing largely to introduction of alien mammalian predators, by accident (rats) and from fur-farming (foxes, raccoons). Magnitude of regional declines estimated at c. 50% in Queen Charlotte Is (since early 1960's), 80% in Aleutians (since early 1900's), and probably high throughout Asia from lengthy exposure to human predation and introduced mammals, especially rats; extirpation of small, unprotected populations in Kuril Is and Sea of Japan seems imminent. Other threats include oil pollution (high mortality from oiling in Sea of Japan; vulnerable elsewhere at sea owing to winter concentrations in regions of high tanker traffic) and human disturbance (adverse effects of tourism near colonies and fatal attraction to lights on fishing boats and other craft). Present management needs are: continued programmes to eradicate introduced foxes and rats from both active and former colony sites in British Columbia and Alaska; effective control programme to remove raccoons from key sites in Queen Charlotte Is (urgent requirement to safeguard population in British Columbia, the single most important site for the species); rapid development and implementation of conservation action plans for key islands in W Pacific, by national and international partnerships; and establishment of integrated international monitoring programme to assess population size and status throughout breeding range.
Bibliography. Armstrong (1983), Austin (1948), Austin & Kuroda (1953), Bailey (1993a, 1993b), Bailey & Kaiser (1993), Beebe (1960), Bent (1919), Brazil (1991), Briggs, Tyler *et al.* (1987), Campbell *et al.* (1990), Chen (1988), Cheng Tsohsin (1987), Étchécopar & Hüe (1978), Flint & Golovkin (1990), Flint *et al.* (1984), Fujimaki (1986), Gaston (1990, 1992a, 1994, 1995), Gaston & Powell (1989), Gaston, Carter & Sealy (1993), Gaston, Jones & Noble (1988), Gaston, Jones, Noble & Smith (1988), Gore & Pyong-oh (1971), Hasegawa (1984), Hobson (1991), Howell & Webb (1995a), Jones & Byrd (1979), Kazama (1971), Knystautas (1993), Kondratiev (1991), Kozlova (1957), Kuroda (1967), Lensink (1984), Litvinenko & Shibaev (1987, 1991), Manuwal (1984), Nazarov & Trukhin (1985), Nechaev (1986), Nysewander *et al.* (1982), Rodway (1991), Rodway *et al.* (1988), Sanger (1987), Sealy (1973a, 1975a, 1975c, 1976), Shuntov (1986), Small (1994), Sowls *et al.* (1978), Speich & Wahl (1989), Springer *et al.* (1993), Vermeer & Lemon (1986), Vermeer, Fulton & Sealy (1985), Vermeer, Sealy *et al.* (1984), Vyatkin (1986), White *et al.* (1973).

13. Japanese Murrelet

Synthliboramphus wumizusume

French: Guillemot du Japon **German**: Japanalk **Spanish**: Mérgulo Japonés
Other common names: Crested Murrelet

Taxonomy. *Uria wumizusume* Temminck, 1835, Japan.
Monotypic.
Distribution. Coasts and islands off E & S Japan (Izu Is S to Shikoku and Kyushu) and South Korea. Winters mostly offshore from breeding locations.

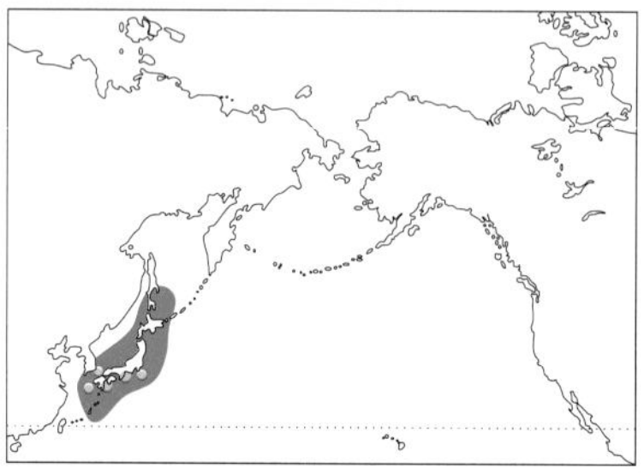

Descriptive notes. 26 cm; 183 g. Short, thick, pale bluish grey bill with dark culmen; iris dark brown, almost blackish; black head with crest of long, narrow black feathers, and with white stripes on sides from top of eye meeting on nape; blackish and bluish grey upperparts; white throat and underparts, with greyish black flanks; yellowish grey legs and feet. Distinguished from *S. antiquus* by crest and by lack of black on throat. In winter, lacks crest and head stripes; resembles *S. antiquus*. Juvenile as winter adult, but head and upperparts appear browner.
Habitat. Offshore and along sea coasts in boreo-cool subtropical waters of NW Pacific. Breeds on small rocky islets and sea coasts. Forages mainly offshore, to edge of continental shelf, also inshore where upwellings or converging currents concentrate food near surface. Winters offshore, mostly in temperate, cool subtropical waters.
Food and Feeding. Mostly planktonic crustaceans, especially euphausiids, and small larval fish throughout year. Summer foods probably similar to those of *S. antiquus* in Sea of Japan and S Sea of Okhotsk, mainly crangonid shrimps (*Sabinea*, *Sclerocrangon*) and Pacific herring (*Clupea harengus*), Pacific saury (*Hypoptychus dybowskii*), sandeels (*Ammodytes*), smelt (*Osmerus*) and sculpin (*Triglops*). Winter diet unknown, probably largely euphausiids. Feeds mainly over continental shelf, usually in small groups, with diving times and depths as for *S. antiquus*.
Breeding. Phenology and reproductive biology poorly known. Spring arrival mid- to late Feb; laying normally mid-Mar to late Jun or early Jul, and fledging mostly by late Apr to end of May. Probably monogamous, with high mate and site fidelity. Colonial, in small and localized groups owing to small population size. Nocturnal at colony. Nests primarily in rock crevices and cavities and under boulders, but also excavates short burrows in soil and under roots of trees and tussock grasses, sometimes in debris and stone walls; may use existing burrow of other species. 2 eggs, sometimes 1, laid at night, laying interval probably 7-8 days; incubation period unknown, probably c. 32-33 days, by both sexes for periods of 24-72 hours; hatching synchronous, within a few hours; downy chick brownish grey above, white below, precocial, unfed until leaving at night with parents for sea, c. 1-2 days after hatching, when family immediately swims offshore, often travelling non-stop for 10-20 hours; parents guard and feed young until fully grown, probably at least 1 month later. Breeding success relatively low, c. 38% of eggs laid produce chicks that go to sea. Most losses at egg stage, occasionally young chicks, usually taken by introduced predators e.g. rats (*Rattus*) and other small rodents when left unattended. Survival rates and age of first breeding unknown; probably as for *S. antiquus*.
Movements. Winters mainly offshore, mostly close to breeding areas. General post-breeding dispersal normally within warm currents flowing NE off E coast (Kuroshio Current) and W coast (Tsushima Current) of Kyushu and Honshu; birds reported N to S Sakhalin and Kuril Is and S to Taiwan. Most return to vicinity of colonies by mid- to late Feb, reoccupying nesting sites shortly thereafter. Movements between post-breeding exodus and spring return comprise short distances. Winter distribution poorly known, but likely determined by relative abundance of small fish and planktonic crustaceans.
Status and Conservation. VULNERABLE. Rarest and most threatened alcid, and probably second-most threatened seabird species in N Hemisphere. Population small, estimated at c. 5000-6000 birds (1995), restricted to 5 small areas off SE Japan: Izu Is, with c. 1670+ birds at 8 sites; Honshu, with 200+ at Mimiana I and small numbers at Kutsujima and Nanatsujima in Sea of Japan; Shikoku, with small numbers on Koshima I; Kyushu, with 3000 at Biro I, 60 at Eboshi I, and 30 at Okinoshima Is; and Danjo Is, with small numbers at 2 sites. Minute population of under 10 pairs reported in South Korea; may also nest in very small numbers (under 100 birds) in Peter the Great Bay, but fledglings and adults collected at sea in region may have migrated there from Japanese colonies. Small population concentrated at only a few locations during and outside breeding season makes species highly vulnerable to disturbance from human activities. Historically, believed to be more widespread and numerous, but human exploitation for food, habitat destruction and alteration, and introduction of alien predators to breeding colonies have undoubtedly caused extirpation of many island populations. In Izu archipelago, once considered the stronghold of the species, current total is under 2000 birds, with breeding at only 3 of 10 islands that had active populations in early 1950's. Rats and feral cats continue to be the major threat. Immediate conservation need for species' survival is protection of existing breeding sites by: regulation and control of human activity; initiation of programme to eradicate all alien predators at active and former colonies; establishment of control measures to prevent spread of alien predators to predator-free islands; and a comprehensive survey and monitoring programme to determine present distribution and numbers, assess population trends, and identify factors responsible for changes observed. Highest priority must be given to this conservation goal by national and international agencies responsible for protection and management of marine birds and their habitats.
Bibliography. Anon. (1993d, 1994i, 1995n), Austin & Kuroda (1953), Brazil (1991), Collar & Andrew (1988), Collar *et al.* (1994), DeSanto & Nelson (1995), Étchécopar & Hüe (1978), Hasegawa (1984), Higuchi (1979), Kostenko *et al.* (1989), Kozlova (1957), Litvinenko & Shibaev (1991), Mochizuki & Ueta (1995), Nagata & Onagamitsu (1995),

Nazarov & Shibaev (1987), Ono (1993), Ono & Nakamura (1993, 1994), Piatt & Gould (1994), Springer *et al.* (1993), Takeishi (1987).

Genus *PTYCHORAMPHUS* M. Brandt, 1837

14. **Cassin's Auklet**

Ptychoramphus aleuticus

French: Starique de Cassin **German**: Aleutenalk **Spanish**: Mérgulo Sombrío
Other common names: Aleutian Auk

Taxonomy. *Uria Aleutica* Pallas, 1811, north Pacific Ocean.
Apparent racial variation may be clinal. Two subspecies provisionally recognized.
Subspecies and Distribution.
P. a. aleuticus (Pallas, 1811) - Aleutian Is to SW & SE Alaska, then S to N Baja California (San Geronimo, San Martin and Guadalupe Is).
P. a. australis van Rossem, 1939 - W Baja California from San Benito Is S to Asuncion and San Roque Is.
Winters within breeding range, mostly offshore, from S British Columbia to S Baja California, with some N to SE Alaska.

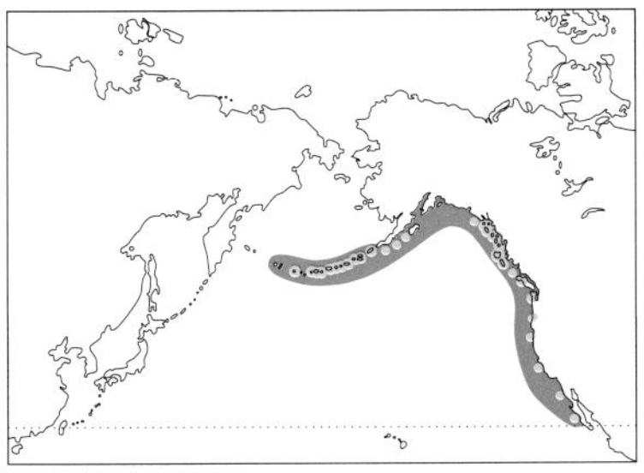

Descriptive notes. 23 cm; 150-200 g. Small, plump alcid; short blackish grey bill with base of lower mandible yellowish; white iris; dark greyish brown head, fading to paler brown chin and throat; white crescent above eye; blackish to slate grey upperparts; greyish brown breast and flanks, white belly; legs and feet bluish pink, with black claws. No marked seasonal variation. Juvenile has whiter throat, browner wings and tail, and dark brown iris. Races nearly identical, with *australis* smaller in linear measurements and mass.

Habitat. Offshore and along sea coasts, mostly over continental shelf to edge, but often beyond into deep ocean. Breeds on coastal islands, with or without trees, using wide range of nesting habitat from steep rocky sea cliffs and slopes to flattish ground. Mostly offshore in winter, sometimes remaining inshore near colony sites, particularly in S of range. Utilizes coastal upwellings in spring and summer, and these probably important throughout year, but winter ecology poorly known.

Food and Feeding. Mostly crustaceans throughout year, supplemented by other invertebrates and small larval fish. Quantitative information largely restricted to chick diet during summer: mainly copepods (*Neocalanus cristatus*) and euphausiids (*Thysanoessa spinifera*, *T. longipes*) in British Columbia; *T. spinifera*, amphipods (*Phromema*) and squid (*Loligo opalescens*) in N California, and diet similar in C California (Farallon Is) but also some fish, mainly rockfish (*Sebastes*) and larval sanddab (*Citharicthys*); diet in other regions unknown. Chicks fed 1-2 meals/day, each averaging 17-25 g of mostly crustaceans; adults bring in food at night, carried in specialized sublingual gular pouch. Often forages in small groups, occasionally large aggregations but rarely alone, both day and night, probably at considerable distances (over 50 km) from colony. Dives average 42 seconds, to depths of 20-80 m.

Breeding. Arrival at colony and start of laying vary greatly with latitude, due largely to differences in oceanographic conditions; nests late Nov to Apr in Baja California; elsewhere, laying period earliest and longest in S of range, in C California (Farallon Is) generally from early Mar to late Apr, rarely to late May; later farther N, normally mid-Apr to late May in British Columbia and early Jun to early Jul in Alaska (Sanak I). Only alcid species known to produce 2 broods in single breeding season, reported only for Farallon Is, with median dates of 2nd clutch mid-Jun to early Jul, c. 90 days after 1st clutch. Monogamous, with high mate and site fidelity. Highly colonial, in small to immense aggregations (under 500 to 1,100,000 birds), usually at high densities (0·7-1·1 pairs/m^2) on optimal maritime grassy slopes, lower on inland flattish bare ground or with shrubs and trees (less than 0·2 pairs/m^2); nocturnal at colonies. Nest placed in crevice, cavity, cave or hole, or in burrow (c. 1 m long) dug into soft soil; lays on rough scrape on bare chamber floor, occasionally lined with bits of vegetation. 1 egg; incubation averages 38-39 days (37-57), by both sexes; early egg losses replaced after c. 17 days (9-25); downy chick black to darkish grey above, grey to pale grey below, c. 18 g, semi-precocial; chick-rearing averages 43 days (41-50), with feeding by both parents only at night, fledgling departing to sea alone, mostly before dawn, just under adult size. Annual variation in breeding success relatively low, except in unusually warm-water years, normally 60-65% of eggs laid produce fledglings (C California, British Columbia); strongly influenced (positively) by occurrence of cold-water upwellings near colonies. Most egg and chick losses due to removal by gulls from short burrows or crevices, also by introduced rats (*Rattus*) and foxes (*Alopex lagopus*, *Vulpes vulpes*) at some colonies. Adult annual survival 86%; estimated survival of fledglings to breeding age c. 65%. Age of first breeding usually 3 years, sometimes 2 or 4.

Movements. Winters mainly offshore within breeding range. S populations relatively sedentary, staying at sea in vicinity of colonies, often visiting colony at night in any month; birds from Alaska and British Columbia migratory, moving S along coast as far as California, where build-up of 500,000-1,000,000 birds occurs during autumn, numbers far exceeding total population from Washington to Baja California. Exodus from wintering areas begins as early as Dec, mostly later during Jan-Feb, with birds reaching N parts of range during Mar-Apr. In general, dispersal patterns and timing of spring influx and autumn exodus require additional study. Distribution largely determined by abundance of small crustaceans, squid and fish.

Status and Conservation. Not globally threatened. Population sizes and trends relatively well known, though distribution and estimates of Alaskan and Mexican populations incomplete. Estimated total population at least 3,600,000 breeding birds, with centre of abundance in British Columbia. Regional totals of c. 600,000 birds in Alaska, with 100,000 on Nigrud Is, Umga I and Chagulak; c. 2,700,000 in British Columbia, with 1,095,000 on Triangle I; c. 88,000 in Washington, with 54,600 on Alexander I; 500 in Oregon; c. 131,000 in California, with 105,000 on SE Farallon I; and 20,000-40,000 in Baja California on islands of San Benito, San Geronimo, Asuncion, San Roque. Population formerly much larger in range and size; reduced as result of widespread human activity from at least 19th century through first half of 20th century, particularly from egging and hunting at colonies and introduction of mammalian predators (foxes, rats, cats) and herbivores (goats). Many colonies in Aleutians and Gulf of Alaska extirpated as result of fox-farming industry, as was probably the case too at several locations W of Buldir I (suspected former colonies at Near Is, Commander Is, Kamchatka and Kuril Is). Rats have destroyed large colonies from British Columbia (e.g. Langara I) to extreme S limit of range, as have introduced foxes and cats (e.g. Channel Is, California) and domestic grazers (e.g. goats on Guadalupe I). Natural factors also important; population declines reported due to increases in Bald Eagles (*Haliaeetus leucocephalus*) and Peregrine Falcons (*Falco peregrinus*) in British Columbia and Washington, and Western Gulls (*Larus occidentalis*) in California; both decreases and increases in N California (e.g. Farallon Is) at least partially explained by intrusion and withdrawal of anomalous warm-water conditions. Overall, introduced mammals (foxes, rats, cats, goats) remain the most serious threat, followed by oil pollution at sea, commercial fisheries, habitat destruction, and colony disturbance (tourism developments and research). Immediate management actions required include: protection of large and small colonies from direct human disturbance; initiation of control programmes to eradicate introduced predators and remove domestic livestock at active and former breeding sites; measures to restore historical populations, particularly in Alaska and Baja California; restrictions on gill-net fishing close to colonies; and continued development of monitoring programmes to assess changes in population size and status in Alaska, Oregon and Baja California.

Bibliography. Ainley & Boekelheide (1990), Ainley & Lewis (1974), Ainley, Boekelheide *et al.* (1990), Ainley, DeGange *et al.* (1981), Ainley, Grau *et al.* (1981), Ainley, Sydeman *et al.* (1994), Armstrong (1983), Astheimer (1986, 1991), Bent (1919), Briggs, Ainley *et al.* (1987), Briggs, Tyler *et al.* (1987), Burger & Powell (1990), Byrd & Day (1986), Clapp *et al.* (1982), DeGange *et al.* (1993), Emslie, Henderson *et al.* (1990), Emslie, Sydeman & Pyle (1992), Everett & Anderson (1991), Gaston (1992b), Howell, A.B. (1917), Howell, S.N.G. & Webb (1995a), Jehl & Everett (1985), Klimkiewicz & Futcher (1989), Lensink (1984), Manuwal (1972, 1974a, 1974b, 1974c, 1978a, 1978b, 1979, 1984), Manuwal & Thoresen (1993), Murie (1959), Page *et al.* (1990), Paine *et al.* (1990), Rodway (1991), van Rossem (1939), Roudybush *et al.* (1980), Sanger (1987), Sowls, DeGange *et al.* (1980), Sowls, Hatch & Lensink (1978), Speich & Manuwal (1974), Speich & Wahl (1989), Springer *et al.* (1993), Thoresen (1960, 1964), Vermeer (1981, 1984, 1987), Vermeer & Cullen (1982), Vermeer & Lemon (1986), Vermeer, Fulton & Sealy (1985), Vermeer, Sealy, Lemon & Rodway (1984), Vermeer, Sealy & Sanger (1987), Vermeer, Vermeer *et al.* (1979).

Genus *CYCLORRHYNCHUS* Kaup, 1829

15. **Parakeet Auklet**

Cyclorrhynchus psittacula

French: Starique perroquet **German**: Rotschnabelalk **Spanish**: Mérgulo Lorito

Taxonomy. *Alca psittacula* Pallas, 1769, Kamchatka.
Monotypic.
Distribution. Chukotskiy Peninsula S to Commander Is, Kamchatka, Sea of Okhotsk (Matykyl I) and Kuril Is, and W Alaska from Diomede Is and Norton Sound S to Aleutians and E to N Gulf of Alaska (Prince William Sound). Winters mostly at sea and along coasts, often at limit of open water near breeding locations, from Bering Sea S to N Japan and casually to S California. General pattern of distribution and limits poorly known.

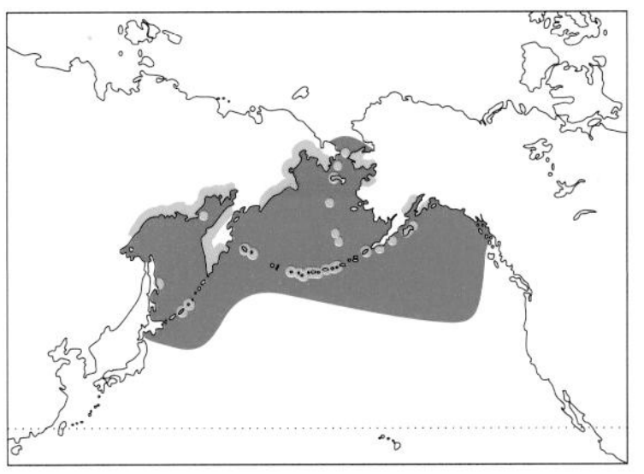

Descriptive notes. 23-25 cm; 297 g. Short, stubby orangish red bill, deep and laterally compressed, with upturned lower mandible producing circular appearance, yellowish at gape; sooty black head with white nuptial plume extending back from eye, and yellowish white iris; black upperparts and chin and throat; mostly white underparts; legs and feet pale grey, with blackish webs and black claws. Differs from much smaller *Aethia pusilla* in distinctly larger bill and black throat. In winter, bill dull brownish red, facial streak less distinct or absent, and throat white. Juvenile similar to winter adult.

Habitat. Marine, occurring offshore and along rocky sea coasts. Breeds mainly on offshore islands, using steep sea cliffs, rocky talus slopes, often turf-covered (mosses, grasses, herbs), and beach boulder fields, usually in association with other auklet species. Mostly pelagic during winter, some remaining in ice-free regions within breeding range (Aleutians, Pribilofs), but most disperse into N Pacific oceanic boreal waters as far S as Japan and California.

Food and Feeding. During breeding season, feeds mainly on planktonic crustaceans, particularly euphausiids and amphipods early and calanoid copepods during chick-rearing, supplemented with varying amounts of other invertebrates (cephalopods, polychaetes) and small fish; overall, the most diverse diet of all auklets and therefore considered a food generalist. Diet information largely from chick meals (adult summer diet probably similar); major prey (St Lawrence I and Pribilofs) includes hyperiid amphipods (*Parathemisto libellulu*, *P. pacifica*), euphausiids (*Thysanoessa*), copepods (*Neocalanus cristatus*), decapod larvae, Ctenophora, Scyphomedusae, and juvenile fish, mostly sandeels (*Ammodytes hexapterus*) and walleye pollock (*Theragra*). Chick fed 2-4 meals/day, food carried by parents in sublingual throat pouch. Foods usually obtained at considerable distances from colony, sometimes closer on shallow inner shelf and coastal regions. Winter diet not known, probably mostly macrozooplankton. Dives normally under 60 seconds to depths usually above 30 m.

Breeding. Spring arrival and start of laying variable, earliest in S and latest in extreme N, with differences between regions c. 4-5 weeks; normally returns to colonies between Apr and May (St Lawrence I mid-May, Diomede Is late May or sometimes early Jun), with start of laying 3-4 weeks later, May to mid-Jul, but can be delayed in N by late snow-melt; hatching to dispersal usually synchronous, mostly mid-Aug to end Sept. Monogamous, with site fidelity high; mate retention uncertain, probably also high. Small, loose to large colonies, largely determined by availability of suitable nesting sites; usually with other auklets, especially *Aethia cristatella* and *A. pusilla*. Nests deep inside dark crevices and cavities; lays in rough scrape on bare ground, sometimes lined with small pebbles. 1 egg; incubation averages 35-36 days, by both sexes for periods of probably 24 hours (uncertain); replacement of lost eggs rare, but some early losses replaced after 16 days; downy chick blackish brown above, head paler than back, pale brownish grey below, c. 28 g, semi-precocial; chick-rearing averages 35 days (34-37), with care and feeding by both parents until fledging, when chick flies to sea alone at night. Breeding success not well known, but c. 65-68% of eggs laid hatch, and limited studies indicate c. 76% of hatchlings fledge, giving total success of c. 50-51%. Most egg and chick losses due to predation by voles (*Microtus*, *Clethrionomys*); some eggs lost by accidental breakage. Adult and juvenile survival unknown. Age of first breeding estimated at 3 years.

Movements. Migratory movements poorly known. Dispersal from late Aug to early Oct. Some birds overwinter in open waters near breeding locations (Pribilofs, Aleutians), but most birds probably move considerable distances S to winter offshore in oceanic waters of N Pacific, S as far as Japan (Hokkaido, and irregularly to Honshu) and casually to S California. No winter sightings from Gulf of Alaska, few from SE Alaska and British Columbia, and regular records from Washington to California; similar exodus from E Bering Sea, Kamchatka and Sea of Okhotsk S and offshore of Kurils to Japan. Most birds return to colonies Apr-May, late May and early Jun at northernmost sites; arrives Commander Is and Aleutians late Apr, St Lawrence I by mid-May, and Bering Strait (N Chukotskiy, Diomede Is, Seward Peninsula) late May to early Jun. Migratory movements and patterns complex, requiring further study; apparently influenced by fluctuations in surface temperatures and salinities.
Status and Conservation. Not globally threatened. Breeding population sizes and trends only roughly known. Estimated total population c. 1,200,000 individuals, with c. 800,000 (400,000-1,000,000) in W Alaska and c. 400,000 (380,000-500,000) in E Siberia. Centres of abundance: Sea of Okhotsk, with 350,000 birds at 15 colonies, of which 200,000 on Matykyl I (Yamskie Is); E Bering Sea, with 180,000 at Pribilofs and 20,000-40,000 at Diomedes; and NW Gulf of Alaska, with 58,000 at Chowiet I (Semidi Is). Information on breeding numbers incomplete for many regions, particularly along W Bering, Kamchatka and Okhotsk coasts, and at more than 20% of sites in Alaska. Trends unknown throughout breeding range, but abundance of birds and colonies probably much reduced from earlier times by negative impacts of human exploitation for food, fox farming, and other introduced predators (rats, voles, feral cats and dogs) in all regions. Current threats within breeding range come from continued human disturbance and predation, introduced mammalian predators, commercial fisheries and marine pollution (particularly offshore oil developments in Sea of Okhotsk); principal threats in winter include oil fouling at sea (beached birds recorded regularly through winter range) and ingestion of small plastic particles in N Pacific. High priority should be given to: eradication of introduced predators at present and former colonies; establishment of monitoring system to assess population size and status; better understanding of post-breeding distribution and movements, and ecological requirements at sea; and magnitude of mortality associated with oiling, consumption of plastic particles, and drowning in gill-nets. Concentration at only a few locations makes species particularly vulnerable to human activities.
Bibliography. Armstrong (1983), Bailey (1948, 1993a, 1993b), Bailey & Kaiser (1993), Bédard (1969a, 1969b), Bédard & Sealy (1984), Bent (1919), Biderman & Drury (1978), Brazil (1991), Byrd & Day (1986), Flint *et al.* (1984), Gabrielson & Lincoln (1959), Gould *et al.* (1982), Harrison, C. (1978), Harrison, N.M. (1990), Hipfner & Byrd (1993), Hunt, Burgeson & Sanger (1981), Hunt, Eppley *et al.* (1981), Hunt, Mayer *et al.* (1978), Johnsgard (1987), Johnson (1976), Kessel (1989), Knystautas (1993), Kondratiev (1991), Kondratiev *et al.* (1993), Kozlova (1957), Lehnhausen (1980), Lensink (1984), Litvenko (1993), Litvinenko & Shibaev (1991), Manuwal (1984), Manuwal & Manuwal (1979), Oehler *et al.* (1995), Portenko (1973), Preble & McAtee (1923), Sealy (1968, 1972, 1975c), Sealy & Bédard (1973), Searing (1977), Sowls *et al.* (1978), Springer *et al.* (1993), Watson & Divoky (1972).

Genus *AETHIA* Merrem, 1788

16. **Crested Auklet**

Aethia cristatella

French: Starique cristatelle **German**: Schopfalk **Spanish**: Mérgulo Empenachado

Taxonomy. *Alca cristatella* Pallas, 1769, Hokkaido to Kamchatka.
Monotypic.
Distribution. Chukotskiy Peninsula S through Diomede Is to N Sea of Okhotsk, Sakhalin and Kuril Is, and W Alaska S through St Lawrence I, St Matthew I and Pribilofs to Aleutians E to Shumagin Is. Winters at sea and along coasts in Bering Sea, often close to breeding areas where open water exists, S to Gulf of Alaska and N Japan; N and S limits poorly known.

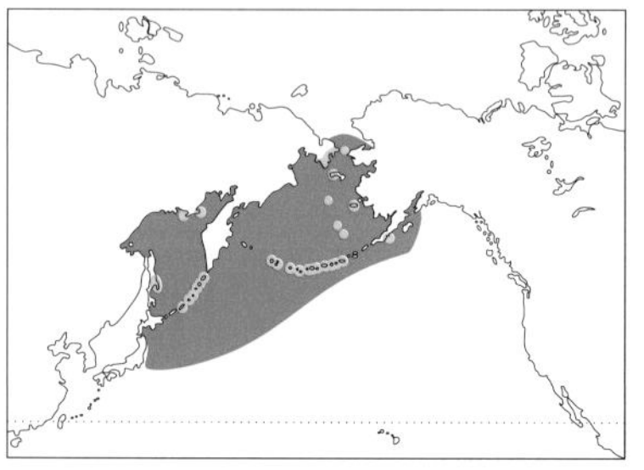

Descriptive notes. 18-20 cm; c. 260 g; wingspan 40-50 cm. Distinctive forward-coiled ornamental facial plumes and crest, striking bright reddish orange and yellow-tipped bill, yellowish white iris, and white auricular plumes from eye across ear-coverts; dark sooty grey upperparts, wings and tail, brownish grey underparts; legs and feet grey, with black claws. Sexes similar, female with slightly smaller and less recurved bill, possibly shorter crest. Distinguished from all other auklets by all-dark body plumage. In winter, bill smaller and dull yellow, lacking accessory plates; crest and auricular plumes somewhat reduced. Juvenile similar to winter adult, but lacks crest and auricular plumes; bill smaller, dull brownish yellow.
Habitat. Offshore and along sea coasts. Breeds on remote islands and coasts, utilizing scree slopes, boulder fields, lava flows and sea cliffs, sometimes with partial vegetative cover (mosses, grasses, herbs), usually in association with other auklet species; density highest on unvegetated scree. Forages in deep water, often far offshore, concentrating in areas where physical dynamics of water system cause dense aggregations of zooplankton to occur: regions of converging currents, upwellings, tidal pumps, stratified waters. Mostly pelagic in winter, usually in large flocks, remaining in ice-free waters of breeding range S to Japan and Gulf of Alaska, particularly near Kodiak I.
Food and Feeding. Forages mainly offshore in deep water, sometimes in near-shore regions, almost always in large flocks throughout year. Adult diet during summer believed similar to chick diet; adults in N Sea of Okhotsk ate chiefly euphausiids (*Thysanoessa*; 88% by number). Chicks fed high diversity of invertebrates, mostly planktonic crustaceans, especially *Thysanoessa*, but also copepods, gammarids, hyperiids, mysids, infrequently small fish and squid; at St Lawrence I mainly *Thysanoessa* (56-80% by number), supplemented by varying amounts of *Calanus finmarchicus*, *C. marshallae*, *Neocalanus plumchrus*, *N. cristatus*, Caridea, Mysidacea and other crustaceans; 1-4 meals/day, average meal size 21 g (4·7-36·3 g) and daily total of c. 80 g; food carried by both parents in sublingual throat pouch, feeding rate higher in female than in male. Summer foods usually obtained at considerable distance from colony, often 50 km away, sometimes closer (5 km), at depths to 30 m. Winter foods unknown, suspected to be largely marine invertebrates.
Breeding. Spring arrival Mar-May, with colony attendance from late Apr (Aleutians), early May (Pribilofs), late May (St Matthew I) or early Jun (St Lawrence I); peak laying late May in W Aleutians, early Jun in Pribilofs, mid- to late Jun at St Matthew I, early Jul at St Lawrence I; late snow-melt can delay laying at N colonies; fledging peaks early Aug (Aleutians), mid-Aug (Pribilofs) and early Sept (St Lawrence). Monogamous, with high site and mate fidelity throughout breeding life; both sexes prefer mates with large crests (correlates with agonistic superiority). Colonial, normally in large groups, with some colonies larger than 100,000 pairs (e.g. Talan, Matykyl, Talus Is); densities determined largely by availability of suitable rock crevices and cavities for nesting, highest on unvegetated scree; usually synchronous (e.g. 80% of hatchings within 10-day period). 1 egg; incubation averages c. 34-35 days, shared equally between sexes, shift length unknown; lost first eggs rarely replaced; downy chick c. 25 g, semi-precocial, brooded more frequently by male to 10th day but female delivers more meals; chick-rearing averages 33 days (27-36). Breeding success variable, average c. 52-55% (48-57%) of eggs laid producing fledglings, with annual productivity c. 0·50-0·55 young fledged/pair. Most egg and chick losses due to predation by foxes (*Alopex lagopus*, *Vulpes vulpes*), voles (*Microtus*) and rats (*Rattus*); fledglings vulnerable to avian predators at time of departure. Information on survival limited: adult annual survival estimated at 86% (1-year data) or lifespan of c. 8 years; pre-breeding survival unknown. Age of first breeding not known, probably 3-4 years.
Movements. Very little known of migratory movements. Autumn exodus occurs in Sept, but winter range poorly documented. Believed to be pelagic, remaining largely within ice-free waters of breeding range except for movements SW to Japan and SE into Gulf of Alaska (Kodiak I region). Birds concentrated into flocks, often in large numbers, up to 15,000 birds, at predictably food-rich offshore locations. Reoccupation of colony areas begins in Mar through May, with first landings from late Apr (Aleutians) to early Jun (St Lawrence I).
Status and Conservation. Not globally threatened. Breeding population size unknown, but North American population estimated at c. 3,000,000 individuals (roughly 2,100,000 pairs) and Russian population around 2,900,000 birds (c. 2,000,000 pairs): total of almost 6,000,000 breeding birds, or 4,100,000 pairs. Largest numbers are at Talan I (1,000,000 birds) and Matykyl I (300,000-400,000 birds) in W (N Sea of Okhotsk), and Kiska I, C Aleutians (Sirius Point: 332,000 birds), and St Lawrence I (Kongkok Bay: 455,000 birds) in E. Estimates very approximate, however, and considerably more census work required; values for Alaska likely low (suspected to be c. 6,000,000 birds) and for Russia high (suspected to be c. 3,000,000 birds). Population sizes and trends little known throughout breeding range. Local changes, however, indicate overall population either stable at reduced level, or in decline. Certain large Alaskan colonies have recently become extinct (e.g. Kagamil and Uliaga in Aleutians) or substantially reduced (e.g. Kiska in Shumigan Is) owing to introduced foxes and rats; present total Aleutian population probably only small fraction of past numbers. Suspected increases at St Lawrence I during 1964-1987 and St George I in 1976-1982 are encouraging, but both may merely reflect differing census techniques or change in adult colony attendance, or both. In NE & SE Russia, human predation and disturbance combined with introduction of foxes, rats, mink (*Mustela*) and cats were serious threats during first half of 20th century, with unknown effects on populations, though major colony declines and extirpations probably occurred (e.g. Kurils and elsewhere). Current threats in both regions come from continued impacts of human predation and habitat disturbance, introduced mammalian predators, commercial fishing, and oil pollution. Species is particularly vulnerable to oil pollution through habit of forming large concentrations at sea all year round. Further studies urgently required on effects of marine pollution and commercial fisheries; also continued examination of effects of introduced predators and prevention of future introductions, particularly rats. Considerable effort required to enhance census methods to permit better assessments of colony-specific changes and to allow meaningful monitoring system to be established.
Bibliography. Anon. (1993e), Armstrong (1983), Bailey (1990, 1993a, 1993b), Bédard (1969a, 1969b), Bédard & Sealy (1984), Bent (1919), Brazil (1991), Byrd *et al.* (1983), Craighead & Oppenheim (1985), Cramp (1985), Flint & Golovkin (1990), Flint *et al.* (1984), Haney (1991), Hipfner & Byrd (1993), Hunt, Harrison & Piatt (1993), Johnsgard (1987), Jones (1993b, 1993c), Knudtson & Byrd (1982), Knystautas (1993), Kondratiev (1991), Kondratiev *et al.* (1993), Lensink (1984), Litvinenko & Shibaev (1991), Manuwal (1984), Piatt, Roberts & Hatch (1990), Piatt, Roberts, Lidster *et al.* (1990), Portenko (1972), Sealy (1975d, 1982), Searing (1977), Sowls *et al.* (1978), Springer *et al.* (1993), Zubakin (1990), Zubakin & Zubakin (1994).

17. **Whiskered Auklet**

Aethia pygmaea

French: Starique pygmée **German**: Bartalk **Spanish**: Mérgulo Bigotudo
Other common names: Pygmy Auklet

Taxonomy. *Alca pygmæa* Gmelin, 1789, Bering Sea.
Race *camtschatica* proposed for birds from Kuril Is based on differences in body size, but recent studies confirm existence of simple clinal variation only, with size increasing from E to W. Monotypic.
Distribution. NE Sea of Okhotsk (Yamskie Is, Penzhin Gulf, Jona I) and Commander Is S to at least C Kuril Is, and throughout Aleutians E to Krenitzen Is and Four Mountains Is. Winters mostly near breeding locations, but S as far as Japan (Honshu, Shikoku), and casual in N Bering Sea (e.g. St Lawrence I).

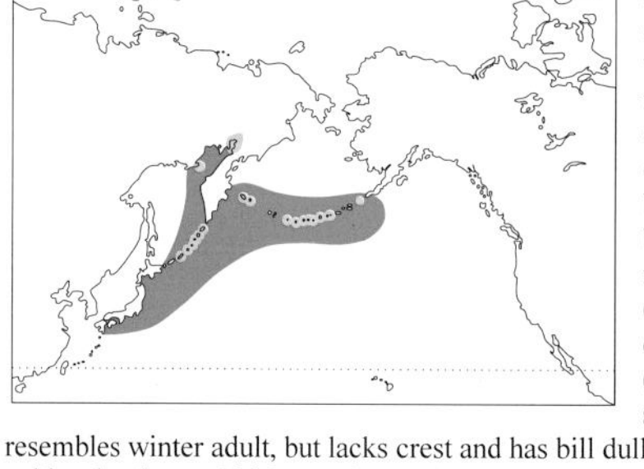

Descriptive notes. 17-18 cm; c. 116 g (99-136 g). Unique head pattern, with long recurved crest on forehead drooping forward over small white-tipped scarlet bill; two white facial plumes running back from near base of upper mandible, and third white plume extending from back of eye across ear-coverts; blackish upperparts and breast, white belly; legs and feet greyish, with blackish webs and dark grey-black claws. Female usually smaller in most measurements (weight, culmen, wing, tarsus). Differs from all other species by head pattern, and small size (only *A. pusilla* is smaller). In winter, crest shorter and facial plumes less distinct. Juvenile resembles winter adult, but lacks crest and has bill dull yellow with blackish tip; separable from other auklets by three whitish streaks on side of face.
Habitat. Offshore and along sea coasts. Breeds on bare to partially covered talus slopes and beach boulder fields, and lava flows on high slopes of rocky islands and sea cliffs, usually with other *Aethia* but in lower numbers, habitats ranging from immediately above high water mark to tops of maritime rocky slopes and cliffs; density highest in unvegetated talus. Forages in near-shore waters close to breeding site, in areas of upwelling and converging currents. In winter mostly near-shore off rocky sea coasts and islands within breeding range, sometimes pelagic.
Food and Feeding. Diet throughout year marine zooplankton. Detailed information lacking, but summer foods at Buldir I (Aleutians) showed high diversity of crustaceans, with copepod *Neocalanus plumchrus* dominant (76% frequency), followed by euphausiids and chaetognaths (probably *Thysanoessa inermis* and *Sagitta elegans*, respectively). Food delivered by both parents, usually at night, carried in sublingual throat pouch and regurgitated to chick; meal size unknown, but 2 meals/

day is suspected maximum. Winter food poorly known, but limited information indicates euphausiids and gammarid amphipods are principal prey outside breeding season, with euphausiids (mostly *Thysanoessa inermis*) comprising over 90% (wet weight) during Sept-Apr (E Aleutians). Forages near-shore, in summer usually within 10 km of colony, sometimes farther off, most often in flocks concentrated at food-rich locations. Diving depths unknown, but normally found in waters not exceeding 100 m.

Breeding. Breeding phenology poorly known. Spring arrival Apr to early May; laying probably late May and early Jun, sometimes advanced; hatching appears synchronous, usually late Jun to early Jul, with fledging mid-Jul to mid-Aug, sometimes earlier. Probably monogamous. Colonial in high numbers, often with other crevice-nesting species (usually *A. cristatella*, *A. pusilla*), but always in lower numbers than congeners in mixed colonies; density determined largely by availability of suitable habitat, highest in unvegetated talus. Nests in rock crevices, also in mixed rock-soil substrates. 1 egg; incubation period uncertain, probably c. 35-36 days, by both sexes, with early egg losses probably replaced; downy chick 12-14 g, semi-precocial; chick-rearing period poorly known, probably longer than for other *Aethia*, at least 39-42 days, with fledged chick departing after dark by flying to sea, usually fully feathered and alone. Annual breeding success 73%, with normally high hatching (82%) and fledging (85%) success. Some egg and chick losses due to aggressive encounters with other *Aethia*, also predation by introduced rats (*Rattus*) and foxes (*Alopex lagopus*, *Vulpes vulpes*). Adults vulnerable to Peregrine Falcon (*Falco peregrinus*), Bald Eagle (*Haliaeetus leucocephalus*) and Glaucous-winged Gulls (*Larus glaucescens*), but mortality low owing to nocturnal behaviour. Adult survival estimated at 80%, pre-breeding survival rate not known. Age of first breeding unknown, probably 3-4 years.

Movements. Distribution and movements outside breeding season poorly known. Returns to colonies Apr to early May, with reproduction complete by mid-Aug, and most birds gone by early Sept. Most birds probably remain near-shore close to breeding areas (e.g. Aleutians), others possibly undergo local movements to adjacent seas (e.g. some Kuril birds to S Japan). Often concentrated in large flocks in winter, presumably at food-rich locations, particularly in E Aleutians.

Status and Conservation. Not globally threatened. Total population small, second rarest alcid in Alaska. Numbers poorly known, but coarse estimates indicate minimum of 100,000 birds, with 75,000 in North America (mostly E Aleutians) and 25,000 in Russia; alternatively something under 100,000 pairs. Largest concentrations at Buldir I (30,000 pairs), Krenitzen Is, Four Mountains Is, and several sites from Atka Pass to E Sitkin Sound; few count data in W, but probably significant numbers at Commander Is (Yama I, 2000 birds), Kurils (Chirinkotan, Matua, Ushishir), and N Sea of Okhotsk (Yamskie Is, c. 1000 pairs). Although estimates coarse, particularly W of Buldir I, sufficient to indicate high vulnerability to human activity. Information on population trends unavailable; incidence of accidental introductions of rats and persistence of introduced foxes on some breeding sites give cause for concern. Most serious current threats from introduced mammalian predators on colonies, oil pollution at sea, and fatal attraction to ship lights at night, particularly near colonies. Protection of breeding habitat critical, as is development of monitoring system capable of determining breeding performance and status at major breeding locations (a formidable task owing to species' nocturnal colony behaviour and breeding habitat characteristics).

Bibliography. Armstrong (1983), Bailey (1993a, 1993b), Bailey & Kaiser (1993), Bent (1919), Brazil (1991), Byrd (1994), Byrd & Day (1986), Byrd & Gibson (1980), Byrd & Williams (1993b), Byrd *et al.* (1983), Day & Byrd (1989), Dementiev & Gladkov (1951b), Feinstein (1959), Flint & Golovkin (1990), Flint *et al.* (1984), Gizenko (1955), Golovkin (1984), Gould *et al.* (1982), Haney, Hood *et al.* (1991), Hipfner & Byrd (1993), Hunt, Harrison & Piatt (1993), Johnsgard (1987), Knudtson & Byrd (1982), Knystautas (1993), Kondratiev (1991), Kozlova (1957), Lensink (1984), Litvinenko & Shibaev (1991), Manuwal (1984), Murie (1959), Sowls *et al.* (1978), Springer *et al.* (1993), Stejneger (1885), Troy (1989), Troy & Bradstreet (1991).

18. **Least Auklet**

Aethia pusilla

French: Starique minuscule **German**: Zwergalk **Spanish**: Mérgulo Mínimo
Other common names: Knob-billed Auklet

Taxonomy. *Uria pusilla* Pallas, 1811, Kamchatka.
Monotypic.

Distribution. Chukotskiy Peninsula S to Sea of Okhotsk (Yamskie Is) and C Kuril Is, and W Alaska from Diomede Is and Cape Lisburne S to Aleutians and E to NW Gulf of Alaska (Sumigan and Semidi Is). Winters at sea and along coasts in Bering Sea, often near breeding areas, from N limits of open water S to Gulf of Alaska and N Japan (Hokkaido).

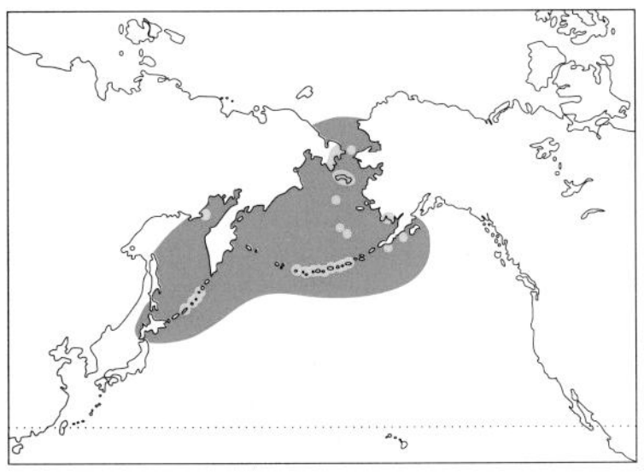

Descriptive notes. 12-14 cm; c. 85 g; wingspan 33-36 cm. Smallest alcid; short, dull red bill with narrow pale tip and blackish base, small horny knob from base of upper mandible; head dark, with white bristly feathers on forehead and lores, and white streak behind eye; white throat and dark breast band diagnostic; dark grey upperparts with white scapular streaks; underparts variably white to blackish grey, with mottled grey commonest. Female has slightly shallower bill. Distinguished from other species by tiny size, and head pattern. In winter, underparts entirely white, bill blackish without knob, and most facial plumes absent. Juvenile resembles winter adult, but lacks white auricular streak.

Habitat. Marine offshore and along coasts. Breeds on remote islands and sea coasts in talus slopes, beach boulder rubble, sea cliffs and lava fields where crevices suitable for breeding are abundant, usually in bare talus (where breeding density highest), occasionally in partially vegetated talus slopes or cliffs, almost always in association with other auklet species. Forages offshore in open ocean, often where upwelling, tidal pumps, etc. concentrate zooplankton (particularly copepods) near surface. Winter range and movements poorly known, but mostly pelagic and along sea coasts within breeding range.

Food and Feeding. Forages on planktonic crustaceans near-shore to offshore throughout year, almost always in large flocks and at open ocean locations with certain physical characteristics, especially stratified waters with strong thermoclines and upwellings. During breeding season, major foods of adults and chicks are calanoid copepods, principally *Neocalanus* (especially *N. plumchrus*), supplemented by numerous other small crustaceans: euphausiids, gammarids, hyperiids and mysids (St Lawrence I, Pribilofs, King I studies). Parents carry food in sublingual throat pouches and deliver 1-4 meals each daily (mean 2·6 meals/parent/day); average meal size from 5·4 g (0·9-12·3 g) at St George I to 8·2 g (6-10 g) at St Paul I, giving daily chick food intake of 28-43 g. Summer foods obtained at varying distances from colony, up to c. 50 km. Winter food not examined, probably variety of planktonic invertebrates. Dives to depths usually above c. 15 m, infrequently 25 m.

Breeding. Spring arrival at colonies variable, earliest towards extreme S, latest at N limit: late Apr to early May in Aleutians, early to mid-May at Pribilofs, late May at St Matthew I, and early to mid-Jun at St Lawrence I and Bering Strait site. Peak laying also earliest in S: usually late May in W Aleutians, early Jun in Pribilofs, mid- to late Jun at St Matthew, eary Jul at St Lawrence; laying at N colonies can be delayed by late snow-melt; fledging peaks early Aug (Aleutians), mid-Aug (Pribilofs), and late Aug to early Sept (St Lawrence). Monogamous, with shared mate choice and relatively low mate fidelity between years; both sexes prefer partners with elaborate facial ornaments (no relationship between degree of ornamentation and bird quality documented). Highly colonial, in large to enormous colonies, many exceeding 100,000 birds and some more than 1,000,000; numbers and density determined largely by availability of suitable habitat and crevices; usually highly synchronous (80% of hatchings within 10-day period). 1 egg; incubation averages c. 30-31 days, by both sexes in shifts of 12-36 hours (mean 23·6); egg losses rarely, if ever, replaced; downy chick brown above, greyish brown below, c. 11 g, semi-precocial, brooded continuously by parents during 1st week, infrequently thereafter; chick-rearing averages 29 days (25-33), chick independent at departure. Breeding success variable within and between colonies, with overall averages of eggs laid producing fledglings 56·5% at Buldir (1976, 1988-1991), 69·7% at St George (1981/82) and 37·6-49·6% at St Lawrence (1987); variation partly due to differences in human disturbance. Overall average annual productivity probably c. 0·5-0·6 young fledged/pair. Most egg and chick losses due to foxes (*Alopex lagopus*, *Vulpes vulpes*) and small voles (*Microtus*) and rats (*Rattus*); chicks especially vulnerable to gulls and foxes at time of fledging. Mean adult annual survival 75-77%, giving life expectancy of 7-8 years; pre-breeding survival rates not known. Sexual maturity at 3 years, but proportion of 3-year-olds that breed is unknown.

Movements. Migratory movements and winter range poorly known. Normally departs from colonies Aug to early Sept (exodus latest in N), wintering largely in seas within breeding range where waters remain ice-free, with some S movement into N Pacific, infrequently S to N British Columbia and N Japan (Hokkaido). Arrives back on land at colonies from late Apr to mid-Jun, non-breeders appearing 3-4 weeks later than breeders.

Status and Conservation. Not globally threatened. Size of breeding population unknown, but believed to be most abundant seabird in Bering Sea and most numerous auklet in Pacific. Estimates for North American population c. 9,000,000 birds or c. 6,300,000 pairs, and of and Russian population minimum c. 8,000,000 birds or c. 5,600,000 pairs, giving total of 17,000,000 birds or c. 12,000,000 pairs. Concentrated at small number of huge colonies: Matykyl I (Yamskie Is, N Sea of Okhotsk), at least 6,000,000 individuals and possibly as many as 10,000,000; St Lawrence I, 1,300,000 birds; Kiska I, 1,200,000 birds; Diomede Is, c. 1,000,000 birds; and St Matthew and Hall Is, c. 300,000 birds each. Absence of adequate census methods limits estimates to educated best guesses, offering little opportunity to assess population trends. In Alaska, local changes at some individual colonies are known: large increases at Skruis Point (Kiska I) and decreases elsewhere; marked declines at St George I (Ulakaia Hill) and St Paul I due to habitat destruction and alteration, and possible increases at St Lawrence I (Kongkok Bay, 1964-1987). Hunting, habitat destruction and disturbance, introduced predators, and effects of marine pollution (oil and fish-waste discharges) suspected prime causes of declines. Introduced rats and foxes serious threats, especially in Aleutians and Pribilofs; increases on St Lawrence may be related to reduced predation pressures from foxes and humans owing to declines in fox abundance and in importance of auklets in subsistence economies of local residents, and also to oceanographic changes in Bering Sea. Populations in NE Russia similarly affected; most serious current threats in NW Pacific include continued mortality from human predation and colony disturbance, alien predators, oil pollution and industrial developments (e.g. E Sakhalin, Sea of Okhotsk) and commercial fisheries. Overall, present conservation needs for this abundant, but vulnerable, species are: development of statistically meaningful census methods to monitor size and status of representative breeding populations throughout range; further examination of effects of introduced predators and human exploitation on populations, and enactment of necessary control measures; careful assessment of possible impacts of oil pollution and commercial fishery developments; and enforcement of existing laws and regulations to reduce disturbance and destruction of seabird colonies and habitat.

Bibliography. Anon. (1991b, 1993e), Armstrong (1983), Bailey (1993a, 1993b), Bailey & Kaiser (1993), Bédard (1969a, 1969b), Bédard & Sealy (1984), Bent (1919), Bradstreet (1985), Brazil (1991), Byrd *et al.* (1983), Flint *et al.* (1984), Godfrey (1986), Haney (1991), Harrison (1978), Hatch & Hatch (1983), Hipfner & Byrd (1993), Hunt & Harrison (1990), Hunt, Burgeson & Sanger (1981), Hunt, Eppley *et al.* (1981), Hunt, Harrison & Cooney (1990), Hunt, Harrison & Piatt (1993), Johnsgard (1987), Jones (1989, 1990, 1992a, 1992b, 1993a), Jones & Montgomerie (1991, 1992), Knudtson & Byrd (1982), Knystautas (1993), Kondratiev (1991), Konratiev *et al.* (1993), Lensink (1984), Litvinenko (1993), Litvinenko & Shibaev (1991), Manuwal (1984), Piatt, Roberts & Hatch (1990), Piatt, Roberts, Lidster *et al.* (1990), Roby (1991), Roby & Brink (1986a, 1986b), Roby & Ricklefs (1986), Sealy (1968, 1975d, 1982), Searing (1977), Sowls *et al.* (1978), Springer & Roseneau (1985), Springer *et al.* (1993).

Genus *CERORHINCA* Bonaparte, 1828

19. **Rhinoceros Auklet**

Cerorhinca monocerata

French: Macareux rhinocéros **German**: Nashornalk **Spanish**: Alca Unicórnea
Other common names: Horn-billed/Unicorn Auk

Taxonomy. *Alca monocerata* Pallas, 1811, Cape St Elias, Alaska.
Monotypic.

Distribution. Akademii Gulf, S Sakhalin and S Kuril Is to Japan (Teuri I) and extreme NE Korea; C Aleutians; S & SE Alaska (W to Barren I, Middleton I, St Lazaria I, Forrester I) S to British Columbia (Triangle I), W Washington (Destruction I) and N California (Castle I, Farallon Is). Winters mostly offshore and along coasts, in Asia near breeding areas, and in North America mainly from S British Columbia (casually from SE Alaska) S to Baja California (Santa Margarita I).

Descriptive notes. 35-38 cm; c. 533 g. Yellowish orange bill, with short, vertical whitish knob or "horn" at base of upper mandible; darkish brown head with yellow iris, and with two long white facial plumes extending backwards, one from above eye to nape and the other from gape to upper throat; brownish upperparts, with pale buff edges giving faint scaled appearance; brownish upper breast, whitish belly, flanks with broken pale brown barring; legs and feet greyish yellow, with black webs and claws. In winter, knob of upper mandible absent, and white facial plumes less distinct; resembles immature *Fratercula cirrhata*, but has smaller, more pointed bill and pointed wings. Juvenile similar to winter adult, but bill smaller and no facial streaks.

Habitat. Marine offshore and along sea coasts and islands. Breeds on maritime and inland grassy slopes, sometimes on flattish ground, on small forested and unforested predator-free islands, rarely on steep island or mainland cliffs; also occurs in large aggregations at sea, and often forms dense roosting

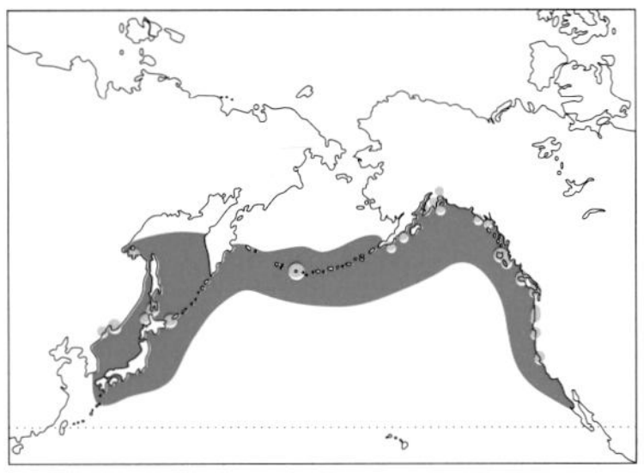

flocks at night in sheltered bays. In winter, normally pelagic in waters offshore from breeding areas, sometimes in near-shore coastal waters where coastal oceanographic conditions (upwellings, converging currents, tidal pumps) concentrate food. Winter ecology poorly known, but mostly pelagic within breeding range.

Food and Feeding. Mostly fish throughout year, supplemented in winter by small amounts of invertebrates (squid, euphausiids and other crustaceans); generally opportunistic, with diverse and seasonably variable diet, including relatively high consumption of crustaceans. Chick diet almost exclusively fish, but invertebrates may appear for late-hatched young; c. 2 meals/day, delivered by both parents at night, averaging c. 30 g of fish/meal or c. 60 g daily, usually of species high in fat, e.g. sandeels (*Ammodytes hexapterus*), capelin (*Mallotus villosus*). Food studies limited, but principal prey fed to young known to vary geographically: e.g. sandeels, bluethroat argentines (*Nansenia candeda*), Pacific saury (*Cololabris saira*) and rockfish (*Sebastes*) predominated in British Columbia (Triangle I), whereas main foods in nearby Washington (Destruction I) were sandeels, Pacific herring (*Clupea harengus*) and northern anchovy (*Engraulis mordax*) with lesser amounts of surf smelt (*Hypomesus pretiosus*) and night smelt (*Spirinchus starksi*); capelin important at N colonies. Adult summer diet appears similar to foods delivered to chick; winter diet little known, but available information indicates small fish (anchovies, rockfish), crustaceans and squid. Generally forages inshore, often in mixed-species flocks, at locations near colony or far offshore. Pelagic schooling fish obtained by pursuit-diving, mostly at depths above 30-40 m.

Breeding. Arrival at colony normally late Mar and early Apr, slightly later in N; laying from end Apr to mid-Jun, with fledging mostly late Jul to early Sept. Monogamous, with site and mate fidelity probably high, but degree of mate retention unconfirmed. Highly colonial, in small to very large concentrations (some exceeding 100,000 birds), usually with other alcids; usually at high densities on optimal grassy-turf habitat, averaging 0·2-1·2 pairs/m^2, sometimes higher; laying often highly synchronous within colony (80% of eggs laid within 14-16 days), but timing variable between populations. Lays in nest chamber at end of burrow, usually 2-3 m long (up to c. 6 m), excavated by both sexes, primarily in exposed grassy maritime slopes or flat ground on forest floor. 1 egg; incubation averages 35 days, by both sexes for stints of 24 hours; early egg losses may be replaced after 9-14 days; downy chick mostly dark greyish brown, slightly paler below, c. 54-57 g, semi-precocial; chick-rearing averages 52 days (annual variations 48-60 days, likely related to food supply), with care and feeding by both parents until fledging, when chick leaves burrow at night and flies to sea unaccompanied, usually fully feathered. Breeding success variable within and between colonies, overall average 56% eggs laid producing fledglings; hatching 81% (65-94%), fledging 69% (27-97%), with lower variation in hatching success than chick survival probably related to inter-year differences in food supply during chick rearing. Egg losses due to breakage, neglect, and predation by gulls and, locally, introduced mammals; chick losses due mainly to food shortage (starvation, or increased exposure to predators). Adult annual survival and recruitment rates not known. Age of first breeding uncertain, probably 5 years.

Movements. Winters mostly offshore, sometimes near-shore and coastal, usually within breeding range. S populations somewhat sedentary, often remaining in coastal and offshore waters adjacent to colony; N birds (Alaska) mostly migratory, moving S to at least S British Columbia. N and inshore movements from wintering areas begin as early as Feb-Mar, most birds reaching colonies in late Mar and Apr.

Status and Conservation. Not globally threatened. Total breeding population estimated at 1,250,000 birds, with c. 347,000 (300,000-400,000) in Asia and c. 903,000 (800,000-1,000,000) in North America, mostly in boreal waters, with centre of abundance in British Columbia. Largest single colonies in Japan (Teuri I, c. 350,000 birds), SE Alaska (Forrester I, 108,000 birds) and British Columbia (Pine I, 90,000 birds). Regional totals of c. 334,000 birds in Sea of Japan (Hokkaido), 10,000 in Kurils, 3000 in Sea of Okhotsk, 119,000 in Alaska (110,000 in SE), 903,000 in British Columbia, 61,000 in Washington, 1000 in Oregon, and under 2000 in California. Historically, population probably much larger than at present, though data insufficient to define precise trends in most regions. In general, populations from Kurils NE to Alaska drastically reduced during 19th and first half of 20th centuries through introduction onto nesting colonies by Japanese and Russian fur-farmers of foxes (*Alopex lagopus*, *Vulpes vulpes*), sable (*Martes zibellina*), ermine (*Mustela erminea*) and mink (*Mustela vison*, *M. lutreola*), and associated rats (*Rattus norvegicus*), voles (*Microtus*), feral cats and dogs, and use of the birds for animal feed. Many colonies extinct, and pressures from alien predators continue today. Numbers in Russia declined from c. 14,000 birds in 1938 to 1500 in 1949, from which level they have not recovered. In Alaska, many former island populations were probably extirpated by introduced foxes throughout SW, SC & SE regions including Aleutians, where now restricted to Buldir I (fewer than 1000), the only fox-free island. Populations farther S in North America were also seriously affected, mostly by human disturbance (egging and hunting, destruction of nesting habitat, lighthouse construction and operation) and by introduced mammals, both predators and domestic livestock. Many extant populations remain threatened by continued presence of introduced ground predators (especially Kurils, Russia, Alaska), but some have shown or are showing significant increases: California, Farallon Is recolonized in early 1970's after extirpation in 1860's, and substantial increase since rabbits removed in 1974; Washington, 700+% increase on Protection I after removal of sheep in 1968; British Columbia, on Cleland I; and Japan, on Teuri I during 1950-1970. Currently, numbers believed relatively stable in Japan, decreasing in Russia, stable or slightly increasing elsewhere. Major threats remain continued predation by introduced mammalian predators at nesting colonies, oil spills in vicinity of major colonies during breeding season and where birds concentrate at sea during winter, commercial fisheries (direct mortality in gill-nets, food shortages during chick-rearing from overfishing), and disturbance at colonies during summer (tourism, researchers). Immediate conservation needs include: increased effort to control and eradicate introduced predators on extant and former breeding colonies; establishment of widespread monitoring system to obtain accurate information on population size and reproductive performance; refinement of existing census techniques; initiation of studies to examine pelagic ecology and winter requirements; further assessment of direct and indirect impacts of commericial fisheries; and development and implementation of more effective system of protection of major breeding colonies.

Bibliography. Ainley & Boekelheide (1990), Ainley, Morrell & Boekelheide (1990), Armstrong (1983), Bailey (1993a, 1993b), Bailey & Kaiser (1993), Bent (1919), Bertram (1988), Bertram & Kaiser (1988), Bertram *et al.* (1991), Brazil (1991), Byrd *et al.* (1993), Campbell *et al.* (1990), Carter *et al.* (1990), Étchécopar & Hüe (1978), Flint *et al.* (1984), Fujimaki (1986), Gaston & Dechesne (1996), Gizenko (1955), Golovkin (1984), Hasegawa (1984), Hatch (1984), Howell & Webb (1995a), Hunt, Burgeson & Sanger (1981), Johnsgard (1987), Knystautas (1993), Lensink (1984), Leschner (1976), Litvinenko (1993), Litvinenko & Shibaev (1991), Manuwal (1984), McChesney *et al.* (1995), Nechaev (1975), Richardson (1961), Rodway (1991), Sealy (1972), Shibaev (1987), Shuntov (1986), Sowls, DeGange *et al.* (1980), Sowls, Hatch & Lensink (1978), Speich & Wahl (1989), Summers & Drent (1979), Takahasi (1939), Thompson *et al.* (1985), Thorenson (1983), Vermeer (1979, 1980), Vermeer & Cullen (1979), Watanuki (1987, 1990), Wehle (1980), Wilson (1986), Wilson & Manuwal (1986).

Genus *FRATERCULA* Brisson, 1760

20. **Atlantic Puffin**

Fratercula arctica

French: Macareux moine **German**: Papageitaucher **Spanish**: Frailecillo Atlántico
Other common names: (Common) Puffin

Taxonomy. *Alca arctica* Linnaeus, 1758, northern Norway.
Recorded differences separating *grabae* from nominate *arctica* may reflect clinal variation only. Three races recognized.

Subspecies and Distribution.
F. a. naumanni Norton, 1901 - NE Canada (high E Arctic) and NW & E Greenland to Jan Mayen, Spitsbergen and N Novaya Zemlya.
F. a. arctica (Linnaeus, 1758) - SE Baffin I and Hudson Bay S to Maine, and E through SW & S Greenland and Iceland to Bear I, C & N Norway, Kola Peninsula and S Novaya Zemlya.
F. a. grabae (C. L. Brehm, 1831) - Faeroes, S Norway and SW Sweden S through British Is to Channel Is and NW France.
Winters at sea, mostly in boreal waters S to New Jersey, Azores, Canary Is, and W Mediterranean, rarely to Virginia and NW Africa.

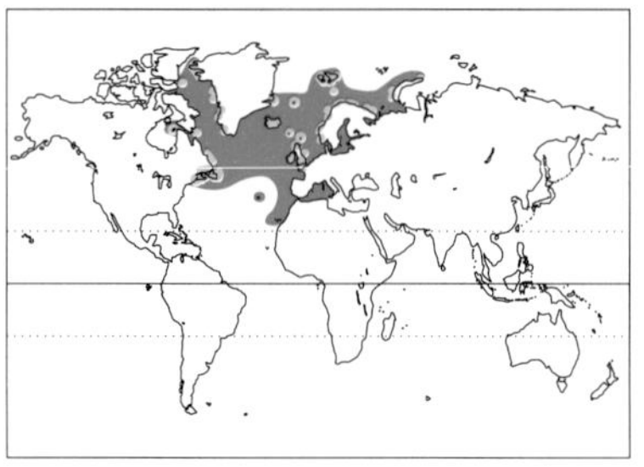

Descriptive notes. 26-36 cm; 460 g; wingspan 47-63 cm. Large, triangular red bill, laterally compressed, with distinct transverse ridges across upper mandible, bluish grey at base with pale yellow cere, and orange-yellow rictal rosette at gape, yellowish mouth and tongue; mostly white to greyish white face, with narrow black band from forehead to nape, greyish chin, and pronounced dark post-ocular stripe; small fleshy-grey protuberances above and below orange-red eye-ring, and soft brown iris; mostly black upperparts; black from neck across throat, with snow white breast, flanks and belly; legs and feet orange to yellowish orange or reddish, with sharply recurved black claws. Differs from larger *F. corniculata* by bill and facial ornaments. In winter, eye ornaments, basal-plate sheath of mandible and cere absent, making bill smaller; face darker grey, bare part colours less distinct. Juvenile resembles adult, but generally smaller (overlap between small adult females and large juveniles); bill and legs duller; fewer than 2 transverse ridges on upper mandible. Races differ only in size, but with much individual variation and overlap.

Habitat. Exclusively marine, occurring along rocky coasts and offshore islands. Breeds on grassy-turfed maritime slopes or adjacent flattish ground, also on sea cliffs, and boulder fields and scree slopes. Almost 60% breed in boreal water zone, 40% in low Arctic waters and less than 1% in high Arctic marine zone. In winter, wide-ranging in offshore and pelagic habitats, normally within open-water regions of breeding range to edge and slope of continental shelf, only infrequently into open ocean, and rarely beyond S limit of boreal waters into cool subtropical waters. Winter distributions poorly known, but principal determinants probably sea surface water temperatures and distribution patterns of key pelagic fish species.

Food and Feeding. Mostly fish throughout year, supplemented mainly late summer to spring by small crustaceans (euphausiids, copepods), polychaetes (nereids) and squid; daily food intake estimated at c. 15-20% of adult body weight. Typically neritic feeder during breeding, obtaining food inshore out to edge of continental shelf, with foraging patterns highly variable between areas and water systems during chick-rearing, from feeding close (3-5 km) to colony to travelling considerable distances (50-100 km) away; birds often gather offshore at edges of banks where water-mass boundaries or fronts and flow gradients concentrate fish prey. Food brought to chicks almost exclusively fish, except late in rearing period when invertebrates may appear, with principal prey species varying between area and water type, but all with relatively high calorific values, primarily small pelagic fish: capelin (*Mallotus villosus*) in low Arctic waters (Labrador, Newfoundland); sandeels (*Ammodytes*, *Hyperoplus*), Atlantic herring (*Clupea harengus*), Atlantic mackerel (*Scomber scombrus*) and gadids in N boreal waters (N Norway); sandeels, sprat (*Sprattus sprattus*) and gadids in S boreal regions (Britain). In general, all colonies of race *grabae* are in areas with sprat, whereas most colonies of race *arctica* are where there is a capelin fishery, and movements of birds from these low Arctic sites seem associated with capelin movements. Chick fed by both parents, c. 3-9 meals/day, averaging total of 43-62 g daily. Winter diet poorly known. Feeds by underwater pursuit-diving, usually after schools of fish (rather than single individuals), to depths normally above 20 m, with average dive times under 30 seconds.

Breeding. Arrival and start of laying variable between regions, usually earlier and with more extended pre-laying and laying periods at extreme S locations, later and with time periods reduced in low Arctic zone; average arrival in boreal waters mid- to late Feb (E Scotland) and late Mar to early Apr (Wales, Scotian Shelf, Gulf of Maine), in low Arctic normally mid-Apr (Murmansk, N Norway, Newfoundland, N Gulf of St Lawrence), sometimes 1st half Jun (Labrador), in high Arctic waters unknown (probably later than low Arctic); most laying early to late May or early Jun, earlier in E Scotland and later in Labrador and high Arctic; fledging normally through Jul and early Aug, later in low and high Arctic. Monogamous, with high mate and site fidelity. Highly colonial, in small to large aggregations; densities highest on seaward-facing slopes, averaging 2·0 pairs/m^2 (1·7-2·8); usually highly synchronous within a colony, often most precisely so among birds on slope habitat. Nests mostly in burrows excavated (1-2 m long) in turf-covered maritime steep slopes and level tops, also in rock crevices and interstices on cliffs and cavities in boulder fields and scree slopes; males spend more time defending and maintaining burrow than females; usually lays on scrape, often lined with dry grass and feathers, in nest chamber at end of tunnel. 1 egg; incubation averages 42 days (36-45 days), by both sexes (females slightly longer) for variable periods averaging c. 32 hours (23-70); early egg losses may be replaced after c. 13-23 days, but replacement rate low (c. 9%); downy chick silvery grey above, white on belly, with black legs and bill, c. 48 g, semi-precocial; chick-rearing variable, averages 38-59 days (39-83), with care and feeding by both parents, chick normally fledging at night soon after dark and flying out to sea unaccompanied, usually fully feathered except late-hatched young, which often depart with considerable down. Breeding success highly variable, averaging from 28% to 93% at different colonies and years through N Atlantic (excluding years of total failure owing to severe food shortages); in average conditions c. 53%, with mean survival of eggs (72% laid hatch) and chicks (73% hatched fledge) very similar; higher in regions of unusual population growth (e.g. Isle of May, E Scotland) and lower on low-quality habitat (e.g. flattish ground in presence of gulls, Great I, Newfoundland) or where fish-stock collapses have occurred (Norway, Atlantic Canada). Factors causing egg and chick losses variable, from parental neglect or mishandling during incubation and brooding to gull predation and food shortages during chick-rearing; human predation and disturbance significant in many regions. Adult survival c. 95%; survival of fledglings to breeding age variable, 13-39%. First breeding normally at 5 years, sometimes 3 or 4 when population expanding.

Movements. Winters largely offshore, widely dispersed at relatively low densities, sometimes off continental shelf and slope into pelagic zone. Post-breeding dispersal complex, with four basic patterns: Greenland and Newfoundland birds remain in W Atlantic, well offshore and dispersed widely; Irish Sea birds and some from N Britain move S to Bay of Biscay, and probably Mediterranean; birds from E Britain, SW Norway and some from N Britain winter mostly in North Sea; those from Murmansk, N Norway, Iceland and European high Arctic and some 1st-winter birds from N Britain move W or SW; younger cohorts from all these regions move longest distances, as far as Greenland and Newfoundland. Extent and magnitude of S movement during winter poorly known, but birds from S colonies appear to migrate farthest S, recorded regularly to W Mediterranean and NW Africa (Morocco) in E Atlantic and to New Jersey in W Atlantic. Return to breeding areas prolonged, with colonies usually occupied by breeders between mid-Mar and mid-May, indicating that spring movements begin during Feb and early Mar. Considerably more work required to identify main wintering areas and clarify patterns of movement.

Status and Conservation. Not globally threatened. Total breeding population estimated at c. 6,000,000 pairs (3,800,000-8,200,000), of which c. 60% in boreal zone (S Iceland to France and Norway), 40% in low Arctic waters (most of E Canada and W Greenland, N Iceland, Bear I, Kola Peninsula, S Novaya Zemlya), and less than 1% in high Arctic marine zone (N Canada, NW & E Greenland, Jan Mayen, Spitsbergen, N Novaya Zemlya). Main concentration in Iceland, with c. 3,000,000 pairs (c. 50%); Norway holds 1,200,000 (20%), Britain 675,000 (11%), Faeroes 500,000 (8%), E Canada 365,000 (6%), Ireland 45,000 (under 1%), smaller numbers elsewhere. Big concentrations during breeding season make species highly vulnerable to direct and indirect effects of disturbance from human activities. Total population significantly reduced through 18th, 19th and first half of 20th centuries, mainly through egging, hunting, uncontrolled killing of birds at colonies for food, and introduced alien predators (rats, feral cats and dogs) and grazing animals (goats, sheep, rabbits); many populations extirpated or severely reduced by expanding human populations, particularly in boreal regions and S low Arctic waters, including S parts of continental W Europe, British Is, E Canada and New England. Slow recovery occurred in some regions from 1920's to 1940's, when marine pollution began to limit and reverse trend of increasing numbers in most regions. More recently, major international fisheries developments in Barents Sea-Norwegian Sea, Irminger Sea and NW Atlantic (Grand Banks of Newfoundland) since early 1960's have resulted in overfishing causing collapses of key forage-fish species, with ensuing reproductive failure and declines of many populations of present species, e.g. Røst (Norway) 64% decline 1979-1988, and Great I (Newfoundland) c. 30% decline 1972-1989; also unknown impacts on winter survival and longevity. Food shortages combined with entanglement and drowning in fishing gear, chronic oil fouling throughout year, disturbance on nesting grounds (uncontrolled "harvesting", livestock grazing, tourism), and winter hunting pose serious threats. Populations decreasing in France, Channel Is, Norway, Kola Peninsula and E Canada, and parts of British Is and Faeroes; status in Iceland uncertain, mainly due to difficulty of monitoring the large and widespread population, though local declines highly probable. Major conservation actions required include: control of human disturbance at breeding colonies; control and removal of alien animals from colonies; major examination of impact of food shortages on populations, particularly those suspected or known to involve commercial fisheries; establishment of enhanced system to monitor and predict impacts of offshore oil developments on major populations, particularly those on critical international bird wintering areas, e.g. Hibernia and Ben Nevis fields, Grand Banks of Newfoundland; increased effort to identify ecological requirements at sea during winter; and initiation of monitoring system to determine status and population trends in Iceland and Faeroes, probably through international partnership.

Bibliography. Anker-Nilssen (1987, 1992), Anker-Nilssen & Lorentsen (1990), Ashcroft (1976, 1979), Barrett & Rikardsen (1992), Barrett, Anker-Nilssen *et al.* (1987), Barrett, Fieler *et al.* (1985), Bédard (1985), Belopol'skii (1957), Bent (1919), Birkhead (1985b), Birkhead & Harris (1985), Birkhead & Nettleship (1995), Bradstreet & Brown (1985), Brown (1985), Brown & Nettleship (1984b), Buckley & Buckley (1984b), Corkhill (1973), Cramp (1985), Cramp *et al.* (1974), Creelman & Storey (1991), Evans (1984a, 1984b), Evans & Nettleship (1985), Flint *et al.* (1984), Gaston (1985c), Grant (1971), Grant & Nettleship (1971), Harris, M.P. (1983a, 1983b, 1984, 1994), Harris, M.P. & Bailey (1992), Harris, M.P. & Birkhead (1985), Harris, M.P. & Hislop (1978), Harris, M.P. & Wanless (1991), Harris, M.P., Heubeck & Suddaby (1991), Hislop & Harris (1983), Hori (1994), Hudson (1979, 1985), Kartaschew (1960), Knystautas (1993), Kozlova (1957), Kress & Nettleship (1988), Lid (1981), Lloyd *et al.* (1991), Lockley (1934, 1962), Løvenskiold (1964), Martin (1989), Mehlum & Bakken (1994), Moen (1991), Myrberget (1959, 1962, 1963, 1973), Nettleship (1970, 1972, 1975, 1976, 1977b, 1980, 1991b), Nettleship & Evans (1985), Perry (1946), Petersen (1976a, 1976b), Piatt (1990), Piatt & Nettleship (1985, 1987), Piatt, Nettleship & Threlfall (1984), Richards (1990), Salmansohn (1995), Salomonsen (1944, 1950, 1967b), Schneider, Pierotti & Threlfall (1990), Tasker *et al.* (1987), Tuck (1971), Urban *et al.* (1986), Uspenski (1956).

21. Horned Puffin

Fratercula corniculata

French: Macareux cornu **German**: Hornlund **Spanish**: Frailecillo Corniculado

Taxonomy. *Mormon corniculata* J. F. Naumann, 1821, Kamchatka.
Monotypic.

Distribution. Wrangel I, Heard I and Chukotskiy Peninsula S through Kamchatka and Commander Is to Sea of Okhotsk, Sakhalin and N Kuril Is, and W Alaska (Diomede Is, Cape Lisburne) S through Bering Sea to Aleutians and E through Gulf of Alaska S to British Columbia (Queen Charlotte Is). Winters offshore and along sea coasts mostly within breeding range, but casually S to C Japan, rarely to W Hawaiian Is, also to S British Columbia and N Washington and rarely to Oregon and California.

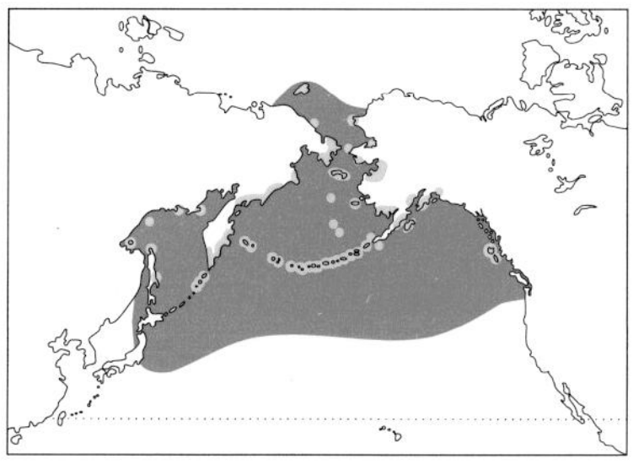

Descriptive notes. 36-41 cm; 612 g; wingspan 56-58 cm. Large, triangular red-tipped yellow bill, laterally compressed, with orangy rictal rosette at gape, yellowish mouth and tongue; white face, with black forehead, crown, nape and chin, dark post-ocular stripe; small elongated, upright, triangular fleshy dark horn above reddish eye-ring; iris dark brown, almost black; black upperparts, snowy white breast and belly; legs and feet orange or reddish, with sharp, recurved black claws. Differs from *F. cirrhata* in white underparts and no nuptial facial plumes. In winter, lacks basal yellow bill plate; face greyish; orangy red of bare parts less pronounced. Juvenile similar to winter adult, but considerably smaller, with shorter and narrower, darker bill.

Habitat. Marine, occurring along sea coasts on rocky cliffs and offshore islands. Breeds mainly on rocky cliffs, boulder areas and talus slopes, less frequently in burrows on grassy-turfed maritime slopes of islands. Occurs mainly on glaciated and rocky coastlines, usually associated with relatively cold water systems. In winter, mostly offshore within open-water areas of breeding range to edge of continental shelf, only infrequently penetrating open ocean (unlike *F. cirrhata*), and rarely S beyond N half of boreal zone; winter distribution largely influenced by sea surface temperatures and associated concentrations of pelagic fish.

Food and Feeding. Predominantly inshore feeder during breeding season, usually within 1-2 km from shore, but sometimes 16 km or more out. Diet throughout year mostly fish of wide diversity of species, supplemented with significant quantities of squid, crustaceans and polychaetes. Overall, more generalized feeder than *F. cirrhata*. Chick diet almost exclusively fish, primarily sandeels (*Ammodytes hexapterus*) and capelin (*Mallotus villosus*), both unusually high in fat and calorific value, and their availability during chick-rearing a major determinant of breeding success; secondary chick foods include greenling (*Hexagrammos*), cod (*Gadus*), sandfish (*Trichondon*) and squid. Chick fed by both parents, 2-6 meals/day averaging 12 g each (8-17 g), or 24-72 g daily. Adult diet through entire breeding season mostly fish (48%), followed by squid (31%), polychaetes (12%) and crustaceans (8%); winter foods poorly known, but available information suggests similar to summer. Food obtained by underwater pursuit-diving, probably at depths above 40 m.

Breeding. Spring arrival and start of breeding variable, with major movement through Bering Sea during May and reoccupation of colonies usually mid-May to early Jun; peak laying mid-Jun to mid-Jul, with fledging mostly early Sept and continuing to end Sept. Few breeding studies, but likely monogamous, with high site and mate fidelity. Colonial, in small to large aggregations; densities largely determined by availability of suitable rock crevices and cavities, highest in less favoured vegetated talus slopes, probably reaching maximum of c. 0·2-0·5 pairs/m²; laying highly synchronous within a colony (most eggs laid within 1 week of each other). Nest typically in crevice or crack in rock substrate, usually on cliff face, also in cavities under beach boulders and talus slopes, and less frequently in burrows excavated on grassy-turfed maritime slopes of islands; lays in scrape on bare floor at end of crevice or cavity tunnel, sometimes sparsely lined with feathers or dry plant material. 1 egg; incubation averages 41 days (38-43), by both sexes; early egg losses may be replaced; downy chick pale grey-brown to dark brown above, greyish white to yellowish white on belly, with blackish bill, legs and feet, c. 59 g, semi-precocial; chick-rearing averages 40 days (38-43, but higher variation likely in relation to food supply), with care and feeding by both parents; chick normally fledging at night, flying out to sea unaccompanied, usually fully feathered. Breeding success averages 57%, with mean survival of eggs (76%) and chicks (71%) similar, though chick mortality usually more variable than egg survival. Most egg and chick losses probably due to parental neglect or food shortages, although foxes (*Alopex lagopus*, *Vulpes fulva*) significant predators at some locations, as are rats (*Rattus*). Adult survival and recruitment rates unknown, but longevity probably high. Age of first breeding uncertain, probably 4-5 years.

Movements. Winters largely offshore adjacent to breeding areas in areas of open water; widespread over continental shelf at relatively low densities. Post-breeding dispersal Sept-Oct, with N populations from Chukchi and Bering Seas mostly moving S to at least Aleutians, some remaining farther N at Commander and Pribilof Is; S populations more sedentary, including large numbers overwintering in Gulf of Alaska, but significant numbers move S to C Japan, and some regularly to S British Columbia and Washington, even to Oregon and California. In general, timing and pattern of movements poorly known, but main spring influx occurs late Apr to mid-May throughout breeding range.

Status and Conservation. Not globally threatened. Total breeding population estimated at 1,220,000 birds, with c. 292,000 (250,000-350,000) in Asia and c. 928,000 (880,000-980,000) in North America, mostly in low Arctic and boreal water zones. Centre of abundance in Alaskan Peninsula, with c. 762,000 birds, including largest known single colony of c. 250,000 breeding birds (Suklik, Semidi Is); this total combined with individuals in Aleutians (c. 92,000), Alaskan Bering Sea (58,000) and SC Alaska (c. 16,000) accounts for 76% of world population. Only other major concentration in Sea of Okhotsk, where 200,000 birds breed, with smaller numbers in Arctic Ocean (48,000 birds), Siberian Bering Sea (40,000), Kurils (c. 4000), SE Alaska (under 1000) and British Columbia (under 1000). Few quantitative data on recent population trends, but probably decimated by introduced foxes over most of range through most of 19th and 20th centuries; both Arctic and red foxes have likely had major impact on species' selection of nesting habitat, by restricting it to rock crevices and cavities inaccessible to foxes. Current threats: predation by introduced predators on nesting grounds, oil spills, direct mortality in gill-nets, and food competition with commercial fisheries. Most pressing conservation needs are: control and eradication of introduced mammalian predators at colonies; design and implementation of monitoring system at representative set of colonies throughout range to assess population trends; detailed examination of summer and winter feeding ecology, including pelagic distribution and water-habitat usage; and initiation of systematic survey and census programme for all regions.

Bibliography. Amaral (1977), Armstrong (1983), Bailey (1993a, 1993b), Bailey & Kaiser (1993), Bent (1919), Brazil (1991), Byrd & Day (1986), Byrd & Douglas (1990), Byrd, Climo & Fuller (1989), Byrd, Douglas *et al.* (1990), Byrd, Murphy *et al.* (1993), Campbell *et al.* (1990), DeGange *et al.* (1993), Flint *et al.* (1984), Fujimaki (1986), Gabrielson & Lincoln & (1959), Golovkin (1984), Hunt, Burgeson & Sanger (1981), Hunt, Eppley *et al.* (1981), Johnsgard (1987), Kessel (1989), Knystautas (1993), Kondratiev (1991), Kondratiev *et al.* (1993), Lensink (1984), Leschner & Burrell (1977), Litvinenko (1993), Litvinenko & Shibaev (1991), Manuwal (1984), Manuwal & Boersma (1978), Moe & Day (1979), Nechaev (1986), Portenko (1973), Richards (1990), Rodway (1991), Sealy (1969, 1972, 1973b), Shuntov (1986), Sowls, DeGange *et al.* (1980), Sowls, Hatch & Lensink (1978), Swartz (1966, 1967), Wehle (1976, 1980, 1983).

22. Tufted Puffin

Fratercula cirrhata

French: Macareux huppé **German**: Gelbschopflund **Spanish**: Frailecillo Coletudo

Taxonomy. *Alca cirrhata* Pallas, 1769, Bering Sea.
Monotypic.

Distribution. N Japan (Hokkaido) through Kuril Is, Sakhalin and Sea of Okhotsk to N Chukotskiy Peninsula, and W Alaska (Diomede Is, Cape Thompson) S to Aleutians, E through Gulf of Alaska (Kodiak Archipelago) and S to British Columbia (Queen Charlotte Is, Triangle I) and C California (Farallon Is). Winters mostly at sea and along coasts from Kamchatka Peninsula and S Alaska S through breeding range, rarely to S Japan and S California.

Descriptive notes. 36-41 cm; 773 g. Large, parrot-like red bill, laterally compressed, basal third of upper mandible with yellowish to greenish base and yellow ridge; white face and chin, with black crown, nape and throat, and long golden to creamy-buff post-ocular tufts descending to nape; red eye-ring, yellow iris; black upperparts and underparts; legs and feet reddish orange, with sharp, curved black claws. Differs from *F. corniculata* and other puffin-like species in dark underparts, pale head plumes, and massive bill. In winter, head entirely dark, with no tufts; bill appears smaller and less triangular, as basal sheath absent. Juvenile has smaller yellowish bill, brown eye, and paler chin, throat and underparts.

Habitat. Marine, along rocky coasts and offshore islands. Breeds mainly in N boreal water zone, usually on maritime slopes and tops of islands, less often on cliffs or slopes of coastal cliffs and islands.

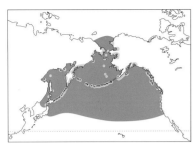

Mostly offshore during winter; one of most pelagic Pacific alcids, moving off continental shelf into oceanic zone to mid-ocean, dispersing over vast regions at very low densities; S limit usually S boreal waters, but sometimes into N cool subtropical zone.

Food and Feeding. Feeds mostly offshore on small fish, cephalopods and crustaceans throughout year. Adult diet averages c. 52% fish, 38% squid, 7% crustaceans and 3% polychaetes (by frequency of occurrence). During breeding season, often forages inshore and close to colony. Chick diet almost exclusively fish, with wide diversity over range, but Pacific sandeels (*Ammodytes hexapterus*) or capelin (*Mallotus villosus*) predominate in many E Bering Sea and Gulf of Alaska regions, often comprising 80-90%; other foods include walleye pollock (*Theragra chalcogramma*), greenling (*Hexagrammos monopoterygius*), mackerel (*Pleurogrammus monopoterygius*), cod (*Eleginus gracilis*), sculpins (*Hemilepidotus jordani*), euphausiids (*Thysanoessa*), squid and octopus, with cephalopods and pollock most important as supplementary foods. Chick fed by both parents, c. 2-4 meals/day averaging 8-20 g each, or 16-80 g daily. Little information available for E Asia; winter food poorly known throughout range. Prey obtained by pursuit-diving to considerable depths, probably above 40-50 m.

Breeding. Spring arrival latest at northernmost sites in Chukchi and Bering Seas, usually late May to early Jun, in most other regions late Apr to mid-May; laying normally peaks end May to mid-Jun, but at N sites may be 1-2 weeks later and in S is earlier, early May to early Jun, with laying period usually 1-3 weeks earlier than for *F. corniculata*; fledging mostly mid-Aug to mid-Sept, to late Sept in N. Believed monogamous, with high site and mate fidelity. Colonial, in small to immense aggregations; densites highest on steep sea-facing grassy slopes, averaging as high as 1·1 pairs/m² (Triangle I, British Columbia), normally 0·2-0·7 pairs/m² across range of habitats; laying usually highly synchronous within a colony, (often 90% eggs laid within 2-week period), variable between regions. Typically nests in shallow burrows excavated in maritime grassy-turfed slopes and flats, sometimes in crevices and cavities on cliffs, slopes and boulder beaches; lays on bare ground in rough scrape at end of burrow tunnel or crevice, usually lined with dry plant material and feathers. 1 egg; incubation averages 45-46 days (42-53 days), apparently shared equally by both sexes for periods of 12-24 hours; early egg losses may be replaced after 10-21 days; downy chick dark sooty black above, slightly paler sooty grey below, infrequently some white on underparts, 64 g, semi-precocial; chick-rearing averages 49 days, with care and feeding by both parents, chick usually fledging at night by going to sea apparently unaccompanied. Breeding success averages c. 46%, with mean survival of eggs (63%) and chicks (71%), and failure rates of each, highly variable between years (since species extremely sensitive to human disturbance, measured reproductive rates may be artificially low). Most losses of eggs due to infertility or damage during incubation, and of chicks to exposure soon after hatching or later from food shortages; egg and chick predation by large gulls occurs, as does kleptoparasitism through-

out chick-rearing period. Adult survival unmeasured, but probably high. Age of first breeding unknown, likely 5-6 years.

Movements. Winters at sea well offshore, often to NC Pacific, normally adjacent to breeding areas except N populations, which move relatively long distances S through Bering Sea into N Pacific. Post-breeding dispersal widespread, occurring mostly solitarily or in pairs, rarely in flocks, at very low densities, some birds moving S to waters off S Japan and S California. Returns to colonies in late Apr and May, with spring migratory movements probably beginning late Feb through Mar, but precise details of pattern and timing unknown. Spring and autumn movements probably complex, requiring further examination.

Status and Conservation. Not globally threatened. Total breeding population estimated at 3,502,000 birds, with c. 764,000 (710,000-810,000) in Asia (c. 22%) and 2,738,000 (2,200,000-3,200,000) in North America (c. 78%); mostly in boreal water zone. Centre of abundance in Aleutians and Alaskan Peninsula region, with 2,340,000 breeding birds (67% of world population), with largest known single colony at Kaligagan I (Unimak) containing c. 375,000 birds. Apart from Sea of Okhotsk (500,000 birds), Kurils (200,000) and SC & SE Alaska (196,000), populations relatively small: Arctic Ocean (4000 birds), Siberian Bering Sea (59,000), Alaskan Bering Sea (99,000), British Columbia (77,000), Washington (23,000), with smallest groups in Oregon (5000 birds), California (under 1000) and Hokkaido (under 1000). Precise data on population levels too few to determine recent trends, but historical record indicates severe declines over last 150 years through most of breeding range, mostly result of introduced predators, i.e. rats (*Rattus*), Arctic fox (*Alopex lagopus*), red fox (*Vulpes vulpes*), mink (*Mustela vison, M. lutreola*), feral cats and dogs, and direct human disturbance on breeding islands associated with fur industry and domestic livestock (goats, sheep, rabbits). Best evidence is extirpation of numerous Alaskan colonies by introduced Arctic foxes by late 1930's, and slow, but steady, decreases at colonies in California since 1900. Immediate conservation actions required are: continued eradication and control of alien predators at present and former colonies (particularly in light of recent recolonizations on Alaskan islands following removal of foxes); removal of all domestic livestock from breeding islands, past and present; enhancement of current monitoring system at Alaskan colonies and establishment of similar systems in other regions to enable effective assessment of breeding population size and status; further studies of pelagic ecology of the species to improve understanding of its ecological requirements at sea throughout annual cycle; and protection of colonies during breeding season by minimizing disturbance (e.g. control of tourism, research, fishing activity) through public education and enforcement of existing regulations.

Bibliography. Ainley & Lewis (1974), Ainley, Morrell & Boekelheide (1990), Amaral (1977), Armstrong (1983), Bailey (1993a, 1993b), Bailey & Kaiser (1993), Baird & Moe (1978b), Bent (1919), Boone (1986), Brazil (1991), Byrd & Douglas (1990), Byrd, Douglas *et al*. (1990), Byrd, Murphy *et al*. (1993), Campbell *et al*. (1990), Flint *et al*. (1984), Fujimaki (1986), Golovkin (1984), Gould *et al*. (1982), Hasegawa (1984), Hunt, Burgeson & Sanger (1981), Hunt, Eppley *et al*. (1981), Kessel (1989), Knystautas (1993), Kondratiev (1986, 1991), Kondratiev *et al*. (1993), Lensink (1984), Leschner & Burrell (1977), Litvinenko (1993), Litvinenko & Shibaev (1991), Manuwal (1980, 1984), McChesney *et al*. (1995), Mikhtaryantz (1986), Moe & Day (1979), Nechaev (1986), Nysewander & Hoberg (1978), Richards (1990), Rodway (1991), Roslyakov (1986), Sealy (1972), Sowls, DeGange *et al*. (1980), Sowls, Hatch & Lensink (1978), Speich & Wahl (1989), Vermeer (1979), Vermeer & Cullen (1979), Vermeer, Cullen & Porter (1979), Vyatkin (1986), Wehle (1976, 1980, 1983).

REFERENCES

REFERENCES OF SCIENTIFIC DESCRIPTIONS

Abdulali (1978). *J. Bombay Nat. Hist. Soc.* **75**: 754.
Aldrich (1972). *Proc. Biol. Soc. Washington* **85**: 67.
Allen (1876). *Bull. Mus. Comp. Zool.* **3**: 357.
Allen (1892). *Bull. Amer. Mus. Nat. Hist.* **4**: 57.
Anthony (1898). *Auk* **15**: 36.
Audubon (1834). *Birds Amer.* **3**: pl. 203.
Audubon (1838). *Birds Amer.* **4**: pls. 409, 427.
Audubon (1839). *Orn. Biog.* **5**: 249, 320.
Baird (1858). *Rep. Expl. Surv. R.R. Pac.* **9**: xxii, xlvii, 714-734.
Baird (1869). *Trans. Chicago Acad. Sci.* **1(2)**: 321.
Bancroft (1929). *Trans. San Diego Soc. Nat. Hist.* **5**: 284.
Bangs (1898). *Proc. Biol. Soc. Washington* **12**: 171.
Bangs (1899). *Proc. New Engl. Zoöl. Cl.* **1**: 45.
Bangs (1907). *Amer. Naturalist* **41**: 178.
Bangs (1910). *Proc. New Engl. Zoöl. Cl.* **4**: 81.
Bangs (1915). *Proc. New Engl. Zoöl. Cl.* **5**: 96.
Bangs & Kennard (1920). *Handb. Jamaica*: 684.
Bangs & Peck (1908). *Proc. Biol. Soc. Washington* **21**: 43.
Bangs & Penard (1918). *Bull. Mus. Comp. Zool.* **62**: 41.
Bangs & Zappey (1905). *Amer. Naturalist* **39**: 193.
Bannerman (1913). *Bull. Brit. Orn. Club* **31**: 33.
Bannerman (1914). *Ibis*: 277.
Bannerman (1922). *Bull. Brit. Orn. Club* **43**: 7.
Bannerman (1930). *Ibis*: 432, 433. [*Ardeotis arabs lynesi, Ardeotis arabs butleri*].
Bannerman (1930). *Bull. Brit. Orn. Club* **50**: 60. [*Neotis denhami jacksoni*].
Bannerman (1931). *Bull. Brit. Orn. Club* **51**: 70.
Barbour & Peters, J.L. (1927). *Proc. New Engl. Zoöl. Cl.* **9**: 95.
Bartlett (1880). *Proc. Zool. Soc. London* 1879: 772.
Bartsch (1917). *Proc. Biol. Soc. Washington* **30**: 131.
Bechstein (1803). *Orn. Taschenbuch Deutschland* **2**: 292, 336.
Bechstein (1812). In: Latham *Allgem. Ueb. Vög.* **4(2)**: 432, 453.
Begbie (1834). *The Malay Peninsula*: 2.
van Bemmel & Hoogerwerf (1941). *Treubia* **17**: 470.
Bennett, E.T. (1834). *Proc. Zool. Soc. London* 1833: 118.
Bennett, F.D. (1840). *Narr. Whaling Voy.* **2**: 248.
Berlepsch & Stolzmann (1902). *Proc. Zool. Soc. London*: 50, 51.
Berlepsch & Taczanowski (1884). *Proc. Zool. Soc. London* 1883: 576.
Bishop (1910). *Auk* **27**: 59.
Blanford (1895). *Bull. Brit. Orn. Club* **5**: 7.
Blasius, A.W.H. (1886). In: Russ' *Isis*: 103.
Blasius, A.W.H. (1888). *Ornis* **4**: 317.
Bloxham (1826). *Voy. "Blonde"*: 251.
Blyth (1842). *J. Asiatic Soc. Bengal* **11**: 587.
Blyth (1843). *J. Asiatic Soc. Bengal* **12**: 180.
Blyth (1848). *J. Asiatic Soc. Bengal* **17**: 252, 254.
Blyth (1849). *J. Asiatic Soc. Bengal* **18**: 820.
Blyth (1852). *Cat. Birds Mus. Asiatic. Soc. Bengal* 1849: 256, 283, 293.
Blyth (1856). *J. Asiatic Soc. Bengal* **24**: 305.
Blyth (1863). *J. Asiatic Soc. Bengal* **32**: 80. [*Turnix tanki blanfordii*].
Blyth (1863). *Ibis*: 119. [*Rallina canningi*].
Bocage (1868). *J. Acad. Sci. Lisboa* **5**: 49.
Boddaert (1783). *Table Planches Enlum*: 13, 48-58.
Böhm (1884). *J. Orn.* **32**: 176.
Boie (1822). *Isis von Oken* **1**: col. 563.
Boie (1826). In: Brehm's *Ornis oder das Neueste und Wichtigate der Vogelkunde* **2**: 127.
Boie (1844). *Isis*: col. 188.
Bonaparte (1825). *J. Acad. Nat. Sci. Philadelphia* **5**: 98.
Bonaparte (1826). *Ann. Lyceum Nat. Hist. New York* **2**: 157.
Bonaparte (1827). *Ann. Lyceum Nat. Hist. New York* **2**: 323.
Bonaparte (1828). *Ann. Lyceum Nat. Hist. New York* **2**: 427.
Bonaparte (1830). *Ann. Stor. Nat. Bologna* **4**: 335.
Bonaparte (1839). *Icon. Fauna Ital., Ucc.* **25**: 3, 4.
Bonaparte (1850). *Compt. Rend. Acad. Sci. Paris* **31**: 562.
Bonaparte (1853). *Compt. Rend. Acad. Sci. Paris* **37**: 925.
Bonaparte (1854). *Naumannia*: 213.
Bonaparte (1855). *Compt. Rend. Acad. Sci. Paris* **41**: 660. [*Gallinago jamesoni*].
Bonaparte (1855). *Rev. Mag. Zool.* (Series 2) **7**: 484. [*Mesitornis*].
Bonaparte (1856). *Compt. Rend. Acad. Sci. Paris* **42**: 773. **43**: 579, 599, 600, 1020.
Bonaparte (1857). *Consp. Av.* **2**: 207, 224.
Bond (1954). *Notulae Naturae* **264**: 1.
Bonnaterre (1791). *Tabl. Encyc. Méth. Orn.* pt. 1: lxxxii, lxxxiv, 5, 64.
Brandt, M. (1837). *Bull. Sci. Acad. Imp. Sci. St. Pétersb.* **2**: cols. 346, 347.
Bree (1876). *Birds Europe* **5**: 58.
Brehm, A.E. (1857). *Allg. Deutsche Naturhist. Zeitung, N.F.* **3**: 483.
Brehm, C.L. (1822). *Beitr. Vögelkd.* **3**: 355, 781.
Brehm, C.L. (1824). *Lehrb. Naturg. eur. Vög.* **2**: 923.
Brehm, C.L. (1830). *Isis von Oken* **23**: col. 994.
Brehm, C.L. (1831). *Naturg. Vög. Deutschl.*
Brème (1839). *Rev. Zool.*: 321.
Brewster (1883). *Bull. Nuttall Orn. Club* **8**: 216.
Brewster (1887). *Auk* **4**: 145.

Brewster (1890). *Auk* **7**: 377.
Brewster (1899). *Proc. New Engl. Zoöl. Cl.* **1**: 50.
Brisson (1760). *Orn.* **1**: 46-56. **5**. **6**.
Brodkorb (1934). *Occas. Pap. Mus. Zool. Univ. Michigan*: 293.
Brooks, W.S. (1915). *Bull. Mus. Comp. Zool.* **59**: 373.
Brooks, W.S. (1920). *Proc. New Engl. Zoöl. Cl.* **7**: 53.
Bruch (1853). *J. Orn.* **1**: 102, 103, 106, 108.
Bruch (1855). *J. Orn.*: 287.
Brünnich (1764). *Orn. Boreal.*: 32, 33, 49, 54.
Bryan (1903). *Occas. Pap. Bishop Mus.* **2**: 101.
Bryant, H. (1861). *Proc. Boston Soc. Nat. Hist.* **8**: 142.
Buller (1869). *Ibis*: 41.
Buller (1888). *Birds New Zealand* **2**: 105.
Buller (1896). *Trans. & Proc. New Zealand Inst.* **28**: 348.
Burchell (1822). *Trav. S. Afr.* **1**: 393, 501.
Burleigh & Lowery (1942). *Occas. Pap. Mus. Zool. Louisiana State Univ.* **10**: 173-177.
Buturlin (1910). *Orn. Mitt.* **1**: 36.
Buturlin (1934). *Ibis*: 171. [*Larus armenicus*].
Buturlin (1934). *Polnyi Opredelitel Ptitsy SSSR* **1**: 88. [*Tringa totanus ussuriensis*].
Cabanis (1857). *J. Orn.* **4**: 418, 419.
Cabanis (1868). *J. Orn.* **16**: 413.
Cabanis (1872). *J. Orn.* **20**: 158.
Cabanis (1873). *J. Orn.* **23**: 449.
Cabanis (1877). *J. Orn.* **25**: 349.
Cabanis (1882). *Orn. Centralbl.* **7**: 14.
Cabanis (1884). *J. Orn.* **32**: 437.
Cabot (1848). *Proc. Boston Soc. Nat. Hist.* **2**: 257.
Carriker (1935). *Proc. Acad. Nat. Sci. Philadelphia* **87**: 343.
Cassin (1852). *Proc. Acad. Nat. Sci. Philadelphia* **6**: 187.
Cassin (1858). In: *Rep. Expl. Surv. R.R. Pac.* **9**: xlvi, 696.
Castelnau & Ramsay (1877). *Proc. Linn. Soc. New South Wales* **1**: 385.
Chapin (1954). *Amer. Mus. Novit.* **1659**: 8.
Chapman (1914). *Bull. Amer. Mus. Nat. Hist.* **33**: 169, 170.
Chapman (1920). *Auk* **37**: 106.
Chapman (1922). *Amer. Mus. Novit.* **31**: 3.
Chasen (1938). *Orn. Monatsber.* **46**: 5-8.
Children (1826). In: Denham & Clapperton's *Travels*: 199.
Chubb (1917). *Bull. Brit. Orn. Club* **38**: 33.
Chubb (1918). *Bull. Brit. Orn. Club* **38**: 41.
Chubb (1919). *Ibis*: 50.
Clancey (1971). *Durban Mus. Novit.* **9(9)**: 113-118.
Clancey (1979). *Durban Mus. Novit.* **12**: 6.
Conover (1934). *Auk* **51**: 365. [*Laterallus xenopterus*].
Conover (1934). *Proc. Biol. Soc. Washington* **47**: 120. [*Psophia viridis dextralis*].
Conover (1949). *Proc. Biol. Soc. Washington* **62**: 173-174.
Cory (1881). *Bull. Nuttall Orn. Club* **6**: 130.
Cory (1883). *Quart. J. Boston Zool. Soc.* **2**: 46.
Coues (1861). *Proc. Acad. Nat. Sci. Philadelphia*: 189, 194.
Coues (1862). *Proc. Acad. Nat. Sci. Philadelphia*: 296.
Coues (1873). In: H.W. Elliott *Rep. Seal Ids. Alaska.*
Cretzschmar (1826). In: Rüppell's *Atlas, Vög.*: 1.
Cretzschmar (1827). In: Rüppell's *Atlas, Vög.* 1826: 21.
Cretzschmar (1829). In: Rüppell's *Atlas, Vög.*: 46.
Cuvier (1829). *Règne Animal* **1**: 500.
D'Albertis & Salvadori (1879). *Ann. Mus. Civ. Genova* **14**: 129, 130.
Darlington (1931). *Bull. Mus. Comp. Zool.* **71**: 372.
Deignan (1946). *J. Washington Acad. Sci.* **36**: 390.
Delacour (1928). *Bull. Brit. Orn. Club* **49**: 49.
Delacour & Jabouille (1930). *Rev. Hist. Nat., 2ème partie, L'Oiseau* **11**: 407.
Des Murs (1845). *Rev. Zool.*: 176 bis.
Desfontaines (1787). *Mém. Acad. Roy. Sci. Paris*: 500.
Diamond (1969). *Amer. Mus. Novit.* **2362**: 3-4.
Diamond (1991). *Auk* **108**: 461-470.
Dickermann (1966). *Condor* **68**: 215.
Dickey (1923). *Auk* **40**: 90.
Dickey (1929). *Condor* **31**: 33.
Dickey & van Rossem (1925). *Condor* **27**: 163.
Dowding (1994). *Notornis* **41**: 221-233.
Dresser (1876). *Proc. Zool. Soc. London*: 674.
Du Bus de Gisignies (1840). *Bull. Acad. Roy. Sci. Bruxelles* **7**: 214.
Durnford (1877). *Ibis*: 194.
Dwight (1919). *Proc. Biol. Soc. Washington* **32**: 11.
Dwight (1922). *Amer. Mus. Novit.* **44**: 1.
Erlanger (1905). *J. Orn.* **53**: 58, 60.
Eschscholtz (1829). *Zool. Atlas* **1**: 2.
Eydoux & Souleyet (1841). *Voy. "La Bonite" Zool.* **1**: 102.
Eyton (1839). *Proc. Zool. Soc. London*: 107.
Falla (1937). *BANZ Antarctic Res. Exp. 1929-1931 Rep.*
Falla (1978). *Notornis* **25**: 101-108.
Fischer (1842). *Bull. Soc. Imp. Nat. Moscou* **15**: 314.
Fischer & Reichenow (1884). *J. Orn.* **32**: 178.

Fisher, W.K. (1903). *Proc. US Natl. Mus.* **26**: 559.
Fjeldså (1983). *Bull. Brit. Orn. Club* **103**: 22. [*Fulica ardesiaca atrura*].
Fjeldså (1983). *Steenstrupia* **8**: 277-282. [*Laterallus jamaicensis tuerosi*].
Forbes (1882). *Ibis*: 428.
Forster, J.R. (1772). *Philos. Trans.* **62**: 411, 431.
Forster, J.R. (1788). *Enchirid. Hist. Nat.*: 37.
Forster, J.R. (1795). *Faunula Indica*: 11.
Forster, J.R. (1844). *Descr. Anim.*: 106, 112.
Forster, T. (1817). *Syn. Cat. Brit. Birds*: 20.
Fraser (1843). *Proc. Zool. Soc. London*: 26.
Fraser (1845). *Proc. Zool. Soc. London* 1844: 157.
Friedmann (1928). *Proc. New Engl. Zoöl. Cl.* **10**: 97.
Gambel (1849). *Proc. Acad. Nat. Sci. Philadelphia* **4**: 129.
Garnot (1826). *Ann. Sci. Nat., Paris* **7**: 47.
Geoffroy Saint-Hilaire, I. (1832). *Mag. Zool.* **2**: pl. 6.
Geoffroy Saint-Hilaire, I. (1838). *Compt. Rend. Acad. Sci. Paris* **6**: 444.
Geoffroy Saint-Hilaire, I. & Lesson (1831). *Cent. Zool.* 1830: 130, 135, 137.
Gibson & Kessel (1989). *Condor* **91(2)**: 436-443.
Gilliard (1961). *Amer. Mus. Novit.* **2031**: 1-2.
Gloger (1842). *Hand-und Hilfsbuch Naturgeschichte* 1841: 440.
Gmelin (1789). *Syst. Nat.* **1**.
Gosse (1847). *Birds Jamaica*: 369.
Gould (1834). *Proc. Zool. Soc. London*: 45.
Gould (1837). *Synop. Birds Australia* pt. 2: pls. 30, 31, 34, 37. [*Turnix melanogaster*, *Turnix maculosa melanota*, *Himantopus himantopus leucocephalus*, *Gelochelidon nilotica macrotarsa*].
Gould (1837). *Proc. Zool. Soc. London* 1836: 81, 85. [*Gallinula ventralis*, *Cursorius rufus*].
Gould (1838). *Synop. Birds Australia* pt. 4: 6, pl. 73.
Gould (1840). *Proc. Zool. Soc. London* 1839: 145.
Gould (1841). *Birds Austr.* pt. 2: pls. 14, 15. pt. 4: pl. 7. [*Turnix pyrrhothorax*, *Turnix velox*, *Himantopus novaezelandiae*].
Gould (1841). In: Darwin's *Zool. Voy. "Beagle"* pt. 3: 132, 141. [*Coturnicops notatus*, *Laterallus spilonotus*, *Larus fuliginosus*].
Gould (1841). *Proc. Zool. Soc. London* 1840: 114, 174, 176. [*Porphyrio porphyrio bellus*, *Peltohyas australis*, *Numenius minutus*, *Pedionomus*, *Pedionomus torquatus*].
Gould (1843). *Proc. Zool. Soc. London* 1842: 139, 140.
Gould (1844). *Proc. Zool. Soc. London*: 56.
Gould (1845). *Proc. Zool. Soc. London*: 2, 62, 76. [*Turnix varia scintillans*, *Fulica atra australis*, *Sterna dougallii gracilis*].
Gould (1845). *Birds Austr.* pt. 18: pl. 15. [*Haematopus fuliginosus*].
Gould (1846). *Birds Austr.* pt. 22: pl. 14. [*Gallinula tenebrosa*].
Gould (1846). *Proc. Zool. Soc. London*: 84, 103. [*Limosa limosa melanuroides*, *Anous tenuirostris melanops*].
Gould (1848). *Proc. Zool. Soc. London*: 38.
Gould (1869). *Birds Austr.* pt. 5(Suppl.): pl. 79.
Gould (1871). *Ann. and Mag. Nat. Hist.* **8(4)**: 192.
Grandidier & Berlioz (1929). *Bull. Acad. Malgache* **10**: 83.
Grant & Mackworth-Praed (1934). *Bull. Brit. Orn. Club* **55**: 17.
Gray, G.R. (1840). *List Gen. Birds*: 69.
Gray, G.R. (1843). In: Dieffenbach's *Trav. New Zealand* **2**: 197.
Gray, G.R. (1845). *Voy. "Erebus" and "Terror", Birds*: 13, 19, pl. 23.
Gray, G.R. (1846). *Gen. Birds* **3**: 545-595, pl. 182.
Gray, G.R. (1849). *Proc. Zool. Soc. London*: 63, 90.
Gray, G.R. (1855). *Cat. Gen. Subgen. Birds*: 109, 111, 119, 120.
Gray, G.R. (1858). *Proc. Zool. Soc. London*: 188.
Gray, G.R. (1860). *Proc. Zool. Soc. London*: 365.
Gray, G.R. (1862). *Proc. Zool. Soc. London* 1861: 432.
Gray, J.E. (1829). In: Griffith's *Animal Kigdom* **8(3)**: 304, 305, 410, 542.
Gray, J.E. (1831). *Zool. Misc.*: 12, 16. [*Gallinago hardwickii*, *Neotis denhami stanleyi*].
Gray, J.E. (1831). In: Hardwicke's *Ill. Ind. Zool.* **1(5)**: pl. 69. [*Sterna aurantia*].
Gray, J.E. (1832). In: Hardwicke's *Ill. Ind. Zool.* **1(6)** 1831: pl. 70. **2(12)**: pl. 47.
Gray, J.E. (1846). *Zool. Voy. "Erebus" and "Terror", Birds*: 14.
Gray, J.E. & Gray, G.R. (1863). *Cat. etc. Mamm. Birds Nepal and Tibet, Brit. Mus.*: 70.
Green & Arnold (1939). *Condor* **41**: 28.
Greenway (1935). *Proc. New England Zool. Club* **14**: 28-29.
Grote (1922). *J. Orn.* **70**: 41.
Guérin-Méneville (1843). *Rev. Zool.*: 322.
Guillemard (1885). *Proc. Zool. Soc. London*: 511.
Güldenstädt (1774). *Novi Comm. Sci. Petropol.* **19**: 473.
Gunnerus (1767). In: Leem *Beskr. Finm. Lapper*: 226, 251.
Günther (1879). *Ann. and Mag. Nat. Hist.* **3(5)**: 168.
Gurney (1877). *Ibis*: 352.
Gyldenstolpe (1955). *Arkiv. Zool. (Ser. 2)* **8**: 34.
Hagen (1952). *The Birds of Tristan da Cunha* **20**: 138.
Hale (1971). *Zool. J. Linn. Soc.* **50**: 259, 260.
Hartert (1898). *Nov. Zool.* **5**: 50, 476.
Hartert (1916). *Bull. Brit. Orn. Club* **36**: 64. [*Scolopax mira*].
Hartert (1916). *Nov. Zool.* **23**: 298. [*Sterna repressa*].
Hartert (1917). *Nov. Zool.* **24**: 266, 268.
Hartert (1920). *Vögel Pal. Fauna* **2**: 1524. [*Cursorius cursor exsul*].
Hartert (1920). *Nov. Zool.* **27**: 137. [*Calidris ptilocnemis quarta*].
Hartert (1921). *Vögel Pal. Fauna* **2**: 1698.
Hartert (1926). *Nov. Zool.* **33**: 172.
Hartert (1927). *Nov. Zool.* **34**: 17.
Hartert (1930). *Nov. Zool.* **36**: 121, 123, 124.
Hartert & Jackson (1915). *Ibis*: 529.
Harting (1873). *Ibis*: 260, 262, 266.
Hartlaub (1841). *Rev. Zool.*: 5.
Hartlaub (1844). *Syst. Verz. Mus. Bremen, Vögel*: 108.
Hartlaub (1852). *Abh. Naturwiss. Ver. Hamburg* **2**: 62.
Hartlaub (1855). *J. Orn.* **3**: 357, 427.
Hartlaub (1857). *Syst. Orn. West-Afr.*: 241.
Hartlaub (1859). *Ibis*: 344.
Hartlaub (1860). *Proc. Zool. Soc. London*: 335.
Hartlaub (1861). *Fauna Madagascar*: 72.
Hartlaub (1865). *Proc. Zool. Soc. London*: 87.
Hartlaub (1866). *Ibis*: 171.
Hartlaub & Finsch (1872). *Proc. Zool. Soc. London*: 107.
Heine (1890). In: Heine & Reichenow, *Nomencl. Mus. Hein. Orn.*: 319.
Heller & Snodgrass (1901). *Condor* **3**: 76.
Hellmayr (1932). *Field Mus. Nat. Hist. Publ. (Zool. Ser.)* **19**: 351.
Hermann (1804). *Obs. Zool.*: 198.
Heuglin (1863). *J. Orn.* **11**: 10. [*Lissotis hartlaubii*].
Heuglin (1863). *Ibis*: 31. [*Rhinoptilus cinctus*].
Hodgson (1831). *Gleanings in Science* **3**: 238.
Hodgson (1836). *Proc. Zool. Soc. London*: 8.
Hodgson (1837). *Bengal Sport Mag.* **9**: 346.
Holyoak & Thibault (1976). *Alauda* **44**: 457-473.
Homeyer (1853). *Naumannia*: 129.
Hoogerwerf (1962). *Ardea* **50**: 199.
Hørring (1937). *Rep. 5th Thule Exped. II* **6**: 87.
Horsfield (1821). *Trans. Linn. Soc. London* **13**: 191-198.
Hume (1874). *Stray Feathers* **2**: 302, 318.
Hume (1877). *Stray Feathers* **5**: 324, 325.
Hume (1878). *Stray Feathers* **7**: 142.
Hutton (1871). *Cat. Birds New Zealand*: 41.
Hutton (1874). *Trans. New Zealand Inst.* **6**: 110.
Illiger (1811). *Prodromus Syst. Mammalium Avium*: 239, 250, 257, 262.
Ingram (1909). *Bull. Brit. Orn. Club* **23**: 65.
Irwin (1963). *Durban Mus. Novit.* **7**: 7.
Jacquin (1784). *Beytr. Gesch. Vög.*: 24.
Jardine & Selby (1827). *Ill. Orn.* **1**: pl. 28.
Jardine & Selby (1835). *Ill. Orn.* **3**: pl. 151.
Jehl (1987). *Auk* **104**: 422.
Jerdon (1840). *Madras J. Lit. Sci.* **12**: 225.
Jerdon (1864). *Birds India* **3**: 648, 725.
Johansen (1960). *J. Orn.* **101**: 325.
Junge (1952). *Zool. Meded. Rijksmus. Nat. Hist. Leiden* **31**: 247.
Kaup (1829). *Skizz. Entw.-Gesch. Eur. Thierw.*
Kennedy & Ross (1987). *Proc. Biol. Soc. Washington* **100**: 459.
King (1827). *Survey Coasts of Australia*. **2**, App. B: 423.
King (1828). *Zool. J.* **4**: 93, 95.
Kittlitz (1858). *Reise Russ. Amerika* **2**: 30.
Koch (1816). *Syst. Baier. Zool.*: 316.
Koelz (1939). *Proc. Biol. Soc. Washington* **52**: 82.
L'Herminier (1837). *Mag. Zool.* **7**: pl. 84.
Lafresnaye (1841). *Rev. Zool.*: 234, 242.
Lafresnaye (1842). *Mag. Zool.*: 1.
Lafresnaye (1845). *Rev. Zool.*: 368.
Latham (1787). *Gen. Syn.* Suppl. 1: 292, 293, 296.
Latham (1790). *Index Orn.* **2**: 712-765.
Latham (1801). *Index Orn.* Suppl.: lxiii, lxvi, lxviii.
Laubman (1913). *Falco* **9**: 30.
Lawrence (1854). *Ann. Lyceum Nat. Hist. New York* **6**: 79.
Lawrence (1861). *Ann. Lyceum Nat. Hist. New York* **7**: 302.
Lawrence (1863). *Proc. Acad. Nat. Sci. Philadelphia*: 106, 107.
Lawrence (1867). *Proc. Acad. Nat. Sci. Philadelphia*: 234.
Lawrence (1871). *Ann. Lyceum Nat. Hist. New York* **10**: 19.
Lawrence (1872). *Proc. Boston Soc. Nat. Hist.* **14**: 285.
Lawrence (1875). *Ann. Lyceum Nat. Hist. New York* **11**: 90.
Le Mahout (1853). *Hist. Nat. Oiseaux*: 339, 340.
Leach (1819). In: Ross' *Voy. Disc.* **2**: lvii.
Legge (1880). *Proc. Zool. Soc. London*: 39.
Leisler (1812). *Nachträge zu Bechstein's Naturg. Deutschl.*: 64, 74.
Lesson (1826). *Dict. Sci. Nat. (éd. Levrault)* **42**: 36, 38.
Lesson (1827). *Voy. "Coquille", Zool., Atlas* **3**: pl. 47.
Lesson (1831). *Traité d'Orn.* **7**: 547, 553. **8**: 596, 616, 621. [*Podica*, *Esacus*, *Bartramia*, *Catharacta antarctica*, *Thalasseus bengalensis*, *Sterna hirundinacea*, *Sterna anaethetus antarctica*].
Lesson (1831). *Bull. Sci. Nat. Géol.* **25**: 343. [*Attagis gayi latreillii*].
Lesson (1839). *Rev. Zool.*: 47.
Lesson (1847). *Compl. Oeuvres Buffon* **20**: 256.
Lichtenstein (1793). *Cat. Rerum Rariss.*: 28.
Lichtenstein (1818). *Verz. Säugeth. und Vög. Berliner Mus.*: 36.
Lichtenstein (1823). *Verz. Doubl.*: 69-83. [*Burhinus capensis*, *Charadrius modestus*, *Thalasseus bergii*, *Larus dominicanus*, *Larus maculipennis*, *Sterna fuscata infuscata*].
Lichtenstein (1823). In: Eversmann's *Reise von Orenburg nach Buchara*: 137. [*Vanellus leucurus*].
Lichtenstein (1844). In: Forster *Descr. Anim.*: 276.
Link (1806). *Beschr. Naturh. Samml. Univ. Rostock* **1**: 46.
Linnaeus (1758). *Syst. Nat.* **10**: 130-155.
Linnaeus (1766). *Syst. Nat.* **12(1)**: 225-263, 345.
Linnaeus (1767). Addendum, page 253 in: *Syst. Nat.* **12(1)**.
Ljungh (1813). *Kungl. Svenska Vet.-Akad. nya Handl.* **34**: 258.
Lönnberg (1921). In: Skottsberg's *Nat. Hist. Juan Fernandez and Easter Ids.* **3(1)**: 20.
Lönnberg (1931). *Ark. Zool.* **23B(2)**: 2.
Løppenthin (1932). *Medd. Grønland* **91(6)**: 85, 93.
Lowe (1915). *Bull. Brit. Orn. Club* **36**: 7.
Lowe (1921). *Bull. Brit. Orn. Club* **41**: 109, 110.
Lowe (1923). *Bull. Brit. Orn. Club* **43**: 174, 175.
Lynes (1920). *Bull. Brit. Orn. Club* **41**: 51.
MacGillivray (1824). *Mem. Wernerian Nat. Hist. Soc.* **5**: 249.
MacGillivray (1842). *Man. Brit. Orn.* **2**: 252.
Madaràsz & Neumann (1911). *Orn. Monatsber.* **19**: 186.
Mandt (1822). *Obs. Hist. Nat. Itin. Groenl.*: 30.
Martens (1897). *Orn. Monatsber.* **5**: 190.
Mathews (1911). *Birds Austr.* **1**: 189, 197, 198, 199. [*Gallirallus philippensis andrewsi*, *Gallirallus philippensis wilkinsoni*, *Gallirallus philippensis lesouefi*, *Gallirallus philippensis swindellsi*, *Gallirallus philippensis sethsmithi*, *Gallirallus philippensis goodsoni*, *Lewinia pectoralis clelandi*].
Mathews (1911). *Nov. Zool.* **18**: 7. [*Irediparra*].
Mathews (1912). *Nov. Zool.* **18**: 192, 208, 209, 212. [*Gallirallus philippensis mellori*, *Catharacta antarctica lonnbergi*, *Thalasseus bergii gwendolenae*, *Sterna striata incerta*, *Sterna nereis horni*].
Mathews (1912). *Birds Austr.* **2**. [*Gelochelidon nilotica addenda*, *Gelochelidon nilotica groenvoldi*, *Sterna dougallii arideensis*, *Sterna dougallii bangsi*, *Sterna nereis exsul*, *Sterna anaethetus recognita*, *Chlidonias hybridus swinhoei*, *Anous minutus americanus*, *Anous minutus atlanticus*, *Procelsterna cerulea nebouxi*, *Procelsterna albivitta imitatrix*, *Larus novaehollandiae forsteri*].
Mathews (1913). *Birds Austr.* **3**: 270, 273.
Mathews (1914). *Av. Rec.* **2**: 87.
Mathews (1916). *Austr. Av. Rec.* **3**: 55.
Mathews (1929). *Bull. Brit. Orn. Club* **50**: 19.
Mathews & Iredale (1912). *Birds Austr.* **2**: 320.
Mathews & Iredale (1913). *Ibis*: 245.
Maynard (1887). *Amer. Exch. and Mart* **3(3)**.
Mayr (1931). *Mitt. Zool. Mus. Berlin* **17**: 709.
Mayr (1933). *Amer. Mus. Novit.* **590**: 1. **609**: 3.
Mayr (1938). *Amer. Mus. Novit.* **1007**: 1-3, 6, 7.
Mayr (1949). *Amer. Mus. Novit.* **1417**: 5-7, 15-16, 21.
Mayr & Gilliard (1951). *Amer. Mus. Novit.* **1524**: 2-3.
McGregor (1904). *Bull. Phil. Mus.* **4**: 8.
McGregor (1907). *Phil. J. Sci.* **2**, Sect. A: 292, 317.
McGregor (1911). *Phil. J. Sci.* **6**, Sect. D: 183.
Mearns (1905). *Proc. Biol. Soc. Washington* **18**: 83.
Mearns (1915). *Smiths. Misc. Coll.* **65(13)**: 7.
Mearns (1916). *Proc. Biol. Soc. Washington* **19**: 71.
Meinertzhagen, R. & Meinertzhagen, A.C. (1926). *Bull. Brit. Orn. Club* **46**: 85.
Merrem (1788). *Vers. Grundr. Allg. Gesch. nat. Eintheil. Vög., Tentamen Nat. Syst. Av.* **1**: 7, 13, 20.
Merrem (1804). *Allg. Lit. Zeitung* **2**: col. 542.
Meyen (1834). *Nova Acta Acad. Caes. Leop. Carol.* **16**(Suppl. 1): 109.

Meyer, B. (1822). In: Meyer & Wolf *Taschenb. Deutschl. Vögelkunde*: 197.
Meyer, A.B. (1883). *Abbild. Vög. Skelett.* **4 & 5**: 28.
Meyer, F.A.A. (1794). *Zool. Annalen* **1**: 286, 287, 296.
Meyer de Schauensee (1938). *Proc. Acad. Nat. Sci. Philadelphia* **89**: 340.
Middendorff (1853). *Reise Nord. und Ost. Siberien* **2**: 222.
Miller, A.H. & Griscom (1921). *Amer. Mus. Novit.* **25**: 11.
Miller, J.F. (1782). *Icones Animalium*: pl. 33.
Miller, J.F. (1783). *Icones Animalium*: pl. 47.
Mitchell (1904). *Abstr. Proc. Zool. Soc. London* **10**: 13.
Molina (1782). *Stagg. Stor. Nat. Chili*: 258.
Montagu (1813). *Orn. Dict.* Suppl.
Mougin & de Naurois (1981). *Oiseau* **51**: 201-204.
Müller, P.L.S. (1776). *Natursyst.* Suppl.: 110-125.
Müller, S. (1842). *Verh. nat. gesch. Ned., Land-en Volkenk* **4**: 158.
Müller, S. (1847). *Verh. nat. gesch. Ned., Land-en Volkenk* **2**: 454.
Murphy (1938). *Amer. Mus. Novit.* **917**: 9, 13.
Naumann, J.F. (1821). *Isis von Oken* **2**: col. 782.
Naumann, J.F. (1836). *Naturg. Vög. Deutschl.* **8**: 429.
Naumann, J.F. (1840). *Naturg. Vög. Deutschl.* **10**: 282, 351.
Naumburg (1930). *Bull. Amer. Mus. Nat. Hist.* **60**: 72.
Néboux (1846). *Voy. "Venus", Atlas Zool., Ois.*: pl. 10.
Nechaev & Tomkovich (1988). *Zoologischeskii Zhurnal* **67**: 1596.
Nelson (1904). *Proc. Biol. Soc. Washington* **17**: 151.
Nelson (1905). *Proc. Biol. Soc. Washington* **18**: 141.
Neumann (1907). *J. Orn.* **55**: 306, 307.
Neumann (1908). *Bull. Brit. Orn. Club* **21**: 45.
Neumann (1910). *Orn. Monatsber.* **18**: 10.
Neumann (1914). *Orn. Monatsber.* **22**: 8.
Neumann (1920). *J. Orn.* **68**: 78.
Neumann (1929). *Orn. Monatsber.* **37**: 117.
Neumann (1934). *Anz. Orn. Ges. Bayern* **2**: 331.
Neumann (1939). *Bull. Brit. Orn. Club* **59**: 91.
Newton, A. (1861). *Proc. Zool. Soc. London*: 19.
Nilsson (1821). *Orn. Svecica* **2**: 29.
Nordmann (1835). In: Erman's *Reise, Naturh. Atlas*: 17. [*Tringa guttifer*].
Nordmann (1835). In: Erman's *Verz. Thier. Pflanz.*: 17. [*Sterna hirundo longipennis*].
North (1908). *Rec. Austr. Mus.* **7**: 31.
Norton (1901). *Proc. Portland Soc. Nat. Hist.* **2**: 144.
Nuttall (1834). *Man. Orn. US & Canada* **2**: 274.
Oberholser (1899). *Proc. Acad. Nat. Sci. Philadelphia*: 202.
Oberholser (1900). *Proc. US Natl. Mus.* **22**: 207.
Oberholser (1905). *Proc. US Natl. Mus.* **28**: 836.
Oberholser (1924). *J. Washington Acad. Sci.* **14**: 295.
Oberholser (1937). *Proc. US Natl. Mus.* **84**: 323, 335.
Ogilvie-Grant (1889). *Ann. and Mag. Nat. Hist.* **4(6)**: 320.
Ogilvie-Grant (1893). *Cat. Birds Brit. Mus.* **22**: 552.
Ogilvie-Grant (1897). *Handb. Game Bds.* **2**: 276.
Ogilvie-Grant (1899). *Bull. Brit. Orn. Club* **10**: 19.
Ogilvie-Grant (1905). *Bull. Brit. Orn. Club* **15**: 78.
Ogilvie-Grant (1913). *Bull. Brit. Orn. Club* **31**: 104.
Olrog (1958). *Acta Zool. Lilloana* **15**: 8.
Olson (1973). *Proc. Biol. Soc. Washington* **86**: 404.
Ord (1814). In: Wilson's *Amer. Orn.* **9**: 77.
Ord (1815). In: Guthrie's *Geogr.* **2**: 319.
Ord (1824). In reprint: Wilson's *Amer. Orn.* **7**: 71.
Ord (1825). In reprint: Wilson's *Amer. Orn.* **9**: ccxviii.
Oustalet (1881). *Bull. Soc. Philom. Paris* **5(7)**: 164.
Oustalet & Grandidier, G. (1903). *Bull. Mus. Hist. Nat. Paris* **9**: 11, 12.
Owen (1848). *Trans. Zool. Soc. London* **3**: 347.
Pallas (1764). In: Vroeg's *Cat. Raisonné Coll. Oiseaux, Audumbr.*: 6, 7.
Pallas (1766). *Misc. Zool.*: 66.
Pallas (1769). *Spic. Zool.* **1(5)**: 7, 13, 18, 33.
Pallas (1770). *Novi Comm. Sci. Petropol.* **14**: 582.
Pallas (1771). *Reise Verschiedene Provinzen Russischen Reichs* **1**: 456.
Pallas (1773). *Reise Verschiedene Provinzen Russischen Reichs* **2**: 713, 714, 715.
Pallas (1776). *Reise Verschiedene Provinzen Russischen Reichs* **3**: 700, 702.
Pallas (1781). *Neue Nord. Beytr.* **2**: 48.
Pallas (1811). *Zoographia Rosso-Asiat.* **2**: 111, 318-373.
Palmén (1887). In: *Nordenskiöld, Vega-Exped. Vetensk. Iakttag* **5**: 370.
Parkes (1949). *Auk* **66**: 84.
Parkes (1968). *Bull. Brit. Orn. Club* **88**: 24.
Parkes & Amadon (1959). *Wilson Bull.* **71**: 303-306.
Paykull (1805). *Kongl. Vet.-Acad. nya Handl.* **26**: 182, 188.
Paynter (1950). *Condor* **52**: 139-140.
Payraudeau (1826). *Ann. Sci. Nat.* **8**: 462.
Peale (1848). *US Expl. Exped.* **8**: 220-277.
Pelzeln (1857). *Sitzungsb. K. Akad. Wiss. Wien, Math-nathurw. Cl.* **24**: 371, 373.
Pelzeln (1865). *Reise "Novara", Zool.* **1**: 133.
Pennant (1769). *Indian Zool.*: 10.
Perry (1810). *Arcana* pt. 6: pl. 22.
Peters, J.L. (1925). *Auk* **42**: 122. [*Grus canadensis tabida*].
Peters, J.L. (1925). *Occas. Pap. Boston Soc. Nat. Hist.*
5: 143, 144. [*Aramus guarauna elucus, Aramus guarauna dolosus*].
Peters, J.L. (1932). *Auk* **49**: 348. [*Nesoclopeus*].
Peters, J.L. (1932). *Proc. New Engl. Zoöl. Cl.* **13**: 64. [*Aenigmatolimnas*].
Peters, J.L. (1934). *Check-list of the Birds of the World.* Vol. 2: 166.
Peters, W.K.H. (1854). *Monatsb. K. Akad. Berlin*: 134.
Philippi (1857). *Anales Univ. Chile* **14**: 180.
Philippi & Landbeck (1861). *Anales Univ. Chile* **19**: 507, 612, 618.
Philippi & Landbeck (1866). *Archiv Naturgeschichte* **32(1)**: 176.
Phillips (1947). *Auk* **64**: 126.
Phipps (1774). *Voy. N. Pole*: 187.
Pitelka (1950). *Univ. Calif. Publ. Zool.* **50**: 43.
du Pont (1976). *Nemouria* **17**: 6.
Pontoppidan (1763). *Danske Atlas* **1**: 621, 622, 623, 624.
Portenko (1936). *Auk* **58**: 195.
Portenko (1937). *Mitt. Zool. Mus. Berlin* **22**: 219-229.
Portenko (1939). *Fauna Anadyr. Kraya*: 159. [*Charadrius mongolus stegmanni*].
Portenko (1939). *Ibis*: 266, 268. [*Larus hyperboreus pallidissimus, Xema sabini tschuktschorum, Xema sabini woznesenskii*].
Portenko (1944). *Doklady Akad. Nauk SSSR* **43**: 226.
Pratt (1982). *Emu* **82**: 117-125.
Przevalski (1876). *Mongol i Strana Tangut* **2**: 135.
Pucheran (1845). *Rev. Zool.*: 277, 279.
Pucheran (1851). *Rev. Mag. Zool. (Series 2)* **3**: 279.
Quoy & Gaimard (1830). *Voy. "Astrolabe", Zool.* **1**: 250, 252.
Raffles (1822). *Trans. Linn. Soc. London* **13**: 328, 329.
Rafinesque (1822). *Kentucky Gazette* **1(8)**: 3.
Ramsay (1878). *Proc. Linn. Soc. New South Wales* **3**: 298.
Rand (1938). *Amer. Mus. Novit.* **990**: 4.
Rand (1940). *Amer. Mus. Novit.* **1072**: 3, 4.
Reichenbach (1848). *Syn. Av.* **3**: 6, pl. 256.
Reichenbach (1853). *Av. Syst. Nat.* 1852: xxi.
Reichenow (1881). *Orn. Centralbl.* **6**: 79.
Reichenow (1886). *J. Orn.* **34**: 116.
Reichenow (1889). *J. Orn.* **37**: 265.
Reichenow (1892). *J. Orn.* **40**: 126.
Reichenow (1894). *J. Orn.* **42**: 102.
Reichenow (1898). *Orn. Monatsber.* **6**: 182.
Reichenow (1900). *Vög. Afr.* **1**: 272.
Reichenow (1904). *Orn. Monatsber.* **12**: 47.
Reichenow (1905). *Vög. Afr.* **3**: 801, 802.
Reichenow (1908). *Deutsche Südpolar-Exped., Zool.* **1**: 566.
Richardson (1831). In: Wilson & Bonaparte *Amer. Orn.* **4**: 352.
Richmond (1896). *Proc. Biol. Soc. Washington* **10**: 53. [*Charadrius thoracicus*].
Richmond (1896). *Proc. US Natl. Mus.* **1089**: 589. [*Charadrius mongolus pamirensis*].
Ridgway (1874). *Amer. Naturalist* **8**: 111.
Ridgway (1880). *Bull. Nutall Orn. Club* **5**: 140, 160.
Ridgway (1882). *Proc. US Natl. Mus.* **5**: 345.
Ridgway (1884). *Proc. US Natl. Mus.* **7**: 358. [*Fulica caribaea*].
Ridgway (1884). *Waters Birds No. Amer.* **2**: 202. [*Rissa tridactyla pollicaris*].
Ridgway (1886). *Auk* **3**: 330, 331.
Ridgway (1919). *Bull. US Natl. Mus.* **50(8)**: 108-113, 487, 514.
Riley (1913). *Proc. Biol. Soc. Washington* **26**: 83.
Riley (1916). *Proc. Biol. Soc. Washington* **29**: 104.
Riley (1921). *Proc. Biol. Soc. Washington* **34**: 55.
Riley (1938). *Proc. Biol. Soc. Washington* **51**: 95.
Roberts (1922). *Ann. Transvaal Mus.* **8**: 202.
Roberts (1926). *Ann. Transvaal Mus.* **11**: 220.
Roberts (1932). *Ann. Transvaal Mus.* **15**: 24.
Roberts (1937). *Ostrich* **8**: 92.
Robinson (1900). *Bull. Brit. Orn. Club* **10**: 43.
Robinson & Stuart Baker (1928). *Bull. Brit. Orn. Club* **48**: 60.
von Rosenberg (1866). *Natuurk. Tijdsch. Nederlandsch Indie* **29**, Ser. 6 **4**, Afl. 2-4: 144.
van Rossem (1934). *Condor* **36**: 243.
van Rossem (1939). *Ann. Mag. Nat. Hist. (Ser. 11)* **4**: 443.
Rothschild (1893). *Bull. Brit. Orn. Club* **1**: 40.
Rothschild (1895). *Nov. Zool.* **2**: 481.
Rothschild (1902). *Bull. Brit. Orn. Club* **12**: 75.
Rothschild (1906). *Bull. Brit. Orn. Club* **16**: 81.
Rothschild (1921). *Bull. Brit. Orn. Club* **41**: 63.
Rothschild (1927). *Nov. Zool.* **34**: 15.
Rothschild (1934). *Orn. Monatsber.* **43**: 46.
Rothschild & Hartert (1894). *Nov. Zool.* **1**: 689.
Rothschild & Hartert (1907). *Nov. Zool.* **14**: 451.
Rowan (1932). *Auk* **49**: 22.
Rüppell (1835). *Neue Wirbelth. Vög.*: 16.
Rüppell (1837). *Mus. Senckenb.* **2**: 223.
Rüppell (1845). *Syst. Uebers. Vög. N.-O. Afr.*: 115, 123.
Sabine (1819). *Trans. Linn. Soc. London* **12(2)**: 522.
Salomonsen (1931). *Vidensk. Medd. Dan. Naturhist. Foren.* **90**: 360.
Salomonsen (1932). *Ibis*: 128, 130.
Salomonsen (1934). *Ibis*: 386-388.
Salvadori (1865). *Atti Soc. Ital. Sci. Nat. Milano* **8**: 381, 387.
Salvadori (1875). *Ann. Mus. Civ. Genova* **7**: 675, 678, 975.
Salvadori (1882). *Orn. Pap. Mol.* **3**: 309.
Salvadori & Festa (1910). *Bull. Mus. Zool. Torino* **25**: 1.
Sassi (1908). *Orn. Jahrb.* **19**: 32.
Saunders (1876). *Proc. Zool. Soc. London*: 649, 654, 668.
Saunders (1893). *Bull. Brit. Orn. Club* **3**: 12.
Saunders (1895). *Bull. Brit. Orn. Club* **4**: 26.
Say (1823). In: Long's *Exped. Rocky Mts.* **1**: 335.
Schiøler (1919). *Dan. Orn. Foren. Tidssk.* **13**: 211.
Schiøler (1922). *Dan. Orn. Foren. Tidssk.* **16**: 19, 21.
Schleep (1819). *Neue Annalen der Wetteranischen Gesellschaft* **1**: 314-320. **2**: 314.
Schlegel (1863). *Mus. Pays-Bas* **6**: 9.
Schlegel (1865). *Mus. Pays-Bas* **4**: 33. **5**: 16.
Schlegel (1866). *Nederlandsch Tijdschrift Dierkunde* **3**: 212, 254.
Schlegel (1871). *Nederlandsch Tijdschrift Dierkunde* **4**: 54, 55.
Schlegel (1881). *Notes Leyden Mus.* **3**: 58.
Schodde (1988). *Canberra Bird Notes* **13(4)**: 119-122.
Schodde & de Naurois (1982). *Notornis* **29**: 131-142.
Schomburgk (1848). *Reisen Brit. Guiana* **2**: 245.
Sclater, P.L. (1856). *Proc. Zool. Soc. London*: 31.
Sclater, P.L. (1857). *Proc. Zool. Soc. London* 1856: 282, 283.
Sclater, P.L. (1861). *Proc. Zool. Soc. London*: 261.
Sclater, P.L. (1867). *Proc. Zool. Soc. London*: 343.
Sclater, P.L. (1869). *Proc. Zool. Soc. London*: 472.
Sclater, P.L. (1880). *Proc. Zool. Soc. London*: 66.
Sclater, P.L. & Salvin (1860). *Proc. Zool. Soc. London*: 300.
Sclater, P.L. & Salvin (1867). *Proc. Zool. Soc. London*: 981.
Sclater, P.L. & Salvin (1868). *Proc. Zool. Soc. London*: 452, 453, 457.
Sclater, P.L. & Salvin (1869). *Proc. Zool. Soc. London*: 419.
Sclater, P.L. & Salvin (1873). *Nomencl. Avium Meotrop.*: 141, 162.
Sclater, P.L. & Salvin (1878). *Proc. Zool. Soc. London*: 439.
Sclater, P.L. & Salvin (1880). *Proc. Zool. Soc. London*: 161.
Sclater, W.L. (1921). *Bull. Brit. Orn. Club* **41**: 132.
Scopoli (1769). *Annus I Hist.-Nat.*: 108.
Scopoli (1786). *Deliciae Florae Faunae Insubricae* **2**: 88, 92, 93.
Seebohm (1894). *Bull. Brit. Orn. Club* **4**: 7.
Sennett (1888). *Auk* **5**: 305.
Severtsov (1873). *Izvest. Imp. Obshch. Estestr. Antr. i Etnogr. Moskva* **3(2)**: 146.
Sharpe (1870). *Proc. Zool. Soc. London*: 400.
Sharpe (1879). *Philos. Trans. Roy. Soc. London* **168**: 468, 469.
Sharpe (1887). In: Gould's *Birds New Guinea* pt. 23: pl. 70.
Sharpe (1893). *Bull. Brit. Orn. Club* **1**: 28, 37, 50, 54. **3**: 13, 14.
Sharpe (1894). *Cat. Birds Brit. Mus.* **23**: 7, 18, 121, 162.
Sharpe (1896). *Cat. Birds Brit. Mus.* **24**: 307. [*Peltohyas*].
Sharpe (1896). *Bull. Brit. Orn. Club* **5**: 44. [*Chionis minor crozettensis*].
Shelley (1883). *Ibis*: 560.
Shelley (1885). *Ibis*: 415.
Sims (1954). *Bull. Brit. Orn. Club* **74**: 37-40.

Sjöstedt (1893). *Orn. Monatsber.* **1**: 42.
Slater (1891). *Ibis*: 44.
Smith, A. (1828). *South African Commercial Advertiser* **3**: 144.
Smith, A. (1831). *Proc. Com. Sci. Corresp. Zool. Soc. London*: 11.
Smith, A. (1836). *Rep. Exped. Explor. Central Africa*: 55, 56.
Smith, A. (1839). *Illus. Zool. South Africa, Aves*: pls. 22, 23, 32.
van Someren (1919). *Bull. Brit. Orn. Club* **40**: 20.
Sparrman (1786). *Mus. Carlsonianum* **1(11)**. **1(14)**: pl. 14.
Sparrman (1788). *Mus. Carlsonianum* **3(63)**.
Spix (1825). *Av. Bras.* **2**: 66-80.
Stegman (1934). *Orn. Monatsber.* **42**: 25.
Stejneger (1884). *Auk* **1**: 231.
Stejneger (1886). *Proc. US Natl. Mus.* **9**: 363.
Stejneger (1887). *Proc. US Natl. Mus.* **10**: 81, 394, 395.
Stejneger (1897). *Auk* **14**: 201.
Stenhouse (1930). *Scottish Naturalist* **182**: 47.
Stepanyan (1972). *Ornitologiia* **10**: 388.
Stephens (1819). In: Shaw's *Gen. Zool.* **11(2)**: 516.
Stephens (1826). In: Shaw's *Gen. Zool.* **13(1)**: 139-196.
Storer (1950). *Condor* **52**: 28-31.
Streets (1877). *Ibis*: 25.
Stresemann (1914). *Nov. Zool.* **21**: 57, 60.
Stresemann (1929). *Orn. Monatsber.* **37**: 190.
Strickland (1852). *Proc. Zool. Soc. London* 1850: 220. [*Rhinoptilus*].
Strickland (1852). *Jardine's Contr. Orn.*: 158, 160. [*Charadrius pallidus, Sterna balaenarum*].
Stuart Baker (1920). *Bull. Brit. Orn. Club* **43**: 9.
Stuart Baker (1927). *Bull. Brit. Orn. Club* **47**: 73.
Sundevall (1851). *Öfversigt K. Vetenskaps-Akad. Förhandlingar, Stockholm* 7(1850): 110.
Sushkin (1925). *Birds of the Russian Altai*: 63, 64.
Sutter (1955). *Verh. Nat. Gesellschaft Basel* **66**: 85-139.
Swainson (1822). *Zool. Illustr.* **2**: pl. 106.
Swainson (1837). *Birds W. Afr.* **2**: 228, 244, 245, 249.
Swainson (1838). *Animals Menageries* 1837: 335, 336, 337, 360.
Swinhoe (1861). *Ibis*: 343.
Swinhoe (1865). *Ibis*: 543.
Swinhoe (1870). *Proc. Zool. Soc. London*: 138.
Swinhoe (1871). *Proc. Zool. Soc. London*: 273, 401, 405.
Swinhoe (1873). *Ann. and Mag. Nat. Hist.* **12(4)**: 376.
Sykes (1832). *Proc. Com. Sci. Corresp. Zool. Soc. London* **2**: 155, 164.
Taczanowski (1874). *J. Orn.* **22**: 331.
Taczanowski (1875). *Proc. Zool. Soc. London* 1874: 561.
Taczanowski (1877). *Proc. Zool. Soc. London*: 747.
Taczanowski (1886). *Orn. Pérou* **3**: 313.
Temminck (1807). *Cat. Syst. Cab. Orn.*: 175.
Temminck (1815). *Pig. et Gall.* **3**: 631, 634, 636, 757. [*Turnix maculosa, Turnix hottentotta, Turnix suscitator fasciata*].
Temminck (1815). *Man. d'Orn.*: 483, 514. [*Stercorarius pomarinus, Chlidonias leucopterus*].
Temminck (1820). *Man. d'Orn.* **2**: 503, 532, 701, 777.
Temminck (1822). *Planches Color* **8**: pl. 47.
Temminck (1823). *Planches Color* **31**: pl. 183. **34**: pl. 202.
Temminck (1824). *Planches Color* **49**: pl. 292. **50**: pl. 298.
Temminck (1825). *Planches Color* **62**: pl. 366.
Temminck (1826). *Planches Color* **68**: pls. 403, 405.
Temminck (1828). *Planches Color* **76**: pl. 454. **78**: pl. 464.
Temminck (1831). *Planches Color* **88**: pl. 523.
Temminck (1835). *Planches Color* **94**: pl. 555. **98**: pl. 579.
Temminck (1840). *Man. d'Orn.* **4**: 464.
Temminck & Schlegel (1849). In: Siebold's *Fauna Jap., Aves*: 121.
Thomson (1842). *Ann. and Mag. Nat. Hist.* **10**: 204.
Todd (1913). *Proc. Biol. Soc. Washington* **26**: 174.

Todd (1932). *Proc. Biol. Soc. Washington* **45**: 216.
Todd (1953). *J. Washington Acad. Sci.* **43**: 86, 87.
Tomkovich (1986). *Byull. Mosk. O-va Ispyt Prir. Otd. Biol.* **91**: 3-15.
Tomkovich (1990). *Byull. Mosk. O-va Ispyt Prir. Otd. Biol.* **95**: 59-72.
Townsend, J.K. (1837). *J. Acad. Nat. Sci. Philadelphia* **7**: 192.
Traill (1823). *Mem. Wernerien Nat. Hist. Soc.* **4**: 514.
Tristram (1893). *Bull. Brit. Orn. Club* **1**: 47.
Tschudi (1843). *Archiv Naturgeschichte* **9(1)**: 387, 388, 389.
Tschudi (1844). *Archiv Naturgeschichte* **10(1)**: 314.
Tweeddale (1878). *Proc. Zool. Soc. London* 1877: 765.
Vaurie (1963). *Amer. Mus. Novit.* **2131**: 2.
Verreaux, J. (1833). *S. Afr. Quart. J.* **2**: 80.
Verreaux, J. & Des Murs (1860). *Rev. et Mag. Zool.* **12(2)**: 437, 439, 440.
Vieillot (1816). *Analyse*: 55-61, 69. [*Anthropoides, Aramus, Porzana, Rostratula, Pluvianus, Stiltia isabella*].
Vieillot (1816). *Nouv. Dict. Hist. Nat.* **3**: 103, 338, 356, 359. **6**: 402, 410. [*Nycticryphes semicollaris, Cladorhynchus leucocephalus, Recurvirostra novaehollandiae, Gallinago paraguaiae, Heteroscelus brevipes, Calidris alpina sakhalina, Rynchops flavirostris*].
Vieillot (1817). *Nouv. Dict. Hist. Nat.* **8**: 302. **10**: 42. **12**: 47, 48. **14**: 277. **15**: 410.
Vieillot (1818). *Nouv. Dict. Hist. Nat.* **21**: 502, 508. **23**: 231. **24**: 124. **27**: 136, 138, 139, 147.
Vieillot (1819). *Nouv. Dict. Hist. Nat.* **28**: 29, 549-568. **32**: 136, 157, 171, 176. **34**: 461, 462, 465, 466. **35**: 49.
Vieillot (1820). *Tabl. Encyc. Méth. Orn.* pt. 1: 333, 334.
Vieillot (1825). *Gal. Ois.* **2**: 91.
Vieillot & Oudart (1825). *Gal. Ois.* **2**: 88.
Vigors (1829). *Zool. J.* **4**: 356, 357, 358.
Vigors (1831). *Proc. Com. Sci. Corresp. Zool. Soc. London*: 35.
Vigors (1832). *Proc. Com. Sci. Corresp. Zool. Soc. London* 1830-1831: 174.
Wagler (1827). *Systema Avium* pt. 1: 48, 77.
Wagler (1829). *Isis von Oken* cols. 648, 650, 653.
Wagler (1830). *Natursyst. Amphib.*: 89.
Wagler (1831). *Isis von Oken* cols. 515, 517.
Wagler (1832). *Isis von Oken* cols. 279, 1223, 1224.
Wahlberg (1856). *Öfversigt K. Vetenskaps-Akad. Förhandlingar, Stockholm* **13**: 174.
Walden (1872). *Ann. and Mag. Nat. Hist.* **9(4)**: 47.
Walkinshaw (1965). *Canadian Field-Nat.* **79**: 181.
Wallace (1863). *Proc. Zool. Soc. London* 1862: 35, 345, 346.
Wallace (1865). *Proc. Zool. Soc. London*: 480.
Wetmore (1941). *Proc. Biol. Soc. Washington* **54**: 203.
Wetmore (1946). *Proc. Biol. Soc. Washington* **59**: 50.
Wetmore (1958). *Proc. Biol. Soc. Washington* **71**: 1-2.
Wetmore (1967). *Proc. Biol. Soc. Washington* **80**: 229.
Wetmore & Borrero (1964). *Auk* **81**: 231.
Wetmore & Peters (1923). *Proc. Biol. Soc. Washington* **36**: 143.
White (1945). *Bull. Brit. Orn. Club* **65**: 47.
Wied (1833). *Beitr. Naturg. Brasil* **4**: 716.
Wilson (1813). *Amer. Orn.* **7**: 43, 53.
Wilson (1814). *Amer. Orn.* **8**: 143.
Witherby (1923). *British Birds* **16**: 324.
Xántus de Vesey (1860). *Proc. Acad. Nat. Sci. Philadelphia* 1859: 299.
Yamashina (1932). *Tori* **7**: 414.
Yamashina & Mano (1981). *J. Yamshina Inst. Orn.* **13**: 1-6.
Zarudny (1885). *Bull. Soc. Imp. Nat. Moscou* **76(1)**: 327.
Zarudny (1905). *Orn. Monatsber.* **13**: 209.
Zarudny & Härms (1911). *J. Orn.* **59**: 240.
Zarudny & Loudon (1902). *Orn. Monatsber.* **10**: 150.
Zedlitz (1908). *Orn. Monatsber.* **16**: 180.
Zedlitz (1914). *J. Orn.* **62**: 624.
Zeledon (1888). *An. Mus. Nac. Costa Rica* **2**: 3.
Zimmer (1930). *Field Mus. Nat. Hist. Publ. (Zool. Ser.)* **17**: 253.
Zimmer & Phelps (1944). *Amer. Mus. Novit.* **1270**: 1, 3.

GENERAL LIST OF REFERENCES

Abbott, C.C. (1940). Notes from the Salton Sea, California. *Condor* **42**: 264-265.

Abbott, J.M. (1982). Hordes of Buff-breasted Sandpipers in Virginia. *Raven* **53**: 33-34.

Abdulali, H. (1951). Extension of breeding range of the Stilt (*Himantopus h. himantopus*) and some notes on its habits and plumage. *J. Bombay Nat. Hist. Soc.* **49(4)**: 789-791.

Abdulali, H. (1952). The Whitetailed Lapwing (*Chettusia leucura*) near Bombay. *J. Bombay Nat. Hist. Soc.* **50(4)**: 947.

Abdulali, H. (1970). On the occurrence of Swinhoe's Snipe, *Capella megala* (Swinhoe), near Bombay, and a note on its identification. *J. Bombay Nat. Hist. Soc.* **67(1)**: 108-109.

Abdulali, H. (1978). The birds of Great and Car Nicobars with some notes on wildlife conservation in the islands. *J. Bombay Nat. Hist. Soc.* **75**: 744-772.

Abe, N. (1989). Population of the cranes in Izumi in 1987-88 winter. *J. Environm. Sci. Lab., Senshu Univ.* **1**: 67-72.

Abe, N., Kohno, H. & Mano, T. (1986). [Estimation of the breeding population of the Sooty Tern *Sterna fuscata* on Nakanokami-shima, South Ryukyu, Japan]. *J. Yamashina Inst. Orn.* **18**: 28-40. In Japanese.

Abensperg-Traun, M. & Dickman, C.R. (1989). Distributional ecology of Red-capped Plover, *Charadrius ruficapillus* (Temminck, 1822), on Western Australian salt lakes. *J. Biogeogr.* **16(2)**: 151-157.

Abraham, D.M. & Ankney, C.D. (1984). Partitioning of foraging habitat by breeding Sabine's Gulls and Arctic Terns. *Wilson Bull.* **96**: 161-172.

Abramson, I.J. (1977). Photographic confirmation of Giant Snipe in Argentina. *Auk* **94(2)**: 357.

Abramson, M. (1979). Vigilance as a factor influencing flock formation among Curlew *Numenius arquata*. *Ibis* **121**: 213-216.

Abreus, E. & Criado, J. (1994). *Distribution and Conservation Approach to Zapata Rail* Cyanolimnas cerverai *and Zapata Wren* Ferminia cerverai, *Zapata Swamp, Cuba*. BP Conservation Expedition Award 1994. BirdLife International & the Flora and Fauna Preservation Society.

Abuladze, A. (1995). Seasonal migrations of Demoiselle Cranes in Georgia. Pp. 302-304 in: Prange *et al.* (1995).

Achtermann, S. (1992). Die Bestimmung von Kleinem Gelbschenkel *Tringa flavipes* und Grossem Gelbschenkel *T. melanoleuca*. [Identification of Lesser *Tringa flavipes* and Greater Yellowlegs *T. melanoleuca*]. *Limicola* **6(2)**: 53-79. In German with English summary.

Adams, D.A. & Quay, T.L. (1958). Ecology of the Clapper Rail in southeastern North Carolina. *J. Wildl. Manage.* **22**: 149-156.

Addy, C.E. (1945). Great Black-backed Gull kills adult Black Duck. *Auk* **62**: 142-143.

Ade, B. (1976). The Crowned Plover: an open space nester. *Honeyguide* **86**: 32-34.

Ade, B. (1979). Some observations on the breeding of Crowned Plovers (1977). *Bokmakierie* **31(1)**: 9-16.

Adret, A. (1982). The sound signals of the adult Avocet *Recurvirostra avosetta* during the perinatal phase. *Ibis* **124**: 275-287.

Aebischer, N.J. & Coulson, J.C. (1990). Survival of the Kittiwake in relation to sex, year, breeding experience and position in the colony. *J. Anim. Ecol.* **59**: 1063-1071.

Aguilar, J.S., Monbailliu, X. & Paterson, A.M. eds. (1993). *Estatus y Conservación de Aves Marinas. Ecogeografía y Plan de Acción para el Mediterráneo. Status and Conservation of Seabirds. Ecogeography and Mediterranean Action Plan.* Actas del II Simposio MEDMARAVIS, SEO, Madrid. In Spanish and English.

Aguon, C.F. (1983). Survey and inventory of native landbirds on Guam. In: *Research Project Report, Guam Aquatic and Wildlife Resources, FY 1983 Annual Report*. Department of Agriculture, Guam.

Ahlquist, J.E. (1974a). *The Relationships of the Shorebirds (Charadriiformes)*. PhD dissertation, Yale University, New Haven, Connecticut.

Ahlquist, J.E. (1974b). Godwits, curlews and Tringine sandpipers: new evidence challenges old classifications. *Discovery* **10**: 15-25.

Ailes, I.W. (1976). *Ecology of the Upland Sandpiper in Central Wisconsin*. MSc thesis, University of Wisconsin, Stevens Point, Wisconsin.

Ailes, I.W. (1980). Breeding biology and habitat use of the Upland Sandpiper in central Wisconsin. *Passenger Pigeon* **42**: 53-63.

Ailes, I.W. & Toepfer, J.E. (1977). Home range and daily movement of radio-tagged Upland Sandpipers in central Wisconsin. *Inl. Bird Banding News* **49**: 203-212.

Ainley, D.G. & Boekelheide, R.J. eds. (1990). *Seabirds of the Farallon Islands: Ecology, Dynamics and Structure of an Upwelling-system Community*. Stanford University Press, Stanford, California.

Ainley, D.G. & Hunt, G.L. (1991). Status and conservation of seabirds in California. Pp. 103-114 in: Croxall (1991).

Ainley, D.G. & Lewis, T.J. (1972). Colony attendance of Farallon Pigeon Guillemots. *Pt. Reyes Bird Obs. Newsl.* **21**: 4-5.

Ainley, D.G. & Lewis, T.J. (1974). The history of Farallon Island marine bird populations, 1854-1972. *Condor* **76**: 432-446.

Ainley, D.G., Allen, S.G. & Spear, L.B. (1995). Offshore occurrence patterns of Marbled Murrelet in central California. Pp. 361-369 in: Ralph *et al.* (1995).

Ainley, D.G., Boekelheide, R.J., Morrell, S.H. & Strong, C.S. (1990). Cassin's Auklet. Pp. 306-338 in: Ainley & Boekelheide (1990).

Ainley, D.G., DeGange, A.R., Jones, L.L. & Beach, R.J. (1981). Mortality of birds in high-seas salmon gillnets. *Fisheries Bull.* **79**: 800-806.

Ainley, D.G., Grau, C.R., Roudybush, T.E., Morrell, S.H. & Utts, J.M. (1981). Petroleum ingestion reduces reproduction in Cassin's Auklets. *Marine Pollution Bull.* **9**: 314-317.

Ainley, D.G., Morrell, S.H. & Boekelheide, R.J. (1990). Rhinoceros Auklet and Tufted Puffin. Pp. 338-348 in: Ainley & Boekelheide (1990).

Ainley, D.G., Morrell, S.H. & Wood, R.C. (1986). South Polar Skua breeding colonies in the Ross Sea region, Antarctica. *Notornis* **33(3)**: 155-163.

Ainley, D.G., O'Connor, E.F. & Boekelheide, R.J. (1984). *The Marine Ecology of Birds in the Ross Sea, Antarctica*. Ornithological Monographs **32**. American Ornithologists' Union, Washington, D.C.

Ainley, D.G., Ribic, C.A. & Wood, R.C. (1990). A demographic study of the South Polar Skua *Catharacta maccormicki* at Cape Crozier. *J. Anim. Ecol.* **59(1)**: 1-20.

Ainley, D.G., Spear, L.B. & Boekelheide, R.J. (1986). Extended parental care in the Red-tailed Tropicbird and Sooty Tern. *Condor* **88(1)**: 101-102.

Ainley, D.G., Spear, L.B. & Wood, R.C. (1985). Sexual color and size variation in the South Polar Skua. *Condor* **87**: 427-428.

Ainley, D.G., Sydeman, W.J., Hatch, S.A. & Wilson, U.W. (1994). Seabird population trends along the west coast of North America: causes and the extent of regional concordance. Pp. 119-133 in: Jehl & Johnson (1994).

Akinyemi, J.O. & Iyoha, M.O. (1983). A case of suspected poisoning of west African Crowned Cranes *Balearica pavonina pavonina* with diazinon, an organophosphate insecticide. *Zool. Garten* **53(3/5)**: 317-319.

Akriotis, T. (1991). Weight-changes in the Wood-sandpiper *Tringa glareola* in south-eastern Greece during the spring migration. *Ringing & Migration* **12(2)**: 61-66.

Al-Hussaini, A.H. (1939). Further notes on the birds of Ghardaqa (Hurghada) Red Sea. *Ibis* **Ser. 14, no. 3**: 342-347.

Alberghetti, S., Cester, D., Cherubini, G., de Faveri, A., Manzi, R. & Panzarin, F. (1992). [Capture of a Buff-breasted Sandpiper, *Tryngites subruficollis*, in the lagoon of Venice (NE Italy)]. *Riv. ital. Orn.* **62(3-4)**: 187-188. In Italian.

Alberico, J.A.R. (1993). Drought and predation cause avocet and stilt breeding failure in Nevada. *Western Birds* **24(1)**: 43-52.

Alberico, J.A.R., Reed, J.M. & Oring, L.W. (1991). Nesting near a Common Tern colony increases and decreases Spotted Sandpiper nest predation. *Auk* **108(4)**: 904-910.

Alberico, J.A.R., Reed, J.M. & Oring, L.W. (1992). Non-random philopatry of sibling Spotted Sandpipers *Actitis macularia*. *Ornis Scand.* **23(4)**: 504-508.

Albignac, R. (1970). Mammifères et oiseaux du Massif du Tsaratanana (Madagascar Nord). *Mém. ORSTOM* **37**: 223-229.

Albrecht, J.S.M. (1986). Some notes on the field characteristics of the Great Snipe *Gallinago media* with reference to the Common Snipe G. gallinago. *Bull. Orn. Soc. Middle East* **16**: 30-33.

Albrecht, S. (1989). Identification of Slender-billed Curlew. *Bull. Orn. Soc. Middle East* **22**: 49-51.

Albrecht, W. (1992). [Successional broods of *Charadrius dubius* in the same nest]. *Falke* **39(3)**: 78-79. In German.

Alcorn, G. (1958). Nesting of the Caspian Tern in Grays Harbor, Washington. *Murrelet* **39**: 19-20.

Alcorn, M. & Alcorn, R. (1990). Banded Stilts on Wimmera wetlands in 1990. *Stilt* **16**: 57.

Alcorn, M., Alcorn, R. & Fleming, M. (1994). *Wader Movements in Australia. Final Report of the Regular Counts Project 1981-1990*. Australasian Wader Studies Group/RAOU Report **94**. Melbourne.

Alcorn, R. (1985). 50,000 Banded Stilts. *RAOU Newsl.* **66**: 4.

Alcorn, R. (1986). A WSG regular counts report, December 1986. *Stilt* **10**: 4-5.

Alcorn, R. (1988). A WSG regular wader counts project. Interim report to June 1987: migratory waders. *Stilt* **12**: 7-23.

Alcorn, R. (1989). Regular wader counts project report: Red-necked Avocet. *Stilt* **14**: 21-32.

Alcorn, R. (1990). Regular counts project report. *Stilt* **16**: 9-22.

Aldrich, J. (1972). A new subspecies of Sandhill Cranes from Mississippi. *Proc. Biol. Soc. Washington* **85(5)**: 63-70.

Alekseev, A.F. (1985). The Houbara Bustard in the north-west Kyzylkum (USSR). *Bustard Studies* **3**: 87-92.

Alerstam, T. (1975). Crane *Grus grus* migration over sea and land. *Ibis* **117(4)**: 489-495.

Alerstam, T. (1990). *Bird Migration*. Cambridge University Press, Cambridge.

Alerstam, T. & Högstedt, G. (1980). Spring predictability and leap-frog migration. *Ornis Scand.* **11**: 196-200.

Alerstam, T. & Högstedt, G. (1982). Bird migration and reproduction in relation to habitats for survival and breeding. *Ornis Scand.* **13**: 25-37.

Alerstam, T. & Högstedt, G. (1985). Leap-frog arguments: reply to Pienkowski, Evans and Townshend. *Ornis Scand.* **16**: 71-74.

Alerstam, T., Gudmundsson, G.A. & Johannesson, K. (1992). Resources for long distance migration: intertidal exploitation of *Littorina* and *Mytilus* by Knots *Calidris canutus* in Iceland. *Oikos* **65**: 179-189.

Alerstam, T., Gudmundsson, G.A., Jönsson, P.E., Karlsson, J. & Lindström, Å. (1990). Orientation, migration routes and flight behavior of Knots, Turnstones and Brant Geese departing from Iceland in spring. *Arctic* **43**: 201-214.

Alessandria, G., della Toffola, M. & Carpegna, F. (1990). [First observation of Spurwinged Plover, *Hoplopterus spinosus*, in Italy]. *Riv. ital. Orn.* **60(3-4)**: 197-198. In Italian.

Alexander, W.B. (1923). A week on the Upper Barcoo, central Queensland. *Emu* **23**: 82-95.

Alexander, W.B. (1947). The Woodcock in the British Isles. *Ibis* **89**: 1-28.

Alexandersson, H. (1987). [Distribution and density of Golden Plover *Pluvialis apricaria* on raised bogs in southwest Sweden. The importance of area and distance between bogs]. *Acta Regiae Soc. Sci. Litt. Gothob. Zool.* **14**: 9-19. In Swedish with English summary.

Ali, S. (1953). *The Birds of Travancore & Cochin*. Oxford University Press, London.

Ali, S. (1958). Notes on the Sarus Crane. *J. Bombay Nat. Hist. Soc.* **55**: 166-168.

Ali, S. (1977). *Field Guide to the Birds of the Eastern Himalayas*. Oxford University Press, Delhi.

Ali, S. (1979). *The Book of Indian Birds*. Bombay Natural History Society, Bombay.

Ali, S. & Rahmani, A.R. (1982). *Study of Ecology of Certain Endangered Species of Wildlife and their Habitats. The Great Indian Bustard*. Annual Report **1** (1981-82). Bombay Natural History Society, Bombay.

Ali, S. & Rahmani, A.R. (1985). *Study of Ecology of Certain Endangered Species of Wildlife and their Habitats. The Great Indian Bustard*. Annual Report **2** (1982-84). Bombay Natural History Society, Bombay.

Ali, S. & Ripley, S.D. (1980). *Handbook of the Birds of India and Pakistan*. Vol. 2. 2nd edition. Oxford University Press, Delhi.

Ali, S. & Ripley, S.D. (1982). *Handbook of the Birds of India and Pakistan*. Vol. 3. 2nd edition. Oxford University Press, Delhi.

Ali, S., Daniel, J.C. & Rahmani, A.R. eds. (1985). *Study of Ecology of Certain Endangered Species of Wildlife and their Habitats. The Floricans*. Annual Report **1** (1984-85). Bombay Natural History Society, Bombay.

Alisauskas, R.T. (1987). Morphological correlates of age and breeding status in American Coots. *Auk* **104**: 640-646.

Alisauskas, R.T. & Arnold, T.W. (1994). American Coot. In: Tacha & Braun (1994).

Allan, D. (1983). Black-winged Plover (R243) in the Transvaal. *Witwatersrand Bird Club News* **120**: 8.

Allan, D.G. (1988). The world's bustards: a looming crisis. *Quagga* **24**: 5-9.

Allan, D.G. (1992). Distribution, relative abundance, and habitats of the Blue Crane in the Karoo and the Southwestern Cape. Pp. 29-46 in: Porter *et al.* (1992).

Allan, D.G. (1993). *Aspects of the Biology and Conservation Status of the Blue Crane* Anthropoides paradiseus *and the Ludwig's* Neotis ludwigii *and Stanley's* N. denhami stanleyi *Bustards in Southern Africa*. MSc thesis, University of Cape Town, Cape Town.

Allan, D.G. (1994a). *Cranes and Farmers*. Endangered Wildlife Trust, Parkview, South Africa.

Allan, D.G. (1994b). The abundance and movements of Ludwig's Bustard *Neotis ludwigii*. *Ostrich* **65**: 95-105.

Allan, D.G. & Davies, R.A.G. (1995). The field identification of the bustards and korhaans (Otididae) of southern Africa. *Bull. African Bird Club* **2**: 16-23.

Allan, L.J. (1978). *Food of the Ring-billed and Herring Gulls Nesting on the Chantry Islands, Lake Huron, 1978*. Canadian Wildlife Service Wildlife Tox. Division Report **39**.

Allanson, B.R. (1953). A note on the behavior of Hartlaub's Gull. *Ostrich* **24**: 183-184.

Allen, A.A. & Kyllingstad, H. (1949). The eggs and young of the Bristle-thighed Curlew. *Auk* **66**: 343-350.

Allen, G.G. (1984). Black-billed food preferences. *Notornis* **31(3)**: 224.

Allen, G.M. (1925). *Birds and their Attributes*. Marshall Jones, Boston.

Allen, J.N. (1980). The ecology and behavior of the Long-billed Curlew in southeastern Washington. *Wildl. Monogr.* **73**: 1-67.
Allen, P.M. & Clifton, M.P. (1972). Aggressive behaviour of Kori Bustard *Otis kori*. *Bull. East Afr. Nat. Hist. Soc.* **1972**: 188-189.
Allen, R.P. (1952). *The Whooping Crane*. Research Report **3**. National Audubon Society, New York.
Allen, R.P. (1956). *A Report on the Whooping Crane's Northern Breeding Grounds*. Supplement to Research Report **3**. National Audubon Society, New York.
Allen, R.P. (1961). *Birds of the Caribbean*. Viking Press, New York.
Alleng, G.P. & Whyte-Alleng, C.A.M. (1993). Survey of Least Tern nesting sites on the south coast of Jamaica. *Colonial Waterbirds* **16(2)**: 190-193.
Alley, R. & Boyd, H. (1950). Parent-young recognition in the Coot *Fulica atra*. *Ibis* **92**: 46-51.
Allouche, L. (1988). *Strategies d'Hivernage Comparées du Canard Chipeau et de la Foulque Macroule pour un Partage Spatio-temporel des Milieux Humides de Camargue*. PhD thesis, Université des Sciences et Techniques du Languedoc, Montpellier.
Allport, G. (1995). Merja Zerga, Morocco. *World Birdwatch* **17(2)**: 6-7.
Almeida, A.C.C. (1988). Comportamento reprodutivo de *Cariama cristata* Sharpe 1874 (Gruiformes, Cariamidae) no Parque Zoobotânico Getulio Vargas, Salvador, Bahia. Page 497 in: *XV Congresso Brasileiro de Zoologia, Curitiba 1988*. Universidade Federal do Paraná, Curitiba. (Abstract).
Alonso, J.A. & Alonso, J.C. eds. (1990). *Distribución y Demografía de la Grulla Común (*Grus grus*) en España*. ICONA, Madrid.
Alonso, J.A., Alonso, J.C., Martín, E. & Morales, M.B. (1995). *La Avutarda en la Reserva de las Lagunas de Villafáfila*. Instituto de Estudios Zamoranos "Florián de Ocampo" (CSIC), Diputación de Zamora, FEPMA (Fundación para la Ecología y la Protección del Medio Ambiente), Zamora.
Alonso, J.A., Alonso, J.C., Martínez-Vicente, I.S. & Bautista, L.M. (1991). Simulation of a Common Crane population model. Pp. 277-283 in: Harris (1991b).
Alonso, J.A., Alonso, J.C. & Muñoz-Pulido, R. (1990). Áreas de invernada de la Grulla Común (*Grus grus*) en España. Pp. 7-162 in: Alonso & Alonso (1990).
Alonso, J.C. & Alonso, J.A. eds. (1990). *Parámetros Demográficos, Selección de Hábitat y Distribución de la Avutarda (*Otis tarda*) en Tres Regiones Españolas*. ICONA, Madrid.
Alonso, J.C. & Alonso, J.A. (1991). Costs and benefits of flocking in wintering Common Cranes. Pp. 271-276 in: Harris (1991b).
Alonso, J.C. & Alonso, J.A. (1992a). Daily activity and intake rate patterns of wintering Common Cranes *Grus grus*. *Ardea* **80(3)**: 343-351.
Alonso, J.C. & Alonso, J.A. (1992b). Male-biased dispersal in the Great Bustard *Otis tarda*. *Ornis Scand.* **23**: 81-88.
Alonso, J.C. & Alonso, J.A. (1993). Age-related differences in time budget and parental care in wintering Common Cranes. *Auk* **110(1)**: 76-88.
Alonso, J.C., Alonso, J.A. & Bautista, L.M. (1994). Carrying capacity of staging areas and facultative migration extension in Common Cranes. *J. Appl. Ecol.* **31(2)**: 212-222.
Alonso, J.C., Alonso, J.A., Cantos, F.J. & Bautista, L.M. (1990). Spring crane migration through Gallocanta, Spain. I. Daily variations in migration volume. II. Timing and pattern of daily departure. *Ardea* **78(3)**: 365-388.
Alonso, J.C., Alonso, J.A., Martín, E. & Morales, M. (1995). Range and patterns of Great Bustard movements at Villafáfila, NW Spain. *Ardeola* **42(1)**: 69-76.
Alonso, J.C., Veiga, J.P. & Alonso, J.A. (1984). Familienauflösung und Abzug aus dem Winterquartier beim Kranich *Grus grus*. *J. Orn.* **125**: 69-74.
Alonso, J.C., Veiga, J.P. & Alonso, J.A. (1987). Possible effects of recent agricultural development on the wintering and migratory patterns of *Grus grus* in Iberia. Pp. 277-299 in: Archibald & Pasquier (1987a).
Alonzo-Pasicolan, S. (1992). The bird-catchers of Dalton Pass. *Bull. Oriental Bird Club* **15**: 33-36.
Alström, P. (1985). Fältbestämning av gulbröstad snäppa *Calidris bairdii* och vitgumpsnäppa *C. fuscicollis*. *Vår Fågelvärld* **44(8)**: 479-484.
Alström, P. (1987). The identification of Baird's and White-rumped Sandpipers in juvenile plumage. *Birding* **19(2)**: 10-13.
Alström, P. (1990). Calls of American and Pacific Golden Plovers. *British Birds* **83(2)**: 70-72.
Alström, P. (1991). Fältbestämning av mongolpipare, *Charadrius mongolus*. *Vår Fågelvärld* **2**: 33-37.
Alström, P. & Olsson, U. (1985). First record of Iceland Gull *Larus glaucoides* from Japan. *Strix* **4**: 70-72.
Alström, P. & Olsson, U. (1989). Identification of juvenile Red-necked and Long-toed Stints. *British Birds* **82(8)**: 360-372.
Alström, P., Barthel, P.H. & Schmidt, C. (1989). Die Bestimmung von Weißbürzel *Calidris fuscicollis* und Bairdstrandläufer *C. bairdii*. [Identification of White-rumped *Calidris fuscicollis* and Baird's Sandpiper *C. bairdii*]. *Limicola* **3(2)**: 49-61. In German with English summary.
Altenburg, W. & van der Kamp, J. (1985). *Importance des Zones Humides de la Mauritanie du Sud, du Sénégal et de la Guinée-Bissau pour la Barge à Queue Noire* Limosa l. limosa. Ned. Sticht. Int. Vogelbesch./RIN Contribution 85-1, Leersum, Netherlands.
Altenburg, W., Engelmoer, M., Mes, R. & Piersma, T. (1982). *Wintering Waders on the Banc D'Arguin*. Communication **6** of the Wadden Sea Working Group. 283 pp.
Altenburg, W., van der Kamp, J. & Beintema, A. (1985). The wintering grounds of the Black-tailed Godwit in west Africa. *Wader Study Group Bull.* **44**: 18-20.
Altevogt, R. & Davis, T.A. (1980). Nocturnal activity of the Turnstone (*Arenaria interpres*) on South Sentinel (Andaman Islands). *J. Bombay Nat. Hist. Soc.* **77(3)**: 508-510.
Altman, R.L. & Gano, R.D. (1984). Least Terns nest alongside Harrier Jet pad. *J. Field Orn.* **55**: 108-109.
Alvarenga, H.M.F. (1985). Um novo Psilopteridae (Aves: Gruiformes) dos sedimentos terciários de Itaboraí, Rio de Janeiro, Brasil. VIII Congr. Bras. Paleont., 1983. MME-DNPM, sér. Geologia **27**. *Paleont. Estratig.* **2**: 17-20.
Álvarez, G. (1994). Ecología y situación de la Gaviota de Audouin en España. *Quercus* **100**: 4-11.
Álvarez, V.B. & Canet, R.S. (1983). Aspectos ecológicos de la nidificación de *Sterna hirundo* y *S. albifrons*. *Cienc. Biol. Acad. Cienc. Cuba* **9**: 128-131.
Álvarez del Toro, M. (1970). Notas para la biología del Pájaro Cantil (*Heliornis fulica*). *Inst. Cienc. Artes Chiapas, Tuxtla Gutiérrez* **1**: 7-13.
Álvarez del Toro, M. (1971). On the biology of the American Finfoot in southern Mexico. *Living Bird* **10**: 79-88.
Amadon, D. & DuPont, J.E. (1970). Notes on Philippine birds. *Nemouria* **1**: 1-14.
Amaral, M.J. (1977). *Comparative Breeding Biology of the Tufted and Horned Puffins in the Barren Islands, Alaska*. MSc thesis, University of Washington, Seattle, Washington.
Amat, J.A. (1986). Information on the diet of the Stone Curlew *Burhinus oedicnemus* in Doñana, southern Spain. *Bird Study* **33(2)**: 71-73.
Ambrose, W.G. (1986). Estimate of removal rate of *Nereis virens* (Polychaeta: Nereidae) from an intertidal mudflat by gulls (*Larus* spp.). *Mar. Biol.* **90**: 243-247.
Ameels, M., Lafontaine, R.M. & Lafontaine, D. (1989). Première observation d'un Bécasseau à queue pointue (*Calidris acuminata*) en Belgique. *Aves* **26(3-4)**: 231-232.
Amerson, A.B. (1966). *Ornithodoros capensis* (Acarina: Argasidae) infesting Sooty Tern (*Sterna fuscata*) nasal cavities. *J. Parasitol.* **52**: 1220-1221.
Amerson, A.B. (1971). *The Natural History of French Frigate Shoals, Northwestern Hawaiian Islands*. Atoll Research Bulletin **150**. 383 pp.
Amerson, A.B. & Shelton, P.C. (1976). *The Natural History of Johnson Atoll, Central Pacific Ocean*. Atoll Research Bulletin **192**. 476 pp.
Amerson, A.B., Clapp, R.B. & Wirtz, W.O.I. (1974). *The Natural History of Pearl and Hermes Reef, Northwestern Hawaiian Islands*. Atoll Research Bulletin **174**. 306 pp.
Ametov, M.B. (1985). [On the ecology of the European Pratincole in the cultivated landscape of the lower River Amu-Darya]. Pp. 52-53 in: Mitropolskii, O.V. ed. (1985). [*Mammals and Birds of Uzbekistan*]. FAN, Tashkent. In Russian.
Ametov, M.B. (1987). [On the ecology of the White-tailed Plover in cultured landscape of the lower part of Amudarya river]. *Uzb. Biol. Zh.* **3**: 44-47. In Russian.
Amiet, L. (1957). A wader survey of some Queensland coastal localities. *Emu* **57**: 236-254.
Amlaner, C.J. & Stout, J.F. (1978). Aggressive communication by *Larus glaucescens*. Part VI: interactions of territory residents with remotely controlled, locomotory model. *Behaviour* **66**: 223-251.
Amlaner, C.K. & McFarland, D.J. (1981). Sleep in the Herring Gull (*Larus argentatus*). *Anim. Behav.* **29**: 551-556.
Amon, A. (1978). *Roadrunners and other Cuckoos*. Atheneum, New York.
Amos, E.J.R. (1991). *A Guide to the Birds of Bermuda*. Warwick.
Amos, E.J.R. & Wingate, D.B. (1983). First record of the Wood Sandpiper, *Tringa glareola*, from Bermuda. *Amer. Birds* **37(1)**: 115-116.
Andell, P. & Jönsson, P.E. (1986). The Kentish Plover in Sweden - a presentation of a conservation project. *Vår Fågelvärld* **45(2)**: 85-92.
Anders, W. & Andersson, A. (1990). [Second and third record of Red-necked Stint, *Calidris ruficollis*, in Sweden]. *Vår Fågelvärld* **49(1)**: 31-34. In Swedish with English summary.
Andersen, F.S. (1944). Contributions to the breeding biology of the Ruff (*Philomachus pugnax*). I. *Dan. Orn. Foren. Tidssk.* **38**: 26-30.
Andersen, F.S. (1948). Contributions to the biology of the Ruff (*Philomachus pugnax* L.). II. *Dan. Orn. Foren. Tidssk.* **42**: 125-148.
Andersen, F.S. (1951). Contributions to the biology of the Ruff (*Philomachus pugnax* L.). III. *Dan. Orn. Foren. Tidssk.* **45**: 145-173.
Andersen, F.S. (1959). Bill, eggs and nests of captured Arctic Terns (*Sterna paradisaea* Pont.) and Common Terns (*Sterna hirundo* L.). *Dan. Orn. Foren. Tidssk.* **53**: 84-100.
Andersen-Harild, P. (1969). [Some results of ringing Black Guillemot (*Cepphus grylle*) in Denmark]. *Dan. Orn. Foren. Tidssk.* **63**: 105-110. In Danish with English summary.
Anderson, A. (1975). A method of sexing moorhens. *Waterfowl* **26**: 77-82.
Anderson, B.W. & Ohmart, R.D. (1985). Habitat use by Clapper Rails in the lower Colorado River valley. *Condor* **87**: 116-126.
Anderson, D.A. & Bellin, B. (1988). Inland records of Ruddy and Black Turnstones in Oregon. *Oregon Birds* **14(1)**: 47-50.
Anderson, D.W. (1983). The seabirds. Pp. 246-264 in: Case, T.J. & Cody, M.L. eds. (1983). *Island Biogeography in the Sea of Cortez*. University of California Press, Los Angeles, California.
Anderson, D.W., Mendoza, J.E. & Keith, J.O. (1976). Seabirds in the Gulf of California: a vulnerable, international resource. *Nat. Resour. J.* **16**: 483-505.
Anderson, E. (1993). The Killdeer. *Bird Watcher's Digest* **15(6)**: 32-37.
Anderson, G.J. (1991). The breeding biology of the Bush Thick-knee *Burhinus magnirostris* and notes on its distribution in the Brisbane area. *Sunbird* **21(2)**: 33-61.
Anderson, J.M. (1977). Yellow Rail (*Coturnicops noveboracensis*). In: Sanderson (1977).
Anderson, K.R. (1974). The biometrics, moult and recoveries of British-ringed Ruff. *Wader Study Group Bull.* **11**: 5-14.
Anderson, K.R. & Minton, C.D.T. (1978). Origins and movements of Oystercatchers on the Wash. *British Birds* **71**: 439 447.
Anderson, M. (1993). A possible attack by a Whistling Kite, *Haliastur sphenurus*, on a Sooty Oystercatcher, *Haematopus fuliginosus*. *Austr. Bird Watcher* **15(4)**: 167.
Anderson, M.G. (1974). American Coots feeding in association with Canvasbacks. *Wilson Bull.* **86**: 462-463.
Anderson, P.C. & Kok, O.B. (1990). [Gonadal cycle of the Crowned Plover *Vanellus coronatus* on some inland airfields]. *S. Afr. Tydskr. Dierk.* **25(1)**: 54-60. In Afrikaans.
Anderson, P.C. & Kok, O.B. (1991). The Crowned Plover problem at airports: a simple solution. *Afr. Wildl.* **45(6)**: 299-301. In English and Afrikaans.
Anderson, P.C. & Kok, O.B. (1992). [Aspects of the anatomy, morphology and moult of the Crowned Plover (*Vanelus coronatus*)]. *S. Afr. Tydskr. Natuurwetensk. Tegn.* **11**: 4-9. In Afrikaans with English summary.
Anderson, R.A. (1968). Notes on the Snares Island Snipe. *Notornis* **15**: 223-227.
Andersson, Å. (1970). Food habits and predation of an inland-breeding population of the Herring Gull *Larus argentatus* in southern Sweden. *Ornis Scand.* **1**: 75-81.
Andersson, B. & Breife, B. (1986). [First record of Baird's Sandpiper, *Calidris bairdii*, in Sweden]. *Vår Fågelvärld* **45(6)**: 347-349. In Swedish with English summary.
Andersson, C.J. & Gurney, J.H. (1872). *Notes on the Birds of Damara Land and the Adjacent Countries of South-West Africa*. John van Voorst, London.
Andersson, G. (1971). Dvargspov, *Numenius minutus*, i Finnmark. *Sterna* **10**: 63-64.
Andersson, M. (1971). Breeding behaviour of the Long-tailed Skua *Stercorarius longicaudus* (Vieillot). *Ornis Scand.* **2**: 35-54.
Andersson, M. (1973). Behaviour of the Pomarine Skua *Stercorarius pomarinus* Temm. with comparative remarks on Stercorariinae. *Ornis Scand.* **4**: 1-16.
Andersson, M. (1976a). Clutch size in the Long-tailed Skua *Stercorarius longicaudus*: some field experiments. *Ibis* **118**: 586-588.
Andersson, M. (1976b). Population ecology of the Long-tailed Skua (*Stercorarius longicaudus* Vieill.). *J. Anim. Ecol.* **45**: 537-559.
Andersson, M. (1976c). Predation and kleptoparasitism by skuas in a Shetland seabird colony. *Ibis* **118**: 208-217.
Andersson, M. (1981). Reproductive tactics of the Long-tailed Skua *Stercorarius longicaudus*. *Oikos* **37**: 287-294.
Andersson, M., Götmark, F. & Wiklund, C.G. (1981). Food information in the Black-headed Gull, *Larus ridibundus*. *Behav. Ecol. Sociobiol.* **9**: 199-202.
André, R. (1985). Some aspects of reproduction in the Little Bustard and a contribution to an estimate of its population in France in 1978/1979. *Bustard Studies* **2**: 153-159.
Andreenkov, V.I. (1986). [Problems of protection of breeding and wintering places of the Ibisbill (*Ibidorhyncha struthersii*) in Issyk Kul Depression]. *Ornitologiya* **21**: 146-147. In Russian.
Andreev, A.V. (1980a). [Biology of the Grey-rumped Sandpiper (*Tringa brevipes*)]. In: Flint (1980a). In Russian.
Andreev, A.V. (1980b). [The study of the nesting biology of Great Knot (*Calidris tenuirostris*) in the Kolyma River Basin]. *Ornitologiya* **15**: 207-208. In Russian.
Andreev, A.V. & Kondratiev, A.Y. (1981). [New data on the biology of the Ross Gull]. *Zoologischeskii Zhurnal* **60**: 418-425. In Russian.
Andreev, B.N. (1974). [*Birds of the Vilvuysk Basin*]. Yakutsk Book Publishers, Yakutsk. In Russian.
Andreeva, T.R. (1991). Trophic relations of the Terek Sandpiper (*Xenus cinereus*) in the Stchuch River Basin, Yamal Peninsula. *Ornitologiya* **25**: 35-39.
Andres, B.A. (1994). *Year-round Residency in Northern Populations of the Black Oystercatcher*. US Fish & Wildlife Service, Anchorage, Alaska.
Andres, B.A. & Falxa, G.A. (1995). Black Oystercatcher (*Haematopus bachmani*). No. **155** in: Poole & Gill (1994-1995).
Andresen, K. & Thomas, L. (1986). The moult of Glaucous Gull *Larus hyperboreus* and Iceland Gull *Larus glaucoides* in Disko, Greenland. *Bird Study* **33**: 49-51.
Andrew, D. (1992). Observations of Chestnut-backed Button-quail. *Wingspan* **8**: 14.
Andrew, I.G. (1975). Black-fronted Dotterel in the Manawatu. *Notornis* **22(3)**: 244-246.
Andrew, P. (1985a). A Sabine's Gull *Larus sabini* off the coast of Sumatra. *Kukila* **2(1)**: 9.
Andrew, P. (1985b). An annotated checklist of the birds of the Cibodas-Gunung Gede Nature Reserve. *Kukila* **2(1)**: 10-28.
Andrew, P. (1992). *The Birds of Indonesia. A Checklist (Peter's Sequence)*. Kukila Checklist **1**. Indonesian Ornithological Society, Jakarta.
Andrew, P. & Holmes, D.A. (1990). Sulawesi bird report. *Kukila* **5(1)**: 4-26.
Andrews, D.A. (1973). *Habitat Utilization by Sora, Virginia Rails and King Rails Near Southwestern Lake Erie*. MSc thesis, Ohio State University, Columbus, Ohio.
Andrews, J. (1991). Restoration of gravel pits for wildlife. *RSPB Conserv. Rev.* **5**: 78-81.
Andrews, M. (1991). A 'flock' of pratincoles. *Bird Obs.* **712**: 89.
Andriamampianina, J. (1981). Les réserves naturelles et la protection de la nature à Madagascar. Pp. 105-111 in: Oberlé, P. ed. (1981). *Madagascar, un Sanctuaire de la Nature*. Lechevalier, Paris.
Andronov, V.A. (1988). [The current status of the Red-crowned Crane (*Grus japonensis*) and White-naped Crane (*Grus vipio*) in the Amur Region]. Pp. 187-190 in: Litvinenko & Neufeldt (1988). In Russian.
Andronov, V.A., Andronova, R.S. & Petrova, L.K. (1988). [Distribution of Red-crowned Crane nesting territories in Arkharinski Lowland]. Pp. 59-62 in: Litvinenko & Neufeldt (1988). In Russian.
Androsenko, N.N. (1981). [Dynamics of populations of colonies of shorebirds in nesting period on Lake Tengiz]. Pp. 118-120 in: Flint (1981). In Russian.
Andryushchenko, N.N. (1995). The current status of the Demoiselle Crane in central Kazakhstan. Page 298 in: Prange *et al.* (1995).
Anegay, K. (1994). Diurnal and nocturnal activity patterns of semi-captive Houbara Bustards *Chlamydotis undulata*. *Sandgrouse* **16**: 41-46.
Anker-Nilssen, T. (1987). The breeding performance of Puffins *Fratercula arctica* on Røst, northern Norway in 1979-1985. *Fauna Norvegica (Ser. C, Cinclus)* **10**: 21-38.
Anker-Nilssen, T. (1992). *Food Supply as a Determinant of Reproduction and Population Development in Norwegian Puffins* Fratercula arctica. PhD thesis, University of Trondheim, Trondheim, Norway.

Anker-Nilssen, T. & Lorentsen, S.H. (1990). Distribution of Puffins *Fratercula arctica* feeding off Røst, northern Norway, during the breeding season, in relation to chick growth, prey and oceanographical parameters. *Polar Res.* **8**: 67-76.
Ankney, C.D. & Hopkins, J. (1985). Habitat selection by roof-nesting Killdeer. *J. Field Orn.* **56(3)**: 284-286.
Annenkov, B.P. (1988). [Habitat of Ibis-bill (*Ibidorhyncha struthersii*) in Alakolskaya Hollow]. *Ornitologiya* **23**: 198. In Russian.
Annett, C. & Pierotti, R. (1989). Chick hatching as a trigger for dietary switching in the Western Gull. *Colonial Waterbirds* **12**: 4-11.
Anon. (1971a). Dunlin bibliography. *Wader Study Group Bull.* **4**: 7-9.
Anon. (1971b). Our diminishing heritage - Australian Bustard *Eupodotis australis*. *State Wildl. Advis. Serv.* **2(2)**: 40-41.
Anon. (1976). [A preliminary study on the breeding of the Japanese Crane *Grus japonensis* in the zoo]. *Chinese J. Zool.* **1**: 41-43. In Chinese.
Anon. (1978). *Red Data Book of Kazakh SSR*. Part 1. Vertebrates. Kainar, Alma Ata.
Anon. (1981a). Erstzucht des Grünflügel-Trompetervogels (*Psophia viridis*). *Gefiederte Welt* **105**: 79-80.
Anon. (1981b). [Quantitative distribution of the Red-crowned Crane *Grus japonensis*]. *Wildlife* **1**: 19-21. In Chinese.
Anon. (1982). [Pheasant-tailed Jacana]. *Yacho* **47(2)**: 28-29. In Japanese.
Anon. (1983a). *The A.O.U. Check-list of North American Birds*. 6th edition. American Ornithologists' Union, Washington, D.C.
Anon. (1983b). *Yuma Clapper Rail Recovery Plan*. US Fish & Wildlife Service, Albuquerque, New Mexico.
Anon. (1984). *Salt Marsh Harvest Mouse and California Clapper Rail Recovery Plan*. US Fish & Wildlife Service, Region 1, Portland, Oregon.
Anon. (1985a). *Light-footed Clapper Rail Recovery Plan (Revised)*. US Fish & Wildlife Service, Region 1, Portland, Oregon.
Anon. (1985b). *Hawaiian Waterbirds Recovery Plan*. US Fish & Wildlife Service, Portland, Oregon.
Anon. (1986). Jerdon's Courser rediscovered in India. *World Birdwatch* **8(1)**: 3.
Anon. (1988). Cryptic gull uncovered in China. *BBC Wildlife* **6(3)**: 118-119.
Anon. (1989a). [The Great Bustard, *Otis tarda*, an endangered species]. *Chinese Wildlife* **5**: 40-42, 20. In Chinese.
Anon. (1989b). The St. Helena Plover. *ICBP Ann. Rep.* **1989**: 7-8.
Anon. (1989c). The Slender-billed Curlew. *ICBP Ann. Rep.* **1989**: 8-10.
Anon. (1990). *American Woodcock Management Plan*. US Fish & Wildlife Service, Laurel, Maryland.
Anon. (1991a). *Mississippi Sandhill Crane Recovery Plan*. US Fish & Wildlife Service, Atlanta, Georgia.
Anon. (1991b). *Seabird Colony Data Base 1991. Version 1*. US Fish & Wildlife Service, Homer, Alaska.
Anon. (1992a). *Mississippi Sandhill Crane (*Grus candensis pulla*) Population and Habitat Viability Assessment Workshop Report*. IUCN/SSC Captive Breeding Specialist Group.
Anon. (1992b). *The Joint Monitoring Project for Breeding Birds in the Wadden Sea: Annual Report 1990*. Common Secretariat for the Cooperation on the Protection of the Wadden Sea.
Anon. (1993a). *Hawaii's Birds*. 4th edition. Hawaii Audubon Society, Honolulu.
Anon. (1993b). Le Courlis à bec grêle. Un courlis en danger. *Oiseau et RFO* **32**: 25-27.
Anon. (1993c). From the field. Hong Kong. *Bull. Oriental Bird Club* **17**: 50-51.
Anon. (1993d). Proceedings of Society. *Bull. Japan Alcid Soc.* **1993**: 1-32.
Anon. (1993e). *Catalog of Alaskan Seabird Colonies-computer Archives*. US Fish & Wildlife Service, Anchorage, Alaska.
Anon. (1993f). *Estudio Geográfico Integral de la Ciénaga de Zapata*. Academia de Ciencias de Cuba, ICGC, la Habana.
Anon. (1994a). *Whooping Crane Recovery Plan*. US Fish & Wildlife Service, Albuquerque, New Mexico.
Anon. (1994b). *List of the Birds of Oman*. 4th edition. Oman Bird Records Committee (OBRC), Muscat.
Anon. (1994c). Bengal Floricans refound. *Bull. Oriental Bird Club* **19**: 18.
Anon. (1994d). New Chinese Black-necked Crane population discovered. *Bull. Oriental Bird Club* **19**: 18-19.
Anon. (1994e). More Saunder's Gull colonies found in north China. *Bull. Oriental Bird Club* **19**: 19.
Anon. (1994f). From the field. Hong Kong. *Bull. Oriental Bird Club* **19**: 65-66.
Anon. (1994g). Cambodia. Major wetland survey. *Bull. Oriental Bird Club* **20**: 17.
Anon. (1994h). Observations de Sternes incas *Larosterna inca* en France. *Ornithos* **1(2)**: 98.
Anon. (1994i). Proceedings of Society. *Bull. Japan Alcid Soc.* **1994**: 1-24.
Anon. (1995a). Siberian Crane project: a five year plan. Pp. 305-307 in: Prange *et al.* (1995).
Anon. (1995b). Blue Crane counts. *Bull. African Bird Club* **2(1)**: 8.
Anon. (1995c). Recent reports. Ethiopia. *Bull. African Bird Club* **2(1)**: 61-62.
Anon. (1995d). Recent reports. The Gambia. *Bull. African Bird Club* **2(1)**: 62.
Anon. (1995e). Recent reports. Malawi. *Bull. African Bird Club* **2(1)**: 63.
Anon. (1995f). Recent reports. Niger. *Bull. African Bird Club* **2(1)**: 63.
Anon. (1995g). Recent reports. South Africa. *Bull. African Bird Club* **2(1)**: 64.
Anon. (1995h). Recent reports. Zambia. *Bull. African Bird Club* **2(1)**: 64.
Anon. (1995i). Whooping Crane (*Grus americana*). *Endangered Species Bull.* **20(5)**: 24.
Anon. (1995j). Improved survival for Florida Whoopers. *ICF Bugle* **21(4)**: 5.
Anon. (1995k). 1993 Eskimo Curlew record is erroneous. *Cotinga* **3**: 69.
Anon. (1995l). Canadian "Eskimo Curlew" nest now thought to be Whimbrel's. *Cotinga* **4**: 7-8.
Anon. (1995m). A nest thought to be of the extremely rare Eskimo Curlew. *World Birdwatch* **17(4)**: 3.
Anon. (1995n). Status and conservation of rare alcids in Japan. *Bull. Japan Alcid Soc.* **1995**: 1-24.
Anon. (1995o). Corncrakes: better news from Scottish islands. *Birdwatch* **41**: 7.
Anon. (1995p). Inaccessible Island. *Bull. African Bird Club* **2(1)**: 10-11.
Anon. (1995q). The Invisible Rail. *World Birdwatch* **17(3)**: 3.
Anon. (1996). Birds get worst of two worlds. *BBC - Wildlife* **14(1)**: 60.
Ansingh, F.H., Koelers, H.F., van der Werf, P.A. & Voous, K.H. (1960). The breeding of the Cayenne or Yellow-billed Sandwich Tern in Curaçao in 1958. *Ardea* **48**: 51-65.
Antas, P.T.Z. (1983). Migration of Nearctic shorebirds (Charadriidae and Scolopacidae) in Brazil - flyways and their different seasonal use. *Wader study Group Bull.* **39**: 52-56.
Antas, P.T.Z. (1988). [Moult and weight analyses for *Pluvialis squatarola*, *Calidris fuscicollis*, *C. alba*, *C. canutus*, *Limosa haemastica*, *Charadrius falklandicus* and *Zonibyx modestus* in Lagoa do Peixe National Park, S. Brazil]. *Anais ENAV, Univ. Vale do Rio dos Sinos* **3**: 63. In Portuguese.
Antas, P.T.Z. (1991). Status and conservation of seabirds breeding in Brazilian waters. Pp. 141-158 in: Croxall (1991).
Antoniazza, M. (1995). Reprises de jeunes Goélands leucophées (*Larus cachinnans*) bagués au Fanel, lac de Neuchâtel. *Nos Oiseaux* **43**: 155-161.
Anzigitova, N.V. & Zubakin, V.A. (1975). [On individual recognition among Arctic Terns (*Sterna paradisaea* Pontopp.) nesting on Great Ainov Island]. Pp. 77-79 in: [*Questions of Zoopsychol., Ethology & Comp. Psychol.*]. Moscow University, Moscow. In Russian.
Appayya, M.K. (1982). Breeding of bustards - an observation in Australia. *J. Bombay Nat. Hist. Soc.* **79**: 195-197.
Appert, O. (1968). Beobachtungen an *Monias benschi* in Südwest-Madagaskar. *J. Orn.* **109(4)**: 402-417.
Appert, O. (1971). Die Limikolen des Mangokygebietes in Südwest-Madagaskar. [The waders of the Mangoky area in Southwest-Madagascar]. *Orn. Beob.* **68(2)**: 53-77.
Appert, O. (1972). Relation entre biotope et endémisme chez les oiseaux de la région du Mongoky, sud-ouest de Madagascar (Communication 27). Pp. 183-189 in: *C.R. Conférence Internationale sur la Conservation de la Nature et de ses Ressources à Madagascar*. IUCN (NS) Doc. Suppl. **36**.
Appert, O. (1985). Zur Biologie der Mesitornithiformes (Nakas oder "Stelzenrallen") Madagaskars und erste fotografische Dokumente von Vertretern der Ordnung. [Notes on the biology of the Mesitornithiformes of Madagascar (Roatelos), with the first photographic documentation of the group]. *Orn. Beob.* **82(1)**: 31-54. In German with French and English summaries.
Appleby, G. (1992). The Double-banded Plover in the Western District, Victoria, 1990-1991. *Stilt* **20**: 26-29.
Appleton, C.C. & Randall, R.M. (1986). Schistosome infection in the Kelp Gull, *Larus dominicanus* from Port Elizabeth, Republic of South Africa. *J. Helminthol.* **60**: 143-146.
Arango, G. (1986). Distribución del género *Gallinago* Brisson 1760 (Aves: Scolopacidae) en los Andes orientales de Colombia. *Caldasia* **15**: 669-706.
Aravena, R.O. (1927). Notas sobre la alimentación de las aves. *Hornero* **4**: 38-49.
Arballo, E. (1990). Nuevos registros para avifauna Uruguaya. *Hornero* **13**: 179-187.
Arcamone, E., Baccetti, N., Mainardi, R. & Spina, F. (1982). Nidificazione della Pernice di Mare *Glareola pratincola* in Toscana. *Riv. ital. Orn.* **52(3-4)**: 187-190.
Archer, G.F. & Godman, E.M. (1937-1961). *The Birds of British Somaliland and the Gulf of Aden*. Vols. 1-2. Gurney & Jackson, London. Vols. 3-4. Oliver & Boyd, Edinburgh & London.
Archibald, G.W. (1974). The Australian Brolga - Crane of the desert. *Brolga Bugle* **1(1)**: 2-3.
Archibald, G.W. (1976). Crane taxonomy as revealed by the unison call. Pp. 225-251 in: Lewis (1976a).
Archibald, G.W. (1981). Cranes wintering in the Republic of Korea. Pp. 66-69 in: Lewis & Masatomi (1981).
Archibald, G.W. (1988). Whooping Crane update. *ICF Bugle* **14(1)**: 4-6.
Archibald, G.W. (1992a). African cranes for the future. Pp. 7-9 in: Porter *et al.* (1992).
Archibald, G.W. (1992b). Meeting develops plans for Siberians. *ICF Bugle* **18(1)**: 4-5.
Archibald, G.W. (1992c). A bird's eye view of Cambodia. *ICF Bugle* **18(2)**: 1-3.
Archibald, G.W. (1992d). Amur River workshop. *ICF Bugle* **18(3)**: 1, 4-5.
Archibald, G.W. (1994). Siberian Cranes. *Natl. Geogr.* **185(5)**: 124-136.
Archibald, G.W. (1995). Meeting coordinates help for Siberian Crane. *ICF Bugle* **21(3)**: 1, 4.
Archibald, G.W. & Landfried, S. (1993). Conservation measures for the Siberian Crane. Pp. 85-87 in: Moser, M. & van Vessem, J. eds. (1993). *Wetland and Waterfowl Conservation in South and West Asia. Proceedings of an International Symposium, Karachi, Pakistan, 14-20 December 1991*. IWRB Special Publication **25**. AWB Publication **85**.
Archibald, G.W. & Mirande, C. (1985). Population status and management efforts for endangered cranes. *Trans. North Amer. Wildl. Nat. Resour. Conf.* **50**: 586-602.
Archibald, G.W. & Oesting, M. (1981). Black-necked Crane: a review. Pp. 190-196 in: Lewis & Masatomi (1981).
Archibald, G.W. & Pasquier, R.F. eds. (1987a). *Proceedings of the 1983 International Crane Conference*. International Crane Foundation, Baraboo, Wisconsin.
Archibald, G.W. & Pasquier, R.F. (1987b). Editor's introduction: African cranes. Page 305 in: Archibald & Pasquier (1987a).
Archibald, G.W. & Swengel, S. (1987). Comparative ecology and behavior of Eastern Sarus Cranes and Brolgas in Australia. Pp. 107-116 in: Lewis (1987).
Archibald, K. (1987). Environmental status on the breeding ground of the Red-crowned Crane (*Grus japonensis*) in Hokkaido, Japan. Pp. 63-86 in: Archibald & Pasquier (1987a).
Ardamatskaya, T.B. (1992). Experience from work on the conservation of the Great Bustard abroad. *Bustard Studies* **5**: 107-121.
Argabrite, W.L. (1988). Another Marbled Godwit in west Virginia. *Redstart* **55(4)**: 105-106.
Argeloo, M. & Stegeman, L. (1988). [Cream-coloured Courser in Noordholland in October 1986]. *Dutch Birding* **10(1)**: 16-19. In Dutch with English summary.
Armbruster, M.J. (1990). *Characterization of Habitat Used by Whooping Cranes During Migration*. Biological Report **90(4)**. US Fish & Wildlife Service, Washington, D.C.
Armistead, H.T. (1978). American Oystercatcher and Herring Gull breed in Dorchester County. *Maryland Birdlife* **33**: 111-112.
Armistead, H.T. (1985). Nesting season: Middle Atlantic Coast Region. *Amer. Birds* **39**: 895-898.
Armistead, H.T. (1989). Nesting season: Middle Atlantic Coast region. *Amer. Birds* **43(5)**: 1299-1303.
Armstrong, A.P. & Nol, E. (1993). Spacing behavior and reproductive ecology of the Semipalmated Plover at Churchill, Manitoba. *Wilson Bull.* **105(3)**: 455-464.
Armstrong, R.H. (1983). *A New, Expanded Guide to the Birds of Alaska*. Alaska Northwest Publishing Company, Anchorage, Alaska.
Arnason, E. (1978). Apostatic selection and kleptoparasitism in the Parasitic Jaeger. *Auk* **95**: 377-381.
Arnason, E. & Grant, P.R. (1978). The significance of kleptoparasitism during the breeding season in a colony of Arctic Skuas *Stercorarius parasiticus* in Iceland. *Ibis* **120**: 38-54.
Arnol, J.D., White, D.M. & Hastings, I. (1984). *Management of the Brolga (*Grus rubicundus*) in Victoria*. Technical Report Series **5**. Victoria Fisheries and Wildlife Service, Department of Conservation, Forests and Lands, Victoria, Australia.
Arnold, K.A. (1978). First United States record of Paint-billed Crake (*Neocrex erythrops*). *Auk* **95**: 745-746.
Arnold, T.W. (1989). Conspecific egg discrimination in American Coots. *Condor* **89**: 675-676.
Arnold, T.W. (1990). *Food Limitation and the Adaptive Significance of Clutch Size in American Coots (*Fulica americana*)*. PhD thesis, University of Western Ontario, London, Canada.
Arnold, T.W. (1992). Continuous laying by American Coots in response to partial clutch removal and total clutch loss. *Auk* **109**: 407-421.
Arnold, T.W. (1993). Factors affecting renesting in American Coots. *Condor* **95**: 273-281.
Arthur, M.J. (1987). First record of the Buff-breasted Sandpiper in South Australia. *S. Austr. Orn.* **30(3)**: 74.
Arthur, S.C. (1921). The feeding habits of the Black Skimmer. *Auk* **38**: 566-574.
Artmann, J.W. & Martin, E.M. (1975). Incidence of ingested shot in Sora Rails. *J. Wildl. Manage.* **39**: 514-519.
Artyukhov, A.I. (1988). [New nesting grounds of Little Curlew]. Pp. 40-41 in: Kondratiev, A.Y. ed. (1988). [*Bulletin of Working Group of Waders*]. Vladivostok. In Russian.
Asbirk, S. (1979). The adaptive significance of the reproductive pattern in the Black Guillemot, *Cepphus grylle*. *Vidensk. Medd. Dan. Naturhist. Foren.* **141**: 29-80.
Asensio, B. (1992). Migración e invernada de la Avefría (*Vanellus vanellus*) en la Península Ibérica. [Migration of Lapwing wintering in the Iberian Peninsula]. *Doñana Acta Vertebrata* **19**: 71-84.
Asensio, B. & Carrascal, L.M. (1987). Migratología de las Agachadizas Comunes (*Gallinago gallinago*, L.) invernantes en la Península Ibérica. [Migration of Common Snipe (*Gallinago gallinago*) wintering in the Iberian Peninsula]. *Ardeola* **34(2)**: 225-242. In Spanish with English summary.
Ash, J.S. (1970). Black Terns feeding round surfacing fish and dolphins. *Seabird Report* **1969**: 40.
Ash, J.S. (1977). Four species of birds new to Ethiopia and other notes. *Bull. Brit. Orn. Club* **97(1)**: 4-9.
Ash, J.S. (1978a). Inland and coastal occurences of Broad-billed Sandpipers *Limicola falcinellus* in Ethiopia and Djibouti. *Bull. Brit. Orn. Club* **98(1)**: 24-26.
Ash, J.S. (1978b). *Sarothrura* crakes in Ethiopia. *Bull. Brit. Orn. Club* **98(1)**: 26-29.
Ash, J.S. (1980a). Common and Lesser Noddy *Anous stolidus* and *A. tenuirostris* in Somalia. *Scopus* **4**: 6-9.
Ash, J.S. (1980b). The Lesser Golden Plover *Pluvialis dominica* in northeast Africa and the southern Red Sea. *Scopus* **4**: 64-66.
Ash, J.S. (1981). Spring migration of Whimbrel *Numenius phaeopus* and other waders off the coast of Somalia. *Scopus* **5**: 71-76.
Ash, J.S. (1989). An atlas of the past and present distribution of bustards in Ethiopia and Somalia. *Bustard Studies* **4**: 1-34.
Ash, J.S. (1990). Additions to the avifauna of Nigeria, with notes on distributional changes and breeding. *Malimbus* **11**: 104-116.
Ash, J.S. & Ashford, O.M. (1977). Great Black-headed Gull *Larus ichthyaetus* and Red-necked Phalaropes *Phalaropus lobatus* inland in Ethiopia. *J. East Afr. Nat. Hist. Soc. & Natl. Mus.* **31**: 1-3.
Ash, J.S. & Gullick, T.M. (1989). The present situation regarding the endemic breeding birds of Ethiopia. *Scopus* **13**: 90-96.
Ash, J.S. & Karani, A.A. (1981). Roseate and Sooty Terns *Sterna dougallii* and *fuscata* breeding on islets in southern Somalia. *Scopus* **5**: 22-27.
Ash, J.S. & Miskell, J.E. (1983). *Birds of Somalia: their Habitat, Status and Distribution*. Scopus Special Supplement **1**. Nairobi. 97 pp.
Ash, J.S. & Miskell, J.E. (1989). Madagascar Pratincoles *Glareola ocularis* and other pratincoles in Somalia. *Scopus* **12(3-4)**: 65-68.
Ashby, R. (1991). Waders of far north-west Tasmania. *Stilt* **19**: 44-49.
Ashcroft, R.E. (1976). *Breeding, Biology and Survival of Puffins*. PhD thesis, University of Oxford, Oxford.
Ashcroft, R.E. (1979). Survival rates and breeding biology of puffins on Skomer Island, Wales. *Ornis Scand.* **10**: 100-110.
Ashkenazie, S. & Safriel, U.N. (1979a). Breeding cycle and behavior of the Semipalmated Sandpiper at Barrow, Alaska. *Auk* **96**: 56-67.
Ashkenazie, S. & Safriel, U.N. (1979b). Time-energy budget of the Semipalmated Sandpiper *Calidris pusilla* at Barrow, Alaska. *Ecology* **60**: 783-799.
Ashmole, M.J. (1970). Feeding of Western and Semipalmated Sandpipers in Peruvian winter quarters. *Auk* **87**: 131-135.
Ashmole, N.P. (1962). The Black Noddy *Anous tenuirostris* on Ascension Island. Part 1. General Biology. *Ibis* **103B(3)**: 235-273.
Ashmole, N.P. (1963a). The biology of the Wideawake or Sooty Tern *Sterna fuscata* on Ascension Island. *Ibis* **103B(4)**: 297-364.
Ashmole, N.P. (1963b). Molt and breeding in populations of the Sooty Tern *Sterna fuscata*. *Yale Peabody Mus. (Postilla)* **76**: 1-18.
Ashmole, N.P. (1965). Adaptive variation in the breeding regime of a tropical sea bird. *Proc. Natl. Acad. Sci. USA* **53**: 311-318.

Ashmole, N.P. (1968a). Breeding and molt in the White Tern (*Gygis alba*) on Christmas Island, Pacific Ocean. *Condor* **70**: 35-55.

Ashmole, N.P. (1968b). Body size, prey size and ecological segregation in five sympatric tropical terns (Aves: Laridae). *Syst. Zool.* **17**: 292-304.

Ashmole, N.P. (1971). Seabird ecology and the marine environment. Pp. 223-286 in: Farner, D.S. & King, J.R. (1971). *Avian Biology*. Vol. 1. Academic Press, London.

Ashmole, N.P. & Ashmole, M.J. (1967). *Comparative Feeding Ecology of Sea Birds of a Tropical Oceanic Island*. Peabody Museum of Natural History Yale University Bulletin **24**. New Haven, Connecticut. 131 pp.

Ashmole, N.P. & Tovar, F.H. (1968). Prolonged parental care in Royal Terns and other birds. *Auk* **85**: 90-100.

Ashmole, N.P., Ashmole, M.J. & Simmons, K.E.L. (1994). Seabird conservation and feral cats on Ascension Island, South Atlantic. Pp. 94-121 in: Nettleship *et al.* (1994).

Ashtiani, M.A. (1987). Siberian Crane as a wintering bird in Iran. Pp. 135-137 in: Archibald & Pasquier (1987a).

Askaner, T. (1959). Några iakttagelser över häckningsbeteende och häckningsresultat hos sothönan (*Fulica atra*). *Vår Fågelvärld* **18**: 285-310.

Aspinall, S. (1993). A wintering or passage population of Great Knot *Calidris tenuirostris* in the Arabian Gulf? *Wader Study Group Bull.* **72**: 43-47.

Aspinall, S., Samour, J. & Howlett, J. (1994). First confirmed breeding of Cream-coloured Courser in the United Arab Emirates. *Emirates Bird Rep.* **18**: 105-106.

Aspinwall, D.R. (1973). Sight record of Great Sandplover *Charadrius leschenaultii*: a species new to Zambia. *Bull. Zambia Orn. Soc.* **5(1)**: 29.

Aspinwall, D.R. (1975). Great Sandplover (*Charadrius leschenaultii*) and Eastern Golden Plovers (*Pluvialis dominica*) at Lusaka. *Bull. Zambia Orn. Soc.* **7(2)**: 101-102.

Aspinwall, D.R. (1977). Black-winged Pratincoles (*Glareola nordmanni*) at Mwinilunga and Liuwa Plain. *Bull. Zambian Orn. Soc.* **9(2)**: 58-59.

Aspinwall, D.R., Moulton, J.P. & Stjernstedt, B.R. (1995). Record of Solitary Sandpiper in Zambia. *Bull. African Bird Club* **2(2)**: 106-107.

Astheimer, L. (1986). Egg formation in Cassin's Auklet *Ptychoramphus aleuticus*. *Auk* **103**: 682-693.

Astheimer, L. (1991). Embryo metabolism and egg neglect in Cassin's Auklets. *Condor* **93**: 486-495.

Astley-Maberly, C.T. (1935a). Notes on *Sarothrura elegans*. *Ostrich* **6**: 39-42.

Astley-Maberly, C.T. (1935b). Further notes upon *Sarothrura elegans*. *Ostrich* **6**: 101-104.

Astley-Maberly, C.T. (1967). An unusual display of the Red-crested Korhaan. *Bokmakierie* **19**: 41.

Aston, P. (1993). Birds new to Hong Kong - Grey Phalarope: the first records for Hong Kong. *Hong Kong Bird Rep. 1993*: 117-120.

Atkins, J.D. & Johnston-Stewart, N. (1989). White-fronted Sandplover near Chikwawa. *Nyala* **13(1/2)**: 77-78.

Atkins, J.D., Johnston-Stewart, N., Atkins, M. & Killick, J.W. (1989). Second record of the White-crowned Plover in Malawi. *Nyala* **13(1/2)**: 76.

Atkins, J.D., Johnston-Stewart, N. & Killick, J.W. (1989). Another African Skimmer breeding record. *Nyala* **13(1/2)**: 79-80.

Atkinson, J.M.S. (1976). Inland wintering and urban roosting by Redshanks. *Bird Study* **23**: 51-55.

Atkinson, N.K., Davies, M. & Prater, A.J. (1978). The winter distribution of Purple Sandpipers in Britain. *Bird Study* **25**: 223-228.

Atkinson, N.K., Summers, R.W., Nicoll, M. & Greenwood, J.J.D. (1981a). Population, movements and biometrics of the Purple Sandpiper *Calidris maritima* is eastern Scotland. *Ornis Scand.* **12(1)**: 18-27.

Atkinson, N.K., Summers, R.W., Nicoll, M. & Greenwood, J.J.D. (1981b). Population, movement and biometrics of the Curlew Sandpiper *Calidris ferruginea* in eastern Scotland. *Ornis Scand.* **12**.

Atkinson, P., Robertson, P., Dellelegn, Y., Wondafrash, M. & Atkins, J. (1996). The recent rediscovery of White-winged Flufftails in Ethiopia. *Bull. African Bird Club* **3(1)**: 34-36.

Atta, G.A.M. (1992). First record of Great Bustard *Otis tarda* in Egypt. *Sandgrouse* **14(2)**: 111-112.

Attwell, R.I.G. (1959). The African Skimmer, *Rynchops flavirostris*: population counts and breeding in the Nsefu Game Reserve. *Ostrich* **30**: 69-72.

Atwood, J.L. (1986). Delayed nocturnal occupation of breeding colonies by Least Terns (*Sterna antillarum*). *Auk* **103**: 242-244.

Atwood, J.L. & Kelly, P.R. (1984). Fish dropped on breeding colonies as indicators of Least Tern food habits. *Wilson Bull.* **96**: 34-37.

Atwood, J.L. & Massey, B.W. (1982). The pikei plumage of the Least Tern. *J. Field Orn.* **53**: 47.

Atwood, J.L. & Massey, B.W. (1988). Site fidelity of Least Terns in California. *Condor* **90**: 389-394.

Atwood, J.L. & Minsky, D. (1983). Least Tern foraging ecology at three major California breeding colonies. *Western Birds* **14**: 57-72.

Au, D.W. & Pitman, R.L. (1988). Seabird relationships with tropical Tunas and Dolphina. Pp. 166-204 in: Burger (1988c).

Aubrey, Y. (1984). First nests of the Common Black-headed Gull in North America. *Amer. Birds* **38**: 366-367.

Aucamp, E. (1994). Blue Crane update. *Vision (Endangered Wildl. Trust Ann.)* **1994**: 58-62.

Aucamp, E. (1996). The breeding biology of the Blue Crane, *Anthropoides paradiseus*, in the Southern Cape, South Africa. In: Beilfuss *et al.* (1996).

Aumann, T. (1991). Notes on the birds of the upper and middle reaches of Kimberley rivers during the dry season 1989. *Austr. Bird Watcher* **14**: 51-67.

Aurioles, D. & Llinas, J. (1987). Western Gulls as a possible predator of California sea lion pups. *Condor* **89**: 923-924.

Austin, O.L. (1940). Some aspects of individual distribution in the Cape Cod tern colonies. *Bird-Banding* **11**: 155-169.

Austin, O.L. (1942). The life span of the Common Tern (*Sterna hirundo*). *Bird-Banding* **13**: 159-176.

Austin, O.L. (1944). The status of Tern Island and the Cape Cod terns in 1943. *Bird-Banding* **15**: 133-139.

Austin, O.L. (1945). The role of longevity in successful breeding by the Common Tern (*Sterna hirundo*). *Bird-Banding* **16**: 21-28.

Austin, O.L. (1947). A study of the mating of the Common Tern. *Bird-Banding* **18**: 1-16.

Austin, O.L. (1948). *The Birds of Korea*. Bulletin of the Museum of Comparative Zoology **101**. Cambridge, Massachusetts. 301 pp.

Austin, O.L. (1949). Site tenacity, a behaviour trait of the Common Tern (*Sterna hirundo* Linn.). *Bird-Banding* **20**: 1-39.

Austin, O.L. (1951). Group adherence in the Common Tern. *Bird-Banding* **22**: 1-60.

Austin, O.L. (1953). The migration of the Common Tern (*Sterna hirundo*) in the western hemisphere. *Bird-Banding* **24**: 39-55.

Austin, O.L. & Kuroda, N. (1953). *Birds of Japan. Their Status and Distribution*. Bulletin of the Museum of Comparative Zoology **109**. Cambridge, Massachusetts.

Autorowe, A. (1992). The occurence of the Marsh Sandpiper (*Tringa stagnatilis*) in Poland. *Notatki Orn.* **33**: 240.

Auzzov, E.M. (1970). [On the discovery of a colony of Relict Gulls *Larus relictus* Lönnberg]. *Bull. Acad. Sciences Kazakhstan SSR* **1**: 59-60. In Russian.

Auzzov, E.M. (1971). [Taxonomic evaluation and systematics of the status of the Relict Gull *Larus relictus* Lönnberg]. *Zoologischeskii Zhurnal* **50**: 235-242. In Russian.

Auzzov, E.M. (1974). [North Vietnam - a new place for finding *L. relictus*]. *Zoologischeskii Zhurnal* **53**: 139. In Russian.

Auzzov, E.M. (1975). [*Larus relictus* at lake Alakol]. Pp. 58-59 in: [*Colonies of Water Birds and their Protection*]. Moscow. In Russian.

Auzzov, E.M. (1977). [On the biology of the Relict Gull]. Pp. 119-130 in: [*Rare and Disappearing Birds and Animals of Kazakhstan*]. Nauka, Alma Ata. In Russian.

Auzzov, E.M., Gabrielov, E.E. & Sima, A.M. (1981). [Dynamics of the population of Relict Gulls on Lake Alakol]. Pp. 23-25 in: Flint (1981). In Russian.

Avery, G. (1977). Report on the marine bird remains from the Paternoster midden. *S. Afr. Archaeol. Bull.* **32**: 74-76.

Avery, G., Brooke, R.K. & Komen, J. (1988). Records of the African Crake *Crex egregia* in western southern Africa. *Ostrich* **59**: 25-29.

Avery, M. & Sherwood, G. (1982). The lekking behaviour of Great Snipe. *Ornis Scand.* **13(1)**: 72-78.

Avery, M.I., Coulthard, N.D., del Nevo, A.J., Leroux, A., Medeiros, F., Merne, O., Monteiro, L., Moralee, A., Ntiamoa-Baidu, Y., O'Briain, M. & Wallace, E. (1995). A recovery plan for Roseate Terns in the east Atlantic: an international programme. *Bird Conserv. Int.* **5(4)**: 441-453.

Avery, M.I., Suddaby, D., Ellis, P.M. & Sim, I.M.W. (1992). Exceptionally low body weights of Arctic Terns *Sterna paradisaea* on Shetland. *Ibis* **134**: 87-88.

Avery, M.L., Pavelka, M.A., Bergman, D.L., Decker, D.G., Knittle, C.E. & Linz, G.M. (1995). Aversive conditioning to reduce raven predation on California Least Tern eggs. *Colonial Waterbirds* **18(2)**: 131-138.

Avise, J.C. & Zink, R.M. (1988). Molecular genetic divergence between avian sibling species; King and Clapper Rails, Long-billed and Short-billed Dowitchers, Boat-tailed and Great-tailed Grackles and Tufted and Black-crested Titmice. *Auk* **105**: 516-528.

Ayers, C. (1982). *Gulls: an Ecological History*. Van Nostrand, New York.

Ayres, J.M., Lima, D.M., Martins, E.S. & Barreiros, J.L.K. (1991). On the track of the road: changes in subsistence hunting in a Brazilian Amazonian village. Pp. 82-92 in: Robinson, J.G. & Redford, K.H. eds. (1991). *Neotropical Wildlife Use and Conservation*. University of Chicago Press, Chicago.

Azarov, V.I. (1977). Siberian Cranes in northern Kazakhstan and Tiumen Province. Pp. 188-189 in: *Abstr. VII USSR Nat. Orn. Congr.* Naukova Dumka, Kiev.

Azevedo-Junior, S.M. (1988). [Ringing summary and plumage analyses for *Calidris pusilla*, *C. alba*, *Charadrius semipalmatus* and *Arenaria interpres* trapped 17 Januari 1987 at Coroa do Aviao, Pernambuco]. *Anais ENAV, Univ. Vale do Rio dos Sinos* **3**: 109. In Portuguese.

Baccetti, N. (1987). Pintail Snipe, *Gallinago stenura*, ringed in central Somalia. *Riv. ital. Orn.* **57(3-4)**: 249-251. In English with Italian summary.

Baccetti, N. (1991). [Occurrence and conservation of the Slender-billed Curlew in Italy]. *Ricerche Biol. Selvaggina* **17(1)**(Suppl.): 497-500. In Italian with English summary.

Baccetti, N. (1995). Revisione delle catture italiane di una specie giunta all'orlo dell'estinzione: *Numenius tenuirostris* (Aves, Scolopacidae). *Ricerche Biol. Selvaggina* **94**: 1-18.

Baccetti, N., Cherubini, G., Magnani, A. & Serra, L. (1995). Homing performances of adult and immature Dunlins *Calidris alpina* (Aves Scolopacidae) displaced from their wintering area. *Ethology, Ecology & Evolution* **7**: 257-264.

Baccetti, N., De Faveri, A. & Serra, L. (1992). Spring migration and body condition of Common Sandpipers *Actitis hypoleucos* on a small Mediterranean island. *Ringing & Migration* **13(2)**: 90-94.

Backhurst, G.C. (1969). A record of *Gallinago stenura* from Kenya. *Bull. Brit. Orn. Club* **89**: 95-96.

Badman, F.J. (1979). Birds of southern and western Lake Eyre drainage. *S. Austr. Orn.* **28**: 29-54.

Baerends, G.P. & Drent, R.H. eds. (1970). *The Herring Gull and its Egg*. Behaviour **17**(Supplement).

Baerends, G.P. & van Rhijn, J.G. (1975). The effect of colour in egg recognition by the Black-headed Gull, *Larus r. ridibundus*. L. II. *Proc. Nederland. Akad. Wetensch.* **78**: 13-20.

Baggerman, B., Baerends, G.P., Heikens, H.S. & Mook, J.H. (1956). Observations on the behaviour of the Black Tern, *Chlidonias n. niger* (L.), in the breeding area. *Ardea* **44**: 1-71.

Baha el Din, S. (1993). *The Catching of Corncrakes Crex crex and Other Birds in Northern Egypt*. BirdLife Study Report **55**. BirdLife International, Cambridge.

Baha el Din, S. & Saleh, M.A. (1983). *Report on the Ornithological Results of the Egyptian Red Sea Pollution Expedition October-December 1982*. Ornithological Society of Egypt, Cairo.

Bailey, A.M. (1934). The haunts of the wailing bird. *Nat. Hist.* **34**: 702-710.

Bailey, A.M. (1948). *Birds of Arctic Alaska*. Colorado Museum of Natural History Popular Series **8**. 317 pp.

Bailey, A.M. (1961). Dusky and Swallow-tailed Gulls of the Galapagos Islands. *Denver Mus. Nat. Hist. Museum Pictorial* **15**.

Bailey, A.M. (1962). Nesting of the Galapagos Penguin and the Galapagos Sooty Gull. *Condor* **64**: 159-161.

Bailey, A.M. & Sorensen, J.H. (1962). *Subantarctic Campbell Island*. Denver Museum of Natural History Proceedings **10**. 305 pp.

Bailey, E.E., Woolfenden, G.E. & Robertson, W.B. (1987). Abrasion and loss of bands from Dry Tortugas Sooty Terns. *J. Field Orn.* **58**: 413-424.

Bailey, E.P. (1973). Discovery of a Kittlitz's Murrelet nest. *Condor* **75**: 457.

Bailey, E.P. (1990). Fox introductions on Aleutian Islands: history, impacts on avifauna and eradication. Unpublished report to US Fish & Wildlife Service, Homer, Alaska.

Bailey, E.P. (1993a). Introduction of foxes to Alaskan Islands-history, effects on avifauna and eradication. *US Fish Wildl. Serv. Resour. Publ.* **191**: 1-53.

Bailey, E.P. (1993b). Alaska's alien animals. *Pacific Seabird Group Bull.* **20**: 5-8.

Bailey, E.P. & Kaiser, G.W. (1993). Impacts of introduced predators on nesting seabirds in the northeast Pacific. Pp. 218-226 in: Vermeer, Briggs *et al.* (1993).

Bailey, R.F. (1935). Field notes on the Australian Pratincole. *Emu* **35**: 1-10.

Bailey, R.S. (1966). The sea-birds of the southeast coast of Arabia. *Ibis* **108**: 224-264.

Baillie, S.R., Clark, N.A. & Ogilvie, M.A. (1986). *Cold Weather Movements of Waterfowl and Waders: an Analysis of Ringing Recoveries*. CSD Report **650**. Nature Conservancy Council, Peterborough.

Baillon, F. (1989). [New wintering record of Audouin's Gull *Larus audouinii* Payr. in Senogambia]. *Oiseau et RFO* **59**: 296-304. In French.

Bainbridge, I.P. & Minton, C.D.T. (1978). The migration and mortality of the Curlew in Britain and Ireland. *Bird Study* **25**: 39-50.

Bainbridge, W.R. (1965). Nesting behaviour of the White-headed Wattled Plover. *Puku* **3**: 171-173.

Baines, D. (1988). The effect of improvement of upland marginal grasslands on the distribution and density of breeding wading birds (Charadriiformes) in northern England. *Biol. Conserv.* **45**: 221-236.

Baines, D. (1989). The effects of improvements of upland, marginal grasslands on the breeding success of Lapwings *Vanellus vanellus* and other waders. *Ibis* **131(4)**: 497-506.

Baines, D. (1990). The roles of predation, food and agricultural practice in determining the breeding success of the Lapwing (*Vanellus vanellus*) on upland grasslands. *J. Anim. Ecol.* **59(3)**: 915-929.

Baird, D.A. (1979). Twenty-eight additions to Archer & Godman's *Birds of British Somaliland and the Gulf of Aden*. *Bull. Brit. Orn. Club* **99**: 6-9.

Baird, K.E. (1974). *A Field Study of the King, Sora and Virginia Rails at Cheyenne Bottoms in West-central Kansas*. MSc thesis, Kansas State College, Fort Hayes, Kansas.

Baird, P.A. & Moe, R.A. (1978a). The breeding biology and feeding ecology of marine birds in the Sitkalidak Strait area, Kodiak Island, 1977. Pp. 30-37 in: *Environmental Assessment of the Alaskan Continental Shelf*. Vol. 3. Receptor - Birds. US Department of Commerce, Washington, D.C.

Baird, P.A. & Moe, R.A. (1978b). The breeding biology and feeding ecology of marine birds in the Sitkalidak Strait area, Kodiak Island, 1978. Pp. 313-524 in: *Environmental Assessment of the Alaskan Continental Shelf*. Vol. 3. Receptor - Birds. US Department of Commerce, Washington, D.C.

Baird, P.H. (1990). Influence of abiotic factors and prey distribution on diet and reproductive success of three seabird species in Alaska. *Ornis Scand.* **21**: 224-235.

Baird, P.H. (1994). Black-legged Kittiwake (*Rissa tridactyla*). No. **92** in: Poole & Gill (1994).

Baird, R.F. (1984). The Pleistocene distribution of the Tasmanian Native Hen *Gallinula mortierii mortierii*. *Emu* **84**: 119-123.

Baird, R.F. (1986). Tasmanian Native-hen *Gallinula mortierii*: the first late Pleistocene record from Queensland. *Emu* **86**: 121-122.

Baird, R.F. (1991). The dingo as a possible factor in the disappearance of *Gallinula mortierii* from the Australian mainland. *Emu* **91**: 121-122.

Bak, B. & Ettrup, H. (1982). Studies on the migration and mortality of the Lapwing (*Vanellus vanellus*) in Denmark. *Dan. Rev. Game Biol.* **12**: 1-20.

Bakaev, S. (1979). [The nesting records of the White-tailed Plover (*Chettusia leucura*) at the lower reaches of the Zeravshan River]. *Ornitologiya* **14**: 185-186. In Russian.

Baker, A.J. (1972). *Systematics and Affinities of New Zealand Oystercatchers*. PhD thesis, University of Canterbury, Christchurch.

Baker, A.J. (1973a). Distribution and numbers of New Zealand oystercatchers. *Notornis* **20**: 128-144.

Baker, A.J. (1973b). Genetics of plumage variability in the Variable Oystercatcher (*Haematopus unicolor*). *Notornis* **20(4)**: 330-345.

Baker, A.J. (1974a). Ecological and behavioural evidence for the systematic status of New Zealand oystercatchers (Charadriiformes: Haematopodidae). *Life Sci. Contr. Royal Ontario Museum* **96**: 1-34.

Baker, A.J. (1974b). Criteria for ageing and sexing New Zealand oystercatchers. *New Zealand J. Mar. Freshwater Res.* **8**: 11-21.

Baker, A.J. (1974c). Melanin pigmentation in the dorsal plumage of New Zealand oystercatchers. *New Zealand J. Zool.* **1(2)**: 159-164.

Baker, A.J. (1974d). Prey specific feeding methods of New Zealand oystercatchers. *Notornis* **21(3)**: 219-233.

Baker, A.J. (1975a). Systematics and evolution of Australasian oystercatchers. *Emu* **74**: 277.

Baker, A.J. (1975b). Lipid levels in the South Island Pied Oystercatcher (*Haematopus ostralegus finschi*). *New Zealand J. Zool.* **2**: 425-434.

Baker, A.J. (1975c). Age structure and sex ratio of live trapped samples of South Island Pied Oystercatchers (*Haematopus ostralegus finschi*). *Notornis* **22**: 189-194.

Baker, A.J. (1975d). Morphological variation, hybridization and systematics of New Zealand oystercatchers (Charadriiformes: Haematopodidae). *J. Zool., London* **175**: 357-390.
Baker, A.J. (1977). Multivariate assessment of the phenetic affinities of Australasian oystercatchers (Aves: Charadriiformes). *Bijdragen tot de Dierkunde* **47**: 156-164.
Baker, A.J. (1991). A review of New Zealand ornithology. *Curr. Orn.* **8**: 1-67.
Baker, A.J. & Cadman, M. (1980). Breeding schedule, clutch size and egg size of American Oystercatchers (*Haematopus palliatus*) in Virginia. *Wader Study Group Bull.* **30**: 32-33.
Baker, A.J. & Hockey, P.A.R. (1984). Behavioural and vocal affinities of the African Black Oystercatcher (*Haematopus moquini*). *Wilson Bull.* **96(4)**: 656-671.
Baker, A.J. & Miller, E.H. (1978). Research on Patagonian oystercatchers. *Wader Study Group Bull.* **23**: 46 47.
Baker, A.J. & Strauch, J.G. (1988). Genetic variation and differentiation in shorebirds. Pp. 1639-1645 in: *Proc. XIX Int. Orn. Congr.* Ottawa, 1986.
Baker, A.J., Parslow, M. & Chambers, D. (1981). Karyological studies of a female Variable Oystercatcher (*Haematopus unicolor*). *Can. J. Gen. Cytol.* **23**: 611 619.
Baker, A.J., Piersma, T. & Rosenmeier, L. (1994). Unraveling the intraspecific phylogeography of Knots *Calidris canutus*: a progress report on the search for genetic markers. *J. Orn.* **135(4)**: 599-608. In English with German summary.
Baker, D.G., Child, R.J. & Taylor, M.J. (1986). A Japanese Snipe at Mangere. *Notornis* **33(3)**: 149-150.
Baker, E.C.S. (1911). The Game Birds of India, Burma and Ceylon. *J. Bombay Nat. Hist. Soc.* **20**: 1-32.
Baker, E.C.S. (1921). *The Game Birds of India, Burma and Ceylon*. Vol. 2. British Museum of Natural History, London.
Baker, E.C.S. (1928a). Note on the races of *Sterna albifrons*. *Bull. Brit. Orn. Club* **49**: 37-39.
Baker, E.C.S. (1928b). *The Fauna of British India, Including Ceylon and Burma*. Vol. 5. Birds. Taylor & Francis, London.
Baker, E.C.S. (1929). *The Fauna of British India, Including Ceylon and Burma*. Vol. 6. Birds. Taylor & Francis, London.
Baker, E.C.S. (1930). *Indian Game Birds, Pheasants, Bustard, Quail*. Vol. 3. Bombay Natural History Society, London.
Baker, E.C.S. (1935). *The Nidification of Birds of the Indian Empire*. Vol. 4. Taylor & Francis, London.
Baker, M.C. (1974). Foraging behavior of Black-bellied Plovers (*Pluvialis squatarola*). *Ecology* **55**: 162-167.
Baker, M.C. (1977). Shorebird food habits in the eastern Canadian arctic. *Condor* **79**: 56-62.
Baker, M.C. (1979). Morphological correlates of habitat selection in a community of shorebirds (Charadriiformes). *Oikos* **33**: 121-126.
Baker, M.C. (1982). Individuality of vocalizations in Dunlin: a possible acoustic basis for recognition of parent by offspring. *Auk* **99**: 771-774.
Baker, M.C. & Baker, A.E.M. (1973). Niche relationships among six species of shorebirds on their wintering and breeding ranges. *Ecol. Monogr.* **43**: 193-212.
Baker, N.E. (1989). The distribution and legal status of bustards in Tanzania. *Bustard Studies* **4**: 35-40.
Baker, N.E. & Boswell, E.M. (1989). Black-naped Tern *Sterna sumatrana*: first record for east Africa. *Scopus* **13**: 123-124.
Baker, N.E., Beakbane, A.J. & Boswell, E.M. (1984). Streaky-breasted Pygmy Crake *Sarothrura boehmi*: first documented records for Tanzania. *Scopus* **8**: 64-66.
Baker, R.H. (1951). *The Avifauna of Micronesia, its Origin, Evolution and Distribution*. University of Kansas Publications of the Museum of Natural History **3**. 359 pp.
Baker-Gabb, D.J. (1987). The conservation and management of the Plains-wanderer *Pedionomus torquatus*. *World Wildl. Fund. Rep.* **49**.
Baker-Gabb, D.J. (1988). The diet and foraging behaviour of the Plains-wanderer *Pedionomus torquatus*. *Emu* **88(2)**: 115-118.
Baker-Gabb, D.J. (1989). *The Conservation and Management of the Plains-wanderer in New South Wales*. RAOU, Melbourne.
Baker-Gabb, D.J. (1990a). The biology and management of the Plains-wanderer (*Pedionomus torquatus*) in NSW. *New South Wales Natl. Parks Wildl. Serv. Species Manage. Rep.* **3**.
Baker-Gabb, D.J. (1990b). Draft management plan for the Plains-wanderer (*Pedionomus torquatus*) in NSW. *New South Wales Natl. Parks Wildl. Serv. Species Draft Manage. Plan* **3**.
Baker-Gabb, D.J. (1993). Managing native grasslands to maintain biodiversity and conserve the Plains-wanderer. *RAOU Conservation Statement* **8**.
Baker-Gabb, D.J., Benshemesh, J. & Maher, P.N. (1990). A revision of the distribution, status and management of the Plains-wanderer *Pedionomus torquatus*. *Emu* **90**: 161-168.
Bakewell, D.N., Carey, G.J., Duff, D.G., Palfery, J., Parker, A. & Williams, M.D. (1989). Observations of Relict Gulls *Larus relictus* on passage at Beidaihe, People's Republic of China. *Forktail* **4**: 77-87.
Bakker, B.J. & Fordham, R.A. (1993). Diving behaviour of the Australian Coot in a New Zealand lake. *Notornis* **40**: 131-136.
Balachandran, S. & Natarajan, V. (1992). Possible occurrence of four subspecies of Lesser Sand Plover *Charadrius mongolus* at Pt. Calimere Wildlife Sanctuary, Tamil Nadu. *J. Bombay Nat. Hist. Soc.* **89(1)**: 118-119.
Balch, L.G. (1980). Some notes on Red-legged Kittiwake identification. *Birding* **12**: 78-82.
Baldassarre, G.A. & Fischer, D.H. (1984). Food habits of fall migrant shorebirds on the Texas high plains. *J. Field Orn.* **55**: 220-229.
Baldwin, J.H. (1977). *A Comparative Study of Sandhill Crane Subspecies*. PhD dissertation, University of Wisconsin-Madison, Wisconsin.
Baldwin, W.P. (1950). Clam catches oystercatcher. *Auk* **63**: 589.
van Balen, J.H. (1959). Over de voortplanting van de Grutto. *Ardea* **47**: 76-86.
van Balen, S. (1991). Jaegers in Indonesian waters. *Kukila* **5(2)**: 117-124.
Bales, B.R. (1919). Twenty-four hours in a Black Skimmer colony. *Wilson Bull.* **31**: 83-87.
Ballmann, P. (1979). Fossile Glareolidae aus dem Miozän des Nördlinger Ries (Aves: Charadriiformes). *Bonn. zool. Beitr.* **30**: 52-101.
Ballot, J.N., Clerc, P. & Yésou, P. (1981). Un Pluvier asiatique *Charadrius asiaticus* en Bretagne: première donnée française. *Oiseau et RFO* **51(3)**: 239-243.
Balmford, R. (1990). Beach Thick-knee in north-west Queensland. *Austr. Bird Watcher* **13(6)**: 203-204.
Balogh, E. (1989). Hand raising of Banded Stilts. Unpublished report to SANPWS.
Balouet, J.C. & Olson, S.L. (1989). *Fossil Birds from Late Quaternary Deposits in New Caledonia*. Smithsonian Contributions to Zoology **469**.
Baltz, D.M., Morejohn, G.V. & Antrim, B.S. (1979). Size selective predation and food habits of two California Terns. *Western Birds* **10**: 17-24.
Baltzer, M.C. (1990). A report on the wetland avifauna of South Sulawesi. *Kukila* **5(1)**: 27-55.
Bamford, M. (1992). The impact of predation by humans upon waders in the Asian/Australian flyway: evidence from the recovery of bands. *Stilt* **20**: 38-40.
Bamford, M.J. (1989). The Little Curlew *Numenius minutus* in Australia: what happens in the wet season? *Stilt* **14**: 66.
Bamford, M.J. (1990). *RAOU Survey of Migratory Waders in Kakadu National Park: Phase III*. RAOU Report **70**. Royal Austalasian Ornithologists' Union, Melbourne.
Bancroft, G. (1927). Breeding birds of Scammons Lagoon, Lower California. *Condor* **29**: 29 57.
Bancroft, G. (1930). Eggs of Xantus' and Craveri's Murrelets. *Condor* **32**: 247-254.
Banda, H. (1996). Status of the Nyika Wattled Crane and management recommendations. In: Beilfuss *et al*. (1996).
Banerjee, V. & Banerjee, M. (1977). Variations of erythrocyte number and haemoglobin content of a migratory bird: *Philomachus pugnax* (Linnaeus). *Zool. Anz.* **199**: 261-264.
Banfield, G.E.A. (1987). Common or Red-winged Pratincole at Aisleby. *Honeyguide* **33(1)**: 15.
Bang, B.G. (1968). Olfaction in Rallidae (Gruiformes), a morphological study of thirteen species. *J. Zool., London* **156**: 97-107.
Bangs, O. (1918). Vertebrata from Madagascar. Aves. *Bull. Mus. Comp. Zool.* **61**: 489-511.
Bankovics, A. (1987a). Some data on the distribution and habitat of the Demoiselle Crane in Mongolia. Pp. 33-34 in: Archibald & Pasquier (1987a).
Bankovics, A. ed. (1987b). *Proceedings of the International Crane Foundation Working Group on European Cranes, 1st Meeting. 21-26 October 1985. Orosháza-Kardoskút, Hungary*. Aquila **93-94**. Budapest. 326 pp.
Banks, R.C. (1977). The decline and fall of the Eskimo Curlew, or why did the curlew go extaille? *Amer. Birds* **31**: 127-134.
Banks, R.C. (1984). Bird specimens from American Samoa. *Pacif. Sci.* **38**: 150-169.
Banks, R.C. & Tomlinson, R.E. (1974). Taxonomic studies of certain Clapper Rails of southwestern United States and northwestern Mexico. *Wilson Bull.* **86**: 325-335.
Bannerman, D.A. (1911). Three new birds from south-western Abyssinia. *Bull. Brit. Orn. Club* **29**: 37-39.
Bannerman, D.A. (1914). An ornithological expedition to the eastern Canary Islands. *Ibis* **Ser. 10, no. 2**: 38-90, 228-293.
Bannerman, D.A. (1919-1920). List of the birds of the Canary Islands, with detailed reference to the migratory species and the accidental visitors. *Ibis* **Ser. 11, no. 1**: 84-131, 291-321, 457-495, 708-764; **Ser. 11, no. 2**: 97-132, 323-360, 519-569.
Bannerman, D.A. (1922). *The Canary Islands, their History, Natural History and Scenery*. Gurney & Jackson, London.
Bannerman, D.A. (1931). *The Birds of Tropical West Africa*. Vol. 2. Crown Agents for the Colonies, London.
Bannerman, D.A. (1951). *The Birds of Tropical West Africa*. Vol. 8. Crown Agents for the Colonies, London.
Bannerman, D.A. (1953). *The Birds of West and Equatorial Africa*. Vols. 1-2. Oliver & Boyd, Edinburgh.
Bannerman, D.A. (1963). *The Birds of the Atlantic Islands. A History of the Birds of the Canary Islands and of the Salvages*. Vol. 1. Oliver & Boyd, Edinburgh & London.
Bannerman, D.A. (1969). A probable sight record of a Canarian Black Oystercatcher. *Ibis* **111**: 257.
Bannerman, D.A. & Bannerman, W.M. (1965). *The Birds of the Atlantic Islands*. Vol. 2. Oliver & Boyd, Edinburgh.
Bannikov, A.G. ed. (1978). [*Red Data Book of USSR: Rare and Endangered Species of Animals and Plants*]. Lesnaya Promyshlennost, Moscow. In Russian.
Bannon, P. (1983). First nesting of the Little Gull (*Larus minutus*) in Quebec. *Amer. Birds* **37**: 838-839.
Barash, D.P., Donovan, P. & Myrick, R. (1975). Clam dropping behavior of the Glaucous-winged Gull (*Larus glaucescens*). *Wilson Bull.* **87**: 60-64.
Barber, R.D. (1986). Little Stints at Brigantine National Wildlife Refuge, New Jersey. *Cassinia* **61**: 77-78.
Barbera, G.G., Calvo, J.F., Estere, M.A., Hernández, V. & Robledano, F. (1990). Importance of small man-made wetlands for breeding waders in south-east Spain. *Wader Study Group Bull.* **60**: 24-26.
Barbosa, A. (1993). Morphometric variation of the hindlimb of waders and its evolutionary implications. *Ardeola* **40(1)**: 65-75.
Barbour, B. (1978). Species of special concern, Royal Tern, *Sterna maxima*. Pp. 91-92 in: Kale (1978).
Barbour, T. (1923). *The Birds of Cuba*. Memoirs of the Nuttall Ornithological Club **6**. Cambridge, Massachusetts. 141 pp.
Barbour, T. (1943). *Cuban Ornithology*. Publications of the Nuttall Ornithological Club **9**. Cambridge, Massachusetts. 144 pp.
Barbour, T. & Peters, J.L. (1927). Two more remarkable new birds from Cuba. *Proc. New England Zool. Club* **9**: 95-97.
Bárcena, F., Teixeira, A.M. & Bermejo, A. (1984). Breeding seabirds populations in the Atlantic sector of the Iberian Peninsula. Pp. 335-345 in: Croxall, Evans & Schreiber (1984).
Bardon, K. (1991). Western Sandpiper documentation. *Loon* **63(3)**: 196-197.
Barker, R.D. & Vestjens, W.J.M. (1989). *The Food of Australian Birds*. Vol. 1. Non-passerines. CSIRO, Melbourne.
Barlow, J.C. (1967). Autumnal breeding of the Paraguay Snipe in Uruguay. *Auk* **84**: 421-422.
Barlow, J.C. & Cuello, J. (1964). New records of Uruguayan birds. *Condor* **66**: 516-517.
Barlow, M. & Sutton, R.R. (1975). Nest of a Marsh Crake. *Notornis* **22**: 178-180.
Barlow, M.L. (1972). The establishment, dispersal and distribution of the Spur-winged Plover in New Zealand. *Notornis* **19(3)**: 201-211.
Barlow, M.L. (1978). Spur-winged Plover longevity record. *Notornis* **25(2)**: 160.
Barlow, M.L. (1988a). Brooding of a Banded Dotterel fledgling. *Notornis* **35(2)**: 158-159.
Barlow, M.L. (1988b). Spur-winged Plover longevity record. *Notornis* **35(3)**: 195-196.
Barlow, M.L. (1989). Establishment of the Black-fronted Dotterel in Southland. *Notornis* **36(1)**: 76-78.
Barlow, M.L. (1993). New Zealand Dotterel: South Island historical notes and recent Southland records. *Notornis* **40(1)**: 15-25.
Barlow, M.L., Mutter, P.M. & Sutton, R.R. (1972). Breeding data on the Spur-winged Plover in New Zealand. *Notornis* **19(3)**: 212-249.
Barnard, C.J. & Stephens, H. (1981). Prey size selection by Lapwings in Lapwing/gull associations. *Behaviour* **77(1-2)**: 1-22.
Barnard, C.J. & Thompson, D.B.A. (1985). *Gulls and Plovers. The Ecology and Behaviour of Mixed-species Feeding Groups*. Croom Helm, London.
Barnard, H.G. (1911). Field notes from Cape York. *Emu* **11**: 17-32.
Barnard, H.G. (1914). Northern Territory birds. *Emu* **14**: 39-57.
Barnes, A. & Hill, G.J.E. (1989). Census and distribution of Black Noddy *Anous minutus* nests on Heron Island, November 1985. *Emu* **89**: 129-134.
Barnes, J.A.G. (1952). The status of the Lesser Black-backed Gull. *British Birds* **45**: 3-17.
Barrantes, G. & Pereira, A. (1992). Abundance and seasonality of Mud-flat birds (Charadriiformes) in a muddy beach at Chomes, Costa Rica. *Rev. Biol. Trop.* **40**: 303-307.
Barrau, J. (1963). Present status of the Kagu *Rhynochetos jubatus* in New Caledonia. *Bull. ICBP* **9**: 90.
Barré, H. (1976). Le Skua subantarctique *Stercorarius skua lonnbergi* (Îles Crozet). *Com. Natl. Fr. Rech. Antarct.* **40**: 77-103.
Barrett, R.T. (1978a). *The Breeding Biology of the Kittiwake (*Rissa tridactyla *(L)) in Tromsø, North Norway*. PhD dissertation, Tromsø University, Tromsø.
Barrett, R.T. (1978b). Adult body temperature and the development of endothermy in the Kittiwake (*Rissa tridactyla*). *Astarte* **11**: 113-115.
Barrett, R.T. (1980). Temperature of Kittiwake (*Rissa tridactyla*) eggs and nests during incubation. *Ornis Scand.* **11(1)**: 50-59.
Barrett, R.T. & Mehlum, F. (1989). Bird observations and seabird census at Hopen, Svalbard. *Fauna Norvegica (Ser. C, Cinclus)* **12**: 21-29.
Barrett, R.T. & Rikardsen, F. (1992). Chick growth, fledging periods and adult mass loss of Atlantic Puffins *Fratercula arctica* during years of prolonged food stress. *Colonial Waterbirds* **15**: 24-32.
Barrett, R.T. & Runde, O.J. (1980). Growth and survival of nestling Kittiwakes (*Rissa tridactyla*) in Norway. *Ornis Scand.* **11**: 228-235.
Barrett, R.T., Anker-Nilssen, T., Rikardsen, F., Valde, K., Röv, N. & Vader, W. (1987). The food, growth and fledging success of Norwegian Puffin chicks *Fratercula arctica* in 1980-1983. *Ornis Scand.* **18**: 73-83.
Barrett, R.T., Fieler, R., Anker-Nilssen, T., Rikardsen, F. (1985). Measurements and weight changes of Norwegian adult Puffins *Fratercula arctica* and Kittiwakes *Rissa tridactyla* during the breeding season. *Ringing & Migration* **6**: 102-112.
Barros, C. (1991). El Alcaraván. [The Eurasian Thick-knee]. *Garcilla* **82**: 10-11. In Spanish.
Barrow, K.M. (1910). *Three Years in Tristan de Cunha*. Skeffington & Son, London.
Bart, J.R., Stehn, A., Herrick, J.A., Heaslip, N.A., Bookhout, T.A. & Stenzel, J.R. (1984). Survey methods for breeding Yellow Rails. *J. Wildl. Manage.* **48**: 1382-1386.
Barter, L. & Barter, M.A. (1988). Biometrics, moult and migration of Large Sand Plovers *Charadrius leschenaultii* spending the non-breeding season in north-western Australia. *Stilt* **12**: 33-40.
Barter, M.A. (1984a). Weight variations and migration strategy of Curlew Sandpiper (*Caldiris ferruginea*) wintering in Tasmania. *Occas. Stint* **3**: 7-18.
Barter, M.A. (1984b). Weight variation in Red-necked Stint (*Calidris ruficollis*) whilst wintering in Tasmania. *Occas. Stint* **3**: 69-80.
Barter, M.A. (1985). Sex determination by bill-length of live Curlew Sandpipers (*Calidris ferruginea*). *Stilt* **7**: 8-17.
Barter, M.A. (1986a). Primary moult in adult Curlew Sandpipers (*Calidris ferruginea*) wintering in the Hobart area. *Occas. Stint* **4**: 1-12.
Barter, M.A. (1986b). Sex-related differences in adult Curlew Sandpipers *Calidris ferruginea* caught in Victoria. *Stilt* **8**: 2-5.
Barter, M.A. (1986c). Great Knots partly undone. *Stilt* **9**: 5-20.
Barter, M.A. (1987a). Morphometrics of Victorian Great Knot. *Victoria Wader Study Group Bull.* **11**: 13-26.
Barter, M.A. (1987b). Are Curlew Sandpipers sexist - and if so, why? *Stilt* **11**: 14-17.
Barter, M.A. (1988). Biometrics and moult of Lesser Golden Plovers *Pluvialis dominica fulva* in Victoria. *Stilt* **13**: 15-19.
Barter, M.A. (1989a). Bar-tailed Godwit *Limosa lapponica* in Australia. Part 1: races, breeding areas and migration routes. *Stilt* **14**: 43-48.
Barter, M.A. (1989b). Bar-tailed Godwit *Limosa lapponica* in Australia. Part 2: weight, moult and breeding success. *Stilt* **14**: 49-53.

Barter, M.A. (1989c). Addendum to "Biometrics and moult of Lesser Golden Plovers *Pluvialis dominica fulva* in Victoria". *Stilt* **14**: 65.
Barter, M.A. (1989d). Further information concerning the breeding grounds of Red Knot *Calidris canutus rogersi*. *Stilt* **14**: 65-66.
Barter, M.A. (1989e). Survival rate of Double-banded Plovers *Charadrius bicinctus bicinctus* spending the non-breeding season in Victoria. *Stilt* **15**: 34-36.
Barter, M.A. (1990). Morphometrics of the Eastern Curlew *Numenius madagascariensis*. *Stilt* **16**: 36-42.
Barter, M.A. (1991a). Morphometrics of Victorian Black-fronted Plover *Charadrius melanops*. *Stilt* **18**: 13-14.
Barter, M.A. (1991b). Biometrics and moult of Mongolian Plovers *Charadrius mongolus* spending the non-breeding season in Australia. *Stilt* **18**: 15-20.
Barter, M.A. (1991c). Addendum to "Survival rate of Double-banded Plovers *Charadrius bicinctus bicinctus* spending the non-breeding season in Victoria". *Stilt* **19**: 5.
Barter, M.A. (1991d). Mongolian Plovers *Charadrius mongolus* in Australia: need for more biometric and breeding plumage information. *Stilt* **19**: 5-6.
Barter, M.A. (1992a). Biometrics and moult of Red-kneed Dotterels *Erythrogonys cinctus* in Australia. *Stilt* **20**: 30-32.
Barter, M.A. (1992b). Changing wader numbers in Swan Bay, Victoria: a cause for concern? *Stilt* **21**: 8-12.
Barter, M.A. (1992c). Morphometrics and moult of Little Curlew *Numenius minutus* in north Western Australia. *Stilt* **21**: 20-21.
Barter, M.A. (1992d). Morphometrics and moult of Victorian Masked Lapwings *Vanellus miles novaehollandiae*. *Stilt* **21**: 24-25.
Barter, M.A. (1992e). Distribution, abundance, migration and moult of the Red Knot *Calidris canutus rogersi*. Pp. 64-70 in: Piersma & Davidson (1992b).
Barter, M.A. & Davies, J. (1991). Mongolian Plover, *Charadrius mongolus* in Australia - need for more biometric and breeding plumage information. *Stilt* **19**: 5-6.
Barter, M.A. & Minton, C. (1987). Biometrics, moult and migration of Double-banded Plovers *Charadrius bicinctus* spending the non-breeding season in Victoria. *Stilt* **10**: 9-14.
Barter, M.A. & Wang Tianhou (1990). Can waders fly non-stop from Australia to China? *Stilt* **17**: 36-39.
Barter, M.A., Jessop, A.E. & Minton, C.D.T. (1988a). Red Knot (*Calidris canutus rogersi*) in Australia. Part 1: subspecies confirmation, distribution and migration. *Stilt* **12**: 29-32.
Barter, M.A., Jessop, A.E. & Minton, C.D.T. (1988b). Red Knot (*Calidris canutus rogersi*) in Australia. Part 2: biometrics and moult in Victoria and north-western Australia. *Stilt* **13**: 20-27.
Barth, E.K. (1955). Egg-laying, incubation and hatching of the Common Gull (*Larus canus*). *Ibis* **97**: 222-239.
Barth, E.K. (1966). Mantle colour as a taxonomic feature in (*Larus argentatus*) and (*Larus fuscus*). *Nytt. Mag. Zool.* **13**: 56-82.
Barth, E.K. (1967a). Standard body measurements in *Larus argentatus, L. fuscus, L. canus* and *L. marinus*. *Nytt. Mag. Zool.* **14**: 7-83.
Barth, E.K. (1967b). Egg dimensions and laying dates of *Larus marinus, L. argentatus, L. fuscus*, and *L.canus*. *Nytt. Mag. Zool.* **15**: 5-34.
Barth, E.K. (1968). The circumpolar systematics of *Larus argentatus* and *Larus fuscus* with special reference to the Norwegian populations. *Nytt. Mag. Zool.* **15(1)**(Suppl.): 1-50.
Barth, E.K. (1975). Moult and taxonomy of the Herring Gull *Larus argentatus* and the Lesser Black-backed Gull *L. fuscus* in northwestern Europe. *Ibis* **117**: 384-387.
Barthel, P.H. (1988). [The Asiatic Dowitcher (*Limnodromus semipalmatus*)]. *Limicola* **2(4)**: 152-155. In German.
Barthel, P.H. (1989). Corrections concerning the winter plumage of White-rumped Sandpiper *Calidris fuscicollis* and Broad-billed Sandpiper *Limicola falcinellus*. *Limicola* **3(6)**: 300-306.
Barthel, P.H. (1992). [Remarks on the occurrence of the Yellowlegs *Tringa flavipes* and *T. melanoleuca* in central Europe]. *Limicola* **6(2)**: 85-90. In German with English summary.
Barthel, P.H. (1994). Die Bestimmung der Fischmöwe *Larus ichthyaetus*. *Limicola* **8(2)**: 64-78.
Barthel, P.H. & Königstedt, D.G.W. (1993). Die Kennzeichen der Dünnschnabelmöwe *Larus genei*. *Limicola* **7(4)**: 165-177.
Bartholomew, G.A. & Dawson, W.R. (1979). Thermoregulatory behavior during incubation in Heermann's Gulls. *Physiol. Zool.* **52(4)**: 422-487.
Bartlett, A.D. (1862). Note on the habits and affinities of the Kagu (*Rhinochetus jubatus*). *Proc. Zool. Soc., London* **1862**: 218-219.
Bartlett, A.D. (1866). Notes on the breeding of several species of birds in the Society's Gardens during 1865. *Proc. Zool. Soc., London* **1866**: 76-79.
Bartlett, E. (1877). Remarks on the affinities of *Mesites*. *Proc. Zool. Soc., London* **1877**: 292-293.
Bartlett, E. (1879). Second list of mammals and birds collected by Mr Thomas Waters in Madagascar. *Proc. Zool. Soc., London* **1879**: 767-773.
Barton, D. (1982). Notes on skuas and jaegers in the western Tasman Sea. *Emu* **82**: 56-59.
Bartonek, J.C. & Nettleship, D.N. eds. (1979). *Conservation of Marine Birds of Northern North America*. Wildlife Research Report **11**. US Department Interior, US Fish & Wildlife Service, Washington, D.C.
Barzen, J. (1991). Restoration mixes science, people & luck in Vietnam. *ICF Bugle* **17(2)**: 2-3.
Barzen, J. (1994). ICF team discovers rare wildlife in Cambodia. *ICF Bugle* **20(4)**: 3-4.
Basilewsky, P. (1970). La faune terrestre de l'île de Sainte Hélène. 1.- Vertébrés. *Ann. Mus. Roy. Afr. Centr. (Ser. 8, Sci. Zool.)* **181**: 77-130.
Basilio, A. (1963). *Aves de la Isla de Fernando Poo*. Coculsa, Madrid.
Bates, G.M. (1927). Notes on some birds of Cameroon and the Lake Chad region; their status and breeding-times. *Ibis* **Ser. 12, no. 3**: 1-64.
Bates, R.S.P. & Lowther, E.H.N. (1952). *Breeding Birds of Kashmir*. Oxford University Press, Bombay.
Bateson, P.P. & Barth, E.K. (1957). Notes on the geographical variation of the Ringed Plover *Charadrius hiaticula* L. *Nytt. Mag. Zool.* **5**: 20-25.
Bateson, P.P.G. & Plowright, R.C. (1959a). Some aspects of the reproductive behavior of the Ivory Gull. *Ardea* **47**: 157-174.
Bateson, P.P.G. & Plowright, R.C. (1959b). The breeding biology of the Ivory Gull in Spitsbergen. *British Birds* **52**: 105-114.
Batten, L.A., Bibby, C.J., Clement, P., Elliott, G.D. & Porter, R.F. eds. (1990). *Red Data Birds in Britain. Action for Rare, Threatened and Important Species*. T. & A.D. Poyser, London.
Battley, P. (1991). Marsh Sandpipers in New Zealand. *Stilt* **19**: 28-29.
Baudraz, M. & Guillaume, T. (1993). [First nesting of the Little Ringed Plover (*Charadrius dubius*) at Vallee de Joux]. *Nos Oiseaux* **42(4)**: 229-230. In French.
Bauer, H.G. (1990). Ein Weißschwanzkiebitz *Chettusia leucura* am Bodensee. [A White-tailed Plover *Chettusia leucura* at lake Constance]. *Limicola* **4(5)**: 265-269. In German with English summary.
Bauer, K. (1953). Die Mittelmeer-Silbermöwe (*Larus argentatus michahellis*) in Osterreich. *Vogelkundl. Nachrichten Osterreich* **3**: 1-2.
Bauer, K. (1960a). Studies of less familiar birds 108. Little Crake. *British Birds* **53**: 518-524.
Bauer, K. (1960b). Variabilitat und Rassengliederung des Haselhuhnes (*Tetarstes bonasia*) in Mitteleuropa. *Bonn. zool. Beitr.* **11**: 1-18.
Bauer, U. (1989). [Breeding of the Common Sandpiper *Actitis hypoleucos* on the Middle Reaches of the River Lech, Bavaria (West Germany)]. *Anz. Orn. Ges. Bayern* **28**: 15-24. In German with English summary.
Baumanis, J. (1989). [Nesting of the Marsh Sandpiper and the Terek Sandpiper in Latvia]. *Putni Daba* **2**: 166-171. In Latvian with Russian and English summaries.
Baumgart, P. & Baumgart, W. (1993). Mornellregenpfeifer, *Eudromias morinellus* - Brutvogel im Nationalpark Hohe Tauern. *Falke* **40**: 163-164.
Bautista, L.M., Alonso, J.C. & Alonso, J.A. (1992). A 20-year study of wintering Common Crane fluctuations using time series analysis. *J. Wildl. Manage.* **56(3)**: 563-572.
Bayer, R.D. (1980). Birds feeding on herring eggs at the Yaquina estuary, Oregon. *Condor* **82**: 193-198.
Bayer, R.D. (1983). Nesting success of Western Gulls at Yaquina Head and on man-made structures in Yaquina estuary, Oregon. *Murrelet* **64**: 87-91.
Bayer, R.D. (1994). Identifying Long-billed Curlews along the Oregon coast: a caution. *Oregon Birds* **20(4)**: 121-122.
Bayer, R.D., Lowe, R.W. & Loeffel, R.E. (1991). Persistent summer mortalities of Common Murres along the Oregon central coast. *Condor* **93**: 516-525.
Bayes, J.C., Dawson, M.J., Joensen, A.H. & Potts, G.R. (1964). The distribution and numbers of the Great Skua breeding in the Faeroes in 1961. *Dan. Orn. Foren. Tidssk.* **58**: 36-41.
Bayes, J.C., Dawson, M.J. & Potts, G.R. (1964). The food and feeding behaviour of the Great Skua in the Faeroes. *Bird Study* **11**: 272-279.
Beall, F.C. (1996). Captive status and management of Wattled Cranes for conservation. In: Beilfuss *et al.* (1996).
Beaman, M. (1994). *Palearctic Birds. A Checklist of the Birds of Europe, North Africa and Asia North of the Foothills of the Himalayas*. Harrier Publications, Stonyhurst, UK.
Beaman, M.A.S. (1978). The feeding and population ecology of the Great Black-backed Gull in Northern Scotland. *Ibis* **120**: 126-127.
Beardslee, C.S. (1944). Bonaparte's Gull on the Niagara River and eastern lake Erie. *Wilson Bull.* **56**: 9-14.
Beaubrun, P.C. (1983). Le Goéland d'Audouin (*Larus audouinii* Payr.) sur les côtes de Maroc. *Oiseau et RFO* **53**: 209-226.
Beaubrun, P.C. (1993). Status of Yellow-legged Gull (*Larus cachinnans*) in Morocco and in the western Mediterranean. Pp. 47-55 in: Aguilar *et al.* (1993).
Beauchamp, A.J. (1986). A case of co-operative rearing in Wekas. *Notornis* **33**: 51-52.
Beauchamp, A.J. (1987a). *A Population Study of the Weka* Gallirallus australis *on Kapiti Island*. PhD thesis, Victoria University.
Beauchamp, A.J. (1987b). The social structure of the Weka (*Gallirallus australis*) at Double Cove, Marlborough Sounds. *Notornis* **34**: 317-325.
Beauchamp, A.J. (1988). Status of the Weka *Gallirallus australis* on Cape Brett, Bay of Islands. *Notornis* **35**: 282-284.
Beauchamp, A.J., Chambers, R. & Kendrick, J.L. (1993). North Island Weka on Rakitu Island. *Notornis* **40**: 309-312.
Bech, C., Martini, S., Brent, R. & Rasmussen, J. (1984). Thermoregulation in newly hatched Black-legged Kittiwakes. *Condor* **86**: 339-341.
Beck, R.E. (1985). First record of the Marsh Sandpiper (*Tringa stagnatilis*) on Guam. *Elepaio* **46(3)**: 20.
Beck, R.E. (1988). Survey and inventory of the native landbirds on Guam. In: *Research Project Report, Guam Aquatic and Wildlife Resources, FY 1988 Annual Report*. Department of Agriculture, Guam.
Beck, R.E. & Savidge, J.A. (1990). *Recovery Plan for the Native Forest Birds of Guam and Rota of the Northern Mariana Islands*. US Fish & Wildlife Service, Honolulu, Hawaii.
Becker, P. (1995). Identification of Water Rail and *Porzana* crakes in Europe. *Dutch Birding* **17**: 181-211.
Becker, P. & Kollibay, F.J. (1976). Erster Brutnachweis der Schwarzflügel-Brachschwalbe (*Glareola nordmanni* Fischer) für Deutschland. *Beitr. Naturkd. Niedersachsens* **29(1-2)**: 14-18.
Becker, P., Jensen, R.A.C. & Berry, H.H. (1974). Broadbilled Sandpiper *Limicola falcinellus* in south west Africa. *Madoqua* **1(8)**: 67-71.
Becker, P.H. (1976). Raubseeschwalbe (*Hydroprogne caspia*) als Brutvogel an der Sudwestafrikanischen Küste. *Namib und Meer* **7**: 21-23.
Becker, P.H. (1984). [How a Common Tern (*Sterna hirundo*) colony defends itself against Herring Gulls (*Larus argentatus*)]. *Z. Tierpsychol.* **66(4)**: 265-288. In German with English summary.
Becker, P.H. (1987). Kann sich die Flußseeschwalben auf Mellum vor Brutverlusten durch Silbermöwen schützen? Pp. 281-292 in: Gerdes, G., Krumbein, W.E. & Reineck, H.E. eds. (1987). *In Mellum - Portrait einer Insel*. Kramer Publications, Frankfurt.
Becker, P.H. (1991). Population and contamination studies in coastal birds: the Common Tern (*Sterna hirundo*). Pp. 433-460 in: Perrins *et al.* (1991).
Becker, P.H. (1995). Effects of coloniality on gull predation on Common Tern (*Sterna hirundo*). *Colonial Waterbirds* **18(1)**: 11-22.
Becker, P.H. & Anlauf, A. (1988a). Nistplatzwahl und Bruterfolg der Flußseeschwalbe (*Sterna hirundo*) im Deichvorland. I. Nestdichte. *Ökol. Vögel* **10**: 27-44.
Becker, P.H. & Anlauf, A. (1988b). Nistplatzwahl und Bruterfolg der Flußseeschwalbe (*Sterna hirundo*) im Deichvorland. II. Hochwasser-Uberflutung. *Ökol. Vögel* **10**: 45-58.
Becker, P.H. & Erdelen, M. (1982). Windrichtung und Vegetationsdeckung am Nest der Silbermöwe (*Larus argentatus*). *J. Orn.* **123**: 117-130.
Becker, P.H. & Erdelen, M. (1987). Die Bestandsentwicklung von Brutvogeln der deutschen Nordseeküste 1950-1979. *J. Orn.* **128**: 1-32.
Becker, P.H. & Finck, P. (1985). Witterung und Ernahrungssituation als entscheidende Faktoren des Bruterfolgs der Flußseeschwalbe (*Sterna hirundo*). *J. Orn.* **126**: 393-404.
Becker, P.H. & Finck, P. (1986). Die Bedeutung von Nestdichte und Neststandort für den Bruterfolg der Flußseeschwalbe (*Sterna hirundo*) in Kolonien einer Wattenmeerinsel. *Vogelwarte* **33**: 192-207.
Becker, P.H. & Specht, R. (1991). Body mass fluctuations and mortality in Common Tern *Sterna hirundo* chicks dependent on weather and tide in the Wadden Sea. *Ardea* **79**: 45-56.
Becker, P.H., Conrad, B. & Sperveslage, H. (1980). [Comparison of quantities of chlorinated hydrocarbons and PCBs in Herring Gull eggs]. *Vogelwarte* **30(4)**: 294-296. In German with English summary.
Becker, P.H., Finck, P. & Anlauf, A. (1985). Rainfall preceding egg-laying - a factor of breeding success in Common Terns (*Sterna hirundo*). *Oecologia* **65**: 431-436.
Becker, P.H., Frank, D. & Sudmann, S.R. (1992). Temporal and spatial pattern of Common Tern (*Sterna hirundo*) foraging in the Wadden Sea. *Oecologia* **93**: 389-393.
Bédard, J. (1969a). Feeding of the Least, Crested and Parakeet Auklets around St. Lawrence Island. *Can. J. Zool.* **47**.
Bédard, J. (1969b). The nesting of Crested, Least and Parakeet Auklets on St. Lawrence Island, Alaska. *Can. J. Zool.* **47**.
Bédard, J. (1969c). Adaptive radiation in Alcidae. *Ibis* **111**: 189-198.
Bédard, J. (1985). Evolution and characteristics of the Atlantic Alcidae. Pp. 1-51 in: Nettleship & Birkhead (1985).
Bédard, J. & Sealey, S.G. (1984). Moults and feather generations of the Least, Crested and Parakeet Auklets. *J. Zool., London* **202**: 461-488.
Beddard, F.E. (1889a). Contributions to the anatomy of the Hoatzin (*Opisthocomus hoazin*), with particular reference to the structure of the wing in the young. *Ibis* **Ser. 6, no. 1**: 283-293.
Beddard, F.E. (1889b). On the anatomy of Burmeister's Cariama (*Chunga burmeisteri*). *Proc. Zool. Soc., London* **1889**: 594-602.
Beddard, F.E. (1890). On the anatomy of *Podica senegalensis*. *Proc. Zool. Soc., London* **1890**: 425-443.
Beddard, F.E. (1891). Contributions to the anatomy of the Kagu (*Rhinochetus jubatus*). *Proc. Zool. Soc., London* **1891**: 9-21.
Beddard, F.E. (1901). On some anatomical differences between the Common Snipe (*Gallinago coelestis*) and the Jack Snipe (*Gallinago gallinula*). *Proc. Zool. Soc., London* **1901(2)**: 596-602.
Beddard, F.E. (1902). Notes on the osteology of *Aramus scolopaceus*. *Ibis* **Ser. 8, no. 2**: 33-54.
Bedggood, G.W. (1977). Field notes on the Southern Stone Curlew in Victoria. *Austr. Bird Watcher* **7(2)**: 35-40.
Bednall, D.K. & Williams, J.G. (1989). Range retraction of the White-eyed Gull *Larus leucophtalmus* from the eastern coast of Africa. *Scopus* **13**: 122-123.
Beebe, F.L. (1960). The marine peregrines of the northwest Pacific coast. *Condor* **62**: 145-189.
Beebe, M.B. & Beebe, C.W. (1910). *Our Search for Wilderness*. Henry Holt & Co., New York.
Beebe, W.C. (1909a). A contribution to the ecology of the adult Hoatzin. *Zoologica* **1**: 45-66. Reprinted in *Smithsonian Report* **1910**: 527-543.
Beebe, W.C. (1909b). An ornithological reconnaissance of northeastern Venezuela. *Zoologica* **1**: 75-76.
Beebe, W.C., Hartley, G.I. & Howes, P.G. (1917). *Tropical Wildlife in British Guiana*. New York Zoological Society, New York.
Beehler, B.M. (1978). *Upland Birds of Northeastern New Guinea*. Wau Ecology Institute Handbook **4**. Wau, Papua New Guinea.
Beehler, B.M. & Forster, M.S. (1988). Hotshots, hotspots, and female preferences in the organization of lek mating systems. *Amer. Naturalist* **131**: 203-219.
Beehler, B.M., Pratt, T.K. & Zimmerman, D.A. (1986). *Birds of New Guinea*. Princeton University Press, Princeton, New Jersey.
Beel, C. (1991). First spring record of Pectoral Sandpiper in Zambia. *Zambian Orn. Soc. Newsl.* **21(4)**: 29-30.
Beer, C.G. (1961). Incubation and nest-building behavior of Black-headed Gull. I: Incubation behavior in the incubation period. *Behaviour* **18**: 62-106.
Beer, C.G. (1962). Incubation and nest-building behavior of Black-headed Gull. II: Incubation behavior in the laying period. *Behaviour* **19**: 283-304.
Beer, C.G. (1963a). Incubation and nest building behavior of Black-headed Gulls. III: The pre-laying period. *Behaviour* **21**: 13-77.
Beer, C.G. (1963b). Incubation and nest building behavior of Black-headed Gulls. IV: Nest building in the incubation and laying periods. *Behaviour* **21**: 259-263.
Beer, C.G. (1965). Clutch size and incubation behavior in the Black-billed Gulls (*Larus bulleri*). *Auk* **82(1)**: 1-18.
Beer, C.G. (1966). Adaptations to nesting habitat in the reproductive behaviour of the Black-billed Gull (*Larus bulleri*). *Ibis* **108**: 394-410.

Beer, C.G. (1969). Laughing Gull chicks: recognition of their parents' voices. *Science* **166**: 1030-1032.
Beer, C.G. (1970a). On the responses of Laughing Gull chicks (*Larus atricilla*) to the calls of adults. I. Recognition of the voices of the parents. *Anim. Behav.* **18**: 652-660.
Beer, C.G. (1970b). On the responses of Laughing Gull chicks (*Larus atricilla*) to the calls of adults. II. Age changes and responses to different types of call. *Anim. Behav.* **18**: 661-677.
Beer, C.G. (1975). Multiple functions and gulls displays. Pp. 16-54 in: Baerends, G.P., Beer, C.G. & Manning, A. eds. (1975). *Function and Evolution in Behaviour-Essays in Honour of Professor Niko Tinbergen*. Clarendon Press, Oxford.
Beer, C.G. (1976). Some complexities in the communication behavior of gulls. *Ann. New York Acad. Sci.* **280**: 413-432.
Beer, C.G. (1979). Vocal communication between Laughing Gull parents and chicks. *Behaviour* **70**: 118-146.
Beer, C.G. (1980). The communication behavior of gulls and other seabirds. Pp 169-206 in: Burger, Olla & Winn (1980).
Beere, W. (1981). Camouflage of crouching Jack Snipe. *British Birds* **74(10)**: 440-441.
Beesley, J.S.S. (1977). Wattled Plover *Vanellus senegallus* in Tanzania. *Scopus* **1(2)**: 45.
Bege, L.A. do Rosário & Pauli, B.T. (1988). *As Aves nas Ilhas Moleques do Sul - Santa Catarina; Aspectos da Ecologia, Etologia e Anilhamento de Aves Marinhas*. FATMA, Florianópolis, Brazil.
Begg, G.W. (1973). The feeding habits of the Whitewinged Black Tern on Lake Kariba. *Ostrich* **44**: 149-153.
Begg, G.W. & Maclean, G.L. (1976). Belly-soaking in the Whitecrowned Plover. *Ostrich* **47(1)**: 65.
Behle, W.H. & Goates, W.A. (1957). Breeding biology of the California Gull. *Condor* **59**: 235-246.
Behn, F. & Millie, G. (1959). Beitrag zur Kenntnis des Rüsselbläßhuhns (*Fulica cornuta* Bonaparte). *J. Orn.* **100**: 119-131.
Behrstock, R.A. (1983). Colombian Crake (*Neocrex colombianus*) and Paint-billed Crake (*N. erythrops*): first breeding records for Central America. *Amer. Birds* **37(6)**: 956-957.
Beijersbergen, J. (1980). Een vondst van de Woestijnplevier *Charadrius leschenaultii*. [First record of greater sandplover in the netherlands]. *Limosa* **53(1)**: 34. In Dutch with English summary.
Beijersbergen, R. (1991). [Black-heaed Gulls and Common Terns plunder chicks of the Little Tern]. *Vogeljaar* **39**: 33. In Dutch.
Beilfuss, R. (1995). Wattled Cranes in the great Zambezi Delta. *ICF Bugle* **21(3)**: 3.
Beilfuss, R., Gichuki, N. & Tarboton, W. eds. (1996). *Proceedings of the 1993 African Crane and Wetland Training Workshop*. International Crane Foundation, Baraboo, Wisconsin.
Beintema, A.J. (1972). The history of the Island Hen (*Gallinula nesiotis*), the extinct flightless gallinule of Tristan da Cunha. *Bull. Brit. Orn. Club* **92**: 106-113.
Beintema, A.J. (1985). A shift in the timing of breeding in meadow birds. *Ardea* **73**: 83-89.
Beintema, A.J. (1986a). Man-made polders in the Netherlands: a traditional habitat for shorebirds. *Colonial Waterbirds* **9**: 196-202.
Beintema, A.J. (1986b). Where in Africa do subadult Black-tailed Godwits spend the summer? *Wader Study Group Bull.* **47**: 10.
Beintema, A.J. (1991a). *Breeding Ecology of Meadow Birds (Charadriiformes); Implications for Conservation and Management*. PhD thesis, Universiteit Groningen, Groningen, the Netherlands.
Beintema, A.J. (1991b). What makes a meadow bird a meadow bird? Pp. 3-5 in: Hötker (1991).
Beintema, A.J. (1991c). Status and conservation of meadow birds in the Netherlands. Pp. 12-13 in: Hötker (1991).
Beintema, A.J. (1994). Condition indices for wader chicks derived from body-weight and bill-length. *Bird Study* **41(1)**: 68-75.
Beintema, A.J. & Drost, N. (1986). Migration of the Black-tailed Godwit. *Gerfaut* **76**: 37-72.
Beintema, A.J. & Müskens, G.J.D.M. (1983). Changes in the migration pattern of the Common Snipe. Pp. 146-160 in: Kalchreuter (1983b).
Beintema, A.J. & Müskens, G.J.D.M. (1987). Nesting succes of birds breeding in Dutch agricultural grasslands. *J. Appl. Ecol.* **24**: 743-758.
Beintema, A.J. & Visser, G.H. (1989a). Growth parameters in chicks of charadriiform birds. *Ardea* **77**: 169-180.
Beintema, A.J. & Visser, G.H. (1989b). The effect of weather on time budgets and development of chicks of meadow birds. *Ardea* **77**: 181-192.
Beintema, A.J., Beintema-Hietbrink, R.J. & Müskens, G.J.D.M. (1985). A shift in the timing of breeding in meadow birds. *Ardea* **73(1)**: 83-89. In English with Dutch summary.
Beintema, A.J., Moedt, O. & Ellinger, D. (1995). *Ecologische Atlas van de Nederlandse Weidevogels*. Schuyt & Co., Haarlem, the Netherlands.
Beintema, A.J., Thissen, J.B., Tensen, D. & Visser, G.H. (1991). Feeding ecology of charadriiform chicks in agricultural grassland. *Ardea* **79**: 31-44.
Bekaert, L. (1989). [Collared Pratincole near Terneuzen in October-November 1987]. *Dutch Birding* **11(1)**: 23-25. In Dutch with English summary.
Bekaert, L. (1991). [Sharp-tailed Sandpiper at Philippine in September 1989]. *Dutch Birding* **13(4)**: 125-127. In Dutch with English summary.
Beklova, M. (1991). Migration of the Czechoslovak population of *Larus ridibundus*. *Prirodoved. Pr. ustavu Cesk. Akad. Ved Brne* **25**: 1-41.
Beland, P. (1975). Enquête sur les oiseaux de Calédonie. Le Cagou. *Nature Calédonienne* **8**: 31-34.
Belant, J.L. & Dolbeer, R.A. (1993a). Migration and dispersal of Laughing Gulls in the United States. *J. Field Orn.* **64**: 557-565.
Belant, J.L. & Dolbeer, R.A. (1993b). Population status of nesting Laughing Gulls in the United States 1977-1991. *Amer. Birds* **47(2)**: 220-224.
Belant, J.L., Seamans, T.W., Garbrey, S.W. & Ickes, S.K. (1993). Importance of landfills to nesting Herring Gulls. *Condor* **95**: 817-830.
Belik, V. (1994a). Black-winged Pratincole. *Glareola nordmanni*. Pp. 250-251 in: Tucker & Heath (1994).
Belik, V. (1994b). Sociable Plover. *Chettusia gregaria*. Pp. 258-259 in: Tucker & Heath (1994).
Belik, V.P. (1985). [Some peculiarities of lek behaviour of the Little Bustard (*Otis tetrax*)]. *Ornitologiya* **20**: 180-181. In Russian.
Belik, V.P. (1989). [Further range expansion by the White-tailed Lapwing]. Pp. 29-31 in: Davygora, A.V. & Gavlyuk, E.V. eds. (1989). [*Birds of the Ural Mountains and their Distribution*]. Orenburg. In Russian.
Belik, V.P. (1992). Distribution, numbers and some features of the ecology of the Little Bustard in the southeast of the European part of the USSR. *Bustard Studies* **5**: 73-77.
Belik, V.P. (1994). Where on earth does the Slender-billed Curlew breed? *Wader Study Group Bull.* **75**: 37-38.
Bell, B.D. (1974). Mangere Island. *Wildlife - A Review* **5**: 31-34.
Bell, B.D. (1975). The rare and endangered species of the New Zealand region and the policies that exist for their management. *Bull. ICBP* **12**: 165-172.
Bell, B.D. (1986). *The Conservation Status of New Zealand Wildlife*. New Zealand Wildlife Service Occasional Publications **12**. Wellington.
Bell, B.D., Cossee, R.O., Flux, J.E.C., Heather, B.C., Hitchmough, R.A., Robertson, C.J.R. & Williams, M.J. eds. (1991). *Acta XX Congressus Internationalis Ornithologici*. Vol. 4. New Zealand Ornithological Congress Trust Board, Wellington.
Bell, J. (1970). The White-quilled Black Bustard. *Animal Kingdom* **73(6)**: 25-28.
Belopol'skii, L.O. (1957). *Ecology of Sea Colony Birds of the Barents Sea*. (English translation 1961). Israel Program for Scientific Translations, Jerusalem.
Belopol'skii, L.O., Gorobets, L.N. & Polonik, N.N. (1976). Growth in the number of nesting colonies of Kittiwakes in eastern Murmansk and factors determining this. *Seabird Report* **1975-76**: 41-45.
Belopol'skii, L.O., Goryainova, G.P. & Milovanova, N.I. (1977). [Particulars of the breeding of Arctic Terns on the Barents, White and Baltic Seas]. *Ornitologiya* **13**: 95-99. In Russian.
Below, T.H. (1979). First reports of pellet ejection in 11 species. *Wilson Bull.* **91**: 626-628.
Belterman, R. & King, C.E. (1993). Captive management and husbandry of Red-crowned Cranes in Europe. *Int. Zoo News* **40(1)**: 7-20.
Belterman, R.H.R. & De Boer, L.E.M. (1984). A karyological study of 55 species of birds, including karyotypes of 39 species new to cytology. *Genetica* **65**: 39-82.
Belton, W. (1984). *Birds of Rio Grande do Sul, Brazil*. Part 1. Rheidae through Furnariidae. Bulletin of the American Museum of Natural History **178(4)**, New York. 267 pp.
Beltzer, A.H. (1986a). Ecología alimentaria de *Calidris fuscicollis* (Aves: Scolopacidae) en la Laguna del Cristal (Cuenca de Saladillo, Santa Fe, Argentina). *Iheringia, Ser. Zool.*
Beltzer, A.H. (1986b). Nota sobre la alimentación de *Charadrius collaris* "Chorlito de Collar" (Aves: Charadriidae) en la Laguna Del Cristal (Santa Fe, Argentina). *Bol. Asoc. Cienc. Nat. Litoral* **6**: 5-9.
Beltzer, A.H. (1991). Aspects of the foraging ecology of the waders *Tringa flavipes*, *Calidris fuscicollis* and *Charadrius collaris* (Aves: Scolopacidae; Charadriidae) in Del Cristal Pond (Santa Fe, Argentina). *Stud. Neotrop. Fauna Environm.* **26(2)**: 65-73.
Beltzer, A.H., Sabattini, R.A. & Marta, M.C. (1991). Ecología alimentaria de la Polla de Agua Negra *Gallinula chloropus galeata* (Aves: Rallidae) en un ambiente lenítico del río Paraná medio, Argentina. *Orn. Neotropical* **2**: 29-36. In Spanish with English summary.
Bengtson, S.A. (1962). Småfläckiga sumphönans (*Porzana porzana*) förekomst och häckningsbiologi i nordöstra Skåne. *Vår Fågelvärld* **21**: 253-266.
Bengtson, S.A. (1967). Revirförhällenden hos vattenrall (*Rallus aquaticus*) tidigt pä våren. *Vår Fågelvärld* **26**: 6-18.
Bengtson, S.A. (1968). Breeding behaviour of the Grey Phalarope in west Spitsbergen. *Vår Fågelvärld* **27**: 1-13.
Bengtson, S.A. (1970). Breeding behaviour of the Purple Sandpiper *Calidris maritima* in west Spitsbergen. *Ornis Scand.* **1**: 17-25.
Bengtson, S.A. (1971). Breeding success of the Arctic Tern (*Sterna paradisaea* (Pontoppidan) in the Kongsfjord area, Spitsbergen in 1967. *Norw. J. Zool.* **19**: 77-82.
Bengtson, S.A. (1975a). Timing of the moult of the Purple Sandpiper *Calidris maritima* in Spitsbergen. *Ibis* **117**: 100-102.
Bengtson, S.A. (1975b). Observations on the breeding biology of the Purple Sandpiper *Calidris maritima* on Svalbard. *Fauna* **28**: 81-86.
Bengtson, S.A. (1984). Breeding ecology and extinction of the Great Auk (*Alca impennis*): anecdotal evidence and conjectures. *Auk* **101**: 1-12.
Bengtson, S.A. & Rundgren, S. (1978). Selective predation on lumbricids by Golden Plover *Pluvialis apricaria*. *Oikos* **31(2)**: 164-168.
Bengtson, S.A. & Svensson, B. (1968). Feeding habits of *Calidris alpina* L. and *C. minuta* Leisl. (Aves) in relation to the distribution of marine shore invertebrates. *Oikos* **19**: 152-157.
Benirschke, R.J. (1977). Karyological difference between *Sagittarius* and *Cariama*. *Experientia* **33(8)**: 1021-1022.
Benito-Espinal, E. & Hautcastel, P. (1988). Les oiseaux menacés de Guadeloupe et de Martinique. Pp. 37-60 in: Thibault & Guyot (1988). In French with English summary.
Bennett, A.J. (1989). Movements and home ranges of Florida Sandhill Cranes. *J. Wildl. Manage.* **53(3)**: 830-836.
Bennett, C.J.L. (1992). Kittlitz's Plover (*Charadrius pecuarius*). *Cyprus Orn. Soc. Newsl.* **1992**(Sep.): 5.
Bennett, G. (1863). Notes on the Kagu (two specimens in captivity). *Proc. Zool. Soc., London* **1863**: 385-386, 439-440.
Bennett, S. (1983). A review of the distribution, status and biology of the Plains-wanderer *Pedionomus torquatus*, Gould. *Emu* **83(1)**: 1-11.
Bennett, S. (1985). The distribution and status of the Black-breasted Button-quail *Turnix melanogaster* (Gould, 1837). *Emu* **85(3)**: 157-162.
Bennett, W.W. & Ohmart, R.D. (1978). *Habitat Requirements and Population Characteristics of the Clapper Rail (*Rallus longirostris yumanensis*) in the Imperial Valley of California*. University of California, Lawrence Livermore Laboratory, Livermore, California.
Benson, C.W. (1950). A contribution to the ornithology of St. Helena and other notes from a sea-voyage. *Ibis* **92**: 75-83.
Benson, C.W. (1956). New or unusual birds from northen Rhodesia. *Ibis* **98**: 595-605.
Benson, C.W. (1960). *The Birds of the Comoro Islands*. Results of the British Ornithologists' Union Centenary Expedition 1958. Ibis **103B**.
Benson, C.W. (1961). Jacanas and other birds perching on hippo. *Bull. Brit. Orn. Club* **81**: 85-86.
Benson, C.W. (1964a). The European and African races of Baillon's Crake, *Porzana pusilla*. *Bull. Brit. Orn. Club* **84**: 2-5.
Benson, C.W. (1964b). Some intra-African migratory birds. *Puku* **2**: 53-56.
Benson, C.W. (1967). The birds of Aldabra and their status. *Atoll Res. Bull.* **118**: 68-111.
Benson, C.W. (1968a). Finfoots. Pp. 111-112 in: Grzimek (1968).
Benson, C.W. (1968b). Kittlitz's Sandplover *Charadrius pecuarius* Temminck, in Angola. *Ostrich* **39(1)**: 41.
Benson, C.W. (1978). The Madagascar Pratincole *Glareola ocularis* in Somalia. *Scopus* **2(1)**: 21.
Benson, C.W. (1981). Les oiseaux: des espèces uniques au monde. Pp. 63-74 in: Oberlé, P. ed. (1981). *Madagascar, un Sanctuaire de la Nature*. Lechevalier, Paris.
Benson, C.W. (1982). Migrants in the Afrotropical region south of the equator. *Ostrich* **53**: 31-49.
Benson, C.W. (1985). Mesite. Page 346 in: Campbell & Lack (1985).
Benson, C.W. & Benson, F.M. (1975). *The Birds of Malawi*. Montfort Press, Limbe, Malawi.
Benson, C.W. & Holliday, C.S. (1964). *Sarothrura affinis* and some other species on the Nyika Plateau. *Bull. Brit. Orn. Club* **84**: 131-132.
Benson, C.W. & Irwin, M.P.S. (1965). Some intra-African migratory birds II. *Puku* **3**: 45-55.
Benson, C.W. & Irwin, M.P.S. (1967). A contribution to the ornithology of Zambia. *Zambia Mus. Pap.* **1**.
Benson, C.W. & Irwin, M.P.S. (1971). A South African male of *Sarothrura ayresi* and other specimens of the genus in the Leiden Museum. *Ostrich* **42**: 227-228.
Benson, C.W. & Irwin, M.P.S. (1972). Variation in tarsal and other measurements in *Otis denhami*, with some distributional notes. *Bull. Brit. Orn. Club* **92**: 70-77.
Benson, C.W. & Pitman, C.R.S. (1959). Further breeding records from Northern Rhodesia. Part 3. *Bull. Brit. Orn. Club* **79**: 18-22.
Benson, C.W. & Pitman, C.R.S. (1964). Further breeding records from Northern Rhodesia. Part 4. *Bull. Brit. Orn. Club* **84**: 54-60.
Benson, C.W. & Pitman, C.R.S. (1966). On the breeding of Baillon's Crake *Porzana pusilla* (Pallas) in Africa and Madagascar. *Bull. Brit. Orn. Club* **86**: 141-143.
Benson, C.W. & Schuz, E. (1967). The African Finfoot in Ethiopia. *Bull. Brit. Orn. Club* **87**: 149-150.
Benson, C.W. & Wagstaffe, R. (1972). *Porzana olivieri* and *Limnocorax flavirostris*; a likely affinity. *Bull. Brit. Orn. Club* **92**: 160-164.
Benson, C.W. & Winterbottom, J.M. (1968). The relationship of the Striped Crake *Crecopsis egregia* (Peters) and the White-throated Crake *Porzana albicollis* (Vieillot). *Ostrich* **39**: 177-179.
Benson, C.W., Beamish, H.H., Jouanin, C., Salvin, J. & Watson, G.E. (1975). The birds of the Isles Glorieuses. *Atoll Res. Bull.* **176**: 1-30.
Benson, C.W., Brooke, R.K., Dowsett, R.J. & Irwin, M.P.S. (1971). *The Birds of Zambia*. Collins, London.
Benson, C.W., Colebrook-Robjent, J.F.R. & Williams, A. (1976-1977). A contribution to the ornithology of Madagascar. *Oiseau et RFO* **46**: 103-134, 209-242, 368-386; **47**: 41-64, 168-191.
Bent, A.C. (1919). *Life Histories of North American Diving Birds*. US National Museum Bulletin **107**. Smithsonian Institution, Washington, D.C. 239 pp.
Bent, A.C. (1921). *Life Histories of North American Gulls and Terns*. US National Museum Bulletin **113**. Smithsonian Institution, Washington, D.C. 337 pp.
Bent, A.C. (1926). *Life Histories of North American Marsh Birds*. US National Museum Bulletin **135**. Smithsonian Institution, Washington, D.C. (Reprinted by Dover Publications, New York). 490 pp.
Bent, A.C. (1927-1929). *Life Histories of North American Shorebirds*. Part 1 & 2. US National Museum Bulletin **142** & **146**. Smithsonian Institution, Washington, D.C. (Reprinted by Dover Publications, New York).
Bent, A.C. (1929). A flight of Ross's Gulls. *Auk* **46**: 224-225.
Beretzk, P., Keve, A., Nagy, B. & Szijj, J. (1959). Economic importance of the Curlews and taxonomic position of the Hungarian populations. *Aquila* **65**: 89-126.
Berezovikov, N.N. (1980). [Occurrence of Ibis-bill (*Ibidorhyncha struthersii*) in Altai]. *Ornitologiya* **15**: 192-193. In Russian.
Berezovikov, N.N. (1992). The present status of the Great Bustard in Kazakhstan. *Bustard Studies* **5**: 52-56.
Berg, Å. (1991). *Ecology of Curlews* Numenius arquata *and Lapwings* Vanellus vanellus *on Farmland*. PhD thesis, Swedish University of Agricultural Sciences, Uppsala.
Berg, Å. (1992a). Factors affecting nest-site choice and reproductive success of Curlews *Numenius arquata* on farmland. *Ibis* **134(1)**: 44-51.
Berg, Å. (1992b). Habitat selection by breeding Curlews *Numenius arquata* on mosaic farmland. *Ibis* **134(4)**: 355-360.
Berg, Å. (1993a). Food resources and foraging success of Curlews *Numenius arquata* in different farmland habitats. *Ornis Fenn.* **70(1)**: 22-31.
Berg, Å. (1993b). Habitat selection by monogamous and polygamous Lapwings on farmland: the importance of foraging habitats and suitable nest sites. *Ardea* **81(2)**: 99-105.
Berg, Å. (1994). Maintenance of populations and causes of population changes of Curlews *Numenius arquata* breeding on farmland. *Biol. Conserv.* **67(3)**: 233-238.
Berg, Å., Lindberg, T. & Kallebrink, K.G. (1992). Hatching success of Lapwings on farmland: differences between habitats and colonies of different sizes. *J. Anim. Ecol.* **61(2)**: 469-476.

van den Berg, A.B. (1984). Occurrence of Sociable Plover in western Europe. *Dutch Birding* **6(1)**: 1-8.
van den Berg, A.B. (1985). Juvenile plumage of Black-winged Pratincole. *Dutch Birding* **7(4)**: 143-144.
van den Berg, A.B. (1988a). Identification of Slender-billed Curlew and its occurrence in Morocco in winter of 1987/88. *Dutch Birding* **10(2)**: 45-53.
van den Berg, A.B. (1988b). *Moroccan Slender-billed Curlew Survey, Winter 1987-88*. ICBP Study Report **29**/WIWO Report **29**. ICBP & WIWO, Girton & Zeist.
van den Berg, A.B. (1990). Habitat of Slender-billed Curlews in Morocco. *British Birds* **83(1)**: 1-7.
van den Berg, A.B., Bosman, C.A.W. & Rozendaal, F.G. (1982). Notes on seabirds: mass movement of Bridled Terns *Sterna anaethetus* and Wilson's Petrels *Oceanites oceanicus* off Colombo, Sri Lanka. *Ardea* **70**: 81-82.
van den Berg, A.B., Hoogendoorn, W. & Mullarney, K. (1991). Wing and tail moult in first-year Brown-headed Gulls wintering in Thailand. *Dutch Birding* **13(2)**: 58-63.
Berg, H.M. (1987). Ein Rotkehlstrandläufer *Calidris ruficollis* in Österreich sowie Anmerkungen zu seinem Auftreten in Europa. *Limicola* **1(2)**: 37-44.
van den Berg, L.M.J. (1989). [Increase of the Curlew as a meadowbird]. *Limosa* **62**: 49. In Dutch with English summary.
Bergan, J.F. & Smith, L.M. (1986). Food robbery of wintering Ring-necked Ducks by American Coots. *Wilson Bull.* **98**: 306-308.
Berger, A.J. (1951). Nesting density of Virginia and Sora Rails in Michigan. *Condor* **53**: 203.
Berger, A.J. (1972). *Hawaiian Birdlife*. University Press of Hawai, Honolulu.
van den Bergh, L. (1991). Status, distribution and research on Corncrakes in the Netherlands. *Vogelwelt* **112**: 78-83.
Bergman, G. (1946). Der Steinwälzer in seiner Beziehung zur Umwelt. *Acta Zool. Fennica* **47**: 1-151.
Bergman, G. (1953). Verhalten und Biologie der Raubseeschwalbe (*Hydroprogne tschegrava*). *Acta Zool. Fennica* **77**: 1-50.
Bergman, G. (1956). Beteendestudier over ungar av skrantarna (*Hydroprogne tschegrava*). [On the development of behavior in chicks of Caspian Tern (*Hydroprogne tschegrava*)]. *Vår Fågelvärld* **15**: 223-245.
Bergman, G. (1971). Gryllteisten *Cepphus grylle* in einen Randgebiet: nahrung, brutresultat, tagesrhythmus und ansiedlung. *Commentationes Biologicae* **42**: 1-26.
Bergman, G. (1978). Av naringsbrist fovorsakade stormingar i tejsterns (tobisgrisslans) *Cepphus grylle* hackning. *Mem. Soc. Fauna Flora Fenn.* **54**: 31-32.
Bergman, G. (1980). Single-breeding versus colonial breeding in the Caspian Tern *Hydroprogne caspia*, the Common Tern *Sterna hirundo* and the Arctic Tern *Sterna paradisaea*. *Ornis Fenn.* **57**: 141-152.
Bergman, G. (1982a). Inter-relationship between ducks and gulls. Pp. 241-248 in: Scott, D.A. ed. (1982). *Managing Wetlands and their Birds. A Manual of Wetland and Waterfowl Management*. IWRB, Slimbridge, UK.
Bergman, G. (1982b). Population dynamics, colony formation and competition in *Larus argentatus*, *fuscus* and *marinus* in the archipelago of Finland. *Ann. Zool. Fennici* **19**: 143-164.
Bergman, G. (1982c). Why are the wings of *Larus f. fuscus* so dark? *Ornis Fenn.* **59**: 77-83.
Bergman, G. (1986). Feeding habits, accommodation to man, breeding success and aspects of coloniality in the Common Gull *Larus canus*. *Ornis Fenn.* **63**: 65-78.
Bergman, R.D. (1973). Use of southern boreal lakes by postbreeding canvasbacks and redheads. *J. Wildl. Manage.* **37**: 160-170.
Bergman, R.D., Swain, P. & Weller, M.W. (1970). A comparative study of nesting Forster's and Black Terns. *Wilson Bull.* **82**: 435-444.
Bergstrom, P.W. (1981). Male incubation in Wilson's Plover (*Charadrius wilsonia*). *Auk* **98(4)**: 835-839.
Bergstrom, P.W. (1982). *Ecology of Incubation in Wilson's Plover (*Charadrius wilsonia*)*. PhD thesis, University of Chicago, Chicago, Illinois.
Bergstrom, P.W. (1986). Daylight incubation sex roles in Wilson's Plover. *Condor* **88(1)**: 113-115.
Bergstrom, P.W. (1988a). Breeding biology of Wilson's Plover. *Wilson Bull.* **100(1)**: 25-35.
Bergstrom, P.W. (1988b). Breeding displays and vocalization of Wilson's Plovers. *Wilson Bull.* **100(1)**: 36-49.
Bergstrom, P.W. (1989). Incubation temperatures of Wilson's Plover and Killdeers. *Condor* **91(3)**: 634-641.
Bergstrom, P.W. & Terwilliger, K. (1987). Nest sites and aggressive behavior of Piping and Wilson's Plovers in Virginia: some preliminary results. *Wader Study Group Bull.* **50**: 35-39.
van Berkel, H. & van Dijken, K. (1985). [White-tailed Plover near Klazienaveen in June 1984]. *Dutch Birding* **7(3)**: 98-99. In Dutch with English summary.
Berlich, H. & Kalchreuter, H. (1983). A study on harvesting roding Woodcock in spring. Pp. 92-99 in: Kalchreuter (1983b).
Berlijn, M. (1991). Jufferkraanvogels bij Asten in augustus-september 1989. [Demoiselle Cranes near Asten in August-September 1989]. *Dutch Birding* **13(3)**: 81-82. In Dutch with English summary.
Berlijn, M. & Luijendijk, T.J.C. (1995). Poelsnip in Workumerwaard in juli-augustus 1994. [Great Snipe in Workumerwaard in July-August 1994]. *Dutch Birding* **17(4)**: 146-148. In Dutch with English summary.
Berlioz, J. (1946). *Oiseaux de la Réunion*. Vol. 4. Faune de l'Empire Français. Larose, Paris.
Berlioz, J. (1948). Le peuplement de Madagascar en oiseaux. *Mém. Inst. Sci. Madagascar (Sér. A)* **1(2)**: 181-192.
Berman, D.I. & Dorogoy, I.V. (1993). [The distribution of the Mongolian Plover (*Charadrius mongolus*) in the north-eastern Asia]. *Russ. J. Orn.* **2(1)**: 55-59. In Russian with English summary.
Berman, D.I. & Kuz'min, I.F. (1965). [The Pintail Snipe in the Tuva, USSR]. *Ornitologiya* **7**: 209-216. In Russian.
Berndt, R.K. (1986). Zur Brutverbreitung des Brachvogels *Numenius arquata* in Schleswig-Holstein auf landwirtschaftlich genutztem Grünland. *Corax* **11**: 311-317.
Berney, F.L. (1907). Field notes on birds of the Richmond District, North Queensland. IV. *Emu* **6**: 106-115.
Bernstein, N.P. (1983). Influence of pack ice on non-breeding Southern Black-backed Gulls (*Larus dominicanus*) in Antarctica. *Notornis* **30**: 1-6.
Berruti, A. & Harris, A. (1976). Breeding schedules of Antarctic and Kerguelen Terns at Marion Island. *Notornis* **23(3)**: 243-245.
Berry, H.H. & Berry, C.U. (1975). A checklist and notes on the birds of Sandvis, South West Africa. *Madoqua* **9(2)**: 5 18.
Berry, P. (1995). Southern Crowned Crane teaches baboon a lesson. *Zambian Orn. Soc. Newsl.* **25(7)**: 76.
Berry, R.J. & Davis, J.W.F. (1970). Polymorphism and behaviour in the Arctic Skua. *Proc. Royal Soc. London* **175B**: 255-267.
Bertault, Y., Dubois, P.J. & Fremont, J.Y. (1988). Some comments on the Armenian Gull in Turkey. *Bull. Orn. Soc. Middle East* **20**: 20-21.
Bertoni, A. de W. (1929). Notas sobre la *Chunga burmeisteri* hallada en el Chaco Paraguayo. *Rev. Soc. Cient. Paraguay* **2(6)**: 228.
Bertram, D.F. (1988). *The Provisioning of Nestlings by Parent Rhinoceros Auklets (*Cerorhinca monocerata*)*. MSc thesis, Simon Fraser University, Burnaby, Canada.
Bertram, D.F. & Kaiser, G.W. (1988). *Monitoring Growth and Diet of Nestling Rhinoceros Auklets to Gauge Prey Availability*. Canadian Wildlife Service Technical Report **48**.
Bertram, D.F., Kaiser, G.W. & Ydenberg, R.C. (1991). Patterns in the provisioning and growth of nestling Rhinoceros Auklets. *Auk* **108**: 842-852.
Beruldsen, G.R. (1975). The Bush-hen in south-eastern Queensland. *Austr. Bird Watcher* **6**: 75-76.
Beruldsen, G.R. (1976). Further notes on the Bush-hen in south-eastern Queensland. *Sunbird* **7**: 53-58.
Beruldsen, G.R. (1980). *A Field Guide to Nests and Eggs of Australian Birds*. Rigby, Adelaide.
Berutti, A., Miller, D.G. & Silbernagl, P. (1979). Kelp Gulls catching crayfish. *Cormorant* **7**: 30.
Beser, H.J. (1977). Zur Brutoekologie des Flußregenpfeifers (*Charadrius dubius*) in zwei Kiesgruben am Niederrhein. [On the breeding ecology of the Little-ringed Plover (*Charadrius dubius*) in two gravel pits in the lower Rhine]. *Charadrius* **13(3)**: 65-70.
Beser, H.J. (1983). Mauserbeginn bei brutenden Kiebitzen (*Vanellus vanellus* L.). *Charadrius* **19**: 11-13.
Beser, H.J. (1987). [On the clutch-size of Lapwings (*Vanellus vanellus*)]. *Charadrius* **23(3)**: 174-182. In German with English summary.
Beser, H.J. & Beser, M. (1989). [Egg measurements of the Lapwing]. *Charadrius* **25**: 255-235. In German.
Beser, H.J. & von Helden Sarnowski, S. (1974). Zur Ökologie und Biologie des Austernfischers am südlichsten Punkt seiner Verbreitung in Deutschland. *Charadrius* **10**: 37 54.
Beser, H.J. & von Helden Sarnowski, S. (1982). Zur Ökologie Einer Ackerpopulation des Kiebitzes *Vanellus vanellus*. *Charadrius* **18**: 93-113.
Beser, M. (1986). Buff-breasted Sandpiper on Texel in September 1985. *Dutch Birding* **8(3)**: 101-102. In Dutch with English summary.
Best, B.J., Clarke, C.T., Checker, M., Broom, A.L., Thelwis, R.M., Duckworth, W. & McNab, A. (1993). Distributional records, natural history notes and conservation of some poorly known birds from southwestern Ecuador and northwestern Peru. *Bull. Brit. Orn. Club* **113**: 108-119.
Beste, H. (1970). The sighting of a Painted Snipe. *Austr. Bird Watcher* **3**: 220-222.
Betham, R.M. (1931). Does Hartlaub's Gull breed twice a year? *Ostrich* **2**: 13-15.
Betterton, F.A. (1947). The altitudinal limit of the Pheasant-tailed Jacana (*Hydrophasianus chirurgus* Scopoli). *J. Bombay Nat. Hist. Soc.* **47(2)**: 384.
Betts, B.J. (1973). A possible hybrid Wattled Jacana x Northern Jacana in Costa Rica. *Auk* **90**: 687-689.
Betts, B.J. & Jenni, D.A. (1991). Time budgets and the adaptiveness of polyandry in Northern Jacanas. *Wilson Bull.* **103(4)**: 578-597.
Beven, G. (1944). Nesting of African Skimmer. *Ostrich* **15**: 138-139.
Beven, G. & Chiazzari, W.L. (1943). Waders, dikkops, coursers and Common Larks at Oudtshoorn. *Ostrich* **14**: 139-151.
Beven, G. & England, M.D. (1977). Studies of less familiar birds. 181. Turnstone. *British Birds* **70**: 23-32.
Beven, J.O. (1913). Notes and observations on the Painted Snipe (*Rostratula capensis*) in Ceylon. *Ibis* **Ser. 10, no. 1**: 527-534.
Beyerbach, M. & Heidmann, W.A. (1990). Characterization of PCB mixtures found in biological samples by evaluating the stability of the phenyl components towards environmental influences. *Chemosphere* **21**: 613-625.
Beyerbach, M., Büthe, A., Heidmann, W.A., Knüwer, H. & Rüssel-Sinn, H.A. (1988). [The burden of Diedrin and other chlorinated hydrocarbons on the Lapwing (*Vanellus vanellus*)]. *J. Orn.* **129**: 353-361. In German with English summary.
Bezzel, E. (1986). Lesser Sandplover, *Charadrius mongolus*, in Turkey. *Zool. Middle East* **1**: 24-26.
Bezzel, E. & Schöpf, H. (1991). Der Wachtelkönig im Murnauer Moos: Artenschutzerfolg durch Ausweisung eines Naturschutzgebietes? *Vogelwelt* **112**: 83-90.
Bharucha, E.K. & Samant, J.S. (1984). On the sighting of a flock of Crab Plovers at Kolhapur. *J. Bombay Nat. Hist. Soc.* **81(3)**: 698.
Bharucha, E.K., Gogte, P.P. & Gole, T.P. (1988). A new nesting colony of River Terns and pratincoles. *J. Bombay Nat. Hist. Soc.* **85(1)**: 191-193.
Bhunya, S.P. & Mohanty, M.K. (1990). Chromosome evolution in two families of charadriiform birds. *Caryologia* **43**: 79-86.
Bhushan, B. (1985). Jerdon's or Double-banded Courser *Cursorius bitorquatus* (Blyth), Pennar Valley areas: Andhra Pradesh: Surveys and discussion. Pp. 86-99 in: Ali *et al.* (1985).
Bhushan, B. (1986a). Rediscovery of the Jerdon's or Double-banded Courser *Cursorius bitorquatus* (Blyth). *J. Bombay Nat. Hist. Soc.* **83(1)**: 1-14.
Bhushan, B. (1986b). Photographic record of the Jerdon's or Double-banded Courser *Cursorius bitorquatus*. *J. Bombay Nat. Hist. Soc.* **83**(Suppl.): 159-162.
Bhushan, B. (1990). Jerdon's Courser, rediscovery and survey. Pp. 127-134 in: *Status and Ecology of the Lesser and Bengal Floricans with Reports on Jerdon's Courser and Mountain Quail*. Bombay Natural History Society, Bombay.
Bhushan, B. (1992a). Jerdon's Coursers at Cuddapah. *Newsl. Birdwatchers* **32(5-6)**: 20.
Bhushan, B. (1992b). Red Data bird: Jerdon's Courser. *World Birdwatch* **14(4)**: 12.
Bhushan, B. & Rahmani, A.R. (1992). Food and feeding behaviour of the Great Indian Bustard *Ardeotis nigriceps* (Vigors). *J. Bombay Nat. Hist. Soc.* **89(1)**: 27-40.
Biaggi, V. (1983). *Las Aves de Puerto Rico*. Editorial de la Universidad de Puerto Rico, Río Piedras, Puerto Rico.
Bianki, V.V. (1967). *Gulls, Shorebirds and Alcids of Kandalaksha Bay*. Proc. Kandalaksha State Reservation **6**. (English translation 1977). Israel Program for Scientific Translation, Jerusalem.
Biber, J.P. (1993). Status and distribution of the Gull-billed Tern (*Sterna nilotica*) in the western Palearctic. (Preliminary results of an inquiry). Pp. 87-95 in: Aguilar *et al.* (1993).
Biber, J.P. (1994). Gull-billed Tern. *Gelochelidon nilotica*. Pp. 292-293 in: Tucker & Heath (1994).
Bicak, T.K. (1977). *Some Eco-ethological Aspects of a Breeding Population of Long-billed Curlews in Nebraska*. MSc thesis, University of Nebraska, Omaha, Nebraska.
Bickart, K.J. (1990). *The Birds of the Late Miocene-Early Pliocene Big Sandy Formation, Mohave County, Arizona*. Ornithological Monographs **44**. American Ornithologists' Union, Washington, D.C. 70 pp.
Biddulph, C.H. (1954). The status of the Pheasant-tailed Jacana (*Hydrophasianus chirurgus*) in south India. *J. Bombay Nat. Hist. Soc.* **52(2-3)**: 606-607.
Biderman, J.O. & Drury, W.O. (1978). Ecological studies in the northern Bering Sea: studies of seabirds in the Bering Strait. Pp. 751-838 in: *Annual Reports of Principal Investigators. Environmental Assessment of the Alaskan Continental Shelf*. Vol. 2. NOAA-BLM, Boulder, Colorado.
Bie, de S. & Zijlstra, M. (1979). Some remarks on the behaviour of the Avocet (*Recurvirostra avosetta* L.) in relation to difficult breeding places. *Ardea* **67**: 68-69.
Bierman, W.H. (1966). Sabine's Gulls (*Larus sabini*) in the North Atlantic. *Ardea* **54**: 271.
Bigalke, R. (1933). Observations on the breeding habits of the Cape Thick-knee *Burhinus capensis capensis* in captivity. *Ostrich* **4**: 41-48.
Bigg, R. (1981). Oriental Plovers near Newcastle. *Austr. Birds* **15(3)**: 54.
Bigg, R. (1988). Bush Stone-curlew breeding near Glossodia. *Austr. Birds* **21(3)**: 78.
Bijlsma, R.G. (1985). Foraging and hunting efficiency of Caspian Terns. *British Birds* **78**: 146-147.
Bijlsma, R.G. & de Roder, F.E. (1986). Notes on Nordmann's Greenshank *Tringa guttifer* in Thailand. *Forktail* **2**: 92-94.
Bijlsma, R.G. & de Roder, F.E. (1991). Foraging behaviour of Terek Sandpipers *Xenus cinereus* in Thailand. *Wader Study Group Bull.* **61**: 22-26.
Billard, R.S. (1948). *An Ecological Study of the Virginia Rail (*Rallus limicola*) and the Sora (*Porzana carolina*) in Some Connecticut Swamps*. MSc thesis, Iowa State College, Ames, Iowa.
Binford, L.C. (1973). Virginia Rail and Cape May Warbler in Chiapas, Mexico. *Condor* **75**: 350-351.
Binford, L.C. (1978). Lesser Black-backed Gull in California, with notes on field identification. *Western Birds* **9**: 141-150.
Binford, L.C., Elliot, B.G. & Singer, S.W. (1975). Discovery of a nest and the downy young of Marbled Murrelet. *Wilson Bull.* **87**: 303-319.
Binkley, C.S. & Miller, R.S. (1983). Population characteristics of the Whooping Crane, *Grus americana*. *Can. J. Zool.* **61**: 2768-2776.
Biondi, M., Pietrelli, L., Guerrieri, G. & Martucci, O. (1992). [Habitat selection and breeding distribution of Little Ringed Plover *Charadrius dubius* along the Latium Coast (Italy)]. *Avocetta* **16(1)**: 41-43. In Italian with English summary.
Birkenholz, D.E. & Jenni, D.A. (1964). Observations on the Spotted Rail and Pinnated Bittern in Costa Rica. *Auk* **81**: 558-559.
Birkenmajer, K. (1969). [Observations of Ivory Gull, *Pagophila eburnea* (Phipps) in the south of West Spitsbergen (Vestspitsbergen)]. *Acta Orn., Varszawa* **11(13)**: 461-476. In Polish.
Birkenmajer, K. & Skreslet, S. (1963). Breeding colony of Ivory Gulls in Torell Land, Vestspitsbergen. *Norsk Polarinstitutt Arbok* **1962**: 120-126.
Birkhead, T.R. (1976). *The Breeding Biology and Survival of Guillemots* Uria aalge. PhD thesis, University of Oxford, Oxford.
Birkhead, T.R. (1977). The effect of habitat and density on breeding success in the Common Guillemot *Uria aalge*. *J. Anim. Ecol.* **46**: 751-764.
Birkhead, T.R. (1978). Behavioural adaptations to high density nesting in the Common Guillemot *Uria aalge*. *Anim. Behav.* **26**: 321-331.
Birkhead, T.R. (1985a). Auk. Pp. 27-28 in: Campbell & Lack (1985).
Birkhead, T.R. (1985b). Coloniality and social behaviour in the Atlantic Alcidae. Pp. 355-382 in: Nettleship & Birkhead (1985).
Birkhead, T.R. (1994). How collectors killed the Great Auk. *New Scientist* **141(1927)**: 24-27.
Birkhead, T.R. & Harris, M.P. (1985). Ecological adaptations for breeding in the Atlantic Alcidae. Pp. 205-231 in: Nettleship & Birkhead (1985).
Birkhead, T.R. & Hudson, P.J. (1977). Population parameters for the Common Guillemot *Uria aalge*. *Ornis Scand.* **8**: 145-154.
Birkhead, T.R. & Nettleship, D.N. (1980). Census methods for murres *Uria* species - a unified approach. *Can. Wildl. Serv. Occas. Pap.* **43**: 1-25.
Birkhead, T.R. & Nettleship, D.N. (1981). Reproductive biology of Thick-billed Murres *Uria lomvia*: an inter-colony comparison. *Auk* **98**: 258-269.
Birkhead, T.R. & Nettleship, D.N. (1982). The adaptive significance of egg size and laying date in Thick-billed Murres *Uria lomvia*. *Ecology* **63**: 300-306.
Birkhead, T.R. & Nettleship, D.N. (1984). Egg size, composition and offspring quality in some Alcidae (Aves: Charadriiformes). *J. Zool., London* **202**: 177-194.

Birkhead, T.R. & Nettleship, D.N. (1985). Plumage variation in young Razorbills and Murres. *J. Field Orn.* **56**: 246-250.
Birkhead, T.R. & Nettleship, D.N. (1987a). Ecological relationships between Common Murres *Uria aalge* and Thick-billed Murres *Uria lomvia* at the Gannet Islands, Labrador. I. Morphometrics and timing of breeding. *Can. J. Zool.* **7**: 1621-1629.
Birkhead, T.R. & Nettleship, D.N. (1987b). Ecological relationships between Common Murres *Uria aalge* and Thick-billed Murres *Uria lomvia* at the Gannet Islands, Labrador. II. Breeding success and site characteristics. *Can. J. Zool.* **7**: 1630-1637.
Birkhead, T.R. & Nettleship, D.N. (1987c). Ecological relationships between Common Murres *Uria aalge* and Thick-billed Murres *Uria lomvia* at the Gannet Islands, Labrador. III. Feeding ecology of the young. *Can. J. Zool.* **7**: 1638-1649.
Birkhead, T.R. & Nettleship, D.N. (1995). Arctic Fox influence on a seabird community in Labrador: a natural experience. *Wilson Bull.* **107**: 397-412.
Birkhead, T.R., Johnson, S.D. & Nettleship, D.N. (1985). Extra-pair matings and mate guarding in the Common Murre *Uria aalge*. *Anim. Behav.* **33**: 608-619.
Birrer, S. & Schmid, H. (1989). [Breeding population and distribution of the Lapwing *Vanellus vanellus* in Switzerland, 1985-1988]. *Orn. Beob.* **86(2)**: 145-154. In German with French and English summaries.
Bishop, K.D. (1983). Some notes on non-passerine birds of west New Britain. *Emu* **83**: 235-241.
Bishop, K.D. (1985). Australian Pratincoles in Timor. *Interwader* **5**: 3.
Bishop, K.D. (1988). The Long-legged Pratincole *Stiltia isabella* in Bali. *Kukila* **3(3-4)**: 141.
Bishop, M.A. (1988a). *Factors Affecting Productivity and Habitat Use of Florida Sandhill Cranes: an Evaluation of Three Areas in Central Florida for a Non-migratory Population of Whooping Cranes*. PhD dissertation. University of Florida, Gainesville, Florida.
Bishop, M.A. (1988b). An evaluation of three areas in central Florida as potential reintroduction sites for a non-migratory flock of Whooping Cranes. A preliminary report submitted to the Whooping Crane Recovery Team. University of Florida, Gainesville, Florida. 56 pp.
Bishop, M.A. (1989). First winter count for Black-necked Cranes. *ICF Bugle* **15(2)**: 4-6.
Bishop, M.A. (1991). A new tune for an ancient harmony. *ICF Bugle* **17(4)**: 2-3.
Bishop, M.A. (1993). The Black-necked Crane winter count, 1991-1992. *J. Ecol. Soc.* **3**: 55-64.
Björklund, M. (1994). Phylogenetic relationships among Charadriiformes: reanalysis of previous data. *Auk* **111**: 825-832.
Blaber, S.J.M. (1990). A checklist and notes on the current status of birds of New Georgia, Western Province, Solomon Islands. *Emu* **90**: 205-214.
Blaber, S.J.M. (1993). Waders at Suva Point, Fiji, during a cyclone. *Notornis* **40**: 225-226.
Blaber, S.J.M. & Milton, D.A. (1991). A note on habitat decline and the status of the Spotted Button-quail *Turnix maculosa salomonis* on Guadalcanal, Solomon Islands. *Emu* **91(1)**: 64-65.
Blaber, S.J.M. & Wassenberg, T.J. (1989). Feeding ecology of the piscivorous birds *Phalacrocorax varius*, *P. melanoleucos* and *Sterna bergii* in Moreton Bay, Australia: diets and dependence on trawler discards. *Mar. Biol.* **101**: 1-10.
Black, B.B. & Harris, L.D. (1981). Winter foraging patterns of gulf coast Black Skimmers. *Colonial Waterbirds* **4**: 187-193.
Black, B.B. & Harris, L.D. (1983). Feeding habitat of Black Skimmers wintering on the Florida Gulf coast. *Wilson Bull.* **95**: 404-415.
Black, J. (1919). Pajingo notes. *Emu* **18**: 206-207.
Black, M.S. (1955). Some notes on the Black-billed Gull (*Larus bulleri*) at Lake Rotorua with special reference to the breeding cycle. *Notornis* **6**: 167-170.
Blackburn, A. (1968). The birdlife of Codfish Island. *Notornis* **15(2)**: 51-65.
Blackman, J.G. (1971). Sex determination of Australian Cranes (Gruidae). *Queensland J. Agric. Anim. Sci.* **28**: 281-286.
Blackman, J.G. (1977). *The Development and Application of Aerial Survey Methods for Population and Ecological Studies of the Brolga* Grus rubicundus *(Perry) Gruidae*. MS thesis, James Cook University of North Queensland, Townsville, Australia.
Blake, E.R. (1959). New and rare Colombian birds. *Lozania* **11**: 1-10.
Blake, E.R. (1977). *Manual of Neotropical Birds*. Vol. 1. Spheniscidae (Penguins) to Laridae (Gulls and Allies). The University of Chicago Press, Chicago & London.
Blake, R.W. (1985). A model of foraging efficiency and daily energy budget in the Black Skimmer (*Rynchops nigra*). *Can. J. Zool.* **63**: 42-48.
Blaker, D. (1966). Notes on the sandplovers *Charadrius* in southern Africa. *Ostrich* **37**: 95-102.
Blaker, D. (1967). An outbreak of botulinus poisoning among waterbirds. *Ostrich* **38**: 144-147.
Blakers, M., Davies, S.J.J.F. & Reilly, P.N. (1984). *The Atlas of Australian Birds*. Royal Australasian Ornithologists Union & Melbourne University Press, Carlton, Victoria.
Blanco, D.E. & Canevari, P. (1992). *Censo Neotropical de Aves Acuáticas*. Programa de Ambientes Acuáticos Neotropicales (NWP), Buenos Aires, Argentina.
Blanco, D.E., Banchs, R., Canavari, P. & Osterheld, M. (1993). Critical sites for the Eskimo Curlew (*Numenius borealis*), and other Nearctic grassland shorebirds in Argentina and Uruguay. Wetlands for the Americas report to US Fish & Wildlife Service.
Blanco, D.E., Rodríguez, H. & Pugnali, G. (1992). La importancia de Punta Rasa, Buenos Aires, en la migración del Playero Rojizo (*Calidris canutus*). [The importance of Punta Rasa, Buenos Aires, in the migration of the Red Knot (*Calidris canutus*)]. *Hornero* **13**: 203-206.
Blanco, P., Goossen, J.P., González, H. & Sirois, J. (1993). Occurrences of the Piping Plover in Cuba. *J. Field Orn.* **64(4)**: 520-526. In English with Spanish summary.
den Blanken, G., Boere, G.C. & Nieboer, E. (1981). Primary moult of the Redshank *Tringa totanus* in the Dutch Waddenzee studied by collecting shed feathers; a test. *Ardea* **69**: 115-124.
Blankert, J.J. (1980). [Identification of Great Snipe and occurrence in the Netherlands]. *Dutch Birding* **2(3)**: 106-115. In Dutch with English summary.
Blankinship, D.R. (1976). Studies of Whooping Cranes on the wintering grounds. Pp. 197-206 in: Lewis (1976a).
Blankinship, D.R. (1987). Research and management programs for wintering Whooping Cranes. Pp. 381-385 in: Archibald & Pasquier (1987a).
Blankley, W.O. (1981). Marine food of Kelp Gulls, Lesser Sheathbills and Imperial Cormorants at Marion Island (Subantarctic). *Cormorant* **9(2)**: 77-84.
Blaszyk, P. (1953). Zum Brüten des Austernfischers im Binnenland. *Vogelwelt* **74**: 41 45.
Blechschmidt, K., Peter, H.U., Korte, J., Wink, M., Seibold, I. & Helbig, A.J. (1993). Untersuchungen zur molekularen Systematik der Raubmöwen (Stercorariidae). *Zool. Jb. Syst. Bd.* **120**: 379-387.
Bledsoe, A.H. (1988). Status and hybridization of Clapper and King Rails in Connecticut. *Connecticut Warbler* **8(1)**: 61-65.
Bledsoe, A.H. & Sibley, D. (1985). Patterns of vagrancy of Ross' Gull. *Amer. Birds* **39**: 219-227.
Blem, C.R. (1980). A Paint-billed Crake in Virginia. *Wilson Bull.* **92**: 393-394.
Blitzblau, S. (1990). [Migration of waders along the Carmel Coast, spring 1990]. *Torgos* **8**: 59-68, 73. In Hebrew with English summary.
Block, B., Block, P., Jaschke, W., Litzbarski, B., Litzbarski, H. & Petrick, S. (1993). Komplexer Artenschutz durch extensive Landwirtschaft im Rahmen des Schutzprojektes 'Grosstrappe'. *Nat. Landschaft* **68**: 565-576.
Blodget, B.G. (1978). The effect of off-road vehicles on Least Terns and other shorebirds. *US Natl. Park Serv. Coop. Res. Unit Report* **26**: 1-17.
Blodget, B.G. (1988). The half-century battle for gull control. *Massachusetts Wildlife* **38**: 4-10.
Blokpoel, H. (1977). Gulls and terns nesting in northern Lake Ontario and the upper St. Lawrence River. *Can. Wildl. Serv. Program Note* **75**: 1-2.
Blokpoel, H. (1981). An attempt to evaluate the impact of cannon-netting in Caspian Tern colonies. *Colonial Waterbirds* **4**: 61-67.
Blokpoel, H. & Courtney, P. (1980). Site tenacity in a new Ring-billed Gull colony. *J. Field Orn.* **51**: 1-5.
Blokpoel, H. & Haymes, G.T. (1979a). Origins of Ring-billed Gulls at a new colony. *Bird-Banding* **50**: 210-215.
Blokpoel, H. & Haymes, G.T. (1979b). Small mammals and birds as food items of Ring-billed Gulls on the lower Great Lakes. *Wilson Bull.* **91**: 623-625.
Blokpoel, H. & Scharf, W.C. (1991a). The Ring-billed Gull in the Great Lakes of North America. Pp. 2372-2377 in: Bell *et al.* (1991).
Blokpoel, H. & Scharf, W.C. (1991b). Status and conservation of seabirds nesting in the Great Lakes of North America. Pp. 17-41 in: Croxall (1991).
Blokpoel, H. & Spaans, A.L. (1991). Introductory remarks: superabundance in gulls: causes, problems and solutions. Pp. 2361-2364 in: Bell *et al.* (1991).
Blokpoel, H. & Tessier, G.D. (1986). The Ring-billed Gull in Ontario: a review of a new problem species. *Can. Wildl. Serv. Occas. Pap.* **57**: 1-34.
Blokpoel, H., Blancher, P.J. & Fetterolf, P.M. (1985). On the plumage of nesting Ring-billed Gulls of different ages. *J. Field Orn.* **56**: 113-124.
Blokpoel, H., Boersma, D.C., Hughes, R.A. & Tessier, G.D. (1989). Field observations of the biology of Common Terns and Elegant Terns wintering in Peru. *Colonial Waterbirds* **12**: 90-97.
Blokpoel, H., Boersma, D.C., Hughes, R.A. & Tessier, G.D. (1992). Foraging by larids on sand crabs *Emerita analoga* along the coast of southern Peru. *Ardea* **80**: 99-104.
Blokpoel, H., Morris, R.D. & Tessier, G.D. (1984). Field investigations of the biology of Common Terns wintering in Trinidad. *J. Field Orn.* **55**: 424-434.
Blokpoel, H., Weller, W.F., Tessier, G.D. & Smith, B. (1990). Roof-nesting by Ring-billed Gulls and Herring Gulls in Ontario in 1989. *Ontario Birds* **8**: 55-60.
Blom, E.A.T. (1990). Possible delayed molt in an adult Laughing Gull. *Maryland Birdlife* **46**: 28-29.
Blomert, A.M., Engelmoer, M. & Ntiamoa-Baidu, Y. (1990). The Banc d'Arguin, Mauritania, as a meeting point for Avocets during spring migration. *Ardea* **78(1/2)**: 185-192. In English with Spanish and Dutch summaries.
Blomqvist, D. & Johansson, O.C. (1991). Distribution, reproductive success, and population trends in the Dunlin *Calidris alpina schinzii* on the Swedish west coast. *Ornis Svecica* **1**: 39-46.
Blomqvist, D. & Johansson, O.C. (1994). Double clutches and uniparental care in Lapwing *Vanellus vanellus*, with a comment on the evolution of double-clutching. *J. Avian Biol.* **25(1)**: 77-79.
Blomqvist, D. & Johansson, O.C. (1995). Trade-offs in nest site selection in coastal populations of Lapwings *Vanellus vanellus*. *Ibis* **137(4)**: 550-558.
Blomqvist, S. (1983a). *Bibliography of the Gena* Calidris *and* Limicola. Special Report **3**. Ottenby Bird Observatory, Degerhamn, Sweden.
Blomqvist, S. (1983b). *Bibliography of the Genus* Phalaropus. Special Report **4**. Ottenby Bird Observatory, Degerhamn, Sweden.
Blomqvist, S. & Elander, M. (1981). Sabine's Gull (*Xema sabini*) Ross' Gull (*Rhodostethia rosea*) and Ivory Gull (*Pagophila eburnea*) in the Arctic: a review. *Arctic* **34**: 122-132.
Blomqvist, S. & Elander, M. (1988). King Eider (*Somateria spectabilis*) nesting in association with Long-tailed Skua (*Stercorarius longicaudus*). *Arctic* **41(2)**: 138-142.
Blomqvist, S. & Lindström, Å. (1992). Routes of spring migrant siberian and nearctic Knots *Calidris canutus* diverge over Sweden. Pp. 91-94 in: Piersma & Davidson (1992b).
Blomqvist, S., Frank, A. & Petersson, L.R. (1987). Metals in liver and kidney tissues of autumn-migrating Dunlin *Calidris alpina* and Curlew Sandpiper *Calidris ferriginea* staging at the Baltic Sea. *Mar. Ecol. Prog. Ser.* **35**: 1-13.
Blondel, J. (1963). Le problème du contrôle des effectifs du Goéland argenté (*Larus argentatus michahellis*) en Camargue. *Rev. Ecol. (Terre Vie)* **17**: 301-315.
Blösch, M. (1971). Über den Einfluß von Phenobarbital auf das Brutverhalten der Silbermöwe (*Larus argentatus argentatus* Pontopp). *Z. Tierpsychol.* **28**: 487-493.
Blossom, J.B. (1992). Fecund African Crowned Cranes. *Avicult. Mag.* **98(2)**: 67-70.
Blus, L.J. & Prouty, R.M. (1979). Organochlorine pollutants and population status of Least Terns in South Carolina. *Wilson Bull.* **91**: 62-71.
Blus, L.J. & Stafford, C.J. (1980). Breeding biology and relation of pollutants to Black Skimmers and Gull-billed Terns in South Carolina. *US Fish Wildl. Serv. Spec. Sci. Rep. Wildl.* **230**.
Blus, L.J., Locke, L.N. & Cromartie, E. (1978). Avian cholera and organochlorine residues in an American Oystercatcher. *Estuaries* **1**: 128-129.
Board, R.G. & Perrott, H.R. (1979). The plugged pores of tinamou (Tinamidae) and jacana (Jacanidae) eggshells. *Ibis* **121**: 469-474.
Boates, J.S. (1988). *Foraging and Social Behaviour of the Oystercatcher (*Haematopus ostralegus*) in Relation to Diet Specialization*. PhD thesis, University of Exeter and Cornwall County Council, UK.
Boates, J.S. & Goss-Custard, J.D. (1989). Foraging behaviour of Oystercatchers *Haematopus ostralegus* during a diet switch from worms *Nereis diversicolor* to clams *Scrobicularia plana*. *Can. J. Zool.* **76**: 2225-2231.
Boates, J.S. & Smith, P.C. (1989). Crawling behaviour of the amphipod *Corophium volutator* and foraging by Semipalmated Sandpipers, *Calidris pusila*. *Can. J. Zool.* **67**: 457-462.
Bocage, J.V.B. (1877). *Ornithologie d'Angola*. Imprimerie Nationale, Lisbon.
Bochenski, Z. & Tomek, T. (1991). Late holocene bird fauna from Duza Sowa Cave (south Poland). *Acta Zool. Cracoviensia* **34**: 553-561.
Bock, W.J. (1958). A generic review of the plovers (Charadriinae, Aves). *Bull. Mus. Comp. Zool. Harvard Coll.* **118**: 27-97.
Bock, W.J. (1959). The status of the Semipalmated Plover. *Auk* **76**: 98-100.
Bock, W.J. (1964). The systematic position of the Australian Dotterel, *Peltohyas australis*. *Emu* **63**: 383-404.
Bock, W.J. (1992). Methodology in avian macrosystematics. Pp. 53-72 in: Monk (1992).
Bock, W.J. & McEvey, A. (1969). *Osteology of* Pedionomus torquatus *(Aves: Pedionomidae) and its Allies*. Proceedings Royal Society of Victoria (New Series) **82(2)**. 45 pp.
Boecker, M. (1967). Vergleichende Untersuchungen zur Nahrungs - und Niskökologie der Flußseeschwalbe (*Sterna hirundo* L) und der Küstenseeschwalbe (*Sterna paradisaea* Pont.). *Bonn. zool. Beitr.* **18**: 15-126.
Boecker, M. (1969). Beziehungen zwischen Nistmaterial und Umgebungsvegetation der Nester bei der Flußseeschwalbe. *Bonn. zool. Beitr.* **20**: 125-129.
Boehm, E.F. (1961). Status of Pacific Gull in South Australia. *Emu* **61**: 210.
Boekel, C. (1980). Birds of Victoria River Downs Station and of Varradin, Northern Territory. Part 1. *Austr. Bird Watcher* **8**: 171-193.
Boere, G.C. (1976). The significance of the Dutch Waddenzee in the annual life cycle of arctic, subarctic and boreal waders. Part 1. The function as a moulting area. *Ardea* **64**: 210-291.
Boere, G.C., Roselaar, K. & Engelmoer, M. (1984). The breeding origins of Purple Sandpipers *Calidris maritima* present in the Netherlands. *Ardea* **72**: 101-109.
Boersma, D. & Ryder, J.P. (1983). Reproductive performance and body condition of earlier and later nesting Ring-billed Gulls. *J. Field Orn.* **54**: 374-380.
Boertmann, D., Meltofte, H. & Forchhammer, M. (1991). Population densities of birds in central northeast Greenland. *Dan. Orn. Foren. Tidssk.* **85**: 151-160.
Boesman, P. (1992). Sierlijke Stern te Zeebrugge in juni-juli 1988. [Elegant Tern at Zeebrugge in June-July 1988]. *Dutch Birding* **14**: 161-169. In Dutch with English summary.
Boettcher, R., Haig, S.M. & Bridges, W.C. (1994). Behavioral patterns and nearest neighbor distances among nonbreeding American Avocets. *Condor* **96(4)**: 973-986.
Boggus, T.G. & Whiting, R.M. (1982). Effects of habitat variables on foraging of American Woodcock wintering in east Texas. Pp. 148-153 in: Dwyer & Storm (1982).
Bogliani, G. & Barbieri, F. (1982). Nidificazione di Sterna Comune, *Sterna hirundo* e Fraticello, *S. albifrons*, sul Fiume Po. *Riv. ital. Orn.* **52**: 91-109.
Bogliani, G., Fasola, M., Canova, L. & Saino, N. (1990). Food and foraging rhythm of a specialized Gull-billed Tern population *Gelochelidon nilotica*. *Ethology, Ecology & Evolution* **2**: 175-182.
Bohlen, H.D. (1993). Melanistic Bonaparte's Gull in central Illinois. *Amer. Birds* **47(3)**: 378.
Böhm, D. (1987). [Multiple breeding of Black-headed Plover *Lobivanellus tectus tectus* (Boddaert)]. *Gefiederte Welt* **111(3)**: 73-74. In German.
Bohmke, B.W. ed. (1992). *International Hooded Crane Studbook:* Grus monachus. St. Louis Zoological Park, St. Louis, Missouri.
Boise, C.M. (1976). *Breeding Biology of the Lesser Sandhill Crane* Grus canadensis canadensis *(L.) on the Yukon-Kuskokwim Delta, Alaska*. MSc thesis, University of Alaska, Fairbanks, Alaska.
Boland, J.M. (1990). Leapfrog migration in North American shorebirds: intra- and interspecific examples. *Condor* **92**: 284-290.
Boland, J.M. (1991). An overview of the seasonal distribution of the North American shorebirds. *Wader Study Group Bull.* **62**: 39-43.
Bold, A., Zvonov, B.M. & Seveenmyadag, N. (1995). [Cranes of Mongolia]. Pp. 41-42 in: Halvorson *et al.* (1995). In Russian.
Bolle, C. (1854-1855). Bemerkungen über die Vögel der Canarischen Inseln. *J. Orn.* **2**: 447-462, **3**: 171-181.
Bolle, C. (1857). Mein zweiter Beitrag zur Vogelkunde der Canarischen Inseln. *J. Orn.* **5**: 305-307.
Bollinger, P.B. (1994). Relative effects of hatching order, egg-size variation, and parental quality on chick survival in Common Terns. *Auk* **111**: 263-273.

Bollinger, P.B., Bollinger, E.K. & Malecki, R.A. (1990). Tests of three hypotheses of hatching asynchrony in the Common Tern. *Auk* **107**: 696-706.
Bologna, G. & Petretti, F. (1978). Sur Cavaliere d'Italia (*Himantopus himantopus*). *Riv. ital. Orn.* **48**: 179-180.
Bolster, D.C. & Robinson, S.K. (1990). Habitat use and relative abundance of migrant shorebirds in a western Amazonian site. *Condor* **92**: 239-242.
Bolton, D.A. (1993). Breeding the Peruvian Thick-knee. *Avicult. Mag.* **99(1)**: 24-26.
Bolton, M. (1991). Determinants of chick survival in Lesser Black-backed Gull: relative contributions of egg size and parental quality. *J. Anim. Ecol.* **60**: 949-960.
Bolze, G. (1968). Anordnung und Bau der Herbstschen Körperchen in Limicolen-schnäbeln im Zusammenhang mit der Nahrungsfindung. *Zool. Anz.* **181**: 313-355.
Bomberger, M.L. (1984). Quantitative assessment of the nesting habitat of Wilson's Phalarope. *Wilson Bull.* **96**: 126-128.
Bomford, M. (1978). *The Behaviour of the Banded Dotterel* Charadrius bicinctus. MSc thesis, University of Otago, Dunedin, New Zealand.
Bomford, M. (1986). Breeding displays and calls of the Banded Dotterel (*Charadrius bicinctus*). *Notornis* **33(4)**: 219-232.
Bomford, M. (1988). Breeding of the Banded Dotterel *Charadrius bicinctus*, on the Cass River Delta, Canterbury. *Notornis* **35(1)**: 6-14.
Bond, J. (1971). *Sixteenth Supplement to the Check-list of Birds of the West Indies (1956)*. Academy of Natural Sciences, Philadelphia.
Bond, J. (1973). *Eighteenth Supplement to the Check-list of Birds of the West Indies (1956)*. Academy of Natural Sciences, Philadelphia.
Bond, J. (1980). *Twenty-third Supplement to the Check-list of Birds of the West Indies (1956)*. Academy of Natural Sciences, Philadelphia.
Bond, J. (1984). *Twenty-fifth Supplement to the Check-list of Birds of the West Indies (1956)*. Academy of Natural Sciences, Philadelphia.
Bond, J. (1985). *Birds of the West Indies*. 5th edition. Collins, London.
Bond, J. & Ripley, S.D. (1960). The Black Noddy at Los Roques, Venezuela. *Auk* **77**: 473-474.
Bond, S.I. (1971). Red Phalarope mortality in southern California. *Calif. Birds* **2**: 97.
Bonde, K. (1993). *Birds of Lesotho*. University of Natal Press, Pietermaritzburg, South Africa.
Bongiorno, S.F. (1968). Egg puncturing behavior in Laughing Gulls. *Auk* **85(4)**: 697-699.
Bongiorno, S.F. (1970). Nest-site selection by adult Laughing Gulls (*Larus atricilla*). *Anim. Behav.* **18**: 434-444.
Bonhote, J.L. (1903). Bird migration at some of the Bahama lighthouses. *Auk* **20**: 169-175.
Bonisch, R., Leibl, F. & Mohrlein, E. (1991). [The breeding of the Green Sandpiper (*Tringa ochropus*) in Bavaria]. *Anz. Orn. Ges. Bayern* **30(1/2)**: 11-20. In German with English summary.
Bonnin, J.M. (1982). Conserving lapwings' eggs. *Austr. Bird Watcher* **9(5)**: 177.
Bonnin, J.M. & Angove, R.C. (1989). Plains-wanderers near Robe. *S. Austr. Orn.* **30(8)**: 215-216.
Boobyer, M.G. (1988). Denizens of the desert. *Bokmakierie* **40**: 47-50.
Boobyer, M.G. (1989). *The Eco-ethology of the Karoo Korhaan* Eupodotis vigorsii. MSc thesis, University of Cape Town, Cape Town.
Boobyer, M.G. (1990). The diet of Ludwig's Bustard. *Ostrich* **61**: 152.
Boobyer, M.G. & Hockey, P.A.R. (1994). Dietary opportunism in the Karoo Korhaan: consequence of a sedentary lifestyle in an unpredictable environment. *Ostrich* **65**: 32-38.
Bookhout, T.A. (1995). Yellow Rail (*Coturnicops novaboracensis*). No. **139** in: Poole & Gill (1994-1995).
Bookhout, T.A. & Stenzel, J.R. (1987). Habitat and movements of breeding Yellow Rails. *Wilson Bull.* **99**: 441-447.
Boone, D.L. (1986). *Breeding Biology and Early Life History of the Tufted Puffin* Fratercula cirrhata. MSc thesis, Oregon State University, Corvallis, Oregon.
Bopp, R. (1959). *Das Bläßhuhn (*Fulica atra*)*. Wittenberg - Lutherstadt.
Borkowski, M. (1990). Great Snipe in Poland. *Birding World* **3(2)**: 54-60.
Borodin, A.M., Bannikov, A.G. & Sokolov, V.E. eds. (1984). [*Red Data Book of the USSR: Rare and Endangered Species of Animals and Plants*]. Vol. 1. Animals. 2nd edition. Lesnaya Promyshlennost, Moscow. In Russian.
Borodulina, T.L. (1953a). [The biology of the Common Tern and its importance for the fishing economy]. *Trudy Inst. Morfol. Zhivotnykh, AN SSSR* **9**: 1-17. In Russian.
Borodulina, T.L. (1953b). [On the biology of marsh terns]. *Trudy Inst. Morfol. Zhivotnykh, AN SSSR* **9**: 18-37. In Russian.
Borodulina, T.L. (1960). *Biology and Economic Importance of Gulls and Terns of Southern-USSR Water Bodies*. Transactions of the Institute of Animal Morphology of the Academy of Sciences of the USSR **32**. (English translation 1966). Israel Program for Scientific Translation, Jerusalem. 132 pp.
Boschert, M. & Rupp, J. (1993). [Breeding biology of Curlew *Numenius arquata* at a breeding site in the southern upper Rhine Valley]. *Vogelwelt* **114(5)**: 199-221. In German with English summary.
Bosman, A.L. (1987). *Avian Determinants of Rocky Intertidal Community Structure in South Africa*. PhD thesis, University of Cape Town, Cape Town.
Bosman, A.L. & Hockey, P.A.R. (1988). Life-history patterns of populations of the limpet *Patella granularis*: the dominant roles of food supply and mortality rate. *Oecologia* **75**: 412-419.
Bosman, A.L., Hockey, P.A.R. & Underhill, L.G. (1989). Oystercatcher predation and limpet mortality: the importance of refuges in enhancing the reproductive output of prey populations. *Veliger* **32(2)**: 120-129.
Bossley, M.I. & Boord, S.K. (1992). Seabird-dolphin associations. *S. Austr. Orn.* **31(4)**: 95-96.
Boswall, J. (1978). The birds of the San Benito Islands, Lower California, Mexico. *Bristol Orn.* **11**: 23-30.
Boswall, J. & Barrett, M. (1978). Notes on the breeding birds of Isla Raza, Baja California. *Western Birds* **9**: 93-108.
Boswall, J. & Veprintsev, B.N. (1985). Keys to identifying Little Curlew. *Amer. Birds* **39**: 251-254.
Bottema, S. (1987). A breeding record of the Greater Sand Plover in Syria. *Bull. Orn. Soc. Middle East* **18**: 8-9.
Bottom, M.L. (1984). Effects of Laughing Gull and shorebird predation on intertidal fauna at Cape May, New Jersey. *Estuarine, Coastal and Shelf Science* **18(2)**: 209-220.
Botton, M.L., Loveland, R.E. & Jacobsen, T.R. (1994). Site selection by migratory shorebirds in Delaware Bay, and its relationship to beach characteristics and abundance of horseshoe crab (*Limulus polyphemus*) eggs. *Auk* **111(3)**: 605-616.
Bouche, S. (1991). Partage des ressources et succès reproducteur d'une cologne d'Avocettes à manteau noir *Recurvirostra avosetta*. [Resource partition and reproductive success of an Avocet *Recurvirostra avosetta* colony]. *Alauda* **59(1)**: 39-40.
Boulinier, T. (1988). [Feeding behaviour and employment of time of a pair of Bonxies *Stercorarius skua* parasitizing Puffins *Fratercula arctica*]. *Alauda* **56(4)**: 409-410. In French.
Bourgeois, A. (1977). Quantitative analysis of American Woodcock nest and brood habitat. Pp. 109-118 in: Keppie & Owen (1977).
Bourget, A.A. (1973). Relation of eiders and gulls nesting in mixed colonies in Penobscot Bay, Maine. *Auk* **90(4)**: 809-820.
Bourke, P.A. (1956). Notes on the Whiskered Tern. *Emu* **56**: 339-348.
Bourke, P.A., Lowe, V.T. & Lowe, T.G. (1973). Notes on the Gull-billed Tern. *Austr. Bird Watcher* **5**: 69.
Bourne, G.R. (1993). Differential snail-size predation by Snail Kites and Limpkins. *Oikos* **68(2)**: 217-223.
Bourne, J.M. (1982). Remarks on the status of the Painted, Little and Red-chested Button-quails in the south-east of South Australia. *S. Austr. Orn.* **29(1)**: 5-6.
Bourne, W.R.P. (1976). Seabirds and pollution. Pp. 403-502 in: Johnson, R. ed. (1976). *Marine Pollution*. Academis Press, London.
Bourne, W.R.P. (1991). Arabian seabirds. *Ibis* **133**(Suppl.): 136-137
Bourne, W.R.P. (1993a). The relationship between the Armenian and Heuglin's Gull. Pp. 57-58 in: Aguilar *et al.* (1993).
Bourne, W.R.P. (1993b). The story of the Great Auk *Pinguinis impennis*. *Arch. Nat. Hist.* **20**: 257-278.
Bourne, W.R.P. & Bundy, G. (1990). Records of Brown-headed Gull *Larus brunnicephalus* and Grey-headed Gull *L. cirrocephalus* around Arabia. *Sandgrouse* **12**: 37-42.
Bourne, W.R.P. & Bundy, G. (1993). Post-juvenile moult and western limit of Brown-headed Gull. *Dutch Birding* **15(4)**: 173-176.
Bourne, W.R.P. & Curtis, W.F. (1994). Bonxies, barnacles and bleached blondes. *British Birds* **87(6)**: 289-298.
Bourne, W.R.P. & David, A.C.F. (1983). Henderson Island, central south Pacific, and its birds. *Notornis* **30**: 233-243.
Bourne, W.R.P. & Lee, D.S. (1994). The first record of McCormick's (or the South Polar) Skua for Europe and the northern hemisphere. *Sea Swallow* **43**: 74-76.
Bourne, W.R.P. & Patterson, I.J. (1962). The spring departure of Common Gulls *Larus canus* from Scotland. *Scottish Birds* **2**: 1-15.
Bourne, W.R.P. & Smith, A.J.M. (1974). Threats to Scottish Sandwich Terns. *Biol. Conserv.* **6**: 222-224.
Bourne, W.R.P., Bogan, J.A., Bullock, D., Diamond, A.W. & Feare, C.J. (1977). Abnormal terns, sick sea and shore birds, organochlorines and arboviruses in the Indian Ocean. *Marine Pollution Bull.* **8**: 154-158.
de Bournonville, D. (1964). Observations sur une importante colonie de Goélands d'Audouin *Larus audouinii* Payraudeau au large de la Corse. *Gerfaut* **54**: 439-453.
Bousfield, M.A., Kirkham, I.R. & McRae, R.D. (1986). Breeding of Wilson's Phalarope, *Phalaropus tricolor*, at Churchil, Manitoba. *Can. Field-Nat.* **100**: 392-393.
Bousfield, R. (1986). Wattled Cranes in the Okavango Delta. *The Crowned Crane* **2**(Aug. 1988): 10.
Boutin, J.M. & Métais, M. (1995). *L'Outarde Canepetière*. Eveil Editeur, Saint Yrieix, France.
Bouwman, R.G. (1987). Crab Plover in Turkey in July 1986. *Dutch Birding* **9(2)**: 65-67.
Bowen, B.S. & Kruse, A.D. (1993). Effects of grazing on nesting by Upland Sandpipers in southcentral North Dakota. *J. Wildl. Manage.* **57**: 291-301.
Bowen, D.E. (1977). *Coloniality, Reproductive Success and Habitat Interactions in Upland Samdpipers,* Bartramia longicauda. PhD thesis, Kansas State University, Manhattan, Kansas.
Bowen, P.J. (1979). Brown-chested Wattled Plover *Vanellus superciliosus* at Mwinilunga: a new species for Zambia. *Bull. Zambia Orn. Soc.* **11(2)**: 33-35.
Bowen, P.J. (1980). The Common Pratincole *Glareola pratincola* in Mwinilunga District. *Bull. Zambian Orn. Soc.* **12(2)**: 46.
Bowler, J. & Taylor, J. (1989). An annotated checklist of the birds of Manusela National Park - Seram. (Birds recorded on the operation Raleigh Expedition). *Kukila* **4(1-2)**: 3-29.
Bowman, R.I. (1960). *Report on a Biological Reconnaisance of the Galápagos Islands During 1957*. UNESCO, Paris.
Boyce, M.S. & Miller, R.S. (1985). Ten-year periodicity in Whooping Crane census. *Auk* **102(3)**: 658-660.
Boyd, H. (1962). Mortality and fertility of Eurasian Charadrii. *Ibis* **104**: 368-387.
Boyd, H. (1992). Arctic summer conditions and British Knot numbers: an exploratory analysis. Pp. 144-152 in: Piersma & Davidson (1992b).
Boyd, H.J. & Alley, R. (1948). The function of the head-coloration of the nestling Coot and other nestling Rallidae. *Ibis* **90**: 582-593.
Boyd, J.M. (1956). Fluctuations of the Common Snipe, Jack Snipe and Golden Plover in Tiree, Argyllshire. *Bird Study* **3**: 105-118.
Boyd, R. (1991). First nesting record for the Piping Plover in Oklahoma. *Wilson Bull.* **103**: 305-308.
Boyd, R.L. (1972). *Breeding Biology of the Snowy Plover at Cheyenne Bottoms Wildlife Management area, Barton County, Kansas*. MSc thesis, Kansas State Teachers College, Emporia, Kansas.
Boyd, R.L. & Thompson, B.C. (1985). Evidence for reproductive mixing of Least Tern populations. *J. Field Orn.* **56**: 406-406.
Boyle, H.S. (1917). Field notes on the Seriema (*Chunga burmeisteri*). *Auk* **34(3)**: 294-296.
Boyle, W.J., Paxton, R.O. & Cutler, D.A. (1987). The winter season, Hudson-Delaware Region. *Amer. Birds* **41**: 260-263.
Braaksma, S. (1960). [The spread of the Curlew *Numenius arquata* as a breeding bird]. *Ardea* **48**: 65-90. In Dutch with English summary.
Braaksma, S. (1962). Voorkomen en levensgewoonten van de Kwartelkoning (*Crex crex* L.) *Limosa* **35**: 230-259.
Braby, R., Braby, S.J. & Braby, R.E. (1992). 5000 Damara Terns in the northern Namib Desert: a reassessment of the world population numbers. *Ostrich* **63**: 133-135.
Brackney, A.W. & Bookhout, T.A. (1982). Population ecology of Common Gallinules in southwestern Lake Erie marshes. *Ohio J. Sci.* **82**: 229-237.
Bradbury, J.P. (1981). The evolution of leks. Pp. 138-169 in: Alexander, R.D. & Tinkle, D.W. eds. (1981). *Natural Selection and Social Behaviour*. Chiron Press, New York.
Brader, M. (1991). [The Bar-tailed Godwit (*Limosa lapponica*) in Austria]. *Egretta* **34(2)**: 86-96. In German with English summary.
Bradley, P. (1986). The breeding biology of Audouin's Gull at the Chafarinas Islands. Pp. 221-230 in: MEDMARAVIS & Monbailliu (1986).
Bradley, R.A. & Bradley, D.W. (1993). Wintering shorebirds increase after kelp (Macrocystis) recovery. *Condor* **95**: 372-376.
Bradshaw, C. (1993a). Brown-headed Gulls in Uzbekistan in May 1985. *Dutch Birding* **15**: 69-70.
Bradshaw, C. (1993b). Separating juvenile Little and Baillon's Crakes in the field. *British Birds* **86**: 303-311.
Bradstreet, M.S.W. (1976). *Summer Feeding Ecology of Seabirds in Eastern Lancaster Sound, 1976*. LGL Ltd, Report for Norlands Petroleums, Calgary, Alberta.
Bradstreet, M.S.W. (1977). *Feeding Ecology of Seabirds along Fast-ice Edges in Wellington Channel and Resolute Passage, N.W.T.* LGL Ltd, Report for Polar Gas Project, Toronto, Ontario.
Bradstreet, M.S.W. (1980). Thick-billed Murres and Black Guillemots in the Barrow Strait area, N.W.T., during spring: diets and food availability along ice edges. *Can. J. Zool.* **58**: 2120-2140.
Bradstreet, M.S.W. (1982). Pelagic feeding ecology of Dovekies *Alle alle* in Lancaster Sound and western Baffin Bay. *Arctic* **35**: 126-140.
Bradstreet, M.S.W. (1985). Feeding studies. Pp. 249-296 in: Johnson, S.R. ed. (1985). *Population Estimation, Productivity and Food Habits of Nesting Seabirds at Cape Pierce and the Pribilof Islands, Bering Sea, Alaska*. LGL Ecol. Res. Assoc., Anchorage, Alaska.
Bradstreet, M.S.W. & Brown, R.G.B. (1985). Feeding ecology of the Atlantic Alcidae. Pp. 263-318 in: Nettleship & Birkhead (1985).
Brady, A. (1994). Kleptoparasitism of Long-tailed Jaeger on Wilson's Storm-petrel. *Cassinia* **65**: 19-20.
Bräger, S. (1995). Vorkommen von Tordalk *Alca torda*, Trottellumme *Uria aalge* und Gryllteiste *Cepphus grylle* auf der Ostsee in Schleswig-Holstein. [Abundance and distribution of non-breeding Razorbill *Alca torda*, Common Guillemot *Uria aalge* and Black Guillemot *Cepphus grylle* on the Baltic Sea of Schleswig-Holstein]. *Vogelwelt* **116**: 305-310. In German with English summary.
Brager, S. & Meissner, J. (1990). Does the Black-tailed Godwit (*Limosa limosa*) prefer intensively or extensively managed meadows for reproduction?. *Corax* **13**: 387-393.
Braine, S. (1987). Extension of the breeding range of the African Black Oystercatcher *Haematopus moquini*. *Madoqua* **15(1)**: 87-88.
Braine, S. & Loutit, R. (1987). Hartlaub's Gull breeding at Swakopmund and Walvis Bay in 1983 and 1984. *Laniouturdus* **23**: 80-83.
Braithwaite, D.H. (1950). Notes on the breeding of Variable Oystercatchers. *Notornis* **4**: 22-24.
Brandel, M. (1976). Sumpvipa (*Vanellus leucurus*) antraffad I Sverige. [First record of White-tailed Plover (*Vanellus leucurus*) in Sweden]. *Vår Fågelvärld* **35(4)**: 298-300. In Swedish with English summary.
Brandl, R. & Gorke, M. (1988). How to live in colonies: foraging range and patterns of density around a colony of Black-headed Gulls *Larus ridibundus* in relation to the gulls' energy balance. *Ornis Scand.* **19**: 305-308.
Brandt, H. (1943). *Alaska Bird Trails*. Bird Research Foundation, Cleveland.
Bransbury, J. (1983). A study of the Hooded Plover in the south-east of South Australia. Unpublished report to South Australian Department of Environment and Planning, Adelaide.
Bransbury, J. (1988). The status and distribution of the Hooded Plover in South Australia. Unpublished report to South Australian Department of Environment and Planning, Adelaide.
Bransbury, J. (1990). A late breeding record of the Hooded Plover. *S. Austr. Orn.* **31(2)**: 55-56.
Bransbury, J. (1991). *The Brolga in South-Eastern South Australia*. Department of Enviroment and Planning, South Australia.
Bransbury, J. (1992). Fairy Tern breeding records from south-eastern South Australia. *S. Austr. Orn.* **31**: 97.
Branson, N.J.B.A. & Minton, C.D.T. (1976). Moult, measurements and migrations of the Grey Plover. *Bird Study* **23**: 257-266.
Branson, N.J.B.A., Ponting, E.D. & Minton, C.D.T. (1978). Turnstone migrations in Britain and Europe. *Bird Study* **25**: 181-187.
Branson, N.J.B.A., Ponting, E.D. & Minton, C.D.T. (1979). Turnstone populations on the Wash. *Bird Study* **26**: 47-54.
Braune, B.M. (1987a). Body morphometrics and molt of Bonaparte's Gulls in the Quoddy Region, New Brunswick, Canada. *Condor* **89**: 150-157.
Braune, B.M. (1987b). Seasonal aspects of the diet of Bonaparte's Gulls (*Larus philadelphia*) in the Quoddy Region, New Brunswick, Canada. *Auk* **104**: 167-172.
Braune, B.M. (1989). Autumn migration and comments on the breeding range of Bonaparte's Gull, *Larus philadelphia*, in Eastern North America. *Can. Field-Nat.* **103**: 524-530.
Braune, B.M. & Gaskin, D.E. (1982). Feeding methods and diving rates of migrating larids off Deer Island, New Brunswick. *Can. J. Zool.* **60**: 2190-2197.

Braune, B.M. & Gaskin, D.E. (1987a). A mercury budget for the Bonaparte's Gull during Autumn moult. *Ornis Scand.* **18**: 244-250.
Braune, B.M. & Gaskin, D.E. (1987b). Mercury levels in Bonaparte's Gull (*Larus philadelphia*) during autumn molt in the Quoddy region, New Brunswick, Canada. *Arch. Environm. Contam. Toxicol.* **16**: 539-549.
Braune, B.M. & Hunt, G.L. (1983). Brood reduction in Black-legged Kittiwakes. *Auk* **100**: 469-476.
Bravery, J.A. (1962). Notes on the Australian Pratincole. *North Queensland Nat.* **30(132)**: 6.
Bravery, J.A. (1970). The birds of Atherton Shire, Queensland. *Emu* **70**: 49-63.
Brazier, F.H. (1991a). Mountain Plover sighting near Regina. *Blue Jay* **49(2)**: 88-89.
Brazier, F.H. (1991b). Black-tailed Godwit sighted near Regina - first for interior North America. *Blue Jay* **49(2)**: 90-92.
Brazil, M.A. (1983). A sight record of a Yellow-legged Herring Gull from Kyushu Japan. *Tori* **32**: 112-113.
Brazil, M.A. (1984). Observations on the behaviour and vocalizations of the Okinawa Rail *Rallus okinawae*. *J. Coll. Dairying (Ebetsu)* **10**: 437-449.
Brazil, M.A. (1985). Notes on the Okinawa Rail *Rallus okinawae*: observations at night and at dawn. *Tori* **33**: 125-127.
Brazil, M.A. (1991). *The Birds of Japan*. Christopher Helm, London.
Brazil, M.A. (1994). Arasaki: Japan's wintering crane capital. *Birding World* **7**: 67-70.
Brazil, M.A. & Ikenaga, H. (1987). The Amami Woodcock *Scolopax mira*: its identity and identification. *Forktail* **3**: 3-16.
Brazil, M.A. & Moores, N. (1993). The importance of the Japanese wetlands as wintering grounds for the endangered Saunders's Gull *Larus saundersi*. *Forktail* **8**: 113-118.
Brearey, D.M. (1979). The breeding biology and foraging behaviour of the Turnstone *Arenaria interpres* in Finland. *Wader Study Group Bull.* **26**: 24. (Abstract).
Brearey, D.M. & Hildén, O. (1985). Nesting and egg-predation by Turnstones *Arenaria interpres* in larid colonies. *Ornis Scand.* **16**: 283-292.
Breckenridge, W.J. (1966). Dovekie on Little Diomede Island, Alaska. *Auk* **83**: 680.
Breese, D., Tershy, B.R. & Craig, D.P. (1993). Craveri's Murrelet: confirmed nesting and fledging age at San Pedro Mártir Island, Gulf of California. *Colonial Waterbirds* **16**: 92-94.
Bregnballe, T. (1986). [Icelandic Redshanks *Tringa totanus robusta* at Esbjerg 1965/66-1984/85]. *Dan. Orn. Foren. Tidssk.* **80**: 103-112. In Danish with English summary.
Bregnballe, T., Halberg, K., Hansen, L.N., Petersen, I.K. & Thorup, O. (1990). *Ornithological Winter Surveys on the Coast of Tanzania 1988-89*. ICBP Study Report **43**, Cambridge.
Bregulla, H.L. (1987). Zur Biologie des Kagu, *Rhinochetus jubatus*. *Zool. Garten* **57(5/6)**: 349-365. In German with English and French summary.
Bregulla, H.L. (1992). *Birds of Vanuatu*. Anthony Nelson, Oswestry, UK.
Breiehagen, T. (1989). Nesting biology and mating system in an alpine population of Temminck's Stint *Calidris temminckii*. *Ibis* **131(3)**: 389-402.
Breife, B. (1989). [Mass migration of Pomarine Skuas *Stercorarius pomarinus* in southern Scandinavia. Are they related to lemming cycles in the high Arctic of Russia?]. *Calidris* **18(1)**: 3-10. In Swedish with English summary.
Breife, B. & Alind, P. (1990). [First record of Red-necked Stint, *Calidris ruficollis*, in Sweden]. *Vår Fågelvärld* **49(1)**: 27-31. In Swedish with English summary.
Bremond, J.C. & Aubin, T. (1992). The role of amplitude modulation in distress-call recognition by the Black-headed Gull (*Larus ridibundus*). *Ethology, Ecology & Evolution* **4**: 187-191.
Brennan, L.A., Finger, M.A., Buchanan, J.B., Schick, C.T. & Herman, S.G. (1990). Stomach contents of Dunlins collected in western Washington. *Northwestern Naturalist* **71**: 99-102.
Brenning, U. (1989). Der Zug des Alpenstrandläufers (*Calidris alpina*) auf der Grundlage von Beringungen, Wiederfunden und Kontrollen in der DDR. *Ber. Vogelwarte Hiddensee* **9**: 16-33.
Brent, R., Rasmussen, J.G., Bech, C. & Martini, S. (1983). Temperature dependence of ventilation and O_2 extraction in the Kittiwake, *Rissa tridactyla*. *Experientia* **39**: 1092-1093.
Brewster, C. (1994). Apparent influx of several species to the Tswapong South area of eastern Botswana in the 1993/94 summer. *Babbler* **28**: 35-36.
Briain, M.O. & Farrelly, P. (1990). Breeding biology of Little Terns at Newcastle, Co. Wicklow and the impact of conservation action, 1985-1990. *Irish Birds* **4**: 149-168.
Brichetti, P. (1986). Beccapesci *Sterna sandvicensis*. *Ricerche Biol. Selvaggina* **9**(Suppl.): 83-92.
Brichetti, P. & Foschi, U. (1985). Prima nidificazione di Sterna del Rüppel *Sterna bengalensis*, in Italia e attuale frequenza nel Mediterraneo occidentale. *Riv. ital. Orn.* **55(3-4)**: 161-170.
Brichetti, P. & Foschi, U. (1987). The Lesser Crested Tern in the western Mediterranean and Europe. *British Birds* **80**: 276-280.
Briggs, K. (1983). The distribution and reproduction of Ringed Plovers breeding coastally and inland in north-west England. *Bird Study* **30**: 222-228.
Briggs, K.B. (1984a). The breeding ecology of coastal and inland Oystercatchers in north Lancashire. *Bird Study* **31**: 141-147.
Briggs, K.B. (1984b). Repeated polygyny by Oystercatchers. *Wader Study Group Bull.* **40**: 42-44.
Briggs, K.T., Ainley, D.G., Spear, L.B., Adams, P.B. & Smith, S.E. (1987). Distribution and diet of Cassin's Auklet and Common Murre in relation to central California upwellings. Pp. 982-990 in: *Proc. XIX Int. Orn. Congr.* Ottawa, 1986.
Briggs, K.T., Dettman, K.F., Lewis, D.B. & Tyler, W.B. (1984). Phalaropes feeding in relation to autumn upwelling off California. In: Nettleship *et al.* (1984).
Briggs, K.T., Tyler, W.B., Lewis, D.B. & Carlson, D.R. (1987). Bird communities at sea off California: 1975 to 1983. *Studies in Avian Biology* **11**: 1-74.
Briggs, K.T., Tyler, W.B., Lewis, D.B. & Dettman, K.F. (1983). *Seabirds of Central and Northern California, 1980-1983: Status, Abundance and Distribution. Investigator's Final Report, Marine Mammal and Seabird Study, Central and Northern California*. Vol 3. Part 3. Minerals Management Service, US Department Interior, Pacific OCS Region, Los Angeles, California.
Briggs, S.V. (1989). Food addition, clutch size and the timing of laying in American Coots. *Condor* **91**: 493-494.
Bright, J. (1935a). Some habits of the Southern Stone-curlew. *Emu* **34**: 159-163.
Bright, J. (1935b). Notes on a few birds of the Rochester District. *Emu* **34**: 295.
Bright, J. & Taysom, A.R. (1932). Birds of Lake Cooper, Victoria, and surroundings. *Emu* **32**: 42-48.
Brindley, E. & del Nevo, A. (1994a). Little Gull. *Larus minutus*. Pp. 284-285 in: Tucker & Heath (1994).
Brindley, E. & del Nevo, A. (1994b). Sandwich Tern. *Sterna sandvicensis*. Pp. 296-297 in: Tucker & Heath (1994).
Brinkman, J. (1980). Greater Sand Plover *Charadrius leschenaultii* near Korba, Tunisia. *Dutch Birding* **1(4)**: 106.
Britt, T.L. (1971). *Studies of Woodcock on the Louisiana Wintering Ground*. MSc thesis, Louisiana State University, Baton Rouge, Louisiana.
Britton, D. (1980). Identification of Sharp-tailed Sandpipers. *British Birds* **73(8)**: 333-345.
Britton, P.L. (1970). Some non-passerine bird weights from East Africa. *Bull. Brit. Orn. Club* **90**: 142-144, 152-154.
Britton, P.L. (1971). Breeding sea-birds at the Kiunga Islands, Kenya. *Ibis* **113**: 364-366.
Britton, P.L. (1977). The Madagascar Pratincole *Glareola ocularis* in Africa. *Scopus* **1(4)**: 94-97.
Britton, P.L. ed. (1980). *Birds of East Africa. Their Habitat, Status and Distribution*. East African Natural History Society, Nairobi.
Britton, P.L. (1982a). Identification of sand plovers. *British Birds* **75(2)**: 94-96.
Britton, P.L. (1982b). Identification of White-cheeked Tern. *Dutch Birding* **4(2)**: 55-57.
Britton, P.L. & Britton, H.A. (1974). Pomarine Skua on the Kenya coast. *Bull. East Afr. Nat. Hist. Soc.* **1974**: 4-5.
Britton, P.L. & Brown, L.H. (1974). The status and breeding behaviour of east African Lari. *Ostrich* **45**: 63-82.
Britton, P.L. & Osborne, T.O. (1976). The race of *Sterna bergii* in Kenya. *Bull. Brit. Orn. Club* **96**: 132-134.
Brock, K.J. (1990). Temporal separation of certain adult and juvenile shorebirds during fall migration. *Indiana Audubon Quarterly* **68**: 67-74.
Brodkorb, P. (1953). A Pliocene gull from Florida. *Wilson Bull.* **65**: 94-96.
Brodkorb, P. (1967). Catalogue of fossil birds. *Bull. Florida State Mus. Biol. Sci.* **11**: 155-156.
Broekhuysen, G.J. (1948). Breeding record of the Blacksmith Plover *Hoplopterus armatus* for the neighbourhood of Capetown. *Ostrich* **19**: 237-239.
Broekhuysen, G.J. (1964). A description and discussion of threat and anxiety behaviour of *Burhinus capensis* (Lichtenstein) during incubation. *Zool. Med.* **39**: 240-248.
Broekhuysen, G.J. & Elliott, C.C.H. (1974). Hartlaub's Gulls breeding on the roof of a building. *Bokmakierie* **26**: 66-67.
Broekhuysen, G.J. & Macleod, J.G.R. (1948). Avocets (*Recurvirostra avosetta*) breeding in the vicinity of Cape Town. *Ostrich* **19(2)**: 148-149.
Broekhuysen, G.J. & Macnae, W. (1949). Observations on the birds of Tristan da Cunha Islands and Gough Island in February and early March, 1948. *Ardea* **37**: 97-113.
Broekhuysen, G.J. & Stanford, W.P. (1953). Notes on the displacement activities of the male Painted Snipe near its nest. *Ostrich* **24**: 182-183.
Broekhuysen, G.J. & Stanford, W.P. (1955). Display in Ringed Plover (*Charadrius hiaticula*) while in the winter quarter. *Ostrich* **26**: 41-43.
Broekhuysen, G.J., Lestrange, G.K. & Myburgh, N. (1964). The nest of the Red-chested Flufftail (*Sarothrura rufa* Vieillot). *Ostrich* **35**: 117-120.
Brogger-Jensen, S. (1977). First record of Temminck's Stint in Zambia. *Bull. Zambia Orn. Soc.* **9(1)**: 23.
Brook, D. & Beck, J.R. (1972). Antarctic Petrels, Snow Petrels and South Polar Skuas breeding in the Theron Mountains. *Bull. Brit. Antarct. Surv.* **27**: 131-137.
Brooke, R.K. (1967). On the food of the Senegal Wattled Plover. *Ostrich* **38**: 202-203.
Brooke, R.K. (1968). On the distribution, movements and breeding of the Lesser Reedhen *Porphyrio alleni* in southern Africa. *Ostrich* **39**: 259-262.
Brooke, R.K. (1974). The Spotted Crake *Porzana porzana* (Aves: Rallidae) in south-central and southern Africa. *Durban Mus. Novit.* **10**: 43-52.
Brooke, R.K. (1975). Cooperative breeding, duetting, allopreening and swimming in the Black Crake. *Ostrich* **46**: 190-191.
Brooke, R.K. (1976). Field discrimination of *Larus fuscus* and *L. dominicanus*. *Ibis* **118**: 594.
Brooke, R.K. (1978). The *Catharacta* skuas (Aves: Laridae) occurring in South African waters. *Durban Mus. Novit.* **11(18)**: 295-308.
Brooke, R.K. (1984a). *South African Red Data Book - Birds*. South African National Scientific Programmes Report **97**. Council for Scientific and Industrial Research, Pretoria.
Brooke, R.K. (1984b). Taxonomic subdivisions within the Heliornithidae. *Ostrich* **55(3)**: 171-173.
Brooke, R.K. & Cooper, J. (1979a). The distinctiveness of Southern African *Larus dominicanus* (Aves: Laridae). *Durban Mus. Novit.* **12**: 27-37.
Brooke, R.K. & Cooper, J. (1979b). What is the feeding niche of the Kelp Gull in South Africa? *Cormorant* **7**: 27-29.
Brooke, R.K. & Dowsett, R.J. (1969). The original name of the bustard *Eupodotis afra*. *Bull. Brit. Orn. Club* **89**: 103-104.
Brooke, R.K. & Vernon, C.J. (1988). Historical records of the Wattled Crane *Bugeranus carunculatus* (Gmelin) in the Cape Province and the Orange Free State, South Africa. *Ann. Cape Prov. Mus. (Nat. Hist.)* **16(15)**: 363-371.
Brooke, R.K., Avery, G. & Brown, P.C. (1982). First specimen of the nominate race of the Kelp Gull *Larus dominicanus* in Africa. *Cormorant* **10**: 117.
Brooker, M.G., Ridpath, M.G., Estbergs, A.J., Bywater, J., Hart, D.S. & Jones, M.S. (1979). Bird observations on the north-western Nullarbor Plain and neighbouring regions, 1967-1978. *Emu* **79**: 176-190.
Brooks, D.J., Evans, M.I., Martins, R.P. & Porter, R.F. (1987). The status of birds in North Yemen and the records of the OSME Expedition in autumn 1985. *Sandgrouse* **9**: 4-66.
Brooks, D.M. (1995). Ecological partitioning between Seriema species in the Paraguayan Chaco with comments on *Chunga* biology. Page 11 in: *V Congreso de Ornitología Neotropical*. Sociedad de Biología del Paraguay, Asunción. (Abstract).
Brooks, W.S. (1915). Notes on birds from east Siberia and arctic Alaska. *Bull. Mus. Comp. Zool.* **59**: 361-413.
Brooks, W.S. (1967). Food and feeding habits of autumn migrant shorebirds at a small midwestern pond. *Wilson Bull.* **79**: 307-315.
Broome, A. (1987). Identification of juvenile Pomarine Skua. *British Birds* **80(9)**: 426-427.
Brosselin, M. (1968). Observation d'un Courlis à bec grêle *Numenius tenuirostris* en Vendée. *Nos Oiseaux* **29**: 274.
Brosset, A. (1963). La reproduction des oiseaux de mer des Îles Galápagos en 1962. *Alauda* **31**: 81-109.
Brosset, A. (1979). Le cycle de reproduction de la glaréole, *Glareola nuchalis*: ses determinants écologiques et comportementaux. [The breeding cycle of *Glareola nuchalis*: its ecological and behavioural determinants]. *Rev. Ecol. (Terre Vie)* **33(1)**: 95-108. In French with English summary.
Brosset, A. & Érard, C. (1986). *Les Oiseaux des Régions Forestières du Nord-est du Gabon*. Vol. 1. Société Nationale du Protection de la Nature, Paris.
Brosset, A. & Olier, A. (1966). Les îles Chaffarines, lieu de reproduction d'une importante colonie de Goélands d'Audouin, *Larus audouinii*. *Alauda* **34**: 187-190.
Brothers, N.P. & Skira, I.J. (1984). The Weka on Macquarie Island. *Notornis* **31**: 145-154.
Broun, M. (1941). Gulls eat fruit of the cabbage palmetto. *Auk* **58(4)**: 579.
Brouwer, A., Spaans, A.L., de Wit, A.A.N. (1995). Survival of Herring Gull *Larus argentatus* chicks: an experimental analysis of the need for early breeding. *Ibis* **137**: 272-278.
Brouwer, J. (1991). Mixed breeding of waders at Bendigo Sewage Farm, Victoria. *Stilt* **19**: 19-23.
Brouwer, J. & Garnett, S.T. eds. (1990). *Threatened Birds of Australia. An Annotated List*. RAOU Report **68**. Royal Australasian Ornithologists' Union, Victoria.
Brown, A. (1977). Hartlaub's Gulls and Swift Terns. *Promerops* **129**: 4.
Brown, A. (1990). Hartlaub's Gull breeding inland. *Promerops* **192**: 11.
Brown, A. (1992). Unusually large clutch for Threebanded Plover. *Promerops* **202**: 8.
Brown, A.F. (1993). The status of Golden Plover *Pluvialis apricaria* in the south Pennines. *Bird Study* **40(3)**: 196-202.
Brown, B. (1980). A Great Knot in Manukau Harbour. *Notornis* **27(1)**: 91.
Brown, C. & Ward, D. (1990). The morphology of the syrinx in the Charadriiformes (Aves): possible phylogenetic implications. *Bonn. zool. Beitr.* **41**: 95-107.
Brown, C.J. (1992). The status of cranes in Namibia. Pp. 73-78 in: Porter *et al.* (1992).
Brown, C.J. (1993). The birds of Owambo, Namibia. *Madoqua* **18**: 147-161.
Brown, J.N.B., Verhage, M. & Morris, R.P. (1991). Crab Plovers on Jazirat Abu Al Abyad. *Tribulus* **1(2)**: 13-15. In English with Arabic summary.
Brown, K.M. & Morris, R.D. (1994). The influence of investigator disturbance on the breeding success of Ring-billed Gulls (*Larus delawarensis*). *Colonial Waterbirds* **17(1)**: 7-17.
Brown, L.H. (1948). Notes on birds of the Kabba, Ilorin and N. Benin Provinces of Nigeria. *Ibis* **90**: 525-537.
Brown, L.H. & Britton, P.L. (1980). *The Breeding Seasons of East African Birds*. East Africa Natural History Society, Nairobi.
Brown, M. & Dinsmore, J.D. (1986). Implications of marsh size and isolation for marsh bird management. *J. Wildl. Manage.* **50**: 392-397.
Brown, P.B. (1974). Breeding the Ypecaha Wood Rail at Harewood Bird Garden. *Avicult. Mag.* **80**: 11-13.
Brown, P.P. & Harris, S.W. (1988). Foods found in 103 Red-necked Phalaropes. *Western Birds* **19**: 79-80.
Brown, R.A. & O'Connor, R.J. (1974). Some observations on the relationships between Oystercatchers and cockles *Cardium edule* L. in Strangford Lough. *Irish Nat. J.* **18**: 73 80.
Brown, R.G. & Engleman, D. (1986). First record of Hudsonian Godwit in Panama. *Amer. Birds* **40(3)**: 429.
Brown, R.G. & Engleman, L. (1988). First record of American Avocet from the Republic of Panama. *Amer. Birds* **42(1)**: 28.
Brown, R.G.B. (1962). The aggressive and distraction behaviour of the Western Sandpiper *Ereunetes mauri*. *Ibis* **104**: 1-12.
Brown, R.G.B. (1967a). Species isolation between the Herring Gull, *Larus argentatus* and Lesser Black-backed Gull, *L. fuscus*. *Ibis* **109**: 310-317.
Brown, R.G.B. (1967b). Breeding success and population growth in a colony of Herring and Lesser Black-backed Gulls *Larus argentatus* and *L. fuscus*. *Ibis* **109**: 502-515.
Brown, R.G.B. (1967c). Courtship behavior in the Lesser Black-backed Gull, *Larus fuscus*. *Behaviour* **29**: 122-153.
Brown, R.G.B. (1976a). Ivory Gulls off Labrador in summer. *Amer. Birds* **30**: 774.
Brown, R.G.B. (1976b). The foraging range of breeding Dovekies *Alle alle*. *Can. Field-Nat.* **90**: 166-168.
Brown, R.G.B. (1979). Seabirds of the Senegal upwelling and adjacent waters. *Ibis* **121**: 283-292.
Brown, R.G.B. (1985). The Atlantic Alcidae at sea. Pp. 383-426 in: Nettleship & Birkhead (1985).
Brown, R.G.B. & Gaskin, D.E. (1988). The pelagic ecology of the Grey and Red-necked Phalaropes *Phalaropus fulicarius* and *P. lobatus* in the Bay of Fundy, eastern Canada. *Ibis* **103**: 234-250.
Brown, R.G.B. & Nettleship, D.N. (1981). The biological significance of polynyas to arctic colonial seabirds. Pp. 59-65 in: Sterling, I. & Cleater, H. eds. (1981). *Polynyas in the Canadian Arctic*. Occasional Papers **45**. Canadian Wildlife Service Ottawa, Ontario.
Brown, R.G.B. & Nettleship, D.N. (1984a). Capelin and seabirds in the northwest Atlantic. Pp. 184-194 in: Nettleship *et al.* (1984).
Brown, R.G.B. & Nettleship, D.N. (1984b). The seabirds of northeastern North America: their present status and conservation requirements. Pp. 85-100 in: Croxall, Evans & Schreiber (1984).
Brown, R.G.B., Blurton-Jones, N.G. & Hussell, D.J.T. (1967). The breeding behavior of Sabine's Gull (*Xema sabini*). *Behaviour* **28**: 110-140.
Brown, R.G.B., Davis, T. & Nettleship, D.N. (1974). Ivory Gulls, *Pagophila eburnea*, on the water. *Can. Field-Nat.* **88**: 363-364.

Brown, R.H. (1938). Notes on the Land-Rail. *British Birds* **32**: 13-16.
Brown, R.J. & Brown, M.N. (1977). Observations on Swamphens breeding near Manjimup, Western Australia. *Corella* **1**: 82-83.
Brown, R.J. & Brown, M.N. (1980). Eurasian Coots breeding on irrigation dams near Manjimup, Western Australia. *Corella* **4**: 33-36.
Brown, R.K. (1972). Partial burying of eggs by a Blacksmith Plover. *Ostrich* **43**: 130.
Brown, S. (1987). *Comparative Breeding Biology of the Piping Plover and Spotted Sandpiper*. MSc thesis, University of Michigan, Ann Arbor, Michigan.
Brown, S.C. (1973). Common Sandpiper biometrics. *Wader Study Group Bull.* **11**: 18-23.
Brown, W.Y. (1975a). Parental feeding of young Sooty Terns (*Sterna fuscata* (L.)) and Brown Noddies (*Anous stolidus* (L.)) in Hawaii. *J. Anim. Ecol.* **44**: 731-742.
Brown, W.Y. (1975b). Artifactual clutch size in Sooty Terns and Brown Noddies. *Wilson Bull.* **87**: 115-116.
Brown, W.Y. (1976a). Prolonged parental care in the Sooty Tern and Brown Noddy. *Condor* **78**: 128-129.
Brown, W.Y. (1976b). Growth and fledging age of the Brown Noddy in Hawaii. *Condor* **78**: 263-264.
Brown, W.Y. (1976c). Growth and fledging age of Sooty Tern chicks. *Auk* **93**: 179-183.
Brown, W.Y. (1976d). Egg specific gravity and incubation in the Sooty Tern and Brown Noddy. *Auk* **93**: 371-374.
Brown, W.Y. (1977). Temporal patterns in laying, hatching and incubation of Sooty Terns and Brown Noddies. *Condor* **79**: 133-136.
Brown, W.Y. & Robertson, W.B. (1975). Longevity of the Brown Noddy. *Bird-Banding* **46**: 250-251.
Browne, P.W.P. (1981). Breeding of six Palaearctic birds in southwest Mauritania. *Bull. Brit. Orn. Club* **101(2)**: 306-310.
Browning, M.R. (1977). Geographic variation in Dunlins, *Calidris alpina*, of North America. *Can. Field-Nat.* **91**: 391-393.
Browning, M.R. (1991). Taxonomic comments on the Dunlin, *Calidris alpina*, from northern Alaska and eastern Siberia. *Bull. Brit. Orn. Club* **111**: 140-145.
Brownsmith, C.B. (1978). Sarus Cranes dominant over Brolgas in captivity. *Emu* **78(2)**: 98.
Broyer, J. (1987). L'habitat du Râle de Genêts *Crex crex* en France. *Alauda* **3**: 161-186.
Broyer, J. (1991). Situation des Wachtelkönigs in Frankreich. *Vogelwelt* **122**: 71-77.
Broyer, J. (1994). La régression du Râle de genêts *Crex crex* en France et la gestation des milieux prairiaux. *Alauda* **62**: 1-7.
Broyer, J. & Rocamora, G. (1994). Enquête nationale Râle de genêts 1991-92. Principaux résultats. *Ornithos* **1(1)**: 55-56.
Broyer, J. & Roché, J. (1991). [The nesting population of Curlew *Numenius arquata* in the Saone Basin]. *Alauda* **59(3)**: 129-135. In French with English summary.
Bruce, M.D. (1987). Additions to the birds of Wallacea. 1. Bird records from smaller islands in the Lesser Sundas. *Kukila* **3(1-2)**: 38-44.
Bruemmer, F. (1993). Low, lean killing machine. *Nat. hist.* **102(1)**: 55-60.
Bruijns, W.F.J.M. & Bruijns, M.F.M. (1957). Waarnemingen van de Grauwe Frangepoot, *Phalaropus lobatus* (L.), in de Indische Oceaan. *Ardea* **45(1-2)**: 72-84. In Dutch with English summary.
de Bruin, A.B. & Dietzen, C. (1995). Bonapartes Strandloper bij Holwerd in augustus 1994. [White-Rumped Sandpiper near Holwerd in August 1994]. *Dutch Birding* **17(4)**: 148-151. In Dutch with English summary.
Bruner, P.L. (1972). *Birds of French Polynesia*. BP Bishop Museum, Honolulu.
Bruning, D. (1985). Buttonquail. Pp. 76-77 in: Campbell & Lack (1985).
Bruning, D. & Clare, M.L. (1977). Inca Terns (*Larosterna inca*) at the New York Zoological Park. *Int. Zoo Yb.* **17**: 153-155.
Brunner, H. (1994). Die Jungendentwicklung beim alpinen Mornellregenpfeifer *Charadrius morinellus*. *Limicola* **8(1)**: 15-27.
Bruns, H. (1991). Zur feldornitogische Unterscheidung der Brachvögel, insbesondere des Dünnschnabelbrachvögels (*Numenius tenuirostris*). *Orn. Mitt.* **43**: 269-277.
Brunton, D.H. (1986). Fatal antipredator behavior of a Killdeer. *Wilson Bull.* **98(4)**: 605-607.
Brunton, D.H. (1987). *Reproductive Effort of Male and Female Killdeer (*Charadrius vociferus*)*. PhD dissertation, University of Michigan, Ann Arbor, Michigan.
Brunton, D.H. (1988a). Energy expenditure in reproductive effort of male and female Killdeer (*Charadrius vociferus*). *Auk* **105(3)**: 553-564.
Brunton, D.H. (1988b). Sexual differences in reproductive effort: time-activity budgets of monogamous Killdeer (*Charadrius vociferus*). *Anim. Behav.* **36(3)**: 705-717.
Brunton, D.H. (1988c). Sequential polyandry by a female Killdeer. *Wilson Bull.* **100(4)**: 670-672.
Brunton, D.H. (1990). The effects of nesting stage, sex and type of predator on parental defense by Killdeer (*Charadrius vociferus*): testing models of avian parental defense. *Behav. Ecol. Sociobiol.* **26(3)**: 181-190.
Brush, A.H. (1979). Comparison of egg-white proteins: effect of electrophoretic conditions. *Biochem. Syst. Evol.* **7**: 155-165.
Bruster, K.H. (1990). On the importance of gravel pits for resting Jack Snipe (*Lymnocryptes minimus*). *Hamburger Avifaunist. Beitr.* **22**: 209-212.
Bryan, D.C. (1981). *Territoriality and Pair Bonding in the Limpkin (*Aramus guarauna*)*. MSc thesis, Florida State University, Tallahassee, Florida.
Bryan, D.C. (1992). Limpkin. In: Kale, H.W., Pranty, B., Stith, B. & Biggs, W. eds. (1992). An atlas of Florida breeding birds. Final report. Non-game Wildlife Program, Florida Game and Fresh Water Fish Commission, Tallahassee, Florida.
Bryan, D.C. (1996). Limpkin. In: Rodgers, Kale & Smith (1996).
Bryant, C.E. (1940a). A note on the Australian Dotterel. *Emu* **39**: 153-155.
Bryant, C.E. (1940b). Photography in the swamps: the Eastern Swamphen. *Emu* **39**: 236-239.
Bryant, C.E. (1942). Photography in the swamps: the Marsh Crake. *Emu* **42**: 31-35.
Bryant, C.E. (1947). Notes on avocets nesting near Melbourne. *Emu* **46**: 241-245.
Bryant, C.E. (1948). More observations on nesting avocets. *Emu* **48**: 89-92.
Bryant, C.E. & Amos, B. (1949). Notes on the crakes of the genus *Porzana* around Melbourne, Victoria. *Emu* **48**: 249-275.
Bub, H. (1962). Planberingungen am Sandregenpfeifer (*Charadrius hiaticula*). *J. Orn.* **103**: 243-249.
Bub, H. (1985a). Avocet. Pp. 31-33 in: Campbell & Lack (1985).
Bub, H. (1985b). Ibisbill. Page 300 in: Campbell & Lack (1985).
Buchanan, J.B. (1988). Migration and winter populations of Greater Yellowlegs, *Tringa melanoleuca*, in western Washington. *Can. Field-Nat.* **102(4)**: 611-616.
Buchanan, J.B., Herman, S.G. & Bulger, J.B. (1991). Observations of courtship and copulatory behavior of the Snowy Plover in the Western Great Basin. *Northwestern Naturalist* **72**: 72-74.
Buchanan, J.B., Schick, C.T., Brennan, L.A. & Herman, S.G. (1988). Merlin predation on wintering Dunlins: hunting success and Dunlin escape tactics. *Wilson Bull.* **100**: 108-118.
Bucher, E.H. & Nores, M. (1988). Present status of birds in steppes and savannas of northern and central Argentina. Pp. 71-79 in: Goriup (1988).
Bucher, J.E. (1978). On sexing American Avocets and Long-billed Curlews. *Inl. Bird Banding News* **50(1)**: 15-18.
Buckley, F. (1980). Broad-billed Sandpiper in Co. Cork. *Irish Birds* **1(4)**: 548-54.
Buckley, F.G. & Buckley, P.A. (1972). The breeding ecology of Royal Terns (*Sterna (Thalasseus) maxima maxima*). *Ibis* **114**: 344-359.
Buckley, F.G. & Buckley, P.A. (1974). Comparative feeding ecology of wintering adult and juvenile Royal Terns (Aves: Laridae, Sterninae). *Ecology* **55**: 1053-1063.
Buckley, F.G. & Buckley, P.A. (1979). Do Aleutian Terns exhibit extraordinary anti-predator adaptations? *Proc. Colonial Waterbird Group* **3**: 99-107.
Buckley, F.G. & Buckley, P.A. (1982). Microenvironmental determinants of success in saltmarsh-nesting Common Terns. *Colonial Waterbirds* **5**: 39-48.
Buckley, F.G., Gochfeld, M. & Buckley, P.A. (1978). Breeding Laughing Gulls return to Long Island. *Kingbird* **28**: 202-207.
Buckley, P.A. & Buckley, F.G. (1970). Color variation in the soft parts and down of Royal Tern chicks. *Auk* **87**: 1-13.
Buckley, P.A. & Buckley, F.G. (1972). Individual egg and chick recognition by adult Royal Terns *Sterna maxima maxima*. *Anim. Behav.* **20**: 457-462.
Buckley, P.A. & Buckley, F.G. (1977). Hexagonal packing of Royal Tern nests. *Auk* **94**: 36-43.
Buckley, P.A. & Buckley, F.G. (1980). Population and colony site trends of Long Island waterbirds for five years in the mid 1970's. *Trans. Linn. Soc., New York* **9**: 23-56.
Buckley, P.A. & Buckley, F.G. (1981). The endangered status of North American Roseate Terns. *Colonial waterbirds* **4**: 166-173.
Buckley, P.A. & Buckley, F.G. (1984a). Cayenne Tern new to North America, with comments on its relationship to Sandwich Tern. *Auk* **101**: 396-398.
Buckley, P.A. & Buckley, F.G. (1984b). Seabirds of the North and Middle Atlantic Coast of the United States: their status and conservation. Pp. 101-133 in: Croxall, Evans & Schreiber (1984).
Buckley, P.A. & Hailman, J.P. (1970). Black-headed Gull and five species of terns skimming water. *British Birds* **63**: 210-212.
Buckley, P.A., Foster, M.S., Morton, E.S., Ridgely, R.S. & Buckley, F.G. eds. (1985). *Neotropical Ornithology*. Ornithological Monographs **36**. American Ornithologists' Union, Washington, D.C.
Buckton, S. & Morris, P. (1993). Observations of Wood Snipe *Gallinago nemoricola* in Nepal. *Bull. Oriental Bird Club* **17**: 31-35.
Buddle, G.A. (1941a). The birds of the Poor Knights. *Emu* **41**: 56-68.
Buddle, G.A. (1941b). Photographing the Spotless Crake. *Emu* **41**: 130-134.
Buden, D.W. (1987). The birds of Cat Island, Bahamas. *Wilson Bull.* **99**: 579-600.
Buhnerkempe, J.E. & Westemeier, R.L. (1988). Breeding biology and habitat of Upland Sandpipers on Prairie-chicken Sanctuaries in Illinois. *Trans. Illinois State Acad. Sci.* **81(1-2)**: 153-162.
Buick, A. & Paton, D.C. (1989). Impact of off-road vehicles on the nesting success of Hooded Plovers *Charadrius rubricollis* in the Coorong region of South Australia. *Emu* **89**: 212-276.
Bukacinska, M. & Bukacinski, D. (1993). The effect of habitat structure and density of nests on territory size and territorial behavior in the Black-headed Gull (*Larus ridibundus* L.). *Ethology* **94**: 306-316.
Buker, J.B. & Groen, N.M. (1989). [Distribution of Black-tailed Godwits *Limosa limosa* in different grassland types during the breeding season]. *Limosa* **62**: 183-190. In Dutch with English summary.
Bull, P.C. (1948). Field notes on waders in the south-west Pacific with special reference to the Russell Islands. *Emu* **47**: 165-176.
Bull, P.C., Gaze, P.B. & Robertson, C.J.R. (1985). *The Atlas of Bird Distribution in New Zealand*. Ornithological Society of New Zealand, Wellington.
Buller, W.L. (1878). Further notes on the ornithology of New Zealand. *Trans. New Zealand Inst.* **10**: 201-209.
Bullock, I. (1990). *Birds of the Republic of Seychelles*. Seychelles Ministry of Education & ICBP.
Bullock, I.D. & Gomersall, C.H. (1981). The breeding populations of terns in Orkney and Shetland in 1980. *Bird Study* **28**: 187-200.
Bundy, G. (1976). *The Birds of Libya. An Annotated Checklist*. BOU Chek-list **1**. British Ornithologists' Union, London.
Bundy, G. (1982). Field characters of first-year White-winged Black Terns. *British Birds* **75(3)**: 129-131.
Bundy, G. (1983). Call of Pintail Snipe. *British Birds* **76(12)**: 575-576.
Bundy, G. (1988). Immature White-cheeked Tern helping to defend chicks. *British Birds* **79**: 295-296.
Bunni, M.K. (1959). *The Killdeer,* Charadrius v. vociferus *Linnaeus, in the Breeding Season: Ecology, Behavior and the Development of Homoiothermism*. PhD thesis, University of Michigan, Ann Arbor, Michigan.
Burbidge, A.A. & Fuller, P.J. (1982). Banded Stilt breeding at Lake Barlee, Western Australia. *Emu* **82(4)**: 212-216.
Burbidge, A.A. & Fuller, P.J. (1989). Numbers of breeding seabirds on Pelsaert Island, Houtman Abrolhos, Western Australia. *Corella* **13**: 57-61.
Burcar, K. (1992). Purple Sandpiper: 4 November 1991, Sheboygan Co., Northpoint Park. *Passenger Pigeon* **54(4)**: 355-356.
Bureau, L. (1879). Récherches sur la mue du bec des oiseaux de la famile des Mermonides. *Bull. Soc. Zool. Fr.* **4**: 1-68.
Burger, A.E. (1978). Terrestrial invertebrates: a food resource for birds at Marion Island. *S. Afr. J. Antarct. Res.* **8**: 87-99.
Burger, A.E. (1979). Breeding biology, moult and survival of Lesser Sheathbills *Chionis minor* at Marion Island. *Ardea* **67**: 1-14. In English with Dutch summary.
Burger, A.E. (1980a). Sexual size dimorphism and aging character in the Lesser Sheathbill at Marion Island. *Ostrich* **51(1)**: 39-43.
Burger, A.E. (1980b). An analysis of the displays of Lesser Sheathbills *Chionis minor*. *Z. Tierpsychol.* **52(4)**: 381-396.
Burger, A.E. (1980c). *Behavioural Ecology of Lesser Sheathbills,* Chionis minor, *at Marion Island*. PhD dissertation, University of Cape Town, Cape Town.
Burger, A.E. (1981a). Food and foraging behaviour of Lesser Sheathbills at Marion Island. *Ardea* **69**: 167-180.
Burger, A.E. (1981b). Time budgets, energy needs and kleptoparasitism in breeding Lesser Sheathbills (*Chionis minor*). *Condor* **83(2)**: 106-112.
Burger, A.E. (1982). Foraging behaviour of Lesser Sheathbills *Chionis minor* exploiting invertebrates on a sub-Antarctic island. *Oecologia* **52(2)**: 236-245.
Burger, A.E. (1984). Winter territoriality in Lesser Sheathbills on breeding grounds at Marion Island. *Wilson Bull.* **96(1)**: 20-33.
Burger, A.E. (1991). Sneak thief of the sub-Antarctic. *Afr. Wildl.* **45**: 188-192.
Burger, A.E. (1995). Marine distribution, abundance and habitats of Marbled Murrelets in British Columbia. Pp. 295-312 in: Ralph *et al.* (1995).
Burger, A.E. & Millar, R.P. (1980). Seasonal changes of sexual and territorial behaviour and plasma testosterone levels in male Lesser Sheathbills (*Chionis minor*). *Z. Tierpsychol.* **52(4)**: 397-406.
Burger, A.E. & Piatt, J.F. (1990). Flexible time budgets in breeding Common Murres: buffers against variable prey abundance. Pp. 71-83 in: Sealy (1990).
Burger, A.E. & Powell, D.W. (1990). Diving depth and diet of Cassin's Auklet at Reef Island, British Columbia. *Can. J. Zool.* **68**: 1572-1577.
Burger, A.E. & Simpson, M. (1986). Diving depths of Atlantic Puffins and Common Murres. *Auk* **103**: 828-830.
Burger, J. (1967). Roosting behavior of the Bonaparte's Gull. *Kingbird* **17**: 4.
Burger, J. (1971). A method for marsh trapping breeding Franklin's Gulls. *Bird-Banding* **42**: 78-79.
Burger, J. (1972a). The use of a fish-eye lens to study nest placement in Franklin's Gulls. *Ecology* **53**: 362-364.
Burger, J. (1972b). Dispersal and post-fledgling survival of Franklin's Gull. *Bird-Banding* **43**: 267-275.
Burger, J. (1973a). Competition for nest sites between Franklin's Gull and the American Coot. *Wilson Bull.* **85**: 449-451.
Burger, J. (1973b). Egg size and shell thickness in the Franklin's Gull. *Auk* **90**: 423-426.
Burger, J. (1974a). Breeding adaptations of the Franklin's Gull (*Larus pipixcan*) to a marsh habitat. *Anim. Behav.* **22**: 521-567.
Burger, J. (1974b). Breeding biology and ecology of the Brown-hooded Gull in Argentina. *Auk* **91(3)**: 601-613.
Burger, J. (1976a). Nest-site selection in the Black-headed Gull, *Larus ridibundus*. *Bird Study* **23**: 27-32.
Burger, J. (1976b). Daily and seasonal activity patterns in breeding Laughing Gulls. *Auk* **93(2)**: 308-323.
Burger, J. (1977a). The role of visibility in the nesting behavior of 5 species of *Larus* gulls. *J. Comp. Physiol. Psychol.* **91**: 1347-1358.
Burger, J. (1977b). Nesting behavior of Herring Gulls: invasion into *Spartina* salt marsh areas of New Jersey. *Condor* **79**: 162-169.
Burger, J. (1978a). Determinants of nest repair in Laughing Gulls. *Anim. Behav.* **26**: 856-861.
Burger, J. (1978b). Great Black-backed Gulls breeding in salt marsh in New Jersey. *Wilson Bull.* **90**: 304-305.
Burger, J. (1979a). Competition and predation: Herring Gulls versus Laughing Gulls. *Condor* **81**: 269-277.
Burger, J. (1979b). Colony size: a test for breeding synchrony in Herring Gulls (*Larus argentatus*). *Auk* **96(4)**: 694-703.
Burger, J. (1980a). Nesting adaptation of Herring Gull (*Larus argentatus*) to salt marsh and storm tides. *Biol. Behav.* **5**: 147-152.
Burger, J. (1980b). Age differences in foraging Black-necked Stilts in Texas. *Auk* **97(3)**: 633-636.
Burger, J. (1980c). Territory size differences in relation to reproductive stage and type of intruder in Herring Gulls. *Auk* **97(4)**: 733-741.
Burger, J. (1980d). The transition to independence and postfledging care in seabirds. Pp. 367-448 in: Burger, Olla & Winn (1980).
Burger, J. (1981a). Behavioral responses of Herring Gulls (*Larus argentatus*) to aircraft noise. *Environm. Pollut.* **24**: 177-184.
Burger, J. (1981b). On becoming independent in Herring Gulls: Parent-young conflict. *Amer. Naturalist* **117**: 444-456.
Burger, J. (1981c). Feeding competition between Laughing Gulls and Herring Gulls at a Sanitary landfill. *Condor* **83**: 328-335.
Burger, J. (1981d). Movements of juvenile Herring Gulls hatched at Jamaica Bay Refuge, New York. *J. Field Orn.* **53**: 285-290.
Burger, J. (1981e). Super-territories: a comment. *Amer. Naturalist* **118**: 578-580.
Burger, J. (1981f). Sexual differences in parental activities of breeding Black Skimmers. *Amer. Naturalist* **117**: 975-984.

Burger, J. (1981g). Aggressive behaviour of Black Skimmers (*Rynchops niger*). *Behaviour* **76**: 207-222.

Burger, J. (1982a). The role of reproductive success in colony-site selection and abandonment in Black Skimmers (*Rynchops niger*). *Auk* **99**: 109-115.

Burger, J. (1982b). Jamaica Bay studies: 1. Environmental determinants of abundance and distribution of Common Terns (*Sterna hirundo*) and Black Skimmers (*Rynchops niger*) at an east coast estuary. *Colonial Waterbirds* **5**: 148-160.

Burger, J. (1983a). Jamaica Bay Studies III: abiotic determinants of distribution and abundance of gulls (*Larus*). *Estuarine Coastal & Shelf Science* **16**: 191-216.

Burger, J. (1983b). Competition between two nesting species of gulls: on the importance of timing. *Behavioral Neuroscience* **97**: 492-501.

Burger, J. (1984a). Grebes nesting in gull colonies: protective associations and early warning. *Amer. Naturalist* **123**: 327-337.

Burger, J. (1984b). *Pattern, Mechanism and Adaptive Significance of Territoriality in Herring Gulls (*Larus argentatus*).* Ornithological Monographs **34**. 192 pp.

Burger, J. (1984c). Shorebirds as marine animals. Pp. 17-81 in: Burger & Olla (1984).

Burger, J. (1984d). Colony stability in Least Terns. *Condor* **86**: 143-167.

Burger, J. (1987a). Selection for equitability in some aspects of reproductive investment in Herring Gulls (*Larus argentatus*). *Ornis Scand.* **18(1)**: 17-23.

Burger, J. (1987b). Foraging efficiency in gulls: a congeneric comparison of age differences in efficiency and age of maturity. Pp. 83-90 in: Hand *et al.* (1987).

Burger, J. (1987c). Physical and social determinants of nest-site selection in Piping Plover in New Jersey. *Condor* **89**: 811-818.

Burger, J. (1988a). Foraging behavior of gulls: differences in method, prey, and habitat. *Colonial Waterbirds* **11**: 9-23.

Burger, J. (1988b). Effects of age on foraging in birds. Pp. 1126-1140 in: *Proc. XIX Int. Orn. Congr.* Ottawa, 1986.

Burger, J. ed. (1988c). *Seabirds and other Marine Vertebrates: Competition, Predation and other Interactions.* Columbia University Press, New York.

Burger, J. (1988d). Social attraction in nesting Least Terns: effects of numbers, spacing and pair bonds. *Condor* **90**: 579-582.

Burger, J. (1989). Least Tern populations in coastal New Jersey: monitoring and management of a regionally-endangered species. *J. Coastal Res.* **5**: 801-811.

Burger, J. (1991). Foraging behavior and the effect of human disturbance on the Piping Plover (*Charadrius melodus*). *J. Coastal Res.* **7(1)**: 39-52.

Burger, J. (1994). The effect of human disturbance on foraging behavior and habitat use in Piping Plover (*Charadrius melodus*). *Estuaries* **17**: 695-701.

Burger, J. & Beer, C.G. (1975). Territoriality in the Laughing Gull (*Larus atricilla*). *Behaviour* **55**: 301-319.

Burger, J. & Brownstein, R. (1968a). The status of Bonaparte's Gull in New York State. *Kingbird* **18**: 9-20.

Burger, J. & Brownstein, R. (1968b). The Little Gull in Western New York. *Kingbird* **18**: 187-194.

Burger, J. & Galli, J. (1987). Factors affecting distribution of gulls (*Larus* spp.) on two New Jersey coastal bays. *Environm. Cons.* **14**: 59-65.

Burger, J. & Gochfeld, M. (1979). Age differences in Ring-billed Gulls kleptoparasitism on Starlings. *Auk* **96(4)**: 806-808.

Burger, J. & Gochfeld, M. (1981a). Nest-site selection by Kelp Gulls in Southern Africa. *Condor* **83**: 243-251.

Burger, J. & Gochfeld, M. (1981b). Discrimination of the threat of direct versus tangential approach to the nest by incubating Herring and Great Black-backed Gulls. *J. Comp. Physiol. Psychol.* **95**: 676-684.

Burger, J. & Gochfeld, M. (1981c). Consequences of unequal sex ratios in Herring Gulls. *Behav. Ecol. Sociobiol.* **8**: 125-128.

Burger, J. & Gochfeld, M. (1981d). Age-related differences in piracy behavior of four species of gulls, *Larus*. *Behaviour* **77**: 242-267.

Burger, J. & Gochfeld, M. (1981e). Colony and habitat selection of six Kelp Gull *Larus dominicanus* colonies in South Africa. *Ibis* **123**: 298-310.

Burger, J. & Gochfeld, M. (1983a). Behavioral responses of Herring (*Larus argentatus*) and Great Black-backed (*L. marinus*) Gulls to variation in the amount of human disturbance. *Behavioural Processes* **8**: 327-344.

Burger, J. & Gochfeld, M. (1983b). Behavior of nine avian species at a Florida garbage dump. *Colonial Waterbirds* **6**: 54-63.

Burger, J. & Gochfeld, M. (1983c). Feeding behavior in Laughing Gulls: compensatory site selection by young. *Condor* **85**: 467-473.

Burger, J. & Gochfeld, M. (1984a). Great Black-backed Gull (*Larus marinus*) predation on Kittiwake (*Rissa tridactyla*) fledglings in Norway. *Bird Study* **31**: 139-141.

Burger, J. & Gochfeld, M. (1984b). The effects of relative numbers on aggressive interactions and foraging efficiency in gulls: the cost of being outnumbered. *Bird Behaviour* **5**: 81-89.

Burger, J. & Gochfeld, M. (1984c). Seasonal variation in size and function of the nasal salt gland of the Franklin's Gull. *Comp. Biochem. Physiol.* **77A**: 103-110.

Burger, J. & Gochfeld, M. (1985a). Nesting habitat of Andean Gull. *Colonial Waterbirds* **8**: 74-78.

Burger, J. & Gochfeld, M. (1985b). Nest site selection by Laughing Gulls (*Larus atricilla*): comparison of tropical colonies (Culebra, Puerto Rico) with temperate New Jersey colonies. *Condor* **87**: 364-373.

Burger, J. & Gochfeld, M. (1985c). Age-related differences in foraging in the Masked Lapwing *Vanellus miles* in Australia. *Emu* **85(1)**: 47-48.

Burger, J. & Gochfeld, M. (1985d). Early post-natal lead exposure: behavioral defects in Common Tern chicks (*Sterna hirundo*). *J. Toxicol. Environm. Health* **16**: 869-886.

Burger, J. & Gochfeld, M. (1986a). Age differences in foraging efficiency of American Avocets *Recurvirostra americana*. *Bird Behaviour* **6(2)**: 66-71.

Burger, J. & Gochfeld, M. (1986b). Nest site selection in Sooty Terns (*Sterna fuscata*) in Puerto Rico and Hawaii. *Colonial waterbirds* **9**: 31-45.

Burger, J. & Gochfeld, M. (1987a). Colony and nest site selection behavior in Silver Gulls *Larus novaehollandiae* in Queensland, Australia. *Bird Behaviour* **7**: 1-21.

Burger, J. & Gochfeld, M. (1987b). Nest-site selection by Mew Gulls (*Larus canus*): a comparison of marsh and dry-land colonies. *Wilson Bull.* **99**: 673-687.

Burger, J. & Gochfeld, M. (1988a). Habitat selection in Mew Gulls: small colonies and site plasticity. *Wilson Bull.* **100**: 395-410.

Burger, J. & Gochfeld, M. (1988b). Effect of lead on growth in young Herring Gulls (*Larus argentatus*). *J. Toxicol. Environm. Health* **25**: 227-236.

Burger, J. & Gochfeld, M. (1988c). Nest-site selection by Roseate Terns in two tropical colonies on Culebra, Puerto Rico. *Condor* **90**: 843-851.

Burger, J. & Gochfeld, M. (1988d). Defensive aggression in terns: effect of species, density and isolation. *Aggressive Behavavior* **14**: 169-178.

Burger, J. & Gochfeld, M. (1988e). Nest site selection and temporal patterns of habitat use in Roseate and Common Terns. *Auk* **105**: 433-438.

Burger, J. & Gochfeld, M. (1988f). Metals in tern eggs: a decade of change. *Environ. Monitor. Assessment* **11**: 127-135.

Burger, J. & Gochfeld, M. (1990a). Nest site selection in Least Terns (*Sterna antillarum*) in New Jersey and New York. *Colonial Waterbirds* **13**: 31-40.

Burger, J. & Gochfeld, M. (1990b). *The Black Skimmer: Social Dynamics of a Colonial Species.* Columbia University Press, New York.

Burger, J. & Gochfeld, M. (1991a). Lead, mercury and cadmium in feathers of Tropical terns in Puerto Rico and Australia. *Arch. Enviornm. Contam. Toxicol.* **21**: 311-315.

Burger, J. & Gochfeld, M. (1991b). Vigilance and feeding behavior in large feeding flocks of Laughing Gulls, *Larus atricilla* on Delaware Bay. *Estuarine Coastal and Shelf Science* **32**: 207-212

Burger, J. & Gochfeld, M. (1991c). *The Common Tern: its Breeding Biology and Social Behavior.* Columbia University Press, New York.

Burger, J. & Gochfeld, M. (1991d). Reproductive vulnerability: parental attendance around hatching in Roseate (*Sterna dougallii*) and Common (*S. hirundo*) Terns. *Condor* **93**: 125-129.

Burger, J. & Gochfeld, M. (1991e). Human activity influence and diurnal and nocturnal foraging of Sanderlings (*Calidris alba*). *Condor* **93(2)**: 259-265.

Burger, J. & Gochfeld, M. (1992a). Experimental evidence for aggressive antipredator behavior in Black Skimmers (*Rynchops niger*). *Aggressive Behavior* **18(3)**: 241-248.

Burger, J. & Gochfeld, M. (1992b). Heavy metal and selenium concentrations on Black Skimmers (*Rynchops niger*): gender differences. *Arch. Environm. Contam. Toxicol.* **23(4)**: 431-434.

Burger, J. & Gochfeld, M. (1993a). Lead and cadmium accumulation in eggs and fledgling seabirds in the New York Bight. *Environm. Toxicol. Chem.* **12**: 261-267.

Burger, J. & Gochfeld, M. (1993b). *Nest Site Selection in Swallow-tailed Gull* Creagrus furcatus *on Genovesa (= Tower) Island in the Galapagos.* Rutgers University Report, New Brunswick, New Jersey.

Burger, J. & Gochfeld, M. (1994a). Behavioral impairments of lead-injected young Herring Gulls in nature. *Fund. Appl. Toxicol.* **23**: 553-561.

Burger, J. & Gochfeld, M. (1994b). Franklin's Gull (*Larus pipixcan*). No. 116 in: Poole & Gill (1994).

Burger, J. & Gochfeld, M. (1994c). Predation and effects of humans on island-nesting seabirds. Pp. 39-67 in: Nettleship *et al.* (1994).

Burger, J. & Gochfeld, M. (1995). Nest site selection of Eared Grebe *Podiceps nigricollis* in a Franklin's Gull *Larus pipixcan* colony: structural stability parasites. *Condor* **97**: 577-580.

Burger, J. & Gochfeld, M. (1996). Use of space by nesting Black-billed Gulls (*Larus bulleri*): behavioural changes during the reproductive cycle. *Emu* **96**: 143-149.

Burger, J. & Howe, M. (1975). Notes on winter feeding behavior and molt in Wilson's Phalaropes. *Auk* **92**: 442-451.

Burger, J. & Lesser, F. (1977). Determinants of colony site selection in Common Terns. *Proc. Colonial Waterbird Group* **1**: 118-127.

Burger, J. & Lesser, F. (1978). Selection of colony sites and nest sites by Common Terns *Sterna hirundo* in Ocean County, New Jersey. *Ibis* **120**: 433-449.

Burger, J. & Lesser, F. (1979). Breeding behavior and success in salt marsh Common Tern colonies. *Bird-Banding* **50(4)**: 322-337.

Burger, J. & Lesser, L. (1980). Nest site selection in an expanding population of Herring Gulls. *Bird-Banding* **51**: 270-280.

Burger, J. & Olla, B.L. eds. (1984). *Shorebirds: Breeding Behavior and Populations.* Plenum Press, New York & London.

Burger, J. & Shisler, J. (1978a). Nest site selection of Willets in a New Jersey salt marsh. *Wilson Bull.* **90**: 599-607.

Burger, J. & Shisler, J. (1978b). Nest site selection and competitive interactions of Herring and Laughing Gulls in New Jersey. *Auk* **95**: 252-266.

Burger, J. & Shisler, J. (1979). Immediate effects of ditching a marsh on breeding Herring Gulls. *Biol. Conserv.* **15**: 85-104.

Burger, J. & Shisler, J. (1980a). The process of colony formation among Herring Gull (*Larus argentatus*) nesting in New Jersey. *Ibis* **122(1)**: 15-26.

Burger, J. & Shisler, J. (1980b). Colony site and nest selection in Laughing Gulls in response to tidal flooding. *Condor* **82**: 251-258.

Burger, J. & Staine, K.S. (1993). Nocturnal behavior of gulls in coastal New Jersey. *Estuaries* **16**: 809-814.

Burger, J. & Wagner, L. (1995). Laughing Gull *Larus atricilla*. Pp. 375-379 in: Dove, L. & Nyman, R. eds. (1995). *Living Resources of the Delaware Estuary.* US Environmental Protection Agency, New York.

Burger, J., Fitch, M., Shugart, G. & Werther, W. (1980). Piracy in *Larus* gulls at a dump in New Jersey. *Proc. Colonial Waterbird Group* **3**: 87-98.

Burger, J., Gochfeld, M. & Boarman, W.I. (1988). Experimental evidence for sibling recognition in Common Terns (*Sterna hirundo*). *Auk* **105**: 142-148.

Burger, J., Hahn, D.C. & Chase, J. (1979). Aggressive interactions in mixed-species flocks of migrating shorebirds. *Anim. Behav.* **27**: 459-469.

Burger, J., Nisbet, I.C.T., Safina, C. & Gochfeld, M. (1995). Temporal patterns in reproductive success in the endangered Roseate Tern (*Sterna dougallii*) nesting on Long Island, New York and Bird Island, Massachusetts. *Auk* **112**: 131-142.

Burger, J., Nisbet, I.C.T., Zingo, J.M., Spendelow, J.A., Safina, C. & Gochfeld, M. (1995). Colony differences in response to trapping in Roseate Terns. *Condor* **97**: 263-266.

Burger, J., Olla, B.L. & Winn, H.E. eds. (1980). *Behavior of Marine Animals: Current Perspectives in Research.* Vol. 4. Marine Birds. Plenum Press, New York.

Burger, J., Parsons, K., Wartenberg, D., Safina, C., O'Connor, J. & Gochfeld, M. (1994). Biomonitoring using Least Terns and Black Skimmers in the northeastern United States. *J. Coastal Res.* **10**: 39-47.

Burger, J., Shealer, D.A. & Gochfeld, M. (1993). Defensive aggression in terns: discrimination and response to individual researchers. *Aggressive Behavior* **19**: 303-311.

Burger, J., Shisler, J. & Lesser, F. (1982). Avian utilization on six salt marshes in New Jersey. *Biol. Conserv.* **23**: 187-212.

Burggraeve, G. (1977). Observations on a probable mised pair of Roseate Tern *Sterna dougallii* x Common Tern *Sterna hirundo* at Knokke(). *Gerfaut* **67**: 75-80.

Burke, T. & Thompson, D.B.A. (1988). Breeding and social systems of birds of the western Palearctic. In: O'Connor, J. ed. (1988). *Sourcebook of Ornithological Data.* T. & A.D. Poyser Ltd, Calton, UK.

Burlando, B., Fadat, C. & Spano, S. (1994). [Working hypothesis on the question of Short-billed Woodcock]. Pp. 61-65 in: Kalchreuter (1994). In French with English summary.

Burleigh, T.D. (1958). *Georgian Birds.* University Oklahoma Press, Norman, Oklahoma.

Burmeister, H. (1937). Contribuição para a historia natural da seriema. (Translated from German by A. de Miranda-Ribeiro). *Rev. Mus. Paulista* **23**: 91-152.

Burness, G.P., Morris, R.D. & Bruce, J.P. (1994). Seasonal and annual variation in brood attendance, prey type delivered to chicks and foraging patterns of male Common Terns (*Sterna hirundo*). *Can. J. Zool.* **72**: 1243-1251.

Burnett, C. (1985). Behaviour of Red-necked Avocets in strong wind. *S. Austr. Orn.* **29(7)**: 194.

Burnier, E. (1977). Sur l'hivernage du Pluvier guignard en Algérie. *Nos Oiseaux* **34**: 74.

Burns, D.W. (1993). Oriental Pratincole: new to the Western Palearctic. *British Birds* **86(3)**: 115-120.

Burt, W. (1994). *Shadowbirds. A Quest for Rails.* Lyons & Burford Publishers, New York.

Burton, J.H. (1959). Some population mechanics of the American Coot. *J. Wildl. Manage.* **2**: 203-210.

Burton, P.J.K. (1971). Comparative anatomy of head and neck in the Spoon-billed Sandpiper, *Eurynorhynchus pygmeus* and its allies. *J. Zool., London* **163**: 145-163.

Burton, P.J.K. (1972a). Some anatomical notes on the Wrybill. *Notornis* **19(1)**: 26-32.

Burton, P.J.K. (1972b). The feeding techniques of Stilt Sandpipers and Dowitchers. *Trans. San Diego Soc. Nat. Hist.* **17**: 63-68.

Burton, P.J.K. (1974). *Feeding and the Feeding Apparatus in Waders. A Study of Anatomy and Adaptions in the Charadrii.* British Museum Natural History, London.

Burton, P.J.K. (1986). Curlews' *Numenius* bills: some anatomical notes. *Bird Study* **33**: 70.

Burton, P.J.K. & Thurston, M.H. (1959). Observations on Arctic Terns in Spitsbergen. *British Birds* **52**: 149-161.

Burton, R.W. (1968a). Breeding biology of the Brown Skua, *Catharacta skua lonnbergi* (Mathews), at Signy Island, South Orkney Islands. *Bull. Brit. Antarct. Surv.* **15**: 9-28.

Burton, R.W. (1968b). Agonistic behaviour of the Brown Skua *Catharacta skua lonnbergi* (Mathews). *Bull. Brit. Antarct. Surv.* **16**: 15-39.

Busche, G. (1995). Zum Niedergang von Wiesenvögeln in Schleswig-Holstein 1950 bis 1992. [The decline of wet-meadow birds in Schleswig-Holstein/Germany from 1950 to 1992]. *J. Orn.* **135**: 167-177. In German with English summary.

Busching, W.D. (1989). [The wing pattern of immature Black-winged Stilts *Himantopus himantopus*]. *Limicola* **3(3)**: 143-145. In German with English summary.

Busse, K. & Busse, K. (1977). Prägungsbedingte Bindung von Küstenseeschwalbenkuken (*Sterna paradisaea* Pont.) an die Eltern und ihre Fähigkeit, sie an der Stimme zu erkennen. *Z. Tierpsychol.* **43**: 287-294.

Busse, K.V. (1983). [The conjugal, family and social life of the Arctic Tern (*Sterna paradisaea* Pont.) with special regard to the long term changes in the inter-individual relationships]. *Ökol. Vögel* **5**: 73-110. In German.

Butchko, P.H. (1990). Predator control for the protection of endangered species in California. *Proc. Vertebrate Pest Conf.* **14**: 237-240.

Butkauskas, N.V. (1981). [Breeding biology of Common Terns in Central Latvia]. Pp. 31-38 in: *Proceedings 10th Baltic Ornithological Conference, Riga.* Biological Institute Latvian Academy of Sciences **2**. In Russian.

Butler, A.L. (1899). The birds of the Andaman and Nicobar Islands. *J. Bombay Nat. Hist. Soc.* **12**: 684-696.

Butler, A.L. (1931). The chicks of the Egyptian Plover. *Ibis* **13(1)**: 345-347.

Butler, R.G. & Janes-Butler, S. (1982). Territoriality and behavioral correlates of reproductive success of Great Black-backed Gulls. *Auk* **99**: 58-66.

Butler, R.G. & Janes-Butler, S. (1983). Sexual differences in the behavior of adult Great Black-backed Gulls, *Larus marinus* during the pre- and post- hatch periods. *Auk* **100**: 63-75.

Butler, R.G. & Trivelpiece, W. (1981). Nest spacing, reproductive success, and behavior of the Great Black-backed Gull (*Larus marinus*). *Auk* **98(1)**: 99-107.

Butler, R.W. & Kaiser, G.H. (1988). Western Sandpiper migration studies along the west coast of Canada. *Wader Study Group Bull.* **52**: 16-17.

Butler, R.W. & Kaiser, G.W. (1995). Migration chronology, sex ratio and body mass of Least Sandpiper in British Columbia. *Wilson Bull.* **107**: 413-422.

Butler, R.W. & Kirbyson, J.W. (1979). Oyster predation by the Black Oystercatcher in British Columbia. *Condor* **81(4)**: 433 435.

Butler, R.W., Kaiser, G.W. & Smith, G.E.J. (1987). Migration chronology, length of stay, sex ratio, and weights of Western Sandpipers (*Calidris mauri*) on the south coast of British Columbia. *J. Field Orn.* **58**: 103-111.

Butler, R.W., Verbeek, N.A.M. & Footit, R.G. (1980). Mortality and dispersal of the Glaucous-winged Gulls of southern British Columbia. *Can. Field-Nat.* **94**: 315-320.

Butler, T.Y. (1979). *The Birds of Ecuador and the Galapagos Archipelago*. The Ramphastos Agency, Portsmouth, New Hampshire.

Buttemer, W.A. & Astheimer, L.B. (1990). Thermal and behavioural correlates of nest site location in Black Noddies. *Emu* **90**: 114-118.

Butts, K.O. (1994). American Woodcock activity in the Wichita Mountains Wildlife Refuge. *Bull. Okla. Orn. Soc.* **27(4)**: 28-29.

Buturlin, S.A. (1906). The breeding grounds of the Rosy Gull. *Ibis* **Ser. 8, no. 6**: 131-139, 333-337, 661-666.

Buturlin, S.A. (1934). *Larus taimyrensis armenicus*. subsp. nov. *Ibis* **Ser. 13, no. 4**: 171-172.

Butyev, V.T. (1983). *Numenius minutus*. Pp. 267-269 in: *The RSFSR Red Data Book*. Russian Agricultural Publications, Moscow.

Buxton, E.J.M. (1939). The breeding of the Oystercatcher. *British Birds* **33**: 184 193.

Buxton, E.J.M. (1957). Migrations of the Oystercatcher in the area of Britain: results of ringing. *British Birds* **50**: 519 524.

Buxton, E.J.M. (1985). Oystercatcher. Pp. 423-424 in: Campbell & Lack (1985).

Buzun, V.A. (1993). [History of study of the Armenian Gull *Larus armenicus* Buturlin, 1934]. *Russ. J. Orn.* **2(3)**: 383-388. In Russian with English summary.

Buzun, V.A. & Golovach, O.F. (1992). The Great Bustard in the Crimea: preliminary information about its distribution and numbers, the structure of the population and behaviour. *Bustard Studies* **5**: 33-51.

Buzun, V.A. & Mierauskas, P. (1987). [Behavior of the Mediterranean Gull *Larus melanocephalus* during colony formation and early breeding]. *Byull. Mosk. Ova. Ispyt. Prir. Otd. Biol.* **92**: 27-36. In Russian.

Buzun, V.A. & Mierauskas, P. (1988). [Development of trophical strategies and evolution of foraging behaviour of Herring Gulls]. *Acta Orn. Lituanica* **1**: 3-66. In Russian.

Bylin, K. (1987). The Common Crane in Sweden: distribution, numerical status, habitats, breeding success, and need of protection. Pp. 215-223 in: Archibald & Pasquier (1987a).

Byrd, G.V. (1978). Red-legged Kittiwake colonies in the Aleutian Islands, Alaska. *Condor* **80**: 250.

Byrd, G.V. (1994). A closer look: Whiskered Auklet. *Birding* **26(6)**: 424-425.

Byrd, G.V. & Day, R.H. (1986). The avifauna of Buldir Island, Aleutian Islands, Alaska. *Arctic* **39**: 109-118.

Byrd, G.V. & Douglas, H. (1990). Results of monitoring studies for puffins in three locations in the Aleutian Islands in summer 1989. Unpublished report to US Fish & Wildlife Service, Adak, Alaska.

Byrd, G.V. & Gibson, D.D. (1980). Distribution and population status of Whiskered Auklet in the Aleutian Islands, Alaska. *Western Birds* **11**: 135-140.

Byrd, G.V. & Tobish, T.G. (1978). Wind-caused mortality in a Kittiwake colony at Buldir Island, Alaska. *Murrelet* **59**: 37.

Byrd, G.V. & Williams, J.C. (1993a). Red-legged Kittiwake (*Rissa brevirostris*). No. **60** in: Poole & Gill (1993).

Byrd, G.V. & Williams, J.C. (1993b). Whiskered Auklet (*Aethia pygmaea*). No. **76** in: Poole & Gill (1993).

Byrd, G.V. & Zeillemaker, G.F. (1981). Ecology of nesting Hawaiian Common Gallinules at Hanali, Hawaii. *Western Birds* **12**: 105-116.

Byrd, G.V., Climo, L. & Fuller, J.P. (1989). Results of monitoring studies for puffins in the western Aleutian Islands in summer 1988. Unpublished report to US Fish & Wildlife Service, Adak, Alaska.

Byrd, G.V., Coleman, R.A., Shallenberger, R.J. & Arume, C.S. (1985). Notes on the breeding biology of the Hawaiian race of the American Coot. *Elepaio* **45**: 57-63.

Byrd, G.V., Day, R.H. & Knudtson, J.C. (1983). Patterns of colony attendance and censusing of auklets at Buldir Island, Alaska. *Condor* **85**: 274-280.

Byrd, G.V., Douglas, H., Maycock, E., Odaniel, D. & Williams, J. (1990). The status of Tufted and Horned Puffins in the western Aleutian Islands following a ban on salmon driftnets. Unpublished report to US Fish & Wildlife Service, Adak, Alaska.

Byrd, G.V., Murphy, E.C., Kaiser, G.W., Kondratyev, A.Y. & Shibaev, Y.V. (1993). Status and ecology of offshore fish-feeding alcids (murres and puffins) in the North Pacific. Pp. 176-186 in: Vermeer, Briggs *et al.* (1993).

Byrkjedal, I. (1978a). Altitudinal differences in breeding schedules of Golden Plovers *Pluvialis apricaria* (L.) in South Norway. *Sterna* **17**: 1-20.

Byrkjedal, I. (1978b). Variation and secondary intergradation in SW-Norwegian Golden Plover *Pluvialis apricaria* populations. *Ornis Scand.* **9**: 101-110.

Byrkjedal, I. (1978c). Autumn diet of Golden Plovers *Pluvialis apricaria* on farmland and on a coastal heather moor in South Norway. *Cinclus* **1**: 22-28.

Byrkjedal, I. (1980). Summer food of the Golden Plover *Pluvialis apricaria* at Hardangervidda, southern Norway. *Holarctic Ecol.* **3**: 40-49.

Byrkjedal, I. (1985a). Time-activity budget for breeding Greater Golden-Plovers in Norwegian mountains. *Wilson Bull.* **97(4)**: 486-501.

Byrkjedal, I. (1985b). Time budget and parental labour division in breeding Black-tailed Godwits *Limosa l. limosa*. *Fauna Norvegica (Ser. C, Cinclus)* **8**: 24-34.

Byrkjedal, I. (1987a). Antipredator behaviour and breeding success in Greater Golden-Plover and Eurasian Dotterel. *Condor* **89(1)**: 40-47.

Byrkjedal, I. (1987b). Short-billed Dowitchers associate closely with Lesser Golden Plovers. *Wilson Bull.* **99**: 494-495.

Byrkjedal, I. (1989a). Habitat use and resource overlap by breeding Golden Plovers and Dotterel (*Pluvialis apricaria*, *Charadrius morinellus*). *J. Orn.* **130(2)**: 197-206.

Byrkjedal, I. (1989b). Time constraints and vigilance: breeding season diet of the Dotterel (*Charadrius morinellus*). *J. Orn.* **130(3)**: 293-302. In English with German summary.

Byrkjedal, I. (1989c). Nest habitat and nesting success of Lesser Golden-Plovers. *Wilson Bull.* **101(1)**: 93-96.

Byrkjedal, I. (1989d). Nest defense behavior of Lesser Golden-plovers. *Wilson Bull.* **101(4)**: 579-590.

Byrkjedal, I. (1990). Song flight of the Pintail Snipe *Gallinago stenura* on the breeding grounds. *Ornis Scand.* **21(4)**: 239-247.

Byrkjedal, I. (1991). The role of drive conflicts as a mechanism for nest-protection behaviour in the shorebird *Pluvialis dominica*. *Ethology* **87(1-2)**: 149-159.

Byrkjedal, I. & Kålås, J.A. (1983). Plover's Page turns into Plover's Parasite: a look at the Dunlin/Golden Plover association. *Ornis Fenn.* **60(1)**: 10-15.

Byrkjedal, I. & Kålås, J.A. (1985). Seasonal variation in egg size in Golden Plover *Pluvialis apricaria* and Dotterel *Charadrius morinellus* populations. *Ornis Scand.* **16(2)**: 108-112.

Byrkjedal, I., Larsen, T. & Moldsvor, J. (1988). Song and mating behaviour of the Spotted Redshank *Tringa erythropus*. *Fauna Norvegica (Ser. C, Cinclus)* **11(2)**: 51-56.

Byrkjedal, I., Larsen, T. & Moldsvor, J. (1989). Sexual and antagonistic behaviour of Bar-tailed Godwits on the breeding grounds. *Ornis Scand.* **20**: 169-175.

Bywater, J. & McKean, J.L. (1987). A record of Latham's Snipe *Gallinago hardwickii* in the Northern Territory. *Austr. Bird Watcher* **12(2)**: 65.

Cabot, J. (1988). *Dinámica Anual de la Comunidad de Aves en Cinco Hábitats del Altiplano Norte de Bolivia*. PhD thesis, Universidad de Córdoba, Córdoba, España.

Cadbury, C.J. & Olney, R.J.S. (1978). Avocet population dynamics in England. *British Birds* **71**: 102-121.

Cadbury, C.J., Hill, D., Patridge, J. & Sorensen, J. (1989). The history of the Avocet population and its management in England since recolonisation. *RSBP Conserv. Rev.* **3**: 9-13.

Cade, M. (1982). Plumage variability of immature Common and Ring-billed Gulls. *British Birds* **75**: 580.

Cadée, G.C. (1994). Mya shell manipulating by Turnstones (Aves) results in concave-up position and left/right sorting. *Palaios* **9**: 307-309.

Cadman, M.D. (1979). Territorial behaviour in American Oystercatchers *Haematopus palliatus*. *Wader Study Group Bull.* **27**: 40 41.

Cadman, M.D. (1980). *Age Related Foraging Efficiency of the American Oystercatcher* Haematopus palliatus. MSc thesis, University of Toronto, Toronto.

Cain, A.J. & Galbraith, I.C.J. (1956). Field notes on birds of the eastern Solomon Islands. *Ibis* **98**: 100-134.

Cairns, D.K. (1978). *Some Aspects of the Biology of the Black Guillemot* Cepphus grylle *in the Estuary and the Gulf of St. Lawrence*. MSc thesis, Université de Laval, Québec.

Cairns, D.K. (1980). Nesting density, habitat structure and human disturbance as factors in Black Guillemot reproduction. *Wilson Bull.* **92**: 352-361.

Cairns, D.K. (1981). Breeding, feeding and chick growth of the Black Guillemot *Cepphus grylle* in southern Quebec. *Can. Field-Nat.* **95**: 312-318.

Cairns, D.K. (1982). Black Guillemot investigations near the Nuvuk Islands, N.W.T., in 1981. Studies on northern seabirds. *Can. Wildl. Serv. Unpublished Rep.* **147**: 1-59.

Cairns, D.K. (1987a). Diet and foraging ecology of Black Guillemots in north-eastern Hudson Bay. *Can. J. Zool.* **65**: 1257-1263.

Cairns, D.K. (1987b). The ecology and energetics of chick provisioning by Black Guillemots. *Condor* **89**: 627-635.

Cairns, D.K. & Schneider, D.C. (1990). Hot spots in cold water: feeding habitat selection by Thick-billed Murres. Pp. 52-60 in: Sealy (1990).

Cairns, D.K., Bredin, K.A. & Montevecchi, W.A. (1987). Activity budgets and foraging ranges of breeding Common Murres. *Auk* **104**: 218-224.

Cairns, D.K., Montevecchi, W.A., Birt-Friesen, V.L. & Macko, S.A. (1990). Energy expenditures, activity budgets and prey harvest of breeding Common Murres. Pp. 84-92 in: Sealy (1990).

Cairns, J. (1953). Studies of Malayan birds. *Malay. Nat. J.* **7**: 173-179.

Cairns, W.E. (1977). *Breeding Biology and Behaviour of the Piping Plover (*Charadrius melodus*) in Southern Nova Scotia*. MSc thesis, Dalhousie University, Halifax, Canada.

Cairns, W.E. (1982). Biology and behavior of breeding Piping Plovers. *Wilson Bull.* **94**: 531-545.

Cairns, W.E. & McLaren, I.A. (1980). Status of the Piping Plover on the east coast of North America. *Amer. Birds* **34**: 206-208.

Calado, M. (1996). Little Tern (*Sterna albifrons*) status and conservation at Ria Formosa Natural Park, Algarve, Portugal. *Colonial Waterbirds* **19**(Spec. Publ. 1): 78-80.

Caldow, R.W.G. & Furness, R.W. (1991). The relationship between kleptoparasitism and plumage polymorphism in the Arctic Skua *Stercorarius parasiticus* (L.). *Functional Ecology* **5(3)**: 331-339.

Calinin, S.S. (1987). [The Sociable Plover in the Kurgan region]. Page 138 in: [*The Problems of Rare Wildlife Conservation*]. Moscow. In Russian.

Calvario, E., Fraschetti, F., Sarrocco, S. & Sestieri, L. (1986). [New data about the breeding status of the Stone Curlew, *Burhinus oedicnemus*, in Latium, central Italy]. *Riv. ital. Orn.* **56(3-4)**: 266-267. In Italian.

Calvo, B. (1993a). *Influences of Agricultural Land-use and Habitat Modification on the Breeding Biology and Conservation of Collared Pratincoles (*Glareola pratincola*) in SW Spain*. PhD thesis, Glasgow University, Glasgow.

Calvo, B. (1993b). Nota breve sobre la población nidificante de *Glareola pratincola* en la provincia de Sevilla. [Short note on the nesting population of *Glareola pratincola* in the province of Sevilla]. *Ecologia* **7**: 455-456.

Calvo, B. (1994a). Effects of agricultural land-use on the breeding of Collared Pratincoles *Glareola pratincola* in south-west Spain. *Biol. Conserv.* **70**: 77-83.

Calvo, B. (1994b). Medidas para conservar el hábitat de reproducción de la Canastera. *Quercus* **106**: 10-14.

Calvo, B. & Alberto, L.J. (1990). Nest-site selection of the Collared Pratincole *Glareola pratincola* in the province of Sevilla, Spain. *Wader Study Group Bull.* **58**: 13-15.

Calvo, B. & Furness, R.W. (1995). Colony and nest-site selection by Collared Pratincoles *Glareola pratincola* in southwest Spain. *Colonial Waterbirds* **18(1)**: 1-10.

Calvo, B., Máñez, M. & Alberto, L.J. (1993). The Collared Pratincole in the National Park of Doñana, south west Spain. *Wader Study Group Bull.* **67**: 81-87.

Campbell, A.J. (1905a). The Kagu of New Caledonia. *Emu* **4**: 166-168.

Campbell, A.J. (1905b). Notes from H.E. Finckh with description of downy young of *Rhynochetos jubatus*. *Emu* **5**: 32.

Campbell, A.J. (1906). Oological notes and further description of new Fruit-pigeon. *Emu* **5**: 195-199.

Campbell, A.J. & Barnard, H.G. (1917). Birds of the Rockingham Bay district, north Queensland. *Emu* **17**: 2-38.

Campbell, B. & Lack, E. eds. (1985). *A Dictionary of Birds*. T. & A. D. Poyser, Calton, UK.

Campbell, J. (1985). Charadriiformes of a north-western Victorian wheat farm. *Stilt* **7**: 21-22.

Campbell, K.E. (1971). First report of Sandwich Terns in Peru. *Auk* **88**: 676.

Campbell, K.R. (1976). The late Pleistocene avifauna of La Carolina, southwestern Ecuador. Pp. 155-168 in: Olson, S.L. ed. (1976). *Collected Papers in Avian Paleontology Honoring the 90th Birthday of Alexander Wetmore*. Smithsonian Contributions to Paleobiology **27**.

Campbell, K.R. (1979). *The Non-passerine Pleistocene Avifauna of the Talara Tar Seeps, Northwestern Peru*. Life Sciences Contributions, Royal Ontario Museum **118**. 203 pp.

Campbell, L. (1972). Caspian Plover *Charadrius asiaticus* at the coast. *Bull. East Afr. Nat. Hist. Soc.* **1972**: 65.

Campbell, R.W. (1970). The Sabine's Gull in southwestern British Columbia. *Can. Field-Nat.* **84**: 310-311.

Campbell, R.W. (1972). The American Avocet (*Recurvirostra americana*) in British Columbia (1908-70). *Syesis* **5**: 173-178.

Campbell, R.W. (1975). Hunting tactics of a Peregrine Falcon on Black Turnstones. *Condor* **77(4)**: 485.

Campbell, R.W. & Gregory, P.T. (1976). The Buff-breasted Sandpiper in British Columbia, with notes on its migration in North America. *Syesis* **9**: 123-130.

Campbell, R.W., Dawe, N.K., McTaggart-Cowan, I., Cooper, J.M., Kaiser, G.W. & McNall, M.C.E. (1990). *The Birds of British Columbia*. Royal British Columbia Museum & Canadian Wildlife Service, Victoria, Canada.

Camphuysen, K.C.J. (1991a). [Aerial courtship of Arctic Terns at sea]. *Sula* **5**: 59-61. In Dutch.

Camphuysen, K.C.J. (1991b). [Distribution, diet and feeding behaviour of the Ivory Gull *Pagophila eburnea* around west Spitsbergen]. *Sula* **5**: 125-137. In Dutch.

Camphuysen, K.C.J. (1994). Ivory Gull. *Pagophila eburnea*. Pp. 290-291 in: Tucker & Heath (1994).

Camphuysen, K.C.J. & van Dijk, J. (1983). Zee-en kustvogels langs de Nederlandse kust, 1974-1979. *Limosa* **56**: 81-230.

Camphuysen, K.C.J. & van Ijzendoorn, E.J. (1988). Influx of Pomarine Skua in northwestern Europe in autumn 1985. *Dutch Birding* **10(2)**: 54-70. In English with Dutch summary.

Campredon, P. (1978). Reproduction de la Sterne caugek, *Thalasseus sandvicensis* Lath., sur le Band d'Arguin (Gironde). Aperçu de la distribution hivernale. *Oiseau et RFO* **48**: 263-280.

Cane, C. (1980). Observations on the behaviour of the Purple Sandpiper during incubation and hatching. Pp. 59-66 in: Innes, J. ed. (1980). *Cambridge University Norwegian Expedition 1978 Report*. Cambridge.

Cane, W.P. (1994). Ontogenic evidence for relationships within the Laridae. *Auk* **111**: 873-880.

Canevari, M., Canevari, P., Carrizo, B.R., Harris, G., Mata, J.R. & Straneck, R.J. (1991). *Nueva guía de las Aves Argentinas*. Vol. 1-2. Fundación Acindar, Buenos Aires.

Canevari, P. & Blanco, D.E. (1994). Literature search for the Eskimo Curlew. Report to US Fish & Wildlife Service Conservation International.

Canova, L. & Saino, N. (1983). Conferma della nidificazione della Pernice di Mare *Glareola pratincola* nella bonifica del mezzano (Emilia-Romagna). *Riv. ital. Orn.* **53(3-4)**: 196-197.

Cao Yuping, Yu Dehai *et al.* (1989). [First discovery and raising of the Houbara Bustard *Chlamydotis undulata* in Hebei Province]. *Chinese Wildlife* **4**: 32. In Chinese.

Caravacho, A., Ríos, R., León, C. & Escofet, A. (1989). *Sterna antillarum browni* en el Golfo de California: observaciones sobre una colonia reproductora en una zona vulnerable al impacto turístico. *Southwest Nat.* **34**: 124-130.

Carballo, C. (1995). Alimentación de la Becada (*Scolopax rusticola*) en período de invernada en Galicia. [Some data on the diet of Woodcocks (*Scolopax rusticola*) wintering in Galicia (NW Spain)]. Pp. 125-130 in: Munilla, I. & Mouriño, J. eds. (1995). *Actas do II Congreso Galego de Ornitoloxía*. Universidade de Santiago de Compostela, Santiago de Compostela. In Spanish with English summary.

Carbonell, M. (1987). [A new locality for the Sungrebe, *Heliornis fulica*, from the province of Corrientes, Argentina (Aves, Heliornithidae)]. *Not. Faun.* **5**: 2. In Spanish.

Cardiff, S.W. & Remsen, J.V. (1994). Type specimens of birds in the Museum of Natural Science, Louisiana State University. *Occas. Pap. Mus. Nat. Sci. Lousiana State Univ.* **68**: 1-32.

Cardno, R. (1979). Black-winged Pratincole in Aberdeenshire. *Scottish Birds* **10(8)**: 314-315.

Carey, C., Leon-Velarde, F., Castro, G. & Monge, C. (1987). Shell conductance, daily water loss, and water content of Andean Gull and Puna Ibis eggs. *J. Exper. Zool. Suppl.* **1**: 247-252.

Carey, G.J. (1993). The status and field identification of Snipe in Hong Kong. *Hong Kong Bird Rep.* **1992**: 139-152.

Carlisle, M.J. & Tacha, T.C. (1983). Fall migration of Sandhill Cranes in west central North Dakota. *J. Wildl. Manage.* **47**: 818-821.

Carlson, G. & Trost, C.H. (1992). Sex determination of the Whooping Crane by analysis of vocalization. *Condor* **94(2)**: 532-536.

Carnaby, I.C. (1946). A further nesting record of the Banded Stilt. *Emu* **46**: 156-158.

Carp, E. (1980). *Directory of Wetlands of International Importance in the Western Palearctic*. IUCN/UNEP, Gland, Switzerland.

Carp, E. (1991). *Censo Neotropical de Aves Acuáticas 1990*. IWRB, Slimbridge, UK.

Carpenter, R.E. & Stafford, M.A. (1970). The secretory rates and the chemical stimulus for secretion of the nasal salt glands in the Rallidae. *Condor* **72**: 316-324.

Carranza, J. & Hidalgo, S.J. (1993). Condition-dependence and sex traits in the male Great Bustard. *Ethology* **94(3)**: 187-200.

Carranza, J., Hidalgo, S.J. & Ena, V. (1989). Mating system flexibility in the Great Bustard: a comparative study. *Bird Study* **36**: 192-198.

Carreker, R.G. (1985). Habitat suitability index models: Least Tern. *US Fish Wildl. Serv. Biol. Rep.* **82**: 1-29.

Carrera, E. (1987). *Gavines*. Cyan Edicions, Barcelona.

Carrera, E. & García, J. (1986). The importance of the Iberian Mediterranean coast as a wintering area for gulls and terns. Pp. 315-331 in: MEDMARAVIS & Monbailliu (1986).

Carrera, E., Monbailliu, X. & Torre, A. (1993). Ringing recoveries of Yellow-legged Gulls in northern Europe. Pp. 181-194 in: Aguilar *et al.* (1993).

Carrera, E., Nebot, M.R. & Vilagrasa, F.X. (1981). Comentaris sobre els desplaçaments erràtics de la població catalana de Gavià Argentat (*Larus argentatus michahellis*). *Butll. Inst. Catalana Hist. Nat.* **47**: 143-153.

Carrick, R. & Murray, M.D. (1964). Social factors in population regulation of the Silver Gull *Larus novaehollandiae* Stephens. *CSIRO Wildl. Res.* **9**: 189-199.

Carrick, R., Wheeler, W.R. & Murray, M.D. (1957). Seasonal dispersal and mortality in the Silver Gull *Larus novaehollandiae* Stephens and Crested Tern *Sterna bergii* Lichtenstein. *CSIRO Wildl. Res.* **2**: 116-144.

Carroll, A.L.K. (1963a). Food habits of the North Island Weka. *Notornis* **10(6)**: 281-284, 289-300.

Carroll, A.L.K. (1963b). Breeding cycle of the North Island Weka. *Notornis* **10(6)**: 300-302.

Carroll, A.L.K. (1963c). Sexing of Wekas. *Notornis* **10(6)**: 302-203.

Carroll, A.L.K. (1966). Food habits of the Pukeko (*Porphyrio melanotus*, Temminck). *Notornis* **13**: 133-144.

Carroll, A.L.K. (1969). The Pukeko (*Porphyrio melanotus*) in New Zealand. *Notornis* **16**: 101-120.

Carroll, J.R. (1988). The status and breeding ecology of the Black Tern (*Chlidonias niger*) in New York State. NY Department of Environment Conservation, Delmar, New York. 20 pp.

Carroll, R.L. (1988). *Vertebrate Paleontology and Evolution*. W.H. Freeman, New York.

Carroll, R.W. (1988). Birds of the Central African Republic. *Malimbus* **10**: 177-200.

Carruthers, R.K. (1968). Notes on an influx of Oriental Pratincole at Mount Isa. *Emu* **68**: 216-217.

Carstairs, D.N. (1989). The status of the Rufous-chested Dotterel *Zonibyx modestus* in the Falkland Islands. *Bull. Brit. Orn. Club* **109(3)**: 166-169.

Cartar, R.V. (1984). A morphometric comparison of Western and Semipalmated Sandpipers. *Wilson Bull.* **96**: 277-286.

Cartar, R.V. (1985). Testis size in sandpipers. The fertilization frequency hypothesis. *Naturwissenschaften* **72**: 157-158.

Cartar, R.V. & Lyon, B.E. (1988). The mating system of the Buff-breasted Sandpiper: lekking and resource defense polygamy. *Ornis Scand.* **19(1)**: 74-76.

Cartar, R.V. & Montgomerie, R.D. (1985). The influence of weather on incubation scheduling of the White-rumped Sandpiper: a uniparental incubator in a cold environment. *Behaviour* **95**: 261-290.

Cartar, R.V. & Montgomerie, R.D. (1987). Day-to-day variation in nest attentiveness of White-rumped Sandpiper. *Condor* **89**: 252-260.

Carter, D.S., Davis, R.E., LeGrand, H.E. & Lynch, J.M. (1992). First record of Little Stint in North Carolina. *Chat* **56(2)**: 35-36.

Carter, H.R. (1984). *At-sea Biology of the Marbled Murrelet* Brachyramphus marmorantus *in Barkley Sound, British Columbia*. MSc thesis, University of Manitoba, Winnipeg, Canada.

Carter, H.R. & Erickson, R.A. (1992). Status and conservation of the Marbled Murrelet in California, 1892-1987. Pp. 92-108 in: Carter & Morrison (1992).

Carter, H.R. & Morrison, M.L. eds. (1992). *Status and Conservation of the Marbled Murrelet in North America*. Proceedings of the Western Foundation of Vertebrate Zoology **5(1)**. Camarillo, California.

Carter, H.R. & Sealy, S.G. (1986). Year-round use of coastal lakes by Marbled Murrelets. *Condor* **88**: 473-477.

Carter, H.R. & Sealy, S.G. (1987). Fish-holding behavior of Marbled Murrelets. *Wilson Bull.* **99**: 289-291.

Carter, H.R. & Sealy, S.G. (1990). Daily foraging behavior of Marbled Murrelets. Pp. 93-102 in: Sealy (1990).

Carter, H.R. & Spear, L.B. (1986). Costs of adoption in Western Gulls. *Condor* **88**: 253-256.

Carter, H.R., Jaques, D.L., McChesney, G.J., Strong, C.S., Parker, M.W. & Takekawa, J.E. (1990). Breeding populations of seabirds on the northern and central California coasts in 1989 and 1990. Unpublished report to US Fish & Wildlife Service, Dixon, California.

Carter, H.R., McChesney, G.J., Jaques, D.L., Strong, C.S., Parker, M.W., Takekawa, J.E., Jory, D.L. & Whitworth, D.L. (1992). Breeding populations of seabirds in California, 1989-1992. Vol. 1. Populations estimates. Unpublished report to US Fish & Wildlife Service, Northern Prairie Wildlife Research Center, Dixon, California.

Carter, M. & Sudbury, A. (1993). Spotted Redshank *Tringa erythropus* in Australia. *Austr. Bird Watcher* **15(4)**: 149-159.

Carter, T. (1904). Birds occurring in the region of the north-west Cape. *Emu* **3**: 171-177.

Carver, J. & Carver, J. (1979). Peters' Finfoot nest. *Bull. East Afr. Nat. Hist. Soc.* **1979**: 113-114.

Casini, L. (1986). [Nesting of a Black-winged Stilt and Avocet in the Salina di Cervia, Ravenna (NE Italy)]. *Riv. ital. Orn.* **56(3-4)**: 181-196. In Italian with English summary.

Caspers, F.J. (1984). Spornkiebitz (*Hoplopterus spinosus*) im Westlichen Rheinland. [*Hoplopterus spinosus* in western Rheinland]. *Charadrius* **20(1)**: 58.

Cassels, K.A.H. & Elliott, H.F.I. (1975). An undescribed display of the Red-crested Korhaan *Lophotis ruficrista*. *Bull. Brit. Orn. Club* **95(3)**: 116-117.

Cassidy, J. ed. (1990). *Book of North American Birds*. Reader's Digest, Pleasantville, New York.

Cassidy, R., Salinger, T. & Wolhuter, D. (1984). The Three-banded Courser in South Africa. *Ostrich* **55(1)**: 34.

Castan, R. (1964). Capture d'un Becasseau rousset *Tryngites subruficollis* (Vieillot) dans le sud Tunisien. *Alauda* **32**: 129-132.

Castellanos, A. (1935). Observaciones de algunas aves de Tierra del Fuego e Isla de los Estados. *Hornero* **6**: 22-37.

Castilla, A.M. (1995). Intensive predation of artificial Audouin's Gull nests by the Yellow-legged Gull in the Columbretes Islands, Spain. *Colonial Waterbirds* **18(2)**: 226-230.

Castilla, A.M. & Pérez, J.J. (1995). Relationships between fishery activities and presence of the Audouin's Gull (*Larus audouinii*) in the Columbretes Islands. *Colonial Waterbirds* **18(1)**: 108-112.

Castro, G. & Myers, J.P. (1989). Flight range estimates for shorebirds. *Auk* **106**: 474-475.

Castro, G. & Myers, J.P. (1990). Validity of predictive equations for total body fat in Sanderlings from different nonbreeding areas. *Condor* **92**: 205-209.

Castro, G., Myers, J.P. & Place, A.R. (1989). Assimilation efficiency of Sanderlings (*Calidris alba*) feeding on horseshoe crab (*Limulus polyphemus*) eggs. *Physiol. Zool.* **62**: 702-715.

Castro, G., Myers, J.P. & Ricklefs, R.E. (1992). Ecology and energetics of Sanderlings migrating to four latitudes. *Ecology* **73(3)**: 833-844.

Catley, G.P. (1984). Feeding behaviour and plumage of an adult Sharp-tailed Sandpiper. *British Birds* **77(4)**: 156-157.

Catley, G.P. & Hume, R.A. (1994). A Golden Plover: but which one? *British Birds* **87(1)**: 16-21.

Caughley, G. (1960). Observations on breeding and chick rearing in the Antarctic Skua. *Notornis* **8**: 194-195.

Causey, M.K., Hudson, M.K. & Mack, T.P. (1987). Breeding activity of American Woodcock in Alabama as related to temperature. *Proc. Ann. Conf. Southeastern Assoc. Fish. & Wildl. Agencies* **41**: 373-377.

Cavanagh, P.M. & Griffin, C.R. (1993). Responses of nesting Common Terns and Laughing Gulls to flyovers by large gulls. *Wilson Bull.* **105**: 333-338.

Cave, B. (1982). Forster's Tern: new to Britain and Ireland. *British Birds* **75**: 55-61.

Cave, F.O. & Macdonald, J.D. (1955). *Birds of the Sudan: their Identification and Distribution*. Oliver & Boyd, Edinburgh & London.

Cawkill, E.M. & Hamilton, J.E. (1961). The birds of the Falkland Islands. *Ibis* **103a**: 1-27.

Cayford, J.T. (1988a). A field test of the accuracy of estimating prey-size selection in oystercatchers from recovered mussel shells. *Wader Study Group Bull.* **54**: 29-32.

Cayford, J.T. (1988b). *The Foraging Behaviour of Oystercatchers (*Haematopus ostralegus*) Feeding on Mussels*. PhD thesis, University of Exeter and Cornwall County Council, UK.

Cayford, J.T. & Goss-Custard, J.D. (1990). Seasonal changes in the size selection of mussels, *Mytilus edulis*, by Oystercatchers, *Haematopus ostralegus*: an optimality approach. *Anim. Behav.* **40**: 609-624.

Cederroth, C. (1995). Gulfotad trut. En nygammal art (?) i trutflockarna. *Vår Fågelvärld* **6-7**: 14-22.

Cempulik, P. (1991). Bestandsentwicklung, Schutzstatus und aktuelle Untersuchungen am Wachtelkönig in Polen. *Vogelwelt* **112**: 40-45.

Cepeda, F. & Cruz, J.B. (1994). Status and management of seabirds on the Galapagos Islands, Ecuador. Pp. 268-278 in: Nettleship *et al.* (1994).

Cezilly, F. & Quenette, P.Y. (1988). Rôle des écrans naturels attenant au nid chez le Goéland leucophée (*Larus cachinnans michahellis*). *Alauda* **56**: 41-50.

Cha Meiwah & Young, L. (1990). Food of the Spoon-billed Sandpiper in Hong Kong. *Hong Kong Bird Rep.* **1990**: 192-193.

Chabrzyk, B. & Coulson, J.C. (1976). Survival and recruitment in the Herring Gull, *Larus argentatus*. *J. Anim. Ecol.* **45**: 187-203.

Chacko, R.T. (1992). Black-necked Cranes wintering in Bhutan. *Bull. Oriental Bird Club* **16**: 36-38.

Chacko, R.T. (1994). [Wintering Black-necked Crane in Bhutan]. *Falke* **41(1)**: 27-31. In German.

Chacón, G. (1993). El Guión de Codornices en la península Ibérica y Baleares. *Quercus* **83**: 26-29.

Chadwick, D.H. (1991). Heavenly goats: the mysterious and musical Common Snipe. *Birder's World* **5(2)**: 10-14.

Chafer, C. (1984). Northern distribution of the Hooded Plover in NSW. *Stilt* **5**: 27.

Chafer, C.J. (1989). A Little Stint at Comerong Island. *Austr. Birds* **22(3/4)**: 89-90.

Chafer, C.J. (1992a). The foraging ecology of the Sooty Oystercatcher *Haematopus fuliginosus* on the Rocky Shores of the Illawarra Region of New South Wales: a preliminary analysis. Unpublished report to the Department of Biological Sciences, University of Wollongong, Australia.

Chafer, C.J. (1992b). Ascidian predation by the Sooty Oystercatcher *Haematopus fuliginosus*: further observations. *Stilt* **20**: 20-21.

Chaffer, N. (1940). Photographing the Avocet - and other birds - at Lake Migdeon. *Emu* **40**: 126-128.

Chaffer, N. (1949). Photographing the Australian Pratincole. *Emu* **49**: 1-5.

Chamberlin, S. & Dowding, J. (1985). Fairy Terns at Tapora, Kaipara Harbour. *Notornis* **32**: 324-325.

Chambers, S. (1989). *Birds of New Zealand. Locality Guide*. Arun Books, Hamilton, New Zealand.

Chandler, R. (1995). Salt lake stilt city. *BBC Wildlife* **13(12)**: 34-37.

Chandler, R.J. (1987a). Yellow orbital ring of Semipalmated and Ringed Plovers. *British Birds* **80(5)**: 241-242.

Chandler, R.J. (1987b). Plumages of breeding female Ruffs. *British Birds* **80(5)**: 246-248.

Chandler, R.J. (1990). Plumage variations of juvenile Ruffs and Greenshanks. *British Birds* **83(3)**: 117-121.

Chandler, R.M. (1990). Fossil birds of the San Diego Formation, Late Pliocene, Blancan, San Diego County, California. *Orn. Monogr.* **44**: 77-161.

Chandler, R.M. & Wilds, C. (1994). Little, Least and Saunder's Terns. *British Birds* **87**: 60-66.

Chandra, J. (1990). Unique Karera Great Indian Bustard sanctuary. *Tigerpaper* **17(1)**: 16-20.

Chaney, A.H., Chapman, B.R., Karges, J.P., Nelson, D.A., Schmidt, R.R. & Thebeau, L.C. (1978). *Use of Dredged Material Islands by Colonial Seabirds and Wading Birds in Texas*. US Army Engineer Waterways Experimental Station, Technical Report D-78-8, Vicksburg, Mississippi.

Chang Jiachuan (1989). New records of birds in China, the Long-tailed Skua *Stercorarius longicaudus*. *Chinese Wildlife* **4**: 43.

Chaniot, G. (1970). Notes on color variation in downy Caspian Terns. *Condor* **72**: 460-465.

Chapdelaine, G. & Brousseau, P. (1989). Size and trends of Black-legged Kittiwake (*Rissa tridactyla*) populations in the Gulf of St. Lawrence (Quebec) 1974-1985. *Amer. Birds* **43**: 21-24.

Chapdelaine, G., Brousseau, P., Anderson, R. & Marsan, R. (1985). Breeding ecology of Common and Arctic Terns in the Mingan Archipelago, Quebec. *Colonial Waterbirds* **8**: 166-177.

Chapin, J.P. (1939). *The Birds of the Belgian Congo*. Part 2. Bulletin of the American Museum of Natural History **75**. 632 pp.

Chapin, J.P. (1948). The mystery of the Mabira Banshee. *Audubon Magazine* **50**: 341-349.

Chapin, J.P. (1954a). Races of the African Finfoot (Aves, Heliornithidae). *Amer. Mus. Novit.* **1659**: 1-10.

Chapin, J.P. (1954b). The calendar of Wideawake Fair. *Auk* **71**: 1-15.

Chapin, J.P. & Wing, L.W. (1959). The Wideawake calendar 1953-1958. *Auk* **76**: 153-158.

Chapman, B. & Parker, J. (1985). Foraging areas, techniques, and schedules of wintering gulls on southeastern Lake Erie. *Colonial Waterbirds* **8**: 135-141.

Chapman, B.A. & Forbes, L.S. (1984). Observations on detrimental effects of Great Blue Herons on breeding Black Terns. *J. Field Orn.* **55**: 251-252.

Chapman, B.A., Goossen, J.P. & Ohanjanian, I. (1985). Occurrences of Black-necked Stilts, *Himantopus mexicanus*, in Western Canada. *Can. Field-Nat.* **99(2)**: 254-257.

Chapman, P. & Stewart, P. (1987). The White-breasted Mesite. Pp. 25-27 in: Walters, R. (1987). The Crocodile Caves of Ankarana 1986. Unpublished report to the Bristol City Museum and Art Gallery, Bristol.

Chapman, S.E. (1969). The Pacific winter quarters of Sabine's Gull. *Ibis* **111**: 615-617.

Chappuis, C. (1975). Illustration sonore de problèmes bioacoustiques posés par les oiseaux de la zone éthiopienne. *Alauda* **43**(Suppl.): 427-474.

Chappuis, C., Érard, C. & Morel, G.J. (1979). Données comparatives sur la morphologie et les vocalisations des diverses formes d'*Eupodotis ruficrista* (Smith). *Malimbus* **1**: 74-89.

Chardine, J.W. (1987). The influence of pair-status on the breeding behaviour of the Kittiwake *Rissa tridactyla* before egg-laying. *Ibis* **129**: 515-526.

Chardine, J.W. & Morris, R.D. (1983). Nocturnal desertion patterns: influence on hatching synchrony in Ring-billed Gulls *Larus delawarensis*. *Ibis* **125**: 389-396.

Chardine, J.W. & Morris, R.D. (1989). Sexual size dimorphism and assortative mating in the Brown Noddy. *Condor* **91**: 868-874.

Chardine, J.W. & Morris, R.D. (1996). Brown Noddy (*Anous stolidus*). No. 220 in: Poole & Gill (1996).

Chartier, B. & Cooke, F. (1980). Ross' Gulls (*Rhodostethia rosea*) nesting at Churchill, Manitoba, Canada. *Amer. Birds* **34**: 839-841.

Chatto, R. (1987). Masked Lapwings kill Kestrel. *Austr. Raptor Assoc. News* **8(3)**: 54.

Chattopadhyay, S. (1980). Observations on parental care of a wounded chick of the Bronzewinged Jacana, *Metopidius indicus* (Latham). *J. Bombay Nat. Hist. Soc.* **77(2)**: 325-326.

Chattopadhyay, S.K. & Chattopadhyay, S. (1988). Molt, gonadal status and body weight in relation to vernal migration in the Spotted Sandpiper, *Tringa glareola* (Linnaeus). *Proc. Zool. Soc.* **41**: 19-24.

Chattopadhyay, S.K., Maji, T.K., Some, K. & Sarkar, A.K. (1994). Body weight, fat deposition and gonadal conditions in the males of three migratory avian species during wintering months in India. *Proc. Zool. Soc.* **47**: 33-39.

Chebez, J.C. & Maletti, E.R. (1990). Una población relictual de la Chuña Real, *Cariama cristata* (Linné, 1766) (Aves: Gruiformes: Cariamidae) en la Mesopotamia Argentina. *Bol. Cient. Aprona* **18**: 5-9.

Chebez, J.C. (1994). *Los Que Se Van. Especies Argentinas en Peligro*. Albatros.

Cheesman, R.E. & Sclater, W.L. (1935). On a collection of birds from north-western Abyssinia - Part II. *Ibis* Ser. 13, no. 5: 297-329.

Cheke, A.S. (1987). An ecological history of the Mascarene Islands. Pp. 5-89 in: Diamond, A.W. ed. (1987). *Studies of Mascarene Island Birds*. Cambridge University Press, Cambridge.

Cheke, R.A. (1980). A small breeding colony of the Rock Pratincole *Glareola nuchalis liberiae* in Togo. *Bull. Brit. Orn. Club* **100(3)**: 175-178.

Cheke, R.A. (1982). Additional information on the Rock Pratincole *Glareola nuchalis* in Togo. *Bull. Brit. Orn. Club* **102(3)**: 116-117.

Cheke, R.A. & Walsh, J.F. (1980). Bird records from the Republic of Togo. *Malimbus* **2**: 112-120.

Chekmenev, D.I. (1960). [On the biology of the Demoiselle Crane in Central Kazakhstan]. *Trudy Inst. Zool. Akad. Nauk Kazhs. SSR* **13**: 142-147. In Russian.

Chekmenev, D.I. (1961). [On the biology of the Sociable Plover]. *Trudy Inst. Zool. Akad. Nauk Kazhs. SSR* **15**: 143-146. In Russian.

Cheltsov-Bebutov, A.M. (1976). [Geographical variability of the Greater Sand Plover (*Charadrius leschenaultii*) and its possible causes]. *Ornitologiya* **12**: 200-206. In Russian.

Chen, Z. (1988). Niche selection of breeding seabirds on Chenlushan Island in the Yellow Sea, China. *Colonial Waterbirds* **11**: 306-307.

Chen Bin & Wang Zuoyi (1991). Observation on wintering ecology of cranes at Poyang Lake. Pp. 105-108 in: Harris (1991b).

Chen Bin, Liu Zhiyong & Tao Fuzhong (1987). [The habits of the wintering White-naped Crane]. Pp. 57-60 in: [*Report on the Rare Birds Winter Ecology Study at Poyang Lake Migratory Birds Reserve*]. Jiangxi Scientific Technical Press, Nanchang, Jiangxi, China. In Chinese.

Chenaux-Repond, R. (1975). White-collared Pratincole at Mazoe. *Honeyguide* **82**: 39-40.

Cheng, L. & Harrison, C.S. (1983). Seabird predation on halobates [(Heteroptera): Gerridae]. *Mar. Biol.* **72**: 303-309.

Cheng Tsohsin (1981). Cranes in China. Pp. 47-48 in: Lewis & Masatomi (1981).

Cheng Tsohsin (1986). Systematic keys for the cranes of the world. *Acta Zool. Sinica* **32(2)**: 189-193.
Cheng Tsohsin (1987). *A Synopsis of the Avifauna of China*. Science Press & Paul Parey, Beijing & Hamburg.
Cheng Zhaoqin (1990). Behavior of nesting Black-tailed Gulls (*Larus crassirostris*). *Colonial Waterbirds* **13**: 103-107.
Chernichko, I.I. (1985). [Trophic adaptation and origin of colonial nesting in precocial and altricial Charadriiformes]. *Bull. Moscow Soc. Nat. Study (Biol. Section)* **90**: 157-162. In Russian.
Chernichko, I.I., Chernichko, R., Diadicheva, E., van der Have, T.M., van de Sant, S. (1993). Biometry of waders in the Sivash, Ukraine. Pp. 65-85 in: van der Have, T.M., van de Sant, S., Verkuil, Y. & van der Winden, J. eds. (1993). *Waterbirds in the Sivash, Spring 1992*. WIWO-Report **36**. Zeist, the Netherlands.
Chernichko, I.I., Grinchenko, A.B. & Siokhin, V.D. (1991). Waders of the Sivash Gulf, Azov-Black Sea, USSR. *Wader Study Group Bull.* **63**: 37-38.
Chernyaev, A.B. (1986). [Food of the Red-necked Phalarope and the Little Stint during autumn migration in southeast Kazakhstan]. Pp. 322-323 in: [*Study of the USSR Birds, their Conservation and Rational Use*]. Abstracts of the papers. I. All-Union Congress of the All-Union Ornithological Society and IX All-Union Ornithological Conference. Part 2. In Russian.
Chestney, R. (1970). Notes on the breeding habits of Common and Sandwich Terns on Scolt Head Island. *Trans. Norfolk Norwich Nat. Soc.* **21**: 353-363.
Chikina, O.D. (1985). [On the ecology of the Little Ringed Plover (*Charadrius dubius curonicus* Gm.)]. Pp. 86-92 in: The investigations of the flora and fauna of Middle Asia. Materials of the research conference "Regional aspects of the flora and fauna of Middle Asia and South Kazakhstan", Tashkent, 18 Februari 1985. Tashkent. In Russian.
Child, P. (1973). Wrybills in Central Otago: further records. *Notornis* **20(1)**: 77-78.
Child, P. (1982). A new breeding species for Central Otago: Black-fronted Dotterel. *Notornis* **29(2)**: 99-100.
Child, P. (1983). Decline of the Pied Stilt in Central Otago. *Notornis* **30**: 243-244.
Child, P. (1986). Black-fronted Tern breeding at high altitude. *Notornis* **33(3)**: 193-194.
Child, P. & Child, M. (1984). The Alexandra Black-fronted Dotterels: 1982/83 season. *Notornis* **31(1)**: 31-39.
Chiweshe, N.C. & Dale, J. (1993). Unusual Kori Bustard food item. *Honeyguide* **39**: 22.
Cho, S. & Won, P. (1990). Wintering ecology of the Hooded Crane (*Grus monacha* Temminck) in Korea. *Bull. Inst. Orn., Kyung Hee Univ.* **3**: 1-22.
Chodkov, G.I. (1979). [Black-headed Gull and Caspian Terns on Lake Chan (Western Siberia)]. Pp. 189-191 in: [*Migration and Ecology of the Birds of Siberia*]. Report to Orn. Conf. Yakustsk Acad Sci., Yakutsk. In Russian.
Chojnacki, I. & Stawarczyk, T. (1988). Wood Sandpipers using tail-pattern as visual signal in aggressive encounters. *British Birds* **81(9)**: 466-468.
Chong, J.R. (1987). [*Rare Birds of the Korean Peninsula*]. Chosum University Natural History Museum. In Japanese.
Chong, J.R. (1988). [Number of cranes wintering in and migrating through the D.P.R. Korea]. Pp. 9-16 in: Masatomi (1988). In Japanese.
Chong, J.R., Higuchi, H. & Pak, U. (1992). [The migration routes and the important resting areas of cranes in the Korean peninsula - from the results of satellite tracking]. *Strix* **11**: 21-34. In Japanese with English summary.
Chong, M.N.H. (1994). Masked Finfoot *Heliopais personata* in Peninsular Malaysia. *Bull. Oriental Bird Club* **20**: 28-31.
Christen, W. (1980a). Späte Brut del Flußregenpfeifers. [Late breeding in the Little Ringed Plover]. *Orn. Beob.* **77(3)**: 197-198.
Christen, W. (1980b). Entwicklung und Ökologie der Trielpopulation *Burhinus oedicnemus* im Elsaß. [Status and ecology of the Stone Curlew *Burhinus oedicnemus* population in the Alsace]. *Orn. Beob.* **77(4)**: 201-208.
Christen, W. (1982). Der Durchzug des Triels *Burhinus oedicnemus* in der Schweiz. [Migration of the Stone Curlew *Burhinus oedicnemus* in Switzerland]. *Orn. Beob.* **79(3)**: 214-216.
Christian, E.J. (1909). Notes on the Black-tailed Native Hen (*Microtribonyx ventralis*). *Emu* **9**: 95-97.
Christian, P.D., Christidis, L. & Schodde, R. (1992a). Biochemical systematics of the Australian dotterels and plovers (Charadriiformes: Charadriidae). *Austr. J. Zool.* **40(2)**: 225-233.
Christian, P.D., Christidis, L. & Schodde, R. (1992b). Biochemical systematics of the Charadriiformes (shorebirds): relationships between the Charadrii, Scolopaci and Lari. *Austr. J. Zool.* **40(3)**: 291-302.
Christidis, L. & Boles, W.E. (1994). *The Taxonomy and Species of Birds of Australia and its Territories*. RAOU **2**. Royal Australasian Ornithologists Union Monograph, Melbourne.
Chu, P.C. (1995). Phylogenetic reanalysis of Strauch's osteological data set for the Charadriiformes. *Condor* **97**: 174-196.
Chubb, C. (1916). *The Birds of British Guiana*. Vol. 1. Bernard Quaritch, London.
Chubb, E.C. (1908). On the nesting of *Podica petersi* Hartl. (Peters' Finfoot) in Rhodesia. *J. S. Afr. Orn. Union* **4**: 107.
Chudzik, J.M., Graham, K.D. & Morris, R.D. (1994). Comparative breeding success and diet of Ring-billed and Herring Gulls on South Limestone Island, Georgian Bay. *Colonial Waterbirds* **17(1)**: 18-27.
Chylarecki, P. & Sikora, A. (1990). Sexual differences in biometrics and moult of Grey Plovers breeding in West Siberia. *Wader Study Group Bull.* **59**: 7.
Cicchino, A.C. (1982). Sobre *Colpocephalum wernecki* Orfila, 1953 y las especies del género *Colpocephalum* Nitzsch, 1818 parásitas de Cariamidae. *Neotropica* **27(79)**: 59-60.
Cikutovic, M.A. & Guerra, C.G. (1983). Bioecología de la migración de la Gaviota de Franklin (*Larus pipixcan*) en los 23° sur (Antofagasta-Chile). Pp. 105-113 in: *Proc. Primier Symp. Orn. Neotropica*. Arequipa, Peru.
Cikutovic, M.A., Guerra, C.G. & Fitzpatrick, L.C. (1988). Gonadal cycle of Gray Gulls *Larus modestus* in northern Chile. *Gerfaut* **78**: 209-216.
Claassen, J. & Claassen, R. (1991). [Caspian Plover in the Karoo]. *Promerops* **197**: 11. In Afrikaans.
Clancey, P.A. (1962). Chestnut-banded Sandplover *Charadrius pallidus pallidus* Strickland in southern Mozambique. *Ostrich* **33(1)**: 26.
Clancey, P.A. (1964a). On the races of the Whimbrel wintering in southeastern Africa. *Bull. Brit. Orn. Club* **84**: 138-140.
Clancey, P.A. (1964b). *The Birds of Natal and Zululand*. Oliver & Boyd, Edinburgh & London.
Clancey, P.A. (1964c). The first records of the Red-necked Stint *Calidris ruficollis* from the Ethiopian region. *Ibis* **106**: 254-255.
Clancey, P.A. (1965). The Knot *Calidris canutus* in Natal. *Ostrich* **36**: 143-144.
Clancey, P.A. (1967). *Gamebirds of Southern Africa*. Purnell, Cape Town.
Clancey, P.A. (1971a). A handlist of the birds of southern Moçambique. *Inst. Invest. Cientifica Moçambique (Ser. A)* **10**: 145-302.
Clancey, P.A. (1971b). On the race of the Oystercatcher *Haematopus ostralegus* occurring in South Africa. *Ostrich* **42**: 72 73.
Clancey, P.A. (1971c). Miscellaneous taxonomic notes on African birds. 33. Variation in Kittlitz's Sandplover *Charadrius pecuarius* Temminck. *Durban Mus. Novit.* **9**: 109-112.
Clancey, P.A. (1971d). Miscellaneous taxonomic notes on African birds. 33. The southern races of the White-fronted Sandplover *Charadrius marginatus* Vieillot. *Durban Mus. Novit.* **9**: 113-118.
Clancey, P.A. (1975a). Miscellaneous taxonomic notes on African birds. 43. On the relationship of *Charadrius marginatus* Vieillot of Ethiopian Africa to *Charadrius alexandrinus* Linnaeus. *Durban Mus. Novit.* **11**: 1-9.
Clancey, P.A. (1975b). *Sterna bergii* and *Sterna maxima* in the South African sub-region, with observations on their relationship. *Durban Mus. Novit.* **10**: 191-206.
Clancey, P.A. (1977a). Notes on recent tern 'wrecks' on the Natal Coast. *Bokmakierie* **29**: 17.
Clancey, P.A. (1977b). Data from Sooty Terns from Natal and Zululand. *Ostrich* **48**: 43-44.
Clancey, P.A. (1977c). Miscellaneous taxonomic notes on African birds. 48-50. *Durban Mus. Novit.* **11**: 223-238.
Clancey, P.A. (1979). Miscellaneous taxonomic notes on African birds. 55. An additional African race of Collared Pratincole. *Durban Mus. Novit.* **12(5)**: 49-50.
Clancey, P.A. (1981a). On birds from Gough Island, central south Atlantic. *Durban Mus. Novit.* **12**: 187-200.
Clancey, P.A. (1981b). Miscellaneous taxonomic notes on African birds. 59. On geographical variation in the Terek Sandpiper *Xenus cinereus* (Güldenstädt). *Durban Mus. Novit.* **12(19)**: 223-229.
Clancey, P.A. (1981c). Miscellaneous taxonomic notes on African birds. 60. Variation in the Afrotropical populations of *Charadrius tricollaris* Vieillot. *Durban Mus. Novit.* **13**: 1-6.
Clancey, P.A. (1982a). Miscellaneous taxonomic notes on African birds. 63. On the Ringed Plover *Charadrius hiaticula* Linnaeus in southern Africa. *Durban Mus. Novit.* **13**: 127-130.
Clancey, P.A. (1982b). Miscellaneous taxonomic notes on African birds. 63. The Great Sandplover *Charadrius leschenaultii* Lesson in southern and eastern Africa. *Durban Mus. Novit.* **13**: 131-132.
Clancey, P.A. (1982c). The Little Tern in southern Africa. *Ostrich* **53**: 102-106.
Clancey, P.A. (1984). Geographical variation and post-breeding dispersal in Temminck's Courser of the Afrotropics. *Gerfaut* **74(4)**: 361-374.
Clancey, P.A. (1985). *The Rare Birds of Southern Africa*. Winchester Press, Johannesburg.
Clancey, P.A. (1986). Endemicity in the southern African avifauna. *Durban Mus. Novit.* **13**: 245-284.
Clancey, P.A. (1989). Four additional species of southern African birds. *Durban Mus. Novit.* **14**: 140-152.
Clancey, P.A. (1995). The name of a proposed eastern race of the Greenshank. *Bull. Brit. Orn. Club* **115(3)**: 190.
Clancey, P.A., Brooke, R.K., Crowe, T.M. & Mendelsohn, J.M. (1991). *SAOS Checklist of Southern African Birds: Second Updating Report 1991*. Southern African Ornithological Society, Johannesburg.
Clancy, G.P. (1986). Observations on nesting Beach Thick-knees *Burhinus neglectus* at Red Rock, New South Wales. *Corella* **10(4)**: 114-118.
Clancy, G.P. (1987). The breeding status of the Little Tern *Sterna albifrons* on the New South Wales north coast, 1979 to 1982. *Corella* **11(2)**: 59-64.
Clancy, G.P. & Christiansen, M. (1980). A breeding record of the Beach Stone-curlew at Red Rock New South Wales. *Austr. Birds* **14(3)**: 55.
Clapham, C.S. (1964). The birds of the Dahlac Archipelago. *Ibis* **106**: 376-388.
Clapp, R.B. (1989). First record of the Little Tern, *Sterna albifrons* from Hawaii. *Elepaio* **49**: 41-43.
Clapp, R.B. & Buckley, P.A. (1984). Status and conservation of seabirds in the southeastern United States. Pp. 135-155 in: Croxall, Evans & Schreiber (1984).
Clapp, R.B. & Kridler, E. (1977). The natural history of Necker Island, northwestern Hawaiian Islands. *Atoll Res. Bull.* **206**: 1-91.
Clapp, R.B., Klimkiewicz, M.K. & Kennard, J.H. (1982). Longevity records of North American birds: Gaviidae through Alcidae. *J. Field Orn.* **53**: 81-124.
Clapp, R.B., Kridler, E. & Fleet, R.R. (1977). The natural history of Nihoa Islands, northwestern Hawaiian Islands. *Atoll Res. Bull.* **207**: 1-147.
Clapp, R.B., Morgan-Jacobs, D. & Banks, R.C. (1983). *Marine Birds of the Southeastern United States and Gulf of Mexico*. Part 3. Charadriiformes. US Fish & Wildlife Service, Washington, D.C.
Clapperton, K. (1983). Sexual differences in Pukeko calls. *Notornis* **30**: 69-70.
Clapperton, K. & Jenkins, P.F. (1984). Vocal repertoire of the Pukeko (Aves: Rallidae). *New Zealand J. Zool.* **11**: 71-84.
Clapperton, K. & Jenkins, P.F. (1987). Individuality in contact calls of the Pukeko (Aves: Rallidae). *New Zealand J. Zool.* **14**: 19-28.
Claridge, G. & Johnson, R. (1988). Possible unusual movement of Red-necked Avocets into northern Australia. *Stilt* **12**: 53.
Clark, A. (1982a). Some observations on the breeding behaviour of Kittlitz's Sandplover. *Ostrich* **53(2)**: 120-122.
Clark, A. (1982b). Some observations on the behaviour of the Threebanded Plover. *Ostrich* **53(4)**: 222-227.
Clark, C.T. (1985). Caribbean Coot? *Birding* **17(2/3)**: 84-86.
Clark, K.E., Niles, L.J. & Burger, J. (1993). Abundance and distribution of migrant shorebirds in Delaware Bay. *Condor* **95**: 694-705.
Clark, N.A. (1978). The weight, moult and morphometrics of Spotted Redshanks in Britain. *Wader Study Group Bull.* **22**: 22-26.
Clark, N.A. (1983). *The Ecology of Dunlin (*Calidris alpina *L.) Wintering on the Severn Estuary*. PhD thesis, University of Edinburgh, Edinburgh.
Clark, N.A. (1984). Ageing criteria for Dunlins. *Wader Study Group Bull.* **42**: 39.
Clark, N.A. (1994). Dunlin. *Calidris alpina*. Pp. 262-263 in: Tucker & Heath (1994).
Clark, R. (1986). *Aves de Tierra del Fuego y Cabo de Hornos. Guia de Campo*. Literature of Latin America, Buenos Aires.
Clarke, G. (1985). Bird observations from northwest Somalia. *Scopus* **9**: 24-42.
Clarke, J.D. (1936). The Brown-chested Wattled Plover, *Anomalophrys superciliosus*. *Nigerian Field* **5**: 72-73.
Clarke, J.H. (1975). Observations on the Bush-hen at Camp Mountain, south-east Queensland. *Sunbird* **6**: 15-21.
Clarke, W.E. (1898). On the avifauna of Franz Josef Land. *Ibis* **Ser. 7, no. 4**: 249-277.
Clausager, I. (1974). Migration of Scandinavian Woodcock (*Scolopax rusticola*) with special reference to Denmark. *Dan. Rev. Game Biol.* **8**: 1-38.
Clausen, M.K. (1990). Mountain Plover sighted in Kimball County. *Nebr. Bird Rev.* **58(4)**: 98-99.
Clay, R.P., Jack, S.R. & Vincent, J.P. (1994). A survey of the birds and large mammals of the proposed Jatun Sacha Bilsa Biological Reserve, north-western Ecuador. Project Esmeraldas '94 preliminary report.
Clay, T. (1981). The ischnoceran lice (Phthiraptera) of the oystercatchers (Aves: Haematopodidae). *Can. J. Zool.* **59**: 933-938.
Cleghorn, J.D. (1942). Great Black-backed Gull killing American Goldeneye. *Auk* **59(4)**: 584-585.
Clements, F.A. & Bradbear, N.J. (1986). Status of wintering Black-necked Cranes *Grus nigricollis* in Bhutan. *Forktail* **2**: 103-107.
Clements, J.F. (1979). Viva Zapata! *Birding* **11**: 2-6.
Clinning, C.F. (1978a). Breeding of the Caspian Tern in southwest Africa. *Cormorant* **6**: 15-16.
Clinning, C.F. (1978b). The biology and conservation of the Damara Tern in south west Africa. *Madoqua* **11**: 31-39.
Clive, J.M.C. (1928). Occurrence of the Wood Snipe in the Central Provinces. *J. Bombay Nat. Hist. Soc.* **32(3)**: 600.
Close, D.H. (1982). Recent records of the Oriental Plover. *S. Austr. Orn.* **28(8)**: 205-206.
Close, D.H. & Newman, O.M.G. (1984). The decline of the Eastern Curlew in south-eastern Australia. *Emu* **84(1)**: 38-40.
Clout, M.N. & Craig, J.L. (1995). The conservation of critically endangered flightless birds in New Zealand. *Ibis* **137(1)(Suppl.)**: S181-S190.
Coates, B. (1978). Black-winged Pratincole (*Glareola nordmanni*) at Kitwe. *Bull. Zambian Orn. Soc.* **10(2)**: 76.
Coates, B.J. (1985). *The Birds of Papua New Guinea*. Vol. 1. Non Passerines. Dove Publications, Alderley, Australia.
Cobb, A.F. (1910). *Birds of the Falkland Islands*. H.F. & G. Witherby, London.
Cobb, S. (1957). Great Black-backed Gull (*Larus marinus*). *Auk* **74**: 498.
Cochran, J.F. & Anderson, S.H. (1987). Comparison of habitat attributes at sites of stable and declining Long-billed Curlew populations. *Great Basin Nat.* **47(3)**: 459-466.
Cochrane, B. (1978). Sabine's Gull. *Promerops* **133**: 4.
Cochrane, K.L., Crawford, R.J.M. & Kriel, F. (1991). Tern mortality caused by collision with a cable at Table Bay, Cape Town, South Africa in 1989. *Colonial Waterbird* **14(1)**: 63-65.
Cohen, C. (1992). Two sheathbills at Granger Bay. *Promerops* **206**: 14.
Coimbra-Filho, A.F. (1965). Notas sobre a reproduçao em caliviero de "*Eurypyga h. helias* (Palas [sic] 1781)". *Rev. Bras. Biol.* **25**: 149-156.
Colahan, B.D. (1990). Cranes wintering in the Harrismith District, O.F.S. *Mirafra* **7(4)**: 109-111.
Coleman, J.D., Warburton, B. & Green, W.Q. (1983). Some population statistics and movements of the Western Weka. *Notornis* **30**: 93-107.
Coleman, R.A. (1981). *The Reproductive Biology of the Hawaiian Subspecies of the Black-necked Stilt* Himantopus mexicanus knudseni. PhD dissertation, Pennsylvania State University, Pennsylvania.
Coles, C.L. & Collar, N.J. eds. (1979). *Symposium Papers: The Great Bustard [and] The Houbara Bustard*. The Game Conservancy, Fordingbridge, UK.
Collar, N.J. (1979a). Bustard Group general report. *Bull. ICBP* **13**: 129-134.
Collar, N.J. (1979b). The world status of the Houbara: a preliminary review. 12 pp. (Unpaginated) in: Coles & Collar (1979).
Collar, N.J. (1983a). A history of the Houbara in the Canaries. *Bustard Studies* **1**: 9-29.
Collar, N.J. (1983b). The bustards and their conservation. Pp. 244-257 in: Goriup & Vardhan (1983).
Collar, N.J. (1985a). The world status of the Great Bustard. *Bustard Studies* **2**: 1-20.
Collar, N.J. (1985b). Bustard. Pp. 74-75 in: Campbell & Lack (1985).
Collar, N.J. (1985c). Crane. Pp. 117-118 in: Campbell & Lack (1985).
Collar, N.J. (1994). The conservation status in 1982 of the Aldabra White-throated Rail, *Dryolimnas cuvieri aldabranus*. *Bird Conserv. Int.* **3(4)**: 299-305.
Collar, N.J. & Andrew, P. (1988). *Birds to Watch. The ICBP World Checklist of Threatened Birds*. ICBP Technical Publication **8**, Cambridge.
Collar, N.J. & Goriup, P.D. (1980). Problems and progress in the captive breeding of Great Bustards *Otis tarda* in quasi-natural conditions. *Avicult. Mag.* **86**: 131-140.
Collar, N.J. & Stuart, S.N. (1985). *Threatened Birds of Africa and Related Islands*. The ICBP/IUCN Red Data Book. Part 1. 3rd edition. ICBP & IUCN, Cambridge.
Collar, N.J. & Stuart, S.N. (1988). *Key Forests for Threatened Birds in Africa*. ICBP Monograph **3**, Cambridge.
Collar, N.J., Crosby, M.J. & Stattersfield, A.J. (1994). *Birds to Watch 2: the World List of Threatened Birds*. BirdLife Conservation Series **4**. BirdLife International, Cambridge.
Collar, N.J., Gonzaga, L.P., Krabbe, N., Madroño, A., Naranjo, L.G., Parker, T.A. & Wege, D.C. (1992). *Threatened Birds of the Americas*. The ICBP/IUCN Red Data Book. Part 2. 3rd edition. ICBP, Cambridge.

Collett, S.F. (1977). Sizes of snails eaten by Snail Kites and Limpkins in a Costa Rican marsh. *Auk* **94(2)**: 365-367.

Collias, E.C. & Collias, N.E. (1957). The response of chicks of the Franklin's Gull to parental bill-color. *Auk* **74(3)**: 371-375.

Collias, N.E. (1988). Progressive analysis of avian vocal repertoires with special reference to the Brown Noddy. *Auk* **5**: 589-590.

Collinge, W.E. (1936). The food and feeding habits of the Coot (*Fulica atra* Linn.). *Ibis* **Ser. 13, no. 6**: 35-39.

Collins, C.T. & LeCroy, M. (1972). Analysis of measurements, weights and composition of Common and Roseate Tern eggs. *Wilson Bull.* **84**: 187-192.

Collins, C.T., Schew, W.A. & Burkett, E. (1991). Elegant Terns breeding in Orange County, California. *Amer. Birds* **45**: 393-395.

Collins, D.R. (1984). *A Study of the Canarian Houbara (*Chlamydotis undulata fuertaventurae*), with Special Reference to its Behaviour and Ecology*. PhD thesis, London University, London.

Collins, D.R. (1994). The diet of the Houbara Bustard *Chlamydotis undulata fuertaventurae* in the Canary Islands. *Bol. Mus. Municipal Funchal* **2**(Suppl.): 57-67.

Collins, P.W. (1979). Vertebrate zoology: the biology of introduced black rats on Anacapa and San Miguel islands. Pp. 14.1-14.49 in: Power, D.M. ed. (1979). *Natural Resources Study of the Channel Islands National Monument, California*. Santa Barbara Museum of Natural History, Santa Barbara, California

Colón, J.A. (1982). Notas sobre una colonia de Gaviota Chica, *Sterna albifrons*, en el Tuque, Ponce, Puerto Rico. Pp. 116-122 in: *Memorias del Tercer Simposio sobre la Fauna de Puerto Rico*.

Colston, P.R. (1975). Occurrence of the Western Sandpiper *Calidris mauri* at Lake Baikal USSR. *Bull. Brit. Orn. Club* **95**: 140-141.

Colwell, M.A. (1986). Intraspecific brood parasitism in three species of prairie-breeding shorebirds. *Wilson Bull.* **98**: 473-475.

Colwell, M.A. (1987). *Breeding Biology, Intrasexual Competition and Philopatry in Wilson's Phalarope (*Phalaropus tricolor*)*. PhD dissertation, University of North Dakota, Grand Forks, North Dakota.

Colwell, M.A. (1991). Effects of fluctuating wetland conditions on prairie shorebirds. Pp. 173-180 in: Holroyd, G.L., Burns, G. & Smith, H.C. eds. (1991). *Proceedings of the Second Endangered Species and Prairie Conservation Workshop*. Provincial Museum of Alberta, Edmonton, Canada.

Colwell, M.A. (1992). Wilson's Phalarope nest success is not influenced by vegetation concealment. *Condor* **94(3)**: 767-772.

Colwell, M.A. (1993). Shorebird community patterns in a seasonally dynamic estuary. *Condor* **95**: 104-114.

Colwell, M.A. & Jehl, J.R. (1994). Wilson's Phalarope (*Phalaropus tricolor*). No. **83** in: Poole & Gill (1994).

Colwell, M.A. & Landrum, S.L. (1993). Nonrandom shorebird distribution and fine-scale variation in prey abundance. *Condor* **95**: 94-103.

Colwell, M.A. & Oring, L.W. (1988a). Variable female mating tactics in a sex-role reversed shorebird, Wilson's Phalarope (*Phalaropus tricolor*). *Natl. Geogr. Res.* **4**: 408-415.

Colwell, M.A. & Oring, L.W. (1988b). Sex ratios and intrasexual competition for mates in a sex-role reversed shorebird, Wilson's Phalarope (*Phalaropus tricolor*). *Behav. Ecol. Sociobiol.* **22**: 165-173.

Colwell, M.A. & Oring, L.W. (1988c). Return rates of prairie shorebirds: sex and species differences. *Wader Study Group Bull.* **55**: 21-24.

Colwell, M.A. & Oring, L.W. (1988d). Wing fluttering display by incubating male Wilson's Phalaropes. *Can. J. Zool.* **66(10)**: 2315-2317.

Colwell, M.A. & Oring, L.W. (1988e). Habitat use by breeding and migrating shorebirds in south central Saskatchewan. *Wilson Bull.* **100**: 554-566.

Colwell, M.A. & Oring, L.W. (1988f). Breeding biology of Wilson's Phalarope in southcentral Saskatchewan. *Wilson Bull.* **100**: 567-582.

Colwell, M.A. & Oring, L.W. (1989a). Extra-pair mating in the Spotted Sandpiper: a female mate acquisition tactic. *Anim. Behav.* **38**: 675-684.

Colwell, M.A. & Oring, L.W. (1989b). Return rates of prairie shorebirds: sex and species differences. *Wader Study Group Bull.* **55**: 21-24.

Colwell, M.A. & Oring, L.W. (1990). Nest site characteristics of prairie shorebirds. *Can. J. Zool.* **68(2)**: 297-302.

Colwell, M.A., Gerstenberg, R.H., Williams, O.E. & Dodd, M.G. (1995). Four Marbled Godwits exceed the North American longevity record for Scolopacids. *J. Field Orn.* **66(2)**: 181-183.

Conant, S., Clapp, R., Hiruki, L. & Choy, B. (1991). A new tern (*Sterna*) breeding record for Hawaii. *Pacif. Sci.* **45**: 348-354.

Condamin, M. (1978). Redécouverte d'*Esacus magnirostris* (Burhinidae) en Nouvelle Calédonie. [Rediscovery of *Esacus magnirostris* (Burhinidae) in New Caledonia]. *Oiseau et RFO* **48(4)**: 381-382.

Condamin, M. (1987). [*Charadrius leschenaultii* - in new species for Senegal]. *Malimbus* **9(2)**: 131-133. In French.

Congdon, B.C. (1990). Brood enlargement and post-natal development in the Black Noddy, *Anous minutus*. *Emu* **90**: 241-247.

Congdon, B.C. (1991). Parent-offspring recognition in the Black Noddy *Anous minutus*. *Emu* **91**: 158-163.

Congdon, B.C. & Catterall, C.P. (1994). Factors influencing the Eastern Curlew's distribution and choice of foraging sites among tidal flats of Moreton Bay, south-eastern Queensland. *Wildlife Research* **21(5)**: 507-518.

Connors, C.S. (1977). *Foraging Ecology of Black Turnstones and Surfbirds on their Wintering Grounds at Bodega Bay, California*. MA thesis, University of California, Berkeley, California.

Connors, J.I. & Doerr, P.D. (1982). Woodcock use of agricultural fields in coastal North Carolina. Pp. 139-147 in: Dwyer & Storm (1982).

Connors, P.G. (1983). Taxanomy, distribution and evolution of Golden Plovers (*Pluvialis dominica* and *Pluvialis fulva*). *Auk* **100(3)**: 607-620.

Connors, P.G. & Smith, K.G. (1982). Oceanic plastic particle pollution: suspected effect on fat deposition in Red Phalaropes. *Marine Pollution Bull.* **13**: 18-20.

Connors, P.G., McCaffery, B.J. & Maron, J.L. (1993). Speciation in Golden Plovers, *Pluvialis dominica* and *P. fulva*: evidence from the breeding grounds. *Auk* **110(1)**: 9-20.

Connors, P.G., Myers, J.P., Connors, C.S.W. & Pitelka, F.A. (1981). Interhabitat movements by Sanderlings in relation to foraging profitability and the tidal cycle. *Auk* **98**: 49-64.

Conover, B. (1944). The North Pacific allies of the Purple Sandpiper. *Field Mus. Nat. Hist. (Zool. Ser.)* **29**: 169-179.

Conover, H.B. (1926). Game birds of the Hooper Bay region, Alaska (concluded). *Auk* **43**: 303-318.

Conover, H.B. (1934). A new species of rail from Paraguay. *Auk* **51**: 365-366.

Conover, H.B. (1941). A study of the dowitchers. *Auk* **58**: 376-380.

Conover, H.B. (1944). The races of the Solitary Sandpiper. *Auk* **61**: 537-544.

Conover, M.R. (1983a). Female-female pairings in Caspian Terns. *Condor* **85**: 343-349.

Conover, M.R. (1983b). Recent changes in Ring-billed and California Gull populations in the western United States. *Wilson Bull.* **95**: 362-383.

Conover, M.R. (1984a). Occurrence of supernormal clutches in the Laridae. *Wilson Bull.* **96**: 249-267.

Conover, M.R. (1984b). Consequences of mate loss to incubating Ring-billed and California Gulls. *Wilson Bull.* **97**: 714-716.

Conover, M.R. (1987). Acquisition of predator information by active and passive mobbers in Ring-billed Gull colonies. *Behaviour* **102**: 41-57.

Conover, M.R. & Conover, D.O. (1981). A documented history of Ring-billed Gull and California Gull colonies in the western United States. *Colonial Waterbirds* **4**: 37-43.

Conover, M.R. & Hunt, G.L. (1984a). Female-female pairs and sex ratios in gulls: an historical perspective. *Wilson Bull.* **96**: 619-625.

Conover, M.R. & Hunt, G.L. (1984b). Experimental evidence that female-female pairs in gulls result from a shortage of breeding males. *Condor* **86**: 472-476.

Conover, M.R. & Miller, D.E. (1978). Acoustical properties of the swoop and soar call of the Ring-billed Gull. *Auk* **95**: 599-602.

Conover, M.R. & Miller, D.E. (1979). Reaction of Ring-billed Gulls to predators and human disturbances at their breeding colonies. *Proc. Colonial Waterbird Group* **2**: 41-47.

Conover, M.R. & Miller, D.E. (1980). Daily activity patterns of breeding Ring-billed and California Gulls. *J. Field Orn.* **51**: 329-339.

Conover, M.R., Miller, D.E. & Hunt, G.L. (1979). Female-female pairs and other unusual reproductive associations in Ring-billed and California Gulls. *Auk* **96**: 6-9.

Conover, M.R., Thompson, B.C., Fitzner, R.E. & Miller, D.E. (1979). Increasing populations of Ring-billed and California Gulls in Washington State. *Western Birds* **10**: 31-36.

Considine, M.T. (1979). *The Feeding Behaviour of the Sooty Oystercatcher (*Haematopus fuliginosus*) on Rocky Shores in Victoria*. Honours thesis, Monash University, Melbourne.

Considine, M.T. (1982). Notes on the seasonal movements of the Sooty Oystercatcher (*Haematopus fuliginosus*) in southern Victoria. *Victoria Wader Study Group Bull.* **5**: 11-15.

Contreras, A. (1988). A review of the status of the Sharp-tailed Sandpiper in Oregon. *Oregon Birds* **14(4)**: 383-387.

Contreras, A. (1992). Winter status of the Sora in the Pacific northwest. *Western Birds* **23(3)**: 137-142.

Contreras, J.F. (1980). Avifauna Mendocina. IV. *Gallinago paraguaiae magellanica* (King) (Aves: Scolopacidae). *Hist. Nat., Mendoza* **1(13)**: 91-92. In Spanish with English summary.

Contreras, J.R. (1978). Ecología de la avifauna de la región de Puerto Lobos, provincias de Río Negro y del Chubut. *Ecosur* **10**: 169-181.

Contreras, J.R. (1980). Nota acerca del límite Rionegrino de la distribución de las subespecies de *Rallus sanguinolentus* en la Argentina (Aves, Rallidae). *Historia Natural* **1**: 149-152.

Contreras, J.R. & Contreras, A.O. (1990). *Atlas Ornitogeográfico de la Provincia de Corrientes, República Argentina*. Literature of Latin America, Buenos Aires.

Contreras, J.R. & Contreras, A.O. (1994). Acerca de *Laterallus exilis* (Temminck, 1831) y de *Calidris bairdii* (Coues, 1861) en la República del Paraguay (Aves: Rallidae y Scolopacidae). *Not. Faun.* **51**: 1-4.

Contreras, J.R., Berry, L.M., Contreras, A.O., Bertonatti, C.C. & Utges, E.E. (1990). *Atlas Ornitogeográfico de la Provincia del Chaco-República Argentina*. Vol. 1. No Passeriformes. Cuadernos Técnicos "Félix de Azara" 1.

Converse, J.D., Hoogstraal, H., Moussa, M.I., Feare, C.J. & Kaiser, M.N. (1975). Soldado virus (Hughes group) from *Ornithodoros (Alectrobius) capensis* (Ixodoidae: Argasidae) infesting Sooty Tern colonies in the Seychelles, Indian Ocean. *Amer. J. Trop. Med. Hyg.* **24**: 1010-1018.

Conway, C.J. (1990). *Seasonal Changes in Movements and Habitat Use by Three Sympatric Species of Rails*. MSc thesis, University of Wyoming, Laramie, Wyoming.

Conway, C.J. (1995). Virginia Rail (*Rallus limicola*). No. **123** in: Poole & Gill (1995).

Conway, C.J. & Eddlemann, W.R. (1994). Virginia Rail. In: Tacha & Braun (1994).

Conway, C.J., Eddleman, W.R. & Anderson, S.H. (1994). Nesting success and survival of Virginia Rails and Soras. *Wilson Bull.* **106(3)**: 466-473.

Conway, C.J., Eddleman, W.R., Anderson, S.H. & Hanebury, L.R. (1993). Seasonal changes in Yuma Clapper Rail vocalization rate and habitat use. *J. Wildl. Manage.* **57**: 282-290.

Conway, W.G. & Bell, J. (1969). Observations on the behaviour of Kittlitz's Sandplovers at the New York Zoological Park. *Living Bird* **7**: 57-70.

Conway, W.G. & Hamer, A. (1977). A 36-year laying record of a Wattled Crane at the New York Zoological Park. *Auk* **94(4)**: 786-787.

Cooch, F.G., Dolan, W., Goossen, J.P., Holroyd, G.L., Johns, B.W., Kuyt, E. & Townsend, G.H. (1988). *Canadian Whooping Crane Recovery Plan*. Environment Canada, Ottawa. 56 pp.

Cook, W.E. (1986). Marbled Godwit inland in upstate New York. *Kingbird* **36(3)**: 138.

Cooke, M.D. (1977). Nesting avocets. *Pacific Discovery* **30(4)**: 13-17.

Cooley, C. (1993). *The Book of Cranes*. Pomegranate Artbooks, Petaluma, California.

Coomans de Ruiter, L. (1947a). Over de wederontdekking van *Aramidopsis plateni* in de Minahasa en het voorkomen van *Gymnocrex rosenbergii* aldaar. *Limosa* **19**: 65-75.

Coomans de Ruiter, L. (1947b). Roofvogel waar nemingen in Zuid-Celebes. *Limosa* **20**: 213-229.

Coon, R.A., Caldwell, P.D. & Storm, G.L. (1976). Some characteristics of fall migration of female Woodcock. *J. Wildl. Manage.* **40**: 91-95.

Coon, R.A., Dwyer, T.J. & Artmann, J.W. (1977). Identification of potential harvest units in the United States for the American Woodcock. Pp. 147-153 in: Keppie & Owen (1977).

Coon, R.A., Williams, B.K., Lindzey, J.S. & George, J.L. (1982). Examination of Woodcock nest sites in central Pennsylvania. Pp. 55-62 in: Dwyer & Storm (1982).

Cooper, D., Hays, H. & Pessino, C. (1970). Breeding of the Common and Roseate Terns on Great Gull Island. *Proc. Linn. Soc. N.Y.* **71**: 83-104.

Cooper, J. (1969). Observations at a nest of the Wattled Crane. *Honeyguide* **60**: 17-20.

Cooper, J. (1976a). Hartlaub's Gull breeding on mainland. *Cormorant* **1**: 9.

Cooper, J. (1976b). Seasonal and spatial distribution of the Antarctic Tern in South Africa. *S. Afr. Trans Antarkt. Nav.* **6**: 30-32.

Cooper, J. (1977a). Food, breeding and coat colour of feral cats on Dassen Island. *Zool. Afr.* **12**: 250 252.

Cooper, J. (1977b). Kelp Gull killing Hartlaub's Gull. *Cormorant* **3**: 18.

Cooper, J. ed. (1981). *Proceedings Symposium of Birds of the Sea and Shore, 1979*. African Seabird Group, Cape Town.

Cooper, J. & Pringle, J.S. (1977). Swift Terns and Hartlaub's Gulls breeding at Strandfontein sewage works. *Cormorant* **2**: 23.

Cooper, J. & Ryan, P.G. (1994). *Management Plan for the Gough Island Wildlife Reserve*. Government of Tristan da Cunha.

Cooper, J., Brooke, R.K., Cyrus, D.P., Martin, A.P., Taylor, R.H. & Williams, A.J. (1992). Distribution, population size and conservation of the Caspian Tern *Sterna caspia* in southern Africa. *Ostrich* **63**: 58-67.

Cooper, J., Crawford, R.J.M., Suter, W. & Williams, A.J. (1990). Distribution, population size and conservation of the Swift Tern *Sterna bergii* in southern Africa. *Ostrich* **61**: 56-65.

Cooper, J., Hockey, P.A.R. & Brooke, R.K. (1985). Introduced mammals on south and south west African islands: history, effects on birds and control. Pp. 179-203 in: Bunning, L.J. ed. (1985). *Proc. Symp. Birds and Man*. Southern African Ornithological Society, Johannesburg.

Cooper, J., Shaughnessy, P.D. & Clinning, C.F. (1977). Hartlaub's Gull and Swift Tern breeding in South West Africa. *Cormorant* **3**: 10-12.

Cooper, J., Williams, A.J. & Britton, P.L. (1984). Distribution, population sizes and conservation of breeding seabirds in the Afrotropical Region. Pp. 403-419 in: Croxall, Evans & Schreiber (1984).

Cooper, J.M. (1983). Recent occurrences of the American Avocet in British Columbia. *Murrelet* **64(2)**: 47-48.

Cooper, J.M. (1993). *The Breeding Biology of the Least Sandpiper on the Queen Charlotte Is*. MSc thesis, University of Victoria, Victoria, Canada.

Cooper, J.M. (1994). Least Sandpiper (*Calidris minutilla*). No. **115** in: Poole & Gill (1994).

Cooper, J.M. & Miller, E.H. (1992). Brood amalgation and alloparental care in Least Sandpipers, *Calidris minutilla*. *Can. J. Zool.* **70(2)**: 403-405.

Cooper, M.R. (1984). Taxonomic relationships and zoogeography within the Cursoriinae: a cladistic approach. *Honeyguide* **30(1)**: 9-12.

Cooper, R. (1993). Hooded Plover - a measure of breeding success in north east Tasmania. *Tasmanian Bird Report* **22**: 12-13.

Cooper, R.P. (1948). Bridled Tern. *Emu* **48**: 107-126.

Cooper, R.P. (1964). The Oriental Pratincole near Melbourne. *Austr. Bird Watcher* **2**: 111-112.

Cooper, R.P. (1971). Little Tern/Fairy Tern in East Gippsland. *Austr. Bird Watcher* **4**: 1-3.

Cooper, S. & Tove, M.H. (1989). Spotted Redshank from North Carolina. *Chat* **53(2)**: 38-41.

Cooper, W. (1991). Harrier attacking Black-billed Gull. *Notornis* **38**: 72.

Cooper, W. & Morrison, K. (1984). Solander Island birds. *Notornis* **31**: 182-183.

Cooper, W.J., Miskelly, C.M., Morrison, K. & Peacock, R.J. (1986). Birds of the Solander Islands. *Notornis* **33**: 77-89.

Coppinger, M.P., Williams, G.D. & Maclean, G.L. (1988). Distribution and breeding biology of the African Skimmer on the upper and middle Zambezi River. *Ostrich* **59(3)**: 85-96.

Corben, C. (1972). Oriental Pratincoles in south-east Queensland. *Sunbird* **3**: 6-8.

Corkhill, P. (1973). Food and feeding ecology of puffins. *Bird Study* **20**: 207-220.

Cormons, G.D. (1976). Roseate Tern bill color change in relation to nesting status and food supply. *Wilson Bull.* **88**: 377-389.

Cornwallis, L. (1983a). A review of the bustard situation in Iran. Pp. 81-88 in: Goriup & Vardhan (1983).

Cornwallis, L. (1983b). Notes on a post-symposium tour to survey the position of bustards (Otididae) in India. Pp. 353-365 in: Goriup & Vardhan (1983).

Corrick, A.H. (1981). Wetlands of Victoria II. Wetlands and waterbirds of South Gippsland. *Proc. Royal Soc. Victoria* **92**: 187-200.

Corrick, A.H. (1982). Wetlands of Victoria III. Wetlands and waterbirds between Port Phillip Bay and Mount Emu Creek. *Proc. Royal Soc. Victoria* **94**: 69-87.

Cosens, S.E. (1981). Development of vocalizations in the American Coot *Fulica americana*. *Can. J. Zool.* **59**: 1921-1928.

Costas, R. (1990). Aves nuevas para España: Chorlitejo Culirrojo *Charadrius vociferus*. [New birds for Spain: the Killdeer *Charadrius vociferus*]. *Garcilla* **77**: 16-17. In Spanish.

Cottam, C. (1936). Food of the Limpkin. *Wilson Bull.* **48**: 11-13.

Cottrell, C.B. (1949). Notes on some nesting habits of the Buff-spotted Pigmy Rail. *Ostrich* **20**: 168-170.
Coues, E. (1868). A monograph of the Alcidae. *Proc. Acad. Nat. Sci. Philadelphia* **20**: 3-81.
Coulson, J.C. (1958). The effect of age on the breeding biology of the Kittiwake *Rissa tridactyla*. *Ibis* **100**: 40-51.
Coulson, J.C. (1959). The post-fledging mortality of the Kittiwake. *Bird Study* **6**: 97-102.
Coulson, J.C. (1961). An analysis of factors influencing the clutch-size of the Kittiwake. *Proc. Zool. Soc., London* **139**: 207-217.
Coulson, J.C. (1963). Egg size and shape in the Kittiwake (*Rissa tridactyla*) and their use in estimating age composition of populations. *Proc. Zool. Soc., London* **140**: 211-227.
Coulson, J.C. (1966). The influence of the pair-bond and age on the breeding biology of the Kittiwake *Rissa tridactyla*. *J. Anim. Ecol.* **35**: 269-279.
Coulson, J.C. (1968). Differences in the quality of birds nesting in the centre and on the edges of a colony. *Nature* **217**: 478-479.
Coulson, J.C. (1983). The changing status of the Kittiwake in the British Isles, 1969-1979. *Bird Study* **30**: 9-16.
Coulson, J.C. (1987). The population and breeding biology of the Arctic Tern *Sterna paradisaea* in Shetland, 1986. *Nat. Conserv. Council Chief Sci. Dir. Rep.* **688**: 1-33.
Coulson, J.C. (1991). The population dynamics of culling Herring Gulls and Lesser Black-backed Gulls. Pp. 479-497 in: Perrins *et al.* (1991).
Coulson, J.C. & Butterfield, J. (1985). Movements of British Herring Gulls. *Bird Study* **32**: 91-103.
Coulson, J.C. & Butterfield, J. (1986). Studies on a colony of colour-ringed Herring Gulls *Larus argentatus*: adult survival rates. *Bird Study* **33**: 51-54.
Coulson, J.C. & Horobin, J. (1976). The influence of age on the breeding biology and survival of the Arctic Tern *Sterna paradisaea*. *J. Zool., London* **178**: 247-260.
Coulson, J.C. & MacDonald, A. (1962). Recent changes in the habits of the Kittiwake. *British Birds* **55**: 171-177.
Coulson, J.C. & Nève de Mévergnies, G. (1992). Where do young Kittiwakes *Rissa tridactyla* breed; philopatry or dispersal? *Ardea* **80**: 187-197.
Coulson, J.C. & Porter, J.M. (1985). Reproductive success of the Kittiwake *Rissa tridactyla*: the roles of clutch size, chick growth rates, and parental quality. *Ibis* **127**: 450-466.
Coulson, J.C. & Thomas, C.S. (1980). A study of the factors influencing the duration of the pair-bond in the Kittiwake Gull *Rissa tridactyla*. Pp. 823-833 in: Nohring, R. ed. (1980). *Acta XVII Congr. Int. Orn.* Berlin, 1978.
Coulson, J.C. & Thomas, C.S. (1983). Mate choice in the Kittiwake Gull. Pp. 361-376 in: Bateson, P.P.G. ed. (1983). *Mate Choice*. Cambridge University Press, Cambridge.
Coulson, J.C. & Thomas, C.S. (1985). Changes in the biology of the Kittiwake, *Rissa tridactyla*: a 31 year study of a breeding colony. *J. Anim. Ecol.* **54**: 9-26.
Coulson, J.C. & White, E. (1956). A study of colonies of the Kittiwake *Rissa tridactyla*. *Ibis* **98**: 63-79.
Coulson, J.C. & White, E. (1958a). The effect of age on the breeding biology of the Kittiwake *Rissa tridactyla*. *Ibis* **100**: 40-51.
Coulson, J.C. & White, E. (1958b). Observations on the breeding of the Kittiwake. *Bird Study* **5**: 74-83.
Coulson, J.C. & White, E. (1959). The post-fledgling mortality of the Kittiwake. *Bird Study* **6**: 97-102.
Coulson, J.C. & White, E. (1960). The effect of age and density of breeding birds on the time of breeding of the Kittiwake *Rissa tridactyla*. *Ibis* **102**: 71-86.
Coulson, J.C. & White, E. (1961). An analysis of the factors determining the clutch size of the Kittiwake. *Proc. Zool. Soc., London* **136**: 207-217.
Coulson, J.C. & Wooller, R.D. (1976). Differential survival rates among breeding Kittiwake Gulls *Rissa tridactyla* (L.). *J. Anim. Ecol.* **45**: 205-213.
Coulson, J.C. & Wooller, R.D. (1984). Incubation under natural conditions in the Kittiwake Gull, *Rissa tridactyla*. *Anim. Behav.* **32**: 1204-1215.
Coulson, J.C., Duncan, N. & Thomas, C. (1982). Changes in the breeding biology of the Herring Gull (*Larus argentatus*) introduced by reduction in size and density of the colony. *J. Anim. Ecol.* **51**: 739-756.
Coulson, R. & Coulson, G. (1993). Diets of the Pacific Gull *Larus pacificus* and Kelp Gull *Larus dominicanus* in Tasmania. *Emu* **93**: 50-53.
Coulter, M.C. (1970). Limits to egg size in the Western Gull, *Larus occidentalis*. *J. Field Orn.* **51**: 75-77.
Coulter, M.C. (1975). Post-breeding movements and mortality in the Western Gull *Larus occidentalis*. *Condor* **77**: 243-249.
Coulter, M.C. (1977). *Growth, Mortality and the Third Chick Disadvantage in the Western Gull,* Larus occidentalis. PhD dissertation, University of Pennsylvania, Pennsylvania.
Coulter, M.C. (1980). Stones: an important incubation stimulus for gulls and terns. *Auk* **97**: 898-899.
Coulter, M.C. (1984). Seabird conservation in the Galapagos Islands, Ecuador. Pp. 237-244 in: Croxall, Evans & Schreiber (1984).
Coulter, M.C. (1986). Assortative mating and sexual dimorphism in the Common Tern. *Wilson Bull.* **98**: 93-100.
Court, G.S. & Davis, L.S. (1990). First report of the Southern Great Skua (*Stercorarius skua lonnbergi*) at Cape Bird, Ross Island, Antarctica. *Notornis* **37(1)**: 25-26.
Courtenay-Latimer, M. (1957). On the breeding of *Sterna vittata tristanensis* Murphy off the coast of Cape Province, South Africa. *Bull. Brit. Orn. Club* **77**: 82-83.
Courtney, P.A. & Blokpoel, H. (1980). Behavior of Common Terns nesting near Ring-billed Gulls. *Can. Field-Nat.* **94**: 336-338.
Courtney, P.A. & Blokpoel, H. (1983). Distribution and numbers of Common Terns on the Lower Great Lakes during 1900-1980: a review. *Colonial Waterbirds* **6**: 107-120.
Couto, J.T. & Couto, F.M. (1994). African Skimmers breeding on the highveld. *Honeyguide* **40**: 95-96.
Couture, R., Babin, M. & Perras, S. (1993). Survey of woodcock habitat with landsat: possibilities and limitations of remote sensing. Pp. 50-56 in: Longcore & Sepik (1993).
Coverdale, M.A.C. (1987). Display of Black-bellied Bustard *Eupodotis melanogaster*. *Scopus* **11**: 52.
Coverdale, M.A.C., Archer, A.L. & Pearson, D.J. (1991). Arabian Bustard *Ardeotis arabs* in northern Kenya. *Scopus* **15**: 50.
Coverley, H.W. (1931). Notes on Portuguese birds. *Ibis* **Ser. 13, no. 1**: 94-96.
Cowan, I. & Martin, P.W. (1954). A new northern record for Xantus Murrelet. *Murrelet* **35**: 50.
Cowan, P.J. (1990). The Crab Plover in Kuwait and the northern Arabian Gulf: a brief review and some new counts. *Bull. Orn. Soc. Middle East* **25**: 6-9.
Cowgill, R.W. (1989). Nesting success of Least Terns on two South Carolina barrier islands in relation to human disturbance. *Chat* **53**: 81-87.
Cowley, J.C. (1981). Some breeding birds of the Red Sea and the Persian Gulf. *Bull. Jourdain Soc.* **141**: 21-26.
Cox, J., Kautz, R., MacLaughlin, M. & Gilbert, T. (1994). *Closing the Gaps in Florida's Wildlife Habitat Conservation System*. Florida Game & Fresh Water Fish Commission, Tallahassee, Florida.
Cox, J.B. (1988a). Some south Australian records of the Little Stint. *S. Austr. Orn.* **30(5)**: 113-116.
Cox, J.B. (1988b). Some records and notes on the identification of the Oriental Plover. *S. Austr. Orn.* **30(5)**: 120-121.
Cox, J.B. (1990). Observations of a Hudsonian Godwit in South Australia. *S. Austr. Orn.* **31(2)**: 48-50.
Cox, J.B. & Close, D.H. (1977). Interbreeding of Little and Fairy Terns. *Emu* **77**: 28-32.
Cox, J.B. & Pedler, L.P. (1977). Birds recorded during three visits to the far north-east of South Australia. *S. Austr. Orn.* **27**: 231-250.
Cracraft, J. (1968). A review of the Bathornithidae (Aves Gruiformes) with remarks on the relationships of the Suborder Cariame. *Amer. Mus. Novit.* **2326**: 1-46.
Cracraft, J. (1971). A new family of Hoatzin-like birds (Order Opisthocomiformes) from the Eocene of South America. *Ibis* **113**: 229-233.
Cracraft, J. (1973). *Systematics and Evolution of the Gruiformes (Class Aves)*. Part 3. Phylogeny of the suborder Grues. Bulletin of the American Museum of Natural History **151**, New York. 128 pp.
Cracraft, J. (1981). Toward a phylogenetic classification of the recent birds of the world (class Aves). *Auk* **98**: 681-714.
Cracraft, J. (1982). Phylogenetic relationships and transantarctic biogeography of some gruiform birds. *Geobios* **6**: 393-402.
Craig, A. (1974). Whiskered Terns feeding on arum frogs. *Ostrich* **45**: 142.
Craig, J.L. (1976). An interterritorial hierarchy: an advantage for a subordinate in a communal territory. *Z. Tierpsychol.* **42**: 200-205.
Craig, J.L. (1977). The behaviour of the Pukeko, *Porphyrio porphyrio melanotus*. *New Zealand J. Zool.* **4**: 413-433.
Craig, J.L. (1979). Habitat variation in the social organization of a communal gallinule, the Pukeko *Porphyrio porphyrio melanotus*. *Behav. Ecol. Sociobiol.* **5**: 331-358.
Craig, J.L. (1980a). Pair and group breeding behavior of a communal gallinule, the Pukeko, *Porphyrio porphyrio melanotus*. *Anim. Behav.* **28**: 593-603.
Craig, J.L. (1980b). Breeding success of a communal gallinule. *Behav. Ecol. Sociobiol.* **6**: 289-295.
Craig, J.L. (1982). On the evidence for a "pursuit deterrent" function of alarm signals of Swamphens. *Amer. Naturalist* **119**: 753-755.
Craig, J.L. & Jamieson, I.G. (1990). Pukeko: different approaches and some different answers. In: Stacey, P.B. & Koenig, W.D. eds. (1990). *Co-operative Breeding in Birds: Long-term Studies of Ecology and Behaviour*. Cambridge University Press, Cambridge.
Craig, J.L., McArdle, B.H. & Wettin, P.D. (1980). Sex determination of the Pukeko or Purple Swamphen. *Notornis* **27**: 287-291.
Craighead, F.L. & Oppenheim, J. (1985). Population estimates and temporal trends of Pribilof Islands seabirds. *US Dept. Commerce, NOAA, OCSEAP Final Rep.* **30**: 307-356.
Craik, J.C.A. & Becker, P.H. (1992). Temporal and spatial variations in body-weights of Common Terns and Arctic Terns. *Seabird* **14**: 43-47.
Craik, J.C.A. & Harvey, S.M. (1984). Biometrics and colour forms of chicks of Common Terns and Arctic Terns. *Ringing & Migration* **5**: 40-48.
Cramp, S. ed. (1985). *The Birds of the Western Paleartic*. Vol. 4. Terns to Woodpeckers. Oxford University Press, Oxford.
Cramp, S. & Reynolds, J.F. (1972). Studies of less familiar birds: 168. Cream-coloured Courser. *British Birds* **65(3)**: 120-124.
Cramp, S. & Simmons, K.E.L. eds. (1980). *The Birds of the Western Palearctic*. Vol. 2. Hawks to Bustards. Oxford University Press, Oxford.
Cramp, S. & Simmons, K.E.L. eds. (1983). *The Birds of the Western Palearctic*. Vol. 3. Waders to Gulls. Oxford University Press, Oxford.
Cramp, S., Bourne, W.R.P. & Saunders, D. eds. (1974). *The Seabirds of Britain and Ireland*. Collins, London.
Crawford, D.N. (1972). Birds of Darwin Area with some records from other parts of Northern Territory. *Emu* **72**: 131-148.
Crawford, D.N. (1977). Notes on the feeding of two *Chlidonias* terns. *Emu* **77**: 146-147.
Crawford, D.N. (1978). Notes on Little Curlew on the subcoastal plains, Northern Territory. *Austr. Bird Watcher* **7(8)**: 270-272.
Crawford, D.N. (1979). Effects of drought on Green Pygmy-geese and Comb-crested Jacanas in Northern Territory. *Emu* **79(1)**: 37-39.
Crawford, R.D. (1978). Tarsal colour of American Coots in relation to age. *Wilson Bull.* **90**: 536-543.
Crawford, R.D. (1980). Effects of age on reproduction in American Coots. *J. Wildl. Manage.* **44**: 183-189.
Crawford, R.J.M. (1995). Conservation of southern Africa's breeding seabirds. *Birding in SA* **47(4)**: 106-109.
Crawford, R.J.M. & Dyer, B.M. (1995). Responses by four seabird species to a fluctuating availability of cape anchovy *Engraulis capensis* off South Africa. *Ibis* **137**: 329-339.
Crawford, R.J.M., Cooper, J. & Shelton, P.A. (1982). Distribution, population size, breeding and conservation of the Kelp Gull in southern Africa. *Ostrich* **53(3)**: 166-177.
Crawford, R.L., Olson, S.L. & Kingsley Taylor, W. (1983). Winter distribution of subspecies of Clapper Rails (*Rallus longirostris*) in Florida with evidence for long-distance and overland movements. *Auk* **100**: 198-200.
Crawshay, R. (1907). *The Birds of Tierra del Fuego*. Bernard Quaritch, London.
Creelman, E. & Storey, A.E. (1991). Sex differences in reproductive behavior of Atlantic Puffins. *Condor* **93**: 390-398.
Cresswell, B.H. & Summers, R.W. (1988). A study of breeding Purple Sandpipers *Calidris maritima* on the Hardangervidda using radio-telemetry. *Fauna Norvegica (Ser. C, Cinclus)* **11**: 1-6.
Cresswell, W. (1994a). Age-dependent choice of Redshank (*Tringa totanus*) feeding location: profitability or risk? *J. Anim. Ecol.* **63**: 589-600.
Cresswell, W. (1994b). Flocking is an effective anti-predation strategy in Redshanks, *Tringa totanus*. *Anim. Behav.* **47**: 433-442.
Cresswell, W. (1994c). The function of alarm calls in Redshanks, *Tringa totanus*. *Anim. Behav.* **47**: 736-738.
Cresswell, W. & Whitfield, D.P. (1994). The effects of raptor predation on wintering wader populations at the Tyninghame estuary, southeast Scotland. *Ibis* **136**: 223-232.
Creutz, G. (1983). Die Wetterabhängigkeit des Zugablaufes bei der Waldschnepfe (*Scolopax rusticola* L.) in Mitteleuropa. *Beitr. Vogelkd.* **29**: 107-117.
Criado, J., Abreus, E., Gómez, T., Ardá, M., Fiaio, J. & Cotayo, L. (1995). La Ciénaga de Zapata, maravilla natural cubana. *Garcilla* **93**: 32-37.
Crick, H.O.P. (1992). *Trends in the Breeding Performance of Golden Plover in Britain*. BTO Research Report **76**. British Trust for Ornithology, Thetford.
Croll, D.A. (1990). Physical and biological determinants of the abundance, distribution and diet of the Common Murre in Monterey Bay, California. Pp. 139-148 in: Sealy (1990).
Croll, D.A., Gaston, A.J., Burger, A.E. & Konnoff, D. (1992). Foraging behavior and physiological adaptation for diving in Thick-billed Murres. *Ecology* **73**: 344-356.
Croll, D.A., Gaston, A.J. & Noble, D.G. (1991). Adaptive loss of mass in Thick-billed Murres. *Condor* **93**: 496-502.
Crome, F.H.H. & Rushton, D.K. (1975). Development of plumage in the Plains-wanderer. *Emu* **75(4)**: 181-184.
Cronan, J.Z. (1974). *Heat Energy Exchange between the Killdeer, its Eggs and the Environment*. MSc thesis, Oregon State University, Corvallis, Oregon.
Crossin, R.S. & Huber, L.N. (1970). Sooty Tern egg predation by Ruddy Turnstones. *Condor* **72**: 372-373.
Crossland, A.C. (1995). A probable case of intraspecific killing in Turnstones (*Arenaria interpres*). *Notornis* **43**: 281-282.
Crouchley, D. (1994). *Takahe Recovery Plan*. Department of Conservation, Wellington.
Crouther, M.M. (1994). Spotless Crake grounded at Eungella, North Queensland. [Includes discussion about nocturnal movements of *Turnix* in Australia and Africa]. *Sunbird* **24**: 28-29.
Crowe, A.A. (1981). The comparative feeding behaviour of the Whitefronted Sandplover *Charadrius marginatus* and the Sanderling *Calidris alba* in the southwestern Cape, South Africa. Page 42 in: Cooper (1981). (Abstract).
Crowe, A.A. (1986). *Aspects of the Behaviour and Ecology of Whitefronted Plovers and Sanderlings on a South African Sandy Beach*. MSc thesis, University of Cape Town, Cape Town.
Crowe, A.A. & Crowe, T.M. (1984). Variation in the breeding season of the White-fronted Sandplover in southern Africa. Pp. 787-798 in: Ledger (1984).
Crowe, J. (1993). Recent Bronze-winged Courser sighting in Gaborone. *Babbler* **25**: 41.
Crowe, T.M., Essop, M.F., Allan, D.G., Brooke, R.K. & Komen, J. (1994). "Overlooked" units of comparative and conservation biology: a case study of small African bustard, the Black Korhaan *Eupodotis afra*. *Ibis* **136**: 166-175.
Crowell, E.M. & Crowell, S. (1946). The displacement of terns by Herring Gulls at the Weepecket Islands. *Bird-Banding* **17**: 1-10.
Croxall, J.P. ed. (1987). *Seabirds Feeding Ecology and Role in Marine Ecosystems*. Cambridge University Press, Cambridge.
Croxall, J.P. ed. (1991). *Seabird Status and Conservation: a Supplement*. ICBP Technical Publication **11**, Cambridge.
Croxall, J.P. & Rothery, P. (1991). Population regulation of seabirds: implications of their demography for conservation. Pp. 272-296 in: Perrins *et al.* (1991).
Croxall, J.P., Evans, P.G.H. & Schreiber, R.W. eds. (1984). *Status and Conservation of the World's Seabirds*. ICBP Technical Publication **2**, Cambridge.
Croxall, J.P., McInnes, S.J. & Prince, P.A. (1984). The status and conservation of seabirds at the Falkland Islands. Pp. 271-291 in: Croxall, Evans & Schreiber (1984).
Croxall, J.P., Prince, P.A., Hunter, I., McInnes, S.J. & Copestake, P.G. (1984). The seabirds of the Antarctic peninsula, islands of the Scotia Sea, and Antarctic continent between 80° W and 20° W: their status and conservation. Pp. 637-666 in: Croxall, Evans & Schreiber (1984).
Crozier, J. & Argelich, J. (1993). [The presence of Dotterel *Charadrius morinellus* in Andorra (Pyrenees) during the breeding season]. *Alauda* **61(4)**: 214. In French.
Ctyroký, P. (1992). [The White-tailed Lapwing (*Chettusia leucura* Lichtenstein) - the endemic lapwing of southwest Asia]. *Beitr. Vogelkd.* **38(2)**: 92-98. In German.
Ctyroký, P. (1994). [*Chettusia leucura* (Lichtenstein, 1823) - a native of southwestern Asia]. *Falke* **41(5)**: 167-170. In German.
Cuello, J.P. (1994). *Aves Uruguayas. (Síntesis de las Familias)*. No Passeriformes. Museo Dámaso Antonio Larrañaga **4**. Tendencia Municipal de Montevideo, Montevideo. 87 pp.
Cuello, J.P. & Gergenstien, E. (1962). *Las Aves del Uruguay*. Vol. 4. Museo de Historia Natural, Montevideo.
Culbert, R.A. (1991). *The Effects of Nest Visibility and Nest Crypticness on Predators of Kildeer Nests*. MSc thesis, University of Michigan, Ann Arbor, Michigan.
Cullen, E. (1957). Adaptations in the Kittiwake to cliff nesting. *Ibis* **99**: 275-302.

Cullen, J.M. (1957). Plumage, age and mortality in the Arctic Tern. *Bird Study* **4**: 197-207.

Cullen, J.M. (1960a). Some adaptations in nesting behavior of terns. Pp. 153-157 in: *Proc. XII Int. Orn. Congr.* Helsinki, 1958.

Cullen, J.M. (1960b). The aerial display of the Arctic Tern and other species. *Ardea* **48**: 1-37.

Cullen, J.M. & Ashmole, N.P. (1963). The Black Noddy *Anous tenuirostris* on Ascension Island. Part 2. Behaviour. *Ibis* **103B**: 423-446.

Cullen, S.A. (1994). Black-necked Stilt foraging site selection and behavior in Puerto Rico. *Wilson Bull.* **106(3)**: 508-513.

Cumming, G.A. (1981). Nesting of Australian Pratincole. *Bird Obs.* **598**: 89, 93.

Cunningham, J.M. (1946). A new Red-billed Gull colony. *New Zealand Bird Notes* **2**: 12.

Cunningham, J.M. (1973). The Banded Dotterel, *Charadrius bicinctus*: pohowera or tuturiwhatu? Call notes and behaviour. *Notornis* **20(1)**: 21-27.

Cunningham-van Someren, G.R. (1971). On the nesting of the 'Chestnut-banded' or 'Magadi' Plover *Charadrius pallidus venestus* Fischer and Reichenow, at Lake Nakuru. *Bull. East Afr. Nat. Hist. Soc.* **1971**: 130-131.

Cunningham-van Someren, G.R. & Robinson, C. (1962). Notes on the African Lilytrotter *Actophilornis africanus* (Gmelin). *Bull. Brit. Orn. Club* **82**: 67-72.

Curry, P. (1984). Long-toed Stints on the way out? *RAOU Newsl.* **60**: 11.

Curry, P.J. & Sayer, J.A. (1979). The inundation zone of the Niger as an environment for Palearctic migrants. *Ibis* **121**: 20-40.

Curry-Lindahl, K. (1981). *Bird Migration in Africa*. Academic Press, London.

Curtis, D.J. & Thompson, D.B.A. (1985). Spacing and foraging behavior of Black-headed Gulls *Larus ridibundus* in an estuary. *Ornis Scand.* **16**: 245-252.

Cushwa, C.T., Barnard, J.E. & Barnes, R.B. (1977). Trends in Woodcock habitat in the United States. Pp. 31-38 in: Keppie & Owen (1977).

Custer, T.W. & Mitchell, C.A. (1987). Organochlorine contaminants and reproductive success of Black Skimmers in south Texas, 1984. *J. Field Orn.* **58(4)**: 480-489.

Custer, T.W. & Mitchell, C.A. (1991). Contaminant exposure of Willets feeding in agricultural drainages of the Lower Rio Grande Valley of south Texas (USA). *Environm. Monitor. Assessment* **16**: 189-200.

Custer, T.W. & Pitelka, F.A. (1987). Nesting by Pomarine Jaegers near Barrow, Alaska, 1971. *J. Field Orn.* **58(2)**: 225-230.

Custer, T.W., Nisbet, I.C.T. & Krynitsky, A.J. (1983). Organochlorine residues and shell characteristics of Roseate Tern eggs, 1981. *J. Field Orn.* **54**: 394-400.

Cuthbert, F.J. (1985a). Mate retention in Caspian Terns. *Condor* **87**: 74-78.

Cuthbert, F.J. (1985b). Intraseasonal movement between colony sites by Caspian Terns in the Great Lakes. *Wilson Bull.* **97**: 502-510.

Cuthbert, F.J. (1988). Reproductive success and colony-site tenacity in Caspian Terns. *Auk* **105**: 339-344.

Cuthbert, N.L. (1954). A nesting study of the Black Tern in Michigan. *Auk* **71**: 36-63.

Cyrus, D.P. (1982). Blackwinged Plovers nesting on the coastal plain of Zululand. *Ostrich* **53(4)**: 248.

Cyrus, D.P. & MacLean, S. (1994). Water temperature and the reproductive success of Caspian Tern *Sterna caspia* at Lake St. Lucia, southern coast of Africa. *Mar. Orn.* **22(2)**: 193-203.

Cyrus, D.P. & Robson, N. (1980). *Bird Atlas of Natal*. University of Natal Press, Pietermaritzburg.

Czackes-Rado, H. & Yom-Tov, Y. (1987). On the incubation biology of the Spur-winged Plover *Hoplopterus spinosus* (Aves: Charadriidae) in Israel. *Israel J. Zool.* **34(3-4)**: 155-157.

Czechura, G.V. (1983). The rails of the Blackall-Conondale Range region with additional comments on Latham's Snipe *Gallinago hardwickii*. *Sunbird* **13**: 31-35.

Czikeli, H. (1976). Beobachtung eines Dünnschnabelbrachvogels (*Numenius tenuirostris*) in Steirischen Ennstal. *Egretta* **19(1-2)**: 61-62.

D'Eath, J.O. (1972). Some notes on breeding the Stanley Crane (*Anthropoides paradisea*). *Avicult. Mag.* **78(5)**: 165-169.

D'Ombrain, A.F. (1944). Behaviour of the Painted Snipe in captivity. *Emu* **43**: 247-248.

D'Ombrain, E.A. (1926). The vanishing Plain Wanderer. *Emu* **26**: 59.

Daan, S. & Koene, P. (1981). On the timing of foraging flights by Oystercatchers *Haematopus ostralegus* on tidal mudflats. *Netherlands J. Sea Res.* **15**: 1 22.

Dabelsteen, T. (1978). Analysis of the song-flight of the Lapwing (*Vanellus vanellus* L.) with respect to causation, evolution and adaptation to signal function. *Behaviour* **66**: 136-178.

Daciuk, J. (1973). Notas faunísticas y bioecológicas de Península Valdés y Patagonia. IX. Colonia de nidificación del Gaviotín Brasileño en Caleta Valdés (Chubut) y sugerencias para su protección. *Physis (Sec. C)* **32**: 71-82.

Daciuk, J. (1976). Notas faunísticas y bioecológicas de Península Valdés y Patagonia. XVII. Colonias de nidificación de *Egretta alba egretta* (Gmelin) y *Sterna eurygnatha* Saunders recientemente encontradas en las costas de Chubut (Rep. Argentina). *Physis (Secc. C.)* **35**: 341-347.

Daddy, F. & Ayeni, J.S.O. (1996). The status of Nigerian freshwater wetlands and their potential for Black Crowned Crane reintroduction. In: Beilfuss *et al.* (1996).

Daguerre, J.B. (1933). Dos aves nuevas para la fauna argentina. *Hornero* **5**: 213-214.

Dale, J. (1990). The Kori Bustard in central Zimbabwe. *Honeyguide* **36**: 123-128.

Dale, P., Hulsman, K., Jahnke, B.R. & Dale, M.B. (1984). Vegetation and nesting preferences of Black Noddies on Masthead Island, Great Barrier Reef. Part 1. Patterns at the macro level. *Austr. J. Ecol.* **9**: 335-341.

Dalgety, C.T. (1932). The Ivory Gull in Spitsbergen. *British Birds* **26**: 2-7.

Danchin, É. (1987). The behavior associated with the occupation of breeding site in the Kittiwake Gull *Rissa tridactyla*. The social status of landing birds. *Anim. Behav.* **35**: 81-93.

Danchin, É. (1988a). Social interactions in Kittiwakes colonies: social facilitation and/or favourable social environment. *Anim. Behav.* **36**: 443-451.

Danchin, É. (1988b). *Role of Behavioural Processes in the Mechanisms of Regulation of Population of Colonial Birds. Case of the Kittiwake (*Rissa tridactyla*)*. Thèse d'Etat, Université Paris VI, Paris.

Danchin, É. & Monnat, J.Y. (1992). Population dynamics modelling of two neighbouring Kittiwake *Rissa tridactyla* colonies. *Ardea* **80**: 171-180.

Danchin, É. & Nelson, J.B. (1991). Behavioral adaptations to cliff nesting in the Kittiwake (*Rissa tridactyla*): convergence with the Gannet (*Sula bassana*) and the Black Noddy (*Anous tenuirostris*). *Colonial Waterbirds* **14(2)**: 103-107.

Daniel, M.J. (1963). Observations on chick mortality in a colony of Black-billed Gulls in the thermal area at Whakarewarewa. *Notornis* **10(6)**: 277-278, 285-289.

Daniels, D., Heath, J. & Rawson, W. (1984). A declaration of intent in the Kittiwake Gull *Rissa tridactyla*. *Anim. Behav.* **32**: 1151-1156.

Daniels, G.F. (1972). Possible sight record of Eskimo Curlew on Martha's Vineyard, Mass. *Amer. Birds* **26**: 907-908.

Danielsen, F. & Skov, H. (1988). The importance of south-east Sumatra as a summering area for non-breeding waders, especially the Bar-tailed Godwit *Limosa lapponica*. *Wader Study Group Bull.* **53**: 8-10.

Danielsen, F., Balete, D.S., Christensen, T.D., Heegaard, M., Jakobsen, O.F., Jensen, A., Lund, T. & Poulsen, M.K. (1994). *Conservation of Biological Diversity in the Sierra Madre Mountains of Isabela and Southern Cagayan Province, the Philippines*. Department of Environment and Natural Resources, BirdLife International & Danish Ornithological Society, Manila & Copenhagen.

Dann, P. (1977). A further note on the nomenclature of New Zealand Spur-winged Plovers. *Notornis* **24(4)**: 284-285.

Dann, P. (1981). Breeding of the Banded and Masked Lapwing in Southern Victoria. *Emu* **81(3)**: 121-127.

Dann, P. (1983). Feeding behaviour of four species of Calidridine sandpiper at Lake Reeve in east Gippsland. *Victoria Wader Study Group Bull.* **7**: 2-6.

Dann, P. (1991a). Breeding territories, nesting and the timing of breeding of the Double-banded Plover *Charadrius bicinctus*. *Corella* **15(1)**: 13-18.

Dann, P. (1991b). Feeding behaviour and diet of Double-banded Plovers *Charadrius bicinctus* in Western Port, Victoria. *Emu* **91(3)**: 179-184.

Dann, P. (1993a). Abundance, diet and feeding of the Whimbrel *Numenius phaeopus variegatus* in Rhyll Inlet, Victoria. *Corella* **17**: 52-57.

Dann, P. (1993b). Data exchange: sexual dimorphism in bill lengths of Whimbrel *Numenius phaeopus variegatus*. *Corella* **17**: 57.

Dare, P.J. (1966). *The Breeding and Wintering Populations of the Oystercatcher (*Haematopus ostralegus *L.) in the British Isles*. M.A.A.F. Fishery Investigations, London (Series 2) **25(5)**.

Dare, P.J. (1970). *The Movements of Oystercatchers* Haematopus ostralegus *L.* M.A.A.F. Fishery Investigations, London (Series 2) **25(9)**.

Dare, P.J. (1977). Seasonal changes in body-weight of Oystercatchers *Haematopus ostralegus*. *Ibis* **119**: 494-506.

Dare, P.J. & Mercer, A.J. (1973). Food of the Oystercatcher in Morecambe Bay, Lancashire. *Bird Study* **20**: 173 184.

Dare, P.J. & Mercer, A.J. (1974a). The timing of wing moult in the Oystercatcher *Haematopus ostralegus* in Wales. *Ibis* **116**: 211 214.

Dare, P.J. & Mercer, A.J. (1974b). White collar of the Oystercatcher. *Bird Study* **21**: 180 184.

Darling, F.F. (1938). *Bird Flocks and the Breeding Cycle. A Contribution to the Study of Avian Sociality*. Cambridge University Press, Cambridge.

Darling, P. (1991). Great Skua killing Brent Goose. *British Birds* **84(11)**: 507.

Darlington, P.J. (1931). Notes on the birds of the Río Frío (near Santa Marta), Magdalena, Colombia. *Bull. Mus. Comp. Zool., Harvard* **71**: 349-421.

Dathe, H. (1970). Der Graurückentrompetervogel. *Falke* **17**: 34.

Dathe, H. (1974). Der Grünflügeltrompetervogel. *Falke* **21**: 214-215.

Davenport, D.L. (1982). The spring passage of the Pomarine Skua on British and Irish coasts. *British Birds* **68**: 456-462.

Davenport, D.L. (1987). Behaviour of Arctic and Pomarine Skuas and identification of immatures. *British Birds* **80(4)**: 167-168.

Davenport, D.L. (1991). The spring passage of Long-tailed Skuas off north Uist in 1991. *Scottish Birds* **16(2)**: 85-89.

David, R.E. (1991). The status of the Spotted Sandpiper (*Actitis macularia*) in the Hawaiian Islands. *Elepaio* **51(6)**: 33-35.

Davidova, G.U. & Korotitskaya, L.N. (1977). [Joint defensive behaviour of the Common Tern and Kamchatka Tern]. Report to the 7th All Union Ornithological Congress in Kiev. *Nauka* **2**: 8-9. In Russian.

Davidson, D. (1989). American Avocets in Franklin County, Tennessee. *Migrant* **60(4)**: 96-97.

Davidson, N. (1982). Changes in the body-condition of Redshanks during mild winters: an inability to regulate reserves? *Ringing & Migration* **4**: 51-62.

Davidson, N. (1991). Body condition of Purple Sandpipers *Calidris maritima* wintering in north-east England. *Wader Study Group Bull.* **58**: 22-24.

Davidson, N.C. (1981). Survival of shorebirds (Charadrii) during severe weather: the role of nutritional reserves. Pp. 231-249 in: Jones, N.V. & Wolff, W.J. eds. (1981). *Feeding and Survival Strategies of Estuarine Organisms*. Plenum Press, New York.

Davidson, N.C. (1994). Knot. *Calidris canutus*. Pp. 260-261 in: Tucker & Heath (1994).

Davidson, N.C. & Evans, P.R. (1982). Mortality of Redshanks and Oystercatchers from starvation during severe weather. *Bird Study* **29**: 183 188.

Davidson, N.C. & Evans, P.R. eds. (1986). *The Ecology of Migrant Knots in North Norway During May 1985*. Durham University, Durham.

Davidson, N.C. & Morrison, R.I.G. (1992). Time budgets of pre-breeding Knots on Ellesmere Island, Canada. Pp. 137-143 in: Piersma & Davidson (1992b).

Davidson, N.C. & Pienkowski, M.W. eds. (1987). *The Conservation of International Flyway Populations of Waders*. Wader Study Group Bulletin **49**(Supplement). IWRB Special Publication 7. 151 pp.

Davidson, N.C. & Piersma, T. (1992). The migration of Knots: conservation needs and implications. Pp. 198-209 in: Piersma & Davidson (1992b).

Davidson, N.C. & Wilson, J.R. (1992). The migration system of European-wintering Knots *Calidris canutus islandica*. Pp. 39-51 in: Piersma & Davidson (1992b).

Davidson, N.C., Townshend, D.J., Pienkowski, M.W. & Speakman, J.R. (1986). Why do curlews have decurved bills? *Bird Study* **33**: 61-69.

Davidson, P., Stones, T. & Lucking, R. (1995). The conservation status of key bird species on Taliabu and the Sula Islands, Indonesia. *Bird Conserv. Int.* **5(1)**: 1-20.

Davidson, P.E. (1967). *A Study of the Oystercatcher in Relation to the Fishery for Cockles in the Burry Inlet, South Wales*. M.A.A.F. Fishery Investigations, London (Series 2) **25(7)**.

Davidson, P.E. (1968). The Oystercatcher a pest of shellfisheries. Discussion. Pp. 141 155, 174 189 in: Murton, R.K. & Wright, E.N. eds. (1968). *The Problem of Birds as Pests*. Academic Press, London.

Davies, K. (1992). *A Molecular Assessment of the Taxonomic Status of Cox's Sandpiper (*Calidris paramelanotos*)*. Honours thesis, Latrobe University, Latrobe, Australia.

Davies, S. (1981). Development and behaviour of Little Tern chicks. *British Birds* **74**: 291-298.

Davies, S. (1991). Longevity, breeding success and faithfulness to wintering sites of Wrybill - as suggested by banding data. *Stilt* **19**: 26-27.

Davies, S. & Carrick, R. (1962). On the ability of Crested Terns, *Sterna bergii*, to recognize their own chicks. *Austr. J. Zool.* **10**: 171-177.

Davies, S.J.J.F. (1988). Nomadism in the Australian Gull-billed Tern. Pp. 744-753 in: *Proc. XIX Int. Orn. Congr.* Ottawa, 1986.

Davis, A.M. (1987). *The Behavioural Ecology and Management of New Zealand Shore Plover*. MSc thesis, University of Auckland, Auckland, New Zealand.

Davis, A.M. (1994a). Status, distribution and population trends of the New Zealand Shore Plover *Thinornis novaeseelandiae*. Pp. 179-194 in: Holdaway, R.N. ed. (1994). *Chatham Island Ornithology*. Notornis **41**(Supplement).

Davis, A.M. (1994b). Breeding biology of the New Zealand Shore Plover *Thinornis novaeseelandiae*. Pp. 195-208 in: Holdaway, R.N. ed. (1994). *Chatham Island Ornithology*. Notornis **41**(Supplement).

Davis, C.A. & Vohs, P.A. (1993). Role of macroinvertebrates in spring diet and habitat use of Sandhill Cranes. *Trans. Nebr. Acad. Sci.* **20**: 81-86.

Davis, F.W. (1970). Territorial conflict in the American Woodcock. *Wilson Bull.* **82**: 327-328.

Davis, G. & Mykytowycz, M. (1982). Further breeding records of White-fronted Terns in Tasmania. *Austr. Bird Watcher* **9**: 158-159.

Davis, J.W.F. (1975a). Age, egg-size and breeding success in the Herring Gull *Larus argentatus*. *Ibis* **117**: 460-473.

Davis, J.W.F. (1975b). Specialization in feeding location by Herring Gulls. *J. Anim. Ecol.* **44**: 795-804.

Davis, J.W.F. (1976). Breeding success and experience in the Arctic Skua, *Stercorarius parasiticus* (L.). *J. Anim. Ecol.* **45**: 531-554.

Davis, J.W.F. & Dunn, E.K. (1976). Intraspecific predation and colonial breeding in Lesser Black-backed Gulls *Larus fuscus*. *Ibis* **118**: 65-77.

Davis, J.W.F. & O'Donald, P. (1976). Territory size, breeding time and mating preference in the Arctic Skua. *Nature* **260**: 774-775.

Davis, L.I. (1951). Fishing efficiency of the Black Skimmer. *Condor* **53**: 259-260.

Davis, L.I. (1972). *A Field Guide to the Birds of Mexico and Central America*. University of Texas Press. Austin & London.

Davis, M.E. (1974). Experiments on the nesting behavior of the California Least Tern. *Proc. Linn. Soc. N.Y.* **72**: 25-43.

Davis, M.M. (1980). Red-capped Dotterel in North Canterbury. *Notornis* **27(4)**: 367-368.

Davis, T.A. & Ackerman, R.A. (1985). Adaptations of Black Tern (*Chlidonias niger*) eggs for water loss in moist nests. *Auk* **102**: 640-643.

Davis, T.A.W. (1935). Some nesting notes from the savannas of the Rupununi District, British Guiana. *Ibis* **Ser. 13, no. 5**: 530-537.

Davis, W.M. & Knight, G. (1989). First Mississippi record of the Mountain Plover. *Miss. Kite* **19(1)**: 2-3.

Davygora, A.V., Gavlyuk, E.V. & Kornev, S.V. (1989). [Sociable Plover in steppes of Preural area]. Pp. 88-90 in: Ilyashenko, V.I. & Mazin, L.N. eds. (1989). [*Rare and Endangered Animal Species*]. TSNIL Glavokhota RSFSR, Moscow. In Russian.

Dawson, E.W. (1958). Food of young Black-billed Gulls (*Larus bulleri*) in a breeding colony, North Canterbury. *Notornis* **8**: 32-38.

Dawson, W.R., Bennett, A.F. & Hudson, J.W. (1976). Metabolism and thermoregulation in hatchling Ring-billed Gulls. *Condor* **78**: 50-60.

Day, K.S. (1994). Observations on Mountain Plover (*Charadrius montanus*) breeding in Utah. *Southwest. Nat.* **39(3)**: 298-300.

Day, R.H. (1995) New information on Kittlitz's Murrelet nests. *Condor* **97**: 271-273.

Day, R.H. (1996) Nesting phenology of Kittlitz's Murrelet (*Brachyramphus brevirostris*). *Condor* **98**.

Day, R.H. & Byrd, G.V. (1989). Food habits of the Whiskered Auklet at Buldir Island, Alaska. *Condor* **91**: 65-72.

Day, R.H., DeGange, A.R., Divoky, G.J. & Troy, D.M. (1988). Distribution and subspecies of the Dovekie in Alaska. *Condor* **90**: 712-714.

Day, R.H., Oakley, K.L. & Barnard, D.R. (1983). Nest sites and eggs of Kittlitz's and Marbled Murrelets. *Condor* **85**: 265-273.

De Villiers, D. & Simmons, R. (1994). The high incidence and origin of two-egg clutches in a Damara Tern colony in south western Namibia. *Madoqua*.

Dean, A.R., Fortey, J.E. & Phillips, E.G. (1977). White-tailed Plover: new to Britain and Ireland. *British Birds* **70(11)**: 465-470.
Dean, W.R.J. (1977a). Moult of Little Stints in South Africa. *Ardea* **65**: 73-79.
Dean, W.R.J. (1977b). Moult of the Curlew Sandpiper at Barberspan. *Ostrich* **12**(Suppl.): 97-101.
Dean, W.R.J. (1980). Brood division by Redknobbed Coot. *Ostrich* **51**: 125-127.
Dean, W.R.J. (1986). On the validity of breeding records for Long-toed Plover *Vanellus crassirostris* in South Africa. *Bull. Brit. Orn. Club* **106(2)**: 87-88.
Dean, W.R.J. & Skead, D.M. (1979a). Whiskered Terns breeding in western Transvaal. *Ostrich* **50**: 118.
Dean, W.R.J. & Skead, D.M. (1979b). Moult and mass of the Redknobbed Coot. *Ostrich* **50**: 199-202.
Debout, C. & Debout, G. (1988). Nidification d'un couple mixte Sterne pierregarin x Sterne arctique. *Cormoran* **6**: 110-117.
Deceuninck, B. (1995). Programme LIFE-Râle des genêts. Bilan des opérations d'études et de conservation menées en France. *Ornithos* **2(4)**: 188-189.
Dee, T.J. (1986). *The Endemic Birds of Madagascar*. ICBP, Cambridge.
DeGange, A.R. (1978). Threatened, American Oystercatcher, *Haematopus palliatus*. Pp. 37-39 in: Kale (1978).
DeGange, A.R. & Day, R.H. (1991). Mortality of seabirds in the Japanese land-based gillnet fishery for Salmon. *Condor* **93**: 251-258.
DeGange, A.R., Day, R.H., Takekawa, J.E. & Mendenhall, V.M. (1993). Losses of seabirds in gill nets in the North Pacific. Pp. 204-211 in: Vermeer, Briggs *et al.* (1993).
DeGroot, D.S. (1931). History of a nesting colony of Caspian Terns on San Francisco Bay. *Condor* **33**: 188-192.
Degtyaryev, A.G. (1991). A method of airborne census of Ross's Gull, *Rodostethia rosea*, in Yakut tundras. *Zoologischeskii Zhurnal* **70**: 81-85.
Degtyaryev, A.G. & Labutin, Y.V. (1991). [Siberian Crane in Yakutia: range, migration, numbers]. *Zoologischeskii Zhurnal* **70(1)**: 63-75. In Russian with English summary.
Deignan, H.G. (1936). Notes on a small collection of birds from the Republic of Honduras. *Auk* **53**: 186-193.
Deignan, H.G. (1945). *The Birds of Northern Thailand*. US National Museum Bulletin **186**. Smithsonian Institution, Washington, D.C.
Dekinga, A. & Piersma, T. (1993). Reconstructing diet composition on the basis of faeces in a mollusc-eating wader, the Knot *Calidris canutus*. *Bird Study* **40(2)**: 144-156.
Delacour, J. (1923). Notes on the birds of the states of Guarico and Apure in Venezuela. *Ibis* **Ser. 11, no. 5**: 136-150.
Delacour, J. (1925). Le grue à cou noir. *Oiseau et RFO* **6**: 233-236.
Delacour, J. (1932). Les oiseaux de la Mission Franco-Anglo-Américaine à Madagascar. *Oiseau et RFO* **2**: 1-96.
Delacour, J. (1947). *Birds of Malaysia*. Macmillan, New York.
Delacour, J. (1966). *Guide des Oiseaux de la Nouvelle-Calédonie et de ses Dépendances*. Delachaux & Niestlé, Neuchâtel, Switzerland.
Delacour, J. & Mayr, E. (1946). *Birds of the Philippines*. Macmillan Co., New York.
Delehanty, D.J. (1991). *The Effects of Clutch Size on Prolactin, Testosteron, and Incubation Persistence in Male Wilson's Phalaropes*, Phalaropus tricolor. MSc thesis, University of North Dakota, Grand Forks, North Dakota.
Delehanty, D.J. & Oring, L.W. (1993). Effect of clutch size on incubating persistance in male Wilson's Phalarope (*Phalaropus tricolor*). *Auk* **110(3)**: 521-528.
Delgushin, I.A. (1962). [Order Lariformes]. Pp. 246-327 in: [*Birds of Kazakhstan*]. Vol. 2. Alma Ata. In Russian.
Delude, A.M., Baron, G. & McNeil, R. (1987). Role of male and female Ring-billed Gulls in the care of young and territorial defense. *Can. J. Zool.* **65**: 1535-1540.
Delude, A.M., McNeil, R. & Baron, G. (1988). Do young Ring-billed Gulls *Larus delawarensis* participate in territorial defence? *Bird Study* **35**: 153-158.
Demaree, S.R. (1975). Observations on roof-nesting Killdeers. *Condor* **77**: 487-488.
Demartis, A.M. (1986). Seabirds of the southern Sardinia islets. Pp. 19-30 in: MEDMARAVIS & Monbailliu (1986).
Dementiev, G.P. & Gladkov, N.A. eds. (1951a). *The Birds of the Soviet Union*. Vol. 2. (English translation 1968). US Department of Commerce, Springfield, Virginia.
Dementiev, G.P. & Gladkov, N.A. eds. (1951b). *The Birds of the Soviet Union*. Vol. 3. (English translation 1969). Israel Program for Scientific Translation, Jerusalem.
Demey, R. & Fishpool, L.D.C. (1991). Additions and annotations to the avifauna of Côte d'Ivoire. *Malimbus* **12**: 61-86.
Demey, R. & Fishpool, L.D.C. (1994). The birds of Yapo Forest, Ivory Coast. *Malimbus* **16**: 100-122.
Dempsey, J. (1991). A King Rail observation. *Loon* **63(1)**: 73-74.
Dennis, M.K. (1995). Yellow-legged Gulls along the River Thames in Essex. *British Birds* **88**: 8-14.
Dennis, N. & Tarboton, W. (1993). *Waterbirds: Birds of Southern Africa's Wetlands*. New Holland, London.
Dennison, M.D. (1979). Sharp-tailed Sandpiper displays. *Notornis* **26(3)**: 319.
Denny, M. (1992). Black Turnstone seen eating millet. *Oregon Birds* **18(3)**: 74.
Densley, M. (1977a). The Ross's Gull (*Rhodostethia rosea*) in Arctic Alaska. *Polar Record* **18**: 604-605.
Densley, M. (1977b). Ross's Gull in Britain. *Scottish Birds* **9(7)**: 334-342.
Densley, M. (1979). Ross's Gull in Alaska. *British Birds* **72(1)**: 23-28.
Densley, M. (1991). Ross's Gull in Siberia. *Dutch Birding* **13**: 168-175.
Densmore, R.J. (1990). Gull-billed Tern predation on a Least Tern chick. *Wilson Bull.* **102**: 180-181.
Dentesani, B. & Genero, F. (1987). [Breeding of the Stone Curlew, *Burhinus oedicnemus*, in Friuli (NE Italy)]. *Riv. ital. Orn.* **57(1/2)**: 69-72. In Italian with English summary.
Deppe, H.J. (1991). Spring migration of Cranes (*Grus grus*) in Mecklenburg and weather conditions. *Vogelwarte* **36(1)**: 62-67. In German with English summary.
Derenne, P.J., Mougin, J.L., Steinberg, C. & Voisin, J.F. (1976). Les oiseaux de l'île aux Cochons, archipel Crozet (46° 06' S, 50° 14' E). *Com. Natl. Fr. Rech. Antarct.* **40**: 107-148.
Derleth, E.L. & Sepik, G.F. (1990). Summer-fall survival of American Woodcock in Maine. *J. Wildl. Manage.* **54**: 97-106.
Derrickson, S. (1996). Reintroduced Guam Rail breeds on Rota Island. *Endangered Species Update* **13(1 & 2)**: 15.
Derrickson, S.R. & Carpenter, J.W. (1982). Whooping Crane production at the Patuxent Wildlife Research Center, 1967-1981. Pp. 190-198 in: Lewis (1982).
Desai, J.H. & Malhotra, A.K. (1976). A note on incubation period and reproductive success of the Redwattled Lapwing, *Vanellus indicus* at Delhi Zoological Park. *J. Bombay Nat. Hist. Soc.* **73(2)**: 392-394.
Desai, R.M. (1980). *Studies in the Biology of the Indian Sarus Crane*. MS thesis, Gujarat University, Ahmedabad, India.
DeSante, D.F. & Ainley, D.G. (1980). The avifauna of the South Farallon Islands, California. *Studies in Avian Biology* **4**: 1-104.
DeSanto, T.L. & Nelson, S.K. (1995). Comparative reproductive ecology of the auks (Family Alcidae) with emphasis on the Marbled Murrelet. Pp. 33-48 in: Ralph *et al.* (1995).
Desbrosse, A. (1988). La conservation des oiseaux de l'Archipel Saint-Pierre et Miquelon. Pp. 27-36 in: Thibault & Guyot (1988).
Desender, K. (1983). Curlew (*Numenius arquata*) food preference on an inland roosting place during autumn. *Gerfaut* **73**: 407-409.
Desmots, D. & Yésou, P. (1994). La Mouette de Sabine *Larus sabini* sur le littoral atlantique français. Situation générale et afflux de septembre 1993. [Sabine's Gulls in western coast of France after the September 1993 storm]. *Ornithos* **1(1)**: 31-33. In French with English summary.
Desmots, D. & Yésou, P. (1996). Un nouvel afflux de Mouettes de Sabine *Larus sabini* aux Sables d'Olonne (Vendée). *Ornithos* **3(1)**: 11-13.
Despin, B., Mougin, J.L. & Segonzac, M. (1972). Oiseaux et mammifères de l'Île de l'Est, Archipel Crozet (46° 25' S, 52° 12' E). *Com. Nat. Fr. Rech. Antarct.* **31**: 1-106.
Desroschers, B.A. & Ankney, C.D. (1986). Effect of brood size and age on the feeding behaviour of adult and juvenile American coots (*Fulica americana*). *Can. J. Zool.* **64**: 1400-1406.
Devillers, P. (1977a). Observations at a breeding colony of *Larus (belcheri) atlanticus*. *Gerfaut* **67**: 22-43.
Devillers, P. (1977b). Comments on plumages and behavior of Scoresby's Gull. *Gerfaut* **67**: 254-265.
Devillers, P. (1977c). The skuas of the North American Pacific coast. *Auk* **94(3)**: 417-429.
Devillers, P. (1978a). Illustration du plumage juvenile des Sternes arctique (*Sterna paradisaea*). *Gerfaut* **68**: 91-96.
Devillers, P. (1978b). Distribution and relationships of South American skuas. *Gerfaut* **68**: 374-417.
Devillers, P. (1985). Gull. Pp. 268-269 in: Campbell & Lack (1985).
Devillers, P. & Terschuren, J.A. (1976a). Desertion of the Grey Gull (*Larus modestus*) colony of Pedro de Valdivia (Chile). *Gerfaut* **66**: 132-137.
Devillers, P. & Terschuren, J.A. (1976b). Observations de la Sterne peruvienne (*Sterna lorata*) au Chile et illustration de son plumage juvenile. *Gerfaut* **66**: 261-265.
Devillers, P. & Terschuren, J.A. (1977). Some distributional records of migrant North American Charadriiformes in coastal South America (continental Argentina, Falkland, Tierra del Fuego, Chile and Ecuador). *Gerfaut* **67**: 107-125.
Devillers, P., McCaskie, G. & Jehl, J.R. (1971). The distribution of certain large gulls (*Larus*) in southern California and Baja California. *Calif. Birds* **2**: 11-26.
Devort, M. (1988). [Comparative study of the Snipe and Woodcock displays]. Pp. 27-28 in: Havet & Hirons (1988). In French with English summary.
Devort, M. (1993). *Contribution a l'Étude des Migrations et de la Biologie des Bécassines. Saisons 1991-1992*. CICB, Paris. In French and English.
Devort, M. (1994). Some aspects of biology and migration of the Common Snipe by wing and tail sampling. Pp. 98-17 in: Kalchreuter (1994).
Devort, M. (1995). *Contribution a l'Étude des Migrations et de la Biologie des Bécassines. Saisons 1992/93 et 1993/94*. CICB, Paris. In French and English.
Devort, M. & Paloc, R. (1994). Some aspects of the moult and migration of the Great Snipe. Pp. 89-97 in: Kalchreuter (1994).
Dewar, J.M. (1922). Ability of the Oystercatcher to open oysters, and its bearing upon the history of the species. *British Birds* **16**: 118 125.
Dewar, J.M. (1940). Identity of specialized feeding habits of the Turnstone and Oystercatcher. *British Birds* **34**: 26 28.
DeWeese, L.R. & Anderson, D.W. (1976). Distribution and breeding biology of Craveri's Murrelet. *Trans. San Diego Soc. Nat. Hist.* **18**: 155-186.
Dexheimer, M. & Southern, W.E. (1974). Breeding success relative to nest location and density in Ring-billed Gull colonies. *Wilson Bull.* **86(3)**: 288-290.
Dey, S.C. (1993). Siberian Crane - Status report and Indian situation. *Indian For.* **119(10)**: 783-792. In English with Hindi summary.
Dharmakumarsinhji, R.S. (1950). The Lesser Florican (*Sypheotides indica* Miller): its courtship display, behaviour and habits. *J. Bombay Nat. Hist. Soc.* **49**: 201-216.
Dharmakumarsinhji, R.S. (1957). Ecological study of the Great Indian Bustard *Ardeotis nigriceps* Vigors (Aves: Otididae) in Kathiawar Peninsula, western India. *J. Zool. Soc. India* **9**: 140-152.
Dharmakumarsinhji, R.S. (1964). Some observations on the Small Indian Pratincole (*Glareola lactea* Temminck) and some other waders breeding in Bhavnagar, Gujarat. *Pavo* **2**: 1-11.
Dharmakumarsinhji, R.S. (1965). Hatching of an Indian Stone Curlew's egg. *Peacock* **2(6)**: 65-66.
Dharmakumarsinhji, R.S. (1971). Study of the Great Indian Bustard. Final report to WWF, Morges, Switzerland.
Dharmakumarsinhji, R.S. (1983). Indian bustard protection strategy. Pp. 258-265 in: Goriup & Vardhan (1983).
Dhindsa, M.S. (1983). Yellow-wattled Lapwing: a rare species in Haryana and Punjab. *Pavo* **21**: 103-104.
Dhondt, A.A. (1975). Notes sur les échassiers (Charadrii) de Madagascar. *Oiseau et RFO* **45**: 73-82.
Diamond, A.W. (1976). Subannual breeding and molt in the Bridled Tern *Sterna anaethetus* in the Seychelles. *Ibis* **118**: 414-419.
Diamond, A.W. (1978). Feeding strategies and population size in tropical seabirds. *Amer. Naturalist* **112**: 215-223.
Diamond, A.W. (1984). Feeding overlap in some tropical and temperate seabird communities. *Studies in Avian Biology* **8**: 24-46.
Diamond, A.W. (1994). Seabirds of the Seychelles, Indian Ocean. Pp. 258-267 in: Nettleship *et al.* (1994).
Diamond, J.M. (1969). Preliminary results of an ornithological exploration of the North Coastal Range, New Guinea. *Amer. Mus. Novit.* **2362**: 1-57.
Diamond, J.M. (1972a). Further examples of dual singing by southwest Pacific birds. *Auk* **89**: 180-183.
Diamond, J.M. (1972b). *Avifauna of the Eastern Highlands of New Guinea*. Publications of the Nuttall Ornithological Club **12**. Cambridge, Massachusetts. 438 pp.
Diamond, J.M. (1975). The island dilemma: lessons of modern biogeographical studies for the design of natural reserves. *Biol. Conserv.* **7**: 129-146.
Diamond, J.M. (1985). New distributional records and taxa from the outlying mountain ranges of New Guinea. *Emu* **85**: 65-91.
Diamond, J.M. (1987). Extant unless proven extinct? Or, extinct unless proven extant? *Conserv. Biol.* **1**: 77-79.
Diamond, J.M. (1991). A new species of rail from the Solomon Islands and convergent evolution of insular flightlessness. *Auk* **108(3)**: 461-470.
Diamond, J.M. & Terborgh, J.W. (1968). Dual singing by New Guinea birds. *Auk* **85**: 62-82.
Dick, W.J.A. (1979). Results of the WSG project on the spring migration of Siberian Knot *Calidris canutus* 1979. *Wader Study Group Bull.* **27**: 8-13.
Dick, W.J.A., Pienkowski, M.W., Waltner, M. & Minton, C.D.T. (1976). Distribution and geographical origins of Knot *Calidris canutus* wintering in Europe and Africa. *Ardea* **64**: 22-47.
Dickerman, R.W. (1968a). Notes on the Red Rail (*Laterallus ruber*). *Wilson Bull.* **80**: 94-99.
Dickerman, R.W. (1968b). Notes on the Ocellated Rail (*Micropygia schomburgkii*) with first record from Central America. *Bull. Brit. Orn. Club* **88**: 25-30.
Dickerman, R.W. (1971). Notes on various rails in Mexico. *Wilson Bull.* **83**: 49-56.
Dickerman, R.W. & Haverschmidt, F. (1971). Further notes on the juvenal plumage of the Spotted Rail (*Rallus maculatus*). *Wilson Bull.* **83**: 444-446.
Dickerman, R.W. & Parkes, K.C. (1969). Juvenal plumage of the Spotted Rail. *Wilson Bull.* **81**: 207-209.
Dickerman, R.W. & Warner, C.W. (1961). Distribution records from Tecolutla, Veracruz, with the first record of *Porzana flaviventer* for Mexico. *Wilson Bull.* **73**: 336-340.
Dickey, D.R. & van Rossem, A.J. (1938). *The Birds of El Salvador*. Field Museum of Natural History (Zoological Series) **23**. Chicago.
Dickinson, E.C. (1984). Notes on Philippine birds, 1. The status of *Porzana paykullii* in the Philippines. *Bull. Brit. Orn. Club* **104**: 71-72.
Dickinson, E.C. & Eck, S. (1984). Notes on Philippine birds. 2. A second record of *Sterna bernsteini*. *Bull. Brit. Orn. Club* **104**: 72.
Dickinson, E.C., Kennedy, R.S. & Parkes, K.C. (1991). *The Birds of the Philippines. An Annotated Checklist*. BOU Check-list **12**. British Ornithologists' Union, Tring, UK.
Dickinson, E.C., Kennedy, R.S., Read, D.K. & Rozendaal, F.G. (1989). Notes on the birds collected in the Philippines during the Steere expedition of 1887-1888. *Nemouria* **32**: 1-19.
DiCostanzo, J. (1980). Population dynamics of a Common Tern colony. *J. Field Orn.* **51**: 229-243.
Didiuk, A. (1976). Whooping Cranes in Manitoba? *Blue Jay* **34(4)**: 234-236.
Diefenbach, D.R., Derleth, E.L., Vander Haegen, W.M., Nichols, J.D. & Hines, J.E. (1990). American Woodcock winter distribution and fidelity to wintering areas. *Auk* **107**: 745-749.
Dierschke, V. (1987). [Interspecific aggression of the Grey Plover *Pluvialis squatarola*]. *Limicola* **1(2)**: 55-56. In German with English summary.
Dierschke, V. (1993). Food and feeding ecology of Purple Sandpipers *Calidris maritima* on rocky intertidal habitats (Helgoland, German Bight). *Netherlands J. Sea Res.* **31**: 309-317.
Dierschke, V. (1994). Einfluss von Gefiederverölung auf die Überlebensrate und Körpermasse von Meerstrandläufern *Calidris maritima* auf Helgoland. *Vogelwelt* **115**: 253-255.
Dietrich, S. & Hoetker, H. (1991). [Where do north Frisian Avocets moult?]. *Vogelwelt* **112(3)**: 140-147. In German with English summary.
van Dijk, A.J. (1976). [Investigation of the occurence of the Whimbrel - *Numenius phaeopus* - in the Netherlands]. *Watervogels* **4**: 7-13. In Dutch with English summary.
van Dijk, A.J. (1980). [Observations on the moult of the Black-tailed Godwit *Limosa limosa*]. *Limosa* **53**: 49-57. In Dutch with English summary.
van Dijk, A.J., van Dijk, K., Dijksen, L.J., van Spanje, T.M. & Wymenga, E. (1986). *Wintering Waders and Waterfowl on the Gulf of Gabès, Tunisia, January-March 1984*. WIWO Report **11**. Zeist, the Netherlands.
van Dijk, A.J., de Roder, F.E., Marteijn, E.C.L. & Spiekman, H. (1990). Summering waders on the Banc d'Arguin, Mauritania: a census in June 1988. *Ardea* **78**: 145-156.
Dijksen, L. (1980). [Some data on the breeding season and breeding success of Oystercatchers *Haematopus ostralegus* in the dunes]. *Watervogels* **5**: 3 7. In Dutch.
Ding Hanlin, Yu Guohai *et al.* (1987). [The breeding ecology of Demoiselle Crane *Anthropoides virgo*]. *Chinese Wildlife* **2**: 22-24. In Chinese.
Ding Tieming (1988). [Wintering ecology of the Great Bustard, *Otis tarda*]. *Chinese Wildlife* **4**: 9-10. In Chinese.
Ding Wenning (1986). [Siberian Crane]. *Chinese Wildlife* **2**: 2. In Chinese.
Ding Wenning & Zhou Fuzhang (1991). [The distribution of the wintering Siberian Crane]. Pp. 1-4 in: [*Bird Studies in China*]. Science Press, Beijing, China. In Chinese.
Dinsmore, J.J. (1972). Sooty Tern behavior. *Bull. Florida State Mus. Biol. Sci.* **16**: 129-179.

Dinsmore, J.J. (1977). Notes on avocets and stilts in Tampa Bay, Florida. *Florida Field Nat.* **5(2)**: 25-30.
Dinsmore, J.J. (1988). Eskimo Curlews - a possible recovery. *Iowa Bird Life* **58(2)**: 32-34.
Dinsmore, J.J. & Schreiber, R.W. (1974). Breeding and annual cycle of Laughing Gulls in Tampa Bay, Florida. *Wilson Bull.* **86**: 419-427.
Dinsmore, S. & Humphrey, R.C. (1987). A Wilson's Plover (*Charadrius wilsonia*) on north Monomoy Island. *Bird Obs.* **15(5)**: 267-268.
van Dinteren, G. (1989). [Migration behaviour, distribution and survival of Ruffs (*Philomachus pugnax*)]. Unpublished report RIN 89/16, the Netherlands. 175 pp. In Dutch.
Dinzl, L. (1990). American Avocets in Pine County. *Loon* **62(3)**: 153-154.
Dircksen, R. (1932). Die Biologie des Austernfischers, des Brandseeschwalbe und der Küstenseeschwalbe nach Beobachtungen und Untersuchungen auf Noorderoog. *J. Orn.* **80**: 427-485.
Disher, P. (1990). A Wilson's Phalarope at Tullakool, new for New South Wales. *Austr. Birds* **24(2)**: 38-39.
Disney, H.J. de S. (1974a). Woodhen. *Austr. Nat. Hist.* **18**: 70-73.
Disney, H.J. de S. (1974b). Survey of the Woodhen. In: Recher, H.F. & Clark, S.S. eds. (1974). *Environmental Survey of Lord Howe Island.* Appendix G, 73-76. Lord Howe Island Board, Sydney.
Disney, H.J. de S. (1976). Report on the Woodhen of Lord Howe Island. Unpublished MS. Australian National Parks and Wildlife Service, Canberra.
Disney, H.J. de S. & Fullagar, P.J. (1984). Saved from the extinction: Lord Howe Island Woodhen. *Austr. Nat. Hist.* **21**: 259.
Disney, H.J. de S. & Smithers, C.N. (1972). The distribution of terrestrial and freshwater birds on Lord Howe Island, in comparison with Norfolk Island. *Austr. Zool.* **17**: 1-11.
Dittberner, H. & Dittberner, W. (1991). [Epimeletic behavior in *Vanellus vanellus*]. *Beitr. Vogelkd.* **37(5/6)**: 346-347. In German.
Dittberner, H. & Dittberner, W. (1993). [Ecology of *Pluvialis apricaria* in stop-over area in Uckermark]. *Beitr. Vogelkd.* **39(4)**: 227-247. In German.
Dittberner, H. & Otto, W. (1986). [The Skua *Stercorarius skua* in the Berlin area, East Germany, in spring]. *Beitr. Vogelkd.* **32(5/6)**: 332-334. In German.
Dittmann, D.L. & Zink, R.M. (1991). Mitochondrial DNA variation among phalaropes and allies. *Auk* **108**: 771-779.
Dittmann, D.L., Zink, R.M. & Gerwin, J.A. (1989). Evolutionary genetics of phalaropes. *Auk* **106**: 326-331.
Divoky, G.J. (1976). The pelagic feeding habits of Ivory and Ross' Gulls. *Condor* **78**: 85-90.
Divoky, G.J., Sanger, G.A., Hatch, S.A. & Haney, J.C. (1988). *Fall Migration of Ross' Gull (*Rhodostethia rosea*) in Alaskan Chukchi and Beaufort Seas.* US Fish & Wildlife Service OCS Study MMS 88-0023, Anchorage, Alaska.
Divoky, G.J., Watson, G.E. & Bartonek, J.C. (1974). Breeding of the Black Guillemot in northern Alaska. *Condor* **76**: 339-343.
Dixon, J. (1917). The home life of the Baird Sandpiper. *Condor* **19**: 77-84.
Dixon, J. (1918). The nesting grounds and nesting habits of the Spoon-billed Sandpiper. *Auk* **35**: 387-404.
Dixon, J. (1927). The Surfbird's secret. *Condor* **29**: 3-16.
Dixon, J.E.W. (1975). Nasal salt secretion from Burchell's Courser. *Madoqua* **9(1)**: 63-64.
Dixon, J.S. (1933). Nesting of the Wandering Tattler. *Condor* **35**: 173-179.
Dobrowolski, K.A. (1970). The occurrence of the Caspian Tern, *Hydroprogne caspia* (Pall.) in Poland during the last 150 years. *Acta Orn., Varszawa* **12**: 159-178. (Smithsonian Institution translation).
Docampo, F. & Velando, A. (1994). Análisis de las recuperaciones de Gaviota Tridáctila *Rissa tridactyla* en la Península Ibérica. [Ringing recoveries of Kittiwakes *Rissa tridactyla* in the Iberian Peninsula]. *Butll. Grup Català d'Anellament* **11**: 39-44.
Docherty, D.E., Converse, K.A., Hansen, W.R. & Norman, G.W. (1994). American Woodcock (*Scolopax minor*) mortality associated with a reovirus. *Avian Diseases* **38**: 899-904.
Dod, A.S. (1980). First records of Spotted Rail *Pardirallus maculatus* on the Island of Hispaniola. *Auk* **97**: 407.
Dod, A.S. (1992). *Endangered and Endemic Birds of the Dominican Republic.* Cypress House, Fort Bragg, California.
Dodman, T. (1996). Present status and distribution of cranes in the Kafue Flats, Zambia with reference to population estimates of the 1980s. In: Beilfuss *et al.* (1996).
Dodson, S.I. & Egger, D.L. (1980). Selective feeding of Red Phalaropes on zooplankton of arctic ponds. *Ecology* **61**: 755-763.
Doherty, P. (1991). Identification of Long-toed Stint and Least Sandpiper. *Birding World* **4(8)**: 279-281.
Dolan, B. (1939). Zoological results of the second Dolan Expedition to western China and eastern Tibet, 1934-1936. Part I. *Proc. Acad. Nat. Sci. Philadelphia* **90**: 159-185.
Dolbeer, R.A., Chevalier, M., Woronecki, P.P. & Butler, E.B. (1989). Laughing Gulls at JFK Airport: safety hazard or wildlife resource. Pp. 37-44 in: *Proc. 4th Eastern Wildlife Damage Control Conf.*
Dolgushin, I.A. ed. (1962). [*Birds of Kazakhstan*]. Vol. 3. Alma Ata. In Russian.
Dolz, J.C. (1994). Collared Pratincole. *Glareola pratincola*. Pp. 248-249 in: Tucker & Heath (1994).
Dolz, J.C., Dies, I. & Belliure, J. (1989). Las colonias de Canastera (*Glareola pratincola* Linn 1766) en la Comunidad Valenciana. *Medi Natural* **1-2**: 69-80.
Dombrowolski, K.A. & Halba, R. (1987). The Common Crane in Poland. Pp. 231-238 in: Archibald & Pasquier (1987a).
Domínguez, F. (1989). The Houbara Bustard in the Canary Islands: towards a recovery plan. *Bustard Studies* **4**: 42-51.
Domínguez, F. & Díaz, G. (1985). Plan de recuperación de la Hubara Canaria. [Plan for the recuperation of the Canarian Houbara]. Unpublished report to Ministerio de Agricultura, Pesca y Alimentación & ICONA, Santa Cruz de Tenerife. 89 pp.
Domínguez-Bello, M.G., Lovera, M., Suárez, P. & Michelangeli, F. (1993). Microbial digestive symbionts of the crop of the Hoatzin (*Opisthocomus hoazin*): an avian foregut fermenter. *Physiol. Zool.* **66(3)**: 374-383.
Domínguez-Bello, M.G., Michelangeli, F., Ruiz, M.C., García, A. & Rodríguez, E. (1994). Ecology of the folivorous Hoatzin (*Opisthocomus hoazin*) on the Venezuelan plains. *Auk* **111(3)**: 643-651.
Domínguez-Bello, M.G., Ruiz, M.C. & Michelangeli, F. (1993). Evolutionary significance of foregut fermentation in the Hoatzin (*Opisthocomus hoazin*; Aves: Opisthocomidae). *J. Comp. Physiol. B Biochem. Syst. Environm. Physiol.* **163(7)**: 594-601.
Domm, S. & Recher, H.F. (1973). Silver Gull piracy on Lesser Crested Tern. *Sunbird* **4**: 63-86.
Donahue, P. (1994). *Birds of Tambopata. A Checklist.* Tambopata Reserve Society, London.
Donahue, P.K. & Petersen, W.R. (1980). First record of Snowy-crowned Tern (*Sterna trudeaui*) for Peru. *Amer. Birds* **34**: 213.
Donaldson, G. (1968). Bill color changes in adult Roseate Terns. *Auk* **86**: 662-668.
Donnelly, B.G. (1966). An aberrant colour variety of the Southern Black-backed Gull *Larus dominicanus*. *Ostrich* **37**: 56.
Donnelly, B.G. (1974). The Lesser Black-backed Gull *Larus fuscus* in southern and central Africa. *Bull. Brit. Orn. Club* **94**: 63-68.
Dontschev, S. (1975). Neue Angaben ueber das Auffinden von /*Phalaropus lobatus*/ (L.), /*Glareola nordmanni*/ Fisch.-Waldh. und /*Arenaria interpres*/ (L.) an der Bulgarischen Schwarzmeerkueste. [New data upon the discovery of /*Phalaropus lobatus*/, /*Glareola nordmanni*/ and /*Arenaria interpres*/ in the Bulgarian Black Sea coast]. *Larus* **26-28**: 183-187. In German with Serbo-Croatian summary.
Dorio, J.C. & Grewe, A.E. (1979). Nesting and brood rearing habitat of the Upland Sandpiper. *J. Minnesota Acad. Sci.* **45**: 8-11.
Dorji, P. (1987). Bhutan's Black-necked Cranes. *Oryx* **21**: 71-72.
Dorogoy, I.V. (1982). [Materials on Knot biology on Vrangel Island]. *Vestnik Zoologii* **5**: 65-69. In Russian.
Dorogoy, I.V. (1983). [Biological data on the Buff-breasted Sandpiper (*Tryngites subruficollis*)]. *Bull. Moscow Soc. Nat. Study (Biol. Section)* **88**: 50-55. In Russian with English summary.
Dorogoy, I.V. (1984). [Material on the biology of the Sabine's Gull]. *Ornitologyia* **19**: 198. In Russian.
Dorst, J. (1968). Stilted rails. Pp. 109-110 in: Grzimek (1968).
Dorward, D.F. (1963). The Fairy Tern (*Gygis alba*) on Ascension Island. *Ibis* **103B**: 365-378.
Dorward, D.F. & Ashmole, N.P. (1963). Notes on the biology of the Brown Noddy *Anous stolidus* on Ascension Island. *Ibis* **103B**: 447-457.
Dostine, P.L. & Morton, S.R. (1989a). Feeding ecology of the Whiskered Tern, *Chlidonias hybrida* in the Alligator Rivers Region, Northern Territory. *Austr. Wildl. Res.* **16**: 549-562.
Dostine, P.L. & Morton, S.R. (1989b). Food of the Black-winged Stilt *Himantopus himantopus* in the Alligator Rivers Region, Northern Territory. *Emu* **89(4)**: 250-253.
Dott, H.E.M. (1985). North American migrants in Bolivia. *Condor* **87**: 343-345.
Doughty, C. & Carter, M.J. (1977). American race (*dominica*) of the Eastern Golden Plover (*Pluvialis dominica*) in Westernport Bay, Victoria. *Austr. Bird Watcher* **7(1)**: 23-24.
Doughty, R.W. (1989). *Return of the Whooping Crane.* University of Texas Press, Austin, Texas.
Douthwaite, R.J. (1974). An endangered population of Wattled Cranes. *Biol. Conserv.* **6(2)**: 134-142.
Douthwaite, R.J. (1978). Geese and Red-knobbed Coot on the Kafue Flats in Zambia, 1970-1974. *East Afr. Wildl. J.* **16**: 29-47.
Douthwaite, R.J. & Miskell, J.E. (1991). Additions to *Birds of Somalia, their Habitat, Status and Distribution* (Ash & Miskell 1983). *Scopus* **14**: 37-60.
Dowding, J.E. (1989). An introduction to the New Zealand Dotterel. *Stilt* **14**: 61-63.
Dowding, J.E. (1993). *New Zealand Dotterel Recovery Plan.* Threatened Species Unit, Department of Conservation. Threatened Species Recovery Plan Series **10**. Wellington.
Dowding, J.E. (1994). Morphometrics and ecology of the New Zealand Dotterel (*Charadrius obscurus*), with a description of a new subspecies. *Notornis* **41**: 221-233.
Dowding, J.E. & Chamberlin, S.P. (1991). Annual movement patterns and breeding-site fidelity of the New Zealand Dotterel (*Charadrius obscurus*). *Notornis* **38(2)**: 89-102.
Dowding, J.E. & Kennedy, E.S. (1993). Size, age structure and morphometrics of the Shore Plover population on South East Island. *Notornis* **40(3)**: 213-222.
Dowding, J.E. & Murphy, E.C. (1993a). Decline of the Stewart Island population of the New Zealand Dotterel. *Notornis* **40(1)**: 1-14.
Dowding, J.E. & Murphy, E.C. (1993b). Distribution and breeding of the Spur-winged Plover on Stewart Island. *Notornis* **40(3)**: 227-229.
Downes, M. (1975). *A Bibliography of the Bustards: First Working Draft.* Wildlife Branch, Department of Agriculture, Stock and Fisheries, Papua New Guinea.
Downes, M.C., Ealey, E.H.M., Gwynn, A.M. & Young, P.S. (1959). *The Birds of Heard Island.* Austr. Nat. Antarct. Res. Exped. Rep. (Ser. B) **1**: 1-135.
Downing, R.L. (1973). A preliminary nesting survey of Least Terns and Black Skimmers in the east. *Amer. Birds* **27**: 946-949.
Dowsett, R.J. (1965). Weights of some Zambian birds. *Bull. Brit. Orn. Club.* **85(8)**: 150-152.
Dowsett, R.J. (1969). Greater Sandplovers *Charadrius leschenaultii* Lesson at Lake Chad. *Bull. Brit. Orn. Club* **89(3)**: 73-74.
Dowsett, R.J. (1975). How does the Skimmer wet its eggs? *Bull. East Afr. Nat. Hist. Soc.* **1975**: 13.
Dowsett, R.J. (1980). The migration of coastal waders from the Palaearctic across Africa. *Gerfaut* **70**: 3-36.
Dowsett, R.J. & Dowsett-Lemaire, F. (1976). A second Zambian record of Mongolian Sandplover. *Bull. Zambia Orn. Soc.* **8(2)**: 68-69.
Dowsett, R.J. & Dowsett-Lemaire, F. (1980). The systematic status of some Zambian birds. *Gerfaut* **70**: 151-199.
Dowsett, R.J. & Dowsett-Lemaire, F. (1989). Liste preliminaire des oiseaux du Congo. *Tauraco Res. Rep.* **2**: 29-51.
Dowsett, R.J. & Dowsett-Lemaire, F. eds. (1991). *Flore et Faune du Bassin du Kouilou (Congo) et leur Exploitation.* Tauraco Research Report **4**. Tauraco Press, Liège, Belgium.
Dowsett, R.J. & Dowsett-Lemaire, F. (1993). *A Contribution to the Distribution and Taxonomy of Afrotropical and Malagasy Birds.* Tauraco Research Report **5**. Tauraco Press, Liège, Belgium.
Dowsett, R.J. & Forbes-Watson, A.D. (1993). *Checklist of Birds of the Afrotropical and Malagasy Regions.* Vol. 1. Species Limits and Distribution. Tauraco Press, Liège, Belgium.
Dowsett, R.J., Dowsett-Lemaire, F. & Stjernstedt, R. (1977). The voice of the courser *Rhinoptilus cinctus*. *Bull. Brit. Orn. Club* **97(3)**: 73-75.
Dowsett-Lemaire, F., Dowsett, R.J. & Bulens, P. (1993). Additions and corrections to the avifauna of Congo. *Malimbus* **15**: 68-80.
Doyle, M., Drake, A. & Von Behrens, D. (1985). A Wandering Tattler at Windang Island, Wollongong, NSW. *Austr. Birds* **19(2)**: 39-40.
Draffan, R.D.W., Garnett, S.T. & Malone, G.J. (1983). Birds of the Torres Strait: an annotated list and biogeographical analysis. *Emu* **83**: 207-234.
Dragesco, J. (1960). Notes biologiques sur quelques oiseaux d'Afrique Equatoriale. *Alauda* **28**: 262-273.
Dragesco, J. (1961). Observations éthologiques sur les oiseaux du Banc d'Arguin. *Alauda* **2**: 81-98.
Drake, J.R. (1980). Inland breeding of Black-billed Gulls in southern Hawkes Bay and northern Wairarapa. *Notornis* **27(1)**: 86-88.
Drenckhahn, D. (1968). Die Mauser des Kampfläufers, *Philomachus pugnax*, in Schleswig-Holstein. *Corax* **2**: 130-150.
Drent, R. & Piersma, T. (1990). An exploration of the energetics of leap-frog migration in arctic breeding waders. Pp. 399-412 in: Gwinner (1990).
Drent, R.H. (1965). Breeding biology of the Pigeon Guillemot *Cepphus columba*. *Ardea* **53**: 99-160.
Drent, R.H., Klaassen, M. & Zwaan, B. (1992). Predictive growth budgets in terns and gulls. *Ardea* **80**: 5-18.
Drewien, R.C. (1973). *Ecology of Rocky Mountain Greater Sandhill Cranes.* PhD dissertation, University of Idaho, Moscow, Idaho.
Drewien, R.C. & Bizeau, E.G. (1974). Status and distribution of Greater Sandhill Cranes in the Rocky Mountains. *J. Wildl. Manage.* **38**: 720-742.
Drewien, R.C. & Bizeau, E.G. (1978). Cross-fostering Whooping Cranes to Sandhill Crane foster parents. Pp. 201-221 in: Temple, S. ed. (1978). *Endangered Birds: Management Techniques for Preserving Threatened Species.* University of Wisconsin Press, Madison, Wisconsin.
Drewien, R.C. & Bizeau, E.G. (1981). Use of radiotelemetry to study the movements of juvenile Whooping Cranes. Pp. 130-134 in: Lewis & Masatomi (1981).
Drewien, R.C. & Kuyt, E. (1979). Teamwork helps the Whooping Crane. *Natl. Geogr.* **155**: 680-693.
Drewien, R.C. & Lewis, J. (1987). Status and distribution of cranes in North America. Pp. 469-477 in: Archibald & Pasquier (1987a).
Drewien, R.C., Brown, W.M., Kendall, W.L. (1995). Recruitment in Rocky Mountain Greater Sandhill Cranes and comparison with other crane populations. *J. Wildl. Manage.* **59(2)**: 339-356.
Drewien, R.C., Littlefield, C.D., Walkinshaw L.H. & Braun, C.E. (1975). Conservation committee report on the status of Sandhill Cranes. *Wilson Bull.* **87(2)**: 297-302.
Driedzic, W.R., Crowe, H.L., Hicklin, P.W. & Sephton, D.H. (1993). Adaptations in pectoralis muscle, heart mass, and energy metabolism during premigratory fattening in Semipalmated Sandpipers (*Calidris pusilla*). *Can. J. Zool.* **71(8)**: 1602-1608.
van den Driessche, R., McConnell, S.D. & Hooper, T.D. (1994). First confirmed breeding record for the Upland Sandpiper, *Bartramia longicauda*, in British Columbia. *Can. Field-Nat.* **108(1)**: 89-91.
Driessens, G. & van Rossum, R. (1988). [Buff-breasted Sandpipers in Belgium and the Netherlands in Summer of 1986]. *Dutch Birding* **10(1)**: 27-29. In Dutch with English summary.
Drinnan, R.E. (1957). The winter feeding of the Oystercatcher, (*Haematopus ostralegus*) on the cockle (*Cardium edule*). *J. Anim. Ecol.* **26**: 441 469.
Drinnan, R.E. (1958a). Observations on the feeding of Oystercatchers in captivity. *British Birds* **51**: 139 149.
Drinnan, R.E. (1958b). *The Winter Feeding of the Oystercatcher (*Haematopus ostralegus*) on the Edible Mussel (*Mytilus edulis*) in the Conway Estuary.* M.A.A.F. Fishery Investigations, London (Series 2) **22(4)**.
Driver, E.A. (1988). Diet and behaviour of young American Coots. *Wildfowl* **39**: 34-42.
Dronen, N.O., Schmidt, G.D., Allison, B.R. & Mellen, J.W. (1988). Some parasitic helminths from the American Oystercatcher, *Haematopus palliatus* Temminck, from the Texas Gulf coast and the Common Pied Oystercatcher, *Haematopus ostralegus* Linnaeus, from New Zealand, including *Dildotaenia latovarium* n. gen. and n. sp. (Cestoda: Hymenolepidae). *J. Parasitol.* **74**: 864-867.
Drost, C.A. & Lewis, D.B. (1995). Xantus' Murrelet (*Synthliboramphus hypoleucus*). No. **164** in: Poole & Gill (1995).
Drost, R. (1968). Auf dem Lebenslauf eines Teichhuhns (*Gallinula chloropus*). *Bonn. zool. Beitr.* **19**: 346-349.
Drost, R. & Schilling, L. (1951). Beobachtungen an einer kleinen Silbermöwen-Population in Jahreslauf. Ein Beitrag zur Sociologie von *Larus argentatus*. *Vogelwarte* **16**: 44-48.
Drost, R. & Schilling, L. (1952). Das Verhalten der männlichen und weiblichen Silbermöwen *Larus a. argentatus* P. außerhalb der Brutzeit. *Vogelwarte* **16**: 108-116.
Drury, W.H. (1960). Breeding activities of Long-tailed Jaeger, Herring Gull and Arctic Tern on Bylot Island, Northwest Territories, Canada. *Bird-Banding* **31**: 63-78.
Drury, W.H. (1961). The breeding biology of shorebirds on Bylot Island, Northwest Territories, Canada. *Auk* **78**: 176-219.
Drury, W.H. (1965). Gulls vs terns. *Mass. Audubon* **1965**(Summer): 1-5.
Drury, W.H. (1973-1974). Population changes in New England seabirds. *Bird-Banding* **44**: 267-313, **45**: 1-15.
Drury, W.H. (1984). Gulls. Pp. 130-145 in: Haley (1984).
Drury, W.H. & Kadlec, J.A. (1974). The current status of the Herring Gull population in the northeastern United States. *Bird-Banding* **45**: 297-306.

Drury, W.H. & Smith, W.J. (1968). Defense of feeding areas by adult Herring Gulls and intrusion by young. *Evolution* **22**: 193-201.
Duan Wenrui, Fen Lingfei & Du Xiandong (1991). [Cranes of Inner Mongolia]. *J. Inner Mongolia Teachers Univ. (Nat. Sci. Edition)* **1**: 41-45. In Chinese.
Dubois, P.J. (1985). Considérations sur le Goéland d'Arménie *Larus armenicus* Buturlin en Israël. *Alauda* **53**: 226-228.
Dubois, P.J. (1992). [Migration and overwintering of Black-winged Stilts (*Himantopus himantopus*) in the west Palearctic and Africa]. *Nos Oiseaux* **41(6)**: 347-366. In French with German and English summaries.
Dubois, P.J. (1994a). La Sterne élégante *Sterna elegans* en France. [Elegant Tern in France]. *Ornithos* **1(2)**: 74-79. In French with English summary.
Dubois, P.J. (1994b). Identification du Goéland à ailes blanches *Larus glaucoides*. *Ornithos* **1(2)**: 84-90.
Dubois, P.J. & Frémont, J.Y. (1996). Identification du Goéland à bec cerclé *Larus delawarensis*. *Ornithos* **3(1)**: 22-32.
Dubois, P.J. & Maheo, R. (1986). *Limicoles Nicheurs de France*. Ministere de l'Environnement & Ligue Française pour la Protection des Oiseaux Bureau International de Recherche sur les Oiseaux d'Eau.
Dubs, B. (1992). *Birds of Southwestern Brazil: Catalogue and Guide to the Birds of the Pantanal of Mato Grosso and its Border Areas*. Betrona Verlag, Kusnacht, Switzerland.
Duc, L.D. (1990). *Hôi Thao Quôc tê Sêu cô Trui va Dât Ngâp Nuoc*. Proceedings of the International Sarus Crane and Wetland Workshop. 11-17 January 1990. Tam Nong, Vietnam. Nha Xuât Ban Nông Nghiêp, Ha Noi. In Vietnamese.
Duc, L.D. (1991). Eastern Sarus Cranes in Indochina. Pp. 317-318 in: Harris (1991b).
Duckworth, W. & Kelsh, R. (1988). *A Bird Inventory of Similajau National Park*. ICBP Study Report **31**, Cambridge.
Duff, D.G., Bakewell, D.N. & Williams, M.D. (1991). The Relict Gull *Larus relictus* in China and elsewhere. *Forktail* **6**: 43-65.
Duffy, D.C. (1977). Breeding populations of terns and skimmers on Long Island Sound and eastern Long Island: 1972-1975. *Proc. Linn. Soc. N.Y.* **73**: 1-48.
Duffy, D.C. (1983). The foraging ecology of Peruvian seabirds. *Auk* **100(4)**: 800-810.
Duffy, D.C. (1986). Foraging at patches: interactions between Common and Roseate Terns. *Ornis Scand.* **17**: 47-52.
Duffy, D.C. (1987). Multiple fish carrying in Swift Terns *Sterna bergii*. *Cormorant* **14**: 45-49.
Duffy, D.C. (1995). Apparent river otter predation at an Aleutian Tern colony. *Colonial Waterbirds* **18(1)**: 91-92.
Duffy, D.C. & Atkins, N. (1979). A second breeding record for the Grey-hooded Gull (*Larus cirrocephalus*) on the coast of Peru. *Condor* **81**: 219.
Duffy, D.C. & Hurtado, M. (1984). The conservation and status of seabirds of the Ecuadorian mainland. Pp. 231-236 in: Croxall, Evans & Schreiber (1984).
Duffy, D.C. & Nettleship, D.N. (1992). Seabirds: management problems and research opportunities. Pp. 525-546 in: McCullough & Barrett (1992).
Duffy, D.C., Hays, C. & Plenge, M.A. (1984). The conservation status of Peruvian seabirds. Pp. 245-259 in: Croxall, Evans & Schreiber (1984).
Dufourny, H. & Lebailly, J.L. (1991). Première observation d'un Bécasseau de Bonaparte (*Calidris fuscicollis*) en Belgique. *Aves* **28(4)**: 220-223.
Dugan, P. (1993). *Wetlands in Danger*. Mitchell Beazley & IUCN, London.
Dugan, P.J. (1982). Seasonal changes in patch use by a territorial Grey Plover: weather-dependent adjustments in foraging behaviour. *J. Anim. Ecol.* **51(3)**: 849-858.
Dugan, P.J., Evans, P.R., Goodyer, L.R. & Davidson, N.C. (1981). Winter fat reserves in shorebirds: disturbance of regulated levels by severe weather conditions. *Ibis* **123**: 359-363.
Dujardin, J.L. & Tostain, O. (1990). Les oiseaux de mer nicheurs de Guyane Française. *Alauda* **58**: 107-134.
Dumas, J.V. & Witman, J.D. (1993). Predation by Herring Gulls on two rocky intertidal crab species. *J. Exper. Mar. Biol. Ecol.* **169**: 89-101.
DuMont, P.A. (1940). Relation of Franklin's Gull colonies to agriculture on the Great Plains. *Trans. North Amer. Wildl. Nat. Resour. Conf.* **5**: 183-189.
Duncan, C.D. (1995). The migration of the Red-necked Phalaropes: ecological mysteries and conservation concerns. *Bird Obs.* **23(4)**: 200-207.
Duncan, N. (1978). The effect of culling Herring Gulls (*Larus argentatus*) on recruitment and population dynamics. *J. Appl. Ecol.* **15**: 697-713.
Duncan, R.A. (1973). Ventriloquism in a Wilson's Plover. *Auk* **90(3)**: 680.
Dunford, R.D. & Owen, R.B. (1973). Summer behavior of immature radio-equipped Woodcock in central Maine. *J. Wildl. Manage.* **37**: 462-469.
Dunlop, C.L., Blokpoel, H. & Jarvie, S. (1991). Nesting rafts as a management tool for a declining Common Tern (*Sterna hirundo*) colony. *Colonial Waterbirds* **14**: 116-120.
Dunlop, J.N. (1985a). Reproductive periodicity in a population of Crested Terns *Sterna bergii* Lichtenstein, in southwestern Australia. *Austr. Wildl. Res.* **12**: 95-102.
Dunlop, J.N. (1985b). The relationship between moult and the reproductive cycle in a population of Crested Terns, *Sterna bergii* Lichtenstein. *Austr. Wildl. Res.* **12**: 487-494.
Dunlop, J.N. (1986). Seasonal variations in prey selection, prey availability and egg size in a population of Crested Terns *Sterna bergii*. *Austr. Wildl. Res.*
Dunlop, J.N. & Jenkins, J. (1992). Known age birds at a subtropical breeding colony of the Bridled Tern (*Sterna anaethetus*): a comparison with the Sooty Tern. *Colonial Waterbirds* **15**: 75-82.
Dunlop, J.N., Cheshire, N.G. & Wooler, R.D. (1988). Observations on the marine distribution of tropicbirds, Sooty and Bridled Terns and Gadfly Petrels from the eastern Indian Ocean. *Records West. Austr. Mus.* **14**: 237-252.
Dunlop, R.R. (1970). Behaviour of the Banded Rail, *Rallus philippensis*. *Sunbird* **1**: 3-15.
Dunn, E. (1994). Species of European conservation concern, category 4. Species with a favourable conservation status but concentrated in Europe (more than half their global population or range in Europe). Pp. 439-469 in: Tucker & Heath (1994).
Dunn, E.H. (1976). The development of endothermy and existence energy expenditure in Herring Gull chicks. *Condor* **78**: 493-498.
Dunn, E.H. (1979). Nesting biology and development of young in Ontario Black Terns. *Can. Field-Nat.* **93**: 276-281.
Dunn, E.H. & Agro, D.J. (1995). Black Tern (*Chlidonias niger*). No. **147** in: Poole & Gill (1994-1995).
Dunn, E.H. & Brisbin, I.L. (1980). Age-specific changes in the major body components and caloric values of Herring Gull chicks. *Condor* **82**: 398-401.
Dunn, E.K. (1972). Effect of age on the fishing ability of Sandwich Terns *Sterna sandvicensis*. *Ibis* **114**: 360-366.
Dunn, E.K. (1973a). Changes in fishing ability of terns associated with windspeed and sea surface conditions. *Nature* **244**: 520-521.
Dunn, E.K. (1973b). Robbing behavior of Roseate Terns. *Auk* **90**: 641-651.
Dunn, E.K. (1975). The role of environmental factors in the growth of tern chicks. *J. Anim. Ecol.* **44**: 743-754.
Dunn, E.K. (1985). Tern. Pp. 587-588 in: Campbell & Lack (1985).
Dunn, E.K. & Mead, C.J. (1982). Relationship between sardine fisheries and recovery rates of ringed terns in West Africa. *Seabird Report* **6**: 98-104.
Dunn, J.L. (1993). The identification of Semipalmated and Common Ringed Plovers in alternate plumage. *Birding* **25(4)**: 238-243.
Dunn, J.L., Morlan, J. & Wilds, C.P. (1987). Field identification of forms of Lesser Golden-Plover. Pp. 28-33 in: *International Identification Meeting*. Proceedings of the 4th International Identification Meeting, 1986. International Birdwatching Center, Eilat, Israel.
Dunn, P.J. & Hirschfeld, E. (1991). Long-tailed Skuas in Britain and Ireland in autumn 1988. *British Birds* **84(4)**: 121-136.
Dunn, P.O., May, T.A., McCollough, M.A. & Howe, M.A. (1988). Length of stay and fat content of migrant Semipalmated Sandpipers in eastern Maine. *Condor* **90**: 824-835.
Dunnett, J.B. (1992). Long-toed Stint: new to Britain and Ireland. *British Birds* **85(8)**: 429-436.
Dunning, J.B. (1984). *Body Weights of 686 Species of North American Birds*. Western Bird Banding Association Monograph **1**.
Dunning, J.B. (1988). Yellow-footed Gull kills Eared Grebe. *Colonial Waterbirds* **11**: 117-118.
Dunning, J.B. ed. (1993). *CRC Handbook of Avian Body Masses*. CRC Press, Boca Raton, Florida.
Dunning, J.S. (1982). *South American Land Birds. A Photographic Aid to Identification*. Harrowood Books, Newtown Square, Pennsylvania.
Duplaix-Hall, N. ed. (1974). Census of rare animals in captivity, 1973. *Int. Zoo Yb.* **14**: 396-429.
DuPont, J.E. (1971). *Philippine Birds*. Monograph Serie **2**. Delaware Museum Natural History, Greenville, Delaware.
Dupuy, A.R. (1977). Reproduction importante de Glaréoles à collier *Glareola pratincola* au Parc national des Oiseaux du Djoudj, Sénégal. *Oiseau et RFO* **47(1)**: 108-109.
Duquet, M. (1995). Des Sternes incas *Larosterna inca* en France 1994. [Inca Tern in France in 1994]. *Ornithos* **2(4)**: 184-185. In French with English summary.
Durell, S.E.A. & Goss-Custard, J.D. (1984). Prey selection within a size class of mussels, *Mytilus edulis*, by Oystercatchers, *Haematopus ostralegus*. *Anim. Behav.* **32**: 1197-1203.
Durell, S.E.A. & Kelly, C.P. (1990). Diets of Dunlin *Calidris alpina* and Gray Plover *Pluvialis squatarola* on the Wash as determined by dropping analysis. *Bird Study* **37(1)**: 44-47.
Durell, S.E.A., Goss-Custard, J.D. & Caldow, R.W.G. (1993). Sex-related differences in diet and feeding method in the Oystercatcher *Haematopus ostralegus*. *J. Anim. Ecol.* **62**: 205-215.
Durinck, J., Skov, H. & Danielsen, F. (1991). Fødevalg hos overvintrende Lomvier *Uria aalge* i Skagerrak. [Winter food of Guillemots *Uria aalge* in the Skagerrak]. *Dan. Orn. Foren. Tidssk.* **85**: 145-150. In Danish with English summary.
Durnford, H. (1877). Notes on the birds of the Province of Buenos Aires. *Ibis* **Ser. 4, no. 1**: 166-203.
Dvorsky, M. & Dvorská, J. (1980). Neobvykla snuska kulika Ricniho (*Charadrius dubius* Gm.). [Unusual clutch size for *Charadrius dubius*]. *Zpravy Morav. Ornitolo. Sdruzeni* **38**: 125-126. In Czech with German summary.
Dwight, J. (1919). A new subspecies of the Western Gull. *Proc. Biol. Soc. Washington* **32**: 11-14.
Dwight, J. (1920). The plumages of gulls in relation to age as illustrated by the Herring Gull (*Larus argentatus*) and other species. *Auk* **18**: 49-63.
Dwight, J. (1925). *The Gulls (Laridae) of the World: their Plumages, Moults, Variations, Relationships and Distribution*. Bulletin of the American Museum of Natural History **52**, New York. 339 pp.
Dwyer, N.C., Bishop, M.A., Harkness, J.S. & Zhang Yao Zhong (1992). Black-necked Cranes nesting in Tibet Autonomous Region, China. Pp. 75-80 in: Stahlecker (1992).
Dwyer, T.J. & Nichols, J.D. (1982). Regional population inferences for the American Woodcock. Pp. 12-21 in: Dwyer & Storm (1982).
Dwyer, T.J. & Storm, G.L. eds. (1982). *Woodcock Ecology and Management*. Wildlife Research Report **14**. US Fish & Wildlife Service, Washington, D.C.
Dwyer, T.J., Derleth, E.L. & McAuley, D.G. (1982). Woodcock brood ecology in Maine. Pp. 63-70 in: Dwyer & Storm (1982).
Dwyer, T.J., Sepik, G.F., Derleth, E.L. & McAuley, D.G. (1988). *Demographic Characteristics of a Maine Woodcock Population and Effects of Habitat Management*. Fish Wildlife Research **4**. US Fish & Wildlife Service, Washington, D.C.
Dybro, T. (1970). [The Kentish Plover *Charadrius alexandrinus* as a breeding bird in Denmark]. *Dan. Orn. Foren. Tidssk.* **64**: 205-222. In Danish with English summary.
Dyer, J.M. (1976). *An Evaluation of Diurnal Habitat Requirements for the American Woodcock (*Philohela minor *Gmelin) in Southern Louisiana*. PhD dissertation, Louisiana State University, Baton Rouge, Louisiana.
Dyer, J.M. & Hamilton, R.B. (1974). An analysis of feeding habits of the American Woodcock (*Philohela minor*) in southern Athens, Louisiana. Page 11 in: *Proc. 5th American Woodcock Workshop, Athens, 1974*.
Dyer, M. (1992). Observations on Wattled Cranes nesting on Nyika Plateau, Malawi. *Nyala* **15(2)**: 57-62.
Dyer, R.W. (1993). The Piping Plover: conservation needs in the eastern United States. *Underwater Nat.* **21(3-4)**: 19-23.
Dyer, R.W., Hecht, A., Melvin, S.M., Raithel, C. & Terwilliger, K. (1988). *Atlantic Coast Piping Plover Recovery Plan*. US Fish & Wildlife Service, Boston, Massachusetts. 81 pp.
Ealey, E.H.M. (1954a). Ecological notes on the birds of Heard Island. *Emu* **54**: 91-112.
Ealey, E.H.M. (1954b). Analysis of stomach contents of some Heard Island birds. *Emu* **54**: 204-210.
Earlé, R.A. & Grobler, N. (1987). *First Atlas of Bird Distribution in the Orange Free State*. National Musuem, Bloemfontein, South Africa.
Earlé, R.A., Louw, S. & Herholdt, J.J. (1988). Notes on the measurements and diet of Ludwig's Bustard *Neotis ludwigii*. *Ostrich* **59(4)**: 178-179.
Eason, D. & Rasch, G. (1993). *Takahe Management 1992/93*. Internal report. Department of Conservation, Wellington.
Eason, P.K. & Sherman, P.T. (1995). Dominance status, mating strategies and copulation success in cooperatively polyandrous White-winged Trumpeters, *Psophia leucoptera* (Aves: Psophiidae). *Anim. Behav.* **49**: 725-736.
Easterla, D.A. (1962). Some foods of the Yellow Rail in Missouri. *Wilson Bull.* **74**: 94-95.
Easterla, D.A. & Damman, D.L. (1977). Unusual food item of Franklin's Gull. *Auk* **94**: 163.
Eaton, R.J. (1931). Great Black-backed Gull (*Larus marinus*) breeding in Essex County, Massachusetts. *Auk* **48**: 588-589.
Eber, G. (1961). Vergleichende Untersuchungen am flugfähigen Teichhuhn *Gallinula chl. chloropus* und an der flugunfähigen Inselralle *Gallinula nesiotis*. *Bonn. zool. Beitr.* **12**: 247-315.
Eck, S. (1976a). Die Vögel der Banggai-Inseln, insbesondere Pelengs. *Zool. Abh., Dresden* **34**: 53-100.
Eck, S. (1976b). [Marginal notes on the taxonomy of the Ringed Plover]. *Beitr. Vogelkd.* **22**: 38-48. In German.
Eckert, J. (1967). The Pectoral Sandpiper in South Australia. *S. Austr. Orn.* **24**: 135-136.
Eckert, J. (1970). An extension of the geographic and breeding range of the Little Tern. *S. Austr. Orn.* **25**: 142-144.
Eckert, J. (1972). Further notes on the Little Quail. *S. Austr. Orn.* **26**: 34-36.
Eckert, K. (1981). First record of Wilson's Plover for Minnesota. *Loon* **53(3)**: 123-125.
Eddleman, W.R. (1983). *A Study of Migratory American Coots,* Fulica americana, *in Oklahoma*. PhD thesis, Oklahoma State University, Stillwater, Oklahoma.
Eddleman, W.R. & Conway, C.J. (1994). Clapper Rail. In: Tacha & Braun (1994).
Eddleman, W.R. & Knopf, F.L. (1985). Determining age and sex of American Coots. *J. Field Orn.* **56**: 41-55.
Eddleman, W.R., Flores, R.E. & Legare, M.L. (1994). Black Rail (*Lateralllus jamaicensis*). In: Poole & Gill (1994-1995).
Eddleman, W.R., Knopf, F.L., Meanley, B., Reid, F.A. & Zembal, R. (1988). Conservation of North American rallids. *Wilson Bull.* **100**: 458-475.
Eddleman, W.R., Knopf, F.L. & Patterson, C.T. (1985). Chronology of migration by American Coots in Oklahoma. *J. Wildl. Manage.* **49**: 241-246.
Eden, S.F. (1987). When do helpers help? Food availability and helping in the Moorhen, *Gallinula chloropus*. *Behav. Ecol. Sociobiol.* **21**: 191-195.
Edgar, A.T. (1968). Oriental Dotterel in Northland. *Notornis* **15(3)**: 211-212.
Edgar, A.T. (1969). Estimated population of the Red-breasted Dotterel. *Notornis* **16(2)**: 85-100.
Edwards, E.P. (1989). *A Field Guide to the Birds of Mexico*. Published privately, Sweet Briar, Virginia.
Edwards, P.J. (1982). Plumage variation, territoriality and breeding displays of the Golden Plover *Pluvialis apricaria* in southwest Scotland. *Ibis* **124**: 88-96.
Edwards, R., Brechtel, S., Bromley, R., Hjertaas, D., Johns, B., Kuyt, E., Lewis, J., Manners, N., Stardom, R. & Tarry, G. eds. (1994). *National Recovery Plan for the Whooping Crane*. RENEW Report **6**. Canadian Whooping Crane Recovery Team, Ottawa.
Eenshuistra, O. (1973). *Goudplevier en Wilstervangst*. Fryske Akademy, Leeuwarden, the Netherlands.
van Eerden, M. & Key, P. (1978). [Results of two Golden Plover (*Pluvialis apricaria*) surveys in the Netherlands in November 1976 and April 1977]. *Watervogels* **4**: 182-190. In Dutch.
van Eerden, M., Key, P. & Tanger, D. (1979). [The Golden Plover survey in November 1978 and the inland wader survey in general]. *Watervogels* **5**: 226-231. In Dutch.
Egensteiner, E.D., Smith, H.T. & Rodgers, J.A. (1996). Royal Tern. In: Rodgers, Kale & Smith (1996).
Egnell, G. & Elmberg, J. (1990). [The migration of skuas through Norra Kvarken in the spring of 1989]. *Vår Fågelvärld* **49(2)**: 95-97. In Swedish with English summary.
Eguchi, K., Nagata, H., Takeishi, M., Henmi, Y. & Takatsuka, M. (1991). Foraging and time budget of the Hooded Cranes in a wintering area at Yashiro, Japan. Pp. 305-310 in: Harris (1991b).
Ehrlich, P.R, Dobkins, D.S. & Wheye, D. (1992). *Birds in Jeopardy. The Imperiled and Extinct Birds of the United States & Canada*. Stanford University Press, Stanford, California.
Eigenhuis, K.J. (1991). Yellow-legged Gulls in Poland. *Dutch Birding* **13(6)**: 209-210.
Eigenhuis, K.J. (1992). [Great Knot in Oostvaardersplassen and near Camperduin in September-October 1991]. *Dutch Birding* **14(4)**: 126-131. In Dutch with English summary.
Einemann, L. (1991). A nesting report of a Wilson's Phalarope in Lancaster County. *Nebr. Bird Rev.* **59(3)**: 59-61.
Eisentraut, M. (1935). Biologische Studien im bolivianischen Chaco. VI. Beitrag zur Biologie der Vogelfauna. *Mitt. Zool. Mus. Berlin* **20**: 367-443.
Eklund, C.R. (1961). Distribution and life history studies of the South Polar Skua. *Bird-Banding* **32**: 187-223.
Eley, T.J. (1976). Extension of the breeding range of the Black Oystercatcher in Alaska. *Condor* **78(1)**: 115.
Elgood, J.H. & Donald, R.G. (1962). Breeding of the Painted Snipe *Rostratula benghalensis* in southwest Nigeria. *Ibis* **104**: 253-256.
Elgood, J.H., Fry, C.H. & Dowsett, R.J. (1973). African migrants in Nigeria. *Ibis* **115**: 1-45.

Elgood, J.H., Heigham, J.B., Moore, A.M., Nason, A.M., Sharland, R.E. & Skinner, N.J. (1994). *The Birds of Nigeria. An Annotated Checklist*. BOU Check-list **4**. British Ornithologists' Union, Tring, UK.
Elkowe, K.D. & Payne, S. (1979). Aging young Herring Gulls from measurements of body parts. *Bird-Banding* **50**: 49-55.
Ellenbrook, F. & Schekkerman, H. (1985). [Greater Sand Plover on Terschelling in August 1984]. *Dutch Birding* **7(2)**: 59-65. In Dutch with English summary.
Eller, G.J. (1989). Grey Ternlets in the Andaman Sea. *Notornis* **36(2)**: 159-160.
Ellingwood, M.R., Shissler, B.P., Samuel, D.E. & Cromer, J.I. (1993). Evidence of leks in the mating strategy of the American Woodcock. Pp. 108-114 in: Longcore & Sepik (1993).
Elliot, H.F.J. (1956). Some field-notes on the Caspian Plover. *British Birds* **49**: 282-283.
Elliot, R.D. (1985). The effects of predation risk and group size on the anti-predator responses of nesting Lapwings *Vanellus vanellus*. *Behaviour* **92(1-2)**: 168-187.
Elliot, R.D. & Morrison, R.I.G. (1979). The incubation period of the Yellow Rail. *Auk* **96**: 422-423.
Elliot, R.D., Collins, B.T., Hayakawa, E.G. & Metras, L. (1991). The harvest of murres in Newfoundland from 1977-78 to 1987-88. Pp. 36-44 in: Gaston & Elliot (1991).
Elliot, R.D., Ryan, P.C. & Lidster, W.W. (1990). The winter diet of Thick-billed Murres in coastal Newfoundland waters. Pp. 125-138 in: Sealy (1990).
Elliott, C.C.H. (1975). Oystercatcher islands. *Cape Bird Club Newsletter* **115**: 3 4.
Elliott, C.C.H., Waltner, M., Underhill, L.G., Pringle, J.S. & Dick, W.J.A. (1976). The migration system of the Curlew Sandpiper *Calidris ferruginea* in Africa. *Ostrich* **47**: 191-213.
Elliott, G., Walker, K. & Buckingham, R. (1991). The Auckland Island Rail. *Notornis* **38**: 199-209.
Elliott, G.P. (1983). *The Distribution and Habitat Requirements of the Banded Rail (*Rallus philippensis*) in Nelson and Marlborough*. Victoria University, Wellington.
Elliott, G.P. (1987). Habitat use by the Banded Rail. *New Zealand J. Ecol.* **10**: 109-115.
Elliott, G.P. (1989). The distribution of Banded Rails and Marsh Crakes in coastal Nelson and Marlborough Sounds. *Notornis* **36**: 117-123.
Elliott, H.F.I. (1953). The fauna of Tristan da Cunha. *Oryx* **2**: 41-53.
Elliott, H.F.I. (1957). A contribution to the ornithology of the Tristan da Cunha group. *Ibis* **99**: 545-586.
Elliott, H.F.I. (1985). Finfoot. Pp. 215-216 in: Campbell & Lack (1985).
Ellis, B.A. (1975). Rare and endangered New Zealand birds: the role of the Royal Forest and Bird Protection Society of New Zealand Inc. *Bull. ICBP* **12**: 173-186.
Ellis, D.H., Lewis, J.C., Gee, G.F. & Smith, D.G. (1992). Population recovery of the Whooping Crane with emphasis on reintroduction efforts: past and future. Pp. 142-150 in: Stahlecker (1992).
Ellis, D.H., Olsen, G.H., Gee, G.F., Nicolich, J.M., O'Malley, K.E., Nagendran, M., Hereford, S.G., Range P., Harper, W.T., Ingram, R.P. & Smith, D.G. (1992). Techniques for rearing and releasing nonmigratory cranes: lessons from the Mississippi Sandhill Crane program. Pp. 135-141 in: Stahlecker (1992).
Ellis, H.I. & Jehl, J.R. (1991). Total body water and body composition in phalaropes and other birds. *Physiol. Zool.* **64**: 973-984.
Ellis, M. (1971). Chestnut-banded Plover at Baringo. *Bull. East Afr. Nat. Hist. Soc.* **1971**: 82.
Ellis, P.M. (1992). Great Knot: new to Britain and Ireland. *British Birds* **85(8)**: 426-429.
Elmberg, J. (1992). Cooperative nest defence by trios of Arctic Skuas *Stercorarius parasiticus*. *Ibis* **134(3)**: 298.
van der Elst, D. (1987). [A remark on the identification of the juvenile Long-tailed Skua (*Stercorarius longicaudus*)]. *Aves* **24(3)**: 112-119. In French.
van der Elst, D. (1991a). [The status of the Common Stilt (*Himantopus himantopus*) in Walloon and in Brussels]. *Aves* **28(1)**: 40-42. In French.
van der Elst, D. (1991b). [The status of Temminck's Stint (*Calidris temminckii*) in Walloon and in Brussels]. *Aves* **28(1)**: 43-45. In French.
van der Elst, P. & Prys-Jones, R.P. (1987). Mass killing by rats of roosting Common Noddies. *Oryx* **21**: 219-222.
Elston, S.F. & Southern, W.E. (1983). Effects of intraspecific piracy on breeding Ring-billed Gulls. *Auk* **100**: 217-220.
Elsukov, S.V. (1984). [On the seacoast avifauna of northern Primorye]. Pp. 34-43 in: [*Faunistics and Biology of Birds in the Soviet Far East*]. USSR Academy of Sciences, Vladivostok. In Russian.
Elsukov, S.V. & Labzyuk, V.I. (1981). Nesting of the Latham's Snipe *Gallinago hardwickii* (Gray) in Primorye. Pp. 108-111 in: *Rare Birds of the Far East*. Nauka: Far East Scientific Center of Acad. Sci USSR, Vladivostok.
Elveland, J. & Tjernberg, M. (1984). [The vegetation on some display grounds of the Great Snipe, *Gallinago media*, in Sweden]. *Mem. Soc. Fauna Flora Fenn.* **60(4)**: 152-140. In Swedish with English summary.
Elvers, H. (1988). Ein Großer Schlammläufer *Limnodromus scolopaceus* in Berlin (West). *Limicola* **2(4)**: 145-147.
Elwell, N.H. (1976). Whiskered Terns breed in the Transvaal. *Bokmakierie* **28**: 9-11.
Emanuel, V.L. (1962). Texans rediscover the near extinct Eskimo Curlew. *Audubon Magazine* **64**: 162-165.
Emanuel, V.L. (1980). First documented Panama record of Spotted Rail (*Pardirallus maculatus*). *Amer. Birds* **34**: 214-215.
Eminov, A.K. (1964a). [Breeding biology of the Least Tern]. *Publ. Biol. Series Turkmen Acad. Sci.* **6**: 84-86. In Russian.
Eminov, A.K. (1964b). [Ecology of the Caspian Tern in south Turkmania]. Pp. 747-749 in: [*Ornithology in the USSR*]. Vol. 2. Bull. Institute Zool. Acad. Sci. Turkan Acad. Sci., Ashkabad. In Russian.
Eminov, A.K. (1974). [Ecology of Gull-billed Tern in south Turkmenia]. Pp. 149-161 in: [*Fauna & Ecology of Birds of Turkmenistan*]. In Russian.
Emison, W.B., Beardsell, C.M., Norman, F.I., Loyn, R.H. & Bennet, S.C. (1987). *Atlas of Victorian Birds*. Department of Conservation, Forest & Lands, and Royal Australasian Ornithologists Union, Melbourne.
Emlen, J.T. (1956). Juvenile mortality in a Ring-billed Gull colony. *Wilson Bull.* **68**: 232-238.
Emlen, J.T. (1964). Determinants of cliff edge and escape responses in Herring Gull chicks in nature. *Behaviour* **22**: 1-15.
Emlen, J.T. & Miller, D.E. (1969). Pace-setting mechanisms in the nesting cycle of the Ring-billed Gull. *Behaviour* **33**: 237-261.
Emlen, J.T., Miller, D.E., Evans, R.M. & Thompson, D.H. (1966). Predator-induced parental neglect in a Ring-billed Gull colony. *Auk* **83**: 677-679.
Emlen, S.T., Demong, N.J. & Emlen, D.J. (1989). Experimental induction of infanticide in female Wattled Jacanas. *Auk* **106(1)**: 1-7.
Emmerson, K.W. (1983). Actual and potential threats to the Canarian Houbara. *Bustard Studies* **1**: 51-56.
Emms, S.K. (1987). *The Adaptive Significance of the Pattern of Nesting Dispersion in the Pigeon Guillemot*. MSc thesis, Simon Fraser University, Burnaby, Canada.
Emms, S.K. & Morgan, K.H. (1989). The breeding biology and distribution of the Pigeon Guillemot *Cepphus columba* in the Strait of Georgia. Pp. 100-106 in: Vermeer, K. & Butler, R.W. eds. (1989). *The Ecology and Status of Marine and Shoreline Birds in the Strait of Georgia, British Columbia*. Canadian Wildlife Service Special Publication, Ottawa.
Emms, S.K. & Verbeek, N.A.M. (1989). Significance of the pattern of nest distribution in the Pigeon Guillemot *Cepphus columba*. *Auk* **106**: 193-202.
Emms, S.K. & Verbeek, N.A.M. (1991). Brood size, food provisioning and chick growth in the Pigeon Guillemot *Cepphus columba*. *Condor* **93**: 943-951.
Emslie, S.D., Henderson, R.P., Carter, H.R. & Ainley, D.G. (1990). Annual variation of primary molt with age and sex in Cassin's Auklet. *Auk* **107**: 689-695.
Emslie, S.D., Sydeman, W.J. & Pyle, P. (1992). The importance of mate retention and experience on breeding success in Cassin's Auklet *Ptychoramphus aleuticus*. *Behav. Ecol.* **3**: 189-195.
Ena, V. & Martínez, A. (1985). Fertilidad de la Avutarda (*Otis tarda* L.) en Villafáfila (Zamora) en 1984. *Misc. Zool.* **9**: 325-329.
Ena, V. & Martínez, A. (1988). Distribución y comportamiento social de la Avutarda. *Quercus* **31**: 12-20.
Ena, V., Lucio, A.J. & Purroy, F.J. (1985). The Great Bustard in León, Spain. *Bustard Studies* **2**: 35-52.
Ena, V., Martínez, A. & Thomas, D.H. (1987). Breeding success of the Great Bustard *Otis tarda* in Zamora Province, Spain, in 1984. *Ibis* **129**: 364-370.
Endersby, I. (1994). Vagrancy, or another migration path, of the Double-banded Plover *Charadrius bicinctus*? *Stilt* **24**: 20-23.
Endo, K. & Hirano, T. (1986). [The habitat and distribution of Latham's Snipe (*Gallinago hardwickii*) in Toguchi Prefecture]. *Strix* **5**: 47-52. In Japanese.
Endo, K., Takahashi, H. & Fujita, S. (1987). [Breeding record of the Indian Pratincole *Glareola maldivarum* in Tochigi Prefecture, central Honshu]. *Jap. J. Orn.* **35(4)**: 166-168. In Japanese with English summary.
Engbring, J. & Engilis, A. (1988). Rediscovery of the Sooty Rail (*Porzana tabuensis*) in American Samoa. *Auk* **105**: 391.
Engbring, J. & Pratt, H.D. (1985). Endangered birds in Micronesia; their history, status and future prospects. *Bird Conserv.* **2**: 71-105.
Engelmoer, M. & Blomert, A.M. (1985). [*Breeding Biology of the Avocet along the Frisian Wadden Sea Coast, 1983 Season*]. Rijksdienst voor de Ijsselmeerpolders, Lelystad, the Netherlands. In Dutch.
Engilis, A. & Pratt, T.K. (1993). Status and population trends of Hawaii's native waterbirds, 1977-1987. *Wilson Bull.* **105(1)**: 142-158.
Engstrom, R.T., Butcher, G.S. & Lowe, J.D. (1990). Population trends in the Least Tern (*Sterna antillarum*) from Maine to Virginia. *US Fish Wildlife Serv. Biol. Rep.* **90(1)**: 130-138.
Ens, B.J. (1982). Size selection in mussel feeding Oystercatchers. *Wader Study Group Bull.* **34**: 16 20.
Ens, B.J. (1992). *The Social Prisoner. Causes of Natural Variation in Reproductive Success of the Oystercatcher*. PhD thesis, Universiteit Groningen, Groningen, Netherlands.
Ens, B.J. & Goss-Custard, J.D. (1984). Interference among Oystercatchers, *Haematopus ostralegus*, feeding on mussels, *Mytilus edulis*, on the Exe estuary. *J. Anim. Ecol.* **53**: 217-231.
Ens, B.J. & Goss-Custard, J.D. (1986). Piping as a display of dominance by wintering Oystercatchers *Haematopus ostralegus*. *Ibis* **128**: 382-391.
Ens, B.J. & Zwarts, L. (1980). [Territorial behaviour in Curlew outside the breeding season]. *Watervogels* **5**: 155-169. In Dutch.
Ens, B.J., Duiven, P., Smit, C.J. & van Spanje, T.M. (1990). Spring migration of Turnstones from the Banc d'Arguin in Mauritania. *Ardea* **78**: 301-314.
Ens, B.J., Esselink, P. & Zwarts, L. (1990). Kleptoparasitism as a problem of prey choice: a study on mudflat-feeding Curlews, *Numenius arquata*. *Anim. Behav.* **39**: 219-230.
Ens, B.J., Kersten, M., Benninkmeijer, A. & Hulscher, J.B. (1992). Territory quality, parental effort and reproductive success of Oystercatchers (*Haematopus ostralegus*). *J. Anim. Ecol.* **61**: 703-715.
Ens, B.J., Piersma, T. & Drent, R.H. (1994). The dependence of waders and waterfowl migrating along the east Atlantic flyway on their coastal food supplies: what is the most profitable research programme? *Ophelia* **6**(Suppl.): 127-151.
Ens, B.J., Piersma, T., Wolff, W.J. & Zwarts, L. eds. (1990). *Homeward Bound: Problems Waders Face when Migrating from the Banc d'Arguin, Mauritania, to their Northern Breeding Grounds in Spring*. Ardea **78**(Special issue). 364 pp.
Ens, B.J., Piersma, T., Wolff, W.J. & Zwarts, L. eds. (1989). *Report of the Dutch-Mauritanian Project Banc d'Arguin 1985-1986*. WIWO-report **25**/RIN-rapport **89/6**. Texel, the Netherlands.
Ens, B.J., Safriel, U.N. & Harris, M.P. (1993). Divorce in the long-lived and monogamous Oystercatcher, *Haematopus ostralegus*: incompatibility or choosing a better option? *Anim. Behav.* **45**: 1199-1217.
Ens, B.J., Wintermans, G.J.M. & Smit, C.J. (1993). [Distribution of wintering waders in the Dutch Waddensea]. *Limosa* **66**: 137-144. In Dutch with English summary.
Eppley, Z.A. (1984). Development of thermoregulatory abilities in Xantus' Murrelet chicks *Synthliboramphus hypoleucus*. *Physiol. Zool.* **57**: 307-317.
Érard, C. (1974). Les oiseaux d'Ethiopie. *Bonn. zool. Beitr.* **25**: 76-78.
Érard, C. & Benson, C.W. (1975). The race of the African Finfoot *Podica senegalensis* (Vieillot) in Ethiopia. *Bull. Brit. Orn. Club* **95**: 147-148.
Érard, C. & Sabatier, D. (1988). Rôle des oiseaux frugivores terrestres dans la dynamique forestière en Guyane française. [The relationship of frugivorous birds to forest dynamics in French Guiana]. Pp. 803-815 in: *Proc. XIX Int. Orn. Congr.* Ottawa, 1986.
Érard, C. & Théry, M. (1994). Frugivorie et ornithochorie en forêt Guyanaise: l'exemple des grands oiseaux terrestres et de la Pénélope Marail. [Fruit eating and ornithochory in the forests of Guyana: the example of large terrestrial birds and Marail Guan]. *Alauda* **62**: 27-31. In French with English summary.
Érard, C., Guillou, J. & Mayaud, N. (1984). Sur l'identité de spécifique de certains Laridés nicheurs au Sénégal. *Alauda* **52(3)**: 184-188.
Érard, C., Hemery, G. & Pasquet, E. (1993). [Geographic variation of *Cursorius cinctus* (Heuglin, 1863), Aves: Glareolidae]. *Bonn. zool. Beitr.* **44(3-4)**: 165-192. In French with English and German summaries.
Érard, C., Théry, M. & Sabatier, D. (1991). Régime alimentaire de *Tinamus major* (Tinamidae), *Crax alector* (Cracidae) et *Psophia crepitans* (Psophiidae) en forêt Guyanaise. [Diets of *Tinamus major* (Tinamidae), *Crax alector* (Cracidae) and *Psophia crepitans* (Psophiidae) in the French Guiana rain forest]. *Gibier Faune Sauvage* **8**: 183-210. In French with English, German and Spanish summaries.
Erhart, F.C. (1994). [Breeding of the Common Sandpiper *Actitis hypoleucos* in the Netherlands]. *Limosa* **67(3)**: 95-99. In Dutch with English summary.
Erickson, H.T. (1992). Spring migration of Lesser Golden-plovers in Benton County, Indiana. *Indiana Audubon Quarterly* **70(2)**: 87-91.
Erickson, R.C. (1976). Whooping Crane studies at the Patuxent Wildlife Research Center. Pp. 166-176 in: Lewis (1976a).
Erickson, R.C. & Derrickson, S.R. (1981). The Whooping Crane. Pp. 104-118 in: Lewis & Masatomi (1981).
von Erlanger, C. (1905). Beitrage zur Vogelfauna Nordostafrikas. *J. Orn.* **53**: 42-158.
Erritzoe, J. (1993). *The Birds of CITES and How to Identify Them*. The Lutterworth Press, Cambridge.
Erskine, A.J. (1963). The Black-headed Gull (*Larus ridibundus*) in North America. *Audubon Field Notes* **17**: 334-338.
Erwin, R.M. (1971). The breeding success of two sympatric gulls, the Herring Gull and the Great Black-backed Gull. *Wilson Bull.* **83(2)**: 152-158.
Erwin, R.M. (1977a). Foraging and breeding adaptations to different food regimes in three seabirds: the Common Tern, *Sterna hirundo*, Royal Tern, *Sterna maxima*, and Black Skimmer, *Rynchops niger*. *Ecology* **58**: 389-397.
Erwin, R.M. (1977b). Black Skimmer breeding ecology and behavior. *Auk* **94**: 709-717.
Erwin, R.M. (1978). Coloniality in terns: the role of social feeding. *Condor* **80**: 211-215.
Erwin, R.M. (1979). Species interactions in a mixed colony of Common Terns (*Sterna hirundo*) and Black Skimmers (*Rynchops niger*). *Anim. Behav.* **27**: 1054-1062.
Erwin, R.M. (1980). Breeding habitat use by colonially nesting waterbirds in two mid-Atlantic US regions under different regimes of human disturbance. *Biol. Conserv.* **18**: 39-51.
Erwin, R.M. (1990). Feeding activities of Black Skimmers in Guyana. *Colonial Waterbirds* **13(1)**: 70-71.
Erwin, R.M. & Smith, D.C. (1985). Habitat comparisons and productivity in nesting Common Terns on the mid-Atlantic coast. *Colonial Waterbirds* **8**: 155-165.
Erwin, R.M., Galli, J. & Burger, J. (1981). Colony site dynamics and habitat use in Atlantic coast seabirds. *Auk* **98**: 550-561.
Erwin, R.M., Smith, G.J. & Clapp, R.B. (1986). Winter distribution and oiling of Common Terns in Trinidad: a further look. *J. Field Orn.* **57**: 300-308.
Escalante, R. (1962). Frequency of occurrence of some seabirds in Uruguay. *Condor* **64**: 510-512.
Escalante, R. (1966). Notes on the Uruguayan population of *Larus belcheri*. *Condor* **68**: 507-510.
Escalante, R. (1968). Notes on the Royal Tern in Uruguay. *Condor* **70**: 243-247.
Escalante, R. (1970a). Notes on the Cayenne Tern in Uruguay. *Condor* **72**: 89-94.
Escalante, R. (1970b). The Yellow-billed Tern (*Sterna superciliaris*) in Uruguay. *Auk* **87**: 574-577.
Escalante, R. (1970c). *Aves Marinas del Río de la Plata y Aguas Vecinas del Océano Atlántico*. Barreiro y Ramos SA, Montevideo.
Escalante, R. (1972). First Pomarine Jaeger specimen from Brazil. *Auk* **89(3)**: 663-665.
Escalante, R. (1973). The Cayenne Tern in Brazil. *Condor* **75**: 470-472.
Escalante, R. (1985). Taxonomy and conservation of Austral-breeding Royal Terns. Pp. 935-942 in: Buckley *et al.* (1985).
Escalante, R. (1991). Status and conservation of seabirds breeding in Uruguay. Pp. 159-164 in: Croxall (1991).
Escott, C.J. & Holmes, D.A. (1980). The avifauna of Sulawesi, Indonesia: faunistic notes and additions. *Bull. Brit. Orn. Club* **100**: 189-194.
Eskell, R. & Garnett, S. (1979). Notes on the colours of the legs, wings and flanks of the Dusky Moorhen *Gallinula tenebrosa*. *Emu* **79**: 143-146.
Espin, P.M.J., Mather, R.M. & Adams, J. (1983). Age and foraging success in Black-winged Stilts *Himantopus himantopus*. *Ardea* **71**: 225-228.
Essenberg, G. (1984). De Braziliaanse dwergral. *Onze Vogels* **45**: 8-9.
Estafiev, A.A. (1989). [Biology of Rudy Turnstone (*Arenaria interpres* L.) in the European north-east of the USSR]. Pp. 29-38 in: [*Ecology of Rare, Less Familiar and Economic Valuable Animals of the USSR European North-East*]. Proceedings Komi Science Centre Ural Branch USSR Academy of Science **100**. Syktyvkar. In Russian.
Estelle, V.B. (1991). Spring foraging of Sanderling (*Calidris alba*) in response to aggregations of *Emerita analoga megalopae*. MSc thesis, San Jose State University, San Jose, California.

Étchécopar, R.D. & Hüe, F. (1964). *Les Oiseaux du Nord de l'Afrique de la Mer Rouge aux Canaries*. Éditions N. Boubée, Paris.
Étchécopar, R.D. & Hüe, F. (1966). Présence de *Larus brunnicephalus* Jerdon à Penang (Malaisie). *Oiseau et RFO* **36**: 65-67.
Étchécopar, R.D. & Hüe, F. (1978). *Les Oiseaux de Chine, de Mongolie et de Corée. Non Passereaux*. Les Éditions du Pacifique, Papeete, Tahiti.
Étchécopar, R.D. & Morel, G. (1960). Notes on the clutch size of Black-headed Plover. *Ool. Rec.* **34**: 6-8.
Ettrup, H. & Bak, B. (1985). Breeding season, clutch size and young production of Danish Lapwings *Vanellus vanellus*. *Dan. Orn. Foren. Tidssk.* **79**: 43-55.
Eubanks, T.L. & Collins, G.F. (1993). *Status of the Eskimo Curlew along the Upper Texas Coast*. US Fish & Wildlife Service Division Technical Service Order No. 2018110522.
Evanich, J. (1989). Identification and status of *fulva* and *dominica* golden-plovers. *Oregon Birds* **15(2)**: 91-95.
Evans, A. (1986). Experimental evidence for the use of visual cues by foraging Dunlins. *Wader Study Group Bull.* **48**: 14-15.
Evans, D.R., Cavanagh, P.M., French, T.W. & Blodget, B.G. (1995). Identifying the sex of Massachusetts Herring Gulls by linear measurements. *J. Field Orn.* **66**: 128-132.
Evans, D.R., Hoopes, E.M. & Griffin, C.R. (1993). Discriminating the sex of Laughing Gulls by linear measurements. *J. Field Orn.* **64**: 472-476.
Evans, M.I. (1988). Observations on the behaviour of the Crab Plover. *Bull. Orn. Soc. Middle East* **20**: 5-7.
Evans, M.I. ed. (1994). *Important Bird Areas in the Middle East*. BirdLife Conservation Series **2**. BirdLife International, Cambridge.
Evans, M.I. & Balmford, A. (1992). Birds in the Ishasha sector of Queen Elizabeth National Park, Uganda. *Scopus* **16**: 34-49.
Evans, M.I. & Keijl, G.O. (1993a). Spring migration of coastal waders through the Saudi Arabian Gulf in 1991. *Sandgrouse* **15(1-2)**: 56-84.
Evans, M.I. & Keijl, G.O. (1993b). Impact of Gulf War oil spills on wader populations of the Saudi Arabian Gulf Coast. *Sandgrouse* **15(1-2)**: 85-105.
Evans, M.I., Duckworth, J.W., Hawkins, A.F.A., Safford, R.J., Sheldon, B.C. & Wilkinson, R.J. (1992). Key bird species of Marojejy Strict Nature Reserve, Madagascar. *Bird Conserv. Int.* **2**: 201-220.
Evans, P.G.H. (1981). Ecology and behaviour of the Little Auk *Alle alle* in west Greenland. *Ibis* **123**: 1-18.
Evans, P.G.H. (1984a). Seabirds of Greenland: their status and conservation. Pp. 49-84 in: Croxall, Evans & Schreiber (1984).
Evans, P.G.H. (1984b). Status and conservation of seabirds in northwest Europe (excluding Norway and USSR). Pp. 293-321 in: Croxall, Evans & Schreiber (1984).
Evans, P.G.H. & Nettleship, D.N. (1985). Conservation of the Atlantic Alcidae. Pp. 427-488 in: Nettleship & Birkhead (1985).
Evans, P.R. (1975). Moult of Red-necked Stints at Westernport Bay, Victoria. *Emu* **75(4)**: 227-229.
Evans, P.R. (1976). Energy balance and optimal foraging strategies in shorebirds: some implications for their distributions and movements in the non-breeding season. *Ardea* **64**: 117-139.
Evans, P.R. (1979). Adaptations shown by foraging shorebirds to cyclical variations in the activity and availability of their intertidal invertebrate prey. Pp. 357-366 in: Naylor, E. & Hartnall, R.G. eds. (1979). *Cyclic Phenomena in Marine Plants and Animals*. Pergamon Press, Oxford.
Evans, P.R. (1985). Plover. Pp. 467-469 in: Campbell & Lack (1985).
Evans, P.R. (1991). Seasonal and annual patterns of mortality in migratory shorebirds: some conservation implications. Pp. 346-359 in: Perrins *et al.* (1991).
Evans, P.R. & Davidson, N.C. (1990). Migration strategies and tactics of waders breeding in Arctic and north temperate latitudes. Pp. 387-398 in: Gwinner (1990).
Evans, P.R. & Pienkowski, M.W. (1984). Population dynamics of shorebirds. Pp. 83-123 in: Burger & Olla (1984).
Evans, P.R. & Smith, P.C. (1975). Studies of shorebirds at Lindisfarne, Northumberland. 2. Fat and pectoral muscle as indicators of body condition in the Bar-tailed Godwit. *Wildfowl* **26**: 64-76.
Evans, P.R., Brearey, D.M. & Goodyer, L.R. (1980). Studies on Sanderling at Teesmouth, NE England. *Wader Study Group Bull.* **30**: 18-20.
Evans, P.R., Goss-Custard, J.D. & Hale, W.G. eds. (1984). *Coastal Waders and Wildfowl in Winter*. Cambridge University Press, Cambridge.
Evans, R.M. (1970a). Imprinting and the control of mobility in young Ring-billed Gulls (*Larus delawarensis*). *Anim. Behav. Monogr.* **3**: 193-248.
Evans, R.M. (1970b). Parental recognition and the "Mew Call" in Black-billed Gulls (*Larus bulleri*). *Auk* **87(3)**: 503-513.
Evans, R.M. (1973). Differential responsiveness of young Ring-billed Gulls and Herring Gulls to adult vocalizations of their own and other species. *Can. J. Zool.* **51**: 759-770.
Evans, R.M. (1975). Responsiveness to adult mew calls in young Ring-billed Gulls (*Larus delawarensis*): effects of exposure to calls alone and in the presence of visual imprinting stimuli. *Can. J. Zool.* **53**: 953-959.
Evans, R.M. (1977). Auditory discrimination learning in young Ring-billed Gulls (*Larus delawarensis*). *Anim. Behav.* **25**: 140-146.
Evans, R.M. (1980). Development of individual call recognition in young Ring-billed Gulls (*Larus delawarensis*): an effect of feeding. *Anim. Behav.* **28**: 60-67.
Evans, R.M. (1982a). Foraging-flock recruitment at a Black-billed Gull colony: implications for the information center hypothesis. *Auk* **99**: 24-30.
Evans, R.M. (1982b). Efficient use of food patches at different distances from a breeding colony in Black-billed Gulls. *Behaviour* **79**: 28-38.
Evans, R.M. (1982c). Colony desertion and reproductive synchrony of Black-billed Gulls *Larus bulleri*. *Ibis* **124**: 491-501.
Evans, R.M. (1982d). Roosts at foraging sites in Black-billed Gulls. *Notornis* **29(2)**: 109-112.
Evans, R.M. (1983). Do secondary roosts function as information centers in Black-billed Gulls? *Wilson Bull.* **95**: 461-462.
Evans, R.M. & McKnicholl, M.K. (1972). Variations in the reproductive activities of Arctic Terns at Churchill, Manitoba. *Arctic* **25**: 131-141.
Evans, R.M. & Welham, C.V.J. (1985). Aggregative mechanisms and behavior in Ring-billed Gulls departing from a colony. *Can. J. Zool.* **63**: 2767-2774.
Evans, R.M., Whitaker, A. & Wiebe, M.O. (1994). Development of vocal regulation of temperature by embryos in pipped eggs of Ring-billed Gulls. *Auk* **111**: 596-604.
Evans, T.J. (1988). *Habitat Use and Behavioral Ecology of American Avocets Wintering at Humboldt Bay, California*. MSc thesis, Humboldt State University, Arcata, California.
Evans, T.J. & Harris, S.W. (1994). Status and habitat use by American Avocets wintering at Humboldt Bay, California. *Condor* **96(1)**: 178-189.
Evens, J.G. & Page, G.W. (1986). Predation on Black Rails during high tides in salt marshes. *Condor* **88**: 107-109.
Evens, J.G., Page, G.W., Laymon, S.A. & Stallcup, R.W. (1991). Distribution, relative abundance and status of the California Black Rail in western North America. *Condor* **93**: 952-966.
Evens, J.G., Page, G.W., Stenzel, L. & Warnock, N. (1986). Distribution, abundance and habitat of California Black Rails in tidal marshes of Marin and Sonoma counties, California. Unpublished report to Point Reyes Bird Observatory, Contribution no. **336**.
Everett, M.J. (1980). Little Terns. Pp. 1-7 in: Everett, M.J. ed. (1980). *Proceedings of a Symposium on Little Terns*. Royal Society for Bird Protection, Sandy, UK.
Everett, W.T. & Anderson, D.W. (1991). Status and conservation of the breeding seabirds on offshore Pacific islands of Baja California and the Gulf of California. Pp. 115-140 in: Croxall (1991).
Everhart, S.H., Parnell, J.F., Soots, R.F. & Doerr, P.D. (1980). Natural and dredged material nesting habitats of Gull-billed Terns, Common Terns and Black Skimmers in North Carolina. *UNC-Sea Grant, Raleigh NC* **79-05**. 48 pp.
Everitt, C. (1962). Breeding the Red-legged Water-Rail. *Avicult. Mag.* **68**: 179-181.
Every, B. (1989). A possible display tactic by the African Jacana? *Bee-eater* **40(2)**: 20.
Ewald, P.W., Hunt, G.L. & Warner, M. (1980). Territory size in Western Gulls: importance of intrusion pressure, defense investments, and vegetative structure. *Ecology* **61**: 80-87.
Ewins, P.J. (1985a). Colony attendance and censusing of Black Guillemots *Cepphus grylle* in Shetland. *Bird Study* **32**: 176-185.
Ewins, P.J. (1985b). Growth, diet and mortality of Arctic Tern chicks in Shetland. *Seabird* **8**: 59-69.
Ewins, P.J. (1986). *The Ecology of Black Guillemots* Cepphus grylle *in Shetland*. PhD thesis, University of Oxford, Oxford.
Ewins, P.J. (1988a). The timing of moult of Black Guillemots *Cepphus grylle* in Shetland. *Ringing & Migration* **9**: 5-10.
Ewins, P.J. (1988b). An analysis of ringing recoveries of Black Guillemots *Cepphus grylle* in Britain and Ireland. *Ringing & Migration* **9**: 95-102.
Ewins, P.J. (1989). Slender-billed Curlews in Morocco in February 1979. *Dutch Birding* **11(3)**: 119-120.
Ewins, P.J. (1990). The diet of the Black Guillemots *Cepphus grylle* in Shetland. *Holarctic Ecol.* **13**: 90-97.
Ewins, P.J. (1992). Growth of Black Guillemot *Cepphus grylle* chicks in Shetland in 1983-84. *Seabird* **14**: 3-14.
Ewins, P.J. (1993). Pigeon Guillemot (*Cepphus columba*). No. **48** in: Poole & Gill (1993).
Ewins, P.J. & Kirk, D.A. (1988). The distribution of Shetland Black Guillemots *Cepphus grylle* outside the breeding season. *Seabird* **11**: 50-61.
Ewins, P.J. & Tasker, M.L. (1985). Breeding distribution of Black Guillemot *Cepphus grylle* in Orkney and Shetland, 1982-1984. *Bird Study* **32**: 186-193.
Ewins, P.J., Carter, H.R. & Shibaev, Y.V. (1993). The status, distribution and ecology of inshore fish-feeding alcids (*Cepphus* guillemots and *Brachyramphus* murrelets) in the north Pacific. Pp. 164-175 in: Vermeer, Briggs *et al.* (1993).
Ewins, P.J., Ellis, P.M., Bird, D.B. & Prior, A. (1988). The distribution and status of Arctic and Great Skuas in Shetland 1985-86. *Scottish Birds* **15(1)**: 9-20.
Ey, A. (1984). Queensland records of Chinese Snipe (*Gallinago megala*). *Sunbird* **14(1)**: 14-15.
Faanes, C.A. (1983). Aspects of the nesting ecology of Least Terns and Piping Plovers in central Nebraska. *Prairie Nat.* **15**: 145-154.
Faanes, C.A. (1990a). A recent record of Eskimo Curlew in Nebraska. *Prairie Nat.* **22(2)**: 137-138.
Faanes, C.A. (1990b). Cuban Sandhills still declining. *ICF Bugle* **16(3)**: 2.
Faanes, C.A. & Senner, S.E. (1991). Status and conservation of the Eskimo Curlew. *Amer. Birds* **45(2)**: 237-239.
Faanes, C.A., Douglas H.J. & Lingle, G.R. (1992). Characteristics of Whooping Crane roost sites in the Platte River. Pp. 90-94 in: Stahlecker (1992).
Fadat, C. (1994a). [Is Woodcock abundance a cyclic phenomenon?]. Pp. 1-7 in: Kalchreuter (1994). In French with English summary.
Fadat, C. (1994b). [Hunting management proposals for the European Woodcock populations]. Pp. 71-80 in: Kalchreuter (1994). In French with English summary.
Fadat, C. (1995). *La Bécasse des Bois en Hiver*. Published privately, Clermont-l'Hérault, France.
Fagan, M.J., Schmitt, M.B. & Whitehouse, P.J. (1976). Moult of Purple Gallinule and Moorhen in the southern Transvaal. *Ostrich* **47**: 226-227.
Faggio, G. (1991). Note sur l'évolution de la repartition des effectifs nicheurs de Goéland leucophée (*Larus cachinnans*) sur l'île Lavezzi. *Trav. Scient. Parc Nat. Reg. Réserves Nat. Corse* **32**: 93-99.
Fairall, R. (1995). The ultimate migrant. Life and travels of the extraordinary Arctic Tern. *Birder's World* **9(4)**: 38-42.
Fairon, J. (1975). Contribution à l'ornithologie de l'Air (Niger). *Gerfaut* **65**: 107-134.
Fairweather, J.A. & Coulson, J.C. (1995). The influence of forced site change on the dispersal and breeding of the Black-legged Kittiwake *Rissa tridactyla*. *Colonial Waterbirds* **18(1)**: 30-40.
Falk, K. & Durinck, J. (1991). The by-catch of Thick-billed Murres in salmon drift nets off west Greenland in 1988. Pp. 23-28 in: Gaston & Elliot (1991).
Falk, K. & Durinck, J. (1992). Thick-billed Murre hunting in West Greenland, 1988-89. *Arctic* **45**: 167-178.
Falk, K. & Durinck. J. (1993). The winter diet of Thick-billed Murres in western Greenland, 1988-89. *Can. J. Zool.* **71**: 264-272.
Fall, B.A. (1988). Deletion of Mountain Plover from Minnesota state list. *Loon* **60(4)**: 146-148.
Falla, R.A. (1937). *Birds*. BANZARE 1929-1931. Report Series B **2**. 304 pp.
Falla, R.A. (1939). New Zealand oystercatchers. *Records Canterbury Mus.* **4**: 259 266.
Falla, R.A. (1949). *Notornis* rediscovered. *Emu* **48**: 316-322.
Falla, R.A. (1951). The nesting season of *Notornis*. *Notornis* **4**: 97-100.
Falla, R.A. (1967). An Auckland Island Rail. *Notornis* **14**: 107-113.
Falla, R.A. (1970). Grey Ternlets in the Bay of Plenty. *Notornis* **17(2)**: 83-86.
Falla, R.A. (1978). Banded Dotterel at the Auckland Islands: description of a new subspecies. *Notornis* **25(2)**: 101-108.
Falla, R.A., Sibson, R.B. & Turbott, E.G. (1981). *The New Guide to the Birds of New Zealand and Outlying Islands*. Collins, Auckland & London.
Falxa, G.A. (1992). *Prey Choice and Habitat Use by Foraging Black Oystercatchers: Interactions between Prey Quality, Habitat Availability and Age of Bird*. PhD dissertation, University of California, Davis, California.
Fan Zhongmin, Liang Yu, Zhang Yaowen & Jin Liankui (1994). Distribution and conservation of cranes and wetlands in Jilin and Liaoning Provinces, northeast China. Pp. 136-140 in: Higuchi & Minton (1994).
Fannucchi, W.A., Fannucchi, G.T. & Naumann L.E. (1986). Effects of harvesting wild rice *Zizania equatica* on Sora Rails. *Can. Field-Nat.* **100**: 533-536.
Fanshawe, J.H. & Kelsey, M.G. (1989). Observations on the behaviour and call of Hartlaub's Bustard *Eupodotis hartlaubii*. *Scopus* **12**: 98-99.
Faragó, S. (1985). Investigations on the nesting ecology of the Great Bustard (*O. tarda* L. 1758) in the Dévaványa Nature Conservation District. I. Comparative studies of microclimate. *Aquila* **92**: 133-173.
Faragó, S. (1992). Clutch size of the Great Bustard (*Otis tarda*) in Hungary. *Aquila* **99**: 69-84. In English with Hungarian summary.
Faragó, S. (1993). Development of Great Bustard populations in Hungary in the period 1981-1990. *Folia Zoologica* **42**: 221-236.
Farhadpour, H. (1987). Wintering Common Cranes in Iran. Pp. 301-304 in: Archibald & Pasquier (1987a).
Farmer, R. (1979). Checklist of birds of the Ile-Ife area, Nigeria. *Malimbus* **1**: 56-64.
Farnell, G. (1983). Artificial incubation and hand rearing of Black-legged Seriema (*Chunga burmeisteri*) at Audubon Zoo. Pp. 221-233 in: *Amer. Assoc. Zool. Parks Aquariums Ann. Conf. Proc.*
Farrand, J. (1977). What to look for: Eskimo and Little Curlews compared. *Amer. Birds* **31(2)**: 137-138, 138A.
Fasola, M. ed. (1986). *Distribuzione e Popolazione dei Laridi e Sternidi Nidifianti in Italia*. Ricerche di Biologia della Selvaggina **11**(Supplement). 179 pp.
Fasola, M. & Bogliani, G. (1984). Habitat selection and distribution of nesting Common and Little Terns on the Po River (Italy). *Colonial Waterbirds* **7**: 127-133.
Fasola, M. & Bogliani, G. (1990). Foraging ranges of an assemblage of Mediterranean seabirds. *Colonial Waterbirds* **13**: 72-74.
Fasola, M. & Canova, L. (1992). Nest habitat selection by eight syntopic species of Mediterranean gulls and terns. *Colonial Waterbirds* **15(2)**: 169-178.
Fasola, M. & Saino, N. (1990). Mono-dimensional and multi-dimensional niches in a Mediterranean seabirds community. *Avocetta* **14**: 37-48.
Fasola, M., Bogliani, G., Saino, N. & Canova, L. (1989). Foraging, feeding and time-activity niches of eight species of seabirds in the coastal wetlands of the Adriatic Sea. *Boll. Zool.* **56**: 61-72.
Fasola, M., Goutner, V. & Walmsley, J. (1989). Comparative breeding biology of the gulls and terns in the four main deltas of North Mediterranean. *Ardeola* **2**(Suppl.).
Favaloro, N. (1944). Notes on two resident Victorian plovers. *Emu* **43**: 145-153.
Favero, M. (1993a). Biologia reproductiva de la Paloma Antártica *Chionis alba* (Charadriiformes) en las Islas Shetland del Sur, Antártida. [Breeding biology of Greater Sheathbill, *Chionis alba* (Charadriiformes) at South Shetland Islands, Antarctica]. *Riv. ital. Orn.* **63(1)**: 33-40. In Spanish with English and Italian summaries.
Favero, M. (1993b). Asociaciones alimentarias de la Paloma Antártica *Chionis alba* en las Islas 25 de Mayo (King George Is.) y Media Luna (Halfmoon Is.), Shetland del Sur. Pp. 55-57 in: *Actas II Jorn. Invest. Cient. Antarct.*
Favero, M. (1995). Kleptoparasitism of Imperial Cormorants *Phalacrocorax atriceps* by Palefaced Sheathbills *Chionis alba* in Antarctica. *Mar. Orn.* **23**.
Favero, M. (1996). Foraging ecology of Pale-faced Sheathbills in colonies of southern elephant seals at King George Island, Antarctica. *J. Field Orn.* **67(2)**: 292-299. In English with Spanish summary.
Favero, M., Bellagamba, P.J. & Farenga, M. (1991). Abundancia y distribución espacial de las poblaciones de aves de Punta Armonía y Punta Dedo, Isla Nelson, Shetland del Sur. [Abundance and spatial distribution of the bird populations at Harmony and Toe Points, Nelson Island, S. Shetland (Antarctica)]. *Riv. ital. Orn.* **61(3-4)**: 85-96. In Spanish with English summary.
Feare, C.J. (1966). The winter feeding of the Purple Sandpiper. *British Birds* **59**: 165-179.
Feare, C.J. (1969). Arctic Terns feeding on earthworms. *British Birds* **62**: 137.
Feare, C.J. (1971). Predation of limpets and dogwhelks by Oystercatcher. *Bird Study* **18**: 121 129.
Feare, C.J. (1975). Post-fledging parental care in Crested and Sooty Terns. *Condor* **77**: 368-370.
Feare, C.J. (1976a). Desertion and abnormal development in a colony of Sooty Terns *Sterna fuscata* infected by virus-infected ticks. *Ibis* **118**: 112-115.

Feare, C.J. (1976b). The breeding of the Sooty Tern *Sterna fuscata* in Seychelles and the effects of experimental removal of its eggs. *J. Zool., London* **179**: 317-360.
Feare, C.J. (1976c). The exploitation of Sooty Tern eggs in the Seychelles. *Biol. Conserv.* **10(3)**: 169-181.
Feare, C.J. (1979a). Ecology of Bird Island, Seychelles. *Atoll Res. Bull.* **226**: 1-29.
Feare, C.J. (1979b). Ecological observations on African Banks, Amirantes. *Atoll Res. Bull.* **227**: 1-7.
Feare, C.J. (1984). Seabird status and conservation in the tropical Indian Ocean. Pp. 457-471 in: Croxall, Evans & Schreiber (1984).
Feare, C.J. (1985). Crab-Plover. Pp. 116-117 in: Campbell & Lack (1985).
Feare, C.J. & Bourne, W.R.P. (1978). The occurrence of "portlandica" Little Terns and absence of Damara Terns and British Storm Petrels in the Indian Ocean. *Ibis* **49**: 64-66.
Feare, C.J. & Summers, R.W. (1985). Birds as predators on rocky shores. Pp. 249-264 in: Moore, P.G. & Seed, R. eds. (1985). *The Ecology of Rocky Coasts*. Hodder & Stoughton, London.
Feare, C.J., Gill, E.L. & Masanobu, F. (1995). Behavioural defence by Sooty Terns *Sterna fuscata* against tick infestation? *Ibis* **137**: 116-119.
Fearnside, J.D. (1990). Camouflage posture of Jack Snipe. *British Birds* **83(7)**: 281-282.
Fedorenko, A.P. (1992). The reasons for the decline in numbers of bustards and means of their conservation in the Ukraine Soviet Socialist Republic. *Bustard Studies* **5**: 8-15.
Feduccia, A. (1980). *The Age of Birds*. Harvard University Press, Cambridge, Massachusetts.
Feduccia, A. (1995). Explosive evolution in tertiary birds and mammals. *Science* **267**: 637-638.
Feduccia, A. (1996). *The Origin and Evolution of Birds*. Yale University Press, New Haven, Connecticut.
Fefer, S.I., Harrison, C.S., Naughton, M.B. & Shallenberger, R.J. (1984). Synopsis of results of recent seabird research conducted in the northwestern Hawaiian Islands. Pp. 9-76 in: Grigg, R.W. & Thomas, K.Y. eds. (1984). *Resource Investigations in the Northwestern Hawaiian Islands*. Vol. 1. University Hawaii Sea Grant Program, Honolulu.
Feindt, P. (1968). *Vier Europäische Rallenarten*. (Record). Hildesheim.
Feinstein, B. (1958). Xantus' Murrelet *Endomychura hyupoleuca scrippsi* from the state of Washington. *Auk* **75**: 90-91.
Feinstein, B. (1959). Geographic variation in the Whiskered Auklet. *Auk* **76**: 60-67.
Feng Kemin & Li Jinlu (1985). [Aerial surveys on the Red-crowned Cranes and other rare water birds]. Pp. 17-36 in: Masatomi (1985a). In Japanese.
Feng Kemin & Li Jinlu (1986). The reproductive ecology of the Red-crowned Crane *Grus japonensis*. *J. Northeast Forestry Univ.* **14(4)**: 39-45.
Fennell, J., Fennell, J., Crossland, A. & Langlands, P. (1985). Asiatic Dowitcher at the Heathcote-avon Estuary, Christchurch. *Notornis* **32(4)**: 322-323.
Ferdinand, L. (1966). Display of the Great Snipe (*Gallinago media* Latham). *Dan. Orn. Foren. Tidssk.* **60**: 14-34.
Ferdinand, L. & Gensbøl, B. (1966). Maintenance of territory in the Great Snipe (*Gallinago media* Latham) on the display ground. *Dan. Orn. Foren. Tidssk.* **60**: 35-40.
Fergenbauer-Kimmel, A. (1992). Vogelbeobachtungen im Norden Australiens. *Trop. Vogel* **13(4)**: 117-124.
Ferguson-Lees, I.J. (1965). Studies of less familiar birds. 132: Spur-winged Plover. *British Birds* **58**: 47-51.
Ferguson-Lees, I.J. (1967). Studies of less familiar birds: Little Bustard. *British Birds* **60**: 80-84.
Ferguson-Lees, I.J. (1971). Studies of less familiar birds. 164: Wood Sandpiper. *British Birds* **64**: 114-117.
Ferguson-Lees, I.J. & Faull, E. (1992). *Endangered Birds*. George Philip, London.
Fernández-Cruz, M. (1974). Observaciones de la Gaviota de Audouinii (*Larus audouinii*) en la costa de Alicante. *Ardeola* **20**: 359-360.
Fernández-Cruz, M. (1981). La migración e invernada de la Grulla Común (*Grus grus*) en España. Resultados del proyecto Grus (Crane Project). *Ardeola* **26-27**: 3-164.
Fernández-Cruz, M. & Araújo, J. (1987). The situation of the Common Crane in Spain. Pp. 251-263 in: Archibald & Pasquier (1987a).
Fernández-Palacios, J. (1994). Crested Coot. *Fulica cristata*. Pp. 232-233 in: Tucker & Heath (1994).
Fernández-Palacios, J. & Raya, C. (1991). Biología de la Focha Común (*Fulica atra*) en Cádiz y otros humedales del Bajo Guadalquivir. Pp. 97-117 in: *Plan de Uso y Manejo de las Reservas Naturales de las Lagunas de Cádiz*. [Biology of the Crested Coot (*Fulica atra*) in Cádiz and other wetlands in Bajo Guadalquivir]. Pp. 97-117 in: [*Plan for the Use and Management of Nature Reserves in Cádiz Lagoons*]. Agencia de Medio Ambiente, Junta de Andalucía, Sevilla. In Spanish.
Ferns, P.N. (1978). Individual differences in the head and neck plumage of Ruddy Turnstones (*Arenaria interpres*) during the breeding season. *Auk* **95(4)**: 753-755.
Ferns, P.N. (1981). Identification, subspecific variation, ageing and sexing in European Dunlins. *Dutch Birding* **3**: 85-98.
Ferns, P.N. & Green, G.H. (1979). Observations on the breeding plumage and prenuptial moult of Dunlins, *Calidris alpina*, captured in Britain. *Gerfaut* **69(3)**: 286-303.
Ferns, P.N. & Siman, H.Y. (1994). Utility of the curved bill of the Curlew *Numenius arquata* as a foraging tool. *Bird Study* **41(2)**: 102-109.
Ferns, P.N. & Worrall, D.H. (1984). Feeding and foraging in the Dunlin. *Ibis* **126**: 457.
Ferrand, Y. (1983). A behavioural hypothesis derived from 5-year's observations of roding Woodcock. Pp. 68-82 in: Kalchreuter (1983b).
Ferrand, Y. (1988). [Individual sound recognition of the roding Woodcock (*Scolopax rusticola*)]. Pp. 29-33 in: Havet & Hirons (1988). In French with English summary.
Ferrand, Y. & Gossmann, F. (1988). [Spatial distribution of Woodcock in their nocturnal habitats in Brittany]. Pp. 48-52 in: Havet & Hirons (1988). In French with English summary.
Ferreira, I. (1983). *Comportamento Reproductivo da jaçanã,* Jacana jacana *no Est. do Rio de Janeiro*. Thesis, Universidade Federal de Rio de Janeiro, Rio de Janeiro.
Fetterolf, P.M. (1979). Nocturnal behaviour of Ring-billed Gulls during the early incubation period. *Can. J. Zool.* **57**: 1190-1195.
Fetterolf, P.M. (1983a). Effects of investigator activity on Ring-billed Gull behavior and reproductive performance. *Wilson Bull.* **95**: 23-41.
Fetterolf, P.M. (1983b). Infanticide and non-fatal attacks on chicks by Ring-billed Gulls. *Anim. Behav.* **31**: 1018-1028.
Fetterolf, P.M. (1984a). An assessment of possible nest parasitism in Ring-billed Gulls. *Can. J. Zool.* **62**: 1680-1684.
Fetterolf, P.M. (1984b). Aggression, nesting synchrony and reproductive fitness in Ring-billed Gulls. *Anim. Behav.* **32**: 1004-1010.
Fetterolf, P.M. (1984c). Pairing behavior and pair dissolution by Ring-billed Gulls during the postbreeding period. *Wilson Bull.* **96**: 711-714.
Fevold, H.R., Pfeiffer, E.W. & Rice, J.S. (1973). Steroid biosynthesis by phalarope (*Steganopus tricolor* and *Lobipes lobatus*) adrenal tissue. *Gen. Comp. Endocrin.* **21**: 353-357.
ffrench, R.P. (1973) *A Guide to the Birds of Trinidad and Tobago*. Livingston, Wynnewood, Pennsylvania.
ffrench, R.P. (1985). Changes in the avifauna of Trinidad. In: Buckley *et al.* (1985).
ffrench, R.P. (1990). Synchronous breeding and moult in the Brown Noddy Tern on Soldado Rock, Trinidad. *Living World*. Special Centenary Issue: 39-41.
ffrench, R.P. & Collins, C.T. (1965). Royal and Cayenne Terns breeding in Trinidad, West Indies. *Auk* **82**: 277.
Fiebig, J. & Jander, G. (1985). Der Steppenschlammläufer, *Limnodromus semipalmatus*, als Mongolischer Brutvogel. *Ann. Orn.* **9**: 107-111.
Field, D. (1978). First aerial survey for Wattled Cranes. *Bokmakierie* **30(1)**: 18-20.
Field, G. (1995). Unpublished notes on birds of Sierra Leone. Ms.
Figuerola, J. & Martí, J. (1994). Autumn migration of the Ringed Plover *Charadrius hiaticula* in north-east Spain. *Butll. Grup Català d'Anellament* **11**: 31-37.
Filchagov, A.V. (1993). The Armenian Gull in Armenia. *British Birds* **86**: 550-560.
Filchagov, A.V. & Semashko, V.J. (1987). [Distribution and ecology of the West-Siberian Herring Gull (*Larus argentatus heuglini* Bree, 1876) in the Kola Peninsula]. *Byull. Mosk. Ova. Ispyt. Prir. Otd. Biol.* **92(3)**: 37-42. In Russian.
Filchagov, A.V., Yésou, P., Grabovsky, V.I. (1992). Le Goéland du Taïmir *Larus heuglini taimyrensis*: répartition et biologie estivales. *Oiseau et RFO* **62**: 128-148.
Filmer, R.J. & Holtshausen, G.R. (1992). The Southern African crane census, 1985-1986. Pp. 132-141 in: Porter *et al.* (1992).
Finch, B.W. (1981). Asiatic Dowitcher *Limnodromus semipalmatus* at Moitaka Settling Ponds: second record for the New Guinea region. *Papua New Guinea Bird Soc. Newsl.* **183-184**: 36-39.
Finch, B.W. (1982a). Black-winged Stilt (*Himantopus himantopus*) nesting at Kanosia Lagoon, Central Province - a new breeding species for the island of New Guinea. *Papua New Guinea Bird Soc. Newsl.* **193-194**: 10.
Finch, B.W. (1982b). Red-kneed Dotterel (*Erythrogonys cinctus*) at Kanosia Lagoon, first record for Central Province. *Papua New Guinea Bird Soc. Newsl.* **193-194**: 11.
Finch, B.W. (1982c). Spur-winged Lapwings *Vanellus miles novaehollandiae* at Moitaka Settling Ponds, Central Province. *Papua New Guinea Bird Soc. Newsl.* **193-194**: 26-28.
Finch, B.W. (1983). The northern race of Little Ringed Plover *Charadrius dubius curonicus* in the Port Moresby region. *Papua New Guinea Bird Soc. Newsl.* **201-202**: 9-10.
Finch, B.W. (1985). Noteworthy observations in Papua New Guinea and the Solomons. *Papua New Guinea Bird Soc. Newsl.* **215**: 6-10.
Finch, B.W. (1986a). Black Tern *Chlidonias niger* at Moitaka Settling Ponds, Central Province - First record for the New Guinean region. *Muruk* **1(1)**: 27-29.
Finch, B.W. (1986b). Baird's Sandpiper *Calidris bairdii* at Kanosia Lagoon - First record for the New Guinea region. *Muruk* **1(3)**: 86-89.
Fincher, F. (1985). Roding at night and vertical escape flight of Woodcock. *British Birds* **78**: 195.
Finckh, H.E. (1915). Notes on Kagus. *Emu* **14**: 168-170.
Finlayson, M. & Moser, M. (1991). *Wetlands*. Facts on File, Oxford.
Finnlund, M., Hissa, R., Koivusaari, J., Merila, E. & Nuuja, I. (1985). Eggshells of Arctic Terns from Finland: effects of incubation and geography. *Condor* **87**: 79-86.
Firsova, L.V. (1978). [Breeding biology of the Red-legged Kittiwake, *Rissa brevirostris* (Bruch) and the Common Kittiwake, *Rissa tridactyla* (Linnaeus) on the Commander Islands]. Pp. 36-45 in: [*Systematics and Biology of Rare and Little-studied Birds*]. Zoological Institute of Academy of Sciences of the USSR, Leningrad. In Russian.
Firsova, L.V. (1983). [Breeding and behavior of the Glaucous-winged Gull (*Larus glaucescens*) on the Komandorski Islands]. *Bull. Moscow Soc. Nat. Study (Biol. Section)* **88**: 39-52. In Russian.
Firsova, L.V. (1986). To the question about variability of the plumage in Slaty Black-backed Gull *Larus schistisagus* Stejneger. Pp. 135-143 in: Litvinenko (1986).
Firsova, L.V., Lobkov, E.G. & Vyatkin, P.V. (1982). [The Slaty-backed Gull *Larus schistisagus* in the Kamchatka Oblast]. *Bull. Moscow Soc. Nat. Study (Biol. Section)* **87**: 30-35. In Russian.
Fisher, D.J. (1985). Observations on Relict Gull in Mongolia. *Dutch Birding* **7**: 117-120.
Fisher, D.J. (1989). Relict Gulls in Japan. *Birding World* **2**: 216-217.
Fisher, J. & Lockley, R.M. (1954). *Sea-birds*. Collins, London, England.
Fisher, J., Simon, N. & Vincent, J. (1969). *Wildlife in Danger*. Viking Press & Collins, New York & London.
Fisher, W.K. (1903). A new *Procelsterna* from the Leeward Islands, Hawaiian Group. *Proc. US Natl. Mus.* **26**: 559-563.
Fisk, E.J. (1978a). Roof-nesting terns, skimmers and plovers in Florida. *Florida Field Nat.* **6**: 1-8.
Fisk, E.J. (1978b). Threatened, Least Tern, *Sterna albifrons*. Pp. 40-43 in: Kale (1978).
Fiske, P. & Kålås, J.A. (1995). Mate sampling and copulation behavior of Great Snipe females. *Anim. Behav.* **49**: 209-219.
Fiske, P., Kålås, J.A., Saether, S.A. (1994). Correlates of male mating success in the lekking Great Snipe (*Gallinago media*): results from a four-year study. *Behav. Ecol.* **5(2)**: 210-218.
Fitch, M.A. & Shugart, G.W. (1983). Comparative biology and behavior of monogamous pairs and one male-two female trios of Herring Gulls. *Behav. Ecol. Sociobiol.* **14**: 1-7.
Fitzherbert, K. (1978). *Observations on Breeding and Display in a Colony of Captive Australian Bustards* Ardeotis australis. BSc thesis, Monash University, Melbourne.
Fitzherbert, K. (1983). Seasonal weight changes and display in captive Australian Bustards (*Ardeotis australis*). Pp. 210-225 in: Goriup & Vardhan (1983).
Fitzner, J.N. (1978). *The Ecology and Behaviour of the Long-billed Curlew (*Numenius americanus*) in Southeastern Washington*. PhD thesis, Washington State University, Pullman, Washington.
Fitzpatrick, L.C., Guerra, C.G. & Aguilar, R.E. (1989). [Microclimatic features of Gray Gull *Larus modestus* nests in the Atacama Desert]. *Gerfaut* **78**: 421-428. In German.
Fivizzani, A.J., Oring, L.W. & El Halawani, M.E. (1987). Changes in prolactin and testosterone related to male incubation in the sex role reversed Spotted Sandpiper and Wilson's Phalarope. *Amer. Zool.* **27**: 155A. (Abstract).
Fivizzani, A.J., Oring, L.W., El Halawani, M.E. & Schlinger, B.A. (1990). Hormonal basis of male parental care and female intrasexual competition in sex-role reversed birds. Pp. 273-286 in: Wada, M. ed. (1990). *Endocrinology of Birds: Molecular to Behavioral*. Springer-Verlag, Berlin.
Fjeldså, J. (1973). Territorial regulation of the progress of breeding in a population of Coots *Fulica atra*. *Dan. Orn. Foren. Tidssk.* **67**: 115-127.
Fjeldså, J. (1975). Entaksering of Haettemage *Larus ridibundus* og Havterne *Sterna paradisaea* i Myratn-omradet, N.O. island. [A census of Black-headed Gull *Larus ridibundus* and Arctic Tern *Sterna paradisaea* in the Lake Myratn area, N.E. Iceland]. *Dans. Orn. Foren. Tidsk.* **69**: 65-72. In Danish with English summary.
Fjeldså, J. (1977). *Guide to the Young of European Precocial Birds*. Skarv Nature Publications, Tisvildeleje, Denmark.
Fjeldså, J. (1981). Biological notes on the Giant Coot *Fulica gigantea*. *Ibis* **123**: 423-437.
Fjeldså, J. (1982). Biology and systematic relations of the Andean Coot *Fulica americana ardesiaca* (Aves, Rallidae). *Steenstrupia* **8**: 1-21.
Fjeldså, J. (1983a). Geographic variation in the Andean Coot *Fulica ardesiaca*. *Bull. Brit. Orn. Club* **103**: 18-22.
Fjeldså, J. (1983b). A Black Rail from Junín, central Peru: *Laterallus jamaicensis tuerosi* ssp. n. (Aves, Rallidae). *Steenstrupia* **8**: 277-282.
Fjeldså, J. (1983c). Systematic and biological notes on the Colombian Coot *Fulica americana columbiana* (Aves: Rallidae). *Steenstrupia* **9**: 209-215.
Fjeldså, J. (1988). Status of birds of steppe habitats of the Andean zone and Patagonia. Pp. 81-95 in: Goriup (1988).
Fjeldså, J. (1990). Systematic relations of an assembly of allopatric rails from western South America (Aves: Rallidae) *Steenstrupia* **16(7)**: 109-116.
Fjeldså, J. & Jensen, J.K. (1985). "Invasion" af Hvidvingede og Kumlien's Måger *Larus glaucoides glaucoides* og kumlieni på Nolsø på Foerøerne. *Dan. Orn. Foren. Tidssk.* **79(3-4)**: 103-106.
Fjeldså, J. & Krabbe, N. (1990). *Birds of the High Andes*. Apollo Books, Svendborg & Zoological Museum, Copenhagen.
Flack, J.A.D. (1976). The Shore Plover. *Wildl. - Rev. New Zealand Wildl. Serv.* **7**: 41-44.
Flade, M. (1991). Die Habitate des Wachtelkönig *Crex crex*: eine kurze biologische Charakterisierung. *Vogelwelt* **112**: 16-40.
Flather, C.H., Joyce, L.A., Bloomgarden, C.A. (1994). *Species Endangerment Patterns in the United States*. US Forest Service. General Technical Reports **241**.
Fleetwood, R.J. (1973). Jacana breeding in Brazoria county, Texas. *Auk* **90(2)**: 422-423.
Flegg, J. & Madge, S. (1995). *Photographic Field Guide. Birds of Australia*. New Holland, London.
Flegg, J.J.M. & Cox, C.J. (1972). Movements of Black-headed Gulls from colonies in England and Wales. *Bird Study* **19**: 228-240.
Flegg, J.J.M. & Cox, C.J. (1975). Mortality in the Black-headed. Gull. *British Birds* **658**: 437-449.
Fleischer, R.C. (1983). Relationships between tidal oscillations and Ruddy Turnstone flocking, foraging and vigilance behavior. *Condor* **85**: 22-29.
Fleming, A. (1976). Multiple feeding by Dusky Moorhens. *Austr. Bird Watcher* **6(8)**: 325-326.
Fleming, A. (1987). Pacific Gulls inland. *Austr. Bird Watcher* **12**: 102.
Fleming, C.A. (1939a). Birds of the Chatham Islands. *Emu* **38**: 492 509.
Fleming, C.A. (1939b). Birds of the Chatham Islands. Part 3. The Shore Plover. *Emu* **39**: 1-15.
Fleming, C.A. (1946). Breeding of Red-billed Gulls. *New Zealand Bird Notes* **2**: 27-29.
Fleming, C.A. (1951). Notornis in February, 1950. Some general reflections on Notornis. *Notornis* **4(5)**: 101-106.
Fleming, C.A. (1962). New Zealand biogeography. A paleontologist's approach. *Tuatara* **10**: 53-108.
Fleming, C.A. & Falconer, M.L. (1974). A Variable Oystercatcher family at Waikanae. *Notornis* **21(3)**: 261 262.
Fleming, P. (1990). Variable Oystercatchers nesting at Waikanae Estuary, 1971-1989. *Notornis* **37(1)**: 73-76.
Flemming, S.P. (1987). Natural and experimental adoption of Piping Plover chicks. *J. Field Orn.* **58**: 270-273.
Flemming, S.P. (1991). Arctic Tern, *Sterna paradisaea*, kills Piping Plover, *Charadrius melodus*. *Canadian Field-Nat.* **105(3)**: 389-390.
Flemming, S.P. (1994). The 1991 International Piping Plover Census in Canada. *Can. Wildl. Serv. Occas. Pap.* 55 pp.
Flemming, S.P., Chaisson, R.D., Smith, P.C., Austin-Smith, P.J. & Bancroft, R.P. (1988). Piping Plover status in Nova Scotia related to its reproductive and behavioral responses to human disturbance. *J. Field Orn.* **59(4)**: 321-330.
Fletcher, A.W. & Fletcher, M. (1989). An apparent New Zealand Stilt in Tasmania. *Stilt* **15**: 37.
Fletcher, J.A. (1909). Bird notes from Cleveland, Tasmania. *Emu* **8**: 210-214.
Fletcher, J.A. (1912). Notes on the Native Hen (*Tribonyx mortieri*). *Emu* **11**: 250-252.

Fletcher, J.A. (1913). Field notes on some Rallinae. *Emu* **13**: 45-47.
Fletcher, J.A. (1914). Field notes on the Spotless Crake (*Porzana immaculata*). *Emu* **13**: 197-202.
Fletcher, J.A. (1916a). Spotless Crake. *Emu* **15**: 188.
Fletcher, J.A. (1916b). Further notes on the Spotless Crake (*Porzana immaculata*). *Emu* **16**: 46-48.
Fletcher, M.R. (1989). Notes on gulls and terns. *Werkgroep Int. Wad-Watervogel Report* **25**: 104-110.
Flieg, G.M. (1973). Breeding biology and behaviour of the South African hemipode in captivity. *Avicult. Mag.* **79**: 55-59.
Flint, E.N. (1991). Time and energy limits to the foraging radius of Sooty Terns *Sterna fuscata*. *Ibis* **133**: 43-46.
Flint, E.N. & Nagy, K.A. (1984). Flight energetics of free living Sooty Terns. *Auk* **101**: 288-294.
Flint, J.H. (1967). Conservation problems on Tristan da Cunha. *Oryx* **9**: 28-32.
Flint, V.E. ed. (1973a). [*Fauna and Ecology of Waders*]. Vol. 1. Moscow State University, Moscow. In Russian.
Flint, V.E. ed. (1973b). [On the biology of the Broad-billed Sandpiper, *Limicola falcinellus sibiricus*]. Pp. 98-99 in: Flint (1973a). In Russian.
Flint, V.E. (1978). [Strategy and tactics for the conservation of rare birds]. *Priroda* **756(8)**: 14-29. In Russian.
Flint, V.E. ed. (1980a). [*New Studies on the Biology and Distribution of Waders*]. Nauka, Moscow. In Russian.
Flint, V.E. (1980b). [New information on spreading and breeding biology of the Rufous-necked Stint (*Calidris ruficollis*)]. Pp. 178-180 in: Flint (1980a). In Russian.
Flint, V.E. ed. (1981). [*Distribution and Status of Nesting Shorebirds on Territory of USSR*]. Nauka, Moscow. In Russian.
Flint, V.E. (1984a). [*Grus leucogeranus*]. Pp. 139-140 in: Borodin *et al*. (1984). In Russian.
Flint, V.E. (1984b). [*Anthropoides virgo*]. Pp. 142-143 in: Borodin *et al*. (1984). In Russian.
Flint, V.E. & Golovkin, A.N. eds. (1990). *Birds of the USSR: Auks, Murres and Puffins (Alcidae)*. Nauka Press, Moscow, Russia. (Translated into English by Department Secretary of State, Government of Canada, Ottawa).
Flint, V.E. & Kistchinski, A.A. (1973). [On the biology of the Sharp-tailed Sandpiper, *Calidris acuminata*]. Pp. 100-105 in: Flint (1973a). In Russian.
Flint, V.E. & Kistchinski, A.A. (1981). The Siberian Crane in Yakutia. Pp. 136-145 in: Lewis and Masatomi (1981).
Flint, V.E. & Kondratiev, A.J. (1977). Materialien zur Biologie des Kiebitzregenpfeifers (*Pluvialis squatarola* L.). *Beitr. Vogelkd.* **23**: 265-277.
Flint, V.E. & Mishchenko, A.L. (1991). The Great Bustard in the USSR: status and conservation. Pp. 89-92 in: Goriup. P.D., Batten, L.A. & Norton, J.A. eds. (1991). *The Conservation of Lowland Dry Grassland Birds in Europe*. Joint Nature Conservation Committee, Peterborough, UK.
Flint, V.E. & Smirenski, S. (1977). [Rare species of cranes of the USSR fauna and prospects of their protection]. Pp. 139-162 in: *Some Problems of Wildlife Conservation in the USSR*. USSR Ministry of Agriculture. In Russian.
Flint, V.E. & Sorokin, A.G. (1981). The biology of the Siberian Crane (Sterkh) in Yakutia. Pp. 146-149 in: Lewis & Masatomi (1981).
Flint, V.E. & Tomkovich, P.S. (1982). [Ecological and ethological isolation in the Pectoral Sandpiper and the Sharp-tailed Sandpiper]. Pp. 241-261 in: Gavrilov, V.M. & Potapov, R.L. eds. (1982). [*Ornithological Studies of the USSR*]. Vol. 2. Zoological Institute, USSR Academy of Sciences, Moscow. In Russian.
Flint, V.E. & Tomkovich, P.S. (1988). eds. [*Waders in the USSR: their Distribution, Biology and Protection*]. Nauka, Moscow. In Russian.
Flint, V.E., Boehme, R.L., Kostin, Y.V. & Kuznetsov, A.A. (1984). *A Field Guide to the Birds of the USSR*. Princeton University Press, Princeton, New Jersey.
Flint, V.E., Gabuzov, O.S. & Khrustov, A.V. (1992). Strategy for the conservation of bustards. *Bustard Studies* **5**: 2-7.
Flint, V.E., Kistchinski, A.A. & Tomkovich, P.S. (1980). [Breeding biology of the Great Knot (*Calidris tenuirostris*)]. Pp. 176-178 in: Flint (1980a). In Russian.
Flodin, L.A., Noren, L.G. & Hirsimaki, H. (1990). [Nest site selection and hatching success of Lapwing, *Vanellus vanellus*, at Getteron]. *Vår Fågelvärld* **49(4)**: 221-229. In Swedish with English summary.
Flohart, G. (1995). Première mention française du Bécasseau à cou roux *Calidris ruficollis*. [Red-necked Stint, a new species record for France]. *Ornithos* **2(4)**: 183-184. In French with English summary.
Flore, B.O., Frölich, J. & Südbeck, P. (1994). [Autumn numbers of Golden Plover (*Pluvialis apricaria*) in Niedersachsen - results of a country-wide survey on 30/31 October 1993]. *Vogelkdl. Ber. Niedersachsen* **26**: 17-26. In German with English summary.
Flores, R.E. (1991). *Ecology of the California Black Rail in Southwestern Arizona*. MSc thesis, University of Rhode Island, Kingston, Rhode Island.
Flores, R.E. & Eddleman, W.R. (1992). *Ecology of the California Black Rail in Southwestern Arizona*. Final Report, US Bure. Reclam., Yuma Proj. Off. & Arizona Department of Game & Fish. Yuma, Arizona.
Flores, R.E. & Eddleman, W.R. (1993). Nesting biology of the California Black Rail in southwestern Arizona. *Western Birds* **24(2)**: 81-88.
Flores, R.E. & Eddleman, W.R. (1995). California Black Rail use of habitat in southwestern Arizona. *J. Wildl. Manage.* **59(2)**: 357-363.
Flowers, T.L. (1985). Recent breeding of the Mountain Plover in Cimarron County, Oklahoma. *Bull. Okla. Orn. Soc.* **18(2)**: 9-12.
Fog, J. (1978). Studies in migration and mortality of Common Snipe (*Gallinago gallinago*) ringed in Denmark. *Dan. Rev. Game Biol.* **11**: 1-12.
Fogden, M.P.L. (1964). The reproductive behaviour and taxonomy of Hemprich's Gull *Larus hemprichii*. *Ibis* **106**: 299-320.
Folk, M.J. & Tacha, T.C. (1990). Sandhill Crane roost site characteristics in the North Platte River valley. *J. Wildl. Manage.* **54(3)**: 480-486.
Follestad, A. (1990). The pelagic distribution of Little Auk *Alle alle* in relation to a frontal system off central Norway, March/April 1988. *Polar Res.* **8**: 23-28.
Follet, W.I. & Ainley, D.G. (1976). Fishes collected by Pigeon Guillemots *Cepphus columba* Pallas, nesting on southeastern Farallon Island, California. *Calif. Fish & Game* **62**: 28-31.
Forbes-Watson, A.D. & Turner, D.A. (1973). Report on bird preservation in Madagascar. Unpublished report to ICBP.
Forchammer, M. & Maagaard, L. (1991). Breeding biology of Sabine's Gull *Larus sabini* in northeast Greenland. *Dan. Orn. Foren. Tidssk.* **85**: 52-62.
Ford, C. & Brown, M. (1995). Unusual Marbled Murrelet nest. *Wilson Bull.* **107**: 178-179.
Ford, F.B.C. (1906). Longbreach (Q.) notes. *Emu* **5**: 158.
Ford, J. (1987). Hybrid zones in Australian birds. *Emu* **87**: 158-178.
Ford, J.R. (1962). Northern extension for the ranges of the Spotless and Spotted Crakes. *Emu* **62**: 61-62.
Fordham, R.A. (1963). Individual and social behaviour of the Southern Black-backed Gull. *Notornis* **10**: 206-222, 229-232.
Fordham, R.A. (1964a). Breeding biology of the Southern Black-backed Gull. I. Pre-egg and egg stage. *Notornis* **11**: 3-34.
Fordham, R.A. (1964b). Breeding biology of the Southern Black-backed Gull. II. Incubation and the chick stage. *Notornis* **11**: 110-126.
Fordham, R.A. (1967). History and status of the Dominican Gull in Wellington. *Notornis* **14**: 144-153.
Fordham, R.A. (1968). Dispersion and dispersal of the Dominican Gull in Wellington, New Zealand. *Proc. New Zealand Ecol. Soc.* **15**: 40-50.
Fordham, R.A. (1970). Mortality and population change of Dominican Gulls in Wellington New Zealand with a statistical appendix by R.M. Cormack. *J. Anim. Ecol.* **39**: 13-27.
Fordham, R.A. (1983). Seasonal dispersion and activity of the Pukeko *Porphyrio p. melanotus* (Rallidae) in swamp and pasture. *New Zealand J. Ecol.* **6**: 133-142.
Foreman, G. (1991). New Zealand Dotterels breeding in northern Hawke's Bay. *Notornis* **38(3)**: 246-247.
Formozov, N.A. & Smirin, J.M. (1987). [Occurrences of White-naped and Hooded Cranes in Kerulen River Valley (Mongolia)]. Pp. 114-115 in: Neufeldt & Kespaik (1987). In Russian.
Forrester, B.C. (1993). *Birding Brazil. A Check-list and Site Guide*. B.C. Forrester, Rankinston, UK.
Forristal, B. (1991). Snipe feeding on Teasel. *British Birds* **84(5)**: 194-195.
Forsberg, F.R., Sachet, M.H. & Stoddart, D.R. (1983). Henderson Island (southeastern Polynesia): summary of current knowledge. *Atoll. Res. Bull.* **272**.
Forsell, D.J. & Gould, P.J. (1981). *Distribution and Abundance of Marine Birds and Mammals Wintering in the Kodiak Area of Alaska*. US Fish & Wildlife Service Biological Service Prog. Rep. FWS/OBS-81/13, Washington, D.C.
Forsman, D. (1991). Aspects of identification of Crested Coot. *Dutch Birding* **13**: 121-125.
Forsythe, D.M. (1970). Vocalizations of the Long-billed Curlew. *Condor* **72**: 213-224.
Forsythe, D.M. (1972). Observations on the nesting biology of the Long-billed Curlew. *Great Basin Nat.* **32**: 88-90.
Forsythe, D.M. (1973). Growth and development of Long-billed Curlew chicks. *Auk* **90**: 435-438.
Foschi, U. (1986). Sterna Zampenere *Gelochelidon nilotica*. *Ricerche Biol. Selvaggina* **9**(Suppl.): 73-82.
Foster, D.J. (1987). First breeding record of Black-winged Stilt in Oman. *Phoenix* **4**: 6.
Foster, D.J. & Greaves, C.M. (1986). First record of Long-billed Dowitcher in the sultanate of Oman. *Sandgrouse* **8**: 113-114.
Fotso, R.C. (1990). Notes sur les oiseaux d'eau de la région de Yaoundé. *Malimbus* **12**: 25-30.
Fox, A.D. & Aspinall, S.J. (1987). Pomarine Skuas in Britain and Ireland in autumn 1985. *British Birds* **80(9)**: 404-421.
Fox, G.A. & Boersma, D. (1983). Characteristics of supernormal Ring-billed Gull clutches and their attending adults. *Wilson Bull.* **95**: 552-559.
Fox, G.A., Allan, L.J., Weseloh, D.V. & Mineau, P. (1990). The diet of Herring Gulls during the nesting period in Canadian waters of the Great Lakes. *Can. J. Zool.* **68**: 1075-1085.
Fox, G.A., Weseloh, D.V., Kubiak, T.J. & Erdman, T.C. (1991). Reproductive outcomes in colonial fish-eating birds: a biomarker for developmental toxicants in Great Lakes food chains. *J. Great Lakes Res.* **17**: 153-157.
Fox, J.L. & Hall, J.E. (1982). A Kittlitz's Murrelet nest in southeast Alaska. *Murrelet* **63**: 27.
Foxall, R.A. (1979). Presumed hybrids of the Herring Gull and Great Black-backed Gull. *Amer. Birds* **33**: 838.
Frame, G.W. (1982). East African Crowned Crane (*Balearica regulorum gibbericeps*): ecology and behavior in Tanzania. *Scopus* **6**: 60-69.
Frame, G.W. (1985). Topknots and tails. *Animal Kingdom* **88(2)**: 26-31.
Francis, J.T. (1991). Red-winged Pratincoles at Lake Robertson. *Honeyguide* **37(2)**: 77.
Frandsen, J. (1982). *Birds of the South Western Cape*. Sable Publishers, Sloane Park, South Africa.
Frank, D. (1992). The influence of feeding conditions on food provisioning of chicks in Common Terns *Sterna hirundo* nesting in the German Wadden Sea. *Ardea* **80**: 45-55.
Frank, D. & Becker, P.H. (1992). Body mass and nest reliefs in Common Terns *Sterna hirundo* exposed to different feeding conditions. *Ardea* **80**: 57-69.
Frank, P.W. (1981). A condition for sessile strategy. *Amer. Naturalist* **118**: 288 290.
Frank, P.W. (1982). Effects of winter feeding on limpets by Black Oystercatchers *Haematopus bachmani*. *Ecology* **63(5)**: 1352 1362.
Franklin, A.B., Clark, D.A. & Clark, D.B. (1979). Ecology and behaviour of the Galapagos Rail. *Wilson Bull.* **91**: 202-221.
Fraser, E. (1972). Some notes on the Spotless Crake. *Notornis* **19**: 87-88.
Fraser, G.C. & Mendel, G.J. (1976). The Bush-hen in New South Wales. *Austr. Birds* **11**: 25-27.
Fraser, M. (1989). The Inaccessible Island Rail: smallest flightless bird in the world. *Afr. Wildl.* **43(1)**: 14-19.
Fraser, M.W. (1984). Foods of Subantarctic Skuas on Inaccessible Island. *Ostrich* **55**: 192-195.
Fraser, M.W., Dean, W.R.J. & Best, I.C. (1992). Observations on the Inacessible Island Rail *Atlantisia rogersi*: the world's smallest flightless bird. *Bull. Brit. Orn. Club* **112**: 12-22.
Fraser, W. (1969). Chestnut-banded Sandplover *Charadrius pallidus*. *Ostrich* **40(3)**: 161.
Fredrickson, L.H. (1970). Breeding biology of American Coots in Iowa. *Wilson Bull.* **82**: 445-457.
Fredrickson, L.H. (1971). Common Gallinule breeding biology and development. *Auk* **88**: 914-919.
Fredrickson, L.H. (1977). American Coot (*Fulica americana*). In: Sanderson (1977).
Freeman, R.J. (1970). Feeding behaviour of a Treble-banded Plover. *Ostrich* **41**: 263-264.
Freer, J. (1981). Bronze-winged Courser. *Witwatersrand Bird Club News* **112**: 9.
Freese, C.H. (1975). Notes on the nesting of the Double-striped Thick-knee. *Condor* **77(3)**: 353-354.
Freethy, R. (1987). *Auks: an Ornithologist's Guide*. Facts on File Publications, New York.
Freitag, R. & Ryder, J.P. (1973). An annotated list of arthropods collected from Ring-billed Gull nests on granite island, Black Bay, Lake Superior, 1972 and 1973. *Entomol. Soc. Ontario* **104**: 38-46.
French, H.J. & Young, H.G. (1992). Captive breeding and management of White-naped Cranes at Jersey Wildlife Preservation Trust. *Avicult. Mag.* **98(2)**: 58-66.
Friedmann, H. (1927). *Notes on some Argentina Birds*. Bulletin of the Museum of Comparative Zoology **68(4)**. Cambridge, Massachusetts.
Friedmann, H. (1949). The status of the Spotted Rail, *Pardirallus maculatus*, in Chiapas. *Auk* **66**: 86-87.
Friedmann, H. & Smith, F.D. (1950). A contribution to the ornithology of northeastern Venezuela. *Proc. US Natl. Mus.* **100**: 411-538.
Friedmann, H. & Smith, F.D. (1955). A further contribution to the ornithology of northeastern Venezuela. *Proc. US Natl. Mus.* **104**: 463-524.
Frieling, H. (1936). *Cariama cristata* L. als Anpassungsform an das Savannenleben. *Z. Morph. Öekol. Tiere* **30**: 673-730.
Frikke, J. & Laursen, K. (1992). Occurrence of the Knot *Calidris canutus* in Denmark, with special reference to the Danish Wadden Sea. Pp. 155-160 in: Piersma & Davidson (1992b).
Frisch, J.D. (1981). *Aves Brasileiras*. Vol. 1. Dalgas Ecoltec, São Paulo.
von Frisch, O. (1956). Zur Brutbiologie und Jugendentwicklung des Brachvogels (*Numenius arquata* L.). *Z. Tierpsychol.* **13**: 50-81.
von Frisch, O. (1961). Zur Jugendentwicklung und Ethologie des Stelzenläufers (*Himantopus himantopus*) und der Brachschwalbe (*Glareola pratincola*). *Z. Tierpsychol.* **18**: 67-70.
von Frisch, O. (1976). Zur Biologie der Zwergtrappe (*Tetrax tetrax*). *Bonn. zool. Beitr.* **27**: 21-38.
Frisch, R. (1978). Surfbirds in Ogilvie and Richardson Mountains, Yukon Territory. *Can. Field-Nat.* **92(4)**: 401-403.
Frisch, T. & Morgan, W.C. (1979). Ivory Gull colonies in southeastern Ellesmere Island, Arctic Canada. *Can. Field-Nat.* **93**: 173-179.
Frith, C.B. (1977). Life history notes on some Aldabra land birds. *Atoll Res. Bull.* **201**: 3-5.
Frith, C.B. (1978). The function of display and coloration in the Sunbittern. *Avicult. Mag.* **84(3)**: 150-157.
Frith, C.B. & Frith, D.W. (1988). The Chestnut Forest-Rail, *Rallina rubra* (Rallidae), at Tari Gap, Southern Highlands Province, Papua New Guinea and its vocalizations. *Muruk* **3**: 48-50.
Frith, C.B. & Frith, D.W. (1990). Nidification of the Chestnut Forest-Rail *Rallina rubra* (Rallidae) in Papua New Guinea and a review of *Rallina* nesting biology. *Emu* **90**: 254-259.
Frith, C.R. (1976). Crane habitat on the Platte River. Pp. 151-156 in: Lewis (1979a).
Frith, H.J. ed. (1969). *Birds in the Australian High Country*. A.H. & A.W. Reed, Sydney.
Frith, H.J. (1976). *Complete Book of Australian Birds*. Reader's Digest Services Ltd, Sydney.
Frith, H.J. (1985). Plains-wanderer. Pp. 465-466 in: Campbell & Lack (1985).
Frith, H.J., Crome, F.H.J. & Brown, B.K. (1977). Aspects of the biology of the Japanese Snipe, *Gallinago hardwickii*. *Austr. J. Ecol.* **2**: 341-368.
Fritzell, E.K., Swanson, G.A. & Meyer, M.I. (1979). Fall foods of migrant Common Snipe in North Dakota. *J. Wildl. Manage.* **43**: 253-257.
Fröbel, F. (1982). Spitzschwanzstrandläufer *Calidris acuminata* am Ammersee beobachtet. [Sharp-tailed Sandpiper *Calidris acuminata* observed at Ammer See]. *Anz. Orn. Ges. Bayern* **21(3)**: 182-183.
Frodin, P., Haas, F. & Lindström, Å. (1994). Mate guarding by Curlew Sandpipers (*Calidris ferruginea*) during spring migration in north Siberia. *Arctic* **47(2)**: 142-144.
Frohring, P.C. & Kushlan, J.A. (1986). Nesting status and colony site variability of Laughing Gulls in southern Florida. *Florida Field Nat.* **14**: 1-17.
Frost, P.G.H. & Shaughnessy, G. (1976). Breeding adaptations of the Damara Tern *Sterna balaenarum*. *Madoqua* **9**: 33-39.
Fry, C.H. (1966). On the feeding of Allen's Gallinule. *Bull. Niger. Orn. Soc.* **3**: 97.
Fry, C.H. (1981). West African Crowned Crane status. Pp. 251-253 in: Lewis & Masatomi (1981).
Fry, C.H. (1983a). The jacanid radius and *Microparra*, a neotenic genus. *Gerfaut* **73**: 173-184.
Fry, C.H. (1983b). Incubation, brooding and a structural character of the African Jacana. *Ostrich* **54(3)**: 175-176.
Fry, C.H. (1987). New data on the West African status of the Black Crowned Crane. Pp. 331-335 in: Archibald & Pasquier (1987a).
Fry, D.M. (1992). Point-source and non-point source problems affecting seabird populations. Pp. 547-562 in: McCullough & Barrett (1992).
Fry, D.M. & Toone, C.K. (1981). DDT-induced feminization of gull embryos. *Science* **213**: 922-924.
Fry, G. (1989). Biometrics, moult and migration of Broad-billed Sandpipers *Limicola falcinellus* spending the non-breeding season in north-west Australia. *Stilt* **15**: 29-33.
Fry, G. (1990). Biometrics, moult and migration of Terek Sandpipers *Tringa terek* spending the non-breeding season in north west Australia. *Stilt* **17**: 24-28.
Fry, K. (1980). *Aspects of the Winter Ecology of the Dunlin (*Calidris alpina*) on the Fraser River Delta*. Canadian Wildlife Service, Pacific & Yukon Region.

Fryer, G. (1972). Conservation of the great lakes of east Africa: a lesson and a warning. *Biol. Conserv.* **4**: 256-262.
Fuchs, E. (1977a). Predation and anti-predator behaviour in a mixed colony of terns *Sterna* sp. and Black-headed Gulls *Larus ridibundus* with special reference to the Sandwich Tern *Sterna sandvicensis*. *Ornis Scand.* **8**: 17-32.
Fuchs, E. (1977b). Kleptoparasitism of Sandwich Terns *Sterna sandvicensis* by Black-headed Gulls *Larus ridibundus*. *Ibis* **119(2)**: 183-190.
Fuchs, E. (1977c). Parasitism of food from Sandwich Terns *Sterna sandvicensis* by Black-headed Gulls *Larus ridibundus*. *Ibis* **119**.
Fuggles-Couchman, N.R. (1962). Nesting of Whiskered Tern *Chlidonias hybrida sclateri* in Tanganyika. *Ibis* **104**: 563-564.
Fujimaki, Y. (1986). Seabird colonies on Hokkaido Island. Pp. 82-87 in: Litvinenko (1986).
Fujimaki, Y. (1994). [Distribution and abundance of the Latham's Snipe in south-eastern Hokkaido]. *Strix* **13**: 73-78. In Japanese with English summary.
Fujimaki, Y. & Haneda, K. (1976). Additional records of the Spoon-billed Sandpiper (*Eurynorhynchus pygmaeus*) from Hokkaido. *Misc. Rep. Yamashina Inst. Orn.* **8(3)**: 276-281. In English with Japanese summary.
Fujimaki, Y. & Skira, I.J. (1984). Notes on the Latham's Snipe *Gallinago hardwickii* in Japan. *Emu* **84(1)**: 49-51.
Fujita, G., Harris, J., Bold, A., Tveenmayadag, N. & Chuluunbatar, S. (1994). Habitat preference of Demoiselle and White-naped Cranes breeding in Mongolia. Pp. 93-96 in: Higuchi & Minton (1994).
Fulgenhauer, J. (1980). Behaviour of button-quail. *Sunbird* **11(2)**: 25-39.
Fullagar, P.J. (1985). The Woodhens of Lord Howe Island. *Avicult. Mag.* **91**: 15-30.
Fullagar, P.J. & Disney, H.J. de S. (1975). The birds of Lord Howe Island: a report on the rare and endangered species. *Bull. ICBP* **12**: 187-202.
Fullagar, P.J. & Disney, H.J. de S. (1981). Discriminant functions for sexing woodhens. *Corella* **5**: 106-108.
Fullagar, P.J., Disney, H.J. de S. & de Naurois, R. (1982). Additional specimens of two rare rails and comments on the genus *Tricholimnas* of New Caledonia and Lord Howe Island. *Emu* **82**: 131-136.
Fuller, E. (1987). *Extinct Birds*. Viking/Rainbird, London.
Fuller, M. (1992). [Extension of breeding range of charadriids, notably, the Lapwing (*Vanellus vanellus*) in the Gutersloh district and in the town of Bielefeld - 1991 status]. *Charadrius* **28(2)**: 69-81. In German with English summary.
Fuller, R.J. & Lloyd, D. (1981). The distribution and habitats of wintering Golden Plovers in Britain 1977-78. *Bird Study* **28**: 169-185.
Fuller, R.J. & Youngman, R.E. (1979). The utilisation of farmland by Golden Plovers wintering in southern England. *Bird Study* **26**: 37-46.
Furness, B.L. (1980). *Territoriality and Feeding Behaviour in the Arctic Skua (*Stercorarius parasiticus *(L.))*. PhD thesis, University of Aberdeen, Aberdeen, UK.
Furness, B.L. (1983). The feeding behaviour of Arctic Skuas *Stercorarius parasiticus* wintering off South Africa. *Ibis* **125(2)**: 245-251.
Furness, B.L. & Furness, R.W. (1982). Biometrics of Sabine's Gulls *Larus sabini* in the South Atlantic during the northern winter. *Cormorant* **10(1)**: 31-34.
Furness, R.W. (1977). Effects of Great Skuas on Arctic Skuas in Shetland. *British Birds* **70**: 96-107.
Furness, R.W. (1978a). Kleptoparasitism by Great Skuas (*Catharacta skua* Brünn.) and Arctic Skuas (*Stercorarius parasiticus* L.) at a Shetland seabird colony. *Anim. Behav.* **26**: 1167-1177.
Furness, R.W. (1978b). Movements and mortality rates of Great Skuas ringed in Scotland. *Bird Study* **25**: 229-238.
Furness, R.W. (1979). Foods of Great Skuas at North Atlantic breeding localities. *Ibis* **121**: 86-92.
Furness, R.W. (1981). The impact of predation by Great Skuas (*Catharacta skua*) on other seabirds populations at a Shetland colony. *Ibis* **123**: 534-539.
Furness, R.W. (1983). Variations in size and growth of Great Skua *Catharacta skua* chicks in relation to adult age, hatching date, egg volume, brood size and hatching sequence. *J. Zool., London* **199**: 101-116.
Furness, R.W. (1984). Influences of adult age and experience, nest location, clutch size and laying sequence on the breeding success of the Great Skua *Catharacta skua*. *J. Zool., London* **202**: 565-576.
Furness, R.W. (1985). Skua. Pp. 547-549 in: Campbell & Lack (1985).
Furness, R.W. (1987a). Kleptoparasitism in seabirds. Pp. 77-100 in: Croxall (1987).
Furness, R.W. (1987b). *The Skuas*. T. & A.D. Poyser, Calton, UK.
Furness, R.W. & Hislop, J.R.G. (1981). Diets and feeding ecology of Great Skuas *Catharacta skua* during the breeding season in Shetland. *J. Zool., London* **195**: 1-23.
Furness, R.W. & Monaghan, P. (1987). *Seabird Ecology*. Blackie, Glasgow & London.
Furness, R.W. & Nettleship, D.N. (1991). Seabirds as monitors of changing marine environments. Pp. 2237-2279 in: *Proc. XX Int. Orn. Congr.* Christchurch, 1990.
Furness, R.W., Hudson, A.V. & Ensor, K. (1988). Interactions between scavenging seabirds and commercial fisheries around the British Isles. Pp. 240-268 in: Burger (1988c).
Furniss, O.C. (1933). Observations on the nesting of the Killdeer Plover in the Prince Albert district in central Saskatchewan. *Can. Field-Nat.* **47**: 135-138.
Furniss, S. (1983). Status of the seabirds of the Culebra Archipelago, Puerto Rico. *Colonial Waterbirds* **6**: 121-125.
Furse, C. (1979). *Elephant Island*. Nelson, Shropshire, UK.
Futter, K. (1989). *Age and Sex Differences in the Foraging Behaviour of Lapwings (*Vanellus vanellus*) in Mixed Species Flocks*. PhD dissertation, University of Nottingham, Nottingham, UK.
Gabrielsen, G.W., Taylor, J.R.E., Konarzewski, M. & Mehlum, F. (1991). Field and laboratory metabolism and thermoregulation in Dovekies *Alle alle*. *Auk* **108**: 71-78.
Gabrielson, I.N. (1933). An Oregon record of the Red-legged Kittiwake (*Rissa brevirostris*). *Auk* **50**: 216.
Gabrielson, I.N. & Lincoln, F.C. (1959). *The Birds of Alaska*. The Stackpole Co., Harrisburg, Pennsylvania.
Gaines, E.P. (1986). *Habitat Selection and Productivity of Piping Plovers in Central North Dakota*. MSc thesis, University of Missouri, Columbia, Missouri.
Gaines, E.P. & Ryan, M.R. (1988). Piping Plover habitat use and reproductive success in North Dakota. *J. Wildl. Manage.* **52(2)**: 266-273.
Galbraith, C.A. & Thompson, P.S. (1981). [Wood Sandpiper *Tringa glareola* breeding in Iceland]. *Natturufraedingurinn* **51(4)**: 164-168. In Icelandic with English summary.
Galbraith, C.A. & Thompson, P.S. (1982). The Wood Sandpiper *Tringa glareola* breeding in Iceland, 1981. *Dan. Orn. Foren. Tidssk.* **76(1-2)**: 72. In English with Danish summary.
Galbraith, H. (1986). *The Effects of Agricultural Land-use on the Breeding Ecology of Lapwings* vanellus vanellus. PhD dissertation, University of Glasgow, Glasgow.
Galbraith, H. (1988a). Effects of egg size and composition on the size, quality and survival of Lapwing chicks. *J. Zool., London* **214(3)**: 383-398.
Galbraith, H. (1988b). Adaptation and constraint in the growth patterns of Lapwing *Vanellus vanellus* chicks. *J. Zool., London* **215(3)**: 537-548.
Galbraith, H. (1988c). Effects of agriculture on the breeding ecology of Lapwings *Vanellus vanellus*. *J. Appl. Ecol.* **25(2)**: 487-503.
Galbraith, H. (1988d). The effects of territorial behaviour on Lapwing populations. *Ornis Scand.* **19(2)**: 134-138.
Galbraith, H. (1989a). The diet of Lapwing *Vanellus vanellus* chicks on Scottish farmland. *Ibis* **131(1)**: 80-84.
Galbraith, H. (1989b). Arrival and habitat use by Lapwings *Vanellus vanellus* in the early breeding season. *Ibis* **131(3)**: 377-388.
Galbraith, H. & Watson, A. (1991). A flight characteristic of recently fledged Lapwings. *British Birds* **84(4)**: 151-152, 289.
Galbraith, H., Murray, S., Duncan, K., Smith, R., Whitfield, D.P. & Thompson, D.B.A. (1993). Diet and habitat use of the Dotterel *Charadrius morinellus* in Scotland. *Ibis* **135(2)**: 148-155.
Galbraith, H., Murray, S., Rae, S., Whitfield, D.P. & Thompson, D.B.A. (1993). Numbers and distribution of Dotterel *Charadrius morinellus* breeding in Great Britain. *Bird Study* **40(3)**: 161-169.
Galbreath, R. & Miskelly, C.M. (1988). The Hakawai. *Notornis* **35(3)**: 215-216.
Galindo, J.M. (1987). Prey selection and foraging behaviour of Wilson's Plover (*Charadrius wilsonia*) in La Paz inlet, Baja California Sur, Mexico. *Pacific Seabird Group Bull.* **14**: 27. (Abstract).
Gallagher, M.D. & Price, K.S. (1990). The Spotted Thick-knee *Burhinus capensis* and Stone Curlew *B. oedicnemus* in Arabia. *Sandgrouse* **12**: 8-24.
Gallagher, M.D. & Rogers, T.D. (1980). On some birds of Dhofar and other parts of Oman. *J. Oman Stud. Spec. Rep.* **22**: 347-385.
Gallagher, M.D. & Woodcock, M.W. (1980). *The Birds of Oman*. Quartet Books, London.
Gallagher, M.D., Scott, D.A., Ormond, R.F.G., Connor, R.J. & Jennings, M.C. (1984). The distribution and conservation of seabirds breeding on the coasts and islands of Iran and Arabia. Pp. 421-456 in: Croxall, Evans & Schreiber (1984).
Gallegos, D. (1984). Aspectos de la biologia reproductiva del Tero Común *Vanellus chilensis* (Gmelin). 1: Comportamiento y territorialidad. [Biological aspects of reproduction of the Southern Lapwing (*Vanellus chilensis*). 1: Behaviour and territoriality]. *Hornero* **12(3)**: 150-155. In Spanish with English summary.
Gallucci, T. (1980). Third Texas nest of the Mountain Plover. *Bull. Texas Orn. Soc.* **13(2)**: 51-52.
Galusha, J.G. & Stout, J.F. (1977). Aggressive communication by *Larus glaucescens*. Part IV. Experiments on visual communication. *Behaviour* **62**: 222-235.
Galván, G.M. (1974). *Las Aves del Valle del Cuzco*. PhD thesis, Universidad Nacional de San Antonio Abad del Cuzco, Cuzco, Peru.
Gálvez, X. & Perera, A. (1995). A crane conservation revival in Cuba. *ICF Bugle* **21(1)**: 2-3.
Ganguli, U. (1975). *A Guide to the Birds of the Delhi Area*. Indian Council of Agricultural Research, Delhi.
Ganguli-Lachungpa, U. & Rahmani, A.R. (1990). Former distribution of the Lesser Florican. Pp. 95-100 in: *Status and Ecology of the Lesser and Bengal Floricans with Reports on Jerdon's Courser and Mountain Quail*. Bombay Natural History Society, Bombay.
Gantz, A. (1985). [The Great Snipe - behavior and identification]. *Sunbird* **3**: 81-85, 95. In Hebrew with English summary.
Gao Zhongxin & Pan Weili (1986). [Preliminary study on ecology of the Demoiselle Crane]. Pp. 203-207 in: Ma Yiqing (1986). In Chinese.
Garba, B. (1996). Status and reintroduction potential of the Black Crowned Crane in Nigeria. In: Beilfuss *et al.* (1996).
Garcher, M.L. & Carroll, J.P. (1991). Comparative diet study of male and female Wilson's Phalaropes in North Dakota. *J. Pennsylvania Acad. Sci.* **64**(Suppl.): 190.
Garcias, P. (1991). Seguiment de la colònia d'Avisadors (*Himantopus himantopus*) al Salobrar de Campos, 1981. *Anuari Orn. Balears* **6**: 29-34.
Gardiner, N. (1975). How does the Skimmer wet its eggs? *Bull. East Afr. Nat. Hist. Soc.* **1975**: 96-97.
Garnett, M.C. (1984). Conservation of seabirds in the South Pacific: a review. Pp. 547-558 in: Croxall, Evans & Schreiber (1984).
Garnett, S. (1985a). Evidence for polyandry in the Comb-crested Jacana. *Stilt* **7**: 24.
Garnett, S. (1985b). Nesting behaviour of the Bush Thick-knee. *Stilt* **7**: 24-25.
Garnett, S. (1992). *The Action Plan for Australian Birds*. Australian National Parks & Wildlife Service, Canberra.
Garnett, S. ed. (1993). *Threatened and Extinct Birds of Australia*. 2nd corrected edition. RAOU Report **82**. Royal Australasian Ornithologists' Union, Victoria.
Garnett, S.T. (1978). The behaviour patterns of the Dusky Moorhen *Gallinula tenebrosa* Gould (Aves: Rallidae). *Austr. Wildl. Res.* **5**: 363-384.
Garnett, S.T. (1980). The social organization of the Dusky Moorhen, *Gallinula tenebrosa* Gould (Aves: Rallidae). *Austr. Wildl. Res.* **7(1)**: 103-112.
Garnett, S.T. & Minton, C.D.T. (1985). Notes on the movements and distribution of the Little Curlew *Numenius minutus* in northern Australia. *Austr. Bird Watcher* **11(3)**: 69-73.
Garrett, K. & Dunn, J. (1981). *Birds of Southern California: Status and Distribution*. Los Angeles Audubon Society, Los Angeles.
Garrido, O.H. (1985). Cuban endangered birds. In: Buckley *et al.* (1985).
Garrod, A.H. (1876). On the anatomy of *Aramus scolopaceus*. *Proc. Zool. Soc., London* **1876**: 275-277.
Garrod, A.H. (1879). Notes on points in the anatomy of the Hoatzin (*Opisthocomus cristatus*). *Proc. Zool. Soc., London* **1879**: 109-114.
Garrod, J.D. (1991). Pectoral Sandpiper's reaction when alarmed. *British Birds* **84(6)**: 222.
Garton, E.O., Drewien, R.C., Brown, W.M., Bizeau, E.G. & Hayward, P.H. (1989). Survival rates and population prospects of Whooping Cranes at Grays Lake NWR (draft). Unpublished draft for US Fish & Wildlife Service, Albuquerque, New Mexico. 18 pp.
Garzón, J. (1981). El censo de Avutardas confirma la regresión de esta especie. *Quercus* **1**: 17-19.
van Gasteren, H. (1984). [Foraging success in Ringed Plovers]. *Aythya* **22**: 17-21. In Dutch.
Gaston, A.J. (1980). Population, movements and wintering areas of Thick-billed Murres *Uria lomvia* in eastern Canada. *Can. Wildl. Serv. Program Note* **110**: 1-10.
Gaston, A.J. (1985a). The diet of Thick-billed Murre chicks in the eastern Canadian Arctic. *Auk* **102**: 727-734.
Gaston, A.J. (1985b). Energy invested in reproduction by Thick-billed Murres *Uria lomvia*. *Auk* **102**: 447-458.
Gaston, A.J. (1985c). Development of the young in the Atlantic Alcidae. Pp. 319-354 in: Nettleship & Birkhead (1985).
Gaston, A.J. (1990). Population paramaters of the Ancient Murrelet. *Condor* **92**: 998-1011.
Gaston, A.J. (1991). Seabirds of Hudson Strait, Hudson Bay and adjacent waters. Pp. 7-16 in: Croxall (1991).
Gaston, A.J. (1992a). *The Ancient Murrelet: a Natural History in the Queen Charlotte Islands*. T. & A.D. Poyser, London, England.
Gaston, A.J. (1992b). Annual survival of breeding Cassin's Auklets in the Queen Charlotte Islands, British Columbia. *Condor* **94**: 1019-1021.
Gaston, A.J. (1994). Ancient Murrelet (*Synthliboramphus antiquus*). No. **132** in: Poole & Gill (1994-1995).
Gaston, A.J. (1995). Status of the Ancient Murrelet *Synthliboramphus antiquus*, in Canada and the effect of introduced predators. *Can. Field-Nat.* **109**.
Gaston, A.J. & Bradstreet, M.S.W. (1993). Intercolony differences in the summer diet of Thick-billed Murres in the eastern Canadian arctic. *Can. J. Zool.* **71**: 1831-1840.
Gaston, A.J. & Dechesne, S.B.C. (1996). Rhinoceros Auklet (*Cerorhinca monocerata*). No. **212** in: Poole & Gill (1996).
Gaston, A.J. & Decker, R. (1985). Interbreeding of Thayer's Gull, *Larus thayeri* and Kumlien's Gull, *Larus glaucoides kumlieni* on Southampton Island, Northwest Territories. *Can. Field-Nat.* **99**: 257-259.
Gaston, A.J. & Elliot, R.D. (1990). Kumlien's Gull, *Larus glaucoides kumlieni*, on Coat's Island, Northwest Territory. *Can. Field-Nat.* **104**: 477-479.
Gaston, A.J. & Elliot, R.D. eds. (1991). *Studies of High-latitude Seabirds*. Vol. 2. Conservation biology of Thick-billed Murres in the northwest Atlantic. Occasional Paper **69**. Canadian Wildlife Service, Ottawa.
Gaston, A.J. & McLaren, P.L. (1990). Winter observations of Black Guillemots in Hudson Bay and Davis Strait. Pp. 67-70 in: Sealy (1990).
Gaston, A.J. & Nettleship, D.N. (1981). *The Thick-billed Murres of Prince Leopold Island - a Study of the Breeding Ecology of a Colonial High Arctic Seabird*. Monograph Series **6**. Canadian Wildlife Service, Ottawa.
Gaston, A.J. & Nettleship, D.N. (1982). Factors determining seasonal changes in attendance at colonies of the Thick-billed Murre *Uria lomvia*. *Auk* **99**: 468-473.
Gaston, A.J. & Powell, D.W. (1989). Natural incubation, egg neglect and hatchability in the Ancient Murrelet. *Auk* **106**: 433-438.
Gaston, A.J., Cairns, D.K., Elliot, R.D. & Noble, D.G. (1985). A natural history of Digges Sound. *Can. Wildl. Serv. Rep. Ser.* **46**: 1-61.
Gaston, A.J., Carter, H.R. & Sealy, S.G. (1993). Winter ecology and diet of Ancient Murrelets off Victoria, British Columbia. *Can. J. Zool.* **71**: 64-70.
Gaston, A.J., de Forest, L.N., Donaldson, G. & Noble, D.G. (1994). Population parameters of Thick-billed Murres at Coats Island, Northwest Territories, Canada. *Condor* **96**: 935-948.
Gaston, A.J., de Forest, L.N., Gilchrist, G. & Nettleship, D.N. (1993). Monitoring Thick-billed Murre populations at colonies in northern Hudson Bay, 1972-1992. *Can. Wildl. Serv. Occas. Pap.* **80**: 1-16.
Gaston, A.J., Jones, I.L. & Noble, D.G. (1988). Monitoring Ancient Murrelet breeding populations. *Colonial Waterbirds* **11**: 58-66.
Gaston, A.J., Jones, I.L., Noble, D.G. & Smith, S.A. (1988). Orientation of Ancient Murrelet *Synthliboramphus antiquus*, chicks during their passage from the burrow to the sea. *Anim. Behav.* **36**: 300-303.
Gatter, W. (1971a). Aufenthalt und Raeumliche Bewegungen Einer Flußregen-pfeifer-population (*Charadrius dubius*). [Cojourn and local movements of a Little Ringed Plover population (*Charadrius dubius*)]. *Anz. Orn. Ges. Bayern* **10(2)**: 100-106. In German with English summary.
Gatter, W. (1971b). Wassertransport beim Flußregenpfeifer (*Charadrius dubius*). [Water transport by Little Ringed Plovers (*Charadrius dubius*)]. *Vogelwelt* **92**: 100-103. In German with English summary.
Gatter, W. (1988). The birds of Liberia (west Africa). A preliminary list with status and open questions. *Verh. orn. Ges. Bayern* **24**: 689-723.
Gatter, W. & Hodgson, G. (1987). Veränderte Verhaltensmuster brutender Landvögel (*Glareola nuchalis*, *Streptopelia semitorquata* und *Ploceus aurantius*) auf Felsen im Atlantik vor Liberia/Westafrika. [Changed patterns of behaviour of breeding land birds (*Glareola nuchalis*, *Streptopelia semitorquata* and *Ploceus aurantius*) on rocks in the Atlantic offshore of West Africa]. *Vogelwarte* **34(2)**: 138-140. In German with English summary.
Gaucher, P. (1991). On the feeding ecology of the Houbara *Chlamydotis undulata undulata*. *Alauda* **59(2)**: 120-121. In English with French summary.
Gaucher, P., Paillat, P., Chappuis, C., Saint Jalme, M., Lotfikhah, F. & Wink, M. (1996). Taxonomy of the Houbara Bustard *Chlamydotis undulata* subspecies considered on the basis of sexual display and genetic divergence. *Ibis* **138(2)**: 273-282.

Gauzer, M.E. (1981a). [Social conditions of chick mortality in colonies of Sandwich Tern (*Thalasseus sandvicensis*) on islands in the Gulf Krasnovodsk. 1. General characteristics of juvenile mortality and its probable causes]. *Zoologischeskii Zhurnal* **60**: 530-539. In Russian.
Gauzer, M.E. (1981b). [Social conditions of chick mortality in colonies of Sandwich Tern (*Thalasseus sandvicensis*) on islands in the Gulf Krasnovodsk. 2. Role of the organization and structure of the colonies]. *Zoologischeskii Zhurnal* **60**: 879-886. In Russian.
Gauzer, M.E. & Ter-Mikhaelyan, M.T. (1987). [Spatial and temporal population structure of Common Terns on islands of Krasnovodsk Bay]. *Zoologischeskii Zhurnal* **66**: 110-118. In Russian.
Gauzer, M.E. & Vassiliev, V.I. (1979). [Phenological aspect of the biology of the Sandwich Tern on the eastern shores of the Caspian Sea]. Pp. 56-60 in: [*Nesting Ecology for Birds and Methods for its Study*]. Report to All Union Conference of Young Scientists, Samarkand. In Russian.
Gauzer, M.Y. (1989). [Asynchronous hatching of chicks as a factor of juvenile mortality of Sandwich Tern, *Sterna sandvicensis*]. *Zoologischeskii Zhurnal* **68**: 103-112. In Russian.
Gavrilov, A.E. (1986). [Some aspects of the autumn migration of the Marsh Sandpiper in central and southeast Kazakhstan]. Pp. 141-142 in: [*Study of the USSR Birds, their Conservation and Rational Use*]. Abstracts of the papers. I. All-Union Congress of the All-Union Ornithological Society and IX All-Union Ornithological Conference. Part 1. In Russian.
Gavrilov, A.E. & Beresovski, V.G. (1988). [Broad-billed Sandpiper (*Limicola falcinellus*) in Tengiz-Kurgaldzhinsk hollow]. *Ornitologiya* **23**: 204-205. In Russian.
Gavrilov, A.E. & Gavrilov, E.I. (1990). [On the interruptive moult of primaries in the Kentish Plover (*Charadrius alexandrinus*)]. *Ornitologiya* **24**: 170-171. In Russian with English summary.
Gavrilov, E.I. (1977). [Population and migration routes of the Demoiselle Crane in Kazakhstan]. Pp. 167-175 in: [*Rare and Vanishing Animals and Birds of Kazakhstan*]. Alma Ata, USSR. In Russian.
Gavrilov, E.I. (1991). [Energetical maintenance in the Little Stint (*Calidris minuta* Leisler) during autumn migration in Kazakhstan]. *Ornitologiya* **25**: 15-25. In Russian.
Gavrilov, E.I. & Bekbayev, E.Z. (1988). [Assessment of energy resources on live waders of several species during their autumn migration]. *Zoologischeskii Zhurnal* **67(12)**: 1900-1903. In Russian with English summary.
Gavrilov, E.I., Beresovski, V.G., Gavrilov, A.E., Erokhov, S.N. & Khrokov, V.V. (1982). [On data of autumn passage of males and females of the Red-necked Phalarope in Kazakhstan]. *Vestnik Zoologii* **5**: 65-67. In Russian with English summary.
Gavrilov, E.I., Beresovski, V.G., Gavrilov, A.E., Erokhov, S.N. & Khrokov, V.V. (1988). [Share and duration of stoppings of the Little Stint in spring migration on waterbodies of Kazakhstan]. Pp. 213-220 in: [*Ecology and Bird Behaviour*]. Nauka, Moscow. In Russian.
Gavrilov, E.I., Jerochov, S.N., Gavrilov, A.E. & Khrokov, V.V. (1983). Über den Herbstzug des Odinswassertreters (*Phalaropus lobatus*) in Kasachstan. *Vogelwarte* **32**: 103-116.
Gavrilov, V.V. (1988). [Territorial distribution, diurnal activity, time and energy budget in Wood Sandpiper males - *Tringa glareola* (Charadriidae) during pre-nesting period]. *Zoologischeskii Zhurnal* **67(10)**: 1549-1560. In Russian with English summary.
Gavrilov, V.V. & Keskpaik, Y.E. (1992). Variations of postnatal growth in Ruff *Philomachus pugnax* (Scolopacidae, Aves). *Izv. Akad. Nauk Ser. Biol.*: 908-914.
Gaza, P.D. (1994). *Rare and Endangered New Zealand Birds: Conservation and Management*. Canterbury University Press, Christchurch.
Gebauer, A. & Nadler, T. (1992). Verhalten und Stimme des Mongolenregenpfeifers *Charadrius mongolus*. *Limicola* **6(3)**: 105-125.
Gee, G.F., Hatfield, J.S., Howey, P.W. (1995). Remote monitoring of parental incubation conditions in the Greater Sandhill Crane. *Zoo Biology* **14(2)**: 159-172.
Gee, J.P. (1984). The birds of Mauritania. *Malimbus* **6**: 31-66.
Geldenhuys, J.N. (1984). The status of cranes (Aves: Gruidae) in the Orange Free State. *S. Afr. J. Wildl. Res.* **14**: 15-18.
Gemperle, M.E. & Preston, F.W. (1955). Variation of shape in the eggs of the Common Tern in the clutch sequence. *Auk* **72**: 184-198.
Génard, M. & Lanusse, D. (1992). Use of marshlands by Common Cranes in winter in south-western France. *Ornis Fenn.* **69(1)**: 19-28.
Génard, M., Lanusse, D. & Béreyziat, T. (1991). Ressources en maïs et stationnement des Grues cendrées (*Grus grus*) dans les sud-ouest de la France. [Corn resources and winter settlement of Common Cranes (*Grus grus*) in southwest France]. *Can. J. Zool.* **69(9)**: 2295-2299. In French with English summary.
George, K. (1993). [Migrating Cranes (*Grus grus*) attack Skua (*Stercorarius* sp.)]. *Vogelwarte* **37(2)**: 145. In German with English summary.
George, N.J. (1985). On the parental care of Yellow-wattled Lapwing *Vanellus malabaricus*. *J. Bombay Nat. Hist. Soc.* **82(3)**: 655-656.
Gerasimov, N.N. (1980). [Spring migration of the Great Knot (*Calidris tenuirostris*) and Knot (*C. canutus*) along the western coast of Kamchatka]. Pp. 96-98 in: Flint (1980a). In Russian.
Gerasimov, N.N. (1988). [Spring record of Spoon-billed Sandpiper (*Eurynorhynchus pygmeus*) at the west coast of Kamchatka]. *Ornitologiya* **23**: 205. In Russian with English summary.
Gerhart, J.D. (1980). Finfoot eating snake. *Scopus* **4(3)**: 69.
Géroudet, P. (1968). L'expansion du Goéland argenté (*Larus argentatus michahellis*) dans le bassin du Rhône et en Suisse. *Nos Oiseaux* **29**: 313-335.
Géroudet, P. (1974). Notes marcassines sur la parade nuptiale de l'Outarde houbara *Chlamydotis undulata*. *Oiseau et RFO* **44**: 149-152.
Géroudet, P. (1982). Le Goéland d'Arménie, *Larus (cachinnans) armenicus*, en Israël. *Alauda* **50**: 310-311.
Géroudet, P. & Juillard, M. (1990). [Attack of Saker Falcons on migrant Avocets off the coast of Palestine]. *Nos Oiseaux* **40(7)**: 429-430. In French.
Géroudet, P. & Landenbergue, D. (1977). Deuxième observation de la Sterna voyageuse *Sterna bengalensis* à Genève et en Suisse. *Nos Oiseaux* **34(4)**: 164-167.
Gerritsen, A.F.C. (1988). *Feeding Techniques and the Anatomy of the Bill in Sandpipers (*Calidris*)*. PhD thesis, University of Leiden, the Netherlands.
Gerritsen, A.F.C. & van Heezik, Y.M. (1985). Substrate foraging and substrate related foraging behaviour in three *Calidris* species. *Netherlands J. Zool.* **35**: 671-692.
Gerritsen, A.F.C. & Meiboom, A. (1986). The role of touch in prey density estimation by *Calidris alba*. *Netherlands J. Zool.* **36**: 530-562.
Gerritsen, A.F.C. & Sevenster, J.G. (1985). Foraging behaviour and bill anatomy in sandpipers. *Fortschr. Zool.* **30**: 237-239.
Gerritsen, G.J. (1990). [Night-time roosts of Black-tailed Godwits *Limosa limosa* in the Netherlands in 1984-1985]. *Limosa* **63**: 51-63. In Dutch with English summary.
Gerritsen, T. (1992). [Ecomorphology: tactile sense and taste in sandpipers]. *Limosa* **65**: 128-129. In Dutch with English summary.
Gewalt, W. (1959). *Die Grosstrappe*. Neue Brehm-Bücherei, Wittenburg-Lutherstadt.
Gewalt, W. (1992). [Advanced age of *Haematopus ater* in the Duisburg Zoo]. *Beitr. Vogelkd.* **38(2)**: 140-141. In German.
Gewalt, W. & Gewalt, I. (1966). Über Haltung und Zucht der Grosstrappe *Otis tarda* L. *Zool. Garten* **32**: 265-322.
Gibbon, G. (1989). Long-tailed Flufftail at Dzalanyama: first record for Malawi. *Nyala* **14(1)**: 46-47.
Gibbons, D., Reid, J.B. & Chapman, R.A. (1993). *The New Atlas of Breeding Birds in Britain and Ireland 1988-1991*. Poyser, Calton.
Gibbons, D.W. (1986). Brood parasitism and cooperative nesting in the Moorhen, *Gallinula chloropus*. *Behav. Ecol. Sociobiol.* **19**: 221-232.
Gibbons, D.W. (1987). Juvenile helping in the Moorhen, *Gallinula chloropus*. *Anim. Behav.* **35**: 170-181.
Gibbons, D.W. (1989). Seasonal reproductive success of the Moorhen *Gallinula chloropus*: the importance of male weight. *Ibis* **131**: 57-68.
Gibbs, D. (1990). *Wallacea. A Site Guide for Birdwatchers*. Published privately, Berks.
Gibbs, D. (1996). Notes on Solomon Islands birds. *Bull. Brit. Orn. Club* **116(1)**: 18-25.
Gibbs, J.P., Shriver, W.G. & Melvin, S.M. (1991). Spring and summer records of the Yellow Rail in Maine. *J. Field Orn.* **62**: 509-516.
Gibson, D.D. & Kessel, B. (1989). Geographical variation in the Marbled Godwit and description of an Alaskan subspecies. *Condor* **91(2)**: 436-443.
Gibson, E. (1920). Further ornithological notes from the neighbourhood of Cape San Antonio, Province of Buenos Aires, III. *Ibis* **Ser. 11, no. 2**: 1-97.
Gibson, F. (1971a). The breeding biology of the American Avocet (*Recurvirostra americana*) in Central Oregon. *Condor* **73(4)**: 444-454.
Gibson, F. (1971b). *Behavioral Patterns and their Temporal Organization in Breeding American Avocets*. PhD thesis, Oregon State University, Corvallis, Oregon.
Gibson, F. (1978). Ecological aspects of the time budget of the American Oystercatcher. *Amer. Midl. Nat.* **99(1)**: 65-82.
Gibson, J.D. (1956). Display flights of the Crested Tern. *Emu* **56**: 131-132.
Gibson, J.D. (1979). Growth in the population of the Silver Gull on the Five Islands group, New South Wales. *Corella* **3**: 103-104.
Gibson, L. (1979). Breeding *Laterallus leucopyrrhus*. *Avicult. Mag.* **85**: 63-67.
Gibson-Hill, C.A. (1947). Notes on the birds of Christmas Island. *Bull. Raffles Mus., Singapore* **18**: 87-165.
Gichuki, N. (1989). Spotted Thick-knee *Burhinus capensis* in Arabuko-sokoke Forest. *Bull. East Afr. Nat. Hist. Soc.* **19(4)**: 56.
Gichuki, N.N. (1993). *Factors Affecting the Reproductive Success of the Grey Crowned Crane*. PhD dissertation, University of Cambridge, Cambridge.
Gichuki, N.N. & Gichuki, C.M. (1991). Relationships between habitat selection and flock characteristics in foraging Grey Crowned Cranes, *Balearica regulorum*, in Kenya. Pp. 357-361 in: Harris (1991b).
Gifford, E.W. (1913). *Expedition of the California Academy of Sciences to the Galapagos Islands, 1905 1906. VIII. The Birds of the Galapagos Islands with Observations on the Birds of the Cocos and Clipperton Islands (Columbiformes to Pelecaniformes)*. Proceedings of the California Academy of Sciences (Series 4) **2**. 132 pp.
Gilbert, P.A. (1936). Field notes on *Rallus pectoralis*. *Emu* **36**: 72-73.
Gill, F.B. (1964). The shield color and relationships of certain Andean Coots. *Condor* **66**: 209-211.
Gill, F.B. (1970). Birds of Innisfall and Hinterland. *Emu* **70**: 105-116.
Gill, H.B. (1969). First record of the Sarus Crane in Australia. *Emu* **69**: 49-52.
Gill, R.E. (1986). What won't Turnstones eat? *British Birds* **79**: 402-403.
Gill, R.E. & Handel, C.M. (1981). Shorebirds of the eastern Bering Sea. In: Hood, D.W. & Calder, J.A. eds. (1981). *The Eastern Bering Sea Shelf: Oceanography and Resources*. University Washington Press, Seattle, Washington.
Gill, R.E. & Handel, C.M. (1990). The importance of subarctic intertidal habitats to shorebirds: a study of the central Yukon-Kuskokwim Delta, Alaska (USA). *Condor* **92**: 709-725.
Gill, R.E. & Mewaldt, L.R. (1983). Pacific Coast Caspian Terns: dynamics of an expanding population. *Auk* **100**: 369-381.
Gill, R.E. & Redmond, R.L. (1992). Distribution, numbers and habitat of Bristle-thighed Curlews (*Numenius tahitiensis*) on Rangiroa Atoll. *Notornis* **39(1)**: 17-26.
Gill, R.E., Handel, C.M. & Shelton, L.A. (1983). Memorial to a Black Turnstone: an exemplar of breeding and wintering site fidelity. *North Amer. Bird Bander* **8(3)**: 98-101.
Gill, R.E., Lanctot, R.B., Mason, J.B. & Handel, C.M. (1991). Observations on habitat use, breeding chronology and parental care in Bristle-thighed Curlews on the Seward Peninsula, Alaska. *Wader Study Group Bull.* **61**: 28-36.
Gill, R.E., McCaffery, B.J. & Tobish, T.G. (1988). Bristle-thighed Curlews, biologists and bird tours - a place for all. *Birding* **20**: 148-155.
Gill, R.G. (1965). Some observations on the Red-necked Rail. *Emu* **64**: 321-322.
Gillett, W.H., Hayward, J.L. & Stout, J.F. (1975). Effects of human activity on egg and chick mortality in a Glaucous-winged Gull colony. *Condor* **77**: 492-495.
Gilliard, E.T. & Lecroy, M. (1961). Birds of the Victor Emmanuel and Hindenburg Mountains, New Guinea. Results of the American Museum of Natural History expedition to New Guinea in 1954. *Bull. Amer. Mus. Nat. Hist.* **125**: 1-86.
Gilliard, E.T. & Lecroy, M. (1966). Birds of the Middle Sepik Region, New Guinea. *Bull. Amer. Mus. Nat. Hist.* **132**: 247-275.
Gilliard, E.T. & Lecroy, M. (1967). Results of the 1958-1959 Gilliard New Britain expedition. *Bull. Amer. Mus. Nat. Hist.* **135**: 175-216.
Gilliland, K.M. (1992). *Foraging Ecology and Body Condition of Migrant Semipalmated Sandpipers,* Calidris pusilla*, on Three Mudflats in the Bay of Fundy Hemispheric Shorebird Reserve, Nova Scotia*. MSc thesis, Acadia University, Nova Scotia, Canada.
Gilmour, J.G. (1972). Corncrakes breeding in Stirlingshire. *Scottish Birds* **7**: 52.
Ginn, P.J. (1977a). The bellyflop bird. *Afr. Wildl.* **31**: 38-39.
Ginn, P.J. (1977b). The elusive African Finfoot. *Fauna & Flora* **28**: 12-14.
Ginn, P.J. (1991). Temminck's Courser breeding on unburnt land. *Honeyguide* **37(1)**: 15-16.
Ginn, P.J., McIlleron, W.G. & Milstein, P. le S. eds. (1989). *The Complete Book of Southern African Birds*. Struik Publishers Ltd, Cape Town.
Girard, O. (1992). Wader migration in continental France: synthesis of the literature. *Alauda* **60**: 13-33.
Girard, O. & Yésou, P. (1989). [The breeding biology of the Avocet (*Recurvirostra avosetta*) in the Olonne marsh: chronology, nest success]. *Gibier Faune Sauvage* **6**: 225-243. In French with English and German summaries.
Girard, O. & Yésou, P. (1991). [Spatial development of an Avocet colony (*Recurvirostra avosetta*)]. *Gibier Faune Sauvage* **8**: 31-42. In French with English and German summaries.
Giraudoux, P., Degauquier, R., Jones, P.J., Weigel, J. & Isenmann, P. (1988). Avifaune du Niger: état des connaissances en 1986. *Malimbus* **10**: 1-140.
Giroux, J.F. (1985). Nest sites and superclutches of American Avocets on Artificial Islands. *Can. J. Zool.* **63(6)**: 1302-1305. In English with French summary.
Givens, T.V. (1948). Notes on the White-browed Crake. *Emu* **48**: 141-147.
Gizenko, A.I. (1955). [*Birds of Sakhalin Province*]. Academy of Sciences Press, Moscow, Russia. In Russian.
Gladkov, N.A. (1949). [Observations of birds on Komsomolsky Island on the Aral Sea]. Pp. 29-43 in: [*Nature Preservation*]. Vol. 8. Society for Nature Preservation. In Russian.
Gladkov, N.A. (1957). Der Rotkehlige Strandläufer ist eine Selbstandige Art. *J. Orn.* **98**: 195-203.
Glahn, J.F. (1974). Study of breeding rails with recorded calls in north-central Colorado. *Wilson Bull.* **86**: 206-214.
Glasgow, L.L. (1958). *Contributions to the Knowledge of the Ecology of the American Woodcock,* Philohela minor *(Gmelin), on the Wintering Range in Louisiana*. PhD dissertation, Texas A & M College, College Station, Texas.
Glayre, D. & Magnenat, D. (1977). Nidifications de la Marouette de baillon et de la Marouette poussin à Chavornay. [Nesting of *Porzana pusilla* and *Porzana parva* at Chavornay]. *Nos Oiseaux* **34(1)**: 3-22. In French with English summary.
Gleeson, N.M., Fogarty, S.M., Player, J.L. & McKenzie, H.R. (1972). Black-billed Gulls extend breeding range north. *Notornis* **19(4)**: 330-334.
Glen, R.M. (1994). Notes and new distribution records of the Quail Plover *Ortyxelos meiffrenii*. *Scopus* **18**: 50-51.
Glenny, F.H. (1967). Main arteries in the neck and thorax of three Sun Grebes (Heliornithidae). *Auk* **84**: 431-432.
Gloe, P. & Busche, G. (1974). Zum Brutvorkommen des Austernfischers in Dithmarschen. *Orn. Mitt.* **26(8)**: 147 151.
Glue, D. & Morgan, R. (1974). Breeding statistics and movements of the Stone Curlew. *Bird Study* **21(1)**: 21-28.
Glustchenko, Y.N. & Dorogoi, I.V. (1986). [The Greater Yellowlegs (*Tringa melanoleuca*) - new species of avifauna of the USSR]. *Ornitologiya* **21**: 131-132. In Russian.
Glustchenko, Y.N. & Shibnev, Y.B. (1979). [New materials on the Asiatic Dowitchers on the Khanka Lake]. Pp. 67-74 in: [*Bird Biology of Southern Far East USSR*]. Vladivostok. In Russian.
Glutz von Blotzheim, U.N. (1972). [On the moult of *Charadrius hiaticula*, *dubius* and *alexandrinus*]. *J. Orn.* **113(3)**: 323-333. In German.
Glutz von Blotzheim, U.N. & Bauer, K.M. eds. (1982). *Handbuch der Vögel Mitteleuropas*. Vol. 8. Akademische Verlagsgesellschaft, Wiesbaden.
Glutz von Blotzheim, U.N., Bauer, K.M. & Bezzel, E. eds. (1973). *Handbuch der Vögel Mitteleuropas*. Vol. 5. Akademische Verlagsgesellschaft, Frankfurt am Main.
Glutz von Blotzheim, U.N., Bauer, K.M. & Bezzel, E. eds. (1975). *Handbuch der Vögel Mitteleuropas*. Vol. 6. Akademische Verslagsgesellschaft, Wiesbaden.
Glutz von Blotzheim, U.N., Bauer, K.M. & Bezzel, E. eds. (1977). *Handbuch der Vögel Mitteleuropas*. Vol. 7. Charadriiformes (2. Teil). Akademische Verlagsgesellschaft, Wiesbaden.
Goater, C.P. & Bush, A.O. (1986). Nestling birds as prey of breeding Long-billed Curlews, *Numenius americanus*. *Can. Field-Nat.* **100(2)**: 263-264.
Goater, C.P. & Bush, A.O. (1988). Intestinal helminth communities in Long-billed Curlews: the importance of congeneric host-specialists. *Holarctic Ecol.* **11**: 140-145.
Gochfeld, M. (1971a). Notes on a nocturnal roost of Spotted Sandpipers in Trinidad, West Indies. *Auk* **88**: 167-168.
Gochfeld, M. (1971b). Premature feather-loss - a 'new disease' of Common Terns on Long Island, New York. *Kingbird* **21**: 206-211.
Gochfeld, M. (1972). Observations on the status, ecology and behaviour of Soras wintering in Trinidad, West Indies. *Wilson Bull.* **84**: 200-201.

Gochfeld, M. (1973a). Observations on new or unusual birds from Trinidad, West Indies, and comments on the genus *Plegadis* in Venezuela. *Condor* **75**: 474-478.
Gochfeld, M. (1973b). Recent status of the Least Tern, *Sterna albifrons*, on the south shore of western Long Island. *Engelhardti* **6**: 1-9.
Gochfeld, M. (1975a). Developmental defects in Common Terns of western Long Island, New York. *Auk* **92**: 58-65.
Gochfeld, M. (1975b). Hazards of tail-first fish swallowing by young terns. *Condor* **75**: 345-346.
Gochfeld, M. (1976). Waterbird colonies of Long Island, New York. 3. Cedar Beach ternery. *Kingbird* **26**: 62-80.
Gochfeld, M. (1977a). Intraclutch variation and the uniqueness of the Common Tern's third egg. *Bird-Banding* **48**: 325-332.
Gochfeld, M. (1977b). Incipient distraction displays of the Least Tern. *Proc. Linn. Soc. N.Y.* **73**: 80-82.
Gochfeld, M. (1978a). Observations on feeding ecology and behavior of Common Terns. *Kingbird* **28**: 84-89.
Gochfeld, M. (1978b). Incubation behaviour in Common Terns: influence of wind speed and direction on orientation of incubation adults. *Anim. Behav.* **26**: 848-851.
Gochfeld, M. (1978c). Colony and nest site selection by Black Skimmers. *Proc. Colonial Waterbird Group* **1**: 78-90.
Gochfeld, M. (1979a). Prevalence of oiled plumage of terns and skimmers on western Long Island, New York: baseline data prior to petroleum exploration. *Environm. Pollut.* **20**: 123-130.
Gochfeld, M. (1979b). Breeding synchrony in Black Skimmers: colony vs. subcolonies. *Proc. Colonial Waterbird Group* **2**: 171-177.
Gochfeld, M. (1979c). Learning to eat by young Common Terns: consistency of presentation as an early cue. *Proc. Colonial Waterbird Group* **3**: 108-118.
Gochfeld, M. (1979d). Group adherence in emigration of Common Terns. *Bird-Banding* **50**: 365-366.
Gochfeld, M. (1980). Mechanisms and adaptive value of reproductive synchrony in colonial seabirds. Pp. 207-271 in: Burger, Olla & Winn (1980).
Gochfeld, M. (1981a). Responses of young Black Skimmers to high-intensity distress notes. *Anim. Behav.* **29**: 1137-1145.
Gochfeld, M. (1981b). Differences of behavioral responses of young Common Terns and Black Skimmers to intrusion and handling. *Colonial Waterbirds* **4**: 47-53.
Gochfeld, M. (1983a). The Roseate Tern: world distribution and status of a threatened species. *Biol. Conserv.* **25**: 103-125.
Gochfeld, M. (1983b). Colony site selection by Least Terns: the influence of physical characteristics. *Colonial Waterbirds* **6**: 205-213.
Gochfeld, M. & Burger, J. (1981). Age related differences in piracy of frigatebirds from Laughing Gulls. *Condor* **83**: 79-82.
Gochfeld, M. & Burger, J. (1982). Feeding enhancement by social attraction in the Sandwich Tern. *Behav. Ecol. Sociobiol.* **10**: 15-17.
Gochfeld, M. & Burger, J. (1987). Nest site selection: comparison of Roseate and Common Terns (*Sterna dougalli* and *S. hirundo*) in a Long Island, New York colony. *Bird Behaviour* **7**: 58-66.
Gochfeld, M. & Burger, J. (1994). Black Skimmer (*Rynchops niger*). No. **108** in: Poole & Gill (1994).
Gochfeld, M. & Ford, D.B. (1974). Reproductive success in Common Tern colonies near Jones Beach, Long Island, New York, in 1972: a hurricane year. *Proc. Linn. Soc. N.Y.* **72**: 63-76.
Gochfeld, M., Burger, J. & Jehl, J.R. (1984). The classification of the shorebirds of the world. Pp. 1-15 in: Burger & Olla (1984).
Gochfeld, M., Saliva, J., Lesser, F., Schukla, T., Bertrand, D. & Burger, J. (1991). Effects of color on cadmium and lead levels in avian contour feathers. *Arch. Environm. Contam. Toxicol.* **20**: 523-526.
Godfrey, W.E. (1986). *The Birds of Canada*. Revised edition. National Museum of Canada, Ottawa.
Godfrey, W.E. (1992). Subspecies of the Red Knot *Calidris canutus* in the extreme north-western Canadian arctic islands. Pp. 24-25 in: Piersma & Davidson (1992b).
Godman, F.C. (1872). Notes on the resident and migratory birds of Madeira and the Canaries. *Ibis* **Ser. 3, no. 2**: 209-224.
Goede, A.A. (1993). Longevity in homeotherms, the high lifespan and lifespan energy potential in Charadriiformes. *Ardea* **81**: 81-88.
Goede, A.A. (1994). Variation in the energy intake of captive Oystercatchers *Haematopus ostralegus*. *Ardea* **81**: 89-97.
Goede, A.A. & Nieboer, E. (1983). Weight variation of Dunlins *Calidris alpina* during post-nuptial moult, after application of weight data transformations. *Bird Study* **30**: 157-163.
Goede, A.A., Nieboer, E. & Zegers, P.M. (1990). Body mass increase, migration pattern and breeding grounds of Dunlins, *Calidris alpina alpina*, staging in the Dutch Wadden Sea in spring. *Ardea* **78**: 135-144.
Goeldi, E.A. (1896). A cigana (*Opisthocomus cristatus*), resenha ornithológica. *Bol. Mus. Paraense Hist. Nat. (Pará)* **1**: 167-184.
Goethe, F. (1937). Beobachtungen und Untersuchungen zur Biologie der Silbermöwe (*Larus a. argentatus* P.) auf der Vogelinsel Memmertsand. *J. Orn.* **85**: 1-119.
Goethe, F. (1963). Verhaltensunterschiede zwischen europäischen Formen der Silbermöwengruppe (*Larus argentatus-cachinnanas-fuscus*). *J. Orn.* **104**: 129-141.
Goethe, F. (1966). Austernfischer mit 36 Jahren altester freilebender Ringvogel. [Oystercatcher 36 years old - the oldest free living ringed bird]. *Vogelwarte* **23**: 313.
Goethe, F. (1969). Zur Einwanderung der Lachmöwe, *Larus ridibundus*, in das Gebiet der deutschen Nordseekuste und ihrer Inseln. *Bonn. zool. Beitr.* **20**: 164-169.
Goethe, F. (1973). Austernfischer (*Haematopus ostralegus*) brütet auf Hausdächen. [Oystercatcher breeding on the roof tops of houses]. *Vogelkdl. Ber. Niedersachsen* **5(1)**: 13 15.
Goetz, R.E., Rudden, W.M. & Snetsinger, P.B. (1986). Slaty-backed Gull winters on the Mississippi River. *Amer. Birds* **40**: 207-216.
Goldin, M.R. (1993). *Effects of Human Distrubance and Off-road Vehicles on Piping Plover Reproductive Success and Behavior at Breezy Point, Gateway National Recreation Area, New York*. MSc thesis, University of Massachusetts, Amherst, Massachusetts.
Goldizen, A.W., Goldizen, A.R. & Devlin, T. (1993). Unstable social structure associated with a population crash in the Tasmanian Native Hen *Tribonyx mortierii*. *Anim. Behav.* **46**: 1013-1016.
Goldstraw, P.W. & DuGuesclin, P.B. (1991). Bird casualties from collisions with a 500 kv transmission line in southwestern Victoria, Australia. Pp. 219-224 in: Harris (1991b).
Gole, P. (1981a). Black-necked Cranes in Ladakh. Pp. 197-203 in: Lewis & Masatomi (1981).
Gole, P. (1981b). Status survey of the Black-necked Crane wintering in Bhutan, February 1981. Unpublished report to WWF India.
Gole, P. (1987). Observing the Sarus. Pp. 107-114: in Archibald & Pasquier (1987a).
Gole, P. (1989a). *The Status and Ecological Requirements of the Sarus Crane. Phase I*. Ecological Society, Pune, India.
Gole, P. (1989b). The pair beside the lake. *ICF Bugle* **15(4)**: 1, 4-5.
Gole, P. (1991). Welfare of the tallest flying bird in the world. *J. Ecol. Soc.* **4**: 29-42.
Gole, P. (1992). *The Status and Ecological Requirements of the Sarus Crane. Phase II*. Ecological Society, Pune, India.
Gole, P. (1993a). *A Field Guide to the Cranes of India*. Ecological Society, Pune, India.
Gole, P. (1993b). On the trail of wintering Blacknecked Cranes in India. *J. Ecol. Soc.* **6**: 7-22.
Gole, P. (1995). The Black-necked Crane in the Indian subcontinent. Pp. 326-329 in: Prange *et al*. (1995).
Golley, M. & Stoddart, A. (1991). Identification of American and Pacific Golden Plovers. *Birding World* **4**: 195-204.
Gollop, B. (1989). The season June 1 - July 31 1989. Prairie provinces region. *Amer. Birds* **43**: 1330-1332.
Gollop, J.B. (1988). The Eskimo Curlew. Pp. 583-595 in: Chandler, W.J., Labate, L. & Wille, C. eds. (1988). *Audubon Wildlife Report*. Academic Press, New York.
Gollop, J.B., Barry, T.W. & Iversen, E.H. (1986). *Eskimo Curlew. A Vanishing Species?* Saskatchewan Natural History Society, Special Publications **17**.
Gollop, M.A. (1978). Status report on endangered wildlife in Canada: Whooping Crane. Committee on the Status of Endangered Wildlife in Canada. Environment Canada, Ottawa. 19 pp.
Golovach, O.F. & Dikiy, A.V. (1992). Changes in the range of the Great Bustard in the Ukraine during the last 100 years. *Bustard Studies* **5**: 20-30.
Golovina, N.M. (1988). [Distribution and breeding biology of the Black-tailed Godwit (*Limosa limosa*) and the Marsh Sandpiper (*Tringa stagnatilis*) in the southeastern part of Western Siberia]. Pp. 38-40 in: Flint & Tomkovich (1988). In Russian.
Golovkin, A.N. (1963). Murre *Uria* species and Black-legged Kittiwake *Rissa tridactyla* fish consumption during the nesting period in the Barents Sea. *Zoologicheskii Zhurnal* **42**: 408-416. (Translated into English by Environment Canada, 1983).
Golovkin, A.N. (1984). Seabirds nesting in the U.S.S.R.: the status and protection of populations. Pp. 473-486 in: Croxall, Evans & Schreiber (1984).
Golovushkin, M.I. (1988). [*Larus relictus* in north-west Mongolia]. *Vestnik Zoologica* **1988(3)**: 87. In Russian.
Golovushkin, M.I. & Ossipova, M.A. (1989). [On the colour polymorphism of the downy cover of the Relict Gull *Larus relictus*]. *Vestnik Zoologica* **1989(2)**: 61-63. In Russian.
Gómez, G.M. (1992). Whooping Cranes in southwest Louisiana: history and human attitudes. Pp. 19-23 in: Stahlecker (1992).
Gómez-Tejedor, H. & De Lope, F. (1995). Cleptoparasitismo en la Gaviota Sombría (*Larus fuscus*): selección de víctimas y diferencias entre clases de edad. [Kleptoparasitism in the Lesser Black-backed Gull (*Larus fuscus*): host selection and age-class differences]. *Ardeola* **42(1)**: 77-81. In Spanish with English summary.
Gonzales, P.C. & Rees, C.P. (1988). *Birds of the Philippines*. Haribon Foundation, Manila.
González, H., Blanco, P., Morera, F., Hernández, D. (1995). Registro de una población de Grullas (*Grus canadensis nesiotes*) en la provincia de Sanctí Spíritus. *El Pitirre* **8(1)**: 3.
González-García, F. (1993). *Avifauna de la Reserva de la Biosfera "Montes Azules", Selva Lacandona, Chiapas, México*. Acta Zoológica Mexicana (Nueva Serie) **55**. 86 pp.
González-Kirchner, J.P. & Sainz, M. (1990). Algunos datos sobre la alimentación de los pollos de la Cigüeñuela (*Himantopus himantopus*) en humedales de la provincia de Ciudad Real. [Some data on the food of Black-winged Stilt (*Himantopus himantopus*) chicks in wetlands of Ciudad Real (central Spain)]. *Doñana Acta Vertebrata* **17(1)**: 113-116. In Spanish with English summary.
Good, T.P. (1992). Experimental assessment of gull predation on the Jonah crab *Cancer borealis* (Stimpson) in New England rocky intertidal and shallow subtidal zones. *J. Exp. Mar. Biol. Ecol.* **157**: 275-284.
Goodall, J.D., Johnson, A.W. & Philippi, R.A. (1957). *Las Aves de Chile*. Vol. 2. Platt Establecimientos Gráficos, Buenos Aires.
Goodall, J.D., Philippi, R.A.B. & Johnson, A.W. (1945). Nesting habits of the Peruvian Gray Gull. *Auk* **62(3)**: 450-451.
Goodbody, I.M. (1955). The breeding of the Black-headed Gull. *Bird Study* **2**: 192-199.
Goodman, J.D. & Goodman, J.M. (1985). African Jacana carries young in Uganda. *Bull. East Afr. Nat. Hist. Soc.* **1985**: 53-54.
Goodman, P.S. (1992). Wattled Cranes on the Marromeu Floodplain. Page 155 in: Porter *et al*. (1992).
Goodman, S.M. & Storer, R.W. (1987). The seabirds of the Egyptian Red Sea and adjacent waters, with notes on selected Ciconiiformes. *Gerfaut* **77**: 109-145.
Goodman, S.M., Meininger, P.L., Baha el Din, S.M., Hobbs, J.J. & Mullié, W.C. eds. (1989). *The Birds of Egypt*. Oxford University Press, Oxford & New York.
Goossen, J.P. (1989). Surveys and conservation of Piping Plovers in Canada. *Wader Study Group Bull.* **57**: 53-57.
Goossen, J.P. (1990a). Piping Plover research and conservation in Canada. *Blue Jay* **48(3)**: 139-153.
Goossen, J.P. (1990b). Prairie Piping Plover conservation; annual report 1989. Canadian Wildlife Service, Ottawa. 34 pp.
Goossen, J.P., Butler, R.W., Stushnoff, B. & Stirling, D. (1982). Distribution and breeding status of Forster's Tern, *Sterna forsteri*, in British Columbia. *Can. Field-Nat.* **96**: 345-346.
Gordienko, N.S. (1991). [Biology and numbers of the Sociable Lapwing (*Chettusia gregaria*) in Kustanai steppe, Northern Kazakhstan]. *Orntiologiya* **25**: 54-61. In Russian with English summary.
Gore, J.A. (1987). Black Skimmers nesting on roofs in northwestern Florida. *Florida Field Nat.* **15**: 77-79.
Gore, J.A. (1991). Distribution and abundance of nesting Least Terns and Black Skimmers in northwest Florida. *Florida Field Nat.* **19(3)**: 65-72.
Gore, J.A. (1996). Least Tern. In: Rodgers, Kale & Smith (1996).
Gore, J.A. & Kinnison, M.J. (1991). Hatching success on roof and ground colonies of Least Terns. *Condor* **93**: 759-762.
Gore, M.E.J. (1989). First Malawi record of the White-crowned Plover. *Nyala* **13(1/2)**: 75-76.
Gore, M.E.J. (1990). *The Birds of the Gambia. An Annotated Checklist*. BOU Check-list **3**. 2nd revised edition. British Ornithologists' Union, London.
Gore, M.E.J. & Gepp, A.R.M. (1978). *Las Aves del Uruguay*. Mosca Hnos., Montevideo.
Gore, M.E.J. & Pyong-oh, W. (1971). *The Birds of Korea*. Royal Asiatic Society, Korea.
Gorenzel, W.P., Ryder, R.A. & Braun, C.E. (1981a). American Coot distribution and migration in Colorado. *Wilson Bull.* **93**: 115-118.
Gorenzel, W.P., Ryder, R.A. & Braun, C.E. (1981b). American Coot response to habitat changes in a Colorado marsh. *Southwest. Nat.* **26**: 59-65.
Gorenzel, W.P., Ryder, R.A. & Braun, C.E. (1982). Reproduction and nest site characteristics of American Coots at different altitudes in Colorado. *Condor* **84**: 59-65.
Goriup, P.D. (1981). Houbara Bustard research and conservation in Pakistan. *World Wildl. Fund. Yb.* **1980/81**: 214-217.
Goriup, P.D. (1982a). Behaviour of Black-winged Stilts. *British Birds* **75(1)**: 12-24.
Goriup, P.D. (1982b). Distraction behaviour of Great Bustard. *British Birds* **75(6)**: 288-289.
Goriup, P.D. (1983a). The decline of the Great Indian Bustard (*Ardeotis nigriceps*): a literature review. Pp. 20-38 in: Goriup & Vardhan (1983).
Goriup, P.D. (1983b). Houbara Bustard (*Chlamydotis undulata*) research and conservation in Pakistan. Pp. 267-272 in: Goriup & Vardhan (1983).
Goriup, P.D. ed. (1983c). *The Houbara Bustard in Morocco*. Al-Areen Wildlife Park, Bahrain.
Goriup, P.D. ed. (1985). *Proceedings of the International Symposiem on Bustards. Peshawar, Pakistan, 4-6 October, 1983*. Bustard Studies **3**.
Goriup, P.D. (1987). Selling out Africa's bustards. *Swara* **10(6)**: 20-22.
Goriup, P.D. ed. (1988). *Ecology and Conservation of Grassland Birds*. ICBP Technical Publication **7**, Cambridge.
Goriup, P.D. (1989). Status and conservation of bustards in the Arabian region with reference to falconry and population management. Pp. 271-280 in: Abdulaziz, H., Abu-Zinada, Goriup, P.D. & Nader, I.K. eds. (1989). *Wildlife Conservation and Development in Saudi Arabia*. National Commission for Wildlife Conservation and Development, Riyadh, Saudi Arabia.
Goriup, P.D. (1992a). The status, conservation and management of bustards. Unpublished report to ICBP Steppe and Grassland Bird Group.
Goriup, P.D. (1992b). Bustards in Russia and neighbouring countries. *Bustard Studies* **5**.
Goriup, P.D. (1994a). Little Bustard. *Tetrax tetrax*. Pp. 236-237 in: Tucker & Heath (1994).
Goriup, P.D. (1994b). Houbara Bustard. *Chlamydotis undulata*. Pp. 238-239 in: Tucker & Heath (1994).
Goriup, P.D. (1994c). Great Bustard. *Otis tarda*. Pp. 240-241 in: Tucker & Heath (1994).
Goriup, P.D. & Karpowicz, Z.J. (1983a). Short note on a study tour of Gujarat for the Lesser Florican (*Sypheotides indica*). Pp. 367-368 in: Goriup & Vardhan (1983).
Goriup, P.D. & Karpowicz, Z.J. (1983b). In search of Lesser Florican (*Sypheotides indica*). Pp. 369-371 in: Goriup & Vardhan (1983).
Goriup, P.D. & Karpowicz, Z.J. (1985). A review of the past and recent status of the Lesser Florican. *Bustard Studies* **3**: 163-182.
Goriup, P.D. & Mundkur, T. (1990). Good news about Bengal Floricans. *Bull. Oriental Bird Club* **12**: 10.
Goriup, P.D. & Parr, D.F. (1983). *Results of a Survey of Bustards in Turkey*. ICBP Study Report **1**, Cambridge.
Goriup, P.D. & Parr, D.F. (1985). Results of the ICBP bustard survey of Turkey, 1981. *Bustard Studies* **2**: 77-97.
Goriup, P.D. & Vardhan, H. eds. (1983). *Bustards in Decline*. Tourism and Wildlife Society of India, Jaipur.
Goriup, P.D., Osborne, P. & Everett, S.J. (1989). Bustards in Meru National Park, Kenya: a preliminary survey. *Bustard Studies* **4**: 52-67.
Gorman, G. (1995). Cranes on the Hungarian Hortobágy: Europe's most spectacular migration. *Birding World* **8(12)**: 453-455.
Gosling, A.P., Christmas, T.J., Parr, A.J. & Christmas, S.E. (1990). Origins of Black-headed Gulls (*Larus ridibundus*) wintering in central London. *Colonial Waterbirds* **13(2)**: 129-132.
Goss-Custard, J.D. (1969). The winter feeding ecology of the Redshank, *Tringa totanus*. *Ibis* **111**: 338-356.
Goss-Custard, J.D. (1970a). Feeding dispersion in some overwintering wading birds. Pp. 3-35 in: Crook, J.H. ed. (1970). *Social Behaviour in Birds and Mammals*. Academic Press, London.
Goss-Custard, J.D. (1970b). The responses of Redshank to spatial variations on the density of their prey. *J. Anim. Ecol.* **39**: 91-113.
Goss-Custard, J.D. (1976). Variation in the dispersion of Redshank *Tringa totanus* on their winter feeding grounds. *Ibis* **118**: 257-263.
Goss-Custard, J.D. (1977a). The ecology of the Wash. III. Density-related behaviour and the possible effects of a loss of feeding grounds on wading birds (Charadrii). *J. Appl. Ecol.* **14**: 721-739.

Goss-Custard, J.D. (1977b). Predator responses and prey mortality in Redshank, *Tringa totanus* (L.), and a preferred prey, *Corophium volutator* (Pallas). *J. Anim. Ecol.* **46**: 21-35.
Goss-Custard, J.D. (1985). Foraging behaviour of wading birds and the carrying capacity of estuaries. Pp. 169-188 in: Sibly & Smith (1985).
Goss-Custard, J.D. (1993). The effect of migration and scale on the study of bird populations: 1991 Witherby Lecture. *Bird Study* **40**: 81-96.
Goss-Custard, J.D. ed. (1996). *The Oystercatcher: from Individuals to Populations*. Oxford University Press, Oxford.
Goss-Custard, J.D. & Durell, S.E.A. (1983). Individual and age differences in the feeding ecology of Oystercatchers *Haematopus ostralegus* wintering on the Exe estuary, Devon. *Ibis* **125**: 155-171.
Goss-Custard, J.D. & Durell, S.E.A. (1987a). Age-related effects in Oystercatchers, *Haematopus ostralegus*, feeding on mussels, *Mytilus edulis*. 1. Foraging efficiency and interference. *J. Anim. Ecol.* **56**: 521-536.
Goss-Custard, J.D. & Durell, S.E.A. (1987b). Age-related effects in Oystercatchers, *Haematopus ostralegus*, feeding on mussels, *Mytilus edulis*. 2. Aggression. *J. Anim. Ecol.* **56**: 537-548.
Goss-Custard, J.D. & Durell, S.E.A. (1987c). Age-related effects in Oystercatchers, *Haematopus ostralegus*, feeding on mussels, *Mytilus edulis*. 3. The effect of interference on overall intake rate. *J. Anim. Ecol.* **56**: 549-558.
Goss-Custard, J.D. & Durell, S.E.A. (1988). The effect of dominance and feeding method on the intake rates of Oystercatchers, *Haematopus ostralegus*, feeding on mussels. *J. Anim. Ecol.* **57**: 827-844.
Goss-Custard, J.D. & Jones, R.E. (1976). The diets of Redshank and Curlew. *Bird Study* **23**: 233-243.
Goss-Custard, J.D. & Moser, M.E. (1988). Rates of change in the numbers of Dunlin, *Calidris alpina*, wintering in British estuaries in relation to the spread of *Spartina anglica*. *J. Appl. Ecol.* **25**: 95-109.
Goss-Custard, J.D., Caldow, R.W.G., Clarke, R.T., Durell, S.E.A., Urfi, J. & West, A.D. (1994). Consequences of habitat loss and change to populations of wintering migratory birds: predicting the local and global effects from studies of individuals. *Ibis* **137**(Suppl.): 56-66.
Goss-Custard, J.D., Clarke, R.T. & Durell, S.E.A. (1984). Rates of food intake and aggression of Oystercatchers *Haematopus ostralegus* on the most and least preferred mussel *Mytilus edulis* beds of the Exe estuary. *J. Anim. Ecol.* **53**: 233-245.
Goss-Custard, J.D., Durell, S.E.A. & Ens, B.J. (1982). Individual differences in aggressiveness and food stealing among wintering Oystercatchers, *Haematopus ostralegus* L. *Anim. Behav.* **30**: 917-928.
Goss-Custard, J.D., Durell, S.E.A., McGrorty, S. & Reading, C.J. (1982). Use of mussel *Mytilus edulis* beds by Oystercatchers *Haematopus ostralegus* according to age and population size. *J. Anim. Ecol.* **51**: 543 554.
Goss-Custard, J.D., Durell, S.E.A., McGrorty, S., Reading, C.J. & Clarke, R.J. (1981). Factors affecting the occupation of mussel (*Mytilus edulis*) beds by Oystercatchers (*Haematopus ostralegus*) on the Exe Estuary, Devon. Pp. 217 229 in: Jones, N.V. & Wolff, W.J. eds. (1981). *Feeding and Survival Strategies of Estuarine Organism*. Plenum Press, London.
Goss-Custard, J.D., Durell, S.E.A., Sitters, H. & Swinfen, R. (1982). Age structure and survival of a wintering population of Oystercatchers *Haematopus ostralegus*. *Bird Study* **29**: 83 98.
Goss-Custard, J.D., McGrorty, S., Reading, C.J. & Durell, S.E.A. (1980). Oystercatchers and mussels on the Exe Estuary. Pp. 161-185 in: *Essays on the Exe Estuary*. Devon Ass. Special Volume **2**.
Gosse, P.H. (1847). *The Birds of Jamaica*. John Van Voorst, London.
Gosselin, M. & David, N. (1975). Field identification of Thayer's Gull (*Larus thayeri*) in eastern North America. *Amer. Birds* **29**: 1059-1066.
Gossmann, F., Ferrand, Y. & Bastat, C. (1994). [Winter mortality of Woodcocks in France from ring recoveries]. Pp. 8-14 in: Kalchreuter (1994). In French with English summary.
Götmark, F. (1982). Coloniality in five *Larus* gulls: a comparative study. *Ornis Scand.* **13**: 211-224.
Götmark, F. (1984). Food and foraging in five European *Larus* gulls in the breeding season. *Ornis Fenn.* **61**: 9-18.
Götmark, F. (1989). Costs and benefits to eiders nesting in gull colonies: a field experiment. *Ornis Scand.* **20**: 283-288.
Götmark, F. (1990). A test of the information-centre hypothesis in a colony of Sandwich Terns *Sterna sandvicensis*. *Anim. Behav.* **39**: 487-489.
Götmark, F. & Ahlund, M. (1988). Nest predation and nest site selection among Eiders *Somateria mollissima*: the influence of gulls. *Ibis* **130**: 111-123.
Götmark, F. & Andersson, M. (1980). Breeding association between Common Gull *Larus canus* and Arctic Skua *Stercorarius parasiticus*. *Ornis Scand.* **11**: 121-124.
Götmark, F. & Andersson, M. (1984). Colonial breeding reduces nest predation in the Common Gull (*Larus canus*). *Anim. Behav.* **32**: 485-492.
Götmark, F., Andersson, M. & Hildén, O. (1981). Polymorphism in the Arctic Skua *Stercorarius parasiticus* in NE Norway. *Ornis Fenn.* **58**: 49-55.
Gould, P.J. (1967). Nocturnal feeding of *Sterna fuscata* and *Puffinus pacificus*. *Condor* **69**: 529.
Gould, P.J. (1974). Sooty Tern *Sterna fuscata*. *Smithsonian Contrib. Zool.* **158**: 6-52.
Gould, P.J., Forsell, D.J. & Lensink, C.J. (1982). *Pelagic Distribution and Abundance of Seabirds in the Gulf of Alaska and Eastern Bering Sea*. US Fish & Wildlife Service Biological Service Prog. Rep. FWS/OBS-82-/48, Washington, D.C.
Goulding, M. (1980). *The Fishes and the Forest*. University of California Press, Berkeley.
Goutner, V. (1984). Belly-soaking in the Avocet. *Ostrich* **55(3)**: 167-168.
Goutner, V. (1985). Breeding ecology of the Avocet *Recurvirostra avosetta* in the Evros delta (Greece). *Bonn. zool. Beitr.* **36**: 37-50.
Goutner, V. (1986). Distribution, status and conservation of the Mediterranean Gull (*Larus melanocephalus*) in Greece. Pp. 431-447 in: MEDMARAVIS & Monbailliu (1986).
Goutner, V. (1987). Vegetation preferences by colonies of Mediterranean Gulls (*Larus melanocephalus*) and Gull-billed Terns (*Gelochelidon nilotica*) in the Evros delta. *Seevoegel* **8**: 29-31.
Goutner, V. (1989). Habitat selection by Black-winged Stilts *Himantopus himantopus* in a Macedonian wetland, Greece. *Avocetta* **13(2)**: 127-131.
Goutner, V. (1990). Habitat selection of Little Terns in the Evros Delta, Greece. *Colonial Waterbirds* **13**: 108-114.
Goutner, V. & Handrinos, G. (1990). The occurrence of Slender-billed Curlews *Numenius tenuirostris* in Greece. *Biol. Conserv.* **53(1)**: 47-60.
Goutner, V. & Isenmann, P. (1993). Breeding status of the Mediterranean Gull (*Larus melanocephalus*) in the Mediterranean Basin. Pp. 59-63 in: Aguilar *et al.* (1933).
Gowthorpe, P. (1979). Reproduction de Laridés et d'Ardéidès dans la delta du Siné-Saloum (Sénégal). *Oiseau et RFO* **49**: 105-112.
Grace, J.W. (1980). Cleptoparasitism by Ring-billed Gulls of wintering waterfowl. *Wilson Bull.* **92**: 246-248.
Graczyk, R. (1980). [Current problems of protection and rehabilitation of the Great Bustard (*Otis tarda*) in Europe]. *Z. Jagdwiss.* **26(1)**: 22-32. In German.
Graeme, A. (1989). Minding the New Zealand Dotterel's business. *For. Bird* **20(3)**: 30-32.
Graham, F. (1982). *Gulls: an Ecological History*. Van Nostrand Reinhold, New York.
Graham, G.L., Graves, G.R., Schulenberg, T.S. & O'Neill, J.P. (1980). Seventeen bird species new to Peru from the Pampas de Heath. *Auk* **97**: 366-370.
Graham, J.M.D. & Brooke, R.K. (1985). Hartlaub's Gull. *Promerops* **169**: 13.
Graig, T.H., Craig, E.H. & Steele, E. (1985). Recent nesting and sight records of Mountain Plovers in northwestern New Mexico. *Southwest. Nat.* **30(3)**: 451-452.
Grajal, A. (1991). *The Nutritional Ecology and Digestive Physiology of the Hoatzin,* Opisthocomus hoazin*, a Folivorous Bird with Foregut Fermentation*. PhD dissertation, University of Florida, Gainesville, Florida.
Grajal, A. (1995a). Digestive efficiency of the Hoatzin, *Opisthocomus hoazin*: a folivorous bird with foregut fermentantion. *Ibis* **137(3)**: 383-388.
Grajal, A. (1995b). Structure and function of the digestive tract of the Hoatzin (*Opisthocomus hoazin*): a folivorus bird with foregut fermentation. *Auk* **112**: 20-28.
Grajal, A. & Parra, O. (1995). Passage rates of digesta markers in the gut of the Hoatzin, a folivorus bird with foregut fermentation. *Condor* **97**: 675-683.
Grajal, A. & Strahl, S.D. (1991). A bird with the guts to eat leaves. *Natural History* **8**: 48-54.
Grajal, A., Strahl, S.D., Parra, R., Domínguez, M.G. & Neher, A. (1989). Foregut fermentation in the Hoatzin, a neotropical leaf-eating bird. *Science* **245**: 1236-1238.
Granberg, B. (1978). Spetsstjartad snappa (*Calidris acuminata*) antraffad I sverige. [First record of the Sharp-tailed Sandpiper (*Calidris acuminata*) in Sweden]. *Vår Fågelvärld* **37(1)**: 63-66. In Swedish with English summary.
le Grand, G., Emmerson, K. & Martín, A. (1984). The status and conservation of seabirds in the Macaronesian islands. Pp. 377-391 in: Croxall, Evans & Schreiber (1984).
Grandidier, G. & Berlioz, J. (1929). Description d'une espèce nouvelle de Madagascar de la famille des Rallidés. *Bull. Acad. Malagache* **10**: 83.
Grant, G.S. (1978). Foot-wetting and belly-soaking by incubating Gull-billed Terns and Black Skimmers. *J. Bombay Nat. Hist. Soc.* **75**: 148-152.
Grant, G.S. (1979). Ring-billed Gulls feeding on date fruits. *Condor* **81**: 432-433.
Grant, G.S. (1981). Belly-soaking by incubating Common, Sandwich, and Royal Terns. *J. Field Orn.* **52**: 244-245.
Grant, G.S. & Hogg, N. (1976). Behavior of late-nesting Black Skimmers at Salton Sea, California. *Western Birds* **7**: 73-80.
Grant, G.S., Paganelli, C.V. & Rahn, H. (1984). Microclimate of Gull-billed Tern and Black Skimmer nests. *Condor* **86**: 337-338.
Grant, M.C. (1991a). Nesting densities, productivity and survival of breeding Whimbrel *Numenius phaeopus* in Shetland. *Bird Study* **38(3)**: 160-169.
Grant, M.C. (1991b). Relationships between egg size, chick size at hatching and chick survival in the Whimbrel *Numenius phaeopus*. *Ibis* **133(2)**: 127-133.
Grant, M.C. (1992). The effects of re-seeding heathland on breeding Whimbrel *Numenius phaeopus* in Shetland: I. Nest distributions. *J. Appl. Ecol.* **29(2)**: 501-508.
Grant, M.C., Chambers, R.E. & Evans, P.R. (1992a). The effects of re-seeding heathland on breeding Whimbrel *Numenius phaeopus* in Shetland: II. Habitat use by adults during the pre-laying period. *J. Appl. Ecol.* **29(2)**: 509-515.
Grant, M.C., Chambers, R.E. & Evans, P.R. (1992b). The effects of re-seeding heathland on breeding Whimbrel *Numenius phaeopus* in Shetland: III. Habitat use by broods. *J. Appl. Ecol.* **29(2)**: 516-523.
Grant, P.J. (1981). Identification of Semipalmated Sandpipers. *British Birds* **74(12)**: 505-509.
Grant, P.J. (1986). *Gulls: a Guide to Identification*. 2nd edition. Buteo Books, Vermillion, South Dakota.
Grant, P.J. (1988). Relict Gulls in China. *Birding World* **1**: 240-241.
Grant, P.J. & Scott, R.E. (1967). Identification of immature Mediterranean Gulls. *British Birds* **60**: 364-368.
Grant, P.J. & Scott, R.E. (1969). Field identification of juvenile Common, Arctic and Roseate Terns. *British Birds* **62**: 297-299.
Grant, P.J., Scott, R.E. & Wallace, D.I.M. (1971). Further notes on the 'portlandica' plumage phase of terns. *British Birds* **64**: 19-22.
Grant, P.R. (1971). Interactive behaviour of puffins (*Fratercula arctica* L.) and skuas (*Stercorarius parasiticus* L.). *Behaviour* **40**: 263-281.
Grant, P.R. & Nettleship, D.N. (1971). Nesting habitat selection by Puffins *Fratercula arctica* L. in Iceland. *Ornis Scand.* **2**: 81-87.
Grant-Mackie, J.A. (1980). Acquisition of a specimen of the New Caledonian Kagu (Cagou). *Notornis* **27(3)**: 292-293.
Granval, P. (1988a). Influence of the availability and accessibility of earthworms on the choice of habitats used by Woodcock (*Scolopax rusticola*, L.). Pp. 60-66 in: Havet & Hirons (1988).
Granval, P. (1988b). [Changes in the diet of the wintering Woodcock (*Scolopax rusticola* L.)]. Pp. 67-77 in: Havet & Hirons (1988). In French with English summary.
Granval, P. & Muys, B. (1992). Management of forest soils and earthworms to improve Woodcock (*Scolopax* sp.) habitats: a literature survey. *Gibier Faune Sauvage* **9**: 243-255.
Granval, P., Aliaga, R. & Soto, P. (1993). The impact of agricultural management on earthworms (Lumbricidae), Common Snipe (*Gallinago gallinago*) and the environmental value of grasslands in the Dives marshes (Calvados). *Gibier Faune Sauvage* **10**: 59-73.
Gratto, C.L. (1983). *Migratory and Reproductive Strategies of the Semipalmated Sandpiper*. MSc thesis, Queen's University, Kingston, Canada.
Gratto, C.L. (1988). Natal philopatry and age at first breeding of Semipalmated Sandpiper. *Wilson Bull.* **100**: 660-663.
Gratto, C.L. (as Gratto-Trevor, C.L.) (1991). Parental care in Semipalmated Sandpipers *Calidris pusilla*: brood desertion by females. *Ibis* **133**: 394-399.
Gratto, C.L. (as Gratto-Trevor, C.L.) (1992). Semipalmated Sandpiper (*Calidris pusilla*). No. **6** in: Poole *et al.* (1992-1993).
Gratto, C.L. & Cooke, F. (1987). Geographic variation in the breeding biology of the Semipalmated Sandpiper. *Ornis Scand.* **18**: 233-235.
Gratto, C.L. & Dickson, H.L. (as Gratto-Trevor, C.L.) (1994). Confirmation of eleptical migration in a population of Semipalmated Sandpipers. *Wilson Bull.* **106(1)**: 78-90.
Gratto, C.L. & Morrison, R.I.G. (1981). Partial postjuvenile wing moult of the Semipalmated Sandpiper *Calidris pusilla*. *Wader Study Group Bull.* **33**: 33-37.
Gratto, C.L., Cooke, F. & Morrison, R.I.G. (1983). Nesting success of yearling and older breeders in the Semipalmated Sandpiper *Calidris pusilla*. *Can. J. Zool.* **61**: 1133-1137.
Gratto, C.L., Fivizzani, A.J., Oring, L.W. & Cooke, F. (as Gratto-Trevor, C.L.) (1990). Seasonal changes in gonadal steroids of a monogamous versus a polyandrous shorebird. *Gen. Comp. Endocrin.* **80**: 407-418.
Gratto, C.L., Morrison, R.I.G. & Cooke, F. (1985). Philopatry, site tenacity, and mate fidelity in the Semipalmated Sandpiper. *Auk* **102**: 16-24.
Gratto, C.L., Oring, L.W., Fivizzani, A.J., El Halawani, M.E. & Cooke, F. (as Gratto-Trevor, C.L.) (1990). The role of prolactin in parental care in a monogamous and a polyandrous shorebird. *Auk* **107**: 718-729.
Gratto, G.W., Thomas, M.L.H. & Gratto, C.L. (1984). Some aspects of the foraging ecology of migrant juvenile sandpipers in the outer Bay of Fundy. *Can. J. Zool.* **62**: 1889-1892.
Graul, W.D. (1971). Observations at a Long-billed Curlew nest. *Auk* **88**: 182-184.
Graul, W.D. (1973a). Adaptive aspects of the Mountain Plover social system. *Living Bird* **12**: 69-94.
Graul, W.D. (1973b). Possible functions of head and breast markings in Charadriinae. *Wilson Bull.* **85**: 60-70.
Graul, W.D. (1973c). *Breeding Adaptations in the Mountain Plover (*Charadrius montanus*)*. PhD dissertation, University of Minnesota, St. Paul, Minnesota.
Graul, W.D. (1974). Vocalizations of the Mountain Plover. *Wilson Bull.* **86(3)**: 221-229.
Graul, W.D. (1975). Breeding biology of the Mountain Plover. *Wilson Bull.* **87(1)**: 6-31.
Graul, W.D. (1976). Food fluctuations and multiple clutches in the Mountain Plover. *Auk* **93(1)**: 166-167.
Graul, W.D. & Webster, L.E. (1976). Breeding status of the Mountain Plover. *Condor* **78(2)**: 265-267.
Graves, G.R. (1981). New Charadriiform records from coastal Peru. *Gerfaut* **71**: 75-79.
Graves, G.R. (1982). First record of Brown Wood Rail (*Aramides wolfi*) for Peru. *Gerfaut* **72**: 237-238.
Graves, G.R. (1992). The endemic land birds of Henderson Island, southeastern Polynesia; notes on natural history and conservation. *Wilson Bull.* **104**: 32-43.
Gray, R.D. & Craig, J.L. (1991). Theory really matters: hidden assumptions in the concept of 'habitat requirements'. Pp. 2553-2560 in: Bell *et al.* (1991).
Grazhdankin, A.V. (1985). [The artificial eggs incubation and postembryonic development of the Sociable Plover's chick]. Pp. 24-29 in: [*Ecological Peculiarities of the Animals Conservation*]. Moscow. In Russian.
Grazhulyavichius, G.B. & Machalov, S.I. (1988). [Nesting of Little Stint (*Calidris minuta*) in the lower Big Chukochya river]. *Ornitologiya* **23**: 206-207. In Russian.
Grebmeier, J.M. & Harrison, N.M. (1992). Seabird feeding on benthic amphipods facilitated by gray whale activity in the northern Bering Sea. *Mar. Ecol. Prog. Ser.* **80**: 125-133.
Green, A.A. (1983). The birds of Bamingui-Bangoran National Park, Central African Republic. *Malimbus* **5**: 17-30.
Green, A.A. (1984). Additional bird records from Bamingui-Bangoran National Park, Central African Republic. *Malimbus* **6**: 70-72.
Green, A.A. & Carroll, R.W. (1991). The avifauna of Dzanga-Ndoki National Park and Dzanga-Sangha Rainforest reserve, Central African Republic. *Malimbus* **13**: 49-66.
Green, G.H., Greenwood, J.J.D. & Lloyd, C.S. (1977). The influence of snow conditions on the date of breeding in waders in north-east Greenland. *J. Zool., London* **183**: 311-328.
Green, I. & Moorhouse, N. (1995). *A Birdwatchers' Guide to Turkey*. Prion Ltd, Perry, UK.
Green, R. (1956). Notes on the inland breeding of the Red-capped Dotterel. *Emu* **56**: 140-143.
Green, R.E. (1984). Feeding and breeding of Common Snipe. *Ibis* **126**: 457.
Green, R.E. (1985). Growth of Snipe chicks *Gallinago gallinago*. *Ringing & Migration* **6**: 1-5.
Green, R.E. (1988a). Effects of environmental factors on the timing and success of breeding of Common Snipe *Gallinago gallinago* (Aves: Scolopacidae). *J. Appl. Ecol.* **25**: 79-93.
Green, R.E. (1988b). Stone-curlew conservation. *RSPB Conserv. Rev.* **2**: 30-33.
Green, R.E. (1991). Sex differences in the behaviour and measurements of Common Snipes *Gallinago gallinago* breeding in Cambridgeshire, England. *Ringing & Migration* **12(2)**: 57-60.
Green, R.E. & Bowden, C.G.R. (1986). Field characters for ageing and sexing Stone-curlews. *British Birds* **79(9)**: 419-422.
Green, R.E. & Tyler, G.A. (1989). Determination of the diet of the Stone Curlew (*Burhinus oedicnemus*) by faecal analysis. *J. Zool., London* **217(2)**: 311-320.

Green, R.E., Cadbury, C.J. & Williams, J. (1987). Floods threaten Black-tailed Godwits breeding in the Ouse Washes. *RSPB Conserv. Rev.* **1**: 14-16.
Green, R.E., Hirons, G.J.M. & Cresswell, B.H. (1990). Foraging habitats of female Common Snipe *Gallinago gallinago* during the incubation period. *J. Appl. Ecol.* **27**: 325-335.
Green, R.E., Hirons, G.J.M. & Kirby, J.S. (1990). The effectiveness of nest defense by Black-tailed Godwits *Limosa limosa*. *Ardea* **78**: 405-413.
Green, R.H. (1963). A forgotten record. *Emu* **62**: 240.
Green, R.H. (1965). Impact of rabbits on predators and prey. *Tasmanian Nat.* **3**: 2.
Green, R.H. (1989). *The Birds of Tasmania*. Potaroo Press, Launceston.
Greenhalgh, C.M. (1952). Food habits of the California Gull in Utah. *Condor* **54**: 302-308.
Greenhalgh, M.E. (1974). Population growth and breeding success in a saltmarsh Common Tern colony. *Scottish Naturalist* **931**: 121-127.
Greenhalgh, M.E. & Greenwood, M.S. (1976). Observations on the establishment of a Herring Gull and Lesser Black-backed Gull colony. *Seabird Report* **1975-76**: 21-27.
Greenham, R. & Greenham, L.M. (1975). Blackhead Plover nesting. *Bull. East Afr. Nat. Hist. Soc.* **1975**: 66-67.
Greenlaw, J.S. & Miller, R.F. (1982). Breeding Soras on a Long Island salt marsh. *Kingbird* **32**: 78-84.
Greenway, J.C. (1952). *Tricholimnas conditicius* is probably a synonym of *Tricholimnas sylvestris*. *Breviora* **5**: 1-4.
Greenway, J.C. (1967). *Extinct and Vanishing Birds of the World*. Dover Publications, New York.
Greenwood, J.G. (1979). *Geographical Variation in the Dunlin* Calidris alpina *(L.)*. PhD thesis, Liverpool Polytechnic, Liverpool.
Greenwood, J.G. (1983). Post-nuptial primary moult in Dunlin *Calidris alpina*. *Ibis* **125**: 223-228.
Greenwood, J.G. (1984). Migrations of Dunlin *Calidris alpina*: a worldwide overview. *Ringing & Migration* **5**: 35-39.
Greenwood, J.G. (1986). Geographical variation and taxonomy of the Dunlin *Calidris alpina* (L.). *Bull. Brit. Orn. Club* **106**: 43-56.
Greenwood, J.G. (1987). Winter visits by Black Guillemots *Cepphus grylle* to an Irish breeding site. *Bird Study* **34**: 135-136.
Greer, J.K. & Greer, M. (1967). Notes on hatching and growth of the Southern Lapwing in Chile. *Auk* **84**: 121-122.
Gregory, J.F. (1987). *Food Habits and Preferences of American Woodcock Wintering in Young Pine Plantations of East Texas*. MSc thesis, Stephen F. Austin State University, Nacogdoches, Texas.
Gregory, M. (1907). The Trumpeter bird (*Psophia crepitans*). *Avicult. Mag.* **6**: 31-32.
Gregory, P. (1995a). Memorable Myola, October 1995. *Muruk* **7(3)**: 107-112.
Gregory, P. (1995b). *The Birds of the OK Tedi Area*. National Library of Papua New Guinea, Tabubil, Papua New Guinea.
Gregory, P.A. (1992). A first record of Black-winged Pratincole (*Glareola nordmanni*) from Seychelles. *Tauraco* **2(1)**: 24. In English with French summary.
Gregory, R.D. (1987). Comparative winter feeding ecology of Lapwings *Vanellus vanellus* and Golden Plovers *Pluvialis apricaria* on cereals and grasslands in the lower Derwent valley, North Yorkshire. *Bird Study* **34(3)**: 244-250.
Gregson, J. (1986). Breeding the Little Black Bustard *Eupodotis afra* at the Paignton Zoological & Botanical Gardens. *Avicult. Mag.* **92**: 61-63.
Greij, E.D. (1994). Common Moorhen. In: Tacha & Braun (1994).
Gretton, A. (1990). Red data bird. Slender-billed Curlew. *World Birdwatch* **12(3)**: 11.
Gretton, A. (1991). *The Ecology and Conservation of the Slender-billed Curlew (*Numenius tenuirostris*)*. ICBP Monograph **6**, Cambridge.
Gretton, A. (1994). Slender-billed Curlew. *Numenius tenuirostris*. Pp. 276-277 in: Tucker & Heath (1994).
Gretton, A. (1995). Europe's rarest bird? *Birdwatch* **37**: 36-37.
Grice, D., Caughley, G. & Short, J. (1986). Density and distribution of the Australian Bustard *Ardeotis australis*. *Biol. Conserv.* **35**: 259-267.
Grieg, S.A., Coulson, J.C. & Monaghan, P. (1983). Age-related differences in foraging success in the Herring Gull (*Larus argentatus*). *Anim. Behav.* **31**: 1237-1243.
Griese, H.J., Ryder, R.A. & Braun, C.E. (1980). Spatial and temporal distribution of rails in Colorado. *Wilson Bull.* **92**: 96-102.
Grieve, A. (1987). Hudsonian Godwit: new to the Western Palearctic. *British Birds* **80(10)**: 466-473.
Grieve, S. (1885). *The Great Auk, or Garefowl* Alca impennis*, its History, Archaeology and remains*. Thomas C. Jack, London.
Griffiths, C.L. & Hockey, P.A.R. (1987). A model describing the interactive roles of predation, competition and tidal elevation in structuring mussel populations. *S. Afr. J. Mar. Sci.* **5**: 547-556.
Grimes, L.G. (1969). The Spotted Redshank in Ghana. *Ibis* **111**: 246-251.
Grimes, L.G. (1977). A radar study of tern movements along the coast of Ghana. *Ibis* **119**: 28-36.
Grimes, L.G. (1987). *The Birds of Ghana. An Annotated Checklist*. BOU Check-list **9**. British Ornithologists' Union, London.
Grimm, H. (1991). [Collectively fishing of Spotted Redshanks (*Tringa erythropus*)]. *Acta Ornithoecol.* **2**: 10. In German with English summary.
Grimmer, J.L. (1962). Strange little world of the Hoatzin. *Natl. Geogr.* **122**: 391-401.
Grimmett, R.F.A. & Jones, T.A. (1989). *Important Bird Areas in Europe*. ICBP Technical Publication **9**, Cambridge.
Grinnell, J. (1910). Birds of the 1908 Alexander Alaska Expedition with a note on the avifaunal relationships of the Prince William Sound District. *Univ. Calif. Publ. Zool.* **5**: 361 428.
Grinnell, J. (1921). Concerning the status of the supposed two races of the Long-billed Curlew. *Condor* **23**: 21-27.
Grisser, P. (1983). Observation d'un Vanneau sociable *Chettusia gregaria* (Pall.) en Dordogne. *Alauda* **51(3)**: 231-233.
Grisser, P. (1988). [Habitat use by the Snipe (*Gallinago gallinago*) in the inter-breeding season]. Pp. 20-22 in: Havet & Hirons (1988). In French with English summary.
Gristchenko, V.N. & Serebryakov, V.V. (1988). [Motion of spring migration of Lapwing (*Vanellus vanellus*) over Ukraine according to the phenological observations]. Pp. 41-44 in: Flint & Tomkovich (1988). In Russian.
Griveaud, P. (1960). Une mission de recherche de l'I.R.S.M. au lac Ihotry (S.E. Morombe, province de Tuléar). *Naturaliste Malgache* **12**: 33-41.
Groen, N.M. (1991). Origin of Black-tailed Godwits *Limosa limosa* wintering in Morocco. *Limosa* **64(2)**: 47-50.
Groen, N.M. (1993). Breeding site tenacity and natal philopatry in the Black-tailed Godwit *Limosa l. limosa*. *Ardea* **81(2)**: 107-113.
Gromadzka, J. (1983). Distribution of breeding sites and numbers of Southern Dunlin *Calidris alpina schinzii* on southern Baltic coast. *Not. Orn.* **24**: 31-36.
Gromadzka, J. (1985a). [Curlew Sandpiper]. In: Ilicev, V.O., Viksne, J.A. & Micheljson, H.A. eds. (1985). [*Migration of Birds of Eastern Europe and Northern Asia*]. Nauka, Moscow. In Russian.
Gromadzka, J. (1985b). Further observations on the wing plumage of Dunlins. *Wader Study Group Bull.* **44**: 32-33.
Gromadzka, J. (1986). Primary moult for adult Dunlins *Calidris alpina* of different age during autumn migration. *Vår Fågelvärld* **11**(Suppl.): 51-56.
Gromadzka, J. (1989). Breeding and wintering areas of Dunlin migrating through southern Baltic. *Ornis Scand.* **20**: 132-144.
Gromadzka, J. (1992). Knots on the Polish Baltic coast. Pp. 161-166 in: Piersma & Davidson (1992b).
Gromadzka, J. & Przystupa, B. (1984). Problems with ageing of Dunlins in autumn. *Wader Study Group Bull.* **41**: 19-20.
Gronow, R.W. (1969). Notes on breeding the Rufous-sided Crake (*Laterallus melanophaius*). *Avicult. Mag.* **75**: 100.
Groom, M.J. (1992). Sand-colored Nighthawks parasitize the antipredator behavior of three nesting species. *Ecology* **73(3)**: 785-793.
Grooms, S. (1992). *The Cry of the Sandhill Crane*. Northword Press, Minoqua, Wisconsin.
de Groot, T. (1993). [Long-billed Dowitcher at Oudega in August-October 1991]. *Dutch Birding* **15(2)**: 63-66. In Dutch with English summary.
Groothuis, T. (1989). On the ontogeny of display behavior in the Black-headed Gull. I. The gradual emergence of the adult form. *Behaviour* **109**: 76-124.
Groothuis, T. (1992). The influence of social experience on the development and fixation of the form of displays in the Black-headed Gull. *Anim. Behav.* **43**: 1-14.
Groothuis, T. & Mulekom, L.V. (1991). The influence of social experience on the ontogenetic change in the relation between aggression, fear and display behavior in Black-headed Gulls. *Anim. Behav.* **42**: 873-881.
Gross, A.O. (1945). The present status of the Great Black-backed Gull on the coast of Maine. *Auk* **62**: 241-256.
Grosskopf, G. (1958). Zur Biologie des Rotschenkels (*Tringa t. totanus*). *J. Orn.* **99**: 1-17.
Grosskopf, G. (1959). Zur Biologie des Rotschenkels (*Tringa t. totanus*). *J. Orn.* **100**: 210-236.
Grosskopf, G. (1963). Weitere Beiträge zur Biologie des Rotschenkels. *Vogelwelt* **84**: 65-83.
Grossler, K. (1977). Der Durchzug des Flußregenpfeifers, (*Charadrius dubius curonicus*), im Flut- und Klaerbeckengebiet von Leipzig. [The migration of (*Charadrius dubius curonicus*) in the Floodplain and adjacent areas of Leipzig]. *Beitr. Vogelkd.* **23(2)**: 107-116.
Grote, H. (1932). Über die Lebensweise von *Glareola nordmanni* Nordm. *Beitr. Fortpflanzungsbiol. Vögel* **8**: 14-17.
Grote, H. (1951). Zur Lebensweise und Verbreitung von *Haematopus ostralegus longipes* Burturl. *J. Orn.* **79**: 346 349.
Grover, P.B. & Knopf, F.L. (1982). Habitat requirements and breeding success of Charadriiform birds nesting at Salt Plains National Wildlife Refuge, Oklahoma. *J. Field Orn.* **53**: 139-148.
Groves, F.H. (1977). Chick retrieval by Black Skimmer. *Florida Field Nat.* **5**: 48-49.
Groves, S. (1978a). Age-related differences in Ruddy Turnstone foraging and aggressive behavior. *Auk* **95**: 95-103.
Groves, S. (1978b). Sibling rivalry and its effect on growth of Black Oystercatcher chicks. *Pacific Seabird Group Bull.* **5(2)**: 69.
Groves, S. (1982). *Aspects of Foraging in Black Oystercatchers (Aves: Haematopodidae)*. PhD thesis, University of British Columbia, Vancouver.
Groves, S. (1984). Chick growth, sibling rivalry, and chick production in American Black Oystercatchers. *Auk* **101(3)**: 525-531.
Grow, R. (1978). A kleptoparasitic action by Bonaparte's Gulls on Yellowlegs. *Indiana Audubon Quarterly* **56**: 178-179.
Gruber, D. (1995). Die Kennzeichen und das Vorkommen der Weißkopfmöwe *Larus cachinnans* in Europa. [Identification and remarks on the occurrence of *Larus cachinnans* in Europe]. *Limicola* **9(3)**: 121-165. In German with English summary.
Grubh, B.R. (1968). Greyheaded Lapwing *Vanellus cinereus* (Blyth): new record for Rajasthan. *J. Bombay Nat. Hist. Soc.* **65(2)**: 484.
Grzimek, B. ed. (1968). *Animal Life Encyclopedia*. Vol. 8. Birds, 2. Van Nostrand Reinhold Company, New York.
Guay, J.W. (1968). *The Breeding Biology of Franklin's Gull (*Larus pipixcan*)*. PhD dissertation, University of Alberta, Edmonton, Canada.
Gubin, B.M. (1992). The numbers, distribution and state of protection of the Houbara Bustard in the south of Kazakhstan. *Bustard Studies* **5**: 98-103.
Gubkin, A.A. (1988). [Black-winged Stilt (*Himantopus himantopus*) in Dnepropetrovsk Country and perspectives of its protection]. *Ornitologiya* **23**: 207-208. In Russian.
Gudmundsson, G.A. (1993). The spring migration pattern of arctic birds in SW Iceland, as recorded by radar. *Ibis* **135**: 166-176.
Gudmundsson, G.A. (1994). Spring migration of the Knot *Calidris c. canutus* over southern Scandinavia, as recorded by radar. *J. Avian Biol.* **25(1)**: 15-26.
Gudmundsson, G.A. & Alerstam, T. (1992). Spring staging of nearctic Knot in Iceland. Pp. 110-113 in: Piersma & Davidson (1992b).
Gudmundsson, G.A. & Gardarsson, A. (1992). The number and distribution of Knots in Iceland in May 1990: preliminary results of an aerial survey. Pp. 118-120 in: Piersma & Davidson (1992b).
Gudmundsson, G.A. & Lindström, Å. (1992). Spring migration of Sanderlings *Calidris alba* through SW Iceland: where from and where to? *Ardea* **80(3)**: 315-326.
Gudmundsson, G.A., Lindström, Å. & Alerstam, T. (1991). Optimal fat loads and long-distance flights by migrating Knots *Calidris canutus*, Sanderlings *Calidris alba* and Turnstones *Arenaria interpres*. *Ibis* **133(2)**: 140-152.
Guerra, C.G. & Cikutovic, M.A. (1983a). Un nuevo sitio de nidificación para la Garuma *Larus modestus* (Aves, Charadriiformes; Laridae). *Estudios Oceanológicos* **3**: 13-20.
Guerra, C.G. & Cikutovic, M.A. (1983b). Alimentación y morfología comparada entre adultos y juveniles de la Garuma *Larus modestus*. *Memorias Asoc. Latino Amer. Acuicultura ALA* **5**: 41.
Guerra, C.G. & Fitzpatrick, L.C. (1987). Albinism in the Gray Gull *Larus modestus* in northern Chile. *Gerfaut* **77**: 275-279.
Guerra, C.G., Aguilar, R.E. & Fitzpatrick, L.C. (1988). Water vapor conductance in Gray Gulls (*Larus modestus*) eggs: adaptation to desert nesting. *Colonial Waterbirds* **11(1)**: 107-109.
Guerra, C.G., Fitzpatrick, L.C. & Aguilar, R.E. (1988). Growth rates in Gray Gulls *Larus modestus*: influence of desert nesting and foraging distance. *Auk* **105**: 779-783.
Guerra, C.G., Fitzpatrick, L.C., Aguilar, R.E. & Luna, G.S. (1988). Location and description of new nesting sites for Gray Gulls *Larus modestus* in the Atacama Desert, northern Chile. *Gerfaut* **78**: 121-129.
Guerra, C.G., Fitzpatrick, L.C., Aguilar, R.E. & Venables, B.J. (1988). Reproductive consequences of El Niño-Southern Oscillation in Gray Gulls (*Larus modestus*). *Colonial Waterbirds* **11(2)**: 170-175.
Gui Xiaojie (1991). Cranes wintering at East Dongting Lake. Pp. 113-114 in: Harris (1991b).
Guichard, G. (1955). Notes sur la biologie de la Sterne de Dougall (*Sterna d. dougallii*, Mont.). *Oiseau et RFO* **25**: 75-86.
Guichard, K.M. (1948). Notes on *Sarothrura ayresi* and three birds new to Abyssinia. *Bull. Brit. Orn. Club* **68**: 102-104.
Guillen, V. (1988). Variaciones de la población del Zarcillo (*Larosterna inca*: Aves) 1963 y 1985 en el litoral Peruano, con énfasis en la Isla Asia. Pp. 335-340 in: Salzwedel, H. & Landa, A.S. (1988). *Recursos y Dinámica del Ecosistema de Alforamiento Peruano*. Boletín Instituto del Mar Perú. Extraordinario.
Gullion, G.W. (1952). The displays and calls of the American Coot. *Wilson Bull.* **64**: 83-97.
Gullion, G.W. (1953a). Observation on molting of the American Coot. *Condor* **55**: 102-103.
Gullion, G.W. (1953b). Territorial behaviour in the American Coot. *Condor* **55**: 169-186.
Gullion, G.W. (1954). The reproductive cycle of American Coots in California. *Auk* **71**: 366-412.
Gunderson, M., Gunderson, E., Lease, E. & Moriarty, P. (1992). Nesting American Avocets in Big Stone County. *Loon* **64(2)**: 125-126.
Gunther, R. & Gunther, V. (1987). [The 1985 nesting of the Green Sandpiper (*Tringa ochropus*) in the northern suburbs of Berlin]. *Beitr. Vogelkd.* **33(1)**: 37-40. In German.
Guo Juting (1981). [The ecology of the Black-necked Crane *Grus nigricollis*]. *Wildlife* **4**: 35-38. In Chinese.
Guömundsson, F. (1954). Islenzkir Fuglar X: Svartbakur (*Larus marinus*). *Natturufraedingurinn* **24**: 177-183. In Icelandic with English Summary.
Guömundsson, F. (1955). Islenzkir Fuglar XI: Hvitmafur (*Larus hyperboreus*). *Natturufraedingurinn* **25**: 24-35.
Gupta, P.D. (1975). Stomach contents of the Great Indian Bustard, *Choriotis nigriceps* (Vigors). *J. Bombay Nat. Hist. Soc.* **71**: 303-304.
Gurney, J.H. (1872). *Andersson's Notes on the Birds of Damaraland and the Adjacent Countries of South West Africa*. John Van Voorst, London.
Gurr, L. (1967). Interbreeding of *Larus novaehollandiae scopulinus* and *Larus bulleri* in the wild in New Zealand. *Ibis* **109**: 552-555.
Gurr, L. & Kinsky, F.C. (1965). The distribution of breeding colonies and status of the Red-billed Gull in New Zealand and its outlying islands. *Notornis* **12**: 223-240.
Gustafson, M.E. & Peterjohn, B.G. (1994). Adult Slaty-backed Gulls: variability in mantle color and comments on identification. *Birding* **26**: 243-249.
Guthery, F.S. & Lewis, J.C. (1979). Sandhill Cranes in coastal counties of Texas: taxonomy, distribution, and populations. Pp. 121-128 in: Lewis (1979a).
Guthova, Z. (1993). Variations in reproduction parameters of Black-headed Gulls (*Larus ridibundus*) living in different conditions in the Czech and Slovak Republics. *Environm. Cons.* **20(4)**: 347-351.
Guthrie-Smith, H. (1910). *Birds of Wood, Water and Waste*. Whitcombe & Tombs, Wellington.
Guthrie-Smith, H. (1914). *Mutton Birds and Other Birds*. Whitcombe & Tombs, Christchurch.
Guthrie-Smith, H. (1925). *Bird Life on Island and Shore*. Blackwood, Edinburgh.
Gutzwiller, K.J., Kinsley, K.R., Storm, G.L., Tzilkowski, W.M. & Wakeley, J.S. (1983). Relative value of vegetation structure and species composition for identifying American Woodcock breeding habitat. *J. Wildl. Manage.* **47**: 535-540.
Gwinner, E. ed. (1990). *Bird Migration: Physiology and Ecophysiology*. Springer-Verlag, Berlin.
Gyldenstolpe, N. (1945). The fauna of Rio Jurua in Western Brazil. *Kung. Svenska Vet. Handl.* **22**: 1-338.
Gyldenstolpe, N. (1955). Notes on a collection of birds made in the Western Highlands, central New Guinea, 1951. *Ark. Zool., Ser. 2* **8**: 1-181.
Haagner, A. & Ivy, R.H. (1908). *Sketches of South African Bird-life*. R.H. Porter, London.
Haagner, A.K. (1948). A list of the birds observed in Beira and neighbourhood with some notes on habits, etc. Part 2. *Ostrich* **19**: 211 217.
Haagner, G.V. & Reynolds, D.S. (1988). Notes on the nesting of the African Crake at Manyeleti Game Reserve, Eastern Transvaal. *Ostrich* **59**: 45.

de Haan, G.A.L. (1950). Notes on the Invisible Flightless Rail of Halmahera (*Habroptila wallacii* Gray). *Amsterdam Nat.* **1**: 57-60.
von Haartman, L. (1980). Nest sites of the Common Gull *Larus canus* in relation to ice age geology and other factors. *Ornis Fenn.* **57**: 11-16.
von Haartman, L. (1982). The Arctic Tern *Sterna paradisaea* - a new inhabitant of the inshore Archipelago. *Ornis Fenn.* **59**: 63-76.
Haas, V., Mach, P., Lucchesi, J.L. & Boutin, J. (1988). La migration postnuptiale du Pluvier guignard *Eudromias morinellus*, Charadriidae dans le sud de la France. [The post-breeding migration of the Dotterel *Eudromias morinellus* in the south of France]. *Alauda* **56(4)**: 433-435.
Haasch, S.J. (1979). *Habitat Use and Ecology of the American Woodcock in Central Wisconsin*. MSc thesis, University of Wisconsin, Stevens Point, Wisconsin.
Haase, B.J.M. (1993). Sight record of Black-legged Kittiwake in Peru. *Amer. Birds* **47(3)**: 382-383.
Habraken, A. (1980). New Zealand Dotterel takes fish. *Notornis* **27(2)**: 159.
Hachisuka, M. (1931). *The Birds of the Philippines Islands, with Notes on the Mammal Fauna*. Vol. 1. Part 1. Witherby, London.
Hachisuka, M.U. (1952). What is the Amami Woodcock? *Bull. Brit. Orn. Club* **72**: 77-81.
Hackett, J. & Hackett, M. (1988). Broad-billed Sandpipers at Clinton Conservation Park. *S. Austr. Orn.* **30(5)**: 117.
Hackett, S.J. (1989). Effects of varied electrophoretic conditions on detections of evolutionary patterns in the Laridae. *Condor* **91**: 73-90.
Hackl, E. & Burger, J. (1988). Factors affecting kleptoparasitism in Herring Gulls at a New Jersey landfill. *Wilson Bull.* **100**: 424-430.
Hackney, M.J. (1940). Wood Snipe (*Capella nemoricola*) near Bombay. *J. Bombay Nat. Hist. Soc.* **41(3)**: 665.
Haddane, B. (1985). The Houbara Bustard in Morocco: a brief review. *Bustard Studies* **3**: 109-111.
Hadden, D. (1970). Notes on the Spotless Crake in the Waingaro District. *Notornis* **17**: 200-213.
Hadden, D. (1972). Further notes on the Spotless Crake. *Notornis* **19**: 323-329.
Hadden, D. (1981). *Birds of the North Solomons*. Vol. 8. Wau Ecological Institute, Wau, Papua New Guinea.
Hadden, D. (1993). First Spotless Crake's nest for the South Island. *Notornis* **40**: 231-232.
Haddon, P.C. & Knight, R.C. (1983). *A Guide to Little Tern Conservation*. Royal Society for Bird Protection, Sandy, UK.
Haefelin, K. (1987). [Propagation of the Red-wattled Lapwing (*Vanellus indicus*)]. *Gefiederte Welt* **111(10)**: 260-261. In German.
Haensel, J. (1991). Das Hindublatthühnchen. *Falke* **38(8)**: 278-279.
Haffer, J. (1968). Notes on the wing and tail molt of the Screamers and Sunbittern and immature guans. *Auk* **85**: 633-638.
Haffer, J. (1974). *Avian Speciation in Tropical South America*. Publications of the Nuttall Ornithological Club **14**. Cambridge, Massachusetts.
Hagar, J.A. (1937). Least Tern studies - 1935 and 1936. *Bull. Mass. Audubon Soc.* **21**: 5-8.
Hagar, J.A. (1966). Nesting of the Hudsonian Godwit at Churchill, Manitoba. *Living Bird* **5**: 5-43.
Hagar, J.A. (1983). The flight of the godwit. *Sanctuary* **22**: 3-6.
Hagar, J.A. & Anderson, K.S. (1977). Sight record of Eskimo Curlew (*Numenius borealis*) on west coast of James Bay, Canada. *Amer. Birds* **31**: 135-136.
Hagen, Y. (1952). *The Birds of Tristan da Cunha*. Results of the Norwegian Scientific Expedition to Tristan da Cunha 1937-38. No. **20**. Kommisjon Hos Jacob Dybwad, Oslo.
Hahn, D.C. (1981). Asynchronous hatching in the Laughing Gull: cutting losses and reducing rivalry. *Anim. Behav.* **29**: 421-427.
Hahn, T. & Denny, M. (1989). Tenacity-mediated selective predation by oystercatchers on intertidal limpets and its role in maintaining habitat partitioning by *'Collisella' scabra* and *Lottia digitalis*. *Mar. Ecol. Prog. Ser.* **53(1)**: 1-10.
Haig, S.M. (1985). *The Status of the Piping Plover in Canada*. National Museum of Canada, Ottawa.
Haig, S.M. (1986). *Piping Plover Distribution and Biology*. Endangered Species Information System Workbooks. US Fish & Wildlife Service, Washington, D.C.
Haig, S.M. (1987). *The Population Biology and Life History Patterns of the Piping Plover*. PhD dissertation, University of North Dakota, Grand Forks, North Dakota.
Haig, S.M. (1991). *Population Estimates for Piping Plovers*. Report to US Fish & Wildlife Service, Twin Cities, Minnesota.
Haig, S.M. (1992). Piping Plover (*Charadrius melodus*). No. **2** in: Poole *et al.* (1992-1993).
Haig, S.M. & Oring, L.W. (1985). The distribution and status of the Piping Plover throughout the annual cycle. *J. Field Orn.* **56**: 334-345.
Haig, S.M. & Oring, L.W. (1988a). Genetic differentiation of Piping Plovers across North America. *Auk* **105(2)**: 260-267.
Haig, S.M. & Oring, L.W. (1988b). Mate, site and territory fidelity in Piping Plovers. *Auk* **105(2)**: 268-277.
Haig, S.M. & Oring, L.W. (1988c). Distribution and dispersal in the Piping Plover. *Auk* **105(4)**: 630-638.
Haig, S.M. & Plissner, J.H. (1993). Distribution and abundance of Piping Plovers: results and implications of the 1991 international census. *Condor* **95(1)**: 145-156.
Haig, S.M., Ballou, J.D. & Derrickson, S.R. (1990). Management options for preserving genetic diversity: reintroduction of Guam Rails to the wild. *Conserv. Biol.* **4**: 290-300.
Haig, S.M., Ballou, J.D. & Derrickson, S.R. (1993). Genetic considerations for the Guam Rail. *Re-introduction News* **7**: 11-12.
Haig, S.M., Harrison, W., Lock, R., Pfannmuller, L., Pike, E., Ryan, M.R. & Sidle, J. (1988). *Recovery Plan for Piping Plover* Charadrius melodus *of the Great Lakes and Northern Great Plains*. US Fish & Wildlife Service, Jamestown, North Dakota.
Hailman, J.P. (1961). Age of Laughing Gull chicks indicated by tarsal length. *Bird-Banding* **32**: 223-226.
Hailman, J.P. (1963). Why is the Galapagos Lava Gull the color of Lava? *Condor* **65**: 528.
Hailman, J.P. (1964a). Breeding synchrony in the equatorial Swallow-tailed Gull. *Amer. Naturalist* **98**: 79-83.
Hailman, J.P. (1964b). The Galapagos Swallow-tailed Gull is nocturnal. *Wilson Bull.* **76**: 347-354.
Hailman, J.P. (1965). Cliff-nesting adaptations of the Galapagos Swallow-tailed Gull. *Wilson Bull.* **77**: 346-362.
Hailman, J.P. (1968a). Behavioral studies of the Swallow-tailed Gull. *Noticias de Galápagos* **11**: 9-11.
Hailman, J.P. (1968b). Visual-cliff responses of newly-hatched chicks of the Laughing Gull *Larus atricilla*. *Ibis* **110**: 197-200.
Hailman, J.P. & Reed, J.R. (1982). Head wind promotes skimming in Laughing Gulls. *Wilson Bull.* **94**: 223-225.
Hakala, A.V.K. (1975). An Ivory Gull colony at Lardyfjellet, Spitsbergen. *Sterna* **14**: 91-94.
Hale, W.G. (1971). A revision of the taxonomy of the Redshank *Tringa totanus*. *Zool. J. Linn. Soc.* **50**: 199-268.
Hale, W.G. (1973). The distribution of the Redshank *Tringa totanus* in the winter range. *Zool. J. Linn. Soc.* **53**: 177-236.
Hale, W.G. (1974). The taxonomic status of the Redshank in Hungary. *Aquila* **78/79**: 199-207.
Hale, W.G. (1980). *Waders*. Collins, London.
Hale, W.G. (1985). Sandpiper. Pp. 521-523 in: Campbell & Lack (1985).
Hale, W.G. & Ashcroft, R.P. (1982). Pair formation and pair maintenance in the Redshank (*Tringa totanus*). *Ibis* **124**: 471-490.
Hale, W.G. & Ashcroft, R.P. (1983). Studies of the courtship behaviour of the Redshank *Tringa totanus*. *Ibis* **125**: 3-23.
van Halewijn, R. (1990). [Voous' favourite species of the Antilles: the Yellow-billed Sandwich Tern]. *Vogeljaar* **38**: 127-133. In Dutch.
van Halewijn, R. & Norton, R.L. (1984). The status and conservation of seabirds in the Caribbean. Pp. 169-222 in: Croxall, Evans & Schreiber (1984).
Haley, D. ed. (1984). *Seabirds of Eastern North Pacific and Arctic Waters*. Pacific Search Press, Seattle, Washington.
Halkin, S.L. (1983). Resting birds tuck bills toward outside of group. *Auk* **100**: 997-998.
Hall, G.A. (1992). Lesser Golden-plover on Allegheny Front Mountain, West Virginia. *Redstart* **59(2)**: 46-47.
Hall, H.M. (1950). Wakulla Limpkins. *Audubon Magazine* **52**: 308-314.
Hall, J.A. (1988). Early chick mobility and brood movements in the Forster's Tern (*Sterna forsteri*). *J. Field Orn.* **59**: 247-251.
Hall, J.A. (1989). Aspects of Forster's Tern (*Sterna forsteri*) reproduction on Cobblestone Islands in southcentral Washington. *Northwest Science* **63**: 90-95.
Hall, J.A. & Miller, D.E. (1991). Orientation to the nest site by incubating Forster's Terns (*Sterna forsteri*) in a landmark-sparse habitat. *Northwestern Naturalist* **72**: 70-72.
Hall, K.R.L. (1958). Observations on the nesting sites and nesting behaviour of the Kittlitz's Sandplover *Charadrius pecuarius*. *Ostrich* **29**: 113-125.
Hall, K.R.L. (1959a). Nest records and additional behaviour for Kittlitz's Sand Plover *Charadrius pecuarius* in the S.W. Cape Province. *Ostrich* **30**: 33-38.
Hall, K.R.L. (1959b). A study of the Blacksmith Plover (*Hoplopterus armatus* Burchel) in the Cape Town area. *Ostrich* **30**: 117-125.
Hall, K.R.L. (1959c). Observations on the nest-sites and nesting behaviour of the Black Oystercatcher *Haematopus moquini* in the Cape Peninsula. *Ostrich* **30**: 143-154.
Hall, K.R.L. (1964). A study of the Blacksmith Plover (*Hoplopterus armatus* Burchel) in the Cape Town area. *Ostrich* **35**: 3-16.
Hall, K.R.L. (1965). Nest records and behaviour notes for three species of plovers in Uganda. *Ostrich* **36**: 107-108.
Hallager, S.L. (1994). Drinking methods in two species of bustards. *Wilson Bull.* **106**: 763-764.
Hallett, C.E., Casler, B.R. & Stern, M.A. (1995). Semipalmated Plover nesting on the Oregon coast. *Western Birds* **26(3)**: 161-164.
Halleux, D. (1994). Annotated bird list of Macenta Prefecture, Guinea. *Malimbus* **16**: 10-29.
Halpin, M. & Paul, D. (1989). Survey of Snowy Plovers in northern Utah - 1988. *Utah Birds* **5(2)**: 21-32.
Halse, S.A. & Jaensch, R.P. (1989). Breeding seasons of waterbirds in south-western Australia - the importance of rainfall. *Emu* **89**: 232-249.
Halvorson, C.H. & Kaliher, F. (1995). [A current assessment of cranes wintering in South Korea, January-March, 1992: needs and opportunities]. Pp. 81-85 in: Halvorson *et al.* (1995). In Russian.
Halvorson, C.H., Harris, J.T. & Smirenski, S.M. eds. (1995). [*Cranes and Storks of the Amur Basin: the Proceedings of the International Workshop*]. Arts Literature Publishers, Moscow. In Russian.
Hamann, M. (1988). [Breeding dispersal of the Little Ringed Plover (*Charadrius dubius*) in Gelsenkirchen in 1987 and a proposal for a species protection plan]. *Charadrius* **24(2)**: 61-66. In German with English summary.
Hamas, M.J. (1988). Delayed egg laying by Killdeer in northeastern Colorado. *Colorado Field Orn. J.* **22(4)**: 137-139.
Hamas, M.J. & Graul, W.D. (1985). A four-egg clutch of the Mountain Plover. *Wilson Bull.* **97(3)**: 388-389.
Hambler, C., Newing, J. & Hambler, K. (1993). Population monitoring for the Flightless Rail *Dryolimnas cuvieri aldabranus*. *Bird Conserv. Int.* **3**: 307-318.
Hamer, K.C. & Furness, R.W. (1991a). Age-specific breeding performance and reproductive effort in Great Skuas *Catharacta skua*. *J. Anim. Ecol.* **60(2)**: 693-704.
Hamer, K.C. & Furness, R.W. (1991b). Sexing Great Skuas *Catharacta skua* by discriminant analysis using external measurements. *Ringing & Migration* **12(1)**: 16-22.
Hamer, K.C. & Furness, R.W. (1993). Parental investment and brood defence by male and female Great Skuas *Catharacta skua*: the influence of food supply, laying date, body size and body condition. *J. Zool., London* **230(1)**: 7-18.
Hamer, K.C., Furness, R.W. & Caldow, R.W.G. (1991). The effects of changes in food availability on the breeding ecology of Great Skuas *Catharacta skua* in Shetland. *J. Zool., London* **223(2)**: 197-188.
Hamer, T.E. & Cummins, E.B. (1995). Relationships between forest characteristics and use of inland sites by Marbled Murrelets in northern Washington. Unpublished report, Nongame program, Washington Department of Wildlife, Olympia, Washington.
Hamilton, J. (1981). Recoveries of wintering Roseate Terns. *J. Field Orn.* **52**: 36-41.
Hamilton, J.E. (1934). The subantarctic forms of the Great Skua (*Catharacta s. skua* Brünn). *Discovery Rep.* **9**: 161-174.
Hamilton, R.B. (1969). *Comparative Behavior of the American Avocet (*Recurvirostra americana*) and the Black-winged Stilt (*Himantopus h. mexicanus*)*. PhD dissertation, University of California, Berkeley, California.
Hamilton, R.B. (1975). *Comparative Behaviour of the American Avocet and the Black-necked Stilt (Recurvirostridae)*. Ornithological Monographs **17**. American Ornithologists' Union, Washington, D.C.
Hamilton, W.J. (1959). Aggressive behavior in migrant Pectoral Sandpipers. *Condor* **61**: 161-179.
Hamling, H.H. (1949). King Reed-hen or Purple Gallinule. *Ostrich* **20**: 91-94.
Hamsch, S. (1987). Zur Biologie der Mesitornithiformes Madagaskars. *Falke* **5**: 160-162.
Hand, J.L. (1980). Human disturbance in Western Gulls *Larus occidentalis* living in colonies and possible amplification by intraspecific predation. *Biol. Conserv.* **18**: 59-63.
Hand, J.L. (1981a). Sociobiological implications of unusual sexual behaviors of gulls: the genotype/behavioral phenotype problem. *Ethol. Sociobiol.* **2**: 135-145.
Hand, J.L. (1981b). A comparison of vocalizations of Western Gulls (*Larus occidentalis occidentalis* and *L. o. livens*). *Condor* **83**: 289-301.
Hand, J.L. (1985). Egalitarian resolution of social conflicts: a study of pair-bonded gulls in nest duty and feeding contexts. *Z. Tierpsychol.* **70**: 123-147.
Hand, J.L. (1986). Territory defense and associated vocalizations of Western Gulls. *J. Field Orn.* **57**: 1-15.
Hand, J.L., Hunt, G.L. & Warner, M. (1981). Thermal stress and predation: influences on the structure of a gull colony and possibly on breeding distributions. *Condor* **83**: 193-203.
Hand, J.L., Southern, W.E. & Vermeer, K. eds. (1987). *Ecology and Behaviour of Gulls*. Studies in Avian Biology **10**.
Handel, C.M. (1982). *Breeding Ecology of the Black Turnstone: a Study in Behavior and Energetics*. MSc thesis, University of California, Davis, California.
Handel, C.M. & Dau, C.P. (1988). Seasonal occurrence of migrant Whimbrels and Bristle-thighed Curlews on the Yukon-Kuskokwim Delta, Alaska. *Condor* **90(4)**: 782-790.
Handel, C.M. & Gill, R.E.J. (1992a). Breeding distribution of the Black Turnstone. *Wilson Bull.* **104(1)**: 122-135.
Handel, C.M. & Gill, R.E.J. (1992b). Roosting behavior of premigratory Dunlins (*Calidris alpina*). *Auk* **109**: 57-72.
Haney, J.C. (1985). Wintering phalaropes off the southeastern United States: application of remote sensing imagery to seabird habitat analysis at Oceanic fronts. *J. Field Orn.* **56**: 321-484.
Haney, J.C. (1991). Influence of pycnocline topography and water-column structure on marine distributions of alcids (Aves: Alcidae) in Anadyr Strait, northern Bering Sea, Alaska. *Mar. Biol.* **110**: 419-435.
Haney, J.C. (1993). A closer look: Ivory Gull. *Birding* **25(5)**: 330-338.
Haney, J.C. & Eiswerth, M.E. (1992). The plight of cranes: a case study for conserving biodiversity. Pp. 12-18 in: Stahlecker (1992).
Haney, J.C. & Lee, D.S. (1994). Air-sea heat flux, ocean wind fields and offshore dispersal of gulls. *Auk* **111**: 427-440.
Haney, J.C. & MacDonald, S.D. (1995). Ivory Gull (*Pagophila eburnea*). No. **175** in: Poole & Gill (1995).
Haney, J.C. & Stone, A.E. (1988). Littoral foraging by Red Phalaropes during spring in the northern Bering Sea. *Condor* **90**: 723-726.
Haney, J.C., Andrew, J.M. & Lee, D.S. (1991). A closer look: Aleutian Tern. *Birding* **23**: 347-351.
Haney, J.C., Hood, D.W., Saupe, S.S. & Troy, D.M. (1991). Physical processes in hydrography. Pp. 2-44 in: Truitt, J.C. & Kertell, K. eds. (1991). *Marine Birds and Mammals of the Unimak Pass Area: Abundance, Habitat Use and Vulnerability*. Outer Continental Shelf Study, Minerals Management Studies 91-0038, Anchorage, Alaska.
Hanley, A.W.D. (1983). The 1982/1983 breeding season of the Humewood Kiewietjies. *Bee-eater* **34**: 9-11.
Hanley, A.W.D. (1988). The 1987/1988 breeding season on the Humewood Kiewietjies. *Bee-eater* **39**: 36-37.
Hanley, A.W.D. (1990). Report on the 1989/1990 breeding season of the Humewood Kiewietjies. *Bee-eater* **41(3)**: 36-37.
Hanmer, D.B. (1982). First record of the African Skimmer breeding in Malawi. *Ostrich* **53(3)**: 189.
Hanmer, D.B. (1988). Red-winged Pratincoles in Malawi. *Honeyguide* **34(2)**: 74-75.
Hanmer, D.B. (1989). The African Skimmer breeding in Malawi. *Nyala* **13(1/2)**: 78-79.
Hanmer, D.B. (1994). Kittlitz's Plover in the lower Shire Valley of Malawi. *Safring News* **23(1)**: 3-9.
Hanna, G.D. (1921). The Pribilof Sandpiper. *Condor* **23**: 50-57.
Hannecart, F. (1988). Les oiseaux menacés de la Nouvelle Calédonie et des îles proches. Pp. 143-165 in: Thibault & Guyot (1988).
Hannecart, F. & Létocart, Y. (1980). *Oiseaux de Nouvelle Calédonie et des Loyautés. New Caledonian Birds*. Vol. 1. Les Editions Cardinalis, Nouméa. In French and English.
Hannecart, F. & Létocart, Y. (1983). *Oiseaux de Nouvelle Calédonie et des Loyautés. New Caledonian Birds*. Vol. 2. Les Editions Cardinalis, Nouméa. In French and English.
Hanners, L.A. & Patton, S.R. (1985). Sexing Laughing Gulls using external measurements and discriminant analysis. *J. Field Orn.* **56**: 158-164.
Hansen, J.M. (1984). The population of Long-tailed Skuas *Stercorarius longicaudus* at Kaerelv, Scoresby Sund, East Greenland, 1979. *Dan. Orn. Foren. Tidssk.* **78**: 99-104.
Hansen, S. (1986). [First record of Lesser Golden Plover *Pluvialis dominica fulva* in Denmark]. *Dan. Orn. Foren. Tidssk.* **80(1)**: 1-4. In Danish with English summary.
Hanssen, O.J. (1980). Spring migration of Ringed Plovers *Charadrius hiaticula* (L.) in Østfold, southeastern Norway. *Fauna Norvegica (Ser. C, Cinclus)* **3**: 70-72.

Hara, K. (1990). Breeding the Kagu. *Anim. Zoos* **42**: 8-12.
Hara, K. & Hori, H. (1992). Breeding the Kagu at Yokohama Nogeyama Zoo. *Int. Zoo News* **39(2)**: 17-21.
Harato, T. & Ozaki, K. (1993). Roosting behaviour of the Okinawa Rail. *J. Yamashina Inst. Orn.* **25**: 40-53.
Harber, D.D. (1962). Slender-billed Gull in Sussex: a bird new to Britain. *British Birds* **55**: 169-171.
Hardee, D. (1988). Long-billed Curlews on Jekyll Island. *Oriole* **53(2/3)**: 28-29.
Harden, R.H. & Robertshaw, J.D. (1987). Lord Howe Island Woodhen census 1986. Unpublished Report to New South Wales National Parks and Wildlife Service, Sydney.
Harden, R.H. & Robertshaw, J.D. (1988). Lord Howe Island Woodhen census 1987. Unpublished Report to New South Wales National Parks and Wildlife Service, Sydney.
Hardy, J.W. (1957). The Least Tern in the Mississippi Valley. *Publ. Mus. Michigan State Univ. Biol. Series* **1**: 1-60.
Hario, M. (1984). Onset and pattern of primary moult in the Lesser Black-backed Gull *Larus f. fuscus* - a comparison with the Herring Gull *Larus argentatus*. *Ornis Fenn.* **61**: 19-23.
Hario, M. (1990). Breeding failure and feeding conditions of Lesser Black-backed Gulls *Larus f. fuscus* in the Gulf of Finland. *Ornis Fenn.* **67**: 113-129.
Hario, M. (1992). Myyttinen *heuglini* - tietoja ja otaksumia. *Lintumies* **3**: 113-117.
Hario, M. (1994). Reproductive performance of the nominate Lesser Black-backed Gull under the pressure of Herring Gull population. *Ornis Fenn.* **71**: 1-10.
Hario, M., Kilpi, M. & Selin, K. (1991). Parental investment by the sexes in the Herring Gull: the use of energy reserves during early breeding. *Ornis Scand.* **22**: 308-312.
Harllee, H.L. (1933). Great Black-backed Gull on the South Carolina coast. *Auk* **50(2)**: 217.
Harlow, R.A. (1971). Roseate Tern breeds during its third year. *Bird-Banding* **42**: 50.
Harmsen, H.H. (1989). [Lesser Yellowlegs near Oosterland in November 1979]. *Dutch Birding* **11(1)**: 1-4. In Dutch with English summary.
Harper, C.A. (1971). Breeding biology of a small colony of Western Gulls (*Larus occidentalis wymani*) in California. *Condor* **73**: 337-341.
Harper, F. (1936). The distribution of the Limpkin and its staple food. *Oriole* **1**: 21-23.
Harper, F. (1941). Further notes on the food of the Limpkin. *Nautilus* **55**: 3-4.
Harpum, J. (1978). Wattled Plover in central Tanzania. *Scopus* **2(1)**: 20.
Harradine, J. (1988). The Woodcock production survey in the United Kingdom and Ireland. Pp. 87-91 in: Havet & Hirons (1988).
Harrap, S. (1990). Temminck's Stint. *Birding World* **3(5)**: 176-177.
Harrap, S. (1993). Purple patches. *Bird Watching* **93**: 25-28.
Harrap, S. & Fisher, T. (1994). A mystery woodcock in the Philippines. *Bull. Oriental Bird Club* **19**: 54-56.
Harrington, B.A. (1974). Colony visitation behavior and breeding ages of Sooty Terns (*Sterna fuscata*). *Bird-Banding* **45**: 115-144.
Harrington, B.A. (1982). Morphometric variation and habitat use of Semipalmated Sandpipers during a migratory stopover. *J. Field Orn.* **53(3)**: 258-262.
Harrington, B.A. (1983). The migration of the Red Knot. *Oceanus* **26**: 44-48.
Harrington, B.A. (1996). *The Flight of the Red Knot. A Natural History Account of a Small Bird's Annual Migration from the Arctic Circle to the Tip of South America and Back.* W.W. Norton & Co., New York.
Harrington, B.A. & Groves, S. (1977). Aggression in foraging migrant Semipalmated Sandpipers. *Wilson Bull.* **89**: 336-338.
Harrington, B.A. & Haase, B. (1994). Latitudinal differences in sex ratios among nonbreeding Western Sandpipers in Puerto Rico and Ecuador. *Southwest. Nat.* **39(2)**: 188-189.
Harrington, B.A. & Morrison, R.I.G. (1979). Semipalmated Sandpiper migration in North America. Pp. 83-100 in: Pitelka (1979).
Harrington, B.A. & Taylor, A.L. (1982). Methods for sex identification and estimation of wing area in Semipalmated Sandpipers. *J. Field Orn.* **53(2)**: 174-177.
Harrington, B.A., Hagan, J.M. & Leddy, L.E. (1988). Site fidelity and survival differences between two groups of New World Red Knots (*Calidris canutus*). *Auk* **105**: 439-445.
Harrington, B.A., Leeuwenberg, F.J., Resende, S.L., McNeil, R., Thomas, B.T., Grear, J.S. & Martínez, E.F. (1991). Migration and mass change of White-rumped Sandpipers in North and South America. *Wilson Bull.* **103(4)**: 621-636.
Harrington, B.A., Picone, C., Resende, S.L. & Leeuwenberg, F. (1993). Hudsonian Godwit *Limosa haemastica* migration in southern Argentina. *Wader Study Group Bull.* **67**: 41-44.
Harrington, G.N., Maher, P.N. & Baker-Gabb, D.J. (1988). The biology of the Plains-wanderer *Pedionomus torquatus* on the Riverine Plain of New South Wales during and after drought. *Corella* **12(1)**: 7-13.
Harris, G. & Yorio, P. (1996). Actualización de la distribución reproductiva, estado poblacional y de conservación de la Gaviota de Olrog (*Larus atlanticus*). *Hornero*.
Harris, J. (1986). To live with the cranes. *ICF Bugle* **12(2)**: 1-3.
Harris, J. (1987). Southeast Asians conserve Eastern Sarus Crane. *ICF Bugle* **13(4)**: 1, 4-5.
Harris, J. (1991a). An international reserve where three countries meet. *ICF Bugle* **17(4)**: 1, 4-6.
Harris, J. ed. (1991b). *Proceedings of the 1987 International Crane Workshop*. International Crane Foundation, Baraboo, Wisconsin.
Harris, J. (1992a). A sacred home for the Sarus Crane. *ICF Bugle* **18(2)**: 4-5.
Harris, J. (1992b). Managing nature reserves for cranes in China. Pp. 1-11 in: Stahlecker (1992).
Harris, J. (1994). Sanjiang: end of a wetland frontier. *ICF Bugle* **20(3)**: 4-5.
Harris, J.G.K. (1984). Mortality rates of Curlew Sandpiper (*Calidris ferruginea*) determined from rocket-net catches. *Occas. Stint* **3**: 41-51.
Harris, M.P. (1962a). Difficulties in the ageing of the Herring Gull and Lesser Black-backed Gull. *Bird Study* **9**: 100-103.
Harris, M.P. (1962b). Migration of the British Lesser Black-backed Gull as shown by ringing data. *Bird Study* **9**: 174-182.
Harris, M.P. (1964). Aspects of the breeding biology of the gulls, *Larus argentatus*, *L. fuscus* and *L. marinus*. *Ibis* **106**: 432-456.
Harris, M.P. (1965). The food of some *Larus* Gulls. *Ibis* **107**: 43-53.
Harris, M.P. (1967). The biology of Oystercatchers *Haematopus ostralegus* on Skokholm Island, S. Wales. *Ibis* **109**: 180 193.
Harris, M.P. (1969). Effect of laying date on chick production in Oystercatchers and Herring Gulls. *British Birds* **62**: 70 75.
Harris, M.P. (1970a). Abnormal migration and hybridisation of *Larus argentatus* and *L. fuscus* after interspecies cross-fostering experiments. *Ibis* **112**: 448-498.
Harris, M.P. (1970b). Breeding ecology of the Swallow-tailed Gull, *Creagrus furcatus*. *Auk* **87(2)**: 215-243.
Harris, M.P. (1970c). Territory limiting size of the breeding population of the Oystercatcher (*Haematopus ostralegus*) a removal experiment. *J. Anim. Ecol.* **39**: 707 713.
Harris, M.P. (1971). Ecological adaptations of moult in some British gulls. *Bird Study* **18**: 113-118.
Harris, M.P. (1973). The Galápagos avifauna. *Condor* **75**: 265-278.
Harris, M.P. (1981). The waterbirds of Lake Junin, Central Peru. *Wildfowl* **32**: 137-145.
Harris, M.P. (1982). *A Field Guide to the Birds of Galapagos*. Collins, London.
Harris, M.P. (1983a). Biology and survival of the immature Puffin *Fratercula arctica*. *Ibis* **125**: 56-73.
Harris, M.P. (1983b) Parent-young communication in the Puffin *Fratercula arctica*. *Ibis* **125**: 109-114.
Harris, M.P. (1984). *The Puffin*. T & A.D. Poyser, Calton, UK.
Harris, M.P. (1994). Puffin. *Fratercula arctica*. Pp. 308-309 in: Tucker & Heath (1994).
Harris, M.P. & Bailey, R.S. (1992). Mortality rates of Puffin *Fratercula arctica* and Guillemot *Uria aalge* and fish abundance in the North Sea. *Biol. Conserv.* **60**: 39-46.
Harris, M.P. & Birkhead, T.R. (1985). Breeding ecology of the Atlantic Alcidae. Pp. 155-204 in: Nettleship & Birkhead (1985).
Harris, M.P. & Hislop, J.R.G. (1978). The food of young Puffins *Fratercula arctica*. *J. Zool.* **185**: 213-236.
Harris, M.P. & Plumb, W.J. (1965). Experiments on the ability of Herring Gulls *Larus argentatus* and Lesser Black-backed Gulls *L. fuscus* to raise larger than normal broods. *Ibis* **107**: 256-257.
Harris, M.P. & Wanless, S. (1988). The breeding biology of Guillemots *Uria aalge* on the Isle of May over a six year period. *Ibis* **130**: 172-192.
Harris, M.P. & Wanless, S. (1989). Fall colony attendance and breeding success in the Common Murre. *Condor* **91**: 139-146.
Harris, M.P. & Wanless, S. (1991). Population studies and conservation of Puffins *Fratercula arctica*. Pp. 230-248 in: Perrins *et al.* (1991).
Harris, M.P. & Wanless, S. (1995a). The food consumption of young Common Murres (*Uria aalge*) in the wild. *Colonial Waterbirds* **18(2)**: 209-213.
Harris, M.P. & Wanless, S. (1995b). Survival and non-breeding of adult Common Guillemots *Uria aalge*. *Ibis* **137**: 192-197.
Harris, M.P., Halley, D.J. & Swann, R.L. (1994). Age of first breeding in Common Murres. *Auk* **111**: 206-211.
Harris, M.P., Heubeck, M. & Suddaby, D. (1991). Results of an examination of Puffins *Fratercula arctica* washed ashore in Shetland in winter 1990-91. *Seabird* **13**: 63-66.
Harris, M.P., Morley, C. & Green, G.H. (1978). Hybridization of Herring and Lesser Black-backed Gulls in Britain. *Bird Study* **25**: 161-166.
Harris, M.P., Webb, A. & Tasker, M.L. (1991). Growth of young Guillemots *Uria aalge* after leaving the colony. *Seabird* **13**: 40-44.
Harris, P.R. (1979). The winter feeding of the Turnstone in north Wales. *Bird Study* **26**: 259-266.
Harrison, C. (1978). *A Field Guide to the Nests, Eggs and Nestlings of North American Birds*. Collins, New York.
Harrison, C.J.O. (1963). Eggs of the Great Sand Plover, *Charadrius leschenaultii* Lesson, from Somaliland. *Bull. Brit. Orn. Club* **83(9)**: 158-159.
Harrison, C.J.O. (1975). The Australian subspecies of Lewin's Rail. *Emu* **75**: 39-40.
Harrison, C.J.O. (1983a). A new wader, Recurvirostridae, (Charadriiformes) from the Early Eocene of Portugal. *Crencias Terr. Univ. Nova Lisboa* **7**: 9-16.
Harrison, C.J.O. (1983b). The occurrence of Saunder's Little Tern in the Upper Arabian Gulf. *Sandgrouse* **5**: 100-101.
Harrison, C.J.O. & Parker, S.A. (1967). The eggs of Woodford's Rail, Rouget's Rail and the Malayan Banded Crake. *Bull. Brit. Orn. Club* **87**: 14-16.
Harrison, C.S. (1982). Spring distribution of marine birds in the Gulf of Alaska. *Condor* **84**: 245-254.
Harrison, C.S. (1984a). Terns. Pp. 146-160 in: Haley (1984).
Harrison, C.S. (1984b). Skimmers. Pp. 162-167 in: Haley (1984).
Harrison, C.S. (1990). *Seabirds of Hawaii: Natural History and Conservation*. Comstock Publishing Associates, Ithaca & London.
Harrison, C.S. & Stoneburner, D.L. (1981). Radiotelemetry of the Brown Noddy in Hawaii. *J. Wildl. Manage.* **45**: 421-425.
Harrison, C.S., Hida, T.S. & Seki, M.P. (1983). Hawaiian seabird feeding ecology. *Wildl. Monogr.* **85**: 1-71.
Harrison, C.S., Naughton, M.B. & Fefer, S.I. (1984). The status and conservation of seabirds in the Hawaiian Archipelago and Johnston Atoll. Pp. 513-526 in: Croxall, Evans & Schreiber (1984).
Harrison, H.H. (1975). *A Field Guide to Birds' Nests*. Houghton Mifflin, Boston.
Harrison, K.C. & Mulligan, S. (1987). Painted Snipe (*Rostratula benghalensis*) at Lake Ellesmere. *Notornis* **34(1)**: 78-79.
Harrison, N.M. (1990). Galatinous zookplankton in the diet of the Parakeet Auklet: comparisons with other auklets. Pp. 114-124 in: Sealy (1990).
Harrison, N.M., Hunt, G.L. & Cooney, R.T. (1990). Front affecting the distribution of seabirds in the northern Bering Sea. *Polar Res.* **8**: 29-31.
Harrison, P. (1985). *Seabirds. An Identification Guide*. Croom & Helm Ltd, Beckenham, UK.
Harrison, P. (1987). *Seabirds of the World. A Photographic Guide*. Christopher Helm, London.
Harrop, H.R., Mellor, M. & Suddaby, D. (1993). Spring passage of Pomarine Skuas off Shetland in May 1992. *Scottish Birds* **17(1)**: 50-55.
Hartert, E. (1903). The birds of the Obi group, Central Moluccas. *Novit. Zool.* **10**: 1-17.
Hartert, E. (1912). On some unfigured birds. *Novit. Zool.* **19**: 373-374.
Hartert, E. & Venturi, S. (1909). Notes sur les oiseaux de la République Argentine. *Novit. Zool.* **16**: 159-267.
Hartlaub, G. (1877). *Die Vögel Madagascars und der benachbarten Inselgruppen*. Halle, Germany.
Hartman, F.A. (1961). *Locomotor Mechanisms of Birds*. Smithsonian Miscellaneous Collections **143(1)**. Smithsonian Instituiion, Washington, D.C. 91 pp.
Hartwick, E.B. (1973). *Foraging Strategy of the Black Oystercatcher*. PhD thesis, University of British Columbia, Vancouver.
Hartwick, E.B. (1974). Breeding ecology of the Black Oystercatcher (*Haematopus bachmani* Audubon). *Syesis* **7**: 83-92.
Hartwick, E.B. (1976). Foraging strategy of the Black Oystercatcher *Haematopus bachmani*. *Can. J. Zool.* **54(2)**: 142 155.
Hartwick, E.B. (1978a). Some observations on foraging by Black Oystercatchers. *Syesis* **11**: 55 60.
Hartwick, E.B. (1978b). The use of feeding areas outside the territory of breeding Black Oystercatchers. *Wilson Bull.* **90(4)**: 650 652.
Hartwick, E.B. (1981). Size gradients and shell polymorphism of limpets with consideration of the role of predation. *Veliger* **23**: 254 264.
Hartwick, E.B. & Blaylock, W. (1979). Winter ecology of a Black Oystercatcher population. Pp. 207-215 in: Pitelka (1979).
Harty, S.T. (1964). The discovery of the Black Rail (*Laterallus jamaicensis*) in Panama and the first breeding record. *Cassinia* **48**: 19-20.
Harvey, T.E. (1988). Breeding biology of the California Clapper Rail in south San Francisco Bay. *Trans. West. Sect. Wildl. Soc.* **24**: 98-104.
Harvey, W.G. (1971). A breeding record of the Black-winged Stilt in coastal Tanzania. *Bull. East Afr. Nat. Hist. Soc.* **1971**: 176-177.
Harvey, W.G. (1972). Caspian Plover *Charadrius asiaticus* at the coast. *Bull. East Afr. Nat. Hist. Soc.* **1972**: 175.
Harvey, W.G. (1973). A recent breeding record of Skimmers *Rynchops flavirostris* - Tanzania. *Bull. East Afr. Nat. Hist. Soc.* **1973**: 139.
Harvey, W.G. (1990). *Birds in Bangladesh*. University Press Ltd, Dhaka.
Harvey, W.G. (1994). Chestnut-banded Sandplover *Charadrius pallidus* breeding at Amboseli in 1993. *Scopus* **17**: 139-140.
Harz, M. & Luge, J. (1990). [Inland brood by *Charadrius hiaticula* in 1988 near Wulfen]. *Beitr. Vogelkd.* **36(5)**: 269-272. In German.
Hasan, S.M. (1983). Status of the Great Indian Bustard (*Choriotis nigriceps*) in Madhya Pradesh. Pp. 44-50 in: Goriup & Vardhan (1983).
Hasegawa, H. (1984). Status and conservation of seabirds in Japan, with special attention to the Short-tailed Albatross. Pp. 487-500 in: Croxall, Evans & Schreiber (1984).
Hashimoto, M. (1977). [Observations on breeding behavior of the Slaty-backed Gull *Larus schistisagus* in Kushiro, East Hokkaido]. *Mem. Kushiro Municipal Mus.* **7**: 11-17. In Japanese.
Hashmi, D. (1991). Bestand und Verbreitung des Wachtelkönigs in der Bundesrepublik Deutschland vor 1990. *Vogelwelt* **112**: 66-71.
Hasson, O. (1991). Chronological orientation of a pursuit deterrent signal: head bobbing of the Spur-winged Plover *Vanellus spinosus*. *Israel J. Zool.* **37(3)**: 188-189.
Hatch, J.J. (1970). Predation and piracy by gulls at a ternery in Maine. *Auk* **87**: 244-254.
Hatch, J.J. (1975). Piracy by Laughing Gulls *Larus atricilla*: an example of the selfish group. *Ibis* **117**: 357-365.
Hatch, S.A. (1983). The fledging of Common and Thick-billed Murres on Middleton Island, Alaska. *J. Field Orn.* **54**: 266-274.
Hatch, S.A. (1984). Nestling diet and feeding rates of Rhinoceros Auklets in Alaska. Pp. 106-115 in: Nettleship *et al.* (1984).
Hatch, S.A. & Hatch, M.A. (1983). Populations and habitat use of marine birds in the Semidi Islands, Alaska. *Murrelet* **64**: 39-46.
Hatch, S.A., Byrd, G.V., Irons, D.B. & Hunt, G.L. (1993). Status and ecology of Kittiwakes (*Rissa tridactyla* and *R. brevirostris*) in the North Pacific. Pp. 82-91 in: Vermeer, Briggs *et al.* (1993).
Hatchwell, B.J. & Birkhead, T.R. (1991). Population dynamics of Common Guillemots *Uria aalge* on Skomer Island, Wales. *Ornis Scand.* **22**: 55-59.
Hattingh, R. (1993). Spotted Dikkop in city. *Promerops* **210**: 11.
Hausmann, A. & Hausmann, K. (1972). Die Austernfischer (*Haematopus ostralegus*) der Insel Mellum 1971. *Orn. Mitt.* **24(5)**: 87 95.
Hausmann, A. & Hausmann, K. (1973a). Zur Frage der Haltbarkeit von Austerfischerringen der Vogelwarte Helgoland. *Orn. Mitt.* **25**: 142 143.
Hausmann, A. & Hausmann, K. (1973b). Die Austernfischer (*Haematopus ostralegus*) der Hallig Norderoog, 1973. *Orn. Mitt.* **26**: 89 94.
van der Have, T.M., Nieboer, E. & Boere, G.C. (1984). Age related distribution of Dunlin in the Dutch Wadden Sea. Pp. 160-176 in: Evans *et al.* (1984).

Haverschmidt, F. (1933). Gegevens over de verspreiding en de getalsterkte van de broedkolonies van de Zwarte Stern (*Chlidonias n. niger* L.) in Nederland. *Ardea* **22**: 92-105.
Haverschmidt, F. (1944). De broedduur van de Zwarte Stern (*Chlidonias n. niger* L.). *Ardea* **33**: 239-240.
Haverschmidt, F. (1952). Beobachtungen an einem frei gehaltenem Trumpetervogel *Psophia crepitans*. *Vogelwelt* **73**: 168-170.
Haverschmidt, F. (1963a). Die Eier von *Psophia crepitans*. *J. Orn.* **104**: 443.
Haverschmidt, F. (1963b). *The Black-tailed Godwit*. E.J. Brill, Leiden, the Netherlands.
Haverschmidt, F. (1966). The migration and wintering of the Upland Plover in Surinam. *Wilson Bull.* **78**: 319-320.
Haverschmidt, F. (1968). *Birds of Surinam*. Oliver & Boyd, Edinburgh & London.
Haverschmidt, F. (1972a). Notes on the Yellow-billed Tern *Sterna superciliaris*. *Bull. Brit. Orn. Club* **92**: 93-95.
Haverschmidt, F. (1972b). The migration of the Buff-breasted Sandpiper through Surinam. *Wilson Bull.* **84**: 341-342.
Haverschmidt, F. (1974a). Notes on the Grey-breasted Crake *Laterallus exilis*. *Bull. Brit. Orn. Club* **94**: 2-3.
Haverschmidt, F. (1974b). The occurrence of the Giant Snipe *Gallinago undulata* in Surinam. *Bull. Brit. Orn. Club* **94**: 132-134.
Haverschmidt, F. (1976). The Common Snipe in Surinam. *Auk* **93(2)**: 379-381.
Haverschmidt, F. (1985). Trumpeter. Pp. 611-612 in: Campbell & Lack (1985).
Haverschmidt, F. & Mees, G.F. (1995). *Birds of Suriname*. Vaco, Paramaribo.
Havet, P. & Hirons, G. eds. (1988). *Third European Woodcock and Snipe Workshop*. IWRB, Slimbridge.
Haward, P. & Barter, M. (1991). Biometrics and moult of Grey-tailed Tattlers *Tringa brevipes* in Australia. *Stilt* **19**: 10-13.
Hawkins, A. & Silvius, M. (1986). West coast Peninsular Malaysia. *Interwader* **7**: 4-5.
Hawkins, A.F.A. (1993). Relations among vegetation structure and White-breasted Mesite *Mesitornis variegata* presence and foraging site choice. Pp. 155-163 in: Wilson, R.T. (1993).
Hawkins, A.F.A. (1994). Conservation status and regional population estimates of the White-breasted Mesite (*Mesitornis variegata*), a rare Malagasy endemic. *Bird Conserv. Int.* **4**: 279-303.
Hawkins, A.F.A., Chapman, P., Ganzhorn, J.U., Bloxham, Q.M.C., Barlow, S.C. & Tonge, S.J. (1990). Vertebrate conservation in Ankarana Special Reserve, northern Madagascar. *Biol. Conserv.* **54**: 83-110.
Hawkins, F. (1993). Black-naped Tern *Sterna sumatrana* in Madagascar. *Bull. Brit. Orn. Club* **144**: 130.
Hawksley, G. (1974). African Skimmer on the highveld. *Honeyguide* **79**: 44-45.
Hawksley, O. (1957). Ecology of a breeding population of Arctic Terns. *Bird-Banding* **28**: 57-92.
Hay, J.R. (1984). *The Behavioural Ecology of the Wrybill Plover* Anarhynchus frontalis. PhD thesis, University of Auckland, Auckland, New Zealand.
Hay, R. (1984). The Tuamotu Sandpiper: little known, little cared for. *For. Bird* **15**: 17.
Hay, R. (1986). *Bird Conservation in the Pacific Islands*. ICBP Study Report **7**, Cambridge.
Haycock, K.A. & Threlfall, W. (1975). The breeding biology of the Herring Gull in Newfoundland. *Auk* **92**: 678-697.
Haydock, E.L. (1954). A survey of the birds of St. Helena. *Ostrich* **25**: 62-75.
Haye, L. (1989). Breeding the Sun-bittern *Eurypyga helias* at the San Diego Zoo, USA. *Avicult. Mag.* **95(1)**: 1-4.
Hayes, F.E. (1995). *Status, Distribution and Biogeography of the Birds of Paraguay*. Monographs in Field Ornithology **1**. American Birding Association. 224 pp.
Hayes, F.E. & Baker, W.S. (1989). Seabird distribution at sea in the Galapagos Islands: environmental correlations and associations with upwelled water. *Colonial Waterbirds* **12(1)**: 60-66.
Hayes, F.E. & Bennett, G.H. (1985). Escape diving by an American Oystercatcher chick. *J. Field Orn.* **56(4)**: 415-416.
Hayes, F.E. & Fox, J.A. (1991). Seasonality, habitat use and flock sizes of shorebirds at the Bahia de Asuncion, Paraguay. *Wilson Bull.* **103**: 637-649.
Hayes, F.E., Goodman, S.M., Fox, J.A., Tamayo, T.G. & López, N.E. (1990). North American bird migrants in Paraguay. *Condor* **92**: 947-960.
Hayman, P. (1956). A note on field-identification of pratincoles. *British Birds* **49**: 312-313.
Hayman, P., Marchant, J. & Prater, T. (1986). *Shorebirds. An Identification Guide to the Waders of the World*. Croom Helm, London.
Haymes, G.T. & Blokpoel, H. (1978a). Food of Ring-billed Gull chicks at the eastern headland of the Toronto outer harbour. *Can. Field-Nat.* **92**: 392-395.
Haymes, G.T. & Blokpoel, H. (1978b). Seasonal distribution and site tenacity of the Great Lakes Common Tern. *Bird-Banding* **49**: 142-151.
Haymes, G.T. & Blokpoel, H. (1980). The influence of age on the breeding biology of Ring-billed Gulls. *Wilson Bull.* **92**: 221-228.
Hays, H. (1970). Sand-kicking camouflages young Black Skimmers. *Wilson Bull.* **82**: 100.
Hays, H. (1972). Polyandry in the Spotted Sandpiper. *Living Bird* **11**: 43-57.
Hays, H. (1975). Probable Common x Roseate Tern hybrids. *Auk* **92**: 219-234.
Hays, H. (1978). Timing and breeding success in three- to seven-year-old Common Terns. *Ibis* **120**: 127-128.
Hays, H. (1993). Roseate Tern trio fledges three young. *Auk* **110**: 653-658.
Hays, H. & LeCroy, M. (1971). Field criteria for determining incubation stage in eggs of the Common Tern. *Auk* **89**: 595-611.
Hays, H. & Parkes, K.C. (1993). Erythristic eggs in the Common Tern. *J. Field Orn.* **64**: 341-345.
Hayward, C.L. (1935). The breeding status and migration of the Caspian Tern in Utah. *Condor* **37**: 140-144.
Hayward, J.L., Miller, D.E. & Hill, C.R. (1982). Mount St. Helens ash: its impact on breeding Ring-billed and California Gulls. *Auk* **99**: 623-631.
Hazarika, R. (1981). The status and problems of the Bengal and Lesser Floricans in Assam. Unpublished report to ICBP Bustard Group.
Hazevoet, C.J. (1987). Breeding range of Brown-headed Gull. *Dutch Birding* **9(4)**: 176-177.
Hazevoet, C.J. (1988). Cape Verde Islands coursers. *Dutch Birding* **10(1)**: 30-32.
Hazevoet, C.J. (1995). *The Birds of the Cape Verde Islands. An Annotated Cheklist*. BOU Check-list **13**. British Ornithologists' Union, Tring, UK.
He Fenqi, Zhang Yinsun, Wu Yong & Gao Tiejun (1992). The distribution of the Relict Gull *Larus relictus* in Maowusu Desert, Inner Mongolia, China. *Forktail* **7**: 151-154.
Heard, C.D.R. (1994). First record of Black-winged Pratincole *Glareola nordmanni* in Yemen. *Sandgrouse* **16(1)**: 57-58.
Heath, M. (1994). Stone Curlew. *Burhinus oedicnemus*. Pp. 244-245 in: Tucker & Heath (1994).
Heather, B.D. (1973). The Black-fronted Dotterel (*Charadrius melanops*) in the Wairarapa. *Notornis* **20(3)**: 251-261.
Heather, B.D. (1977). Foot-trembling by the Black-fronted Dotterel. *Notornis* **24(1)**: 1-8.
Heather, B.D. (1980). Brown Teal, New Zealand Dotterel and Variable Oystercatcher an unusual rock group. *Notornis* **27(2)**: 164 167.
Heather, B.D. & Robertson, H.A. (1981). A Mongolian Dotterel in breeding plumage. *Notornis* **28(1)**: 82-83.
Hebard, F.V. (1945). Recent new or interesting winter records from interior southeastern Georgia. *Oriole* **10**: 4-6.
Hébert, P.N. (1988). Adoption behaviour by gulls: a new hypothesis. *Ibis* **130**: 216-220.
Hébert, P.N. & Barclay, R.M.R. (1986). Asynchronous and synchronous hatching effect on early growth and survivorship of Herring Gull *Larus argentatus* chicks. *Can. J. Zool.* **64**: 2357-2362.
Hecht, A. (1995). Coastal Plover on the rise. *Endangered Species Tech. Bull.* **20(5)**: 14-16.
Hedenström, A. (1985). [Notes on a population of Little Ringed Plover, *Charadrius dubius*, in Sweden]. *Vår Fågelvärld* **44(8)**: 458-464. In Swedish with English summary.
Hedenström, A. (1987). Assortative mating in the Little Ringed Plover *Charadrius dubius*. *Ornis Scand.* **18(4)**: 325-327.
Hedenström, A. & Alerstam, T. (1994). Optimal climbing flight in migrating birds: predictions and observations of Knots and Turnstones. *Anim. Behav.* **48(1)**: 47-54.
Hedgren, S. (1976). Om sillgrisslans *Uria aalge* foda vid Stora Karlsö. *Vår Fågelvårld* **35**: 287-290.
Hedgren, S. (1980). Reproductive success of guillemots *Uria aalge* on the island of Stora Karlsö. *Ornis Fenn.* **57**: 49-57.
Hedley, R., Tibbett, S. & Midgley, R. (1986). Wilson's Phalarope in Oman: the first record for Arabia. *Sandgrouse* **8**: 115-116.
de Heer, P. (1979). Woestijnplevier *Charadrius leschenaultii* in Nederland. [Greater Sand Plover *Charadrius leschenaultii* in the Netherlands]. *Dutch Birding* **1(2-3)**: 56-57. In Dutch with English summary.
van Heezik, Y.M., Gerritsen, A.F.C. & Swennen, C. (1983). The influence of chemoreception on the foraging behaviour of two species of sandpiper, *Calidris alba* and *Calidris alpina*. *Netherlands J. Sea Res.* **17**: 47-56.
Heg, D. (1988). [Wintering of the Green Sandpiper *Tringa ochropus* around Nijmegen]. *Limosa* **61(3/4)**: 113-118. In Dutch with English summary.
Heg, D. (1991). [Adult Great Black-backed Gull (*Larus marinus*) seizes juvenile Avocet *Recurvirostra avosetta*]. *Limosa* **64(1)**: 26-27. In Dutch with English summary.
Heidemann, M.K. & Oring, L.W. (1976). Functional analysis of Spotted Sandpiper (*Actitis macularia*) song. *Behaviour* **56**: 181-193.
Heilmann, G. (1926). *The Origin of Birds*. Witherby, London.
Heim de Balsac, H. & Mayaud, N. (1962). *Les Oiseaux du Nord-est de l'Afrique*. Editions Paul Lechevalier, Paris.
Heimsath, S.F., López, J., Cueto, V.R. & Cittadino, E.A. (1993). [Habitat use by *Fulica armillata*, *Fulica leucoptera* and *Gallinula chloropus* during spring]. *Hornero* **13(4)**: 286-289. In Spanish with English summary.
Heinrich, G. (1932). *Der Vögel Schnarch. Zwei Jahre Rallenfang und Urwaldforschung in Celebes*. D. Reimer, Berlin.
Heinrich, G. (1956). Biologische Aufzeichnungen Über Vögel von Halmahera und Batjan. *J. Orn.* **97**: 31-40.
Heinroth, O. (1924). Die Jugendentwicklung von *Cariama cristata*. *J. Orn.* **72(1)**: 119-124.
Heinroth, O. & Heinroth, M. (1928). *Die Vögel Mitteleuropas*. Vol. 3. Hugo Bermuhler, Berlin.
Heiser, F. (1992). [Lesser Yellowlegs *Tringa flavipes* in winter Bavaria]. *Limicola* **6(2)**: 81-84. In German with English summary.
Heisler, D. & Weston, M. (1993). An examination of the efficacy of counting Hooded Plovers in autumn in eastern Victoria, Australia. *Stilt* **23**: 20-22.
Helbig, A.J. (1985). Occurrence of White-tailed Plover in Europe. *Dutch Birding* **7(3)**: 79-84.
Helbig, A.J., Barth, R. & Bauer, H.G. (1991). [First record of Spotted Sandpiper *Actitis macularia* for Austria]. *Limicola* **5(6)**: 299-302. In German with English summary.
Helbing, G.L. (1977). *Maintenance Activities of the Black Oystercatcher,* Haematopus bachmani *Audubon, in Northwestern California*. MSc thesis, Humbolt State University, Arcata, California.
Hellebrekers, W.P.J. & Hoogerwerf, A. (1967). *A Further Contribution to our Zoological Knowledge of the Island of Java (Indonesia)*. Zoologische Verhandelingen **88**. 164 pp.
Heller, J. (1991). Marbled Godwit *Limosa fedoa*, Lancaster County. *Pennsylvania Birds* **5(3)**: 120.
Hellmayr, C.E. & Conover, B. (1942). *Catalogue of the Birds of the Americas and Adjacents Islands*. Publications of the Field Museum of Natural History (Zoological Series) **13 pt. 1(1)**. Chicago.
Hellmayr, C.E. & Conover, B. (1948). *Catalogue of the Birds of the Americas and Adjacents Islands*. Publications of the Field Museum of Natural History (Zoological Series) **13 pt. 1(3)**. Chicago.
Hellmich, J. (1988). Zum Balz-Verhalten der Riesentrappe (*Ardeotis kori*). *Zool. Garten* **58**: 345-352.
Hellmich, J. (1991). *La Avutarda en Extremadura*. Alytes Monografía **2**. ADENEX, Mérida.
Hellmich, J. (1992). Impacto del uso de pesticidas sobre las aves: el caso de la Avutarda. *Ardeola* **39**: 7-22.
Helm, R.N. (1982). *Chronological Nesting Study of Common and Purple Gallinules in the Marshlands and Rice Fields of Southwest Louisiana*. MSc thesis, Louisiana State University, Baton Rouge.
Helm, R.N. (1994). Purple Gallinule. In: Tacha & Braun (1994).
Helm, R.N., Pashley, D.N. & Zwank, P.J. (1987). Notes on the nesting of the Common Moorhen and Purple Gallinule in southwestern Louisiana. *J. Field. Orn.* **58**: 55-61.
Helms, O. (1926). The birds of Angmagssalik. Based upon the collections and notes of Johan Petersen. *Medd. Grønland* **58(4)**: 205-274.
von Helversen, O. (1963). Beobachtungen zum Verhalten und zur Brutbiologie des Spornkiebitzes (*Hoplopterus spinosus*). *J. Orn.* **104**: 89-96.
van Helvoort, B.E. (1985). A breeding record of Great Thick-knee *Esacus magnirostris* (Vieillot) on Bali. *Kukila* **2(3)**: 68-69.
Hemmings, A.D. (1984). Aspects of the breeding biology of McCormick's Skua, *Catharacta maccormicki*, at Signy Island, South Orkney Islands. *Bull. Brit. Antarct. Surv.* **65**: 65-79.
Hemmings, A.D. (1989). Communally breeding skuas: breeding success of pairs, trios and groups of *Catharacta lonnbergi* on the Chatham Islands, New Zealand. *J. Zool., London* **218**: 393-405.
Hemmings, A.D. (1990). Winter territory occupation and behavior of Great Skuas at the Chatham Islands, New Zealand. *Emu* **90(2)**: 108-113.
Hempel, K. & Rudolph, B. (1991). [About *Burhinus oedicnemus* in the district of Brandenburg]. *Falke* **38(4)**: 112-113. In German.
Henderson, D. (1982). The Banded Stilt in Tasmania. *Tasmanian Bird Report* **11**: 14-15.
Henderson, I.G. & Harper, D.M. (1992). Bird distribution and habitat structure on Lake Naivasha, Kenya. *Afr. J. Ecol.* **30**: 223-232.
Henderson, I.G., Peach, W.J. & Baillie, S.R. (1993). *The Hunting of Snipe and Woodcock in Europe: a Ringing Recovery Analysis*. BTO Research Report **115**. British Trust for Ornithology, Thetford.
Hendrickson, H.T. (1969). A comparative study of the egg white proteins of some species of the avian order Gruiformes. *Ibis* **111**: 80-91.
Henriksen, K. (1985). [The postnuptial moult of the remiges in the Golden Plover *Pluvialis apricaria*]. *Dan. Orn. Foren. Tidssk.* **79(3-4)**: 141-150. In Danish with English summary.
Henriksen, K. (1991a). Breeding performance of Ringed Plovers *Charadrius hiaticula* on filled-up areas in Arhus Harbor, eastern Jutland (Denmark). *Dan. Orn. Foren. Tidssk.* **85(1-2)**: 63-66.
Henriksen, K. (1991b). [*Population Status and Trends of Curlew (*Numenius arquata*) in Northern Europe*]. Danske Vildtundersøgelser **46**. In Danish.
Henry, G.M. (1971). *A Guide to the Birds of Ceylon*. 2nd edition. Oxford University Press, London.
Heppleston, P.B. (1968). *An Ecological Study of the Oystercatcher (*Haematopus ostralegus *L.) in Coastal and Inland Habitats of North east Scotland*. PhD thesis, University of Aberdeen, UK.
Heppleston, P.B. (1970). Anatomical observations on the bill of the Oystercatcher (*Haematopus ostralegus occidentalis*) in relation to feeding behaviour. *J. Zool., London* **161**: 519 524.
Heppleston, P.B. (1971a). The feeding ecology of Oystercatchers (*Haematopus ostralegus* L.) in winter in northern Scotland. *J. Anim. Ecol.* **40**: 651 672.
Heppleston, P.B. (1971b). Feeding techniques of the Oystercatcher. *Bird Study* **18**: 15 20.
Heppleston, P.B. (1971c). Nest site selection by Oystercatchers (*Haematopus ostralegus*) in the Netherlands and Scotland. *Netherlands J. Zool.* **21**: 208 211.
Heppleston, P.B. (1972). The comparative breeding ecology of Oystercatchers (*Haematopus ostralegus* L.) in inland and coastal habitats. *J. Anim. Ecol.* **41**: 23 51.
Heppleston, P.B. (1973a). The distribution and taxonomy of oystercatchers. *Notornis* **20**: 102 112.
Heppleston, P.B. (1973b). Oystercatcher etymology. *Notornis* **20**: 120 122.
Heppleston, P.B. & Kerridge, D.F. (1970). Sexing oystercatchers from bill measurements. *Bird Study* **17**: 48 49.
Heredia, B. & Máñez, M. (1985). Primera cita del Chorlito Social (*Vanellus gregarius*) en las marismas del Guadalquivir. [First sighting of *Vanellus gregarius* in marismas del Guadalquivir]. *Doñana Acta Vertebrata* **12(1)**: 182-183.
Herholdt, J.J. (1987). Some notes on the behaviour of the Ludwig's Bustard *Neotis ludwigii* in the Orange Free State and northern Cape Province. *Mirafra* **4(2)**: 34-35.
Herholdt, J.J. (1988). The distribution of Stanley's and Ludwig's Bustards in southern Africa: a review. *Ostrich* **59(1)**: 8-13.
Herholdt, J.J. & Bernitz, Z. (1995). Wattled Crane monitoring in the southeastern Transvaal. *Birding in SA* **47(3)**: 68-69.
Herklots, G.A.C. (1961). *The Birds of Trinidad and Tobago*. Collins, London.
Herman, S.G., Bulger, J.B. & Buchanan, J.B. (1988). The Snowy Plover in southeastern Oregon and western Nevada. *J. Field Orn.* **59(1)**: 13-21.
Hermenau, B. & Pannach, G. (1993). Migration and hibernation of the Jack Snipe *Lymnocryptes minimus* in comparison to the Snipe. *Braunschw. Naturkd. Schr.* **4**: 217-228.
Hermes, N. (1980). Endangered species. In: Haigh, C. ed. (1980). *Endangered Animals of New South Wales*. National Parks and Wildlife Service, Sydney.
Hermes, N. (1985). *Birds of Norfolk Island*. Wonderland Publications, Norfolk Island.
Heron, M. (1977). First New Guinea record of the Asiatic Dowitcher. *Papua New Guinea Bird Soc. Newsl.* **129**: 9.
Herremans, M.L.J. (1984). Head pattern of Broad-billed Sandpiper. *Dutch Birding* **6(4)**: 142.
Herrmann, C. & Holz, R. (1988). [About mortality of the Ringed Plover, *Charadrius hiaticula*, comparison of methods]. *Ökol. Vögel* **10(1)**: 13-26. In German with English summary.
Herrmann, J. (1977). *The Nest Relief of Laughing Gulls: a Study of Mate Relations During the Incubation Period*. PhD dissertation, Rutgers University, New Brunswick, New Jersey.
Herroelen, P. (1983). Un Labbe parasite *Stercorarius parasiticus* au Katanga: une nouvelle espèce pour le Zaïre. *Malimbus* **5**: 78.
Herroelen, P. (1987). Bill and leg colour in Forbes' Plover. *Malimbus* **9(1)**: 57-58.
Herter, D.R. (1982). Staging of Sandhill Cranes on the eastern Copper River Delta, Alaska. Pp. 273-280 in: Lewis (1982).
Hertzel, A. (1990). Summer record for a Long-billed Curlew. *Loon* **62(1)**: 58-59.
Hervieux, D.P. (1987). *Acoustical Characteristics of Male American Woodcock Breeding Territories in Relation to Site Use*. MSc thesis, University of New Brunswick, Fredericton, Canada.

Hesch, C.G. (1987). Importance of pen size in raising crane chicks. Pp. 406-411 in: Lewis (1987).
Heslop, I.R.P. (1937). *Anomalophrys superciliosus* in Nigeria. *Ibis* **Ser. 14, no. 1**: 174-175.
Hesse, A. (1988). Die Messelornithidae - eine neue Familie der Kranichartigen (Aves: Gruiformes, Rhynocheti) aus dem Tertiär Europas und Nordamericas. *J. Orn.* **129**: 83-96.
Heubeck, M. (1992). Great Skuas attacking a flock of Moulting Eiders. *Scottish Birds* **16(4)**: 284-285.
Heubeck, M., Harvey, P.V. & Okill, J.D. (1991). Changes in the Shetland Guillemot *Uria aalge* population and the pattern of recoveries of ringed birds, 1959-1990. *Seabird* **13**: 3-21.
Hewish, M. (1987). Report on the winter 1986 population monitoring count: a bumper year for Red Knots and Grey Plovers. *Stilt* **11**: 18-22.
Hewish, M. (1988). The winter 1987 population monitoring count: Lesser Golden Plover over-wintering in Australia. *Stilt* **12**: 41-46.
Hewish, M. (1989). The summer 1988 population monitoring count: Banded Stilts at monitored sites in south-eastern Australia. *Stilt* **14**: 14-20.
Hewish, M. (1990). The winter 1989 population monitoring count: Pied and Sooty Oystercatchers at monitored sites. *Stilt* **17**: 5-16.
Hicklin, P.W. (1983). Influence of prey density and biomass on migration timing of Semipalmated Sandpipers in the Bay of Fundy. *Wader Study Group Bull.* **39**: 59.
Hicklin, P.W. & Smith, P.C. (1979). The diets of five species of migrant shorebirds in the Bay of Fundy. *Proc. Nova Scotia Inst. Sci.* **29**: 482-488.
Hicklin, P.W. & Smith, P.C. (1984). Selection of foraging sites and invertebrate prey by migrant Semipalmated Sandpipers, *Calidris pusilla* (Pallas), in Minas Basin, Bay of Fundy. *Can. J. Zool.* **62**: 2201-2210.
Hicks, R.K. & Burrows, I. (1994). A red Little Curlew (*Numenius minutus*) or something else? *Muruk* **6(3)**: 15.
Hidalgo, S.J. (1990). World status of the Great Bustard (*Otis tarda*) with special attention to the Iberian peninsula populations. *Misc. Zool.* **14**: 167-180.
Hidalgo, S.J. & Carranza, J. (1990a). *Ecologia y Comportamiento de la Avutarda (*Otis tarda *L.)*. Universidad de Extremadura, Cáceres, Spain.
Hidalgo, S.J. & Carranza, J. (1990b). Sistemática, distribución y origen de Otididae. Pp. 29-39 in: Hidalgo & Carranza (1990a).
Hidalgo, S.J. & Carranza, J. (1991). Timing, structure and functions of the courtship display in male Great Bustard. *Ornis Scand.* **22(4)**: 360-366.
Higgins, K.F. & Kirsch, L.M. (1975). Some aspects of the breeding biology of the Upland Sandpiper in North Dakota. *Wilson Bull.* **87**: 96-102.
Higgins, K.F., Kirsch, L.M., Ryan, M.R. & Renken, R.B. (1979). Some ecological aspects of Marbled Godwits and Willets in North Dakota. *Prairie Nat.* **11**: 114-118.
Higuchi, H. (1990). Winter counts of endangered cranes. *ICF Bugle* **16(3)**: 8.
Higuchi, H. (1991a). Cooperative work on crane migration from Japan to the USSR through Korea and China. Pp. 189-201 in: Salathé, T. ed. (1991). *Conserving Migratory Birds*. ICBP Technical Publication **12**, Cambridge.
Higuchi, H. (1991b). Winter counts of endangered cranes. *ICF Bugle* **17(4)**: 8.
Higuchi, H. (1993). Tracking cranes by satellite in eastern Asia. *ICF Bugle* **19(4)**: 4-6.
Higuchi, H. & Minton, J. eds. (1994). *The Future of Cranes and Wetlands: Proceedings of the International Symposium*. Wild Bird Society of Japan, Tokyo.
Higuchi, H., Nagendren, M., Sorokin, A.G. & Ueta, M. (1994). Satellite tracking of Common Cranes *Grus grus* migrating north from Keoladeo National Park, India. Pp. 26-31 in: Higuchi & Minton (1994).
Higuchi, H., Ozaki, K., Golovushkin, K., Goroshko, O., Krever, V., Minton, J., Ueta, M., Andronov, V., Ilyashenko, V., Kanmuri, N. & Archibald, G.W. (1994). The migration routes and important rest sites of crane satellite tracked from south-central Russia. Pp. 15-25 in: Higuchi & Minton (1994).
Higuchi, H., Ozaki, K., Soma, M., Kanmuri, N. & Ueta, M. (1992). Satellite tracking of the migration routes of cranes from southern Japan. *Strix* **11**: 1-20. In English with Japanese summary.
Higuchi, Y. (1979). [Breeding ecology and distribution of the Japanese Crested Murrelet]. *Aquatic Biology* **1**: 20-24. In Japanese.
Hildén, O. (1971). Occurrence, migration and colour phases of the Arctic Skua (*Stercorarius parasiticus*) in Finland. *Ann. Zool. Fennici* **8**: 223-230.
Hildén, O. (1975). Breeding system of Temminck's Stint *Calidris temminckii*. *Ornis Fenn.* **52(4)**: 117-146.
Hildén, O. (1978). Population dynamics in Temminck's Stint *Calidris temminckii*. *Oikos* **30(1)**: 17-28.
Hildén, O. (1979a). The timing of arrival and departure of the Spotted Redshank *Tringa erythropus* in Finland. *Ornis Fenn.* **56**: 18-23.
Hildén, O. (1979b). Territoriality and site tenacity of Temminck's Stint *Calidris temminckii*. *Ornis Fenn.* **56**: 56-74.
Hildén, O. (1983). Mating system and breeding biology of the Little Stint *Calidris minuta*. *Wader Study Group Bull.* **39**: 47. (Abstract).
Hildén, O. & Vuolanto, S. (1972). Breeding biology of the Red-necked Phalarope *Phalaropus lobatus* in Finland. *Ornis Fenn.* **49**: 57-85.
Hill, D. (1988). Population dynamics of the Avocet (*Recurvirostra avosetta*) breeding in Britain. *J. Anim. Ecol.* **57**: 669-683.
Hill, D. (1989). The Avocet. *Shire Nat. Hist. Ser.* **34**: 1-24.
Hill, D. & Carter, N. (1991). An empirical simulation model of an Avocet *Recurvirostra avosetta* population. *Ornis Scand.* **22(1)**: 65-72.
Hill, D. & Player, A. (1992). Behavioural responses of Black-headed Gulls and Avocets to two methods of control of gull productivity. *Bird Study* **39(1)**: 34-42.
Hill, G. & Rosier, J. (1989). Wedgetailed Shearwaters, White-capped Noddies and tourist development on Heron Island, Great Barrier Reef Marine Park. *J. Environm. Manage.* **29**: 107-114.
Hill, J.K. & Hamer, K.C. (1994). Do Great Skuas *Catharacta skua* respond to changes in the nutritional needs of their chicks? *Seabird* **16**: 3-7.
Hill, L.A. (1985). *Breeding Ecology of Interior Least Tern, Snowy Plovers and American Avocets at Salt Plains National Wildlife Refuge*. MSc thesis, Oklahoma State University, Stillwater, Oklahoma.
Hill, L.A. & Talent, L.G. (1990). Effects of capture, handling, banding and radio-marking on breeding Least Terns and Snowy Plovers. *J. Field Orn.* **61(3)**: 310-319. In English with Spanish summary.
Hill, W.L. (1986). Clutch overlap in American Coots. *Condor* **88**: 96-97.
Hill, W.L. (1988). The effect of food abundance on the reproductive patterns of coots. *Condor* **90**: 324-331.
Hill, W.L. (1991). Correlates of male mating success in the Ruff *Philomachus pugnax*, a lekking shorebird. *Behav. Ecol. Sociobiol.* **29(5)**: 367-372.
Hilty, S.L. (1985). Distribution changes in the Colombian avifauna: a preliminary blue list. Pp. 1000-1012 in: Buckley *et al.* (1985).
Hilty, S.L. & Brown, W.L. (1986). *A Guide to the Birds of Colombia*. Princeton University Press, Princeton, New Jersey.
Himmatsinhji, M.K. (1968). Some interesting migrants in Kutch. *J. Bombay Nat. Hist. Soc.* **65(1)**: 225.
Hindwood, H.A. (1940). Notes on the distribution and habits of the Jacana or lotusbird. *Emu* **39**: 261-267.
Hindwood, K.A. (1940). Birds of Lord Howe Island. *Emu* **40**: 1-86.
Hindwood, K.A. (1946). The White-fronted Tern in Australia. *Emu* **45**: 197-200.
Hindwood, K.A. (1953). River pollution and birds. *Emu* **53**: 90-91.
Hindwood, K.A. (1960). The Painted Snipe and its nestlings. *Austr. Bird Watcher* **1**: 66-69.
Hindwood, K.A. & Hoskin, E.S. (1954). The waders of Sydney (County of Cumberland), New South Wales. *Emu* **54**: 217-255.
Hines, C.J. (1993). Temporary wetlands of Bushmanland and Kavango, northeast Namibia. *Madoqua* **18**: 57-69.
Hines, C.J. (1996). Cranes in Namibia. In: Beilfuss *et al.* (1996).
Hingston, R.W.G. (1932). Habits of the Indian Spur-winged Plover (*Hoplopterus ventralis*). *J. Bombay Nat. Hist. Soc.* **32**: 219-220.
Hinz, C. & Heiss, E.M. (1989). The activity patterns of Houbara Bustards: aspects of a field study in the Canary Islands. *Bustard Studies* **4**: 68-79.
Hiom, L., Bolton, M., Monaghan, P. & Worrall, D. (1991). Experimental evidence for food limitation of egg production in gulls. *Ornis Scand.* **22**: 94-97.
Hipfner, J.M. & Byrd, G.V. (1993). Breeding biology of the Parakeet Auklet compared to other crevice-nesting species at Buldir Island, Alaska. *Colonial Waterbirds* **16(2)**: 128-138.
Hirons, G. (1980). The significance of roding by Woodcock, *Scolopax rusticola*: an alternative explanation based on observations of marked birds. *Ibis* **122**: 350-354.
Hirons, G. (1982). Conclusion of the studies on Woodcock. *Game Conservancy Ann. Rev.* **13**: 35-42.
Hirons, G. (1983). A five-year study of the breeding behaviour and biology of the Woodcock in England - a first report. Pp. 51-67 in: Kalchreuter (1983b).
Hirons, G. (1988). Habitat use by Woodcock (*Scolopax rusticola*) during the breeding season. Pp. 42-47 in: Havet & Hirons (1988).
Hirons, G. & Bickford-Smith, P. (1983). The diet and behaviour of Eurasian Woodcock wintering in Cornwall. Pp. 11-17 in: Kalchreuter (1983b).
Hirons, G. & Johnson, T.H. (1987). A quantitative analysis of habitat preferences of Woodcock, *Scolopax rusticola*, in the breeding season. *Ibis* **129**: 371-381.
Hirons, G. & Linsey, M. (1989). Counting Woodcock. *Game Conservancy Ann. Rev.* **20**: 47-48.
Hirsch, K.V. & Fouchi, C.M. (1984). American Avocets nesting in Traverse County. *Loon* **56(3)**: 204-205.
Hirschfeld, E. (1990). Black-winged Stilts breeding for the first time in Bahrain. *Phoenix* **7**: 3-4.
Hirschfeld, E. (1991). First record of Long-toed Stint *Calidris subminuta* in Bahrain. *Sandgrouse* **13(2)**: 108-110.
Hirschfeld, E. (1992). First records of Pintail Snipe *Gallinago stenura* in Bahrain. *Sandgrouse* **14(2)**: 116-119.
Hirschfeld, E. (1995). Tundrapipare i Sverige. *Vår Fågelvärld* **4**: 28-30.
Hislop, J.R.G. & Harris, M.P. (1983). Recent changes in the food of young Puffins *Fratercula arctica* on the Isle of May in relation to fish stocks. *Ibis* **127**: 234-239.
Hitchcock, W.B. (1959). A review of "Least" Terns in Australian waters. *S. Austr. Orn.* **22**: 87-106.
Hitchcock, W.B. & Favaloro, N.F. (1951). Victorian records of *Sterna striata* Gm. and *Sterna hirundo longipennis* Nordm. *Mem. Natl. Mus. Victoria* **17**: 207-214.
Hjort, C. (1976). An observation of Ivory Gull *Pagophila eburnea* migration along the East Greenland Current. *Dan. Orn. Foren. Tidssk.* **70**: 72-73.
Hjort, C. (1980). Ross's Gull *Rhodostethia rosea* breeding in Peary Land, North Greenland. 1979. *Dan. Orn. Foren. Tidssk.* **74**: 75-76.
Hjort, C., Håkansson, E. & Stemmerik, L. (1983). Bird observations around the Nordøstvandet polynya, Northeast Greenland, 1980. *Dan. Orn. Foren. Tidssk.* **77**: 107-114.
Hoath, R. (1994). Interaction between Wood Sandpipers and diced water snake in Egypt. *Bull. Orn. Soc. Middle East* **32**: 24-25.
Hobbs, J.N. (1967). Distraction display by two species of crakes. *Emu* **66**: 299-300.
Hobbs, J.N. (1972). Breeding of Red-capped Dotterel at Fletcher's Lake, Dareton, New South Wales. *Emu* **72**: 121-125.
Hobbs, J.N. (1973a). The Oriental Pratincole in NSW. *Austr. Bird Watcher* **5**: 1-4.
Hobbs, J.N. (1973b). Reaction to predators by Black-tailed Native Hen. *Austr. Bird Watcher* **5**: 29-30.
Hobbs, J.N. (1981). Grey Butcherbird taking a Painted Button-quail. *Austr. Birds* **16(2)**: 31.
Hobcroft, D. (1987). A Buff-breasted Sandpiper at Richmond, New South Wales. *Austr. Birds* **21(2)**: 56-57.
Hobson, K.A. (1990). Stable isotope analysis of Marbled Murrelets: evidence for freshwater feeding and determination of trophic level. *Condor* **92**: 897-903.
Hobson, K.A. (1991). Stable isotopic determinations of the trophic relationships of seabirds: preliminary investigations of alcids from coastal British Columbia. Pp. 16-20 in: Montevecchi, W.A. & Gaston, A.J. eds. (1991). *Studies of High-latitude Seabirds*. Vol. 1. Behavioral, Energetic and Oceanographic Aspects of Seabird Feeding Ecology. Occasional Paper **68**. Canadian Wildlife Service, Ottawa.
Hobson, K.A. & Montevecchi, W.A. (1991). Stable isotopic determination of trophic relationships of Great Auks. *Oecologia* **87**: 528-531.
Hobson, W. (1972). The breeding biology of the Knot. *Proc. West. Found. Vert. Zool.* **2**: 5-26.
Hochbaum, G. & Ball, G. (1978). An aggressive encounter between a Pintail with a brood and a Franklin's Gull. *Wilson Bull.* **90**: 455.
Hockey, P.A.R. (1980). Kleptoparasitism by Kelp Gulls *Larus dominicanus* of African Black Oystercatchers (*Haematopus moquini*). *Cormorant* **8(2)**: 97.
Hockey, P.A.R. (1981a). Feeding techniques of the African Black Oystercatcher *Haematopus moquini*. Pp. 99-115 in: Cooper (1981).
Hockey, P.A.R. (1981b). Morphometrics and sexing of the African Black Oystercatcher. *Ostrich* **52(4)**: 244 247.
Hockey, P.A.R. (1982a). The taxonomic status of the Canary Islands Oystercatcher *Haematopus meadewaldoi*. *Bull. Brit. Orn. Club* **102(2)**: 77-83.
Hockey, P.A.R. (1982b). Adaptiveness of nest site selection and egg coloration in the African Black Oystercatcher *Haematopus moquini*. *Behav. Ecol. Sociobiol.* **11(2)**: 117-123.
Hockey, P.A.R. (1982c). A further observation of Whitewinged Black Terns *Chlidonias leucopterus* foraging at sea. *Cormorant* **10**: 47.
Hockey, P.A.R. (1983a). Aspects of the breeding biology of the African Black Oystercatcher *Haematopus moquini*. *Ostrich* **54(1)**: 26-35.
Hockey, P.A.R. (1983b). The distribution, population size, movements and conservation of the African Black Oystercatcher *Haematopus moquini*. *Biol. Conserv.* **25(3)**: 233-262.
Hockey, P.A.R. (1983c). *Ecology of the African Black Oystercatcher* Haematopus moquini. PhD dissertation, University of Cape Town.
Hockey, P.A.R. (1984a). Behaviour patterns of non-breeding African Black Oystercatchers *Haematopus moquini* at offshore islands. Pp. 707-727 in: Ledger (1984).
Hockey, P.A.R. (1984b). Growth and energetics of the African Black Oystercatcher *Haematopus moquini*. *Ardea* **72(1)**: 111-117.
Hockey, P.A.R. (1985). Observations on the communal roosting of African Black Oystercatchers. *Ostrich* **56(1-3)**: 52-57.
Hockey, P.A.R. (1986a). Meade-Waldo's Black Oystercatcher - a path to extinction. *Afr. Wildl.* **40(4)**: 140-151.
Hockey, P.A.R. (1986b). The Canary Islands expedition. *Quagga* **16**: 22-23.
Hockey, P.A.R. (1987). The influence of coastal utilization by man on the presumed extinction of the Canarian Black Oystercatcher *Haematopus meadewaldoi*. *Biol. Conserv.* **39(1)**: 49-62.
Hockey, P.A.R. & Boobyer, M.G. (1994). Territoriality and determinants of group size in the Karoo Korhaan *Eupodotis vigorsii* (Otididae). *J. Arid Environm.* **28(4)**: 325-332.
Hockey, P.A.R. & Bosman, A.L. (1988). Stabilizing processes in bird-prey interactions on rocky shores. Pp. 297-315 in: Vannini, M. & Chelazzi, G. eds. (1988). *Behavioural Adaptations to Intertidal Life*. Plenum Press, New York.
Hockey, P.A.R. & Branch, G.M. (1983). Do oystercatchers influence limpet shell shape? *Veliger* **26**: 139-141.
Hockey, P.A.R. & Branch, G.M. (1984). Oystercatchers and limpets: impacts and implications. A preliminary assessment. *Ardea* **72(2)**: 199-206. In English with Dutch summary.
Hockey, P.A.R. & Cooper, J. (1980). Paralytic shellfish poisoning a controlling factor in Black Oystercatcher populations? *Ostrich* **51(3)**: 188 190.
Hockey, P.A.R. & Cooper, J. (1982). Occurrence of the European Oystercatcher *Haematopus ostralegus* in southern Africa. *Ardea* **70**: 55 58.
Hockey, P.A.R. & Douie, C. (1995). *Waders of Southern Africa*. Struik, Cape Town.
Hockey, P.A.R. & van Erkom Schurink, C. (1992). The invasive biology of the mussel *Mytilus galloprovincialis* on the southern African coast. *Trans. Roy. Soc. S. Afr.* **48**: 123-139.
Hockey, P.A.R. & Hockey, C.T. (1980). Notes on Caspian Terns *Sterna caspia* breeding near the Berg River, Southwestern Cape. *Cormorant* **8**: 7-10.
Hockey, P.A.R. & Underhill, L.G. (1984). Diet of the African Black Oystercatcher on rocky shores: spatial, temporal and sex-related variation. *S. Afr. J. Zool.* **19(1)**: 1-11. In English with Afrikaans summary.
Hockey, P.A.R., Ryan, P.G. & Bosman, A.L. (1989). Age-related intraspecific kleptoparasitism and foraging success of Kelp Gulls *Larus dominicanus*. *Ardea* **77**: 205-210.
Hockey, P.A.R., Underhill, L.G. & Neatherway, M. (1989). *Atlas of the Birds of the Southwestern Cape*. Cape Bird Club, Cape Town.
Hodder, J. & Graybill, M.R. (1985). Reproduction and survival of seabirds in Oregon during the 1982-83 El Niño. *Condor* **87**: 535-541.
Hodges, A.F. (1969). A time lapse study of Kittiwake incubation rhythms. *Ibis* **111**: 442-443.
Hodges, A.F. (1974). The orientation of adult Kittiwakes *Rissa tridactyla* at the nest site in Northumberland. *Ibis* **117**: 235-240.
Hodgson, R. (1983). Rearing the African Jacana *Actophilornis africana* at the Wildfowl Trust, Slimbridge, Glos. *Avicult. Mag.* **89(2)**: 67-68.
Hoelzinger, J., Mickley, M. & Schilhansl, K. (1973). Zur Ueberwinterung des Waldwasserlaeufers (*Tringa ochropus*) im Donaubereich bei Ulm. [Wintering of Green Sandpipers (*Tringa ochropus*) in the Donau Valley near Ulm]. *Anz. Orn. Ges. Bayern* **12(1)**: 57-64. In German with English summary.
Hoerschelmann, H. & Jacob, J. (1992). Ein Beitrag zur Chemotaxonomie der Wat-, Möwen- und Alkenvögel (Aves: Charadriiformes). *Mitt. Hamb. Zool. Mus. Inst.* **89**: 319-350.
Hoesch, W. (1959). Zur Biologie des sudafrikanischen Laufhühnchens *Turnix sylvatica lepurana*. *J. Orn.* **100**: 341-349.

Hoesch, W. (1960). Zum Brutverhalten des Laufhühnchens *Turnix sylvatica lepurana*. *J. Orn.* **101**: 265-275.
Hoetker, H. & Dietrich, S. (1992). Aspects of the migration of north Frisian Avocets. *Wader Study Group Bull.* **64**: 9.
Hoffman, K. & Hoffman, M. (1992). Purple Sandpiper in Grand Marais. *Loon* **64(1)**: 56-57.
Hoffman, P.W. (1927). Home life of the Black Tern in Wisconsin. *Wilson Bull.* **39**: 78-80.
Hoffman, T.W. (1990). Breeding of the Common Tern *Sterna hirundo* in Sri Lanka. *J. Bombay Nat. Hist. Soc.* **87**: 68-72.
Hoffman, W. (1984). *Phylogeny, Feeding Behavior, and Wing Structure in Gulls, Terns, and Allies (Laroidea)*. PhD thesis, University of South Florida, Tampa, Florida.
Hoffman, W., Sprunt, A., Kalla, P. & Robson, M. (1993). Bridled Tern breeding record in the United States. *Amer. Birds* **47(3)**: 379-381.
Hoffman, W., Wiens, J.A. & Scott, J.M. (1978). Hybridization between gulls (*Larus glaucescens* and *L. occidentalis*) in the Pacific Northwest. *Auk* **95(3)**: 441-458.
Hoffmann, A. (1949). Über die Brutpflege des polyandrischen Wasserfasans, *Hydrophasianus chirurgus* (Scop.). *Zool. Jahrb.* **78**: 367-403.
Hoffmann, A. (1950). Zur Brutbiologie des polyandrischen Wasserfasans *Hydrophasianus chirurgus* Scop. *Orn. Ber.* **2**: 119-126.
Hoffmann, L. (1957). Le passage d'autumne du Chevalier sylvian (*Tringa glareola*) en France Mediterranéenne. *Alauda* **25**: 30-57.
Hofmeyr, J. (1991). Hartlaub's Gulls (316) nesting. *Promerops* **200**: 17.
Hogan-Warburg, A.J. (1966). Social behavior of the Ruff, *Philomachus pugnax* (L.). *Ardea* **54**: 109-229.
Hogan-Warburg, A.J. (1992). Female choice and the evolution of mating strategies in the Ruff *Philomachus pugnax* (L.). *Ardea* **80(3)**: 395-403.
Hogg, P., Dare, P.J. & Rintoul, J.V. (1984). Palaearctic migrants in the central Sudan. *Ibis* **126**: 307-331.
Höglund, J. (1989a). *Sexual Selection and the Evolution of Leks in the Great Snipe (*Gallinago media*)*. Acta Universitatis Upsaliensis **184**.
Höglund, J. (1989b). Size and plumage dimorphism in lek-breeding birds: a comparative analysis. *Amer. Naturalist* **134**: 72-87.
Höglund, J. & Alatalo, R.V. (1995). *Leks*. Princeton University Press, Princeton.
Höglund, J. & Lundberg, A. (1987). Sexual selection in a monomorphic lek-breeding birds: correlates of male mating success in the Great Snipe *Gallinago media*. *Behav. Ecol. Sociobiol.* **21(4)**: 211-216.
Höglund, J. & Lundberg, A. (1989). Plumage color correlates with body size in the Ruff (*Philomachus pugnax*). *Auk* **106**: 336-339.
Höglund, J. & Robertson, J.G.M. (1990a). Female preference, male decision rules and the evolution of leks in the Great Snipe *Gallinago media*. *Anim. Behav.* **40(1)**: 15-22.
Höglund, J. & Robertson, J.G.M. (1990b). Spacing of leks in relation to female home ranges, habitat requirements and male attractiveness in the Great Snipe (*Gallinago media*). *Behav. Ecol. Sociobiol.* **26(3)**: 173-180.
Höglund, J., Eriksson, M. & Lindell, L.E. (1990). Females of the lek-breeding Great Snipe, *Gallinago media*, prefer males with white tails. *Anim. Behav.* **40(1)**: 23-32.
Höglund, J., Kålås, J.A. & Fiske, P. (1992). The costs of secondary sexual characteristics in the lekking Great Snipe (*Gallinago media*). *Behav. Ecol. Sociobiol.* **30(5)**: 309-315.
Höglund, J., Kålås, J.A. & Løfaldli, L. (1990). Sexual dimorphism in the lekking Great Snipe. *Ornis Scand.* **21(1)**: 1-6.
Höglund, J., Montgomerie, R. & Widemo, F. (1993). Costs and consequences of variation in the size of Ruff leks. *Behav. Ecol. Sociobiol.* **32**: 31-39.
Högstedt, G. (1974). Length of the pre-laying period in the Lapwing *Vanellus vanellus* L. in relation to its food resources. *Ornis Scand.* **5**: 1-4.
Höhn, E.O. (1965). *Die Wassertreter*. [*The Phalaropes*]. Zeimsen Verlag, A. Wittenberg, Germany.
Höhn, E.O. (1967). Observations on the breeding biology of Wilson's Phalarope *Steganopus tricolor* in central Alberta. *Auk* **84**: 220-244.
Höhn, E.O. (1968). Some observations on the breeding of the Northern Phalarope at Scammon Bay, Alaska. *Auk* **85**: 316-317.
Höhn, E.O. (1971). Observations on the breeding behaviour of Grey and Red-necked Phalaropes. *Ibis* **113**: 335-348.
Höhn, E.O. (1975). Notes on Black-headed Ducks, Painted Snipe and Spotted Tinamous. *Auk* **92(3)**: 566-575.
Höhn, E.O. & Barron, J.R. (1963). The food of Wilson's Phalarope during the breeding season. *Can. J. Zool.* **41**: 1171-1173.
Holdgate, M.W. (1957). Gough Island - a possible sanctuary. *Oryx* **4**: 168-175.
Holdgate, M.W. & Wace, N.M. (1961). The influence of man on the floras of southern islands. *Polar Record* **10**: 475-493.
Holdsworth, M.C. & Park, P. (1993). 1992 survey of the Hooded Plover in Tasmania. *Stilt* **22**: 37-40.
Holgersen, H. (1962). Ringing and recoveries of Norwegian oystercatchers. *Stavanger Mus. Arbok* **1962**: 175 180.
Holland, P.K. & Yalden, D.W. (1983). Common Sandpiper food requirements. *Wader Study Group Bull.* **37**: 7-8. (Abstract).
Holland, P.K. & Yalden, D.W. (1991a). Growth of Common Sandpiper chicks. *Wader Study Group Bull.* **62**: 13-15.
Holland, P.K. & Yalden, D.W. (1991b). Population dynamics of Common Sandpipers *Actitis hypoleucos* breeding along an upland river system. *Bird Study* **38(3)**: 151-159.
Holland, P.K. & Yalden, D.W. (1994). An estimate of lifetime reproductive success for the Common Sandpiper *Actitis hypoleucos*. *Bird Study* **41(2)**: 110-119.
Holland, P.K., Robson, J.E. & Yalden, D.W. (1982). The breeding biology of the Common Sandpiper *Actitis hypoleucos* in the Peak District. *Bird Study* **29**: 99-110.
Holley, A.J.F. (1984). Adoption, parent-chick recognition and maladaptation in the Herring Gull *Larus argentatus*. *Z. Tierpsychol.* **64**: 9-14.
Hollom, P.A.D., Porter, R.F., Christensen, S. & Willis, I. (1988). *Birds of the Middle East and North Africa*. Poyser, Calton, UK.
Holloway, J. (1995). Semipalmated Sandpiper in Orkney. *British Birds* **88(3)**: 196-200.
Holloway, M. (1993). The variable breeding success of the Little Tern *Sterna albifrons* in south-east India and protective measures needed for its conservation. *Biol. Conserv.* **65**: 1-8.
Hollyer, J.N. (1984). Camouflage postures of Jack Snipe at day roost. *British Birds* **77(7)**: 319-320.
Holmes, D. & Nash, S. (1991). *The Birds of Java and Bali*. Oxford University Press, Singapore.
Holmes, D.A. (1995). Additions to the avifauna of Pulau Alor, Nusatenggara. *Kukila* **7(2)**: 155-157.
Holmes, D.A. & Rusila Noor, Y. (1995). Discovery of waterbirds colonies in north Lampung, Sumatra. *Kukila* **7(2)**: 121-128.
Holmes, G. (1987). Status of rare birds in the Tweed Volcano Region. Report to New South Wales National Parks and Wildlife Service.
Holmes, R.T. (1966a). Breeding ecology and annual cycle adaptations of the Red-backed Sandpiper (*Calidris alpina*) in northern Alaska. *Condor* **68**: 3-46.
Holmes, R.T. (1966b). Feeding ecology of the Red-backed Sandpiper (*Calidris alpina*) in arctic Alaska. *Ecology* **47**: 32-45.
Holmes, R.T. (1971a). Density, habitat and the mating system of the Western Sandpiper (*Calidris mauri*). *Oecologia* **7**: 191-208.
Holmes, R.T. (1971b). Latitudinal differences in the breeding and molt schedules of Alaskan Red-backed Sandpipers (*Calidris alpina*). *Condor* **73**: 93-99.
Holmes, R.T. (1972). Ecological factors influencing the breeding season schedule of Western Sandpipers (*Calidris mauri*) in subarctic Alaska. *Amer. Midl. Nat.* **87**: 472-491.
Holmes, R.T. (1973). Social behaviour of breeding Western Sandpipers *Calidris mauri*. *Ibis* **115**: 107-123.
Holmes, R.T. & Pitelka, F.A. (1962). Behavior and taxonomic position of the White-rumped Sandpiper. *Proc. Alaska Sci. Conf.* **12**: 19-20.
Holmes, R.T. & Pitelka, F.A. (1964). Breeding behaviour and taxonomic relationships of the Curlew Sandpiper. *Auk* **81**: 362-379.
Holmes, R.T. & Pitelka, F.A. (1968). Food overlap among coexisting sandpipers on northern Alaskan tundra. *Syst. Zool.* **17**: 305-318.
Holmgren, N., Ellegren, H. & Pettersson, J. (1993a). Stopover length, body mass and fuel deposition rate in autumn migrating adult Dunlins *Calidris alpina*: evaluating the effects of moulting status and age. *Ardea* **81(1)**: 9-20.
Holmgren, N., Ellegren, H. & Pettersson, J. (1993b). The adaptation of moult pattern in migratory Dunlins *Calidris alpina*. *Ornis Scand.* **24(1)**: 21-27.
Holt, D.W. (1994). Effects of Short-eared Owls on Common Tern colony desertion, reproduction and mortality. *Colonial Waterbirds* **17**: 1-6.
Holthuijzen, Y.A. (1979). [The food of the Spotted Redshank *Tringa erythropus* in the Dollard]. *Limosa* **52**: 22-33. In Dutch with English summary.
Holtshausen, G. & Ledger, J. (1985). Southern African crane census 1985/86. *Bokmakierie* **39**: 196-199.
Holyoak, D.T. (1970). The behaviour of captive Purple Gallinules. *Avicult. Mag.* **76**: 98-109.
Holyoak, D.T. (1973). Notes on the birds of Rangiroa, Tuamotu Archipelago, and the surrounding ocean. *Bull. Brit. Orn. Club* **93**: 26-32.
Holyoak, D.T. (1979). Notes on the birds of Vita Levu and Taveuni, Fiji. *Emu* **79**: 7-18.
Holyoak, D.T. & Thibault, J.C. (1976). La variation géographique de *Gygis alba*. *Alauda* **44**: 457-473.
Holyoak, D.T. & Thibault, J.C. (1984). *Contribution à l'Étude des Oiseaux de Polynésie Orientale*. Mémoires du Muséum National d'Histoire Naturelle Série A, Zoologie **127**. Éditions du Muséum d'Histoire Naturelle, Paris.
Holz, R. (1987a). [Age characteristics of Ringed Plover (*Charadrius hiaticula*) of the south-west Baltic coast]. *Beitr. Vogelkd.* **33(5-6)**: 233-243. In German with English summary.
Holz, R. (1987b). [*Development of Ringed Plover Population (*Charadrius hiaticula*) in the Southwest Baltic Region: Causes and Consequences of the Changed Habitat Utilization*]. Natur und Naturschutz in Mecklenburg **25**. Greifswald, Waren. In German with English summary.
Hölzinger, J. (1975a). Verhalten und Nahrungsgrundlage der Flußregenpfeifer *Charadrius dubius* in wasserführenden und wasserlosen Brutrevieren. [Behaviour and food basis of Little Ringed Plover in breeding grounds with and without water]. *Orn. Beob.* **72(1)**: 9-17.
Hölzinger, J. (1975b). Untersuchungen zum Verhalten des Flußregenpfeifers (*Charadrius dubius*) bei Gestoertem und Ungestoertem Brutablauf. [Investigations on the behaviour of Little Ringed Plover (*Charadrius dubius*) during disturbed and undisturbed incubation]. *Anz. Orn. Ges. Bayern* **14(2)**: 166-173. In German with English summary.
Hölzinger, J. & Schilhansl, K. (1971). Zur Gewichtsentwicklung Junger Flußregepfeifer (*Charadrius dubius*). [On the increase of body weight of young Little Ringed Plovers (*Charadrius dubius*)]. *Anz. Orn. Ges. Bayern* **10(2)**: 107-109. In German with English summary.
Hölzinger, J. & Schilhansl, K. (1972). Untersuchungen zur Brutbiologie an Einer Suedwestdeutschen Population des Flußregenpfeifers (*Charadrius dubuis*). [Observations of a population of *Charadrius dubius* in southwestern Germany]. *Beitr. Naturkd. Forsch. Suedwestdtsch.* **31**: 93-101.
Hon, T., Odum, R.R. & Belcher, D.P. (1977). Results of Georgia's Clapper Rail banding program. *Proc. Ann. Conf. Southeastern Assoc. Fish & Wildl. Agencies* **31**: 72-76.
Hoodless, A.N. (1993). Understanding Woodcock populations: results from ring recoveries. *Game Conservancy Ann. Rev.* **24**: 89-91.
Hoodless, A.N. (1994). Woodcock. *Scolopax rusticola*. Pp. 270-271 in: Tucker & Heath (1994).
Hoodless, A.N. & Coulson, J.C. (1994). Survival rates and movements of British and Continental Woodcock *Scolopax rusticola* in the British Isles. *Bird Study* **41(1)**: 48-60.
Hoogendoorn, W. (1991a). Western border of non-breeding range of Brown-headed Gull. *Dutch Birding* **13(3)**: 102-103.
Hoogendoorn, W. (1991b). Record of Brown-headed Gull in Israel in May 1985. *Dutch Birding* **13(3)**: 104-106.
Hoogendoorn, W. (1993). First record of Laughing Gull in Chile. *Amer. Birds* **47**: 156-158.
Hoogendoorn, W. (1995a). The Audouin's Gull in northern France. *Birding World* **8(7)**: 263-265.
Hoogendoorn, W. (1995b). Un Goéland d'Audouin *Larus audouinii* dans le Boulonnais. [Audouin's Gull in Boulonnais, northern France]. *Ornithos* **2(3)**: 136-139. In French with English summary.
Hoogendoorn, W. & Mackrill, E.J. (1987). Audouin's Gull in southwestern Paleartic. *Dutch Birding* **9**: 99-107.
Hoogendoorn, W., van den Berg, A.B. & Mullarney, K. (1991). Brown-headed Gulls with mirrors on three primaries. *Dutch Birding* **13**: 63-64.
Hoogendoorn, W., Moerbeek, D.J., Meininger, P.L. & Berrevoets, C.M. (1992). Spring head-moult in Mediterranean Gull in north-western France. *Dutch Birding* **14(6)**: 207-214.
Hoogerwerf, A. (1936). On the nidification of some Javan birds. *Bull. Raffles Mus., Singapore* **12**: 118-124.
Hoogerwerf, A. (1949). *Bijdrage tot de Oölogie van Java*. Limosa **22**. 277 pp.
Hoogerwerf, A. (1964). On birds for New Guinea or with a larger range than previously known. *Bull. Brit. Orn. Club* **84**: 70-77, 94-96, 118-124, 142-148, 153-161.
Hoogerwerf, A. (1966). On the validity of *Charadrius alexandrinus javanicus* Chasen, and the occurrence of *Ch. a. ruficapillus* Temm. and of *Ch. peronii* Schl. on Java and New Guinea. *Philippine J. Sci.* **95**: 209-214.
Hoogerwerf, A. (1969). On the ornithology of the Rhino sanctuary Udjung Kulon in west Java (Indonesia). I Part. *Nat. Hist. Bull. Siam Soc.* **23**: 9-65.
Hoogerwerf, A. & Siccama, G.F.H.W. (1937). Rengers Hora. De avifauna van Batavia en omstreken. 2. *Ardea* **26**: 116-159.
Hooper, T.D. (1988). Habitat, reproductive parameters and nest-site tenacity of urban-nesting Glaucous-winged Gulls at Victoria, British Columbia. *Murrelet* **69**: 10-14.
Hoopes, E.M. (1993). *Relationships between Human Recreation and Piping Plover Foraging Ecology and Chick Survival*. MSc thesis, University of Massachusetts, Amherst, Massachusetts.
Hopcraft, J.B.D. (1968). Some notes on the chick-carrying behavior of the African Jacana. *Living Bird* **7**: 85-88.
Hopkins, C.D. & Wiley, R.H. (1972). Food parasitism and competition in two terns. *Auk* **89**: 583-594.
Hopkins, N. (1976). Further notes on the Australian Pratincole. *North Queensland Nat.* **168**. 2 pp. (Unpaginated).
Hopkinson, G. & Masterson, A.N.B. (1975). Notes on the Striped Crake. *Honeyguide* **84**: 12-21.
Hopkinson, G. & Masterson, A.N.B. (1977). On the occurrence near Salisbury of the White-winged Flufftail. *Honeyguide* **91**: 25-28.
Hopkinson, G. & Masterson, A.N.B. (1984). The occurrence and ecological preferences of certain Rallidae near Salisbury, Zimbabwe. In: Ledger (1984).
Hopson, A.J. & Hopson, J. (1974). A Buff-breasted Sandpiper *Tryngites subruficollis* at Kerio Bay, Lake Rudolf. *Bull. East Afr. Nat. Hist. Soc.* **1974**: 17-18.
Hopson, J. & Hopson, A.J. (1972). Broad-billed Sandpiper at Lake Rudolf. *Bull. East Afr. Nat. Hist. Soc.* **1972**: 170-171.
Hopwood, J.C. (1921). The nidification of the Masked Finfoot (*Heliopais personata*). *J. Bombay Nat. Hist. Soc.* **27**: 634.
Horak, G.J. (1970). A comparative study of the foods of the Sora and Virginia Rail. *Wilson Bull.* **82**: 206-213.
Hori, H. (1994). International zoo news. Tokyo Sea Life Park, Japan. *Int. Zoo News* **255**: 58.
Horlyk, N.O. & Lind, H. (1978). Pecking response of artificially hatched Oystercatcher (*Haematopus ostralegus*) young. *Ornis Scand.* **9**: 138 145.
Horn, C.L. (1990). A Marbled Godwit in Minneapolis. *Loon* **62(2)**: 114.
Hornbuckle, J. (1994). *Birdwatching in the Philippines*. Published privately.
Horning, C.L., Hutchins, M. & English, W. (1988). Breeding and management of the Common Trumpeter (*Psophia crepitans*). *Zoo Biology* **7(3)**: 193-210.
Horsfall, J.A. (1984a). Brood reduction and brood division in Coots. *Animal Behav.* **32**: 216-225.
Horsfall, J.A. (1984b). The "dawn chorus" and incubation in the Coot (*Fulica atra* L.). *Behav. Ecol. Sociobiol.* **15**: 69-71.
Horsfall, J.A. (1984c). Food supply and egg mass variation in the European Coot. *Ecology* **65**: 89-95.
Horton, G.I. & Causey, M.K. (1979). Woodcock movements and habitat utilization in central Alabama. *J. Wildl. Manage.* **43**: 414-420.
Horton, G.I. & Causey, M.K. (1982). Association among Woodcock brood members after brood breakup. Pp. 71-74 in: Dwyer & Storm (1982).
Horton, N., Brough, T., Fletcher, M.R., Rochard, J.B.A. & Stanley, P.I. (1984). The winter distribution of foreign Black-headed Gulls in the British Isles. *Bird Study* **31**: 171-186.
Horwich, R. (1986). Reintroduction of Sandhill Cranes to the wild. *ICF Bugle* **12(4)**: 1, 4-5.
Horwood, J.W. & Goss-Custard, J.D. (1977). Predation by Oystercatchers, *Haematopus ostralegus* L., in relation to the cockle, *Cerastoderma edule* L. fishery in the Burry Inlet, South Wales. *J. Appl. Ecol.* **14**: 139 158.
Hosey, G.R. & Goodridge, F. (1980). Establishment of territories in two species of gull on Walney Island, Cumbria. *Bird Study* **27**: 73-80.
Hosken, J.H. (1966). Food of Peters' Finfoot *Podica senegalensis*. *Ostrich* **37**: 235.
Hötker, H. (1985). Migration studies of Ruffs wintering in Senegal. *Wader Study Group Bull.* **45**: 7.
Hötker, H. (1989). Waders breeding on wet grasslands in the countries of the European Community - a brief summary of current knowledge on population sizes and population trends. Pp. 50-55 in: Hötker (1991).
Hötker, H. (1990). Territorial behaviour of wintering Marsh Sandpipers *Tringa stagnatilis*. *Wader Study Group Bull.* **60**: 20.
Hötker, H. ed. (1991). *Waders Breeding on Wet Grasslands*. Wader Study Group Bulletin **61**(Supplement). 107 pp.
Houde, P. & Braun, M.J. (1988). Museum collections as a source of DNA for studies of avian phylogeny. *Auk* **105**: 773-776.

Hounsell, R.G. (1992). *Status of the Woodcock in Canada 1991*. Canadian Wildlife Service, Sackville, Canada.
Houston, D.C. (1979). Why do Fairy Terns *Gygis alba* not build nests? *Ibis* **121**: 102-104.
Houston, D.C., Jones, P.J. & Sibly, R.M. (1983). The effect of female body condition on egg-laying in Lesser Black-backed Gulls *Larus fuscus*. *J. Zool., London* **200**: 509-520.
Houston, P. & Barter, M. (1990). Morphometrics of Ruddy Turnstone *Arenaria interpres* in Australia. *Stilt* **17**: 17-23.
How, R.A. & Dell, J. (1990). Vertebrate fauna of Bold Park, Perth. *West. Austr. Nat.* **18(4/5)**: 122-131.
Howard, H. (1950). Fossil evidence of avian evolution. *Ibis* **92**: 1-21.
Howe, F.E. & Ross, J.A. (1931). Eggs of the Banded Stilt. *Emu* **31**: 63-65.
Howe, M.A. (1974). Observations on the terrestrial wing displays of breeding Willets. *Wilson Bull.* **86**: 286-288.
Howe, M.A. (1975a). Behavioral aspects of the pair bond in Wilson's Phalarope. *Wilson Bull.* **87**: 248-270.
Howe, M.A. (1975b). Social interactions in flocks of courting Wilson's Phalaropes (*Phalaropus tricolor*). *Condor* **77**: 24-33.
Howe, M.A. (1982). Social organization in a nesting population of Eastern Willets (*Catoptrophorus semipalmatus*). *Auk* **99**: 88-102.
Howe, M.A. (1987). Habitat use by migrating Whooping Cranes in the Aransas-Wood Buffalo corridor. Pp. 303-311 in: Lewis (1987).
Howe, M.A. (1989). *Migration of Radio-marked Whooping Cranes from the Aransas-Wood Buffalo Population: Patterns of Habitat Use, Behavior, and Survival*. Fish and Wildlife Technical Report **21**. US Fish & Wildlife Service, Washington, D.C.
Howe, M.A., Geissler, P.H. & Harrington, B.A. (1989). Population trends of North American shorebirds based on the International Shorebird Survey. *Biol. Conserv.* **49(3)**: 185-199.
Howell, A.B. (1917). Birds of the islands off the coast of southern California. *Pacific Coast Avifauna* **12**: 1-137.
Howell, A.H. (1932). *Bird Life*. Florida Game & Fresh Water Fish Commission & US Bureau Biol. Surv. Coward-McCann, New York.
Howell, J., Laclergue, D., Paris, S., Boarman, W., DeGange, A.R. & Binford, L.C. (1983). First nests of Heermann's Gull in the United States. *Western Birds* **14**: 39-46.
Howell, S.N.G. (1990). The seabirds of Las Islas Revillagigedo, Mexico. *Wilson Bull.* **102**: 140-146.
Howell, S.N.G. (1993). Status of the Piping Plover in Mexico. *Euphonia* **2(3)**: 51-54.
Howell, S.N.G. & Webb, S. (1994). Occurrence of Snowy and Collared Plovers in the interior of Mexico. *Western Birds* **25(3)**: 146-150.
Howell, S.N.G. & Webb, S. (1995a). *A Guide to the Birds of Mexico and Northern Central America*. Oxford University Press, New York.
Howell, S.N.G. & Webb, S. (1995b). Noteworthy bird observations from Chile. *Bull. Brit. Orn. Club* **115(1)**: 57-66.
Howell, S.N.G., Dowell, B.A., James, D.A., Behrstock, R.A. & Robbins, C.S. (1992). New and noteworthy bird records from Belize. *Bull. Brit. Orn. Club* **112**: 235-244.
Howell, S.N.G., Webb, S. & de Montes, B.M. (1990). Notes on tropical terns in Mexico. *Amer. Birds* **44**: 381-383.
Howell, T.R. (1978). Breeding biology of the Egyptian plover *Pluvianus aegyptius*. *Bull. Niger. Orn. Soc.* **14(46)**: 51-53.
Howell, T.R. (1979). Breeding biology of the Egyptian Plover *Pluvianus aegyptius*. *Univ. Calif. Publ. Zool.* **113**: 1-76.
Howell, T.R. (1983a). Desert-nesting sea gulls. *Nat. Hist.* **93**: 52-59.
Howell, T.R. (1983b). Buried treasure of the Egyptian Plover. *Nat. Hist.* **93(9)**: 60-67.
Howell, T.R. (1984). Reproductive adaptations of the Egyptian Plover, *Pluvianus aegyptius*. *Natl. Geogr. Soc. Res. Rep.* **17**: 475-484.
Howell, T.R. & Bartholmew, G.A. (1962). Temperature regulation in the Sooty Tern *Sterna fuscata*. *Ibis* **104**: 98-105.
Howell, T.R., Araya, B. & Millie, W.R. (1974). Breeding biology of the Gray Gull, *Larus modestus*. *Univ. Calif. Publ. Zool.* **104**: 1-57.
Howells, R.J. (1968). Ring-billed Gulls displaying in West Glamorgan. *British Birds* **79**: 42.
Howells, W.W. (1977). Lesser Blackwinged Plovers in Wankie National Park. *Honeyguide* **92**: 48.
Howells, W.W. & Fynn, K.J. (1979). The occurrence of Denham's Bustard at Wankie National Park and in north west Rhodesia with notes on movements and behaviour. *Honeyguide* **97**: 4-12.
Howes, J.R. (1988). Nordmann's Greenshank *Tringa guttifer*: status and trends. *Asian Wetland News* **1**: 12.
Howes, J.R. & Bakewell, D. (1989). *Shorebird Studies Manual*. Asian Wetland Bureau Publications **55**. Kuala Lumpur.
Howes, J.R. & Lambert, F. (1987). Some notes on the status, field identification and foraging characteristics of Nordmann's Greenshank *Tringa guttifer*. *Wader Study Group Bull.* **49**: 14-17.
Howes, J.R. & Parish, D. (1989). *New Information on Asian Shorebirds: a Preliminary Review of the INTERWADER Programme 1983-1989 and Priorities for the Future*. Asian Wetland Bureau Publication **42**. Kuala Lumpur. 32 pp.
Hoxie, W.J. (1887). An egg lifter. *Ornithologist and Oologist* **12**: 129.
Hoy, G. (1967). The eggs and nesting ground of the Puna Plover. *Auk* **84**: 130-131.
Hu Yaoguang & Wang Jiao (1989). [Studies on the breeding ecology of the Kentish Plover *Charadrius alexandrinus*]. *Trans. Liaoning Zool. Soc.* **7(1)**: 125-127. In Chinese.
Huang Guozhu (1990). [A newly discovered wintering area of Black-necked Cranes]. *Da Ziran* **2(40)**: 11. In Chinese.
Huang Zhengyi & Tang Ziying (1984). The discovery of a Long-tailed Skua *Stercorarius longicaudus* Vieillot from Changle, Fujian Province. *J. Fudan Univ. (Nat. Sci.)* **23(1)**: 118.
Hubaut, D. (1984). Première observation d'un Bécasseau rousset (*Tryngites subruficollis*) en Belgique. *Aves* **21(4)**: 237-243.
Hudon, J. & Brush, A.H. (1990). Carotenoids produce flush in the Elegant Tern plumage. *Condor* **92**: 798-801.
Hudson, A.V. & Furness, R.W. (1988). Utilization of discarded fish by scavenging seabirds behind whitefish trawlers in Shetland. *J. Zool., London* **215**: 151-166.
Hudson, A.V., Stowe, T.J. & Aspinall, S.J. (1990). Status and distribution of Corncrakes in Britain. *British Birds* **83**: 173-186.
Hudson, G.E., Hoff, K.M., Vanden Berge, J. & Trivette, E.C. (1969). A numerical study of the wing and leg muscles of Lari and Alcae. *Ibis* **111**: 459-524.
Hudson, P.J. (1979). The parent-chick fledging relationship of the Puffin, *Fratercula arctica*. *J. Anim. Ecol.* **48**: 889-898.
Hudson, P.J. (1985). Population parameters for the Atlantic Alcidae. Pp. 233-261 in: Nettleship & Birkhead (1985).
Hudson, R. (1974). Allen's Gallinule in Britain and the Palaearctic. *British Birds* **67**: 405-413.
Hudson, W.H. (1920). *Birds of La Plata*. Vol. 2. Dent, London.
Hüe, F. & Étchécopar, R.D. (1970). *Les Oiseaux du Proche et du Moyen Orient de la Méditerranée aux Contreforts de l'Himalaya*. Editions N. Boubée, Paris.
Hughes, B.J. (1991). Mapping the Sooty Terns. *Adjutant (J. Army Bird Watch. Soc.)* **21**: 10-13.
Hughes, M.R. (1984). Osmoregulation in nestling Glaucous-winged Gulls. *Condor* **86**: 390-395.
Hughes, P. & Hughes, B. (1991). Notes on the Black-breasted Button-quail at Widgee, Queensland. *Austr. Bird Watcher* **14(4)**: 113-118.
Hughes, R.A. (1968). Notes on the occurrence of the Grey-hooded Gull *Larus cirrocephalus* on the west coast of South America. *Ibis* **110**: 357-358.
Hughes, R.A. (1977). Franklin's Gull (*Larus pipixcan*) at Lake Titicaca, Peru. *Biotropica* **9**: 52.
Hughes, R.A. (1980). Additional puna zone bird species on the coast of Peru. *Condor* **82**: 475.
Hughes, R.A. (1984). Further notes on Puna bird species on the coast of Peru. *Condor* **86(1)**: 93.
Hughey, K.F.D. (1985). The relationship between riverbed flooding and non-breeding Wrybills on northern grounds in summer. *Notornis* **32(1)**: 42-50.
Hughey, K.F.D. (1989). The status of the Red-caped Dotterel in New Zealand. *Notornis* **36(1)**: 24-26.
Hulscher, J.B. (1971). The Oystercatcher and the Wadden Sea. *Waddenbulletin* **1971(2)**: 9 13.
Hulscher, J.B. (1973). Enkele waarnemingen over de wegtrek van de Scholekster van de broedgebieden na de broedtijd in Friesland. *Vanellus* **26**: 35-39.
Hulscher, J.B. (1974). An experimental study of the food intake of the Oystercatcher *Haematopus ostralegus* L. in captivity during the summer. *Ardea* **62**: 155 171.
Hulscher, J.B. (1975a). De trek van de Scholekster in Friesland aan de hand van ringgegevens. *De Levende Natuur* **78**: 218-230.
Hulscher, J.B. (1975b). Het voorkomen in de winter en het begin van de voorjaarstrek van de Scholekster in het binneland van Friesland. *Vanellus* **28**: 141-147.
Hulscher, J.B. (1976). Localisation of cockles (*Cardium edule* L.) by the Oystercatcher (*Haematopus ostralegus* L.) in darkness and daylight. *Ardea* **64**: 292 310.
Hulscher, J.B. (1977a). The progress of wing moult of Oystercatchers *Haematopus ostralegus* at Drachten, Netherlands. *Ibis* **119**: 507 512.
Hulscher, J.B. (1977b). Wat verkeerschlachtoffers van Scholeksters ons nog kunnen leren. *Vanellus* **30**: 170 179.
Hulscher, J.B. (1982). The Oystercatcher *Haematopus ostralegus* as a predator of the bivalve *Macoma balthica* in the Dutch Wadden Sea. *Ardea* **70**: 89 152.
Hulscher, J.B. (1985). Growth and abrasion of the Oystercatcher bill in relation to dietary switches. *Netherlands J. Zool.* **35**: 124-154.
Hulscher, J.B. (1988). Mossel doodt Scholekster *Haematopus ostralegus*. *Limosa* **61**: 42-45.
Hulscher, J.B. (1989). Sterfte en overleving van Scholeksters *Haematopus ostralegus* bij strenge vorst. *Limosa* **62**: 177-181.
Hulscher, J.B. (1990). Survival of oystercatchers during hard winter weather. *Ring Bull.* **13**: 167-172.
Hulscher, J.B. & Ens, B.J. (1991). Somatic modifications of feeding system structures due to feeding on different foods with emphasis of changes in bill shape in oystercatchers. Pp. 889-896 in: *Proc. XX Int. Orn. Congr.* Christchurch, 1990.
Hulscher, J.B. & Ens, B.J. (1992). Is the bill of the male Oystercatcher a better tool for attacking mussels than the bill of the female? *Netherlands J. Zool.* **42**: 85-100.
Hulsman, K. (1974). Notes on the behaviour of terns at One Tree Island. *Sunbird* **5**: 44-49.
Hulsman, K. (1976). The robbing behaviour of gulls and terns. *Emu* **76**: 143-149.
Hulsman, K. (1977). The breeding success and mortality of terns at One Tree Island, Great Barrier Reef. *Emu* **77**: 49-60.
Hulsman, K. (1981). Width of gape as a determinant of size of prey eaten by terns. *Emu* **81**: 29-32.
Hulsman, K. (1984). Selection of prey and success of Silver Gulls robbing Crested Terns. *Condor* **86**: 130-138.
Hulsman, K. (1987). Resource partitioning among sympatric species of terns. *Ardea* **75**: 255-262.
Hulsman, K. (1988). The structure of seabird communities: an example from Australian waters. Pp. 59-92 in: Burger (1988c).
Hulsman, K. & Langham, N.P.E. (1985). Breeding biology of the Bridled Tern *Sterna anaethetus*. *Emu* **85**: 240-249.
Hulsman, K. & Smith, G.C. (1988). Biology and growth of the Black-naped Tern *Sterna sumatrana*, a hypothesis to explain the relative growth rates of inshore, offshore and pelagic feeders. *Emu* **88**: 234-242.
Hulsman, K., Dale, P. & Jahnke, B.R. (1984). Vegetation and nesting preferences of Black Noddies at Masthead Island, Great Barrier Reef. II. Patterns at the micro-scale. *Austr. J. Ecol.* **9**: 343-352.
Hulsman, K., Langham, N.P.E. & Bluhdorn, D. (1989). Factors affecting the diet of Crested Terns, *Sterna bergii*. *Austr. Wildl. Res.* **16**: 475-489.
Humblot, L. (1882). Rapport sur un mission à Madagasar. *Arch. Miss. Sci. Litt.* **(3)8**: 153-157.
Hume, A.O. (1890). *The Nests and Eggs of Indian Birds*. Vol. 3. R.H. Porter, London.
Hume, R.A. (1975). Identification and aging of Glaucous and Iceland Gulls. *British Birds* **68**: 24-37.
Hume, R.A. & Grant, P.J. (1974). The upperwing pattern of adult Common and Arctic Terns. *British Birds* **67**: 133-136.
Hummel, D. (1990). [Influx of Great Bustards *Otis tarda* in western Europe during the winter of 1986/87]. *Limicola* **4(1)**: 1-8, 10-21. In German with English summary.
Humphrey, P.S., Bridge, D., Reynolds, P.W. & Peterson, R.T. (1970). *Birds of Isla Grande (Tierra del Fuego)*. Museum of Natural History, University of Kansas, Lawrence, Kansas.
Humphrey, R.C. (1988). *Ecology and Range Expansion of American Oystercatchers in Massachusetts*. MSc thesis, University of Massachusetts, Amherst, Massachusetts.
Hunt, G.L. (1972). Influence of food distribution and human disturbance on the reproductive success of Herring Gulls. *Ecology* **53**: 1051-1061.
Hunt, G.L. & Butler, J.L. (1980). Reproductive ecology of Western Gulls and Xantus' Murrelets with respect to food resources in the southern California Bight. *Calif. Coop. Oceanic Fish. Invest. Rep.* **21**: 62-67.
Hunt, G.L. & Harrison, N.M. (1990). Foraging habitat and prey taken by Least Auklets at King Island, Alaska. *Mar. Ecol. Prog. Ser.* **65**: 141-150.
Hunt, G.L. & Hunt, M.W. (1973). Clutch size, hatching success and eggshell thinning in Western Gulls. *Condor* **75**: 483-486.
Hunt, G.L. & Hunt, M.W. (1975). Reproductive ecology of the Western Gull: the importance of nest spacing. *Auk* **92**: 270-279.
Hunt, G.L. & Hunt, M.W. (1976a). Exploitation of fluctuating food resources by Western Gulls. *Auk* **93**: 301-307.
Hunt, G.L. & Hunt, M.W. (1976b). Gull chick survival: the significance of growth rates, timing of breeding and territory size. *Ecology* **57**: 62-75.
Hunt, G.L. & Hunt, M.W. (1977). Female-female pairing in Western Gulls (*Larus occidentalis*) in southern California. *Science* **196**: 1466-1467.
Hunt, G.L. & Smith, W.J. (1963). The swallowing of fish by young Herring Gulls *Larus argentatus*. *Ibis* **106**: 457-461.
Hunt, G.L., Burgeson, B. & Sanger, G.A. (1981). Feeding ecology of seabirds of the eastern Bering Sea. Pp. 629-648 in:Hood, D.W. & Calder, J.A. eds. (1981). *The Eastern Bering Sea Shelf: Oceanography and Resources*. University Washington Press, Seattle, Washington.
Hunt, G.L., Eppley, Z.A., Burgeson, B. & Squibb, R. (1981). *Reproductive Ecology, Foods and Foraging Areas of Seabirds Nesting on the Pribilof Islands, 1975-1979*. US Department of Commerce, NOAA, OCSEAP Final Report Biological Studies **12**. 258 pp.
Hunt, G.L., Eppley, Z.A. & Schneider, D.C. (1986). Reproductive performance of seabirds: the importance of population and colony size. *Auk* **103**: 306-317.
Hunt, G.L., Harrison, N.M. & Cooney, R.T. (1990). The influence of hydrographic structure and prey abundance on foraging Least Auklets. Pp. 7-22 in: Sealy (1990).
Hunt, G.L., Harrison, N.M. & Piatt, J.F. (1993). Foraging ecology as related to the distribution of planktivorous auklets in the Bering Sea. Pp. 18-26 in: Vermeer, Briggs *et al.* (1993).
Hunt, G.L., Mayer, B., Rodstrom, W. & Squibb, R. (1978). The reproductive ecology, foods and foraging areas of seabirds nesting on St. Spaul Island, Pribilof Islands. Pp. 570-775 in: *Annual Reports of Principal Investigators. Environmental Assessment of the Alaskan Continental Shelf*. Vol. 1. NOAA-BLM, Boulder, Colorado.
Hunt, G.L., Pitman, R.I., Naughton, M., Winnet, K., Newman, A., Kelly, P.R. & Briggs, K.T. (1981). *Distribution, Status, Reproductive Ecology and Foraging Habits of Breeding Seabirds. Summary of Marine Mammal and Seabird Surveys of the Southern California Bight Area, 1975-1978*. US Department of Commerce, Natl. Tech. Inf. Serv. Publ. PB-81-248-205. Springfield, Virginia.
Hunt, G.L., Wingfield, J.D., Newman, A. & Farner, D.S. (1980). Sex ratio of Western Gulls on Santa Barbara Island, California. *Auk* **97(3)**: 473-479.
Hunt, G.R. (1992). Census of Kagus (*Rhynochetos jubatus*) on the main island of New Caledonia during 1991/1992. Unpublished report to ASNNC/SRETIE, Nouméa, New Caledonia.
Hunt, G.R. (1993). Preliminary report on the Kagu deaths at Pic Nigua. Unpublished report to BirdLife International.
Hunt, G.R. (1994). Kagu. *World Birdwatch* **16(1)**: 20-21.
Hunt, G.R. (1995). Kagu project phase II: final report summarizing the phase II fieldwork research programme, 1/8/92-31/3/95. Unpublished report to ASNNC/BirdLife International/LPO/RSPB.
Hunt, G.R. (1996). Environmental variables associated with population patterns of the Kagu *Rhynochetos jubatus* of New Caledonia. *Ibis* **138**.
Hunt, G.R., Hay, R. & Veltman, C.J. (1996). Multiple Kagu *Rhynochetos jubatus* deaths caused by dog attacks at a high altitude study site on Pic Ningua, New Caledonia. *Bird Conservation International* **6**.
Hunt, M.C. (1994). Analysis of the relationship between egg order (1-15) and egg quality as determined by hatching and fledging rates in Siberian, Florida Sandhill, White-naped and Red-crowned Cranes. *Avicult. Mag.* **100(1)**: 29-34.
Hunter, L., Canevari, P., Myers, J.P. & Payne, L.X. (1991). Shorebird and wetland conservation in the western hemisphere. Pp. 279-290 in: Salathé, T. ed. (1991). *Conserving Migratory Birds*. ICBP Technical Publication **12**, Cambridge.
Hunter, L.A. (1987a). Acquisition of territories by floaters in cooperatively breeding Purple Gallinules. *Anim. Behav.* **35**: 402-410.
Hunter, L.A. (1987b). Cooperative breeding in Purple Gallinules: the role of helpers in feeding chicks. *Behav. Ecol. Sociobiol.* **20**: 171-177.
Hüppop, O. (1996). Nestling der Dreizehenmöwe (*Rissa tridactyla*) verhindert erste erfolgreiche Felsbrut einer Schwarzkopfmöwe (*Larus melanocephalus*) auf Helgoland. *Seevögel* **17(1)**: 1-2.
Hurford, C. (1989). Lesser-crested Tern: new to Britain and Ireland. *British Birds* **82(9)**: 396-398.
Hurlbert, S.H., López, M. & Keith, J.O. (1984). Wilson's Phalarope in the central Andes and its interaction with the Chilean Flamingo. *Rev. Chilena Hist. Nat.* **57**: 47-57.
Hurter, H.U. (1972). Nahrung und Ernährungsweise des Bläßhuhns *Fulica atra* am Sempachersee. *Orn. Beob.* **69**: 125-149.
Hussain, S.A. (1985). Black-necked Crane in Ladakh - 1983: problems and prospects. *J. Bombay Nat. Hist. Soc.* **82**: 449-458.
Hussell, D.J.T. & Page, G.W. (1976). Observations on the breeding biology of Black-bellied Plovers on Devon Island, N.W.T., Canada. *Wilson Bull.* **88**: 632-653.

Hutchinson, C.D. & Neath, B. (1978). Little Gulls in Britain and Ireland. *British Birds* **71**: 563-582.
Hutchison, R.E., Stevenson, J.G. & Thorpe, W.H. (1968). The basis for individual recognition by voice in the Sandwich Tern (*Sterna sandvicensis*). *Behaviour* **32**: 150-157.
Hutson, G.D. (1977a). Agonistic display and spacing in the Black-headed Gull *Larus ridibundus*. *Anim. Behav.* **25**: 765-773.
Hutson, G.D. (1977b). Observations on the swoop and soar display of the Black-headed Gull *Larus ridibundus*. *Ibis* **119**: 67-73.
Hutton, K. (1992). Long-toed Stints in New South Wales. *Austr. Birds* **26(1)**: 20-28.
Hutton, M. & Sloan, B. (1993). Variable Oystercatchers cope with gulls. *Notornis* **40(2)**: 144.
Huxley, C.R. & Wilkinson, R. (1977). Vocalizations of the Aldabra White-throated Rail *Dryolimnas cuvieri aldabranus*. *Proc. Royal Soc. London* **197B**: 315-331.
Huxley, C.R. & Wilkinson, R. (1979). Duetting and vocal recognition by Aldabra White-throated Rails *Dryolimnas cuvieri aldabranus*. *Ibis* **212**: 265-273.
Huxley, C.R. & Wood, N.A. (1976). Aspects of the breeding of the Moorhen in Britain. *Bird Study* **23**: 1-10.
Huxley, J.S. & Fisher, J. (1940). Hostility reactions in Black-headed Gulls. *Proc. Zool. Soc., London* **110**: 1-10.
Ibáñez, F. (1990). [The Dotterel *Eudromias morinellus* regular breeder in the Pyrénées]. *Oiseau et RFO* **60**: 303-306. In French.
van Iersel, J.J.A. & Bot, A.C.A. (1958). Preening of two tern species. A study on displacement activities. *Behaviour* **13**: 1-87.
Igou, T.D. (1986). Marbled Godwit: first observation in west Virginia. *Redstart* **53(4)**: 138.
Iida, T. (1991). [The breeding behaviour and habitat of the Latham's Snipe]. *Strix* **10**: 31-50. In Japanese with English summary.
van Ijzendoorn, E.J. (1981). On identification of immature Arctic Skua and Long-tailed Skua. *Dutch Birding* **3**: 10-12.
Ikenaga, H. (1983). Appearance time and behaviour of the Okinawa Rail *Rallus okinawae* at a water site in the late afternoon. *Strix* **2**: 11.
Ikenaga, H. & Gima, T. (1993). Vocal repertoire and duetting in the Okinawa Rail *Rallus okinawae*. *J. Yamashina Inst. Orn.* **25**: 28-39.
Ilicev, V.D. & Zubakin, V.A. eds. (1988). *Handbuch der Vögel der Sowjetunion*. Vol. 6/1. Charadriiformes (Lari). A. Ziemsen Verlag, Wittenberg Lutherstad.
Ilyashenko, V. (1988). [Red-crowned Crane on Kunashiri Island]. Pp. 199-203 in: Litvinenko & Neufeldt (1988). In Russian.
Ilyenko, A.I. & Burov, K.N. (1985). [Egg-size variability in colonies of Black-headed Gulls (*Larus ridibundus*) and Black-necked Grebes (*Podiceps nigricollis*) as an index of breeding condition]. *Ornitologiya* **20**: 170-172. In Russian.
Imai, M., Ozawa, S. & Shinba, T. (1986). [The first record of the Bonaparte's Gull in Japan]. *Jap. J. Orn.* **35**: 33-34. In Japanese.
Imber, M.J. & Crockett, D.E. (1970). Seabirds found dead in New Zealand in 1968. *Notornis* **17**.
Imbert, G. (1988). [Use of bag statistics for the evaluation of the diurnal habitat of wintering Woodcock (*Scolopax rusticola*)]. Pp. 53-59 in: Havet & Hirons (1988). In French with English summary.
Imboden, C. (1974). [Migration, dispersion and breeding period of the Lapwing *Vanellus vanellus* in Europe]. *Orn. Beob.* **71**: 5-134. In German.
van Impe, J. (1988). [A comparing study of breeding biology of Lapwing, *Vanellus vanellus*, on fallow and on farmland]. *Gerfaut* **78**: 287-314. In Dutch with English summary.
van Impe, J. (1995). [Considerations on the causes of disappearance of the Slender-billed Curlew *Numenius tenuirostris*]. *Alauda* **63(2)**: 111-114. In French with English summary.
van Impe, J. & Lieckens, H. (1993). Aspects of the breeding biology of the Coot *Fulica atra* in an uncommon habitat. *Oriolus* **59**: 3-13.
Impekoven, M. (1971). Prenatal experience of parental calls and pecking in the Laughing Gull (*Larus atricilla*). *Anim. Behav.* **19**: 475-480.
Impekoven, M. (1973). The response of incubating Laughing Gulls (*Larus atricilla* L.) to calls of hatching chicks. *Behaviour* **46**: 94-113.
Indrawan, M. (1991). A winter flock of Pheasant-tailed Jacanas at Ciamis, west Java. *Kukila* **5(2)**: 138-140.
Ingalls, E.A. (1972). *Aspects of the Ethology of Limpkins (*Aramus guarauna*)*. MSc thesis, University of South Florida, Tampa, Florida.
Inglis, C.M. (1940). The Painted Snipe. *Rostratula benghalensis benghalensis* (Linn). *J. Bengal Nat. Hist. Soc.* **15**: 1-7.
Ingold, J.L., Vaughn, J.C., Guttman, S.I. & Maxson, L.R. (1989). Phylogeny of the cranes (Aves: Gruidae) as deduced from DNA-DNA hybridization and albumin micro-complement fixation analyses. *Auk* **106**: 592-602.
Ingold, R. (1930). Weiteres vom Wachtelkönig. *Orn. Beob.* **28**: 23-24.
Ingolfsson, A. (1970a). The moult of remiges and rectrices in Great Black-backed Gulls *Larus marinus* and Glaucous Gulls *L. hyperboreus* in Iceland. *Ibis* **112**: 83-92.
Ingolfsson, A. (1970b). Hybridization of Glaucous Gull *Larus hyperboreus* and Herring Gull *L. argentatus* in Iceland. *Ibis* **112**: 340-362.
Ingolfsson, A. (1976). The feeding habits of Great Black-backed Gulls, *Larus marinus*, and Glaucous Gull, *L. hyperboreus*, in Iceland. *Acta Naturalia Islandica* **24**: 1-19.
Ingram, C. (1978). Carriage of the young and related adaptations in the anatomy of the Woodcock *Scolopax rusticola*. *Ibis* **120**: 67.
Inouye, M. (1981). A historical review of conservation of Red-crowned Crane (Tancho) in Hokkaido. Pp. 99-101 in: Lewis & Masatomi (1981).
Insfram, F. (1929). Observaciones biológicas sobre la (Saria Hû) *Chunga burmeisteri*. *Rev. Soc. Cient. Paraguay* **2**: 225-227.
Inskipp, C. & Collar, N.J. (1984). The Bengal Florican: its conservation in Nepal. *Oryx* **18**: 30-35.
Inskipp, C. & Inskipp, T. (1983). *Results of a Preliminary Survey of Bengal Floricans* Houbaropsis bengalensis *in Nepal and India, 1982*. ICBP Study Report **2**, Cambridge.
Inskipp, C. & Inskipp, T. (1985). A survey of Bengal Floricans in Nepal and India, 1982. *Bustard Studies* **3**: 141-160.
Inskipp, C. & Inskipp, T. (1991). *A Guide to the Birds of Nepal*. Croom Helm, London.
Inskipp, C. & Inskipp, T. (1994). Birds recorded during a visit to Bhutan in spring 1993. *Forktail* **9**: 121-143.
Inskipp, T. & Collins, L. (1993). *World Checklist of Threatened Birds*. Joint Nature Conservation Committee, Peterborough, UK.
Inskipp, T. & Round, P.D. (1989). A review of the Black-tailed Crake *Porzana bicolor*. *Forktail* **5**: 3-15.
Iqubal, P. (1992). *Breeding Behaviour in the Sarus Crane (*Grus antigone antigone*)*. MS thesis, Aligarh Muslim University, Aligarh, India.
Irish, J. (1974). Postbreeding territorial behaviour of Soras and Virginia Rails in several Michigan marshes. *Jack-Pine Warbler* **52**: 115-124.
Irisov, E. & Irisova, N. (1995). The present distribution of the Demoiselle Crane in the Altai territory. Pp. 295-297 in: Prange *et al.* (1995).
Irisov, E.I. (1976). [Notes on the Solitary Snipe in the Altai]. Pp. 141-142 in: [*Rare, Threatened and Inadequately-known Birds of the USSR*]. Moscow. In Russian.
Irons, D.B. (1987). Diets of Glaucous-winged Gulls: a comparison of methods for collecting and analyzing data. Page 103 in: Hand *et al.* (1987).
Irons, D.B. (1988). Black-legged Kittiwakes nest on advancing glacier. *Wilson Bull.* **100**: 324-325.
Irons, D.B., Anthony, R.G. & Estes, J.A. (1986). Foraging strategies of Glaucous-winged Gulls in a rocky intertidal community. *Ecology* **67**: 1460-1474.
Irvine, K. (1996). Understanding proposed changes to the endangered species act: the case of the Marbled Murrelet. *Endangered Species Update* **13(1 & 2)**: 17-21.
Irwin, M.P.S. (1976). Some little known and inadequately documented Rhodesian birds. *Honeyguide* **90**: 9-13.
Irwin, M.P.S. (1981). *The Birds of Zimbabwe*. Quest Publishing, Harare.
Isakov, Y.A. (1974). Present distribution and population status of the Great Bustard *Otis tarda* Linnaeus. *J. Bombay Nat. Hist. Soc.* **71**: 433-444.
Isenmann, P. (1972). Aire de repartition de la Sterne caugek *Sterna sandvicensis* en Méditerranée et données sur sa biologie en Camargue. *Nos Oiseaux* **31**: 150-162.
Isenmann, P. (1975a). [Passage of the Caspian Tern *Hydroprogne caspia* in 1971 and 1972 in Camargue]. *Alauda* **41**: 365-370. In French.
Isenmann, P. (1975b). Contribution à l'étude de la biologie de reproduction et d'écologie de la Mouette mélanocephale *Larus melanocephalus*. *Nos Oiseaux* **33**: 66-73.
Isenmann, P. (1976a). Contribution à l'étude de la biologie de la reproduction et de l'écologie du Goéland argenté à pieds jaunes (*Larus argentatus michahellis*) en Camargue. *Rev. Ecol. (Terre Vie)* **20**: 551-563.
Isenmann, P. (1976b). Contribution à l'étude de la biologie de la reproduction et de l'étho-écologie du Goéland railleur, *Larus genei*. *Ardea* **64**: 48-61.
Isenmann, P. (1976c). Observations sur le Guifette noire *Chlidonias niger* en Camargue. *Alauda* **44**: 319-327.
Isenmann, P. (1977a). Stratégie spatio-temporelle d'alimentation de la Mouette rieuse (*Larus ridibundus*) en Camargue. *Gerfaut* **67**: 235-252.
Isenmann, P. (1977b). L'essor démographique et spatial de la Mouette rieuse (*Larus ridibundus*) en Europe. *Oiseau et RFO* **47**: 25-40.
Isenmann, P. (1977c). À propos de *Larus relictus*. *Alauda* **45**: 235-236.
Isenmann, P. & Goutner, V. (1993). Breeding status of the Slender-billed Gull (*Larus genei*) in the Mediterranean Basin. Pp. 65-70 in: Aguilar *et al.* (1993).
Isenmann, P., Lebreton, J.D. & Brandl, R. (1991). The Black-headed Gull in Europe. Pp. 2384-2389 in: Bell *et al.* (1991).
Isleib, M.E. (1979). Migratory shorebird populations on the Copper River delta and eastern Prince William Sound, Alaska. Pp. 125-129 in: Pitelka (1979).
Ivanov, A.I. (1969). [*Birds of Pamir-Alai*]. Nauka, Leningrad. In Russian.
Ivanov, A.I., Kozlova, E.V., Portenko, L.A. & Tugarinov, A.J. (1953). [*Birds of the USSR*]. Vol. 2. Academy of Sciences of the USSR, Leningrad. In Russian.
Ivanova, N.S. (1973). [Postembryonic development in the Ruff (*Philomachus pugnax*)]. *Zoologischeskii Zhurnal* **52**: 1677-1682. In Russian.
Iversen, E. (1976). On the brink of extinction. *Texas Parks Wildl.* **34**: 24-26.
Iversen, E. (1989a). El Chorlo Esquimal; una de las aves americanas más raras. *Nuestras Aves* **20**: 24-27.
Iversen, E. (1989b). Survival; the uncertain future of the Eskimo Curlew. *Birder's World* **3(4)**: 20-23.
Iversen, E. (1995). Eskimo Curlew; bird on the edge of forever. In: Luquer, H. ed. (1995). *Wetlands for the Americas, Manoment*.
Iverson, G.C., Vohs, P.A. & Tacha, T.C. (1985). Distribution and abundance of Sandhill Cranes wintering in western Texas. *J. Wildl. Manage.* **49**: 250-255.
Iverson, G.C., Vohs, P.A. & Tacha, T.C. (1987). Habitat use by mid-continent Sandhill Cranes during spring migration. *J. Wildl. Manage.* **51**: 448-458.
Iverson, G.C., Warnock, S.E., Butler, R.W., Bishop, M.A. & Warnock, N. (1996). Spring migration of Western Sandpipers (*Calidris mauri*) along the Pacific coast of North America: a telemetry study. *Condor* **98**: 10-21.
Ivey, G.L. & Baars, C. (1990). A second Semipalmated Plover nest in Oregon. *Oregon Birds* **16(3)**: 207-208.
Ivey, G.L., Fothergill, K.A. & Yates-Mills, K.L. (1988). A Semipalmated Plover nest in Oregon. *Western Birds* **19(1)**: 35-36.
Jablonski, B. (1986). Distribution, abundance and biomass of a summer community of birds in the region of the Admiralty Bay (King George Island, South Shetland Islands, Antarctic) in 1978/79. *Polar Res.* **7(3)**: 217-260.
Jackson, C.F. & Allan, P.F. (1932). Additional notes on the breeding in Maine of the Great Black-backed Gull (*Larus marinus*). *Auk* **49**: 349-350.
Jackson, D.B. (1994). Breeding dispersal and site-fidelity in three monogamous wader species in the Western Isles, U.K. *Ibis* **136**: 463-473.
Jackson, F.J. & Sclater, W.L. (1938). *The Birds of Kenya Colony and the Uganda Protectorate*. Vol. 1. Gurney & Jackson, London.
Jackson, J.A. (1976). Some aspects of the nesting ecology of Least Terns on the Mississippi Gulf coast. *Miss. Kite* **6**: 25-35.
Jackson, J.A. & Jackson, B.J.S. (1985). Status, dispersion and population changes of the Least Tern in coastal Mississippi. *Colonial Waterbirds* **8(1)**: 54-62.
Jackson, J.A. & Key, J.P. (1992). Lethal mobbing of a Laughing Gull by Least Terns. *Miss. Kite* **22**: 13-15.
Jackson, J.A., Rowe, B.E., Hetrick, M.S. & Schardien, B.J. (1982). Site-specific nest defense behavior of Black Skimmers and Least Terns. *Condor* **84**: 120.
Jackson, R. & Lyall, H. (1964). An account of the establishment of the Australian Coot in the Rotorua District with some notes on its nesting habits. *Notornis* **11**: 82-86.
Jackson, T.H. (1887). The Limpkin and its nest and eggs. *Ornithologist and Oologist* **12(10)**: 159-160.
Jacob, J. (1978). Chemotaxonomic relationships within the order Charadriiformes. *Biochem. Syst. Ecol.* **6(4)**: 347-350.
Jacob, J.P. & Courbet, B. (1980). Oiseaux de mer nicheurs sur la côte Algérienne. *Gerfaut* **70**: 385-401.
Jacob, J.P. & Fouarge, J.P. (1992). Evolution de l'effectif nicheur et habitats du Petit gravelot (*Charadrius dubius*) en Wallonie et dans la région bruxelloise. [Evolution in numbers and habitats of the Little Ringed Plover (*Charadrius dubius*) in Wallonia and the Brussels region]. *Aves* **29(3-4)**: 113-136.
Jacob, J.P. & Lardinois, O. (1982). Hivernage d'un jeune Goéland bourgmestre (*Larus hyperboreus*) à Mont-Saint-Guibert (Brabant Wallon). *Aves* **19(3)**: 193-197.
Jaensch, R.P. (1982). Little Ringed Plover at Little Bool Lagoon. *S. Austr. Orn.* **28(8)**: 201-204.
Jaensch, R.P. (1983a). Australian Pratincoles near Bool Lagoon. *S. Austr. Orn.* **29(3)**: 72.
Jaensch, R.P. (1983b). The Asian Dowitcher in north-western Australia. *Stilt* **4**: 2-5.
Jaensch, R.P. (1986). *Rostratula* at Vasse. *West. Austr. Bird Notes* **37**: 6.
Jaensch, R.P. (1988). Pectoral Sandpipers and Long-toed Stints in south-western Australia: notes on abundance and distribution. *Stilt* **12**: 54-57.
Jaensch, R.P. (1989). *Birds of Wetlands and Grasslands in the Kimberley Division, Western Australia: some Records of Interest, 1981-88*. RAOU Report **61**. Royal Australasian Ornithologists' Union, Victoria.
Jaensch, R.P. (1990). Pin-tailed Snipe *Gallinago stenura* in south-western Australia. *Stilt* **16**: 55-56.
Jaensch, R.P. (1994). Lake Finniss: an internationally significant site for Little Curlew. *Stilt* **25**: 21.
Jaensch, R.P. & Vervest, R.M. (1990). *Waterbirds at Remote Wetlands in Western Australia, 1986-88. Part One: Lake Argyle and Lake Gregory*. Royal Australasian Ornithologists Union, Canning Bridge, Western Australia.
Jaensch, R.P., Vervest, R.M. & Hewish, M.J. (1988). *Waterbirds in Nature Reserves of South-western Australia 1981-1985: Reserve Accounts*. RAOU Report **30**. Royal Australasian Ornithologists' Union.
James, D. (1995). Picking a gull-friend: Identification and ageing of Black-backed Gulls. *Wingspan* **5(2)**: 34-37.
James, R.A. (1991). *Sex Roles in Parental Care of the Black-necked Stilt (*Himantopus mexicanus*) in Southern California*. MSc thesis, California State University, Long Beach, California.
James-Veitch, E. & Booth, E.S. (1954). Behavior and life history of the Glaucous-winged Gull. *Walla Walla College Publ.* **12**: 1-39.
Jamieson, I.G. & Craig, J.L. (1987a). Dominance and mating in a communal polygynandrous bird: cooperation or indifference towards mating competitors? *Ethology* **75**: 317-327.
Jamieson, I.G. & Craig, J.L. (1987b). Male-male and female-female courtship and copulation behaviour in a communally breeding bird. *Anim. Behav.* **35**: 1251-1252.
Jansen, F.H. & Haase, B.J.M. (1981). Het patroon van de trek van de Scholekster (*Haematopus ostralegus*) voor Scheveningen. [The migration pattern of the Oystercatcher past Scheveningen]. *Watervogels* **6**: 25 39.
Jansen, F.H. & Remeeus, A. (1978). Naar een definitieve vestiging van de Zwartkopmeeuw *Larus melanocephalus* in Nederland? *Limosa* **51(3-4)**: 88-106.
Janssen, R.B. (1986). Minnesota's first Mountain Plover record. *Loon* **58(4)**: 154-158.
Jaramillo, A. & Henshaw, B. (1995). Identification of breeding plumaged Long- and Short-billed Dowitchers. *Birding World* **8(6)**: 221-228.
Jaramillo, A., Pittaway, R. & Burke, P. (1991). The identification and migration of breeding plumaged dowitchers in southern Ontario. *Birders J.* **1**: 8-25.
Jarvis, W.L. & Southern, W.E. (1976). Food habits of Ring-billed Gulls breeding in the Great Lakes region. *Wilson Bull.* **88**: 621-631.
Jayakar, S.D. & Spurway, H. (1965a). The Yellow-wattled Lapwing, a tropical dry-season nester (*Vanellus malabaricus* Boddaert, Charadriidae). I. The locality and the incubatory adaptations. *Zool. Jb. Syst. Bd.* **92**: 53-72.
Jayakar, S.D. & Spurway, H. (1965b). The Yellow-wattled Lapwing, *Vanellus malabaricus* (Boddaert) a tropical dry-season nester. II. Additional data on breeding biology. *J. Bombay Nat. Hist. Soc.* **62**: 1-14.
Jayakar, S.D. & Spurway, H. (1968). The Yellow-wattled Lapwing, *Vanellus malabaricus* (Boddaert), a tropical dry-season nester. III. Two further seasons' breeding. *J. Bombay Nat. Hist. Soc.* **65**: 369-383.
Jeffery, R.G. (1987). Influence of human disturbance on the nesting success of African Black Oystercatchers. *S. Afr. J. Wildl. Res.* **17(2)**: 71-72.
Jeffery, R.G. & Liversidge, R. (1951). Notes on the Chestnut-banded Sandplover *Charadrius pallidus pallidus*. *Ostrich* **22**: 68-76.
Jeggo, D. (1978). A preliminary survey report on the Kagu *Rhynochetos jubatus* of New Caledonia. *Dodo* **15**: 20-28.

Jehl, J.R. (1963). An investigation of fall-migrating dowitchers in New Jersey. *Wilson Bull.* **75**: 250-261.
Jehl, J.R. (1968a). The systematic position of the Surfbird *Aphriza virgata*. *Condor* **70**: 206-210.
Jehl, J.R. (1968b). Relationships in the Charadrii (shorebirds): a taxonomic study based on color patterns of the downy young. *San Diego Soc. Nat. Hist. Memoir* **3**: 1-54.
Jehl, J.R. (1968c). Review of *The Shorebirds of North America* by G. Stout, P. Matthiesen & R.V. Clem. *Auk* **85**: 515-520.
Jehl, J.R. (1970). Sexual selection for size differences in two species of sandpipers. *Evolution* **24**: 311-319.
Jehl, J.R. (1973a). Breeding biology and systematic relationships of the Stilt Sandpiper. *Wilson Bull.* **85**: 115-147.
Jehl, J.R. (1973b). The distribution of marine birds in Chilean waters in winter. *Auk* **90**: 114-135.
Jehl, J.R. (1974). A specimen of *Larus glaucescens* from Hudson Bay. *Wilson Bull.* **86**: 168-169.
Jehl, J.R. (1975a). Breeding biology of the Magellanic Plover *Pluvianellus socialis*. *Emu* **74**: 193-210. (Abstract).
Jehl, J.R. (1975b). *Pluvianellus socialis*: biology, ecology and relationships of an enigmatic Patagonian shorebird. *Trans. San Diego Soc. Nat. Hist.* **18**: 29-73.
Jehl, J.R. (1976). The northernmost colony of Heermann's Gull. *Western Birds* **7**: 25-26.
Jehl, J.R. (1978). A new hybrid oystercatcher from South America, *Haematopus leucopodus* x *H. ater*. *Condor* **80(3)**: 344-346.
Jehl, J.R. (1979). The autumnal migration of Baird's Sandpiper. Pp. 55-68 in: Pitelka (1979).
Jehl, J.R. (1984). Conservation problems of seabirds in Baja California and the Pacific northwest. Pp. 41-48 in: Croxall, Evans & Schreiber (1984).
Jehl, J.R. (1985). Hybridization and evolution of oystercatchers on the Pacific coast of Baja California. Pp. 484-504 in: Buckley *et al.* (1985).
Jehl, J.R. (1986). Biology of Red-necked Phalaropes *Phalaropus lobatus* at the western edge of the Great Basin in fall migration. *Great Basin Nat.* **46**: 185-197.
Jehl, J.R. (1987a). Moult and moult migration in a transequatorially migrating shorebird: Wilson's Phalarope. *Ornis Scand.* **18**: 173-178.
Jehl, J.R. (1987b). Geographic variation and evolution in the California Gull (*Larus californicus*). *Auk* **104**: 421-428.
Jehl, J.R. (1987c). A historical explanation for polyandry in Wilson's Phalarope. *Auk* **104**: 555-556.
Jehl, J.R. (1988). Biology of the Eared Grebe and Wilson's Phalarope in the nonbreeding season: a study of adaptation to saline lakes. Pp. 1-74 in: Pitelka, F.A. ed. (1988). *Studies in Avian Biology* **12**.
Jehl, J.R. (1989). Nest-site tenacity and patterns of adult mortality in nesting California Gulls (*Larus californicus*). *Auk* **106**: 102-106.
Jehl, J.R. (1990). Aspects of the molt migration. Pp. 102-113 in: Gwinner (1990).
Jehl, J.R. (1994a). Absence of nest density effects in a growing colony of California Gulls. *J. Avian Biol.* **25**: 224-230.
Jehl, J.R. (1994b). Changes in saline lake avifaunas in the past 150 years. Pp. 258-272 in: Jehl & Johnson (1994).
Jehl, J.R. & Bond, S.I. (1975). Morphological variation and species limits in murrelets of the genus *Endomychura*. *Trans. San Diego Soc. Nat. Hist.* **18**: 9-24.
Jehl, J.R. & Chase, C. (1987). Foraging patterns and prey selection by avian predators: a comparative study in two colonies of California Gulls. Pp. 91-101 in: Hand *et al.* (1987).
Jehl, J.R. & Everett, W.T. (1985). History and status of the avifauna of Isla Guadalupe, Mexico. *Trans. San Diego Soc. Nat. Hist.* **20**: 313-336.
Jehl, J.R. & Hussell, D.J.T. (1966). Incubation periods of some subarctic shorebirds. *Can. Field-Nat.* **80**: 179-180.
Jehl, J.R. & Johnson, N.K. eds. (1994). *A Century of Avifaunal Change in Western North America*. Studies in Avian Biology **15**.
Jehl, J.R. & Mahoney, S.A. (1987). The roles of thermal environment and predation in habitat choice in the California Gull. *Condor* **89**: 850-862.
Jehl, J.R. & Murray, B.G. (1986). The evolution of normal and reverse sexual size dimorphism in shorebirds and other birds. *Curr. Orn.* **3**: 1-86.
Jehl, J.R. & Rumboll, M.A.E. (1976). Notes on the avifauna of Isla Grande and Patagonia, Argentina. *Trans. San Diego Soc. Nat. Hist.* **18**: 145 154.
Jehl, J.R. & Smith, B.A. (1970). *Birds of the Churchill Region, Manitoba*. Special Publication **1**. Manitoba Museum of Man and Nature, Winnipeg, Canada.
Jehl, J.R., Babb, D.E. & Power, D.M. (1984). History of the California Gull colony at Mono Lake, California. *Colonial Waterbirds* **7**: 94-104.
Jehl, J.R., Babb, D.E. & Power, D.M. (1988). On interpretation of historical data with reference to the California Gull colony at Mono Lake. *Colonial Waterbirds* **11**: 322-327.
Jehl, J.R., Francine, J. & Bond, S.I. (1990). Growth patterns of two races of California Gull raised in a common environment. *Condor* **92**: 732-738.
Jehl, J.R., Rumboll, M.A.E. & Winter, J.P. (1973). Winter bird populations of Golfo San José, Argentina. *Bull. Brit. Orn. Club* **93**: 56-63.
Jehl, J.R., Todd, F.S., Rumboll, M.A.E. & Schwartz, D. (1979). Pelagic birds in the South Atlantic Ocean and at South Georgia in the Austral autumn. *Gerfaut* **69(1)**: 13-28.
Jenkins, A.R. & Meiklejohn, M.F.M. (1960). Song of the Water Rail. *Scottish Birds* **1**: 187-188.
Jenkins, J.M. (1979). Natural history of the Guam Rail. *Condor* **81**: 404-408.
Jenkins, J.M. (1983). The native forest birds of Guam. *Orn. Monogr.* **31**: 1-61.
Jenks-Jay, N. (1980). Chick shelters decrease avian predators in Least Tern colonies on Nantucket Island, Massachusetts. *J. Field. Orn.* **53**: 58-60.
Jenni, D.A. (1974). Evolution of polyandry in birds. *Amer. Zool.* **14**: 129-144.
Jenni, D.A. (1979). Female chauvinist birds. *New Scientist* **82**: 896-899.
Jenni, D.A. (1983). *Jacana spinosa*. Pp. 584-586 in: Janzen, D.H., ed. (1983). *Costa Rican Natural History*. University of Chicago Press, Chicago.
Jenni, D.A. (1985). Jacana. Pp. 311-313 in: Campbell & Lack (1985).
Jenni, D.A. & Betts, B.J. (1978). Sex differences in nest construction, incubation and parental behaviour in the polyandrous American Jacana (*Jacana spinosa*). *Anim. Behav.* **26**: 207-218.
Jenni, D.A. & Collier, G. (1972). Polyandry in the American Jacana (*Jacana spinosa*). *Auk* **89**: 743-765.
Jenni, D.A., Gambs, R.D. & Betts, B.J. (1975). Acoustic behavior of the Northern Jacana. *Living Bird* **13**: 193-210.
Jennings, M.C. (1981a). *Birds of the Arabian Gulf*. George Allen & Unwin, London.
Jennings, M.C. (1981b). *The Birds of Saudi Arabia: a Check-list*. Published privately, Cambridge.
Jennings, M.C. (1985). New breeding species. *Glareola pratincola* Collared Pratincole. *Phoenix* **1**: 3.
Jennings, M.C. (1988). A note on the birds of the Farasan Islands, Red Sea, Saudi Arabia. *Fauna of Saudi Arabia* **9**: 457-467.
Jennings, M.C., Heathcote, P.C., Parr, D. & Baha el Din, S.M. (1985). *Ornithological Survey of the Ras Dib Area and the Islands at the Mouth of the Gulf of Suez, Egypt*. Report to BP Petroleum Development Co. Ltd, Egypt.
Jensen, J.V. & Kirkeby, J. (1980). *The Birds of The Gambia. An Annotated Checklist & Guide to the Localities in The Gambia*. Aros Nature Guides, Århus.
Jerrentrup, H. (1993). [On the status of the Spur-winged Plover (*Hoplopterus spinosus*) in the Nestos delta in 1993]. Unpublished report to European Natural Heritage Fond, Hrysoupolis. In German.
Jerrentrup, H. (1994). Spur-winged Plover. *Hoplopterus spinosus*. Pp. 256-257 in: Tucker & Heath (1994).
Jesson, R.A. & Maclean, G.L. (1976). Salt glands in the neonatal Australian Pratincole. *Emu* **76(4)**: 227.
Jessop, A.E. (1987). Foraging strategies of the family Recurvirostridae. *Stilt* **10**: 15-19.
Jessop, R. (1990). Biometrics and moult of the Red-capped Plover in Victoria, Tasmania, South Australia and north west Australia. *Stilt* **17**: 29-35.
Jessop, R. (1992). Biometrics of Sanderling *Calidris alba* caught in Victoria, Australia. *Stilt* **21**: 22-23.
Jiang Fulin (1984). [Mate selection of the Red-crowned Crane *Grus japonensis*]. *Chinese Wildlife* **6**: 54-55. In Chinese.
Jin Ni Wang (1988). Caohai: in search of a resting place for the Black-necked Crane. *Bird World* **11(3)**: 24-25.
Jo, S. & Won, P. (1989). [Wintering ecology of Hooded Cranes, *Grus monacha* Temminck, in the Taegu area]. *J. Environm. Sci. Lab., Senshu Univ.* **1**: 83-92. In Korean.
Johansen, H. (1961). Die Superspecies *Larus canus*. *Vogelwarte* **21**: 152-155.
Johns, A.D. & Thorpe, R.I. (1981). On the occurrence of long-distance movement in the Yellow-wattled Lapwing, *Vanellus* (=*Lobipluvia*) *malabaricus*. *J. Bombay Nat. Hist. Soc.* **78**: 597-598.
Johns, B.W. (1986). Spring Whooping Crane migration: prairie provinces. *Blue Jay* **44(3)**: 174-176.
Johns, B.W. (1987). Whooping Crane sightings in the prairie provinces, 1979-1985. *Can. Wildl. Serv. Progress Notes* **169**. 6 pp.
Johns, J.E. (1969). Field studies of Wilson's Phalarope. *Auk* **86**: 660-670.
Johnsgard, P.A. (1981). *The Plovers, Sandpipers and Snipes of the World*. University of Nebraska Press, Lincoln & London.
Johnsgard, P.A. (1983). *Cranes of the World*. Indiana University Press, Bloomington, Indiana.
Johnsgard, P.A. (1987). *Diving Birds of North America*. University of Nebraska Press, Lincoln, Nebraska.
Johnsgard, P.A. (1990). Bustards: stalkers of the dry plains. *Zoonooz* **63(7)**: 4-11.
Johnsgard, P.A. (1991a). *Crane Music: A Natural History of North American Cranes*. Smithsonian Institution Press, Washington, D.C.
Johnsgard, P.A. (1991b). *Bustards, Hemipodes and Sandgrouse: Birds of Dry Places*. Oxford University Press, Oxford.
Johnson, A.R. & Isenmann, P. (1971). La nidification et le passage de la Mouette mélanocéphale (*Larus melanocephalus*) en Camargue. *Alauda* **39**: 105-111.
Johnson, A.W. (1964a). Notes on Mitchell's Plover *Phegornis mitchellii*. *Ibis* **106**: 249-251.
Johnson, A.W. (1964b). Notes on the African Finfoot, *Podica senegalensis* (Vieillot) and the Chilean Torrent Duck, *Merganetta a. armata* (Gould). *Bull. Brit. Orn. Club* **84**: 148-149.
Johnson, A.W. (1964c). The Giant Coot *Fulica gigantea* Eydoux and Souleyet. *Bull. Brit. Orn. Club* **84**: 170-172.
Johnson, A.W. (1965a). The Horned Coot, *Fulica cornuta* Bonaparte. *Bull. Brit. Orn. Club* **85**: 84-88.
Johnson, A.W. (1965b). *The Birds of Chile and Adjacent Regions of Argentina, Bolivia and Peru*. Vol. 1. Platt Establecimientos Gráficos, Buenos Aires.
Johnson, A.W. (1967). *The Birds of Chile and Adjacent Regions of Argentina, Bolivia and Peru*. Vol. 2. Platt Establecimientos Gráficos, Buenos Aires.
Johnson, A.W. (1972). *Supplement to the Birds of Chile and Adjacent Regions of Argentina, Bolivia and Peru*. Platt Establecimientos Gráficos, Buenos Aires.
Johnson, A.W., Millier, W.R. & Moffett, G. (1970). Notes on the birds of Easter Island. *Ibis* **112**: 532-538.
Johnson, C.M. (1987). *Aspects of the Wintering Ecology of the Piping Plover in Coastal Alabama*. MSc thesis, Auburn University, Auburn, Alabama.
Johnson, C.M. & Baldassarre, G.A. (1988). Aspects of the wintering ecology of Piping Plovers in coastal Alabama. *Wilson Bull.* **100(2)**: 214-223.
Johnson, D.H. & Stewart, R.E. (1973). Racial composition of migrant populations of Sandhill Cranes in the northern plains states. *Wilson Bull.* **85**: 148-162.
Johnson, D.N. (1992). The status of cranes in Natal in 1992. Pp. 20-28 in: Porter *et al.* (1992).
Johnson, D.N. & Barnes, P.R. (1985). The conservation of the Wattled Crane in South Africa. *Afr. Wildl.* **39(5)**: 188-195.
Johnson, D.N. & Barnes, P.R. (1986). The Natal crane census. *Lammergeyer* **37**: 40-49.
Johnson, D.N. & Barnes, P.R. (1991). The breeding biology of the Wattled Crane in Natal. Pp. 377-385 in: Harris (1991b).
Johnson, D.N. & Sinclair, J.C. (1983). A Wattled Crane mortality. *Lammergeyer* **34**: 64.
Johnson, G. & Baker-Gabb D.J. (1993). Technical Report Arthur Rylah Institute of Environmental Research **129(A)**.
Johnson, J. (1987). Oregon's first Little Stint. *Oregon Birds* **13(3)**: 283-285.
Johnson, O.W. (1979). Biology of shorebirds summering on Enewetak Atoll. Pp. 193-205 in: Pitelka (1979).
Johnson, O.W. (1985). Timing of primary molt in first-year Golden-Plovers and some evolutionary implications. *Wilson Bull.* **97(2)**: 237-239.
Johnson, O.W. (1993). The Pacific Golden-plover (*Pluvialis fulva*): discovery of the species and other historical notes. *Auk* **110(1)**: 136-141.
Johnson, O.W. & Connors, P.G. (1996). American Golden-plover (*Pluvialis dominica*), Pacific Golden-plover (*Pluvialis fulva*). No. **201-202** in: Poole & Gill (1996).
Johnson, O.W. & Johnson, P.M. (1983). Plumage-molt-age relationships in over-summering and migratory Lesser Golden Plovers. *Condor* **85(4)**: 406-419.
Johnson, O.W., Connors, P.G., Bruner, P.L. & Maron, J.L. (1993). Breeding ground fidelity and mate retention in the Pacific Golden-plover. *Wilson Bull.* **105(1)**: 60-67.
Johnson, O.W., Johnson, P.M. & Bruner, P.L. (1981a). Wintering behaviour and site faithfulness of American Golden Plovers *Pluvialis dominica fulva* in Hawaii. *Wader Study Group Bull.* **31**: 44.
Johnson, O.W., Johnson, P.M & Bruner, P.L. (1981b). Wintering behavior and site-faithfulness of Golden Plovers on Oahu. *Elepaio* **41(12)**: 123-130.
Johnson, O.W., Morton, M.L., Bruner, P.L. & Johnson, P.M. (1989). Fat cyclicity, predicted migratory flight ranges and features of wintering behavior in Pacific Golden-Plovers. *Condor* **91(1)**: 156-177.
Johnson, P. (1979). Third census of the Damara Tern at Elizabeth Bay, south west Africa, December 1978. *Cormorant* **7**: 32.
Johnson, P. & Frost, P. (1978). Conserving the Damara Tern. *Optima* **27**: 106-107.
Johnson, R. (1990). Waders feeding on flood-displaced prey. *Stilt* **17**: 74.
Johnson, R., Lawler, W. & Barter, M. (1991). Biometrics and moult of Oriental Pratincole *Glareola maldivarum* in the Indramayu-Cirebon region, West Java, Indonesia. *Stilt* **19**: 14-18.
Johnson, R., Lawler, W., Noor, Y.R. & Barter, M. (1992). *Migratory Waterbird Survey and Bird Banding Project in the Indramayu-Cirebon Region, West Java: the Oriental Pratincole* Glareola maldivarum *as a Case Study*. PHPA/AWB/AWSG, Bogor, Indonesia. 34 pp.
Johnson, R.R. & Dinsmore, J.J. (1985). Brood-rearing and postbreeding habitat use by Virginia Rails and Soras. *Wilson Bull.* **97**: 551-554.
Johnson, R.R. & Dinsmore, J.J. (1986a). Habitat use by breeding Virginia Rails and Soras. *J. Wildl. Manage.* **50**: 387-392.
Johnson, R.R. & Dinsmore, J.J. (1986b). The use of tape-recorded calls to count Virginia Rails and Soras. *Wilson Bull.* **98**: 303-306.
Johnson, R.W. (1973). *Observations on the Ecology and Management of the Northern Clapper Rail,* Rallus longirostris crepitans *Gmelin, in Nassau County, N.Y.* PhD thesis, Cornell University, Ithaca, New York.
Johnson, S. & Carter, H.R. (1985). Cavity-nesting Marbled Murrelets. *Wilson Bull.* **97**: 1-3.
Johnson, S.R. (1976). Spring movements and abundance of birds at Northwest Cape, St. Lawrence Island, Bering Sea, Alaska. *Syesis* **9**: 31-44.
Johnson, S.R. & Herter, D.R. (1989). *The Birds of the Beaufort Sea*. PB Exploration (Alaska) Inc., Anchorage, Alaska.
Johnson, T.B. & Spicer, R.B. (1981). Mountain Plovers on the New Mexico-Arizona border. *Cont. Birdl.* **2(3)**: 69-73.
Johnson, T.H. & Stattersfield, A.J. (1990). A global review of island endemic birds. *Ibis* **132**: 167-180.
Johnston, D.W. (1956a). The annual reproductive cycle of the California Gull. I. Criteria of age and the testis cycle. *Condor* **58**: 134-162.
Johnston, D.W. (1956b). The annual reproductive cycle of the California Gull. II. Histology and female reproductive system. *Condor* **58**: 206-221.
Johnston, D.W. (1979). The uropygial gland of the Sooty Tern. *Condor* **82**: 430-432.
Johnston, D.W. & Foster, M.E. (1954). Interspecific relations of breeding gulls at Honey Lake, California. *Condor* **56**: 38-42.
Johnston, D.W. & McFarlane, R.W. (1967). Migration and bioenergetics of flight in the Pacific Golden Plover. *Condor* **69**: 156-168.
Johnston, V.H. & Ryder, J.P. (1987). Divorce in Larids: a review. *Colonial Waterbirds* **10(1)**: 16-26.
Johnston-Stewart, J.B., Heigham, P.E.O. & Sawyer, F.W. (1981). A first breeding record of Rock Pratincoles (*Glareola nuchalis*) in Malawi. *Nyala* **7(2)**: 141-142.
Johnstone, G.W. (1985). Threats to birds in the subantarctic islands. Pp. 101-121 in: Moors, P.J. ed. (1985). *Conservation of Island Birds. Case Studies for the Management of Threatened Island Species*. ICBP Technical Publication **3**, Cambridge.
Johnstone, R.E. (1982). Distribution, status and variation of the Silver Gull *Larus novaehollandiae* Stephens, with notes on the *Larus cirrocephalus* species-group. *Records West. Austr. Mus.* **10(2)**: 133-165.
Johst, E. (1972). Die Haltung und künstliche Aufzucht der Senegal-Trappe (*Eupodotis senegalensis* Vieillot). *Gefiederte Welt* **96**: 61-64.
Joiris, C. (1978). Seabirds recorded in the northern North Sea in July: the ecological implications of their distribution. *Gerfaut* **68**: 419-440.
Jolivet, C. (1996). L'Outarde canepetière *Tetrax tetrax* en déclin en France. Situation en 1995. *Ornithos* **3(2)**: 73-77.
Jones, A. (1979). Notes on the behaviour of Variable Oystercatchers. *Notornis* **26(1)**: 47 52.
Jones, E. & Skira, I.J. (1979). Breeding distribution of the Great Skua at Macquarie Island in relation to numbers of rabbits. *Emu* **79**: 19-23.
Jones, I.L. (1989). *Status Signalling, Sexual Selection and the Social Signals of Least Auklets* Aethia pusilla. PhD thesis, Queen's University, Kingston, Canada.
Jones, I.L. (1990). Plumage variability functions for status signalling in Least Auklets. *Anim. Behav.* **39**: 967-975.
Jones, I.L. (1992a). Colony attendance of Least Auklets *Aethia pusilla* at St. Paul Island, Alaska: implications for population monitoring. *Condor* **94**: 93-100.

Jones, I.L. (1992b) Factors affecting adult survival of Least Auklets at St. Paul Island, Alaska. *Auk* **109**: 576-584.

Jones, I.L. (1993a) Least Auklet (*Aethia pusilla*). No. **69** in: Poole & Gill (1993).

Jones, I.L. (1993b). Sexual differences in bill shape and external measurements of Crested Auklets *Aethia cristatella*. *Wilson Bull.* **105**: 525-529.

Jones, I.L. (1993c). Crested Auklet (*Aethia cristatella*). No. **70** in: Poole & Gill (1993).

Jones, I.L. & Montgomerie, R.D. (1991). Mating and remating of Least Auklets *Aethia pusilla* relative to ornamental traits. *Behav. Ecol.* **2**: 249-257.

Jones, I.L. & Montgomerie, R.D. (1992). Least Auklet ornaments: do they function as quality indicators? *Behav. Ecol. Sociobiol.* **30**: 43-52.

Jones, J. (1945). The Banded Stilt. *Emu* **45**: 1-36, 110-118.

Jones, J.C. (1940). Food habits of the American Coot with notes on distribution. *US Dep. Inter. Wildl. Res. Bull.* **2**: 1-52.

Jones, J.M.B. (1987). A breeding colony of Rock Pratincoles on the Zambezi River. *Honeyguide* **33(2)**: 60.

Jones, M.J., Juhaeni, D., Banjaransari, H., Banham, W., Lace, L., Linsley, M.D. & Marsden, S.J. (1994). *The Status, Ecology and Conservation of the Forest Birds and Butterflies of Sumba*. Manchester Metropolitan University, Manchester.

Jones, M.J., Linsley, M.D. & Marsden, S.J. (1995). Population sizes, status and habitat associations of the restricted-range bird species of Sumba, Indonesia. *Bird Conserv. Int.* **5(1)**: 21-52.

Jones, N.V. (1963). The sheathbill, *Chionis alba* (Gmelin), at Signy Island, South Orkney Islands. *Bull. Brit. Antarct. Surv.* **2**: 53-71.

Jones, P., Schubel, S., Jolly, J., Brooke, M. de L. & Vickery, J. (1995). Behaviour, natural history and annual cycle of the Henderson Island Rail *Porzana atra* (Aves: Rallidae). *Biol. J. Linn. Soc.*

Jones, R.D. & Byrd, G.V. (1979). Inter-relationships between seabirds and introduced animals. Pp. 221-226 in: Bartonek & Nettleship (1979).

Jones, R.E. (1975). Food of Turnstones in the Wash. *British Birds* **68**: 339-341.

Jones, R.E. (1980). Interspecific copulation between Slender-billed and Black-headed Gulls. *British Birds* **73**: 474-475.

Jones, T. (1987). Techniques used for hand-rearing the Double-striped Thick-knee *Burhinus bistriatus* at the Dallas Zoo. *Avicult. Mag.* **93(3)**: 121-129.

de Jong, J. (1993). *Robusta, totanus* of toch *britannica*? *Op het Vinkentouw* **71**: 8-13.

Jonsson, L. & Grant, P.J. (1984). Identification of stints and peeps. *British Birds* **77**: 293-315.

Jönsson, P.E. (1983). [The Kentish Plover in Sweden, its status and breeding ecology]. *Anser* **22**: 209-230. In Swedish.

Jönsson, P.E. (1986a). The migration and wintering of Baltic Dunlins *Calidris alpina schinzii*. *Vår Fågelvärld* **11**(Suppl.): 71-78.

Jönsson, P.E. (1986b). [The Kentish Plover *Charadrius alexandrinus* in Scania 1986 - a report from a conservation project]. *Anser* **25(4)**: 237-244. In Swedish with English summary.

Jönsson, P.E. (1987a). Sexual size dimorphism and disassortative mating in the Dunlin *Calidris alpina schinzii* in southern Sweden. *Ornis Scand.* **18**: 257-264.

Jönsson, P.E. (1987b). The wintering and migration of Baltic Dunlins *Calidris alpina schinzii*. *Får Fågelvärld* **11**(Suppl.): 71-78.

Jönsson, P.E. (1987c). [The Kentish Plover *Charadrius alexandrinus* in Scania, south Sweden, in 1987 - a report from a conservation project]. *Anser* **26(4)**: 259-264. In Swedish with English summary.

Jönsson, P.E. (1988). [*Ecology of the Southern Dunlin*]. PhD thesis, Lund University, Lund. In Swedish.

Jönsson, P.E. (1989). [The Kentish Plover *Charadrius alexandrinus* in Scania, south Sweden, 1988 - a report from a conservation project]. *Anser* **28(1)**: 25-36. In Swedish with English summary.

Jönsson, P.E. (1990). [The Dunlin *Calidris alpina schinzii* as a breeding bird in Scania in 1990 - numbers, hatching success and population trends]. *Anser* **29**: 261-272. In Swedish.

Jönsson, P.E. (1991a). Reproduction and survival in a declining population of the southern Dunlin *Calidris alpina schinzii*. Pp. 56-68 in: Hötker (1991).

Jönsson, P.E. (1991b). [The Kentish Plover *Charadrius alexandrinus* in Scania, south Sweden, 1990 - a report from a conservation project]. *Anser* **30(1)**: 41-50. In Swedish with English summary.

Jönsson, P.E. (1992). [The Kentish Plover *Charadrius alexandrinus* in Scania, south Sweden, 1991 - a report from a conservation project]. *Anser* **31(1)**: 1-10. In Swedish with English summary.

Jönsson, P.E. (1993). [The Kentish Plover project - report for 1992]. *Anser* **32(1)**: 29-34. In Swedish with English summary.

Jönsson, P.E. (1994). Kentish Plover. *Charadrius alexandrinus*. Pp. 252-253 in: Tucker & Heath (1994).

Jönsson, P.E. (1995). [The Kentish Plover in Scania, south Sweden, 1993-1995 - a report from a conservation project]. *Anser* **34**: 203-213. In Swedish with English summary.

Jönsson, P.E. & Alerstam, T. (1990). The adaptive significance of parental role division and sexual size dimorphism in breeding shorebirds. *Biol. J. Linn. Soc.* **41**: 301-314.

Jorgensen, P.D. (1975). *Habitat Preference of the Light-footed Clapper rail in Tijuana Marsh, California*. PhD thesis, San Diego State University, San Diego, California.

Joubert, C.S.W. (1974). Black-winged Stilts breeding on Lake Kariba. *Honeyguide* **80**: 28-31.

Jouventin, P. (1994). Past, present and future of Amsterdam Island (Indian Ocean) and its avifauna. Pp. 122-132 in: Nettleship *et al*. (1994).

Jouventin, P. & Guillotin, M. (1979). Socio-écologie du Skua antarctique a Pointe Géologie. *Rev. Ecol. (Terre Vie)* **33**: 109-127.

Jouventin, P., Stahl, J.C. & Weimerskirch, H. (1988). La conservation des oiseaux des terres Australes et Antarctiques Françaises. Pp. 225-252 in: Thibault & Guyot (1988).

Józefik, M. (1969). Caspian Tern *Hydroprogne caspia* (Pallas) in Poland: the biology of the migration period. *Acta Orn., Varszawa* **11**: 381-443.

de Juana, E. (1984). The status and conservation of seabirds in the Spanish Mediterranean. Pp. 347-361 in: Croxall, Evans & Schreiber (1984).

de Juana, E. (1986). The status of the seabirds of the extreme western Mediterranean. Pp. 39-106 in: MEDMARAVIS & Monbailliu (1986).

de Juana, E. (1994). Audouin's Gull. *Larus audouinii*. Pp. 286-287 in: Tucker & Heath (1994).

de Juana, E. & Martínez, C. (1996). Distribution abundance and conservation status of the Little Bustard *Tetrax tetrax* in the Iberian Peninsula. *Ardeola* **43**.

de Juana, E. & Varela, J. (1987). Audouin's Gull, Chafarinas, 1987. *Seabird Group Newsletter* **50**: 16.

de Juana, E. & Varela, J. (1993). La población mundial reproductora de la Gaviota de Audouin (*Larus audouinii*). [The world breeding population of the Audouin's Gull (*Larus audouinii*)]. Pp. 71-85 in: Aguilar *et al*. (1993). In Spanish with English summary.

de Juana, E., Bradley, P.M., Varela, J. & Witt, H.H. (1987). Sobre los movimientos migratorios de la Gaviota de Audouin (*Larus audouinii*). [On the migratory movements of *Larus audouinii*]. *Ardeola* **34(1)**: 15-24. In Spanish with English summary.

de Juana, E., Bueno, J.M., Carbonell, M., Pérez-Mellado, V. & Varela, J. (1979). Aspectos de la alimentación y biología de reproducción de *Larus audouinii* Payr. en su gran colonia de cría de las Islas Chafarinas (año 1976). *Boletín de la Estación Central de Ecología* **8(16)**: 53-65.

de Juana, E., Varela, J. & Witt, H.H. (1984). The conservation of seabirds at the Chafarinas Islands. Pp. 363-370 in: Croxall, Evans & Schreiber (1984).

Jubb, R.A. (1981). The stately Kori Bustard. *Naturalist* **25(3)**: 9-11.

Jubb, R.A. (1982). Peters' Finfoot: a rather shy bird. *Naturalist* **26(1)**: 7-9.

Judin, K.A. (1965). Phylogeny and classification of Charadriiforme birds. Pp. 1-261 in: *Fauna of the U.S.S.R., Birds*. Vol. 2. Section 1. Part 1. USSR Academy of Science, Science Publications New Series **91**. Moscow & Leningrad.

Judin, K.A. (1981). [The systematic status of the Australian Pratincole (*Stiltia isabella* Vieillot, Charadriiformes, Aves)]. *Trudy Zool. Inst. Leningr.* **102**: 40-55. In Russian.

Jukema, J. (1982). [Moult and biometry of the Golden Plover *Pluvialis apricaria*]. *Limosa* **55**: 79-84. In Dutch with English summary.

Jukema, J. (1986). [Spring moult in Golden Plovers *Pluvialis apricaria* in Friesland]. *Limosa* **59(3)**: 111-113. In Dutch with English summary.

Jukema, J. (1987). Were Lesser Golden Plovers *Pluvialis fulva* regular visitors to Friesland, the Netherlands, in the first half of the 20th century? *Wader Study Group Bull.* **51**: 56-68.

Jukema, J. (1988a). Were Lesser Golden Plovers *Pluvialis fulva* regular visitors to Friesland, the Netherlands, in the first half of the 20th century? *Wader Study Group Bull.* **51**: 56-58.

Jukema, J. (1988b). [On the Pacific Lesser Golden Plover *Pluvialis fulva* as a migrant in Friesland]. *Limosa* **61(3/4)**: 189-190. In Dutch with English summary.

Jukema, J. (1989). [Plumage characteristics of northern and southern Eurasian Golden Plovers *Pluvialis apricaria* migrating through the Netherlands]. *Limosa* **62(3)**: 147-152. In Dutch with English summary.

Jukema, J. (1994). [Not all small golden plovers are Lesser Golden Plovers]. *Limosa* **68**: 35-36. In Dutch with English summary.

Jukema, J. & Hulscher, J.B. (1988). [Recovery rate of ringed Golden Plovers *Pluvialis apricaria* in relation to the severity of the winter]. *Limosa* **61(2)**: 85-90. In Dutch with English summary.

Jukema, J. & Piersma, T. (1987). Special moult of breast and belly feathers during breeding in Golden Plovers *Pluvialis apricaria*. *Ornis Scand.* **18(3)**: 157-162.

Jukema, J. & Piersma, T. (1992). [Golden Plovers *Pluvialis apricaria* do not show sexual dimorphy in external and internal linear dimensions]. *Limosa* **65(4)**: 147-154. In Dutch with English summary.

Jukema, J. & van der Veen, B. (1992). [Pacific Golden Plover near Abbega in November 1990]. *Dutch Birding* **14(1)**: 14-17. In Dutch with English summary.

Jukema, J., Piersma, T., Louwsma, L., Monkel, C., Rijpma, U., Visser, K. & van der Zee, D. (1995). [Moult and mass changes of northward migrating Ruffs in Friesland, March-April 1993 and 1994]. *Vanellus* **3**: 55-61. In Dutch.

Junge, G.C.A. & Voous, K.H. (1955). The distribution and relationship of *Sterna eurygnatha* Saunders. *Ardea* **43**: 226-247.

Jungfer, W. (1954). Über Paartreue, Nistplaztreue und Alter der Austernfischer (*Haematopus ostralegus*) auf Mellum. *Vogelwarte* **17**: 6 15.

Jyrkkanen, J.A. (1975). Glaucous-winged Gull predation on Feral Rock Doves. *Can. Field-Nat.* **89**: 77-78.

Kaczmarek, J. & Winjecki, A. (1980). Ponowne stwierdzenie sieweczki pustynnej (*Charadrius leschenaultii*) w Polsce. [The second observation of Great Sand Plover in Poland]. *Notatki Orn.* **21(1-4)**: 77-78. In Polish with English summary.

Kadlec, J.A. & Drury, W.H. (1968). Structure of the New England Herring Gull population. *Ecology* **49**: 644-676.

Kadlec, J.A., Drury, W.H. & Onion, D.K. (1969). Growth and mortality of Herring Gull chicks. *Bird-Banding* **40**: 222-233.

Kaestner, P. (1987). Some observations from lowland swamp forest in south Bougainville. *Muruk* **2**: 34-38.

Kaftanovskii, Y.M. (1951). [*Birds of the Murre Group of the Eastern Atlantic. Studies of the Fauna and Flora of the USSR*]. Moscow Society of Naturalists, New Series, Zoology Section **28(13)**. 170 pp. In Russian.

Kagarise, C.M. (1979). Breeding biology of the Wilson's Phalarope in North Dakota. *Bird-Banding* **50**: 12-22.

Kahl, H. (1989). [Oldest Great Skua (*Stercorarius skua*) in nature]. *Vogelwarte* **35(1)**: 81. In German with English summary.

Kaigler, C.G. (1968). Red-necked Avocet in Westland. *Notornis* **15(2)**: 123.

Kaiser, G.W., Barcley, H.J., Burger, A.E., Kangasniemi, D., Lindsay, D.J., Munro, W.T., Pollard, W.R., Redhead, R., Rice, J. & Seip, D. (1994). *National Recovery Plan for the Marbled Murrelet*. Recovery of Nationally Endangered Wildlife Committee Report **8**. Canadian Wildlife Service, Ottawa.

Kaiser, M. (1986). Scheidenschnäbel - "Haushühner" der Antarktis? *Urania* **62**: 34-38.

Kaiser, M. (1995). Bemerkungen zur Handaufzucht und zur Thermoregulation von Küken der Antarktis- und Küstenseeschwalbe (*Sterna vittata* und *S. paradisaea*). *Milu* **8**: 635-653.

Kaiser, M. (1996). *Untersuchungen zur Biologie und Ökologie der Antarktisseschwalbe (Sterna vittata Gmelin, 1789) Während der Brutzeit auf King George Island, Südshetlandinseln*. Dissertation, Humboldt Universität, Berlin.

Kakebeeke, B. (1993). Striped Flufftail found breeding in Somerset West. *Birding in SA* **45**: 9-11.

Kålås, J.A. (1980). Migration of Common Snipe *Gallinago gallinago* ringed in Fennoscandia. *Fauna Norvegica (Ser. C, Cinclus)* **3**: 84-88.

Kålås, J.A. (1986). Incubation schedules in different parental care systems in the Dotterel *Charadrius morinellus*. *Ardea* **74(2)**: 185-190.

Kålås, J.A. (1988). Sexual dimorphism in size and plumage of the polyandrous Dotterel (*Charadrius morinellus*): sex roles and constraints on sexual selection. *Can. J. Zool.* **66(6)**: 1334-1341.

Kålås, J.A. & Byrkjedal, I. (1984). Breeding chronology and mating system of the Eurasian Dotterel (*Charadrius morinellus*). *Auk* **101(4)**: 838-847.

Kålås, J.A. & Løfaldli, L. (1987). Clutch size in the Dotterel *Charadrius morinellus*: an adaptation to parental incubation behaviour? *Ornis Scand.* **18(4)**: 316-319.

Kålås, J.A., Fiske, P. & Saether, S.A. (1995). The effect of mating probability on risk taking: an experimental study in lekking Great Snipe. *Amer. Naturalist* **146(1)**: 59-71.

Kålås, J.A., Løfaldli, L. & Fiske, P. (1989). Effects of radio packages on Great Snipe during breeding. *J. Wildl. Manage.* **53(4)**: 1155-1158.

Kalchreuter, H. (1983a). *The Woodcock*. Verlag Dieter Hoffmann, Mainz.

Kalchreuter, H. ed. (1983b). *Proceedings of the Second European Woodcock and Snipe Workshop, 1982*. IWRB, Slimbridge, UK.

Kalchreuter, H. ed. (1994). *Fourth European Woodcock and Snipe Workshop*. IWRB Publication **31**, Slimbridge.

Kale, H.W. ed. (1978). *Rare and Endangered Biota of Florida*. Vol. 2. Birds. University Presses of Florida, Gainesville, Florida.

Kale, H.W. & Loftin, R.W. (1982). A longevity record for the Black Skimmer. *North Amer. Bird Bander* **7**: 54.

Kale, H.W., Sciple, G.W. & Tomkins, I.R. (1965). The Royal Tern colony of Little Egg Island, Georgia. *Bird-Banding* **36**: 21-26.

Kalejta, B. (1992). Time budgets and predatory impact of waders at the Berg River estuary, South Africa. *Ardea* **80**: 327-342.

Kalejta, B. (1993). Intense predation cannot always be detected experimentally: a case study of shorebird predation on nereid polychaetes in South Africa. *Netherlands J. Sea Res.* **31**: 385-393.

Kalejta, B. & Hockey, P.A.R. (1994). Distribution of shorebirds at the Berg River estuary, South Africa, in relation to foraging mode, food supply and environmental features. *Ibis* **136**: 233-239.

Kalejta, B., Underhill, L.G. & Summers, R.W. (1994). Leaving no stone unturned - the secrets of Turnstone migration. *Birding in SA* **46(1)**: 23-27.

Kaliher, F. (1993). A peace park and nature reserve for Korea's DMZ? *ICF Bugle* **19(4)**: 3, 8.

Källander, H. (1977). Piracy by Black-headed Gulls on Lapwings. *Bird Study* **24(3)**: 186-194.

Källander, H. (1988). Starlings (*Sturnus vulgaris*) kleptoparasitising Lapwings (*Vanellus vanellus*). *Ecol. Birds* **10(1)**: 113-114. In English with German summary.

Källander, H. (1991). Differences in prey capture efficiency of adult and juvenile Common *Sterna hirundo* and Arctic *S. paradisaea* Terns. *Ornis Svecica* **1**: 121-122.

van Kalsbeek, A. & Meijer, P.C. (1986). [Greater Sand Plover at Den Oever in August 1985]. *Dutch Birding* **8(1)**: 25-26. In Dutch with English summary.

Kalsi, R.S. & Khera, S. (1986). Some observations on breeding and displacement behaviour of the Redwattled Lapwing, *Vanellus indicus indicus* (Aves: Charadriidae). *Res. Bull. Panjab Univ. Sci.* **37(3-4)**: 131-141.

Kalsi, R.S. & Khera, S. (1987). Agonistic and distraction behaviour of the Redwattled Lapwing, *Vanellus indicus indicus*. *Pavo* **25**: 43-56.

Kalsi, R.S. & Khera, S. (1990). Growth and development of the Red-wattled Lapwing *Vanellus indicus*. *Stilt* **17**: 57-64.

Kalsi, R.S. & Khera, S. (1992). Some observations on maintenance behaviour of the Redwattled Lapwing *Vanellus indicus* (Boddaert). *J. Bombay Nat. Hist. Soc.* **89(3)**: 368-372.

Kamata, M. & Tomioka, T. (1991). [Breaking up of the family of the Red-crowned Crane *Grus japonensis* at the Tsurui-ito Tancho Sanctuary in eastern Hokkaido]. *Strix* **10**: 21-30. In Japanese with English summary.

Kampp, K. (1982). Notes on the Long-tailed Skua *Stercorarius longicaudus* in West Greenland. *Dan. Orn. Foren. Tidssk.* **76**: 129-135.

Kampp, K. (1990). The Thick-billed Murre population of the Thule District, Greenland. *Arctic* **43(2)**: 115-120. In English with French summary.

Kampp, K. & Kristensen, R.M. (1980). Ross's Gull *Rhodostethia rosea* breeding in Disko Bay, West Greenland, 1979. *Dan. Orn. Foren. Tidssk.* **74**: 65-74.

Kampp, K., Nettleship, D.N. & Evans, P.G.H. (1994). Thick-billed Murres of Greenland: status and prospects. Pp.133-154 in: Nettleship *et al*. (1994).

Kamweneshe, D.N. (1996). Management and natural resource utilization patterns in the Bangweulu Swamps, Zambia. In: Beilfuss *et al*. (1996).

Kanai, Y. & Isobe, S. (1990). [Distribution of breeding colonies of the Little Tern *Sterna albifrons* along the coast of Tokyo Bay]. *Strix* **9**: 177-190. In Japanese.

Kane, R., Buckley, P.A. & Golub, J. (1989). Large-billed Tern in New Jersey: North America's first confirmed occurrence. *Amer. Birds* **43**: 1275-1726.

Kania, W. (1990). The primary moult of breeding Dunlins *Calidris alpina* in the central Taymyr in 1989. *Wader Study Group Bull.* **60**: 17-19.

Kanyawimba, S. (1996). Gray Crowned Cranes as indicators for wetlands conservation in Rwanda. In: Beilfuss *et al.* (1996).
Kapoor, J.P. & Bhatia, H.M. (1983). Ecology of the Great Indian Bustard. Pp. 137-145 in: Goriup & Vardhan (1983).
Karavaev, A.A. (1977). The nestling of the White-tailed Plover. *Ornitologiya* **13**: 207. In Russian.
Karhu, S. (1973). On the development stages of chicks and adult Moorhens *Gallinula chloropus* at the end of a breeding season. *Ornis Fenn.* **50**: 1-17.
Karim, F. (1985). A note on the disappearance of the Bengal Florican from Bangladesh. *Bustard Studies* **3**: 161-162.
Karl, S.A., Zink, R.M & Jehl, J.R. (1987). Allozyme analysis of the California Gull (*Larus californicus*). *Auk* **104(4)**: 767-769.
Karpov, F.F. (1994). [Behaviour of the Broad-billed Sandpipers *Limicola falcinellus* at stopover sites in south and south-east Kazakhstan during autumn migration]. *Russ. J. Orn.* **3(1)**: 47-51. In Russian with English summary.
Karpovitch, V.N., Solovieva-Volinskaya, T.N. & Shekht, H.H. (1958). [Ecology of the Black Tern along the Middle Reaches of the Oka River]. Pp. 78-101 in: [*Report of Oskov Reserve*]. Moscow. In Russian.
Kartaschew, N.N. (1960). *Die Alkenvogel des Nordatlantiks*. A. Ziemsen Verlag, Wittenberg, Germany.
Kashkarov, L.Y. & Ostapenko, M.M. eds. (1990). *Birds of Uzbekistan*. Vol. 2. FAN, Tashkent, Uzbekistan.
Kasparek, M. (1982). Zur Zuggeschwindigkeit der Flußseeschwalbe *Sterna hirundo*. *J. Orn.* **123**: 297-305.
Kasparek, M. (1988). The Demoiselle Crane, *Anthropoides virgo*, in Turkey: distribution and population of a highly endangered species. *Zoology in the Middle East* **2**: 31-38.
Kasparek, M. (1989). Status and distribution of the Great Bustard and Little Bustard in Turkey. *Bustard Studies* **4**: 80-113.
Kasparek, M. (1990). On the migration of the Whimbrel, *Numenius phaeopus*, in Turkey. *Zool. Middle East* **4**: 25-32.
Kasparek, M. (1992a). Status of Sociable Plover *Chettusia gregaria* and White-tailed Plover *C. leucura* in Turkey and the Middle East. *Sandgrouse* **14(1)**: 2-15.
Kasparek, M. (1992b). Zum Zug der Steinwälzer, *Arenaria interpres*, in der Türkei. *Beitr. Vogelkd.* **38**: 200-208. In German with English summary.
Katenekwa, K. (1996). Reduction in distribution of the Crowned Crane: a case study of the Barotse flood plains. In: Beilfuss *et al.* (1996).
Katondo, J. (1996). An overview of the status and distribution of the Gray Crowned Cranes in Tanzania. In: Beilfuss *et al.* (1996).
Kaufman, K. (1987). The practiced eye: Pectoral Sandpiper and Sharp-tailed Sandpiper. *Amer. Birds* **41(5)**: 1356-1358.
Kaufman, K. (1989). The practiced eye: Black-legged Kittiwake and Red-legged Kittiwake. *Amer. Birds* **43**: 3-6.
Kaufman, K. (1995). Field identification: Black-bellied Plover. *Birder's World* **9(4)**: 68-69.
Kaufman, K. (1996). Field identification: Sanderling. *Birder's World* **10(1)**: 72-73.
Kaufmann, G.W. (1971). *Behaviour and Ecology of the Sora (*Porzana carolina*) and Virginia Rail (*Rallus limicola*)*. PhD dissertation, University of Minnesota, Minnesota.
Kaufmann, G.W. (1977). Breeding requirements of the Virginia Rail and the Sora in captivity. *Avicult. Mag.* **83**: 135-141.
Kaufmann, G.W. (1983). Displays and vocalizations of the Sora and the Virginia Rail. *Wilson Bull.* **95**: 42-59.
Kaufmann, G.W. (1987a). Swamp habitat use by Spotless Crakes and Marsh Crakes at Pukepuke Lagoon. *Notornis* **34**: 207-216.
Kaufmann, G.W. (1987b). Growth and development of Sora and Virginia Rail chicks. *Wilson Bull.* **99(3)**: 432-440.
Kaufmann, G.W. (1988a). The usefulness of taped Spotless Crake calls as a census technique. *Wilson Bull.* **100**: 682-686.
Kaufmann, G.W. (1988b). Development of Spotless Crake chicks. *Notornis* **35**: 324-327.
Kaufmann, G.W. (1988c). Social preening in Soras and in Virginia Rails. *Loon* **60(2)**: 59-63.
Kaufmann, G.W. (1989). Breeding ecology of the Sora *Porzana carolina* and the Virginia Rail *Rallus limicola*. *Can. Field-Nat.* **103**: 270-282.
Kaufmann, G.W. & Lavers, R. (1987). Observations of breeding behaviour of Spotless Crake (*Porzana tabuensis*) and Marsh Crake (*P. pusilla*) at Pukepuke lagoon. *Notornis* **34**: 193-205.
Kautesk, B.M. (1985). "Caribbean Coots" in British Columbia? *Discovery* **14(2)**: 49-51.
Kautesk, B.M., Scott, R.E., Aldcroft, D.S. & Ireland, J. (1983). Temminck's Stint at Vancouver, British Columbia. *Amer. Birds* **37(3)**: 347-349.
Kaverkina, N.P. (1979). Defensive audio signals of the Kamchatka Tern. Pp. 96-97 in: *Nesting Ecology for Birds and Methods for its Study*. Report to All Union Conference of Young Scientists, Samarkand.
Kaverkina, N.P. (1982). [Nesting of current tern populations on Karaginsk Island]. Pp. 86-88 in: [*Ecological Reserves and Preservation of Birds in the Baltic Republics. (Konaus)*]. In Russian.
Kaverkina, N.P. (1983). [Nature of spontaneous flight of the Polar Tern]. *Bull. Leningrad Univ.* **15**: 31-35. In Russian.
Kaverkina, N.P. (1984). [Defensive behaviour of *Sterna paradisaea*]. *Bull. Leningrad Univ.* **15**: 19-25. In Russian.
Kaverkina, N.P. (1986a). [Pairing behavior of terns]. *Bull. Moscow Soc. Nat. Hist. Res. (Biol. Section)* **91**: 40-47. In Russian.
Kaverkina, N.P. (1986b). Nesting biology of the Kamchatka Tern *Sterna camtschatica* Pallas. Pp. 101-107 in: Livinenko (1986).
Kaverkina, N.P. (1988). [On the breeding biology of the Collared Pratincole (*Glareola pratincola*) in southeastern Kazakhstan]. Pp. 53-55 in: Flint & Tomkovich (1988). In Russian.
Kaverkina, N.P. (1989). [Feeding and foraging behavior in terns]. *Bull. Zool. Leningrad Univ.* **1**: 50-53. In Russian.
Kaverkina, N.P. (1990). [To the problem of Pallas' priority in the first description of the Aleutian Tern (*Sterna camtschatica*)]. *Ornitologiya* **24**: 182-185. In Russian.
Kaverkina, N.P. & Babitsch, N.V. (1987). [Nesting biology of the Sandwich Tern]. *Byull. Mosk. Ova. Ispyt. Prir. Otd. Biol.* **92**: 19-27. In Russian.
Kaverkina, N.P. & Roschevski, U.K. (1984). [Defensive behavior of the Arctic Tern]. *Bull. Leningrad Univ.* **15**: 19-25. In Russian.
Kawamura, N. (1981). The Hooded Crane at Yashiro, Yamaguchi prefecture, Japan. Pp. 244-249 in: Lewis & Masatomi (1981).
Kawamura, N. (1991). Conservation of the Hooded Crane at Yashiro, Japan. Pp. 301-303 in: Harris (1991b).
Kay, G.T. (1947). The Glaucous Gull in winter. *British Birds* **40**: 369-373.
Kay, G.T. (1950). The Iceland Gull in winter. *British Birds* **43**: 399-402.
Kazama, T. (1971). Mass destruction of *Synthliboramphus antiquus* by oil pollution of Japan Sea. *Yamashina Chorui Kenkyusho Kenyuko Hokoku* **6**: 389-398.
Kazmierczak, K.J., Balachandran, S. & Rosalind, L. (1992). Caspian Plover *Charadrius asiaticus* Pallas at Pt. Calimere, Tamil Nadu. *J. Bombay Nat. Hist. Soc.* **89(3)**: 373.
Keartland, G.A. (1901). Notes on the Plain Wanderer. *Victorian Naturalist* **17**: 167-168.
Keast, J.A. (1949). Field notes on the Grey-tailed Tattler. *Records Austr. Mus.* **22**: 207-211.
Keeley, B.R. (1985). Red-billed Gulls robbing Wrybills. *Notornis* **32(4)**: 270.
Keep, M.E. (1985). The occurrence of and breeding attempts by Blue Cranes *Tetrapteryx paradisea* in Umfolozi Game Reserve. *Lammergeyer* **35**: 28-32.
Kefford, H.K. (1945). Peculiar behaviour of the Bronze-winged Jacana (*Metopidius indicus* Latham). *J. Bombay Nat. Hist. Soc.* **45(2)**: 238-239.
Keijl, G.O. (1994a). Greater Sand Plover. *Charadrius leschenaultii*. Page 254 in: Tucker & Heath (1994).
Keijl, G.O. (1994b). Caspian Plover. *Charadrius asiaticus*. Page 255 in: Tucker & Heath (1994).
Keijl, G.O., Eggenhuizen, A.H.V. & Ruiters, P.S. (1993). Identification of Red-knobbed Coot. *Dutch Birding* **15**: 22-25.
Keijl, G.O., van Roomen, M.W.J., Ruiters, P.S. & Wijker, A. (1992). *Migration of Waders and other Waterbirds along the Mediterranean Coast of Israel, Spring 1989*. WIWO Report **30**. Zeist, the Netherlands.
Keith, G.S. (1973). The voice of *Sarothrura insularis*, with further notes on members of the genus. *Bull. Brit. Orn. Club* **93**: 130-136.
Keith, G.S. (1980). Origins of the avifauna of the Malagasy Region. Pp. 99-108 in: *Proc. IV Pan-Afr. Orn. Congr.*
Keith, J.A. (1966). Reproduction in a population of Herring Gulls (*Larus argentatus*) contaminated by DDT. *J. Appl. Ecol.* **3**(Suppl.): 57-60.
Keith, S. (1978). Review: Rails of the world. *Wilson Bull.* **90**: 322-325.
Keith, S., Benson, C.W. & Irwin, M.P.S. (1970). The genus *Sarothrura* (Aves, Rallidae). *Bull. Amer. Mus. Nat. Hist.* **143(1)**: 1-84.
Kelly, P.R. & Cogswell, H.R. (1979). Movements and habitat use by wintering populations of Willets and Marbled Godwits. Pp. 69-82 in: Pitelka (1979).
Kelsey, M.G. & Hassall, M. (1989). Patch selection by Dunlin on a heterogeneous mudflat. *Ornis Scand.* **20**: 250-254.
Kemf, E. (1988). Dance of a thousand cranes. *New Scientist* **120(1633)**: 34-36.
Kemp, A.C. (1980). The importance of the Kruger National Park for bird conservation in the Republic of South Africa. *Koedoe* **23**: 99-122.
Kemp, A.C. & Maclean, G.L. (1973). Nesting of the Three-banded Courser. *Ostrich* **44**: 82-83.
Kemp, A.C. & Tarboton, W.L. (1976). Small South African bustards. *Bokmakierie* **28**: 40-43.
Kemp, J.B. (1984). Identification of first-winter Pomarine Skua. *British Birds* **77**: 27.
Kennedy, R.S. & Ross, C.A. (1987). A new subspecies of *Rallina euryzonoides* (Aves: Rallidae) from the Batan Islands, Philippines. *Proc. Biol. Soc. Washington* **100**: 459-461.
Kennerley, P.R. (1987). Little Stint *Calidris minuta* at Tsim Bei Tsui. A new species for Hong Kong. *Hong Kong Bird Rep.* **1986**: 69-71.
Kennerley, P.R. & Bakewell, D.N. (1987). Nordmann's Greenshank in Hong Kong: a review of the identification and status. *Hong Kong Bird Rep.* **1986**: 83-100.
Kennerley, P.R. & Bakewell, D.N. (1991). Identification and status of Nordmann's Greenshank. *Dutch Birding* **13(1)**: 1-8.
Kennerley, P.R. & Hoogendoorn, W. (1991). Slender-billed Gull at Mai Po and Starling Inlet. The first record for Hong Kong. *Hong Kong Bird Rep.* **1990**: 100-102.
Kennerley, P.R., Leader, P.J. & Leven, M.R. (1993). Aleutian Tern: the first records for Hong Kong. *Hong Kong Bird Rep.* **1992**: 107-113.
Kent, T.H. (1991). Sharp-tailed Sandpiper at Coralville Reservoir. *Iowa Bird Life* **61(4)**: 122-123.
Kenyon, K.W. (1949). Observations on behaviour and populations of oystercatchers in Lower California. *Condor* **51**: 193-199.
Kepler, C.B. (1976). Dominance and dominance-related behavior in the Whooping Crane. Pp. 177-196 in: Lewis (1976a).
Kepler, C.B. (1978). Captive propagation of Whooping Cranes: a behavioral approach. Pp. 231-242 in: Temple, S. ed. (1978). *Endangered Birds: Management Techniques for Preserving Threatened Species*. University of Wisconsin Press, Madison, Wisconsin.
Kepp, T., Melter, J. & Reinke, E. (1991). *Report of the Ornithological Expedition to Northern Cameroon January/ February 1991*. O.A.G. Münster, Münster.
Keppie, D.M. & Owen, R.B. eds. (1977). *Proceedings of the Sixth Woodcock Symposium*. New Brunswick Department of Natural Resources, Fredericton, Canada.
Keppie, D.M. & Redmond, G.W. (1985). Body weight and possession of territory for male American Woodcock. *Condor* **87**: 287-290.
Keppie, D.M. & Redmond, G.W. (1988). A review of possible explanations for reverse size dimorphism of American Woodcock. *Can. J. Zool.* **66**: 2390-2397.
Keppie, D.M. & Whiting, R.M. (1994). American Woodcock (*Scolopax minor*). No. **100** in: Poole & Gill (1994).
Kerlinger, P. & Wiedner, D.S. (1990). Vocal behaviour and habitat use of Black Rails in south Jersey. *Rec. New Jersey Birds* **16**: 58-62.
Kersten, M. & Brenninkmeijer, A. (1995). Growth, fledging success and post-fledging survival of juvenile Oystercatchers *Haematopus ostralegus*. *Ibis* **137** 396-404.
Kersten, M. & Piersma, T. (1984). [Prey choice and food intake of Grey Plovers *Pluvialis squatarola* in the Wadden Sea during spring and autumn migration]. *Limosa* **57**: 105-111. In Dutch with English summary.
Kersten, M. & Piersma, T. (1987). High levels of energy expenditure in shorebirds; metabolic adaptations to an energetically expensive way of life. *Ardea* **75**: 175-187.
Kessel, B. (1984). Migration of Sandhill Cranes in east-central Alaska, with routes through Alaska and western Canada. *Can. Field-Nat.* **98(3)**: 279-292.
Kessel, B. (1989). *Birds of the Seward Peninsula, Alaska*. University of Alaska Press, Fairbanks, Alaska.
Kessel, B. & Gibson, D.D. (1978). *Status and Distribution of Alaska Birds*. Studies in Avian Biology **1**. 100 pp.
Key, E.M. (1991). Greater Yellowlegs in central Oklahoma in winter. *Bull. Okla. Orn. Soc.* **24(4)**: 31-32.
Khachar, S., Patankar, H.R., Gaekwad, A., Mundkur, T., Pravez, R. & Naik, R.M. (1991). Wintering cranes in Gujarat State, India. Pp. 327-333 in: Harris (1991b).
Khacher, L. (1978). The Bronzewinged Jacana *Metopidius indicus* (Latham) in Saurashtra at Jamnagar. *J. Bombay Nat. Hist. Soc.* **75(3)**: 923.
Khacher, L. (1981). Conservation needs of Black-necked Cranes of Bhutan, Arunachal Pradesh, and Ladakh. Pp. 204-211 in: Lewis & Masatomi (1981).
Khajuria, H. (1970). Nestlings of the Redwattled Lapwing, *Vanellus i. indicus* (Boddaert). *Pavo* **8**: 82-83.
Kharitonov, S.P. (1978). [Questions on territoriality and regulation of colony density of the Common Black-headed Gull (*Larus ridibundus*)]. *Lindude Kaitumine Orn. Kogumik, Tallinn, Estonia* **8**: 82-98. In Russian.
Kharitonov, S.P. (1981a). [On the formation of microcolonies in the Black-headed Gull, *Larus ridibundus*]. *Zoologischeskii Zhurnal* **60**: 540-546. In Russian.
Kharitonov, S.P. (1981b). [Interrelations of the Black-headed Gull (*Larus ridibundus*) in the local groups within the colony]. *Zoologischeskii Zhurnal* **60**: 871-877. In Russian.
Kharitonov, S.P. (1983). [On the evolution of coloniality in birds]. Pp. 93-104 in: Zubakin *et al.* (1983). In Russian.
Kharitonov, S.P. (1993). [Breeding-site fidelity and movements of Black-headed Gulls *Larus ridibundus* within a colony]. *Russ. J. Orn.* **2(3)**: 361-382. In Russian with English summary.
Khlebosolov, E.I. (1989). [Mechanisms of nesting density regulation and adaptive significance of the lek mating system in Ruff (*Philomachus pugnax*)]. *Zoologischeskii Zhurnal* **68**: 77-88. In Russian with English summary.
Khodkov, G.I. & Totunov, V.M. (1979). [Black-headed Gull and Caspian Tern on Lake Chani (western Siberia)]. Pp. 189-191 in: [*Migration and Ecology of Birds of Siberia*]. Academy of Science, Yakutsk. In Russian.
Khokhlov, A.N. (1987). [The Sociable Plover in the Stavropol region]. Page 137 in: [*The Problems of Rare Wildlife Conservation*]. Moscow. In Russian.
Khrokov, V.V. (1973). [Nest displacement of *Charadrius dubius*]. *Ekologiya* **4(2)**: 107-108. In Russian.
Khrokov, V.V. (1978). [The Sociable Plover, *Chettusia gregaria*]. *Priroda* **1978(12)**: 92-96. In Russian.
Khrokov, V.V. (1983). [Material on the biology of the Black-winged Pratincole *Glareola nordmanni* Nordm. in the Tengiz-Kurgaldzhinsk region (central Kazakhstan)]. *Aquila* **90**: 117-137. In Russian with Hungarian summary.
Khrokov, V.V., Avezov, E.M., Berezowski, V.G. & Grachev, A.V. (1979). [Expansion of the nesting range of the White-tailed Plover in Kazakhstan]. *Ornitologiya* **14**: 200-202. In Russian.
Khrokov, V.V., Avezov, E.M. & Gubin, B.M. (1980). [Materials on the nesting biology of the Oystercatcher (*Haematopus ostralegus*) in Kazakhstan]. In: Flint (1980a). In Russian.
Kiel, W.H. (1955). Nesting studies of the Coot in southwestern Manitoba. *J. Wildl. Manage.* **19**: 189-198.
Kieser, J.A. & Kieser, G.A. (1982). Field identification of common waders: Marsh Sandpiper and Greenshank. *Bokmakierie* **34(3)**: 63-66.
Kieser, J.A. & Liversidge, R. (1981). Identification of White-fronted Sandplover. *Dutch Birding* **3(3)**: 81-84.
Kieser, J.A. & Smith, F.T.H. (1982). Field identification of the Pectoral Sandpiper *Calidris melanotos*. *Austr. Bird Watcher* **9**: 137-146.
Kiff, L.F. (1975). Notes on southwestern Costa Rican birds. *Condor* **77**: 101-103.
Kiff, L.F. (1981). Eggs of the Marbled Murrelet. *Wilson Bull.* **93**: 400-403.
Kiis, A. (1984). Time-budgets of transient Greenshanks in Denmark. *Wader Study Group Bull.* **42**: 23-24.
Kilham, L. (1979). Location and fate of oystercatcher nests on Sapelo and Cabretta Islands. *Oriole* **44**: 45 46.
Kilham, L. (1980). Cocked tail display and evasive behaviour of American oystercatchers. *Auk* **97(1)**: 205.
Kilham, L. (1981). Courtship feeding and copulation of Royal Terns. *Wilson Bull.* **93**: 390-391.
Kilham, L.A. (1979). Snake and pond snails as food of Grey-necked Wood-Rails. *Condor* **81**: 100-101.
Kilpi, M. (1989). The effect of varying pair numbers and reproduction and use of space in a small Herring Gull *Larus argentatus* colony. *Ornis Scand.* **20**: 204-210.
Kilpi, M. (1990). Breeding biology of the Herring Gull *Larus argentatus* in the northern Baltic. *Ornis Fenn.* **67**: 130-140.
Kilpi, M. (1992). Responses of Herring Gulls *Larus argentatus* and Common Gulls *L. canus* to warm years: early migration and early breeding. *Ornis Fenn.* **69**: 82-87.
Kilpi, M. (1995a). Egg size asymmetry within Herring Gull clutches predicts fledging success. *Colonial Waterbirds* **18**: 41-46.
Kilpi, M. (1995b). Variation in laying synchrony in a small Herring Gull colony. *Ornis Fenn.* **72**: 37-42.
Kilpi, M. & Byholm, P. (1995a). The odd colour of the last laid egg in Herring Gull *Larus argentatus* clutches: does it reflect egg quality? *Ornis Fenn.* **72**: 85-88.
Kilpi, M. & Byholm, P. (1995b). Diet of courtship feeding Herring Gulls in the Gulf of Finland. *Ornis Fenn.* **72**: 135-137.
Kilpi, M. & Hario, M. (1986). Wing-tip pattern and possible affinities of coastal Finnish Herring Gulls *Larus argentatus*. *Ornis Fenn.* **63**: 52-54.
Kilpi, M. & Saurola, P. (1983). Pre-migration movements of coastal Finnish Herring Gulls (*Larus argentatus*) in Autumn. *Ann. Zool. Fennici* **20**: 245-254.

Kilpi, M. & Saurola, P. (1984a). Migration and wintering strategies of juvenile and adult *Larus marinus*, *L. argentatus* and *L. fuscus* from Finland. *Ornis Fenn.* **61**: 1-8.
Kilpi, M. & Saurola, P. (1984b). Migration and survival areas of Caspian Terns *Sterna caspia* from the Finnish coast. *Ornis Fenn.* **61(1)**: 24-29.
Kilpi, M. & Saurola, P. (1985). Movements and survival areas of Finnish Common Gulls. *Ann. Zool. Fennici* **22**: 157-168.
Kilpi, M., Hillstrom, L. & Lindstrom, K. (1996). Egg-size variation and reproductive success in the Herring Gull, *Larus argentatus*: adaptive or constrained size of the last egg? *Ibis* **138**: 212-217.
Kilpi, M., Lindstrom, K. & Wuorinen, J.D. (1992). A change in clutch size in the Arctic Tern *Sterna paradisaea* in the northern Baltic. *Ornis Fenn.* **69**: 88-91.
King, B. (1973). Probable Sandwich Tern showing runt and albinistic characters. *British Birds* **66**: 538-539.
King, B. (1980). Individual recognition and winter behaviour of Water Rails. *British Birds* **73**: 33-35.
King, B., Balch, L., Dunn, J., Finch, D.W., Hall, G.E. & Tobish, T. (1980). First Green Sandpipers, *Tringa ochropus*, for North America. *Amer. Birds* **34(3)**: 319-321.
King, B.F. & Gallagher, M.D. (1983). First record of Great Knot *Calidris tenuirostris* in Oman, Eastern Arabia. *Bull. Brit. Orn. Club* **103(4)**: 139-140.
King, B.F., Woodcock, M. & Dickinson, E.C. (1975). *A Field Guide to the Birds of South-east Asia*. Collins, London.
King, J. & Shirihai, H. (1996). Identification and ageing of Audouin's Gull. *Birding World* **9(2)**: 52-61.
King, K.A. (1989). Food habits and organochlorine contaminants in the diet of Black Skimmers, Galveston Bay, Texas, USA. *Colonial Waterbirds* **12(1)**: 109-112.
King, K.A. & Cromartie, E. (1986). Mercury, cadmium, lead, and selenium in three waterbird species nesting in Galveston Bay, Texas, USA. *Colonial Waterbirds* **9**: 90-94.
King, K.A., Lefever, D.A. & Mulhern, B.M. (1983). Organochlorine and metal residues in Royal Terns nesting on the Central Texas Coast. *J. Field Orn.* **54**: 295-303.
King, W.B. ed. (1978/79). *Endangered Birds of the World. The ICBP Bird Red Data Book*. Vol. 2. Aves. 2nd edition. IUCN, Morges, Switzerland.
King, W.B. (1984). Incidental mortality of seabirds in gillnets in the North Pacific. Pp. 709-721 in: Croxall, Evans & Schreiber (1984).
King, W.B. & Sanger, G.A. (1979). Oil vunerability index for marine oriented birds. Pp. 227-239 in: Bartonek & Nettleship (1979).
Kingston, A.H. (1912). Painted Snipe (*Rostratula capensis*) in large numbers. *J. Bombay Nat. Hist. Soc.* **21**: 667.
Kinkel, L.K. & Southern, W.E. (1978). Adult female Ring-billed Gulls sexually molest juveniles. *Bird-Banding* **49**: 184-186.
Kinsky, F. (1963). The Southern Black-backed Gull (*Larus dominicanus*) Lichtenstein. *Rec. Dominion Mus.* **4**: 149-219.
Kinsky, F. & Yaldwyn, J.C. (1981). The bird fauna of Niue Island, south-west Pacific, with special notes on the White-tailed Tropic Bird and Golden Plover. *Natl. Mus. New Zealand (Misc. Ser.)* **2**: 1-49.
Kipp, M. (1991). [On the breeding pair status of the Curlew (*Numenius arquata*) in the Steinfurt District]. *Charadrius* **27(2)**: 72-80. In German with English summary.
Kirby, J.S. & Green, R.E. (1991). Nest defence by Black-tailed Godwits on the Ouse Washes, Cambridgeshire, England. *Wader Study Group Bull.* **61**: 71-72.
Kirby, J.S. & Lack, P.C. (1993). Spatial dynamics of wintering Lapwings and Golden Plovers in Britain and Ireland, 1981/1982 to 1983/1984. *Bird Study* **40(1)**: 38-50.
Kirby, J.S., Ferns, P.R., Waters, R.J. & Prys-Jones, R.P. (1991). *Wader and Wildfowl Counts 1990-1991*. Wildfowl and Wetlands Trust, Slimbridge, UK.
Kirchner, H. (1972). Zur Brut des Waldwasserläufers (*Tringa ochropus*) in Schleswig-Holstein. [On the breeding of the Green Sandpiper (*Tringa ochropus*) in Schleswig-Holstein]. *Orn. Mitt.* **24(12)**: 268-271.
Kirchner, K. (1969). *Die Uferschnepfe*. Neue Brehm-Bücherei **413**.
Kirchner, K. (1978). *Bruchwasserläufer und Waldwasserläufer,* Tringa glareola *und* Tringa ochropus. Neue Brehm-Bücherei **309**.
Kirkconnell, A., Sánchez, B. & Rodríguez, D. (1992). Notas sobre *Charadrius melodus* (Aves: Charadriidae) en Cayo Paredón Grande del archipiélago Sabana-camaguey, Cuba. [Notes on *Charadrius melodus* (Aves: Charadriidae) in Cayo Paredón Grande of the Sabana-camaguey archipelago, Cuba]. *Volante Migratorio* **19**: 29-30.
Kirkham, I.R. & Morris, R.D. (1979). Feeding ecology of Ring-billed Gull (*Larus delawarensis*) chicks. *Can. J. Zool.* **57**: 1086-1090.
Kirkham, I.R. & Nettleship, D.N. (1987). Status of the Roseate Tern in Canada. *J. Field Orn.* **58**: 505-515.
Kirkham, I.R. & Nisbet, I.C.T. (1987). Feeding techniques and field identification of Arctic, Common and Roseate Terns. *British Birds* **80**: 41-47.
Kirkman, F.B. (1937). *Bird Behaviour*. Nelson & Sons Ltd, London.
Kirkman, F.B. (1940). The inner territory of the Black-headed Gull. *British Birds* **34**: 100-104.
Kirkpatrick, K.M. (1952). Occurrence of the Pheasant-tailed Jacana (*Hydrophasianus chirurgus* Scop.) in Nellore district, Madras. *J. Bombay Nat. Hist. Soc.* **50(4)**: 947-948.
Kirsch, E.M. (1993). Observations of aggression in Piping Plover adults in Nebraska. *Prairie Nat.* **25(1)**: 77-79.
Kirsch, L.M. & Higgins, K.F. (1976). Upland Sandpiper nesting and management in North Dakota. *Wildl. Soc. Bull.* **4**: 16-20.
Kirwan, G. (1992). The migration of the Great Snipe, *Gallinago media*, through Turkey. *Zool. Middle East* **7**: 11-19.
Kirwan, G. (1994). First record of White-breasted Waterhen *Amaurornis phoenicurus* in Yemen. *Sandgrouse* **16**: 55.
Kiselev, F.A. (1951). [The agricultural importance of the Herring Gull in northwestern Crimea]. *Trudy Krymskogo Filiala An SSR* **2**: 21-30. In Russian.
Kiss, J.B., Rékási, J. & Sterbetz, I. (1988). [Data on the diet of the Woodcock (*Scolopax rusticola*) in northern Dobruja (Rumania)]. Pp. 78-82 in: Havet & Hirons (1988). In French with English summary.
Kist, J. (1961). "Systematische" beschouwingen naar anleiding van de waarneming van Heuglins geelpootzilvermeeuw, *Larus cachinnans heuglini* Bree in Nederland. *Ardea* **49**: 1-51.
Kistchinski, A.A. (1974). [The biology and behaviour of Pectoral Sandpiper in the tundras of eastern Siberia]. *Byull. Mosk. Ova. Ispyt. Prir. Otd. Biol.* **79**: 73-88. In Russian.
Kistchinski, A.A. (1975). Breeding biology and behaviour of the Grey Phalarope *Phalaropus fulicarius* in east Siberia. *Ibis* **117**: 285-301.
Kistchinski, A.A. (1980). *Birds of Koryak Highlands*. Nauka, Moscow.
Kistyakovski, A.B. (1980). [Does the Slender-billed Curlew (*Numenius tenuirostris*) still exist?]. In: Flint (1980a). In Russian.
Kitagawa, T. (1988a). Ethosociological studies of the Black-winged Stilt *Himantopus himantopus himantopus*. II. Social structure in an overwintering population. *Jap. J. Orn.* **37(2)**: 45-62. In English with Japanese summary.
Kitagawa, T. (1988b). Ethosociological studies of the Black-winged Stilt *Himantopus himantopus himantopus*. III. Female-female pairing. *Jap. J. Orn.* **37(2)**: 63-67. In English with Japanese summary.
Kitagawa, T. (1989). Ethosociological studies of the Black-winged Stilt *Himantopus himantopus himantopus*. I. Ethogram of the agonistic behaviours. *J. Yamashina Inst. Orn.* **21**: 52-75. In English with Japanese summary.
Kitazawa, H. & Watanabe, T. (1992). [Molting of the Spotted Redshank *Tringa erythropus* at Oguti lotus fields]. *Strix* **11**: 329-332. In Japanese with English summary.
Kitson, A.R. (1980). *Larus relictus* - a review. *Bull. Brit. Orn. Club* **100(3)**: 178-185.
Kitson, A.R., Marr, B.A.E. & Porter, R.F. (1980). Greater Sand Plover: new to Britain and Ireland. *British Birds* **73(12)**: 568-573.
Kittle, T. (1975). Weights and moult of Green Sandpipers in Britain. *Ringing & Migration* **1(1)**: 52-55.
Klaassen, M. (1994). Growth and energetics of tern chicks from temperate and polar environments. *Auk* **111(3)**: 525-544.
Klaassen, M. & Bech, C. (1992). Resting and peak metabolic rates of Arctic Tern nestlings and their relations to growth rate. *Physiol. Zool.* **65**: 803-814.
Klaassen, M., Bech, C., Masman, D. & Slagsvold, G. (1989). Growth and energetics of Arctic Tern chicks (*Sterna paradisaea*). *Auk* **106**: 240-248.
Klaassen, M., Bech, C. & Slagsvold, G. (1989). Basal metabolic rate and thermal conductance in Arctic Tern chicks and the effect of heat increment of feeding on thermoregulatory expenses. *Ardea* **77**: 193-200.
Klaassen, M., Habekotte, B., Schinkelshoek, P., Stienen, E. & Van Tienen, P. (1994). Influence of growth rate retardation on time budgets and energetics of Arctic Tern *Sterna paradisaea* and Common Tern *S. hirundo* chicks. *Ibis* **136**: 197-204.
Klaassen, M., Kersten, M. & Ens, B.J. (1990). Energetic requirements for maintenance and premigratory body mass gain of waders wintering in Africa. *Ardea* **78**: 209-220.
Klaassen, M., Zwaan, B., Heslenfeld, P., Lucas, P. & Luijckx, B. (1992). Growth rate associated changes in the energy requirements of tern chicks. *Ardea* **80**: 19-28.
Klapste, J. (1977). A large concentration of Oriental and Australian Pratincoles in northern Queensland. *Austr. Bird Watcher* **7(2)**: 65-67.
Kleefisch, T. (1984). Die Weiß-brustalle (*Laterallus leucopyrrhus*). [The Red-and-white Crake (*Laterallus leucopyrrhus*)]. *Gefiederte Welt* **108(4)**: 100-103.
Klemp, S. (1993). [Population trends of the Lapwing (*Vanellus vanellus*) in Schleswig-Holstein]. *Corax* **15**: 147-155. In German with English summary.
Kliebe, A. & Kliebe, K. (1985). Beobachtungen zur Flugbalz und zum Verhalten des Sumpfläufers (*Limicola f. falcinellus*) in Nordskandinavien. *Vogelwelt* **106(2)**: 62-65.
Kliebe, K. (1974). Beobachtungen zur Flugbalz der Zwergschepfe. *Vogelwelt* **95**: 30-33.
Klimaitis, J.F. & Moschione, F.N. (1984). Observaciones sobre nidificación asociada en *Charadrius collaris*, *Sterna superciliaris* y *Rynchops nigra* en el Río Uruguay, Entre Ríos, Argentina. [Report of observations of the nesting association between *Charadrius collaris*, *Sterna superciliaris* and *Rynchops nigra* in Río Uruguay, Entre Ríos, Argentina]. *Hornero* **12(3)**: 197-202.
Klimaitis, J.F. & Moschione, F.N. (1987). *Aves de la Reserva Integral de Selva Marginal de Punta Lara y sus Alrededores*. Dirección de Servicios Generales del Ministerio, Argentina.
Klimenko, M.I. (1950). [Ecology of the Laridae on the north coast of the Black Sea]. *Trudy Chernomorskovo Zapovednika* **1**: 53-69. In Russian.
Klimkiewicz, M.K. & Futcher, A.G. (1989). Longevity records of North American birds, Supplement 1l. *J. Field Orn.* **60**: 469-494.
Klimov, S.M. & Sarychev, V.S. (1987). [Nesting of the Terek Sandpiper (*Xenus cinereus*) on the Upper Don river]. *Ornitologiya* **22**: 183. In Russian.
Klomp, H. (1954). [Habitat selection by the Lapwing]. *Ardea* **42**: 1-139. In Dutch.
Klomp, H. & Speek, B.J. (1971). Survival of young Lapwings in relation to time of hatching. *Bird Study* **18**: 229-231.
Klomp, N.I. & Furness, R.W. (1990). Variations in numbers of nonbreeding Great Skuas attending a colony. *Ornis Scand.* **21(4)**: 270-276.
Klomp, N.I. & Furness, R.W. (1992a). Non-breeders as a buffer against environmental stress: declines in numbers of Great Skuas on Foula, Shetland, and prediction of future recruitment. *J. Appl. Ecol.* **29**: 341-348.
Klomp, N.I. & Furness, R.W. (1992b). The dispersal and philopatry of Great Skuas from Foula, Shetland. *Ringing & Migration* **13(2)**: 73-82.
de Knijff, P. (1981). The occurence of the Great Bustard (*O. tarda*) in the Netherlands during the winter of 1978/79. *Vogeljaar* **29(1)**: 1-8.
Knolle, P. & Balten, B. (1993). [Buff-breasted Sandpiper at Lauwersmeer in June 1993]. *Dutch Birding* **15(5)**: 218-220. In Dutch with English summary.
Knopf, F.L. (1994). Avian assemblages on altered grasslands. Pp. 247-257 in: Jehl & Johnson (1994).
Knopf, F.L. (1996a). Prairie legacies - Birds. In: Samson, F.B. & Knopf, F.L. eds. (1996). *Prairie Conservation: Preserving North America's Most Endangered Ecosystem*. Island Press, Covelo, California.
Knopf, F.L. (1996b). Mountain Plover (*Charadrius montanus*). No. **211** in: Poole & Gill (1996).
Knopf, F.L. & Miller, B.J. (1994). *Charadrius montanus* - Montane, grassland, or bare-ground plover? *Auk* **111(2)**: 504-506.
Knopf, F.L. & Rupert, J.R. (1995). Habits and habitats of Mountain Plovers in California. *Condor* **97(3)**: 743-751.
Knopf, F.L. & Rupert, J.R. (1996a). Reproduction and movements of Mountain Plovers breeding in Colorado. *Wilson Bull.* **108**: 28-35.
Knopf, F.L. & Rupert, J.R. (1996b). Use of crop fields by breeding Mountain Plovers. In: Herkert, J.R. & Vickery, P. eds. (1996). *Grassland Bird Symposium*. Journal of Field Ornithology **67**(Supplement).
Knowles, C.J. & Knowles, P.R. (1984). Additional records of Mountain Plovers using prairie dog towns in Montana. *Prairie Nat.* **16(4)**: 183-186.
Knowles, C.J., Stoner, C.J. & Gieb, S.P. (1982). Selective use of black-tailed prairie dog towns by Mountain Plovers. *Condor* **84(1)**: 71-74.
Knox, A. (1987). Taxanomic status of Lesser Golden Plovers. *British Birds* **80(10)**: 482-487.
Knudtson, E.P. & Byrd, G.V. (1982). Breeding biology of Crested, Least and Whiskered Auklets on Buldir Island, Alaska. *Condor* **84**: 197-202.
Knutson, M.G. (1991). Characteristics of Black Tern (*Chlidonias niger*) nesting habitat at Lakeview Wildlife Management area, New York. *Kingbird* **41**: 228-236.
Knystautas, A. (1987). *The Natural History of the USSR*. Century, London.
Knystautas, A. (1993). *The Birds of Russia*. Harper Collins Publishers, London.
Kobayashi, H. (1948). Breeding of *Bubulcus ibis coromandus* and *Rostratula b. benghalensis* near Himeji city. *Tori* **12**: 67-69.
Kobayashi, H. (1954). Observations of the Painted Snipe. *Tori* **13**: 31-39.
Kobayashi, H. (1955). Observations of the Painted Snipe *Rostratula benghalensis*. *Tori* **14**: 1-13.
Kobayashi, H. (1960). A note on *Glareola pratincola*. *Tori* **15(75)**: 232-235.
Kochan, Z. (1992). Wintering of the Coot (*Fulica atra*) on the Gulf of Gdansk during the seasons of 1984/1985-1986/1987. *Notatki Orn.* **34**: 125-130.
Kock, A.C. & de Randall, R.M. (1984). Organochlorine insecticide and polychlorinated biphenyl residues in eggs of coastal birds from the eastern Cape, South Africa. *Environm. Pollut.* **A35**: 193-201.
Koelink, A.F. (1972). *Bioenergetics of Growth in the Pigeon Guillemot*. MSc thesis, University of British Columbia, Vancouver.
Koeman, J.H. (1972). Side-effects of persistent pesticides and other chemicals on birds and mammals in the Netherlands. *TNO Nieuws* **27**: 527-532.
Koen, R. (1983). Spotted Dikkop (R 275). *Witwatersrand Bird Club News* **120**: 19.
Koene, P. (1978). De Scholekster Aantalseffecten op Devoedselopname. *Dieroecologie Rug.* **60**: 1 123.
Koenig, O. (1943). *Rallen und Bartmeisen*. Niederdonau Nat. Kult., Wien.
Koepcke, H.W. & Koepcke, M. (1971). *Las Aves Silvestres de Importancia Económica del Perú*. Ministerio de Agricultura, Servicio Forestal y de Caza y Servicio de Pesquería, Lima.
Koepcke, M. (1970). *The Birds of the Department of Lima, Peru*. Livingston Publishing Company, Wynnewood, Pennsylvania.
Koerkamp, G.G. (1987). Common Gulls with pale iris. *British Birds* **80**: 628-629.
Kohno, H. & Kishimoto, H. (1991). Prey of the Bridled Tern on Nakanokamishima Island, South Ryukyus, Japan. *Jap. J. Orn.* **40**: 15-25.
Kohno, H., Abe, N. & Mano, T. (1986). Chick mortality of the Sooty Tern *Sterna fuscata* caused by Typhoon-8211 on Nakamokami-shima, South Ryukyu, Japan. *J. Yamashina Inst. Orn.* **18**: 41-50.
Kok, O.B. (1993). Diet of the Spotted Dikkop *Burhinus capensis*. *Ostrich* **64(4)**: 182-184.
Kok, O.B. & Anderson, P.C. (1989). Diet composition of Crowned Plovers in open grassland. *S. Afr. J. Wildl. Res.* **19(3)**: 122-125.
Kok, O.B. & Earlé, R.A. (1990). Diet of the Black Korhaan *Eupodotis afra* in the Orange Free State and North-west Cape. *Ostrich* **61**: 107-110.
Kok, O.B. & Van Ee, C.A. (1989). [Diet composition of several Gruiformes in the Orange-free State and northwest Cape]. *Mirafra* **6(2)**: 47-51. In Afrikaans with English summary.
Kokhanov, V.D. (1993). [The breeding of the Little Gull *Larus minutus* in the Kola Peninsula]. *Russ. J. Orn.* **2(2)**: 256-257. In Russian with English summary.
Koli, L. & Soikkeli, M. (1974). Fish prey of breeding Caspian Terns in Finland. *Ann. Zool. Fennici* **11**: 304-308.
Kolichis, N. (1976). New breeding records of the Banded Stilt in Western Australia. *West. Austr. Nat.* **13**: 114-119.
Kollar, H.P. (1988). *Arten-und Biotopschutz am Beispiel der Großtrappe (*Otis tarda *L.)*. Verein für Ökologie und Umweltforschung **11**. Wien. 56 pp.
Kollar, H.P. & Seiter, M. (1991). Sex ratio and population dynamics of Great Bustards, *Otis tarda*. *Ibis* **133**(Suppl.): 135-136.
Kolmodin, U. & Risberg, L. (1994). Wood Sandpiper. *Tringa glareola*. Pp. 282-283 in: Tucker & Heath (1994).
Kolomijtsev, N.P. (1988). [On the ecology of the Long-billed Plover (*Charadrius placidus*)]. Pp. 62-67 in: Flint & Tomkovich (1988). In Russian.
Komeda, S. (1983). Nest attendance of parent birds in the Painted Snipe (*Rostratula benghalensis*). *Auk* **100(1)**: 48-55.
Komen, J., Williams, A.J. & Myer, E. (1986). Hartlaub's Gulls and Swift Terns in Luderitz: a conservation problem. *Lanioturdus* **22**: 10-13.
Komolphalin, P. (1993). Bird survey of Tarutao National Park, Thailand. *Bull. Oriental Bird Club* **18**: 13-14.
Kondla, N.G. (1977). An unusual American Avocet nest. *Blue Jay* **35(2)**: 94-95.
Kondla, N.G. & Pinel, H.W. (1978). Clutch size of the American Avocet in the Prairie Provinces. *Blue Jay* **36(3)**: 150-153.
Kondratiev, A.J. (1986). Seabird colonies on the arctic coast of the Soviet Far North-East. Pp. 37-47 in: Litvinenko (1986).

Kondratiev, A.J. (1991). Status of the seabirds nesting in northeast USSR. Pp. 165-173 in: Croxall (1991).

Kondratiev, A.J. & Kondratieva, L.K. (1984). [Growth and development of Sabine's Gull chicks]. *Ornitologyia* **19**: 81-87. In Russian.

Kondratiev, A.J., Zubakin, V.A., Kharitonov, S.P., Tarkhov, S.V. & Kharitonova, I.A. (1993). Study of bird seashore colonies on Matykil and Kokontse Islands (Yamskie Islands) and Pyagin Peninsula. *Bull. Moscow Soc. Nat. Study (Biol. Section)* **98(5)**: 21-32.

Kondratyva, L.F. (1994). Prey selection by the Slaty-backed Gull on Talan Island, Sea of Okhotsk. *Pacific Seabird Group Bull.* **21**: 44. (Abstract).

Königstedt, D. (1986). [On field characters and courtship display of Swinhoe's Snipe (*Gallinago megala*)]. *Mitt. Zool. Mus. Berlin* **62**(Suppl.): *Ann. Orn.* **10**: 127-136. In German with English summary.

Königstedt, D. & Langbehn, H. (1990). Zum Brutbestand der Rotflügel-Brachschwalbe (*Glareola pratincola*) in Bulgarien. *Orn. Mitt.* **42(3)**: 73-75.

Konrad, P.M. (1981). Status and ecology of Wattled Crane in Africa. Pp. 220-237 in: Lewis & Masatomi (1981).

Konrad, P.M. (1987). Rainy season ecology of South African Grey Crowned Cranes in the Luangwa Valley, Zambia. Pp. 337-344: in Archibald & Pasquier (1987a).

Konyukhov, N.B. & Kitaysky, A.S. (1995). The Asiatic race of the Marbled Murrelet. Pp. 23-29 in: Ralph *et al.* (1995).

Konyukhov, N.B. & McCaffery, B.J. (1993). Second record of a Bristle-thighed Curlew from Asia and first record for the former Soviet Union. *Wader Study Group Bull.* **70**: 22-23.

Kooiker, G. (1984). Brutökologische Untersuchungen an Einer Population des Kiebitzes *Vanellus vanellus*. *Vogelwelt* **105**: 121-137.

Kooiker, G. (1987). [Clutch-size, hatching rate, hatching success and breeding success in the Lapwing (*Vanellus vanellus*)]. *J. Orn.* **128(1)**: 101-107. In German with English summary.

Kooiker, G. (1990). [Population dynamics and breeding success of the Lapwing *Vanellus vanellus* in an agricultural area near Osnabruck, Lower Saxony]. *Vogelwelt* **111(6)**: 202-216. In German with English summary.

Kooiker, G. (1993). [Phenology and breeding biology of Lapwing (*Vanellus vanellus*): results of a 17 years' study in NW-Germany]. *J. Orn.* **134(1)**: 43-58. In German with English summary.

Kooiman, J.G. (1940). Mededeelingen over het voorkomen in Oostjava voor dit gewest nog niet in de literatuur genoemde vogels. *Ardea* **29**: 98-108.

Koolhaas, A., Dekinga, A. & Piersma, T. (1993). Disturbance of foraging Knots by aircraft in the Dutch Wadden Sea in August-October 1992. *Wader Study Group Bull.* **68**: 20-22.

Koonz, W.H. (1982). Vandalism in a Manitoba Caspian Tern colony. *Blue Jay* **40**: 48-49.

Koonz, W.H. (1986). Possible Bonaparte's Gull colonies in Manitoba. *Blue Jay* **44**: 118-119.

Koopman, K. (1986). Primary moult and weight changes of Ruffs in the Netherlands in relation to migration. *Ardea* **74**: 69-77.

Koopman, K. (1987). Verschillen in overwinteringsgebied van Friese Scholeksters *Haematopus ostralegus*. *Limosa* **60**: 179-183.

Koopman, K. (1992). Biometrie, gewichtsverloop en handpenrui van een binnenlandse populatie Scholeksters *Haematopus ostralegus*. *Limosa* **65**: 103-108.

Kopachena, J.G. (1987). Variations in the temporal spacing of
Franklin's Gull (*Larus pipixcan*) flocks. *Can. J. Zool.* **65**: 2450-2457.

Kopachena, J.G. & Evans, R.M. (1990). Flock recruitment in Franklin's Gulls. *Colonial Waterbirds* **13**: 92-95.

Kopij, G. & Kok, O.B. (1994). Distribution, numbers and habitat preference of Crowned *Vanellus coronatus* and Blacksmith Plovers *V. armatus* in Inner Bloemfontein. *Mirafra* **11(3)**: 48-50.

Korducki, M. (1992). Purple Sandpiper (*Calidris maritima*) - 29 November 1991, Racine County, at Myers Park. *Passenger Pigeon* **54(2)**: 176-177.

Kornowski, G. (1957). Beiträge zur Ethologie des Bläßhuhns (*Fulica atra* L.). *J. Orn.* **98**: 318-355.

de Korte, J. (1977). Ecology of the Long-tailed Skua (*Stercorarius longicaudus* Vieillot, 1819) at Scoresby Sund, East Greenland. 1. Distribution and density. *Beaufortia* **25**: 201-219.

de Korte, J. (1984). Ecology of the Long-tailed Skua (*Stercorarius longicaudus* Vieillot, 1819) at Scoresby Sund, East Greenland. 2. Arrival, site tenacity and departure. *Beaufortia* **34**: 1-14.

de Korte, J. (1985). Ecology of the Long-tailed Skua (*Stercorarius longicaudus* Vieillot, 1819) at Scoresby Sund, East Greenland. 3. Clutch size, laying date and incubation in relation to energy reserves. *Beaufortia* **35**: 93-127.

de Korte, J. (1986). Ecology of the Long-tailed Skua (*Stercorarius longicaudus* Vieillot, 1819) at Scoresby Sund, East Greenland. 4. Breeding success and growth of young. *Bijdragen tot de Dierkunde* **56**: 1-23.

de Korte, J. & Volkov, A. (1993). Large colony of Ivory Gulls *Pagophila eburnea* at Domastiny Island, Severnaya Zemlya. *Sula* **7**: 107-110.

de Korte, J. & Wattel, J. (1988). Food and breeding success of the Long-tailed Skua at Scoresby Sund, northeast Greenland. *Ardea* **76(1)**: 27-41. In English with Dutch summary.

Korzyakov, A.I. & Petrovskeya, L.P. (1988). [Breeding biology and distribution of the Black-winged Stilt (*Himantopus himantopus*) in the extreme south-western part of the USSR]. Pp. 82-87 in: Flint & Tomkovich (1988). In Russian.

Koshelev, A.I. (1994). Baillon's Crake. *Porzana pusilla*. Pp. 226-227 in: Tucker & Heath (1994).

Kosinski, R.J. & Podolsky, R.H. (1979). An analysis of breeding and mortality in a maturing kittiwake colony. *Auk* **96**: 537-543.

Koskimies, J. (1952). Observations on the development of mobility in young Common Gulls *Larus canus* and Lesser Black-backed Gulls *L. fuscus*. *Ornis Fenn.* **29**: 83-87.

Koskimies, J. (1957). Terns and gulls as features of habitat recognition for birds nesting in their colonies. *Ornis Fenn.* **34**: 1-6.

Koskimies, P. (1994). Broad-billed Sandpiper. *Limicola falcinellus*. Pp. 264-265 in: Tucker & Heath (1994).

Kostenko, V.A., Ler, P.A., Nechaev, V.A. & Shibaev, Y.V. (1989). *Rare Vertebrates of the Soviet Far East and their Protection*. Nauka Publishing House, Leningrad.

Koster, S.H. & Grettenberger, J.F. (1983). A preliminary survey of birds in W Park, Niger. *Malimbus* **5**: 62-72.

Kostin, G.N. & Panov, E.N. (1982). [Mortality of downy chicks and personal bonds between chicks and parents among Great Black-headed Gulls]. *Zoologischeskii Zhurnal* **61**: 1531-1542. In Russian.

Kotagama, S. & Fernando, P. (1994). *A Field Guide to the Birds of Sri Lanka*. Wildlife Heritage Trust of Sri Lanka, Colombo.

Kotliar, N.B. & Burger, J. (1984). The use of decoys to attract Least Terns (*Sterna antillarum*) to abandoned colony sites in New Jersey. *Colonial Waterbirds* **7**: 134-138.

Kotliar, N.B. & Burger, J. (1986). Colony site selection and abandonment by Least Terns *Sterna antillarum* in New Jersey, USA. *Biol. Conserv.* **37**: 1-21.

Kovács, G. (1985). [The Golden Plover (*Pluvialis apricaria* L.) on the Hortobágy (1975-1984)]. *Aquila* **92**: 97-103. In Hungarian with English summary.

Kovács, G. (1987). Staging and summering of Cranes (*Grus grus*) in the Hortobágy in 1975-1985. *Aquila* **93-94**: 153-169.

Kovács, G. (1991). Migration of Dotterels (*Eudromias morinellus* L., 1758) in the Hortobágy. *Aquila* **98**: 83-95.

Kovacs, K.M. & Ryder, J.P. (1981). Nest-site tenacity and mate fidelity in female-female pairs of Ring-billed Gulls. *Auk* **98(3)**: 625-627.

Kovacs, K.M. & Ryder, J.P. (1983). Reproductive performance of female-female pairs and polygynous trios of Ring-billed Gull. *Auk* **100**: 658-669.

Kovalev, A.H., Kaverkina, N.P., Davidova, G.U., Koritítskaya, L.N. & Roschevsky, V. (1980). [On the nesting of the Aleutian Tern on Lake Nevsky]. *Ornitologiya* **15**: 196-197. In Russian.

Kovshar, A.F. (1974). *Larus relictus*. Pp. 407-411 in: [*Birds of Kazakhstan*]. Alma Ata. In Russian.

Kovshar, A.F. (1980a). [On the breeding biology of Ibisbill (*Ibidorhyncha struthersii* Vigors]. *Byull. Mosk. Ova. Ispyt. Prir. Otd. Biol.* **85**: 25-33. In Russian.

Kovshar, A.F. (1980b). Zur Brutbiologie des Ibisschnabels *Ibidorhyncha struthersii* Vig., 1832. *Mitt. Zool. Mus. Berlin* **56**(Suppl.): 33-40.

Kovshar, A.F. (1982). Der Ibisschnabel *Ibidorhynchus struthersii*. [The Ibisbill *Ibidorhynchus struthersii*]. *Falke* **29(8)**: 275-276. In German.

Kovshar, A.V. (1987). The Demoiselle Crane in Kazakhstan and Central Asia. Pp. 23-31: in Archibald & Pasquier (1987a).

Kovshar, A.V. & Neufeldt, E.A. eds. (1991). [*The Demoiselle Crane in the USSR*]. Institute of Zoology, Kazakhstan Academy of Sciences, Gylym, Alma Ata. In Russian.

Kovshar, A.V., Winter, S.V., Baranov, A.A., Berezovikov, M.N., Golovushkin, M.I., Kidiraliev, A.K., Moseikin, V.N., Osipova, M.A., Sotnikova, E.I., Khakhin, G.V. & Khokhlov, A.N. (1995). The status of the Demoiselle Crane in the former USSR. Pp. 278-284 in: Prange *et al.* (1995).

Kowalczyk, E. & McNeal, J. (1984). Captive breeding of the Common Trumpeter (*Psophia crepitans*) at Woodland Park Zoological Gardens. *Anim. Keepers' Forum* **11(12)**: 461-465.

Kozicky, E.L. & Schmidt, F.L. (1949). Nesting habits of the Clapper Rail in New Jersey. *Auk* **66**: 355-364.

Kozlova, E.V. (1938). Field observations on the breeding of the Herring Gull (*Larus argentatus ponticus*) on the Caspian Sea. *Ibis* **Ser. 14, no. 2**: 245-254.

Kozlova, E.V. (1957). *Fauna of USSR*. Vol. 2(3). Birds: Charadriiformes, suborder Alcae. (English translation 1961). Israel Program for Scientific Translations, Jerusalem.

Kozlova, E.V. (1961a). [*Fauna of USSR*]. Vol. 2. Birds: Charadriiformes, suborder Charadrii. Academy of Sciences of the USSR, Leningrad. In Russian.

Kozlova, E.V. (1961b). [Direction of evolutionary process in waders of family Charadridae]. *Proc. Zool. Inst. Acad. Sci. USSR* **29**. Leningrad. In Russian.

Kozlova, E.V. (1966). Discovery of the nesting of the Sharp-tailed Sandpiper. *Emu* **66**: 252.

Kozlova, E.V. (1975). [*Birds of Zonal Steppes and Deserts of Central Asia*]. Nauka, Leningrad. In Russian.

Kraatz, S. & Beyer, K.H. (1982). Zur Brutbiologie des Waldwasserläufers (*Tringa ochropus*). *Beitr. Vogelkd.* **28(6)**: 231-256.

Kraatz, S. & Beyer, K.H. (1984). [Further observations on the breeding biology of the Green Sandpiper (*Tringa ochropus* L.)]. *Beitr. Vogelkd.* **30(1)**: 33-47. In German with English summary.

Kraft, M. (1993). [Breeding and resting population of the Lapwing *Vanellus vanellus* in the Lahn-valley near Marburg from 1962 to 1991]. *Vogelwelt* **114(3)**: 113-124. In German with English summary.

Kragh, W.D., Kautesk, B.M., Ireland, J. & Sian, E. (1986). Far Eastern Curlew in Canada. *Amer. Birds* **40(1)**: 13-15.

Krajewski, C. (1989). Phylogenetic relationships among cranes (Gruiformes: Gruidae) based on DNA hybridization. *Auk* **106**: 603-618.

Krajewski, C. & Fetzner, J.W. (1994). Phylogeny of cranes (Gruiformes: Gruidae) based on cytochrome-B DNA (deoxyribonucleic acid) sequences. *Auk* **111(2)**: 351-365.

Kramer, D. (1994). Aggressive behaviour of Northern Lapwing towards corpse of Black-headed Gull. *British Birds* **87(2)**: 90-91.

Krannitz, P.G. (1989). Nesting biology of Black Skimmers, Large-billed Terns and Yellow-billed Terns in Amazonian Brazil. *J. Field Orn.* **60(2)**: 216-223.

Krapu, G.L., Facey, D.E., Fritzell, E.K. & Johnson, D.H. (1984). Habitat use by migrant Sandhill Cranes in Nebraska. *J. Wildl. Manage.* **48**: 407-417.

Kraus, C., Bernath, O., Zbinden, K. & Pilleri, G. (1975). Zum Verhalten und Vokalisation von *Tribonyx mortierii* du Bois, 1840 (Aves, Rallidae). *Rev. Suisse Zool.* **82**: 6-13.

Kraus, M. & Lischka, W. (1956). Zum Vorkommen der *Porzana*-Arten im Fränkischen Weihergebiet. *J. Orn.* **97**: 190-201.

Krebs, A. (1956). Kentish Plover (*Charadrius alexandrinus*) and Little Ring Plover (*Charadrius dubius*) nesting in south India. *J. Bombay Nat. Hist. Soc.* **53(4)**: 702-703.

Krechmar, A.V., Andreev, A.V. & Kondratev, A.Y. (1978). [Ecology and distribution of Sandhill Cranes in north-eastern USSR]. Pp. 140-142 in: Krechmar, A.V. ed. (1978). [*Ecology and Distribution of Birds of Northeastern USSR*]. Izdatelstvo, Moscow. In Russian.

Krementz, D.G. & Pendleton, G.W. (1994). Diurnal habitat use of American Woodcock wintering along the Atlantic coast. *Can. J. Zool.* **72**: 1945-1950.

Krementz, D.G., Seginak, J.T. & Pendleton, G.W. (1994). Winter movements and spring migration of American Woodcock along the Atlantic coast. *Wilson Bull.* **106(3)**: 482-493.

Krementz, D.G., Seginak, J.T. & Smith, D.R. (1994). Survival rates of American Woodcock wintering along the Atlantic coast. *J. Wildl. Manage.* **58(1)**: 147-155.

Kress, S.W. & Nettleship, D.N. (1988). Re-establishment of Atlantic Puffins *Fratercula arctica* at a former breeding site in the Gulf of Maine. *J. Field Orn.* **59**: 161-170.

Kress, S.W., Weinstein, E.H. & Nisbet, I.C.T. (1983). The status of tern populations in northeastern United States and adjacent Canada. *Colonial Waterbirds* **6**: 84-106.

Krey, W. (1991). Singt der Seeregenpfeifer (*Charadrius alexandrinus*) wie der Alpenstrandläufer (*Calidris alpina*)? Ein historischer Fall von Verwechslung. [Is there no difference between the songs of Kentish Plover (*Charadrius alexandrinus*) and Dunlin (*Calidris alpina*)? A historical case of confusion]. *Vogelwarte* **36**: 99-109. In German with English summary.

Krienke, W. (1943). *Podica senegalensis petersi*, Peters' Finfoot. *Ostrich* **14**: 25-26.

Krohn, W.B. (1970). Woodcock feeding habits as related to summer field usage in central Maine. *J. Wildl. Manage.* **34**: 769-775.

Krohn, W.B. (1971). Some patterns of Woodcock activities on Maine summer fields. *Wilson Bull.* **83**: 396-407.

Król, E. (1985). Numbers, reproduction and breeding behaviour of Dunlin *Calidris alpina schinzii* at the Red Mouth, Poland. *Acta Orn., Varszawa* **21**.

Kruuk, H. (1964). *Predators and Anti-predator Behavior of the Black-headed Gull (*Larus ridibundus *L.)*. Behaviour **11**(Supplement).

Krych, S. (1992). Long-billed Curlew in Mcleod County. *Loon* **64(1)**: 61-63.

Kube, J. (1991). [Migration of the Great Snipe (*Gallinago media*) in the former GDR]. *Beitr. Vogelkd.* **37(5/6)**: 325-336. In German with English summary.

Kube, J. (1994). Aspects of the feeding ecology of migrating waders along the coast of the southern Baltic. *Corax* **15**: 57-72.

Kube, J., Graumann, G. & Grube, B. (1994). [The phenology of autumn migration of Golden Plovers (*Pluvialis apricaria*) at the German Baltic coast and in inland northeastern Germany]. *Corax* **15(2)**(Suppl.): 83-92. In German.

Kubiak, T.J., Harris, H.J., Smith, L.M., Schwartz, T.R., Stalling, D.L., Trick, J.A., Sileo, L., Docherty, D.E. & Erdman, T.C. (1989). Microcontaminants and reproductive impairment of the Forster's Tern on Green Bay, Lake Michigan-1983. *Arch. Environm. Contam. Toxicol.* **18**: 706-727.

Kuchin, A.P. & Chekcheev, I.P. (1987a). [The Sociable Plover in the Kulunda lakes hollow]. Pp. 138-139 in: [*The Problems of Rare Wildlife Conservation*]. Moscow. In Russian.

Kuchin, A.P. & Chekcheev, I.P. (1987b). [The Asiatic Dowitcher in the Kulunda lakes hollow]. Page 145 in: [*The Problems of Rare Wildlife Conservation*]. Moscow. In Russian.

Kuenzel, W.J. & Wiegert, R.G. (1973). Energetics of a Spotted Sandpiper feeding on brine fly larvae (*Paracoenia*; *Diptera*; *Ephydridae*) in a thermal spring community. *Wilson Bull.* **85**: 473-476.

Kuerzi, R.G. (1936). The Black-backed Gull as a predator. *Proc. Linn. Soc. N.Y.* **48**: 98-99.

Kuhnapfel, K.H. (1991). [Evidence of a clutch of six in *Charadrius dubius*]. *Charadrius* **27(4)**: 202-204. In German with English summary.

Kulkarni, B.S. (1981). Ecology and behaviour of Great Indian Bustard (Fam. Otididae). *J. Bombay Nat. Hist. Soc.* **78(2)**: 375-377.

Kulkarni, B.S. (1983). Ecology and behaviour of Great Indian Bustard (*Choriotis nigriceps*). Pp. 146-151 in: Goriup & Vardhan (1983).

Kull, R.C. (1978). Color selection of nesting material by Killdeer. *Auk* **94**: 602-604.

Kumari, E. (1976). The increase in the numbers of the Common Gull *Larus canus* and its colonization of Estonian peat-bogs in recent decades. *Ornis Fenn.* **53**: 33-39.

Kumari, E. (1977). *Der Regenbrachvogel* Numenius phaeopus. Neue Brehm-Bücherei **501**.

Kumerloeve, H. (1961). *Zur Kenntnis der Avifauna des Kleinasiens*. Bonner zoologische Beitraege, Sonderheft.

Kummer, J. (1990). [On the breeding of *Charadrius hiaticula* in the Mark Brandenburg District]. *Beitr. Vogelkd.* **36(5)**: 291-292. In German.

Kuroda, N. (1936a). *The Birds of the Island of Java*. Vol. 2. Tokyo.

Kuroda, N. (1936b). On a new breeding ground for *Pseudototanus guttifer*. *Tori* **9(43)**: 232-238.

Kuroda, N. (1954). On some osteological and anatomical characters of Japanese *Alcidae* Aves. *Jap. J. Zool.* **11**: 311-327.

Kuroda, N. (1955). Additional notes on the osteology of the Alcidae (Aves). *Annotationes Zool. Jap.* **28**: 110-113.

Kuroda, N. (1967). Morpho-anatomical analysis of parallel evolution between Diving-Petrel and Ancient Auk, with comparative osteological data of other species. *Misc. Rep. Yamashina Inst. Orn.* **5**: 111-137.

Kuroda, N. (1993). Morpho-anatomy of the Okinawa Rail. *J. Yamashina Inst. Orn.* **25**: 12-27.

Kuroda, N., Mano, T. & Ozaki, K. (1984). The Rallidae, their insular distribution and conservation, with special note around discovery of *Rallus okinawae*. *50 Years' Retrospect of Yamashina Inst. Orn.* **14**: 36-57.

Kurotshkin, E.N. (1970). Taxonomic position and morphological peculiarities of the genus *Pagophila*. *Acta Orn., Varszawa* **12**: 269-291.

Kürschner, W. (1976). Beobachtung eines Steppenkiebitzes - *Chettusia gregaria* - in Hessen. [Observation of a White-tailed Plover *Chettusia gregaria* in Hessen]. *Luscinia* **43(1/2)**: 33-34. In German.

Kury, C.R. & Gochfeld, M. (1975). Human interference and gull predation in cormorant colonies. *Biol. Conserv.* **8**: 23-34.

Kus, B.E., Ashman, P., Page, G.W. & Stenzel, L.E. (1984). Age-related mortality in a wintering population of Dunlin. *Auk* **101**: 69-73.
Kutilek, M.J. (1974). Notes on Kittlitz's Sandplover and Blacksmith Plover at Lake Nakuru. *East Afr. Wildl. J.* **12(1)**: 87-91.
Kuyt, E. (1976). Whooping Cranes: the long road back. *Nature Canada* **5**: 2-9.
Kuyt, E. (1981). Population status, nest site fidelity, and breeding habitat of Whooping Cranes. Pp. 119-125 in: Lewis & Masatomi (1981).
Kuyt, E. (1987). Whooping Crane migration studies, 1981-1982. Pp. 371-379 in: Archibald & Pasquier (1987a).
Kuyt, E. (1989). A recent record of American Avocet in the Northwest Territories. *Alberta Nat.* **19(1)**: 28-29.
Kuyt, E. (1992). *Aerial Radio-tracking of Whooping Cranes Migrating between Wood Buffalo National Park and Aransas National Wildlife Refuge, 1981-1984*. Occasional Papers **74**. Canadian Wildlife Service, Ottawa.
Kuyt, E. (1993). Whooping Crane, *Grus americana*, home range and breeding range expansion in Wood Buffalo National Park, 1970-1991. *Can. Field-Nat.* **107(1)**: 1-12.
Kuyt, E. & Johns, B.W. (1992). Recent American Avocet, *Recurvirostra americana*, breeding records in the Northwest Territories, with notes on avocet parasitism of Mew Gull, *Larus canus*, nests. *Can. Field-Nat.* **106(4)**: 507-510.
Kuzniak, S. & Pugacewicz, E. (1992). [The occurrence of the Marsh Sandpiper (*Tringa stagnatilis*) in Poland]. *Notatki Orn.* **33**: 227-240. In Polish.
Kuzyakin, V. (1994). Principal points of the Russian Woodcock programme. Pp. 66-70 in: Kalchreuter (1994).
Kvitek, R.G. (1991). Sequestered paralytic shellfish poisoning toxins mediate Glaucous-winged Gull predation on bivalve prey. *Auk* **108**: 381-392.
Kwater, E. (1992). Identifying a problem Yellowlegs. *Birding* **24(1)**: 18-20.
Kydyraliyev, A. (1990). *Birds of Lakes and Montane Rivers of Kirgiziya*. Ylim, Frunze, Kirgiziya.
Kydyraliyev, A. (1995). The Demoiselle Crane in Central Asia. Pp. 299-301 in: Prange *et al.* (1995).
Kyllingstad, H.C. (1948). The secret of the Bristle-thighed Curlew. *Arctic* **1**: 113-118.
L'Arrivee, L. & Blokpoel, H. (1988). Seasonal distribution and site fidelity in Great Lakes Caspian Terns. *Colonial Waterbirds* **11**: 202-214.
L'Hyver, M.A. (1985). *Intraspecific Variation in Nesting Phenology, Clutch Size and Egg Size in the Black Oystercatcher* Haematopus bachmani. MSc thesis, University of Victoria, Victoria, Canada.
L'Hyver, M.A. & Miller, E.H. (1991). Geographic and local variation in nesting phenology and clutch size of Black Oystercatcher. *Condor* **93(4)**: 892-903.
Labitte, A. (1955). La reproduction d'*Otis tetrax* (L.) dans la partie nord du Département d'Eure-et-Loir. *Oiseau et RFO* **25**: 144-147.
Labuda, S.E. & Butts, K.O. (1979). Habitat use by wintering Whooping Cranes on the Aransas National Wildlife Refuge. Pp. 151-157 in: Lewis (1979a).
Labutin, Y.V. & Dregayev, A.G. (1988). [*Grus canadensis* (Linnaeus) near the western boundary of their range: distribution and numbers]. Pp. 161-164 in: Litvinenko & Neufeldt (1988). In Russian.
Labutin, Y.V., Leonovitch, V.V. & Veprintsev, B.N. (1982). The Little Curlew, *Numenius minutus*, in Siberia. *Ibis* **124(3)**: 302-319.
Lacan, F. & Mougin, J.L. (1974). Les oiseaux des Îles Gambier et de quelques atolls orientaux de l'archipel des Tuamotu (Océan Pacifique). *Oiseau et RFO* **44**: 192-280.
Lack, D.L. (1968). *Ecological Adaptations for Breeding in Birds*. Methuen, London.
Lack, P.C. (1975). Range expansion of the Quail Plover. *Bull. East Afr. Nat. Hist. Soc.* **1975**: 110.
Lack, P.C. (1983). The Canarian Houbara: survey results 1979. *Bustard Studies* **1**: 45-50.
Lagrenade, M. & Mousseau, P. (1983). Female-female pairs and polygynous associations in Quebec Ring-billed Gull colony. *Auk* **100**: 210-212.
Lahrman, F.W. (1972). A rare observation of the Eskimo Curlew (on Padre Island, Texas). *Blue Jay* **30**: 87-88.
Lainer, H. (1991). Grey-headed Lapwing *Vanellus cinereus* (Blyth) in Goa. *J. Bombay Nat. Hist. Soc.* **88(1)**: 111.
Lal, R. (1993). Bustards and floricans: bird conservation in India. *Witwatersrand Bird Club News* **160**: 9-10.
Lalas, C. (1979). Seasonal movements of Black-fronted Terns. *Notornis* **26(1)**: 69-72.
Lalas, C. & Heather, B.D. (1980). The morphology, moult and taxonomic status of the Black-fronted Tern. *Notornis* **27(1)**: 45-67.
Lall, S. & Raman, L. (1994). The Siberian Cranes' last Indian winter. *Asian Wetlands News* **7(2)**: 23.
Lamarche, B. (1980). Liste commentée des oiseaux du Mali. 1ère partie: Non-passereaux. *Malimbus* **2**: 121-158.
Lamarche, B. (1988). *Liste Commentée des Oiseaux de Mauritanie*. Études Sahariennes et Ouest-Africaines **1(4)**. 164 pp.
Lambeck, R.H.D. (1991). Changes in abundance, distribution and mortality of wintering Oystercatchers after habitat loss in the Delta area, SW Netherlands. Pp. 2208-2218 in: *Proc. XX Int. Orn. Congr.* Christchurch, 1990.
Lambert, A. & Ratcliff, B. (1981). Present status of the Piping Plover in Michigan. *Jack-Pine Warbler* **59**: 44-52.
Lambert, F.R. (1985). Large-scale movements of Common Pratincole *Glareola pratincola* at Juba, Sudan. *Malimbus* **7(2)**: 136.
Lambert, F.R. (1987). New and unusual bird records from the Sudan. *Bull. Brit. Orn. Club* **107(1)**: 17-19.
Lambert, F.R. (1989). Some field observations of the endemic Sulawesi rails. *Kukila* **4**: 34-36.
Lambert, F.R. (1994). Notes on the avifauna of Bacan, Kasiruta and Obi, north Moluccas. *Kukila* **7(1)**: 1-9.
Lambert, K. (1967). Beobachtungen zum Zug under Winterquartier der Schwalbenmöwe (*Xema sabini*) in östlichen Atlantik. *Vogelwarte* **24**: 99-106.
Lambert, K. (1975). Schwalbenmöwen-Beobachtungen, *Xema sabini* (Sabine 1819), im Südsommer 1972/73 im Südafrikanischen Winterquartier. *Beitr. Vogelkd.* **21**: 410-415.
Lambert, K. (1980). Ein Überwinterungsgebiet der Falkenraubmöwe, *Stercorarius longicaudus* Vieill. 1819 vor Südwest mid Südafrica entdeckt. *Beitr. Vogelkd.* **26**: 199-212.
Lambert, K. (1983). Zum Zug des Zwergstrandläufers (*Calidris minuta*) nach Beringungsergebnissen aus der DDR. *Ber. Vogelwarte Hiddensee* **4**: 79-86.
Lambert, K. (1984). Zum Zug des Brachwasserläufers (*Tringa glareola*) nach Beringungsergebnissen aus der DDR. *Ber. Vogelwarte Hiddensee* **5**: 6-14.
Lambertini, M. (1993). The ecology and conservation of Audouin's Gull (*Larus audouinii*) at the northern limits of its breeding range. Pp. 261-272 in: Aguilar *et al.* (1993).
Lambertini, M. (1995). Audouin's Gull - the future in fishermen's hands. *Birding World* **8(7)**: 261-262.
Lamey, C.S. (1992). *Chick Loss in the Brown Skua (*Catharacta skua lonnbergi*)*. MSc thesis, Oklahoma State University, Stillwater, Oklahoma.
Lamey, C.S. (1995). Chick loss in the Falkland Skua *Catharacta skua antarctica*. *Ibis* **137**: 231-236.
Lamm, D.W. & Horwood, M.T. (1958). Species recently added to the list of Ghana birds. *Ibis* **100**: 175-178.
Lanctot, R.B. (1994). Blood sampling in juvenile Buff-breasted Sandpipers: movement, mass change and survival. *J. Field Orn.* **65(4)**: 534-542.
Lanctot, R.B. (1995). A closer look: Buff-breasted Sandpiper. *Birding* **27(5)**: 384-390.
Lanctot, R.B. & Laredo, C.D. (1994). Buff-breasted Sandpiper (*Tryngites subruficollis*). No. **91** in: Poole & Gill (1994).
Lanctot, R.B., Gill, R.E., Tibbitts, T.L. & Handel, C.M. (1995). Brood amalgamation in the Bristle-thighed Curlew *Numenius tahitiensis*: process and function. *Ibis* **137**: 559-569.
Land, H.C. (1970). *Birds of Guatemala*. Livingston Publishing Company, Wynnewood, Pennsylvania.
Landfried, S.E., Chaudry, A.A., Malik, M.M. & Ahmad, A. (1995). Integrated crane conservation activities in Pakistan: education, research, and publicity - a case study. In: Jacobson, S. ed. (1995). *Wildlife Conservation: International Case Studies of Education and Communication Programs*. Columbia University Press, New York.
Landmann, A. (1979). Zur Überwinterung des Waldwasserläufers *Tringa ochropus* in Nordtirol. [On the overwintering of the Green Sandpiper *Tringa ochropus* in northern Tyrol]. *Anz. Orn. Ges. Bayern* **18(2/3)**: 183-184.
Landry, P. (1978). *Modélisation et Comparison de l'Impact Énergétique de Deux Populations Françaises de Mouette Rieuse,* Larus ridibundus. *L.* Thèse 3ème cycle Lyon I.
Lane, B.A. (1981). The Hooded Plover survey, October 1980. *Victoria Wader Study Group Bull.* **3**: 6-8.
Lane, B.A. (1982). Hooded Plover survey, October 1981. *Stilt* **2**: 46.
Lane, B.A. (1986). The subspecies of Mongolian Plover *Charadrius mongolus* in Australia. *Stilt* **8**: 14-17.
Lane, B.A. (1991). Survey of Victorian beaches for Hooded Plovers - October 1990. *Stilt* **19**: 7-8.
Lane, B.A. & Davies, J. (1987). *Shorebirds in Australia*. Nelson, Melbourne.
Lane, B.A. & Forest, B.S. (1984). Preliminary results from banding Lathams Snipe *Gallinago hardwickii* in Southern Victoria. *Victoria Wader Study Group Bull.* **8**: 2-12.
Lane, B.A. & Jessop, A.E. (1983). Distribution and habitat of the Red-capped Plover in Victoria. *Victoria Wader Study Group Bull.* **7**: 35-40.
Lane, B.A. & Jessop, A.E. (1985). Report on the 1985 North-west Australia Wader Studies Expedition. *Stilt* **6**: 2-16.
Lane, S.G. (1978). Some results from banding Japanese Snipe near Sydney, New South Wales. *Corella* **2(3)**: 49-51.
Lane, S.G. (1985). The Hooded Plover - northern distribution in Eastern Australia. *Stilt* **6**: 35.
Lane, S.G. (1986). Nesting behaviour of Sooty Terns *Sterna fuscata* on Pelsart Island, Western Australia. *Corella* **10**: 28-29.
Lane, S.G. (1994). Feeding association between Comb-crested Jacana *Irediparra galllinacea* and Australasian Grebe *Tachybaptus novaehollandiae*. *Austr. Bird Watcher* **15(7)**: 324.
Lang, A.L. (1991). Status of the American Coot in Canada. *Can. Field-Nat.* **105**: 530-541.
Lange, G. (1968). Über Nahrung, Nahrungsaufnahme und Verdauungstrakt mitteleuropäischer Limicolen. *Beitr. Vogelkd.* **13**: 225-334.
Langham, N.P. (1972). Chick survival in the terns (*Sterna* spp.) with particular reference to the Common Tern. *J. Anim. Ecol.* **41**: 385-395.
Langham, N.P. (1983). Growth strategies in marine terns. *Studies in Avian Biology* **8**: 73-83.
Langham, N.P. (1986). The effect of cyclone 'Simon' on terns nesting on One Tree Island, Great Barrier Reef, Australia. *Emu* **86**: 53-57.
Langham, N.P. & Hulsman, K. (1986). The breeding biology of the Crested Tern *Sterna bergii*. *Emu* **86**: 23-32.
Langham, N.P.E. (1971). Seasonal movements of British terns in the Atlantic Ocean. *Bird Study* **18**: 155-175.
Langham, N.P.E. (1974). Comparative breeding biology of the Sandwich Tern. *Auk* **91**: 255-277.
Langrand, O. (1990). *Guide to the Birds of Madagascar*. Yale University Press, New Haven & London.
Langridge, H.P. & Hunter, G.S. (1986). Inland nesting of Black Skimmers. *Florida Field Nat.* **14(3)**: 73-74.
Lanier, H. (1990). On the status of the Sandwich Tern *Sterna sandvicensis* on India's West Coast. *J. Bombay Nat. Hist. Soc.* **87**: 298-299.
Lank, D. (1983). *Migrating Behavior of the Semipalmated Sandpiper at Inland and Coastal Staging Areas*. PhD thesis, Cornell University, Ithaca, New York.
Lank, D.B. (1989). Why fly by night? Inferences from tidally-induced migratory departures of sandpipers. *J. Field Orn.* **60**: 154-161.
Lank, D.B. & Smith C.M. (1987). Conditional lekking in Ruff (*Philomachus pugnax*). *Behav. Ecol. Sociobiol.* **20**: 137-145.
Lank, D.B. & Smith, C.M. (1992). Females prefer larger leks: field experiments with Ruffs (*Philomachus pugnax*). *Behav. Ecol. Sociobiol.* **30(5)**: 323-329.
Lank, D.B., Smith, C.M., Hanotte, O., Burke, T. & Cooke, F. (1995). Genetic polymorphism for alternative mating behaviour in lekking male Ruff *Philomachus pugnax*. *Nature* **378**: 59-62.
Lansdown, P. (1993). Separation of South Polar Skua from Great Skua. *British Birds* **86(4)**: 176-177.
Larionov, V.F. & Cheltsov-Bebutov, A.M. (1972). [Discovery of *L. relictus* on the Torey lakes, Transbaikalia]. *Ornitologiya* **10**: 277-279. In Russian.
Larkins, D. (1989). Bush Stone-curlews: recollections of their occurrence at Preston, New South Wales. *Austr. Birds* **22(3/4)**: 82-83.
Larkins, D. & McGill, A. (1978). Oriental Dotterels at Bankstown Airport, NSW. *Austr. Birds* **12(3)**: 59-60.
Larousse, A. (1995). Nidification de l'Avocette élégante *Recurvirostra avosetta* dans le centre de la France. *Ornithos* **2(3)**: 139-141.
Larsen, R.T. & Ralph, C.J. (1984). The arrival, departure and residency of a small population of the Lesser Golden-plover in Hawaii. *Elepaio* **45(2)**: 12-13.
Larsen, T. (1993). Information parasitism in foraging Bar-tailed Godwits *Limosa lapponica*. *Ibis* **135**: 271-276.
Larsen, T. & Moldsvor, J. (1992). Antipredator behavior and breeding associations of Bar-tailed Godwits and Whimbrels. *Auk* **109(3)**: 601-608.
Larson, S. (1955). Tertiär och pleistocen artbildning inom underordningen Charadrii. *Vår Fågelvärld* **2**: 65-78.
Larson, S. (1957). The suborder Charadrii in Arctic and Boreal areas during the Tertiary and Pleistocene. *Acta Vertebratica* **1**: 1 84.
LaRue, C. (1979). Breeding the Brolga. *Avicult. Mag.* **85(3)**: 139-140.
Latham, P.C.M. (1979). New Zealand Dotterels catching fish. *Notornis* **26(1)**: 36.
Latham, P.C.M. (1981). Black-fronted Terns wintering in the Bay of Plenty. *Notornis* **28(4)**: 221-239.
Latham, P.C.M. & Parrish, R. (1987). Notes on the feeding habits of the New Zealand Dotterel. *Notornis* **34(1)**: 9-10.
LaTouche, J.D.D. (1931). *Handbook of the Birds of Eastern China*. Taylor & Francis, London.
LaTour, M. (1973). Nidification de cinq espèces de Laridés au voisinage de l'embouchure du Fleuve Sénégal. *Oiseau et RFO* **43**: 90-96.
Launay, F. & Loughland, R. (1995). Breeding system of Houbara Bustard *Chlamydotis undulata macqueenii*: preliminary observations. *Bull. Orn. Soc. Middle East* **35**: 14-17.
Launay, F. & Paillat, P. (1990). A behavioural repertoire of the adult Houbara Bustard (*Chlamydotis undulata macqueenii*). *Rev. Ecol. (Terre Vie)* **45(1)**: 65-88. In English with French summary.
Lauro, A.J. (1980). The winter ecology of Bonaparte's Gull on the south shore of Long Island. *Linn. Soc. N.Y. Newsletter* **34(1)**: 1-3.
Lauro, A.J. & Spencer, B.J. (1980). A method for separating juvenile and first-winter Ring-billed Gulls (*Larus delawarensis*) and Common Gulls (*Larus canus*). *Amer. Birds* **34**: 111-117.
Lauro, B. & Burger, J. (1989). Nest-site selection of American Oystercatchers (*Haematopus palliatus*) in salt marshes. *Auk* **106(2)**: 185-192.
Lauro, B. & Nol, E. (1993). The effect of prevailing wind direction and tidal flooding on the reproductive success of Pied Oystercatchers *Haematopus longirostris*. *Emu* **93(3)**: 199-202.
Lauro, B., Nol, E. & Vicari, M. (1992). Nesting density and communal breeding in American Oystercatchers. *Condor* **94(1)**: 286-289.
Lavauden, L. (1931). Note préliminaire sur les oiseaux appartenant aux genres *Mesoenas* et *Monias*. *Alauda* **3**: 395-400.
Lavauden, L. (1932). Étude d'une petite collection d'oiseaux de Madagascar. *Bull. Mus. Natl. Hist. Nat. (2e Sér.)* **4(6)**: 629-640.
Lavauden, L. (1937). Supplément. In: Milne-Edwards, A. & Grandidier, A. (1885). *Histoire Physique, Naturelle et Politique de Madagascar*. Vol. 12. Histoire Naturelle des Oiseaux. Société d'Editions Géographiques, Maritimes et Coloniales, Paris.
Lavauden, L. & Poisson, H. (1929). Contribution à l'étude de l'anatomie du *Monias benschi*. *Nos Oiseaux* **10**: 665-670.
Lavee, D. (1985). The influence of grazing and intensive cultivation on the population size of the Houbara Bustard in the northern Negev in Israel. *Bustard Studies* **3**: 103-107.
Lavee, D. (1988). Why is the Houbara *Chlamydotis undulata macqueenii* still an endangered species in Israel? *Biol. Conserv.* **45(1)**: 47-54.
Lavee, D. (1994). [The Houbara Bustard *Chlamydotis undulata* in the Western Negev]. *Torgos* **23**: 24-27, 66. In Hebrew with English summary.
Lavers, R. & Mills, J. (1984). *Takahe*. John McIndoe & New Zealand Wildlife Service, Dunedin.
Lavery, H.G. (1965). The Brolga, *Grus rubicundus* (Perry), on some coastal areas in north Queensland: fluctuations in number and economic status. *Queensland J. Agric. Sci.* **21**: 261-264.
Lavery, H.G. & Blackman, J.G. (1969). The cranes of Australia. *Queensland Agric. J.* **95**: 156-162.
Lawrence, D. (1993). Spotted Sandpiper displaying to and mating with Common Sandpiper. *British Birds* **86**: 628.
Lawson, W.J. (1966). Peters Finfoot. *Bokmakierie* **18**: 47.
Layard, E.L. (1875). Notes on Fijian birds. *Proc. Zool. Soc., London* **1875**: 423-442.
Layard, E.L. (1876). Notes on some little known birds of the Fiji Islands. *Ibis* **Ser. 3, no. 6**: 137-156.
Layard, E.L. & Layard, E.C.L. (1882). Notes on the avifauna of New Caledonia. *Ibis* **Ser. 4, no. 6**: 493-550.
Laybourne, S. (1978). Ivory Gull bathing and settling on water. *British Birds* **71**: 39.
Le Roux, S.F. (1965). Some observations on the Black Oystercatcher. *Afr. Wildl.* **19**: 256 257.
Le Souëf, D. (1903). Descriptions of birds' eggs from the Port Darwin district, northern Australia. *Emu* **2**: 139-159.
Leach, G.J. (1988). Birds of Narayen Research Station, Mundubbera, south-east Queensland. *Sunbird* **18(3)**: 55-75.
Leach, G.J. & Hines, H.B. (1992). Waterbirds at Minden Dam, southeast Queensland, 1979-1987, and factors influencing their abundance. *Corella* **16**: 111-118.
Leach, G.J., Lloyd, C.G. & Hines, H.B. (1987). Observations at the nest of the Painted Snipe *Rostratula benghalensis* in south-east Queensland. *Austr. Bird Watcher* **12(1)**: 15-19.
Leavitt, B.B. (1957). Food of the Black Skimmer (*Rynchops nigra*). *Auk* **74**: 394.
Lebreton, J.D. & Isenmann, P. (1976). Dynamique de la population Camarguaise de Mouettes rieuses *Larus ridibundus* L: un modèle mathématique. *Rev. Ecol. (Terre Vie)* **30**: 529-549.
Lebreton, J.D. & Landry, P. (1979). Fécondité de la Mouette rieuse (*Larus ridibundus*) dans une colonie importante de la Plaine du Forez (Loire, France). *Gerfaut* **69**: 159-194.

Leck, C.F. (1971). Nocturnal habits of Ring-billed Gulls (*Larus delawarensis*) at Thimble Shoals, Virginia. *Chesapeake Sci.* **12**: 188.
Leck, C.F. (1979). Avian extinction in an isolated tropical wet forest preserve, Ecuador. *Auk* **96**: 343-352.
LeCroy, M. (1972). Young Common and Roseate Terns learning to fish. *Wilson Bull.* **84**: 201-202.
LeCroy, M. (1976). Bird observation in Los Roquest, Venezuela. *Amer. Mus. Novit.* **2599**: 1-30.
LeCroy, M. & Collins, C.T. (1972). Growth and survival of Roseate and Common Tern chicks. *Auk* **89**: 595-611.
LeCroy, M. & LeCroy, S. (1974). Growth and fledging in the Common Tern (*Sterna hirundo*). *Bird-Banding* **45**: 326-340.
Ledant, J.P., Jacob, J.P., Jacobs, P., Malher, F., Ochando, B. & Roché, J. (1981). Mise à jour de l'avifaune algérienne. *Gerfaut* **71**: 295-398.
Ledger, J.A. ed. (1984). *Proceedings of the V Pan-African Ornithological Congress*. Southern African Ornithological Society, Johannesburg.
Lee, D.S. (1992). Specimen records of Aleutian Terns from the Philippines. *Condor* **94**: 276-279.
Lee, D.S. & Cardiff, S.W. (1993). Status of the Arctic Tern in the coastal and offshore waters of the southeastern United States. *J. Field Orn.* **64**: 158-168.
Lee, G.C. (1989). *Breeding Ecology and Habitat Use Patterns of Snowy and Wilson's Plovers at the Cabo Rojo Salt Flats, Puerto Rico*. MSc thesis, Clemson University.
Lees, A. (1991). *A Protected Forests System for the Solomon Islands*. Maruia Society, Nelson, New Zealand.
Leger, D.W. (1982). Effects of contextual information on behavior of *Calidris* sandpipers following alarm calls. *Wilson Bull.* **94**: 322-328.
Legg, K. (1954). Nesting and feeding of the Black Oystercatcher near Monterey, California. *Condor* **56**: 359 360.
Lehman, P. (1980). The identification of Thayer's Gull in the field. *Birding* **12**: 198-210.
Lehmann, H. (1969). The Greater Sand Plover in Asia Minor. *Ool. Rec.* **43**: 30-54.
Lehmann, H. (1971). Der Wüstenregenpfeifer (*Charadrius leschenaultii* Lesson), ein Bewohner der Steppe Inneranatoliens. *Jahresber. Naturwiss. Ver. Wuppertal* **24**: 101-120.
Lehnhausen, W.A. (1980). *Nesting Habitat Relationships of Four Species of Alcids at Fish Island, Alaska*. MSc thesis, University of Alaska, Fairbanks, Alaska.
Leicester, M. (1960). Some notes on the Lewin Rail. *Emu* **60**: 20-24.
Leinaas, H.P. & Ambrose, W.G. (1992). Utilization of different foraging habitats by the Purple Sandpiper *Calidris maritima* on a Spitsbergen beach. *Fauna Norvegica (Ser. C, Cinclus)* **15(2)**: 85-91. In English with Norwegian summary.
Lekagul, B. & Round, P.D. (1991). *A Guide to the Birds of Thailand*. Saha Karn Bhaet, Bangkok.
Lelek, A. (1958). Contribution to the bionomy of the Coot (*Fulica atra* L.). *Folia Zoologica* **7**: 143-168.
Lemmetyinen, R. (1971). Nest defence behaviour of Common and Arctic Terns and its effect on the success achieved by predators. *Ornis Fenn.* **48**: 13-24.
Lemmetyinen, R. (1972). Growth and mortality in the chicks of Arctic Terns in the Kongsfjord area, Spitsbergen in 1970. *Ornis Fenn.* **49**: 45-53.
Lemmetyinen, R. (1973a). Clutch size and timing of breeding in the Arctic Tern in the Finnish archipelago. *Ornis Fenn.* **50**: 18-28.
Lemmetyinen, R. (1973b). Feeding ecology of *Sterna paradisaea* Pohntopp. and *S. hirundo* L. in the archipelago of southwestern Finland. *Ann. Zool. Fennici* **10**: 507-525.
Lemmetyinen, R. (1973c). Breeding success in *Sterna paradisaea* Pontopp. and *S. hirundo* L. in southern Finland. *Ann. Zool. Fennici* **10**: 526-535.
Lemmetyinen, R. (1974). Comparative breeding biology of the Arctic and the Common Tern with special reference to feeding. *Rep. Dept. Zool. Univ. Turku, Finland* **3**: 1-19.
Lemmetyinen, R. (1976). Feeding segregation in the Arctic and Common Terns in southern Finland. *Auk* **93**: 636-640.
Lemmetyinen, R., Portin, P. & Vuolanto, S. (1974). Polymorphism in relation to the substrate in chicks of *Sterna paradisaea* Pontopp. *Ann. Zool. Fennici* **11**: 265-270.
Lemnell, P.A. (1978). Social behaviour of the Great Snipe *Capella media*, at the arena display. *Ornis Scand.* **9(2)**: 146-163.
Lendon, A. (1938). The breeding in captivity of the Little Button-quail (*Turnix velox*). *Avicult. Mag.* **3(5)**: 78-79.
Lenington, S. (1980). Bi-parental care in Killdeer: an adaptive hypothesis. *Wilson Bull.* **92**: 8-20.
Lenington, S. & Mace, T. (1975). Mate fidelity and nesting site tenacity in the Killdeer. *Auk* **92**: 149-150.
Lensink, C.J. (1984). The status and conservation of seabirds in Alaska. Pp. 13-27 in: Croxall, Evans & Schreiber (1984).
Leonard, M.L., Horn, A.G. & Eden, S.F. (1989). Does juvenile helping enhance breeder reproductive success? A removal experiment on moorhens. *Behav. Ecol. Sociobiol.* **25**: 357-362.
Leonovitch, V.V. (1973). [On the distribution and biology of *Calidris subminuta* Midd]. Pp. 78-83 in: Flint (1973a). In Russian.
Leonovitch, V.V. (1976a). [Asiatic Dowitcher in the Primorski Krai]. Pp. 164-167 in: [*Rare, Threatened and Inadequately-known Birds of the USSR*]. Moscow. In Russian.
Leonovitch, V.V. (1976b). [New nesting site of Kamchatka Terns]. Pp. 171-172 in: [*Rare, Disappearing and Little Studied Birds of the U.S.S.R.*]. Vol. 13. Oksk. Wildlife Preserve, Ryazan. In Russian.
Leonovitch, V.V. & Kretzschmar, A.W. (1966). Zur Biologie des Graubürzelwasserläufers. *Falke* **13**: 154-156.
Leopold, M.F., Swennen, C. & de Bruijn, L.L.M. (1989). Experiments on selection of feeding site and food size in Oystercatchers, *Haematopus ostralegus*, of different social status. *Netherlands J. Sea Res.* **23**: 333-346.
Leroux, A. & Thomas, A. (1989). Evolution de la population bretonne de la Sterne de Dougall et stratégie de protection. *Penn Bed* **135**: 16-18.
Leschner, L.L. (1976). *The Breeding Biology of the Rhinoceros Auklet on Destruction Island*. MSc thesis, University of Washington, Seattle, Washington.
Leschner, L.L. & Burrel, G. (1977). Populations and ecology of marine birds of the Semidi Islands. Pp. 13-109 in: *Annual Reports of Principal Investigators. Environmental Assessment of the Alaskan Continental Shelf.* Vol. 4. NOAA-BLM, Boulder, Colorado.
Leschner, L.L. & Cummins, E.B. (1992). Breeding records, inland distribution and threats of the Marbled Murrelet in Washington from 1905 to 1987. Pp.42-47 in: Carter & Morrison (1992).
Lessells, C.M. (1984). The mating system of Kentish Plovers *Charadrius alexandrinus*. *Ibis* **126**: 474-483.
Lethaby, N. (1995). Undertail-coverts of Solitary Sandpipers. *Birding World* **8(11)**: 426-427.
Lethaby, N. & Gilligan, J. (1991). An occurrence of the Great Knot in Oregon. *Oregon Birds* **17(2)**: 35-37.
Lethaby, N. & Gilligan, J. (1992). Great Knot in Oregon. *Amer. Birds* **46(1)**: 46-47.
Létocart, Y. (1984). Sauvegarde du Cagou. Unpublished report to Circonscription du Dévelopment de l'Économie Rurale, Païta.
Létocart, Y. (1989). Étude sur la biologie du Cagou huppé (*Rhynochetus jubatus*) dans le Parc Territorial de la Rivière Bleue. Internal unpublished report to Eaux et Forêts de la Nouvelle-Calédonie, Nouméa, New Caledonia.
Létocart, Y. (1991). Mise en évidence par biotélémétrie de l'habitat utilisé, du comportement territorial et social, et de la reproduction chez le Cagou huppé (*Rhynochetus jubatus*) dans le Parc Territorial de la Rivière Bleue. Internal unpublished report to Service de l'Environnement et de la Gestion des Parcs et Réserves de la Province Sud, Nouméa, New Caledonia.
Létocart, Y. (1992). Sauvegarde du Cagou huppé (*Rhynochetos jubatus*) dans le Parc Provincial de la Rivière Bleue. Internal unpublished report to Service de l'Environnement et de la Gestion des Parcs et Réserves de la Province Sud, Nouméa, New Caledonia.
Leuzinger, H. & Jenni, L. (1993). [Migration of Wood Sandpipers *Tringa glareola* at Ägelsee, Switzerland]. *Orn. Beob.* **90(3)**: 169-188. In German with English summary.
Lévêque, R. (1964). Notes sur la reproduction des oiseaux aux Îles Galapagos. [Notes on the breeding of birds on the Galapagos Islands]. *Alauda* **32**: 5 44.
Lever, C. (1987). *Naturalized Birds of the World*. Longman Scientific & Technical, Harlow, UK.
Levi, P.J. (1966). Observations on the Southern White-breasted Crake in captivity. *Avicult. Mag.* **72**: 24-26.
Levi, P.J. (1968). Some notes on the Sun-bittern (*Eurypyga helias*). *Avicult. Mag.* **74**: 206-209.
Levings, S.C., Garrity, S.D. & Ashkenas, L.R. (1986). Feeding rates and prey selection of oystercatchers in the Pearl Islands of Panama. *Biotropica* **18(1)**: 62-71.
Levy, N. & Yom-Tov, Y. (1991). Activity and status of Cranes *Grus grus* wintering in Israel. *Sandgrouse* **13(2)**: 58-72.
Lewartowski, Z. (1983). Ostatnie stanowisko legowe kulona *Burhinus oedicnemus* w wielkopolsce. [The last breeding locality of the Stone-curlew, *Burhinus oedicnemus*, in major Poland]. *Chronmy Przyr. Ojczysta* **39(4)**: 68-71. In Polish.
Lewington, I., Alström, P. & Colston, P. (1991). *A Field Guide to the Rare Birds of Britain and Europe*. Harper Collins, London.
Lewis, A. (1990). Spur-winged Plover flushing prey from dry ground with its feet. *Bull. East Afr. Nat. Hist. Soc.* **20(1)**: 11.
Lewis, A.D. & Pomeroy, D.E. (1989). *A Bird Atlas of Kenya*. A.A. Balkema, Rotterdam.
Lewis, J.C. (1974). *Ecology of the Sandhill Crane in the Southeastern Central Flyway*. PhD dissertation. Oklahoma State University, Stillwater, Oklahoma.
Lewis, J.C. ed. (1976a). *Proceedings of the International Crane Workshop*. Oklahoma State University Publishing and Printing, Stillwater, Oklahoma.
Lewis, J.C. (1976b). Roost habitat and roosting behavior of Sandhill Cranes in the southern central flyway. Pp. 93-104 in: Lewis (1976a).
Lewis, J.C. ed. (1979a). *Proceedings, 1978 Crane Workshop*. Colorado State University & National Audubon Society, Fort Morgan, Colorado.
Lewis, J.C. (1979b). Taxonomy, food, and feeding habitat of Sandhill Cranes, Platte Valley, Nebraska. Pp. 21-27 in: Lewis (1979a).
Lewis, J.C. ed. (1982). *Proceedings of the 1981 International Crane Workshop*. National Audubon Society, Tavernier, Florida.
Lewis, J.C. (1986). The Whooping Crane. Pp. 659-676 in: Di Silvestro, R.L. ed. (1986). *Audubon Wildlife Report 1986*. National Audubon Society, New York.
Lewis, J.C. ed. (1987). *Proceedings, 1985 Crane Workshop*. Platte River Whooping Crane Habitat Maintenance Trust and US Fish & Wildlife Service, Grand Island, Nebraska.
Lewis, J.C. (1991). International cooperation in recovery of Whooping Cranes: a model for other nations. Pp. 389-394 in: Harris (1991b).
Lewis, J.C. (1992). The contingency plan for federal-state cooperative protection of Whooping Cranes. Pp. 293-300 in: Wood (1992).
Lewis, J.C. (1995). Whooping crane (*Grus americana*). No. **153** in: Poole & Gill (1994-1995).
Lewis, J.C. & Cooch, F.G. (1992). Introduction of Whooping Cranes in eastern North America. Pp. 301-305 in: Wood (1992).
Lewis, J.C. & Garrison, R.L. (1983). *Habitat Suitability Index Models: Clapper Rail*. US Fish & Wildlife Service FWS/OBS-82/10.51.
Lewis, J.C. & Masatomi, H. eds. (1981). *Crane Research Around the World*. International Crane Foundation, Baraboo, Wisconsin.
Lewis, M. (1991). The status of the Long-tailed Jaeger *Stercorarius longicaudus* in Australian waters. *Austr. Bird Watcher* **14(4)**: 119-122.
Li Dehao (1987). The distribution and status of the Black-necked Crane in the Tibetan Plateau. Pp. 45-50 in: Archibald & Pasquier (1987a).
Li Fangman & Li Peixun (1991). The spring migration of Siberian Cranes at Lindian County, Heilongjiang Province, China. Pp. 133-134 in: Harris (1991b).
Li Fangman, Li Peixun & Yu Xuefeng (1991). [The primary study on territories of White-naped Cranes]. *Zool. Res.* **12(1)**: 29-34. In Chinese with English summary.
Li Jinlu & Feng Kemin (1985). [Overwintering of Red-crowned Crane and Siberian Crane in China]. *J. Northeast Forestry Univ.* **13(3)**: 135-142. In Chinese.
Li Jinlu & Feng Kemin (1990). [Siberian Cranes at lower reaches of the Wuyuer River]. Pp. 18-20 in: Gao Zhiyuan ed. (1990). [*Collections of the Academic Theses of the Wildlife Institute, Heilongjiang Province*]. Forest Press, Beijing, China. In Chinese.
Li Lin (1993). [The first breeding record of the Hooded Crane in China]. *Chinese Wildlife* **5**: 16. In Chinese.
Li Peixun, Li Fangman & Yu Xuefeng (1991). Selection of nesting sites and territories by White-naped Cranes in Lindian County, China. Pp. 59-60 in: Harris (1991b).
Li Peixun, Yuan Tao, Li Fangman & Yu Xuefeng (1987). [A preliminary study of copulatory behavior and territory of the White-naped Crane]. *Chinese Wildlife* **3**: 11-12. In Chinese.
Liang, Y.L.J. (1989). [Observations on the breeding habits of the Whiskered Tern *Chlidonias hybrida*]. *Trans. Liaoning Zool. Soc.* **7**: 121-124. In Chinese.
Liang Qihui (1986). [The Button Quail, *Turnix tanki*, a species in which the females dominate the males]. *Chinese Wildlife* **3**: 61. In Chinese.
Liao Yanfa (1986). [Investigating Black-necked Cranes (*Grus nigricollis*) at Longbaotan (Qinghai Province)]. *Nature* **4**: 6-11. In Chinese.
Liao Yanfa (1987). The Black-necked Cranes of Longbaotan. *ICF Bugle* **13(1)**: 1, 4-5.
Liao Yanfa & Wang Xia (1983). [The breeding of the Brown-headed Gull *Larus brunnicephalus*]. *Wildlife* **2**: 45-50. In Chinese.
Liao Yanfa, Nian Guangcan & Qiu Lidong (1991). The study of breeding techniques for Black-necked Cranes. Page 199 in: Harris (1991b).
Lid, G. (1981). Reproduction of the Puffin on Røst in the Lofoten Islands in 1964-1980. *Fauna Norvegica (Ser. C, Cinclus)* **4**: 30-39.
Lida, T. (1991). [Breeding behaviour and habitat of Latham's Snipe]. *Strix* **10**: 31-50. In Japanese.
Liddy, J. (1959). The Australian Pratincole in north-west Queensland. *Emu* **59**: 136-140.
Liedel, K. (1982). Verbreitung und Ökologie des Steppenschlammläufers. *Mitt. Zool. Mus. Berlin* **58**(Suppl.): *Ann. Orn.* **6**: 147-162.
Liedel, K. (1987). *Limnodromus semipalmatus* (Blyth). In: Stresemann, E. & Portenko, L.A. eds. (1987). *Atlas der Verbreitung Palaearktischer Vögel*. Vol. 14. Akademie Verlag, Berlin.
Lien, J. (1975). Aggression between Great Black-backed Gulls and Bald Eagles. *Auk* **92**: 584-585.
Lifjeld, J.T. (1984). Prey selection in relation to body size and bill length of five species of waders feeding in the same habitat. *Ornis Scand.* **15**: 217-226.
Liker, A. (1992). [Breeding biology of Lapwing (*Vanellus vanellus*) in alkaline grassland]. *Ornis Hungarica* **2(2)**: 61-66. In Hungarian with English summary.
Lim Kimseng (1994). Birds to watch: threatened birds in Singapore. *Bull. Oriental Bird Club* **19**: 52-54.
Lind, H. (1961). *Studies on the Behaviour of the Black-tailed Godwit*. Medd. Naturfredningsrådets Reservatudvalg **66**. Munksgaard, Copenhagen.
Lind, H. (1963a). The reproductive behaviour of the Gull-billed Tern, *Sterna nilotica* Gmelin. *Vidensk. Medd. Dan. Naturhist. Foren.* **125**: 407-448.
Lind, H. (1963b). [Notes on social behaviour in terns]. *Dan. Orn. Foren. Tidssk.* **57**: 157-175. In Danish.
Lind, H. (1965). Parental feeding in the Oystercatcher. *Dan. Orn. Foren. Tidssk.* **59**: 1 31.
Lindberg, D.R., Warheit, K.I. & Estes, J.A. (1987). Prey preference and seasonal predation by oystercatchers on limpets at San Nicolas Island, California, USA. *Mar. Ecol. Prog. Ser.* **39(2)**: 105-113.
Lindgren, E. (1971). Records of new and uncommon species for the island of New Guinea. *Emu* **71**: 134-136.
Lindsay, C.J., Phillipps, W.J. & Watters, W.A. (1959). Birds of Chatham Island and Pitt Island. *Notornis* **8**: 99-106.
Lindsey, T.R. (1992). *Encyclopedia of Australian Animals*. Birds. Angus & Robertson, NPIAW, Sydney.
Lingle, G.R. (1987). Status of Whooping Crane migration habitat within the Great Plains of North America. Pp. 331-340 in: Lewis (1987).
Lingle, G.R., Wingfield, G.A. & Ziewitz, J.W. (1991). The migration ecology of Whooping Cranes in Nebraska, USA. Pp. 395-401 in: Harris (1991b).
Lint, K.C. (1968). A rail of Guam. *Zoo Nooz* **41(5)**: 16-17.
Linz, G.M., Bergman, D.L., Blixt, D.G. & Bleier, W.J. (1994). Response of Black Terns (*Chlidonias niger*) to glyphosphate-induced habitat alterations on wetlands. *Colonial Waterbirds* **17(2)**: 160-167.
Linz, G.M., Knittle, C.E. & Johnson, R.E. (1990). Activity of Common Ravens in relation to a California Least Tern colony on Camp Pendleton, California. Pp. 323-324 in: *52nd Midwest Fish & Wildlife Conference Program.*
Lippens, L. & Wille, H. (1976). *Les Oiseaux du Zaïre*. Editions Lannoo Tielt, Belgium.
Lisetski, A.S. & Gudina, A.N. (1983). [Record of the Black-winged Stilt in Kharkov Region]. *Ornitologiya* **18**: 167-168. In Russian.
Lissak, W. & Willy, J. (1991). [A Spotted Sandpiper *Actitis macularia* in Bavaria]. *Limicola* **5(2)**: 75-77. In German with English summary.
Lister, S.M. (1981). Le Grand maubèche *Calidris tenuirostris* nouveau pour l'ouest du Paléarctique. *Alauda* **49(3)**: 227-228.
Little, J.V. (1966). Sight record of the Chestnut-banded Sandplover *Charadrius pallidus* Strickland at Lake Chrissie, Eastern Transvaal. *Ostrich* **37(4)**: 238.
Little, J.V. (1967). Some aspects of the behaviour of the Wattled Plover *Afribix senegallus* (Linnaeus). *Ostrich* **38**: 259-280.
Littlefield, C.D. (1981). The Greater Sandhill Crane. Pp. 163-166 in: Lewis & Masatomi (1981).
Littlefield, C.D. (1995). Female Greater Sandhill Crane continues to incubate after the loss of her mate. *J. Field Orn.* **66(2)**: 296-298.
Littlefield, C.D. & Thompson, S.P. (1979). Distribution and status of the central valley population of Greater Sandhill Cranes. Pp. 113-120 in: Lewis (1979a).

Littlefield, C.D. & Thompson, S.P. (1981). History and status of the Franklin's Gull on Malheur National Wildlife Refuge, Oregon. *Great Basin Nat.* **41**: 440-444.
Littler, F.M. (1910). *A Handbook of the Birds of Tasmania and its Dependencies*. Published privately, Launceston, Tasmania.
Litvinenko, N.M. (1980). *Black-tailed Gull*. Academy of Sciences USSR, Nauka, Moscow.
Litvinenko, N.M. ed. (1986). *Seabirds of the Far East*. Far East Science Center, Russian Academy of Sciences, Vladivostok. (Translated into English by Canadian Wildlife Service 1988).
Litvinenko, N.M. ed. (1987). *Distribution and Biology of Seabirds of the Far East*. Far East Science Center, USSR Academy of Sciences, Vladivostok. (Translated into English by Canadian Wildlife Service 1989).
Litvinenko, N.M. (1993). Effects of disturbance by people and introduced predators on seabirds in the northwest Pacific. Pp. 227-231 in: Vermeer, Briggs *et al.* (1993).
Litvinenko, N.M. & Neufeldt, I.A. eds. (1982). [*Cranes of East Asia*]. Far East Branch, Academy of Sciences of the USSR, Vladivostock, USSR. In Russian.
Litvinenko, N.M. & Neufeldt, I.A. eds. (1988). [*Palearctic Cranes*]. Far East Branch, Academy of Sciences of the USSR, Vladivostock, USSR. In Russian.
Litvinenko, N.M. & Shibaev, Y.V. (1987). The Ancient Murrelet *Synthliboramphus antiquus* (Gm.): reproductive biology and raising of young. Pp. 72-84 in: Litvinenko (1987).
Litvinenko, N.M. & Shibaev, Y.V. (1991). Status and conservation of the seabirds nesting in southeast USSR. Pp. 175-204 in: Croxall (1991).
Litzbarski, H. (1993). Das Schutzprojekt 'Grosstrappe' in Brandenburg. *Ber. Vogelschutz* **31**: 61-66.
Liu Bowen & Sun Zhaofeng (1992). [The first record of the Hooded Crane in Yichun (Heilongjiang)]. *Chinese Wildlife* **4**: 47. In Chinese.
Liu Peiqi (1988). [Influence of capturing and banding colour bands on the behaviour of the Sandhill Crane *Grus canadensis*]. *Chinese Wildlife* **3**: 26-27, 15. In Chinese.
Liu Zhiyong & Chen Bin (1991). The wintering ecology of the Siberian Crane. Pp. 109-112 in: Harris (1991b).
Liu Zhiyong, Chen Bin & Wang Zuyou (1987a). [Observation of wintering behavior of Siberian Cranes]. Pp. 47-56 in: [*Report on Rare Birds Winter Ecology Study at Poyang Lake Migratory Birds Reserve*]. Jiangxi Scientific Technical Press, Nanchang, Jiangxi, China. In Chinese.
Liu Zhiyong, Chen Bin & Wang Zuyou (1987b). [The habits of the wintering Hooded and Common Cranes]. Pp. 61-68 in: [*Report on Rare Birds Winter Ecology Study at Poyang Lake Migratory Birds Reserve*]. Jiangxi Scientific Technical Press, Nanchang, Jianxi, China. In Chinese.
Liu Zuomo (1988). [Cranes found in Shanxi Province and distribution of Common Crane *Grus grus* in China]. *J. Shanxi Univ. (Nat. Sci. Ed.)* **3**: 96-99. In Chinese.
Liversidge, R. (1957). On the status of the Tristan Tern in South Africa. *Ostrich* **28**: 176-177.
Liversidge, R. (1965). Egg-covering in *Charadrius marginatus*. *Ostrich* **36(2)**: 59-61.
Liversidge, R. (1968). The first plumage of *Sarothrura rufa*. *Ostrich* **39**: 200.
Liversidge, R. & Courtenay-Latimer, M. (1963). Sabine's Gull in South Africa. *Ann. Cape Prov. Mus. (Nat. Hist.)* **3**: 57-60.
Livingstone, D.A. & Melack, J.M. (1984). Some lakes of subsaharan Africa. Pp. 467-497 in: Taub, F.B. ed. (1984). *Ecosystems of the World 23: Lakes and Reservoirs*. Elsevier, Amsterdam.
Llewellyn, L.C. (1975). Recent observations of the Plains-wanderer with a review of its past and present status. *Emu* **75(3)**: 137-142.
Llinas, J. & Galindo, J.M. (1990). [Some aspects of feeding behaviour of *Catoptrophorus semipalmatus* (Scolopacidae), in Baja California Sur, Mexico]. *Southwest. Nat.* **35(2)**: 237-240. In Spanish.
Lloyd, C., Tasker, M.L. & Partridge, K. (1991). *The Status of Seabirds in Britain and Ireland*. T. & A.D. Poyser, London.
Lloyd, C.A. (1897). Nesting of some Guiana birds. *Timehri* **11**: 1-10.
Lloyd, C.S., Bibby, C.J. & Everett, M.J. (1975). Breeding terns in Britain and Ireland in 1969-74. *British Birds* **68**: 221-237.
Lloyd, R.I. & Lloyd, H.J. (1991). An Oriental Pratincole at the Dry Creek Saltfields. *S. Austr. Orn.* **31(3)**: 74.
Lobkov, E.G. (1976). [Distribution and ecology of Kamchatka Tern (*Sterna camtschatica*)]. *Zoologischeskii Zhurnal* **55**: 1368-1374. In Russian.
Lobkov, E.G. (1989). [Solitary Snipe in eastern Kamtchatka]. Page 91 in: Ilyashenko, V.I. & Mazin, L.N. eds. (1989). [*Rare and Endangered Animal Species*]. TSNIL Glavokhota RSFSR, Moscow. In Russian.
Lobkov, E.G. & Golovina, N.M.A. (1978). [A comparative analysis of the biology of Kamchatka and Common Terns in Kamchatka]. *Byull. Mosk. Ova. Ispyt. Prir. Otd. Biol.* **83**: 27-37. In Russian.
Lobkov, E.G. & Nechaev, V.A. (1986). [Current status of the population of Kamchatka Tern (*Sterna camtschatica*) on the territory of the USSR]. Pp. 189-190 in: *Trans. XVIII Int. Orn. Congr.* Moscow, 1982. In Russian.
Lock, A.R. (1988). Recent increases in the breeding population of Ring-billed Gulls, *Larus delawarensis* in Atlantic Canada. *Can. Field-Nat.* **102**: 627-633.
Lockley, R.M. (1934). On the breeding habits of the Puffin: with special reference to the incubation- and fledging-period. *British Birds* **27**: 214-223.
Lockley, R.M. (1962). *Puffins*. The American Museum of Natural History & The Natural History Library Anchor Books Doubleday & Company, Garden City, New York.
Loegering, J.P. (1992). *Piping Plover Breeding Biology, Foraging Ecology and Behavior on Assateague Island National Seashore, Maryland*. MSc thesis, Virginia Polytechnic Institute & State University, Blacksburg, Virginia.
Loery, G. (1993). The ups and downs of a Virginia Rail population. *Connecticut Warbler* **13(2)**: 54-56.
Løfaldli, L. (1981). On the breeding season biometrics of the Common Sandpiper. *Ringing & Migration* **3**: 133-136.
Løfaldli, L. (1985). Incubation rhythm in the Great Snipe *Gallinago media*. *Holarctic Ecol.* **8(2)**: 107-112.
Løfaldli, L., Kålås, J.A. & Fiske, P. (1990). Food and habitat use of Great Snipe during the breeding season. *Trans. Congr. Int. Union Game Biol.* **19**: 129-129. (Abstract).
Løfaldli, L., Kålås, J.A. & Fiske, P. (1992). Habitat selection and diet of Great Snipe *Gallinago media* during breeding. *Ibis* **134(1)**: 35-43.
Löfgren, L. (1984). *Oceanic Birds. Their Breeding Biology and Behaviour*. Croom Helm, Beckenham, UK.
Loftin, H. (1962). A study of boreal shorebirds summering on Apalachee Bay, Florida. *Bird-Banding* **33**: 21-42.
Loftin, H. (1991). An annual cycle of pelagic birds in the Gulf of Panama. *Orn. Neotropical* **2(2)**: 85-94.
Loftin, R.W. (1982). Diet of Black Skimmers and Royal Terns in northeastern Florida. *Florida Field Nat.* **10**: 19-20.
Loftin, R.W. & Sutton, S. (1979). Ruddy Turnstones destroy Royal Tern colony. *Wilson Bull.* **91**: 133-135.
Longcore, J.R. & Sepik, J.F. eds. (1993). *Proceedings of the Eighth Woodcock Symposium*. Biological Report **16**. US Fish & Wildlife Service, Washington, D.C.
Longrigg, T.D. (1992). Red-winged Pratincole (304) in the Cape Peninsula. *Promerops* **204**: 10.
Lönnberg, E. (1931). A remarkable gull from the Gobi Desert. *Arkiv. fur Zool.* **23B**: 1-5.
Lönnberg, E. (1933). Some remarks on the systematic status of the Yellow-legged Herring-Gulls. *Ibis* **Ser. 13, no. 3**: 47-50.
Lord, E.A.R. (1936). Notes on the Dusky Moorhen. *Emu* **36**: 128-129.
Lord, E.A.R. (1956). The birds of Murphy's Creek District, southern Queensland. *Emu* **56**: 100-128.
Lorenzo, J.A. (1994). Cream-coloured Courser. *Cursorius cursor*. Pp. 246-247 in: Tucker & Heath (1994).
Lorenzo, J.A. & Emmerson, K.W. (1993). Hubara Canaria. *Garcilla* **88**: 22-25.
Lotter, W.J. (1975). Is Kraanvoels ware landlewende voels? [Are cranes terrestrial birds?]. *Bokmakierie* **27(4)**: 75-78. In Afrikaans with English summary.
Louette, M. (1981). *The Birds of Cameroon. An annotated Check-list*. Paleis der Academien, Brussel.
Louette, M. (1988). *Les Oiseaux des Comores*. Musée Royal de l'Afrique Centrale, Tervuren, Belgique.
Lourie-Fraser, G. (1982). Captive breeding of the Lord Howe Island Woodhen: an endangered rail. *A.F.A. Watchbird* **10**: 30-44.
Lovegrove, R. (1971). BOU supported expedition to northeast Canary Islands. *Ibis* **113**: 269-272.
Lovegrove, R., Mann, I., Morgan, G. & Williams, I. (1989). Tuamotu Islands expedition report. Report on an expedition to ascertain the status of Red Data Book species in the Tuamotu Archipelago (French Polynesia). Unpublished report. 21 pp.
Løvenskiold, H.L. (1964). *Avifauna Svalbardensis with a Discussion on the Geographical Distribution of the Birds in Spitsbergen and Adjacent Islands*. Norsk Polarinstitutt Skrifter **129**. 460 pp.
Loveridge, A. (1969). A Sheathbill, *Chionis alba* on St. Helena. *Bull. Brit. Orn. Club* **89(2)**: 48-49.
Lovvorn, J.R. & Kirkpatrick, C.M. (1981). Roosting behavior and habitat preference of migrant Greater Sandhill Cranes. *J. Wildl. Manage.* **45(4)**: 842-857.
Lovvorn, J.R. & Kirkpatrick, C.M. (1982). Recruitment and socially-specific flocking tendencies of Eastern Sandhill Cranes. *Wilson Bull.* **94(3)**: 313-321.
Low, G.C. (1923a). Note on the nomenclature of the South American Black Oystercatcher, *Haematopus townsendi*. *Bull. Brit. Orn. Club* **44**: 16 18.
Low, G.C. (1923b). Notes on the classification of the species and subspecies of *Haematopus*. *Bull. Brit. Orn. Club* **44**: 18 20.
Lowe, P.R. (1915). Studies on the Charadriiformes. II. On the osteology of the Chatham Island Snipe (*Coenocorypha pusilla* Buller). *Ibis* **Ser. 10, no. 3**: 690-716.
Lowe, P.R. (1923). Notes on the systematic position of *Ortyxelus*, together with some remarks on the relationships of the Turnicomorphs and the position of the seed-snipe (Thinocoridae) and sand-grouse. *Ibis* **Ser. 11, no. 5**: 276-299.
Lowe, P.R. (1924). On the anatomy and systematic position of the Madagascar bird Mesites (*Mesoenas*), with a preliminary note on the osteology of *Monias*. *Proc. Zool. Soc., London* **1924**: 1131-1154.
Lowe, P.R. (1925). On the systematic position of the Jacanidae (Jaçanás), with some notes on a hitherto unconsidered anatomical character of apparent taxonomic value. *Ibis* **Ser. 12, no. 1**: 132-144.
Lowe, P.R. (1928). A description of *Atlantisia rogersi*, the diminutive and flightless rail of Inaccessible Island (Southern Atlantic), with some notes on flightless rails. *Ibis* **Ser. 12, no. 4**: 99-131.
Lowe, P.R. (1931). On the relations of the Gruimorphae to the Charadriimorphae and Rallimorphae, with special reference to the taxonomic position of Rostratulidae, Jacanidae, and Burhinidae; with a suggested new order (Telmatomorphae). *Ibis* **Ser. 13, no. 1**: 491-534.
Lowe, V.T. (1963). Observations on the Painted Snipe. *Emu* **62**: 221-237.
Lowe, V.T. (1970). Notes on the behaviour of the Painted Snipe. *Austr. Bird Watcher* **3**: 218-220.
Lowe, V.T. (1976). Sharp-tailed Sandpiper in captivity. *Austr. Bird Watcher* **6(7)**: 251-252.
Lowe, W.P. (1933). A report on birds collected by the Vernay expedition to Tenasserim and Siam, Part II. *Ibis* **Ser. 13, no. 3**: 473-493.
Lowen, J.C., Clay, R.P., Brooks, T.M., Esquivel, E.Z., Bartrina, L., Barnes, R., Butchart, S.H.M. & Etcheverry, N.I. (1995). Bird conservation in the Paraguayan atlantic forest. *Cotinga* **4**: 58-64.
Lowery, G.H. & Dalquest, W.W. (1951). *Birds from the State of Veracruz, Mexico*. University of Kansas Publications, Museum of Natural History **3(4)**. University of Kansas, Lawrence, Kansas. 119 pp.
Lowther, E.H.N. (1941). Notes on some Indian birds. *J. Bombay Nat. Hist. Soc.* **42**: 782-795.
Lowther, E.H.N. (1949). *A Bird Photographer in India*. Oxford University Press, London.
Lowther, J.K. (1977). Nesting biology of the Sora at Vermilion, Alberta. *Can. Field-Nat.* **91**: 63-67.
Lozano, I.E. (1993). Observaciones sobre la ecología y el comportamiento de *Rallus semiplumbeus* en el Humedal de la Florida, Sabana de Bogotá. Unpublished report.
Lu Zhongbao (1983). The wintering habits of the Black-necked Crane, *Grus nigricollis*. *Wildlife* **2**: 35-36.
Lu Zhongbao (1986). [Ecological study of the Black-necked Crane]. *La Animala Mondo* **3(1)**: 37-51. In Chinese.
Lu Zhongbao, Yao Jiunchu & Liao Yanfa (1980). [An examination of the reproductive ecology of the Black-necked Crane]. *Chinese J. Zool.* **1**: 19-24. In Chinese.
Lucas, F.A. (1890). The expedition to the Funk Island, with observations upon the history and anatomy of the Great Auk. *Rep. US Natl. Mus.* **1887-88**: 493-529.
Lucio, A.J. (1985). Datos sobre la alimentación de la Avutarda (*Otis tarda* L., 1758) en la Cuenca del Duero. *Alytes* **3**: 69-86.
Lucio, A.J. & Purroy, F.J. (1985). Protección de la Avutarda. *Garcilla* **65**: 28-30.
Lucio, A.J., Purroy, F.J. & Sáenz de Buruaga, M. (1994). The Woodcock project: preliminary hunting bag data of the Woodcock in Spain. Pp. 15-23 in: Kalchreuter (1994).
Lucker, H. (1987). [Hoatzins (*Ophistocoma hoatzin*) in Ecuadorean rain forests]. *Z. Kölner Zoo* **30(2)**: 43-46. In German with English summary.
Luckner, G.D. (1992). Marbled Godwit. *Spoonbill* **41(8)**: 7.
Ludlow, F. (1928). Birds of the Gyantse neighbourhood, southern Tibet - Part III. *Ibis* **Ser. 12, no. 4**: 211-232.
Ludwig, F.E. (1942). Migration of Caspian Terns banded in the Great Lakes area. *Bird-Banding* **13**: 1-9.
Ludwig, J.P. (1965). Biology and population structure of the Caspian Tern (*Hydroprogne caspia*) population of the Great Lakes from 1896-1964. *Bird-Banding* **36**: 217-233.
Ludwig, J.P. (1974). Recent changes in the Ring-billed Gull population and biology in the Laurentian Great Lakes. *Auk* **91(3)**: 575-594.
Ludwig, J.P. (1979). Present status of the Caspian Tern population of the Great Lakes. *Mich. Acad.* **12**: 64-77.
Ludwig, J.P. (1981). Band wear and band loss in the Great Lakes Caspian Tern population and a generalized model of band loss. *Colonial Waterbirds* **4**: 174-186.
Ludwig, J.P. & Tomoff, C.S. (1966). Reproductive success and insecticide residues in Lake Michigan Herring Gulls. *Jack-Pine Warbler* **44**: 77-84.
Luge, J. (1992). [On the status and protection of the Eurasian Curlew in the Kothen District]. *Beitr. Vogelkd.* **38(2)**: 113-117. In German.
Lukschanderl, L. (1971). Zur Verbreitung und Ökologie und Schutz der Großtrappe (*Otis tarda* L.) in Osterreich. *J. Orn.* **112**: 70-93.
Lund-Hansen, L.C. & Lange, P. (1991). The numbers and distribution of the Great Skua *Stercorarius skua* breeding in Iceland 1984-1985. *Acta Naturalia Islandica* **34**: 1-16.
Lundberg, C.A. & Vaisanen, R.A. (1979). Selective correlation of egg size with chick mortality in the Black-headed Gull (*Larus ridibundus*). *Condor* **81(2)**: 146-156.
Lunt, I. (1992). Historical records of Australian Bustards (*Ardeotis australis*) in eastern Victoria. *Victorian Naturalist* **109(2)**: 56-57.
Luthin, C.S., Archibald, G.W., Hartman, L., Mirande, C.M. & Swengel, S. (1986). Captive breeding of endangered cranes, storks, ibises and spoonbills. *Int. Zoo Yb.* **24/25**: 25-39.
Luttik, R. & Wassink, A. (1980). Voorkomen van Poelruiter *Tringa stagnatilis* in Nederland. [Occurence of Marsh Sandpiper *Tringa stagnatilis* in the Netherlands]. *Dutch Birding* **2(1)**: 13-14. In Dutch with English summary.
Luttrell, J. (1991). Spurwings retrieve their eggs. *Notornis* **38(2)**: 151.
Lynes, H. (1925). On the birds of North and Central Darfur, with notes on the West-Central Kordofan and North Nuba Provinces of British Sudan. Part V. *Ibis* **Ser. 12, no. 1**: 541-590.
Lyon, B.E. (1991). Brood parasitism in American Coots: avoiding the constraints of parental care. Pp. 1023-1030. in: *Proc. XX Int. Orn. Congr.* Christchurch, 1990.
Lyon, B.E. & Fogden, M.P.L. (1989). Breeding biology of the Sunbittern (*Eurypyga helias*) in Costa Rica. *Auk* **106(3)**: 503-507.
Lythgoe, J.N. (1979). *The Ecology of Vision*. Clarendon Press, Oxford.
Ma Guoen (1982). [A preliminary study on the breeding habits of Red-crowned Crane *Grus japonensis*]. *Wildlife* **1**: 10-16. In Chinese.
Ma Ming, Ca Dai, Jing Changlin & Ma Jun (1993). [Breeding ecology of the Common and Demoiselle Cranes in Xinjiang]. *Arid Zone Research* **10(2)**: 56-60. In Chinese.
Ma Yiqing ed. (1986). [*Crane Research and Conservation in China*]. Heilongjiang Education Press, Harbin, China. In Chinese.
Ma Yiqing (1991). Status and conservation of cranes in China. Pp. 27-33 in: Harris (1991b).
Ma Yiqing & Jin Longrong (1987). Distribution and numbers of Red-crowned Cranes in northeast China. Pp. 57-60 in: Archibald & Pasquier (1987a).
Ma Yiqing & Li Xiaomin (1991). The numerical distribution of Red-crowned Cranes in China. Pp. 41-45 in: Harris (1991b).
Ma Yiqing & Li Xiaomin (1995). The status of the Red-crowned Crane in China. Pp. 316-324 in: Prange *et al.* (1995).
Macartney, P. (1968). Wattled Cranes in Zambia. *Bokmakierie* **20(2)**: 38-41.
Maccarone, A.D., Brzorad, J.N. & Parsons, K.C. (1993). Nest site selection by Herring Gulls in an urban estuary. *Colonial Waterbirds* **16(2)**: 216-220.
Macdonald, J.D. (1957). *Contribution to the Ornithology of Western South Africa*. Trustees of the British Museum, London.
Macdonald, J.D. (1971). Validity of the Buff-breasted Quail. *Sunbird* **2**: 1-5.
Macdonald, J.D. (1988). *Birds of Australia. A Summary of Information*. Reed, Frenchs Forest, Australia.
Macdonald, J.D. & Hall, B.P. (1957). Ornithological results of the Bernard Carp/Transvaal Museum Expedition to the Kaokoveld, 1951. *Ann. Transvaal Mus.* **23**: 1-39.
Macdonald, R. (1966). Australian Coots on Virginia Lake, Wanganui. *Notornis* **13**: 165.
Macdonald, R. (1968). The Australian Coot established on Virginia Lake, Wanganui. *Notornis* **15**: 234-237.
MacDonald, S.D. (1979). First breeding record of Ross' Gull in Canada. *Proc. Colonial Waterbird Group* **2**: 16.
MacDonald, S.D. & Macpherson, A.H. (1962). Breeding places of Ivory Gull in Arctic Canada. *Natl. Mus. Can. Bull.* **183**: 111-117.
MacDonald, S.D. & Parmelee, D.F. (1962). Feeding behaviour of the Turnstone in arctic Canada. *British Birds* **55**: 241-244.
Mace, T.R. (1978). Killdeer breeding densities. *Wilson Bull.* **90**: 442-443.
Mace, T.R. (1981). *Causation, Function and Variation of the Vocalizations of the Northern Jacana,* Jacana spinosa. PhD dissertation, University of Montana, Missoula, Montana.

MacGillivray, W. (1914). Notes on some north Queensland birds. *Emu* **13**: 132-186.
MacGillivray, W. (1917). Ornithologists in north Queensland. *Emu* **17**: 63-87.
MacGillivray, W. (1918). Ornithologists in north Queensland. *Emu* **17**: 145-148.
MacGillivray, W. (1924). A contribution on the life-story of the Australian Pratincole. *Emu* **24**: 81-85.
MacGillivray, W. (1928). Bird life of the Bunker and Capricorn Islands. *Emu* **27**: 230-239.
Macikunas, A. (1981). [Some factors affecting mortality of the Black Tern chicks]. Pp. 149-150 in: [*Ecology and Protection of Birds*]. Proc. 8th Soviet Union Orn. Conf., Kishinev. In Russian.
Macikunas, A. (1990). Internal volume determination from linear dimensions for the Black Tern (*Chlidonias nigra* L) egg. *Acta Orn. Lituanica* **2**: 131-133, 170.
Macikunas, A. (1993). Hatching success and replacement clutches of the Black Tern (*Chlidonias niger*) of the Kaunas Sea. *Acta Orn. Lituanica* **7-8**: 107-114.
MacIvor, L.H. (1990). *Population Dynamics, Breeding Ecology and Management of Piping Plovers on Outer Cape Cod, Massachusetts*. MSc thesis, University of Massachusetts, Amherst, Massachusetts.
MacIvor, L.H., Melvin, S.M. & Griffin, C.R. (1990). Effects of research activity on Piping Plover nest predation. *J. Wildl. Manage.* **54(3)**: 443-447.
MacKay, B.K. (1996). The Eskimo Curlew. *Bird Watcher's Digest* **18(4)**: 22-33.
Mackereth, B. (1992). Avian pox in Variable Oystercatcher chick. *Notornis* **39(4)**: 248.
MacKinnon, G.E. & Coulson, J.C. (1987). The temporal and geographic distribution of Continental Black-headed Gulls *Larus ridibundus* in the British Isles. *Bird Study* **34**: 1-9.
MacKinnon, J. (1988). *Field Guide to the Birds of Java and Bali*. Gadjah Mada University Press, Yogyakarta, Indonesia.
MacKinnon, J. & Phillipps, K. (1993). *A Field Guide to the Birds of Borneo, Sumatra, Java and Bali*. Oxford University Press, Oxford.
Mackrill, E. (1989). First-year plumages of Audouin's Gull. *British Birds* **82(2)**: 73-77.
Mackworth-Praed, C.W. & Grant, C.H.B. (1957). *African Handbook of Birds. Series One. Birds of Eastern and North Eastern Africa*. Vol. 1. Longman, London.
Mackworth-Praed, C.W. & Grant, C.H.B. (1962). *African Handbook of Birds. Series Two. Birds of the Southern Third of Africa*. Vol. 1. Longman, London & New York.
Mackworth-Praed, C.W. & Grant, C.H.B. (1970). *African Handbook of Birds. Series Three. Birds of West Central and Western Africa*. Vol. 1. Longman, London & New York.
MacLachlan, A., Wooldridge, T., Schramm, M. & Kuhn, M. (1980). Seasonal abundance, biomass and feeding of shore birds on sandy beaches in the Eastern Cape, South Africa. *Ostrich* **51**: 44-52.
MacLean, A. (1986). Age-specific foraging ability and the evolution of deferred breeding in three species of gulls. *Wilson Bull.* **98**: 267-279.
MacLean, D.C., Litwin, T.S., Ducey-Ortiz, A.M. & Lent, R.A. (1991). Nesting biology, habitat use, and inter-colony movements of the Least Tern (*Sterna antillarum*) on Long Island, N.Y. Pp. 1-70 in: *Seatuck Research Program, Islip, NY*.
Maclean, G.L. (1965). Nest transfer in the Three-banded Sandplover *Charadrius tricollaris* Vieillot. *Ostrich* **36**: 62-63.
Maclean, G.L. (1966). Studies on the behaviour of a young Cape Dikkop *Burhinus capensis* (Lichtenstein) reared in captivity. *Ostrich* **6**(Suppl.): 155-170.
Maclean, G.L. (1967). The breeding biology and behaviour of the Double-banded Courser *Rhinoptilus africanus* (Temminck). *Ibis* **109**: 556-569.
Maclean, G.L. (1969). A study of seedsnipe in southern South America. *Living Bird* **8**: 33-80.
Maclean, G.L. (1970a). A study of seedsnipe in southern South America. *Bird-Banding* **41(3)**: 258-259.
Maclean, G.L. (1970b). The neonatal plumage of the Double-banded Courser. *Ostrich* **41**: 215-216.
Maclean, G.L. (1972a). Problems of display postures in the Charadrii (Aves: Charadriiformes). *Zool. Afr.* **7**: 57 74.
Maclean, G.L. (1972b). Clutch size and evolution in the Charadrii. *Auk* **89**: 299-324.
Maclean, G.L. (1973). A review of the biology of the Australian desert waders, *Stiltia* and *Peltohyas*. *Emu* **73(2)**: 61-70.
Maclean, G.L. (1974). Egg-covering in the Charadrii. *Ostrich* **45**: 167-174.
Maclean, G.L. (1975). Belly-soaking in the Charadriiformes. *J. Bombay Nat. Hist. Soc.* **72**: 74-82.
Maclean, G.L. (1976a). A field study of the Australian Pratincole. *Emu* **76(4)**: 171-182.
Maclean, G.L. (1976b). A field study of the Australian Dotterel. *Emu* **76(4)**: 207-215.
Maclean, G.L. (1977). Comparative notes on Black-fronted and Red-kneed Dotterel. *Emu* **77(4)**: 199-207.
Maclean, G.L. (1982). Opportunistic breeding of plovers under manipulated conditions. *Ostrich* **53(1)**: 52-54.
Maclean, G.L. (1985a). Courser. Pp. 115-116 in: Campbell & Lack (1985).
Maclean, G.L. (1985b). Pratincole. Pp. 484-485 in: Campbell & Lack (1985).
Maclean, G.L. (1985c). Seedsnipe. Page 529 in: Campbell & Lack (1985).
Maclean, G.L. (1993). *Roberts' Birds of Southern Africa*. 6th edition. Trustees of the John Voelcker Bird Book Fund, Cape Town.
Maclean, G.L. & Kemp, A.C. (1973). Neonatal plumage patterns of Three-banded and Temminck's Coursers and their bearing on courser genera. *Ostrich* **44**: 80-81.
Maclean, G.L. & Moran, V.C. (1965). The choice of nest site in the White-fronted Sandpiper *Charadrius marginatus* Vieillot. *Ostrich* **36(2)**: 63-72.
Maclean, G.L., Maclean, C.M., Geldenhuys, J.N. & Allan, D.G. (1983). Group size in the Blue Korhaan. *Ostrich* **54**: 243-244.
MacLean, S.F. & Verbeek, N.A.M. (1968). Nesting of the Black Guillemot at Point Barrow, Alaska. *Auk* **85**: 139-140.
Macmillan, B.W.H. (1990). Attempts to re-establish Wekas, Brown Kiwis and Red-crowned Parakeets in the Waitakere Ranges. *Notornis* **37**: 45-51.
MacMillen, R.E., Whittow, G.C., Christopher, E.A. & Ebisu, R.J. (1977). Oxygen consumption, evaporative water loss and body temperature in the Sooty Tern. *Auk* **94**: 72-79.
Macpherson, A.H. (1961). Observations on Canadian Arctic *Larus* gulls and on the taxonomy of *L. thayeri* Brooks. *Arctic Inst. North America Tech. Pap.* **7**: 1-40.
MacRoberts, B.R. & MacRoberts, M.H. (1972). Social stimulation of reproduction in Herring and Lesser Black-backed Gulls. *Ibis* **114**: 495-506.
MacRoberts, M.H. (1973). Extramarital courting in Lesser Black-backed and Herring Gulls. *Z. Tierpsychol.* **32**: 62-74.
MacRoberts, M.H. & MacRoberts, B.R. (1972). The relationship between laying date and incubation period in Herring and Lesser Black-backed Gulls. *Ibis* **114**: 93-97.
Madge, S. (1990). Eine Armenienmöwe *Larus (cachinnans) armenicus* ohne schwarze Schnabelzeichnung. *Limicola* **4(4)**: 216-217.
Madge, S.C. (1977). Field identification of Pintail Snipe. *British Birds* **70(4)**: 146-152.
Madge, S.C. (1989a). Swinhoe's Snipe *Gallinago megala*: a new species for Nepal. *Forktail* **4**: 121-123.
Madge, S.C. (1989b). Swinhoe's Snipe *Gallinago megala*: a new species for Nepal. *J. Bombay Nat. Hist. Soc.* **86(2)**: 243.
Madoc, G.C. (1976). *An Introduction to Malayan Birds*. Malayan Nature Society, Kuala Lumpur, Malaysia.
Madsen, K.K. (1981). Search for the Eastern Sarus Crane on Luzon, Philippines. Pp. 216-218 in: Lewis & Masatomi (1981).
Mafabi, P. (1991). The ecology and conservation status of the Gray Crowned Crane in Uganda. Pp. 363-367 in: Harris (1991b).
Magarry, D. (1991). Red-necked Crakes in Cairns. *Queensland Orn. Soc. Newsl.* **22(6)**: 5.
Magrath, R.D., Ridley, M.W. & Woinarski, J.Z. (1985). Status and habitat requirements of Lesser Floricans in Kathiawar, western India. *Bustard Studies* **3**: 185-193.
Magyar, G. (1988). [The first observation of the Killdeer (*Charadrius vociferus* L., 1758) in Hungary]. *Aquila* **95**: 182-184. In Hungarian.
Mahan, T.A. & Simmers, B.S. (1992). Social preference of four cross-foster reared Sandhill Cranes. Pp. 114-119 in: Stahlecker (1992).
Maher, P.N. & Baker-Gabb, D.J. (1994). *Surveys and Conservation of the Plains-wanderer in Northern Victoria*. ARI Technical Report **132**. DCNR, Melbourne.
Maher, W.J. (1970a). The Pomarine Jaeger as a brown lemming predator in northern Alaska. *Wilson Bull.* **82**: 130-157.
Maher, W.J. (1970b). Ecology of the Long-tailed Jaeger at Lake Hazen, Ellesmere Island. *Arctic* **23**: 112-129.
Maher, W.J. (1974). Ecology of Pomarine, Parasitic and Long-tailed Jaegers in northern Alaska. *Pacific Coast Avifauna* **37**: 1-148.
Maher, W.J. (1984). Skuas and Jaegers. Pp. 120-129 in: Haley (1984).
Mahoney, S.A. & Jehl, J.R. (1985a). Physiological ecology and salt loading of California Gulls at an alkaline, hypersaline lake. *Physiol. Zool.* **58**: 553-563.
Mahoney, S.A. & Jehl, J.R. (1985b). Adaptations of migratory shorebirds to highly saline and alkaline lakes: Wilson's Phalarope and American Avocet. *Condor* **87(4)**: 520-527.
Mainardi, R. (1988). Turnover-annuale del gabbiano corallino *Larus melanocephala* al Calambrone (Livorno). *Quad. Mus. Stor. Nat. Livorno* **9**: 91-94.
Maisonneuve, C. (1993). Is population decline in Short-billed Dowitchers *Limnodromus griseus*, related to hydroelectric projects? *Can. Field-Nat.* **107(2)**: 253-255.
Maisonneuve, C., Brousseau, P. & Lehoux, D. (1990). Critical fall staging sites for shorebirds migrating through the St. Lawrence system, Quebec (Canada). *Can. Field-Nat.* **104**: 372-378.
Majnep, I.S. & Bulmer, R. (1977). *Birds of my Kalam Country*. Oxford University Press, Auckland.
Majumdar, N. & Brahmachari, G.K. (1988). Major grassland types of India and their bird communities: a conservation perspective. Pp. 205-214 in: Goriup (1988).
Majumdar, N. & Roy, C.S. (1993). Extension of range of the Indian Skimmer, *Rynchops albicollis* Swainson (Aves: Laridae). *J. Bombay Nat. Hist. Soc.* **90**: 511.
Makatsch, W. (1952). Ein Beitrag zur Biologie der Brachschwalbe *Glareola p. pratincola* (L.). *Larus* **4-5**: 89-97.
Makatsch, W. (1962). [Some observations at the breeding grounds of the Spur-winged Plover (*Hoplopterus spinosus*)]. *J. Orn.* **103**: 219-228. In German.
Makatsch, W. (1968). Beobachtungen an einem Brutplatz der Korallenmöwe (*Larus audouinii*). [Observations at a breeding site of Audouin's Gull (*Larus audouinii*)]. *J. Orn.* **109**: 43-56.
Makatsch, W. (1969a). [The Spur-winged Plover, one of the most recent additions to Europe's breeding avifauna]. *Natur und Museum* **99**: 379-385. In German.
Makatsch, W. (1969b). Studies of less familiar birds. 154. Audouin's Gull. *British Birds* **62**: 230-232.
Makatsch, W. (1987). The status of the Common Crane in the German Democratic Republic. Pp. 239-241 in: Archibald & Pasquier (1987a).
Makkink, G.F. (1936). An attempt at an ethogram of the European Avocet (*Recurvirostra avosetta* L.) with ethological and psychological remarks. *Ardea* **25**: 1-63.
Makkink, G.F. (1942). Contribution to the knowledge of the behaviour of the Oystercatcher (*Haematopus ostralegus* L.). *Ardea* **31**: 23 74.
Malambo, C.H. & Chabwela, H. (1992). Preliminary observations on the distribution and abundance of Wattled Cranes in Zambian wetlands. Pp. 71-74 in: Bennun, L. ed. (1992). *Proc. VII Pan-Afr. Orn. Congr.* Nairobi, 1988.
Male, J.P. (1989). Foster parenting, growth and management of the Common Trumpeter *Psophia crepitans* at the National Zoological Park, Washington. *Int. Zoo Yb.* **28**: 240-244.
Malik, M.M. (1985). The distribution and conservation of Houbara Bustards in North West Frontier Province. *Bustard Studies* **3**: 81-85.
Malkov, N.P., Belikov, V.I. & Malkov, V.N. (1983). [On ecology of *Gallinago stenura* during a breeding period in Central Altai]. Pp. 197-199 in: *Ptitsy Sibiri*. Tez. Dokl. K 2. Sib. Orn. Konf., Gorno-Altaisk. In Russian.
Mallory, E.P. (1982). Territoriality of Whimbrels *Numenius phaeopus hudsonicus* wintering in Panama. *Wader Study Group Bull.* **34**: 37-39.
Mallory, E.P. & Schneider, D.C. (1979). Agonistic behavior in Short-billed Dowitchers feeding on a patchy resource. *Wilson Bull.* **91**: 271-278.
Malvaud, F. (1985). [The Stone Curlew in Val de Seine]. *Cormoran* **5(4)**: 338-343. In French with English summary.
Malvaud, F. (1993). Un oiseau mystérieux l'Oedicnème criard. *L'Oiseau Magazine* **32**: 34-37.
Malvaud, F. (1995). L'Oedicnème criard *Burhinus oedicnemus* en France: répartition et effectifs. [Status of Stone Curlew in France]. *Ornithos* **2(2)**: 77-81. In French with English summary.
Manakadan, R. (1991). Greenshank *Tringa nebularia* (Gunner) feeding on large fish. *J. Bombay Nat. Hist. Soc.* **88(3)**: 451-452.
Manakadan, R. & Rahmani, A.R. eds. (1986). *Study of Ecology of Certain Endangered Species of Wildlife and their Habitats. Great Indian Bustard*. Annual Report **3** (1985-86). Bombay Natural History Society, Bombay.
Manakadan, R. & Rahmani, A.R. (1989). Rollapadu Wildlife Sanctuary, with special reference to the Great Indian Bustard *Ardeotis nigriceps* (Vigors). *J. Bombay Nat. Hist. Soc.* **86(3)**: 368-380.
Manakadan, R. & Rahmani, A.R. (1990). Growth and development of a captive Great Indian Bustard *Choriotis nigriceps* chick. *Avicult. Mag.* **96(3)**: 133-140.
Mangubuli, M.J.J. (1996). Wattled Cranes in Botswana: their status and needs for conservation. In: Beilfuss *et al.* (1996).
Manley, G.H. (1960a). *The Agonistic Behaviour of the Black-headed Gull*. PhD thesis, Bodleian Library, Oxford.
Manley, G.H. (1960b). The swoop and soar performance of the Black-headed Gull, *Larus ridibundus* L. *Ardea* **48**: 37-51.
Mann, C.F. (1974). A second Pomarine Skua on the Kenya Coast. *Bull. East Afr. Nat. Hist. Soc.* **1974**: 31.
Mann, C.F. (1987). Notable bird observations from Brunei, Borneo. *Forktail* **3**: 51-56.
Mann, C.F. (1990). More notable bird observations from Brunei, Borneo. *Forktail* **5**.
Manning, T.H., Höhn, E.O. & Macpherson, A.H. (1956). *The Birds of Banks Island*. National Museum Canadian Bulletin **143**. 143 pp.
Manseau, M. & Ferron, J. (1991). Nocturnal feeding activity of Semipalmated Sandpipers (*Calidris pusilla*) during a migratory stopover in the Bay of Fundy (Canada). *Can. J. Zool.* **69(2)**: 380-384.
Manson, A.J. (1986). Notes on the breeding of the Buff-spotted Flufftail at Seldomseen, Vumba. *Honeyguide* **32**: 137-142.
Mantlik, F.W. (1986). First documented Sharp-tailed Sandpiper in Connecticut. *Connecticut Warbler* **6(2)**: 15-17.
Manuwal, D.A. (1972). *The Population Ecology of Cassin's Auklet on Southeast Farallon Island, California*. PhD thesis, University of California, Los Angeles, California.
Manuwal, D.A. (1974a). The natural history of Cassin's Auklet *Ptychoramphus aleuticus*. *Condor* **76**: 421-431.
Manuwal, D.A. (1974b). The incubation patches of Cassin's Auklet. *Condor* **76**: 481-484.
Manuwal, D.A. (1974c). Effects of territoriality on breeding in a population of Cassin's Auklet. *Ecology* **55**: 1399-1406.
Manuwal, D.A. (1978a). Criteria for aging Cassin's Auklet. *Bird-Banding* **49**: 157-161.
Manuwal, D.A. (1978b). *Effect of Man on Marine Birds: a Review*. Proceedings John S. Wright Forestry Conference, Wildlife & People. Purdue University, W. Lafayette, Indiana.
Manuwal, D.A. (1979). Reproductive commitment and success of Cassin's Auklet. *Condor* **81**: 111-121.
Manuwal, D.A. (1980). *Breeding Biology of Seabirds on the Barren Islands, Alaska*. US Fish & Wildlife Service Report Contract No. 14-16-008-2054. Anchorage, Alaska.
Manuwal, D.A. (1984). Alcids. Pp. 168-187 in: Haley (1984).
Manuwal, D.A. & Boersma, D. (1978). Dynamics of marine bird populations on the Barren Islands, Alaska. *US Dept. Commerce, NOAA, OCSEAP Annual Rep.* **4**: 294-420.
Manuwal, D.A. & Manuwal, R.W. (1979). Habitat specific behavior of the Parakeet Auklet in the Barren Islands. *Western Birds* **10**: 189-200.
Manuwal, D.A. & Thoresen, A.C. (1993). Cassin's Auklet (*Ptychoramphus aleuticus*). No. **50** in: Poole & Gill (1993).
Manuwal, D.A., Mattocks, P.W. & Richter, K.O. (1979). First Arctic Tern colony in the contiguous western United States. *Amer. Birds* **33**: 144-145.
Máñez, M. (1994). Purple Gallinule. *Porphyrio porphyrio*. Pp. 230-231 in: Tucker & Heath (1994).
Maozeka, F. (1993). Breeding Kori Bustard at Central Estates, Mvuma. *Honeyguide* **39**: 133-137.
Maranini, N., Cornara, L., Burlando, B. & Borgo, E. (1991). [A record of Purple Sandpiper, *Calidris maritima*, in Liguria, NW Italy]. *Riv. ital. Orn.* **61(1-2)**: 67-68. In Italian.
Marcström, V. (1988). A study on display activities of Woodcock in Sweden. Pp. 83-85 in: Havet & Hirons (1988).
Marcström, V. & Mascher, J.W. (1979). Weights and fat in lapwings (*Vanellus vanellus*) and Oystercatchers (*Haematopus ostralegus*) starved to death during a cold spell in spring. *Ornis Scand.* **10**: 235 240.
Marchant, J., Carter, S. & Balmer, D. (1993). Waterways bird survey 1991-1992 population changes. *BTO News* **186**: 6-7.
Marchant, J.H. (1984). Identification of Slender-billed Curlew. *British Birds* **77(4)**: 135-140.
Marchant, J.H. (1986). Identification, habits and status of Great Knot. *British Birds* **79(3)**: 123-135.
Marchant, J.H., Hudson, R., Carter, S.P. & Whittington, P. (1990). *Population Trends in British Breeding Birds*. British Trust for Ornithology, Tring, UK.
Marchant, S. (1956). Occurrence of the Piping Plover (*Charadrius melodus*), in Ecuador. *Ibis* **98**: 533-534.
Marchant, S. & Higgins, P.J. eds. (1993). *Handbook of Australian, New Zealand and Antarctic Birds*. Vol. 2. Raptors to Lapwings. Oxford University Press, Melbourne.

Marchant, S. & Higgins, P.J. eds. (1996). *Handbook of Australian, New Zealand and Antarctic Birds*. Vol. 3. Pratincoles to Pigeons. Oxford University Press, Melbourne.
Marcus, M.J. (1985). Feeding associations between capybaras and jacanas: a case of interspecific grooming and possibly mutualism. *Ibis* **127(2)**: 240-243.
Margolis, R.L., Mariscal, S.K., Gordon, J.D., Dolinger, J. & Gould, J.L. (1987). The ontogeny of the pecking response of Laughing Gull chicks. *Anim. Behav.* **35**: 101-111.
Marin, M.A. & Sheldon, F.H. (1987). Some new nesting records of padi-dwelling birds in Sabah, east Malaysia (north Borneo). *Bull. Brit. Orn. Club* **107**: 23-25.
Marion, L., Yésou, P., Dubois, P.J. & Nicolau-Guillaumet, P. (1985). Coexistence progressive de la reproduction de *Larus argentatus* et de *Larus cachinnans* sur les côtes atlantiques françaises. *Alauda* **53**: 81-89.
Marks, J.S. (1992). Longevity record for the Bristle-thighed Curlew: an extension. *J. Field Orn.* **63(3)**: 309-310.
Marks, J.S. (1993). Molt of Bristle-thighed Curlews in the northwestern Hawaiian Islands. *Auk* **110(3)**: 573-587.
Marks, J.S. & Hall, C.S. (1992). Tool use by Bristle-thighed Curlews feeding on albatross eggs. *Condor* **94(4)**: 1032-1034.
Marks, J.S. & Hendricks, P. (1989). On the flushing behavior of incubating White Terns. *Condor* **91**: 997-998.
Marks, J.S. & Redmond, R.L. (1994a). Conservation problems and research needs for Bristle-thighed Curlews *Numenius tahitiensis* on their wintering grounds. *Bird Conserv. Int.* **4**: 329-341.
Marks, J.S. & Redmond, R.L. (1994b). Migration of Bristle-thighed Curlews on Laysan Island: timing, behavior and estimated flight range. *Condor* **96(2)**: 316-330.
Marks, J.S. & Underhill, L.G. (1994). Moult, migration and mass of a handicapped Bristle-thighed Curlew *Numenius tahitiensis*. *Ardea* **82**: 153-155.
Marks, J.S., Redmond, R.L., Hendricks, P., Clapp, R.B. & Gill, R.E. (1990). Notes on longevity and flightlessness in Bristle-thighed Curlew. *Auk* **107(4)**: 779-781.
van Marle, J.G. & Voous, K.H. (1988). *The Birds of Sumatra. An Annotated Checklist*. BOU Check-list **10**. British Ornithologists' Union, Tring, UK.
Maron, J.L. (1982). Shell-dropping behavior of Western Gulls (*Larus occidentalis*). *Auk* **99**: 565-569.
Maron, J.L. & Myers, J.P. (1984). A description and evaluation of two techniques for sexing wintering Sanderlings. *J. Field Orn.* **55(3)**: 336-342.
Maron, J.L. & Myers, J.P. (1985). Seasonal changes in feeding success, activity patterns, and weights of non-breeding Sanderlings (*Calidris alba*). *Auk* **102**: 580-586.
Marples, G. & Marples, A. (1934). *Sea Terns or Sea Swallows*. Country Life Ltd, London.
Marsden, S. & Peters, S. (1992). Little-known bird: Sumba Buttonquail. *Bull. Oriental Bird Club* **15**: 24-26.
Marsh, C.P. (1984). *The Role of Avian Predators in an Oregon Rocky Intertidal Community*. PhD thesis, Oregon State University, Corvallis, Oregon.
Marsh, C.P. (1986a). Impact of avian predators on high intertidal limpet populations. *J. Exper. Mar. Biol. Ecol.* **104**: 185-201.
Marsh, C.P. (1986b). Rocky intertidal community organization: the impact of avian predators on mussel recruitment. *Ecology* **67**: 771-786.
Marshall, D.B. (1989). A review of the status of the Snowy Plover in Oregon. *Oregon Birds* **15(1)**: 57-76.
Marshall, W.H. (1982). Minnesota Woodcock. *Loon* **54**: 203-211.
Martín, A., Nogales, M., Hernández, M.A., Lorenzo, J.A., Medina, F.A. & Rando, J.C. (1996). Status, conservation and habitat selection of the Houbara Bustard *Chlamydotis undulata fuertaventurae* in Lanzarote (Canary Islands). *Bird Conserv. Int.* **6**.
Martin, A.C., Zim, H.S. & Nelson, A.L. (1951). *American Wildlife and Plants*. Dover, New York.
Martin, A.P. (1991). *Feeding Ecology of Birds on the Swartkops Estuary, South Africa*. PhD thesis, University of Port Elizabeth, Port Elizabeth.
Martin, A.P. & Baird, D. (1987). Seasonal abundance and distribution of birds on the Swartkops estuary, Port Elizabeth. *Ostrich* **58**: 122-134.
Martin, A.P. & Martin, J.A. (1988). Hudsonian Godwit at Port Elizabeth - first African record. *Ostrich* **59(3)**: 144.
Martin, A.R. (1989). The diet of the Atlantic Puffin *Fratercula arctica* and Northern Gannet *Sula bassana* chicks at a Shetland colony during a period of changing prey availability. *Bird Study* **36**: 170-180.
Martin, E.M. & Perry, M.C. (1981). Yellow Rail collected in Maryland. *Maryland Birdlife* **37**: 15-16.
Martin, G.R. & Katzir, G. (1994). Visual fields in the Stone-curlew *Burhinus oedicnemus*. *Ibis* **136(4)**: 448-453.
Martin, J. (1971). Nesting habits of our three resident sandplovers. *Bokmakierie* **24**: 40-41.
Martin, J.L. (1983). Adaptive significance of changes in migratory routes and wintering grounds: two examples. *Ornis Fenn.* **3**(Suppl.): 54-55.
Martin, M. & Berry, T.W. (1978). Nesting behaviour and food habits of Parasitic Jaegers at Anderson River delta, Northern Territories. *Can. Field-Nat.* **92**: 45-50.
Martin, P. & Martin, J. (1987). Hudsonian Godwit - first record for Africa. *Bokmakierie* **39(2)**: 51-52.
Martin, P. & Martin, J. (1992). Too late the phalarope. *Bee-eater* **43(1)**: 6-7.
Martin, P.R., Thompson, B.G. & Witts, S.J. (1979). Niche separation in three species of water birds. *Corella* **3**: 1-5.
Martin, R. & Zwank, P.J. (1986). Habitat suitability index models: Forster's Tern (breeding). *US Fish Wildl. Serv. Biol. Rep.* **82(10)**: 1-15.
Martínez, A. & Muntaner, J. (1979). [Migration of the Caspian Tern (*Hydroprogne caspia*) in the Ebro Delta]. *Alauda* **47(1)**: 29-33. In French with Spanish and English summaries.
Martínez, C. (1988). Size and sex composition of Great Bustard (*Otis tarda*) flocks in Villafáfila, Northwest Spain. *Ardeola* **35(1)**: 125-133.
Martínez, C. (1991a). Patterns of distribution and habitat selection of a Great Bustard (*Otis tarda*) population in northwestern Spain. *Ardeola* **38(1)**: 137-147.
Martínez, C. (1991b). Relaciones espaciales en una población de avutarda (*Otis tarda*) del noroeste de España. *Ardeola* **38(2)**: 265-276.
Martínez, C. (1994). Habitat selection by the Little Bustard *Tetrax tetrax* in cultivated areas of central Spain. *Biol. Conserv.* **67**: 125-128.
Martínez, C. & de Juana, E. (1993). Estado de conservación y requerimientos de hábitat del Sisón (*Tetrax tetrax*) en España. [Conservation status and habitat requirements of the Little Bustard *Tetrax tetrax* in Spain]. Unpublished report to Sociedad Española de Ornitología (SEO), Madrid. In Spanish and English.
Martínez, C. & de Juana, E. (1995). El Sisón. *Garcilla* **92**: 16-19.
Martínez, F., Rodríguez, R. & Velasco, T. (1996). Características de la población de Avefría nidificante en España. *Quercus* **119**: 16-19.
Martínez-Vilalta, A. (1991). Primer censo nacional de limícolas coloniales y Pagaza Piconegra, 1989. *Ecología* **5**: 321-327.
Martínez-Vilalta, A. & Motis, A. (1982). Quelques observations sur la presénce de Goéland d'Audouini (*Larus audouinii*) pendant le période postnuptial au Delta de l'Ebre. *Misc. Zool.* **6**: 158-161.
Martínez-Vilalta, A., Motis, A., Matheu, E. & Llimosa, F. (1983). Data on the breeding biology of the Oystercatcher *Haematopus ostralegus* L. in the Ebro Delta. *Ardea* **71**: 229-234.
Martini, E. (1964). Otolithen in Gewollen der Raubseeschwalbe *Hydroprogne caspia*. *Bonn. zool. Beitr.* **15**: 59-71.
Masatomi, H. (1981). The Red-crowned Crane. Pp. 89-93 in: Lewis & Masatomi (1981).
Masatomi, H. ed. (1985a). [*International Spring Censuses on* Grus japonensis *(Red-crowned Crane) in 1984*]. Wild Bird Society of Japan, Tokyo. In Japanese.
Masatomi, H. (1985b). [Numerical status of Tancho, *Grus japonensis* - a resume]. Pp. 67-71 in: Masatomi (1985a). In Japanese.
Masatomi, H. ed. (1988). [*International Censuses of* Grus japonensis*, the Tancho or Red-crowned Crane, in the Wintering Grounds, 1986-87*]. International Crane Research Unit in Eastern Asia, Bibai, Japan. In Japanese.
Masatomi, H. (1991). Population dynamics of Red-crowned Cranes in Hokkaido since the 1950s. Pp. 297-299 in: Harris (1991b).
Masatomi, H. (1993). [*The Tancho of Kushiro Shitsugen*]. Japanese Society for Preservation of Birds, Kushiro, Japan. In Japanese.
Masatomi, H. & Kitagawa, T. (1974). Binomics and sociology of Tancho or the Japanese Crane, *Grus japonensis*. I. Distribution, habitat and outline of annual cycle. *J. Fac. Sci., Hokkaido Univ. (Ser. VI, Zool.)* **19(3)**: 777-802.
Masatomi, H. & Kitagawa, T. (1975). Binomics and sociology of Tancho or the Japanese Crane, *Grus japonensis*. II. Ethogram. *J. Fac. Sci., Hokkaido Univ. (Ser. VI, Zool.)* **19(4)**: 834-878.
Masatomi, H., Momose, K. & Hanawa, S. (1985). [Aerial surveys of Tancho (*Grus japonensis*) breeding in Eastern Hokkaido in 1984]. Pp. 37-66 in: Masatomi (1985a). In Japanese.
Mascher, J.W. & Marcström, V. (1976). Measures, weights and lipid levels in migrating Dunlins *Calidris a. alpina* at Ottenby Bird Observatory, south Sweden. *Ornis Scand.* **7**: 49-59.
Mason, A.G. (1940). On some experiments with Corncrakes. *Irish Nat. J.* **7**: 226-237.
Mason, A.G. (1941). Further experiments with Corncrakes. *Irish Nat. J.* **7**: 321-332.
Mason, A.G. (1944). Combat display of Corncrake. *Irish Nat. J.* **8**: 200-202.
Mason, A.G. (1945). The display of the Corn-Crake. *British Birds* **38**: 351-352.
Mason, A.G. (1947). Aggressive behaviour of Corn-Crake and Ringed Plover. *British Birds* **40**: 191-192.
Mason, A.G. (1950). The behaviour of Corn-Crakes. *British Birds* **43**: 70-78.
Mason, A.G. (1951). Aggressive display of the Corncrake. *British Birds* **44**: 162-166.
Mason, C.F. & Macdonald, S.M. (1976). Aspects of the breeding biology of the Snipe. *Bird Study* **23**: 33-38.
Mason, I.J. & Wolfe, T.O. (1975). First record of Marsh Crake for the Northern Territory. *Emu* **75**: 235.
Mason, I.J., Gill, H.B. & Young, J.H. (1981). Observations on the Red-necked Crake *Rallina tricolor*. *Austr. Bird Watcher* **9**: 69-77.
Mason, V. (1988). The Oriental pratincole *Glareola maldivarum* in Bali. *Kukila* **3(3-4)**: 141.
Massey, B.W. (1974). Breeding biology of the California Least Tern. *Proc. Linn. Soc. N.Y.* **72**: 1-24.
Massey, B.W. (1976). Vocal differences between American Least Terns and the European Little Tern. *Auk* **93**: 760-773.
Massey, B.W. (1977). Occurrence and nesting of the Least Tern and other endangered species in Baja California, Mexico. *Western Birds* **8**: 67-70.
Massey, B.W. & Atwood, J.L. (1978). Plumages of the Least Tern. *Bird-Banding* **49**: 360-317.
Massey, B.W. & Atwood, J.L. (1981). Second-wave nesting of the California Least Tern: age composition and reproductive success. *Auk* **98**: 596-605.
Massey, B.W. & Fancher, J.M. (1989). Renesting by California Least Terns. *J. Field Orn.* **60**: 350-357.
Massey, B.W. & Zembal, R. (1987). Vocalizations of the Light-footed Clapper Rail. *J. Field Orn.* **58**: 32-40.
Massey, B.W., Bradley, D.W. & Atwood, J.L. (1992). Demography of a California Least Tern colony including effects of the 1982-1983 El Niño. *Condor* **94**: 976-983.
Massey, B.W., Keane, K. & Bordman, C. (1988). Adverse effects of radio transmitters on the behavior of nesting Least Terns. *Condor* **90**: 945-947.
Massey, B.W., Zembal, R. & Jorgensen, P.D. (1984). Nesting habitat of the Light-footed Clapper Rail in southern California. *J. Field Orn.* **55**: 67-80.
Massias, A. & Becker, P.H. (1990). Nutritive value of food and growth in Common Tern *Sterna hirundo* chicks. *Ornis Scand.* **21**: 187-194.
Massoli-Novelli, R. (1987). [Contribution to the knowledge of the migration of Great Snipe *Gallinago media*]. *Riv. ital. Orn.* **57(1/2)**: 14-20. In Italian.
Massoli-Novelli, R. (1988a). Status and habitat of Great Snipe in Ethiopia and its movements in Africa. Pp. 12-15 in: Havet & Hirons (1988).
Massoli-Novelli, R. (1988b). Migration, ringing recoveries and some bag statistics of Common, Great and Jack Snipe in Italy. Pp. 16-19 in: Havet & Hirons (1988).
Massoli-Novelli, R. (1988c). Segnalazione di Schiribilla Alibianche, *Sarothrura ayresi*, in Ethiopia. *Riv. ital. Orn.* **58**: 40-42.
Masters, J.R. & Milhinch, A.L. (1974). Birds of the shire of Northam, about 100 km east of Perth, W.A. *Emu* **74**: 228-244.
Masterson, A. (1986). Wattled Cranes - hot seating? *Honeyguide* **32**: 154-155.
Masterson, A.N.B. (1969). Flufftails and button quails. *Honeyguide* **59**: 15-17.
Masterson, A.N.B. (1973). Notes on the Hottentot Button-quail. *Honeyguide* **74**: 12-16.
Masterson, A.N.B. (1991). Notes on the African Crake *Crecopsis egregia*. Unpublished MS. Harare, Zimbabwe.
Masterson, A.N.B. & Child, G.F.T. (1959). Ornithological notes on an expedition to the Chimanimani Mountains. *Ostrich* **30**: 22-32.
Mather, M. & Rounsevell, D. (1991). Painted Button-quail on Maria Island. *Tasmanian Bird Report* **20**: 18-20.
Matheson, W.E. (1974). The irruption of Native Hens in South Australia in 1972-73. *S. Austr. Orn.* **26**: 151-156.
Matheson, W.E. (1978). A further irruption of Native Hens in 1975. *S. Austr. Orn.* **27**: 270-273.
Mathew, D.N. (1964). Observations on the breeding habits of the Bronzewinged Jacana (*Metopidius indicus* Latham). *J. Bombay Nat. Hist. Soc.* **61**: 295-302.
Mathews, G.M. (1913-1914). *The Birds of Australia*. Vol. 3. Part 1. Witherby, London.
Mathews, G.M. (1928). *The Birds of Norfolk and Lord Howe Islands*. Witherby, London.
Mathiasson, S. (1980). Sandwich Tern *Sterna sandvicensis* in a changing bird community and the need for alternative breeding sites. *Acta Orn., Varszawa* **17**: 87-106.
Mathiu, P.M., Dawson, W.R. & Whittow, G.C. (1991). Development of thermoregulation in Hawaiian Brown Noddies. *J. Therm. Biol.* **16**: 317-325.
Mathiu, P.M., Dawson, W.R. & Whittow, G.C. (1994). Thermal responses of late embryos and hatchlings of the Sooty Tern. *Condor* **96**: 280-295.
Mathiu, P.M., Johnson, O.W., Johnson, P.M. & Whittow, G.C. (1989). Basal metabolic rate of Pacific Golden-Plovers. *Wilson Bull.* **101(4)**: 652-654.
Mathur, C.M. (1983). Strategy for the preservation of the Great Indian Bustard. Pp. 283-287 in: Goriup & Vardhan (1983).
Matos, J.G. (1974). *Las Aves del Valle del Cuzco*. PhD thesis, Universidad Nacional San Antonio Abad del Cuzco, Peru.
Matsunaga, C., Mathiu, P.M., Whittow, G.C. & Tazawa, H. (1989). Oxygen consumption of Brown Noddy (*Anous stolidus*) embryos in a quasiequilibrium state at lowered ambient temperatures. *Comp. Biochem. Physiol.* **93A**: 707-710.
Matter, H. (1982). [The effect of intensive agricultural activities on the breeding success of Lapwings *Vanellus vanellus* in central Europe]. *Orn. Beob.* **79**: 1-24. In German.
Matthews, S.L., Boates, J.S. & Walde, S.J. (1992). Shorebird predation may cause discrete generations in an amphipod prey. *Ecography* **15**: 393-400.
Matthews, W.C. (1983). *Home Range, Movements and Habitat Selection of Nesting Gallinules in a Louisiana Freshwater Marsh*. Louisiana State University, Baton Rouge, Louisiana.
Matthiessen, P. (1994). *The Wind Birds. Shorebirds of North America*. Chapters Publishing Ltd, Shelburne, Vermont.
Mattingley, A.H.E. (1929). The love-display of the Australian Bustard. *Emu* **28**: 198.
Mauer, K.A. & van Ijzendoorn, E.J. (1987). Terekruiters in Nederland en Europa. [Terek Sandpipers in the Netherlands and Europe]. *Dutch Birding* **9(3)**: 89-98. In Dutch with English summary.
Mauersberger, G. (1975). The first records of the Mongolian Plover, *Charadrius mongolus* Pallas, for Mongolia. *Bull. Brit. Orn. Club* **95(4)**: 131-133.
Mauersberger, G. (1978). Aggressive Verhaltensmuster des Uferläufers, *Tringa hypoleucos*. *Orn. Jber. Mus. Heineanum, Halberstadt* **3**: 73-74.
Mauersberger, G. (1990). Zur Feldkennzeichnung von Schwarzflügelbrachschwalbe *Glareola nordmanni*. [On the field marks of *Glareola nordmanni*]. *Beitr. Vogelkd.* **36(6)**: 321-326. In German with English summary.
Mauersberger, G., Wagner, S., Wallschlager, D. & Warthold, R. (1982). Neue Daten zur Avifauna Mongolica. *Mitt. Zool. Mus. Berlin* **58**: 11-74.
Maumary, L. & Duflon, J.M. (1989). Le Pluvier guignard (*Eudromias morinellus*): migration en Europe et synthèse des observations en Suisse de 1927 à 1988. *Nos Oiseaux* **40**: 207-216. In French with English summary.
Maunder, J.E. & Threlfall, W. (1972). The breeding biology of the Black-legged Kittiwake in Newfoundland. *Auk* **89**: 789-816.
Mauro, I. (1994). Enkele bemerkingen bij nieuwe gegevens over het Porseleinhoen *Porzana porzana* te Molsbroek-Lokeren (Oost-Vlaanderen) tijdens het broedseizoen 1992. [Some remarks on new data on Spotted Crakes at Molsbroek-Lokeren (East-Flanders) during the 1992 breeding season]. *Oriolus* **60(2)**: 30-33. In Dutch with English summary.
Mawby, S. (1988). Sociable Plover in Northamptonshire. *Birding World* **1(9)**: 310-311.
Mawhinney, K., Hicklin, P.W. & Boates, J.S. (1993). A re-evaluation of the numbers of migrant Semipalmated Sandpipers, *Calidris pusilla*, in the Bay of Fundy during fall migration. *Can. Field-Nat.* **107(1)**: 19-23.
Maxson, S.J. & Bernstein, N.P. (1980). Ecological studies of Southern Black-backed Gulls, Blue-eyed Shags and Adelie Penguins at Palmer Station. *Antarct. J. US* **15**: 157.
Maxson, S.J. & Bernstein, N.P. (1984). Breeding season time budgets of the Southern Black-backed Gull in Antarctica. *Condor* **86(4)**: 401-409.
Maxson, S.J. & Oring, L.W. (1980). Breeding season time and energy budgets of the polyandrous Spotted Sandpiper. *Behaviour* **74**: 200-263.
Maxwell, G.R. & Smith, G.A. (1983). Reproductive success of island nesting Ring-Billed Gulls and Common Terns in the St. Lawrence River. *Kingbird* **28**: 26-33.
May, P.L. (1992). *The Feasibility of Establishing a Breeding Whooping Crane Flock on the Canadian Prairies*. ME Des. thesis, The University of Calgary, Calgary. 182 pp.

May, P.L. & Henry, J.D. (1995). A Whooping Crane reintroduction project on the Canadian prairies: identifying relevant issues using expert consultation. *Endangered Species UPDATE* **12(7-8)**: 1-7.
Mayaud, N. (1954). Sur les migrations et l'hivernage de *Larus melanocephalus*. *Alauda* **22**: 225-245.
Mayaud, N. (1956a). Nouvelles données sur *Larus melanocephalus*. *Alauda* **24**: 123-131.
Mayaud, N. (1956b). Étude sur la migration et les zones d'hivernage des Sternes caspiennes *Hydroprogne caspia* (Pallas) d'Eurasie. *Alauda* **24**: 206-218.
Mayaud, N. (1961). Sur les migrations de la Mouette de Sabini *Xema sabini* (Sabine) et la question de ses zones d'hivernage. *Alauda* **29**: 165-174.
Mayaud, N. (1965). Sur la zone d'hivernage atlantique de la Mouette de Sabini *Xema sabini* (Sabine). *Alauda* **33**: 81-83.
Mayaud, N. (1982). Les oiseaux du nord-ouest de l'Afrique. Notes complémentaires. *Alauda* **50(1)**: 45-67.
Mayer, P.M. (1991). *Conservation Biology of Piping Plovers in the Northern Great Plains*. MSc thesis, University of Missouri, Columbia, Missouri.
Mayer, P.M. & Ryan, M.R. (1991a). Survival rates of artificial Piping Plover nests in American Avocet colonies. *Condor* **93(3)**: 753-755.
Mayer, P.M. & Ryan, M.R. (1991b). Electric fences reduce mammalian predation on Piping Plover nests and chicks. *Wildl. Soc. Bull.* **19(1)**: 59-63.
Mayer, S. (1995). First record of Giant Snipe *Gallinago undulata* for Bolivia. *Bull. Brit. Orn. Club* **115(3)**: 188-189.
Mayes, E. (1993). The decline of the Corncrake *Crex crex* in Britain and Ireland in relation to habitat. *J. Appl. Ecol.* **30**: 53-62.
Mayes, E. & Stowe, T.J. (1989). The status and distribution of the Corncrake in Ireland in 1988. *Irish Birds* **4**: 1-12.
Mayfield, H.F. (1973). Black-bellied Plover incubation and hatching. *Wilson Bull.* **85**: 82-85.
Mayfield, H.F. (1978a). Red Phalaropes breeding on Bathurst Island. *Living Bird* **17**: 7-40.
Mayfield, H.F. (1978b). Undependable breeding conditions in the Red Phalarope. *Auk* **95**: 590-592.
Maynard Smith, J. & Ridpath, M.G. (1972). Wife sharing in the Tasmanian Native Hen, *Tribonyx mortierii*: a case of kin selection. *Amer. Nat.* **106**: 447-452.
Mayol, J. (1978). Observaciones sobre la Gaviota de Audouin, *Larus audouinii* Payr., en el Mediterráneo occidental (primavera de 1978). *Naturalia Hispanica* **20**. 34 pp.
Mayr, E. (1933). Birds collected during the Whitney South Sea expedition. XXII. *Amer. Mus. Novit.* **590**: 1-6.
Mayr, E. (1944). *The Birds of Timor and Sumba*. Bulletin of the American Museum of Natural History **83(2)**, New York.
Mayr, E. (1945). *Birds of the Southwest Pacific*. Macmillan, New York.
Mayr, E. (1949). Notes on the birds of Northern Melanesia, 2. *Amer. Mus. Novit.* **1417**: 1-38.
Mayr, E. & Gilliard, E.T. (1954). Birds of central New Guinea. Results of the American Museum of Natural History expedition to New Guinea in 1950 and 1952. *Bull. Amer. Mus. Nat. Hist.* **103**: 315-374.
Mayr, E. & Rand, A.L. (1937). *Results of the Archibold Expeditions. 14. Birds of the 1933-1934 Papuan Expedition*. Bulletin of the American Museum of Natural History **73**, New York. 248 pp.
Mayr, E. & Short, L.L. (1970). *Species Taxa of North American Birds. A Contribution to Comparative Systematics*. Publications of the Nuttall Ornithological Club **9**. Cambridge, Masschusetts. 127 pp.
McAllan, I.A.W. & Bruce, M.D. (1988). *The Birds of New South Wales. A working list*. Biocon Research Group, Turramurra, Australia.
McAlpine, D.F., Phinney, M. & Makepeace, S. (1988). New Brunswick breeding of Wilson's Phalarope, *Phalaropus tricolor*, confirmed. *Can. Field-Nat.* **102**: 77-78.
McAuley, D.G., Longcore, J.R. & Sepik, G.F. (1990). Renesting by American Woodcocks (*Scolopax minor*) in Maine. *Auk* **107**: 407-410.
McAuley, D.G., Longcore, J.R. & Sepik, G.F. (1993). Behavior of radio-marked breeding American Woodcocks. Pp. 115-124 in: Longcore & Sepik (1993).
McCaffery, B.J. (1983). Breeding flight display of the female White-rumped Sandpiper (*Caldiris fuscicollis*). *Auk* **100**: 500-501.
McCaffery, B.J. & Gill, R.E. (1992). Antipredator strategies in breeding Bristle-thighed Curlews. *Amer. Birds* **46**: 378-383.
McCaffery, B.J. & Peltola, G. (1986). The status of the Bristle-thighed Curlew on the Yukon Delta National Wildlife Refuge, Alaska. *Wader Study Group Bull.* **47**: 22-25.
McCaffery, B.J., Sordahl, T.A. & Zahler, P. (1984). Behavioral ecology of the Mountain Plover in northeastern Colorado. *Wader Study Group Bull.* **40**: 18-21.
McCaskie, G. (1983). Another look at the Western and Yellow-footed Gulls. *Western Birds* **14**: 85-107.
McCaskie, G., Liston, S. & Rapley, W.A. (1974). First nesting of Black Skimmer in California. *Condor* **76**: 337-338.
McChesney, G.J., Carter, H.R. & Whitworth, D.L. (1995). Reoccupation and extension of southern breeding limits of Tufted Puffins and Rhinoceros Auklets in California. *Colonial Waterbirds* **18(1)**: 79-90.
McCleery, R.H. & Sibly, R.M. (1986). Feeding specialization and preference in Herring Gulls. *J. Anim. Ecol.* **55**: 245-259.
McClure, D. & McClure, P. (1983). Lesser Golden Plover observed in south Fulton County. *Oriole* **48(1)**: 6-7.
McClure, H.E. (1974). *Migration and Survival of Birds in Asia*. US Army Medical Component, SEATO Medical Project, Bangkok, Thailand.
McClure, H.E. & Leelavit, L.P. (1972). *Birds Banded in Asia During the MAPS Program, by Locality, 1963-1971*. US Army Research & Development Group, Far East, Report No. FE-315-7. 478 pp.
McColl, J.G. & Burger, J. (1976). Chemical input by a colony of Franklin's Gulls nesting in Cattails. *Amer. Midl. Nat.* **96**: 270-280.
McCollough, M.A. (1981). *Feeding Ecology of Semipalmated Sandpipers, Semi-palmated Plovers, Black-bellied Plovers and Short-billed Dowitchers on Coastal Staging Areas in Eastern Maine*. MSc thesis, University of Maine, Orono, Maine.
McConkey, B.F. (1971). *Bionomics of the Pied Stilt in New Zealand: with Special Reference to Breeding Behaviour*. MSc thesis, Massey University, Palmerston North.
McCrie, N. (1984). Further records of the Oriental Plover and a reassessment of some problems in field identification. *S. Austr. Orn.* **29(4)**: 106-107.
McCulloch, M.N. (1991). Status, habitat and conservation of the St Helena Wirebird *Charadrius sanctaehelenae*. *Bird Conserv. Int.* **1**: 361-392.
McCulloch, M.N. (1992). *The Status and Ecology of the St Helena Wirebird*. BTO Research Report **97**. British Trust for Ornithology, Thetford.
McCullough, D.R. & Barrett, R.H. eds. (1992). *Wildlife 2001: Populations*. Elsevier Applied Science, London.
McDaniel, T.H. & Beckett, T.A.I. (1971). Caspian Terns nesting in South Carolina. *Chat* **35**: 39-41.
McFarland, D. (1993). Notes on the Pied Oystercatcher *Haematopus longirostris* in the Cooloola-Fraser Island area. *Sunbird* **23(4)**: 109-113.
McFarlane, R.W. (1975). Notes on the Giant Coot (*Fulica gigantea*). *Condor* **77**: 324-327.
McGeehan, A. (1995). Telling tails. *Birdwatch* **37**: 23-29.
McGeehan, A. (1996). Awkward auks. *Birdwatch* **43**: 28-33.
McGill, A.R. (1944). The Red-kneed Dotterel in coastal south-eastern Australia. *Emu* **43**: 225-228.
McGill, A.R. (1951). An Australian review of the Sanderling. *Emu* **50**: 197-206.
McGill, A.R. (1955). The two larger gulls in Eastern Australia. *Emu* **55**: 90-96.
McGill, A.R. (1960). The Little Whimbrel. *Emu* **60**: 89-94.
McGill-Harelstad, P.A. (1985). *Mechanisms and Consequences of Interspecific Interactions among Gulls*. PhD dissertation, Cornell University, Ithaca, New York.
McGilp, J. (1934). The nesting of the Painted Snipe (*Rostratula australis*). *S. Austr. Orn.* **12**: 167-169.
McGilp, J. & Morgan, A.M. (1931). The nesting of the Banded Stilt. *S. Austr. Orn.* **11**: 37-53.
McGilp, J.N. (1923). Birds of Lake Frome district, South Australia. *Emu* **22**: 237-243.
McGuigan, C.C. (1990). Hybrid Lesser Crested x Sandwich Tern at Musselburgh. *Lothian Bird Rep.* **1989**: 95-96.
McIvor, D.E. & Conover, M.R. (1994). Habitat preference and diurnal use among Greater Sandhill Cranes. *Great Basin Nat.* **54(4)**: 329-334.
McKean, J.L. (1978). Some remarks on the taxonomy of Australasian oystercatchers *Haematopus* spp. *Sunbird* **9**: 3 6.
McKean, J.L. & Hindwood, K.A. (1965). Additional notes on the birds of Lord Howe Island. *Emu* **64**: 79-97.
McKean, J.L. & Read, M. (1979). Further sightings of the Bush-Hen *Gallinula olivacea* from sub-coastal Northern Territory. *Sunbird* **10**: 73-74.
McKean, J.L., Evans, O. & Lewis, J.H. (1976). Notes on the birds of Norfolk Island. *Notornis* **23**: 299-301.
McKean, J.L., Shurcliff, K.S. & Thompson, H.A.F. (1986). Notes on the status of the Little Curlew *Numenius minutus* in the Darwin area, Northern Territory, 1974-1985. *Austr. Bird Watcher* **11(8)**: 258-260.
McKee, J. (1982). The winter feeding of Turnstones and Purple Sandpipers in Strathclyde. *Bird Study* **29**: 213-216.
McKenzie, H.R. (1978). New Zealand Dotterel banding report number one. *Notornis* **25(3)**: 186-194.
McKenzie, H.R. (1980). Some Red-capped Dotterel records. *Notornis* **27(3)**: 291-292.
McKenzie, H.R., Sibson, R.B. & Rutheford, V.M. (1956). Probable recent occurrences of Oriental Dotterel in New Zealand. *Notornis* **7(1)**: 25-27.
McKenzie, M.E., Reed, S.M. & McKenzie, H.R. (1977). Variation in hatching to flying period of New Zealand Dotterel chicks. *Notornis* **24(2)**: 136-137.
McKibben, L.A. & Hofmann, P. (1985). Breeding range and population studies of Common Snipe in California. *Calif. Fish & Game* **71**: 68-75.
McLachlan, A., Wooldridge, T., Schramm, M. & Kühn, M. (1979). Seasonal abundance, biomass and feeding of shore birds on sandy beaches in the east Cape, South Africa. *Ostrich* **51**: 44 52.
McLachlan, G.R. (1955). Nesting of the Grey-headed Gull (*Larus cirrocephalus*). *Ostrich* **26**: 39.
McLachlan, G.R. & Jeffery, R.G. (1949). Nesting of the Chestnut-banded Sandplover. *Ostrich* **20(1)**: 36-37.
McLannahan, H.M.C. (1973). Some aspects of the ontogeny of cliff nesting behavior in the Kittiwake (*Rissa tridactyla*) and the Herring Gull (*Larus argentatus*). *Behaviour* **44**: 36-86.
McMahon, J. (1982). A new bird for Oklahoma: Wilson's Plover. *Bull. Okla. Orn. Soc.* **15(4)**: 25-27.
McMillen, J.L. (1988). Conservation of North American cranes. *Amer. Birds* **42**: 1213-1221.
McNair, D.B. (1988). Second record of American Avocet from the Mountain Region of North Carolina. *Chat* **52(4)**: 79-80.
McNair, D.B. (1991). Agonistic behavior of Ruddy Turnstones toward Short-billed Dowitchers foraging for horseshoe crab eggs. *Florida Field-Nat.* **19(3)**: 83-84.
McNamara, J.A. (1980). Nocturnal feeding of the Inland Dotterel (*Peltohyas australis*). *Emu* **80(1)**: 39-40.
McNeil, R. (1970). Hivernage et estivage d'oiseaux aquatiques nord-américains dans le nord-est du Venezuela (mue, accumulation de graisse, capacité de vol et routes de migration). *Oiseau et RFO* **40**: 185-302.
McNeil, R. & Burton, J. (1973). Dispersal of some southbound migrating North American shorebirds away from the Magdalen Islands, Gulf of St. Lawrence, and Sable Island, Nova Scotia. *Caribb. J. Sci.* **13**: 257-278.
McNeil, R. & Robert, M. (1988). Nocturnal feeding strategies of some shorebirds species in a tropical environment. Pp. 2328-2336 in: *Proc. XIX Int. Orn. Congr.* Ottawa, 1986.
McNeil, R. & Rodríguez, J.R. (1990). When does the Willet 'plough' the water to catch fish? *Wader Study Group Bull.* **58**: 50-51.
McNeil, R. & Rompré, G. (1995). Day and night feeding territoriality in Willets *Catoptrophorus semipalmatus* and Whimbrels *Numenius phaeopus* during the the non-breeding season in tropical environment. *Ibis* **137(2)**: 169-176.
McNeil, R., Drapeau, P. & Goss-Custard, J.D. (1992). The occurrence and adaptive significance of nocturnal habits in waterfowl. *Biol. Rev.* **67**: 381-419.
McNeil, R., Lemoges, B., Mercier, F. & Rodríguez, J.R. (1987). Wilson's Phalarope in South America. *Amer. Birds* **41**: 391.
McNeil, R., Rodríguez, S.J.R. & Mercier, F. (1985). Eastward range expansion of the Marbled Godwit in South America. *Wilson Bull.* **97**: 243-244.
McNicholl, M.K. (1975). Larid site tenacity and group adherence in relation to habitat. *Auk* **92(1)**: 98-104.
McNicholl, M.K. (1979). Territories of Forster's Terns. *Proc. Colonial Waterbird Group* **3**: 196-203.
McNicholl, M.K. (1981). Interactions between Forster's Terns and Yellow-headed Blackbirds. *Colonial Waterbirds* **4**: 150-152.
McNicholl, M.K. (1982). Factors affecting reproductive success of Forster's Terns at Delta Marsh, Manitoba. *Colonial Waterbirds* **5**: 32-38.
McNicholl, M.K. (1983). Hatching of Forster's Tern. *Condor* **85**: 50-52.
McNicholl, M.K. (1985). Profiles on risk status of Canadian birds: 2. Piping Plover. *Alberta Nat.* **15(4)**: 135-138.
McNicholl, M.K. (1990). Temporary feeding territories among Caspian Terns. *Colonial Waterbirds* **13**: 133-135.
McNulty, F. (1966). *The Whooping Crane: The Bird that Defies Extinction*. E.P. Dutton, New York.
McRae, R.D. (1984). First nesting of the Little Gull in Manitoba. *Amer. Birds* **38**: 368-369.
McWhirter, D.W. (1987). Feeding methods and other notes on the Spoon-billed Sandpiper *Eurynorhynchus pygmeus* in Okinawa. *Forktail* **3**: 60-61.
Mead, C. (1973). Feeling the crunch: Little Tern. *BTO News* **59**: 1.
Meade-Waldo, E.G. (1889a). Notes on some birds of the Canary Islands. *Ibis* **Ser. 6, no. 1**: 1-13.
Meade-Waldo, E.G. (1889b). Further notes on the birds of the Canary Islands. *Ibis* **Ser. 6, no. 1**: 503-520.
Meade-Waldo, E.G. (1890). Further notes on the birds of the Canary Islands. *Ibis* **Ser. 6, no. 2**: 429-438.
Meade Waldo, E.G. (1893). List of birds observed in the Canary Islands. *Ibis* **Ser. 6, no. 5**: 185 207.
Meadows, B.S. (1977). Exceptional numbers of Black-tailed Godwits *Limosa limosa* wintering at Lake Naivasha during 1976/77. *Scopus* **1**: 49-50.
Meanley, B. (1953). Nesting of the King Rail in the Arkansas ricefields. *Auk* **70**: 262-269.
Meanley, B. (1956). Food habits of the King Rail in the Arkansas rice fields. *Auk* **73**: 252-258.
Meanley, B. (1957). Notes on the courtship behavior of the King Rail. *Auk* **74**: 433-440.
Meanley, B. (1960). Fall food of the Sora Rail in the Arkansas rice fields. *J. Wildl. Manage.* **24**: 339.
Meanley, B. (1965a). Early fall food and habitat of the Sora in the Patuxent River Marsh, Maryland. *Chesapeake Sci.* **6**: 226-237.
Meanley, B. (1965b). King and Clapper Rails of Broadway Meadows. *Delaware Conservationist* (winter issue): 3-7.
Meanley, B. (1969). Natural history of the King Rail. *Bur. Sports, Fisheries & Wildl.: North American Fauna* **67**: 1-108.
Meanley, B. (1992). King Rail (*Rallus elegans*). No. **3** in: Poole *et al.* (1992-1993).
Meanley, B. & Meanley, A.G. (1958). Growth and development of the King Rail. *Auk* **75**: 381-386.
Meanley, B. & Wetherbee, D.K. (1962). Ecological notes on mixed populations of King Rails and Clapper Rails in Delaware Bay marshes. *Auk* **79**: 453-457.
Meathrel, C.E. & Ryder, J.P. (1987a). Sex ratios of Ring-billed Gulls in relation to egg size, egg sequence and female body condition. *Colonial Waterbirds* **10(1)**: 72-77.
Meathrel, C.E. & Ryder, J.P. (1987b). Intra-clutch variation in the size, mass and composition of Ring-billed Gull eggs. *Condor* **89**: 364-368.
Meathrel, C.E., Mills, J.A. & Wooller, R.D. (1991). The Silver Gull in Australia and New Zealand. Pp. 2390-2395 in: Bell *et al.* (1991).
Medland, R.D. (1988). White-fronted Sandplover, *Charadrius marginatus*, at Lumbadzi Sewage Works, Lilongwe. *Nyala* **12(1/2)**: 73-74.
Medland, R.D. (1989a). Probable Three-banded Courser on the Viphya Mountains. *Nyala* **13(1/2)**: 81.
Medland, R.D. (1989b). White-crowned Plover in Malawi. *Nyala* **14(1)**: 40-41.
Medland, R.D. (1991). First record of Pacific Golden Plover, *Pluvialis fulva*, in Malawi. *Nyala* **15(1)**: 48-49.
MEDMARAVIS & Monbailliu, X. eds. (1986). *Mediterranean Marine Avifauna. Population Studies and Conservation*. NATO ASI Series, Series G: Ecological Sciences **12**, Springer-Verlag, Berlin.
Meduna, A.J., Stopfords, G.P. & Garba, B. (1988). Status and distribution of the Northern Crowned Crane in Kano State. *Nigerian Field* **53(4)**: 157-160.
Medway, Lord & Wells, D.R. (1976). *The Birds of the Malay Peninsula*. Vol. 5. Conclusions and Survey of Every Species. Witherby & Penerbit University Malaya, London & Kuala Lumpur.
Meek, E.R., Sim, I.M.W. & Ribbands, B. (1994). Breeding skuas in Orkney: the results of the 1992 census. *Seabird* **16**: 34-40.
Mees, G.F. (1965). The avifauna of Misool. *Nova Guinea, Zool.* **31**: 139-203.
Mees, G.F. (1975). Identiteit en status van *Sterna bernsteini* Schlegel 1863. *Ardea* **63**: 78-86.
Mees, G.F. (1977). The subspecies of *Chlidonias hybridus* (Pallas), their breeding distribution and migration (Aves, Laridae, Sterninae). *Zool. Verhand.* **157**: 1-64.
Mees, G.F. (1982). Birds from the lowlands of southern New Guinea (Merauke and Koembe). *Zool. Verhand.* **191**: 1-188.
Meese, R.J. (1993). Effects of predation by birds on gooseneck barnacle *Pollicipes polymerus* Sowerby distribution and abundance. *J. Exper. Mar. Biol. Ecol.* **166**: 47-64.
Meeth, P. (1969). Sabine's Gulls (*Larus sabini*) in West African Ross's Gulls in the Arctic pack-ice. *British Birds* **74**: 316-320.
Meeth, P. & Meeth, K. (1989). Long-billed Plover on Bali in November 1973. *Dutch Birding* **11(3)**: 114-115.
Meeus, H., van Dooren, J. & Voet, H. (1985). Whimbrels *Numenius phaeopus* ejecting the lining membrane of their gizzard. *Wielewaal* **51**: 305-309.
Mehlum, F. (1991). The incubation behaviour of the Gray Phalarope *Phalaropus fulicarius* on Svalbard (Arctic Ocean). *Fauna Norvegica (Ser. C, Cinclus)* **14(1)**: 33-38.
Mehlum, F. & Bakken, V. (1994). Seabirds in Svalbard (Norway): status, recent changes and management. Pp. 155-171 in: Nettleship *et al.* (1994).

Mehlum, F. & Gabrielsen, G.W. (1993). The diet of high-arctic seabirds in coastal and ice-covered, pelagic areas near the Svalbard archipelago. *Polar Res.* **12**: 1-20.

Meijer, A.W.J. (1995). Bristle-thighed Curlew. *Dutch Birding* **17(1)**: 21-22.

Meine, C.D. (1993). The calling of cranes. *World Birdwatch* **15(4)**: 14-17.

Meine, C.D. & Archibald, G.W. eds. (1996). *The Cranes: Status Survey and Conservation Action Plan*. IUCN/Species Survival Comission, Gland & Cambridge.

Meinertzhagen, A.C. (1927). A review of the family Cursoridae. *Ibis* **Ser. 12, no. 4**: 469-501.

Meinertzhagen, R. (1930). *Nicoll's Birds of Egypt*. Hugh Rees Ltd, London.

Meinertzhagen, R. (1954). *Birds of Arabia*. Oliver & Boyd, Edinburgh & London.

Meinertzhagen, R. (1959). *Pirates and Predators*. Oliver & Boyd, Edinburgh.

Meininger, P.L. (1988). *A Preliminary Investigation of Tern Catching in Senegal, Winter 1987/88*. ICBP, Cambridge.

Meininger, P.L. (1991). [Breeding Black-winged Stilts, *Himantopus himantopus*, in the Netherlands in 1990]. *Limosa* **64(2)**: 72-73. In Dutch with English summary.

Meininger, P.L. (1993). Breeding Black-winged Stilts in the Netherlands in 1989-93, including one paired with Black-necked Stilt. *Dutch Birding* **15(5)**: 193-197.

Meininger, P.L. (1995). Little Gulls breeding in south-western Netherlands. *Dutch Birding* **17(4)**: 152-154.

Meininger, P.L. & Schekkerman, H. (1990). [Breeding Black-winged Stilts *Himantopus himantopus* in the Netherlands in 1989]. *Limosa* **63(1)**: 11-15. In Dutch with English summary.

Meininger, P.L. & Sørensen, U.G. (1986). The occurrence of skuas (*Stercorariidae*) in the Middle East, with special reference to Egypt and the northern Red Sea. *Vogelwarte* **33**: 281-294.

Meininger, P.L., Berrevoets, C., Schekkerman, H., Strucker, R. & Wolf, P. (1991). [Food and feeding areas of breeding Mediterranean Gulls in the SW-Netherlands]. *Sula* **5**: 109-110. In Dutch.

Meininger, P.L., Blomert, A.M. & Marteijn, E.C.L. (1991). Watervogelsterfte in het Deltagebied, ZW-Nederland, gedurende de drie koude winters van 1985, 1986 en 1987. *Limosa* **64**: 89-102.

Meininger, P.L., Wolf, P.A., Hadoud, D.A. & Essghaier, M.F.A. (1994). Rediscovery of Lesser Crested Terns breeding in Libya. *British Birds* **87**: 160-170.

Meire, P.M. & Kuyken, E. (1984). Relations between the distribution of waders and the intertidal benthic fauna of the Oosterschelde, Netherlands. Pp. 57-68 in: Evans *et al.* (1984).

Meise, W. (1934). Zur Brutbiologie der Ralle *Laterallus leucopyrrhus* (Vieill.). *J. Orn.* **82**: 257-268.

Meise, W. (1968a). Button quails. Pp.137-140 in: Grzimek (1968).

Meise, W. (1968b). Sheathbills. Pp. 197-198 in: Grzimek (1968).

Meissner, W. (1992). Knots' autumn migration in the western part of the gulf of Gdansk, Poland: preliminary results. Pp. 167-171 in: Piersma & Davidson (1992b).

Meissner, W. & Skakuj, M. (1986). [Next records of Greater Sand Plover in Poland and some remarks on its identification in post-nuptial plumage]. *Notatki Orn.* **27(1-2)**: 92-97. In Polish with English summary.

Meissner, W. & Skakuj, M. (1988). [Field identification of Common, Great, Pintail and Swinhoe's Snipes]. *Notatki Orn.* **29(1-2)**: 67-75. In Polish.

Meissner, W., Sikora, A. & Skakuj, M. (1989). [The first record of a Greater Yellowlegs in Poland]. *Notatki Orn.* **30(3-4)**: 91-93. In Polish with English summary.

Melde, F. (1991). Zur Biologie des Flußregenpfeifers. *Falke* **38(7)**: 226-230.

Melnikov, I.I. (1994). On Common Crane predation behavior. *Byull. Mosk. Ova. Ispyt. Prir. Otd. Biol.* **99(6)**: 72-73.

Melnikov, U.I. & Sadkov, V.S. (1977). [On the breeding biology of the Common Tern on Lake Baikal]. Pp. 92-109 in: [*Ecology Birds Eastern Siberia*]. Irkutsk Univ., Irkutsk. In Russian.

Melnikov, Y.I. (1985). [About the ecology of the Asiatic Dowitcher in the delta of the Selenga river]. *Byull. Mosk. Ova. Ispyt. Prir. Otd. Biol.* **90**: 16-25. In Russian.

Melnikov, Y.I. (1988). [Spatial structure and dynamics of the Asiatic Dowitcher range in Eastern Siberia]. Pp. 146-152 in: [*Rare Terrestrial Vertebrate of Siberia*]. Nauka, Novosibirsk. In Russian.

Melnikov, Y.I. (1990a). [Data on the Asiatic Dowitcher]. Pp. 57-64 in: [*Results of the Studies of Rare Animals*]. Moscow. In Russian.

Melnikov, Y.I. (1990b). [Oological characteristic of the Asian Dowitcher (*Limnodromus semipalmatus*) in Selenga River Delta, Baikal Lake]. *Ornitologiya* **24**: 131-132. In Russian.

Melnikov, Y.I. (1991a). Ecology of the Dowitcher, *Limnodromus semipalmatus*, at the limit of its range in eastern Siberia. *Ekologiya* **22(3)**: 52-58.

Melnikov, Y.I. (1991b). Ecology of the Asian Snipe-billed Godwit and its range boundary in Eastern Siberia. *Ekologiya* **22(3)**: 176-181.

Melnikov, Y.I. (1994). [Distraction display of Asian Dowitcher *Limnodromus semipalmatus* during breeding period]. *Russ. J. Orn.* **3(1)**: 31-46. In Russian with English summary.

Melter, J. (1995). Daily and annual activity budgets of migrating Ruff, *Philomachus pugnax*, at the sewage farms of Muenster, Germany. *Vogelwelt* **116(1)**: 19-33.

Meltofte, H. (1985). Populations and breeding schedules of waders, Charadrii, in high arctic Greenland. *Medd. Grønland* **16**: 3-43.

Meltofte, H. (1986). Hunting as a possible factor in the decline of Fenno-Scandian populations of Curlews *Numenius arquata*. *Vår Fågelvärld* **11**(Suppl.): 135-140.

Meltofte, H. (1987). The occurrence of staging waders Charadrii at the Tipperne reserve, western Denmark, 1928-1982. *Dan. Orn. Foren. Tidssk.* **81**: 1-108.

Meltofte, H. (1991). The northern Dunlin puzzle. *Wader Study Group Bull.* **62**: 15-17, **63**: 32.

Meltofte, H. (1993). Wader migration through Denmark: populations, non-breeding phenology and migratory strategies. *Dan. Orn. Foren. Tidssk.* **87**: 1-180.

Meltofte, H., Blew, J., Frikke, J., Rösner, H.U. & Smit, C.J. (1994). *Numbers and Distribution of Waterbirds in the Wadden Sea. Results and Evaluation of 36 Simultaneous Counts in the Dutch-German-Danish Wadden Sea 1980-1991*. IWRB Publication **34**. Wader Study Group Bulletin **74**(Special issue).

Meltofte, H., Edelstam, C., Granstrøm, G., Hammar, J. & Hjort, C. (1981). Ross's Gulls in the arctic pack-ice. *British Birds* **74**: 316-320.

Melville, D.S. (1977). Gray-rumped Tattlers catching fish. *Auk* **94(3)**: 604.

Melville, D.S. (1981). Spring measurements, weight and plumage status of *Calidris ruficollis* and *C. ferruginea* in Hong Kong. *Wader Study Group Bull.* **33**: 18-21.

Melville, D.S. (1984). Seabirds of China and the surrounding seas. Pp. 501-511 in: Croxall, Evans & Schreiber (1984).

Melville, D.S. (1985). Long-tailed Skuas *Stercorarius longicaudus* in New Zealand. *Notornis* **32(1)**: 51-73.

Melville, D.S. (1990). *Management Plant for* Larus saundersi. Worldwide Fund. for Nature (Hong Kong) Project Report **4527**.

Melville, D.S. & Round, P.D. (1982). Further records of the Asian Dowitcher *Limnodromus semipalmatus* from Thailand, with notes on its distribution and identification. *Nat. Hist. Bull. Siam Soc.* **30(2)**: 119-204.

Melvin, S.M. & Gibbs, J.P. (1994). Sora. In: Tacha & Braun (1994).

Melvin, S.M. & Temple, S.A. (1982). Migration ecology of Sandhill Cranes: a review. Pp. 73-87 in: Lewis (1982).

Melvin, S.M., Griffin, C.R. & MacIvor, L.H. (1991). Recovery strategies for Piping Plovers in managed coastal landscapes. *Coastal Manage.* **19(1)**: 21-34.

Melvin, S.M., Hecht, A. & Griffin, C.R. (1994). Piping Plover mortalities caused by off-road vehicles on Atlantic coast beaches. *Wildl. Soc. Bull.* **22(3)**: 409-414.

Mendelsohn, J.M., Sinclair, J.C. & Tarboton, W.R. (1983). Flushing flufftails out of vleis. *Bokmakierie* **35**: 9-11.

Mendelssohn, H. (1983). Observations on the Houbara (*Chlamydotis undulata*) in Israel. Pp. 91-96 in: Goriup & Vardhan (1983).

Mendelssohn, H., Marder, U. & Stavy, M. (1979). Captive breeding of the Houbara *Chlamydotis undulata macqueenii* and a description of its display. *Bull. ICBP* **13**: 134-149.

Mendelssohn, H., Marder, U. & Stavy, M. (1983). Captive breeding of the Houbara (*Chlamydotis undulata macqueenii*) and the development of the young bird. Pp. 288-292 in: Goriup & Vardhan (1983).

Mendenhall, V.M. (1992). Distribution, breeding records and conservation problems of the Marbled Murrelet in Alaska. Pp. 5-16 in: Carter & Morrison (1992).

Mercer, A.J. (1968). Individual weight change in breeding Oystercatchers. *Bird Study* **15**: 93 98.

Mercier, F., McNeil, R. & Rodríguez, J.S. (1987). First occurrence of Bar-tailed Godwit in South America and status of the Marbled Godwit in northeastern Venezuela. *J. Field Orn.* **58(1)**: 78-80. In English with Spanish summary.

Mercier, F.M. (1985). Fat reserves and migration of Red-necked Phalaropes (*Phalaropus lobatus*) in the Quoddy region, New Brunswick, Canada. *Can. J. Zool.* **63**: 2810-2816.

Meretsy, V.J. (1988). *Population Size and Feeding Ecology of Marbled Godwits on North Humboldt Bay, CA - July to December 1987*. MSc thesis, Humboldt State University, Arcata, California.

Merilees, W.J. (1969). Longevity of Dominican Gulls. *Austr. Bird Bander* **1969**(Sept.): 60-61.

Merilees, W.J. (1974). A Glaucous-winged Gull mated to a Herring Gull on Okanagan Lake, British Columbia. *Can. Field-Nat.* **88**: 485-486.

Merton, D.V. (1970). Kermadec Islands expedition reports: a general account of birdlife. *Notornis* **17**: 147-199.

van der Merwe, D. (1987). *The Ecology of the White-fronted Plover (*Charadrius marginatus*) in an Eastern Cape Dunefield*. MSc thesis, University of Port Elizabeth, Port Elizabeth.

van der Merwe, D., McLachlan, A. & De Ruyck, A.M.C. (1992). Partitioning of feeding habitats by Whitefronted Plovers *Charadrius marginatus* at a dune/beach interface. *Ostrich* **63(2-3)**: 49-57.

van der Merwe, D., McLachlan, A. & De Ruyck, A.M.C. (1994). Seasonal movements between habitats of Whitefronted Plovers *Charadrius marginatus* in a coastal dunefield. *J. Coastal Res.* **10(3)**: 747-751.

Mes, R., Schuckard, R. & Wattel, J. (1978). [Cooling behaviour in Common Terns *Sterna hirundo*]. *Limosa* **51(1-2)**: 64-68. In Dutch with English summary.

Meschini, A. (1991). [Migratory aspects of Stone Curlew (*Burhinus oedicnemus*) in Lazio]. *Ricerche Biol. Selvaggina* **17(1)**(Suppl.): 467-470. In Italian with English summary.

Meschini, A. & Fraschetti, F. (1989). [Distribution, population and habitat of the Stone Curlew *Burhinus oedicnemus* in central Italy]. *Avocetta* **13(1)**: 15-20. In Italian with English summary.

Meschini, E., Arcamone, E. & Mainardi, R. (1979). Una colonia di Gabbiano Corso (*Larus audouinii*) nell'isola di Capraia. *Avocetta* **3**: 47-49.

Metcalfe, N.B. (1984a). The effects of habitat on the vigilance of shorebirds: is visibility important? *Anim. Behav.* **32**: 981-985.

Metcalfe, N.B. (1984b). The effects of mixed-species flocking on the vigilance of shorebirds: who do they trust? *Anim. Behav.* **32**: 986-993.

Metcalfe, N.B. (1985). Prey detection by intertidally feeding Lapwing. *Z. Tierpsychol.* **67**: 45-57.

Metcalfe, N.B. (1986). Variations in winter flocking associations and dispersion patterns in the Turnstone *Arenaria interpres*. *J. Zool., London* **209**: 385-403.

Metcalfe, N.B. (1989). Flocking preferences in relation to vigilance benefits and aggression costs in mixed-species shorebird flocks. *Oikos* **56**: 91-98.

Metcalfe, N.B. & Furness, R.W. (1984). Changing priorities: the effect of pre-migratory fattening on the trade-off between foraging and vigilance. *Behav. Ecol. Sociobiol.* **15**: 203-206.

Metcalfe, N.B. & Furness, R.W. (1985). Survival, winter population stability and site fidelity in the Turnstone *Arenaria interpres*. *Bird Study* **32**: 207-214.

Metcalfe, N.B. & Furness, R.W. (1987). Aggression in shorebirds in relation to flock density and composition. *Ibis* **129**: 553-563.

van Meurs, R.A. (1989). Possible breeding of African Skimmer in Egypt in June 1987. *Dutch Birding* **11(2)**: 77-78.

Mey, E. (1993). Zwei neue ischnocere Federlinge (Insecta, Phthiraptera) der Stelzenrallen (Mesitornithidae) von Madagascar. [Two new Ischnoceran Chewing Lice (Insecta, Phthiraptera) of the Mesites (Mesitornithidae) from Madagascar]. *Mitt. Zool. Mus. Berlin* **69**(Suppl. Ann. Orn. 17): 147-164.

Meyer, P.O. (1936). *Die Vögel des Bismarckarchipel*. Catholic Mission, Kokopo, New Britain.

Meyer de Schauensee, R. (1962). Notes on Venezuelan birds, with a history of the rail *Coturnicops notata*. *Notulae Naturae* **357**: 1-8.

Meyer de Schauensee, R. (1966). *The Species of Birds of South America and their Distribution*. Livingston, Narberth, Pennsylvania.

Meyer de Schauensee, R. (1982). *A Guide to the Birds of South America*. Livingston Publishing Company for the Academy of Natural Sciences of Philadelphia (reprinted with addenda by ICBP Pan-American Section), Wynnewood, Pennsylvania.

Meyer de Schauensee, R. (1984). *The Birds of China*. Smithsonian Institution Press, Washington, D.C.

Meyer de Schauensee, R. & Phelps, W.H. (1978). *A Guide to the Birds of Venezuela*. Princeton University Press, Princeton, New Jersey.

Meyer de Schauensee, R. & Ripley, S.D. (1940). *Zoological Results of the George Vanderbilt Sumatran Expedition, 1936-1939*. Part 1. Birds from Atjeh. Proceedings of Natural Sciences of Philadelphia **91**.

Mian, A. (1984). A contribution to the biology of Houbara: 1982-83 wintering population in Baluchistan. *J. Bombay Nat. Hist. Soc.* **81**: 537-545.

Mian, A. (1985). A contribution to the biology of Houbara: some evidences of breeding in Baluchistan. Pp. 261-269 in: *Proc. 5th Pakistan Congr. Zool.*

Mian, A. (1986a). Ecological impact of Arab falconry on Houbara Bustard in Baluchistan. *Environm. Cons.* **13(1)**: 41-46.

Mian, A. (1986b). A contribution to the biology of Houbara: some studies on gizzard contents from 1983-84 wintering population in the western Baluchistan. *Pakistan J. Zool.* **18**: 363-370.

Mian, A. (1988). A contribution to the biology of the Houbara (*Chlamydotis undulata macqueenii*): some observations on 1983-84 wintering population in Baluchistan. *J. Bombay Nat. Hist. Soc.* **81**: 9-25.

Mian, A. & Dasti, A.A. (1985). The Houbara Bustard in Baluchistan, 1982-83: a preliminary review. *Bustard Studies* **3**: 45-49.

Mian, A. & Surahio, M.I. (1983). Biology of Houbara Bustard (*Chlamydotis undulata macqueenii*) with reference to western Baluchistan. *J. Bombay Nat. Hist. Soc.* **80**: 111-118.

Mian, A., Warsi, S.S.T. & Rana, M.U. (1994). Radioactivity in some waders of southern Punjab Pakistan: a preliminary report. *Pakistan J. Zool.* **26**: 83-85.

Michael, C.W. (1938). Black Oystercatchers at Point Lobos. *Condor* **40**: 125 126.

Michaud, G. & Ferron, J. (1986). [Comparative study of feeding behavior of four species of shorebirds]. *Naturaliste Canadien* **113(3)**: 281-292. In French with English summary.

Michaud, G. & Ferron, J. (1990). [Prey-selection by four species of migratory shorebirds (Charadrii) in the estuary of the St. Lawrence River during southward migration]. *Can. J. Zool.* **68(6)**: 1154-1162. In French with English summary.

Michelutti, P.L. (1991). ¿*Numenius borealis* en Córdoba? *Nuestras Aves* **25**: 25.

Middlemiss, E. (1961). Biological aspects of *Calidris minuta* while wintering in south-west Cape. *Ostrich* **32**: 107-121.

Midura, A.M., Beyer, S.M. & Kilpatrick, H.J. (1991). An observation of human-induced adoption in Piping Plovers. *J. Field Orn.* **62(4)**: 429-431. In English with Spanish summary.

Mienis, H.K. (1985). Spur-winged Plovers killing a White-breasted Kingfisher. *Bull. Orn. Soc. Middle East* **15**: 5-6.

Mierauskas, P. & Buzun, V. (1991). Competitive interactions between the Herring Gull *L. a. cachinnans* and the Great Black-headed Gull *L. ichthyaetus* at Sivash Lake (South Ukraine). *Seevoegel* **12**: 34-35.

Mierauskas, P. & Greimas, E. (1992). Taxonomic status of Yellow-legged Herring Gulls in eastern Baltic. *Dutch Birding* **11**: 91-94.

Mierauskas, P., Greimas, E. & Buzun, V. (1991). A comparison of morphometrics, wing-tip pattern & vocalizations between Yellow-legged Herring Gulls (*Larus argentatus*) from Eastern Baltic and *Larus cachinnans*. *Acta Orn. Lituanica* **4**: 3-26.

Mikhalkin, K.F. & Bascakov, V.V. (1987). [The Asiatic Dowitcher in the Baikalski Strict nature reserve]. Page 145 in: [*The Problems of Rare Wildlife Conservation*]. Moscow. In Russian.

Mikhtaryantz, E.A. (1986). The breeding biology of Tufted Puffins - *Lunda cirrhata* (Pall.) - in the Commander Islands. Pp. 108-118 in: Litvinenko (1986).

Miles, D.H. (1986). White Terns breeding on Oahu, Hawaii. *Elepaio* **46**: 171-175.

Millar, C.D., Anthony, I., Lambert, D.M., Stapleton, P.M., Bergmann, C.C., Bellamy, A.R. & Young, E.C. (1994). Patterns of reproductive success determined by DNA fingerprinting in a communally breeding oceanic bird. *Biol. J. Linn. Soc.* **52**: 31-48.

Millar, C.D., Lambert, D.M., Bellamy, A.R., Stapleton, P.M. & Young, E.C. (1992). Sex-specific restriction fragments and sex ratios revealed by DNA fingerprinting in the Brown Skua. *J. Heredity* **83**: 350-355.

Milledge, D. (1972). The birds of Maatsuyker Island, Tasmania. *Emu* **72**: 167-170.

Millenbah, K. (1995). Working together for the Great Lakes Piping Plover. *Endangered Species Tech. Bull.* **19(6)**: 6.

Miller, A.H. (1931). Observations on the incubation and care of the young in the Jacanas. *Condor* **33**: 32-33.

Miller, A.H. (1943). Census of a colony of Caspian Terns. *Condor* **45**: 220-225.

Miller, A.H. (1953). A fossil Hoatzin from the Miocene of Colombia. *Auk* **70**: 484-489.

Miller, A.H. (1963). Seasonal activity and ecology of the avifauna of an American equatorial cloud forest. *Univ. Calif. Publ. Zool.* **66**: 1-74.

Miller, A.H. & Sibley, C.G. (1941). A Miocene gull from Nebraska. *Auk* **58**: 563-566.

Miller, B. & Kingston, T. (1980). Lord Howe Island Woodhen. *Parks & Wildl.* **1980**(Aug.): 17-26.

Miller, B. & Mullette, K.J. (1985). Rehabilitation of an endangered Australian bird: the Lord Howe Island Woodhen *Tricholimnas sylvestris* (Sclater). *Biol. Conserv.* **34**: 55-95.

Miller, B.J. & Knopf, F.L. (1993). Growth and survival of Mountain Plovers. *J. Field Orn.* **64**: 500-506, **65**: 193.

Miller, B.W. & Tilson, R.L. (1985). Snail Kite kleptoparasitism of Limpkins. *Auk* **102(1)**: 170-171.

Miller, D.E. & Conover, M.R. (1979). Differential effects of chick vocalizations and bill-pecking on parental behavior in the Ring-billed Gull. *Auk* **96**: 284-295.

Miller, D.E. & Emlen, J.T. (1975). Individual chick recognition and family integrity in the Ring-billed Gull. *Behaviour* **52**: 124-144.
Miller, D.L. & Causey, M.K. (1985). Food preferences of American Woodcock wintering in Alabama. *J. Wildl. Manage.* **49**: 492-496.
Miller, E.H. (1977). *Breeding Biology of the Least Sandpiper,* Calidris minutilla *(Vieill.), on Sable Island, Nova Scotia*. PhD dissertation, Dalhouse University, Halifax, Canada.
Miller, E.H. (1979a). Egg size in the Least Sandpiper (*Calidris minutilla*) (Vieill.), on Sable I., Nova Scotia, Canada. *Ornis Scand.* **10**: 10-16.
Miller, E.H. (1979b). Functions of display flights by males of the Least Sandpiper, *Calidris minutilla* (Vieill.), on Sable I., Nova Scotia. *Can. J. Zool.* **57**: 876-893.
Miller, E.H. (1983a). Habitat and breeding cycle of the Least Sandpiper (*Calidris minutilla*) on Sable I., Nova Scotia. *Can. J. Zool.* **61**: 2880-2898.
Miller, E.H. (1983b). Structure of display flights in the Least Sandpiper. *Condor* **85**: 220-242.
Miller, E.H. (1983c). The structure of aerial displays in three species of Calidridinae (Scolopacidae). *Auk* **100**: 440-451.
Miller, E.H. (1984). Communication in breeding shorebirds. Pp. 169-241 in: Burger & Olla (1984).
Miller, E.H. (1985). Parental behavior in the Least Sandpiper (*Calidris minutilla*). *Can. J. Zool.* **63**: 1593-1601.
Miller, E.H. (1986). Components of variation in nuptial calls of the Least Sandpiper (*Calidris minutilla*; Aves, Scolopacidae). *Syst. Zool.* **35**: 400-413.
Miller, E.H. (1992). *Acoustic Signals of Shorebirds. A Survey and Review of Published Information*. Royal British Columbia Museum Technical Report, Victoria, Canada.
Miller, E.H. (1995). Sounds of shorebirds: opportunities for amateurs and an update of published information. *Wader Study Group Bull.* **78**: 18-22.
Miller, E.H. & Baker, A.J. (1980). Displays of the Magellanic Oystercatcher *Haematopus leucopodus*. *Wilson Bull.* **92(2)**: 149-168.
Miller, E.H., Gunn, W.W.H. & Harris, R.E. (1983). Geographic variation in the aerial song of the Short-billed Dowitcher (Aves, Scolopacidae). *Can. J. Zool.* **61**: 2191-2198.
Miller, E.H., Gunn, W.W.H. & MacLean, S.F. (1987). Breeding vocalizations of the Surfbird. *Condor* **89(2)**: 406-412.
Miller, E.H., Gunn, W.W.H., Myers, J.P. & Veprintsev, B.N. (1984). Species-distinctiveness of Long-billed Dowitcher song (Aves: Scolopacidae). *Proc. Biol. Soc. Washington* **97**: 804-811.
Miller, E.H., Gunn, W.W.H. & Veprintsev, B.N. (1988). Breeding vocalizations of Baird's Sandpiper *Calidris bairdii* and related species, with remarks on phylogeny and adaption. *Ornis Scand.* **19(4)**: 257-267.
Miller, J.R. & Miller, J.T. (1948). Nesting of the Spotted Sandpiper at Detroit, Michigan. *Auk* **65**: 558-567.
Miller, R.S., Botkin, D.B. & Mendelssohn, R. (1974). The Whooping Crane (*Grus americana*) population of North America. *Biol. Conserv.* **6**: 106-111.
Miller, W.D. & Griscom, L. (1921). Descriptions of proposed new birds from Central America, with notes on other little-known forms. *Amer. Mus. Novit.* **25**: 1-13.
Miller, W.T. (1951). The Grey-headed Gull. *Bokmakierie* **3**: 30-31.
Millington, R. (1993). Identification and status of Kumlien's Gull. *Birding World* **6**: 101-106.
Mills, J.A. (1969). The distribution of breeding Red-billed Gull colonies in New Zealand in relation to areas of plankton enrichment. *Notornis* **16**: 180-186.
Mills, J.A. (1970). *The Population Ecology of Red-billed Gulls (*Larus novaehollandiae scopulinus*)*. PhD thesis, University of Canterbury, New Zealand.
Mills, J.A. (1971). Sexing Red-billed Gulls from standard measurements. *New Zealand J. Mar. Freshwater Res.* **5**: 326-328.
Mills, J.A. (1973a). Takahe research. *Wild. - Rev. New Zealand Wildl. Serv.* **4**: 24-27.
Mills, J.A. (1973b). The influence of age and pair-bond on the breeding biology of the Red-billed Gull *Larus novaehollandiae scopulinus*. *J. Anim. Ecol.* **42**: 147-162.
Mills, J.A. (1975). Population studies on Takahe, *Notornis mantelli* in Fiordland, New Zealand. *Bull. ICBP* **12**: 140-146.
Mills, J.A. (1976). Takahe-red Deer. *Wildl. - Rev. New Zealand Wildl. Serv.* **7**: 24-30.
Mills, J.A. (1979). Factors affecting the egg size of Red-billed Gulls *Larus novaehollandiae scopulinus*. *Ibis* **121**: 53-67.
Mills, J.A. (1989). Red-billed Gull. Pp. 387-404 in: Newton, I. ed. (1989). *Lifetime Reproduction in Birds*. Academic Press, London.
Mills, J.A. (1991). Lifetime reproduction in the Red-billed Gull. Pp. 1522-1527 in: Bell, B.D., Cossee, R.O., Flux, J.E.C., Heather, B.C., Hitchmough, R.A., Robertson, C.J.R. & Williams, M.J. eds. (1991). *Acta XX Congressus Internationalis Ornithologici*. Vol. 3. New Zealand Ornithological Congress Trust Board, Wellington.
Mills, J.A. & Lavers, R.B. (1974). Preliminary results of research into the present status of Takahe (*Notornis mantelli*) in the Murchison Mountains. *Notornis* **21**: 312-317.
Mills, J.A. & Mark, A.F. (1977). Food preferences of Takahe in Fiordland National Park, New Zealand, and the effect of competition from introduced Red Deer. *J. Animal Ecol.* **46**: 939-958.
Mills, J.A., Lavers, R.B. & Lee, W.G. (1984). The Takahe - a relict of the Pleistocene grassland avifauna of New Zealand. *New Zealand J. Ecol.* **7**: 57-70.
Mills, J.A., Lee, W.G., Mark, A.F. & Lavers, R.B. (1980). Winter use by Takahe (*Notornis mantelli*) of the Summer-green Fern (*Hypolepis millefolium*) in relation to its annual cycle of carbohydrates and minerals. *New Zealand J. Ecol.* **3**: 131-137.
Milne-Edwards, A. & Grandidier, A. (1885). *Histoire Physique, Naturelle et Politique de Madagascar*. Vol. 12. Histoire Naturelle des Oiseaux. Tome 1. Société d'Editions Géographiques, Maritimes et Coloniales, Paris.
Milon, P. (1947). Note on the nidification in Madagascar of the South African Whiskered Tern. *Ostrich* **18**: 183-187.
Milon, P. (1948). Notes d'observation à Madagascar. *Alauda* **16**: 55-74.
Milon, P. (1951). Notes sur l'avifaune actuelle de l'île de la Réunion. *Terre Vie* **98**: 129-178.
Milon, P. & Jouanin, C. (1953). Contribution à l'ornithologie de l'Île Kerguelen. *Oiseau et RFO* **23**: 4-53.
Milon, P., Petter, J.J. & Randrianasolo, G. (1973). *Faune de Madagascar*. Vol. 35. Oiseaux. ORSTOM & CNRS, Tananarive & Paris.
Milsom, T.P. (1984). Diurnal behaviour of Lapwings in relation to moonphase during winter. *Bird Study* **31**: 117-120.
Milsom, T.P. (1990). Lapwings *Vanellus vanellus* on aerodromes and the birdstrike hazard. *Ibis* **132(2)**: 218-231.
Milsom, T.P., Holditch, R.S. & Rochard, J.B.A. (1985). Diurnal use of an airfield and adjacent agricultural habitats by Lapwings *Vanellus vanellus*. *J. Appl. Ecol.* **22**: 313-326.
Milsom, T.P., Rochard, J.B.A. & Poole, S.J. (1990). Activity patterns of Lapwings *Vanellus vanellus* in relation to the lunar cycle. *Ornis Scand.* **21(2)**: 147-156.
Milton, G.R. (1985). Notes on the distribution of the Masked Finfoot *Heliopais personata* in Indonesia. *Kukila* **2**: 41-43.
Minaya, N.G. (1968). Informe sobre estudios ornitológicos realizados en el laboratorio de la Puntilla (Pisco) en Septiembre de 1965/55. *Instituto del Mar (Perú) Informes Especiales* **31**: 18-19.
Minton, C. (1983). Further sightings of colour marked birds. *Victorian Wader Study Group Bull.* **3**: 10-11.
Minton, C. (1987). Report on visit to N.W. Australia 21 March to 5 April 1987. *Stilt* **11**: 6-12.
Minton, C. (1989). Banded Stilts do breed. *RAOU Newsl.* **80**: 3.
Minton, C. (1993). Migratory departure dates for Eastern Curlew. *Victorian Wader Study Group Bull.* **17**: 21-23.
Minton, C. & Campbell, J. (1995). Long-billed Dowitcher: a new species for Australia? *Wingspan* **5(3)**: 40.
Minton, C., Lane, J. & Pearson, G. (1995). Update on Banded Stilt breeding event. *Wingspan* **5(3)**: 9.
Minton, C., Pearson, G. & Lane, J. (1995). History in the mating: Banded Stilts do it again! *Wingspan* **5(2)**: 13-15.
Minton, C.D.T. (1987a). Double-banded Plover finale. *Stilt* **10**: 7.
Minton, C.D.T. (1987b). Trans-Tasman movements of Double-banded Plovers. *Victorian Wader Study Group Bull.* **11**: 27-34.
Minton, C.D.T. & Pierce, R.J. (1986). Migration studies of Double-banded Plovers. *Stilt* **8**: 27.
Miranda-Ribeiro, A. (1937). A seriema. *Rev. Mus. Paulista* **23**: 35-90.
Mirande, C., Lacy, R. & Seal, U. (1993). *Whooping Crane Conservation Viability Assessment Workshop Report*. IUCN Captive Breeding Specialist Group. Apple Valley, Minnesota.
Miskelly, C.M. (1981). Leg colour and dominance in Buff Wekas. *Notornis* **28**: 47-48.
Miskelly, C.M. (1987). The identity of the Hakawai. *Notornis* **34**: 95-116.
Miskelly, C.M. (1988). The Little Barrier Island Snipe. *Notornis* **35(4)**: 273-281.
Miskelly, C.M. (1989). Flexible incubation system and prolonged incubation in New Zealand Snipe. *Wilson Bull.* **101(1)**: 127-132.
Miskelly, C.M. (1990a). Breeding systems of New Zealand Snipe *Coenocorypha aucklandica* and Chatham Snipe *C. pusilla*; are they food limited? *Ibis* **132(3)**: 366-379.
Miskelly, C.M. (1990b). Effects of the 1982-83 El Niño event on two endemic landbirds on the Snares Islands, New Zealand. *Emu* **90(1)**: 24-27.
Miskelly, C.M. (1990c). Aerial displaying and flying ability of Chatham Island Snipe *Coenocorypha pusilla* and New Zealand Snipe *C. aucklandica*. *Emu* **90(1)**: 28-32.
Miskelly, C.M., Cooper, W.J., Morrison, K. & Morrison, J.V. (1985). Snipe in Southland. *Notornis* **32(4)**: 327-328.
Mitchell, C.A. & Custer, T.W. (1986). Hatching success of Caspian Terns nesting in the lower Laguna Madre, Texas, USA. *Colonial Waterbirds* **9**: 86-89.
Mitchell, M.H. (1957). *Observations on Birds of Southeastern Brazil*. University of Toronto Press, Toronto.
Mitchell, P.C. (1915). Anatomical notes on the Gruiform birds *Aramus giganteus* Bonap. and *Rhinochetus kagu*. *Proc. Zool. Soc., London* **1915**: 413-423.
Mitchell, S. (1977). Apparently atypical habitat and behaviour of Peters' Finfoot. *Honeyguide* **92**: 43.
Miyagi, K. (1989). Conservation of Okinawa Rail and Okinawa Woodpecker. Proceedings Joint Meeting of International Council for Bird Preservation Asian Section and East Asia Bird Protection Conference, Bangkok, Thailand. Unpublished.
Mjelstad, H. & Saetersdal, M. (1986). Density, population size and breeding distribution of Spotted Redshank *Tringa erythropus*, Bar-tailed Godwit *Limosa lapponica* and Jack Snipe *Lymnocryptes minimus* in Norway. *Fauna Norvegica (Ser. C, Cinclus)* **9(1)**: 13-16. In English with Norwegian summary.
Mjelstad, H. & Saetersdal, M. (1987). When does the female Spotted Redshank *Tringa erythropus* leave the breeding grounds? *Fauna Norvegica (Ser. C, Cinclus)* **10(1)**: 57-58. In English with Norwegian summary.
Mlody, B.V. & Becker, P.H. (1991). [The development of body mass and mortality in chicks of the Common Tern (*Sterna hirundo*) under unfavourable environmental conditions]. *Vogelwarte* **36(2)**: 110-131. In German with English summary.
Mmari, E.D.J. (1996). The effects of pastoralism on Gray Crowned Cranes at West Kilimanjaro Ranch. In: Beilfuss *et al.* (1996).
Mochizuki, H. & Ueta, M. (1995). [Decrease of Japanese Murrelets in Izu Islands, central Japan]. *Strix* **14**. In Japanese with English summary.
Modafferi, R.D. (1967). *A Population Behavior Study of Male American Woodcock on Central Massachusetts Singing Grounds*. MSc thesis, University of Massachusetts, Amherst, Massachusetts.
Modesto, V.M. (1943). [Ecology of nesting period of gulls in the Volga Delta]. *Zoologischeskii Zhurnal* **22**: 92-101. In Russian.
Modha, M.L. & Coe, M.J. (1969). Notes on the breeding of the African Skimmer *Rynchops flavirostris* on Central Island, Lake Rudolf. *Ibis* **111**: 593-598.
Mödlinger, P. (1973-1974). A zarttéri tenyésztés mint a veszélyeztetett fajok megmentésének egyik jarhato utja - az ugartyuk (*Burhinus oedicnemus*) tenyésztése. [The breeding in captivity by one of the rearing methods for restoring endangered species: breeding of the Stone Curlew *Burhinus oedicnemus*]. *Aquila* **80-81**: 189-196. In Hungarian with German summary.
Mödlinger, P. (1978). Az ugarty'uk (*Burhinus oedicnemus*) elöfordul'asa 'es ökol'ogiai viszonyai magyarorsz'agon. [Occurrence and ecology of *Burhinus oedicnemus* in Hungary]. *Aquila* **85**: 59-75. In Hungarian with German summary.
Moe, R.A. & Day, R.H. (1979). Populations and ecology of seabirds of the Koniuju Group, Shumagin Islands, Alaska. *US Dept. Commerce., NOAA, OCSEAP Annual Rep.* **2**: 395-516.
Moen, S.M. (1991). Morphologic and genetic variation among breeding colonies of the Atlantic Puffin *Fratercula arctica*. *Auk* **108**: 755-763.
Moerbeek, D.J. (1993). Ross' Meeuw te Ijmuiden in november 1992. *Dutch Birding* **15(1)**: 7-13.
Moksnes, A. (1987). Food biology of Ringed Plovers *Charadrius hiaticula* and Temmink's Stints *Calidris temminckii* in the regulation zone of a hydroelectric power reservoir. *Fauna Norvegica (Ser. C, Cinclus)* **10(2)**: 103-113.
Moksnes, A. (1988). Grit in the stomachs of Ringed Plovers *Charadrius hiaticula* and Temminck's Stints *Calidris temminckii* during breeding. *Fauna Norvegica (Ser. C, Cinclus)* **11(1)**: 7-10.
Møller, A.P. (1975a). Europaeiske Sandterners (*Gelochelidon nilotica nilotica*) traek belyst ved hjaelp af ringmaerkning. [Migration of European Gull-billed Terns (*Gelochildon nilotica nilotica*) according to recoveries]. *Danske Fugle* **27**: 61-73.
Møller, A.P. (1975b). Ynglebstanden af Sandterne (*Gelochelidon nilotica nilotica*) Gmel. i 1972 i Europa, Afrika og det vestlige Asien med en oversight over bestandsaendringer i dette arhundred. [The breeding population of Gull-billed Tern (*Gelochelidon nilotica nilotica*) Gmel. in 1972 in Europe, Africa, and Western Asia, with a review of fluctuations during the present century]. *Dan. Orn. Foren. Tidssk.* **69**: 1-8.
Møller, A.P. (1975c). Sandternens (*Gelochelidon n. nilotica* Gm) ynglebiologi i Danmark. [The breeding biology of the Gull-billed Tern *Gelochelidon n. nilotica* Gm.) in Denmark]. *Dan. Orn. Foren. Tiddsk.* **69**: 9-18.
Møller, A.P. (1978a). Deserting flights in the Gull-billed Tern (*Gelochelidon nilotica nilotica*) with specieal reference to the Danish population. *Dan. Orn. Foren. Tidssk.* **72**: 119-126.
Møller, A.P. (1978b). [Feeding areas of the Gull-billed Tern *Gelochelidon n. nilotica* Gmel. during the breeding season]. *Dan. Orn. Foren. Tidsk.* **72**: 145-147. In Danish.
Møller, A.P. (1981). Breeding cycle of the Gull-billed Tern (*Gelochelidon nilotica*) especially in relation to colony size. *Ardea* **69**: 193-198.
Møller, A.P. (1982). Coloniality and colony structure in Gull-billed Tern *Gelochelidon nilotica*. *J. Orn.* **123**: 41-53.
Molodan, G.N. (1988). [Black-winged Pratincole]. Pp. 117-118 in: Voinstvenskiy, M.A. ed. (1988). [*Colonial Waterbirds of South Ukraine: the Waders*]. Naukova Dumka, Kiev. In Russian.
Molodan, G.N. & Pozhidayeva, S.I. (1991). [The state of the Black-winged Pratincole population in the Ukraine and the methods for its preservation]. Pp. 85-86 in: Galushin, V.M. ed. (1991). [*Abstracts 10th USSR Ornithological Conference. Part 2*]. Nauka i Tekhnika, Vitebsk & Minsk. In Russian.
Momiyama, T.T. (1930). On the birds of Bonin and the Iwo-Islands. *Bull. Bio-Geogr. Soc. Japan* **1**: 89-186.
Momose, K. & Nakamura, R. (1983). Present status and protection of Japanese Cranes in Hokkaido. *Strix* **2**: 121-130.
Monaghan, P. (1979). Aspects of the breeding biology of Herring Gulls *Larus argentatus* in urban colonies. *Ibis* **121**: 475-481
Monaghan, P. (1980). Dominance and dispersal between feeding sites in the Herring Gull (*Larus argentatus*). *Anim. Behav.* **28**: 521-527.
Monaghan, P., Metcalfe, N.B. & Hansell, M.H. (1986). The influence of food availability and competition on the use of a feeding site by Herring Gulls *Larus argentatus*. *Bird Study* **33**: 87-90.
Monaghan, P., Uttley, J.D. & Burns, M.D. (1988). The relationship between food supply, reproductive effort and breeding success in Arctic Terns. Pp. 1-57 in: Tasker (1988).
Monaghan, P., Uttley, J.D. & Burns, M.D. (1992). Effect of changes in food availability on reproductive effort in Arctic Terns. *Ardea* **80**: 71-81.
Monaghan, P., Uttley, J.D. & Okill, J.D. (1989). Terns and sandeels: seabirds as indicators of changes in marine fish populations. *J. Fish. Biol.* **35**(Suppl. A): 339-340.
Monbailliu, X. & Torre, A. (1986). Nest-site selection and interaction of Yellow-legged and Audouin's Gulls at Isola dell'Asinara. Pp. 245-263 in: MEDMARAVIS & Monbailliu (1986).
Moncrieff, P. (1928). Bird migration in New Zealand. *Emu* **28**: 138-149.
Monk, J.F. ed. (1992). *Avian Systematics and Taxonomy*. Bulletin of the British Ornithologists' Club. Centenary Supplement **112A**.
Monroe, B.L. (1955). A gull new to North America. *Auk* **72**: 208.
Monroe, B.L. (1956). Observations of Elegant Terns at San Diego, California. *Wilson Bull.* **68**: 239-244.
Monroe, B.L. (1968). *A Distributional Survey of the Birds of Honduras*. Ornithological Monographs **7**. American Ornithologists' Union, Washington, D.C. 458 pp.
Monroe, B.L. (1989). The correct name of the Terek Sandpiper. *Bull. Brit. Orn. Club* **109**: 106-107.
Montalti, D. & Coria, N.R. (1993). The use of the stomach-flushing technique to obtain stomach contents samples of Antarctic seabirds. *Riv. ital. Orn.* **63(1)**: 69-73.
Montevecchi, W.A. (1975). *Behavioral and Ecological Factors Influencing the Reproductive Success of a Tidal Salt Marsh Colony of Laughing Gulls (*Larus atricilla*)*. PhD dissertation, Rutgers University, New Brunswick, New Jersey.
Montevecchi, W.A. (1976). Eggshell removal by Laughing Gull. *Bird-Banding* **47**: 219-135.
Montevecchi, W.A. (1977). Predation in a salt marsh Laughing Gull colony. *Auk* **94**: 583-585.
Montevecchi, W.A. (1978). Nest site selection and its survival value among Laughing Gulls. *Behav. Ecol. Sociobiol.* **4**: 148-161.
Montevecchi, W.A. (1979). The seasonal timing and dispersion of egg-laying among Laughing Gulls *Larus atricilla*. *Ibis* **121**: 337-344.
Montevecchi, W.A., Cairns, D.K., Burger, A.E., Elliot, R.D. & Wells, J. (1987). The status of the Common Black-headed Gull in Newfoundland and Labrador. *Amer. Birds* **41**: 197-203.

Moody, A.F. (1932). *Water-fowl and Game-birds in Captivity*. Witherby, London.
Moojen, J., Carvalho, J.C. de M. & Lopes, H. de S. (1941). Observações sobre o conteúdo gástrico das aves brasileiras. *Mem. Inst. Oswaldo Cruz* **36(3)**: 405-444.
Moon, G.J.H. (1960). *Focus on New Zealand Birds*. Wellington.
Moon, S.J. (1983). Little Whimbrel: new to Britain and Ireland. *British Birds* **76(10)**: 438-445.
Moore, C.C. (1996). Ship-attending movements of Atlantic Yellow-legged Gulls in Portuguese waters. *Dutch Birding* **18(1)**: 17-18.
Moore, M.E. (1954). Probable Australian Avocet at Catlins River. *Notornis* **5(7)**: 239.
Moore, P.J. (1983). Marsh Crake at Lake Wairarapa. *Notornis* **30(3)**: 246-249.
Moore, R. & Vernon, C. (1973). Crowned Plover nesting in loose colonies. *Ostrich* **44(3-4)**: 262.
Moore, R.D. (1981). Long-tailed Skuas *Stercorarius longicaudus* at the Kenya coast. *Scopus* **5**: 79.
Moore, R.J. & Balzarotti, M.A. (1983). Observations of sea birds nesting on islands of the Sudanese Red Sea. *Bull. Brit. Orn. Club* **103(2)**: 65-71.
Moors, P.J. (1980). Southern Great Skuas on Antipodes Island, New Zealand: observations on foods, breeding and growth of chicks. *Notornis* **27(2)**: 133-146.
Moreau, R.E. (1946). Coition of Three-banded Plover *Charadrius tricollaris tricollaris* Vieillot. *Ibis* **88**: 524-525.
Moreau, R.E. (1972). *The Palaearctic-African Bird Migration Systems*. Academic Press, London.
Moreira, F. (1994). Diet, prey-sized selection and intake rates of Black-tailed Godwits *Limosa limosa* feeding on mudflats. *Ibis* **136(3)**: 349-355.
Moreira, F. (1995a). The winter feeding ecology of Avocets *Recurvirostra avosetta* on intertidal areas. I. Feeding strategies. *Ibis* **137(1)**: 92-98.
Moreira, F. (1995b). The winter feeding ecology of Avocets *Recurvirostra avosetta* on intertidal areas. II. Diet and feeding mechanisms. *Ibis* **137(1)**: 99-108.
Morel, G.J. & Chappuis, C. (1992). Past and future taxonomic research in West Africa. Pp. 217-224 in: Monk (1992).
Morel, G.J. & Morel, M.Y. (1990). *Les Oiseaux de Sénégambie*. Editions de l'ORSTOM, Paris.
Morel, G.J. & Roux, F. (1966). Les migrateurs paléarctiques au Sénégal. *Terre Vie* **113**: 19-72, 143-176.
Morel, R. (1989). A note on the status of bustards in Mali, Mauritania and Senegal. *Bustard Studies* **4**: 123-124.
Morell, V. (1994). The really secret life of plants. *New York Times Magazine* **18**(Dec.): 50-53.
Moreno, A. (1953). Consideration about the systematic value of *Laterallus jamaicensis jamaicensis* (Gmelin) and *Laterallus jamaicensis pygmaeus* (Blackwell). *Torreia* **20**. 8 pp.
Morgan, B. & Morgan, J. (1968). The Bush-hen in southeastern Queensland. *Emu* **68**: 150.
Morgan, K.H. (1994). Underwater swimming behavior of American Black Oystercatcher chicks. *J. Field Orn.* **65(3)**: 406-409. In English with Spanish summary.
Morgan, K.H., Paganelli, C.V. & Rahn, H. (1978). Egg weight loss and nest humidity during incubation in two Alaskan gulls. *Condor* **80**: 272-275.
Morgan, R.A. (1985). Thickknee. Pp. 590-591 in: Campbell & Lack (1985).
Morgan, R.A. & Shorten, M. (1974). Breeding of the Woodcock in Britain. *Bird Study* **21**: 193-199.
Morgan-Davies, A.M. (1960a). A nesting colony of Avocets at Lake Manyara, Tanganyika. *J. East Afr. & Uganda Nat. Hist. Soc.* **23(6)**: 241-243.
Morgan-Davies, A.M. (1960b). The Chestnut-banded Plover at Lake Manyara, Tanganyika. *J. East Afr. & Uganda Nat. Hist. Soc.* **23(7)**: 299.
Morgan-Davies, A.M. (1965). On the Kori Bustard, *Ardeotis kori* (Burchell) in north-western Tanzania. *Bull. Brit. Orn. Club* **85(8)**: 145-147.
Morozov, V.V. (1988). [Breeding biology and space using by the Marsh Sandpiper (*Tringa stagnatilis*) and the Redshank (*Tringa totanus*)]. Pp. 100-110 in: Flint & Tomkovich (1988). In Russian.
Morozov, V.V. (1993a). Zonal peculiarities of the ecology of Whimbrel. *Russ. J. Ecol.* **24(2)**: 118-122.
Morozov, V.V. (1993b). [Territoriality and mating behaviour of the Pintail Snipe *Gallinago stenura* males in the European tundra]. *Russ. J. Orn.* **2(2)**: 181-189. In Russian with English summary.
Morozov, V.V. (1994). Great Snipe. *Gallinago media*. Pp. 268-269 in: Tucker & Heath (1994).
Morozov, V.V. & Tomkovich, P.S. (1984). [Regularities of distribution and nesting habitats of Red-necked Stint (*Calidris ruficollis* Pall.)]. *Biologicheskie Nauki* **4**: 42-48. In Russian.
Morozov, V.V. & Tomkovich, P.S. (1986). [Dynamics of spatial organization of a population of the Red-necked Stint (*Calidris ruficollis*) in the reproductive period]. *Ornitologiya* **21**: 38-47. In Russian.
Morozov, V.V. & Tomkovich, P.S. (1988). [Breeding biology of Red-necked Stint (*Calidris ruficollis*) on eastern Chukotski Peninsula]. *Arch. Zool. Mus. Moscow State Univ.* **26**: 184-206. In Russian.
Morrell, S.H., Huber, H.R., Lewis, T.J. & Ainley, D.G. (1979). Feeding ecology of Black Oystercatchers on South Farallon Island, California. Pp. 185-186 in: Pitelka (1979).
Morrier, A. & McNeil, R. (1991). Time activity budget of Wilson's and Semipalmated Plovers in a tropical environment. *Wilson Bull.* **103(4)**: 598-620.
Morris, A. (1986). An account of New York state's first Rufous-necked Stint. *Kingbird* **36(1)**: 3-5.
Morris, A. (1987). The status of cranes in Zimbabwe. Pp. 345-348 in: Archibald & Pasquier (1987a).
Morris, A.K. (1971). The Red-chested Quail in New South Wales. *Emu* **71(4)**: 178-181.
Morris, A.K. (1972). The Grey Noddy in Australia. *Austr. Bird Watcher* **5**: 203.
Morris, A.K. (1975). The birds of Gosford, Wyong and Newcastle (County of Northumberland). *Austr. Birds* **9**: 37-76.
Morris, A.K. (1989). Hooded Plover survey - New South Wales. *Stilt* **14**: 37.
Morris, A.K. (1991). Hudsonian Godwit: first Australian and New South Wales record. *Austr. Birds* **25(1)**: 24-25.
Morris, A.K. & Kurtz, N. (1977). Red-chested and Little Button-quail in the Mudgee district of New South Wales. *Corella* **1(4)**: 77-79.
Morris, P. (1992). A record of Great Black-headed Gull (*Larus ichthyaetus*) in Thailand. *Nat. Hist. Bull. Siam Soc.* **40**: 193-195.
Morris, P. (1993). The first record of Pied Avocet (*Recurvirostra avosetta*) for Thailand. *Nat. Hist. Bull. Siam Soc.* **41(1)**: 69.
Morris, R.B. (1976). Stoat predation at a Red-billed Gull colony, Kaikoura. *Notornis* **23**: 354.
Morris, R.B. (1977). Observations of Takahe nesting behaviour at Mount Bruce. *Notornis* **24(1)**: 54-58.
Morris, R.D. (1984). Breeding chronology and reproductive success of seabirds on Little Tobago, Trinidad, 1975-76. *Colonial Watebirds* **7**: 1-9.
Morris, R.D. (1986). Seasonal differences in courtship feeding rates of male Common Terns. *Can. J. Zool.* **64**: 501-507.
Morris, R.D. (1987). Time-partitioning of clutch and brood care activities in Herring Gulls: a measure of parental quality? Pp. 58-73 in: Hand *et al*. (1987).
Morris, R.D. & Bidochka, M.J. (1983). Mate-guarding in Herring Gulls. *Colonial Waterbirds* **5**: 124-130.
Morris, R.D. & Chardine, J.W. (1985). The effects of ice cover over the colony site on reproductive activities in Herring Gulls. *Can. J. Zool.* **63**: 607-611.
Morris, R.D. & Chardine, J.W. (1990). Costs of parental neglect in the Brown Noddy (*Anous stolidus*). *Can. J. Zool.* **68**: 2025-2027.
Morris, R.D. & Chardine, J.W. (1992). The breeding biology and aspects of the foraging ecology of Brown Noddies nesting near Culebra, Puerto Rico 1985-1989. *J. Zool., London* **226**: 65-79.
Morris, R.D. & Hunter, R.A. (1976). Factors influencing desertion of colony sites by Common Terns (*Sterna hirundo*). *Can. Field-Nat.* **90**: 137-143.
Morris, R.D. & Wiggins, D.A. (1986). Ruddy Turnstones, Great Horned Owls and egg loss from Common Tern clutches. *Wilson Bull.* **98**: 101-109.
Morris, R.D., Blokpoel, H. & Tessier, G.D. (1992). Management efforts for the conservation of Common Tern colonies: two case histories. *Biol. Conserv.* **60**: 7-14.
Morris, R.D., Kirkham, I.R. & Chardine, J.W. (1980). Management of a declining Common Tern colony. *J. Wildl. Manage.* **44**: 241-245.
Morris, R.D., Woufle, M. & Wichert, G.D. (1991). Hatching asynchrony, chick care and adoption in the Common Tern: can disadvantaged chicks win? *Can. J. Zool.* **69**: 661-668.
Morris, R.P. (1992). Observations on a colony of Crab Plovers *Dromas ardeola* in Abu Dhabi. *Sandgrouse* **14(1)**: 34-47.
Morrison, A. (1939a). Notes on birds of Lake Junin, central Peru. *Ibis* **Ser. 14, no. 3**: 643-654.
Morrison, A. (1939b). A new coot from Peru. *Bull. Brit. Orn. Club* **59**: 56-57.
Morrison, R.I.G. (1975). Migration and morphometrics of European Knot and Turnstone on Ellesmere Island, Canada. *Bird Banding* **46**: 290-301.
Morrison, R.I.G. (1976). Moult of the Purple Sandpiper *Calidris maritima* in Iceland. *Ibis* **118**: 237-246.
Morrison, R.I.G. (1977). Migration of arctic waders wintering in Europe. *Polar Record* **18**: 475-486.
Morrison, R.I.G. (1980). First specimen of the Little Stint (*Calidris minuta*) for North America. *Auk* **97(3)**: 627-628.
Morrison, R.I.G. (1991). Research requirements for shorebird conservation. *Trans. North Amer. Wildl. Nat. Resour. Conf.* **56**: 473-480.
Morrison, R.I.G. (1992). Early records of Knot migration in Iceland. Pp. 95-100 in: Piersma & Davidson (1992b).
Morrison, R.I.G. & Harrington, B.A. (1992). The migration system of the Red Knot in the New World. *Wader Study Group Bull.* **64**(Suppl.): 71-84.
Morrison, R.I.G. & Manning, T.H. (1976). First breeding records of Wilson's Phalarope for James Bay, Ontario. *Auk* **93**: 656-657.
Morrison, R.I.G. & Myers, J.P. (1989). *Shorebird Flyways in the New World*. IWRB Special Publication **9**, Slimbridge, UK.
Morrison, R.I.G. & Ross, R.K. (1989). *Atlas of Nearctic Shorebirds on the Coast of South America*. Vol 1. Canadian Wildlife Service Special Publication, Ottawa.
Morrison, R.I.G. & Wilson, J.R. (1992). Observations of Knot migration in Iceland 1970-1972. Pp. 101-109 in: Piersma & Davidson (1992b).
Morrison, R.I.G., Antas, P.T.Z. & Ross, R.K. (1987). Migratory routes in the Amazon coast. Pp. 159-199 in: de Freitas, M. de L.D. ed. (1987). *Anais Seminario Desenvolvimento Impacto Ambiental Areas Tropico Umido Brasileiro - a Experencia da CVRD, Belem, Para*. Companhia Vale do Rio Doce, Rio de Janeiro.
Morrison, R.I.G., Downes, C. & Collins, B. (1994). Population trends on shorebirds on fall migration in eastern Canada 1974-1991. *Wilson Bull.* **106**: 431-447.
Morton, E.S. (1979). Status of endemic birds of the Zapata Swamp, Cuba. Unpublished memorandum to S.D. Ripley, 6 November.
Morton, H.J. (1953). Notes on Spotless Crake (*Porzana plumbea*). *S. Austr. Orn.* **21**: 5.
Morton, S.R., Brennan, K.G. & Armstrong, M.D. (1990). Distribution and abundance of waterbirds in the Alligator Rivers region, Northern Territory. Report to the Australian National Parks & Wildlife Service.
Morton, S.R., Brennan, K.G. & Armstrong, M.D. (1993). Distribution and abundance of Brolgas and Black-necked Storks in the Alligator Rivers Region, Northern Territory. *Emu* **93(2)**: 88-92.
Morvan, P., Mougin, J.L. & Prévost, J. (1967). Écologie du Skua antarctique (*Stercorarius skua maccormicki*) dans l'Archipel de Pointe Geologie (Terre Adelie). *Oiseau et RFO* **37**: 193-220.
Mosansky, A. (1977). Prve hniezdenie sisily bocianovitej (*Himantopus himantopus* L. 1758) na Slovensku a poznamky k teritorialnym zmenam jej populacie v Europe. [First nesting of a Black-winged Stilt (*Himantopus himantopus* L., 1758) in Slovakia and notes on territorial changes of its population in Europe]. *Biologia* **32(4)**: 881-892. In Czech with Russian and English summaries.
Moseley, L.J. (1979). Individual auditory recognition in the Least Tern (*Sterna albifrons*). *Auk* **96**: 31-39.
Moser, M.E. (1988). Limits to the numbers of Grey Plovers *Pluvialis squatarola* wintering on British estuaries: an analysis of long-term population trends. *J. Appl. Ecol.* **25(2)**: 473-485.
Moser, M.E. & Carrier, M. (1983). Patterns of population turnover in Ringed Plovers and Turnstones during their spring passage through the Solway Firth in 1983. *Wader Study Group Bull.* **39**: 37-41.
Moser, M.L. & Lee, D.S. (1992). A fourteen-year survey of plastic ingestion by western North Atlantic seabirds. *Colonial Waterbirds* **15**: 83-94.
Moseykin, V.N. (1992). Ecology and protection of the Little Bustard in the Saratov region. *Bustard Studies* **5**: 78-91.
Moskoff, W. (1995). Solitary Sandpiper (*Tringa solitaria*). No. **156** in: Poole & Gill (1994-1995).
Mossman, A.S. (1958). Selective predation of Glaucous-winged Gulls upon adult red salmon. *Ecology* **39**: 482-486.
Mosso, E.D. & Beltzer, A.H. (1993). Nota sobre la dieta de *Fulica leucoptera* en el valle aluvial del Río Paraná medio, Argentina. *Orn. Neotropical* **4**: 91-93.
Mougin, J.L. & de Naurois, R. (1981). Le Noddi bleu des îles Gambier *Procelsterna caerulea murphyi* ssp. nov. *Oiseau et RFO* **51**: 201-204.
Mountfort, G. (1988). *Rare Birds of the World*. Collins, London.
Mourer-Chauviré, C. (1981). Première indication de la présence de Phorusrhacidés, famille d'oiseaux géants d'Amerique do Sud, dans le Tertiaire européan: *Ameghinornis* nov. gen. *Geobios* **14**: 637-647.
Mouritsen, K.N. (1992). Predator avoidance in night-feeding Dunlins *Calidris alpina*: a matter of concealment. *Ornis Scand.* **23**: 195-198.
Mouritsen, K.N. (1993). Diurnal and nocturnal prey detection by Dunlins *Calidris alpina*. *Bird Study* **40(3)**: 212-215.
Mouritsen, K.N. (1994). Day and night feeding in Dunlins *Calidris alpina*: choice of habitat, foraging technique and prey. *J. Avian Biol.* **25(1)**: 55-62.
Mouritsen, K.N. & Jensen, K.T. (1992). Choice of microhabitat in tactile foraging Dunlins *Calidris alpina*: the importance of sediment penetrability. *Mar. Ecol. Progr. Ser.* **85**: 1-8.
Mousley, H. (1937). A study of Virginia and Sora Rails at their nests. *Wilson Bull.* **49**: 80-84.
Mousley, H. (1940). Further notes on the nesting habits of the Virginia Rail. *Wilson Bull.* **52**: 87-90.
Moyle, P. (1966). Feeding behavior of the Glaucous-winged Gull on an Alaskan salmon stream. *Wilson Bull.* **78**: 175-190.
Moynihan, M.M. (1955). *Some Aspects of Reproductive Behavior in the Black-headed Gull (*Larus ridibundus ridibundus *L.) and Related Species*. Behaviour **4**(Supplement). 201 pp.
Moynihan, M.M. (1959). A revision of the family Laridae (Aves). *Amer. Mus. Novit.* **1928**: 1-42.
Moynihan, M.M. (1962). *Hostile and Sexual Behaviour Patterns of South American and Pacific Laridae*. Behaviour **8**(Supplement). 365 pp.
Mudge, G.P. & Ferns, P.N. (1982). The feeding ecology of five species of gulls (Aves: Larini) in the inner Bristol Channel. *J. Zool., London* **197**: 497-510.
Mueller, H. (1959). Die Zugerhaltnisse der europäischen Brandseeschwalben (*Sterna sandvicensis*) nach Beringungsergebnissen. *Vogelwarte* **20**: 91-115.
Mukherjee, A.K. (1975). Food-habits of water-birds of Sundarban, 24 Parganas District, West Bengal, India-V. Lapwing, Sandpiper, Stint, Tern, Kingfisher. *J. Bombay Nat. Hist. Soc.* **72**: 422-447.
Mukhina, Y.A. (1990). [*Chlamydotis undulata macqueenii* in the Bukhara Gazelle Nursery: settlement pattern, population dynamics, and ecology]. *Zoologischeskii Zhurnal* **69(7)**: 107-116. In Russian with English summary.
Mulder, J.L. & Swaan, A.H. (1992). Body-weight changes of egg-laying Curlews *Numenius arquata*, as monitored by an automatic weighing system. *Ardea* **80(2)**: 273-279.
Mulder, T. (1972). *De Grutto in Nederland*. Wetenschappelijke Mededelingen Koninklijke Nederlandse Natuurhistorische Vereniging **90**. 52 pp.
Mulholland, R. (1983). *Feeding Ecology of the Common Moorhen and Purple Gallinule on Orange Lake, Florida*. MSc thesis, University of Florida, Gainesville, Florida.
Mulholland, R. & Percival, H.F. (1982). Food habits of the Common Moorhen and Purple Gallinule in north-central Florida. *Proc. Ann. Conf. Southeastern Assoc. Fish. & Wildl. Agencies* **36**: 527-536.
Mullarney, K. (1988). Short-billed Dowitcher in Count Wexford, an addition to the Irish list. *Irish Birds* **3(4)**: 596-600.
Mullarney, K. (1992). The Western Sandpiper in County Wexford. *Birding World* **5(9)**: 341-343.
Müller, E.J. (1995). Siberian Cranes for America? Pp. 311-313 in: Prange *et al*. (1995).
Müller, H.E.J. (1988a). [Ground display of Green Sandpiper *Tringa ochropus*]. *Limicola* **2(1)**: 27-29. In German with English summary.
Müller, H.E.J. (1988b). [Nest relocation by a Great Snipe (*Gallinago media*) following a disturbance]. *Beitr. Vogelkd.* **34(2/3)**: 147-153. In German.
Müller, H.E.J. & Königstedt, D.G.W. (1987). [On the field characters of the Great Snipe (*Gallinago media*) - a photographic documentation]. *Zool. Abh., Dresden* **42(2)**: 181-194. In German with English summary.
Müller, H.E.J. & Königstedt, D.G.W. (1989). [Biology and identification of the Great Snipe *Gallinago media*]. *Limicola* **3(4)**: 197-216. In German with English summary.
Müller, H.E.J. & Königstedt, D.G.W. (1990). [Protective defecation at the nest of Snipe (*Gallinago gallinago*) and Great Snipe (*G. media*)]. *Ecol. Birds* **12(1)**: 85-89. In German with English summary.
Muller, K. (1975). Threat display of the Australian Painted Snipe. *Emu* **75(1)**: 28-30.
Müller, P. (1973). *The Dispersal Centres of Terrestrial Vertebrates in the Neotropical Realm*. W. Junk, the Hague.
Müller-Schwarze, D., Butler, R., Belanger, P., Bekoff, M. & Bekoff, A. (1975). Feeding territories of South Polar Skuas at Cape Crozier. *Antarct. J. US* **10**: 121-122.
Mullié, W.C. & Meininger, P.L. (1981). Numbers, measurements and stomach contents of Dunlins, Little Stints and Kentish Plovers from Lake Manzala, Egypt. *Wader Study Group Bull.* **32**: 25-29.
Mundahl, J.T. (1982). Role specialization in the parental and territorial behavior of the Killdeer. *Wilson Bull.* **94(4)**: 515-530.
Mundkur, T. (1985). Observations on the roof-nesting habit of the Red-wattled Lapwing (*Vanellus indicus*) in Poona, Maharashtra. *J. Bombay Nat. Hist. Soc.* **82(1)**: 194-196.
Mundkur, T. (1988). Time to pull the alarm - for the Blackbellied Tern. *Newsl. Birdwatcher* **28**: 6-7.
Mundkur, T. (1990). Indian River Tern *Sterna aurantia*, a coastal species or a case of mistaken identity? *J. Bombay Nat. Hist. Soc.* **87(2)**: 298.

Mundkur, T. (1991). Prey items of the Great Thick-knee *Esacus recurvirostris*. *Forktail* **6**: 71-72.

Mundkur, T. (1992). Breeding by one-year-old Indian River Terns. *Colonial Waterbirds* **15**: 144-147.

Mundkur, T., Carr, P., Sun Hean & Chhim Somean (1995). *Surveys for Large Waterbirds in Cambodia, March-April 1994*. IUCN Species Survival Commission, Gland & Cambridge.

Mundy, P.J. (1994). Crowned Crane - with murderous intent. *Honeyguide* **40**: 24.

Munro, G.C. (1960). *Birds of Hawaii*. Charles E. Tuttle Co., Rutland, Vermont.

Münster, O.A.G. (1975). Migration, moult and biometrics of the Snipe *G. gallinago* in the sewage farms of Münster. *J. Orn.* **116**: 455-488.

Münster, O.A.G. (1989a). Zum Wintervorkommen des Waldwasserläufers *Tringa ochropus* in den Rieselfeldern Münster. [Winter occurrence of Green Sandpipers (*Tringa ochropus*) in the sewage farms of Münster]. *Vogelwelt* **110(4)**: 130-142.

Münster, O.A.G. (1989b). Beobachtungen zur Heimzugstrategie des Kampfläufers *Philomachus pugnax*. *J. Orn.* **130**: 175-182.

Münster, O.A.G. (1990). Mensural data of the Ruff *Philomachus pugnax* in both migration periods. *Vogelwelt* **111**: 2-18.

Münster, O.A.G. (1991). The molt of the Ruff (*Philomachus pugnax*) and the intra-individual variation of the primary molt patterns. *J. Orn.* **132(1)**: 1-28.

Muñoz-Pulido, R. (1989). Ecologia invernal de la grulla en España. *Quercus* **45**: 10-21.

Muñoz-Pulido, R., Alonso, J.A., Alonso, J.C., Román, J.A., Sánchez, A. & Ferrero, J.J. (1988). Censo de la Grulla Común (*Grus grus*) en España: Invierno 1987-1988. *Ecologia* **2**: 269-274.

Murie, O.J. (1924). Nesting records of the Wandering Tattler and Surf-bird in Alaska. *Auk* **41**: 213-237.

Murie, O.J. (1959). *Fauna of the Aleutian Islands and Alaska Peninsula*. North American Fauna **61**. US Fish & Wildlife Service, Washington, D.C. 406 pp.

Murobushi, Y. (1986). [Observations of Latham's Snipes at the Sengokubara Moor, central Honshu]. *Jap. J. Orn.* **35(1)**: 38-39. In Japanese with English summary.

Murphy, D.W. & Thompson, F.R. (1993). Breeding chronology and habitat of the American Woodcock in Missouri. Pp. 12-18 in: Longcore & Sepik (1993).

Murphy, E.C., Day, R.H., Oakley, K.L. & Hoover, A.A. (1984). Dietary changes and poor reproductive performance in Glaucous-winged Gulls. *Auk* **101**: 532-541.

Murphy, E.C., Hoover-Miller, A.A., Day, R.H. & Oakley, K.L. (1992). Intracolony variability during periods of poor reproductive performance at a Glaucous-winged Gull colony. *Condor* **94(3)**: 598-607.

Murphy, E.C., Springer, A.M. & Roseneau, D.G. (1991). High annual variability in reproductive success of Kittiwakes (*Rissa tridactyla* L.) at a colony in western Alaska. *J. Anim. Ecol.* **60**: 515-534.

Murphy, R.C. (1924). Birds collected during the Whitney South Sea Expedition. II. *Amer. Mus. Novit.* **124**: 1-13.

Murphy, R.C. (1925). Notes on certain species and races of oystercatchers. *Amer. Mus. Novit.* **194**: 5 15.

Murphy, R.C. (1936). *Oceanic Birds of South America*. 2 Vols. American Museum of Natural History, New York.

Murphy, R.C. (1938). Birds collected during the Whitney South Sea Expedition 37: on Pan-Antarctic Terns. *Amer. Mus. Novit.* **977**: 1-17.

Murphy, W.L. (1991). Second record of Baird's Sandpiper (*Calidris bairdii*) for Trinidad, with notes on its occurrence in the Caribbean Basin. *Pitirre* **4(1)**: 3-5.

Murphy, W.L., Hoi, T.Y. & James, A. (1991). First record of Wilson's Phalarope, *Phalaropus tricolor*, for Tobago. *Pitirre* **4(2)**: 2-3.

Murray, B.G. (1983). Notes on the breeding biology of Wilson's Phalarope. *Wilson Bull.* **95(3)**: 472-475.

Murray, B.G. (1991). Measuring annual reproductive success, with comments on the evolution of reproductive behavior. *Auk* **108**: 942-952.

Murray, K.G. (1980). *Predation by Deer Mice on Xantus' Murrelet Eggs on Santa Barbara Island, California*. MSc thesis, California State University, Northridge, California.

Murray, K.G., Winnett-Murray, K., Eppley, A., Hunt, G.L. & Schwartz, D.B. (1983). Breeding biology of the Xantus' Murrelet. *Condor* **85**: 12-21.

Murray, K.G., Winnett-Murray, K. & Hunt, G.L. (1980). Egg neglect in Xantus' Murrelet. *Proc. Colonial Waterbird Group* **3**: 186-195.

Murray, M.D. & Carrick, R. (1964). Seasonal movements and habitats of the Silver Gull, *Larus novaehollandiae* Stephens in southeastern Australia. *CSIRO Wildl. Res.* **9**: 160-188.

Muse, C. & Muse, S. (1982). *The Birds and Birdlore of Samoa*. Pioneer Press, Walla Walla, Washington.

Muselet, D. (1983). Repartition et effectif de la Sterna pierregarin (*Sterna hirundo*) et de la Sterne naine (*Sterna albifrons*) nicheuses en France pour l'année 1982. *Oiseau et RFO* **53**: 309-322.

Muselet, D. (1985). Les quartiers d'hivernage des Sternes naines européennes. *Oiseau et RFO* **55**: 183-193.

Muselet, D. (1990). Choix et chronologie de l'occupation du site de reproduction chez la Sterne naine *Sterna albifrons albifrons*. *Oiseau et RFO* **60**: 299-303.

Mustafa, H. & Durbunde, A.A. (1992). Status and distribution of the Black Crowned Crane in West and Central Africa. Unpublished report presented at the International Conference on the Black Crowned Crane and Its Wetlands Habitat in West and Central Africa, Kano, Nigeria, February 1992.

Mwangi, E.M. & Karanja, W.K. (1989). Home range, group size and sex composition in White-bellied and Kori Bustards. *Bustard Studies* **4**: 114-122.

Mwangi, E.M. & Karanja, W.K. (1992). Bustard population densities and habitat utilisation in Nairobi National Park and its environs. Pp. 489-494 in: Bennun, L. ed. (1992). *Proc. VII Pan-Afr. Orn. Congr.* Nairobi, 1988.

Mwangi, E.M. & Karanja, W.K. (1993). Diurnal activity of White-bellied *Eupodotis senegalensis* and Kori *Ardeotis kori* Bustards near Nairobi, Kenya. Pp. 417-420 in: Wilson, R.T. (1993).

Myers, J.P. (1978). One deleterious effect of mobbing in the Southern Lapwing. *Auk* **95(2)**: 419-420.

Myers, J.P. (1979). Leks, sex and Buff-breasted Sandpipers. *Amer. Birds* **33**: 823-825.

Myers, J.P. (1980a). Sanderlings *Calidris alba* at Bodega Bay: facts, inferences and shameless speculations. *Wader Study Group Bull.* **30**: 26-32.

Myers, J.P. (1980b). Territoriality and flocking by Buff-breasted Sandpiper: variations in non-breeding dispersal. *Condor* **82**: 241-250.

Myers, J.P. (1980c). The Pampas shorebird community: interactions between breeding and nonbreeding members. Pp. 37-49 in: Keast, A. & Morton, E.S. eds. (1980). *Migrant Birds in the Neotropics: Ecology, Behavior, Distribution and Conservation*. Smithsonian Institution Press, Washington, D.C.

Myers, J.P. (1981a). A test of three hypotheses for latitudinal segregation of the sexes in wintering birds. *Can. J. Zool.* **59**: 1527-1534.

Myers, J.P. (1981b). Cross-seasonal interactions in the evolution of sandpiper social systems. *Behav. Ecol. Sociobiol.* **8**: 195-202.

Myers, J.P. (1982). The promiscuous Pectoral Sandpiper. *Amer. Birds* **36**: 119-122.

Myers, J.P. (1983). Space, time and the pattern of individual associations in a group-living species; Sanderlings have no friends. *Behav. Ecol. Sociobiol.* **12**: 129-134.

Myers, J.P. (1988). The Sanderling. *Audubon Wildl. Rep.* **1988/1989**: 651-666.

Myers, J.P. & Myers, L.P. (1979). Shorebirds of coastal Buenos Aires Province, Argentina. *Ibis* **121(2)**: 186-200.

Myers, J.P., Connors, P.G. & Pitelka, F.A. (1979a). Territoriality in non-breeding shorebirds. Pp. 231-246 in: Pitelka (1979).

Myers, J.P., Connors, P.G. & Pitelka, F.A. (1979b). Territory size in wintering Sanderlings: the effect of prey abundance and intruder density. *Auk* **96**: 551-561.

Myers, J.P., Connors, P.G & Pitelka, F.A. (1980). Optimal territory size and the Sanderling: compromises in a variable environment. Pp. 135-158 in: Kamil, A.C. & Sargent, T.D. eds. (1980). *Mechanisms of Foraging Behavior*. Garland Press, New York.

Myers, J.P., Hildén O. & Tomkovich, P. (1982). Exotic *Calidris* species of the Siberian tundra. *Ornis Fenn.* **59**: 175-182.

Myers, J.P., Maron, J.L. & Sallaberry, M. (1985). Going to extremes: why do Sanderlings migrate to the Neotropics? *Orn. Monogr.* **36**: 520-535.

Myers, J.P., Morrison, R.I.G., Antaz, P.A., Harrington, B.A., Lovejoy, T.E., Sallaberry, M., Senner, S.E. & Tarak, A. (1987). Conservation strategy for migratory species. *Amer. Sci.* **75**: 19-26.

Myers, J.P., Sallaberry, A.M., Ortiz, E., Castro, G., Gordon, L.M., Maron, J.L., Schick, C.T., Tabilo, E., Antas, P. & Below, T. (1990). Migration routes of New World Sanderlings (*Calidris alba*). *Auk* **107**: 172-183.

Myers, J.P., Schick, C.T. & Castro, G. (1988). Structure in Sanderling (*Calidris alba*) populations: the magnitude of intra- and inter-year dispersal during the nonbreeding season. Pp. 604-615 in: *Proc. XIX Int. Orn. Congr.* Ottawa, 1986.

Myers, J.P., Schick, C.T. & Hohenberger, C.J. (1984). Notes on the 1983 distribution of Sanderlings along the United States' Pacific coast. *Wader Study Group Bull.* **40**: 22-26.

Myers, J.P., Williams, S.L. & Pitelka, F.A. (1980). An experimental analysis of prey availability for Sanderlings *Calidris alba* Pallas feeding on sandy beach crustaceans. *Can. J. Zool.* **58**: 1564-1574.

Myers, P. & Hansen, R.L. (1980). Rediscovery of the Rufous-faced Crake (*Laterallus xenopterus*) *Auk* **97**: 901-902.

Myrberget, S. (1959). Lundeura på Lovunden, og lundebestanden der. *Fauna* **12**: 143-156.

Myrberget, S. (1962). [Contribution to the breeding biology of the Puffin *Fratercula arctica*: eggs, incubation and young]. *Pap. Norwegian State Game Res. Inst. (2d Ser.)* **11**: 1-49. In Norwegian with English summary.

Myrberget, S. (1963). Systematic position of *Fratercula arctica* from a North Norwegian colony. *Nytt. Mag. Zool.* **11**: 74-84.

Myrberget, S. (1973). Merking av toppskarv og lunde på Røst. *Sterna* **12**: 307-315.

Naarding, J.A. (1986). *Latham's Snipe* Gallinago hardwickii *in Australia and Japan*. RAOU Report **24**. Royal Australasian Ornithologists' Union, Victoria.

Nadler, T. (1969). Zur Biologie der Brachschwalbe. *Falke* **16**: 232-236.

Nadler, T. (1983). Die Brachschwalbennachweise auf dem Gebiet der DDR. *Falke* **30(5)**: 157-159.

Nadler, T. (1990). Einflüge von Brachschwalben (*Glareola pratincola* und *Glareola nordmanni*) nach Mittel- und Nord-europa, ihre Abhängigkeiten und Ursachen. *Rudolstaedter Naturhist. Schr.* **3**: 75-88.

Nadler, T. & Königstedt, D. (1986). Zur Unterschiedung von Mongolenregenpfeifer (*Charadrius mongolus*) und Wüstenregenpfeifer (*Charadrius leschenaultii*) und zu ihrem Vorkommen in der Mongolei (MVR) (Aves, Charadriiformes, Charadriidae). [On the separation of Lesser Sand Plover (*Charadrius mongolus*) and Greater Sand Plover (*Charadrius leschenaultii*) and their occurrence in Mongolia]. *Zool. Abh., Dresden* **42(1)**: 79-106. In German with English summary.

Nagano, Y., Ohsako, Y., Nishida, S. & Mizoguchi, F. (1992). [Reactions of Hooded and White-naped Cranes to men and cars]. *Strix* **11**: 179-187. In Japanese with English summary.

Nagata, H. & Onagamitsu, J. (1995). Rediscovery of a breeding population of the Japanese Murrelet *Synthliboramphus wumizusume* on Eboshi-Jima Island in the Sea of Genkai, Kyushu. *Bull. Japan Alcid Soc.* **1993**: 24.

Naik, R.M., George, P.V. & Dixit, D.B. (1961). Some observations on the behaviour of the incubating Red-wattled Lapwing, *Vanellus indicus indicus* (Bodd.). *J. Bombay Nat. Hist. Soc.* **58**: 223-230.

Nakamura, H. & Shigemori, K. (1990). Diurnal change of activity and social behaviour of Latham's Snipe *Gallinago hardwickii*. *J. Yamashina Inst. Orn.* **22**: 85-113.

Nameer, P.O. (1992). Great Stone Plover *Esacus magnirostris* (Vieillot) in Kerala. *J. Bombay Nat. Hist. Soc.* **89(1)**: 118.

Nankinov, D. (1985). Migration route of the European Broad-billed Sandpiper (*Limicola f. falcinellus* Pontoppidan, 1763). *Orn. Inf. Byull.* **17**: 37-51.

Nankinov, D. (1991). Sightings of Slender-billed Curlew *Numenius tenuirostris* (Vieillot, 1817) in the Balkan countries. *Wader Study Group Bull.* **62**: 24-32.

Napier, J.R. (1969). Birds of the Break O'Day Valley, Tasmania. *Austr. Bird Watcher* **3**: 179-192.

Napier, J.R. (1982). Note on the breeding of the White-fronted Tern in Franklin Sound, Furneaux Group, Tasmania. *Austr. Bird Watcher* **9**: 210-212.

Napolitano, G.E., Ackman, R.G. & Parrish, C.C. (1992). Lipids and lipophilic pollutants in three species of migratory shorebirds and their food in Shepody Bay (Bay of Fundy, New Brunswick). *Lipids* **27**: 785-790.

Naranjo, L.G. (1991a). Nest, eggs and young of the Blackish Rail. *Orn. Neotropical* **2**: 47-48.

Naranjo, L.G. (1991b). Notes on reproduction of the Southern Lapwing in Colombia. *Orn. Neotropical* **2**: 95-96.

Naranjo, L.G., Franke, R. & Beltrán, W. (1994). Migration and wintering of Western Sandpipers on the Pacific Coast. *J. Field Orn.* **65(2)**: 194-200.

Narayan, G. (1990). General ecology and behaviour of the Bengal Florican. Pp. 17-33 in: *Status and Ecology of the Lesser and Bengal Floricans with Reports on Jerdon's Courser and Mountain Quail*. Bombay Natural History Society, Bombay.

Narayan, G. (1992). *Ecology, Distribution and Conservation of the Bengal Florican* Houbaropsis bengalensis *(Gmelin) in India*. PhD thesis, University of Bombay, Bombay.

Narayan, G. & Rosalind, L. (1990a). An introduction to the Bengal Florican. Pp. 9-16 in: *Status and Ecology of the Lesser and Bengal Floricans with Reports on Jerdon's Courser and Mountain Quail*. Bombay Natural History Society, Bombay.

Narayan, G. & Rosalind, L. (1990b). The Bengal Florican at Manas Wildlife Sanctuary. Pp. 35-43 in: *Status and Ecology of the Lesser and Bengal Floricans with Reports on Jerdon's Courser and Mountain Quail*. Bombay Natural History Society, Bombay.

Narayan, G., Akhtar, A., Rosalind, L. & D'Cunha, E. (1986). Black-necked Crane *Grus nigricollis* in Ladakh - 1986. *J. Bombay Nat. Hist. Soc.* **83**: 180-195.

Narayan, G., Sankaran, R. Rosalind, L. & Rahmani, A.R. (1989). *Study of Ecology of Certain Endangered Species of Wildlife and their Habitats. The Floricans:* Houbaropsis bengalensis *and* Sypheotides indica. Annual Report **4** (1988-89). Bombay Natural History Society, Bombay.

Narita, A. (1994). [Adoption of chicks by Black-tailed Gulls *Larus crassirostris*]. *Strix* **13**: 218-220. In Japanese with English summary.

Naroski, S. (1969). Nidificación de algunas aves en la región central de la provincia de Buenos Aires. *Hornero* **11**: 27-31.

Narosky, T. (1985). *Aves Argentinas: Guía para el Reconocimiento de la Avifauna Bonaerense*. Editorial Albatros, Buenos Aires.

Narosky, T. & Yzurieta, D. (1987). *Guía para la Identificación de las Aves de Argentina y Uruguay*. Vázquez Mazzini, Buenos Aires.

Narosky, T., Di Giacomo, A.G. & Babarskas, M. (1993). Winter presence of Magellanic Plover (*Pluvianellus socialis*) in Buenos Aires Province, Argentina. *Hornero* **13(4)**: 309-310.

Naslund, N.L. (1993). Why do Marbled Murrelets attend old-growth forest nesting areas year-round? *Auk* **110**: 594-602.

Naslund, N.L., Piatt, J.F. & van Pelt, T. (1994). *Breeding Behavior and Nest Site Fidelity of Kittlitz's Murrelet*. Abstracts of Pacific Seabird Group meeting, 26-29 January 1994, Sacramento, California.

Naumov, R.L. (1962). [On the biology of *Gallinago megala* Swinh. in central Siberia]. *Ornitologiya* **4**: 160-168. In Russian.

de Naurois, R. (1969). Peuplements et cycles de reproduction des oiseaux de la côte occidentale d'Afrique. *Mem. Mus. Natl. Hist. Nat. Ser. A* **56**: 1-312.

de Naurois, R. (1983). Le courvite de l'Archipel Cap-Vert *Cursorius cursor exsul* Hartert 1920. *Cyanopica* **3**: 5-15.

de Naurois, R. (1986). [On the ecology and biology of *Himantopus himantopus*, *Charadrius alexandrinus* and *Columba livia* on the Cape Verde Islands]. *Cyanopica* **3(4)**: 539-552. In French with English summary.

de Naurois, R. (1994). *Les Oiseaux des Îles du Golfe de Guinée (São Tomé, Prince et Annobon. As Aves das Ilhas do Golfo da Guiné (São Tomé, Príncipe e Ano Bom)*. Instituto de Investigação Científica Tropical, Lisboa. In French and Portuguese.

Navarro, R.A., Velásquez, C.R. & Schlatter, R.P. (1989). Diet of the Surfbird in southern Chile. *Wilson Bull.* **101(1)**: 137-141.

Navas, J.R. (1956). Manifestaciones vocales de las gallaretas. *Hornero* **10**: 119-135.

Navas, J.R. (1960). Comportamiento aggresivo de *Fulica armillata* Vieillot. *Rev. Mus. Arg. Cienc. Nat. Bernardino Ricadavio* **6**: 103-129.

Navas, J.R. (1962). Reciente hallazgo de *Rallus limicola antarcticus* King (Aves, Rallidae). *Neotropica* **8**: 73-76.

Navas, J.R. (1970). Desarollo y secuencias de plumajes en *Fulica armillata* Vieillot (Aves, Rallidae). *Rev. Mus. Arg. Cienc. Nat. Bernardino Ricadavio* **16**: 65-85.

Navas, J.R. & Bo, N.A. (1993). Aves nuevas o poco conocidas de Misiones, Argentina. V. (Addenda). *Rev. Mus. Arg. Cienc. Nat. Bernardino Rivadavia* **16(4)**: 37-50.

Nazarov, Y.N. & Labzyuk, V.I. (1972). On the biology of Spectacled Guillemot in South Ussuriland. *Nauchn. Dokl. Vyssh. Shk. Biol. Nauki* **15(3)**: 32-35. (Translated into English by Edward Grey Institute Library, University of Oxford University)

Nazarov, Y.N. & Shibaev, Y.V. (1987). Crested Murrelet *Synthliboramphus wumizusume*, nesting on the northwestern shore of the sea of Japan. Pp. 87-88 in: Litvinenko (1987).

Nazarov, Y.N. & Trukhin, A.M. (1985). On the biology of *Falco peregrinus* and *Bubo bubo* on islands of the Great Peter's Bay, South Primoriye. Pp. 70-76 in: Litvinenko, N.M. ed. (1985). *Rare and Endangered Birds of the Far East*. Far East Science Centre, USSR Academy of Sciences, Vladivostok. (Translated into English by Canadian Wildlife Service).

Nebelung, F. (1993). [The occurence and migration patterns of the Spotted Redshank (*Tringa erythropus*, Pallas 1764) in the Schleswig-Holstein part of the Waddensea, considering ecological facts and conservation on the main roosting-sites]. Zool. Inst. Mus., University of Hamburg. In German with English summary.

Nechaev, V.A. (1975). [Birds of Moneron Island]. Pp. 5-25 in: [*Ornithological Studies in the Soviet Far East*]. Far East Science Center, USSR Academy of Sciences, Vladivostok. In Russian.

Nechaev, V.A. (1977). [Comparative nesting characteristics of the Kamchatka Tern and the Common Tern on Sakhalin Island]. Report to All Union Ornithological Congress in Kiev. *Nauka* **1**: 291-293. In Russian.

Nechaev, V.A. (1978). A contribution to the biology and behaviour of *Tringa guttifer* on Sakhalin Island. *Zoologischeskii Zhurnal* **57(5)**: 727-737.

Nechaev, V.A. (1981). [Distribution and biology of the Kamchatka Tern - *Sterna camtschatica* Pall. on Sakhalin Island]. Pp. 47-55 in: [*Rare Birds of the Far East*]. Nauka: Far East Scientific Center of Acad. Sci USSR, Vladivostok. In Russian.

Nechaev, V.A. (1982). [Nesting biology of the Spotted Greenshank (*Tringa guttifer*) in the Sakhalin Island]. Pp 138-147 in: [*Ornithological Studies in the USSR, Collection of Papers*]. Vol. 1. Zoological Institute, USSR Academy of Sciences, Moscow. In Russian.

Nechaev, V.A. (1986). New data about seabirds on Sakhalin Island. Pp. 71-81 in: Litvinenko (1986).

Nechaev, V.A. (1988). [Nesting of Red-necked Phalarope (*Phalaropus lobatus*) at Sachalin Island]. *Ornitologiya* **23**: 219-220. In Russian with English summary.

Nechaev, V.A. (1989). The status of Nordmann's Greenshank (*Tringa guttifer*) in the USSR. *Asian Wetland News* **2(2)**: 11, 14.

Nechaev, V.A. (1994). Latham's Snipe in the Russian Far East. *Stilt* **25**: 37-39.

Nechaev, V.A. & Tomkovich, P.S. (1987). [A new subspecies of the Dunlin, *Calidris alpina litoralis* ssp. n. (Charadriidae, Aves), from the Sakhalin Island]. *Zoologischeskii Zhurnal* **66**: 1110-1113. In Russian with English summary.

Nechaev, V.A. & Tomkovich, P.S. (1988). [A new name for Sakhalin Dunlin (Aves: Charadriidae)]. *Zoologischeskii Zhurnal* **67**: 1596. In Russian with English summary.

Nedelman, J., Thompson, J.A. & Taylor, R.J. (1987). The statistical demography of Whooping Cranes. *Ecology* **68(5)**: 1401-1411.

Neelakantan, K.K. (1953a). Strange habit of terns breeding on Godavari sand-flats. *J. Bombay Nat. Hist. Soc.* **51(3)**: 740-741.

Neelakantan, K.K. (1953b). Occurrence of the Pheasant-tailed Jacana (*Hydrophasianus chirurgus*) in Madras state. *J. Bombay Nat. Hist. Soc.* **51(3)**: 741-742.

Neelakantan, K.K. (1990). Breeding of the River Tern *Sterna aurantia* in Kerala. *J. Bombay Nat. Hist. Soc.* **87(1)**: 144-145.

Neelakantan, K.K. (1991). Bluebreasted Banded Rail *Rallus striatus* Linn. nesting in Kerala. *J. Bombay Nat. Hist. Soc.* **88(3)**: 448-450.

Neelakantan, K.K., Sreenivasan, K.V. & Sureshkumar, V.K. (1980). The Crab Plover (*Dromas ardeola*) in Kerala. *J. Bombay Nat. Hist. Soc.* **77(3)**: 508.

Neginhal, S.G. (1983a). Status and distribution of the Great Indian Bustard in Karnataka. Pp. 76-80 in: Goriup & Vardhan (1983).

Neginhal, S.G. (1983b). Ecology and behaviour of the Great Indian Bustard (*Choriotis nigriceps*). Pp. 155-163 in: Goriup & Vardhan (1983).

Negret, A. & Teixeira, D.M. (1984a). Notas sobre duas espécies de aves raras: *Micropygia schomburgkii* e *Laterallus xenopterus* (Rallidae) na região de Brasilia-DF. Page 337 in: *Resumos, XI Congresso Brasileiro de Zoologia*. Imprensa Universitária, Belo Horizonte.

Negret, A. & Teixeira, D.M. (1984b). The Ocellated Crake (*Micropygia schomburgkii*) of central Brazil. *Condor* **86**: 220.

Nehls, G. & Tiedemann, R. (1993). What determines the densities of feeding birds on tidal flats? A case study on Dunlin, *Calidris alpina*, in the Wadden Sea. *Netherlands J. Sea Res.* **31**: 375-384.

Nehls, H. (1989). A review of the status and distribution of dowitchers in Oregon. *Oregon Birds* **15(2)**: 97-102.

Nehls, H.W. (1969). Zur Umsiedlung, Brutortstreue und Brutreife der Brandseeschwalbe (*Sterna sandvicensis*) nach Ringfunden auf Langenwerder. *Vogelwarte* **25**: 52-57.

Nehls, H.W. (1973). [Common Gull]. *Falke* **20**: 380-387. In German.

Nehls, H.W. & Schmeckebier, D. (1988). [Great Knot (*Calidris tenuirostris*) on the Baltic coast of East Germany in August, 1987]. *Beitr. Vogelkd.* **34(2/3)**: 194-196. In German with English summary.

Neill, W. (1987). Wood sandpiper's reactions to passing raptors. *British Birds* **80(9)**: 426.

Neithammer, G. (1966). Sexualdimorphismus am Ösophagus von *Rostratula*. *J. Orn.* **107(2)**: 201-204.

Nelson, B. (1973). *Azraq: Desert Oasis*. Allen Lane, London.

Nelson, D.A. (1982). *The Communication Behavior of the Pigeon Guillemot* Cepphus columba. PhD thesis, University of Michigan, Ann Arbor, Michigan.

Nelson, D.A. (1987). Factors influencing colony attendance by Pigeon Guillemot on Southeast Farallon Island, California. *Condor* **89**: 340-348.

Nelson, D.A. (1991). Demography of the Pigeon Guillemot on southeast Farallon Island, California. *Condor* **93**: 765-768.

Nelson, D.L. (1993). Piping Plovers: a case for how they colonized southeast Colorado and implications based on that scenario for their future as a breeding species. *Colorado Field Orn. J.* **27(2)**: 81-88.

Nelson, J.B. (1968a). *Galapagos, Islands of Birds*. Longmans, Green & Co., London.

Nelson, J.B. (1968b). Breeding behavior of the Swallow-tailed Gull in the Galapagos. *Behaviour* **30**: 146-173.

Nelson, J.B. (1980). *Seabirds. Their Biology and Ecology*. Hamlyn, London.

Nelson, J.T., Small, C.R., Ellis, D.H. (1995). Quantitative assessment of pair formation behavior in captive Whooping Cranes (*Grus americana*). *Zoo Biology* **14(2)**: 107-114.

Nelson, S.K. & Hamer, T.E. (1995). Nesting biology and behavior of the Marbled Murrelet. Pp. 57-67 in: Ralph *et al.* (1995).

Nelson, S.K., McAllister, M.L.C., Stern, M.A., Varoujean, D.H. & Scott, J.M. (1992). The Marbled Murrelet in Oregon, 1899-1987. Pp. 61-91 in: Carter & Morrison (1992).

Nero, R.W. (1977). The American Woodcock in Manitoba. *Blue Jay* **35**: 240-256.

Nero, R.W. (1986). American Woodcock breeding range extension. *Blue Jay* **44**: 120-122.

Nesbitt, S.A. (1975). Spring migration of Sandhill Cranes from Florida. *Wilson Bull.* **87**: 424-426.

Nesbitt, S.A. (1978). Species of special concern, Limpkin, *Aramus guarauna*. Pp. 86-88 in: Kale (1978).

Nesbitt, S.A. (1982). The past, present and future of the Whooping Crane in Florida. Pp. 151-154 in: Lewis (1982).

Nesbitt, S.A. (1987). A technique for aging Sandhill Cranes using wing molt - preliminary finding. Pp. 224-229 in: Lewis (1987).

Nesbitt, S.A. (1988). Nesting, renesting, and manipulating nesting of Florida Sandhill Cranes. *J. Wildl. Manage.* **52**: 758-763.

Nesbitt, S.A. (1989). The significance of mate loss in Florida Sandhill Cranes. *Wilson Bull.* **101**: 648-651.

Nesbitt, S.A. (1992). First reproductive success and individual productivity in Sandhill Cranes. *J. Wildl. Manage.* **56(3)**: 573-577.

Nesbitt, S.A. (1994). Whooping Cranes return to Florida. *ICF Bugle* **20(3)**: 1-3.

Nesbitt, S.A. & Carpenter, J.W. (1993). Survival and movements of Greater Sandhill Cranes experimentally released in Florida. *J. Wildl. Manage.* **57(4)**: 673-679.

Nesbitt, S.A. & Williams, K.S. (1990). Home range and habitat use of Florida Sandhill Cranes. *J. Wildl. Manage.* **54**: 92-96.

Nesbitt, S.A., Gilbert, D.T. & Barbour, D.B. (1976). Capturing and banding Limpkins in Florida. *Bird-Banding* **47(2)**: 164-165.

Nethersole-Thompson, D. (1973). *The Dotterel*. William Collins Sons & Co., Glasgow.

Nethersole-Thompson, D. & Nethersole-Thompson, M. (1979). *Greenshanks*. T. & A.D. Poyser, Berkhamsted.

Nethersole-Thompson, D. & Nethersole-Thompson, M. (1986). *Waders: their Breeding Haunts and Watchers*. T. & A.D. Poyser, Calton, UK.

Nettleship, D.N. (1970). *Breeding Success of the Common Puffin* Fratercula arctica *on Different Habitats at Great Island, Newfoundland*. PhD thesis, McGill University, Montreal.

Nettleship, D.N. (1972). Breeding success of the Common Puffin *Fratercula arctica* (L.) on different habitats at Great Island, Newfoundland. *Ecol. Monogr.* **42**: 239-268.

Nettleship, D.N. (1973). Breeding ecology of Turnstones *Arenaria interpres* at Hazen Camp, Ellesmere Island, N.W.T. *Ibis* **115**: 202-217.

Nettleship, D.N. (1974a). Seabird colonies and distributions around Devon Island and vicinity. *Arctic* **27**: 95-103.

Nettleship, D.N. (1974b). The breeding of the Knot *Calidris canutus* at Hazen Camp, Ellesmere Island, N.W.T. *Polarforschung* **44**: 8-26.

Nettleship, D.N. (1975). Effects of *Larus* gulls on breeding performance and nest distribution in Atlantic Puffins. Pp. 47-69 in: *Proceedings of Gull Seminar*. Canadian Wildlife Service, Sackville.

Nettleship, D.N. (1976). Census techniques for seabirds of arctic and eastern Canada. *Can. Wildl. Serv. Occas. Pap.* **25**: 1-33.

Nettleship, D.N. (1977a). Studies of seabirds at Prince Leopold Island and vicinity, Northwest Territories. Preliminary report of biological investigations in 1975. *Can. Wildl. Serv. Program Note* **73**: 1-11.

Nettleship, D.N. (1977b). Seabird resources of eastern Canada: status, problems and prospects. Pp. 96-108 in: Mosquin, T. & Suchal, C. eds. (1977). *Proceedings of Symposium Canada's Endangered Species and Habitats*. Canadian Nature Fed. Spec. Publ. **6**. Ottawa.

Nettleship, D.N. (1980). A guide to the major seabird colonies of eastern Canada: identity, distribution and abundance. Studies on Northern Seabirds. *Can. Wildl. Serv. Manuscript Rep.* **97**: 1-133.

Nettleship, D.N. (1991a). Seabird management and future research. *Colonial Waterbirds* **14**: 77-84.

Nettleship, D.N. (1991b). The diet of Atlantic Puffin chicks in Newfoundland before and after the initiation of an international capelin fishery, 1967-1984. Pp. 2263-2271 in: *Proc. XX Int. Orn. Congr.* Christchurch, 1990.

Nettleship, D.N. & Birkhead, T.R. eds. (1985). *The Atlantic Alcidae. The Evolution, Distribution and Biology of the Auks Inhabiting the Atlantic Ocean and Adjacent Water Areas*. Academic Press, London.

Nettleship, D.N. & Duffy, D.C. (1992). Seabird populations. Pp. 523-632 in: McCullough & Barrett (1992).

Nettleship, D.N. & Evans, P.G.H. (1985). Distribution and status of the Atlantic Alcidae. Pp. 53-154 in: Nettleship & Birkhead (1985).

Nettleship, D.N. & Gaston, A.J. (1978). Patterns of pelagic distribution of seabirds in western Lancaster Sound and Barrow Strait, Northwest Territories, in August and September 1976. *Can. Wildl. Serv. Occas. Pap.* **39**: 1-40.

Nettleship, D.N. & Hunt, G.L. eds. (1988). Reproductive biology of seabirds at high latitudes in the northern and southern hemispheres. Pp. 1141-1219 in: *Proc. XIX Int. Orn. Congr.* Ottawa, 1986.

Nettleship, D.N. & Smith, P.A. (1975). *Ecological Sites in Northern Canada*. Canadian Committee for the International Biological Programme, Conservation Terrestrial, Panel 9, Ottawa.

Nettleship, D.N., Burger, J. & Gochfeld, M. eds. (1994). *Seabirds on Islands. Threats, Case Studies and Action Plans*. BirdLife Conservation Series **1**. BirdLife International, Cambridge.

Nettleship, D.N., Sanger, G.A. & Springer, P.F. eds. (1984). *Marine Birds: their Feeding Ecology and Commercial Fisheries Relationships*. Canadian Wildlife Service Special Publication, Ottawa.

Neubauer, W. (1990). Die Nährung nestjunger Flußseeschwalben (*Sterna hirundo*) am Krakower See. *Acta Orn. Lituanica* **2**: 171-179.

Neuby Varty, B.V. (1953). Reichenow Striped Flufftail. *Bokmakierie* **5**: 52.

Neuchterlein, G.L. (1981). "Information parasitism" in mixed colonies of Western Grebes and Forster's Terns. *Anim. Behav.* **29**: 985-989.

Neufeldt, I. (1974). [The Siberian White Crane]. *Okhota i Okhotniche Khozaistvo* **12**: 26-27. In Russian.

Neufeldt, I. (1977). [Recent distribution of the Hooded Crane]. *Ornitologiya* **13**: 56-61. In German.

Neufeldt, I. (1981). The Hooded Crane in the USSR. Pp. 206-215 in: Lewis & Masatomi (1981).

Neufeldt, I. ed. (1982). [*Cranes of the USSR*]. Papers presented at the 2nd Meeting of the Soviet Working Group on Cranes. 16-18 February 1981. Leningrad. Zoological Institute of the Academy of Sciences of the USSR, Leningrad. In Russian with English titles.

Neufeldt, I. & Kespaik, J. eds. (1987). [*Crane Study in the USSR*]. Academy of Sciences of the Stonian SSR, (Communications of the Baltic Commission for the Study of Bird Migration **19**), Tartu. 224 pp. In Russian.

Neufeldt, I. & Kespaik, J. eds. (1989). [*Common Crane Researches in the USSR*]. Academy of Sciences of the USSR, (Communications of the Baltic Commission for the Study of Bird Migration **21**), Tartu. 185 pp. In Russian with English summaries.

Neufeldt, I., Krechmar, A.V. & Ivanov, A.I. (1961). Studies of less familiar birds. 110. Grey-rumped Sandpiper. *British Birds* **54**: 30-33.

Neufeldt, I.A. (1978). [Extinct birds in the collection of the Zoological Institute of Academy of Sciences of the USSR]. Pp. 101-110 in: Skarlato, O.A. ed. (1978). [*Systematics and Life History of Rare and Little Known Birds*]. Proceedings of the Zoological Institute **76**.

Neufeldt, I.A. & Vietinghoff-Scheel, E.V. (1983). *Tringa guttifer* (Nordmann). In: Stresemann, E. & Portenko L.A. eds. (1983). *Atlas der Verbreitung Palaearktischer Vögel*. Vol. 11. Akademie Verlag, Berlin.

Neufeldt, I.A. & Wunderlich, K. (1980). *Larus relictus* Lönnberg. In: Dathe, H. & Neufeldt, I.A. eds. (1980). *Atlas der Verbreitung Palearktischer Vögel*. Vol. 9. Akademie Verlag, Berlin.

Neufeldt, I.A. & Wunderlich, K. (1986). *Larus brunnicephalus* Jerdon. In: Dathe, H. & Neufeldt, I.A. eds. (1986). *Atlas der Verbreitung Palearktischer Vögel*. Vol. 13. Akademie Verlag, Berlin.

Neumann, T. (1987). Breeding status of the Common Crane in the Federal Republic of Germany. Pp. 243-245 in: Archibald & Pasquier (1987a).

del Nevo, A. (1994). Roseate Tern. *Sterna dougallii*. Pp. 298-299 in: Tucker & Heath (1994).

del Nevo, A., Rodwell, S., Sim, I.M.W., Saunders, C.R. & Wacher, T. (1994). Audouin's Gulls *Larus audouinii* in Senegambia. *Seabird* **16**: 57-61.

Newby, J.E. (1979). The birds of the Ouadi Rimé - Ouadi Achim Faunal Reserve: a contribution to the study of the Chadian avifauna. Part 1. *Malimbus* **1(2)**: 90-109.

Newby, J.E. (1980). The birds of the Ouadi Rimé - Ouadi Achim Faunal Reserve: a contribution to the study of the Chadian avifauna. Part 2. *Malimbus* **2(1)**: 29-50.

Newby, J.E. (1990). The slaughter of Sahelian wildlife by Arab falconers. *Oryx* **24**: 6-8.

Newby, J.E., Grettenberger, J. & Watkins, J. (1987). The birds of northern Air. *Malimbus* **9**: 4-16.

Newman, C.J. & Vinicombe, K.E. (1980). Greater Sand Plover in Avon. *British Birds* **73(12)**: 583-586.

Newman, K. (1980). *Birds of Southern Africa 1: Kruger National Park*. Macmillan, Johannesburg.

Newman, K. (1983). *Newman's Birds of Southern Africa*. Macmillan, Johannesburg.

Newman, O.M.G. (1982a). Wader studies in the Hobart area - past and future. *Occas. Stint* **1**: 3-10.

Newman, O.M.G. (1982b). Dispersal of immature Pied Oystercatchers in the Hobart area. *Occas. Stint* **1**: 51-58.

Newman, O.M.G. (1982c). Sooty Oystercatcher, evaluation of Hobart area count data, 1964-72. *Occas. Stint* **1**: 65-72.

Newman, O.M.G. (1982d). Hooded Plover: is Tasmania the real stronghold? *Stilt* **3**: 8-9.

Newman, O.M.G. (1983). Pied Oystercatcher - replacement clutches. *Occas. Stint* **2**: 49-52.

Newman, O.M.G. (1984). Survival of Pied Oystercatchers banded as pulli. *Occas. Stint* **3**: 45-51.

Newman, O.M.G. (1986). Pied Oystercatcher - exceptions to pair fidelity. *Occas. Stint* **4**: 13-15.

Newman, O.M.G. (1991). A forecast of population decline in Pied Oystercatchers based on breeding disturbance. *Tasmanian Bird Report* **20**: 21-24.

Newman, O.M.G. (1992a). Nesting association between Hooded Plover and Pied Oystercatcher. *Stilt* **21**: 26.

Newman, O.M.G. (1992b). Pied Oystercatcher breeding at Mortimer Bay, Tasmania. *Emu* **92(2)**: 87-92.

Newman, O.M.G. & Fletcher, A.W.J. (1982). Fluctuations in Hobart area wader populations, 1964-1981. *Tasmanian Bird Report* **10**: 4-11.

Newman, O.M.G. & Park, P. (1992a). Egg laying interval: Pied Oystercatcher and Hooded Plover. *Stilt* **20**: 22-23.

Newman, O.M.G. & Park, P. (1992b). Pied Oystercatcher breeding success in the 1991/92 summer. *Tasmanian Bird Report* **21**: 13-22.

Newman, O.M.G. & Park, P. (1993). Hooded Plovers - further breeding information including association with Pied Oystercatchers. *Stilt* **23**: 12-14.

Newman, O.M.G. & Patterson, R.M. (1984). A population survey of the Hooded Plover *Charadrius rubricollis* in Tasmania, October 1982. *Stilt* **3**: 1-6.

Newman, O.M.G., Patterson, R.M. & Barter, M.A. (1985). A study of the northward migration from southern Tasmania of Red-necked Stint *Calidris ruficollis* and Curlew Sandpiper *C. ferruginea* using colour-dyed birds. *Stilt* **7**: 18-20.

Newton, A. (1889). *Cariama cristata*, its breeding in Zoological Society Gardens. *Proc. Zool. Soc., London* **1889**: 25-26.

Newton, A. & Gadow, H. (1893-1896). *A Dictionary of Birds*. A. & C. Black, London.

Newton, S.F. (1996a). Crane and wetland action plan of the North and Northeast African Crane and Wetland Working Group. In: Beilfuss *et al.* (1996).

Newton, S.F. (1996b). Establishing a monitoring program for the African wintering population of Demoiselle Cranes during their spring migration through Saudi Arabia. In: Beilfuss *et al.* (1996).

Newton, S.F. & Symons, P. (1993). A survey of African Demoiselle Cranes, *Anthropoides virgo*, migrating through Saudi Arabia in Spring 1992. Pp. 595-596 in: Wilson, R.T. (1993).

Neyrolles, J.N. (1978). Rapport d'étude sur le kagou huppé: Le comportement. *Nature Calédonienne* **15**: 57-58.

Neyrolles, J.N. & de Naurois, R. (1985). Kagu. Page 314 in: Campbell & Lack (1985).

Nhlane, M.E.D. (1993). Notes on the Wattled Crane *Bugeranus carunculatus* in Nyika National Park, Malawi. Page 404 in: Wilson, R.T. (1993).

Nicéforo, M.H. & Olivares, A. (1965). Adiciones a la avifauna Colombiana, II (Cracidae-Rnychopidae). *Bol. Soc. Venez. Cienc. Nat.* **110**: 370-393.

Nicholls, E.B. (1905). A trip to the west. *Emu* **5**: 78-82.

Nicholls, G. (1988). A Franklin's Gull in Western Australia. *Austr. Birds* **21**: 93-94.

Nicholls, G.H. (1977). Studies of less familiar birds: Bridled Tern. *Bokmakierie* **29**: 20-23.
Nicholls, J.L. (1989). *Distribution and other Ecological Aspects of the Piping Plover Wintering along the Atlantic and Gulf Coasts*. MSc thesis, Auburn University, Auburn, Alabama.
Nicholls, J.L. & Baldassarre, G.A. (1990a). Winter distribution of Piping Plovers along the Atlantic and Gulf coasts of the United States. *Wilson Bull.* **102(3)**: 400-412.
Nicholls, J.L. & Baldassarre, G.A. (1990b). Habitat association of Piping Plovers wintering in the USA. *Wilson Bull.* **102(4)**: 581-590.
Nichols, C.A. (1974). Double-brooding in a Western Australian population of the Silver Gull, *Larus novaehollandiae* Stephens. *Austr. J. Zool.* **22**: 63-70.
Nicholson, D.J. (1928). Habits of the Limpkin in Florida. *Auk* **45**: 305-309.
Nicholson, D.J. (1948). Nocturnal fresh-water wandering of the Black Skimmer. *Auk* **65**: 299-300.
Nickell, W.P. (1943). Observations on the nesting of the Killdeer. *Wilson Bull.* **55**: 23-28.
Nicolau-Guillaumet, P. (1977). Mise au point et reflexions sur la repartition des Goélands argentés *Larus argentatus* de France. *Alauda* **45**: 53-73.
Nicoll, M. & Kemp, P. (1983). Partial primary moult in first-spring/summer Common Sandpipers *Actitis hypoleucos*. *Wader Study Group Bull.* **37**: 37-38.
Nicoll, M., Rae, R., Summers, R.W., Strann, K.B. & Brockie, K. (1991). The biometrics of Norwegian and Svalbard Purple Sandpipers *Calidris maritima*. *Ringing & Migration* **12(2)**: 67-71.
Nicoll, M., Summers, R.W., Underhill, L.G., Brockie, K. & Rae, R. (1988). Regional, seasonal and annual variations in the structure of Purple Sandpiper *Calidris maritima* populations in Britain. *Ibis* **130**: 221-233.
Nicoll, M.E. & Langrand, O. (1989). *Madagascar: Revue de la Conservation et des Aires Protégées*. WWF, Gland, Switzerland.
van Niekerk, D.J. (1993). [Ludwig's Bustard near Reddersburg]. *Mirafra* **10(2)**: 26-27. In Afrikaans with English summary.
van Niekerk, D.J. & Kotze, A.J. (1993). [Stanley's Bustard near Reddersburg]. *Mirafra* **10(1)**: 19-20. In Afrikaans with English summary.
Nielsen, B.P. (1971). Migration and relationships of four Asiatic plovers Charadriinae. *Ornis Scand.* **2(2)**: 137-142.
Nielsen, B.P. (1975). Affinities of *Eudromias morinellus* (L.) to the genus *Charadrius* L. *Ornis Scand.* **6**: 65-82.
Nielsen, B.P. (1986). [Notes on phenology and moult of Danish Dotterel *Charadrius morinellus* during spring migration]. *Dan. Orn. Foren. Tidssk.* **80(3-4)**: 132-133. In Danish with English summary.
Nielsen, B.P. & Colston, P.R. (1984). Breeding plumage of female Caspian Plover. *British Birds* **77**: 356-357.
Nielsen, O.K. (1991). [A territorial Broad-billed Sandpiper on Tjornes, NE Iceland]. *Bliki* **10**: 51-54. In Icelandic with English summary.
Niemi, G.J. & Davis, T.E. (1979). Notes on the nesting ecology of the Piping Plover. *Loon* **51**: 74-79.
Niethammer, G. (1961). Sonderbildungen an Oesophagus und Trachea beim Weibchen von *Turnix sylvatica lepurana*. *J. Orn.* **102**: 75-79.
Niethammer, G. (1966). Sexualdimorphismus am Ösophagus von *Rostratula*. *J. Orn.* **107**: 201-204.
Niethammer, K.R., Megyesi, J.L. & Hu, D. (1992). Incubation periods for 12 seabird species at French Frigate Shoals, Hawaii. *Colonial Waterbirds* **15**: 124-127.
Nightingale, T. (1986). Little Stints feeding by hovering. *British Birds* **79(3)**: 136.
Nikiforov, L.P. & Hybet, L.A. (1981). [Regulation of numbers and distribution of Great Snipe in natural and anthropogenic habitats]. In: Mikhelson, H.A. ed. (1981). [*Abstracts 10th Baltic Ornithological Conference, 2*]. Institute of Biology, Latvian Academy of Sciences, Riga. In Russian.
Nikiforov, M.E., Kozulin, A.V., Yaminski, B.V. & Zuyrnok, S.V. (1991). [New data on breeding of the Ringed Plover (*Charadrius hiaticula*), the Oystercatcher (*Haematopus ostralegus*) and the Terek Sandpiper (*Xenus cinereus*) in Belorussia]. *Ornitologiya* **25**: 168-169. In Russian.
Nikolaev, V.I. (1990). [Peculiarities of life of the Greater Golden Plover (*Pluvialis apricaria*) and the Whimbrel (*Numenius phaeopus*) in the Upper Volga River]. *Ornitologiya* **24**: 157-158. In Russian with English summary.
Nikolaus, G. (1981). Palaearctic migrants new to the north Sudan. *Scopus* **5**: 121-124.
Nikolaus, G. (1987). *Distribution Atlas of Sudan's Birds with Notes on Habitat and Status*. Bonner Zoologische Monographieren **25**. Zoologisches Forschungsinstitut und Museum Alexander Koenig, Bonn.
Nikolaus, G. & Hamed, D.M. (1984). Distinct status changes of certain Palearctic migrants in the Sudan. *Scopus* **8**: 36-38.
Nikolskii, I.D. (1987). Acoustical signalization in Sabine's Gull (*Xema sabini*) during the nesting period. *Zoologischeskii Zhurnal* **66**: 412-417.
Nilsson, S.G. & Nilsson, I.N. (1978). Population, habitat and display activity of the Jack Snipe *Lymnocryptes minimus* in southern Sweden. *Vår Fågelvärld* **37(1)**: 1-8.
Nipkow, M. (1989). [Early returning of the Stone Curlew *Burhinus oedicnemus* from winter habitat]. *Vogelwelt* **110(6)**: 238-239. In German with English summary.
Nipkow, M. (1990). [Habitat selection of the Stone Curlew (*Burhinus oedicnemus*) in the Alsace]. *J. Orn.* **131(4)**: 371-380. In German with English summary.
Nisbet, I.C.T. (1961). Studies of less familiar birds. 113. Broad-billed Sandpiper. *British Birds* **54**: 320-323.
Nisbet, I.C.T. (1963). Western Sandpiper on Fair Isle, Shetland (1956). *British Birds* **56**: 55-58.
Nisbet, I.C.T. (1971). The Laughing Gull in the northeast. *Amer. Birds* **25**: 677-683.
Nisbet, I.C.T. (1972). The tern-eating garter snakes of Nomans Land. *Man & Nature (Mass.)* **1972**: 27-29.
Nisbet, I.C.T. (1973a). Terns in Massachusetts: present numbers and historical changes. *Bird-Banding* **44**: 27-55.
Nisbet, I.C.T. (1973b). Courtship-feeding, egg-size and breeding success in Common Terns. *Nature* **241**: 141-142.
Nisbet, I.C.T. (1975). Selective effects of predation in a tern colony. *Condor* **77**: 221-226.
Nisbet, I.C.T. (1976). The colonization of Monomoy by Laughing Gulls. *Cape Naturalist* **5**: 4-8.
Nisbet, I.C.T. (1978a). Dependence of fledging success on egg-size, parental performance and egg-composition among Common and Roseate Terns, *Sterna hirundo* and *S. dougallii*. *Ibis* **120**: 207-215.
Nisbet, I.C.T. (1978b). Population models for Common Terns in Massachusetts. *Bird-Banding* **49**: 50-58.
Nisbet, I.C.T. (1980). *Status and Trends of the Roseate Tern in North America and the Caribbean*. US Fish & Wildlife Service, Laurel, Maryland. 131 pp.
Nisbet, I.C.T. (1981a). Behavior of Common and Roseate Terns after trapping. *Colonial Waterbirds* **4**: 44-46.
Nisbet, I.C.T. (1981b). *Biological Characteristics of the Roseate Tern (*Sterna dougalii*) in North America and the Caribbean*. US Fish & Wildlife Service, Laurel, Maryland.
Nisbet, I.C.T. (1983a). Territorial feeding by Common Terns. *Colonial Waterbirds* **6**: 64-70.
Nisbet, I.C.T. (1983b). Paralytic shellfish poisoning: effects on breeding terns. *Condor* **85**: 338-345.
Nisbet, I.C.T. (1984). Migration and winter quarters of North American Roseate Terns as shown by banding recoveries. *J. Field Orn.* **55**: 1-17.
Nisbet, I.C.T. (1989). *Status and Biology of the Northeastern Population of the Roseate Tern (*Sterna dougalii*): a Literature Survey and Update: 1981-1989*. US Fish & Wildlife Service, Newton Corner, Massachusetts.
Nisbet, I.C.T. (1994). Effects of pollutants on marine birds. Pp. 8-25 in: Nettleship *et al.* (1994).
Nisbet, I.C.T. & Cohen, M.E. (1975). Asynchronous hatching in Common and Roseate Terns, *Sterna hirundo* and *S. dougallii*. *Ibis* **117**: 374-379.
Nisbet, I.C.T. & Drury, W.H. (1972a). Measuring breeding success in Common and Roseate Terns. *Bird-Banding* **43**: 97-106.
Nisbet, I.C.T. & Drury, W.H. (1972b). Post-fledging survival in Herring Gulls in relation to brood size and date of hatching. *Bird-Banding* **43**: 161-172.
Nisbet, I.C.T. & Welton, M. (1984). Seasonal variations in breeding success of Common Terns: consequences of predation. *Condor* **86**: 53-60.
Nisbet, I.C.T., Burger, J., Safina, C. & Gochfeld, M. (1990). Estimating fledging success and productivity in Roseate Terns (*Sterna dougallii*). *Colonial Waterbirds* **13**: 85-91.
Nisbet, I.C.T., Spendelow, J.A. & Hatfield, J.S. (1995). Variations in growth of Roseate Tern chicks. *Condor* **97**: 335-344.
Nisbet, I.C.T., Winchell, J.M. & Heise, A.E. (1984). Influence of age on the breeding biology of Common Terns. *Colonial Waterbirds* **7**: 117-126.
Nitta, K. & Fujimaki, Y. (1985). [Seasonal variation in daily activity of *Gallinago hardwickii* in the breeding season]. *Tori* **34(2/3)**: 49-55. In Japanese with English summary.
Nixon, A. (1987). Spurs on the wings of the Blacksmith Plover. *Bee-eater* **38(4)**: 58-59.
Noble, G.K. & Lehrman, D.S. (1940). Egg recognition by the Laughing Gull. *Auk* **57**: 22-43.
Noble, G.K. & Wurm, M. (1943). The social behavior of the Laughing Gull. *Ann. New York Acad. Sic.* **45**: 179-220.
Nogueira-Neto, P. (1973). *A Criação de Animais Indígenas Vertebrados*. Tecnaspis, São Paulo.
Nol, E. (1984). *Reproductive Strategies in the Oystercatchers (Aves: Charadriiformes)*. PhD thesis, University of Toronto, Toronto.
Nol, E. (1985). Sex roles in the American Oystercatcher. *Behaviour* **95**: 232-260.
Nol, E. (1986). Incubation period and foraging technique in shorebirds. *Amer. Naturalist* **128**: 115-119.
Nol, E. (1989). Food supply and reproductive performance of the American Oystercatcher in Virginia. *Condor* **91(2)**: 429-435.
Nol, E. & Blokpoel, H. (1983). Incubation period of Ring-billed Gulls and the egg immersion technique. *Wilson Bull.* **95**: 283-286.
Nol, E. & Brooks, R.J. (1982). Effects of predator exclosures on nesting success of Killdeer. *J. Field Orn.* **53(3)**: 263-268.
Nol, E. & Humphrey, R.C. (1994). American Oystercatcher (*Haematopus palliatus*). No. **82** in: Poole & Gill (1994).
Nol, E. & Lambert, A. (1984). Comparison of Killdeer, *Charadrius vociferus*, breeding in mainland and peninsular sites in southern Ontario. *Can. Field-Nat.* **98(1)**: 7-11.
Nol, E., Baker, A.J. & Cadman, M.D. (1984). Clutch initiation dates, clutch size, and egg size of the American Oystercatcher in Virginia. *Auk* **101(4)**: 855-867.
Noordhuis, R. & Spaans, A.L. (1992). Intraspecific competition for food between Herring *Larus argentatus* and Lesser Black-backed Gulls *L. fuscus* in the Dutch Wadden Sea area. *Ardea* **80**: 115-132.
Norderhaug, M. (1964). Studier av rednebbternas (*Sterna macrura*'s) biologi pa Vestspitsbergen. *Fauna* **17**: 137-154.
Norderhaug, M. (1967). Trekkforhold, stedstrohet og pardannelse hos alkekonge på Svalbard. *Fauna* **20**: 236-244.
Norderhaug, M. (1970). The role of the Little Auk *Plautus alle* (L.) in arctic ecosystems. Pp. 558-560 in: Holdgate, M.W. ed. (1970). *Antarctic Ecology*. Vol. 1. Academic Press, London.
Norderhaug, M. (1980). Breeding biology of the Little Auk *Plautus alle* in Svalbard. *Norsk Polarinstitutt Skrifter* **173**: 1-45.
Norderhaug, M., Brun, E. & Møllen, G.U. (1977). *Seabird Resources of the Barents Sea*. Norsk Polarinstitutt Meddelelser **104**. 119 pp. (Translated into English by R.G.B. Brown, Canadian Wildlife Service 1981).
Nordin, T. (1995). Snötranan. Går en osäker framtid till mötes. *Vår Fågelvärd* **4**: 18-21.
Nordstrom, L.H. (1990). *Evaluation of Piping Plover Habitat and Food Availability in the Great Lakes National Seashores*. MSc thesis, University of Missouri, Columbia, Missouri.
Nores, M. & Yzurieta, D. (1980). *Aves de Ambientes Acuáticos de Córdoba y Centro de Argentina*. Secretaría de Estado de Agricultura y Ganadería. Provincia de Córdoba, Córdoba, Argentina.
Nores, M., Yzurieta, D. & Miatello, R. (1983). *Lista y Distribución de las Aves de Córdoba, Argentina*. Boletín de la Academia Nacional de Ciencias **56(1-2)**.
Norman, D. (1992). The growth rate of Little Tern *Sterna albifrons* chicks. *Ringing & Migration* **13**: 98-102.
Norman, D. (1994). The importance of the Mersey estuary for waders in the cold weather of February 1991. *Ringing & Migration* **15**: 91-97.
Norman, F.I. & Mumford, L. (1985). Studies on the Purple Swamphen, *Porphyrio porphyrio*, in Victoria. *Austr. Wildl. Res.* **12**: 263-278.
Norman, F.I. & Ward, S.J. (1990). Foods of the South Polar Skua at Hop Island, Rauer Group, East Antarctica. *Polar Biol.* **10**: 489-493.
Norman, F.I., McFarlane, R.A. & Ward, S.J. (1994). Carcasses of Adelie Penguins as a food source for South Polar Skuas: some preliminary observations. *Wilson Bull.* **106(1)**: 26-34.
Norrdahl, K., Suhonen, J., Hemminki, O. & Korpimaki, E. (1995). Predator presence may benefit; Kestrels protect Curlew nests against nest predators. *Oecologia* **101**: 105-109.
Norris, C.A. (1947). Report on the distribution and status of the Corncrake. *British Birds* **40**: 226-244.
North, A.J. (1901-1903). Description of the eggs of the Kagu, *Rhinochetus jubatus*, Verreaux et Des Murs. *Records Austr. Mus.* **4**: 310-311.
North, A.J. (1913-1914). *Nests and Eggs of Birds Found Breeding in Australia and Tasmania*. Vol. 4. Australian Museum, Sydney.
North, M.E.W. (1936). Breeding habits of the Crested Wattled Plover (*Sarciophorus tectus latifrons*). *J. East Afr. & Uganda Nat. Hist. Soc.* **13**: 132-145.
North, M.R. (1986). Piping Plover nesting success on Mallard Island, central North Dakota and implications for water level management. *Prairie Nat.* **18**: 117-122.
Norton, D.W. (1965). Notes on some non-passerine birds from eastern Ecuador. *Breviora* **230**: 1-11.
Norton, D.W. (1972). Incubation schedules of four species of Calidrine sandpipers at Barrow, Alaska. *Condor* **74**: 164-176.
Norton, D.W., Senner, S.E., Gill, R.E., Martin, P.D., Wright, J.M. & Fukuyama, A.K. (1990). Shorebirds and Herring Roe in Prince William Sound, Alaska. *Amer. Birds* **44**: 367-371, 508.
Norton, R.I. (1986). Case of botulism in Laughing Gulls at landfill in the Virgin Islands. *Florida Field Nat.* **14**: 97-98.
Norton, R.L. (1984). Cayenne x Sandwich Terns nesting in Virgin Islands, Greater Antilles. *J. Field Orn.* **55**: 243-246.
Norton, R.L. (1988). Extra-egg clutches and interspecific egg-dumping of the Roseate Tern (*Sterna dougallii*) in the West Indies. *Florida Field Nat.* **16**: 67-70.
Norton, R.L. (1989). First West Indian record of the Black Noddy and nesting of Masked Booby at Sombrero Island, Lesser Antilles. *Colonial Waterbirds* **12**: 120-122.
Norton Griffiths, M. (1967a). Some ecological aspects of the feeding behaviour of the Oystercatcher *Haematopus ostralegus* on the Edible Mussel *Mytilis edulis*. *Ibis* **109**: 412-424.
Norton Griffiths, M. (1967b). *A Study of the Feeding Behaviour of the Oystercatcher (*Haematopus ostralegus*)*. PhD thesis, Oxford University, Oxford.
Norton Griffiths, M. (1969). The organization, control and development of parental feeding in the Oystercatcher *Haematopus ostralegus*. *Behaviour* **34**: 55 114.
Noseworthy, C.M. & Lien, J. (1976). Ontogeny of nesting habitat recognition and preference in neonatal Herring Gull chicks, *Larus argentatus*. Pontopiddan. *Anim. Behav.* **24**: 637-651.
Noszály, G. & Székely, T. (1993). [Clutch and egg-size variation in the Kentish Plover (*Charadrius alexandrinus*) during the breeding season]. *Aquila* **100**: 161-179. In Hungarian with English summary.
Novakowski, N.S. (1966). *Whooping Crane Population Dynamics on the Nesting Grounds, Wood Buffalo National Park, Northwest Territories, Canada*. Canadian Wildlife Society Report Series **1**.
Nowald, G. (1994). [*Habitat Use by Spring Migrant Common Cranes* Grus grus *in the Rügen-Bock Area, Germany*]. Dissertation, Univeristy of Osnabrück, Germany. In German.
Nowicki, T. (1973). *A Behavioral Study of the Marbled Godwit in North Dakota*. MSc thesis, Central Michigan University.
Ntiamoa-Baidu, Y. (1993). Trends in the use of Ghanaian coastal wetlands by migrating Knots *Calidris canutus*. *Ardea* **81**: 71-79.
Nudds, T.D. (1981). The effects of coots on duck densities in Saskatchewan parkland. *Wildfowl* **32**: 19-22.
Nur, N. (1984). Increased reproductive success with age in the California Gull: due to increased effort or improvement of skill? *Oikos* **43**: 407-408.
Nuttall, R.J. & de Swardt, D.H. (1993). Temminck's Courser *Cursorius temminckii* breeding near Jagersfontein, Orange Free State. *Mirafra* **10(3)**: 57-58.
Nyenhuis, H. (1990). Zugwege der Waldschnepfe (*Scolopax rusticola* L.) in Nordwesteuropa. *Vogelwarte* **35**: 208-214.
Nysewander, D.R. (1974). Preliminary report on Black Oystercatcher studies. Pp. 213-217 in: *Small Game Management Report 1973 1974*. Washington Game Department, Olympia, Washington.
Nysewander, D.R. (1977). *Reproductive Success of the Black Oystercatcher in Washington State*. MSc thesis, University of Washington, Seattle, Washington.
Nysewander, D.R. (1978). Reproductive success of the Black Oystercatcher in Washington State. *Pacific Seabird Group Bull.* **5(1)**: 44 45.
Nysewander, D.R. & Barbour, D.B. (1979). The breeding biology of marine birds associated with Chiniak Bay, Kodiak Island, 1975 1978. Pp. 21-106 in: *Annual Reports of Principal Investigators. Environmental Assessment of the Alaskan Continental Shelf*. Vol. 2. NOAA-BLM, Boulder, Colorado.
Nysewander, D.R. & Hoberg, E. (1978). The breeding biology of marine birds associated with Chiniak Bay, Kodiak Island, 1977. Pp. 525-574 in: *Annual Reports of Principal Investigators. Environmental Assessment of the Alaskan Continental Shelf*. Vol. 3. NOAA-BLM, Boulder, Colorado.
Nysewander, D.R. & Knudtson, P. (1977). The population ecology and migration of seabirds, shorebirds and waterfowl associated with Constantine Harbour, Hinchinbrook Island, Prince William Sound, 1976. Pp. 500-575 in: *Annual Reports of Principal Investigators. Environmental Assessment of the Alaskan Continental Shelf*. Vol. 4. NOAA-BLM, Boulder, Colorado.
Nysewander, D.R., Forsell, D.J., Baird, P.A., Shields, D.J., Weiler, G.J. & Kogan, G.H. (1982). Marine Bird and Mammal Survey of the Eastern Aleutian Islands, Summers of 1980-81. Unpublished report to US Fish & Wildlife Service, Anchorage, Alaska.
O'Brian, M. & Smith, K.W. (1992). Changes in the status of waders breeding on wet lowland graslands in England and Wales between 1982 and 1989. *Bird Study* **39**: 165-176.

O'Connor, R.J. (1974). Feeding behavior of the Kittiwake. *Bird Study* **21**: 185-191.
O'Connor, R.J. & Brown, R.A. (1977). Prey depletion and foraging strategy in the Oystercatcher *Haematopus ostralegus*. *Oecologia* **27**: 75 92.
O'Connor, R.J. & Shrubb, M. (1986). *Farming and Birds*. Cambridge University Press, Cambridge.
O'Donald, P. (1983). *The Arctic Skua: a Study of the Ecology and Evolution of a Seabird*. Cambridge University Press, Cambridge.
O'Donald, P. & Davis, J.W.F. (1975). Demography and selection in a population of Arctic Skuas. *Heredity* **35**: 75-83.
O'Donald, P., Wedd, N.S. & Davis, J.W.F. (1974). Mating preferences and sexual selection in the Arctic Skua. *Heredity* **33**: 1-16.
O'Donnell, C.F.J. (1988). Black Stilts nesting at Lake Ellesmere. *Notornis* **35(3)**: 247-248.
O'Donnell, C.F.J. (1994). Distribution and habitats of Spotless Crakes in Canterbury. *Notornis* **41**: 211-213.
O'Donnell, C.F.J. & Moore, S.G.M. (1983). *The Wildlife and Conservation of Braided River Systems in Canterbury*. Fauna Survey Unit Report **33**. New Zealnd Wildlife Service, Wellington.
Oakley, K.L. (1981). *Determinants of Population Size of Pigeon Guillemots on Naked Island, Prince William Sound, Alaska*. MSc thesis, University of Alaska, Fairbanks, Alaska.
Oates, E.W. (1901). *Catalogue of the Collection of Birds' Eggs in the British Museum*. Vol. 1. Taylor & Francis, London.
Oatley, T.B. (1969). Unusual breeding behaviour of Blue Cranes *Tetrapteryx paradisea*. *Lammergeyer* **10**: 87-88.
Oberholser, H.C. (1915). A synopsis of the races of the Crested Tern, *Thalasseus bergii* (Lichtenstein). *Proc. US Natl. Mus.* **49**: 515-526.
Obst, B.S. (1985). Densities of Antarctic seabirds at sea and the presence of the krill *Euphausia superba*. *Auk* **102**: 540-549.
Obst, B.S. & Hunt, G.L. (1990). Marine birds feed at gray whale mud plumes in the Bering Sea. *Auk* **107**: 678-688.
Oehler, D.A., Schmid, S.C. & Miller, M.P. (1995). Maintaining Parakeet Auklets, at the Cincinnati Zoo & Botanical Gardens; hand-rearing protocol with development and behavioural observations. *Avicult. Mag.* **101(1)**: 3-12.
Ogden, J. (1979). Estimates of the population sizes of the Black Noddy and Wedge-tailed Shearwater at Heron Island in 1978. *Sunbird* **10**: 33-39.
Ogden, J. (1993). On Cyclones, *Pisonia grandis* and the mortality of Black Noddy *Anous minutus* on Heron Island. *Emu* **93**: 281-283.
Ogi, H. & Shiomi, K. (1991). Diet of murres caught incidentally during winter in northern Japan. *Auk* **108**: 184-185.
Ogi, H., Tanaka, H. & Tsujita, T. (1985). The distribution and feeding ecology of murres in the northwestern Bering Sea. *J. Yamashina Inst. Orn.* **17**: 44-56.
Ogilvie, M.A. (1963). The migration of European Redshank and Dunlin. *Ann. Rep. Wildfowl Trust* **14**: 141-149.
Ohata, K. (1988). [Migration of the Japanese Snipe *Gallinago hardwickii* at Tokisata River, the mouth of Lake Utonai, Hokkaido]. *Strix* **8**. In Japanese.
Ohlendorf, H.M., Custer, T.W., Lowe, R.W., Rigney, M. & Cromartie, E. (1988). Organochlorines and mercury in eggs of coastal terns and herons in California, USA. *Colonial Waterbirds* **11**: 85-94.
Ohlendorf, H.M., Schaffner, F.C., Custer, T.W. & Stafford, C.J. (1985). Reproduction and organochlorine contaminants in terns at San Diego Bay, California. *Colonial Waterbirds* **8**: 42-53.
Ohmart, R.D. & Tomlinson, R.E. (1977). Foods of western Clapper Rails. *Wilson Bull.* **89**: 332-336.
Ohsako, Y. (1987). Effects of artificial feeding of cranes wintering in Izumi and Akune, Kyushu, Japan. Pp. 89-98 in: Archibald & Pasquier (1987a).
Ohsako, Y. (1989). Flock organization, dispersion and territorial behaviour of wintering Hooded Cranes *Grus monacha* in Izumi and Akune, Kyushu. *Jap. J. Orn.* **38(1)**: 15-29. In English with Japanese summary.
Okugawa, K.T., Ishii, T., Mitsuno, M., Hasegawa, S., Tsukamoto, K., Aoki, M., Yamashita, S. & Yamamoto, S. (1973). [An ecological study of *Macrosarcops cinereus* (Blyth), Grey-headed Lapwing (Charadriidae), of the Ogura Farm area, Kyota]. *Bull. Kyoto Univ. Educ. (Ser. B)* **37**: 3-87. In Japanese with English summary.
Okulewicz, J. & Witkowski, J. (1979). Jack Snipe *Lymnocryptes minimus* (Brünn., 1764), again a breeding bird in Poland. *Przeglad Zoologiczny* **23**: 255-257.
Olioso, G. (1992). [The Marsh Sandpiper *Tringa stagnatilis* in France]. *Alauda* **60(3)**: 143-147. In French with English summary.
Olivares, A. (1957). Aves de la costa del Pacífico, Municipio de Guápi, Cauca, Colombia, II. *Caldasia* **8**: 217-251.
Olivares, A. (1959). Cinco aves que aparentemente no habían sido registradas en Colombia. *Lozania* **12**: 51-56.
Olivares, A. (1969). *Aves de Cundinamarca*. Universidad Nacional de Colombia, Bogotá.
Olivares, A. (1974). *Aves de la Orinoquia Colombiana*. Instittuto de Ciencias Naturales Ornitología, Universidad Nacional de Colombia. 127 pp.
de Oliveira, R.G. & Rech, F.G. (1988). [*Vanellus chilensis*: history, biology and folklore]. Page 30 in: Assembleia Legislativa Estado Rio Grande do Sul. In Portuguese.
Oliver, W.R.B. (1974). *New Zealand Birds*. Reed, Wellington.
Ollson, M. (1979). Seriemas: their natural history, captive management and propagation. *Game Bird Breeders Conserv. Gaz.* **28(6-7)**: 8-9, 11-12.
Olmos, F., Martuscelli, P., Silva, R. & Neves, T.S. (1995). The sea-birds of São Paulo, southeastern Brazil. *Bull. Brit. Orn. Club* **115(2)**: 117-128.
Olney, P.J.S. (1970). Studies of Avocet behaviour. *British Birds* **63**: 206-209.
Olrog, C.C. (1958). Notas ornitológicas sobre la colección del Instituto Miguel Lillo, Tucumán. III. *Acta Zool. Lilloana* **15**: 5-18.
Olrog, C.C. (1967). Breeding of the Band-tailed Gull (*Larus belcheri*) on the Atlantic coast of Argentina. *Condor* **69**: 42-48.
Olrog, C.C. (1984). *Las Aves Argentinas*. Administración de Parques Nacionales, Buenos Aires.
Olsen, D.L., Blankinship, D.R., Erickson, R.C., Drewien, R., Irby, H.D., Lock, R. & Smith, L.S. (1980). *Whooping Crane Recovery Plan*. US Fish & Wildlife Service, Washington, D.C.
Olsen, K.M. (1989a). Field identification of the smaller skuas. *British Birds* **82(4)**: 143-176.
Olsen, K.M. (1989b). [Field identification of skuas Stercorariidae]. *Limicola* **3(3)**: 93-136. In German with English summary.
Olsen, K.M. (1995). Svarthuvad mås en allt mer regelbunden raritet. *Vår Fågelvärld* **4**: 34-38.
Olsen, K.M. & Christensen, S. (1984). Field identification of juvenile skuas. *British Birds* **77**: 448-450.
Olsen, K.M. & Larssen, H. (1995a). Field identification of Little and Saunder's Tern. *Bull. African Bird Club* **2(2)**: 81-85.
Olsen, K.M. & Larssen, H. (1995b). *Terns of Europe and North America*. Princeton University Press, Princeton, New Jersey.
Olsen, P.D., Crome, F. & Olsen, J. (1993). *Birds of Prey and Ground Birds of Australia*. Australian Museum and Angus & Robertson, Sydney.
Olson, C.S. (1976). Band-tailed Gull photographed in Florida. *Auk* **93**: 176-177.
Olson, S.L. (1970). The relationships of *Porzana flaviventer*. *Auk* **87**: 805-808.
Olson, S.L. (1973a). Evolution of the rails of the South Atlantic Islands (Aves: Rallidae). *Smithsonian Contrib. Zool.* **152**: 1-53.
Olson, S.L. (1973b). A classification of the Rallidae. *Wilson Bull.* **85**: 381-446.
Olson, S.L. (1973c). A plumage aberration of *Cariama cristata*. *Auk* **90(4)**: 912-914.
Olson, S.L. (1974a). The pleistocene rails of North America. *Condor* **76**: 169-175.
Olson, S.L. (1974b). A new species of *Nesotrochis* from Hispaniola, with notes on other fossil rails from the West Indies (Aves: Rallidae). *Proc. Biol. Soc. Washington* **87**: 439-450.
Olson, S.L. (1974c). Purple Gallinule carrying young. *Florida Field Nat.* **2**: 15-16.
Olson, S.L. (1975a). The fossil rails of C.W. de Vis, being mainly an extinct form of *Tribonyx mortierii* from Queensland. *Emu* **75**: 49-54.
Olson, S.L. (1975b). The South Pacific gallinules of the genus *Pareudiastes*. *Wilson Bull.* **87**: 1-5.
Olson, S.L. (1984). *Density and Distribution, Nest Site Selection, and Activity of the Mountain Plover on the Charles M. Russell National Wildlife Refuge*. MSc thesis, University of Montana, Missoula, Montana.
Olson, S.L. (1985a). Mountain Plover food items on and adjacent to a prairie dog town. *Prairie Nat.* **17(2)**: 83-90.
Olson, S.L. (1985b). The fossil record of birds. Pp. 80-238 in: Farner, D.S., King, J.R. & Parkes, K.C. eds. (1985). *Avian Biology*. Vol. 8. Academic Press, New York.
Olson, S.L. (1986). *Gallirallus sharpei* (Büttikofer) nov. comb. A valid species of rail (Rallidae) of unknown origin. *Gerfaut* **76**: 263-269.
Olson, S.L. (1989). Extinction on islands: man as a catastrophe. In: Western, D. & Pearl, M.C. eds. (1989). *Conservation for the Twenty-first Century*. Oxford University Press, New York.
Olson, S.L. (1991). Requiescat for *Tricholimnas conditicius*, a rail that never was. *Bull. Brit. Orn. Club* **112**: 174-179.
Olson, S.L. (1992). A new family of primitive landbirds from the Lower Eocene Green River Formation of Wyoming. Pp. 127-136 in: Campbell, K.E. ed. (1992). *Papers in Avian Paleontology*. Natural History Museum of Los Angeles County, Science Series **36**. Los Angeles, California.
Olson, S.L. & Edge, D. (1985). Nest-site selection by Mountain Plovers in northcentral Montana. *J. Range Manage.* **38**: 278-280.
Olson, S.L. & Feduccia, A. (1980). *Relationships and Evolution of Flamingos (Aves, Phoenicopteridae)*. Smithsonian Contributions to Zoology **316**. 73 pp.
Olson, S.L. & Steadman, D.W. (1979). The fossil record of the Glareolidae and Haematopodidae (Aves: Charadriiformes). *Proc. Biol. Soc. Washington* **91(4)**: 972-981.
Olson, S.L. & Steadman, D.W. (1981). The relationships of the Pedionomidae (Aves: Charadriiformes). *Smithsonian Contrib. Zool.* **337**: 1-25.
Olson-Edge, S.L. & Edge, W.D. (1987). Density and distribution of the Mountain Plover on the Charles M. Russell National Wildlife Refuge. *Prairie Nat.* **19**: 223-238.
Olsson, U. (1987). Separation of Pintail Snipe from Snipe. *British Birds* **80(5)**: 248-249.
van Ommen, E.G.C. & van Ijzendoorn, E.J. (1988). [Red-necked Stint at Lauwersmeer in May 1987]. *Dutch Birding* **10(4)**: 178-182. In Dutch with English summary.
Oniki, Y. (1987). Nesting of the Southern Lapwing *Vanellus chilensis* in São Paulo, Brazil. *Avicult. Mag.* **92(3)**: 151-156.
Onley, D. (1982a). The Spotless Crake (*Porzana tabuensis*) on Aorangi, Poor Knights Island. *Notornis* **29**: 9-21.
Onley, D. (1982b). The nomenclature of the Spotless Crake (*Porzana tabuensis*). *Notornis* **29**: 75-79.
Onnen, J. (1985). [New discovery of *Calidris temminckii* in Spain]. *Vogelwarte* **33(2)**: 166. In German.
Onnen, J. (1989). [The ecology of a lapwing-population (*Vanellus vanellus*) in the Weser-Ems-area]. *Ecol. Birds* **11(2)**: 209-249. In German with English summary.
Onnen, J. (1991). Zugphänologie, Biometrie und Gewicht des Alpenstrandläufers (*Calidris alpina*) im Nordwestlichen Niedersachsen. *Vogelwelt* **36**: 132-145.
Onno, S.K. (1965). [On nesting conservatism (ortstreue) of the Mew Gull, Common Tern and the Arctic Tern]. Pp. 140-162 in: [*Communic. Baltic Commission Study Bird Migration*]. Vol. 3. Estonian Acad. Science, Tartu. In Russian.
Ono, K. (1993). The biology of nesting Japanese Murrelets on Kojine reef (Hachijo Island). In: Ono, K. ed. (1993). *Symposium on the Japanese Murrelet: its Status and Conservation*. Annual meeting of Japanese Ornithological Society; October 11, 1993, Ehine University. Japanese Ornithological Society, Tokyo.
Ono, K. & Nakamura, Y. (1993). The biology of nesting Japanese Murrelets on Biroto Island (Kadokawa-cho, Miyazaki pref.). In: Ono, K. ed. (1993). *Symposium on the Japanese Murrelet: its Status and Conservation*. Annual meeting of Japanese Ornithological Society; October 11, 1993, Ehine University. Japanese Ornithological Society, Tokyo.
Ono, K. & Nakamura, Y. (1994). Current status and breeding ecology of Japanese Murrelets. *Pacific Seabird Group Bull.* **21**: 47. (Abstract).
Opie, M.J. (1974). A further sighting of the Oriental Pratincole. *S. Austr. Orn.* **26**: 166-167.
Oreel, G.J. (1976). Short note: on the alleged occurrence of the Brown-headed Gull *Larus brunnicephalus* in Tanzania. *Ardea* **64**: 80.
Oreel, G.J. (1984). Caspian Plover, *Charadrius asiaticus*. *Cyprus Orn. Soc.* **31**: 61-62.
Oreel, G.J. (1986). Caspian Plover in Cyprus in April 1984. *Dutch Birding* **8(1)**: 26-28.
Orians, G.H. & Paulson, D.R. (1969). Notes on Costa Rican birds. *Condor* **71**: 426-431.
Oring, L.W. (1964). Displays of the Buff-breasted Sandpiper at Norman, Oklahoma. *Auk* **81**: 83-86.
Oring, L.W. (1968). Vocalizations of the Green and Solitary Sandpipers. *Wilson Bull.* **80**: 395-420.
Oring, L.W. (1973). Solitary Sandpiper early reproductive behavior. *Auk* **90**: 652-663.
Oring, L.W. (1986). Avian polyandry. Pp. 309-351 in: Johnston, R.F. ed. (1986). *Current Ornithology*. Vol. 3. Plenum Press, New York.
Oring, L.W. (1988). Dispersal of juvenile Spotted Sandpipers: distance, sex bias and consequences. Pp. 575-584 in: *Proc. XIX Int. Orn. Congr.* Ottawa, 1986.
Oring, L.W. & Knudson, M.L. (1972). Monogamy and polyandry in the Spotted Sandpiper. *Living Bird* **11**: 59-73.
Oring, L.W. & Lank, D.B. (1982). Sexual selection, arrival times, philopatry and site fidelity in the polyandrous Spotted Sandpiper. *Behav. Ecol. Sociobiol.* **10**: 185-191.
Oring, L.W., Colwell, M.A. & Reed, J.M. (1991). Lifetime reproductive success in the Spotted Sandpiper (*Actitis macularia*): sex differences and variance components. *Behav. Ecol. Sociobiol.* **28(6)**: 425-432.
Oring, L.W., Fivizzani, A.J., Colwell, M.A. & El Halawani, M.E. (1988). Hormonal changes associated with natural and manipulated incubation in the sex-role reversed Wilson's Phalarope. *Gen. Comp. Endocrin.* **72**: 247-256.
Oring, L.W., Fleischer, R.C., Reed, J.M. & Marsden, K.E. (1992). Cuckoldry through stored sperm in the sequentially polyandrous Spotted Sandpiper. *Nature* **359**: 631-633.
Oring, L.W., Lank, D.B. & Maxson, S.J. (1983). Population studies of the polyandrous Spotted Sandpiper. *Auk* **100**: 272-285.
Oring, L.W., Reed, J.M. & Alberico, J.A.R. (1994). Mate acquisition tactics in polyandrous Spotted Sandpipers (*Actitis macularia*): the role of age and experience. *Behav. Ecol.* **5(1)**: 9-16.
Oring, L.W., Reed, J.M., Colwell, M.A., Lank, D.B. & Maxson, S.J. (1991). Factors regulating annual mating success and reproductive success in Spotted Sandpiper (*Actitis macularia*). *Behav. Ecol. Sociobiol.* **28(6)**: 433-442.
Oring, L.W., Reed, J.M. & Maxson, S.J. (1994). Copulation patterns and mate guarding in the sex-role reversed, polyandrous Spotted Sandpiper, *Actitis macularia*. *Anim. Behav.* **47(5)**: 1065-1072.
Ormerod, S.J. & Tyler, S.J. (1988). The diet of Green Sandpipers *Tringa ochropus* in contrasting areas of their winter range. *Bird Study* **35(1)**: 25-30.
Oró, D. (1995). The influence of commercial fisheries in daily activity of Audouin's Gull *Larus audouinii* in the Ebro Delta, NE Spain. *Ornis Fenn.* **72**: 154-158.
Oró, D. (1996). Interspecific kleptoparasitism in Audouin's Gull *Larus audouinii* at the Ebro Delta, northeast Spain: a behavioural response to low food availability. *Ibis* **138(2)**: 218-221.
Oró, D. & Martínez-Vilalta, A. (1992). The colony of the Audouin's Gull at the Ebro Delta. *Avocetta* **16**: 36-39.
Oró, D. & Martínez-Vilalta, A. (1994). Factors affecting kleptoparasitism and predation rates upon a colony of Audouin's Gull (*Larus audouinii*) by Yellow-legged Gulls (*Larus cachinnans*) in Spain. *Colonial Waterbirds* **17(1)**: 35-41.
Oró, D., Bosch, M. & Ruiz, X. (1995). Effects of trawl moratorium on the breeding parameters of the Yellow-legged Gull *Larus cachinnans*. *Ibis* **137**: 547-549.
Orr, C.D. & Parsons, J.L. (1982). Ivory Gulls, *Pagophila eburnea* and ice edges in Davis Strait and the Labrador Sea. *Can. Field-Nat.* **96**: 323-328.
Orr, C.D., Ward, R.M.P., Williams, N.A. & Brown, R.G.B. (1982). Migration patterns of Red and Northern Phalaropes in southwest Davis Strait and in the northern Labrador Sea. *Wilson Bull.* **94**: 303-312.
Orsini, P. (1980). Première observation hivernale du Phalarope à bec étroit *Phalaropus lobatus* dans le Moyen-Atlas (Maroc). *Alauda* **48**: 258-259.
Ortali, A. (1977). Il nido del Fraticello *Sterna albifrons* (Pallas) visto attraverso l'obiettivo. *Riv. ital. Orn.* **47**: 53-109.
Ortega, V.R., Almeida, F.S.C. & Audi, A. (1988). [Ringing of aquatic birds by CESP. Preliminary results (Oct. 1983 and Dec. 1986)]. *Anais ENAV, Univ. Vale do Rio dos Sinos* **3**: 85-86. In Portuguese.
Ortiz, F. & Carrión, J.M. (1991). *Introducción a las Aves del Ecuador*. FECODES, Quito.
Osborne, B.C. (1982). Foot-trembling and feeding behaviour in the Ringed Plover *Charadrius hiaticula*. *Bird Study* **29**: 209-212.
Osborne, B.C. (1985). Aspects of the breeding biology and feeding behaviour of the Brown Skua *Catharacta lönnbergi* on Bird Island, South Georgia. *Bull. Brit. Antarct. Surv.* **66**: 57-71.
Osborne, D.R. (1982). Replacement nesting and polyandry in the Wattled Jacana. *Wilson Bull.* **94(2)**: 206-208.
Osborne, D.R. (1983). Habitat factors affecting polyandry in Wattled Jacanas. *Wader Study Group Bull.* **39**: 60.
Osborne, D.R. & Beissinger, S.R. (1979a). Long-winged Harrier predation on Wattled Jacana eggs. *Wilson Bull.* **91(3)**: 470-471.
Osborne, D.R. & Beissinger, S.R. (1979b). The Paint-billed Crake in Guyana. *Auk* **96**: 425.
Osborne, D.R. & Bourne, G.R. (1977). Breeding behavior and food habits of the Wattled Jacana. *Condor* **79(1)**: 98-105.
Osborne, L. (1985). Progress toward the captive rearing of Great Bustards. *Bustard Studies* **2**: 123-130.
Osborne, P. ed. (1986). *Survey of the Birds of Fuerteventura, Canary Islands, with Special Reference to the Status of the Canarian Houbara Bustard* Chlamydotis undulata. ICBP Study Report **10**, Cambridge.
Osborne, P. (1989). The bustards morphometrics database: an introduction and some preliminary findings. *Bustard Studies* **4**: 125-134.
Osborne, P., Collar, N. & Goriup, P.D. (1984). *Bustards*. Dubai Wildlife Research Centre, Dubai, United Arabs Emirates.
Osieck, E. (1994). Avocet. *Recurvirostra avosetta*. Pp. 242-243 in: Tucker & Heath (1994).

Osing, H. (1992). [On the breeding of *Charadrius dubius* at the Great Dhunntal Dam]. *Falke* **39(3)**: 80-81. In German.
Osing, H. (1993a). *Der Flußregenpfeifer (*Charadrius dubius*)*. Verlag Natur & Wissenschaft, Solingen, Germany.
Osing, H. (1993b). [Between humans and nature - Golden Plover - bird of the year 1993]. *Falke* **40(12)**: 423-429. In German.
Osmundson, B.C. (1989). American Avocets in Utah wetlands. *Utah Birds* **5(2)**: 33-37.
Ossipova, M.A. (1987a). [Status of the Baikal Region population of Relict Gulls (*Larus relictus* Lonnb.) in 1982]. *Vestnik Zoologica* **1987(1)**: 84-86. In Russian.
Ossipova, M.A. (1987b). [The study of the molting of the Relict Gull (*Larus relictus* Lonnb.)]. *Vestnik Zoologica* **1987(2)**: 15-17. In Russian.
Ostapenko, V.A., Gavrilov, V.M., Fomin. V.E., Bold, A. & Tsevenmyadag, N. (1980). State, distribution and some ecological features of waders in Mongolia. *Ornitologiya* **15**: 49-62.
Ostergaard, E. (1986). [The breeding population of the Wood Sandpiper in Denmark 1982-84]. *Dan. Orn. Foren. Tidssk.* **80(3-4)**: 134-136. In Danish with English summary.
Ottaway, J.R., Carrick, R. & Murray, M.D. (1984). Evaluation of leg bands for visual identification of free-living Silver Gulls. *J. Field Orn.* **55**: 287-308.
Ottaway, J.R., Carrick, R. & Murray, M.D. (1985). Dispersal of Silver Gulls, *Larus novaehollandiae* Stephens, from breeding colonies in South Australia. *Austr. Wildl. Res.* **12**: 279-298.
Ottaway, J.R., Carrick, R. & Murray, M.D. (1988). Reproductive ecology of Silver Gulls, *Larus novaehollandiae* Stephens, in South Australia. *Austr. Wildl. Res.* **15**: 541-560.
Ouellet, H., McNeil, R. & Burton, J. (1973). The Western Sandpiper in Quebec and the Maritime Provinces, Canada. *Can. Field-Nat.* **87**: 291-300.
Owen, R.B. & Galbraith, W.J. (1989). Earthworm biomass in relation to forest types, soil and land use: implications for Woodcock management. *Wildl. Soc. Bull.* **17**: 130-136.
Owen, R.B. & Krohn, W.B. (1973). Molt patterns and weight changes of the American Woodcock. *Wilson Bull.* **85**: 31-41.
Owen, R.B. & Moran, J.W. (1975). Summer behavior of adult radio-equipped Woodcock in central Maine. *J. Wildl. Manage.* **39**: 179-182.
Owens, I.P.F., Burke, T. & Thompson, D.B.A. (1994). Extraordinary sex roles in the Eurasian Dotterel - female mating arenas, female-female competition and female mate choice. *Amer. Naturalist* **144(1)**: 76-100.
Owens, I.P.F., Dixon, A., Burke, T. & Thompson, D.B.A. (1995). Strategic paternity assurance in the sex-role reversed Eurasian Dotterel (*Charadrius morinellus*): behavioral and genetic evidence. *Behav. Ecol.* **6**: 14-21.
Owens, N.W. (1984). Why do Curlew have curved beaks? *Bird Study* **31**: 230-231.
Oyarzo, H. & Ruiz, V. (1983). *Charadrius collaris* (Veillot 1818) inverna en la Bahía de Concepción, Chile. *Bol. Soc. Biol. Concepción* **54**: 153-157.
Ozaki, K. (1991). Returns and recoveries of Hooded and White-naped Cranes banded in winter at Izumi, Japan. Pp. 311-314 in: Harris (1991b).
Ozaki, K. & Baba, T. (1994). Recoveries and resightings of color banded Hooded (*Grus monacha*) and White-naped (*G. vipio*) Cranes in Northeast Asia. Pp. 33-40 in: Higuchi & Minton (1994).
Pace, R.M. (1980). *Aspects of the Ecology of American Woodcock Wintering in Coastal South Carolina*. MSc thesis, Clemson University, Clemson, South Carolina.
Pace, R.M. & Wood, G.W. (1993). Use of daytime microhabitat by wintering woodcocks in coastal South Carolina. Pp. 66-74 in: Longcore & Sepik (1993).
Pacheco, J.F. & Whitney, B.M. (1995). Range extensions for some birds in northeastern Brazil. *Bull. Brit. Orn. Club* **115**: 157-163.
Pae, S. & Pyong-Oh Won (1994). Ecology of Red-crowned Cranes and White-naped Cranes, *Grus japonensis* and *G. vipio*, in the Choelwon Basin, Korea. Pp. 97-106 in: Higuchi & Minton (1994).
Page, D. (1978). Distinctive feeding action of Baird's Sandpiper. *British Birds* **71(2)**: 78-79.
Page, G.W. (1974a). Age, sex, moult and migration of Dunlins at Bolinas Lagoon. *Western Birds* **5(1)**: 1-12.
Page, G.W. (1974b). Molt of wintering Least Sandpipers. *Bird-Banding* **45(2)**: 93-105.
Page, G.W. & Bradstreet, M. (1968). Size and composition of a fall population of Least and Semipalmated Sandpipers at Long Point, Ontario. *Ont. Bird Band.* **4**: 80-88.
Page, G.W. & Gill, R.E. (1994). Shorebirds in western North America: late 1800's to late 1900's. Pp. 147-160 in: Jehl & Johnson (1994).
Page, G.W. & Middleton, A.L.A. (1972). Fat deposition during autumn migration in the Semipalmated Sandpiper. *Bird-Banding* **43(2)**: 85-96.
Page, G.W. & Ribic, C.A. (1985). Nest site selection and clutch predation in the Snowy Plover. *Auk* **102**: 347-353.
Page, G.W. & Salvadori, A. (1969). Weight changes of Semipalmated and Least Sandpipers pausing during autumn migration. *Ont. Bird Band.* **5**: 52-58.
Page, G.W. & Stenzel, L.E. eds. (1981). The breeding status of the Snowy Plover in California. *Western Birds* **12**: 1-40.
Page, G.W. & Whiteacre, D.F. (1975). Raptor predation on wintering shorebirds. *Condor* **77(1)**: 73-83.
Page, G.W., Bidstrup, F.C., Ramer, R.J. & Stenzel, L.E. (1986). Distribution of wintering Snowy Plovers in California and adjacent states. *Western Birds* **17(4)**: 145-170.
Page, G.W., Carter, H.R. & Ford, R.G. (1990). Numbers of seabirds killed or debilitated in the 1986 Apex Houston oil spill in central California. Pp. 164-174 in: Sealy (1990).
Page, G.W., Quinn, P.L. & Warriner, J.C. (1989). Comparison of the breeding of hand- and wild-reared Snowy Plovers. *Conserv. Biol.* **3(2)**: 198-201. In English with Spanish summary.
Page, G.W., Shuford, W.D. & Bruce, C.R. (1991). Distribution and abundance of Snowy Plover on its western North American breeding grounds. *J. Field Orn.* **62**: 184-205.
Page, G.W., Stenzel, L.E. & Ribic, C.A. (1985). Nest site selection and clutch predation in the Snowy Plover. *Auk* **102**: 347-353.
Page, G.W., Stenzel, L.E., Shuford, W.D. & Bruce, C.R. (1991). Distribution and abundance of the Snowy Plover on its western North American breeding grounds. *J. Field Orn.* **62(2)**: 245-255. In English with Spanish summary.
Page, G.W., Stenzel, L.E., Winkler, D.W. & Swarth, C.W. (1983). Spacing out at Mono Lake: breeding success, nest density and predation in the Snowy Plover. *Auk* **100**: 13-24.
Page, G.W., Stern, M.A. & Paton, P.W.C. (1995). Differences in wintering areas of Snowy Plovers from inland breeding sites in western North America. *Condor* **97**: 258-262.
Page, G.W., Warriner, J.S., Warriner, J.C. & Paton, P.W.C. (1995). Snowy Plover (*Charadrius alexandrinus*). No. **154** in: Poole & Gill (1994-1995).
Paige, J.P. (1965). Field identification and winter range of the Asiatic Dowitcher. *Ibis* **107**: 95-97.
Paine, R.T., Wootton, J.T. & Boersma, P.D. (1990). Direct and indirect effects of Peregrine Falcon predation on seabird abundance. *Auk* **107**: 1-9.
Pakenham, R.H.W. (1943). Field notes on the birds of Zanzibar and Pemba. *Ibis* **85**: 165-189.
Pakenham, R.H.W. (1979). *The Birds of Zanzibar and Pemba. An Annotated Checklist*. BOU Check-list **2**. British Ornithologists' Union, London.
Palacios, E. & Alfaro, L. (1992). Occurrence of Black Skimmers in Baja California. *Western Birds* **23(4)**: 173-176.
Palacios, E. & Mellink, E. (1996). Status of the Least Tern in the Gulf of California. *J. Field Orn.* **67(1)**: 48-58.
Palacios, E., Alfaro, L. & Page, G.W. (1994). Distribution and abundance of breeding Snowy Plovers on the Pacific coast of Baja California. *J. Field Orn.* **65(4)**: 490-497. In English with Spanish summary.
Palacios, F., Garzón, J. & Castroviejo, J. (1975). La alimentación de la Avutarda en España, especialmente en primavera. *Ardeola* **21(1)**: 347-406.
Palfery, J. (1988). A note on the feeding behaviour of Greater Sand Plover. *Sandgrouse* **10**: 105-106.
Palindant, R., Land, V. & Weseloh, D.V. (1973). First authenticated record of the Western Sandpiper for Alberta. *Can. Field-Nat.* **87**: 315-316.
Palmer, R.S. (1941). A behavior study of the Common Tern. *Proc. Boston Soc. Nat. Hist.* **42**: 1-119.
Palmer, R.S. (1967). Buff-breasted Sandpiper (*Tryngites subruficollis*). Pp. 212-214 in: Stout, G.D. ed. (1967). *The Shorebirds of North America*. Viking Press, New York.
Palmer, R.S. (1985). Limpkin. Pp.328-329 in: Campbell & Lack (1985).
Palmer, T.S. (1897). Nansen's discovery of the breeding grounds of the Rosy Gull. *Science* **5**: 175-176.
Palmer-Ball, B. & Bennett, M. (1993). First reported nesting of Black-necked Stilt in Kentucky. *Kentucky Warbler* **69(4)**: 65-68.
Palmes, P. & Briggs, C. (1986). Crab-plovers *Dromas ardeola* in the Gulf of Kutch. *Forktail* **1**: 21-28.
Palmgren, J. (1983). Field identification of Great Snipe *Gallinago media* and the occurrence in Finland in the years 1970-1981. *Lintumies* **18**: 58-66.
Palsson, K. (1992). [Black-tailed Godwit *Limosa limosa* colonization in Hunavatnssyslur Counties, N. Iceland]. *Bliki* **12**: 59-60. In Icelandic with English summary.
Paludan, K. (1951). Contributions to the breeding biology of *Larus argentatus* and *Larus fuscus*. *Vidensk. Meed. Dan. Naturhist. Foren.* **114**: 1-128.
Paludan, K. (1955). Some behaviour patterns of *Rissa tridactyla*. *Vidensk. Meed. Dan. Naturhist. Foren.* **117**: 1-24.
Paludan, K. (1959). *On the Birds of Afghanistan*. Dansk Naturhistorisk Forenings Videnskabelige Meddelelser **122**. 332 pp.
Pampush, G.J. & Anthony, R.G. (1993). Nest success, habitat utilization and nest-site selection of Long-billed Curlews in the Columbia Basin, Oregon. *Condor* **95(4)**: 957-967.
Pande, P., Kothari, A. & Singh, S. (1991). *Andaman and Nicobar Islands*. Indian Institute of Public Administration, Delhi.
Pandolfi, M.M. (1986). *Étude sur le Kagou (*Rhinochetus jubatus*)*. PhD thesis, Paul Sabatier University, Toulouse.
Pang Bingzhang (1981). [Ecology of the Common Snipe *Capella gallinago*]. *Wildlife* **2**: 31-32. In Chinese.
Panov, E. (1963). [Taxonomic position of the Ussuri Plover, *Charadrius hiaticula placidus*, on the basis of ethological data]. *Zoologischeskii Zhurnal* **42**: 1546-1553. In Russian.
Panov, E.N. & Zikova, L.U. (1982). [Social determinants for mortality in Great Black-headed Gull colonies (*Larus ichthyaetus*) - dynamics and extent of juvenile mortality in various sized colonies]. *Zoologischeskii Zhurnal* **61**: 1396-1411. In Russian.
Panov, E.N. & Zikova, L.U. (1987). [Influence of ecological and social factors on the reproductive success of the Great Black-headed Gull (*Larus ichthyaetus*)]. *Zoologischeskii Zhurnal* **66**: 883-894. In Russian.
Panov, E.N., Zikova, L.U., Zikova Kostina, G.N. & Andrusenko, N.N. (1980). [Social factors involved in the mortality of chicks and cannibalism in Great Black-headed Gull colonies: the scope and reasons for juvenile mortality]. *Zoologischeskii Zhurnal* **59**: 1694-1705. In Russian.
Papacotsia, A., Soreau, A. & Thibault, J.C. (1980). La situation du Goéland d'Audouin en Corse. *Nos Oiseaux* **35**: 219-226.
Pareigis, V. (1989). [The breeding of the Ringed Plover in Gargzdai Gravelpits]. *Acta Orn. Lituanica* **1**: 133-134. In Russian with Lithuanian summary.
Parera, A. (1987). [New data about *Heliornis fulica* (Boddaert, 1783) in the province of Corrientes, Argentina (Aves: Heliornithidae)]. *Not. Faun.* **1**: 2. In Spanish.
Parish, D. & Howes, J.R. (1989). Waterbird hunting and management in SE Asia. Paper presented at the Symposium on Wildlife, Tokyo, April 5-6.
Parish, D. & Wells, D.R. (1984). *Interwader '83 Report*. Interwader Publication **1**. Kuala Lumpur.
Park, P. (1986). A cooling mechanism in Little Curlew? *Stilt* **8**: 22.
Park, P. (1993). Observations on the breeding of Hooded Plover. *Tasmanian Bird Report* **22**: 14.
Parker, R.H. (1971). Priorities in bird conservation in Nigeria. *IUCN Publications* **22**: 34-37.
Parker, T.A. (1982). Observations of some unusual rainforest and marsh birds in southeastern Peru. *Wilson Bull.* **94**: 477-493.
Parker, T.A. & Remsen, J.V. (1987). Fifty-two Amazonian bird species new to Bolivia. *Bull. Brit. Orn. Club* **107**: 94-107.
Parker, T.A., Castillo, U.A., Gell-Mann, M. & Rocha, O.O. (1991). Records of new and unusual birds from northern Bolivia. *Bull. Brit. Orn. Club* **111**: 120-138.
Parker, T.A., Parker, S.A. & Plenge, M.A. (1982). *An Annotated Checklist of Peruvian Birds*. Buteo Books, Vermillion, South Dakota.
Parker, T.A., Schulenberg, T.S., Kessler, M. & Wust, W.H. (1995). Natural history and conservation of the endemic avifauna in north-west Peru. *Bird Conserv. Int.* **5(2/3)**: 201-231.
Parkes, K.C. (1968). An undescribed subspecies of button-quail from the Philippines. *Bull. Brit. Orn. Club* **88(2)**: 24-25.
Parkes, K.C. (1971). Taxonomic and distributional notes on Philippine birds. *Nemouria* **4**: 1-67.
Parkes, K.C. & Amadon, D. (1959). A new species of rail from the Philippine Islands. *Wilson Bull.* **71**: 303-306.
Parkes, K.C., Kibbe, D.P. & Roth, E.L. (1978). First records of the Spotted Rail (*Pardirallus maculatus*) for the United States, Chile, Bolivia and western Mexico. *Amer. Birds* **32**: 295-299.
Parkes, K.C., Poole, A. & Lapham, H. (1971). The Ruddy Turnstone as an egg predator. *Wilson Bull.* **83**: 306-308.
Parmelee, D.F. (1970). Breeding behavior of the Sanderling in the Canadian high arctic. *Living Bird* **9**: 97-146.
Parmelee, D.F. (1985). Polar adaptations in the South Polar Skua (*Catharacta maccormicki*) and the Brown Skua (*Catharacta lonnbergi*) of Anvers Island, Antarctica. Pp. 520-529 in: *Proc. XVIII Int. Orn. Congr.* Moscow, 1982.
Parmelee, D.F. (1988a). The hybrid skua: a southern ocean enigma. *Wilson Bull.* **100**: 345-356.
Parmelee, D.F. (1988b). Unexpected weight gain in resident Antarctic Terns *Sterna vittata* during the austral winter. *Ibis* **130**: 438-443.
Parmelee, D.F. (1992). White-rumped Sandpiper (*Calidris fuscicollis*). No. **29** in: Poole *et al.* (1992-1993).
Parmelee, D.F. & MacDonald, S.D. (1960). *The Birds of West-central Ellesmere Island and Adjacent Areas*. National Museum of Canada Bulletin **169**. Ottawa. 101 pp.
Parmelee, D.F. & Maxson, S.J. (1975). The Antarctic Terns of Anvers Island. *Living Bird* **13**: 233-250.
Parmelee, D.F. & Payne, R.B. (1973). On multiple broods and the breeding stategy of arctic Sanderlings. *Ibis* **115**: 218-226.
Parmelee, D.F. & Pietz, P.J. (1987). Philopatry, mate and nest-site fidelity in the Brown Skuas of Anvers Island, Antarctica. *Condor* **89(4)**: 916-919.
Parmelee, D.F., Greiner, W.D. & Graul, D.W. (1968). Summer schedule and breeding biology of the White-rumped Sandpiper in the central Canadian arctic. *Wilson Bull.* **80**: 5-29.
Parmelee, D.F., Schwilling, M.D. & Stephens, H.A. (1969). Charadriiform birds of Cheyenne Bottoms. *Kansas Orn. Soc. Bull.* **20**: 17-24.
Parmelee, D.F., Stephens, H.A. & Schmidt, R.H. (1967). *The Birds of South-eastern Victoria Island and Adjacent Small Islands*. National Museum of Canada Bulletin **222**. Ottawa. 229 pp.
Parnell, G.W. (1967). Spotted Crake at Marandellas. *Honeyguide* **50**: 10.
Parnell, G.W. (1968). Behaviour and breeding of the Senegal Wattled Plover. *Honeyguide* **55**: 28.
Parnell, J.F. & Soots, R.F. (1975). Herring and Great Black-backed Gulls nesting in North Carolina. *Auk* **92**: 154-157.
Parnell, J.F., Erwin, R.M. & Molina, K.C. (1995). Gull-billed Tern, *Sterna nilotica*. No. **140** in: Poole & Gill (1994-1995).
Parr, R. (1980). Population study of Golden Plovers *Pluvialis apricaria* using marked birds. *Ornis Scand.* **11**: 179-189.
Parr, R. (1992). The decline to extinction of a population of Golden Plover in north-east Scotland. *Ornis Scand.* **23(2)**: 152-158.
Parr, R. (1993). Nest predation and numbers of Golden Plovers, *Pluvialis apricaria*, and other moorland birds. *Bird Study* **40(3)**: 223-231.
Parrinder, E.D. (1989). Little Ringed Plover *Charadrius dubius* in Britain in 1984. *Bird Study* **36(3)**: 147-153.
Parrinder, E.R. & Parrinder, E.D. (1969). Little Ringed Plovers in Britain in 1963-1967. *British Birds* **62**: 219-223.
Parrinder, E.R. & Parrinder, E.D. (1975). Little Ringed Plovers in Britain in 1968-73. *British Birds* **68(9)**: 359-368.
Parrish, G.R. & Pulham, G.W. (1995a). *Observations on the Breeding Ecology of the New Zealand Fairy Tern*. Department of Conservation, Auckland, New Zealand.
Parrish, G.R. & Pulham, G.W. (1995b). The population status, productivity and post breeding movements of the New Zealand Fairy Tern. Report to the Department of Conservation, Auckland.
Parrish, T.L., Anderson, S.H. & Oelklaus, W.F. (1993). Mountain Plover habitat selection in the Powder River Basin, Wyoming. *Prairie Nat.* **25(3)**: 219-226.
Parrott, J. (1979). Kaffir Rail *Rallus caerulescens* in west Africa. *Malimbus* **1**: 145-146.
Parsons, J. (1970). Relationship between egg size and post hatching chick mortality in the Herring Gull (*Larus argentatus*). *Nature* **228**: 1221-1222.
Parsons, J. (1971). Cannibalism in Herring Gulls. *British Birds* **64**: 528-537.
Parsons, J. (1972). Egg size, laying date and incubation period in the Herring Gull. *Ibis* **114**: 536-541.
Parsons, J. (1975a). Asynchronous hatching and chick mortality in the Herring Gull *Larus argentatus*. *Ibis* **117**: 517-520.
Parsons, J. (1975b). Seasonal variation in the breeding success of the Herring Gull: an experimental approach to pre-fledging success. *J. Anim. Ecol.* **44**: 553-573.
Parsons, J. (1976a). Factors determining the number and size of eggs laid by the Herring Gull. *Condor* **78**: 481-492.
Parsons, J. (1976b). Nesting density and breeding success in the Herring Gull *Larus argentatus*. *Ibis* **118**: 537-546.
Pascoe, J.G. (1984). A census of the South Polar Skua at Cape Hallett, Antarctica. *Notornis* **31(4)**: 312-319.
Paterson, A.J. (1986). Kleptoparasitic feeding by migrating skuas in Malaga Bay, Spain. *Ringing & Migration* **7(1)**: 51-55.
Paterson, A.M., Martínez-Vilalta, A. & Dies, J.I. (1992). Partial breeding failure of Audouin's Gull in two Spanish colonies in 1991. *British Birds* **85**: 97-100.

Paton, D.C. & Wykes, B.J. (1978). Re-appraisal of moult of Red-necked Stints in southern Australia. *Emu* **78(2)**: 54-60.
Paton, D.C., Wykes, B.J. & Dann, P. (1982). Moult of juvenile Curlew Sandpipers in southern Australia. *Emu* **82**: 54-56.
Paton, P.W.C. (1994a). *Breeding Biology of the Snowy Plover at Great Salt Lake, Utah*. PhD dissertation, Utah State University, Logan, Utah.
Paton, P.W.C. (1994b). Survival estimates for Snowy Plovers breeding at Great Salt Lake, Utah. *Condor* **96(4)**: 1106-1109.
Paton, P.W.C. (1995). Breeding biology of Snowy Plovers at Great Salt Lake, Utah. *Wilson Bull.* **107**: 275-288.
Paton, P.W.C. & Dalton, J. (1994). Breeding ecology of Long-billed Curlews at Great Salt Lake, Utah. *Great Basin Nat.* **54(1)**: 79-85.
Paton, P.W.C. & Edwards, T.C. (1990). Status and nesting ecology of the Snowy Plover at Great Salt Lake - 1990. *Utah Birds* **6(4)**: 49-66.
Paton, P.W.C., Ralph, C.J. & Erickson, R.A. (1992). Use of an inland site in northwestern California by Marbled Murrelets. Pp. 109-116 in: Carter & Morrison (1992).
Paton, P.W.C., Scott, J.M. & Burr, T.A. (1985). American Coot and Black-necked Stilt on the island of Hawaii. *Western Birds* **16(4)**: 175-181.
Patrikeev, M.V. (1995). *The Birds of Azerbaijan*. Draft MS.
Patten, S. & Weisbrod, A.R. (1974). Sympatry and interbreeding of Herring and Glaucous-winged Gulls in south-eastern Alaska. *Condor* **76**: 343-344.
Patterson, I.J. (1965). Timing and spacing of broods in the Black-headed Gull. *Ibis* **107**: 433-459.
Patterson, M.E., Fraser, J.D. & Roggenbuck, J.W. (1990). Piping Plover ecology, management and research needs. *Virginia J. Sci.* **41(4A)**: 419-426.
Patterson, M.E., Fraser, J.D. & Roggenbuck, J.W. (1991). Factors affecting Piping Plover productivity on Assateague Island (USA). *J. Wildl. Manage.* **55(3)**: 525-531.
Patterson, R.M. (1989a). Twenty five years of waders research in southeast Tasmania. *Stilt* **15**: 7-8.
Patterson, R.M. (1989b). A Black-tailed Native Hen near Hobart. *Tasmanian Bird Report* **18**: 29-30.
Patterson, R.M., Wakefield, W.C. & Wakefield, M. (1994). A Hudsonian Godwit *Limosa haemastica* in south-eastern Tasmania. *Austr. Bird Watcher* **15(7)**: 283-286.
Patton, S.R. & Southern, W.E. (1978). The effect of nocturnal red fox predation on the nesting success of colonial gulls. *Proc. Colonial Waterbird Group* **1**: 91-101.
Paul, R.T. (1995). Caspian Tern. In: Rodgers, J.A. (1995). *Endangered Birds of Florida*.
Pauler, K. (1968). Eine Brut des Tüpfelsumpfhuhns (*Porzana porzana*) in Gefangenschaft. *Egretta* **11**: 16-19.
Paulian, P. (1953). Pinnepèdes, cétacés, oiseaux des Îles Kerguelen et Amsterdam. Mission Kerguelen 1951. *Mém. Inst. Sci. Madagascar (Sér. A)* **8**: 111-234.
Paullin, D.C. (1987). Cannibalism in American Coots induced by severe spring weather and avian cholera. *Condor* **89**: 442-443.
Paulson, D.R. (1983). Fledging dates and southward migration of juveniles of some *Calidris* sandpipers. *Condor* **85**: 99-101.
Paulson, D.R. (1986). Identification of juvenile Tattlers, and a Gray-tailed Tattler record from Washington. *Western Birds* **17(1)**: 33-36.
Paulson, D.R. (1989). Surfbirds eating large edible mussels. *Wash. Birds* **1**: 35-36.
Paulson, D.R. (1990). Sandpiper-like feeding in Black-bellied Plovers. *Condor* **92(1)**: 245.
Paulson, D.R. (1995). Black-bellied Plover (*Pluvialis squatarola*). No. **186** in: Poole & Gill (1995).
Paulson, D.R. & Erckmann, W.J. (1985). Buff-breasted Sandpipers nesting in association with Black-bellied Plovers. *Condor* **87**: 429-430.
Paulson, D.R. & Erckmann, W.J. (1993). *Shorebirds of the Pacific Northwest*. University of Washington Press, Seattle, Washington.
Paulson, D.R. & Lee, D.S. (1992). Wintering of Lesser Golden-plovers in eastern North America. *J. Field Orn.* **63(2)**: 121-128. In English with Spanish summary.
Paynter, R.A. (1949). Clutch-size and the egg and chick mortality of Kent Island Herring Gulls. *Ecology* **30**: 146-166.
Paynter, R.A. (1955). *The Ornithogeography of the Yucatán Peninsula*. Peabody Museum of Natural History Yale University Bulletin **9**. New Haven, Connecticut.
Paynter, R.A. (1963). Birds from Flores, Lesser Sunda Islands. *Breviora* **182**: 1-5.
Paz, U. (1987). *The Birds of Israel*. Christopher Helm, Bromley, UK.
Peabody, P.B. (1922). Haunts and breeding habits of the Yellow Rail *Coturnicops noveboracensis*. *J. Mus. Comp. Oology* **2**: 33-44.
Peach, H.C. (1981). *The Foraging Ecology of Adult and Juvenile Semipalmated Plover (*Charadrius semipalmatus bonaparte*) on the Starrs Point Mudflat, Minas Basin*. BSc thesis, Acadia University, Nova Scotia, Canada.
Peach, W.J., Thompson, P.S. & Coulson, J.C. (1994). Annual and long-term variation in the survival rates of British Lapwings *Vanellus vanellus*. *J. Anim. Ecol.* **63(1)**: 60-70.
Peakall, D.B. (1967). Recent changes in the status of the Great Black-backed Gull. *Kingbird* **17**: 69-73.
Peakall, D.B., Fox, G.A., Gilman, A.P., Hallett, D.J. & Norstrom, R.J. (1980). The Herring Gull as a monitor of Great Lakes contaminants. Pp. 337-344 in: Afghan, B.K. & MacKay, D. (1980). *Hydrocarbons and Halogenated Hydrocarbon in the Aquatic Environment*. Plenum Press, New York.
Pearman, M. (1995a). Neotropical notebook. Bolivia. *Cotinga* **3**: 62.
Pearman, M. (1995b). Neotropical notebook. Falkland Islands/Islas Malvinas. *Cotinga* **3**: 63.
Pearse, T. (1946). Nesting of the Western Gull of the coast of Vancouver Island, British Columbia, and possible hybridization with the Glaucous-winged Gull. *Murrelet* **27**: 39-40.
Pearson, D. (1989). Breeding of the Banded Stilt in the Western Australian goldfields during 1986. *West. Austr. Nat.* **18(2)**: 34-36.
Pearson, D.J. (1974). The timing of wing moult in some Palaearctic waders wintering in east Africa. *Wader Study Group Bull.* **12**: 6-12.
Pearson, D.J. (1977). The first year moult of the Common Sandpiper *Tringa hypoleucos* in Kenya. *Scopus* **1**: 89-94.
Pearson, D.J. (1981). The wintering and moult of Ruffs *Philomachus pugnax* in the Kenyan Rift Valley. *Ibis* **123**: 158-182.
Pearson, D.J. (1984a). The moult of the Little Stint *Calidris minuta* in the Kenyan Rift Valley. *Ibis* **126**: 1-15.
Pearson, D.J. (1984b). A Pintail Snipe *Gallinago stenura* at Naivasha. *Scopus* **8**: 45-46.
Pearson, D.J. (1986). East African bird report. *Scopus* **8**: 101-123.
Pearson, D.J. (1987). The status, migrations and seasonality of the Little Stint in Kenya. *Ringing & Migration* **8(2)**: 91-108.
Pearson, D.J., Philips, J.H. & Backhurst, G.C. (1970). Weights of some Palearctic waders wintering in Kenya. *Ibis* **112**: 199-208.
Pearson, D.L. (1975). Range extensions and new records for bird species in Ecuador, Peru and Bolivia. *Condor* **77**: 96-99.
Pechuán, L. (1974). La colonia de *Larus audouinii* de las Islas Columbretes. *Ardeola* **20**: 358-359.
Pechuán, L. (1975). Nidificación de *Larus audouinii* en las Islas Columbretes. *Ardeola* **21(1)**: 407-408.
Peckover, W.S. & Filewood, L.W.C. (1976). *Birds of New Guinea and Tropical Australia*. A.H. & A.W. Reed, Sydney.
Pedersen, M.B. (1989a). [Wintering strategy of the Jack Snipe in Denmark]. *Dan. Orn. Foren. Tidssk.* **83(1-2)**: 69-73. In Danish with English summary.
Pedersen, M.B. (1989b). [Changes in the occurrence of the roosting and moulting Snipes and Jack Snipes on inland habitats in Denmark]. *Dan. Orn. Foren. Tidssk.* **83(1-2)**: 75-82. In Danish with English summary.
Pedersen, M.B. (1990). [Project Jack Snipe]. *Vår Fågelvärld* **49**: 485-487. In Swedish.
Pedersen, M.B. (1991). Vinterforekomsten af Enkeltbekkasin *Lymnocryptes minimus* og Dobbeltbekkasin *Gallinago gallinago* i Danmark. [Winter population estimates of Jack Snipe *Lymnocryptes minimus* and Common Snipe *Gallinago gallinago* in Denmark]. *Dan. Orn. Foren. Tidssk.* **85(3-4)**: 173-174. In Danish with English summary.
Pedersen, M.B. (1992). Breeding status of the Jack Snipe in south Baltic: a preliminary study in Lithuania. WWF Project **326**(Suppl. 1992). 2 pp.
Pedersen, M.B. (1994). Jack Snipe. *Lymnocryptes minimus*. Pp. 266-267 in: Tucker & Heath (1994).
Pedersen, M.B. (1995). Opportunistic behaviour as key-determinant in the winter strategy of the Jack Snipe *Lymnocryptes minimus* in southern Scandinavia. *Wader Study Group Bull.* **78**: 23-26.
Pedler, L. (1982a). An Oriental Plover in the mid-north of South Australia. *S. Austr. Orn.* **28(8)**: 207.
Pedler, L. (1982b). Northern records of the Painted Button-quail in South Australia. *S. Austr. Orn.* **29(1)**: 1-5.
Peero, M., Michiels, G. & Jacob, P.J. (1985). Statut des Guifette moustac (*Chlidonias hybridus*) et leucoptère (*Chlidonias leucopterus*) en Belgique. Rappel des critères d'identification. *Aves* **22(2)**: 89-106.
Pellow, K. (1990). Caspian Plover in Scilly: first British record this century. *British Birds* **83(12)**: 549-551.
Penard, F.B. & Penard, A.P. (1908-1910). *De Vogels van Guyana (Suriname, Cayenne en Demarara)*. N.J. Boon, Amsterdam.
Pendleton, R.C. (1947). Field observations on the Spotted Button-quail on Guadalcanal. *Auk* **64**: 418-421.
Penland, S. (1981). Natural history of the Caspian Tern in Grays Harbor, Washington. *Murrelet* **62**: 66-72.
Penland, S. (1984). An alternative origin of supernormal clutches in Caspian Terns. *Condor* **86**: 496.
Pennie, I.D. (1946). Common Gulls nesting on birch trees. *British Birds* **39**: 61.
Penniman, T.M., Coulter, M., Spear, L.B. & Boekelheide, R.J. (1990). Western Gull. Pp. 218-244 in: Ainley & Boekelheide (1990).
Penny, M.J. (1974). *The Birds of Seychelles and the Outlying Islands*. Collins, London.
Penny, M.J. & Diamond, A.W. (1971). The White-throated Rail *Dryolimnas cuvieri* on Aldabra. *Phil. Trans. Roy. Soc., London B* **260**: 529-548.
Penrith, E. (1992). Grey Phalarope - what's in a name? *Bee-eater* **43(1)**: 4-6.
Penry, E.H. (1979). The Rock Pratincole (*Glareola nuchalis*) at Greystone, Kitwe and a review of its migratory movements. *Bull. Zambian Orn. Soc.* **11(2)**: 20-32.
Penry, E.H. (1980). Blacksmith Plover *Vanellus armatus* breeding on the Copperbelt. *Bull. Zambia Orn. Soc.* **12(1)**: 10-12.
Penry, E.H. (1987). Recent records of Wattled Plover (*Vanellus senegallus*) in the Orange Free State and western Transvaal. Mirafra **4(1)**: 3-4.
Penry, E.H. (1994). *A Bird Atlas of Botswana*. University of Natal Press, Pietermaritzburg, South Africa.
Penry, E.H. & Tarboton, W.R. (1990). Red-winged Pratincoles breeding at Lake Ngami. *Babbler* **19**: 7-11.
de la Peña, M.R. (1981a). Nidificación de aves en la República Argentina. [Nesting of birds in the Republic of Argentina]. *Centzontle* **1(3/4)**: 193-201.
de la Peña, M.R. (1981b). Nidificación de ostreros Haematopodidae en la República Argentina. [Nesting of oyster-catchers in the Republic of Argentina]. *Centzontle* **1(3/4)**: 203-207.
de la Peña, M.R. (1987). *Nidos y Huevos de Aves Argentinas*. M.R. de la Peña, Santa Fe, Argentina.
de la Peña, M.R. (1992). *Guía de Aves Argentinas*. Vol. 2. 2nd edition. Falconiformes-Charadriiformes. Literature of Latin America, Buenos Aires.
Percy, W. (1963). Further notes on the African Finfoot, *Podica senegalensis* (Vieillot). *Bull. Brit. Orn. Club* **83**: 127-132.
Perdeck, A.C. (1960). Observations on the reproductive behaviour of the Great Skua or Bonxie, *Stercorarius skua skua* (Brünn), in Shetland. *Ardea* **48**: 111-136.
Perdeck, A.C. (1963). The early reproductive behaviour of the Arctic Skua, *Stercorarius parasiticus* (L.). *Ardea* **51**: 1-15.
Perennou, C. (1991). *Les Recensements Internationaux d'Oiseaux d'Eau en Afrique Tropicale*. IWRB Special Publication **15**, Slimbridge, UK.
Perennou, C., Mundkur, T., Scott, D.A., Follestad, A. & Kvenild, L. (1994). *The Asian Waterfowl Census 1987-91: Distribution and Status of Asian Waterfowl*. AWB Publication **86**. IWRB Publication **24**. AWB & IWRB, Kuala Lumpur & Slimbridge.
Peres, C.A. & Whittaker, A. (1991). Annotated checklist of the bird species of the upper Rio Urucu, Amazonas, Brazil. *Bull. Brit. Orn. Club* **111**: 156-171.
Pereyra, J.A. (1923). Aves de la región ribereña de la provincia de Buenos Aires. *Hornero* **3**: 159-174.
Pereyra, J.A. (1931). Los Cresciscus. *Hornero* **4**: 414-415.
Pérez, G.S.A. (1968). Notes on the breeding season of Guam Rails (*Rallus owstoni*). *Micronesica* **4**: 133-135.
Pérez, J.L. (1964). Nidificación de Canasteras y Charrancitos en el río Guadiana. *Ardeola* **10**: 37-38.
Perfiliev, V.I. (1963). [New data on the ecology of Siberian White Crane]. *Byull. Mosk. Ova. Ispyt. Prir. Otd. Biol.* **68(1)**: 25-28. In Russian.
Perfiliev, V.I. (1965). [The Siberian Crane and its preservation in Yakutia]. Pp. 99-113 in: *Priroda Yakutii i Okhrana*. Yakutsk, USSR. In Russian.
Peris, S.J. & Alabarce, E.A. (1992). The post-breeding avifauna of the montane pasture lands (Tafí Valley, Aconquija Mountains Tucuman). *Acta Zool. Lilloana* **40(2)**: 125-133.
Peris, S.J., Corrales, L., González, N. & Velasco, J.C. (1992). Surveys of wintering Great Bustards in West-Central Spain. *Biol. Conserv.* **60(2)**: 109-114.
Perkins, S. (1992). Skua identification. *Bird Observer* **20(2)**: 91-93.
van Perlo, B. (1995). *Birds of Eastern Africa*. Harper Collins Publishers, London.
Perrins, C.M., Lebreton, J.D. & Hirons, G.J.M. eds. (1991). *Bird Population Studies. Relevance to Conservation and Management*. Oxford University Press, Oxford.
Perry, I.A. (1975). Chestnut-banded Sandplover at Aiselby, Bulawayo. *Honeyguide* **84**: 44-45.
Perry, P. (1992). Feeding behaviour of Little Stints. *British Birds* **85(6)**: 309-310.
Perry, R. (1946). *Lundy, Isle of Puffins*. Lindsay Drummond, London.
Persson, H. (1991). [The Great Bustard and the Greylag Goose - a conservation problem]. *Anser* **30(2)**: 119-124. In Swedish with English summary.
Peter, H.U., Kaiser, M. & Gebauer, A. (1990). Ecological and morphological investigations on South Polar Skuas (*Catharacta maccormicki*) and Brown Skuas (*Catharacta skua lonnbergi*) on Fildes Peninsula, King George Island, South Shetland Islands. *Zool. Jb. Syst. Bd.* **117**: 201-218.
Peter, H.U., Kaiser, M., Gebauer, A. & Zippel, D. (1988). Zur Dynamik der Winterbestände des Weißgesicht-Scheidenschnabels (*Chionis alba*) auf King George Island (South Shetland Islands). [The dynamics of wintering groups of *Chionis alba* at King George Island (South Shetland Islands)]. *Beitr. Vogelkd.* **34**: 205-220. In German with English summary.
Peters, J.L. (1925). A Review of the Limpkins (*Aramus* Vieillot). *Occas. Pap. Boston Soc. Nat. Hist.* **5**: 141-144.
Peters, J.L. (1934). *Check-list of Birds of the World*. Vol. 2. Museum of Comparative Zoology, Harvard University Press, Cambridge, Massachusetts.
Peters, J.L. & Griscom, L. (1928). A new rail and a new dove from Micronesia. *Proc. New England Zool. Club* **10**: 99-106.
Petersen, A. (1976a). Size variables in Puffins *Fratercula arctica* from Iceland and bill features as criteria of age. *Ornis Scand.* **7**: 185-192.
Petersen, A. (1976b). Age of first breeding in Puffin *Fratercula arctica* L. *Astarte* **9**: 43-50.
Petersen, A. (1979). [The breeding birds of Flatey and some adjoining islets in Breidafjördur, northwest Iceland]. *Natturufraedingurinn* **49**: 229-256. In Icelandic with English summary.
Petersen, A. (1981). *Breeding Biology and Feeding Ecology of Black Guillemots*. PhD thesis, University of Oxford, Oxford.
Petersen, A. (1992). [Turnstone *Arenaria interpres* holding territory in Iceland]. *Bliki* **12**: 57-58. In Icelandic with English summary.
Petersen, A. (1994). Black Guillemot. *Cepphus grylle*. Pp. 306-307 in: Tucker & Heath (1994).
Petersen, K.H. (1928). Rosenmaagen, *Larus roseus*, Mcgill., i Grønland. *Dan. Orn. Foren. Tidssk.* **22**: 76-90.
Petersen, P.C. (1989). Sharp-tailed Sandpiper at Davenport. *Iowa Bird Life* **59(3)**: 90-91.
Peterson, B. (1995). Elegant encounter: exploring a tern colony in Orange County, California. *Bird Watcher's Digest* **17(6)**: 69-71.
Peterson, R.T. & Chalif, E.L. (1973). *A Field Guide to Mexican Birds*. Houghton Mifflin, Boston.
Petit, P. (1976). Presence et nidification d'une Sterne voyageuse (*Sterna bengalensis*) dans une colonie de Sterne caugek (*Sterna sandvicensis*) sur le Banc d'Arguin (France). *Ardea* **64**: 81-83.
Petretti, F. (1985). Preliminary data on the status of the Little Bustard in Italy. *Bustard Studies* **2**: 165-170.
Petrie, M. (1983). Female Moorhens compete for small fat males. *Science* **220**: 413-414.
Petrie, M. (1984). Territory size in the Moorhen (*Gallinula chloropus*): an outcome of RHP asymmetry between neighbours. *Anim. Behav.* **32**: 861-870.
Petter, A.J., Chermette, R. & Vassart, M. (1988). *Cagourakis dorsalata* n. g., n. sp., Heterakidae (Nematoda) parasite du Cagou (*Rhynochetos jubatus*) (Ralliformes) en Nouvelle-Calédonie. *Bull. Mus. Natl. Hist. Nat.* **10**: 675-683.
Pettet, A. (1982). Feeding behaviour of White-tailed Plover. *British Birds* **75(4)**: 182.
Pettigrew, J.D. & Frost, B.J. (1985). A tactile fovea in the Scolopacidae? *Brain Behav. Evol.* **26**: 185-195.
Pettingill, E.R. (1960). *Penguin Summer*. Clarkson N. Potter Inc, New York.
Pettingill, O.S. (1937). Behavior of Black Skimmers at Cardwell Island, Virginia. *Auk* **54**: 237-244.
Pettingill, O.S. (1939). History of one hundred nests of Arctic Tern. *Auk* **56**: 420-427.
Pettit, T.N. & Whittow, G.C. (1983). Embryonic respiration and growth in two species of noddy terns. *Physiol. Zool.* **83**: 355-361.
Pettit, T.N., Grant, G.S. & Whittow, G.C. (1984). Nestling metabolism and growth in the Black Noddy and White Tern. *Condor* **86**: 83-85.

Pettit, T.N., Grant, G.S., Whittow, G.C., Rahn, H. & Paganelli, C.V. (1981). Respiratory gas exchange and growth of White Tern embryos. *Condor* **83**: 355-361.
Petursson, G. (1992). The first Semipalmated Sandpiper *Calidris pusilla* found in Iceland. *Bliki* **12**: 1-8. In Icelandic with English summary.
Pfeifer, R. (1993). Spatial differences in the seasonal pattern of migrating Common Sandpipers *Actitis hypoleucos*. *Orn. Anz.* **32(3)**: 141-145.
Pfister, C., Harrington, B.A. & Levine, M. (1992). The impact of human disturbance on shorebirds at a migration staging area. *Biol. Conserv.* **60**: 115-126.
Philippi, R.A., Johnson, A.W., Goodall, J.D. & Behn, F. (1954). Notas sobre aves de Magallanes y Tierra del Fuego. *Bol. Mus. Nac. Hist. Nat.* **26**: 1-56.
Philips, R.L. (1988). Observations on the Lesser Black-winged Plover in the South-east Lowveld. *Honeyguide* **34**: 124.
Phillips, A.R. (1975). Semipalmated Sandpiper: identification, migrations, summer and winter ranges. *Amer. Birds* **29**: 799-806.
Phillips, B.T. (1945). Photographing the Ibis-bill. *J. Bombay Nat. Hist. Soc.* **45(3)**: 347-352.
Phillips, N.J. (1984). Migrant species new to the Seychelles. *Bull. Brit. Orn. Club* **104**: 9-10.
Phillips, R.E. (1972). Sexual and agonistic behavior in the Killdeer, *Charadrius vociferus*. *Anim. Behav.* **20**: 1-9.
Phillips, R.E. (1977). Notes on the behaviour of the New Zealand Shore Plover. *Emu* **77(1)**: 23-27.
Phillips, R.E. (1980). Behaviour and systematics of New Zealand plovers. *Emu* **80**: 177-197.
Phillips, T.J. (1961a). The Pheasant-tailed Jacana. *Malay. Nat. J.* **15**: 66-67.
Phillips, T.J. (1961b). Wigeon, jacanas and dabchicks. *Malay. Nat. J.* **15**: 72-73.
Phillips, W.R. (1989). Life atop the lilypads. *Birds International* **1**: 18-24.
Phillips, W.W.A. (1942). Some observations on the nesting habits of the Indian Courser, *Cursorius coromandelicus* (Gmelin). *J. Bombay Nat. Hist. Soc.* **43**: 200-205.
Phillips, W.W.A. (1978). *Annotated Checklist of the Birds of Ceylon*. Revised edition. Wildlife & Nature Protection Society of Ceylon in association with the Ceylon Bird Club.
Phipps, G. (1976). Breeding the Black-breasted Turnix. *Austr. Avicult.* **30**: 130-134.
Phythian-Adams, E.G. (1934). Woodsnipe (*Capella nemoricola* Hodgs.) in Malabar. *J. Bombay Nat. Hist. Soc.* **37(1)**: 220-221.
Phythian-Adams, E.G. (1940). Eggs of Yellow-wattled Lapwing *Lobipluvia malabarica* (Bodd.). *J. Bombay Nat. Hist. Soc.* **41(4)**: 899.
Piao Renzhu (1989). Nursing of the Whooping Crane *Grus americana* by the Sandhill Crane *Grus canadensis*. *Chinese Wildlife* **3**: 35-37, 6.
Piatt, J.F. (1990). The aggregative response of Common Murres and Atlantic Puffins to schools of capelin. Pp. 36-51 in: Sealy (1990).
Piatt, J.F. & Ford, R.G. (1993). Distribution and abundance of Marbled Murrelets in Alaska. *Condor* **95**: 662-669.
Piatt, J.F. & Gould, P.J. (1994). Postbreeding dispersal and drift-net mortality of endangered Japanese Murrelets. *Auk* **111**: 953-961.
Piatt, J.F. & Naslund, N.L. (1995). Abundance, distribution, and population status of Marbled Murrelets in Alaska. Pp. 285-294 in: Ralph *et al*. (1995).
Piatt, J.F. & Nettleship, D.N. (1985). Diving depths of four alcids. *Auk* **102**: 293-297.
Piatt, J.F. & Nettleship, D.N. (1987). Incidental catch of marine birds and mammals in fishing nets off Newfoundland, Canada. *Marine Pollution Bull.* **18**: 344-349.
Piatt, J.F., Carter, H.R. & Nettleship, D.N. (1991). Effects of oil pollution on marine bird populations. Pp. 125-141 in: White, J. ed. (1991). *The Effects of Oil on Wildlife: Research, Rehabilitation and General Concerns*. Sheridan Press, Hanover, Pennsylvania.
Piatt, J.F., Hatch, S.A., Roberts, B.D., Lidster, W.W., Wells, J.L. & Hainey, C.J. (1988). *Populations Productivity and Feeding Habits of Seabirds on St. Lawrence Island, Alaska*. US Fish & Wildlife Service, Anchorage, Alaska.
Piatt, J.F., Lensink, C.J., Butler, W., Kendziorek, M. & Nysewander, D.R. (1990). Immediate impact of the 'Exxon Valdez' oil spill on marine birds. *Auk* **107**: 387-397.
Piatt, J.F., Naslund, N.L. & van Pelt, T.I. (1994). Nest-site selection and fidelity in Kittlitz's Murrelet. *Beringian Seabird Bull.* **2**: 54-56.
Piatt, J.F., Nettleship, D.N. & Threlfall, W. (1984). Net mortality of Common Murres *Uria aalge* and Atlantic Puffins *Fratercula arctica* in Newfoundland, 1951-1981. Pp. 196-206 in: Nettleship *et al*. (1984).
Piatt, J.F., Roberts, B. & Hatch, S. (1990). Colony attendance and population monitoring of Least and Crested Auklets at St. Lawrence Island, Alaska. *Condor* **92**: 97-106.
Piatt, J.F., Roberts, B., Lidster, W., Wells, J. & Hatch, S.A. (1990). Effects of human disturbance on breeding Least and Crested Auklets at St. Lawrence Island, Alaska. *Auk* **107**: 342-350.
Piatt, J.F., Wells, J.J., MacCharles, A. & Fadely, B.S. (1991). The distribution of seabirds and fish in relation to ocean currents in the southeastern Chukchi Sea. Pp. 21-31 in: Montevecchi, W.A. & Gaston, A.J. eds. (1991). *Studies of High-latitude Seabirds*. Vol. 1. Behavioural, Energetic and Oceanographic Aspects of Seabird Feeding Ecology. Occasional Paper **68**. Canadian Wildlife Service, Ottawa.
Pickett, P.E., Maxson, S.J. & Oring, L.W. (1988). Interspecific interactions of Spotted Sandpipers. *Wilson Bull.* **100**: 297-302.
Pienkowski, M.W. (1978/79). Difference in habitat requirements and distribution patterns of plovers and sandpipers as investigated by studies of feeding behaviour. *Verh. orn. Ges. Bayern* **23**: 105-124.
Pienkowski, M.W. (1982). Diet and energy intake of Grey and Ringed Plovers, *Pluvialis squatarola* and *Charadrius hiaticula*, in the non-breeding season. *J. Zool., London* **197(4)**: 511-549.
Pienkowski, M.W. (1983a). Changes in the foraging pattern of plovers in relation to environmental factors. *Anim. Behav.* **31**: 244-264.
Pienkowski, M.W. (1983b). Development of feeding and foraging behaviour in young Ringed Plovers *Charadrius hiaticula*, in Greenland and Britain. *Dan. Orn. Foren. Tidssk.* **77(3-4)**: 133-147.
Pienkowski, M.W. (1983c). The effects of environmental conditions on feeding rates and prey-selection of shore plovers. *Ornis Scand.* **14**: 227-238.
Pienkowski, M.W. (1983d). Surface activity of some intertidal invertebrates in relation to temperature and the foraging behaviour of their shorebird predators. *Mar. Ecol. Prog. Ser.* **11**: 141-150.
Pienkowski, M.W. (1983e). Breeding biology and population dynamics of Ringed Plovers *Charadrius hiaticula* in Britain and Greenland: nest-predation as a possible factor limiting distribution and timing of breeding. *J. Zool., London* **202(1)**: 83-114.
Pienkowski, M.W. (1984a). Behaviour of young Ringed Plovers *Charadrius hiaticula* and its relationship to growth and survival to reproductive age. *Ibis* **126(2)**: 133-135.
Pienkowski, M.W. (1984b). Breeding biology and population dynamics of Ringed Plovers *Charadrius hiaticula* in Britain and Greenland: nest-predation as a possible factor limiting distribution and timing of breeding. *J. Zool., London* **202**: 83-114.
Pienkowski, M.W. & Dick, W.J.A. (1975). The migration and wintering of Dunlin *Calidris alpina* in north-west Africa. *Ornis Scand.* **6**: 151-167.
Pienkowski, M.W. & Evans, P.R. (1985). The role of migration in the population dynamics of birds. Pp. 331-352 in: Sibly & Smith (1985).
Pienkowski, M.W. & Green, G.H. (1976). Breeding biology of Sanderlings in north-east Greenland. *British Birds* **69**: 165-177.
Pienkowski, M.W. & Greenwood, J.J.D. (1979). Why change mates? *Biol. J. Linn. Soc.* **12**: 85-94.
Pienkowski, M.W. & Pienkowski, A.E. (1983). WSG project on the movement of wader populations in western Europe: eighth progress report. *Wader Study Group Bull.* **38**: 13-22.
Pienkowski, M.W. & Pienkowski, A.E. (1989). Limitation by nesting habitat of the density of breeding Ringed Plovers *Charadrius hiaticula*: a natural experiment. *Wildfowl* **40**: 115-126.
Pienkowski, M.W., Lloyd, C.S. & Minton, C.D.T. (1979). Seasonal and migrational weight changes in Dunlins. *Bird Study* **26**: 134-148.
Pierce, R. (1990a). Feeding observations on the Magellanic Plover *Pluvianellus socialis* at Peninsula Valdés, Chubut, Argentina. *Hornero* **13**: 166-167.
Pierce, R. (1990b). Observations on the Diademed Sandpiper Plover *Phegornis mitchellii* in Peru. *Hornero* **13**: 168-169.
Pierce, R.J. (1974). Presumed attempted breeding of White-winged Black Tern in New Zealand. *Notornis* **21(2)**: 129-134.
Pierce, R.J. (1978). Feeding methods of an Oriental Pratincole. *Notornis* **25(4)**: 290.
Pierce, R.J. (1979). Foods and feeding of the Wrybill (*Anarhynchus frontalis*) on its riverbed breeding grounds. *Notornis* **26(1)**: 1-21.
Pierce, R.J. (1980a). Habitats and feeding of the Auckland Island Banded Dotterel (*Charadrius bicinctus exilis* Falla 1978) in autumn. *Notornis* **27(4)**: 309-324.
Pierce, R.J. (1980b). The Black Stilt - endangered bird of the high country. *Forest Bird* **13**: 15-18.
Pierce, R.J. (1982). *A Comparative Ecological Study of Pied and Black Stilts in South Canterbury*. PhD thesis, University of Otago, Otago, New Zealand.
Pierce, R.J. (1983). Charadriiforms of a high country river valley. *Notornis* **30**: 169-185.
Pierce, R.J. (1984a). The changed distribution of stilts in New Zealand. *Notornis* **31(1)**: 7-18.
Pierce, R.J. (1984b). Plumage, morphology and hybridization of New Zealand stilts *Himantopus* spp. *Notornis* **31(2)**: 106-130.
Pierce, R.J. (1984c). Breeding success of isolated pairs of Caspian Terns in Canterbury. *Notornis* **31(3)**: 185-190.
Pierce, R.J. (1985). Feeding methods of stilts (*Himantopus* spp.). *New Zealand J. Zool.* **12**: 467-472.
Pierce, R.J. (1986a). Foraging responses of stilts (*Himantopus* spp.) to changes in abundance of their riverbed prey. *New Zealand J. Mar. Freshwater Res.* **12**: 467-472.
Pierce, R.J. (1986b). Differences in susceptibility to predation between Pied and Black Stilts (*Himantopus* spp., Aves). *Auk* **103(2)**: 273-280.
Pierce, R.J. (1986c). Observations on behaviour and foraging of the Ibisbill *Ibidorhyncha struthersii* in Nepal. *Ibis* **128(1)**: 37-47.
Pierce, R.J. (1987). Observations on distribution and numbers of Double-banded Plovers in Tasmania. *Stilt* **11**: 32-35.
Pierce, R.J. (1989). Breeding and social patterns of Banded Dotterels (*Charadrius bicinctus*) at Cass River. *Notornis* **36**: 13-23.
Pierotti, R. (1981). Male and female parental roles in the Western Gull under different environmental conditions. *Auk* **98**: 532-549.
Pierotti, R. (1982). Habitat selection and its effect on reproductive output in the Herring Gull in Newfoundland. *Ecology* **63**: 854-868.
Pierotti, R. (1983). Gull-puffin interactions on Great Island, Newfoundland. *Biol. Conserv.* **26**: 1-14.
Pierotti, R. (1987). Behavioral consequences of habitat selection in the Herring Gull. Pp. 119-128 in: Hand *et al.* (1987).
Pierotti, R. (1988a). Associations between marine birds and mammals in the northwest Atlantic Ocean. Pp. 31-58 in: Burger (1988c).
Pierotti, R. (1988b). Interactions between gulls and otariid pinnipeds: competition, commensalism, and cooperation. Pp. 205-231 in: Burger (1988c).
Pierotti, R. & Annett, C. (1991). Diet choice in the Herring Gull: constraints imposed by reproductive and ecological factors. *Ecology* **72**: 319-328.
Pierotti, R. & Annett, C. (1995). Western Gull (*Larus occidentalis*). No. **174** in: Poole & Gill (1995).
Pierotti, R. & Bellrose, C.A. (1986). Proximate and ultimate causation of egg size and the "third-chick disadvantage" in the Western Gull. *Auk* **103**: 401-407.
Pierotti, R. & Good, T.P. (1994). Herring Gull (*Larus argentatus*). No. **124** in: Poole & Gill (1994-1995).
Pierotti, R. & Murphy, E.C. (1987). Intergenerational conflicts in gulls. *Anim. Behav.* **35**: 435-444.
Pierre, J.P. (1994). Effects of sexual dimorphism on feeding behaviour of the Bar-tailed Godwit (*Limosa lapponica*) at a southern hemisphere wintering site. *New Zealand Nat. Sci.* **21**: 109-112.
Piersma, T. (1983). [Communal roosting Black-tailed Godwits *Limosa limosa* on the Mokkebank]. *Limosa* **56**: 1-8. In Dutch with English summary.
Piersma, T. (1985). Foot-vibration and crouching in foraging Mongolian Plovers and a 'crocodile-posture' in Grey-tailed Tattlers. *Stilt* **6**: 29-30.
Piersma, T. (1986a). Coastal waders on three Canary Islands in March-April 1986. *Wader Study Group Bull.* **48**: 19-20.
Piersma, T. ed. (1986b). *Breeding Waders in Europe. A Review of Population Size Estimates and a Bibliography of Information Sources*. Wader Study Group Bulletin **48**(Supplement). 116 pp.
Piersma, T. (1986c). Foraging behaviour of Terek Sandpipers *Xenus cinereus* feeding on sand-bubbling crabs *Scopimera globosa*. *J. Orn.* **127**: 475-486.
Piersma, T. (1986d). Feeding method of Spoon-billed Sandpipers on a mudflat in South Korea. *J. Bombay Nat. Hist. Soc.* **83**(Suppl.): 206-208.
Piersma, T. (1986e). Eastern Curlews *Numenius madagascariensis* feeding on *Macrophthalmus* and other ocypodid crabs in the Nakdong Estuary, South Korea. *Emu* **86(3)**: 155-160.
Piersma, T. (1987). Hop, skip or jump? Constraints on migration of arctic waders by feeding, fattening and flight speed. *Limosa* **60**: 185-194.
Piersma, T. (1989a). Knot (*Calidris canutus*). Pp. 264-275 in: Ens *et al*. (1989).
Piersma, T. (1989b). Bar-tailed Godwit (*Limosa lapponica*). Pp. 315-319 in: Ens *et al*. (1989).
Piersma, T. (1989c). Redshank (*Tringa totanus*). Pp. 323-326 in: Ens *et al*. (1989).
Piersma, T. (1994). *Close to the Edge: Energetic Bottlenecks and the Evolution of Migratory Pathways in Knots*. PhD thesis, Universiteit Groningen, Texel, the Netherlands.
Piersma, T. (1995). Morph and sex composition of Ruffs on Russian tundra in June 1994: are satellite males more prone to migrate northwards than resident males? *Wader Study Group Bull.* **78**: 31-32.
Piersma, T. & Barter, M. (1991). Wader catching casualties for body condition analysis: rationale and first results for Great Knots. *Stilt* **19**: 36-38.
Piersma, T. & Beukema, J.J. eds. (1993). Trophic interactions between shorebirds and their invertebrate prey. *Neth. J. Sea Res.* **31**(Special issue): 299-512.
Piersma, T. & Davidson, N.C. (1992a). The migrations and annual cycles of five subspecies of Knots in perspective. *Wader Study Group Bull.* **64**: 187-197.
Piersma, T. & Davidson, N.C. eds. (1992b). *The Migration of Knots*. Wader Study Group Bulletin **64**(Supplment). 209 pp.
Piersma, T. & Jukema, J. (1990). Budgeting the flight of a long-distance migrant: changes in nutrient reserve levels of Bar-tailed Godwits at successive spring staging sites. *Ardea* **78**: 315-337.
Piersma, T. & Jukema, J. (1993). Red breasts as honest signals of migratory quality in a long-distance migrant, the Bar-tailed Godwit. *Condor* **95(1)**: 163-177.
Piersma, T. & Morrison, R.I.G. (1994). Energy expenditure and water turnover of incubating Ruddy Turnstones: high costs under high arctic climatic conditions. *Auk* **111(2)**: 366-376.
Piersma, T. & Ntiamoa-Baidu, Y. (1995). *Waterbird Ecology and the Management of Coastal Wetlands in Ghana*. NIOZ-report 1995-6, Texel, the Netherlands.
Piersma, T. & Zegers, P. (1983). Aspects of the foraging behaviour of Grey Plovers. Pp. 27-43 in: Kersten, M., Piersma, T., Smit, C. & Zegers, P. eds. (1983). *Wader Migration along the Atlantic Coast of Morocco, March 1981*. RIN Report **83/20**. Texel, the Netherlands.
Piersma, T., Beintema, A.J., Davidson, N.C., Münster, O.A.G. & Pienkowski, M.W. (1987). Wader migration systems in the East Atlantic. *Wader Study Group Bull.* **49**(Suppl.), *IWRB Spec. Publ.* **7**: 35-56.
Piersma, T., Bruinzeel, L., Drent, R., Kersten, M., van der Meer, J. & Wiersma, P. (1996). Variability in basal metabolic rate of a long-distance migrant shorebird (Red Knot *Calidris canutus*) reflects shifts in organ sizes. *Physiol. Zool.* **69**: 191-217.
Piersma, T., Cadée, N. & Daan, N. (1995). Seasonality in basal metabolic rate and thermal conductance in a long-distance migrant shorebird, the Knot (*Calidris canutus*). *J. Comp. Physiol. B Biochem. Syst. Environm. Physiol.* **165(1)**: 37-45.
Piersma, T., Drent, R.H. & Wiersma, P. (1991). Temperate versus tropical wintering in the world's northernmost breeder, the Knot: a metabolic scope and resource levels restrict subspecific options. Pp. 761-772 in: Bell, B.D., Cossee, R.O., Flux, J.E.C., Heather, B.C., Hitchmough, R.A., Robertson, C.J.R. & Williams, M.J. eds. (1991). *Acta XX Congressus Internationalis Ornithologici*. Vol. 2. New Zealand Ornithological Congress Trust Board, Wellington.
Piersma, T., van Gils, J., de Goeij, P. & van der Meer, J. (1995). Holling's functional response model as a tool to link the food-finding mechanism of a probing shorebird with its spatial distribution. *J. Anim. Ecol.* **64**: 493-504.
Piersma, T., de Goeij, P. & Tulp, I. (1993). An evaluation of intertidal feeding habitats from a shorebird perspective: towards relevant comparisons between temperate and tropical mudflats. *Netherlands J. Sea Res.* **31**: 503-512.
Piersma, T., Hoekstra, R., Dekinga, A., Koolhaas, A., Wolf, P., Battley, P. & Wiersma, P. (1993). Scale and intensity of intertidal habitat use by Knots *Calidris canutus* in the western Wadden Sea in relation to food, friends and foes. *Netherlands J. Sea Res.* **31**: 331-357.
Piersma, T., Klaassen, M., Bruggemann, J.H., Blomert, A.M., Gueye, A., Ntiamoa-Baidu, Y. & van Brederode, N.E. (1990). Seasonal timing of the spring departure of waders from the Banc d'Arguin, Mauritania. *Ardea* **78(1/2)**: 123-134.
Piersma, T., Koolhaas, A. & Dekinga, A. (1993). Interactions between stomach structure and diet choice in shorebirds. *Auk* **110**: 552-564.

Piersma, T., Ott, C., Scheele, A. & Jukema, J. (1991). [Body fat of *Pluvialis apricaria*]. *Limosa* **64(4)**: 173-175. In Dutch.
Piersma, T., Prokosch, P. & Bredin, D. (1992). The migration system of Afro-Siberian Knots *Calidris canutus canutus*. Pp. 52-63 in: Piersma & Davidson (1992b).
Piersma, T., Tulp, I., Verkuil, Y., Wiersma, P., Gudmundsson, G.A. & Lindström, Å. (1991). Arctic sounds on temperate shores: the occurrence of song and ground display in Knots *Calidris canutus* at spring staging sites. *Ornis Scand.* **22**: 404-407.
Piersma, T., Verkuil, Y. & Tulp, I. (1994). Resources for long-distance migration of Knots *Calidris canutus islandica* and *C. c. canutus*: how broad is the temporal exploitation window of benthic prey in the western and eastern Wadden Sea. *Oikos* **71**: 393-407.
Piersma, T., Zwarts, L. & Bruggemann, J.H. (1990). Behavioural aspects of the departure of waders before long-distance flights: flocking, vocalizations, flight paths and diurnal timing. *Ardea* **78**: 157-184.
Pietz, P.J. (1985). Long call displays of sympatric South Polar and Brown Skuas. *Condor* **87**: 316-326.
Pietz, P.J. (1986). Daily activity patterns of South Polar and Brown Skuas near Palmer Station, Antarctica. *Auk* **103**: 726-736.
Pietz, P.J. (1987). Feeding and nesting ecology of sympatric South Polar and Brown Skuas. *Auk* **104**: 617-627.
Pietz, P.J. & Parmelee, D.F. (1994). Survival, site and mate fidelity in South Polar Skuas *Catharacta maccormicki* at Anvers Island, Antarctica. *Ibis* **136(1)**: 32-38.
Pilcher, C.W. & Sexton, D.B. (1993). Effects of the Gulf War oil spills and well-head fires on the avifauna and environment of Kuwait. *Sandgrouse* **15**: 6-17.
Pineau, O. (1993). Notes on the breeding biology of the Kentish Plover in the Nile Delta. *Wader Study Group Bull.* **67**: 63-66.
Pinto, A.A. da Rosa (1983). *Ornitologia de Angola*. Vol. 1. Non Passeres. Instituto de Investigação Cientifica Tropical, Lisboa.
Pinto, O.M. de Oliveira (1964). *Ornitologia Brasiliense*. Vol. 1. Parte Introdutória e Familias Rheidae a Cuculidae. Departamento de Zoologia da Secretaria da Agricultura do Estado de São Paulo, São Paulo.
Pirow, P.C. (1981). Ethiopian Snipe (R 250). *Witwatersrand Bird Club News* **115**: 10.
Pitelka, F.A. (1943). Territoriality, display and certain ecological relations of the American Woodcock. *Wilson Bull.* **55**: 88-114.
Pitelka, F.A. (1948). Problematic relationships of the Asiatic shorebird *Limnodromus semipalmatus*. *Condor* **50**: 259-269.
Pitelka, F.A. (1950). Geographic variation and the species problem in the shore-bird genus *Limnodromus*. *Univ. Calif. Publ. Zool.* **50**: 1-108.
Pitelka, F.A. (1959). Numbers, breeding schedule and territoriality in Pectoral Sandpipers of northern Alaska. *Condor* **61**: 233-264.
Pitelka, F.A. ed. (1979). *Shorebirds in Marine Environments*. Studies in Avian Biology **2**. Cooper Ornithological Society.
Pitelka, F.A., Holmes, R.T. & MacLean, S.F. (1974). Ecology and evolution of social organization in arctic sandpipers. *Amer. Zool.* **14**: 185-204.
Pitman, C.R.S. (1912). The Painted Snipe *Rostratula capensis*. *J. Bombay Nat. Hist. Soc.* **21**: 666-667.
Pitman, C.R.S. (1928). The breeding of the *Burhinus vermiculatus büttikoferi* - the West African Water Dikkop, on the shores and islands of the Victoria Nyanza. *Ool. Rec.* **7(4)**: 102-105.
Pitman, C.R.S. (1929). Notes on the breeding habits and nesting of *Limnocorax flavirostra* - the Black Rail. *Ool. Rec.* **9**: 37-41.
Pitman, C.R.S. (1931). Notes from Uganda on the breeding of *Burhinus s. senegalensis* (Swainson). *Ool. Rec.* **11**: 62-64.
Pitman, C.R.S. (1932a). Notes on the breeding habits and eggs of *Rhinoptilus chalcopterus*. *Ool. Rec.* **12(1)**: 16-23.
Pitman, C.R.S. (1932b). Notes on the breeding habits and eggs of *Rynchops flavirostris* (Vieill.) - African Skimmer or Scissor-bill. *Ool. Rec.* **12**: 51-54.
Pitman, C.R.S. (1960). A note on the African Jacana, *Actophilornis africanus* (Gmelin). *Bull. Brit. Orn. Club* **80**: 103-105.
Pitman, C.R.S. (1962). Notes on the African Finfoot, *Podica senegalensis* (Vieillot) with particular reference to Uganda. *Bull. Brit. Orn. Club* **82**: 156-160.
Pitman, C.R.S. (1965a). The nest and eggs of the Striped Crake, *Porzana marginalis* Hartlaub. *Bull. Brit. Orn. Club* **85**: 32-40.
Pitman, C.R.S. (1965b). The eggs and nesting habits of the St. Helena Sand-Plover or Wirebird, *Charadrius pecuarius sanctae-helenae* (Harting). *Bull. Brit. Orn. Club* **85**: 121-129.
Pitman, C.R.S. (1967). Seafowl and land migrants observed on a voyage, London to Capetown, 26th April-12th May 1966. *Bull. Brit. Orn. Club* **87**: 41-45.
Pittaway, R. (1992). Short-billed Dowitchers subspecies. *Birding* **24(5)**: 309-311.
Pizzey, G. & Doyle, R. (1980). *A Field Guide to the Birds of Australia*. Collins, Sydney.
Pleske, T. (1928). Birds of the Eurasian Tundra. *Mem. Boston Soc. Nat. Hist.* **6**: 217-222.
du Plessis, D. (1987). [Observations of Wattled Plovers (*Vanellus senegallus*) in the Orange Free State]. *Mirafra* **4(2)**: 36-37. In Afrikaans with English summary.
du Plessis, G.J. (1994). Coursers in the Kroonstad area, Orange Free State. *Mirafra* **11(1)**: 1-5.
du Plessis, G.J. (1995). Large aggregation of Black-winged Pratincoles *Glareola nordmanni* in the northern Orange Free State. *Ostrich* **66(1)**: 40-41.
Plotnick, R. (1951). Costumbres de la Gaviota de Capucho Café. *Com. Inst. Nac. Invest. Cienc. Nat. (Mus. Argent.)* **2**: 113-129.
Plumb, W.J. (1978). The Lesser Golden Plover in Kenya. *Scopus* **2(3)**: 72-73.
Pocock, T.N. (1962). Red-necked Phalarope *Phalaropus lobatus* and other birds at Iscor Dams, Vanderbijl Park. *Ostrich* **33**: 41-44.
Pollard, C.J.W. (1980). A visual record of Chestnut-banded Sandplover at the Victoria Falls. *Honeyguide* **102**: 37.
Pollard, C.J.W. (1982). Status of the Rock Pratincole in the Victoria Falls area. *Honeyguide* **109**: 29-30.
Pollard, C.J.W. (1986). Toleration between Kori and Denham's Bustards. *Honeyguide* **32**: 156.
Polozov, S.A., Shubin, A.O. & Mustapha, L.R. (1990). [The Red-wattled Lapwing (*Lobivanellus indicus*) record in Daghestan]. *Ornitologiya* **24**: 158. In Russian.
Poluszynski, J. (1979). Some observations of breeding kittiwakes on Helgoland. *Abh. Geb. Vogelk.* **6**: 113-120.
Pomeroy, D.E. (1980a). Aspects of the ecology of the Crowned Crane (*Balearica regulorum*) in Uganda. *Scopus* **4(2)**: 29-35.
Pomeroy, D.E. (1980b). Growth and plumage changes of the Grey Crowned Crane (*Balearica regulorum gibbericeps*). *Bull. Brit. Orn. Club* **100(4)**: 219-223.
Pomeroy, D.E. (1987). The ecology and status of Crowned Cranes in East Africa. Pp. 323-330 in: Archibald & Pasquier (1987a).
Ponomarena, T.S. (1985). [The Demoiselle Crane in Buryatia]. *Bull. Moscow Soc. Nat. Study (Biol. Section)* **90(4)**: 47-49. In Russian.
Ponomareva, T.T. (1983). [Reproductive behaviour and distribution of Houbara Bustard *Chlamydotis undulata macqueenii*]. *Zoologischeskii Zhurnal* **62**: 592-602. In Russian.
Ponomareva, T.T. (1985). The Houbara Bustard: present status and conservation prospects (in the USSR). *Bustard Studies* **3**: 93-96.
Ponomareva, T.T. (1992). The status and conservation of the eastern Great Bustard. *Bustard Studies* **5**: 57-62.
Pook, J. (1992). Banding round-up complete list. Australian bird and bat banding scheme. *Stilt* **20**: 51-76.
Poole, A.F. & Gill, F.B. eds. (1993). *The Birds of North America*. Vol. 2. Academy of Natural Sciences & American Ornithologists' Union, Philadelphia & Washington, D.C.
Poole, A.F. & Gill, F.B. eds. (1994). *The Birds of North America*. Vol. 3. Academy of Natural Sciences & American Ornithologists' Union, Philadelphia & Washington, D.C.
Poole, A.F. & Gill, F.B. eds. (1994-1995). *The Birds of North America*. Vol. 4. Academy of Natural Sciences & American Ornithologists' Union, Philadelphia & Washington, D.C.
Poole, A.F. & Gill, F.B. eds. (1995). *The Birds of North America*. Vol. 5. Academy of Natural Sciences & American Ornithologists' Union, Philadelphia & Washington, D.C.
Poole, A.F. & Gill, F.B. eds. (1996). *The Birds of North America*. Vol. 6. Academy of Natural Sciences & American Ornithologists' Union, Philadelphia & Washington, D.C.
Poole, A.F., Setetteneheim, P. & Gill, F.B. eds. (1992-1993). *The Birds of North America*. Vol. 1. Academy of Natural Sciences & American Ornithologists' Union, Philadelphia & Washington, D.C.
Poor, H.H. (1946). Plumage and soft-part variations in the Herring Gull. *Auk* **63**: 135-151.
Poore, G.C.B., Corrick, A.H. & Norman, F.I. (1979). Food of three waders at Lake Reeve, Victoria. *Emu* **79**: 228-229.
Pörner, H. (1987). Beringungsergebnisse von in der DDR Markierten Bekassinen (*Gallinago gallinago*). II. Vögel unbekannter Herkunft. *Ber. Vogelwarte Hiddensee* **8**: 20-33.
Pörner, H. (1989). Beringungsergebnisse von in der DDR Markierten Bekassinen (*Gallinago gallinago*). III. Vögel unbekannter Herkunft. *Ber. Vogelwarte Hiddensee* **9**: 42-56.
Portenko, L. (1939). On some new forms of Arctic gulls. 2. On two new races of Sabine's Gull. *Ibis* **Ser. 14, no. 3**: 266-269.
Portenko, L.A. (1933). Some new materials adding to the knowledge of breeding ranges and life history of Eastern Knot, *Calidris tenuirostris* (Horsf.). *Arctica* **1**: 75-98.
Portenko, L.A. (1957). Studien an einigen selten Limicolen aus dem nördlichen und östlichen Sibirien. I. Die Löffelschnepfe - *Eurynorhynchus pygmeus* (L.). *J. Orn.* **198**: 454-466.
Portenko, L.A. (1959). [Studies on some rare waders from northern and eastern Siberia. II. The Curlew Sandpiper - *Erolia ferruginea* (Pontopp.)]. *J. Orn.* **100**: 141-172. In German.
Portenko, L.A. (1963). [Taxonomic status and systematic situation of the Slaty-backed Gull (*L. argentatus schistisagus* Stejn)]. Pp. 61-64 in: *Fauna Kamchatka Oblast*. Academy Science USSR, Moscow. In Russian.
Portenko, L.A. (1972). *Birds of the Chukchi Peninsula and Wrangel Island*. Vol. 1. (English translation 1981). Delhi.
Portenko, L.A. (1973). *Birds of the Chukchi Peninsula and Wrangel Island*. Vol. 2. (English translation 1989). Smithsonian Institution Libraries & National Science Foundation, Washington, D.C.
Porter, D.J., Craven, H.S., Johnson, D.N. & Porter, M.J. eds. (1992). *Proceedings of the First Southern African Crane Conference*. The southern African Crane Foundation, Durban, South Africa.
Porter, J.M. (1988). Prerequisites for recruitment of Kittiwakes *Rissa tridactyla*. *Ibis* **130**: 204-215.
Porter, J.M. & Coulson, J.C. (1987). Long term changes in recruitment to the breeding group, and the quality of recruits at a Kittiwake *Rissa tridactyla* colony. *J. Anim. Ecol.* **56**: 675-689.
Porter, R.J. & Goriup, P.D. (1985). Recommendations for the conservation of the Arabian Bustard and Houbara Bustard in Saudi Arabia. Unpublished report to IUCN.
Portmann, A. (1947). Études sur la cérébralisation chez les oiseaux. *Alauda* **15**: 1-15.
Portnoy, J.W. (1977). Colonial waterbird population status and management on the north Gulf of Mexico coast. *Proc. Colonial Waterbird Group* **1**: 38-43.
Portnoy, J.W. (1978). Black Skimmer abundance on the Louisiana-Mississippi-Alabama coast. *Wilson Bull.* **90**: 438-441.
Poslavsky, A.N. (1969). [Migration and moult of the Curlew at the north shore of the Caspian Sea and adjacent deserts]. *Falke* **16**: 184-188. In German.
Poslavsky, A.N. (1978). On the biology of the Caspian Plover. *Vestnik Zoologii* **2**: 85-87.
Poslavsky, A.N. & Krivonosov, G.A. (1976). [Ecology of the Sandwich Tern (*Thalasseus sandvicensis*) on the boundaries of its range]. *Ekologia* **3**: 51-56. In Russian.
Poslavsky, A.N. & Sokolov, A.I. (1980). [Number and biology of the Swinhoe's Snipe (*Gallinago megala*) in the south Kuzbass]. In: Flint (1980a). In Russian.
Pospichal, L.B. & Marshall, W.H. (1954). A field study of Sora Rail and Virginia Rail in central Minnesota. *Flicker* **26**: 2-32.
Post, P.W. (1971). Additional observations of Sabine's Gull from coastal Peru and Chile. *Ibis* **113**: 517.
Post, P.W. & Gochfeld, M. (1978). Recolonization by Common Terns at Breezy Point, New York. *Proc. Colonial Waterbird Group* **2**: 128-136.
Post, P.W. & Lewis, R.H. (1995a). Lesser Black-backed Gull in the Americas: occurrence and subspecific identity. Part 1. Taxonomy, distribution and migration. *Birding* **27**: 283-290.
Post, P.W. & Lewis, R.H. (1995b). Lesser Black-backed Gull in the Americas: occurrence and subspecific identity. Part 2. Field identification. *Birding* **27**: 371-383.
Post, P.W. & Riepe, D. (1980). Laughing Gulls colonize Jamaica Bay. *Kingbird* **30**: 11-13.
Postage, A. (1984). The behaviour of breeding African Jacanas. *Bokmakierie* **36(1)**: 12-14.
Potapov, E. (1992). Some breeding observations on the Siberian White Crane *Grus leucogeranus* in the Kolyma lowlands. *Bird Conserv. Int.* **2(2)**: 149-156.
Potapov, R.L. (1966). [Nesting of the Brown-headed Gull (*Larus brunnicephalus* Jerd.) in the USSR]. *Doklady Akademii Nauk SSR* **167**: 1409-1410. In Russian.
Potapov, R.L. & Flint, V.E. eds. (1987). *Handbuch der Vögel der Sowjetunion*. Vol. 4. Galliformes-Gruiformes. A. Ziemsen Verlag, Wittenberg Lutherstadt.
Potts, G.R. & Hirons, G.J.M. (1983). Towards a realistic simulation model for Woodcock populations. Pp. 83-91 in: Kalchreuter (1983b).
Potts, T.H. (1869). On the birds of New Zealand. *Trans. New Zealand Inst.* **2**: 40-78.
Potts, T.H. (1872). On the birds of New Zealand. Part 3. *Trans. New Zealand Inst.* **5**: 171-205.
Pouget, P. (1875). Note sur le kagou. *Bulletin de la Société d'Acclimatation* **2**: 162-171.
Poulsen, H. (1950). Bidrag til Mudderklirens ethologi. *Vår Fågelvärld* **9**: 4-10.
Poulsen, M.K. (1995). The threatened and near-threatened birds of Luzon, Philippines, and the role of the Sierra Madre mountains in their conservation. *Bird Conser. Int.* **5(1)**: 79-115.
Pourreau, J. & Guennec, H. (1992). [First record of the Green Sandpiper *Tringa ochropus* nesting in France]. *Alauda* **60(4)**: 222. In French.
Powell, A.N. (1990). Eastern Wood-pewee attempts to feed Killdeer chicks. *J. Field Orn.* **61(2)**: 214-216. In English with Spanish summary.
Powell, A.N. (1993). Brood rearing and chick behavior in Killdeer *Charadrius vociferus* and Piping Plover *C. melodus*. *Wader Study Group Bull.* **71**: 15-16. (Abstract).
Powell, A.N. & Cuthbert, F.J. (1992). Habitat and reproductive success of Piping Plovers nesting on Great Lakes islands. *Wilson Bull.* **104(1)**: 155-161.
Powell, A.N. & Cuthbert, F.J. (1993). Augmenting small populations of plovers: an assessment of cross-fostering and captive-rearing. *Conserv. Biol.* **7**: 160-168.
Powers, E. (1971). *Waders in New Zealand*. Collins, Auckland.
Pracy, L.T. (1969). Weka liberations in the Palliser Bay region. *Notornis* **26**: 212-213.
van Praet, L. (1980). Breeding *Laterallus leucopyrrhus*. *Avicult. Mag.* **86**: 60.
Prainsson, G. (1995). [The first Baird's Sandpiper *Calidris bairdii* found in Iceland]. *Bliki* **15**: 52-56. In Icelandic with English summary.
Prakash, I. (1983). Current status of the Great Indian Bustard (*Choriotis nigriceps*) in the Thar Desert. Pp. 39-43 in: Goriup & Vardhan (1983).
Prange, H. ed. (1989). *Der Graue Kranisch*. Die Neue Brehm-Bücherei. A. Ziemsen Verlag, Wittenberg, Germany.
Prange, H. (1991). [Migration and resting of the Common Crane (*Grus grus*) in East Germany in 1988]. *Vogelwarte* **36**: 35-47. In German.
Prange, H. (1994). Crane. *Grus grus*. Pp. 234-235 in: Tucker & Heath (1994).
Prange, H. ed. (1995). *Crane Research and Protection in Europe*. European Crane Working Group and Martin-Luther-Universität, Halle-Wittenberg, Germany.
Prange, H. & Mewes, W. (1989). [The situation of the Common Crane (*Grus grus*) in central Europe]. *Beitr. Vogelkd.* **15**: 1-32. In German.
Prange, H. & Mewes, W. (1991a). The Common Crane in the German Democratic Republic. Pp. 263-269 in: Harris (1991b).
Prange, H. & Mewes, W. (1991b). [Migration and resting in the Common Crane (*Grus grus*) in east Germany in 1988]. *Vogelwarte* **36(1)**: 35-47. In German with English summary.
Prange, H. & Petersen, J.E. eds. (1995). Conservation of the Common Crane in Europe - Towards a long-term strategy: International Conference in Orellano la Vieja, Spain, 21-24 January 1994. In: Prange (1995).
Prange, H., Alonso, J.C., Alonso, J.A. eds. (1995). Proceedings of the 1989 Paleartic Crane Workshop in Tallinn, Estonia. In: Prange (1995).
Prater, A. (1974). Breeding biology of the Ringed Plover. Pp. 241-251 in: *Proc. IWRB Wader Symp.* Warsow, 1974.
Prater, A.J. (1972). The ecology of Morecambe Bay. III. The food and feeding habits of the Knot (*Calidris canutus* L.) in Morecambe Bay. *J. Appl. Ecol.* **9**: 179-194.
Prater, A.J. (1975). The wintering population of the Black-tailed Godwit. *Bird Study* **22**: 169-176.
Prater, A.J. (1981a). *Estuary Birds of Britain and Ireland*. T. & A.D. Poyser Ltd, Carlton, UK.
Prater, A.J. (1981b). A review of the patterns of primary moult in Palaearctic waders (Charadrii). Pp. 393-409 in: Cooper (1981).
Prater, A.J. (1982). Identification of Ruff. *Dutch Birding* **4**: 8-14.
Prater, A.J. & Marchant, J.H. (1975). Primary moult of *Tringa brevipes* and *T. incana*. *Bull. Brit. Orn. Club* **95**: 120-122.
Prater, A.J., Marchant, J.H. & Vuorinen, J. (1977). *Guide to the Identification and Ageing of Holarctic Waders*. BTO Guide **17**. British Trust for Ornithology, London.

Pratt, H.D. (1978). Do mainland coots occur in Hawaii? *Elepaio* **38**: 73.
Pratt, H.D. (1987). Occurrence of the North American Coot (*Fulica americana americana*) in the Hawaiian Islands, with comments on the taxonomy of the Hawaiian Coot. *Elepaio* **47**: 25-28.
Pratt, H.D. (1993). *Enjoying Birds in Hawaii: a Birdfinding Guide to the Fiftieth State*. Mutual Publishing, Honolulu.
Pratt, H.D. & Bruner, P.L. (1981). Noteworthy records of nonbreeding birds in Micronesia. *Micronesica* **17(1-2)**: 195-198.
Pratt, H.D., Bruner, P.L. & Berrett, D.G. (1979). America's unknown avifauna: the birds of the Marianas Islands. *Amer. Birds* **33**: 227-235.
Pratt, H.D., Bruner, P.L. & Berrett, D.G. (1987). *A Field Guide to the Birds of Hawaii and the Tropical Pacific*. Princeton University Press, Princeton, New Jersey.
Pratt, H.D., Engbring, J., Bruner, P.L. & Berrett, D.G. (1980). Notes on the taxonomy, natural history and status of the resident birds of Palau. *Condor* **82**: 117-131.
Pratt, T.K. (1982). Additions to the avifauna of the Adelbert Range, Papua New Guinea. *Emu* **82**: 117-125.
Preble, E.A. & McAtee, W.L. (1923). *A Biological Survey of the Pribilof Islands, Alaska. Part I. Birds and Mammals*. North American Fauna **46**. 255 pp.
Prellwitz, D.M. (1993). Additional Mountain Plover sightings in Montana. *Prairie Nat.* **25(1)**: 23-26.
Preston, F.W. (1962). A nesting of Amazonian terns and skimmers. *Wilson Bull.* **74**: 286-287.
Preston, W.C. (1968). *Breeding Ecology and Social Behaviour of the Black Guillemot* Cepphus grylle. PhD thesis, University of Michigan, Ann Arbor, Michigan.
Preuss, N.O. (1961). The migration of the Oystercatcher across the North Sea. *Dan. Orn. Foren. Tidssk.* **55**: 140 151.
Prevett, J.P. & Barr, J.F. (1976). Lek behavior of the Buff-breasted Sandpiper. *Wilson Bull.* **88**: 500-503.
Prévost, J. & Mougin, J.L. (1970). *Guide des Oiseaux et Mammifères des Terres Australes et Antarctiques Françaises*. Delachaux et Niestlé Éditeurs, Paris.
Price, J. (1985). *The Ecology and Behavior of an Avian Terrestrial Frugivore; the White-winged Trumpeter (*Psophia leucoptera*) in Southeastern Peru*. Senior thesis, Princeton University, Princeton, New Jersey.
Price, L.W. (1973). The local ecological effect of Long-tailed Jaegers nesting in the subArctic. *Arctic* **26**: 253-255.
Prigogine, A. (1971). *Les Oiseaux de l'Itombwe et de son Hinterland*. Musée Royal de l'Afrique Centrale Annales (Série 8) **185**.
Priklonski, S. & Markin, Y. (1982). [The number and fluctuation of the Common Crane in the center of European Russia]. Pp. 84-88 in: Neufeldt, I.A. ed. (1982). [*Cranes of the USSR*]. Zoological Institute of Leningrad. In Russian.
Pringle, J.D. (1987). *The Shorebirds of Australia*. Angus & Robertson, North Ryde, Australia.
Pringle, J.S. & Pringle, W.S. (1971). Red-necked Phalarope *Phalaropus lobatus* at Strandfontein. *Ostrich* **42(3)**: 228-229.
Pringle, W.S. (1971). Oystercatcher episode. *Bokmakierie* **23**: 22 23.
Prinzinger, R., Misovic, A. & Schleucher, E. (1993). [Energy turnover and body temperature in the Painted Quail *Coturnix chinensis* (Galliformes /Phasianidae) and the Barred Button-quail *Turnix suscitator* (Gruiformes/ Turnicidae)]. *J. Orn.* **134(1)**: 79-84. In German with English summary.
Proctor, D.L. (1975). The problem of chick loss in the South Polar Skua (*Catharacta maccormicki*). *Ibis* **117**: 452-459.
Prokofiev, S.M. (1995). The Demoiselle Crane in the Minusinsk basin. Pp. 293-294 in: Prange *et al*. (1995).
Prokosch, P. (1988). [The Schleswig-Holstein Wadden Sea as spring staging area for Arctic wader populations demonstrated by Grey Plover (*Pluvialis squatarola*, L. 1758), Knot (*Calidris canutus*, L. 1758) and Bar-tailed Godwit (*Limosa lapponica*, L. 1758)]. *Corax* **12(4)**: 273-442. In German with English summary.
Prozesky, O.P.M. (1977). Kori Bustard heaviest flier. *Custos* **6(4)**: 4-5.
Pruett-Jones, S.G. (1988). Lekking versus solitary display: temporal variations in dispersion in the Buff-breasted Sandpiper. *Anim. Behav.* **36(6)**: 1740-1752.
Pryor, G.R. (1969). Breeding the Blackish Rail (*Rallus nigricans*). *Avicult. Mag.* **75**: 164-165.
Prys-Jones, R.P. & Wilson, J.R. (1986). Migrant and vagrant snipe on western Indian Ocean islands. *Bull. Brit. Orn. Club* **106(1)**: 9-12.
Prys-Jones, R.P., Corse, C.J. & Summers, R.W. (1992). The role of the Orkney Islands as a spring staging post for Turnstones *Arenaria interpres*. *Ringing & Migration* **13(2)**: 83-89.
Prys-Jones, R.P., Underhill, L.G. & Waters, R.J. (1994). Index numbers for waterbird populations. II. Coastal wintering waders in the United Kingdom, 1970/71-1990/91. *J. Appl. Ecol.* **31**: 481-492.
Ptacek, J. & Schwilling, M. (1983). Mountain Plover reintroduction in Kansas. *Kansas Orn. Soc. Bull.* **34(2)**: 21-22.
Ptaszyk, J. (1981). [Food of the Black-headed Gull, *Larus ridibundus*]. *Przeglad Zoologiczny* **25**: 267-272. In Polish.
Pugesek, B.H. (1981). Increased reproductive effort with age in California Gull (*Larus californicus*). *Science* **212**: 822-823.
Pugesek, B.H. (1983). The relationship between parent age and reproductive effort in the California Gull, *Larus californicus*. *Behav. Ecol. Sociobiol.* **13**: 161-171.
Pugesek, B.H. (1984). Age-specific reproductive tactics in the California Gull. *Oikos* **43**: 409-410.
Pugesek, B.H. (1987). Age-specific survivorship in relation to clutch size and fledging success in California Gulls. *Behav. Ecol. Sociobiol.* **21**: 217-221.
Pugesek, B.H. (1990). Parental effort in the California Gull: tests of parent-offspring conflict theory. *Behav. Ecol. Sociobiol.* **27**: 211-215.
Pugesek, B.H. (1993). Chick growth in the California Gull: relationships with hatching asynchrony and parental age. *Colonial Waterbirds* **16(2)**: 183-189.
Pugesek, B.H. & Diem, K.L. (1983). A multivariate study of the relationship of parental age to reproductive success in California Gulls. *Ecology* **64**: 829-839.
Pugesek, B.H. & Diem, K.L. (1986). Ages of mated pairs of California Gulls. *Wilson Bull.* **98**: 610-612.
Pugesek, B.H. & Diem, K.L. (1990). The relationship between reproduction and survival in known-aged California Gulls. *Ecology* **71**: 811-817.
Pukinski, Y.B. (1977). [The Hooded Crane in Primorye]. *Okhota i Okhotnichye Kozyaistvo* **1**: 28-30. In Russian.
Pukinski, Y.B. & Ilyinski, I.V. (1977). [On the biology and behavior of the Hooded Crane during the nesting period, Primorye Territory, Bikin River Basin]. *Bull. Moscow Soc. Nat. Study (Biol. Section)* **82**: 5-17. In Russian.
Pulcher, C. (1986a). Mignattino *Chlidonias niger*. *Ricerche Biol. Selvaggina* **9**(Suppl.): 129-136.
Pulcher, C. (1986b). Mignattino alibianche *Chlidonias leucopterus*. *Ricerche Biol. Selvaggina* **9**(Suppl.): 137-142.
Pulich, W.M. (1962). A record of the Yellow Rail from Dallas County, Texas. *Auk* **78**: 639-640.
Pulido, V. (1991). *El Libro Rojo de la Fauna Silvestre del Perú*. INIAA, WWF & US Fish & Wildlife Service, Lima.
Pulliainen, E. (1970). On the breeding biology of the Dotterel *Charadrius morinellus*. *Ornis Fenn.* **47**: 69-73.
Pulliainen, E. & Marjakangas, A. (1980). Eggshell thickness in sea and shorebird species of the Botnian Bay. *Ornis Fenn.* **57**: 65-70.
Pulliainen, E. & Saari, L. (1991). Breeding biology of the Wood Sandpiper *Tringa glareola* in eastern Finnish Lapland. *Ornis Fenn.* **68(3)**: 127-128.
Pulliainen, E. & Saari, L. (1992a). Body mass and physical condition of the breeding Dotterel (*Charadrius morinellus*) in Finland. *Oecol. Montana* **1**: 1-4.
Pulliainen, E. & Saari, L. (1992b). Breeding biology of the Dotterel *Charadrius morinellus* in eastern Finnish Lapland. *Ornis Fenn.* **69(2)**: 101-107.
Pulliainen, E. & Saari, L. (1993a). Breeding biology of the Golden Plover *Pluvialis apricaria* in eastern Finnish Lapland. *Ornis Fenn.* **70(1)**: 40-43. In English with Finnish summary.
Pulliainen, E. & Saari, L. (1993b). Egg size of the Dotterel *Charadrius morinellus* in Finland. *Ornis Fenn.* **70(1)**: 44-46. In English with Finnish summary.
Pulliainen, E. & Saari, L. (1993c). Ring recoveries of Finnish Dotterels *Charadrius morinellus*. *Wader Study Group Bull.* **67**: 54-56.
Pulliainen, E. & Saari, L. (1993d). Breeding biology of the Whimbrel *Numenius phaeopus* in eastern Finnish Lapland. *Ornis Fenn.* **70(2)**: 110-116.
Purchase, D. (1973). Breeding of the Crested Tern. *CSIRO Wildl. Res. Tech. Pap.* **27**: 1-4.
Purdue, J.R. (1976a). Adaptations of the Snowy Plover of the Great Salt Plains, Oklahoma. *Southwest. Nat.* **21**: 347-357.
Purdue, J.R. (1976b). Thermal environment of the nest and related parental behaviors of Snowy Plovers, *Charadrius alexandrinus*. *Condor* **78**: 180-185.
Purdue, J.R. & Haines, H. (1977). Salt water tolerance and water turnover in the Snowy Plover. *Auk* **94**: 248-255.
Purdy, M.A. (1985). *Parental Behaviour and Role Differentiation in the Black Oystercatcher* Haematopus bachmani. MSc thesis, University of Victoria, Victoria, Canada.
Purdy, M.A. & Miller, E.H. (1988). Time budget and parental behaviour of breeding American Black Oystercatchers (*Haematopus bachmani*) in British Columbia. *Can. J. Zool.* **66(8)**: 1742-1751.
Putnam, M.S. & Archibald, G.W. (1987). The Siberian Crane: its history and biology in captivity. Pp. 173-195 in: Archibald & Pasquier (1987a).
Puttick, G.M. (1978). Diet of the Curlew Sandpiper at Langebaan Lagoon, South Africa. *Ostrich* **49**: 158-167.
Puttick, G.M. (1979). Foraging behaviour and activity budgets of Curlew Sandpipers. *Ardea* **67**: 111-122.
Puttick, G.M. (1980). Energy budgets of Curlew Sandpipers at Langebaan Lagoon, South Africa. *Estuar. Coastal Mar. Sci.* **11**: 207-215.
Puttick, G.M. (1981). Sex-related differences in foraging behaviour of Curlew Sandpipers. *Ornis Scand.* **12**: 13-17.
Puzovic, S. (1994). On the Woodcock in former Yugoslavia. Pp. 35-41 in: Kalchreuter (1994).
Pycraft, W.P. (1895). On the pterylography of the Hoatzin *Opisthocomus cristatus*. *Ibis* **Ser. 7, no.1**: 345-373.
Pye-Smith, G. (1950). The nest and eggs of the Uganda White-spotted Crake (*Sarothrura pulchra centralis*). *Ool. Rec.* **24**: 48-49.
Pyle, P., Spear, L.B., Sydeman, W.J. & Ainley, D.G. (1991). The effects of experience and age on the breeding performance of Western Gulls. *Auk* **108**: 25-33.
Pyle, R.L. (1991). The winter season. Hawaiian Islands region. *Amer. Birds* **45**: 324-325.
Pym, A. (1982). Identification of Lesser Golden Plover and status in Britain and Ireland. *British Birds* **75**: 112-124.
Qiu Guoxin (1990). [Discovery of the new hibernaculum of *Grus nigricollis* in the northeast Yunnan]. *Zool. Res.* **11(4)**: 272. In Chinese.
Quäbicker, G. (1939). Die Graukopfmöwe (*Larus cirrocephalus*) an der Westküste Sudamerikas. *Orn. Monatsber.* **47**: 57-58.
Quale, T.R. (1976). Interchick aggression in Sandhill Cranes. Pp. 263-267 in: Lewis (1976a).
de Queiroz, K. & Good, D.A. (1988). The scleral ossicles of *Opisthocomus* and their phylogenetic significance. *Auk* **105(1)**: 29-35.
Quelch, J.J. (1888). Notes on the breeding of the Hoatzin. *Ibis* **Ser. 5, no. 6**: 378-379.
Quelch, J.J. (1890). On the habits of the Hoatzin. *Ibis* **Ser. 6, no. 2**: 327-335.
Quine, D.A. & Cullen, J.M. (1964). The pecking response of young Arctic Terns *Sterna macrura* and the adaptiveness of the "releasing mechanism". *Ibis* **106**: 146-173.
Quinlan, S.E. & Hughes, J.H. (1990). Location and description of a Marbled Murrelet tree nest site in Alaska. *Condor* **92**: 1068-1073.
Quinlan, S.E. & Hughes, J.H. (1992). Techniques for capture and radio tagging of Marbled Murrelets. Pp. 117-121 in: Carter & Morrison (1992).
Quinn, J.S. (1985). Caspian Terns respond to rattlesnake predation in a colony. *Wilson Bull.* **97**: 233-234.
Quinn, J.S. (1988). *Sexual Size Dimorphism and Parental Care: a Comparative Study of Black Skimmers and Caspian Terns, and a Computer Simulation Model*. PhD dissertation, University of Oklahoma, Stillwater, Oklahoma.
Quinn, J.S. (1989). Black Skimmer parental defense against chick predation by gulls. *Anim. Behav.* **38**: 534-541.
Quinn, J.S. (1990). Sexual size dimorphism and parental care patterns in a monomorphic and a dimorphic larid. *Auk* **107(2)**: 260-274.
Quinn, J.S. & Morris, R.D. (1986). Intra-clutch egg weight apportionment and chick survival in Caspian Terns. *Can. J. Zool.* **64**: 2116-2122.
Quinn, J.S. & Wiggins, D.A. (1990). Differences in prey delivered to chicks by individual Gull-billed Terns. *Colonial Waterbirds* **13**: 67-69.
Quinn, J.S., Whittingham, L.A. & Morris, R.D. (1994). Infanticide in skimmers and terns: side effects of territorial attacks or inter-generational conflict? *Anim. Behav.* **47(2)**: 363-367.
Quinton, W.F. (1948). The Karoo Korhaan (*Eupodotis vigorsi vigorsi*). *Ostrich* **19**: 235-236.
Rabe, D.L., Prince, H.H. & Beaver, D.L. (1983). Feeding-site selection and foraging strategies of American Woodcock. *Auk* **100**: 711-716.
Rabe, D.L., Prince, H.H. & Goodman, E.D. (1983). The effect of weather on bioenergetics of breeding American Woodcock. *J. Wildl. Manage.* **47**: 762-771.
Rabor, D.S. (1955). Notes on mammals and birds of the central northern Luzon highlands, Philippines. Part II. Notes on birds. *Silliman J.* **2**: 253-311.
Rabor, D.S. (1977). *Philippine Birds & Mammals*. University of the Philippines Press, Quezon City.
Radamaker, K. & Ludden, C. (1993). A record of Bar-tailed Godwit for Mexico. *Euphonia* **2(3)**: 58-65. In English with Spanish summary.
Radetzky, J. (1976). A feh'erfark'u lileb'ibic (*Chettusia leucura*) elsö magyarorsz'agi Megfigyel'ese. [First observations on the White-tailed Plover *Chettusia leucura* in Hungary]. *Aquila* **83**: 189-190. In Hungarian with German summary.
Radford, D.J. (1985). Arctic Terns incubating Ringed Plover eggs to hatching. *British Birds* **78(9)**: 454-455.
Rafaelli, D., Hull, S. & Milne, H. (1989). Long-term changes in nutrients, weed mats and shorebirds in an estuarine system. *Cah. Biol. Mar.* **30**: 259-270.
Raffaele, H.A. (1989). *A Guide to the Birds of Puerto Rico and the Virgin Islands*. Princeton University Press, Princeton & London.
Ragless, G.B. (1977). The Chestnut Rail at Darwin. *S. Austr. Orn.* **27**: 254-255.
Rahmani, A.R. (1984). Return of the Great Indian Bustard. *Hornbill* **3**: 7-14.
Rahmani, A.R. (1986). *Status of the Great Indian Bustard in Rajasthan*. Bombay Natural History Society Technical Report **11**. 324 pp.
Rahmani, A.R. (1987). Protection for the Great Indian Bustard. *Oryx* **21**: 174-179.
Rahmani, A.R. (1988a). Grassland birds of the Indian subcontinent: a review. Pp. 187-204 in: Goriup (1988).
Rahmani, A.R. (1988b). The conservation of the Great Indian Bustard *Ardeotis nigriceps* (Vigors) in the Karera Bustard Sanctuary. *Biol. Conserv.* **46(2)**: 135-144.
Rahmani, A.R. (1989). The Great Indian Bustard. Final report in the study of ecology of certain endangered species of wildlife and their habitats. Bombay Natural History Society, Bombay.
Rahmani, A.R. (1991). Flocking behaviour of a resident population of the Great Indian Bustard *Ardeotis nigriceps* (Vigors). *Rev. Ecol. (Terre Vie)* **46(1)**: 53-64.
Rahmani, A.R. (1992). Interaction between Great Indian Bustard and vultures. *Vulture News* **26**: 4-6.
Rahmani, A.R. & Manakadan, R. (1985). Present status of the Great Indian Bustard. *Bustard Studies* **3**: 123-131.
Rahmani, A.R. & Manakadan, R. (1986). Movement and flock composition of the Great Indian Bustard *Ardeotis nigriceps* (Vigors) at Nanaj, Solapur District, Maharashtra, India. *J. Bombay Nat. Hist. Soc.* **83(1)**: 17-31.
Rahmani, A.R. & Manakadan, R. (1987). Interspecific behaviour of the Great Indian Bustard *Ardeotis nigriceps* (Vigors). *J. Bombay Nat. Hist. Soc.* **84(2)**: 317-331.
Rahmani, A.R. & Manakadan, R. (1989). Breeding records of Cream-coloured Courser from India. *J. Bombay Nat. Hist. Soc.* **86(3)**: 447-448.
Rahmani, A.R. & Manakadan, R. (1990). The past and present distribution of the Great Indian Bustard *Ardeotis nigriceps* (Vigors) in India. *J. Bombay Nat. Hist. Soc.* **87**: 175-194.
Rahmani, A.R. & Sankaran, R. (1988). *The Bengal Florican, Status and Ecology*. Annual Report **3** (1986-87). Bombay Natural History Society, Bombay.
Rahmani, A.R. & Shobrak, M. (1987). Arabian Bustard survey 1987. Technical Report **1**. Report to National Commission for Wildlife Conservation and Development, Riyadh, Saudi Arabia. 13 pp.
Rahmani, A.R. & Shobrak, M. (1990). Arabian Bustard project - Progress report (December 1989 to February 1990). Report to National Commission for Wildlife Conservation and Development, Riyadh, Saudi Arabia. 21 pp.
Rahmani, A.R. & Shobrak, M.Y. (1992). Glossy Ibises (*Plegadis falcinellus*) and Black-tailed Godwits (*Limosa limosa*) feeding on sorghum in flooded fields in southwestern Saudi Arabia. *Colonial Waterbirds* **15(2)**: 239-240.
Rahmani, A.R., Narayan, G., Rosalind, L. & Sankaran, R. (1990). Status of the Bengal Florican *Houbaropsis bengalensis* in India. Pp. 55-82 in: *Status and Ecology of the Lesser and Bengal Floricans with Reports on Jerdon's Courser and Mountain Quail*. Bombay Natural History Society, Bombay.
Rahmani, A.R., Narayan, G., Rosalind, L., Sankaran, R. & Ganguli-Lachungpa, U. (1991). Status of the Bengal Florican *Houbaropsis bengalensis* in India. *J. Bombay Nat. Hist. Soc.* **88**: 349-375.
Rahmani, A.R., Narayan, G., Sankaran, R. & Rosalind, L. eds. (1988). *The Bengal Florican: Status and Ecology*. Annual Report. Bombay Natural History Society, Bombay.
Rahn, H. & Dawson, W.R. (1979). Incubation water loss in eggs of Heermann's and Western Gulls. *Physiol. Zool.* **52**: 451-460.
Rahn, H., Paganelli, C.V., Nisbet, I.C.T. & Whittow, G.C. (1976). Regulation of incubation water loss in eggs of seven species of terns. *Physiol. Zool.* **49**: 245-259.
Raju, K.S.R. (1978). Ecological notes on some migrant waders in India. *J. Bombay Nat. Hist. Soc.* **75**(Suppl.): 1080-1089.
Ralph, C.J. (1994). Evidence of changes in population of the Marbled Murrelet in the Pacific Northwest. Pp. 286-292 in: Jehl & Johnson (1994).
Ralph, C.J., Hunt, G.L., Raphael, M.G. & Piatt, J.F. eds. (1995). *Ecology and Conservation of the Marbled Murrelet*. Gen. Tech. Rep. PSW-GTR-152. Pacific Southwest Research Station, Forest Service, US Department of Agriculture, Albany, California.

Ramadan-Jaradi, G. & Ramadan-Jaradi, G. (1989). Breeding the Houbara Bustard at the Al Ain Zoo & Aquarium, Abu Dhabi, UAE. *Zool. Garten* **59**: 229-240.
Ramo, C. & Busto, B. (1984). La Chenchena (*Opisthocomus hoazin*): algunos datos sobre su nidificación en Venezuela. [The Hoatzin (*Opisthocomus hoazin*): some data on nesting in Venezuela]. *Biotropica* **16(4)**: 330-331.
Ramos, J.A. & del Nevo, A.J. (1995). Nest-site selection by Roseate Terns and Common Terns in the Azores. *Auk* **112**: 580-589.
Ramsay, G. (1992). White-tailed Plovers breed in the Eastern Province of Saudi Arabia in 1992. *Phoenix* **9**: 3-4.
Ramsay, S. & Ramsay, B. (1990). Sighting of a Comb-crested Jacana at Long Swamp, Bermagui, New South Wales. *Austr. Birds* **24(2)**: 42-43.
Rand, A.L. (1936). *The Distribution and Habits of Madagascar Birds: a Summary of Field Notes of the Mission Zoologique Franco-Anglo-Américaine à Madagascar*. Bulletin of the American Museum of Natural History **72**, New York. 357 pp.
Rand, A.L. (1942). Results of the Archibold expeditions. No. 43. Birds of the 1938-1939 expedition. *Bull. Amer. Mus. Nat. Hist.* **79**: 425-515.
Rand, A.L. (1951a). Birds from Liberia, with a discussion of barriers between upper and lower Guinea sub-species. *Fieldiana Zool.* **32(9)**: 558-653.
Rand, A.L. (1951b). The nests and eggs of *Mesoenas unicolor* of Madagascar. *Auk* **68(1)**: 23-26.
Rand, A.L. & Gilliard, E.T. (1967). *Handbook of New Guinea Birds*. Weidenfeld & Nicolson, London.
Rand, A.L. & Rabor, S.S. (1960). *Birds of the Philippine Islands: Siquijor, Mount Malindang, Bohol and Samar*. Fieldiana Zoology **35(7)**. 117 pp.
Rand, R.W. (1949). Notes on birds observed on Sinclairs Island, South West Africa. *Ostrich* **20**: 130 136.
Rand, R.W. (1950). Weight and culmen changes in *Haematopus moquini*. *Ostrich* **21**: 72 76.
Randall, R.D. (1994a). Huge flocks of Red-winged Pratincoles *Glareola pratincola* and Brownthroated Martins *Riparia paludicola* near Kasane. *Babbler* **26-27**: 33.
Randall, R.D. (1994b). Important numbers of African Skimmers *Rynchops flavirostris* on the Chobe River. *Babbler* **26-27**: 31.
Randall, R.M. & Hosten, L.W. (1983). First breeding records of Greyheaded Gulls *Larus cirrocephalus* from the eastern Cape, South Africa. *Cormorant* **11**: 59-60.
Randall, R.M. & McLachlan, A. (1982). Damara Terns breeding in the Eastern Cape South Africa. *Ostrich* **53**: 50-51.
Randall, R.M. & Randall, B.M. (1978). Diet of Roseate Tern during the breeding season at St. Croix Island, Algoa Bay. *Cormorant* **5**: 4-10.
Randall, R.M. & Randall, B.M. (1980). Status and distribution of the Roseate Tern in South Africa. *Ostrich* **51**: 14-20.
Randall, R.M. & Randall, B.M. (1981). Roseate Tern breeding biology and factors responsible for low chick production in Algoa Bay, South Africa. *Ostrich* **52**: 17-24.
Randall, R.M. & Randall, B.M. (1982). The hard shelled diet of African Black Oystercatcher chicks at St. Croix Island, South Africa. *Ostrich* **53(3)**: 157 163.
Rands, M.R.W., Rands, G.F. & Porter, R.F. (1987). *Birds in the Yemen Arab Republic*. Report of the Ornithological Society of the Middle East Expedition 1985. ICBP, Cambridge.
Raner, L. (1972). [Polyandry in the Red-necked Phalarope, *Phalaropus lobatus*, and the Spotted Redshank, *Tringa erythropus*]. *Fauna och Flora* **67**: 135-138. In Swedish with English summary.
Ranftl, H. (1983). Zum Brutvorkommen des Flußregenpfeifers *Charadrius dubius* in Nordbayern. [On the occurrence of Little Ringed Plover in northern Bavaria]. *Anz. Orn. Ges. Bayern* **22(1/2)**: 103-106.
Rank, M. (1990). New wintering area for Black-necked Cranes found. *Bull. Oriental Bird Club* **12**: 9-10.
Rao, P. & Mohapatra, K.K. (1992). Biometrics of the Collared Pratincole *Glareola pratincola maldivarum* J.R. Forster. *J. Bombay Nat. Hist. Soc.* **89(2)**: 248-250.
Rapin, P. & Versel, C. (1988). [Springtime observation of a Broad-billed Sandpiper in Fanel, Switzerland]. *Nos Oiseaux* **39(6)**: 295-296. In French.
Rasmussen, J.F., Rahbek, C., Poulsen, B.O., Poulsen, M.K. & Bloch, H. (1996). Distributional records and natural history notes on threatened and little known birds of southern Ecuador. *Bull. Brit. Orn. Club* **116(1)**: 26-46.
Ratcliffe, D.A. (1976). Observations on the breeding of the Golden Plover in Great Britain. *Bird Study* **23**: 63-116.
Rathbone, P. & Rathbone, M. (1992). Stone-curlew killing adult Linnet. *British Birds* **85(3)**: 135.
Rattiste, K. & Lilleleht, V. (1987). Population ecology of the Common Gull *Larus canus* in Estonia. *Ornis Fenn.* **64**: 25-26.
Rattiste, K. & Lilleleht, V. (1990). Breeding success and genealogical structure in Common Gull colonies. *Baltic Birds* **5**: 89-97.
Rattner, B.A., Capizzi, J.L., King, K.A., Lecaptain, L.J. & Melancon, M.J. (1995). Exposure and effects of oil field brine discharges on Western Sandpipers (*Calidris mauri*) in Nueces Bay, Texas. *Bull. Environm. Contam. Toxicol.* **54**: 683-689.
Rauzon, M.J. (1988). Red-kneed Dotterel in Belau: first record for Micronesia. *Elepaio* **48(7)**: 56-57.
Rauzon, M.J. & Kenyon, K.W. (1984). White Tern nest sites in altered habitat. *Elepaio* **44**: 1-2.
Rauzon, M.J., Harrison, C.S. & Clapp, R.B. (1984). Breeding biology of the Blue-gray Noddy. *J. Field Orn.* **55**: 309-321.
Razdan, T. & Mansoori, J. (1989). A review of the bustard situation in the Islamic Republic of Iran. *Bustard Studies* **4**: 135-145.
Reagan, W.W. (1977). *Resource Partitioning in the North American Gallinules in Southern Texas*. MSc thesis, Utah State University, Logan, Utah.
Reay, P.J. (1991). Wintering Avocets in Cornwall and Devon. *Devon Birds* **44**: 3-11.
Reay, P.J. (1992). Behaviour of a flock of wintering Avocets, *Recurvirostra avosetta*. *Wader Study Group Bull.* **64**: 11.
Recher, H.F. (1966). Some aspects of the ecology of migrant shorebirds. *Ecology* **47**: 393-407.
Recher, H.F. & Clark, S.S. (1974). A biological survey of Lord Howe Island, with recommendations for the conservation of the island's wildlife. *Biol. Conserv.* **6**: 263-273.
Recorbet, B. (1994). [A case of the Black-winged Stilt *Himantopus himantopus* breeding in Corsica]. *Alauda* **62(3)**: 139-140. In French.
Reddig, E. (1981). *Die Bekassine* Capella gallinago. A. Ziemsen Verlag, Wittenberg Lutherstadt, Germany.
Redfern, C.P.F. (1982). Lapwing nest sites and chick mobility in relation to habitat. *Bird Study* **29**: 201-208.
Redfern, C.P.F. (1983). Aspects of growth and development of Lapwings *Vanellus vanellus*. *Ibis* **125**: 266-272.
Redford, K.H. & Peters, G. (1986). Notes on the biology and song of the Red-legged Seriema (*Cariama cristata*). *J. Field Orn.* **57(4)**: 261-269.
Redford, K.H. & Shaw, P. (1989). The terror bird still screams. *Int. Wildl.* **19(3)**: 14-16.
Redmond, G.W. (1983). *A Male Removal and Vegetation Study at Woodcock Display Sites in Coniferous Forest*. MSc thesis, University of New Brunswick, Fredericton, Canada.
Redmond, G.W. & Keppie, D.M. (1988). Variation in occupancy of coniferous territories by male American Woodcock. *Can. J. Zool.* **66**: 2029-2035.
Redmond, R.L. (1986). Egg size and laying date of Long-billed Curlew (*Numenius americanus*): implications for female reproductive tactics. *Oikos* **46(3)**: 330-338.
Redmond, R.L. & Jenni, D.A. (1982). Natal philopatry and breeding area fidelity of Long-billed Curlew (*Numenius americanus*): patterns and evolutionary consequences. *Behav. Ecol. Sociobiol.* **10**: 277-279.
Redmond, R.L. & Jenni, D.A. (1986). Population ecology of the Long-billed Curlew (*Numenius americanus*) in western Idaho. *Auk* **103(4)**: 755-767.
Redmond, R.L., Bicak, T.K. & Jenni, D.A. (1981). An evaluation of breeding season census techniques for Long-billed Curlews (*Numenius americanus*). *Studies in Avian Biology* **6**: 197-201.
Redpath, S. (1988). Vigilance levels in preening Dunlin *Calidris alpina*. *Ibis* **130**: 555-557.
Reeber, S. (1995). Le Goéland railleur *Larus genei* en France. [Status of Slender-billed Gull in France]. *Ornithos* **2(3)**: 103-106. In French with English summary.
Reeber, S. (1996). Premières tentatives de nidification de la Mouette pygmée *Larus minutus* en France. [First breeding attempts of Little Gull in France]. *Ornithos* **3(1)**: 41-43. In French with English summary.
Reed, C.E.M. (1986). *The Maintenance and Reproductive Behaviour of Black Stilts* Himantopus novaezealandiae *in Captivity, and Implications for Management of this Rare Species*. MSc thesis, Massey University, Palmerston North, New Zealand.
Reed, C.E.M. (1994a). Hand-rearing and breeding the endangered Black Stilt *Himantopus novaezelandiae* at Twizel. *Int. Zoo Yb.* **33**: 125-128.
Reed, C.E.M. (1994b). Causes of mortality in Black Stilts *Himantopus novaezealandiae* in captivity. *Int. Zoo Yb.* **33**: 129-135.
Reed, C.E.M. (1995). Release of captive-reared stilts into the wild, New Zealand. *Re-introduction News* **11**: 5-6.
Reed, C.E.M. & Merton, D. (1991). Behavioural manipulation of endangered New Zealand birds as an aid towards species recovery. Pp. 2514-2522 in: Bell *et al.* (1991).
Reed, C.E.M., Murray, D.P. & Butler, D.J. (1993). *Black Stilt Recovery Plan*. Threatened Species Recovery Plan **4**. Department of Conservation, Wellington.
Reed, C.E.M., Nilsson, R.J. & Murray, D.P. (1993). Cross-fostering New Zealand's Black Stilt. *J. Wildl. Manage.* **57**: 608-611.
Reed, J.M. (1985). Relative energetics of two foraging behaviors of Forster's Terns. *Colonial Waterbirds* **8**: 79-82.
Reed, J.M. & Ha, S.J. (1983). Enhanced foraging efficiency in Forster's Terns. *Wilson Bull.* **95**: 479-481.
Reed, J.M. & Oring, L.W. (1992). Reconnaissance for future breeding sites by Spotted Sandpipers. *Behav. Ecol.* **3**: 310-317.
Reed, J.M. & Oring, L.W. (1993). Philopatry, site fidelity, dispersal and survival of Spotted Sandpipers. *Auk* **110**: 541-551.
Reed, J.M., Hays, H.E. & Zegers, D.A. (1982). Feeding behaviors and efficiencies of Common and Forster's Terns. *Wilson Bull.* **94**: 567-569.
Reed, S.M. (1980). The birds of Savai'i, Western Samoa. *Notornis* **27(2)**: 151-159.
Reed, S.M. (1981). New Zealand Dotterel (*Charadrius obscurus*) - an endangered species? *Notornis* **28(2)**: 129-132.
Reel, S. (1989). Upland Sandpiper, *Bartramia longicauda*. Pp. 77-78 in: Clark, T.W. & Harvey, A.H. eds. (1989). *Rare, Sensitive and Threatened Species of the Greater Yellowstone Ecosystem*. Northern Rockies Conservation Cooperative, Montana Natural Heritage Program, the Nature Conservancy-Idaho, Montana and Wyoming Field Offices, Mountain West Environmental Services.
Regalado, P. (1981). El género *Torreornis* (Aves: Fringillidae), descripción de una nueva subespecie en Cayo Coco, Cuba. *Centro Agricola* **2**: 87-112.
Regan, E.R. (1994). The king of Huntley Meadows. *Birder's World* **8(5)**: 42-45.
Rego, L.H.A. (1983). The status of bustards in Maharashtra. Pp. 60-75 in: Goriup & Vardhan (1983).
Rehfisch, M., Clark, N.A., Langston, R.H.W. & Greenwood, J.J.D. (1996). A guide to the provision of refuges for waders: an analysis of thirty years of ringing data from the Wash, England. *J. Appl. Ecol.* **33**.
Reichel, J.D., Aldan, D.T. & Glass, P.O. (1989). Range extension for the Little Tern in the Western Pacific. *Colonial Waterbirds* **12**: 218-219.
Reichenow, A. (1900-1901). *Die Vögel Afrikas*. Vol. 1. Neumann, Neudamm.
Reicherzer, S. (1986). [Passage of Golden Plovers *Pluvialis apricaria* through the Ries/Bavaria]. *Anz. Orn. Ges. Bayern* **24(2/3)**: 135-149. In German wtih English summary.
Reichholf, J. (1989). [Why did the Gull-billed Tern *Gelochelidon nilotica* and Stone Curlew *Burhinus oedicnemus* vanish from Bayern?]. *Anz. Orn. Ges. Bayern* **28**: 8-14. In German.
Reid, B.E. (1966). The growth and development of the South Polar Skua (*Catharacta maccormicki*). *Notornis* **13(2)**: 71-89.
Reid, B.E. (1967). Some featues of recent research on the Takahe (*Notornis mantelli*). *Proc. New Zeland Ecol. Soc.* **14**: 79-87.
Reid, B.E. (1971). Takahe - a vanishing species. *Wildlife - Rev. New Zealand Wildl. Serv.* **3**: 39-42.
Reid, B.E. (1974a). Sightings and records of the Takahe (*Notornis mantelli*) prior to its "official rediscovery" by Dr. G.B. Orbell in 1948. *Notornis* **21(4)**: 277-295.
Reid, B.E. (1974b). Feaces of Takahe (*Notornis mantelli*): a general discussion relating the quantity of feaces to the type food and to the estimated energy requirements of the bird. *Notornis* **21(4)**: 306-311.
Reid, B.E. (1977). Takahe at Mt. Bruce. *Wildl. - Rev. New Zealand Wildl. Serv.* **8**: 56-73.
Reid, D. & Reid, B. (1965). The Sulphur Point (Lake Rotorua) gull colony. *Notornis* **12**: 138-157.
Reid, F.A. (1989). *Differential Habitat Use by Waterbirds in a Managed Wetland Complex*. PhD dissertation, University of Missouri, Columbia, Missouri.
Reid, F.A., Meanley, B. & Fredrickson, L.H. (1994). King Rail. In: Tacha & Braun (1994).
Reid, M.L. & Montgomerie, R.D. (1985). Seasonal patterns of nest defence by Baird's Sandpipers. *Can. J. Zool.* **63**: 2207-2211.
Reid, W.V. (1987a). Constraints on clutch size in the Glaucous-winged Gull. Pp. 8-25 in: Hand *et al.* (1987).
Reid, W.V. (1987b). The cost of reproduction in the Glaucous-winged Gull. *Oecologia* **74**: 458-467.
Reid, W.V. (1988a). Age-specific patterns of reproduction in the Glaucous-winged Gull: increased effort with age. *Ecology* **69**: 1454-1465.
Reid, W.V. (1988b). Population dynamics of the Glaucous-winged Gull. *J. Wildl. Manage.* **52**: 763-770.
Reid, W.V. (1988c). Fledging success of experimentally enlarged broods of the Glaucous-winged Gull. *Wilson Bull.* **100**: 476-482.
Reinecke, K.J. & Krapu, G.L. (1986). Feeding ecology of Sandhill Cranes during spring migration in Nebraska. *J. Wildl. Manage.* **50**: 71-79.
Reithmüller, E. (1931). Nesting notes from Willis Island. *Emu* **31**: 142-246.
Remsen, J.V. (1990). Community ecology of Neotropical Kingfishers. *Univ. Calif. Publ. Zool.* **124**: 1-116.
Remsen, J.V. & Parker, T.A. (1990). Seasonal distribution of the Azure Gallinule (*Porphyrula flavirostris*), with comments on vagrancy in rails and gallinules. *Wilson Bull.* **102**: 380-399.
Remsen, J.V. & Traylor, M.A. (1983). Additions to the avifauna of Bolivia, part 2. *Condor* **85**: 95-98.
Remsen, J.V. & Traylor, M.A. (1989). *An Annotated List of the Birds of Bolivia*. Buteo Books, Vermillion, South Dakota.
Remsen, J.V., Traylor, M.A. & Parkes, K.C. (1985). Range extensions for some Bolivian birds, 1 (Tinamiformes to Charadriiformes). *Bull. Brit. Orn. Club* **105**: 124-130.
Renaud, J. (1989). Captive propagation of Houbara Bustards at the National Wildlife Research Centre, Tãif. Pp. 335-339 in: Abdulaziz, H., Abu-Zinada, Goriup, P.D. & Nader, I.K. eds. (1989). *Wildlife Conservation and Development in Saudi Arabia*. National Commission for Wildlife Conservation and Development, Riyadh, Saudi Arabia.
Renaud, W.E. & MacLaren, P.L. (1982). Ivory Gull (*Pagophila eburnea*) distribution in late summer and autumn in eastern Lancaster Sound and western Baffin Bay. *Arctic* **35**: 141-148.
Renken, R.B. & Smith, J.W. (1995a). Annual adult survival of interior Least Terns. *J. Field Orn.* **66**: 117-127.
Renken, R.B. & Smith, J.W. (1995b). Interior Least Tern site fidelity and dispersal. *Colonial Waterbirds* **18(2)**: 193-198.
Rennie, F.W. (1988). The status and distribution of the Great Skua in the Western Isles. *Scottish Birds* **15(2)**: 80-82.
Rensch, B. (1931). Die Vogelwelt von Lombok, Sumbawa und Flores. *Mitt. Zool. Mus. Berlin* **17**: 451-637.
Repking, C.F. (1975). *Distribution and Habitat Requirements of the Black Rail (*Laterallus jamaicensis*) Along the Lower Colorado River*. MSc thesis, Arizona State University, Tempe, Arizona.
Repking, C.F. & Ohmart, R.D. (1977). Distribution and density of Black Rail populations along the lower Colorado River. *Condor* **79**: 486-489.
Resende, S.L. & Leeuwenberg, F. (1989). A first breeding record of the Two-banded Plover *Charadrius falklandicus* in Brazil. *Wader Study Group Bull.* **56**: 38-39.
Retallick, R.W.R. & Bolitho, E.E. (1993). Disturbance of Hooded Plovers by domestic dogs. *Stilt* **23**: 23.
Reynard, G.B. (1974). Some vocalizations of the Black, Yellow and Virginia Rails. *Auk* **91**: 747-756.
Reynolds, J.D. (1985). Philandering phalaropes. *Nat. Hist.* **94(8)**: 58-65.
Reynolds, J.D. (1987). Mating system and nesting biology of the Red-necked Phalarope *Phalaropus lobatus*: what constrains polyandry? *Ibis* **129**: 225-242.
Reynolds, J.D. & Cooke, F. (1988). The influence of mating systems on philopatry: a test with polyandrous Red-necked Phalaropes. *Anim. Behav.* **36**: 1788-1795.
Reynolds, J.D., Colwell, M.A. & Cooke, F. (1986). Sexual selection and spring arrival times of Red-necked and Wilson's Phalaropes. *Behav. Ecol. Sociobiol.* **18**: 303-310.
Reynolds, J.F. (1968). Observations on the White-headed Plover. *East Afr. Wildl. J.* **6**: 142-144.
Reynolds, J.F. (1975a). Chestnut-banded Sand Plover responding to a supernormal stimulus. *Bull. East Afr. Nat. Hist. Soc.* **1975**: 130.
Reynolds, J.F. (1975b). Coursers of the dry savannahs. *Wildlife* **17**: 274-278.
Reynolds, J.F. (1977a). Wattled Plovers *Vanellus senegallus* in Tanzania. *Scopus* **1(1)**: 22-23.
Reynolds, J.F. (1977b). Pratincole *Glareola pratincola* catching flies at ground level. *Scopus* **1(1)**: 23.
Reynolds, J.F. (1977c). Thermo-regulatory problems of birds nesting in areas in east Africa: a review. *Scopus* **1(3)**: 57-68.
Reynolds, J.F. (1980). Sympatry of Blacksmith and Spur-winged Plover *Vanellus armatus* and *spinosus* at Amboseli. *Scopus* **4(2)**: 43.
Reynolds, J.F. (1984). Response of a Blacksmith Plover *Vanellus armatus* to ants attacking a hatching egg. *Scopus* **8**: 79.
Reynolds, J.W., Krohn, W.B. & Jordan, G.A. (1977). Earthworm populations as related to Woodcock habitat usage in central Maine. Pp. 135-146 in: *Proceedings of the Sixth Woodcock Symposium*.

Reynolds, P.W. (1935). Notes on the birds of Cape Horn. *Ibis* **Ser. 13, no. 5**: 65-101.
Rezanov, A.G. & Khorokov, V.V. (1988a). [Feeding behaviour of the Redshanks (*Tringa totanus*) during autumn migration]. Pp. 118-123 in: Flint & Tomkovich (1988). In Russian.
Rezanov, A.G. & Khrokov, V.V. (1988b). [Distribution and behaviour of Redshank on feeding areas in autumn migration]. *Izv. Akad. Nauk Kaz. SSR Ser. Biol.* **1**: 43-47. In Russian.
van Rhijn, J.G. (1973). Behavioural dimorphism in male Ruffs *Philomachus pugnax* (L.). *Behaviour* **47**: 153-229.
van Rhijn, J.G. (1981). Units of behavior in the Black-headed Gull, *Larus ridibundus* L. *Anim. Behav.* **29**: 586-597.
van Rhijn, J.G. (1983). On the maintenance and origin of alternative strategies in the Ruff *Philomachus pugnax*. *Ibis* **125**: 482-498.
van Rhijn, J.G. (1985a). A scenario for the evolution of social organization in Ruffs *Philomachus pugnax* and other charadriiform species. *Ardea* **73**: 25-37.
van Rhijn, J.G. (1985b). Black-headed Gull or Black-headed Girl? On the advantage of concealing sex by gulls and other colonial birds. *Netherlands J. Zool.* **35**: 87-102.
van Rhijn, J.G. (1990). Unidirectionality in the phylogeny of social organization, with special reference to birds. *Behaviour* **115**: 153-174.
van Rhijn, J.G. (1991). *The Ruff. Individuality in a Gregarious Wading Bird*. T. & A.D. Poyser, London.
van Rhijn, J.G. & Groothuis, T. (1985). Biparental care and the basis for alternative bond-types among gulls with special reference to Black-headed Gulls. *Ardea* **73**: 159-174.
van Rhijn, J.G. & Groothuis, T. (1987). On the mechanism of mate selection in Black-headed Gulls. *Behaviour* **100**: 134-169.
Rich, E. (1973). Black-tailed Native Hen in desert country. *Austr. Bird Watcher* **5**: 28-29.
Richards, A. (1990). *Seabirds of the Northern Hemisphere*. Dragon's World Ltd, Surrey, UK.
Richards, B. (1989). Red-necked Stint: new to Britain and Ireland. *British Birds* **82(9)**: 391-395.
Richards, D.K. (1980). Distribution of the Chestnut-banded Plover *Charadrius pallidus* in Tanzania. *Scopus* **4**: 24.
Richards, M.H. & Morris, R.D. (1984). An experimental study of nest site selection in Common Terns. *J. Field Orn.* **55**: 457-466.
Richards, M.W. & Boswall, J. (1985). Some Egyptian Plover nests in Senegal. *Malimbus* **7(2)**: 128.
Richardson, C. (1990). *The Birds of the United Arab Emirates*. Hobby Publications, Dubai & Warrington.
Richardson, F. (1961). Breeding biology of the Rhinoceros Auklet on Protection Island, Washington. *Condor* **63**: 456-473.
Richardson, F. (1967). Black Tern nest and egg moving experiments. *Murrelet* **48**: 52-56.
Richardson, F. & Fisher, H.I. (1950). Birds of Moku Manu and Manana Islands off Oahu, Hawaii. *Auk* **67**: 285-306.
Richardson, M.E. (1984). Aspects of the ornithology of the Tristan da Cunha group and Gough Island, 1972-1974. *Cormorant* **12**: 123-201.
Richardson, M.G. (1990). The distribution and status of Whimbrel *Numenius phaeopus phaeopus* in Shetland and Britain (UK). *Bird Study* **37**: 61-68.
Richford, A.S. (1985). Painted Snipe. Pp. 425-426 in: Campbell & Lack (1985).
Richter, D. (1967). Deutungsversuch zur Nahrungsaufnahme eines schnabelverletzten Austernfischers. *J. Orn.* **108**: 328 334.
Ricklefs, R.E. (1983). Some considerations on the reproductive energetics of pelagic seabirds. *Studies in Avian Biology* **8**: 84-94.
Ricklefs, R.E. (1987). Characterizing the development of homeothermy by rate of body cooling. *Functional Ecology* **1**: 151-157.
Ricklefs, R.E. & White, S.E. (1981). The growth and energetics of chicks of the Sooty Tern (*Sterna fuscata*) and Common Tern (*S. hirundo*). *Auk* **98**: 361-378.
Ricklefs, R.E. & White-Schuler, S.C. (1978). Growth rate of the Brown Noddy on the Dry Tortugas. *Bird-Banding* **49**: 301-312.
Ricklefs, R.E., Hahn, D.C. & Montevecchi, W.A. (1978). The relationship between egg size and chick size in the Laughing Gull and Japanese Quail. *Auk* **95**: 135-144.
Riddiford, N. (1983). Call of tundra Ringed Plover. *British Birds* **76(11)**: 534-535.
Ridgely, R.S. (1981). *A Guide to the Birds of Panama*. Princeton University Press, Princeton, New Jersey.
Ridgely, R.S. & Gaulin, S.J.C. (1980). The birds of Finca Merenberg, Huila Department, Colombia. *Condor* **82**: 379-391.
Ridgely, R.S. & Gwynne, J.A. (1989). *A Guide to the Birds of Panama with Costa Rica, Nicaragua and Honduras*. Princeton University Press, Princeton, New Jersey.
Ridgely, R.S. & Wilcove, D.S. (1979). First nesting record of Grey-hooded Gull. *Condor* **81**: 438-439.
Ridgway, R. (1886). Description of a new species of oystercatcher from the Galapagos Islands. *Auk* **3**: 331.
Ridgway, R. (1897). Birds of the Galapagos Archipelago. *Proc. US Natl. Mus.* **19**: 459 670.
Ridgway, R. & Friedmann, H. (1941). *The Birds of North America and Middle America*. US National Museum Bulletin **50(9)**. Smithsonian Institution, Washington, D.C.
Ridley, E. (1985). First breeding of the Plains-wanderer. *Bird Keep. Austr.* **28**: 49-53.
Ridley, M.W. (1980). The breeding behaviour and feeding ecology of Grey Phalarope *Phalaropus fulicarius* in Svalbard. *Ibis* **122**: 210-226.
Ridley, M.W. (1983). A review of the ecology and behaviour of button-quails. *World Pheasant Assoc. J.* **8**: 50-61.
Ridley, M.W., Magrath, R.D. & Woinarzki, J.C.Z. (1985). Display leap of the Lesser Florican *Sypheotides indica*. *J. Bombay Nat. Hist. Soc.* **82(2)**: 271-277.
Ridpath, M.G. (1964). The Tasmanian Native Hen. *Austr. Nat. Hist.* **14**: 346-350.
Ridpath, M.G. (1972a). The Tasmanian Native Hen, *Tribonyx mortierii*. I. Patterns of behaviour. *CSIRO Wildl. Res.* **17**: 1-51.
Ridpath, M.G. (1972b). The Tasmanian Native Hen, *Tribonyx mortierii*. II. The individual, the group and the population. *CSIRO Wildl. Res.* **17**: 53-90.
Ridpath, M.G. (1972c). The Tasmanian Native Hen, *Tribonyx mortierii*. III. Ecology. *CSIRO Wildl. Res.* **17**: 91-118.
Ridpath, M.G. & Meldrum, G.K. (1968a). Damage to pasture by the Tasmanian Native Hen *Tribonyx mortierii*. *CSIRO Wildl. Res.* **13**: 11-24.
Ridpath, M.G. & Meldrum, G.K. (1968b). Damage to oat crops by the Tasmanian Native Hen *Tribonyx mortierii*. *CSIRO Wildl. Res.* **13**: 25-54.
Riegen, A. (1994). National Wrybill census - 29 May 1994. *Orn. Soc. New Zealand News* **72**: 2-3.
Riggs, C.D. (1948). The family Eurypgidae: a review. *Wilson Bull.* **60**: 75-80.
Riley, J.W. & Rooke, K.B. (1962). Sociable Plover in Dorset. *British Birds* **55**: 233-235.
Rimmer, D.W. & Deblinger, R.D. (1990). Use of predator exclosures to protect Piping Plover nests. *J. Field Orn.* **61(2)**: 217-223. In English with Spanish summary.
Rinke, D. (1987). The avifauna of 'Eua and its off-shore islet Kalau, Kingdom of Tonga. *Emu* **87**: 26-34.
Ripley, S.D. (1957a). Notes on the Horned Coot, *Fulica cornuta* Bonaparte. *Postilla* **30**: 1-8.
Ripley, S.D. (1957b). Additional notes on the Horned Coot, *Fulica cornuta* Bonaparte. *Postilla* **32**: 1-2.
Ripley, S.D. (1964). *A Systematic and Ecological Study of Birds of New Guinea*. Peabody Museum of Natural History Yale University Bulletin **19**. New Haven, Connecticut.
Ripley, S.D. (1977). *Rails of the World*. Godine, Boston.
Ripley, S.D. (1982). *A Synopsis of the Birds of India and Pakistan*. Bombay Natural History Society, Bombay.
Ripley, S.D. (1985). Rail. Pp. 495-496 in: Campbell & Lack (1985).
Ripley, S.D. & Beehler, B.M. (1985). Rails of the world, a compilation of new information, 1975-1983 (Aves: Rallidae). *Smithsonian Contrib. Zool.* **417**: 1-28.
Ripley, S.D. & Beehler, B.M. (1989). Systematics, biogeography and conservation of Jerdon's Courser *Rhinoptilus bitorquatus*. *J. Yamashina Inst. Orn.* **21(2)**: 165-174.
Risen, K.W. (1992). Unusual feeding behavior observed for King Rail. *Loon* **64(3)**: 162-163.
Riska, D.E. (1984). Experiments on nestling recognition by Brown Noddies (*Anous stolidus*). *Auk* **101**: 605-609.
Riska, D.E. (1986a). An analysis of vocal communication in young Brown Noddies (*Anous stolidus*). *Auk* **103**: 351-358.
Riska, D.E. (1986b). An analysis of vocal communication in the adult Brown Noddy (*Anous stolidus*). *Auk* **103**: 359-369.
Ritchie, L. (1990). A Long-billed Curlew at the farm. *Loon* **62(3)**: 167-168.
Ritter, M. & Fuchs, E. (1980). Das Zugverhalten der Lachmöwe *Larus ridibundus*. *Orn. Beob.* **77**: 219-229.
Ritter, M.W. & Sweet, T.M. (1993). Rapid colonization of a human-made wetland by Mariana Common Moorhen on Guam. *Wilson Bull.* **105**: 685-687.
Rittinghaus, H. (1956). Untersuchungen am Seeregenpfeifer (*Charadrius alexandrinus* L.) auf der Insel Oldeoog. *J. Orn.* **97**: 117-155.
Rittinghaus, H. (1961). Der Seeregenpfeifer (*Charadrius alexandrinus* L.). A. Ziemsen Verlag, Wittenberg, East Germany.
Rittinghaus, H. (1963). Sonderbare Nistplätze des Austernfischers. *Natur und Museum* **93**: 155 164.
Rittinghaus, H. (1964). Betrachtungen zu den Nistgewohnheiten der Zwergseeschwalbe. *Natur und Museum* **9**: 231-237.
Rivadeneira, G.V. (1987). Nota sobre el comportamiento de la gaviota *Larus pipixcan* en Chucuito-Callao. *Bol. Lima* **9**: 15-18.
Rivadeneira, G.V., Vásquez, P.C. & la Rosa, M.M. (1986). Aves de la Isla 'El Frontón' (Callao-Perú): nota preliminar. *Bol. Lima* **8**: 35-47.
Robbins, C.R. (1974). Probable interbreeding of Common and Roseate Terns. *British Birds* **67**: 168-170.
Robbins, C.S., Bruun, B. & Zim, H.S. (1983). *Birds of North America*. Golden Press, New York.
Robel, D. (1982). Nachweise von Brachschwalben in der DDR. [Reports of pratincoles in east Germany]. *Falke* **29(1)**: 24-25.
Robel, D. (1991). [Are identifications in the field hopeless? On the identifying characteristics of juvenile *Stercorarius longicaudus*]. *Falke* **38(6)**: 184-189. In German.
Robel, D. & Beschow, R. (1994). Eine Fischmöwe *Larus ichthyaetus* in Brandenburg. *Limicola* **8(2)**: 51-62.
Robel, D. & Königstedt, D. (1979). Zum Durchzug des Mornellregenpfeifers, *Eudromias morinellus* (L.), in Südosteuropa. *Beitr. Vogelkd.* **25**: 356-358.
Roberson, D. & Baptista, L.F. (1988). White-shielded Coots in North America: a critical evaluation. *Amer. Birds* **42**: 1241-1246.
Robert, H.C. & Ralph, C.J. (1975). Effects of human disturbance on the breeding success of gulls. *Condor* **77**: 495-499.
Robert, J.C. (1983). Un Gravelot de leschenault *Charadrius leschenaultii* Lesson (1826) en Baie de Somme. [A Greater Sand Plover *Charadrius leschenaultii* in Somme Bay]. *Alauda* **51(2)**: 151-152. In French.
Robert, M. & Laporte, P. (1993). *Le Râle Jaune (*Coturnicops noveboracensis*) à l'Ile aux Grues et à Cacouna.* Rapport d'activités estivales - 1993. Service Canadien de la Faune, Sainte-Foy, Quebec.
Robert, M. & Laporte, P. (1994). *Plan d'Action pour le Rétablissement du Râle Jaune au Québec*. Service Canadien de la Faune, Sainte-Foy, Quebec.
Robert, M. & McNeil, R. (1989). Comparative day and night feeding strategies of shorebird species in a tropical environment. *Ibis* **131**: 69-79.
Robert, M. & McNeil, R. & Leduc, A. (1989). Conditions and significance of night feeding in shorebirds and other water birds in a tropical lagoon. *Auk* **106**: 94-101.
Roberts, B. (1985). Glaucous-winged Gulls prey on feral rabbits on Middleton Island, Alaska. *Murrelet* **66**: 24.
Roberts, B.D. & Hatch, S.A. (1994). Chick movements and adoption in a colony of Black-legged Kittiwakes. *Wilson Bull.* **106**: 289-298.
Roberts, G. (1991). Winter movements of Sanderlings (*Calidris alba*) between feeding sites. *Acta Oecol.* **12(2)**: 281-294.
Roberts, G. & Evans, P.R. (1993). A method for the detection of non-random associations among flocking birds and its application to Sanderlings *Calidris alba* wintering in N.E. England. *Behav. Ecol. Sociobiol.* **32(5)**: 349-354.
Roberts, G.J. (1975). Observations of water birds in south west Queensland. *Sunbird* **6**: 69-75.
Roberts, G.J. (1979). *The Birds of South-east Queensland*. Queensland Conservation Council, Brisbane.
Roberts, G.J. (1980). Records of interest from the Alice Springs region. *S. Austr. Orn.* **28**: 99-102.
Roberts, M.G. (1976). Belly-soaking and chick transport in the African Skimmer. *Ostrich* **47**: 126.
Roberts, M.G. (1977). Belly-soaking in the Whitefronted Plover. *Ostrich* **48(3-4)**: 111-112.
Roberts, T.H. (1980). Sexual development during winter in male American Woodcock. *Auk* **97**: 879-881.
Roberts, T.H. (1993). The ecology and management of wintering Woodcocks. Pp. 86-96 in: Longcore & Sepik (1993).
Roberts, T.J. (1985). Zangi Nawar-Portrait of a unique lake in the desert. *J. Bombay Nat. Hist. Soc.* **82**: 540-547.
Roberts, T.J. (1991). *The Birds of Pakistan*. Vol. 1. Non-Passeriformes. Oxford University Press, Karachi.
Roberts, T.J. & Landfried, S. (1987). Hunting pressures on cranes migrating through Pakistan. Pp. 139-145 in: Archibald & Pasquier (1987a).
Roberts, T.S. (1900). An account of the nesting habits of Franklin's Rosy Gull (*Larus pipixcan*), as observed at Heron Lake, in southern Minnesota. *Auk* **17**: 272-283.
Robertshaw, P.T. (1977). Excavations at Paternoster, South western Cape. *S. Afr. Archeol. Bull.* **32**: 63 73.
Robertson, C.J.R. (1985). *Reader's Digest Complete Book of New Zealand Birds*. Reader's Digest, Sydney.
Robertson, C.J.R., O'Donnell, C.F.J. & Overmars, F.B. (1983). Habitat requirements of wetland birds in the Ahuriri River catchment. New Zealand Wildlife Service Occasional Publications **3**. Department of Internal Affairs, Wellington.
Robertson, D.B. (1976). Weka liberation in Northland. *Notornis* **23**: 213-219.
Robertson, H.A. & Dennison, M.D. (1977). Red-kneed Dotterel (*Charadrius cinctus*) - first record for New Zealand. *Notornis* **24(3)**: 193-194.
Robertson, H.G. & Wooller, R.D. (1981). Seasonal decrease in the clutch size of Hartlaub's Gulls *Larus hartlaubii* at Strandfontein in 1978. *Cormorant* **9**: 23-26.
Robertson, I.S. (1992). Identification pitfalls and assessment problems. 14. Crane *Grus grus*. *British Birds* **85(11)**: 587-592.
Robertson, J. & Berg, Å. (1992). Status and population changes of farmland birds in southern Sweden. *Ornis Svecica* **2**: 119-130.
Robertson, P. (1992). Some observations on Double-banded Courser. *Witwatersrand Bird Club News* **157**: 22-23.
Robertson, W.B. (1964). Terns of the Dry Tortugas. *Bull. Florida State Mus. Biol. Sci.* **8**: 1-94.
Robertson, W.B. (1969). Transatlantic migration of juvenile Sooty Terns. *Nature* **222**: 632-634.
Robertson, W.B. (1978). Species of special concern, Noddy Tern, *Anous stolidus*. Pp. 95-96 in: Kale (1978).
Robertson, W.B. (1996). Brown Noddy. In: Rodgers, Kale & Smith (1996).
Robertson, W.B. & Robertson, M.J. (1996). Sooty Tern. In: Rodgers, Kale & Smith (1996).
Robertson, W.B., Paulson, D.R. & Mason, C.R. (1961). A tern new to the United States. *Auk* **78**: 423-424.
Robiller, F. (1983). Bade- und Huderverhalten des Temminckstrandläufers (*Calidris temmincki*). [Bathing and "huder" behaviour of *Calidris temmincki*]. *Beitr. Vogelkd.* **29(3)**: 180-182.
Robiller, F. & Borrmann, K. (1988). [Observations on the nest of the Snowy Plover (*Charadrius alexandrinus* L.) in southern Hungary]. *Beitr. Vogelkd.* **34(2/3)**: 85-92. In German.
Robin, K. (1981). Brut des Spornkibitzes *Hoplopterus spinosus* im Tierpark Bern. [Breeding the Spur-winged Plover *Hoplopterus spinosus* in the zoo of Berne]. *Orn. Beob.* **78(3)**: 209-210. In German with English summary.
Robinson, A.C. (1995). Breeding pattern in the Banded Rail (*Gallirallus philippensis*) in western Samoa. *Notornis* **42**: 46-48.
Robinson, G.P. (1975). Breeding records for the Black-winged Stilt at Mufulira. *Bull. Zambian Orn. Soc.* **7(1)**: 32-33.
Robinson, J.R. & Robinson, C.S.M. (1951). Some notes on the Chestnut-banded Sandplover *Charadrius venustus*. *Ostrich* **22(3)**: 198.
Robinson, S.R. (1981). Head-scratching and yawning in Black Skimmers. *J. Field Orn.* **52**: 59-60.
Robinson, T. & Minton, C. (1989). The enigmatic Banded Stilt. *Birds International* **1**: 72-85.
Robson, C. (1992). From the field. Thailand. *Bull. Oriental Bird Club* **16**: 51-52.
Roby, D.D. (1991). Diet and post-natal energetics in convergent taxa of plankton-feeding seabirds. *Auk* **108**: 131-146.
Roby, D.D. & Brink, K.L. (1986a). Breeding biology of Least Auklets on the Pribilof Islands, Alaska. *Condor* **88**: 336-346.
Roby, D.D. & Brink, K.L. (1986b). Decline of breeding Least Auklets on St. George Island, Alaska. *J. Field Orn.* **57**: 57-59.
Roby, D.D. & Ricklefs, R.E. (1986). Energy expenditure in adult Least Auklets and diving petrels during the chick-rearing period. *Physiol. Zool.* **59**: 661-678.
Roby, D.D., Brink, K.L. & Nettleship, D.N. (1981). Measurements, chick meals and breeding distribution of Dovekies *Alle alle* in northwest Greenland. *Arctic* **34**: 241-248.
Rocha, O. & Peñaranda, E. (1995). Avifauna de Huaraco: una localidad de la puna semiárida del altiplano central, Departamento de La Paz, Bolivia. *Cotinga* **3**: 17-25. In Spanish with English summary.
Roché, J. (1988). [Distribution of the Common Sandpiper *Actitis hypoleucos* in France and in Europe]. *Alauda* **56(4)**: 410. In French.
Roché, J. (1993). The use of historical data in the ecological zonation of rivers: the case of the 'Tern zone'. *Vie Milieu* **43**: 27-41.
Roché, J. & Frochot, B. (1993). Ornithological contribution to river zonation. *Acta Oecol.* **14**: 415-434.
Rockingham-Gill, A. (1992). Black-bellied Bustard eating Little Bee-eater. *Honeyguide* **38**: 185-186.
Rockingham-Gill, D. (1983). On the distribution of the Kori Bustard (*Otis kori*) in Zimbabwe. Pp. 97-103 in: Goriup & Vardhan (1983).
Rockingham-Gill, D. (1989). Status of bustards in Zimbabwe. *Bustard Studies* **4**: 146-150.
Rockwell, E.D. (1982). Intraspecific food robbing in Glaucous-winged Gulls. *Wilson Bull.* **94**: 282-288.

Rodenko, N.V. & Molodan, G.N. (1990). [On the behaviour of the Little Ringed Plover (*Charadrius dubius*) at nests]. *Ornitologiya* **24**: 133-134. In Russian with English summary.
Rodgers, J.A., Kale, H.W.I. & Smith, H.T. (1996). *Rare and Endangered Biota of Florida*. Vol. 5. University Press of Florida, Gainesville, FLorida.
Rodgers, J.A., Smith, H.T. & Paul, R.T. (1996). Sandwich Tern. In: Rodgers, Kale & Smith (1996).
Rodrigues, A.A.F. & Lopes, A.T.L. (1992). Ocorrência da reprodução de *Charadrius wilsonia* (Charadriiformes: Charadriidae), na Ilha de Curupu, município de Paço do Lumiar, Maranhão, Brasil. Resumos **042**. Cong. Bras. Orn. Campo Grande, Brazil.
Rodrigues, H. (1962). Duas novas espécies do gênero *Oxyspirura*. *Rev. Bras. Biol.* **22**: 371-376.
Rodríguez, F., Díaz, G., Almeida, R.S. & Nogales, I. (1987). Noticiario ornitológico. Corredor (*Cursorius cursor*). *Ardeola* **34(2)**: 284.
Rodríguez, J. & Días, A.B. (1975). Primera nidificación de la Gaviota Tridactila *Rissa tridactyla* en el suroeste de Europa. *Ardeola* **21**: 409-414.
Rodríguez, R. & Hiraldo, F. (1975). [Dietary requirements of *Porphyrio porphyrio* in the Guadalquivir marshes]. *Doñana Acta Vertebrata* **2**: 201-213. In Spanish.
Rodríguez-Estrella, R., Donázar, J.A. & Hiraldo, F. (1995). Yellow-footed Gulls attack Turkey Vultures on Isla Epíritu Santo, Baja California, Mexico. *Colonial Waterbirds* **18(1)**: 100-101.
Rodway, M.S. (1991). Status and conservation of breeding seabirds in British Columbia. Pp. 43-67 in: Croxall (1991).
Rodway, M.S., Carter, H.R., Sealy, S.G. & Campbell, R.W. (1992). Status of the Marbled Murrelet in British Columbia. Pp. 17-41 in: Carter & Morrison (1992).
Rodway, M.S., Lemon, M. & Kaiser, G.W. (1988). *Canadian Wildlife Service Seabird Inventory Report No. 1: East Coast of Moresby Island*. Technical Report Series **50**. Canadian Wildlife Service, Pacific and Yukon Region, Delta.
Rodway, M.S., Regehr, H.M. & Savard, J.L. (1993). Activity patterns of Marbled Murrelets in old-growth forest in the Queen Charlotte Islands, British Columbia. *Condor* **95**: 831-848.
Roe, K.S. (1990). Foragers of the seastrand. *Birder's World* **4(3)**: 30-34.
Roe, N.A. & Rees, W.E. (1979). Notes on the Puna avifauna of Azángaro Province, Department of Puna, southern Peru. *Auk* **96**: 475-482.
Rogacheva, H. (1992). *The Birds of Central Siberia*. Husum-Druck und Verlagsgesellschaft, Husum, Germany.
Roger, B. (1976). Gray-backed Terns eat Lizards. *Wilson Bull.* **88**: 354.
Rogers, D. (1995a). A mystery with history: the Buff-breasted Button-quail. *Wingspan* **5(1)**: 26-31.
Rogers, D. (1995b). Corrections and addendum: Field identification of Buff-breasted Button-quail. *Wingspan* **5(3)**: 36.
Rogers, K.G. (1982). Moult, biometrics and sexing of the Eastern Curlew. *Victorian Wader Study Group Bull.* **5**: 23-26.
Rogers, K.G. (1995). Eastern Curlew biometrics: based on bivariate separation of the sexes. *Stilt* **26**: 23-34.
Röhl, E. (1959). *Fauna Descriptiva de Venezuela*. Nuevas Gráficas, S.A., Madrid.
Rohwer, S., Martin, D.F. & Benson, G.G. (1979). Breeding of the Black-necked Stilt in Washington. *Murrelet* **60(2)**: 67-71.
Rohwer, S.A. & Woolfenden, G.E. (1968). The varied diet of the Gull-billed Tern includes a shrub-inhabiting lizard. *Wilson Bull.* **80**: 330-331.
Rojas, L.M., Tai, S. & McNeil, R. (1993). Comparison of rod/cone ratio in three species of shorebirds having different nocturnal foraging strategies. *Auk* **110**: 141-145.
Romig, T. (1989). A record of Denham's Bustard *Neotis denhami denhami* in north-west Kenya. *Scopus* **13**: 118.
Rompré, G. & McNeil, R. (1994). Seasonal changes in day and night foraging of Willets in northeastern Venezuela. *Condor* **96(3)**: 734-738.
de Roo, A. & van Damme, G. (1970). A first record of the Long-tailed Skua, *Stercorarius longicaudus* Vieillot, from the Ethiopian Region (Aves: Stercorariidae). *Rev. Zool. Bot. Afr.* **82(1/2)**: 157-162.
de Roos, G.T. (1981). The impact of tourism upon some breeding wader species on the Isle of Vlieland in the Netherlands' Wadden Sea. *Meded. Landbouwhogeschool Wageningen* **81(4)**: 1 131.
de Roos, G.T. (1992). Spring tail moult in Purple Sandpiper *Calidris maritima* in the Dutch Wadden Sea. *Wader Study Group Bull.* **64**: 40.
de Roos, G.T. & Schaafsma, W. (1981). Is recreation affecting the numbers of birds' nests. *Stat. Neerl.* **35**: 69-90.
Roos, M.T. & Schrijvershof, P.G. (1993). Red-wattled Lapwing in Israel in winter of 1991/92. *Dutch Birding* **15(1)**: 13-15.
Root, B.G., Ryan, M.R. & Mayer, P.M. (1992). Piping Plover survival in the Great Plains. *J. Field Orn.* **63(1)**: 10-15.
Root, T. (1988). *Atlas of Wintering North American Birds. An Analysis of Christmas Bird Count Data*. The University of Chicago Press, Chicago & London.
Rooth, J. (1989). [Numbers of Sandwich Tern *Sterna sandvicensis* breeding in the Netherlands in 1961-88]. *Limosa* **62**: 121-124. In Dutch with English summary.
Rooth, J. & Jonkers, D.A. (1972). The status of some piscivorous birds in the Netherlands. *TNO Nieuws* **27**: 551-555.
Rosair, D. (1995a). Diademed Sandpiper-plover in focus. *Birding World* **8(7)**: 268.
Rosair, D. (1995b). Bristle-thighed Curlew in focus. *Birding World* **8(8)**: 313.
Rosair, D. (1995c). Spoon-billed Sandpiper in focus. *Birding World* **8(9)**: 344-345.
Rosair, D. (1995d). Shore Plover in focus. *Birding World* **8(10)**: 390.
Rosair, D. (1995e). Tuamotu Sandpiper in focus. *Birding World* **8(11)**: 432-433.
Rosair, D. & Cottridge, D. (1995). *Hamlyn Photographic Guide to the Waders of the World*. Hamlyn, London.
Roschevski, U.K. & Laukhina, L.N. (1980). [Influence of density of colony on clutch size of current tern populations]. *Ornitologiya* **15**: 138-141. In Russian.
Rose, A.B. (1994). Predation of Little Terns by Whimbrels. *Austr. Birds* **28(1)**: 1-4.
Rose, P.M. & Scott, D.A. (1994). *Waterfowl Population Estimates*. IWRB Special Publication **29**, Slimbridge, UK.
Roselaar, C.S. (1979). [Variation in numbers of Curlew Sandpipers (*Calidris ferruginea*)]. *Watervogels* **4**: 202-210. In Dutch with English summary.
Roselaar, C.S. (1983). *Charadrius alexandrinus* geographical variation. Page 165 in: Cramp & Simmons (1983).
Roselaar, C.S. (1990). Identification and occurence of American and Pacific Golden Plover in the Netherlands. *Dutch Birding* **12(5)**: 221-232.
Roselaar, C.S. & Gerritsen, G.J. (1991). Recognition of Icelandic Black-tailed Godwit and its occurrence in the Netherlands. *Dutch Birding* **13(4)**: 128-135.
Roselaar, K. (1993). Ijslandse Tureluurs, wat zijn dat? *Op het Vinkentouw* **71**: 25-35.
Rosenband, G. (1982). Eye-ring of Sharp-tailed Sandpiper. *British Birds* **75(3)**: 128.
Rosenberg, D.K. (1990). The impact of introduced herbivores on the Galapagos Rail (*Laterallus spilonotus*). *Monogr. Syst. Bot. Mo. Bot. Gard.* **32**: 169-178.
Rosendahl, S. & Skovgaard, P. (1971). Recoveries of Danish Oystercatchers (*Haematopus ostralegus* L.). *Danske Fugle* **23**: 65 69.
Roseveare, P. & Allen, T. (1991). A first record of Long-tailed Skuas in the Lesser Sundas. *Kukila* **5(2)**: 151.
Roshier, D.A. (1995). Anecdotal reports on the status of Houbara Bustard *Chlamydotis undulata macqueenii* in Syria. *Bull. Orn. Soc. Middle East* **35**: 18-21.
Roslyakov, G.E. (1979). [Colonial settlement of the White-winged Tern on Lake Everon and Lake Chukchagirskoy]. *Ornitologiya* **14**: 196-199. In Russian.
Roslyakov, G.E. (1986). Coastal birds of the Shantarsky Islands. Pp. 66-70 in: Litvinenko (1986).
Roslyakov, G.Y. (1995). The Hooded Crane on the Khabarovsk territory. Pp. 314-315 in: Prange *et al.* (1995).
Rösner, H.U. (1990). [Are there age dependent differences in migration patterns and choice of resting sites in the Dunlin *Calidris alpina alpina*?]. *J. Orn.* **131**: 121-139. In German with English summary.
van Rossem, A.J. (1939). Some new races of birds from Mexico. *Ann. Mag. Nat. His. Ser.* **11(4)**: 443.
Rossouw, J. (1992). Two illegal immigrants on Malgas Island. *Promerops* **204**: 12.
Rost, V.F. (1995). Der Brutbestand von Bläßhuhn (*Fulica atra*) und Teichhuhn (*Gallinula chloropus*) in Thüringen 1994. *Anz. Ver. Thüring Orn.* **2**: 145-157.
Roth, R.R., Newsom, J.D., Joanen, T. & McNease, L.L. (1972). The daily and seasonal behaviour patterns of the Clapper Rail (*Rallus longirostris*) in the Louisiana coastal marshes. *Proc. Ann. Conf. Southeastern Assoc. Game & Fish Agencies* **26**: 136-159.
Rothschild, Lord (1928). The hitherto unknown egg of the Flightless Rail (*Atlantisia rogersi* Lowe) of Inaccessible Island, Tristan d'Acunha group. *Bull. Brit. Orn. Club* **48**: 121-122.
Rothschild, M. (1962). Development of paddling and other movements in young Black-headed Gull. *British Birds* **55**: 114-120.
Rothschild, W. (1899). On a new species of oystercatcher. *Bull. Brit. Orn. Club* **10**: 4 5.
Rothschild, W. (1930). Sarus Crane breeding at Tring. *Bull. Brit. Orn. Club* **50**: 67-68.
Rothschild, W. & Hartert, E. (1915). The birds of Dampier Island. *Novit. Zool.* **22**: 26-37.
Roudybush, T., Hoffman, L. & Rahn, H. (1980). Conductance, pore geometry and water loss of eggs of Cassin's Auklet. *Condor* **82**: 105-106.
Round, P.D. (1988). *Resident Forest Birds in Thailand: their Status and Conservation*. ICBP Monograph **2**, Cambridge.
Rounsevell, D.E. & Brothers, N.P. (1984). The status and conservation of seabirds at Macquarie Island. Pp. 587-592 in: Croxall, Evans & Schreiber (1984).
Roux, F. (1961). Observations sur la migration de la Mouette de Sabine (*Xema sabini*) dans les eaux cotières de l'Afrique nord-occidentale (Mai 1961). *Alauda* **29**: 161-164.
Roux, F. & Benson, C.W. (1969). A note on *Sarothrura lugens*. *Bull. Brit. Orn. Club* **89**: 67-68.
Roux, F. & Morel, G. (1964). Le Sénegal, région privilégée pour les migrateurs paléarctiques. *Ostrich* **6**(Suppl.): 249-254.
Rowan, M.K. (1962). Mass mortality among European Common Terns in South Africa in April-May 1961. *British Birds* **55**: 103-114.
Rowan, W. (1927). Notes on Alberta waders included in the British list. Part VI: Dowitcher and Spotted Sandpiper. *British Birds* **20**: 210-221.
Rowan, W. (1932). The status of dowitchers with description of a new subspecies from Alberta and Manitoba. *Auk* **49**: 14-35.
Rowlands, J.A. (1994). First record of Oriental Pratincole *Glareola maldivarum* in Cyprus. *Sandgrouse* **16(1)**: 56-57.
de Roy, T.A. (1984). The nighttime gull. *Animal Kingdom* **87(1)**: 38-43.
Rozendaal, F.G. & Dekker, R.W.R.J. (1989). Annotated checklist of the birds of the Dumoga-Bone National Park, north Sulawesi. *Kukila* **4**: 85-109.
Rubega, M.A. (1991). Feeding performance and beak morphology in phalaropes: a comparison of surface tension feeding in two shorebirds. *Amer. Zool.* **31**: 63A.
Rubega, M.A. (1993a). *The Functional Morphology and Ecology of Feeding in* Phalaropus lobatus*, the Red-necked Phalarope*. PhD dissertation, University of California, Irvine, California.
Rubega, M.A. (1993b). Foraging efficiency of freeliving Red-necked Phalaropes at Mono Lake: a test of the usefulness of laboratory measures of feeding performance. *Pacific Seabird Group Bull.* **20**: 50.
Rubega, M.A. & Inouye, C. (1994). Prey switching in Red-necked Phalaropes *Phalaropus lobatus*: feeding limitations, the functional response and water management at Mono Lake, California, USA. *Biol. Conserv.* **70(3)**: 205-210.
Rubega, M.A. & Obst, B.S. (1993). Surface-tension feeding in phalaropes: discovery of a novel feeding mechanism. *Auk* **110(2)**: 169-178.
Rufino, R. & Neves, R. (1991). Snipe on wet grasslands in Portugal. *Wader Study Group Bull.* **61**: 31-32.
Ruiz, G.M., Connors, P.G., Griffin, S.E. & Pitelka, F.A. (1989). Structure of a wintering Dunlin population. *Condor* **91**: 562-570.
Ruiz, M.C., Domínguez-Bello, M.G. & Michelangeli, F. (1994). Gastric lysozyme as a digestive enzyme in the Hoatzin (*Opisthocomus hoazin*), a ruminant-like folivorous bird. *Experientia* **50(5)**: 499-501.
Ruiz, X., Oró, D., Martínez-Vilalta, A. & Jover, L. (1996). Feeding ecology of Audouin's Gulls (*Larus audouinii*) in the Ebro Delta. *Colonial Waterbirds* **19**(Spec. Publ. 1): 68-74.
Rumiz, D.I. (1983). Nuevos registros de *Heliornis fulica* (Boddaert, 1783) (Aves, Heliornithidae) para el noreste argentino. [New records of *Heliornis fulica* (Aves, Heliornithidae) from northeastern Argentina]. *Hist. Nat., Mendoza* **3(18)**: 175-176. In Spanish with English summary.
Runde, O.J. & Barrett, R.T. (1981). Variations in egg size and incubation period of the Kittiwake *Rissa tridactyla* in Norway. *Ornis Scand.* **12**: 80-86.
Rundle, W.D. (1982). A case for esophageal analysis in shorebird food studies. *J. Field Orn.* **53**: 249-257.
Rundle, W.D. & Fredrickson, L.H. (1981). Managing seasonally flooded impoundments for migrant rails and shorebirds. *Wildl. Soc. Bull.* **9**: 80-87.
Rundle, W.D. & Sayre, M.W. (1983). Feeding ecology of migrant Soras in southeastern Missouri. *J. Wildl. Manage.* **47**: 1153-1159.
Rüppell, E. (1845). *Systematische Übersicht der Vögel Nord-Ost-Afrikas*. Schmerber'schen, Frankfurt am Main.
Ruschi, A. (1979). *Aves do Brasil*. Editora Rios, São Paulo.
Rushing, E.L. (1980). *Breeding Biology of the American Woodcock in Piedmont North Carolina*. MSc thesis, North Carolina State University, Raleigh, North Carolina.
Russell, R.P. (1983). The Piping Plover in the Great Lakes Region. *Amer. Birds* **37**: 951-955.
Rutgers, A. & Norris, K.A. (1970). *Encyclopaedia of Aviculture*. Vol. 1. Blanford Press, London.
Rutschke, E. (1976). Zur Struktur der Schallfedern von Bekassinen (*Capella*). *Beitr. Vogelkd.* **22**: 12-25.
Rutschke, R. (1970). Morphologisch-funktionelle Untersuchungen über Reibungsstrukturen an Schwanzfedern. *Zeitschrift für Wissenschaftliche Zoologie* **181(3-4)**: 331-352.
Ruttledge, R.F. (1962). Distraction displays of Common Gulls. *British Birds* **55**: 133.
Ryabitsev, V.K. (1985). [Incubation of clutches by the females of the Red-necked Phalarope (*Phalaropus lobatus*)]. *Ornitologiya* **20**: 193. In Russian.
Ryabov, L.S., Likhatsky, Y.P. & Vorobyov, G.P. (1984). [The Bustard (*Otis tarda*) and the Little Bustard (*Otis tetrax*) in the Voronezh Region]. *Ornitologiya* **19**: 164-170. In Russian with English summary.
Ryan, M. (1955). The Ivory Gull at Manasquan Inlet: an apocryphal account. *Linn. Soc. N.Y. Newsletter* **9(2)**: 2-3.
Ryan, M.R. (1981). Evasive behaviour of American Coots to kleptoparasitism by waterfowl. *Wilson Bull.* **93**: 274-275.
Ryan, M.R. (1982). *Marbled Godwit Habitat Selection in the Northern Prairies*. PhD thesis, Iowa State University, Ames, Iowa.
Ryan, M.R. & Dinsmore, J.J. (1979). A quantitative study of the behaviour of breeding American Coots. *Auk* **96**: 704-713.
Ryan, M.R. & Dinsmore, J.J. (1980). The behavioral ecology of breeding American Coots in relation to age. *Condor* **82**: 320-327.
Ryan, M.R. & Renken, R.B. (1987). Habitat use by breeding Willets in the northern Great Plains. *Wilson Bull.* **99**: 175-189.
Ryan, M.R., Renken, R.B. & Dinsmore, J.J. (1984). Marbled Godwit habitat selection in the Northern Prairie region. *J. Wildl. Manage.* **48**: 1206-1218.
Ryan, M.R., Root, B.G. & Mayer, P.M. (1993). Status of Piping Plovers in the Great Plains of Norh America: a demographic simulation model. *Conserv. Biol.* **7(3)**: 581-585.
Ryan, P.G. (1987). The foraging behavior and breeding seasonality of Hartlaub's Gull *Larus hartlaubii*. *Cormorant* **15**: 23-32.
Ryan, P.G. (1989). The distribution and abundance of Long-tailed Skuas off Southern Africa. *Ostrich* **60(2)**: 89-90.
Ryan, P.G. & Avery, G. (1990). Arctic Skua killed by Sea-barbel Spine. *British Birds* **83(7)**: 282-283.
Ryan, P.G. & Graham, J. (1989). The trials and tribulations of the second Hudsonian Godwit for southern Africa. *Birding in SA* **41(4)**: 103-104.
Ryan, P.G. & Moloney, C.L. (1991). Prey selection and temporal variation in the diet of Subantarctic Skuas at Inaccessible Island, Tristan da Cunha. *Ostrich* **62(1/2)**: 52-58.
Ryan, P.G. & Rose, B. (1989). Migrant seabirds. Pp. 274-287 in: Payne, A.I.L. & Crawford, R.J.M. eds. (1989). *Oceans of Life off Southern Africa*. Vlaeberg, Cape Town.
Ryan, P.G., Watkins, B.P. & Siegfried, W.R. (1989). Morpetrics, metabolic rate and body temperature of the smallest flightless bird: the Inaccessible Island Rail. *Condor* **91**: 465-467.
Ryder, J.P. (1975). Egg-laying, egg size, and success in relation to immature-mature plumage of Ring-billed Gulls. *Wilson Bull.* **87**: 534-542.
Ryder, J.P. (1983). Sex ratio and egg sequence in Ring-billed Gulls. *Auk* **100**: 726-727.
Ryder, J.P. (1993). Ring-billed Gull (*Larus delawarensis*). No. **33** in: Poole *et al.* (1992-1993).
Ryder, J.P. & Somppi, P.L. (1977). Growth and development of known age Ring-billed Gull embryos. *Wilson Bull.* **89**: 243-252.
Ryder, J.P. & Somppi, P.L. (1979). Female-female pairing in Ring-billed Gulls. *Auk* **96**: 1-5.
Ryder, J.P., Orr, D.E. & Saedi, G.H. (1977). Egg quality in relation to nest location in Ring-billed Gulls. *Wilson Bull.* **89**: 473-475.
Ryder, P.L. & Ryder, J.P. (1981). Reproductive performance of Ring-billed Gulls in relation to nest location. *Condor* **83**: 57-60.
Ryder, R.A. (1963). Migration and population dynamics of American Coots in western North America. Pp. 441-453 in: *Proc. XIII Int. Orn. Congr.* Ithaca, New York, 1962.
Rydzewski, W. (1978). The longevity of ringed birds. *Ring* **8(96-97)**: 218-262.
Ryttman, H., Tegelström, H. & Jansson, H. (1978). Egg dimensions of Herring Gulls *Larus argentatus* and Lesser Black-backed Gulls *L. fuscus*. *Ibis* **120**: 353-356.
Saab, V.A. & Petit, D.R. (1992). Impact of pasture development on winter bird communities in Belize, Central America. *Condor* **94(1)**: 66-71.

Sack, R. (1961). On wintering Jack Snipe. *Falke* **8**: 183-187.
Sackl, P. (1993). A review of the current situation of Dotterel *Eudromias morinellus* in the central Alps of Austria. *Wader Study Group Bull.* **71**: 39-40.
Sadleir, R.M.F.S., Taylor, R.H. & Taylor, G.A. (1986). Breeding of Antarctic Terns (*Sterna vittata bethunei*). *Notornis* **33**: 264-265.
Saether, B.E., Kålås, J.A., Løfaldli, L. & Andersen, R. (1986). Sexual dimorphism and reproductive ecology in relation to mating system in waders. *Biol. J. Linn. Soc.* **28(3)**: 273-284.
Saether, S.A. (1994). Vocalizations of female Great Snipe *Gallinago media* at the lek. *Ornis Fenn.* **71(1)**: 11-16.
Saether, S.A., Kålås, J.A. & Fiske, P. (1994). Age determination of breeding shorebirds: quantification of feather wear in the lekking Great Snipe. *Condor* **96(4)**: 959-972.
Safford, R.J. (1992). A record of Great Knot *Calidris tenuirostris* from Mauritius, Indian Ocean. *Bull. Brit. Orn. Club* **112(2)**: 134-135.
Safford, R.J. & Duckworth, J.W. eds. (1990). *A Wildlife Survey of Marojejy Nature Reserve, Madagascar*. ICBP Study Report **40**, Cambridge.
Safina, C. (1990a). Foraging habitat partitioning in Roseate and Common Terns. *Auk* **107**: 351-358.
Safina, C. (1990b). Bluefish mediation of foraging competition between Roseate and Common Terns. *Ecology* **71**: 1804-1809.
Safina, C. & Burger, J. (1983). Effects of human disturbance on reproductive success in the Black Skimmer. *Condor* **85**: 164-171.
Safina, C. & Burger, J. (1985). Common Tern foraging: seasonal trends in prey fish densities and competition with Bluefish. *Ecology* **66**: 1457-1463.
Safina, C. & Burger, J. (1988). Prey dynamics and the breeding phenology of Common Terns (*Sterna hirundo*). *Auk* **105**: 720-726.
Safina, C. & Burger, J. (1989). Inter-annual variation in prey availability for Common Terns at different stages in their reproductive cycle. *Colonial Waterbirds* **12**: 37-42.
Safina, C., Burger, J. & Gochfeld, M. (1994). Occurrence of ants in nests of Roseate Terns and Common Terns at Cedar Beach, New York. *Colonial Waterbirds* **17**: 91-94.
Safina, C., Burger, J., Gochfeld, M. & Wagner, R.H. (1988). Evidence for prey limitation of Common and Roseate Tern reproduction. *Condor* **90**: 852-859.
Safina, C., Wagner, R.H., Witting, D.A. & Smith, K.J. (1990). Prey delivered to Roseate and Common Tern chicks: composition and temporal variability. *J. Field Orn.* **61**: 331-338.
Safina, C., Witting, D. & Smith, K. (1989). Viability of salt marshes as nesting habitat for Common Terns in New York. *Condor* **91**: 571-584.
Safriel, U.N. (1967). *Population and Food Study of the Oystercatcher*. PhD thesis, Oxford University, Oxford.
Safriel, U.N. (1980). The Semipalmated Sandpiper: reproductive strategies and tactics. *Ibis* **122**: 425.
Safriel, U.N. (1981). Social hierarchy among siblings in broods of the Oystercatcher *Haematopus ostralegus*. *Behav. Ecol. Sociobiol.* **9**: 59-63.
Safriel, U.N. (1982). Effect of disease on social hierarchy of young Oystercatchers. *British Birds* **75**: 365-369.
Safriel, U.N. (1985). 'Diet dimorphism' within an Oystercatcher *Haematopus ostralegus* population - adaptive significance and effects on recent distribution dynamics. *Ibis* **127**: 287-305.
Safriel, U.N., Harris, M.P., Brooke, M. de L. & Britton, C.K. (1984). Survival of breeding Oystercatchers *Haematopus ostralegus*. *J. Anim. Ecol.* **53**: 867-877.
Sagar, P. & Pierce, R. (1990). News from the OSNZ: Movements of Pied Stilts. *RAOU Newsl.* **86**: 8.
Sagar, P.M. (1978). Breeding of Antarctic Terns at the Snares Islands, New Zealand. *Notornis* **25(1)**: 59-70.
Sagar, P.M. (1991). Aspects of the breeding and feeding of Kerguelen and Antarctic Terns at the Kerguelen Islands. *Notornis* **38**: 191-198.
Sagar, P.M. & Sagar, J.L. (1989). The effects of wind and sea on the feeding of Antarctic Terns at the Snares Islands, New Zealand. *Notornis* **36(3)**: 171-182.
Sagitov, A.K. & Fundukchiev, S.E. (1988). [Materials to the biology of the White-tailed Plover (*Chettusia leucura*)]. Pp. 126-129 in: Flint & Tomkovich (1988). In Russian.
Sai Daojian, Liu Xiangpu, Yu Xinjian, Wang Xiupu & Li Yinhua (1991). [A survey of the distribution of the wintering Common Crane in the Yellow River Delta]. *J. Sandong For. Sci. Techn.* **1**: 5-8. In Chinese.
Saino, N. & Fasola, M. (1990). Habitat categorization, niche overlap measures, and clustering techniques. *Avocetta* **14**: 27-36.
Saino, N. & Fasola, M. (1993). Egg and nest recognition by two tern species (Sternidae Aves). *Ethology, Ecology & Evolution* **5**: 467-476.
Sakane, M. (1957). Notes on the Grey-headed Lapwing in Kinki, W. Honshu. *Tori* **14**: 25-37.
Sakane, M. (1958). Notes on the Grey-headed Lapwing in Kinki, W. Honshu. *Tori* **15**: 13-17.
Salamolard, M. (1995). Râle des genêts. Au secours du "roi des cailles". *Oiseau et RFO* **39**: 34-37.
Salathé, T. (1991). Möglichkeiten und Probleme eines internationalen Schutzprogramms für den Wachtelkönig. *Vogelvelt* **112**: 108-116.
Salder, D.A.R. & Maher, W.J. (1976). Notes on the Long-billed Curlew in Saskatchewan. *Auk* **93**: 382-384.
Saleh, M.A. (1989). The status of the Houbara Bustard in Egypt. *Bustard Studies* **4**: 151-156.
Saliva, J.E. & Burger, J. (1989). Effect of experimental manipulation of vegetation density on nest site selection in Sooty Terns. *Condor* **91**: 689-698.
Sallaberry, M.A. (1991). Genetic and morphological differentation of Sanderling (*Calidris alba*) populations on the wintering grounds. *Diss. Abstr. Int. B Sci. Eng.* **51**: 5762, Order no. DA9112616.
Salmansohn, P. (1995). Planting Puffins. Puffin restoration project blossoms on Maine's Eastern Egg Rock. *Birder's World* **9(2)**: 20-24.
Salomonsen, F. (1944). *The Atlantic Alcidae. The Seasonal and Geographical Variation of the Auks Inhabiting the Atlantic Ocean and Adjacent Waters*. Göteborgs Kungliga Vetenskaps- och Vitterhets-Samhälles Handlingar, Serie B **3(5)**. 138 pp.
Salomonsen, F. (1950). *Grønlands Fugle*. Ejnar Munksgaard, Copenhagen.
Salomonsen, F. (1961). Ismågen (*Pagophila eburnea*) som yndfuge, Grønland. *Dan. Orn. Foren. Tidssk.* **55**: 177-180.
Salomonsen, F. (1967a). Migratory movements of the Arctic Tern (*Sterna paradisaea* Pontoppidan) in the Southern Ocean. *Det Kongelige Danske Vidensk Selskab Biolog Meddel.* **24**: 1-42.
Salomonsen, F. (1967b). *Fuglene på Grønland*. [*Seabirds of Greenland*]. Rhodos, Copenhagen. In Danish, translated into English by Brown, R.G.B. Canadian Wildlife Service, Dartmouth, Nova Scotia.
Salomonsen, F. (1976). The South Polar Skua *Stercorarius maccormicki* Saunders in Greenland. *Dan. Orn. Foren. Tidssk.* **70**: 81-89.
Salomonsen, F. (1979a). *Ornithological and Ecological Studies in Southwest Greenland (59°46'-62°27'N. Latitude)*. Meddelelser Grønland **204**. 214 pp.
Salomonsen, F. (1979b). Marine birds in the Danish Monarchy and their conservation. Pp. 267-287 in: Bartonek & Nettleship (1979).
Salt, G.W. & Willard, D.E. (1971). The hunting behavior and success of Forster's Tern. *Ecology* **52**: 989-998.
Salter, R.E., Smith, J.A., Koski, W.R. & Barbeau, J.M. (1986). Mongolian Plover, *Charadrius mongolus*, in Alberta. *Can. Field-Nat.* **100(2)**: 257-258.
Salvan, J. (1968). Contribution à l'étude des oiseaux du Tchad. *Oiseau et RFO* **38**: 53-85.
Salvan, J. (1970). Remarques sur l'évolution de l'avifaune malgache depuis 1945. *Alauda* **38**: 191-203.
Salvan, J. (1971). Observations nouvelles à Madagascar. *Alauda* **39**: 37-42.
Salvan, J. (1972a). Essai d'évaluation des densités d'oiseaux dans quelques biotopes malgaches. *Alauda* **40**: 163-170.
Salvan, J. (1972b). Statut, recensement, reproduction des oiseaux dulçaquicoles aux environs de Tananarive. *Oiseau et RFO* **42**: 35-51.
Salvin, O. (1876). On the avifauna of the Galápagos Archipelago. *Trans. Zool. Soc. London* **9**: 447-510.
Salzer, D.W. & Larkin, G.J. (1990). Impact of courtship feeding on clutch and third-egg size in Glaucous-winged Gulls. *Anim. Behav.* **39**: 1149-1162.
Salzman, A.G. (1982). The selective importance of heat stress in gull nest location. *Ecology* **63(3)**: 742-751.
Samaraweera, P. (1967). Young Red-wattled Lapwings. *Loris* **11(2)**: 113-116.
Samorodov, A.V. & Samorodov, Y.A. (1968). [On some results of ringing of *Larus argentatus* and *L. ichthyaetus*]. *Vest. Mosk. Gos. Univ.* **6**: 109-110. In Russian.
Samorodov, A.V. & Samorodov, Y.A. (1972). [Sightings of Black Tern on the eastern shore of the Black Sea]. *Ornitologiya* **10**: 387-388. In Russian.
Samorodov, Y.A. (1971). [Nocturnal behavior of some gulls of the Kustanal region]. *Vest. Mosk. Univ. (Ser. 6 Biol.)* **26(6)**: 22-26. In Russian.
Samorodov, Y.A. & Ryabov, V.F. (1969). [Ecology of the Greater Black-headed Gull *Larus ichthyaetus* Pall. in the Kustanaiskoi Oblast]. *Vest. Mosk. Univ. (Ser. 6 Biol.)* **24**: 32-37. In Russian.
Samorodov, Y.A. & Ryabov, V.F. (1971a). [On the Great Black-headed Gull in Kustanski Province]. *Ornitologiya* **10**: 266-276. In Russian.
Samorodov, Y.A. & Ryabov, V.F. (1971b). [Feeding of the Greater Black-headed Gull *Larus ichthyaetus* in the Kustanaiskoi Oblast]. *Vest. Mosk. Univ. (Ser. 6 Biol.)* **26**: 29-33. In Russian.
Sampath, K. (1990). Food of the Spotted Sandpiper *Tringa glareola* Linn. *J. Bombay Nat. Hist. Soc.* **87(2)**: 297.
Sampath, K. (1991). Food habitats of shorebirds from the Great Vedaranyam Salt Swamp of Tamil Nadu, India. *Stilt* **19**: 50-52.
Samual, D.E. & Beightol, D.R. (1973). The vocal repertoire of male American Woodcock. *Auk* **90**: 906-909.
Sánchez, E. (1992). Reintroducidas por primera vez veintidós Fochas Cornudas criadas en cautividad. *Quercus* **77**: 11.
Sánchez, J.M., Muñoz, A. & de la Cruz, C. (1991). Segregación alimentaria entre adultos y pollos de *Gelochelidon nilotica* (Gm., 1789) en la laguna de Fuente de Piedra. *Ardeola* **38**: 21-27.
Sánchez, J.M., Sánchez, A., Fernández, A. & Muñoz, A. (1993). *La Grulla Común* Grus grus *en Extremadura. Status y Relación con el Uso del Suelo*. [*The Common Crane (*Grus grus*) in Extremadura. Its Status and Relationship with Land Used for Farming*]. Área de Biología Animal, Universidad de Badajoz, Badajoz.
Sánchez-Lafuente, A.M., Rey, P., Valera, F. & Muñoz-Cobo, J. (1992). Past and current distribution of the Purple Swamphen *Porphyrio porphyrio* L. in the Iberian Peninsula. *Biol. Conserv.* **62**: 23-30.
Sanderson, G.C. ed. (1977). *Management of Migratory Shore and Upland Game Birds in North America*. International Association of Fish & Wildlife Agencies, Washington, D.C.
Sanger, G.A. (1986). Diets and food web relationships of seabirds in the Gulf of Alaska and adjacent marine regions. *US Dept. Commerce, NOAA, OSCEAP Final Rep.* **45**: 631-711.
Sanger, G.A. (1987). Trophic levels and trophic relationships of seabirds in the Gulf of Alaska. Pp. 229-257 in: Croxall (1987).
Sangha, H. (1994). Birds recorded in the The Desert National Park. *Bull. Oriental Bird Club* **20**: 10.
Sankaran, R. (1987). The Lesser Florican. *Sanctuary* **7(1)**: 26-37.
Sankaran, R. (1990a). The Bengal Florican in Dudwa National Park. Pp. 45-54 in: *Status and Ecology of the Lesser and Bengal Floricans with Reports on Jerdon's Courser and Mountain Quail*. Bombay Natural History Society, Bombay.
Sankaran, R. (1990b). Ecology and behaviour of the Lesser Florican. Pp. 85-93 in: *Status and Ecology of the Lesser and Bengal Floricans with Reports on Jerdon's Courser and Mountain Quail*. Bombay Natural History Society, Bombay.
Sankaran, R. (1991). *Some Aspects of the Breeding Behaviour of the Lesser Florican* Sypheotides indica *(J. F. Miller) and the Bengal Florican* Houbaropsis bengalensis *(Gmelin)*. PhD thesis, University of Bombay, Bombay.
Sankaran, R. (1993). Lesser Florican. *World Birdwatch* **15(4)**: 18-19.
Sankaran, R. (1994a). Some aspects of the territorial system in Lesser Florican *Sypheotides indica* (J.F. Miller). *J. Bombay Nat. Hist. Soc.* **91**: 173-186.
Sankaran, R. (1994b). Conservation of the Lesser Florican. Unpublished report to Salim Ali Centre for Ornithology and Natural History.
Sankaran, R. (1995). A fresh initiative to conserve the Lesser Florican. *Bull. Oriental Bird Club* **22**: 42-45.
Sankaran, R. & Manakadan, R. (1990). Recent breeding records of the Lesser Florican *Sypheotides indica* (Miller) from Andhra Pradesh. *J. Bombay Nat. Hist. Soc.* **87(2)**: 294-296.
Sankaran, R. & Rahmani, A.R. (1986). *Study of Ecology of Certain Endangered Species of Wildlife and their Habitats: the Lesser Florican*. Annual Report **2** (1985-86). Bombay Natural History Society, Bombay.
Sankaran, R. & Rahmani, A.R. (1990). Status of the Lesser Florican in western India. Pp. 101-112 in: *Status and Ecology of the Lesser and Bengal Floricans with Reports on Jerdon's Courser and Mountain Quail*. Bombay Natural History Society, Bombay.
Sankaran, R., Rahmani, A.R. & Ganguli-Lachungpa, U. (1992). The distribution and status of the Lesser Florican *Sypheotides indica* (J.F. Miller) in the Indian subcontinent. *J. Bombay Nat. Hist. Soc.* **89(2)**: 156-179.
Santharam, V. (1980). Some observations on the nests of Yellow-wattled Lapwing, Stone Curlew, Blackbellied Finch-lark and Redwinged Bush-lark. *Newsl. Birdwatcher* **20(6/7)**: 5-12.
Santoro, V., Gandara, A. & Gandara, E. (1988). Gallareta *Fulica cornuta* en la región de Antofagasta. [Coot (*Fulica cornuta*) in the region Antofagasta]. *Medio Ambiente* **9(1)**: 88-93. In Spanish with English summary.
Sanz-Zuasti, J. & Sierra, G. (1993). Avances en la conservación de la Avutarda en Castilla y León. *Quercus* **92**: 6-12.
Sarasin, F. (1913). Die Vögel Neu-Kaledoniens und der Loyalty-Inseln. Pp. 1-78 in: Sarasin, F. & Roux, J. eds. (1913). *Nova Caledonia*. A: Zoologie 1. C.W. Kreidels, Wiesbaden, Germany.
Sargeant, D.E. (1994). *The Birds of Junglaven, Venezuela. Junglaven Lodge, Amazonas, Venezuela*. Published privately, Junglaven Camp.
Sassoon, S. (1974). Finfoot *Podica senegalensis* in Ethiopia. *Bull. Brit. Orn. Club* **94**: 176.
Satat, N. & Laird, B. (1992). The Armenian Gull. *Birding World* **5**: 32-36.
Sauer, E.G.F. (1962). Ethology and ecology of Golden Plovers on St. Lawrence Island, Bering Sea. *Psychol. Forsch.* **26**: 399-470.
Sauer, E.G.F. (1963). Migration habits of Golden Plovers. Pp. 454-467 in: *Proc. XIII Int. Orn. Congr.* Ithaca, New York, 1962.
Sauer, J.R. & Bortner, J.B. (1991). Population trends from the American Woodcock singing-ground survey, 1970-1988. *J. Wildl. Manage.* **55(2)**: 300-312.
Sauey, R.T. (1976). The behavior of Siberian Cranes wintering in India. Pp. 326-342 in: Lewis (1976a).
Sauey, R.T. (1979). The feeding biology of juvenile Siberian Cranes in India. Pp. 205-210 in: Lewis (1979a).
Sauey, R.T. (1985). *The Range, Status, and Winter Ecology of the Siberian Crane (*Grus leucogeranus*)*. PhD dissertation. Cornell University, Ithaca, New York.
Sauey, R.T. (1987). Disturbance factors affecting Siberian Cranes at Keoladeo National Park, India. Pp. 151-170 in: Archibald & Pasquier (1987a).
Sauey, R.T., Das, P. & Prakash V. (1987). A recent survey of 19th century wintering sites for Siberian Cranes in the Gangetic Basin. Pp. 197-208 in: Archibald & Pasquier (1987a).
Saunders, C.R. (1970). Observations on breeding of the Long-toed or White-winged Plover *Vanellus crassirostris leucoptera* (Reichenow). *Honeyguide* **62**: 27-29.
Saunders, D.A. & de Rebeira, C.P. (1986). Seasonal occurrence of members of the suborder Charadrii (waders or shorebirds) on Rottnest Island, Western Australia. *Austr. Wildl. Res.* **13(2)**: 225-244.
Sauppe, B., MacDonald, B.A. & Mark, D.M. (1978). First Canadian and third North American record of the Spoon-billed Sandpiper (*Eurynorhynchus pygmeus*). *Amer. Birds* **32(5)**: 1062-1064.
Sauvage, A. (1993). Notes complémentaires sur l'avifaune du Niger. *Malimbus* **14**: 44-47.
Savidge, J.A. (1987). Extinction of an island forest avifauna by an introduced snake. *Ecology* **68**: 660-668.
Saxena, R. (1991). River Tern *Sterna aurantia* Gray snatching a fish from Pariah Kite *Milvus migrants* (Boddaert) in flight. *J. Bombay Nat. Hist. Soc.* **88(3)**: 452.
Saxena, V.S. (1983). Shokaliya - The abode of Great Indian Bustard. Pp. 167-177 in: Goriup & Vardhan (1983).
Saxena, V.S. & Meena, B.L. (1985). Occurrence of Lesser Floricans in forest plantations in Rajasthan. *Bustard Studies* **3**: 183-184.
Sayce, J.R. & Hunt, G.L. (1987). Sex ratios of prefledging Western Gulls. *Auk* **104**: 33-37.
Sayre, M.W. & Rundle, W.D. (1984). Comparison of habitat use by migrant Soras and Virginia Rails. *J. Wildl. Manage.* **48**: 599-605.
Scarlett, R.J. (1980). Do oystercatchers have a colour bar? *Notornis* **27**: 20.
Schäfer, E. (1938). *Ornithologische Ergebnisse zweier Forschungreisen nach Tibet*. Journal für Ornithologie **86**: 1-349.
Schaffer, F. & Laporte, P. (1994). Diet of Piping Plovers on the Magdalen Islands, Quebec. *Wilson Bull.* **106(3)**: 531-536.
Schäffer, N. (1995). Rufverhalten und Funktion des Rufens beim Wachtelkönig *Crex crex*. *Vogelwelt* **116**: 141-151.
Schaffner, F.C. (1985). Royal Tern nesting attempts in California: isolated or significant incidents? *Western Birds* **15**: 71-80.
Schaffner, F.C. (1986). Trends in Elegant Tern and northern anchovy populations in California. *Condor* **88**: 347-354.
Schaffner, F.C. (1990). Egg recognition by Elegant Terns (*Sterna elegans*). *Colonial Waterbirds* **13**: 25-30.
Schaldach, W.J. (1963). *The Avifauna of Colima and Adjacent Jalisco, Mexico*. Proceedings of the Western Foundation of Vertebrate Zoology **1(1)**. 100 pp.
Schamel, D. & Tracy, D.M. (1977). Polyandry, replacement clutches and site tenacity in the Red Phalarope (*Phalaropus fulicarius*) at Barrow, Alaska. *Bird-Banding* **48**: 314-325.
Schamel, D. & Tracy, D.M. (1987). Latitudinal trends in breeding Red Phalaropes. *J. Field Orn.* **58**: 126-134.
Schamel, D. & Tracy, D.M. (1988). Are yearlings distinguishable from older Red-necked Phalaropes? *J. Field Orn.* **59**: 235-238.
Schamel, D. & Tracy, D.M. (1991). Breeding site fidelity and natal philopatry in sex role-reversed Red and Red-necked Phalaropes. *J. Field Orn.* **62(3)**: 390-398.

Schardien, B.J. & Jackson, J.A. (1979). Belly-soaking as a thermoregulatory mechanism in nesting Killdeers. *Auk* **96**: 604-606.
Schardien, S. (1981). *Behavioural Ecology of a Southern Population of Killdeer*. PhD dissertation, Mississippi State University.
Scharf, W.C. & Shugart, G.W. (1984). Distribution and phenology of nesting Forster's Terns in eastern Lake Huron and Lake St. Clair. *Wilson Bull.* **96**: 306-309.
van Scheepen, P. & Oreel, G.J. (1995). Herkenning en voorkomen van Ijslandse Grutto in Nederland. [Identification and occurrence of Icelandic Black-tailed Godwit in the Netherlands]. *Dutch Birding* **17(2)**: 54-64.
Schekkerman, H. (1986). Great Knot in Israel in October 1985. *Dutch Birding* **8(3)**: 99-101.
Schekkerman, H. & van Roomen, M. (1995). *Breeding Waders at Pronchishcheva Lake, Northeastern Taimyr, Siberia, in 1991*. WIWO Report **55**. Zeist, the Netherlands.
Schekkerman, H. & van Wetten, J.C.J. (1988). Palearctic Cream-coloured Coursers in Kenya in January-February 1987. *Dutch Birding* **10(1)**: 26.
Schekkerman, H., Meininger, P.L. & Lambeck, R.H.D. (1992). Knots in the Delta Area, southwest Netherlands. Pp. 175-181 in: Piersma & Davidson (1992b).
Schenk, H. & Aresu, M. (1985). On the distribution, number and conservation of the Little Bustard in Sardinia (Italy), 1971-1982. *Bustard Studies* **2**: 161-164.
Schepers, F.J. & Marteijn, E.C.L. eds. (1993). *Coastal Waterbirds in Gabon, Winter 1992*. WIWO Report **41**. Zeist, the Netherlands.
Schew, W.A. & Collins, C.T. (1990). Age and sex determination on Black Skimmer chicks. *J. Field Orn.* **61(2)**: 174-179.
Schew, W.A., Collins, C.T. & Harvey, T.E. (1994). Growth and breeding biology of Caspian Terns (*Sterna caspia*) in two coastal California environments. *Colonial Waterbirds* **17(2)**: 153-159.
Schiefart, G., Ketzenberg, C. & Exo, K.M. (1993). Utilization of the Wadden Sea by waders: differences in the budgets between two populations of Bar-tailed Godwits (*Limosa lapponica*) on spring migration. *Verh. Deutsch. Zool. Ges.* **86**: 287.
Schiefer, T.L. & Hodges, M.F. (1987). Baird's Sandpipers in Oktibbeha County, Mississippi, with a review of previous records for the state. *Miss. Kite* **17(1)**: 8-10.
Schiemann, H. (1980). Wilsonwassertreter (*Phalaropus tricolor*) in Europa und Nordafrika. *Vogelwarte* **30**: 260-268. In German with English summary.
Schiemann, H. (1985). Nahrungsaufnahme der Kuken des Odinswassertreter (*Phalaropus lobatus*). *Orn. Mitt.* **37**: 77-78.
Schiemann, H. (1986). Red-necked Phalaropes *Phalaropus lobatus* off the coast of Somalia and Kenya. *Scopus* **10**: 42-44.
Schiemann, H. (1989). Vom Durchzug und der Übersommerung des Odinswassertreters in Osteuropa. *Falke* **36**: 14-21.
Schiemann, H. (1991). Der Thorwassertreter (*Phalaropus fulicarius*) als Durchzügler und Wintergast in Mittel- und Südeuropa. [*Phalaropus fulicarius* as transient and wintering guest in central and southern Europe]. *Beitr. Vogelkd.* **37(1/2)**: 107-118. In German with English summary.
Schiemann, H. (1992). [Phalaropodidae in Mecklenburg-Vorpommern, 1981-1990]. *Falke* **39(12)**: 417-421. In German.
Schlatter, R.P. (1984). The status and conservation of seabirds in Chile. Pp. 261-269 in: Croxall, Evans & Schreiber (1984).
Schleufler, H. & Stiefel, A. (1985). *Der Kampfläufer,* Philomachus pugnax. Neue Brehms-Bücherei **574**. 212 pp.
Schlinger, B.A., Fivizzani, A.J. & Callard, G.V. (1989). Aromatase, 5-alpha and 5-beta reductase in brain, pituitary and skin of the sex-role reversed Wilson's Phalarope. *J. Endocrinol.* **122**.
Schmid, C.K. (1993). Birds of Nokopo. *Muruk* **6(2)**: 1-62.
Schmidl, D. (1982). *The Birds of the Serengeti National Park, Tanzania*. BOU Check-list **5**. British Ornithologists' Union, London.
Schmidt, C. & Barthel, P.H. (1993). [Plumages of Little Stint *Calidris minuta* and their variation]. *Limicola* **7(3)**: 109-129. In German with English summary.
Schmidt, E. (1988). [Spotted Redshank (*Tringa erythropus*) feeding on backswimmers during a migration rest]. *Charadrius* **24(2)**: 67-72. In German with English summary.
Schmidt, O. & Schmidt, R. (1991). A rare visitor to Cape Town. *Promerops* **200**: 15.
Schmidt, R.K. (1961). Incubation period of the Painted Snipe *Rostratula benghalensis*. *Ostrich* **32(4)**: 183-184.
Schmitt, C.G. & Cole, D.C. (1981). First records of Black-legged Seriema (*Chunga burmeisteri*) in Bolivia. *Condor* **83(2)**: 182-183.
Schmitt, C.G., Schmitt, D.C., Remsen, J.V. & Glick, B.D. (1986). New bird records for Departamento Santa Cruz, Bolivia. *Hornero* **12(4)**: 307-311.
Schmitt, M.B. (1975). Observations on the Black Crake in the southern Transvaal. *Ostrich* **46**: 129-138.
Schmitt, M.B. (1976). Observations on the Cape Rail in the southern Transvaal. *Ostrich* **47**: 16-26.
Schmitt, M.B. & Whitehouse, P.J. (1976). Moult and mensural data of Ruff on the Witwatersrand. *Ostrich* **47(4)**: 179-190.
Schmitt, M.B., Milstein, P.L.S., Hunter, H.C. & Hopcroft, C.J. (1973). Black Terns in the Transvaal. *Bokmakierie* **25**: 91-92.
Schmolz, M. (1991). [Spotted Sandpiper *Actitis macularia* in Baden-Württemberg]. *Limicola* **5(2)**: 74-75. In German with English summary.
Schmutz, E. (1977). *Die Vögel der Manggarai (Flores)*. Published privately, Ruteng, Flores.
Schmutz, E. (1978). *Addenda and Corrigenda*. Published privately, Ruteng, Flores.
Schnakenwinkel, G. (1970). Studien an der Population des Austernfischers (*Haematopus ostralegus*) auf Mellum. *Vogelwarte* **25**: 336-355.
Schneider, D.C. (1992). Thinning and clearing of prey by predators. *Amer. Naturalist* **139**: 148-160.
Schneider, D.C., Harrison, N.M. & Hunt, G.L. (1990). Seabird diet at a front near the Pribilof Islands, Alaska. Pp. 61-66 in: Sealy (1990).
Schneider, D.C., Pierotti, R. & Threlfall, W. (1990). Alcid patchiness and flight direction near a colony in Eastern Newfoundland. Pp. 23-35 in: Sealy (1990).
Schneider, H. & Schneider, P. (1970). Bestandaufnahme des Flußregenpfeifers (*Charadrius dubius*) in Nordbayern. [The Little Ringed Plover in northern Bavaria]. *Anz. Orn. Ges. Bayern* **9(2)**: 105-119. In German with English summary.
Schneider, K.M. (1957). Über gegliederte Rufweisen bei Tieren. *Beitr. Vogelkd.* **5**: 168-183.
Schneider-Jacoby, M. (1991). Verbreitung und Bestand des Wachtelkönigs in Jugoslawien. *Vogelwelt* **112**: 48-57.
Schnell, G.D. (1970). A phenetic study of the suborder Lari (Aves), parts I-II. *Syst. Zool.* **19**: 35-57, 264-302.
Schnell, G.D., Worthen, G.L. & Douglas, M.E. (1985). Morphometric assessment of sexual dimorphism in skeletal elements of California Gulls. *Condor* **87**: 484-493.
Schodde, R. & Mason, I.J. (1980). *Nocturnal Birds of Australia*. Landsdowne, Melbourne.
Schodde, R. & de Naurois, R. (1982). Patterns of variation and dispersal in the Buff-banded Rail (*Gallirallus philippensis*) in the south-west Pacific, with description of a new subspecies. *Notornis* **29**: 131-142.
Schodde, R. & Tidemann, S.C. eds. (1986). *Reader's Digest Complete Book of Australian Birds*. Reader's Digest Services, Sydney.
Schodde, R., Fullagar, P. & Hermes, N. (1983). *A Review of Norfolk Island Birds: Past and Present*. Australian National Parks & Wildlife Service Special Publication **8**. Canberra.
Schomburgk, M.R. (1848). *Reisen in Britisch-Guiana in den Jahren 1840-1844*. Vol. 3. J.J. Weber, Leipzig, Germany.
Schon, S. (1988). Long-billed Curlew visits Ely. *Loon* **60(2)**: 89-90.
Schonert, B. (1990). [Attempted breeding by *Charadrius hiaticula* and *Himantopus himantopus* at the city limits of Berlin]. *Beitr. Vogelkd.* **36(3/4)**: 193-200. In German.
Schonert, C. (1961). Zur Brutbiologie und Ethologie der Zwergseeschwalbe (*Sterna albifrons albifrons* Pallas). Pp. 131-187 in: Schildmacher, H.S. (1961). *Beitrage zur Kenntnis Deutscher Vögel*. Gustav-Fischer-Verlag, Jena.
Schönle, E. (1983). Beobachtungen an Einer kleinen Population des Flußregenpfeifers *Charadrius dubius*. [Observations on a small population of Little Ringed Plovers *Charadrius dubius*]. *Orn. Beob.* **80(3)**: 183-189. In German with English summary.
Schönn, S. & Schiller, C. (1979). Brut des Zwergschnäppers in Oschatz. [Breeding of Jack Snipe in Oschatz]. *Falke* **26(10)**: 344-346. In German.
Schönwetter, M. (1935). Vogeleier aus Neubrittanien. *Beitr. Fortpflanzungsbiol. Vögel* **11**: 129-136.
Schönwetter, M. (1967). *Handbuch der Oologie*. Vol. 1. Akademie-Verlag, Berlin.
Schrader, N.W. (1974). Invasion of Black-tailed Nativehens. *Austr. Bird Watcher* **5**: 234.
Schreiber, E.A. & Schreiber, R.W. (1980). Breeding biology of Laughing Gulls in Florida. Part II. Nesting parameters. *J. Field Orn.* **51**: 340-355.
Schreiber, E.A., Schreiber, R.W. & Dinsmore, J.J. (1979). Breeding biology of Laughing Gulls in Florida. Part I. Nesting, egg and incubation parameters. *Bird-Banding* **50**: 304-321.
Schreiber, R.W. (1970). Breeding biology of Western Gulls (*Larus occidentalis*) on San Nicolas Island, California 1968. *Condor* **72**: 133-140.
Schreiber, R.W. & Ashmole, N.P. (1970). Sea-bird breeding seasons on Christmas Island, Pacific Ocean. *Ibis* **112**: 363-394.
Schreiber, R.W. & Dinsmore, J.J. (1972). Caspian Tern nesting records in Florida. *Florida Nat.* **45**: 161.
Schreiber, R.W. & Schreiber, E.A. (1978). *Colonial Bird Use and Plant Succession on Dredged Material Islands in Florida*. Vol. 1. Sea and Wading Bird Colonies. US Army Eng. Waterways Experimental Station, Technical Report D-78-14, Vicksburg, Mississippi.
Schreiber, R.W. & Schreiber, E.A. (1979). Notes on measurements, mortality, molt and gonad condition in Florida West Coast Laughing Gull. *Florida Field Nat.* **7**: 19-23.
Schreiber, R.W. & Schreiber, E.A. (1984). Central Pacific seabirds and the El Niño-Southern oscillation: 1982-1983 perspectives. *Science* **225**: 713-716.
Schroeder, K. & Zockler, C. (1992). Habitatwahl, Gefährdung und Schutz der Trauerseeschwalbe *Chlidonias niger* im Hadelner Sietland (Cuxhaven). *Vogelwelt* **113**: 144-151.
Schubart, O., Aguirre, A.C. & Sick, H. (1965). Contribuição para o conhecimento da alimentação das aves brasileiras. *Arq. Zool. São Paulo* **12**: 95-249.
Schulenberg, T.S., Parker, T.A., Hughes, R.A. (1987). First record of Least Tern, *Sterna antillarum*, for Peru. *Gerfaut* **77(2)**: 271-273.
Schulz, H. (1980). Zur Bruthabitatwahl der Zwergtrappe *Tetrax t. tetrax* in der Crau (Südfrankreich). *Braunschw. Naturkd. Schr.* **1**: 141-160.
Schulz, H. (1985a). A review of the world status and breeding distribution of the Little Bustard. *Bustard Studies* **2**: 131-151.
Schulz, H. (1985b). On the social behaviour of the Little Bustard: a preliminary report. *Bustard Studies* **2**: 179-182.
Schulz, H. (1985c). Grundlagenforschung zur Biologie der Zwergtrappe *Tetrax tetrax*. Abschlußbericht EG-Forschungsvorhaben Nr. ENV-**628**-D(B), Braunschweig, Germany.
Schulz, H. (1986a). Agonistisches Verhalten, Territorialverhalten und Balz der Zwergtrappe (*Tetrax tetrax*). *J. Orn.* **127**: 125-204.
Schulz, H. (1986b). Zum Geschlechterverhältnis der Zwergtrappe (*Tetrax tetrax*). *Vogelwelt* **107**: 201-210.
Schulz, H. & Schulz, M. (1986). Beitrag zur Biologie der Schwartzbauchtrappe (*Eupodotis melanogaster*) in Senegal. *Vogelwelt* **107**: 140-156.
Schulz, M. (1986a). Foot-trembling in the Red-kneed Dotterel. *Stilt* **8**: 21-22.
Schulz, M. (1986b). The Hooded Plover (*Charadrius rubricollis*) as a reef-forager. *Stilt* **9**: 50-55.
Schulz, M. (1987). Flocking behaviour in the Hooded Plover *Charadrius rubricollis*. *Corella* **11(1)**: 28-29.
Schulz, M. (1988). The Hooded Plover - a natural beachcomber! *Trees & Nat. Resources* **30**: 17-18.
Schulz, M. (1989a). Feeding notes on the Terek Sandpiper *Tringa terek*. *Stilt* **14**: 53-55.
Schulz, M. (1989b). Sooty Oystercatcher feeding on a washed up cunjevoi. *Stilt* **14**: 66-67.
Schulz, M. (1990). The Black-fronted Plover *Charadrius melanops* in the coastal environment of King Island, Tasmania. *Stilt* **17**: 75.
Schulz, M. (1992). Hooded Plover taken by a Peregrine Falcon. *Stilt* **21**: 27.
Schulz, M. (1993). A survey of shorebirds of western Tasmania. Part one, Macquarie Harbour to Bluff Point. *Stilt* **23**: 24-25.
Schulz, M. & Bamford, M. (1987). *The Hooded Plover - a RAOU Conservation Statement*. RAOU Report **35**. Royal Australasian Ornithologists' Union, Victoria.
Schulz, M. & Kristensen, K.A. (1993). A survey of shorebirds of western Tasmania. Part two, North Head, Port Davey entrance to Cape Sorell. *Stilt* **23**: 26-29.
Schulz, M. & Lumsden, L. (1983). Fluctuations of Hooded Plover numbers at Venus Bay in 1981 and 1982. *Victorian Wader Study Group Bull.* **7**: 11-12.
Schulz, M. & Schulz, H. (1991). *Working Bibliography of the Bustards*. National Wildlife Research Center & National Commission for Wildlife Conservation and Development, Tãif & Riyadh, Saudi Arabia.
Schulz, M., Grant, A. & Lumsden, L. (1984). Some aspects of the feeding behaviour and diet in the Hooded Plover, *Charadrius rubricollis* (Charadriidae), during the non-breeding season. *Stilt* **5**: 2-8.
Schulz, R. & Stock, M. (1993). Kentish Plovers and tourists: competitors on sandy coasts? *Wader Study Group Bull.* **68**(Spec. Vol.): 83-91.
Schuster, S. (1994). Untersuchungen zur Mauser des Großen Brachvogels (*Numenius arquata*) im Vorarlberger Rheindelta. [Investigations on the moult of the Curlew (*Numenius arquata*) in the Rhine Delta of Vorarlberger]. *Egretta* **37(2)**: 60-70. In German and English.
Schütz, M. (1991). [Time dependend aggressive behaviour during courtship in Ringed Plovers (*Charadrius hiaticula*)]. *Ökol. Vögel* **13(2)**: 187-191. In German with English summary.
Schwalbach, M.J. (1988). *Conservation of Least Terns and Piping Plovers along the Missouri River and its Major Western Tributaries in South Dakota*. MSc thesis, South Dakota State University, Brookings, South Dakota.
Schwarhoff, H. (1992). [Lesser Yellowlegs *Tringa flavipes*, new to Germany]. *Limicola* **6(2)**: 79-81. In German with English summary.
Schwartz, C.W. & Schwartz, E.R. (1951). The Hawaiian Stilt. *Auk* **68**: 505-506.
Schwartz, C.W. & Schwartz, E.R. (1952). The Hawaiian Coot. *Auk* **69**: 446-449.
Schwartz, T.R. & Satlling, D.L. (1991). Chemometric comparison of polychlorinated biphenyl residues and toxicologically active polychlorinated biphenyl congeners in the eggs of Forster's Terns (*Sterna forsteri*). *Arch. Environm. Contam. Toxicol.* **20**: 183-199.
Schwarze, E. & Schwarze, K. (1981). Zum Vorkommen des Rotkehlstrandläufers (*Calidris ruficollis*) in Europa. [On the occurrence of the Rufous-necked Sandpiper *Calidris ruficollis* in Europe]. *Beitr. Vogelkd.* **27(1)**: 46-48. In German.
Sclater, P.L. (1870). *Chunga burmeisteri* in captivity. *Proc. Zool. Soc., London* **1870**: 666.
Sclater, P.L. (1898). On the *Psophia obscura* of Natterer and Pelzeln. *Ibis* **4**: 520-524.
Sclater, P.L. & Salvin, O. (1879). On the birds collected by T.K. Salmon in the state of Antioquia, United States of Colombia. *Proc. Zool. Soc., London* **1879**: 486-550.
Sclater, W.L. (1906). *The Birds of South Africa*. Vol. 4. R.H. Porter, London.
Scolaro, J.A., Laurenti, S. & Gallelli, H. (1996). The nesting and breeding biology of the South American Tern in northern Patagonia. *J. Field Orn.* **67(1)**: 17-24.
Scott, A. (1993). A conservation programme for the Blue Crane *Anthropoides paradisea* in the Overberg. Cape Nature Conservation and Museums and the Overberg Crane Group, Voëlklip, South Africa.
Scott, A.J. (1983). A Lesser Black-winged Plover *Vanellus lugubris* at Chililabombwe. *Bull. Zambia Orn. Soc.* **13-15**: 123-125.
Scott, D.A. ed. (1989). *A Directory of Asian Wetlands*. IUCN, Gland & Cambridge.
Scott, D.A. (1993). The Black-necked Cranes, *Grus nigricollis*, of Ruoergai Marshes, Sichuan, China. *Bird Conserv. Int.* **3(3)**: 245-259.
Scott, D.A. & Carbonell, M. eds. (1986). *Inventario de Humedales de la Región Neotropical*. IWRB & UICN, Slimbridge & Cambridge.
Scott, G.A. (1963). First nesting of the Little Gull (*Larus minutus*) in Ontario and in the New World. *Auk* **80**: 548-549.
Scott, J.M. (1971). Interbreeding of the Glaucous-winged Gull and Western Gull in the Pacific Northwest. *Calif. Birds* **2**: 129-133.
Scott, J.M. (1973). *Resource Allocation in Four Syntopic Species of Marine Diving Birds*. PhD thesis, Oregon State University, Corvallis, Oregon.
Scott, J.M., Butler, J., Pearcy, W.G. & Bertrand, G.A. (1971). Occurrence of the Xantus' Murrelet off the Oregon coast. *Condor* **73**: 254.
Sealy, S.G. (1968). *A Comparative Study of Breeding Ecology and Timing in Plankton-feeding Alcids* Cyclorrhynchus *and* Aethia *spp. on St. Lawrence Island, Alaska*. MSc thesis, University of British Columbia, Vancouver.
Sealy, S.G. (1969). Incubation and nestling periods of the Horned Puffin. *Condor* **71**: 81.
Sealy, S.G. (1972). *Adaptive Differences in Breeding Biology in the Marine Bird Family Alcidae*. PhD thesis, University of Michigan, Ann Arbor, Michigan.
Sealy, S.G. (1973a). Interspecific feeding assemblages of marine birds off British Columbia. *Auk* **90**: 796-802.
Sealy, S.G. (1973b). Breeding biology of the Horned Puffin on St. Lawrence Island, Bering Sea, with zoogeographical notes on the North Pacific puffins. *Pacif. Sci.* **27**: 99-119.
Sealy, S.G. (1975a). Feeding ecology of Ancient and Marbled Murrelets near Langara Island, British Columbia. *Can. J. Zool.* **53**: 418-433.

Sealy, S.G. (1975b). Aspects of the breeding biology of the Marbled Murrelet in British Columbia. *Bird-Banding* **46**: 141-154.
Sealy, S.G. (1975c). Egg size of murrelets. *Condor* **77**: 500-501.
Sealy, S.G. (1975d). Influence of snow on egg-laying in auklets. *Auk* **92**: 528-538.
Sealy, S.G. (1976). Biology and nesting of Ancient Murrelet. *Condor* **78**: 294-306.
Sealy, S.G. (1982). Voles as a source of egg and nestling loss among nesting auklets. *Murrelet* **63**: 9-14.
Sealy, S.G. ed. (1990). *Auks at Sea*. Studies in Avian Biology **14**.
Sealy, S.G. & Bédard, J. (1973). Breeding biology of the Parakeet Auklet *Cyclorrhynchus psittacula* on St. Lawrence, Island, Alaska. *Astarte* **6**: 59-68.
Sealy, S.G. & Carter, H.R. (1984). At-sea distribution and nesting habitat of the Marbled Murrelet in British Columbia: problems in the conservation of a solitary nesting seabird. Pp. 737-756 in: Croxall, Evans & Schreiber (1984).
Sealy, S.G., Carter, H.R., Shuford, W.D., Powers, K.D. & Chase, C.A. (1991). Long-distance vagrancy of the Asiatic Marbled Murrelet in North America, 1979-1989. *Western Birds* **22(4)**: 145-155.
Searcy, W.A. (1978). Foraging success in three age classes of Glaucous-winged Gulls. *Auk* **95**: 586-588.
Searing, G.F. (1977). Some aspects of the ecology of cliff-nesting seabirds at Kongkok Bay, St. Lawrence Island, Alaska, during 1976. Pp. 263-412 in: *Annual Reports of Principal Investigators. Environmental Assessment of the Alaskan Continental Shelf*. Vol. 5. NOAA-BLM, Boulder, Colorado.
Searle, B. (1984). Foot-paddling by a New Zealand Dotterel. *Notornis* **31(3)**: 208.
Sears, C. (1994). Is it a cow? Is it a bird? *New Scientist* **144(1951)**: 35-39.
Sears, H.F. (1978). Nesting behavior of the Gull-billed Tern. *Bird-Banding* **49**: 1-16.
Sears, H.F. (1981). The display behavior of the Gull-billed Tern. *J. Field Orn.* **52**: 191-209.
Sears, H.F., Moseley, L.J. & Mueller, H.C. (1976). Behavioral evidence on skimmers' evolutionary relationships. *Auk* **93**: 170-174.
Seddon, P. (1995/96). Born to be wild. *Arabian Wildlife* **2(3)**: 16-18.
Seddon, P. & Gelinaud, G. (1995). Saudi Arabia - an overview. Re-introduced Houbara Bustard begin to breed in the Mahazat as-Sayd Reserve, Saudi Arabia. *Re-inroduction News* **11**: 6-7.
Seitre, R. & Seitre, J. (1991). *Causes de Disparition des Oiseaux Terrestres de Polynésie Française*. Occasional Papers Serie 8. South Pacific Region Environment Programme, Nouméa, New Caledonia.
Seki, M.P. & Harrison, C.S. (1989). Feeding ecology of two subtropical seabird species at French Frigate Shoals, Hawaii. *Bull. Mar. Sci.* **45**: 52-67.
Sellin, D. (1983). Beobachtungen zum Beuteerwerb spätziehender Flußseeschwalben, *Sterna hirundo* unter besonderen ökologischen Verhaltnissen. *Beitr. Vogelkd.* **29**: 161-168.
Selman, J. & Goss-Custard, J.D. (1988). Interference between foraging Redshank *Tringa totanus*. *Anim. Behav.* **36**: 1542-1544.
Selous, E. (1900). An observational diary of the habits of the Great Plover (*Oedicnemus crepitans*) during September and October. *Zoologist* **4**: 173-185, 270-277, 458-476.
Selous, E. (1916). The spring habits of the Stone Curlew. *Wild Life* **8**: 51-54, 76-81, 112-115.
Semmler, W. (1983). Dünnschnabel-brachvogel, *Numenius tenuirostris*, im Gebiet des Velencer Sees. [*Numenius tenuirostris* in the Velence Lake Area]. *Beitr. Vogelkd.* **29(5/6)**: 334-335. In German.
Senior, R.J. (1987). Spinning rate of Grey Phalarope. *British Birds* **80**: 18.
Senner, S.E. (1979). An evaluation of the Copper River Delta as critical habitat for migrating shorebirds. Pp. 131-145 in: Pitelka (1979).
Senner, S.E. & Martínez, E.F. (1982). A review of Western Sandpiper migration in interior North America. *Southwest. Nat.* **27**: 149-159.
Senner, S.E. & Mickelson, P.G. (1979). Fall foods of Common Snipe on the Copper River Delta, Alaska. *Can. Field-Nat.* **93**: 171-172.
Senner, S.E., Norton, D.W. & West, G.C. (1989). Feeding ecology of Western Sandpipers, *Calidris mauri*, and Dunlins, *Calidris alpina*, during spring migration at Harney Bay, Alaska (USA). *Can. Field-Nat.* **103**: 372-379.
Senner, S.E., West, G.C. & Norton, D.W. (1981). The spring migration of Western Sandpipers and Dunlins in southcentral Alaska: numbers, timing and sex ratios. *J. Field Orn.* **52**: 271-284.
Sennet, G.B. (1879). Further notes on the ornithology of the Lower Rio Grande of Texas. *Bull. US Geol. & Geogr. Survey* **5**: 371 440.
Sepik, G.F. & Derleth, E.L. (1993a). Premigratory dispersal and fall migration of American Woodcocks in Maine. Pp. 36-40 in: Longcore & Sepik (1993).
Sepik, G.F. & Derleth, E.L. (1993b). Habitat use, home range size and patterns of moves of the American Woodcock in Maine. Pp. 41-49 in: Longcore & Sepik (1993).
Sepik, G.F., McAuley, D.G. & Longcore, J.R. (1993). Critical review of the current knowledge of the biology of the American Woodcock and its management on the breeding grounds. Pp. 98-104 in: Longcore & Sepik (1993).
Seppi, B.E. (1995). Hudsonian Godwit migration at Carter Spit, Alaska. *Western Birds* **26(3)**: 167.
Serasinghe, R. (1992). Communal roosting of the Common Sandpiper (*Actitis hypoleucos*). *Loris* **19(5)**: 174-175.
Serié, P. & Smyth, Y.C.H. (1923). Notas sobre aves de Santa Elena (E. Ríos). *Hornero* **3**: 37-55.
Sériot, J. (1989). [A population study of the Stilt (*Himantopus himantopus*) in Languedoc-Roussillon]. *Nos Oiseaux* **40(1)**: 1-10. In French.
Sériot, J., Pineau, O., de Schatzen, R. & Dubois, P.J. (1986). Black-tailed Crake *Porzana bicolor*: a new species for Thailand. *Forktail* **2**: 101-103.
Serle, W. (1939a). Field observations on some northern Nigerian birds. *Ibis* **Ser. 14, no. 3**: 654-699.
Serle, W. (1939b). Observations on the breeding habits of some Nigerian Rallidae. *Ool. Rec.* **19**: 61-70.
Serle, W. (1950). A breeding colony of *Glareola pratincola* at Niamey, French Sudan. *Ibis* **92**: 479-480.
Serle, W. (1954). A second contribution to the ornithology of the British Cameroons. *Ibis* **96**: 47-80.
Serle, W. (1956a). Exhibition of eggs of *Charadrius forbesi* (Shelley). *Bull. Brit. Orn. Club* **76(5)**: 79.
Serle, W. (1956b). Notes on *Anomalophrys superciliosus* (Reichenow) in west Africa with special reference to its nidification. *Bull. Brit. Orn. Club* **76(6)**: 101-104.
Serle, W. (1957). A contribution to the ornithology of the eastern region of Nigeria. *Ibis* **99**: 371-418.
Serle, W., Morel, G.J. & Hartwig, W. (1977). *A Field Guide to the Birds of West Africa*. Collins, London.
Sermet, E. (1986). Observation d'un Vanneau sociable, *Chettusia gregaria*, près de Mathod. *Nos Oiseaux* **38(5)**: 242-243.
Serra, L. & Baccetti, N. (1991). [Spring migration of Ruff and Black-tailed Godwit across northern Italy: a description of current researches and proposals for a conservation strategy of stopover sites]. *Ist. Nazl. Biol. Selvaggina* **19**: 181-194. In Italian with English summary.
Serra, L., Baccetti, N. & Zenatello, M. (1995). Slender-billed Curlews wintering in Italy in 1995. *Birding World* **8(8)**: 295-299.
Serra, L., Magnani, A. & Baccetti, N. (1990). Weight and duration of stays in Ruff *Philomachus pugnax* during spring migration: some data from Italy. *Wader Study Group Bull.* **58**: 19-24.
Serrano, P., Cabot, J. & Fernández, J. (1983). Dieta de la Cigüeñuela (*Himantopus himantopus*) en las salinas del estuario del Guadiana. [Diet of the Black-winged Stilt (*Himantopus himantopus*) in the salt-pits of the Guadiana estuary (SW Spain)]. *Doñana Acta Vertebrata* **10(1-2)**: 55-69. In Spanish with English summary.
Serventy, D.L. (1953). The southern invasion of northern birds during 1952. *West. Austr. Nat.* **3**: 177-196.
Serventy, D.L. (1958). A new bird for the Australian list: the Malay Banded Crake. *Emu* **58**: 415-418.
Serventy, D.L. & Whittell, H.M. (1976). *Birds of Western Australia*. University Western Australia Press, Perth.
Serventy, D.L., Serventy, V. & Warham, J. (1971). *The Handbook of Australian Seabirds*. A.H. & A.W. Reed, Sydney.
Serventy, V. (1959). The birds of Willis Island. *Emu* **59**: 167-176.
Serventy, V. ed. (1985). *The Waterbirds of Australia*. Angus & Robertson, North Ryde.
Serventy, V. & White, S. (1951). Roseate Tern nesting behaviour. *Emu* **50**: 145-151.
Sessions, P.H.B. (1967). Notes on the birds of Lengetia Farm, Mau Narok. *J. East Afr. Nat. Hist. Soc.* **26**: 18-48.
Seth-Smith, D. (1903). On the breeding in captivity of *Turnix tanki*, with some notes on the habits of the species. *Avicult. Mag.* **(2)1**: 317-324.
Seth-Smith, D. (1912). [On *Cariama cristata*]. *Proc. Zool. Soc., London* **1912**: 557-558.
Severinghaus, L.L. (1982). Nest site selection by the Common Tern *Sterna hirundo* on Oneida Lake, New York. *Colonial Waterbirds* **5**: 11-18.
Seymour, R.S. & Ackerman, R.A. (1980). Adaptations to underground nesting in birds and reptiles. *Amer. Zool.* **20(2)**: 437-447.
Shackford, J.S. (1991). Breeding ecology of the Mountain Plover in Oklahoma. *Bull. Okla. Orn. Soc.* **24(2)**: 9-13.
Shackford, J.S. (1994). Nesting of Long-billed Curlews on cultivated fields. *Bull. Okla. Orn. Soc.* **27**: 17-20.
Shackford, J.S. (1995). Melanistic Mountain Plover in Cimarron County, Oklahoma. *Bull. Okla. Orn. Soc.* **28**: 4-5.
Sharland, M.S.R. (1925). Tasmania's endemic birds. *Emu* **25**: 94-103.
Sharland, M.S.R. (1938). Two small terns: (*Sterna albifrons* and *Sterna nereis*). *Emu* **38**: 1-7.
Sharland, M.S.R. (1981). *A Guide to the Birds of Tasmania*. Oldham, Beddome & Meredith, Hobart.
Sharma, V.D. (1986). Breeding of the Cream-coloured Courser in India. *Sanctuary* **6**: 49-50.
Sharma, V.D. & Sharma, S. (1991). The vanishing Siberian Crane. *Indian For.* **117(10)**: 850-855. In English with Hindi summary.
Sharp, M.H. (1995). Fishing on the fly. *Birder's World* **9(4)**: 16-20.
Sharpe, R.B. (1907). On further collections of birds from the Efulen District of Cameroon, west Africa. *Ibis* **Ser. 9, no. 1**: 416-464.
Sharrock, J.T.R.S. (1976). *The Atlas of Breeding Birds in Britain and Ireland*. T. & A.D. Poyser, Berkhamsted, England.
Sharrock, J.T.R.S. (1980). Rare breeding birds in the United Kingdom in 1978. *British Birds* **73**: 5-26.
Shaughnessy, P.D. (1980). Food of Kelp Gulls *Larus dominicanus* at Square Point, South West Africa. *Cormorant* **8(2)**: 99-100.
Shaw, K. & Webb, A. (1991). The Greater Sand Plover on the Don Estuary, Grampian. *Birding World* **4(11)**: 396-398.
Shaw, P. (1986). The relationship between dominance behaviour, bill size and age group in Greater Sheathbills *Chionis alba*. *Ibis* **128(1)**: 48-56.
Shaw, T.H. (1936). *The Birds of Hopei Province*. Fan Memorial Institute Biology, Peking.
Shcherbakov, V.V. (1979). [The Pin-tailed Snipe (*Gallinago stenura*) at the western Altai]. *Ornitologiya* **14**: 202. In Russian.
Shcherbakov, V.V. (1980). [Biology of the Eastern Solitary Snipe (*Gallinago solitaria*) in the western Altai Mountains]. In: Flint (1980a). In Russian.
Shealer, D.A. & Burger, J. (1992). Differential responses of tropical Roseate Terns to aerial intruders throughout the nesting cycle. *Condor* **94**: 712-719.
Shealer, D.A. & Burger, J. (1993). Effects of interference competition on the foraging activity of tropical Roseate Terns. *Condor* **95**: 322-329.
Shealer, D.A. & Burger, J. (1995). Comparative foraging success between adult and one-year-old Roseate and Sandwich Terns. *Colonial Waterbirds* **18(1)**: 93-99.
Shealer, D.A. & Kress, S.W. (1994). Post-breeding movements and prey selection of Roseate Terns at Stratton Island, Maine. *J. Field Orn.* **65**: 349-362.
Shealer, D.A. & Saliva, J.E. (1992). Northeastern Roseate Terns seen at Puerto Rican colony during breeding season. *Colonial Waterbirds* **15**: 152-154.
Shealer, D.A. & Zurovchak, J.G. (1995). Three extremely large clutches of Roseate Tern eggs in the Caribbean. *Colonial Waterbirds* **18(1)**: 105-107.
Shebareva, T.P. (1962). [New data on the location of banded Caspian Terns (*Hydroprogne tschegrava* Lepechin]. *Animal Migration (Moscow Acad. Sci. USSR)* **3**: 92-105. In Russian.
Sheldon, W.G. (1967). *The Book of the American Woodcock*. University of Massachusetts Press, Amherst, Massachusetts.
Shelley, L.O. (1933). Some feeding habits of the Solitary Sandpiper. *Auk* **50**: 357.
Shenk, T.M. & Ringelman, J.K. (1992). Habitat use by cross-fostered Whooping Cranes in Colorado. *J. Wildl. Manage.* **56(4)**: 769-776.
Shepard, J.M. (1976). Factors influencing female choice in the lek mating system of the Ruff. *Living Bird* **14**: 87-111.
Shephard, M. (1989). *Aviculture in Australia*. Black Cockatoo Press, Melbourne.
Shepherd, K. (1992). Visible migration of Knots at Sheringham, Norfolk: some preliminary results. Pp. 172-174 in: Piersma & Davidson (1992b).
Sherman, P.T. (1991). *The Ecology and Social Behavior of the White-winged Trumpeter (*Psophia leucoptera*)*. PhD dissertation, University of California, Davis, California.
Sherman, P.T. (1995a). Breeding biology of White-winged Trumpeters (*Psophia leucoptera*) in Peru. *Auk* **112(2)**: 285-295.
Sherman, P.T. (1995b). Social organization of cooperatively polyandrous White-winged Trumpeters (*Psophia leucoptera*). *Auk* **112(2)**: 296-309.
Sherrod, C.L. & Medina, R. (1992). Whooping Crane habitat alteration analysis at Aransas National Wildlife Refuge, Texas. Pp. 87-99 in: Wood (1992).
Shevchenko, V.L. & Debelo, P.V. (1991). [Sociable Plover in the northern Cis-Caspian]. Pp. 165-166 in: Kovshar, A.F. ed. (1991). [*Rare Birds and Mammals of Kazakhstan*]. Gylym, Alma Ata. In Russian.
Shewell, E.L. (1951). Notes on the nesting of the Whitefronted Sandplover *Charadrius marginatus* at Gautoos River mouth in 1950. *Ostrich* **22(2)**: 117-119.
Shi Ming & Lu Jianjian (1990). The dynamics of body composition of overwintering Dunlin *Calidris alpina sakhalina*. *Stilt* **16**: 59.
Shi Zerong, Thouless, C.R. & Melville, D.S. (1988). Discovery of the breeding grounds of Saunders' Gull *Larus saundersi*. *Ibis* **130(3)**: 445-446.
Shibaev, Y.V. (1985). [Results of *Grus japonensis* censuses over Khanka Plain]. Pp. 8-16 in: Masatomi (1985a). In Japanese.
Shibaev, Y.V. (1987). Census of bird colonies and survey of certain bird species in Peter the Great Bay (Sea of Japan). Pp. 88-124 in: Litvinenko (1987).
Shibaev, Y.V. & Andronov, V. (1995). The status of the Red-crowned Crane in the former USSR. Page 325 in: Prange *et al.* (1995).
Shibaev, Y.V. & Surmach, S.G. (1994). Autumn migration of Red-crowned and White-naped Cranes, *Grus japonensis* and *G. vipio*, in the Primorye region, far east Russia. Pp. 114-120 in: Higuchi & Minton (1994).
Shields, M.A. & Parnell, J.F. (1990). Marsh nesting by American Oystercatchers in North Carolina. *J. Field Orn.* **61**: 431-433.
Shipley, F.S. (1984). The 4-egg clutch limit in the Charadrii: an experiment with American Avocets. *Southwest. Nat.* **29(2)**: 143-147.
Shirihai, H. (1988). Pintail Snipe in Israel in November 1984 and its identification. *Dutch Birding* **10(1)**: 1-11.
Shirihai, H. (1992). Grey-headed Gulls in Israel and their identification. *Dutch Birding* **14**: 1-6.
Shirihai, H. (1994). Field characters of Senegal Thick-knee. *British Birds* **87(4)**: 183-186.
Shirihai, H. (1996). *The Birds of Israel*. Academic Press, London.
Shirihai, H. & van den Berg, A.B. (1987). Influx of Kittliz's Sand Plover in Israel in 1986-1987. *Dutch Birding* **9(3)**: 85-88.
Shissler, B.P. (1981). *The Breeding Biology of the American Woodcock in West Virginia*. MSc thesis, West Virginia University, Morgantown, West Virginia.
Shobrak, M. (1988). The present status of the Arabian Bustard (*Ardeotis arabs*) in Saudi Arabia. Technical Report **2**. Unpublished report to National Wildlife Research Center, Tãif, Saudi Arabia. 20 pp.
Shobrak, M. & Boug, A. (1990). Arabian Bustard survey. Unpublished report to National Wildlife Research Center, Tãif, Saudi Arabia. 3 pp.
Shobrak, M. & Rahmani, A. (1991). Notes on the Arabian Bustard, *Ardeotis arabs*, in Saudi Arabia. *Sandgrouse* **13(1)**: 14-23.
Shobrak, M. & Rahmani, A. (1993). Conservation of the Arabian Bustard *Ardeotis arabs* in Saudi Arabia. Pp. 350-357 in: Wilson, R.T. (1993).
Shore-Baily, W. (1926). Brazilian rails nesting (*Aramides ypecaha* and *Aramides cayennensis*). *Avicult. Mag.* **Ser 4, no. 4**: 305-310.
Shore-Baily, W. (1929). Breeding the South African Water Rail. *Avicult. Mag.* **Ser. 4, no. 7**: 286-288.
Short, L.L. (1975). *A Zoogeographical Analysis of the South American Chaco Avifauna*. Bulletin of the American Museum of Natural History **154(3)**, New York. 188 pp.
Short, L.L., Horne, J.F.M. & Muringo-Gichuki, C. (1990). *Annotated Check-list of the Birds of East Africa*. Proceedings of the Western Foundation of Vertebrate Zoology **4(3)**. 186 pp.
Shorten, M. (1974). *The European Woodcock (*Scolopax rusticola*): a Search of the Literature since 1940*. Game Conservancy, Fordingbridge, UK.
Shrubb, M. (1988). The influence of crop rotations and field size on a wintering Lapwing *V. vanellus* population in an area of mixed farmland in West Sussex. *Bird Study* **35(2)**: 123-131.
Shrubb, M. (1990). Effects of agricultural change on nesting Lapwings *Vanellus vanellus* in England and Wales. *Bird Study* **37(2)**: 115-127.
Shrubb, M. & Lack, P.C. (1991). The numbers and distribution of Lapwings *V. vanellus* nesting in England and Wales in 1987. *Bird Study* **38(1)**: 20-37.
Shubin, A.O. (1988). [Space, aggressive and feeding behaviour of Red-necked Phalaropes (*Phalaropus lobatus*) during fall migration]. *Biologicheskie Nauki* **2**: 28-34. In Russian with English summary.
Shuel, R. (1938). Notes on the breeding habits of birds near Zaria, Nigeria, with descriptions of their nests and eggs. *Ibis* **Ser. 14, no. 2**: 230-244.

Shufeldt, R.W. (1892). A study of the fossil avifauna of the Equus beds of the Oregon desert described *L. oregonus* from Pleistocene. *J. Acad. Nat. Sci. Philadelphia* **9**: 389-425.
Shufeldt, R.W. (1916). On the comparative osteology of the Limpkin (*Aramus vociferus*) and its place in the system. *Anat. Rec.* **9**: 591-606.
Shuford, W.D., Page, G.W. & Hickey, C.M. (1995). Distribution and abundance of Snowy Plovers wintering in the interior of California and adjacent states. *Western Birds* **26(2)**: 82-98.
Shugart, G.W. (1976). Effects of Ring-billed Gull nesting on vegetation. *Jack-Pine Warbler* **54**: 50-53.
Shugart, G.W. (1977). The development of chick recognition by adult Caspian Terns. *Proc. Colonial Waterbird Group* **1**: 110-117.
Shugart, G.W. (1980). Frequency and distribution of polygyny in Great Lakes Herring Gulls in 1978. *Condor* **82**: 426-429.
Shugart, G.W. (1990). A cue-isolation experiment to determine if Caspian Tern parents learn their offspring's down color. *Ethology* **84**: 155-161.
Shugart, G.W., Scharf, W.C. & Cuthbert, F.J. (1979). Status and reproductive success of the Caspian Tern (*Sterna caspia*) in the U.S. Great Lakes. *Proc. Colonial Waterbird Group* **2**: 146-156.
Shuker, K. (1993). *The Lost Ark. New and Rediscovered Animals of the 20th Century*. Harper Collins, London.
Shukla, R.K. (1983). Field notes on the Great Indian Bustard (*Choriotis nigriceps* Vigors) in Shivpuri. Pp. 54-59 in: Goriup & Vardhan (1983).
Shuntov, V.P. (1972). [*Seabirds and Biological Structure of the Oceans*]. Far East Publishers, Vladivostok. In Russian.
Shuntov, V.P. (1986). Seabirds in the sea of Okhotsk. Pp. 6-19 in: Litvinenko (1986).
Sibley, C.G. (1951). Notes on the birds of New Georgia, central Solomon Islands. *Condor* **53**: 81-92.
Sibley, C.G. (1994). On the phylogeny and classification of living birds. *J. Avian Biol.* **25(2)**: 87-92.
Sibley, C.G. & Ahlquist, J.E. (1972). *A Comparative Study of the Egg White Proteins of Non-passerine Birds*. Peabody Museum of Natural History Yale University Bulletin **39**. New Haven, Connecticut. 276 pp.
Sibley, C.G. & Ahlquist, J.E. (1973). The relationship of the Hoatzin. *Auk* **90(1)**: 1-13.
Sibley, C.G. & Ahlquist, J.E. (1985). The relationships of some groups of African birds, based on comparisons of the genetic material, DNA. Pp. 115-161 in: Schuchmann, K.L. ed. (1985). *Proc. Int. Symp. African Vertebrates*. Forschungsinstitut und Museum Alexander Koening, Bonn.
Sibley, C.G. & Ahlquist, J.E. (1990). *Phylogeny and Classification of Birds: a Study of Molecular Evolution*. Yale University Press, New Haven & London.
Sibley, C.G. & Monroe, B.L. (1990). *Distribution and Taxonomy of Birds of the World*. Yale University Press, New Haven & London.
Sibley, C.G. & Monroe, B.L. (1993). *A Supplement to Distribution and Taxonomy of Birds of the World*. Yale University Press, New Haven & London.
Sibley, C.G., Ahlquist, J.E. & de Benedictis, P. (1993). The phylogenetic relationships of the rails, based on DNA comparisons. *J. Yamashina. Inst. Orn.* **25**: 1-11.
Sibley, C.G., Ahlquist, J.E. & Monroe, B.L. (1988). A classification of the living birds of the world based on DNA-DNA hybridization studies. *Auk* **105**: 409-423.
Sibley, C.G., Corbin, K.W. & Ahlquist, J.E. (1968). The relationships of the seed-snipe (Thinocoridae) as indicated by their egg white proteins and hemoglobins. *Bonn. zool. Beitr.* **19**: 235-248.
Sibly, R. & McCleery, R.H. (1983). The distribution between feeding sites of Herring Gulls breeding at Walney Island, UK. *J. Anim. Ecol.* **52**: 51-68.
Sibly, R. & McCleery, R.H. (1985). Optimal decision rules for Herring Gulls. *Anim. Behav.* **33**: 446-465.
Sibly, R.M. & Smith, R.H. eds. (1985). *Behavioural Ecology. Ecological Consequences of Adaptive Behaviour*. Blackwell Scientific Publications, Oxford.
Sibson, R.B. (1945). Some observations on Southern Island Pied Oystercatchers in Auckland. *New Zealand Bird Notes* **1**: 107 109.
Sibson, R.B. (1963). A population study of the Wry-billed Plover (*Anarhynchus frontalis*). *Notornis* **10(4)**: 146-153.
Sibson, R.B. (1965). A note on Wandering Tattlers in Fiji. *Notornis* **12**: 248-250.
Sibson, R.B. (1966). Increasing numbers of South Island Pied Oystercatchers visiting northern New Zealand. *Notornis* **13(2)**: 94 97.
Sibson, R.B. (1967). The flocking of the Red-breasted Dotterel. *Notornis* **14(4)**: 211-214.
Sibson, R.B. (1978). Banded Dotterels on the village green. *Notornis* **25(1)**: 95-96.
Sibson, R.B. (1982). *Birds at Risk. Rare or Endangered Species of New Zealand*. A.H. & A.W. Reed Ltd, Wellington.
Sibson, R.B., Medway, D.G., Smuts-Kennedy, C., Drew, J. & Grant, G. (1972). The spread of the Black-fronted Dotterel. *Notornis* **19(1)**: 83-85.
Sick, H. (1962). Die Buntschnepfe, *Nycticryphes semicollaris*, in Brasilien. *J. Orn.* **103**: 102-107.
Sick, H. (1968). Trumpeters. Pp. 124-126 in: Grzimek (1968).
Sick, H. (1979). Notes on some Brazilian birds. *Bull. Brit. Orn. Club* **99**: 115-120.
Sick, H. (1985a). Hoatzin. Pp. 284-285 in: Campbell & Lack (1985).
Sick, H. (1985b). Seriema. Page 530 in: Campbell & Lack (1985).
Sick, H. (1985c). *Ornitologia Brasileira, uma Introdução*. Editora Universidade de Brasília, Brasília.
Sick, H. (1993). *Birds in Brazil. A Natural History*. Princeton University Press, Princeton, New Jersey.
Sick, H. & Leao, A.P.A. (1965). Breeding sites of *Sterna eurygnatha* and other seabirds off the Brazilian coast. *Auk* **82**: 507-508.
Sick, H. & Teixeira, D.M. (1979). Notas sobre aves brasileiras raras ou amenaçadas de extinçao. *Publ. Avuls. Mus. Nac.* **62**: 1-39.
Sick, H.L. (1930). The nesting of the Black Rail. *Avicult. Mag.* **8**: 270-273.
Sidle, J.G. & Arnold, P.M. (1982). Nesting of the American Avocet in North Dakota. *Prairie Nat.* **14(3)**: 73-80.
Sidle, J.G. & Kirsch, E.M. (1993). Least Tern and Piping Plover nesting at Sand Pits in Nebraska. *Colonial Waterbirds* **16(2)**: 139-148.
Sidle, J.G., Carlson, D.E., Kirsch, E.M. & Dinan, J.J. (1992). Flooding: mortality and habitat renewal for Least Terns and Piping Plovers. *Colonial Waterbirds* **15(1)**: 132-136.
Sidle, J.G., Mayne, K. & McPhillips, E.N. (1991). Protecting the Piping Plover under section 7 of the endangered species act. *Environm. Manage.* **15(3)**: 349-356.
Siefke, A. (1982). Größe und Struktur eines Brutbestandes des Sandregenpfeifers, *Charadrius hiaticula*, in ihrer Beziehung zu Dismigration und lokalen Umwelteinflüßen (I.). [Size and structure of a breeding population of the Ringed Plover *Charadrius hiaticula* in its relation to "Dismigration" and local environment]. *Beitr. Vogelkd.* **28(1-2)**: 89-106.
Siefke, A. (1983). Beobachtungen zur Tages-brutrhythmik des Sandregenpfeifers, *Charadrius hiaticula*, bei Bigynie. [Observations on the diurnal breeding rhythm of the Ringed Plover *Charadrius hiaticula*]. *Beitr. Vogelkd.* **29(2)**: 103-106.
Siegel-Causey, D. (1991). Foraging habitat selection by American and Magellanic Oystercatchers (*Haematopus palliatus* and *H. leucopodus*) on Patagonian tidal flats. *Can. J. Zool.* **69(6)**: 1636-1643. In English with French summary.
Siegel-Causey, D., Meehan, T.E. (1981). Red-legged Kittiwakes forage in mixed-species flocks in southeastern Alaska. *Wilson Bull.* **93**: 111-112.
Siegfried, W.R. (1977). Mussel-dropping behaviour of Kelp Gulls. *S. Afr. J. Sci.* **79**: 337-341.
Siegfried, W.R. (1985). Relative abundance of cranes (Gruidae) in the Cape Province. *Ostrich* **56(1/3)**: 101-103.
Siegfried, W.R. & Batt, B.D.J. (1972). Wilson's Phalaropes forming feeding associations with Shovelers. *Auk* **89**: 667-668.
Siegfried, W.R. & Frost, P.G.H. (1973). Regular occurrence of *Porphyrula martinica* in South Africa. *Bull. Brit. Orn. Club* **93**: 36-38.
Siegfried, W.R. & Frost, P.G.H. (1975). Continuous breeding and associated behaviour in the Moorhen *Gallinula chloropus*. *Ibis* **117**: 102-109.
Siegfried, W.R. & Johnson, P. (1977). The Damara Tern and other seabirds on the Diamond Coast, south west Africa, December 1977. *Cormorant* **3**: 13.
Sierra, J. (1993). El Alcaraván (*Burhinus oedicnemus*), centinela de los llanos. [The Eurasian Thick-knee (*Burhinus oedicnemus*), sentinel of the plains]. *Vida Silvestre* **73**: 15-19. In Spanish.
Sigmund, L. (1959). Mechanik und anatomische Grundlagen der Fortbewegung bei Wasser-ralle (*Rallus aquaticus* L.), Teichhuhn (*Gallinula chloropus* L.) und Bläßhuhn (*Fulica atra* L.). *J. Orn.* **100**: 3-24.
Sikora, A. (1986). [Next record of Lesser Golden Plover in Poland]. *Notatki Orn.* **27(1-2)**: 97-98. In Polish with English summary.
Silbernagl, H.P. (1982). Seasonal and spatial distribution of the American Purple Gallinule in South Africa. *Ostrich* **53**: 236-240.
Silcock, W.R. (1991). Long-billed Curlew in Pottawattamie County. *Iowa Bird Life* **61(4)**: 120-121.
de Silva, R.I. (1991). A new specimen of the Subantarctic Skua *Catharacta antarctica lonnbergi* from Sri Lanka. *Mar. Orn.* **19(2)**: 139.
de Silva, R.I. (1992). First record of Nordmann's Greenshank *Tringa guttifer* from Sri Lanka. *Loris* **19(6)**: 195-196.
de Silva, R.I. & Perera, L. (1993). Long-billed Plover *Charadrius placidus*: a new species for Sri Lanka. *Forktail* **9**: 154.
Silvius, M.J. (1986). *Survey of Coastal Wetlands in Sumatra, Selatan and Jambi, Indonesia*. Interwader Report **1**. Asian Wetland Bureau (AWB-PHPA), Bogor, Indonesia.
Silvius, M.J. (1988). On the importance of Sumatra's east coast for waterbirds, with notes on the Asian Dowitcher *Limnodromus semipalmatus*. *Kukila* **3**: 117-137.
Silvius, M.J. (1994). Beach Thick-knee at Lake Tempe, south Sulawesi. *Kukila* **7(1)**: 74.
Silvius, M.J. & Erftenmeijer, P.L.A. (1989). A further revision of the main wintering range of the Asian Dowitcher *Limnodromus semipalmatus*. *Kukila* **4**: 49-50.
Silvius, M.J., Verheugt, W.J.M. & Iskandar, J. (1986). *Coastal Wetlands Inventory of Southeast Sumatra*. ICBP Study Report **9**. ICBP & University of Utrecht, Cambridge & Utrecht.
Simeonov, S.D., Michev, T. & Nankinov, L. (1990). [*The Fauna of Bulgaria*]. Vol. 20. Part 1. Aves. Bulgarian Academy of Sciences, Sofia. In Bulgarian.
Simmons, K.E.L. (1951). Behaviour of Common Sandpiper in winter quarters. *British Birds* **44**: 415-416.
Simmons, K.E.L. (1953a). Some studies of the Little Ringed Plover. *Avicult. Mag.* **59**: 191-207.
Simmons, K.E.L. (1953b). The aggressive behaviour of three closely related plovers (*Charadrius*). *Ibis* **95**: 115-127.
Simmons, K.E.L. (1956). Territory in the Little Ringed Plover *Charadrius dubius*. *Ibis* **98**: 390-397.
Simmons, K.E.L. (1957). The taxonomic significance of the head-scratching methods of birds. *Ibis* **99**: 178-181.
Simmons, K.E.L. (1972). Some adaptive features of seabird plumage types. *British Birds* **65**: 465-521.
Simmons, K.E.L. (1987). The head-scratching method of the Ibisbill *Ibidorhyncha struthersii*. *Ibis* **129(1)**: 114-115.
Simmons, R.E. (1993a). A census of the desert-breeding Damara Tern, *Sterna balaenarum* in Namibia. Pp. 395-398 in: Wilson, R.T. (1993).
Simmons, R.E. (1993b). Catching and counting the elusive Damara Tern. *Afr. Wildl.* **47**: 150-152.
Simmons, R.E. & Braine, S. (1994). Breeding, foraging, trapping and sexing of Damara Terns in the Skeleton Coast Park, Namibia. *Ostrich* **65**: 264-273.
Simon, D. (1977). Hartlaub's Gulls feeding at night on insects. *Cormorant* **3**: 17.
Simons, T.R. (1980). Discovery of a ground-nesting Marbled Murrelet. *Condor* **82**: 1-9.
Simpson, C.D. (1961). The African Jacana, *Actophilornis africanus* (Gmelin). *Bull. Brit. Orn. Club* **81**: 82-85.
Simpson, K. & Day, N. (1994). *Field Guide to the Birds of Australia*. Christopher Helm, London.
Sims, T.V. (1977). Plovers turn the tables on gulls. *Bird Study* **24**: 195.
Sinclair, I. & Davidson, I. (1995). *Southern African Birds. A Photographic Guide*. Struik Publishers, Cape Town.
Sinclair, I., Hockey, P. & Tarboton, W. (1993). *Birds of Southern Africa*. New Holland, London.
Sinclair, J.C. (1977a). Black-naped Tern in Natal. *Bokmakierie* **29**: 18-19.
Sinclair, J.C. (1977b). Interbreeding of Grey-headed and Hartlaub's Gulls. *Bokmakierie* **29**: 70-71.
Sinclair, J.C. (1980). Subantarctic Skua, *Catharcta antarctica*, predation techniques on land and at sea. *Cormorant* **8(1)**: 3-6.
Sinclair, J.C. (1981). Whitewinged Black Terns *Chlidonias leucopterus* foraging at sea in southern Africa. *Cormorant* **9**: 42.
Sinclair, J.C. (1987). *Ian Sinclair's Field Guide to the Birds of Southern Africa*. Collins, London.
Sinclair, J.C. & Hockey, P.A.R. (1980). Wilson's Phalarope in South Africa. *Bokmakierie* **32**: 114-115.
Sinclair, J.C. & Nicholls, G.H. (1976). Red-necked Stint identification. *Bokmakierie* **28**: 59-60.
Sinclair, J.C. & Nicholls, G.H. (1980). Winter identification of Greater and Lesser Sandplovers. *British Birds* **73(5)**: 206-213.
Sinclair, J.C. & Whyte, I. (1991). *Field Guide to the Birds of the Kruger National Park*. Struik, Cape Town.
Singer, S.W., Naslund, N.L., Singer, S.A. & Ralph, C.J. (1991). Discovery and observation of two tree nests of the Marbled Murrelet. *Condor* **93**: 330-339.
Singh, R., Khan, B.A. & Vardhan, H. (1987). Alternate wintering grounds for Siberian Cranes. Pp. 147-150 in: Archibald & Pasquier (1987a).
Sinha, S.K. (1983). Status of the Great Indian Bustard (*Choriotis nigriceps*) in the Gujarat State. Pp. 51-53 in: Goriup & Vardhan (1983).
Siokhin, V.D. (1981). [Distribution and number of gulls on north shore Sea of Azov and Sivash]. Pp. 17-20 in: Flint (1981). In Russian.
Sirois, J. & Fournier, M.A. (1993). Clarification of the status of the Black Tern (*Chlidonias niger*) in the Northwest territories, Canada. *Colonial Waterbirds* **16(2)**: 208-212.
Sjoberg, G. (1991). [Great Bustard: nobility in a civilized landscape]. *Vår Fågelvärld* **50(3-4)**: 7-11. In Swedish.
Skagen, S.K. & Knopf, F.L. (1993). Towards conservation of midcontinental shorebird migration. *Conserv. Biol.* **7**: 533-541.
Skagen, S.K. & Knopf, F.L. (1994). Residency patterns of migrating sandpipers at a midcontinental stopover. *Condor* **96(4)**: 949-958.
Skagen, S.K., Knopf, F.L. & Cade, B.S. (1993). Estimation of lipids and lean mass of migrating sandpipers. *Condor* **95**: 944-956.
Skead, C.J. (1955). A study of the Crowned Plover *Stephanibyx coronatus coronatus* (Boddaert). *Ostrich* **26**: 88-98.
Skead, C.J. (1962). Peters' Finfoot *Podica senegalensis* (Vieillot) at the nest. *Ostrich* **33**: 31-33.
Skead, C.J. (1967). *Ecology of Birds in the Eastern Cape Province*. Ostrich 7(Supplement). 103 pp.
Skead, D. (1966). Birds frequenting the intertidal zone of the Cape Peninsula. *Ostrich* **37**: 10-16.
Skead, D.M. (1967). Ecology of birds in the eastern Cape Province. *Ostrich* 7(Suppl.): 1-104.
Skead, D.M. (1977). Weights of birds handled at Barberspan. *Ostrich* **12**(Suppl.): 117-131.
Skead, D.M. (1980). Recovery distribution of Redknobbed Coots ringed at Barberspan. *Ostrich* **52**: 126-128.
Skeel, M.A. (1976). *Nesting Strategies and other Aspects of the Breeding Biology of the Whimbrel (*Numenius phaeopus*) at Churchill, Manitoba*. MSc thesis, University of Toronto, Toronto.
Skeel, M.A. (1978). Vocalizations of the Whimbrel on its breeding grounds. *Condor* **80**: 194-202.
Skeel, M.A. (1982). Sex determination of adult Whimbrels. *J. Field Orn.* **53**: 414-416.
Skeel, M.A. (1983). Nesting success, density, philopatry and nest-site selection of the Whimbrel (*Numenius phaeopus*) in different habitats. *Can. J. Zool.* **61**: 218-255.
Skeel, M.A. & Mallory, E.P. (1996). Whimbrel (*Numenius phaeopus*). No. **219** in: Poole & Gill (1996).
Skeen, R.Q. (1991). Spotted Redshank evading attack by diving. *British Birds* **84(6)**: 222-223.
Skemp, J.R. (1955). Notes on the Lewin's Rail. *Emu* **55**: 169-172.
Skinner, J.F. (1979). Fernbird duetting with Spotless Crake. *Notornis* **26**: 22.
Skinner, N.J. & Langham, N.P.E. (1981). Hudsonian Godwit in Fiji. *Notornis* **28(2)**: 138-139.
Skipnes, K. & Slagsvold, T. (1984). The behaviour of Arctic Terns *Sterna paradisaea* during the pre-egg period in relation to time of day, season and environmental factors. *Fauna Norvegica (Ser. C, Cinclus)* **7**: 37-45.
Skira, J. (1984). Breeding distribution of the Brown Skua on Macquarie Island. *Emu* **84(4)**: 248-249.
Skov, H., Durinck, J. & Danielsen, F. (1992). Udbredelse og antal af Lomvie *Uria aalge* i Skagerrak i sensommerperioden. [The distribution and number of Guillemot *Uria aalge* in the Skagerrak during late summer]. *Dan. Orn. Foren. Tidssk.* **86**: 169-176. In Danish with English summary.
Skutch, A.F. (1935). Helpers at the nest. *Auk* **52**: 257-273.
Skutch, A.F. (1947). A nest of the Sun-bittern in Costa Rica. *Wilson Bull.* **59**: 38.
Skutch, A.F. (1966). Life history notes on three tropical American cuckoos. *Wilson Bull.* **78**: 139-165.
Skutch, A.F. (1985). Sunbittern. Pp. 568-569 in: Campbell & Lack (1985).
Skutch, A.F. (1994). The Grey-necked Wood-Rail: habits, food, nesting and voice. *Auk* **111**: 200-204.
Slater, P. (1987). *Australian Waterbirds*. Reed Books, Frenchs Forest, Australia.
Slater, P., Slater, P. & Slater, R. (1989). *The Slater Field Guide to Australian Birds*. Weldon, Sydney.
Slator, C. & Worwood, S. (1995). Post-breeding display by Green Sandpipers on autumn passage. *British Birds* **88(5)**: 225-226.
Slight, D.A. (1966). Mating behaviour of Kittlitz's Sandplover. *Ostrich* **37**: 277.
Slotta-Bachmayr, L. (1992). The situation of the Curlew (*Numenius arquata*) in the northern part of Salzburg County and neighbouring areas. *Egretta* **35(2)**: 173-183. In German with English summary.
Slud, P. (1964). *The Birds of Costa Rica*. Bulletin of the American Museum of Natural History **128**, New York. 430 pp.
Sludski, A.A. (1959). [On the distribution and biology of the Siberian White Crane]. *Ornitologiya* **15**: 26-35. In Russian.
Sluys, R. (1982). Geographical variation of the Kittiwake. *Gerfaut* **72**: 221-230.
Smaby-Stone, M. (1991). The current status of the tern colony on Pulau Tukong Ara. *Sarawak Mus. J.* **42**: 455-461.
Small, A. (1994). *California Birds: their Status and Distribution*. Ibis Publ. Co., Vista, California.
Smart, J.B. & Forbes-Watson, A. (1971). Occurrence of the Asiatic Dowitcher in Kenya. *Bull. East Afr. Nat. Hist. Soc.* **1971**: 74-75.

de Smet, K. (1989). The Houbara Bustard in Algeria: a preliminary report. *Bustard Studies* **4**: 157-159.

de Smet, K. (1992). *Status Report on the Long-billed Curlew* Numenius americanus *in Canada*. Committee on the Status of Endangered Wildlife in Canada. Canadian Wildlife Service, Ottawa. 28 pp.

Smetanin, N.N. & Belikovich, A.V. (1987). [The Solitary Snipe in the Sokhondinski Strict nature reserve]. Pp. 143-144 in: [*The Problems of Rare Wildlife Conservation*]. Moscow. In Russian.

Smirenski, S. (1980). [Geographic range and population number of Red-crowned and White-naped Cranes]. *Ornitologiya* **15**: 26-35. In Russian.

Smirenski, S. (1992a). People and cranes along Russia's Amur River. Pp. 33-35 in: Whitaker (1992).

Smirenski, S. (1992b). Crane Conservation in Russia. Page 44 in: Whitaker (1992).

Smirenski, S., Andronov, V.A. & Roslyakov, G.E. (1988). [Distribution of Red-crowned Cranes in Priamurye during 1984]. Pp. 3-7 in: Masatomi (1988). In Japanese.

Smit, C.J. (1994). Bar-tailed Godwit. *Limosa lapponica*. Pp. 274-275 in: Tucker & Heath (1994).

Smit, C.J. & Piersma, T. (1989). Numbers, midwinter distribution and migration of wader populations using the East Atlantic flyway. Pp. 24-63 in: Boyd, H. & Pirot, J.Y. eds. (1989). *Flyways and Reserve Networks for Water Birds*. IWRB Special Publication **9**, Slimbridge, UK.

Smit, C.J. & van Spanje, T.M. (1989). Sanderling. Pp. 276-283 in: Ens *et al*. (1989).

Smith, A. (1994). American Avocet nesting in Morgan County, Utah. *Utah Birds* **10(3)**: 43-46.

Smith, A.J.M. (1975). Studies of breeding Sandwich Terns. *British Birds* **68**: 142-156.

Smith, E. & Valentine, J.M. (1987). Habitat changes within the Mississippi Sandhill Crane range in Jackson County, Mississippi (1942-1984). Pp. 341-354 in: Lewis (1987).

Smith, F.T.H. (1974). A Victorian record of the Asiatic Dowitcher. *Austr. Bird Watcher* **5**: 111-118.

Smith, F.T.H. (1987). Baird's Sandpiper at lake Connewarre, Victoria. *Austr. Bird Watcher* **12(1)**: 25-27.

Smith, F.T.H. (1992). A second Australian sighting of the Stilt Sandpiper *Micropalama himantopus*. *Austr. Bird Watcher* **14(8)**: 313-317.

Smith, G.A. (1987). *A Selected and Annotated Bibliography for Use in Management of the Caspian Tern (*Sterna caspia*)*. New York Department Environmental Conservation, Delmar, New York.

Smith, G.C. (1990). Factors influencing egg laying and feeding in Black-naped Terns *Sterna sumatrana*. *Emu* **90**: 88-96.

Smith, G.C. (1991a). The Roseate Tern *Sterna dougallii gracilis* breeding on the northern Great Barrier Reef, Queensland. *Corella* **15**: 33-36.

Smith, G.C. (1991b). Kleptoparasitic Silver Gulls *Larus novaehollandiae* on the northern Great Barrier Reef, Queensland. *Corella* **15**: 41-44.

Smith, G.C. (1992a). Observation of Crested Terns with an experimentally added egg in the nest. *Corella* **16**: 38.

Smith, G.C. (1992b). Silver Gulls and emerging problems from increasing abundance. *Corella* **16**: 39-46.

Smith, G.C. (1993). Feeding and breeding of Crested Terns at a tropical locality - comparison with sympatric Black-naped Terns. *Emu* **93**: 65-70.

Smith, G.C. & Carlile, N. (1992a). Silver Gull breeding at two colonies in the Sydney-Wollongong region, New South Wales. *Wildlife Research* **19**: 429-441.

Smith, G.C. & Carlile, N. (1992b). Habitat use by Silver Gulls *Larus novaehollandiae* in the Sydney-Wollongong region, New South Wales. *Wetlands (Australia)* **11**: 33-45.

Smith, G.C. & Carlile, N. (1993). Food and feeding ecology of breeding Silver Gulls in urban Australia. *Colonial Waterbirds* **16**: 9-16.

Smith, G.C., Carlile, N. & Louwerse, I. (1991). The importance of human refuse as a food source for Silver Gulls *Larus novaehollandiae*. *Austr. Bird Watcher* **14**: 24-27.

Smith, G.C., Carlile, N. & Tully, S. (1992a). Breeding and movements by Wing-tagged Silver Gulls (*Larus novaehollandiae*) at the largest colony in New South Wales. *Wildlife Research* **19**: 161-167.

Smith, G.C., Carlile, N. & Tully, S. (1992b). Sexing and ageing Silver Gulls, *Larus novaehollandiae*. *Wildlife Research* **19**: 341-345.

Smith, H.T. (1996). Roseate Tern. In: Rodgers, Kale & Smith (1996).

Smith, J.E. & Diem, K.L. (1972). Growth and development of young California Gulls (*Larus californicus*). *Condor* **74**: 462-470.

Smith, J.H. & King, B. (1988). Strategy of inland feeding Turnstones. *British Birds* **81**: 181.

Smith, J.W. & Renken, R.B. (1991). Least Tern nesting habitat in the Mississippi River Valley adjacent to Missouri. *J. Field Orn.* **62(4)**: 497-504.

Smith, J.W. & Renken, R.B. (1993). Reproductive success of Least Terns in the Mississippi River Valey. *Colonial Waterbirds* **16**: 39-44.

Smith, K.A., Murphy, R.K., Michaelson, D.L. & Viehl, W.C. (1993). Habitat and predation management for nesting Piping Plover Sat Lostwood National Wildlife Refuge, North Dakota. *Prairie Nat.* **25(2)**: 139-147.

Smith, K.D. (1957). An annotated check list of the birds of Eritrea. *Ibis* **99**: 1-26, 307-337.

Smith, K.D. (1963). The identification of the Slender-billed Curlew. *British Birds* **56**: 294-295.

Smith, K.D. (1965). On the birds of Morocco. *Ibis* **107**: 493-526.

Smith, K.W., Reed, J.M. & Trevis, B.E. (1992). Habitat use and site fidelity of Green Sandpipers *Tringa ochropus* wintering in southern England. *Bird Study* **39(3)**: 155-164.

Smith, L.S., Blankenship, D.R., Derrickson, S.R., Drewien, R.C., Cooch, F.G., Lock, R.A. & Thompson, B.C. (1986). *Whooping Crane Recovery Plan*. US Fish & Wildlife Service, Albuquerque, New Mexico.

Smith, M.J. (1987). Observations on Denham's Bustard *Neotis denhami* at Maralal, Kenya. *Scopus* **11**: 47-51.

Smith, M.R. (1990). A Spotted Redshank in Wellfleet. *Bird Obs.* **18(5)**: 280-283.

Smith, N.G. (1966a). Evolution of some Arctic gulls (*Larus*): an experimental study of isolating mechanisms. *Orn. Monogr.* **4**: 1-99.

Smith, N.G. (1966b). Adaptations to cliff-nesting in some Arctic gulls (*Larus*). *Ibis* **108**: 63-83.

Smith, N.G. (1969). Polymorphism in Ringed Plovers. *Ibis* **111**: 177-188.

Smith, N.G. (1991). Arctic gulls 32 years later: a reply to Snell. *Colonial Waterbirds* **14**: 190-195.

Smith, N.J.H. (1985). The impact of cultural and ecological change on Amazonian fisheries. *Biol. Conserv.* **32**: 355-373.

Smith, P. (1991). *The Biology and Management of Waders (Suborder Charadrii) in NSW*. NSW National Parks & Wildlife Service, Hurstville, Australia.

Smith, P.C. & Evans, P.R. (1973). Studies of shorebirds at Lindisfarne, Northumberland. 1. Feeding ecology and behaviour of the Bar-tailed Godwit. *Wildfowl* **24**: 135-139.

Smith, P.C. & Evans, P.R. (1975). Studies of shorebirds at Lindisfarne, Northumberland. 2. Fat and pectoral muscle as indicators of body condition the Bar-tailed Godwit. *Wildfowl* **26**: 64-76.

Smith, P.H. (1975). The changing status of Little Gulls *Larus minutus* in north Merseyside, England. *Seabird* **10**: 12-21.

Smith, P.M. (1975). *Habitat Requirements and Observations on the Clapper Rail (*Rallus longirostris yumanensis*)*. MSc thesis, Arizona State University, Tempe, Arizona.

Smith, P.W. & Houghton, N.T. (1984). Fidelity of Semipalmated Plovers to a migration stopover. *J. Field Orn.* **55(2)**: 247-249.

Smith, R.D. & Whitfield, D.P. (1995). Renesting by male Dotterel *Charadrius morinellus* after successfully rearing chicks. *Bird Study* **42(2)**: 174-175.

Smith, R.W. & Barclay, J.S. (1978). Evidence of westward changes in the range of the American Woodcock. *Amer. Birds* **32**: 1122-1127.

Smythies, B.E. (1981). *The Birds of Borneo*. Sabah Society & Malayan Nature Society, Sabah & Kuala Lumpur.

Smythies, B.E. (1986). *The Birds of Burma*. Nimrod Press Ltd, Liss, Hants, UK.

Snell, R.G.T. (1988). First record of Baird's Sandpiper in South Australia. *S. Austr. Orn.* **30(5)**: 118-119.

Snell, R.R. (1989). Status of *Larus* gulls at Home Bay, Baffin Island. *Colonial Waterbirds* **12(1)**: 12-23.

Snell, R.R. (1991a). Conflation of the observed and the hypothesized: Smith's 1961 research in Home Bay, Baffin Island. *Colonial Waterbirds* **14(2)**: 196-202.

Snell, R.R. (1991b). Variably plumaged Icelandic Herring Gulls reflect founders not hybrids. *Auk* **108**: 329-341.

Snodderly, D.M. (1978). Eggshell removal by the Laughing Gull (*Larus atricilla*): normative data and visual preference behavior. *Anim. Behav.* **26**: 487-506.

Snow, B.K. & Snow, D.W. (1968). Behavior of the Swallow-tailed Gull of the Galapagos. *Condor* **70**: 252-264.

Snow, B.K. & Snow, D.W. (1969). Observations on the Lava Gull *Larus fuliginosus*. *Ibis* **111**: 30-35.

Snow, D.W. (1966). The breeding cycles of some Galapagos seabirds. *Ibis* **108**: 157.

Snow, D.W. ed. (1978). *An Atlas of Speciation in African Non-passerine Birds*. British Museum (Natural History), London.

Snow, D.W. (1979). Atlas of speciation in African non-passerine birds - addenda and corrigenda. *Bull. Brit. Orn. Club* **99**: 66-68.

Snow, D.W. & Snow, B.K. (1967). The breeding cycle of the Swallow-tailed Gull *Creagrus furcatus*. *Ibis* **109**: 14-24.

Snyder, D.E. (1966). *The Birds of Guyana*. Peabody Museum, Salem, Massachusetts.

Snyder, D.L., Riemenschneider, V., Inman, V.W. & Goller, F. (1989). Current status of the Upland Sandpiper breeding area of South Bend, Indiana. *Indiana Audubon Quarterly* **67(4)**: 198-202.

Snyder, N.F.R. & Snyder, H.A. (1969). A comparative study of mollusc predation of Limpkins, Everglade Kites and Boat-tailed Grackles. *Living Bird* **8**: 177-223.

Soikkeli, M. (1962). [On the *Sterna albifrons* population in the Gulf of Bothnia and its migration along the West Coast of Finland]. *Ornis Fenn.* **39**: 60-67. In Finnish.

Soikkeli, M. (1966). On the variation in bill- and wing-length of the Dunlin (*Calidris alpina*) in Europe. *Bird Study* **13**: 256-269.

Soikkeli, M. (1967). Breeding cycle and population dynamics in the Dunlin (*Calidris alpina*). *Ann. Zool. Fennici* **4**: 158-198.

Soikkeli, M. (1970a). Dispersal of Dunlin *Calidris alpina* in relation to sites of birth and breeding. *Ornis Fenn.* **47**: 1-9.

Soikkeli, M. (1970b). Mortality and reproductive rates in a Finnish population of Dunlin *Calidris alpina*. *Ornis Fenn.* **47**: 149-158.

Soikkeli, M. (1970c). Mortality rates of Finnish Caspian Terns (*Hydroprogne caspia*). *Ornis Fenn.* **47**: 177-179.

Soikkeli, M. (1973a). Breeding success of the Caspian Tern in Finland. *Bird-Banding* **44**: 196-204.

Soikkeli, M. (1973b). Long-distance fishing flights of the Caspian Tern *Hydroprogne caspia*. *Ornis Fenn.* **50**: 47-48.

Soikkeli, M. (1974). Size variation of breeding Dunlin in Finland. *Bird Study* **21**: 151-154.

Soikkeli, W. (1990). Breeding success of the Common Gull in a Finnish population. *Baltic Birds* **5**: 159-162.

Solem, J.K. (1986). Limpkin in Howard County, Maryland. *Maryland Birdlife* **42(1)**: 3-4.

Solís, J.C. (1995). La estrategia del Alcavarán: nidos, huevos y pollos que pasan desapercibidos. [Nest, eggs and chicks crypsis in the Stone Curlew]. *Quercus* **117**: 22-26. In Spanish with English summary.

Solís, J.C. & de Lope, F. (1995). Nest and egg crypsis in the ground-nesting Stone Curlew *Burhinus oedicnemus*. *J. Avian Biol.* **26(2)**: 135-138.

Solomatin, A.O. (1973). [Biology of the Sociable Plover]. Pp. 93-94 in: Flint (1973a). In Russian.

van Someren, V.D. (1947). Field notes on some Madagascar birds. *Ibis* **89**: 235-267.

van Someren, V.G.L. (1925-1935). The birds of Kenya and Uganda. *J. East Afr. & Uganda Nat. Hist. Soc.* 21-58.

van Someren, V.G.L. (1956). *Days with Birds*. Fieldiana Zoology **38**. 520 pp.

Somofalov, M.F. (1986). [The Black-winged Pratincole (*Glareola nordmanni*) in Chernigov region]. *Ornitologiya* **21**: 142. In Russian.

Soni, R.G. (1995). The Demoiselle Cranes of Khichan. *ICF Bugle* **21(4)**: 1, 4.

Sonobe, K. ed. (1982). *A Field Guide to the Birds of Japan*. Wild Bird Society of Japan, Tokyo.

Sonobe, K. & Izawa, N. eds. (1987). *Endangered Bird Species in the Korean Peninsula*. Museum of Korean Nature & Wild Bird Society of Japan, Tokyo.

Sonter, C. (1987). A note on the Banded Stilt *Cladorhynchus leucocephalus* in Sunrasia. *Austr. Bird Watcher* **12(3)**: 98-99.

Soothill, E. & Soothill, R. (1982). *Wading Birds of the World*. Blandford Press, Poole, UK.

Soper, M.F. (1967). Some observations on Black Stilts. *Notornis* **14**: 8-10.

Soper, M.F. (1969a). Kermadec Islands Expedition Reports. The White-capped Noddy (*Anous tenuirostris minutus*). *Notornis* **16**: 71-75.

Soper, M.F. (1969b). Kermadec Island Expedition Reports: The Spotless Crake (*Porzana tabuensis plumbea*). *Notornis* **16**: 219-220.

Soper, M.F. (1976). *New Zealand Birds*. Whitcoulls Ltd, Christchurch.

Sordahl, T.A. (1979). Vocalizations and behavior of the Willet. *Wilson Bull.* **91**: 551-574.

Sordahl, T.A. (1980). *Antipredator Behavior and Parental Care in the American Avocet and Black-necked Stilt (Aves: Recurvirostridae)*. PhD dissertation, Utah State University, Utah.

Sordahl, T.A. (1981). Predator-mobbing behaviour in the shorebirds of North America. *Wader Study Group Bull.* **31**: 41-44.

Sordahl, T.A. (1982). Antipredator behavior of American Avocet and Black-necked Stilt chicks. *J. Field Orn.* **53(4)**: 315-325.

Sordahl, T.A. (1988a). Does the downy American Avocet mimic the adult Wilson's Phalarope? *Prairie Nat.* **20(1)**: 39-45.

Sordahl, T.A. (1988b). The American Avocet (*Recurvirostra americana*) as a paradigm for adult automimicry. *Evol. Ecol.* **2(3)**: 189-196.

Sordahl, T.A. (1990). Sexual differences in anti-predator behaviour of breeding American Avocets and Black-necked Stilts. *Condor* **92(2)**: 530-532.

Sordahl, T.A. (1991). Antipredator behavior of Mountain Plover chicks. *Prairie Nat.* **23(3)**: 109-115.

Sordahl, T.A. (1994). Eggshell removal behavior of American Avocets and Black-necked Stilts. *J. Field Orn.* **65(4)**: 461-465. In English with Spanish summary.

Sorensen, E. (1990). Documenting a Buff-breasted Sandpiper: a state first. *Utah Birds* **6(2-3)**: 25-27.

Sorensen, F.E. & Lindberg, D.R. (1991). Preferential predation by American Black Oystercatchers on transitional ecophenotypes of the limpet *Lottia pelta* (Rathke). *J. Exper. Mar. Biol. Ecol.* **154(1)**: 123-136.

Sorenson, M.D. (1995). Evidence of conspecific nest parasitism and egg discrimination in the Sora. *Condor* **97(3)**: 819-821.

Sorokin, A.G. & Kotyukov, Y.V. (1987). Discovery of the nesting ground of the Ob River population of the Siberian Crane. Pp. 209-211 in: Archibald & Pasquier (1987a).

Sotnikov, V.N. & Litun, V.I. (1988). [Record of Broad-billed Sandpiper (*Limicola falcinellus*) in Kirovsk Region]. *Ornitologiya* **23**: 223. In Russian.

Soulen, T.K. (1991). Purple Sandpiper (*Calidris maritima*): 18 March 1991, Sheboygan County, Sheboygan. *Passenger Pigeon* **53(4)**: 356-357.

Southern, H.N. (1944). Dimorphism in *Stercorarius pomarinus* (Temminck). *Ibis* **86**: 1-16.

Southern, H.N. & Lewis, W.A.S. (1938). The breeding behaviour of Temminck's Stint. *British Birds* **31**: 314-321.

Southern, L.K. (1981). Sex-related differences in territorial aggression by Ring-billed Gulls. *Auk* **98**: 179-181.

Southern, L.K. & Southern, W.E. (1978). Absence of nocturnal predator defense mechanisms in breeding gulls. *Proc. Colonial Waterbirds Group* **1**: 157-162.

Southern, L.K. & Southern, W.E. (1980). Mate fidelity in Ring-billed Gulls. *J. Field Orn.* **53**: 170-171.

Southern, L.K. & Southern, W.E. (1982). Effect of habitat decimation on Ring-billed Gull colony and nest-site tenacity. *Auk* **99**: 328-331.

Southern, L.K. & Southern, W.E. (1983). Response of Ring-billed Gulls to cannon netting and wing-tagging. *J. Wildl. Manage.* **47**: 234-237.

Southern, L.K., Patton, S.R. & Southern, W.E. (1982). Nocturnal predation on (*Larus*) gulls. *Colonial Waterbirds* **5**: 169-172.

Southern, W.E. (1967). Colony selection, longevity and Ring-billed Gull populations: preliminary discussion. *Bird-Banding* **38**: 52-60.

Southern, W.E. (1974). Copulatory wing-flagging: a synchronizing stimulus for nesting Ring-billed Gulls. *Bird-Banding* **45**: 210-216.

Southern, W.E. (1977). Colony selection and colony site tenacity in Ring-billed Gulls at a stable colony. *Auk* **94**: 469-478.

Southern, W.E. (1980). Comparative distribution and orientation of North American gulls. Pp. 449-498 in: Burger, Olla & Winn (1980).

Southern, W.E. & Southern, L.K. (1982). Intensification of adult Ring-billed Gull aggression during reproduction and its possible consequences. *Colonial Waterbirds* **5**: 2-10.

Sowl, L.W. (1979). The historical status of nesting seabirds of the northern and western gulf of Alaska. Pp. 47-71 in: Bartonek & Nettleship (1979).

Sowls, A.L., DeGange, A.R., Nelson, J.W. & Lester, G.S. (1980). *Catalog of California Seabird Colonies*. US Department Interior, Fish & Wildlife Service, Biological Services Program, FWS/OBS 37/80, Washington, D.C.

Sowls, A.L., Hatch, S.A. & Lensink, C.J. (1978). *Catalog of Alaskan Seabird colonies*. US Fish & Wildlife Service FWS/OBS 78/78, Anchorage, Alaska.

Spaans, A.L. (1971). On the feeding ecology of the Herring Gull *Larus argentatus* Pont. in the northern part of the Netherlands. *Ardea* **59(3/4)**: 75-188.

Spaans, A.L. (1976). Molt of flight and tail feathers of the Least Sandpiper in Surinam, South America. *Bird-Banding* **47**: 359-364.

Spaans, A.L. (1978). Status and numerical fluctuations of some North American waders along the Suriname coast. *Wilson Bull.* **90**: 60-83.

Spaans, A.L. (1980). Biometrics and moult of Sanderlings *Calidris alba* during the autumn in Surinam. *Wader Study Group Bull.* **28**: 33-35.
Spaans, A.L. ed. (1992). *Population Dynamics of Lari in Relation to Food Resources*. Ardea **80**. 200 pp.
Spaans, A.L. & Autar, L. (1982). First record of Wilson's Phalarope *Phalaropus tricolor* from Suriname. *Bull. Brit. Orn. Club* **102(3)**: 114-115.
Spaans, A.L. & Blokpoel, H. (1991). Concluding remarks: superabundance in gulls: causes, problems and solutions. Pp. 2396-2398 in: Bell *et al.* (1991).
Spaans, A.L., Coulson, J.C., Migot, P., Monaghan, P., Pruter, J. & Vauk, L. (1991). The Herring Gull in North-West Europe. Pp. 2365-2371 in: Bell *et al.* (1991).
Spaans, A.L., de Wit, A.A.N. & van Vlaardingen, D. (1987). Effects of increased population size in Herring Gulls on breeding success and other parameters. Pp. 57-65 in: Hand *et al.* (1987).
van Spanje, T.M., Veel, P. & van den Berg, A.B. (1995). Vangst van Poelsnip te Zandvoort in juli 1994. [Great Snipe at Zandvoort in July 1994]. *Dutch Birding* **17**: 106-113. In Dutch with English summary.
Sparling, D.W. & Krapu, G.L. (1994). Communal roosting and foraging behavior of staging Sandhill Cranes. *Wilson Bull.* **106(1)**: 62-77.
Speakman, J.R. (1987). Apparent absorption efficiencies for Redshank (*Tringa totanus* L.) and Oystercatcher (*Haematopus ostralegus* L.): implications for the predictions of optimal foraging models. *Amer. Naturalist* **130**: 677-691.
Speakman, J.R. & Bryant, D.M. (1993). The searching speeds of foraging shorebirds: Redshank (*Tringa totanus*) and Oystercatcher (*Haematopus ostralegus*). *Amer. Naturalist* **142**: 296-319.
Spear, L. & Ainley, D.G. (1993). Kleptoparasitism by Kermadec Petrels, jaegers and skuas in the eastern tropical Pacific: evidence of mimicry by two species of *Pterodroma*. *Auk* **110(2)**: 222-233.
Spear, L.B. (1980). Band loss from Western Gull on Southeast Farallon Island. *J. Field Orn.* **51**: 319-328.
Spear, L.B. (1987). Hybridization of Glaucous and Herring Gulls at the Mackenzie Delta, Canada. *Auk* **104**: 123-125.
Spear, L.B. (1988). Dispersal patterns of Western Gulls from southeast Farallon Island. *Auk* **105**: 128-141.
Spear, L.B. (1993). Dynamics and effect of Western Gulls feeding in a colony of guillemots and Brandt's Cormorants. *J. Anim. Ecol.* **62**: 399-414.
Spear, L.B. & Anderson, D.W. (1989). Nest-site selection by Yellow-footed Gulls. *Condor* **91**: 91-99.
Spear, L.B. & Nur, N. (1994). Brood size, hatching order and hatching date: effects on four life-history stages from hatching recruitment in Western Gullls. *J. Anim. Ecol.* **63(2)**: 283-298.
Spear, L.B., Henderson, R.P. & Ainley, D.G. (1986). Post-fledging parental care in the Western Gull. *Condor* **88**: 194-199.
Spear, L.B., Penniman, T.M., Penniman, J.F., Carter, H.R. & Ainley, D.G. (1987). Survivorship and mortality factors in a population of Western Gulls. Pp. 44-56 in: Hand *et al.* (1987).
Spear, L.B., Sydeman, W.J. & Pyle, P. (1995). Factors affecting recruitment age and recruitment probability in the Western Gull *Larus occidentalis*. *Ibis* **137**: 352-359.
Speich, S.M. & Manuwal, D.A. (1974). Gular pouch development and population structure of Cassin's Auklet. *Auk* **91**: 291-306.
Speich, S.M. & Wahl, T.R. (1989). *Catalog of Washington Seabird Colonies*. Biological Report **88(6)**. US Fish & Wildlife Service, Washington, D.C.
Speich, S.M. & Wahl, T.R. (1995). Marbled Murrelet populations of Washington - marine habitat preferences and variability of occurrence. Pp. 313-326 in: Ralph *et al.* (1995).
Speich, S.M., Wahl, T.R. & Manuwal, D.A. (1992). The numbers of Marbled Murrelets in Washington marine waters. Pp. 48-60 in: Carter & Morrison (1992).
Speight, J.A. (1981). *The Status of King Rails and Clapper Rails along the Mississippi Gulf Coast*. MSc thesis, Mississippi State University.
van der Spek, A. & van der Spek, V. (1992). [Lesser Yellowlegs near Flaauwersinlaag in October 1991]. *Dutch Birding* **14(2)**: 50-52. In Dutch with English summary.
Spellerberg, I.F. (1970). Body measurements and colour phases of the McCormick Skua *Catharacta maccormicki*. *Notornis* **17(4)**: 280-285.
Spellerberg, I.F. (1971a). Breeding behaviour of the McCormick Skua *Catharacta maccormicki* in Antarctica. *Ardea* **59**: 189-230.
Spellerberg, I.F. (1971b). Aspects of McCormick Skua breeding biology. *Ibis* **113**: 357-363.
Spence, B.R. (1983). Greater Sand Plover in Humberside. *British Birds* **76(12)**: 574-575.
Spence, I.M. (1988). Mortality of Snipe estimated from a mark and recapture study. *Ringing & Migration* **9**: 27-31.
Spencer, B.J. & Lauro, A.J. (1984). Separating first basic Ring-billed and Common Gull. *Dutch Birding* **6**: 55-57.
Spendelow, J.A. (1982). An analysis of temporal variation in, and the effects of habitat modification on the reproductive success of Roseate Terns. *Colonial Waterbirds* **5**: 19-31.
Spendelow, J.A. (1991). Postfledging survival and recruitment of known-origin Roseate Terns (*Sterna dougallii*) at Falkner Island, Connecticut. *Colonial Waterbirds* **14**: 108-115.
Spendelow, J.A. & Nichols, J.D. (1989). Annual survival rates of breeding adult Roseate Terns. *Auk* **106**: 367-374.
Spendelow, J.A., Burger, J., Nisbet, I.C.T., Nichols, J.D., Hines, J.E., Hays, H., Cormons, G.D. & Gochfeld, M. (1994). Sources of variation in loss rates of color bands applied to adult Roseate Terns (*Sterna dougallii*) in the western North Atlantic. *Auk* **111**: 879-885.
Spendelow, J.A., Nichols, J.D., Nisbet, I.C.T., Hays, H., Cormons, G.D., Burger, J., Safina, C., Hines, J.E. & Gochfeld, M. (1995). Estimating annual survival and movement rates of adults within a metapopulation of Roseate Terns. *Ecology* **76**: 2415-2428.
Spillner, W. (1975). Zur Fortpflanzungsbiologie der Trauerseeschwalbe (*Chlidonias niger*). *Beitr. Vogelkd.* **21**: 172-215.
Spina, F. (1982). Contribution to the breeding biology of the Whiskered Tern *Chlidonias hybrida* in Val Campotto (Northern Italy). *Avocetta* **6**: 23-33.
Spina, F. (1986). Mignattino piombato *Chlidonias hybridus*. *Ricerche Biol. Selvaggina* **9**(Suppl.): 121-128.
Spitzer, G. (1978). Zur Reproduktionsrate der Mittelmeer-Silbermöwe (*Larus argentatus michahellis*). *Vogelwarte* **29**: 272-275.
Spitzer, P.R. (1979). The Siberian Crane at Bharatpur. Pp. 249-253 in: Lewis (1979a).
Spitzer, P.R. (1981). The lily of birds. *Animal Kingdom* **84(5)**: 25-30.
Spring, L. (1968). *A Comparison of Functional and Morphological Adaptations in the Common Murre* Uria aalge *and Thick-billed Murre* Uria lomvia. PhD thesis, University of Washington, Seattle, Washington.
Spring, L. (1971). A comparison of functional and morphological adaptations in the Common Murre (*Uria aalge*) and Thick-billed Murre (*Uria lomvia*). *Condor* **73**: 1-27.
Springer, A.M. & Roseneau, D.G. (1985). Copepod-based food webs: auklets and oceanography in the Bering Sea. *Mar. Ecol. Prog. Ser.* **21**: 229-237.
Springer, A.M., Kondratyev, A.Y., Ogi, H., Shibaev, Y.V. & van Vliet, G.B. (1993). Status, ecology and conservation of *Synthliboramphus* murrelets and auklets. Pp. 187-201 in: Vermeer, Briggs *et al.* (1993).
Sprout, G.D. (1937). Migratory behavior of some Glaucous-winged Gulls in the Strait of Georgia, British Columbia. *Condor* **39**: 238-242.
Sprunt, A. (1948a). The tern colonies of the Dry Tortugas keys. *Auk* **65**: 1-19.
Sprunt, A. (1948b). Voice in the wilderness. *Fauna* **10**: 39-42.
Sprunt, A. (1954). *Florida Bird Life*. Coward-McCann, New York.
Squibb, R.C. & Hunt, G.L. (1983). A comparison of nesting-ledges used by seabirds on St. George Island. *Ecology* **64**: 727-734.
Squibb, R.C. & Pitts, M.E. (1982). Copulatory behavior of the cliff-nesting Red-legged Kittiwake. *Anim. Behav.* **30**: 930.
Squire, J. (1990). Some southern records and other observations of the Buff-breasted Button-quail *Turnix olivei*. *Austr. Bird Watcher* **13(5)**: 149-152.
St. Clair, C.C. & St. Clair, R.C. (1992). Weka predation on eggs and chicks of Fiordland Crested Penguins. *Notornis* **39**: 60-63.
Staaland, H. (1967). Anatomical and physiological adaptations of the nasal glands in Charadriiformes birds. *Comp. Biochem. Physiol.* **23A**: 933-944.
Staav, R. (1977). [Study of the migration of Caspian Terns in the Mediterranean by captures of tagged birds in Sweden]. *Alauda* **45(4)**: 265-270. In French with German and English summaries.
Staav, R. (1979). Dispersal of Caspian Tern *Sterna caspia* in the Baltic. *Ornis Fenn.* **56**: 13-17.
Stahl, J.C. & Weimerskirch, H. (1982). La ségrégation écologique entre les deux espèces de sternes des Îles Crozet. *Com. Natl. Fr. Rech. Antarct.* **51**: 449-456.
Stahlecker, D.W. ed. (1992). *Proceedings of the Sixth North American Crane Workshop*. North American Crane Working Group, Grand Island, Nebraska.
Staine, K.J. & Burger, J. (1994). Nocturnal foraging behavior of breeding Piping Plovers (*Charadrius melodus*) in New Jersey. *Auk* **111(3)**: 579-587.
Stairmand, D.A. (1970). Occurrence of the Indian Skimmer or Scissorbill (*Rynchops albicollis* Swainson) in Salsette Island. *J. Bombay Nat. Hist. Soc.* **67(3)**: 571.
Stalheim, P.S. (1974). *Behaviour and Ecology of the Yellow Rail (*Coturnicops noveboracensis*)*. MSc thesis, University of Minnesota, Minneapolis, Minnesota.
Stamm, R.A. (1969). Zum Begattungsverhalten der Lackmöwe (*Larus ridibundus* Linnaeus 1766; Aves, Laridae). *Verhandl. Deutschen Zool. Gesell. Innsbruck* **32**: 318-324.
Stamps, R.T. & Doerr, P.D. (1977). Reproductive maturation and breeding of Woodcock in North Carolina. Pp. 185-190 in: Keppie & Owen (1977).
Stanford, J.K. (1954). A survey of the ornithology of northern Libya. *Ibis* **96**: 449-473.
Stanford, W.P. (1953). Winter distribution of the Grey Phalarope *Phalaropus fulicarius*. *Ibis* **95**: 483-491.
Stanley, P.I. & Minton, C.D.T. (1972). The unprecedented westward migration of Curlew Sandpipers in autumn 1969. *British Birds* **65**: 365-380.
Starck, J.M. (1991). [Biogeography and life history of *Turnix suscitator* Gmelin, 1789. Small adult size as a consequence of selection for rapid growth]. *Z. Zool. Syst. Evolutionsforsch.* **29(3)**: 213-237. In English with German summary.
Starks, J. & Lane, B. (1987). The northward migration of waders from Australia, February to April, 1985. *Stilt* **10**: 20-27.
Staub, F. (1976). *Birds of the Mascarenes and St. Brandon*. Organization Normale des Enterprises Ltée, Port Louis, Mauritius.
Stawarczyk, T. (1984). Aggression and its suppression in mixed-species wader flocks. *Ornis Scand.* **15**: 23-37.
Stead, E.F. (1932). *The Life Histories of New Zealand Birds*. Search, London.
Stedman, S. & Stedman, A. (1989). Feeding association between Bonaparte's Gulls and Hooded Mergansers. *Florida Field Nat.* **17**: 19-20.
Steele, W.K. (1989). Factors influencing inland foraging by gulls. *Ostrich* **60**: 45-47.
Steele, W.K. (1992a). Diet of Hartlaub's Gull *Larus hartlaubii* and the Kelp Gull *L. dominicanus* in the Southwestern Cape Province. *Ostrich* **63**: 68-82.
Steele, W.K. (1992b). Breeding of Hartlaub's Gull *Larus hartlaubii* at Hout Bay Harbour, South Africa. *Mar. Orn.* **20(1/2)**: 75-79.
Steele, W.K. & Hockey, P.A.R. (1990). Population size, distribution and dispersal of Kelp Gulls in the Southwestern Cape, South Africa. *Ostrich* **61**: 97-106.
Steeves, J.B. & Holohan, S. (1994). Semipalmated Sandpiper *Calidris pusilla* southward migration on the Canadian prairie. *Wader Study Group Bull.* **73**: 29-32.
Stegmann, B. (1934). Über die Formen der großen Möwen ("Subgenus *Larus*") und ihre gegenseitigen Beziehungen. *J. Orn.* **82**: 340-380.
Stegmann, B. (1935). Die systematische Stellung der tibetanischen Lachmöwe (*Larus brunnicephalus* Jerd.). *Orn. Monatsber.* **43**: 77-82.
Stegmann, B. (1960). Zur Systematik des Rassenkreises *Larus argentatus*. *J. Orn.* **101**: 498-499.
Stegmann, B.C. (1978). Relationships of the superorders Alectoromorphae and Charadriomorphae. (Aves): a comparative study of the avian hand. *Publ. Nuttall Orn. Club* **17**: 52-57.
Stehn, T.V. (1992a). Unusual movements and behaviors of color-banded Whooping Cranes during winter. Pp. 95-101 in: Stahlecker (1992).
Stehn, T.V. (1992b). Behavior of Whooping Cranes during initiation of migration. Pp. 102-105 in: Stahlecker (1992).
Stehn, T.V. & Johnson, E.F. (1987). Distribution of winter territories of Whooping Cranes on the Texas Coast. Pp. 180-195 in: Lewis (1987).
Stein, G. (1926). Zur Brutbiologie des Flußuferläufers. *Orn. Monatsber.* **34**: 163-169.
Stein, G. (1928). Ein weiterer Beitrag zur Brutbiologie von *Tringa hypoleucos*. *Orn. Monatsber.* **36**: 129-135.
Steinbacher, G. (1931). Beitrage zur Brutbiologie von Silbermöwe und Brandseeschwalbe. *J. Orn.* **79**: 349-353.
Steinbacher, J. (1968). Bemerkungen zur Brutbiologie, Morphologie und Anatomie von Kagu-Jungen (*Rhynochetos jubatus* Verreaux & Des Murs). *Bonn. zool. Beitr.* **19**: 198-205.
Steinbacher, J. (1977). Vogelleben auf Inseln in Indischen Ozean 3. Madagaskar. *Gefiederte Welt* **101**: 193-197.
Steinbacher, J. (1981). Neue Erkenntnisse über den Krokodilwächter. *Natur und Museum* **111(9)**: 286-288.
Stejneger, L. (1885). *Results of Ornithological Explorations in the Commander Islands and in Kamtschatka*. US National Museum Bulletin **29**. Smithsonian Institution, Washington, D.C.
Stempniewicz, L. (1980). Factors influencing the growth of Little Auk *Platus alle* (L.) nestlings on Spitsbergen. *Ekol. Pol.* **28**: 557-581.
Stempniewicz, L. (1981). Breeding biology of the Little Auk *Plautus alle* in the Hornsund region, Spitsbergen. *Acta Orn., Varszawa* **18**: 1-26.
Stempniewicz, L. (1982). Body proportions in adult and fledglings of the Little Auk. *Acta Zool. Cracoviensia* **26**: 149-158.
Stempniewicz, L. (1983). Hunting methods of the Glaucous Gull and escape maneuvers of its prey, the Dovekie. *J. Field Orn.* **54**: 329-331.
Stempniewicz, L. (1986). Factors causing changes in the rhythm of attendance of the Little Auks at a colony during the breeding season in Svalbard. *Ekol. Pol.* **34**: 247-263.
Stempniewicz, L. (1990). The functioning of Southern Spitsbergen coastal ecosystem. Pp. 43-65 in: Klekowski, R.Z. & Weslawski, J.M. eds. (1990). *Atlas of the Marine Fauna of Southern Spitsbergen*. Vol. 1. Vertebrates. Ossolineum PAS Press, Wroclaw, Poland.
Stempniewicz, L. (1993). The polar bear *Ursus maritimus* feeding in a seabird colony in Franz Josef Land. *Polar Res.* **12**: 33-36.
Stempniewicz, L. & Jezierski, J. (1987). Incubation shifts and chick feeding rate in the Little Auk *Alle alle* in Svalbard. *Ornis Scand.* **18**: 152-155.
Stempniewicz, L. & Weslawski, J.M. (1992). Outline of trophic relationships in Hornsund Fiord, SW Spitsbergen (with special consideration of seabirds). Pp. 271-298 in: *Landscape, Life World and Man in High Arctic*. Institute of Ecology, Polish Academy of Sciences, Warszawa.
Stenhouse, J.H. (1930). The Little Auk *Alle alle* (*polaris* sub-species nov.) of Franz Joseph Land. *Scottish Naturalist* **1930**: 47-49.
Stenning, J. & Hirst, P. (1994). The Grey-tailed Tattler in Grampian - the second Western Palearctic record. *Birding World* **7(12)**: 469-472.
Stenzel, J.R. (1982). *Ecology of Breeding Yellow Rails at Seney National Wildlife Refuge*. MSc thesis, Ohio State University, Columbus, Ohio.
Stenzel, L.E., Huber, H.R. & Page, G.W. (1976). Feeding behavior and diet of the Long-billed Curlew and Willet. *Wilson Bull.* **88**: 314-331.
Stenzel, L.E., Warriner, J.C., Warriner, J.S., Wilson, K.S., Bidstrup, F.C. & Page, G.W. (1994). Long-distance breeding dispersal of Snowy Plovers in western North America. *J. Anim. Ecol.* **63(4)**: 887-902.
Stepanjan, L.S. (1979). [Possible relations of *Ibidorhyncha struthersii* and notes on the history of the family Haematopodidae (Aves)]. *Zoologischeskii Zhurnal* **58(11)**: 1671-1679. In Russian with English summary.
Stepanjan, L.S. (1990a). [*Conspectus of the Ornithological Fauna of the USSR*]. Nauka, Moscow. In Russian.
Stepanjan, L.S. (1990b). Remarks on four names of Palaearctic birds. *Zoologischeskii Zhurnal* **69**: 68-73.
Stepanov, E.A. (1986). [Records of the Great Bustard (*Otis tarda*), the Little Bustard (*O. tetrax*) and the Macqueen's Bustard (*O. undulata*) in central Kazakhstan]. *Ornitologiya* **21**: 113-117. In Russian with English summary.
Stephen, W.J.D. (1979). Whooping Crane sighting prairie provinces, 1977 and 1978. *Blue Jay* **37(3)**: 163-168.
Stephens, J. (1974). Kanaha Pond: vital habitat for Hawaii's endangered Coot and Stilt. *Natl. Parks Conserv. Mag.* **48(4)**: 10-13.
Stephens, M.L. (1982). Mate takeover and possible infanticide by a female Northern Jacana (*Jacana spinosa*). *Anim. Behav.* **30(4)**: 1253-1254.
Stephens, M.L. (1984a). Intraspecific distraction display of the polyandrous Northern Jacana *Jacana spinosa*. *Ibis* **126(1)**: 70-72.
Stephens, M.L. (1984b). Interspecific aggressive behavior of the polyandrous Northern Jacana (*Jacana spinosa*). *Auk* **101(3)**: 508-518.
Stephens, M.L. (1984c). Effects of number of mates on maternal care in the polyandrous Northern Jacana (*Jacana spinosa*). *Wader Study Group Bull.* **36**: 61.
Stephens, M.L. (1984d). *Maternal Care and Polyandry in the Northern Jacana (*Jacana spinosa*)*. PhD dissertation, University of Chicago, Chicago, Illinois.
Sterbetz, I. (1974). *Die Brachschwalbe*. A. Ziemsen Verlag, Wittenberg Lutherstadt.
Sterbetz, I. (1979). Investigations into the nutrition of the Great Bustard (*Otis tarda* L.) in the winter aspect of 1977/78. *Aquila* **86**: 93-100.

Sterbetz, I. (1981). Comparative investigations into the reproduction behaviour of monogamous, polygamous and unmated Great Bustard populations in South-eastern Hungary. *Aquila* **87**: 31-47.
Sterbetz, I. (1992). Foods of Dunlin (*Calidris alpina*) in Hungary. *Aquila* **99**: 49-57.
Stern, M.A. & Jarvis, R.L. (1991). Sexual dimorphism and assortative mating in Black Terns. *Wilson Bull.* **103**: 266-271.
Stern, M.A., Morawski, J.F. & Rosenberg, G.A. (1993). Rediscovery and status of a disjunct population of breeding Yellow Rails in southern Oregon. *Condor* **95**: 1024-1027.
Stettenheim, P.R. (1959). *Adaptations for Underwater Swimming in the Common Murre* Uria aalge. PhD thesis, University of Michigan, Ann Arbor, Michigan.
Stevenson, H.M. (1975). Identification of difficult birds: 3. Semipalmated and Western Sandpipers. *Florida Field Nat.* **3**: 39-44.
Stevenson, H.M. & Anderson, B.H. (1994). *The Birdlife of Florida*. University Press of Florida, Gainesville, Florida.
Stevenson, J.O. & Griffith, R.E. (1946). Winter life of the Whooping Crane. *Condor* **48**: 160-178.
Stewart, B.A. & Bally, R. (1985). The ecological role of the Red-knobbed Coot *Fulica cristata* Gmelin at the Bot River Estuary, South Africa: a preliminary investigation. *Trans. Roy. Soc. S. Afr.* **45**: 419-426.
Stewart, I.D. (1989). Hooded Plover survey - South Australian/Victorian border to Murray mouth. *Stilt* **14**: 32-33.
Stewart, I.D. (1991). 1990 spring Hooded Plover survey, South Australia. *Stilt* **19**: 9-10.
Stewart, I.D. (1993). 1992 Hooded Plover survey, South Australia. *Stilt* **22**: 44.
Stewart, J.M. (1987). The 'lily of birds': the success story of the Siberian White Crane. *Oryx* **21**: 6-10.
Stewart, R.E. (1954). Migratory movements of the Northern Clapper Rail. *Bird-Banding* **25**: 1-5.
Stewart, R.E. & Robbins, C.S. (1958). *Birds of Maryland and the District of Columbia*. North American Fauna **62**. Washington.
Steyn, P. (1960). Nesting of Whiskered Tern in Southern Cape. *Bokmakierie* **12**: 35-36.
Steyn, P. (1965). Temminck's Courser. *Afr. Wildl.* **19(1)**: 29-32.
Steyn, P. (1966). White-fronted Sandplover. *Bokmakierie* **18**: 75.
Steyn, P. (1973). African Jacana at last. *Bokmakierie* **25**: 34-37.
Steyn, P. (1992). First record of Red-winged Pratincole in southwestern Cape. *Promerops* **204**: 9.
Steyn, P. & Ellman-Brown, P. (1974). Crowned Crane nesting in a tree. *Ostrich* **45**: 40-42.
Steyn, P. & Myburgh, N. (1986). A tale of two flufftails. *Afr. Wildl.* **40**: 22-27.
Steyn, P. & Tredgold, D. (1977). Crowned Cranes covering eggshells. *Bokmakierie* **29(3)**: 82-83.
Stidolph, R.H.D. (1947). Breeding habits of Red-billed Gulls. *New Zealand Bird Notes* **2**: 121-122.
Stidolph, R.H.D. (1973). Plumage of Variable Oystercatchers. *Notornis* **20(4)**: 311 313.
Stiefel, A. (1991). Situation des Wachtelkönigs in Ostdeutschland (vormalige DDR). *Vogelwelt* **112**: 57-66.
Stiefel, A. & Berg, W. (1975). Geschlechtsunterschiede in einigen Rufen der Wasserralle (*Rallus aquaticus*). *Beitr. Vogelkd.* **21**: 330-339.
Stiefel, A. & Scheufler, H. (1984). *Der Rotschenkel,* Tringa totanus. Neue Brehm-Bücherei **562**.
Stiefel, A. & Scheufler, H. (1989). *Der Alpenstrandläufer,* Calidris alpina. Neue Brehm-Bücherei **592**.
Stiles, F.G. (1981). Notes on the Uniform Crake in Costa Rica. *Wilson Bull.* **93**: 107-108.
Stiles, F.G. (1988). Notes on the distribution and status of certain birds in Costa Rica. *Condor* **90**: 931-933.
Stiles, F.G. & Levey, D.J. (1988). The Gray-breasted Crake (*Laterallus exilis*) in Costa Rica: vocalizations, distribution and interactions with White-throated Crakes (*L. albigularis*). *Condor* **90(3)**: 607-612.
Stiles, F.G. & Skutch, A.F. (1989). *A Guide to the Birds of Costa Rica*. Christopher Helm, London.
Stinson, C.H. (1977). The spatial distribution of wintering Black-bellied Plovers. *Wilson Bull.* **89**: 470-472.
Stinson, D.W., Ritter, M.W. & Reichel, J.D. (1991). The Mariana Common Moorhen: decline of an island endemic. *Condor* **93**: 38-43.
Stishov, M.S. (1989). [*Tryngites subruficollis* Vieill. on the Ayon Island (the western Chukotka Peninsula)]. *Zoologischeskii Zhurnal* **68(11)**: 154-156. In Russian with English summary.
Stishov, M.S. (1994). [On the distribution and habitat of Buff-Breasted Sandpiper *Tryngites subruficollis* (Aves) on Chukotski Peninsula]. *Zoologischeskii Zhurnal* **73**: 83-91. In Russian with English summary.
Stock, M., Herber, R.F.M. & Geron, H.M.A. (1989). Cadmium levels in Oystercatchers *Haematopus ostralegus* from the German Wadden Sea. *Mar. Ecol. Prog. Ser.* **53**: 227-234.
Stock, M., Strotmann, J., Witte, H. & Nehls, G. (1987). Jungvögel sterben im harten Winter zuerst: Winterverluste beim Austernfischer, *Haematopus ostralegus*. *J. Orn.* **128**: 325-331.
Stockton, A. (1978). *Aves de la República Dominicana*. Museo Nacional de Historia Natural, Santo Domingo.
Stoddart, D.R. (1971). White-throated Rail *Dryolimnas cuvieri* on Astove Atoll. *Bull. Brit. Orn. Club* **91(6)**: 145-147.
Stokes, S. (1926). The Grey-winged Trumpeter (*Psophia crepitans*). *Avicult. Mag.* **4**: 1-3.
Stokes, T. (1979). On the possible existence of the New Caledonian Wood Rail *Tricholimnas lafresnayanus*. *Bull. Brit. Orn. Club* **99**: 47-54.
Stokes, T. (1983). Bird casualties in 1975-76 at the Booby Island lightstation, Torres Strait. *Sunbird* **13**: 53-58.
Stokes, T. (1988). *A Review of the Birds of Christmas Island, Indian Ocean*. Occasional Paper **16**. Australian National Parks & Wildlife Service, Canberra. 73 pp.
Stokes, T., Sheils, W. & Dunn, K. (1984). Birds of the Cocos (Keeling) Islands, Indian Ocean. *Emu* **84**: 23-28.
Stolt, B.O., Ekström, L., Fransson, T., Malmgren, B., Staav, R., Sällström, B. & Sällström, U.B. (1992). Dunlin *Calidris alpina* recoveries 1972-1991. Report on Swedish bird ringing for 1989, Swedish Museum of Natural Histoty, Stockholm.
Stone, A.C. (1912). Birds of Lake Boga, Victoria. *Emu* **12**: 112-122.
Stone, W. (1937). *Bird Studies at Old Cape May*. Vol. 2. Delaware Valley Ornithological Club, Philadelphia.
Stonehouse, B. (1956). The Brown Skua *Catharacta skua lonnbergi* (Mathews) of South Georgia. *FIDS Sci. Rep.* **14**: 1-25.
Stonehouse, B. (1985). Sheathbill. Page 533 in: Campbell & Lack (1985).
Storer, R.W. (1945). Structural modifications in the hind limb in the Alcidae. *Ibis* **87**: 433-456.
Storer, R.W. (1950). Geographic variation in the Pigeon Guillemots of North America. *Condor* **52**: 28-31.
Storer, R.W. (1952). A comparison of variation, behaviour and evolution in the seabird genera *Uria* and *Cepphus*. *Univ. Calif. Publ. Zool.* **52(2)**: 121-222.
Storer, R.W. (1960). Evolution in the diving birds. Pp. 694-707 in: *Proc. XII Int. Orn. Congr.* Helsinki, 1958.
Storer, R.W. (1981). The Rufous-faced Crake *Laterallus xenopterus* and its Paraguayan congeners. *Wilson Bull.* **93**: 137-144.
Storer, R.W. (1987). The possible significance of large eyes in the Red-legged Kittiwake. *Condor* **89**: 192-194.
Storey, A.E. (1987a). Characteristics of successful nest sites for marsh-nesting Common Terns. *Can. J. Zool.* **65**: 1411-1416.
Storey, A.E. (1987b). Adaptations for marsh nesting in Common and Forster's Terns. *Can. J. Zool.* **65**: 1417-1420.
Storkersen, O.R. (1986). Pink Black-headed Gulls. *British Birds* **79**: 211-212.
Storr, G.M. (1973). List of Queensland birds. *Spec. Publs. West. Austr. Mus.* **5**.
Storr, G.M. (1977). *Birds of the Northern Territory*. Western Australian Museum Special Publication **7**.
Storr, G.M. (1980). *Birds of the Kimberly Division*. Western Australian Museum Special Publication **11**.
Storr, G.M. (1985). Birds of the Gascoyne Region, Western Australia. *Records West. Austr. Mus.* **21**(Suppl.): 1-66.
Storr, G.M. & Johnstone, R.E. (1984). The subspecific status of the Painted Button-quail of the Houtman Abrolhos, Western Australia. *Records West. Austr. Mus.* **11**: 315.
Stotz, D.F., Bierregaard, R.O., Cohn-Haft, M., Petermann, P., Smith, J., Whittaker, A. & Wilson, S.V. (1992). The status of American migrants in central Amazonian Brazil. *Condor* **94**: 608-621.
Stout, J.F. (1975). Aggressive communication by *Larus glaucescens*. III. Description of the displays related to territorial protection. *Behaviour* **55**: 181-207.
Stout, J.F. & Brass, M.E. (1969). Aggressive communication by *Larus glaucescens*. II. Visual communication. *Behaviour* **34**: 42-54.
Stout, J.F., Wilcox, J.R. & Creitz, L.E. (1969). Aggressive communication by *Larus glaucescens*. I. Sound communication. *Behaviour* **34**: 29-41.
Stowe, T.J. & Becker, D. (1992). Status and conservation of Corncrakes *Crex crex* outside the breeding grounds. *Tauraco* **2**: 1-23.
Stowe, T.J. & Hudson, A.V. (1991a). Radio telemetry studies of Corncrake in Great Britain. *Vogelwelt* **112**: 10-16.
Stowe, T.J. & Hudson, A.V. (1991b). Corncrakes outside the breeding grounds and ideas for a conservation strategy. *Vogelwelt* **112**: 103-107.
Stowe, T.J., Newton, A.V., Green, R.E. & Mayes, E. (1993). The decline of the Corncrake *Crex crex* in Britain and Ireland in relation to habitat. *J. Appl. Ecol.* **30**: 53-62.
Strahl, S.D. (1985). *The Behavior and Socio-ecology of the Hoatzin* Opisthocomus hoazin, *in the Llanos of Venezuela*. PhD dissertation, State University of New York, Albany, New York.
Strahl, S.D. (1988). The social organization and behavior of the Hoatzin *Opisthocomus hoazin* in central Venezuela. *Ibis* **130(4)**: 483-502.
Strahl, S.D. & Schmitz, A. (1990). Hoatzins: cooperative breeding in a folivorous neotropical bird. Pp. 133-155 in: Stacey, P.B. & Koenig, W.D. eds. (1990). *Cooperative Breeding in Long-term Studies of Ecology and Behavior*. Cambridge University Press.
Straka, U. (1991). [Contribution to the occurrence of Golden Plovers (*Pluvialis apricaria*) on farmland in eastern Austria]. *Egretta* **34(2)**: 97-103. In German with English summary.
Strandgaard, K. (1988). Ageing and sexing of the Common Snipe (*Gallinago gallinago*). Pp. 24-26 in: Havet & Hirons (1988).
Strang, C.A. (1974). *The Alaskan Glaucous Gull (*Larus hyperboreus barrovianus *Ridgway): Autecology, Taxonomy, Behavior-1974*. Progress Report Purdue University, West Lafayette, Indiana.
Strang, C.A. (1977). Variation and distribution of Glaucous Gulls in western Alaska. *Condor* **79**: 170-175.
Strang, G.L. (1974). Nesting and feeding ecology of Mew Gulls (*Larus canus*) and Sabine's Gulls (*Xema sabini*) on the Kashunuk River. Unpublished report to Purdue University, West Lafayette, Indiana.
Stranger, R.H. (1991). Breeding of the Red-kneed Plover, *Charadrius cinctus*, at Mayland, W.A. (Western Australia). *West. Austr. Nat.* **18(8)**: 223-224.
Strann, K.B. (1992). Numbers and distribution of Knot *Calidris canutus islandica* during spring migration in north Norway 1983-1989. Pp. 121-125 in: Piersma & Davidson (1992b).
Strann, K.B. & Summers, R.W. (1990). Diet and diurnal feeding activity of Purple Sandpipers *Calidris maritima* wintering in northern Norway. *Fauna Norvegica (Ser. C, Cinclus)* **13**: 75-78.
Strann, K.B. & Vader, W. (1992). The nominate Lesser Black-backed Gull *Larus fuscus fuscus*, a gull with tern-like feeding biology, and its recent decrease in northern Norway. *Ardea* **80**: 133-142.
Strann, K.B., Vader, W. & Barrett, R. (1991). Auk mortality in fishing nets in north Norway. *Seabird* **13**: 22-29.
Strauch, J.G. (1971). Killdeer breeding range extension. *Auk* **88**: 171.
Strauch, J.G. (1976). *The Cladistic Relationships of the Charadriiformes*. PhD dissertation, University of Michigan, Ann Arbor, Michigan.
Strauch, J.G. (1978). The phylogeny of the Charadriiformes (Aves): a new estimate using the method of character compatibility analysis. *Trans. Zool. Soc. London* **34**: 263-345.
Strauch, J.G. (1985). The phylogeny of the Alcidae. *Auk* **102**: 520-539.
Strauch, J.G. & Abele, L.G. (1979). Feeding ecology of three species of plovers wintering on the Bay of Panama, Central America. Pp. 217-230 in: Pitelka (1979).
Strauss, A.E. (1991). Buff-breasted Sandpipers in Middleboro. *Bird Obs.* **19(4)**: 196-198.
Strauss, E.G. (1990). *Reproductive Success, Life History Patterns, and Behavioral Variation in a Population of Piping Plovers Subjected to Human Disturbances*. PhD dissertation, Tufts University.
Straw, J.A. (1993). *American Woodcock Harvest and Breeding Population Status, 1993*. Admin. Rep., US Fish & Wildlife Service, Laurel, Maryland.
Street, J.F. (1923). On the nesting grounds of the Solitary Sandpiper and the Lesser Yellow-legs. *Auk* **40**: 577-583.
Stresemann, E. (1927). Die Schwarzen Austernfischer (*Haematopus*). *Orn. Monatsber.* **35**: 71 77.
Stresemann, E. (1931). Vorläufiges über die ornithologischen Ergebnisse der Expedition Heinrich 1930-1931. *Orn. Monatsber.* **39**: 167-171.
Stresemann, E. (1932). Vorläufiges über die Ornithologischer Ergebnisse der Expedition Heinrich 1930-32. VII. Zur Ornithologie von Südost Celebes. *Orn. Monatsber.* **40**: 104-115.
Stresemann, E. (1941). Die Vögel von Celebes, Teil 3. Systematik und Biologie. *J. Orn.* **89**: 1-112.
Stresemann, E. & Stresemann, V. (1966). *Die Mauser der Vögel*. Journal für Ornithologie **107**(Supplement). 439 pp.
Stresemann, E. & Timofeeff, N.W. (1947). Artentstehung in geographischen Formenkreisen. I. Der Formenkreis *Larus argentatus-cachinnans-fuscus*. *Biol. Zbl.* **66**: 57-76.
Stretton, W.S. (1992). Some thoughts on the decline of the Blue Crane and the role of the farmer in its conservation. Pp. 111-114 in: Porter *et al.* (1992).
Striberny, W. (1981). Elfenbeinmöwe (*Pagophila eburnea*) auf Sylt. *Orn. Mitt.* **33**: 36-40.
Stribling, H.L. & Doerr, P.D. (1985). Nocturnal use of fields by American Woodcock. *J. Wildl. Manage.* **49**: 485-491.
Stromar, L. (1967/68). Biology of the Herring Gull, *Larus argentatus* (Pontopp.), and the Common Tern, *Sterna hirundo* (L.), and their mutual relationships on some of the Kornat Islands. *Larus* **21/22**: 89-98.
Stronach, B. (1983). A report concerning the reproductive organs of Woodcock in the month of February. Pp. 43-50 in: Kalchreuter (1983b).
Strophlet, J.J. (1946). Birds of Guam. *Auk* **65**: 534-540.
Struger, J. & Weseloh, D.V. (1985). Great Lakes Caspian Terns: egg contaminants and biological implications. *Colonial Waterbirds* **8**: 142-149.
Stubbe, M. & Bolod, A. (1971). Möwen und Seeschwalben (Laridae, Aves) der Mongolei. *Mitt. Zool. Mus. Berlin* **47**: 51-62.
Su Liying (1992). Human impacts on cranes in China. Pp. 22-32 in: Whitaker (1992).
Su Liying (1993). *Comparative Feeding Ecology of the Red-crowned and White-naped Cranes*. MA thesis, University of Missouri, Columbia.
Su Liying, Xu Jie & Zhou Desheng (1991). Breeding habits of White-naped Cranes at Zhalong Nature Reserve. Pp. 51-58 in: Harris (1991b).
Su Liying, Xu Jie *et al.* (1987). [The difference in behavior of male and female Red-crowned Crane *Grus japonensis* during the breeding season]. *Chinese Wildlife* **5**: 18-21. In Chinese.
Subramanya, S. (1987). Occurrence of Greyheaded Lapwing, *Vanellus cinereus* (Blyth) in Bangalore. *J. Bombay Nat. Hist. Soc.* **84(1)**: 205-206.
Sueur, F. (1975). Nidification de l'Avocette *Recurvirostra avosetta* en Baie de Somme. *Alauda* **43**: 482-483.
Sueur, F. (1984). Quelques donées sur la reproduction de l'Avocette *Recurvirostra avosetta* dans la Marqueterre (Somme). *Oiseau et RFO* **54**: 131-136.
Sueur, F., Mouronval, J.B. & Vandromme, D. (1990). [Two eastern waders in the Marquenterre: Asiatic Dowitcher (*Limnodromus semipalmatus*), first record for western Europe, and Terek Sandpiper (*Xenus cinereus*), first record for Picardie in the 20th century]. *Avocetta* **14**: 74-77. In French with English summary.
Sugathan, R. (1985). Observations on Spoonbilled Sandpiper (*Eurynorhynchus pygmaeus*) in its wintering ground at Point Caimere, Thanjavur district, Tamil Nadu. *J. Bombay Nat Hist. Soc.* **82(2)**: 407-409.
Sugden, L.G. (1979). Habitat use by nesting American Coots in Saskatchewan parklands. *Wilson Bull.* **91**: 599-607.
Sulley, S.C. & Sulley, M.E. (1992). *Birding in Cuba*. Worldwide Publications, Belper, UK.
Sullivan, K.A. (1984). Cooperative foraging and courtship feeding in the Laughing Gull. *Wilson Bull.* **96**: 710-711.
Sullivan, P. (1988). Whistling Kite takes avocet. *Austr. Raptor Assoc. News* **9(1)**: 13.
Summers, J. (1977). Aerial feeding in Kelp Gulls. *Cormorant* **2**: 21.
Summers, K.R. & Drent, R.H. (1979). Breeding biology and twinning experiments of Rhinoceros Auklets on Cleland Island, British Columbia. *Murrelet* **60**: 16-27.
Summers, R.W. (1978). Results from dye-marking waders in the south-west Cape. *Ostrich* **49**: 48-51.
Summers, R.W. (1994). The migration patterns of the Purple Sandpiper *Calidris maritima*. *Ostrich* **65(2)**: 167-173.
Summers, R.W. & Cooper, J. (1977). The population, ecology and conservation of the Black Oystercatcher *Haematopus moquini*. *Ostrich* **48**: 28-40.
Summers, R.W. & Hockey, P.A.R. (1980). Breeding biology of the White-fronted Plover (*Charadrius marginatus*) in the south-western Cape, South Africa. *J. Nat. Hist.* **14(3)**: 433-445.
Summers, R.W. & Hockey, P.A.R. (1981). Egg-covering behaviour of the Whitefronted Plover *Charadrius marginatus*. *Ornis Scand.* **12(3)**: 240-243.
Summers, R.W. & Rogers, M. (1991). Seasonal and long-term changes in the numbers of Purple Sandpipers *Calidris maritima* at Portland Bill, Dorset. *Ringing & Migration* **12(2)**: 72-74.
Summers, R.W. & Underhill, L.G. (1991). The relationship between body size and time of breeding in Icelandic Redshanks *Tringa t. robusta*. *Ibis* **133**: 134-139.
Summers, R.W. & Waltner, M. (1979). Seasonal variation in the mass of waders in southern Africa, with special reference to migration. *Ostrich* **50**: 21-37.
Summers, R.W., Corse, C.J., Nicoll, M., Smith, R. & Whitfield, D.P. (1988). The biometrics and wintering area of Icelandic Purple Sandpipers. *Ringing & Migration* **9**: 133-138.
Summers, R.W., Ellis, P.M. & Johnstone, J.P. (1988). Waders on the coast of Shetland in winter: numbers and habitat preferences. *Scottish Birds* **15**: 71-79.
Summers, R.W., Nicoll, M., Underhill, L.G. & Petersen, A. (1988). Methods for estimating the proportions of Icelandic and British Redshanks *Tringa totanus* in mixed populations wintering on British coasts. *Bird Study* **35**: 169-180.
Summers, R.W., Smith, S., Nicoll, M. & Atkinson, N.K. (1990). Tidal and sexual differences in the diet of Purple Sandpipers *Calidris maritima* in Scotland (UK). *Bird Study* **37**: 187-194.
Summers, R.W., Strann, K.B., Rae, R. & Heggas, J. (1990). Wintering Purple Sandpipers *Calidris maritima* in Troms County, northern Norway. *Ornis Scand.* **21**: 248-254, 1990.

Summers, R.W., Underhill, L.G., Clinning, C.F. & Nicoll, M. (1989). Populations, migrations, biometrics and moult of the Turnstone *Arenaria i. interpres* on the east Atlantic coastline, with special reference to the Siberian population. *Ardea* **77**: 145-168.

Summers, R.W., Underhill, L.G., Nicoll, M., Rae, R. & Piersma, T. (1992). Seasonal, size- and age-related patterns in body-mass and composition of Purple Sandpipers *Calidris maritima* in Britain. *Ibis* **134(4)**: 346-354.

Summers, R.W., Underhill, L.G., Pearson, D.J. & Scott, D.A. (1987). Wader migration systems in southern and eastern Africa and western Asia. *Wader Study Group Bull.* **49**, *IWRB Spec. Publ.* **7**: 15-34.

Summers, R.W., Underhill, L.G., Waltner, M. & Whitelaw, D.A. (1987). Population, biometrics and movements of Sanderling *Calidris alba* in southern Africa. *Ostrich* **58**: 24-39.

Sundararaman, V. (1989). Belly-soaking and nest wetting behaviour of Redwattled Lapwing, *Vanellus indicus* (Boddaert). *J. Bombay Nat. Hist. Soc.* **86(2)**: 242.

Surahio, M.I. (1985). Ecology and distribution of Houbara Bustards in Sind. *Bustard Studies* **3**: 55-58.

Surman, C.A. & Wooller, R.D. (1995). The breeding biology of the Lesser Noddy on Pelsaert Island, Western Australia. *Emu* **95(1)**: 47-53.

Susanth, C., Suresh, C. & Rajeevan, S. (1986). Breeding of the Painted Snipe (*Rostratula benghalensis*) in Trivandrum, Kerala. *J. Bombay Nat. Hist. Soc.* **83(3)**: 663-664.

Suter, M. (1950). The occurrence of the Wood Snipe (*Gallinago gallinago* Hodgs.) near Poona. *J. Bombay Nat. Hist. Soc.* **49(1)**: 123.

Sutherland, J.M. (1991). Effects of drought on American Coot, *Fulica americana*, reproduction in Saskatchewan parklands. *Can. Field-Nat.* **105**: 267-273.

Sutherland, J.M. & Maher, W.J. (1987). Nest-site selection of the American Coot in the Aspen parklands of Saskatchewan. *Condor* **89**: 804-810.

Sutherland, W.J. (1982a). Do Oystercatchers select the most profitable cockles? *Anim. Behav.* **30**: 857-861.

Sutherland, W.J. (1982b). Spatial variation in the predation of cockles by Oystercatchers at Traeth Melynog, Anglesey. I. The cockle population. *J. Anim. Ecol.* **51**: 481 489.

Sutherland, W.J. (1982c). Spatial variation in the predation of cockles by Oystercatchers at Traeth Melynog, Anglesey. II. The pattern of mortality. *J. Anim. Ecol.* **51**: 491 500.

Sutherland, W.J. (1982d). Food supply and dispersal in the determination of wintering population levels of Oystercatchers, *Haematopus ostralegus*. *Estuarine Coastal and Shelf Science* **14**: 223 230.

Sutherland, W.J. & Ens, B.J. (1987). The criteria determining the selection of mussels *Mytilus edulis* by Oystercatchers *Haematopus ostralegus*. *Behaviour* **103**: 188-202.

Sutherland, W.J. & Koene, P. (1982). Field estimates of the strength of interference between Oystercatchers *Haematopus ostralegus*. *Oecologia* **55**: 108-109.

Sutter, E. (1955). Über die Mauser einiger Laufhühnchen und die Rassen von *Turnix maculosa* und *sylvatica* im indo-australischen Gebiet. *Verh. Naturf. Ges. Basel* **66**: 85-139.

Suttie, J.M. & Fennessy, P.F. (1992). Organ weight and weight relationships in Takahe and Pukeko. *Notornis* **39**: 47-53.

Sutton, G.M. (1967). Behaviour of the Buff-breasted Sandpiper at the nest. *Arctic* **20**: 3-7.

Sutton, G.M. (1968a). Review: Evolution of some Arctic gulls (*Larus*): an experimental study of isolating mechanisms by N.G. Smith. *Auk* **85**: 142-145.

Sutton, G.M. (1968b). Sexual dimorphism in the Hudsonian Godwit. *Wilson Bull.* **80**: 251-252.

Sutton, G.M. (1981). On aerial and ground displays of the world's snipe. *Wilson Bull.* **93**: 457-477.

Sutton, G.M. & Parmelee, D.F. (1955). Breeding of the Semipalmated Plover on Baffin Island. *Bird-banding* **26**: 137-147.

Sutton, G.M. & Parmelee, D.F. (1978). On maturation of Thayer's Gull. *Wilson Bull.* **90**: 479-491.

Sutton, J. (1935). *Gabianus pacificus*. *S. Austr. Orn.* **13**: 54-56.

Suwal, R.N. (1994). Crane ecology and bird conservation. *Bull. Oriental Bird Club* **20**: 13-14.

Svanberg, P.O. (1994). [Speculations and comments on the causes of plumage colorations in *Grus grus*]. *Falke* **41(6)**: 188-189. In German.

Svensson, B.W. (1987). Structure and vocalizations of display flights in the Broad-billed Sandpiper *Limicola falcinellus*. *Ornis Scand.* **18(1)**: 47-52.

Swales, M.K. (1965). The seabirds of Gough Island. *Ibis* **107**: 17-42, 215-229.

Swales, M.K. & Murphy, R.C. (1965). A specimen of *Larus pipixcan* from Tristan da Cunha. *Ibis* **107**: 394.

Swanberg, P.O. (1965). Studies of less familiar birds. 138. Great Snipe. *British Birds* **58**: 504-508.

Swanberg, P.O. (1987). Migrating Common Cranes in Sweden: experiments in farming for cranes and vegetation control in wetlands. Pp. 225-230 in: Archibald & Pasquier (1987a).

Swartz, L.G. (1966). Sea-cliff birds. Pp. 611-678 in: Willimovsky, N.J. & Wolfe, J.N. eds. (1966). *Environment of the Cape Thompson Region, Alaska*. US Atom. Ener. Comm., Oak Ridge, Tennessee.

Swartz, L.G. (1967). Distribution and movements of birds in the Bering and Chuckchi Seas. *Pacif. Sci.* **21**: 332-347.

Swengel, S.R. (1987). A proposed management plan for captive Red-crowned Cranes. Pp. 513-523 in: Archibald & Pasquier (1987a).

Swengel, S.R. (1992). Sexual size dimorphism and size indices of six species of captive cranes at the International Crane Foundation. Pp. 151-158 in: Stahlecker (1992).

Swennen, C. (1971). [The food of the Greenshank *Tringa nebularia* during its stay in the Dutch Waddenzee-area]. *Limosa* **44**: 71-83. In Dutch with English summary.

Swennen, C. (1984). Differences in the quality of roosting flocks of Oystercatchers. Pp. 177-189 in: Evans *et al.* (1984).

Swennen, C. (1990). Oystercatchers feeding on giant bloody cockles on the Banc d'Arguin, Mauritania. *Ardea* **78**: 53-62.

Swennen, C. (1992). Observations on the departure of Knots from the Dutch Wadden Sea in spring. Pp. 87-90 in: Piersma & Davidson (1992b).

Swennen, C. & de Bruijn, L.L.M. (1980). De dichtheid van broedterritoria van de Scholekster (*Haematopus ostralegus*) op Vlieland. *Limosa* **53**: 85 90.

Swennen, C. & Duiven, P. (1977). Size of food objects of three fish-eating seabird species: *Uria aalge*, *Alca torda* and *Fratercula arctica* (Aves, Alcidae). *Netherlands J. Sea Res.* **11**: 92-98.

Swennen, C. & Duiven, P. (1983). Characteristics of Oystercatchers killed by cold-stress in the Dutch Wadden Sea area. *Ardea* **71**: 155-159.

Swennen, C. & Marteijn, E.C.L. (1988). Foraging behaviour of Spoon-billed Sandpipers *Eurynorhynchus pigmeus* on a mudflat in peninsular Thailand. *Nat. Hist. Bull. Siam Soc.* **36(1)**: 85-88.

Swennen, C. & Park, J.Y. (1991). Spotted Greenshank *Tringa guttifer* feeding on an intertidal flat in Korea. *J. Yamashina Inst. Orn.* **23**: 13-19.

Swennen, C., de Bruijn, L.L.M., Duiven, P., Leopold, M.F. & Marteijn, E.C.L. (1983). Differences in bill form of the Oystercatcher *Haematopus ostralegus*: a dynamic adaptation to specific foraging techniques. *Netherlands J. Sea Res.* **17**: 57-83.

Swennen, C., Leopold, M.F. & de Bruijn, L.L.M. (1989). Time-stressed Oystercatchers, *Haematopus ostralegus*, can increase their intake rate. *Anim. Behav.* **38**: 8-22.

Swennen, C., Ruttanadakul, N., Ardseungnurn, S. & Howes, J.R. (1987). Foraging behavior of the Crab Plover (*Dromas ardeola*) at Ko Libon, southern Thailand. *Nat. Hist. Bull. Siam Soc.* **35(1/2)**: 27-34.

Swickard, D.K. (1972). Status of the California Least Tern at Camp Pendelton, California. *Calif. Bids* **3**: 49-58.

Swift, J.J. (1960). Notes on the behaviour of Whiskered Terns. *British Birds* **53**: 559-572.

Swinhoe, R. (1871). On a new Chinese gull. *Proc. Zool. Soc., London* **1871**: 273-275.

Switzer, P., Lewin, V. & Wolfe, F.H. (1971). Shell thickness, DDE levels and reproductive success in Common Terns (*Sterna hyirundo*) in Alberta. *Can. J. Zool.* **49**: 69-73.

Sydeman, W.J. & Emslie, S.D. (1992). Effects of parental age on hatching asynchrony, egg size and third-chick disadvantage in Western Gulls. *Auk* **109**: 242-248.

Sydeman, W.J., Penniman, J.F., Penniman, T.M., Pyle, P. & Ainley, D.G. (1991). Breeding performance in the Western Gull: effects of parental age, timing of breeding and year in relation to food availability. *J. Anim. Ecol.* **60**: 135-149.

Sykes, P.W. (1975). Caribbean Coot collected in southern Florida. *Florida Field Nat.* **3(2)**: 25-27.

Sykes, P.W., Ryman, W.E., Kepler, C.B., Hardy, J.W. (1995). A 24-hour remote surveillance system for terrestrial wildlife studies. *J. Field Orn.* **66(2)**: 199-211.

Symens, P. (1991). The ICBP/NCWCD seabird monitoring survey of offshore islands in the northern Arabian Gulf, Saudi Arabia May-July 1991. *Phoenix* **8**: 4-5.

Symens, P. & Evans, M.I. (1993). Impact of Gulf War oil spills on Saudi Arabian breeding populations of terns *Sterna* in the Arabian Gulf. *Sandgrouse* **15**: 18-36.

Symens, P. & Werner, M. (1994). First record of Senegal Thick-knee *Burhinus senegalensis* in Arabia. *Bull. Orn. Soc. Middle East* **33**: 12-14.

Symmes, T.C.L. (1952). Some observations on the breeding of the Crowned Plover. *Ostrich* **23**: 85-87.

Szabó, L.V. (1970). Vergleichende Untersuchungen der Brutverhältnisse der drei *Porzana*-Arten in Ungarn. *Aquila* **66-67**: 73-113.

Szabó, L.V. (1975). Feketszarnyu szekicser (*Glareola nordmanni*) feszkelese a Hortobagyon. [Nesting of the Black-winged Pratincole (*Glareola nordmanni*) in Hortobagy]. *Aquila* **80-81**: 55-72. In Hungarian with English Summary.

Székely, T. (1991). Status and breeding biology of Kentish Plovers *Charadrius alexandrinus* in Hungary: a progress report. *Wader Study Group Bull.* **62**: 17-23.

Székely, T. (1992). Reproduction of Kentish Plover *Charadrius alexandrinus* in grasslands and fish-ponds: the habitat mal-assessment hypothesis. *Aquila* **99**: 59-68.

Székely, T. & Lessells, C.M. (1993). Mate change by Kentish Plovers *Charadrius alexandrinus*. *Ornis Scand.* **24(4)**: 317-322.

Székely, T. & Williams, T.D. (1994). Factors affecting timing of brood desertion by female Kentish Plovers *Charadrius alexandrinus*. *Behaviour* **130(1-2)**: 17-28.

Székely, T., Karsai, I. & Williams, T.D. (1994). Determination of clutch-size in the Kentish Plover *Charadrius alexandrinus*. *Ibis* **136(3)**: 341-348.

Székely, T., Kozma, J. & Piti, A. (1994). The volume of Snowy Plover eggs. *J. Field Orn.* **65(1)**: 60-64. In English with Spanish summary.

Szep, T. (1991). The present and historical situation of the Corncrake in Hungary. *Vogelwelt* **112**: 45-48.

Tacha, T.C. (1984). Preflight behavior of Sandhill Cranes. *Wilson Bull.* **96**: 471-477.

Tacha, T.C. (1987). Foraging and maintenance behaviors of Sandhill Cranes. Pp. 93-105 in: Lewis (1987).

Tacha, T.C. & Braun, C.E. eds. (1994). *Management of Migratory Shore and Upland Game Birds in North America*. International Association of Fish & Wildlife Agencies, Washington, D.C.

Tacha, T.C. & Nesbitt, S.A. (1994). Sandhill Crane. Pp. 77-94 in: Tacha & Braun (1994).

Tacha, T.C., Nesbitt, S.A. & Vohs, P.A. (1992). Sandhill Crane (*Grus canadensis*). No. **31** in: Poole *et al.* (1992-1993).

Tacha, T.C., Vohs, P.A. & Warde, W.D. (1985). Morphometric variation of Sandhill Cranes from mid-continental North America. *J. Wildl. Manage.* **49**: 246-250.

Takagi, N. & Sasaki, M. (1980). Unexpected karyotypic resemblance between the Burmeister's Seriema, *Chunga burmeisteri* and the Toucan, *Ramphastos toco*. *Chromosome Inf. Serv.* **28**: 10-11.

Takahasi, T. (1939). On birds of Kaibato Islands and breeding *Cerorhinca monocerata* (Pallas). *Rep. Sakhalin Gov. Mus.* **3(3)**: 159-214.

Takeishi, M. (1987). [The mass mortality of Japanese Murrelet *Synthliboramphus wumizusume* on the Koyashima Islet in Fukuoka]. *Bull. Kitakyushu Mus. Nat. Hist.* **7**: 121-131. In Japanese with English summary.

Takekawa, J.E., Carter, H.R. & Harvey, T.E. (1990). Decline of the Common Murre in central California, 1980-1986. Pp. 149-163 in: Sealy (1990).

Takeshita, M. (1994). [Discovery of a new breeding site of the Roseate Tern *Sterna dougallii* at Miike Island, an artificial island, in Fukuoka Prefecture, southern Japan]. *Strix* **13**: 250-253. In Japanese with English summary.

Takeshita, M., Samoto, K. & Hayashi, O. (1993). [Annual and seasonal changes in the number of wintering Saunder's Gull *Larus saundersi* at the tidal mud flat of Sone in Kitakyusyu City, Fukuoka, Japan]. *Strix* **12**: 107-114. In Japanese.

Tallman, D.A. & Tallman, E.J. (1986). Solitary sandpiper breeding records in northwestern Ontario. *Ontario Birds* **4(3)**: 118-119.

Tallman, D.A., Parker, T.A. & Leiter, G.D. (1978). Notes on 2 species of birds previously unreported from Peru. *Wilson Bull.* **90**: 445-446.

Tallman, D.A., Tallman, E.J. & Pearson, D.L. (1977). *The Birds of Limonocha, Napo Province, Ecuador*. Instituto Lingüístico de Verano, Quito.

Talpeanu, M. (1963). Données sur la biologie de *Glareola pratincola pratincola* (L.) et *Motacilla flava feldegg* Mich. (Aves). *Trav. Mus. Hist. Nat. "Grigore Antipa"* **4**: 401-415.

Talposh, V.C. (1977). [Nesting of the Whiskered Tern *Chlidonias hybridus* in the Western Ukraine]. *Bull. Zool., Moscow* **4**: 83-86. In Russian.

Tamar, H. (1983). A Killdeer incubates stones. *Indiana Audubon Quarterly* **61(1)**: 2-3.

Tan Yaokuang (1983). [*The Red-Crowned Crane,* Grus japonensis]. China Pictorial Press. In Chinese.

Tanaka, S. & Lida, T. (1991). [The protection of nesting Grey-headed Lapwings *Microsarcops cinereus* by lifting up and moving their nest]. *Strix* **10**: 229-238. In Japanese with English summary.

Tang Xiyang (1984). [The world's largest flock of White Cranes *Grus leucogeranus* discovered at Poyang Lake (Jiangxi Province)]. *Da Ziran* **2**: 6-10. In Chinese.

Tanner, I. & Jaensch, R. (1988). A Sarus Crane near Karratha, Western Australia. *Austr. Bird Watcher* **12(8)**: 269-270.

Tanner, W.D. & Hendrickson, G.O. (1954). Ecology of the Virginia Rail in Clay County, Iowa. *Iowa Bird Life* **24**: 65-70.

Tanner, W.D. & Hendrickson, G.O. (1956). Ecology of the Sora in Clay County, Iowa. *Iowa Bird Life* **26**: 78-81.

Tarboton, W.R. (1976). Notes on South African jacanas. *Fauna & Flora* **27**: 5-7.

Tarboton, W.R. (1984). The status and conservation of the Wattled Crane in the Transvaal. Pp. 665-678 in: Ledger (1984).

Tarboton, W.R. (1989). Breeding behaviour of Denham's Bustards. *Bustard Studies* **4**: 160-169.

Tarboton, W.R. (1992a). The population status of the Crowned Crane in the Transvaal. Pp. 10-19 in: Porter *et al.* (1992).

Tarboton, W.R. (1992b). Extent and reasons for population declines in South Africa's three crane species. Pp. 117-118 in: Porter *et al.* (1992).

Tarboton, W.R. (1992c). Aspects of the breeding biology of the African Jacana. *Ostrich* **63(4)**: 141-158.

Tarboton, W.R. (1992d). Variability in African Jacana eggs and clutches. *Ostrich* **63(4)**: 158-164.

Tarboton, W.R. (1993). Incubation behaviour of the African Jacana. *S. Afr. J. Zool.* **28(1)**: 32-39.

Tarboton, W.R. (1995). Wattled Cranes in South Africa. *ICF Bugle* **21(3)**: 8.

Tarboton, W.R. & Fry, C.H. (1986). Breeding and other behaviour of the Lesser Jacana. *Ostrich* **57(4)**: 233-243.

Tarboton, W.R. & Johnson, D.N. (1992). Management plan for the conservation of the Wattled Crane in South Africa, 1982. Pp. 127-131 in: Porter *et al.* (1992).

Tarboton, W.R. & Nel, F. (1980). On the occurrence of the White-crowned Plover in the Kruger National Park. *Bokmakierie* **32(1)**: 19-21.

Tarboton, W.R., Barnes, P.R. & Johnson, D.N. (1987). The Wattled Crane in South Africa during 1978-1982. Pp. 353-361 in: Archibald & Pasquier (1987a).

Tarboton, W.R., Kemp, M.I. & Kemp, A.C. (1987). *Birds of the Transvaal*. Transvaal Museum, Pretoria.

Tarburton, M.K. (1981). Seabirds nesting at Norfolk Island. *Notornis* **28(3)**: 209-211.

Tarburton, M.K. (1984). Chick feeding and attendance in the White Tern. *Notornis* **31(1)**: 86-89.

Tarburton, M.K. (1987). Migration and breeding strategies of the Black Noddy, Fiji. *Emu* **87**: 50-52.

Tarburton, M.K. (1989). Feeding behavior of the Black-fronted Dotterel. *Notornis* **36(4)**: 249-259.

Tarsnane, S. (1981). The artificial incubation and hand-rearing of two East African Crowned Cranes. *Ratel* **8(3)**: 15-17.

Tasker, C.R. & Mills, J.A. (1981). A functional analysis of courtship feeding in the Red-billed Gull, *Larus novaehollandiae scopulinus*. *Behaviour* **77**: 221-241.

Tasker, M. (1994). Common Gull. *Larus canus*. Pp. 288-289 in: Tucker & Heath (1994).

Tasker, M.L. ed. (1988). *Seabird Food and Feeding Ecology*. Nature Conservancy Council, Aberdeen.

Tasker, M.L., Jones, P.H., Blake, B.F. & Dixon, T.J. (1985). Distribution and feeding habits of the Great Skua *Catharacta skua* in the North Sea. *Seabird* **8**: 34-43.

Tasker, M.L., Webb, A., Hall, A.J., Pienkowski, M.W. & Langslow, D.R. (1987). *Seabirds in the North Sea*. Nature Conservancy Council, Peterborough, UK.

Tatner, P. & Bryant, D.M. (1993). Interspecific variation in daily energy expenditure during avian incubation. *J. Zool., London* **231**: 215-232.

Taverner, J.H. (1965). Observations on breeding Sandwich and Common Terns. *British Birds* **58**: 5-9.

Taverner, J.H. (1969). Further observations on the breeding behaviour of Sandwich Terns. *Seabird Report* **1969**: 46-47.

Taverner, J.H. (1976). Voice, behavior and display of Mediterranean gulls. *British Birds* **69**: 4-8.

Taverner, J.H. (1982). Feeding behaviour of Spotted Redshank flocks. *British Birds* **75**: 333-334.

Taylor, C. & Harper, D. (1988). The feeding ecology of the African Lily Trotter *Actophilornis africanus* (Gmelin) at Lake Naivasha, Kenya. *Afr. J. Ecol.* **26**: 329-335.

Taylor, I.R. (1979). The kleptoparasitic behaviour of the Arctic Skua *Stercorarius parasiticus* with three species of tern. *Ibis* **121**: 274-282.

Taylor, I.R. (1983). Effects of wind on the foraging behaviour of Common and Sandwich Terns. *Ornis Scand.* **14**: 90-96.

Taylor, K. (1985). Great Black-backed Gull *Larus marinus* predation of seabird chicks on three Scottish islands. *Seabird* **8**: 45-52.

Taylor, N. (1992). Crowned Crane observations. *Promerops* **202**: 11.

Taylor, P. (1993a). Migration of Bonaparte's Gull *Larus philadelphia* in southeastern Manitoba. *Can. Field-Nat.* **107**: 314-318.

Taylor, P. (1993b). Mid-continental jaegers: a Manitoba perspective. *Blue Jay* **51(3)**: 157-164.

Taylor, P.B. (1977). Great Sandplover (*Charadrius leschenaultii*) at Ndola. *Bull. Zambia Orn. Soc.* **9(2)**: 67-68.

Taylor, P.B. (1978). Mongolian Plover (*Charadrius mongolus*) at Ndola. *Bull. Zambia Orn. Soc.* **10(2)**: 79-80.

Taylor, P.B. (1979). Palaearctic and intra-African migrant birds in Zambia: a report for the period May 1971 to December 1976. *Zambian Orn. Soc. Occas. Pap.* **1**.

Taylor, P.B. (1980a). The field separation of Common, Ethiopian and Great Snipe *Gallinago gallinago*, *G. nigripennis* and *G. media*. *Scopus* **4(1)**: 1-5.

Taylor, P.B. (1980b). Pectoral Sandpiper *Calidris melanotos* and Lesser Yellowlegs *Tringa flavipes* in Zambia. *Bull. Brit. Orn. Club* **100**: 233-235.

Taylor, P.B. (1980c). Little Crake *Porzana parva* at Ndola, Zambia. *Scopus* **4**: 93-95.

Taylor, P.B. (1981a). Field characters and habitat preferences of Great Snipe and Snipe. *Dutch Birding* **3(2)**: 52-54.

Taylor, P.B. (1981b). First East African record of the Red-necked Stint *Calidris ruficollis*. *Scopus* **5(4)**: 126-127.

Taylor, P.B. (1982a). Field identification of sand plovers in East Africa. *Dutch Birding* **4(4)**: 113-130.

Taylor, P.B. (1982b). First Zambian records of Chestnut-banded Sandplover *Charadrius pallidus* and observations of White-fronted Sandplovers *C. marginatus* and Cape Teal *Anas capensis* at the same locality. *Bull. Brit. Orn. Club* **102(1)**: 5-7.

Taylor, P.B. (1982c). Further records of Slender-billed Gull *Larus genei* at Lake Turkana. *Scopus* **6**: 22-23.

Taylor, P.B. (1982d). Leg colour of sand plovers. *Dutch Birding* **4(4)**: 139-140.

Taylor, P.B. (1983). Field identification of sand plovers in East Africa. *Dutch Birding* **5(2-3)**: 37-66.

Taylor, P.B. (1984a). A field study of the Corncrake *Crex crex* at Ndola, Zambia. *Scopus* **8**: 53-59.

Taylor, P.B. (1984b). Field identification of Pintail Snipe and recent records in Kenya. *Dutch Birding* **6**: 77-90.

Taylor, P.B. (1985a). Field studies of the African Crake *Crex egregia* in Zambia and Kenya. *Ostrich* **56**: 170-185.

Taylor, P.B. (1985b). Observations of Allen's Gallinule at Mombasa, Kenya. *Malimbus* **7**: 141-150.

Taylor, P.B. (1987). A field study of the Spotted Crake *Porzana porzana* at Ndola, Zambia. *Ostrich* **58**: 107-117.

Taylor, P.B. (1988). The distribution, status, movements and habitat of Jack Snipe and Pintail Snipe in Africa. Pp. 7-11 in: Havet & Hirons (1988).

Taylor, P.B. (1994). *The Biology, Ecology and Conservation of Four Flufftail Species,* Sarothrura *(Aves: Rallidae)*. PhD thesis, University of Natal, Pietermaritzburg, South Africa.

Taylor, P.B. & Hustler, K. (1993). The southern African specimen of the Longtoed Flufftail *Sarothrura lugens*: a case of misidentification. *Ostrich* **64**: 38-40.

Taylor, P.B. & Taylor, C.A. (1986). Field studies of forest flufftails (*Sarothrura* species) in Kenya. Unpublished MS. Nairobi, Kenya.

Taylor, P.B., Smith, E.P. & Herholdt, J.J. (1994). The Striped Crake in southern Africa. *Birding in SA* **46**: 18-21.

Taylor, P.W. (1988). A Plains-wanderer near Nantawarra. *S. Austr. Orn.* **30(6)**: 165.

Taylor, R.C. (1974). A method for sexing adult Ringed Plovers *Charadrius hiaticula* L. in summer plumage. *Wader Study Group Bull.* **11**: 15-17.

Taylor, R.C. (1978). *Geographical Variation in the Ringed Plover* Charadrius hiaticula. PhD dissertation, Liverpool Polytechnic, Liverpool.

Taylor, R.C. (1979). Moult of the Long-billed Ringed Plover *Charadrius placidus*. *Bull. Brit. Orn. Club* **99(3)**: 98-102.

Taylor, R.C. (1980). Migration of the Ringed Plover *Charadrius hiaticula*. *Ornis Scand.* **11**: 30-42.

Taylor, R.H. (1979). Predation on Sooty Terns at Raoul Island by rats and cats. *Notornis* **26(2)**: 199-202.

Taylor, R.H. & Wodzicki, K. (1958). Black-backed Gull - a Gannet predator. *Notornis* **8**: 22-23.

Taylor, R.J. & Mooney, N.J. (1991). Increased mortality of birds on an elevated section of highway in northern Tasmania. *Emu* **91**: 186-188.

Teague, G.W. (1955). Observaciones sobre las aves indígenas y migratorias del orden Charadriiformes (chorlos, gaviotas, gaviotines y sus congéneres) que frecuentan las costas y esteros del litoral del Uruguay. *Com. Zool. Mus. Hist. Nat. Montevideo* **4**: 1-58.

Tehsin, R.H. & Lokhandwala, J. (1982). Unusual nesting of Redwattled Lapwing (*Vanellus indicus*). *J. Bombay Nat. Hist. Soc.* **79(2)**: 414.

Teixeira, D.M. & Puga, M.E.M. (1984). Notes on the Speckled Crake (*Coturnicops notata*) in Brazil. *Condor* **86**: 342-343.

Teixeira, D.M., Méndez, M.E. & Nacinovic, J.B. (1983). [Notes on the biology of the Great Snipe *Gallinago undulata undulata* (Temminck 1826)]. *An. Soc. Sul-Rio Grand. Orn.* **4**: 7-9. In Portuguese with English summary.

Teixeira, D.M., Nacinovic, J.B. & Luigi, G. (1989). Notes on some birds of northeastern Brazil (4). *Bull. Brit. Orn. Club* **109**: 152-157.

Teixeira, D.M., Nacinovic, J.B. & Tavares, M.S. (1986). Notes on some birds of northeastern Brazil. *Bull. Brit. Orn. Club* **106**: 70-74.

Tejedor, O. (1986). Aves nuevas para la avifauna española. Correlimos Zancolín (*Micropalama himantopus*). [New birds for Spanish avifauna. Stilt Sandpiper (*Micropalama himantopus*)]. *Garcilla* **67**: 32-35.

Telfer, T.C. & Shisler, J.K. (1981). Record of movement of a Laughing Gull to Hawaii from New Jersey. *J. Field Orn.* **52**: 340-341.

Temme, M. (1974). New records of Philippine birds on the island of Mindoro. *Bonn. zool. Beitr.* **25**: 292-296.

Temme, M. (1991). Ein weiteres Brutvorkommen der Rotbrust-Brachschwalbe *Glareola maldivarum* auf den Philippinen. [Further breeding and sight records of the pratincole *Glareola maldivarum* in the Philippines]. *Beitr. Vogelkd.* **37(1-2)**: 61-64.

Temple, S. ed. (1979). *Red Data Book*. Vol 2. Aves. IUCN, Morges, Switzerland.

TenBrink, J. (1993). Mountain Plovers (*Charadrius montanus*) nesting north of Byers, Colorado. *Colorado Field Orn. J.* **27(4)**: 165-166.

Terborgh, J. & Weske, J.S. (1972). Rediscovery of the Imperial Snipe in Peru. *Auk* **89(3)**: 497-505.

Terres, J.K. (1982). *The Audubon Society Encyclopedia of North American Birds*. Alfred Knopf, New York.

Terrill, L.M. (1943). Nesting habits of the Yellow Rail in Gaspé County, Quebec. *Auk* **60**: 171-180.

Tessen, D.D. (1991). Purple Sandpiper (*Calidris maritima*), 25 November 1990, Sheboygan Co., near Sheboygan Pt. Along lakeshore. *Passenger Pigeon* **53(2)**: 193-194.

van Tets, G.F. & Fullagar, P.J. (1984). Status of seabirds breeding in Australia. Pp. 559-571 in: Croxall, Evans & Schreiber (1984).

van Tets, G.F., D'Andria, A.H. & Slater, E. (1967). Nesting distribution and nomenclature of Australasian Vanelline plovers. *Emu* **67**: 85-93.

Teyssèdre, A. (1984). Comparaison acoustique de *Larus argentatus argentatus*, *L. fuscus graellsii*, *L. cachinnans (?) michahellis* et du Goéland argenté à pattes jaunes Cantabrique. *Behaviour* **88**: 13-23.

von Thanner, R. (1908). Auf der Suche nach dem Austernfischer (*Haematopus niger* Meade-Waldo [sic]). *Orn. Jahrb.* **24**: 189-193.

Theiss, N., Franz, D. & Glätzer, G. (1992). [The developments of a local population of the Common Sandpiper *Actitis hypoleucos* in the Upper Valley of the River Main between 1981 and 1991]. *Orn. Anz.* **31(1/2)**: 43-49. In German with English summary.

Thelle, T. (1970). Traekket af Strandkade (*Haematopus ostralegus*) fre Vestnorge til Vadehavet. *Dan. Orn. Foren. Tidssk.* **64**: 229-247.

Thévenot, M. (1989). [Wintering of Slender-billed Curlew *Numenius tenuirostris* Vieillot in Morocco]. *Alauda* **57(1)**: 47-59. In French with English summary.

Thibault, J.C. (1973). Notes ornithologiques polynésiennes. I. Les Isles Gambier. *Alauda* **41**: 111-119.

Thibault, J.C. (1988). Menaces et conservation des oiseaux de Polynésie Française. Pp. 87-124 in: Thibault & Guyot (1988).

Thibault, J.C. & Guyot, I. eds. (1988). *Livre Rouge des Oiseaux Menacés des Regions Françaises d'Outre-Mer*. ICBP Monograph **5**. Saint-Claude, France.

Thibault, M. & McNeil, R. (1994). Day/night variation in habitat use by Wilson's Plovers in northeastern Venezuela. *Wilson Bull.* **106(2)**: 299-310.

Thibault, M. & McNeil, R. (1995a). Day- and night-time parental investment by incubating Wilson's Plovers in a tropical environment. *Can. J. Zool.* **73**: 879-886.

Thibault, M. & McNeil, R. (1995b). Predator prey relationship between Wilson Plovers and fiddler crabs in north-eastern Venezuela. *Wilson Bull.* **107**: 73-80.

Thiede, U. (1982). "Yambaru Kuina" (*Rallus okinawae*), eine neu entdeckte Rallenart in Japan. *Vogelwelt* **103**: 143-150.

Thing, H. (1976). Field notes on birds in Thule District, Greenland, 1975. *Dan. Orn. Foren. Tidssk.* **70**: 141-143.

Thingstad, P.G. (1978). Expansion of a wintering population of Oystercatchers in Nord Trondelag, Norway. *Var. Fuglejanna* **1**: 66 68.

Thiollay, J.M. (1985). The birds of Ivory Coast. *Malimbus* **7(1)**: 1-59.

Thiollay, J.M. (1988). Les oiseaux menacés de Guyane. Pp. 61-80 in: Thibault & Guyot (1988).

Thiollay, J.M. (1989). Étude et conservation du Cagou (*Rhynochetos jubatus*). Unpublished report to CNRS/SRETIE, Paris.

Thomas, B.T. (1979). The birds of a ranch in the Venezuelan llanos. Pp. 213-232 in: Eisenberg, J.F. ed. (1979). *Vertebrate Ecology in the Northern Neotropics*. Smithsonian Institution Press, Washington, D.C.

Thomas, B.T. (1987). Spring shorebird migration through central Venezuela. *Wilson Bull.* **99**: 571-578.

Thomas, B.T. & Ingels, J. (1995). On the type specimen, type locality, distribution and clutch size of the Sunbittern *Eurypyga helias* (Pallas 1781). *Bull. Brit. Orn. Club* **115(4)**: 226-228.

Thomas, B.T. & Strahl, S.D. (1990). Nesting behavior of Sunbitterns (*Eurypyga helias*) in Venezuela. *Condor* **95(2)**: 576-581.

Thomas, C.J., Thompson, D.B.A. & Galbraith, H. (1989). Physiognomic variation in Dotterel *Charadrius morinellus* clutches. *Ornis Scand.* **20(2)**: 145-150.

Thomas, C.S. (1983). The relationship between breeding experience, egg volume and reproductive success of the Kittiwake *Rissa tridactyla*. *Ibis* **125**: 567-574.

Thomas, C.S. & Coulson, J.C. (1988). Reproductive success of Kittiwake Gulls, *Rissa tridactyla*. Pp. 251-262 in: Clutton-Brock, T.H. ed. (1988). *Reproductive Success*. The University of Chicago Press, Chicago, Illinois.

Thomas, D. (1970). Wader migration across Australia. *Emu* **70**: 145-154.

Thomas, D. ed. (1989). Regular wader counts project report: Red-necked Avocet. *Stilt* **14**: 21-32.

Thomas, D.G. (1968). Waders of Hobart. *Emu* **68**: 95-125.

Thomas, D.G. (1969). Breeding biology of the Australian Spur-winged Plover. *Emu* **69**: 81-102.

Thomas, D.G. (1972). Moult of the Banded Dotterel (*Charadrius bicinctus*) in winter quarters. *Notornis* **19(1)**: 33-35.

Thomas, D.G. (1979). *Tasmanian Bird Atlas*. Vol. 2. Fauna of Tasmania. University of Tasmania, Hobart.

Thomas, D.G. (1987). The weights of Red-necked and Little Stints. *Stilt* **11**: 36-39.

Thomas, D.G. & Dartnall, A.J. (1970). Pre-migratory deposition of fat in the Red-necked Stint. *Emu* **70**: 87.

Thomas, D.G. & Dartnall, A.J. (1971a). Ecological aspects of the feeding behaviour of two calidritine sandpipers wintering in south-eastern Tasmania. *Emu* **71**: 20-26.

Thomas, D.G. & Dartnall, A.J. (1971b). Moult of the Red-necked Stint. *Emu* **71(2)**: 49-53.

Thomas, D.G. & Dartnall, A.J. (1971c). Moult of the Curlew Sandpiper in relation to its annual cycle. *Emu* **71**: 153-158.

Thomas, D.H. (1983). Aposematic behaviour in the Blacksmith Plover. *Ostrich* **54(1)**: 51-52.

Thomas, D.K. & Elliott, H.F.I. (1973). Nesting of the Roseate Tern (*Sterna dougallii*) near Dar es Salaam. *Bull. Brit. Orn. Club* **93**: 21-23.

Thomas, G.J. (1980). European status and distribution of the Little Tern *Sterna albifrons*. Pp. 6-10 in: Everett, M.J. ed. (1980). *Proceedings of a Symposium on Little Terns* Sterna albifrons. Royal Society for Bird Protection, Sandy, UK.

Thomas, G.J., Underwood, L.A. & Partridge, J.K. (1989). Breeding Terns in Britain and Ireland 1980-1984. *Seabird* **12**: 20-31.

Thomas, P.O. (1988). Kelp Gulls, *Larus dominicanus* are parasites on flesh of the right whale, *Eubalaena australis*. *Ethology* **79**: 89-103.

Thomas, T. (1983). Donées récentes sur l'avifaune des Kerguelen. *Oiseau et RFO* **53**: 133-141.

Thompson, A.L. (1943). The migration of the Sandwich Tern. *British Birds* **37**: 62-69.

Thompson, B.C. & Slack, R.D. (1982). Physical aspects of colony selection by Least Terns on the Texas coast. *Colonial Waterbirds* **5**: 161-168.

Thompson, B.C. & Slack, R.D. (1984). Post-fledging departure from colonies by juvenile Least Terns in Texas: implications for estimating production. *Wilson Bull.* **96**: 309-313.

Thompson, B.C., Schmidt, M.E., Calhoun, S.W., Morizot, D.C. & Slack, R.D. (1992). Subspecific status of Least Tern populations in Texas: North American implications. *Wilson Bull.* **104**: 244-262.

Thompson, D.B.A. (1983). Prey assessment by plovers (Charadriidae): net rate of energy intake and vulnerability to kleptoparasites. *Anim. Behav.* **31**: 1226-1236.

Thompson, D.B.A. & Barnard, C.J. (1983). Anti-predator responses in mixed species associations of Lapwings, Golden Plovers and gulls. *Anim. Behav.* **31(2)**: 585-593.

Thompson, D.B.A. & Barnard, C.J. (1984). Prey selection by plovers: optimal foraging in mixed species groups. *Anim. Behav.* **32**: 554-563.

Thompson, D.B.A. & Lendrem, D.W. (1985). Gulls and plovers: host vigilance, kleptoparasite success and a model of kleptoparasite detection. *Anim. Behav.* **33(4)**: 1318-1324.

Thompson, D.B.A., Thompson, P.S. & Nethersole-Thompson, D. (1986). Timing of breeding and breeding performance in a population of Greenshanks (*Tringa nebularia*). *J. Anim. Ecol.* **55(1)**: 181-200.

Thompson, D.B.A., Thompson, P.S. & Nethersole-Thompson, D. (1988). Fidelity and philopatry in breeding Redshanks (*Tringa totanus*) and Greenshanks (*Tringa nebularia*). Pp. 563-574 in: *Proc. XIX Int. Orn. Congr.* Ottawa, 1986.

Thompson, D.R., Hamer, K.C. & Furness, R.W. (1991). Mercury accumulation in Great Skuas *Catharacta skua* of known age and sex, and its effects upon breeding and survival. *J. Appl. Ecol.* **28(2)**: 672-684.

Thompson, J. (1990). The sex and age-related distribution of Bar-tailed Godwit in Moreton Bay, Queensland, during the northward migration. *Emu* **90**: 169-174.

Thompson, M.C. (1973). Migratory patterns of Ruddy Turnstones in the Central Pacific. *Living Bird* **12**: 5-23.

Thompson, P.M. & Evans, M.I. eds. (1991). *A Survey of Ambatovaky Special Reserve, Madagascar*. Madagascar Environmental Research Group, London.

Thompson, P.M. & Evans, M.I. (1992). The threatened birds of Ambatovaky Special Reserve, Madagascar. *Bird Conserv. Int.* **2**: 221-237.

Thompson, P.M., Harvey, W.G., Johnson, D.L., Millin, D.J., Rashid, S.M.A., Scott, D.A., Stanfield, C. & Woolner, J.D. (1993). Recent notable bird records from Bangladesh. *Forktail* **9**: 13-44.

Thompson, P.S. & Hale, W.G. (1989). Breeding site fidelity and natal philopatry in the Redshank *Tringa totanus*. *Ibis* **131**: 214-224.

Thompson, P.S. & Hale, W.G. (1991). Age-related reproductive variation in the Redshank *Tringa totanus*. *Ornis Scand.* **22**: 353-359.

Thompson, P.S. & Hale, W.G. (1993). Adult survival and numbers in a coastal breeding population of Redshank *Tringa totanus* in northwest England. *Ibis* **135**: 61-69.

Thompson, P.S. & Thompson, D.B.A. (1991). Greenshanks *Tringa nebularia* and long-term studies of breeding waders. *Ibis* **133(1)**(Suppl.): 99-112.

Thompson, P.S., Baines, D., Coulson, J.C. & Longrigg, G. (1994). Age at first breeding, philopatry and breeding site-fidelity in the Lapwing *Vanellus vanellus*. *Ibis* **136(4)**: 474-484.

Thompson, P.S., McCarty, C. & Hale, W.G. (1990). Growth and development of Redshank *Tringa totanus* chicks on the Ribble saltmarshes, N.W. England. *Ringing & Migration* **11**: 57-64.

Thompson, S.P., McDermond, D.K., Wilson, U.W. & Montgomery, K. (1985). Rhinoceros Auklet burrow count on Protection Island, Washington. *Murrelet* **66**: 62-65.

Thomsen, P. & Jacobsen, P. (1979). *The Birds of Tunisia*. Nature-Travels, Copenhagen, Denmark.

Thomson, D.L. (1994). Growth and development in Dotterel chicks *Charadrius morinellus*. *Bird Study* **41(1)**: 61-67.

Thonnerieux, Y., Walsh, J.F. & Bortoli, L. (1989). L'avifaune de la ville d'Ouagadougou et ses environs (Burkina Faso). *Malimbus* **11**: 7-40.

Thorenson, A.C. (1983). Diurnal activity and social displays of Rhinoceros Auklets on Teuri Island, Japan. *Condor* **85**: 373-375.

Thoresen, A. (1960). *Breeding Behavior and Growth Rates of Cassin's Auklet* Ptychoramphus aleuticus, *Pallas*. PhD thesis, Oregon State University, Corvallis, Oregon.

Thoresen, A.C. (1964). The breeding behavior of the Cassin Auklet. *Condor* **66**: 456-476.

Thoresen, A.C. (1984). Breeding phenology and mid-seasonal social behaviour of the Sooty Guillemot on Teuri Island, Japan. *Western Birds* **15**: 145-160.

Thoresen, A.C. (1989). Diving times and behavior of Pigeon Guillemots and Marbled Murrelets off Rosario Head, Washington. *Western Birds* **20**: 33-37.

Thoresen, A.C. & Booth, E.S. (1958). Breeding activities of the Pigeon Guillemot *Cepphus columba columba* (Pallas). *Walla Walla Coll. Publ.* **23**: 1-36.

Tian Xiuhua, Bai Xiaojie & Li Shuxiu (1992). [Captive breeding of the White-naped Crane]. *Chinese Wildlife* **3**: 51-53. In Chinese.
Tibor, H. (1993). First observation of the Greater Sand Plover (*Charadrius leschenaultii*) in Hungary. *Aquila* **100**: 298-300.
Ticehurst, C.B. (1924). The birds of Sind. *Ibis* **Ser. 11, no. 6**: 110-146.
Ticehurst, C.B. (1929). The downy young of *Heliopais personata*. *Bull. Brit. Orn. Club* **49**: 65-66.
Ticehurst, C.B. (1933). The breeding of *Rhodostethia rosea* in Greenland. *Ibis* **Ser. 13, no. 3**: 785-786.
Ticehurst, C.B., Buxton, R.A. & Cheesman, R.E. (1922). The birds of Mesopotamia. *J. Bombay Nat. Hist. Soc.* **28**: 210-250, 381-427, 650-674, 937-956.
Ticehurst, C.B., Cox, P. & Cheesman, R.E. (1926). Additional notes on the birds of Iraq. *J. Bombay Nat. Hist. Soc.* **31**: 91-119.
Tiedemann, R. (1992). The spring migration of the Knot through south-east Iceland. Pp. 114-117 in: Piersma & Davidson (1992b).
Tikhonov, A.V. & Fokin, S.Y. (1980). [Acoustic signalization and the behaviour of Woodcock in early ontogenis. II. The signalization and the behaviour of nestlings]. *Biologicheskie Nauki* **10**: 45-54. In Russian.
Tilba, P.A. (1990). [On the migration of the Dotterel (*Charadrius morinellus*) in Krasnodar region]. *Ornitologiya* **24**: 163-164. In Russian with English summary.
Tima, C.B. (1961). The composition of the food of Gulls in Latvia. Pp. 123-128 in: Lusis, Y.Y., Spurin, Z.D., Taurins, E.J. & Vilka, E.K. eds. (1961). *Birds of the Baltic Region: Ecology and Migrations*. (English translation 1968). Israel Program for Scientific Translations, Jerusalem.
Timmermann, G. (1954-1955). Die verwandtschaftlichen Beziehungen einiger Watvogelgruppen im Lichte der vergleichenden Parasitologie. Pp. 356-361 in: *Proc. XI Int. Orn. Congr.* Basel, 1954.
Timmis, W.H. (1974). The breeding and behaviour of Blue-breasted Banded Rail. *Avicult. Mag.* **80**: 125-131.
Tinarelli, R. (1987a). Wintering biology of the Black-winged Stilt in the Mahgreb region. *Wader Study Group Bull.* **50**: 30-34.
Tinarelli, R. (1987b). Aspetti della biologia invernale dell'Avocetta *Recurvirostra avosetta* in alcune zone umide costiere del nord Adriatico. *Avocetta* **11**: 37-45.
Tinarelli, R. (1990). [*Results of a National Survey on the Black-winged Stilt in Italy*]. Ricerche di Biologia della Selvaggina **87**. In Italian with English summary. 102 pp.
Tinarelli, R. (1992a). Habitat preference and breeding performance of the Black-winged Stilt *Himantopus himantopus* in Italy. *Wader Study Group Bull.* **65**: 58-62.
Tinarelli, R. (1992b). [The wintering of Black-winged Stilts, *Himantopus himantopus*, in the inner delta of Niger (Mali)]. *Riv. ital. Orn.* **62(3-4)**: 105-115. In Italian with English summary.
Tinarelli, R. (1993a). Some aspects of the wintering ecology of the Black-winged Stilt, *Himantopus himantopus*, in the inner Delta of Niger (Mali). *Riv. ital. Orn.* **63(1)**: 3-9.
Tinarelli, R. (1993b). The Kentish Plover project in Italy: report for 1992. *Wader Study Group Kentish Plover Project Newsl.* **2**: 15-18.
Tinbergen, N. (1931). Zur Paarungsbiologie der Flußseeschwalbe (*Sterna h. hirundo* L.). *Ardea* **20**: 1-17.
Tinbergen, N. (1935). Field observations of east Greenland birds. 1. The behaviour of the Red-necked Phalarope (*Phalaropus lobatus* L.) in spring. *Ardea* **24**: 1-42.
Tinbergen, N. (1938). Erganzende Beobachtungen über die Paarbildung der Flußseeschwalbe (*Sterna h. hirundo* L.). *Ardea* **27**: 247-249.
Tinbergen, N. (1940). Die Übersprungbewegung. *Z. Tierpsychol.* **4**: 1-40.
Tinbergen, N. (1953). *The Herring Gull's World*. Collins, New Naturalist, London.
Tinbergen, N. (1956). On the functions of territory in gulls. *Ibis* **98**: 401-411.
Tinbergen, N. (1959). Comparative studies of the behavior of gulls (Laridae) a progress report. *Behaviour* **15**: 1-70.
Tinbergen, N. (1960). The evolution of behaviour in gulls. *Scientific American* **203(6)**.
Tinbergen, N. (1964). On adaptive radiation in gulls (Tribe Larini). *Zool. Med.* **39**: 209-223.
Tinbergen, N. (1967). Adaptive features of the Black-headed Gull *Larus ridibundus*. Pp. 43-59 in: *Proc. XIV Int. Orn. Congr.* Oxford, 1966.
Tinbergen, N. & Broekhuysen, G.J. (1954). On the threat and courtship behavior of Hartlaub's Gull. *Ostrich* **25**: 50-61.
Tinbergen, N. & Moynihan, M. (1952). Head flagging in the Black-headed Gull; its function and origin. *British Birds* **45**: 19-22.
Tinbergen, N. & Norton Griffiths, M. (1964). Oystercatchers and mussels. *British Birds* **57**: 64 70.
Tinbergen, N., Broekhuysen, G.J., Feekes, F., Houghton, J.C.W. Kruuk, H. & Szulc, E. (1962). Egg shell removal by the Black-headed Gull, *Larus ridibundus* L; a behavior component of camouflage. *Behaviour* **19**: 74-117.
Tinbergen, N., Impekoven, M. & Frank, D. (1967). An experiment on spacing-out as a defense against predation. *Behaviour* **28**: 307-321.
Tinbergen, N., Kruuk, H. & Paillette, M. (1962). Egg shell removal by Black-headed Gull (*Larus r. ridibundus*) L. II. The effects of experience on the response to colour. *Bird Study* **9**: 123-131.
Tipper, R. (1993). Waders in Hong Kong. *British Birds* **86**: 231-242.
Tjallingii, S.T. (1970). [Census of breeding Avocets in the Netherlands in 1969]. *Levende Nat.* **73**: 222-229, 251-255. In Dutch.
Toba, E. (1989). [Extra-pair copulations in Little Terns *Sterna albifrons*]. *Jap. J. Orn.* **38**: 67-77. In Japanese.
Tobish, T.G. & Isleib, M.E. (1992). The spring season. Alaska region. *Amer. Birds* **46**: 462-465.
Todd, R.L. (1977). Black Rail, Little Black Rail, Black Crake, Farallon Rail (*Laterallus jamaicensis*). In: Sanderson (1977).
Todd, R.L. (1986). *A Saltwater Marsh Hen in Arizona. A History of the Yuma Clapper Rail (*Rallus longirostris yumanensis*)*. Completion Rept. Fed. Aid Proj. W-95-R, Phoenix, Arizona Game & Fish Department, Arizona.
Toland, B. (1992). Use of Forested Spoil Islands by nesting American Oystercatchers in southeast Florida. *J. Field Orn.* **63(2)**: 155-158. In English with Spanish summary.
Toland, B. & Gilbert, T. (1987). Roof nesting by Royal Terns in Vero Beach, Florida. *Florida Field Nat.* **15**: 80-82.
Tolchin, V.A. (1976). Distribution and ecology of the Marsh Sandpiper in central Siberia. *Nauchn. Dokl. Vyssh. Shk. Biol. Nauki* **5**: 42-48.
Tolchin, V.A. (1980). [Spreading of the Far Eastern Curlew (*Numenius madagascariensis*) in East Siberia]. In: Flint (1980a). In Russian.
Tolchin, V.A. (1983). [Distribution and ecology of the Ruff in south eastern Siberia]. *Ekol. Pozvon. Zhivotnykh Vostochnoi Sibiri Irkutsk*: 75-90. In Russian.
Tolchin, V.A. & Melnikov, U. (1974). [Breeding and ecology of the Black-tailed Godwit in eastern Siberia]. *Biologicheskie Nauki* **1974**: 27-30. In Russian.
Tolchin, V.A. & Melnikov, U. (1977). [Nesting habits of the Snipe-billed Godwit, *Limnodromus semipalmatus*, in eastern Siberia]. *Vestnik Zoologii* **43**: 16-19. In Russian.
Tolle, D.A. (1976). A westward extension in the breeding range of the Mountain Plover. *Wilson Bull.* **88(2)**: 358-359.
Tolonen, K.E. (1970). Ring-billed Gull and Laughing Gull catch fish by ploughing and skimming. *Wilson Bull.* **82**: 222-223.
Tomialojc, L. (1994a). Corncrake. *Crex crex*. Pp. 228-229 in: Tucker & Heath (1994).
Tomialojc, L. (1994b). Black-tailed Godwit. *Limosa limosa*. Pp. 272-273 in: Tucker & Heath (1994).
Tomialojc, L. (1994c). Curlew. *Numenius arquata*. Pp. 278-279 in: Tucker & Heath (1994).
Tomialojc, L. (1994d). Caspian Tern. *Sterna caspia*. Pp. 294-295 in: Tucker & Heath (1994).
Tomialojc, L. (1994e). Little Tern. *Sterna albifrons*. Pp. 300-301 in: Tucker & Heath (1994).
Tomialojc, L. (1994f). Whiskered Tern. *Chlidonias hybridus*. Pp. 302-303 in: Tucker & Heath (1994).
Tomialojc, L. (1994g). Black Tern. *Chlidonias niger*. Pp. 304-305 in: Tucker & Heath (1994).
Tomkins, I.R. (1933). Ways of the Black Skimmer. *Wilson Bull.* **45**: 147-151.
Tomkins, I.R. (1941). Foot-washing by the Black Skimmer. *Auk* **58**: 96.
Tomkins, I.R. (1942). Least Tern watering eggs: Gideon Mabbett's query. *Auk* **59**: 308.
Tomkins, I.R. (1947). The oystercatcher of the Atlantic coast of northern America and its relation to oysters. *Wilson Bull.* **59**: 204 208.
Tomkins, I.R. (1951). Method of feeding of the Black Skimmer, *Rynchops nigra*. *Auk* **68(2)**: 236-239.
Tomkins, I.R. (1959). Life history notes on the Least Tern. *Wilson Bull.* **71**: 313-322.
Tomkins, I.R. (1963). Skimmer-like behavior in the Royal and Caspian Terns. *Auk* **80**: 549.
Tomkins, I.R. (1964). Migrations and habitats of the Long-billed Dowitcher on the coast of Georgia and South Carolina. *Wilson Bull.* **76**: 188-189.
Tomkins, I.R. (1965). The Willets of Georgia and South Carolina. *Wilson Bull.* **77**: 151-167.
Tomkovich, P.C. (1986). [Material on the biology of the Ivory Gull on Graham Bell Island (Franz Joseph Land)]. Pp. 34-39 in: Ilicev, V.D. (1986). [*Current Problems of Ornithology*]. All-Union Ornithological Society of Academy of Sciences USSR, Nauka, Moscow. In Russian.
Tomkovich, P.S. (1980a). [Territorial behavior and pair formation of the Little Stint (*Calidris minuta*) during migration]. Pp. 170-172 in: Flint (1980a). In Russian.
Tomkovich, P.S. (1980b). [The biology of the Long-toed Stint (*Calidris subminuta*)]. *Ornitologiya* **15**: 104-110. In Russian.
Tomkovich, P.S. (1982a). Territoriality of some monogamous species of Calidridinae sandpipers. Abstract symposia and poster presentations of XVIII Congress of International Ornithology. 300. Moscow, 1982.
Tomkovich, P.S. (1982b). Sexual dimorphism of the Rock Sandpiper *Calidris ptilocnemis*. *Zoologischeskii Zhurnal* **61(7)**: 1110-1113.
Tomkovich, P.S. (1982c). [Peculiarities of the autumn migration of the Sharp-tailed Sandpiper]. *Byull. Mosk. Ova. Ispyt. Prir. Otd. Biol.* **87(4)**: 56-61. In Russian.
Tomkovich, P.S. (1985a). Sketch of the Purple Sandpiper (*Calidris maritima*) biology of Franz Josef Land. *Ornitologiya* **20**: 3-17.
Tomkovich, P.S. (1985b). [Biology of the Baird's Sandpiper in Chukotka]. *Byull. Mosk. Ova. Ispyt. Prir. Otd. Biol.* **90**: 26-38. In Russian with English summary.
Tomkovich, P.S. (1986). [Population variability of the Red-necked Stint, *Calidris ruficollis* (Charadriidae), within its nesting range]. *Zoologischeskii Zhurnal* **65**: 156-158. In Russian.
Tomkovich, P.S. (1988a). [Breeding relations and partners role in care for nesting in Curlew Sandpipers]. Pp. 180-184 in: [*Studies and Protection of Birds in Northern Ecosystems*]. Far-Eastern Branch, USSR Academy of Sciences, Vladivostok. In Russian.
Tomkovich, P.S. (1988b). [On the originality at breeding biology of Temminck's Stint (*Calidris temminckii*) at the northern limit of its area]. *Ornitologiya* **23**: 188-193. In Russian.
Tomkovich, P.S. (1989). Parental roles and the mating system of the Long-toed Stint *Calidris subminuta*. *Wader Study Group Bull.* **57**: 42-43.
Tomkovich, P.S. (1990). Analysis of the geographical variability in Knot *Calidris canutus* (L.). *Bull. Moscow Soc. Nat. Study (Biol. Section)* **95**: 59-72.
Tomkovich, P.S. (1991a). Factors of variation in the clutch size, egg size and egg weight in Spoon-billed Sandpiper (*Eurynorhynchus pygmaeus*) (Charadriiformes, Scolopacidae). *Zoologischeskii Zhurnal* **70(4)**: 107-112.
Tomkovich, P.S. (1991b). Three-year study of breeding Spoon-billed Sandpiper. *Asian Wetland News* **4**: 17.
Tomkovich, P.S. (1991c). [External morphology of the Spoon-billed Sandpiper (*Eurynorhynchus pygmeus*) at Chukotski Peninsula]. *Ornitologiya* **25**: 135-144. In Russian.
Tomkovich, P.S. (1992a). An analysis of the geographical variability of Knots *Calidris canutus* based on museum skins. Pp. 17-23 in: Piersma & Davidson (1992b).
Tomkovich, P.S. (1992b). Breeding-range and population changes of waders in the former Soviet Union. *British Birds* **85**: 344-365.
Tomkovich, P.S. (1992c). Migration of the Spoon-billed Sandpiper *Eurynorhynchus pygmeus* in the Far East of the Russian Federation. *Stilt* **21**: 29-33.
Tomkovich, P.S. (1992d). Spoon-billed Sandpiper in north-eastern Siberia. *Dutch Birding* **14(2)**: 37-41.
Tomkovich, P.S. (1994a). [Spatial structure of the Spoon-billed Sandpiper (*Eurynorhynchus pygmeus*) population at the breeding grounds]. Pp. 130-148 in: [*Modern Ornithology 1992*]. Nauka, Moscow. In Russian with English summary.
Tomkovich, P.S. (1994b). [Site fidelity and spatial structure of population in the Rock Sandpiper *Calidris ptilocnemis* and Dunlin *Calidris alpina* on Chukotskyi Peninsula]. *Russ. J. Orn.* **3(1)**: 13-30. In Russian with English summary.
Tomkovich, P.S. (1994c). A preliminary report on research on the Great Knot *Calidris tenuirostris* on the breeding grounds. *Stilt* **24**: 29-30.
Tomkovich, P.S. (1995a). Great Knot on Siberian breeding grounds. *Dutch Birding* **17(1)**: 15-17.
Tomkovich, P.S. (1995b). Second report on research on the Great Knot *Calidris tenuirostris* on the breeding grounds. *Stilt* **26**: 58-60.
Tomkovich, P.S. (1995c). Does the wind influence egg fertility? A probable case with Curlew Sandpiper *Calidris ferruginea*. *Wader Study Group Bull.* **77**: 48-49.
Tomkovich, P.S. (1996). *Calidris* sandpipers of north-eastern Siberia. *Dutch Birding* **18(1)**: 11-12.
Tomkovich, P.S. & Fokin, S.Y. (1983). [On the ecology of Temminck's Stint in northeast Siberia]. *Ornitologiya* **18**: 40-56. In Russian with English summary.
Tomkovich, P.S. & Fokin, S.Y. (1984). [Behaviour of Temminck's Stint (*Calidris temminckii*) during the breeding season]. Pp. 208-226 in: Sokolov, V.E. ed. (1984). [*Signalling and Ecology of Mammals and Birds*]. Nauka, Moscow. In Russian.
Tomkovich, P.S. & Morozov, V.V. (1980). [Breeding biology of the Western Sandpiper (*Calidris mauri*) in Chukotka]. Pp. 173-175 in: Flint (1980a). In Russian.
Tomkovich, P.S. & Morozov, V.V. (1994). Some characteristics of fledgling development in Eastern Little Stint *Calidris ruficollis* and Western Sandpiper *Calidris mauri*. *Byull. Mosk. Ova. Ispyt. Prir. Otd. Biol.* **99**: 29-37.
Tomkovich, P.S. & Soloviev, M.Y. (1994). Site fidelity in high arctic breeding waders. *Ostrich* **65**: 174-180.
Tomkovich, P.S., Soloviev, M.Y. & Syroechkowski, E.E. (1994). Birds of arctic tundras of northern Taimyr, Knipovich Bay area. Pp. 41-107 in: Rogacheva, H.V. ed. (1994). *Arctic Tundras of Taimyr and the Kara Sea Islands: Nature, Wildlife and their Conservation*. Institute of Animal Morphology and Ecology, Russian Academy of Sciences, Moscow.
Tomlinson, R.E. & Todd, R.L. (1973). Distribution of two Western Clapper Rail races as determined by responses to taped calls. *Condor* **75**: 177-183.
Tompkins, I.R. (1944). Wilson's Plover in its summer home. *Auk* **61**: 259-269.
Tong Junchang (1986). [Preliminary observation of the Demoiselle Crane in Xianghai Nature Reserve]. Pp. 198-202 in: Ma Yiqing (1986). In Chinese.
Tonni, E.P. & Tambussi, C.P. (1988). Un nuevo Psilopterinae (Aves: Ralliformes) del Mioceno tardío de la Provincia de Buenos Aires, República Argentina. *Ameghiniana* **25(2)**: 155-160.
Took, J.M.E. (1967). Mating behaviour of Kittlitz's Sandplover. *Ostrich* **38(3)**: 199.
Tordoff, H.B. (1962). Age and plumage of the Black Tern. *Kansas Orn. Soc. Bull.* **13**: 7-8.
Torres, B. (1987). *The Ecology of the Hoatzin (*Opisthocomus hoazin*) in Peru*. MSc thesis, Ohio State University, Columbus, Ohio.
Tostain, O. & Dujardin, J.L. (1989). Mise en place d'une aire d'hivernage néotropicale de Laridés holarctiques: *Larus pipixcan*, *L. ridibundus* & *L. fuscus*. *Alauda* **57**: 189-215.
Tostain, O., Dujardin, J.L., Érard, C. & Thiollay, J.M. (1992). *Oiseaux de Guyane*. Société d'Études Ornithologiques, Brunoy, France.
Tovar, F.H. (1965). *Contribución al Comportamiento de las Aves del Litoral Peruano*. Thesis, Universidad Nacional Mayor de San Marcos, Lima.
Tovar, F.H. (1968). Áreas de reproducción y distribución de las aves marinas en el litoral peruano. *Bol. Inst. Mar Perú* **1**: 525-546.
Tovar, F.H. (1974). *Distribución y Frecuencia Estacional de la Avifauna Marina en las Bahías de Paracas e Independencia*. PhD thesis, Universidad Nacional Mayor de San Marcos, Lima.
Tovar, F.H. & Ashmole, N.P. (1970). A breeding record for the Grey-hooded Gull, *Larus cirrocephalus*, on the Peruvian coast. *Condor* **72**: 119-122.
Tove, M. (1993). Field separation of Ring-billed, Mew, Common and Kamchatka Gulls. *Birding* **25**: 386-403.
Townshend, D.J. (1982). The Lazarus syndrome in Grey Plovers. *Wader Study Group Bull.* **34**: 11-12.
Townshend, D.J. (1984). The effects of predation upon shorebird populations in the non-breeding season. *Wader Study Group Bull.* **40**: 51-54.
Townshend, D.J. (1985). Decisions for a lifetime: establishment of spatial defence and movement patterns by juvenile Grey Plovers (*Pluvialis squatarola*). *J. Anim. Ecol.* **54**: 267-274.
Townshend, D.J., Dugan, P.J. & Pienkowski, M.W. (1984). The unsociable plover - use of intertidal areas by Grey Plovers. Pp. 140-159 in: Evans *et al.* (1984).
Tracy, D.M. & Schamel, D. (1988). Male initiation of pair formation in Red Phalaropes. *Wilson Bull.* **100**: 144-146.
Traneving, B. (1993). [Cranes: passage from Spain to Scandinavia]. *Vår Fågelvärld* **52(2)**: 9-12. In Swedish.
Transue, G.J. & Burger, J. (1989). Responses to mate loss by Herring Gulls *Larus argentatus* and Great Black-backed Gulls *Larus marinus*. *Ornis Scand.* **20**: 53-58.
Trapp, J.L. (1979). Variation in summer diet of Glaucous-winged Gulls in western Aleutian Islands: an ecological interpretation. *Wilson Bull.* **91**: 412-419.
Trapp, J.L. (1985). Populations of waterbirds wintering along the Pacific coast of the United States and Canada: patterns of distribution and abundance. Part 1. State and provincial summary. Unpublished report to US Fish & Wildlife Service, Anchorage, Alaska.
Trawoger, E. & Kurz, H. (1986). [The Buff-breasted Sandpiper, *Tryngites subruficollis* in Chiemsee, West Germany]. *Anz. Orn. Ges. Bayern* **25(1)**: 93-95. In German.

Traylor, M.A. (1958). *Birds of Northeastern Peru*. Fieldiana: Zoology **35(5)**. Chicago Natural History Museum.
Tréca, B. (1983). [The influence of drought on the daily rhythm of Ruffs *Philomachus pugnax* in Senegal]. *Malimbus* **5**: 73-77. In French with English summary.
Tréca, B. (1984). La Barge à queue noire (*Limosa limosa*) dans le delta du Sénégal: régime alimentaire, données biometriques, importance économique. *Oiseau et RFO* **54**: 247-262.
Tréca, B. (1993). Water birds and their energy needs in the Senegal delta. *Alauda* **61**: 73-82.
Tréca, B. & Ndiaye, S. (1996). The Black Crowned Cranes in the Senegal Delta. In: Beilfuss *et al.* (1996).
Tree, A.J. (1964). Forbes' Plover *Charadrius forbesi* in the Central Province. *Puku* **2**: 129-130.
Tree, A.J. (1973). Ageing the Kittlitz Plover. *Safring News* **2**: 23-25.
Tree, A.J. (1974). Ageing and sexing the Little Stint. *Safring News* **3**: 31-33.
Tree, A.J. (1978). Little known plovers in Rhodesia. *Honeyguide* **96**: 23.
Tree, A.J. (1979). Biology of the Greenshank in southern Africa. *Ostrich* **50**: 240-251.
Tree, A.J. (1980a). Migration as an ecological adaptation in Central African Charadrii. *Honeyguide* **102**: 16-25.
Tree, A.J. (1980b). Small plover studies in southern Africa. *Safring News* **9(1-2)**: 3-9.
Tree, A.J. (1981a). Age at which Crowned Plover may breed. *Ostrich* **52**: 64.
Tree, A.J. (1981b). Greater and Lesser Yellowlegs in southern Africa. *Bokmakierie* **33**: 44-46.
Tree, A.J. (1982). Greenshank studies. *Safring News* **11**: 18-20.
Tree, A.J. (1987a). Red-winged Pratincoles breeding on Darwendale Dam in 1986. *Honeyguide* **33(1)**: 15-17.
Tree, A.J. (1987b). Further notes on the 1986 Red-winged Pratincole season on Darwendale Dam. *Honeyguide* **33(2)**: 59-60.
Tree, A.J. (1987c). Ringing recoveries and migration of Greenshank between Europe and Africa. *Safring News* **16(2)**: 51-66.
Tree, A.J. & Kieser, J.A. (1982). Field separation of Lesser Yellowlegs and Wood Sandpiper. *Honeyguide* **2**: 40-41.
Tremauville, Y. (1984). [Observation of a Broad-billed Sandpiper]. *Cormoran* **5(2)**: 134. In French with English summary.
von Treuenfels, C.A. (1989). [*Cranes: Birds of Luck*]. Rasch und Röhring Verlag, Hamburg. In German.
Trillmich, F. (1978). Feeding territories and breeding success of South Polar Skuas. *Auk* **95**: 23-33.
Triplet, P. (1989). Sélectivité alimentaire liée à l'age chex l'Huitrier-pie (*Haematopus ostralegus*) consommateur de *Nereis diversicolor* en Baie de Somme. *Gibier Faune Sauvage* **6**: 427-436.
Triplet, P. & Yésou, P. (1994). Winter breeding and distraction display of the Cream-Coloured Courser. *Wader Study Group Bull.* **72**: 32.
Triplet, P., Debacker, F. & Noyon, C. (1987). Origine et distribution des Huitriers-pies *Haematopus ostralegus* repris en France. *Bull. mens. ONC* **116**: 38-43.
Trivelpiece, W. & Volkman, N.J. (1982). Feeding strategies of sympatric South Polar Skuas *Catharacta maccormicki* and Brown Skuas *C. lönnbergi*. *Ibis* **124(1)**: 50-54.
Trivelpiece, W., Ainley, D.G., Fraser, W.R. & Trivelpiece, S.G. (1990). Skua survival. *Nature* **345**: 211-212.
Trivelpiece, W., Butler, R.G. & Volkman, N.J. (1980). Feeding territories of Brown Skuas *Catharacta lonnbergi*. *Auk* **97(4)**: 669-676.
Trolliet, B. & Girard, O. (1991). On the Ruff *Philomachus pugnax* wintering in the Senegal delta. *Wader Study Group Bull.* **62**: 10-12.
Trolliet, B., Girard, O., Fouquet, M., Ibáñez, F., Triplet, P. & Léger, F. (1992). L'effectif de Combattants *Philomachus pugnax* hivernant dans le delta du Sénégal. [The number of Ruff *Philomachus pugnax* wintering in the Senegal delta, west Africa]. *Alauda* **60(3)**: 159-163. In French with English summary.
Trollope, J. (1970). Behaviour notes on the Barred and Andalusian Hemipodes (*Turnix suscitator* and *Turnix sylvatica*). *Avicult. Mag.* **76**: 219-227.
Trotignon, J. (1994). Statut récent des guifettes nichant en France. *Ornithos* **1(1)**: 53-55.
Trounson, D. (1987). *Australia. Land of Birds*. Collins, Sydney.
Troy, D.M. (1989). Marine birds and mammals of Unimak Pass. Pp. 143-150 in: Jarvela, L.E. & Thorsteinson, L.K. eds. (1989). *Proceedings Gulf of Alaska, Cook Inlet, and North Aleutian Basin Information Update Meeting, 7-8 Feb. 1989, Alaska*. Outer Continental Shelf Study, Minerals Management Service 89-0041, Washington, D.C.
Troy, D.M. & Bradstreet, M.S.W. (1991). Marine bird abundance and habitat use. Pp. 51-68 in: Truett, J.C. & Kertell, K. eds. (1991). *Marine Birds and Mammals of the Unimak Pass Area*. LGL Alaska Research Associates, Inc. Final report to the US Department of the Interior, Minerals Management Service, Anchorage, Alaska.
Truffi, G. & Maranini, N. (1989). [Little Ringed Plover, *Charadrius dubius*, breeding in the river-bed of Bisagno Stream, Genoa (Liguria, NW Italy)]. *Riv. ital. Orn.* **59(1-2)**: 102-104. In Italian.
Trull, P. (1988). The Roseate Tern in Massachusetts. *Massachusetts Wildlife* **38**: 22-31.
Truslow, F.K. (1958). Limpkin, the "crying bird" that haunts Florida swamps. *Natl. Geogr.* **113**: 114-121.
Tubbs, C.R. (1991). The population history of Grey Plovers *Pluvialis squatarola* in the Solent, southern England. *Wader Study Group Bull.* **61**: 15-21.
Tubbs, C.R., Tubbs, J.M. & Kirby, J.S. (1992). Dunlin *Calidris alpina alpina* in The Solent, southern England. *Biol. Conserv.* **60**: 15-24.
Tuck, G.S. & Heinzel, H. (1978). *A Field Guide to the Seabirds of Britain and the World*. William Collins Sons & Co. Ltd, London.
Tuck, L.M. (1961). *The Murres: their Distribution, Populations and Biology - a Study of the Genus* Uria. Monograph Series **1**. Canadian Wildlife Service, Ottawa.
Tuck, L.M. (1968). Laughing Gulls (*Larus atricilla*) and Black Skimmers (*Rynchops nigra*) brought to Newfoundland by hurricane. *Bird-Banding* **39**: 200-208.
Tuck, L.M. (1971). The occurrence of Greenland and European birds in Newfoundland. *Bird-Banding* **42**: 184-209.
Tuck, L.M. (1972). *The Snipes: a Study of the Genus* Capella *by Leslie M. Tuck*. Canadian Wildlife Service Monograph Series **5**.
Tucker, G.M. & Heath, M.F. eds. (1994). *Birds in Europe: their Conservation Status*. BirdLife Conservation Series **3**. BirdLife International, Cambridge.
Tucker, G.M., Davies, S.M. & Fuller, R.J. eds. (1994). *The Ecology and Conservation of Lapwings* Vanellus vanellus. Joint Nature Conservation Committee, Peterborough, UK. 33 pp.
Tucker, J.J. (1973). The field identification of White-winged Black Terns and Whiskered Terns in non-breeding dress. *Honeyguide* **74**: 21-23.
Tucker, J.J. (1979). Some Blacksmith Plover biometrics from Zambia. *Bull. Zambia Orn. Soc.* **11(1)**: 38-40.
Tucker, L. (1982). That sheathbill. *British Birds* **75(12)**: 591.
Tuellinhoff, R. & Bergmann, H.H. (1993). Curlew habitats (*Numenius arquata*) in Lower Saxony: preferred and avoided structures in agricultural landscapes. *Vogelwarte* **37(1)**: 1-11.
Tuljapurkar, V.B. (1986). The Yellow-wattled Lapwing. *Sanctuary* **6(2)**: 236-243.
Tull, C.E., Germain, P. & May, A.W. (1972). Mortality of Thick-billed Murres in the west Greenland salmon fishery. *Nature* **237**: 42-44.
Tulloch, L. & Hartwick, E.B. (1978). Size distribution and shell polymorphism of limpets in relation to predation by Black Oystercatchers. *Pacific Seabird Group Bull.* **5(1)**: 34.
Tulp, I. & de Goeij, P. (1991). Hot news from a hot place: feeding ecology studies on Knots and other waders in Broome, northwest Australia, spring 1991. *Stilt* **19**: 24-26.
Tulp, I. & de Goeij, P. (1994). Evaluating wader habitats in Roebuck Bay (north-western Australia) as a springboard for northbound migration in waders, with a focus on Great Knots. *Emu* **94(2)**: 78-95.
Tulp, I., McChesney, S. & de Goeij, P. (1994). Migratory departures of waders from north-western Australia: behaviour, timing and possible migration routes. *Ardea* **82**: 201-221.
Tulp, I., McChesney, S. & de Goeij, P. (1995). Hop, skip or jump revisited: size-related dichotomy of travel strategies in waders migrating from northwestern Australia to East China in spring. *Ardea* **82**: 201-221.
Tunnicliffe, G.A. (1985). High altitude records of Pukeko in the southern Alps. *Notornis* **32**: 81-82.
Tunnicliffe, G.A. & Langlands, P.A. (1990). First record of the Bridled (Brown-winged) Tern (*Sterna anaethetus*) in New Zealand. *Notornis* **37**: 131-139.
Tupiza, A. & Gordillo, J. (1978). El Tero Real (*Himantopus himantopus*) en las Islas Galápagos. [The Black-necked Stilt (*Himantopus himantopus*) in the Galapagos Islands]. *Noticias de Galápagos* **28**: 13-16. In Spanish with English summary.
Turbott, E.G. (1967). *Buller's Birds of New Zealand*. Whitcombe & Tombs, Auckland.
Turbott, E.G. (1970). The Wrybill: a feeding adaptation. *Notornis* **17(1)**: 25-27.
Turbott, E.G. (1990). *Checklist of the Birds of New Zealand*. 3rd edition. Ornithological Society of New Zealand, Wellington.
Turner, D.A. (1981). A note on Bensch's Rail *Monias benschi* from Madagascar. *Bull. Brit. Orn. Club* **101(1)**: 240-241.
Turner, D.A. (1982). The status and distribution of the Arabian Bustard *Otis arabs* in northeastern Africa and its possible occurrence in northern Kenya. *Scopus* **6**: 20-21.
Turner, D.A. & Gerhart, J. (1971). 'Foot-wetting' by incubating African Skimmers *Rynchops flavirostris*. *Ibis* **113(2)**: 244.
Turner, D.A. & Goriup, P.D. (1989). The status of Denham's Bustard in Kenya. *Bustard Studies* **4**: 170-173.
Turpie, J.K. (1994). Why do plovers have a stereotyped behaviour? *Wader Study Group Bull.* **75**: 39.
Turpie, J.K. (1995). Non-breeding territoriality: causes and consequences of seasonal and individual variation in Grey Plover *Pluvialis squatarola* behaviour. *J. Anim. Ecol.* **64**: 429-438.
Turpie, J.K. & Hockey, P.A.R. (1993). Comparative diurnal and nocturnal foraging behaviour and energy intake of premigratory Grey Plovers *Pluvialis squatarola* and Whimbrels *Numenius phaeopus* in South Africa. *Ibis* **135(2)**: 156-165.
Turton, J.M. (1993). A record of Black-tailed Gull (*Larus crassirostris*) at Bang Poo, Thailand. *Nat. Hist. Bull. Siam Soc.* **41(2)**: 141-142.
Twomey, A.C. (1934). Breeding habits of Bonaparte's Gull. *Auk* **51**: 291-296.
Tye, A. (1983). Caspian Tern feeding young in winter quarters. *Malimbus* **5**: 91.
Tyler, S. (1978). Observations on the nesting of Three-banded Plover *Charadrius tricollaris*. *Scopus* **2(2)**: 39-41.
Tyler, S.J. & Ormerod, S.J. (1987). Dietary overlap between Mountain Wagtails *Motacilla clara*, Grey Wagtails *M. cinerea* and Green Sandpipers *Tringa ochropus* in Ethiopia. *Scopus* **11**: 33-37.
Tyrberg, T. (1993). [History of the swedish Crocodile-bird]. *Vår Fågelvärld* **52(7)**: 38-39. In Swedish.
Tyrberg, T. & Hernández, F. (1995). First fossil record of the Great Skua. *Bull. Brit. Orn. Club* **115(3)**: 167-168.
Udvardy, M.D.F. (1960). Movements and concentrations of the Hawaiian Coot on the island of Oahu. *Elepaio* **21**: 20-22.
Udvardy, M.D.F. (1963). Zoogeographical study of the Pacific Alcidae. Pp. 85-111 in: Gressit, J.L. ed. (1963). *Pacific Basin Biography*. Bishop Museum, Honolulu, Hawaii.
Uhlig, R. (1989). Zum Status der Rotflügel-Brachschwalbe (*Glareola pratincola*) in Südosteuropa. *Orn. Mitt.* **41(7)**: 155-159.
Uhlig, R. (1990a). New observations on migration and winter guest status of the Broad-billed Sandpiper, *Limicola falcinellus* (Pont.) in Bulgaria (Aves, Charadriiformes: Scolopacidae). *Faun. Abh.* **17(2)**: 135-140.
Uhlig, R. (1990b). On the migration of the Whimbrel, *Numenius phaeopus*, in Bulgaria. *Zool. Middle East* **4**: 33-38.
Uhlig, R. (1990c). Zum Vorkommen des Terekwasserläufers (*Xenus cinereus*) in Südosteuropa. [On the occurrence of *Xenus cinereus* in southeastern Europe]. *Beitr. Vogelkd.* **36(3/4)**: 234-236.
Uhlig, R. (1990d). Herkunft und Verhältnis der in Mitteleuropa beobachteten Brachschwalben (*Glareola pratincola* u. *Glareola nordmanni*). *Orn. Mitt.* **42(1)**: 17-19.
Uhlig, R. & Baumgart, W. (1995). Distribution and population status of the Stone Curlew, *Burhinus oedicnemus*, in Bulgaria. *Vogelwelt* **116(1)**: 11-17.
Ulbricht, J. (1979). Zur Territorialstruktur einer "Kolonie" des Flußregenpfeifers. [On the territorial structure on a "colony" of Little Ringed Plover]. *Falke* **26(10)**: 351-354.
Ulfstrand, S. (1979). Age and plumage associated differences of behavior among Black-headed Gulls (*Larus ridibundus*): foraging success, conflict, victoriousness and reaction to disturbance. *Oikos* **33**: 160-166.
Ulfvens, J. (1993). Population and colony site dynamics in Black-headed Gulls *Larus ridibundus* breeding on the Finnish West Coast. *Ornis Fenn.* **70**: 96-101.
Ullman, M. (1991). Distinguishing Demoiselle Crane from Crane. *Dutch Birding* **13(3)**: 90-93.
Ullman, M. (1994). [Field identification of the Common Pratincole in flight]. *Vår Fågelvärld* **53(4)**: 28-30. In Swedish.
Ulrich, T.J. (1984). *Birds of the Northern Rockies*. Mountain Press Publishing Company, Missoula, Montana.
Underhill, L.G. (1987). Changes in the age structure of Curlew Sandpiper populations at Langebaan Lagoon, South Africa, in relation to lemming cycles in Siberia. *Trans. Roy. Soc. S. Afr.* **46**: 209-214.
Underhill, L.G. (1990). Breeding productivity of Siberian Knots and Curlew Sandpipers, 1987-1989. *Safring News* **19**: 3-6.
Underhill, L.G. (1991). Ringed Sanderling recovered in Russia. *Promerops* **197**: 13-14.
Underhill, L.G. & Summers, R.W. (1992). Knots in Southern Africa. Pp. 182-183 in: Piersma & Davidson (1992b).
Underhill, L.G. & Underhill, G.D. (1986). An analysis of the mortality and survival of Hartlaub's Gull. *Ostrich* **57**: 216-223.
Underhill, L.G., Prys-Jones, R.P., Syroechkovski, E.E., Groen, N.M., Karpov, V., Lappo, H.G., van Roomen, M.W.J., Rybkin, A., Schekkerman, H., Spiekman, H. & Summers, R.W. (1993). Breeding of waders (Charadrii) and Brent Geese *Branta bernicla bernicla* at Pronchishcheva Lake, northeastern Taimyr, Russia, in a peak and a decreasing lemming year. *Ibis* **135**: 277-292.
Underhill, L.G., Waltner, M. & Summers, R.W. (1989). Three-year cycles in breeding productivity of Knots *Calidris canutus* wintering in southern Africa suggest Taimyr Peninsula provenance. *Bird Study* **36**: 83-87.
Urban, E.K. (1959). *Birds from Coahuila, México*. University of Kansas Publications, Museum of Natural History **11(8)**. University of Kansas, Lawrence, Kansas. 74 pp.
Urban, E.K. (1980). *Ethiopia's Endemic Birds*. Ethiopian Tourist Commission, Addis Ababa.
Urban, E.K. (1981). The Sudan Crowned Crane. Page 254 in: Lewis & Masatomi (1981).
Urban, E.K. (1985). Monitoring cranes in Botswana. *Babbler* **10**: 6-7.
Urban, E.K. (1987). The cranes of Africa - an overview. Pp. 307-315 in: Archibald & Pasquier (1987a).
Urban, E.K. (1996). Status of cranes in Africa, 1994. In: Beilfuss *et al.* (1996).
Urban, E.K. & Brown, L.H. (1971). *A Checklist of the Birds of Ethiopa*. Haile Selassie I University Press, Addis Ababa.
Urban, E.K. & Gichuki, N. (1991). Recent research and conservation activities with cranes in Africa. Pp. 351-355 in: Harris (1991b).
Urban, E.K. & Walkinshaw, L.H. (1967). The Wattled Crane in Ethiopia. *Auk* **84(2)**: 263-264.
Urban, E.K., Brown, L.H., Buer, C.E. & Page, G.D. (1970). Four descriptions of nesting, previously undescribed, for Ethiopia. *Bull. Brit. Orn. Club* **90(6)**: 162-164.
Urban, E.K., Fry, C.H. & Keith, S. eds. (1986). *The Birds of Africa*. Vol. 2. Academic Press, London & New York.
Urdiales, C. (1993). Estudio preliminar para el inicio de un plan de manejo del Torillo en el Parque Nacional de Doñana: informe final. [Prospective study for the initiation of a management plan for the Andalusian Hemipode in the Doñana National Park: final report]. Unpublished report to ICONA, Parque Nacional de Doñana.
Urdiales, C. (1994). Andalusian Hemipode. *Turnix sylvatica*. Pp. 224-225 in: Tucker & Heath (1994).
Urrutia, L.P. & Drummond, H. (1990). Brood reduction and parental infanticide in Heermann's Gulls. *Auk* **107**: 772-774.
Uspenski, S.M. (1956). *The Bird Bazaars of Novaya Zemlya*. (English translation 1958). Canadian Wildlife Service Translations of Russian Game Reports, Vol. 4, Ottawa.
Uttley, J. (1992). Food supply and the allocation of parental effort in Arctic Terns *Sterna paradisaea*. *Ardea* **80**: 83-91.
Uttley, J., Monaghan, P. & White, S. (1989). Differential effects of reduced sandeel availabilty on two sympatrically breeding species of tern. *Ornis Scand.* **20**: 273-277.
Uttley, J., Tatner, T. & Monaghan, P. (1994). Measuring the daily energy expenditure of free-living Arctic Terns (*Sterna paradisaea*). *Auk* **111**: 453-459.
Uttley, J.D., Thomas, C.J., Green, M.G., Suddaby, D. & Platt, J.B. (1988). The autumn migration of waders and other waterbirds through the northern United Arabs Emirates. *Sandgrouse* **10**: 58-70.
Uys, C.J. (1963). Some observations on the Stanley Bustard (*Neotis denhami*) at the nest. *Bokmakierie* **15**: 2-4.
Uys, C.J. (1978). Swift Terns breeding along the western Cape Coast. *Bokmakierie* **30**: 64-66.
Uys, C.J. & Underhill, G.D. (1977). Nesting of the Double-banded Courser in the Worcester district. *Bokmakierie* **29(2)**: 43-45.
Vader, W. (1980). The Great Skua *Stercorarius skua* in Norway and the Spitsbergen area. *Fauna Norvegica (Ser. C, Cinclus)* **3**: 49-55.
Vader, W., Barrett, R.T., Erikstad, K.E. & Strann, K.B. (1990). Differential responses of Common and Thick-billed Murres to a crash in the capelin stock in the southern Barents Sea. Pp. 175-180 in: Sealy (1990).
Väisänen, R.A. (1969). *Evolution of the Ringed Plover (*Charadrius hiaticula *L.) During the Last Hundred Years in Europe*. Annales Academiae Scientiarum Fennicae (Series A IV Biologica) **149**. 90 pp.
Väisänen, R.A. (1973). Establishment of colonies of Caspian Tern *Hydroprogne caspia* by deserting flights in the northern Gulf of Bothnia. *Ornis Scand.* **4**: 47-53.
Väisänen, R.A. (1977). Geographic variation in the timing of breeding and egg size in eight European species of waders. *Ann. Zool. Fennici* **14**: 1-25.
Valentine, J.M. (1981). The Mississippi Sandhill Crane, 1980. Pp. 167-174 in: Lewis & Masatomi (1981).
Valentine, J.M. (1982). Breeding ecology of the Mississippi Sandhill Crane in Jackson County, Mississippi. Pp. 63-72 in: Lewis (1982).
Valentine, J.M. & Noble, R.E. (1970). A colony of Sandhill Cranes in Mississippi. *J. Wildl. Manage.* **34**: 761-768.
Van, D.D., McConnell, S.D. & Hooper, T.D. (1994). First confirmed breeding record for the Upland Sandpiper, *Bartramia longicauda*, in British Columbia. *Can. Field-Nat.* **108**: 89-91.

Van de Weghe, J.P. & Monfort-Braham, N. (1975). Quelques aspects de la séparation écologique des vanneaux du Parc National de l'Akagera. *Alauda* **43**: 143-166.
Van Ee, C.A. (1966). Notes on the breeding behaviour of the Blue Crane *Tetrapteryx paradisea*. *Ostrich* **37(1)**: 23-29.
Van Ee, C.A. (1981). Status of the Blue Crane in south and southwest Africa. Page 259 in: Lewis & Masatomi (1981).
Van Tyne, J. & Berger, A.J. (1959). *Fundamentals of Ornithology*. John Wiley & Sons, New York.
Van Tyne, J. & Drury, W.H. (1959). The birds of southern Bylot Island, 1954. *Occas. Pap. Mus. Zool Univ. Mich.* **615**: 1-37.
Vandenbuicke, P. (1989). Herkomst, hand penrui en biometrie van de Grote Mantelmeeuw, *Larus marinus*, aan de Belgische kust. *Gerfaut* **79(1-4)**: 31-53.
Vander Haegen, W.M. (1992). *Bioenergetics of American Woodcock During the Breeding Season on Moosehorn National Wildlife Refuge, Maine*. PhD dissertation, University of Maine, Orono, Maine.
Vander Haegen, W.M., Krohn, W.B. & Owen, R.B. (1993). Care, behavior and growth of captive-reared American Woodcocks. Pp. 57-65 in: Longcore & Sepik (1993).
Vander Haegen, W.M., Owen, R.B. & Krohn, W.B. (1993). Effects of weather on earthworm abundance and spring food habits of American Woodcock. Pp. 26-31 in: Longcore & Sepik (1993).
Vander Haegen, W.M., Owen, R.B. & Krohn, W.B. (1994). Metabolic rate of American Woodcock. *Wilson Bull.* **106(2)**: 338-343.
Vanderwerf, E.A. & Strahl. S.D. (1990). Effects of unit size and territory defense on communal nest care in the Hoatzin (*Opisthocomus hoazin*). *Auk* **107(3)**: 626-628.
Vangeluwe, D. & Snethlage, M. (1986). [Observation of a *Cursorius cursor* at Cabo de Gata (Andalusia, Spain)]. *Aves* **23(1)**: 65. In French.
Vardhan, H. (1985). A report on the status of bustard in India. *Bustard Studies* **3**: 113-115.
Varela, J.M. & de Juana, E. (1986). The *Larus cachinnans michahellis* colony of Chafarinas Islands. Pp. 231-244 in: MEDMARAVIS & Monbailliu (1986).
Varela, J.M. & de Juana, E. (1987). Comparación de los plumajes neoptilos de *Larus audouinii* y *Larus cachinnans michahellis*. [Comparison of the neoptyle plumage of *Larus audouinii* and *Larus cachinnans michahellis*]. *Ardeola* **34(1)**: 113-122. In Spanish with English summary.
Varela, J.M., Pérez-Mellado, V. & de Juana, E. (1980). Nuevos datos sobre la ecología de la Gaviota de Audouin (*Larus audouinii* Payrandeau). *Ardeola* **25**: 71-92.
Varty, N., Adams, J., Espin, P. & Hambler, C. eds. (1986). *An Ornithological Survey of Lake Tota, Colombia, 1982*. ICBP Study Report **12**, Cambridge.
Vasilchenko, A. (1995). Distribution and numbers of the Demoiselle Crane in the former Tuva ASSR. Pp. 290-292 in: Prange *et al.* (1995).
Vasilchenko, A.A. & Unzhakov, V.V. (1977). [Biology of the Dotterel (*Charadrius morinellus*) in the Baikal Reserve]. *Ornitologiya* **13**: 201-202. In Russian.
Vaske, J.J., Rimmer, D.W. & Deblinger, R.D. (1994). The impact of different predator exclosures on Piping Plover nest abandonment. *J. Field Orn.* **65(2)**: 201-209. In English with Spanish summary.
Vassart, M. (1988). Premiers resultats d'une investigation relative à la biologie et à la pathologie des cagous (*Rhinochetos jubatus*) en Nouvelle-Calédonie. *Revue d'élevage et de médecine vétérinaire de la Nouvelle-Calédonie* **11**: 17-21.
von Vauk, G., Hartwig, E., Reineking, B. & Vauk-Hentzelt, E. (1989). Losses of seabirds by oil pollution at the German North Sea coast. *Scientia Marina* **53**: 749-754.
Vaurie, C. (1961). A new subspecies of the Nubian Bustard. *Bull. Brit. Orn. Club* **81**: 26-27.
Vaurie, C. (1962). The status of *Larus relictus* and other hooded gulls from Central Asia. *Auk* **79**: 303-309.
Vaurie, C. (1963). Systematic notes on Palearctic birds. No. 51. A review of *Burhinus oedicnemus*. *Amer. Mus. Novit.* **2131**: 1-13.
Vaurie, C. (1965). *The Birds of the Palearctic Fauna: Non-passeriformes*. Witherby, London.
Vaurie, C. (1972). *Tibet and its Birds*. H.F. & G. Witherby, London.
Veen, J. (1977). *Functional and Causal Aspects of Nest Distribution in Colonies of the Sandwich Tern (*Sterna s. sandvicensis *Lath.)*. Behaviour **20**(Supplement). 193 pp.
Veen, J. (1980). Breeding behavior and breeding success of a colony of Little Gulls *Larus minutus* in the Netherlands. *Limosa* **53**: 73-83.
Veen, J. (1985). On the functional significance of long call components in the Little Gull. *Netherlands J. Zool.* **35**: 63-86.
Veen, J. (1987). Ambivalence in the structure of display vocalizations of gulls and terns: new evidence in favour of Tinbergen's conflict hypothesis? *Behaviour* **100**: 33-49.
Veen, J. & Piersma, T. (1986). Causation and function of different vocal reactions of Little Gulls *Larus minutus* to intruders near the nest. *Behaviour* **96**: 241-264.
Veiga, J. (1985). Contribution a l'étude du régime alimentaire de la Bécassine sourde (*Lymnocryptes minimus*). [Diet of the Jack Snipe (*Lymnocryptes minimus*)]. *Gibier Faune Sauvage* **1985(1)**: 75-84. In French with English and German summaries.
Veiga, J. (1986). [Estimation of the food requirements of the Common Snipe determined through energy partitioning]. *Gibier Faune Sauvage* **3**: 423-439. In French with English summary.
Veiga, J. (1988). Some aspects of the diet of snipes. Page 23 in: Havet & Hirons (1988). (Abstract).
Veit, R.R. (1978). Some observations of South Polar Skuas (*Catharacta maccormicki*) on Georges Bank. *Amer. Birds* **32**: 300-302.
Veit, R.R. (1985). Long-tailed Jaegers wintering along the Falkland Current. *Amer. Birds* **39**: 873-877.
Veit, R.R. (1988). Identification of the Salton Sea Rufous-necked Sandpiper. *Western Birds* **19(4)**: 165-169.
Veit, R.R. & Petersen, W.R. (1982). First and second records of Rufous-necked Sandpiper (*Calidris ruficollis*) for Massachusetts. *Bird Obs.* **10(2)**: 75-77.
Veitch, C.R. (1974). Bristle-thighed Curlew records from the Kermadec Islands. *Notornis* **21**: 83-84.
Velarde, E. (1992). Predation of Heermann's Gull (*Larus heermanni*) by Yellow-footed Gulls (*Larus livens*) in dense and scattered nesting sites. *Colonial Waterbirds* **15(1)**: 8-13.
Velarde, E. (1993). Predation of nesting larids by Peregrine Falcons at Rasa Island, Gulf of California, Mexico. *Condor* **95**: 706-708.
Velarde, E. & Anderson, D.W. (1994). Conservation and management of seabird islands in the Gulf of California: setbacks and successes. Pp. 229-243 in: Nettleship *et al.* (1994).
Velarde, E., Anderson, D.W. & Beebe, S.B. (1985). *Conservation of the Islands in a Desert Sea*. Conservation International, Portland, Oregon.
Velasco, T. (1992a). Migración e hivernada del Corremolinos de Temminck (*Calidris temminckii*) en España. [Migration and overwintering of Temminck's Stint (*Calidris temminckii*) in Spain]. *Ecología* **6**: 207-214. In Spanish with English summary.
Velasco, T. (1992b). El Archibebe Fino (*Tringa stagnatilis*) en España. [The Marsh Sandpiper (*Tringa stagnatilis*) in Spain]. *Ardeola* **39(1)**: 55-62. In Spanish with English summary.
Velasco, T. & Alberto, J. (1994). Wintering of Kentish Plover *Charadrius alexandrinus* in Spain: numbers, distribution and habitat selection. *Wader Study Group Bull.* **73**: 54-55.
Velásquez, C.R. & Navarro, R.A. (1993). The influence of water depth and sediment type on the foraging behavior of Whimbrels. *J. Field Orn.* **64(2)**: 149-157.
Veling, E.J.M. (1977). Waarnemingen van een Siberische Gestreepte Strandloper *Calidris acuminata* en een Amerikaanse Gestreepte Strandloper *Calidris melanotos* een vergelijking. *Limosa* **50(1-2)**: 22-26.
Velizhanin, A.G. (1969). [Colonial seabirds of the Kuril Islands]. Pp. 112-115 in: *Ornitologiya v SSSR*. Vol. 2. Ashkhabad, USSR. In Russian.
Velizhanin, A.G. (1975). [Bird colonies of the Yama Islands]. *Okhota i Okhotniche khozaistvo* **7**: 18. In Russian.
Velizhanin, A.G. (1977). [On certain rare and little known birds of the Kurile Islands]. *Ornitologiya* **13**: 25-32. In Russian.
van Velzen, A. & Kreitzer, J.F. (1975). The toxicity of p,p'-DDT to the Clapper Rail. *J. Wildl. Manage.* **39**: 305-309.
van Velzen, W.T. & Benedict, R.D. (1972). Recoveries of Royal Terns banded in Virginia. Part I. The Caribbean. *Raven* **43**: 38-41.
van der Ven, J.A. (1981). Common Cranes in Europe. Pp. 181-183 in: Lewis & Masatomi (1981).
Venegas, C.C. (1973). El Ostrero Americano *Haematopus ostralegus* sp. en el estrecho de Magallanes. *Anales Inst. Patagonia* **4**: 281 289.
Veprintsev, B.N. & Zablotskaya, M.M. (1982). [Acoustic signalling of the Little Curlew, *Numenius minutus* Gould]. Libr. Wildlife Sounds Publications. In Russian.
Verbeek, N.A.M. (1977a). Comparative feeding behavior of immature and adult Herring Gulls. *Wilson Bull.* **89**: 415-421.
Verbeek, N.A.M. (1977b). Interactions between Herring and Lesser Black-backed Gulls feeding on refuse. *Auk* **94(4)**: 726-735.
Verbeek, N.A.M. (1979a). Timing of primary molt and egg-laying in the Glaucous-winged Gull. *Wilson Bull.* **91**: 420-425.
Verbeek, N.A.M. (1979b). Some aspects of the breeding biology and behavior of the Great Black-backed Gull. *Wilson Bull.* **91**: 575-582.
Verbeek, N.A.M. (1984). The effects of adult faecal material on egg hatchability in Glaucous-winged Gulls (*Larus glaucescens*). *Auk* **101**: 824-829.
Verbeek, N.A.M. (1986). Aspects of the breeding biology of an expanded population of Glaucous-winged Gulls in British Columbia. *J. Field Orn.* **57**: 22-33.
Verbeek, N.A.M. (1988). Differential predation of eggs in clutches of Glaucous-winged Gulls *Larus glaucescens*. *Ibis* **130**: 512-518.
Verbeek, N.A.M. (1993). Glaucous-winged Gull (*Larus glaucescens*). No. **59** in: Poole & Gill (1993).
Verboven, N. & Piersma, T. (1995). Is the evaporative water loss of Knots *Calidris canutus* higher in tropical than in temperate climates? *Ibis* **137(3)**: 308-316.
Vercruijsse, H. (1995). In Frankrijk geringde Geelpootmeeuw gepaard met Zilvermeeuw op Neeltje Jans in 1992-94. [French-ringed Yellow-legged Gull paired with Herring Gull on Neeltje Jans]. *Dutch Birding* **17(6)**: 246-247. In Dutch with English summary.
Verhage, M., Chapman, A. & Brown, B. (1990). Crab Plovers breed in the Gulf. *Phoenix* **7**: 4-5.
Verheugt, W.J.M. (1988). Red data bird: Asian Dowitcher. *World Birdwatch* **10(1)**: 5.
Verheugt, W.J.M., Danielsen, F., Skov, H., Purwoko, A., Kadarisman, R. & Suwarman, U. (1990). Seasonal variations in the wader populations of the Banyuasin Delta, south Sumatra, Indonesia. *Wader Study Group Bull.* **58**: 28-35.
Verheugt, W.J.M., Skov, H. & Danielsen, F. (1993). Notes on the birds of the tidal lowlands and floodplains of south Sumatra province, Indonesia. *Kukila* **6(2)**: 53-84.
Verheyden, C. (1988). La formation de couples hivernaux chez le Petit bec-en-fourreau (*Chionis minor*) et sa signification biologique. [Winter pairing in Lesser Sheathbills (*Chionis minor*); its biological significance]. *Rev. Ecol. (Terre Vie)* **43(4)**: 375-387. In French with English summary.
Verheyden, C. (1993). Kelp Gulls exploit food provided by active right whales. *Colonial Waterbirds* **16**: 88-91.
Verheyden, C. & Jouventin, P. (1991). Over-wintering strategies of the Lesser Sheathbill *Chionis minor* in an impoverished and insular environment. *Oecologia* **86**: 132-139.
Verheyen, R. (1953). *Exploration du Parc National de l'Upemba. Oiseaux*. Institut des Parcs Nationaux du Congo Belge, Bruxelles.
Verheyen, R. (1958). Contribution à la systématique des Alciformes. *Bull. Inst. Roy. Sci. Nat. Belgique* **34**: 1-15.
Verkuil, Y., Koolhaas, A. & van der Winden, J. (1993). Wind effects on prey availability: how northward migrating waders use brackish and hypersaline lagoons in the Sivash, Ukraine. *Netherlands J. Sea Res.* **31**: 359-374.
Verkuil, Y., van de Sant, S., Stikvoort, E., van der Winden, J. & Zwinselman, B. (1993). Feeding ecology of waders in the Sivash, Ukraine. Pp. 39-63 in: van der Have, T.M., van de Sant, S., Verkuil, Y. & van der Winden, J. eds. (1993). *Waterbirds in the Sivash, Spring 1992*. WIWO-Report **36**. Zeist, the Netherlands.
Vermeer, K. (1963). The breeding ecology of the Glaucous-winged Gull (*Larus glaucescens*) on Mandarte Island. *Occas. Pap. Brit. Col. Prov. Mus.* **13**: 1-100.
Vermeer, K. (1969). Egg measurements of California and Ring-billed Gull eggs at Miguelon Lake, Alberta. *Wilson Bull.* **81**: 102-103.
Vermeer, K. (1973a). Food habitats and breeding range of Herring Gulls in the Canadian prairie provinces. *Condor* **75**: 478-480.
Vermeer, K. (1973b). Comparison of egg laying chronology of Herring and Ring-billed Gull at Kawinaw Lake, Manitoba. *Can. Field-Nat.* **87**: 306-308.
Vermeer, K. (1979). Nesting requirements, food and breeding distribution of Rhinoceros Auklets, *Cerorhinca monocerata*, and Tufted Puffins, *Lunda cirrhata*. *Ardea* **67**: 22-27.
Vermeer, K. (1980). The importance of timing and type of prey to reproductive success of Rhinoceros Auklets *Cerorhinca monocerata*. *Ibis* **122**: 343-350.
Vermeer, K. (1981). The importance of plankton to Cassin's Auklets during breeding. *J. Plankton Res.* **3**: 315-329.
Vermeer, K. (1982). Comparison of the diet of the Glaucous-winged Gull on the east and west coast of Vancouver Island. *Murrelet* **63**: 80-85.
Vermeer, K. (1984). The diet and food consumption of nestling Cassin's Auklets during summer and a comparison with other plankton-feeding alcids. *Murrelet* **65**: 65-77.
Vermeer, K. (1987). *Growth and Nestling Periods of Cassin's Auklets: Adaptations of Planktivorous Auklets to Breeding at Northern Latitudes*. Canadian Technical Report Hydrology Ocean Sciences **93**. Institute of Ocean Sciences, Sidney, Canada.
Vermeer, K. & Cullen, L. (1979). Growth of Rhinoceros Auklet and Tufted Puffin, Triangle Island, British Columbia. *Ardea* **67**: 22-27.
Vermeer, K. & Cullen, L. (1982). Growth comparison of a plankton- and a fish-feeding alcid. *Murrelet* **63**: 34-39.
Vermeer, K. & Devito, K. (1986). The nesting biology of Mew Gulls (*Larus canus*) on Kennedy Lake, British Columbia, Canada: comparison with Mew Gulls in northern Europe. *Colonial Waterbirds* **9**: 95-103.
Vermeer, K. & Devito, K. (1987). Habitat and nest-site selection of Mew and Glaucous-winged Gulls in coastal British Columbia. Pp. 105-118 in: Hand *et al.* (1987).
Vermeer, K. & Irons, D.B. (1991). The Glaucous-winged Gull on the Pacific coast of North America. Pp. 2378-2383 in: Bell *et al.* (1991).
Vermeer, K. & Lemon, M. (1986). Nesting habits and habitats of Ancient Murrelets and Cassin's Auklets in the Queen Charlotte Islands, British Columbia. *Murrelet* **67**: 33-44.
Vermeer, K. & Sealy, S.G. (1984). Status of nesting seabirds of British Columbia. Pp. 29-40 in: Croxall, Evans & Schreiber (1984).
Vermeer, K., Briggs, K.T., Morgan, K.H. & Siegel-Causey, D. eds. (1993). *The Status, Ecology and Conservation of Marine Birds of the North Pacific*. Canadian Wildlife Service Special Publication, Ottawa.
Vermeer, K., Cullen, L. & Porter, M. (1979). A provisional explanation of the reproductive failure of Tufted Puffins *Lunda cirrhata* on Triangle Island, British Columbia. *Ibis* **121**: 348-354.
Vermeer, K., Ewins, P.J., Morgan, K.H. & Smith, G.E.J. (1991). Population, nesting habitat and reproductive success of American Black Oystercatchers on the west coast of Vancouver Island. *Can. Wildl. Serv. Occas. Pap.* **75**: 65-70. In English with French summary.
Vermeer, K., Fulton, J.D. & Sealy, S.G. (1985). Differential use of zooplankton prey by Ancient Murrelets and Cassin's Auklets in the Queen Charlotte Islands. *J. Plankton Res.* **7**: 443-459.
Vermeer, K., Morgan, K.H. & Smith, G.E.J. (1992). Black Oystercatcher habitat selection, reproductive success, and their relationship with Glaucous-winged Gulls. *Colonial Waterbirds* **15**: 14-23.
Vermeer, K., Morgan, K.H. & Smith, G.E.J. (1993a). Colony attendance of Pigeon Guillemots as related to tide height and time of day. *Colonial Waterbirds* **16**: 1-8.
Vermeer, K., Morgan, K.H. & Smith, G.E.J. (1993b). Nesting biology and predation of Pigeon Guillemots in the Queen Charlotte Islands, British Columbia. *Colonial Waterbirds* **16**: 119-127.
Vermeer, K., Morgan, K.H., Smith, G.E.J. & York, B.A. (1991). Effects of egging on the reproductive success of Glaucous-winged Gulls. *Colonial Waterbirds* **14**: 158-165.
Vermeer, K., Power, D. & Smith, G.E.J. (1988). Habitat selection and nesting biology of roof-nesting Glaucous-winged Gulls. *Colonial Waterbirds* **11**: 189-201.
Vermeer, K., Sealy, S.G., Lemon, M. & Rodway, M. (1984). Predation and potential environmental perturbances on Ancient Murrelets nesting in British Columbia. Pp. 757-770 in: Croxall, Evans & Schreiber (1984).
Vermeer, K., Sealy, S.G. & Sanger, G.A. (1987). Feeding ecology of Alcidae in the eastern North Pacific Ocean. Pp. 189-227 in: Croxall (1987).
Vermeer, K., Szabo, I. & Greisman, P. (1987). The relationship between plankton-feeding Bonaparte's and Mew Gulls and tidal upwelling at Active Pass, British Columbia. *J. Plankton Res.* **9**: 483-501.
Vermeer, K., Vermeer, R.A., Summers, K.R. & Billings, R.R. (1979). Numbers and habitat selection of Cassin's Auklet breeding on Triangle Island, British Columbia. *Auk* **96**: 143-151.
Vernon, C.J. (1973). Polyandrous *Actophilornis africanus*. *Ostrich* **44**: 85.
Vernon, C.J. (1983a). Notes from the border– 11. Blue Korhaan group size. *Bee-eater* **10**(Suppl.): 1-2.
Vernon, C.J. (1983b). Display of the Finfoot. *Bee-eater* **10**(Suppl.): 12.
Vernon, C.J. & Boshoff, A.F. (1986). The status and conservation of the Wattled Crane, *Grus carunculatus*, in the Cape Province and Transkei. *Bontebok* **5**: 37-41.
Vernon, C.J., Boshoff, A.F. & Stretton, W.S. (1992). The status and conservation of cranes in the Eastern Cape Province. Pp. 47-58 in: Porter *et al.* (1992).
Vernon, J.D.R. (1970). Feeding habitats and food of the Black-headed and Common Gulls. Part I. Feeding habitats. *British Birds* **17**: 287-295.

Vernon, J.D.R. (1972). Feeding habitats and food of the Black-headed and Common Gulls. Part II. Foods. *British Birds* **19**: 173-185.
Verrill, A.E. & Verrill. A.H. (1909). Notes on the birds of San Domingo, with a list of the species, including a new hawk. *Proc. Acad. Nat. Sci. Philadelphia* **61**: 352-356.
Verschuren, J. (1977). Note sur la faune ornithologique du Burundi, principalement près de Bujumbura. *Gerfaut* **67**: 3-20.
Verschuren, J. (1978). Observations ornithologiques dans les parcs nationaux du Zaire, 1968-1974. *Gerfaut* **68**: 3-24.
Verspoor, E., Birkhead, T.R. & Nettleship, D.N. (1987). Incubation and brooding shift duration in the Common Murre *Uria aalge*. *Can. J. Zool.* **2**: 247-252.
Vesey-Fitzgerald, D. (1941). Further contributions to the ornithology of the Seychelles Islands. *Ibis* **Ser. 14, no. 5**: 518-531.
Vestjens, W.J.M. (1963). Remains of the extinct Banded Rail at Macquarie Island. *Emu* **62**: 249-250.
Vestjens, W.J.M. (1977). Status, habitats and food of vertebrates at Lake Cowal. *Tech. Memo Div. Wildl. Res. CSIRO* **12**: 1-87.
Vides-Almonacid, R. (1988). [Notes on the status of the populations of Horned Coot (*Fulica cornuta*) in the province of Tucuman, Argentina]. *Hornero* **13(1)**: 34-38. In Spanish with English summary.
Vieillard, J. (1974). The Purple Gallinule in the marismas of the Guadalquivir. *British Birds* **67**: 230-236.
Viet, R. & Peterson, W. (1993). *Birds of Massachusetts*. Massachusetts Audubon Society, Lincoln, Massachusetts.
Vigil, C. (1973). *Aves Argentinas y Sudamericanas*. Editorial Atlántida, Buenos Aires.
Vijayagopal, K. & Chacko, S. (1991). Hitherto unrecorded nesting site of Yellow-wattled Lapwing *Vanellus malabaricus* (Boddaert). *J. Bombay Nat. Hist. Soc.* **88(3)**: 451.
Viksne, J. (1961). Problems of migration of the Black-headed Gull in Latvia. Pp. 208-214 in: Lusis, Y.Y., Spurin, Z.D., Taurins, E.J. & Vilka, E.K. eds. (1961). *Birds of the Baltic Region: Ecology and Migrations*. (English translation 1968). Israel Program for Scientific Translations, Jerusalem.
Viksne, J. (1968a). [On the structure of the nesting population of the Black-headed Gull (*Larus ridibundus* L.) on maritime lakes of Latvia]. Pp. 207-228 in: Viksne, J. ed. (1968). [*Ecology of the Waterbirds of Latvia*]. Zenatnia, Riga. In Russian.
Viksne, J. (1968b). [On the significance of post-breeding movements in the territorial distribution of nests of Black-headed Gull (*Larus ridibundus*): example Baltic population]. Pp. 229-248 in: Viksne, J. ed. (1968). [*Ecology of the Waterbirds of Latvia*]. Zenatnia, Riga. In Russian.
Viksne, J. (1968c). [Link to the nesting territory and dispersion of young birds and formation of new colonies of the Black-headed Gull (*Larus ridibundus* L.)]. Pp. 116-133 in: [*Migration of Animals*]. Vol. 5. Nauka, Riga. In Russian.
Viksne, J. (1980). Some problems in Black-headed Gull (*Larus ridibundus*) research and the necessity of international cooperation in this respect. *Acta Ornitologica* **17**: 72-80.
Viksne, J. (1985). Long-term study of population demography of the Black-headed Gull (*Larus ridibundus* L.) in Latvia. Page 1187 in: *Acta XVIII Int. Orn. Congr.* Moscow, 1982.
Viksne, J. & Janaus, M. (1980). Breeding success of the Black-headed Gull. *Ornis Fenn.* **57**: 1-10.
Viksne, J. & Janaus, M. (1990). What is important for the survival of the Black-headed Gull chicks. *Baltic Birds* **5**: 220-230.
Vilina, Y. & Droully, P. (1990). New information on the distribution of the Collared Plover *Charadrius collaris* in Chile. *Wader Study Group Bull.* **59**: 29.
Vilina, Y. & Teillier, S. (1990). The Tawny-throated Dotterel *Oreopholus ruficollis* in northern Chile. *Wader Study Group Bull.* **60**: 32-33.
Vilina, Y., Larrea, A. & Gibbons, J.E. (1992). First record of the Bristle-thighed Curlew *Numenius tahitiensis* in Easter Island, Chile. *Wader Study Group Bull.* **66**: 43-44.
Viljoen, P.C. & Viljoen, S.B. (1987). Notes on the foraging association between Carmine Bee-eaters and Kori Bustards in the Chobe National Park, Botswana. *Ostrich* **58**: 187-188.
Viljoen, P.J. (1983). Distribution, numbers and group size of the Karoo Korhaan in Kaokoland, South West Africa. *Ostrich* **54**: 50-51.
Villaseñor, J.F. & Phillips, A.R. (1994). A new puzzling American route of the Arctic Tern and its implications. *Bull. Brit. Orn. Club* **114**: 249-258.
Vincent, A.W. (1945). On the breeding habits of some African birds. *Ibis* **87**: 345-365.
Vincent, J. (1934). Birds of northern Portuguese east Africa. *Ibis* **Ser. 13, no. 4**: 495-527.
Vine, A.E. & Sergeant, D.E. (1948). Arboreal nesting by Black-headed Gull colony. *British Birds* **41**: 158-159.
Vines, G. (1979). Spatial distributions of territorial aggressiveness in Oystercatchers *Haematopus ostralegus*. *Anim. Behav.* **27**: 300 308.
Vines, G. (1980). Spatial consequences of aggressive behaviour in flocks of Oystercatchers *Haematopus ostralegus*. *Anim. Behav.* **28**: 1175 1183.
Vinicombe, K. (1971). Sabine's Gull hawking flying insects inland. *British Birds* **64**: 503-504.
Vinicombe, K. (1980). Tern showing mixed characters of Black Tern and White-winged Black Tern. *British Birds* **73**: 223-225.
Vinicombe, K. (1995). Nice race shame about the legs. *Birdwatch* **38**: 24-29.
Vinicombe, K. & Hopkin, P.J. (1993). The Great Black-headed Gull in Britain. *British Birds* **86(5)**: 201-205.
Vinicombe, K., Wright, B., Stagg, A., Scott, M., Siddle, J. & Muddeman, J. (1995). Yellow-legged Gulls. So much more to learn about a complicated group of birds. *Birdwatch* **40**: 22-23.
Vinokurov, A.A. (1976a). [On the Solitary Snipe in the central Tien Shan]. Pp. 139-141 in: [*Rare, Threatened and Inadequately-known Birds of the USSR*]. Moscow. In Russian.
Vinokurov, A.A. (1976b). [On *Numenius minutus*]. Page 149 in: [*Rare, Endangered and Insufficiently Studied Birds of the USSR*]. Moskovsky Rabochiy Publications, Ryanzan' Sect., Ryazan'. In Russian.
Vinter, S.V. (1980). [The Far Eastern Curlew (*Numenius madagascariensis*) on the lower Bureya river]. In: Flint (1980a). In Russian.
Violani, C. & Boano, G. (1990). L'Uria di Craveri *Synthliboramphus craveri* (Aves, Alcidae). *Riv. Piem. St. Nat.* **11**: 155-162. In Italian with English summary.
Violani, C.G. & Massa, B. (1993). Extinction of the Andalusian Hemipode *Turnix s. sylvatica* (Desf.) in the Mediterranean region. *Bull. Brit. Orn. Club* **113(4)**: 225-229.
Visser, G.H. & Ricklefs, R.E. (1993a). Development of temperature regulation in shorebirds. *Physiol. Zool.* **66**: 771-792.
Visser, G.H. & Ricklefs, R.E. (1993b). Temperature regulation in neonates of shorebirds. *Auk* **110**: 445-457.
Visser, J. (1974). The post-embryonic development of the Coot *Fulica atra*. *Ardea* **62**: 172-189.
Voipio, P. (1968). Zur Verbeitung der *argentatus*- und *cachinnans*- Möwen. *Ornis Fenn.* **45**: 73-83.
Voipio, P. (1972). Silbermöwen der *Larus argentatus cachinnans* Gruppe als Besiedler des baltischen Raumes. *Ann. Zool. Fennici* **9**: 131-136.
Voisin, J.F. (1979). Observations ornithologiques aux îles Tristan da Cunha et Gough. *Alauda* **47**: 73-82.
Volet, B. (1994). Sternes arctiques (*Sterna paradisea*) à la rade de Genève: notes sur la coloration du bec en plumage juvénile. *Nos Oiseaux* **42(6)**: 335-347.
von Volker, K. (1994). Kennzeichen des Dünnschnabelbrachvogels (*Numenius tenuirostris*). *Orn. Mitt.* **46(11)**: 291-295.
Volkov, A.E. (1986). [Nesting of Little Curlew on the Anabar Plateau]. *Ornitologiya* **21**: 129-130. In Russian.
Volsøe, H. (1950). *Spring Observations on Migrant Birds in the Canary Islands*. Videnskabelige Meddelelser fra Dansk Naturhistorisk Forening **112**. 43 pp.
Von Heuglin, T. (1869-1873). *Ornithologie Nordost-Afrikas*. Kassel.
Vooren, C.M. & Chiaradia, A. (1989). *Stercorarius longicaudus* and *S. parasiticus* in southern Brazil. *Ardea* **77(2)**: 233-235. In English with Dutch summary.
Vooren, C.M. & Chiaradia, A. (1990). Seasonal abundance and behaviour of coastal birds on Cassino Beach, Brazil. *Orn. Neotropical* **1(1-2)**: 9-24.
Voous, K.H. (1959). Geographical variation of the Herring Gull, *Larus argentatus*, in Europe and North America. *Ardea* **47**: 176-187.
Voous, K.H. (1960). *Atlas of European Birds*. Nelson, London.
Voous, K.H. (1961a). Micro-geographical variation in Netherlands Herring Gulls *Larus argentatus*. *Ardea* **49**: 69-72.
Voous, K.H. (1961b). The generic distinction of the Gough Island Flightless Gallinule. *Bijdragen tot de Dierkunde* **31**: 75-79.
Voous, K.H. (1962). Notes on a collection of birds from Tristan da Cunha and Gough Island. *Beaufortia* **9**: 105-114.
Voous, K.H. (1963). Tern colonies in Aruba, Curaçao and Bonaire, South Caribbean Sea. Pp. 1214-1216 in: *Proc. XIII Int. Orn. Congr.* Ithaca, New York, 1962.
Voous, K.H. (1968a). *Larus audouinii* en el sur de España. *Ardeola* **14**: 219-220.
Voous, K.H. (1968b). Geographical variation in the Cayenne Tern. *Ardea* **56**: 184-187.
Voous, K.H. (1983). *Birds of the Netherlands Antilles*. De Walburg Pers, Zutphen.
Voous, K.H. (1993). Over de Ijslandse Tureluur. *Op het Vinkentouw* **71**: 4-8.
Vorbiev, K.A. (1963).[*The Birds of Yakutia*]. Moscow. In Russian.
Vorobyova, T.D. (1992). Wintering of the Little Bustard on the southwestern coast of the Caspian Sea. *Bustard Studies* **5**: 92-94.
Voronov, G.A. & Eremin, U.P. (1982). [On the nesting of the Aleutian Tern (*Sterna camtschatica*) on Sakhalin Island]. Pp. 26-35 in: [*Ecology and Faunistic Study of Certain of Vertebrates of Sakhalin and the Kurile Islands*]. Vladivostok. In Russian.
Voronov, V.G. (1980). [Observation on the feeding of the Spoon-bill Stint (*Eurynorhynchus pygmaeus*)]. Pp. 138-139 in: Flint (1980a). In Russian.
Votier, S.C. (1992). Semipalmated Sandpiper on Fair Isle: a first record for Scotland. *Scottish Birds* **16(4)**: 277-279.
Vuilleumier, F. (1969). Field notes on some birds from the Bolivian Andes. *Ibis* **111**: 599-608.
Vuilleumier, F. (1995). A large colony of Ivory Gulls on Victoria Island, Russia. *Alauda* **63(2)**: 135-148.
Vuilleumier, F. & Gochfeld, M. (1976). Notes sur l'avifaune de Nouvelle-Calédonie. *Alauda* **44**: 237-273.
Vuilleumier, F., LeCroy, M. & Mayr, E. (1992). New species of birds described from 1981 to 1990. Pp. 267-309 in: Monk (1992).
Vuolanto, S. (1968). On the breeding biology of the Turnstone (*Arenaria interpres*) at Norrskär, Gulf of Bothnia. *Ornis Fenn.* **45**: 19-24.
Vuosalo-Tavakoli, E. (1991). The Siberian Crane in Iran. Pp. 341-347 in: Harris (1991b).
Vuosalo-Tavakoli, E. (1995). Some observations on the Siberian Crane wintering at Fereidoonkenar, Iran. Pp. 308-310 in: Prange *et al.* (1995).
Vyas, D.K., Mathur, D.J. & Mathur, K.M. (1983). Some aspects of the ecology, behaviour and breeding biology of the Great Indian Bustard. Pp. 184-193 in: Goriup & Vardhan (1983).
Vyatkin, P.S. (1986). Nest cadastre of colonial seabirds of Kamchatka. Pp. 20-36 in: Litvinenko (1986).
Vyshkvartsev, D.I. & Lebedev, E.B. (1986). Analysis of the distribution and role of birds in the ecological system of Novgorod and Ekspeditsiya bays in Posiet Gulf (Sea of Japan). Pp. 144-151 in: Litvinenko (1986).
Wace, N.M. & Holdgate, M.W. (1976). *Man and Nature in Tristan da Cunha*. IUCN Monograph **6**, Morges, Switzerland.
Wacher, T. (1993). Some new observations of forest birds in The Gambia. *Malimbus* **15**: 24-37.
Wada, M.Y., Hori, H., Suzuki, T., Tsuchiya, K. & Wurster-Hill, D.H. (1993). The chromosomes of the kagu (*Rhynochetos jubatus*). *Caryologia* **46**: 91-98.
Wadewitz, O. (1952). Ein Beitrag zur Biologie des Flußuferläufers, *Actitis hypoleucos*. *Beitr. Vogelkd.* **3**: 1-20.
Wadewitz, O. (1955). Zur Brutbiologie des Triels, *Burhinus oedicnemus* (L.). *Beitr. Vogelkd.* **4**: 86-107.
Wadewitz, O. (1957). Weitere Beobachtungsergebnisse am Flußuferläufer, *Actitis hypoleucos*. *Beitr. Vogelkd.* **6**: 2-10.
Wadewitz, O. (1968). Stone Curlews. Pp. 202-204 in: Grzimek (1968).
Wadsack, J.A. & Alaoui, Y. (1994). [Provisional analysis of data and weights of Woodcock wintering in Morocco]. Pp. 24-26 in: Kalchreuter (1994). In French with English summary.
Wagner, R.H. & Safina, C. (1989). Relative contribution of the sexes to chick feeding in Roseate and Common Terns. *Wilson Bull.* **101**: 497-500.
Wagner, S. (1980). Sumpfläufer (*Limicola falcinellus*) an der Drauschleife bei Villach. [Broad-billed Sandpiper *Limicola falcinellus* in Drauschleife near Villach]. *Egretta* **23(2)**: 61-62.
Wahl, T.R. (1977). Notes on behavior of California Gulls and South Polar Skuas off the Washington coast. *Murrelet* **58**: 47-49.
Wakefield, W.C. & Robertson, B.I. (1988). Breeding resource partitioning of a mixed population of Pied and Sooty Oystercatchers. *Stilt* **13**: 39-40.
Waki, R. & Tomioka, T. (1992). [Pair formation by a male individual (T-02) of the Red-crowned Crane, *Grus japonensis*, at Tsurui-ito Tancho Sanctuary in eastern Hokkaido, Japan]. *Strix* **11**: 109-118. In Japanese with English summary.
Walbeck, D.E. (1989). Observations of roof-nesting Killdeer and Common Nighthawks in Frostburg, Maryland. *Maryland Birdlife* **45(1)**: 3-9.
Walker, A.J. & Chandler, D.F. (1985). Family group movements by breeding Redshanks on South Uist. *Wader Study Group Bull.* **45**: 29-31.
Walker, D. & Turley, R. (1989). White-cheeked Tern in Kent - a new British bird. *Birding World* **3**: 173-174.
Walker, K., Moore, P. & Elliott, E. (1991). The Auckland Island Banded Dotterel has apparently increased. *Notornis* **38(4)**: 257-265.
Walker, R.J. & Gregory, J. (1987). Little Whimbrel in Norfolk. *British Birds* **80(10)**: 494-497.
Walker, T.A. (1986). Black-naped Terns *Sterna sumatrana* on the Southern Great Barrier Reef, 1985-1986. *Corella* **10**: 123-124.
Walker, T.A. (1988). Population of the Silver Gull *Larus novaehollandiae* on the Capricorn and Bunker Islands, Great Barrier Reef. *Corella* **12**: 113-118.
Walker, T.A. (1992). A record Crested Tern *Sterna bergii* colony and concentrated breeding by seabirds in the Gulf of Carpentaria. *Emu* **93**: 152-156.
Walkinshaw, L.H. (1937). The Virginia Rail in Michigan. *Auk* **54**: 464-475.
Walkinshaw, L.H. (1939). The Yellow Rail in Michigan. *Auk* **56**: 227-237.
Walkinshaw, L.H. (1940). Summer life of the Sora Rail. *Auk* **57**: 153-168.
Walkinshaw, L.H. (1949). The Sandhill Cranes. *Cranbrook Inst. Sci. Bull.* **29**: 1-22.
Walkinshaw, L.H. (1963). Some life history studies of the Stanley Crane. Pp. 344-353 in: *Proc. XIII Int. Orn. Congr.* Ithaca, New York, 1962.
Walkinshaw, L.H. (1964). The African Crowned Cranes. *Wilson Bull.* **76(4)**: 355-377.
Walkinshaw, L.H. (1965). The Wattled Crane, *Bugeranus carunculatus*. *Ostrich* **36**: 73-81.
Walkinshaw, L.H. (1966). The Crowned Crane on the Jos Plateau, Northern Nigeria. *Bull. Niger. Orn. Soc.* **3(9)**: 6-10.
Walkinshaw, L.H. (1973). *Cranes of the World*. Winchester Press, New York.
Walkinshaw, L.H. (1981a). The Sandhill Cranes. Pp. 151-162 in: Lewis & Masatomi (1981).
Walkinshaw, L.H. (1981b). West African Crowned Crane observations. Pp. 255-257 in: Lewis & Masatomi (1981).
Walkinshaw, L.H. (1982a). Nesting of the Florida Sandhill Crane in Central Florida. Pp. 53-62 in: Lewis (1982).
Walkinshaw, L.H. (1982b). Observations on Limpkin nesting. *Florida Field Nat.* **10(3)**: 45-54.
Walkinshaw, L.H. (1991). Yellow Rail. In: Brewer, R., Mcpeek, G.A. & Adams, R.J. eds. (1991). *The Atlas of Breeding Birds of Michigan*. Michigan State University Press, East Lansing, Michigan.
Wall, L.E. (1990). Letter to the editor. *Stilt* **17**: 76.
Wall, L.E. & Harris, J.G.K. (1978). Banded Stilt in Tasmania. *Emu* **78(3)**: 163.
Wallace, D.I.M. (1964). Studies of less familiar birds. 128. Slender-billed Gull. *British Birds* **57**: 242-247.
Wallace, D.I.M. (1969). Observations on Audouin's Gull in Majorca. *British Birds* **62**: 223-229.
Wallace, D.I.M. (1977). Further definition of Great Snipe characters. *British Birds* **70(7)**: 283-289.
Wallace, D.I.M. (1979). Review of British records of Semipalmated Sandpipers and claimed Red-necked Stints. *British Birds* **72(6)**: 264-274.
Wallace, D.I.M. (1989). Field characters and voice of Swinhoe's Snipe. *British Birds* **82(6)**: 269-271.
Wallace, R.A. (1966). Nesting and defensive behavior of the Black-naped Tern in the Maldive Islands. *Auk* **83**: 138.
Wallis, C.A. (1986). Mountain Plover. *Prov. Mus. Alberta Nat. Hist. Occas. Pap.* **9**: 263-264.
Wallis, C.A. & Wershler, C.R. (1981). Status and breeding of Mountain Plover (*Charadrius montanus*) in Canada. *Can. Field-Nat.* **95(2)**: 133-136.
Walmsley, J.G. (1970). Une Glaréole de Nordmann *Glareola nordmanni* en Camargue, première observation et premier cas de nidification pour la France. *Alauda* **38(4)**: 292-305.
Walmsley, J.G. (1976). Une Glaréole à ailes noires *Glareola nordmanni* en Camargue. *Alauda* **44**: 334-335.
Walmsley, J.G. (1988). [Another observation of a Black-winged Pratincole *Glareola nordmanni* in the Camargue, southern France]. *Alauda* **56(4)**: 430-432. In French.
Walmsley, J.G. (1991). Feral cat predation on Sooty Terns (*Sterna fuscata* on Ascension Island, South Atlantic Ocean - March 1990. *Army Orn. Soc. Bull.* **1**: c43-c52.
Walpole-Bond, J. (1938). *A History of Sussex Birds*. Vol 3. London.
Walter, C.B. (1984). Fish prey remains in Swift Tern and Hartlaub's Gull pellets at Possession Island, off Namibia. *Ostrich* **55**: 166-167.
Walter, C.B., Cooper, J. & Suter, W. (1987). Diet of Swift Tern chicks in the Saldanha Bay Region, South Africa. *Ostrich* **58**: 49-53.
Walter, C.B., Duffy, D.C., Cooper, J. & Suter, W. (1987). Cape anchovy in Swift Tern diets and fishery landings in the Benguela upwelling region, South Africa. *S. Afr. J. Wildl. Res.* **17**: 139-149.
Walter, D.M. (1984). Adaptable oystercatchers. *Notornis* **31(4)**: 278.

Walter, J.C. (1983). An unexpected sighting of Red-necked Avocet *Recurvirostra novaehollandiae* and chicks. *Sunbird* **13(2)**: 40-41.
Walters, J. (1978). The primary moult in four gull species near Amsterdam. *Ardea* **66**: 32-47.
Walters, J. (1979). The onset of the postnuptial moult in the Common Tern *Sterna hirundo* near Amsterdam. *Ardea* **67**: 62-67.
Walters, J. (1984). The onset of primary moult in breeding *Charadrius* plovers. *Bird Study* **31(1)**: 43-48.
Walters, J. (1985). On the primary moult in adult Common Tern, *Sterna hirudno*. *Gerfaut* **75**: 323-326.
Walters, J. & Walters, B.J. (1980). Cooperative breeding by Southern Lapwings (*Vanellus chilensis*). *Ibis* **122(4)**: 505-509.
Walters, J.R. (1979). Interspecific aggressive behaviour by Long-toed Lapwings (*Vanellus crassirostris*). *Anim. Behav.* **27(4)**: 969-981.
Walters, J.R. (1982). Parental behaviour in lapwings (Charadriidae) and its relationship with clutch sizes and mating systems. *Evolution* **36**: 1030-1040.
Walters, J.R. (1984). The evolution of parental behavior and clutch size in shorebirds. Pp. 243-287 in: Burger & Olla (1984).
Walters, J.R. (1990). Anti-predatory behavior of lapwings: field evidence of discriminative abilities. *Wilson Bull.* **102**: 49-70.
Walters, M. (1987). The provenance of the Gilbert Rail *Tricholimnas conditicius* (Peters & Griscom). *Bull. Brit. Orn. Club* **107**: 181-184.
Walters, M. (1993). On the status of the Christmas Island Sandpiper, *Aechmorhynchus cancellatus*. *Bull. Brit. Orn. Club* **113(2)**: 97-102.
Waltner, M. & Sinclair, J.C. (1981). Distribution, biometrics and moult of the Terek Sandpiper *Xenus cinereus* in southern Africa. Pp. 233-266 in: Cooper (1981).
Walton, H.J. (1946). On the birds of southern Tibet. *Ibis* **88**: 57-84, 225-226.
Waltz, E.C. (1987). A test of the information-centre hypothesis in two colonies of Common Terns, *Sterna hirundo*. *Anim. Behav.* **35**: 28-39.
Wander, W. (1981). Red Phalarope eating carrion. *Wilson Bull.* **93**: 557.
Wang, L.E.A. (1991). [The reproductive ecology of Black-tailed Gull]. *Chinese Wildlife* **61**: 29-30. In Chinese.
Wang, T., Tang, S. & Ma, J. (1991). *Survey of Shorebirds and Coastal Wetlands in Yellow River Delta, Shangong Province, Autumn 1991*. East China Waterbird Ecology Study Group Report, Shanghai.
Wang, Z. & Norman, F.I. (1993). Timing of breeding, breeding success and chick growth in South Polar Skuas (*Catharacta maccormicki*) in the eastern Larsemann Hills, Princess Elizabeth Land, east Antarctica. *Notornis* **40(3)**: 189-203.
Wang Haichang (1984). [A preliminary observation on the breeding behaviour of the Common Sandpiper *Tringa hypoleucos*]. *Chinese J. Zool.* **2**: 9-13. In Chinese.
Wang Haichang & Deng Minglu (1966). [Preliminary observations on the breeding ecology of the Little Ringed Plover *Charadrius dubius*]. *Chinese J. Zool.* **8(3)**: 123-124. In Chinese.
Wang Hui (1992). [A field study of spring migratory population of Nordmann's Greenshank (*Tringa guttifer*) in Yancheng Nature Reserve]. *Zool. Res.* **13(1)**: 36. In Chinese.
Wang Junsen & He Baichuan (1983). [A preliminary study on the breeding ecology of the Coot *Fulica atra* in the Zhalong Protecting Area (Heilongjiang Province)]. *Nat. Resour. Res.* **3**: 47-52. In Chinese.
Wang Liantie & Du Wei (1989). [The first record of Hooded-cranes *Grus monacha* in Shenyang (Liaoning Province)]. *Trans. Liaoning Zool. Soc.* **7(1)**: 79-82. In Chinese.
Wang Qishan (1988). [The Hooded Crane *Grus monacha*]. *Chinese J. Zool.* **4**: 30-34. In Chinese.
Wang Qishan (1991). The conservation and management of cranes at Shengjin Lake in Anhui Province. Pp. 97-100 in: Harris (1991b).
Wang Qishan & Hu Xiaolong (1987). Status and ecology of wintering Hooded Cranes in the lower reaches of the Yangtze River of China. Pp. 105-106 in: Archibald & Pasquier (1987a).
Wang Tianhou & Qian Gouzhen (1988). *Shorebirds in the Estuary of the Yangtze River and Hangzhou Bay*. East China Normal University Press, Shanghai.
Wang Tianhou & Tong Sixian (1991). *Survey of Shorebirds and Coastal Wetlands in Shanghai. Autumn 1990*. Asian Wetland Bureau, Kuala Lumpur.
Wang Youhui (1991). A preliminary study of the winter ecology of Common Cranes in Caohai. Pp. 119-122 in: Harris (1991b).
Wang Youhui, Wu Zhigang, Li Zhumei, Li Dehao & Zhou Zhijun (1991). [An observation on the nest, the egg and the chick of Black-necked Cranes]. *Acta Biol. Plateau Sinica* **10**: 117-124. In Chinese with English summary.
Wanink, J. & Zwarts, L. (1985). Does an optimally foraging Oystercatcher obey the functional response? *Oecologia* **67**: 98-106.
Warakagoda, D. (1994). The Oriental Plover (*Charadrius veredus*) a new record for Sri Lanka. *Ceylon Bird Club Notes* **1994**: 7-8.
Ward, D. (1987). What do plovers know about competition? *Bokmakierie* **39(2)**: 62-64.
Ward, D. (1988). Belly-soaking in the Blacksmith Plover *Vanellus armatus*. *Ostrich* **59**: 142.
Ward, D. (1989a). Habitat selection of Crowned, Blackwinged and Lesser Blackwinged Plovers. *Ostrich* **60(2)**: 49-54.
Ward, D. (1989b). Feeding ecology of Crowned, Blackwinged and Lesser Blackwinged Plovers. *Ostrich* **60(3)**: 97-102.
Ward, D. (1989c). Behaviour associated with breeding of Crowned, Blackwinged and Lesser Blackwinged Plovers. *Ostrich* **60(4)**: 141-150.
Ward, D. (1990a). Incubation temperatures and behavior of Crowned, Black-winged and Lesser Black-winged Plovers. *Auk* **107(1)**: 10-17.
Ward, D. (1990b). The demography, diet and reproductive success of African Black Oystercatchers on a sandy beach. *Ostrich* **61(3-4)**: 125-133.
Ward, D. (1991). The size selection of clams by African Black Oystercatchers and Kelp Gulls. *Ecology* **72(2)**: 513-522.
Ward, D. (1992). The behavioural and morphological affinities of some Vanelline plovers (Vannellinae: Charadriiformes: Aves). *J. Zool., London* **228**: 625-640.
Ward, D. (1993). African Black Oystercatchers (*Haematopus moquini*) feeding on wedge clams (*Donax serra*): the effects of non-random prey availability in the intertidal on the predictions of an optimal diet model. *Ethology, Ecology & Evolution* **5(4)**: 457-466.
Ward, D. & Maclean, G. (1988). Coexistence of Crowned and Blackwinged Plovers. *Oecologia* **77(3)**: 400-406.
Warham, J. (1958). Bridled Tern. *British Birds* **51**: 303-308.
Warham, J. & Bell, B.D. (1979). The birds of Antipodes Island, New Zealand. *Notornis* **26**: 121-169.
Warheit, K.I., Lindberg, D.R. & Boekelheide, R.J. (1984). Pinniped disturbance lowers reproductive success of Black Oystercatcher *Haematopus bachmani* (Aves). *Mar. Ecol. Prog. Ser.* **17(1)**: 101-104.
Warman, S.R. (1979). The Roseate Tern *Sterna dougallii arideensis* on Aride Island, Seychelles. *Bull. Brit. Orn. Club* **99**: 124-128.
Warner, D.W. (1947). *The Ornithology of New Caledonia and the Loyalty Islands*. PhD thesis, Cornell University, Ithaca, New York.
Warner, D.W. (1948). The present status of the Kagu, *Rhynochetos jubatus*, on New Caledonia. *Auk* **65**: 287-288.
Warner, D.W. & Dickerman, R.W. (1959). The status of *Rallus elegans tenuirostris* in Mexico. *Condor* **61**: 49-51.
Warnock, N.D. (1994). *Biotic and Abiotic Factors Affecting the Distribution and Abundance of a Wintering Population of Dunlin*. PhD dissertation, University of California, Davis, California.
Warnock, N.D. & Gill, R.E.J. (1996). Dunlin (*Calidris alpina*). No. **203** in: Poole & Gill (1996).
Warnock, N.D., Page, G.W. & Stenzel, L.E. (1995). Nonmigratory movements of Dunlins on their California wintering grounds. *Wilson Bull.* **107**: 131-139.
Warnock, S.E. & Takekawa, J.Y. (1996). Wintering site fidelity and movements patterns of Western Sandpipers *Calidris mauri* in the San Francisco Bay estuary. *Ibis* **138(2)**: 160-167.
Warriner, J.S., Warriner, J.C., Page, G.W. & Stenzel L.E. (1986). Mating system and reproductive success of a small population of polygamous Snowy Plovers. *Wilson Bull.* **98(1)**: 15-37.
Watanuki, Y. (1982). Size selective hunting by Slaty-backed Gulls *Larus schistisagus* and influence on fledging success of Black-tailed Gulls *L. crassirostris*. *J. Yamashina Inst. Orn.* **14**: 25-34.
Watanuki, Y. (1983). Predation and anti-predation behavior in seabirds on Teuri Island, Hokkaido. *J. Yamashina Inst. Orn.* **15**: 167-174.
Watanuki, Y. (1987). Breeding biology and foods of Rhinoceros Auklets on Teuri Island, Japan. *Natl. Inst. Polar Res. (NIPR) Symposium Polar Biological Proceedings* **1**: 175-183.
Watanuki, Y. (1988a). Regional difference in the diet of Slaty-backed Gulls breeding around Hokkaido. *J. Yamashina Inst. Orn.* **20**: 71-81.
Watanuki, Y. (1988b). Intraspecific predation and chick survival: comparison among colonies of Slaty-backed Gull. *Oikos* **53**: 194-202.
Watanuki, Y. (1989). [Sex and individual variations in the diet of Slaty-backed Gulls breeding on Teuri Island, Hokkaido]. *Jap. J. Orn.* **38**: 1-13. In Japanese.
Watanuki, Y. (1990). Daily activity pattern of Rhinoceros Auklets and kleptoparasitism by Black-tailed Gulls. *Ornis Scand.* **21**: 28-36.
Watanuki, Y. (1992). Individual diet difference, parental care and reproductive success in Slaty-backed Gulls. *Condor* **94**: 159-171.
Watanuki, Y. (1994). Responses of breeding seabirds to the crash of sardine stocks in Japan. *Pacific Seabird Group Bull.* **21**: 51.
Watanuki, Y., Kondo, N. & Nakagawa, H. (1988). [Status of seabirds breeding in Hokkaido]. *Jap. J. Orn.* **37**: 17-32. In Japanese.
Watier, J.M. & Fournier, O. (1980). Eléments de démographie de la population d'Avocettes *Recurvirostra avosetta* de la côte atlantique française. *Oiseau et RFO* **50**: 307-321.
Watkins, B.P. & Furness, R.W. (1986). Population status, breeding and conservation of the Gough Moorhen. *Ostrich* **57**: 32-36.
Watkins, D. (1993). *A National Plan for Shorebird Conservation in Australia*. RAOU Report **90**. Australasian Wader Study Group, Royal Australasian Ornithologists Union & World Wide Fund for Nature.
Watling, D. (1982). *Birds of Fiji, Tonga and Samoa*. Millwood Press, Wellington, New Zealand.
Watling, D. (1983). Ornithological notes from Sulawesi. *Emu* **83**: 247-261.
Watson, A. (1988). Dotterel *Charadrius morinellus* numbers in relation to human impact in Scotland. *Biol. Conserv.* **43(4)**: 245-256.
Watson, A. (1989). Dotterel populations and spacing on three Scottish areas in 1967-1986. *Ornis Fenn.* **66**: 85-99.
Watson, A. & Rae, R. (1987). Dotterel numbers, habitat and breeding success in Scotland. *Scottish Birds* **14**: 191-198.
Watson, G.E. (1962). Notes on the Spotted Rail in Cuba. *Wilson Bull.* **74**: 349-356.
Watson, G.E. (1971). Slender-billed Gull *Larus genei* at Lake Manyara, Tanzania. *Bull. Brit. Orn. Club* **91**: 167.
Watson, G.E. (1973). Sea-bird colonies in the islands of the Aegean Sea. *Natl. Geogr. Soc. Res. Rep.* **1966**(Projects): 299-305.
Watson, G.E. (1975). *Birds of the Antarctic and Sub-Antarctic*. American Geophysical Union, Washington, D.C.
Watson, G.E. & Divoky, G.J. (1972). Pelagic bird and mammal observations in the eastern Chukchi Sea, early fall 1970. Pp. 111-172 in: Merton, C.I. ed. (1972). *An Ecological Survey in the Eastern Chukchi Sea, September-October 1970*. US Coast Guard Oceanographic Report **50**.
Watson, G.E., Zusi, R.L. & Storer, R.E. (1963). *Preliminary Guide to the Birds of the Indian Ocean*. US National Museum, Smithsonian Institution, Washington, D.C.
Watson, I.M. (1955). Some species seen at the Laverton Saltworks, Victoria, 1950-1953, with notes on seasonal changes. *Emu* **55**: 224-248.
Watson, J.B. (1908). The behavior of Noddy and Sooty Terns. *Papers Tortugas Lab.* **2**: 187-225.
Watson, J.J. (1992). Dune breeding birds and off-road vehicles. *Naturalist* **36**: 8-12.
Watson, J.J. & Kerley, G.I.H. (1995). A survey of the dune-breeding in the eastern Cape, South Africa. *Ostrich* **66(1)**: 15-20.
Watson, J.L. (1969). Aviary breeding of the Black Crake. *Honeyguide* **59**: 11-12.
Watson, R.M., Singh, T. & Parker, I.S.C. (1970). The diet of duck and coot on Lake Naivasha. *East Afr. Wildl. J.* **8**: 131-144.
Watt, J. (1955). Territory threat display of the Black Oystercatcher (*Haematopus unicolor unicolor*). *Notornis* **6**: 175.
Waugh, J. (1988). An Oriental Pratincole in Tasmania. *Stilt* **12**: 58, 60.
Weaver, D.J. (1990). Survey of Sukla Phanta for Bengal Floricans. *Bull. Oriental Bird Club* **12**: 4-7.
Weaver, D.J. (1991). A survey of Bengal Floricans *Houbaropsis bengalensis* at Royal Sukla Phanta Wildlife Reserve and Royal Bardia National Park, western Nepal, 1990. Unpublished report to the Oriental Bird Club.
Weaver, D.K. (1970). *Parental Behavior of the Herring Gull (*Larus argentatus smithsonianus*) and its Effect on Reproductive Success*. PhD dissertation, University of Michigan, Ann Arbor, Michigan.
Weaver, P. (1987). *The Lapwing*. Shire Publications, Ltd, Bucks, UK.
Webb, A., Harrison, N.M., Leaper, G.M., Steele, R.D., Tasker, M.L. & Pienkowski, M.W. (1990). *Seabird Distribution West of Britain*. Nature Conservancy Council, Peterborough, UK.
Webb, B.E. & Conry, J.A. (1979). A Sharp-tailed Sandpiper in Colorado, with notes on plumage and behaviour. *Western Birds* **10(2)**: 86-91.
Webb, C. (1965). The Hoatzin. *Animals* **7**: 222-223.
Webb, C.S. (1954). *A Wanderer in the Wind*. Hutchinson, London.
Webb, H.P. (1992). Field observations of the birds of Santa Isabel, Solomon Islands. *Emu* **92**: 52-57.
Webber, G.L. (1968). Solitary Sandpiper in Wiltshire. *British Birds* **61**: 265-267.
Weber, C. (1989). Ein Weißbürzel-Strandläufer *Calidris fuscicollis* in Niedersachsen. *Limicola* **3(2)**: 61-64.
Weber, J.W. & Fitzner, R.E. (1986). Nesting of the Glaucous-winged Gull east of the Washington Cascades. *Amer. Birds* **40**: 567-569.
Weber, L.M. & Martin, B.H. (1991). Piping Plover nest on dry and nearly dry alkali wetland in the northern Great Plains: 1986-90. *Prairie Nat.* **23**: 209-21.
Webster, C.G. (1964). Fall foods of Soras from two habitats in Connecticut. *J. Wildl. Manage.* **28**: 163-165.
Webster, J.D. (1941a). The breeding of the Black Oystercatcher. *Wilson Bull.* **53**: 141 156.
Webster, J.D. (1941b). The feeding habits of the Black Oystercatcher. *Condor* **43** 175-180.
Webster, J.D. (1942). Notes on the growth and plumages of the Black Oystercatcher. *Condor* **44**: 205 211.
Webster, J.D. (1943). The downy young of oystercatchers. *Wilson Bull.* **55**: 40-46.
Webster, J.D. (1951). Corrections concerning data on Alaskan birds. *Condor* **53**: 54.
Webster, R.E., Morlan, J. & Roberson, D. (1990). First record of the Sooty Tern in California. *Western Birds* **21(1)**: 25-32.
Weeden, R.B. (1959). A new breeding record of the Wandering Tattler in Alaska. *Auk* **76**: 230-232.
Weeden, R.B. (1965). Further notes on Wandering Tattlers in central Alaska. *Condor* **67**: 87-89.
Wege, D.C. & Long, A.J. (1995). *Key Areas for Threatened Birds in the Neotropics*. BirdLife Conservation Series **5**. BirdLife International, Cambridge.
Weggler, M. (1992). [Foraging behaviour of four species of waders: patterns of locomotion, foraging success and spatial distribution]. *Orn. Beob.* **89(3)**: 177-190. In German with English summary.
Wehle, D.H.S. (1976). *Summer Food and Feeding Ecology of Tufted and Horned Puffins on Buldir Island, Alaska, 1975*. MSc thesis, University of Alaska, Fairbanks, Alaska.
Wehle, D.H.S. (1980). *The Breeding Biology of the Puffins: Tufted Puffin* Lunda cirrhata, *Horned Puffin* Fratercula corniculata *and Rhinoceros Auklet* Cerorhinca nonocerata. PhD thesis, University of Alaska, Fairbanks, Alaska.
Wehle, D.H.S. (1983). The food, feeding and development of young Tufted and Horned Puffins in Alaska. *Condor* **85**: 427-442.
Wehner, R. (1966). Einfluße der Weißflügelseeschwalbe (*Chlidonias leucopterus*) nach Mitteleuropa. *Vogelwarte* **23**: 173-180.
Weid, R. (1991). Verhalten und Habitatansprüche des Wachtelkönigs im intensiv genutzen Grünland in Franken. *Vogelwelt* **112**: 90-96.
Weidmann, R. & Weidmann, U. (1958). An analysis of the stimulus situation releasing food-begging in the Black-headed Gull. *Anim. Behav.* **6**: 114.
Weidmann, U. (1955). Some reproductive activities of the Common Gull, *Larus canus* L. *Ardea* **43**: 85-132.
Weidmann, U. (1956). Observations and experiments on egg-laying in the Black-headed Gull (*Larus ridibundus* L.). *Brit. J. Animal Behav.* **4**: 150-161.
Weimerskirch, H. & Stahl, J.C. (1988). The breeding and feeding ecology of the Kerguelen Tern *Sterna virgata*. *Ornis Scand.* **19**: 199-204.
Weimerskirch, H., Zotier, R. & Jouventin, P. (1989). The avifauna of the Kergulen Islands. *Emu* **89**: 15-29.
Weir, N.L. & Graves, H.B. (1982). Discriminant analysis of the peent call for identification of individual male American Woodcock. Pp. 34-39 in: Dwyer & Storm (1982).
Welch, G. & Welch, H. (1989). A preliminary survey of the Arabian Bustard in Djibouti. *Bustard Studies* **4**: 177-184.
Welham, C.V.J. (1987). Diet and foraging behavior of Ring-billed Gulls breeding at Dog Lake, Manitoba. *Wilson Bull.* **99**: 233-239.
Welham, C.V.J. & Ydenberg, R.C. (1993). Efficiency maximizing flight speeds in parent Black Terns. *Ecology* **74(6)**: 1893-1901.
Weller, M.W. (1967). Notes on some marsh birds of Cape San Antonio, Argentina. *Ibis* **109**: 391-411.
Weller, M.W. & Fredrickson, L.H. (1974). Avian ecology of a managed glacial marsh. *Living Bird* **12**: 269-291.
Wells, D.R. (1990). Malayan bird report: 1986 and 1987. *Malay. Nat. J.* **43**: 172-210.

Wells, J.V. & Vickery, P.D. (1990). Willet nesting in Sphagnum Bog in eastern Maine. *J. Field Orn.* **61(1)**: 73-75. In English with Spanish summary.

Wenink, P.W., Baker, A.J. & Tilanus, M.G.J. (1993). Hypervariable control region sequences reveal global population structuring in a long-distance migrant shorebird, the Dunlin (*Calidris alpina*). *Proc. Natl. Acad. Sci. USA* **90**: 94-98.

Wenink, P.W., Baker, A.J. & Tilanus, M.G.J. (1994). Mitochondrial control region sequences in two shorebird species, the Turnstone and the Dunlin, and their utility in population genetic studies. *Mol. Biol. Evol.* **11**: 22-31.

Wenink, P.W., Baker, A.J. & Tilanus, M.G.J. (1996). Global mitochondrial DNA phylogeography of Holarctic breeding Dunlins (*Calidris alpina*). *Evolution* **50**: 318-330.

Wenner, A.S. & Nesbitt, S.A. (1987). Wintering of Greater Sandhill Cranes in Florida. Pp. 196-200 in: Lewis (1987).

Wennrich, G. (1981). Zuchterfolge und Verhalten von Sonnerallen (*Eurypyga helias*) im Vogelpark Walsrode. *Gefiederte Welt* **105**: 145-150, 167-172.

Wennrich, G. (1985). [Measurements and behavioral observations of a newly hatched *Bugeranus carunculatus*]. *Zool. Garten* **55(2/3)**: 97-112. In German with English summary.

Werder, J.P. & Gillieron, G. (1978). Site de nidification étonnant pour le Petit gravelot (*Charadrius dubius*). [Astonishing nesting site of the Little Ringed Plover (*Charadrius dubius*)]. *Nos Oiseaux* **34(8)**: 354-355.

Wershler, C.R. (1986). The Mountain Plover in Canada. *Prov. Mus. Alberta Nat. Hist. Occas. Pap.* **9**: 259-261.

Weseloh, D.V. (1981). A probable Franklin x Ring-billed Gull pair nesting in Alberta. *Can. Field-Nat.* **95**: 474-476.

Weseloh, D.V. & Mineau, P. (1986). Apparent hybrid Common Black-headed Gull nesting in Lake Ontario. *Amer. Birds* **40**: 18-20.

Weseloh, D.V. & Myers, M.T. (1981). Seasonal fluctuations in gull numbers at Calgary, Alberta, Canada and a model for estimating their numbers. *Colonial Waterbirds* **4**: 132-137.

Weseloh, D.V. & Weseloh, L.M. (1983). Numbers and nest site characteristics of the Piping Plover in central Alberta, 1974-77. *Blue Jay* **41**: 155-161.

Weseloh, D.V., Sutherland, R.B. & Mineau, P. (1983). Utilization of garbage dumps by Ring-billed and Herring Gulls on the lower Great Lakes (abstract). *Colonial Waterbirds* **6**: 72.

Weske, J.S. (1969). *An Ecological Study of the Black Rail in Dorchester County, Maryland*. MSc thesis, Cornell University, Ithaca, New York.

Wesley, H.D. (1986). Courtship behavior of Painted Snipe in Tiruchirapalli, Tamilnadu. *J. Bombay Nat. Hist. Soc.* **83(2)**: 435-436.

Wesley, H.D. (1990). Breeding habits and habitat of the Painted Snipe as observed in Tiruchirapalli, Tamilnadu, south India. Pp. 456-462 in: Daniel, J.C. & Serrao, J.S. eds. (1990). *Conservation in Developing Countries: Problems and Prospects - Proceedings of the Centenary Seminar of the Bombay Natural History Society*. Bombay Natural History Society & Oxford University Press, Bombay & Delhi.

West, O. (1963). Notes on the Wattled Crane, *Bugeranus carunculatus* (Gmelin). *Ostrich* **34**: 63-77.

West, O. (1976). Notes on the distribution and status of the southern population of Wattled Crane in Africa. Pp. 347-349 in: Lewis (1976a).

West, O. (1982). The Wattled Crane *Grus carunculatus* (Gmelin), an endangered species. *Naturalist* **27(1)**: 2-9.

Weston, F.M. & Williams, E.A. (1965). Recent records of the Eskimo Curlew. *Auk* **82**: 493-496.

Weston, M. (1993). Twelve years of counting the Hooded Plover in Victoria, Australia. *Stilt* **23**: 15-19.

Weston, M. & Rush, M. (1992). Probable pseudo copulation of Red-necked Avocet. *Stilt* **21**: 28.

Westwood, N.J. (1983). Breeding of the Stone-curlews at Weeting Heath, Norfolk. *British Birds* **76(7)**: 291-304.

Wetmore, A. (1916). *Birds of Puerto Rico*. US Department of Agriculture Bulletin **326**. Washington, D.C.

Wetmore, A. (1926). *Observations on the Birds of Argentina, Paraguay, Uruguay and Chile*. US National Museum Bulletin **133**. Smithsonian Institution, Washington, D.C.

Wetmore, A. (1944). The subspecific characters and distribution of the New World skimmers (*Rynchops nigra*). *Caldasia* **3(2)**: 111-118.

Wetmore, A. (1965). *The Birds of the Republic of Panama*. Part 1. Tinamidae (Tinamous) to Rynchopidae (Skimmers). Smithsonian Miscellaneous Collections **150**. Smithsonian Institution, Washington, D.C. 483 pp.

Wetmore, A. & Borrero, H. (1964). Description of a race of the Double-striped Thick-knee (Aves, family Burhinidae) from Colombia. *Auk* **81**: 231-233.

Wetmore, A. & Swales, B.H. (1931). *The Birds of Haiti and the Dominican Republic*. US National Museum Bulletin **155**. Smithsonian Instituion, Washington, D.C.

Wetmore, A. & Watson, G.E. (1969). The generic name for the Dovekie or Little Auk. *Bull. Brit. Orn. Club* **89**: 6-7.

Whateley, A. (1982). Anting in the African Finfoot. *Ostrich* **53(3)**: 177.

Wheeler, P. (1989). Geographical variation in Royal Terns. *Birding World* **2**: 326-327.

Wheeler, R. (1948). More notes from 'The Bend'. *Emu* **48**: 1-7.

Wheeler, R. (1959). The RAOU camp-out at Noosa Heads, Queensland, 1958. *Emu* **59**: 229-249.

Wheeler, R. (1973). The Black-tailed Native Hen recent invasion. *Geelon Nat.* **10**: 45-50.

Wheeler, W.R. (1946). Pacific Gulls and mussels. *Emu* **45**: 307.

Wheeler, W.R. (1955). Charadriiformes at the Laverton Saltworks, Victoria, 1950-1953. *Emu* **55**: 279-295.

Wheeler, W.R. & Watson, I. (1963). The Silver Gull *Larus novaehollandiae* Stephens. *Emu* **63**: 99-173.

Whinray, J.S. (1978). Painted Button-quail feeding. *Austr. Bird Watcher* **7(6)**: 204.

Whinray, J.S. (1980). The first Australian breeding record of the White-fronted Tern. *Austr. Bird Watcher* **8**: 137-146.

Whinray, J.S. (1982). More Australian breeding records of the White-fronted Tern. *Austr. Bird Watcher* **9**: 160-164.

Whistler, H. (1949). *Popular Handbook of Indian Birds*. 4th edition. Gurney & Jackson, London.

Whitaker, H. ed. (1992). *People, Water, and Wildlife: Human Population Impacts on Cranes*. National Audubon Society, Kearney, Nebraska.

White, C.M., Emison, W.B. & Williamson, F.S.L. (1973). DDE in a resident Aleutian Island peregrine population. *Condor* **75**: 306-311.

White, C.M., Williamson, F.S.L. & Emison, W.B. (1974). *Tringa glareola* - a new breeding species for North America. *Auk* **91(1)**: 175-177.

White, C.M.N. (1945). The ornithology of the Kaonde-Lunda Province, northern Rhodesia. Part III. Systematic list (contd.). *Ibis* **87**: 309-345.

White, C.M.N. (1965). *A Revised Check-list of African non-Passerine Birds*. Government Press, Lusaka.

White, C.M.N. (1976). Comments on the Dusky Moorhen *Gallinula tenebrosa*. *Bull. Brit. Orn. Club* **96**: 125-128.

White, C.M.N. (1983). Distribution and habitat preference of the Upland Sandpiper *Bartramia longicauda* in Wisconsin. *Amer. Birds* **37**: 16-22.

White, C.M.N. & Bruce, M.D. (1986). *The Birds of Wallacea (Sulawesi, the Moluccas and the Lesser Sunda Islands, Indonesia)*. BOU Check-list **7**. British Ornithologists' Union, London.

White, D.H. & James, D. (1978). Differential use of fresh water environments by wintering waterfowl of coastal Texas. *Wilson Bull.* **90**: 99-111.

White, D.H. & Kolbe, E.J. (1985). Secondary poisoning of Franklin's Gulls in Texas by monocrotophos. *J. Wildl. Diseases* **21**: 76-78.

White, D.H. & Mitchell, C.A. (1990). Body mass and lipid content of shorebirds overwintering on the south Texas coast (USA). *J. Field Orn.* **61**: 445-452.

White, D.H., Mitchell, C.A. & Prouty, R.M. (1983). Nesting biology of Laughing Gulls in relation to agricultural chemicals in South Texas, 1978-81. *Wilson Bull.* **95**: 540-551.

White, D.H., Mitchell, C.A. & Swineford, D.M. (1984). Reproductive success of Black Skimmers in Texas relative to environmental pollutants. *J. Field Orn.* **55**: 18-30.

White, D.M. (1985). A report on the captive breeding of Australian Bustards at Serendip Wildlife Research Station. *Bustard Studies* **3**: 195-212.

White, D.M. (1987). The status and distribution of the Brolga (*Grus rubicundus*) in Victoria, Australia. Pp. 115-131 in: Archibald & Pasquier (1987a).

White, E. & Gittins, J.C. (1965). The value of measurements in the study of wader migration with particular reference to the Oystercatcher. *Bird Study* **11**: 257 261.

White, H.L. (1922a). Description of nests and eggs of *Turnix olivii* (Robinson). *Emu* **22**: 2-3.

White, H.L. (1922b). A collecting trip to Cape York Peninsula. *Emu* **22**: 99-116.

White, L.M. (1985). *Body Composition and Fat Deposition of Migrant Semipalmated Sandpipers During Autumn Migration in the Bay of Fundy*. MSc thesis, University of Guelph, Guelph, Canada.

White, R.P. (1988). Wintering grounds and migration patterns of the Upland Sandpiper. *Amer. Birds* **42(5)**: 1247-1253.

White, S.A. (1918). Birds of Lake Victoria and the Murray River for 100 miles down stream. *Emu* **18**: 8-25.

White, S.C., Robertson, W.B. & Ricklefs, R.E. (1976). The effect of hurricane Agnes on growth and survival of tern chicks in Florida. *J. Field Orn.* **47(1)**: 54-71.

White, S.R. (1946). Notes on the bird life of Australia's heaviest rainfall region. *Emu* **46**: 81-122.

Whitfield, D.P. (1985). Raptor predation on wintering waders in southeast Scotland. *Ibis* **127**: 544-558.

Whitfield, D.P. (1986). Plumage variability and territoriality in breeding Turnstone *Arenaria interpres*: status signalling or individual recognition? *Anim. Behav.* **34**: 1471-1482.

Whitfield, D.P. (1987). Plumage variability, status signalling and individual recognition in avian flocks. *Trends Ecol. Evol.* **2**: 13-18.

Whitfield, D.P. (1988a). The social significance of plumage variability in wintering Turnstone *Arenaria interpres*. *Anim. Behav.* **36**: 408-415.

Whitfield, D.P. (1988b). Sparrowhawks *Accipiter nisus* affect the spacing behaviour of wintering Turnstone *Arenaria interpres* and Redshank *Tringa totanus*. *Ibis* **130**: 284-287.

Whitfield, D.P. (1989). [Sexual conflict in the Red-necked Phalarope]. *Bliki* **7**: 59-62. In Icelandic.

Whitfield, D.P. (1990a). Individual feeding specializations of wintering Turnstone *Arenaria interpres*. *J. Anim. Ecol.* **59**: 193-212.

Whitfield, D.P. (1990b). Male choice and sperm competition as constraints on polyandry in the Red-necked Phalarope *Phalaropus lobatus*. *Behav. Ecol. Sociobiol.* **27**: 247-254.

Whitfield, D.P. & Brade, J.J. (1991). The breeding behavior of the Knot *Calidris canutus*. *Ibis* **133**: 246-255.

Whiting, R.M. & Boggus, T.G. (1982). Breeding biology of American Woodcock in east Texas. Pp. 132-138 in: Dwyer & Storm (1982).

Whitlock, F.L. (1914). Notes on the Spotless Crake and Western Ground-Parrot. *Emu* **13**: 202-205.

Whitman, P.L. (1988). Biology and conservation of the endangered Interior Least Tern: a literature review. *US Fish Widl. Serv. Biol. Rep.* **88**: 3.

Whitten, A.J., Bishop, K.D., Nash, S.V. & Clayton, L. (1987). One or more extinctions from Sulawesi, Indonesia? *Conserv. Biol.* **1**: 42-48.

Whittle, J. (1992). Marbled Godwit. *Spoonbill* **41(8)**: 6.

Whittow, G.C. (1980). Physiological and ecological correlates of prolonged incubation in seabirds. *Amer. Zool.* **20**: 427-436.

Whittow, G.C. (1984). Physiological ecology of incubation in tropical seabirds. *Studies in Avian Biology* **8**: 47-72.

Whittow, G.C. (1985). Partition of water loss from the eggs of the Sooty Tern between the pre-pipping and pipped periods. *Wilson Bull.* **97**: 240-241.

Whittow, G.C., Grant, G.S. & Flint, E.N. (1985). Egg water loss, shell water-vapor conductance, and the incubation period of the Grey-backed Tern (*Sterna lunata*). *Condor* **87**: 269-279.

Whittow, G.C., Kurata, L.M. & Zhange, Q.G. (1992). Failure of the 1989 Sooty Tern breeding season on Manan Island, following heavy rain. *Elepaio* **52**: 36-37.

Whoriskey, F.G. & Fitzgerald, G.J. (1985). The effects of bird predation on an estuarine stickleback (Pisces: Gasterosteidae) community. *Can. J. Zool.* **63**: 301-307.

Whyte, A.J. (1985). *Breeding Ecology of the Piping Plover (*Charadrius melodus*) in Central Saskatchewan*. MSc thesis, University of Saskatchewan, Saskatoon, Canada.

Widgery, D.E. (1982). *Over the Arabian Gulf: a View of Birds and Places*. De Mont Publications, Hamilton, New Zealand.

Widrig, R.S. (1980). November nesting of the Collared Plover *Charadrius collaris* in western Mexico. *Wader Study Group Bull.* **29**: 30-31.

Widrig, R.S. (1983a). December nesting of the Collared Plover in western Mexico. *Amer. Birds* **37(3)**: 273-274.

Widrig, R.S. (1983b). A Bristle-thighed Curlew at Leadbetter Point, Washington. *Western Birds* **14(4)**: 203-204.

Wied-Neuwied, M. Prinz zu (1820-1821). *Reise nach Brasilien in den Jahren 1815-1817*. Heinrich Ludwig Broenner, Frankfurt am Main.

Wied-Neuwied, M. Prinz zu (1833a). *Beiträge zur Naturgeschichte von Brasilien*. Vol. 3. Part 2. Landes-Industrie-Comptoirs, Weimar, Germany.

Wied-Neuwied, M. Prinz zu (1833b). *Beiträge zur Naturgeschichte von Brasilien*. Vol. 4. Part 2. Landes-Industrie-Comptoirs, Weimar, Germany.

Wiens, J., Patten, D.T. & Botkin, D.B. (1993). Assessing ecological impact assessment: lessons from Mono Lake, California. *Ecol. Appl.* **3**: 595-609.

Wiens, J.A. (1966). Notes on the distraction display of the Virginia Rail. *Wilson Bull.* **78**: 229-231.

Wiens, T.P. (1986). *Nest-site Tenacity and Mate Retention in the Piping Plover*. MSc thesis, University of Minnesota, Duluth, Minnesota.

Wiens, T.P. & Cuthbert, F.J. (1988). Nest-site tenacity and mate retention of the Piping Plover. *Wilson Bull.* **100(4)**: 545-553.

Wiersma, P. & Piersma, T. (1994). Effects of microhabitat, flocking, climate and migratory goal on energy expenditure in the annual cycle of Red Knots. *Condor* **96**: 257-279.

Wiersma, P., Bruinzeel, L. & Piersma, T. (1993). [Energy savings in waders: studies on the insulation of Knots]. *Limosa* **66(2)**: 41-52. In Dutch with English summary.

Wiggins, D.A. (1989). Consequences of variation in brood size on the allocation of parental care in Common Terns (*Sterna hirundo*). *Can. J. Zool.* **67**: 2411-2413.

Wiggins, D.A. & Morris, R.D. (1986). Criteria for female choice of mates: courtship feeding and parental care in the Common Tern. *Amer. Naturalist* **128**: 126-129.

Wiggins, D.A. & Morris, R.D. (1987). Parental care of the Common Tern *Sterna hirundo*. *Ibis* **129**: 533-540.

Wiggins, D.A. & Morris, R.D. (1988). Courtship feeding and copulatory behaviour in the Common Tern *Sterna hirundo*. *Ornis Scand.* **19**: 163-165.

Wiggins, D.A., Morris, R.D., Nisbet, I.C.T. & Custer, T.W. (1984). Occurrence and timing of second clutches in Common Terns. *Auk* **101**: 281-287.

Wightman, J. (1968). Bustards (behaviour, display, reproduction, habitat). *Animals* **11**: 341-343.

Wijesinghe, D.P. (1994). *Checklist of the Birds of Sri Lanka*. Ceylon Bird Club, Colombo.

Wymenga, E. & van Dijk, K. (1985). Slender-billed Curlew in Tunisia in February 1984. *Dutch Birding* **7(2)**: 67-68.

Wilbur, S.R. (1974a). The literature of the California Least Tern. *Bur. Sport Fisheries & Wildlf. Spec. Scient. Rep.* **175**: 1-18.

Wilbur, S.R. (1974b). The status of the Light-footed Clapper Rail. *Amer. Birds* **28**: 868-870.

Wilbur, S.R. (1987). *Birds of Baja California*. University of California Press, Berkeley & Los Angeles, California.

Wilbur, S.R. & Tomlinson, R.E. (1976). *The Literature of the Western Clapper Rails*. US Fish & Wildlife Service Special Scientific Report - Wildlife **194**.

Wilbur, S.R., Jorgensen, P.D., Massey, B.W. & Basham, V.A. (1979). The Light-footed Clapper Rail: an update. *Amer. Birds* **33**: 251.

Wilcox, L. (1944). Great Black-backed Gull breeding in New York. *Auk* **61**: 653-654.

Wilcox, L. (1959). A twenty year banding study of the Piping Plover. *Auk* **76**: 129-152.

Wilcox, L. (1980). Observations on the life history of Willets on Long Island, New York. *Wilson Bull.* **92**: 253-258.

Wildash, P. (1968). *Birds of South Vietnam*. Tultle, Rutland, Vermont.

Wilds, C. (1982). Separating the Yellowlegs. *Birding* **14**: 172-188.

Wilds, C. & Czaplak, D. (1994). Yellow-legged Gulls (*Larus cachinnans*) in North America. *Wilson Bull.* **106**: 344-356.

Wilds, C. & Newton, M. (1983). The identification of dowitchers. *Birding* **15(4/5)**: 151-165.

Wilds, C.P. (1978). Mountain Plover at Chincoteague. *Raven* **49(2)**: 34-35.

Wilkie, A.O.M. (1981). Incubation rhythm and behaviour of a dotterel *Charadrius morinellus* nesting in Norway. *Ornis Fenn.* **58(1)**: 11-20. In English with Finnish summary.

Wilkinson, A.S. (1927). Birds of Kapiti Island. *Emu* **26**: 237-258.

Wilkinson, R. & Huxley, C.R. (1978). Vocalizations of chicks and juveniles and the development of adult calls in the Aldabra White-throated Rail *Dryolimnas cuvieri aldabranus* (Aves: Rallidae). *J. Zool., London* **186**: 487-505.

Wilkinson, R., Beecroft, R. & Aidley, D.J. (1982). Nigeria: a new wintering area for the Little Crake *Porzana parva*. *Bull. Brit. Orn. Club* **102**: 139-140.

Willard, D.E. (1985). Comparative feeding ecology of twenty-two tropical piscivores. *Orn. Monogr.* **36**: 788-797.

Willi, P. (1983). [*Calidris acuminata* in Rhein Delta]. *Egretta* **26(2)**: 67-68. In German with English summary.

Williams, A.H. (1988). Eskimo Curlew: on the road to recovery at last perhaps. *Bird Obs.* **16(2)**: 73.

Williams, A.J. (1977a). Midwinter diurnal activity and energetics of Kelp Gulls. *Cormorant* **3**: 4-9.

Williams, A.J. (1977b). Notes on the breeding biology of the Hartlaub's Gull. *Cormorant* **3**: 15.

Williams, A.J. (1980a). The effect of attendance by three adults upon nest contents and chick growth in the Southern Great Skua. *Notornis* **27**: 79-85.

Williams, A.J. (1980b). Aspects of the breeding biology of the Subantarctic Skua at Marion Island. *Ostrich* **51**: 160-167.

Williams, A.J. (1980c). Variation in weight of eggs and its effect on the breeding biology of the Great Skua. *Emu* **80**: 198-202.

Williams, A.J. (1986). African Skimmers breeding in the Okavango River. *Lanioturdus* **22(3)**: 53-54.
Williams, A.J. (1989). Courtship feeding and copulation by Hartlaub's Gulls *Larus hartlaubii* and probable Hartlaub's Greyheaded Gull *L. cirrocephalus* hybrids. *Cormorant* **17**: 73-76.
Williams, A.J. (1990). Hartlaub's Gull: eggs and incubation. *Ostrich* **61**: 93-96.
Williams, A.J., Cooper, J. & Hockey, P.A.R. (1984). Aspects of the breeding biology of the Kelp Gull at Marion Island and in South Africa. *Ostrich* **55**: 147-157.
Williams, A.J., Siegfried, W.R., Burger, A.E. & Berruti, A. (1979). The Prince Edward Islands: a sanctuary for seabirds in the southern ocean. *Biol. Conserv.* **15(1)**: 59-71.
Williams, A.J., Steele, W.K., Cooper, J. & Crawford, R.J.M. (1990). Distribution, population size and conservation of the Hartlaub's Gull *Larus hartlaubii*. *Ostrich* **61**: 667-87.
Williams, B., Akers, B., Beck, R. & Via, J. (1993). The 1992 colonial and beach-nesting waterbird survey of the Virginia barrier islands. *Raven* **64**: 24-29.
Williams, G., Holmes, J. & Kirby, J. (1995). Action plans for United Kingdom and European rare, threatened and internationally important birds. *Ibis* **137(1)**(Suppl.): S201-S213.
Williams, G.D., Coppinger, M.P. & Maclean, G.L. (1989). Distribution and breeding of the Rock Pratincole on the upper and middle Zambezi River. *Ostrich* **60(2)**: 55-64.
Williams, G.R. (1952). Notornis in March, 1951. A report of the sixth expedition. *Notornis* **4(8)**: 202-208.
Williams, G.R. (1957). Some preliminary data on the population dynamics of the Takahe (*Notornis mantelli* Owen, 1848). *Notornis* **7**: 165-171.
Williams, G.R. (1960). The Takahe (*Notornis mantelli* Owen, 1848). A general survey. *Trans. Roy. Soc. New Zealand* **88**: 235-258.
Williams, G.R. (1975). *Birds of New Zealand*. A.H. & A.W. Reed, Wellington.
Williams, G.R. (1979). Review: Rails of the world. *Notornis* **26**: 102-103.
Williams, G.R. & Given, D.R. (1981). *The Red Data Book of New Zealand*. Nature Conservation Council, Wellington.
Williams, G.R. & Miers, K.H. (1958). A five year banding study of the Takahe (*Notornis mantelli* Owen). *Notornis* **8**: 1-12.
Williams, J. (1987). Wattled Crane survey in Caprivi. *Quagga* **18**: 22-23.
Williams, J.G. (1941). On the birds of the Varanger Peninsula, East Finmark. *Ibis* **Ser. 14, no. 5**: 245-264.
Williams, L. (1927). Notes on the Black Oystercatcher. *Condor* **29**: 80 81.
Williams, L.E. (1978). Threatened, Florida Sandhill Crane, *Grus canadensis*. Pp. 36-37 in: Kale (1978).
Williams, L.E. & Phillips, R.W. (1972). North Florida Sandhill Crane populations. *Auk* **89**: 541-548.
Williams, M.D. (1981). Description of the nest and eggs of the Peruvian Thick-knee (*Burhinus superciliaris*). *Condor* **83(2)**: 183-184.
Williams, M.D. ed. (1986). *Report on the Cambridge Ornithological Expedition to China 1985*. Cambridge Ornithological Expedition to China 1985, Scarborough, UK.
Williams, M.D., Bakewell, D.N., Carey, G.J. & Holloway, S.J. (1986). On the bird migration at Beidaihe, Hebei province, China, during spring 1985. *Forktail* **2**: 3-20.
Williams, M.D., Bakewell, D.N., Carey, G.J., Xu Weishu & Jin Longrong (1991). Migration of cranes at Beidaihe Beach, Hebei Province, China. Pp. 139-147 in: Harris (1991b).
Williams, M.D., Carey, G.J., Duff, D.G. & Xu Weishu (1992). Autumn bird migration at Beidaihe, China, 1986-1990. *Forktail* **7**: 3-55.
Williams, M.L., Hothem, R.L. & Ohlendor, H.M. (1989). Recruitment failure in American Avocets and Black-winged Stilts nesting at Kesterson Reservoir, California, 1984-1985. *Condor* **91(4)**: 797-802.
Williams, R. (1995a). Neotropical notebook. Chile. *Cotinga* **4**: 67.
Williams, R. (1995b). Neotropical notebook. Falkland Islands/Malvinas. *Cotinga* **4**: 67-68.
Williams, S.O. (1969). *Population Dynamics of Woodcock Wintering in Louisiana*. MSc thesis, Louisiana State University, Baton Rouge, Louisiana.
Williams, S.O. (1982). Black Skimmers on the Mexican plateau. *Amer. Birds* **36**: 255-257.
Williams, S.O. (1987). A Northern Jacana in Trans-pecos Texas. *Western Birds* **18(2)**: 123-124.
Williams, S.O. (1989). Notes on the rail *Rallus longirostris tenuirostris* in the highlands of central Mexico. *Wilson Bull.* **101**: 117-120.
Williamson, F.S.L. & Peyton, L.J. (1963). Interbreeding of Glaucous-winged and Herring Gulls in the Cook Inlet Region of Alaska. *Condor* **65**: 24-28.
Williamson, F.S.L. & Smith, M.A. (1964). The distribution and breeding status of the Hudsonian Godwit in Alaska. *Condor* **66**: 41-50.
Williamson, K. (1943). The behaviour pattern of the Western Oystercatcher in defense of nests and young. *Ibis* **85**: 486 490.
Williamson, K. (1946). Field-notes on the breeding-biology of the Whimbrel. *Northwestern Naturalist* **21**: 167-184.
Williamson, K. (1950). The pseudo sleeping attitude of the Oystercatcher. *British Birds* **43**: 1-4.
Williamson, K. (1952). Regional variation in the distraction displays of the Oystercatcher. *Ibis* **94**: 85 96.
Williamson, K. (1960). Juvenile and winter plumages of marsh terns. *British Birds* **53**: 243-252.
Willis, E.O. (1983). Tinamous, chickens, guans, rails and trumpeters as army ant followers. *Rev. Bras. Biol.* **43**: 9-22.
Willis, E.O. (1994). Are *Actitis* sandpipers inverted flying fishes? *Auk* **111(1)**: 190-191.
Willis, E.O. & Oniki, Y. (1993). New and reconfirmed birds from the state of São Paulo, Brazil, with notes on disappearing species. *Bull. Brit. Orn. Club* **113**: 23-34.
Wills, R.G. (1958). The dowitcher problem. *Passenger Pigeon* **20**: 95-105.
Wilmé, L. & Langrand, O. (1990). Rediscovery of Slender-billed Flufftail *Sarothrura watersi* (Bartlett, 1879), and notes on the genus *Sarothrura* in Madagascar. *Biol. Conserv.* **51**: 211-223.
Wilson, A.E. & Swales, M.K. (1958). Flightless Moorhens *Porphyrio c. comeri* from Gough Island breed in captivity. *Avicult. Mag.* **64**: 43-45.
Wilson, E.M. (1988). Long-billed Curlew in Prince Georges County. *Maryland Birdlife* **44(1)**: 29-32.
Wilson, E.M. & Harriman, B.R. (1989). First record of the Terek Sandpiper in California. *Western Birds* **20(2)**: 63-69.
Wilson, G. (1974). Incubation behaviour of the African Jacana. *Ostrich* **45(3)**: 185-188.
Wilson, G. (1989). Notes on the Bush Thick-knee on the Capricornia Institute Campus. *Stilt* **15**: 27-28.
Wilson, G.E. (1976). Spotted Sandpipers nesting in Scotland. *British Birds* **69**: 288-292.
Wilson, H.J. (1982). Movements, home ranges and habitat use of wintering Woodcock in Ireland. *Wildl. Res. Rep.* **14**: 168-178.
Wilson, J. (1983). Wintering site fidelity of Woodcock in Ireland. Pp. 18-27 in: Kalchreuter (1983b).
Wilson, J.H. (1977). Camouflage posture of Bronze-wing Courser. *Honeyguide* **92**: 48.
Wilson, J.R. & Morrison, R.I.G. (1981). Primary moult in Oystercatcher in Iceland. *Ornis Scand.* **12**: 211 215.
Wilson, J.R. & Morrison, R.I.G. (1992). Staging studies of Knots *Calidris canutus islandica* in Iceland in the early 1970s: body mass patterns. Pp. 129-136 in: Piersma & Davidson (1992b).
Wilson, J.R., Czajkowski, M.A. & Pienkowski, M.W. (1980). The migration through Europe and wintering in west Africa of the Curlew Sandpiper. *Wildfowl* **31**: 107-122.
Wilson, M.A. (1993). Distribución temporal de *Phalaropus tricolor* en el interior de la bahía de la ciudad de Puno. [Temporal distribution of *Phalaropus tricolor* in the interior bay of the city of Puno]. *Volante Migratorio* **20**: 27-29.
Wilson, R.T. ed. (1993). *Birds and the African Environment: Proceedings of the VIII Pan-African Ornithological Congress*. Annales du Musée Royal de l'Afrique Centrale (Zoologie) **268**.
Wilson, U.W. (1986). Breeding biology of the Rhinoceros Auklet in Washington. *Condor* **88**: 143-155.
Wilson, U.W. & Manuwal, D.A. (1986). Breeding biology of the Rhinoceros Auklet in Washington. *Condor* **88**: 143-155.
Wilson, V.J. (1972). Notes on *Otis denhami jacksoni* from the Nyika Plateau. *Bull. Brit. Orn. Club* **92**: 77-81.
Wilson, W.H. (1990). Relationship between prey abundance and foraging site selection by Semipalmated Sandpipers on a Bay of Fundy (Canada) mudflat. *J. Field Orn.* **61**: 9-19.
Wilson, W.H. (1993). Conservation of stop-over areas for migratory waders: Grays Harbor, Washington. *Wader Study Group Bull.* **67**: 37-40.
Wilson, W.H. (1994a). Western Sandpiper (*Calidris mauri*). No. **90** in: Poole & Gill (1994).
Wilson, W.H. (1994b). The effects of episodic predation by migratory shorebirds in Grays Harbor, Washington. *J. Exp. Mar. Biol. Ecol.* **177**: 15-25.
Wiltraut, R. (1991). A late adult Hudsonian Godwit (*Limosa haemastica*): first Lehigh County record. *Pennsylvania Birds* **5(4)**: 155-156.
van der Winden, J., Chernichko, I.I., van der Have, T.M., Siokhin, V.D. & Verkuil, Y. (1993). The migration of Broad-billed Sandpiper *Limicola falcinellus* during May 1992 in the Sivash, Ukraine. *Wader Study Group Bull.* **71**: 41-43.
Windingstad, R.M. (1988). Nonhunting mortality in Sandhill Cranes. *J. Wildl. Manage.* **52**: 260-263.
Wingate, D.B. (1993). First photo-confirmed record of a Sandhill Crane, *Grus canadensis*, on Bermuda. *Bermuda Dep. Agric. Fish. Parks Monthly Bull.* **64(11)**: 85-87.
Wink, M., Kahl, U. & Heidrich, P. (1994). Genetic distinction of *Larus argentatus*, *L. fuscus*, and *L. cachinnans*. *J. Orn.* **135**: 73-80.
Winkelman, J.E. (1994). Redshank. *Tringa totanus*. Pp. 280-281 in: Tucker & Heath (1994).
Winkler, D.W. (1985). Factors determining clutch-size reduction in California Gulls (*Larus californicus*): a multi-hypothesis approach. *Evolution* **39**: 667-677.
Winkler, D.W. & Shuford, W.D. (1988). Changes in the numbers and locations of California Gulls nesting at Mono Lake, California, in the period 1863-1986. *Colonial Waterbirds* **11**: 263-274.
Winkler, H. (1980). [On the feeding of Terek Sandpipers in winter quarters]. *Egretta* **23(2)**: 56-60. In German with English summary.
Winn, H.E. (1950). The Black Guillemots of Kent Island, Bay of Fundy. *Auk* **67**: 477-485.
Winter, S.V. (1981). Nesting of Red-crowned Cranes in the central Amur Region. Pp. 74-80 in: Lewis & Masatomi (1981).
Winter, S.V. (1991). The Demoiselle Crane in the agricultural landscape of the Ukrainian steppe zone. Pp. 285-294 in: Harris (1991b).
Winter, S.V., Andryshchenko, Y.A. & Gorlov, P.I. (1995). The Demoiselle Crane in Ukraine: status, ecology and conservation prospects. Pp. 285-289 in: Prange *et al.* (1995).
Winterbottom, J.M. (1961a). African Jacana in the Richtersveld. *Ostrich* **32**: 99.
Winterbottom, J.M. (1961b). Systematic notes on birds of the Cape Province. XVII. *Larus cirrocephalus* Vieil. *Ostrich* **32**: 139-140.
Winterbottom, J.M. (1963). Comments on the ecology and breeding of sandplovers *Charadrius* in southern Africa. *Rev. Zool. Bot. Afr.* **67**: 11-16.
Winterbottom, J.M. (1966). Some notes on the Red-knobbed Coot *Fulica cristata* in South Africa. *Ostrich* **37**: 92-94.
Winterbottom, J.M. (1968). *A Check List of the Land and Fresh Water Birds of the Western Cape Province*. Annals of the South African Museum **53**. 276 pp.
Winterbottom, J.M. (1971). Birds following ploughs. *Bokmakierie* **23**: 68-69.
Wintle, C.C. (1975). Notes on the breeding habits of the Kurrichane Buttonquail. *Honeyguide* **82**: 27-30.
Wintle, C.C. (1988). Crakes and flufftails in captivity. Unpublished MS. Bromley, Zimbabwe.
Wintle, C.C. & Taylor, P.B. (1993). Sequential polyandry, behaviour and moult in captive Striped Crakes *Aenigmatolimnas marginalis*. *Ostrich* **64**: 115-122.
Wishart, R.A. & Bider, J.R. (1976). Habitat preferences of Woodcock in southwestern Quebec. *J. Wildl. Manage.* **40**: 523-531.
Wishart, R.A. & Spencer, G.S. (1980). Late summer time budget and feeding behaviour of Marbled Godwits (*Limosa fedoa*) in southern Manitoba. *Can. J. Zool.* **58**: 1277-1282.
de Wit, A.A.N. & Spaans, A.L. (1984). Veranderingen in de broedibiologie van de Zilvermeeuw *Larus argentatus* door toegenomen aantallen. *Limosa* **57**: 87-90.
Witherby, H.F., Jourdain, F.C.R., Ticehurst, N.F. & Tucker, B.W. (1941). *The Handbook of British Birds*. Vol. 5. Witherby, London.
Withers, P.C. & Timko, P.L. (1977). The significance of ground effect to the aerodynamic cost of flight and energetics of the Black Skimmer (*Rynchops nigra*). *J. Exper. Biol.* **70**: 13-26.
Witt, H. (1992). Reproduktionserfolge von Rotschenkel (*Tringa totanus*), Uferschnepfe (*Limosa limosa*) und Austernfischer (*Haematopus ostralegus*) in intensiv genutzten Grünlandgebieten - Beispiele für eine "irrtümliche" Biotopwahl sog. Wiesenvögel. *Corax* **11**: 262-300.
Witt, H.H. (1974a). Zur Nahrungsökologie der Mittelmeer-Silbermöwe (*Larus argentatus michahellis*) in einem Brutplatz auf Sardinien. *Vogelwelt* **95**: 148-150.
Witt, H.H. (1974b). Audouin's Gull *Larus audouinii*. *Ibis* **116**: 416-417.
Witt, H.H. (1975). Status of Audouin's Gull. *British Birds* **68**: 304.
Witt, H.H. (1976). *Zur Biologie der Korallenmöwe* L. audouinii. Friedrich-Wilhelms-Universitat, Bonn.
Witt, H.H. (1977a). Zur Biologie der Korallenmöwe *Larus audouinii* Brut und Ernährung. *J. Orn.* **118**: 134-155.
Witt, H.H. (1977b). Zur Verhaltensbiologie der Korallenmöwe *Larus audouinii*. *Z. Tierpsychol.* **43**: 46-67.
Witt, H.H., Crespo, J., de Juana, E. & Varela, J. (1981). Comparative feeding ecology of Audouin's Gull *Larus audouinii* and the Herring Gull *L. argentatus* in the Mediterranean. *Ibis* **123**: 519-526.
Witt, H.H., Stempel, N., de Juana, E. & Varela, J. (1982). Geschlechtsunterschiede bei der Korallenmöwe (*Larus audouinii*) nach meßbaren Merkmalen. *Vogelwarte* **31**: 457-460.
Witteman, G.J. & Beck, R.E. (1991). Decline and conservation of the Guam Rail. In: Maruyama, N. *et al.* eds. (1991). *Wildlife Conservation: Present Trends and Perspectives for the 21st Century*. Proceedings International Symposium on Wildlife Conservation in Tsukuba and Yokohama, Japan, August 21-25 1990. Japan Wildlife Research Centre, Tokyo.
Witteman, G.J., Beck, R.E., Pimm, S.L. & Derrickson, S.R. (1991). The decline and restoration of the Guam Rail *Rallus owstoni*. *Endangered Species Update* **8**: 36-39.
Wittling, N. (1984). Verhaltensbeobachtungen an einer Braunflügel-brachschwalbe (*Glareola pratincola*) bei Zülpich. [Behavioral observations on the Collared Pratincole (*Glareola pratincola*) near Zülpich]. *Charadrius* **20(1)**: 54-56.
Wizeman, R.A. (1972). An extended sojourn and a state record of a Wandering Tattler in Arizona. *Calif. Birds* **3(1)**: 13-15.
Woehler, E.J. (1991). Status and conservation of the seabirds of Heard Island and the McDonald Islands. Pp. 263-277 in: Croxall (1991).
Woehler, E.J. & Johnstone, G.W. (1991). Status and conservation of the seabirds of the Australian Antarctic territory. Pp. 279-308 in: Croxall (1991).
Woehler, E.J., Wakefield, W.C. & Wakefield, M. (1991). Preliminary investigations into the morphology of the Crested Tern *Sterna bergii* in south-east Tasmania. *Corella* **15**: 37-40.
Wolf, L.L. & Gill, F.B. (1961). Flock feeding behavior in migrant Bonaparte's Gulls. *Wilson Bull.* **73**: 389-390.
Wolfe, L.R. (1954). The Australian Snipe in Japan. *Emu* **54**: 198-203.
Wolff, S.W. & Milstein, P. le S. (1976). Rediscovery of the Whitewinged Flufftail in South Africa. *Bokmakierie* **28**: 33-36.
Wolk, R.G. (1959). *Some Reproductive Behavior Patterns of the Black Skimmer,* Rynchops nigra nigra *Linnaeus*. PhD thesis, Cornell University, Ithaca, New York.
Wolk, R.G. (1974). Reproductive behavior of the Least Tern. *Proc. Linn. Soc. N.Y.* **72**: 44-62.
Wolters, H.E. (1982). *Die Vogelarten der Erde* (1975-1982). Paul Parey, Hamburg & Berlin.
Won, P.O. (1981). Status and conservation of cranes wintering in Korea. Pp. 61-65 in: Lewis & Masatomi (1981).
Won, P.O. (1988). [Present status of cranes wintering in Korea, 1986-87]. Pp. 17-35 in: Masatomi (1988). In Japanese.
Won, P.O. (1993). [*A Field Guide to the Birds of Korea*]. Kyo-Hak Publishing Co. Ltd, Seoul. In Korean.
Won, P.O. & Koo, T.H. (1986). [*Wintering Habitat and Conservation of the White-naped Crane,* Grus vipio *Pallas, on the Han River Estuary*]. Bulletin of the Institute of Ornithology, Kyunghee University, Seoul, South Korea. In Korean.
Wong, F.K.O. (1994). Status and distribution of Saunders' Gull *Larus saundersi*. Pp. 24-29 in: *Waterbird Research in China*. East China Normal University Press, Hong Kong.
Wong, P.L. & Anderson, R.C. (1990). *Ancyracanthopsis winegardi* n. sp. (Nematoda: Acuarioidea) from *Pluvialis squatarola* (Aves: Charadriidae) and *Acyracanthus heardi* n. sp. from *Rallus longirostris* (Aves: Rallidae), and a review of the genus. *Can. J. Zool.* **68**: 1297-1306.
Wood, A.G. (1986). Diurnal and nocturnal territories in the Grey Plover at Teesmouth, as revealed by radio telemetry. *J. Field Orn.* **57(3)**: 213-221.
Wood, A.G. (1987). Discriminating the sex of Sanderling *Calidris alba*: some results and their implications. *Bird Study* **34**: 200-204.
Wood, D.A. ed. (1992). *Proceedings of the 1988 North American Crane Workshop*. Nongame Wildlife Program Technical Report **12**. State of Florida Game & Fresh Water Fish Commission. 305 pp.
Wood, D.S. (1979). Phenetic relationships within the family Gruidae. *Wilson Bull.* **91(3)**: 384-399.
Wood, K.A. (1989). Seasonal abundance, marine habitats and behaviour of skuas of central New South Wales. *Corella* **13**: 97-104.
Wood, N. (1977). A feeding technique of Allen's Gallinule *Porphyrio alleni*. *Ostrich* **48**: 120-121.
Wood, N.A. (1974). The breeding biology and behaviour of the Moorhen. *British Birds* **67**: 104-115, 135-158.
Wood, N.A. (1975). Habitat preference and behaviour of Crested Coot in winter. *British Birds* **68**: 116-118.
Wood, R.C. (1971). Population dynamics of breeding South Polar Skuas of unknown age. *Auk* **88**: 805-814.
Wood, R.C. (1972). A population study of South Polar Skuas (*Catharacta maccormicki*) aged one to eight years. Pp. 705-706 in: *Proc. XV Int. Orn. Congr.* the Hague, 1970.

Wood, T.C. (1991). Purple Sandpiper (*Calidris maritima*): 2 December 1991, Sheboygan Co., Sheboygan. *Passenger Pigeon* **53(3)**: 279-280.
Wood-Mason, J. (1878). On the structure and development of the trachea in the Indian Painted Snipe (*Rhynchaea capensis*). *Proc. Zool. Soc., London* **1878**: 745-751.
Woodall, P.F. & Woodall L.B. (1989). Daily activity and feeding behaviour of the Beach Thick-knee *Burhinus neglectus* on north Keppel Island. *Queensland Nat.* **29(3-6)**: 71-75.
Woodbury, A.M. & Knight, H. (1951). Results of the Pacific Gull colorbanding project. *Condor* **53**: 57-77.
Woods, R.W. (1988). *Guide to Birds of the Falkland Islands*. Anthony Nelson, Oswestry, UK.
Woodward, P.W. (1972). *The Natural History of Kure Atoll, Northwestern Hawaiian Islands*. Atoll Research Bulletin **164**. 318 pp.
Woolcock, D. (1983a). Wattled Cranes at Paradise Park, Hayle, Cornwall. *Ratel* **10(3)**: 70-73.
Woolcock, D. (1983b). Wattled Cranes at Paradise Park, Hayle, Cornwall. Part two. *Ratel* **10(4)**: 106-109.
Woolcock, D. (1984a). Wattled Cranes - Breeding notes from Paradise Park, Hayle, Cornwall. *Proc. Symp. Assoc. Brit. Wildl. Anim. Keep.* **9**: 20-22.
Woolcock, D. (1984b). Wattled Cranes at Paradise Park, Hayle, Cornwall. *Ratel* **11(1)**: 25-28.
Woolfenden, G.E. (1978). Species of special concern, Piping Plover, *Charadrius melodus*. Page 88 in: Kale (1978).
Woolfenden, G.E. (1979). Winter breeding by the American Coot at Tampa, Florida. *Florida Field Nat.* **7**: 26.
Wooller, R.D. (1978). Individual vocal recognition in the Kittiwake Gull *Rissa tridactyla*. *Z. Tierpsychol.* **48**: 68-86.
Wooller, R.D. (1979). Seasonal, diurnal and area differences in calling activity within a colony of Kittiwakes *Rissa tridactyla*. *Z. Tierpsychol.* **51**: 329-336.
Wooller, R.D. & Coulson, J.C. (1977). Factors affecting the age of first breeding of the Kittiwake *Rissa tridactyla*. *Ibis* **119**: 339-349.
Wooller, R.D. & Dunlop, J.N. (1979). Multiple laying by the Silver Gull *Larus novaehollandiae* Stephens, on Carnac Island, Western Australia. *Austr. Wildl. Res.* **6**: 325-335.
Wooller, R.D. & Dunlop, J.N. (1981a). Annual variation in the clutch and egg sizes of Silver Gulls, *Larus novaehollandiae*. *Austr. Wildl. Res.* **8**: 431-433.
Wooller, R.D. & Dunlop, J.N. (1981b). The use of a single external measurement for determining sex in a population of Silver Gulls, *Larus novaehollandiae*. *Austr. Wildl. Res.* **8**: 679-680.
Worrall, D.H. (1984). Diet of the Dunlin, *Calidris alpina*, in the Severn estuary. *Bird Study* **31**: 203-212.
van't Woudt, B.D. & Dobbs, R.A. (1988). Wetland wildlife tracks. *Notornis* **35**: 27-34.
Wozniak, I. (1992). [Dotterel (*Charadrius morinellus*) breeding in Tatra Mountain]. *Notatki Orn.* **33(1-2)**: 168-169. In Polish with English summary.
Wragg, G.M. & Weisler, M.I. (1994). Extinctions and new records of birds from Henderson Island, Pitcairn Group, South Pacific Ocean. *Notornis* **41**: 61-70.
Wren, J. (1988). Unusual behaviour of four Sharp-tailed Sandpipers (*Calidris acuminata*). *Stilt* **12**: 60.
Wright, B.K. (1995). Observations on copulating Crab Plovers *Dromas ardeola* in Kuwait. *Bull. Orn. Soc. Middle East* **34**: 14-15.
Wright, G. (1987). Hudsonian Godwit in Devon. *British Birds* **80(10)**: 492-494.
Wright, N.J.R. & Matthews, D.W. (1980). New nesting colonies of the Ivory Gull (*Pagophila eburnea*) in southern East Greenland. *Dan. Orn. Foren. Tidssk.* **74**: 59-64.
Wu Zhigang & Li Ruoxian (1985). [A preliminary study on the wintering ecology of the Black-necked Crane (*Grus nigricollis*)]. *Acta Ecol. Sinica* **5(1)**: 71-75. In Chinese.
Wu Zhigang & Wang Youhui (1986). [Observation on ecology of the Common Crane in Caohai (Guizhou)]. Pp. 208-211 in: Ma Yiqing (1986). In Chinese.
Wu Zhigang, Han Xiaodong & Wang Li (1991). Observations of migratory Siberian Cranes at Momoge Nature Reserve. Pp. 135-138 in: Harris (1991b).
Wu Zhigang, Li Zhumei, Wang Youhui, Jang Ya-Meng, Li Ruoxian, Li Dehao, Zhou Zhijun & Li Lai-Xing (1993). [Migration of Black-necked Crane in China]. *Acta Zool. Sinica* **39(1)**: 105-106. In Chinese.
Wu Zhigang, Li Zhumei, Wang Youhui & Li Ruoxian (1991). The wintering ecology of the Black-necked Crane in Caohai. Pp. 115-118 in: Harris (1991b).
Wu Zhigang, Wang Youhui, Jiang Yameng, Li Zhumei, Li Ruoxian, Li Dehao & Zhou Zhijun (1991). Distribution and abundance of Black-necked Cranes (*Grus nigricollis* Przewalski) in China. *Acta Biol. Plateau Sinica* **10**: 109-116. In English with Chinese summary.
Wuorinen, J.D. (1992). Do Arctic Skuas *Stercorarius parasiticus* exploit and follow terns during the fall migration? *Ornis Fenn.* **69(4)**: 198-200. In English with Finnish summary.
Wymenga, E. & Altenburg, W. (1989). [Spring migration of Black-tailed Godwits in the west of France]. *Vogeljaar* **37**: 77-79. In Dutch.
Wymenga, E., Engelmoer, M., Smit, C.J. & van Spanje, T.M. (1990). Geographical breeding origin and migration of waders wintering in West Africa. *Ardea* **78**: 83-112.
Wyndham, C. (1942). Nest and eggs of the Avocet (*Recurvirostra avosetta*). *Ostrich* **13(2)**: 70-74.
Wynne-Edwards, V.C. (1935). On the habits and distribution of birds on the North Atlantic. *Proc. Boston Soc. Nat. Hist.* **40**: 233-346.
Xantus, de V. (1860). Descriptions of supposed new species of birds from Cape St. Lucas, lower California. *Proc. Acad. Nat. Sci. Philadelphia* **11**: 297-299.
Xian Yaohua (1983). [The Brown-headed Gull *Larus brunnicephalus* at Qinghai Lake (Qinghai Province)]. *Wildlife* **3**: 6-7. In Chinese.
Xu Jie, Jiang Xingxing & Song Shengli (1986). [Observation on the habits of the migration and wintering of the Siberian Crane]. Pp. 121-124 in: Ma Yiqing (1986). In Chinese.
Xu Weishu & Melville, D.S. (1994). Seabirds of China and adjacent seas: status and conservation. Pp. 210-218 in: Nettleship *et al.* (1994).
Xu Xinjie, Liu Hongxi, Wang Jiangtang & Zhang Wancang (1991). Cranes in the place where the Yellow River flowed long ago in Henan Province. Pp. 153-154 in: Harris (1991b).
Xue Jie, Su Liying & Jiang Xingxing (1991). A way of expediting the recovery of the Red-crowned Crane. Pp. 47-50 in: Harris (1991b).
Yahya, H.S.A. (1990). An assessment of the present distribution and population status of the Lesser Florican. Pp. 446-455 in: Daniel, J.C. & Serrao, J.S. eds. (1990). *Conservation in Developing Countries: Problems and Prospects - Proceedings of the Centenary Seminar of the Bombay Natural History Society*. Bombay Natural History Society & Oxford University Press, Bombay & Delhi.
Yalden, D.W. (1986a). Diet, food availabilty and habitat selection of breeding Common Sandpipers *Actitis hypoleucos*. *Ibis* **128(1)**: 23-36.
Yalden, D.W. (1986b). The status of Golden Plovers in the Peak Park, England in relation to access and recreational disturbance. *Wader Study Group Bull.* **46**: 34-35.
Yalden, D.W. (1986c). The habitat and activity of Common Sandpipers *Actitis hypoleucos* breeding by upland rivers. *Bird Study* **33(3)**: 214-222.
Yalden, D.W. (1991). Radio-tracking of Golden Plover *Pluvialis apricaria* chicks. *Wader Study Group Bull.* **63**: 41-44.
Yalden, D.W. (1992). The influence of recreational disturbance on Common Sandpipers *Actitis hypoleucos* breeding by an upland reservoir, in England. *Biol. Conserv.* **61(1)**: 41-49.
Yalden, D.W. & Dougall, T.W. (1994). Habitat, weather and growth rates of Common Sandpiper *Actitis hypoleucos* chicks. *Wader Study Group Bull.* **73**: 33-35.
Yalden, D.W. & Holland, P.K. (1992). Relative contributions of Common Sandpiper *Actitis hypoleucos* parents to guarding their chicks. *Ringing & Migration* **13(2)**: 95-97.
Yalden, D.W. & Yalden, P.E. (1989a). Estimating the date of hatching of eggs of Golden Plovers *Pluvialis apricaria*. *Wader Study Group Bull.* **55**: 19-20.
Yalden, D.W. & Yalden, P.E. (1989b). The sensitivity of breeding Golden Plovers *Pluvialis apricaria* to human intruders. *Bird Study* **36(1)**: 49-55.
Yalden, D.W. & Yalden, P.E. (1991). Efficiency of censusing Golden Plovers. *Wader Study Group Bull.* **62**: 32-36.
Yalden, P.E. & Yalden, D.W. (1988). Plover's page or plover's parasite? Aggressive behaviour of Golden Plover toward Dunlin. *Ornis Fenn.* **65(4)**: 169-171. In English with Finnish summary.
Yalden, P.E. & Yalden, D.W. (1990). Recreational disturbance of breeding Golden Plovers *Pluvialis apricaria*. *Biol. Conserv.* **51(4)**: 243-262.
Yamashina, Y. (1961). *Birds in Japan: a Field Guide*. Tokyo News Service Ltd, Tokyo.
Yamashina, Y. & Mano, T. (1981). A new species of rail from Okinawa Island. *J. Yamashina Inst. Orn.* **13**: 1-6.
Yan Anhou (1982). [Ecological studies and hunting of the Great Bustard *Otis tarda* in winter]. *Chinese J. Zool.* **1**: 37-39. In Chinese.
Yan Anhou (1986). [Preliminary observations on the ecology of Grey-headed Lapwing *Microsarcops cinereus*]. *Sichuan J. Zool.* **5(3)**: 34-35. In Chinese.
Yan Anhou & Pang Bingzhang (1986). [Ecology of the White-breasted Waterhen, *Amaurornis phoenicurus*]. *Chinese Wildlife* **6**: 31-33. In Chinese.
Yanagisawa, N., Fujimaki, Y. & Higuchi, H. (1994). Japanese data on waterbird population sizes, summarised for IWRB. In: Rose & Scott (1994).
Yang Dehua (1982). [Ecological observations of the Common Crane in winter]. *Chinese J. Zool.* **3**: 6-7. In Chinese.
Yang Lan (1987). [Current distribution of the Sarus Crane (*Grus antigone*) in Yunnan]. *Zool. Res.* **8(3)**: 338. In Chinese.
Yang Lan (1991). The distribution and habitats of the cranes in Yunnan Province. Pp. 127-129 in: Harris (1991b).
Yang Ruoli, Xu Jie & Su Liying (1991). [The distribution and migration of the White-naped Crane]. *Forest Research* **4(3)**: 253-256. In Chinese.
Yang Xueming & Tong Junchang (1991). Preliminary study on the breeding habits and domestication of the Demoiselle Crane. Pp. 79-82 in: Harris (1991b).
Yang Xueming, Tong Junchang & Gou Jinsheng (1986). [Study of the breeding ecology and domestication of the White-naped Crane]. Pp. 169-177 in: Ma Yiqing (1986). In Chinese.
Yao Jianchu (1982). [The distribution of the Black-necked Cranes in Qinghai Province]. *Chinese Wildlife* **1**: 20-22. In Chinese.
Yao Jianchu (1986). [The distribution of the Black-necked Crane in Qinghai Province]. Pp. 141-146 in: Ma Yiqing (1986). In Chinese.
Yao Jianchu & Liao Yanfa (1984). [Observation on the reproductive habits of Black-necked Cranes *Grus nigricollis*]. *Acta Biol. Plateau Sinica* **3**: 141-147. In Chinese.
Yarbrough, C.G. (1970). Summer lipid levels of some subarctic birds. *Auk* **87**: 100-110.
Yawetz, A., Zook Rimon, Z. & Dotan, A. (1993). Cholinesterase profiles in two species of wild birds exposed to insecticide sprays in their natural habitat. *Arch. Insect Biochem. Physiol.* **22**: 501-509.
Yeates, G.K. (1948). Quelques notes sur la reproduction de la Glaréole *Glareola pratincola pratincola* (L) en France. *Oiseau et RFO* **18**: 98-103.
Yeatman, L.J. (1976). *Atlas des Oiseaux Nicheurs de France*. Paris.
Yeatman-Berthelot, D. (1991). *Atlas of Wintering Birds in France*. Société Ornithologique de France, Paris.
Yen, C.W. (1991). First breeding record of the Black-winged Stilt (*Himantopus himantopus himantopus*) in Taiwan. *J. Taiwan Mus.* **44**: 309-320.
Yésou, P. (1982). Les limnodromes *Limnodromus griseus* et *L. scolopaceus*: identification, synthèse des données françaises. *Alauda* **50(3)**: 220-227.
Yésou, P. (1985). Separating Ring-billed and Common Gull. *Dutch Birding* **7**: 105-106.
Yésou, P. (1991). The sympatric breeding of *Larus fuscus*, *L. cachinnans* and *L. argentatus* in western France. *Ibis* **133**: 256-263.
Yésou, P., Chupin, I.I. & Grabovsky, V.I. (1992). Notes on th breeding biology of the Bar-tailed Godwit *Limosa lapponica* in Taimyr. *Wader Study Group Bull.* **66**: 45-47.
Yi, J.Y., Yoo, J.C. & Won, P.O. (1994). Foraging behavior and energy intake of premigratory Australian Curlews *Numenius madagascariensis* on Kanghwa Island, Korea. *Kor. J. Orn.* **1**: 1-12.
Ylimaunu, O., Ylimaunu, J., Hemminki, O. & Liehu, H. (1987). [Breeding ecology and size of the breeding Curlew *Numenius arquata* population in Finland]. *Lintumies* **22**: 98-103. In Finnish.
Yogev, A. & Yom-Tov, Y. (1994). The Spur-winged Plover (*Vanellus spinosus*) is a determinate egg layer. *Condor* **96(4)**: 1109-1110.
Yorio, P., Boersma, P.D. & Swann, S. (1994). Breeding biology of the Dolphin Gull (*Larus scoresbii*) at Punta Tombo, Argentina. Unpublished MS.
Yosef, R. (1994). Sex-related differences in distraction-displays by Florida Sandhill Cranes. *Condor* **96(1)**: 222-224.
Yosef, R. (1995). Foraging behaviour of Arctic, Pomarine and Long-tailed Skua on migration in the Red Sea. *Bull. Orn. Soc. Middle East* **34**: 12-13.
Young, C.G. (1929). A contribution to the ornithology of the coastland of British Guiana. *Ibis* **Ser. 12, no. 5**: 1-38.
Young, D.P. (1991). Least Terns and Killdeer on rooftop in Chatham County. *Oriole* **56(4)**: 80-82.
Young, E.C. (1963a). The breeding behaviour of the South Polar Skua *Catharacta maccormicki*. *Ibis* **105**: 203-233.
Young, E.C. (1963b). Feeding habits of the South Polar Skua *Catharacta maccormicki*. *Ibis* **105**: 301-318.
Young, E.C. (1972). Territory establishment and stability in McCormick's Skua. *Ibis* **114**: 234-244.
Young, E.C. (1977). Egg-laying in relation to latitude in southern hemisphere skuas. *Ibis* **119**: 191-195.
Young, E.C. (1978). Behavioural ecology of *lönnbergi* skuas in relation to environment on the Chatham Islands, New Zealand. *New Zealand J. Zool.* **5(2)**: 401-416.
Young, E.C. (1990). Diet of the South Polar Skua *Catharacta maccormicki* from regurgitated pellets: limitations of a technique. *Polar Record* **26**: 124-125.
Young, E.C. (1994). *Skua and Penguin: Predator and Prey*. Cambridge University Press, Cambridge.
Young, R.T. (1952). The status of the California Gull colony at Mono Lake, California. *Condor* **54**: 206-207.
Yovanovich, G.D.L. (1995). Collared Plover in Uvalde, Texas. *Birding* **27(2)**: 102-104.
Ytreberg, N.J. (1956). Contribution to the breeding biology of the Black-headed Gull (*Larus ridibundus* L.) in Norway. Nest, eggs and incubation. *Nytt. Mag. Zool.* **4**: 5-106.
Ytreberg, N.J. (1960). Some observations on egg-laying in the Black-headed Gull (*Larus ridibundus* L.) and the Common Gull (*Larus canus* L.). *Nytt. Mag. Zool.* **9**: 5-15.
Yu Changyun & Gao Wei (1983). [The breeding of the Great Bustard *Otis tarda*]. *Wildlife* **3**: 2-5. In Chinese.
Yu Yuqun, Liu Wulin & Sang Jie (1993). [A preliminary study on the overwintering ecology of Black-necked Crane (*Grus nigricollis*) in the Upper Lhasa River]. *Zool. Res.* **14(3)**: 251-250. In Chinese.
Yuan, H. (1993). Possible evidence of double-brooding in Common Terns (*Sterna hirundo*) at Oneida Lake, New York. *Colonial Waterbirds* **16**: 83-87.
Yuan Tao & Li Peixun (1991). Observations of mating behavior of the White-naped Crane in the wild. Pp. 63-66 in: Harris (1991b).
Yudin, K.A. (1965). [*Fauna of the USSR, Birds*]. Vol. 2. Part 1. Section 1. Phylogeny and Classification of the Waders. Science Publishers, Moscow. In Russian.
Yurlov, A.K. (1981). [Asiatic Dowitcher *Limnodromus semipalmatus* in the Lake Chany region (Western Siberia)]. Pp. 102-109 in: Yurlov, K.T. ed. (1981). *Ekologiya i biotsenoticheskie svyazi pereletnykh ptits zapadnoi sibiri*. Novosibirsk. In Russian.
Yurlov, A.K. (1986). [Breeding ecology of the Little Ringed Plover in the forest-steppe zone of western Siberia]. Pp. 31-36 in: [*The Ecology of the Ural's Bird Species and Adjacent Territory*]. In Russian.
Zapata, A.R.P. (1965). Nuevas localidades de nidificación de *Leucophaeus scoresbii* (Traill) y *Sterna sandvicensis eurygnatha* Saunders. (Aves, Laridae). *Physis* **25**: 383-385.
Zapata, A.R.P. (1967). Observaciones sobre aves de Puerto Deseado, Provincia de Santa Cruz. *Hornero* **10**: 351-378.
Zarudsky, J.D. (1985). Breeding status of the American Oystercatcher in the town of Hempstead. *Kingbird* **35(2)**: 105-113.
Zembal, R. & Fancher, J.M. (1988). Foraging behaviour and foods of the Light-footed Clapper Rail. *Condor* **90**: 959-962.
Zembal, R. & Massey, B.W. (1985). Function of a rail "mystery" call. *Auk* **102**: 179-180.
Zembal, R. & Massey, B.W. (1987). Seasonality of vocalizations by Light-footed Clapper Rails. *J. Field Orn.* **58**: 41-48.
Zhang, Y. & He, F. (1990). *Breeding Population of the Relict Gull* Larus relictus *in Inner Mongolia*. Proc. ICBP World Conference, Hamilton, New Zealand.
Zhang Weigong & Chen Zuoping (1985). [Button Quails *Turnix tanki* breeding in Xi'an (Shaanxi Province)]. *Chinese J. Zool.* **4**: 56. In Chinese.
Zhang Yinsun (1991). [A new finding of the breeding population of Relict Gull in Ordos]. *Chinese J. Zool.* **26(3)**: 32-33. In Chinese.
Zhang Yinsun, Ding Wenning, Bu He & Tian Lu (1992). Breeding ecology of the Relict Gull *Larus relictus* in Ordos, Inner Mongolia, China. *Forktail* **7**: 131-137.
Zhang Yinsun, Liu Changjiang, Tian Lu & Bu He (1991). Recent records of the Relict Gull *Larus relictus* in western Nei Mongol autonomous region, China. *Forktail* **6**: 66-67.
Zhang Yuewen, Jin Liankui & Zheng Jimin (1993). [A discovery of the wintering flock of the Common Crane in Liaoning]. *Chinese Wildlife* **5**: 26. In Chinese.
Zhao Diansheng (1986). [Present status and the future of the Great Bustards, *Otis tarda*, of the world]. *Chinese Wildlife* **1**: 49-51, 54. In Chinese.
Zhao Haizhong (1991). Winter ecology of Hooded Cranes. Pp. 101-103 in: Harris (1991b).
Zheng Zuoxin (1955). Natural enemy of the locusts, the Indian Pratincole *Glareola maldivarum*. *Bull. Biol.* **5**: 10-11.
Zhmud, M.E. (1988). [Breeding philopatry and dispersion in the Redshanks (*Tringa totanus*) in southern Ukraine]. Pp. 47-53 in: Flint & Tomkovich (1988). In Russian.

Zhmud, M.Y. (1992). Territorial relations and population structure of the Redshank *Tringa totanus* during the nesting period in the south of Ukraine. *Wader Study Group Bull.* **64**: 45-46.

Zhou Chenyao (1986). [Observation of the mating behavior of the White-naped Crane on its wintering grounds]. Pp. 178-183 in: Ma Yiqing (1986). In Chinese.

Zhou Fuzhang & Ding Wenning (1982). [Siberian Crane (*Grus leucogeranus*) wintering habits]. *Chinese J. Zool.* **17(4)**: 19-21. In Chinese.

Zhou Fuzhang & Ding Wenning (1987). Siberian Crane wintering in the lower Yangtze in China. Pp. 171-172 in: Archibald & Pasquier (1987a).

Zhou Fuzhang, Ding Wenning & Wang Ziyu (1981). [A large flock of the Siberian Crane (*Grus leucogeranus*) wintering in China]. *Acta Zool. Sinica* **27(2)**: 179. In Chinese.

Zhou Fuzhang, Ding Wenning & Wang Ziyu (1987). Observations on the wintering habitat of the Black-necked Crane. Pp. 41-44 in: Archibald & Pasquier (1987a).

Zhou Haizhong, Chen Bin & Yan Li (1986). [The wintering habits of the Siberian Crane at Poyang Lake]. Pp. 112-115 in: Ma Yiqing (1986). In Chinese.

Zhou Shie (1988). [Observations on the wintering habits of the Red-crowned Crane in Jiangsu Province of China]. Pp. 5-7 in: Masatomi (1988). In Japanese.

Zhou Zonghan & Huan Baoqing (1984). [Wintering habits of the Red-crowned Crane *Grus japonensis*]. *Chinese Wildlife* **6**: 15-16. In Chinese.

Zhukov, V.S. (1988). [Marsh Sandpiper (*Tringa stagnatilis*) in the forest-steppe of the Middle Siberia]. *Ornitologiya* **23**: 208-209. In Russian.

Zhuravlev, M.N. (1975). [Observations of *Larus relictus*]. Pp. 165-167 in: [*Colonies of Water Birds and their Protection*]. Moscow. In Russian.

Zielinski, M. (1992a). Egyptian Plover in Poland in October-November 1991. *Dutch Birding* **14(3)**: 99.

Zielinski, M. (1992b). [The Egyptian Plover (*Pluvianus aegyptius*) observed in Poland]. *Notatki Orn.* **33(3-4)**: 319-321. In Polish with English summary.

Ziewitz, J.W., Sidle, J.G. & Dinan, J.J. (1992). Habitat conservation for nesting Least Terns and Piping Plovers on the Platte River, Nebraska. *Prairie Nat.* **24(1)**: 1-20.

Zikova, L.U. & Panov, E.N. (1983). [Influence of the number and density of nesting colonies on the reproductive success of the Yellow-legged Gull *Larus argentatus cachinnans*]. *Zoologischeskii Zhurnal* **62**: 1533-1540. In Russian.

Zikova, L.U., Panov, E.N. & Gauser, M.E. (1986). [Asynchronous hatching as one of the reasons for juvenile mortality in the Slender-billed Gull *Larus genei*]. *Zoologischeskii Zhurnal* **65**: 1373-1378. In Russian.

Zimmer, J.T. (1930). *Birds of the Marshall Field Peruvian Expedition*. Field Museum of Natural History (Zoological Serie) **17**. 480 pp.

Zimmer, J.T. & Phelps, W.H. (1944). New species and subspecies of birds from Venezuela. *Amer. Mus. Novit.* **1270**: 1-16.

Zimmer, K.J. (1991). Plumage variation in "Kumlien's" Iceland Gull. *Birding* **23**: 254-269.

Zimmerman, D.R. (1975). *To Save a Bird in Peril*. Coward, McCann & Geoghegan, New York.

Zimmerman, J.L. (1984). Distribution, habitat and status of the Sora and Virginia Rail in interior Kansas. *J. Field Orn.* **55**: 38-47.

Zink, R.M. & Winkler, D.W. (1983). Genetic and morphological similarity of two California Gull populations with different life history trains. *Biochem. Syst. Ecol.* **11**: 497-403.

Zollner, T. (1995). [Lapwings (*Vanellus vanellus*) copulate during breeding relief]. *J. Orn.* **136(3)**: 296-299. In German with English summary.

Zonfrillo, B. (1981). Food of a Jack Snipe. *Wader Study Group Bull.* **33**: 10.

Zotta, A. (1934). Sobre el contenido estomacal de aves argentinas. *Hornero* **5**: 376-383.

Zoutendyk, P. (1965). The occurrence of Sabine's Gull *Xema sabini* off the coast of southern Africa. *Ostrich* **31**: 15-16.

Zoutendyk, P. (1968). The occurrence of Sabine's Gull *Xema sabini* off the Cape Peninsula. *Ostrich* **39**: 9-11.

Zoutendyk, P. & Feely, J. (1953). Note on Grey-headed Gull in a breeding colony of Hartlaub's Gulls. *Ostrich* **24**: 188.

Zubakin, V.A. (1975a). [Index of nesting density of certain gull species and method of their calculation]. *Zoologischeskii Zhurnal* **54**: 1386-1389. In Russian.

Zubakin, V.A. (1975b). [On the demonstrative behavior of the Great Black-headed Gull (*Larus ichthyaetus* Pall.)]. Pp. 55-57 in: [*Questions of Zoopsychology, Ethology, and Comparative Psychology*]. Moscow University, Moscow. In Russian.

Zubakin, V.A. (1975c). [Cannibalism in Gull-billed Terns (*Gelochelidon nilotica* Gm.)]. *Bull. Moscow Univ. (Biology)* **16**: 32-36. In Russian.

Zubakin, V.A. (1976). [Some questions of individual recognition in Gulls (Laridae)]. *Bull. Moscow Soc. Nat. Study (Biol. Section)* **81**: 31-37. In Russian.

Zubakin, V.A. (1979a). [Display and nesting behavior of the Relict Gull (*Larus relictus*) on Barun-Tor Lake]. *Byull. Mosk. Ova. Ispyt. Prir. Otd. Biol.* **84**: 15-20. In Russian.

Zubakin, V.A. (1979b). [Nesting of the Black-winged Stilt (*Himantopus himantopus*) in the southern part of the Chita District]. *Ornitologiya* **14**: 191-192. In Russian.

Zubakin, V.A. (1982a). [Ecology and behavior of the Brown-headed Gull *Larus brunnicephalus* in the Pamirs]. *Byull. Mosk. Ova. Ispyt. Prir. Otd. Biol.* **87**: 45-56. In Russian.

Zubakin, V.A. (1982b). Density index of nesting of some species of Larids and method of its calculation. Pp. 483-493 in: Gavrilov, V.M. & Potapov, R.L. eds. (1982). [*Ornithological Studies of the USSR*]. Vol. 2. Zoological Institute, USSR Academy of Sciences, Moscow.

Zubakin, V.A. (1983). [The role of different factors in the origin and evolution of Laridae coloniality]. Pp. 37-64 in: Zubakin *et al.* (1983). In Russian.

Zubakin, V.A. (1985). [Parallelisms in the evolution of coloniality in birds]. Pp. 42-47 in: Zubakin, V.A., Ivanitsky, B.B., Stotskaya, E.E. & Kharitonov, S.P. (1985). [*Theoretical Aspects of Coloniality in Birds*]. Nauka, Moscow. In Russian.

Zubakin, V.A. (1990). Some aspects of the nesting biology and social behaviour of the Crested Auklet (*Aethia cristatella*). Pp. 9-13 in: *Study of Colonial Seabirds of the USSR*. USSR Academy of Sciences, Magadan.

Zubakin, V.A. & Avdanin, V.O. (1983). [The peculiarities of colonial nesting of Ross' Gull (*Rhodostethia rosea*)]. *Zoologischeskii Zhurnal* **62**: 1754-1756. In Russian.

Zubakin, V.A. & Flint, W.E. (1980). Ökologie und Verhalten der Reliktmöwe (*Larus relictus*). *Beitr. Vogelkd.* **26**: 253-275.

Zubakin, V.A. & Kharitonov, S.P. (1981). [Nesting of Black-headed Gulls on Lake Kievo, Moscow Region]. Pp. 45-49 in: Viksne, J. ed. (1981). [*Distribution and Number of Black-headed Gulls*]. Nauka, Moscow. In Russian.

Zubakin, V.A. & Zubakin, E.V. (1994). Some results of a marked population study of Crested Auklets, Parakeet Auklets and Tufted Puffins at Talan Island (Tauyskaia Bay, Sea of Okhotsk). *Beringian Seabird Bull.* **1**.

Zubakin, V.A., Mozgovoy, D.P., Panov, E.N., Roschevsky, U.K. eds. (1983). *Collected Papers. Coloniality in Birds: Structure, Function, Evolution*. Kuibyshev Univ., Kuibyshev. In Russian.

Zubarovskij, V.M. (1976). On the biology of the Eastern Solitary Snipe (*Gallinago solitaria*) in the Altai. *Ornitologiya* **12**: 114-117.

Zuquim, P.T. (1991). Status and conservation of seabirds breeding in Brazilian waters. Pp. 141-158 in: Croxall (1991).

Zusi, R.L. (1958). Laughing Gull takes fish from Black Skimmer. *Condor* **60**: 647-648.

Zusi, R.L. (1959). Fishing rates in the Black Skimmer. *Condor* **61**: 298.

Zusi, R.L. (1962). *Structural Adaptations of the Head and Neck in the Black Skimmer*. Publications of the Nuttall Ornithological Club **3**. Cambridge, Massachusetts. 101 pp.

Zusi, R.L. (1968). "Ploughing" for fish by the Greater Yellowlegs. *Wilson Bull.* **80**: 491-492.

Zusi, R.L. (1985). Skimmer. Pp. 546-547 in: Campbell & Lack (1985).

Zusi, R.L. & Bridge, D. (1981). On the slit pupil of the Black Skimmer (*Rynchops niger*). *J. Field Orn.* **52**: 338-340.

Zusi, R.L. & Jehl, J.R. (1970). The systematic position of *Aechmorhynchus*, *Prosobonia* and *Phegornis* (Charadriiformes: Charadrii). *Auk* **87**: 760-780.

Zwarts, L. (1974). *Vogels van het Brakke Getij-gebied. Ecologische Onderzoekingen op de Ventjagersplaten*. Jeugdbondsuitgeverij, Amsterdam.

Zwarts, L. (1985). The winter exploitation of fiddler crabs *Uca tangeri* by waders in Guinea-Bissau. *Ardea* **73**: 3-12.

Zwarts, L. (1988). Numbers and distribution of coastal waders in Guinea-Bissau. *Ardea* **76**: 42-55.

Zwarts, L. (1990). Increased prey availability drives premigration hyperphagia in Whimbrels and allows them to leave the Banc d'Arguin, Mauritania, in time. *Ardea* **78**: 279-300.

Zwarts, L. & Blomert, A.M. (1990). Selectivity of Whimbrels feeding on fiddler crabs explained by components of specific digestibility. *Ardea* **78**: 193-208.

Zwarts, L. & Blomert, A.M. (1992). Why Knot *Calidris canutus* take medium-sized *Macoma balthica* when six prey species are available. *Mar. Ecol. Progr. Ser.* **83**: 113-128.

Zwarts, L. & Dirksen, S. (1990). Digestive bottleneck limits the increase in food intake of Whimbrels preparing for spring migration from the Banc d'Arguin, Mauritania. *Ardea* **78**: 257-278.

Zwarts, L. & Drent, R.H. (1981). Prey depletion and the regulation of predator density: Oystercatcher (*Haematopus ostralegus*) feeding on mussels (*Mytilis edulis*). Pp. 193 216 in: Jones, N.V. & Wolff, W.J. eds. (1981). *Feeding and Survival Strategies of Estuarine Organisms*. Plenum Press, New York & London.

Zwarts, L. & Esselink, P. (1989). Versatility of male Curlews *Numenius arquata* preying upon *Nereis diversicolor*: deploying contrasting capture modes dependent on prey availability. *Mar. Ecol. Progr. Ser.* **56**: 255-269.

Zwarts, L. & Wanink, J. (1984). How Oystercatchers and Curlews successively deplete clams. Pp. 69-83 in: Evans *et al.* (1984).

Zwarts, L., Blomert, A.M. & Wanink, J.H. (1992). Annual and seasonal variation in the food supply harvestable by Knot *Calidris canutus* staging in the Wadden Sea in late summer. *Mar. Ecol. Progr. Ser.* **83**: 129-139.

Zwarts, L., Ens, B.J., Kersten, M. & Piersma, T. (1990). Moult, mass and flight range of waders ready to take off for long-distance migrations. *Ardea* **78**: 339-364.

Zweers, G.A. (1991). Pathways and space for evolution of feeding mechanisms in birds. Pp. 530-547 in: Dudley, E.C. ed. (1991). *The Unity of Evolutionary Biology*. Dioscorides Press, Portland, Oregon.

Zykova, L.U. (1983). [The role of social factors in the reproductive behavior of the Herring Gull *Larus argentatus*]. Pp. 143-157 in: Zubakin *et al.* (1983). In Russian.

INDEX

INDEX